ROTH
FOOTBALL
YEARBOOK
1995-96

EDITOR: JACK ROLLIN
ASSISTANT EDITOR: GLENDA ROLLIN

HEADLINE

First published in 1995
by HEADLINE BOOK PUBLISHING

10 9 8 7 6 5 4 3 2 1

Cover photographs: (top left) Steve Bould (Arsenal) and Jürgen Klinsmann (Tottenham Hotspur)—*Colorsport*; (bottom left) Alan Shearer (Blackburn Rovers)—*Colorsport*; (top right) Robert Lee (Newcastle United)—*Action Images*; (bottom right) Maurizio Gaudino (Manchester City) and Andy Cole (Manchester United)—*Colorsport*.

British Library Cataloguing in Publication Data
Rothmans Football Yearbook.—1995–96
1. Association Football—Serials
796.334′05

ISBN 0 7472 1413 1 (hardback)
0 7472 7823 7 (softback)

Typeset by BPC Whitefriars Ltd,
Tunbridge Wells

Printed and bound in Great Britain by
BPC Hazell Books Ltd
Member of BPC Ltd

HEADLINE BOOK PUBLISHING
A division of Hodder Headline PLC
338 Euston Road
London NW1 3BH

CONTENTS

INTERNATIONAL FOOTBALL

EUROPEAN FOOTBALL

NON-LEAGUE FOOTBALL

INFORMATION AND RECORDS

INTRODUCTION

The 26th Edition of Rothmans Yearbook includes an up-to-date list of all qualifying results in the 1996 European Championship, the finals of which will be held in England next summer. There are goalscorers, teams, times of goals, attendances and referees for the competition.

On the domestic scene there is a radical change in the presentation of players for the 92 English League clubs (*see page 33*). The new Players Directory includes all previous items of information in an easy-to-read A-Z guide. There are now four pages for each English club in the FA Carling Premiership and Endsleigh Insurance League. Again squad numbers have been ignored, the more familiar 1 to 11, 12, 14 and 15 (representing the goalkeeper substitute) have been utilised.

Information which previously featured on the sixth club page has now been moved elsewhere, with both the Managers and Did You Know sections now separately listed, while other data has been incorporated into the extended page two. As a consequence of this, the club badge has been moved to the top of the third club page and the fourth one in this section now features initials of the players making appearances in 1994-95.

The performances of British clubs in Europe are monitored and special articles include those on the Football Trust, Football and the Law, Referees and the work of Football in the Community. Also the special work carried out by Chaplains to clubs is again included.

Amateur, schools, university and women's football plus coverage of non-league soccer, awards, records and the International Directory of all member countries in FIFA are among the regular items.

Transfer fees are given where known. When two clubs have differed as to the amount of a record move, the lower figure has been quoted in both instances. Also the date when a player is signed often varies from one given as his registration.

The Editor would also like to thank Alan Elliott for the Scottish section, Norman Barrett for the Milestones Diary and Ian Vosper for the Obituaries. Thanks are also due to John English who provided his usual painstaking and conscientious reading of the proofs. Appreciation, too, for the fine editorial assistance of Christine Forrest.

The Editor would like to pay tribute to the various organisations who have helped to make this edition complete, especially Sheila Andrew of the Football League, Mike Foster of the FA Premier League and the secretaries of all the FA Premier, Football League and Scottish League clubs for their kind co-operation. The ready availability of Football League secretary David Dent and his staff to answer queries was as usual most appreciated especially Chris Hull and thanks are due in equal measure to the Scottish Football League as well as Adrian Cook and Neil Harrison of the FA Premier League.

ACKNOWLEDGEMENTS

The Editor would also like to express his appreciation of the following individuals and organisations for their co-operation: Glynis Firth, Sandra Whiteside, Lorna Parnell, Debbie Birch (all from the Football League), David C. Thompson of the Scottish League, Alan Dick, Malcolm Brodie, Bob Hennessy, Peter Hughes (English Schools FA), W.P. Goss (AFA), Ken Scott for Vauxhall Conference information, Rev. Nigel Sands, Edward Grayson, Ken Goldman and Andy Howland.

Special thanks are due to Lorraine Jerram of Headline Book Publishing Ltd for her constant support, unflagging patience, sincerity, understanding and appreciation.

Finally sincere thanks to Allan Wyatt, David Prebble and Trevor Stevens and the production staff at BPC Whitefriars for their efforts in the production of this book which was much appreciated throughout the year.

DON ALDRIDGE

A few days after the 25th edition went to press, Don Aldridge, a valued Rothmans contributor over many years, died in hospital following a short illness. He had completed his work on the book before being taken ill. Formerly editor of the FA News, he was, until shortly before his death also responsible for editing programmes at Wembley Stadium. A first-class researcher, his other speciality was successfully harrassing errant organisations for their Rothmans copy.

EDITORIAL

Two days after Eric Cantona's infamous Bruce Lee impression at Crystal Palace, one of those early morning radio programmes cuttingly posed the rhetorical question: "How can you bring soccer into disrepute". Then you know the image of the game is flawed.

That was not the end of the problem. There was the disaster in Dublin and as a result of this, all English teams playing abroad have been designated as 'high risk' affairs. Allegations of managers accepting 'bungs', players accused of involvement in fixing matches, it seemed that the list of scandal was endless. Greed and corruption would appear to be widespread.

All this is so sad, particularly when the game is making strenuous efforts to improve its stature. Ground redevelopments, the unsung work of the various supporters organisations, the Football Trust, Football in the Community programmes, signs of closer liaison between the authorities and the fans, encouragement of families at football etc., all point to the positive aspect of our national sport.

Alas football's answer to the outbreaks of hooliganism is that it is society's problem. But the game is a crucial part of the fabric of many people's leisure activities and those connected with the game cannot divorce themselves from what is happening in the world. More importantly, how we have allowed events to drift to a degree with which we are dissatisfied, affects each and everyone of us.

In an era when there is a proliferation of bad language and violence on television, we can scarcely be surprised when a minority of spectators fail to observe the decencies at matches. The human species may have become wretched and miserable; advanced in technology, but forever slipping back on a moral plane. Parental responsibility is probably politically incorrect, but it is necessary. No one should underestimate the pressures of raising children in present circumstances, but when it is often abrogated completely or at best privatised, only a total re-think can alter the situation.

After all if we want to foster family enclosures at football, there will have to be sufficient numbers to make it viable.

While numbers of spectators and the standard of behaviour they display must play a leading role in the future, there are other statistics to be noted. While the FA Carling Premiership showed a further welcome increase in attendances at matches in 1994-95, there was a less encouraging set of figures for goalscoring.

Going back to 1924-25 when the offside law was about to be changed, the number of goals scored in the then First Division had fallen to 1,192. The following season under the new rules, it had increased to 1,703. In 1994-95 it was just 1,195, the same figure as in 1993-94.

Perhaps we have come to expect fewer goals in the modern era of tighter defences and the danger is that there will be a panic towards implementing the type of idea, like the kick-in experiment which had to be seen to be disapproved, that will further erode the standing of the beautiful game.

Bill Shankly's oft quoted remarks about life and death and football were much nearer the truth than we might have imagined. The best evidence is that while death is likely to strike just once, losing matches is a certainty more than once.

The game of life has few enough free kicks but frequent penalties. One must gratefully accept the former and face the latter with as much dignity as possible. But then is sudden death preferable to penalties...?

ROTHMANS FOOTBALL HONOURS

BIRMINGHAM CITY FOOTBALL CLUB. Though the midland club were regularly involved in the transfer market during the 1994-95 season, and called upon the services of more players than any other in the four English divisions -37 in all -they could reflect on a successful outcome and a double which produced the Second Division championship and the Auto Windscreens Shield Trophy. Ebullient manager Barry Fry shuffled his pack shrewdly enough to bring promotion and the crowds flocked to St Andrews. Indeed the attendance for their final at Wembley was bettered there by just one other during the entire season and that for the FA Cup Final itself, as City fans alone accounted for well over 40,000 spectators.

MATTHEW LE TISSIER. Discovered while touring with the Guernsey Under-15's, he was once the youngest Southampton player to score a hat-trick. While he has delved deeply into his resources to contrive goals from various angles and positions, it is his inherent flair and vision which has made him one of the most gifted of present day players, despite just a handful of full England international opportunities. Last season he did much to stifle the cry that consistency was not one of his attributes. His almost unerring accuracy from the penalty spot is also confirmed: he has never failed to hit the target and only once in March 1993 did he have a shot saved in 36 overall attempts.

BRYAN ROBSON. The 1994-95 season must have seemed like a fairy story come true for Middlesbrough and Bryan Robson. Striving to regain their Premier League status and with a newly-installed player-manager anxious to prove himself, they emerged as worthy champions of the Endsleigh Insurance First Division. Now they are taking their place among the elite and about to settle into a new £6 million home. Robson's first season at the helm was all that he might have wished for himself and his calculated moves into the transfer arena were well-judged and rewarding. He also succeeded in overcoming injury problems to combine his demanding midfield role with well executed off-field duties.

JOE ROYLE. That Joe Royle would won day become manager of Everton was possibly not the wildest of dreams for anyone to contemplate. Merseyside born, he had been their youngest senior debutant at only 16 years of age in 1966. In ten seasons he scored 119 League and Cup goals for the club and won England honours in their colours. After playing spells elsewhere, he became Oldham Athletic's manager in 1982 and was generally acknowledged to have distinguished himself in their cause. Taking over at Goodison Park last season when Everton were staring relegation in the face, he put the smiles back with his commitment and enthusiasm, banishing fear of the drop and adding the FA Cup as an endorsement of his fine efforts.

ALAN SHEARER. The Geordie who came south to make his name and then move to the north-west, Alan Shearer is probably best described as an old-fashioned leader of the attack, who in a previous era would have contributed 40 or 50 goals a season. That in 1994-95 with Blackburn Rovers he equalled the record for the FA Premier League with 34 goals, merely emphasises his value among tighter modern defences. In only his second game for Southampton, he scored three goals to become the youngest to do so in a First Divison game. Accuracy on the ground and in the air, the ability to initiate attacks and clinically finish them off, has earned him international honours for England. Another personal milestone: his 100th League goal on 18 March.

WOKING FOOTBALL CLUB. Under the astute managership of Geoff Chapple, Woking have become one of the most consistent teams outside the four English divisions in recent years, consolidating their position in the Vauxhall Conference, enjoying spirited FA Cup runs and achieving the unusual feat of winning the FA Trophy in successive years 1994 and 1995. The club's ambitions do not lie dormant there, however, for there are advance plans to break into the Football League once suitable headquarters have been prodcued. Importantly the Cards have an excellent deal with the local Council. In addition to their Cup triumph in 1994-95, they were well in the hunt for championship honours in the League, finishing a creditable second in the final analysis.

AN EXCLUSIVE GOALSCORING CLUB

Hat-tricks are few and far between—last season there were less than 75 in Premier and Endsleigh League matches. Players scoring four or more goals in League football are naturally very rare. Usually less than five players manage four goals in a single match and last season just one player—Andy Cole of Manchester United—scored five, the first five in the top division since 1983.

Since the Football League was formed in 1888, there have been over 440,000 goals scored. A list of players scoring six goals or more in a single league match will take up far less room. The following players belong to this rather exclusive 'club'.

Name	Club	Date	Goals Scored	
Southworth	Everton	30/12/1893	Six	WBA
Capes Adr.	Bolton W	21/1/1895	Six	Walsall
McCairns	Grimsby T	11/4/1896	Six	Leicester F
Glover	Southport	22/10/1921	Six	Grimsby T
Duncan	Leicester C	25/12/1924	Six	Port Vale
Page	Burnley	10/4/1926	Six	Birmingham
Walsh	Bristol C	15/1/1927	Six	Gillingham
Cookson	WBA	17/9/1927	Six	Blackpool
Waring	Tranmere R	7/1/1928	Six	Durham C
Chandler	Leicester C	20/10/1928	Six	Portsmouth
Watson	West Ham U	9/2/1929	Six	Leeds U
Keetley	Doncaster R	16/2/1929	Six	Ashington
Whitehurst	Bradford C	6/3/1929	Seven	Tranmere R
Tippett	Rochdale	21/4/1930	Six	Hartlepool U
Cheesemuir	Gillingham	26/4/1930	Six	Merthyr T
Simpson	Crystal Palace	4/10/1930	Six	Exeter C
Bacon	Reading	3/4/1931	Six	Stoke C
Keetley	Lincoln C	16/1/1932	Six	Halifax T
Littlewood	Port Vale	24/9/1932	Six	Chesterfield
Drake	Arsenal	14/12/1935	Seven	Aston Villa
Bell	Tranmere R	26/12/1935	Nine	Oldham Ath
Payne	Luton T	13/4/1936	Ten	Bristol R
Hartson	Mansfield T	23/1/1937	Seven	Hartlepool U
Henson	Bradford PA	29/1/1938	Six	Blackburn R
Hunt	Sheffield W	19/11/1938	Six	Norwich C
Shackleton	Newcastle U	5/10/1946	Six	Newport Co
Graver	Lincoln C	29/9/1951	Six	Crewe Alex
Gemmell	Oldham Ath	19/1/1952	Seven	Chester
Briggs	Blackburn R	5/2/1955	Seven	Bristol R
Coleman	Stoke C	23/2/1957	Seven	Lincoln C
Lister	Oldham Ath	26/12/1962	Six	Southport
Hurst	West Ham U	19/10/1968	Six	Sunderland

This represents 32 occasions out of almost 150,000 League games since 1888. And the last time some 27 years ago.

The Association of Football Statisticians.

NUMBER OF PLAYERS SENT OFF IN ENGLISH LEAGUE MATCHES 1946–47 TO 1994–95

1946–47	12	1963–64	45	1980–81	107
1947–48	5	1964–65	46	1981–82	133
1948–49	10	1965–66	46	1982–83	221
1949–50	14	1966–67	50	1983–84	152
1950–51	7	1967–68	48	1984–85	165
1951–52	14	1968–69	51	1985–86	185
1952–53	15	1969–70	37	1986–87	193
1953–54	14	1970–71	28	1987–88	195
1954–55	13	1971–72	36	1988–89	172
1955–56	20	1972–73	83	1989–90	161
1956–57	15	1973–74	76	1990–91	202
1957–58	27	1974–75	97	1991–92	244
1958–59	20	1975–76	89	1992–93	226
1959–60	19	1976–77	100	1993–94	233
1960–61	18	1977–78	98	1994–95	314
1961–62	25	1978–79	108		
1962–63	35	1979–80	111		

MILESTONES DIARY 1994–95

June 1994

Spurs banished from Cup and docked 12pts in League . . . Celtic sack Lou Macari . . . 5-goal Oleg . . . Maradona chucked out of World Cup

13 FIFA deny Irish claims that players would not be allowed water during World Cup matches, maintaining that instructions insist only that they come to the touchline to drink.
14 Found guilty of financial irregularities, Spurs receive swingeing punishments from the FA - banishment from next season's FA Cup, 12 points deducted at the start of the Premiership season, and £600,000 fine. The Diadora League will be the first in the world to operate FIFA's 'kick-in' experiment.
15 Spurs chairman Alan Sugar accuses FA of a personal vendetta against him. Rangers complete the signing of Danish international Brian Laudrup from Fiorentina for 'quite a lot less than £3m', and Middlesbrough sign Villa's U-21 defender Neil Cox for £1m.
16 Celtic sack Lou Macari after less than 8 months in charge, citing his failure to move to Scotland as a major reason. Joao Havelange is re-elected FIFA president unopposed.
17 Holders Germany beat Bolivia 1-0 in the opening World Cup match (Chicago 3.00pm).
18 A Ray Houghton goal gives Ireland victory over Italy in their first World Cup match.
20 Hearts' new chairman Chris Robinson performs his first duty - sacking manager Sandy Clark.
21 Millwall are found guilty of misconduct regarding the pitch invasion in the play-off against Derby last month, but instead of the feared ground closure for the 6th time they receive a suspended (until December) punishment of two games behind closed doors, 3 League points deducted and a £100,000 fine to be imposed in the event of further serious misconduct.
22 Man City complete the signing of defender Nicky Summerbee, son of their former star Mike, from Swindon for £1.5m. In the World Cup, FIFA general secretary Sepp Blatter is unhappy about two things - some of the refereeing and Jack Charlton's attitude.
24 Ireland manager Jack Charlton is involved in row with FIFA official over delay in substitution of John Aldridge, who goes on to score a vital goal in their 2-1 defeat by Mexico.
25 Jack Charlton is banned by FIFA disciplinary committee from the touchline for Ireland's last group match and is fined £10,000, as is the Irish FA, and John Aldridge is fined £1,250, for the altercation during the game against Mexico.
27 Germany's manager Bertie Vogts sends Stefan Effenberg home from the World Cup after the aptly named midfielder shows his middle finger to German fans in their stuttering 3-2 victory over S.Korea.
28 Despite the sensational World Cup record of 5 goals achieved by Oleg Salenko in their 6-1 thrashing of Cameroon, Russia go out. Sweden striker Martin Dahlin, who has 3 goals to his credit, turns down a transfer from Borussia to Everton at the last moment after two weeks of negotiations.
29 FIFA announce that a World Cup player has tested positive for drugs, but refuse to name him or his country until the second sample is analysed.
30 FIFA drop a bombshell - the player whose second sample has now tested positive is Diego Maradona, and the Argentina captain is expelled from the tournament. Argentina are not punished, however, and even though they lose their evening match to Bulgaria, they go through to the 2nd round. Leeds sign Carlton Palmer from Sheff Wed for £2.6m and intend to use him in defence.

July

Colombian captain assassinated after own goal . . . Ireland out of World Cup . . . Blackburn sign Chris Sutton for record £5m . . . Brazil win 4th World Cup . . . Spurs sign World Cup stars Dumitrescu and Klinsmann

1 Maradona determines to fight possible life ban. Fans in Ireland have so far raised more than £100,000 to pay Jack Charlton's World Cup fine, but any money collected will go to charity.
2 Andreas Escobar, captain of the disappointingly eliminated Colombian team, is gunned down in a Medellin car park after his return home, apparently because of the own goal he scored in the match they lost to the USA.
4 The Irish World Cup bubble is burst as two defensive mistakes hand Holland a 2-0 victory in Orlando.
6 The FA Appeals Board reduce Tottenham's 12-point deduction to 6 points, but increase their fine from £600,000 to £1.5m and maintain their ban from next season's FA Cup. FIFA's disciplinary committee suspend Brazil left-back Leonardo for 4 matches, which rules him out of the World Cup finals.
8 FIFA president Joao Havelange denies there has been a FIFA conspiracy against Diego Maradona to wreck his career after the Argentine had failed a drug test.
9 Kilmarnock block Celtic's attempt to lure player-manager Tommy Burns back to Parkhead.
10 Norwich chairman Robert Chase announces that uncapped striker Chris Sutton is available at a British record £5m, provided the deal is ratified by next Friday (15th).
11 Man Utd bow out of the chase for Norwich's Chris Sutton, leaving Blackburn and Arsenal as favourites for his signature.

12 After studying video evidence, FIFA hand Italy's defender Mauro Tassotti an 8-game suspension and a £10,000 fine for elbowing Luis Enrique of Spain in the face, an off-the-ball incident that escaped punishment on the field. Kilmarnock's Tommy Burns is appointed Celtic manager.
13 Man Utd star Eric Cantona, working for French TV, is arrested at the Rose Bowl and misses the Brazil-Sweden semi-final after a scuffle with a Press Box official, but is released without being charged. In Norwich, Chris Sutton is arrested and spends a night in a police cell after an incident involving damage to a car outside a night club. Leeds agree a club record of £3m for Genoa's Czech international striker Tomas Skuhravy. Dutch winger Bryan Roy completes his £2.5m signing for Forest. Spurs keeper Erik Thorstvedt has a shoulder operation and will be out till October. Alex McLeish is confirmed as Motherwell manager.
14 Brazilian criminal Peralta, the mastermind behind the theft 9 years ago of the Jules Rimet Trophy - won outright by the last Brazilian team to reach the World Cup final (in 1970) and believed to have been melted down - is recaptured after 8 years on the run. Arsenal withdraw from the race for Chris Sutton, leaving the field to Blackburn.
15 Blackburn complete the signing of Chris Sutton from Norwich for £5m - at a reputed weekly salary of £12,000 - £1m more than the previous British record paid by Rangers for Duncan Ferguson.
17 Brazil become the first country to win 4 World Cups, beating Italy on penalties after a 0-0 draw.
20 In the draw for the new-style European Cup, seeded Man Utd find themselves in the same group as Barcelona, with a possible return clash with Galatasaray, who knocked them out last season.
21 Liverpool's new assistant manager is old-boy Doug Livermore, who resigned from Spurs earlier in the week.
22 England will play the USA in a friendly at Wembley on 7 September. Premiership debutants Leicester sign Notts County midfielder Mark Draper, the fee to go to tribunal.
25 Liverpool transfer-list midfielder Don Hutchison after his third disciplinary lapse in a year. Blackburn's David Batty will be out for about 3 months with a broken bone in his foot.
26 Spurs captain Gary Mabbutt, now fully recovered from the effects of John Fashanu's elbow, announces that he will not be taking legal action. Richard Thompson quits as chairman of QPR, retaining his controlling interest and his seat on the board, while director Peter Ellis takes his place. Peter Johnson is confirmed as Everton chairman. The proposed £3m transfer of Czech international Tomas Skuhravy from Genoa to Leeds has collapsed.
27 Ossie Ardiles finally gets to spend some of the £9m promised him by chairman Alan Sugar, as Spurs agree a fee with Steaua Bucharest of £2.6m for Romanian World Cup star Ilie Dumitrescu. Liverpool manager Roy Evans gets tough with his players after their 4-1 defeat by 1st Div Bolton in a friendly, pulling defenders Mark Wright and Julian Dicks out of the squad to tour Germany, the former for his 'attitude', the latter for his 'fitness'. Extrovert US World Cup defender Alexi Lalas punctures Coventry's hopes by signing for Padova, and will be the first American to play in the Italian League. A 10-day tournament is planned in England next summer called Euro 95, in which the 1996 European Championship hosts will compete with Brazil, Japan and 3 other countries.
28 Ardiles loses out in his quest for Brazilian World Cup defender Marcio Santos, who joins Fiorentina in Italy for about £2m. Former Chelsea manager Ian Porterfield leaves Zambia to take over as coach for Saudi Arabia.
29 Spurs' spending spree gathers momentum with the acquisition of German star World Cup striker Jurgen Klinsmann, 30, from Monaco for £2m.

August

West Ham discard Billy Bonds . . . Bruce Grobbelaar goes to Southampton . . . Spurs fraud inquiry dropped . . . Celtic fined for poaching manager . . . Rangers' early exit from Coca-Cola Cup

1 Wolves winger Tony Daley needs a cartilage op and will miss the start of the season. Scarborough sack manager Steve Wicks after 9 months. Liverpool defender Torben Piechnik returns to Denmark.
2 Everton sign unsettled Spurs midfielder Vinny Samways, 25, for £2.2m.
3 PSV Eindhoven sign teenage Brazilian international striker Ronaldo from Cruzeiro for £4m.
4 Wimbledon striker John Fashanu goes to Villa in a surprise £1.35m deal.
5 Man Utd tell Paul Ince to sign a new contract or leave the club. Arsenal announce record profits of £5.63m for a turnover of £21.5m, with commercial profits overtaking gate receipts for the first time. Bournemouth sack manager Tony Pulis. Former Newcastle midfielder Terry Hibbitt dies of cancer at 46.
6 Man United's Eric Cantona is sent off in the Ibrox pre-season tournament. Sampdoria beat Newcastle 3-1 in the final. Sheff Wed complete the signing of Romanian World Cup defender Dan Petrescu for £1.3m from Genoa.
7 Arsenal beat Napoli 1-0 to win the Makita tournament.
8 The dreadlocked Cobi Jones, US World Cup winger, joins Coventry for a fee to be agreed with the USSF, who hold his registration.
9 In the UEFA Cup Preliminary Round, Aberdeen draw away and Motherwell win 3-0 at home, but the Welsh and Irish clubs in action all lose.
10 After 27 years at Upton Park as player, coach and manager, Billy Bonds is asked to step down, with his place being taken by his assistant Harry Redknapp, who earlier in the week turned down the Bournemouth job. Newcastle complete the signing of Belgian World Cup defender Philippe Albert from Anderlecht for £2.6m. Rangers lose their preliminary round 1st leg European Cup tie 2-0 at AEK Athens, while Galatasaray's 5-1 victory over Avenir Beggen in Luxembourg virtually sets up another meeting with Man Utd. Hearts transfer-list captain Craig Levein and Graeme Hogg, who were sent off for fighting in a friendly against Raith, Hogg having to be stretchered off. Mario Zagalo takes over as Brazil coach for the third time.

11 Chelsea sign former England midfielder David Rocastle from Man City for £1.25m. Keeper Bruce Grobbelaar leaves Liverpool after 13 years to sign for Southampton. Newcastle fail to get a work permit for US keeper Brad Friedel.

12 The fraud inquiry into bribery allegations at Spurs involving England manager Terry Venables is finally dropped, removing also the clouds hanging over Brian Clough and Frank McLintock. Eric Cantona, who was fined 2 weeks' wages (£20,000) by Man Utd, is banned for 3 matches, while the Broadcast Advertising Clearance Centre ban, for being offensive, a Nike advert featuring Cantona making a 'four-letter boast' about his 'dirty tricks' on the field.

13 The English season starts with a full Endsleigh League programme but not the Premiership, and 10 players are dismissed, all in Divs 2 and 3. Hibs make the best start in the Scottish Premier with a 5-0 home win over Cup-winners Dundee Utd, whose manager Ivan Golac condemns referee Joe Timmins for sending off Alex Cleland - 9 players are booked, 6 of them from United. Motherwell's Rab Shannon is sent off at Ibrox and in the 5 Premier League matches 26 players are cautioned. The initial reaction to kick-ins in the Diadora League is unfavourable, and St Albans City general manager Allan Cockram threatens his players with substitution and fines if any opt for them.

14 Man Utd beat Blackburn 2-0 in the Charity Shield, Cantona scoring his 3rd penalty in consecutive games at Wembley. World Cup referee Philip Don flourishes 7 yellow cards.

15 Spurs will not start the season 6 points behind the rest of the Premiership, but will have the points deducted after the completion of the programme. Brechin City player-manager Ian Redford resigns as the result of their 5-1 home defeat by Meadowbank on Saturday.

16 Twelve players are sent off in 21 1st-round Coca-Cola Cup ties. Newcastle and Man Utd chairmen, Sir John Hall and Martin Edwards, launch scathing attacks on PFA chief Gordon Taylor for his claim that English clubs are bringing foreigners in to the detriment of national interests.

17 Apart from Aberdeen, who need a late goal to scrape through against Stranraer at Pittodrie, all the big guns in Scotland ease through the Coca-Cola Cup 2nd round, Rangers winning 6-1 at Arbroath, where Duncan Ferguson hits 3.

18 The Scottish League fine Celtic a record £100,000 for poaching Kilmarnock manager Tommy Burns. Sheff Wed sign full-back Ian Nolan from Tranmere for £1.5m.

19 Paul Ince finally re-signs for Man Utd, on a 3-year contract. A tribunal decides Leicester must pay Notts County £1.25m for midfielder Mark Draper.

20 The Premiership start is marked by a 6-1 Liverpool win at Palace. Champions Man Utd beat QPR 2-0, both sides finishing with 10 men. Jurgen Klinsmann scores in Spurs' 4-3 win at Hillsborough. Wendy Toms is the Football League's first female linesman, officiating at the Torquay-Carlisle match in Div 3. After only two games, Rangers are the only 100% side in the Scottish Premier.

21 Newcastle begin their Premiership programme with a 3-1 win at Leicester.

22 Man Utd draw 1-1 at Forest. Newcastle's Peter Beardsley and Palace's Ray Wilkins expect to be out for several weeks with cheekbone and foot fractures, respectively.

23 Aberdeen make a shock exit from the UEFA Cup in the Preliminary Round, losing on away goals to Skonto Riga (Latvia) after a 1-1 draw at Pittodrie, but Motherwell steam through 7-1 on aggregate over Havnar Boltfelag in the Faroes. Of the Irish and Welsh sides, only Linfield progress. Man Utd fine Paul Ince and he is warned about conduct in the Charity Shield match in which he 'overdid' celebrations after scoring. £5m Chris Sutton scores his first for Blackburn in their 3-0 Premiership defeat of Leicester.

24 FIFA slap their second 15-month ban on Diego Maradona since 1991, for testing positive for drugs during the World Cup in June. AEK Athens win 1-0 at Ibrox to put Rangers out of the European Cup in the Preliminary Round. Newcastle beat Coventry 4-0 to go top of the Premiership after two games, on goal difference above Spurs, for whom Klinsmann scores both goals in their 2-1 defeat of Everton. Other 100% teams, Liverpool and Chelsea do not have a game. Barcelona fine Brazilian star Romario £50,000 for returning 3 weeks late from the World Cup. Sheff Utd have 3 players sent off at Bramall Lane in an Anglo-Italian Cup match against Udinese.

25 Sligo Rovers reach the 1st round of the Cup-Winners' Cup with a 3-2 aggregate victory over Floriana of Malta, but Barry Town and Bangor City are hammered out.

26 Norwich sign Man City forward Mike Sheron for £1m.

27 Chairman Alan Sugar states that England coach Terry Venables is still persona non grata at Spurs, after manager Ossie Ardiles had yesterday said he was welcome. Newcastle go 2pts clear in the Premiership after beating Southampton 5-1, Spurs losing 1-0 at home to Man Utd. Chris Sutton scores a hat-trick in Blackburn's 4-0 defeat of Coventry. Leicester are still pointless. Everton complete the £3m signing of Nigeria's World Cup striker Daniel Amokachi, 21, from Bruges. Hibs go top of the Scottish Premier on goal difference over Celtic, whose 2-0 win at Ibrox ruins Rangers 100% record.

28 Liverpool retain their 100% Premiership record after 2 matches as Robbie Fowler hits all 3 in their 3-0 win over Arsenal.

29 West Ham sign Liverpool's troubled midfielder Don Hutchison for £1.5m. The Scottish FA fine Dundee £10,000 for their poor disciplinary record, doubling last year's similar punishment.

30 Terry Venables, who brings John Barnes back into the England reckoning and introduces Newcastle midfielder Robert Lee into the squad for the match with USA, dismisses as outrageous Alan Sugar's claims that he hired a PR company to stage a demonstration against the Spurs chairman. Forest go top of the Premiership with a 2-1 win at Everton, and Klinsmann scores another 2 for Spurs who move up to 3rd with a 3-1 win at Ipswich.

31 Newcastle go back to the Premiership summit with a 3-1 win at West Ham, while both Chelsea and Liverpool maintain their 100% records. There are shocks galore in the Scottish Coca-Cola Cup as Rangers go down 2-1 at home to Falkirk and Premier clubs Hearts, Motherwell and Kilmarnock all go out to Div 1 sides.

September

Littlewoods to sponsor FA Cup . . . Liverpool spend £7m on two defenders . . . Billy Wright of England and Wolves dies . . . Newcastle win first 6 in Premiership . . . Blackburn out of UEFA Cup

1 The FA Cup is to be sponsored in a 4-year deal with Pools giants Littlewoods out of which Wembley will take a considerable - though undisclosed - share. The competition will be called, officially, 'The FA Cup, sponsored by Littlewoods Pools'. Liverpool pay Coventry £3.75m for Irish World Cup central defender Phil Babb, who becomes the most expensive defender in British football. Mel Machin, 49, former Man City manager, takes over the job at Bournemouth, replacing Tony Pulis.

2 Liverpool take spending on their central defence to nearly £7m in 24 hours as John Scales joins them from Wimbledon for £3m. Two Div 3 managers are sacked, Kenny Hibbit of Walsall and Kenny Swain of Wigan. UEFA fine AEK Athens £25,000 for the violent behaviour of their fans at their European Cup match with Rangers in August.

3 Billy Wright, former England and Wolves captain, first man to win 100 caps, dies at 70. There are no Premier division matches because of England and Scotland's midweek matches. Preston, the last English team to play on 'plastic', beat Lincoln 4-0 in the first match on their new grass pitch.

6 Venables gives Newcastle's Barry Venison his first England cap, against the USA tomorrow. An exchange deal sees striker Tony Cottee back at West Ham together with an undisclosed sum, while David Burrows returns to Merseyside, to Everton.

7 Ireland and Scotland enjoy good away victories over Latvia and Finland respectively in European Championship qualifiers, while Wales beat Albania, but N.Ireland go down 2-1 at home to Portugal. Alan Shearer scores both goals in England's comfortable 2-0 defeat of the USA at Wembley. Vinny Jones takes over the Wimbledon captaincy from transfer-seeking Dean Holdsworth.

8 Stoke and manager Joe Jordan agree to part company. Spurs' profits last season slumped to less than £0.9m from £3.4m the previous year owing largely to the big FA fine and a deficit on transfer deals.

9 Spurs take their summer spending on foreign stars to £7.5m with the signing for £2.9m from Dutch side PSV of another Romanian World Cup star, central defender Gheorge Popescu, 26, while Sheff Wed complete the signing, from the same club, of Sweden's midfielder Klas Ingesson for £2m. Man Utd get £2m for striker Dion Dublin from Coventry, double what they paid Cambridge Utd in 1992 for a player who has started only 4 League games for them. Celtic break their club record by paying £1.75m for Motherwell midfielder Phil O'Donnell. Hartlepool manager of less than a year John MacPhail is sacked. Man City's new youth coach Neil McNab is banned for 5 weeks for abusing the referee after his first game in charge. National captain Eric Cantona is in trouble with the French Football Federation for his belligerent attitude to the French press in midweek.

10 Newcastle make it 5 wins out of 5 with a 4-2 victory at St James' Park to destroy Chelsea's 100% record, and Liverpool lose theirs when they are surprisingly held at Anfield 0-0 by West Ham, who have Tony Cottee sent off after 55min. This leaves Newcastle with the only 100% record in the League. Wimbledon's new captain Vinnie Jones is sent off, but they notch their first win as Leicester lose two players and the match 2-1 - all in the first half.

11 Pre-publication extracts from Terry Venables' autobiography reopen the dispute with Spurs chairman Alan Sugar. Leeds beat Man Utd 2-1 at Elland Road, their first victory over the champions for 13 matches that go back to the early 1980s.

13 Newcastle make a sensational return to Europe after 17 years with a brilliant 5-0 victory in the UEFA Cup over Royal Antwerp in Belgium, midfielder Robert Lee hitting a hat-trick, but Blackburn lose on their European debut 1-0 at home to Trelleborgs of Sweden.

14 Man Utd enjoy a convincing 4-2 win at Old Trafford over IFK Gothenburg in their first Champions League Group A match. Notts Co sack manager Mick Walker. Archie Gemmill and John McGovern are confirmed as the new managerial team at Rotherham in place of Phil Henson, who becomes chief executive.

15 Paul Merson scores 2 as Arsenal begin their defence of the Cup-Winners' Cup with a 3-1 victory over Omonia Nicosia in Cyprus, while Chelsea beat Czech side Viktoria Zizkov 4-2. Dundee Utd beat Tatran Presov of Slovakia 3-2 at Tannadice Park. In the UEFA Cup, Villa return from Milan 1-0 down to Inter. Everton's long-drawn-out efforts to sign Brazilian star Muller collapse at Goodison when they refuse to pay his annual tax bill. Assistant manager Russell Slade moves up to take the vacant manager's post at Notts Co. Hereford manager Greg Downs leaves by mutual agreement and assistant John Layton takes over.

17 With Newcastle engaged tomorrow, Forest miss their chance to sneak top spot in the Premiership when they only draw at The Dell, and Man Utd beat Liverpool 2-0 to go 3rd. The last two pointless teams in the League, Bournemouth and Chester of Div 2, draw 1-1. Celtic are still the only unbeaten side in the Scottish Premier League, but a home draw with bottom club Kilmarnock allows Rangers to go top.

18 Newcastle beat Arsenal 3-2 at Highbury to make it 6 out of 6 and take a 4-pt lead in the Premiership over Blackburn, who win 2-1 at Chelsea.

20 In Coca-Cola Cup 2nd round first-leg matches, three Div 3 sides enjoy home wins over Premiership clubs, Barnet 1-0 over Man City with a goal by Dougie Freedman in 27sec, Walsall 2-1 over West Ham, and Lincoln 1-0 over Palace. Premiership bottom club Everton lose 3-2 at home to Div 1 Portsmouth. Dane Whitehouse scores 3 for Sheff Utd in their 5-1 victory at Stockport. Raith reach the semi-finals of the Scottish Coca-Cola Cup.

21 Wednesday night thrills in the Coca-Cola Cup include Jurgen Klinsmann's hat-trick in Spurs' 6-3 win at Watford, the 1-0 home defeat of Leeds by Mansfield, 4th from bottom of the League, and Div 1 Bolton's 3-0 win at Ipswich. Arsenal away to Hartlepool and Villa at home to Wigan make their 2nd legs redundant with 5-0 victories. Leicester go down 1-0 at Brighton of Div 2. Man Utd manager Alec Ferguson, controversially fielding a largely inexperienced young side at Port Vale, justifies his

selection with a 2-1 victory despite going behind in the first minute. In the Scottish Coca-Cola Cup, Div 1 Airdrie, who win 2-1 at Hibs, reach the semi-finals along with Celtic and Aberdeen. Injury-plagued Gary Lineker will retire from Japanese football in November and join the BBC.

22 As Terry Venables launches his autobiography, Alan Sugar says he will not be allowed into the Spurs ground until he apologises for 'slagging' Sugar off and stops suing for wrongful dismissal.

23 Liverpool spoil Newcastle's 100% record in the Premiership with a 1-1 draw at St James' Park. The other two unbeaten sides win to move within 2pts of the leaders, Blackburn beating Villa 3-1 and Forest winning 4-1 at Spurs. Man Utd go down to a shock 3-2 defeat at Ipswich. Newcastle finally sign striker Paul Kitson from Derby for £2.25 after prolonged negotiations. Celtic go back to the top of the Scottish Premier.

27 Blackburn, costing some £27m, go out of the UEFA Cup to a team of Swedish part-timers as Trelleborgs, playing most of the second half with 10 men, score 5min from time to earn a draw and win 3-2 on aggregate. It's a different story at St James' Park, where Andy Cole is the hat-trick man this time as the Magpies slam Antwerp 5-2 for a 10-2 aggregate. But the European hero of the night is Fabrizi Ravanelli, who scores all 5 as Juventus thrash CSKA Sofia 5-1 (7-4 on agg). In the Coca-Cola Cup, Swindon stage a splendid recovery with a 4-1 win at Charlton after extra time and a 5-4 aggregate victory, Norwegian striker Jan-Aage Fjortoft scoring 3. Belgium and Holland will co-host the European Championship in 2000.

28 Man Utd come through their intimidating Euro tie in Turkey unscathed with a 0-0 draw against Galatasaray and lead Group A as Gothenburg beat Barcelona 2-1. After two matches, the only 100% sides are Paris St Germain and Ajax Amsterdam. Holders AC Milan beat Salzburg 3-0 but face an inquiry after the Austrian keeper is hit by a bottle from the crowd. In the UEFA Cup, Motherwell lose 2-0 at home to Borussia Dortmund and go out 3-0 on aggregate. Transfer-listed Hearts players Craig Levein and Graeme Hogg are now banned for 10 matches by the SFA for their violent brawl in a friendly last month.

29 Villa beat Inter Milan on penalties after a nail-biting 1-0 victory and go through to the 2nd Round of the UEFA Cup. Chelsea earn a safe passage in the Cup-Winners' Cup with a goalless away draw, while Arsenal ease through 6-1 on aggregate. Lou Macari is appointed manager of Stoke for the second time. Portsmouth defender Andy Awford is out for the season with a multiple fracture of his leg sustained last night in a Div 1 match at West Brom.

30 Man Utd announce pre-tax profits of £10.7m to the year ending 31 July.

October

Tony Adams captains England . . . Raich Carter dies . . . John Aldridge scores goal No.400 . . . English fair play earns extra UEFA Cup place . . . Terry Venables again attacked in *Panorama*

1 Thursday's European victors Arsenal and Villa lose at home in the Premiership, the latter 2-0 to Newcastle, who extend their lead to 5pts as Blackburn lose their unbeaten record at Norwich. In Palace's first win of the season and first League victory at Highbury, Ian Wright scores his 100th goal for Arsenal against his old club. Steve McManaman hits a second-half hat-trick as Liverpool beat Sheff Wed 4-1. In the Scottish Premier, Rangers regain the lead from Celtic.

2 Forest go 2nd in the Premiership, 2pts behind Newcastle, with a 3-2 win over QPR.

3 Terry Venables makes Arsenal's Tony Adams captain of England for the first time, in the absence of injured David Platt, and includes Newcastle's in-form midfielder Robert Lee in his squad for the game against Romania, but there is controversy about the omission of Andy Cole, who feels his manager Kevin Keegan has exaggerated his shin-splints injury to the England coach. Leicester PRO Alan Birchenall strongly criticises the referee over the PA system at Filbert Street at half-time after the dismissal of a player from each side in the 2-2 draw with Coventry. Bottom Premiership club Everton sign two Glasgow Rangers players on loan - Ian Durrant for 1 month, after his transfer collapsed when he failed a medical, and £4m striker Duncan Ferguson for 3 months.

4 Lowly Div 3 club Mansfield knock Leeds out of the Coca-Cola Cup, holding them 0-0 at Field Mill to retain their 1-0 advantage from the 1st leg. Watford embarrass Spurs with a 3-2 win at White Hart Lane but lose 8-6 on aggregate.

5 Three Premiership teams go out of the Coca-Cola Cup to Div 1 sides - Everton to Portsmouth, Leicester to Brighton and Ipswich to Bolton - while Man City and West Ham reverse their 1st-leg deficits against Barnet and Walsall respectively. Matt Le Tissier scores all 4 for Southampton as they beat Huddersfield 5-0 on aggregate.

6 The FA have sent videos of matches to referees asking for comments on certain incidents they are unhappy with.

8 Forest draw 3-3 at Man City to climb to within a point of Newcastle, who play tomorrow.

9 Newcastle retain their unbeaten record in the Premiership with a late goal from Steve Howey to draw 1-1 with Blackburn at St James' Park, but Peter Beardsley has to withdraw from the England squad with a thigh strain. Liverpool's Steve McManaman replaces the injured Darren Anderton in the squad.

10 Raich Carter, legendary England, Sunderland and Derby inside-forward, dies at 80.

11 Liverpool's Jamie Redknapp scores a hat-trick for England Under-21s as they beat Austria 3-1 in Kapfenberg in Group 6 of the European U-21 Championship, but club-mate Robbie Fowler is sent off for dissent. Wales U-21s lose 1-0 in Moldova. Northampton play their last match at the County Ground. Wimbledon sign Nigerian striker Efan Ekoku from Norwich for £1m.

12 Robert Lee keeps Venables' unbeaten record intact with the equaliser in England's 1-1 draw with Romania at Wembley, in which Matt Le Tissier also makes his debut. In European Championship qualifiers, Scotland and Ireland enjoy easy wins against Faroe Is and Liechtenstein respectively and N.Ireland a splendid 2-1 victory in Austria, but a depleted Wales are beaten 3-2 in Moldova.

14 UEFA dock AC Milan 2pts from their Champions League total for the bottle-throwing incident but allow the result, a 3-0 win over Casino Salzburg, to stand. They must also play their next two home matches in the tournament at least 185 miles from Milan.

15 A Peter Beardsley goal in the 89th minute gives Newcastle a 1-0 win at Palace, their 5th away victory out of 5, and stretches their Premiership lead to 5pts. Blackburn beat Liverpool 3-2 to go 2nd, above Forest who play on Monday. Man City hold out for a 2-1 win at QPR despite playing the last 14min with 9 men and a replacement keeper. Everton, still winless, lose 2-0 at home to Coventry and are 4pts adrift at the bottom. John Aldridge scores the 400th goal of his career in a hat-trick for Tranmere. Celtic, beaten at Hearts, lose the last unbeaten record in the Scottish Premier.

17 Forest beat Wimbledon 3-1 and close the gap at the top to 3pts. West Brom sack manager Keith Burkinshaw after exactly a year of his 4-year contract.

18 In the UEFA Cup 2nd round, Newcastle are pegged back from 3-0 at St James' Park by 2 late goals from Athletic Bilbao, while Villa incur a 1-0 deficit to Trabzonspor in Turkey. Everton reveal they are paying Rangers £35,000 a week for the loan of Duncan Ferguson in addition to his wages (probably £5,000 a week).

19 Lee Sharpe earns Man Utd a 2-2 draw with Barcelona in a classic at Old Trafford and they retain their lead in Group A on goal difference over IFK, who beat Galatasaray 1-0. Paris retain their 100% record in Group B. The FA reduce to a caution the sending-off of Spurs defender Kevin Scott against QPR 11 days ago after seeing a video of the incident and asking the referee to reconsider.

20 Holders Arsenal come away from Copenhagen with a 2-1 edge over Brondby in the 2nd round of the Cup-Winners' Cup, but Chelsea are held 0-0 at home by Austria Vienna. Alan Buckley leaves Grimsby to become the new West Brom manager, their 11th in 13 years. After 13 mostly unhappy months at Anfield, full-back Julian Dicks moves back to West Ham.

21 The first UEFA Fair Play Ranking List, produced from club and national fixtures, recognizes England, Norway and Luxembourg for their sportsmanlike conduct, and the three associations are awarded an extra place in next season's UEFA Cup, upping England's contingent to 4. But the winner of the Coca-Cola Cup will cease to qualify in 3 years' time - unless the domestic championship has been limited to 34 matches (18-team league). Rangers striker Duncan Ferguson's court hearing on an assault charge is postponed till 9 Jan, so he will be able to complete his loan period with Everton.

22 Newcastle and Forest both win, so the gap at the top of the Premiership is still 2pts. Spurs suffer another heavy defeat, 5-2 at Man City, and Everton are still stranded at the bottom after their 4th straight defeat, 1-0 at Palace, puts more pressure on manager Mike Walker.

23 Referee Gerald Ashby has Kenny Dalglish fuming when he awards Man Utd a penalty and sends off Henning Berg just before half time, enabling Cantona to equalise from the spot and United eventually to win 4-2, ruining Blackburn's 100% home record and jumping above them into 3rd place. Ian Wright hits both of Arsenal's goals in their 2-1 defeat of Coventry, making it his 10th consecutive game on Arsenal's scoresheet to beat their record set in 1931 by David Jack, but his 7th booking of the season earns him a 3-match ban and a groin injury puts him out at half-time.

24 The Football League decide not to fine Man Utd for fielding weakened teams in their 2nd round Coca-Cola ties, and are to recommend that clubs involved in European competition should be exempt in future until the 3rd round.

25 In the Coca-Cola Cup 3rd round, Kevin Gallen scores for QPR after 13sec, but in-form Man City come away from Loftus Road with a 4-3 win. In the semi-final of the Scottish equivalent at Perth, Raith beat Airdrie 5-4 on penalties to reach their first final since 1948-49.

26 Notts Co humiliate Spurs 3-0 in the Coca-Cola Cup, any chance Spurs had of clawing back an early 2-0 deficit disappearing when Dumitrescu is sent off after 36min - the knives are out for manager Ossie Ardiles. In the big tie of the round, at St James' Park, Newcastle beat an again under-strength Man Utd 2-0 with goals in the last 10min. Celtic central defender Brian O'Neil scores in extra time against Aberdeen at Ibrox to take them into the Scottish Coca-Cola Cup final.

27 FIFA decree that from next season all member countries' domestic leagues must employ the 3pts for a win system. In FIFA's distribution of the 8 extra places for the 1998 World Cup finals in France, the zones Europe, Africa and Asia/Oceania have been allotted two places each, and South America and Concacaf one each.

28 Newcastle's Andy Cole is sidelined for a month to rest his troublesome shin splints.

29 Saturday sees the clash of the top 4 in the Premiership and something has to give - it turns out to be the last two unbeaten records in the League, as Newcastle go down 2-0 at Old Trafford and Forest 2-0 at home to Blackburn. The positions stay the same, but now there are only 6pts between 1st and 5th, as Liverpool win 3-1 at Ipswich to come into contention with still a game in hand. Spurs beat West Ham 3-1, but there seems little hope for manager Ossie Ardiles, who has to face a board meeting on Thursday. Beleaguered Mike Walker at Everton is in a similar position, as they grab a rare point at Goodison from Arsenal, but Albion Rovers' victory in the Scots Div 3 leaves the Toffeemen as the only team in Britain without a win. In Div 2, Linton Brown hits a 7min 2nd-half hat-trick as Hull blast Crewe 7-1. With Rangers playing tomorrow, Hibs and Motherwell overtake them at the top of the Scottish Premier.

30 Rangers beat Celtic 3-1 at Parkhead to go back on top in Scotland.

31 New allegations of financial chicanery are levelled at England coach Terry Venables in a second BBC *Panorama* investigation, which accuses him of unlawfully obtaining over £430,000 which he used in connection with purchasing Tottenham shares. QPR's Les Ferdinand, back after a 3-match suspension, punctures Liverpool's revival with a late winner at Loftus Road.

November
Ossie Ardiles and Mike Walker out, Gerry Francis and Joe Royle in . . . Bruce Grobbelaar in bribe allegations . . . Ron Atkinson out, Brian Little in . . . Paul Merson confesses to drug, drink and gambling problems . . . Raith Rovers win Coca-Cola Cup

1 Inevitably, Ossie Ardiles is sacked from the Spurs job, learning the news last night at chairman Alan Sugar's home, and assistant manager Steve Perryman becomes caretaker manager. Ardiles had 3 years of his contract to run, and should get over £500,000 in compensation. The FA stand by Terry Venables despite allegations on *Panorama*. Villa and Newcastle both go out of the UEFA Cup on away goals. Everton chalk up their first Premiership win, 1-0 over West Ham at Goodison, but is it too late for Mike Walker?

2 Man Utd are humbled and outclassed 4-0 by Barcelona at the Nou Camp as World Cup stars Stoichkov and Romario run riot, and with Gothenburg winning in Turkey, United are now 3rd in their group of the Champions League with an awful lot to do. Paris qualify for the last 8. In the Premiership, Blackburn win 1-0 at Sheff Wed to go 2nd. On the managerial front, QPR's Gerry Francis was expected to resign because the offer of the post of chief executive (with full control over transfers) to former star Rodney Marsh would compromise the manager's job - but he doesn't. Villa chairman Doug Ellis goes on air to give his manager a vote of confidence - which must have Ron Atkinson worried. And Derby fans turn on manager Roy McFarland after the Rams lose 2-1 at home to improving Reading.

3 Both London clubs get through to the 3rd round of the Cup-Winners' Cup, Arsenal getting a fright at Highbury as Brondby draw 2-2 but winning 4-3 on aggregate, and Chelsea winning on away goals. QPR back down over Marsh and won't accept Francis's resignation. Former Spurs manager David Pleat, now with Luton, has talks at White Hart Lane.

5 At the top of the Premiership, Newcastle and Blackburn both win.

6 Man Utd put their Barcelona defeat behind them and win 2-1 at Villa to go 3rd in the Premiership.

7 Forest and Newcastle play out an entertaining goalless draw at the City Ground, so the Magpies extend their lead over Blackburn in the Premiership to 3pts. The Premier League launch a code to prevent the practice of managers moving to another club without the consent of their employers. Paul Gascoigne has some pins removed and sets a spring comeback target.

8 The sensational claim published in the *Sun* that Southampton keeper Bruce Grobbelaar has taken bribes to fix matches almost obscures the news of Mike Walker's sacking as Everton manager. Ironically, the two clubs, Everton and Spurs, who have been fined in the last year for seducing managers from other clubs, have now given those managers the chop within a week of each other. Southend chairman Vic Jobson warns that 16 clubs are about to serve notice on the Football League to form an elite First Division attached to the FA Premiership.

9 The Grobbelaar bribe allegations, which go back to 1992 and refer to specific matches involving former club Liverpool as well as Southampton and involve Malaysian betting syndicates, have caused a furore, and the FA promise a swift investigation. Meanwhile Liverpool take advantage of their game in hand, beating Chelsea 3-1 to move up to 3rd in the Premiership, 4pts behind Newcastle. In Coca-Cola Cup replays, all three home teams reach the 4th round, Arsenal, Swindon and Norwich, who come back from 2-0 down to beat Tranmere 4-2. Rangers draw at Hearts to take a 3pt lead in the Scottish Premier. Dutch star Ruud Gullit leaves AC Milan after 2 months and returns to Sampdoria.

10 While hysteria mounts over the Grobbelaar 'scandal', with the police to open an inquiry and the accused denying any wrongdoing as he flies out to play for Zimbabwe, Aston Villa sack manager Ron Atkinson and Everton appoint their former star striker Joe Royle. Meanwhile, a most significant move is made at the top end of the Premiership, Man Utd using their game in hand to thrash neighbours City 5-0 at Old Trafford (Kanchelskis 3) - their biggest ever derby win - to go 2nd, just 2pts behind Newcastle. FA chairman Sir Bert Millichip is appointed to FIFA's World Cup Organising Committee. Newcastle's uncapped defender Steve Howey is drafted into the England squad in place of the injured Tony Adams.

11 David Pleat decides not to join Spurs as general manager and Gerry Francis, now granted his release from QPR, is the new favourite for the job. Villa are fined £9,000 for the pitch invasion after their UEFA Cup defeat by Trabzonspor, who are fined £6,000. The FA inform FIFA that Bruce Grobbelaar will not be suspended pending a hearing, and FIFA clear him to play for Zimbabwe.

12 With no Premier games, the 1st Round of the FA Cup takes centre stage, and Enfield and Kingstonian are non-League conquerors of League sides Cardiff and Brighton respectively. Paul Miller scores 4 in Bristol Rovers' 5-0 win at Bath, Ashley Ward 3 in Crewe's 7-1 thrashing of Gresley, and Martin Foyle 3 in Div 1 Port Vale's 6-0 beating of Hartlepool. Barnet come back from a 3-0 half-time deficit at Underhill to draw 4-4 with Woking. Sheff Utd chairman Reg Brealey announces at half-time in their 2-1 victory over Derby that the club is up for sale.

13 More giant-killing in the FA Cup as Marlow - 3rd from bottom of the Diadora League - knock out neighbours Oxford United with 2 goals from John Caesar.

14 After studying documents and videos provided by the *Sun* and coming to the conclusion that there is a case to answer, the FA charge Bruce Grobbelaar with offences relating to match-fixing, but do not suspend him and stress that he is innocent until proved guilty. Bristol City sack manager Russell Osman.

15 Gerry Francis signs a one-year rolling contract as manager of Spurs, making his first act to dispense with the services of caretaker-manager Steve Perryman, while Ray Wilkins takes over at former club QPR as player-manager. Joe Jordan also returns to manage a former club, Bristol City. Newcastle suffer another injury blow, midfielder Scott Sellars out for 6-8 weeks after a knee op. Sheff Wed

captain Des Walker is banned for 3 matches and fined £1,200, having been found guilty of misconduct regarding his dismissal at Ipswich.

16 Terry Venables' gamble on Dennis Wise pays off as the Chelsea forward is instrumental in England's 1-0 victory over African champions Nigeria at Wembley in a friendly in which Newcastle's Steve Howey and Liverpool's Neil Ruddock win their first caps and Steve McManaman wins his as a 25min sub. In European Championship qualifiers, Wales are humiliated 5-0 in Georgia, but no less so than Italy, who go down 2-1 at home to Croatia, or Belgium, held at home by Macedonia. The Republic beat N.Ireland 4-0 in Belfast, but Scotland can only draw 1-1 with Russia at Hampden Park. Oldham striker Graeme Sharp is appointed player-manager of the club.

17 Leicester chairman Martin George demands £1.5m compensation from Villa if they want his manager Brian Little and two assistants. Quashing rumours, Football League president Gordon McKeag states that neither the FA nor the Premier League would sanction the formation of a 2nd Division. As a result of the 3rd meeting with referees, players and managers, the Premier League announce a plan designed to cut out the two-footed tackle and provide more consistency in the application of the laws, especially the punishments for tackles from behind and player dissent.

19 With most of Saturday's interest elsewhere, Man Utd beat Palace 3-0 at Old Trafford to go top of the Premiership, a point in front of Blackburn, who win 3-1 at Ipswich, and Newcastle, who go down 3-2 at Wimbledon and lose 1st place for the first time since the start of the season. Wimbledon captain Vinnie Jones is sent off again, 15min from time. The media crowd into The Dell, where Bruce Grobbelaar puts on an immaculate performance, watches Paul Dickov put a penalty over his bar and sees Southampton beat Arsenal 1-0. Elsewhere, the new managers have a mixed day, Gerry Francis watching Spurs stage a magnificent recovery from 3-0 down to managerless Villa at White Hart Lane only for Dean Saunders to spoil it with a last-minute winner, while his old side QPR, now under Ray Wilkins, beat Leeds 3-2. In Scotland, Falkirk draw with Rangers at Ibrox fielding a debut-making goalkeeper - for his 21st club in England and Scotland - 42-year-old John Burridge.

20 Leicester, under reluctant manager Brian Little, lose 1-0 at home to Man City and stay 2nd from bottom of the Premiership. In the crucial Div 1 clash at Ayresome Park, Middlesbrough beat Wolves 1-0 to take their place at the top.

21 Joe Royle could not have wished for a better start at Goodison as Everton - with keeper Neville Southall making a record 35th Merseyside derby appearance and on-loan striker Duncan Ferguson scoring his first goal for the club - beat Liverpool 2-0 and climb off the bottom of the Premiership. John Lyall, manager of 2nd-bottom club Ipswich, is ominously given a vote of confidence by chairman John Kerr. Div 1 Swindon sack manager John Gorman.

22 Leicester manager Brian Little resigns for 'personal' reasons. In FA Cup 1st round replays, non-League Hitchin and Woking beat League opposition, Hereford (4-2) and Barnet (1-0) respectively, but Yeading come a 7-1 cropper at Colchester. Bury need penalties to beat Bishop Auckland, and Fulham extra time to account for Ashford 5-3. Bobby Davison scores a 10sec goal in Rotherham's 3-0 win over York.

23 Man Utd, with Paul Ince sent off late on, go down 3-1 in Gothenburg and only Barcelona's shock 2-1 defeat by Galatasaray leaves the Reds with just a chance of reaching the knock-out stage of the European Cup. Ajax clinch their place in the last 8, beating AC Milan - whose home tie is played in Trieste - 2-0, and the Italian club must win their remaining game to go through. Managerless Leicester lift themselves off the bottom of the Premiership by beating Arsenal 2-1.

25 Arsenal's England international Paul Merson, 26, confesses in the *Daily Mirror* that he has been taking cocaine for about a year, has been on 8-hour drinking binges and has amassed huge gambling debts: the FA's first reaction is to provide help rather than take immediate disciplinary action, while his club also promise total support. Spurs may be allowed to play in the Cup after all, as the independent arbiters studying their punishment for irregular payments rule that an FA commission must reassess the penalties imposed. Brian Little is named as Villa's new manager. Meanwhile, the FA, in the shape of chief executive Graham Kelly and England coach Terry Venables, unveil a far-reaching plan for raising the standards of English football, including the creation of a post for a technical director in charge of long-term strategy. Man Utd announce an £11.45m trading profit. In Scotland, Rangers beat Aberdeen to boost their lead over Motherwell to 4pts, at least until tomorrow.

26 Blackburn go top of the Premiership after beating QPR 4-0 helped by an Alan Shearer hat-trick, while Man Utd draw 0-0 at Highbury and to compound a week's misery have Mark Hughes sent off near the end.

27 Raith Rovers of Scottish Div 1 win their first major trophy, beating Celtic 6-5 on penalties after a 2-2 draw at Ibrox to take the Coca-Cola Cup and leave the Glasgow giants 5 years without one.

28 More grief for Arsenal as the Premier League look into allegations in a book published in Denmark that a top official received payment as part of the John Jensen transfer deal in 1992; other Scandinavian transfers are also being looked into. Man City's midfielder Steve McMahon is appointed Swindon player-manager. Cardiff sack manager Eddie May, and Rochdale Dave Sutton.

29 Brian Laws is the new manager of Grimsby.

30 Ian Rush celebrates his 600th appearance for Liverpool by scoring a hat-trick as they win 3-1 at Blackburn in the 4th round of the Coca-Cola Cup. Forest and West Ham both suffer two-goal home defeats to Div 1 sides, Millwall and, inevitably, Bolton, respectively. A goal down at half-time, Palace come back to smash Villa 4-1, while Steve Morrow scores in Arsenal's 2-0 win over Sheff Wed at Highbury - his only other goal for Arsenal having been the winner against the same side in the 1993 final. The Scottish FA and League agree a £10.5m deal with Sky TV for the screening of 17 League and Cup matches a season.

December

Paul Merson escapes punishment . . . John Lyall forced out at Ipswich . . . Man Utd out of European Cup . . . Spurs reinstated . . . George Graham 'bung' allegations . . . Everton sign Duncan Ferguson for £4m . . . John Jensen scores for Arsenal!

1 After a meeting with Paul Merson and club and PFA representatives, the FA decide to take no action against the errant Arsenal forward, although he must undergo a 4-6 week rehabilitation programme away from home. On the basis of a long-dead Welsh grandfather, Watford-born Vinnie Jones of Wimbledon is drafted into the Welsh international squad. Martin O'Neill turns down the Leicester job to stay with Wycombe.

2 Preston manager John Beck resigns rather than change his notorious long-ball game, and his assistant Gary Peters is appointed in his place. Arsenal captain Tony Adams has an Achilles op and will be out for 2 months, while striker Ian Wright's goal against Newcastle in September is validated by the Premier League giving him a club record of scoring in 12 consecutive League and Cup matches.

3 Blackburn's splendid 3-0 win at Wimbledon keeps them a point ahead of Man Utd in the Premiership, but Newcastle slip back again, 4pts adrift, after losing 4-2 at Spurs, where Teddy Sheringham hits 3. Brian Little's immediate return to Leicester with his new club Aston Villa brings a 1-1 draw - and a constant stream of abuse from the fans directed at the former manager. Chris Waddle comes on as a 75th-min sub for Sheff Wed, his first League appearance of the year after a long-term injury. In Div 1, new Swindon player-manager Steve McMahon is sent off in his first match as his side lose 2-0 at Southend. In Scotland, Div 1 bottom club Stranraer are hammered 8-1 at leaders Airdrie after scoring in the 1st minute, but create a Scottish League record - 4 players in one team sent off, the maximum before a referee must abandon the match.

4 Rangers go 4pts clear in Scotland, beating Dundee Utd 3-0 at Tannadice.

5 Under increasing pressure from the fans, manager of bottom club Ipswich, John Lyall, resigns after 4 years and coach Paul Goddard becomes caretaker manager. The PFA, having spent a year and £100,000 compiling a report on coaching, condemn FA director of coaching Charles Hughes and his 'formula football'. Altrincham, of the Vauxhall Conference, who were drawn against 'Tottenham or bye' in the 3rd round of the Cup, will be compensated if Spurs are not reinstated and the tie at White Hart Lane does not take place.

7 Despite a stirring 4-0 victory over Galatasaray with a scratch side containing several fledglings, Man Utd are out of the European Cup. Barcelona only draw at home to Gothenburg but it is enough to see them through. Milan get their win, 1-0, at Salzburg to scrape through despite their 2pt penalty.

8 'Green Flag' will be plastered all over England's training kit in the next 4 years after a sponsorship deal is agreed with the parent company of National Breakdown.

9 It's Spurs 2 the FA 0 and they're still playing - Spurs have been reinstated in the Cup and their 6pt Premiership penalty annulled by the investigating tribunal, who feel that it was unreasonable to impose any penalty other than a fine, and this might still be reduced. UEFA want to stage experimental matches with two referees.

10 The Premiership's major contenders Blackburn and Man Utd both win 3-2. Rangers begin to draw clear in Scotland, their 2-1 win at Kilmarnock extending their lead to 7pts over Motherwell, beaten at home by Aberdeen.

11 Reports that Arsenal manager George Graham has been under investigation by the IR have again brought to the surface accusations regarding Scandinavian players signing for English clubs - specifically that Graham is alleged to have received a secret payment of £285,000 via a Norwegian agent from the £1.57m transfer of John Jensen in 1992 - although Graham denies he has profited from any transfers. Former Scotland striker Frank McAvennie, now with St Mirren, admits he took cocaine when with West Ham. Scottish football enters its first official winter shut-down, with clubs not due to play again till Boxing Day.

12 FIFA president Joao Havelange, not for the first time, comes under attack for his dictatorial ways, with UEFA chief Lennart Johansson threatening UEFA's secession, now backed by Peter Velappan of the Asian Football Confederation, who resents the autocratic manner in which at FIFA's October meeting all the general secretaries of the continental confederations except the S.American one were excluded from the executive committee - Havelange having resorted to photocopying lists of the new members personally, distributing them, and then immediately declaring the meeting closed.

13 Everton sign their on-loan striker Duncan Ferguson from Rangers for £4m despite the fact that the controversial Scottish international has a 12-match suspension hanging over his head, pending the resolution of an alleged criminal assault. Plymouth manager Peter Shilton is given 4 matches to improve the team's performances and 7 days to answer the club solicitor's letter regarding an unpaid tax bill Plymouth are being pressed for by the IR. Newcastle's Andy Cole and Liverpool's Rob Fowler, as substitute, make their goalscoring marks at B-international level as England beat Ireland 2-0 at Anfield. Non-League Enfield win their FA Cup replay at Torquay 1-0.

14 Wales suffer their 3rd successive defeat in the Euro Championship qualifiers, going down 3-0 at Cardiff to Bulgaria despite the debut of adopted Vinnie Jones. Mark McGhee decides to wrench himself away from promotion-chasing Reading and take his chance as manager of relegation-haunted Leicester. Billy Ayre resigns after just 4 months with the League's bottom club Scarborough. Portsmouth are refused planning permission for the projected new stadium.

15 The Premier League's 3-man commission begins its inquiry into the Scandinavian 'bung' allegations, examining evidence and documents from Arsenal. Hampshire County Council refuse Southampton permission to buy land at Stoneham to build a new stadium.

17 Premiership leaders Blackburn, after 7 straight League wins, are held 0-0 at Leicester but go 2pts clear of Man Utd, who not only lose their 100% home record but suffer their first defeat at Old

Trafford, 2-1 to Forest, conceding their first League goals at home since 4 April. With their goalless draw at Goodison with Spurs, Everton set a club record 7th game without conceding a goal. The Plymouth board warn manager Peter Shilton before their Div 2 game at Brentford that he faces the sack unless they collect 8pts from the next 4 matches - they lose 7-0.

18 As the FA commission inquiry widens to cover 23 transfers, further revelations appear to stick the knife deeper into Arsenal manager George Graham's back, in that he is said to have admitted during Thursday's meeting with the commission handing over more than £400,000 to Arsenal, not just the £285,000 allegedly received from Norwegian agent Rune Hauge for the Jensen deal. Other allegations are published implying that Graeme Souness received similar 'bungs' while with both Rangers and Liverpool. On the football pitch, Scotland suffer a crucial defeat in Athens, going down to an 18th-min penalty by group leaders Greece. Ray McHale, sacked last year, is back as Scarborough manager.

19 Beleaguered manager George Graham receives unanimous backing from the Arsenal board. Steve Coppell, a member of the FA's 3-man investigating commission, is to remain despite calls from Graham for his withdrawal in the light of comments published that appeared to prejudge the issue. Merthyr chairman John Reddy claims to have encountered 'foul and abusive language' from chief executive Alun Evans when presenting a petition on behalf of 25 clubs calling for a vote of no confidence in the FA of Wales Council. Another 10 footballers are arrested in Malaysia. bringing the total to nearly 40 detained as the police wrap up their two-year probe into match-fixing - a 'cottage industry' said by Mr Peter Velappan, Asian Football Confederation chief, to be worth more than £300m a year in South-East Asia.

20 PFA's Gordon Taylor says that Forest captain Stuart Pearce is going to apologise for allegedly racist remarks made to Man Utd's Paul Ince. League Managers' Association chairman Howard Wilkinson defends Steve Coppell against calls for him to resign from the FA commission, suggesting his comments 'reflected a hypothetical outcome to a hypothetical question'. Liverpool's Stig Bjornebye, who was signed from Norwegian club Rosenborg for £600,000 in 1992, says he will be paying a reported £33,000 tax bill, 40% of the sum allegedly received from agent Rune Hauge's company.

21 Man City reach the Coca-Cola Cup quarter-finals with a shock 2-0 replay win at Newcastle. FIFA admit that transfer irregularities have become a world problem, but new regulations concerning the registration of agents that come into force on Jan 1 will bring some order. Orient chairman Tony Wood says he will listen to any reasonable offer for the club.

22 Spurs manager Gerry Francis transfer-lists Romanian star Ilie Dumitrescu. Villa and Sheff Wed complete an exchange deal that takes midfielder Ian Taylor to Villa Park for £700,000 rated striker Guy Whittingham and £300,000.

24 George Burley resigns as manager of Colchester.

26 Boxing Day away wins for Blackburn, 3-1 at Man City, and Man Utd, 3-2 at Chelsea, maintain the status quo at the top of the Premiership. Joe Royle suffers his first serious setback as Everton go down 4-1 at home to Sheff Wed, for whom new boy Whittingham scores 2. High scoring in Div 3 includes Mansfield's 7-1 thrashing of Hereford and Carlisle's 5-1 victory at Hartlepool which takes them 8pts clear of 2nd club Bury. Rangers retain their 7pt lead over Motherwell in Scotland, with the rest dropping further behind. Celtic set an unwanted club record with their 11th League game without a win when they chalk up their 7th successive draw.

27 Only 4 Premiership clubs are asked to play two days running, and only Forest produce a goal as they beat Norwich. The Endsleigh League offers almost a full programme again, and in Div 3 Mansfield make it 12 goals in 2 days with a 5-2 win at Scarborough.

28 With Blackburn's home match against Leeds postponed because of a mini-monsoon, Man Utd miss their chance to go top as they are held 1-1 at home by lowly Leicester. Villa provide new manager Brian Little with his first win in 7 games, beating Chelsea 3-0. George Burley, who made exactly 500 appearances for Ipswich, is appointed manager and watches the team chosen by caretaker-manager Paul Goddard go down 2-0 to Arsenal at Portman Road.

29 Northampton sack manager John Barnwell.

30 Spurs loan Ilie Dumitrescu to Spanish club Sevilla for the rest of the season.

31 John Jensen scores for Arsenal! The Danish midfielder who has become a cult figure at Highbury for his inability to score in 97 games, and whose transfer in 1992 is currently giving his manager much grief, finally puts the ball in the net with a spectacular effort, but QPR spoil the show and run out 3-1 winners. Blackburn win 1-0 at Palace to take a 3pt lead in the Premiership as Man Utd draw 2-2 at Southampton. Birmingham go top of Div 2, thrashing Blackpool 7-1 after being a goal down. Rangers win 3-1 at their nearest challengers Motherwell to open up a 10pt lead in Scotland. Bristol Rovers mourn the death of their only England international, Geoff Bradford, 67.

January
Wrexham knock Ipswich out of Cup . . . £7 million Cole for Man Utd . . . Cantona goes berserk - suspended for season . . . Death in Genoa . . . Romario World Player of the Year

1 UEFA offer places in the UEFA Cup for semi-finalists in the long-established (1953) but peripheral Inter Toto Cup, a summer competition geared to accommodate 64 clubs, and the FA apply for 4 places, while most western European countries continue to abstain.

2 An Alan Shearer hat-trick (including 2 pens) gives Blackburn a 4-2 win over West Ham and a 6pt lead in the Premiership over Man Utd, who play tomorrow.

3 Man Utd beat Coventry 2-0, the second a penalty for the incident that sees central defender Steve Pressley dismissed. FIFA announce that official bids for the 2002 World Cup have been lodged by Japan, Mexico and S.Korea.

4 Plymouth suspend manager Peter Shilton for up to 2 weeks for his failure to meet the deadline set for repayment of a tax debt esimated at about £50,000. Celtic hold Rangers 1-1 at Ibrox.

5 In a letter to all members of the FA Council, FA chairman Sir Bert Millichip stresses that the FA remain the power in English football whatever some Premiership moguls might be hinting at.

6 Villa sign Tommy Johnson and Gary Charles from Derby for £2.9m. Southampton pay a club record £1.2m for Chelsea's Neil Shipperley. On the eve of Arsenal's Cup tie at the New Den, Ian Wright accuses the Millwall fans of racism.

7 Ipswich, who lose 2-1 at 2nd Div Wrexham, are the only Premiership side to go down to lower-division opposition in today's 3rd round FA Cup ties, although Leeds' equaliser comes in the last 5 minutes of their 1-1 draw at Walsall. All four non-League sides go out without scoring a goal. In Scotland, Rangers increase their lead to 12pts in the Premier despite only drawing at Partick. Celtic pay Dutch club NAC Breda £1.2m for striker Pierre van Hooijdonk.

8 In the big Cup match, Blackburn hold Newcastle 1-1 at St James'.

9 FA Cup holders Man Utd win 2-0 at Sheff Utd after the home side have midfielder Charlie Hartfield dismissed in the 13th minute. Leeds pay a club record £3.4m for Frankfurt's Ghanaian striker Anthony Yeboah, top Bundesliga scorer for the last two seasons. Malaysian officials identify a 50-year-old blind man with no knowledge of football as the mastermind behind their match-fixing scandal.

10 Man Utd manager Alex Ferguson brings off a sensational coup, signing striker Andy Cole from rivals Newcastle for a British record fee of £7m - £6m plus N.Ireland winger Keith Gillespie. Mike Pejic, manager for only 7 months, leaves struggling Div 2 side Chester. Ian Atkins takes over at Northampton.

11 In the Coca-Cola Cup quarter-finals, Liverpool beat Arsenal 1-0, Bolton claim another Premiership scalp with a 1-0 victory over Norwich, and Palace slam 4 goals past Man City without reply, including 3 in the last 10min. Swindon beat Millwall 3-1 in the other tie, and respective managers Steve McMahon and Mick McCarthy have to be separated by the police and admonished by the referee in the 2nd half. Peter Shilton and Plymouth part in confusion, the club chairman Don McCauley insisting he resigned, Shilton's solicitors claiming he did not.

12 Howard Kendall takes charge at struggling Notts Co, replacing Russell Slade, who stays as assistant manager. Plymouth appoint caretaker manager Steve McCall in Peter Shilton's place, while Colchester appoint former player Steve Wignall as manager and Mick Docherty takes over at Rochdale.

13 In an emotional press conference, a tearful Paul Merson, discharged today from an addiction clinic, admits to being an alcoholic, apart from being addicted to gambling, although the FA confirm that cocaine abuse was a 'minimal problem'. Meanwhile his club Arsenal pay Luton £2m (rising to £2.5m) for 19-year-old Welsh striker John Hartson and also sign Ipswich striker Chris Kiwomya, offering half the £2m asking fee, and a Premier League inquiry team investigating the George Graham 'kickback' allegations spend three hours interviewing Norwegian agent Rune Hauge.

14 Blackburn extend their Premiership lead to 6pts over Man Utd with equal games played, beating Forest 3-0, while Ipswich's first ever win at Anfield dents Liverpool's title aspirations. A last-minute goal from Stuart McCall gives Rangers a 3-2 win at Falkirk and a 14pt lead in the Scottish Premier.

15 Man Utd, by agreement without newly signed Andy Cole, are held 1-1 by Newcastle at St James' and have Mark Hughes stretchered off with damaged knee ligaments, dashing Everton's immediate expectations of securing his services. The Football Writers' Association celebrate the birthday of Sir Stanley Matthews (80 on 1 Feb).

16 Leeds veteran Gordon Strachan, 37, retires from first-team football to concentrate on coaching. Leicester complete the £1m signing of Norwich striker Mark Robins.

17 In 3rd-round FA Cup replays, Leeds beat Walsall 5-2 thanks to a hat-trick by South African striker Phil Masinga who comes on as a sub in extra-time, and 2nd Div Swansea win 2-1 at 1st Div leaders Middlesbrough.

18 An eventful evening of Cup replays sees Newcastle win 2-1 at Blackburn, Millwall shock Arsenal 2-0 at gloom-laden Highbury, Liverpool scrape through 2-0 on penalties over Birmingham at Anfield and Man City welcomed former manager Howard Kendall back to Maine Road by thrashing his new side Notts Cty 5-2, German striker Uwe Rosler snaffling 4.

20 Steve Nicol leaves Liverpool after 13 years to join Notts Co as player-coach on a free transfer.

21 Torrential rain washes out all but 16 English League fixtures. In Scotland, where only 3 matches, all in the lower divisions, are lost, Rangers beat Hearts 1-0 to stay 14pts ahead, while Motherwell drop back to 3rd after a 6-1 thrashing at Dundee Utd.

22 Man Utd beat Blackburn 1-0 at Old Trafford to move within 2pts of them at the top of the Premiership, but have played one more game. More embarrassment for Arsenal as *The Mail on Sunday* alleges a 'secret kickback' of £145,000 paid to a 'mysterious Swiss company' out of the transfer of Pal Lyderson from Norwegian club IK Start in September 1991.

23 West Ham's relegation worries are not helped by the dismissals of Alvin Martin and Tim Breacker in their 2-0 defeat by Sheff Wed at Upton Park. New Zealander Linda Black, 36, is the first woman to referee a men's international, officiating in New Zealand's 2-1 defeat of Denmark's Olympic side.

24 Everton earn a goalless draw at Anfield and Liverpool manager Roy Evans criticises their 'tough tactics'. Celtic's £8.9m share issue is oversubscribed, making it £21m raised in 10 months.

25 Eric Cantona really goes over the top this time - sent off at Selhurst Park for kicking Richard Shaw, he leaps the barrier with a two-footed attack on a spectator and then wades in with fists before he can be dragged away. Palace earn a 1-1 draw which leaves Man Utd still 1pt behind Blackburn, having played 2 more games, both home fixtures. Wimbledon manager Joe Kinnear calls the ref a cheat after their 2-1 defeat at Newcastle. Jurgen Klinsmann is carried off after a rash aerial challenge from Mark Bosnich outside the area, but the Villa keeper goes unpunished and Spurs lose 1-0. A

transfer tribunal sets Chris Kiwomya's fee at £1.25m (rising to a maximum £1.55m after 60 first-team appearances), Arsenal having offered £0.5m, while Ipswich asked for £2.5m. Paul Merson makes his comeback in Arsenal's reserves.

26 The 'Cantona affair' takes up an extraordinary amount of media space and time, as the errant Man Utd star is given 14 days by the FA to answer their charges, but his club have not yet spoken. The police receive a complaint from the Palace fan involved in the incident, and will also interview United captain Paul Ince, who was allegedly involved in a separate scuffle. Five players in France, 4 from Bordeaux, are suspended for up to 2 months for fighting in a Div 1 match last week at St Etienne. Former Spurs and West Brom player Vic Buckingham dies at 79.

27 Man Utd suspend Cantona from the rest of the season's first-team games and fine him the maximum 2 weeks' wages (about £20,000), while in France Cantona is stripped of the national team captaincy and dropped for the season. The Palace fan involved, season-ticket holder 20-year-old Matthew Simmons (who, it is revealed, has a conviction for assault with intent to rob), is banned from the club for the rest of the season.

28 In the FA Cup 4th round, Man Utd recover their composure to beat 2nd Div Wrexham 5-2 at Old Trafford despite going a goal down, while they go 4pts behind in the Premiership as Blackburn, still with a game in hand, beat Ipswich 4-1, Alan Shearer scoring a hat-trick. Other Cup results include Newcastle's 3-0 defeat of Swansea, Paul Kitson scoring all 3, and Palace's 2-1 win at Forest. Burnley hold Liverpool 0-0 at Turf Moor, and Leicester win 1-0 at Portsmouth, who have two men sent off including keeper Alan Knight. At the New Den, 3 policemen are taken to hospital and 5 arrests are made as trouble flares up between respective fans during Millwall's 0-0 draw with Chelsea. With the leaders Birmingham's game postponed, Brentford go top of Div 2, beating Cambridge 6-0, all the goals coming in the last 25min, 4 in the last 10. In the 3rd round of Scottish Cup, holders Dundee Utd are held 0-0 at home by 2nd Div Clyde, Kilmarnock likewise by Morton, while Huntly win the non-League clash 7-0 against Burntisland Shipyard, 7 ties being snowed off.

29 All 3 FA Cup ties go to Premiership sides playing away to Div 1 clubs, Spurs leading the way with a 4-1 win at Sunderland, who lose defender Gary Bennett after 49min for handling on the line. The Genoa v AC Milan fixture in Italy is abandoned at half-time because of crowd trouble caused by the death of a Genoa fan in a stabbing incident before the start.

30 The FA appoint Don Howe full-time Technical Co-ordinator on a 2-year contract, and he will be responsible for overseeing England's progress at all levels and co-ordinating the development of techniques and tactics. Everton complete the signing of defender Earl Barrett from Villa for £1.7m. Arsenal striker Ian Wright is banned for 4 matches and fined a record £1,000 for accumulating 41 penalty points, and Fulham midfielder Terry Hurlock, on 51pts, has a 4-match ban extended to 6. Italian sports authorities cancel events scheduled for next Sunday in deference to the death of the fan killed yesterday.

31 Vauxhall Labour MP Kate Hoey's call for an independent inquiry into the 'backhanders, bungs and fixes' of football is rejected by Sports Minister Iain Sproat, who feels confident that the FA can deal with the problem. West Ham's Alvin Martin has his sending-off against Sheff Wed on Saturday cancelled, as referee Paul Danson, after studying the video, allows the FA to rescind his decision. Cambridge terminate the contract of Billy Manuel, sent off on Saturday for the 3rd time in 6 games. FIFA name Brazil's Romario Player of the Year after a poll of national team coaches.

February

Sir Stanley Matthews 80 . . . Aberdeen sack manager Willie Miller . . . Rioting as Millwall knock Chelsea out of Cup . . . Cantona attacks ITN reporter in Guadeloupe . . . Dublin international abandoned after England fans riot . . . Arsenal sack George Graham

1 Paul Merson makes his return for Arsenal after his enforced rehabilitation, coming on at Highbury for the last 15min of the 0-0 draw with AC Milan in the 1st leg of the European Super Cup. In the two Premiership games to survive the weather, 14 players are booked, and Blackburn's keeper Tim Flowers is dismissed after 2min of their 1-1 draw with Leeds at Ewood Park, both goals coming from disputed penalties, and referee Rodger Gifford is attacked by a fan at the end of the game. Blackburn go 5pts ahead of Man Utd in the Premiership. In the other match, Everton have two players sent off, their new signing Earl Barrett and Barry Horne, before going down 2-0 to Newcastle at St James' Park in a match that sees David Elleray brandish his yellow card 12 times to 10 different players. Sir Stanley Matthews, never booked in his long career, celebrates his 80th birthday. Former Liverpool chairman Sir John Smith dies at 74. Portsmouth sack manager Jim Smith and replace him with Terry Fenwick.

4 Andy Cole's first goal for Man Utd is enough to give his new club victory over Villa and take them to within 2pts of Blackburn, who play tomorrow. Is there no end to Arsenal's woes? Tony Adams and John Hartson are sent off at Hillsborough as they lose 3-1 to Sheff Wed. Bolton slam rivals Wolves 5-1 to go top of Div 1 as leaders Middlesbrough are beaten 1-0 at home by Reading, another promotion challenger. Despite being held at home by lowly Dundee Utd, Rangers increase their lead of the Scottish Premier League to 15pts as Hibs go down at home to bottom club Partick.

5 A comprehensive 3-1 defeat by Spurs at White Hart Lane leaves Blackburn only 2pts ahead of Man Utd, who are now favourites to retain the Premiership title.

6 Terry Venables looks to his old club Spurs for new talent, promoting Nick Barmby and Sol Campbell to the senior squad for next week's international in Dublin. Aberdeen sack manager Willie Miller, with them since he joined the club as a player in 1971. Jimmy Allen, former Portsmouth, Villa and England defender, dies at 85.

7 Chelsea captain Dennis Wise is found guilty of assaulting a taxi driver and faces possible prison; the FA drop him from the England squad, but Chelsea will keep him in tomorrow's Cup side. Liverpool beat Burnley 1-0 at Anfield in their 4th round FA Cup replay.

8 AC Milan beat Arsenal 2-0 in the return tie to win the European Super Cup. Millwall beat Chelsea on penalties in their 4th round FA Cup replay at Stamford Bridge, where some of the worst scenes witnessed in recent years take place, with fans fighting on the pitch and in the stands at the finish, and two dozen police horses needed to keep rival fans apart - 11 policemen are injured and 38 arrests made. In other replays, Wolves beat Sheff Wed on penalties - with Chris Waddle missing a vital sudden-death spot-kick to bring back unwanted World Cup '90 memories, and Southampton enjoy an easy passage, beating Luton 6-0. Man United's suspended French striker Eric Cantona is involved in further controversy, allegedly completing a Caribbean family holiday instead of turning up for a police interview. English clubs earn an extra place in next season's UEFA Cup because of their prominence in the fair-play ranking list. Sacked Portsmouth manager Jim Smith will take over from Steve Coppell as chief executive of the League Managers' Association on 1 April.

9 The police attach no blame to Chelsea for yesterday's Cup tie riots, stating that their security arrangements could not be faulted.

10 Peter Shilton signs for Wimbledon as keeper cover.

11 Eric Cantona hits the front pages again, as well as, allegedly, an ITN reporter trying to film him on the holiday island of Guadeloupe, with a repeat of the 'kung-fu kick' that felled a Crystal Palace fan two weeks ago. With Blackburn playing tomorrow, Man Utd go top with a flourish, winning the Maine Road local derby 3-0. Villa slam 7 past Wimbledon after going a goal down, Tommy Johnson hitting 3. The pressure builds on manager George Graham, who has to deny reports that he is going to quit, as Arsenal are held at home by bottom club Leicester and Ian Selley breaks a leg. Bad weather and waterlogged pitches see 12 English games called off and another 8 in Scotland.

12 Blackburn restore their 2pt Premiership lead with a 3-1 win over Sheff Wed, who have keeper Kevin Pressman sent off after 44min. Swindon beat Bolton 2-1 in the 1st leg of their Coca-Cola Cup semi-final. Rangers suffer a rare defeat in the Scottish Premier, 2-0 by lowly Aberdeen under new manager Roy Aitken. Keeper Ian Walker is the fifth Spurs player in Terry Venables' England squad, drafted in to replace injured Tim Flowers.

13 As Eric Cantona's lawyer announces that he is to sue ITN over the Guadeloupe incident for 'invasion of privacy', Man Utd manager Alex Ferguson comes out strongly in support of his player.

14 Coventry manager Phil Neal loses his job after just 15 months. Arsenal sign Dutch winger Glenn Helder from Vitesse Arnhem for £2m.

15 Rioting England soccer followers, in what is thought to have been an orchestrated incident, bring shame on their country and force the Dublin friendly to be abandoned after 27min, with Ireland leading 1-0; there are 43 arrests and 20 people are taken to hospital. A last-minute goal gives Liverpool a 1-0 lead from their Coca-Cola Cup semi-final 1st leg against Palace at Anfield. Ron Atkinson takes over as manager at Coventry.

16 Reactions to last night's Dublin riot: the FA launch an inquiry and call on true fans to identify the troublemakers; FIFA president Joao Havelange supports England's right to retain Euro '96; Ireland manager Jack Charlton pleads for the game to be put back on; and the National Football Intelligence Unit blame the Irish authorities for not heeding the warnings and detailed briefings sent to them more than a week ago.

18 In the FA Cup 5th round, Everton slam Norwich 5-0, and the visitors' captain Jon Newsome becomes the 289th player sent off this season, an English record. Millwall go out at last to their third London Premiership opponents when QPR's Clive Wilson converts a disputed last-minute penalty. Hibs beat Motherwell 2-0 in the big clash of the Scottish Cup 4th round, while Aberdeen lose 2-0 to Div 2 leaders Stenhousemuir.

19 Holders Man Utd score twice in the first 4min and a 2nd half goal from the fit-again Mark Hughes eases them to a 3-1 win over Leeds in the Cup.

20 Behind-the-scenes reports emerge that the Premier League Commission have found Arsenal manager George Graham guilty of taking a 'bung' - a cut of some £285,000 from the John Jensen transfer - and have made their finding known to the club directors. Thanks to the FA's 'hooligan hotline', at least 40 Dublin riot suspects are claimed to have been identified. Another shock in the Scottish Cup - Hearts knock Rangers out by 4-2.

21 Arsenal sack manager George Graham as a result of the Premier League Commission findings for failing to 'act in the best interests of the club', and Graham promises to 'vigorously contest' his dismissal; 7 hours later, under assistant manager Stewart Houston who has been offered the job as caretaker, Arsenal beat Forest 1-0, their first League win at Highbury for 4 months. After being questioned at South Norwood police station, Man United's Eric Cantona is charged with common assault over the infamous incident at Crystal Palace. Peterborough keeper John Keeley, 33, has quit the game because of verbal abuse from supporters..

22 Man Utd enjoy a comprehensive 2-0 victory at Carrow Road, while leaders Blackburn struggle to beat Wimbledon 2-1 at Ewood Park. At the other end of the Premiership table, Leicester scrape themselves off the bottom with 3 goals in the last 13 minutes for a 4-4 draw at Villa Park, enough to take them above Ipswich, 2-0 losers at Maine Road. Several matches are off because of rain and snow, including both Coca-Cola Cup semi-final 2nd legs. Southend manager Peter Taylor has been told to take a month's holiday, and it is thought he will return in a coaching capacity.

23 Premier League chief executive Rick Parry confirms the leaked reports concerning the George Graham inquiry, namely that the Arsenal manager received a total of £425,500 from agent Rune Hauge, and had returned this plus £40,000 interest to the club; Parry warns that Graham is not the only culprit. Ex-Lincoln manager Steve Thompson takes over at Southend.

24 An FA disciplinary ruling on the Cantona incident at Selhurst Park extends his ban until 30 Sep (worldwide) and fines him £10,000; Man Utd confirm the player intends to remain with them.

25 Blackburn stretch their Premiership lead to 3pts but fail to take full advantage of Man United's defeat at Everton, being held at home by Norwich.

28 Chelsea lose their Cup-Winners' Cup quarter-final 1st leg 1-0 at Bruges. Liverpool win their 5th round Cup replay 2-0 at Wimbledon.

March

Chris Armstrong fails drugs test . . . Man Utd beat Ipswich 9-0 . . . Three outfield subs . . . Paul Ince charged with common assault . . . Grobbelaar, Fashanu and Segers arrested . . . Cantona jail sentence reduced to community service . . .

1 In a thrill-packed Cup replay at the Dell, 2nd-half sub Ronnie Rosenthal pulls Spurs back from a 2-0 deficit, completes his hat-trick to put them ahead in extra time and the final result is Southampton 2 Spurs 6.. Mike Walker wins his case against Everton for breach of contract, having been sacked with 32 months still to run, damages to be assessed later. With Mexico withdrawing, only Japan and S.Korea are left as applicants to host the 2002 World Cup finals.

2 A 1-1 draw against Auxerre at Highbury in the Cup-Winners' Cup leaves Arsenal with a stiff task in the 2nd leg. David Burrows joins Coventry for £1.1m after only 6 months at Everton. Darlington sack manager Alan Murray.

3 Palace striker Chris Armstrong, it is revealed, failed a random drugs test on 23 Jan in which traces of cannabis were found, and will have to undergo counselling. Boxing and snooker promoter Barry Hearn agrees to buy a controlling interest in ailing Orient. The FA warn players not to take their shirts off when celebrating a goal.

4 Man Utd run riot against Ipswich to the tune of 9-0, a Premiership record, with 5 from Andy Cole, and although Blackburn squeeze a 1-0 win at Villa Park to maintain their 3pts Premiership lead, the overall result switches goal advantage to the champions. In a relegation battle at Filbert Street, Leicester claw back a 2-goal deficit after Everton are reduced to 9 men, having had Vinny Samways and Duncan Ferguson sent off. Ex-ref Ken Aston claims he was offered £25,000 by a Far Eastern syndicate for addresses and telephone numbers of Premiership referees and players. New Laws passed by the International Board at Turnberry, Scotland, include provision for 3 subs (including keeper or not) and rewording of the offside law to prevent penalising a player not interfering with play; there will also be an experiment with time-outs in a FIFA tournament in the next 12 months.

6 Graeme Souness has started libel proceedings against the *Today* newspaper for allegations concerning Torben Piechnik's transfer to Liverpool in 1992. MP David Mellor makes a scathing TV attack on the Belgian police for their indiscriminate use of water cannon and riot squads to control fans at the Bruges-Chelsea European tie last week and is bluntly dismissive not only of Bruges' ground but of the Belgian nation.

7 A late Steve Bruce goal at Wimbledon gives Man Utd a 1-0 win and the Premiership lead on goal difference over Blackburn, who now have a game in hand, and leaves Wimbledon manager Joe Kinnear, ordered off the bench, fuming at the referee for the dismissal of Alan Kimble shortly before the goal. The FA finally charge sacked Arsenal manager with misconduct over the Scandinavian transfers and the police charge Man United's Paul Ince with common assault over an incident alleged to have occurred at Selhurst Park after the infamous Cantona foray into the front stalls.

8 Blackburn beat Arsenal 3-1 to go back on top of the Premiership. Bolton win a stirring Coca-Cola Cup semi-final against Swindon after going 2-0 down on aggregate, with 3 goals in the last half hour, and in the final they will meet Liverpool, 1-0 victors at Palace (2-0 agg).

9 Wimbledon manager Joe Kinnear bans himself from the touchline.

10 Aston Villa pay Blackburn £1m for Under-21 defender Alan Wright. Bolton take on Peter Shilton as their third keeper till the end of the season.

11 Spurs march into the FA Cup semi-finals with a 2-1 victory at Anfield, Jurgen Klinsmann scoring a late winner after Liverpool had initially gone ahead. In the other tie Palace are held 1-1 at home by 1st Div Wolves. A late Alan Shearer equaliser gives Blackburn a point at Coventry and takes them 4 clear of Man Utd, who now have a game in hand. Rangers are held at home by Falkirk but still lead the Scottish Premier by 16pts.

12 Both home sides go through to the FA Cup semi-finals, Everton beating Newcastle 1-0, Man Utd beating QPR 2-0. Hearts reach the Scottish Cup semis, beating holders Dundee Utd 2-1.

13 The FA clear Palace striker Chris Armstrong to resume playing. Wimbledon manager Joe Kinnear is charged with bringing the game into disrepute.

14 In melodramatic raids, three footballers are arrested on claims of match-fixing by a Far-Eastern syndicate - Bruce Grobbelaar (Southampton), John Fashanu (Villa) and Hans Segers (Wimbledon) - and, together with Fashanu's wife Melissa Kassa-Mapsi and London-based Malaysian businessman Heng Suan Lim, are held overnight at separate police stations in Hampshire. Chelsea beat Bruges 2-0 (agg 2-1) to reach the Cup-Winners' Cup semis. In the Premiership, Palace climb out of the bottom 4 with a 2-1 win over Sheff Wed, Chris Armstrong scoring on his return, and a Peter Ndlovu hat-trick gives Coventry a 3-2 victory at Anfield. Dundee Utd part company with manager Ivan Golac.

15 All five arrested yesterday by police investigating match-fixing allegations are released after questioning. Man United's title hopes take a knock as Spurs hold them to a 0-0 draw at Old Trafford. Blackburn sign Southampton's Irish international defender Jeff Kenna for £1.5m.

16 A spectacular Ian Wright goal at Auxerre is enough to put Arsenal into the Cup-Winners' Cup semis. Sampdoria beat Porto on penalties, but David Platt, sent off 4 minutes from the end of extra time, will miss both semi-final legs. FIFA cancel the World Youth Championships to be held in Nigeria owing to concern over security, and will probably transfer the competition to Qatar.

18 Blackburn, with Alan Shearer scoring his 100th League goal, beat Chelsea 2-1 after going behind early on and go 6pts ahead of Man Utd, who play tomorrow. Rangers lose 2-1 at Hearts and their Scottish Premier lead is cut to 12pts by Motherwell, who have a game in hand.

19 Man Utd go down 2-0 to Liverpool, a severe blow to their Premiership ambitions. Relegation-threatened Swindon gain an invaluable win at West Brom by 5-2, twice coming from

behind, with all the goals scored in the 2nd half. Notts Co beat Ascoli 2-1 in the Anglo-Italian Cup final at Wembley.

20 Terry Venables leaves Paul Ince, facing a court appearance this week, out of his England squad for the Uruguay game, as well as the 'out of form' Matt Le Tissier, while both Ian Walker and Nick Barmby of Spurs and Jamie Redknapp of Liverpool are in. Another Spurs man, central defender Colin Calderwood, is a surprise inclusion in the Scottish squad for the Euro qualifier in Moscow.

21 Liverpool sign Millwall's Dublin-born winger Mark Kennedy, 18, for £1.5m, with another £0.5m linked to appearances. Middlesbrough win 1-0 at Sunderland to go top of Div 1.

22 Crystal Palace outclass Wolves 4-1 in their FA Cup 6th round replay at Molineux, with 2 goals from a rampant Chris Armstrong. Man Utd beat Arsenal 3-0 to cut Blackburn's Premiership lead to 3pts, but have now played one game more. Southampton, with 3 goals in the last 5min, beat Newcastle 3-1, but remain in the bottom 4. Gordon Strachan rejoins his old Man Utd boss Ron Atkinson to become assistant at Coventry, with a clause in his contract that he will be offered the manager's job in 1997.

23 Eric Cantona is bailed pending appeal after being sentenced by Croydon magistrates to 2 weeks' jail for his assault on a spectator at Selhurst Park on 25 Jan. Man Utd team-mate Paul Ince, who pleaded 'not guilty' to an assault charge at the same game, is bailed to his trial on 25 May. Clydebank and former Scotland and Rangers winger Davie Cooper, 39, dies in hospital after collapsing yesterday with a brain haemorrhage while making a coaching video. Man United striker Andy Cole is called up to replace the injured Alan Shearer in the England squad. Blackburn sign £1.5m-rated Dutch midfielder Richard Witschge on loan. Middlesbrough sign Swindon's Norwegian striker Jan Aage Fjortoft for £1.3m.

24 The Palace fan, Matthew Simmons, attacked by Eric Cantona pleads not guilty to charges of using threatening behaviour and is remanded on bail by Croydon magistrates until 23 May.

25 With no Premiership soccer, the spotlight is on Div 1, where gameless Middlesbrough stay top as Tranmere lose and Bolton draw away from home. Only 5pts now cover the top 6 teams. In 30 Endsleigh League matches only Div 3 Gillingham, who have been in receivership for 2 months, score more than 2 goals, beating fellow-strugglers Exeter 3-0.

26 Middlesbrough, with player-manager Bryan Robson scoring his first goal for the club, beat Port Vale 3-0 to extend their Div 1 lead to 4pts.

27 In a European U-21 group match, England beat Ireland 2-0 in Dublin in front of 6,000 spectators, marshalled by some 700 stewards and police, none of whom are troubled. Charlton suspend two teenagers who failed random drug tests, both Dean Chandler and Lee Bowyer admitting taking cannabis.

28 Man United's half-yearly accounts show a pre-tax profit of £7.3m but throw up a mystery in that winger Keith Gillespie, a supposed £1m makeweight in the Andy Cole deal with Newcastle, is valued at only £0.25m. Former Dundee Utd player and coach Billy Kirkwood takes over as manager.

29 As England and Uruguay play out a disappointing 0-0 draw at Wembley, Nick Barmby and Andy Cole win their first caps as 2nd-half subs. In Euro Championship matches, Ireland miss their chance to go top of Gp 6, held frustratingly to a 1-1 draw in Dublin by N.Ireland, Wales's 3-1 defeat in Bulgaria leaves them bottom of Gp 7, and Scotland manage a 0-0 draw away to Russia. Peter Reid replaces Mick Buxton in charge of struggling Sunderland, their fifth managerial change in little over 3 years, his position to be reviewed in the summer. Plymouth manager Steve McCall, in charge less than 3 months, resigns.

30 Man Utd captain Steve Bruce will miss the FA Cup semi against Palace because of a 41-pt suspension. Cardiff team manager and director Terry Yorath, a member of a consortium trying to buy the club, resigns. Sporting impresario Barry Hearn takes over officially as Orient chairman. Gillingham chairman Bernard Baker quits. Millwall chairman Reg Burr, the recipient of death threats against his family, will step down at the end of the season.

31 Eric Cantona wins his appeal against his jail sentence, receiving 120 hours' community service instead, and a subsequent press conference is reduced to farce by his pseudo-philosophic utterances. Stockport's Uruguayan manager Danny Bergara is sacked after 6 years in the job, reportedly after an altercation with chairman Brendan Elwood. Eddie May returns to take charge of Cardiff 4 months after being sacked.

April

Owls' record 7-1 home defeat . . . Liverpool win Coca-Cola Cup . . . Palace fan killed in brawl . . . Alan Shearer PFA Player of Year . . . Paul Gascoigne makes his comeback . . . Roy Keane in stamping incident . . . Leicester and Ipswich relegated . . . 7th Championship running for Rangers . . . Seaman saves 3 penalties to put Arsenal in Euro final . . . Graham Taylor spat at . . . Klinsmann Footballer of the Year . . . Carlisle win Div 3 title

1 Blackburn go 6pts clear again in the Premiership with an important 2-1 victory at Everton. Forest shatter Sheff Wed 7-1 at Hillsborough, the Owls' heaviest ever home defeat. Notts Co, beaten at home 3-1 by Barnsley and now 4pts adrift at the bottom of Div 1, sack manager Howard Kendall after only 10 weeks - not because of the results but for the way the club was being run. In the Scottish Premier, a 1-0 defeat at home to Kilmarnock leaves Aberdeen in deep relegation trouble.

2 Bolton put up a brave fight at Wembley but lose 2-1 to Liverpool in a Coca-Cola Cup final graced by two outstanding goals from Steve McManaman. Man Utd stutter again in the Championship race, held 0-0 at home by Leeds, and are 5pts behind Blackburn who have a game in hand.

3 The FA complete another sponsorship package, this time with brewers Carlsberg for £5m, which includes what will now be called the FA Carlsberg Vase. Cambridge Utd sack manager Gary Johnson, putting former West Ham defender Tommy Taylor in temporary charge.

4 A 1-0 victory at QPR gives Blackburn an 8pt lead over Man Utd at the top of the Premiership and, with only 6 games to go, the title is theirs for the taking. Partick's 3-1 defeat of Hearts pushes Aberdeen to bottom spot in the Scottish Premier.

5 Liverpool spoil Bruce Grobbelaar's emotional return to Anfield and to football, beating Southampton 3-1. Leeds' Ghanaian striker Anthony Yeboah scores a hat-trick as they crush hapless Ipswich 4-0 and send the East Anglians to the bottom. Middlesbrough lose 1-0 at Oldham, but remain 4pts clear in Div 1. But Bolton win 1-0 at Swindon, whose player-manager Steve McMahon is sent off for the second time, to go 3rd, 4pts behind with 2 games in hand, despite having Mixu Paatelainen sent off in the last minute. But the most sensational dismissal is that of the club's PA announcer Pete Lewis, whose half-time criticism of the referee earns him a warning from a senior police officer followed by the sack from the club.

6 In the Cup-Winners' Cup semis, Chelsea crash 3-0 to Real Zaragoza in Spain, where some of their fans rip up and throw seats at police during the match, while Arsenal will take a slender 3-2 lead to Italy as Sampdoria rally after central defender Steve Bould gives the Gunners a 2-0 half-time lead.

7 Hibs' veteran keeper Jim Leighton saves an Andy Walker penalty to earn them a 0-0 draw with Celtic and a replay in their Scottish Cup semi at Ibrox. Disgraced 1993 European Cup winners Marseille hit a new low - no longer able to pay their debts, they are placed into receivership.

8 Div 1 Airdrie reach the Scottish Cup final, beating Hearts with a goal from Englishman Steve Cooper on his first visit to Hampden. Rangers' 3-2 victory over a desperate Aberdeen takes them out of reach of all challengers except 4th-placed Celtic. In England, Leicester lose 1-0 at Sheff Wed, which means, barring miracles, they are relegated to Div 1. Chester, bottom of Div 2, are the first club to be relegated.

9 In the first FA Cup semi at Leeds, Everton surprise Spurs to the tune of 4-1, Nigerian striker Daniel Amokachi coming on by mistake for Paul Rideout and scoring 2 late goals to make sure Spurs get no further in the competition they were originally banned from. Later in the day Man Utd have to come back twice, once in extra time, at Villa Park to force a 2-2 draw and a replay against Palace. It later emerges that a Palace fan, Paul Nixon, was killed by a coach while trying to escape from a brawl between rival fans at a pub 8 miles from Villa Park before the match. Alan Shearer (Blackburn) is voted PFA Player of the Year, Robbie Fowler (Liverpool), Young Player of the Year. In Italy, Paul Gascoigne lasts the full 90min in his comeback after a year out through injury, helping Lazio to a 2-0 win over Reggiana.

10 The 6 South Yorkshire police officers who claimed their career was ruined by the trauma suffered in witnessing the 1989 Hillsborough disaster fail to win damages against their own chief constable at Sheffield High Court.

11 Celtic beat Hibs 3-1 in their replayed Scottish Cup semi.

12 Man Utd beat Palace 2-0 in the Cup semi replay, but Roy Keane, who has 7 stitches in an ankle gash at half-time, may miss the final after being red-carded for stamping on Gareth Southgate; Palace's Darren Patterson is also sent off for getting into the argument. Newport AFC, Caernarfon and Colwyn Bay win their restraint of trade action as the High Court reject FA of Wales claims that banning them from playing from Welsh bases was necessary to protect the Konica League representation in Europe.

13 The FA charge yesterday's culprits Keane and Patterson with bringing the game into disrepute. West Ham climb out of the relegation frame with a 3-0 win over Wimbledon, and send Leicester back to Div 1 in the process.

14 In Friday night matches, a late Klinsmann equaliser for Spurs at Selhurst Park robs Palace of vital points they need in their fight against relegation, while fellow strugglers Everton and Man City both notch valuable wins, condemning Ipswich to relegation.

15 Man Utd show they still have title - and double - aspirations with a 4-0 victory at Leicester to go within 6pts of Blackburn, who are stunned by a last-minute Brian Deane goal at Elland Road that gives Leeds a draw; only 5 matches remain. In Div 1 Steve Bull scores his 200th League goal in Wolves' 3-2 defeat at Charlton. In Div 2, Orient lose 2-0 at Swansea and are relegated. In Scotland, Aberdeen gain on the clubs directly above them with a 2-0 win over Celtic - handing the title to Rangers, their 7th in succession. Forfar clinch promotion from Div 3.

17 The Easter Monday fixtures expose jangling nerves in the Premiership race as Man Utd apparently blow their outside chance when held 0-0 at Old Trafford by Chelsea, but then in the evening Blackburn lose 3-2 at home to Man City - so the gap is reduced to 5pts. Newcastle lose 2-1 at home to Leeds, their first Premiership defeat at St James' since Jan '94. Arsenal win 4-0 at Villa, who are now in serious trouble, only 1pt above Palace in the relegation zone but having played 2 games more. Norwich lose at Spurs and look doomed, 3rd from bottom with only 3 games left, while Palace's 1-0 win at QPR gives them new hope. In Div 1, Tranmere's hopes of the automatic promotion spot take a nose-dive with a 5-0 defeat at Derby, who appear to have left their effort too late to win a play-off spot. In Div 3, leaders Carlisle suffer their first home defeat, 1-0 to lowly Hartlepool, but are still 8pts clear at the top.

18 Dundee Utd win at Partick in an important Scottish relegation battle, but Aberdeen lose 2-1 at Motherwell and are now 4pts adrift. Terry Venables includes 13 uncapped Premiership players in the 19-strong England squad for next week-end's get-together, including central midfielders Jamie Redknapp (Liverpool), Garry Flitcroft (Man City) and Mark Draper (Leicester). Middlesbrough lose their British Steel sponsorship because their new stadium is being built from cheaper German steel.

19 Ajax impressively beat Bayern Munich 5-2 (5-2 agg) to reach the final of the European Cup, where they will play AC Milan. England captain David Platt signs for another year with Sampdoria.

20 David Seaman is Arsenal's hero in their Cup-Winners' Cup semi as he makes 3 penalty saves in a shoot-out against Sampdoria after Stefan Schwarz had kept Arsenal in the game with a late goal to make the aggregate score 5-5. In the final, Arsenal will play Real Zaragoza, who, although losing 3-1 to a courageous Chelsea at Stamford Bridge, win the tie 4-3. Blackburn take another shaky step towards the Premiership title with a 2-1 win at home to Palace and now go 8pts clear - they need 5pts from their last 3 games. Former Coventry striker Keith Houchen takes over at Hartlepool from David McCreery, who resigned when told his contract would not be renewed in the summer, and former Welsh international Kevin Ratcliffe becomes caretaker manager of Chester, Derek Mann stepping down to become youth development officer. Billy Bonds rejects an offer to take over at Orient, who have sacked their joint managers John Sitton and Chris Turner.

21 Bolton miss a chance of going top of Div 1 when they lose 2-1 at Reading.

22 There are no Saturday Premier games in England or Scotland. A 1-1 draw at Barnsley gives Middlesbrough a 3pt lead in Div 1 and ensures them at least a play-off place. After his side draw 3-3 at Sheff Utd, Wolves manager Graham Taylor tries unsuccessfully to make a citizen's arrest on a spectator who spits on him. At the bottom, Bristol City lose 1-0 at Watford and are relegated - along with Burnley, who go down 2-1 to Portsmouth at Turf Moor. In Div 2, jittery leaders Brentford manage to beat Cardiff 2-0 and send the Welshmen down. Chelsea's Robert Fleck has been banned from receiving Cup final tickets for 5 years.

23 A crowd of 76,000 see Birmingham make history with an extra-time sudden-death victory over Carlisle in the final of the Auto Windscreens Shield, sub Paul Tait making the score 1-0 in the 103rd minute. The safety officer at Bramall Lane, Tom Broomhead, criticises Wolves manager Graham Taylor for trying to grab a spectator who spat on him, but the former England manager is unrepentant.

24 The FA charge Birmingham's Paul Tait with bringing the game into disrepute for revealing an offensive T-shirt during the celebrations of his sudden-death winner at Wembley yesterday. Spurs veteran midfielder Micky Hazard, 35, has been forced to retire because of a persistent back problem.

25 Blackburn's unfortunate Paul Warhurst breaks a leg in a reserve-team work-out.

26 In Euro Championship qualifiers, Wales are the only British Isles team not to win, but their performance takes pride of place - an improbable 1-1 draw with Germany in Dusseldorf that takes them off bottom spot in Gp 7 and deprives the Germans of their 100% record. Ireland's important 1-0 victory over Portugal in Dublin takes them to the top of Gp 6, above their hitherto 100% opponents, while N.Ireland's 1-0 win in Latvia takes them into 3rd place. Scotland should have recorded more than a 2-0 victory from their away tie with San Marino. The only domestic match was of great significance, Birmingham beating Brentford 2-0 to leapfrog above them on goals at the top of Div 2 with a game in hand. The Sheff Utd supporter, Robert Hollister, who spat at Graham Taylor is released on bail after being questioned by police and travels to Wolverhampton to apologise in person to the Wolves manager.

27 Ill-advised verbal utterances cost Wimbledon personnel - manager Joe Kinnear a £1,500 fine and a touchline ban for recent remarks about two referees, and midfielder Vinnie Jones a £1,750 fine for comments after the game at Newcastle. Fulham midfielder Terry Hurlock, having become the first player to register 61 disciplinary points in a season since the present system started 21 years ago, is fined £400 and banned for 4 matches. Spurs youth team coach Pat Holland takes over as manager of Orient.

28 Eric Cantona signs a new 3-year contract with Man Utd rather than accept an offer from Inter-Milan.

29 Jurgen Klinsmann, who scores Spurs' equaliser in the 1-1 draw at Highbury, his 28th goal of the season, is voted Footballer of the Year. Palace and Norwich dig themselves into deeper relegation trouble, both losing 2-1 at home, to Forest and Liverpool respectively, and Villa's 1-0 defeat at Leeds leaves them on the precipice. An angry protest outside Carrow Road after Norwich's defeat, in which two police officers are injured, leads to 13 arrests and 5 charges for public order offences. Derby decide to part company with manager Roy McFarland in the wake of their home defeat by in-form Southend. All 4 relegation places are now decided as Portsmouth, having done for Burnley last week, repeat the dose at Swindon, whose 2-0 defeat sends them down. Sunderland's draw at Burnley ensures their safety. Nerve-ends are showing in Div 2, where leaders Birmingham lose a 2-goal lead and are lucky to salvage a point from their home game with Brighton, Brentford go down 2-1 at home to lowly Bournemouth, and Huddersfield's draw at struggling Cambridge now puts them out of the running for the automatic promotion place. Carlisle clinch the Div 3 title with a 1-0 win at Colchester. In Scotland, Aberdeen's 2-1 victory at Hearts enables them to make ground on their relegation rivals.

30 Blackburn's shock 2-0 defeat at relegation-haunted West Ham suddenly leaves their 8pt Premiership lead looking vulnerable as Man Utd now have 2 games in hand. While Div 1 leaders Middlesbrough almost clinch automatic promotion with a 2-1 win over Luton in the last match they will play at Ayresome Park, Tranmere blow their chances of that luxury in their 5-1 defeat at West Brom, where Lee Ashcroft hits a hat-trick and the visitors have defender David Higgins sent off in the 45th minute. Meanwhile at Tranmere's ground, Arsenal beat Liverpool 3-2 in the FA Women's Cup final. H.E. Bert McGhee, 77, former Sheff Wed chairman (1975-90), dies.

May

Robson's Middlesbrough promoted . . . Norwich go down . . . Arsenal beaten in Cup-Winners' Cup final . . . Klinsmann to leave Spurs . . . Dundee Utd relegated . . . Blackburn win the Premiership . . . Everton win Cup, Man Utd miss out twice . . . Owls sack Trevor Francis . . . Crewe win Fair Play trophy . . . Ajax win European Cup . . . Celtic win Scottish Cup . . . Bolton promoted . . . Ted Drake dies . . . Chelsea sign Ruud Gullit

1 Despite having 6 first-choice players suspended or injured, Man Utd keep up the pressure on Blackburn with an inspired 3-2 victory at Coventry, Andy Cole scoring twice.

2 Birmingham, held at home 0-0 by Bradford, miss their first chance to clinch promotion from Div 2, while Bournemouth's 3-0 victory over Shrewsbury ensures their survival and at the same time the relegation of both Cambridge and Plymouth.

3 The Premiership relegation battle is the Wednesday night focus, and home draws for West Ham, Everton and Villa bring important points in view of Palace's 3-1 defeat by Southampton. Bolton's failure to get more than a draw at Stoke hands Middlesbrough the Div 1 title and promotion.

4 A 0-0 draw at Bury is enough for Walsall to clinch the second automatic promotion place to Div 2. Jurgen Klinsmann signs a boot deal with Reebok worth £3m over 4 years, but has not yet decided whether to stay with Spurs next season.

6 One of the two remaining Premiership relegation spots is filled when Norwich suffer their 7th successive defeat, 2-1 at Leeds. Palace keep their hopes alive by beating West Ham 1-0, and Villa by beating Liverpool 2-0. A 1-0 win over Man City ensures Forest 3rd or 4th place and a spot in next season's UEFA Cup. Div 1 is playing tomorrow, but the Div 2 programme is completed, with Birmingham finally clinching the title, winning 2-1 at Huddersfield, where one person is injured and several arrested as rival fans clash before the match. Aberdeen win their crucial home match with Dundee Utd to leapfrog above them at the bottom of the Scottish Premier with one round of matches left. Greenock Morton clinch promotion from Div 2, Montrose from Div 3. Noel Brotherston, 38, former N.Ireland winger, dies suddenly from a heart attack in Blackburn.

7 David May, the defender acquired from Blackburn last summer, scores a 5th-minute goal that is enough to beat Sheff Wed and take Man Utd to within 2pts of the leaders with 2 games to play. One fan is killed and several seriously injured when they fall from a stand after a railing collapses at the Jose de Alvalade stadium, home ground of Sporting Lisbon, before the match with Bobby Robson's Porto; Porto's 1-0 victory clinches the Portuguese title.

8 Blackburn clear their penultimate hurdle, beating Newcastle 1-0 in their last home match with a typical far-post header from Alan Shearer after 28min - his 36th goal of the season - but may have to win at Anfield to clinch the Premiership.

9 The 3 Premiership evening games all have a bearing on relegation, Coventry and Everton winning respectively at Spurs and Ipswich to ensure safety, but Palace losing at Leeds to leave themselves on the precipice.

10 Arsenal are cruelly defeated in the Cup-Winners' Cup final 2-1 by Real Zaragoza with the last kick of extra time, as keeper David Seaman, hero of their semi-final penalty shoot-out, is beaten by a brilliant, speculative 40-yard looping shot from former Spurs midfielder Nayim. Man Utd take the Premiership struggle right down to the wire as Denis Irwin converts a late penalty to give them a 2-1 victory over Southampton at Old Trafford. West Ham, who entertain United in their last match next Sunday, beat Liverpool, who entertain Blackburn, by 3-0 to ensure safety.

11 The 'Will he?, Won't he?' saga of Jurgen Klinsmann is finally resolved when Spurs' inspirational striker confirms he is going back to Germany, to join Bayern Munich, but the good news, revealed in another press conference, is that manager Gerry Francis is staying. Villa join Rangers in a £5m bid for Paul Gascoigne.

12 Chelsea director Matthew Harding, who has already committed more than £7m to the club in the last 18 months, buys the freehold of Stamford Bridge from the Royal Bank of Scotland for £16.5m, but neither takes nor wants control of the club.

13 Saturday sees the completion of the Scottish programme, with Dundee Utd, beaten 1-0 at home by Celtic, relegated, and Aberdeen having to play off with Div 1 runners-up Dunfermline, as Raith claim the title with a goalless draw at Hamilton. In Div 2, Dumbarton win 2-0 at Stirling to pip them for the second promotion place.

14 Blackburn win the Carling Premiership, their first Championship for 81 years, despite losing 2-1 at Liverpool, as Man Utd are held 1-1 by West Ham at Upton Park; Blackburn chief Kenny Dalglish thus joins Herbert Chapman and Brian Clough in managing two clubs to the Championship. Palace are relegated after a brave fight at Newcastle, but Wednesday's and Villa's positive results would have consigned them to Div 1 anyway. Chelsea player-manager Glenn Hoddle marks the end of an era as he celebrates his last game with a 2-1 victory over Arsenal at Stamford Bridge. At White Hart Lane, Jurgen Klinsmann, captain for the day, fails to get the goal the Spurs fans wanted, but he is given a standing ovation at the end and the 1-1 draw is sufficient for Leeds to clinch a UEFA Cup place. In Div 1 play-offs, runners-up Reading gain a comprehensive 3-1 1st-leg victory at Tranmere, while Wolves will take a 2-1 lead to Bolton.

15 Palace manager Alan Smith, publicly at loggerheads with his chairman, Ron Noades, for much of the season, is finally sacked. Man Utd win the FA Youth Cup final on penalties from Spurs after Terry Cooke puts them level on aggregate in the last seconds of normal time.

16 As expected, Man City fire manager Brian Horton after 21 months - he is the 12th Premier League manager to get the chop this season, the 52nd League manager to part company with a total of 43 clubs. Mark Kennedy, 18, is called into the Irish senior squad only 2 months after his £2m transfer from Millwall to Liverpool. AC Milan sign Paris SG's Liberian striker George Weah for £5m, with the player getting £1.5m over the 2-year contract.

17 Luckless England keeper David Seaman breaks an ankle playing for Arsenal on their Far Eastern tour. Parma beat fellow Italians Juventus 2-1 on aggregate to win the UEFA Cup. Ilie Dumitrescu, on loan to Sevilla, is returning to Spurs because the Spanish club will not pay the £2m asking fee. Two goals by John McGinlay against Wolves, the second in extra time, put Bolton through to the final of the Div 1 play-offs against Reading. In Div 2, Huddersfield beat Brentford on penalties, while Bristol Rovers beat Crewe on away goals. Chesterfield, with 3 goals in extra time, win their Div 3 play-off 6-3 on aggregate against Mansfield - who have 2 players sent off - and will play Bury at Wembley.

18 Man United's Ukrainian winger Andrei Kanchelskis, who has not played in the team since returning from international duty in April suffering from a stomach problem, announces he no longer wants to play for Alex Ferguson. Aberdeen appoint Roy Aitken as their new manager.

20 Having averted relegation, Joe Royle's Everton win the Cup with a Paul Rideout goal after 30min to deprive Man Utd of their second trophy in a week. Sheff Wed announce that manager Trevor Francis's contract has been terminated by mutual agreement with still a year to run.

21 Wrexham beat Cardiff 2-1 in the National Stadium to win the Welsh Cup for a record 23rd time. Scotland play a goalless draw with Japan in Hiroshima, both teams having a man sent off and Scotland finishing with 9 men.

22 The consortium taking over Cardiff City replace manager Eddie May with Colin Murphy. Arsenal return home from their tour of China and Hong Kong with young midfielder Ray Parlour in disgrace, having been fined around £170 by a Hong Kong court after an incident in which a taxi driver was injured. An arbitration tribunal orders Celtic to pay Kilmarnock £200,000 compensation for poaching manager Tommy Burns and his assistant last year. Graeme Souness returns to the game, agreeing to manage Turkish club Galatasaray on a 1-year contract worth a reported £0.5m. Barcelona complete the £2.8m signing of Spurs' Romanian defender Gica Popescu.

23 Paul Gascoigne is back in England's international squad for the upcoming Umbro Cup, while Ray Parlour is dropped from the U-21s for his misdemeanours in Hong Kong. Southampton manager Alan Ball, one of only 9 Premiership managers to keep their job this season, is given a new 3-year contract. Crewe win the Bobby Moore Fair Play Trophy for the second year running, with only 89 disciplinary points.

24 Ajax lift the European Cup for the 4th time, beating holders AC Milan 1-0 with an 86th-min goal from 18-year-old Patrick Kluivert. Man United's Paul Ince is cleared of threatening behaviour and assaulting a fan. UEFA alter the method of qualifying direct into next season's Champions League, which means Blackburn, as English champions, are seeded 5th and will not have to pre-qualify.

25 UEFA threaten to ban all English clubs from their competitions if the FA do not persuade 3 teams to take part in the Inter Toto Cup. Paul Ince withdraws from the England squad after consultation with Terry Venables, who replaces him with Liverpool's Jamie Redknapp. Aberdeen beat Dunfermline 3-1 to win their play-off 6-2 on aggregate and remain in the Premier League.

26 Man United's Roy Keane is fined a further £5,000 for his red-card offence in the Cup semi replay against Palace, the FA deciding to make a special case of the incident. Everton's uncapped defender David Unsworth, 21, replaces the injured Tony Adams in the England squad.

27 Celtic beat Airdrie 1-0 to win the Scottish Cup, their first major trophy for 6 years, with a goal scored by Dutchman Pierre van Hooijdonk. Chesterfield beat Bury 2-0 in the Div 3 play-off final.

28 Huddersfield beat Bristol Rovers 2-1 in the Div 2 play-off final.

29 The English domestic season, one of the most troubled in the history of the game, concludes with a stirring Wembley final, as Bolton, 2-0 down at half-time, come back to beat Reading 4-3 after extra time to win the Div 1 play-offs and return to the top division after 15 years in the wilderness. Former Sunderland defender Tom Gilbert, only 36, collapses and dies while coaching.

30 Euro '96 matches that go to extra time will be decided by sudden death, or, failing that, penalties. Former Southampton, Arsenal and England centre-forward and Chelsea manager Ted Drake dies at 82. Bobby Stokes, scorer of Southampton's winning goal in the 1976 Cup final, dies of natural causes at the age of 44.

31 Chelsea manager Glenn Hoddle pulls off an audacious coup, signing 32-year-old Dutch goalscoring midfielder Ruud Gullit from Sampdoria on a free transfer; the former shining star of Holland and AC Milan is set to receive about £1.5m over 2 years and play as a sweeper. Sheff Wed, Spurs and Wimbledon have agreed to play in the unpopular Inter Toto Cup.

June

Irish setbacks in Euro qualifiers . . . £6m Ferdinand for Newcastle . . . Bruce Rioch Arsenal's new manager . . . England no match for Brazil in Umbro Cup

2 Chelsea captain Dennis Wise wins his appeal against a 3-month prison sentence for attacking a taxi driver, but receives scathing criticism from the judge and is not awarded costs. Bristol City midfielder Martin Kuhl is banned from driving for 18 months as a result of a near miss with a police car and being over twice the legal alcohol limit. It appears that the 3 clubs persuaded to take part in the Inter Toto Cup have been promised £250,000 each, and the Premier League are demanding £50,000 from each of the other Premiership clubs to fund the entrants.

3 Ireland suffer a severe setback to their Euro '96 qualifying campaign as they are held to a shock 0-0 draw in Liechtenstein. England put up an embarrassing performance at Wembley in the opening match of the Umbro Cup, just scraping a 2-1 win over Japan with a late penalty by captain David Platt, albeit with a makeshift side including 4 new caps - defenders Gary Neville (Man Utd), David Unsworth (Everton) and John Scales (Liverpool) and striker Stan Collymore (Forest); Paul Gascoigne, on his way to Rangers to confirm his end-of-the-month transfer from Lazio, comes on as a 68th-min sub. Newcastle sign England full-back Warren Barton from Wimbledon for £4m (plus £1m after 50 games)

4 Brazil beat Sweden 1-0 at Villa Park in the Umbro Cup.
5 Neil Warnock, manager of promoted Huddersfield, resigns. Notts Co appoint a managerial partnership - Colin Murphy as general manager, Steve Thompson responsible for team affairs.
6 Brazil brush Japan aside 3-0 in the Umbro Cup with a masterly display of football, while their Under-21s beat England 2-0 in the Toulon Tournament. Bobby Robson accepts that his contract with Porto cannot be broken and declines a £2m offer from Arsenal.
7 Newcastle sign England striker Les Ferdinand, 28, from QPR for £6m, 10% of which will go to Diadora League club Hayes. A poor night for British clubs in the Euro Championship sees Wales return to the bottom of Gp 7 after losing 1-0 at home to Georgia and having Vinnie Jones sent off for stamping on an opponent, N.Ireland blow their chances in Gp 6 with a 2-1 home defeat by Latvia, and Scotland making a meal of their 2-0 win away to the Faroes in Gp 8, where Russia show how it should be done, winning 7-0 in San Marino. Germany lose 3-2 to Gp 7 runaway leaders Bulgaria after leading 2-0, but the biggest shock is Luxembourg's 1-0 defeat of the Czechs.
8 Arsenal appoint Bolton's Bruce Rioch as their new manager. Two goals in the last 2min, including a spectacular equaliser from Darren Anderton, give England a lucky draw against a superior Swedish side in the Umbro Cup at Elland Road. Former manager Steve Coppell returns to Palace as technical director. Paul Ince is stunned by Man United's decision to accept a reported offer of £8m from Inter-Milan.
10 England beat Nigeria 3-2 to reach the quarter-finals of the Women's World Championships.
11 Ireland stutter to a disastrous 3-1 defeat in Dublin by Austria after taking a 65th-min lead and their once odds-on chances of qualifying for Euro '96 take a nose-dive. Brazil come back from 1-0 down with a fluent display to beat England 3-1 at Wembley and win the Umbro Cup. UEFA back the joint Holland-Belgium bid to host Euro 2000.
12 Last season's Spurs love affair with Jurgen Klinsmann looks like ending in acrimony as the German striker accuses chairman Alan Sugar (who reportedly wants him suspended until FIFA have investigated their contractual dispute) of attempting to sour his relationship with English supporters. England and Scotland are beaten in the semis of the Toulon U-21 Tournament by France and Brazil respectively.

Jack Rollin about to receive a Rothmans Award of a crystal decanter from the then Arsenal manager George Graham to mark the 25th edition of Rothmans Football Yearbook. In the background, Master of Ceremonies Jim Rosenthal.

Review of the season

Blackburn Rovers may not have been the most scintillating championship winners of all time, but there was an admirable balance and adaptability about a team which was maintained despite several forced and unforced changes. Moreover, they fully deserved to celebrate their first title success for 81 years.

The key roles were undoubtedly found in defence and attack with centre-back Colin Hendry and striker Alan Shearer outstanding. Hendry intelligently covered large areas of ground at the rear, organising on the ground and commanding in the air, while Shearer effectively kept the attack flowing as well as contributing 34 goals. He was well supported by £5 million capture Chris Sutton and these two accounted for all but 31 of Blackburn's League total.

Oddly enough Blackburn lost both matches to their nearest rivals from Old Trafford. On 23 October they crashed 4-2 at home and were lying fourth at the time of the defeat. However this proved to be something of a spur, as they embarked on a run of 12 unbeaten games which took them into first place. The sequence was ended — by United! This time they went down to a single goal defeat at Old Trafford.

Blackburn called upon the services of 21 different players during the season. Shearer was the only ever present in the ranks, Hendry and Tim Sherwood each missed four matches, Henning Berg and Chris Sutton two each, while Graeme Le Saux and Tim Flowers were absent on three occasions.

Shearer scored three hat-tricks and ten penalties, Sutton one treble. At the back, United's success in scoring four times against the Blackburn defence was an isolated event; no other team in the Premiership managed to score as many in one game, though the Mancunian connection across at Manchester City was responsible for a 3-2 win at Ewood Park in the middle of April, a reverse which then gave United some cause for hope that they might still catch their opponents.

Blackburn failed to score in just five games, three of these finishing as goalless draws. The defence produced 16 clean sheets, eight at home and eight away. Their highest wins were 4-0 against both Coventry and Queens Park Rangers. Significantly, they did not have more than a two-match gap without a win.

Arguably the biggest disappointment of the season was the failure to reach beyond the first round in the UEFA Cup, though this might well have proved a blessing in their ultimate aim of the championship title.

Manager Kenny Dalglish was always mindful of using the full width of the pitch in his preferred 4-4-2 formation and though he did not have a large pool of players on whom to call, one or two judicious moves into the transfer market at crucial moments proved well justified. The club owed much to the money lavished on it by millionaire Jack Walker, but the overall approach by everyone connected with Blackburn proved a winning formula. Yet in some respects, the last game of the season became almost anti-climatic.

Manchester United had to win at West Ham and hope Liverpool defeated Blackburn at Anfield. A draw would have been enough for Blackburn, who took the lead, lost it and the game in the last seconds, only for news to filter through almost immediately that United had only managed a draw themselves.

Six days later, Manchester United were to lose the FA Cup Final. Over the season they could point to the loss of the suspended Eric Cantona, injuries to wingers Andrei Kanchelskis and Ryan Giggs, plus loss of form elsewhere in the team for failure to retain the title. At Old Trafford they were practically invincible. Peter Schmeichel conceded just two goals there, Gary Walsh letting in the other two in the United's only home defeat 2-1 to Nottingham Forest on 17 December. All told, United boasted 24 clean sheets.

Forest, in fact, were 11 points behind in third place. Stan Collymore scored freely for a team who often looked the most attractive the League. They finished the season in style: 13 games unbeaten. Collymore joined Liverpool in the summer for an English record £8.5 million, his new team having finished a respectable fourth and winners of the Coca-Cola Cup. Their attitude in the final match of the season against Blackburn was both a credit to themselves and the competition as a whole. Top scorer Robbie Fowler hit the fastest Premier League hat-trick in five minutes against Arsenal in August.

Leeds made several useful signings from Africa, the most successful of them being Tony Yeboah, the Ghana international striker from Germany, but Newcastle United fell away after a perfect start and the sale of Andy Cole to Manchester United. Tottenham Hotspur improved after the psychological barrier of points deduction was removed and German striker Jurgen Klinsmann enjoyed his brief season in English football.

Attractive Queens Park Rangers ended the campaign in eighth place, their highest all season and Wimbledon tailed off after causing several notable upsets. Southampton equalled the number of draws in the Premier League and seven of their 18 came in successive matches. A spell of ten games ending in mid-February upset Chelsea and Arsenal, who had a mid-table look all season, did best in Europe, just failing to retain the Cup-Winners' Cup.

Disappointing Sheffield Wednesday even suffered their heaviest home defeat when losing 7-1 to Nottingham Forest on April Fools' Day, but West Ham made up six places in the last two months to avoid relegation. A change of manager had a dramatic effect on Everton's season and they climbed to 15th themselves in the latter stages. Any inflated hopes that Coventry had ended from early December with 11 matches without a win. Manchester City had similar problems around the same time and showed inconsistency in attack, while Aston Villa contrived only one win in the last 11 matches.

However, the four relegated clubs were Crystal Palace, Norwich City, Leicester City and Ipswich Town. Palace scraped only 34 goals and went nine successive games without scoring even one. Norwich plummeted with only one win from their last 20, Leicester were never out of the bottom two from November and Ipswich produced fewest points, the heaviest defeat-9-0 at Manchester United -and more reverses than anyone else.

Middlesbrough justifiably emerged as champions of the Endsleigh First Division, finishing with only one defeat in their last ten. But the play-off system dealt cruelly to second placed Reading, who reached the final against Bolton Wanderers at Wembley to become involved in one of the most exciting matches of the 1994-95 season. They led 2-0, missed a penalty and were beaten 4-3 in extra time. Third placed Bolton, who had finished as runners-up to Liverpool in the Coca-Cola Cup, had incredibly failed to score more than one goal in any of their last 13 League games in the regular season.

Wolverhampton Wanderers were handicapped by drawing seven of their last nine matches and losing one of the other two, while Tranmere failed to win any of the last five. Barnsley, as high as third on Boxing Day, were unable to stay the course, Watford had little to show for 20 clean sheets and Sheffield United, fourth on 18 March, managed only one other win. Derby also faltered with a single victory among the last seven games, Grimsby were fourth on 3 December and a late revival for Stoke only took them to half-way.

Millwall reached the fifth round of both major cup competitions, yet had one run of ten in the League without a win and nine without defeat. Southend won eight of their last 12, Oldham scored them freely and conceded goals just as easily, Charlton Athletic were as high as sixth by the end of October and Luton snatched just one win from the final ten games.

Alan Shearer turns to acknowledge the cheers of Blackburn supporters at Anfield after his opening goal against Liverpool. Though Rovers were beaten by a last minute goal from Jamie Redknapp, Manchester United's failure to win at West Ham was enough for Blackburn to take the title. (Action Images)

Matt Le Tissier avoids Norwich City's tackling duo of Jon Newsome (left) and Ian Crook. Both Southampton matches with Norwich were drawn last season. In fact the Saints were the draw specialists of the Premiership, while Le Tissier was their inspiration. (Colorsport)

Inconsistency prevented Port Vale from making any substantial impact, but Portsmouth showed a second-half improvement after a string of nine matches without victory.

West Bromwich were handicapped by having to play their first five games away because of ground improvements and had to struggle up to reach even 19th. Sunderland hauled themselves out of trouble following the appointment of Peter Reid as manager, but it was relegation for Swindon Town, Burnley, Bristol City and Notts County.

Swindon's season collapsed having been as high as fifth on 29 October. Burnley's leaky defence prevented the opposition from scoring only four times, Bristol City won one of their last 11 as did Notts County, whose consolation was winning the Anglo-Italian Cup.

Birmingham City survived one stumbling period to lose just once in the last third of the season and as Second Division champions were excellently supported. Brentford failed in the play-offs but had a free-scoring attacking duo in Nicky Forster and Robert Taylor, while the defence produced 22 clean sheets, 14 of them at home.

Crewe Alexandra were also unable to overcome the play-offs, despite finishing strongly with ten undefeated games and a similar fate befell Bristol Rovers with one defeat in the last 15. However, fifth placed Huddersfield Town, who had slipped slightly after a splendid opening when they suffered just one defeat in 15 -and that on their debut at the new ground -came through to join Birmingham in promotion.

Wycombe Wanderers' hopes were dashed with five successive scoreless games in March, Oxford United failed to live up to early-season promise as did Hull who were fourth on 5 November. York City improved too late for the play-offs, and Swansea City never appeared to mount a serious challenge of their own. Goalkeeper Roger Freestone even converted a late season penalty. Injury to Kevin Francis and his subsequent move to Birmingham affected Stockport County and Blackpool in spite of reaching fifth on several occasions, lacked consistency.

Wrexham were unable to improve on 13th place despite having in Gary Bennett, the country's leading goalscorer. Bradford City had a good opening spell and a poor late one, Peterborough went 12 games without a win at the turn of the year and Brighton were never as convincing after the transfer of Kurt Nogan to Burnley. Rotherham United hovered just above the relegation zone as did Shrewsbury Town, but Bournemouth showed distinct improvement in the New Year.

Jan Aage Fjortoft (right), Middlesbrough's late season capture from Swindon Town at £1.3 million, celebrates Alan Moore's goal on the way towards the Ayresome Park club winning a place back in the top echelon. (Action Images)

The five clubs demoted were Cambridge United, Plymouth Argyle, Cardiff City, Chester City and Leyton Orient. Cambridge never recovered from a run of ten games without a win, Plymouth had a wretched start with only two points from a possible 21, Cardiff were never higher than 19th, Chester had a disastrous sequence of 16 games without a win from November and Leyton Orient lost their last nine games.

At one stage, Carlisle United seemed capable of breaking several records in Division Three. They suffered only their second defeat of the season on 18 February losing 1-0 at Preston and twice had crowds of over 12,000. They were joined in automatic promotion by Walsall, who produced several strong runs of consecutive wins.

Third placed Chesterfield were able to give some logic to the play-offs and owed much to their defence which enjoyed 22 clean sheets. Bury themselves managed one fewer, but lost out to Chesterfield at Wembley despite a late run of 11 games without defeat. Preston, back on grass, again found the play-offs too difficult but had improved under a new manager. Free-scoring Mansfield were third on 11 March but had some defensive frailties.

Scunthorpe, as high as fifth in January, also missed out on the play-offs as did Fulham, whose best sequence was one of ten unbeaten matches, starting on New Year's Eve. Doncaster Rovers were as high as third on 10 December but they too faltered along with Colchester fifth in February after winning 1-0 at Barnet, who had been hit by eight games without a win prior to the New Year.

Lincoln had a mid-table look throughout the season, though they were the last to fail to score a goal at home, Torquay never improved after a fine beginning and Wigan were never higher than 12th all season. Rochdale's lack of scoring power was evident after a useful start and 16th place was as high as Hereford managed all season.

Northampton were never higher than one place lower than this, but were well supported at their new ground from the middle of October. Hartlepool pulled themselves together after a run of 12 games without a win, Gillingham's financial position never kept them far from the bottom and Darlington won only one of their last 14 games.

Scarborough completed a club record 16 matches without a win ending in January and Exeter, who also faced serious financial problems, finished last after a run of 16 unsuccessful games of their own at the end of the season. They escaped demotion as Vauxhall Conference champions Macclesfield had been informed much earlier that their ground did not meet Football League requirements, despite providing Chester with a home two years earlier!

INTRODUCTION TO THE CLUB SECTION

For the first time since Rothmans Football Yearbook was originally formulated, this edition introduces a complete change in the way in which players in the 92 League clubs are presented. Instead of the names appearing under the club with whom they were last with in the previous season, there is an A-Z of all such players (see pages 404-532). However, in an easy-to-read guide, the name of the player's last club is indicated in black. All other aspects of the players' details are kept intact as in previous editions.

Because of this alteration to the club section, this now comprises four instead of six pages. The first page again features the team photograph depicting those players and officials taken at the beginning of the 1994-95 season. On the second page which gives historical and record details for each club, the information which was previously to be found on the sixth page of this section is now incorporated here. As a result of this, the club badge has been moved to page three while page four has an added piece of information with the initials of all players appearing for that club during the 1994-95 season.

Again, the third and fourth pages give a complete record of the League season, including date, venue, opponents, result, half-time score, League position, goalscorers, attendance and complete line-ups, including substitutes where used, for every League game in the 1994-95 season. Once again, squad numbers have been ignored; those used are familar ones, 1-11, 12, 14 and 15. The No. 15 represents the substitute goalkeeper. Players replaced are respectively given a light type figure, an italic one with a bold italic for the goalkeeper. These two pages also include consolidated lists of goalscorers for the club in League, Coca-Cola and FA Cup matches and a summary of results in these two main domestic cups.

Due to the increase in the number of matches played on Sundays, the League positions shown after every League result takes into consideration the final standings on this day. Full holiday programmes are also recorded, but the position after mid-week fixtures will not normally be updated. Attendance figures quoted for each Endsleigh Insurance League game are those which appeared in the Press at the time. But those in the FA Carling Premiership are official. The attendance statistics published on pages 574 and 575 are those officially issued by the Football League at the end of the season. However, the figures for each League games are those used in conjunction with the Daily Telegraph and Jack Rollin's weekly statistics in that newspaper.

In the totals at the top of each column on page four, substitute appearances are listed separately by the '+', but have been amalgamated in the totals which feature in the player's historical section in the directory mentioned above. Thus these appearances include those as substitute. In fact the players directory again features those whose names appear on the FA Premier League and Football League's 'Retained' list, which is published at the end of May. Each player's height and weight where known, plus birth place, birth date and source together with total League goals and appearances for each club he has represented can be found as in previous editions. The player's details remain under the club which retain him at the end of the season. An asterisk * by a player's name indicates that he was given a free transfer at the end of the 1994-95 season, a dagger against a name means that he is a non-contract player, a double dagger indicates that the player's registration was cancelled during the season and a SS indicates either a Trainee or an Associated Schoolboy who has made FA Premier League or Football League apperances. Appearances by players in the play-offs are not included in their career totals.

There is also a directory of all League club managers and a separate section with new stories in the 'Did you know' series.

ARSENAL 1994-95 *Back row (left to right):* Pat Rice (Youth Team Coach), Gary Lewin (Physio), Lee Harper, Steve Morrow, Paul Merson, Martin Keown, Andy Linighan, David Seaman, Nigel Winterburn, Alan Smith, Scott Marshall, Ray Parlour, Alan Miller, Stewart Houston (First Team Coach), George Armstrong (Reserve Team Coach).
Front row: Steve Bould, Stefan Schwarz, David Hillier, Kevin Campbell, Jimmy Carter, Eddie McGoldrick, Ian Wright, George Graham (Manager), Tony Adams, John Jensen, Paul Davis, Lee Dixon, Paul Dickov, Ian Selley, Mark Flatts.

FA Premiership **ARSENAL**

Arsenal Stadium, Highbury, London N5 1BU. Telephone: (0171) 226 0304. Box Office: (0171) 354 5404. Commercial and Marketing (0171) 359 0808. Recorded information on (0171)359 0131. Clubline: 0891 20 20 20. Mail Order (0171) 354 8397.

Ground capacity: 38,500 all seated.

Record attendance: 73,295 v Sunderland, Div 1, 9 March 1935.

Record receipts: £392,726.50 v Sampdoria, European Cup-Winners Cup, semi-final first leg, 6 April 1995.

Pitch measurements: 110yd × 71yd.

Chairman: P. D. Hill-Wood. ***Vice-Chairman:*** D. Dein.

Directors: Sir Robert Bellinger CBE, DSC, R. G. Gibbs, C. E. B. L. Carr, R. C. S. Carr, D. D. Fiszman.

Managing Director: K. J. Friar.

Manager: Bruce Rioch. ***Assistant Manager/Coach:*** Stewart Houston.

Physio: Gary Lewin. ***Reserve Coach:*** George Armstrong. ***Youth Coach:*** Pat Rice.

Secretary: K. J. Friar. ***Assistant Secretary:*** David Miles. ***Commercial Manager:*** John Hazell. ***Marketing Manager:*** Phil Carling.

Year Formed: 1886. ***Turned Professional:*** 1891. ***Ltd Co.:*** 1893.

Previous Names: 1886, Dial Square; 1886–91, Royal Arsenal; 1891–1914, Woolwich Arsenal.

Club Nickname: 'Gunners'.

Previous Grounds: 1886–87, Plumstead Common; 1887–88, Sportsman Ground; 1888–90, Manor Ground; 1890–93, Invicta Ground; 1893–1913, Manor Ground; 1913, Highbury.

Foundation: Formed by workers at the Royal Arsenal, Woolwich in 1886 they began as Dial Square (name of one of the workshops) and included two former Nottingham Forest players Fred Beardsley and Morris Bates. Beardsley wrote to his old club seeking help and they provided the new club with a full set of red jerseys and a ball. The club became known as the "Woolwich Reds" although their official title soon after formation was Woolwich Arsenal.

First Football League game: 2 September, 1893, Division 2, v Newcastle U (h) D 2-2 – Williams; Powell, Jeffrey; Devine, Buist, Howat; Gemmell, Henderson, Shaw (1), Elliott (1), Booth.

Record League Victory: 12–0 v Loughborough T, Division 2, 12 March 1900 – Orr; McNichol, Jackson; Moir, Dick (2), Anderson (1); Hunt, Cottrell (2), Main (2), Gaudie (3), Tennant (2).

Record Cup Victory: 11–1 v Darwen, FA Cup, 3rd rd, 9 January 1932 – Moss; Parker, Hapgood; Jones, Roberts, John; Hulme (2), Jack (3), Lambert (2), James, Bastin (4).

Record Defeat: 0–8 v Loughborough T, Division 2, 12 December 1896.

Most League Points (2 for a win): 66, Division 1, 1930–31.

Most League Points (3 for a win): 83, Division 1, 1990–91.

Most League Goals: 127, Division 1, 1930–31.

Highest League Scorer in Season: Ted Drake, 42, 1934–35.

Most League Goals in Total Aggregate: Cliff Bastin, 150, 1930–47.

Most Capped Player: Kenny Sansom, 77 (86), England.

Most League Appearances: David O'Leary, 558, 1975–93.

Record Transfer Fee Received: £2,000,000 from Leeds U for David Rocastle.

Record Transfer Fee Paid: £7,500,000 to Internazionale for Dennis Bergkamp, June 1995.

Football League Record: 1893 Elected to Division 2; 1904–13 Division 1; 1913–19 Division 2; 1919–92 Division 1; 1992– FA Premier League.

Honours: *Football League:* Division 1 – Champions 1930–31, 1932–33, 1933–34, 1934–35, 1937–38, 1947–48, 1952–53, 1970–71, 1988–89, 1990–91; Runners-up 1925–26, 1931–32, 1972–73; Division 2 – Runners-up 1903–04. *FA Cup:* Winners 1930, 1936, 1950, 1971, 1979, 1993; Runners-up 1927, 1932, 1952, 1972, 1978, 1980. *Double performed:* 1970–71. *Football League Cup:* Winners 1987, 1993; Runners-up 1968, 1969, 1988. **European Competitions:** *Fairs Cup:* 1963–64, 1969–70 (winners), 1970–71; *European Cup:* 1971–72, 1991–92; *UEFA Cup:* 1978–79, 1981–82, 1982–83; *European Cup-Winners' Cup:* 1979–80 (runners-up), 1993–94 (winners), 1994–95 (runners-up).

Colours: Red shirts with white sleeves, white shorts, red and white hooped stockings. **Change colours:** Navy shirts with teal sleeves, navy shorts, navy and teal hooped stockings.

ARSENAL 1994–95 LEAGUE RECORD

Match No.	Date	Venue	Opponents	Result	H/T Score	Lg. Pos.	Goalscorers	Attendance
1	Aug 20	H	Manchester C	W 3-0	2-0	—	Campbell, Coton (og), Wright	38,368
2	23	A	Leeds U	L 0-1	0-0	—		34,318
3	28	A	Liverpool	L 0-3	0-3	14		30,017
4	31	H	Blackburn R	D 0-0	0-0	—		37,629
5	Sept 10	A	Norwich C	D 0-0	0-0	12		17,768
6	18	H	Newcastle U	L 2-3	1-2	15	Adams, Wright	36,819
7	25	A	West Ham U	W 2-0	1-0	14	Adams, Wright	18,495
8	Oct 1	H	Crystal Palace	L 1-2	0-2	14	Wright	34,136
9	8	A	Wimbledon	W 3-1	1-0	12	Wright, Smith, Campbell	10,842
10	15	H	Chelsea	W 3-1	1-1	11	Wright 2, Campbell	38,234
11	23	H	Coventry C	W 2-1	2-0	9	Wright 2	31,725
12	29	A	Everton	D 1-1	1-1	10	Schwarz	32,005
13	Nov 6	H	Sheffield W	D 0-0	0-0	10		33,705
14	19	A	Southampton	L 0-1	0-0	11		15,201
15	23	A	Leicester C	L 1-2	1-2	—	Wright (pen)	20,774
16	26	H	Manchester U	D 0-0	0-0	12		38,301
17	Dec 3	A	Nottingham F	D 2-2	0-1	12	Keown, Davis	21,662
18	12	A	Manchester C	W 2-1	2-0	—	Smith, Schwarz	20,500
19	17	H	Leeds U	L 1-3	0-1	11	Linighan	38,100
20	26	H	Aston Villa	D 0-0	0-0	11		34,452
21	28	A	Ipswich T	W 2-0	1-0	9	Wright, Campbell	22,047
22	31	H	QPR	L 1-3	0-1	13	Jensen	32,393
23	Jan 2	A	Tottenham H	L 0-1	0-1	13		28,747
24	14	H	Everton	D 1-1	1-1	13	Wright	34,743
25	21	A	Coventry C	W 1-0	0-0	,11	Hartson	14,557
26	24	H	Southampton	D 1-1	1-0	—	Hartson	27,213
27	Feb 4	A	Sheffield W	L 1-3	1-2	11	Linighan	23,468
28	11	H	Leicester C	D 1-1	0-0	12	Merson	31,373
29	21	H	Nottingham F	W 1-0	0-0	—	Kiwomya	35,441
30	25	A	Crystal Palace	W 3-0	2-0	8	Merson, Kiwomya 2	17,063
31	Mar 5	H	West Ham U	L 0-1	0-1	9		36,295
32	8	A	Blackburn R	L 1-3	0-2	—	Morrow	23,452
33	19	A	Newcastle U	L 0-1	0-0	13		35,611
34	22	A	Manchester U	L 0-3	0-2	—		43,623
35	Apr 1	H	Norwich C	W 5-1	3-1	10	Hartson 2, Dixon, Merson, Newman (og)	36,942
36	8	A	QPR	L 1-3	0-1	12	Adams	16,341
37	12	H	Liverpool	L 0-1	0-0	—		38,036
38	15	H	Ipswich T	W 4-1	1-0	10	Merson, Wright 3	36,818
39	17	A	Aston Villa	W 4-0	2-0	10	Hartson 2, Wright 2 (1 pen)	32,005
40	29	H	Tottenham H	D 1-1	0-0	10	Wright (pen)	38,377
41	May 4	H	Wimbledon	D 0-0	0-0	—		32,822
42	14	A	Chelsea	L 1-2	1-1	12	Hartson	29,542

Final League Position: 12

GOALSCORERS

League (52): Wright 18 (3 pens), Hartson 7, Campbell 4, Merson 4, Adams 3, Kiwomya 3, Linighan 2, Schwarz 2, Smith 2, Davis 1, Dixon 1, Jensen 1, Keown 1, Morrow 1, own goals 2.
Coca-Cola Cup (11): Dickov 3, Wright 3, Adams 1, Campbell 1, Merson 1, Morrow 1, Smith 1.
FA Cup (0).

Seaman D.A. 31	Dixon L.M. 39	Winterburn N. 39	Schwarz S. 34	Bould S.A. 30 + 1	Adams T.A. 27	Campbell K.J. 19 + 4	Wright I.E. 30 + 1	Smith A.M. 17 + 2	Merson P.C. 24	Jensen J. 24	Keown M.R. 24 + 7	Dickov P. 4 + 5	Linighan A. 13 + 7	Davis P. 3 + 1	Selley I. 10 + 3	Parlour R. 22 + 8	McGoldrick E.J.P. 9 + 2	Hillier D. 5 + 4	Carter J.W.C. 2 + 1	Morrow S.J. 11 + 4	Bartram V.L. 11	Flatts M. 1 + 2	Shaw P. — + 1	Hughes S.J. 1	Clarke A.J. — + 1	Hartson J. 14 + 1	Kiwomya C.M. 5 + 9	Helder G. 12 + 1	McGowan G.G. 1	*Match No.*
1	2	3	4	5	6	7	8	9	*10*	11	12	14																		1
1	2	3	4	5	6	7	8	9	10	11	12																			2
1	2	3	4		6	7	8	9	*10*	11	5		12	14																3
1	2	3	4		*6*	7	8	9	10	11	5	12	14																	4
1	2	3	4		6	9	8	12			5				7	10	11													5
1	2	3	4		6	12	8	9	10	7	5				14	*11*														6
1	2	3	4		6		8	9	10		5		12	11	7															7
1	2	3	4		6	12	8	9	10				5	11	7															8
1	2	3	4	5	6	10	8	9		7						11		12												9
1	2	3	4	5	6	10	8	9		7	12				14	11														10
1	2	3	4	5		10	8	9			6				7	11	12													11
1		*3*	4		6	8		9	10	7	5		12		14	11	2													12
1		3	4	5	6	12		9			2	10			7	8	11													13
1	2	3	4	5	6	9					10	8			7		11		12											14
1	2	3	4	5		12	8				10	9	6		*7*				11	14										15
1	2	3		5	6		8	9		*7*	14	12					11		10	4										16
	2	3	4	5		9					6			10		11		7			1	8	12							17
	2	3	4	5		8		9		7	6					11				10	1									18
	2	3	4	5		8		*9*		7	6		12			11				10	1	14								19
	2	3	4	5		9					6	8				11				10	1	12		7						20
	2	3	4	5		10	*8*	9		7	6	14	12			11					1									21
	2	3	4	5		10	8	9		7	6					11					1				12					22
1	2	3	4	5		9	8	12		7			6		10	11														23
1	2	3	4				8			7	5		6			*11*		10		12						9	14			24
1	2		4	5		7	*8*				11		6			12		10		3						9	14			25
1	2		4	5			8			7	*3*		6			11		14		10						9	12			26
1	2	3			6	8			10	7	12		5		*4*	14										9	11			27
1	2	3			6				10	*4*	12		5		7	14	11									9	8			28
1	2	3	4	5					10	7			6				11										9	8		29
1	2	3	4	5					10	7			6			14	11			*12*							9	8		30
	2	3	4	5			8		10	7			6			11				12	1						14	*9*		31
	2	3	4	14	6		12		10				*5*			11				7	1					9		8		32
	2	3		5	6		8		10	7						12	14			4	1					*9*		11		33
	2	3		5	6		8		10		7					11				4	1						9	12		34
	2	3		5	6		8		10		12							4		7	1					*9*	14	11		35
1	2	3	4	5	6		8		10									14		*7*						9	12	11		36
1		3	4	5	6		8		*10*		7					14	2	11								12		9		37
1	2	3	4	5	6		*8*		10		7					12										9	14	11		38
1	2	3	4	5	6		*8*		10		7					11		12								9	14			39
1	2	3	4	5	6		8		10		7					12										9		11		40
1	2	3			6		8		10	7			5			4										9	12	11		41
1	2			5	6		8		10	7		12	14			4										9		11	*3*	42

Coca-Cola Cup

Second Round	Hartlepool U (a)	5-0
	(h)	2-0
Third Round	Oldham Ath (a)	0-0
	(h)	2-0
Fourth Round	Sheffield W (h)	2-0
Fifth Round	Liverpool (a)	0-1

FA Cup

Third Round	Millwall (a)	0-0
	(h)	0-2

ASTON VILLA 1994–95 *Back row (left to right):* David Farrell, Ugo Ehiogu, Paul McGrath, John Fashanu, Shaun Teale, Andy Townsend, Garry Parker.
Centre row: Jim Walker, Graham Fenton, Guy Whittingham, Nigel Spink, Mark Bosnich, Michael Oakes, Bryan Small, Earl Barrett, Jim Barron.
Front row: Dwight Yorke, Nii Lamptey, Ray Houghton, Kevin Richardson, Ron Atkinson, Dean Saunders, Dalian Atkinson, Phil King, Steve Staunton.
(Photograph: Mike Smith)

FA Premiership ASTON VILLA

Villa Park, Trinity Rd, Birmingham B6 6HE. Telephone: (0121) 327 2299. Fax: (0121) 322 2107. Commercial Dept: (0121) 327 5399. Clubcall: 0891 121148. Ticketline: 0891 121848. Ticket office: (0121) 327 5353. Club shop: (0121) 327 2800.

Ground capacity: 40,310.

Record attendance: 76,588 v Derby Co, FA Cup 6th rd, 2 March 1946.

Record receipts: £1,005,402 Manchester U v Crystal Palace, FA Cup semi-final, 9 April 1995.

Pitch measurements: 115yd × 75yd.

President: H. J. Musgrove. ***Chairman:*** H. D. Ellis.

Directors: J. A. Alderson, Dr D. H. Targett, P. D. Ellis.

Manager: Brian Little. ***Assistant Manager:*** Allan Evans. ***First Team Coach:*** John Gregory.

Secretary: Steven Stride. ***Director of Youth:*** Peter Withe.

Physio: Jim Walker. ***Youth Coach:*** Tony McAndrew. ***Chief Scout:*** Malcolm Beard. ***Fitness Consultant:*** Paul Barron.

Commercial Manager: Abdul Rashid.

Year Formed: 1874. ***Turned Professional:*** 1885. ***Ltd Co.:*** 1896.

Previous Grounds: 1874–76, Aston Park; 1876–97, Perry Barr; 1897, Villa Park.

Club Nickname: 'The Villans'.

Foundation: Cricketing enthusiasts of Villa Cross Wesleyan Chapel, Aston, Birmingham decided to form a football club during the winter of 1873–74. Football clubs were few and far between in the Birmingham area and in their first game against Aston Brook St. Mary's Rugby team they played one half rugby and the other soccer. In 1876 they were joined by a Scottish soccer enthusiast George Ramsay who was immediately appointed captain and went on to lead Aston Villa from obscurity to one of the country's top clubs in a period of less than 10 years.

First Football League game: 8 September, 1888, Football League, v Wolverhampton W, (a) D 1-1 – Warner; Cox, Coulton; Yates, H. Devey, Dawson; A. Brown, Green (1), Allen, Garvey, Hodgetts.

Record League Victory: 12–2 v Accrington S, Division 1, 12 March 1892 – Warner; Evans, Cox; Harry Devey, Jimmy Cowan, Baird; Athersmith (1), Dickson (2), John Devey (4), L. Campbell (4), Hodgetts (1).

Record Cup Victory: 13–0 v Wednesbury Old Ath, FA Cup, 1st rd, 30 October 1886 – Warner; Coulton, Simmonds; Yates, Robertson, Burton (2); R. Davis (1), A. Brown (3), Hunter (3), Loach (2), Hodgetts (2).

Record Defeat: 1–8 v Blackburn R, FA Cup, 3rd rd, 16 February 1889.

Most League Points (2 for a win): 70, Division 3, 1971–72.

Most League Points (3 for a win): 78, Division 2, 1987–88.

Most League Goals: 128, Division 1, 1930–31.

Highest League Scorer in Season: 'Pongo' Waring, 49, Division 1, 1930–31.

Most League Goals in Total Aggregate: Harry Hampton, 215, 1904–15.

Most Capped Player: Paul McGrath, 45 (76), Republic of Ireland.

Most League Appearances: Charlie Aitken, 561, 1961–76.

Record Transfer Fee Received: £5,500,000 from Bari for David Platt, August 1991.

Record Transfer Fee Paid: £3,500,000 to Partizan Belgrade for Savo Milosevic, June 1995.

Football League Record: 1888 Founder Member of the League; 1936–38 Division 2; 1938–59 Division 1; 1959–60 Division 2; 1960–67 Division 1; 1967–70 Division 2; 1970–72 Division 3; 1972–75 Division 2; 1975–87 Division 1; 1987–88 Division 2; 1988–92 Division 1; 1992– FA Premier League.

Honours: *FA Premier League:* – Runners-up 1992–93. *Football League:* Division 1 – Champions 1893–94, 1895–96, 1896–97, 1898–99, 1899–1900, 1909–10, 1980–81; Runners-up 1888–89, 1902–03, 1907–08, 1910–11, 1912–13, 1913–14, 1930–31, 1932–33, 1989–90; Division 2 – Champions 1937–38, 1959–60; Runners-up 1974–75, 1987–88; Division 3 – Champions 1971–72. *FA Cup:* Winners 1887, 1895, 1897, 1905, 1913, 1920, 1957; Runners-up 1892, 1924. *Double Performed:* 1896–97. *Football League Cup:* Winners 1961, 1975, 1977, 1994; Runners-up 1963, 1971. **European Competitions:** *European Cup:* 1981–82 (winners), 1982–83; *UEFA Cup:* 1975–76, 1977–78, 1983–84, 1990–91, 1993–94, 1994–95. *World Club Championship:* 1982; European Super Cup: 1982–83 (winners).

Colours: Claret body, sky blue sleeves, sky blue collar with trim, white shorts, claret stockings with sky blue top. **Change colours:** Dark blue body, sky blue trim & collar, sky blue shorts, dark blue stockings, sky blue top.

ASTON VILLA 1994–95 LEAGUE RECORD

Match No.	Date	Venue	Opponents	Result		H/T Score	Lg. Pos.	Goalscorers	Attendance
1	Aug 20	A	Everton	D	2-2	0-1	—	Fashanu, Saunders	35,552
2	24	H	Southampton	D	1-1	1-0	—	Saunders	24,179
3	27	H	Crystal Palace	D	1-1	0-0	12	Staunton	23,305
4	29	A	Coventry C	W	1-0	1-0	—	Yorke	12,218
5	Sept 10	H	Ipswich T	W	2-0	1-0	9	Staunton, Saunders	22,241
6	17	A	West Ham U	L	0-1	0-0	8		18,326
7	24	A	Blackburn R	L	1-3	0-1	9	Ehiogu	22,694
8	Oct 1	H	Newcastle U	L	0-2	0-0	12		29,960
9	8	A	Liverpool	L	2-3	1-2	14	Whittingham, Staunton	32,158
10	15	H	Norwich C	D	1-1	0-0	16	Saunders	22,468
11	22	H	Nottingham F	L	0-2	0-1	16		29,217
12	29	A	QPR	L	0-2	0-1	19		16,073
13	Nov 6	H	Manchester U	L	1-2	1-1	19	Atkinson	32,136
14	9	A	Wimbledon	L	3-4	2-1	—	Parker, Saunders 2	6221
15	19	A	Tottenham H	W	4-3	3-1	19	Atkinson, Fenton 2, Saunders	26,899
16	27	H	Sheffield W	D	1-1	1-0	19	Atkinson	25,082
17	Dec 3	A	Leicester C	D	1-1	0-1	19	Whittingham	20,896
18	10	H	Everton	D	0-0	0-0	20		29,678
19	19	A	Southampton	L	1-2	0-1	—	Houghton	13,874
20	26	A	Arsenal	D	0-0	0-0	20		34,452
21	28	H	Chelsea	W	3-0	2-0	19	Sinclair (og), Yorke, Taylor	32,901
22	31	A	Manchester C	D	2-2	0-1	20	Brightwell I (og), Saunders	22,513
23	Jan 2	H	Leeds U	D	0-0	0-0	19		35,038
24	14	H	QPR	W	2-1	1-0	18	Fashanu, Ehiogu	26,578
25	21	A	Nottingham F	W	2-1	1-0	14	Fashanu, Saunders	24,598
26	25	H	Tottenham H	W	1-0	1-0	—	Saunders	40,017
27	Feb 4	A	Manchester U	L	0-1	0-1	14		43,795
28	11	H	Wimbledon	W	7-1	4-1	11	Reeves (og), Johnson 3, Saunders 2 (1 pen), Yorke	23,982
29	18	A	Sheffield W	W	2-1	2-0	9	Saunders 2	24,063
30	22	H	Leicester C	D	4-4	2-0	—	Saunders, Staunton, Yorke, Johnson	30,825
31	25	A	Newcastle U	L	1-3	1-1	11	Townsend	34,637
32	Mar 4	H	Blackburn R	L	0-1	0-1	11		40,114
33	6	H	Coventry C	D	0-0	0-0	—		26,186
34	18	H	West Ham U	L	0-2	0-1	15		28,682
35	Apr 1	A	Ipswich T	W	1-0	0-0	13	Swailes (og)	15,895
36	4	A	Crystal Palace	D	0-0	0-0	—		12,949
37	15	A	Chelsea	L	0-1	0-1	16		17,015
38	17	H	Arsenal	L	0-4	0-2	16		32,005
39	29	A	Leeds U	L	0-1	0-0	18		32,973
40	May 3	H	Manchester C	D	1-1	1-0	—	Ehiogu	30,133
41	6	H	Liverpool	W	2-0	2-0	15	Yorke 2	40,154
42	14	A	Norwich C	D	1-1	1-0	18	Staunton	19,374

Final League Position: 18

GOALSCORERS

League (51): Saunders 15 (1 pen), Yorke 6, Staunton 5, Johnson 4, Atkinson 3, Ehiogu 3, Fashanu 3, Fenton 2, Whittingham 2, Houghton 1, Parker 1, Taylor 1, Townsend 1, own goals 4.
Coca-Cola Cup (10): Atkinson 3, Lamptey 3, Saunders 1, Townsend 1, Whittingham 1, Yorke 1.
FA Cup (2): Saunders 1, Yorke 1.

Bosnich M.J. 30	Richardson K. 18 + 1	Staunton S. 34 + 1	Townsend A.D. 32	McGrath P. 36 + 4	Ehiogu U. 38 + 1	Houghton R.J. 19 + 7	Fashanu J. 11 + 2	Saunders D.N. 39	Parker G.S. 12 + 2	Yorke D. 33 + 4	King P.G. 13 + 3	Atkinson D.R. 11 + 5	Barrett E.D. 24 + 1	Spink N.P. 12 + 1	Teale S. 28	Lamptey N. 1 + 5	Fenton G.A. 7 + 10	Whittingham G. 4 + 3	Small B. 5	Boden C.D. — + 1	Taylor I.K. 22	Johnson T. 11 + 3	Charles G.A. 14 + 2	Carr F.A. — + 2	Wright A. 8	Match No.
1	2	3	4	5	6	7	8	9	10	11	12															1
1	2		4	5	6	7	8	9	*10*	11	3	12	14													2
1	6	3	11	5	4	7	8	9		12		10	2													3
1	6	11	10	5	4		8	9		7	3		2													4
	6	11	10	5	4		8	9		7	3	12	2	1												5
1	6	3	10		5	7	8	9		11		12	2		4											6
1	6	3	8	5	7			9		11		10	2		4	*12*	14									7
		12	8	5	4	7			6	11	3		2	1		14	*9*	10								8
1		3	8	5	4	7		9	6	11	12		2			14		10								9
1	6	11		5	4	12		9	8	7	3	*10*	2					14								10
		6	8	5	4	7		9	12	11	*3*		2	1			10	14								11
1	6	3	8	5	4			9	11	7			2			10	12									12
	6	11	8	5	4	7		9	14	12	3	10	2	1												13
1	12		8	5	4	7		*9*	6	11	3	10	2				14									14
1	6			5	4	7		9	8		3	10	2			12	11									15
1	6			5	4	7		9	8		3	10	2				11	12								16
				12	5	7		9	6		*11*		2	1	4		8	10	3	14						17
	6				5	7			8		11		2	1	4	12	9	10	3							18
	6			5		7	8	9	10	12	11		2	1	4				3							19
	6	3	10	12	5	7	8	9					2	1	4						11					20
	6	3	8	12	5	7		9		11			2	1	4						10					21
	6	*3*	8	12	5	7	14	9		11			2	1	4						10					22
	6	3		5	8	7	12	9		11			2	1	4						10					23
1		3		5	6	12	8	9		7			2		4						10	11				24
1		3		5	6	12	8	9		7			2		4						10	*11*	14			25
1		3	8	5	6	12		9		*7*			2		4						10	11	14			26
1		6	11	5		12	*8*	9		7					4				3		10	14	2			27
1		6	11	5				9		7					4				3		10	8	2			28
1		6	11	5	4			9		7					3						10	8	2			29
1		6	11	5	4			9		*7*		12			3						10	8	2	14		30
1		6	11	5	4			9		7		12			3						10	8	2			31
1		6	11	5	4	12		9		7					3		14				10	*8*	2			32
1		6		5	4	*7*		9		11					3		12				10	8	2	14		33
1		6	11	5	14	12		9		*7*					4						10	8	2		3	34
1		11	7	5	6			9		12		*8*			4		14				10		2		3	35
1		11	8	5	6					7		9			4		12				10		2		3	36
1		6	11	5	2			9		7		*8*			4		12				10	14			3	37
1		3	11	5	2			9		7		10			4						6	8				38
1		11	8	5	6			9		*7*				15	4		12				10		2		3	39
1		11	8	5	6			9		7					4						10		2		3	40
1		11	8	5	6			9		7					4		12				10		2		3	41
		11	8	5	6			*9*		7	12			1	4		10					14	2		3	42

Coca-Cola Cup

Second Round	Wigan Ath (h)	5-0
	(a)	3-0
Third Round	Middlesbrough (h)	1-0
Fourth Round	Crystal Palace (a)	1-4

FA Cup

Third Round	Barnsley (a)	2-0
Fourth Round	Manchester C (a)	0-1

BARNET 1994–95 *Back row (left to right):* Shaun Gale, Mark Cooper, Carl Hoddle, Alan Walker, Tim Alexander, Lee Hodges, Linvoy Primus, Geoff Cooper.
Centre row: Terry Bullivant (Coach), Laird Budge (Kit Manager), Gary Smith, Mark Newson, Paul Newell, Gary Phillips, Dougie Freedman, David McDonald, Barry Frankham (Physio).
Front row: Micky Tomlinson, Terry Gibson, Peter Scott, Ray Clemence (Manager), Paul Wilson, Robert Mutchell, Louis Affor.

Division 3 BARNET

Underhill Stadium, Barnet Lane, Barnet, Herts EN5 2BE. Telephone: (0181) 441 6932. Fax: (0181)447 0655. Credit Card Bookings: (0181)441 1677.

Ground capacity: 3924.

Record attendance: 11,026 v Wycombe Wanderers. FA Amateur Cup 4th Round 1951–52.

Record Receipts: £31,202 v Portsmouth FA Cup 3rd Round 5th January 1991.

Pitch measurements: 112yd × 72yd.

Chairman: A. Kleanthous. ***Vice-Chairman:*** D. J. Buchler FCA. ***Chief Executive:*** D. B. Edwards OBE.

Directors: S. Glynne, F. Higgins FCA.

Manager: Ray Clemence MBE. ***Player-Manager:*** Gary Phillips. ***Physio:*** David Mott.

Coach: Terry Bullivant. ***Secretary:*** Miss P. J. Sawford. ***Sales and Commercial Manager:*** Brian Wheeler. ***Marketing Manager:*** Tessa Bills.

Year Formed: 1888. ***Turned Professional:*** 1965. ***Ltd Co:***

Club Nickname: The Bees.

Previous Names: 1906–19 Barnet Alston FC.

Previous Grounds: Queens Road (1888–1901) Totteridge Lane (1901–07).

Foundation: Barnet Football Club was formed in 1888, disbanded in 1901. A club known as Alston Works FC was then formed and in 1906 changed its name to Barnet Alston FC. In 1912 it combined with The Avenue to become Barnet and Alston.

First Football League game: 17 August, 1991, Division 4, v Crewe Alex (h) L 4-7 – Phillips; Blackford, Cooper (Murphy), Horton, Bodley (Stein), Johnson, Showler, Carter (2), Bull (2), Lowe, Evans.

Record League Victory: 6–0 v Lincoln C (away), Division 4, 4 September 1991 – Pape; Poole, Naylor, Bodley, Howell, Evans (1), Willis (1), Murphy (1), Bull (2), Lowe, Showler (1 og).

Record Defeat: 1–5 v York C, Division 3, 13 March 1993.

Most League Points (3 for a win): 79, Division 3, 1992–93.

Most League Goals: 81, Division 4, 1991–92.

Highest League Scorer in Season: Gary Bull, 20, Division 4, 1991–92.

Most League Goals in Total Aggregate: Gary Bull 37, 1991–93.

Most League Appearances: Gary Phillips, 117, 1991–95.

Record Transfer Fee Received: £350,000 from Wimbledon for Andy Clarke, February 1991.

Record Transfer Fee Paid: £40,000 to Barrow for Kenny Lowe, January 1991 and £40,000 to Runcorn for Mark Carter, February 1991.

Football League Record: Promoted to Division 4 from GMVC 1991; 1991–92 Division 4; 1992–93 Division 3; 1993–94 Division 2; 1994– Division 3.

Honours: *Football League:* best season 24th, Division 2, 1993–94. *FA Amateur Cup:* Winners 1946. *GM Vauxhall Conference:* Winners 1990–91. *FA Cup:* best season; never past 3rd rd. *League Cup:* never past 2nd rd.

Colours: Amber and black striped shirts, black shorts, black stockings. **Change colours:** Green and white striped shirts, green shorts, green stockings.

BARNET 1994–95 LEAGUE RECORD

Match No.	Date	Venue	Opponents	Result		H/T Score	Lg. Pos.	Goalscorers	Attendance
1	Aug 13	H	Scunthorpe U	L	1-2	0-2	—	Cooper	2208
2	20	A	Scarborough	W	1-0	0-0	14	Cooper	1471
3	27	H	Preston NE	W	2-1	0-0	7	Freedman, Hodges	2441
4	30	A	Hartlepool U	W	1-0	1-0	—	Freedman	2095
5	Sept 3	A	Wigan Ath	W	2-1	1-1	3	Cooper, Wilson (pen)	1438
6	10	H	Doncaster R	D	0-0	0-0	5		2625
7	13	H	Rochdale	W	6-2	4-1	—	Freedman 4, Cooper, Gale	1688
8	17	A	Scunthorpe U	L	0-1	0-0	3		2481
9	24	A	Torquay U	W	2-1	2-0	3	Newson, Hodges	3280
10	Oct 1	H	Fulham	D	0-0	0-0	3		3579
11	8	H	Hereford U	D	2-2	1-1	3	Newson, Hodges	2116
12	15	A	Northampton T	D	1-1	0-0	4	Freedman	7461
13	22	A	Carlisle U	L	0-4	0-1	5		6155
14	29	H	Chesterfield	W	4-1	2-1	4	Freedman 2, McMahon, Dyche (og)	2130
15	Nov 5	A	Lincoln C	W	2-1	1-1	4	Cooper, Freedman	2741
16	19	H	Bury	D	1-1	1-0	4	McMahon	3006
17	26	A	Darlington	W	1-0	0-0	4	Gregan (og)	2157
18	Dec 10	H	Scarborough	W	3-1	0-0	4	Wilson (pen), Cooper, Freedman	1988
19	17	A	Preston NE	L	0-1	0-0	4		6429
20	26	A	Walsall	L	0-4	0-2	5		5392
21	27	H	Gillingham	W	1-0	0-0	4	Freedman	3074
22	31	A	Mansfield T	L	0-3	0-1	4		2891
23	Jan 14	A	Colchester U	D	1-1	1-0	6	Hodges	3706
24	24	H	Carlisle U	L	0-2	0-0	—		2413
25	Feb 4	H	Darlington	L	2-3	0-2	10	Walker, Cooper	2034
26	14	A	Chesterfield	L	0-2	0-0	—		2978
27	18	H	Colchester U	L	0-1	0-1	11		2242
28	25	A	Fulham	L	0-4	0-3	12		6195
29	28	H	Exeter C	D	1-1	1-0	—	Gibson	1325
30	Mar 4	H	Torquay U	W	2-0	1-0	11	Freedman, Gale	1816
31	11	A	Doncaster R	D	1-1	0-0	12	Freedman	1979
32	14	A	Bury	L	0-3	0-3	—		2380
33	18	H	Hartlepool U	W	4-0	1-0	10	Freedman 3, Tomlinson	1557
34	25	H	Wigan Ath	D	1-1	1-1	11	Freedman	2362
35	Apr 1	A	Rochdale	D	2-2	1-1	11	Freedman 2	1834
36	4	H	Lincoln C	W	2-1	1-1	—	Freedman, Wilson (pen)	1616
37	8	H	Mansfield T	D	2-2	1-1	9	Cooper 2	2115
38	15	A	Gillingham	L	1-2	1-2	10	Freedman	3448
39	17	H	Walsall	L	1-3	1-2	11	Inglethorpe	2078
40	22	A	Exeter C	W	2-1	1-0	11	Inglethorpe, Cooper	1903
41	29	H	Northampton T	L	2-3	1-2	11	Freedman, Inglethorpe	2796
42	May 6	A	Hereford U	L	2-3	1-3	11	Cooper, Freedman	2069

Final League Position: 11

GOALSCORERS

League (56): Freedman 24, Cooper M 11, Hodges 4, Inglethorpe 3, Wilson 3 (3 pens), Gale 2, McMahon 2, Newson 2, Gibson 1, Tomlinson 1, Walker 1, own goals 2.
Coca-Cola Cup (7): Freedman 5, Cooper M 2.
FA Cup (4): Cooper 2, Hodges 1, McMahon 1.

Phillips G.C. 27	McDonald D.H. 35	Gale S.M. 25 + 2	Hoddle C. 26 + 4	Walker A. 21	Newson M.J. 29 + 1	Tomlinson M.L. 21 + 6	Freedman D.A. 42	Hodges L.L. 32 + 2	Cooper M.D. 32 + 2	Wilson P.R. 35 + 1	Scott P.R. 23 + 5	Primus L.S. 39	Alexander T.M. 2 + 2	Haynes J.L.A. 2 + 4	Carmichael M. 2 + 1	Mutchell R.D. 7 + 1	McMahon G.J. 10	Newell P.C. 15	Hamlet A.G. 3	Smith G.N. 3 + 1	Adams K.C. 2 + 2	Gibson T.B. 4 + 8	Watson K.E. 13	Inglethorpe A.M. 5 + 1	Thomas G.A. 6 + 1	Brady M.J. — + 1	Cooper G.V. 1	Match No.
1	2	3	4	5	6	7	8	9	10	11	12																	1
1	2	3	4	5		7	8	9	10	11	12	6																2
1	2	3	4	5		7	8	9	10	11		6																3
1	2	3	4	5		7	8	9	10	11	12	*6*	14															4
1	2	3	4	*5*		7	8	9	10	11	12	6	14															5
1	2	3	4			7	8	9	10	11		6	5															6
1	2	3	4			7	8	9	10	11	12	6	5	14														7
1	2	3	4	5	12		8	9		11	10	6		7														8
1	2	3	4		5		8	9		11	7	6		12	10													9
1	2	3	4		5	12	8	9		11	10	6			7													10
1	2		4		5	7	8	9	12	11	10	6				3												11
1	2	3	*4*		5	7	8	9	10	11		6		12	14													12
1	2	3	4		5	12	8	9	10	11		6					7											13
1	2		4	3	5		8	9	10		11	6					7											14
1			4	2	5		8	9	10		11	6				3	7											15
1	2		4	3	5		8		10	9	11	6				12	7											16
	2		4	5		10	8			9	11	6		12		3	7	1										17
	2		4	3	5		8		10	9	11	6					7	1										18
	2		4	3	5		8	12	10	9	11	6					7	1										19
	2		*4*	3	5	14	8	9	10	12	11	6					7	1										20
	2				5	12	8	4	10	9	11	6				3	7	1										21
						12	8	4		9		6		11		*3*	7	1	2	10	14						5	22
			4	5		7	8	9		11		6				3		1	2	10								23
	2		4	5		7	8	9	10	11		6				3		1				12						24
	2		4	5		7	8	9	10	11	3	6						1				12						25
	2		4	5		7	8	9	10	11	3	6						1				12						26
1	2	14		5	3	7	8	9	10		*11*	6										12	4					27
1	2	7	11	5	3		8	9	10			6											4					28
1	2	3			5		8	9	10	11		6										7	4					29
1	2	3	12		5		*8*	9	14	11	10	6										7	4					30
1		3		2	5	12	8	9		11	10	6										7	4					31
1		3		5	2	7	8			10	11	6								12		9	4					32
1	2	3	12		5	9	*8*		10	11		6								7	14		4					33
1	2	3	7		5	9	8		10	11		6											4	12				34
1	2	3			5	9	8		10	11	7	6										12	4					35
1	2	*3*			5	7	8		10	11	9	6										12	4		14			36
1	2	3			5	7	8	12	10	11		6										14	9		4			37
		2	12		5		8	9	10	11		6						1					4	7	3			38
	2	3			5		8	9	10		11							1				12	4	7	6			39
	2	3	12		5		8	9	10		11							1			4			7	6			40
	2	12			5		8	9	10	3	11	4						1						7	6			41
					5		8	9	10	11		6						1	2		4			7	3	12		42

Coca-Cola Cup

First Round	Leyton Orient (h)	4-0
	(a)	1-1
Second Round	Manchester C (h)	1-0
	(a)	1-4

FA Cup

First Round	Woking (h)	4-4
	(a)	0-1

BARNSLEY 1994–95 *Back row (left to right):* Chris Jackson, Richard Hanby, Steve Davis, Lee Butler, Dean Fearon, Gerry Taggart, Dave Watson, Adrian Moses, Andy Rammell, Glynn Hurst.

Centre row: Malcolm Shotton (Reserve Team Coach), Eric Winstanley (First Team Coach), Darren Field, Gary Fleming, Andy Payton, Andy Liddell, Nicky Eaden, Mark Burton, Troy Bennett, David Brooke, Simon Bochenski, Scott Jones, Norman Rimmington (Kit Manager), Steve Stafford (Physio).

Front row: Glynn Snodin, Martin Bullock, Brendan O'Connell, Danny Wilson (Player/Manager), Neil Redfearn, Darren Sheridan, Owen Archdeacon, Mark Feeney.

Division 1 **BARNSLEY**

Oakwell Ground, Grove St, Barnsley, South Yorkshire S71 1ET. Telephone:(01226) 295353. Fax: (01226) 201000. Clubcall: 0891 121152. Commercial Office: (01226) 286718.

Ground capacity: 19,101.

Record attendance: 40,255 v Stoke C, FA Cup 5th rd, 15 February 1936.

Record receipts: Not disclosed.

Pitch measurements: 110yd × 75yd.

President: Arthur Raynor. ***Chairman:*** J. A. Dennis.

Directors: C. B. Taylor (Vice-Chairman), C. H. Harrison, M. R. Hayselden, J. N. Kelly, S. M. Hall, I. D. Potter.

Player-Manager: Danny Wilson.

First Team Coach: Eric Winstanley. ***Physio:*** Stephen Redmond.

General Manager/Secretary: Michael Spinks. ***Lotteries Manager:*** Gerry Whewall. ***Marketing Manager:*** Ian Davies.

Year Formed: 1887. ***Turned Professional:*** 1888. ***Ltd Co.:*** 1899.

Previous Name: Barnsley St Peter's, 1887–97.

Club Nickname: 'The Tykes', 'Reds' or 'Colliers'.

Foundation: Many clubs owe their inception to the church and Barnsley are among them, for they were formed in 1887 by the Rev. T. T. Preedy, curate of Barnsley St. Peter's and went under that name until it was dropped in 1897 a year before being admitted to the Second Division of the Football League.

First Football League game: 1 September, 1898, Division 2, v Lincoln C (a) L 0-1 – Fawcett; McArtney, Nixon; King, Burleigh, Porteous; Davis, Lees, Murray, McCullough, McGee.

Record League Victory: 9–0 v Loughborough T, Division 2, 28 January 1899 – Greaves; McCartney, Nixon; Porteous, Burleigh, Howard; Davis (4), Hepworth (1), Lees (1), McCullough (1), Jones (2). 9–0 v Accrington S, Division 3 (N), 3 February 1934 – Ellis; Cookson, Shotton; Harper, Henderson, Whitworth; Spence (2), Smith (1), Blight (4), Andrews (1), Ashton (1).

Record Cup Victory: 6–0 v Blackpool, FA Cup, 1st rd replay, 20 January 1910 – Mearns; Downs, Ness; Glendinning, Boyle (1), Utley; Bartrop, Gadsby (1), Lillycrop (2), Tufnell (2), Forman. 6–0 v Peterborough U, League Cup, 1st rd, 2nd leg, 15 September 1981 – Horn; Joyce, Chambers, Glavin (2), Banks, McCarthy, Evans, Parker (2), Aylott (1), McHale, Barrowclough (1).

Record Defeat: 0–9 v Notts Co, Division 2, 19 November 1927.

Most League Points (2 for a win): 67, Division 3 (N), 1938–39.

Most League Points (3 for a win): 74, Division 2, 1988–89.

Most League Goals: 118, Division 3 (N), 1933–34.

Highest League Scorer in Season: Cecil McCormack, 33, Division 2, 1950–51.

Most League Goals in Total Aggregate: Ernest Hine, 123, 1921–26 and 1934–38.

Most Capped Player: Gerry Taggart, 35, Northern Ireland.

Most League Appearances: Barry Murphy, 514, 1962–78.

Record Transfer Fee Received: £1,500,000 from Nottingham F for Carl Tiler, May 1991.

Record Transfer Fee Paid: £310,000 to Celtic for Andy Payton, November 1993.

Football League Record: 1898 Elected to Division 2; 1932–34 Division 3 (N); 1934–38 Division 2; 1938–39 Division 3 (N); 1946–53 Division 2; 1953–55 Division 3 (N); 1955–59 Division 2; 1959–65 Division 3; 1965–68 Division 4; 1968–72 Division 3; 1972–79 Division 4; 1979–81 Division 3; 1981–92 Division 2; 1992– Division 1.

Honours: *Football League:* best season: 3rd, Division 2, 1914–15, 1921–22; Division 3 (N) – Champions 1933–34, 1938–39, 1954–55; Runners-up 1953–54; Division 3 – Runners-up 1980–81; Division 4 – Runners-up 1967–68; Promoted 1978–79. *FA Cup:* Winners 1912; Runners-up 1910. *Football League Cup:* best season: 5th rd, 1982.

Colours: Red shirts, white shorts, red stockings. **Change colours:** Navy and turquoise striped shirts, black shorts, black stockings.

BARNSLEY 1994–95 LEAGUE RECORD

Match No.	Date	Venue	Opponents	Result	H/T Score	Lg. Pos.	Goalscorers	Attendance
1	Aug 13	H	Derby Co	W 2-1	2-1	—	Rammell 2	8737
2	20	A	Charlton Ath	D 2-2	0-0	3	Payton, Davis	8171
3	27	H	Reading	L 0-2	0-1	11		4771
4	30	A	Port Vale	L 1-2	0-1	—	O'Connell	7228
5	Sept 3	A	Burnley	W 1-0	0-0	10	Payton	11,968
6	10	H	Watford	D 0-0	0-0	12		4251
7	13	H	Notts Co	D 1-1	0-0	—	Rammell	3928
8	17	A	Sunderland	L 0-2	0-0	18		16,145
9	24	A	Oldham Ath	L 0-1	0-0	21		7941
10	Oct 1	H	Swindon T	W 2-1	1-0	18	Redfearn 2	3911
11	8	H	Southend U	D 0-0	0-0	19		3659
12	16	A	Sheffield U	D 0-0	0-0	20		12,317
13	22	H	WBA	W 2-0	1-0	16	O'Connell, Redfearn	5082
14	29	A	Luton T	W 1-0	0-0	9	Rammell	7212
15	Nov 1	A	Tranmere R	L 1-6	0-2	—	Rammell	5592
16	5	H	Stoke C	W 2-0	1-0	7	O'Connell, Sheridan	5117
17	19	A	Millwall	W 1-0	1-0	9	Liddell	7040
18	26	H	Bolton W	W 3-0	2-0	6	Eaden, Davis, Redfearn	8507
19	Dec 3	A	WBA	L 1-2	0-1	9	Jackson	13,921
20	7	H	Bristol C	W 2-1	1-1	—	Liddell, Archdeacon	4305
21	10	H	Charlton Ath	W 2-1	1-0	5	Redfearn, Liddell	5465
22	17	A	Derby Co	L 0-1	0-0	6		13,205
23	26	H	Grimsby T	W 4-1	2-1	3	Payton 3, Liddell	8669
24	27	A	Portsmouth	L 0-3	0-3	4		6751
25	31	H	Wolverhampton W	L 1-3	1-2	7	Redfearn (pen)	9207
26	Jan 14	H	Luton T	W 3-1	0-0	6	Redfearn, Liddell 2	4808
27	Feb 4	A	Bristol C	L 2-3	0-0	9	Rammell, Wilson	6408
28	11	H	Tranmere R	D 2-2	1-1	9	Rammell, Redfearn	5506
29	18	A	Bolton W	L 1-2	0-2	10	Liddell	12,463
30	21	H	Millwall	W 4-1	1-0	—	Redfearn 2, Payton 2	4733
31	25	A	Swindon T	D 0-0	0-0	9		8158
32	Mar 7	H	Burnley	W 2-0	1-0	—	Taggart, Payton	5537
33	11	A	Reading	W 3-0	1-0	7	O'Connell, Taggart, Payton	7556
34	14	A	Middlesbrough	D 1-1	0-1	—	Payton	19,655
35	18	H	Port Vale	W 3-1	2-0	7	Liddell 2, Sheridan	6878
36	21	A	Watford	L 2-3	0-1	—	Liddell 2	6883
37	24	H	Sunderland	W 2-0	0-0	—	Shotton, Payton	7803
38	Apr 1	A	Notts Co	W 3-1	1-1	7	O'Connell, Wilson, Liddell	6834
39	8	A	Wolverhampton W	D 0-0	0-0	6		26,385
40	12	A	Stoke C	D 0-0	0-0	—		10,752
41	15	H	Portsmouth	W 1-0	0-0	5	Payton	6825
42	17	A	Grimsby T	L 0-1	0-1	6		7277
43	22	H	Middlesbrough	D 1-1	0-1	6	Liddell	11,711
44	29	H	Sheffield U	W 2-1	1-1	6	O'Connell 2	10,844
45	May 2	H	Oldham Ath	D 1-1	1-1	—	Taggart	9838
46	7	A	Southend U	L 1-3	0-1	6	Redfearn	6425

Final League Position: 6

GOALSCORERS

League (63): Liddell 13, Payton 12, Redfearn 11 (1 pen), O'Connell 7, Rammell 7, Taggart 3, Davis 2, Sheridan 2, Wilson 2, Archdeacon 1, Eaden 1, Jackson 1, Shotton 1.
Coca-Cola Cup (3): Redfearn 2, Taggart 1.
FA Cup (0).

Watson D.N. 37	Eaden N.J. 44 + 1	Fleming J.G. 46	Wilson D.J. 34	Taggart G.P. 41	Bishop D.C. 7 + 1	O'Connell B. 44 + 1	Redfearn N.D. 37 + 2	Rammell A.V. 17 + 7	Payton A.P. 38 + 5	Snodin G. 11 + 3	Davis S.P. 34 + 2	Liddell A.M. 31 + 8	Bullock M.J. 17 + 12	Jackson C.D. 7 + 1	Sheridan D.S. 35	Archdeacon O.D. 6 + 3	Butler L.S. 9	Moses A.P. 3 + 1	Shotton M. 8	Hurst G. — + 2	*Match No.*
1	2	3	4	5	6	7	8	9	10	11											1
1	2	3	4	5	6	7	8	9	10	11	12										2
1	2	3	4	5		7	8	9	10	11	6	12	14								3
1	2	*3*	4	5	6	7	8	9	10	11	12		14								4
1	2	3	4	5		7	8	9	10	11	6										5
1	2	3	4	5		7	8	9	10	11	6	12									6
1	2	3	4	5		7	8	9	10	11	6	12									7
1		3	4	5	2	7	8	9	10	11	6	12									8
1	14	3	4	5	*2*	7	8	9	10	11	6	12									9
1	2	3	4	5	6		8		10	11		7	12	9							10
1	2	3	4	5		7	8	12	10		6	14		9	11						11
1	2	3	4	5		7	8	9	10		6				11						12
1	2	3	4	5		7	8	9	10		6				11						13
1	2	3	4	5		7	8	9	10		6				11						14
1	2	3	4	5		7	8	9	*10*		6	12			11	14					15
1	2	3	4	5		7	8				6	10		9	11						16
	2	3	*4*	5		7	8		12		6	10		9	11	14	1				17
	2	3		5		7	8		12		6	10		9	11	4	1				18
	2	3		5		7	8		14		6	10	12	9	11	4	1				19
	2	3		5		7	8		14		6	10	12	*9*	11	4	1				20
	2	3		5		7	8		9		6	10			11	4	1				21
	2	3		5		7	8		9		6	10	12		11	4	1				22
	2	3		5		7	8		9		6	10	4		11		1				23
	2	3		*5*	14	7	8	12	9		6	10	4		11		1				24
	2	3			5	7	8	12	9		6	10	4		11		1				25
1	2	3	4			7	8	9			6	10			11			5			26
1	2	3	4			7	8	9				10	12		11			5	6		27
1	2	3	4	5		7	8	9	14			*10*	12		11				6		28
1	2	*3*	4	5		7	8		9	14	6	10	12		11						29
1	2	3	4	5		7	*8*		9	14	6	10	12		11						30
1	2	3	4	5		7	8		9		6	10	12		11						31
1	2	3	4	5		7	*8*		9	14	6	10	12		11						32
1	2	3	4	5		7			9		6	10	8		11						33
1	2	3	4	5		7			9		6	10	8		11	12					34
1	2	3	4	5		7		12	9			10	8		11	*6*		14			35
1	2	3	4	5		7		12	9			10	8		11			6			36
1	2	3	4	5		7			9			10	8		11				6		37
1	2	3	4	5		7			9			10	8		11				6		38
1	2	3	4	5		7	12		9			10	8		11				6		39
1	2	3	4	5		7		12	9			10	8		11				6		40
1	2	3	4	5		7	12		9	11	6	10	8								41
1	2	3		5		7	4	12	9		6	10	8		11						42
1	2	3				7	4		9		6	10	8		11				5	12	43
1	2	3				7	4		9		6	10	8		11				5		44
1	2	3		5		7	8		9		6	*10*	4	12	11					14	45
1	2	3	*4*	5		12	8	10	9		6	14	7		11						46

Coca-Cola Cup

First Round	Darlington (a)	2-2
	(h)	0-0
Second Round	Newcastle U (a)	1-2
	(h)	0-1

FA Cup

Third Round	Aston Villa (h)	0-2

BIRMINGHAM CITY 1994–95 *Back row (left to right):* Neil McDairmid (Physio), Danny Wallace, Paul Tait, Kenny Lowe, Miguel De Souza, Steve McGavin, Chris Whyte, Peter Shearer, Paul Harding, Richard Scott, Lil Fuccillo (Chief Scout).
Centre row: Kevan Broadhurst (Coach), Andy Saville, Dave Barnett, Dave Regis, Ian Bennett, Richard Dryden, Liam Daish, Harry Willis, David Howell (Coach).
Front row: Jose Dominguez, Louie Donowa, Gary Cooper, John Frain, Mark Ward (Player Coach), Barry Fry (Manager), Edwin Stein (Assistant Manager), Scott Hiley, Steve Claridge, Paul Moulden, Neil Doherty.

Division 1 **BIRMINGHAM CITY**

St Andrews, Birmingham B9 4NH. Telephone: (0121) 772 0101. Fax: (0121) 766 7866. Lottery Office/Souvenir Shop: (0121) 772 1245. Clubcall: 0891 121188. Club Soccer Shop: (0121) 766 8274.

Ground capacity: 25,936.

Record attendance: 66,844 v Everton, FA Cup 5th rd, 11 February 1939.

Record receipts: £230,000 v Aston Villa, Coca Cola Cup 2nd rd 1st leg, 21 September 1993.

Pitch measurements: 115yd × 75yd.

Directors: J. F. Wiseman (Chairman), K. R. Brady (Managing Director), D. Sullivan, D. Gold, R. Gold, B. Gold, H. Brandman, A. G. Jones.

Manager: Barry Fry. ***Assistant Manager:*** Edwin Stein. ***Coach:*** David Howell. ***Physio:*** N. McDiarmid. ***Commercial Manager:*** Allan Robson.

Secretary: A. G. Jones BA, MBA.

Year Formed: 1875. ***Turned Professional:*** 1885. ***Ltd Co.:*** 1888.

Previous Names: 1875–88, Small Heath Alliance; 1888, dropped 'Alliance'; became Birmingham 1905; became Birmingham City 1945.

Club Nickname: 'Blues'.

Previous Grounds: 1875, waste ground near Arthur St; 1877, Muntz St, Small Heath; 1906, St Andrews.

Foundation: In 1875 cricketing enthusiasts who were largely members of Trinity Church, Bordesley, determined to continue their sporting relationships throughout the year by forming a football club which they called Small Heath Alliance. For their earliest games played on waste land in Arthur Street, the team included three Edden brothers and two James brothers.

First Football League game: 3 September, 1892, Division 2, v Burslem Port Vale (h) W5-1 – Charsley; Bayley, Speller; Ollis, Jenkyns, Devey; Hallam (1), Edwards (1), Short (1), Wheldon (2), Hands.

Record League Victory: 12–0 v Walsall T Swifts, Division 2, 17 December 1892 – Charnley; Bayley, Jones; Ollis, Jenkyns, Devey; Hallam (2), Walton (3), Mobley (3), Wheldon (2), Hands (2). 12–0 v Doncaster R, Division 2, 11 April 1903 – Dorrington; Goldie, Wassell; Beer, Dougherty (1), Howard; Athersmith (1), Leonard (3), McRoberts (1), Wilcox (4), Field (1). Aston. (1 og).

Record Cup Victory: 9–2 v Burton W, FA Cup, 1st rd, 31 October 1885 – Hedges; Jones, Evetts (1); F. James, Felton, A. James (1); Davenport (2), Stanley (4), Simms, Figures, Morris (1).

Record Defeat: 1–9 v Sheffield W, Division 1, 13 December 1930 and v Blackburn R, Division 1, 5 January 1895.

Most League Points (2 for a win): 59, Division 2, 1947–48.

Most League Points (3 for a win): 89, Division 2, 1994–95.

Most League Goals: 103, Division 2, 1893–94 (only 28 games).

Highest League Scorer in Season: Joe Bradford, 29, Division 1, 1927–28.

Most League Goals in Total Aggregate: Joe Bradford, 249, 1920–35.

Most Capped Player: Malcolm Page, 28, Wales.

Most League Appearances: Frank Womack, 491, 1908–28.

Record Transfer Fee Received: £975,000 from Nottingham F for Trevor Francis, February 1979.

Record Transfer Fee Paid: £800,000 to Southend U for Ricky Otto, December 1994.

Football League Record: 1892 elected to Division 2; 1894–96 Division 1; 1896–1901 Division 2; 1901–02 Division 1; 1902–03 Division 2; 1903–08 Division 1; 1908–21 Division 2; 1921–39 Division 1; 1946–48 Division 2; 1948–50 Division 1; 1950–1955 Division 2; 1955–65 Division 1; 1965–72 Division 2; 1972–79 Division 1; 1979–80 Division 2; 1980–84 Division 1; 1984–1985 Division 2; 1985–86 Division 1; 1986–89 Division 2; 1989–92 Division 3; 1992–94 Division 1; 1994–95 Division 2; 1995– Division 1.

Honours: *Football League:* Division 1 best season: 6th, 1955–56; Division 2 – Champions 1892–93, 1920–21, 1947–48, 1954–55, 1994–95; Runners-up 1893–94, 1900–01, 1902–03, 1971–72, 1984–85.Division 3 Runners-up 1991–92. *FA Cup:* Runners-up 1931, 1956. *Football League Cup:* Winners 1963. *Leyland Daf Cup:* Winners 1991. *Auto Windscreens Shield:* Winners 1995. **European Competitions:** *European Fairs Cup:* 1955–58, 1958–60 (runners-up), 1960–61 (runners-up), 1961–62.

Colours: Blue shirts, white shorts, blue and white hooped stockings. **Change colours:** All red.

BIRMINGHAM CITY 1994–95 LEAGUE RECORD

Match No.	Date	Venue	Opponents	Result	H/T Score	Lg. Pos.	Goalscorers	Attendance
1	Aug 13	A	Leyton Orient	L 1-2	1-1	—	Claridge	7578
2	20	H	Chester C	W 1-0	1-0	14	Donowa	12,188
3	27	A	Swansea C	W 2-0	0-0	10	Claridge 2	5797
4	30	H	Wycombe W	L 0-1	0-0	—		14,305
5	Sept 3	H	Plymouth Arg	W 4-2	2-0	8	Regis 2, Wallace, Tait	13,202
6	10	A	Oxford U	D 1-1	0-0	11	Claridge	8077
7	13	A	Rotherham U	D 1-1	0-1	—	Bull	3799
8	18	H	Peterborough U	W 4-0	3-0	6	Bull 2, Tait, Dominguez	10,600
9	24	H	Hull C	D 2-2	1-1	9	Claridge (pen), Dominguez	12,192
10	Oct 1	A	Wrexham	D 1-1	0-1	9	Claridge	6002
11	8	H	Huddersfield T	D 1-1	1-1	9	Bull	15,265
12	15	A	Brighton & HA	W 1-0	0-0	9	Donowa	11,004
13	22	A	Brentford	W 2-1	1-0	9	Shearer, Ward	7779
14	29	H	Bristol R	W 2-0	2-0	6	Bull, Claridge	15,886
15	Nov 1	H	Crewe Alex	W 5-0	3-0	—	Hunt 3, Donowa, Claridge	14,212
16	5	A	Shrewsbury T	W 2-0	1-0	3	Bull, Hunt	5942
17	19	H	Bournemouth	D 0-0	0-0	3		15,477
18	26	A	Stockport Co	W 1-0	0-0	3	Hunt	5577
19	Dec 10	A	Chester C	W 4-0	2-0	2	Daish, Claridge, McGavin, Lowe	3946
20	17	H	Leyton Orient	W 2-0	1-0	2	Donowa 2	20,022
21	26	H	Cambridge U	D 1-1	1-0	2	Otto	20,098
22	28	A	Cardiff C	W 1-0	0-0	—	Otto	7420
23	31	H	Blackpool	W 7-1	3-1	1	Bradshaw (og), Donowa 2, Claridge 2, Lowe, Parris	18,025
24	Jan 2	A	Bradford C	D 1-1	0-1	1	Cooper	10,539
25	14	A	York C	L 0-2	0-1	1		6828
26	Feb 4	H	Stockport Co	W 1-0	0-0	1	Dinning (og)	17,160
27	11	A	Crewe Alex	L 1-2	0-1	3	Donowa	6359
28	18	H	York C	W 4-2	2-0	3	Francis 2, Otto, Shearer	14,846
29	21	A	Bournemouth	L 1-2	0-1	—	Francis	6024
30	25	H	Wrexham	W 5-2	1-2	2	Francis 2, Shearer, Otto, Donowa	18,884
31	Mar 4	A	Hull C	D 0-0	0-0	3		9854
32	11	H	Swansea C	L 0-1	0-1	4		16,191
33	18	A	Wycombe W	W 3-0	2-0	4	Shearer, Claridge, Evans (og)	7289
34	21	H	Oxford U	W 3-0	1-0	—	Francis, Claridge, Daish	19,781
35	25	A	Peterborough U	D 1-1	0-0	3	Shearer	8796
36	29	A	Bristol R	D 1-1	0-1	—	Claridge	8010
37	Apr 1	H	Rotherham U	W 2-1	0-1	3	Francis, Shearer	16,077
38	4	A	Blackpool	D 1-1	1-1	—	Claridge	4494
39	11	H	Shrewsbury T	W 2-0	1-0	—	Claridge 2	18,366
40	15	H	Cardiff C	W 2-1	1-1	2	Tait, Ward (pen)	17,455
41	17	A	Cambridge U	L 0-1	0-0	3		5317
42	19	A	Plymouth Arg	W 3-1	0-0	—	Whyte, Claridge 2	8550
43	26	H	Brentford	W 2-0	0-0	—	Francis, Daish	25,581
44	29	H	Brighton & HA	D 3-3	2-1	1	Dominguez, Shearer, Ward	19,006
45	May 2	H	Bradford C	D 0-0	0-0	—		25,139
46	6	A	Huddersfield T	W 2-1	0-0	1	Claridge, Tait	18,775

Final League Position: 1

GOALSCORERS

League (84): Claridge 20 (1 pen), Donowa 9, Francis 8, Shearer 7, Bull 6, Hunt 5, Otto 4, Tait 4, Daish 3, Dominguez 3, Ward 3 (1 pen), Lowe 2, Regis 2, Cooper 1, McGavin 1, Parris 1, Wallace 1, Whyte 1, own goals 3.
Coca-Cola Cup (4): Claridge 1 (pen), Daish 1, McGavin 1, Saville 1.
FA Cup (7): McGavin 3, Shearer 2, Cooper 1, Otto 1.

Bennett I.M. 46	Hiley S.P. 9	Dryden R.A. 3	Ward M.W. 41	Shearer P.A. 20 + 3	Whyte C.A. 31	Lowe K. 4 + 3	Claridge S.E. 41 + 1	Saville A.V. 3 + 7	Willis R.C. 1 + 2	Donowa B.L. 21 + 10	Regis D. 4 + 2	Dominguez J.M.M. 12 + 18	Frain J.W. 6 + 1	Daish L.S. 37	Harding P. 5 + 1	Doherty N. 3 + 5	Scott R.P. 5	De Souza J.M. 4 + 4	Tait P.R. 18 + 7	Wallace D.L. 4 + 2	Small B. 3	Bull G.W. 10	Poole G.J. 34	Hunt J.R. 18 + 2	McGavin S.J. 10 + 5	Barnett D. 31	Cooper G. 26	Howell D.C. 2	Otto R. 18 + 6	Parris G. 1 + 1	Bodley M.J. 3	Francis K.D.M. 15	Robinson S.E. 5 + 1	Webb M.L. — + 1	Williams P.A. 8 + 3	Hendon I.M. 4	*Match No.*
1	2	3	4	5	6	7	*8*	9	10	11	12	14																									1
1	2		4		5		8	9		7		12	*3*	6	10	11																					2
1	2		4		5		8	9		11	12	14		6	10		3	*7*																			3
1	2		4		5		8	12		14	9	*11*		6			3	7	10																		4
1	2		*4*		5		8			12	9	14		6	7		3		10	11																	5
1			*4*		5		8		12		9	14		6	7		2		10	11	3																6
1		4			5		8		12		9	14	3		7		2		10	*11*		6															7
1		5	4		6		8					14			12				10	*11*	3	9	2	7													8
1			4		5		8					11		6					*10*	12	3	9	2	7	14												9
1			4				8					11	3	6				12	*10*	14		9	2	7		5											10
1			*4*	11			8			12		10	3	6				14				9	2	7		5											11
1			4	11			8			12				6				10				9	2	7		5	3										12
1			4	11	3		8			10		12		6								9	2	7		5											13
1			4	11	3		*8*			10		12		6								9	2	7	14	5											14
1			4	11	3		8			10		12		6								*9*	2	7	14	5											15
1			4	11	3		*8*			10		12		6								9	2	7	14	5											16
1			4	11	3		8			12		10		6					14				2	7	*9*	5											17
1			4	11	3		8			10		12		6					14				2	7	*9*	5											18
1					3	12	8			7		*10*		6		14			11				2		9	5	4										19
1			4		3	12	8	14		7				6		11							2		*9*	5	10										20
1			4		3	12	8	14		7													2		*9*	5	11	6	10								21
1			4		3		8									7		9					2			5	11	6	10								22
1			4		*3*	9	8			7				6									2		12	5	11		10	14							23
1			4			*10*	8			7				6		14		12					2		9	5	3			11							24
1			4			11	8			7			12	6				14					2		*9*	5	3		10								25
1			4		2		8			7		12							11							5	3		10		6	9					26
1			4	12	3					7		14		6					11				2			5	*8*		10			9					27
1			4	12				14		7									11				2		*8*	5	3		10		6	9					28
1			4	12				14		7									11				2		*8*	5	3		10		6	9					29
1			4	11	*3*			12		7		*10*		6									2			5	8		14			9					30
1				11	3		8	12		*7*				6					4				2			5			10			9	14				31
1			4		3		8							6		12			11				2		*9*	5			10				7	14			32
1			4	11			8							6									2			5	3		12			9	7		10		33
1			4	11			8							6		12							2			5	3		14			9	7		10		34
1			*4*	11			8							6		12			14				2			5	3		10			9			7		35
1				11	3		12					14							6				2				4		10			9	7		8	5	36
1	2		4	11	3		8					12		6										7					*10*			9			14	5	37
1				11			8					12		6					4					7		5	3		14			9			*10*	2	38
1	2		4	11			8					7		6					12							5	3		10			*9*			14		39
1			4				8			12		7		6					*11*				2	14		5	3		10						9		40
1	2		4				8			12		7		6									11	14		5	3		10						*9*		41
1			4		5		8					12	3	6									2	7			10		14			9	11				42
1			*4*	11			8			12				6					14				2	7		5	3		10			9					43
1	2		4	*11*	5		8			12		9		6					14					7			3		10								44
1			4		5		8			9		*10*		6					11				2	7			3		12						14		45
1			4		5		8			12			3	6					14				2	7			11								*10*	9	46

Coca-Cola Cup

First Round	Shrewsbury T (a)	1-2
	(h)	2-0
Second Round	Blackburn R (a)	0-2
	(h)	1-1

FA Cup

First Round	Slough (a) (at Birmingham)	4-0
Second Round	Scunthorpe U (h)	0-0
	(a)	2-1
Third Round	Liverpool (h)	0-0
	(a)	1-1

BLACKBURN ROVERS 1994–95 *Back row (left to right):* Peter Thorne, Mark Atkins, Paul Harford, Frank Talia, Tim Flowers, Matt Dickins, Bobby Mimms, Seamus Given, Nicky Marker, Andy Morrison, Chris Malone.
Centre row: Tony Parkes, Jason Wilcox, Stuart Ripley, Henning Berg, Tim Sherwood, Tony Gale, Ian Pearce (First Team Coach), Chris Sutton, Colin Hendry, Mike Newell, Paul Warhurst, Alan Shearer, Danny Goodall, Mike Pettigrew (Physio).
Front row: Gary Tallon, Wayne Gill, Kevin Gallacher, Graeme Le Saux, Richard Brown, Ray Harford (Assistant Manager), Kenny Dalglish (Manager), Robbie Slater, Lee Makel, David Batty, Alan Wright, Paul Ainscough.
(Photograph: Action Images)

FA Premiership BLACKBURN ROVERS

Ewood Park, Blackburn BB2 4JF. Telephone: (01254) 698888. Fax: (01254) 671042. Ticket Office: (01254) 696767. Club Shop-Mail Order: (01254) 672137.

Ground capacity: 31,089.

Record attendance: 61,783 v Bolton W, FA Cup 6th rd, 2 March, 1929.

Record receipts: £333,067 v Liverpool, Coca-Cola Cup 4th rd, 30 November 1994.

Pitch measurements: 115yd × 72yd.

Chairman: R. D. Coar BSC. ***Vice-Chairman:*** R. L. Matthewman. ***Directors:*** K. C. Lee, I. R. Stanners, G. R. Root FCMA.

Director of Football: Kenny Dalglish MBE. ***Manager:*** Ray Harford. ***Physio:*** Steve Foster. ***Coach:*** Tony Parkes.

Commercial Manager: Ken Beamish.

Secretary: John W. Howarth FAAI.

Year Formed: 1875. ***Turned Professional:*** 1880. ***Ltd Co.:*** 1897.

Club Nickname: Rovers.

Previous Grounds: 1875/6, all matches played away; 1876, Oozehead Ground; 1877, Pleasington Cricket Ground; 1878, Alexandra Meadows; 1881, Leamington Road; 1890, Ewood Park.

Foundation: It was in 1875 that some Public School old boys called a meeting at which the Blackburn Rovers club was formed and the colours blue and white adopted. The leading light was John Lewis, later to become a founder of the Lancashire FA, a famous referee who was in charge of two FA Cup Finals, and a vice-president of both the FA and the Football League.

First Football League game: 15 September, 1888, Football League, v Accrington (h) D 5-5 – Arthur; Beverley, James Southworth; Douglas, Almond, Forrest; Beresford (1), Walton, John Southworth (1), Fecitt (1), Townley (2).

Record League Victory: 9–0 v Middlesbrough, Division 2, 6 November 1954 – Elvy; Suart, Eckersley; Clayton, Kelly, Bell; Mooney (3), Crossan (2), Briggs, Quigley (3), Langton (1).

Record Cup Victory: 11–0 v Rossendale, FA Cup 1st rd, 13 October 1884 – Arthur; Hopwood, McIntyre; Forrest, Blenkhorn, Lofthouse; Sowerbutts (2), J. Brown (1), Fecitt (4), Barton (3), Birtwistle (1).

Record Defeat: 0–8 v Arsenal, Division 1, 25 February 1933.

Most League Points (2 for a win): 60, Division 3, 1974–75.

Most League Points (3 for a win): 89, FA Premier League, 1994–95.

Most League Goals: 114, Division 2, 1954–55.

Highest League Scorer in Season: Ted Harper, 43, Division 1, 1925–26.

Most League Goals in Total Aggregate: Simon Garner, 168, 1978–92.

Most Capped Player: Bob Crompton, 41, England.

Most League Appearances: Derek Fazackerley, 596, 1970–86.

Record Transfer Fee Received: £900,000 from Aston Villa for Alan Wright, March 1995.

Record Transfer Fee Paid: £5,000,000 to Norwich C for Chris Sutton, July 1994.

Football League Record: 1888 Founder Member of the League; 1936–39 Division 2; 1946–48 Division 1; 1948–58 Division 2; 1958–66 Division 1; 1966–71 Division 2; 1971–75 Division 3; 1975–79 Division 2; 1979–80 Division 3; 1980–92 Division 2; 1992– FA Premier League.

Honours: *FA Premier League:* – Champions 1994–95; Runners-up 1993–94. *Football League:* Division 1 – Champions 1911–12, 1913–14; Division 2 – Champions 1938–39; Runners-up 1957–58; Division 3 – Champions 1974–75; Runners-up 1979–80. *FA Cup:* Winners 1884, 1885, 1886, 1890, 1891, 1928; Runners-up 1882, 1960. *Football League Cup:* Semi-final 1962, 1993. *Full Members' Cup:* Winners 1987. **European Competitions:** *UEFA Cup:* 1994–95.

Colours: Blue and white halved shirts, white shorts with blue trim, blue stockings with white trim. **Change colours:** Red and black shirts, red shorts, black and red stockings.

BLACKBURN ROVERS 1994–95 LEAGUE RECORD

Match No.	*Date*	*Venue*	*Opponents*	*Result*		*H/T Score*	*Lg. Pos.*	*Goalscorers*	*Attendance*
1	Aug 20	A	Southampton	D	1-1	0-1	—	Shearer	14,209
2	23	H	Leicester C	W	3-0	1-0	—	Sutton, Berg, Shearer	21,050
3	27	H	Coventry C	W	4-0	0-0	2	Sutton 3, Wilcox	21,657
4	31	A	Arsenal	D	0-0	0-0	—		37,629
5	Sept 10	H	Everton	W	3-0	2-0	3	Shearer 2 (1 pen), Wilcox	26,548
6	18	A	Chelsea	W	2-1	1-0	2	Johnsen (og), Sutton	17,513
7	24	H	Aston Villa	W	3-1	1-0	2	Shearer 2 (1 pen), Sutton	22,694
8	Oct 1	A	Norwich C	L	1-2	1-1	3	Sutton	18,146
9	9	A	Newcastle U	D	1-1	0-0	3	Shearer (pen)	34,344
10	15	H	Liverpool	W	3-2	0-1	2	Atkins, Sutton 2	30,263
11	23	H	Manchester U	L	2-4	1-1	4	Warhurst, Hendry	30,260
12	29	A	Nottingham F	W	2-0	1-0	4	Sutton 2	22,131
13	Nov 2	A	Sheffield W	W	1-0	0-0	—	Shearer	24,207
14	5	H	Tottenham H	W	2-0	1-0	2	Wilcox, Shearer (pen)	26,933
15	19	A	Ipswich T	W	3-1	2-1	2	Sutton, Sherwood, Shearer	17,607
16	26	H	QPR	W	4-0	1-0	1	Sutton, Shearer 3 (1 pen)	21,302
17	Dec 3	A	Wimbledon	W	3-0	0-0	1	Atkins, Wilcox, Shearer	12,341
18	10	H	Southampton	W	3-2	2-0	1	Atkins, Shearer 2	23,372
19	17	A	Leicester C	D	0-0	0-0	1		20,559
20	26	A	Manchester C	W	3-1	2-1	1	Shearer, Atkins, Le Saux	23,387
21	31	A	Crystal Palace	W	1-0	0-0	1	Sherwood	14,232
22	Jan 2	H	West Ham U	W	4-2	1-1	1	Shearer 3 (2 pens), Le Saux	25,503
23	14	H	Nottingham F	W	3-0	0-0	1	Warhurst, Wilcox, Chettle (og)	27,510
24	22	A	Manchester U	L	0-1	0-0	1		43,742
25	28	H	Ipswich T	W	4-1	2-0	1	Shearer 3 (1 pen), Sherwood	21,325
26	Feb 1	H	Leeds U	D	1-1	1-0	—	Shearer (pen)	28,561
27	5	A	Tottenham H	L	1-3	0-1	1	Sherwood	28,124
28	12	H	Sheffield W	W	3-1	2-1	1	Sherwood, Atkins, Shearer	22,223
29	22	H	Wimbledon	W	2-1	2-1	—	Shearer, Atkins	20,586
30	25	H	Norwich C	D	0-0	0-0	1		25,579
31	Mar 4	A	Aston Villa	W	1-0	1-0	1	Hendry	40,114
32	8	H	Arsenal	W	3-1	2-0	—	Shearer 2 (1 pen), Le Saux	23,452
33	11	A	Coventry C	D	1-1	0-1	1	Shearer	18,556
34	18	H	Chelsea	W	2-1	2-1	1	Shearer, Sherwood	25,490
35	Apr 1	A	Everton	W	2-1	2-1	1	Sutton, Shearer	37,905
36	4	A	QPR	W	1-0	0-0	—	Sutton	16,508
37	15	A	Leeds U	D	1-1	1-0	1	Hendry	39,426
38	17	H	Manchester C	L	2-3	2-1	1	Shearer, Hendry	27,851
39	20	H	Crystal Palace	W	2-1	0-0	—	Kenna, Gallacher	28,005
40	30	A	West Ham U	L	0-2	0-0	1		24,202
41	May 8	H	Newcastle U	W	1-0	1-0	—	Shearer	30,545
42	14	A	Liverpool	L	1-2	1-0	1	Shearer	40,014

Final League Position: 1

GOALSCORERS

League (80): Shearer 34 (10 pens), Sutton 15, Atkins 6, Sherwood 6, Wilcox 5, Hendry 4, Le Saux 3, Warhurst 2, Berg 1, Gallacher 1, Kenna 1, own goals 2.
Coca-Cola Cup (6): Sutton 3, Shearer 2, Wilcox 1.
FA Cup (2): Sutton 2.

Flowers T.D. 39	Berg H. 40	Le Saux G.P. 39	Slater R. 12 + 6	Hendry E.C.J. 38	Gale A.P. 15	Ripley S.E. 36 + 1	Sherwood T.M. 38	Shearer A. 42	Sutton C.R. 40	Wilcox J.M. 27	Warhurst P. 20 + 7	Pearce I.A. 22 + 6	Atkins M.N. 30 + 4	Newell M.C. 2 + 10	Wright A. 4 + 1	Mimms R.A. 3 + 1	Kenna J.J. 9	Batty D. 4 + 1	Gallacher K.W. 1	Witschge R. 1	Match No.
1	2	3	4	5	6	7	8	9	10	11											1
1	2	3	4	5	6	7	8	9	*10*	11	12	14									2
1		3	4	5	*6*	7	8	9	10	11	2	14	12								3
1	2	3	4	5	6	7	8	9	10	11	12										4
1	2	3	4	5	6	7	8	9	*10*	11		12	14								5
1	2	3	4	5	6	7	8	9	10		12		11								6
1	2	3		5	6	7	4	9	10	11	12		8								7
1	2	3	12	5		7	4	9	10	11	6		8								8
1	2	3		5		7	4	9	10	11	6		8								9
1	2	3		5	4	7		9	10	11	6		8								10
1	2	3	12	5	*6*	7		9	10	11	4	14	8								11
1	2	3		5		7	4	9	10	11	6	12	8								12
1	2	3		5	6	7	8	9	10	11	4										13
1	2	3		5	6	7	8	9	10	11	4										14
1		3	11		6	7	4	9	10		2	5	8								15
1	6	3	11			7	4	9	10		2	5	8	12	14						16
1	6	3		5		7	4	9	10	11	2		8								17
1	6	3	12	5		7	4	9	*10*	11	2		8	14							18
1	2	3			6	7	4	9	10	11		5	8								19
1	2	3		5	6	7	4	9	10	11			8								20
1	2	3		5		7	4	9	10	11		6	8								21
1	2	3		5	6	7	4	*9*	10	11	12		8	14							22
1	2		7	5				9	10	11	4	6	8	12	3						23
1	2	3		5			4	9	10	*11*	6	14	8	12	7						24
1	2	3	7	5			8	9	*10*	11	4	6	12	14							25
1	2	3		5			4	9	10	11	7	6	*8*			15					26
	2			5		7	4	9	10	11	8	6	12	14	3	1					27
	2		11	5			4	9	10		7	6	8		3	1					28
	2	3	11	5		12	4	9			7	6	8	10		1					29
1	2	3		5		7	4	9		11	12	6	8	10							30
1	2	3		5		7	4	9	10	11		6	8								31
1	2	3		5		7	4	9	*10*	11	12	6	8	14							32
1	2	3	12	5		7	4	9	*10*		11	6	8	14							33
1	2	11		5		7	4	9	10			6	8				3				34
1	2	11		5		7	4	9	10			6	8				3				35
1	2	11		5		7	4	9	10			6	8				3				36
1	2	11		5		7	4	9	10			6	8				3				37
1	2	11		5		7	4	9	10			6	8				3	12			38
1	5	3	12			7		9	10			6	8				2	4	11		39
1	2	6		5		7	8	9	10					12			3	4		11	40
1	2	11	12	5		7	8	9	10			6					3	4			41
1	2	11		5		7	8	9	10			6					3	4			42

Coca-Cola Cup

Second Round	Birmingham C (h)	2-0
	(a)	1-1
Third Round	Coventry C (h)	2-0
Fourth Round	Liverpool (h)	1-3

FA Cup

Third Round	Newcastle U (a)	1-1
	(h)	1-2

BLACKPOOL 1994–95 *Back row (left to right):* Stuart Parkinson, Graeme Craggs, Andy Watson, Kevin Sheedy, Paul Symons, Ian Gore, Mitch Cook, Jonathan Sunderland, Mike Davies, Lee Thorpe, Jamie Sheppard.
Centre row: Fred O'Donoghue (Youth Liaison Scout), Tony Rodwell, Bryan Griffiths, Paul Stoneman, Tony Ellis, Jamie Murphy, David Thompson, Melvin Capleton, Les Sealey, Lee Martin, Phil Horner, Darren Bradshaw, David Burke, Andy Gouck, Neil Mitchell, Steve Redmond (Physio).
Front row: Mark Bonner, Phil Brown, Bobby Saxton (Chief Scout/Coach), Sam Allardyce (Manager), Billy Bingham (Director of Football), Neil Bailey (Youth Team Coach), Chris Beech, James Quinn.

Division 2 **BLACKPOOL**

Bloomfield Rd Ground, Blackpool FY1 6JJ. Telephone: (01253) 404331. Fax: (01253) 405011. Clubcall: 0891 121648.

Ground capacity: 10,337.

Record attendance: 38,098 v Wolverhampton W, Division 1, 17 September 1955.

Record receipts: £72,949 v Tottenham H, FA Cup 3rd rd, 5 January 1991.

Pitch measurements: 112yd × 74yd.

President: C. A. Sagar BEM.

Chairman: Owen J. Oyston. ***Deputy Chairman:*** Mrs V. Oyston.

Managing Director: Mrs G. Bridge.

Directors: G. Warburton, J. Wilde MBE, W. Bingham MBE.

Manager: Sam Allardyce.

Secretary: Carol Banks.

Commercial Manager: Geoffrey Warburton.

Coach: Neil Bailey. ***Physio:*** Stephen Redmond.

Year Formed: 1887. ***Turned Professional:*** 1887. ***Ltd Co.:*** 1896.

Previous Name: 'South Shore' combined with Blackpool in 1899, twelve years after the latter had been formed on the breaking up of the old 'Blackpool St John's' club.

Club Nickname: 'The Seasiders'.

Previous Grounds: 1887, Raikes Hall Gardens; 1897, Athletic Grounds; 1899, Raikes Hall Gardens; 1899, Bloomfield Road.

Foundation: Old boys of St. John's School who had formed themselves into a football club decided to establish a club bearing the name of their town and Blackpool FC came into being at a meeting at the Stanley Arms Hotel in the summer of 1887. In their first season playing at Raikes Hall Gardens, the club won both the Lancashire Junior Cup and the Fylde Cup.

First Football League game: 5 September, 1896, Division 2, v Lincoln C (a) L 1-3 – Douglas; Parr, Bowman; Stuart, Stirzaker, Norris; Clarkin, Donnelly, R. Parkinson, Mount (1), J. Parkinson.

Record League Victory: 7–0 v Preston NE (away), Division 1, 1 May 1948 – Robinson; Shimwell, Crosland; Buchan, Hayward, Kelly; Hobson, Munro (1), McIntosh (5), McCall, Rickett (1).

Record Cup Victory: 7–1 v Charlton Ath, League Cup, 2nd rd, 25 September 1963 – Harvey; Armfield, Martin; Crawford, Gratrix, Cranston; Lea, Ball (1), Charnley (4), Durie (1), Oakes (1).

Record Defeat: 1–10 v Small Heath, Division 2, 2 March 1901 and v Huddersfield T, Division 1, 13 December 1930.

Most League Points (2 for a win): 58, Division 2, 1929–30.

Most League Points (3 for a win): 86, Division 4, 1984–85.

Most League Goals: 98, Division 2, 1929–30.

Highest League Scorer in Season: Jimmy Hampson, 45, Division 2, 1929–30.

Most League Goals in Total Aggregate: Jimmy Hampson, 247, 1927–38.

Most Capped Player: Jimmy Armfield, 43, England.

Most League Appearances: Jimmy Armfield, 568, 1952–71.

Record Transfer Fee Received: £750,000 from QPR for Trevor Sinclair, August 1993.

Record Transfer Fee Paid: £200,000 to Crystal Palace for Andy Preece, June 1995.

Football League Record: 1896 Elected to Division 2; 1899 Failed re-election; 1900 Re-elected; 1900–30 Division 2; 1930–33 Division 1; 1933–37 Division 2; 1937–67 Division 1; 1967–70 Division 2; 1970–71 Division 1; 1971–78 Division 2; 1978–81 Division 3; 1981–85 Division 4; 1985–90 Division 3; 1990–92 Division 4; 1992– Division 2.

Honours: *Football League:* Division 1 – Runners-up 1955–56; Division 2 – Champions 1929–30; Runners-up 1936–37, 1969–70; Division 4 – Runners-up 1984–85. *FA Cup:* Winners 1953; Runners-up 1948, 1951. *Football League Cup:* Semi-final 1962. *Anglo-Italian Cup:* Winners 1971; Runners-up 1972.

Colours: Tangerine shirts with navy and white trim, white shorts, tangerine stockings with navy blue tops. **Change colours:** Navy and sky blue stripes, navy shorts, navy stockings.

BLACKPOOL 1994–95 LEAGUE RECORD

Match No.	Date	Venue	Opponents	Result		H/T Score	Lg. Pos.	Goalscorers	Attendance
1	Aug 13	H	Huddersfield T	L	1-4	0-2	—	Gouck	8343
2	20	A	Bournemouth	W	2-1	1-1	13	Ellis 2	3098
3	27	H	Shrewsbury T	W	2-1	0-1	9	Horner, Ellis (pen)	4428
4	31	A	Bristol R	D	0-0	0-0	—		3762
5	Sept 3	A	Crewe Alex	L	3-4	2-2	12	Beech, Watson, Griffiths (pen)	4915
6	10	H	Cardiff C	W	2-1	0-1	10	Brown, Ellis (pen)	4189
7	13	H	Brighton & HA	D	2-2	2-2	—	Brown, Beech	3438
8	17	A	Brentford	L	2-3	1-0	13	Horner, Quinn	4157
9	24	H	Wrexham	W	2-1	0-0	10	Brown 2 (1 pen)	5015
10	Oct 1	A	Rotherham U	W	2-0	2-0	7	Quinn, Ellis	3517
11	8	A	Hull C	L	0-1	0-1	10		3829
12	15	H	Bradford C	W	2-0	0-0	8	Ellis, Watson	6156
13	22	H	Swansea C	W	2-1	2-0	8	Ellis (pen), Watson	4911
14	29	A	Plymouth Arg	W	2-0	1-0	5	Ellis, Watson	6285
15	Nov 1	A	Oxford U	L	2-3	1-1	—	Watson 2	5610
16	5	H	Leyton Orient	W	2-1	1-1	6	Ellis, Watson	4653
17	19	A	Chester C	L	0-2	0-1	6		3114
18	26	H	Wycombe W	L	0-1	0-0	8		4846
19	Dec 10	H	Bournemouth	W	3-1	2-1	6	Ellis 2, Mitchell	3847
20	17	A	Huddersfield T	D	1-1	0-0	8	Watson	11,536
21	26	A	York C	L	0-4	0-2	11		4542
22	27	H	Stockport Co	L	1-2	0-1	12	Mitchell	5745
23	31	A	Birmingham C	L	1-7	1-3	13	Bradshaw	18,025
24	Jan 2	H	Peterborough U	W	4-0	1-0	12	Quinn 2, Watson, Ellis	3692
25	7	A	Cardiff C	W	1-0	1-0	8	Watson	3467
26	14	H	Cambridge U	L	2-3	1-1	9	Mellon, Murphy	4076
27	28	H	Plymouth Arg	W	5-2	0-1	7	Watson 2, Ellis, Mellon 2	3599
28	Feb 4	A	Wycombe W	D	1-1	0-1	8	Quinn	6380
29	7	A	Leyton Orient	W	1-0	1-0	—	Watson	3301
30	11	H	Oxford U	W	2-1	0-0	6	Gouck, Quinn	5206
31	18	A	Cambridge U	D	0-0	0-0	6		3192
32	21	H	Chester C	W	3-1	2-1	—	Mitchell, Alsford (og), Mellon (pen)	4649
33	25	H	Rotherham U	D	2-2	1-1	5	Mitchell, Ellis	5043
34	28	A	Swansea C	L	0-1	0-0	—		2308
35	Mar 4	A	Wrexham	W	1-0	0-0	5	Watson	4251
36	7	H	Crewe Alex	D	0-0	0-0	—		5859
37	11	A	Shrewsbury T	D	0-0	0-0	6		4261
38	18	H	Bristol R	L	0-2	0-0	7		4484
39	25	H	Brentford	L	1-2	0-2	8	Brown	4663
40	Apr 1	A	Brighton & HA	D	2-2	1-1	10	Ellis, Watson	7157
41	4	H	Birmingham C	D	1-1	1-1	—	Quinn	4494
42	15	A	Stockport Co	L	2-3	0-2	11	Quinn 2	5021
43	18	H	York C	L	0-5	0-3	—		3517
44	22	A	Peterborough U	L	0-1	0-0	13		5716
45	29	A	Bradford C	W	1-0	1-0	12	Ellis	5036
46	May 6	H	Hull C	L	1-2	1-1	12	Ellis	4251

Final League Position: 12

GOALSCORERS

League (64): Ellis 17 (3 pens), Watson 15, Quinn 9, Brown 5 (1 pen), Mellon 4 (1 pen), Mitchell 4, Beech 2, Gouck 2, Horner 2, Bradshaw 1, Griffiths 1 (pen), Murphy 1, own goal 1.
Coca-Cola Cup (3): Brown 1, Ellis 1, Quinn 1.
FA Cup (0).

Sealey L.J. 7	Brown P. 28 + 3	Burke D.I. 23	Bonner M. 9 + 8	Horner P.M. 33 + 1	Gore I.G. 3 + 1	Rodwell A. 7 + 2	Gouck A.S. 35 + 4	Bamber J.D. 2	Ellis A.J. 40	Griffiths B.K. 12 + 2	Quinn S.J. 37 + 4	Gibson C.J. 1 + 1	Briggs G. 1	Beech C.S. 25 + 3	Stoneman P. 4	Watson A.A. 24 + 9	Cook M. 4 + 2	Thompson D. 17	Moore N. 7	Martin L.B. 31	Thorpe L.A. — + 1	Mitchell N.N. 25 + 5	Bradshaw D.S. 26	Capleton M.D.R. 8 + 2	Murphy J.A. 6	Mellon M.J. 26	Sunderland J. — + 2	Morrison A.C. 18	Davies M.J. 1	Rowett G. 17	Darton S.R. 18	Lydiate J.L. 11	Parkinson S.G. — + 1	Match No.
1	2	3	4	5	6	7	*8*	9	10	11	12	14																						1
1	2	3		4	6	12			10	11	9	8	5	7																				2
1	2	3		4		7	11	9	10		8			6	5																			3
1	2	3	4	6		7	11		10	12	9			8	5																			4
1	2	3	14	4	6	7	*11*			12	9			8	5	10																		5
1	2			4		7	11		10		9			8			3	5	6															6
1	2		12	4		7	11			10	9			8			3	5	6															7
	2		6	4	12	7	11			10	9			8			3		5	1	14													8
	2			4					10	11	9			8	7		3	5	6	1		12												9
	2	*3*		4		12	7		10		9			8			14	5	6	1		11												10
	2	3		4			*7*			10	9			8		12	14	5	6	1		11												11
	2	3	12	5			4		10	11	9			8		7			6	1														12
	2	3		6			12		10	11	9			8		7		5		1			4											13
	2	3		6					10	11	12			8		9		5		1		7	4											14
	2	3		6					10	11				8		9		5		1		7	4											15
	2	3		6					10	11				8		9		5		1		7	4											16
	2	3	8	6			12		10	11	14					*9*		5		*1*		7	4	15										17
		3	11	6					10		9							5				7	8	1	2	4	12							18
		3	7	6			12		10		*9*					14		5				11		1	2	8		4						19
		3	7	6					10		9					12		5				11		1	2	8		4						20
	12	3	*7*	6			14		10					4		9		5				11		1	2	8								21
	2	3		6			7		10					4		9		5				11		1		8								22
	2	3	12				4		10		7					9						11	6	1	5	8								23
	2	3					11		10		7			4		9				1			6			8		5						24
	2	3		6			11		10		7			4		9				1		12				8		5						25
				6			11		10		7			4		9				1		12			3	8		5	2					26
				6			11		10		7					9				1			4			8		5		2	3			27
				4			11		10		7					9				1			6			8		5		2	3			28
				4			11		10		7					9				1		12	6			8		5		2	3			29
				4			11		10		7					9				1			6			8		5		2	3			30
	12		14	4			11				7					9				1		*10*	6			8		5		2	3			31
	6		12	4			11				*7*					9		5		1		10				8				2	3			32
	6		12	4			11		10		7							5		1		9				8				2	3			33
			12	4			11		10		7					9				1		5	6			8				2	3			34
			4				11		10		7					9				1			6			8				2	3	5		35
			12				11		10		*7*					9				1		14	6			8		4		2	3	5		36
							11		10		*7*			12						1		9	6			8		4		2	3	5		37
							11		10		7			12						1		9	6			8		4		2	3	5		38
	2			5			8		10		9			*4*		12				1		11	6							7	3		14	39
	2						8		10		9			4		12				1		11	6							7	3	5		40
	14						8		10		9			*4*		12				1		11	6					7		2	3	5		41
							7		10		9					12				1		11	6			8		4		2	3	5		42
							7		10		9					12						11	6	1		8		4		2	3	5		43
	2						7		10		*9*			12		14						11	6	1		8		4			3	5		44
	2	3					11		10		12			7		9				1			6			8		4				5		45
	2	3					11		10					4		9				1		7	6	15		8	12					5		46

Coca-Cola Cup First Round	Chesterfield (h)	1-2	**FA Cup** First Round	Preston NE (a)	0-1
	(a)	2-4			

BOLTON WANDERERS 1994–95 *Back row (left to right):* Mark Winstanley, Andy Mason, Jason Lydiate, Mark Seagraves, Scott Green.
Third row: Jason McAteer, David Lee, Aidan Davison, Keith Branagan, Jimmy Phillips, Owen Coyle.
Second row: Ewan Simpson (Physio), Steve Carroll (Reserve Team Manager), Stuart Whittaker, Neil Fisher, Andy McKay, Gary Martindale, Neil McDonald, Tony Kelly, Colin Todd (Coach), Ian McNeil (Chief Scout)
Front row: Andy Roscoe, Alan Thompson, John McGinlay, Bruce Rioch (Manager), Alan Stubbs, Nicky Spooner, Mark Patterson.

FA Premiership **BOLTON WANDERERS**

Burnden Park, Bolton BL3 2QR. Telephone: (01204) 389200. Fax: (01204) 382334. Ticket Office: (01204) 521101. Ticket Office Fax: (01204) 392474. Commercial Dept: (01204) 24518.

Ground capacity: 20,500.

Record attendance: 69,912 v Manchester C, FA Cup 5th rd, 18 February 1933.

Record receipts: £159,290.50 v Swindon T, Coca-Cola Cup semi-final, 8 March 1995.

Pitch measurements: 113yd × 76yd.

President: Nat Lofthouse.

Chairman: G. Hargreaves.

Directors: P. A. Gartside, G. Ball, G. Seymour, G. Warburton, W. B. Warburton, B. Scowcroft.

Team Manager: Roy McFarland. ***Assistant Manager:*** Colin Todd. ***Physio:*** E. Simpson.

Chief Executive & Secretary: Des McBain. ***Commercial Manager:*** T. Holland.

Year Formed: 1874. ***Turned Professional:*** 1880. ***Ltd Co.:*** 1895.

Previous Name: 1874–77, Christ Church FC; 1877 became Bolton Wanderers.

Club Nickname: 'The Trotters'.

Previous Grounds: Park Recreation Ground and Cockle's Field before moving to Pike's Lane ground 1881; 1895, Burnden Park.

Foundation: In 1874 boys of Christ Church Sunday School, Blackburn Street, led by their master Thomas Ogden, established a football club which went under the name of the school and whose president was Vicar of Christ Church. Membership was 6d (two and a half pence). When their president began to lay down too many rules about the use of church premises, the club broke away and formed Bolton Wanderers in 1877, holding their earliest meetings at the Gladstone Hotel.

First Football League game: 8 September, 1888, Football League, v Derby C (h), L 3-6 – Harrison; Robinson, Mitchell; Roberts, Weir, Bullough, Davenport (2), Milne, Coupar, Barbour, Brogan (1).

Record League Victory: 8–0 v Barnsley, Division 2, 6 October 1934 – Jones; Smith, Finney; Goslin, Atkinson, George Taylor; George T. Taylor (2), Eastham, Milsom (1), Westwood (4), Cook. (1 og).

Record Cup Victory: 13–0 v Sheffield U, FA Cup, 2nd rd, 1 February 1890 – Parkinson; Robinson (1), Jones; Bullough, Davenport, Roberts; Rushton, Brogan (3), Cassidy (5), McNee, Weir (4).

Record Defeat: 1–9 v Preston NE, FA Cup 2nd rd, 10 December 1887.

Most League Points (2 for a win): 61, Division 3, 1972–73.

Most League Points (3 for a win): 90, Division 2, 1992–93.

Most League Goals: 96, Division 2, 1934–35.

Highest League Scorer in Season: Joe Smith, 38, Division 1, 1920–21.

Most League Goals in Total Aggregate: Nat Lofthouse, 255, 1946–61.

Most Capped Player: Nat Lofthouse, 33, England.

Most League Appearances: Eddie Hopkinson, 519, 1956–70.

Record Transfer Fee Received: £550,000 from Celtic for Andy Walker, July 1994.

Record Transfer Fee Paid: £450,000 to Leeds U for Chris Fairclough, July 1995.

Football League Record: 1888 Founder Member of the League; 1899–1900 Division 2; 1900–03 Division 1; 1903–05 Division 2; 1905–08 Division 1; 1908–09 Division 2; 1909–10 Division 1; 1910–11 Division 2; 1911–33 Division 1; 1933–35 Division 2; 1935–64 Division 1; 1964–71 Division 2; 1971–73 Division 3; 1973–78 Division 2; 1978–80 Division 1; 1980–83 Division 2; 1983–87 Division 3; 1987–88 Division 4; 1988–92 Division 3; 1992–93 Division 2; 1993–95 Division 1; 1995– FA Premier League.

Honours: *Football League:* Division 1 best season: 3rd, 1891–92, 1920–21, 1924–25, 1994–95; Division 2 – Champions 1908–09, 1977–78; Runners-up 1899–1900, 1904–05, 1910–11, 1934–35, 1992–93; Division 3 – Champions 1972–73. *FA Cup:* Winners 1923, 1926, 1929, 1958; Runners-up 1894, 1904, 1953. *Football League Cup:* Runners-up 1995. *Freight Rover Trophy:* Runners-up 1986. *Sherpa Van Trophy:* Winners 1989.

Colours: White shirts, navy blue shorts, blue stockings. **Change colours:** Dark/sky blue shirts, navy blue shorts, blue stockings.

BOLTON WANDERERS 1994–95 LEAGUE RECORD

Match No.	Date		Venue	Opponents	Result		H/T Score	Lg. Pos.	Goalscorers	Atten-dance
1	Aug	13	A	Grimsby T	D	3-3	2-1	—	Paatelainen 2, McGinlay (pen)	8393
2		20	H	Bristol C	L	0-2	0-1	17		12,127
3		27	A	Middlesbrough	L	0-1	0-1	19		19,570
4		30	H	Millwall	W	1-0	0-0	—	Patterson	9519
5	Sept	3	H	Stoke C	W	4-0	1-0	9	McGinlay (pen), McAteer 2, Paatelainen	11,515
6		10	A	Sheffield U	L	1-3	0-1	15	McGinlay	14,116
7		13	A	Luton T	W	3-0	1-0	—	McGinlay 2, Sneekes	5764
8		17	H	Portsmouth	D	1-1	1-0	10	McGinlay	11,284
9		24	A	Southend U	L	1-2	1-0	12	Sneekes	4507
10	Oct	1	H	Derby Co	W	1-0	0-0	8	McGinlay	12,015
11		8	A	Burnley	D	2-2	1-0	9	McGinlay, Coleman	16,687
12		16	H	Oldham Ath	D	2-2	2-0	10	Paatelainen, Lee	11,106
13		22	A	Port Vale	D	1-1	0-0	12	Green	10,003
14		29	H	Watford	W	3-0	1-0	7	Paatelainen, McGinlay 2 (1 pen)	10,483
15	Nov	1	H	Swindon T	W	3-0	1-0	—	Coleman, Thompson, De Freitas	10,046
16		5	A	Charlton Ath	W	2-1	1-0	5	Sneekes 2	9793
17		19	H	Notts Co	W	2-0	1-0	3	De Freitas, Paatelainen	11,698
18		23	A	Wolverhampton W	L	1-3	1-0	—	Paatelainen	25,903
19		26	A	Barnsley	L	0-3	0-2	4		8507
20	Dec	6	H	Port Vale	W	1-0	0-0	—	Patterson	10,324
21		10	A	Bristol C	W	1-0	1-0	4	Patterson	6144
22		17	H	Grimsby T	D	3-3	1-2	3	Coyle 2, Lee	10,522
23		26	A	Sunderland	D	1-1	0-0	5	Paatelainen	19,758
24		27	H	Tranmere R	W	1-0	1-0	2	Thompson	16,782
25		31	A	WBA	L	0-1	0-1	6		18,184
26	Jan	2	H	Reading	W	1-0	1-0	4	Coleman	14,705
27		14	A	Watford	D	0-0	0-0	3		9113
28		21	H	Charlton Ath	W	5-1	2-1	3	McGinlay 2, McAteer, Coyle, Paatelainen	10,516
29	Feb	4	H	Wolverhampton W	W	5-1	2-1	1	Sneekes, Coleman, Phillips, Coyle, Thompson	16,964
30		7	A	Notts Co	D	1-1	0-0	—	Coyle	7553
31		18	H	Barnsley	W	2-1	2-0	1	Thompson, Sneekes	12,463
32		26	A	Derby Co	L	1-2	1-0	3	McAteer	11,003
33	Mar	4	H	Southend U	W	3-0	1-0	3	Thompson, Lee, McAteer	10,766
34		11	H	Middlesbrough	W	1-0	1-0	3	Paatelainen	18,370
35		19	A	Millwall	W	1-0	0-0	2	McGinlay	6103
36		22	H	Sheffield U	D	1-1	1-1	—	Stubbs	16,756
37		25	A	Portsmouth	D	1-1	1-0	2	Paatelainen	7765
38	Apr	5	A	Swindon T	W	1-0	0-0	—	Thompson	8100
39		8	H	WBA	W	1-0	0-0	3	Thompson	16,207
40		11	H	Luton T	D	0-0	0-0	—		13,619
41		14	A	Tranmere R	L	0-1	0-1	—		14,959
42		17	H	Sunderland	W	1-0	0-0	2	McGinlay	15,030
43		21	A	Reading	L	1-2	0-1	—	Lee	13,223
44		29	A	Oldham Ath	L	1-3	1-2	3	McGinlay	11,901
45	May	3	A	Stoke C	D	1-1	1-1	—	McGinlay	15,557
46		7	H	Burnley	D	1-1	0-0	3	Paatelainen	16,853

Final League Position: 3

GOALSCORERS

League (67): McGinlay 16 (3 pens), Paatelainen 12, Thompson 7, Sneekes 6, Coyle 5, McAteer 5, Coleman 4, Lee 4, Patterson 3, De Freitas 2, Green 1, Phillips 1, Stubbs 1.
Coca-Cola Cup (15): McGinlay 4, Lee 2, McAteer 2, Paatelainen 2, Thompson 2, Sneekes 1, Stubbs 1, own goal 1.
FA Cup (1): Sneekes 1.

Branagan K.G. 43	McDonald N.R. 4	Phillips J.N. 46	McAteer J.W. 41 + 2	Lydiate J.L. 17 + 1	Stubbs A. 37 + 2	Lee D.M. 35 + 4	Patterson M.A. 23 + 3	Paatelainen M. 43 + 1	McGinlay J. 34 + 3	Thompson A. 34 + 3	Coyle O.C. 8 + 11	Sneekes R. 37 + 1	Kernaghan A.N. 9 + 2	Fisher N.J. 10 + 1	De Freitas F. 7 + 6	Kelly A.G. 4	Spooner N.M. 1	Coleman S. 22	Green S.P. 26 + 5	Whitaker S. — + 1	Davison A.J. 3 + 1	Seagraves M. 13	Bergsson G. 8	Dreyer J.B. 1 + 1	Shilton P.L. — + 1	Match No.
1	2	3	4	5	6	7	8	9	10	*11*	12	14														1
1	*2*	3	4		6	7	8	9	10	14	12	11	5													2
1		3	4	2	6		11	9	12			8	5	7	10											3
1		3	4	2	6		11	9	12			8	5	7	10											4
1		3	4	2	6			9	10			8	5	7		11										5
1		*3*	4	2	6			9	10	14	12	8	5	7		11										6
1		3	4	2	6			9	10			8	5	7		11										7
1		3	4	2	6	12		9	10			8	5	7		11										8
1		3	4	2	6	11		*9*	10	5		8	12	7	14											9
1		3	4	2		11		9	10	5		8	6	7												10
1		3	4	2		11		9	10	*5*		8		12	14		6	7								11
1		3	4	2		11		9	10	5		8	12	7				6								12
1		3	4			11		9	10	5		8	2	*7*	12			6	14							13
1		3		2		11	4	9	10	5		8						6	7							14
1		3	12	2		11	4	9		5	14	8			*10*			7	6							15
1		3	12	2		11	4	9		5	14	8			*10*			7	6							16
1		3		2	12	11	4	9		5	14	8			*10*			7	6							17
1		3		2	12	11	4	9		5	14	8			*10*			7	6							18
1		3	11	2	4	12		9	10	*5*	14	8						7	6							19
1		3	4		6	7	11	9	10			8						5	2							20
1		3	4		6	7	11	9	10		12	8						5	2							21
1		3	4		6	7	11	9		12	10	8						5	2							22
1		3	4		6	7		9		11	10	8						5	2							23
1		3	4		6	7	8	9	10	11	12							5	2							24
1		3	4		6	7	12	9	10	11		8						5	2							25
1		3	4		6	7	9	12	10		11	*8*						5	2	14						26
1		3	4		6	7		9	10	11		8						5	2							27
1		3	4	14	6	7		9	10	11	*12*	8						5	2							28
1		3	4		6	7		9		11	10	8						5	2							29
1		3	4		6	7		9		11	10	8			12			5	2		15					30
1		3	4		6	7		9	10	11		8						5	2							31
		3	4		6	7	12	9	*10*	11		8			14			5	2		1					32
1		3	4		6	7	8		10	11	9								2			5				33
1		3	4		6	12	8	9	10	11		7							2			5				34
1	8	3	4		6			9	10	11		7							2			5				35
1		3	4		6	7		9	10	11		8							2			5				36
1	8	3	4		6	12		9		11	10	7							2			5				37
1		3	4		6	7	8	9	10	11									12			5	2			38
1		3	4		6	7	8	9	*10*	11					14				12			5	2			39
1		3	4		6			9	12	11		8			10				7			5	2			40
1		3	4		6	7	12	9	10	11		8										5	2			41
1		3	4		6	7	11	9	10			8							12			5	2	14		42
1		3	4		6	7	8		10	11	9											5		2		43
1		3	4		6	7	8	9	10	11												5	2			44
		3	4		6	7	8	9	10	11									12		1	5	2		15	45
		3	4		6	7	8	9	10	11									2		1		5			46

Coca-Cola Cup

Second Round	Ipswich T (a)	3-0
	(h)	1-0
Third Round	Sheffield U (a)	2-1
Fourth Round	West Ham U (a)	3-1
Fifth Round	Norwich C (h)	1-0
Semi-final	Swindon T (a)	1-2
	(h)	3-1
Final at Wembley	Liverpool	1-2

FA Cup

Third Round	Portsmouth (a)	1-3

AFC BOURNEMOUTH 1994–95 *Back row (left to right):* Sean O'Driscoll (Physio/Player), Chris Leadbitter, Mark Morris, Michael McElhatton, Robert Murray.
Centre row: Steve Hardwick (Physio), Gary Chivers, Scott Mean, Neil Moss, Ian Andrews, Alex Watson, Steve Fletcher, John Williams (Youth Manager).
Front row: Mark O'Connor, Kevin Russell, Steve Cotterill, Mel Machin (Manager), Warren Aspinall, Adrian Pennock, Russell Beardsmore.

Division 2 **AFC BOURNEMOUTH**

Dean Court Ground, Bournemouth, Dorset BH7 7AF. Telephone: (01202) 395381. Fax: (01202) 309797.

Ground capacity: 11,880.

Record attendance: 28,799 v Manchester U, FA Cup 6th rd, 2 March 1957.

Record receipts: £33,723 v Manchester U, FA Cup 3rd rd, 7 January 1984.

Pitch measurements: 112yd × 75yd.

Chairman: K. Gardiner.

Directors: B. E. Willis (vice-chairman), G. M. C. Hayward, E. G. Keep, C. W. Legg, N. Hayward.

Secretary: K. R. J. MacAlister.

Manager: Mel Machin. ***First Team Coach:*** John Williams. ***Youth Team Coach:*** Sean O'Driscoll. ***Physio:*** Steve Hardwick. ***Commercial Manager:*** Terry Lovell.

Year Formed: 1899. ***Turned Professional:*** 1912. ***Ltd Co.:*** 1914.

Previous Names: Boscombe St Johns, 1890–99; Boscombe FC, 1899–1923; Bournemouth & Boscombe Ath FC, 1923–71.

Club Nickname: 'Cherries'.

Previous Grounds: 1899–1910, Castlemain Road, Pokesdown; 1910, Dean Court.

Foundation: There was a Bournemouth FC as early as 1875, but the present club arose out of the remnants of the Boscombe St John's club (formed 1890). The meeting at which Boscombe FC came into being was held at a house in Gladstone Road in 1899. They began by playing in the Boscombe and District Junior League.

First Football League game: 25 August, 1923, Division 3(S), v Swindon T (a), L 1-3 – Heron; Wingham, Lamb; Butt, C. Smith, Voisey; Miller, Lister (1), Davey, Simpson, Robinson.

Record League Victory: 7–0 v Swindon T, Division 3 (S), 22 September 1956 – Godwin; Cunningham, Keetley; Clayton, Crosland, Rushworth; Siddall (1), Norris (2), Arnott (1), Newsham (2), Cutler (1). 10–0 win v Northampton T at start of 1939–40 expunged from the records on outbreak of war.

Record Cup Victory: 11–0 v Margate, FA Cup, 1st rd, 20 November 1971 – Davies; Machin (1), Kitchener, Benson, Jones, Powell, Cave (1), Boyer, MacDougall (9 incl. 1p), Miller, Scott (De Garis).

Record Defeat: 0–9 v Lincoln C, Division 3, 18 December 1982.

Most League Points (2 for a win): 62, Division 3, 1971–72.

Most League Points (3 for a win): 97, Division 3, 1986–87.

Most League Goals: 88, Division 3 (S), 1956–57.

Highest League Scorer in Season: Ted MacDougall, 42, 1970–71.

Most League Goals in Total Aggregate: Ron Eyre, 202, 1924–33.

Most Capped Player: Gerry Peyton, 7 (33), Republic of Ireland.

Most League Appearances: Sean O'Driscoll, 423, 1984–95.

Record Transfer Fee Received: £800,000 from Everton for Joe Parkinson, March 1994.

Record Transfer Fee Paid: £210,000 to Gillingham for Gavin Peacock, August 1989.

Football League Record: 1923 Elected to Division 3 (S). Remained a Third Division club for record number of years until 1970; 1970–71 Division 4; 1971–75 Division 3; 1975–82 Division 4; 1982–87 Division 3; 1987–90 Division 2; 1990– 92 Division 3; 1992– Division 2.

Honours: *Football League:* Division 3 – Champions 1986–87; Division 3 (S) – Runners-up 1947–48. Promotion from Division 4 1970–71 (2nd), 1981–82 (4th). *FA Cup:* best season: 6th rd, 1957. *Football League Cup:* best season: 4th rd, 1962, 1964. *Associate Members' Cup:* Winners 1984.

Colours: Red shirts with black 4″ stripe, black shorts, black stockings. **Change colours:** Blue shirts, with black 4″ stripe, white shorts, white stockings.

AFC BOURNEMOUTH 1994–95 LEAGUE RECORD

Match No.	Date	Venue	Opponents	Result		H/T Score	Lg. Pos.	Goalscorers	Attendance
1	Aug 13	A	Wrexham	L	0-2	0-2	—		3580
2	20	H	Blackpool	L	1-2	1-1	21	Cotterill	3098
3	27	A	Rotherham U	L	0-4	0-0	24		2306
4	30	H	Peterborough U	L	0-3	0-2	—		2649
5	Sept 3	H	York C	L	1-4	0-3	24	Aspinall (pen)	3181
6	10	A	Stockport Co	L	0-1	0-0	24		4054
7	13	A	Leyton Orient	L	2-3	1-1	—	Aspinall, Leadbitter	2536
8	17	H	Chester C	D	1-1	0-1	24	Leadbitter	3025
9	24	H	Cardiff C	W	3-2	1-1	23	Beardsmore 2, Aspinall (pen)	3177
10	Oct 1	A	Hull C	L	1-3	1-2	23	Aspinall	3056
11	8	A	Shrewsbury T	L	0-3	0-1	24		3684
12	15	H	Brentford	L	0-1	0-1	24		4411
13	22	H	Bradford C	L	2-3	1-2	24	Mean (pen), Morris	3037
14	29	A	Huddersfield T	L	1-3	0-2	24	Jones	11,251
15	Nov 2	A	Brighton & HA	D	0-0	0-0	—		5631
16	5	H	Cambridge U	W	1-0	0-0	24	Robinson	3272
17	19	A	Birmingham C	D	0-0	0-0	24		15,477
18	26	H	Oxford U	L	0-2	0-1	24		4277
19	Dec 10	A	Blackpool	L	1-3	1-2	24	Jones	3847
20	16	H	Wrexham	L	1-3	1-1	—	Hughes (og)	2505
21	26	A	Bristol R	L	1-2	0-1	24	Pennock	6913
22	27	H	Crewe Alex	D	1-1	1-0	24	Beardsmore	3325
23	31	A	Wycombe W	D	1-1	1-0	24	Robinson	5990
24	Jan 2	H	Swansea C	W	3-2	2-1	23	Fletcher 2, Pennock	3816
25	7	A	Bradford C	W	2-1	0-0	22	Robinson, Leadbitter (pen)	5426
26	14	H	Plymouth Arg	D	0-0	0-0	22		4913
27	21	A	Cambridge U	D	2-2	0-1	22	Pennock, McElhatton	2834
28	28	H	Huddersfield T	L	0-2	0-0	22		4427
29	Feb 4	A	Oxford U	W	3-0	2-0	21	Jones 2, Fletcher	5473
30	11	H	Brighton & HA	L	0-3	0-2	21		5247
31	18	A	Plymouth Arg	W	1-0	1-0	21	McElhatton	5435
32	21	H	Birmingham C	W	2-1	1-0	—	Jones, Mean	6024
33	25	H	Hull C	L	2-3	2-3	21	Jones, Pennock	4345
34	Mar 4	A	Cardiff C	D	1-1	1-1	20	Fletcher	3008
35	7	A	York C	L	0-1	0-0	—		2301
36	11	H	Rotherham U	D	1-1	0-0	20	Morris	5666
37	18	A	Peterborough U	D	0-0	0-0	21		4495
38	21	H	Stockport Co	W	2-0	1-0	—	Fletcher, Jones	2892
39	25	A	Chester C	D	1-1	0-0	20	Fletcher	1618
40	Apr 1	H	Leyton Orient	W	2-0	1-0	20	Pennock, Holland	4118
41	8	H	Wycombe W	W	2-0	1-0	20	Mean 2 (2 pens)	8615
42	15	A	Crewe Alex	L	0-2	0-1	20		3906
43	18	H	Bristol R	W	2-0	1-0	—	Morris, Jones	7020
44	22	A	Swansea C	L	0-1	0-0	20		2664
45	29	A	Brentford	W	2-1	0-0	19	Mean, Jones	10,079
46	May 2	H	Shrewsbury T	W	3-0	3-0	—	Robinson 2, Mean	10,737

Final League Position: 19

GOALSCORERS

League (49): Jones 9, Fletcher 6, Mean 6 (3 pens), Pennock 5, Robinson 5, Aspinall 4 (2 pens), Beardsmore 3, Leadbitter 3 (1 pen), Morris 3, McElhatton 2, Cotterill 1, Holland 1, own goal 1.
Coca-Cola Cup (3): Cotterill 2, Russell 1.
FA Cup (4): Jones 1, McElhatton 1, Morris 1, Russell 1.

Moss N.G. 8	O'Driscoll S.M. 10	O'Connor M.A. 11 + 2	Morris M.J. 38	Watson A.F. 16 + 6	Leadbitter C.J. 25 + 2	Beardsmore R.P. 43	Aspinall W. 8 + 1	Fletcher S.M. 37 + 3	Cotterill S. 8	Russell K.J. 13	Mean S. 32 + 8	Reeve J.M. 2 + 5	McElhatton M.T. 13 + 14	Murray R.J. 28 + 3	Andrews I.E. 38	Russell L. 3	Town D.E. — + 5	Williams G.J. — + 1	Barfoot S.J. — + 2	Brooks S. 1	Ferrett C.A. — + 1	Young N.A. 32	Chivers G.P.S. 5	Pennock A.B. 31	Scully A.D.T. 6 + 4	Jones S.G. 27 + 3	Robinson S. 30 + 2	Vincent J.R. 8	Wells D. — + 1	Brissett J.C. 24 + 1	Holland M.R. 9 + 7	Strong S.G. — + 1	*Match No.*
1	2	3	4	5	6	7	8	9	10	11	12																						1
1	2	3	4	5	6	7		9	10	11	8	12																					2
1	2	3	4	5	6	7		9	10	11	8																						3
1	2	3	4	*5*	6	7	12	9	10	11			8	14																			4
1	2	3			8	7	6	5	10	11	12	14	4	*9*																			5
	2	3			11	7	8	6	10	4	12		5		1	9	14																6
	2	3		5	11		8	6	10	9	12	14	*7*		1	4																	7
		3		5	11	7		6	10	9	8	12	2		1	4		14															8
	2	3		5	11	7	9	6		10	8		4		1																		9
	2	3		5	11	7	9	6		10	8	12	*4*		1				14														10
	2			5	11	7	9	6			8	10	4		1				12	*3*	14												11
			4	5		7	*9*	12			8	10	14		1							2	3	6	11								12
			4			7		12			8		14	*5*	1							2	3	6	11	9	10						13
			4		6	7		5		9	8				1							2	3		11	10	12						14
			4	5	6	7				11	8				1							2	3		12	10	9						15
			4	5	6	7					8		12	14	1							2	3		11	10	9						16
			4	5	6	7					8		12		1							3		2	11	10	9						17
				5	6	7					8			12	1							2		4	11	10	9	3					18
		12	4	5	6	7					8				1							*2*		11	14	10	9	3					19
1			4	5		7				11	8											2		6	12	10	*9*	3	15				20
			4		6	7		12						5	1							2		11	14	10	*9*	3		8			21
		12	4		8	7		*10*						5	1		14					2		6			9	3		11			22
			4		9	7		10			12		14	5	1							2		6			8	3		*11*			23
			4		*9*	7		10			12			5	1							2		6		14	8	3		11			24
			4		9	7		10						5	1							2		6		12	8	3		11			25
		3	4	12				10			9		7	5	1							2		6		14	8			11			26
			4	12		3		10			9		14	5	1							2		6		7	8			11			27
			4		9	3		10					12	5	1							2		6		7	8			*11*	14		28
			4		9	3		10					12	5	1							2		6		7	8				11		29
			4		9	3		10			12			5	1							2		6		7	8			14	11		30
			4			3		10			12		2	5	1									6		9	8			11	7		31
1			4	12		3		10			6		2	5												9	8			11	7		32
1			*4*	12				10			6		2	5			14					3		8		9				11	7		33
			4			3		10			*6*		12	5	1							2		8		9	14			11	7		34
			4			3		10			6		12	5	1							2		8		9				11	7		35
			4	12	14	3		10			6			5	1							2		9			8			11	7		36
			4		12	3		10			6			5	1							2		9			8			11	7		37
			4			3		10			6		12	5	1							2		8		9	7			11			38
			4			3		10			6			5	1		12					2		7		9	8			11	14		39
			4			3		10			6			5	1							2		7		9	8			11	12		40
			4			3		10			6			5	1							2		7		9	8			11	12		41
			4			3		10			6			5	1		12					2		7		9	*8*			11	14		42
			4			3		10			6		12	5	1							2		7		9	8			11			43
			4	12		3		10			6		*2*	5	1									7		9	8			11	14		44
			4			3		10			6		12	5	1							2		7		9	*8*			11	14		45
			4			3		10			6		12	5	1							2		7		*9*	8			11		14	46

Coca-Cola Cup

First Round	Northampton T (h)	2-0
	(a)	1-0
Second Round	Chelsea (a)	0-1
	(h)	0-1

FA Cup

First Round	Worthing (h)	3-1
Second Round	Plymouth Arg (a)	1-2

BRADFORD CITY 1994–95 *Back row (left to right):* Leena Stocks (Physio), Wayne Jacobs, Chris Kamara, Neil Tolson, John Taylor, Ian Bowling, Paul Tomlinson, Lee Sinnott, Dean Richards, Des Hamilton, Paul Showler, Steve Smith (Youth Development Officer).
Front row: Wayne Benn, Gary Robson, Lee Power, Gavin Oliver, Lennie Lawrence (Manager), Lee Duxbury, George Shipley (Assistant Manager), Paul Jewell, Richard Liburd, Neil Grayston, Shaun Murray.

Division 2 **BRADFORD CITY**

The Pulse Stadium, Bradford BD8 7DY. Telephone: (01274) 306062 (Office). Fax: (01274) 307457.

Ground capacity: 14,359.

Record attendance: 39,146 v Burnley, FA Cup 4th rd, 11 March 1911.

Record receipts: £74,213 v Sheffield W, Coca-Cola Cup 2nd rd 2nd leg, 4 October 1994.

Pitch measurements: 110yd × 73yd.

Chairman: Geoffrey Richmond. ***Vice-Chairman:*** David Thompson FCA.

Directors: David Richmond, Elizabeth Richmond, Terry Goddard.

Manager: Lennie Lawrence. ***Assistant Manager:*** Chris Kamara.

Youth Coach: Steve Smith. ***Physio:*** S. Redmond.

Secretary: Shaun A. Harvey. ***Commercial Manager:*** Allan Gilliver.

Year Formed: 1903. ***Turned Professional:*** 1903. ***Ltd Co.:*** 1908.

Club Nickname: 'The Bantams'.

Foundation: Bradford was a rugby stronghold around the turn of the century but after Manningham RFC held an archery contest to help them out of financial difficulties in 1903, they were persuaded to give up the handling code and turn to soccer. So they formed Bradford City and continued at Valley Parade. Recognising this as an opportunity of spreading the dribbling code in this part of Yorkshire, the Football League immediately accepted the new club's first application for membership of the Second Division.

First Football League game: 1 September, 1903, Division 2, v Grimsby T (a), L 0-2 – Seymour; Wilson, Halliday; Robinson, Millar, Farnall; Guy, Beckram, Forrest, McMillan, Graham.

Record League Victory: 11–1 v Rotherham U, Division 3 (N), 25 August 1928 – Sherlaw; Russell, Watson; Burkinshaw (1), Summers, Bauld; Harvey (2), Edmunds (3), White (3), Cairns, Scriven (2).

Record Cup Victory: 11–3 v Walker Celtic, FA Cup, 1st rd (replay), 1 December 1937 – Parker; Rookes, McDermott; Murphy, Mackie, Moore; Bagley (1), Whittingham (1), Deakin (4 incl. 1p), Cooke (1), Bartholomew (4).

Record Defeat: 1–9 v Colchester U, Division 4, 30 December 1961.

Most League Points (2 for a win): 63, Division 3 (N), 1928–29.

Most League Points (3 for a win): 94, Division 3, 1984–85.

Most League Goals: 128, Division 3 (N), 1928–29.

Highest League Scorer in Season: David Layne, 34, Division 4, 1961–62.

Most League Goals in Total Aggregate: Bobby Campbell, 121, 1981–84, 1984–86.

Most Capped Player: Harry Hampton, 9, Northern Ireland.

Most League Appearances: Cec Podd, 502, 1970–84.

Record Transfer Fee Received: £1,850,000 from Wolverhampton W for Dean Richards, June 1995.

Record Transfer Fee Paid: £300,000 to Bristol R for John Taylor, July 1994.

Football League Record: 1903 Elected to Division 2; 1908–22 Division 1; 1922–27 Division 2; 1927–29 Division 3 (N); 1929–37 Division 2; 1937–61 Division 3; 1961–69 Division 4; 1969–72 Division 3; 1972–77 Division 4; 1977–78 Division 3; 1978–82 Division 4; 1982–85 Division 3; 1985–90 Division 2; 1990–92 Division 3; 1992– Division 2.

Honours: *Football League:* Division 1 best season: 5th, 1910–11; Division 2 – Champions 1907–08; Division 3 – Champions 1984–85; Division 3 (N) – Champions 1928–29; Division 4 – Runners-up 1981–82. *FA Cup:* Winners 1911 (first holders of the present trophy). *Football League Cup:* best season: 5th rd, 1965, 1989.

Colours: Claret and amber striped shirts, black shorts, black stockings. **Change colours:** Light blue shirts and shorts, blue stockings.

THE BANTAMS

BRADFORD CITY 1994–95 LEAGUE RECORD

Match No.	Date	Venue	Opponents	Result		H/T Score	Lg. Pos.	Goalscorers	Attendance
1	Aug 13	A	Chester C	W	4-1	1-0	—	Jewell 3, Taylor	4459
2	20	H	Leyton Orient	W	2-0	1-0	3	Jewell 2	7473
3	27	A	Plymouth Arg	W	5-1	4-0	1	Jewell 3, Shutt 2	6469
4	30	H	Oxford U	L	0-2	0-1	—		9005
5	Sept 3	H	Wycombe W	W	2-1	1-0	3	Jewell, Shutt	8010
6	10	A	Swansea C	D	0-0	0-0	5		3445
7	13	A	Wrexham	W	1-0	1-0	—	Jewell	4179
8	17	H	York C	D	0-0	0-0	3		8670
9	24	H	Huddersfield T	L	3-4	0-1	3	Jewell, Kamara, Taylor	11,300
10	Oct 1	A	Cambridge U	L	1-4	1-2	6	Liburd	3338
11	8	H	Brighton & HA	W	2-1	1-0	6	Kamara, Taylor	6970
12	15	A	Blackpool	L	0-2	0-0	7		6156
13	22	A	Bournemouth	W	3-2	2-1	7	Kamara, Jewell, Huxford	3037
14	30	H	Cardiff C	L	2-3	1-2	10	Murray, Perry (og)	5937
15	Nov 2	H	Brentford	W	1-0	1-0	—	Jewell	4105
16	5	A	Bristol R	L	0-4	0-2	9		4247
17	19	H	Crewe Alex	L	0-2	0-2	11		5520
18	26	A	Shrewsbury T	W	2-1	1-0	9	Sinnott, Murray	3776
19	Dec 10	A	Leyton Orient	D	0-0	0-0	10		2553
20	17	H	Chester C	D	1-1	1-0	12	Taylor	4555
21	26	A	Rotherham U	L	1-3	0-3	13	Taylor	5400
22	28	H	Hull C	W	1-0	0-0	—	Taylor	7312
23	31	A	Stockport Co	W	2-1	1-0	9	Shutt, Taylor	4613
24	Jan 2	H	Birmingham C	D	1-1	1-0	9	Taylor	10,539
25	7	H	Bournemouth	L	1-2	0-0	10	Young (og)	5426
26	14	A	Peterborough U	D	0-0	0-0	11		4400
27	Feb 4	H	Shrewsbury T	D	1-1	1-0	12	Jacobs	4817
28	7	H	Bristol R	W	2-1	1-0	—	Murray, Verveer	4243
29	11	A	Brentford	L	3-4	1-1	11	Robson, Murray, Power	6019
30	18	H	Peterborough U	W	4-2	2-0	10	Taylor 2, Youds 2	4806
31	21	A	Crewe Alex	W	1-0	0-0	—	Taylor	4214
32	25	H	Cambridge U	D	1-1	0-0	8	Jewell	6075
33	Mar 4	A	Huddersfield T	D	0-0	0-0	9		17,404
34	11	H	Plymouth Arg	W	2-0	0-0	10	Power 2 (1 pen)	5399
35	18	A	Oxford U	L	0-1	0-0	12		5363
36	21	H	Swansea C	L	1-3	0-1	—	Richards	4417
37	25	A	York C	D	0-0	0-0	12		5431
38	28	A	Cardiff C	W	4-2	1-2	—	Tolson 2, Murray, Showler	2560
39	Apr 1	H	Wrexham	D	1-1	1-1	11	Showler	4461
40	4	A	Wycombe W	L	1-3	0-3	—	Hamilton	4522
41	8	H	Stockport Co	L	1-2	1-0	12	Youds	3927
42	15	A	Hull C	L	0-2	0-2	13		4368
43	17	H	Rotherham U	L	0-3	0-2	14		3535
44	29	H	Blackpool	L	0-1	0-1	14		5036
45	May 2	A	Birmingham C	D	0-0	0-0	—		25,139
46	6	A	Brighton & HA	L	0-1	0-0	14		7701

Final League Position: 14

GOALSCORERS

League (57): Jewell 14, Taylor 11, Murray 5, Shutt 4, Kamara 3, Power 3 (1 pen), Youds 3, Showler 2, Tolson 2, Hamilton 1, Huxford 1, Jacobs 1, Liburd 1, Richards 1, Robson 1, Sinnott 1, Verveer 1, own goals 2.
Coca-Cola Cup (6): Taylor 2, Duxbury 1, Murray 1, Richards 1, Shutt 1.
FA Cup (3): Power 1, Richards 1, Tolson 1.

Tomlinson P. 37	Benn W. 8 + 2	Jacobs W.G. 38	Robson G. 22 + 1	Sinnott L. 16	Richards D.I. 30	Shutt C.S. 28 + 4	Kamara C. 22 + 1	Taylor J.P. 35 + 1	Jewell P. 32 + 6	Murray S. 38 + 3	Duxbury L.E. 19 + 1	Liburd R.J. 9	Hamilton D.V. 23 + 7	Power L.M. 12 + 15	Tolson N. 4 + 6	Oliver G.R. 11	Huxford R.J. 33	Bowling I. 6	Dow A. 5	Showler P. 17 + 6	Scargill W. 1	Petterson A.K. 3	Mitchell G.L. 26	Youds E.P. 17	Verveer E. 9	Stabb C.J. 1	Johnson I. 1 + 1	Midgley C.S. — + 3	Grayston N.J. 3	*Match No.*
1	2	3	4	5	6	7	8	9	10	11	12																			1
1		3	8	5	6	7	12	9	10	11	4	2																		2
1		3		5	6	7	8	9	10	11	4	2																		3
1		3		5	6	7	8	9	10	*11*	4	2	12	14																4
1		3		5	6	7	8	9	10	11	4	2																		5
1		3		5	6	7	8	9	10	11	4	2	12																	6
1		3		5	6		8	9	10	11	4	2		7	12															7
1		3		5	6	7	8	9	10	11	4	2		12																8
1	5	3			6	7	8	9	10	11	4	2		12	14															9
1	12	3				7	8	9	10	11	4	2		*6*	14	5														10
1	12	3	6			7	8	9	10		4		*11*	14		5	2													11
			6			7	8	9	10	11	4			12		5	2	1	3											12
1				5	6	7	8	9	10	11	4			12			2		3											13
1				5	6	7	8	9	10	11	4		14	12			2		3											14
1				5			8	9	10		4		7		12	6	2		3	11										15
1				5			8	9	*10*	12	4		7		14	6			3	11	2									16
1		3		6	5	12	8	14			4		7	*9*	10		2			11										17
1		3		5	6	7		9	10	11	4			12		8	2													18
	8	3		5	6	7		9		11	4			10			2			12		1								19
	8	3		5	6	7		9		11	4		12	*10*	14		2					1								20
	8	3	4		6	7		9		11			10				2					1	5							21
1		3	4			7		9	10	11			8			6	2			12			5							22
1		3			6	7		9	10	11			8			4	2						5							23
1		3			6	7		9	10	11			8			4	2			12			5							24
1		3	8		6	7		9	10	11			12			4	2			14			5							25
1		3	8		6	7		9	10	11			12			4	2						5							26
1		3	4		6	7		9	10	11			8							12			5	2						27
1		3	8		6			9	12	11			7	14						*10*			5	2	4					28
1		3	*4*		6			9	12	11			7	14			2						5	10	8					29
1		3			6			9		11			7				2			8			5	10	4					30
1		3	4		6			9	12	11							2			7			5	10	8					31
1		3	4		6			9	12	*11*				14			2			7			5	10	8					32
1		3	4		6			9					11				2			7			5	10	8					33
1		3	4		6	12		9		*11*			10	14			2			7			5		8					34
1		3			6	12		9		14			11	10			2			7			5	4	*8*					35
1		3	12		6			9	14				7	10			2			11			5	4	*8*					36
1		3	6			9			10	11			7		8		2						5	4						37
1		3	4			9			10	11			7	12	8		2			14			5	6						38
1		3	4			9	*6*		12	11			14	10	8		2			7			5							39
1		3	4			12	9		8	10			11				2			7			5			6				40
1		3	4			9	8		*10*	12			11	14			2			7			5	6						41
		3	4			9	8		10	7			*11*	12			2	1					5	6			14			42
		3	4				8		10	7				9			2	1					5	6			11	12		43
	4						8		10	11				9			2	1		7			5	6				12	3	44
	4								10	11			8	9			2	1		7			5	6					3	45
	4								10	11			8	9			2	1		7			5	6				12	3	46

Coca-Cola Cup

First Round	Grimsby T (h)		2-1
		(a)	2-1
Second Round	Sheffield W (a)		1-2
		(h)	1-1

FA Cup

First Round	Scunthorpe U (h)		1-1
		(a)	2-3

BRENTFORD 1994–95 *Back row (left to right):* Robert Taylor, Simon Ratcliffe, David Thompson, Alan Judge, Tamar Fernandes, Kevin Dearden, Shane Westley, Barry Ashby, Jamie Bates.

Centre row: Bob Booker (Youth Team Manager), Kevin Lock (Assistant Manager), David McGhee, Robert Peters, Paul Smith, Ian Benjamin, Corey Campbell, Gus Hurdle, Billy Manuel, Carl Hutchings, Roy Johnson (Physio), Neil Mason (Physio).

Front row: Martin Grainger, Brian Statham, Darren Annon, Denny Mundee, David Webb (Manager), Nick Forster, Craig Ravenscroft, Paul Stephenson, Lee Harvey.

Division 2 BRENTFORD

Griffin Park, Braemar Rd, Brentford, Middlesex TW8 0NT. Telephone: (0181) 847 2511. Fax: (0181) 568 9940. Commercial Dept: (0181) 560 6062. Press Office: (0181) 574 3047. Clubcall: 0891 21108.

Ground capacity: 13,870.

Record attendance: 39,626 v Preston NE, FA Cup 6th rd, 5 March 1938.

Record receipts: £79,838 v Tottenham H, Coca Cola Cup 2nd rd 2nd leg, 7 October 1992.

Pitch measurements: 111yd × 74yd.

President: W. Wheatley. ***Deputy President:*** E. White.

Chairman: M. M. Lange.

Directors: B. Evans, J. Herting, E. J. Radley-Smith MS, FRCS, LRCP, D. Tana.

Chief Executive: Keith Loring.

Manager: David Webb. ***Assistant Manager:*** Kevin Lock.

Youth Team Manager: Bob Booker.

Community Officer: Lee Doyle.

Secretary: Polly Kates.

Press Officer/Programme Editor: Eric White (0181)–574 3047. ***Safety officer:*** Jill Dawson.

Year Formed: 1889. ***Turned Professional:*** 1899. ***Ltd Co.:*** 1901.

Club Nickname: 'The Bees'.

Previous Grounds: 1889–91, Clifden Road; 1891–95, Benns Fields, Little Ealing; 1895–98, Shotters Field; 1898–1900, Cross Road, S. Ealing; 1900–04, Boston Park; 1904, Griffin Park.

Foundation: Formed as a small amateur concern in 1889 they were very successful in local circles. They won the championship of the West London Alliance in 1893 and a year later the West Middlesex Junior Cup before carrying off the Senior Cup in 1895. After winning both the London Senior Amateur Cup and the Middlesex Senior Cup in 1898 they were admitted to the Second Division of the Southern League.

First Football League game: 28 August, 1920, Division 3, v Exeter C (a), L 0-3 – Young; Rosier, Hodson; Amos, Levitt, Elliott; Henery, Morley, Spredbury, Thompson, Smith.

Record League Victory: 9–0 v Wrexham, Division 3, 15 October 1963 – Cakebread; Coote, Jones; Slater, Scott, Higginson; Summers (1), Brooks (2), McAdams (2), Ward (2), Hales (1). (1 og).

Record Cup Victory: 7–0 v Windsor & Eton (away), FA Cup, 1st rd, 20 November 1982 – Roche; Rowe, Harris (Booker), McNichol (1), Whitehead, Hurlock (2), Kamara, Bowles, Joseph (1), Mahoney (3), Roberts.

Record Defeat: 0–7 v Swansea T, Division 3 (S), 8 November 1924 and v Walsall, Division 3 (S), 19 January 1957.

Most League Points (2 for a win): 62, Division 3 (S), 1932–33 and Division 4, 1962–63.

Most League Points (3 for a win): 85, Division 2, 1994–95.

Most League Goals: 98, Division 4, 1962–63.

Highest League Scorer in Season: Jack Holliday, 38, Division 3 (S), 1932–33.

Most League Goals in Total Aggregate: Jim Towers, 153, 1954–61.

Most Capped Player: John Buttigieg, (63), Malta.

Most League Appearances: Ken Coote, 514, 1949–64.

Record Transfer Fee Received: £720,000 from Wimbledon for Dean Holdsworth, August 1992.

Record Transfer Fee Paid: £275,000 to Chelsea for Joe Allon, November 1992.

Football League Record: 1920 Original Member of Division 3; 1921–33 Division 3 (S); 1933–35 Division 2; 1935–47 Division 1; 1947–54 Division 2; 1954–62 Division 3 (S); 1962–63 Division 4; 1963–66 Division 3; 1966–72 Division 4; 1972–73 Division 3; 1973–78 Division 4; 1978–92 Division 3; 1992–93 Division 1; 1993– Division 2.

Honours: *Football League:* Division 1 best season: 5th, 1935–36; Division 2 – Champions 1934–35; Division 3 – Champions 1991–92; Division 3 (S) – Champions 1932–33; Runners-up 1929–30, 1957–58; Division 4 – Champions 1962–63. *FA Cup:* best season: 6th rd, 1938, 1946, 1949, 1989. *Football League Cup:* best season: 4th rd, 1983. *Freight Rover Trophy;* Runners-up 1985.

Colours: Red and white vertical striped shirts, red shorts, red stockings. **Change colours:** Blue shirts, dark blue shorts, dark blue stockings.

BRENTFORD 1994–95 LEAGUE RECORD

Match No.	Date	Venue	Opponents	Result		H/T Score	Lg. Pos.	Goalscorers	Attendance
1	Aug 13	A	Plymouth Arg	W	5-1	3-1	—	Smith, Forster 2, Stephenson, Taylor	7976
2	20	H	Peterborough U	L	0-1	0-1	11		5516
3	27	A	Stockport Co	W	1-0	1-0	7	Taylor	4399
4	30	H	Rotherham U	W	2-0	1-0	—	Taylor, Forster	4031
5	Sept 3	H	Wrexham	L	0-2	0-2	7		5820
6	10	A	Wycombe W	L	3-4	1-1	13	Taylor, Stephenson, Cousins (og)	6847
7	13	A	York C	L	1-2	1-1	—	Taylor	2836
8	17	H	Blackpool	W	3-2	0-1	11	Forster, Smith, Grainger (pen)	4157
9	24	A	Crewe Alex	W	2-0	1-0	8	Forster, Taylor	3839
10	Oct 1	H	Shrewsbury T	W	1-0	1-0	5	Taylor	4556
11	8	H	Bristol R	W	3-0	2-0	5	Forster 2, Taylor	5330
12	15	A	Bournemouth	W	1-0	1-0	4	Forster	4411
13	22	H	Birmingham C	L	1-2	0-1	5	Ward (og)	7779
14	29	A	Cambridge U	D	0-0	0-0	7		3102
15	Nov 2	A	Bradford C	L	0-1	0-1	—		4105
16	5	H	Hull C	L	0-1	0-0	10		5455
17	19	A	Huddersfield T	L	0-1	0-0	13		10,889
18	26	H	Brighton & HA	W	2-1	0-1	11	Ashby, Ansah	4728
19	Dec 10	A	Peterborough U	D	2-2	1-2	12	Taylor, Forster	4102
20	17	H	Plymouth Arg	W	7-0	2-0	9	Annon, Smith, Taylor 2, Forster, Mundee, Harvey	4492
21	26	H	Leyton Orient	W	3-0	3-0	8	Mundee, Ratcliffe, Forster	6125
22	27	A	Chester C	W	4-1	3-1	6	Forster 3, Grainger	2266
23	31	H	Oxford U	W	2-0	1-0	5	Forster, Taylor	7125
24	Jan 2	A	Cardiff C	W	3-2	2-0	5	Harvey, Forster, Taylor	5235
25	14	H	Swansea C	D	0-0	0-0	5		7211
26	21	A	Hull C	W	2-1	0-0	2	Mundee, Grainger	3823
27	28	H	Cambridge U	W	6-0	0-0	1	Taylor 2, Forster, Grainger (pen), Bailey 2	6390
28	Feb 4	A	Brighton & HA	D	1-1	1-0	2	Bailey	9499
29	11	H	Bradford C	W	4-3	1-1	1	Mundee, Taylor, Grainger (pen), Forster	6019
30	17	A	Swansea C	W	2-0	1-0	—	Forster 2	3935
31	21	H	Huddersfield T	D	0-0	0-0	—		9562
32	25	A	Shrewsbury T	L	1-2	1-1	1	Forster	4570
33	Mar 4	H	Crewe Alex	W	2-0	1-0	2	Mundee, Taylor	7143
34	7	A	Wrexham	D	0-0	0-0	—		2834
35	11	H	Stockport Co	W	1-0	1-0	1	Taylor	6513
36	18	A	Rotherham U	W	2-0	2-0	1	Forster, Abrahams	2968
37	21	H	Wycombe W	D	0-0	0-0	—		9530
38	25	A	Blackpool	W	2-1	2-0	2	Bates, Taylor	4663
39	Apr 1	H	York C	W	3-0	1-0	1	Grainger, Forster, Taylor	6474
40	8	A	Oxford U	D	1-1	1-1	2	Taylor	7800
41	15	H	Chester C	D	1-1	0-1	3	Abrahams	8020
42	17	A	Leyton Orient	W	2-0	1-0	1	Bates, Forster	4459
43	22	H	Cardiff C	W	2-0	0-0	1	Grainger (pen), Taylor	8268
44	26	A	Birmingham C	L	0-2	0-0	—		25,581
45	29	H	Bournemouth	L	1-2	0-0	2	Abrahams	10,079
46	May 6	A	Bristol R	D	2-2	0-1	2	McGhee, Taylor	8501

Final League Position: 2

GOALSCORERS

League (81): Forster 24, Taylor 23, Grainger 7 (4 pens), Mundee 5, Abrahams 3, Bailey 3, Smith 3, Bates 2, Harvey 2, Stephenson 2, Annon 1, Ansah 1, Ashby 1, McGhee 1, Ratcliffe 1, own goals 2.
Coca-Cola Cup (4): Parris 1, Smith 1, Stephenson 1, Taylor 1.
FA Cup (3): Annon 1, Grainger 1, Taylor 1.

Fernandes T.H. 3 + 1	Hurdle A.A.J. 7 + 2	Hutchings C.E. 38 + 1	Westley S.L.M. 15 + 1	Bates J. 38	Smith P.W. 35	Parris G. 5	Harvey L.D. 24 + 1	Taylor R.A. 43	Forster N.M. 46	Stephenson P. 34	Dearden K.C. 43	Annon D.C. 9 + 1	Ashby B.J. 40	Mundee D.W.J. 22 + 17	Grainger M.R. 36 + 1	Statham B. 26 + 10	Ratcliffe S. 24 + 1	Benjamin I.T. 1	Ravenscroft C. 1	Ansah A. 2 + 1	Hooker J.W. — + 1	McGhee D. 1 + 6	Bailey D.L. 6	Abrahams P. 7 + 3	Match No.
1	2	3	4	5	6	7	8	9	10	11															1
	2	3	4	5	6	7	8	9	10	11	1	12													2
	2	3		4	6	7	8	9	10	11	1		5	12											3
	2	3		4	6	7		9	10	11	1		5	8											4
	2	3		4	6	7	12	9	10	11	1		5	8	14										5
	2	7		4	6		8	9	10	11	1		5	12	3										6
		7		4	6		8	9	10	11	1		5		3	2	12								7
		7	14	4	6		8		10	11	1		5	12	3	2		9							8
		7	4		6		8	9	10	11	1		5	12	3	2									9
		7	4		6		8	9	10		1		5	12	3	2			11						10
	12	7		4	6		8	9	10	11	1		5	14	3	2									11
15		7	4		6		8	9	10	11	1		5	12	3	2									12
		7	4		6		8	9	10	11	1		5	12	3	2									13
1			4		6		8	9	10	11			5		3	2	7								14
			4		6		8	9	10	11	1		5	12	3	2	7								15
			4		6		8	9	10		1		5	12	3	2	7			11					16
	12	7	4		6		8	9	10		1		5		3	2				11					17
			4	7	6		8	9	10		1	11	5	12	3	2				14					18
1	3			4	6		8	9	10			7	5	11		2					12				19
		2		4	6		8	9	10		1	11	5	12	3		7								20
		2		4			8	9	10		1	7	5	11	3		6								21
		2		4			8	9	10		1	7	5	11	3		6								22
		2	4	5			8	9	10		1	7		11	3	12	6								23
		2	4	5			8	9	10		1	7		11	3	12	6								24
		2		4			8	9	10		1	7	5	11	3	12	6								25
		2		4			8	9	10		1	7	5	11	3	12	6					14			26
		2		4				9	10	7	1		5	11	3	12	6						8		27
		2		4				9	10	7	1		5	11	3	12	6					14	8		28
		2		4				9	10	7	1		5	11	3	12	6						8		29
		2		4				9	10	7	1		5	11	3		6						8		30
		2		4					10	11	1		5	9	3	12	6					7	8		31
		2		4	6				10	11	1		5	9	3	12	7					14	8		32
		2		4	6			9	10	11	1		5	8	3	12	7								33
		2	4	5	6			9	10	11	1			8		3	7								34
		2	4	5	6			9	10	11	1			8		3	7								35
		2		4	6			9	10	7	1		5		3	8								11	36
		2		4	6			9	10	7	1		5	11	3	8								12	37
		2		4	6			9	10	7	1		5	12	3	8								11	38
		2		4	6			9	10	7	1		5		3	8								11	39
		2		4	6			9	10	7	1		5	12	3	8								11	40
		2		4	6			9	10	7	1		5	12	3	8						14		11	41
				4	6			9	10	11	1		5	8	3	2	7								42
		12		4	6			9	10	11	1		5	8	3	2	7							14	43
				4	6			9	10	11	1		5	8	3	2	7							12	44
		3		4	6			9	10	7	1		5	12		2	8					14		11	45
		3		4	6			9	10	7	1		5	12		2	8					14		11	46

Coca-Cola Cup

First Round	Colchester U (a)		2-0
		(h)	2-0
Second Round	Tranmere R (a)		0-1
		(h)	0-0

FA Cup

First Round	Cambridge U (a)		2-2
		(h)	1-2

BRIGHTON AND HOVE ALBION 1994–95 *Back row (left to right):* George Petchey (Youth Development Officer), Junior McDougald, Nicky Bisset, Simon Funnell, Nicky Rust, Paul McCarthy, Mark Ormerod, Mark Fox, Kevin McGarrigle, Ross Yorke-Johnson, Malcolm Stuart (Physio).
Third row: Gerry Ryan (Assistant Manager), Stuart Munday, Danny Simmonds, Stuart Tuck, Stuart Myall, Steven Scott, Jeffrey Minton, Nicky Henderson, Lee MacAulay, John Ryan, Jimmy Case (Player/Coach).
Second row: John Crumplin, Kurt Nogan, Ian Chapman, Steve Foster, Liam Brady (Manager), Raphael Meade, Colin Pates, Robert Codner, Dean Wilkins.
Front row: Philip Andrews, Robert Cox, Garrett Doyle, Ian Earles, Simon Fox, Kerry Mayo, Jay Pickering, Danny Smith, Anthony Tilley, Tim Whitehouse.

Division 2 BRIGHTON & HOVE ALBION

Goldstone Ground, Newtown Rd, Hove, East Sussex BN3 7DE. Telephone: (01273) 778855 (all departments). Fax: (01273) 321095. Recorded information (team & ticket news etc): Seagull Line 0891 800609.

Ground capacity: 16,254.

Record attendance: 36,747 v Fulham, Division 2, 27 December 1958.

Record receipts: £109,615.65 v Crawley T, FA Cup 3rd rd, 4 January 1992.

Pitch measurements: 111yd × 74yd.

Directors: G. A. Stanley (Chairman), W. Archer, R. A. Bloom, B. E. Clarke, P. Kent, D. Sizen, D. Stanley, D. Sullivan.

Manager: Liam Brady. ***Assistant Manager:*** Gerry Ryan.

Secretary: Derek Allan. ***Chief Executive/Deputy Chairman:*** David Bellotti.

Coach: Jimmy Case. ***Physio:*** Malcolm Stuart.

Promotions Executive: Ray Woodford.

Year Formed: 1901. ***Turned Professional:*** 1901. ***Ltd Co.:*** 1904.

Previous Grounds: 1901, County Ground; 1902, Goldstone Ground.

Club Nickname: 'The Seagulls'.

Foundation: A professional club Brighton United was formed in November 1897 at the Imperial Hotel, Queen's Road, but folded in March 1900 after less than two seasons in the Southern League at the County Ground. An amateur team, Brighton & Hove Rangers was then formed by some prominent United supporters and after one season at Withdean, decided to turn semi-professional and play at the County Ground. Rangers were accepted into the Southern League but then also folded June 1901. John Jackson the former United manager organised a meeting at the Seven Stars public house, Ship Street on 24 June 1901 at which a new third club Brighton & Hove United was formed. They took over Rangers' place in the Southern League and pitch at County Ground. The name was changed to Brighton & Hove Albion before a match was played because of objections by Hove FC.

First Football League game: 28 August, 1920, Division 3, v Southend U (a), L 0-2 – Hayes; Woodhouse, Little; Hall, Comber, Bentley; Longstaff, Ritchie, Doran, Rodgerson, March.

Record League Victory: 9–1 v Newport C, Division 3 (S), 18 April 1951 – Ball; Tennant (1p), Mansell (1p); Willard, McCoy, Wilson; Reed, McNichol (4), Garbutt, Bennett (2), Keene (1). 9–1 v Southend U, Division 3, 27 November 1965 – Powney; Magill, Baxter; Leck, Gall, Turner; Gould (1), Collins (1), Livesey (2), Smith (3), Goodchild (2).

Record Cup Victory: 10–1 v Wisbech, FA Cup, 1st rd, 13 November 1965 – Powney; Magill, Baxter; Collins (1), Gall, Turner; Gould, Smith (2), Livesey (3), Cassidy (2), Goodchild (1). (1 og).

Record Defeat: 0–9 v Middlesbrough, Division 2, 23 August 1958.

Most League Points (2 for a win): 65, Division 3 (S), 1955–56 and Division 3, 1971–72.

Most League Points (3 for a win): 84, Division 3, 1987–88.

Most League Goals: 112, Division 3 (S), 1955–56.

Highest League Scorer in Season: Peter Ward, 32, Division 3, 1976–77.

Most League Goals in Total Aggregate: Tommy Cook, 114, 1922–29.

Most Capped Player: Steve Penney, 17, Northern Ireland.

Most League Appearances: 'Tug' Wilson, 509, 1922–36.

Record Transfer Fee Received: £900,000 from Liverpool for Mark Lawrenson, August 1981.

Record Transfer Fee Paid: £500,000 to Manchester U for Andy Ritchie, October 1980.

Football League Record: 1920 Original Member of Division 3; 1921–58 Division 3 (S); 1958–62 Division 2; 1962–63 Division 3; 1963–65 Division 4; 1965–72 Division 3; 1972–73 Division 2; 1973–77 Division 3; 1977–79 Division 2; 1979–83 Division 1; 1983–87 Division 2; 1987–88 Division 3; 1988– Division 2.

Honours: *Football League:* Division 1 best season: 13th, 1981–82; Division 2 – Runners-up 1978–79; Division 3 (S) – Champions 1957–58; Runners-up 1953–54, 1955–56; Division 3 – Runners-up 1971–72, 1976–77, 1987–88; Division 4 – Champions 1964–65. *FA Cup:* Runners-up 1983. *Football League Cup:* best season: 5th rd, 1979.

Colours: Blue and white striped shirts, blue shorts, white stockings. **Change colours:** All yellow.

BRIGHTON & HOVE ALBION 1994–95 LEAGUE RECORD

Match No.	Date	Venue	Opponents	Result		H/T Score	Lg. Pos.	Goalscorers	Attendance
1	Aug 13	A	Swansea C	D	1-1	0-1	—	Nogan (pen)	4640
2	20	H	Plymouth Arg	D	1-1	0-0	16	Chamberlain	8309
3	27	A	Wrexham	L	1-2	0-1	17	McDougald	3339
4	31	H	York C	W	1-0	0-0	—	Nogan (pen)	6996
5	Sept 3	H	Leyton Orient	W	1-0	0-0	10	Nogan	8581
6	10	A	Chester C	W	2-1	1-0	8	Nogan 2	2063
7	13	A	Blackpool	D	2-2	2-2	—	Bissett, Chamberlain	3438
8	17	H	Oxford U	D	1-1	1-0	10	Nogan	9970
9	24	H	Cambridge U	W	2-0	1-0	6	McDougald, Nogan	8280
10	Oct 1	A	Huddersfield T	L	0-3	0-1	11		10,321
11	8	A	Bradford C	L	1-2	0-1	13	McDougald	6970
12	15	H	Birmingham C	L	0-1	0-0	14		11,004
13	22	A	Bristol R	L	0-3	0-2	15		4107
14	29	H	Rotherham U	D	1-1	0-1	15	Smith	6734
15	Nov 2	H	Bournemouth	D	0-0	0-0	—		5631
16	5	A	Cardiff C	L	0-3	0-0	17		5004
17	19	H	Peterborough U	L	1-2	1-2	18	Codner	6445
18	26	A	Brentford	L	1-2	1-0	18	Chapman	4728
19	Dec 10	A	Plymouth Arg	W	3-0	0-0	17	Codner 2, Akinbiyi	6091
20	17	H	Swansea C	D	1-1	0-1	18	Codner	6817
21	26	A	Wycombe W	D	0-0	0-0	17		7085
22	27	H	Shrewsbury T	W	2-1	0-1	16	McDougald, Akinbiyi	7290
23	31	A	Hull C	D	2-2	1-1	17	Minton, Akinbiyi	5099
24	Jan 2	H	Stockport Co	W	2-0	0-0	15	Minton, Akinbiyi	8842
25	14	A	Crewe Alex	L	0-4	0-1	17		4286
26	Feb 4	H	Brentford	D	1-1	0-1	17	Bates (og)	9499
27	11	A	Bournemouth	W	3-0	2-0	16	Minton 2, McDougald	5247
28	14	H	Bristol R	L	1-2	1-0	—	Chapman	5232
29	18	H	Crewe Alex	L	0-1	0-1	17		6986
30	21	A	Peterborough U	L	1-2	0-1	—	McDougald	3870
31	25	H	Huddersfield T	D	0-0	0-0	18		7751
32	Mar 4	A	Cambridge U	W	2-0	1-0	18	Chapman, Myall	3856
33	7	A	Leyton Orient	W	3-0	1-0	—	Minton, McDougald, Fox M	2983
34	11	H	Wrexham	W	4-0	0-0	15	Byrne J, McCarthy, Parris, McDougald	7514
35	15	H	Cardiff C	D	0-0	0-0	—		6956
36	18	A	York C	L	0-1	0-1	15		2915
37	22	H	Chester C	W	1-0	1-0	—	McDougald	5979
38	25	A	Oxford U	D	0-0	0-0	15		6725
39	28	A	Rotherham U	L	3-4	1-3	—	Byrne J, Byrne P, Myall	2316
40	Apr 1	H	Blackpool	D	2-2	1-1	15	McCarthy, Byrne J	7157
41	8	H	Hull C	W	1-0	0-0	15	McDougald	6038
42	15	A	Shrewsbury T	D	1-1	1-1	16	Byrne J	3597
43	19	H	Wycombe W	D	1-1	1-0	—	Parris	8094
44	22	A	Stockport Co	L	0-2	0-1	16		3789
45	29	A	Birmingham C	D	3-3	1-2	16	Munday, Storer, Chapman	19,006
46	May 6	H	Bradford C	W	1-0	0-0	16	Munday	7701

Final League Position: 16

GOALSCORERS

League (54): McDougald 10, Nogan 7 (2 pens), Minton 5, Akinbiyi 4, Byrne J 4, Chapman 4, Codner 4, Chamberlain 2, McCarthy 2, Munday 2, Myall 2, Parris 2, Bissett 1, Byrne P 1, Fox M 1, Smith 1, Storer 1, own goal 1.
Coca-Cola Cup (10): Nogan 5, McDougald 2, Chamberlain 1, McCarthy 1, Munday 1.
FA Cup (1): Codner 1.

Rust N.C.I. 44	Munday S.C. 18 + 13	Pates C.G. 15 + 1	Chapman I.R. 38 + 2	Foster S.B. 38	McCarthy P.J. 37	Minton J.T. 37 + 2	McDougald D.E. 37 + 4	Nogan K. 26	Codner R.A.G. 21 + 2	Wilkins D.M. 11 + 3	Chamberlain M.V. 12 + 7	Bissett N. 12	Case J.R. 9	Simmonds D.B. 2 + 2	Smith P. 35 + 3	Tuck S.G. 18 + 5	Funnell S.P. — + 1	Meade R.J. — + 3	Kerr S. 2	Stapleton F.A. 1 + 1	Andrews P.D. — + 5	Myall S.T. 23 + 4	Akinbiyi A.P. 7	McGarrigle K. 16 + 1	Parris G. 18	Fox M.S. 4 + 5	Byrne J.F. 14	Byrne P. 8	Fox S.M. 1 + 1	Storer S.J. 2	Match No.
1	2	3	4	5	6	7	8	9	10	11																					1
1	2	3	4	5	6	7	8	9	10	11	12																				2
1		3		5	6	11	8	9	10		7	2	4	12																	3
1		3		5	6	11	8	9	*10*	12	7	2	4	14																	4
1		6	12	5		*10*	8	9	14		7		4	11	2	3															5
1		3	*11*	5		12	8	9	10		7	6	4		2	14															6
1		3	11	5		8		9	10		7	6	*4*		2	12	14														7
1	12	3	11	5		8		9	10	4	*7*	6			2			14													8
1	12	3	11	5		7	8	9	*10*	4		6			2			14													9
1	4		11	5		7	8	9	10			6			2	3		12													10
1		12	11		5	7	8	9	10			6		4	2	3															11
1	10	3	*11*		5	7	8	9			12	6	4		2	14															12
1	12	3	*11*	5	6	10	8	9			7	2	4			14															13
1	12	3	11	5	6	7	8	9	10		14	*2*			4																14
	7	3	11	*5*	6		8	9	10		12	2			4				1	14											15
	4	5	12		6	7	*8*	9	10		14				2	3			1	11											16
1	12	5	11		6	4	8	9	10		*7*				2	3					14										17
1			3		6	4		9	10	11					2	5						7	8								18
1	11		3		6	4		9	10						2	5						7	8	12							19
1			3		6	4	12	9	10	11					2	5						7	8								20
1	12		3	5	6	4		9	10	11					2							7	8								21
1			3	5	6		12	9	10	11	14		4		*2*							7	8								22
1	4		3	5	6	10	12	9		*11*					2	14						7	8								23
1			3	5	6	11	12	9	*10*	14			4		2							7	8								24
1	2		3	5	6	4	8	9	10	11	12											7									25
1	12		11	5	6	10	8	9			4				2	3						7									26
1			11	5	6	10	8				9				2	3					12	7			4						27
1	12		11	5	6	10	8			14	*9*				2	3						7			4						28
1	12		3	5	6	10	8		14	11	*9*				2							7			4						29
1	11		3	5	6	10	8								2						12	7			4	9					30
1	12		3	5	6	10	9								2						14	7		11	4		*8*				31
1			3	5	6	10	9								2							7		11	4		8				32
1			3	5	6	10	9								2							7		11	4	12	8				33
1	12		3	5	6		9								2							7		11	4	14	8	10			34
1	2		3	5	6	12	9								14							7		11	4		8	10			35
1	2		3	5	6		9															7		11	4	12		10	8		36
1	2		3	5	6		9								12									11	4	7	8	10			37
1	2		3	5	6		9															7		11	4	8		10	12		38
1	2		3	5	6		9								12							7		11	4	14	8	10			39
1				5	6	*10*	9								2	3						12		11	4	14	8	7			40
1				5	6	10	9								2	3								11	4		8	7			41
1	7			5	6	10	9								2	3						12		11	4		8				42
1	12			5	6	10	9								2	3						7		11	4		8				43
1	5		3			10	9								2	6					12	7		11		4	8				44
1	4		3	5		10	9								2	6						12		11			8			7	45
1	12		*3*	5		10	9								2	6						14		11	4		8			7	46

Coca-Cola Cup

First Round	Wycombe W (h)	2-1
	(a)	3-1
Second Round	Leicester C (h)	1-0
	(a)	2-0
Third Round	Swindon T (h)	1-1
	(a)	1-4

FA Cup

First Round	Kingstonian (a)	1-2

BRISTOL CITY 1994–95 *Back row (left to right):* Marvin Harriott, Scott Partridge, Stuart Duffin, Colin Loss, Mike Wyatt, Ian Brown, Rodney McAree, Junior Bent.
Centre row: Russell Osman (Manager), Clive Whitehead (First Team Coach), Martin Scott, Jason Fowler, Scott Paterson, Wayne Allison, Keith Welch, Richard Rowe, Henry McKop, Paul Milsom, Matt Hewlett, Leroy Rosenior (Reserve Team Coach), Buster Footman (Physio).
Front row: Tony Fawthrop (Assistant Manager), Liam Robinson, Matt Bryant, Brian Tinnion, Stuart Munro, Mark Shail, Dave Martin, Ian Baird, Rob Edwards, Gerry Sweeney (Coach).

Division 2 **BRISTOL CITY**

Ashton Gate, Bristol BS3 2EJ. Telephone: (0117) 962812 (5 lines). Fax: (0117) 9639574. Commercial: (0117) 9633876. Shop: (0117) 9538566. Clubcall: 0891 121176. Supporters Club: (0117) 9665554. Community Dept: (0117) 9664685.

Ground capacity: 20,000 approx.

Record attendance: 43,335 v Preston NE, FA Cup 5th rd, 16 February 1935.

Record receipts: £148,282 v Everton, FA Cup 4th rd, 29 January 1995.

Pitch measurements: 115yd × 75yd.

Chairman: D. A. Russe. ***Vice-Chairman:*** M. Fricker.

Directors: J. Clapp, D. Coller, S. Davidson, R. Neale, G. Williams. ***Commercial Manager:*** John Cox.

Manager: Joe Jordan. ***Assistant Manager:*** John Gorman.

Physio: H. Footman. ***Secretary:*** Jean Harrison. ***Commercial Manager:*** John Cox.

Year Formed: 1894. ***Turned Professional:*** 1897. ***Ltd Co.:*** 1897. BCFC (1982) PLC.

Previous Name: Bristol South End 1894–97.

Club Nickname: 'Robins'.

Previous Grounds: 1894, St John's Lane; 1904, Ashton Gate.

Foundation: The name Bristol City came into being in 1897 when the Bristol South End club, formed three years earlier, decided to adopt professionalism and apply for admission to the Southern League after competing in the Western League. The historic meeting was held at The Albert Hall, Bedminster. Bristol City employed Sam Hollis from Woolwich Arsenal as manager and gave him £40 to buy players. In 1901 they merged with Bedminster, another leading Bristol club.

First Football League game: 7 September, 1901, Division 2, v Blackpool (a) W 2-0 – Moles; Tuft, Davies; Jones, McLean, Chambers; Bradbury, Connor, Boucher, O'Brien (2), Flynn.

Record League Victory: 9–0 v Aldershot, Division 3 (S), 28 December 1946 – Eddols; Morgan, Fox; Peacock, Roberts, Jones (1); Chilcott, Thomas, Clark (4 incl. 1p), Cyril Williams (1), Hargreaves (3).

Record Cup Victory: 11–0 v Chichester C, FA Cup, 1st rd, 5 November 1960 – Cook; Collinson, Thresher; Connor, Alan Williams, Etheridge; Tait (1), Bobby Williams (1), Atyeo (5), Adrian Williams (3), Derrick. (1 og).

Record Defeat: 0–9 v Coventry C, Division 3 (S), 28 April 1934.

Most League Points (2 for a win): 70, Division 3 (S), 1954–55.

Most League Points (3 for a win): 91, Division 3, 1989–90.

Most League Goals: 104, Division 3 (S), 1926–27.

Highest League Scorer in Season: Don Clark, 36, Division 3 (S), 1946–47.

Most League Goals in Total Aggregate: John Atyeo, 314, 1951–66.

Most Capped Player: Billy Wedlock, 26, England.

Most League Appearances: John Atyeo, 597, 1951–66.

Record Transfer Fee Received: £1,750,000 from Newcastle U for Andy Cole, March 1993.

Record Transfer Fee Paid: £500,000 to Arsenal for Andy Cole, July 1992.

Football League Record: 1901 Elected to Division 2; 1906–11 Division 1; 1911–22 Division 2; 1922–23 Division 3 (S); 1923–24 Division 2; 1924–27 Division 3 (S); 1927–32 Division 2; 1932–55 Division 3 (S); 1955–60 Division 2; 1960–65 Division 3; 1965–76 Division 2; 1976–80 Division 1; 1980–81 Division 2; 1981–82 Division 3; 1982–84 Division 4; 1984–90 Division 3; 1990–92 Division 2; 1992– Division 1.

Honours: *Football League:* Division 1 – Runners-up 1906–07; Division 2 – Champions 1905–06; Runners-up 1975–76; Division 3 (S) – Champions 1922–23, 1926–27, 1954–55; Runners-up 1937–38; Division 3 – Runners-up 1964–65, 1989–90. *FA Cup:* Runners-up 1909. *Football League Cup:* Semi-final 1971, 1989. *Welsh Cup:* Winners 1934. *Anglo-Scottish Cup:* Winners 1978. *Freight Rover Trophy:* Winners 1986; Runners-up 1987.

Colours: Red shirts, white shorts, red and white stockings. **Change colours:** Green, black, red repeat hooped shirts, black shorts with red trim, green stockings with black trim.

BRISTOL CITY 1994–95 LEAGUE RECORD

Match No.	Date		Venue	Opponents	Result		H/T Score	Lg. Pos.	Goalscorers	Attendance
1	Aug	13	H	Sunderland	D	0-0	0-0	—		11,127
2		20	A	Bolton W	W	2-0	1-0	4	Baird, Allison	12,127
3		27	H	Port Vale	D	0-0	0-0	8		8588
4		30	A	Burnley	D	1-1	0-1	—	Allison	11,067
5	Sept	3	A	Charlton Ath	L	2-3	0-1	16	Allison 2	9019
6		10	H	Notts Co	W	2-1	1-1	10	Bent, Scott (pen)	6670
7		13	H	Derby Co	L	0-2	0-1	—		8029
8		17	A	Southend U	L	1-2	0-1	17	Baird	3663
9		24	H	Middlesbrough	L	0-1	0-0	20		8642
10	Oct	1	A	Luton T	W	1-0	0-0	17	Baird	6633
11		8	H	Millwall	W	1-0	0-0	13	Baird	7499
12		15	A	Reading	L	0-1	0-0	16		9389
13		22	A	Grimsby T	L	0-1	0-0	20		4024
14		29	H	Portsmouth	D	1-1	1-0	21	Scott (pen)	7238
15	Nov	1	H	Wolverhampton W	L	1-5	1-2	—	Baird	10,401
16		5	A	Sheffield U	L	0-3	0-2	22		11,568
17		20	H	Swindon T	W	3-2	0-0	22	Bent, Allison 2	9086
18		26	A	Oldham Ath	L	0-2	0-0	22		7277
19	Dec	3	H	Grimsby T	L	1-2	0-0	23	Partridge	6030
20		7	A	Barnsley	L	1-2	1-1	—	Bent	4305
21		10	H	Bolton W	L	0-1	0-1	23		6144
22		17	A	Sunderland	L	0-2	0-0	23		11,661
23		26	A	WBA	L	0-1	0-0	23		21,071
24		27	H	Stoke C	W	3-1	0-0	23	Bryant, Allison 2	8500
25		31	A	Tranmere R	L	0-2	0-2	23		7439
26	Jan	2	H	Watford	D	0-0	0-0	23		9423
27		14	A	Portsmouth	D	0-0	0-0	23		8803
28		21	H	Sheffield U	W	2-1	0-0	23	Gayle (og), Shail	10,211
29	Feb	4	H	Barnsley	W	3-2	0-0	22	Dryden, Bryant, Allison	6408
30		11	A	Wolverhampton W	L	0-2	0-1	22		25,451
31		15	A	Swindon T	W	3-0	1-0	—	Bent, Fleck, Bryant	9881
32		18	H	Oldham Ath	D	2-2	2-1	20	Allison 2	7851
33		25	H	Luton T	D	2-2	0-1	21	Owers, Bent	7939
34	Mar	4	A	Middlesbrough	L	0-3	0-1	21		17,371
35		7	H	Charlton Ath	W	2-1	1-0	—	Kuhl, Tinnion	6118
36		11	A	Port Vale	L	1-2	1-1	21	Owers	7646
37		18	H	Burnley	D	1-1	1-0	22	Partridge	6717
38		21	A	Notts Co	D	1-1	0-0	—	Baird	5692
39		25	H	Southend U	D	0-0	0-0	21		6159
40	Apr	1	A	Derby Co	L	1-3	1-2	21	Allison	14,555
41		8	H	Tranmere R	L	0-1	0-1	23		6723
42		15	A	Stoke C	L	1-2	1-1	23	Shail	10,172
43		17	H	WBA	W	1-0	0-0	23	Bent	8777
44		22	A	Watford	L	0-1	0-0	23		7190
45		29	H	Reading	L	1-2	0-1	23	Tinnion	9474
46	May	7	A	Millwall	D	1-1	1-1	23	Allison	8805

Final League Position: 23

GOALSCORERS

League (42): Allison 13, Baird 6, Bent 6, Bryant 3, Owers 2, Partridge 2, Scott 2 (2 pens), Shail 2, Tinnion 2, Dryden 1, Fleck 1, Kuhl 1, own goal 1.
Coca-Cola Cup (0).
FA Cup (3): Baird 1, Bent 1, Tinnion 1.

Welch K.J. 44	Harriott M.L. 19	Scott M. 18	Shail M.E.D. 37 + 1	Bryant M. 37	Fowler J.K.G. 10 + 3	McAree R.J. 4 + 2	Bent J.A. 40 + 1	Baird I.J. 28 + 9	Allison W. 37	Edwards R.W. 29 + 1	Partridge S.M. 14 + 19	Munro S. 29 + 2	Loss C.P. 3 + 2	Brown I.O. — + 1	McKop H.G. — + 1	Tinnion B. 33 + 2	Simpson F. 4	Seal D. 5 + 4	Wyatt M.J. 1 + 2	Humphries M. 4	Paterson S. 2 + 1	Kite P.D. 2	Hansen V. 29	Parris G. 6	Watson K.E. 1 + 1	Owers G. 21	Dryden R.A. 15 + 4	Kuhl M. 17	Fleck R. 10	Flatts M. 4 + 2	Martin D. 3 + 1	Hewlett P.M. — + 1	Match No.
1	2	3	4	5	6	7	8	9	10	11	12																						1
1	2	3	4	5	6	7	8	9	10	11	12	14																					2
1	2	3	4	5	6		8	9	10	11	12		7	14																			3
1	2	3	4	5	6		8	9	10	11	12		7																				4
1	2	3	4	5	6		8	9	10	11	12		7																				5
1	2	3	4	5	6		8	9	10	11	7		12		14																		6
1	2	3	4	5	6		8	9	10	11	7		12																				7
1	2	3	4	5			8	9		11	7					6	10																8
1	2	3	4	5		7	8	9		11	12					6	10																9
1	2	3	4	5			8	9		11	12	6				10	7																10
1	2	3	4	5		11		9			12	6				10	7	8	14														11
1	2		4	5				9	10	11	12	7				6		8		3													12
1	2		4	5		12		9	10	11	14	7				6		8		3													13
1	2	3	4	5			7	9	10	11	8	12				6		14															14
1			4	5	12		7	9		11		3				6		8		2	10												15
1	2		4	5	6		12	9		11	14							8	7	3	10												16
	2	3		5	6		8		10	11	7					9						1	4										17
	2	3	4		7	12	8		10	11	9					6						1	5										18
1		3	4	5	12		8		10	11	9					6								2	7								19
1	2	3	4				8	9	10	11	12					6							5	7									20
1	2	3	4				8	9	10	11	12					6							5	7	14								21
1		3	4				8	9	10	11	6	2				12							5	7									22
1			4	5			8	9	10		12	3				6							2	7		11							23
1			4	5			8	9	10		12	3				6							2	7		11	14						24
1			4	5			8	9	10		12	3				6							2			11		7					25
1			4	5			8	9	10	11		3				6		12					2					7					26
1			4	5			8	12	10			3				6							2			11	14	7	9				27
1			4	5			8		10	7	12					6							2			11	3		9				28
1				5			8	12	10			3				6							2			11	4	7	9				29
1			4	5			8	12	10			3				6							2			11		7	9				30
1			4	5			8	12	10			3				6							2			11		7	9				31
1			4	5			8	12	10			3				6							2			11	14	7	9				32
1				5			8		10			3				6							2			11	4	7	9				33
1			4	5			8	12	10			3				6							2			11	14	7	9				34
1				5			8	12	10			3				6							2			11	4	7	9				35
1			12	5			8		10			3				6		14					2			11	4	7	9				36
1				5			8	9		6	10	3							12				2			11	4	7					37
1				5			8	9		7	10	3				6							2			11	4						38
1				5			8	9		7	10	3				6							2			11	4			12			39
1			4				8	9	10			3				6							2			11	5	7		12			40
1			4				8		10		12	3				6							2			11	5	7		9			41
1			4				8	12	10	14		3				6							2			11	5			9	7		42
1			4				8		10	6	12	3											2			11	5	7		9	14		43
1			4				8	12	10		9	3				14							2			11	5	7		6			44
1			4	8	12				10	11	9	3				6		14					2				5				7		45
1				4				9	10	11	6	3									12		2				5	8			7	14	46

Coca-Cola Cup

Second Round	Notts Co (h)	0-1
	(a)	0-3

FA Cup

Third Round	Stoke C (h)	0-0
	(a)	3-1
Fourth Round	Everton (h)	0-1

BRISTOL ROVERS 1994–95 *Back row (left to right):* Ian Wright, Billy Clark, Andy Tillson, Ian McLean, Gareth Taylor, Marcus Browning, Tom White, Lee Maddison.
Third row: Ian Alexander, Justin Channing, Gary Waddock, Marcus Law, Brian Parkin, Paul Hardyman, David Pritchard, Marcus Stewart.
Second Row: Roy Dolling (Youth Development Manager), Keith James (Physio), Dennis Booth (Assistant Manager), John Ward (Manager), Steve Cross (Reserve Team Manager), Tony Gill (Youth Coach), Ray Kendall (Kit Manager), Terry Connor (Community Officer).
Front Row: Lee Archer, Paul Tovey, Andrew Gurney, Mike Davis, Martin Paul, Worrell Sterling, Matt Hayfield.

Division 2 BRISTOL ROVERS

Twerton Park, Twerton, Bath, BA2 1DB. Telephone: (0117) 352508. Fax: (0117) 353477. Training Ground: (0117) 861743. Match Day Ticket Office: (01225) 312327. Offices: Avonfields House, Somerdale, Keynsham, Bristol BS18 2DJ. (0117) 9869999. Pirates Hotline: 0891 338345. Fax: (0117) 9864030. Community Office: (0117) 9860809.

Ground capacity: 8943.

Record attendance: 9464 v Liverpool, FA Cup 4th rd, 8 February 1992 (Twerton Park). 38,472 v Preston NE, FA Cup 4th rd, 30 January 1960 (Eastville).

Record receipts: £62,480 v Liverpool, FA Cup 4th rd, 8 February 1992.

Pitch measurements: 110yd × 75yd.

President: Marquis of Worcester.

Vice-Presidents: Dr W. T. Cussen, A. I. Seager, H. E. L. Brown, R. Redmond.

Chairman: D. H. A. Dunford. ***Vice-Chairman:*** G. M. H. Dunford.

Directors: R. Craig, B. Andrews, V. Stokes.

Manager: John Ward. ***Assistant Manager:***–.

Reserve Team Manager: Steve Cross. ***Physio:*** Keith James. ***Youth Team Coach:*** Tony Gill. ***Commercial Manager:*** R. Miller.

Secretary: Ian Wilson. ***Assistant Secretary:*** I. I. Wilson. ***Office Manager:*** Mrs Angela Mann.

Year Formed: 1883. ***Turned Professional:*** 1897. ***Ltd Co.:*** 1896.

Previous Names: 1883, Black Arabs; 1884, Eastville Rovers; 1897, Bristol Eastville Rovers; 1898, Bristol Rovers.

Club Nickname: 'Pirates'.

Previous Grounds: Purdown, Three Acres, Ashley Hill, Rudgeway, Eastville.

Foundation: Bristol Rovers were formed at a meeting in Stapleton Road, Eastville, in 1883. However, they first went under the name of the Black Arabs (wearing black shirts). Changing their name to Eastville Rovers in their second season, they won the Gloucestershire Senior Cup in 1888–89. Original members of the Bristol & District League in 1892, this eventually became the Western League and Eastville Rovers adopted professionalism in 1897.

First Football League game: 28 August, 1920, Division 3, v Millwall (a) L 0-2 – Stansfield; Bethune, Panes; Boxley, Kenny, Steele; Chance, Bird, Sims, Bell, Palmer.

Record League Victory: 7–0 v Brighton & HA, Division 3 (S), 29 November 1952 – Hoyle; Bamford, Geoff Fox; Pitt, Warren, Sampson; McIlvenny, Roost (2), Lambden (1), Bradford (1), Peterbridge (2). (1 og). 7–0 v Swansea T, Division 2, 2 October 1954 – Radford; Bamford, Watkins; Pitt, Muir, Anderson; Petherbridge, Bradford (2), Meyer, Roost (1), Hooper (2). (2 og). 7–0 v Shrewsbury T, Division 3, 21 March 1964 – Hall; Hillard, Gwyn Jones; Oldfield, Stone (1), Mabbutt; Jarman (2), Brown (1), Biggs (1p), Hamilton, Bobby Jones (2).

Record Cup Victory: 6–0 v Merthyr Tydfil, FA Cup, 1st rd, 14 November 1987 – Martyn; Alexander (Dryden), Tanner, Hibbitt, Twentyman, Jones, Holloway, Meacham (1), White (2), Penrice (3) (Reece), Purnell.

Record Defeat: 0–12 v Luton T, Division 3 (S), 13 April 1936.

Most League Points (2 for a win): 64, Division 3 (S), 1952–53.

Most League Points (3 for a win): 93, Division 3, 1989–90.

Most League Goals: 92, Division 3 (S), 1952–53.

Highest League Scorer in Season: Geoff Bradford, 33, Division 3 (S), 1952–53.

Most League Goals in Total Aggregate: Geoff Bradford, 245, 1949–64.

Most Capped Player: Neil Slatter, 10 (22), Wales.

Most League Appearances: Stuart Taylor, 545, 1966–80.

Record Transfer Fee Received: £1,000,000 from Crystal Palace for Nigel Martyn, November 1989.

Record Transfer Fee Paid: £370,000 to QPR for Andy Tillson, November 1992.

Football League Record: 1920 Original Member of Division 3; 1921–53 Division 3 (S); 1953–62 Division 2; 1962–74 Division 3; 1974–81 Division 2; 1981–90 Division 3; 1990– 92 Division 2. 1992–93 Division 1; 1993– Division 2.

Honours: *Football League:* Division 2 best season: 4th, 1994–95; Division 3 (S) – Champions 1952–53; Division 3 – Champions 1989–90; Runners-up 1973–74. *FA Cup:* best season: 6th rd, 1951, 1958. *Football League Cup:* best season: 5th rd, 1971, 1972.

Colours: Blue and white quartered shirts, white shorts, blue stockings. **Change colours:** Green shirts, black shorts, black stockings.

BRISTOL ROVERS 1994–95 LEAGUE RECORD

Match No.	Date	Venue	Opponents	Result		H/T Score	Lg. Pos.	Goalscorers	Attendance
1	Aug 13	A	Peterborough U	D	0-0	0-0	—		5695
2	20	H	York C	W	3-1	1-1	8	Clark, Miller, Stewart	3957
3	27	A	Wycombe W	D	0-0	0-0	11		5895
4	31	H	Blackpool	D	0-0	0-0	—		3762
5	Sept 3	H	Stockport Co	D	2-2	2-1	13	Tillson, Archer	4263
6	10	A	Rotherham U	W	3-0	3-0	12	Miller 2, Wilder (og)	2596
7	13	A	Swansea C	D	0-0	0-0	—		3226
8	17	H	Wrexham	W	4-2	1-0	7	Clark 2, Taylor, Miller	4441
9	24	A	Shrewsbury T	L	0-1	0-1	11		4596
10	Oct 1	H	Crewe Alex	D	2-2	0-2	12	Taylor 2	4862
11	8	A	Brentford	L	0-3	0-2	15		5330
12	15	H	Cardiff C	D	2-2	0-1	13	Channing, Clark	3936
13	22	H	Brighton & HA	W	3-0	2-0	12	Stewart, Miller 2	4107
14	29	A	Birmingham C	L	0-2	0-2	12		15,886
15	Nov 1	A	Cambridge U	D	1-1	0-0	—	Tillson	2328
16	5	H	Bradford C	W	4-0	2-0	12	Stewart 2, Oliver (og), Browning	4247
17	19	A	Hull C	W	2-0	1-0	10	Stewart 2	4450
18	26	H	Huddersfield T	D	1-1	1-1	12	Miller	5679
19	Dec 10	A	York C	W	3-0	1-0	9	Skinner, Stewart 2	3094
20	17	H	Peterborough U	W	3-1	0-1	7	Stewart 2 (1 pen), Gurney	4635
21	26	H	Bournemouth	W	2-1	1-0	7	Miller, Stewart	6913
22	31	H	Chester C	W	3-0	2-0	8	Archer 2, Stewart	5629
23	Jan 14	H	Oxford U	W	3-2	0-2	8	Taylor, Miller, Stewart	5875
24	Feb 4	A	Huddersfield T	D	1-1	1-0	9	Sterling	10,389
25	7	A	Bradford C	L	1-2	0-1	—	Heggs	4243
26	14	A	Brighton & HA	W	2-1	0-1	—	Stewart, Archer	5232
27	18	A	Oxford U	D	0-0	0-0	8		6349
28	25	A	Crewe Alex	L	1-2	0-2	11	Miller	4222
29	Mar 1	H	Hull C	L	0-2	0-1	—		3707
30	4	H	Shrewsbury T	W	4-0	1-0	10	Taylor, Archer, Browning, Miller (pen)	4338
31	7	A	Stockport Co	L	1-2	1-1	—	Miller	3580
32	11	H	Wycombe W	W	1-0	1-0	11	Taylor	5118
33	15	H	Cambridge U	W	2-1	2-1	—	Miller, Taylor	3734
34	18	A	Blackpool	W	2-0	0-0	6	Miller, Skinner	4484
35	22	H	Rotherham U	W	2-0	0-0	—	Taylor, Clark	4420
36	25	A	Wrexham	D	1-1	1-0	5	Archer	3170
37	29	H	Birmingham C	D	1-1	1-0	—	Whyte (og)	8010
38	Apr 1	H	Swansea C	W	1-0	0-0	4	Taylor	7062
39	4	A	Plymouth Arg	D	1-1	0-1	—	Miller	6743
40	8	A	Chester C	D	0-0	0-0	4		2241
41	11	A	Leyton Orient	W	2-1	1-0	—	Miller, Channing	2338
42	15	H	Plymouth Arg	W	2-0	0-0	4	Taylor, Wright	7068
43	18	A	Bournemouth	L	0-2	0-1	—		7020
44	22	H	Leyton Orient	W	1-0	0-0	4	Clark	4838
45	29	A	Cardiff C	W	1-0	0-0	4	Stewart	5462
46	May 6	H	Brentford	D	2-2	1-0	4	Taylor 2	8501

Final League Position: 4

GOALSCORERS

League (70): Miller 16 (1 pen), Stewart 15 (1 pen), Taylor 12, Archer 6, Clark 6, Browning 2, Channing 2, Skinner 2, Tillson 2, Gurney 1, Heggs 1, Sterling 1, Wright 1, own goals 3.
Coca-Cola Cup (2): Stewart 1, Tillson 1.
FA Cup (8): Millar 4, Stewart 4.

Parkin B. 40	Pritchard D.M. 43	Maddison L.R. 12 + 2	Channing J.A. 35 + 5	Clark W.R. 42	Tillson A. 40	Sterling W.R. 46	Stewart M.P. 26 + 1	Paul M.L. 2 + 3	Skinner J. 38	Archer L. 32 + 10	Browning M.T. 31 + 10	Taylor G.K. 23 + 16	Gurney A.R. 35 + 3	Miller P. 41 + 1	Waddock G.P. 1	Wright I.M. 6 + 1	Law M.W. 2	Davis M.V. — + 2	McLean I. — + 1	Collett A.A. 4	Hardyman P.G.T. 1 + 4	Heggs C.S. 2 + 3	White T.M. 4	Match No.
1	2	3	4	5	6	7	8	9	10	11	12	14												1
1	2		4	5	6	7	9		10	11	12		3	8										2
1	2		4	5	6	7	9		10	11	12	14	3	8										3
1	2		4	5	6	7				11		9	3	8	10									4
1	2		4	5	6	7			10	11	12	9	3	8										5
1	2		4	5	6	7		12	10	11		9	3	8										6
1	2		4	5	6	7			10	11		9	3	8										7
1	2		4	5	6	7			10	11		9	3	8										8
1	2		4	5	6	7			10	11	12	9	3	8		14								9
1	2	12	4	5		7			10	11	14	9	3	8		6								10
	2	12	4	5		7		8	10	11	9		3			6	1	14						11
	2	3	4	5	6	7			10	11	8	9	14				1		12					12
	2		4	5	6	7	9		10		11	12	3	8						1				13
	2		4	5	6	7	9		10	14	11	12	3	8						1				14
	2		4	5	6	7	9		10		11		3	8						1				15
	2		4	5	6	7	9		10	12	11	14	3	8						1				16
1	2		4	5	6	7	9	14	10	12	11	8	3											17
1	2			5	6	7	9		10	11	4	12	3	8										18
1	2			5	6	7	9		10	11	4		3	8							12			19
1			2	5		7	9		10	11	4		3	8		6					12			20
1		3		5		7	9		10	11	4	12	2	8		6					14			21
1	2			5	6	7	9		10	11	4	12	3	8							14			22
1			2	5	6	7	9	12		11	4	14	3	8							10			23
1	2		11	5	6	7			10		4	12	3	8								9		24
1	2		11		6	7			10		4	12	3	8								9	5	25
1	2		8		5	7	9			11	6	12	3	10								14	4	26
1	2		10		6	7	9			11	4	12	3	8								14	5	27
1	2		10		6	7	9			11	4	8	3	12								14	5	28
1	2		10	6	5	7	9		11	12	4		3	8										29
1	2			5	6	7			10	11	4	9	3	8				12						30
1	2		12	5	6	7			10	11	4	9	3	8										31
1	2			5	6	7			10	11	4	9	3	8										32
1	2		12	5	6	7			10	11	4	9	3	8										33
1	2		12	5	6	7			10	11	4	9	3	8										34
1	2	3	12	5	6	7			10	11	4	9		8										35
1	2	3	12	5	6	7			10	11	4	9		8										36
1	2	3	4	5	6	7	9		10	11		12		8										37
1	2	3	4	5	6	7	9		10	11	12	14		8										38
1	2	3	4	5	6	7	9			11	10			8										39
1	2	3	4	5	6	7	9			11	10	14	12	8										40
1	2	3	10	5	6	7	9			12	4	11	14	8										41
1	2	3	4	5		7	9		10	12	14	11		8		6								42
1	2	3	11	5		7			10	12	4	9		8		6								43
1	2		11	5	6	7	12		10	14	4	9	3	8										44
1	2		11	5	6	7	4		10	12	14	9	3	8										45
1	2		11	5	6	7	4		10	12	14	9	3	8										46

Coca-Cola Cup

First Round	Port Vale (h)	1-3
	(a)	1-1

FA Cup

First Round	Bath C (a)	5-0
Second Round	Leyton Orient (a)	2-0
Third Round	Luton T (a)	1-1
	(h)	0-1

BURNLEY 1994–95 *Back row (left to right):* Andy Farrell, Mark Winstanley, Nathan Peel, Wayne Russell, Marlon Beresford, Mark Monington, John Pender, Tony Philliskirk.
Centre row: Harry Wilson (Reserve Team Coach), Paul Wilson, David Eyres, Adrian Randall, Anthony McCluskey, Paul Smith, Andrew Bannister, Richard Livingstone, Wayne Dowell, John Mullin, Glen Davis, Matthew Taylor, Adrian Heath, Graham Lancashire, Andy Jones (Physio).
Front row: Terry Pashley (Youth Team Coach), Liam Robinson, Chris Vinnicombe, Ted McMinn, Gary Parkinson, Mr Jimmy Mullen (Manager), Steve Davis, Mr Brian Miller (Chief Scout), Chris Brass, Paul Weller, John Deary, Warren Joyce, Clive Middlemass (Assistant Manager).

Division 2 BURNLEY

Turf Moor, Burnley BB10 4BX. Telephone: (01282) 427777. Fax: (01282) 428938. Clubcall: 0891 121153. Credit Card Ticket Sales: (0645) 101010.

Ground capacity: 22,966.

Record attendance: 54,775 v Huddersfield T, FA Cup 3rd rd, 23 February 1924.

Record receipts; £150,000 v Liverpool, FA Cup 4th rd, 28 January 1995.

Pitch measurements: 114yd × 72yd.

Chairman: F. J. Teasdale.

Vice-Chairman: Dr R. D. Iven MRCS (Eng), LRCP (Lond), MRCGP.

Directors: B. Dearing LLB, B. Rothwell JP, C. Holt,R. Blakeborough.

Manager: Jimmy Mullen. ***Assistant Manager:*** Clive Middlemass.

Secretary: Mark Blackbourne. ***Coaches:*** Harry Wilson, Terry Pashley.

Commercial Manager: T. Skelly. ***Physio:*** Andy Jones.

Year Formed: 1882. ***Turned Professional:*** 1883. ***Ltd Co.:*** 1897.

Previous Name: 1881–82, Burnley Rovers.

Club Nickname: 'The Clarets'.

Previous Grounds: 1881, Calder Vale; 1882, Turf Moor.

Foundation: The majority of those responsible for the formation of the Burnley club in 1881 were from the defunct rugby club Burnley Rovers. Indeed, they continued to play rugby for a year before changing to soccer and dropping "Rovers" from their name. The changes were decided at a meeting held in May 1882 at the Bull Hotel.

First Football League game: 8 September, 1888, Football League, v PNE (a), L 2-5 – Smith; Lang, Bury, Abrams, Friel, Keenan, Brady, Tait, Poland (1), Gallocher (1), Yates.

Record League Victory: 9–0 v Darwen, Division 1, 9 January 1892 – Hillman; Walker, McFettridge, Lang, Matthews, Keenan, Nicol (3), Bowes, Espie (1), McLardie (3), Hill (2).

Record Cup Victory: 9–0 v Crystal Palace, FA Cup, 2nd rd (replay) 10 February 1909 – Dawson; Barron, McLean; Cretney (2), Leake, Moffat; Morley, Ogden, Smith (3), Abbott (2), Smethams (1). 9–0 v New Brighton, FA Cup, 4th rd, 26 January 1957 – Blacklaw; Angus, Winton; Seith, Adamson, Miller; Newlands (1), McIlroy (3), Lawson (3), Cheesebrough (1), Pilkington (1). 9–0 v Penrith FA Cup, 1st rd, 17 November 1984 – Hansbury; Miller, Hampton, Phelan, Overson (Kennedy), Hird (3 incl. 1p), Grewcock (1), Powell (2), Taylor (3), Biggins, Hutchison.

Record Defeat: 0–10 v Aston Villa, Division 1, 29 August 1925 and v Sheffield U, Division 1, 19 January 1929.

Most League Points (2 for a win): 62, Division 2, 1972–73.

Most League Points (3 for a win): 83, Division 4, 1991–92.

Most League Goals: 102, Division 1, 1960–61.

Highest League Scorer in Season: George Beel, 35, Division 1, 1927–28.

Most League Goals in Total Aggregate: George Beel, 178, 1923–32.

Most Capped Player: Jimmy McIlroy, 51 (55), Northern Ireland.

Most League Appearances: Jerry Dawson, 522, 1907–28.

Record Transfer Fee Received: £300,000 from Everton for Martin Dobson, August 1974, and from Derby Co for Leighton James, November 1975.

Record Transfer Fee Paid: £250,000 to Bristol C for Liam Robinson, August 1994 and £250,000 to Brighton & HA for Kurt Nogan, February 1995.

Football League Record: 1888 Original Member of the Football League; 1897–98 Division 2; 1898–1900 Division 1; 1900–13 Division 2; 1913–30 Division 1; 1930–47 Division 2; 1947–71 Division 1; 1971–73 Division 2; 1973–76 Division 1; 1976–80 Division 2; 1980–82 Division 3; 1982–83 Division 2; 1983–85 Division 3; 1985–92 Division 4; 1992–94 Division 2; 1994–95 Division 1; 1995– Division 2.

Honours: *Football League:* Division 1 – Champions 1920–21, 1959–60; Runners-up 1919–20, 1961–62; Division 2 – Champions 1897–98, 1972–73; Runners-up 1912–13, 1946–47; Division 3 – Champions 1981–82. Division 4 – Champions 1991–92. Record 30 consecutive Division 1 games without defeat 1920–21. *FA Cup:* Winners 1914; Runners-up 1947, 1962. *Football League Cup:* semi-final 1961, 1969, 1983. *Anglo-Scottish Cup:* Winners 1979. *Sherpa Van Trophy:* Runners-up 1988. **European Competitions;** *European Cup:* 1960–61. *European Fairs Cup:* 1966–67.

Colours: Claret shirts with sky blue sleeves, white shorts and stockings. **Change colours:** Yellow shirts with black pinstripe, yellow shorts, yellow stockings with black band.

BURNLEY 1994–95 LEAGUE RECORD

Match No.	Date	Venue	Opponents	Result		H/T Score	Lg. Pos.	Goalscorers	Attendance
1	Aug 13	A	Middlesbrough	L	0-2	0-2	—		23,343
2	20	H	Stoke C	D	1-1	1-0	20	Davis	15,331
3	27	A	Oldham Ath	L	0-3	0-0	23		11,310
4	30	H	Bristol City	D	1-1	1-0	—	Robinson	11,067
5	Sept 3	H	Barnsley	L	0-1	0-0	23		11,968
6	10	A	Luton T	W	1-0	1-0	21	Robinson	6911
7	14	A	Millwall	W	3-2	0-0	—	Winstanley 2, Robinson	7375
8	17	H	Wolverhampton W	L	0-1	0-0	21		17,766
9	24	A	WBA	L	0-1	0-0	22		13,539
10	Oct 1	H	Tranmere R	D	1-1	0-1	22	Eyres (pen)	12,427
11	8	H	Bolton W	D	2-2	0-1	22	Davis, Deary	16,687
12	15	A	Sunderland	D	0-0	0-0	22		17,700
13	22	A	Charlton Ath	W	2-1	0-0	21	Davis, Robinson	9436
14	29	H	Notts Co	W	2-1	1-0	18	Eyres (pen), Hoyland	12,876
15	Nov 1	H	Watford	D	1-1	0-1	—	Eyres	11,739
16	5	A	Reading	D	0-0	0-0	21		8150
17	20	H	Sheffield U	W	4-2	1-1	15	Robinson, Hoyland, Gayle, Davis	11,475
18	23	A	Swindon T	D	1-1	0-1	—	Gayle	7654
19	26	A	Grimsby T	D	2-2	0-1	15	Davis, Parkinson	7084
20	Dec 10	A	Stoke C	L	0-2	0-0	18		13,040
21	18	H	Middlesbrough	L	0-3	0-1	20		12,049
22	31	H	Southend U	W	5-1	2-0	19	Saville, Gayle, Bressington (og), Davis, Robinson	10,561
23	Jan 2	A	Portsmouth	L	0-2	0-1	20		9097
24	14	A	Notts Co	L	0-3	0-0	22		8702
25	21	H	Reading	L	1-2	0-2	22	Parkinson	9841
26	Feb 4	H	Swindon T	L	1-2	0-1	23	Harrison	10,960
27	11	A	Watford	L	0-2	0-0	23		9297
28	18	H	Grimsby T	L	0-2	0-1	23		10,511
29	21	A	Sheffield U	L	0-2	0-1	—		13,349
30	25	A	Tranmere R	L	1-4	0-1	24	Garnett (og)	9909
31	Mar 4	H	WBA	D	1-1	0-0	24	Robinson	11,885
32	7	A	Barnsley	L	0-2	0-1	—		5537
33	11	H	Oldham Ath	W	2-1	1-0	24	Nogan, Vinnicombe	11,620
34	15	A	Derby Co	L	0-4	0-1	—		13,922
35	18	A	Bristol C	D	1-1	0-1	24	Eyres	6717
36	21	H	Luton T	W	2-1	0-0	—	Mullin, Harrison	9551
37	24	A	Wolverhampton W	L	0-2	0-1	—		25,703
38	28	H	Port Vale	W	4-3	1-1	—	Nogan, Randall, Shaw, Sandeman (og)	10,058
39	Apr 1	H	Millwall	L	1-2	0-1	23	Shaw	10,454
40	4	H	Charlton Ath	W	2-0	1-0	—	Eyres, Shaw	10,045
41	8	A	Southend U	L	1-3	0-2	22	Nogan	5027
42	15	H	Derby Co	W	3-1	2-0	22	Eyres, Shaw, Davis	11,534
43	17	A	Port Vale	L	0-1	0-1	22		9663
44	22	H	Portsmouth	L	1-2	0-1	22	Eyres	10,666
45	29	H	Sunderland	D	1-1	1-1	21	Eyres (pen)	15,121
46	May 7	A	Bolton W	D	1-1	0-0	22	Philliskirk	16,853

Final League Position: 22

GOALSCORERS

League (49): Eyres 8 (3 pens), Davis 7, Robinson 7, Shaw 4, Gayle 3, Nogan 3, Harrison 2, Hoyland 2, Parkinson 2, Winstanley 2, Deary 1, Mullin 1, Philliskirk 1, Randall 1, Saville 1, Vinnicombe 1, own goals 3.
Coca-Cola Cup (4): Robinson 2, Gayle 1, Joyce 1.
FA Cup (8): Eyres 2 (2 pens), Heath 2, Deary 1, Gayle 1, Randall 1, Robinson 1.

Beresford M. 40	Parkinson G. 42 + 1	Vinnicombe C. 29	Davis S.M. 43	Winstanley M.A. 44	Joyce W.G. 4 + 1	Harper A. 27	Deary J.S. 12 + 4	Heath A.P. 21 + 6	Robinson S.L. 29 + 10	McMinn K.C. 17 + 5	Lancashire G. — + 1	Gayle J. 7 + 7	Harrison G.R. 16 + 3	Russell W.L. 6 + 2	Eyres D. 38 + 1	Randall A.J. 32	Philliskirk A. 7 + 6	Hoyland J.W. 30	Francis J.A. — + 2	Dowell W.A. 5	Mullin J. 6 + 6	Armstrong C. 4	Saville A.V. 3 + 1	Brass C.P. 2 + 3	Pender J.P. 5	Stewart P.A. 6	Peel N.J. — + 3	Nogan K. 11 + 4	Thompson S.J. 12	Shaw P. 8 + 1	*Match No.*
1	2	3	4	5	6	7	8	9	10	11	12																				1
1	2	3	4	5	6	7	12	9	10	11		8																			2
1	3		4	5	6	7	12	9	10	11		8	2	15																	3
1	2	3	4	5	6	7		9	10	11		8	12																		4
1	2	3	4	5	14	*6*	8	12	10	7		9			11																5
	2	3	4	5		7		9	10	11			8	1		6															6
1	2	3	4	5		7	6	9	10	11			8																		7
1	2	3	4	5		7	6	9	*10*	11			8		12		14														8
1	2	3	4	5		7	12	9	10	*8*			6		11		14														9
1	2	3	4	5		6		9	10	7			8		11		12														10
1	*2*	3	4	5			9		10	7		12	14		11	6	8														11
1	2	3		5		7	9	12	10			14			11	6	*8*	4													12
1	2	3	4	5		7	9		10						11	6		8													13
1	2	3	4	5		7	9	12	10						11	6		8													14
1	2	3	4	5		7	*9*	12	10						11	6	14	8													15
1	2	*3*	4	5		7	9	8	10			12			11	6			14												16
1	2		4	5		7		8	10			12			11	6		9		3											17
1	2		4	5		7		8	10			12			11	6		9		3											18
1	2		4	5		7		8	*10*			12			11	6		9	14	3											19
1	2		4	5		7		8	10			9			11	*6*	12	3			14										20
1	2		4	5		7		8	*10*			12			11	6		9		3	14										21
1	2		4	5			11	8	10	12		9	6									3	7								22
1	2		4	5			11	8	9				*6*	15	10		12					*3*	7	14							23
1	2		4	5		7	12	8	10	14					3	*6*		11					9								24
	2		4	5		7			10	12		9		1	11	6		8				*3*	14								25
1	2		4	5		7			*10*	12			14		11	6		8			9	3									26
1	2			5		7		9	10	12			6		3			8			11				4						27
1	3			5				12	14	7			*2*		11	6		8			10				4	9					28
1	2		4	5		7		9					6		3			8			11					10	12				29
1	2		4			7		9	12				6		3			5								10		11	8		30
1	2		4			7		12	14						11	6		5		*3*						9		10	8		31
1	2	3	4	5											11	6		7								9	12	10	8		32
1	2	3	4	5											11	6		7								9		10	8		33
1	2	3	4	5											11	6		7			9						12	10	8		34
	12	3	4	5					14				2	1	11	6		7							10			*9*	8		35
		3	4	5					7				2	1	11	6					12				10			9	8		36
		3	4	5					*10*				2	1	11	6		7						12				9	8	14	37
		3	4	5									2	1	11	6		10			14			12				*9*	8	7	38
1	2		4	5					12						11	6		10			14			3				*9*	8	7	39
1	2	3	4	5					12	11					9	6		10											8	7	40
1	2	3	4	5					12	11					9	6		10						8				14		*7*	41
1	2	3	4	5					12	7					11	6	9	10												8	42
1	2	3	4	5					12						11	6	9	10							8			14		*7*	43
1	2	3	4	5					12	7					11	6	*9*	10										14		8	44
1	2	3	4	5						7					11	6	9	10			12							14		*8*	45
1	2	3	4	5											11	6	9				7							8	10		46

Coca-Cola Cup

First Round	York C (h)	1-0
	(a)	2-2
Second Round	Liverpool (a)	0-2
	(h)	1-4

FA Cup

First Round	Shrewsbury T (h)	2-1
Second Round	Chester C (a)	2-1
Third Round	Cambridge U (a)	4-2
Fourth Round	Liverpool (h)	0-0
	(a)	0-1

BURY 1994–95 *Back row (left to right):* Peter Reid, Mark Sertori, David Pugh, Ryan Cross, John Paskin, Tony Kelly.
Centre row: Alan Raw (Physio), Stan Ternent (Assistant Manager), Lee Anderson, Ian Hughes, Ian Stevens, Lee Bracey, Chris Lucketti, Nick Daws, Tony Rigby, Cliff Roberts (Coach), Walter Joyce (Youth Development Officer).
Front row: Mark Carter, Michael Jackson, Ronnie Mauge, Mike Walsh (Manager), Jimmy Mulligan, Roger Stanislaus, Lenny Johnrose.

Division 3 **BURY**

Gigg Lane, Bury BL9 9HR. Telephone: (0161) 764 4881. Fax:(0161) 764 5521. Commercial Dept: (0161) 705 2144. Clubcall: 0898 121197. Community Programme: (0161) 797 5423. Social Club: (0161) 764 6771.

Ground capacity: 12,000 (unofficial).

Record attendance: 35,000 v Bolton W, FA Cup 3rd rd, 9 January 1960.

Record receipts: £37,000 v Bolton W, Division 3 play-off, 19 May 1991.

Pitch measurements: 112yd × 72yd.

Chairman: T. Robinson. ***Vice-Chairman:*** Canon J. R. Smith MA.

Directors: C. H. Eaves, J. Smith, F. Mason.

Manager: Mike Walsh. ***Coaches:*** Stan Ternent and Cliff Roberts. ***Physio:*** Alan Raw. ***Youth Development:*** W. Joyce.

Assistant Secretary: J. Neville. ***Commercial Manager:*** Neville Neville.

Year Formed: 1885. ***Turned professional:*** 1885. ***Ltd Co.:*** 1897. ***Club Nickname:*** 'Shakers'.

Club Sponsors: Birthdays.

Foundation: A meeting at the Waggon & Horses Hotel, attended largely by members of Bury Wesleyans and Bury Unitarians football clubs, decided to form a new Bury club. This was officially formed at a subsequent gathering at the Old White Horse Hotel, Fleet Street, Bury on April 24, 1885.

First Football League game: 1 September, 1894, Division 2, v Manchester C (h) W 4-2 – Lowe; Gillespie, Davies; White, Clegg, Ross; Wylie, Barbour (2), Millar (1), Ostler (1), Plant.

Record League Victory: 8–0 v Tranmere R, Division 3, 10 January 1970 – Forrest; Tinney, Saile; Anderson, Turner, McDermott; Hince (1), Arrowsmith (1), Jones (4), Kerr (1), Grundy. (1 og).

Record Cup Victory: 12–1 v Stockton, FA Cup, 1st rd (replay), 2 February 1897 – Montgomery; Darroch, Barbour; Hendry (1), Clegg, Ross (1); Wylie (3), Pangbourn, Millar (4), Henderson (2), Plant. (1 og).

Record Defeat: 0–10 v Blackburn R, FA Cup, preliminary round, 1 October 1887 and v West Ham U, Milk Cup, 2nd rd, 2nd leg, 25 October 1983.

Most League Points (2 for a win): 68, Division 3, 1960–61.

Most League Points (3 for a win): 84, Division 4, 1984–85.

Most League Goals: 108, Division 3, 1960–61.

Highest League Scorer in Season: Craig Madden, 35, Division 4, 1981–82.

Most League Goals in Total Aggregate: Craig Madden, 129, 1978–86.

Most Capped Player: Bill Gorman, 11 (13), Republic of Ireland and (4), Northern Ireland.

Most League Appearances: Norman Bullock, 506, 1920–35.

Record Transfer Fee Received: £375,000 from Southampton for David Lee, October 1991.

Record Transfer Fee Paid: £175,000 to Shrewsbury T for John McGinlay, July 1990.

Football League Record: 1894 Elected to Division 2; 1895–1912 Division 1; 1912–24 Division 2; 1924–29 Division 1; 1929–57 Division 2; 1957–61 Division 3; 1961–67 Division 2; 1967–68 Division 3; 1968–69 Division 2; 1969–71 Division 3; 1971–74 Division 4; 1974–80 Division 3; 1980–85 Division 4; 1985– Division 3.

Honours: *Football League:* Division 1 best season: 4th, 1925–26; Division 2 – Champions 1894–95; Runners-up 1923–24; Division 3 – Champions 1960–61; Runners-up 1967–68. *FA Cup:* Winners 1900, 1903. *Football League Cup:* Semi-final 1963.

Colours: White shirts, royal blue shorts, royal blue stockings. **Change colours:** Navy/red shirts, white shorts, navy/red stockings.

BURY 1994–95 LEAGUE RECORD

Match No.	Date		Venue	Opponents	Result		H/T Score	Lg. Pos.	Goalscorers	Attendance
1	Aug	13	H	Rochdale	L	0-1	0-0	—		3230
2		20	A	Exeter C	W	4-0	3-0	10	Carter 3, Jackson	2164
3		27	H	Hartlepool U	W	2-0	1-0	6	Carter 2 (1 pen)	2145
4		30	H	Preston NE	D	0-0	0-0	—		3623
5	Sept	3	A	Mansfield T	W	2-0	1-0	5	Carter, Paskin	2576
6		10	H	Scunthorpe U	W	2-0	1-0	3	Johnrose, Carter	2540
7		13	H	Doncaster R	W	2-0	1-0	—	Pugh, Paskin	2395
8		17	A	Rochdale	W	3-0	0-0	2	Carter, Paskin 2	3748
9		24	H	Chesterfield	W	2-1	1-1	1	Pugh, Carter	3031
10	Oct	1	A	Colchester U	L	0-1	0-0	2		3286
11		8	A	Darlington	W	2-0	0-0	2	Carter, Pugh	2352
12		15	H	Lincoln C	W	2-0	2-0	1	Johnrose, Pugh	3139
13		22	H	Gillingham	W	3-2	2-0	1	Carter (pen), Paskin 2	2976
14		29	A	Walsall	W	1-0	0-0	1	Pugh (pen)	5255
15	Nov	5	H	Scarborough	W	1-0	0-0	1	Johnrose	3016
16		19	A	Barnet	D	1-1	0-1	2	Mulligan	3006
17		26	H	Fulham	D	0-0	0-0	2		3323
18	Dec	10	H	Exeter C	D	0-0	0-0	2		2876
19		17	A	Hartlepool U	L	1-3	0-2	2	Daws	1746
20		26	H	Wigan Ath	D	3-3	2-2	2	Lucketti, Carter, Matthews	3616
21		27	A	Carlisle U	L	0-3	0-1	2		12,242
22	Jan	14	H	Hereford U	D	1-1	1-0	4	Carter	2708
23	Feb	4	A	Fulham	L	0-1	0-0	5		3941
24		18	A	Hereford U	L	0-1	0-1	9		1827
25		25	H	Colchester U	W	4-1	1-0	7	Stant, Hughes, Betts (og), Lucketti	2484
26		28	H	Torquay U	W	3-1	1-0	—	Kelly T, Lucketti, Stant	2241
27	Mar	4	A	Chesterfield	D	0-0	0-0	5		4429
28		7	A	Northampton T	W	5-0	1-0	—	Pugh 3 (1 pen), Kelly T, Stant	4208
29		11	A	Scunthorpe U	L	2-3	1-1	5	Pugh, Mulligan	2767
30		14	H	Barnet	W	3-0	3-0	—	Rigby, Stant, Johnrose	2380
31		18	A	Preston NE	L	0-5	0-2	5		9626
32		21	A	Scarborough	W	2-1	1-1	—	Pugh 2	1744
33		25	H	Mansfield T	D	2-2	1-0	4	Kelly T, Pugh (pen)	4188
34	Apr	1	A	Doncaster R	W	2-1	0-1	4	Stant 2	2485
35		4	A	Gillingham	D	1-1	1-1	—	Lancaster	2945
36		8	A	Torquay U	D	2-2	1-1	4	Stant 2	1969
37		15	H	Carlisle U	W	2-0	0-0	4	Stant, Jackson	5507
38		18	A	Wigan Ath	W	3-0	1-0	—	Stant 2, Paskin	2531
39		22	H	Northampton T	W	5-0	1-0	4	Daws, Pugh 2 (1 pen), Rigby, Paskin	2921
40		29	A	Lincoln C	W	3-0	2-0	4	Pugh 2, Stant	3928
41	May	4	H	Walsall	D	0-0	0-0	—		6790
42		6	H	Darlington	W	2-1	1-1	4	Carter (pen), Stant	3612

Final League Position: 4

GOALSCORERS

League (73): Pugh 16 (4 pens), Carter 14 (3 pens), Stant 13, Paskin 8, Johnrose 4, Kelly T 3, Lucketti 3, Daws 2, Jackson 2, Mulligan 2, Rigby 2, Hughes 1, Lancaster 1, Matthews 1, own goal 1.
Coca-Cola Cup (3): Carter 1 (pen), Rigby 1, own goal 1.
FA Cup (5): Johnrose 1, Lucketti 1, Paskin 1, Rigby 1, Stanislaus 1.

Kelly G.A. 38	Cross R. 11 + 1	Stanislaus R.E.P. 33	Mauge R.C. 14 + 4	Lucketti C.J. 39	Jackson M.J. 24	Mulligan J. 9 + 6	Carter M.C. 21 + 5	Hulme K. 24 + 4	Reid P. 1	Pugh D. 42	Daws N.J. 30 + 4	Paskin W.J. 15 + 11	Johnrose L. 23 + 3	Rigby A.A. 24 + 6	Matthewson T. 18	Bracey L.M.I. 4 + 2	Sertori M.A. — + 2	Kelly A.O.N. 19 + 3	Hughes I. 19 + 4	De Souza J.M. 2 + 1	Matthews N. 2	Stant P. 19 + 1	Bimson S.J. 19	Lancaster D. 3 + 2	Rowe R.C. 1 + 2	Woodward A.S. 8	Match No.
1	2	3	4	5	6	7	8	9	10	11	*12*	14															1
1	2	3	4	5	6	7	8	9		11		12	10														2
1	2	3	4	5	6	7	8	*9*		11		14	12	10													3
1	2	3	4	5	6	7	8	9		11		12	14	*10*													4
1	2	3	4	5		7	8	9		11		12	10	14	6												5
		3	*4*	5	2	7	8	9		11		12	10		6	1	14										6
		3		5	2	7	8	9		11	4	12	10		6	1											7
1		3	4	5	2		8	*9*		11	12	7	10	14	6												8
1		3		5	2		8	9		11	4	7	10	12	6												9
1		3		5	2		8	9		11	4	7	10	12	6												10
1		3		5	2		8	9		11	4	7	10		6			12									11
1		3		5	2		8			11	4	7	10	9	6		12										12
1	2	3		5			8	12		11	4	7	10	9	6												13
1	2	3		5		*12*	8	9		11	4		10	7	6				14								14
1		3		5	2	8		9		11	4		10	7	6			12									15
1	2	3	10	5		12				11	4	9	8	7	6	15											16
1	2	3	10	5				8		11		9	4		6			7		12							17
1		3		5	*2*		12			11	10		4	14	6			7	9	8							18
1		3		5	2		8			11	4		10	12	6				7	9							19
1		3	4	5	2		8			11	14		10	*7*	6				12		9						20
1	12	3	4	5	2		8			11	6		10						7		9						21
1	2	3	4			12	8	7		11		9	10		6				5								22
1		3	4	5	2		8			11	12	*9*	10					7	6			14					23
1	2			5				12		11		8	10	4				7	6			9	3				24
1		2		5				12		11	10	8		4				7	6			9	3				25
1		2		5						11	10	8		4				7	6			9	3				26
1		2	12	5				14		11	10	*8*		4				7	6			9	3				27
1		2	12	5		14		8		11	*10*			4				7	6			9	3				28
1		2		5		12		8		11	10			4				7	6			9	3				29
1		2		5		7	14			11	10		12	4					6			9	3	*8*			30
1		2			7			8		11	10			4	5				6			9	3	12			31
1		2		5				8		11	10			4		15		12	6			*9*	3		7		32
1		2		5			12	8		11	10			*4*				7	6			9	3		14		33
1		2		5						11	4		10					7	6			9	3	8			34
				5			12			11	4		10			1		7	6			9	3	8	14	2	35
			12	5			*8*			11	4			10		1		7	6			9	3	14		2	36
1				5	6			8		11	4	12		10				7				9	3			2	37
1			*4*	5	6			8		11	10	12						7	14			9	3			2	38
1				5	6			8		11	4	12		10				7				9	3			2	39
1				5	6			8		11	4	12		10				7	14			9	3			*2*	40
1				5	6		12			11	10	8		4				7				9	3			2	41
1			12		6	14	*8*			11	4			10				7	5			9	3			2	42

Coca-Cola Cup

First Round	Hartlepool U (h)	2-0
	(a)	1-5

FA Cup

First Round	Bishop Auckland (a)	0-0
	(h)	1-1
Second Round	Crewe Alex (a)	2-1
Third Round	Tranmere R (h)	2-2
	(a)	0-3

CAMBRIDGE UNITED 1994–95 *Back row (left to right):* Craig Middleton, Darran Hay, Ollie Morah, Mick Heathcote, Steve Butler, Michael Danzey, Jody Craddock, Simon Livett, Kevin Bartlett, Danny Granville.

Centre row: Ken Steggles (Physio), Roger Parker (Kit Manager), Kofi Nyamah, Andy Jeffrey, Jon Sheffield, John Filan, Micah Hyde, John Fowler, Efon Elad, Paul Ashworth (Youth Development Officer).

Front row: Tommy Taylor (Youth Team Manager), Hakan Hayrettin, Carlo Corazzin, Matthew Joseph, Gary Johnson (Manager), Dean Barrick, Junior Hunter, Jon Rattle, Danny O'Shea (Player/Coach).

Division 3 CAMBRIDGE UNITED

Abbey Stadium, Newmarket Rd, Cambridge, CB5 8LN. Telephone: (01223) 566500. Fax: (01223) 566502. Abbey Update: 0891 555885.

Ground capacity: 9667.

Record attendance; 14,000 v Chelsea, Friendly, 1 May 1970.

Record receipts: £86,308 v Manchester U, Rumbelows Cup 2nd rd 2nd leg, 9 October 1991.

Pitch measurements: 110yd × 74yd.

Chairman: R. H. Smart. ***Vice-Chairman:*** R. F. Hunt. ***Directors:*** G. Harwood, J. Howard, R. Hunt, G. Lowe, R. Summerfield.

Manager: Tommy Taylor. ***Assistant Manager:*** Paul Clark. ***Youth Manager:*** Peter Braybrook.

Physio: Ken Steggles.

Secretary: Steve Greenall. ***Commercial Manager:*** John Holmes. ***Stadium Manager:*** Ian Darler.

Year Formed: 1919. ***Turned Professional:*** 1946. ***Ltd Co.:*** 1948.

Club Nickname: The 'U's'.

Previous Name: Abbey United until 1949.

Foundation: The football revival in Cambridge began soon after World War II when the Abbey United club (formed 1919) decided to turn professional and in 1949 changed their name to Cambridge United. They were competing in the United Counties League before graduating to the Eastern Counties League in 1951 and the Southern League in 1958.

First Football League game: 15 August, 1970, Division 4, v Lincoln C (h) D 1-1 – Roberts; Thompson, Meldrum (1), Slack, Eades, Hardy, Leggett, Cassidy, Lindsey, McKinven, Harris.

Record League Victory: 6–0 v Darlington, Division 4, 18 September 1971 – Roberts; Thompson, Akers, Guild, Eades, Foote, Collins (1p), Horrey, Hollett, Greenhalgh (4), Phillips. (1 og). 6–0 v Hartlepool, Division 4, 11 February 1989 – Vaughan; Beck, Kimble, Turner, Chapple (1), Daish, Clayton, Holmes, Taylor (3 incl. 1p), Bull (1), Leadbitter (1).

Record Cup Victory: 5–1 v Bristol C, FA Cup, 5th rd, second replay, 27 February 1990 – Vaughan; Fensome, Kimble, Bailie (O'Shea), Chapple, Daish, Cheetham (Robinson), Leadbitter (1), Dublin (2), Taylor (1), Philpott (1).

Record Defeat: 0–6 v Aldershot, Division 3, 13 April 1974 and v Darlington, Division 4, 28 September 1974 and v Chelsea, Division 2, 15 January 1983.

Most League Points (2 for a win): 65, Division 4, 1976–77.

Most League Points (3 for a win): 86, Division 3, 1990–91.

Most League Goals: 87, Division 4, 1976–77.

Highest League Scorer in Season: David Crown, 24, Division 4, 1985–86.

Most League Goals in Total Aggregate: Alan Biley, 74, 1975–80.

Most Capped Player: Tom Finney, 7 (15), Northern Ireland.

Most League Appearances: Steve Spriggs, 416, 1975–87.

Record Transfer Fee Received: £1,000,000 from Manchester U for Dion Dublin, August 1992.

Record Transfer Fee Paid: £190,000 to Luton T for Steve Claridge, November 1992.

Football League Record: 1970 Elected to Division 4; 1973–74 Division 3; 1974–77 Division 4; 1977–78 Division 3; 1978–84 Division 2; 1984–85 Division 3; 1985–90 Division 4; 1990–91 Division 3; 1991–92 Division 2; 1992–93 Division 1; 1993– 95 Division 2; 1995– Division 3.

Honours: *Football League:* Division 2 best season: 5th, 1991–92; Division 3 – Champions 1990–91; Runners-up 1977–78; Division 4 – Champions 1976–77. *FA Cup:* best season: 6th rd, 1990, 1991. *Football League Cup:* 5th rd, 1993.

Colours: Amber & black striped shirts, black shorts with amber & black trim, black & amber stockings. **Change colours:** Patterned white & sky blue shirts, royal blue shorts, royal blue stockings.

CAMBRIDGE UNITED 1994–95 LEAGUE RECORD

Match No.	Date	Venue	Opponents	Result		H/T Score	Lg. Pos.	Goalscorers	Attendance
1	Aug 13	A	Wycombe W	L	0-3	0-1	—		5782
2	20	H	Stockport Co	L	3-4	1-2	18	Joseph, Morah, Corazzin	3163
3	27	A	Oxford U	L	0-1	0-1	22		5513
4	30	H	Chester C	W	2-1	0-0	—	Barrick, Corazzin	2520
5	Sept 3	H	Rotherham U	W	2-1	1-0	15	Corazzin 2	2885
6	10	A	Leyton Orient	D	1-1	0-0	15	Morah	3699
7	13	A	Plymouth Arg	D	0-0	0-0	—		3824
8	17	H	Swansea C	L	1-3	1-2	18	Granville	2795
9	24	A	Brighton & HA	L	0-2	0-1	20		8280
10	Oct 1	H	Bradford C	W	4-1	2-1	18	Corazzin, Lillis, Butler 2	3338
11	8	H	Wrexham	L	1-2	0-0	18	Corazzin	3221
12	15	A	Huddersfield T	L	1-3	1-0	19	Butler	10,742
13	22	A	Cardiff C	L	1-3	1-1	20	Jeffrey	3580
14	29	H	Brentford	D	0-0	0-0	21		3102
15	Nov 1	H	Bristol R	D	1-1	0-0	—	Corazzin	2328
16	5	A	Bournemouth	L	0-1	0-0	22		3272
17	19	H	Shrewsbury T	W	3-1	1-1	21	Butler 2, Lillis	2748
18	26	A	Crewe Alex	L	2-4	0-1	21	Corazzin 2	3636
19	Dec 10	A	Stockport Co	L	1-2	0-0	21	Butler	3903
20	16	H	Wycombe W	D	2-2	1-1	—	Butler, Corazzin	3713
21	26	A	Birmingham C	D	1-1	0-1	20	Otto (og)	20,098
22	28	H	York C	W	1-0	0-0	—	Corazzin	3285
23	31	A	Peterborough U	D	2-2	1-1	18	Lillis 2	7412
24	Jan 2	H	Hull C	D	2-2	0-2	18	Hay 2	3569
25	14	A	Blackpool	W	3-2	1-1	18	Butler, Corazzin 2	4076
26	17	H	Cardiff C	W	2-0	1-0	—	Corazzin, Butler (pen)	2460
27	21	H	Bournemouth	D	2-2	1-0	17	Butler 2	2834
28	28	A	Brentford	L	0-6	0-0	17		6390
29	Feb 4	H	Crewe Alex	L	1-2	0-0	18	Corazzin	3339
30	18	H	Blackpool	D	0-0	0-0	19		3192
31	21	A	Shrewsbury T	D	1-1	1-0	—	Hay	3200
32	25	A	Bradford C	D	1-1	0-0	19	Jeffrey	6075
33	Mar 4	H	Brighton & HA	L	0-2	0-1	19		3856
34	7	A	Rotherham U	L	0-1	0-1	—		2208
35	11	H	Oxford U	L	1-2	0-1	19	Corazzin	3558
36	15	A	Bristol R	L	1-2	1-2	—	Kyd	3734
37	18	A	Chester C	W	3-1	3-0	19	Corazzin 2, Butler	1720
38	21	H	Leyton Orient	D	0-0	0-0	—		3048
39	24	A	Swansea C	L	0-1	0-1	—		4007
40	Apr 1	H	Plymouth Arg	D	1-1	0-0	19	Butler (pen)	3913
41	8	H	Peterborough U	W	2-0	1-0	19	Joseph, Butler	5828
42	15	A	York C	L	0-2	0-1	19		3278
43	17	H	Birmingham C	W	1-0	0-0	19	Heathcote	5317
44	22	A	Hull C	L	0-1	0-0	19		3483
45	29	H	Huddersfield T	D	1-1	1-1	20	Granville	5188
46	May 6	A	Wrexham	W	1-0	1-0	20	Corazzin	3172

Final League Position: 20

GOALSCORERS

League (52): Corazzin 19, Butler 14 (2 pens), Lillis 4, Hay 3, Granville 2, Jeffrey 2, Joseph 2, Morah 2, Barrick 1, Heathcote 1, Kyd 1, own goal 1.
Coca-Cola Cup (2): Barrick 1, Craddock 1.
FA Cup (8): Butler 4 (2 pens), Lillis 2, Barrick 1, Hay 1.

Filan J.R. 16	Hunter A.J. 23 + 3	Barrick D. 44	Craddock J.D. 38	Heathcote M. 24	O'Shea D.E. 30 + 1	Hyde M. 18 + 9	Elad D.E. 2 + 1	Butler S. 35 + 2	Corazzin G.M. 45 + 1	Nyamah K. 5 + 4	Morah O. 8 + 6	Fowler J.A. 12 + 4	Rattle J.P. 6	Joseph M.N.A. 39	Livett S.R. 2	Danzey M.J. 7 + 4	Kyd M.R. 10 + 9	Granville D.P. 11 + 5	Lillis J.W. 14 + 5	Rush D. 2	Hayrettin H. 15 + 2	Walker R.K. 5	Hay D.A. 7 + 19	Jeffrey A.S. 25 + 3	Manuel W.A.J. 10	Sheffield J. 28	Campbell D.A. 1	Campbell J. 12	Lomas A. 2	Pack L.J. 3	Thompson D.G. 7	*Match No.*
1	2	3	4	5	6	7	8	9	10	*11*	12	14																				1
1	2	3	4	5	6	7	14	9	10		12		8	*11*																		2
1	2	3	4	5	12	6	8	14	10	*11*	9	7																				3
1	2	3	4		5				10		9	7	11		6	8	12															4
1	2	3	4		5	12			10		9	7	11		6	*8*	14															5
1	2	3	4		5	12			10		9	7	11				14	*6*	8													6
1	2	3	4		5	12			10		14	7	11					6	*8*	9												7
1	2	3	4		5	12			10		14	7	*11*	8				6		9												8
1	2	3	4		5	14		9	10		12	*7*		11							6	8										9
1	2	3	4		5	12		9	10	14				11					*7*		6	8										10
1	2	3	4		5			9	10	14				11			12		7		*6*	8										11
1		3	4		5			9	10	*2*				11		6		14	7			8	12									12
1	4	3			5			*9*	10					11		6		12	7			8	14	2								13
1	6	3	4		5			9	10			12		11				7						2	8							14
1	2	3	4		5	12		9	10			6		*11*				7					14		8							15
1	2	3	4		5	6		9	10			12		11				*7*					14		8							16
		3	4		5	6		9	10			12		2					8				11		7	1						17
		3	4		5	6		9	10	14		7		2					*8*				11	12		1						18
	2	3	4			6		9	10					8					12				11	5	7	1						19
	2	3	4			6		9	10					8					12				11	5	7	1						20
	2	3	4		6	8		9	10					*11*				14	12					5	7	1						21
	2	3	4		6	9			11					10				12	*8*				14	5	7	1						22
	2	3	4		6	8			10			7		11					9				12	5		1						23
	2	3	4		6	9		12	10			7		11					8				14	5		1						24
		3	4	5	6	7		9	10					11					8				12	2		1						25
	12	3	4	5	6	7		9	10					11					*8*				14	2		1						26
		3	4	5	6			9	10		7			11					12				14	2	*8*	1						27
		3	4	5	*6*			9	10		7			11									14	12	8	1	2					28
		3	4			6		9	10					2		5		7			8		12	11		1						29
		3	4	5		7		9	10			8		2							6		12	11		1						30
	7	3	4	5					10		*9*			2			14		12		6		8	11		1						31
	7	3	4	5				9	10		12			2			14				6		*8*	11		1						32
		3	4	5				9	10		7			2			8				6		12	11		1						33
		3	4	5	6	12		9	10					2			8				*7*		14	11		1						34
			4	5	6	14		9	12					2			8		10				7	11		1		3				35
		3		5	6			9	10					2			8	11					12	4		1		7				36
		3	4	5	6			9	10					2			*8*	11			12		14					7	1			37
		3		5	6			9	10					2			8				7		12	14				4	1	*11*		38
		3		5		4		9	10					2			8				7		12			1		6		11		39
	12			5		7		9	10	14				2			*8*				6					1		3		11	4	40
		3		5				9	10	8				2		6	12							11		1		7			4	41
		3	4	5				9	10	*8*				2		14	12							11		1		7			6	42
	12	3	*4*	5					10					2		14	9				8			11		1		7			6	43
		3		5				9	10							2	6	12			8			11		1		7			4	44
		3		5				9	10					2		12	14	*6*			8			11		1		7			4	45
		3	4	5				9	10					2		12		8			14			*11*		1		7			6	46

Coca-Cola Cup

First Round	Portsmouth (a)	0-2
	(h)	2-3

FA Cup

First Round	Brentford (h)	2-2
	(a)	2-1
Second Round	Peterborough U (a)	2-0
Third Round	Burnley (h)	2-4

CARDIFF CITY 1994–95 *Back row (left to right):* Carl Dale, Derek Brazil, Andy Scott, Wayne Fereday
Centre row: Gavin Tait (Youth Development Officer), Jimmy Goodfellow (Physio), Mark Aizlewood (Player Coach), Paul Millar, Lee Baddeley, David Williams, Jason Perry, Steve Williams, Nick Richardson, Scott Young, Gary Thompson, Harry Parsons (Kit Manager).
Front row: Damon Searle, Nathan Wigg, Charlie Oatway, Terry Yorath (Manager), Ryan Nicholls, Darren Adams, Anthony Bird.

Division 3 CARDIFF CITY

Ninian Park, Cardiff CF1 8SX. Telephone: (01222) 398636. Fax: (01222) 341148. Newsline: 0891 888603.

Ground capacity: 20,284.

Record attendance: 61,566, Wales v England, 14 October 1961.

Club record: 57,893 v Arsenal, Division 1, 22 April 1953.

Record receipts: £141,756 v Manchester C, FA Cup 4th rd, 29 January 1994.

Pitch measurements: 114yd × 78yd.

Directors: R. Wright, W. Dixon, D. Henderson, J. Oliver, S. Williams.

Secretary: Jim Finney.

Manager: Eddie May.

Physio: Jimmy Goodfellow. *Coach:* Eddie May.

Year Formed: 1899. *Turned Professional:* 1910. *Ltd Co.:* 1910.

Previous Names: 1899–1902, Riverside; 1902–08, Riverside Albion; 1908, Cardiff City.

Club Nickname: 'Bluebirds'.

Previous Grounds: Riverside, Sophia Gardens, Old Park and Fir Gardens. Moved to Ninian Park, 1910.

Foundation: Credit for the establishment of a first class professional football club in such a rugby stronghold as Cardiff, is due to members of the Riverside club formed in 1899 out of a cricket club of that name. Cardiff became a city in 1905 and in 1908 the local FA granted Riverside permission to call themselves Cardiff City.

First Football League game: 28 August, 1920, Division 2, v Stockport C (a) W 5-2 – Kneeshaw; Brittain, Leyton; Keenor (1), Smith, Hardy; Grimshaw (1), Gill (2), Cashmore, West, Evans (1).

Record League Victory: 9–2 v Thames, Division 3 (S), 6 February 1932 – Farquharson; E. L. Morris, Roberts; Galbraith, Harris, Ronan; Emmerson (1), Keating (1), Jones (1), McCambridge (1), Robbins (5).

Record Cup Victory: 8–0 v Enfield, FA Cup, 1st rd, 28 November 1931 – Farquharson; Smith, Roberts; Harris (1), Galbraith, Ronan; Emmerson (2), Keating (3); O'Neill (2), Robbins, McCambridge.

Record Defeat: 2–11 v Sheffield U, Division 1, 1 January 1926.

Most League Points (2 for a win): 66, Division 3 (S), 1946–47.

Most League Points (3 for a win): 86, Division 3, 1982–83.

Most League Goals: 93, Division 3 (S), 1946–47.

Highest League Scorer in Season: Stan Richards, 30, Division 3 (S), 1946–47.

Most League Goals in Total Aggregate: Len Davies, 128, 1920–31.

Most Capped Player: Alf Sherwood, 39 (41), Wales.

Most League Appearances: Phil Dwyer, 471, 1972–85.

Record Transfer Fee Received: £300,000 from Sheffield U for Nathan Blake, February 1994.

Record Transfer Fee Paid: £180,000 to San Jose Earthquakes for Godfrey Ingram, September 1982.

Football League Record: 1920 Elected to Division 2; 1921–29 Division 1; 1929–31 Division 2; 1931–47 Division 3 (S); 1947–52 Division 2; 1952–57 Division 1; 1957–60 Division 2; 1960–62 Division 1; 1962–75 Division 2; 1975–76 Division 3; 1976–82 Division 2; 1982–83 Division 3; 1983–85 Division 2; 1985–86 Division 3; 1986–88 Division 4; 1988–90 Division 3; 1990–92 Division 4; 1992–93 Division 3; 1993–95 Division 2; 1995– Division 3.

Honours: Football League: Division 1 – Runners-up 1923–24; Division 2 – Runners-up 1920–21, 1951–52, 1959–60; Division 3 (S) – Champions 1946–47; Division 3 – Champions 1992–93. Runners-up 1975–76, 1982–83; Division 4 – Runners-up 1987–88. *FA Cup:* Winners 1927 (only occasion the Cup has been won by a club outside England); Runners-up 1925. *Football League Cup:* Semi-final 1966. *Welsh Cup:* Winners 21 times. *Charity Shield:* 1927. European Competitions: *European Cup-Winners' Cup:* 1964–65, 1965–66, 1967–68, 1968–69, 1969–70, 1970–71, 1971–72, 1973–74, 1974–75, 1976–77, 1977–78, 1988–89, 1991–92, 1992–93, 1993–94.

Colours: Blue shirts, blue shorts, blue stockings. **Change colours:** Yellow shirts, navy shorts, navy stockings.

CARDIFF CITY 1994–95 LEAGUE RECORD

Match No.	Date	Venue	Opponents	Result		H/T Score	Lg. Pos.	Goalscorers	Attendance
1	Aug 13	A	Stockport Co	L	1-4	1-1	—	Stant	5139
2	20	H	Oxford U	L	1-3	1-2	20	Stant	7281
3	27	A	York C	D	1-1	0-0	19	Millar	2861
4	30	H	Wrexham	D	0-0	0-0	—		4903
5	Sept 3	H	Swansea C	D	1-1	0-1	21	Richardson	5523
6	10	A	Blackpool	L	1-2	1-0	21	Richardson	4189
7	13	A	Chester C	W	2-0	0-0	—	Stant, Aizlewood	1671
8	17	H	Plymouth Arg	L	0-1	0-0	21		5674
9	24	A	Bournemouth	L	2-3	1-1	22	Scott, Griffith	3177
10	Oct 1	H	Peterborough U	L	1-2	1-1	22	Fereday	4225
11	8	H	Crewe Alex	L	1-2	1-0	22	Stant	4126
12	15	A	Bristol R	D	2-2	1-2	22	Millar, Richardson	3936
13	22	H	Cambridge U	W	3-1	1-1	22	Stant 3	3580
14	30	A	Bradford C	W	3-2	3-1	20	Millar 2 (1 pen), Stant	5937
15	Nov 1	A	Leyton Orient	L	0-2	0-0	—		2558
16	5	H	Brighton & HA	W	3-0	0-0	19	Baddeley, Stant 2	5004
17	19	A	Wycombe W	L	1-3	0-1	20	Stant	5391
18	25	H	Hull C	L	0-2	0-2	—		4226
19	Dec 10	A	Oxford U	L	0-1	0-1	20		6181
20	17	H	Stockport Co	D	1-1	0-0	21	Dale	3448
21	26	A	Shrewsbury T	W	1-0	0-0	19	Stant (pen)	4933
22	28	H	Birmingham C	L	0-1	0-0	—		7420
23	31	A	Rotherham U	L	0-2	0-1	20		3064
24	Jan 2	H	Brentford	L	2-3	0-2	21	Stant, Bird	5235
25	7	H	Blackpool	L	0-1	0-1	21		3467
26	14	H	Huddersfield T	D	0-0	0-0	21		3808
27	17	A	Cambridge U	L	0-2	0-1	—		2460
28	Feb 4	A	Hull C	L	0-4	0-2	22		3903
29	18	A	Huddersfield T	L	1-5	0-4	22	Brazil	10,035
30	21	H	Wycombe W	W	2-0	0-0	—	Dale, Richardson	3024
31	25	A	Peterborough U	L	1-2	1-1	22	Dale	4226
32	Mar 4	H	Bournemouth	D	1-1	1-1	22	Dale	3008
33	7	A	Swansea C	L	1-4	0-3	—	Wigg	3943
34	11	H	York C	L	1-2	1-2	22	Griffith	2689
35	15	A	Brighton & HA	D	0-0	0-0	—		6956
36	18	A	Wrexham	W	3-0	1-0	22	Nicholls, Griffith, Humes (og)	3023
37	25	A	Plymouth Arg	D	0-0	0-0	22		5611
38	28	H	Bradford C	L	2-4	2-1	—	Perry, Millar	2560
39	Apr 1	H	Chester C	W	2-1	1-0	22	Dale, Millar	4405
40	4	H	Leyton Orient	W	2-1	0-0	—	Bird 2	4324
41	8	H	Rotherham U	D	1-1	1-0	22	Griffith	6412
42	15	A	Birmingham C	L	1-2	1-1	22	Millar	17,455
43	17	H	Shrewsbury T	L	1-2	0-1	22	Bird	4677
44	22	A	Brentford	L	0-2	0-0	22		8268
45	29	H	Bristol R	L	0-1	0-0	22		5462
46	May 6	A	Crewe Alex	D	0-0	0-0	22		4382

Final League Position: 22

GOALSCORERS

League (46): Stant 13 (1 pen), Millar 7 (1 pen), Dale 5, Bird 4, Griffith 4, Richardson 4, Aizlewood 1, Baddeley 1, Brazil 1, Fereday 1, Nicholls 1, Perry 1, Scott 1, Wigg 1, own goal 1.
Coca-Cola Cup (3): Stant 2, Oatway 1.
FA Cup (0).

Williams S.D. 6	Evans T. 7	Scott A.M. 13	Aizlewood M. 17	Perry J. 34	Oatway A.P.D. 27 + 3	Griffith C. 31 + 7	Richardson N.J. 32 + 1	Stant P. 19	Bird A. 7 + 12	Fereday W. 26 + 1	Brazil D.M. 26 + 4	Dale C. 33 + 2	Williams D. 40	Millar W.P. 25 + 10	Adams D.S. 4 + 2	Young S. 15 + 7	Thompson G.L. 11 + 2	Searle D.P. 32	Baddeley L.M. 33 + 3	McLean I. 4	Ramsey P. 11	Wigg N.M. 18 + 1	Evans D.A. 4 + 8	Nicholls R. 6 + 6	Honor C. 10	Pearson J.S. 12	Vick L. 2	Milsom P.J. 1 + 2	Match No.
1	2	3	4	5	6	7	8	9	10	11	12	14																	1
	2		4	5	6		8	9	10	11	3	14	1	7	12														2
	2	3			6	7	8		9	11	5	10	1	12		4													3
	2	3			6	7	8		12	11	5	10	1	9		4													4
	2	3	4		6	7	8				5	10	1	12			9	11	14										5
	2	3	4		7	11	8	9			6	10	1	12			14			5									6
		3	4	6	7	11	8	9	12		2	10	1							5									7
		3	4	6	7	11	8		12		2	10	1				9		14	5									8
	2	3	4	6	7	11	8					10	1	14		12	9		5										9
			4	2	6	8	12	9	14	11		10	1	7				3	5										10
			4	5	6	7	8	9		11	2		1		10			3					12						11
				6	4	7	8	9		11	2		1	14	10			3	5				12						12
		3		6	4	7		9		11	2	10	1	8					5										13
		3		6	4	7		9		11	2	10	1	8					5										14
		3		6	4	7		9		11	2	10	1	8					5										15
		3		6	4	8		9	12	11	2		1	10					5		7	14							16
			4	6	8	12		9					1	11		2	10	3	5		7								17
			4		6	12	8	9	14		5		1	11		2	10	3			7								18
					4	12	8	9		14	6	7	1	11		2	10	3	5										19
			6		4			9		11		8	1	12		2	10	3	5		7								20
				6	4	12		9		11		8	1					3	5	2	7		10						21
				6	4	11		9		2		8	1	12		14		3	5		7		10						22
				6	4	12		9	14	2		8	1	11		7		3	5				10						23
		11		6	4			9	12	2		8	1			14	10	3	5		7								24
				6	8	11				2		9	1			12	10	3	5		7		14	4					25
				6	8				14	2		11	1	12	9		10	3	5		7			4					26
				6	4	12			14			8	1	11	9	2	10	3	5		7								27
			4				8			11		7	1			12	14	3	5		6			10	2	9			28
			4				10			2	6	8	1	12				3	5			11			7	9			29
			4	6		12	10			11		8	1					3	5			7			2	9			30
				6			10			11	4	8	1					3	5			7	9		2				31
			4	6			10			11	14	8	1					3	5			7	12		2	9			32
			4	6		8	10			11	12		1	14				3	5			7			2	9			33
				6		4	10			3	12		1	11					5			7		14	2	9	8		34
				6		4	10			3			1	11		12			5			7		14	2	9	8		35
				6		4	10						1	11		5		3				7		8	2	9			36
				6		4	10				2		1	11		5		3	12			7		8		9		14	37
				6		4	10						1	11		5		3				7		8	2	9		12	38
				6		11	8		12		2	10	1	7				3	5			4		14		9			39
				6		11	8		12		2	10	1	7				3	5			4		14		9			40
				6		11	8		9		2	10	1	7				3	5			4	12	14					41
1				6		11	8		9		2	10		7		12		3	5			4							42
1						11	8		9		2	10		7		6		3	5			4	12	14					43
1					12	11	8		9		2	10		7	14	6		3	5			4							44
1					12	11	10				2	8		7		6		3	5			4	14					9	45
1				6	12	11	8				2	10		9		7		3	5			4	14						46

Coca-Cola Cup
First Round Torquay U (h) 1-0
(a) 2-4

FA Cup
First Round Enfield (a) 0-1

CARLISLE UNITED 1994–95 *Back row (left to right):* David Reeves, Tony Hopper, Jeff Thorpe, Tony Gallimore, Paul Murray, Rory Delap, Richard Prokas, Dave Burgess, Dean Walling. *Centre row:* Peter Hampton (Physio/Coach), David Wilkes (Youth/Reserves Coach), Darren Edmondson, Jamie Robinson, Paul Conway, Tony Caig, Tony Elliott, John Pearson, Derek Mountfield, David Currie, Mick Wadsworth (Director of Coaching), Mervyn Day (Coach).
Front row: Neil Dalton, Joe Joyce (Player Coach), Simon Davey, Albert Doweck (Director), Barry Chaytow (Vice Chairman), Michael Knighton (Chairman & Chief Executive), Bob McKnight (Director), Rod Thomas, Ian Arnold, Shane Reddish.

Division 2 CARLISLE UNITED

Brunton Park, Carlisle CA1 1LL. Telephone: (01228) 26237. Fax: (01228) 30138. Commercial Dept: (01228) 24014. Information Line: 0891 230011.

Record attendance: 27,500 v Birmingham C, FA Cup 3rd rd, 5 January 1957 and v Middlesbrough, FA Cup 5th rd, 7 February 1970.

Record receipts: £104,410 v Sunderland, FA Cup 3rd rd replay, 18 January 1994.

Ground capacity: 13,288 (will increase to 17,500).

Pitch measurements: 117yd × 72yd.

Directors: M Knighton (Chairman), B. Chaytow, R. McKnight, A. Doweck.

Director of Coaching: Mick Wadsworth ***Player-Coach:*** Joe Joyce. ***Coach:*** Mervyn Day.

Physio: Peter Hampton.

Commercial Manager: Martin Hudson.

Acting Secretary: A. Ritchie.

Year Formed: 1903. ***Ltd Co.:*** 1921.

Previous Grounds: 1903–5, Milholme Bank; 1905–9, Devonshire Park; 1909– Brunton Park.

Previous Name: Shaddongate United.

Club Nickname: 'Cumbrians' or 'The Blues'.

Foundation: Carlisle United came into being in 1903 through the amalgamation of Shaddongate United and Carlisle Red Rose. The new club was admitted to the Second Division of the Lancashire Combination in 1905–06, winning promotion the following season.

First Football League game: 25 August, 1928, Division 3(N), v Accrington S (a) W 3-2 – Prout; Coulthard, Cook; Harrison, Ross, Pigg; Agar, Hutchison, McConnell (1), Ward (1), Watson. 1 o.g.

Record League Victory: 8–0 v Hartlepools U, Division 3 (N), 1 September 1928 – Prout; Smiles, Cook; Robinson (1) Ross, Pigg; Agar (1), Hutchison (1), McConnell (4), Ward (1), Watson. 8–0 v Scunthorpe United, Division 3 (N), 25 December 1952 – MacLaren; Hill, Scott; Stokoe, Twentyman, Waters; Harrison (1), Whitehouse (5), Ashman (2), Duffett, Bond.

Record Cup Victory: 6–1 v Billingham Synthonia, FA Cup, 1st rd, 17 November 1956 – Fairley; Hill, Kenny; Johnston, Waters, Thompson; Mooney, Broadis (1), Ackerman (2), Garvie (3), Bond.

Record Defeat: 1–11 v Hull C, Division 3 (N), 14 January 1939.

Most League Points (2 for a win): 62, Division 3 (N), 1950–51.

Most League Points (3 for a win): 91, Division 3, 1994–95.

Most League Goals: 113, Division 4, 1963–64.

Highest League Scorer in Season: Jimmy McConnell, 42, Division 3 (N), 1928–29.

Most League Goals in Total Aggregate: Jimmy McConnell, 126, 1928–32.

Most Capped Player: Eric Welsh, 4, Northern Ireland.

Most League Appearances: Alan Ross, 466, 1963–79.

Record Transfer Fee Received: £275,000 from Vancouver Whitecaps for Peter Beardsley, April 1981.

Record Transfer Fee Paid: £121,000 to Notts Co for David Reeves, December 1993.

Football League Record: 1928 Elected to Division 3 (N); 1958–62 Division 4; 1962–63 Division 3; 1963–64 Division 4; 1964–65 Division 3; 1965–74 Division 2; 1974–75 Division 1; 1975–77 Division 2; 1977–82 Division 3; 1982–86 Division 2; 1986–87 Division 3; 1987–92 Division 4; 1992–95 Division 3; 1995– Division 2.

Honours: *Football League:* Division 1 best season: 22nd, 1974–75; Promoted from Division 2 (3rd) 1973–74; Division 3 – Champions 1964–65, 1994–95; Runners-up 1981–82; Division 4 – Runners-up 1963–64. *FA Cup:* 6th rd 1975. *Football League Cup:* Semi-final 1970. *Auto Windscreens Shield:* Runners-up 1995.

Colours: Blue shirts, white shorts, blue stockings. **Change colours:** Red shirts, green shorts, white stockings.

CARLISLE UNITED 1994–95 LEAGUE RECORD

Match No.	Date	Venue	Opponents	Result		H/T Score	Lg. Pos.	Goalscorers	Attendance
1	Aug 13	H	Wigan Ath	W	2-1	1-0	—	Reeves, Walling	6231
2	20	A	Torquay U	D	1-1	0-0	5	Reeves	3506
3	27	H	Scarborough	W	2-0	2-0	4	Mountfield, Reeves	5720
4	30	A	Walsall	W	2-1	1-1	—	Reeves 2	3610
5	Sept 3	A	Scunthorpe U	W	3-2	0-2	1	Gallimore, Thorpe 2	3217
6	10	H	Exeter C	W	1-0	1-0	1	Thomas	6213
7	13	H	Mansfield T	W	2-1	0-0	—	Thomas, Currie	6136
8	17	A	Wigan Ath	W	2-0	0-0	1	Edmondson, Reeves	3003
9	24	A	Northampton T	L	1-2	0-1	2	Reeves	3508
10	Oct 1	H	Darlington	W	2-1	0-1	1	Gallimore (pen), Walling	6100
11	8	A	Lincoln C	D	1-1	0-0	1	Reeves	3097
12	15	H	Colchester U	D	0-0	0-0	2		5817
13	22	H	Barnet	W	4-0	1-0	2	Reeves, Conway, Davey, Thomas	6155
14	29	A	Fulham	W	3-1	2-0	2	Reeves, Mountfield, Conway	5563
15	Nov 5	H	Rochdale	W	4-1	1-0	2	Davey 2, Reeves, Edmondson	5984
16	19	A	Hereford U	W	1-0	1-0	1	Conway	2531
17	26	H	Doncaster R	D	1-1	0-0	1	Walling	7781
18	Dec 10	H	Torquay U	W	1-0	1-0	1	Thomas	5141
19	17	A	Scarborough	W	2-1	1-1	1	Gallimore (pen), Currie	1910
20	26	A	Hartlepool U	W	5-1	1-0	1	Mountfield, Conway, Reeves 2, Gallimore (pen)	3854
21	27	H	Bury	W	3-0	1-0	1	Currie, Conway, Reeves	12,242
22	31	A	Gillingham	W	1-0	0-0	1	Walling	3682
23	Jan 14	H	Preston NE	D	0-0	0-0	1		10,684
24	21	A	Rochdale	D	1-1	0-0	1	Walling	3289
25	24	A	Barnet	W	2-0	0-0	—	Currie, Davey	2413
26	28	H	Fulham	D	1-1	1-1	1	Thomas	6891
27	Feb 4	A	Doncaster R	D	0-0	0-0	1		3587
28	11	H	Hereford U	W	1-0	1-0	1	Gallimore (pen)	5676
29	18	A	Preston NE	L	0-1	0-1	1		11,867
30	25	A	Darlington	W	2-0	1-0	1	Thomas, Reeves	3992
31	Mar 4	H	Northampton T	W	2-1	2-0	1	Walling 2	6755
32	11	A	Exeter C	D	1-1	1-1	1	Reeves	2673
33	18	H	Walsall	W	2-1	0-1	1	Reeves 2	7769
34	25	H	Scunthorpe U	W	2-1	0-0	1	Aspinall, Hayward	6704
35	Apr 1	A	Mansfield T	W	2-1	1-1	1	Prokas, Thorpe	5197
36	4	H	Chesterfield	D	1-1	0-0	—	Robinson	8478
37	8	H	Gillingham	W	2-0	2-0	1	Thorpe, Hayward	6786
38	15	A	Bury	L	0-2	0-0	1		5507
39	17	H	Hartlepool U	L	0-1	0-1	1		10,242
40	29	A	Colchester U	W	1-0	0-0	1	Reeves	3333
41	May 2	A	Chesterfield	W	2-1	1-1	—	Reeves 2	7283
42	6	H	Lincoln C	L	1-3	0-1	1	Conway	12,412

Final League Position: 1

GOALSCORERS

League (67): Reeves 21, Walling 7, Conway 6, Thomas 6, Gallimore 5 (4 pens), Currie 4, Davey 4, Thorpe 4, Mountfield 3, Edmondson 2, Hayward 2, Aspinall 1, Prokas 1, Robinson 1.
Coca-Cola Cup (3): Reeves 2, Walling 1.
FA Cup (8): Conway 2, Reeves 2, Currie 1, Davey 1, Mountfield 1, Walling 1.

Caig A. 40	Joyce J.P. 17 + 4	Gallimore A.M. 40	Walling D.A. 41	Mountfield D.N. 30 + 1	Edmondson D.S. 36 + 2	Thomas R.C. 36	Currie D.N. 38	Reeves D. 42	Davey S. 25	Reddish S. 2	Thorpe J.R. 7 + 21	Pearson J.S. — + 1	Prokas R. 37 + 2	Peacock L.A. 2 + 5	Valentine P. 9	Robinson J. 6 + 8	Arnold I. 1 + 3	Lowe K. 1 + 1	Murray P. 2 + 3	Conway P.J. 24	Peters R.A.A. 5 + 3	Delap R.J. 2 + 1	Elliott A.R. 2 + 1	Aspinall W. 6 + 1	Hayward S.L. 9	Hopper T. 2 + 3	Match No.
1	2	3	4	5	6	7	*8*	9	10	11	12	14															1
1	2	3	4	5	6	7	8	9		10	12		11														2
1	2	3	4	5	6	7	8	9	10		12		11	14													3
1	2	3	4		6	7	8	9	10		12		*11*		5	14											4
1	2	3	4		6	7	*8*	9	10		12		11		5	14											5
1	2	3	4		12	7	*8*	9	10		6		11		5		14										6
1	2	3	4		6	7	8	9	10		12		11		5												7
1	2	3	4		6	7	8	9	10		12		11		5												8
1	2	3	4	6	12	7	8	9	10				14		5			*11*									9
1	2	3	4		6	7	8	9	10		12		11		5		14										10
1	2	3	4	12	6	7	*8*	9	10		14		11		5												11
1	2	3	4		*6*	7		9	10				11	12	5		8	14									12
1			4	5	2	7	8	9	10		12		11						3	6							13
1		3	4	5	2	7	8	9	10				11							6							14
1		3	4	5	2	7	8	9	10				11				12		14	*6*							15
1	12	3	4	5	2	7	8	9	10				11							6							16
1		3	4	5	2	7	8	9	10				11							6							17
1		3	4	5	2	7	8	9					11							6	10						18
1		3	4	5	2	7	*8*	9			12		11							6	10		15				19
1	12	3	4	5	2		*8*	9			7		11							6	10	14					20
1		3	4	5	2	7	8	9	10		12		11							6							21
		3	4	5	2		8	9	10		7		11							6	12		1				22
1		3	4	5	2	7	8	9	10		12		11							6							23
1		3	4	5	2	7	8	9	10		12		11							6							24
1	2	3	4	5		7	8	9	10				11			12				6							25
1		3	4	5	2	7	8	9	10		12		11							6							26
1		3	4	5	2	7	8	9	10				11			12				6							27
1		3	4	5	2	7	8	9	10				11							6	12						28
1		3	4	5	2	7	8	9	10				12						11	*6*	14						29
1		3	4	5	2	7	8	9					11			12				10	6						30
1		3	4	5	*2*	7	8	9			12		11			14				10	6						31
1		3	4	5	2	7	8	9			12		11							10				6			32
1		3	4	5	2		8	9			12		11							10				6	7		33
1		3		5	2		*8*	9			14		11	12		4				10				6	7		34
1	2	3	4	5		7	8	9			12		11	14										*6*	10		35
1	*11*	3	4		2	7		9			8			6		5			12						10	14	36
1	12		4	5	2	7		9			8		11	6		3									10	14	37
1	2	3	4	5			8	9			7		11			12						10				6	38
1	2	3	4	5		7	8	9					11			12								*6*	10	14	39
1	12	3	4		2	7	8	9			14		11			5				6					10		40
		3	4		2			9			11			14		5			12			7	1	*6*	10	8	41
1		3	4		2	7	8	9					11			5				6				12	10		42

Coca-Cola Cup

First Round	Rotherham U (a)	0-1
	(h)	3-1
Second Round	QPR (h)	0-1
	(a)	0-2

FA Cup

First Round	Guiseley (a) (at Bradford)	4-1
Second Round	Darlington (h)	2-0
Third Round	Sunderland (a)	1-1
	(h)	1-3

CHARLTON ATHLETIC 1994–95 *Back row (left to right):* Scott McGleish, Steve Brown, Richard Rufus, Mike Ammann, Mike Salmon, Andy Petterson, Carl Leaburn, Dean Chandler, Danny Mills.
Centre row: Jimmy Hendry (Physio), Lee Bowyer, Shaun Newton, Mickey Bennett, Paul Sturgess, Phil Chapple, Kim Grant, David Whyte, Mark Robson, Paul Linger, Neil Banfield (Youth Development Officer).
Front row: Paul Mortimer, Alan Pardew, Garry Nelson, Alan McLeary, Keith Peacock (Reserve Team Coach), Steve Gritt (Player/Manager), Alan Curbishley (Player/Manager), Stuart Balmer, Colin Walsh, Peter Garland, John Robinson.
(Photograph: Tom Morris)

Division 1 CHARLTON ATHLETIC

The Valley, Floyd Road, Charlton, London SE7 8BL. Telephone: (0181) 293 4567. Fax: (0181) 293 5143. Box Office: (0181) 858 5888. Clubcall 0891 121146.

Ground capacity: 15,000.

Record attendance: 75,031 v Aston Villa, FA Cup 5th rd, 12 February 1938 (at The Valley).

Record receipts: £114,618.70 v Liverpool (at Selhurst Park), Division 1, 23 January 1988.

Pitch measurements: 110yd × 73yd.

President: R. D. Collins.

Chairman: M. A. Simons. ***Vice-Chairman:*** R. A. Murray.

Directors: R. N. Alwen, G. P. Bone, S. T. Clarke, R. D. Collins, J. T. T. Fuller, M. C. Stevens, D. G. Ufton.

Manager: Alan Curbishley.

Reserve team manager: Keith Peacock. ***Youth Team Manager:*** Neil Banfield. ***Youth Development Officer:*** Steve Watts. ***Physio:*** Jimmy Hendry.

Secretary: Chris Parkes.

Marketing Manager: Steve Dixon.

Year Formed: 1905. ***Turned Professional:*** 1920. ***Ltd Co.:*** 1919.

Club Nickname: 'Addicks'.

Previous Grounds: 1906, Siemen's Meadow; 1907, Woolwich Common; 1909, Pound Park; 1913, Horn Lane; 1920, The Valley; 1923, Catford (The Mount); 1924, The Valley; 1985 Selhurst Park; 1991 Upton Park; 1992 The Valley.

Foundation: The club was formed on 9 June 1905, by a group of 14 and 15-year-old youths living in streets by the Thames in the area which now borders the Thames Barrier. The club's progress through local leagues was so rapid that after the First World War they joined the Kent League where they spent a season before turning professional and joining the Southern League in 1920. A year later they were elected to the Football League's Division 3 (South).

First Football League game: 27 August, 1921, Division 3(S), v Exeter C (h) W 1-0 – Hughes; Mitchell, Goodman; Dowling (1), Hampson, Dunn; Castle, Bailey, Halse, Green, Wilson.

Record League Victory: 8–1 v Middlesbrough, Division 1, 12 September 1953 – Bartram; Campbell, Ellis; Fenton, Ufton, Hammond; Hurst (2), O'Linn (2), Leary (1), Firmani (3), Kiernan.

Record Cup Victory: 7–0 v Burton A, FA Cup, 3rd rd, 7 January 1956 – Bartram; Campbell, Townsend; Hewie, Ufton, Hammond; Hurst (1), Gauld (1), Leary (3), White, Kiernan (2).

Record Defeat: 1–11 v Aston Villa, Division 2, 14 November 1959.

Most League Points (2 for a win): 61, Division 3 (S), 1934–35.

Most League Points (3 for a win): 77, Division 2, 1985–86.

Most League Goals: 107, Division 2, 1957–58.

Highest League Scorer in Season: Ralph Allen, 32, Division 3 (S), 1934–35.

Most League Goals in Total Aggregate: Stuart Leary, 153, 1953–62.

Most Capped Player: John Hewie, 19, Scotland.

Most League Appearances: Sam Bartram, 583, 1934–56.

Record Transfer Fee Received: £750,000 from Newcastle U for Robert Lee, September 1992.

Record Transfer Fee Paid: £600,000 to Chelsea for Joe McLaughlin, August 1989.

Football League Record: 1921 Elected to Division 3 (S); 1929–33 Division 2; 1933–35 Division 3 (S); 1935–36 Division 2; 1936–57 Division 1; 1957–72 Division 2; 1972–75 Division 3; 1975–80 Division 2; 1980–81 Division 3; 1981–86; Division 2; 1986–90 Division 1; 1990–92 Division 2; 1992– Division 1.

Honours: *Football League:* Division 1 – Runners-up 1936–37; Division 2 – Runners-up 1935–36, 1985–86; Division 3 (S) – Champions 1928–29, 1934–35; Promoted from Division 3 (3rd) 1974–75, 1980–81. *FA Cup:* Winners 1947; Runners-up 1946. *Football League Cup:* best season: 4th rd, 1963, 1966, 1979. *Full Members Cup:* Runners-up 1987.

Colours: Red shirts, white shorts, red stockings. **Change colours:** White shirts, black shorts, white stockings.

CHARLTON ATHLETIC 1994–95 LEAGUE RECORD

Match No.	Date		Venue	Opponents	Result		H/T Score	Lg. Pos.	Goalscorers	Attendance
1	Aug	13	A	Oldham Ath	L	2-5	2-2	—	Whyte, Robinson	8924
2		20	H	Barnsley	D	2-2	0-0	16	Whyte, Chapple	8171
3		27	A	Portsmouth	D	1-1	1-1	18	Nelson	10,566
4		30	H	Sheffield U	D	1-1	1-1	—	Brown (pen)	8678
5	Sept	3	H	Bristol C	W	3-2	1-0	14	Mortimer, Whyte 2	9019
6		10	A	Grimsby T	W	1-0	0-0	8	Robson	3970
7		14	A	Stoke C	L	2-3	0-2	—	Nelson, Whyte	10,643
8		17	H	Swindon T	W	1-0	1-0	8	Whyte	9794
9		24	A	Notts Co	D	3-3	1-2	7	Nelson 2, Whyte	5726
10	Oct	1	H	Watford	W	3-0	0-0	6	Nelson, Grant, Whyte	8169
11		8	H	Reading	L	1-2	0-1	6	Robson	10,544
12		15	A	Port Vale	W	2-0	0-0	6	Chapple, Whyte	7707
13		22	H	Burnley	L	1-2	0-0	6	Whyte	9436
14		29	A	Derby Co	D	2-2	1-1	6	Grant 2	12,588
15	Nov	1	A	Sunderland	D	1-1	0-1	—	Grant	14,085
16		5	H	Bolton W	L	1-2	0-1	10	Brown (pen)	9793
17		13	H	WBA	D	1-1	1-0	11	Grant	10,876
18		19	A	Tranmere R	D	1-1	1-0	11	Nelson	7567
19		26	H	Middlesbrough	L	0-2	0-1	16		10,019
20	Dec	10	A	Barnsley	L	1-2	0-1	19	Mortimer	5465
21		17	H	Oldham Ath	W	2-0	0-0	17	Whyte, Jones	8970
22		26	H	Southend U	W	3-1	0-1	16	Whyte, Leaburn 2	9525
23		28	A	Wolverhampton W	L	0-2	0-2	—		26,738
24	Jan	1	H	Millwall	D	1-1	0-1	16	Robinson	10,655
25		2	A	Luton T	W	1-0	1-0	15	Whyte	7642
26		14	H	Derby Co	L	3-4	3-1	17	Whyte, Pardew, Robson	9389
27		21	A	Bolton W	L	1-5	1-2	17	Whyte	10,516
28	Feb	5	A	WBA	W	1-0	0-0	14	Nelson	12,084
29		11	H	Sunderland	W	1-0	0-0	12	Whyte	12,380
30		18	A	Middlesbrough	L	0-1	0-1	12		16,301
31		21	H	Tranmere R	L	0-1	0-0	—		11,860
32	Mar	4	H	Notts Co	W	1-0	1-0	14	Mortimer	13,638
33		7	A	Bristol C	L	1-2	0-1	—	Pardew	6118
34		11	H	Portsmouth	W	1-0	1-0	13	Leaburn	9443
35		18	A	Sheffield U	L	1-2	0-0	13	Pardew	11,862
36		21	H	Grimsby T	W	2-1	1-1	—	Robinson, Balmer	9601
37		25	A	Swindon T	W	1-0	0-0	12	Grant	9106
38	Apr	1	H	Stoke C	D	0-0	0-0	13		10,008
39		4	A	Burnley	L	0-2	0-1	—		10,045
40		8	A	Millwall	L	1-3	1-2	14	Balmer	9506
41		15	H	Wolverhampton W	W	3-2	1-1	14	Whyte, Walsh, Mortimer	10,922
42		18	A	Southend U	L	1-2	0-0	—	Whyte	6397
43		22	H	Luton T	W	1-0	0-0	13	Whyte	10,867
44		29	H	Port Vale	D	1-1	1-1	13	Brown	12,596
45	May	2	A	Watford	L	0-2	0-0	—		6024
46		7	A	Reading	L	1-2	0-1	15	Chandler	12,137

Final League Position: 15

GOALSCORERS

League (58): Whyte 19, Nelson 7, Grant 6, Mortimer 4, Brown 3 (2 pens), Leaburn 3, Pardew 3, Robinson 3, Robson 3, Balmer 2, Chapple 2, Chandler 1, Jones 1, Walsh 1.
Coca-Cola Cup (4): Nelson 2, Whyte 2.
FA Cup (0).

Salmon M.B. 20	Brown S.B. 42	Sturgess P.C. 23	Mortimer P.H. 26	Chapple P.R. 21	McLeary A.T. 22	Robinson J.R.C. 16 + 5	Nelson G.P. 21 + 6	Pardew A.S. 22 + 2	Whyte D.A. 36 + 2	Walsh C.D. 23 + 5	Grant K.T. 14 + 12	Robson M.A. 40	Garland P.J. 6 + 4	Linger P.H. 3 + 5	Ammann M.A. 18 + 1	Newton S.O. 10 + 16	Balmer S.M. 28 + 1	Petterson A.K. 8 + 1	Jones K.A. 31	Leaburn C.W. 22 + 5	Bowyer L.D. 5	McGleish S. — + 6	Bennett M.R. 9 + 5	Rufus R.R. 27 + 1	Hovi T.H. — + 2	Stuart J.C. 12	Chandler D.A.R. 1	*Match No.*
1	2	3	4	5	6	7	8	9	10	11	12																	1
1	2	3	4	5	6	7	8	9	10			*11*	12	14	15													2
	2	3	4	5	6	7	8		10		12	*11*	9		1	14												3
	2	3	*4*	5	6	7	8		10		12	11	9		1		14											4
	2	3	4	5	6		8		10	14	12	*11*	9		1	7												5
	2	3	4	5	6		8		10	14	12	*11*	9		1	7												6
	2	3		5	6		8	14	10	4	12	11	*9*		1	7												7
	2	3		5			8	12	10	9		*11*				7	6	1	4	14								8
	2	3		5			8		10	*9*	12	11	14			7	6	1	4									9
	2	3		5			8		10	9	12	11				14	6	1	*4*		7							10
	2	3		5			8		10	*9*	12	11				14	6	1	4		7							11
	2	3		5					10	9	8	11					6	1	4		7	12						12
	2	3		5					10	9	8	11					6	1	4		7	12						13
	2	3		5	6	*11*			10	9	8				1	12			4				7	14				14
	2	3		5	6	11		10		9	*8*			14	1	12							7	4				15
	2	3		9	6	*11*		10			8	7			1	14			4	12				5				16
	2	3			6		10	4		11	8	7			1	12				9				5				17
	2	3			6		10			11	8	7			1	12			4	9				5				18
	2	3			6		10		12	*11*	8	7			1	14			4	9				5				19
	2	3	11		6		12		10						1	7	8		4	9				5				20
1	2	3	11		6				10	12		7					8		4	9				5				21
1	2	3	11		6		14		10	12		7					*8*		4	9				5				22
1	*2*		3	5	6		12		10	11		7					8		4	9			14					23
1			3	5	6	8	12		10	*11*		7				14			4	9			2					24
1	2		4	5	6	8	12	11	10			7								9			3					25
1	2		*3*	5	6		12	8	10	11		7								9			4		14			26
	2		3		6		8	9	10	11	12	7			1								4	5	14			27
1	2		11				8	9	*10*			7					6		4			14	12	5		3		28
1	2					12	*8*	9	10			7					6		4			14	11	5		3		29
1	2					12	8	9	10			7					6		4			14	*11*	5		3		30
1	2					12	*8*	9	10			7					6		4	14			11	5		3		31
1	2		*11*			12	8	9	10			7					6		4	14				5		3		32
1	2		11			12	8	9	10			7					6		4	14				5		*3*		33
1	2		3			11		9	10			7				12	6		4	8				5				34
1			3	2		11		9	10	4	12	7					6			8				5				35
1	2		3			11		9			10	7		12		14	6		4	8				5				36
1	*2*		3			11		9			10	7		12		14	6		4	8				5				37
1	2		3			11		9	12		10	7				14	6		4	8				5				38
1	2		3			11		9			*10*	7				12	6	15	4	8			14	5				39
		3	7		*2*	11		9		12	10			4			6	1		8			14	5				40
	2		11					9	10	4		7			1	12	6			8				5		3		41
	2								10	11	8	7	12	9	1	5	6		4							3		42
	2		11						10	9		7			1		6		4	8		12		5		3		43
	2								10	9		7	12		1	11	6		4	8				5		3		44
	2								10	9			11	12	1	7	6		4	8				5		3		45
									10		12	7		*11*		2		1	4	8	9		14	5		3	6	46

Coca-Cola Cup

Second Round	Swindon T (a)	3-1
	(h)	1-4

FA Cup

Third Round	Chelsea (a)	0-3

CHELSEA 1994–95 *Back row (left to right):* David Collyer (Youth Development Officer), Anthony Barness, Neil Shipperley, Nigel Spackman, Michael Duberry, Jacob Kjeldbjerg, Erland Johnsen, Paul Furlong, Paul Hughes, Craig Norman, Mustafa Izzett, Gwyn Williams (Chief Scout/Youth Development Officer).
Centre row: Eddie Niedzwiecki (Reserve Team Manager), Bob Ward (Physio), Scott Minto, Darren Barnard, Zeke Rowe, Andy Myers, Kevin Hitchcock, Dmitri Kharine, Nick Colgan, Steve Clarke, Terry Skiverton, David Hopkin, Craig Burley, Graham Rix (Youth Team Manager), Terry Byrne (Kit Manager/Club Masseur).
Front row: Eddie Newton, Andy Dow, Gareth Hall, Mark Stein, Dennis Wise, Glenn Hoddle (Manager), Peter Shreeves (Assistant Manager), Gavin Peacock, David Rocastle, Robert Fleck, John Spencer, Frank Sinclair
(Photograph: Action Images)

FA Premiership **CHELSEA**

Stamford Bridge, London SW6 1HS. Telephone: (0171) 385 5545. Fax: (0171) 381 4831. Clubcall: 0891 121159. Ticket News and Promotions: 0891 121011. Ticket credit card service: (0171) 386 7799.

Ground capacity: 31,791 (during ground development); 41,000 (eventually).

Record attendance: 82,905 v Arsenal, Division 1, 12 Oct 1935.

Record receipts: £465,324 v Manchester U, FA Premier League, 11 September 1993.

Pitch measurements: 110yd × 74yd.

President: G. M. Thomson.

Chairman: K. W. Bates.

Directors: C. Hutchinson (Managing), Y. S. Todd, M. Harding.

Team Manager: Glenn Hoddle. ***Assistant Manager:*** Peter Shreeves.

Physio: Michael Banks. ***Reserve Team Manager:*** Eddie Niedzwiecki.

Company Secretary/Director: Yvonne Todd. ***Match Secretary:*** Keith Lacy. ***Commercial Manager:*** Carole Phair.

Year Formed: 1905. ***Turned Professional:*** 1905. ***Ltd Co.:*** 1905.

Club Nickname: 'The Blues'.

Foundation: Chelsea may never have existed but for the fact that Fulham rejected an offer to rent the Stamford Bridge ground from Mr. H. A. Mears who had owned it since 1904. Fortunately he was determined to develop it as a football stadium rather than sell it to the Great Western Railway and got together with Frederick Parker, who persuaded Mears of the financial advantages of developing a major sporting venue. Chelsea FC was formed in 1905, and when admission to the Southern League was denied, they immediately gained admission to the Second Division of the Football League.

First Football League game: 2 September, 1905, Division 2, v Stockport C (a) L 0-1 – Foulke; Mackie, McEwan; Key, Harris, Miller; Moran, J.T. Robertson, Copeland, Windridge, Kirwan.

Record League Victory: 9–2 v Glossop N E, Division 2, 1 September 1906 – Byrne; Walton, Miller; Key (1), McRoberts, Henderson; Moran, McDermott (1), Hilsdon (5), Copeland (1), Kirwan (1).

Record Cup Victory: 13–0 v Jeunesse Hautcharage, ECWC, 1st rd 2nd leg, 29 September 1971 – Bonetti; Boyle, Harris (1), Hollins (1p), Webb (1), Hinton, Cooke, Baldwin (3), Osgood (5), Hudson (1), Houseman (1).

Record Defeat: 1–8 v Wolverhampton W, Division 1, 26 September 1953.

Most League Points (2 for a win): 57, Division 2, 1906–07.

Most League Points (3 for a win): 99, Division 2, 1988–89.

Most League Goals: 98, Division 1, 1960–61.

Highest League Scorer in Season: Jimmy Greaves, 41, 1960–61.

Most League Goals in Total Aggregate: Bobby Tambling, 164, 1958–70.

Most Capped Player: Ray Wilkins, 24 (84), England.

Most League Appearances: Ron Harris, 655, 1962–80.

Record Transfer Fee Received: £2,200,000 from Tottenham H for Gordon Durie, July 1991.

Record Transfer Fee Paid: £2,300,000 to Norwich C for Robert Fleck, July 1992.

Football League Record: 1905 Elected to Division 2; 1907–10 Division 1; 1910–12 Division 2; 1912–24 Division 1; 1924–30 Division 2; 1930–62 Division 1; 1962–63 Division 2; 1963–75 Division 1; 1975–77 Division 2; 1977–79 Division 1; 1979–84 Division 2; 1984–88 Division 1; 1988–89 Division 2; 1989–92 Division 1; 1992– FA Premier League.

Honours: *Football League:* Division 1 – Champions 1954–55; Division 2 – Champions 1983–84, 1988–89; Runners-up 1906–7, 1911–12, 1929–30, 1962–63, 1976–77. *FA Cup:* Winners 1970; Runners-up 1915, 1967, 1994. *Football League Cup:* Winners 1965; Runners-up 1972. *Full Members' Cup:* Winners 1986. *Zenith Data Systems Cup:* Winners 1990. **European Competitions:** *European Fairs Cup:* 1958–60, 1965–66, 1968–69; *European Cup-Winners' Cup:* 1970–71 (winners), 1971–72, 1994–95.

Colours: Royal blue, amber shirts, royal blue, white shorts, white stockings. **Change colours:** Graphite, tangerine and navy shirts, tangerine, navy and graphite shorts, tangerine, navy and graphite stockings.

CHELSEA 1994–95 LEAGUE RECORD

Match No.	Date	Venue	Opponents	Result		H/T Score	Lg. Pos.	Goalscorers	Attendance
1	Aug 20	H	Norwich C	W	2-0	1-0	—	Sinclair, Furlong	23,098
2	27	A	Leeds U	W	3-2	1-2	7	Wise (pen), Spencer 2	32,212
3	31	H	Manchester C	W	3-0	1-0	—	Peacock, Wise, Vonk (og)	21,740
4	Sept 10	A	Newcastle U	L	2-4	2-2	7	Peacock, Furlong	34,435
5	18	H	Blackburn R	L	1-2	0-1	7	Spencer	17,513
6	24	A	Crystal Palace	W	1-0	0-0	5	Furlong	16,064
7	Oct 2	H	West Ham U	L	1-2	0-0	7	Furlong	18,696
8	8	H	Leicester C	W	4-0	2-0	6	Spencer 2, Peacock, Shipperley	18,397
9	15	A	Arsenal	L	1-3	1-1	7	Wise	38,234
10	23	H	Ipswich T	W	2-0	0-0	7	Wise, Shipperley	15,068
11	29	A	Sheffield W	D	1-1	1-0	7	Wise	25,356
12	Nov 6	H	Coventry C	D	2-2	0-1	8	Spencer, Kjeldbjerg	17,090
13	9	A	Liverpool	L	1-3	1-3	—	Spencer	32,855
14	19	A	Nottingham F	W	1-0	1-0	7	Spencer	22,092
15	23	A	Tottenham H	D	0-0	0-0	—		27,037
16	26	H	Everton	L	0-1	0-1	8		28,115
17	Dec 3	A	Southampton	W	1-0	0-0	7	Furlong	14,404
18	10	A	Norwich C	L	0-3	0-2	8		18,246
19	18	H	Liverpool	D	0-0	0-0	8		27,050
20	26	H	Manchester U	L	2-3	0-1	9	Spencer (pen), Newton	31,139
21	28	A	Aston Villa	L	0-3	0-2	10		32,901
22	31	H	Wimbledon	D	1-1	0-0	10	Furlong	16,009
23	Jan 14	H	Sheffield W	D	1-1	1-0	12	Spencer	17,285
24	21	A	Ipswich T	D	2-2	0-0	12	Stein, Burley	17,619
25	25	H	Nottingham F	L	0-2	0-1	—		17,890
26	Feb 4	A	Coventry C	D	2-2	2-2	12	Stein, Spencer (pen)	13,423
27	11	H	Tottenham H	D	1-1	0-1	13	Wise	30,812
28	25	A	West Ham U	W	2-1	0-1	13	Burley, Stein	21,500
29	Mar 5	H	Crystal Palace	D	0-0	0-0	13		14,130
30	8	A	Manchester C	W	2-1	1-1	—	Stein 2	21,880
31	11	H	Leeds U	L	0-3	0-2	11		20,174
32	18	A	Blackburn R	L	1-2	1-2	14	Stein	25,490
33	22	A	QPR	L	0-1	0-0	—		15,103
34	Apr 1	H	Newcastle U	D	1-1	1-0	15	Peacock	22,987
35	10	A	Wimbledon	D	1-1	1-0	—	Sinclair	7022
36	12	H	Southampton	L	0-2	0-2	—		16,739
37	15	H	Aston Villa	W	1-0	1-0	14	Stein	17,015
38	17	A	Manchester U	D	0-0	0-0	14		43,728
39	29	H	QPR	W	1-0	0-0	12	Sinclair	21,704
40	May 3	A	Everton	D	3-3	1-1	—	Furlong 2, Hopkin	33,180
41	6	A	Leicester C	D	1-1	1-1	12	Furlong	18,140
42	14	H	Arsenal	W	2-1	1-1	11	Furlong, Stein	29,542

Final League Position: 11

GOALSCORERS

League (50): Spencer 11 (2 pens), Furlong 10, Stein 8, Wise 6 (1 pen), Peacock 4, Sinclair 3, Burley 2, Shipperley 2, Hopkin 1, Kjeldbjerg 1, Newton 1, own goal 1.
Coca-Cola Cup (2): Peacock 1, Rocastle 1.
FA Cup (4): Peacock 1, Sinclair 1, Spencer 1, Stein 1.

Kharine D.V. 31	Clarke S. 29	Sinclair F.M. 35	Kjeldbjerg J. 23	Johnsen E. 33	Spackman N. 36	Rocastle D.C. 26 + 2	Shipperley N.J. 6 + 4	Furlong P.A. 30 + 6	Peacock G.K. 38	Wise D.F. 18 + 1	Newton E.J.I. 22 + 8	Hoddle G. 3 + 9	Spencer J. 26 + 3	Barness A. 10 + 2	Lee D.J. 9 + 5	Hall G.D. 4 + 2	Hopkin D. 7 + 8	Myers A. 9 + 1	Hitchcock K. 11 + 1	Burley C.W. 16 + 9	Minto S.C. 19	Stein M.E.S. 21 + 3	Rix G. — + 1	Match No.
1	2	3	4	5	6	7	8	9	10	11	12	14												1
1	2	3	4	5	6	7		9	10	11	12		8											2
1	2	3	4	5	6	7		9	10	11	12		8											3
1	2	3	4	5	6	7		9	10	11	12	14	8											4
1	2	3	4	5	6	7		9	10	11	12		8											5
1	2	3	4	5	6	7		9	10		11		8											6
1	2	3	4	5		7	12	9	10		6		8	11	14									7
1	2	3	4	5	6	7	14	9	10	11	12		8											8
1	2	3	4	5	6	7	12	9	10	11	8													9
1			4	5		7	8	9	10	11	6			3	12	2	14							10
1			4	5	6	7	9			11	8			3		2	10	12						11
			4	5	6	7	9				11		8	2			10	3	1	12				12
			4	5	6	7	9			11	10		8	2			12	3	1	14				13
1			4	5	6	7	12		10	11	9		8	2						14	3			14
1		5	4		6	7	9			11	10		8	2	14					12	3			15
1		5	4		6			12	10	11	9	14	8	2						7	3			16
1		5	4		6			12	10	11	9		8	2			14			7	3			17
1		4		5	6			9	10	11	7		8	2						12	3			18
1		4		5	6	7		9	10	11	2	8		12							3	14		19
1	2	4		5	6			9	10		12	7	8					3		11		14		20
1	2	6		5	11			9	10		8		7					3		4		12		21
1	2	3	4	5	6			8	10		11	12	7									9		22
1	2	6	4	5	11			8	10		12		7								3	9		23
1		6	4	5	11			8	10		2		7				12			14	3	9		24
1		4		5	6			8	10	12	11		7							2	3	9		25
1	2	6		5	8	12		14	10	11			7							4	3	9		26
1	2	6				7		12	10	11	4	14	8		5						3	9		27
1	2			5		7		12	10		6		8		4				15	11	3	9		28
	2	6		5	4	12			10		7		8					3	1	11		9		29
	2	6		5		7		8	10		4						12	3	1	11		9		30
	2	6		5		7		8	10		4			14			12	3	1	11		9		31
	2	6		5	4	7		8	10						12	14		3	1	11		9		32
	2			5	6	7		8	10			12			4			3	1	11		9		33
	2	6		5	4	11		8	10				7				14		1	12	3	9		34
		6	4		5			8	10				12			2	11		1	7	3	9		35
1	2	6	4		5			12	10				8		14		11			7	3	9		36
1	2	3	4	5	11	7		8	10				12		6	14						9		37
	2	6		5	11	7		8	10				12		4	3			1	14		9		38
1	2	6		5	11	7		8	10			12			4		14				3	9		39
1	2	6			5			8	10			12			4		7			11	3	9		40
	2	6			5			8	10			12			4		7		1	11	3	9		41
1	2	6			5			8	10			7			4		11			12	3	9	14	42

Coca-Cola Cup

Second Round	Bournemouth (h)	1-0
	(a)	1-0
Third Round	West Ham U (a)	0-1

FA Cup

Third Round	Charlton Ath (h)	3-0
Fourth Round	Millwall (a)	0-0
	(h)	1-1

CHESTER CITY 1994–95 *Back row (left to right):* Iain Cannon, Don Page, Jason Burnham, Julian Aisford, Dave Feigate, Spencer Whelan, Ray Newland, Chris Lightfoot, Andy Milner, Leroy Chambers, Brett Bariow.
Centre row: Dave Turner, Gary Shelton, Roger Preece, Eddie Bishop, Kevin Ratcliffe, Mike Pejic, Dave Flitcroft, Iain Jenkins, Stuart Rimmer, John Murphy.
Front row: Ian Bold, Greg Briggs, Philip Wood, Steven Spence, Roy Sweeney, Greg Brown, Steven Moss.

Division 3 CHESTER CITY

The Deva Stadium, Bumpers Lane, Chester, CH1 4LT. Telephone: (01244) 371376, 371809. Fax: (01244) 390265. Commercial: (01244) 390243.

Ground capacity: 6000.

Record attendance: 20,500 v Chelsea, FA Cup 3rd rd (replay), 16 January, 1952 (at Sealand Road).

Record receipts: £30,609 v Sheffield W, FA Cup 4th rd, 31 January 1987.

Pitch measurements: 115yd × 78yd.

Club Patron: Duke of Westminster.

Chairman: M. S. Guterman. ***Director:*** I. G. Morris. ***Manager:*** Kevin Ratcliffe. ***General Manager:*** Bill Wingrove.

Secretary: Derek Barber JP, AMITD. ***Physio:*** Derek Mann.

Year Formed: 1884. ***Turned Professional:*** 1902. ***Ltd Co.:*** 1909.

Previous Name: Chester until 1983.

Club Nickname: 'Blues' and 'City'.

Previous Grounds: Faulkner Street; Old Showground; 1904, Whipcord Lane; 1906, Sealand Road; 1990, Moss Rose Ground, Macclesfield; 1992, The Stadium, Bumpers Lane.

Foundation: All students of soccer history have read about the medieval games of football in Chester, but the present club was not formed until 1884 through the amalgamation of King's School Old Boys with Chester Rovers. For many years Chester were overshadowed in Cheshire by Northwich Victoria and Crewe Alexandra who had both won the Senior Cup several times before Chester's first success in 1894–95.

First Football League game: 2 September, 1931, Division 3(N), v Wrexham (a) D 1-1 – Johnson; Herod, Jones; Keeley, Skitt, Reilly; Thompson, Ranson, Jennings (1), Cresswell, Hedley.

Record League Victory: 12–0 v York C, Division 3 (N), 1 February 1936 – Middleton; Common, Hall; Wharton, Wilson, Howarth; Horsman (2), Hughes, Wrightson (4), Cresswell (2), Sargeant (4).

Record Cup Victory: 6–1 v Darlington, FA Cup, 1st rd, 25 November 1933 – Burke; Bennett, Little; Pitcairn, Skitt, Duckworth; Armes (3), Whittam, Mantle (2), Cresswell (1), McLachlan.

Record Defeat: 2–11 v Oldham Ath, Division 3 (N), 19 January 1952.

Most League Points (2 for a win): 56, Division 3 (N), 1946–47 and Division 4, 1964–65.

Most League Points (3 for a win): 84, Division 4, 1985–86.

Most League Goals: 119, Division 4, 1964–65.

Highest League Scorer in Season: Dick Yates, 36, Division 3 (N), 1946–47.

Most League Goals in Total Aggregate: Stuart Rimmer, 110, 1985–88, 1991–95.

Most Capped Player: Bill Lewis, 7 (30), Wales.

Most League Appearances: Ray Gill, 408, 1951–62.

Record Transfer Fee Received: £300,000 from Liverpool for Ian Rush, May 1980.

Record Transfer Fee Paid: £94,000 to Barnsley for Stuart Rimmer, August 1991.

Football League Record: 1931 Elected Division 3 (N); 1958–75 Division 4; 1975–82 Division 3; 1982–86 Division 4; 1986–92 Division 3; 1992–93 Division 2; 1993–94 Division 3; 1994–95 Division 2; 1995– Division 3.

Honours: *Football League:* Division 3 – Runners-up 1993–94; Division 3 (N) – Runners-up 1935–36; Division 4 – Runners-up 1985–86. *FA Cup:* best season: 5th rd, 1977, 1980. *Football League Cup:* Semi-final 1975. *Welsh Cup:* Winners 1908, 1933, 1947. *Debenhams Cup:* Winners 1977.

Colours: Blue and white striped shirts, blue shorts, blue stockings. **Change colours:** Jade and black striped shirts, black shorts, black stockings.

CHESTER CITY 1994–95 LEAGUE RECORD

Match No.	*Date*	*Venue*	*Opponents*	*Result*		*H/T Score*	*Lg. Pos.*	*Goalscorers*	*Attendance*
1	Aug 13	H	Bradford C	L	1-4	0-1	—	Milner	4459
2	20	A	Birmingham C	L	0-1	0-1	22		12,188
3	27	H	Huddersfield T	L	1-2	0-1	23	Bishop	2895
4	30	A	Cambridge U	L	1-2	0-0	—	Page	2520
5	Sept 3	A	Hull C	L	0-2	0-1	23		3615
6	10	H	Brighton & HA	L	1-2	0-1	23	Page	2063
7	13	H	Cardiff C	L	0-2	0-0	—		1671
8	17	A	Bournemouth	D	1-1	1-0	23	Lightfoot	3025
9	24	A	Plymouth Arg	L	0-1	0-1	24		5329
10	Oct 1	H	Oxford U	W	2-0	1-0	24	Hackett, Priest	2324
11	8	H	Swansea C	D	2-2	1-1	23	Page (pen), Shelton	2186
12	15	A	Leyton Orient	L	0-2	0-1	23		3309
13	22	A	York C	L	0-2	0-1	23		2820
14	30	H	Wrexham	D	1-1	1-0	23	Hackett	4974
15	Nov 2	H	Stockport Co	W	1-0	0-0	—	Shelton	2400
16	5	A	Peterborough U	L	0-2	0-1	23		4610
17	19	H	Blackpool	W	2-0	1-0	23	Milner, Page	3114
18	26	A	Rotherham U	L	0-2	0-0	23		2947
19	Dec 10	H	Birmingham C	L	0-4	0-2	23		3946
20	17	A	Bradford C	D	1-1	0-1	23	Milner	4555
21	26	A	Crewe Alex	L	1-2	1-0	23	Page (pen)	5428
22	27	H	Brentford	L	1-4	1-3	23	Richardson	2266
23	31	A	Bristol R	L	0-3	0-2	23		5629
24	Jan 7	H	York C	L	0-4	0-0	24		1844
25	14	A	Shrewsbury T	L	0-1	0-0	24		3879
26	28	H	Peterborough U	D	1-1	0-0	24	Hackett	1501
27	31	H	Wycombe W	L	0-2	0-2	—		1524
28	Feb 4	H	Rotherham U	D	4-4	3-2	24	Hackett, Rimmer, Milner, Preece	1794
29	11	A	Stockport Co	D	2-2	2-0	24	Preece, Dinning (og)	4405
30	14	A	Wrexham	D	2-2	1-2	—	Bishop (pen), Milner	5698
31	18	H	Shrewsbury T	L	1-3	0-1	24	Bishop (pen)	2720
32	21	A	Blackpool	L	1-3	1-2	—	Milner	4649
33	25	A	Oxford U	L	0-1	0-0	24		4930
34	Mar 4	H	Plymouth Arg	W	1-0	1-0	24	Rimmer	1823
35	11	A	Huddersfield T	L	1-5	1-3	24	Booth (og)	9606
36	18	H	Cambridge U	L	1-3	0-3	24	Milner	1720
37	22	A	Brighton & HA	L	0-1	0-1	—		5979
38	25	H	Bournemouth	D	1-1	0-0	24	Jackson	1618
39	28	H	Hull C	L	1-2	0-0	—	Lightfoot	1191
40	Apr 1	A	Cardiff C	L	1-2	0-1	24	Hackett	4405
41	8	H	Bristol R	D	0-0	0-0	24		2241
42	15	A	Brentford	D	1-1	1-0	24	Lightfoot	8020
43	17	H	Crewe Alex	L	0-1	0-0	24		3054
44	22	A	Wycombe W	L	1-3	1-2	24	Whelan	5284
45	29	H	Leyton Orient	W	1-0	0-0	23	Bishop	1596
46	May 6	A	Swansea C	W	1-0	1-0	23	Milner	2065

Final League Position: 23

GOALSCORERS

League (37): Milner 8, Hackett 5, Page 5 (2 pens), Bishop 4 (2 pens), Lightfoot 3, Preece 2, Rimmer 2, Shelton 2, Jackson 1, Priest 1, Richardson 1, Whelan 1, own goals 2.
Coca-Cola Cup (2): Chambers 1, Whelan 1.
FA Cup (3): Alsford 1, Milner 1, Page 1.

Felgate D.W. 37 + 1	Jenkins I. 40	Burnham J.J. 22 + 2	Ratcliffe K. 23	Alsford J. 32 + 3	Whelan S.R. 23	Flitcroft D.J. 20 + 12	Rimmer S.A. 22 + 3	Preece R. 42 + 1	Milner A.J. 32 + 4	Chambers L.D. 6 + 7	Page D.R. 22 + 8	Lightfoot C.I. 26 + 2	Bishop E.M. 16 + 3	Newland R.J. 9 + 1	Anthrobus S.A. 7	Hackett G.S. 30 + 5	Priest C. 22 + 2	Shelton G. 31 + 2	Jackson P.A. 32	Murphy J.J. — + 5	Richardson N.J. 6	Aunger G.E. 1 + 4	Tolson N. 3 + 1	Gardiner M.C. 2 + 1	*Match No.*
1	2	3	4	5	6	7	*8*	9	10	11	12	14													1
1	2	3	4	9	5	12	*10*	6	7	14	11		8												2
	2	3	4	5	11	7		6	9	12	*8*		14	1	10										3
	2	3	4	8	5	7		6	*9*	14	11	12		1	10										4
1	2	3		4	5			6		12	11	9	8	15	10	7									5
	2	3		4	5						11	9	8	1	10	7	6								6
	2	3		4	5	8			12	14	11	9		1	10	*7*	6								7
	2	3		4	5					12	11	9		1	10	7	8	6							8
	2	3		4	5	14		12		10	7	9		1	11		*8*	6							9
	2		3	4		12		7			10	9		1		11	8	6	5						10
1	2		3	4		12		7	14		10	*9*				11	8	6	5						11
	2		3			9		7	12		10	4		1		11	8	6	5						12
1	2		4			12		9	14	7	10	5				11	8	6	3						13
1	2		3	4		12		9		7	10					11	8	6	5	14					14
1	2		3	4		12		9		7	10					11	8	6	5	14					15
1	2		3	4		12		9		7	10					11	8	6	5	14					16
1	2		3	4		8	12	9	7		10					11		6	5						17
1	2		3	4		8	12	9	7		*10*					11		6	5	14					18
1	2	3		4		8		9		12	*10*	7				11		6	5	14					19
1			3	4				2	7		10	9				11		6	5		8	12			20
1			3	4				2	7		10	9				11		6	5		8	12			21
1			3	4				2	7		12	9				11		6	5		8	10			22
1			3	4				2	7		*10*	9	11			12		6	5		8	14			23
1	2		3	4				7	11			9	12					*6*	5		8	14	10		24
1	3			2		7		4	9		12	6	14			*11*			5		8		10		25
1	3			2		7	12	4	9			6	8			11			5				10		26
1	3			2		7	10	4	*9*			6	8			11		12	5				14		27
1	3			2			10	4	9		12	6	8			11		7	5						28
1	2		3	5			10	4	9		12	6	8			*11*	14	7							29
1	3	12		5		7	*10*	2	9		14	6	11				8	4							30
1	3			2		7	10	4	9			6	11				8		5						31
1	2		3	5		12	10	7	9			4	8				11		6						32
1	2	12	3		6	7	10	4	9							11	*8*	14	5						33
1	2		3		5	12	10	4			9					11	*7*	8	6					14	34
1		3	6	2	5		10	4	9		12					14	7	8						*11*	35
15		3		2	6	12	10	4	9					*1*		11	14	7	5					*8*	36
1	2	3		12	6		10	4	9							11	7	8	5						37
1	2	3			6		10	4	9							11	7	8	5						38
1	2	3			6	12	10	4	9			8				11	7		5						39
1	2	3			6	8	10	4	9		12	5				11	7								40
1	2	3			6		10	4	9							11	7	8	5						41
1	2	3		12	6	7	10	4	9			5	11					8							42
1	2	3			6	7	10	4	9				11			12		8	5						43
1	2	3		12	6	7	10	4	*9*				11			14		8	5						44
1	2	3			6	7	10	4	9				11					8	5						45
1	2	3			6	7	10	4	9				11			12		8	5						46

Coca-Cola Cup

First Round	Lincoln C (a)	0-2
	(h)	2-3

FA Cup

First Round	Witton Alb (h)	2-0
Second Round	Burnley (h)	1-2

CHESTERFIELD 1994–95 *Back row (left to right):* Dave Moss, Kevin Davies, Mick Leonard, Lyndly Brocklehurst, Chris Marples, Nicky Law, Darren Carr.
Third row: Mark Jules, Wayne Fairclough, Lee Rogers, Andy Morris, Sean Dyche, Darren Roberts, Steve Spooner, Steve Norris.
Second row: Steve Williams, Chris Perkins, Jamie Hewitt, Kevin Randall (Assistant Manager), John Duncan (Manager), Dave Rushbury (Physio), Tony Dennis, Michael Cheetham, Tom Curtis.
Front row: Andrew Kuchta, Lee Ashton, Richard Hopkinson.

Division 2 **CHESTERFIELD**

Recreation Ground, Chesterfield S40 4SX. Telephone: (01246) 209765. Fax: (01246) 556799. Commercial Dept: (01246) 231535.

Ground capacity: 8880.

Record attendance: 30,968 v Newcastle U, Division 2, 7 April 1939.

Record receipts: £45,000 v Mansfield T, Division 3 play-off semi-final, 17 May 1995.

Pitch measurements: 113yd × 71yd.

President: His Grace the Duke of Devonshire MC, DL, JP.

Chairman: J. Norton Lea. ***Vice-Chairman:*** B. W. Hubbard.

Directors: R. F. Pepper, M. L. Warner.

Manager: John Duncan.

Physio: Dave Rushbury. ***Assistant Manager:*** Kevin Randall.

Secretary: Mrs N. J. Bellamy. ***Commercial Manager:*** Jim Brown.

Year Formed: 1866. ***Turned Professional:*** 1891. ***Ltd Co:*** 1871.

Previous Names: Chesterfield Town.

Club Nickname: 'Blues' or 'Spireites'.

Foundation: Chesterfield are fourth only to Stoke, Notts County and Nottingham Forest in age for they can trace their existence as far back as 1866, although it is fair to say that they were somewhat casual in the first few years of their history playing only a few friendlies a year. However, their rules of 1871 are still in existence showing an annual membership of 2s (10p), but it was not until 1891 that they won a trophy (the Barnes Cup) and followed this a year later by winning the Sheffield Cup, Barnes Cup and the Derbyshire Junior Cup.

First Football League game: 2 September, 1899, Division 2, v Sheffield W (a) L 1-5 – Hancock; Pilgrim, Fletcher; Ballantyne, Bell, Downie; Morley, Thacker, Gooing, Munday (1), Geary.

Record League Victory: 10–0 v Glossop, Division 2, 17 January 1903 – Clutterbuck; Thorpe, Lerper; Haig, Banner, Thacker; Tomlinson (2), Newton (1), Milward (3), Munday (2), Steel (2).

Record Cup Victory: 5–0 v Wath Ath (away), FA Cup, 1st rd, 28 November 1925 – Birch; Saxby, Dennis; Wass, Abbott, Thompson; Fisher (1), Roseboom (1), Cookson (2), Whitfield (1), Hopkinson.

Record Defeat: 0–10 v Gillingham, Division 3, 5 September 1987.

Most League Points (2 for a win): 64, Division 4, 1969–70.

Most League Points (3 for a win): 91, Division 4, 1984–85.

Most League Goals: 102, Division 3 (N), 1930–31.

Highest League Scorer in Season: Jimmy Cookson, 44, Division 3 (N), 1925–26.

Most League Goals in Total Aggregate: Ernie Moss, 161, 1969–76, 1979–81 and 1984–86.

Most Capped Player: Walter McMillen, 4 (7), Northern Ireland.

Most League Appearances: Dave Blakey, 613, 1948–67.

Record Transfer Fee Received: £200,000 from Wolverhampton W for Alan Birch, August 1981.

Record Transfer Fee Paid: £150,000 to Carlisle U for Phil Bonnyman, March 1980.

Football League Record: 1899 Elected to Division 2; 1909 failed re-election; 1921–31 Division 3 (N); 1931–33 Division 2; 1933–36 Division 3 (N); 1936–51 Division 2; 1951–58 Division 3 (N); 1958–61 Division 3; 1961–70 Division 4; 1970–83 Division 3; 1983–85 Division 4; 1985–89 Division 3; 1989–92 Division 4; 1992–95 Division 3; 1995– Division 2.

Honours: *Football League:* Division 2 best season: 4th, 1946–47; Division 3 (N) – Champions 1930–31, 1935–36; Runners-up 1933–34; Division 4 – Champions 1969–70, 1984–85. *FA Cup:* best season: 5th rd, 1933, 1938, 1950. *Football League Cup:* best season: 4th rd, 1965. *Anglo-Scottish Cup:* Winners 1981.

Colours: Blue shirts, white shorts, blue stockings. **Change colours:** Green and white striped shirts, navy shorts, navy stockings.

CHESTERFIELD 1994–95 LEAGUE RECORD

Match No.	Date	Venue	Opponents	Result		H/T Score	Lg. Pos.	Goalscorers	Attendance
1	Aug 13	H	Scarborough	L	0-1	0-1	—		3099
2	20	A	Rochdale	L	1-4	0-1	17	Norris	2122
3	27	H	Mansfield T	L	0-1	0-0	19		4210
4	30	A	Wigan Ath	W	3-2	2-1	—	Robertson (og), Morris, Moss	1231
5	Sept 3	A	Hartlepool U	W	2-0	0-0	11	Morris, Moss	2173
6	10	H	Walsall	D	0-0	0-0	12		3027
7	13	H	Exeter C	W	2-0	1-0	—	Davies, Norris	2136
8	17	A	Scarborough	W	1-0	1-0	10	Curtis	1475
9	24	A	Bury	L	1-2	1-1	12	Davies	3031
10	Oct 1	H	Torquay U	W	1-0	0-0	9	Burton (og)	2465
11	8	A	Colchester U	W	3-0	1-0	8	Davies, Moss, Morris	3476
12	15	H	Darlington	D	0-0	0-0	6		2836
13	22	H	Fulham	D	1-1	1-0	7	Roberts	2860
14	29	A	Barnet	L	1-4	1-2	9	Hewitt	2130
15	Nov 5	H	Hereford U	W	1-0	1-0	7	Norris	2448
16	19	A	Gillingham	D	1-1	1-0	7	Davies	2722
17	26	H	Preston NE	W	1-0	0-0	7	McAuley	3191
18	Dec 10	H	Rochdale	D	2-2	2-1	7	Hewitt 2	2457
19	18	A	Mansfield T	L	2-4	0-2	7	Davies, Robinson	3519
20	26	H	Doncaster R	W	2-0	1-0	7	Robinson 2	4226
21	27	A	Northampton T	W	3-2	2-1	7	Moss 2, Madden	6329
22	31	H	Lincoln C	W	1-0	0-0	5	Robinson	3325
23	Jan 8	A	Fulham	D	1-1	1-0	4	Moss	3927
24	14	H	Scunthorpe U	W	3-1	3-0	3	Lormor, Moss 2	3245
25	24	A	Hereford U	W	2-0	1-0	—	Lormor, Davies	1673
26	Feb 4	A	Preston NE	D	0-0	0-0	3		8544
27	11	H	Gillingham	W	2-0	2-0	2	Lormor, Law	3070
28	14	H	Barnet	W	2-0	0-0	—	Moss, Davies	2978
29	18	A	Scunthorpe U	W	1-0	0-0	2	Robinson	3566
30	25	A	Torquay U	D	3-3	1-1	2	Lormor, Davies 2	3236
31	Mar 4	H	Bury	D	0-0	0-0	2		4429
32	11	A	Walsall	W	3-1	1-0	2	Carr, Lormor, Howard	6219
33	18	H	Wigan Ath	D	0-0	0-0	2		3808
34	25	H	Hartlepool U	W	2-0	1-0	2	Lormor 2 (1 pen)	4125
35	Apr 1	A	Exeter C	W	2-1	0-0	2	Davies, Morris	2144
36	4	A	Carlisle U	D	1-1	0-0	—	Moss	8478
37	8	A	Lincoln C	W	1-0	1-0	2	Robinson	5141
38	15	H	Northampton T	W	3-0	1-0	2	Morris 2, Robinson	4884
39	17	A	Doncaster R	W	3-1	1-1	2	Robinson, Carr, Curtis	4796
40	29	A	Darlington	W	1-0	1-0	2	Lormor	3387
41	May 2	H	Carlisle U	L	1-2	1-1	—	Davies	7283
42	6	H	Colchester U	D	2-2	1-1	3	Lormor 2 (1 pen)	4133

Final League Position: 3

GOALSCORERS

League (62): Davies 11, Lormor 10 (2 pens), Moss 10, Robinson 8, Morris 6, Hewitt 3, Norris 3, Carr 2, Curtis 2, Howard 1, Law 1, McAuley 1, Madden 1, Roberts 1, own goals 2.
Coca-Cola Cup (8): Cheetham 1, Curtis 1, Davies 1, Jules 1, Morris 1, Moss 1, Norris 1, Perkins 1.
FA Cup (0).

Marples C. 21	Hewitt J.R. 38	Rogers L.J. 39	Fairclough W.R. 12 + 1	Carr D. 35	Law N. 35	Curtis T. 39 + 1	Norris S.M. 5 + 2	Davies K.C. 41	Moss D. 27 + 5	Cheetham M.M. 5	Perkins C.P. 17 + 1	Roberts D.A. 4 + 7	Spooner S.A. 6 + 1	Marshall D. — + 1	Morris A.D. 21 + 5	Hill D.M. 3	Jules M.A. 10 + 13	Madden L.D. 10	Reddish S. 2 + 1	Dyche S.M. 22	McAuley S. 1	Beasley A. 20 + 1	Robinson P.J. 22	Howard J. 1 + 11	Lormor A. 23	Narbett J.V. 2 + 1	Bibbo S. — + 1	Stewart W.I. 1	Match No.
1	2	3	4	5	6	7	8	9	10	11	12	14																	1
1	2	3	4	5		7	8	9		11	6		10	12															2
1	2	3	4	5	6	7	8	9		10					11														3
1	2	3		5	6	7		9	10						8	4	11												4
1	2	3		5	6	7		9	10						8	4	11												5
1	2	3		5	6	7		9	10			12	14		8	4	11												6
1	2	3		5	6	7	12	9				10	11		8			4											7
1	2	3		5	6	7		9	10			12	11		8			4											8
1	2	3	14	5	6	7		9	10			12	4		8		11												9
1	2			5	6	7		10				8	4		9		11	3	12										10
1		3	2		6	7		8	10			12	4		9		14	5	11										11
1	2	3	6			7		8	10			12			9		14	5	4	11									12
1	2	3	6	5		7		8	12	10	4	9					14			11									13
1	2	3	6	5		7		8	10		4				9		12			11									14
1	2	3	6	5		7	8				4	10			9					11									15
1		3	6	5		7	8	9	10		4						11			2									16
	11	3	7	5	6			8			4				9					2	10	1							17
	2	3			6		12	8	10		4						14	5		11		1	7	9					18
	2	3			6	12		9	10	8	4	14						5		11		1	7						19
1	2	3		5	6	4		9	10								12			11			7		8				20
1	2			5	6	4		8	10								12	3		11			7		9				21
1	2		5		6	4		8	10		3						12			11			7		9				22
1	2	3		5	6	4		8	10								12			11			7		9				23
1	2	3		5	6	4		8	10								12			11		15	7		9				24
	2	3		5	6	4		8							10		12			11		1	7		9	14			25
	2	3		5	6	4		8	10						12					11		1	7		9				26
	2	3		5	6	4		8	10						12					11		1	7		9				27
	2	3		5	6	4		8	10						12					11		1	7		9				28
	2	3		5	6	4		8	10		11											1	7		9				29
	2	3		5	6	4		8	10								11					1	7	12	9				30
	2	3		5	6	4		8	10						12					11		1	7		9		15		31
	2	3		5	6	4		8	10								7			11		1		12	9				32
	2	3		5	6	4		8	10								12			11				14	9	7		1	33
		3			6	4		8			2				10		12	5		11		1		14	9	7			34
		3			6	4		8							10		2	5		11		1	7	12	9				35
	2	3		5	6	4		8	12						10		11					1	7	14	9				36
	2	3		5	6	4		8	10		11											1	7	12	9				37
	2	3		5	6	4		8	12		11				10							1	7	14	9				38
	2	3		5	6	4		8			11				10							1	7		9				39
	2	3		5	6	4		8	12		11				10							1	7	14	9				40
	2	3		5	6	4		8	10		11				12							1	7	14	9				41
	2	3	6	5		4		8	12		11				10							1	7	14	9				42

Coca-Cola Cup

First Round	Blackpool (a)	2-1
	(h)	4-2
Second Round	Wolverhampton W (h)	1-3
	(a)	1-1

FA Cup

First Round	Scarborough (h)	0-0
	(a)	0-2

COLCHESTER UNITED 1994–95 *Back row (left to right):* Steve Whitton (Player/Coach), Chris Fry, Scott Walters, Paul Champ, Steve Brown, Andy Partner, David Schultz, Peter Cawley, Tony English, Tim Allpress, Paul Abrahams, Brian Owen (Physio).
Front row: Simon Betts, Danny Roberts, Neil Butler, Justin Gentle, John Cheesewright, George Burley (Manager), Carl Emberson, Steve Ball, Mark Kinsella, Christian Hyslop, Justin Booty.

Division 3 COLCHESTER UNITED

Layer Rd Ground, Colchester, Essex CO2 7JJ. Telephone: (01206) 574042. Fax: (01206) 48700. Club Shop: (01206) 561180. Soccer Centre: (01206) 571581. Commercial Dept: (01206) 574042.

Ground capacity: 7190.

Record attendance: 19,072 v Reading, FA Cup 1st rd, 27 Nov, 1948.

Record receipts: £26,330 v Barrow, GM Vauxhall Conference, 2 May 1992.

Pitch measurements: 110yd × 71yd.

Patron: The Mayor of Colchester.

Directors: Gordon Parker (Chairman), Peter Heard (vice-chairman), John Worsp, Peter Powell.

Manager: Steve Wignall. ***Player-Coach:*** Steve Whitton. ***Youth Coach:*** Steve Foley.

Physio: Brian Owen. ***Consultant Physio:*** Ray Cole.

Secretary: Sue Smith.

Commercial Manager: Marie Partner. ***Lottery Manager:*** Liz Blacknall.

Year Formed: 1937. ***Turned Professional:*** 1937. ***Ltd Co.:*** 1937.

Club Nickname: 'The U's'.

Foundation: Colchester United was formed in 1937 when a number of enthusiasts of the much older Colchester Town club decided to establish a professional concern as a limited liability company. The new club continued at Layer Road which had been the amateur club's home since 1909.

First Football League game: 19 August, 1950, Division 3(S), v Gillingham (a) D 0-0 – Wright; Kettle, Allen; Bearryman, Stewart, Elder; Jones, Curry, Turner, McKim, Church.

Record League Victory: 9–1 v Bradford C, Division 4, 30 December 1961 – Ames; Millar, Fowler; Harris, Abrey, Ron Hunt; Foster, Bobby Hunt (4), King (4), Hill (1), Wright.

Record Cup Victory: 7–1 v Yeovil T (away), FA Cup, 2nd rd (replay), 11 December 1958 – Ames; Fisher, Fowler; Parker, Milligan, Hammond; Williams (1), McLeod (2), Langman (4), Evans, Wright.

Record Defeat: 0–8 v Leyton Orient, Division 4, 15 October 1989.

Most League Points (2 for a win): 60, Division 4, 1973–74.

Most League Points (3 for a win): 81, Division 4, 1982–83.

Most League Goals: 104, Division 4, 1961–62.

Highest League Scorer in Season: Bobby Hunt, 37, Division 4, 1961–62.

Most League Goals in Total Aggregate: Martyn King, 131, 1959–65.

Most Capped Player: None.

Most League Appearances: Micky Cook, 613, 1969–84.

Record Transfer Fee Received: £100,000 from Birmingham C for Steve McGavin, January 1994.

Record Transfer Fee Paid: £40,000 to Lokeren for Dale Tempest, August 1987.

Football League Record: 1950 Elected to Division 3(S); 1958–61 Division 3; 1961–62 Division 4; 1962–65 Division 3; 1965–66 Division 4; 1966–68 Division 3; 1968–74 Division 4; 1974–76 Division 3, 1976–77 Division 4; 1977–81 Division 3; 1981–90 Division 4; 1990–92 GM Vauxhall Conference; 1992– Division 3.

Honours: *Football League:* Division 3(S) best season: 3rd , 1956–57; Division 4 – Runners-up 1961–62. *FA Cup* best season: 1971, 6th rd (record for a Fourth Division club shared with Oxford United and Bradford City). *Football League Cup:* best season 5th rd 1975. *GM Vauxhall Conference winners* 1991–92. *FA Trophy winners* 1992.

Colours: Blue and white striped shirts, white shorts, white stockings. **Change colours:** White shirts, black shorts black stockings white trim.

COLCHESTER UNITED 1994–95 LEAGUE RECORD

Match No.	Date		Venue	Opponents	Result		H/T Score	Lg. Pos.	Goalscorers	Atten-dance
1	Aug	13	H	Torquay U	L	1-3	1-2	—	Kinsella	3175
2		20	A	Mansfield T	L	0-2	0-0	18		2247
3		27	H	Doncaster R	L	0-3	0-2	21		2320
4		30	A	Exeter C	L	0-1	0-1	—		1804
5	Sept	3	A	Scarborough	W	1-0	0-0	20	Dennis	1494
6		10	H	Hartlepool U	W	1-0	0-0	18	Whitton	2428
7		13	H	Walsall	W	3-2	0-1	—	Kinsella 2, Whitton	2239
8		17	A	Torquay U	D	3-3	0-1	12	Whitton, Brown, Dennis	3390
9		24	A	Darlington	W	3-2	2-1	11	Whitton 2, Brown	2260
10	Oct	1	H	Bury	W	1-0	0-0	8	Cawley	3286
11		8	H	Chesterfield	L	0-3	0-1	9		3476
12		15	A	Carlisle U	D	0-0	0-0	11		5817
13		22	H	Preston NE	W	3-1	1-0	9	Brown 2, Whitton	3015
14		29	A	Wigan Ath	W	2-1	2-0	6	Kinsella, Fry	1621
15	Nov	5	H	Gillingham	D	2-2	1-2	6	Fry, Kinsella	3817
16		19	A	Rochdale	D	0-0	0-0	6		1903
17		26	H	Scunthorpe U	W	4-2	2-0	6	Brown, Abrahams 2, Whitton	2904
18	Dec	10	H	Mansfield T	D	1-1	1-0	6	Fry	3016
19		16	A	Doncaster R	W	2-1	0-0	—	Cawley, Brown	2460
20		26	H	Northampton T	L	0-1	0-1	6		5064
21		27	A	Fulham	W	2-1	1-1	6	Kinsella, Blake (og)	4243
22		31	H	Hereford U	D	2-2	0-2	7	Stoneman, Whitton	3322
23	Jan	10	A	Preston NE	L	1-2	0-1	—	Fry	6377
24		14	H	Barnet	D	1-1	0-1	8	Putney	3706
25		28	H	Wigan Ath	L	0-1	0-0	11		3067
26	Feb	4	A	Scunthorpe U	W	4-3	2-3	9	Locke, English, Thompson 2	2748
27		11	H	Rochdale	D	0-0	0-0	7		3080
28		18	A	Barnet	W	1-0	1-0	5	Asaba	2242
29		21	A	Lincoln C	L	0-2	0-0	—		1969
30		25	A	Bury	L	1-4	0-1	9	Fry	2484
31	Mar	4	H	Darlington	W	1-0	1-0	7	Asaba	6055
32		11	A	Hartlepool U	L	1-3	1-2	9	Fry	1371
33		18	H	Exeter C	W	3-1	1-0	8	Thompson, Betts (pen), Lock	2375
34		25	H	Scarborough	L	0-2	0-0	8		3025
35	Apr	1	A	Walsall	L	0-2	0-0	9		3622
36		8	A	Hereford U	L	0-3	0-2	11		1669
37		11	A	Gillingham	W	3-1	0-1	—	Betts (pen), Thompson 2	3328
38		15	H	Fulham	W	5-2	4-1	8	Cheetham, English, Caesar, Fry 2	3448
39		17	A	Northampton T	D	1-1	0-1	8	Whitton	5011
40		22	H	Lincoln C	L	1-2	1-1	9	McCarthy	2654
41		29	H	Carlisle U	L	0-1	0-0	10		3333
42	May	6	A	Chesterfield	D	2-2	1-1	10	Whitton, Putney (pen)	4133

Final League Position: 10

GOALSCORERS

League (56): Whitton 10, Fry 8, Brown 6, Kinsella 6, Thompson 5, Abrahams 2, Asaba 2, Betts 2 (2 pens), Cawley 2, Dennis 2, English 2, Putney 2 (1 pen), Caesar 1, Cheetham 1, Lock 1, Locke 1, McCarthy 1, Stoneman 1, own goal 1.
Coca-Cola Cup (0).
FA Cup (11): Abrahams 3, Whitton 3, Brown 2, Kinsella 2, English 1.

Cheesewright J. 23	Culling G. 2	Dalli J. 1	English A.K. 33	Caesar G. 39	Dennis J.A. 32 + 1	Fry C.D. 24 + 9	Brown S.R. 26 + 2	Whitton S.P. 36	Kinsella M.A. 42	Abrahams P. 20 + 8	Allpress T.J. 3 + 8	Davis A. 4	Burley G. 5 + 2	Putney T.A. 28	Partner A.N. — + 1	Cawley P. 23	Allen L.G. — + 2	Betts S.R. 34 + 1	Locke A.S. 20 + 2	Stoneman P. 3	Emberson C.W. 19 + 1	Thompson N. 5 + 8	Lock A.C. — + 3	Asaba C. 9 + 3	Gibbs P. 8 + 1	Williams M.K. 3	McCarthy A.P. 10	Cheetham M.M. 8 + 1	Reinelt R.S. 2 + 3	*Match No.*
1	2	3	4	5	6	7	8	9	10	11	12																			1
1	2		6	5	7	12	9	10	8	11	4	3																		2
1				5	6		8	9	10	11	4	3	2	7																3
1				*5*	6	12	8	9	10	11	4	3	2	7	14															4
1			2	5	6	12	8	9	10	11		3		7		4														5
1			3	5	6		8	9	10	11			2	7		4	12													6
1			3	5	6		8	9	10	11			2	7		4		12												7
1			3	5	6		8	9	10	11			12	7		4		2												8
1			3	5	6	*11*	8	9	10					7		4	12	2	14											9
1			3	5	6		8	9	10	11						4		2	7											10
1			3	5	6	12	8	9	10	*11*			14			4		2	7											11
1			3	5	*6*	11	8	9	10	12				7		4		2	14											12
1			3	5		11	8	9	10	12				7		4		2	6											13
1			3	5	12	*11*	8	9	10	14				7		4		2	6											14
1			3	5		11	8	9	10	12				7		4		2	6											15
1			3	5	6	12	8	9	10	11						4		2	7											16
1			3	5			8	9	10	11				7		4		2	6											17
1				5	3	7	8	9	10	11						4		2	6											18
1				*5*	11	7	8	9	10	12	14		2			4		3	6											19
1			3	5	4	12	8	9	10	11				7				2	6											20
1			3		4	11	8	9	10	12	14			7				2	6	5										21
1			3			11	8	9	10	12	14			7		4		2	6	5										22
1			3	5	6	12	8	9	10	11				7		4		2			15									23
			3	5	8	12			10	11				7		4		2	6		1	9								24
				5	8		12		10	11				7		4		2	6	3	1	*9*	14							25
			2	5	8	7	11	9	10							4		3	6		1	12								26
			3	5	*6*	7	8	9	10	12	14					4		2			1	11								27
			4	5	6	7		9	10	*11*	12							3	2		1	14		8						28
			4	5	6	7			10	11								3	2		1	9	12	8						29
			4	5	6	7			10	11	12			8				3	2		1			9						30
				5	6	7	12	9	10					8		4		3	2		1			11						31
				5	6	7	*8*		10		12					4		2			1	14		9	3	11				32
			4		6	7			10									2			1	8	12	9	3	11	5			33
			4	6				9	10					7				2			1	12		8	3	*11*	5	14		34
			3	5	6			9	10									2	8		1			11			4	7		35
			3	5	6	12		11	10					8				2			1	14		*9*			4	7		36
			8	5		7		9	2					6				3			1	12			*11*		4	10	14	37
			8	5		7		*9*	2					6				3			1	12			11		4	10	14	38
			8	5		7		9	2					6				3			1	14		12	*11*		4	10		39
			8	5		7		9	2					6				*3*			1			12	11		4	10	14	40
				5	6	7		11	2					8							1			12	3		4	10	9	41
				5	6	7		11	2					8				3			1				12		4	10	9	42

Coca-Cola Cup

First Round	Brentford (h)	0-2
	(a)	0-2

FA Cup

First Round	Yeading (a)	2-2
	(h)	7-1
Second Round	Exeter C (a)	2-1
Third Round	Wimbledon (a)	0-1

COVENTRY CITY 1994–95 *Back row (left to right):* Jason Smith, David Busst, Mick Harford, Jim Blythe (Goalkeeping Coach), Steve Sims (Youth Development Officer), Tim Exeter (Fitness Coach), John Williams, Steve Morgan, Julian Darby.
Centre row: George Dalton (Physio), Brian Roberts (Reserve Team Manager), Paul Williams, Tony Sheridan, Stewart Robson, Jamie Barnwell-Edinboro, Jonathan Gould, Steve Ogrizovic, Martin Davies, Tim Blake, Marcus Hall, Gavin O'Toole, Sandy Robertson, Trevor Gould (Youth Team Manager), Bert Edwards (Recruitment Officer).
Front row: Willie Boland, Brian Borrows, Roy Wegerle, Leigh Jenkinson, Mick Quinn, Mick Brown (Assistant Manager), Phil Neal (Manager), Phil Babb, David Rennie, Sean Flynn, Peter Ndlovu, Ally Pickering.
(Photograph: Action Images)

FA Premiership COVENTRY CITY

Highfield Road Stadium, King Richard Street, Coventry CV2 4FW. Telephone: (01203) 223535. Fax: (01203) 630318. Ticket Office Fax: (01203) 258856. Sales & Marketing: (01203) 633823. Clubcall: 0891 121166.

Ground capacity: 23,500.

Record attendance: 51,455 v Wolverhampton W, Division 2, 29 April 1967.

Record receipts: £250,065.38 v Manchester U, FA Premiership, 1 May 1995 (£216,126 actual receipts excluding season tickets).

Pitch measurements: 110yd × 75yd.

Life President: Derrick H. Robbins.

Chairman: B. A. Richardson. ***Deputy Chairman:*** M. C. McGinnity.

Directors: E. W. Grove, A. M. Jepson, J. F. W Reason, P. D. H. Robins.

Secretary: Graham Hover.

Manager: Ron Atkinson. ***Assistant Manager:*** Gordon Strachan. ***Physio:*** George Dalton.

Sales & Marketing Manager: Mark Jones.

Club Statistician: Jim Brown.

Year Formed: 1883. ***Turned Professional:*** 1893. ***Ltd Co.:*** 1907.

Previous Names: 1883–98, Singers FC; 1898, Coventry City FC.

Club Nickname: 'Sky Blues'.

Previous Grounds: Binley Road, 1883–87; Stoke Road, 1887–99; Highfield Road, 1899–.

Foundation: Workers at Singer's cycle factory formed a club in 1883. The first success of Singers' FC was to win the Birmingham Junior Cup in 1891 and this led in 1894 to their election to the Birmingham and District League. Four years later they changed their name to Coventry City and joined the Southern League in 1908 at which time they were playing in blue and white quarters.

First Football League game: 30 August, 1919, Division 2, v Tottenham H (h) L 0-5 – Lindon; Roberts, Chaplin, Allan, Hawley, Clarke, Sheldon, Mercer, Sambrooke, Lowes, Gibson.

Record League Victory: 9–0 v Bristol C, Division 3 (S), 28 April 1934 – Pearson; Brown, Bisby; Perry, Davidson, Frith; White (2), Lauderdale Bourton (5), Jones (2), Lake.

Record Cup Victory: 7–0 v Scunthorpe U, FA Cup, 1st rd, 24 November 1934 – Pearson; Brown, Bisby; Mason, Davidson, Boileau; Birtley (2), Lauderdale (2), Bourton (1), Jones (1), Liddle (1).

Record Defeat: 2–10 v Norwich C, Division 3 (S), 15 March 1930.

Most League Points (2 for a win): 60, Division 4, 1958–59 and Division 3, 1963–64.

Most League Points (3 for a win): 63, Division 1, 1986–87.

Most League Goals: 108, Division 3 (S), 1931–32.

Highest League Scorer in Season: Clarrie Bourton, 49, Division 3 (S), 1931–32.

Most League Goals in Total Aggregate: Clarrie Bourton, 171, 1931–37.

Most Capped Player: Dave Clements, 21 (48), Northern Ireland and Ronnie Rees, 21 (39) Wales.

Most League Appearances: George Curtis, 486, 1956–70.

Record Transfer Fee Received: £3,600,000 from Liverpool for Phil Babb, September 1994.

Record Transfer Fee Paid: £1,950,000 to Manchester U for Dion Dublin, September 1994.

Football League Record: 1919 Elected to Division 2; 1925–26 Division 3 (N); 1926–36 Division 3 (S); 1936–52 Division 2; 1952–58 Division 3 (S); 1958–59 Division 4; 1959–64 Division 3; 1964–67 Division 2; 1967–92 Division 1; 1992– FA Premier League.

Honours: *Football League:* Division 1 best season: 6th, 1969–70; Division 2 – Champions 1966–67; Division 3 – Champions 1963–64; Division 3 (S) – Champions 1935–36; Runners-up 1933–34; Division 4 – Runners-up 1958–59. *FA Cup:* Winners 1987. *Football League Cup:* best season: Semi-final 1981, 1990. **European Competitions:** *European Fairs Cup:* 1970–71.

Colours: All Sky blue. **Change colours:** Purple and mauve striped shirts with gold pinstripe, purple and gold shorts, gold stockings with purple trim.

COVENTRY CITY 1994–95 LEAGUE RECORD

Match No.	Date	Venue	Opponents	Result		H/T Score	Lg. Pos.	Goalscorers	Attendance
1	Aug 20	H	Wimbledon	D	1-1	0-0	—	Busst	11,005
2	24	A	Newcastle U	L	0-4	0-3	—		34,163
3	27	A	Blackburn R	L	0-4	0-0	21		21,657
4	29	H	Aston Villa	L	0-1	0-1	—		12,218
5	Sept 10	A	QPR	D	2-2	1-2	20	Cook, Dublin	11,398
6	17	H	Leeds U	W	2-1	0-0	18	Dublin, Cook (pen)	15,383
7	24	H	Southampton	L	1-3	1-1	20	Dublin	11,798
8	Oct 3	A	Leicester C	D	2-2	1-1	—	Wegerle, Dublin	19,372
9	10	H	Ipswich T	W	2-0	1-0	—	Wark (og), Cook (pen)	9509
10	15	A	Everton	W	2-0	2-0	14	Dublin, Wegerle	28,219
11	23	A	Arsenal	L	1-2	0-2	15	Wegerle (pen)	31,725
12	29	H	Manchester C	W	1-0	0-0	13	Dublin	15,802
13	Nov 2	H	Crystal Palace	L	1-4	1-2	—	Dublin	10,729
14	6	A	Chelsea	D	2-2	1-0	15	Dublin, Ndlovu	17,090
15	19	H	Norwich C	W	1-0	0-0	13	Jones	11,891
16	26	A	West Ham U	W	1-0	0-0	10	Busst	17,251
17	Dec 3	H	Liverpool	D	1-1	0-1	10	Flynn	21,032
18	10	A	Wimbledon	L	0-2	0-2	16		7349
19	17	H	Newcastle U	D	0-0	0-0	12		17,237
20	26	H	Nottingham F	D	0-0	0-0	12		19,116
21	28	A	Sheffield W	L	1-5	1-3	15	Ndlovu (pen)	26,056
22	31	H	Tottenham H	L	0-4	0-1	17		19,965
23	Jan 3	A	Manchester U	L	0-2	0-1	—		43,120
24	14	A	Manchester C	D	0-0	0-0	17		20,232
25	21	H	Arsenal	L	0-1	0-0	19		14,557
26	25	A	Norwich C	D	2-2	1-1	—	Dublin, Jenkinson	14,024
27	Feb 4	H	Chelsea	D	2-2	2-2	20	Flynn, Burley (og)	13,423
28	11	A	Crystal Palace	W	2-0	0-0	17	Jones, Dublin	12,076
29	18	H	West Ham U	W	2-0	1-0	13	Ndlovu, Marsh	17,563
30	25	H	Leicester C	W	4-2	2-0	12	Flynn 2, Marsh, Ndlovu	20,650
31	Mar 4	A	Southampton	D	0-0	0-0	12		14,505
32	6	A	Aston Villa	D	0-0	0-0	—		26,186
33	11	H	Blackburn R	D	1-1	1-0	12	Dublin	18,556
34	14	A	Liverpool	W	3-2	2-0	—	Ndlovu 3 (1 pen)	27,183
35	18	A	Leeds U	L	0-3	0-1	10		29,179
36	Apr 1	H	QPR	L	0-1	0-0	12		15,751
37	15	H	Sheffield W	W	2-0	1-0	12	Dublin, Ndlovu	15,733
38	17	A	Nottingham F	L	0-2	0-2	15		26,253
39	May 1	H	Manchester U	L	2-3	1-1	—	Ndlovu, Pressley	21,858
40	6	A	Ipswich T	L	0-2	0-0	18		12,342
41	9	A	Tottenham H	W	3-1	1-0	—	Ndlovu 2 (1 pen), Dublin	24,930
42	14	H	Everton	D	0-0	0-0	16		21,787

Final League Position: 16

GOALSCORERS

League (44): Dublin 13, Ndlovu 11 (3 pens), Flynn 4, Cook 3 (2 pens), Wegerle 3 (1 pen), Busst 2, Jones 2, Marsh 2, Jenkinson 1, Pressley 1, own goals 2.
Coca-Cola Cup (5): Dublin 2, Darby 1, Flynn 1, Wegerle 1.
FA Cup (4): Ndlovu 2, Dublin 1, Wegerle 1 (pen).

Ogrizovic S. 33	Borrows B. 33 + 2	Morgan S. 26 + 2	Busst D.J. 20	Rennie D. 28	Babb P.A. 3	Darby J.T. 27 + 2	Jenkinson L. 10 + 1	Flynn S. 32	Quinn M. 3 + 3	Boland W.J. 9 + 3	Wegerle R.C. 21 + 5	Cook P.A. 33 + 1	Pickering A.G. 27 + 4	Williams J.N. 1 + 6	Dublin D. 31	Jones C. 16 + 5	Gillespie G.T. 2 + 1	Ndlovu P. 28 + 2	Pressley S. 18 + 1	Marsh M.A. 15	Hall M.T.J. 2 + 3	Richardson K. 14	Gould J.A. 7	Burrows D. 11	Robertson A. — + 1	Strachan G.D. 5	Filan J.R. 2	Williams P.R. 5	Match No.
1	2	3	4	5	6	7	*8*	9	10	11	12	14																	1
1	2	3	4	5		7	8	*6*	10	12	9	11	14																2
1	2	3	4	5	6	7		11	10		9	8		12															3
1	2	3	4	5	6	7		9		11	10	8		12															4
1		3	6	5		7	*10*	11		12	8	4	2	14	9														5
1		3	6	5		7		10		11		4	2		9	8													6
1		3	6	*5*		7		10		11	12	4	2		9	8	14												7
1	12	3	6			7		11			10	4	2		9	8	5												8
1		3	6	5		7		11			10	4	2		9	8		12											9
1		3	6	5		7		11			10	4	2		9	8													10
1	12	3	6	5		7		11			10		2		9	*8*		14	4										11
1	2		6	5		7		11			10	4	3		9			8											12
1	3	12	6	5		7		*4*		11	10		2		9	14		8											13
1	2	3	6			7					10	4			9	11		8	5										14
1	2	3	6			7		11				4			9	10		8	5										15
1	2	3	6			7	12	11				4			9	10		8	5										16
1	2	3	6			7	10	9				4	12			11		8	5										17
1	2	3	6			7		9			10	4		12		11		8	5										18
1	2	3	6			7		9		12	10	4				11		8	5										19
1	2	3	*6*			7		9	12		10	4	14			11		8	5										20
1	*2*	3				7		9	12		10	4	14			11	6	8	5										21
1	2	3				7		9	12		8	*4*	5			11				10	14							6	22
1		3				12	11	7			8	4	2		9	14			5	10								6	23
1	2	3				7	11	4							9			8	5	10								6	24
1	2			5		7	11				8	4	3		9	12				10								6	25
1	2			5		7	11				12	4	3		9			8		10								6	26
1	2	6		5			11	7			12		3		9			8	4	10									27
1	2	3		5		12		7					6		9	11		8	4	10									28
1	2	3		5				11				7	6		9			8		10		4							29
1	2	3		5				11				7	6		9			8		10		4							30
	2			5				11				7	6		9			8		10		4	1	3					31
	2			5				7		11		10	6		9			8				4	1	3					32
	2			5				7		11			6		9			8	12	10		4	1	3					33
	6			5						11		7	2		9			8		10		4	1	3					34
	6	12		5				9		*11*		7	2	14				8		10		4	1	3					35
1				5				11				7	2		9			8	6	10		4		3	12				36
1	6										10	11	2	12	9			8	5		14	4		3		7			37
1	6										12	*7*	2	11	9			8	5	10	14	4		3					38
	2			5							10	11			9			8	6		3	4	1			7			39
	2			5								11			9	12		8	6		10	4	1	3		7			40
	6			5		11					10		2		9	12		8				4		3		7	1		41
	6			5		11	10						2		9			8				4		3		7	1		42

Coca-Cola Cup

Second Round	Wrexham (a)	2-1
	(h)	3-2
Third Round	Blackburn R (a)	0-2

FA Cup

Third Round	WBA (h)	1-1
	(a)	2-1
Fourth Round	Norwich C (h)	0-0
	(a)	1-3

CREWE ALEXANDRA 1994–95 *Back row (left to right):* Phil Clarkson, Gus Wilson, Anthony Hughes, Steve Macauley, Danny Collier, Dele Adebola, Anthony Woodward, Rob Savage, Steve Walters.
Centre row: John Fleet (Kit Man), Steve Holland (Youth Coach), Billy Barr, Wayne Collins, Francis Tierney, Mark Smith, Ian Wilkinson, Mark Gayle, Ashley Ward, Shaun Smith, Rob Edwards, Neil Baker (Assistant Manager).
Front row: Mark Gardiner, Martyn Booty, Neil Lennon, Darren Rowbotham, Dario Gradi (Manager), Steve Garvey, Gareth Whalley, Danny Murphy, Richard Annan.
(Photograph: Steve Finch L.R.P.S.)

Division 2 CREWE ALEXANDRA

Football Ground, Gresty Rd, Crewe, CW2 6EB. Telephone: (01270) 213014.

Ground capacity: 6000.

Record attendance: 20,000 v Tottenham H, FA Cup 4th rd, 30 January 1960.

Record receipts: £41,093 v Liverpool, FA Cup 3rd rd, 6 January 1992.

Pitch measurements: 112yd × 74yd.

President: N. Rowlinson.

Chairman: J. Bowler. ***Vice-Chairman:*** N. Hassall.

Directors: K. Potts, D. Rowlinson, R. Clayton, J. McMillan, E. Weetman, J. R. Holmes, D. Gradi.

Manager: Dario Gradi.

Secretary/Commercial Manager: Mrs Gill Palin.

Year Formed: 1877. ***Turned Professional:*** 1893. ***Ltd Co.:*** 1892.

Club Nickname: 'Railwaymen'.

Foundation: Crewe Alexandra played cricket and probably rugby before they decided to form a football club in 1877. They took the name "Alexandra" after Princess Alexandra. Crewe's first trophy was the Crewe and District Cup in 1887 and it is worth noting that they reached the semi-finals of the FA Cup the following year.

First Football League game: 3 September, 1892, Division 2, v Burton Swifts (a) L 1-7 – Hickton; Moore, Cope; Linnell, Johnson, Osborne; Bennett, Pearson (1), Bailey, Barnett, Roberts.

Record League Victory: 8–0 v Rotherham U, Division 3 (N), 1 October 1932 – Foster; Pringle, Dawson; Ward, Keenor (1), Turner (1); Gillespie, Swindells (1), McConnell (2), Deacon (2), Weale (1).

Record Cup Victory: 7–1 v Gresley R, FA Cup, 1st rd, 12 November 1994 – Smith M; Booty, Smith S (1), Wilson, Macauley, Whalley, Garvey (1), Collins, Ward (3), Lennon, Rowbotham (2).

Record Defeat: 2–13 v Tottenham H, FA Cup 4th rd replay, 3 February 1960.

Most League Points (2 for a win): 59, Division 4, 1962–63.

Most League Points (3 for a win): 83, Division 2, 1994–95.

Most League Goals: 95, Division 3 (N), 1931–32.

Highest League Scorer in Season: Terry Harkin, 35, Division 4, 1964–65.

Most League Goals in Total Aggregate: Bert Swindells, 126, 1928–37.

Most Capped Player: Bill Lewis, 12 (30), Wales.

Most League Appearances: Tommy Lowry, 436, 1966–78.

Record Transfer Fee Received: £600,000 from Liverpool for Rob Jones, October 1991.

Record Transfer Fee Paid: £80,000 to Barnsley for Darren Foreman, March 1990.

Football League Record: 1892 Original Member of Division 2; 1896 Failed re-election; 1921 Re-entered Division 3 (N); 1958–63 Division 4; 1963–64 Division 3; 1964–68 Division 4; 1968–69 Division 3; 1969–89 Division 4; 1989–91 Division 3; 1991–92 Division 4; 1992–94 Division 3; 1994– Division 2.

Honours: *Football League:* Division 2 best season: 3rd, 1994–95. *FA Cup:* best season: semi-final 1888. *Football League Cup:* best season: 3rd rd, 1975, 1976, 1979, 1993. *Welsh Cup:* Winners 1936, 1937.

Colours: Red shirts, white shorts, red stockings. **Change colours:** Blue and green shirts, white shorts, blue stockings.

CREWE ALEXANDRA 1994–95 LEAGUE RECORD

Match No.	Date	Venue	Opponents	Result		H/T Score	Lg. Pos.	Goalscorers	Attendance
1	Aug 13	A	York C	W	2-1	0-0	—	Macauley 2	4420
2	20	H	Rotherham U	W	3-1	2-0	4	Rowbotham, Tierney, Ward	3505
3	27	A	Peterborough U	W	5-1	3-0	2	Rowbotham 2, Collins, Smith S (pen), Ward	4579
4	30	H	Stockport Co	W	2-1	0-0	—	Booty, Collins	5050
5	Sept 3	H	Blackpool	W	4-3	2-2	1	Garvey, Smith S (pen), Barr, Booty	4915
6	10	A	Wrexham	L	0-1	0-0	1		6399
7	13	A	Oxford U	L	1-2	0-2	—	Savage	6499
8	17	H	Wycombe W	L	1-2	0-2	5	Walters	4466
9	24	H	Brentford	L	0-2	0-1	7		3839
10	Oct 1	A	Bristol R	D	2-2	2-0	8	Ward, Garvey	4862
11	8	A	Cardiff C	W	2-1	0-1	7	Ward, Edwards	4126
12	15	H	Shrewsbury T	W	1-0	1-0	6	Ward	4296
13	22	H	Huddersfield T	D	3-3	3-2	6	Garvey, Macauley, Edwards	5352
14	29	A	Hull C	L	1-7	0-2	9	Ward	4694
15	Nov 1	A	Birmingham C	L	0-5	0-3	—		14,212
16	5	H	Swansea C	L	1-2	0-1	11	Smith S (pen)	3242
17	19	A	Bradford C	W	2-0	2-0	8	Ward, Adebola	5520
18	26	H	Cambridge U	W	4-2	1-0	6	Smith S (pen), Collins 2, Ward	3636
19	Dec 10	A	Rotherham U	D	2-2	2-0	8	Collins, Lennon	2907
20	16	H	York C	W	2-1	2-0	—	Adebola, Lennon	3432
21	26	H	Chester C	W	2-1	0-1	6	Adebola, Lennon	5428
22	27	A	Bournemouth	D	1-1	0-1	7	Collins	3325
23	31	H	Leyton Orient	W	3-0	0-0	6	Clarkson, Murphy, Bellamy (og)	3792
24	Jan 2	A	Plymouth Arg	L	2-3	2-1	7	Murphy, Clarkson	6802
25	7	A	Huddersfield T	W	2-1	1-1	6	Smith S, Collins	11,466
26	14	H	Brighton & HA	W	4-0	1-0	3	Adebola, Collins, Smith S, Clarkson	4286
27	Feb 4	A	Cambridge U	W	2-1	0-0	4	Murphy, Collins	3339
28	11	H	Birmingham C	W	2-1	1-0	4	Clarkson, Murphy	6359
29	18	A	Brighton & HA	W	1-0	1-0	4	Savage	6986
30	21	H	Bradford C	L	0-1	0-0	—		4214
31	25	H	Bristol R	W	2-1	2-0	4	Adebola, Murphy	4222
32	Mar 4	A	Brentford	L	0-2	0-1	4		7143
33	7	A	Blackpool	D	0-0	0-0	—		5859
34	11	H	Peterborough U	L	1-3	0-2	5	Rowbotham	3983
35	18	A	Stockport Co	L	1-3	0-1	5	Lennon	4946
36	21	H	Wrexham	L	1-3	0-0	—	Smith S (pen)	3632
37	25	A	Wycombe W	D	0-0	0-0	7		6288
38	Apr 1	H	Oxford U	W	3-2	1-2	6	Rowbotham, Smith S, Adebola	3928
39	8	A	Leyton Orient	W	4-1	2-1	6	Whalley, Rowbotham, Tierney, Lennon	2797
40	15	H	Bournemouth	W	2-0	1-0	6	Collins, Tierney	3906
41	17	A	Chester C	W	1-0	0-0	5	Tierney	3054
42	22	H	Plymouth Arg	D	2-2	2-1	7	Lennon, Adebola	3786
43	25	A	Swansea C	W	1-0	1-0	—	Clarkson	2600
44	29	A	Shrewsbury T	W	2-1	2-1	5	Collins, Barr	4381
45	May 2	H	Hull C	W	3-2	2-2	—	Macauley, Clarkson, Adebola	3870
46	6	H	Cardiff C	D	0-0	0-0	3		4382

Final League Position: 3

GOALSCORERS

League (80): Collins 11, Adebola 8, Smith S 8 (5 pens), Ward 8, Clarkson 6, Lennon 6, Rowbotham 6, Murphy 5, Macauley 4, Tierney 4, Garvey 3, Barr 2, Booty 2, Edwards 2, Savage 2, Walters 1, Whalley 1, own goal 1.
Coca-Cola (2): Garvey 1, Ward 1.
FA Cup (8): Ward 4, Rowbotham 2, Garvey 1, Smith S 1.

Smith M.A. 22 + 2	Booty M.J. 44	Gardiner M.C. 9 + 2	Wilson E. 20 + 1	Macauley S.R. 43	Barr W.J. 29 + 5	Tierney F. 13 + 7	Walters S.P. 8 + 3	Ward A.S. 16	Whalley G. 40	Rowbotham D. 20 + 1	Adebola B. 25 + 5	Smith G.S. 45	Garvey S.H. 22 + 6	Gayle M.S.R. 24 + 1	Collier D.J. 3 + 2	Collins W.A. 38 + 2	Murphy D.B. 20 + 15	Savage R.W. 5 + 1	Edwards R. 8 + 9	Lennon N.F. 31	Clarkson P.I. 19 + 4	McCarthy A.P. 2	Woodward A.S. — + 2	*Match No.*
1	2	3	4	5	6	7	8	9	10	11	12													1
1	2	3		5	6	7	8	9	10	11		4	12											2
	2			5	6	7		*9*	10	11	12	4		1	3	8	14							3
	2			5	6			9	10	11		3	7	1	4	8	12							4
	2			5	6		12	9	3	11		4	7	1		8	10							5
	2			5	6		4		10	11		3	7	1	12	8		*9*	14					6
	2			5	6		4	9	10			3	7	1		8	12	11						7
	2			5	6		4	9	10			3	7	1	12		8	*11*	14					8
	2	10			6		4	9			14	3	7	1	*5*	8	12		11					9
15	2	10		5	6			9	4	11		3	7	*1*		8	12							10
	2		4	5				9	6	11		3	7	1		8	10		12					11
15	2		4	5	12		14	*9*		11		3	7	*1*		8	10		6					12
	2		4	5					6	11	9	3	7	1		8	12		10					13
	2		4	5			12	9	*6*	11	14	3	7	1		8	10							14
	2		4	5		12	8	9	6	11		3		1		14	10			*7*				15
	2		4	5			8	9	*6*	11		3	12	1		14	10			7				16
1	2		4	5				9	6		11	3	7			8				10				17
1	2		4	5				9	6		11	3	7			8				10				18
1	2		4	5					6		11	3	7			8				10	9			19
1	2	12	4	5					6		11	3	7			8				10	9			20
1	2		4						6		11	3	7			8	12			10	*9*	5	14	21
1	2	6	4								11	3	7			*8*	12	14		10	9	5		22
1	2	6	4	5	12	14						3	7			8	11			10	9			23
1	2	6	4	5	12	7						3				8	11		14	10	*9*			24
1	2		4	5					6		9	3		15		8	7		11	10	12			25
1	2		4	5	12				6		9	3				8	7			10	11			26
1	2		4	5	12	14			6		9	3				8	*7*			10	11			27
1	2			5	4	8			6		9	3	12				7			10	11			28
1	2			5	4	12			6			3	8				7	9		10	11			29
1	2			5	4	12			6			3	8				7	*9*		10	11		14	30
1	2			5	4				6		*9*	3	12			8	7		14	10	11			31
1			2	5	4	12			6		9	3				8	7		14	10	*11*			32
1	2			5	4				6		9	3				8	7		11	10	12			33
1	*2*		14	5	4				6	12		3				8	7		11	10	9			34
1			4	5	2				6	9	14	3	12			8			7	10	*11*			35
1	2			5	4				6	11	9	3	12			8			7	10				36
	2			5	4				6	11	9	3	7	1		8	12			10				37
	2			5	4	12			6	*11*	9	3	7	1		8				10	14			38
	2			5	4	7			6	11	9	3		1		8	12			10				39
	2	12		5	4	7			6	*11*	9	3		1		8	14			10				40
	2			5	4	7			6	11	9	3		1		8	12			10				41
	2	6		5	4	7					9	3		1		8	12		14	10	*11*			42
	2	10		5	4	7			6		9	3		1		8			12		11			43
	2			5	4	7			6		9	3		1		8	12			10	11			44
	2			5	4	7			6		9	3		1		8	12			10	11			45
	2			5	4	7			6		*9*	3		1		8	11		12	10	14			46

Coca-Cola Cup

First Round	Wigan Ath (h)	2-1
	(a)	0-3

FA Cup

First Round	Gresley R (h)	7-1
Second Round	Bury (h)	1-2

CRYSTAL PALACE 1994–95 *Back row (left to right):* Paul Sparrow, Glen Little, Eric Smith, Eddie Dixon.
Third row: Kevin Hall, Brian Launders, George Ndah, Darren Patterson, Andrew Preece, Ian Cox, Andy Thorn, Bobby Bowry, Ricky Newman, Jamie Vincent, Anthony Scully
Second row: Spike Hill, David Kemp, Bruce Dyer, Ray Wilkins, Damian Matthew, Dean Gordon, Jimmy Glass, Nigel Martyn, Richard Shaw, Darren Pitcher, Paul Williams, Ray Lewington, Peter McLean.
Front row: John Salako, John Humphrey, Chris Armstrong, Ron Noades, Alan Smith, Gareth Southgate, Chris Coleman, Simon Rodger, Eric Young.

Division 1 CRYSTAL PALACE

Selhurst Park, London SE25 6PU. Telephone: (0181) 653 1000. Fax: (0181) 771 5311. Lottery Office: (0181) 771 9502. Club Shop: (0181) 653 5584. Dial-A-Seat Ticketline: (0181) 771 8841. Palace Publications: (0181) 771 8299. Fax: (0181) 653 6312. Palace Clubline: 0891 400 333. Palace Ticket Line: 0891 400 334 (normal 0891 charges apply for these services).

Ground capacity: 26,400.

Record attendance: 51,482 v Burnley, Division 2, 11 May 1979.

Record receipts: £327,124 v Manchester U, FA Premier League, 21 April 1993 (League); £336,583 v Chelsea, Coca-Cola Cup 5th rd, 6 January 1993.

Pitch measurements: 110yd × 74yd.

Chairman: R. G. Noades.

Directors: R. G. Noades (Chairman and Managing), B. Coleman OBE, A. S. C. De Souza, M. E. Lee, S. Hume-Kendall, P. H. J. Norman, R. E. Anderson, V. E. Murphy, C. L. Noades, S. R. Ebbs MS, FRCS, D. A. Miller, P. L. Morley CBE, JP.

Technical Director: Steve Coppell. ***First Team Coaches:*** Ray Lewington, Peter Nicholas. ***Physio:*** Peter McClean.

Company Secretary: Doug Miller. ***Club Secretary:*** Mike Hurst. ***Assistant Secretary:*** Terry Byfield. ***Sales and Marketing Manager:*** Mike Ryan.

Year Formed: 1905. ***Turned Professional:*** 1905. ***Ltd Co.:*** 1905.

Club Nickname: 'The Eagles'.

Club Sponsor: TDK.

Previous Grounds: 1905, Crystal Palace; 1915, Herne Hill; 1918, The Nest; 1924, Selhurst Park.

Foundation: There was a Crystal Palace club as early as 1861 but the present organisation was born in 1905 after the formation of a club by the company that controlled the Crystal Palace (the building that is), had been rejected by the FA who did not like the idea of the Cup Final hosts running their own club. A separate company had to be formed and they had their home on the old Cup Final ground until 1915.

First Football League game: 28 August, 1920, Division 3, v Merthyr T (a) L 1-2 – Alderson; Little, Rhodes; McCracken, Jones, Feebury; Bateman, Conner, Smith, Milligan (1), Whibley.

Record League Victory: 9–0 v Barrow, Division 4, 10 October 1959 – Rouse; Long, Noakes; Truett, Evans, McNichol; Gavin (1), Summersby (4 incl. 1p), Sexton, Byrne (2), Colfar (2).

Record Cup Victory: 8–0 v Southend U, Rumbelows League Cup, 2nd rd (1st leg), 25 September 1990 – Martyn; Humphrey (Thompson (1)), Shaw, Pardew, Young, Thorn, McGoldrick, Thomas, Bright (3), Wright (3), Barber (Hodges (1)).

Record Defeat: 0–9 v Burnley, FA Cup, 2nd rd replay, 10 February 1909 and 0–9 v Liverpool, Division 1, 12 September 1990.

Most League Points (2 for a win): 64, Division 4, 1960–61.

Most League Points (3 for a win): 90, Division 1, 1993–94.

Most League Goals: 110, Division 4, 1960–61.

Highest League Scorer in Season: Peter Simpson, 46, Division 3 (S), 1930–31.

Most League Goals in Total Aggregate: Peter Simpson, 153, 1930–36.

Most Capped Player: Eric Young, 19 (20), Wales.

Most League Appearances: Jim Cannon, 571, 1973–88.

Record Transfer Fee Received: £4,500,000 from Tottenham H for Chris Armstrong, June 1995.

Record Transfer Fee Paid: £1,800,000 to Sunderland for Marco Gabbiadini, September 1991.

Football League Record: 1920 Original Members of Division 3; 1921–25 Division 2; 1925–58 Division 3 (S); 1958–61 Division 4; 1961–64 Division 3; 1964–69 Division 2; 1969–73 Division 1; 1973–74 Division 2; 1974–77 Division 3; 1977–79 Division 2; 1979–81 Division 1; 1981–89 Division 2; 1989–92 Division 1; 1992–93 FA Premier League; 1993–94 Division 1; 1994–95 FA Premier League; 1995– Division 1.

Honours: *Football League:* Division 1 – Champions 1993–94; 3rd 1990–91; Division 2 – Champions 1978–79; Runners-up 1968–69; Division 3 – Runners-up 1963–64; Division 3 (S) – Champions 1920–21; Runners-up 1928–29, 1930–31, 1938–39; Division 4 – Runners-up 1960–61. *FA Cup:* best season: Runners-up 1990. *Football League Cup:* best season; semi-final 1993, 1995. *Zenith Data System Cup:* Winners: 1991.

Colours: Red and blue shirts, red shorts, red stockings. **Change colours:** White shirts, red or blue shorts, red or blue stockings.

CRYSTAL PALACE 1994–95 LEAGUE RECORD

Match No.	Date	Venue	Opponents	Result		H/T Score	Lg. Pos.	Goalscorers	Attendance
1	Aug 20	H	Liverpool	L	1-6	0-3	—	Armstrong	18,084
2	24	A	Norwich C	D	0-0	0-0	—		19,015
3	27	A	Aston Villa	D	1-1	0-0	18	Southgate	23,305
4	30	H	Leeds U	L	1-2	0-1	—	Gordon	14,453
5	Sept 10	A	Manchester C	D	1-1	1-1	17	Dyer	19,971
6	17	H	Wimbledon	D	0-0	0-0	21		12,366
7	24	H	Chelsea	L	0-1	0-0	21		16,064
8	Oct 1	A	Arsenal	W	2-1	2-0	17	Salako 2	34,136
9	8	A	West Ham U	L	0-1	0-0	19		16,959
10	15	H	Newcastle U	L	0-1	0-0	20		17,739
11	22	H	Everton	W	1-0	0-0	17	Preece	15,026
12	29	A	Leicester C	W	1-0	1-0	16	Preece	20,022
13	Nov 2	A	Coventry C	W	4-1	2-1	—	Preece 2, Salako, Newman	10,729
14	5	H	Ipswich T	W	3-0	1-0	11	Newman, Armstrong, Salako	13,450
15	19	A	Manchester U	L	0-3	0-2	12		43,788
16	26	H	Southampton	D	0-0	0-0	13		14,186
17	Dec 3	A	Sheffield W	L	0-1	0-1	15		21,930
18	11	A	Liverpool	D	0-0	0-0	13		30,972
19	17	H	Norwich C	L	0-1	0-0	16		12,473
20	26	H	QPR	D	0-0	0-0	17		16,699
21	27	A	Tottenham H	D	0-0	0-0	—		27,730
22	31	H	Blackburn R	L	0-1	0-0	18		14,232
23	Jan 2	A	Nottingham F	L	0-1	0-0	18		21,326
24	14	H	Leicester C	W	2-0	2-0	16	Newman, Ndah	12,707
25	21	A	Everton	L	1-3	0-1	17	Coleman	23,734
26	25	H	Manchester U	D	1-1	0-0	—	Southgate	18,224
27	Feb 4	A	Ipswich T	W	2-0	0-0	16	Dowie, Gordon (pen)	15,361
28	11	H	Coventry C	L	0-2	0-0	18		12,076
29	25	H	Arsenal	L	0-3	0-2	19		17,063
30	Mar 5	A	Chelsea	D	0-0	0-0	20		14,130
31	14	H	Sheffield W	W	2-1	0-1	—	Armstrong, Dowie	10,964
32	18	A	Wimbledon	L	0-2	0-1	19		8835
33	Apr 1	H	Manchester C	W	2-1	1-0	19	Armstrong, Patterson	13,451
34	4	H	Aston Villa	D	0-0	0-0	—		12,949
35	14	H	Tottenham H	D	1-1	1-0	—	Armstrong	18,068
36	17	A	QPR	W	1-0	0-0	19	Dowie	14,227
37	20	A	Blackburn R	L	1-2	0-0	—	Houghton	28,005
38	29	H	Nottingham F	L	1-2	0-1	19	Dowie	16,335
39	May 3	A	Southampton	L	1-3	1-2	—	Southgate	15,151
40	6	H	West Ham U	W	1-0	0-0	19	Armstrong	18,224
41	9	A	Leeds U	L	1-3	0-2	—	Armstrong	30,963
42	14	A	Newcastle U	L	2-3	0-3	19	Armstrong, Houghton	35,626

Final League Position: 19

GOALSCORERS

League (34): Armstrong 8, Dowie 4, Preece 4, Salako 4, Newman 3, Southgate 3, Gordon 2 (1 pen), Houghton 2, Coleman 1, Dyer 1, Ndah 1, Patterson 1.
Coca-Cola Cup (12): Armstrong 5, Southgate 2, Dyer 1, Gordon 1, Pitcher 1, Preece 1, Salako 1.
FA Cup (15): Armstrong 5, Dowie 4, Salako 2, Coleman 1, Gordon 1 (pen), Ndah 1, Pitcher 1.

Martyn A.N. 37	Pitcher D.E.J. 21 + 4	Gordon D.D. 38 + 3	Southgate G. 42	Young E. 13	Coleman C. 35	Rodger S.L. 4	Wilkins R.C. 1	Armstrong C.P. 40	Preece A.P. 17 + 3	Salako J.A. 39	Bowry R. 13 + 5	Dyer B.A. 7 + 9	Patterson D.J. 22	Shaw R.E. 41	Newman R.A. 32 + 3	Cox I.G. 1 + 10	Matthew D. 2 + 2	Ndah G.E. 5 + 7	Launders B.T. 1 + 1	Humphrey J. 19 + 2	Williams P.A. 2 + 2	Wilmot R.J. 5 + 1	Dowie I. 15	Houghton R.J. 10	Match No.
1	2	3	4	5	6	7	8	9	*10*	11	12	14													1
1		3	4		6	7		9		11	8	*10*	2	5	12	14									2
1	12	3	4		6	*7*		9		11		10	2	5	8	14									3
1		3	4		6	7		9	10	11		8	2	5	12										4
1		2	4		6			9		11		7	3	5	8		10								5
1	2	3	4		6			9		11		7		5	8		10	12							6
1		2	4		6			9		11		12	3	5	8			10	7						7
1		2	4		6			9		11	7		3	5	8			10							8
1		3	4		6			9		11	7	12	*2*	5	8			10	14						9
1		3	4		6			9	10	11	7			5	8					2					10
1	12	3	4		6			9	10	11	7			5	8					2					11
1	12	3	4		6			9	10	11	7			5	8					2					12
1		3	4		6			9	10	11			2	5	8					7					13
1		3	4		6			9	10	11	7			5	8					2					14
1		3	4		6			9	10	11	12		2	5	8					7					15
1		3	4		6			9	10	11	7	12		5	8					2					16
1		3	4		6			9	10	11	7			5	8			12		2					17
1	6	3	4					9	10	11	7			5	8					2					18
1	14	3	4		6			9	10	11	7	12		*5*	8					2					19
1		3	4		6			9	10	11				5	8	7				2	12				20
1	10	3	4		6			9		11	7		2	5	8						12				21
1		3	4		6			9	10				2	5	8			12		7	11				22
1	10	3	4		6			9					2	5	8			12		7	11	15			23
1	10	3	4		6			9	12	11				5	8			*7*		2					24
1	10	3	4		6			9		11				5	8			12		2			7		25
1	10	3	4		6			9	12	11			2	5	8								7		26
1	10	3	4		6			9		11	12		2	5	8								7		27
1	10	3	4		6				12	11	7		2	5				8					9		28
1	10	3	4		6			9		11		12	2	5	*8*		14			7					29
1	7	3	4	*6*					10	11			2	5	8		14	12					9		30
1	2	12	4	6	3			9	10	11				5	8								7		31
1	2	12	4	6	3			9	10	11				5	*8*					14			7		32
1	10		4	6	3			9		*11*		7	2	5		14		12						8	33
1	10	12	4	6	3			9		11		*7*	2	5		14								8	34
	10	3	4	6				9		*11*			2	5	12	14						1	7	8	35
		3	4	6	5			9		11	14			2	7	*12*						1	10	8	36
		11	4	6	3			9					2	5	7	14				*12*		1	10	8	37
		3	4		6			9		11	14			5	*7*	12				2		1	10	8	38
	10	3	4	6				9		11		12		5						2		1	7	8	39
1	10	3	4	6				9		11				5						2			7	8	40
1	10	3	4	6				9		11		12	2	5		14							7	*8*	41
1	2	3	4	6				9		11		12		5	*10*	14							7	8	42

Coca-Cola Cup

Second Round	Lincoln C (a)	0-1
	(h)	3-0
Third Round	Wimbledon (a)	1-0
Fourth Round	Aston Villa (h)	4-1
Fifth Round	Manchester C (h)	4-0
Semi-final	Liverpool (a)	0-1
	(h)	0-1

FA Cup

Third Round	Lincoln C (h)	5-1
Fourth Round	Nottingham F (a)	2-1
Fifth Round	Watford (a)	0-0
	(h)	1-0
Sixth Round	Wolverhampton W (h)	1-1
	(a)	4-1
Semi-final	Manchester U at Villa Park	2-2
	Replay at Villa Park	0-2

DARLINGTON 1994–95 *Back row (left to right):* Darren Collier, Mike Pollitt, Ryan Scott.
Third row: Matty Appleby, Robbie Painter, Steve Gaughan, Andy Crosby, Sean Gregan, Adam Reed, Ian Banks.
Second row: Simon Shaw, Paul Cross, Nigel Carnel (Physio), Alan Murray, Eddie Kyle, Paul Olsson, Bernie Slaven.
Front row: Gary Himsworth, Peter Kirkham, Robert Blake, Andy Ripley, Gary Chapman, Paul Mattison.

Division 3 DARLINGTON

Feethams Ground, Darlington, DL1 5JB. Telephone: (01325) 465097. Fax: (01325) 381377.

Ground capacity: 7046.

Record attendance: 21,023 v Bolton W, League Cup 3rd rd, 14 November 1960.

Record receipts: £32,300 v Rochdale, Division 4, 11 May 1991.

Pitch measurements: 110yd × 74yd.

President: A. Noble.

Chairman: S. Weeks. ***Vice-Chairman:*** G. Hodgson.

Director: S. Morgon.

Directors of Coaching: David Hodgson, Jim Platt. ***Coach:*** J. Hope.

Chief Executive: T. D. Hughes.

Secretary: S. Morgon. ***Physio:*** Nigel Carnell.

Year Formed: 1883. ***Turned Professional:*** 1908. ***Ltd Co.:*** 1891.

Club Nickname: 'The Quakers'.

Foundation: A football club was formed in Darlington as early as 1861 but the present club began in 1883 and reached the final of the Durham Senior Cup in their first season, losing to Sunderland in a replay after complaining that they had suffered from intimidation in the first. The following season Darlington won this trophy and for many years were one of the leading amateur clubs in their area.

First Football League game: 27 August, 1921, Division 3(N), v Halifax T (h) W 2-0 – Ward; Greaves, Barbour; Dickson (1), Sutcliffe, Malcolm; Dolphin, Hooper (1), Edmunds, Wolstenholme, Winship.

Record League Victory: 9–2 v Lincoln C, Division 3 (N), 7 January 1928 – Archibald; Brooks, Mellen; Kelly, Waugh, McKinnell; Cochrane (1), Gregg (1), Ruddy (3), Lees (3), McGiffen (1).

Record Cup Victory: 7–2 v Evenwood T, FA Cup, 1st rd, 17 November 1956 – Ward; Devlin, Henderson; Bell (1p), Greener, Furphy; Forster (1), Morton (3), Tulip (2), Davis, Moran.

Record Defeat: 0–10 v Doncaster R, Division 4, 25 January 1964.

Most League Points (2 for a win): 59, Division 4, 1965–66.

Most League Points (3 for a win): 85, Division 4, 1984–85.

Most League Goals: 108, Division 3 (N), 1929–30.

Highest League Scorer in Season: David Brown, 39, Division 3 (N), 1924–25.

Most League Goals in Total Aggregate: Alan Walsh, 90, 1978–84.

Most Capped Player: None.

Most League Appearances: Ron Greener, 442, 1955–68.

Record Transfer Fee Received: £200,000 from Leicester C for Jim Willis, December 1991.

Record Transfer Fee Paid: £95,000 to Motherwell for Nick Cusack, January 1992.

Football League Record: 1921 Original Member Division 3 (N); 1925–27 Division 2; 1927–58 Division 3 (N); 1958–66 Division 4; 1966–67 Division 3; 1967–85 Division 4; 1985–87 Division 3; 1987–89 Division 4; 1989–90 GM Vauxhall Conference; 1990–91 Division 4; 1991– Division 3.

Honours: *Football League:* Division 2 best season: 15th, 1925–26; Division 3 (N) – Champions 1924–25; Runners-up 1921–22; Division 4 Champions 1990–91 – Runners-up 1965–66. *FA Cup:* best season: 3rd rd, 1911, 5th rd, 1958. *Football League Cup:* best season: 5th rd, 1968. *GM Vauxhall Conference:* Champions 1989–90.

Colours: Black and white. **Change colours:** All red.

DARLINGTON 1994–95 LEAGUE RECORD

Match No.	Date	Venue	Opponents	Result		H/T Score	Lg. Pos.	Goalscorers	Attendance
1	Aug 13	H	Preston NE	D	0-0	0-0	—		3800
2	20	A	Hartlepool U	L	0-1	0-0	16		3035
3	27	H	Exeter C	W	2-0	0-0	13	Gaughan, Painter	1861
4	30	A	Mansfield T	W	1-0	0-0	—	Gaughan	2427
5	Sept 3	A	Doncaster R	D	0-0	0-0	9		2967
6	10	H	Torquay U	W	2-1	1-1	8	Painter, Gaughan	2161
7	13	H	Scunthorpe U	L	1-3	1-2	—	Painter	2181
8	17	A	Preston NE	W	3-1	1-0	7	Appleby, Olsson, Chapman	8884
9	24	H	Colchester U	L	2-3	1-2	9	Chapman, Himsworth	2260
10	Oct 1	A	Carlisle U	L	1-2	1-0	12	Painter	6100
11	8	H	Bury	L	0-2	0-0	14		2352
12	15	A	Chesterfield	D	0-0	0-0	13		2836
13	22	H	Hereford U	W	3-1	0-0	11	Gregan, Olsson, Painter	1996
14	29	A	Gillingham	L	1-2	1-1	13	Painter	2785
15	Nov 5	H	Walsall	D	2-2	1-0	13	Painter, Gregan	2186
16	19	A	Wigan Ath	L	1-4	1-2	15	Worboys	1785
17	26	H	Barnet	L	0-1	0-0	16		2157
18	Dec 10	H	Hartlepool U	L	1-2	1-1	16	Burgess (og)	3193
19	17	A	Exeter C	W	2-0	1-0	15	Gaughan, Worboys	2338
20	26	H	Scarborough	W	1-0	1-0	14	Slaven	2958
21	27	A	Lincoln C	L	1-3	1-1	15	Slaven	2964
22	31	H	Northampton T	W	4-1	1-0	13	Slaven, Banks, Gaughan, Shaw	2250
23	Jan 7	A	Hereford U	D	0-0	0-0	13		2237
24	14	H	Fulham	D	0-0	0-0	13		2113
25	Feb 4	A	Barnet	W	3-2	2-0	14	Worboys 2, Gaughan	2034
26	11	H	Wigan Ath	L	1-3	0-1	15	Worboys	1780
27	18	A	Fulham	L	1-3	0-1	15	Slaven	3864
28	21	H	Gillingham	W	2-0	0-0	—	Slaven, Painter	1548
29	25	H	Carlisle U	L	0-2	0-1	16		3992
30	Mar 4	A	Colchester U	L	0-1	0-1	16		6055
31	11	A	Torquay U	L	0-1	0-0	16		2332
32	14	A	Walsall	L	0-2	0-1	—		3154
33	18	H	Mansfield T	D	0-0	0-0	16		1613
34	21	A	Rochdale	L	0-2	0-0	—		1471
35	25	H	Doncaster R	L	0-2	0-0	16		2017
36	Apr 1	A	Scunthorpe U	L	1-2	1-1	17	Olsson	2449
37	8	A	Northampton T	L	1-2	0-1	18	Painter	4496
38	15	H	Lincoln C	D	0-0	0-0	17		1664
39	18	A	Scarborough	L	1-3	0-1	—	Olsson	2182
40	22	H	Rochdale	W	4-0	2-0	17	Worboys (pen), Gaughan 2, Himsworth	1886
41	29	H	Chesterfield	L	0-1	0-1	19		3387
42	May 6	A	Bury	L	1-2	1-1	20	Reed	3612

Final League Position: 20

GOALSCORERS

League (43): Painter 9, Gaughan 8, Worboys 6 (1 pen), Slaven 5, Olsson 4, Chapman 2, Gregan 2, Himsworth 2, Appleby 1, Banks 1, Reed 1, Shaw 1, own goal 1.
Coca-Cola Cup (2): Cross 1, Slaven 1.
FA Cup (3): Worboys 2, Slaven 1.

Pollitt M.F. 40	Appleby M.W. 35 + 1	Cross P. 13	Crosby A. 35	Gregan S.M. 22 + 3	Banks I.F. 39	Slaven B. 24 + 2	Painter P.R. 34 + 4	Gaughan S.E. 39 + 2	Olsson P. 42	Mattison P. 4 + 6	Himsworth G.P. 32 + 6	Chapman G.A. 19 + 14	Reed A.M. 34 + 4	Collier D. 2	Taylor M.S. 8	Worboys G. 24 + 3	Kirkham P.J. 3 + 1	Shaw S.R. 9 + 3	Blake R.J. 3 + 6	Bolton N.A. 1 + 1	*Match No.*
1	2	3	4	5	6	7	8	9	10	11	12										1
1	2	3	5	*6*	4	7	8	9	10		12	11	14								2
1	2	3	5			7	8	9	10		11	4	6								3
1	2	3	5		4	7	8	9	10			11	6								4
1	2	3	5		4	7	8	9	10		12	11	6								5
1	2	3	5		4	7	8	9	10	14	*12*	11	6								6
1	2	3	5		4	7	8	9	10		12	11	6								7
1	2	3	5		4		8	9	10		7	11	6								8
1	2	3	5		4	12	8	9	10		7	11	6								9
1	2	3	5	6	4	7	8	9	10		11	12									10
1	2	3	5	6	4	7		9	10	12	11	8	14								11
1	2	3	5	6	4		8	9	10	7		11	12								12
		3	5	6	4	12	8	9	10	14	7	11	2	1							13
	2		5	6	4	7	8	9	10		11	12		1	3						14
1	2		5	6	4		8	9	10		11		12		3	7					15
1	2			6	4		8	9	10		7		5		3	11					16
1	2			6	4	7	8	12	10		11		5		3	9					17
1	2		5		4	7	8	12	10		11	14	6		3	*9*					18
1	2		5		4	7	8	11	10		12	14	6		3	9					19
1			5		4	7	8	*11*	10	14	2	12	6		3	9					20
1			5		4	7	8	*11*	10	14	2	12	6		3	9					21
1	2		5		*4*	7		8	10		3	12	6			9	11	14			22
1	2		5	12	4	7	8	11	*10*		3	14	6			9					23
1	2		5		4		8	11	10		3		6			9	7				24
1	2		5	12	4	7	8	11	10		3	14	6			9					25
1	2		5		4	7	8	11	10		3	12	6			9					26
1	2		5	3	4	7	8	11	10			12	6			9					27
1			5	3		7	8	11	10		4	2	6			9					28
1	12		5	3		7	8	11	10		4	2	6			9					29
1	2			5	4	7	8	11	10		3	9						6	12		30
1	2				4		8	11	10		3	12	5			9	7	6	14		31
1	2		5		4		8	11	10		3	12	6			*9*		7	14		32
1			5	2	4		*8*	11	10	7	3	12	6			14			9		33
1			5	2	4	7	12		10	*8*	3		6			11		14	9		34
1	7		5	2	4		8	11	10		3		6			*9*		12		14	35
1	7		5	2	4		8	11	10		3		6			9			12		36
1	7			5	4		*8*	11	10	12	3		6			9		2	14		37
1	7			5	4			11	10		3	9	6			12		2	8		38
1	7			5	4			11	10		3	9	6			12	14	*2*		8	39
1	7		5		*4*		12	11	10		3	8	6			9		2	14		40
1	7		5	12	4		14	11	10		3	*8*	6			9		2			41
1	7		5	3	4		12	11	10			8	6			9		2			42

Coca-Cola Cup

First Round	Barnsley (h)	2-2
	(a)	0-0

FA Cup

First Round	Hyde (a)	3-1
Second Round	Carlisle U (a)	0-2

DERBY COUNTY 1994–95 *Back row (left to right):* Jason Kavanagh, Darren Wassall, Michael Forsyth, Craig Short, Paul Williams, Shane Nicholson, Martin Kuhl.
Centre row: Billy McEwan (Coach), Alan Durban (Assistant Manager), Steve Hayward, Mark Stallard, Martin Taylor, Steve Sutton, Tommy Johnson, John Harkes, Gary Charles, Gordon Guthrie (Physio).
Front row: Dean Sturridge, Paul Simpson, Marco Gabbiadini, Roy McFarland (Manager), Gordon Cowans, Paul Kitson, Mark Pembridge.

Division 1 **DERBY COUNTY**

Baseball Ground, Shaftesbury Crescent, Derby DE3 8NB. Telephone: (01332) 340505. Fax: (01332) 293514. Ramtique Sports Shop: (01332) 292081. Clubcall: 0891 121187.

Ground capacity: 19,500 (15,000 seated).

Record attendance: 41,826 v Tottenham H, Division 1, 20 September 1969.

Record receipts: £146,651 v Aston Villa, FA Cup 4th rd, 5 February 1992.

Pitch measurements: 110yd × 71yd.

President:

Chairman: L. V. Pickering. ***Vice-Chairman:*** P. J. Gadsby.

Directors: J. N. Kirkland, A. S. Webb.

Manager: Jim Smith. ***Chief Scout:*** Alan Durban.

Coach: Billy McEwan. ***Physio:*** Gordon Guthrie.

Secretary: Lance Luckhurst. ***Commercial Manager:*** Colin Tunnicliffe.

Year Formed: 1884. ***Turned Professional:*** 1884. ***Ltd Co.:*** 1896.

Club Nickname: 'The Rams'.

Previous Grounds: 1884–95, Racecourse Ground; 1895, Baseball Ground.

Foundation: Derby County was formed by members of the Derbyshire County Cricket Club in 1884, when football was booming in the area and the cricketers thought that a football club would help boost finances for the summer game. To begin with, they sported the cricket club's colours of amber, chocolate and pale blue, and went into the game at the top immediately entering the FA Cup.

First Football League game: 8 September, 1888, Football League, v Bolton W (a) W 6-3 – Marshall; Latham, Ferguson, Williamson; Monks, W. Roulstone; Bakewell (2), Cooper (2), Higgins, H. Plackett, L. Plackett (2).

Record League Victory: 9–0 v Wolverhampton W, Division 1, 10 January 1891 – Bunyan; Archie Goodall, Roberts; Walker, Chalmers, Roulston (1); Bakewell, McLachlan, Johnny Goodall (1), Holmes (2), McMillan (5). 9–0 v Sheffield W, Division 1, 21 January 1899 – Fryer; Methven, Staley; Cox, Archie Goodall, May; Oakden (1), Bloomer (6), Boag, McDonald (1), Allen. (1 og).

Record Cup Victory: 12–0 v Finn Harps, UEFA Cup, 1st rd 1st leg, 15 September 1976 – Moseley; Thomas, Nish, Rioch (1), McFarland, Todd (King), Macken, Gemmill, Hector (5), George (3), James (3).

Record Defeat: 2–11 v Everton, FA Cup 1st rd, 1889–90.

Most League Points (2 for a win): 63, Division 2, 1968–69 and Division 3 (N), 1955–56 and 1956–57.

Most League Points (3 for a win): 84, Division 3, 1985–86 and Division 3, 1986–87.

Most League Goals: 111, Division 3 (N), 1956–57.

Highest League Scorer in Season: Jack Bowers, 37, Division 1, 1930–31 and Ray Straw, 37 Division 3 (N), 1956–57.

Most League Goals in Total Aggregate: Steve Bloomer, 292, 1892–1906 and 1910–14.

Most Capped Player: Peter Shilton, 34 (125), England.

Most League Appearances: Kevin Hector, 486, 1966–78 and 1980–82.

Record Transfer Fee Received: £2,900,000 from Liverpool for Dean Saunders, July 1991.

Record Transfer Fee Paid: £2,500,000 to Notts Co for Craig Short, September 1992.

Football League Record: 1888 Founder Member of the Football League; 1907–12 Division 2; 1912–14 Division 1; 1914–15 Division 2; 1915–21 Division 1; 1921–26 Division 2; 1926–53 Division 1; 1953–55 Division 2; 1955–57 Division 3 (N); 1957–69 Division 2; 1969–80 Division 1; 1980–84 Division 2; 1984–86 Division 3; 1986–87 Division 2; 1987–91 Division 1; 1991–92 Division 2; 1992– Division 1.

Honours: *Football League:* Division 1 – Champions 1971–72, 1974–75; Runners-up 1895–96, 1929–30, 1935–36; Division 2 – Champions 1911–12, 1914–15, 1968–69, 1986–87; Runners-up 1925–26; Division 3 (N) Champions 1956–57; Runners-up 1955–56. *FA Cup:* Winners 1946; Runners-up 1898, 1899, 1903. *Football League Cup:* Semi-final 1968. *Texaco Cup:* 1972. **European Competitions:** *European Cup:* 1972–73, 1975–76; *UEFA Cup:* 1974–75, 1976–77. *Anglo-Italian Cup:* Runners-up 1993.

Colours: White shirts, black shorts, white stockings. **Change colours:** All Petrol blue.

DERBY COUNTY 1994–95 LEAGUE RECORD

Match No.	Date	Venue	Opponents	Result		H/T Score	Lg. Pos.	Goalscorers	Attendance
1	Aug 13	A	Barnsley	L	1-2	1-2	—	Pembridge	8737
2	20	H	Luton T	D	0-0	0-0	19		13,060
3	27	A	Millwall	L	1-4	0-1	21	Sturridge	8809
4	31	H	Middlesbrough	L	0-1	0-1	—		14,659
5	Sept 3	H	Grimsby T	W	2-1	1-0	21	Charles, Pembridge	12,027
6	11	A	Swindon T	D	1-1	1-1	20	Kitson	9054
7	13	A	Bristol C	W	2-0	1-0	—	Kitson, Carsley	8029
8	17	H	Oldham Ath	W	2-1	1-0	11	Carsley, Short	13,746
9	25	H	Stoke C	W	3-0	2-0	6	Hodge, Gabbiadini, Charles	11,782
10	Oct 1	A	Bolton W	L	0-1	0-0	8		12,015
11	8	H	Watford	D	1-1	0-1	11	Hodge	13,413
12	16	A	Southend U	L	0-1	0-0	15		4218
13	23	A	Notts Co	D	0-0	0-0	18		6389
14	29	H	Charlton Ath	D	2-2	1-1	16	Short, Johnson	12,588
15	Nov 2	H	Reading	L	1-2	0-1	—	Gabbiadini	10,585
16	6	A	Portsmouth	W	1-0	0-0	17	Gabbiadini	5507
17	12	A	Sheffield U	L	1-2	0-0	18	Simpson (pen)	15,001
18	19	H	Port Vale	W	2-0	1-0	14	Johnson 2	13,357
19	27	A	Wolverhampton W	W	2-0	1-0	11	Johnson, Stallard	22,768
20	Dec 3	H	Notts Co	D	0-0	0-0	13		14,278
21	11	A	Luton T	D	0-0	0-0	14		6400
22	17	H	Barnsley	W	1-0	0-0	10	Johnson	13,205
23	26	A	Tranmere R	L	1-3	0-1	14	Johnson	11,581
24	31	A	Sunderland	D	1-1	0-0	15	Johnson	13,979
25	Jan 2	H	WBA	D	1-1	0-1	16	Trollope	16,035
26	14	A	Charlton Ath	W	4-3	1-3	13	Short, Gabbiadini 2, Stallard	9389
27	22	H	Portsmouth	W	3-0	0-0	8	Simpson 3	11,143
28	Feb 4	H	Sheffield U	L	2-3	1-1	12	Williams, Kavanagh	15,882
29	11	A	Reading	L	0-1	0-1	13		8834
30	21	A	Port Vale	L	0-1	0-0	—		9387
31	26	H	Bolton W	W	2-1	0-1	12	Yates, Mills	11,003
32	Mar 4	A	Stoke C	D	0-0	0-0	13		13,462
33	7	A	Grimsby T	W	1-0	0-0	—	Pembridge	5310
34	11	H	Millwall	W	3-2	1-1	10	Pembridge, Trollope, Gabbiadini	12,490
35	15	H	Burnley	W	4-0	1-0	—	Mills, Trollope, Simpson (pen), Gabbiadini	13,922
36	18	A	Middlesbrough	W	4-2	3-0	8	Mills 2, Pembridge, Gabbiadini	18,168
37	22	H	Swindon T	W	3-1	1-1	—	Simpson (pen), Pembridge, Mills	16,839
38	25	A	Oldham Ath	L	0-1	0-1	8		7696
39	Apr 1	H	Bristol C	W	3-1	2-1	8	Gabbiadini, Williams, Wrack	14,555
40	8	H	Sunderland	L	0-1	0-1	8		15,442
41	12	H	Wolverhampton W	D	3-3	1-1	—	Simpson 2 (1 pen), Gabbiadini	16,040
42	15	A	Burnley	L	1-3	0-2	8	Trollope	11,534
43	17	H	Tranmere R	W	5-0	2-0	7	Pembridge 2, Mills, Williams, Gabbiadini	13,957
44	22	A	WBA	D	0-0	0-0	7		15,265
45	29	H	Southend U	L	1-2	0-2	7	Mills	12,528
46	May 7	A	Watford	L	1-2	0-1	9	Pembridge	8492

Final League Position: 9

GOALSCORERS

League (66): Gabbiadini 11, Pembridge 9, Simpson 8 (4 pens), Johnson 7, Mills 7, Trollope 4, Short 3, Williams 3, Carsley 2, Charles 2, Hodge 2, Kitson 2, Stallard 2, Kavanagh 1, Sturridge 1, Wrack 1, Yates 1.
Coca-Cola Cup (5): Gabbiadini 2, Simpson 1, Stallard 1, Williams 1.
FA Cup (0).

Taylor M.J. 12	Charles G.A. 18	Forsyth M.E. 21 + 1	Hayward S.L. 3	Short C.J. 37	Williams P.D. 37	Cowans G.S. 17	Gabbiadini M. 30 + 2	Kitson P. 8	Pembridge M.A. 27	Simpson P.D. 37 + 5	Harkes J.A. 29 + 4	Wassall D.P. 25 + 7	Johnson T. 14	Nicholson S.M. 15	Kuhl M. 9	Kavanagh J.C. 20 + 5	Sturridge D.C. 7 + 5	Hodge S.B. 10	Stallard M. 13 + 3	Carsley L.K. 22 + 1	Davies W. 1 + 1	Sutton S.J. 19 + 1	Trollope P.J. 23 + 1	Wrack D. 2 + 14	Sutton W.F. 3 + 3	Yates D.R. 11	Mills R.L. 16	Hoult R. 15	Boden C.D. 4 + 2	Ashbee I. 1	Cooper K.L. — + 1	*Match No.*
1	2	3	4	5	6	7	8	9	10	11	12	14																				1
1	2	3	4	5		7	12	9	10	11		6	8																			2
1	2	5	8			7		*9*	10	11		6		3	4	12	14															3
1	2	3		5		7		9	10	11		6				12	8	4	14													4
1	2	3		5		7		9	10	12	11	6					8	4														5
1	2	3		5	6	7	8	9	10									4		11												6
1	2	3		5	6	7	8	9	10	12								4		11												7
1	2	3		5	6	7	8	9	10	12	14							4		*11*												8
1	2	3		5	6	7	8		10	12	14		9					4		*11*												9
1	2	3		5	6	7			10	9	*11*	12					8	4		14												10
1	2	3			6	7			10		11	5					8	4			9											11
1	2	3		5	6	7			10	*12*	11	14					8	4		9		15										12
	2	3		5	6	7					11		10				9	4	12	8		1										13
	2	3		5	6	7	10			11		4	9							8		1										14
	2	3		5	6	7	10			11		4	9							8		1										15
	2	3		5	6	7	10			11			9		4	12				8		1										16
	2	*3*			6	7	10			11		5	9		4	12			14	8		1										17
				5	6					11	7		9	3	4	2			10	8		1										18
				5	6					11	7		9	3	4	2			10	8		1										19
				5	6					11	7		9	3	4	2			10	8		1										20
				5	6					11	7		9		4	2	3		10	8		1										21
		3			6					11	7	5	9		4	2			10	8		1	12									22
	2				6		12			11	7	5	9		4	3			10	8		1										23
		3		5	6						7	12	9	4		2			10	8		1	11	14								24
				5	6					11	7			3		2			10	8	12	1	4	9								25
		6		5			10			11		7		3		2			9	8		1	4									26
		3		2			11			7		5		4		6			10			1	9	12	8							27
		12		5	6		10			11		7		3		2			9			1	4	14	*8*							28
				5	6		10			11		12		3		7			*9*	8		1	4	14		2						29
				5	6		10			11	12	2		3					*9*	8		1	7	14		4						30
				5			10			11	7			3		2				8			4	12		6	9	1				31
				5			10		8	11	7	12		3		2							4			6	9	1				32
				5			10		8	11	7	2		3									4			6	9	1				33
				5	6		10		*8*	11	7	12		3									4	14		2	9	1				34
				5	6		10		8	11	7	3											4	12	14	*2*	9	1				35
				5	6		10		8	11	7	3											4	12		2	9	1				36
				5	6		10		8	11	7	3											4	12		2	9	1				37
				5	6		10		8	11	7	3				12							4	14		2	*9*	1				38
					6		10		8	11	7	3				5	12						4	14		*2*	9	1				39
					6		10		8	*11*	7	3				5	12						4	2			9	1	14			40
				5	6		10		8	11	7	3				2							4				9	1				41
				5	6		10		8	*11*	7	3				2							4	12			9	1	14			42
				5	6		10		8	11	7	3											4		12		9	1	2			43
				5	6		10		8	11	7	3											4	12			9	1	2			44
					6		10		8	11	7					5	12						4		14		9	1	2	*3*		45
					6		10		8	7	2					5	12					1	4		*3*		9		11		14	46

Coca-Cola Cup

Second Round	Reading (a)	1-3
	(h)	2-0
Third Round	Portsmouth (a)	1-0
Fourth Round	Swindon T (a)	1-2

FA Cup

Third Round	Everton (a)	0-1

DONCASTER ROVERS 1994–95 *Back row (left to right):* Lee Warren, Graeme Jones, Sam Kitchen, Russ Wilcox, Andy Beasley, Perry Suckling, Paul Marquis, David Roche, Gary Brabin, Ryan Kirby.

Centre row: Andy Sibson, Nicky Limber, Lee Thew, Scott Maxfield, Khristian Hoy, Sean Parrish, Steve Harper, James Lawrence, Warren Hackett.

Front row: Gudmunder Torfason, Steve Gallen, James Meara, Jimmy Golze (Youth Coach), George Smith (Assistant Manager/Coach), Sammy Chung (Team Manager), Steve Beaglehole (Youth Manager), Darren Finlay, Paul Williams, Chris Swailes.

Division 3 DONCASTER ROVERS

Belle Vue Ground, Doncaster, DN4 5HT. Telephone: (01302) 539441. Fax: (01302) 539679.

Ground capacity: 7794.

Record attendance: 37,149 v Hull C, Division 3 (N), 2 October 1948.

Record receipts: £22,000 v QPR, FA Cup 3rd rd, 5 January 1985.

Pitch measurements: 110yd × 76yd.

Chairman: –. ***Directors:*** K. Haran, C. Dunn, L. Mabbett, J. Richardson.

Manager: Sammy Chung. ***Coach:*** John McClelland.

Secretary: Mrs K. J. Oldale. ***Physio:*** Phil McLoughlin. ***Youth Team Coach:*** Jim Golze.

Commercial Executive: Terry Burdass.

Year Formed: 1879. ***Turned Professional:*** 1885. ***Ltd Co.:*** 1905 and 1920.

Club Nickname: 'Rovers'.

Previous Grounds: 1880–1916, Intake Ground; 1920–22, Benetthorpe Ground; 1922, Low Pasture, Belle Vue.

Foundation: In 1879 Mr. Albert Jenkins got together a team to play a game against the Yorkshire Institution for the Deaf. The players stuck together as Doncaster Rovers joining the Midland Alliance in 1889 and the Midland Counties League in 1891.

First Football League game: 7 September, 1901, Division 2, v Burslem Port Vale (h) D 3-3 – Eggett; Simpson, Layton; Longden, Jones, Wright; Langham, Murphy, Price, Goodson (2), Bailey (1).

Record League Victory: 10–0 v Darlington, Division 4, 25 January 1964 – Potter; Raine, Meadows; Windross (1), White, Ripley (2); Robinson, Book (2), Hale (4), Jeffrey, Broadbent (1).

Record Cup Victory: 7–0 v Blyth Spartans, FA Cup, 1st rd, 27 November 1937 – Imrie; Shaw, Rodgers; McFarlane, Bycroft, Cyril Smith; Burton (1), Kilourhy (4), Morgan (2), Malam, Dutton.

Record Defeat: 0–12 v Small Heath, Division 2, 11 April 1903.

Most League Points (2 for a win): 72, Division 3 (N), 1946–47.

Most League Points (3 for a win): 85, Division 4, 1983–84.

Most League Goals: 123, Division 3 (N), 1946–47.

Highest League Scorer in Season: Clarrie Jordan, 42, Division 3 (N), 1946–47.

Most League Goals in Total Aggregate: Tom Keetley, 180, 1923–29.

Most Capped Player: Len Graham, 14, Northern Ireland.

Most League Appearances: Fred Emery, 417, 1925–36.

Record Transfer Fee Received: £250,000 from QPR for Rufus Brevett, February 1991.

Record Transfer Fee Paid: £60,000 to Stirling Albion for John Philliben, March 1984.

Football League Record: 1901 Elected to Division 2; 1903 Failed re-election; 1904 Re-elected; 1905 Failed re-election; 1923 Re-elected to Division 3 (N); 1935–37 Division 2; 1937–47 Division 3 (N); 1947–48 Division 2; 1948–50 Division 3 (N); 1950–58 Division 2; 1958–59 Division 3; 1959–66 Division 4; 1966–67 Division 3; 1967–69 Division 4; 1969–71 Division 3; 1971–81 Division 4; 1981–83 Division 3; 1983–84 Division 4; 1984–88 Division 3; 1988– 92 Division 4; 1992– Division 3.

Honours: *Football League:* Division 2 best season: 7th, 1901–02; Division 3 (N) Champions 1934–35, 1946–47, 1949–50; Runners-up 1937–38, 1938–39; Division 4 – Champions 1965–66, 1968–69; Runners-up 1983–84. Promoted 1980–81 (3rd). *FA Cup:* best season: 5th rd, 1952, 1954, 1955, 1956. *Football League Cup:* best season: 5th rd, 1976.

Colours: All red. **Change colours:** All blue.

Doncaster Rovers Football Club Ltd.
(Founded 1879)

DONCASTER ROVERS 1994–95 LEAGUE RECORD

Match No.	Date	Venue	Opponents	Result		H/T Score	Lg. Pos.	Goalscorers	Attendance
1	Aug 13	A	Hereford U	W	1-0	1-0	—	Jones	3076
2	20	H	Northampton T	W	1-0	1-0	2	Jones	2194
3	27	A	Colchester U	W	3-0	2-0	1	Jones, Donaldson 2	2320
4	30	H	Fulham	D	0-0	0-0	—		3003
5	Sept 3	H	Darlington	D	0-0	0-0	4		2967
6	10	A	Barnet	D	0-0	0-0	6		2625
7	13	A	Bury	L	0-2	0-1	—		2395
8	16	H	Hereford U	W	3-0	2-0	—	Brabin, Thew, Harper	1938
9	24	H	Preston NE	W	2-1	0-0	4	Harper, Brabin	3321
10	Oct 1	A	Rochdale	L	0-2	0-0	5		2445
11	8	H	Wigan Ath	W	5-3	3-1	4	Roche (pen), Brabin 2, Harper 2	2060
12	15	A	Scarborough	D	2-2	0-2	5	Roche 2 (2 pens)	1641
13	22	A	Mansfield T	W	1-0	0-0	3	Jones (pen)	2988
14	29	H	Torquay U	W	3-0	0-0	3	Hackett, Jones, Lawrence	2697
15	Nov 5	A	Exeter C	W	5-1	4-0	3	Parrish 2, Turner, Harper, Jones	2813
16	19	H	Hartlepool U	W	3-0	1-0	3	Brabin, Harper, Meara	2507
17	26	A	Carlisle U	D	1-1	0-0	3	Lawrence	7781
18	Dec 10	A	Northampton T	D	0-0	0-0	3		4538
19	16	H	Colchester U	L	1-2	0-0	—	Brabin	2460
20	26	A	Chesterfield	L	0-2	0-1	4		4226
21	27	H	Scunthorpe U	D	1-1	1-0	5	Bryan	3852
22	31	A	Walsall	L	0-1	0-0	6		4561
23	Jan 10	H	Mansfield T	L	0-2	0-0	—		2577
24	14	A	Lincoln C	L	0-1	0-0	9		2771
25	28	A	Torquay U	W	1-0	0-0	8	Hackett	2852
26	31	H	Exeter C	W	1-0	0-0	—	Brabin	1611
27	Feb 4	H	Carlisle U	D	0-0	0-0	4		3587
28	7	H	Gillingham	L	1-2	1-1	—	Schofield	1740
29	18	H	Lincoln C	W	3-0	1-0	4	Wilcox, Finlay, Harper	2291
30	25	H	Rochdale	L	0-1	0-1	5		2246
31	Mar 4	A	Preston NE	D	2-2	1-0	6	Jones, Wilcox	9624
32	11	H	Barnet	D	1-1	0-0	7	Harper	1979
33	18	A	Fulham	W	2-0	1-0	7	Jones, Parrish	4031
34	21	A	Hartlepool U	L	1-2	0-2	—	Jones	1354
35	25	A	Darlington	W	2-0	0-0	7	Wilcox (pen), Brabin	2017
36	Apr 1	H	Bury	L	1-2	1-0	7	Wilcox (pen)	2485
37	8	H	Walsall	L	0-2	0-1	8		2368
38	15	A	Scunthorpe U	W	5-0	3-0	7	Norbury 3, Warren, Harper	4366
39	17	H	Chesterfield	L	1-3	1-1	7	Jones	4796
40	22	A	Gillingham	L	2-4	2-3	8	Norbury, Warren	2826
41	29	H	Scarborough	W	1-0	0-0	7	Jones	1710
42	May 6	A	Wigan Ath	L	2-3	0-0	9	Jones, Norbury	1576

Final League Position: 9

GOALSCORERS

League (58): Jones 12 (1 pen), Harper 9, Brabin 8, Norbury 5, Wilcox 4 (2 pens), Parrish 3, Roche 3 (3 pens), Donaldson 2, Hackett 2, Lawrence 2, Warren 2, Bryan 1, Finlay 1, Meara 1, Schofield 1, Thew 1, Turner 1.
Coca-Cola Cup (3): Jones 1, Swailes 1, Torfason 1.
FA Cup (1): Jones 1.

Suckling P.J. 9	Kitchen D.E. 7 + 1	Hackett W.J. 39	Brabin G. 27 + 1	Wilcox R. 37	Swailes C.W. 32	Lawrence J.H. 14 + 2	Thew L. 15 + 6	Jones G.A. 25 + 7	Finlay D.J. 6 + 2	Parrish S. 25	Kirby R. 41 + 1	Donaldson O.M. 7 + 2	Torfason G. 1 + 3	Harper S.J. 31 + 2	Meara J.S. 14 + 1	Williams D.P. 33 + 2	Warren L.A. 10 + 4	Roche D. 19 + 1	Williams D.A. 1	Marquis P.R. 1 + 1	Turner A.P. 4	Schofield J.D. 25 + 2	Norbury M.S. 17 + 5	Bryan M.L. 5	Maxfield S. 10	Williams P.L. 6 + 1	Hoy K. — + 1	Measham I. 1	*Match No.*
1	2	3	4	5	6	7	8	*9*	10	11	12	14																	1
1		3	4	5	6	7	8	9			2	12	10	11															2
1		3		5	6	7	8	9		11	2	10	12		4	15													3
		3		5	6	7		9		11	2	*10*	12	14	4	1	8												4
		3	14	5	6	7		9		11	2	10	12		*4*	1	8												5
		3	4	5	6	7	12	9		11	2	10				1		8											6
		3	4	5	6		7	9		*11*	2	10		14		1	12	8											7
		3	4	5	6		7			11	2	10		9		1		8											8
		3	4	5	6		7	12		11	2			9		1		8	10										9
		3	4		6		7	9		11	2			10		1		8		5									10
		3	4	5	6		7	9	11		2			10		1		8		12									11
		3	4	5	6	12	7			11	2			10		1		8			9								12
		3	4	5	6	7		12		11	2			10		1		8			9								13
		3	4	5	6	7		12		11	2			10		1		8			9								14
		3	4	5	6	7		12		11	2			10		1		8			9								15
		3	4	5	6	7		12		11	2			10	9	1						8							16
		3	4	5	6	7		12		*11*	2	10			8	1						14	9						17
		3		5	6	7		9		11	2				8	1						12	10	4					18
		3	4	5	6		12				2			9	11	1						8	10	7					19
		3	4	5	6	12	14				2			*10*	11	1						8	9	7					20
	6		4	5		7	11		10		2					1	12					8		9	3				21
	6	3	4	5		7	11		12		2					1		10				8		9					22
	5	3	4		6		7			11	2			9	12	1		10				8	14						23
		3			6		7	12	4	11	2			9	5	1	14	10				8							24
		3	4	5	6			9			2			7		1		10				8	12		11				25
		3	4	5	6			9			2			7		1		10				8	12		11				26
		3		5	6			9		11	2			7	4	1		10				8	12						27
		3		5	6		11				2			7	4	1	12	10				8	9						28
1				5	6				11		2			7	4							8	9		3	10			29
1				5	6		12		11		2			7	4							8	9		3	10			30
1		3	4	5	6			9		11	2			7								8	10						31
1		3	4	5	6			9		11	2			7		15		12				8	10						32
		3	4		6		12	9		11	2			7		1		5				8	10						33
		3	4		6			9		11	2			7		1		5				8	10						34
	6	3	4	5				9		11	2			7		1	10					8							35
	6	3		5			12	9		11	2			7		1	4					8	10						36
	6	3		5			11	9			2			7		1	4					8	12			10			37
		3		5				9			2			7		1	4					8	10		6	11	12		38
		3		5				9			2			7		1	4					8	10		6	11			39
		3		5				9	12		2			7		1	4					8	10		6	11			40
1		3	4	5				9			2			7			11					8	10		6	12			41
1	12	3		5				9			2				11		4					8	10		6			7	42

Coca-Cola Cup

First Round	Wrexham (h)	2-4
	(a)	1-1

FA Cup

First Round	Huddersfield T (h)	1-4

EVERTON 1994–95 *Back row (left to right):* Gary Ablett, Graham Stuart, John Ebbrell, Gary Rowett, Joe Parkinson, Matt Jackson, Paul Rideout, Andy Hinchcliffe, Paul Holmes, Neil Moore.
Centre row: Jim Martin (Kit Manager), Jim Gabriel (Reserve Team Coach), Duncan Ferguson, Vinny Samways, Jason Kearton, Neville Southall, Stephen Reeves, Tony Grant, Chris Priest, Willie Donachie (First Team Coach), Les Helm (Physiotherapist).
Front row: David Unsworth, Stuart Barlow, Barry Horne, Anders Limpar, Joe Royle (Manager), Dave Watson, David Burrows, Daniel Amokachi, Brett Angell.

FA Premiership **EVERTON**

Goodison Park, Liverpool L4 4EL. Telephone: (0151) 521 2020. Fax: (0151) 523 9666. Ticket Infoline: 0891 121599. Clubcall 0891 121199. Dial-A-Seat Service: (0151) 525 1231.

Ground capacity: 39,655.

Record attendance: 78,299 v Liverpool, Division 1, 18 September 1948.

Record receipts: £330,000 v Liverpool, FA Premiership, 21 November 1994.

Pitch measurements: 112yd × 78yd.

Chairman: Peter R. Johnson.

Directors: Sir Desmond Pitcher, Clifford Finch, Richard Hughes, Sir Philip Carter CBE, Dr. David M. Marsh, Keith Tamlin, David Newton, Bill Kenwright, Arthur Abercromby, John C. Suenson-Taylor.

Manager: Joe Royle. ***Assistant Manager:*** Willie Donachie. ***Coach:*** Jimmy Gabriel.

Physio: Les Helm.

Secretary: Michael J. Dunford.

Commercial Manager: Andrew Watson. ***Sales Promotion Manager:*** Colum Whelan.

Year Formed: 1878. ***Turned Professional:*** 1885. ***Ltd Co.:*** 1892.

Previous Name: St Domingo FC, 1878–79.

Club Nickname: 'The Toffees'.

Previous Grounds: 1878, Stanley Park; 1882, Priory Road; 1884, Anfield Road; 1892, Goodison Park.

Foundation: St. Domingo Church Sunday School formed a football club in 1878 which played at Stanley Park. Enthusiasm was so great that in November 1879 they decided to expand membership and changed the name to Everton playing in black shirts with a white sash and nicknamed the "Black Watch". After wearing several other colours, royal blue was adopted in 1901.

First Football League game: 8 September, 1888, Football League, v Accrington (h) W 2-1 – Smalley; Dick, Ross; Holt, Jones, Dobson; Fleming (2), Waugh, Lewis, E. Chadwick, Farmer.

Record League Victory: 9–1 v Manchester C, Division 1, 3 September 1906 – Scott; Balmer, Crelley; Booth, Taylor (1), Abbott (1); Sharp, Bolton (1), Young (4), Settle (2), George Wilson. 9–1 v Plymouth Arg, Division 2, 27 December 1930 – Coggins; Williams, Cresswell; McPherson, Griffiths, Thomson; Critchley, Dunn, Dean (4), Johnson (1), Stein (4).

Record Cup Victory: 11–2 v Derby Co, FA Cup, 1st rd, 18 January 1890 – Smalley; Hannah, Doyle(1); Kirkwood, Holt (1), Parry; Latta, Brady (3), Geary (3), Chadwick, Millward (3).

Record Defeat: 4–10 v Tottenham H, Division 1, 11 October 1958.

Most League Points (2 for a win): 66, Division 1, 1969–70.

Most League Points (3 for a win): 90, Division 1, 1984–85.

Most League Goals: 121, Division 2, 1930–31.

Highest League Scorer in Season: William Ralph 'Dixie' Dean, 60, Division 1, 1927–28 (All-time League record).

Most League Goals in Total Aggregate: William Ralph 'Dixie' Dean, 349, 1925–37.

Most Capped Player: Neville Southall, 81, Wales.

Most League Appearances: Neville Southall, 494, 1981–95.

Record Transfer Fee Received: £2,750,000 from Barcelona for Gary Lineker, July 1986.

Record Transfer Fee Paid: £4,000,000 to Rangers for Duncan Ferguson, December 1994.

Football League Record: 1888 Founder Member of the Football League; 1930–31 Division 2; 1931–51 Division 1; 1951–54 Division 2; 1954–92 Division 1; 1992– FA Premier League.

Honours: *Football League:* Division 1 – Champions 1890–91, 1914–15, 1927–28, 1931–32, 1938–39, 1962–63, 1969–70, 1984–85, 1986–87; Runners-up 1889–90, 1894–95, 1901–02, 1904–05, 1908–09, 1911–12, 1985–86; Division 2 Champions 1930–31; Runners-up 1953–54. *FA Cup:* Winners 1906, 1933, 1966, 1984, 1995; Runners-up 1893, 1897, 1907, 1968, 1985, 1986, 1989. *Football League Cup:* Runners-up 1977, 1984. *League Super Cup:* Runners-up 1986. *Simod Cup:* Runners-up 1989. *Zenith Data System Cup:* Runner-up 1991. **European Competitions:** *European Cup:* 1963–64, 1970–71. *European Cup-Winners' Cup:* 1966–67, 1984–85 (winners). *European Fairs Cup:* 1962–63, 1964–65, 1965–66. *UEFA Cup:* 1975–76, 1978–79, 1979–80.

Colours: Blue shirts, white shorts, black/blue hooped stockings. **Change colours:** White shirts, black shorts, black stockings.

EVERTON 1994–95 LEAGUE RECORD

Match No.	Date	Venue	Opponents	Result		H/T Score	Lg. Pos.	Goalscorers	Attendance
1	Aug 20	H	Aston Villa	D	2-2	1-0	—	Stuart, Rideout	35,552
2	24	A	Tottenham H	L	1-2	0-2	—	Rideout	24,553
3	27	A	Manchester C	L	0-4	0-0	20		19,867
4	30	H	Nottingham F	L	1-2	0-1	—	Rideout	26,689
5	Sept 10	A	Blackburn R	L	0-3	0-2	22		26,548
6	17	H	QPR	D	2-2	2-1	22	Amokachi, Rideout	27,291
7	24	H	Leicester C	D	1-1	0-0	22	Ablett	28,015
8	Oct 1	A	Manchester U	L	0-2	0-1	22		43,803
9	8	A	Southampton	L	0-2	0-1	22		15,163
10	15	H	Coventry C	L	0-2	0-2	22		28,219
11	22	A	Crystal Palace	L	0-1	0-0	22		15,026
12	29	H	Arsenal	D	1-1	1-1	22	Unsworth	32,005
13	Nov 1	H	West Ham U	W	1-0	0-0	—	Ablett	28,353
14	5	A	Norwich C	D	0-0	0-0	22		18,377
15	21	H	Liverpool	W	2-0	0-0	—	Ferguson, Rideout	39,866
16	26	A	Chelsea	W	1-0	1-0	20	Rideout	28,115
17	Dec 5	H	Leeds U	W	3-0	1-0	—	Rideout, Ferguson, Unsworth (pen)	25,906
18	10	A	Aston Villa	D	0-0	0-0	18		29,678
19	17	H	Tottenham H	D	0-0	0-0	19		32,813
20	26	H	Sheffield W	L	1-4	1-2	19	Ferguson	37,089
21	31	H	Ipswich T	W	4-1	1-1	19	Ferguson, Rideout 2, Watson	25,667
22	Jan 2	A	Wimbledon	L	1-2	1-2	20	Rideout	9506
23	14	A	Arsenal	D	1-1	1-1	20	Watson	34,743
24	21	H	Crystal Palace	W	3-1	1-0	18	Ferguson 2, Rideout	23,734
25	24	A	Liverpool	D	0-0	0-0	—		39,505
26	Feb 1	A	Newcastle U	L	0-2	0-0	—		34,465
27	4	H	Norwich C	W	2-1	1-0	18	Stuart, Rideout	23,295
28	13	A	West Ham U	D	2-2	1-1	—	Rideout, Limpar	21,081
29	22	A	Leeds U	L	0-1	0-0	—		30,793
30	25	H	Manchester U	W	1-0	0-0	16	Ferguson	40,011
31	Mar 4	A	Leicester C	D	2-2	2-0	17	Limpar, Samways	20,447
32	8	A	Nottingham F	L	1-2	1-1	—	Barlow	24,526
33	15	H	Manchester C	D	1-1	0-1	—	Unsworth (pen)	28,485
34	18	A	QPR	W	3-2	0-1	17	Barlow, McDonald (og), Hinchcliffe	14,488
35	Apr 1	H	Blackburn R	L	1-2	1-2	18	Stuart	37,905
36	14	H	Newcastle U	W	2-0	1-0	—	Amokachi 2	34,628
37	17	A	Sheffield W	D	0-0	0-0	17		27,880
38	29	H	Wimbledon	D	0-0	0-0	17		31,567
39	May 3	H	Chelsea	D	3-3	1-1	—	Hinchcliffe, Ablett, Amokachi	33,180
40	6	H	Southampton	D	0-0	0-0	17		36,851
41	9	A	Ipswich T	W	1-0	0-0	—	Rideout	14,940
42	14	A	Coventry C	D	0-0	0-0	15		21,787

Final League Position: 15

GOALSCORERS

League (44): Rideout 14, Ferguson 7, Amokachi 4, Ablett 3, Stuart 3, Unsworth 3 (2 pens), Barlow 2, Hinchcliffe 2, Limpar 2, Watson 2, Samways 1, own goal 1.
Coca-Cola Cup (3): Samways 1, Stuart 1 (pen), Watson 1.
FA Cup (13): Amokachi 2, Jackson 2, Rideout 2, Stuart 2, Ferguson 1, Hinchcliffe 1, Limpar 1, Parkinson 1, Watson 1.

Southall N. 41	Jackson M.A. 26 + 3	Ablett G.I. 26	Ebbrell J.K. 26	Watson D. 38	Unsworth D.G. 37 + 1	Samways V. 14 + 5	Stuart G.C. 20 + 8	Cottee A.R. 3	Rideout P.D. 25 + 4	Limpar A. 19 + 8	Parkinson J.S. 32 + 2	Angell B.A.M. 3 + 1	Hinchcliffe A.G. 28 + 1	Burrows D. 19	Amokachi D. 17 + 1	Snodin I. 2 + 1	Holmes P. 1	Rowett G. 2	Barlow S. 7 + 4	Durrant I. 4 + 1	Ferguson D. 22 + 1	Horne B. 31	Kearton J.B. 1	Grant A.J. 1 + 4	Barrett E.D. 17	*Match No.*
1	2	3	4	5	6	7	8	9	10	11	12															1
1	2	3	4	5	6	7	8	9	10		*11*	12	14													2
1	2	3	4	5	6	7	8	9	10	12	11															3
1	2		4	5	6	7	8		10	11		9	3													4
1	2		4	5	6	7	8		10	11				3	9											5
1	2		4	5	6	7	8		10	11				3	9	12										6
1		4		5	6	7	8					10		3	9	11	2									7
1				5	6	7	8				4		11	3	9	2		10	12							8
1	2			*5*	6	7	12		10		4		11	3	9			8		14						9
1	2	5			6	7	12				4			3	9					11	10	8				10
1	2	5			6	7	8				12			3	9					11	10	4				11
1	2	5			6		8		12	14	4			3	9					*11*	10	7				12
1	2	6		5			*8*		12	14	4			3	9					11	10	7				13
1	2	4		5	6		8		10	12	11			3							9	7				14
1	2	3	4	5	6				12	14	8		11		*9*						10	7				15
1	2	4		5	6				10	11	8		3								9	7				16
1	2	3	4	5	6		12		10		8		11								9	7				17
	2		4	5	6				10	7	8		11	3							9		1			18
1	2		4	5	6				10	12	8		11	3					9			7				19
1	2		4	5	6		12		10	7			11	3							9	8				20
1	2		4	5	6				10		8		11	3							9	7				21
1	2		4	5	6				10		8		11	3					12		9	7				22
1	2		4	5	6				10		8		11	3							9	7				23
1	2		4	5	6				10		8		11	3							9	7				24
1	2		4	5	6				10		8		11	3							9	7				25
1	2		4	5	6	12	9			7	10			11								8		14	3	26
1		3	4	5	6	12	9		10		8		11									7			2	27
1		3	4	5	6		8		10	12			11								9	7			2	28
1		6	4	5			12		10	11	8		3								9	7			2	29
1			4	5	6	12				11	8		3						10		9	7			2	30
1	12			5	6	7	14			*11*	4		3						10		9	8			2	31
1		3		5	6	7	12			11	4								10		9	8			2	32
1		*6*	4	5	12		14			11	8		3						10		9	7			2	33
1	12	6	4	5						11		*10*	3	14					9			7		8	2	34
1	2	6		5			8				11		3		9				10			7		12	4	35
1		3		5	6		8			7	4		11		9							10		12	2	36
1	12	3		5	6				10	7	4		11								*9*	8		14	2	37
1		3		5	6		10		12	7	4		11		9							8			2	38
1		3		5	6		8		10		4		11		9				12			7			2	39
1		3	4	5	6	12			10	14	8		*11*		9							7			2	40
1		3	4	5	6	12			10	7			11		*9*				14			8			2	41
1	5	3	4		6	7	8			11	10				9						12				2	42

Coca-Cola Cup

Second Round	Portsmouth (h)	2-3
	(a)	1-1

FA Cup

Third Round	Derby Co (h)	1-0
Fourth Round	Bristol C (a)	1-0
Fifth Round	Norwich C (h)	5-0
Sixth Round	Newcastle U (h)	1-0
Semi-final	Tottenham H at Elland Road	4-1
Final at Wembley	Manchester U	1-0

EXETER CITY 1994–95 *Back row (left to right):* Mark Gavin, Mark Cooper, David Cooper, Anthony Thirlby, Gary Rice, Martin Phillips, Danny Bailey, Micky Ross, Jason Minett.
Centre row: Russell Coughlin, Ronnie Robinson, Peter Whiston, Mark Came, Peter Fox, Robbie Turner, Andy Woodman, Stuart Storer, Scott Daniels, Jonathan Richardson, Richard Pears, Jonathan Brown.
Front row: Michele Cecere, Mike Chapman (Physio), Trevor Morgan, Terry Cooper (Manager), George Kent, Mark Radfort (YTS Manager), Colin Anderson.

Division 3 EXETER CITY

St James Park, Exeter EX4 6PX. Telephone: (01392) 54073. Fax: (01392) 425885. Training Ground: (01395) 232784.

Ground capacity: 10,570.

Record attendance: 20,984 v Sunderland, FA Cup 6th rd (replay), 4 March 1931.

Record receipts: £59,862.98 v Aston Villa, FA Cup 3rd rd 8 January 1994.

Pitch measurements: 114yd × 73yd.

Honorary President: W. C. Hill.

Chairman: A. I. Doble.

Directors: P. Carter, M. Couch, S. W. Dawe, L. G. Vallance, M. Shelbourne.

Manager: Peter Fox. ***Assistant Manager/Coach:*** Trevor Morgan. ***Physio:*** Mike Chapman.

Secretary: Margaret Bond. ***Company Secretary:*** P. Carter.

Commercial Manager: –.

Year Formed: 1904. ***Turned Professional:*** 1908. ***Ltd Co.:*** 1908.

Club Nickname: 'The Grecians'.

Foundation: Exeter City was formed in 1904 by the amalgamation of St. Sidwell's United and Exeter United. The club first played in the East Devon League and then the Plymouth & District League. After an exhibition match between West Bromwich Albion and Woolwich Arsenal was held to test interest as Exeter was then a rugby stronghold, Exeter City decided at a meeting at the Red Lion Hotel to turn professional in 1908.

First Football League game: 28 August, 1920, Division 3, v Brentford (h) W 3-0 – Pym; Coleburne, Feebury (1p); Crawshaw, Carrick, Mitton; Appleton, Makin, Wright (1), Vowles (1), Dockray.

Record League Victory: 8–1 v Coventry C, Division 3 (S), 4 December 1926 – Bailey; Pollard, Charlton; Pullen, Pool, Garrett; Purcell (2), McDevitt, Blackmore (2), Dent (2), Compton (2). 8–1 v Aldershot, Division 3 (S), 4 May 1935 – Chesters; Gray, Miller; Risdon, Webb, Angus; Jack Scott (1), Wrightson (1), Poulter (3), McArthur (1), Dryden (1). (1 og).

Record Cup Victory: 9–1 v Aberdare, FA Cup 1st rd, 26 November 1927 – Holland; Pollard, Charlton; Phoenix, Pool, Gee; Purcell (2), McDevitt, Dent (4), Vaughan (2), Compton (1).

Record Defeat: 0–9 v Notts Co, Division 3 (S), 16 October 1948 and v Northampton T, Division 3 (S), 12 April 1958.

Most League Points (2 for a win): 62, Division 4, 1976–77.

Most League Points (3 for a win): 89, Division 4, 1989–90.

Most League Goals: 88, Division 3 (S), 1932–33.

Highest League Scorer in Season: Fred Whitlow, 33, Division 3 (S), 1932–33.

Most League Goals in Total Aggregate: Tony Kellow, 129, 1976–78, 1980–83, 1985–88.

Most Capped Player: Dermot Curtis, 1 (17), Eire.

Most League Appearances: Arnold Mitchell, 495, 1952–66.

Record Transfer Fee Received: £500,000 from Rangers for Chris Vinnicombe, November 1989.

Record Transfer Fee Paid: £65,000 to Blackpool for Tony Kellow, March 1980.

Football League Record: 1920 Elected Division 3; 1921–58 Division 3 (S); 1958–64 Division 4; 1964–66 Division 3; 1966–77 Division 4; 1977–84 Division 3; 1984–90 Division 4; 1990–92 Division 3; 1992–94 Division 2; 1994– Division 3.

Honours: *Football League:* Division 3 best season: 8th, 1979–80; Division 3 (S) – Runners-up 1932–33; Division 4 – Champions 1989–90; Runners-up 1976–77. *FA Cup:* best season: 6th rd replay, 1931. *Football League Cup:* never beyond 4th rd. *Division 3 (S) Cup:* Winners 1934.

Colours: Red and white striped shirts, black shorts, red stockings. **Change colours:** Blue and white striped shirts, blue shorts, blue stockings.

EXETER CITY 1994–95 LEAGUE RECORD

Match No.	Date	Venue	Opponents	Result		H/T Score	Lg. Pos.	Goalscorers	Attendance
1	Aug 13	A	Lincoln C	L	0-2	0-2	—		3439
2	20	H	Bury	L	0-4	0-3	22		2164
3	27	A	Darlington	L	0-2	0-0	22		1861
4	30	H	Colchester U	W	1-0	1-0	—	Bailey	1804
5	Sept 3	H	Gillingham	W	3-0	2-0	14	Cooper M 2, Dunne (og)	2241
6	10	A	Carlisle U	L	0-1	0-1	17		6213
7	13	A	Chesterfield	L	0-2	0-1	—		2136
8	17	H	Lincoln C	W	1-0	0-0	15	Thirlby	2180
9	24	A	Mansfield T	D	1-1	0-0	14	Morgan	2468
10	Oct 1	H	Hartlepool U	W	2-1	1-1	14	Gavin, Cooper M	2390
11	8	H	Northampton T	D	0-0	0-0	15		3015
12	15	A	Fulham	L	0-4	0-2	16		4314
13	22	H	Scunthorpe U	D	2-2	1-1	15	Came, Cecere	2511
14	29	A	Preston NE	W	1-0	1-0	14	Cecere	6808
15	Nov 5	H	Doncaster R	L	1-5	0-4	15	Turner	2813
16	19	A	Walsall	L	0-1	0-1	16		3629
17	26	H	Scarborough	W	5-2	2-1	14	Cecere 2, Gavin, Phillips, Storer	2179
18	Dec 10	A	Bury	D	0-0	0-0	15		2876
19	17	H	Darlington	L	0-2	0-1	16		2338
20	26	H	Torquay U	L	1-2	1-0	16	Storer	5538
21	27	A	Hereford U	L	0-3	0-2	17		2567
22	Jan 7	A	Scunthorpe U	L	0-3	0-2	18		2463
23	14	H	Rochdale	D	0-0	0-0	17		2316
24	31	A	Doncaster R	L	0-1	0-0	—		1611
25	Feb 4	A	Scarborough	W	2-0	1-0	17	Anderson, Pears	1512
26	18	A	Rochdale	W	1-0	1-0	17	Cooper M	1945
27	21	H	Wigan Ath	L	2-4	1-2	—	Richardson, Cecere	2370
28	25	A	Hartlepool U	D	2-2	1-1	18	Cecere, Thirlby	1440
29	28	A	Barnet	D	1-1	0-1	—	Cooper M	1325
30	Mar 4	H	Mansfield T	L	2-3	1-1	18	Phillips, Minett (pen)	2458
31	11	H	Carlisle U	D	1-1	1-1	18	Brown	2673
32	18	A	Colchester U	L	1-3	0-1	19	Cecere	2375
33	21	H	Preston NE	L	0-1	0-0	—		2057
34	25	A	Gillingham	L	0-3	0-2	21		3332
35	Apr 1	H	Chesterfield	L	1-2	0-0	21	Brown	2144
36	4	H	Walsall	L	1-3	0-1	—	Cecere	1551
37	8	A	Wigan Ath	L	1-3	0-2	21	Cecere	1417
38	15	H	Hereford U	D	1-1	0-1	21	Cecere	2083
39	18	A	Torquay U	D	0-0	0-0	—		4155
40	22	H	Barnet	L	1-2	0-1	21	Cooper M	1903
41	29	H	Fulham	L	0-1	0-0	22		3388
42	May 6	A	Northampton T	L	1-2	0-1	22	Minett (pen)	6734

Final League Position: 22

GOALSCORERS

League (36): Cecere 10, Cooper M 6, Brown 2, Gavin 2, Minett 2 (2 pens), Phillips 2, Storer 2, Thirlby 2, Anderson 1, Bailey 1, Came 1, Morgan 1, Pears 1, Richardson 1, Turner 1, own goal 1.
Coca-Cola Cup (2): Cecere 1, Turner 1.
FA Cup (2): Cecere 1, Morgan 1.

Woodman A.J. 6	Daniels S. 6 + 1	Anderson C.R. 21	Cooper M.N. 31 + 9	Came M.R. 32	Richardson J.D.P. 38	Storer S.J. 21 + 2	Coughlin R. 23 + 2	Turner R.P. 10 + 1	Ross M.P. 1	Gavin M.W. 37	Thirlby A.D. 20 + 7	Brown J. 32 + 5	Rice G.J. 5 + 5	Bailey D.S. 14	Phillips M.J. 18 + 6	Cecere M.J. 27 + 1	Pears R.J. 12 + 7	Fox P.D. 31	Minett J. 38	Robinson R. 16 + 1	Morgan T.J. 4 + 5	Bellotti R.C. 1 + 1	Barrett M.J. 4	Cooper D.B.E. 14	*Match No.*
1	2	3	4	5	6	7	8	*9*	10	11	12	14													1
1	2		12	5				9		11	8	6	3	4	7	*10*	14								2
			7	5	6	12				11	8	14	3	4		9	*10*	1	2						3
		3	9	5	6	7	10			11	8	12		4				1	2						4
			9	5	6	7	10			11	8			4	12			1	2	3					5
			9	5	6	7	10				8	11	12	4				1	2	3					6
			9	5	6	7	10			11	8	4	14		12			1	2	3					7
				5	6	7	10			11	8	4				12		1	2	3	9				8
			10		6	7	5	9			8	4	11					1	2	3	12				9
		10	4	5	6		7	9		11	*8*	12						1	2	3	14				10
			4	5		7	10	9		11	8	6						1	2	3	12				11
			4	5	6	7	10	9		11	8							1	2	3					12
1			4	5		7	10	9		11	8	3				6			2						13
1			4	5	6	7	10	9		11						8			2	3					14
1			4	5	6	7	10	12		11		3	14		*8*	9			2						15
			12	5	6		8	9		11	7	3		4	14	10		1	2						16
1			12		6	7	*10*	*9*		11		3	14	4	5	8			2			15			17
	10		9	5	6	7	8			11		3		4					2	12		1			18
	12		*9*	5	6	7				11	8	3		4					2	10	14		1		19
		8	12	5	6	7				11		10		4					2	3	9		1		20
	5	8	10		6	7				11				4	12		9		2	3			1		21
	5	10	8		6	7				11				4		3			2	9			1		22
	5	10	8		6	7				9		12		4		*11*	14	1	2	3					23
		3	8	5	6	7	4			11		9				10	12	1	2						24
		4	8	5	6	7				11	12	3				10	9	1	2						25
		4	8	5	6					11	7	3			12	10	9	1	2						26
		4	8	5	6	12				11	7	3			14	10	*9*	1	2						27
			8		6		4			11	12	2			7	10	9	1		5	14			3	28
			8		6		4			11	12	5			7	10	9	1	2					3	29
			8		6		4			11	12	9			7	10		1	2	5				3	30
			12	5	6					11	8	4			7	10	9	1	2					3	31
		4	12	5						11	10	6			7	8	9	1	2					3	32
		4	12	5	6					11	*10*	9			7	8	14	1	2					3	33
		4	12	5	6					11		8			7	10		1	2		9			3	34
		4	8	5	6		12				11	10			7		14	1	2		*9*			3	35
		4	8	5	6					11		9			7	10		1	2					3	36
		4	8	5	6							11	12		7	10	9	1	2					3	37
		4	8		6		11				12	2	3	9	7	10		1						5	38
		4		5	6		8			11		9			7	10	12	1	2					3	39
			12	5	6		4			11		8			7	10	9	1	2					3	40
		3	8	5	6		12			11	14	4			7	10	*9*	1	2						41
		10	9		6					11		4	3		7	8	12	1	2					5	42

Coca-Cola Cup
First Round — Swansea C (h) — 2-2
(a) — 0-2

FA Cup
First Round — Crawley (h) — 1-0
Second Round — Colchester U (h) — 1-2

FULHAM 1994–95 *Back row (left to right):* Micky Adams (Player/Coach), Chris Smith (Physio), Julian Hails, Duncan Jupp, Robert Haworth, Michael Mison, Jim Stannard, Lee Harrison, Terry Angus, Glen Thomas, Alan Cork, Martin Ferney, Len Walker (Assistant Manager).
Front row: Danny Bolt, Martin Thomas, Gary Bazil, John Marshall, Kevin Moore, Ian Branfoot (Manager), Simon Morgan, Ara Bedrossian, Robbie Herrera, Nicky Andrews, Terry Hurlock.

Division 3 **FULHAM**

Craven Cottage, Stevenage Rd, Fulham, London SW6 6HH. Telephone: (0171) 736 6561. Fax: (0171) 731 7047. Call Line: 0891 440044.

Ground capacity: 14,969.

Record attendance: 49,335 v Millwall, Division 2, 8 October 1938.

Record receipts: £80,247 v Chelsea, Division 2, 8 October 1983.

Pitch measurements: 110yd × 75yd.

Chief Executive: R.J. Summers.

Chairman: Jimmy Hill.

Directors: W. F. Muddyman (vice-chairman), C. A. Swain, A. Muddyman, T. Wilson, D. E. Shrimpton.

Manager: Ian Branfoot. ***Assistant Manager:*** Len Walker.

Player-Coach: Micky Adams. ***Physio:*** Chris Smith. ***Community Officer:*** Gary Mulcahey.

Club Secretary: Mrs Janice O'Doherty.

Commercial Manager: Ken Myers.

Year Formed: 1879. ***Turned Professional:*** 1898. ***Ltd Co.:*** 1903. ***Reformed:*** 1987.

Club Nickname: 'Cottagers'.

Previous Name: 1879–88, Fulham St Andrew's.

Previous Grounds: 1879 Star Road, Fulham; c.1883 Eel Brook Common, 1884 Lillie Road; 1885 Putney Lower Common; 1886 Ranelagh House, Fulham; 1888 Barn Elms, Castelnau; 1889 Purser's Cross (Roskell's Field), Parsons Green Lane; 1891 Eel Brook Common; 1891 Half Moon, Putney; 1895 Captain James Field, West Brompton; 1896 Craven Cottage.

Foundation: Churchgoers were responsible for the foundation of Fulham, which first saw the light of day as Fulham St. Andrew's Church Sunday School FC in 1879. They won the West London Amateur Cup in 1887 and the championship of the West London League in its initial season of 1892–93. The name Fulham had been adopted in 1888.

First Football League game: 3 September, 1907, Division 2, v Hull C (h) L 0-1 – Skene; Ross, Lindsay; Collins, Morrison, Goldie; Dalrymple, Freeman, Bevan, Hubbard, Threlfall.

Record League Victory: 10–1 v Ipswich T, Division 1, 26 December 1963 – Macedo; Cohen, Langley; Mullery (1), Keetch, Robson (1); Key, Cook (1), Leggat (4), Haynes, Howfield (3).

Record Cup Victory: 6–0 v Wimbledon (away), FA Cup, 1st rd (replay), 3 December 1930 – Iceton; Gibbon, Lilley; Oliver, Dudley, Barrett; Temple, Hammond (1), Watkins (1), Gibbons (2), Penn (2). 6–0 v Bury, FA Cup, 3rd rd, 7 January 1938 – Turner; Bacuzzi, Keeping; Evans, Dennison, Tompkins; Higgins, Worsley, Rooke (6), O'Callaghan, Arnold.

Record Defeat: 0–10 v Liverpool, League Cup 2nd rd, 1st leg, 23 September 1986.

Most League Points (2 for a win): 60, Division 2, 1958–59 and Division 3, 1970–71.

Most League Points (3 for a win): 78, Division 3, 1981–82.

Most League Goals: 111, Division 3 (S), 1931–32.

Highest League Scorer in Season: Frank Newton, 43, Division 3 (S), 1931–32.

Most League Goals in Total Aggregate: Gordon Davies, 159, 1978–84, 1986–91.

Most Capped Player: Johnny Haynes, 56, England.

Most League Appearances: Johnny Haynes, 594, 1952–70.

Record Transfer Fee Received: £333,333 from Liverpool for Richard Money, May 1980.

Record Transfer Fee Paid: £150,000 to Orient for Peter Kitchen, February 1979, and to Brighton & HA for Teddy Maybank, December 1979.

Football League Record: 1907 Elected to Division 2; 1928–32 Division 3 (S); 1932–49 Division 2; 1949–52 Division 1; 1952–59 Division 2; 1959–68 Division 1; 1968–69 Division 2; 1969–71 Division 3; 1971–80 Division 2; 1980–82 Division 3; 1982–86 Division 2; 1986–92 Division 3; 1992–94 Division 2; 1994– Division 3.

Honours: *Football League:* Division 1 best season: 10th, 1959–60; Division 2 – Champions 1948–49; Runners-up 1958–59; Division 3 (S) – Champions 1931–32; Division 3 – Runners-up 1970–71. *FA Cup:* Runners-up 1975. *Football League Cup:* best season: 5th rd, 1968, 1971.

Colours: White shirts, red and black trim, black shorts, white stockings red and black trim. **Change colours:** Red and black halved shirts, white shorts, black stockings with red trim.

FULHAM 1994–95 LEAGUE RECORD

Match No.	Date	Venue	Opponents	Result		H/T Score	Lg. Pos.	Goalscorers	Attendance
1	Aug 13	H	Walsall	D	1-1	0-1	—	Moore	5308
2	20	A	Scunthorpe U	W	2-1	1-1	6	Cork 2	3165
3	27	H	Wigan Ath	W	2-0	1-0	5	Morgan, Cork	4241
4	30	A	Doncaster R	D	0-0	0-0	—		3003
5	Sept 3	A	Torquay U	L	1-2	1-2	8	Moore	4739
6	10	H	Preston NE	L	0-1	0-0	10		5001
7	13	H	Scarborough	L	1-2	1-2	—	Hails	2729
8	17	A	Walsall	L	1-5	0-3	17	Brazil	3378
9	24	H	Hereford U	D	1-1	0-1	15	Brazil	3740
10	Oct 1	A	Barnet	D	0-0	0-0	17		3579
11	8	A	Rochdale	W	2-1	0-1	16	Brazil, Hurlock	2573
12	15	H	Exeter C	W	4-0	2-0	12	Stallard 3, Morgan	4314
13	22	A	Chesterfield	D	1-1	0-1	12	Moore	2860
14	29	H	Carlisle U	L	1-3	0-2	15	Morgan	5563
15	Nov 5	A	Northampton T	W	1-0	1-0	12	Adams	7366
16	19	H	Lincoln C	D	1-1	1-0	13	Adams	3955
17	26	A	Bury	D	0-0	0-0	11		3323
18	Dec 10	H	Scunthorpe U	W	1-0	1-0	8	Morgan	3358
19	17	A	Wigan Ath	D	1-1	0-1	10	Marshall	1791
20	26	A	Gillingham	L	1-4	0-1	12	Morgan	4677
21	27	H	Colchester U	L	1-2	1-1	13	Hamill	4243
22	31	A	Hartlepool U	W	2-1	1-1	12	Cusack, Brazil	1698
23	Jan 2	H	Mansfield T	W	4-2	1-1	12	Hamill, Cusack, Blake, Thomas M	4091
24	8	H	Chesterfield	D	1-1	0-1	11	Brazil	3927
25	14	A	Darlington	D	0-0	0-0	12		2113
26	28	A	Carlisle U	D	1-1	1-1	12	Walling (og)	6891
27	Feb 4	H	Bury	W	1-0	0-0	12	Thomas M	3941
28	14	H	Northampton T	D	4-4	2-1	—	Morgan 2, Adams (pen), Hamill	3423
29	18	H	Darlington	W	3-1	1-0	8	Adams 2, Hamill	3864
30	25	H	Barnet	W	4-0	3-0	6	Cusack, Marshall, Morgan, Hamill	6195
31	Mar 4	A	Hereford U	D	1-1	1-0	8	Jupp	2895
32	11	A	Preston NE	L	2-3	1-1	10	Jupp, Blake (pen)	8601
33	18	H	Doncaster R	L	0-2	0-1	11		4031
34	25	H	Torquay U	W	2-1	0-1	9	Adams, Cusack	4941
35	Apr 1	A	Scarborough	L	1-3	0-0	10	Adams	2050
36	8	H	Hartlepool U	W	1-0	0-0	10	Blake	3465
37	11	A	Lincoln C	L	0-2	0-1	—		2932
38	15	A	Colchester U	L	2-5	1-4	11	Morgan, Mison	3448
39	17	H	Gillingham	W	1-0	0-0	10	Morgan	3612
40	22	A	Mansfield T	D	1-1	0-1	10	Morgan	2861
41	29	A	Exeter C	W	1-0	0-0	9	Brazil	3388
42	May 6	H	Rochdale	W	5-0	3-0	8	Cusack 3, Thomas M, Brazil	4342

Final League Position: 8

GOALSCORERS

League (60): Morgan 11, Adams 7 (1 pen), Brazil 7, Cusack 7, Hamill 5, Blake 3 (1 pen), Cork 3, Moore 3, Stallard 3, Thomas M 3, Jupp 2, Marshall 2, Hails 1, Hurlock 1, Mison 1, own goal 1.
Coca-Cola Cup (5): Haworth 2, Moore 2, Blake 1.
FA Cup (9): Adams 4 (2 pens), Hamill 2, Blake 1, Cork 1, Morgan 1.

Stannard J. 36	Morgan S.C. 42	Marshall J.P. 25 + 2	Mison M. 17 + 7	Moore K.T. 31	Thomas G.A. 7	Thomas M.R. 21 + 2	Bedrossian A. 3	Cork A.G. 11 + 4	Brazil G.N. 30 + 2	Herrera R. 26 + 1	Haworth R.J. 3 + 7	Jupp D.A. 35 + 1	Ferney M.J. 5 + 2	Hurlock T.A. 27	Hails J. 6 + 2	Angus T.N. 21 + 2	Adams M.R. 18 + 3	Blake M.C. 34 + 1	Stallard M. 4	Finnigan A. 7 + 4	Cusack N.J. 26 + 1	Harrison L.D. 6 + 1	Hamill R. 18 + 5	Bartley C.A. 1	Gregory J.G. — + 1	Bolt D.A. 2	*Match No.*
1	2	3	4	5	6	7	8	9	10	11	12	14															1
1	2	7	4	5	6			9	10	3	11	8	12														2
1	2	7	11	5	6			9	10	3		8		4	12												3
1	2	7	11	5	6				10			8		4	9	3											4
1	2	7	11	5	6			9	10		12	8		4	14		3										5
1	2	7		5	6			9	10		12	8		4	11		3										6
1	2	12	7	5	6	14		9	10			8		4	11		*3*										7
1	2	7		5		*6*		9	10	3	12	8		4	11			14									8
1	2	7	4	5				9	12	3		8					10	6	11								9
1	6	3	4			11	7		10		14			8		12		5	9	2							10
1	6		8			11	7		10		12	2		4		3		5	9								11
1	8		7	5		11			10			2		4		3		6	9								12
1	8		7	5					10		9	2		4	*11*	3	12	6		14							13
1	8		7	5					10		9	2		4	*11*	3	12	6		14							14
1	8	4	7					12	10	3						5	11	6		2	9						15
1	8	10	7	5						3		2		4			11	6			9	15					16
1	8	7		5				10		3		2		4			11	6			9						17
1	8	7		5				11	10	3		2		4				6			9		12				18
1	8	7	4	5					10	3		2	12					6			9		11				19
1	8		12	5					10	3		2	7	4		14		6			9		11				20
1	8			5					10			2		4		3		6		7	9		11				21
1	8			5		7			10			2		4		3		6			9		11				22
1	8			5		7			10	12		2		4		3		6			9		11				23
1	8			5		7			10	3	12	2		4				6			9		11				24
1	8			5		7			10	3			4					6		2	9		11				25
1	8			5		7			10				4			3		6		2	9		11				26
1	8	4		5		7			10			2				3		6			9		11				27
1	8	4		5		7			10			2				3	12	6			9		11				28
1	8	4				7				3		2				5	10	6		12	9		11				29
1	8	4	12			7				3		2				5	*10*	6		14	9		11				30
1	8	7	12						14	3		2		4		5	*10*	6			9		11				31
1	8	7	10					12		3		2		4		5		6			9		11				32
1	8	7		5		12				3		2		4			10	6			9		11				33
1	8			5		7				3		2		4			10	6			9		11				34
1	8	11		5		7						2		4		3	10	6			9		12				35
	8	7		5				12		3		2		4			10	6				1	11	*9*	15		36
	8	12		5		7		9		3		2		4			10	6			14	1	*11*				37
	8	7	12	5				14	*11*	3		2		4			10	6			9	1					38
	8	7	12			4			*11*	3		2				5	10	6			9	1	14				39
1	8		4			7			11	3		2				5	10	6			9		12				40
	8		12			7			11	3			4			5		6		2	9	1				10	41
	8		12			7			11	3			4			5		6		2	9	1	14			*10*	42

Coca-Cola Cup

First Round	Luton T (a)	1-1
	(h)	1-1
Second Round	Stoke C (h)	3-2
	(a)	0-1

FA Cup

First Round	Ashford T (a)	2-2
	(h)	5-3
Second Round	Gillingham (a)	1-1
	(h)	1-2

GILLINGHAM 1994–95 *Back row (left to right):* Andy Ramage, Paul Hague, Tony Butler, Steve Banks, Lee Osborne, Scott Barrett, Robin Trott, Andy Arnott, Lee Palmer.
Third row: Paul Baker, Sam Comer, Danny Lander, Lee Spiller, Marc Hills, Neil Smillie (Coach), Kevin Clifford, Scott Clarke, Paul Wilson, Lee Quigley, Javed Mughal (Physio).
Second row: Joe Dunne, Richard Carpenter, Paul Watson, Robert Reinelt, Mike Flanagan (Manager), Richard Green, Gary Micklewhite, Neil Smith, Scott Lindsey.
Front row: Lee Williams, Richard Corbyn, Karl Emerick, John Carney, Danny Francis, Mark Barnes, Lee Bacon, Adam Flanagan, Paul Sykes.

Division 3 **GILLINGHAM**

Priestfield Stadium, Gillingham, ME7 4DD. Telephone: (01634) 851854/576828. Fax: (01634) 850986.

Ground capacity: 10,412.

Record attendance: 23,002 v QPR, FA Cup 3rd rd 10 January 1948.

Record receipts: £80,184 v Sheffield W, FA Cup 3rd rd, 7 January 1995.

Pitch measurements: 114yd × 75yd.

President: J. W. Leech. ***Vice-Presidents:*** G. B. Goodere, G. V. W. Lukehurst.

Chairman: A. Smith.

Directors: M. G. Lukehurst, Mrs. V. Smith.

Manager: Tony Pulis. ***Coach:*** Gary Micklewhite.

Physio: Javed Mughal.

Acting Secretary: S. Close. ***Commercial Manager:*** M. Ling.

Year Formed: 1893. ***Turned Professional:*** 1894. ***Ltd Co.:*** 1893.

Club Nickname: 'The Gills'.

Previous Name: New Brompton, 1893–1913.

Foundation: The success of the pioneering Royal Engineers of Chatham excited the interest of the residents of the Medway Towns and led to the formation of many clubs including Excelsior. After winning the Kent Junior Cup and the Chatham District League in 1893, Excelsior decided to go for bigger things and it was at a meeting in the Napier Arms, Brompton, in 1893 that New Brompton FC came into being as a professional concern, securing the use of a ground in Priestfield Road.

First Football League game: 28 August, 1920, Division 3, v Southampton (h) D 1-1 – Branfield; Robertson, Sissons; Battiste, Baxter, Wigmore; Holt, Hall, Gilbey (1), Roe, Gore.

Record League Victory: 10–0 v Chesterfield, Division 3, 5 September 1987 – Kite; Haylock, Pearce, Shipley (2) (Lillis), West, Greenall (1), Pritchard (2), Shearer (2), Lovell, Elsey (2), David Smith (1).

Record Cup Victory: 10–1 v Gorleston, FA Cup, 1st rd, 16 November 1957 – Brodie; Parry, Hannaway; Riggs, Boswell, Laing; Payne, Fletcher (2), Saunders (5), Morgan (1), Clark (2).

Record Defeat: 2–9 v Nottingham F, Division 3 (S), 18 November 1950.

Most League Points (2 for a win): 62, Division 4, 1973–74.

Most League Points (3 for a win): 83, Division 3, 1984–85.

Most League Goals: 90, Division 4, 1973–74.

Highest League Scorer in Season: Ernie Morgan, 31, Division 3 (S), 1954–55 and Brian Yeo, 31, Division 4, 1973–74.

Most League Goals in Total Aggregate: Brian Yeo, 135, 1963–75.

Most Capped Player: Tony Cascarino, 3 (56), Republic of Ireland.

Most League Appearances: John Simpson, 571, 1957–72.

Record Transfer Fee Received: £300,000 from Tottenham H for Peter Beadle, June 1992.

Record Transfer Fee Paid: £102,500 to Tottenham H for Mark Cooper, October 1987.

Football League Record: 1920 Original Member of Division 3; 1921 Division 3 (S); 1938 Failed re-election; Southern League 1938–44; Kent League 1944–46; Southern League 1946–50; 1950 Re-elected to Division 3 (S); 1958–64 Division 4; 1964–71 Division 3; 1971–74 Division 4; 1974–89 Division 3; 1989–92 Division 4; 1992– Division 3.

Honours: *Football League:* Division 3 best season: 4th, 1978–79, 1984–85; Division 4 – Champions 1963–64; Runners-up 1973–74. *FA Cup:* best season: 5th rd, 1970. *Football League Cup:* best season: 4th rd, 1964.

Colours: Blue shirts, white shorts, white stockings. **Change colours:** Red shirts, white shorts, red stockings.

GILLINGHAM 1994–95 LEAGUE RECORD

Match No.	Date	Venue	Opponents	Result		H/T Score	Lg. Pos.	Goalscorers	Attendance
1	Aug 13	H	Hartlepool U	D	0-0	0-0	—		2956
2	20	A	Wigan Ath	W	3-0	1-0	4	Foster, Reinelt, Watson	1514
3	27	H	Rochdale	D	1-1	0-1	9	Butler	3015
4	30	A	Scunthorpe U	L	0-3	0-0	—		2098
5	Sept 3	A	Exeter C	L	0-3	0-2	16		2241
6	10	H	Scarborough	W	3-1	1-0	9	Palmer, Ritchie, Baker	2414
7	13	H	Preston NE	L	2-3	2-2	—	Smith, Baker	2555
8	17	A	Hartlepool U	L	0-2	0-1	16		1756
9	24	A	Walsall	L	1-2	0-1	17	Micklewhite	3654
10	Oct 1	H	Mansfield T	L	0-2	0-1	20		2555
11	8	H	Torquay U	W	1-0	1-0	17	Pike	2439
12	15	A	Hereford U	L	1-2	0-1	19	Arnott	2472
13	22	A	Bury	L	2-3	0-2	20	Pike 2 (1 pen)	2976
14	29	H	Darlington	W	2-1	1-1	17	Pike, Smillie	2785
15	Nov 5	A	Colchester U	D	2-2	2-1	17	Reinelt, Pike	3817
16	19	H	Chesterfield	D	1-1	0-1	17	Reinelt	2722
17	26	A	Lincoln C	D	1-1	0-0	17	Arnott	2919
18	Dec 10	H	Wigan Ath	L	0-1	0-0	19		2257
19	17	A	Rochdale	L	1-2	0-2	19	Foster	1665
20	26	H	Fulham	W	4-1	1-0	18	Reinelt, Micklewhite, Foster 2	4677
21	27	A	Barnet	L	0-1	0-0	18		3074
22	31	H	Carlisle U	L	0-1	0-0	19		3682
23	Jan 14	A	Northampton T	L	0-2	0-0	21		5529
24	Feb 4	H	Lincoln C	D	0-0	0-0	20		4196
25	7	A	Doncaster R	W	2-1	1-1	—	Pike 2	1740
26	11	A	Chesterfield	L	0-2	0-2	19		3070
27	18	H	Northampton T	W	3-1	1-0	19	Ramage, Green, Foster	4075
28	21	A	Darlington	L	0-2	0-0	—		1548
29	25	A	Mansfield T	L	0-4	0-1	20		3182
30	Mar 4	H	Walsall	L	1-3	0-0	20	Foster	3669
31	11	A	Scarborough	D	0-0	0-0	21		1949
32	18	H	Scunthorpe U	D	2-2	0-1	20	Foster, Pike	2459
33	25	H	Exeter C	W	3-0	2-0	19	Foster, Pike (pen), Butler	3332
34	Apr 1	A	Preston NE	D	1-1	0-1	19	Dunne	9100
35	4	H	Bury	D	1-1	1-1	—	Brown	2945
36	8	A	Carlisle U	L	0-2	0-2	19		6786
37	11	H	Colchester U	L	1-3	1-0	—	Watson	3328
38	15	H	Barnet	W	2-1	2-1	18	Brown, Pike	3448
39	17	A	Fulham	L	0-1	0-0	19		3612
40	22	H	Doncaster R	W	4-2	3-2	18	Kirby (og), Pike 3	2826
41	29	H	Hereford U	D	0-0	0-0	17		4208
42	May 6	A	Torquay U	L	1-3	0-1	19	Stamps (og)	2638

Final League Position: 19

GOALSCORERS

League (46): Pike 13 (2 pens), Foster 8, Reinelt 4, Arnott 2, Baker 2, Brown 2, Butler 2, Micklewhite 2, Watson 2, Dunne 1, Green 1, Palmer 1, Ramage 1, Ritchie 1, Smillie 1, Smith 1, own goals 2.
Coca-Cola Cup (0).
FA Cup (6): Pike 4 (1 pen), Reinelt 2.

Barrett S. 4	Dunne J.J. 35	Palmer L.J. 10	Micklewhite G. 33 + 2	Green R.E. 37	Butler P.A. 31 + 2	Smillie N. 15	Smith N.J. 32 + 1	Foster A.M. 27 + 2	Arnott A.J. 24 + 4	Watson P.D. 39	Ramage A.W. 8 + 5	Baker D.P. 7 + 1	Reinelt R.S. 18 + 9	Carpenter R. 26 + 3	Wilson P.A.F. — + 2	Banks S. 38	Watts G.S. 2 + 1	Ritchie P. 5	Kennedy A.J. — + 2	Trott R.F. 7 + 2	Pike C. 26 + 1	Hutchinson I.N. 1 + 4	Bodley M.J. 6 + 1	Lindsey S. 11 + 1	Knott G.R. 5	Freeman D.B.A. — + 2	Martin E.J. 7	Brown S.R. 8	*Match No.*
1	2	3	4	5	6	*7*	8	9	*10*	11	12	14																	1
1	2	3	4	5	6		8	9		11		10	7																2
1	2	3	4	5	6		8	*9*	12	11		10	7	14															3
1	2	*3*	4	5	6		8		9	11		*10*	7	12	14														4
	2		4	5	6	11	8		9	3			7	12	14	1	*10*												5
	2	3		5	6		8			11		9	7	4		1		10											6
	2	*3*	*12*	5	6		8			11		9	7	4		1		10	14										7
	2			5	6		8			11		9	7	4		1		10	12	3									8
	2		7	5	6	11	8			3		9	12	4		1		10											9
	2	3	7	5	6		8			11			12	4		1		10			9								10
	2	3	7	5	6		8		12	11			10	4		1	14				*9*								11
	2	3	7	5	6		8		12	11			10	*4*		1	9					14							12
	2	3	7	5	6		*8*		12	11	14		10	4		1					9								13
	2		7	5	6	11	8			3			10	4		1					9								14
	2		7	5	6	11			8	3			10	4		1					9	12							15
	2		7		6	11	12	8	5	3			10	4		1				14	9								16
			7			11	2	8	5	3			10	4		1					9	12	6						17
			12		5	11	7	9	2	3			8	4		1					10		6						18
			7	5	*6*	11	8	9	2	3			12	4		1					10		14						19
			7	6	5		8	9	2				11	4		1					10		3						20
			7	6	5		8	9	2				11	4		1						10	3						21
			7	6	5		8	9	2				11	4		1					10	12	*3*	14					22
			7	6	5		8	9	2	11			12	4		1					10		3						23
	2		7	5		11		10		3	4		12			1				6	9			8					24
	2		7	5		11		9		3	4					1				6	10			8					25
	2		7	5		11		9		3	4		12			1				6	10			8					26
	2		8	5	11			10		3	4					1				6	9				7				27
	2		7	5	8			10		3	4		12			1				6	9				11				28
	2		7	5	6			9	8	11	4		12			1				3	10								29
	7		8	5	*6*		4	10	2	3			12			1					9				11	14			30
	7		8	5	6		4	10	2	3	12					1					9				11				31
	2		8	5	6		4	10		3				7		1					9				11	12			32
	2		8	5	6		4	10		11				7		1					9						3		33
	4			5				10	6	11	8			7		1					9			2			3		34
	7		8	5				10	6	11				4		1								2			3	9	35
	7			5	12		4	*10*	6	11				8		1					14			2			3	9	36
	2		8	5			4	10	6	11				7		1											3	9	37
	7			5		11	4		6	3	12			8		1					10			2				9	38
	7			5		11	4	10	6	3	12			8		1				14				*2*				9	39
	7		8	5	12		4	14	*6*	11						1					9			2			3	10	40
	7		8		5		4	10	6	11						1								2			3	9	41
	7				5	11	4	12	6	3	8					1					10			2				9	42

Coca-Cola Cup

First Round	Reading (h)	0-1	
	(a)	0-3	

FA Cup

First Round	Heybridge S (a)	2-0
Second Round	Fulham (h)	1-1
	(a)	2-1
Third Round	Sheffield W (h)	1-2

GRIMSBY TOWN 1994–95 *Back row (left to right):* Paul Groves, Paul Futcher, Steve Livingstone, Graham Rodger, Mark Lever, Peter Handyside, Neil Woods, Joby Gowshall, Clive Mendonca.

Centre row: Richard O'Kelly (Youth Coach), Tony Rees, Jim Dobbin, John Cook, Jimmy Neil, Paul Crichton, Rhys Wilmot, Simon Buckley, Jack Lester, Paul Agnew, Gary Croft, Paul Mitchell (Physio), Arthur Mann (Reserve Coach).

Front row: Darren Lambert, Tommy Watson, David Gilbert, Alan Buckley (Manager), Gary Childs, John McDermott, Kevin Jobling.

Division 1 **GRIMSBY TOWN**

Blundell Park, Cleethorpes, South Humberside DN35 7PY. Telephone: (01472) 697111. Fax: (01472) 693665. Clubcall: 0891 121576.

Ground capacity: 8,500 (approx).

Record attendance: 31,657 v Wolverhampton W, FA Cup 5th rd, 20 February 1937.

Record receipts: £119,799 v Aston Villa, FA Cup 4th rd, 29 January 1994.

Pitch measurements: 111yd × 75yd.

Presidents: T. J. Lindley, T. Wilkinson.

Chairman: W. H. Carr. ***Vice-Chairman:*** T. A. Aspinall.

Directors: P. W. Furneaux, G. Lamming, J. Mager.

Manager: Brian Laws. ***Assistant Manager:*** Kenny Swain.

Youth Team Coach: John Cockerill.

Company Secretary: Ian Fleming. ***Commercial Manager:*** Tony Richardson.

Lottery Manager: T. E. Harvey.

Physio: Paul Mitchell.

Year Formed. 1878. ***Turned Professional:*** 1890. ***Ltd Co.:*** 1890.

Previous Name: Grimsby Pelham.

Club Nickname: 'The Mariners'.

Previous Grounds: Clee Park; Abbey Park.

Foundation: Grimsby Pelham FC as they were first known, came into being at a meeting held at the Wellington Arms in September 1878. Pelham is the family name of big landowners in the area, the Earls of Yarborough. The receipts for their first game amounted to 6s. 9d. (approx. 39p). After a year, the club name was changed to Grimsby Town.

First Football League game: 3 September, 1892, Division 2, v Northwich Victoria (h) W 2-1 – Whitehouse; Lundie, T. Frith; C. Frith, Walker, Murrell; Higgins, Henderson, Brayshaw, Riddoch (2), Ackroyd.

Record League Victory: 9–2 v Darwen, Division 2, 15 April 1899 – Bagshaw; Lockie, Nidd; Griffiths, Bell (1), Nelmes; Jenkinson (3), Richards (1), Cockshutt (3), Robinson, Chadburn (1).

Record Cup Victory: 8–0 v Darlington, FA Cup, 2nd rd, 21 November 1885 – G. Atkinson; J. H. Taylor, H. Taylor; Hall, Kimpson, Hopewell; H. Atkinson (1), Garnham, Seal (3), Sharman, Monument (4).

Record Defeat: 1–9 v Arsenal, Division 1, 28 January 1931.

Most League Points (2 for a win): 68, Division 3 (N), 1955–56.

Most League Points (3 for a win): 83, Division 3, 1990–91.

Most League Goals: 103, Division 2, 1933–34.

Highest League Scorer in Season: Pat Glover, 42, Division 2, 1933–34.

Most League Goals in Total Aggregate: Pat Glover, 182, 1930–39.

Most Capped Player: Pat Glover, 7, Wales.

Most League Appearances: Keith Jobling, 448, 1953–69.

Record Transfer Fee Received: £650,000 from Sunderland for Shaun Cunnington, July 1992.

Record Transfer Fee Paid: £150,000 to Blackpool for Paul Groves, August 1992.

Football League Record: 1892 Original Member Division 2; 1901–03 Division 1; 1903 Division 2; 1910 Failed re-election; 1911 re-elected Division 2; 1920–21 Division 3; 1921–26 Division 3 (N); 1926–29 Division 2; 1929–32 Division 1; 1932–34 Division 2; 1934–48 Division 1; 1948–51 Division 2; 1951–56 Division 3 (N); 1956–59 Division 2; 1959–62 Division 3; 1962–64 Division 2; 1964–68 Division 3; 1968–72 Division 4; 1972–77 Division 3; 1977–79 Division 4; 1979–80 Division 3; 1980–87 Division 2; 1987–88 Division 3; 1988–90 Division 4; 1990–91 Division 3; 1991– 92 Division 2; 1992– Division 1.

Honours: *Football League:* Division 1 best season: 5th, 1934–35; Division 2 – Champions 1900–01, 1933–34; Runners-up 1928–29; Division 3 (N) – Champions 1925–26, 1955–56; Runners-up 1951–52; Division 3 – Champions 1979–80; Runners-up 1961–62; Division 4 – Champions 1971–72; Runners-up 1978–79; 1989–90. *FA Cup:* Semi-finals, 1936, 1939. *Football League Cup:* best season: 5th rd, 1980, 1985. *League Group Cup:* Winners 1982.

Colours: Black and white striped shirts, black shorts, white stockings. **Change colours:** Red and blue striped shirts, blue shorts, red stockings.

GRIMSBY TOWN 1994–95 LEAGUE RECORD

Match No.	Date	Venue	Opponents	Result		H/T Score	Lg. Pos.	Goalscorers	Attendance
1	Aug 13	H	Bolton W	D	3-3	1-2	—	Mendonca 3 (1 pen)	8393
2	20	A	Watford	D	0-0	0-0	13		6324
3	27	H	Tranmere R	W	3-1	2-0	6	Livingstone 2, Groves	4087
4	30	A	Sunderland	D	2-2	1-1	—	Childs, Mendonca (pen)	15,788
5	Sept 3	A	Derby Co	L	1-2	0-1	13	Mendonca	12,027
6	10	H	Charlton Ath	L	0-1	0-0	17		3970
7	13	H	Port Vale	W	4-1	1-0	—	Woods, Mendonca 2, Gilbert	3216
8	17	A	WBA	D	1-1	0-1	12	Shakespeare	14,496
9	24	A	Swindon T	L	2-3	1-1	14	Woods, Groves	8219
10	Oct 1	H	Portsmouth	W	2-0	1-0	11	Mendonca (pen), Woods	4172
11	8	H	Sheffield U	D	0-0	0-0	14		8930
12	15	A	Wolverhampton W	L	1-2	1-1	17	Groves	24,447
13	22	H	Bristol C	W	1-0	0-0	11	Childs	4024
14	29	A	Southend U	D	0-0	0-0	13		5086
15	Nov 1	A	Luton T	W	2-1	0-0	—	Gilbert 2	5839
16	5	H	Middlesbrough	W	2-1	2-0	6	Woods, Dobbin	8488
17	12	H	Millwall	W	1-0	0-0	5	Woods	5261
18	19	A	Stoke C	L	0-3	0-2	6		12,055
19	26	H	Burnley	D	2-2	1-0	7	Woods, Gilbert	7084
20	Dec 3	A	Bristol C	W	2-1	0-0	4	Gilbert, Childs	6030
21	10	H	Watford	D	0-0	0-0	8		6288
22	17	A	Bolton W	D	3-3	2-1	8	Woods, Jobling, Groves	10,522
23	26	A	Barnsley	L	1-4	1-2	9	Woods	8669
24	27	H	Oldham Ath	L	1-3	0-2	13	Woods	6958
25	31	A	Reading	D	1-1	1-0	13	Shakespeare	8526
26	Jan 14	H	Southend U	W	4-1	1-1	10	Shakespeare, Groves, Woods, Croft	3915
27	21	A	Middlesbrough	D	1-1	0-0	9	Woods	15,360
28	28	H	Notts Co	W	2-1	1-0	7	Woods, Mendonca	5161
29	Feb 4	A	Millwall	L	0-2	0-1	8		7397
30	11	H	Luton T	W	5-0	2-0	8	Dobbin, Gilbert, Woods, Watson 2	4615
31	18	A	Burnley	W	2-0	1-0	7	Mendonca 2	10,511
32	21	H	Stoke C	D	0-0	0-0	—		6384
33	25	A	Portsmouth	L	1-2	1-1	7	Rodger	8274
34	Mar 4	H	Swindon T	D	1-1	1-0	7	Watson	4934
35	7	H	Derby Co	L	0-1	0-0	—		5310
36	11	A	Tranmere R	L	0-2	0-2	9		15,810
37	19	H	Sunderland	W	3-1	1-0	9	Livingstone 2, Forrester	5697
38	21	A	Charlton Ath	L	1-2	1-1	—	Childs	9601
39	25	H	WBA	L	0-2	0-1	10		7393
40	Apr 1	A	Port Vale	W	2-1	2-0	9	Livingstone, Laws	7150
41	8	H	Reading	W	1-0	0-0	9	Livingstone	4519
42	15	A	Oldham Ath	L	0-1	0-1	10		6757
43	17	H	Barnsley	W	1-0	1-0	9	Woods	7277
44	22	A	Notts Co	W	2-0	1-0	9	Livingstone, Reece (og)	5286
45	29	H	Wolverhampton W	D	0-0	0-0	9		10,112
46	May 6	A	Sheffield U	L	1-3	1-2	10	Livingstone	14,323

Final League Position: 10

GOALSCORERS

League (62): Woods 14, Mendonca 11 (3 pens), Livingstone 8, Gilbert 6, Groves 5, Childs 4, Shakespeare 3, Watson 3, Dobbin 2, Croft 1, Forrester 1, Jobling 1, Laws 1, Rodger 1, own goal 1.
Coca-Cola Cup (2): Gilbert 1, Groves 1.
FA Cup (0).

Crichton P.A. 43	Jobling K.A. 37 + 1	Croft G. 44	Futcher P. 6 + 1	Lever M. 31	Shakespeare C.R. 16 + 3	Watson T.R. 20 + 1	Gilbert D.J. 40	Livingstone S. 29 + 5	Mendonca C.P. 21 + 1	Groves P. 46	Agnew P. 7 + 3	Lester J. 1 + 6	Handyside P.D. 34 + 1	Woods N.S. 33 + 4	Childs G.P.C. 18 + 7	Dobbin J. 35 + 3	McDermott J. 8 + 4	Rodger G. 20 + 1	Laws B. 6 + 10	Forrester J. 7 + 2	Fickling A. 1	Pearcey J.K. 3	Match No.
1	2	3	4	5	6	7	8	9	10	11	12												1
1		2	4	5	6		8	9	10	11	3		7	12									2
1		2	4	5	6		8	9	10	11	3	12			7								3
1	3	2	4	5	6		8	*9*	10	11			12	14	7								4
1	3	2	4	5	6		8	*9*	10	11	12			14	7								5
1		2		5	6		8		10	11	3		4	9	7	12							6
1		2		5	6		8	12	10	11	3		4	9	7								7
1		2		5	6		8	12	10	11	3		4	9	7	14							8
1		2		5	6		8	12	10	11	3		4	9		7							9
1	12	2		5	6		8		10	11	3		4	9		7							10
1	3	2		5	6	8			10	11		12	4	9		7							11
1	3	2	12	5	6	*8*		10		11			4	9	14	7							12
1	3	2		5	6	7		9		11			4	10	12	8							13
1	3	2		5		7	11	9		6			4	10		8							14
1	3	2		5		7	11	9		6	12		4	10		8							15
1	3	2		5		7	11	9		6			4	10		8							16
1	3	2		5		7	11	9		6			4	10		8							17
1	3	2		5		7	11	*9*		6			4	10	12	8	14						18
1	3	2		5			11	9		6			4	10	7	8							19
1	3	2		*5*			11	9		6		12	4	10	7	8		14					20
1	3	2					11	9		6			4	10	7	8	12	5					21
1	3	2					11	9		6			4	10	7	8	12	5					22
1	3	2			12		11	*9*		6		14	4	10	7	8	5						23
1		3	5		12	7	*11*		14	6		9	4	10		8	2						24
1		3			8	7	11		9	6		12	4	10			2	5					25
1	2	3			8	7	11		9	6			4	10				5					26
1	*2*	3		5		7	11	12	10	6			4	9		8	14						27
1	2	3		5		7	11		10	6			4	9		8			12				28
1	2	3		5		7	11		10	6			4	9	12	*8*			14				29
1	3			*5*		7	11		10	6			4	9	12	8	2		14				30
1	3					7	11		10	6			4	9		8	2	5	12				31
1	3	2				7	11		10	6			4	9		8		5	12				32
1	3	11				7		12	10	6			4	9		8	*2*	5	14				33
1	3	11				7			10	6			4	9		8	2	5					34
1	3	11				12	10	9		6			4		7	*8*	2	5	14				35
1	3	2					11	9		6			4		7	8		5	12	10			36
1	3	2					11	9		6			4		7	8		5		10			37
1	3	2					11	9		6			4		7	8		5	12	10			38
1	3	2		4	12		*11*	9		6					7	8		5	14	10			39
1	3	11		4				9		6					7	8		5	2	10			40
1	3	7		4			11	9		6		12				8		5	2	10			41
1	3	7					11	9		6				12		8		5	2	10	4		42
1	3	7		4			11	10		6				*9*	12	8		5	2	14			43
	3	7		4			11	10		6				9		8		5	2			1	44
	3	7		4			11	10		6				9	12	8		5	2			1	45
	3	2		4	8		11	*10*		6				9	7	12		5		14		1	46

Coca-Cola Cup
First Round Bradford C (a) 1-2
(h) 1-2

FA Cup
Third Round Norwich C (h) 0-1

HARTLEPOOL UNITED 1994–95 *Back row (left to right):* Nicky Southall, Phil Gilchrist, Keith Houchen, Steven Jones, Ian McGuckin, Brian Horne, Matty Hyson, Jason Ainsley, Paul Thompson, Gary Henderson (Physio).
Front row: Scott Garrett, Chris Lynch, Denny Ingram, John MacPhail (Manager), Brian Honour, Alan Hay (Assistant Manager), Anthony Skedd, Stephen Halliday, Keith Oliver.

Division 3 HARTLEPOOL UNITED

The Victoria Ground, Clarence Road, Hartlepool, TS24 8BZ. Telephone: (01429) 272584. Commercial Dept: (01429) 222077. Fax: (01429) 863007. Football in the Community: (01429) 862595.

Ground capacity: 7985.

Record attendance: 17,426 v Manchester U, FA Cup 3rd rd, 5 January 1957.

Record receipts: £42,300 v Tottenham H, Rumbelows Cup, 2nd rd 2nd leg, 9 October 1990.

Pitch measurements: 110yd × 75yd.

President: E. Leadbitter.

Chairman: H. Hornsey.

Directors: A. Bamford, D. Jukes.

Manager: Keith Houchen. ***Coach:*** Mick Tait.

Youth/Reserve Coach: Eric Gates. ***Physio:*** Gary Henderson. ***Commercial Manager:*** Frank Baggs. ***Secretary:*** Stuart Bagnall.

Year Formed: 1908. ***Turned Professional:*** 1908. ***Ltd Co.:*** 1908.

Club Nickname: 'The Pool'.

Previous Names: Hartlepools United until 1968; Hartlepool until 1977.

Foundation: The inspiration for the launching of Hartlepool United was the West Hartlepool club which won the FA Amateur Cup in 1904–05. They had been in existence since 1881 and their Cup success led in 1908 to the formation of the new professional concern which first joined the North-Eastern League. In those days they were Hartlepools United and won the Durham Senior Cup in their first two seasons.

First Football League game: 27 August, 1921, Division 3(N), v Wrexham (a) W 2-0 – Gill; Thomas, Crilly; Dougherty, Hopkins, Short; Kessler, Mulholland (1), Lister (1), Robertson, Donald.

Record League Victory: 10–1 v Barrow, Division 4, 4 April 1959 – Oakley; Cameron, Waugh; Johnson, Moore, Anderson; Scott (1), Langland (1), Smith (3), Clark (2), Luke (2). (1 og).

Record Cup Victory: 6–0 v North Shields, FA Cup, 1st rd, 30 November 1946 – Heywood; Brown, Gregory; Spelman, Lambert, Jones; Price, Scott (2), Sloan (4), Moses, McMahon.

Record Defeat: 1–10 v Wrexham, Division 4, 3 March 1962.

Most League Points (2 for a win): 60, Division 4, 1967–68.

Most League Points (3 for a win): 82, Division 4, 1990–91.

Most League Goals: 90, Division 3 (N), 1956–57.

Highest League Scorer in Season: William Robinson, 28, Division 3 (N), 1927–28 and Joe Allon, 28, Division 4, 1990–91.

Most League Goals in Total Aggregate: Ken Johnson, 98, 1949–64.

Most Capped Player: Ambrose Fogarty, 1 (11), Republic of Ireland.

Most League Appearances: Wattie Moore, 447, 1948–64.

Record Transfer Fee Received: £300,000 from Chelsea for Joe Allon, August 1991.

Record Transfer Fee Paid: £60,000 to Barnsley for Andy Saville, March 1992.

Football League Record: 1921 Original Member of Division 3 (N); 1958–68 Division 4; 1968–69 Division 3; 1969–91 Division 4; 1991–92 Division 3; 1992–94 Division 2; 1994– Division 3.

Honours: *Football League:* Division 3 best season: 22nd, 1968–69; Division 3 (N) – Runners-up 1956–57. *FA Cup:* best season: 4th rd, 1955, 1978, 1989, 1993. *Football League Cup,* best season: 4th rd, 1975.

Colours: Blue and white striped shirts. **Change colours:** Red shirts with white trim.

HARTLEPOOL UNITED 1994–95 LEAGUE RECORD

Match No.	Date	Venue	Opponents	Result		H/T Score	Lg. Pos.	Goalscorers	Atten-dance
1	Aug 13	A	Gillingham	D	0-0	0-0	—		2956
2	20	H	Darlington	W	1-0	0-0	9	Lynch	3035
3	27	A	Bury	L	0-2	0-1	14		2145
4	30	H	Barnet	L	0-1	0-1	—		2095
5	Sept 3	H	Chesterfield	L	0-2	0-0	18		2173
6	10	A	Colchester U	L	0-1	0-0	20		2428
7	13	A	Northampton T	D	1-1	0-0	—	Halliday	2466
8	17	H	Gillingham	W	2-0	1-0	18	Houchen, Walsh (pen)	1756
9	24	H	Lincoln C	L	0-3	0-3	19		1419
10	Oct 1	A	Exeter C	L	1-2	1-1	21	Halliday	2390
11	8	A	Mansfield T	L	0-2	0-1	21		2545
12	15	H	Preston NE	W	3-1	2-1	20	Houchen, Ainsley, Foster	2002
13	22	H	Walsall	D	1-1	1-1	19	Houchen	1704
14	29	A	Scunthorpe U	D	0-0	0-0	20		2624
15	Nov 5	H	Wigan Ath	L	0-1	0-1	20		1683
16	19	A	Doncaster R	L	0-3	0-1	22		2507
17	26	H	Rochdale	W	1-0	1-0	19	Sloan	1387
18	Dec 10	A	Darlington	W	2-1	1-1	17	Southall, Houchen	3193
19	17	H	Bury	W	3-1	2-0	17	Houchen 3	1746
20	26	H	Carlisle U	L	1-5	0-1	17	Caig (og)	3854
21	27	A	Torquay U	D	2-2	1-1	16	Southall (pen), Thompson	3172
22	31	H	Fulham	L	1-2	1-1	16	Southall (pen)	1698
23	Jan 14	H	Scarborough	D	3-3	0-1	16	Thompson 2, Sloan	1784
24	28	H	Scunthorpe U	L	1-4	0-1	17	Thompson	1660
25	Feb 4	A	Rochdale	L	0-1	0-1	19		1848
26	18	A	Scarborough	D	2-2	1-1	21	McGuckin, Houchen	1517
27	21	A	Hereford U	L	0-1	0-0	—		1685
28	25	H	Exeter C	D	2-2	1-1	21	Houchen, McGuckin	1440
29	28	A	Wigan Ath	L	0-2	0-1	—		1452
30	Mar 4	A	Lincoln C	L	0-3	0-0	21		6477
31	7	A	Walsall	L	1-4	1-1	—	McGuckin	3314
32	11	H	Colchester U	W	3-1	2-1	20	Southall 3 (2 pens)	1371
33	18	A	Barnet	L	0-4	0-1	21		1557
34	21	H	Doncaster R	W	2-1	2-0	—	Houchen 2	1354
35	25	A	Chesterfield	L	0-2	0-1	20		4125
36	Apr 1	H	Northampton T	D	1-1	1-0	20	Houchen	2113
37	8	A	Fulham	L	0-1	0-0	20		3465
38	15	H	Torquay U	D	1-1	0-0	20	Henderson	1770
39	17	A	Carlisle U	W	1-0	1-0	20	Houchen	10,242
40	22	H	Hereford U	W	4-0	0-0	19	Holmes 2, Henderson 2	1596
41	29	A	Preston NE	L	0-3	0-2	20		9129
42	May 6	H	Mansfield T	W	3-2	1-0	18	Halliday 3	3049

Final League Position: 18

GOALSCORERS

League (43): Houchen 13, Southall 6 (4 pens), Halliday 5, Thompson 4, Henderson 3, McGuckin 3, Holmes 2, Sloan 2, Ainsley 1, Foster 1, Lynch 1, Walsh 1 (pen), own goal 1.
Coca-Cola Cup (5): Southall 2, Houchen 1, Thompson 1, own goal 1.
FA Cup (0).

Horne B. 41	Ingram S.D. 35	Sweeney P.M. 1	Gilchrist P.A. 23	McGuckin T.I. 34	Oliver K. 18	Ainsley J. 14 + 1	Sloan S.M. 26 + 3	Houchen K.M. 32	Honour B. 1	Southall L.N. 37	Skedd A.S. 17 + 6	Thompson P.D.Z. 24 + 4	Lynch C.J. 8 + 3	Halliday S.W. 19 + 9	Hyson M.A. 1 + 4	Tait M.P. 20	Garrett S. — + 1	Gourlay A.M. — + 1	Burgess D.J. 11	Walsh A. 4	McCreery D. 7 + 2	Foster W.P. 4	Cook M. 22 + 2	Reddish S. 23	MacPhail J. 6	Daughtry P.W. 14 + 1	Peverell N.J. — + 1	Jones S. 1 + 1	Sunley M. 1 + 1	Henderson D.M. 12	Holmes S.P. 5	Homer C. 1	*Match No.*
1	2	3	4	5	6	7	8	9	10	11																							1
1	2		4	5	6		8	9		11	3	7	10	12																			2
1	2		4	5		6		9		11	3	7	10	8	12																		3
1	2		4	5	6			9		11	3	7	10	8	12																		4
1	2		4	*5*	6	8		9		11	3	7	10	12	14																		5
1	2		4		6	8	11	9			*3*	7	10		12	5	14																6
1	2		4		6	8	11	9				7	3	10		5		12															7
1			4	5	6		11	9				7	12	10		8			2	3													8
1			4	5	6			9			14	7	12	10	*11*	8			2	3													9
1	8		4	5	6	11	12	9				7		10					2	3													10
1	8		4	5	6	11	14	9		7		12		10					2	*3*													11
1	3		4	5		6	7	9		11									2		8	10											12
1	3		4	5		6	7	9		11		12							2		8	10											13
1	3		4	5		6	7	9		11									2		8	10											14
1	3		4	5		6	*7*	9		11	14	12							2		8	10											15
1	10		4	5		*6*	9			11		7		12					2		14		3	8									16
1			4				10			11	6	9		12					2				3	8	5	7							17
1			4	5			10	9		11	6					8			2				3			7							18
1	2		4	5			10	9		11	6					8							3			7							19
1	2		4				10			11	6	9		12		5							3	8		7							20
1	2		4			8	10			11		9				6							3		5	7							21
1	2		4	5		8	10			11	3	9				6										7	12						22
1	2			5			*10*			11		9		12		6							3	8	4	7		15					23
	2			5			10			11		9		12		6							3	8	4	7		1					24
1	2		4	5		12	10			11		9		14		6							3	8		7							25
1	2			5			10	9		11	14	4				6					12		3	8		7							26
1	2			5			10	9		11		4				6							3	8		7							27
1	2			5			10	9		11	12	4		14		6							3	8		7							28
1	*2*			5			10	9		11	12			7		6							3	8	4				14				29
1					4		10	9		11				7		6							3	8	5				2				30
1				5	4		10			11	12			7		6					8		3	2						9			31
1				5	8			9		11				7		6							3	2						10	4		32
1	2			5				9		11				7									3	6		8				10	4		33
1	8			5			12	9		11	3			7		*6*								2		14				10	4		34
1	6			5				9		11	3	4		7										2		8				10			35
1	6			5				9		11	3	4		7							8		12	2						10			36
1	9									11	10	4	12	7							8		3	2						5		6	37
1	6				4		10	9		11	3	8		7									12	2						5			38
1	2			5	4			9		11	3												7	8						10	6		39
1	2			5	4			9		11			3										7	8						10	6		40
1	2			5	4			9		11	3	12		10									7	8						6			41
1	6			5	4			9		11			3	8									7	2						10			42

Coca-Cola Cup

First Round	Bury (a)	0-2
	(h)	5-1
Second Round	Arsenal (h)	0-5
	(a)	0-2

FA Cup

First Round	Port Vale (a)	0-6

HEREFORD UNITED 1994–95 *Back row (left to right):* Richard Wilkins, Michael Gonzague, Howard Clark, Chris Pike, Chris MacKenzie,Tony Pennock, Brian Thomas, Tony James, Gareth Davies, Paul Eversham.

Front row: Phil Preedy, Tim Steele, John Layton (Assistant Manager), Dean Smith, Greg Downs (Manager), Andy Reece, Nicky Cross.

Division 3 **HEREFORD UNITED**

Edgar Street, Hereford, HR4 9JU. Telephone: (01432) 276666. Fax: (01432) 341359.

Ground capacity: 9022.

Record attendance: 18,114 v Sheffield W, FA Cup 3rd rd, 4 January 1958.

Record receipts: £72,840 v Manchester U, FA Cup 4th rd, 28 January 1990.

Pitch measurements: 110yd × 74yd.

Chairman: P. S. Hill FRICS. ***Vice-Chairman:*** M. B. Roberts.

Directors: J. W. T. Duggan, D. H. Vaughan, R. A. Fry, J. Simmons, K. Benjamin (Assoc).

Manager: ***Assistant Manager:*** Dick Bate.

Physio: S. Shakesaft. ***Coach:*** S. Ritchie.

Secretary: J. Fennessy. ***Commercial Manager:*** M. Tranter.

Year Formed: 1924. ***Turned Professional:*** 1924. ***Ltd Co.:*** 1939.

Club Nickname: 'United'.

Foundation: A number of local teams amalgamated in 1924 under the chairmanship of Dr. E. W. Maples to form Hereford United and joined the Birmingham Combination. They graduated to the Birmingham League four years later.

First Football League game: 12 August, 1972, Division 4, v Colchester U (a) L 0-1 – Potter; Mallender, Naylor; Jones, McLaughlin, Tucker; Slattery, Hollett, Owen, Radford, Wallace.

Record League Victory: 6–0 v Burnley (away), Division 4, 24 January 1987 – Rose; Rodgerson, Devine, Halliday, Pejic, Dalziel, Harvey (1p), Wells, Phillips (3), Kearns (2), Spooner.

Record Cup Victory: 6–1 v QPR, FA Cup, 2nd rd, 7 December 1957 – Sewell; Tomkins, Wade; Masters, Niblett, Horton (2p); Reg Bowen (1), Clayton (1), Fidler, Williams (1), Cyril Beech (1).

Record Defeat: 1-7 v Mansfield T, Division 3, 26 December 1994.

Most League Points (2 for a win): 63, Division 3, 1975–76.

Most League Points (3 for a win): 77, Division 4, 1984–85.

Most League Goals: 86, Division 3, 1975–76.

Highest League Scorer in Season: Dixie McNeil, 35, 1975–76.

Most League Goals in Total Aggregate: Stewart Phillips, 93, 1980–88, 1990–1.

Most Capped Player: Brian Evans, 1 (7), Wales.

Most League Appearances: Mel Pejic, 412, 1980–92.

Record Transfer Fee Received: £440,000 from QPR for Darren Peacock, December 1990.

Record Transfer Fee Paid: £80,000 to Walsall for Dean Smith, June 1994.

Football League Record: 1972 Elected to Division 4; 1973–76 Division 3; 1976–77 Division 2; 1977–78 Division 3; 1978–92 Division 4; 1992– Division 3.

Honours: *Football League:* Division 2 best season: 22nd, 1976–77; Division 3 – Champions 1975–76; Division 4 – Runners-up 1972–73. *FA Cup:* best season: 4th rd, 1972, 1977, 1982, 1990. *Football League Cup:* best season: 3rd rd, 1975. *Welsh Cup:* Winners 1990.

Colours: White and black striped shirts, black shorts, black stockings. **Change colours:** Red and black striped shirts, white shorts, white stockings.

HEREFORD UNITED 1994–95 LEAGUE RECORD

Match No.	Date	Venue	Opponents	Result		H/T Score	Lg. Pos.	Goalscorers	Attendance
1	Aug 13	H	Doncaster R	L	0-1	0-1	—		3076
2	20	H	Preston NE	L	0-2	0-0	21		3039
3	27	H	Walsall	D	0-0	0-0	18		3004
4	30	A	Scarborough	L	1-3	0-1	—	Clark	1490
5	Sept 3	A	Rochdale	W	3-1	1-0	17	Preedy, James, White	2258
6	10	H	Wigan Ath	L	1-2	1-0	19	White	2771
7	13	H	Torquay U	D	1-1	1-0	—	White	2153
8	16	A	Doncaster R	L	0-3	0-2	—		1938
9	24	A	Fulham	D	1-1	1-0	21	White	3740
10	Oct 1	H	Scunthorpe U	W	2-1	1-1	18	Cross, White	2267
11	8	A	Barnet	D	2-2	1-1	18	White, Reece	2116
12	15	H	Gillingham	W	2-1	1-0	17	Cross, Davis	2472
13	22	A	Darlington	L	1-3	0-0	17	Cross	1996
14	29	H	Lincoln C	L	0-3	0-1	19		2485
15	Nov 5	A	Chesterfield	L	0-1	0-1	19		2448
16	19	H	Carlisle U	L	0-1	0-1	21		2531
17	26	A	Northampton T	W	3-1	0-0	18	Pick, Reece (pen), White	5148
18	Dec 10	A	Preston NE	L	2-4	0-3	20	Reece, Cross	6581
19	17	A	Walsall	L	3-4	2-1	20	Cross, James, White	3652
20	26	A	Mansfield T	L	1-7	0-1	21	Wilkins	2887
21	27	H	Exeter C	W	3-0	2-0	20	Lyne, Cross, Wilkins	2567
22	31	A	Colchester U	D	2-2	2-0	18	Brough, Whitton (og)	3322
23	Jan 7	H	Darlington	D	0-0	0-0	19		2237
24	14	A	Bury	D	1-1	0-1	19	Reece (pen)	2708
25	24	H	Chesterfield	L	0-2	0-1	—		1673
26	28	A	Lincoln C	L	0-2	0-0	19		2545
27	Feb 4	H	Northampton T	W	2-1	1-1	18	Lloyd, White	2365
28	11	A	Carlisle U	L	0-1	0-1	18		5676
29	18	H	Bury	W	1-0	1-0	18	Lloyd	1827
30	21	H	Hartlepool U	W	1-0	0-0	—	White	1685
31	25	A	Scunthorpe U	L	0-1	0-1	17		2193
32	Mar 4	H	Fulham	D	1-1	0-1	17	Pick	2895
33	18	H	Scarborough	W	2-1	0-0	17	Smith 2 (1 pen)	1479
34	25	H	Rochdale	D	0-0	0-0	17		1954
35	29	A	Wigan Ath	D	1-1	0-0	—	Pounder	1492
36	Apr 1	A	Torquay U	W	1-0	1-0	16	White	2410
37	8	H	Colchester U	W	3-0	2-0	16	White 2, Smith	1669
38	15	A	Exeter C	D	1-1	1-0	16	White	2083
39	17	H	Mansfield T	D	0-0	0-0	16		2743
40	22	A	Hartlepool U	L	0-4	0-0	16		1596
41	29	A	Gillingham	D	0-0	0-0	16		4208
42	May 6	H	Barnet	W	3-2	3-1	16	White, Pounder, Lloyd	2069

Final League Position: 16

GOALSCORERS

League (45): White 15, Cross 6, Reece 4 (2 pens), Lloyd 3, Smith 3 (1 pen), James 2, Pick 2, Pounder 2, Wilkins 2, Brough 1, Clark 1, Davis 1, Lyne 1, Preedy 1, own goal 1.
Coca-Cola Cup (2): White 2.
FA Cup (4): Lyne 2, Pick 1, White 1.

Pennock A. 13 + 2	Reece A.J. 35 + 2	Preedy P. 15 + 1	Davies G.M. 26 + 2	Smith D. 35	James A.C. 18	Wilkins R.J. 34 + 1	Pick G. 23 + 6	Cross N.J. 24 + 4	Clark H.W. 17 + 1	Steele T.W. 4 + 1	Downs G. 2 + 1	Clarke D.B. 3 + 2	Davis M.V. 1	White S.J. 31 + 5	Mackenzie C.N. 21 + 1	Pounder A.M. 23 + 5	Pike C. 2 + 2	Gonzague M. 2 + 1	Williams C.J. — + 2	Eversham P.J. 3 + 2	Lyne N.G.F. 27 + 4	Sheffield J. 8	Fishlock M.E. 12 + 2	Farrington M.A. — + 1	Llewellyn A.D. 3 + 1	Brough J.R. 16 + 2	Lloyd K. 24	Warner R.M. 15 + 1	Brownrigg A.D. 8	Gregory D. 2	Henderson D.M. 5	Stoker G. 10	Reeve J.M. — + 5	Hall L. — + 1	*Match No.*
1	2	3	4	5	6	7	8	9	*10*	11	12	14																							1
1	2	3	4	5	6	7	12	9		11	8		10																						2
1	6	11	*12*	4	5	7		10	2	8	3			9					14																3
1	4	11	3	5	6	7		9	2			*8*		10	15																				4
1	12	*3*		5	6	7	4	9	2					10		8	11	14																	5
1	4		3	5	6	7		9	2					10		8	11		12																6
	4		3	5	6	7		9	2					10	1	8	12			11	14														7
	4	3		5	6		12	*9*	2	7				10			14			8	11	1													8
	4	3	11	5	6	7	8	9	2					10							12	1													9
	4	11		5	6	12	8	9	2					10						7		1	3												10
	4	11		5	6	7	8	9	2					10								1	3												11
	4	11	12	5	6	7	*8*	9	2					10								1	3	14											12
	4	11	5		6		8	9						10		7		2		12		1	3												13
	4	11	5		6	8		9						10		7		*2*		14	12	1	3												14
	4	11	5		6	8		9						10		7					12	1	3		*2*	14									15
1	6	14	5	4		8	11	9						12		7					10		3			*2*									16
1	2		5	4		8	11							9		7					10		6			12	3								17
1	2		*11*	4	6		8	12						9		7					10		5		14		3								18
1	4	11		5	6	7		8						9							10				2		3								19
1	4	*11*		5	6	7	12	8						9		14					10				2		3								20
	4			5		7	11	8							1	12					10					9	3	2	6						21
	4		7	5			11	8							1	12					10					9	3	2	6						22
	4			5			11		7	12				8	1						10					9	3	2	6						23
15	4			5		7	*11*	12						10	1						9					8	3	2	6						24
	4			5		7		11	*6*					12	1	14					10					9	3	2		8					25
1	4		2	5		6		12						14							10					9	3	7		*8*	11				26
	4		8	5		7								10	1						11						3	2	6		9				27
	4		8			7	12							10	1	14					11					5	*3*	2	6		9				28
	4		8			7								12	1	11					9					5	3	2	6		10				29
	4		8			7								12	1	11					10					5	3	2	6		9				30
	4		8	5		7		9							1	11					10					6	3	2							31
	4		8	5		7	12	14	*3*					9	1	11					10					6		2							32
15			8	5		7	12	9	14						*1*	11					10		3			6		*2*				4			33
			8	5		7	4	*9*						10	1	11							12			6	3					2	14		34
1				5		7	4							9		11					10		3			6	8					2	12		35
			8	5		7	4							9	1	11					10		12			6	*3*					2	14		36
			8	5		7	4							9	1	11					10		3				6	12				2			37
	12		8	5		7	4							9	1	11					*10*						6	3				2	14		38
	6		8	5			4					12		9	1	11					10						3	2				7			39
	4			5			8		6			2		*9*	1	11					10						3					7	14	12	40
	4			5		7	8		6					9	1	11					10						3					2			41
	4					7	8		6			3		9	1	11					10						5					2			42

Coca-Cola Cup

First Round	WBA (h)	0-0
	(a)	1-0
Second Round	Nottingham F (a)	1-2
	(h)	0-0

FA Cup

First Round	Hitchin (h)	2-2
	(a)	2-4

HUDDERSFIELD TOWN 1994–95 *Back row (left to right):* Jon Whitney, Michael Midwood, Rodney Rowe, Robbie Ryan, Kevin Blackwell, Steve Francis, Chris Billy, Gary Glayton, Stephen Payne, Simon Collins.
Centre row: Mick Jones (Assistant Manager), Richard Logan, Jonathan Dyson, Kevin Gray, Pat Scully, Peter Jackson, Andrew Booth, Graham Mitchell, Ronnie Jepson, Dave Wilson (Physio).
Front row: Simon Trevitt, Simon Baldry, Tom Cowan, Phil Starbuck, Neil Warnock (Manager), Darren Bullock, Iain Dunn, Paul Robinson, Paul Reid.

Division 1 HUDDERSFIELD TOWN

The Alfred McAlpine Stadium, Leeds Rd, Huddersfield HD1 6PX. Telephone: (01484) 420335. Fax: (01484) 515122. Ticket Office: (01484) 424444. Club Shop: (01484) 534867. Recorded Information: 0891 121635.

Ground capacity: 19,500.

Record attendance: 67,037 v Arsenal, FA Cup 6th rd, 27 February 1932 (at new ground): 18,775 v Birmingham C, Division 2, 6 May 1995.

Record receipts: £89,081 v Arsenal, Coca-Cola Cup, 2nd rd lst leg, 21 September 1993 (at new ground): £110,850 v Southampton, Coca-Cola Cup, 20 September 1994.

Pitch measurements: 115yd × 76yd.

Chairman: D. G. Headey.

Directors: M. Asquith, D. Taylor, R. Whiteley.

Associate Director: T. J. Cherry.

Manager: Brian Horton. ***Assistant Managers:*** David Moss, Dennis Booth.

Secretary: Alan D. Sykes. ***Commercial Manager:*** Alan Stevenson. ***Chief Executive:*** Paul Fletcher.

Physio: Dave Wilson.

Year Formed: 1908. ***Turned Professional:*** 1908. ***Ltd Co.:*** 1908.

Club Nickname: 'The Terriers'.

Foundation: A meeting, attended largely by members of the Huddersfield & District FA, was held at the Imperial Hotel in 1906 to discuss the feasibility of establishing a football club in this rugby stronghold. However, it was not until a man with both the enthusiasm and the money to back the scheme came on the scene, that real progress was made. This benefactor was Mr. Hilton Crowther and it was at a meeting at the Albert Hotel in 1908, that the club formally came into existence with a capital of £2,000 and joined the North-Eastern League.

First Football League game: 3 September, 1910, Division 2, v Bradford PA (a) W 1-0 – Mutch; Taylor, Morris; Beaton, Hall, Bartlett; Blackburn, Wood, Hamilton (1), McCubbin, Jee.

Record League Victory: 10–1 v Blackpool, Division 1, 13 December 1930 – Turner; Goodall, Spencer; Redfern, Wilson, Campbell; Bob Kelly (1), McLean (4), Robson (3), Davies (1), Smailes (1).

Record Cup Victory: 7–1 v Chesterfield (away), FA Cup, 3rd rd, 12 January 1929 – Turvey; Goodall, Wadsworth; Evans, Wilson, Naylor: Jackson (1), Kelly, Brown (3), Cumming (2), Smith. (1 o.g).

Record Defeat: 1–10 v Manchester C, Division 2, 7 November 1987.

Most League Points (2 for a win): 66, Division 4, 1979–80.

Most League Points (3 for a win): 82, Division 3, 1982–83.

Most League Goals: 101, Division 4, 1979–80.

Highest League Scorer in Season: Sam Taylor, 35, Division 2, 1919–20; George Brown, 35, Division 1, 1925–26.

Most League Goals in Total Aggregate: George Brown, 142, 1921–29 and Jimmy Glazzard, 142, 1946–56.

Most Capped Player: Jimmy Nicholson, 31 (41), Northern Ireland.

Most League Appearances: Billy Smith, 520, 1914–34.

Record Transfer Fee Received: £375,000 from Southampton for Simon Charlton, June 1993.

Record Transfer Fee Paid: £250,000 to Bradford C for Lee Duxbury, December 1994.

Football League Record: 1910 Elected to Division 2; 1920–52 Division 1; 1952–53 Division 2; 1953–56 Division 1; 1956–70 Division 2; 1970–72 Division 1; 1972–73 Division 2; 1973–75 Division 3; 1975–80 Division 4; 1980–83 Division 3; 1983–88 Division 2; 1988–92 Division 3; 1992–95 Division 2; 1995– Division 1.

Honours: *Football League:* Division 1 – Champions 1923–24, 1924–25, 1925–26; Runners-up 1926–27, 1927–28, 1933–34; Division 2 – Champions 1969–70; Runners-up 1919–20, 1952–53; Division 4 – Champions 1979–80. *FA Cup:* Winners 1922; Runners-up 1920, 1928, 1930, 1938. *Football League Cup:* Semi-final 1968. *Autoglass Trophy:* Runners-up 1994.

Colours: Blue and white striped shirts, white shorts, white stockings. **Change colours:** White shirts with black sleeves, black shorts, white stockings.

HUDDERSFIELD TOWN 1994–95 LEAGUE RECORD

Match No.	Date	Venue	Opponents	Result	H/T Score	Lg. Pos.	Goalscorers	Attendance
1	Aug 13	A	Blackpool	W 4-1	2-0	—	Reid 2, Jepson 2	8343
2	20	H	Wycombe W	L 0-1	0-1	12		13,334
3	27	A	Chester C	W 2-1	1-0	8	Booth, Dunn	2895
4	30	H	Leyton Orient	W 2-1	0-1	—	Booth, Reid	8552
5	Sept 3	H	Oxford U	D 3-3	1-2	5	Booth, Starbuck (pen), Bullock	10,122
6	10	A	Plymouth Arg	W 3-0	2-0	4	Booth 3	5464
7	13	A	Peterborough U	D 2-2	1-2	—	Dunn 2	5316
8	17	H	Stockport Co	W 2-1	1-1	2	Booth 2	9526
9	24	A	Bradford C	W 4-3	1-0	2	Booth 2, Jepson, Reid	11,300
10	Oct 1	H	Brighton & HA	W 3-0	1-0	1	Booth, Reid, Logan	10,321
11	8	A	Birmingham C	D 1-1	1-1	1	Bullock	15,265
12	15	H	Cambridge U	W 3-1	0-1	1	Jepson 2 (1 pen), Dunn	10,742
13	22	A	Crewe Alex	D 3-3	2-3	1	Jepson, Billy, Booth	5352
14	29	H	Bournemouth	W 3-1	2-0	1	Booth, Jepson, Scully	11,251
15	Nov 1	H	Wrexham	W 2-1	1-0	—	Bullock, Billy	9639
16	5	A	York C	L 0-3	0-2	1		6345
17	19	H	Brentford	W 1-0	0-0	1	Jepson	10,889
18	26	A	Bristol R	D 1-1	1-1	2	Jepson (pen)	5679
19	Dec 10	A	Wycombe W	L 1-2	1-0	4	Jepson	6790
20	17	H	Blackpool	D 1-1	0-0	4	Booth	11,536
21	26	A	Hull C	L 0-1	0-0	4		10,220
22	27	H	Rotherham U	W 1-0	1-0	4	Booth	15,557
23	31	A	Swansea C	D 1-1	0-0	4	Booth	5438
24	Jan 2	H	Shrewsbury T	W 2-1	1-1	2	Jepson, Duxbury	12,748
25	7	H	Crewe Alex	L 1-2	1-1	2	Booth	11,466
26	14	A	Cardiff C	D 0-0	0-0	2		3808
27	28	A	Bournemouth	W 2-0	0-0	2	Jepson, Duxbury	4427
28	Feb 4	H	Bristol R	D 1-1	0-1	3	Booth	10,389
29	11	A	Wrexham	W 2-1	0-1	2	Booth, Jepson	5894
30	18	H	Cardiff C	W 5-1	4-0	2	Booth, Cowan, Jepson, Reid, Crosby	10,035
31	21	A	Brentford	D 0-0	0-0	—		9562
32	25	A	Brighton & HA	D 0-0	0-0	3		7751
33	28	H	York C	W 3-0	1-0	—	Jepson, Bullock, Crosby	10,468
34	Mar 4	H	Bradford C	D 0-0	0-0	1		17,404
35	7	A	Oxford U	L 1-3	0-0	—	Dyson	7160
36	11	H	Chester C	W 5-1	3-1	2	Cowan, Jepson, Booth 3	9606
37	18	A	Leyton Orient	W 2-0	0-0	2	Dunn, Jepson (pen)	3177
38	21	H	Plymouth Arg	W 2-0	1-0	—	Dyson, Booth	12,099
39	25	A	Stockport Co	W 2-1	1-0	1	Jepson (pen), Gannon (og)	5383
40	Apr 1	H	Peterborough U	L 1-2	0-1	2	Bullock	11,324
41	8	H	Swansea C	W 2-0	1-0	1	Crosby 2	10,105
42	15	A	Rotherham U	D 1-1	0-0	1	Booth	6687
43	17	H	Hull C	D 1-1	0-0	2	Sinnott	12,402
44	22	A	Shrewsbury T	L 1-2	0-2	3	Jepson (pen)	4758
45	29	A	Cambridge U	D 1-1	1-1	3	Booth	5188
46	May 6	H	Birmingham C	L 1-2	0-0	5	Bullock	18,775

Final League Position: 5

GOALSCORERS

League (79): Booth 26, Jepson 19 (5 pens), Bullock 6, Reid 6, Dunn 5, Crosby 4, Billy 2, Cowan 2, Duxbury 2, Dyson 2, Logan 1, Scully 1, Sinnott 1, Starbuck 1 (pen), own goal 1.
Coca-Cola Cup (4): Jepson 2, Reid 1, Scully 1.
FA Cup (4): Booth 1, Bullock 1, Dunn 1, Jepson 1.

Francis S.S. 43	Billy C.A. 30 + 7	Cowan T. 37	Starbuck P.M. 4 + 5	Scully P.J. 38	Mitchell G.L. 11 + 1	Baldry S. 8 + 3	Bullock D.J. 39	Booth A.D. 45 + 1	Jepson R.F. 36 + 5	Reid P.R. 42	Dyson J.P. 23 + 5	Dunn I.G.W. 13 + 26	Logan R.A. 24 + 3	Trevitt S. 20 + 1	Whitington C. 1	Gray K.J. 5	Crosby G. 16 + 3	Blackwell K.P. 3 + 1	Williams P.R. 9	Short C.M. 6	Sinnott L. 25	Duxbury L.E. 26	Clayton G. — + 2	Moulden P.A. — + 2	Collins S. 2 + 2	*Match No.*
1	2	3	4	5	6	7	8	9	10	11	12	14														1
1	2	3	4	5	6	7	8	9	10	11		12														2
1	2	3	*10*	5		7	8	9		11	6	12	4	14												3
1	2	3		5		7	8	9		11	6	12	4		10											4
1	2	3	7		12	14	8	9		11	6	*10*	4			5										5
1	2	3		5	6	7	8	9	14	11	12	*10*	4													6
1	2	3		5	6	7	8	9		11	12	10	4													7
1	2	3	12	5		7	8	9	14	11	6	10	4													8
1	2	3	12	5			8	9	14	11	6	*10*	4	7												9
1		3	12	5			8	9	10	11	6		4	2			7									10
1		3		5			8	9	10	11	6		4	2			7	15								11
		3	12	5			8	9	10	11	6	14	4	2			*7*	1								12
	7	3	14	5			8	9	10	*11*	6	12	4	2				1								13
1	7	3		5	6		8	9	10	11		12	4	2			14									14
1	7	3		5	6		8	9	10	11			4	2												15
1	7	3		5	6		8	9	*10*	11	4	14	12	2												16
1	7			5	6		8	9	10	11		12	4	2					3							17
	7			5	6		8	9	10	11			4	2				1	3							18
1	7	3			6		8	9	10	11		14	12	2		5	4									19
1	7	3			6		8	9	10	*11*		14	4	2		5	12									20
1	12	3		5			8	9	10	11		14	4							2	6	*7*				21
1	7	3						9	10	11	5	12	4							2	6	8				22
1	7	3						9	12	11	5	10	4							2	*6*	8	14			23
1	7	3						9	10	11	5	12	4							2	6	8				24
1		3				*7*	4	9	10	11	5	12					14			2	6	8				25
1	12	3		5				14	*10*	11		9	4				7			2	6	8				26
1	7	3		5				9	10			12	4	2			11				6	8				27
1	7	3		5				9	10			12	*4*	2			11				6	8	14			28
1		3		5			4	9	10	11				2			7				6	8				29
1	12	3		5			4	9	*10*	11		14		2			7				6	8				30
1		3		5			4	9	10	11				2			7				6	8				31
1	12	3		5			4	9	10	11		14		2			7				6	*8*				32
1	2	3		5			*4*	9	10	11	14	12					7				6	8				33
1	2	3		5			4	9	10	11		12					7				6	8				34
1	2	3		5			4	9	*10*	11	14	12					7				6	8				35
1	7	3		5		14	4	9	10	11	2	12									6	8				36
1				5			4	9	10	11	2	7							3		6	8				37
1				5		12	4	9	10	11	2	7							3		6	8				38
1	12			5			4	9	10	11	2	7				6			3			8				39
1	12			5			4	9	10	11	2	7							3		6	8		14		40
1	7						4	9	12	11	2					5	10		3		6	8				41
1	7			5			4	9		11	2	*12*	14				10		3		6	8				42
1	7			5			4	9	10	11	2	12							3		6	8			14	43
1	7	3		5				9	10	*11*	2	12	4								6	8			14	44
1		3		5			4	9	10			11		2							6	8			7	45
1	12	3		5			4	9	10			11		2							6	8		14	*7*	46

Coca-Cola Cup

First Round	Scunthorpe U (a)	1-2
	(h)	3-0
Second Round	Southampton (h)	0-1
	(a)	0-4

FA Cup

First Round	Doncaster R (a)	4-1
Second Round	Lincoln C (a)	0-1

HULL CITY 1994–95 *Back row (left to right):* David Mail, Gary Hobson, Chris Hargreaves, Steve Wilson, Rob Dewhurst, Alan Fettis, Neil Allison, Graeme Atkinson, Matthew Edeson.
Centre row: Billy Legg (Under-16s Manager), Jamie Cass, Dean Windass, Neil Mann, Simon Dakin, Richard Peacock, Jimmy Graham, Brian Mitchell, Bernard Ellison (Chief Scout/Youth Team Manager), Jeff Radcliffe (Physio).
Front row: Steve Moran, Linton Brown, Greg Abbott, Terry Dolan (Manager), Jeff Lee (Assistant Manager), Craig Lawford, Chris Lee, Adam Lowthorpe.

Division 2 HULL CITY

Boothferry Park, Hull HU4 6EU. Telephone: (01482) 351119. Fax: (01482) 565752. Commercial Manager: (01482) 566050. Football in the Community Office: (01482) 565088.

Ground capacity: 16,564.

Record attendance: 55,019 v Manchester U, FA Cup 6th rd, 26 February 1949.

Record receipts: £79,604 v Liverpool FA Cup, 5th rd, 18 February 1989.

Pitch measurements: 115yd × 75yd.

President: T. C. Waite FIMI, MIRTE.

Honorary Vice-President: D. Robinson, H. Bermitz, J. Johnson BA, DPA.

Vice-Presidents: R. Beercock, K. Davis, N. Howe, R. Booth, A. Fetiveau, W. Law.

Chairman: M. W. Fish MCA. ***Vice-Chairman:*** R. M. Chetham.

Directors: G. H. C. Needler MA, FCA, .

Manager: Terry Dolan. ***Assistant Manager:*** Jeff Lee.

Secretary: M. W. Fish. ***Physio:*** Jeff Radcliffe MCSP, SRP.

Commercial Manager: Simon Cawkhill. ***Stadium Manager:*** John Cooper.

Ticket Office/Gate Manager: Wilf Rogerson. ***Hon. Medical Officers:*** G. Hoyle, MBCHB, FRCS, Dr. B. Kell, MBBS.

Year Formed: 1904. ***Turned Professional:*** 1905. ***Ltd Co.:*** 1905.

Club Nickname: 'The Tigers'.

Previous Grounds: 1904, Boulevard Ground (Hull RFC); 1905, Anlaby Road (Hull CC); 1944/5 Boulevard Ground; 1946, Boothferry Park.

Foundation: The enthusiasts who formed Hull City in 1904 were brave men indeed. More than that they were audacious for they immediately put the club on the map in this Rugby League fortress by obtaining a three-year agreement with the Hull Rugby League club to rent their ground! They had obtained quite a number of conversions to the dribbling code, before the Rugby League forbade the use of any of their club grounds by Association Football clubs. By that time, Hull City were well away having entered the FA Cup in their initial season and the Football League, Second Division after only a year.

First Football League game: 2 September, 1905, Division 2, v Barnsley (h) W 4-1 – Spendiff; Langley, Jones; Martin, Robinson, Gordon (2); Rushton, Spence (1), Wilson (1), Howe, Raisbeck.

Record League Victory: 11–1 v Carlisle U, Division 3 (N), 14 January 1939 – Ellis; Woodhead, Dowen; Robinson (1), Blyth, Hardy; Hubbard (2), Richardson (2), Dickinson (2), Davies (2), Cunliffe (2).

Record Cup Victory: 8–2 v Stalybridge Celtic (away), FA Cup, 1st rd, 26 November 1932 – Maddison; Goldsmith, Woodhead; Gardner, Hill (1), Denby; Forward (1), Duncan, McNaughton (1), Wainscoat (4), Sargeant (1).

Record Defeat: 0–8 v Wolverhampton W, Division 2, 4 November 1911.

Most League Points (2 for a win): 69, Division 3, 1965–66.

Most League Points (3 for a win): 90, Division 4, 1982–83.

Most League Goals: 109, Division 3, 1965–66.

Highest League Scorer in Season: Bill McNaughton, 39, Division 3 (N), 1932–33.

Most League Goals in Total Aggregate: Chris Chilton, 195, 1960–71.

Most Capped Player: Terry Neill, 15 (59), Northern Ireland.

Most League Appearances: Andy Davidson, 520, 1952–67.

Record Transfer Fee Received: £750,000 from Middlesbrough for Andy Payton, November 1991.

Record Transfer Fee Paid: £200,000 to Leeds U for Peter Swan, March 1989.

Football League Record: 1905 Elected to Division 2; 1930–33 Division 3 (N); 1933–36 Division 2; 1936–49 Division 3 (N); 1949–56 Division 2; 1956–58 Division 3 (N); 1958–59 Division 3; 1959–60 Division 2; 1960–66 Division 3; 1966–78 Division 2; 1978–81 Division 3; 1981–83 Division 4; 1983–85 Division 3; 1985–91 Division 2; 1991– 92 Division 3; 1992– Division 2.

Honours: *Football League:* Division 2 best season: 3rd, 1909–10; Division 3 (N) – Champions 1932–33, 1948–49; Division 3 – Champions 1965–66; Runners-up 1958–59; Division 4 – Runners-up 1982–83. *FA Cup:* best season: Semi-final 1930. *Football League Cup:* best season: 4th, 1974, 1976, 1978. *Associate Members' Cup:* Runners-up 1984.

Colours: Black and amber striped shirts, black shorts, amber stockings with two black hoops and black turnover. **Change colours:** White and jade.

HULL CITY 1994–95 LEAGUE RECORD

Match No.	Date	Venue	Opponents	Result		H/T Score	Lg. Pos.	Goalscorers	Attendance
1	Aug 13	A	Oxford U	L	0-4	0-4	—		5485
2	20	H	Swansea C	L	0-2	0-0	24		3797
3	27	A	Leyton Orient	D	1-1	0-0	21	Brown	3243
4	30	H	Plymouth Arg	W	2-0	0-0	—	Mann, Lee	3384
5	Sept 3	H	Chester C	W	2-0	1-0	14	Brown, Windass	3615
6	10	A	Peterborough U	L	1-2	1-1	17	Peacock	5044
7	13	A	Wycombe W	W	2-1	1-0	—	Dakin, Abbott	4626
8	17	H	Rotherham U	L	0-2	0-2	16		4431
9	24	A	Birmingham C	D	2-2	1-1	17	Windass (pen), Peacock	12,192
10	Oct 1	H	Bournemouth	W	3-1	2-1	14	Brown, Dewhurst, Atkinson	3056
11	8	H	Blackpool	W	1-0	1-0	12	Gouck (og)	3829
12	15	A	Wrexham	D	2-2	1-0	11	Lawford, Windass	3418
13	22	A	Shrewsbury T	W	3-2	2-0	11	Peacock, Dewhurst, Lawford	3685
14	29	H	Crewe Alex	W	7-1	2-0	8	Windass 2, Peacock, Brown 3, Dewhurst	4694
15	Nov 1	H	York C	W	3-0	3-0	—	Brown, Windass, Lawford	6551
16	5	A	Brentford	W	1-0	0-0	4	Dewhurst	5455
17	19	H	Bristol R	L	0-2	0-1	5		4450
18	25	A	Cardiff C	W	2-0	2-0	—	Brown, Windass (pen)	4226
19	Dec 10	A	Swansea C	L	0-2	0-1	5		4903
20	17	H	Oxford U	W	3-1	2-1	5	Windass 2, Fettis	4884
21	26	H	Huddersfield T	W	1-0	0-0	5	Peacock	10,220
22	28	A	Bradford C	L	0-1	0-0	—		7312
23	31	H	Brighton & HA	D	2-2	1-1	7	Brown, Windass	5099
24	Jan 2	A	Cambridge U	D	2-2	2-0	6	Brown, Windass	3569
25	7	H	Shrewsbury T	D	2-2	0-2	7	Windass (pen), Cox	4369
26	14	A	Stockport Co	L	0-4	0-1	7		4516
27	21	H	Brentford	L	1-2	0-0	7	Joyce	3823
28	Feb 4	H	Cardiff C	W	4-0	2-0	7	Ormondroyd 2, Brown, Joyce	3903
29	18	H	Stockport Co	D	0-0	0-0	9		4576
30	25	A	Bournemouth	W	3-2	3-2	9	Ormondroyd 2, Mann	4345
31	Mar 1	A	Bristol R	W	2-0	1-0	—	Brown, Ormondroyd	3707
32	4	H	Birmingham C	D	0-0	0-0	8		9854
33	11	H	Leyton Orient	W	2-0	1-0	7	Dewhurst, Joyce	4519
34	18	A	Plymouth Arg	L	1-2	1-2	9	Ormondroyd	4839
35	21	H	Peterborough U	D	1-1	1-1	—	Breen (og)	4609
36	25	A	Rotherham U	L	0-2	0-1	11		3692
37	28	A	Chester C	W	2-1	0-0	—	Abbott, Lund	1191
38	Apr 1	H	Wycombe W	D	0-0	0-0	9		5054
39	4	A	York C	L	1-3	0-1	—	Windass	4612
40	8	A	Brighton & HA	L	0-1	0-0	11		6038
41	15	H	Bradford C	W	2-0	2-0	10	Windass 2 (1 pen)	4368
42	17	A	Huddersfield T	D	1-1	0-0	8	Dewhurst	12,402
43	22	H	Cambridge U	W	1-0	0-0	9	Dewhurst	3483
44	29	H	Wrexham	W	3-2	2-1	9	Dewhurst, Lund, Windass	3683
45	May 2	A	Crewe Alex	L	2-3	2-2	—	Abbott, Lund	3870
46	6	A	Blackpool	W	2-1	1-1	8	Windass (pen), Fettis	4251

Final League Position: 8

GOALSCORERS

League (70): Windass 17 (5 pens), Brown 12, Dewhurst 8, Ormondroyd 6, Peacock 5, Abbott 3, Joyce 3, Lawford 3, Lund 3, Fettis 2, Mann 2, Atkinson 1, Cox 1, Dakin 1, Lee 1, own goals 2.
Coca-Cola Cup (2): Lee 1, Peacock 1.
FA Cup (0).

Fettis A. 27 + 1	Dakin S.M. 19 + 2	Graham J. 39	Allison N.J. 11 + 2	Dewhurst R.M. 41	Abbott G.S. 22 + 4	Peacock R.J. 28 + 9	Lee C. 42 + 3	Hargreaves C. 13 + 8	Windass D. 43 + 1	Lawford C.B. 25 + 6	Hobson G. 35 + 1	Brown L. 32 + 1	Lowthorpe A. 21 + 1	Atkinson G. 7 + 2	Mann N. 29 + 2	Mail D. 10 + 4	Wilson S.L. 20	Wallace R.G. 7	Cox P.R. 5	Joyce W.G. 9	Ormondroyd I. 10	Lund G.J. 11	Edeson M.K. — + 3	Fewings P.J. — + 2	Match No.
1	2	3	4	5	6	7	*8*	9	10	11	12	14													1
1		3		5		7	8	6	10	11	4	9	2	12											2
1		3		5		7	8		10	12	4	9	2	11	6										3
1		3		5			8		10	11	4	9	2	7	6										4
1		3		5	12	14	8		10	11	4	9	2	7	6										5
1		3		5		7	8		10	11	4	9	2	12	6										6
1	7	3		5	6		8		10			9	2	11		4									7
1	7	3		5	6	14	8	12	10			9	2	11		4									8
1		3		5	6	7	8	9	10		4			11		2									9
	2	3		5	6	7	8	10			4	9		11			1								10
	2	3		5		7	8	10		11	4	9			6		1								11
	2	3		5		7	8	10	12	11	4	9			6		1								12
		3		5		7	8	12	10	11	4	9	2		6		1								13
		3		5	14	7	*8*	12	10	11	4	9	2		6		1								14
		3		5	14	7	8	12	10	11	4	9	*2*		6		1								15
	2	3		5		7	8	12	10	11	4	9			6		1								16
	2	3		5	14		8	7	10	11	4	9			6	12	1								17
	2	3		5	6	7	8		10	11	4	9					1								18
	2	3	12	5	6	7	8		10	11	4	9			14		1								19
12		3			6	7			10	11	4	9			8		1	2	5						20
		3		5	6	7	12		10	11	4	9			8		1	2							21
		3		*5*	6	7	8	12	10	11	4	9				14	1	2							22
		3			6	7	12		10	11	4	9			8		1	2	5						23
		3				7	6	12	10	11	4	9			8		1	2	5						24
		3				7	6	12	10	11	*4*	9			8	14	1	2	5						25
		3		7		12	6		10	11		9			8	4	1	2	5						26
1		3		5			6	9	10	11	4		2		8					7					27
1		3	6	5		12	14		10		4	9	2		*8*					7	11				28
1		3	6	5			2		10		4	9			8					7	11				29
1		3	6	5			2		10		4	9			8					7	11				30
1		3	6	5			2		10		4	9			8					7	11				31
1		3	6	5		12	2		10		4	9			8					7	11				32
1		3	6	5		12	2		10		4	9			8					7	11				33
1	4	*3*	6	5		12	2		10	14		9			8					7	11				34
1		3	6	5		8	2		10	12	4	9								7	11				35
	12	3	6	5	*8*	7	2		10	14	4						1				11	9			36
	4	*3*		5	8		2		10	14			12		7	6	1				11	9			37
1	5	3			8	12	2		10	14	4		*11*		7	6						9			38
1	5	*3*		6	8		7		10	11	4		2		12	14						9			39
1				5	8	12	7		10	3	6		2		11	4						9			40
1	12			5	6	7	8		10	3	4		2		*11*							9	14		41
1	4			5	6	7	8	11	10				2			3						9			42
1	4			5	6	7	8	11	10				2			3						9	12		43
1	4		12	5	6	7	8	11	10				2			3						9			44
1	4		3	5	6	7	8	11	10				2									9		12	45
8	4			5	*6*	7	2	11	10				3				1					9	12	14	46

Coca-Cola Cup
First Round — Scarborough (h) — 2-1
(a) — 0-2

FA Cup
First Round — Lincoln C (h) — 0-1

IPSWICH TOWN 1994–95 *Back row (left to right):* Geraint Williams, Neil Gregory, David Gregory, Antony Vaughan, Adam Tanner, James Scowcroft, Phil Whelan, Claus Thomsen, Steve Palmer, Eddie Youds, Gavin Johnson, John Wark.

Centre row: Gary Thompson, Graham Connell, Peter Mortley, Kenneth Weston, Clive Baker, Craig Forrest, Philip Morgan, Graham Mansfield, Gavin Dolby, Matthew Weston, Leo Cotterell, David Pirie.

Front row: Mick Stockwell, Lee Norfolk, Lee Durrant, Ian Marshall, Stuart Slater, Paul Mason, David Linighan, Steve Sedgley, Neil Thompson, Frank Yallop, Chris Kiwomya, Simon Milton.

Division 1 IPSWICH TOWN

Portman Road, Ipswich, Suffolk IP1 2DA. Telephone: (01473) 219211 (4 lines). Fax: (01473) 226835. Ticket office: (01473) 221133. Sales & Marketing Dept: (01473) 212202.

Ground capacity: 22,559.

Record attendance: 38,010 v Leeds U, FA Cup 6th rd, 8 March 1975.

Record receipts: £105,950 v AZ 67 Alkmaar, UEFA Cup Final 1st leg, 6 May 1981.

Pitch measurements: 112yd × 70yd.

Chairman: John Kerr MBE.

President: P. M. Cobbold. ***Vice-President:*** J. M. Sangster.

Directors: K. H. Brightwell, P. Hope-Cobbold, J. Kerridge, R. Moore, D. Sheepshanks, H. Smith.

Manager: George Burley. ***Assistant Manager:*** Dale Roberts. ***Coaches:*** Bryan Klug, Paul Goddard. ***Youth Team Coach:*** Peter Trevivian. ***Chief Scout:*** C. Woods. ***Director of Coaching:*** C. Suggett.

Physio: D. Bingham.

Secretary: David C. Rose.

Commercial Manager: C. Turner. ***Sales & Promotions Manager:*** Mike Noye.

Year Formed: 1878. ***Turned Professional:*** 1936. ***Ltd Co.:*** 1936.

Club Nickname: 'Blues' or 'Town'.

Foundation: Considering that Ipswich Town only reached the Football League in 1938, many people outside of East Anglia may be surprised to learn that this club was formed at a meeting held in the Town Hall as far back as 1878 when Mr. T. C. Cobbold, MP, was voted president. Originally it was the Ipswich Association FC to distinguish it from the older Ipswich Football Club which played rugby. These two amalgamated in 1888 and the handling game was dropped in 1893.

First Football League game: 27 August, 1938, Division 3(S), v Southend U (h) W 4-2 – Burns; Dale, Parry; Perrett, Fillingham, McLuckie; Williams, Davies (1), Jones (2), Alsop (1), Little.

Record League Victory: 7–0 v Portsmouth, Division 2, 7 November 1964 – Thorburn; Smith, McNeil; Baxter, Bolton, Thompson; Broadfoot (1), Hegan (2), Baker (1), Leadbetter, Brogan (3). 7–0 v Southampton, Division 1, 2 February 1974 – Sivell; Burley, Mills (1), Morris, Hunter, Beattie (1), Hamilton (2), Viljoen, Johnson, Whymark (2), Lambert (1) (Woods). 7–0 v WBA, Division 1, 6 November 1976 – Sivell; Burley, Mills, Talbot, Hunter, Beattie (1), Osborne, Wark (1), Mariner (1) (Bertschin), Whymark (4), Woods.

Record Cup Victory: 10–0 v Floriana, European Cup, Prel. rd, 25 September 1962 – Bailey; Malcolm, Compton; Baxter, Laurel, Elsworthy (1); Stephenson, Moran (2), Crawford (5), Phillips (2), Blackwood.

Record Defeat: 1–10 v Fulham, Division 1, 26 December 1963.

Most League Points (2 for a win): 64, Division 3 (S), 1953–54 and 1955–56.

Most League Points (3 for a win): 84, Division 1, 1991–92.

Most League Goals: 106, Division 3 (S), 1955–56.

Highest League Scorer in Season: Ted Phillips, 41, Division 3 (S), 1956–57.

Most League Goals in Total Aggregate: Ray Crawford, 203, 1958–63 and 1966–69.

Most Capped Player: Allan Hunter, 47 (53), Northern Ireland.

Most League Appearances: Mick Mills, 591, 1966–82.

Record Transfer Fee Received: £1,900,000 from Tottenham Hotspur for Jason Dozzell, August 1993.

Record Transfer Fee Paid: £1,000,000 to Tottenham H for Steve Sedgley, June 1994.

Football League Record: 1938 Elected to Division 3 (S); 1954–55 Division 2; 1955–57 Division 3 (S); 1957–61 Division 2; 1961–64 Division 1; 1964–68 Division 2; 1968–86 Division 1; 1986–92 Division 2; 1992–95 FA Premier League; 1995– Division 1.

Honours: *Football League:* Division 1 – Champions 1961–62; Runners-up 1980–81, 1981–82; Division 2 – Champions 1960–61, 1967–68, 1991–92; Division 3 (S) – Champions 1953–54, 1956–57. *FA Cup:* Winners 1978. *Football League Cup:* best season: Semi-final 1982, 1985, *Texaco Cup:* 1973. **European Competitions:** *European Cup:* 1962–63. *European Cup-Winners' Cup:* 1978–79. *UEFA Cup:* 1973–74, 1974–75, 1975–76, 1977–78, 1979–80, 1980–81 (winners), 1981–82, 1982–83.

Colours: Blue shirts, white shorts, blue stockings. **Change colours:** Red shirts, thin black stripe, black shorts, red stockings.

IPSWICH TOWN 1994–95 LEAGUE RECORD

Match No.	Date	Venue	Opponents	Result		H/T Score	Lg. Pos.	Goalscorers	Attendance
1	Aug 20	H	Nottingham F	L	0-1	0-1	—		18,763
2	23	A	Wimbledon	D	1-1	0-1	—	Milton	6341
3	27	A	QPR	W	2-1	1-0	9	Yates (og), Guentchev	12,456
4	30	H	Tottenham H	L	1-3	0-3	—	Kiwomya	22,430
5	Sept 10	A	Aston Villa	L	0-2	0-1	16		22,241
6	19	H	Norwich C	L	1-2	1-1	—	Wark (pen)	17,405
7	24	H	Manchester U	W	3-2	2-0	15	Mason 2, Sedgley	22,553
8	Oct 1	A	Southampton	L	1-3	0-0	16	Marshall	13,266
9	10	A	Coventry C	L	0-2	0-1	—		9509
10	16	H	Sheffield W	L	1-2	0-1	21	Wark	12,825
11	23	A	Chelsea	L	0-2	0-0	21		15,068
12	29	H	Liverpool	L	1-3	0-1	21	Paz	22,379
13	Nov 1	H	Leeds U	W	2-0	1-0	—	Sedgley, Williams	15,354
14	5	A	Crystal Palace	L	0-3	0-1	20		13,450
15	19	H	Blackburn R	L	1-3	1-2	20	Thomsen	17,607
16	26	A	Newcastle U	D	1-1	0-0	22	Thomsen	34,459
17	Dec 3	H	Manchester C	L	1-2	0-2	22	Mason	13,754
18	10	A	Nottingham F	L	1-4	1-4	22	Thomsen	21,340
19	16	H	Wimbledon	D	2-2	1-1	—	Milton, Sedgley	11,282
20	26	A	West Ham U	D	1-1	0-1	22	Thomsen	20,562
21	28	H	Arsenal	L	0-2	0-1	22		22,047
22	31	A	Everton	L	1-4	1-1	22	Sedgley	25,667
23	Jan 2	H	Leicester C	W	4-1	1-0	21	Kiwomya 2, Tanner, Yallop	15,817
24	14	A	Liverpool	W	1-0	1-0	21	Tanner	32,733
25	21	H	Chelsea	D	2-2	0-0	21	Slater, Wark (pen)	17,619
26	28	A	Blackburn R	L	1-4	0-2	21	Wark (pen)	21,325
27	Feb 4	H	Crystal Palace	L	0-2	0-0	21		15,361
28	22	A	Manchester C	L	0-2	0-0	—		21,430
29	25	H	Southampton	W	2-1	0-1	21	Mathie, Chapman	15,788
30	28	H	Newcastle U	L	0-2	0-2	—		18,639
31	Mar 4	A	Manchester U	L	0-9	0-3	21		43,804
32	8	A	Tottenham H	L	0-3	0-2	—		24,930
33	20	A	Norwich C	L	0-3	0-0	—		17,510
34	Apr 1	H	Aston Villa	L	0-1	0-0	21		15,895
35	5	A	Leeds U	L	0-4	0-4	—		28,565
36	11	H	QPR	L	0-1	0-0	—		11,736
37	15	A	Arsenal	L	1-4	0-1	22	Marshall	36,818
38	17	H	West Ham U	D	1-1	1-0	22	Thomsen	18,882
39	29	A	Leicester C	L	0-2	0-0	22		15,248
40	May 6	H	Coventry C	W	2-0	0-0	22	Marshall, Pressley (og)	12,342
41	9	H	Everton	L	0-1	0-0	—		14,940
42	14	A	Sheffield W	L	1-4	0-1	22	Mathie	30,307

Final League Position: 22

GOALSCORERS

League (36): Thomsen 5, Sedgley 4, Wark 4 (3 pens), Kiwomya 3, Marshall 3, Mason 3, Mathie 2, Milton 2, Tanner 2, Chapman 1, Guentchev 1, Paz 1, Slater 1, Williams 1, Yallop 1, own goals 2.
Coca-Cola Cup (0).
FA Cup (1): Linighan 1.

Forrest C.L. 36	Stockwell M.T. 14 + 1	Yallop F.W. 41	Mason P.D. 19 + 2	Wark J. 26	Youds E.P. 9 + 1	Williams D.G. 38	Slater S.I. 22 + 5	Milton S.C. 19 + 6	Marshall I.P. 14 + 4	Kiwomya C.M. 13 + 2	Guentchev B.L. 11 + 5	Linighan D. 31 + 1	Johnson G. 14 + 3	Sedgley S.P. 26	Palmer S.L. 10 + 2	Paz A. 13 + 4	Thomsen C. 31 + 2	Cotterell L.S. — + 2	Vaughan A.J. 10	Gregory D.S. — + 1	Whelan P.J. 12 + 1	Gregory N.R. 1 + 2	Tanner A.D. 9 + 1	Chapman L.R. 9 + 7	Thompson N. 9 + 1	Mathie A. 13	Norfolk L.R. 1 + 2	Swailes C.W. 4	Baker C.E. 2	Ellis K.E. 1	Morgan P.J. 1	Wright R.I. 3	*Match No.*
1	2	3	4	5	6	7	8	9	10	11	12																						1
1	2	3	4	5		7	8	9	10	11		6																					2
1	2	3	4	5		7	8	9		11	10	6																					3
1	2	3	4	5		7	8	9		11	10	6																					4
1	2	3	4	5		7	8	9	12	11	10	6																					5
1		2		5		7	8	9	10	11	12	6	3	4																			6
1		2	4	5		7		12			14	6	3	8	9	*10*	11																7
1		2	4	*5*		7			12		10	6	3	8	9		11	14															8
1		2		5		7	8			10		6	3	4	9		11	12															9
1		2		5	12	7		4			8		3	6	9	10	11																10
1	12	2			5	7		9			8			6	4	*10*	11		3	14													11
1	2				5	7					8	12	6	4	9	10	11		3														12
1	2	3			5	7		12		14	*9*	6		8		10	11				4												13
1	2	3			5	7		12		14	*9*	6		8		10	11				4												14
1		2	4		5	7		12	9			6		8		10	11				3												15
1		2	4		5	7	12		9			6		8		10	11				3												16
1		2	4		5	7	12				9	*6*	14	8		10	11				3												17
1		2	4			7	12	14		9		*6*	3	8		10	11				5												18
1		2	4			7		8		10				6		12	11		3		5	9											19
1		2	4	5		7	12	10		9				8			11		3		6												20
1		2	*4*	5		7		8		9	12		10		14		11		3		6												21
1		2	4	*5*			12			9	10	6		7	8		11		3		14												22
1		2	*4*				8			9		6		7	12		11		3		5	14	10										23
1		2		5		7	8					6	3	4		10	11						9										24
1		2		5		7	8					6	3	4		10	11						9	12									25
1		2		5		7	8						12	4			11		3		6		9	10									26
1		2		5		7	8						*11*	4		14	12		6				9	10	3								27
1		2		5		7	8					6	9	4		12	11		*3*					10	14								28
1		2		5					*8*			6	4	7		12							11	10	3	9	14						29
1		2	12	5			8					6		4									9	10	3	7	11						30
1		2		5		7	8		12			6		4	11									10	3	9							31
1		2			5	7		8	14			6		4		*10*	12						9	11	3								32
1		2		5		6	8	7	9								11				4			12	3	10							33
1		2		5		6	8	7	9								11								3	10		4					34
1		2				7	8	4			12	6					11							10	3	9		5					35
1	2	4				6	8		9			5			7		11							12	3	10							36
	2	4				6	8	12	9			5			10		11							14		7			1	3			37
	2	3	12	5		6	8	7	*9*			4					11							14		10			1				38
		2		5		4	8	7	9			6	3				11									10					1		39
	2	3	4	5		7			9			6					11						*8*	12		10	14					1	40
	2	3	4			7		9	*10*			6	12				11							14		8		5				1	41
	2	3	4			7		9				*6*					11					14	12	10		8		5				1	42

Coca-Cola Cup
Second Round — Bolton W (h) 0-3
(a) 0-1

FA Cup
Third Round — Wrexham (a) 1-2

LEEDS UNITED 1994–95 *Back row (left to right):* David White, Carlton Palmer, John Lukic, David Wetherall, Mark Beeney, Brian Deane, Gary McAllister.
Centre row: Mike Hennigan (Assistant Manager), Lucas Radebe, Mark Tinkler, Kevin Sharp, John Pemberton, Philemon Masinga, Chris Fairclough, Noel Whelan, Nigel Worthington, David O'Leary, Geoff Ladley (Physio).
Front row: Gary Kelly, Gary Speed, Gordon Strachan, Howard Wilkinson (Manager), Tony Dorigo, Rod Wallace, Jamie Forrester.

FA Premiership **LEEDS UNITED**

Elland Road, Leeds LS11 0ES. Telephone: (0113) 2716037 (4 lines). Fax: (0113) 2720370. Ticket Office: (0113) 710710. Clubcall: 0891 121181.

Ground capacity: 40,000.

Record attendance: 57,892 v Sunderland, FA Cup 5th rd (replay), 15 March 1967.

Record receipts: £314,063 v Oldham Ath, FA Cup 4th rd, 28 January 1995.

Pitch measurements: 117yd × 72yd.

President: The Right Hon The Earl of Harewood LLD.

Executive Directors: L. H. Silver OBE (Chairman); P. J. Gilman (Vice-chairman); W. J. Fotherby (Managing).

Directors: J. W. G. Marjason, R. Barker, M. Bedford, E. Carlile, R. Feldman, A. Hudson, P. Ridsdale, K. J. Woolmer.

Manager: Howard Wilkinson. *Assistant Manager:* Mick Hennigan.

Company/Club Secretary: Nigel Pleasants.

General Manager: Alan Roberts.

Coaches: Paul Hart, Peter Gunby, David Williams, Robin Wray, Eddie Gray.

Physios: Geoff Ladley, Alan Sutton.

Commercial Manager: Bob Baldwin.

Year Formed: 1919, as Leeds United after disbandment (by FA order) of Leeds City (formed in 1904). *Turned Professional:* 1920. *Ltd Co.:* 1920.

Club Nickname: 'United'.

Foundation: Immediately the Leeds City club (founded in 1904) was wound up by the FA in October 1919, following allegations of illegal payments to players, a meeting was called by a Leeds solicitor, Mr. Alf Masser, at which Leeds United was formed. They joined the Midland League playing their first game in that competition in November 1919. It was in this same month that the new club had discussions with the directors of a virtually bankrupt Huddersfield Town who wanted to move to Leeds in an amalgamation. But Huddersfield survived even that crisis.

First Football League game: 28 August, 1920, Division 2, v Port Vale (a) L 0-2 – Down; Duffield, Tillotson; Musgrove, Baker, Walton; Mason, Goldthorpe, Thompson, Lyon, Best.

Record League Victory: 8–0 v Leicester C, Division 1, 7 April 1934 – Moore; George Milburn, Jack Milburn; Edwards, Hart, Copping; Mahon (2), Firth (2), Duggan (2), Furness (2), Cochrane.

Record Cup Victory: 10–0 v Lyn (Oslo), European Cup, 1st rd 1st leg, 17 September 1969 – Sprake; Reaney, Cooper, Bremner (2), Charlton, Hunter, Madeley, Clarke (2), Jones (3), Giles (2) (Bates), O'Grady (1).

Record Defeat: 1–8 v Stoke C, Division 1, 27 August 1934.

Most League Points (2 for a win): 67, Division 1, 1968–69.

Most League Points (3 for a win): 85, Division 2, 1989–90.

Most League Goals: 98, Division 2, 1927–28.

Highest League Scorer in Season: John Charles, 42, Division 2, 1953–54.

Most League Goals in Total Aggregate: Peter Lorimer, 168, 1965–79 and 1983–86.

Most Capped Player: Billy Bremner, 54, Scotland.

Most League Appearances: Jack Charlton, 629, 1953–73.

Record Transfer Fee Received: £2,700,000 from Blackburn Rovers for David Batty, October 1993.

Record Transfer Fee Paid: £3,400,000 to Eintracht Frankfurt for Tony Yeboah, January 1995.

Football League Record: 1920 Elected to Division 2; 1924–27 Division 1; 1927–28 Division 2; 1928–31 Division 1; 1931–32 Division 2; 1932–47 Division 1; 1947–56 Division 2; 1956–60 Division 1; 1960–64 Division 2; 1964–82 Division 1; 1982–90 Division 2; 1990–92 Division 1; 1992– FA Premier Division.

Honours: Football League: Division 1 – Champions 1968–69, 1973–74, 1991–92; Runners-up 1964–65, 1965–66, 1969–70, 1970–71, 1971–72; Division 2 – Champions 1923–24, 1963–64, 1989–90; Runners-up 1927–28, 1931–32, 1955–56. *FA Cup:* Winners 1972; Runners-up 1965, 1970, 1973. *Football League Cup:* Winners 1968. **European Competitions:** *European Cup:* 1969–70, 1974–75 (runners-up), 1992–93. *European Cup-Winners' Cup:* 1972–73 (runners-up). *European Fairs Cup:* 1965–66, 1966–67 (runners-up), 1967–68 (winners), 1968–69, 1970–71 (winners). *UEFA Cup:* 1971–72, 1973–74, 1979–80.

Colours: All white with yellow and blue trim. **Change colours:** Blue and green striped shirts, blue shorts, green stockings.

LEEDS UNITED 1994–95 LEAGUE RECORD

Match No.	Date	Venue	Opponents	Result		H/T Score	Lg. Pos.	Goalscorers	Attendance
1	Aug 20	A	West Ham U	D	0-0	0-0	—		18,610
2	23	H	Arsenal	W	1-0	0-0	—	Whelan	34,318
3	27	H	Chelsea	L	2-3	2-1	10	Masinga, Whelan	32,212
4	30	A	Crystal Palace	W	2-1	1-0	—	White, Whelan	14,453
5	Sept 11	H	Manchester U	W	2-1	1-0	6	Wetherall, Deane	39,120
6	17	A	Coventry C	L	1-2	0-0	6	Speed	15,383
7	26	A	Sheffield W	D	1-1	1-1	—	McAllister	23,227
8	Oct 1	H	Manchester C	W	2-0	1-0	6	Whelan 2	30,938
9	8	A	Norwich C	L	1-2	0-0	9	Wallace	17,390
10	15	H	Tottenham H	D	1-1	0-1	9	Deane	39,362
11	24	H	Leicester C	W	2-1	1-0	—	McAllister, Whelan	28,479
12	29	A	Southampton	W	3-1	0-1	6	Maddison (og), Wallace 2	15,202
13	Nov 1	A	Ipswich T	L	0-2	0-1	—		15,354
14	5	H	Wimbledon	W	3-1	3-1	6	Wetherall, Speed, White	27,246
15	19	A	QPR	L	2-3	0-2	6	McDonald (og), Deane	17,416
16	26	H	Nottingham F	W	1-0	0-0	6	Whelan	37,709
17	Dec 5	A	Everton	L	0-3	0-1	—		25,906
18	10	H	West Ham U	D	2-2	2-1	7	Worthington, Deane	28,987
19	17	A	Arsenal	W	3-1	1-0	6	Masinga 2, Deane	38,100
20	26	H	Newcastle U	D	0-0	0-0	6		39,337
21	31	H	Liverpool	L	0-2	0-1	8		38,468
22	Jan 2	A	Aston Villa	D	0-0	0-0	7		35,038
23	14	H	Southampton	D	0-0	0-0	8		28,869
24	24	H	QPR	W	4-0	2-0	—	Masinga 2, White, Deane	28,750
25	Feb 1	A	Blackburn R	D	1-1	0-1	—	McAllister (pen)	28,561
26	4	A	Wimbledon	D	0-0	0-0	7		10,211
27	22	H	Everton	W	1-0	0-0	—	Yeboah	30,793
28	25	A	Manchester C	D	0-0	0-0	6		22,892
29	Mar 4	H	Sheffield W	L	0-1	0-1	7		33,774
30	11	A	Chelsea	W	3-0	2-0	7	Yeboah 2, McAllister	20,174
31	15	A	Leicester C	W	3-1	1-1	—	Yeboah 2, Palmer	20,068
32	18	H	Coventry C	W	3-0	1-0	6	Yeboah, Gould (og), Wallace	29,179
33	22	A	Nottingham F	L	0-3	0-3	—		26,299
34	Apr 2	A	Manchester U	D	0-0	0-0	6		43,712
35	5	H	Ipswich T	W	4-0	4-0	—	Yeboah 3, Speed	28,565
36	9	A	Liverpool	W	1-0	1-0	6	Deane	37,454
37	15	H	Blackburn R	D	1-1	0-1	6	Deane	39,426
38	17	A	Newcastle U	W	2-1	2-1	6	McAllister (pen), Yeboah	35,626
39	29	H	Aston Villa	W	1-0	0-0	6	Palmer	32,973
40	May 6	H	Norwich C	W	2-1	0-1	6	McAllister (pen), Palmer	31,981
41	9	H	Crystal Palace	W	3-1	2-0	—	Yeboah 2, Wetherall	30,963
42	14	A	Tottenham H	D	1-1	0-1	5	Deane	33,040

Final League Position: 5

GOALSCORERS

League (59): Yeboah 12, Deane 9, Whelan 7, McAllister 6 (3 pens), Masinga 5, Wallace 4, Palmer 3, Speed 3, Wetherall 3, White 3, Worthington 1, own goals 3.
Coca-Cola Cup (0).
FA Cup (10): Masinga 4, Wetherall 2, Deane 1, Palmer 1, White 1, Yeboah 1.

Lukic J. 42	Kelly G. 42	Worthington N. 21 + 6	Palmer C.L. 39	Wetherall D. 38	Strachan G.D. 5 + 1	White D. 18 + 5	Wallace R.S. 30 + 2	Deane B.C. 33 + 2	McAllister G. 41	Speed G.A. 39	Masinga P. 15 + 7	Whelan N. 18 + 5	Fairclough C.H. 1 + 4	Pemberton J.M. 22 + 5	Tinkler M.R. 3	Radebe L. 9 + 3	Dorigo A.R. 28	Yeboah A. 16 + 2	Couzens A.J. 2 + 2	Sharp K. — + 2	Match No.
1	2	3	4	5	6	7	8	9	10	11	12										1
1	2	3	4	5	6	7	8		10	11	9	12									2
1	2	3	4	5		7	8		6	11	9	10									3
1	2	3	4	5		7	8		6	11	9	10	12								4
1	2	3	4	5		7	8	12	6	11	*9*	10	14								5
1	2	3	4	5	7		8		6	11	*9*	10	12	14							6
1	2	3	4	5			8	9	10	11	7	12			*6*	14					7
1	2	3	4	6			8	9	10	11		7	5	12							8
1	2	11	4	5			8	9	6	7		*10*	12	14			3				9
1	2	11	4	5			8	9	6	7		10		12			3				10
1	2	11	4	5			8	9	6	7		10					3				11
1	2	11	4	5			8	9	6	7		10				12	3				12
1	2	3	4	5		7	8	9	6	11	12	10									13
1	2	3	4	5		7	8	9	6	11	12	10				14					14
1	2	3	4	5		12	8	9	6	11		10				7					15
1	2		4	5		7	8	9	6	11	12	*10*		14			3				16
1	2		4	5		7	8	9	6	11		10					3				17
1	2	11	4	5	7	12		9	6			10			8		3				18
1	2		4	5		12		9		11	8	10		6		7	3				19
1	2	12	4	5	14	7			8	11	*9*	10		6			3				20
1	2	12		5	7	14			8	11	9	10		6		4	3				21
1	2	3		5		7	12	9	10	11	8			6		4					22
1	2	3	4	5		7	12	9	10	11	14			6		*8*					23
1	2	3	4	5		7		9	10	11	8			6				12			24
1	2	12	4			7		9	10	11	*8*			6		5	3	14			25
1	2	11	4			7		9	10		8			6		5	3				26
1	2	12		5		7			10	11	8			6		4	3	9			27
1	2	6	4	5		7		12	10	11	8						3	9			28
1	2		4	5			8	9	10	11	12			6			3	7			29
1	2		4	5			8	9	10	11				6			3	7			30
1	2		4	5			8	9	10	11				6			3	7			31
1	2		4				8	9	10	11					6	5	3	7	12		32
1	2		4			12	8	9	10	11				6			3	7	5		33
1	2	12	4	5			8	*9*	10			14		6			3	7	11		34
1	2		4	5			8	9	10	11				6			3	7	12		35
1	2		4	5			8	9	10	11				6			3	7			36
1	2		4	5			8	9	10	11		12		6			3	7			37
1	2	12	4	5		7		9	10	11	14			6			3	*8*			38
1	2		4	5			8	9	10	11				6			3	7			39
1	2		4	5			*8*	9	10	11		12		6			3	7		14	40
1	2		4	5			8	9	10	11				6			3	7			41
1	2		4	5			8	9	10	11				6			3	7		12	42

Coca-Cola Cup

Second Round	Mansfield T (h)	0-1
	(a)	0-0

FA Cup

Third Round	Walsall (a)	1-1
	(h)	5-2
Fourth Round	Oldham Ath (h)	3-2
Fifth Round	Manchester U (a)	1-3

LEICESTER CITY 1994–95 *Back row (left to right):* Sam McMahon, Jimmy Willis, Scott Eustace, Brian Carey, Steve Walsh, Ian Ormondroyd, Iwan Roberts, Gary Coatsworth, Ian Thompson, Richard Smith, Ian Blyth.

Centre row: Neil Lewis, David Speedie, Colin Gibson, Gary Mills, Nicky Mohan, Russell Hoult, Kevin Poole, Gavin Ward, David Oldfield, Steve Thompson, Lee Philpott, Colin Hill, Neil Maisey.

Front row: Mark Draper, David Lowe, Simon Grayson, Julian Joachim, Allan Evans (Assistant Manager), Brian Little (Manager), John Gregory (First Team Coach), Steve Agnew, Mike Whitlow, Phil Gee, Mark Blake.

Division 1 LEICESTER CITY

City Stadium, Filbert St, Leicester LE2 7FL. Telephone: (0116) 2555000 and (0116) 2854000. Fax: (0116) 2470585. Ticket Office: (0116) 2915232. Club Shop: (0116) 2559455. Ticket line: 0891 121028. Clubcall: 0891 121185.

Ground capacity: 22,517.

Record attendance: 47,298 v Tottenham H, FA Cup 5th rd, 18 February 1928.

Record receipts: £200,613 v Liverpool, FA Premiership, 26 December 1994.

Pitch measurements: 112yd × 75yd.

President: K. R. Brigstock.

Chairman: Martin George. ***Vice-Chairman:*** Tom Smeaton.

Chief Executive: Barrie Pierpoint.

Directors: J. M. Elsom FCA, R. W. Parker, J. E. Sharp, T. W. Shipman, W. K. Shooter FCA.

Manager: Mark McGhee. ***Assistant Manager:*** Colin Lee. ***First Team Coach:*** Mike Hickman.

Youth Team Coach: David Nish.

Football Secretary: Ian Silvester.

Company Secretary: Steve Kind.

Head of Publicity/Press Officer: Paul Mace.

Physio: Alan Smith. ***General Sales Manager:*** Charles Rayner.

Year Formed: 1884.

Club Nickname: 'Fiberts' or 'Foxes'.

Previous Grounds: 1884, Victoria Park; 1887, Belgrave Road; 1888, Victoria Park; 1891, Filbert Street.

Previous Name: 1884–1919, Leicester Fosse.

Foundation: In 1884 a number of young footballers who were mostly old boys of Wyggeston School, held a meeting at a house on the Roman Fosse Way and formed Leicester Fosse FC. They collected 9d (less than 4p) towards the cost of a ball, plus the same amount for membership. Their first professional, Harry Webb from Stafford Rangers, was signed in 1888 for 2s 6d (12p) per week, plus travelling expenses.

First Football League game: 1 September, 1894, Division 2, v Grimsby T (a) L 3-4 – Thraves; Smith, Bailey; Seymour, Brown, Henrys; Hill, Hughes, McArthur (1), Skea (2), Priestman.

Record League Victory: 10–0 v Portsmouth, Division 1, 20 October 1928 – McLaren; Black, Brown; Findlay, Carr, Watson; Adcock, Hine (3), Chandler (6), Lochhead, Barry (1).

Record Cup Victory: 8–1 v Coventry C (away), League Cup, 5th rd, 1 December 1964 – Banks; Sjoberg, Norman (2); Roberts, King, McDerment; Hodgson (2), Cross, Goodfellow, Gibson (1), Stringfellow (2). (1 og).

Record Defeat: 0–12 (as Leicester Fosse) v Nottingham F, Division 1, 21 April 1909.

Most League Points (2 for a win): 61, Division 2, 1956–57.

Most League Points (3 for a win): 77, Division 2, 1991–92.

Most League Goals: 109, Division 2, 1956–57.

Highest League Scorer in Season: Arthur Rowley, 44, Division 2, 1956–57.

Most League Goals in Total Aggregate: Arthur Chandler, 259, 1923–35.

Most Capped Player: John O'Neill, 39, Northern Ireland.

Most League Appearances: Adam Black, 528, 1920–35.

Record Transfer Fee Received: £3,250,000 from Aston Villa for Mark Draper, July 1995.

Record Transfer Fee Paid: £1,250,000 to Notts Co for Mark Draper, July 1994.

Football League Record: 1894 Elected to Division 2; 1908–09 Division 1; 1909–25 Division 2; 1925–35 Division 1; 1935–37 Division 2; 1937–39 Division 1; 1946–54 Division 2; 1954–55 Division 1; 1955–57 Division 2; 1957–69 Division 1; 1969–71 Division 2; 1971–78 Division 1; 1978–80 Division 2; 1980–81 Division 1; 1981–83 Division 2; 1983–87 Division 1; 1987–92 Division 2; 1992–94 Division 1; 1994–95 FA Premier League; 1995– Division 1.

Honours: *Football League:* Division 1 – Runners-up 1928–29; Division 2 – Champions 1924–25, 1936–37, 1953–54, 1956–57, 1970–71, 1979–80; Runners-up 1907–08. *FA Cup:* Runners-up 1949, 1961, 1963, 1969. *Football League Cup:* Winners 1964; Runners-up 1965. **European Competitions:** *European Cup-Winners' Cup:* 1961–62.

Colours: All blue. **Change colours:** All gold.

LEICESTER CITY 1994–95 LEAGUE RECORD

Match No.	Date	Venue	Opponents	Result		H/T Score	Lg. Pos.	Goalscorers	Attendance
1	Aug 21	H	Newcastle U	L	1-3	0-0	—	Joachim	20,048
2	23	A	Blackburn R	L	0-3	0-1	—		21,050
3	27	A	Nottingham F	L	0-1	0-1	22		21,601
4	31	H	QPR	D	1-1	0-1	—	Gee	18,695
5	Sept 10	A	Wimbledon	L	1-2	1-2	21	Lowe	7683
6	17	H	Tottenham H	W	3-1	1-0	20	Joachim 2, Lowe	21,300
7	24	A	Everton	D	1-1	0-0	18	Draper	28,015
8	Oct 3	H	Coventry C	D	2-2	1-1	—	Roberts 2	19,372
9	8	A	Chelsea	L	0-4	0-2	20		18,397
10	15	H	Southampton	W	4-3	2-0	18	Blake 2, Roberts, Carr	20,020
11	24	A	Leeds U	L	1-2	0-1	—	Blake	28,479
12	29	H	Crystal Palace	L	0-1	0-1	20		20,022
13	Nov 5	A	West Ham U	L	0-1	0-0	21		18,780
14	20	H	Manchester C	L	0-1	0-1	21		19,006
15	23	H	Arsenal	W	2-1	2-1	—	Seaman (og), Lowe	20,774
16	26	A	Norwich C	L	1-2	1-0	21	Draper	20,657
17	Dec 3	H	Aston Villa	D	1-1	1-0	21	Gee	20,896
18	10	A	Newcastle U	L	1-3	0-1	21	Oldfield	34,400
19	17	H	Blackburn R	D	0-0	0-0	21		20,559
20	26	H	Liverpool	L	1-2	0-0	21	Roberts	21,393
21	28	A	Manchester U	D	1-1	0-0	21	Whitlow	43,789
22	31	H	Sheffield W	L	0-1	0-1	21		20,624
23	Jan 2	A	Ipwich T	L	1-4	0-1	22	Roberts	15,817
24	14	A	Crystal Palace	L	0-2	0-2	22		12,707
25	25	A	Manchester C	W	1-0	0-0	—	Robins	21,007
26	Feb 4	H	West Ham U	L	1-2	1-2	22	Robins	20,375
27	11	A	Arsenal	D	1-1	0-0	22	Draper	31,373
28	22	A	Aston Villa	D	4-4	0-2	—	Robins, Roberts, Lowe 2	30,825
29	25	A	Coventry C	L	2-4	0-2	22	Lowe, Roberts	20,650
30	Mar 4	H	Everton	D	2-2	0-2	22	Draper, Roberts	20,447
31	8	A	QPR	L	0-2	0-0	—		10,189
32	11	H	Nottingham F	L	2-4	1-1	22	Lowe, Draper	20,423
33	15	H	Leeds U	L	1-3	1-1	—	Roberts	20,068
34	18	A	Tottenham H	L	0-1	0-0	22		30,851
35	Apr 1	H	Wimbledon	L	3-4	1-0	22	Robins, Willis, Lawrence	15,489
36	5	H	Norwich C	W	1-0	0-0	—	Parker	15,992
37	8	A	Sheffield W	L	0-1	0-1	21		22,551
38	15	H	Manchester U	L	0-4	0-2	21		21,281
39	17	A	Liverpool	L	0-2	0-0	21		36,012
40	29	H	Ipswich T	W	2-0	0-0	21	Whitlow, Lowe	15,248
41	May 6	H	Chelsea	D	1-1	1-1	21	Willis	18,140
42	14	A	Southampton	D	2-2	0-1	21	Parker, Robins	15,101

Final League Position: 21

GOALSCORERS

League (45): Roberts 9, Lowe 8, Draper 5, Robins 5, Blake 3, Joachim 3, Gee 2, Parker 2, Whitlow 2, Willis 2, Carr 1, Lawrence 1, Oldfield 1, own goal 1.
Coca-Cola Cup (0).
FA Cup (3): Roberts 2, Oldfield 1.

Ward G.J. 6	Grayson S.N. 34	Whitlow M. 28	Mohan N. 23	Smith R.G. 10 + 2	Hill C.F. 24	Joachim J.K. 11 + 4	Blake M.A. 26 + 4	Walsh S. 5	Agnew S.M. 7 + 4	Draper M.A. 39	Roberts I.W. 32 + 5	Thompson S.J. 16 + 3	Willis J.A. 29	Poole K. 36	Philpott L. 19 + 4	Lowe D.A. 19 + 10	Mills G.R. 1	Gee P. 3 + 4	Lewis N.A. 13 + 3	Carey B.P. 11 + 1	Carr F.A. 12 + 1	Oldfield D.C. 8 + 6	Ormondroyd I. 6	Lawrence J.H. 9 + 8	Robins M.G. 16 + 1	Galloway M. 4 + 1	Parker G.S. 14	Heskey E. 1	McMahon S.K. — + 1	*Match No.*
1	2	3	4	5	6	7	*8*	9	10	11	12	14																		1
1	2	3	4		*6*	7	8	9	10	11	12	14	5																	2
	2	*3*	4	5		7	8		10	11	9	12	6	1	14															3
		3	4	2					10		9	8	5	1	11	7	6	12												4
	2					12	8		14	6	10		5	1	11	9			*3*	4	7									5
	2		4			9	8		14	6	10		5	1	*11*	12			3		7									6
	2		4			9	8			6	10		5	1	11				3		7									7
	2		4	12		9	8		14	6	10		5	1	11				*3*		7									8
	2	3	4	12		9	8			6	10		5	1	*11*	14					7									9
1	2	4					8			6	10		5		11	*9*		14	3		7	12								10
1	2	5	4			9	8			6	10				*11*	12			3		7	14								11
1	2	5	4			9	8			6	10				11	12			3		*7*	14								12
1	2	5	4				8			6	10				11	9			3		7									13
	2	3		5				9		6	12	8	4	1		10					7	14	*11*							14
		3	4				2	9		6		8	5	1		10						7	11							15
		3	4				2	9		6		8	5	1		10		12				7	11							16
		3	4		5	12	2			6	14	8		1				*9*			7	10	11							17
	7	3	4		5	12	2			6		8		1	11			9			14	10								18
	7	3			4	12	2			6		8	5	1	11			9				10								19
	2	3			4		10		14	6	12	*8*	5	1	11						7	9								20
	2	3			4		12		9	6	10	8	5	1	11	14						*7*								21
	2	3			4		12		9	6	10	8	5	1	11	14						*7*								22
	2	3			4				7	6	10	8	5	1	12	*9*			11			14								23
			4	2	5		9			6	10	8		1	3	12						14	*11*	7						24
	2		4	3	5		11			6	10	8		1										7	9					25
	2		4	3	5					6	10	8		1	11									12	9	7				26
	2	3		*5*	4					6	10	8		1	11				12					7	9	14				27
	2	3			4					6	10	8	5	1		14			*12*						9	7	11			28
	2				4					6	10		5	1		8			3						9	7	11			29
	2				4					6	10		5	1		8			3					12	9	7	11			30
			4	2			5			6	9			1	3	8		12						7			10	11		31
			4	2			11			6	10			1	12	8			3	5				7	9					32
	2		4				7			6	*10*			1	14	8			3	5				12	9		11			33
	2		4				3			*7*	*10*		5	1		8			12	6				14	9		11			34
	7	3	4		*6*								2	1		8				5			11	14	9		10		12	35
	2	3			4						10		5	1		8				6				7	9		11			36
	2	3			4		12			7	10		5	1		8				*6*				14	9		11			37
	2	3			4		12			6	10		5	1		*8*				14				7	9		11			38
	2	3			4		8			7	10		5	1						6				12	9		11			39
		3			4		2			7	10		5	1		8				6				12	9		11			40
	3				4	7				8	10		5	1		12				6				2	9		11			41
	2	3			4	9				8	10		5	1		12				*6*				7	14		11			42

Coca-Cola Cup

Second Round	Brighton & HA (a)		0-1
	(h)		0-2

FA Cup

Third Round	Enfield (h)	2-0
Fourth Round	Portsmouth (a)	1-0
Fifth Round	Wolverhampton W (a)	0-1

LEYTON ORIENT 1994–95 *Back row (left to right):* Danny Carter, Darren Purse, Colin West, Glenn Cockerill, Mark Warren, Barry Lakin.
Centre row: Tony Flynn, Andy Gray, Kevin Austin, Paul Heald, Gary Bellamy, Terry Howard, Andy Taylor.
Front row: Gary Barnett, Mark Dempsey, Chris Turner, Ian Hendon, John Sitton, Ian Bogie, Vaughan Ryan.

Division 3 **LEYTON ORIENT**

Leyton Stadium, Brisbane Road, Leyton, London E10 5NE. Telephone: (0181) 539 2223/4. Fax: (0181) 539 4390. Clubcall: 0891 121150.

Ground capacity: 17,065 (7,171 seats).

Record attendance: 34,345 v West Ham U, FA Cup 4th rd, 25 January 1964.

Record receipts: £87,867.92 v West Ham U, FA Cup 3rd rd, 10 January 1987.

Pitch measurements: 110yd × 80yd.

Chairman: Barry Hearn.

Directors: D. L. Weinrabe, Tony Wood, Harry Linney, V. Marsh, J. Goldsmith FR, BA.

Team Manager: Pat Holland. ***Assistant Manager:*** Tom Cunningham. ***Physio:*** A. Taylor.

Secretary: David Burton. ***Asst. Sec.:*** Mrs Sue Tilling. ***Commercial Manager:*** Frank Woolf.

Year Formed: 1881. ***Turned Professional:*** 1903. ***Ltd Co.:*** 1906.

Club Nickname: 'The O's'.

Previous Names: 1881–86, Glyn Cricket and Football Club; 1886–88, Eagle Football Club; 1888–98, Orient Football Club; 1898–1946, Clapton Orient; 1946–66, Leyton Orient; 1966–87, Orient.

Previous Grounds: Glyn Road, 1884–96; Whittles Athletic Ground, 1896–1900; Millfields Road, 1900–30; Lea Bridge Road, 1930–37.

Foundation: There is some doubt about the foundation of Leyton Orient, and, indeed, some confusion with clubs like Leyton and Clapton over their early history. As regards the foundation, the most favoured version is that Leyton Orient was formed originally by members of Homerton Theological College who established Glyn Cricket Club in 1881 and then carried on through the following winter playing football. Eventually many employees of the Orient Shipping Line became involved and so the name Orient was chosen in 1888.

First Football League game: 2 September, 1905, Division 2, v Leicester Fosse (a) L 1-2 – Butler; Holmes, Codling; Lamberton, Boden, Boyle; Kingaby (1), Wootten, Leigh, Evenson, Bourne.

Record League Victory: 8–0 v Crystal Palace, Division 3 (S), 12 November 1955 – Welton; Lee, Earl; Blizzard, Aldous, McKnight; White (1), Facey (3), Burgess (2), Heckman, Hartburn (2). 8–0 v Rochdale, Division 4, 20 October 1987 – Wells; Howard, Dickenson (1), Smalley (1), Day, Hull, Hales (2), Castle (Sussex), Shinners (2), Godfrey (Harvey), Comfort (2). 8–0 v Colchester U, Division 4, 15 October 1988 – Wells; Howard, Dickenson, Hales (1p), Day (1). Sitton (1), Baker (1), Ward, Hull (3). Juryeff, Comfort (1).

Record Cup Victory: 9–2 v Chester, League Cup, 3rd rd, 15 October 1962 – Robertson; Charlton, Taylor; Gibbs, Bishop, Lea; Deeley (1), Waites (3), Dunmore (2), Graham (3), Wedge.

Record Defeat: 0–8 v Aston Villa, FA Cup 4th rd, 30 January 1929.

Most League Points (2 for a win): 66, Division 3 (S), 1955–56.

Most League Points (3 for a win): 75, Division 4, 1988–89.

Most League Goals: 106, Division 3 (S), 1955–56.

Highest League Scorer in Season: Tom Johnston, 35, Division 2, 1957–58.

Most League Goals in Total Aggregate: Tom Johnston, 121, 1956–58, 1959–61.

Most Capped Player: John Chiedozie, 8 (10), Nigeria.

Most League Appearances: Peter Allen, 432, 1965–78.

Record Transfer Fee Received: £600,000 from Notts Co for John Chiedozie, August 1981.

Record Transfer Fee Paid: £175,000 to Wigan Ath for Paul Beesley, October 1989.

Football League Record: 1905 Elected to Division 2; 1929–56 Division 3 (S); 1956–62 Division 2; 1962–63 Division 1; 1963–66 Division 2; 1966–70 Division 3; 1970–82 Division 2; 1982–85 Division 3; 1985–89 Division 4; 1989–92 Division 3; 1992–95 Division 2; 1995– Division 3.

Honours: *Football League:* Division 1 best season: 22nd, 1962–63; Division 2 – Runners-up 1961–62; Division 3 – Champions 1969–70; Division 3 (S) – Champions 1955–56; Runners-up 1954–55. *FA Cup:* Semi-final 1978. *Football League Cup:* best season: 5th rd, 1963.

Colours: Red shirts with white pinstripe, white shorts, red stockings. **Change colours:** Blue and yellow.

LEYTON ORIENT 1994–95 LEAGUE RECORD

Match No.	Date	Venue	Opponents	Result		H/T Score	Lg. Pos.	Goalscorers	Attendance
1	Aug 13	H	Birmingham C	W	2-1	1-1	—	Purse, Bogie	7578
2	20	A	Bradford C	L	0-2	0-1	15		7473
3	27	H	Hull C	D	1-1	0-0	14	Gray	3243
4	30	A	Huddersfield T	L	1-2	1-0	—	Purse	8552
5	Sept 3	A	Brighton & HA	L	0-1	0-0	19		8581
6	10	H	Cambridge U	D	1-1	0-0	19	West	3699
7	13	H	Bournemouth	W	3-2	1-1	—	Cockerill, West 2 (2 pens)	2536
8	17	A	Shrewsbury T	L	0-3	0-3	19		3560
9	24	A	Oxford U	L	2-3	0-0	19	Hague, Howard	5814
10	Oct 1	H	Plymouth Arg	L	0-2	0-2	21		4140
11	8	A	Wycombe W	L	1-2	0-1	20	Gray	5668
12	15	H	Chester C	W	2-0	1-0	20	Cockerill, West	3309
13	22	A	Rotherham U	L	0-2	0-1	21		2700
14	29	H	Stockport Co	L	0-1	0-0	22		3267
15	Nov 1	H	Cardiff C	W	2-0	0-0	—	Purse, West	2558
16	5	A	Blackpool	L	1-2	1-1	21	West	4653
17	19	H	York C	L	0-1	0-0	22		3532
18	26	A	Peterborough U	D	0-0	0-0	22		5114
19	Dec 10	H	Bradford C	D	0-0	0-0	22		2553
20	17	A	Birmingham C	L	0-2	0-1	22		20,022
21	26	A	Brentford	L	0-3	0-3	22		6125
22	27	H	Swansea C	L	0-1	0-1	22		3259
23	31	A	Crewe Alex	L	0-3	0-0	22		3792
24	Jan 7	H	Rotherham U	D	0-0	0-0	23		2796
25	14	A	Wrexham	L	1-4	0-1	23	Bogie (pen)	6616
26	28	A	Stockport Co	L	1-2	0-1	23	West	4250
27	Feb 4	H	Peterborough U	W	4-1	2-0	23	Warren 3, West	3447
28	7	H	Blackpool	L	0-1	0-1	—		3301
29	18	H	Wrexham	D	1-1	1-0	23	Cockerill	3135
30	21	A	York C	L	1-4	1-2	—	Cockerill	2926
31	25	A	Plymouth Arg	L	0-1	0-0	23		5173
32	Mar 4	H	Oxford U	D	1-1	1-0	23	West	4052
33	7	H	Brighton & HA	L	0-3	0-1	—		2983
34	11	A	Hull C	L	0-2	0-1	23		4519
35	18	H	Huddersfield T	L	0-2	0-0	23		3177
36	21	A	Cambridge U	D	0-0	0-0	—		3048
37	25	H	Shrewsbury T	W	2-1	1-1	23	Austin, Gray	2724
38	Apr 1	A	Bournemouth	L	0-2	0-1	23		4118
39	4	A	Cardiff C	L	1-2	0-0	—	McGleish	4324
40	8	H	Crewe Alex	L	1-4	1-2	23	Austin	2797
41	11	H	Bristol R	L	1-2	0-1	—	Dempsey	2338
42	15	A	Swansea C	L	0-2	0-2	23		3277
43	17	H	Brentford	L	0-2	0-1	23		4459
44	22	A	Bristol R	L	0-1	0-0	23		4838
45	29	A	Chester C	L	0-1	0-0	24		1596
46	May 6	H	Wycombe W	L	0-1	0-0	24		4698

Final League Position: 24

GOALSCORERS

League (30): West 9 (2 pens), Cockerill 4, Gray 3, Purse 3, Warren 3, Austin 2, Bogie 2 (1 pen), Dempsey 1, Hague 1, Howard 1, McGleish 1.
Coca-Cola Cup (1): Cockerill 1.
FA Cup (3): Carter 1, Gray 1, West 1.

Heald P.A. 45	Warren M.W. 24 + 7	Austin K. 39	Purse D.J. 37 + 1	Hendon I.M. 29	Lakin B. 17 + 5	Barnett G.L. 15 + 12	Ryan V.W. 6 + 1	Bogie I. 28 + 3	West C. 27 + 3	Dempsey M.A. 43	Gray A. 13 + 12	Cockerill G. 32 + 1	Howard T. 27	Carter D.S. 25 + 4	Martin J.A. 1 + 3	Hague P. 17 + 1	Bellamy G. 32	Brooks S. 8 + 1	Wilkie G. 10 + 1	Read P. 11	McGleish S. 4 + 2	Turner C.R. 1	Barry G. 5 + 1	Perifimou C. 3 + 1	Rufus M.M. 5 + 2	Shearer L.S. 2	*Match No.*
1	2	3	4	5	6	7	*8*	9	10	11	12	14															1
1		3	4	5	12	7	6	14	10	11		8	2	*9*													2
1		3	4	5	12			6	10	11	9	8	2	7													3
1	14	3	4	2	12		6	7	10	11	9	8	5														4
1	2	3	4		6	12	7		10	11	*9*	8	5	14													5
1		3	4	2	6		7		10	11	*9*	8	5	12	14												6
1		3	4	2		12	7		10	11	*9*	8	5	6	14												7
1		3	*4*	2	7		12		10	11		8	5	6	9	14											8
1		3	4	2	7				10	*11*	12	8	6	9	14	5											9
1		3	4		7	12		14	10	11	9	8	2	*6*		5											10
1	12	3	14		7			6	10	11	9	8	2			*5*	4										11
1		3	9	5	7			6	10	11		8	2	12			4										12
1	12	3	9	5	7			6	10	11			2	8			4										13
1		3	9	5	7	12		6	10	11			2	8			4										14
1		3	9	5	7	12		6	10	11			2	8			4										15
1	2	3	*9*		7	12		6	10	11	14	8	5				4										16
1		3		2	12	7		6	10	11	9	8	5				4										17
1		3		2	12	7		6	10	11	9	8	5				4	14									18
1		3	5		7	12		6		11	14	8	2	9			4	*10*									19
1	12		5	2	8	7		6		11	14		3	9			4	10									20
1	12			2				6		11	7	8	3	9		5	4	10									21
1	10			2		12		6		11	7	8	3	9		5	4										22
1	10	3	5			12		6		11	7	8	*2*	9			4		14								23
1	*9*	3	4			7		6		11	14	8	2	12		5		10									24
1	9	3	4	8				6	12	11			2	7		5		10									25
1			5	2				12	10	11	9	8	3	7			4	6									26
1	10		5	2	6			9	12	11		8	3	7			4										27
1	10		5	2	6			9	12	11		8	3	7			4										28
1	9	3	5	2		12		6	10	11		8		7			4										29
1	9	3	5	2				6	10	11		8		7			4										30
1	9	3	5	2				6	10	11		8		7			4										31
1	12	3	5	2				6	*10*	11	14	8		7			4			9							32
1	10	3	5	2		7		6		11		8					4			9	12						33
	12	3	5	2				6	10	11		8					4			9	7	1					34
1	9	3		2	7			6	10	11		8				5	4										35
1	*9*			2		12		6	10	11	14	8				5			4		7		3				36
1	*9*	3	4			12			10	11	14	8				5			6		7		2				37
1	9	3	4			8				11						5	7		6	10	12		2				38
1	9	3	4			8					12					5	7			10	6		2	*11*	14		39
1	10	3	4							11	12	8				5	7		6	9			2				40
1	10	3	4			*8*				11	12						5		2	9			14	7	6		41
1	10	3				8				11						5	4		2	9				7	6		42
1	10	3				7				11				8			4		2	9					6	5	43
1		3	9			8				11				7		5	4		2	10					6		44
1	2	3	9			7								11		5	6	4	8	10					12		45
1	2	3	9			7										5	6	4	8					12	11	10	46

Coca-Cola Cup

First Round	Barnet (a)	0-4
	(h)	1-1

FA Cup

First Round	Tiverton (a)	3-1
Second Round	Bristol R (h)	0-2

LINCOLN CITY 1994–95 *Back row (left to right):* Steve Williams, Neil Matthews, Colin Greenall, Nicky Platnauer, Mark Smith, John Schofield, Alan Johnson, Grant Brown, Trevor Hebberd.
Centre row: Billy Ayre, Ben Dixon, David Johnson, Sean Dunphy, Andy Leaning, Matt Carbon, Steve Parkinson, Udo Onwere, Sam Ellis (Manager).
Front row: Paul Smith, Dean West, Tony Daws, Steve Mardenborough, Steve Foley, David Puttnam, David Hill, Darren Huckerby

Division 3 **LINCOLN CITY**

Sincil Bank, Lincoln LN5 8LD. Telephone: (01522) 522224. Fax: (01522) 520564. Commercial: (01522) 536966. Community Officer: (01522) 539671.

Ground capacity: 10,918.

Record attendance: 23,196 v Derby Co, League Cup 4th rd, 15 November 1967.

Record receipts: £44,184.46 v Everton, Coca-Cola Cup 2nd rd 1st leg, 21 September 1993.

Pitch measurements: 110yd × 75yd.

Hon. Life Presidents: V. C. Withers, D. W. L. Bocock.

President: H. Dove.

Chairman: K. J. Reames. ***Vice-Chairman:*** G. R. Davey (and Managing).

Directors: H. C. Sills, J. Hicks, Mrs E. C. Reames, N. Woolsey, C. J. Thomas.

Hon. Consultant Surgeon: Mr Brian Smith. ***Hon. Club Doctor:*** Nick Huntley.

Secretary: Phil Hough.

Manager: Sam Ellis. ***Assistant Manager:*** Frank Lord. ***Physio:*** Mark Riley. ***Commercial Manager:*** G. R. Davey.

Year Formed: 1883. ***Turned Professional:*** 1892. ***Ltd Co.:*** 1892.

Club Nickname: 'The Red Imps'.

Previous Grounds: 1883, John O'Gaunt's; 1894, Sincil Bank.

Foundation: Although there was a Lincoln club as far back as 1861, the present organisation was formed in 1883 winning the Lincolnshire Senior Cup in only their fourth season. They were Founder members of the Midland League in 1889 and that competition's first champions.

First Football League game: 3 September, 1892, Division 2, v Sheffield U (a) L 2-4 – W. Gresham; Coulton, Neill; Shaw, Mettam, Moore; Smallman, Irving (1), Cameron (1), Kelly, J. Gresham.

Record League Victory: 11–1 v Crewe Alex, Division 3 (N), 29 September 1951 – Jones; Green (1p), Varney; Wright, Emery, Grummett (1); Troops (1), Garvey, Graver (6), Whittle (1), Johnson (1).

Record Cup Victory: 8–1 v Bromley, FA Cup, 2nd rd, 10 December 1938 – McPhail; Hartshorne, Corbett; Bean, Leach, Whyte (1); Hancock, Wilson (1), Ponting (3), Deacon (1), Clare (2).

Record Defeat: 3–11 v Manchester C, Division 2, 23 March 1895.

Most League Points (2 for a win): 74, Division 4, 1975–76.

Most League Points (3 for a win): 77, Division 3, 1981–82.

Most League Goals: 121, Division 3 (N), 1951–52.

Highest League Scorer in Season: Allan Hall, 42, Division 3 (N), 1931–32.

Most League Goals in Total Aggregate: Andy Graver, 144, 1950–55 and 1958–61.

Most Capped Player: David Pugh, 3 (7), Wales and George Moulson, 3, Republic of Ireland.

Most League Appearances: Tony Emery, 402, 1946–59.

Record Transfer Fee Received: £250,000 plus increments from Blackburn R for Matt Dickins, March 1992.

Record Transfer Fee Paid: £63,000 to Leicester City for Grant Brown, January 1990.

Football League Record: 1892 Founder member of Division 2. Remained in Division 2 until 1920 when they failed re-election but also missed seasons 1908–09 and 1911–12 when not re-elected. 1921–32 Division 3 (N); 1932–34 Division 2; 1934–48 Division 3 (N); 1948–49 Division 2; 1949–52 Division 3 (N); 1952–61 Division 2; 1961–62 Division 3; 1962–76 Division 4; 1976–79 Division 3; 1979–81 Division 4; 1981–86 Division 3; 1986–87 Division 4; 1987–88 GM Vauxhall Conference; 1988–92 Division 4; 1992– Division 3.

Honours: *Football League:* Divison 2 best season: 5th, 1901–02; Division 3 (N) – Champions 1931–32, 1947–48, 1951–52; Runners-up 1927–28, 1930–31, 1936–37; Division 4 – Champions 1975–76; Runners-up 1980–81. *FA Cup:* best season: 1st rd of Second Series (5th rd equivalent), 1887, 2nd rd (5th rd equivalent), 1890, 1902. *Football League Cup:* best season: 4th rd, 1968. *GM Vauxhall Conference:* Champions 1987–88.

Colours: Red and white striped shirts, black shorts, red stockings with white trim. **Change colours:** Jade shirts, black shorts, jade stockings.

LINCOLN CITY 1994–95 LEAGUE RECORD

Match No.	Date	Venue	Opponents	Result		H/T Score	Lg. Pos.	Goalscorers	Attendance
1	Aug 13	H	Exeter C	W	2-0	2-0	—	Daws, Johnson D (pen)	3439
2	20	A	Walsall	L	1-2	0-1	11	West	3813
3	27	H	Torquay U	L	1-2	1-1	15	Daley	3154
4	30	A	Rochdale	L	0-1	0-1	—		1974
5	Sept 3	A	Preston NE	L	0-4	0-0	19		8337
6	10	H	Mansfield T	W	3-2	1-1	14	Daley, West, Puttnam	2575
7	13	H	Wigan Ath	W	1-0	0-0	—	Schofield	2030
8	17	A	Exeter C	L	0-1	0-0	13		2180
9	24	A	Hartlepool U	W	3-0	3-0	13	West, Greenall, Puttnam	1419
10	Oct 1	H	Northampton T	D	2-2	1-2	13	Brown, Puttnam	3248
11	8	H	Carlisle U	D	1-1	0-0	12	Bannister	3097
12	15	A	Bury	L	0-2	0-2	15		3139
13	22	H	Scarborough	W	2-0	1-0	13	Bannister (pen), Daley	2396
14	29	A	Hereford U	W	3-0	1-0	11	Matthews, Daley, Puttnam	2485
15	Nov 5	H	Barnet	L	1-2	1-1	11	Matthews	2741
16	19	A	Fulham	D	1-1	0-1	12	Bannister (pen)	3955
17	26	H	Gillingham	D	1-1	0-0	10	West	2919
18	Dec 10	H	Walsall	D	1-1	1-1	11	Brown	2717
19	17	A	Torquay U	L	1-2	0-1	14	Daws	2004
20	26	A	Scunthorpe U	L	0-2	0-0	15		4785
21	27	H	Darlington	W	3-1	1-1	12	Johnson D, Carbon 2	2964
22	31	A	Chesterfield	L	0-1	0-0	14		3325
23	Jan 14	H	Doncaster R	W	1-0	0-0	15	Daws (pen)	2771
24	28	H	Hereford U	W	2-0	0-0	13	Hill, Carbon	2545
25	Feb 4	A	Gillingham	D	0-0	0-0	15		4196
26	7	A	Scarborough	D	1-1	1-0	—	Daws (pen)	1217
27	18	A	Doncaster R	L	0-3	0-1	14		2291
28	21	H	Colchester U	W	2-0	0-0	—	Bannister, Johnson D.	1969
29	25	A	Northampton T	L	1-3	0-1	13	Greenall	4821
30	Mar 4	H	Hartlepool U	W	3-0	0-0	12	Bannister, Carbon, Daws (pen)	6477
31	11	A	Mansfield T	L	2-6	0-1	13	Daws, Brown	3396
32	18	H	Rochdale	D	2-2	2-0	13	West, Johnson D	2939
33	25	H	Preston NE	D	1-1	1-0	14	West	5487
34	Apr 1	A	Wigan Ath	W	1-0	1-0	13	Hill	1696
35	4	A	Barnet	L	1-2	1-1	—	Carbon	1616
36	8	H	Chesterfield	L	0-1	0-1	14		5141
37	11	H	Fulham	W	2-0	1-0	—	Carbon, Hill	2932
38	15	A	Darlington	D	0-0	0-0	13		1664
39	17	H	Scunthorpe U	D	3-3	2-2	12	Carbon, Greenall, Williams	3330
40	22	A	Colchester U	W	2-1	1-1	12	Bannister, Huckerby	2654
41	29	H	Bury	L	0-3	0-2	12		3928
42	May 6	A	Carlisle U	W	3-1	1-0	12	Bannister, Huckerby, Daws	12,412

Final League Position: 12

GOALSCORERS

League (54): Bannister 7 (2 pens), Carbon 7, Daws 7 (3 pens), West 6, Johnson D 4 (1 pen), Daley 4, Puttnam 4, Brown 3, Greenall 3, Hill 3, Huckerby 2, Matthews 2, Schofield 1, Williams 1.
Coca-Cola Cup (6): Johnson D 2 (1 pen), Schofield 2, Carbon 1, West 1.
FA Cup (3): Bannister 1, Greenall 1, Johnson D 1.

Hoult R. 15	Schofield J.D. 12	Platnauer N.R. 13	Hebberd T.N. 20 + 5	Greenall C.A. 39	Brown G.A. 39	West D. 41	Onwere U.A. 7 + 1	Daley P. 19 + 1	Daws A. 20 + 6	Johnson D.A. 23 + 1	Johnson A.K. 24 + 1	Matthews N. 17 + 6	Carbon M.P. 30 + 3	Puttnam D.P. 8 + 9	Foley S. 15 + 1	Bannister G. 25 + 4	Lucas R. 4	Hill D.M. 25 + 1	Leaning A.J. 21	Dixon B. 17 + 1	Smith P.M. 15 + 2	Williams S.R. 3 + 3	Sherwood S. 6 + 1	Huckerby D.C. 4 + 2	Match No.
1	2	3	4	5	6	7	8	9	*10*	11	12	14													1
1	2	3	4	5	6	7		9		11	8	12	10												2
1	2	3	4	5	6	7		9		11	8		10												3
1	2	3	12	5	6	7	4	9	14	11	8		*10*												4
1	2	3	12	5	6	7	4	9		11	8		*10*	14											5
1	2	3		5	6	7		9		11	8			10	4										6
1	2	3	12	5	6	7		9		11	8			10	4										7
1	2	3		5	6	7		9		11	8			10	4	12									8
1	2	3		5	6	7	8						11	10	4	9									9
1	2	3	12	5	6	7	8	14					*11*	10	4	9									10
1	2	3	4	5	6	7	8	9			11		12			10									11
1	2		12	5	6	7	8	*9*					11	14	4	10	3								12
1			7	5	6	2		9			3		11	12	4	10	8								13
1			4	5	6	2		9			3	8		11		10	7	12							14
1			4	5	6	2		9			3	8	12			10	7	11							15
			8	5	6	2		9			3	7	12		4	10		11	1						16
			8	5	6	2		9	14	12	3	7			4	*10*		11	1						17
			8	5	6	2		9	12	*10*	3	7	4			14		11	1						18
			4	5	6	2		9	8	10		7		12		14		*11*	1	3					19
			8	5	6	2		9	10		3		4	12	7	11			1						20
			7	5	6	2		9	14	11	3		4	*10*	12	8			1						21
			8		6	2	12		14	10	3		4	11	7	*9*			1	5					22
			4			2			10	11	3		9		8			7	1	5	6				23
			4		6	2			10	7	3		9		8			11	1	5	12				24
			4	5	6	2			10	7	3	9			8			11	1		12				25
				5	6	2			10	7	3	9			8			11	1		4				26
				5	6	2			10	7	3	*9*	8					11	1	12	4	14			27
			10	5	6	2				7	3		8			12		11	1		4	9			28
			8	5	6	2				7	3		9			10		11	1		4				29
			8	5	6	2			12	7			9			10		11	1	3	4				30
				5	6	2			8	7		12	9			10		11	1	3	4				31
				5	6	2			8	7		12	9			10		11	1	3	4				32
				5	6	2			10	7		12	9			8		11	1	3	4				33
				5	6	2			10			7	9	12		8		11	*1*	3	4		15		34
				5	6	2			10			7	9	12		*8*		11		3	4		1	14	35
				5	6	2			10			7	9	12		8		11		3	4		1		36
				5	6	2			8			7	9			10		11		3	4		1		37
				5	6	2			8			7	9			10		11		3	4	12	1	14	38
				5	*6*	2			8			12	9			10		11		3	4	14	1	7	39
		4		5					8			7	9			10		11		3		6	1	2	40
				5	6	2			8			7	9	12				11	1	3		4		10	41
		4		5		2			8			7	9			6		11	1	3				10	42

Coca-Cola Cup

First Round	Chester C (h)	2-0
	(a)	3-2
Second Round	Crystal Palace (h)	1-0
	(a)	0-3

FA Cup

First Round	Hull C (a)	1-0
Second Round	Huddersfield T (h)	1-0
Third Round	Crystal Palace (a)	1-5

LIVERPOOL 1994–95 *Back row (left to right):* Mark Walters, Dominic Matteo, Mark Wright, Michael Stensgaard, Torben Piechnik, David James, Jan Molby, Phil Charnock, Rob Jones. *Centre row:* Ronnie Moran (Coach), Steve Harkness, Steve Nicol, Nigel Clough, Paul Stewart, Lee Jones, Stig Bjornebye, Michael Thomas, Doug Livermore (Assistant Manager), Sammy Lee (Coach).

Front row: Julian Dicks, Neil Ruddock, Robbie Fowler, Ian Rush, Roy Evans (Team Manager), John Barnes, Jamie Redknapp, Don Hutchison, Steve McManaman.

FA Premiership LIVERPOOL

Anfield Road, Liverpool L4 0TH. Telephone: (0151) 263 2361. Fax: (0151) 260 8813. Clubcall: 0891 121184. Ticket and Match Information: (0151) 260 9999 (24-hour service) or (0151) 260 8680 (office hours) Credit Card Bookings.

Ground Capacity: 41,000.

Record attendance: 61,905 v Wolverhampton W, FA Cup 4th rd, 2 February 1952.

Record receipts: £445,000 v Tottenham H, FA Cup 6th rd, 11 March 1995.

Pitch measurements: 110yd × 74yd.

Chairman: D. R. Moores.

Directors:J. T. Cross, N. White FSCA, T. D. Smith, T. W. Saunders, P. B. Robinson, K. E. B. Clayton FCA.

Vice-Presidents: C. J. Hill, H. E. Roberts, W. D. Corkish FCA, R. Paisley OBE, HON MSC.

Team Manager: Roy Evans. ***Assistant Manager:*** Doug Livermore. ***Coach:*** Ronnie Moran.
Physio: Mark Leather.

Chief Executive/General Secretary: Peter B. Robinson. ***Commercial Manager:*** Mike Turner.

Year Formed: 1892. ***Turned Professional:*** 1892. ***Ltd Co.:*** 1892.

Club Nickname: 'Reds' or 'Pool'.

Foundation: But for a dispute between Everton FC and their landlord at Anfield in 1892, there may never have been a Liverpool club. This dispute persuaded the majority of Evertonians to quit Anfield for Goodison Park, leaving the landlord, Mr. John Houlding, to form a new club. He originally tried to retain the name "Everton" but when this failed, he founded Liverpool Association FC on 15 March, 1892.

First Football League game: 2 September, 1893, Division 2, v Middlesbrough Ironopolis (a) W 2-0 – McOwen; Hannah, McLean; Henderson, McQue (1), McBride; Gordon, McVean (1), M. McQueen, Stott, H. McQueen.

Record League Victory: 10–1 v Rotherham T, Division 2, 18 February 1896 – Storer; Goldie, Wilkie; McCarthy, McQueen, Holmes; McVean (3), Ross (2), Allan (4), Becton (1), Bradshaw.

Record Cup Victory: 11–0 v Stromsgodset Drammen, ECWC 1st rd 1st leg, 17 September 1974 – Clemence; Smith (1), Lindsay (1p), Thompson (2), Cormack (1), Hughes (1), Boersma (2), Hall, Heighway (1), Kennedy (1), Callaghan (1).

Record Defeat: 1–9 v Birmingham C, Division 2, 11 December 1954.

Most League Points (2 for a win): 68, Division 1, 1978–79.

Most League Points (3 for a win): 90, Division 1, 1987–88.

Most League Goals: 106, Division 2, 1895–96.

Highest League Scorer in Season: Roger Hunt, 41, Division 2, 1961–62.

Most League Goals in Total Aggregate: Roger Hunt, 245, 1959–69.

Most Capped Player: Ian Rush, 65 (71), Wales.

Most League Appearances: Ian Callaghan, 640, 1960–78.

Record Transfer Fee Received: £2,750,000 from Juventus for Ian Rush, June 1986.

Record Transfer Fee Paid: £8,500,000 to Nottingham F for Stan Collymore, June 1995.

Football League Record: 1893 Elected to Division 2; 1894–95 Division 1; 1895–96 Division 2; 1896–1904 Division 1; 1904–05 Division 2; 1905–54 Division 1; 1954–62 Division 2; 1962–92 Division 1; 1992– FA Premier Division.

Honours: *Football League:* Division 1 – Champions 1900–01, 1905–06, 1921–22, 1922–23, 1946–47, 1963–64, 1965–66, 1972–73, 1975–76, 1976–77, 1978–79, 1979–80, 1981–82, 1982–83, 1983–84, 1985–86, 1987–88, 1989–90 (Liverpool have a record number of 18 League Championship wins); Runners-up 1898–99, 1909–10, 1968–69, 1973–74, 1974–75, 1977–78, 1984–85, 1986–87, 1988–89, 1990–91; Division 2 – Champions 1893–94, 1895–96, 1904–05, 1961–62. *FA Cup:* Winners 1965, 1974, 1986, 1989, 1992; Runners-up 1914, 1950, 1971, 1977, 1988; *Football League Cup:* Winners 1981, 1982, 1983, 1984, 1995; Runners-up 1978, 1987. *League Super Cup:* Winners 1986. **European Competitions:** *European Cup:* 1964–65, 1966–67, 1973–74, 1976–77 (winners), 1977–78 (winners), 1978–79, 1979–80, 1980–81 (winners), 1981–82, 1982–83, 1983–84 (winners), 1984–85 (runners-up); *European Cup-Winners' Cup:* 1965–66 (runners-up), 1971–72, 1974–75, 1992–93; *European Fairs Cup:* 1967–68, 1968–69, 1969–70, 1970–71; *UEFA Cup:* 1972–73 (winners), 1975–76 (winners), 1991–92; *Super Cup:* 1977 (winners), 1978, 1984; *World Club Championship:* 1981 (runners-up).

Colours: All red. **Change colours:** White and green.

LIVERPOOL 1994–95 LEAGUE RECORD

Match No.	Date		Venue	Opponents	Result		H/T Score	Lg. Pos.	Goalscorers	Attendance
1	Aug	20	A	Crystal Palace	W	6-1	3-0	—	Molby (pen), McManaman 2, Fowler, Rush 2	18,084
2		28	H	Arsenal	W	3-0	3-0	5	Fowler 3	30,017
3		31	A	Southampton	W	2-0	1-0	—	Fowler, Barnes	15,190
4	Sept	10	H	West Ham U	D	0-0	0-0	4		30,907
5		17	A	Manchester U	L	0-2	0-0	5		43,740
6		24	A	Newcastle U	D	1-1	0-0	6	Rush	34,435
7	Oct	1	H	Sheffield W	W	4-1	0-1	5	McManaman 2, Walker (og), Rush	31,493
8		8	H	Aston Villa	W	3-2	2-1	4	Ruddock, Fowler 2	32,158
9		15	A	Blackburn R	L	2-3	1-0	5	Fowler, Barnes	30,263
10		22	H	Wimbledon	W	3-0	2-0	5	McManaman, Fowler, Barnes	31,139
11		29	A	Ipswich T	W	3-1	1-0	5	Barnes, Fowler 2	22,379
12		31	A	QPR	L	1-2	0-1	—	Barnes	18,295
13	Nov	5	H	Nottingham F	W	1-0	1-0	5	Fowler	33,329
14		9	H	Chelsea	W	3-1	3-1	—	Fowler 2, Ruddock	32,855
15		21	A	Everton	L	0-2	0-0	—		39,866
16		26	H	Tottenham H	D	1-1	1-0	4	Fowler (pen)	35,007
17	Dec	3	A	Coventry C	D	1-1	1-0	4	Rush	21,032
18		11	H	Crystal Palace	D	0-0	0-0	4		30,972
19		18	A	Chelsea	D	0-0	0-0	5		27,050
20		26	A	Leicester C	W	2-1	0-0	4	Fowler (pen), Rush	21,393
21		28	H	Manchester C	W	2-0	0-0	3	Phelan (og), Fowler	38,122
22		31	A	Leeds U	W	2-0	1-0	3	Redknapp, Fowler	38,468
23	Jan	2	H	Norwich C	W	4-0	2-0	3	Scales, Fowler 2, Rush	34,709
24		14	H	Ipswich T	L	0-1	0-1	3		32,733
25		24	H	Everton	D	0-0	0-0	—		39,505
26	Feb	4	A	Nottingham F	D	1-1	0-1	4	Fowler	25,418
27		11	H	QPR	D	1-1	0-1	4	Scales	35,996
28		25	A	Sheffield W	W	2-1	1-1	4	Barnes, McManaman	31,964
29	Mar	4	H	Newcastle U	W	2-0	0-0	4	Fowler, Rush	39,300
30		14	H	Coventry C	L	2-3	0-2	—	Molby (pen), Burrows (og)	27,183
31		19	H	Manchester U	W	2-0	1-0	4	Bruce (og), Redknapp	38,906
32		22	A	Tottenham H	D	0-0	0-0	—		31,988
33	Apr	5	H	Southampton	W	3-1	1-1	—	Rush 2, Fowler (pen)	29,881
34		9	H	Leeds U	L	0-1	0-1	5		37,454
35		12	A	Arsenal	W	1-0	0-0	—	Fowler	38,036
36		14	A	Manchester C	L	1-2	1-1	—	McManaman	27,055
37		17	H	Leicester C	W	2-0	0-0	4	Fowler, Rush	36,012
38		29	A	Norwich C	W	2-1	1-1	4	Harkness, Rush	21,843
39	May	2	A	Wimbledon	D	0-0	0-0	—		12,041
40		6	A	Aston Villa	L	0-2	0-2	4		40,154
41		10	A	West Ham U	L	0-3	0-1	—		22,446
42		14	H	Blackburn R	W	2-1	0-1	4	Barnes, Redknapp	40,014

Final League Position: 4

GOALSCORERS

League (65): Fowler 25 (3 pens), Rush 12, Barnes 7, McManaman 7, Redknapp 3, Molby 2 (2 pens), Ruddock 2, Scales 2, Harkness 1, own goals 4.
Coca-Cola Cup (16): Rush 6, Fowler 4, McManaman 2, Redknapp 2, Clough 1, Scales 1.
FA Cup (6): Barnes 2, Fowler 2, Redknapp 1, Rush 1.

James D.B. 42	Jones R.M. 31	Bjornebye S.I. 31	Nicol S. 4	Molby J. 12 + 2	Ruddock N. 37	McManaman S. 40	Redknapp J.F. 36 + 5	Rush I.J. 36	Barnes J.C.B. 38	Fowler R.B. 42	Thomas M.L. 16 + 7	Scales J.R. 35	Babb P.A. 33 + 1	Clough N.H. 3 + 7	Jones P.L. — + 1	Harkness S. 8	Walters M.E. 7 + 11	Matteo D. 2 + 5	Wright M. 5 + 1	Kennedy M. 4 + 2	Match No.
1	2	3	4	5	6	7	8	9	10	11	12										1
1	2	3	4	5	6	7	8	9	10	11	12										2
1	2	3	4	5	6	7	8	9	10	11											3
1	2	3		5	6	7	8	9	10	11		4									4
1	2	3		5	6	7	8	9	10	11		4	12								5
1	2	3		8	6	7		9	10	11		4	5	12							6
1	2	3	4	8	6	7	12	9	10	11			5								7
1	2	3		8	6	7	12	9	10	11		4	5								8
1	2	3		8	6	7	12	9	10	11		4	5								9
1	2	3			6	7	8	9	10	*11*		4	5	12	14						10
1	2	3			6	7	8	9	10	11		4	5								11
1	2	3		12	6	7	8	9	10	11		4	5								12
1	2	3		12	6	7	8	9	10	11		4	5								13
1	2	3		4	6	7	8	9	10	11			5								14
1	2	3		8	6	7	12	9	10	11		4	5								15
1	2	3			6	7	8	9	10	11	12	4	5								16
1		2			6	7	8	9		11	10	4	5			3	12				17
1		2			6		8		10	11	7	4	5	9		3	12				18
1		3			6		8	9	10	11	2	4	5				7				19
1	2	3			6	7	8	9	10	11	12	4	5								20
1	2	3			6	7	8	9	10	11		4	5								21
1	2	3			6	7	8	9	10	11		4	5								22
1	2	3			6	7	8	9	10	11		4	5								23
1	2	3			6	7	8	9		11	10	4	5				12				24
1	2	3			6	7	8	9	10	11		4	5								25
1	2				6	7	8	9	10	11	12	4	5				14	*3*			26
1	2	*3*			6	7	12	9	10	11	8	4	5				14				27
1	2	3				7	6		10	9	8	4	5				11	12			28
1	2				6	7	4	9	10	11	12	5	3				8				29
1	2	3		5	6	7	8	9		11	10	4					12				30
1		3			6	7	8	9	*10*	11	14	4	5				12		2		31
1	2	3			6	7	8			11	9	4	5	12			10				32
1	2	3			6	7	8	9	10	11		4	5				12				33
1	2				6	7	4	9	10	11		5	3				8			12	34
1	*2*				6	7	4		10	8	9	5	3				12		14	11	35
1					6	7	4	9	10	8	5		3	12				14	2	11	36
1					6	7	4	9	10	8	2			12		3			5	11	37
1						7	8	9	10	*11*	2	4	5	12		3	14		6		38
1					6	7	4	9	10	11	2	5				3	8	12			39
1						7	4	9	10	11	2	5		12		3	*8*	14	6		40
1						7	8		10	11	2	4	5	9		6	12	*3*		14	41
1						7	6		10	8	2	4	5	9		3		12		11	42

Coca-Cola Cup

Second Round	Burnley (h)	2-0
	(a)	4-1
Third Round	Stoke C (h)	2-1
Fourth Round	Blackburn R (a)	3-1
Fifth Round	Arsenal (h)	1-0
Semi-final	Crystal Palace (h)	1-0
	(a)	1-0
Final at Wembley	Bolton W	2-1

FA Cup

Third Round	Birmingham C (a)	0-0
	(h)	1-1
Fourth Round	Burnley (a)	0-0
	(h)	1-0
Fifth Round	Wimbledon (h)	1-1
	(a)	2-0
Sixth Round	Tottenham H (h)	1-2

LUTON TOWN 1994–95 *Back row (left to right):* Tony Adcock, Des Linton, Mitchell Thomas, Juergen Sommer, Marvin Johnson, David Greene, John Hartson.
Centre row: Clive Goodyear (Physio), Martin Williams, Richard Harvey, Julian James, Kerry Dixon, Aaron Skelton, Scott Oakes, Dwight Marshall, John Moore (Coach).
Front row: Ceri Hughes, Scott Houghton, David Preece, David Pleat (Manager), Trevor Peake, Tony Thorpe, Paul Telfer.

Division 1 **LUTON TOWN**

Kenilworth Road Stadium, 1 Maple Rd, Luton, Beds. LU4 8AW. Telephone: (01582) 411622. Ticket Office: (01582) 416976. Credit Hotline: (01582) 30748 (24 hrs). Banqueting: (01582) 411526. Clubcall: 0891 121123.

Ground capacity: 9975.

Record attendance: 30,069 v Blackpool, FA Cup 6th rd replay, 4 March 1959.

Record receipts: £115,541.20 v West Ham U, FA Cup 6th rd, 23 March 1994.

Pitch measurements: 110yd × 72yd.

Chairman & Managing Director: D. A. Kohler BSC (HONS), ARICS.

Directors: C. S. Bassett, C. T. F. Green, N. S. Terry.

Secretary: Cherry Newbery.

Commercial Manager: Kathy Leather.

Manager: Terry Westley. ***Assistant Manager:*** Mick McGiven. ***Coaches:*** Wayne Turner, John Moore.

Physio: Clive Goodyear.

Year Formed: 1885. ***Turned Professional:*** 1890. ***Ltd Co.:*** 1897.

Club Nickname: 'The Hatters'.

Previous Grounds: 1885, Excelsior, Dallow Lane; 1897, Dunstable Road; 1905, Kenilworth Road.

Foundation: Formed by an amalgamation of two leading local clubs, Wanderers and Excelsior a works team, at a meeting in Luton Town Hall in April 1885. The Wanderers had three months earlier changed their name to Luton Town Wanderers and did not take too kindly to the formation of another Town club but were talked around at this meeting. Wanderers had already appeared in the FA Cup and the new club entered in its inaugural season.

First Football League game: 4 September, 1897, Division 2, v Leicester Fosse (a) D 1-1 – Williams; McCartney, McEwen; Davies, Stewart, Docherty; Gallacher, Coupar, Birch, McInnes, Ekins (1).

Record League Victory: 12–0 v Bristol R, Division 3 (S), 13 April 1936 – Dolman; Mackey, Smith; Finlayson, Nelson, Godfrey; Rich, Martin (1), Payne (10), Roberts (1), Stephenson.

Record Cup Victory: 9–0 v Clapton, FA Cup, 1st rd (replay after abandoned game), 30 November 1927 – Abbott; Kingham, Graham; Black, Rennie, Fraser; Pointon, Yardley (4), Reid (2), Woods (1), Dennis (2).

Record Defeat: 0–9 v Small Heath, Division 2, 12 November 1898.

Most League Points (2 for a win): 66, Division 4, 1967–68.

Most League Points (3 for a win): 88, Division 2, 1981–82.

Most League Goals: 103, Division 3 (S), 1936–37.

Highest League Scorer in Season: Joe Payne, 55, Division 3 (S), 1936–37.

Most League Goals in Total Aggregate: Gordon Turner, 243, 1949–64.

Most Capped Player: Mal Donaghy, 58 (91), Northern Ireland.

Most League Appearances: Bob Morton, 494, 1948–64.

Record Transfer Fee Received: £2,500,000 from Arsenal for John Hartson, January 1995.

Record Transfer Fee Paid: £850,000 to Odense for Lars Elstrup, August 1989.

Football League Record: 1897 Elected to Division 2; 1900 Failed re-election; 1920 Division 3; 1921–37 Division 3 (S); 1937–55 Division 2; 1955–60 Division 1; 1960–63 Division 2; 1963–65 Division 3; 1965–68 Division 4; 1968–70 Division 3; 1970–74 Division 2; 1974–75 Division 1; 1975–82 Division 2; 1982– Division 1.

Honours: *Football League:* Division 1 best season: 7th, 1986–87; Division 2 – Champions 1981–82; Runners-up 1954–55, 1973–74; Division 3 – Runners-up 1969–70; Division 4 – Champions 1967–68; Division 3 (S) – Champions 1936–37; Runners-up 1935–36. *FA Cup:* Runners-up 1959. *Football League Cup:* Winners 1988; Runners-up 1989. *Simod Cup:* Runners-up 1988.

Colours: White shirts with blue sleeves with white and orange trim, blue collar with orange trim, blue shorts with orange and white trim, blue and white hooped stockings with orange trim. **Change colours:** Black and orange vertical striped shirts, with black collar and orange trim, black shorts with orange stripe down side, black stockings with orange turnover.

LUTON TOWN 1994–95 LEAGUE RECORD

Match No.	Date		Venue	Opponents	Result		H/T Score	Lg. Pos.	Goalscorers	Atten-dance
1	Aug	13	H	WBA	D	1-1	0-1	—	Oakes	8640
2		20	A	Derby Co	D	0-0	0-0	14		13,060
3		27	H	Southend U	D	2-2	1-0	17	Hartson, Hughes	5918
4		30	A	Tranmere R	L	2-4	0-0	—	Hughes, Hartson	5480
5	Sept	3	A	Port Vale	W	1-0	0-0	15	Marshall	8541
6		10	H	Burnley	L	0-1	0-1	18		6911
7		13	H	Bolton W	L	0-3	0-0	—		5764
8		17	A	Watford	W	4-2	3-2	16	Oakes, Dixon, Telfer 2	8880
9		24	A	Millwall	D	0-0	0-0	16		7150
10	Oct	1	H	Bristol C	L	0-1	0-0	20		6633
11		9	A	Stoke C	W	2-1	1-0	18	Marshall, Preece	11,712
12		15	H	Middlesbrough	W	5-1	3-0	11	Wilkinson (og), Marshall 2, Preece, Hartson	8412
13		22	A	Sheffield U	W	3-1	1-1	7	Gayle (og), James, Dixon	13,317
14		29	H	Barnsley	L	0-1	0-0	10		7212
15	Nov	1	H	Grimsby T	L	1-2	0-0	—	Oakes	5839
16		5	A	Wolverhampton W	W	3-2	1-0	8	Preece, Marshall, Dixon	26,749
17		12	A	Oldham Ath	D	0-0	0-0	8		7907
18		19	H	Portsmouth	W	2-0	1-0	8	Dixon, Preece	8214
19		26	A	Swindon T	W	2-1	1-1	5	Dixon, Oakes	9455
20	Dec	3	H	Sheffield U	L	3-6	0-2	8	Hartson, Gayle (og), Johnson (pen)	8516
21		11	H	Derby Co	D	0-0	0-0	10		6400
22		18	A	WBA	L	0-1	0-1	12		14,392
23		26	A	Reading	D	0-0	0-0	12		11,623
24		27	H	Sunderland	W	3-0	2-0	9	Oakes 2, Hartson	8953
25		31	A	Notts Co	W	1-0	0-0	8	Telfer	6249
26	Jan	2	H	Charlton Ath	L	0-1	0-1	8		7642
27		14	A	Barnsley	L	1-3	0-0	11	Dixon	4808
28	Feb	4	H	Oldham Ath	W	2-1	1-0	10	Marshall 2	6903
29		11	A	Grimsby T	L	0-5	0-2	10		4615
30		18	H	Swindon T	W	3-0	1-0	9	Horlock (og), Marshall 2	6595
31		21	A	Portsmouth	L	2-3	1-0	—	Telfer, James	7363
32		25	A	Bristol C	D	2-2	1-0	10	Oakes 2	7939
33	Mar	4	H	Millwall	D	1-1	1-0	10	Marshall	6864
34		7	H	Port Vale	W	2-1	0-0	—	Telfer, Dixon	5947
35		11	A	Southend U	L	0-3	0-1	11		4558
36		18	H	Tranmere R	W	2-0	1-0	10	James, Biggins	6660
37		21	A	Burnley	L	1-2	0-0	—	Marshall	9551
38		26	H	Watford	D	1-1	1-0	11	Telfer	7984
39	Apr	4	H	Wolverhampton W	D	3-3	2-0	—	Telfer 2, Taylor	9651
40		8	H	Notts Co	W	2-0	1-0	12	Telfer, Oakes (pen)	6482
41		11	A	Bolton W	D	0-0	0-0	—		13,619
42		15	A	Sunderland	D	1-1	1-0	11	Taylor	17,292
43		17	H	Reading	L	0-1	0-1	11		8717
44		22	A	Charlton Ath	L	0-1	0-0	12		10,867
45		30	A	Middlesbrough	L	1-2	0-1	16	Taylor	23,903
46	May	7	H	Stoke C	L	2-3	1-0	16	Harvey, Waddock	8252

Final League Position: 16

GOALSCORERS

League (61): Marshall 11, Oakes 9 (1 pen), Telfer 9, Dixon 7, Hartson 5, Preece 4, James 3, Taylor 3, Hughes 2, Biggins 1, Harvey 1, Johnson 1 (pen), Waddock 1, own goals 4.
Coca-Cola Cup (2): Marshall 1, Oakes 1.
FA Cup (3): Biggins 1, Hartson 1, Marshall 1.

Sommer J.P. 37	James J.C. 42	Johnson M.A. 46	Skelton A.M. 3 + 2	Greene D.M. 7 + 1	Peake T. 46	Telfer P.N. 45 + 1	Oakes S.J. 37 + 6	Dixon K.M. 23 + 6	Preece D.W. 42	Houghton S.A. 1	Linton D.M. 5 + 5	Marshall D.W. 36 + 9	Hughes C.M. 8 + 1	Hartson J. 11 + 9	Thomas M.A. 33 + 3	Woodsford J.M. 1 + 6	Waddock G.P. 40	Thorpe A. — + 4	Allen P.K. 4	Williams M.K. — + 2	Adcock A.C. — + 2	Harvey R.G. 9 + 3	Biggins W. 6 + 1	Matthews R. 6 + 5	Davis K.G. 9	Taylor J.P. 9	*Match No.*
1	2	3	4	5	6	7	8	9	10	*11*	12	14															1
1	2	3		5	6	7		9	10		4	8	11														2
1	2	3		5	6	7	8	12	10			*11*	4	9	14												3
1	2	3	4	5	6	7	8		10			12	11	9													4
1	2	3	4	5	6	7	11	9	*10*			8			12	14											5
1	2	3		*5*	6	7	11	12	10			8		9	14		4										6
1	2	3			6	7	8	9	10		12	14		*11*	5		4										7
1	2	3			6	7	8	9	10			11			5		4										8
1	2	3			6	7	8	9	10			11		12	5		4										9
1	2	3			6	7	8	9	10			11	14	12	*5*		4										10
1	2	3			6	7	12		10			11	8	9	5		4										11
1	2	3			6	7	12		10			11	8	9	5		4										12
1	2	3			6	7	12	9	10			11	8		5		4										13
1	2	3			6	7	12	14	10			11	8	9	5		*4*										14
1	2	3			6	7	12		10			11	8	9	5		4										15
1	2	3			6	7	8	9	10			11		12	5		4										16
1	2	3			6	7	8	9	10			11		12	5		4										17
1	2	3			6	7	8	9	10			11			5		4	12									18
1	2	3			6	7	8	9	10		11			12	5		4										19
1	2	3			6	7	8	9	10		*11*	12		14	5		4										20
1	2	3			6	7	8	9	10			14		12	5		4		*11*								21
1	2	3			6	7	8	9	10			11		12	5				4								22
1	2	3			6	7	12	*9*	10			11		14	5		4		8								23
1	2	3	12		6	7	8		10			*11*		9	5		4			14							24
1	2	3			6	7	8		10			11		9	5		4				12						25
1	2	3			6	7	8					11		9	5		4		10		12						26
1	2	3	12		6	7	8	9				11			5		4					10					27
1	2	3			6	7	8	9				11			5		4	12					10				28
1	2	3			6	12	8	*9*	7			11			5	14	4						10				29
1	2	3			6	7	8	12	10			*11*			5	14	4						9				30
1	2	3			6	7	*8*	9	10			11			5	12	4					14					31
1	2	3			6	7	8	9	10			11			5		4			12							32
1	2	3			6	7	8	12	10			11			5		*4*						9	14			33
1	2	3			6	7	8	12	10			11			5		*4*						9	14			34
1	2	3			6	7	8	9				11			5		4						12	10			35
1	2	3			6	7	8		10			11			5		4						9	12			36
1	2	3			6	7		9	10			11			*5*	12	4					14		8			37
	2	3			6	7			10			11					4	12				5		8	1	9	38
	2	3			6	7	8		10			11				12	4					5			1	9	39
	2	3			6	7	8		10		12	*11*					4					5		14	1	9	40
	2	3			6	7	8		10		12	14					4					5		11	1	9	41
		3		12	6	7	8		10		2	14					4					5		*11*	1	9	42
	2	3			6	7	8		10		12	11					*4*					5		14	1	9	43
		3		2	6	7	8		10			12			5		4					14		*11*	1	9	44
		3			6	7	8		10		2	11					4	12				5			1	9	45
		2			6	7	8		10			12			5	11	4					3			1	9	46

Coca-Cola Cup

First Round	Fulham (h)		1-1
		(a)	1-1

FA Cup

Third Round	Bristol R (h)		1-1
		(a)	1-0
Fourth Round	Southampton (h)		1-1
		(a)	0-6

MANCHESTER CITY 1994–95 *Back row (left to right):* Nick Summerbee, Ian Brightwell, Rae Ingram, Adie Mike, Andy Hill, Alan Kernaghan, David Kerr, Mike Sheron, Alphonse Groenendijk, Garry Flitcroft.
Centre row: Les Chapman (Reserve Team Manager), David Moss (Assistant Manager), Paul Lake, Steve Lomas, Michael Vonk, Martyn Margetson, Tony Coton, Andy Dibble, David Brightwell, Niall Quinn, Uwe Rosler, Eamonn Salmon (Physio), Tony Book (Reserve Team Coach).
Front row: Peter Beagrie, Michael Quigley, Carl Griffiths, Richard Edghill, Steve McMahon, Brian Horton (Manager), Keith Curle, Fitzroy Simpson, Jonathan Foster, Terry Phelan, Paul Walsh.

FA Premiership MANCHESTER CITY

Maine Road, Moss Side, Manchester M14 7WN. Telephone: (0161) 226 1191/2. Fax: (0161) 227 9418. Ticket Office: (0161) 226 2224. Dial-A-Seat: (0161) 227 9229. Development Office: (0161) 226 3143. Clubcall: 0891 121191. Ticketcall: 0891 121591.

Ground capacity: 28,053.

Record attendance: 84,569 v Stoke C, FA Cup 6th rd, 3 March 1934 (British record for any game outside London or Glasgow).

Record receipts: £512,235 Manchester U v Oldham Ath, FA Cup semi-final replay, 13 April 1994.

Pitch measurements: 117yd × 78yd.

Chairman: F. H. Lee. ***Vice-Chairman:*** F. Pye. ***Managing Director:*** C. J. Barlow.

Directors: I. L. G. Niven, A. Thomas, J. G. Dunkerley, W. A. Miles, G. Doyle, B. Turnbull, J. Greibach, D. A. Holt, A. M. Lewis, G. J. Grant, B. Jervis.

General Secretary: J. B. Halford. ***Commercial Manager:*** G. Durbin.

Manager: Alan Ball. ***Assistant Manager:***Asa Hartford. ***First Team Coach:*** Tony Book. ***Physio:*** Eamonn Salmon. ***Youth Team Coach:*** Neil McNab.

Year Formed: 1887 as Ardwick FC; 1894 as Manchester City.

Turned Professional: 1887 as Ardwick FC. ***Ltd Co.:*** 1894. ***Club Nickname:*** Blues The Citizens.

Previous Names: 1887–94, Ardwick FC (formed through the amalgamation of West Gorton and Gorton Athletic, the latter having been formed in 1880).

Previous Grounds: 1880–81, Clowes Street; 1881–82, Kirkmanshulme Cricket Ground; 1882–84, Queens Road; 1884–87, Pink Bank Lane; 1887–1923, Hyde Road (1894–1923, as City); 1923, Maine Road.

Foundation: Manchester City was formed as a Limited Company in 1894 after their predecessors Ardwick had been forced into bankruptcy. However, many historians like to trace the club's lineage as far back as 1880 when St. Mark's Church, West Gorton added a football section to their cricket club. They amalgamated with Gorton Athletic in 1884 as Gorton FC. Because of a change of ground they became Ardwick in 1887.

First Football League game: 3 September, 1892, Division 2, v Bootle (h) W 7-0 – Douglas; McVickers, Robson; Middleton, Russell, Hopkins; Davies (3), Morris (2), Angus (1), Weir (1), Milarvie.

Record League Victory: 10–1 Huddersfield T, Division 2, 7 November 1987 – Nixon; Gidman, Hinchcliffe, Clements, Lake, Redmond, White (3), Stewart (3), Adcock (3), McNab (1) Simpson.

Record Cup Victory: 10–1 v Swindon T, FA Cup, 4th rd, 29 January 1930 – Barber; Felton, McCloy; Barrass, Cowan, Heinemann; Toseland, Marshall (5), Tait (3), Johnson (1), Brook (1).

Record Defeat: 1–9 v Everton, Division 1, 3 September 1906.

Most League Points (2 for a win): 62, Division 2, 1946–47.

Most League Points (3 for a win): 82, Division 2, 1988–89.

Most League Goals: 108, Division 2, 1926–27.

Highest League Scorer in Season: Tommy Johnson, 38, Division 1, 1928–29.

Most League Goals in Total Aggregate: Tommy Johnson, 158, 1919–30.

Most Capped Player: Colin Bell, 48, England.

Most League Appearances: Alan Oakes, 565, 1959–76.

Record Transfer Fee Received: £1,700,000 from Tottenham H for Paul Stewart, June 1988.

Record Transfer Fee Paid: £2,500,000 to Wimbledon for Keith Curle, August 1991.

Football League Record: 1892 Ardwick elected founder member of Division 2; 1894 Newly-formed Manchester C elected to Division 2; Division 1 1899–1902, 1903–09, 1910–26, 1928–38, 1947–50, 1951–63, 1966–83, 1985–87, 1989–92; Division 2 1902–03, 1909–10, 1926–28, 1938–47, 1950–51, 1963–66, 1983–85, 1987–89; 1992– FA Premier League.

Honours: *Football League:* Division 1 – Champions 1936–37, 1967–68; Runners-up 1903–04, 1920–21, 1976–77; Division 2 – Champions 1898–99, 1902–03, 1909–10, 1927–28, 1946–47, 1965–66; Runners-up 1895–96, 1950–51, 1987–88. *FA Cup:* Winners 1904, 1934, 1956, 1969; Runners-up 1926, 1933, 1955, 1981. *Football League Cup:* Winners 1970, 1976; Runners-up 1974. **European Competitions:** *European Cup:* 1968–69. *European Cup-Winners' Cup:* 1969–70 (winners), 1970–71. *UEFA Cup:* 1972–73, 1976–77, 1977–78, 1978–79.

Colours: Sky blue shirts, white shorts, white stockings. **Change colours:** Red and black striped shirts, black shorts, black stockings with white top.

MANCHESTER CITY 1994–95 LEAGUE RECORD

Match No.	Date	Venue	Opponents	Result		H/T Score	Lg. Pos.	Goalscorers	Attendance
1	Aug 20	A	Arsenal	L	0-3	0-2	—		38,368
2	24	H	West Ham U	W	3-0	2-0	—	Walsh, Beagrie, Rosler	19,150
3	27	H	Everton	W	4-0	0-0	6	Rosler 2, Walsh 2	19,867
4	31	A	Chelsea	L	0-3	0-1	—		21,740
5	Sept 10	H	Crystal Palace	D	1-1	1-1	10	Walsh	19,971
6	17	A	Sheffield W	D	1-1	1-0	10	Walsh	26,585
7	24	H	Norwich C	W	2-0	0-0	7	Quinn, Rosler	21,031
8	Oct 1	A	Leeds U	L	0-2	0-1	11		30,938
9	8	H	Nottingham F	D	3-3	1-1	11	Quinn 2, Lomas	23,150
10	15	A	QPR	W	2-1	0-0	8	Flitcroft, Walsh	13,631
11	22	H	Tottenham H	W	5-2	3-1	8	Walsh 2, Quinn, Lomas, Flitcroft	25,473
12	29	A	Coventry C	L	0-1	0-0	9		15,802
13	Nov 5	H	Southampton	D	3-3	0-1	9	Walsh 2, Beagrie	21,589
14	10	A	Manchester U	L	0-5	0-2	—		43,738
15	20	A	Leicester C	W	1-0	1-0	8	Quinn	19,006
16	26	H	Wimbledon	W	2-0	1-0	7	Flitcroft, Rosler	21,131
17	Dec 3	A	Ipswich T	W	2-1	2-0	6	Flitcroft, Rosler	13,754
18	12	H	Arsenal	L	1-2	0-2	—	Simpson	20,500
19	17	A	West Ham U	L	0-3	0-2	9		17,286
20	26	H	Blackburn R	L	1-3	1-2	10	Quinn	23,387
21	28	A	Liverpool	L	0-2	0-0	11		38,122
22	31	H	Aston Villa	D	2-2	1-0	11	Rosler 2	22,513
23	Jan 2	A	Newcastle U	D	0-0	0-0	11		34,437
24	14	H	Coventry C	D	0-0	0-0	11		20,232
25	25	H	Leicester C	L	0-1	0-0	—		21,007
26	Feb 4	A	Southampton	D	2-2	1-1	13	Kernaghan, Flitcroft	14,902
27	11	H	Manchester U	L	0-3	0-0	14		26,368
28	22	H	Ipswich T	W	2-0	0-0	—	Quinn, Rosler	21,430
29	25	H	Leeds U	D	0-0	0-0	15		22,892
30	Mar 4	A	Norwich C	D	1-1	0-0	15	Simpson	16,266
31	8	H	Chelsea	L	1-2	1-1	—	Gaudino	21,880
32	15	A	Everton	D	1-1	1-0	—	Gaudino	28,485
33	18	H	Sheffield W	W	3-2	1-2	12	Rosler 2, Walsh	23,355
34	21	A	Wimbledon	L	0-2	0-0	—		5268
35	Apr 1	A	Crystal Palace	L	1-2	0-1	16	Rosler	13,451
36	11	A	Tottenham H	L	1-2	0-0	—	Rosler	27,410
37	14	H	Liverpool	W	2-1	1-1	—	Summerbee, Gaudino	27,055
38	17	A	Blackburn R	W	3-2	1-2	12	Curle (pen), Rosler, Walsh	27,851
39	29	H	Newcastle U	D	0-0	0-0	13		27,389
40	May 3	A	Aston Villa	D	1-1	0-1	—	Rosler	30,133
41	6	A	Nottingham F	L	0-1	0-1	13		28,882
42	14	H	QPR	L	2-3	1-1	17	Quinn, Curle (pen)	27,850

Final League Position: 17

GOALSCORERS

League (53): Rosler 15, Walsh 12, Quinn 8, Flitcroft 5, Gaudino 3, Beagrie 2, Curle 2 (2 pens), Lomas 2, Simpson 2, Kernaghan 1, Summerbee 1.
Coca-Cola Cup (11): Quinn 2, Rosler 2, Summerbee 2, Walsh 2, Beagrie 1, Curle 1 (pen), Lomas 1.
FA Cup (9): Rosler 5, Beagrie 1, Brightwell D 1, Gaudino 1, Walsh 1.

Coton A.P. 22 + 1	Hill A.R. 10 + 3	Phelan T. 26 + 1	McMahon S. 6 + 1	Curle K. 31	Vonk M.C. 19 + 2	Summerbee N. 39 + 2	Walsh P.A. 39	Rosler U. 29 + 2	Flitcroft G.W. 37	Beagrie P.S. 33 + 4	Quinn N.J. 24 + 11	Brightwell I.R. 29 + 1	Lomas S.M. 18 + 2	Edghill R.A. 14	Griffiths C.B. — + 2	Mike A.R. 1 + 1	Dibble A. 14 + 1	Tracey S.P. 3	Brightwell D.J. 9	Kernaghan A.N. 18 + 4	Simpson F. 10 + 6	Kerr D.W. 2	Foster J.C. 9 + 2	Gaudino M. 17 + 3	Burridge J. 3 + 1	Thomas S.L. — + 2	Match No.
1	2	3	4	5	6	7	8	9	*10*	11	12	14															1
1		*3*	4	5	6	7	8	9	10	11	12	2	14														2
1			4	5	6	7	8	9	10	11	12	2	3														3
1			4	5	6	7	8	9	10	11	12	2	3														4
1		3	4	5	6	7	8		10	11	9	2															5
1	5		4		6	7	8	9		11	12	3	10	2													6
1	12	3		5		7	8	*9*	4	11	10	6	14	2													7
1	2	3	12		6	7			4	11	9	5	10		14	*8*											8
	5	3				7	8		4	11	9	6	10	2			1										9
15	12	3		5		7	8		4	11	9	6	10	2			1										10
		3		5		7	8		4	11	9	6	10	2			1										11
	2	3			6	7	8		4	11	9	5	10					1									12
	2	3			6	7	8		4	11	9	5	10			12		1									13
		3			6	7	8		4	11	9	5	10	2				1									14
	2			5		7	8	12	4	11	9	6	10				1		3								15
	2			5		7	8	12	4	11	9	6	10				1		3	14							16
				5		7	*8*	10	4	11	9	6		2			1		3	12	14						17
				5		7	8	10	4	*11*	9	6	3				1			12	14	2					18
					12	7	8	11	4		9	6	10				1		*3*	5		2	14				19
		12				7		10	4	11	9	6	3				1			5			2	8			20
		3			12	7	8	9	4	11		6	2				1			5				10			21
		3				7	8	9	4	11		6	10				1			5			2				22
		3			6	7	8	9	4	11			10				1			5	12		2				23
		3		5		2	8	9	10	11							1		6	4	12			7			24
				5	6	2	8	9	10	11	12	4					1		3					7			25
1				5	6	2	8	9	10	11		7					15		3	4				12			26
1				5		2	8	9	10	11	12	6							3	4				7			27
1		3		5		2	*8*	9	10	11	12	6								4	14			7			28
1	2	3		5	6	7					10	8								4	11			9			29
1	12	3		5	*6*	2	8				9	10			14					4	11			7			30
1		3		5		2	8	9		11	12	6								4	10			7			31
1		3		5	6		8	9		11	10	2									4		12	7			32
1		3		5	6	2	8	9	10	11											4			7			33
1		3		5	6	12	8	9	10	11	14										4		2	*7*			34
1				5	6	12	8	9	10	11									3	4			2	7			35
1	4	3		5		7	8	9	10		12			2									6	11			36
1		*3*		5		7	8	9	4	12	10			2						14			6	11			37
1				5		7	8	9	4	12	10			3						6	11		2				38
1		3		5		7	8	9	4	12	10			2						6	*11*			14	15		39
		3		5		7	8	*9*	4	12	10			2						6	11			14	1		40
				5		2	8		10	11	9			3						4	6			7	1	12	41
				5		7	*8*	9	4		10			2						6	12		3	11	1	14	42

Coca-Cola Cup

Second Round	Barnet (a)	0-1
	(h)	4-1
Third Round	QPR (a)	4-3
Fourth Round	Newcastle U (h)	1-1
	(a)	2-0
Fifth Round	Crystal Palace (a)	0-4

FA Cup

Third Round	Notts County (a)	2-2
	(h)	5-2
Fourth Round	Aston Villa (h)	1-0
Fifth Round	Newcastle U (a)	1-3

MANCHESTER UNITED 1994–95 *Back row (left to right):* Lee Sharpe, Eric Cantona, Peter Schmeichel, Gary Walsh, Gary Pallister, Dion Dublin. *Centre row:* Norman Davies (Kit Manager), Andrei Kanchelskis, Ryan Giggs, Chris Casper, Nicky Butt, David May, Roy Keane, David Fevre (Physio). *Front row:* Brian McClair, Mark Hughes, Steve Bruce, Alex Ferguson, Brian Kidd, Paul Ince, Denis Irwin, Paul Parker.

FA Premiership MANCHESTER UNITED

Old Trafford, Manchester M16 0RA. Telephone: (0161) 872 1661. Fax: (0161) 876 5502. Ticket and Match Information: (0161) 872 0199. Membership Enquiries: (0161) 872 5208. Souvenir shop: (0161) 872 3398.

Ground capacity: 30,000 (all-seater – at start of season due to re-development).

Record attendance: 76,962 Wolverhampton W v Grimsby T, FA Cup semi-final. 25 March 1939.

Club record: 70,504 v Aston Villa, Division 1, 27 December 1920.

Record receipts: £529,827.50 v Leeds U, FA Cup 5th rd, 19 February 1995.

Pitch measurements: 116yd × 76yd.

Chairman/Chief Executive: C. M. Edwards.

Directors: J. M. Edelson, Sir Bobby Charlton CBE, E. M. Watkins LL.M., R. L. Olive, R. P. Launders.

Manager: Alex Ferguson CBE. ***Assistant Manager:*** Brian Kidd.

Secretary: Kenneth Merrett. ***Commercial Manager:*** Danny McGregor.

Year Formed: 1878 as Newton Heath LYR; 1902, Manchester United.

Turned Professional: 1885. ***Ltd Co.:*** 1907.

Previous Name: Newton Heath, 1880–1902.

Club Nickname: 'Red Devils'.

Previous Grounds: 1880–93, North Road, Monsall Road; 1893, Bank Street; 1910, Old Trafford (played at Maine Road 1941–49).

Foundation: Manchester United was formed as comparatively recently as 1902 after their predecessors, Newton Heath, went bankrupt. However, it is usual to give the date of the club's foundation as 1878 when employees of the Lancashire and Yorkshire Railway Company formed Newton Heath L and YR. Cricket and Football Club. They won the Manchester Cup in 1886 and as Newton Heath FC were admitted to the Second Division in 1892.

First Football League game: 3 September, 1892, Division 1, v Blackburn R (a) L 3-4 – Warner; Clements, Brown; Perrins, Stewart, Erentz; Farman (1), Coupar (1), Donaldson (1), Carson, Mathieson.

Record League Victory (as Newton Heath): 10–1 v Wolverhampton W, Division 1, 15 October 1892 – Warner; Mitchell, Clements; Perrins, Stewart (3), Erentz; Farman (1), Hood (1), Donaldson (3), Carson (1), Hendry (1).

Record League Victory (as Manchester U): 9–0 v Ipswich T, FA Premiership, 4 March 1995 – Schmeichel; Keane (1) (Sharpe), Irwin, Bruce (Butt), Kanchelskis, Pallister, Cole (5), Ince (1), McClair, Hughes (2), Giggs.

Record Cup Victory: 10–0 v RSC Anderlecht, European Cup, Prel. rd (2nd leg), 26 September 1956 – Wood; Foulkes Byrne; Colman, Jones, Edwards; Berry (1), Whelan (2), Taylor (3), Viollet (4), Pegg.

Record Defeat: 0–7 v Blackburn R, Division 1, 10 April 1926 and v Aston Villa, Division 1, 27 December 1930 and v Wolverhampton W. Division 2, 26 December 1931.

Most League Points (2 for a win): 64, Division 1, 1956–57.

Most League Points (3 for a win): 92, FA Premier League, 1993–94.

Most League Goals: 103, Division 1, 1956–57 and 1958–59.

Highest League Scorer in Season: Dennis Viollet, 32, 1959–60.

Most League Goals in Total Aggregate: Bobby Charlton, 199, 1956–73.

Most Capped Player: Bobby Charlton, 106, England.

Most League Appearances: Bobby Charlton, 606, 1956–73.

Record Transfer Fee Received: £7,000,000 from Internazionale for Paul Ince, June 1995.

Record Transfer Fee Paid: £6,250,000 to Newcastle U for Andy Cole, January 1995.

Football League Record: 1892 Newton Heath elected to Division 1; 1894–1906 Division 2; 1906–22 Division 1; 1922–25 Division 2; 1925–31 Division 1; 1931–36 Division 2; 1936–37 Division 1; 1937–38 Division 2; 1938–74 Division 1; 1974–75 Division 2; 1975–92 Division 1; 1992– FA Premier League.

Honours: *FA Premier League:* – Champions 1992–93, 1993–94; Runners-up 1994–95. *Football League:* Division 1 – Champions 1907–8, 1910–11, 1951–52, 1955–56, 1956–57, 1964–65, 1966–67; Runners-up 1946–47, 1947–48, 1948–49, 1950–51, 1958–59, 1963–64, 1967–68, 1979–80, 1987–88, 1991–92. Division 2 – Champions 1935–36, 1974–75; Runners-up 1896–97, 1905–06, 1924–25, 1937–38. *FA Cup:* Winners 1909, 1948, 1963, 1977, 1983, 1985, 1990, 1994; Runners-up 1957, 1958, 1976, 1979, 1995. *Football League Cup:* Winners 1992, 1983 (Runners-up), 1991 (Runners-up), 1994 (Runners-up). **European Competitions:** *European Cup:* 1956–57 (s-f), 1957–58 (s-f), 1965–66 (s-f), 1967–68 (winners), 1968–69 (s-f), 1993–94, 1994–95. *European Cup-Winners' Cup:* 1963–64, 1977–78, 1983–84, 1990–91 (winners). 1991–92. *European Fairs Cup:* 1964–65. *UEFA Cup:* 1976–77, 1980–81, 1982–83, 1984–85, 1992–93. *World Club Championship:* 1968. *Super Cup:* 1991 (winners).

Colours: Red shirts, white shorts, black stockings. **Change colours:** Black shirts, black shorts, black stockings.

MANCHESTER UNITED 1994–95 LEAGUE RECORD

Match No.	*Date*	*Venue*	*Opponents*	*Result*	*H/T Score*	*Lg. Pos.*	*Goalscorers*	*Atten-dance*
1	Aug 20	H	QPR	W 2-0	0-0	—	Hughes, McClair	43,214
2	22	A	Nottingham F	D 1-1	1-1	—	Kanchelskis	22,072
3	27	A	Tottenham H	W 1-0	0-0	3	Bruce	24,502
4	31	H	Wimbledon	W 3-0	1-0	—	Cantona, McClair, Giggs	43,440
5	Sept 11	A	Leeds U	L 1-2	0-1	5	Cantona (pen)	39,120
6	17	H	Liverpool	W 2-0	0-0	4	Kanchelskis, McClair	43,740
7	24	A	Ipswich T	L 2-3	0-2	4	Cantona, Scholes	22,553
8	Oct 1	H	Everton	W 2-0	1-0	4	Kanchelskis, Sharpe	43,803
9	8	A	Sheffield W	L 0-1	0-1	5		32,616
10	15	H	West Ham U	W 1-0	1-0	4	Cantona	43,795
11	23	A	Blackburn R	W 4-2	1-1	3	Cantona (pen), Kanchelskis 2, Hughes	30,260
12	29	H	Newcastle U	W 2-0	1-0	3	Pallister, Gillespie	43,795
13	Nov 6	A	Aston Villa	W 2-1	1-1	3	Ince, Kanchelskis	32,136
14	10	H	Manchester C	W 5-0	2-0	—	Cantona, Kanchelskis 3, Hughes	43,738
15	19	H	Crystal Palace	W 3-0	2-0	1	Irwin, Cantona, Kanchelskis	43,788
16	26	A	Arsenal	D 0-0	0-0	2		38,301
17	Dec 3	H	Norwich C	W 1-0	1-0	2	Cantona	43,789
18	10	A	QPR	W 3-2	2-1	2	Scholes 2, Keane	18,948
19	17	H	Nottingham F	L 1-2	0-1	2	Cantona	43,744
20	26	A	Chelsea	W 3-2	1-0	2	Hughes, Cantona (pen), McClair	31,139
21	28	H	Leicester C	D 1-1	0-0	2	Kanchelskis	43,789
22	31	A	Southampton	D 2-2	0-1	2	Butt, Pallister	15,204
23	Jan 3	H	Coventry C	W 2-0	1-0	—	Scholes, Cantona (pen)	43,120
24	15	A	Newcastle U	D 1-1	1-0	2	Hughes	34,471
25	22	H	Blackburn R	W 1-0	0-0	2	Cantona	43,742
26	25	A	Crystal Palace	D 1-1	0-0	—	May	18,224
27	Feb 4	H	Aston Villa	W 1-0	1-0	2	Cole	43,795
28	11	A	Manchester C	W 3-0	0-0	2	Ince, Kanchelskis, Cole	26,368
29	22	A	Norwich C	W 2-0	2-0	—	Ince, Kanchelskis	21,824
30	25	A	Everton	L 0-1	0-0	2		40,011
31	Mar 4	H	Ipswich T	W 9-0	3-0	2	Keane, Cole 5, Hughes 2, Ince	43,804
32	7	A	Wimbledon	W 1-0	0-0	—	Bruce	18,224
33	15	H	Tottenham H	D 0-0	0-0	—		43,802
34	19	A	Liverpool	L 0-2	0-1	2		38,906
35	22	H	Arsenal	W 3-0	2-0	—	Hughes, Sharpe, Kanchelskis	43,623
36	Apr 2	H	Leeds U	D 0-0	0-0	2		43,712
37	15	A	Leicester C	W 4-0	2-0	2	Sharpe, Cole 2, Ince	21,281
38	17	H	Chelsea	D 0-0	0-0	2		43,728
39	May 1	A	Coventry C	W 3-2	1-1	—	Scholes, Cole 2	21,858
40	7	H	Sheffield W	W 1-0	1-0	2	May	43,868
41	10	H	Southampton	W 2-1	1-1	—	Cole, Irwin (pen)	43,479
42	14	A	West Ham U	D 1-1	0-1	2	McClair	24,783

Final League Position: 2

GOALSCORERS

League (77): Kanchelskis 14, Cantona 12 (4 pens), Cole 12, Hughes 8, Ince 5, McClair 5, Scholes 5, Sharpe 3, Bruce 2, Irwin 2 (1 pen), Keane 2, May 2, Pallister 2, Butt 1, Giggs 1, Gillespie 1.
Coca-Cola Cup (4): Scholes 2, McClair 1, May 1.
FA Cup (16): Irwin 4 (1 pen), Bruce 2, Hughes 2, McClair 2, Pallister 2, Cantona 1, Giggs 1, Sharpe 1, own goal 1.

Schmeichel P.B. 32	May D. 15 + 4	Irwin J.D. 40	Bruce S.R. 35	Sharpe L.S. 26 + 2	Pallister G.A. 42	Kanchelskis A. 25 + 5	Ince P.E.C. 36	McClair B.J. 35 + 5	Hughes L.M. 33 + 1	Giggs R.J. 29	Parker P.A. 1 + 1	Keane R.M. 23 + 2	Cantona E. 21	Walsh G. 10	Scholes P. 6 + 11	Butt N. 11 + 11	Gillespie K.R. 3 + 6	Davies S.I. 3 + 2	Pilkington K.W. — + 1	Neville G.A. 16 + 2	Cole A. 17 + 1	Neville P.J. 1 + 1	Beckham D.R.J. 2 + 2	*Match No.*
1	2	3	4	*5*	6	7	8	9	10	11	12	14												1
1	2	3	4	5	6	7	8	9	10	11		12												2
1	2	3	4	5	6	7	8	9	10	11														3
1	2	3	4	5	6	8		9	10	11			7											4
1	2	3	4	12	6	5	8	*9*	10	11			7			14								5
1	2	3	4	5	6	7	8	12	10	11			9											6
		2	4	3	6	7	8	*9*		11		5	10	1	12	14								7
1	2	3	4	5	6	11	8	12	10			9	7											8
1	12	3	4	5	6		8	9	10		2	7			14		*11*							9
1	2	3	4	5	6	7	8		10	11			9			12								10
1		3	4	5	6	7	8	12	10			2	9			11								11
1		3	4		6	5	8	9	10	11		2	7				12							12
		3	4		6	5	8	12		11		2	9	1	*7*	10	14							13
1		3	4		6	5	8	9	10	11		2	7		12									14
1	4	3			6	5	8	9	10				7		14		12	*11*	15	2				15
	4	3			6	5	8	9	10				7	1		12	*11*	14		2				16
	4	3			6	*5*	8	9	10				7	1		14	12	11		2				17
		3	4		6	7	8	9				5		1	10	14	12	*11*		2				18
		3	4		6	*5*	8	9	10	11		2	7	1		12				14				19
		3	4		6	12	*8*	9	10	11		2	7	1		5				14				20
		3	4		6	5		9	10	11		8	7	1	12					2				21
	2		4		6			9	10	11		5	7	1		8	12			3				22
		3	4		6			12		11		8	7	1	9	10	5			2				23
1	12	3	4	5	6			9	*10*	11		2	7		14	8								24
1		3	4	5	6	12	8	9		11		2	7								10			25
1	4	3		5	6	12	8	9		11		2	7								10			26
1	12	3	4	5	6	14	8	9		*11*					7					2	10			27
1	12	3	4	5	6	7	8	9		11					14						10	*2*		28
1			4	3	6	5	8	9	10	11		2									7			29
1		2	4	3	6	12	8	9	10	11		5									7			30
1		3	*4*	12	6	5	8	9	10	11		2				14					7			31
1		3	4	5	6		8	9	10	11										2	7			32
1		2	4	3	6	5	8	9	10	11						12					7			33
1		2	4	3	6	7	8	9	10	11		*5*				14					12			34
1		3	4	5	6	7	8		10	11		2									9			35
1		3			6		8	9	10	11		5								2	7		4	36
1		3	4	*5*	6		8	9	10						12	11				2	7		14	37
1		3	4		6		8	9	10						12	11		14		2	7		*5*	38
1	4	3		5	6			9	10						11	7				2	8		12	39
1	*4*	3		5	6		8	9	10						11	12				2	7	14		40
1		3	4	5	6		8	9	10						12	11				2	7			41
1		3	4	5	6		8	9	12			*10*			14	11				2	7			42

Coca-Cola Cup

Second Round	Port Vale (a)	2-1
	(h)	2-0
Third Round	Newcastle U (a)	0-2

FA Cup

Third Round	Sheffield U (a)	2-0
Fourth Round	Wrexham (h)	5-2
Fifth Round	Leeds U (h)	3-1
Sixth Round	QPR (h)	2-0
Semi-final	Crystal Palace at Villa Park	2-2
Replay at Villa Park		2-0
Final at Wembley	Everton	0-1

MANSFIELD TOWN 1994–95 *Back row (left to right):* Chris Timons, Stewart Hadley, Darren Ward, Paul Holland, Jason Pearcey, Simon Ireland, Lee Howarth.
Centre row: Chris Kerry, Kevin Noteman, Dean Marrows, Lee Wilkinson, Kevin Lampkin, Gary Castledine, Brendan Aspinall.
Front row: Steve Wilkinson, Ian Barraclough, Adey Boothroyd, Barry Statham (Physio), Andy King (Manager), Keith Alexander (Reserve and Youth Team Coach), Steve Parkin, Paul Fleming, Iffy Onoura.

Division 3 MANSFIELD TOWN

Field Mill Ground, Quarry Lane, Mansfield, NG18 5DA. Telephone: (01623) 23567. Fax: (01623) 25014. Marketing: (01623) 658070. Football in the Community: (01623) 25197.

Ground capacity: 7073.

Record attendance: 24,467 v Nottingham F, FA Cup 3rd rd, 10 January 1953.

Record receipts: £46,915 v Sheffield W, FA Cup 3rd rd, 5 January 1991.

Pitch measurements: 115yd × 70yd.

Chairman/Chief Executive: Keith Haslam.

Directors: K. Walker, Mrs M. Haslam. ***Associate Directors:*** T. Hewson, D. Wardman, K. Woodcock, S. Whetton.

Manager: Andy King.

Physio: Barry Statham.

Community Scheme Organiser: D. Bentley Tel: (01623) 25197.

Secretary: Mick Horton. ***Marketing Manager:*** L. Smith.

Year Formed: 1910. ***Turned Professional:*** 1910. ***Ltd Co.:*** 1921.

Previous Name: Mansfield Wesleyans 1891–1910.

Club Nickname: 'The Stags'.

Foundation: Many records give the date of Mansfield Town's formation as 1905. But the present club did not come into being until 1910 when the Mansfield Wesleyans (formed 1891) and playing in the Notts and District League, decided to spread their wings and changed their name to Mansfield Town, joining the new Central Alliance in 1911.

First Football League game: 29 August, 1931, Division 3(S), v Swindon T (h) W 3-2 – Wilson; Clifford, England; Wake, Davis, Blackburn; Gilhespy, Readman (1), Johnson, Broom (2), Baxter.

Record League Victory: 9–2 v Rotherham U, Division 3 (N), 27 December 1932 – Wilson; Anthony, England; Davies, S. Robinson, Slack; Prior, Broom, Readman (3), Hoyland (3), Bowater (3).

Record Cup Victory: 8–0 v Scarborough (away), FA Cup, 1st rd, 22 November 1952 – Bramley; Chessell, Bradley; Field, Plummer, Lewis; Scott, Fox (3), Marron (2), Sid Watson (1), Adam (2).

Record Defeat: 1–8 v Walsall, Division 3 (N), 19 January 1933.

Most League Points (2 for a win): 68, Division 4, 1974–75.

Most League Points (3 for a win): 81, Division 4, 1985–86.

Most League Goals: 108, Division 4, 1962–63.

Highest League Scorer in Season: Ted Harston, 55, Division 3 (N), 1936–37.

Most League Goals in Total Aggregate: Harry Johnson, 104, 1931–36.

Most Capped Player: John McClelland, 6 (53), Northern Ireland.

Most League Appearances: Rod Arnold, 440, 1970–83.

Record Transfer Fee Received: £500,000 from Middlesbrough for Simon Coleman, September 1989.

Record Transfer Fee Paid: £80,000 to Leicester C for Steve Wilkinson, September 1989.

Football League Record: 1931 Elected to Division 3 (S); 1932–37 Division 3 (N); 1937–47 Division 3 (S); 1947–58 Division 3 (N); 1958–60 Division 3; 1960–63 Division 4; 1963–72 Division 3; 1972–75 Division 4; 1975–77 Division 3; 1977–78 Division 2; 1978–80 Division 3; 1980–86 Division 4; 1986–91 Division 3; 1991–92 Division 4; 1992–93 Division 2; 1993– Division 3.

Honours: *Football League:* Division 2 best season: 21st, 1977–78; Division 3 – Champions 1976–77; Division 4 – Champions 1974–75; Division 3 (N) – Runners-up 1950–51. *FA Cup:* best season: 6th rd, 1969. *Football League Cup:* best season: 5th rd, 1976. *Freight Rover Trophy:* Winners 1987.

Colours: Amber and blue striped shirts, blue shorts, white stockings. **Change colours:** Green with purple trim shirts, green shorts, purple stockings.

MANSFIELD TOWN 1994–95 LEAGUE RECORD

Match No.	Date	Venue	Opponents	Result		H/T Score	Lg. Pos.	Goalscorers	Attendance
1	Aug 20	H	Colchester U	W	2-0	0-0	13	Holland, Hadley	2247
2	27	A	Chesterfield	W	1-0	0-0	8	Hadley	4210
3	30	H	Darlington	L	0-1	0-0	—		2427
4	Sept 3	H	Bury	L	0-2	0-1	15		2576
5	10	A	Lincoln C	L	2-3	1-1	15	Wilkinson, Noteman	2575
6	13	A	Carlisle U	L	1-2	0-0	—	Hadley	6136
7	17	H	Northampton T	D	1-1	0-0	19	Holland	2557
8	24	H	Exeter C	D	1-1	0-0	18	Howarth	2468
9	Oct 1	A	Gillingham	W	2-0	1-0	15	Holland, Wilkinson	2555
10	8	H	Hartlepool U	W	2-0	1-0	13	Holland, Wilkinson	2545
11	11	A	Northampton T	W	1-0	1-0	—	Wilkinson	4993
12	15	A	Torquay U	L	1-2	1-1	10	Peters	2800
13	22	H	Doncaster R	L	0-1	0-0	14		2988
14	29	A	Rochdale	D	3-3	2-1	12	Hadley, Noteman (pen), Wilkinson	1968
15	Nov 5	H	Preston NE	L	1-2	1-2	14	Hadley	2602
16	19	A	Scunthorpe U	W	4-3	0-1	11	Holland, Hadley, Noteman, Peters	2975
17	26	H	Walsall	L	1-3	0-2	13	Wilkinson	2733
18	Dec 10	A	Colchester U	D	1-1	0-1	14	Wilkinson	3016
19	18	H	Chesterfield	W	4-2	2-0	11	Campbell, Wilkinson 3	3519
20	26	H	Hereford U	W	7-1	1-0	10	Donaldson 2, Baraclough, Hadley, Howarth, Ireland, Wilkinson	2887
21	27	A	Scarborough	W	5-2	2-1	8	Donaldson 2, Baraclough, Wilkinson, Noteman	1926
22	31	H	Barnet	W	3-0	1-0	8	Donaldson 2, Ireland	2891
23	Jan 2	A	Fulham	L	2-4	1-1	8	Baraclough, Hadley	4091
24	10	A	Doncaster R	W	2-0	0-0	—	Hadley 2	2577
25	14	H	Wigan Ath	W	4-3	1-0	5	Holland, Peters, Wilkinson, Doolan	2618
26	21	A	Preston NE	L	1-2	1-1	5	Lampkin	8448
27	Feb 4	A	Walsall	L	0-1	0-0	8		4369
28	18	A	Wigan Ath	W	4-0	2-0	7	Holland 2, Hadley 2	1884
29	21	H	Scunthorpe U	W	1-0	0-0	—	Wilkinson	3079
30	25	H	Gillingham	W	4-0	1-0	3	Holland, Ireland, Parkin, Wilkinson	3182
31	Mar 4	A	Exeter C	W	3-2	1-1	4	Wilkinson 2, Onuora	2458
32	7	H	Rochdale	D	1-1	0-1	—	Wilkinson	2931
33	11	H	Lincoln C	W	6-2	1-0	3	Noteman 2 (1 pen), Hadley, Onuora 3	3396
34	18	A	Darlington	D	0-0	0-0	4		1613
35	25	A	Bury	D	2-2	0-1	5	Onuora, Wilkinson	4188
36	Apr 1	H	Carlisle U	L	1-2	1-1	5	Lampkin	5197
37	8	A	Barnet	D	2-2	1-1	5	Wilkinson, Phillips (og)	2115
38	15	H	Scarborough	W	3-2	2-2	5	Ireland, Wilkinson, Hadley	2931
39	17	A	Hereford U	D	0-0	0-0	6		2743
40	22	H	Fulham	D	1-1	1-0	5	Peters	2861
41	29	H	Torquay U	D	2-2	1-1	6	Onuora, Wilkinson	3216
42	May 6	A	Hartlepool U	L	2-3	0-1	6	Ireland, Onuora	3049

Final League Position: 6

GOALSCORERS

League (84): Wilkinson 22, Hadley 14, Holland 9, Onuora 7, Donaldson 6, Noteman 6 (2 pens), Ireland 5, Peters 4, Baraclough 3, Howarth 2, Lampkin 2, Campbell 1, Doolan 1, Parkin 1, own goal 1.
Coca-Cola Cup (4): Wilkinson 3, Ireland 1.
FA Cup (7): Holland 3, Aspinall 1, Donaldson 1, Hadley 1, Ireland 1.

Ward D. 35	Boothroyd A.N. 35 + 1	Baraclough I.R. 36	Holland P. 33	Howarth L. 39 + 1	Aspinall B.J. 13 + 7	Ireland S.P. 38 + 2	Parkin S.J. 22	Wilkinson S.J. 41	Hadley S. 28 + 11	Fleming P. 2	Noteman K.S. 27 + 5	Timons C. 4 + 2	Castledine G.J. 3 + 7	Alexander K. — + 2	Doolan J. 21 + 3	Frain D. 4 + 2	Peters M. 25 + 1	Hoyle C.R. 4 + 1	Pearcey J.K. 3	Trinder J.L. 4 + 3	Campbell J. 3	Pearson J.S. — + 2	Donaldson O.M. 4	Lampkin K. 22 + 1	Elad E. — + 2	Onuora I. 10 + 4	Walker R.N. 4	Sherlock P.G. 1 + 1	Clifford M.R. 1	Williams M.J. — + 1	Match No.
1	2	3	4	5	6	7	8	9	10	11	12																				1
1	2		4	5	6	7	8	9	10	3	11	12																			2
1	2		4	5	6	7	8	9	10		11	3	12	14																	3
1	2		4	5	6	7	8	9	10		*11*		12		3	14															4
1	3		4	5	6	7	8	9	10		12				2	11															5
1	2	3	4	5	6	7		9	12		*11*		14		8	10															6
1	2	3	4	5	6	7		9	10		11				8	12															7
1	2	3	4	5	6	7		9	10		11		12			8															8
1	2	3	4	5		7		9	10		11					8	6														9
1	2	3	4	5		7		9			11				10		6	8													10
	2	3	4	5		7		9	12		11	14			10		6	8	1												11
	2	3		5	12	7		9	8		11		4		10		6		1												12
	2	3	4	5		7		9	12		11		*8*		10		6	14	1												13
1	2	3	4	5		7		9	8		11		12		10		6														14
1	2	3	4	5				9	10		11		7				6	8													15
1		3	4	5	12	7	8	9	10		11						6	2		15											16
1	2	3	4	5		12		9	10		*11*	6			8						7	14									17
1	2	3	4		6	7		9			*11*	5	12		8					15	10	14									18
1	2	3	4		5	7		9			11			12	10		6				8										19
1	2	3		5	12	7		9	10		11						6			15			8	4							20
	2	3		5	6	7		9	10		11									1			8	4							21
	2	3	4	5	12	7		9	10		11		14							1			8	*6*							22
	2	3	4	5	12	7		9	10		*11*						14			1			8	6							23
1	2	3	4	5		7	8	9	10						12		6							11							24
1	2		4	5	12	7		9	10		11				3		6							8							25
1	2	3	4	5	12	7		9	10		14				*11*		6							8							26
1	2	3	4	5		7	8	9	10								6							11	12						27
1		3	4	5	2	7	8	9	10								6							11	12	14					28
1		3	4	5		7	8	9	10						2		6							11							29
1		3	4	5		7	8	9	*10*		12				2		6							11		14					30
1		3	4	5		7	8	9	*10*		12				2		6							11		14					31
1	12	3	4	5		7	8	9	*10*						2		6							11		14					32
1	2	3		5		7	*8*	9	12		11				14		6							4		10					33
1	2	3		5			8	9	11						7		6							4		10					34
1	2	3		5		7	8	9	12		11													4		10	6				35
1	2	3		5		12	8	9	14		11				*7*									4		10	6				36
1	2	3	*4*	5		7	8	9	12						14									11		10	6				37
1	2	11	4	5		7	8	9	12								6							14		10	*3*				38
1	2	3		5		7	8	9	12		11						6							4		10					39
1	2	3	4	5		7	8	9	12								6							11		10					40
1	2	3	4	5		7	8	9	12								6							*11*		10		14			41
				12	6	7			9		11	5			3					1				4		10		8	*2*	14	42

Coca-Cola Cup

First Round	Rochdale (a)	2-1
	(h)	1-0
Second Round	Leeds U (a)	1-0
	(h)	0-0
Third Round	Millwall (h)	0-2

FA Cup

First Round	Northwich V (h)	3-1
Second Round	Halifax T (a)	0-0
	(h)	2-1
Third Round	Wolverhampton W (h)	2-3

MIDDLESBROUGH 1994–95 *Back row (left to right):* Andy Todd, Jamie Pollock, Derek Whyte, Steve Vickers, Nigel Pearson, Paul Wilkinson, Robbie Mustoe.
Centre row: Chris Morris, Curtis Fleming, Michael Barron, Ben Roberts, Steve Pears, Andy Collett, Craig Hignett, Graham Kavanagh, Alan Moore.
Front row: Mark Nile (Senior Physio), John Hendrie, Neil Cox, Bryan Robson (Player-Manager), John Pickering (First Team Coach), Viv Anderson (Assistant Manager), Clayton Blackmore, Tommy Wright, Tommy Johnson (Physio).

FA Premiership **MIDDLESBROUGH**

Cellnet Riverside Stadium, Middlesbrough, Cleveland TS3 6RS. Telephone: (01642) 227227. Fax: (01642) 252532. Boro Livewire: 0891 424200.

Ground capacity: 30,000.

Record attendance: 53,596 v Newcastle U, Division 1, 27 December 1949.

Record receipts: £200,351 v Newcastle U, Coca Cola Cup 2nd rd 2nd leg, 7 October 1992.

Pitch measurements: 115yd × 75yd.

Chairman: S. Gibson.

Directors: G. Cooke, R. Corbidge, G. Fordy.

Chief Executive/Secretary: Keith Lamb.

Manager: Bryan Robson. ***Assistant Manager:*** Viv Anderson.

Physio: Bob Ward. ***Coach:*** John Pickering. ***Commercial Director:*** Graham Fordy.

Youth Development Officer: Ron Bone.

Year Formed: 1876. ***Turned Professional:*** 1889; became amateur 1892, and professional again, 1899. ***Ltd Co:*** 1892.

Club Nickname: 'Boro'.

Previous Grounds: 1877, Old Archery Ground, Albert Park; 1879, Breckon Hill; 1882, Linthorpe Road Ground; 1903, Ayresome Park; 1995, Cellnet Riverside Stadium.

Foundation: A previous belief that Middlesbrough Football Club was founded at a tripe supper at the Corporation Hotel has proved to be eroneous. In fact, members of Middlesbrough Cricket Club were responsible for forming it at a meeting in the gymnasium of the Albert Park Hotel in 1875.

First Football League game: 2 September, 1899, Division 2, v Lincoln C (a) L 0-3 – Smith; Shaw, Ramsey; Allport, McNally, McCracken; Wanless, Longstaffe, Gettins, Page, Pugh.

Record League Victory: 9–0 v Brighton & HA, Division 2, 23 August 1958 – Taylor; Bilcliff, Robinson; Harris (2 pens), Phillips, Walley; Day, McLean, Clough (5), Peacock (2), Holliday.

Record Cup Victory: 9–3 v Goole T, FA Cup, 1st rd, 9 January 1915 – Williamson; Haworth, Weir; Davidson, Cook, Malcolm; Wilson, Carr (3), Elliott (3), Tinsley (3), Davies.

Record Defeat: 0–9 v Blackburn R, Division 2, 6 November 1954.

Most League Points (2 for a win): 65, Division 2, 1973–74.

Most League Points (3 for a win): 94, Division 3, 1986–87.

Most League Goals: 122, Division 2, 1926–27.

Highest League Scorer in Season: George Camsell, 59, Division 2, 1926–27 (Second Division record).

Most League Goals in Total Aggregate: George Camsell, 326, 1925–39.

Most Capped Player: Wilf Mannion, 26, England.

Most League Appearances: Tim Williamson, 563, 1902–23.

Record Transfer Fee Received: £2,300,000 from Manchester United for Gary Pallister, August 1989.

Record Transfer Fee Paid: £1,300,000 to Swindon T for Jan-Aage Fjortoft, March 1995.

Football League Record: 1899 Elected to Division 2; 1902–24 Division 1; 1924–27 Division 2; 1927–28 Division 1; 1928–29 Division 2; 1929–54 Division 1; 1954–66 Division 2; 1966–67 Division 3; 1967–74 Division 2; 1974–82 Division 1; 1982–86 Division 2; 1986–87 Division 3; 1987–88 Division 2; 1988–89 Division 1; 1989–92 Division 2; 1992–93 FA Premier League; 1993–95 Division 1; 1995– FA Premier League.

Honours: *Football League:* Division 1 – Champions 1994–95. Division 2 – Champions 1926–27, 1928–29, 1973–74; Runners-up 1901–02, 1991–92. Division 3 – Runners-up 1966–67, 1986–87. *FA Cup:* best season: 6th rd, 1936, 1947, 1970, 1975, 1977, 1978; old last eight 1901, 1904. *Football League Cup:* Semi-final 1976. *Amateur Cup:* Winners 1895, 1898, *Anglo-Scottish Cup:* Winners 1976.

Colours: Red and white. **Change colours:** Royal blue and black.

MIDDLESBROUGH 1994–95 LEAGUE RECORD

Match No.	Date	Venue	Opponents	Result	H/T Score	Lg. Pos.	Goalscorers	Attendance
1	Aug 13	H	Burnley	W 2-0	2-0	—	Hendrie 2	23,343
2	20	A	Southend U	W 2-0	1-0	1	Hendrie 2	5722
3	27	H	Bolton W	W 1-0	1-0	1	Wilkinson	19,570
4	31	A	Derby Co	W 1-0	1-0	—	Blackmore	14,659
5	Sept 3	A	Watford	D 1-1	1-0	1	Blackmore	9478
6	11	H	Sunderland	D 2-2	0-1	1	Moore, Pearson	19,578
7	14	H	WBA	W 2-1	1-1	—	Mustoe, Hignett (pen)	14,878
8	17	A	Port Vale	L 1-2	1-0	2	Pollock	10,313
9	25	A	Bristol C	W 1-0	0-0	2	Hendrie	8642
10	Oct 1	H	Millwall	W 3-0	0-0	2	Hendrie, Wilkinson, Beard (og)	17,229
11	8	H	Tranmere R	L 0-1	0-0	2		18,497
12	15	A	Luton T	L 1-5	0-3	4	Whyte	8412
13	23	A	Portsmouth	D 0-0	0-0	3		7281
14	29	H	Swindon T	W 3-1	1-0	2	Cox, Hendrie, Wilkinson (pen)	17,328
15	Nov 1	H	Oldham Ath	W 2-1	0-1	—	Moore, Hignett	15,929
16	5	A	Grimsby T	L 1-2	0-2	2	Hignett (pen)	8488
17	20	H	Wolverhampton W	W 1-0	0-0	1	Hendrie	19,953
18	26	A	Charlton Ath	W 2-0	1-0	1	Hendrie, Pollock	10,019
19	Dec 3	H	Portsmouth	W 4-0	2-0	1	Wilkinson 2, Hignett 2	17,185
20	6	A	Reading	D 1-1	0-0	—	Wilkinson (pen)	10,301
21	10	H	Southend U	L 1-2	0-1	1	Hendrie	16,843
22	18	A	Burnley	W 3-0	1-0	1	Hendrie 3	12,049
23	26	A	Sheffield U	D 1-1	0-0	1	Hignett	20,693
24	28	H	Notts Co	W 2-1	2-1	—	Hignett, Pearson	21,558
25	31	A	Stoke C	D 1-1	1-1	1	Vickers	15,914
26	Jan 15	A	Swindon T	L 1-2	1-1	1	Hignett	8888
27	21	H	Grimsby T	D 1-1	0-0	1	Mustoe	15,360
28	Feb 4	H	Reading	L 0-1	0-0	3		17,982
29	18	H	Charlton Ath	W 1-0	1-0	3	Fuchs	16,301
30	21	A	Wolverhampton W	W 2-0	0-0	—	Vickers, Fuchs	27,611
31	26	A	Millwall	D 0-0	0-0	2		7247
32	Mar 4	H	Bristol C	W 3-0	1-0	2	Fuchs 3	17,371
33	7	H	Watford	W 2-0	1-0	—	Mustoe, Fuchs	16,630
34	11	A	Bolton W	L 0-1	0-1	2		18,370
35	14	H	Barnsley	D 1-1	1-0	—	Moreno	19,655
36	18	H	Derby Co	L 2-4	0-3	3	Fuchs, Pollock	18,168
37	21	A	Sunderland	W 1-0	0-0	—	Pollock	16,501
38	26	H	Port Vale	W 3-0	2-0	1	Fuchs, Robson, Vickers	17,401
39	Apr 1	A	WBA	W 3-1	0-1	1	Pollock, Raven (og), Moore	20,256
40	5	A	Oldham Ath	L 0-1	0-0	—		11,024
41	8	H	Stoke C	W 2-1	1-1	1	Pearson, Moore	20,867
42	15	A	Notts Co	D 1-1	0-0	1	Fuchs	9377
43	17	H	Sheffield U	D 1-1	1-1	1	Fjortoft	23,225
44	22	A	Barnsley	D 1-1	1-0	1	Fjortoft	11,711
45	30	H	Luton T	W 2-1	1-0	1	Hendrie 2	23,903
46	May 7	A	Tranmere R	D 1-1	0-1	1	Fjortoft	16,377

Final League Position: 1

GOALSCORERS

League (67): Hendrie 15, Fuchs 9, Hignett 8 (2 pens), Wilkinson 6 (2 pens), Pollock 5, Moore 4, Fjortoft 3, Mustoe 3, Pearson 3, Vickers 3, Blackmore 2, Cox 1, Moreno 1, Robson 1, Whyte 1, own goals 2.
Coca-Cola Cup (8): Wilkinson 3, Hendrie 1, Hignett 1, Moore 1, Mustoe 1, Pollock 1.
FA Cup (2): Hendrie 1, Moore 1.

Miller A.J. 41	Cox N.J. 39 + 1	Fleming C. 21	Vickers S. 44	Pearson N.G. 33	Blackmore C.G. 26 + 4	Robson B. 21 + 1	Pollock J. 41	Wilkinson P. 27 + 4	Hendrie J.G. 37 + 2	Moore A. 35 + 2	Mustoe R. 24 + 3	Whyte D. 36	Hignett C. 19 + 7	Pears S. 5	Moreno J. 6 + 8	Kavanagh G.A. 5 + 2	Wright T.E. 1	Todd A.J.J. 5	Morris C.B. 14 + 1	Fuchs U. 13 + 2	Stamp P.L. 1 + 2	O'Halloran K. 1	Anderson V.A. 2	Fjortoft J.A. 8	Freestone C.M. — + 1	Liddle C. 1	Match No.
1	2	3	4	5	6	7	8	9	10	11																	1
1	2	3	4	5	6	7	8	9	10	11																	2
1	2	3	4	5	6	7	8	9	10	11	12																3
1	2	3	4	5	6	7	8	9	10	11	12																4
1	2	3		5	6	7	8	9	10	11		4															5
1	2	3	4	5	6	7	8	9	10	11			12														6
1	2	3	4	5	14	7	8	9	10	11	12		6														7
	2	3	4				8	9	10	11	7	5	6	1													8
	2	3	4				8	9	10	11	7	5	6	1													9
	2	3	4		6		8	9	10		7	5	11	1	12												10
	2	3	4		6		8	9	10		7	5	11	1	12												11
	2	3	4		6		8	9	10			5	7	1		12	11										12
1	2	3	4		6		8	9	10			5	12		11			7									13
1	2	3	4		6		8	9	10	11		5	12					7									14
1	2	3	4		6		8	9	10	11		5	12					7									15
1	2		4		3		8	9	10	11		5	7					6									16
1	2		4		12		8	9	10	11	6	5	7						3								17
1	2		4	6			8	9	10		7	5	11						3								18
1	2		4				8	9	10	11	6	5	7		12				3								19
1	2		4	6			8	9	10	12	11	5	7						3								20
1	7		4	5	12			9	10	11	6	3			14			8	2								21
1	2	3	4	6		7		9	10	11	8	5															22
1	2	3	4	6		7		9	10	11		5	12			8											23
1	2	3		6			8	9	10	11	4	5	7						12								24
1		3	4	5		7	8	9	10		6		11						2								25
1		3	4	5			8		10	11	7	6	9			12			2								26
1		3	4	5	7		8	9	10	12	6		11						2								27
1			4	5		12	8	9	10	11	6	3	7						2	14							28
1			4	5	6	7	8			11	10	3							2	9							29
1			4	5	6	7	8			11	10	3							2	9							30
1	14		4	5	6	7	8	12		11	10	3							2	9							31
1	2		4	5	6	7		12		11	10	3	14		8					9							32
1	2		4	5	6		7			11	10	3			8					9							33
1	2		4	5	6	7	8		11		10	3			14					9	12						34
1	2		4	5			8	12	14	11	6	3	7		10					9							35
1	2		4	5		7	8		10	11	6				12					9		3					36
1	2		4	5		7	8		10	11	6	3								9							37
1	2		4	5	6	7	8		10	11		3			12					9							38
1	2		4		6	7	8			11		3								9			5	10			39
1	2		4	5	6	7	8	12		11		3	14							9				10			40
1	2		4	5	12		8		10	11		3	7		14	6								9			41
1	2		4	5			8		11			3	7		10	6				14	12			9			42
1	2		4	5	6		8		12	11		3				7				9				10			43
1	2		4		6		8		10	11						7			3				5	9			44
1	2		4	5	6	7	8		10	11		3												9			45
1	2		4	5					10			6			11				3		7			9	12	8	46

Coca-Cola Cup

Second Round	Scarborough (a)	4-1
	(h)	4-1
Third Round	Aston Villa (a)	0-1

FA Cup

Third Round	Swansea C (a)	1-1
	(h)	1-2

MILLWALL 1994–95 *Back row (left to right):* John Kerr, Mark Kennedy, Dave Mitchell, Jon Goodman, Greg Berry, Tony McCarthy, Kenny Cunningham, Clive Allen.
Centre row: Keith Johnstone (Physio), Ken Barry (Kit Manager), Keith Stevens, Pat Van Den Hauwe, Kasey Keller, Tim Carter, Richard Huxford, Dave Savage, Ian McDonald (Coach), Peter Melville (Physio).
Front row: Andy May, Andy Roberts, Mark Beard, Alex Rae, Ian Evans (First Team Coach), Mick McCarthy (Manager), Phil Barber, Jermaine Wright, Ian Dawes, Ben Thatcher.

Division 1 **MILLWALL**

Millwall Football & Athletic Company (1985) plc, The Den, Zampa Road, Bermondsey SE16 3LN. Telephone: (0171) 232 1222. Ticket Office: (0171) 231 9999. Club Shop: (0171) 231 5881. Fax: (0171) 231 3663.

Ground capacity: 20,146 (all-seater).

Record Attendance: 20,093 v Arsenal, FA Cup 3rd rd, 10 January 1994.

Record Receipts: (to be advised).

Pitch measurements: 100 metres × 68m.

President: Lord Mellish of Bermondsey.

Chairman: Peter W. Mead. ***Directors:*** R. I. Burr, J. D. Burnige, B. E. Mitchell, Cllr. David Sullivan, J. M. R. Berardo.

Chief Executive Secretary: Graham Hortop. ***Assistant Secretary:*** Yvonne Haines.

Manager: Mick McCarthy. ***First Team Coach:*** Ian Evans.

Reserve Team Coach: Ian McDonald. ***Youth Team Coach:*** Tom Walley. ***Chief Scout:*** Ron Howard. ***Youth Development Officer:*** Allen Batsford. ***Physio:*** Keith Johnstone. ***Hon. Medical Officer:*** Dr. Daniel Baron.

Sales & Promotions Manager: Mike Sullivan. ***Commercial Manager:*** Billy Neil.
Marketing Manager: D. Frazer.

Year Formed: 1885. ***Turned Professional:*** 1893. ***Ltd Co.:*** 1894.

Previous Names: 1885, Millwall Rovers; 1889, Millwall Athletic.

Club Nickname: 'The Lions'.

Previous Grounds: 1885, Glengall Road, Millwall; 1886, Back of 'Lord Nelson'; 1890, East Ferry Road; 1901, North Greenwich; 1910, The Den, Cold Blow Lane; 1993, The Den, Bermondsey.

Foundation: Formed in 1885 as Millwall Rovers by employees of Morton & Co, a jam and marmalade factory in West Ferry Road. The founders were predominantly Scotsmen. Their first headquarters was the The Islanders pub in Tooke Street, Millwall. Their first trophy was the East End Cup in 1887.

First Football League game: 28 August, 1920, Division 3, v Bristol R (h) W 2-0 – Lansdale; Fort, Hodge; Voisey (1), Riddell, McAlpine; Waterall, Travers, Broad (1), Sutherland, Dempsey.

Record League Victory: 9–1 v Torquay U, Division 3 (S), 29 August 1927 – Lansdale; Tilling, Hill; Amos, Bryant (3), Graham; Chance, Hawkins (3), Landells (1), Phillips (2), Black. 9–1 v Coventry C, Division 3 (S), 19 November 1927 – Lansdale; Fort, Hill; Amos, Collins (1), Graham; Chance, Landells (4), Cock (2), Phillips (2), Black.

Record Cup Victory: 7–0 v Gateshead, FA Cup, 2nd rd, 12 December 1936 – Yuill; Ted Smith, Inns; Brolly, Hancock, Forsyth; Thomas (1), Mangnall (1), Ken Burditt (2), McCartney (2), Thorogood (1).

Record Defeat: 1–9 v Aston Villa, FA Cup 4th rd, 28 January 1946.

Most League Points (2 for a win): 65, Division 3 (S), 1927–28 and Division 3, 1965–66.

Most League Points (3 for a win): 90, Division 3, 1984–85.

Most League Goals: 127, Division 3 (S), 1927–28.

Highest League Scorer in Season: Richard Parker, 37, Division 3 (S), 1926–27.

Most League Goals in Total Aggregate: Teddy Sheringham, 93, 1984–91.

Most Capped Player: Eamonn Dunphy, 22 (23), Republic of Ireland.

Most League Appearances: Barry Kitchener, 523, 1967–82.

Record Transfer Fee Received: £2,300,000 from Liverpool for Mark Kennedy, March 1995.

Record Transfer Fee Paid: £800,000 to Derby Co for Paul Goddard, December 1989.

Football League Record: 1920 Original Members of Division 3; 1921 Division 3 (S); 1928–34 Division 2; 1934–38 Division 3 (S); 1938–48 Division 2; 1948–58 Division 3 (S); 1958–62 Division 4; 1962–64 Division 3; 1964–65 Division 4; 1965–66 Division 3; 1966–75 Division 2; 1975–76 Division 3; 1976–79 Division 2; 1979–85 Division 3; 1985–88 Division 2; 1988–90 Division 1; 1990–92 Division 2; 1992– Division 1.

Honours: *Football League:* Division 1 best season: 7th 1992–93; Division 2 – Champions 1987–88; Division 3 (S) – Champions 1927–28, 1937–38; Runners-up 1952–53; Division 3 – Runners-up 1965–66, 1984–85; Division 4 – Champions 1961–62; Runners-up 1964–65. *FA Cup:* Semi-final 1900, 1903, 1937 (first Division 3 side to reach semi-final). *Football League Cup:* best season: 5th rd, 1974, 1977, 1995. *Football League Trophy:* Winners 1983.

Colours: Blue shirts, white shorts, blue stockings. **Change colours:** Green and white shirts, green shorts, green stockings.

MILLWALL 1994–95 LEAGUE RECORD

Match No.	Date	Venue	Opponents	Result		H/T Score	Lg. Pos.	Goalscorers	Attendance
1	Aug 13	H	Southend U	W	3-1	1-0	—	Mitchell, Goodman, Tilson (og)	8283
2	20	A	Sunderland	D	1-1	1-0	2	Rae	17,296
3	27	H	Derby Co	W	4-1	1-0	2	Rae, Kerr 3	8809
4	30	A	Bolton W	L	0-1	0-0	—		9519
5	Sept 3	A	Reading	D	0-0	0-0	5		8715
6	10	H	WBA	D	2-2	1-1	7	Goodman 2	8378
7	14	H	Burnley	L	2-3	0-0	—	Savage, Rae (pen)	7375
8	17	A	Tranmere R	L	1-3	1-1	15	Roberts	6243
9	24	H	Luton T	D	0-0	0-0	15		7150
10	Oct 1	A	Middlesbrough	L	0-3	0-0	19		17,229
11	8	A	Bristol C	L	0-1	0-0	21		7499
12	15	H	Stoke C	D	1-1	1-0	21	Goodman	7856
13	22	A	Wolverhampton W	D	3-3	1-1	22	Goodman 2, Cadette	25,059
14	29	H	Sheffield U	W	2-1	0-0	22	Kennedy (pen), Cadette	8445
15	Nov 2	H	Portsmouth	D	2-2	2-1	—	Goodman, Rae	7108
16	5	A	Swindon T	W	2-1	0-0	18	Goodman, Kennedy	9311
17	12	A	Grimsby T	L	0-1	0-0	19		5261
18	19	H	Barnsley	L	0-1	0-1	20		7040
19	26	A	Port Vale	L	1-2	0-0	20	Kennedy	8016
20	Dec 4	H	Wolverhampton W	W	1-0	0-0	20	Mitchell	8025
21	10	H	Sunderland	W	2-0	0-0	15	Kennedy, Mitchell	7698
22	17	A	Southend U	W	1-0	1-0	15	Cadette	5833
23	26	A	Notts Co	W	1-0	0-0	13	Mitchell	6758
24	27	H	Watford	W	2-1	0-0	10	Rae (pen), Cadette	12,289
25	Jan 1	A	Charlton Ath	D	1-1	1-0	11	Rae	10,655
26	3	H	Oldham Ath	D	1-1	0-1	—	Rae (pen)	7438
27	14	A	Sheffield U	D	1-1	1-0	12	Beard	12,650
28	Feb 4	H	Grimsby T	W	2-0	1-0	11	Kennedy, Roberts	7397
29	21	A	Barnsley	L	1-4	0-1	—	Webber	4733
30	26	H	Middlesbrough	D	0-0	0-0	13		7247
31	Mar 1	H	Swindon T	W	3-1	0-0	—	Rae 2, Van Blerk	5950
32	4	A	Luton T	D	1-1	0-1	11	Mitchell	6864
33	8	H	Reading	W	2-0	1-0	—	Oldfield, Williams (og)	7546
34	11	A	Derby Co	L	2-3	1-1	12	Rae, Mitchell	12,490
35	15	A	Portsmouth	L	2-3	1-1	—	Oldfield, Witter	6032
36	19	H	Bolton W	L	0-1	0-0	12		6103
37	22	A	WBA	L	0-3	0-1	—		11,782
38	25	H	Tranmere R	W	2-1	0-0	13	Dixon, Roberts	7470
39	Apr 1	A	Burnley	W	2-1	1-0	11	Oldfield 2	10,454
40	5	H	Port Vale	L	1-3	0-2	—	Oldfield	5260
41	8	H	Charlton Ath	W	3-1	2-1	11	McRobert, Thatcher, Dixon	9506
42	14	A	Watford	L	0-1	0-1	—		6907
43	19	H	Notts Co	D	0-0	0-0	—		5471
44	22	A	Oldham Ath	W	1-0	0-0	11	Savage	6319
45	29	A	Stoke C	L	3-4	2-2	11	Dixon, Webber, Oldfield	9111
46	May 7	H	Bristol C	D	1-1	1-1	12	Dixon	8805

Final League Position: 12

GOALSCORERS

League (60): Rae 10 (3 pens), Goodman 8, Mitchell 6, Oldfield 6, Kennedy 5 (1 pen), Cadette 4, Dixon 4, Kerr 3, Roberts 3, Savage 2, Webber 2, Beard 1, McRobert 1, Thatcher 1, Van Blerk 1, Witter 1, own goals 2.
Coca-Cola Cup (8): Berry 2, Goodman 2, Kennedy 2, Cadette 1, Mitchell 1.
FA Cup (3): Beard 1, Kennedy 1, Savage 1.

Keller K. 44	Cunningham K.E. 15	Thatcher B.D. 38 + 2	May A.M. 14 + 2	McCarthy A.P. 12	Roberts A.J. 44	Savage D. 31 + 6	Rae A. 38	Mitchell D.S. 23 + 5	Goodman J. 15	Kennedy M. 28 + 2	Beard M. 24 + 7	Kerr J. 7 + 7	Chapman D.G. 4 + 8	Huxford R.J. — + 1	Van Den Hauwe P.W. 4	Van Blerk J. 24 + 3	Carter T.D. 2	Connor J.R. 1	Witter A.J. 26 + 1	Cadette R.R. 12 + 4	Dawes I.R. 12 + 2	Stevens K.H. 20	Kelly A.G. 1 + 1	Webber D. 19 + 3	Berry G.J. 4 + 5	Beckford J.N. 6 + 3	Edwards A.M. 3 + 1	McRobert L. 4 + 3	Oldfield D.C. 16 + 1	Joseph R. 5	Dixon K.M. 9	Taylor S.J. 1 + 5	Forbes S. — + 1	*Match No.*
1	2	3	4	5	6	7	8	*9*	10	11	12	14																						1
1	2	3	4	5	6	7	8	9	10	11		12																						2
1	2	3	4	5	6	7	8	*9*	10	11	12	14																						3
1	2	3		5	6	7	8		10	11		9	4																					4
1	2	3		5	6	7	8		10	11	12	9	4	14																				5
1	2	3		5	6	7	8		10	11		9	4																					6
1	2	3		5	6	7	8	12	10	11	14	*9*	4																					7
1	2	3		5	6	7	8	9	10	11		12			4	14																		8
1	2	3		5	6	7	8	*9*	10	11		12			4	14																		9
1		3		5	6	7	8		10	11	2	9	14		*4*	12																		10
	2	3		5	6	12	8	*10*		11	7	9	14			4	1																	11
1	2	3			6	7	8	12	10	11								4	*5*	9	14													12
1	2	3			6	7		*9*	10	11	12				4				5	14	8													13
1	2				4	7		12	10	11	3								5	9	8	6												14
1	2				4	7	3	12	10	*11*	14								5	9	8	6												15
1	2	8			4	7	3	12	10	*11*									5	9	14	6												16
1		8			4		3	10		11	2								5	9	7	6	12											17
1		8			4	7	3	10		11	2								5	9			6	12										18
1		3			4	7	8	10		11	2								5	9		6			12									19
1		3			4		8	10		11	2								5	12	7	6			9									20
1		3			4	12	8	10		11	2								5	14	7	6			*9*									21
1					4		8	10		*11*			14			3			5	9	2	6			12	7								22
1					4		8	10		*11*			12			3			5	9	2	6		14		7								23
1		3			4	7	8	10			2					11			5	9		6		12										24
1		3			4	7	8	10				12	14			11			5	9	2			6										25
1		3			4		8			12	14	10				11			5	9	2			6		*7*								26
1					4	12	8	10		11	7		14			3					2	6		5			*9*							27
1		6			4	12	8	10		*11*	7					3			5		2					14	9							28
1		3	*8*	11	4	7					2	12				10			5					6			9	14						29
1		3			4	7	8				2					11			5					6		10		12	9					30
1		3	12		4	7	8				2					11			5					6		10	14		*9*					31
1		3	4			7	8	10								11			5					6		12			9	2				32
1		3	4			7	8	10		12						11			5					6		14			*9*	2				33
		12	7		4	14	8	10		*11*						3	1		5					6					9	2				34
1		12	2		4	7	8	10		11						3			5					6					9					35
1		3	12		4	7		10		11	2					8			5			6							9					36
1		3			4	10					7					11			12			6		5	9				8	2				37
1		3	10		4	12					7					11						6		5	14				*8*	2	9			38
1		3	10		4	7					2		12			11						6		5					8		9			39
1		3	10		4						2		12						6					5	11	*7*			9		8	14		40
1		3	10		4		*7*				2					11								5	12			6	8		9	14		41
1		3	7		4		10				2					11						6		5				12	*8*		9	14		42
1			*2*		4	7	8									3						6		5	12			11	14		9	10		43
1		3			4	7	8				2					11						6		5					10		9			44
1		3			4	7	8				2									12		6		5				*11*	10		9	14		45
1		3			4		8				2					11			5			*6*						7	10		9	12	14	46

Coca-Cola Cup

Second Round	Sunderland (h)	2-1
	(a)	1-1
Third Round	Mansfield T (a)	2-0
Fourth Round	Nottingham F (a)	2-0
Fifth Round	Swindon T (a)	1-3

FA Cup

Third Round	Arsenal (h)	0-0
	(a)	2-0
Fourth Round	Chelsea (h)	0-0
	(a)	1-1
Fifth Round	QPR (a)	0-1

NEWCASTLE UNITED 1994–95 *Back row (left to right):* Chris Holland, Nicos Papavasliou, Alan Neilson, Nathan Murray, Stephen Harper, Mike Jeffrey, Alex Mathie, Jason Drysdale, Malcolm Allen.

Centre row: Paul Ferris (Assistant Physio), Derek Fazackerley (First Team Coach), Scott Sellars, Lee Clark, Steve Howey, Mike Hooper, Steve Watson, Pavel Srnicek, Philippe Albert, Marc Hottiger, Steve Guppy, Robbie Elliott, Jeff Clarke (Reserve Team Coach), Derek Wright (Physio).

Front row: Barry Venison, John Beresford, Andy Cole, Peter Beardsley, Terry McDermott (Assistant Manager), Kevin Keegan (Manager), Arthur Cox (Coach), Paul Bracewell, Ruel Fox, Robert Lee, Darren Peacock.

FA Premiership NEWCASTLE UNITED

St James' Park, Newcastle-upon-Tyne NE1 4ST. Telephone: (0191) 232 8361. Club Fax: (0191) 232 9875. Lottery Office: (0191) 230 2861. Commercial Dept: (0191) 232 3050. Ticket Office Hotline: (0191) 261 1571. Club Shop: (0191) 261 6357. Club Shop Mail Order Answering Service: (0191) 232 4080. Football in the Community Scheme: (0191) 261 9715. Conference and Banqueting: (0191) 222 1860. Clubcall: 0891 121590. Clubcall Main Line: 0891 121190. Ticket Line: 0891 121590. Club Shop numbers: St James' Park Club Shop: (0191) 261 6357. Metro Centre Club Shop: (0191) 461 0000. Eldon Square Club Shop: (0191) 230 0808. Travel Club: (0191) 2211000. Junior Magpies: (0191) 232 2571. Lottery Office: (0191) 230 2861.

Ground capacity: 36,649.

Record attendance: 68,386 v Chelsea, Division 1, 3 Sept 1930.

Record receipts: £359,112.12 v Swansea C, FA Cup 4th rd, 28 January 1995.

Pitch measurements: 110yd × 73yd (subject to alteration).

President: T. L. Bennett.

Chairman: Sir John Hall.

Vice-Chairman: W. F. Shepherd. ***Chief Executive:*** A. O. Fletcher.

Directors: D. S. Hall, R. Jones, T. L. Bennett.

Manager: Kevin Keegan. ***Assistant Manager:*** Terry McDermott.

Coach: Jeff Clarke. ***Physios:*** Derek Wright, Paul Ferris.

General Manager/Secretary: R. Cushing.

Assistant Secretary: A. Toward. ***Marketing Control:*** Trevor Garwood.

Year Formed: 1881. ***Turned Professional:*** 1889. ***Ltd Co.:*** 1890.

Club Nickname: 'Magpies'.

Previous Names: Stanley 1881; Newcastle East End 1882–1892.

Previous Grounds: South Byker, 1881; Chillingham Road, Heaton, 1886 to 1892.

Foundation: It stemmed from a newly formed club called Stanley in 1881. In October 1882 they changed their name to Newcastle East End to avoid confusion with Stanley in Co. Durham. Shortly afterwards another club Rosewood merged with them. Newcastle West End had been formed in August 1882 and they played on a ground which is now St. James' Park. In 1889, West End went out of existence after a bad run and the remaining committee men invited East End to move to St. James' Park. They accepted and at a meeting in Bath Lane Hall in 1892, changed their name to Newcastle United.

First Football League game: 2 September, 1893, Division 2, v Royal Arsenal (a) D 2-2 – Ramsay; Jeffery, Miller; Crielly, Graham, McKane; Bowman, Crate (1), Thompson, Sorley (1), Wallace. Graham and not Crate scored according to some reports.

Record League Victory: 13–0 v Newport Co, Division 2, 5 October 1946 – Garbutt; Cowell, Graham; Harvey, Brennan, Wright; Milburn (2), Bentley (1), Wayman (4), Shackleton (6), Pearson.

Record Cup Victory: 9–0 v Southport (at Hillsborough) FA Cup, 4th rd, 1 February 1932 – McInroy; Nelson, Fairhurst; McKenzie, Davidson, Weaver (1); Boyd (1), Jimmy Richardson (3), Cape (2), McMenemy (1), Lang (1).

Record Defeat: 0–9 v Burton Wanderers, Division 2, 15 April 1895.

Most League Points (2 for a win): 57, Division 2, 1964–65.

Most League Points (3 for a win): 96, Division 1, 1992–93.

Most League Goals: 98, Division 1, 1951–52.

Highest League Scorer in Season: Hughie Gallacher, 36, Division 1, 1926–27.

Most League Goals in Total Aggregate: Jackie Milburn, 178, 1946–57.

Most Capped Player: Alf McMichael, 40, Northern Ireland.

Most League Appearances: Jim Lawrence, 432, 1904–22.

Record Transfer Fee Received: £6,250,000 from Manchester U for Andy Cole, January 1995.

Record Transfer Fee Paid: £6,000,000 to QPR for Les Ferdinand, June 1995.

Football League Record: 1893 Elected to Division 2; 1898–1934 Division 1; 1934–48 Division 2; 1948–61 Division 1; 1961–65 Division 2; 1965–78 Division 1; 1978–84 Division 2; 1984–89 Division 1; 1989–92 Division 2; 1992–93 Division 1; 1993– FA Premier League.

Honours: *Football League:* Division 1 – Champions 1904–05, 1906–07, 1908–09, 1926–27, 1992–93; Division 2 – Champions 1964–65; Runners-up 1897–98, 1947–48. *FA Cup:* Winners 1910, 1924, 1932, 1951, 1952, 1955; Runners-up 1905, 1906, 1908, 1911, 1974. *Football League Cup:* Runners-up 1976. *Texaco Cup:* Winners 1974, 1975. **European Competitions:** *European Fairs Cup:* 1968–69 (winners), 1969–70, 1970–71 *UEFA Cup:* 1977–78, 1994–95. *Anglo-Italian Cup:* Winners 1972–73.

Colours: Black and white striped shirts, black shorts, black stockings. **Change colours:** Maroon and navy hooped shirts, cream shorts, maroon stockings.

NEWCASTLE UNITED 1994–95 LEAGUE RECORD

Match No.	Date	Venue	Opponents	Result		H/T Score	Lg. Pos.	Goalscorers	Attendance
1	Aug 21	A	Leicester C	W	3-1	0-0	—	Cole, Beardsley, Elliott	20,048
2	24	H	Coventry C	W	4-0	3-0	—	Lee 2, Watson, Cole	34,163
3	27	H	Southampton	W	5-1	3-0	1	Watson 2, Cole 2, Lee	34,182
4	31	A	West Ham U	W	3-1	2-0	—	Potts (og), Lee, Mathie	17,375
5	Sept 10	H	Chelsea	W	4-2	2-2	1	Cole 2, Fox, Lee	34,435
6	18	A	Arsenal	W	3-2	2-1	1	Keown (og), Beardsley (pen), Fox	36,819
7	24	H	Liverpool	D	1-1	0-0	1	Lee	34,435
8	Oct 1	A	Aston Villa	W	2-0	0-0	1	Lee, Cole	29,960
9	9	H	Blackburn R	D	1-1	0-0	1	Flowers (og)	34,344
10	15	A	Crystal Palace	W	1-0	0-0	1	Beardsley	17,739
11	22	H	Sheffield W	W	2-1	2-0	1	Watson, Cole	34,369
12	29	A	Manchester U	L	0-2	0-1	1		43,795
13	Nov 5	H	QPR	W	2-1	0-1	1	Kitson, Beardsley	34,278
14	7	A	Nottingham F	D	0-0	0-0	—		22,102
15	19	A	Wimbledon	L	2-3	2-3	3	Beardsley, Kitson	14,203
16	26	H	Ipswich T	D	1-1	0-0	3	Cole	34,459
17	Dec 3	A	Tottenham H	L	2-4	2-2	3	Fox 2	28,002
18	10	H	Leicester C	W	3-1	1-0	3	Albert 2, Howey	34,400
19	17	A	Coventry C	D	0-0	0-0	3		17,237
20	26	A	Leeds U	D	0-0	0-0	3		39,337
21	31	A	Norwich C	L	1-2	1-2	4	Fox (pen)	21,172
22	Jan 2	H	Manchester C	D	0-0	0-0	5		34,437
23	15	H	Manchester U	D	1-1	0-1	5	Kitson	34,471
24	21	A	Sheffield W	D	0-0	0-0	4		31,215
25	25	H	Wimbledon	W	2-1	1-0	—	Fox, Kitson	34,374
26	Feb 1	H	Everton	W	2-0	0-0	—	Fox, Beardsley (pen)	34,465
27	4	A	QPR	L	0-3	0-3	3		16,576
28	11	H	Nottingham F	W	2-1	0-0	3	Fox, Lee	34,471
29	25	H	Aston Villa	W	3-1	1-1	3	Venison, Beardsley 2	34,637
30	28	A	Ipswich T	W	2-0	2-0	—	Fox, Kitson	18,639
31	Mar 4	A	Liverpool	L	0-2	0-0	3		39,300
32	8	H	West Ham U	W	2-0	1-0	—	Clark, Kitson	34,595
33	19	H	Arsenal	W	1-0	0-0	3	Beardsley	35,611
34	22	A	Southampton	L	1-3	1-0	—	Kitson	14,666
35	Apr 1	A	Chelsea	D	1-1	0-1	3	Hottiger	22,987
36	8	H	Norwich C	W	3-0	2-0	3	Beardsley 2 (1 pen), Kitson	35,518
37	14	A	Everton	L	0-2	0-1	—		34,628
38	17	H	Leeds U	L	1-2	1-2	5	Elliott	35,626
39	29	A	Manchester C	D	0-0	0-0	5		27,389
40	May 3	H	Tottenham H	D	3-3	2-3	—	Gillespie, Peacock, Beardsley	35,603
41	8	A	Blackburn R	L	0-1	0-1	—		30,545
42	14	H	Crystal Palace	W	3-2	3-0	6	Fox, Lee, Gillespie	35,626

Final League Position: 6

GOALSCORERS

League (67): Beardsley 12 (3 pens), Fox 10 (1 pen), Cole 9, Lee 9, Kitson 8, Watson 4, Albert 2, Elliott 2, Gillespie 2, Clark 1, Hottiger 1, Howey 1, Mathie 1, Peacock 1, Venison 1, own goals 3.
Coca-Cola Cup (6): Cole 2, Albert 1, Fox 1, Jeffrey 1, Kitson 1.
FA Cup (9): Kitson 3, Gillespie 2, Beresford 1, Clark 1, Hottiger 1, Lee 1.

Srnicek P. 38	Hottiger M. 38	Beresford J. 33	Venison B. 28	Peacock D. 35	Albert P. 17	Lee R.M. 35	Beardsley P.A. 34	Cole A. 18	Fox R.A. 40	Sellars S. 12	Elliott R.J. 10 + 4	Mathie A. 3 + 6	Hooper M.D. 4 + 2	Watson S.C. 22 + 5	Howey S.N. 29 + 1	Kitson P. 24 + 2	Neilson A.B. 5 + 1	Clark L.R. 9 + 10	Bracewell P.W. 13 + 3	Gillespie K.R. 15 + 2	Allen M. — + 1	Match No.
1	2	3	4	5	6	7	*8*	9	10	11	12	*14*	15									1
1	2	3	4	5	6	7		9	10	11	12	14		*8*								2
1	2	3	4	5	6	7		9	*10*	11	12	14		8								3
1	2	3	4	5	6	7		9		11	12	10		8								4
	2	3	4	5	6	7		9	10	11			1	8								5
1	2	3		5	6	7	8	9	10	11					4							6
1	2	3	*4*	5	6	7	8	9	10	11				12	14							7
1	2	3		5	6	7	8	9	10	11					4	12						8
1	2	3		5		7	8	9	10	11				6	4	12						9
1		3			6		8	9	10	11				5	4	7	2					10
1	2	3		5	6		8	9	10	11				4		7		12				11
1	2	3		5	6	9	8		*10*	11		12		7	4			14				12
1	2	3		5	6	9	8		10					7	4	11						13
1	2	3		5	6	9	8		10					7		11		4				14
1	2	3	7	*5*	6	9	8		10					12	4	11		14				15
1	2	3	4		*6*	7	8	9	10			12		11			5	14				16
1	2	3	4				8	9	10			7		6			5	11				17
1	2	11	4	5	3		8	9	10					7	6							18
1	2	3	4	5			8	9	10					7	6	11		12				19
1		3	2		6	7		9	10					4	5	11			8			20
1		3	2	5		7		9	10					6	4	11		12	8			21
1		3	2	5		7	8	9	10						6	11			4			22
1	2	3	4	5		7			10		11				6	9		8				23
1	2	3	4	5		7	8		10						6	9		11		12		24
1	2		4	5			8		10		3				6	9			7	11		25
	2		4			7	8		10		3	9	1				5	12	6	11		26
	2					7	8				3	12	1	4		9	5	10	6	11		27
1	2	3	4	5		7	8		10						6	9			12	11		28
1	2	3	4	5		7	8		10						6	9				11		29
1	2	3	4	5		7	8		10						6	9				11		30
1	2	3	4	5		7	8		*10*					12	6	9			14	11		31
1	2	3	4	5		7			10					12	*6*	9		8	14	11		32
1	2		4	5		7	8		10		3					9		12	6	11		33
1	2		4	5		7	8		10		3				6	9				11		34
1	2		4	5		7	8		10		3			14	6	*9*		12	11			35
1	2		4	5		7	8		10		3				6	9			11			36
	2		4	5		7	8		*10*		3		1		6	9		12	11	14		37
1	2					7	8		10		3			5	6	9	12		4	11		38
1	2	3		5			8		10					4	6			11	7	9		39
1	2	3		5		7	8		*10*				15	11	6				4	9	12	40
1	2	3		5		7	8		10					4	6			11		9		41
1	2	3		5		7	8		10					4	6			11		9		42

Coca-Cola Cup

Second Round	Barnsley (h)	2-1
	(a)	1-0
Third Round	Manchester U (h)	2-0
Fourth Round	Manchester C (a)	1-1
	(h)	0-2

FA Cup

Third Round	Blackburn R (h)	1-1
	(a)	2-1
Fourth Round	Swansea C (h)	3-0
Fifth Round	Manchester C (h)	3-1
Sixth Round	Everton (a)	0-1

NORTHAMPTON TOWN 1994–95 *Back row (left to right):* Lee Colkin, Jason Pascoe, Kevin Wilkin, Robbie Curtis, Scott Stackman, Richard Skelly.
Centre row: Dennis Casey (Physio), Ray Byrne, Mark Turner, Dean Trott, Billy Stewart, Ian Sampson, Scott Middlemass, Richard Preston, Paul Curtis (Youth Coach).
Front row: Peter Morris (Assistant Manager), Gary Harrison, Neil Grayson, Ray Warburton, Mickey Bell, Darren Harmon, John Barnwell (Manager).
(Photograph: Pete Norton)

Division 3 NORTHAMPTON TOWN

Sixfields Stadium, Upton Way, Northampton NN1 4PS. Telephone: (01604) 757773. Fax: (01604) 751613/754960. Ticket Office: (01604) 588338. Soccer Line: 0839 664477.

Ground capacity: 7650.

Record attendance (at County Ground): 24,523 v Fulham, Division 1, 23 April 1966.

Record receipts (at County Ground): £47,292.40 v Coventry C, FA Cup 3rd rd, 6 January 1990.

Pitch measurements: 116yd × 72yd.

Chairman: B. J. Ward.

Directors: B. Stonhill, B. Hancock, M. Church, B. Church, D. Kerr, B. Collins, B. Lomax.

Secretary: Barry Collins.

Manager: Ian Atkins. ***Assistant Manager:*** Peter Morris. ***Coach:*** Danny O'Shea.

Physio: Dennis Casey. ***Commercial Manager:*** Bob Gorrill.

Year Formed: 1897. ***Turned Professional:*** 1901. ***Ltd Co.:*** 1901.

Previous Ground: County Ground.

Club Nickname: 'The Cobblers'.

Foundation: Formed in 1897 by school teachers connected with the Northampton and District Elementary Schools' Association, they survived a financial crisis at the end of their first year when they were £675 in the red and became members of the Midland League – a fast move indeed for a new club. They achieved Southern League membership in 1901.

First Football League game: 28 August, 1920, Division 3, v Grimsby T (a) L 0-2 – Thorpe; Sproston, Hewison; Jobey, Tomkins, Pease; Whitworth, Lockett, Thomas, Freeman, MacKechnie.

Record League Victory: 10–0 v Walsall, Division 3 (S), 5 November 1927 – Hammond; Watson, Jeffs; Allen, Brett, Odell; Daley, Smith (3), Loasby (3), Hoten (1), Wells (3).

Record Cup Victory: 10–0 v Sutton T FA Cup pr rd, 7 December 1907 – Cooch; Drennan, Lloyd Davies, Tirrell (1), McCartney, Hickleton, Badenock (3), Platt (3), Lowe (1), Chapman (2), McDiarmid.

Record Defeat: 0–11 v Southampton, Southern League, 28 December 1901.

Most League Points (2 for a win): 68, Division 4, 1975–76.

Most League Points (3 for a win): 99, Division 4, 1986–87.

Most League Goals: 109, Division 3, 1962–63 and Division 3 (S), 1952–53.

Highest League Scorer in Season: Cliff Holton, 36, Division 3, 1961–62.

Most League Goals in Total Aggregate: Jack English, 135, 1947–60.

Most Capped Player: E. Lloyd Davies, 12 (16), Wales.

Most League Appearances: Tommy Fowler, 521, 1946–61.

Record Transfer Fee Received: £265,000 from Watford for Richard Hill, July 1987.

Record Transfer Fee Paid: £85,000 to Manchester C for Tony Adcock, January 1988.

Football League Record: 1920 Original Member of Division 3; 1921 Division 3 (S); 1958–61 Division 4; 1961–63 Division 3; 1963–65 Division 2; 1965–66 Division 1; 1966–67 Division 2; 1967–69 Division 3; 1969–76 Division 4; 1976–77 Division 3; 1977–87 Division 4; 1987–90 Division 3; 1990–92 Division 4; 1992– Division 3.

Honours: *Football League:* Division 1 best season: 21st, 1965–66; Division 2 – Runners-up 1964–65; Division 3 – Champions 1962–63; Division 3 (S) – Runners-up 1927–28, 1949–50; Division 4 – Champions 1986–87; Runners-up 1975–76. *FA Cup:* best season: 5th rd, 1934, 1950, 1970. *Football League Cup:* best season: 5th rd, 1965, 1967.

Colours: Claret with white shirts, yellow shoulder panel (Lotto logo), white shorts, claret stockings. **Change colours:** Reverse of (home) first choice.

NORTHAMPTON TOWN 1994–95 LEAGUE RECORD

Match No.	Date	Venue	Opponents	Result		H/T Score	Lg. Pos.	Goalscorers	Attendance
1	Aug 20	A	Doncaster R	L	0-1	0-1	20		2194
2	27	A	Scunthorpe U	D	1-1	1-1	17	Trott	2499
3	30	A	Torquay U	L	1-2	0-2	—	Sampson	3619
4	Sept 3	A	Walsall	D	1-1	1-1	21	Trott	4249
5	10	H	Rochdale	L	1-2	1-0	22	Trott	3052
6	13	H	Hartlepool U	D	1-1	0-0	—	Aldridge	2466
7	17	A	Mansfield T	D	1-1	0-0	21	Aldridge	2557
8	24	H	Carlisle U	W	2-1	1-0	20	Aldridge, Bell	3508
9	Oct 1	A	Lincoln C	D	2-2	2-1	19	Harmon, Warburton	3248
10	8	A	Exeter C	D	0-0	0-0	20		3015
11	11	H	Mansfield T	L	0-1	0-1	—		4993
12	15	H	Barnet	D	1-1	0-0	21	Aldridge	7461
13	22	H	Wigan Ath	W	1-0	1-0	18	Grayson	6379
14	29	A	Scarborough	D	0-0	0-0	18		1468
15	Nov 5	H	Fulham	L	0-1	0-1	18		7366
16	19	A	Preston NE	L	0-2	0-1	18		7297
17	26	H	Hereford U	L	1-3	0-0	21	Cahill	5148
18	Dec 10	H	Doncaster R	D	0-0	0-0	21		4538
19	16	H	Scunthorpe U	L	0-1	0-1	—		3845
20	26	A	Colchester U	W	1-0	1-0	20	Harmon (pen)	5064
21	27	H	Chesterfield	L	2-3	1-2	21	Brown, Harmon (pen)	6329
22	31	A	Darlington	L	1-4	0-1	21	Grayson	2250
23	Jan 7	A	Wigan Ath	L	1-2	0-1	21	Colkin	1911
24	14	H	Gillingham	W	2-0	0-0	20	Harmon (pen), Trott	5529
25	28	H	Scarborough	L	0-3	0-0	20		5737
26	Feb 4	A	Hereford U	L	1-2	1-1	21	Grayson	2365
27	11	H	Preston NE	W	2-1	0-0	20	Burns, Smith	5195
28	14	A	Fulham	D	4-4	1-2	—	Aldridge 2, Brown, Grayson	3423
29	18	A	Gillingham	L	1-3	0-1	20	Thompson	4075
30	25	H	Lincoln C	W	3-1	1-0	19	Brown (og), Grayson, Aldridge	4821
31	Mar 4	A	Carlisle U	L	1-2	0-2	19	Martin	6755
32	7	H	Bury	L	0-5	0-1	—		4208
33	11	A	Rochdale	D	0-0	0-0	19		1894
34	18	H	Torquay U	W	2-0	0-0	18	Grayson, Brown	3832
35	25	H	Walsall	D	2-2	1-1	18	Grayson, Warburton	6282
36	Apr 1	A	Hartlepool U	D	1-1	0-1	18	Thompson	2113
37	8	H	Darlington	W	2-1	1-0	17	Thompson, Grayson	4496
38	15	A	Chesterfield	L	0-3	0-1	19		4884
39	17	H	Colchester U	D	1-1	1-0	17	Brown	5011
40	22	A	Bury	L	0-5	0-1	20		2921
41	29	A	Barnet	W	3-2	2-1	18	Burns, Thompson, Warburton	2796
42	May 6	H	Exeter C	W	2-1	1-0	17	O'Shea, Sampson	6734

Final League Position: 17

GOALSCORERS

League (45): Grayson 8, Aldridge 7, Brown 4, Harmon 4 (3 pens), Thompson 4, Trott 4, Warburton 3, Burns 2, Sampson 2, Bell 1, Cahill 1, Colkin 1, Martin 1, O'Shea 1, Smith 1, own goal 1.
Coca-Cola Cup (0).
FA Cup (0).

Stewart W.I. 26 + 1	Pascoe J. 11 + 4	Curtis R. 13	Norton D.W. 36 + 2	Warburton R. 39	Sampson I. 42	Harmon D.J. 26 + 7	Byrne R. 2	Trott D. 20 + 2	Grayson N. 34 + 4	Bell M. 12	Colkin L. 28 + 5	Wilkin K. 2 + 2	Aldridge M.J. 18 + 9	Robinson P.J. 14	McNamara B. — + 1	Williams G.J. 13 + 2	Cahill O.F. 5 + 3	Skelly R.B. 3	Ovendale M.J. 6	Harrison G.M. 5	Sedgemore B.R. 1	Brown I.O. 23	Flounders A.J. 2	Patmore W.J. 1 + 3	Hughes D.J. 12 + 1	Burns C. 16 + 1	Smith N. 6	Daniels S. 5 + 3	Thompson G.L. 15	Martin D. 7	Turner G.M. 2 + 2	Woodman A.J. 10	O'Shea D.E. 7	*Match No.*
1	2	3	4	5	6	7	*8*	9	10	11	12	14																						1
1	2		4	5	6	7	8	9	12	11	3	10																						2
1	2	6	8	5	4	7		9	10	11	3		12																					3
1		6	2	5	4	7		9	10	11	3		12	8																				4
1			2	5	4	7		9	10	11	3	8		6	12																			5
1	6		2	5	4	7		9	10	11	3		12	8																				6
1		6	2	5	4	7		9		11	3		10	8																				7
1		6	2	5	4	7		9		11	3		10	8																				8
1		6	2	5	4	7		9		11	3		10	8																				9
1		6	2	5	4	7		9		11	3			8		10																		10
1		*6*	2	5	4	7		9	14	11	3		12	8		10																		11
1	2			5	4	7		9	12	11	3		10	6		8																		12
1	2	6		5	4	7			9		3		10	11		8	12																	13
1	2			5	4	7		9	8		11		12	10		6		3																14
1	2		12	5	4	7			8		3		9	10		6	11																	15
	12		2	5	4	7		9	11		3		8	10		6	14		1															16
1			2	5	4	7		9	12				8	10		6	11	3																17
1	3		2	5	4	7		9	8				12			6	11			10														18
1	12		2	5	4	7		*9*	3			14	8			6	11			10														19
1	12	5	2		4	7			9		3					11					6	8	*10*	14										20
1	2	5	6		4	7			9		3					*11*	12					8	10	14										21
1		6	2	5	4				10		3		12			11				7		8		9										22
1	12	6	2	5	4				11		10		9					3		7		8												23
1			2	5	4	7		12	11		6		9									8			3	10								24
1			2	5	4	7		9	11													8		12	3	10	6							25
			2	5	6	12		9	10										1	11		8			14	7	4	*3*						26
			2	5	4	6			11				7						1			8				10	3		9					27
			2	5	4	12			11				7						1			8				10	3		9	6				28
1			2	5	4	12			11				7									8					3		9	6	10			29
			2	5	4	10			11				7						1			8					3		9	6	12			30
15			2	5	4	12			11		3		7			14			*1*			*8*				10			9	6				31
1			2	5	4	12			11		3		7									8				10			9	6	14			32
			2	5	4				11		12		14									8			3	10			9	6	7	1		33
			2	5	4				11		12		7									8			3	10			9	6		1		34
			2	5	4	12			11		6					14						*8*			3	10		7	9			1		35
			2	5	4				11		12											8			3	10		7	9			1	6	36
			2	5	4				11		7											8			3	10		12	9			1	6	37
	5		2		4	12		14	11		7											8			*3*	10			9			1	6	38
			12	5	4				11		7											8			3	10		2	9			1	6	39
				5	4	10		9	11		7											8			3	12		2				1	6	40
			2	5	4				11		7		12									*8*			3	10		14	9			1	6	41
			2	5	4				*11*		12						7					8			3	10		14	9			1	6	42

Coca-Cola Cup
First Round Bournemouth (a) 0-2
(h) 0-1

FA Cup
First Round Peterborough U (a) 0-4

NORWICH CITY 1994–95 *Back row (left to right):* Efan Ekoku, Keith O'Neill, Andy Johnson, Spencer Prior, Jon Newsome, Rob Newman, Ian Butterworth, Daryl Sutch, Ade Akinbiyi. *Centre row:* Tim Sheppard (Physio), Stacey Kreft, Johnny Wright, Shaun Carey, Mark Robins, Jeremy Goss, John Faulkner, Andy Marshall, Gary Megson, (Assistant Manager), Carl Bradshaw, Mark Bowen, Robert Ullathorne, Alistair Gibb, Justin Harrington, Keith Webb.
Front row: Marcus Oldbury, Darren Eadie, Neil Adams, John Polston, Bryan Gunn, John Deehan (Manager), Scott Howie, Ian Crook, Mike Milligan, Jamie Cureton, Jimmy Simpson.

Division 1 **NORWICH CITY**

Carrow Road, Norwich NR1 1JE. Telephone: (01603) 760760. Fax: (01603) 665510. Box Office: (01603) 761661. Canary Call: 0891 424212.

Ground capacity: 21,994.

Record attendance: 43,984 v Leicester C, FA Cup 6th rd, 30 March 1963.

Record receipts: £261,918 v Internazionale, UEFA Cup 3rd rd 1st leg, 24 November 1993.

Pitch measurements: 114yd × 74yd.

President: G. C. Watling.

Chairman: Robert T. Chase JP. ***Vice-Chairman:*** J. A. Jones.

Directors: B. W. Lockwood, G. A. Paterson.

Manager: Martin O'Neill. ***Assistant Manager:*** Paul Franklin.

Youth Team Coach: Steve Walford.

Commercial Manager: Ray Cossey.

Physio: Tim Sheppard MCSP, SRP.

Secretary: A. R. W. Neville.

Year Formed: 1902. ***Turned Professional:*** 1905. ***Ltd Co.:*** 1905.

Club Nickname: 'The Canaries'.

Previous Grounds: 1902, Newmarket Road; 1908–35, The Nest, Rosary Road.

Foundation: Formed in 1902, largely through the initiative of two local schoolmasters who called a meeting at the Criterion Cafe, they were shocked by an FA Commission which in 1904 declared the club professional and ejected them from the FA Amateur Cup. However, this only served to strengthen their determination. New officials were appointed and a professional club established at a meeting in the Agricultural Hall in March 1905.

First Football League game: 28 August, 1920, Division 3, v Plymouth A (a) D 1-1 – Skermer; Gray, Gadsden; Wilkinson, Addy, Martin; Laxton, Kidger, Parker, Whitham (1), Dobson.

Record League Victory: 10–2 v Coventry C, Division 3 (S), 15 March 1930 – Jarvie; Hannah, Graham; Brown, O'Brien, Lochhead (1); Porter (1), Anderson, Hunt (5), Scott (2), Slicer (1).

Record Cup Victory: 8–0 v Sutton U, FA Cup, 4th rd, 28 January 1989 – Gunn; Culverhouse, Bowen, Butterworth, Linighan, Townsend (Crook), Gordon, Fleck (3), Allen (4), Phelan, Putney (1).

Record Defeat: 2–10 v Swindon T, Southern League, 5 September 1908.

Most League Points (2 for a win): 64, Division 3 (S), 1950–51.

Most League Points (3 for a win): 84, Division 2, 1985–86.

Most League Goals: 99, Division 3 (S), 1952–53.

Highest League Scorer in Season: Ralph Hunt, 31. Division 3 (S), 1955–56.

Most League Goals in Total Aggregate: Johnny Gavin, 122, 1945–54, 1955–58.

Most Capped Player: Mark Bowen, 30 (32), Wales.

Most League Appearances: Ron Ashman, 592, 1947–64.

Record Transfer Fee Received: £5,000,000 from Blackburn R for Chris Sutton, July 1994.

Record Transfer Fee Paid: £1,000,000 to Leeds U for Jon Newsome, June 1994.

Football League Record: 1920 Original Member of Division 3; 1921 Division 3 (S): 1934–39 Division 2; 1946–58 Division 3 (S); 1958–60 Division 3; 1960–72 Division 2; 1972–74 Division 1; 1974–75 Division 2; 1975–81 Division 1; 1981–82 Division 2; 1982–85 Division 1; 1985–86 Division 2; 1986–92 Division 1; 1992–95 FA Premier League; 1995– Division 1.

Honours: *FA Premier League* best season: 3rd 1992–93. *Football League:* Division 2 – Champions 1971–72, 1985–86. Division 3 (S) – Champions 1933–34; Division 3 – Runners-up 1959–60. *FA Cup:* Semi-finals 1959, 1989, 1992. *Football League Cup:* Winners 1962, 1985; Runners-up 1973, 1975. **European Competitions:** *UEFA Cup:* 1993–94.

Colours: Yellow shirts, green shorts, yellow stockings. **Change colours:** All blue.

NORWICH CITY 1994–95 LEAGUE RECORD

Match No.	Date	Venue	Opponents	Result	H/T Score	Lg. Pos.	Goalscorers	Attendance
1	Aug 20	A	Chelsea	L 0-2	0-1	—		23,098
2	24	H	Crystal Palace	D 0-0	0-0	—		19,015
3	27	H	West Ham U	W 1-0	0-0	11	Robins	19,110
4	31	A	Sheffield W	D 0-0	0-0	—		25,072
5	Sept 10	H	Arsenal	D 0-0	0-0	11		17,768
6	19	A	Ipswich T	W 2-1	1-1	—	Newman, Bradshaw	17,405
7	24	A	Manchester C	L 0-2	0-0	11		21,031
8	Oct 1	H	Blackburn R	W 2-1	1-1	9	Bowen, Newsome	18,146
9	8	H	Leeds U	W 2-1	0-0	8	Robins, Adams	17,390
10	15	A	Aston Villa	D 1-1	0-0	6	Milligan	22,468
11	22	H	QPR	W 4-2	0-1	6	Robins, Bowen, Sheron, White (og)	19,431
12	30	A	Wimbledon	L 0-1	0-0	8		8242
13	Nov 2	A	Southampton	D 1-1	0-0	—	Robins	12,876
14	5	H	Everton	D 0-0	0-0	7		18,377
15	19	A	Coventry C	L 0-1	0-0	9		11,891
16	26	H	Leicester C	W 2-1	0-1	9	Newsome, Sutch	20,657
17	Dec 3	A	Manchester U	L 0-1	0-1	9		43,789
18	10	H	Chelsea	W 3-0	2-0	9	Ward 2, Cureton	18,246
19	17	A	Crystal Palace	W 1-0	0-0	7	Ward	12,473
20	26	H	Tottenham H	L 0-2	0-1	7		21,814
21	27	A	Nottingham F	L 0-1	0-0	—		21,010
22	31	H	Newcastle U	W 2-1	2-1	7	Adams, Ward	21,172
23	Jan 2	A	Liverpool	L 0-4	0-2	8		34,709
24	14	H	Wimbledon	L 1-2	1-1	9	Goss	18,261
25	25	H	Coventry C	D 2-2	1-1	—	Adams (pen), Ward	14,024
26	Feb 4	A	Everton	L 1-2	0-1	10	Milligan	23,295
27	11	H	Southampton	D 2-2	1-2	10	Newsome, Ward	18,361
28	22	H	Manchester U	L 0-2	0-2	—		21,824
29	25	A	Blackburn R	D 0-0	0-0	14		25,579
30	Mar 4	H	Manchester C	D 1-1	0-0	14	Cureton	16,266
31	8	H	Sheffield W	D 0-0	0-0	—		13,530
32	11	A	West Ham U	D 2-2	1-0	14	Eadie, Ullathorne	21,464
33	15	A	QPR	L 0-2	0-0	—		10,519
34	20	H	Ipswich T	W 3-0	0-0	—	Cureton, Ward, Eadie	17,510
35	Apr 1	A	Arsenal	L 1-5	1-3	14	Cureton	36,942
36	5	A	Leicester C	L 0-1	0-0	—		15,992
37	8	A	Newcastle U	L 0-3	0-2	14		35,518
38	12	H	Nottingham F	L 0-1	0-0	—		19,005
39	17	A	Tottenham H	L 0-1	0-1	20		32,304
40	29	H	Liverpool	L 1-2	1-1	20	Ullathorne	21,843
41	May 6	A	Leeds U	L 1-2	1-0	20	Ward	31,981
42	14	H	Aston Villa	D 1-1	0-1	20	Goss	19,374

Final League Position: 20

GOALSCORERS

League (37): Ward 8, Robins 4, Cureton 4, Adams 3 (1 pen), Newsome 3, Bowen 2, Eadie 2, Goss 2, Milligan 2, Ullathorne 2, Bradshaw 1, Newman 1, Sheron 1, Sutch 1, own goal 1.
Coca-Cola Cup (9): Polston 2, Adams 1, Bradshaw 1 (pen), Eadie 1, Newman 1, Prior 1, Sheron 1, own goal 1.
FA Cup (4): Sheron 2, Crook 1, Eadie 1.

Gunn B. 21	Bradshaw C. 25 + 1	Bowen M.R. 34 + 2	Newsome J. 35	Polston J.D. 38	Newman R.N. 23 + 9	Crook I.S. 33 + 1	Ullathorne R. 27	Robins M.G. 14 + 3	Ekoku E. 5 + 1	Goss J. 19 + 6	Adams N.J. 23 + 10	Sutch D. 20 + 10	Eadie D.M. 22 + 4	Akinbiyi A.P. 6 + 7	Sheron M.N. 17 + 4	Milligan M.J. 25 + 1	Prior S. 12 + 5	Wright J. 1 + 1	O'Neill K.P. — + 1	Cureton J. 9 + 8	Ward A.S. 25	Marshall A.J. 20 + 1	Tracey S.P. 1	Johnson A.J. 6 + 1	Megson G.J. 1	*Match No.*
1	2	3	4	5	6	7	8	9	*10*	11	12	14														1
1	2	3	4	5		7	8	9	10	6	11		12													2
1	2	3	4	5	12	7	8	9	*10*	6	11			14												3
1	2	3	4	5	12	7	8	9		6	11			*10*	14											4
1	2	3	4	5	9	7	8	12	10	6	*11*	14														5
1	2	3	4	5	9	7			12	6	11		14		10	8										6
1	2	3	4	5	9	7	8	12		6	*11*				10	14										7
1	2	3	4	5	9	6		14	*10*	12	11		7			8										8
1	2	3	*4*		5	6		9		12	11		7		10	8	14									9
1	*2*	3			4	6		9			11		7	12	10	8	5	14								10
1		3	4	5	12	6		9		14	*11*		7		10	8		2								11
1		3		5	8	12	6			11	14	2		*9*	10	7	4									12
1		3		5	*2*	7		9		4	11	12		10		8	6		14							13
1		3		5	8	7		9		6	11	2				10	4			12						14
1		3	5	2	8	4		9		12	*11*	14	7			10	6									15
1		3	4	5	9	6				12	11	2	7		*10*	8				14						16
1	2	3	4	5	8	10	6	9		11		7								12						17
1	2		4	5	12	6	3	*9*				7	11			8				14	10					18
1	2	12	4	5	14	*6*	3	9				7	11			8					10					19
1		2	4	5	12	6	3	9		11	14	7	8								10					20
1			4	5	8	6	3			11	12	2			9					7	10	15				21
			4	5	12	7	3			6	11	2			*9*	8				14	10	1				22
				5	*4*	7	3			11	12	2	14		9	8	6				10	1				23
		3	4	5		7	8			6	*11*	2		12	9		14				10	1				24
		3	4	5	8						11	2	12		9	7	6				10		1			25
		3	4	5		7	6			12	14	*2*	11		9	8					10	1				26
	2	3	4			7	6			11	14	12	8		9		*5*				10	1				27
	2	3	4	5							7		11		9	8					10	1		6		28
	2	3	4	5							7	12	11		9	*8*				14	10	1		6		29
	2	3		5	4						7		11		12	8	14			*9*	10	1		6		30
	2	3	4	5	12	7	6					8	11							9	10	1		14		31
			4	5	8		3				12	2	*11*	14			6			9	10	1		7		32
				5	4		3				12	2	11	14		8	6			*9*	10	1		7		33
		3	4	5	12	2	6				*7*	14	11			8				9	10	1				34
	2	3	4		5		6				7	12	11							9	10	1		8		35
	2	12	4	5	8		3					7	11				14			9	10	1			*6*	36
	2	3	4	*5*		7	8					12	11			10	6			14	9	1				37
	2	3	4	5		6					7		11	14		8	12			*9*	10	1				38
	2	3	4	5	11	7						12		14	*9*	8	6				10	1				39
	2	3	4	5		11	6				12	7		9		8				14	10	1				40
	12	3	4	5	2	11	8			6		7		*9*	14						10	1				41
	2	3	4	5		7	8			6		11		9	12						10	1				42

Coca-Cola Cup

Second Round	Swansea C (h)	3-0
	(a)	0-1
Third Round	Tranmere R (a)	1-1
	(h)	4-2
Fourth Round	Notts Co (h)	1-0
Fifth Round	Bolton W (a)	0-1

FA Cup

Third Round	Grimsby T (a)	1-0
Fourth Round	Coventry C (a)	0-0
	(h)	3-1
Fifth Round	Everton (a)	0-5

NOTTINGHAM FOREST 1994–95 *Back row (left to right):* Des Lyttle, Gary Crosby, Steven Stone, Vance Warner, Neil Webb, Gary Bull, Kingsley Black, Steven Howe.
Centre row: Liam O'Kane (Coach), Richard Money (Reserve Coach), Alf Haaland, Carl Tiler, Mark Crossley, Jason Lee, Robert Rosario, Tommy Wright, Lars Bohinen, Steven Chettle, John Haselden (Physio), Peter Edwards (Fitness Coach).
Front row: Scot Gemmill, Brian Laws, Stan Collymore, Brian Roy, Frank Clark (Manager), Alan Hill (Assistant Manager), Stuart Pearce, Ian Woan, David Philips, Colin Cooper.

FA Premiership NOTTINGHAM FOREST

City Ground, Nottingham NG2 5FJ. Telephone: (0115) 9526000. Fax: (0115) 9526003. Information Desk: (0115) 9526016. Commercial Office: (0115) 9526006. Commercial Office Fax: (0115) 9526007. Ticket Office: (0115) 9526002. Souvenir Shop: (0115) 9526026. Junior Reds: (0115) 9526001. Lottery Office: (0115) 9526005.

Ground capacity: 30,539.

Record attendance: 49,946 v Manchester U, Division 1, 28 October 1967.

Record receipts: £272,735 v Sheffield W, FA Cup 3rd rd replay, 19 January 1994.

Pitch measurements: 115yd × 78yd.

Chairman: Fred Reacher. ***Vice-Chairman:*** I. I. Korn.

Directors: G. E. Macpherson, J. M. Smith, C. Wootton, K. Gibson, R. A. Fairhall.

Manager: Frank Clark. ***Assistant Manager:*** Alan Hill.

Secretary: Paul White. ***Commercial Manager:*** David Pullan.

Coach: Liam O'Kane. ***Physio:*** John Haselden.

Year Formed: 1865. ***Turned Professional:*** 1889. ***Ltd Co.:*** 1982.

Club Nickname: 'Reds'.

Previous Grounds: 1865, Forest Racecourse; 1879, The Meadows; 1880, Trent Bridge Cricket Ground; 1882, Parkside, Lenton; 1885, Gregory, Lenton; 1890, Town Ground; 1898, City Ground.

Foundation: One of the oldest football clubs in the world, Nottingham Forest was formed at a meeting in the Clinton Arms in 1865. Known originally as the Forest Football Club, the game which first drew the founders together was "shinney" a form of hockey. When they determined to change to football in 1865, one of their first moves was to buy a set of red caps to wear on the field.

First Football League game: 3 September, 1892, Division 1, v Everton (a) D 2-2 – Brown; Earp, Scott; Hamilton, A. Smith, McCracken; McCallum, W. Smith, Higgins (2), Pike, McInnes.

Record League Victory: 12–0 v Leicester Fosse, Division 1, 12 April 1909 – Iremonger; Dudley, Maltby; Hughes (1), Needham, Armstrong; Hooper (3), Marrison, West (3), Morris (2), Spouncer (3 incl. 1p).

Record Cup Victory: 14–0 v Clapton (away), FA Cup, 1st rd, 17 January 1891 – Brown; Earp, Scott; A. Smith, Russell, Jeacock; McCallum (2), 'Tich' Smith (1), Higgins (5), Lindley (4), Shaw (2).

Record Defeat: 1–9 v Blackburn R, Division 2, 10 April 1937.

Most League Points (2 for a win): 70, Division 3 (S), 1950–51.

Most League Points (3 for a win): 83, Division 1, 1993–94.

Most League Goals: 110, Division 3 (S), 1950–51.

Highest League Scorer in Season: Wally Ardron, 36, Division 3 (S), 1950–51.

Most League Goals in Total Aggregate: Grenville Morris, 199, 1898–1913.

Most Capped Player: Stuart Pearce, 59, England.

Most League Appearances: Bob McKinlay, 614, 1951–70.

Record Transfer Fee Received: £8,500,000 from Liverpool for Stan Collymore, June 1995.

Record Transfer Fee Paid: £2,900,000 to Foggia for Bryan Roy, August 1994.

Football League Record: 1892 Elected to Division 1; 1906–07 Division 2; 1907–11 Division 1; 1911–22 Division 2; 1922–25 Division 1; 1925–49 Division 2; 1949–51 Division 3 (S); 1951–57 Division 2; 1957–72 Division 1; 1972–77 Division 2; 1977–92 Division 1; 1992–93 FA Premier League; 1993–94 Division 1; 1994– FA Premier League.

Honours: *Football League:* Division 1 – Champions 1977–78; Runners-up 1966–67, 1978–79; Division 2 – Champions 1906–07, 1921–22; Runners-up 1956–57; Division 3 (S) – Champions 1950–51. *FA Cup:* Winners 1898, 1959; Runners-up 1991. *Anglo-Scottish Cup:* Winners 1977; *Football League Cup:* Winners 1978, 1979, 1989, 1990; Runners-up 1980. *Simod Cup:* Winners 1989. *Zenith Data Systems Cup:* Winners: 1992. **European Competitions:** *Fairs Cup:* 1961–62, 1967–68. *European Cup:* 1978–79 (winners), 1979–80 (winners), 1980–81. *Super Cup:* 1979–80 (winners), 1980–81 (runners-up). *World Club Championship:* 1980. *UEFA Cup:* 1983–84, 1984–85.

Colours: Red shirts with black shoulders, white shorts, red stockings. **Change colours:** All blue/green.

NOTTINGHAM FOREST 1994–95 LEAGUE RECORD

Match No.	Date	Venue	Opponents	Result		H/T Score	Lg. Pos.	Goalscorers	Attendance
1	Aug 20	A	Ipswich T	W	1-0	1-0	—	Roy	18,763
2	22	H	Manchester U	D	1-1	1-1	—	Collymore	22,072
3	27	H	Leicester C	W	1-0	1-0	4	Collymore	21,601
4	30	A	Everton	W	2-1	1-0	—	Hinchcliffe (og), Cooper	26,689
5	Sept 10	H	Sheffield W	W	4-1	1-0	2	Black, Bohinen, Pearce (pen), Roy	22,022
6	17	A	Southampton	D	1-1	1-0	3	Collymore	14,185
7	24	A	Tottenham H	W	4-1	1-1	3	Stone, Roy 2, Bohinen	24,558
8	Oct 2	H	QPR	W	3-2	0-0	2	Black, Roy, Collymore	21,449
9	8	A	Manchester C	D	3-3	1-1	2	Collymore, Dibble (og), Woan	23,150
10	17	H	Wimbledon	W	3-1	1-0	—	Bohinen, Collymore, Woan	20,287
11	22	A	Aston Villa	W	2-0	1-0	2	Pearce (pen), Stone	29,217
12	29	H	Blackburn R	L	0-2	0-1	2		22,131
13	Nov 5	A	Liverpool	L	0-1	0-1	4		33,329
14	7	H	Newcastle U	D	0-0	0-0	—		22,102
15	19	H	Chelsea	L	0-1	0-1	5		22,092
16	26	A	Leeds U	L	0-1	0-0	5		37,709
17	Dec 3	H	Arsenal	D	2-2	1-0	5	Pearce (pen), Roy	21,662
18	10	H	Ipswich T	W	4-1	4-1	5	Collymore, Gemmill, Haaland, Pearce	21,340
19	17	A	Manchester U	W	2-1	1-0	4	Collymore, Pearce	43,744
20	26	A	Coventry C	D	0-0	0-0	5		19,116
21	27	H	Norwich C	W	1-0	0-0	—	Bohinen	21,010
22	31	A	West Ham U	L	1-3	0-3	5	McGregor	20,644
23	Jan 2	H	Crystal Palace	W	1-0	0-0	4	Bull	21,326
24	14	A	Blackburn R	L	0-3	0-0	4		27,510
25	21	H	Aston Villa	L	1-2	0-1	5	Collymore (pen)	24,598
26	25	A	Chelsea	W	2-0	1-0	—	Collymore 2	17,890
27	Feb 4	H	Liverpool	D	1-1	1-0	5	Collymore	25,418
28	11	A	Newcastle U	L	1-2	0-0	5	Lee	34,471
29	21	A	Arsenal	L	0-1	0-0	—		35,441
30	26	A	QPR	D	1-1	0-0	5	Stone	13,363
31	Mar 4	H	Tottenham H	D	2-2	0-0	5	Bohinen, Lee	28,711
32	8	H	Everton	W	2-1	1-1	—	Collymore, Pearce	24,526
33	11	A	Leicester C	W	4-2	1-1	5	Pearce (pen), Collymore, Woan, Lee	20,423
34	18	H	Southampton	W	3-0	1-0	5	Roy 2, Collymore	24,146
35	22	H	Leeds U	W	3-0	3-0	—	Roy 2, Collymore	26,299
36	Apr 1	A	Sheffield W	W	7-1	2-0	4	Pearce, Woan, Roy 2, Collymore 2, Bohinen	30,060
37	8	H	West Ham U	D	1-1	0-0	4	Collymore	28,361
38	12	A	Norwich C	W	1-0	0-0	—	Stone	19,005
39	17	H	Coventry C	W	2-0	2-0	3	Woan, Collymore	26,253
40	29	A	Crystal Palace	W	2-1	1-0	3	Roy, Collymore	16,335
41	May 6	H	Manchester C	W	1-0	1-0	3	Collymore	28,882
42	13	A	Wimbledon	D	2-2	1-2	3	Phillips, Stone	15,341

Final League Position: 3

GOALSCORERS

League (72): Collymore 22 (1 pen), Roy 13, Pearce 8 (4 pens), Bohinen 6, Stone 5, Woan 5, Lee 3, Black 2, Bull 1, Cooper 1, Gemmill 1, Haaland 1, McGregor 1, Phillips 1, own goals 2.
Coca-Cola Cup (5): Collymore 2, Roy 2, Pearce 1.
FA Cup (3): Bohinen 1, Collymore 1, Gemmill 1.

Crossley M.G. 42	Lyttle D. 38	Pearce S. 36	Cooper C.T. 35	Chettle S. 41	Stone S.B. 41	Phillips D.O. 38	Gemmill S. 19	Lee J.B. 5 + 17	Woan I.S. 35 + 2	Roy B. 37	Bohinen L. 30 + 4	Rosario R.M. — + 1	Collymore S.V. 37	Black K. 5 + 5	Haaland A-I.R. 18 + 2	McGregor P.A. — + 11	Warner V. 1	Bull G.W. 1	Tiler C. 3	Match No.
1	2	3	4	5	6	7	8	9	10	*11*	12	14								1
1	2	3	4	5	6	7	8		11	9	12		10							2
1	2	3	4	5	6	7	8		11	9			10							3
1	2	3	4	5	6	7	8		11	9	12		10							4
1	2	3	4	5	6	7				8	9		10	11						5
1	2	3	4		6	7				8	9		10	11	5					6
1	2	3	4	5	6	7				8	9		10	11	12					7
1	2	3	4	5	6	7				8	9		10	11						8
1		3	4	5	6	7	8	12	14		9		10	*11*	2					9
1		3	4	5	6	7			11	8	9		10		2					10
1		3	4	5	6	7		12	11	8	9		10		2					11
1	2	3	4	5	6	7		10	11	8	9			12						12
1	2	3	4	5	6	7		10	11	8	9									13
1	2	3	4	5	6	7			11	8	9		10	12						14
1	2	3	4	5	6	7		12	11	8	9		10							15
1	2	3	4	5	6	7		12	11	8	9		10							16
1	2	3		5		4	7		11	8	9		10	12	6					17
1	2	3		5	6		7	12	11	8	*9*		10		4	14				18
1	2	3		5	6	7	8		11	9	12		10		4					19
1	2	3	4	5	6	7	*8*		11		9		10		12	14				20
1	2	3	4	5	6				11	8	9		10	12	7					21
1	2	3	*4*	5	6				11	8	9		10	12	7	14				22
1	2	3		5	6		8		11	10					7	12	4	9		23
1	2			5	6	7	8		11	9			10		3	12			4	24
1	2			5	6	7			11	8	9		10		3				4	25
1	2			5	6	7	8			11	9		10		4	12			3	26
1	2		4	5	6	3	8	12	11	9			10		7					27
1	2	3	4	5	6	7	8	12	11				10		9					28
1	2	3	4	5	6	7	8	10	11		9					12				29
1	2		4	5	6	3	8		12	11	9		10		7					30
1	2		4	5	6	3		12	11	8	9		10		7					31
1	2	3	4	5	6	7		12	11	8	9		10							32
1	2	3	4	5	6	7		12	11	8	9		10							33
1		3	4	5	6	7		12	11	8	9		10		2					34
1	*2*	3	4	5	6	7		12	11	8	9		10			14				35
1	2	3	4	5	6	7			11	8	9		10			12				36
1	2	3	4	5	6	7		12	11	8	*9*		10			14				37
1	2	3	4	5	6	7		12	11	8	9		10							38
1	2	3	4	5	6	7		12	*11*	8	9		10			14				39
1	2	3	4	5	6	7	8	12	11	9			10							40
1	2	3	4	5	6	7	8	12	11	9			10							41
1	2	3	4	5	6	7	8	9	11				10							42

Coca-Cola Cup

Second Round	Hereford U (h)	2-1
	(a)	0-0
Third Round	Wolverhampton W (a)	3-2
Fourth Round	Millwall (h)	0-2

FA Cup

Third Round	Plymouth Arg (h)	2-0
Fourth Round	Crystal Palace (h)	1-2

NOTTS COUNTY 1994–95 *Back row (left to right):* Tony Agana, Shaun Murphy, Steve Cherry, Paul Reece, Steve Slawson, Gary McSwegan.
Centre row: Wayne Jones (Assistant Manager), Tommy Gallagher, Chris Short, Michael Simpson, Paul Cox, Paul Sherlock, Richard Walker, Gary Lund, Dean Yates, Gary Mills, Rob Matthews, Dennis Petitt (Physio), John Gaunt (Youth Coach).
Front row: Peter Butler, Michael Johnson, Michael Emenalo, Dean Thomas, Derek Pavis (Chairman), Russell Slade (Manager), Phil Turner, Paul Devlin, Nigel Jemson, Andy Legg.

Division 2 NOTTS COUNTY

County Ground, Meadow Lane, Nottingham NG2 3HJ. Telephone: (0115) 9529000. Fax: (0115) 9553994. Ticket office: (0115) 9557210. Clubline: 0891 888684. Football in the Community: (0115) 9863656. Supporters Club: (0115) 9557255.

Ground capacity: 20,300.

Record attendance: 47,310 v York C, FA Cup 6th rd, 12 March 1955.

Record receipts: £124,539.10 v Manchester C, FA Cup 6th rd, 16 February 1991.

Pitch measurements: 114yd × 74yd.

Chairman: D. C. Pavis. ***Vice-Chairman:*** J. Mounteney.

Directors: W. A. Hopcroft, D. Ward, F. Sherwood (President), Mrs V. Pavis.

Manager: Colin Murphy. ***Assistant Manager:*** Steve Thompson. ***Commerical Manager:*** Helen Marsh.

Coach: D. Thomas. ***Chief Executive:*** Neal Hook MCIM. AMLD.

Physio: Dennis Pettitt.

Year Formed: 1862 *(*see Foundation).*

Turned Professional: 1885. ***Ltd Co.:*** 1888.

Club Nickname: 'Magpies'.

Previous Grounds: 1862, The Park; 1864, The Meadows; 1877, Beeston Cricket Ground; 1880, Castle Ground; 1883, Trent Bridge; 1910, Meadow Lane.

Foundation: For many years the foundation date of the Football League's oldest club was given as 1862 and the club celebrated its centenary in 1962. However, the researches of Keith Warsop have since shown that the club was on a very haphazard basis at that time, playing little more than practice matches. The meeting which put it on a firm footing was held at the George IV Hotel in December 1864, when they became known as the Notts Football Club.

First Football League game: 15 September, 1888, Football League, v Everton (a) L 1-2 – Holland; Guttridge, McLean; Brown, Warburton, Shelton; Hodder, Harker, Jardine, Moore (1), Wardle.

Record League Victory: 11–1 v Newport C, Division 3 (S), 15 January 1949 – Smith; Southwell, Purvis; Gannon, Baxter, Adamson; Houghton (1), Sewell (4), Lawton (4), Pimbley, Johnston (2).

Record Cup Victory: 15–0 v Rotherham T (at Trent Bridge), FA Cup, 1st rd, 24 October 1885 – Sherwin; Snook, H. T. Moore; Dobson (1), Emmett (1), Chapman; Gunn (1), Albert Moore (2), Jackson (3), Daft (2), Cursham (4). (1 og).

Record Defeat: 1–9 v Blackburn R, Division 1, 16 November, 1889 and v Aston Villa, Division 1, 29 September, 1888 and v Portsmouth, Division 2, 9 April, 1927.

Most League Points (2 for a win): 69, Division 4, 1970–71.

Most League Points (3 for a win): 87, Division 3, 1989–90.

Most League Goals: 107, Division 4, 1959–60.

Highest League Scorer in Season: Tom Keetley, 39, Division 3 (S), 1930–31.

Most League Goals in Total Aggregate: Les Bradd, 124, 1967–78.

Most Capped Player: Kevin Wilson, 15 (42), Northern Ireland.

Most League Appearances: Albert Iremonger, 564, 1904–26.

Record Transfer Fee Received: £2,500,000 from Derby Co for Craig Short, September 1992.

Record Transfer Fee Paid: £685,000 to Sheffield U for Tony Agana, November 1991.

Football League Record: 1888 Founder Member of the Football League; 1893–97 Division 2; 1897–1913 Division 1; 1913–14 Division 2; 1914–20 Division 1; 1920–23 Division 2; 1923–26 Division 1; 1926–30 Division 2; 1930–31 Division 3 (S); 1931–35 Division 2; 1935–50 Division 3 (S); 1950–58 Division 2; 1958–59 Division 3; 1959–60 Division 4; 1960–64 Division 3; 1964–71 Division 4; 1971–73 Division 3; 1973–81 Division 2; 1981–84 Division 1; 1984–85 Division 2; 1985–90 Division 3; 1990–91 Division 2; 1991–95 Division 1; 1995– Division 2.

Honours: *Football League:* Division 1 best season: 3rd, 1890–91, 1900–01; Division 2 – Champions 1896–97, 1913–14, 1922–23; Runners-up 1894–95, 1980–81; Division 3 (S) – Champions 1930–31, 1949–50; Runners-up 1936–37; Division 3 – Runners-up 1972-73; Division 4 – Champions 1970–71; Runners-up 1959–60. *FA Cup:* Winners 1894; Runners-up 1891. *Football League Cup:* best season: 5th rd, 1964, 1973, 1976. *Anglo-Italian Cup:* Winners; 1995; Runners-up 1994.

Colours: Black and white striped shirts, white shorts, black stockings. **Change colours:** Tartan shirts, black shorts, tartan stockings.

NOTTS COUNTY 1994–95 LEAGUE RECORD

Match No.	Date	Venue	Opponents	Result		H/T Score	Lg. Pos.	Goalscorers	Attendance
1	Aug 13	A	Portsmouth	L	1-2	0-1	—	Sherlock	10,487
2	21	H	Wolverhampton W	D	1-1	1-0	—	Simpson	8569
3	27	A	Sheffield U	W	3-1	2-0	10	McSwegan 2, Lund	15,301
4	30	H	Oldham Ath	L	1-3	1-1	—	McSwegan	6603
5	Sept 3	H	Swindon T	L	0-1	0-1	19		6537
6	10	A	Bristol C	L	1-2	1-1	22	Jemson	6670
7	13	A	Barnsley	D	1-1	0-0	—	Lund	3928
8	17	H	Stoke C	L	0-2	0-1	23		8281
9	24	H	Charlton Ath	D	3-3	2-1	24	Agana, Lund, Sturgess (og)	5726
10	Oct 1	A	Reading	L	0-2	0-1	24		7465
11	8	H	Port Vale	D	2-2	1-0	23	Williams, Agana	6903
12	15	A	Watford	L	1-3	0-2	23	Williams	7008
13	23	H	Derby Co	D	0-0	0-0	24		6389
14	29	A	Burnley	L	1-2	0-1	24	Davis (og)	12,876
15	Nov 1	A	Southend U	L	0-1	0-1	—		4302
16	5	H	Sunderland	W	3-2	2-0	24	Devlin 2, Legg	8890
17	19	A	Bolton W	L	0-2	0-1	24		11,698
18	26	H	WBA	W	2-0	1-0	24	Turner, Lund	10,088
19	Dec 3	A	Derby Co	D	0-0	0-0	24		14,278
20	6	H	Tranmere R	W	1-0	0-0	—	Devlin	4703
21	10	A	Wolverhampton W	L	0-1	0-0	24		25,786
22	17	H	Portsmouth	L	0-1	0-0	24		6382
23	26	H	Millwall	L	0-1	0-0	24		6758
24	28	A	Middlesbrough	L	1-2	1-2	—	McSwegan	21,558
25	31	H	Luton T	L	0-1	0-0	24		6249
26	Jan 14	H	Burnley	W	3-0	0-0	24	White, Devlin, McSwegan	8702
27	21	A	Sunderland	W	2-1	1-0	24	Matthews, Lund	14,334
28	28	A	Grimsby T	L	1-2	0-1	24	White	5161
29	Feb 4	A	Tranmere R	L	2-3	0-1	24	Legg, Devlin (pen)	6105
30	7	H	Bolton W	D	1-1	0-0	—	Matthews	7553
31	11	H	Southend U	D	2-2	1-1	24	Legg, Matthews	6768
32	18	A	WBA	L	2-3	0-1	24	Devlin 2	13,748
33	25	H	Reading	W	1-0	0-0	23	Agana	7183
34	Mar 4	A	Charlton Ath	L	0-1	0-1	23		13,638
35	11	H	Sheffield U	W	2-1	1-0	23	White, Simpson	11,102
36	14	A	Oldham Ath	D	1-1	0-1	—	Devlin	5465
37	21	H	Bristol C	D	1-1	0-0	—	White	5692
38	25	A	Stoke C	L	1-2	0-1	24	White	10,204
39	Apr 1	H	Barnsley	L	1-3	1-1	24	Devlin	6834
40	8	A	Luton T	L	0-2	0-1	24		6482
41	15	H	Middlesbrough	D	1-1	0-0	24	White	9377
42	19	A	Millwall	D	0-0	0-0	—		5471
43	22	H	Grimsby T	L	0-2	0-1	24		5286
44	29	H	Watford	W	1-0	1-0	24	White	5083
45	May 3	A	Swindon T	L	0-3	0-1	—		6553
46	7	A	Port Vale	D	1-1	0-1	24	McSwegan	9452

Final League Position: 24

GOALSCORERS

League (45): Devlin 9 (1 pen), White 7, McSwegan 6, Lund 5, Agana 3, Legg 3, Matthews 3, Simpson 2, Williams 2, Jemson 1, Sherlock 1, Turner 1, own goals 2.
Coca-Cola Cup (7): Lund 2, McSwegan 2, Agana 1, Devlin 1, Jemson 1.
FA Cup (4): Matthews 2, McSwegan 1, White 1.

Cherry S.R. 25	Hoyle C.R. 3	Johnson M.O. 27 + 4	Turner P. 37 + 1	Murphy S.P. 31 + 4	Yates D.R. 21	Agana P.A.O. 25 + 6	Legg A. 32 + 2	Lund G.J. 17 + 6	McSwegan G.J. 19 + 3	Simpson M. 15 + 4	Sherlock P.G. 2 + 3	Cox P.R. 3	Emenalo M. 7	Devlin P.J. 37 + 3	Matthews R. 11 + 7	Gallagher T.D. 7	Jemson N.B. 5 + 6	Kuhl M. 2	Walker R.N. 6 + 1	Mills G.R. 33 + 1	Williams J.N. 3 + 2	Butler P.J.F. 20	Reece P.J. 11	Daniel R.C. 5	Marsden C. 7	White D.W. 16 + 4	Kearton J.B. 10	Nicol S. 19	Hogg G.J. 17	Forsyth M.E. 7	Russell K.J. 9 + 2	Short C.M. 11 + 2	Slawson S.M. — + 1	Galloway M.A. 6 + 1	Ridgeway I.D. — + 1	*Match No.*
1	2	3	4	5	6	7	8	9	10	11	12																									1
1	2		4	5	6	7	8	9	10	11			3		12																					2
1			4	5	6	7	8	9	10	12		2	3	11																						3
1			4	5		7	8	9	10		2	6	3	11	12																					4
1			4	5	6	12	8	9	10			2	3	7	11																					5
1		5	3		6		8	12	10				4		9	2	7	11																		6
1		5	4		6		8	12	10					9		2	7	11	3																	7
1		5	4		6		8	12	10	11			3	9		2	7																			8
1		5	4	3	6	11	8	9	12		2			7			10																			9
1		3	4	6	5	11	8	9						7	12		10			2																10
1		3	4	6	5	11		9						7	12				8	2	10															11
1		3		6	5	11		*9*		4				7			12		14	2	10	8														12
		6	4		5	11		9						7			12		3	2	10	8	1													13
			4		5	11	9		10					7		2			3		12	8	1	6												14
			4		5	11			10		14			7	9	2			*6*		12	8	1	3												15
		6	4		5	11	10				12			7	9	2						8	1	3												16
		6	4	5		11		12						7	9					2		8	1	3	10											17
1		6	4		5	11		9						7		10				2		8		3												18
1		6	4	12	5	11	3	9	10					7						2		8														19
1		6		12	5	11	3	9	10					7						2		8			4											20
1		6	*4*	14	5	11	3	9						7			12			2		8			10											21
1		6	4	12	5	11	3	9						7			14			2		8			*10*											22
1		6	4		5	11	3		10					7						2		8				9										23
1		6	4	*5*		11	3		10						14		12			2		8			7	9										24
1		6	4	5			*3*		11					7	14		12			2		8			10	9										25
1		6	4	5		12	3		10					7	11					2		8				9										26
		6	4	5			3	9						7	11					2		8				12	1	10								27
		6	4	5			3	9						7	11					2		8				12	1	10								28
		11	4	5		9	3			12				7						*2*					8	14	1	10	6							29
		11	4	5		9	3			8				7	12					2							1	10	6							30
		11	4	5		9	3	12		14				7	8					2							1	*10*	6							31
		11	4	5			3	14	*9*	12				7	8					2							1	10	6							32
		12	4	5		14	11			10				7	*8*					2							1		6	3	9					33
		12	4	5		*11*								7						2						14	1	10	6	3	9	.8				34
				5		12	11			4				7						2						8	1	10	6	3	*9*	14				35
				5		12	11			4				7						2						8	1	10	6	3	*9*	14				36
1		12	14			9	11							7						2						8		10	6	5	*4*	3				37
1			4	5			*11*						9	7						12						8		10	6	3	14	2				38
1		12	4				11		*9*					7						3						8		10	6	5		2	14			39
1	6	11	4	5						7				12						3						8		10			9	*2*		14		40
			4	5		12				7										3			1			8		10	6		9	2		11		41
			4	5			14			7				12						3			1			8		10	6		9	2		11		42
				5			14			7				12						3		4	1			8		10	6		9	*2*		11		43
				5					12	7				9						3		4	1			8		10	6		14	2		*11*		44
				5					12	7				9						3		4	1			8		10	6			2		*11*	14	45
				5					9	7									4	3			1			8		10	6			2		11		46

Coca-Cola Cup

Second Round	Bristol C (a)	1-0
	(h)	3-0
Third Round	Tottenham H (h)	3-0
Fourth Round	Norwich C (a)	0-1

FA Cup

Third Round	Manchester C (h)	2-2
	(a)	2-5

OLDHAM ATHLETIC 1994–95 *Back row (left to right):* Paul Rickers, John Eyre, Richard Jobson, Jon Hallworth, Ian Olney, Paul Gerrard, Gunnar Halle, Chris Makin, Neil Pointon. *Centre row:* Bill Urmson (Youth Team Coach), Mark Brennan, Richard Graham, Paul Bernard, Ronnie Evans (Kit Manager), Andy Holden (Reserve Team Coach), Jim Cassell (Chief Scout), Darren Beckford, Nicky Banger, Billy Kenny, Colin Harvey (Coach).
Front row: Lee Richardson, Rick Holden, Sean McCarthy, Nick Henry, Graeme Sharp (Manager), Steve Redmond, Craig Fleming, Andy Ritchie, Andy Barlow.

Division 1 OLDHAM ATHLETIC

Boundary Park, Oldham OL1 2PA. Telephone: (0161) 624 4972. Fax: (0161) 652 6501. Ticket Call: 0891 121582. Commercial Office: (0161) 627 1802. Clubcall: 0891 121142.

Ground capacity: 13,544 (all seated).

Record attendance: 47,671 v Sheffield W, FA Cup 4th rd. 25 January 1930.

Record receipts: £138,680 v Manchester U, FA Premier League, 29 December 1993.

Pitch measurements: 110yd × 74yd.

President: R. Schofield.

Chairman & Chief Executive: I. H. Stott, ***Vice-Chairman:*** D. A. Brierley.

Directors: G. T. Butterworth, R. Adams, D. R. Taylor, P. Chadwick, J. Slevin, N. Holden.

Manager: Graeme Sharp. ***Assistant Manager:*** Colin Harvey.

Secretary: Terry Cale. ***Commercial Manager:*** Alan Hardy. ***Public Relations Office:*** Gordon A. Lawton.

Coaches: Billy Urmson, Andy Holden. ***Physio:*** Alex Moreno MCSP.

Year Formed: 1895. ***Turned Professional:*** 1899. ***Ltd Co.:*** 1906.

Previous Name: 1895, Pine Villa; 1899, Oldham Athletic.

Club Nickname: 'The Latics'.

Previous Ground: Sheepfoot Lane; 1905, Boundary Park.

Foundation: It was in 1895 that John Garland, the landlord of the Featherstall and Junction Hotel, decided to form a football club. As Pine Villa they played in the Oldham Junior League. In 1899 the local professional club Oldham County, went out of existence and one of the liquidators persuaded Pine Villa to take over their ground at Sheepfoot Lane and change their name to Oldham Athletic.

First Football League game: 9 September, 1907, Division 2, v Stoke (a) W 3-1 – Hewitson; Hodson, Hamilton; Fay, Walders, Wilson; Ward, W. Dodds (1), Newton (1), Hancock, Swarbrick (1).

Record League Victory: 11–0 v Southport, Division 4, 26 December 1962 – Hollands; Branagan, Marshall; McCall, Williams, Scott; Ledger (1), Johnstone, Lister (6), Colquhoun (1), Whitaker (3).

Record Cup Victory: 10–1 v Lytham, FA Cup, 1st rd, 28 November 1925 – Gray; Wynne, Grundy; Adlam, Heaton, Naylor (1), Douglas, Pynegar (2), Ormston (2), Barnes (3), Watson (2).

Record Defeat: 4–13 v Tranmere R, Division 3 (N), 26 December 1935.

Most League Points (2 for a win): 62, Division 3, 1973–74.

Most League Points (3 for a win): 88, Division 2, 1990–91.

Most League Goals: 95, Division 4, 1962–63.

Highest League Scorer in Season: Tom Davis, 33, Division 3 (N), 1936–37.

Most League Goals in Total Aggregate: Roger Palmer, 141, 1980–94.

Most Capped Player: Gunnar Halle, (46), Norway.

Most League Appearances: Ian Wood, 525, 1966–80.

Record Transfer Fee Received: £1,700,000 from Aston Villa for Earl Barrett, February 1992.

Record Transfer Fee Paid: £700,000 to Aston Villa for Ian Olney, June 1992.

Football League Record: 1907 Elected to Division 2; 1910–23 Division 1; 1923–35 Division 2; 1935–53 Division 3 (N); 1953–54 Division 2; 1954–58 Division 3 (N); 1958–63 Division 4; 1963–69 Division 3; 1969–71 Division 4; 1971–74 Division 3; 1974–91 Division 2; 1991–92 Division 1; 1992–94 FA Premier League; 1994– Division 1.

Honours: *Football League:* Division 1 – Runners-up 1914–15; Division 2 – Champions 1990–91; Runners-up 1909–10; Division 3 (N) – Champions 1952–53; Division 3 – Champions 1973–74; Division 4 – Runners-up 1962–63. *FA Cup:* Semi-final 1913, 1990. *Football League Cup:* Runners-up 1990.

Colours: All blue with red and white trim. **Change colours:** Tangerine and blue shirts, blue shorts, tangerine stockings.

OLDHAM ATHLETIC 1994–95 LEAGUE RECORD

Match No.	Date	Venue	Opponents	Result		H/T Score	Lg. Pos.	Goalscorers	Attendance
1	Aug 13	H	Charlton Ath	W	5-2	2-2	—	McCarthy 2, Richardson 2, Sharp	8924
2	20	A	Port Vale	L	1-3	0-0	7	Sharp	10,051
3	27	H	Burnley	W	3-0	0-0	4	Ritchie, McCarthy 2 (1 pen)	11,310
4	30	A	Notts Co	W	3-1	1-1	—	McCarthy 3	6603
5	Sept 3	A	Southend U	L	0-1	0-0	3		4435
6	10	H	Reading	L	1-3	1-1	6	Richardson	8412
7	13	H	Watford	L	0-2	0-1	—		7243
8	17	A	Derby Co	L	1-2	0-1	14	McCarthy (pen)	13,746
9	24	H	Barnsley	W	1-0	0-0	10	Halle	7941
10	Oct 1	A	Sheffield U	L	0-2	0-1	15		14,223
11	8	H	Portsmouth	W	3-2	1-0	8	Holden R 2 (2 pens), Graham	7683
12	16	A	Bolton W	D	2-2	0-2	9	Bernard, McCarthy	11,106
13	22	H	Stoke C	D	0-0	0-0	13		8954
14	29	A	Sunderland	D	0-0	0-0	14		17,252
15	Nov 1	A	Middlesbrough	L	1-2	1-0	—	Graham	15,929
16	6	H	Tranmere R	D	0-0	0-0	19		6475
17	12	H	Luton T	D	0-0	0-0	15		7907
18	19	A	WBA	L	1-3	0-2	18	Halle (pen)	14,616
19	26	H	Bristol C	W	2-0	0-0	17	Richardson, McCarthy	7277
20	Dec 4	A	Stoke C	W	1-0	0-0	14	McCarthy	12,558
21	10	H	Port Vale	W	3-2	1-1	12	Ritchie 3	7712
22	17	A	Charlton Ath	L	0-2	0-0	14		8970
23	26	H	Wolverhampton W	W	4-1	1-0	11	Ritchie 3, McCarthy	11,962
24	27	A	Grimsby T	W	3-1	2-0	8	Ritchie, Henry, McCarthy	6958
25	31	H	Swindon T	D	1-1	1-1	9	Halle	8917
26	Jan 3	A	Millwall	D	1-1	1-0	—	Richardson (pen)	7438
27	14	H	Sunderland	D	0-0	0-0	8		9742
28	22	A	Tranmere R	L	1-3	1-1	10	Makin	5581
29	Feb 4	A	Luton T	L	1-2	0-1	13	Holden R	6903
30	18	A	Bristol C	D	2-2	1-2	13	Halle, Ritchie	7851
31	21	H	WBA	W	1-0	1-0	—	Richardson	7690
32	25	H	Sheffield U	D	3-3	2-2	11	Banger 2, Ritchie	9640
33	Mar 7	H	Southend U	L	0-2	0-1	—		7168
34	11	A	Burnley	L	1-2	0-1	14	McCarthy	11,620
35	14	H	Notts Co	D	1-1	1-0	—	Henry	5465
36	21	A	Reading	L	1-2	1-0	—	Halle	6921
37	25	H	Derby Co	W	1-0	1-0	15	Graham	7696
38	Apr 1	A	Watford	W	2-1	2-1	14	Banger, Brennan	8090
39	5	H	Middlesbrough	W	1-0	0-0	—	Ritchie	11,024
40	8	A	Swindon T	L	1-3	1-2	13	Ritchie	7488
41	15	H	Grimsby T	W	1-0	1-0	13	McCarthy	6757
42	17	A	Wolverhampton W	L	1-2	1-1	13	Bernard	25,840
43	22	H	Millwall	L	0-1	0-0	15		6319
44	29	H	Bolton W	W	3-1	2-1	12	McCarthy 2, Rickers	11,901
45	May 2	A	Barnsley	D	1-1	1-1	—	Eyre	9838
46	7	A	Portsmouth	D	1-1	1-0	14	McCarthy (pen)	11,002

Final League Position: 14

GOALSCORERS

League (60): McCarthy 18 (3 pens), Ritchie 12, Halle 5 (1 pen), Richardson 6 (1 pen), Banger 3, Graham 3, Holden R 3 (2 pens), Henry 2, Sharp 2, Bernard 2, Brennan 1, Eyre 1, Makin 1, Rickers 1.
Coca-Cola Cup (2): Richardson 1, Ritchie 1.
FA Cup (5): Halle 2, Richardson 1, Sharp 1, own goal 1.

Hallworth J.G. 4 + 2	Makin C. 28	Barlow A.J. 2	Kenny W. 4	Jobson R.I. 20	Fleming C. 5	Halle G. 40	Richardson L.J. 28 + 2	Sharp G.M. 10 + 2	McCarthy S.C. 35 + 4	Holden R.W. 18 + 13	Henry N.I. 33 + 1	Ritchie A.T. 25 + 8	Gerrard P.W. 42	Brennan M.R. 34 + 6	Redmond S. 43	Graham R.E. 29 + 3	Banger N.L. 20 + 8	Pointon N.G. 32	Rickers P.S. 4	Bernard P.R.J. 16 + 1	Eyre J.R. 3 + 5	Holden A.I. 1	Beckford D.R. — + 3	Snodin I. 17	Moore N. 5	Webster S.P. 7	McNiven S.A. 1	Beresford D. — + 2	Match No.
1	2	3	4	5	6	7	8	9	10	11																			1
1	2	3	4	5	6	7	*8*	9	10	11	12	14																	2
	3			5	6	2	7	9	10	11	4	12	1	8															3
	3			5	6	2	7	9	10	11			1	8	4														4
15	3			5	6	2	7	9	10	11		12	1	8	*4*														5
	3		4	5		2	7	9	10	11		12	1	8	6														6
15	3		4			2	7	9	10	11		12	1	*8*	6	5													7
1	3			5		2	7		10	12	4	11		8	6	9													8
	3			5		2	7	14	10	12	4	*11*	1	8	6	9													9
1	3			5		2	12	*9*	10	14	4	11		8	6	7													10
	3			5		2	7	12	10	11	*4*		1	14	6	9	8												11
				5		2	7		10	11	4		1		6	9	8	3		12									12
				5		2			10	11	4		1		6	9	8	3	7										13
				5		2			10	11	4		1		6	9	8	3		7	12								14
				5		2			10	11	4	*8*	1	12	6	9		3		7	14								15
	3			5		2			10	11	4		1		6	9	8			7									16
	2			5		7				11	4	10	1	12	6	9	8	3											17
	2			5		7			9		4	10	1	11	6	8	12	3											18
	2			5			7		9	*11*	4	8	1	14	6	10	12	3											19
	2			5			7		9	*11*	4	8	1	14	6	10	12	3											20
	2			5			7		9	11	4	8	1	14	6	10	12	*3*											21
	3					2			9	14	4	8	1	11	6	10	12			7		5							22
	2					7	10		9		4	8	1	11	6	5		3					12						23
	2					7	10		9		4	8	1	11	6	5		3					12						24
	2					7	10		*9*	14	4	8	1	11	6	5	12	3											25
	2					7	10	9			4		1	11	6	5	8	3					12						26
	2					7	10	9		14		*8*	1	11	6	5	12	3						4					27
	2					7	10			12		8	1	11	6	5	9	3						4					28
						7	10		12	14	*4*	8	1	11	6	5	9	3						2					29
						7	10		12	14	4	8	1	*11*	6		9	3						2	5				30
						7	*10*		12	14	4	8	1	11	6		9	3						2	5				31
						7	10			12	4	8	1	11	6		9	3						2	5				32
						7	10			4		8	1	11	6		9	3			12			2	5				33
						7	10		12	14		8	1	11	6			3		4	9			2	5				34
						7			9	12	4		1	11	6	5	10	3		8				2					35
						7			9		4	12	1	11	6	5	10	3		8				2					36
						7			9			12	1	11	6	4	10	3		8				2		5			37
						7			9		4		1	11	6	12	10	3		8				2		5			38
						7			9		4	12	1	11	6		10	3		8				2		5			39
						7					4	9	1	11	6	12	10	3		8				2		5			40
						7			9		4	10	1	11	6			3		8				2		5			41
						7			9		4	10	1	11	6	12	14	*3*		8				2		5			42
	2					7			9		4	8	1	11	6	10		3			12					5			43
	2						12		9		4		1	11	6	5	*10*	3	7	8	14								44
	3						4		9				1	11	6	5			7	8	10						2	12	45
	2						4		9				1	11	6			3	7	8	10			5				12	46

Coca-Cola Cup

Second Round	Oxford U (a)	1-1
	(h)	1-0
Third Round	Arsenal (h)	0-0
	(a)	0-2

FA Cup

Third Round	Reading (a)	3-1
Fourth Round	Leeds U (a)	2-3

OXFORD UNITED 1994–95 *Back row (left to right):* Paul Wanless, David Collins, John Byrne, Nick Cusack, Mike Ford, Alex Dyer.
Centre row: Maurice Evans (General Manager), Malcolm Crosby (Assistant Manager), Anton Rogan, Paul Moody, Paul Reece, Phil Whitehead, Matt Elliott, Steve Wood, John Clinkard (Physio), Steve McClaren (Reserve/Youth Team Coach).
Front row: Chris Allen, Les Robinson, Stuart Massey, Bobby Ford, Denis Smith (Manager), Dave Smith, Mickey Lewis, Matt Murphy, Mark Druce.

Division 2 OXFORD UNITED

Manor Ground, Headington, Oxford, OX3 7RS. Telephone: (01865) 61503. Fax: (01865) 741820. Supporters Club: (01865) 63063. Clubline: 0891 440055.

Ground capacity: 9572.

Record attendance: 22,750 v Preston NE, FA Cup 6th rd, 29 February 1964.

Record receipts: £103,411 v Leeds U, FA Cup 4th rd, 29 January 1994.

Pitch measurements: 110yd × 75yd.

President: The Duke of Marlborough.

Directors: K. A. Cox (Managing), D. M. Clitheroe, G. E. Coppock, N. J. W. Harris, P. L. Lowe.

Manager: Denis Smith. *Assistant Manager:* Malcolm Crosby. *Physio:* John Clinkard.

Secretary: Mick Brown. *Commercial Manager:* Tony Watson.

Year Formed: 1893. *Turned Professional:* 1949. *Ltd Co.:* 1949.

Club Nickname: 'The U's'.

Previous Names: 1893, Headington; 1894, Headington United; 1960, Oxford United.

Previous Grounds: 1893–94 Headington Quarry; 1894–98 Wootten's Field; 1898–1902 Sandy Lane Ground; 1902–09 Britannia Field; 1909–10 Sandy Lane; 1910–14 Quarry Recreation Ground; 1914–22 Sandy Lane; 1922–25 The Paddock Manor Road; 1925– Manor Ground.

Foundation: There had been an Oxford United club around the time of World War I but only in the Oxfordshire Thursday League and there is no connection with the modern club which began as Headington in 1893, adding "United" a year later. Playing first on Quarry Fields and subsequently Wooton's Fields, they owe much to a Dr. Hitchings for their early development.

First Football League game: 18 August, 1962, Division 4, v Barrow (a) L 2-3 – Medlock; Beavon, Quartermain; R. Atkinson, Kyle, Jones; Knight, G. Atkinson (1), Houghton (1), Cornwell, Colfar.

Record League Victory: 7–0 v Barrow, Division 4, 19 December 1964 – Fearnley; Beavon, Quartermann; Ron Atkinson (1), Kyle, Jones; Morris, Booth (3), Willey (1), Graham Atkinson (1), Harrington (1).

Record Cup Victory: 6–0 v Gillingham, League Cup, 2nd rd (1st leg), 24 September 1986 – Judge; Langan, Trewick, Phillips (Brock), Briggs, Shotton, Houghton (1), Aldridge (4 incl. 1p), Charles (Leworthy), Hebberd, Slatter. (1 og).

Record Defeat: 0–6 v Liverpool, Division 1, 22 March 1986.

Most League Points (2 for a win): 61, Division 4, 1964–65.

Most League Points (3 for a win): 95, Division 3, 1983–84.

Most League Goals: 91, Division 3, 1983–84.

Highest League Scorer in Season: John Aldridge, 30, Division 2, 1984–85.

Most League Goals in Total Aggregate: Graham Atkinson, 77, 1962–73.

Most Capped Player: Jim Magilton, 18 (29), Northern Ireland.

Most League Appearances: John Shuker, 478, 1962–77.

Record Transfer Fee Received: £1,190,000 from Derby Co for Dean Saunders, October 1988.

Record Transfer Fee Paid: £285,000 to Gillingham for Colin Greenall, February 1988.

Football League Record: 1962 Elected to Division 4; 1965–68 Division 3; 1968–76 Division 2; 1976–84 Division 3; 1984–85 Division 2; 1985–88 Division 1; 1988–92 Division 2; 1992–94 Division 1; 1994– Division 2.

Honours: Football League: Division 1 best season: 18th, 1985–86, 1986–87; Division 2 – Champions 1984–85; Division 3 – Champions 1967–68, 1983–84; Division 4 – Promoted 1964–65 (4th). *FA Cup:* best season: 6th rd, 1964 (record for 4th Division club). *Football League Cup:* Winners 1986.

Colours: Gold shirts with blue sleeves, blue shorts, blue stockings. **Change colours:** Red and black striped shirts, black shorts, black stockings.

OXFORD UNITED 1994–95 LEAGUE RECORD

Match No.	Date	Venue	Opponents	Result	H/T Score	Lg. Pos.	Goalscorers	Attendance
1	Aug 13	H	Hull C	W 4-0	4-0	—	Byrne 3, Moody	5485
2	20	A	Cardiff C	W 3-1	2-1	2	Moody 3	7281
3	27	H	Cambridge U	W 1-0	1-0	3	Moody (pen)	5513
4	30	A	Bradford C	W 2-0	1-0	—	Moody, Jacobs (og)	9005
5	Sept 3	A	Huddersfield T	D 3-3	2-1	2	Moody (pen), Druce, Rogan	10,122
6	10	H	Birmingham C	D 1-1	0-0	2	Moody (pen)	8077
7	13	H	Crewe Alex	W 2-1	2-0	—	Byrne 2	6499
8	17	A	Brighton & HA	D 1-1	0-1	1	Moody	9970
9	24	H	Leyton Orient	W 3-2	0-0	1	Moody, Elliott, Rush	5814
10	Oct 1	A	Chester C	L 0-2	0-1	2		2324
11	8	H	Plymouth Arg	W 1-0	1-0	2	Byrne	6550
12	15	A	Swansea C	W 3-1	3-1	2	Byrne 2, Moody	3724
13	22	A	Wrexham	L 2-3	2-2	2	Humes (og), Hunter (og)	3925
14	29	H	Shrewsbury T	D 0-0	0-0	3		6094
15	Nov 1	H	Blackpool	W 3-2	1-1	—	Elliott, Byrne, Rush	5610
16	5	A	Stockport Co	W 2-0	1-0	2	Moody 2 (1 pen)	5132
17	19	H	Rotherham U	W 2-1	2-1	2	Moody 2	5801
18	26	A	Bournemouth	W 2-0	1-0	1	Byrne, Butters	4277
19	Dec 10	H	Cardiff C	W 1-0	1-0	1	Murphy	6181
20	17	A	Hull C	L 1-3	1-2	1	Elliott	4884
21	26	A	Peterborough U	W 4-1	2-1	1	Ford R, Rush 2, Murphy	5803
22	27	H	Wycombe W	L 0-2	0-1	1		9540
23	31	A	Brentford	L 0-2	0-1	2		7125
24	Jan 2	H	York C	L 0-2	0-1	3		6386
25	14	A	Bristol R	L 2-3	2-0	4	Druce 2	5875
26	28	A	Shrewsbury T	D 1-1	1-1	4	Byrne	3768
27	Feb 4	H	Bournemouth	L 0-3	0-2	6		5473
28	11	A	Blackpool	L 1-2	0-0	7	Rush	5206
29	18	H	Bristol R	D 0-0	0-0	7		6349
30	21	A	Rotherham U	D 1-1	1-0	—	Murphy	2833
31	25	H	Chester C	W 1-0	0-0	7	Gilchrist	4930
32	28	H	Stockport Co	W 4-0	1-0	—	Murphy, Lewis, Rush (pen), Allen	4594
33	Mar 4	A	Leyton Orient	D 1-1	0-1	6	Moody	4052
34	7	H	Huddersfield T	W 3-1	0-0	—	Elliott, Murphy, Moody	7160
35	11	A	Cambridge U	W 2-1	1-0	3	Rush 2	3558
36	18	H	Bradford C	W 1-0	0-0	3	Moody	5363
37	21	A	Birmingham C	L 0-3	0-1	—		19,781
38	25	H	Brighton & HA	D 0-0	0-0	4		6725
39	Apr 1	A	Crewe Alex	L 2-3	2-1	5	Moody, Allen	3928
40	4	H	Wrexham	D 0-0	0-0	—		4729
41	8	H	Brentford	D 1-1	1-1	5	Dyer	7800
42	15	A	Wycombe W	L 0-1	0-1	7		7683
43	17	H	Peterborough U	W 1-0	1-0	6	Moody	5163
44	22	A	York C	W 2-0	1-0	6	Murphy 2	3732
45	30	H	Swansea C	L 1-2	1-1	7	Rush	5244
46	May 6	A	Plymouth Arg	D 1-1	0-1	7	Ford R	4953

Final League Position: 7

GOALSCORERS

League (66): Moody 20 (4 pens), Byrne 11, Rush 9 (1 pen), Murphy 7, Elliott 4, Druce 3, Allen 2, Ford R 2, Butters 1, Dyer 1, Gilchrist 1, Lewis 1, Rogan 1, own goals 3.
Coca-Cola Cup (5): Dyer 1, Ford M 1, Massey 1, Moody 1 (pen), Robinson 1.
FA Cup (0).

Whitehead P.M. 38	Robinson L. 46	Ford M.P. 15 + 3	Dyer A.C. 32 + 6	Elliott M.S. 45	Rogan A.G.P. 27 + 2	Massey S.A. 20 + 2	Smith D. 41 + 1	Moody P. 34 + 7	Byrne J.F. 25	Allen C.A. 32 + 4	Lewis M. 30 + 9	Cusack N.J. — + 2	Druce M.A. 9 + 10	Ford R.J. 20 + 3	Murphy M.S. 17 + 5	Deegan M. 2	Marsh S.T. 8	Rush D. 22 + 12	Collins D.D. 3	Butters G. 3	Wanless P.S. 3 + 7	Dobson A.J. 5	Carter J.W.C. 3 + 1	Key L.W. 6	Wood S.A. 2	Gilchrist P.A. 18	*Match No.*
1	2	3	4	5	6	7	8	9	*10*	11	12	14															1
1	2	3	4	5	6	7	8	9	10	11	12																2
1	2	3	4	5	6	7	8	9	10	11			12														3
1	2	3	4	5	6	7	8	9		11			10														4
1	2	3	4	5	6	7	8	9		11			10	12													5
1	2	3	4	5	6	7	8	9		11			10		12												6
1	2	3	4	5	6	7	8	*9*	10	11	12		14														7
	2	3		5		7	8	9	10	11	4					1	6										8
1	2	3		5		7	8	9	10	11	4						6	12									9
1	2	3	6	5		7	8	9	10	11	4							12									10
1	2	3	4	5	6	7	8	*9*	10	11	12							14									11
1	2	3	4	5	6	7	8	9	10	*11*	12							14									12
1	2	3	4	5	6	7	8	9	*10*		12	14		11													13
1	2	3	4	5	6	7	*8*	9	10		12			11				14									14
1	2		4	5		7	8	9	10					11			6	12	3								15
1	2		4	5		7	8	9	*10*		12			11			6	14		3							16
1	2		4	5			8	9	10	7	6			11				12		3							17
1	2		4	5			8	9	10		6		12	11				14		3	*7*						18
1	2		4	5			8	9	*10*		3		12	11	7			14			6						19
1	2		4	5			8	9	10		3		12	*11*	7			14				6					20
1	2		4	5	12		8		10		3			11	14			9				6	7				21
1	2		4	5	12		8	14	10		3			*11*				9				6	7				22
1	2		4	5			8	9	10		*3*			11	12						14	6	7				23
1	2		4	5			8	9		12	3				*7*		11	10				6	14				24
	2		4	5	6		8			*11*			9	7	12	1	3	10			14						25
	2		4	5	6		8	*9*	10	11	12		14	7					3					1			26
	2		4	5	6		8	9	10	11			14	7				12						1	*3*		27
	2		12	5	6		8	14	*10*	11	4			7				9						1	3		28
	2		11	5			8		10	12	4		14		7		3	*9*						1		6	29
	2		11	5			8	12	10	14	4				7		*3*	9						1		6	30
	2		3	5			8	9		11	4				7			10						1		6	31
1	*2*		3	5		12	8			11	4		9		7			10			14					6	32
1	2	3		5			8	12		11	4		9		7			10								6	33
1	2			5	3		8	12		11	4		9		7			10								6	34
1	2		12	5	3		8	*9*		11	4		14		7			10								6	35
1	2		12	5	3		8	14		11	4		*9*		7			10								6	36
1	2		12	5	3		8	14		11	4		*9*		7			10								6	37
1	2		11	5	3		8	9		12	4		14		*7*			10								6	38
1	2		12	5	3	7	*8*	9		11	4				14			10								6	39
1	2		12	5	3	7	*8*	9		11	4			14				10								6	40
1	2		10	5	3	7	*8*	9		11	4			12							14					6	41
1	2	12	10	5	3			9		11	*4*			7				8			14					6	42
1	2	12		5	3			9		11	4			7	8			*10*			14					6	43
1	2			5	3			9		11	4			7	8			10								6	44
1	2	12			3	14		9		11	4			7	*8*			10			5					6	45
1	2			5		9	12			11	4			7	8			10	3		14					*6*	46

Coca-Cola Cup

First Round	Peterborough U (h)	3-1
	(a)	1-0
Second Round	Oldham Ath (h)	1-1
	(a)	0-1

FA Cup

First Round	Marlow (a)	0-2

PETERBOROUGH UNITED 1994–95 *Back row (left to right):* Tony Lormor, Nick Dunphy, David Morrison, Sean Farrell, Gary Breen, Greg Heald, Ashley Warner, Kenny Webster, Liburd Henry.
Centre row: Simon Clark, Kenny Charlery, Fred Barber, Brian McGorry, Scott Cooksey, Jason Brissett, Paul Moran
Front row: Keith Oakes (Physio), Lee Williams, Tony Spearing, Mark Peters, John Still (Manager), Steve Welsh, Marcus Ebdon, Andy Curtis, Michael Halsall (Assistant Manager).

Division 2 **PETERBOROUGH UNITED**

London Road Ground, Peterborough PE2 8AL. Telephone: (01733) 63947. Fax: (01733) 577210.

Ground capacity: 14,300 (rising to 16,300 when completed).

Record attendance: 30,096 v Swansea T, FA Cup 5th rd, 20 February 1965.

Record receipts: £51,315 v Brighton & HA, 5th rd, 15 February 1986.

Pitch measurements: 112yd × 75yd.

Chairman: A. H. Hand. ***Vice-Chairman:*** N. Hards.

Directors: R. Terrell, P. Sagar. ***Company Secretary:*** Miss Caroline Hand.

Chief Executive: Chris Turner.

Manager: John Still. ***Assistant Manager/Coach:*** Mick Halsall.

Physio: Keith Oakes.

Commercial Manager: Michael Vincent.

Year Formed: 1934. ***Turned Professional:*** 1934. ***Ltd Co.:*** 1934.

Club Nickname: 'The Posh'.

Foundation: The old Peterborough & Fletton club, founded in 1923, was suspended by the FA during season 1932–33 and disbanded. Local enthusiasts determined to carry on and in 1934 a new professional club Peterborough United was formed and entered the Midland League the following year.

First Football League game: 20 August, 1960, Division 4, v Wrexham (h) W 3-0 – Walls; Stafford, Walker; Rayner, Rigby, Norris; Halls, Emery (1), Bly (1), Smith, McNamee (1).

Record League Victory: 8–1 v Oldham Ath, Division 4, 26 November 1969 – Drewery; Potts, Noble; Conmy, Wile, Wright; Moss (1), Price (3), Hall (4), Halliday, Robson.

Record Cup Victory: 6–0 v Redditch, FA Cup, 1st rd (replay), 22 November 1971 – Drewery; Carmichael, Brookes; Oakes, Turner, Wright; Conmy, Price (1), Hall (2), Barker (2), Robson (1).

Record Defeat: 1–8 v Northampton T, FA Cup 2nd rd (2nd replay), 18 December, 1946.

Most League Points (2 for a win): 66, Division 4, 1960–61.

Most League Points (3 for a win): 82, Division 4, 1981–82.

Most League Goals: 134, Division 4, 1960–61.

Highest League Scorer in Season: Terry Bly, 52, Division 4, 1960–61.

Most League Goals in Total Aggregate: Jim Hall, 122, 1967–75.

Most Capped Player: Tony Millington, 8 (21), Wales.

Most League Appearances: Tommy Robson, 482, 1968–81.

Record Transfer Fee Received: £400,000 from Notts Co for David Robinson, October 1992.

Record Transfer Fee Paid: £176,000 to Watford for Ken Charlery, December 1993.

Football League Record: 1960 Elected to Division 4; 1961–68 Division 3, when they were demoted for financial irregularities; 1968–74 Division 4; 1974–79 Division 3; 1979–91 Division 4; 1991–92 Division 3; 1992–94 Division 1; 1994– Division 2.

Honours: *Football League:* Division 1 best season: 10th Division 1 1992–93; Division 4 – Champions 1960–61, 1973–74. *FA Cup:* best season: 6th rd, 1965. *Football League Cup:* Semi-final 1966.

Colours: Royal blue shirts, white shorts, white stockings. **Change colours:** All red.

PETERBOROUGH UNITED 1994–95 LEAGUE RECORD

Match No.	Date	Venue	Opponents	Result	H/T Score	Lg. Pos.	Goalscorers	Attendance
1	Aug 13	H	Bristol R	D 0-0	0-0	—		5695
2	20	A	Brentford	W 1-0	1-0	10	Charlery	5516
3	27	H	Crewe Alex	L 1-5	0-3	15	Morrison	4579
4	30	A	Bournemouth	W 3-0	2-0	—	Farrell, Morrison, Charlery	2649
5	Sept 3	A	Shrewsbury T	D 2-2	2-0	9	Henry 2	3879
6	10	H	Hull C	W 2-1	1-1	7	Morrison, Charlery	5044
7	13	H	Huddersfield T	D 2-2	2-1	—	Farrell, Charlery	5316
8	18	A	Birmingham C	L 0-4	0-3	12		10,600
9	24	H	Rotherham U	D 2-2	1-2	13	Henry 2	4894
10	Oct 1	A	Cardiff C	W 2-1	1-1	10	McGorry, Charlery	4225
11	8	A	York C	D 1-1	0-0	11	Williams	3601
12	15	H	Stockport Co	L 0-1	0-0	12		5369
13	22	H	Wycombe W	L 1-3	1-1	13	Henry	5924
14	29	A	Swansea C	L 0-2	0-1	14		2733
15	Nov 1	A	Plymouth Arg	W 1-0	1-0	—	Henry	4145
16	5	H	Chester C	W 2-0	1-0	13	Charlery, Farrell	4610
17	19	A	Brighton & HA	W 2-1	2-1	12	Charlery, Ebdon	6445
18	26	H	Leyton Orient	D 0-0	0-0	13		5114
19	Dec 10	H	Brentford	D 2-2	2-1	14	Henry, Kelly	4102
20	17	A	Bristol R	L 1-3	1-0	14	Farrell	4635
21	26	H	Oxford U	L 1-4	1-2	15	Charlery	5803
22	27	A	Wrexham	D 3-3	2-0	14	Morrison 2, Ebdon	4689
23	31	H	Cambridge U	D 2-2	1-1	14	Charlery 2	7412
24	Jan 2	A	Blackpool	L 0-4	0-1	16		3692
25	14	H	Bradford C	D 0-0	0-0	16		4400
26	28	A	Chester C	D 1-1	0-0	16	Morrison	1501
27	Feb 4	A	Leyton Orient	L 1-4	0-2	16	Ebdon	3447
28	11	H	Plymouth Arg	L 1-2	0-1	18	Farrell	4318
29	18	A	Bradford C	L 2-4	0-2	18	Farrell, Ebdon	4806
30	21	H	Brighton & HA	W 2-1	1-0	—	Charlery, Farrell	3870
31	25	H	Cardiff C	W 2-1	1-1	16	Charlery 2	4226
32	Mar 4	A	Rotherham U	D 0-0	0-0	16		3123
33	7	H	Shrewsbury T	D 1-1	0-0	—	Charlery	3554
34	11	A	Crewe Alex	W 3-1	2-0	16	Ebdon, Morrison, Breen	3983
35	18	H	Bournemouth	D 0-0	0-0	16		4495
36	21	A	Hull C	D 1-1	1-1	—	McGorry	4609
37	25	H	Birmingham C	D 1-1	0-0	16	Charlery	8796
38	28	A	Wycombe W	L 1-3	0-1	—	Gordon	4590
39	Apr 1	A	Huddersfield T	W 2-1	1-0	16	Ebdon, McGorry	11,324
40	4	H	Swansea C	W 1-0	1-0	—	Kelly (pen)	3764
41	8	A	Cambridge U	L 0-2	0-1	16		5828
42	15	H	Wrexham	W 1-0	1-0	15	Manuel	4309
43	17	A	Oxford U	L 0-1	0-1	15		5163
44	22	H	Blackpool	W 1-0	0-0	15	Farrell	5716
45	29	A	Stockport Co	D 1-1	0-1	15	Morrison	4387
46	May 6	H	York C	D 1-1	0-0	15	Charlery (pen)	4983

Final League Position: 15

GOALSCORERS

League (54): Charlery 16 (1 pen), Farrell 8, Morrison 8, Henry 7, Ebdon 6, McGorry 3, Kelly 2 (1 pen), Breen 1, Gordon 1, Manuel 1, Williams 1.
Coca-Cola Cup (1): Morrison 1.
FA Cup (4): Charlery 2 (1 pen), Henry 1, Williams 1.

Cooksey S.A. 12	Ashley K.M. 27	Clark S. 32	Ebdon M. 35	Heald G. 27 + 2	Welsh S. 14	Morrison D.E. 34 + 8	Breen G. 43 + 1	Farrell S.P. 25 + 8	Charlery K. 44	Moran P. 5 + 2	Williams L. 35 + 5	Henry L.A. 22 + 10	McGorry B.P. 30 + 4	Dunphy N. — + 2	Spearing A. 31 + 2	Furnell A.P. 4 + 4	Tyler M.R. 4 + 1	Brissett J.C. 4 + 1	Prudhoe M. 6	Lormor A. 2 + 3	Thomas G.A. 6 + 2	Kelly A.G. 12 + 1	Barber F. 5	Soloman J.R. 4	Keeley J.H. 3	Feuer A.I. 16	Manuel W.A.J. 14	Gordon D.A. 6	Le Bihan N.E.R. 3 + 1	Semple R.E.J. 1 + 1	*Match No.*
1	2	3	4	5	6	7	8	9	10	11	12																				1
1	2	3	4		6	7	5	9	10	11	8	12																			2
1	2	3	4		6	7	5	9	10		*8*	11	12	14																	3
1	2	3		5	6	7		9	*10*			11	4	12	8	14															4
1	2	3		5	6	7	12	9	10		4	11			8																5
1	2	3		5	6	7	8	9	10		4	11	12																		6
1	2	3		5	6	7	8	9	10			11	4		12																7
	2	3		5	6	7	8	*9*	10		12	11	4				1	14													8
	2	3	4	5	6	7	8	12	10		9	11	14				1														9
	2	3	4		6	7	5		10			11	8					9	1												10
	2	3	4		6	7	5		10		12	11	8					9	1	14											11
	2	3	4		6	7	5	12	10		14	11	8					9	1												12
	2	3	4		6	7	5	9	10		12	11	8						1												13
	2	3	4		6	7	5	12	10		9	11	8		14				1												14
	2	6	4				5	7	10		9	11	8		3				1												15
1	2	6	4			12	5	7	10		9	11	8		3																16
1	2	6	4			7	5		10		9	11	8		3					12											17
1	2	6	4			12	5		10		9		*8*		3			7		11	14										18
1	*2*	6	4			7	5	12			9	10			3					11	14	8									19
1	2	6	4			7	5	11			9	10			3					12		8									20
	2		4	12		7	5		10		9	*11*			3	14					6	8	1								21
	2		4	7		9	5		10			12			3	11					6	8	1								22
	2	6	4			7	5	12	10			11			3	9						8	1								23
	2	6		4		7		12	10				11		3	9					5	8	1								24
		6		2		7	5	9	10		11		4			12	15				3		*1*	8							25
		6		2		7	5		10	12	11		4			9	1				3			8							26
	2		9			11	5		10	12	7				3						6	4		8	1						27
	2	6	4			12	5	9	10	11	7				3									8	1						28
		6	4	2		12	5	9	10	11	7		8		3										1						29
		6	4	2		12	5	9	10		7	11	8		3											1					30
		6	4	2		12	5	9	10		7	*11*	8		3							14				1					31
	2	6	4	12			5	9	10		7		8		3											1	11				32
		6	4			7	5	9	10	11	2		12		3											1	8				33
			4	6		7	5	*9*	10		2	12	11		3	14										1	8				34
			4	6		7	5	9	10		2	12	11		3											1	8				35
			4	6		7	5	9	10		2	12	11		3											1	8				36
			4	6		7	5		10		2		11		3											1	8	9			37
			4	6		7	5		10		2	12	11		3											1	8	9			38
			4	6			5		10		2		11		3							7				1	8	9			39
			4	6			5		10		2		11		3							7				1	8	9			40
			4	6		12	5		10		2	14	*11*		3							7				1	8	9			41
			4	6		11	5	12	10		2	9			3							7				1	8				42
				6		11	5	9	10		2	12			3							7				1	8		4		43
		7		6		11	5	12	10		2		8		3		1											9	4	14	44
			8	6		12	5	9	10		2	14	7		3											1	11		*4*		45
		3		6		11	5	9	10		2	12	*4*													1	8		14	7	46

Coca-Cola Cup

First Round	Oxford U (a)		1-3
	(h)		0-1

FA Cup

First Round	Northampton T (h)	4-0
Second Round	Cambridge U (h)	0-2

PLYMOUTH ARGYLE 1994–95 *Back row (left to right):* Craig Skinner, Wayne Burnett, Kevin Nugent, Alan Nicholls, Richard Landon, Michael Evans, Daniel O'Hagan.
Centre row: Paul Sumner (Physio), Marc Edworthy, Chris Twiddy, Marcus Crocker, Jamie Morgan, Dominic Naylor, Martin Barlow.
Front row: Keith Hill, Paul Dalton, Steve Castle, John McGovern (Assistant Manager), Peter Shilton (Team Manager), Ian Bowyer (Youth Team Manager), Andy Comyn, Steve McCall, Mark Patterson.

Division 3 **PLYMOUTH ARGYLE**

Home Park, Plymouth, Devon PL2 3DQ. Telephone: (01752) 562561. Fax: (01752) 606167. Marketing Department: (01752) 569597. Lottery Shop: (01752) 561041. Pilgrim Shop: (01752) 558292.

Ground capacity: 19,630.

Record attendance: 43,596 v Aston Villa, Division 2, 10 October1936.

Record receipts: £128,000 v Burnley, Division 2 play-off, 18 May 1994.

Pitch measurements: 110yd × 72yd.

President: S. J. Rendell.

Chairman: D. McCauley. ***Vice-Chairman:*** P. Bloom.

Directors: D. Angilley, G. Jasper, I. Jones.

Manager: Neil Warnock. ***Assistant Manager:*** Ian Bowyer. ***Physio:*** Paul Sumner.

Secretary: Michael Holladay.

Year Formed: 1886. ***Turned Professional:*** 1903. ***Ltd Co.:*** 1903.

Club Nickname: 'The Pilgrims'.

Previous Name: 1886–1903, Argyle Athletic Club.

Foundation: The club was formed in September 1886 as the Argyle Football Club by former public and private school pupils who wanted to continue playing the game. The meeting was held in a room above the Borough Arms (a Coffee House), Bedford Street, Plymouth. It was common then to choose a local street/terrace as a club name and Argyle or Argyll was a fashionable name throughout the land due to Queen Victoria'great interest in Scotland.

First Football League game: 28 August, 1920, Division 3, v Norwich C (h) D 1-1 – Craig; Russell, Atterbury; Logan, Dickinson, Forbes; Kirkpatrick, Jack, Bowler, Heeps (1), Dixon.

Record League Victory: 8–1 v Millwall, Division 2, 16 January 1932 – Harper; Roberts, Titmuss; Mackay, Pullan, Reed; Grozier, Bowden (2), Vidler (3), Leslie (1), Black (1). (1 og). 8–1 v Hartlepool U (a), Division 2, 7 May 1994 – Nicholls; Patterson (Naylor), Hill, Burrows, Comyn, McCall, Barlow, Castle, Landon, Marshall, Dalton.

Record Cup Victory: 6–0 v Corby T, FA Cup, 3rd rd, 22 January 1966 – Leiper; Book, Baird; Williams, Nelson, Newman; Jones (1), Jackson (1), Bickle (3), Piper (1), Jennings.

Record Defeat: 0–9 v Stoke C, Division 2, 17 December 1960.

Most League Points (2 for a win): 68, Division 3 (S), 1929–30.

Most League Points (3 for a win): 87, Division 3, 1985–86.

Most League Goals: 107, Division 3 (S), 1925–26 and 1951–52.

Highest League Scorer in Season: Jack Cock, 32, Division 3 (S), 1925–26.

Most League Goals in Total Aggregate: Sammy Black, 180, 1924–38.

Most Capped Player: Moses Russell, 20 (23), Wales.

Most League Appearances: Kevin Hodges, 530, 1978–92.

Record Transfer Fee Received: £350,000 from Southend U for Gary Poole, July 1993.

Record Transfer Fee Paid: £250,000 to Hartlepool U for Paul Dalton, June 1992.

Football League Record: 1920 Original Member of Division 3; 1921–30 Division 3 (S); 1930–50 Division 2; 1950–52 Division 3 (S); 1952–56 Division 2; 1956–58 Division 3 (S); 1958–59 Division 3; 1959–68 Division 2; 1968–75 Division 3; 1975–77 Division 2; 1977–86 Division 3; 1986–95 Division 2; 1995– Division 3.

Honours: *Football League:* Division 2 best season: 4th, 1931–32, 1952–53; Division 3 (S) – Champions 1929–30, 1951–52; Runners-up 1921–22, 1922–23, 1923–24, 1924–25, 1925–26, 1926–27 (record of six consecutive years); Division 3 – Champions 1958–59; Runners-up 1974–75, 1985–86. *FA Cup:* best season: Semi-final 1984. *Football League Cup:* Semi-final 1965, 1974.

Colours: Green and black striped shirts, black shorts, black stockings. **Change colours:** All white.

PLYMOUTH ARGYLE 1994–95 LEAGUE RECORD

Match No.	Date	Venue	Opponents	Result		H/T Score	Lg. Pos.	Goalscorers	Attendance
1	Aug 13	H	Brentford	L	1-5	1-3	—	Swan	7976
2	20	A	Brighton & HA	D	1-1	0-0	17	Bradshaw	8309
3	27	H	Bradford C	L	1-5	0-4	20	Dalton	6469
4	30	A	Hull C	L	0-2	0-0	—		3384
5	Sept 3	A	Birmingham C	L	2-4	0-2	22	Castle, Nugent	13,202
6	10	H	Huddersfield T	L	0-3	0-2	22		5464
7	13	H	Cambridge U	D	0-0	0-0	—		3824
8	17	A	Cardiff C	W	1-0	0-0	22	Castle	5674
9	24	H	Chester C	W	1-0	1-0	21	Twiddy	5329
10	Oct 1	A	Leyton Orient	W	2-0	2-0	19	Landon 2	4140
11	8	A	Oxford U	L	0-1	0-1	19		6550
12	15	H	Wycombe W	D	2-2	2-1	18	Skinner (pen), Barlow	6864
13	22	A	Stockport Co	W	4-2	2-1	17	Edworthy, O'Hagan, Landon 2	5652
14	29	H	Blackpool	L	0-2	0-1	19		6285
15	Nov 1	H	Peterborough U	L	0-1	0-1	—		4145
16	5	A	Rotherham U	L	1-3	0-1	20	Skinner	2848
17	19	H	Wrexham	W	4-1	2-1	17	Hughes (og), Burnett, Phillips (og), Barlow	6936
18	26	A	York C	L	0-1	0-0	17		3185
19	Dec 10	H	Brighton & HA	L	0-3	0-0	19		6091
20	17	A	Brentford	L	0-7	0-2	19		4492
21	26	A	Swansea C	L	0-3	0-3	21		4859
22	Jan 2	H	Crewe Alex	W	3-2	1-2	20	Patterson, Evans 2	6802
23	14	A	Bournemouth	D	0-0	0-0	20		4913
24	21	H	Rotherham U	D	0-0	0-0	20		5484
25	28	A	Blackpool	L	2-5	1-0	20	Patterson, Dalton	3599
26	Feb 4	H	York C	L	1-2	1-0	20	Skinner	5572
27	7	A	Shrewsbury T	L	2-3	1-0	—	Nugent, Evans	3029
28	11	A	Peterborough U	W	2-1	1-0	20	McCall, Nugent	4318
29	18	H	Bournemouth	L	0-1	0-1	20		5435
30	21	A	Wrexham	L	1-3	1-0	—	Castle	3030
31	25	H	Leyton Orient	W	1-0	0-0	20	Landon	5173
32	Mar 4	A	Chester C	L	0-1	0-1	21		1823
33	11	A	Bradford C	L	0-2	0-0	21		5399
34	18	H	Hull C	W	2-1	2-1	20	Nugent, Evans	4839
35	21	A	Huddersfield T	L	0-2	0-1	—		12,099
36	25	H	Cardiff C	D	0-0	0-0	21		5611
37	28	H	Stockport Co	L	0-2	0-1	—		4618
38	Apr 1	A	Cambridge U	D	1-1	0-0	21	Landon	3913
39	4	H	Bristol R	D	1-1	1-0	—	Nugent	6743
40	8	H	Shrewsbury T	W	1-0	1-0	21	Patterson	5089
41	15	A	Bristol R	L	0-2	0-1	21		7068
42	17	H	Swansea C	W	2-1	1-1	21	Swan, Nugent	5890
43	19	H	Birmingham C	L	1-3	0-0	—	Dalton	8550
44	22	A	Crewe Alex	D	2-2	1-2	21	Gardiner (og), Dalton (pen)	3786
45	29	A	Wycombe W	W	2-1	1-0	21	Hill, Landon	6850
46	May 6	H	Oxford U	D	1-1	1-0	21	Nugent	4953

Final League Position: 21

GOALSCORERS

League (45): Landon 7, Nugent 7, Dalton 4 (1 pen), Evans 4, Castle 3, Patterson 3, Skinner 3 (1 pen), Barlow 2, Swan 2, Bradshaw 1, Burnett 1, Edworthy 1, Hill 1, McCall 1, O'Hagan 1, Twiddy 1, own goals 3.
Coca-Cola Cup (2): Castle 1, Swan 1.
FA Cup (3): Ross 2, Skinner 1.

Hodge M.J. 17	Patterson M. 37 + 1	Hill K.J. 32 + 2	Comyn A.J. 30	Swan P.H. 24 + 3	Payne I.N. 1	Barlow M.D. 40 + 2	Burnett W. 25 + 7	Nugent K.P. 34 + 3	Evans M.J. 12 + 11	Skinner C.R. 21 + 3	Edworthy M. 24 + 3	Landon R.J. 18 + 6	Naylor D.J. 42	Bradshaw D. 5 + 1	Dalton P. 23 + 3	Castle S.C. 23 + 3	Shaw G.P. 6	Twiddy C. 13 + 2	Nicholls A. 26 + 1	Morgan J.A. 6 + 2	O'Hagan D.A.N. 1 + 2	Dungey J.A. 3 + 1	Crocker M.A. 3 + 2	Quinn M. 3	Ross M.P. 11 + 6	Dawe S. 3 + 1	Shilton S. 1 + 1	Barber P.A. 4	Gee P. 6	McCall S.H. 7	Wotton P.A. 5 + 2	*Match No.*
1	2	3	4	5	*6*	7	8	9	10	11	12	14																				1
1		6	4	5		7	12	9	10		2		3	8	11																	2
1			4	5		7		9			2		3	6	11	8	10	12														3
1	2	4		5			7	9					3	6	11	8	10	12														4
1	2	6	4	5		7		9					3	12		8	10	11														5
1		12	4	5		7	6	9					3	2		8	10	11	15													6
		4	5			7	6	9					3	2		8	10	11	1													7
	2	4	5	12		7	6	9				14	3			8	*10*	11	1													8
1	2	4	5	12		7	6	9	14			*10*	3					11		8												9
	2	4	5			7	6			9	12	10	3					11	1	8												10
	2	4	5			7	6	12		9	14	10	3					11	1	8												11
		2	5	4		7	6			9		10	3					11	1	8	12											12
	2	4	5			7	6			9	8	10	3					*11*	1		12	15										13
	2		5			7	6			9	4	10	3					11	1		8		12									14
	2		5			7	6	12			4	10	3					11	1	8			9									15
1	2		5			7	*6*	9	12	11	4	14	3							8			10									16
	2		5			7	6	9	11	8	4		3						1	12				10								17
	2		5	12		7	6	9		8	4		3					*11*	1					10	14							18
	2		5	4		7	6		12				3						1					9	10	8	11					19
1	2		5	4		7	6	8	9														11		10	3	12					20
	2	3	5	4		7	6	12	*9*										1				14		10	8		11				21
	2	5		4		7		9	12	8	6		3						1						10			11				22
	2	4	5			7	6	9	10	8		12	3						1							14		11				23
		4	5			8	6		10	7	2	9	3		12				1									11				24
	2	4	5			8	12			7	6	*10*	3		14				1										9	11		25
	2	4	5			8	11	10	12	7			3		14				1										9	*6*		26
	2	4	5			7		10	12				3		11	14			1										9	*6*	8	27
	2	4		5		7		10	9	12			3		11	14			1											*6*	8	28
	2	4		5		7		10	12				3		11	8			1										9	*6*	14	29
1	2	4		5		7				12		9	3		11	8													10	6		30
1	2	4	5			7	12			14		9	3		11	8													10		*6*	31
1	2	4	5			7		9	12			10	3		11	8		*6*													14	32
1			5	4			6	9	10		2		3		11	8				12					14						*7*	33
1			5	4			6	9	7		2		3		11	8									10							34
1	14		5	4		12	6	9	7		2		3		11	8									*10*							35
1	2	12		4		6		9	7		5		3		11	8									10							36
1	2			4		7		9	12		5		3		11	8									10						6	37
	2	6		4		7	12	9			5	*10*	3		11	8			1						14							38
	2	6		4		7	12	9			5	*10*	3		11	8			1						14							39
	2	6				8		9		7	5	*10*	3		11	12			1						14					4		40
	2	6				8	4	9		7	5	10			11	3			1						12							41
	2	6		4		12		9		7	5		3		11	8			1						10							42
	2	6		4				9		7	5	12	3		11	8			1						10							43
	2	6		4		5	12	9		7		14	3		11	8						1			*10*							44
	2	4				6		9	12	7	5	10	3		11	8						1										45
	2	4				6	12	9	14	7	5	*10*	3		11	8						1										46

Coca-Cola Cup			**FA Cup**		
First Round	Walsall (a)	0-4	First Round	Kettering T (a)	1-0
	(h)	2-1	Second Round	Bournemouth (h)	2-1
			Third Round	Nottingham F (a)	0-2

PORTSMOUTH 1994–95 *Back row (left to right):* Neil Sillett (Physio), Gorden Neave (Kit Manager), Martin Hinshelwood (Youth Team Manager), Mike Bailey (Reserve Team Manager), Graham Paddon (Assistant Manager).
Third row: Jason Rees, Stuart Doling, Deon Burton, Sam Igoe.
Second row: Darryl Powell, Lee Russell, Tony Dobson, Aaron Flahavan, Mart Poom, Alan Knight, Guy Butters, Robbie Pethick, Ray Daniel.
Front row: Paul Hall, Andy Awford, Pedrag Radosavljevic, Mark Stimson, Gerry Creaney, Bjorn Kristensen, Jim Smith (Manager), Kit Symons, Warren Neill, Alan McLoughlin, Paul Wood, John Durnin, Jon Gittens.

Division 1 **PORTSMOUTH**

Fratton Park, Frogmore Rd, Portsmouth PO4 8RA. Telephone: (01705) 731204. Fax: (01705) 734129. Commercial Dept: (01705) 827111. Ticket Office: (01705) 750825. Lottery Office: (01705) 825016. Clubcall: 0891 338383.

Ground capacity: 26,452.

Record attendance: 51,385 v Derby Co, FA Cup 6th rd, 26 February 1949.

Record receipts: £214,000 v Manchester U, Coca-Cola Cup 5th rd replay, 26 January 1994.

Pitch measurements: 114yd × 72yd.

Chairman: J. A. Gregory.

Directors: M. H. Gregory, D. K. Deacon, B. A. V. Henson, J. S. Hutchison, R. E. Smith.

Manager: Terry Fenwick. ***First Team Coach:*** Keith Waldon.

Secretary: Paul Weld. ***Marketing Manager:*** Julie Baker.

Physio: Neil Sillett. ***Youth Team Coach:*** K. Todd.

Year Formed: 1898. ***Turned Professional:*** 1898. ***Ltd Co.:*** 1898.

Club Nickname: 'Pompey'.

Foundation: At a meeting held in his High Street, Portsmouth offices in 1898, solicitor Alderman J. E. Pink and five other business and professional men agreed to buy some ground close to Goldsmith Avenue for £4,950 which they developed into Fratton Park in record breaking time. A team of professionals was signed up by manager Frank Brettell and entry to the Southern League obtained for the new club's September 1899 kick-off.

First Football League game: 28 August, 1920, Division 3, v Swansea T (h) W 3-0 – Robson; Probert, Potts; Abbott, Harwood, Turner; Thompson, Stringfellow (1), Reid (1), James (1), Beedie.

Record League Victory: 9–1 v Notts Co, Division 2, 9 April 1927 – McPhail; Clifford, Ted Smith; Reg Davies (1), Foxall, Moffat; Forward (1), Mackie (2), Haines (3), Watson, Cook (2).

Record Cup Victory: 7–0 v Stockport Co, FA Cup, 3rd rd, 8 January 1949 – Butler; Rookes, Ferrier; Scoular, Flewin, Dickinson; Harris (3), Barlow, Clarke (2), Phillips (2), Froggatt.

Record Defeat: 0–10 v Leicester C, Division 1, 20 October 1928.

Most League Points (2 for a win): 65, Division 3, 1961–62.

Most League Points (3 for a win): 91, Division 3, 1982–83.

Most League Goals: 91, Division 4, 1979–80.

Highest League Scorer in Season: Guy Whittingham, 42, Division 1, 1992–93.

Most League Goals in Total Aggregate: Peter Harris, 194, 1946–60.

Most Capped Player: Jimmy Dickinson, 48, England.

Most League Appearances: Jimmy Dickinson, 764, 1946–65.

Record Transfer Fee Received: £2,000,000 from Tottenham H for Darren Anderton, May 1992.

Record Transfer Fee Paid: £650,000 to Celtic for Gerry Creaney, January 1994.

Football League Record: 1920 Original Member of Division 3; 1921 Division 3 (S); 1924–27 Division 2; 1927–59 Division 1; 1959–61 Division 2; 1961–62 Division 3; 1962–76 Division 2; 1976–78 Division 3; 1978–80 Division 4; 1980–83 Division 3; 1983–87 Division 2; 1987–88 Division 1; 1988–92 Division 2; 1992– Division 1.

Honours: *Football League:* Division 1 – Champions 1948–49, 1949–50; Division 2 – Runners-up 1926–27, 1986–87; Division 3 (S) – Champions 1923–24; Division 3 – Champions 1961–62, 1982–83. *FA Cup:* Winners 1939; Runners-up 1929, 1934. *Football League Cup:* best season: 5th rd, 1961, 1986.

Colours: Blue shirts, white shorts, red stockings. **Change colours:** Red and black shirts, black shorts, red stockings.

PORTSMOUTH 1994–95 LEAGUE RECORD

Match No.	Date	Venue	Opponents	Result		H/T Score	Lg. Pos.	Goalscorers	Attendance
1	Aug 13	H	Notts Co	W	2-1	1-0	—	Powell, Symons	10,487
2	20	A	Reading	D	0-0	0-0	5		9106
3	27	H	Charlton Ath	D	1-1	1-1	7	Symons	10,566
4	30	A	Southend U	W	2-1	1-1	—	Creaney, Powell	4333
5	Sept 10	H	Port Vale	L	0-2	0-1	13		8989
6	14	H	Tranmere R	D	1-1	0-0	—	Hall	6383
7	17	A	Bolton W	D	1-1	0-1	13	Creaney	11,284
8	24	H	Wolverhampton W	L	1-2	1-1	19	Creaney (pen)	13,466
9	28	A	WBA	W	2-0	1-0	—	Pethick, Hall	13,545
10	Oct 1	A	Grimsby T	L	0-2	0-1	14		4172
11	8	A	Oldham Ath	L	2-3	0-1	17	Creaney, Hall	7683
12	15	H	Swindon T	W	4-3	2-1	12	McLoughlin 2, Powell, Creaney (pen)	10,610
13	23	H	Middlesbrough	D	0-0	0-0	14		7281
14	29	A	Bristol C	D	1-1	0-1	15	Powell	7238
15	Nov 2	A	Millwall	D	2-2	1-2	—	Rees, McLoughlin (pen)	7108
16	6	H	Derby Co	L	0-1	0-0	20		5507
17	19	A	Luton T	L	0-2	0-1	21		8214
18	26	H	Sunderland	L	1-4	0-3	21	Powell	7527
19	30	H	Stoke C	L	0-1	0-0	—		5272
20	Dec 3	A	Middlesbrough	L	0-4	0-2	22		17,185
21	10	H	Reading	D	1-1	1-0	22	Creaney	8578
22	17	A	Notts Co	W	1-0	0-0	22	Wood	6382
23	26	A	Watford	L	0-2	0-0	22		9953
24	27	H	Barnsley	W	3-0	3-0	19	Newhouse, Creaney 2	6751
25	31	A	Sheffield U	L	1-3	1-0	21	Creaney	13,467
26	Jan 2	H	Burnley	W	2-0	1-0	19	Radosavljevic, Creaney	9097
27	14	H	Bristol C	D	0-0	0-0	19		8803
28	22	A	Derby Co	L	0-3	0-0	19		11,143
29	Feb 4	A	Stoke C	W	2-0	0-0	18	Radosavljevic, Creaney	9704
30	18	A	Sunderland	D	2-2	1-2	19	McLoughlin, Doling	12,372
31	21	H	Luton T	W	3-2	0-1	—	McLoughlin, Radosavljevic, Creaney (pen)	7363
32	25	H	Grimsby T	W	2-1	1-1	14	Creaney, Symons	8274
33	Mar 5	A	Wolverhampton W	L	0-1	0-0	16		23,284
34	8	H	WBA	L	1-2	1-1	—	Creaney	7160
35	11	A	Charlton Ath	L	0-1	0-1	20		9443
36	15	H	Millwall	W	3-2	1-1	—	Creaney 2, Hall	6032
37	18	H	Southend U	D	1-1	1-1	15	McLoughlin	6667
38	21	A	Port Vale	L	0-1	0-1	—		7388
39	25	H	Bolton W	D	1-1	0-1	18	Creaney	7765
40	Apr 1	A	Tranmere R	L	2-4	1-3	19	Radosavljevic, Irons (og)	8722
41	8	H	Sheffield U	W	1-0	0-0	19	Creaney	8216
42	15	A	Barnsley	L	0-1	0-0	20		6825
43	17	H	Watford	W	2-1	1-0	18	Durnin (pen), Burton	8396
44	22	A	Burnley	W	2-1	1-0	18	Durnin (pen), Symons	10,666
45	29	A	Swindon T	W	2-0	1-0	18	Radosavljevic, Burton	9220
46	May 7	H	Oldham Ath	D	1-1	0-1	18	Hall	11,002

Final League Position: 18

GOALSCORERS

League (53): Creaney 18 (3 pens), McLoughlin 6 (1 pen), Hall 5, Powell 5, Radosavljevic 5, Symons 4, Burton 2, Durnin 2 (2 pens), Doling 1, Newhouse 1, Pethick 1, Rees 1, Wood 1, own goal 1.
Coca-Cola Cup (9): Creaney 3, Powell 3, Hall 1, Kristensen 1, Stimson 1.
FA Cup (3): Radosavljevic 2, Creaney 1.

Knight A.E. 43	Gittens J. 37 + 1	Stimson M. 15	McLoughlin A.F. 36 + 2	Symons C.J. 40	Dobson A.J. 14	Neill W.A. 7	Pethick R.J. 39 + 5	Powell D.A. 34	Creaney G. 39	Hall P.A. 30 + 13	Daniel R.C. 17 + 5	Lee D.J. 4 + 1	Awford A.T. 3 + 1	Kristensen B. 15 + 10	Radosavljevic P. 30 + 10	Burton D.J. 5 + 2	Rees J.M. 14 + 5	McGrath L.A. 15 + 3	Russell L. 18 + 1	Totten A.R. 3 + 1	Durnin J. 8 + 8	Butters G. 24	Newhouse A.R. 6	Wood P.A. 5	Glass J.R. 3	Doling S.J. 2 + 3	Igoe S.G. — + 1	Match No.
1	2	3	4	5	6	7	8	9	*10*	11	12	14																1
1	2	3	4	5	6	7	14	9	10	11	12	*8*																2
1	2	3	4	5	6	7	14	9	10	11	12	*8*																3
1	2	3	4	5	6	7		9	10	11		8																4
1	2	3	*4*	5	6	7	14	9	10	11	12	8																5
1	2	3	4	5		7		9	10	11	12		6	8														6
1	2	3	4	5	6		12		10	*11*	9		7	8	14													7
1	2	3	4	5			12	9	10	11	7		6	*8*	14													8
1	2	3	4	5	6		9		10	12	*7*		14	11	8													9
1	2	3	4	5	*6*		9		10	11	7				8	12	14											10
1	*2*	3	4	5			6	9	10	11	7			8	12		14											11
1	2	3	4	5			7	9	10	11				12	8			6										12
1	2	3	4	5			7	9	10	11					8			6										13
1	2	3		5	11		7	9	10	12				4	*8*		14	6										14
1	2		4	5	11		7	9		12				3	8		10	*6*	14									15
1		3	4	5			7	9	10					*8*	12		11		6	2	14							16
1	2		4		3		7	9	10					8	5	*11*	12		6	14								17
1	2		4		3	6	7	9	10	8					12	11				5								18
1	2		4	5	6		7	9	10	11	3			8	12													19
1	2			5	6		7	9	10	14				*8*	12				4			3	11					20
1	2		12				7	9	10	14					8			4		3		5	*11*	6				21
1	2		12	5			7	9		14	10				*8*			4				3	11	6				22
1	2			5			*7*	9	10	14	8				12			4				3	11	6				23
1	2			5			7	9	10		3				8			4				6	11					24
1	2			5			7	9	10	12	3				8			4				6	11					25
1	2			5			7	9	10	12	3				8			4				6		11				26
1				5			7	9	10	12	3				8			4	2			6		11				27
1			4				7	9	10	12	3			11	8			5	2			6						28
1	2		4	5			7	9	10	12	3				8		11					6						29
			4	5			2		10	9	3			*7*	8		11				12	6			1	14		30
1			4	5			2		10	9	3				8		11	7				6				12		31
1	2		4	5			7		10	9	3				8		*11*	14			12	6						32
1	2		4	5			7		10	9				12	*8*			11	3		14	6						33
1	2		4	5			7	11	10	*9*					8			12	3			6						34
1	2		4	5			7	9	10	12					8			11	*3*		14	6						35
1	2		4	5			7	9	10	11					8			*12*	3		14	6						36
1	2		4	5			7	9	10	11				12	8		*6*		3		14							37
	2		4	5			7	9	10	11				12	*8*		3				14	6			1			38
	2						7	9	10	11				5	8		3		6		4				1	12		39
1			4				7	9	10	11				5	8				6		3	2						40
1			4	5			7	*9*	10	11				12	8		14		6		3	2						41
1	12		4	5			7			11				14	8		*9*		6		10	3				2		42
1	3		4	5			7			11				12	*8*	14	9		6		10					2		43
1	3		4	5			7			11				14	12	8	9		6		*10*	2						44
1	3		4	5			7			*11*				12	14	8	9		6		10	2						45
1			4	5			2			11				12	*7*	8	9		6		10	3					14	46

Coca-Cola Cup

First Round	Cambridge U (h)	2-0
	(a)	3-2
Second Round	Everton (a)	3-2
	(h)	1-1
Third Round	Derby Co (h)	0-1

FA Cup

Third Round	Bolton W (h)	3-1
Fourth Round	Leicester C (h)	0-1

PORT VALE 1994–95 *Back row (left to right):* Joe Allon, Dean Glover, Peter Billing, Stuart Talbot, Paul Musselwhite, Gareth Griffiths, Arjen van Heusden, Robin van der Laan, Neil Aspin, John Morris, Martin Foyle.

Centre row: Bill Dearden (First Team Coach), Stan Nicholls (Kit Man), Lee Glover, Wayne Corden, Oliver Heald, Paul Kerr, John Jeffers, Allen Tankard, Jim Joyce (Physio), Ian Miller (Youth Team Coach).

Front row: Kevin Kent, Ray Walker, Bradley Sandeman, John Rudge (Manager), Andy Porter, Dean Stokes, Tony Naylor.

Division 1 **PORT VALE**

Vale Park, Burslem, Stoke-on-Trent ST6 1AW. Telephone: (01782) 814134. Fax: (01782) 834981. Commercial Dept: (01782) 835524. Clubcall: 0891 121636. Commercial Fax: (01782) 836875. Valiant Leisure Shop: (01782) 818718.

Ground capacity: 22,359.

Record attendance: 50,000 v Aston Villa, FA Cup 5th rd, 20 February 1960.

Record receipts: £170,022 v Liverpool, Rumbelows Cup 3rd rd replay, 20 November 1991.

Pitch measurements: 116yd × 76yd.

President: J. Burgess.

Chairman: W. T. Bell TECH. ENG, MIMI.

Directors: A. Belfield, I. McPherson, D. Bundy (vice-chairman).

Manager: John Rudge. ***Secretary:*** R. A. Allan. ***Commercial Executive:*** Keith Dale.
Commercial Manager: Mrs Margaret Moran-Smith.

Coach: Bill Dearden. ***Physio:*** Rick Carter. ***Medical Officer:*** Dr. D. Phillips. ***Stadium Manager:*** F. W. Lodey. ***Groundsman:*** R. Fairbanks. ***Community Scheme Officer:*** Jim Cooper (0782 575594).

Year Formed: 1876. ***Turned Professional:*** 1885. ***Ltd Co.:*** 1911.

Club Nickname: 'Valiants'.

Previous Name: Burslem Port Vale; became Port Vale, 1911.

Previous Grounds: 1876, Limekin Lane, Longport; 1881, Westport; 1884, Moorland Road, Burslem; 1886, Athletic Ground, Cobridge; 1913, Recreation Ground, Hanley; 1950, Vale Park.

Foundation: Formed in 1876 as Port Vale, adopting the prefix 'Burslem' in 1884 upon moving to that part of the city. It was dropped in 1911.

First Football League game: 3 September, 1892, Division 2, v Small Heath (a) L 1-5 – Frail; Clutton, Elson; Farrington, McCrindle, Delves; Walker, Scarratt, Bliss (1), Jones. (Only 10 men).

Record League Victory: 9–1 v Chesterfield, Division 2, 24 September 1932 – Leckie; Shenton, Poyser; Sherlock, Round, Jones; McGrath, Mills, Littlewood (6), Kirkham (2), Morton (1).

Record Cup Victory: 7–1 v Irthlingborough (away), FA Cup, 1st rd, 12 January 1907 – Matthews; Dunn, Hamilton; Eardley, Baddeley, Holyhead; Carter, Dodds (2), Beats, Mountford (2), Coxon (3).

Record Defeat: 0–10 v Sheffield U, Division 2, 10 December 1892 and v Notts Co, Division 2, 26 February 1895.

Most League Points (2 for a win): 69, Division 3 (N), 1953–54.

Most League Points (3 for a win): 89, Division 2, 1992–93.

Most League Goals: 110, Division 4, 1958–59.

Highest League Scorer in Season: Wilf Kirkham 38, Division 2, 1926–27.

Most League Goals in Total Aggregate: Wilf Kirkham, 154, 1923–29, 1931–33.

Most Capped Player: Sammy Morgan, 7 (18), Northern Ireland.

Most League Appearances: Roy Sproson, 761, 1950–72.

Record Transfer Fee Received: £925,000 from Norwich C for Darren Beckford, June 1991.

Record Transfer Fee Paid: £375,000 from Oxford U for Martin Foyle, June 1991.

Football League Record: 1892 Original Member of Division 2, Failed re-election in 1896; Re-elected 1898; Resigned 1907; Returned in Oct, 1919, when they took over the fixtures of Leeds City; 1929–30 Division 3 (N); 1930–36 Division 2; 1936–38 Division 3 (N); 1938–52 Division 3 (S); 1952–54 Division 3 (N); 1954–57 Division 2; 1957–58 Division 3 (S); 1958–59 Division 4; 1959–65 Division 3; 1965–70 Division 4; 1970–78 Division 3; 1978–83 Division 4; 1983–84 Division 3; 1984–86 Division 4; 1986–89 Division 3; 1989–94 Division 2; 1994– Division 1.

Honours: *Football League:* Division 2 – Runners-up 1993–94; Division 3 (N) – Champions 1929–30, 1953–54; Runners-up 1952–53; Division 4 – Champions 1958–59; Promoted 1969–70 (4th). *FA Cup:* Semi-final 1954, when in Division 3. *Football League Cup:* never past 2nd rd. *Autoglass Trophy:* Winners: 1993.

Colours: White shirts, black shorts, black and white stockings. **Change colours:** All yellow.

PORT VALE 1994–95 LEAGUE RECORD

Match No.	Date	Venue	Opponents	Result		H/T Score	Lg. Pos.	Goalscorers	Attendance
1	Aug 14	A	Swindon T	L	0-2	0-1	—		10,431
2	20	H	Oldham Ath	W	3-1	0-0	10	Kenny (og), Foyle, Naylor	10,051
3	27	A	Bristol C	D	0-0	0-0	12		8588
4	30	H	Barnsley	W	2-1	1-0	—	Glover L, Burke	7228
5	Sept 3	H	Luton T	L	0-1	0-0	12		8541
6	10	A	Portsmouth	W	2-0	1-0	5	Glover L, Naylor	8989
7	13	A	Grimsby T	L	1-4	0-1	—	Foyle	3216
8	17	H	Middlesbrough	W	2-1	0-1	7	Naylor, Glover L	10,313
9	24	H	Sheffield U	L	0-2	0-0	9		9324
10	Oct 1	A	Wolverhampton W	L	1-2	0-0	12	Allon	27,469
11	8	A	Notts Co	D	2-2	0-1	15	Kelly, Foyle	6903
12	15	H	Charlton Ath	L	0-2	0-0	19		7707
13	22	H	Bolton W	D	1-1	0-0	19	Allon	10,003
14	29	A	Tranmere R	D	1-1	0-0	20	Jeffers	6972
15	Nov 2	A	WBA	D	0-0	0-0	—		14,513
16	5	H	Southend U	W	5-0	2-0	14	Van Der Laan, Allon, Foyle, Walker, Porter	7141
17	19	A	Derby Co	L	0-2	0-1	19		13,357
18	26	H	Millwall	W	2-1	0-0	18	Allon, Burke	8016
19	29	H	Sunderland	D	0-0	0-0	—		8121
20	Dec 6	A	Bolton W	L	0-1	0-0	—		10,324
21	10	A	Oldham Ath	L	2-3	1-1	17	Van Der Laan, Guppy	7712
22	17	H	Swindon T	D	2-2	1-1	18	Foyle 2	7747
23	28	H	Reading	L	0-2	0-1	—		7891
24	31	A	Watford	L	2-3	1-1	22	Foyle 2	7794
25	Jan 15	H	Tranmere R	W	2-0	1-0	21	Tankard, Foyle	7944
26	28	A	Southend U	W	2-1	1-1	18	Foyle, Van Der Laan	3619
27	Feb 4	A	Sunderland	D	1-1	1-1	20	Naylor	13,377
28	11	H	WBA	W	1-0	0-0	17	Guppy	10,751
29	21	H	Derby Co	W	1-0	0-0	—	Kent	9387
30	25	H	Wolverhampton W	L	2-4	1-3	18	Naylor, Kent	13,676
31	Mar 4	A	Sheffield U	D	1-1	0-0	17	Glover L	13,647
32	7	A	Luton T	L	1-2	0-0	—	Porter	5947
33	11	H	Bristol C	W	2-1	1-1	15	Scott, Naylor	7646
34	14	H	Stoke C	D	1-1	1-1	—	Naylor	19,510
35	18	A	Barnsley	L	1-3	0-2	17	Allon	6878
36	21	H	Portsmouth	W	1-0	1-0	—	Allon	7388
37	26	A	Middlesbrough	L	0-3	0-2	17		17,401
38	28	A	Burnley	L	3-4	1-1	—	Foyle 2, Allon	10,058
39	Apr 1	H	Grimsby T	L	1-2	0-2	17	Naylor	7150
40	5	A	Millwall	W	3-1	2-0	—	Van Der Laan, Foyle, Bogie	5260
41	8	H	Watford	L	0-1	0-0	17		7276
42	15	A	Reading	D	3-3	0-3	17	Porter, Bogie (pen), Naylor	8635
43	17	H	Burnley	W	1-0	1-0	16	Van Der Laan	9663
44	22	A	Stoke C	W	1-0	0-0	14	Foyle	20,429
45	29	A	Charlton Ath	D	1-1	1-1	17	Foyle	12,596
46	May 7	H	Notts Co	D	1-1	1-0	17	Foyle	9452

Final League Position: 17

GOALSCORERS

League (58): Foyle 16, Naylor 9, Allon 7, Van Der Laan 5, Glover L 4, Porter 3, Bogie 2 (1 pen), Burke 2, Guppy 2, Kent 2, Jeffers 1, Kelly 1, Scott 1, Tankard 1, Walker 1, own goal 1.
Coca-Cola Cup (5): Glover L 3, Foyle 1, Naylor 1.
FA Cup (6): Foyle 3, Allon 1, Glover D 1, Griffiths 1.

Musselwhite P.S. 44	Sandeman B.R. 37	Tankard A.J. 39	Porter A.M. 43 + 1	Griffiths G.J. 20	Glover D.V. 28 + 1	Kent K.J. 19 + 4	Van Der Laan R.P. 43 + 1	Foyle M.J. 40 + 2	Glover E.L. 21 + 7	Jeffers J.J. 6 + 4	Walker R. 20 + 3	Naylor A.J. 29 + 4	Burke M. 4 + 11	Allon J.B. 10 + 9	Kelly A.G. 3 + 1	Billing P.G. 6	Aspin N. 37	Guppy S.A. 25 + 2	Lawton C.T. — + 1	Scott K.W. 17	Stokes D.A. 3	Bogie I. 7 + 2	Van Heusden A. 2	Talbot S. 2	Burndred J.N. 1	Corden S.W. — + 1	Match No.
1	2	3	4	5	6	7	8	9	10	11	12																1
1	2	3	4	5	6	7	8	9	10			11															2
1	2	3	4	5	6	7	8	9	10			11	12														3
1	2	3	4	5	6	7	8	9	10			11	12														4
1	2	3	*4*	5	6	7	8	9	10		14	11	12														5
1	2	3	4	5	6	7	8	9	10		12	11															6
1	2	3	4	5	6	7	8	9	10			11	12	14													7
1	2	3	4	5	6	7	8	9	10			11															8
1	2	3	4	5	6	7	8	9	10				11		12												9
1	2	3	4		6		14		10			9	11	12	7	*5*	8										10
1	2	3	4				8	9	10			11			7	6	5										11
1	2	3	4				*8*	9	10	12		11	14		7	6	5										12
1		3	4	5		7	8		10	11		*9*	12	14		6	2										13
1		3	4	5	6	7	8	10		12	11			9			2										14
1		3	4	5	6		8	10		7	11			9			2										15
1		3	4	5	6		8	10		7	11			9			2										16
1		3	4	5	6		8	10	12	7	11		14	9			2										17
1		3	4	5	6		*8*	10	12		11		14	9			2	7									18
1		3	4	5	6		8	10			11		12	9			2	7									19
1		3	12	5	6	*11*	8	9	10		4		14				2	7									20
1			4	5	6	7	*8*	9	10	3		12	14				2	11									21
1	3		4	5	6		8	9	10			12	7				2	11									22
1	3		4	5	6		8	9	10			12	7				2	11									23
1	3		4		6	7	8	9	10		11					5	2		12								24
1	2	3	4				8	9			11	10					5	7		6							25
1	2	3	4			12	8	9			11	*10*		14			5	7		6							26
1	2	3	4		12	11	8	9				10					5	7		6							27
1	2	3	4			11	8	9				10					5	7		6							28
1	2	3				11	8	9			4	10		12			5	7		6							29
1	2	3				11	8	9	12		*4*	10		14			5	7		6							30
1	2	3	4				8	9	12		11	10					5	7		6							31
1	2	3	4				8	9	12		11	*10*		14			5	7		6							32
1	2	3	4				8	9	12		11	10					5	7		6							33
1	2	3	4			12	8		*9*		11	10		14		6	5	7									34
1	2	3	4			12	8		*9*		11	10		14			5	7		6							35
1	2		4				8	12		14	11	10		*9*			5	7		6	3						36
1	2		4				8	12			11	10		9			5	7		6	3						37
1	2	3	4				8	10			11			9			5	7		6		12					38
1	2	3	4			11	8	10				12		9			5	7		6		14					39
1	2	3	4		11		8	9				10					5			6		7					40
1	2	*3*	4		11		8	9	12			10					5	14		6		7					41
1	2	3	4		11		8	9				10					5	12		6		7					42
1	2	3	4		6	12	8	9				10					5	11				7					43
1	2	3	4		6		8	9				10					5	11				7					44
	2	3	4		6			9	10								5	11				7	1	8			45
	2		4		6			9		12							5	11			3	7	1	8	*10*	14	46

Coca-Cola Cup

First Round	Bristol R (a)	3-1
	(h)	1-1
Second Round	Manchester U (h)	1-2
	(a)	0-2

FA Cup

First Round	Hartlepool U (h)	6-0
Second Round	Scarborough (a)	0-1

PRESTON NORTH END 1994–95 *Back row (left to right):* Stuart Hicks, Ryan Kidd, Jamie Squires, Neil Trebble, Mark Sale, Steve Holmes, David Moyes, Mike Conroy, Gavin Nebbeling. *Centre row:* Glenn Bonnell, Ian Bryson, Greg Challender, Farrell Kilbane, John Vaughan, Barry Richardson, Kelham O'Hanlon, Neil Whalley, Mickey Norbury, Paul Raynor, Geoff McDougall (Youth Team Scout). *Front row:* Alexis Moreno (Physio), Chris Sulley (Youth Development Officer), Terry Fleming, Kevin Magee, Gary Peters (Manager), John Beck, Gareth Ainsworth, Lee Cartwright, Andy Fensome, Brian Hickson (Kit Man).
(Photograph: Karen Pearson)

Division 3 PRESTON NORTH END

Deepdale, Preston PR1 6RU. Telephone: (01772) 795919. Fax: (01772) 653266. Commercial/Shop: (01772) 795465. Community Office: (01772) 704275.

Ground capacity: 14,659.

Record attendance: 42,684 v Arsenal, Division 1, 23 April 1938.

Record receipts: £68,650 v Sheffield W, FA Cup 3rd rd, 4 January 1992.

Pitch measurements: 110yd × 75yd.

President: Tom Finney OBE, JP.

Vice President: T. C. Nicholson JP, FCIOB.

Chairman: Bryan M. Gray.

Directors: K. W. Leeming, (vice-chairman), M. J. Woodhouse (snr) (vice-chairman), D. Shaw (managing), L. King (company secretary), M. J. Woodhouse (jnr).

Manager: Gary Peters. ***Coach:*** Joe Jakub.

Secretary: Mrs Audrey Shaw.

General Manager: Phil Critchley.

Year Formed: 1881. ***Turned Professional:*** 1885. ***Ltd Co.:*** 1893.

Club Nicknames: 'The Lilywhites' or 'North End'.

Foundation: North End Cricket and Rugby Club which was formed in 1863, indulged in most sports before taking up soccer in about 1879. In 1881 they decided to stick to football to the exclusion of other sports and even a 16–0 drubbing by Blackburn Rovers in an invitation game at Deepdale, a few weeks after taking this decision, did not deter them for they immediately became affiliated to the Lancashire FA.

First Football League game: 8 September, 1888, Football League, v Burnley (h) W 5-2 – Trainer; Haworth, Holmes; Robertson, W. Graham, J. Graham; Gordon (1), Ross (2), Goodall, Dewhurst (2), Drummond.

Record League Victory: 10–0 v Stoke, Division 1, 14 September 1889 – Trainer; Howarth, Holmes; Kelso, Russell (1), Graham; Gordon, Jimmy Ross (2), Nick Ross (3), Thomson (2), Drummond (2).

Record Cup Victory: 26–0 v Hyde, FA Cup, 1st rd, 15 October 1887 – Addision; Howarth, Nick Ross; Russell (1), Thomson (5), Graham (1); Gordon (5), Jimmy Ross (8), John Goodall (1), Dewhurst (3), Drummond (2).

Record Defeat: 0–7 v Blackool, Division 1, 1 May 1948.

Most League Points (2 for a win): 61, Division 3, 1970–71.

Most League Points (3 for a win): 90, Division 4, 1986–87.

Most League Goals: 100, Division 2, 1927–28 and Division 1, 1957–58.

Highest League Scorer in Season: Ted Harper, 37, Division 2, 1932–33.

Most League Goals in Total Aggregate: Tom Finney, 187, 1946–60.

Most Capped Player: Tom Finney, 76, England.

Most League Appearances: Alan Kelly, 447, 1961–75.

Record Transfer Fee Received: £765,000 from Manchester C for Michael Robinson, June 1979.

Record Transfer Fee Paid: £125,000 to Norwich C for Mike Flynn, December 1989.

Football League Record: 1888 Founder Member of League; 1901–04 Division 2; 1904–12 Division 1; 1912–13 Division 2; 1913–14 Division 1; 1914–15 Division 2; 1919–25 Division 1; 1925–34 Division 2; 1934–49 Division 1; 1949–51 Division 2; 1951–61 Division 1; 1961–70 Division 2; 1970–71 Division 3; 1971–74 Division 2; 1974–78 Division 3; 1978–81 Division 2; 1981–85 Division 3; 1985–87 Division 4; 1987–92 Division 3; 1992–93 Division 2; 1993– Division 3.

Honours: *Football League:* Division 1 – Champions 1888–89 (first champions), 1889–90; Runners-up 1890–91, 1891–92, 1892–93, 1905–06, 1952–53, 1957–58; Division 2 – Champions 1903–04, 1912–13, 1950–51; Runners-up 1914–15, 1933–34; Division 3 – Champions 1970–71; Division 4 – Runners-up 1986–87. *FA Cup:* Winners 1889, 1938; Runners-up 1888, 1922, 1937, 1954, 1964. *Double Performed:* 1888–89. *Football League Cup:* best season: 4th rd, 1963, 1966, 1972, 1981.

Colours: White and navy shirts, navy shorts, navy stockings. **Change colours:** Red/navy.

PRESTON NORTH END 1994–95 LEAGUE RECORD

Match No.	Date		Venue	Opponents	Result		H/T Score	Lg. Pos.	Goalscorers	Attendance
1	Aug	13	A	Darlington	D	0-0	0-0	—		3800
2		20	A	Hereford U	W	2-0	0-0	8	Conroy, Sale	3039
3		27	A	Barnet	L	1-2	0-0	12	Sale	2441
4		30	A	Bury	D	0-0	0-0	—		3623
5	Sept	3	H	Lincoln C	W	4-0	0-0	7	Moyes, Sale 2, Ainsworth	8337
6		10	A	Fulham	W	1-0	0-0	7	Trebble	5001
7		13	A	Gillingham	W	3-2	2-2	—	Sale 2, Fleming	2555
8		17	H	Darlington	L	1-3	0-1	6	Trebble	8884
9		24	A	Doncaster R	L	1-2	0-0	8	Fleming	3321
10	Oct	1	H	Walsall	L	1-2	1-0	11	Whalley	7852
11		8	H	Scunthorpe U	L	0-1	0-0	11		6895
12		15	A	Hartlepool U	L	1-3	1-2	14	Atkinson	2002
13		22	A	Colchester U	L	1-3	0-1	16	Trebble	3015
14		29	H	Exeter C	L	0-1	0-1	16		6808
15	Nov	5	A	Mansfield T	W	2-1	2-1	16	Conroy 2	2602
16		19	H	Northampton T	W	2-0	1-0	14	Moyes, Raynor	7297
17		26	A	Chesterfield	L	0-1	0-0	15		3191
18	Dec	10	H	Hereford U	W	4-2	3-0	10	Magee, Conroy, Bryson 2 (2 pens)	6581
19		17	H	Barnet	W	1-0	0-0	9	Kidd	6429
20		26	H	Rochdale	W	3-0	3-0	9	Smart, Kidd, Conroy	10,491
21		31	H	Scarborough	W	1-0	0-0	10	Smart	8407
22	Jan	2	A	Torquay U	L	0-1	0-1	11		3770
23		10	H	Colchester U	W	2-1	1-0	—	Smart, Trebble	6377
24		14	A	Carlisle U	D	0-0	0-0	10		10,684
25		21	H	Mansfield T	W	2-1	1-1	6	Bryson, Smart	8448
26		24	A	Wigan Ath	D	1-1	0-1	—	Cartwright	3618
27	Feb	4	H	Chesterfield	D	0-0	0-0	7		8544
28		11	A	Northampton T	L	1-2	0-0	8	Smart	5195
29		18	H	Carlisle U	W	1-0	1-0	6	Conroy	11,867
30		28	A	Walsall	D	2-2	1-1	—	Conroy, Raynor	4492
31	Mar	4	H	Doncaster R	D	2-2	0-1	9	Davey, Beckham	9624
32		11	H	Fulham	W	3-2	1-1	6	Conroy, Raynor, Beckham	8601
33		18	H	Bury	W	5-0	2-0	6	Carmichael 2, Conroy 2, Moyes	9626
34		21	A	Exeter C	W	1-0	0-0	—	Bryson	2057
35		25	A	Lincoln C	D	1-1	0-1	6	Kidd	5487
36	Apr	1	H	Gillingham	D	1-1	1-0	6	Carmichael	9100
37		8	A	Scarborough	D	1-1	1-1	6	Bryson	4266
38		15	H	Wigan Ath	W	1-0	1-0	6	Smart	10,238
39		17	A	Rochdale	W	1-0	1-0	5	Davey	4012
40		22	H	Torquay U	L	0-1	0-0	6		9173
41		29	H	Hartlepool U	W	3-0	2-0	5	Moyes, Holmes, Davey	9129
42	May	6	A	Scunthorpe U	L	1-2	1-2	5	Sale	3691

Final League Position: 5

GOALSCORERS

League (58): Conroy 10, Sale 7, Smart 6, Bryson 5 (2 pens), Moyes 4, Trebble 4, Carmichael 3, Davey 3, Kidd 3, Raynor 3, Beckham 2, Fleming 2, Ainsworth 1, Atkinson 1, Cartwright 1, Holmes 1, Magee 1, Whalley 1.
Coca-Cola Cup (2): Fensome 1 (pen), Moyes 1.
FA Cup (2): Conroy 1, Smart 1.

Richardson B. 17	Fensome A.B. 42	Fleming T.M. 20 + 7	Whalley D.N. 14 + 1	Hicks S.J. 8	Moyes D.W. 38	Ainsworth G. 16	Cartwright L. 25 + 11	Raynor P.J. 34 + 4	Trebble N.D. 8 + 11	Bryson J.I.C. 41	Kidd R.A. 32	Sale M.D. 10 + 3	Conroy M.K. 22 + 3	Squires J.A. 11	Vaughan J. 25 + 1	Sharp R. 21	Atkinson G. 8 + 7	Holmes S.P. 5	Emerson D. 1 + 1	Smart A. 17 + 2	Magee K. 14	Rimmer S.A. — + 2	Lancashire G. 9 + 8	Davey S. 13	Beckham D.R.J. 4 + 1	Carmichael M. 7 + 3	Match No.
1	2	3	4	5	6	7	8	9	10	11																	1
1	2	11	4	5	6	7	8	9			3	10	12														2
1	2	3	4	5		7	8	12	*9*	11	6	14	10														3
1	2		4		6	7		11		8	3	10	9	5													4
1	2	14	4		6	7	12	9		8	3	10	*11*	5													5
1	2	*11*	4	5	6	7	12	9	14	8	3	10															6
1	2	11	4	5	6	7	12	*9*	14	8	3	10															7
1	2	11	4		6	7	12	9	14	8	*3*	*10*		5													8
1	2	9	4		6	7		11	10	8	3			5													9
1	2	14	4		6	7	12	*11*	10	8	3	9		5													10
1	2	10	4	5	6	7		11	12	8	3	9															11
	2	12	*4*	5		7	14		10	8	6	9			1	3	11										12
	2	14	4	5	6		*7*		9	8		12	10		1	3	11										13
	2	7	*4*		6		14	9		8		12	10		1	3	11	5									14
	2	7	12		6		4	9		8			10	5	1	3	11										15
1	2	12			6	7	4	9	11	*8*			10			3		5	14								16
1	2				6		4	12	7	8	11		10			3		5		9							17
1	2	12			6		4	11		8			10			3		5		*9*	7	14					18
1	2				6		7	11		8	5		10			3			4	9		12					19
1	2				6		4	11		8	5		10			3	12			*9*	7		14				20
1	2				6		4	11		8	5		*10*		15	3	12			9	7		14				21
	2	3			6	7	4		12	8	5		14		1		11			*9*			10				22
	2	3			6		4	11	12	8	5				1		14			9	7		10				23
	2	3			6		4	11	12	8	5				1		14			9	7		10				24
	2	3			6		4	11	12	8	5				1		14			9	7		10				25
	2	12			6	7	4	11	14	8	5				1	*3*				9			10				26
	2				6		4	11	12	8	5				1	3	14			9	7		10				27
	2				6	7	4	11	12	8	5				1	3	10			9							28
	2				6		4	11		8	5		10		1	3	12			*9*	7		14				29
	2				6		4	11		8	5		10		1	3				9			12	7			30
	2				6		4	*11*		8	5		10		1	3				12			9	7	14		31
	2				6		12	9		8	5		10		1	3					11			7	4		32
	2				6					8	5		10		1	3					11			7	4	9	33
	2				6			12		8			10	5	1	3					11			7	4	9	34
	2				6		12	14		8	5		10		1	3					11			7	4	*9*	35
	2				6		12	4		8				5	1	*3*	10			14	11			7		9	36
	2	3			6		11	4		8			10	5	1								12	7		9	37
	2	3			*6*		4	11		8	5		10		1					9			12	7		14	38
	2	3					4	11		8	5		12	6	1					*9*			14	7		10	39
	2	3					4	11		8	*5*		10	6	1					9			12	7		14	40
	2	3			6			4		8					1			5			11		9	7		10	41
	2	3			6		12	4		8	5	*10*			1		11						9	7		14	42

Coca-Cola Cup

First Round	Stockport Co (h)	1-1
	(a)	1-4

FA Cup

First Round	Blackpool (h)	1-0
Second Round	Walsall (h)	1-1
	(a)	0-4

QUEENS PARK RANGERS 1994–95 *Back row (left to right):* Brian Croft, Trevor Chellis, Steve Yates, Daniele Dichio, Alan McCarthy, Tony Witter, Kevin Gallen, Karl Ready, Chris Plummer, Marvin Bryan, Matthre Brazier.
Centre row: Phil Parkes (Goalkeeping Coach), Des Bulpin (Youth Team Manager), Les Boyle (Kit Manager), Dennis Bailey, John Cross, Michael Meaker, Peter Caldwell, Tony Roberts, Sieb Dykstra, Devon White, Danny Maddix, Andrew Impey, Roger Cross (Reserve Team Manager), John Nolan (Assistant Kit Manager), Brian Morris (Physio).
Front row: Bradley Allen, Ian Holloway, David Bardsley, Rufus Brevett, Les Ferdinand, Gerry Francis, Alan McDonald, Frank Sibley (Assistant Manager), Gary Penrice, Mark Graham, Clive Wilson, Maurice Doyle, Trevor Sinclair.
(Photograph: Action Images)

FA Premiership **QUEENS PARK RANGERS**

South Africa Road, W12 7PA. Telephone: (0181) 743 0262. Fax: (0181) 749 0994. Box Office: (0181) 749 5744 (24 hour information service 0181 749 7798). Supporters Club: (0181) 749 6771. Club Shop: (0181) 749 6862. Marketing: (0181) 740 8737.

Ground capacity: 18,919.

Record attendance: 35,353 v Leeds U, Division 1, 27 April 1974.

Record receipts: £218,475 v Manchester U, FA Premier League, 5 February 1994.

Pitch measurements: 112yd × 72yd.

Chairman: P. D. Ellis.

Directors: R. B. Copus ACA, A. Ellis, A. Ingham, R. C. Thompson.

Manager: Ray Wilkins MBE. ***Assistant Manager/Coach:*** Frank Sibley.

Secretary: Miss S. F. Marson. ***Commercial Controller:*** Leon Gold.

Reserve Team Coach: Roger Cross.

Physio: Brian Morris.

Year Formed: 1885 *(*see Foundation*). ***Turned Professional:*** 1898. ***Ltd Co.:*** 1899.

Club Nicknames: 'Rangers' or 'Rs'. ***Previous Name:*** 1885–87, St Jude's.

Previous Grounds: 1885 *(*see Foundation*), Welford's Fields; 1888–99; London Scottish Ground, Brondesbury, Home Farm, Kensal Rise Green, Gun Club Wormwood Scrubs, Kilburn Cricket Ground; 1899, Kensal Rise Athletic Ground; 1901, Latimer Road, Notting Hill; 1904, Agricultural Society, Park Royal; 1907, Park Royal Ground; 1917, Loftus Road; 1931, White City; 1933, Loftus Road; 1962, White City; 1963, Loftus Road.

Foundation: There is an element of doubt about the date of the foundation of this club, but it is believed that in either 1885 or 1886 it was formed through the amalgamation of Christchurch Rangers and St. Jude's Institute FC. The leading light was George Wodehouse, whose family maintained a connection with the club until comparatively recent times. Most of the players came from the Queen's Park district so this name was adopted after a year as St. Jude's Institute.

First Football League game: 28 August, 1920, Division 3, v Watford (h) L 1-2 – Price; Blackman, Wingrove; McGovern, Grant, O'Brien; Faulkner, Birch (1), Smith, Gregory, Middlemiss.

Record League Victory: 9–2 v Tranmere R, Division 3, 3 December 1960 – Drinkwater; Woods, Ingham; Keen, Rutter, Angell; Lazarus (2), Bedford (2), Evans (2), Andrews (1), Clark (2).

Record Cup Victory: 8–1 v Bristol R (away), FA Cup, 1st rd, 27 November 1937 – Gilfillan; Smith, Jefferson; Lowe, James, March; Cape, Mallett, Cheetham (3), Fitzgerald (3) Bott (2). 8–1 v Crewe Alex, Milk Cup, 1st rd, 3 October 1983 – Hucker; Neill, Dawes, Waddock (1), McDonald (1), Fenwick, Micklewhite (1), Stewart (1), Allen (1), Stainrod (3), Gregory.

Record Defeat: 1–8 v Mansfield T, Division 3, 15 March 1965 and v Manchester U, Division 1, 19 March 1969.

Most League Points (2 for a win): 67, Division 3, 1966–67.

Most League Points (3 for a win): 85, Division 2, 1982–83.

Most League Goals: 111, Division 3, 1961–62.

Highest League Scorer in Season: George Goddard, 37, Division 3 (S), 1929–30.

Most League Goals in Total Aggregate: George Goddard, 172, 1926–34.

Most Capped Player: Alan McDonald, 50, Northern Ireland.

Most League Appearances: Tony Ingham, 519, 1950–63.

Record Transfer Fee Received: £6,000,000 from Newcastle U for Les Ferdinand, June 1995.

Record Transfer Fee Paid: £1,000,000 to Luton T for Roy Wegerle, December 1989.

Football League Record: 1920 Original Members of Division 3; 1921–48 Division 3 (S); 1948–52 Division 2; 1952–58 Division 3 (S); 1958–67 Division 3; 1967–68 Division 2; 1968–69 Division 1; 1969–73 Division 2; 1973–79 Division 1; 1979–83 Division 2; 1983–92 Division 1; 1992– FA Premier League.

Honours: *Football League:* Division 1 – Runners-up 1975–76; Division 2 – Champions 1982–83; Runners-up 1967–68, 1972–73; Division 3 (S) – Champions 1947–48; Runners-up 1946–47; Division 3 – Champions 1966–67. *FA Cup:* Runners-up 1982. *Football League Cup:* Winners 1967; Runners-up 1986. (In 1966–67 won Division 3 and Football League Cup). **European Competition:** *UEFA Cup:* 1976–77, 1984–85.

Colours: Blue and white hooped shirts, white shorts, white stockings. **Change colours:** All red with black trim.

QUEENS PARK RANGERS 1994–95 LEAGUE RECORD

Match No.	*Date*		*Venue*	*Opponents*	*Result*		*H/T Score*	*Lg. Pos.*	*Goalscorers*	*Attendance*
1	Aug	20	A	Manchester U	L	0-2	0-0	—		43,214
2		24	H	Sheffield W	W	3-2	1-1	—	Ferdinand, Sinclair, Gallen	12,788
3		27	H	Ipswich T	L	1-2	0-1	15	Ferdinand	12,456
4		31	A	Leicester C	D	1-1	1-0	—	Willis (og)	18,695
5	Sept	10	H	Coventry C	D	2-2	2-1	13	Penrice 2	11,398
6		17	A	Everton	D	2-2	1-2	12	Ferdinand 2	27,291
7		24	H	Wimbledon	L	0-1	0-0	16		11,061
8	Oct	2	A	Nottingham F	L	2-3	0-0	18	Ferdinand, Allen	21,449
9		8	A	Tottenham H	D	1-1	1-0	17	Impey	25,799
10		15	H	Manchester C	L	1-2	0-0	19	Wilson	13,631
11		22	A	Norwich C	L	2-4	1-0	20	Barker, Gallen	19,431
12		29	H	Aston Villa	W	2-0	1-0	18	Dichio, Penrice	16,073
13		31	H	Liverpool	W	2-1	1-0	—	Sinclair, Ferdinand	18,295
14	Nov	5	A	Newcastle U	L	1-2	1-0	17	Dichio	34,278
15		19	H	Leeds U	W	3-2	2-0	18	Ferdinand 2, Gallen	17,416
16		26	A	Blackburn R	L	0-4	0-1	18		21,302
17	Dec	4	H	West Ham U	W	2-1	2-0	16	Ferdinand, Sinclair	12,780
18		10	H	Manchester U	L	2-3	1-2	17	Ferdinand 2	18,948
19		17	A	Sheffield W	W	2-0	0-0	13	Maddix, Ferdinand	23,288
20		26	A	Crystal Palace	D	0-0	0-0	16		16,699
21		28	H	Southampton	D	2-2	1-1	16	Barker, Gallen	16,078
22		31	A	Arsenal	W	3-1	1-0	14	Gallen, Allen, Impey	32,393
23	Jan	14	A	Aston Villa	L	1-2	0-1	15	Yates	26,578
24		24	A	Leeds U	L	0-4	0-2	—		28,750
25	Feb	4	H	Newcastle U	W	3-0	3-0	17	Ferdinand 2, Barker	16,576
26		11	A	Liverpool	D	1-1	1-0	16	Gallen	35,996
27		26	H	Nottingham F	D	1-1	0-0	17	Barker	13,363
28	Mar	4	A	Wimbledon	W	3-1	1-1	16	Ferdinand 2, Holloway	9176
29		8	H	Leicester C	W	2-0	0-0	—	McDonald, Wilson	10,189
30		15	H	Norwich C	W	2-0	0-0	—	Ferdinand, Gallen	10,519
31		18	H	Everton	L	2-3	1-0	11	Ferdinand, Gallen	14,488
32		22	H	Chelsea	W	1-0	0-0	—	Gallen	15,103
33	Apr	1	A	Coventry C	W	1-0	0-0	9	Sinclair	15,751
34		4	H	Blackburn R	L	0-1	0-0	—		16,508
35		8	H	Arsenal	W	3-1	1-0	9	Impey, Gallen, Ready	16,341
36		11	A	Ipswich T	W	1-0	0-0	—	Ferdinand	11,736
37		15	A	Southampton	L	1-2	0-0	8	Ferdinand	15,210
38		17	H	Crystal Palace	L	0-1	0-0	8		14,227
39		29	A	Chelsea	L	0-1	0-0	8		21,704
40	May	3	A	West Ham U	D	0-0	0-0	—		22,923
41		6	H	Tottenham H	W	2-1	0-1	8	Ferdinand 2	18,637
42		14	A	Manchester C	W	3-2	1-1	8	Ferdinand 2, Dichio	27,850

Final League Position: 8

GOALSCORERS

League (61): Ferdinand 24, Gallen 10, Barker 4, Sinclair 4, Dichio 3, Impey 3, Penrice 3, Allen 2, Wilson 2, Holloway 1, McDonald 1, Maddix 1, Ready 1, Yates 1, own goal 1.
Coca-Cola Cup (6): Allen 1, Ferdinand 1, Gallen 1, Penrice 1, Sinclair 1, Wilson 1 (pen).
FA Cup (6): Ferdinand 1, Gallen 1, Impey 1, Maddix 1, Meaker 1, Wilson 1 (pen).

Roberts A.M. 31	Bardsley D.J. 30	Wilson C. 36	Barker S. 37	Yates S. 22 + 1	McDonald A. 39	Impey A.R. 40	Holloway I.S. 28 + 3	Ferdinand L. 37	Gallen K.A. 31 + 6	Sinclair T. 32 + 1	Maddix D.S. 21 + 6	Penrice G.K. 9 + 10	Brevett R.E. 17 + 2	Ready K. 11 + 2	Meaker M.J. 7 + 1	Allen B.J. 2 + 3	Dykstra S. 11	White D.W. 1	Dichio D.S.E. 4 + 5	Hodge S.B. 15	McCarthy A.J. — + 2	Wilkins R.C. 1 + 1	Match No.
1	2	3	4	5	6	7	8	*9*	10	11	12	14											1
1	2	3	4	5	6	7	8	9	10	11	12												2
1	2	3	4	5	6	7	8	9	10	11		12											3
1	2	3	4	5	6	7	8	9	12	11		10											4
1	2		4	5	6	7	8	9	12	11		10	3										5
1	2	11	4	5	6	7	8	9				10	3	12									6
1	2	11	4	5	6	7		9	12			10	3		8								7
1	2		10	5	6	7	8	9		11	4		3			12							8
1	2	3	4	5	6	7	8	9		11	12					10							9
1	2	3	4	5	6	7	8	9	12	11						10							10
	2	3	4	5	6		8		10	11					7	12	1	9					11
	2	3	8	5	6		7		10	11	14	12					1		9	4			12
	2	3	8	5	6	7		9	10	11							1			4			13
	2	3	8	5	6	7		9	10	11							1		12	4			14
		3	8	2	6	7	12	9	10	11				5			1			4			15
		3	8	2	6	7		9	10	11				5			1			4			16
		3	8	5	6	7	12	9	10	11	2						1			4			17
	2	3	8		6	7		9	10	11	5						1			4			18
	2	3	8		6	7	12	9	10	11	5						1			4			19
		3	8	2	6	7		9	10	11	5				12		1			4			20
		3	8	2	6	7		9	10		5		12		11		1			4			21
1	2	3	8		6	7		9	10		5				11	12				4			22
1	2	3		5		7	8	9	10		6				11					4	12		23
1	2			5		7	8	9	*10*	12	6		3		11					4	14		24
1	2		4		6	7	8	9	10	11	5		3						12				25
1	2	3	4		6	7	8	9	10		5		11										26
1		3	4	2	6	7	8	9	10		5	12		14	*11*								27
1		3	4		6	7	8	9	10		5	12	11	2									28
1		3	4		6	7	8		10	11	5	12		2					9				29
1	2	3	4		6	7	8	9	10	11	5												30
1	2	3	4		6	7	8	9	10	11	5	12											31
1	2	3	4		6	7	8		10	11				5					9				32
1		3	4		6	7	8		10	11			2	5					9				33
1		3	4		6	7	8	9	10	11			2	5					12				34
1		3	4		6	7	8	9	10	11		12	2	5									35
1		3	*4*		6	7	8	9	10	11	14	12	2	5									36
1	2	11				7		9	10	8	6	12	3	5						4		14	37
1	2	4			6	7	8	9		11	12	10	*3*	5					14				38
1	2	11			6	7		9	12		5	10	3							4		8	39
1	2	*3*	4		6	7	8	9	12	11	5	10	14										40
1	2		4		6	7	8	9		11	5	10	3										41
1	2		4	12	6	7		9	*10*	11	5	8	3						14				42

Coca-Cola Cup

Second Round	Carlisle U (a)	1-0
	(h)	2-0
Third Round	Manchester C (h)	3-4

FA Cup

Third Round	Aylesbury (a) (at QPR)	4-0
Fourth Round	West Ham U (h)	1-0
Fifth Round	Millwall (h)	1-0
Sixth Round	Manchester U (a)	0-2

READING 1994–95 *Back row (left to right):* Alan Carey, Ray Ranson, James Lambert, Shaka Hislop, Micky Gooding, Scott Taylor, Michael Gilkes.
Centre row: Colin Lee (Assistant Manager), Phil Parkinson, Jeff Hopkins, Andy Bernal, Dariusz Wdowczyk, David Bass, Keith McPherson, Uwe Hartenberger, Jimmy Quinn, Mark McGhee (Manager).
Front row: Lea Barkus, Tom Jones, Dylan Kerr, Adrian Williams, Simon Osborn, Stuart Lovell, Paul Holsgrove.

Division 1 **READING**

Elm Park, Norfolk Road, Reading RG3 2EF. Telephone: (01734) 507878. Fax: (01734) 566628. Community Office: (01734) 560898. Promotions Office: (01734) 464008.

Ground capacity: 14,058.

Record attendance: 33,042 v Brentford, FA Cup 5th rd, 19 February 1927.

Record receipts: £83,671 v Manchester C, FA Cup 3rd rd, 13 January 1993.

Pitch measurements: 112yd × 77yd.

Life President: J. H. Brooks.

Chairman: John Madejski. ***Managing Director:*** M. J. Lewis.

Directors: G. Denton, I. Wood-Smith.

Joint Managers: Jimmy Quinn/Mick Gooding.

Coach: Phil Holder. ***Youth Development Officer:*** Mike Hickman.

Physio: Paul Turner.

Commercial Manager: Kevin Girdler.

Secretary: Ms Andrea Barker.

Year Formed: 1871. ***Turned Professional:*** 1895. ***Ltd Co.:*** 1895.

Club Nickname: 'The Royals'.

Previous Grounds: 1871, Reading Recreation; Reading Cricket Ground; 1882, Coley Park; 1889, Caversham Cricket Ground; 1896, Elm Park.

Foundation: Reading was formed as far back as 1871 at a public meeting held at the Bridge Street Rooms. They first entered the FA Cup as early as 1877 when they amalgamated with the Reading Hornets. The club was further strengthened in 1889 when Earley FC joined them. They were the first winners of the Berks and Bucks Cup in 1878–79.

First Football League game: 28 August, 1920, Division 3, v Newport C (a) W 1-0 – Crawford; Smith, Horler; Christie, Mavin, Getgood; Spence, Weston, Yarnell, Bailey (1), Andrews.

Record League Victory: 10–2 v Crystal Palace, Division 3 (S), 4 September 1946 – Groves; Glidden, Gulliver; McKenna, Ratcliffe, Young; Chitty, Maurice Edelston (3), McPhee (4), Barney (1), Deverell (2).

Record Cup Victory: 6–0 v Leyton, FA Cup, 2nd rd, 12 December 1925 – Duckworth; Eggo, McConnell; Wilson, Messer, Evans; Smith (2), Braithwaite (1), Davey (1), Tinsley, Robson (2).

Record Defeat: 0–18 v Preston NE, FA Cup 1st rd, 1893–94.

Most League Points (2 for a win): 65, Division 4, 1978–79.

Most League Points (3 for a win): 94, Division 3, 1985–86.

Most League Goals: 112, Division 3 (S), 1951–52.

Highest League Scorer in Season: Ronnie Blackman, 39, Division 3 (S), 1951–52.

Most League Goals in Total Aggregate: Ronnie Blackman, 158, 1947–54.

Most Capped Player: Jimmy Quinn, 15 (44), Northern Ireland.

Most League Appearances: Martin Hicks, 500, 1978–91.

Record Transfer Fee Received: £500,000 from Wimbledon for Keith Curle, October 1988.

Record Transfer Fee Paid: £250,000 to Leicester C for Steve Moran, November 1987, £250,000 to Huddersfield T for Craig Maskell, August 1990 and £250,000 to Watford for Lee Nogan, December 1994.

Football League Record: 1920 Original Member of Division 3; 1921–26 Division 3 (S); 1926–31 Division 2; 1931–58 Division 3 (S); 1958–71 Division 3; 1971–76 Division 4; 1976–77 Division 3; 1977–79 Division 4; 1979–83 Division 3; 1983–84 Division 4; 1984–86 Division 3; 1986–88 Division 2; 1988–92 Division 3; 1992–94 Division 2; 1994– Division 1.

Honours: *Football League:* Division 1 – Runners-up 1994–95; Division 2 – Champions 1993–94; Division 3 – Champions 1985–86. Division 3 (S) – Champions 1925–26; Runners-up 1931–32, 1934–35, 1948–49, 1951–52; Division 4 – Champions 1978–79. *FA Cup:* Semi-final 1927. *Football League Cup:* best season: 4th rd, 1965, 1966, 1978. *Simod Cup:* Winners 1988.

Colours: Navy and white hooped shirts, white shorts, white stockings. **Change colours:** All red.

READING 1994–95 LEAGUE RECORD

Match No.	Date	Venue	Opponents	Result		H/T Score	Lg. Pos.	Goalscorers	Attendance
1	Aug 13	A	Wolverhampton W	L	0-1	0-1	—		27,012
2	20	H	Portsmouth	D	0-0	0-0	21		9106
3	27	A	Barnsley	W	2-0	1-0	13	Osborn, Taylor	4771
4	30	H	Stoke C	W	4-0	0-0	—	Lovell, Kerr, Gilkes, Taylor	7103
5	Sept 3	H	Millwall	D	0-0	0-0	6		8715
6	10	A	Oldham Ath	W	3-1	1-1	2	Lovell 2, Osborn	8412
7	14	A	Swindon T	L	0-1	0-0	—		11,551
8	17	H	Sheffield U	W	1-0	0-0	3	Quinn	9036
9	24	A	Watford	D	2-2	0-2	5	Osborn, Lovell	8015
10	Oct 1	H	Notts Co	W	2-0	1-0	3	Lovell, Hartenberger	7465
11	8	A	Charlton Ath	W	2-1	1-0	3	Osborn, Gilkes	10,544
12	15	H	Bristol C	W	1-0	0-0	2	Gilkes	9389
13	22	H	Sunderland	L	0-2	0-1	2		10,757
14	29	A	WBA	L	0-2	0-0	4		14,313
15	Nov 2	A	Derby Co	W	2-1	1-0	—	Taylor, Gilkes	10,585
16	5	H	Burnley	D	0-0	0-0	4		8150
17	19	A	Southend U	L	1-4	1-1	5	Quinn	5511
18	26	H	Tranmere R	L	1-3	0-2	8	Jones	7887
19	Dec 3	A	Sunderland	W	1-0	0-0	5	Taylor	14,021
20	6	H	Middlesbrough	D	1-1	0-0	—	Taylor	10,301
21	10	A	Portsmouth	D	1-1	0-1	6	Quinn (pen)	8578
22	18	H	Wolverhampton W	W	4-2	2-1	5	Osborn, Quinn, Gilkes 2	10,136
23	26	H	Luton T	D	0-0	0-0	6		11,623
24	28	A	Port Vale	W	2-0	1-0	—	Quinn (pen), Taylor	7891
25	31	H	Grimsby T	D	1-1	0-1	4	Lambert	8526
26	Jan 2	A	Bolton W	L	0-1	0-1	6		14,705
27	14	H	WBA	L	0-2	0-0	7		9390
28	21	A	Burnley	W	2-1	2-0	5	Nogan, Taylor	9841
29	Feb 4	A	Middlesbrough	W	1-0	0-0	5	Holsgrove	17,982
30	11	H	Derby Co	W	1-0	1-0	4	Kavanagh (og)	8834
31	18	A	Tranmere R	L	0-1	0-0	5		8744
32	21	H	Southend U	W	2-0	0-0	—	Holsgrove, Nogan	7895
33	25	A	Notts Co	L	0-1	0-0	6		7183
34	Mar 4	H	Watford	W	4-1	1-0	5	Gilkes 2, Holsgrove, Hartenberger	9705
35	8	A	Millwall	L	0-2	0-1	—		7546
36	11	H	Barnsley	L	0-3	0-1	6		7556
37	18	A	Stoke C	W	1-0	1-0	6	Taylor	10,006
38	21	H	Oldham Ath	W	2-1	0-1	—	Nogan, Lovell	6921
39	25	A	Sheffield U	D	1-1	0-0	5	Nogan	19,241
40	Apr 1	H	Swindon T	W	3-0	2-0	4	Lovell 3 (1 pen)	12,565
41	8	A	Grimsby T	L	0-1	0-0	5		4519
42	15	H	Port Vale	D	3-3	3-0	6	Nogan 3	8635
43	17	A	Luton T	W	1-0	1-0	5	Taylor (og)	8717
44	21	H	Bolton W	W	2-1	1-0	—	Lovell, Nogan	13,223
45	29	A	Bristol C	W	2-1	1-0	2	Lovell, Nogan	9474
46	May 7	H	Charlton Ath	W	2-1	1-0	2	Nogan, Williams	12,137

Final League Position: 2

GOALSCORERS

League (58): Lovell 11 (1 pen), Nogan 10, Gilkes 8, Taylor 8, Osborn 5, Quinn 5 (2 pens), Holsgrove 3, Hartenberger 2, Jones 1, Kerr 1, Lambert 1, Williams 1, own goals 2.
Coca-Cola Cup (7): Quinn 4, Holsgrove 1, Lovell 1, Williams 1.
FA Cup (1): Taylor 1.

Hislop N.S. 46	Bernal A. 33	Kerr D. 35 + 1	Wdowczyk D. 37 + 1	Williams A. 20 + 2	Parkinson P.J. 25 + 6	Taylor S.D. 31 + 13	Gooding M.C. 37 + 2	Quinn J.M. 31 + 4	Lovell S.A. 25 + 5	Osborn S.E. 31 + 1	Hopkins J. 20 + 1	Gilkes E.G.M. 37 + 3	Holsgrove P. 23 + 1	Jones T. 18 + 2	Hartenberger U. 8 + 7	Murphy M. — + 1	Lambert C.J.P. 3 + 8	McPherson K.A. 19 + 4	Barnard D.S. 3 + 1	Carey A.W. — + 2	Nogan L.M. 18 + 2	Viveash A.L. 6	*Match No.*
1	2	3	4	5	6	*7*	8	9	10	11	12	14											1
1	2	3	4	5	6	7	8	9	10	11		12											2
1		3	4	5	6	12	8	9	10	11	2	7											3
1		3	4	5	6	12	8	9	10	*11*	2	7	14										4
1		3	4		*6*	12	8	9	10	11	2	7	5	14									5
1		3	4	5			8	9	10	11	2	7	6										6
1	2	3	4	5		12	8	9	10	11		7	6										7
1	2	3	4	5	12	14	8	9	10	11		7	*6*										8
1		12	4	5	3	*10*	8	9	14	11	2	7	6										9
1		3	4	5	8	12		*9*	10	11	2	7	6		14								10
1	2	3	4	5	12	14	8	9		11		7	6		*10*								11
1	2	3	4	5	12		8	9		11		7	6		*10*	14							12
1	2	3	4	5	*6*	10	8	9		11		7					12	14					13
1		3	4	5	*6*	12	8			11	2	7		10	9			14					14
1	2	3	4		6	9	8			11	5	7		10									15
1	2	3	4		6	9	8			11	5	7		10				12					16
1		3	4			7	8	9		11	2			6				5	10	12			17
1	2	3	4			7	8	9		11	*5*			6			12	14	10				18
1	2	3	4			12	8	9	*10*	11				6			14	5	7				19
1	2	3	4			12	8	9	10	11		7		6				5					20
1	2	3			6	4	8	9	10	11		7						5	12				21
1	2	3			6	4	8	9	10	11		7			12			5					22
1	2		5		6	4	8	9	10	11		7		3			12						23
1	2		4		6	12	8	9	10	11		7		3				5					24
1	2		4		6	12	*8*	9	10	11		7		3			14	5					25
1			4		6	3	8	9	10			7		2	12		11	5					26
1	5				6	3	8	9	12		4	7	11	2							10		27
1	2					11	8	10	12		5	7	4	3							9	6	28
1	2		3			12	8	10	14		5	7	4	11							*9*	6	29
1		3	4		12	8		10			2	*7*	6	11			14				9	5	30
1		3	4		7	8		*10*			2		6	11	14		12				9	5	31
1		3			8	11		12			4		6	2	*10*		7			14	9	5	32
1		3		14	8	7		12			5		4	2	*10*		11				9	6	33
1	2	3		5	12	11	8				4	7	6		10						9		34
1	2	3	12	5		11	8	14			6	7	4		*10*						9		35
1	2	3	4			11	8	9	12			7	*6*				14	5			10		36
1	2	3	4		10	11	8	9				7	6					5			12		37
1	2	3	4		8	11	12	*9*	10			7	6					5			14		38
1	2	3	4		8	11			10			7	6		12			5			9		39
1	2	3	4		8	11			10	12		*7*	6		14			5			9		40
1	2	3	4	12		11	14			*8*		7	6		10			5			9		41
1	2	3		5		11	8		10	6		7			12			4			9		42
1	2	3	4	5		11	8		10	7		12						6			9		43
1	2		4	5		11	8		10	3		7						6			9		44
1	2		4	5	12	11	8		10	3		7						6			9		45
1	*2*		4	5		11	8	12	10	3		7		14				6			9		46

Coca-Cola Cup

First Round	Gillingham (a)	1-0
	(h)	3-0
Second Round	Derby Co (h)	3-1
	(a)	0-2

FA Cup

Third Round	Oldham Ath (h)	1-3

ROCHDALE 1994–95 *Back row (left to right):* Kevin Formby, Neil Matthews, Paul Butler, Paul Williams, Alan Reeves, Mark Stuart, Steve Doyle.
Centre row: Darren Ryan, Trevor Jones (Youth Coach), Keith Hicks (Youth Coach), Chris Clarke, John Dawson (Physio), Jimmy Robson (Youth Team Manager), Steve Whitehall.
Front row: Jason Peake, Dave Thompson, Andy Thackeray, Mick Docherty (Assistant Manager), Dave Sutton (Manager), Darren Oliver, Shaun Reid, Alex Russell.

Division 3 **ROCHDALE**

Spotland, Sandy Lane, Rochdale OL11 5DS. Telephone: (01706) 44648. Fax: (01706) 48466. Commercial: (01706) 47521.

Ground capacity: 6655.

Record attendance: 24,231 v Notts Co, FA Cup 2nd rd, 10 December 1949.

Record receipts: £46,000 v Burnley, Division 4, 5 May 1992.

Pitch measurements: 114yd × 76yd.

President: Mrs L. Stoney.

Chairman: D. F. Kilpatrick.

Directors: G. R. Brierley, T. Butterworth, C. Dunphy, M. Mace, J. Marsh, G. Morris.

Manager: Mick Docherty.

Secretary: Keith Clegg. ***Coach:*** Jimmy Robson. ***Commercial Manager:*** S. Walmsley. ***Advertising & Sponsorship Manager:*** L. Duckworth.

Physio: J. Dawson.

Year Formed: 1907. ***Turned Professional:*** 1907. ***Ltd Co.:*** 1910.

Club Nickname: 'The Dale'.

Foundation: Considering the love of rugby in their area, it is not surprising that Rochdale had difficulty in establishing an Association Football club. The earlier Rochdale Town club formed in 1900 went out of existence in 1907 when the present club was immediately established and joined the Manchester League, before graduating to the Lancashire Combination in 1908.

First Football League game: 27 August, 1921, Division 3(N), v Accrington Stanley (h) W 6-3 – Crabtree; Nuttall, Sheehan; Hill, Farrer, Yarwood; Hoad, Sandiford, Dennison (2), Owens (3), Carney (1).

Record League Victory: 8–1 v Chesterfield, Division 3 (N), 18 December 1926 – Hill; Brown, Ward; Hillhouse, Parkes, Braidwood; Hughes, Bertram, Whitehurst (5), Schofield (2), Martin (1).

Record Cup Victory: 8–2 v Crook T, FA Cup, 1st rd, 26 November 1927 – Moody; Hopkins, Ward; Braidwood, Parkes, Barker; Tompkinson, Clennell (3) Whitehurst (4), Hall, Martin (1).

Record Defeat: 0–8 v Wrexham, Division 3 (N), 28 December 1929, 0–8 v Leyton Orient, Division 4, 20 October 1987, and 1–9 v Tranmere R, Division 3 (N), 25 December 1931.

Most League Points (2 for a win): 62, Division 3 (N), 1923–24.

Most League Points (3 for a win): 67, Division 4, 1991–92.

Most League Goals: 105, Division 3 (N), 1926–27.

Highest League Scorer in Season: Albert Whitehurst, 44, Division 3 (N), 1926–27.

Most League Goals in Total Aggregate: Reg Jenkins, 119, 1964–73.

Most Capped Player: None.

Most League Appearances: Graham Smith, 317, 1966–74.

Record Transfer Fee Received: £300,000 from Wimbledon for Alan Reeves, September 1994.

Record Transfer Fee Paid: £80,000 to Scunthorpe U for Andy Flounders, August 1991.

Football League Record: 1921 Elected to Division 3 (N); 1958–59 Division 3; 1959–69 Division 4; 1969–74 Division 3; 1974–92 Division 4; 1992– Division 3.

Football League: Division 3 best season: 9th, 1969–70; Division 3 (N) – Runners-up 1923–24, 1926–27. *FA Cup:* best season: 5th rd, 1990. *Football League Cup:* Runners-up 1962 (record for 4th Division club).

Colours: Blue with red and white chevrons. **Change colours:** White shirts, white shorts, blue stockings.

ROCHDALE 1994–95 LEAGUE RECORD

Match No.	Date	Venue	Opponents	Result		H/T Score	Lg. Pos.	Goalscorers	Attendance
1	Aug 13	A	Bury	W	1-0	0-0	—	Thompson	3230
2	20	H	Chesterfield	W	4-1	1-0	1	Reid, Thompson, Thackeray, Whitehall	2122
3	27	A	Gillingham	D	1-1	1-0	2	Hall	3015
4	30	H	Lincoln C	W	1-0	1-0	—	Whitehall	1974
5	Sept 3	H	Hereford U	L	1-3	0-1	6	Williams	2258
6	10	A	Northampton T	W	2-1	0-1	4	Reid, Thompson	3052
7	13	A	Barnet	L	2-6	1-4	—	Reid (pen), Williams	1688
8	17	H	Bury	L	0-3	0-0	9		3748
9	24	A	Scarborough	W	4-2	1-1	6	Williams 2, Whitehall, Butler	1200
10	Oct 1	H	Doncaster R	W	2-0	0-0	4	Williams, Peake	2445
11	8	H	Fulham	L	1-2	1-0	6	Whitehall	2573
12	15	A	Wigan Ath	L	0-4	0-4	7		2118
13	22	A	Torquay U	L	1-4	0-1	10	Thackeray	2547
14	29	H	Mansfield T	D	3-3	1-2	10	Butler, Whitehall 2	1968
15	Nov 5	A	Carlisle U	L	1-4	0-1	10	Stuart	5984
16	19	H	Colchester U	D	0-0	0-0	10		1903
17	26	A	Hartlepool U	L	0-1	0-1	12		1387
18	Dec 10	A	Chesterfield	D	2-2	1-2	13	Russell, Whitehall (pen)	2457
19	17	H	Gillingham	W	2-1	2-0	12	Stuart, Valentine	1665
20	26	A	Preston NE	L	0-3	0-3	13		10,491
21	27	H	Walsall	L	0-2	0-1	14		2438
22	31	A	Scunthorpe U	L	1-4	0-2	15	Butler	2653
23	Jan 7	H	Torquay U	W	2-0	0-0	14	Sharpe, Thompson	1636
24	14	A	Exeter C	D	0-0	0-0	14		2316
25	21	H	Carlisle U	D	1-1	0-0	13	Peake	3289
26	Feb 4	H	Hartlepool U	W	1-0	1-0	13	Deary	1848
27	11	A	Colchester U	D	0-0	0-0	13		3080
28	18	H	Exeter C	L	0-1	0-1	13		1945
29	25	A	Doncaster R	W	1-0	1-0	14	Sharpe	2246
30	Mar 7	A	Mansfield T	D	1-1	1-0	—	Whitehall	2931
31	11	H	Northampton T	D	0-0	0-0	15		1894
32	18	A	Lincoln C	D	2-2	0-2	15	Thompson, Valentine	2939
33	21	H	Darlington	W	2-0	0-0	—	Thompson, Whitehall	1471
34	25	A	Hereford U	D	0-0	0-0	13		1954
35	Apr 1	H	Barnet	D	2-2	1-1	14	McDonald (og), Thackeray	1834
36	8	H	Scunthorpe U	L	1-2	1-0	15	Ryan	1720
37	15	A	Walsall	D	0-0	0-0	15		3766
38	17	H	Preston NE	L	0-1	0-1	15		4012
39	22	A	Darlington	L	0-4	0-2	15		1886
40	25	H	Scarborough	D	1-1	0-1	—	Ryan	1170
41	29	H	Wigan Ath	W	1-0	1-0	14	Whitehall (pen)	1949
42	May 6	A	Fulham	L	0-5	0-3	15		4342

Final League Position: 15

GOALSCORERS

League (44): Whitehall 10 (2 pens), Thompson 6, Williams 5, Butler 3, Reid 3 (1 pen), Thackeray 3, Peake 2, Ryan 2, Sharpe 2, Stuart 2, Valentine 2, Deary 1, Hall 1, Russell 1, own goal 1.
Coca-Cola Cup (1): Whitehall 1.
FA Cup (0).

Clarke C.J. 24	Thackeray A.J. 41	Formby K. 27 + 1	Reid S. 27 + 1	Reeves A. 5	Matthews N.P. 10 + 3	Thompson D.S. 38 + 2	Peake J.W. 36 + 3	Bowden J.L. 6 + 5	Whitehall S.C. 41 + 1	Stuart M.R. 26 + 5	Ryan D.T. 15 + 10	Williams P.A. 12 + 2	Doyle S.C. 7 + 4	Butler P.J. 39	Hall D.R. 5 + 4	Rimmer S.A. 3	Russell A. 2 + 5	Dunford N. 2	Dickins M.J. 4	Taylor J.L. 1 + 8	Sharpe R. 9 + 7	Oliver D. 8 + 1	Gray I.J. 12	Valentine P. 27	Whitington C. 1	Martin D. 12 + 3	Deary J.S. 17	Shaw G.P. 4	Bayliss D.A. 1	*Match No.*
1	2	3	4	5	6	7	8	9	10	11	12																			1
1	2	3	4	5	6	7	*8*		10	11	12	9	14																	2
1	2	3	4	5		7	12		10	11		9		6	8															3
1	2	3	4	5		7	12		10	11		9	14	6	*8*															4
1	2	3	4	5		7	8		10		14	9	12	6		*11*														5
1	2	3	4		5	7	8		12			9	10	6		11														6
1	2	3	4		5	7	8		10			14	11	6	12	*9*														7
1	2	3	4		5	7			10	11		9		6	8															8
1	2	3	4		5	7	12		10	11		9		6	*8*		14													9
	2	3	12			7	8		10	11	14	9	5	6			4	1												10
	2	3	4			12	8		10	*11*	7	9	5	6			14	1												11
	2	3	4			7	8		10	11	12	9	5	6			14		1											12
	2	3	4			7			10		11	9	*5*	6	8				1	12	14									13
	2		4		5	7	8		10	11				6					1	12	9	3								14
	2	3	4		5	12	8		10	9	11			6					1		14	7								15
	2	3	4		5				10	11		9	7	6						12			1	8						16
	2		4		5		7		10	*11*			12	6							14	3	1	8	9					17
	2					7	*8*	9	10		11	12		6	14		4					3	1	5						18
	2					7	8	9	10	*4*	11			6	12					14		3	1	5						19
	2	*3*				7	8	9	10	4	11			6			12					14	1	5						20
	2		4			7	8	9	*10*	11				6			12				14	3	1	5						21
	2		4			7	8	12	*10*	11	14			6							9	3	1	5						22
	2		4			7	8	9	10					6							11	3	1	5						23
	2	3	4		14	7	8		10	12				6							*11*		1	5		9				24
	2	3	4			7	8		10	11				6									1	5		9				25
	2	3	4			7	8		10	*11*				6							14		1	5		12	9			26
	2	*3*	4			7	8		10	12				6							11		1	5		14	9			27
1	2	3	4		14	7	8		10	11				6						12				5			9			28
1	2	3	4		12	7	*8*		10					6	14						11			5			9			29
1	2	3	4			7	8		10	12	14			6							11			5			*9*			30
1	2	3	4			7	8		10	14	12			6							*11*			5			9			31
1	2	3				7	8		10	12	14			6							*9*			5		4	11			32
1	2					7	8		10	3	9			6							12			5		4	11			33
1	2					7	3		10		11			6							12			5		4	8	9		34
1	2					7	3	12	10		11													5		4	8	9	6	35
1	2					7	*3*	12	10		11			6						14				5		4	8	9		36
1	2					7	3	12	10		11			6										5		4	8	9		37
1	2	12				7	3		10	9	11			6										5		4	8			38
1	2	3				7	4	12	10	9	*11*			6										5		14	8			39
1	2					7	3		10	9	11			6						12				5		4	8			40
1	2					7	3		10	9	11			6						12				5		4	8			41
1		2				7	3		10	9	12			6						11				5		4	8			42

Coca-Cola Cup
First Round Mansfield T (h) 1-2
(a) 0-1

FA Cup
First Round Walsall (a) 0-3

ROTHERHAM UNITED 1994–95 *Back row (left to right):* Andy Williams, Tony Brien, Carey Williams, Neil Richardson, Ian Helliwell, Billy Mercer, Matthew Clarke, Nigel Johnson, Ian Breckin, Shaun Goater, Mark Barnard, Martin Pike.
Centre row: Chris Hutchings, Billy Russell, Jonathan Howard, Paul Green, Karl Marginson, Chris Wilder, Martin James, Des Hazel, John Breckin, Ian Bailey.
Front row: Scott Smith, Glynn Roberts, Mark Todd, Imri Varadi, Phil Henson, Chris Dolby, Shaun Goodwin, Paul Hurst, Chris Hilton.

Division 2 ROTHERHAM UNITED

Millmoor Ground, Rotherham S60 1HR. Telephone: (01709) 562434. Fax: (01709) 563336.

Ground Capacity: 11,533.

Record attendance: 25,000 v Sheffield U, Division 2, 13 December 1952 and v Sheffield W, Division 2, 26 January 1952.

Record receipts: £79,155 v Newcastle U, FA Cup 4th rd, 23 January 1993.

Pitch measurements. 115yd × 75yd.

President: Sir J. Layden.

Chairman: K. F. Booth.

Directors: R. Hull (vice-chairman), C. A. Luckock, J. A. Webb. ***Chief Executive:*** Phil Henson.

Joint Managers: Archie Gemmill/John McGovern. ***Assistant Manager/Coach:*** John Breckin. ***Physio:*** Ian Bailey.

Secretary: N. Darnill.

Commercial Manager: D. Nicholls.

Year Formed: 1884. ***Turned Professional:*** 1905. ***Ltd Co.:*** 1920.

Club Nickname: 'The Merry Millers'.

Previous Names: 1884, Thornhill United; 1905, Rotherham County; 1925, amalgamated with Rotherham Town under Rotherham United.

Previous Ground: Red House Ground; 1907, Millmoor.

Foundation: This club traces its history back to the formation of Thornhill United in 1878 (reformed 1884). They changed their name to Rotherham County in 1905. Confusion exists because of the existence of the Rotherham Town club (founded c. 1885) and in the Football League as early as 1893 but this club was not the one previously mentioned. The Town amalgamated with Rotherham County to form Rotherham United in 1925.

First Football League game: 2 September, 1893, Division 2, Rotherham T v Lincoln C (a) D 1-1 – McKay; Thickett, Watson; Barr, Brown, Broadhead; Longden, Cutts, Leatherbarrow, McCormick, Pickering. 1 o.g. 30 August, 1919, Division 2, Rotherham C v Nottingham F (h) W 2-0 – Branston; Alton, Baines; Bailey, Coe, Stanton; Lee (1), Cawley (1), Glennon, Lees, Lamb.

Record League Victory: 8–0 v Oldham Ath, Division 3 (N), 26 May 1947 – Warnes; Selkirk, Ibbotson; Edwards, Horace Williams, Danny Williams; Wilson (2), Shaw (1), Ardron (3), Guest (1), Hainsworth (1).

Record Cup Victory: 6–0 v Spennymoor U, FA Cup, 2nd rd, 17 December 1977 – McAlister; Forrest, Breckin, Womble, Stancliffe, Green, Finney, Phillips (3), Gwyther (2) (Smith), Goodfellow, Crawford (1). 6–0 v Wolverhampton W, FA Cup, 1st rd, 16 November 1985 – O'Hanlon; Forrest, Dungworth, Gooding (1), Smith (1), Pickering, Birch (2), Emerson, Tynan (1), Simmons (1), Pugh.

Record Defeat: 1–11 v Bradford C, Division 3 (N), 25 August 1928.

Most League Points (2 for a win): 71, Division 3 (N), 1950–51.

Most League Points (3 for a win): 82, Division 4, 1988–89.

Most League Goals: 114, Division 3 (N), 1946–47.

Highest League Scorer in Season: Wally Ardron, 38, Division 3 (N), 1946–47.

Most League Goals in Total Aggregate: Gladstone Guest, 130, 1946–56.

Most Capped Player: Harold Millership, 6, Wales.

Most League Appearances: Danny Williams, 459, 1946–62.

Record Transfer Fee Received: £200,000 from Bristol C for Martin Scott, December 1990.

Record Transfer Fee Paid: £110,000 to Wolverhampton W for Paul Blades, July 1995.

Football League Record: 1893 Rotherham Town elected to Division 2; 1896 Failed re-election; 1919 Rotherham County elected to Division 2; 1923–51 Division 3 (N); 1951–68 Division 2; 1968–73 Division 3; 1973–75 Division 4; 1975–81 Division 3; 1981–83 Division 2; 1983–88 Division 3; 1988–89 Division 4; 1989–91 Division 3; 1991–92 Division 4; 1992– Division 2.

Honours: *Football League:* Division 2 best season: 3rd, 1954–55 (equal points with champions and runners-up); Division 3 – Champions 1980–81; Division 3 (N) – Champions 1950–51; Runners-up 1946–47, 1947–48, 1948–49; Division 4 – Champions 1988–89; Runners-up 1991–92. *FA Cup:* best season: 5th rd, 1953, 1968. *Football League Cup:* Runners-up 1961.

Colours: Red and white. **Change colours:** White shirts with black sleeves, black shorts, black stockings.

ROTHERHAM UNITED 1994–95 LEAGUE RECORD

Match No.	Date	Venue	Opponents	Result		H/T Score	Lg. Pos.	Goalscorers	Attendance
1	Aug 13	H	Shrewsbury T	L	0-4	0-3	—		3762
2	20	A	Crewe Alex	L	1-3	0-2	23	Varadi	3505
3	27	H	Bournemouth	W	4-0	0-0	16	Goater 2, Hayward, Morris (og)	2306
4	30	A	Brentford	L	0-2	0-1	—		4031
5	Sept 3	A	Cambridge U	L	1-2	0-1	20	Goater	2885
6	10	H	Bristol R	L	0-3	0-3	20		2596
7	13	H	Birmingham C	D	1-1	1-0	—	Hazel	3799
8	17	A	Hull C	W	2-0	2-0	20	Goodwin, Goater	4431
9	24	A	Peterborough U	D	2-2	2-1	18	Goodwin, Goater	4894
10	Oct 1	H	Blackpool	L	0-2	0-2	20		3517
11	8	A	Stockport Co	L	0-1	0-0	21		4991
12	15	H	York C	W	2-1	2-0	21	Goater, Goodwin	3380
13	22	H	Leyton Orient	W	2-0	1-0	18	Marginson (pen), Goater	2700
14	29	A	Brighton & HA	D	1-1	1-0	18	Davison	6734
15	Nov 1	A	Swansea C	L	0-1	0-0	—		2511
16	5	H	Plymouth Arg	W	3-1	1-0	16	Goater 2, Varadi	2848
17	19	A	Oxford U	L	1-2	1-2	16	Helliwell	5801
18	26	H	Chester C	W	2-0	0-0	16	Goater 2 (1 pen)	2947
19	Dec 10	H	Crewe Alex	D	2-2	0-2	16	McGlashan, Hayward	2907
20	16	A	Shrewsbury T	L	0-1	0-1	—		3243
21	26	H	Bradford C	W	3-1	3-0	16	Roscoe, Goater (pen), Davison	5400
22	27	A	Huddersfield T	L	0-1	0-1	17		15,557
23	31	H	Cardiff C	W	2-0	1-0	16	Monington, Breckin	3064
24	Jan 7	A	Leyton Orient	D	0-0	0-0	17		2796
25	14	H	Wycombe W	W	2-0	1-0	15	Brown (og), Hayward	3537
26	21	A	Plymouth Arg	D	0-0	0-0	15		5484
27	Feb 4	A	Chester C	D	4-4	2-3	15	Monington, McGlashan 2, Wilder	1794
28	11	H	Swansea C	D	3-3	3-2	15	Roscoe, Hayward, Davison	2858
29	18	A	Wycombe W	L	0-2	0-0	16		5153
30	21	H	Oxford U	D	1-1	0-1	—	Goater	2833
31	25	A	Blackpool	D	2-2	1-1	17	Davison, Goater	5043
32	Mar 4	H	Peterborough U	D	0-0	0-0	17		3123
33	7	H	Cambridge U	W	1-0	1-0	—	Goater	2208
34	11	A	Bournemouth	D	1-1	0-0	17	Goater	5666
35	14	A	Wrexham	L	1-3	1-1	—	Goater	1823
36	18	H	Brentford	L	0-2	0-2	18		2968
37	22	A	Bristol R	L	0-2	0-0	—		4420
38	25	H	Hull C	W	2-0	1-0	18	Peel, Roscoe	3692
39	28	H	Brighton & HA	W	4-3	3-1	—	Breckin, Peel, Roscoe, Goater	2316
40	Apr 1	A	Birmingham C	L	1-2	1-0	17	Goater (pen)	16,077
41	8	A	Cardiff C	D	1-1	0-1	17	Peel	6412
42	15	H	Huddersfield T	D	1-1	0-0	17	Hayward	6687
43	17	A	Bradford C	W	3-0	2-0	17	Farrelly, Hayward, Peel	3535
44	22	H	Wrexham	L	0-1	0-0	17		2628
45	29	A	York C	L	0-2	0-0	17		3183
46	May 6	H	Stockport Co	W	1-0	0-0	17	Farrelly	3469

Final League Position: 17

GOALSCORERS

League (57): Goater 19 (3 pens), Hayward 6, Davison 4, Peel 4, Roscoe 4, Goodwin 3, McGlashan 3, Breckin 2, Farrelly 2, Monington 2, Varadi 2, Hazel 1, Helliwell 1, Marginson 1 (pen), Wilder 1, own goals 2.
Coca-Cola Cup (2): Hayward 1, Varadi 1.
FA Cup (8): Davison 3, Goater 3, Helliwell 1, Hurst 1.

Clarke M.J. 45	Smith S.D. 3 + 1	Hurst P.M. 8 + 5	Wilder C.J. 45	Breckin I. 41	Richardson N.T. 23 + 2	Hazel D.L. 16 + 5	Goodwin S.L. 10	Goater L.S. 45	Varadi I. 6 + 11	James M.J. 40	Brien A.J. 16 + 1	Mercer W. 1	Williams A. 17	Helliwell I. 10 + 2	Hayward A. 33 + 4	Williams C. — + 2	Pike M.R. 7	Foran M.J. 3	Todd M.K. 12 + 2	Dolby C.J. — + 2	Roberts G.S. — + 2	Marginson K.K. 5 + 3	Davison R. 19 + 2	Roscoe A.R. 31	McGlashan J. 27	Monington M.D. 25	Farrelly G. 9 + 1	Peel N.J. 9	*Match No.*
1	2	3	4	5	6	7	8	9	10	11	12																		1
			2		6	7	8	*11*	10	3	5	1	4	9	12	14													2
1			2			7		8		11			4	10	9		3	5	6	12									3
1			2			7		8		11			4	10	9		3	5	6	12									4
1			2			7		8	12	11			4	10	*9*		3	5	6		14								5
1			2	5		7		8		11			4	10	9		3		6										6
1			2	5		7	8	10			6		4	9			3		11		12								7
1			2	5		7	8	10		3	6		4	9					11										8
1			2	5		7	8	10		3	6		4	9					11										9
1			2	5		7	8	10	12	3	6		4	9					11										10
1			2	5			8	10		7	6		4			12	3		11			9							11
1			2	5		7	8	10		11	6		4		12		3						9						12
1			2	5			8	10	12	3	6		4		7							11	9						13
1			2	5			*8*	10	12	3	6		4		7							14	9	11					14
1			2	5				10	9	3	6		4		7							8		11					15
1		12	2	5				10	9	3	6		4		7							8		11					16
1	7		2	5	12			10	9	3	6		4	*8*	14									11					17
1		14	2	5	8			10	12	3	6		*4*		7								9	11					18
1		11	2		4			10		3	6				7								9		8	5			19
1		11	2	6	4			10		3					7								9		8	5			20
1		12	2	6	4			10		3				14	7								*9*	11	8	5			21
1			2	6	4	12		10		3					7								9	11	8	5			22
1		12	2	6	4	14		10		3					7								*9*	11	8	5			23
1			2	6	*4*	10				3				12	7							14	9	11	8	5			24
1			2	6	4	12		10		3					7								9	11	8	5			25
1			2	6	4			10	12	3					7								9	11	8	5			26
1			2	6	4	12		10		3					7								9	11	8	5			27
1			2	6	4	12		10		3					7								9	11	8	5			28
1			2	6	4			10	12	3					7							14	9	11	*8*	5			29
1			2	6	4	7		10		3													9	11	8	5			30
1			2	6	4	7		10		3													9	11	8	5			31
1		12	2	6	4	7		*10*	14	3													9	11	8	5			32
1		3	2	6	4			10	12						7								9	11	8	5			33
1		3	2	6	4			10							7				9					11	8	5			34
1		3	2	6	4			10	12						7				9			8		11		5			35
1	2	3		6	4	7		10	*9*						12				14					11	8	5			36
1		3	2	6	4			10	12						7				9					11	8	5	14		37
1			2	6				10		3					7									11	8	5	4	9	38
1			2	6				10		3	5				7									11	8		4	9	39
1			2	6				10		3					7				12					11	8	5	4	9	40
1			2	6				10		3	5				7									11	8		4	9	41
1			2	6				10		3					7									11	8	5	4	9	42
1			2	6	12			*10*		3					7								14	11	8	5	4	9	43
1			2	6				10		3					7								12	11	8	5	4	9	44
1	12		2	6	5			10		3					7									11	8		4	9	45
1			2	6				10		3					7									11	8	5	4	9	46

Coca-Cola Cup

First Round	Carlisle U (h)	1-0
	(a)	1-3

FA Cup

First Round	York C (a)	3-3
	(h)	3-0
Second Round	Wrexham (a)	2-5

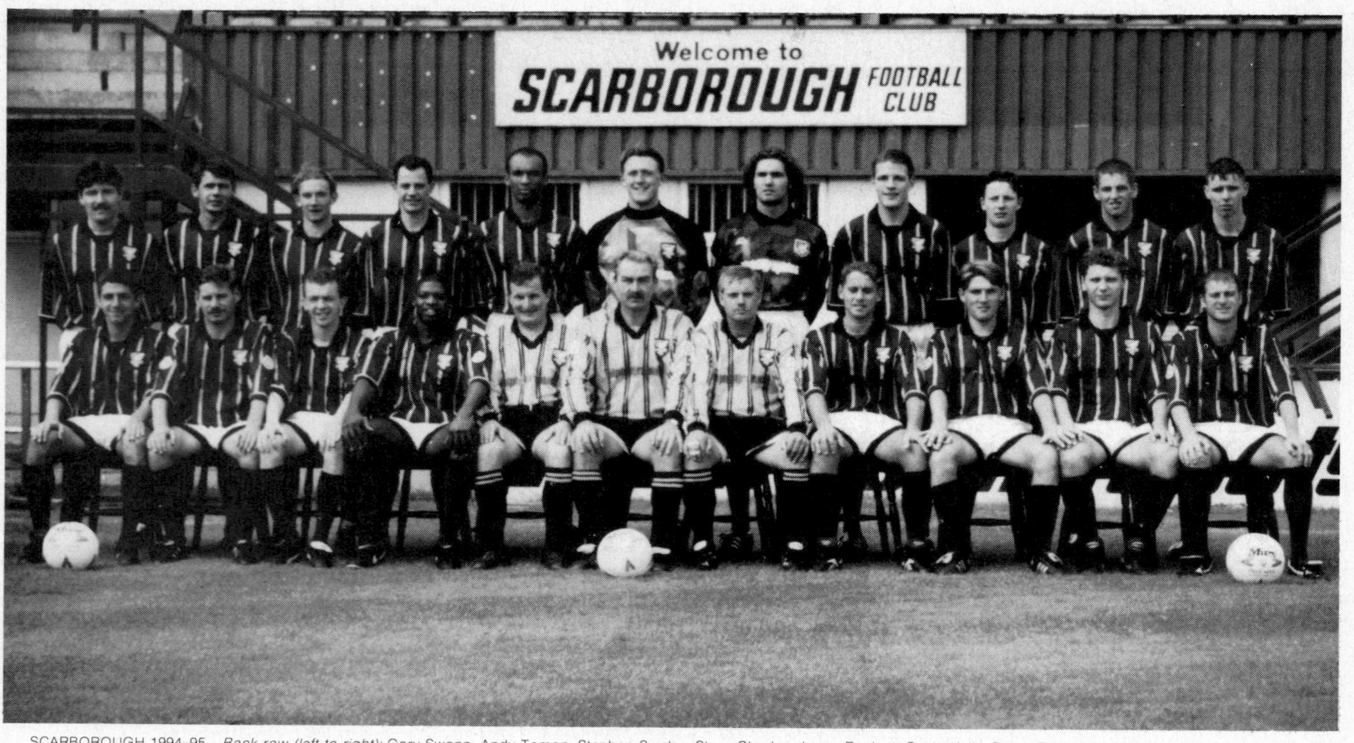

SCARBOROUGH 1994–95 *Back row (left to right):* Gary Swann, Andy Toman, Stephen Swales, Steve Charles, Jason Rockett, Gavin Kelly, Stuart Ford, Adrian Meyer, Alex Willgrass, Lee Harper, Andrew Hudson.
Front row: Mark Wells, Darren Knowles, Michael McHugh, Jason White, John Murray (Physio), Billy Ayre (Manager), Phil Chambers (Assistant Manager), Mark Calvert, Simon Thompson, Stuart Young, Darren Foreman.

Division 3 SCARBOROUGH

The McCain Stadium, Seamer Road, Scarborough YO12 4HF. Telephone: (01723) 375094. Fax: (01723) 378733.

Ground capacity: 6899.

Record Attendance: 11,130 v Luton T, FA Cup 3rd rd, 8 January 1938. Football League: 7314 v Wolverhampton W, Division 4, 15 August 1987.

Record receipts: £37,609.50 v Arsenal, Coca-Cola Cup 4th rd, 6 January 1993.

Pitch measurements: 114yd × 74yd.

President and Chief Executive: John Birley.

Chairman: J. Russell.

Directors: Mrs G. Russell.

Manager: Ray McHale. ***Assistant Manager:*** Phil Chambers.

Secretary: Eric V. Hall. ***Physio:*** J. Murray.

Year Formed: 1879. ***Turned Professional:*** 1926. ***Ltd Co.:*** 1933.

Club Nickname: 'The Boro'.

Previous Grounds: 1879–87, Scarborough Cricket Ground; 1887–98, Recreation Ground; 1898– Athletic Ground.

Foundation: Scarborough came into being as early as 1879 when they were formed by members of the town's cricket club and went under the name of Scarborough Cricketers' FC with home games played on the North Marine Road Cricket Ground.

First Football League game: 15 August, 1987, Division 4, v Wolverhampton W (h) D 2-2 – Blackwell; McJannet, Thompson, Bennyworth, Richards, Kendall, Hamill, Moss, McHale (1), Mell (1), Graham.

Record League Victory: 4–0 v Bolton W, Division 4, 29 August 1987 – Blackwell; McJannet, Thompson, Bennyworth (Walker), Richards (1) (Cook), Kendall, Hamill (1), Moss, McHale, Mell (1), Graham. (1 og). 4–0 v Newport Co (away), Division 4, 12 April 1988 – Ironside; McJannet, Thompson, Kamara, Richards (1), Short (1), Adams (Cook 1), Brook, Outhart (1), Russell, Graham.

Record Cup Victory: 6–0 v Rhyl Ath, FA Cup, 1st rd, 29 November 1930 – Turner; Severn, Belton; Maskell, Robinson, Wallis; Small (1), Rand (2), Palfreman (2), A. D. Hill (1), Mickman.

Record Defeat: 1–16 v Southbank, Northern League, 15 November 1919.

Most League Points (3 for a win): 77, Division 4, 1988–89.

Most League Goals: 69, Division 4, 1990–91.

Highest League Scorer in Season: Darren Foreman, 27, Division 4, 1992–93.

Most League Goals in Total Aggregate: Darren Foreman, 35, 1991–95.

Most Capped Player: None.

Most League Appearances: Steve Richards, 119, 1987–90.

Record Transfer Fee Received: £240,000 from Notts Co for Chris Short, September 1990.

Record Transfer Fee Paid: £102,000 to Leicester C for Martin Russell, March 1989.

Football League Record: Promoted to Division 4 1987; 1992– Division 3.

Honours: *Football League:* Division 4 best season: 5th, 1988–89. *FA Cup:* best seasons: 3rd rd, 1931, 1938, 1976, 1978, 1995. *Football League Cup:* best season: 4th rd 1993. *FA Trophy:* Winners 1973, 1976, 1977. *GM Vauxhall Conference:* Winners 1986–87.

Colours: Red and white. **Change colours:** Yellow and black.

SCARBOROUGH 1994–95 LEAGUE RECORD

Match No.	Date	Venue	Opponents	Result		H/T Score	Lg. Pos.	Goalscorers	Attendance
1	Aug 13	A	Chesterfield	W	1-0	1-0	—	Charles (pen)	3099
2	20	H	Barnet	L	0-1	0-0	15		1471
3	27	A	Carlisle U	L	0-2	0-2	16		5720
4	30	H	Hereford U	W	3-1	1-0	—	Foreman, Rowe, White	1490
5	Sept 3	H	Colchester U	L	0-1	0-0	13		1494
6	10	A	Gillingham	L	1-3	0-1	16	Calvert	2414
7	13	A	Fulham	W	2-1	2-1	—	Swann, D'Auria	2729
8	17	H	Chesterfield	L	0-1	0-1	14		1475
9	24	H	Rochdale	L	2-4	1-1	16	Charles (pen), White	1200
10	Oct 1	A	Wigan Ath	D	1-1	1-1	16	Charles (pen)	1403
11	8	A	Walsall	L	1-4	1-1	19	White	3601
12	15	H	Doncaster R	D	2-2	2-0	18	Rutherford, Swann	1641
13	22	A	Lincoln C	L	0-2	0-1	21		2396
14	29	H	Northampton T	D	0-0	0-0	21		1468
15	Nov 5	A	Bury	L	0-1	0-0	21		3016
16	19	H	Torquay U	D	1-1	1-0	20	White	1241
17	26	A	Exeter C	L	2-5	1-2	22	Young, D'Auria	2179
18	Dec 10	A	Barnet	L	1-3	0-0	22	White	1988
19	17	H	Carlisle U	L	1-2	1-1	22	Rodwell	1910
20	26	A	Darlington	L	0-1	0-1	22		2958
21	27	H	Mansfield T	L	2-5	1-2	22	Griffiths, Thompson	1926
22	31	A	Preston NE	L	0-0	0-0	22		8407
23	Jan 14	A	Hartlepool U	D	3-3	1-0	22	Norris 2 (1 pen), D'Auria	1784
24	28	A	Northampton T	W	3-0	0-0	22	Swann, Norris, D'Auria	5737
25	Feb 4	H	Exeter C	L	0-2	0-1	22		1512
26	7	H	Lincoln C	D	1-1	0-1	—	D'Auria	1217
27	18	H	Hartlepool U	D	2-2	1-1	22	Norris, Wells	1517
28	25	H	Wigan Ath	L	0-1	0-1	22		1416
29	28	H	Scunthorpe U	W	3-0	0-0	—	Trebble, Swales, D'Auria	1179
30	Mar 7	A	Torquay U	L	1-2	1-1	—	White	1492
31	11	H	Gillingham	D	0-0	0-0	22		1949
32	18	A	Hereford U	L	1-2	0-0	22	White	1479
33	21	H	Bury	L	1-2	1-1	—	White	1744
34	25	A	Colchester U	W	2-0	0-0	22	Charles, Trebble	3025
35	Apr 1	H	Fulham	W	3-1	0-0	22	White, D'Auria, Scott	2050
36	8	H	Preston NE	D	1-1	1-1	22	Charles	4266
37	15	A	Mansfield T	L	2-3	2-2	22	White 2	2931
38	18	H	Darlington	W	3-1	1-0	—	Davis, Scott 2	2182
39	22	A	Scunthorpe U	L	1-3	0-1	22	Trebble	2079
40	25	A	Rochdale	D	1-1	1-0	—	Davis	1170
41	29	A	Doncaster R	L	0-1	0-0	21		1710
42	May 2	H	Walsall	L	1-2	0-0	—	Calvert	2841

Final League Position: 21

GOALSCORERS

League (49): White 11, D'Auria 7, Charles 5 (3 pens), Norris 4 (1 pen), Scott 3, Swann 3, Trebble 3, Calvert 2, Davis 2, Foreman 1, Griffiths 1, Rodwell 1, Rowe 1, Rutherford 1, Swales 1, Thompson 1, Wells 1, Young 1.
Coca-Cola Cup (5): Blackstone 2, Charles 1 (pen), Rowe 1, Young 1.
FA Cup (3): Swann 1, Toman 1, White 1.

Kelly G.J. 24	Knowles D.T. 39	Charles S. 40	Calvert M.R. 26 + 4	Meyer A.M. 13	Rockett J. 27	Rowe R.C. 10 + 4	Swann G. 24 + 3	Young S.R. 7 + 6	White J.G. 36 + 3	Blackstone I.K. 11 + 2	Thompson S.L. 14 + 2	Foreman D. 10 + 4	Dunphy S. 10	D'Auria D. 31 + 3	Rutherford P. 6 + 2	Toman J.A. 9 + 7	Davis D.J. 22 + 1	Swales S.C. 21	Ford S.T. 6	Wells M.A. 16 + 2	Martin K. 3	Rodwell A. 6 + 2	Griffiths B.K. 5	Norris S.M. 8	Mardenborough S.A. — + 1	Hicks S.J. 6	Trebble N.D. 15	Scott R. 8	Ironside I. 9	*Match No.*
1	2	3	4	5	6	7	8	9	10	11																				1
1	2	3	4	5	6	7	8	9		11	10	12																		2
1	2	3	4		6	7	8	12	10	11		9	5	14																3
1	2	3	7		6	12	8	14	10	11		*9*	5	4																4
1	2	3	12		6	7	8	14	10	11		*9*	5	4																5
1		3	7		6	12	8		10	11	2		5	4	9															6
1		3	7		6	9	8		10	11	2		5	4		12														7
1		3	7		*6*	9	8	12	10	11	2		5	4		14														8
1	2	9	4	6		7		11	8		3	10	5																	9
1	2	8	4			7	12			*9*	3	10	5	11	14		6													10
1	*2*		4			12	8	7	9		3			11	10	14	6	5												11
1	2	8				12	4	7	9		3			11	10		6	5												12
	2	8	12				4	7	9	14	3			11			6	*5*	1	10										13
	2	8				7	4		12	9			5		10		6	3	1	11										14
	2	8			4	9	7	12	14				5		10		6	*3*		11	1									15
	2	8	*11*		6		7	12	9					14	10	4	5	3			1									16
	2	8			6		7	10	9					12	14	*4*	5	3		11	1									17
	2	8		5			7		9	12				11			6		1	3		4	10							18
	2	8		5	6		7		9		14			11		12			1	3		4	*10*							19
	2	3	4	5	6		10		9		12					14			1			7	11	8						20
	2	3		5	6		10		9		7					4			1				11	8						21
1	2	3		5	6		10		9		7					4	12						11	8						22
1	2	3		5			10		9		7			4			6			11				8						23
1	2	3		5			10		9		7	12		4		14	6			11				8						24
1	2	3	12	5			10		9			*7*		4		14	6			11				8						25
1	2	3	4	5					9					10		7	6			11				8	12					26
1	2	3	4		6		12		14	*9*				7		10	5			11				8						27
1	2	3	4		6		12		9		7	14		8						11						5	10			28
1	2				6		4		9			7		8				3		11						5	10			29
1	2	3			6				9			7		8				4		11						5	10			30
1	2	3	12		6				9			*7*		8				4		11		14				5	10			31
1	2	3	11		6				9					8				4				7				5	10			32
1	2	3	11		6				9			12		8				4		14		7				*5*	10			33
	2	4	11	5	6				9					8				3		12							10	7	1	34
	2	4	11		6				9					8			5	3									10	7	1	35
	2	4	11		6				9					8			5	3									10	7	1	36
	2	4	11						9					8		6	5	3									10	7	1	37
	2	4	11						9					8		6	5	3									10	7	1	38
	2	4	11						9					8		6	5	3									10	7	1	39
	2	4	11		6				9					8			5	3									10	7	1	40
	2	4	11		6				9					8			5	3				12					10	7	1	41
	2	4	11									9		8			5	3		6		7					10		1	42

Coca-Cola Cup

First Round	Hull C (a)	1-2
	(h)	2-0
Second Round	Middlesbrough (h)	1-4
	(a)	1-4

FA Cup

First Round	Chesterfield (a)	0-0
	(h)	2-0
Second Round	Port Vale (h)	1-0
Third Round	Watford (h)	0-0
	(a)	0-2

SCUNTHORPE UNITED 1994–95 *Back row (left to right):* Ian Juryeff, Damian Henderson, Christian Sansam, Timothy Ryan, Wayne Bullimore, Steven Housham.
Centre row: Ian Whyte (Youth Development Officer), Christopher Hope, Russell Bradley, Mark Samways, Alan Knill, Michael Heath, Ian Thompstone, Matthew Carmichael.
Front row (left to right): Dean Martin, Paul Mudd, Graham Alexander, David Moore (Manager), Tony Ford, Stephen Thornber, Mark Smith, Samuel Goodacre.

Division 3 **SCUNTHORPE UNITED**

Glanford Park, Scunthorpe, South Humberside DN15 8TD. Telephone: (01724) 848077. Fax: (01724) 857986.

Ground capacity: 9183.

Record attendance: Old Showground: 23,935 v Portsmouth, FA Cup 4th rd, 30 January 1954. Glanford Park: 8775 v Rotherham U, Division 4, 1 May 1989.

Record receipts: £44,481.50 v Leeds U, Rumbelows Cup 2nd rd lst leg, 24 September 1991.

Pitch measurements: 110yd × 71yd.

Vice-Presidents: I. T. Botham, G. Johnson, A. Harvey, G. J. Alston, R. Ashman.

Chairman: K. Wagstaff.

Vice-Chairman: R. Garton.

Directors: J. B. Borrill, C. Plumtree, S. Wharton, B. Collen, J. A. C. Godfrey.

Team Manager: David Moore. ***Physio:*** D. Moore.

Chief Executive/Secretary: A. D. Rowing. ***Commercial Manager:*** A. D. Rowing.

Year Formed:1899. ***Turned Professional:*** 1912. ***Ltd Co.:*** 1912.

Club Nickname: 'The Iron'.

Previous Names: Amalgamated with Brumby Hall: North Lindsey United to become Scunthorpe & Lindsey United, 1910; dropped '& Lindsey' in 1958.

Previous ground: Old Showground to 1988.

Foundation: The year of foundation for Scunthorpe United has often been quoted as 1910, but the club can trace its history back to 1899 when Brumby Hall FC, who played on the Old Showground, consolidated their position by amalgamating with some other clubs and changing their name to Scunthorpe United. The year 1910 was when that club amalgamated with North Lindsey United as Scunthorpe and Lindsey United. The link is Mr. W. T. Lockwood whose chairmanship covers both years.

First Football League game: 19 August, 1950, Division 3(N), v Shrewsbury T (h) D 0-0 – Thompson; Barker, Brownsword; Allen, Taylor, McCormick; Mosby, Payne, Gorin, Rees, Boyes.

Record League Victory: 8–1 v Luton T, Division 3, 24 April 1965 – Sidebottom; Horstead, Hemstead; Smith, Neale, Lindsey; Bramley (1), Scott, Thomas (5), Mahy (1), Wilson (1).

Record Cup Victory: 9–0 v Boston U, FA Cup, 1st rd, 21 November 1953 – Malan; Hubbard, Brownsword; Sharpe, White, Bushby; Mosby (1), Haigh (3), Whitfield (2), Gregory (1), Mervyn Jones (2).

Record Defeat: 0–8 v Carlisle U, Division 3 (N), 25 December 1952.

Most League Points (2 for a win): 66, Division 3 (N), 1956–57, 1957–58.

Most League Points (3 for a win): 83, Division 4, 1982–83.

Most League Goals: 88, Division 3 (N), 1957–58.

Highest League Scorer in Season: Barrie Thomas, 31, Division 2, 1961–62.

Most League Goals in Total Aggregate: Steve Cammack, 110, 1979–81, 1981–86.

Most Capped Player: None.

Most League Appearances: Jack Brownsword, 595, 1950–65.

Record Transfer Fee Received: £350,000 from Aston Villa for Neil Cox, February 1991.

Record Transfer Fee Paid: £80,000 to York City for Ian Helliwell, August 1991.

Football League Record: 1950 Elected to Division 3 (N); 1958–64 Division 2; 1964–68 Division 3; 1968–72 Division 4; 1972–73 Division 3; 1973–83 Division 4; 1983–84 Division 3; 1984–92 Division 4; 1992– Division 3.

Honours: *Football League:* Division 2 best season: 4th, 1961–62; Division 3 (N) – Champions 1957–58. *FA Cup:* best season: 5th rd, 1958, 1970. *Football League Cup:* never past 3rd rd.

Colours: White shirts, claret and blue trim collar and sleeves, sky blue shorts, claret and white trim, sky blue stockings with claret and white trim. **Change colours:** Red with green, yellow and claret flashes.

SCUNTHORPE UNITED 1994–95 LEAGUE RECORD

Match No.	Date	Venue	Opponents	Result		H/T Score	Lg. Pos.	Goalscorers	Atten-dance
1	Aug 13	A	Barnet	W	2-1	2-0	—	Henderson, Juryeff	2208
2	20	H	Fulham	L	1-2	1-1	12	Juryeff	3165
3	27	H	Northampton T	D	1-1	1-1	11	Bradley	2499
4	30	H	Gillingham	W	3-0	0-0	—	Thornber, Henderson, Smith	2098
5	Sept 3	H	Carlisle U	L	2-3	2-0	10	Juryeff, Thornber	3217
6	10	A	Bury	L	0-2	0-1	11		2540
7	13	A	Darlington	W	3-1	2-1	—	Bullimore, Ford, Alexander	2181
8	17	H	Barnet	W	1-0	0-0	8	Juryeff	2481
9	24	H	Wigan Ath	W	3-1	1-0	5	Thornber, Alexander, Bullimore (pen)	2602
10	Oct 1	A	Hereford U	L	1-2	1-1	6	Bradley	2267
11	8	A	Preston NE	W	1-0	0-0	7	Alexander	6895
12	15	H	Walsall	L	0-1	0-1	8		3609
13	22	A	Exeter C	D	2-2	1-1	8	Henderson, Juryeff	2511
14	29	H	Hartlepool U	D	0-0	0-0	8		2624
15	Nov 5	A	Torquay U	D	1-1	0-1	9	Juryeff	3036
16	19	H	Mansfield T	L	3-4	1-0	9	Bullimore, Nicholson, Juryeff	2975
17	26	A	Colchester U	L	2-4	0-2	9	Thornber, Knill	2904
18	Dec 10	A	Fulham	L	0-1	0-1	12		3358
19	16	A	Northampton T	W	1-0	1-0	—	Knill	3845
20	26	H	Lincoln C	W	2-0	0-0	11	Juryeff, Eyre	4785
21	27	A	Doncaster R	D	1-1	0-1	10	Carmichael	3852
22	31	H	Rochdale	W	4-1	2-0	9	Mudd, Bullimore (pen), Eyre, Thompstone	2653
23	Jan 7	H	Exeter C	W	3-0	2-0	8	Eyre 2, Alexander	2463
24	14	A	Chesterfield	L	1-3	0-3	11	Bullimore (pen)	3245
25	21	H	Torquay U	W	3-2	2-2	8	Smith, Eyre, Carmichael	2229
26	28	A	Hartlepool U	W	4-1	1-0	5	Knill, Young, Thornber, Eyre	1660
27	Feb 4	H	Colchester U	L	3-4	3-2	6	Eyre 2, Bullimore	2748
28	18	H	Chesterfield	L	0-1	0-0	10		3566
29	21	A	Mansfield T	L	0-1	0-0	—		3079
30	25	H	Hereford U	W	1-0	1-0	8	Nicholson	2193
31	28	A	Scarborough	L	0-3	0-0	—		1179
32	Mar 11	H	Bury	W	3-2	1-1	8	Gregory 2, Hughes (og)	2767
33	18	A	Gillingham	D	2-2	1-0	9	Young, Turnbull	2459
34	25	A	Carlisle U	L	1-2	0-0	10	Kiwomya	6704
35	Apr 1	H	Darlington	W	2-1	1-1	8	Gregory 2	2449
36	4	A	Wigan Ath	D	0-0	0-0	—		1307
37	8	A	Rochdale	W	2-1	0-1	7	Turnbull, Kiwomya	1720
38	15	H	Doncaster R	L	0-5	0-3	9		4366
39	17	A	Lincoln C	D	3-3	2-2	9	Turnbull, Gregory, Nicholson	3330
40	22	H	Scarborough	W	3-1	1-0	7	Gregory, Nicholson, Kiwomya	2079
41	29	A	Walsall	L	1-2	0-0	8	Gregory	4539
42	May 6	H	Preston NE	W	2-1	2-1	7	Ford, Knill	3691

Final League Position: 7

GOALSCORERS

League (68): Eyre 8, Juryeff 8, Gregory 7, Bullimore 6 (3 pens), Thornber 5, Alexander 4, Knill 4, Nicholson 4, Henderson 3, Kiwomya 3, Turnbull 3, Bradley 2, Carmichael 2, Ford 2, Smith 2, Young 2, Mudd 1, Thompstone 1, own goal 1.
Coca-Cola Cup (2): Bullimore 1, Henderson 1.
FA Cup (5): Alexander 1, Bullimore 1, Carmichael 1, Hope 1, Thompstone 1.

Samways M. 42	Ford T. 38	Mudd P.A. 35	Thornber S.J. 36 + 1	Knill A.R. 39	Bradley R. 24 + 1	Alexander G. 38 + 2	Bullimore W.A. 34 + 1	Juryeff I.M. 21	Henderson D.M. 16 + 1	Smith M.C. 24 + 8	Carmichael M. 9 + 11	Goodacre S.D. 1 + 4	Hope C.J. 22 + 2	Martin D.S. — + 5	Thompstone I.P. 8 + 11	Nicholson M. 14 + 1	Sansam C. 4 + 2	Eyre J.R. 9	Young S.R. 12 + 2	Eli R. — + 2	Turnbull L.M. 10	Gregory N.R. 10	Kiwomya A.D. 9	Housham S.J. 4	Walsh M.S. 3	*Match No.*
1	2	3	4	5	6	7	8	9	10	11																1
1	2	3	4	5	6	7	8	9	*10*	11	12	14														2
1	2	3	4		6	7	*8*	9	10	11	12		5	14												3
1	2	3	4	5	6	7	8		10	11		9		12												4
1	2	3	4	5	6	7	8	*9*	10	11		14		12												5
1	4	3		5	6	7	8	9	10	11	2															6
1	4	3		5	6	7	8	9	10	11	2			12												7
1	2	3	4	5	6	7	8	9	10	11																8
1	2	3	4	5	6	7	8	9	10	11																9
1	2	3	*4*	5	6	7	8	9	10	11			12	14												10
1	2	3	4	5	6	7	8	9	10				11													11
1	2	3	4	5	6	7	8	9	*10*	12			11		14											12
1	2	3	4	*5*	6	7		9	10	11		12	8		14											13
1	2	3	4	5	6	7		*9*	10	11	12	14	8													14
1	2	3	4	5	6	7		9	10	11	12		8													15
1	4	3		5	6	7	8	9					2			11	10									16
1	2	3	4	5		7	8	9			6		12		14	11	*10*									17
1	2	3	4	5	6	7	8	9	*10*	11	12				14											18
1	2	3	4	5	6	7	8	*9*		11	12						14	10								19
1	2	3	4	5	6	7	8	*9*		11	12				14			10								20
1	2	3	4	5	6	7	8	*9*		11	12				14			10								21
1	2	3	4		6	7	8			11	5				12			10	9							22
1	2	3	4		6	7	8			11	5							10	9							23
1	2	3	4	5	6	7	8			11	12				14			10	*9*							24
1	2	3	4	5	6	7	8			11	12							10	9							25
1	2	3	4	5		7	8			*11*	6				12	14		10	9							26
1	2	3	4	5		7	8			12	6				14	11		*10*	9							27
1	2		4	5		7		10			6		3		8	11			9	12						28
1	2		4	5		7				12	6		3		8	11	*10*		9	14						29
1	2	3	4	5		7	8				12		6		10	11			9							30
1	2	3	4	5		7	11		12	14			6		9	10			*8*							31
1	2	3	4	5						12			6		7	11			9		8	10				32
1	2	3	4	5		7	12			14			6			11			*9*		8	10				33
1	2	3	4	5		7	9						6								8	10	11			34
1	2	3	4	5		7	9						6		12						8	10	11			35
1		3	4	5		7	9						6		2						8	10	11			36
1		3	4	5		7				12			6		2	*9*			14		8	10	11			37
1			4	5	14	7	9			3			6		*2*				12		8	10	11			38
1				5		7	4			3			6			9					8	10	11	2		39
1	7		4	5			8			12			6			9						10	11	2	3	40
1	7			5		12	8						6			9	14				4	10	11	*2*	3	41
1	7		12	5		14	8						6			9	*10*				4		11	2	3	42

Coca-Cola Cup

First Round	Huddersfield T (h)	2-1
	(a)	0-3

FA Cup

First Round	Bradford C (a)	1-1
	(h)	3-2
Second Round	Birmingham C (a)	0-0
	(h)	1-2

SHEFFIELD UNITED 1994–95 *Back row (left to right):* Rob Scott, David Tuttle, Doug Hodgson, Jostein Flo, Alan Kelly, Billy Mercer, Mark Foran, Brian Gayle, Paul Beesley, Paul Rogers.
Centre row: Derek French (Physio), Tony Battersby, Roger Nilsen, Ash Fickling, Carl Veart, Simon Tracey, Glyn Hodges, Charlie Hartfield, Nathan Blake, Andy Scott, Geoff Taylor (Assistant Manager).
Front row: John Gannon, Kevin Gage, Mitch Ward, Dave Bassett (Manager), Dane Whitehouse, John Reed, Adrian Littlejohn.

Division 1 SHEFFIELD UNITED

Bramall Lane Ground, Sheffield S2 4SU. Telephone: (0114) 2738955. Fax: (0114) 2723030. Ticket Office: (0114) 2766771. Pools Office: (0114) 2727901. Club Shop: (0114) 2750596. Community Scheme: (0114) 2769314. Executive Suite: (0114) 2755277. Ticket info line: 0891 332950.

Ground capacity: 23,459.

Record attendance: 68,287 v Leeds U, FA Cup 5th rd, 15 February 1936.

Record receipts: £261,758 v Manchester U, FA Cup 5th rd, 14 February 1993.

Pitch measurements: 112yd × 72yd.

Chairman: R. L. Brealey.

Directors: A. H. Laver, D. Dooley, B. Proctor, J. A. Plant JP.

Team Manager: Dave Bassett. ***Assistant Manager:*** Geoff Taylor. ***Coaches:*** Brian Eastick, Wally Downes. ***Youth Coach:*** Keith Mincher.

Physios: Derek French, Denis Circuit.

Secretary: D. Capper AFA. ***Commercial Manager:*** Andy R. Daykin.

Youth Development Officer: John Dungworth.

Community Programme Organiser: Tony Currie, Tel: (0114) 2769314.

Year Formed: 1889. ***Turned Professional:*** 1889. ***Ltd Co.:*** 1899.

Club Nickname: 'The Blades'.

Foundation: In March 1889, Yorkshire County Cricket Club formed Sheffield United six days after an FA Cup semi-final between Preston North End and West Bromwich Albion had finally convinced Charles Stokes, a member of the cricket club, that the formation of a professional football club would prove successful at Bramall Lane. The United's first secretary, Mr. J. B. Wostinholm was also secretary of the cricket club.

First Football League game: 3 September, 1892, Division 2, v Lincoln C (h) W 4-2 – Lilley; Witham, Cain; Howell, Hendry, Needham (1); Wallace, Dobson, Hammond (3), Davies, Drummond.

Record League Victory: 10–0 v Burslem Port Vale (away), Division 2, 10 December 1892 – Howlett; Witham, Lilley; Howell, Hendry, Needham; Drummond (1), Wallace (1), Hammond (4), Davies (2), Watson (2).

Record Cup Victory: 5–0 v Newcastle U (away), FA Cup, 1st rd, 10 January 1914 – Gough; Cook, English; Brelsford, Howley, Sturgess; Simmons (2), Gillespie (1), Kitchen (1), Fazackerley, Revill (1). 5–0 v Corinthians, FA Cup, 1st rd, 10 January 1925 – Sutcliffe; Cook, Milton; Longworth, King, Green; Partridge, Boyle (1), Johnson 4), Gillespie, Tunstall. 5–0 v Barrow, FA Cup, 3rd rd, 7 January 1956 – Burgin; Coldwell, Mason; Fountain, Johnson, Iley; Hawksworth (1), Hoyland (2), Howitt, Wragg (1), Grainger (1).

Record Defeat: 0–13 v Bolton W, FA Cup 2nd rd, 1 February 1890.

Most League Points (2 for a win): 60, Division 2, 1952–53.

Most League Points (3 for a win): 96, Division 4, 1981–82.

Most League Goals: 102, Division 1, 1925–26.

Highest League Scorer in Season: Jimmy Dunne, 41, Division 1, 1930–31.

Most League Goals in Total Aggregate: Harry Johnson, 205, 1919–30.

Most Capped Player: Billy Gillespie, 25, Northern Ireland.

Most League Appearances: Joe Shaw, 629, 1948–66.

Record Transfer Fee Received: £2,700,000 from Leeds U for Brian Deane, July 1993.

Record Transfer Fee Paid: £700,000 to Ipswich T for Brian Gayle, September 1991.

Football League Record: 1892 Elected to Division 2; 1893–1934 Division 1; 1934–39 Division 2; 1946–49 Division 1; 1949–53 Division 2; 1953–56 Division 1; 1956–61 Division 2; 1961–68 Division 1; 1968–71 Division 2; 1971–76 Division 1; 1976–79 Division 2; 1979–81 Division 3; 1981–82 Division 4; 1982–84 Division 3; 1984–88 Division 2; 1988–89 Division 3; 1989–90 Division 2; 1990–92 Division 1; 1992–94 FA Premier League; 1994– Division 1.

Honours: *Football League:* Division 1 – Champions 1897–98; Runners-up 1896–97, 1899–1900; Division 2 – Champions 1952–53; Runners-up 1892–93, 1938–39, 1960–61, 1970–71, 1989–90; Division 4 – Champions 1981–82. *FA Cup:* Winners 1899, 1902, 1915, 1925; Runners-up 1901, 1936. *Football League Cup:* best season: 5th rd, 1962, 1967, 1972.

Colours: Broad red, thin white striped shirts with large white diamond overlay, black shorts with red/white trim, black stockings with red/white trim. **Change colours:** Purple and yellow halved shirts with matching trim, yellow shorts with purple trim, yellow stockings with purple trim.

SHEFFIELD UNITED 1994–95 LEAGUE RECORD

Match No.	Date	Venue	Opponents	Result		H/T Score	Lg. Pos.	Goalscorers	Attendance
1	Aug 13	H	Watford	W	3-0	2-0	—	Flo, Ward 2	16,820
2	27	H	Notts Co	L	1-3	0-2	15	Whitehouse (pen)	15,301
3	30	A	Charlton Ath	D	1-1	1-1	—	Rogers	8678
4	Sept 3	A	Tranmere R	L	1-2	0-2	18	Hodges (pen)	7253
5	10	H	Bolton W	W	3-1	1-0	14	Veart 2, Davison	14,116
6	13	H	Sunderland	D	0-0	0-0	—		15,239
7	17	A	Reading	L	0-1	0-0	20		9036
8	24	A	Port Vale	W	2-0	0-0	13	Blake, Whitehouse (pen)	9324
9	Oct 1	H	Oldham Ath	W	2-0	1-0	9	Reed, Flo	14,223
10	8	A	Grimsby T	D	0-0	0-0	10		8930
11	16	H	Barnsley	D	0-0	0-0	13		12,317
12	18	A	WBA	L	0-1	0-0	—		12,713
13	22	H	Luton T	L	1-3	1-1	17	Blake	13,317
14	29	A	Millwall	L	1-2	0-0	19	Blake	8445
15	Nov 2	A	Stoke C	D	1-1	1-0	—	Gage	11,556
16	5	H	Bristol C	W	3-0	2-0	15	Hartfield, Gage, Whitehouse	11,568
17	12	H	Derby Co	W	2-1	0-0	9	Blake, Whitehouse	15,001
18	20	A	Burnley	L	2-4	1-1	12	Winstanley (og), Scott A	11,475
19	26	H	Southend U	W	2-0	1-0	10	Whitehouse (pen), Veart	13,405
20	Dec 3	A	Luton T	W	6-3	2-0	6	Gage 2, Veart 2, Hodges, Scott A	8516
21	10	H	WBA	W	2-0	1-0	7	Veart, Scott A	13,891
22	17	A	Watford	D	0-0	0-0	7		8919
23	26	H	Middlesbrough	D	1-1	0-0	7	Hodges	20,693
24	27	A	Swindon T	W	3-1	1-0	6	Reed, Bodin (og), Littlejohn	11,007
25	31	H	Portsmouth	W	3-1	0-1	5	Blake 2, Scott A	13,467
26	Jan 2	A	Wolverhampton W	D	2-2	0-0	5	Blake 2	27,809
27	14	H	Millwall	D	1-1	0-1	5	Gage	12,650
28	21	A	Bristol C	L	1-2	0-0	6	Gayle	10,211
29	Feb 4	A	Derby Co	W	3-2	1-1	6	Veart 2, Whitehouse	15,882
30	11	H	Stoke C	D	1-1	1-1	7	Starbuck	13,900
31	18	A	Southend U	W	3-1	1-1	6	Blake 2, Veart	4700
32	21	H	Burnley	W	2-0	1-0	—	Blake 2	13,349
33	25	A	Oldham Ath	D	3-3	2-2	4	Rogers, Blake, Flo	9640
34	Mar 4	H	Port Vale	D	1-1	0-0	6	Veart	13,647
35	7	H	Tranmere R	W	2-0	1-0	—	Black, Blake	14,127
36	11	A	Notts Co	L	1-2	0-1	5	Beesley	11,102
37	18	H	Charlton Ath	W	2-1	0-0	4	Flo, Beesley	11,862
38	22	A	Bolton W	D	1-1	1-1	—	Blake	16,756
39	25	H	Reading	D	1-1	0-0	6	Blake	19,241
40	Apr 1	A	Sunderland	L	0-1	0-0	6		17,259
41	8	A	Portsmouth	L	0-1	0-0	7		8216
42	15	H	Swindon T	D	2-2	0-1	7	Rogers, Hodges	12,217
43	17	A	Middlesbrough	D	1-1	1-1	8	Blake	23,225
44	22	H	Wolverhampton W	D	3-3	1-0	8	Whitehouse (pen), Foran, Flo	16,714
45	29	A	Barnsley	L	1-2	1-1	8	Rogers	10,844
46	May 6	H	Grimsby T	W	3-1	2-1	8	Whitehouse, Black, Flo	14,323

Final League Position: 8

GOALSCORERS

League (74): Blake 17, Veart 10, Whitehouse 8 (4 pens), Flo 6, Gage 5, Hodges 4 (1 pen), Rogers 4, Scott A 4, Beesley 2, Black 2, Reed 2, Ward 2, Davison 1, Foran 1, Gayle 1, Hartfield 1, Littlejohn 1, Starbuck 1, own goals 2.
Coca-Cola Cup (7): Whitehouse 3 (1 pen), Flo 2, Blake 1, Scott A 1.
FA Cup (0).

Kelly A.T. 38	Gage K.W. 40	Nilsen R. 33	Rogers P.A. 44	Gayle B.W. 35	Beesley P. 26 + 1	Ward M.D. 10 + 4	Flo J. 25 + 7	Blake N.A. 28 + 7	Hodges G.P. 20 + 5	Whitehouse D.L. 35 + 4	Littlejohn A.S. 9 + 7	Hartfield C.J. 23 + 2	Tracey S.P. 5	Marshall S.R. 17	Veart C. 30 + 9	Davison R. 1 + 2	Reed J.P. 11 + 1	Scott A. 18 + 19	Gannon J.S. 12	Hoyland J.W. — + 2	Hodgson D.J.H. — + 1	Starbuck P.M. 20 + 3	Mercer W. 3	Scott R. — + 1	Blount M. 4 + 1	Foran M.J. 4	Anthony G.J. — + 1	Black K. 8 + 3	Tuttle D.P. 6	Davidson R. 1	*Match No.*
1	2	3	4	5	6	7	8	9	*10*	11	12	14																			1
	2	3	4	5		7	8	9	10	11	12		1	6	14																2
	2	3	4	5		7	8	9	10	11			1	6	12																3
	2	3	4	5			12		10		11	*8*	1	6	7	9	14														4
	2	3	6	4				9	10	*11*			1	5	8	12	7	14													5
	2	3	4	5				9	10	11			1	6	8	14	7	12													6
1	2	3	4	5				9		*11*				6	8		7	12	10	14											7
1	2	3	4	5			10	12		11	*9*			6			7		8	14											8
1	2		4	5		12	10	14		11	*9*			6			7	3	8												9
1	2		4	5			10	12		11	9			6	14		7	3	8												10
1	2		4	5			10	9		11		12		6	14		7	3	8												11
1	2		4	5		7	*10*	12		11	9			6	14			3	8												12
1	2		4	5			*10*	9		11	12			6			7	3	8		14										13
1	2	3		5				9		11	10	4		6	8		7					12									14
1	2	3	7		5			10		11		4		6	8			12				9									15
1	2	3	7	5				*10*	14	11		4		6	8			12				9									16
	2	3	7	5				10	14	*11*		4		6	8			12				9	1								17
1	2	3	7	5			10		12	11		4		6	*8*			14				9									18
1	2	3	7	5	6		14		*10*	11		4			8			12				9									19
1	2	3	7	5	6	12	14		10			4			8			*11*				9									20
1	2	3	7	5	6			12	10	14		*4*			8			11				9									21
1	2	3	7	5	6			12	*10*	14		4			8			11				9									22
1	2	3	7	5	6				10	9		4			8			11				12									23
1	2		7	5	6		9				10	4					11	3				8		12							24
1	2	3	7	5				11	10	12		4			8			6				9									25
1	2	6	7	5				12	10	3		4			8			11				9									26
1	2	3	7	5	6				10	12	14	4			8			11				*9*									27
	2	3	7	5	12		14		10	6		4			8			*11*				9	1								28
		3	7	5	6	2	10			11	12				8			14	4			*9*	1								29
1		*3*	7	5	6	2	10			11	12				8			14	4			9									30
1			7		6	2	10	11							8			12	4			9			3	5					31
1	2		7		6	9	10	11							8			5	*4*			12			3		14				32
1	2		7	5	6	12	10	11		*9*					8			14	4						3						33
1	2		7	5	6	12	14	11		3		4			*8*							9						10			34
1	2		7	5	6	8	9	11		3		4													12			10			35
1	2		7	5	6	8	9	11		3		4			12													10			36
1	2	3	7	5	6		9	11		4					12		8	14										*10*			37
1	2	3	7	5	6		12	10		9	14	4			*8*			11													38
1	2		7		6		*9*	10		3		4			12			14				8						11	5		39
1	2	3	7		6			10	12	*9*		4			8			14										11	5		40
1	2	3			6		10		12		9	4			8			14				*7*						11	5		41
1	2	3	7		6		9	11	10	5								12				*8*			4			14			42
1	2	3	7				9	11	10	4					8			12								6			5		43
1		3	7		2		12	11	10	*4*					8			9								6		14	5		44
1		3	7		6		4	11	10		9				8			2								5		12			45
1		3	4		6		8	9	10	*11*					12			14										7	5	2	46

Coca-Cola Cup

Second Round	Stockport Co (a)	5-1
	(h)	1-0
Third Round	Bolton W (h)	1-2

FA Cup

Third Round	Manchester U (h)	0-2

SHEFFIELD WEDNESDAY 1994–95 *Back row (left to right):* Ryan Jones, Brian Linighan, Chris Woods, Simon Coleman, Andy Pearce, Kevin Pressman, Julian Watts, Mark Bright.
Centre row: Richie Barker (Assistant Manager), Chris Waddle, Gordon Watson, John Sheridan, Lee Briscoe, Chris Bart-Williams, Adem Poric, Michael Williams, Ian Taylor, Dave Galley (Physio).
Front row: Ian Nolan, Dan Petrescu, Graham Hyde, Des Walker, Trevor Francis (Manager), David Hirst, Andy Sinton, Peter Atherton, Nigel Jemson.

FA Premiership **SHEFFIELD WEDNESDAY**

Hillsborough, Sheffield, S6 1SW. Telephone: (0114) 2343122. Fax: (0114) 2337145. Ticket Office: (0114) 2337233. Clubcall: 0891 121186.

Ground capacity: 36,020.

Record attendance: 72,841 v Manchester C, FA Cup 5th rd, 17 February 1934.

Record receipts: £533,918 Sunderland v Norwich C, FA Cup semi-final, 5 April 1992.

Pitch measurements: 115yd × 77yd.

Chairman: D. G. Richards. ***Vice-Chairman:*** K. T. Addy.

Directors: G. K. Hulley, R. M. Grierson FCA, J. Ashton MP, G. A. Thorpe.

Manager: David Pleat. ***Assistant Manager:*** Danny Bergara.

Physio: David Galley.

Secretary: Graham Mackrell FCCA. ***Commercial Manager:*** Sean O'Toole.

Year Formed: 1867 (fifth oldest League club).

Turned Professional: 1887. ***Ltd Co.:*** 1899.

Former Names: The Wednesday until 1929.

Club Nickname: 'The Owls'.

Previous Grounds: 1867, Highfield; 1869, Myrtle Road; 1877, Sheaf House; 1887, Olive Grove; 1899, Owlerton (since 1912 known as Hillsborough). Some games were played at Endcliffe in the 1880s. Until 1895 Bramall Lane was used for some games.

Foundation: Sheffield, being one of the principal centres of early Association Football, this club was formed as long ago as 1867 by the Sheffield Wednesday Cricket Club (formed 1825) and their colours from the start were blue and white. The inaugural meeting was held at the Adelphi Hotel and the original committee included Charles Stokes who was subsequently a founder member of Sheffield United.

First Football League game: 3 September, 1892, Division 1, v Notts C (a) W 1-0 – Allan; T. Brandon (1), Mumford; Hall, Betts, H. Brandon; Spiksley, Brady, Davis, R.N. Brown, Dunlop.

Record League Victory: 9–1 v Birmingham, Division 1, 13 December 1930 – Brown; Walker, Blenkinsop; Strange, Leach, Wilson; Hooper (3), Seed (2), Ball (2), Burgess (1), Rimmer (1).

Record Cup Victory: 12–0 v Halliwell, FA Cup, 1st rd, 17 January 1891 – Smith; Thompson, Brayshaw; Harry Brandon (1), Betts, Cawley (2); Winterbottom, Mumford (2), Bob Brandon (1), Woolhouse (5), Ingram (1).

Record Defeat: 0–10 v Aston Villa, Division 1, 5 October 1912.

Most League Points (2 for a win): 62, Division 2, 1958–59.

Most League Points (3 for a win): 88, Division 2, 1983–84.

Most League Goals: 106, Division 2, 1958–59.

Highest League Scorer in Season: Derek Dooley, 46, Division 2, 1951–52.

Most League Goals in Total Aggregate: Andy Wilson, 199, 1900–20.

Most Capped Player: Nigel Worthington, 50 (58), Northern Ireland.

Most League Appearances: Andy Wilson, 502, 1900–20.

Record Transfer Fee Received: £2,650,000 from Blackburn R for Paul Warhurst, September 1993.

Record Transfer Fee Paid: £2,750,000 to Sampdoria for Des Walker, July 1993 and £2,750,000 to QPR for Andy Sinton, August 1993.

Football League Record: 1892 Elected to Division 1; 1899–1900 Division 2; 1900–20 Division 1; 1920–26 Division 2; 1926–37 Division 1; 1937–50 Division 2; 1950–51 Division 1; 1951–52 Division 2; 1952–55 Division 1; 1955–56 Division 2; 1956–58 Division 1; 1958–59 Division 2; 1959–70 Division 1; 1970–75 Division 2; 1975–80 Division 3; 1980–84 Division 2; 1984–90 Division 1; 1990–91 Division 2; 1991–92 Division 1; 1992– FA Premier League.

Honours: *Football League:* Division 1 – Champions 1902–03, 1903–04, 1928–29, 1929–30; Runners-up 1960–61; Division 2 – Champions 1899–1900, 1925–26, 1951–52, 1955–56, 1958–59; Runners-up 1949–50, 1983–84. *FA Cup:* Winners 1896, 1907, 1935; Runners-up 1890, 1966, 1993. *Football League Cup:* Winners 1991; Runners-up 1993. **European Competitions:** *Fairs Cup:* 1961–62, 1963–64, 1992–93.

Colours: Blue and white striped shirts, blue shorts, blue stockings. **Change colours:** All black with yellow and grey trim.

SHEFFIELD WEDNESDAY 1994–95 LEAGUE RECORD

Match No.	Date	Venue	Opponents	Result		H/T Score	Lg. Pos.	Goalscorers	Attendance
1	Aug 20	H	Tottenham H	L	3-4	0-2	—	Petrescu, Calderwood (og), Hirst	34,051
2	24	A	QPR	L	2-3	1-1	—	Sheridan, Hyde	12,788
3	27	A	Wimbledon	W	1-0	0-0	13	Watson	7453
4	31	H	Norwich C	D	0-0	0-0	—		25,072
5	Sept 10	A	Nottingham F	L	1-4	0-1	15	Hyde	22,022
6	17	H	Manchester C	D	1-1	0-1	16	Watson	26,585
7	26	H	Leeds U	D	1-1	1-1	—	Bright	23,227
8	Oct 1	A	Liverpool	L	1-4	1-0	19	Nolan	31,493
9	8	H	Manchester U	W	1-0	1-0	16	Hirst	32,616
10	16	A	Ipswich T	W	2-1	1-0	13	Bright, Hirst	12,825
11	22	A	Newcastle U	L	1-2	0-2	14	Taylor	34,369
12	29	H	Chelsea	D	1-1	0-1	15	Bright	25,356
13	Nov 2	H	Blackburn R	L	0-1	0-0	—		24,207
14	6	A	Arsenal	D	0-0	0-0	16		33,705
15	19	H	West Ham U	W	1-0	1-0	16	Petrescu	25,300
16	27	A	Aston Villa	D	1-1	0-1	15	Atherton	25,082
17	Dec 3	H	Crystal Palace	W	1-0	1-0	14	Bart-Williams	21,930
18	10	A	Tottenham H	L	1-3	1-0	15	Nolan	25,912
19	17	H	QPR	L	0-2	0-0	18		23,288
20	26	A	Everton	W	4-1	2-1	15	Bright, Ingesson, Whittingham 2	37,089
21	28	H	Coventry C	W	5-1	3-1	13	Bright 2, Waddle, Whittingham 2	26,056
22	31	A	Leicester C	W	1-0	1-0	9	Hyde	20,624
23	Jan 2	H	Southampton	D	1-1	1-0	10	Hyde	28,424
24	14	A	Chelsea	D	1-1	0-1	10	Nolan	17,285
25	21	H	Newcastle U	D	0-0	0-0	9		31,215
26	23	A	West Ham U	W	2-0	1-0	—	Waddle, Bright	14,554
27	Feb 4	H	Arsenal	W	3-1	2-1	8	Petrescu, Ingesson, Bright	23,468
28	12	A	Blackburn R	L	1-3	1-2	8	Waddle	22,223
29	18	H	Aston Villa	L	1-2	0-2	8	Bright	24,063
30	25	H	Liverpool	L	1-2	1-1	9	Bart-Williams	31,964
31	Mar 4	A	Leeds U	W	1-0	1-0	8	Waddle	33,774
32	8	A	Norwich C	D	0-0	0-0	—		13,530
33	11	H	Wimbledon	L	0-1	0-0	8		20,395
34	14	A	Crystal Palace	L	1-2	1-0	—	Whittingham	10,964
35	18	A	Manchester C	L	2-3	2-1	9	Whittingham, Hyde	23,355
36	Apr 1	H	Nottingham F	L	1-7	0-2	11	Bright (pen)	30,060
37	8	H	Leicester C	W	1-0	1-0	10	Whittingham	22,551
38	15	A	Coventry C	L	0-2	0-1	11		15,733
39	17	H	Everton	D	0-0	0-0	13		27,880
40	29	A	Southampton	D	0-0	0-0	14		15,189
41	May 7	A	Manchester U	L	0-1	0-1	14		43,868
42	14	H	Ipswich T	W	4-1	1-0	13	Whittingham 2, Williams, Bright	30,307

Final League Position: 13

GOALSCORERS

League (49): Bright 11 (1 pen), Whittingham 9, Hyde 5, Waddle 4, Hirst 3, Nolan 3, Petrescu 3, Bart-Williams 2, Ingesson 2, Watson 2, Atherton 1, Sheridan 1, Taylor 1, Williams 1, own goal 1.
Coca-Cola Cup (4): Bart-Williams 2, Hyde 1, Taylor 1.
FA Cup (3): Bright 2, Waddle 1.

Pressman K.P. 34	Petrescu D. 20 + 9	Nolan I.R. 42	Taylor I.K. 9 + 5	Atherton P. 41	Walker D.S. 38	Sheridan J.J. 34 + 2	Bart-Williams C.G. 32 + 6	Hirst D.E. 13 + 2	Bright M.A. 33 + 4	Sinton A. 22 + 3	Watson G.W.G. 5 + 18	Hyde G. 33 + 2	Jones R.A. 3 + 2	Pearce A.J. 34	Coleman S. 1	Ingesson K. 9 + 4	Briscoe L.S. 6	Waddle C.R. 20 + 5	Whittingham G. 16 + 5	Poric A. 1 + 3	Woods C.C. 8 + 1	Williams M.A. 8 + 2	Donaldson O'.M. — + 1	Match No.
1	2	3	4	5	6	7	8	9	10	11	12													1
1	2	3	4	5	6	7	12	9		*11*	10	8	14											2
1	*8*	3	4	2	6	11	10	9			12	14	7	5										3
1	8	3	*4*	2	6	7	14	9	10	11	12			5										4
1	4	3		2		7	14	9		11	12	8		5	6	10								5
1	2	3		4		7	6	9	10	*11*	12	8		5		14								6
1	2	3	14	5	6	7	4	12	10	*11*	9	8												7
1	2	3		5	6	7	4	12	10	11	9	8												8
1		3	14	2	6	7	*4*	9	10		12	8		5			11							9
1		3	14	2	6	7	*4*	9	10	12		8		5			11							10
1	12	3	4	2	6	7	14	*9*	10	11		8		5										11
1	12	3	4	2	6	7	10		9	11	14	8		5										12
1	12	3	4	2	6	7	*10*		9	11	14	8		5										13
1	12	3	4	2	6	7	10		9	*11*	14	8		5										14
1	4	3	12	2	6	7	*10*		9	11	14	8		5										15
1	4	3	12	2	6	7	10			11	9	8		5										16
1	4	3	6	2		7	10		9	11		8		5				12						17
1		2		4		7	6		9	11		10		5			3	8						18
1	12	3		2	6	7	4		*9*			10	11	5		14		8						19
1		3		2	6	7	4		9			8		5		11			10	12				20
1		3		2	6	7	4		9		12	8		5		*11*		14	10					21
1	14	3		2	6	7	4		9		12	10		5				*8*	11					22
1	14	3		2	6	7	4		9		12	10		5				*8*	11					23
1	14	2		5	6	7	4		9		12					11	*3*	8	10					24
	2	3		5	6	7	4		12		9					11		8	10		1			25
1	14	3		2	6		4		9		12	7		5		11		*8*	10					26
1	4	3		2	6	12	*10*		9			7		5		11		8	14					27
1	*4*	3		2	6	7	10		9	*11*				5				8	12		15	14		28
1	4	2		5	6	7	12		9	11		10					*3*	8	14					29
1	2	3		5	6	14	4		9	11	12	7						*8*	10					30
	4	3		2	6		7		9	12		10		5				8			1	11		31
		3		2	6		4		9		12	10		5			11	8			1	7		32
1	*4*	3		2	6				9	11		10		5				8	12	14		7		33
1		3		2	6				9	11	14	8	*7*	5				12	10			4		34
1		*3*		2	6	7	4		9			10		5				8	11			12	14	35
1	2	3			6	7	4		9	11		10		5				8	12					36
		3		2	6	7		9	12	14				5		*4*		8	10		1	11		37
	4	3		2	6	7	12	9				8		5		11		14	10		1			38
1		3		2	6	7	4	9	12			*10*		5		14		8	11					39
		3		2	6		4		9				12	5		14		*8*	10	7	1	11		40
		3		2	6	7	4		9			8		5				12	*10*	14	1	11		41
		3		2	6	7		*9*	14	11		12		5				8	10		1	4		42

Coca-Cola Cup		
Second Round	Bradford C (h)	2-1
	(a)	1-1
Third Round	Southampton (h)	1-0
Fourth Round	Arsenal (a)	0-2

FA Cup		
Third Round	Gillingham (a)	2-1
Fourth Round	Wolverhampton W (h)	0-0
	(a)	1-1

SHREWSBURY TOWN 1994–95 *Back row (left to right):* Fred Davies (Manager), Paul Edwards, Kevin Summerfield, Wayne Clarke, Tommy Lynch, Dean Spink, Mark Hughes, Gary Patterson, Mark Williams, David Walton, Tim Clarke, Malcolm Musgrove (Physio).
Front row: David Hockaday, Kevin Seabury, Nathan King, Paul Evans, Michael Brown, Mark Smith, Mark Taylor, Ian Reed, Joe Gallen, Chris Withe, Ray Woods.

Division 2 SHREWSBURY TOWN

Gay Meadow, Shrewsbury SY2 6AB. Telephone: (01743) 360111. Commercial Dept: (01743) 56316. Clubcall: 0891 121194.

Ground capacity: 7500.

Record attendance: 18,917 v Walsall, Division 3, 26 April 1961.

Record receipts: £36,240 v Ipswich T, FA Cup 5th rd, 13 February 1982.

Pitch measurements: 116yd × 76yd.

Vice-President: Dr J. Millard Bryson.

Chairman: R. Bailey.

Directors: F. C. G. Fry, M. J. Starkey, G. W. Nelson, W. H. Richards, K. R. Woodhouse.

Manager: Fred Davies. ***Commercial Manager:*** M. Thomas.

Physio: Malcolm Musgrove.

Secretary: M. J. Starkey.

Club Nickname: 'Town' or 'Shrews'.

Year Formed: 1886. ***Turned Professional:*** 1905 (approx). ***Ltd Co.:*** 1936.

Previous Ground: Old Shrewsbury Racecourse.

Foundation: Shrewsbury School having provided a number of the early England and Wales internationals it is not surprising that there was a Town club as early as 1876 which won the Birmingham Senior Cup in 1879. However, the present Shrewsbury Town club was formed in 1886 and won the Welsh FA Cup as early as 1891.

First Football League game: 19 August, 1950, Division 3(N), v Scunthorpe U (a) D 0-0 – Eggleston; Fisher, Lewis; Wheatley, Depear, Robinson; Griffin, Hope, Jackson, Brown, Barker.

Record League Victory: 7–0 v Swindon T, Division 3 (S), 6 May 1955 – McBride; Bannister, Keech; Wallace, Maloney, Candlin; Price, O'Donnell (1), Weigh (4), Russell, McCue (2).

Record Cup Victory: 7–1 v Banbury Spencer, FA Cup, 1st rd, 4 November 1961 – Gibson; Walters, Skeech; Wallace, Pountney, Harley; Kenning (2), Pragg, Starkey (1), Rowley (2), McLaughlin (2).

Record Defeat: 1–8 v Norwich C, Division 3 (S), 1952–53 and v Coventry C, Division 3, 22 October 1963.

Most League Points (2 for a win): 62, Division 4, 1974–75.

Most League Points (3 for a win): 79, Division 3, 1993–94.

Most League Goals: 101, Division 4, 1958–59.

Highest League Scorer in Season: Arthur Rowley, 38, Division 4, 1958–59.

Most League Goals in Total Aggregate: Arthur Rowley, 152, 1958–65 (thus completing his League record of 434 goals).

Most Capped Player: Jimmy McLaughlin, 5 (12), Northern Ireland and Bernard McNally, 5, Northern Ireland.

Most League Appearances: Colin Griffin, 406, 1975–89.

Record Transfer Fee Received: £385,000 from WBA for Bernard McNally, July 1989.

Record Transfer Fee Paid: £100,000 to Aldershot for John Dungworth, November 1979 and £100,000 to Southampton for Mark Blake, August 1990.

Football League Record: 1950 Elected to Division 3 (N); 1951–58 Division 3 (S); 1958–59 Division 4; 1959–74 Division 3; 1974–75 Division 4; 1975–79 Division 3; 1979–89 Division 2; 1989–94 Division 3; 1994– Division 2.

Honours: *Football League:* Division 2 best season: 8th, 1983–84, 1984–85; Division 3 – Champions 1978–79, 1993–94; Division 4 – Runners-up 1974–5. *FA Cup:* best season: 6th rd, 1979, 1982. *Football League Cup:* Semi-final 1961. *Welsh Cup:* Winners 1891, 1938, 1977, 1979, 1984, 1985; Runners-up 1931, 1948, 1980.

Colours: Blue shirts, white trim, blue shorts, blue stockings, white trim. **Change colours:** Red shirts, white shorts, red stockings.

SHREWSBURY TOWN 1994–95 LEAGUE RECORD

Match No.	Date	Venue	Opponents	Result		H/T Score	Lg. Pos.	Goalscorers	Atten-dance
1	Aug 13	A	Rotherham U	W	4-0	3-0	—	Taylor, Spink 2, Clarke W	3762
2	20	H	Wrexham	D	2-2	1-2	6	Clarke W, Brown	5748
3	27	A	Blackpool	L	1-2	1-0	12	Clarke W (pen)	4428
4	Sept 3	H	Peterborough U	D	2-2	0-2	16	Spink, Clarke W	3879
5	6	H	Swansea C	D	3-3	1-0	—	Clarke W, Currie, Stevens	3534
6	10	A	York C	L	0-3	0-1	18		3196
7	13	A	Stockport Co	L	1-2	0-0	—	Patterson	3473
8	17	H	Leyton Orient	W	3-0	3-0	17	Brown, Clarke W, Currie	3560
9	24	H	Bristol R	W	1-0	1-0	14	Stevens	4596
10	Oct 1	A	Brentford	L	0-1	0-1	15		4556
11	8	H	Bournemouth	W	3-0	1-0	14	Brown, Clarke W 2	3684
12	15	A	Crewe Alex	L	0-1	0-1	15		4296
13	22	H	Hull C	L	2-3	0-2	16	Clarke W, Stevens	3685
14	29	A	Oxford U	D	0-0	0-0	16		6094
15	Nov 1	A	Wycombe W	L	0-1	0-1	—		4620
16	5	H	Birmingham C	L	0-2	0-1	18		5942
17	19	A	Cambridge U	L	1-3	1-1	19	Stevens	2748
18	26	H	Bradford C	L	1-2	0-1	19	Stevens	3776
19	Dec 10	A	Wrexham	W	1-0	0-0	18	Evans	5859
20	16	H	Rotherham U	W	1-0	1-0	—	Walton	3243
21	26	H	Cardiff C	L	0-1	0-0	18		4933
22	27	A	Brighton & HA	L	1-2	1-0	18	Clarke W	7290
23	Jan 2	A	Huddersfield T	L	1-2	1-1	19	Withe	12,748
24	7	A	Hull C	D	2-2	2-0	19	Clarke W, Jeffers	4369
25	14	H	Chester C	W	1-0	0-0	19	Evans	3879
26	28	H	Oxford U	D	1-1	1-1	19	Stevens	3768
27	Feb 4	A	Bradford C	D	1-1	0-1	19	Spink	4817
28	7	H	Plymouth Arg	W	3-2	0-1	—	Spink 2, Withe	3029
29	11	H	Wycombe W	D	2-2	1-0	17	Spink, Taylor	3945
30	18	A	Chester C	W	3-1	1-0	15	Evans (pen), Spink, Walton	2720
31	21	H	Cambridge U	D	1-1	0-1	—	Evans	3200
32	25	H	Brentford	W	2-1	1-1	15	Spink, Lynch	4570
33	Mar 4	A	Bristol R	L	0-4	0-1	15		4338
34	7	A	Peterborough U	D	1-1	0-0	—	Spink	3554
35	11	H	Blackpool	D	0-0	0-0	18		4261
36	17	A	Swansea C	D	0-0	0-0	—		4130
37	21	H	York C	W	1-0	1-0	—	Evans	2849
38	25	A	Leyton Orient	L	1-2	1-1	17	Williams	2724
39	Apr 1	H	Stockport Co	D	1-1	0-1	18	Stevens	3655
40	8	A	Plymouth Arg	L	0-1	0-1	18		5089
41	11	A	Birmingham C	L	0-2	0-1	—		18,366
42	15	H	Brighton & HA	D	1-1	1-1	18	Scott	3597
43	17	A	Cardiff C	W	2-1	1-0	18	Smith, Spink	4677
44	22	H	Huddersfield T	W	2-1	2-0	18	Walton, Stevens	4758
45	29	H	Crewe Alex	L	1-2	1-2	18	Smith	4381
46	May 2	A	Bournemouth	L	0-3	0-3	—		10,737

Final League Position: 18

GOALSCORERS

League (54): Clarke W 11 (1 pen), Spink 11, Stevens 8, Evans 5 (1 pen), Brown 3, Walton 3, Currie 2, Smith 2, Taylor 2, Withe 2, Jeffers 1, Lynch 1, Patterson 1, Scott 1, Williams 1.
Coca-Cola Cup (2): Clarke W 1, Spink 1.
FA Cup (1): Spink 1.

Edwards P. 31	Hockaday D. 16	Lynch T.M. 34	Taylor R.M. 44	Williams M.S. 33 + 2	Patterson G. 17 + 1	Brown M.A. 9	Clarke W. 26 + 5	Spink D.P. 36 + 3	Walton D.L. 36	Woods R.G. 15 + 4	Summerfield K. 14 + 4	Withe C. 27 + 4	Hughes M. 18 + 2	Stevens I.D. 26 + 12	Currie D. 15 + 2	Clarke T.J. 15 + 1	Seabury K. 27 + 3	Evans P.S. 27 + 5	Smith M.A. 10 + 7	Slawson S.M. 6	Harford P. 3 + 3	Simkin D.S. 10 + 2	Jeffers J.J. 3	Scott R.P. 7 + 1	Reed I.P. 1 + 3	Match No.
1	2	3	4	5	6	7	8	9	10	11	12															1
1	2	3	4	5	10	7	8	9	6			11														2
1	2	3	4	5	6	7	8	9	10		12	*11*	14													3
1	2	3	4		6		8	9	10	11	7		5	12												4
1	*2*	3	4	14	6		8	9	10	11			5	12	7											5
		3	4	5	6		8	9		*11*		12	10		7	1	2	14								6
		3	4	5	8	*7*		9	10				6	12	11	1	2	14								7
1		3	*4*	5	6	7	8	9	10			2		12	11			14								8
1	2	3	4	5	6	7	8		10					9	11			12								9
1	2	3	4	5	6	7	8		10			12		9	*11*				14							10
1	2	3	4	5	6	7	8		10					9	11				12							11
1		3	4	5	6		8		10					9	11		2	7	12							12
1		3	4	5	6		8	12	10	7				9	11		2									13
1			4	5	6		8		10	7	11	3		9	12		2									14
1		9	4	5	6				10	7	8	3			12		2			11						15
1		3	4	5	6	7		12		14	10		8		*11*		2			9						16
1	2	3	4	5	12			9		7	8		6	10						11						17
1		3	4	5	8			9		7			6	10			2		12	11						18
1	2	*3*	4	5			12	9	10				6	7			14	8		11						19
1	2		8				12	9	4			5	3	10		15	6	7		*11*	14					20
1	2		6				8	9		11		5	3	12			4	10			7					21
1		6	*4*	5			8	9		12	10	3		7				11			14	2				22
1	2		4	5			8	9	10		6	3		7				11			12					23
1	2		4	5			8	9	10	7	6	3		12									11			24
1	2		4	5			8	9	10	7	*6*	3		12				14					11			25
1	2	6		5			8	12		7		3		9				4			10		11			26
1		6	4					9	10			3		7	11		12	8			5	2				27
1		6	4					9	10			3		7	11		12	8	5			2				28
1		6	4					9	10			3		7	11		5	8				2				29
1		6	4				12	9	10			3	14	7	11		5	8				*2*				30
1		6	4					9	10			3		7	11		5	8				2				31
1		6	4					9	10			3	11	7			5	8				2				32
1		6	4	12				9	10		14	3	*11*	7			5	8				2				33
		6	4	5			8	9			11	3		12		1	2	10	7							34
		6	4	5			8	9			11	3	7	12		1	2	10								35
		3	4	5			8	9	10		11		6			1	2	7	12							36
		3	4	5			8		10				7	9		1	2	6	11			12				37
		3	4	5			8	9	10				7	12		1		6	11			*2*		14		38
		3	4	5			8	9	10			12		14		1	2	6	*11*					7		39
		3	4	5			*8*	9	10			12		14		1	2	6	11					7		40
			4	5				9	10	7	12	3	*6*	11		1	2	8	14							41
			4	5				9	10	7		3		8		1	2	*6*	12					11	14	42
			4					9	10		5	3		8		1	2	6	11			12		7	14	43
			4	5				9	10	12		3		7		1	2	6	11					8		44
			4	5			12	9	10			3		8		1	2	6	7					11	14	45
							12	9		14	*10*	3	5			1	2	4	7			6		8	11	46

Coca-Cola Cup

First Round	Birmingham C	(h)	2-1
		(a)	0-2

FA Cup

First Round	Burnley (a)	1-2

SOUTHAMPTON 1994–95 *Back row (left to right):* Nicky Banger, Kevin Doherty, Paul McDonald, Derek Allan, Colin Cramb, Matthew Bound, David Hughes, Frankie Bennett, Neal Bartlett, Matthew Robinson, Paul Tisdale, Paul Sheerin.

Centre row: Dave Merrington (Reserve Team Manager), Jason Dodd, Tommy Widdrington, Craig Maskell, Ian Andrews, Richard Hall, Dave Beasant, Ken Monkou, Neil Hopper, Iain Dowie,, Perry Groves, Neil Heaney, Don Taylor (Physio).

Front row: Lew Chatterley (Assistant Manager), Simon Charlton, Jeff Kenna, Neil Maddison, Lawrie McMenemy (Director of Football), Matthew Le Tissier, Alan Ball (Manager), Francis Benali, Jim Magilton, Paul Allen, John Mortimore (Assistant Manager).

FA Premiership **SOUTHAMPTON**

The Dell, Milton Road, Southampton SO9 4XX. Telephone: (01703) 220505. Fax: (01703) 330360. Recorded Ticket Information: (01703) 228575.

Ground capacity: 15,000.

Record attendance: 31,044 v Manchester U, Division 1, 8 October 1969.

Record receipts: £193,229 v Tottenham H, FA Cup 5th rd replay, 1 March 1995.

Pitch measurements: 110yd × 72yd.

Chairman: F. G. L. Askham FCA.

Vice-Chairman: K. St. J. Wiseman.

Directors: I. L. Gordon, B. H. D. Hunt, L. McMenemy, M. R. Richards FCA.

President: J. Corbett. ***Vice-President:*** E. T. Bates. ***Manager:*** Dave Merrington.

Joint Assistant Managers: John Mortimore, Lew Chatterley.

Coach: Lew Chatterley. ***Physio:*** Don Taylor.

Secretary: Brian Truscott.

Year Formed: 1885. ***Turned Professional:*** 1894. ***Ltd Co.:*** 1897.

Club Nickname: 'The Saints'.

Previous Name: Southampton St Mary's until 1885.

Previous Grounds: 1885, Antelope Ground; 1897, County Cricket Ground; 1898, The Dell.

Foundation: Formed largely by players from the Deanery FC, which had been established by school teachers in 1880. Most of the founders were connected with the young men's association of St. Mary's Church. At the inaugural meeting held in November 1885 the club was named Southampton St. Mary's and the church's curate was elected president.

First Football League game: 28 August, 1920, Division 3, v Gillingham (a) D 1-1 – Allen; Parker, Titmuss; Shelley, Campbell, Turner; Barratt, Dominy (1), Rawlings, Moore, Foxall.

Record League Victory: 9–3 v Wolverhampton W, Division 2, 18 September 1965 – Godfrey; Jones, Williams; Walker, Knapp, Huxford; Paine (2), O'Brien (1), Melia, Chivers (4), Sydenham (2).

Record Cup Victory: 7–1 v Ipswich T, FA Cup, 3rd rd, 7 January 1961 – Reynolds; Davies, Traynor; Conner, Page, Huxford; Paine (1), O'Brien (3 incl. 1p), Reeves, Mulgrew (2), Penk (1).

Record Defeat: 0–8 v Tottenham H, Division 2, 28 March 1936 and v Everton, Division 1, 20 November 1971.

Most League Points (2 for a win): 61, Division 3 (S), 1921–22 and Division 3, 1959–60.

Most League Points (3 for a win): 77, Division 1, 1983–84.

Most League Goals: 112, Division 3 (S), 1957–58.

Highest League Scorer in Season: Derek Reeves, 39, Division 3, 1959–60.

Most League Goals in Total Aggregate: Mike Channon, 185, 1966–77, 1979–82.

Most Capped Player: Peter Shilton, 49 (125), England.

Most League Appearances: Terry Paine, 713, 1956–74.

Record Transfer Fee Received: £3,300,000 from Blackburn R for Alan Shearer, July 1992.

Record Transfer Fee Paid: £1,200,000 to Chelsea for Neil Shipperley, January 1995 and to Sheffield W for Gordon Watson, March 1995.

Football League Record: 1920 Original Member of Division 3; 1921–22 Division 3 (S); 1922–53 Division 2; 1953–58 Division 3 (S); 1958–60 Division 3; 1960–66 Division 2; 1966–74 Division 1; 1974–78 Division 2; 1978–92 Division 1; 1992– FA Premier League.

Honours: *Football League:* Division 1 – Runners-up 1983–84; Division 2 – Runners-up 1965–66, 1977–78; Division 3 (S) – Champions 1921–22; Runners-up 1920–21; Division 3 – Champions 1959–60. *FA Cup:* Winners 1976; Runners-up 1900, 1902. *Football League Cup:* Runners-up 1979. *Zenith Data Systems Cup:* Runners-up 1992. **European Competitions:** *European Fairs Cup:* 1969–70. *UEFA Cup:* 1971–72, 1981–82, 1982–83, 1984–85. *European Cup-Winners' Cup:* 1976–77.

Colours: Red and white striped shirts, black shorts, red and white hooped stockings. **Change colours:** Blue and yellow striped shirts, blue shorts, blue and yellow hooped stockings.

SOUTHAMPTON 1994–95 LEAGUE RECORD

Match No.	Date	Venue	Opponents	Result		H/T Score	Lg. Pos.	Goalscorers	Attendance
1	Aug 20	H	Blackburn R	D	1-1	1-0	—	Banger	14,209
2	24	A	Aston Villa	D	1-1	0-1	—	Le Tissier	24,179
3	27	A	Newcastle U	L	1-5	0-3	17	Banger	34,182
4	31	H	Liverpool	L	0-2	0-1	—		15,190
5	Sept 12	A	Tottenham H	W	2-1	0-1	—	Le Tissier 2 (1 pen)	22,387
6	17	H	Nottingham F	D	1-1	0-1	14	Le Tissier (pen)	14,185
7	24	A	Coventry C	W	3-1	1-1	13	Dowie 2, Ekelund	11,798
8	Oct 1	H	Ipswich T	W	3-1	0-0	8	Maddison, Ekelund, Dowie	13,266
9	8	H	Everton	W	2-0	1-0	7	Ekelund, Le Tissier	15,163
10	15	A	Leicester C	L	3-4	0-2	10	Dowie 2, Le Tissier	20,020
11	22	A	West Ham U	L	0-2	0-0	11		18,853
12	29	H	Leeds U	L	1-3	1-0	12	Maddison	15,202
13	Nov 2	H	Norwich C	D	1-1	0-0	—	Le Tissier (pen)	12,876
14	5	A	Manchester C	D	3-3	1-0	12	Hall, Ekelund 2	21,589
15	19	H	Arsenal	W	1-0	0-0	10	Magilton	15,201
16	26	A	Crystal Palace	D	0-0	0-0	11		14,186
17	Dec 3	H	Chelsea	L	0-1	0-0	13		14,404
18	10	A	Blackburn R	L	2-3	0-2	14	Le Tissier 2	23,372
19	19	H	Aston Villa	W	2-1	1-0	—	Hall, Le Tissier	13,874
20	26	H	Wimbledon	L	2-3	2-2	14	Dodd, Le Tissier	14,603
21	28	A	QPR	D	2-2	1-1	14	Dodd, Hughes	16,078
22	31	H	Manchester U	D	2-2	1-0	15	Magilton, Hughes	15,204
23	Jan 2	A	Sheffield W	D	1-1	0-1	15	Le Tissier (pen)	28,424
24	14	A	Leeds U	D	0-0	0-0	14		28,869
25	24	A	Arsenal	D	1-1	0-1	—	Magilton	27,213
26	Feb 4	H	Manchester C	D	2-2	1-1	15	Coton (og), Le Tissier	14,902
27	11	A	Norwich C	D	2-2	2-1	15	Hall, Magilton	18,361
28	25	A	Ipswich T	L	1-2	1-0	18	Maddison	15,788
29	Mar 4	H	Coventry C	D	0-0	0-0	18		14,505
30	15	H	West Ham U	D	1-1	0-1	—	Shipperley	15,178
31	18	A	Nottingham F	L	0-3	0-1	20		24,146
32	22	H	Newcastle U	W	3-1	0-1	—	Heaney, Watson, Shipperley	14,666
33	Apr 2	H	Tottenham H	W	4-3	2-2	17	Heaney, Le Tissier 2, Magilton	15,105
34	5	A	Liverpool	L	1-3	1-1	—	Hall	29,881
35	12	A	Chelsea	W	2-0	2-0	—	Shipperley, Le Tissier	16,739
36	15	H	QPR	W	2-1	0-0	13	Shipperley, Watson	15,210
37	17	A	Wimbledon	W	2-0	2-0	11	Le Tissier, Magilton	10,521
38	29	H	Sheffield W	D	0-0	0-0	11		15,189
39	May 3	H	Crystal Palace	W	3-1	2-1	—	Wilmot (og), Watson, Le Tissier	15,151
40	6	A	Everton	D	0-0	0-0	10		36,851
41	10	A	Manchester U	L	1-2	1-1	—	Charlton	43,479
42	14	H	Leicester C	D	2-2	1-0	10	Monkou, Le Tissier	15,101

Final League Position: 10

GOALSCORERS

League (61): Le Tissier 19 (4 pens), Magilton 6, Dowie 5, Ekelund 5, Hall 4, Shipperley 4, Maddison 3, Watson 3, Banger 2, Dodd 2, Heaney 2, Hughes 2, Charlton 1, Monkou 1, own goals 2.
Coca-Cola Cup (5): Le Tissier 5 (1 pen).
FA Cup (12): Le Tissier 5 (3 pens), Heaney 2, Shipperley 2, Hughes 1, Magilton 1, Monkou 1.

Grobbelaar B.D. 30	Kenna J.J. 28	Benali F.V. 32 + 3	Charlton S.T. 25	Hall R.A. 36 + 1	Widdrington T. 23 + 5	Le Tissier M.P. 41	Magilton J. 42	Banger N.L. 4	Maddison N.S. 35	Allen P.K. 11	Heaney N. 21 + 13	Whiston P. — + 1	Monkou K.J. 31	Dowie I. 17	Ekelund R. 15 + 2	Dodd J.R. 24 + 2	Beasant D. 12 + 1	Hughes D.R. 2 + 10	McDonald P. — + 2	Maskell C.D. 2 + 4	Tisdale P.R. — + 7	Shipperley N.J. 19	Watson G.W.G. 12	Robinson M.R. — + 1	Oakley M. — + 1	Match No.
1	2	3	4	5	6	7	8	9	10	11	12															1
1	2	3	4	5	6	7	8	9	10	11	12															2
1	2	3	4	5	6	7	8	9	10	11	12	14														3
1	2	4	3	12		7	8	9	10	11	6		5													4
1	2	4	3	5		7	8		10	11	6			9												5
1	2	4	3	5		7	8		10	11	6			9	12											6
1	2	4	3			7	6		10	11			5	9	8											7
1			3	5		7	4		10	11	12		6	9	8	2										8
1	2	5	3			7	4		10		11		6	9	8		15									9
	2	5	3			7	4		10	11	12		6	9	8	14	1									10
	2	12	3	5		7	4		10	11			6	9	8		1	14								11
1	2	12	3	5		7	4		10	11	14		6	9	8											12
1	2	3		5		7	4		10		11		6	9	8				12							13
1	2	3		5	11	7	4		10		12		6	9	8	14										14
1	2	3		5	6	7	4		10		11			9	8											15
1	2	3		5	6	7	4		10		11			9	8											16
1	2	3		5	6	7	4		10		11			9	8											17
1	2	3	4	5	9	7	11		10				6		8			12		14						18
1	2	3		5	10	7	4				11		6		8			12		9						19
1	2			5	10	7	4				11		6	9		3		8	14	12						20
1	2			5	10	7	4				3		6	9	8	11		14		12						21
1	2	3			6	7	4				12		5	9	8	11		10								22
1	2	3		5	10	7	4				12		6	9		11				8	14					23
1	2	3		5	4	7	8		10				6			11		12				9				24
1	2	3		5	14	7	4		10		11		6			8		12				9				25
1	2	3	4	5		7	8		10		6					11						9				26
1	2			5	4	7	8		10		11		6			3		12				9				27
1	2	5			4	7	8		10		11		6			3		12			14	9				28
1	2	3		5		7	8		10		11		6			4				12		9				29
		3		5	4	7	8		10		11		6		12	2	1	14				9				30
		3		5	4	7	8		10		12		6			2	1	14				9	11			31
1		3	4	5		7	8		10		12		6			2						9	11			32
1			3	5	12	7	4		10		11		6			2						9	8			33
1			3	5	6	7	4		10		11					2					12	9	8			34
			3	5	11	7	4		10				6			2	1				12	9	8			35
		12	3	5	4	7	8				11		6			2	1					9	10			36
		6	4	5	11	7	8				3					2	1				12	9	10			37
		3	4	5		7	8		10				6			2	1				12	9	11	14		38
		3	4	5	12	7	8		10				6			2	1				14	9	11			39
		3	4	5	11		8		10				6			2	1					9	7		12	40
		3	4	5	14	7	8		10		12		6			2	1					9	11			41
		3	4	5	14	7	8		10		12		6			2	1					9	11			42

Coca-Cola Cup

Second Round	Huddersfield T (a)	1-0
	(h)	4-0
Third Round	Sheffield W (a)	0-1

FA Cup

Third Round	Southend U (h)	2-0
Fourth Round	Luton T (a)	1-1
	(h)	6-0
Fifth Round	Tottenham H (a)	1-1
	(h)	2-6

SOUTHEND UNITED 1994–95 *Back row (left to right):* Daniel Foot, Andy Sussex, Andy Edwards, Keith Dublin, Paul Sansome, John Cornwell, Simon Royce, Dominic Iorfa, Mark Hone, Graham Bressington, Phil Gridelet.
Centre row: Danny Greaves, Ijah Anderson, Gary Poole, Steve Tilson, Mick Bodley, Chris Powell, Declan Perkins, Gary Jones, Craig Davidson, Mark Hall, John Gowens.
Front row: Andy Ansah, Andy Thomson, Keith Jones, Theo Foley, Vic Jobson, Peter Taylor, Ricky Otto, Jon Hunt, Jae Martin.

Division 1 SOUTHEND UNITED

Roots Hall Football Ground, Victoria Avenue, Southend-on-Sea SS2 6NQ. Telephone: (01702) 340707. Fax: (01702) 330164. Commercial Dept: (01702) 437154/6. Soccerline: 0839 664444. Ticket Office: (01702) 435602. Infoline: 0839 664443.

Ground capacity: 10,350.

Record attendance: 31,090 v Liverpool FA Cup 3rd rd, 10 January 1979.

Record receipts: £83,999 v West Ham U, Division 1, 7 April 1993.

Pitch measurements: 110yd × 74yd.

President: N. J. Woodcock.

Chairman and Managing Director: V. T. Jobson. ***Vice-Chairman and Chief Executive:*** J. W. Adams.

Secretary: J. W. Adams.

Directors: J. A. Bridge, B. R. Gunner, W. R. Kelleway, C. Wooldridge. ***Associate Directors:*** A. W. Jobson, R. J. Osborne, W. E. Parsons.

Manager: Ronnie Whelan. ***Assistant Manager:*** Theo Foley. ***Youth Team Coach:*** Danny Greaves.

Physio: John Cowens. ***Commercial Manager:*** C. Wooldridge. ***Stadium Manager:*** David Jobson.

Club Nickname: 'The Blues or The Shrimpers'.

Year Formed: 1906. ***Turned Professional:*** 1906. ***Ltd Co.:*** 1919.

Previous Grounds: 1906, Roots Hall, Prittlewell; 1920, Kursaal; 1934, Southend Stadium; 1955, Roots Hall Football Ground.

Foundation: The leading club in Southend around the turn of the century was Southend Athletic, but they were an amateur concern. Southend United was a more ambitious professional club when they were founded in 1906, employing Bob Jack as secretary-manager and immediately joining the Second Division of the Southern League.

First Football League game: 28 August, 1920, Division 3, v Brighton & HA (a) W 2-0 – Capper; Reid, Newton; Wileman, Henderson, Martin; Nicholls, Nuttall, Fairclough (2), Myers, Dorsett.

Record League Victory: 9–2 v Newport Co, Division 3 (S), 5 September 1936 – McKenzie; Nelson, Everest (1); Deacon, Turner, Carr; Bolan, Lane (1), Goddard (4), Dickinson (2), Oswald (1).

Record Cup Victory: 10–1 v Golders Green, FA Cup, 1st rd, 24 November 1934 – Moore; Morfitt, Kelly; Mackay, Joe Wilson, Carr (1); Lane (1), Johnson (5), Cheesmuir (2), Deacon (1), Oswald. 10–1 v Brentwood, FA Cup, 2nd rd, 7 December 1968 – Roberts; Bentley, Birks; McMillan (1) Beesley, Kurila; Clayton, Chisnall, Moore (4), Best (5), Hamilton. 10–1 v Aldershot, Leyland Daf Cup, Pr rd, 6 November 1990 – Sansome; Austin, Powell, Cornwell, Prior (1), Tilson (3), Cawley, Butler, Ansah (1), Benjamin (1), Angell (4).

Record Defeat: 1–9 v Brighton & HA, Division 3, 27 November 1965.

Most League Points (2 for a win): 67, Division 4, 1980–81.

Most League Points (3 for a win): 85, Division 3, 1990–91.

Most League Goals: 92, Division 3 (S), 1950–51.

Highest League Scorer in Season: Jim Shankly, 31, 1928–29 and Sammy McCrory, 1957–58, both in Division 3 (S).

Most League Goals in Total Aggregate: Roy Hollis, 122, 1953–60.

Most Capped Player: George Mackenzie, 9, Eire.

Most League Appearances: Sandy Anderson, 451, 1950–63.

Record Transfer Fee Received: £2,000,000 from Nottingham F for Stan Collymore, June 1993.

Record Transfer Fee Paid: £350,000 to Plymouth Arg for Gary Poole, June 1993.

Football League Record: 1920 Original Member of Division 3; 1921–58 Division 3 (S); 1958–66 Division 3; 1966–72 Division 4; 1972–76 Division 3; 1976–78 Division 4; 1978–80 Division 3; 1980–81 Division 4; 1981–84 Division 3; 1984–87 Division 4; 1987–89 Division 3; 1989–90 Division 4; 1990–91 Division 3; 1991–92 Division 2; 1992– Division 1.

Honours: *Football League:* Best season: 15th, Division 1, 1993–94. Division 3 – Runners-up 1990–91; Division 4 – Champions 1980–81; Runners-up 1971–72, 1977–78. *FA Cup:* best season: old 3rd rd, 1921, 5th rd, 1926, 1952, 1976, 1993. *Football League Cup:* never past 3rd rd.

Colours: All royal blue. **Change colours:** All red.

SOUTHEND UNITED 1994–95 LEAGUE RECORD

Match No.	Date	Venue	Opponents	Result		H/T Score	Lg. Pos.	Goalscorers	Attendance
1	Aug 13	A	Millwall	L	1-3	0-1	—	Iorfa	8283
2	20	H	Middlesbrough	L	0-2	0-1	24		5722
3	27	A	Luton T	D	2-2	0-1	20	Dublin, Otto	5918
4	30	H	Portsmouth	L	1-2	1-1	—	Thomson	4333
5	Sept 3	H	Oldham Ath	W	1-0	0-0	20	Otto	4435
6	10	A	Stoke C	L	1-4	0-2	23	Butler (og)	11,808
7	13	A	Wolverhampton W	L	0-5	0-3	—		23,608
8	17	H	Bristol C	W	2-1	1-0	22	Thomson, Whelan	3663
9	24	H	Bolton W	W	2-1	0-1	17	Otto, Thomson	4507
10	Oct 1	A	Sunderland	W	1-0	1-0	13	Thomson	15,520
11	8	A	Barnsley	D	0-0	0-0	16		3659
12	16	H	Derby Co	W	1-0	0-0	8	Regis	4218
13	22	A	Swindon T	D	2-2	2-1	10	Thomson, Otto	9909
14	29	H	Grimsby T	D	0-0	0-0	12		5086
15	Nov 1	H	Notts Co	W	1-0	1-0	—	Thomson	4302
16	5	A	Port Vale	L	0-5	0-2	9		7141
17	12	A	Watford	L	0-1	0-0	12		8551
18	19	H	Reading	W	4-1	1-1	10	Bressington (pen), Jones G 2, Thomson	5511
19	26	A	Sheffield U	L	0-2	0-1	12		13,405
20	Dec 3	H	Swindon T	W	2-0	1-0	11	Willis, Edwards	5803
21	10	A	Middlesbrough	W	2-1	1-0	9	Hails, Gridelet	16,843
22	17	H	Millwall	L	0-1	0-1	11		5833
23	26	A	Charlton Ath	L	1-3	1-0	15	Bressington (pen)	9525
24	27	H	WBA	W	2-1	1-1	12	Gridelet 2	6856
25	31	A	Burnley	L	1-5	0-2	14	Willis	10,561
26	Jan 2	H	Tranmere R	D	0-0	0-0	13		5195
27	14	A	Grimsby T	L	1-4	1-1	15	Chapman	3915
28	28	H	Port Vale	L	1-2	1-1	14	Thomson	3619
29	Feb 4	H	Watford	L	0-4	0-3	15		4914
30	11	A	Notts Co	D	2-2	1-1	15	Edwards, Willis	6768
31	18	H	Sheffield U	L	1-3	1-1	16	Willis	4700
32	21	A	Reading	L	0-2	0-0	—		7895
33	25	H	Sunderland	L	0-1	0-1	20		4686
34	Mar 4	A	Bolton W	L	0-3	0-1	20		10,766
35	7	A	Oldham Ath	W	2-0	1-0	—	Jones G, Thomson	7168
36	11	H	Luton T	W	3-0	1-0	16	Jones G, Thomson, Dublin	4558
37	18	A	Portsmouth	D	1-1	1-1	18	Jones G	6667
38	21	H	Stoke C	W	4-2	2-0	—	Jones G, Tilson, Edwards, Sussex (pen)	4240
39	25	A	Bristol C	D	0-0	0-0	16		6159
40	Apr 1	H	Wolverhampton W	L	0-1	0-0	16		8522
41	8	H	Burnley	W	3-1	2-0	15	Jones G, Hails, Battersby	5027
42	15	A	WBA	L	0-2	0-1	18		14,393
43	18	H	Charlton Ath	W	2-1	0-0	—	Jones G, Tilson	6397
44	21	A	Tranmere R	W	2-0	2-0	—	McGreal (og), Jones G	9971
45	29	A	Derby Co	W	2-1	2-0	14	Gridelet, Jones G	12,528
46	May 7	H	Barnsley	W	3-1	1-0	13	Gridelet, Thomson, Jones G	6425

Final League Position: 13

GOALSCORERS

League (54): Jones G 11, Thomson 11, Gridelet 5, Otto 4, Willis 4, Edwards 3, Bressington 2 (2 pens), Dublin 2, Hails 2, Tilson 2, Battersby 1, Chapman 1, Iorfa 1, Regis 1, Sussex 1 (pen), Whelan 1, own goals 2.
Coca-Cola Cup (0).
FA Cup (0).

Sansome P.E. 33	Poole G.J. 5 + 1	Powell C.G.R. 44	Jones K.A. 7	Edwards A.D. 42 + 2	Dublin K.B.L. 40	Hunt J.R. 5 + 2	Tilson S.B. 17 + 9	Iorfa D. 4 + 4	Otto R. 19	Thomson A. 35 + 4	Hone M. 39 + 1	Royce S. 13	Bressington G. 19 + 1	Martin J.A. — + 4	Sussex A.R. 14 + 1	Forrester J. 3 + 2	Whelan R.A. 33	Gridelet P.R. 26 + 3	Willis R.C. 21	Regis D. 9	Jones G. 19 + 6	Hails J. 20 + 6	Ansah A. 7 + 2	Chapman L.R. 1	Foot D.F. 2 + 1	Westley S.L.M. 4 + 1	Harkness S. 6	Perkins D.O. 1 + 5	Bodley M.J. 12	Battersby T. 6 + 2	Roche D. — + 4	*Match No.*
1	2	3	4	5	6	7	8	9	10	11	12																					1
	2	3	4	11	6	7		9	10		8	1	5	12																		2
1	2	3	4	5	6	12		*9*	10	11	7			14	8																	3
1	2	3	4	5		7			10	9	8		6	12	11																	4
1	2	3	4	5		12			10	9	8		6		11	7																5
1		3	4	5		7			10	9	2		6			11	8															6
1	14	3	4	12	5	7			10	9	2		6			*11*	8															7
1		3		5	6		14		10	9	2					12	8	*4*	7	11												8
1		3		5	6				10	11	2					12	8	4	7	9												9
1		3		5	6				10	11	2						8	4	7	9												10
1		3		5	6		12		10	11	2						8	4	7	9												11
1		3		5	6				10	11	2						8	4	7	9												12
1		3		5	6		12		10	11	2		4				8		7		9											13
1		3		5	6		12		10	11	2		14				8	*4*	7	9												14
1		3		5	6		12		10	11	2		7				8	4		9												15
1		3		5	6		12		10	11	2						8	4	7	*9*	14											16
1		3		5	6				10	11	2		8					4	7	9	12											17
1		3		5	6		12		10	11	2		8					4	7		9											18
1		3		5	6		12		10		2		8				7	4	9		11											19
1		3		5	6		10			11	2						8	4	7		9	12										20
1		3		5	6					11	2		7				8	4			9	10										21
1		3		5	6		12	14		11	2		7				8	4			*9*	10										22
1		3		5	6			14		12	2		7				8	4	9			*11*	10									23
1		3		5	6					11	2						8	4	9			7	10									24
1		3		5						11	2		6		12		8	4	9			7	10									25
1		3			6		11			9	2		5				8	4	10		12	7										26
1		3		5	6					11	2						*8*		10		12	4	7	9	14							27
1		3		5	6		8	12		9	2		4						7		10	*11*	14									28
1		3		5	6			*10*		9	2								7			11	12			4	8	14				29
1				5	6					*9*	2		3					4	7			11	10			14	8	12				30
1		3		5	6			12		9	2		*11*					4	7			14	10				8					31
1				12	6					*9*	2		7					4				11	10		3	5	8	14				32
1		3		6						*9*	2			12	8						14	7			4	5	10	11				33
1		3		6			8			9	2				10		4				12	7				5	11					34
		3		6	11		10			9	2	1			8		4				7								5			35
		3		6	11		*10*			9	2	1			8		4				7	12						14	5			36
		3		6	11		10			9	2	1			8		4				7	12							5			37
		3		6	11		10				2	1			8		4	12			9	7							5			38
		3		6	11		10				2	1			8		4				7	9							5	12		39
		3		6	11		10				*2*	1			8		4	12			7	9							5	14		40
		3			6		10					1			*8*		4	2			7	9						12	5	11	14	41
		3		6	2		10			12		1			*8*		4	14			7	9							5	11		42
		3		6	2		10			9		1					4	8			7	12							5	11		43
		3		6	2		10					1			9		4	8			7	12							5	*11*	14	44
		3		6	2		10			12		1					4	8			7	9							5	*11*	14	45
		3		5	2		10			12		1					4	*8*			7	9							6	11	14	46

Coca-Cola Cup
First Round | Watford (h) | 0-0
(a) | 0-1

FA Cup
Third Round | Southampton (a) | 0-2

STOCKPORT COUNTY 1994–95 *Back row (left to right):* Alun Armstrong, Tony Dinning, Jeff Eckhardt, Michael Flynn, Michael Olliver, Kevin Slinn, Dean Emerson.
Centre row: Dave Philpotts, Dean Connelly, Sean Connelly, Neil Edwards, Ian Ironside, John Keeley, Chris Beaumont, David Miller, John Sainty (Assistant Manager).
Front row: Dave Jones, Deiniol Graham, Kevin Francis, David Frain, Danny Bergara (Manager), Peter Ward, Martyn Chalk, Lee Todd, Rodger Wylde (Physio).

Division 2 STOCKPORT COUNTY

Edgeley Park, Hardcastle Road, Stockport, Cheshire SK3 9DD. Telephone: (0161) 480 8888. Fax: (0161) 480 0230. Club Shop: (0161) 480 8117. Clubcall: 0891 121638.

Ground capacity: 12,500 (approx).

Record attendance: 27,833 v Liverpool, FA Cup 5th rd, 11 February 1950.

Record receipts: £66,807 v Bristol C, FA Cup 4th rd, 9 February 1994.

Pitch measurements: 111yd × 72yd.

Hon. Vice-Presidents: Mike Yarwood OBE, Freddie Pye, Andrew Barlow.

Chairman: Brendan Elwood. ***Vice-Chairman:*** Grahame White.

Directors: Mike Baker, Michael Rains, Brian Taylor, David Jolley.

Secretary: Gary Glendenning BAACA.

Manager: Dave Jones. ***Assistant Manager:*** John Sainty.

Physio: Rodger Wylde.

Assistant Secretary: Andrea Welborn. ***Commercial Manager:*** John Rutter.
Marketing Manager and Programme Editor: Steve Bellis.

Year Formed: 1883. ***Turned Professional:*** 1891. ***Ltd Co.:*** 1908.

Club Nicknames: 'County' or 'Hatters'.

Previous Names: Heaton Norris Rovers, 1883–88; Heaton Norris, 1888–90.

Previous Grounds: 1883 Heaton Norris Recreation Ground; 1884 Heaton Norris Wanderers Cricket Ground; 1885 Chorlton's Farm, Chorlton's Lane; 1886 Heaton Norris Cricket Ground; 1887 Wilkes' Field, Belmont Street; 1889 Nursery Inn, Green Lane; 1902 Edgeley Park.

Foundation: Formed at a meeting held at Wellington Road South by members of Wycliffe Congregational Chapel in 1883, they called themselves Heaton Norris Rovers until changing to Stockport County in 1890, a year before joining the Football Combination.

First Football League game: 1 September, 1900, Division 2, v Leicester Fosse (a) D 2-2 – Moores; Earp, Wainwright; Pickford, Limond, Harvey; Stansfield, Smith (1), Patterson, Foster, Betteley (1).

Record League Victory: 13–0 v Halifax T, Division 3 (N), 6 January 1934 – McGann; Vincent (1p), Jenkinson; Robinson, Stevens, Len Jones; Foulkes (1), Hill (3), Lythgoe (2), Stevenson (2), Downes (4).

Record Cup Victory: 6–2 v West Auckland T (away), FA Cup, 1st rd, 14 November 1959 – Lea; Betts (1), Webb; Murray, Hodder, Porteous; Wilson (1), Holland, Guy (2), Ritchie (1), Davock (1).

Record Defeat: 1–8 v Chesterfield, Division 2, 19 April 1902.

Most League Points (2 for a win): 64, Division 4, 1966–67.

Most League Points (3 for a win): 85, Division 2, 1993–94.

Most League Goals: 115, Division 3 (N), 1933–34.

Highest League Scorer in Season: Alf Lythgoe, 46, Division 3 (N), 1933–34.

Most League Goals in Total Aggregate: Jack Connor, 132, 1951–56.

Most Capped Player: Harry Hardy, 1, England.

Most League Appearances: Andy Thorpe, 489, 1978–86, 1988–92.

Record Transfer Fee Received: £250,000 from WBA for Paul A. Williams, March 1991.

Record Transfer Fee Paid: £125,000 to Preston NE for Mike Flynn, March 1993.

Football League Record: 1900 Elected to Division 2; 1904 Failed re-election; 1905–21 Division 2; 1921–22 Division 3 (N); 1922–26 Division 2; 1926–37 Division 3 (N); 1937–38 Division 2; 1938–58 Division 3 (N); 1958–59 Division 3; 1959–67 Division 4; 1967–70 Division 3; 1970–91 Division 4; 1991–92 Division 3; 1992– Division 2.

Honours: *Football League:* Division 2 best season: 10th, 1905–06; Division 3 (N) – Champions 1921–22, 1936–37; Runners-up 1928–29, 1929-30; Division 4 – Champions 1966–67; Runners-up 1990–91. *FA Cup:* best season: 5th rd, 1935, 1950. *Football League Cup:* best season: 4th rd, 1973. *Autoglass Trophy:* Runners-up 1992, 1993.

Colours: White shirts with double royal pinstripe, white shorts with double royal pinstripe, white stockings. **Change colours:** Red and black striped shirts, black shorts, red and black stockings.

STOCKPORT COUNTY 1994–95 LEAGUE RECORD

Match No.	Date		Venue	Opponents	Result		H/T Score	Lg. Pos.	Goalscorers	Atten-dance
1	Aug	13	H	Cardiff C	W	4-1	1-1	—	Ward, Francis 2, Armstrong	5139
2		20	A	Cambridge U	W	4-3	2-1	1	Francis 2, Armstrong, Gannon	3163
3		27	H	Brentford	L	0-1	0-1	6		4399
4		30	A	Crewe Alex	L	1-2	0-0	—	Armstrong	5050
5	Sept	3	A	Bristol R	D	2-2	1-2	11	Sterling (og), Eckhardt	4263
6		10	H	Bournemouth	W	1-0	0-0	9	Francis	4054
7		13	H	Shrewsbury T	W	2-1	0-0	—	Flynn, Armstrong	3473
8		17	A	Huddersfield T	L	1-2	1-1	9	Chalk	9526
9		24	H	Wycombe W	W	4-1	3-0	4	Francis 2, Armstrong, Chalk	4607
10	Oct	1	A	York C	W	4-2	2-2	3	Tutill (og), Slinn, Francis, Ward	3790
11		8	H	Rotherham U	W	1-0	0-0	3	Francis	4991
12		15	A	Peterborough U	W	1-0	0-0	3	Armstrong	5369
13		22	H	Plymouth Arg	L	2-4	1-2	4	Chalk, Francis	5652
14		29	A	Leyton Orient	W	1-0	0-0	2	Francis	3267
15	Nov	2	A	Chester C	L	0-1	0-0	—		2400
16		5	H	Oxford U	L	0-2	0-1	7		5132
17		19	A	Swansea C	L	0-2	0-0	7		3019
18		26	H	Birmingham C	L	0-1	0-0	10		5577
19	Dec	10	H	Cambridge U	W	2-1	0-0	7	Gannon 2	3903
20		17	A	Cardiff C	D	1-1	0-0	11	Gannon	3448
21		26	H	Wrexham	D	1-1	1-0	10	Todd	5636
22		27	A	Blackpool	W	2-1	1-0	9	Wallace, Gannon	5745
23		31	H	Bradford C	L	1-2	0-1	10	Francis	4613
24	Jan	2	A	Brighton & HA	L	0-2	0-0	11		8842
25		14	H	Hull C	W	4-0	1-0	10	Beaumont, Helliwell 2, Armstrong	4516
26		28	H	Leyton Orient	W	2-1	1-0	10	Ware, Armstrong	4250
27	Feb	4	A	Birmingham C	L	0-1	0-0	10		17,160
28		11	H	Chester C	D	2-2	0-2	10	Wallace, Beaumont	4405
29		18	A	Hull C	D	0-0	0-0	11		4576
30		21	H	Swansea C	L	0-1	0-1	—		3088
31		25	H	York C	L	2-3	1-2	13	Armstrong, Gannon	3570
32		28	A	Oxford U	L	0-4	0-1	—		4594
33	Mar	4	A	Wycombe W	D	1-1	1-0	14	Gannon	5275
34		7	H	Bristol R	W	2-1	1-1	—	Flynn, Armstrong	3580
35		11	A	Brentford	L	0-1	0-1	13		6513
36		18	H	Crewe Alex	W	3-1	1-0	13	Chalk 2, Armstrong	4946
37		21	A	Bournemouth	L	0-2	0-1	—		2892
38		25	H	Huddersfield T	L	1-2	0-1	14	Armstrong	5383
39		28	A	Plymouth Arg	W	2-0	1-0	—	Graham, Dinning	4618
40	Apr	1	A	Shrewsbury T	D	1-1	1-0	14	Graham	3655
41		8	A	Bradford C	W	2-1	0-1	13	Armstrong, Ward	3927
42		15	H	Blackpool	W	3-2	2-0	12	Helliwell 2, Todd	5021
43		17	A	Wrexham	L	0-1	0-0	12		3041
44		22	H	Brighton & HA	W	2-0	1-0	11	Chalk, Davenport	3789
45		29	H	Peterborough U	D	1-1	1-0	11	Armstrong	4387
46	May	6	A	Rotherham U	L	0-1	0-0	11		3469

Final League Position: 11

GOALSCORERS

League (63): Armstrong 14, Francis 12, Gannon 7, Chalk 6, Helliwell 4, Ward 3, Beaumont 2, Flynn 2, Graham 2, Todd 2, Wallace 2, Davenport 1, Dinning 1, Eckhardt 1, Slinn 1, Ware 1, own goals 2.
Coca-Cola Cup (6): Armstrong 1, Beaumont 1, Chalk 1, Emerson 1, Francis 1, Ward 1.
FA Cup (0).

Keeley J.H. 10	Connelly S.P. 37 + 2	Todd L. 37	Eckhardt J.E. 26 + 1	Flynn M.A. 43	Gannon J.P. 43 + 2	Emerson D. 1 + 2	Ward P. 27 + 1	Francis K.D.M. 16 + 1	Armstrong A. 40 + 5	Chalk M.P.G. 24 + 9	Miller D.B. — + 3	Graham D.W. 5 + 6	Frain D. 2	Slinn K.P. 2 + 2	Ironside I. 7 + 1	Beaumont C.P. 33 + 5	Wallace M. 24 + 1	Dinning T. 38 + 2	Ware P.D. 16 + 3	Edwards N.R. 18 + 1	Bound M.T. 14	Helliwell I. 17	Dickins M.J. 11 + 1	Oliver M. 10 + 3	Brown R.A. 1	Davenport P. 3 + 3	Marshall L.A. 1	Williams M. — + 1	*Match No.*
1	2	3	4	5	6	7	8	9	*10*	11	12	14																	1
1	2	3	4	5	6		8	9	*10*	11	12		7	14	15														2
1	5		*4*		6		8	9	10	11		12	7			2	3	14											3
1	2		4		6		8	9	10	11		7					3	5											4
1	2		4		6	14	8	9	10	*11*	12	7					3	5											5
1	2	3	4	5	7		8	9	10	11								6											6
1	2	3	4	5	7		8	9	10	11								6											7
1	2	3	4	5	7	12	8	9	10	11								6											8
1	2	3	4	5	7		8	9	10	11								6	12										9
1	2	3	4	5	7		8	*9*	10					11		12		6	14										10
	2	3	4	5	7		8	9	10	11					1	12		6											11
		3	4	5	7		8	9	10						1	11		6	2										12
	2	*3*	4	5	7		8	9	10	11					*1*	12		6	14	15									13
	2		4	5	7		8	9	10						1	11	3				6								14
	2		4	5	7		*8*	9	10	12					1	11	3	14			6								15
	2		4	5	7				9	11					1	10	3		8		6								16
	2	3	4	5	7				9	11					1	10		8			6								17
	2	3	4	5	7			9	10					12		11		8		1	6								18
	2	3	9	5	7				12	11						10	8	4		1	6								19
	2	3	9	5	7				12	11						10	8	4		1	6								20
	2	3	8	5	7		12		*9*	14						10	11	4		1	6								21
	2	3	9	5	7		8			11						10	12	4		1	6								22
	2	3	9	5	7			12	14	11						10	8	4		1	6								23
		2		5	7				9	12		11				10	3	4	8	1	6								24
	2	3		5	7				10							11	8	6	4	1		9							25
	2	3		5	7				10							11	8	6	4	1		9							26
	2	3	12	5	7				10	14						11	8	6	4	1		9							27
	2	3	7	5	12				*10*	14						11	8	6	4	1		9							28
	2	3	9	5	7				12					10		11	8	6	4	1									29
	2	3	9	5	7				12	11						10	8	6	4	1									30
	2	3		5	7				10	12						11	8	6	4	*1*		9	15						31
				5	7				10	8		12				11	3	2	4		6	9	1	14					32
				5	7				10	12						11	3	6	4			9	1	8	2				33
		2		5	7				10	12						11	3	6	4	1		9		8					34
		2		5	7		8		10							11	3	6	4			9	1	12					35
	2			5	7		8		10	11		12				9	3	6	4				1						36
	6	2		5	7		8		10	11						9	3		4				1	12					37
	2	3		5	7				10			12				9		6			4		1	8		11			38
	2	3		5	7		8		10			11				12		6				9	1	4					39
	2	3		5	7		8		10			11				12		6				9	1	4					40
	2	3		5			8		10			12				7		6				9	1	4		11			41
	2	3		5	12		8		10							7		6				9	1	4		11			42
	2	3		5	7		8		10	12						11		*6*				9	1	4		14			43
	12	3		5	7		8		*10*	11						2		6		1		9		4		14			44
	12	3		5	7		8		10	*11*						2		6		1		9		4		14			45
		3		5	7		8		10	11						2				1	6	9					4	12	46

Coca-Cola Cup

First Round	Preston NE (a)	1-1
	(h)	4-1
Second Round	Sheffield U (h)	1-5
	(a)	0-1

FA Cup

First Round	Wrexham (a)	0-1

STOKE CITY 1994–95 *Back row (left to right):* John Clark, Carl Beeston, Ian Cranson, Graham Potter, John Dreyer, Vince Overson, Nigel Cleghorn, Lee Sandford.
Centre row: Brian Caswell (Youth Coach), Ian Clarkson, Toddy Orlygsson, Mark Prudhoe, Ron Sinclair, Carl Muggleton, Wayne Biggins, John Butler, Richard Gray.
Front row: Graham Shaw, Simon Sturridge, Mick Gynn, Asa Hartford (Coach), Joe Jordan, Dennis Rofe, Martin Carruthers, Paul Peschisolido, Paul Ware.

Division 1 STOKE CITY

Victoria Ground, Stoke-on-Trent ST4 4EG. Telephone: (01782) 413511. Fax: (01782) 745340. Commercial Dept: (01782) 45840. Soccerline Information: 0891 700278. Football in the Community: (01782) 744347.

Ground capacity: 24,071.

Record attendance: 51,380 v Arsenal, Division 1, 29 March 1937.

Record receipts: £97,000 v Liverpool, FA Cup 3rd rd, 9 January 1988.

Pitch measurements: 116yd × 75yd.

Vice-President: J. A. M. Humphries.

Chairman: P. Coates. ***Vice-Chairman:*** K. A. Humphreys.

Directors: D. J. Edwards, M. E. Moors.

Manager: Lou Macari. ***Assistant Manager:*** Asa Hartford.

Physio: David Looms.

Secretary: M. J. Potts.

Chief Executive: Jez Moxey F. INST SMM.

Year Formed: 1863 *(*see Foundation*).

Turned Professional: 1885. ***Ltd Co.:*** 1908.

Club Nickname: 'The Potters'.

Previous Name: Stoke.

Previous Grounds: 1875, Sweeting's Field; 1878, Victoria Ground (previously known as the Athletic Club Ground).

Foundation: The date of the formation of this club has long been in doubt. The year 1863 was claimed, but more recent research by Wade Martin has uncovered nothing earlier than 1868, when a couple of Old Carthusians, who were apprentices at the local works of the old North Staffordshire Railway Company, met with some others from that works, to form Stoke Ramblers. It should also be noted that the old Stoke club went bankrupt in 1908 when a new club was formed.

First Football League game: 8 September, 1888, Football League, v WBA (h) L 0-2 – Rowley; Clare, Underwood; Ramsey, Shutt, Smith; Sayer, McSkimming, Staton, Edge, Tunnicliffe.

Record League Victory: 10–3 v WBA, Division 1, 4 February 1937 – Doug Westland; Brigham, Harbot; Tutin, Turner (1p), Kirton; Matthews, Antonio (2), Freddie Steele (5), Jimmy Westland, Johnson (2).

Record Cup Victory: 7–1 v Burnley, FA Cup, 2nd rd (replay), 20 February 1896 – Clawley; Clare, Eccles; Turner, Grewe, Robertson; Willie Maxwell, Dickson, A. Maxwell (3), Hyslop (4), Schofield.

Record Defeat: 0–10 v Preston NE, Division 1, 14 September 1889.

Most League Points (2 for a win): 63, Division 3 (N), 1926–27.

Most League Points (3 for a win): 93, Division 2, 1992–93.

Most League Goals: 92, Division 3 (N), 1926–27.

Highest League Scorer in Season: Freddie Steele, 33, Division 1, 1936–37.

Most League Goals in Total Aggregate: Freddie Steele, 142, 1934–49.

Most Capped Player: Gordon Banks, 36 (73), England.

Most League Appearances: Eric Skeels, 506, 1958–76.

Record Transfer Fee Received: £1,500,000 from Chelsea for Mark Stein, October 1993.

Record Transfer Fee Paid: £480,000 to Sheffield W for Ian Cranson, July 1989.

Football League Record: 1888 Founder Member of Football League; 1890 Not re-elected; 1891 Re-elected; relegated in 1907, and after one year in Division 2, resigned for financial reasons; 1919 re-elected to Division 2; 1922–23 Division 1; 1923–26 Division 2; 1926–27 Division 3 (N); 1927–33 Division 2; 1933–53 Division 1; 1953–63 Division 2; 1963–77 Division 1; 1977–79 Division 2; 1979–85 Division 1; 1985–90 Division 2; 1990–92 Division 3; 1992–93 Division 2; 1993– Division 1.

Honours: *Football League:* Division 1 best season: 4th, 1935–36, 1946–47; Division 2 – Champions 1932–33, 1962–63, 1992–93; Runners-up 1921–22; Promoted 1978–79 (3rd); Division 3 (N) – Champions 1926–27. *FA Cup:* Semi-finals 1899, 1971, 1972. *Football League Cup:* Winners 1972. *Autoglass Trophy:* Winners: 1992. **European Competitions:** *UEFA Cup:* 1972–73, 1974–75.

Colours: Red and white striped shirts, white shorts, red stockings. **Change colours:** Green and black striped shirts, black shorts, black stockings.

STOKE CITY 1994–95 LEAGUE RECORD

Match No.	Date	Venue	Opponents	Result		H/T Score	Lg. Pos.	Goalscorers	Attendance
1	Aug 13	H	Tranmere R	W	1-0	0-0	—	Gleghorn	15,915
2	20	A	Burnley	D	1-1	0-1	6	Dreyer	15,331
3	27	H	Sunderland	L	0-1	0-1	14		15,159
4	30	A	Reading	L	0-4	0-0	—		7103
5	Sept 3	A	Bolton W	L	0-4	0-1	22		11,515
6	10	H	Southend U	W	4-1	2-0	16	Orlygsson, Edwards (og), Dreyer, Biggins	11,808
7	14	H	Charlton Ath	W	3-2	2-0	—	Gleghorn, Orlygsson, Peschisolido	10,643
8	17	A	Notts Co	W	2-0	1-0	6	Peschisolido 2	8281
9	25	A	Derby Co	L	0-3	0-2	8		11,782
10	Oct 2	H	WBA	W	4-1	2-1	7	Carruthers 2, Wallace, Peschisolido	14,203
11	9	H	Luton T	L	1-2	0-1	7	Carruthers	11,712
12	15	A	Millwall	D	1-1	0-1	7	Peschisolido	7856
13	22	A	Oldham Ath	D	0-0	0-0	9		8954
14	30	H	Wolverhampton W	D	1-1	1-1	11	Keen	15,928
15	Nov 2	H	Sheffield U	D	1-1	0-1	—	Gleghorn	11,556
16	5	A	Barnsley	L	0-2	0-1	16		5117
17	19	H	Grimsby T	W	3-0	2-0	13	Peschisolido 2, Carruthers	12,055
18	26	A	Watford	D	0-0	0-0	14		9126
19	30	A	Portsmouth	W	1-0	0-0	—	Beeston	5272
20	Dec 4	H	Oldham Ath	L	0-1	0-0	12		12,558
21	10	H	Burnley	W	2-0	0-0	11	Orlygsson 2 (1 pen)	13,040
22	17	A	Tranmere R	W	1-0	0-0	9	Carruthers	7601
23	26	H	Swindon T	D	0-0	0-0	8		17,662
24	27	A	Bristol C	L	1-3	0-0	11	Cranson	8500
25	31	H	Middlesbrough	D	1-1	1-1	12	Gleghorn	15,914
26	Jan 14	A	Wolverhampton W	L	0-2	0-1	14		28,298
27	Feb 4	H	Portsmouth	L	0-2	0-0	16		9704
28	11	A	Sheffield U	D	1-1	1-1	16	Peschisolido	13,900
29	21	A	Grimsby T	D	0-0	0-0	—		6384
30	25	A	WBA	W	3-1	1-1	15	Scott, Peschisolido 2	16,591
31	Mar 4	H	Derby Co	D	0-0	0-0	15		13,462
32	11	A	Sunderland	L	0-1	0-0	18		12,282
33	14	A	Port Vale	D	1-1	1-1	—	Sandford	19,510
34	18	H	Reading	L	0-1	0-1	20		10,006
35	21	A	Southend U	L	2-4	0-2	—	Allen, Biggins (pen)	4240
36	25	H	Notts Co	W	2-1	1-0	19	Gleghorn, Sturridge	10,204
37	Apr 1	A	Charlton Ath	D	0-0	0-0	18		10,008
38	4	H	Watford	W	1-0	1-0	—	Sigurdsson	9576
39	8	A	Middlesbrough	L	1-2	1-1	18	Peschisolido	20,867
40	12	H	Barnsley	D	0-0	0-0	—		10,752
41	15	H	Bristol C	W	2-1	1-1	16	Andrade, Peschisolido	10,172
42	17	A	Swindon T	W	1-0	1-0	14	Orlygsson	10,549
43	22	H	Port Vale	L	0-1	0-0	17		20,429
44	29	H	Millwall	W	4-3	2-2	15	Scott, Gleghorn 2, Keen	9111
45	May 3	H	Bolton W	D	1-1	1-1	—	Orlygsson (pen)	15,557
46	7	A	Luton T	W	3-2	0-1	11	Orlygsson, Peschisolido, Scott	8252

Final League Position: 11

GOALSCORERS

League (50): Peschisolido 13, Gleghorn 7, Orlygsson 7 (2 pens), Carruthers 5, Scott 3, Biggins 2 (1 pen), Dreyer 2, Keen 2, Allen 1, Andrade 1, Beeston 1, Cranson 1, Sandford 1, Sigurdsson 1, Sturridge 1, Wallace 1, own goal 1.
Coca-Cola Cup (4): Peschisolido 2, Gleghorn 1, Orlygsson 1 (pen).
FA Cup (1): Scott 1.

Muggleton C. 24	Clark J.B. 5	Sandford L.R. 34 + 1	Dreyer J.B. 16 + 2	Overson V.D. 33 + 2	Orlygsson T. 38	Carruthers M.G. 26 + 6	Wallace R.G. 16 + 4	Biggins W. 8 + 9	Peschisolido P.P. 39 + 1	Gleghorn N.W. 44 + 2	Beckford J.N. 2 + 2	Sturridge S.A. 2 + 6	Butler J.E. 38 + 3	Shaw G.P. 1 + 2	Cranson I. 37	Downing K.G. 16	Keen K.I. 15 + 6	Potter G.S. 1	Beeston C.F. 15 + 1	Wade S.P. — + 1	Clarkson I.S. 15 + 3	Sigurdsson L. 22 + 1	Sinclair R.M. 22 + 2	Williams J.N. 1 + 3	Scott K. 16 + 2	Allen P.K. 17	Leslie S. — + 1	Gayle J. 1 + 3	Andrade J. 2 + 2	Match No.
1	2	3	4	5	6	7	8	9	10	11	12																			1
1	2	3	4	5	6	7	8	9		11		10	12	14																2
1	2	3	4			12	8	9	7	11		10			5	6														3
1	2	3	4	5		12	8	9	7	11			10			6														4
1	2	3	4	5			8	9	7	11	10		12			6														5
1		3	4	5	6	12	14	9	10	11	7		2			8														6
1		3	4		6	9	7		10	11			2		5	8														7
1		3	4		6	9	7		10	11			2		5	8														8
1		3	4		6	9	7	12	10	11			2		5	8														9
1		3	4	14	6	9	2	12	10	11			*7*		5	8														10
1		3	4	12	6	9	*2*		10	11	14		7		5	8														11
1		3	4	2	6	9	12		10	11			7		5	8														12
1		3		5	6	9		12	10	11			2		4		7	*8*	14											13
1		3		5	6	9		12	10	11			2		4		7		8											14
1		3		5	6	9			10	11			2		4		7		8	12										15
1		3		5	6	9			10	11		12			4		7		8		2									16
1		3		5	6	9			10	11			2		4		7		8											17
1		3		5	6	9		12	10	11			2		4		7				8									18
1		3		5	6	9			10	11			2		4				8			7								19
1		3		5	6	9		12	10	11					4		7		8		2									20
1		3		5	6	*9*		12	10	11				7	4				8		2	14								21
1		3	12	5	6	*9*		14	10	11			2		4				8		7		15							22
1		3	5		6	9			10	11			2		4		8				7			12						23
		3	*5*		6			9	12	11			2	14	4						8	7	1	10						24
1		3		5	6	9			10	11			2		4						7		15	12	8					25
		3	*8*	5	6			12	10	11			7		4						2		1	14	9					26
			3		7				8	11			12		4	10					*2*	5	1		9	6	14			27
			12		7				8	11			3		4	10					2	5	1		*9*	6		14		28
		3		5	6		12		8	11			10		4							2	1		9	7				29
		3		5	6				*9*	11		14	7		4		12					2	1		10	8				30
		3		5	6				*9*	12			7		4		14		11			2	1		10	8				31
		3		5		9				11		14	7		4		12		6			2	1		*10*	8				32
		3		5	6	*9*				11			2		4		12		8			7	1		14	10				33
		3		5	6	9				12		14	2		4				8			7	1		*11*	10				34
		3		5	6			9		11		12	2		4				*10*			8	1			7		14		35
				5	6				9	11		12	2		4		14		8			3	1		10	*7*				36
				5		12			10	11			2		4		6		*8*		14	3	1		9	7				37
				5					9	11			2		4	8	6				12	3	1		10	7				38
						8	4		9	11			2			6					5	3	1			7		10	12	39
					6				9	11			2		4	7					3	5	1		10	8			12	40
					6	12	4		9	11			2			8	14				5	3	1			*7*			10	41
				5	6	9	12			11			2				8				4	3	1		14	7			*10*	42
				5		10	3		9	11			2		4		8					6	1			7		12		43
				5	6		7		9	11			2		4		8					3	1		10					44
		12		5	6	14	7		9	11			2		4		8					3	1		*10*					45
		3		5	6		7		9	11			2				8				12	4	1		10					46

Coca-Cola Cup

Second Round	Fulham (a)	2-3
	(h)	1-0
Third Round	Liverpool (a)	1-2

FA Cup

Third Round	Bristol C (a)	0-0
	(h)	1-3

SUNDERLAND 1994–95 *Back row (left to right):* Martin Smith, Gary Bennett, Gordon Armstrong, Ian Sampson, Richard Ord, Andy Melville, Lee Howey, Gary Owers.
Centre row: Jimmy Montgomery, Ian Ross, Derek Ferguson, Don Goodman, John Kay, Anthony Smith, Sean Musgrave, Alec Chamberlain, Tony Norman, David Preece, Sean Cunnington, Michael Gray, David Rush, Phil Gray, Mick Buxton (Manager), Steve Smelt.
Front row: George Herd, Gudni Helgason, Mark Angel, Chris Lawless, Ian Rodgerson, Dariusz Kubicki, Kevin Ball, Craig Russell, Brian Atkinson, Martin Gray, Phillip Brumwell, John Waldock, Stephen Brodie, Trevor Hartley.

Division 1 SUNDERLAND

Roker Park Ground, Sunderland SR6 9SW. Telephone: (0191) 514 0332. Fax: (0191) 514 5854.

Ground capacity: 22,657.

Record attendance: 75,118 v Derby Co, FA Cup 6th rd replay, 8 March 1933.

Record receipts: £186,000 v Tottenham H, Division 1, 28 August 1990.

Pitch measurements: 113yd × 74yd.

Chairman: J. R. Featherstone.

Deputy chairman: G. S. Wood.

Directors: R. S. Murray, G. S. Wood, J. G. Wood, Alec King.

Manager: Peter Reid.

General Manager/Secretary: P. Fiddaman BA (HONS) ACA.

Chief Coach: Paul Bracewell. ***Youth Team Coach:*** Ricky Sbragia.

Physio: Steve Smelt. ***Director of Youth:*** Jimmy Montgomery. ***Commercial Manager:*** Alec King.

Year Formed: 1879. ***Turned Professional:*** 1886. ***Ltd Co.:*** 1906.

Club Nickname: 'Rokermen'.

Previous Name: 1879–80, Sunderland and District Teacher's AFC.

Previous Grounds: 1879, Blue House Field, Hendon; 1882, Groves Field, Ashbrooke; 1883, Horatio Street; 1884, Abbs Field, Fulwell; 1886, Newcastle Road; 1898, Roker Park.

Foundation: A Scottish schoolmaster named James Allan, working at Hendon Boarding School, took the initiative in the foundation of Sunderland in 1879 when they were formed as The Sunderland and District Teachers' Association FC at a meeting in the Adults School, Norfolk Street. Because of financial difficulties, they quickly allowed members from outside the teaching profession and so became Sunderland AFC in October 1880.

First Football League game: 13 September, 1890, Football League, v Burnley (h) L 2-3 – Kirtley; Porteous, Oliver; Wilson, Auld, Gibson; Spence (1), Miller, Campbell (1), Scott, D. Hannah.

Record League Victory: 9–1 v Newcastle U (away), Division 1, 5 December 1908 – Roose; Forster, Melton; Daykin, Thomson, Low; Mordue, Hogg (4), Brown, Holley (3), Bridgett (2).

Record Cup Victory: 11–1 v Fairfield, FA Cup, 1st rd, 2 February 1895 – Doig; McNeill, Johnston; Dunlop, McCreadie (1), Wilson; Gillespie (1), Millar (5), Campbell, Hannah (3), Scott (1).

Record Defeat: 0–8 v West Ham U, Division 1, 19 October 1968 and v Watford, Division 1, 25 September 1982.

Most League Points (2 for a win): 61, Division 2, 1963–64.

Most League Points (3 for a win): 93, Division 3, 1987–88.

Most League Goals: 109, Division 1, 1935–36.

Highest League Scorer in Season: Dave Halliday, 43, Division 1, 1928–29.

Most League Goals in Total Aggregate: Charlie Buchan, 209, 1911–25.

Most Capped Player: Martin Harvey, 34, Northern Ireland.

Most League Appearances: Jim Montgomery, 537, 1962–77.

Record Transfer Fee Received: £1,500,000 from Crystal Palace for Marco Gabbiadini, September 1991.

Record Transfer Fee Paid: £900,000 to WBA for Don Goodman, December 1991.

Football League Record: 1890 Elected to Division 1; 1958–64 Division 2; 1964–70 Division 1; 1970–76 Division 2; 1976–77 Division 1; 1977–80 Division 2; 1980–85 Division 1; 1985–87 Division 2; 1987–88 Division 3; 1988–90 Division 2; 1990–91 Division 1; 1991–92 Division 2; 1992– Division 1.

Honours: *Football League:* Division 1 – Champions 1891–92, 1892–93, 1894–95, 1901–02, 1912–13, 1935–36; Runners-up 1893–94; 1897–98, 1900–01, 1922–23, 1934–35; Division 2 – Champions 1975–76; Runners-up 1963–64, 1979–80; Division 3 – Champions 1987–88. *FA Cup:* Winners 1937, 1973; Runners-up 1913, 1992. *Football League Cup:* Runners-up 1985. **European Competitions:** *Cup-Winners' Cup:* 1973–74.

Colours: Red and white striped shirts, black shorts, red stockings, white turnover. **Change colours:** White shirts, blue and green sleeves, navy blue shorts, white stockings, navy blue trim.

SUNDERLAND 1994–95 LEAGUE RECORD

Match No.	Date	Venue	Opponents	Result		H/T Score	Lg. Pos.	Goalscorers	Attendance
1	Aug 13	A	Bristol C	D	0-0	0-0	—		11,127
2	20	H	Millwall	D	1-1	0-1	15	Goodman	17,296
3	27	A	Stoke C	W	1-0	1-0	9	Gray P	15,159
4	30	H	Grimsby T	D	2-2	1-1	—	Goodman (pen), Gray P	15,788
5	Sept 3	H	Wolverhampton W	D	1-1	1-1	11	Gray P	15,111
6	11	A	Middlesbrough	D	2-2	1-0	11	Russell 2	19,578
7	13	A	Sheffield U	D	0-0	0-0	—		15,239
8	17	H	Barnsley	W	2-0	0-0	9	Gray P, Goodman	16,145
9	24	A	Tranmere R	L	0-1	0-0	11		7500
10	Oct 1	H	Southend U	L	0-1	0-1	16		15,520
11	8	A	WBA	W	3-1	2-0	12	Smith M, Gray P 2	13,717
12	15	H	Burnley	D	0-0	0-0	14		17,700
13	22	A	Reading	W	2-0	1-0	8	Melville, Gray P	10,757
14	29	H	Oldham Ath	D	0-0	0-0	8		17,252
15	Nov 1	H	Charlton Ath	D	1-1	1-0	—	Smith M	14,085
16	5	A	Notts Co	L	2-3	0-2	12	Gray P, Owers	8890
17	19	H	Watford	L	1-3	0-2	17	Smith M	15,063
18	26	A	Portsmouth	W	4-1	3-0	13	Russell, Melville, Gray P (pen), Smith M	7527
19	29	A	Port Vale	D	0-0	0-0	—		8121
20	Dec 3	H	Reading	L	0-1	0-0	15		14,021
21	10	A	Millwall	L	0-2	0-0	16		7698
22	17	H	Bristol C	W	2-0	0-0	16	Howey 2	11,661
23	26	H	Bolton W	D	1-1	0-0	17	Smith M	19,758
24	27	A	Luton T	L	0-3	0-2	17		8953
25	31	H	Derby Co	D	1-1	0-0	17	Gray P	13,979
26	Jan 14	A	Oldham Ath	D	0-0	0-0	18		9742
27	21	H	Notts Co	L	1-2	0-1	18	Armstrong	14,334
28	Feb 4	H	Port Vale	D	1-1	1-1	21	Ball	13,377
29	11	A	Charlton Ath	L	0-1	0-0	21		12,380
30	18	H	Portsmouth	D	2-2	2-1	21	Smith M 2	12,372
31	21	A	Watford	W	1-0	1-0	—	Russell	8189
32	25	A	Southend U	W	1-0	1-0	17	Agnew	4686
33	Mar 5	H	Tranmere R	L	0-1	0-0	18		12,043
34	8	A	Wolverhampton W	L	0-1	0-0	—		25,926
35	11	H	Stoke C	W	1-0	0-0	17	Melville	12,282
36	15	A	Swindon T	L	0-1	0-1	—		8233
37	19	A	Grimsby T	L	1-3	0-1	19	Agnew	5697
38	21	H	Middlesbrough	L	0-1	0-0	—		16,501
39	24	A	Barnsley	L	0-2	0-0	—		7803
40	Apr 1	H	Sheffield U	W	1-0	0-0	20	Russell	17,259
41	8	A	Derby Co	W	1-0	1-0	20	Ball	15,442
42	15	H	Luton T	D	1-1	0-1	19	Gray P	17,292
43	17	A	Bolton W	L	0-1	0-0	20		15,030
44	22	H	Swindon T	W	1-0	1-0	20	Smith M	16,874
45	29	A	Burnley	D	1-1	1-1	20	Smith M	15,121
46	May 7	H	WBA	D	2-2	1-0	20	Smith M, Gray P	18,232

Final League Position: 20

GOALSCORERS

League (41): Gray P 12 (1 pen), Smith M 10, Russell 5, Goodman 3 (1 pen), Melville 3, Agnew 2, Ball 2, Howey 2, Armstrong 1, Owers 1.
Coca-Cola Cup (2): Gray P 1, Russell 1.
FA Cup (5): Armstrong 2, Gray P 2, Russell 1.

Norman A.J. 29	Kubicki D. 46	Martin D Gray 17 + 5	Bennett G.E. 19 + 1	Ferguson D. 23	Melville A.R. 36	Owers G. 18 + 1	Goodman D.R. 17 + 1	Gray P. 41 + 1	Michael Gray 10 + 6	Ball K.A. 42	Atkinson B. 16 + 1	Cunnington S.G. 3 + 5	Ord R.J. 33	Russell C.S. 28 + 10	Smith M. 33 + 2	Rodgerson I. 3 + 3	Chamberlain A.F.R. 17 + 1	Snodin I. 6	Howey L.M. 6 + 9	Armstrong G.I. 10 + 5	Scott M. 24	Agnew S.M. 16	Williams P.A. 3	Brodie S.E. 1 + 7	Matteo D. 1	Angell B.A.M. 8	Smith A. — + 1	Match No.
1	2	3	4	5	6	7	8	9	10	11	12																	1
1	3		4	5	6	2	8	9	10	11	7	12																2
1	3		4	5	6	2	8	9	10	11	7	12																3
1	3		4	5	6	2	8	9	10	11	7	12																4
1	3			5		2	8	9	10	6	7		4	11														5
1	2			5	6	7	8	9	12	4	*11*	14	3	10														6
1	2		12	5	6	7	8	9		4		11	3	10														7
1	2		4	5	6	7	8	9		11			3	10	12													8
1	2	5			6	7	8	9		4			3	10		11												9
1	2	5			6	7	8	9		4			3	11	10	12	15											10
	2	5	4		6		8	9		7			3	11	10	12	1											11
	2	5			6		8	9		7			3	11	10		1	4	12									12
	2	5			6		8	9		7			3	11	10	12	1	4										13
	2	5			6	12	8	9		7			3	11	10		1	*4*	14									14
	2	12			6	7	8	9		5			3	14	10	11	1	*4*										15
	2				6	7	8	9		5			3	12	10	11	1	4										16
	2				6	7	8	9		5	11		*3*	12	10		1	4		14								17
	2	5			6	7		9		4	11		3	8	10		1											18
	2	5			6	7	12	9		4	11		3	8	10		1											19
	2	5			6	7		9		4	*11*		3	8	10		1		14	12								20
	2	5	4			7		9		6			3	8	10		1		12	11								21
	3		4	7	6	2			12	5				8	10		1		9	11								22
	2	12	4	7	6			9		5				8	10		1		11		3							23
	2	5			6			9		4	7	11		8	10		1		12		3							24
	2		4		6			9	12	5	7			8	10		1			11	3							25
	2			5	6			9	12	4				8	10		1			11	3	7						26
	2		4	5	6			9							10		1		12	11	3	7	8					27
1	2			5	6			9		4				12	10					11	3	7	8					28
1	2		6	5				9	12	11			4	8					14		3	7	*10*					29
1	2			5				9	8	4			6	12	10				11		3	7						30
1	2			5	6			9		4			7	8	*10*					12	3	11		14				31
1	2		4	5				9		11			6	8	*10*					12	3	7		14				32
1	2		4	5				9		6			11	8	10				12		3	7						33
1	2		4	5						6			11	8	10				9		3	7		12				34
1	2			5	6					4				8	10				9	11	3	7		12				35
1	2		4	5	6			9		11					*10*				8	12	3	7		14				36
1	2			5	6			9		4		12	*11*	8						10	3	7		14				37
1	2				6			9		4		*5*	11	8					12	10	3	7		14				38
1	2	*12*			6			9					4	14	10					11	3	7			5	8		39
1	2	12	4	5				9			11		6	14	10						3	7				*8*		40
1	2	12	4							5	11		6	8	10						3	7				9		41
1	2	7	*4*					9	14	5	11		6	12	10						3					8		42
1	2	10			6			9	5	7	11		4	14	12						3					*8*		43
1	2	7			6			9	5		11		4		10						3					8	12	44
1	2	7			6			9	5	11			4	12	10						3					8		45
1	2	5			6			12	4	7			11		10						3			9		8		46

Coca-Cola Cup

Second Round	Millwall (a)	1-2
	(h)	1-1

FA Cup

Third Round	Carlisle U (h)	1-1
	(a)	3-1
Fourth Round	Tottenham H (h)	1-4

SWANSEA CITY 1994–95 *Back row (left to right):* David Barnhouse, Martin Hayes, Roger Freestone, Andy McFarlane, Lee Jones, David Penney, Darren Perrett.
Centre row: Jimmy Rimmer (Youth Team Coach), Bobby Smith (Assistant Manager), Michael Basham, Mark Harris, John Ford, Steve Torpey, Steve Jenkins, Shaun Chapple, Ron Walton (Youth Development Officer).
Front row: Mark Clode, Kwame Ampadu, John Hodge, Frank Burrows (Manager), John Cornforth, Colin Pascoe, Jason Bowen.

Division 2 SWANSEA CITY

Vetch Field, Swansea SA1 3SU. Telephone: (01792) 474114. Fax: (01792) 646120. Club Shop: 33 William St, Swansea SA1 3QS. Telephone: (01792) 462584.

Ground capacity: 16,540.

Record attendance: 32,796 v Arsenal, FA Cup 4th rd, 17 February 1968.

Record receipts: £36,477.42 v Liverpool, Division 1, 18 September 1982.

Pitch measurements: 112yd × 74yd.

President: I. C. Pursey MBE.

Chairman: D. J. Sharpe.

Directors: D. G. Hammond FCA, MBIM (vice-chairman), M. Griffiths.

Chief Executive: Robin Sharpe.

Team Manager: Frank Burrows. ***Assistant Manager:*** Bobby Smith.

Youth Team Manager: Jimmy Rimmer. ***Physio:*** Mike Davenport.

Programme Editor: Major Reg Pike.

Year Formed: 1912. ***Turned Professional:*** 1912. ***Ltd Co.:*** 1912.

Secretary: George Taylor.

Previous Name: Swansea Town until February 1970.

Club Nickname: 'The Swans'.

Foundation: The earliest Association Football in Wales was played in the Northern part of the country and no international took place in the South until 1894, when a local paper still thought it necessary to publish an outline of the rules and an illustration of the pitch markings. There had been an earlier Swansea club, but this has no connection with Swansea Town (now City) formed at a public meeting in June 1912.

First Football League game: 28 August, 1920, Division 3, v Portsmouth (a) L 0-3 – Crumley; Robson, Evans; Smith, Holdsworth, Williams; Hole, I. Jones, Edmundson, Rigsby, Spottiswood.

Record League Victory: 8–0 v Hartlepool U, Division 4, 1 April 1978 – Barber; Evans, Bartley, Lally (1) (Morris), May, Bruton, Kevin Moore, Robbie James (3 incl. 1p), Curtis (3), Toshack (1), Chappell.

Record Cup Victory: 12–0 v Sliema W (Malta), ECWC 1st rd 1st leg, 15 September 1982 – Davies; Marustik, Hadziabdic (1), Irwin (1), Kennedy, Rajkovic (1), Loveridge (2) (Leighton James), Robbie James, Charles (2), Stevenson (1), Latchford (1) (Walsh (3)).

Record Defeat: 0–8 v Liverpool, FA Cup 3rd rd, 9 January 1990.

Most League Points (2 for a win): 62, Division 3 (S), 1948–49.

Most League Points (3 for a win): 73, Division 2, 1992–93.

Most League Goals: 90, Division 2, 1956–57.

Highest League Scorer in Season: Cyril Pearce, 35, Division 2, 1931–32.

Most League Goals in Total Aggregate: Ivor Allchurch, 166, 1949–58, 1965–68.

Most Capped Player: Ivor Allchurch, 42 (68), Wales.

Most League Appearances: Wilfred Milne, 585, 1919–37.

Record Transfer Fee Received: £375,000 from Nottingham F for Des Lyttle, July 1993.

Record Transfer Fee Paid: £340,000 to Liverpool for Colin Irwin, August 1981.

Football League Record: 1920 Original Member of Division 3; 1921–25 Division 3 (S); 1925–47 Division 2; 1947–49 Division 3 (S); 1949–65 Division 2; 1965–67 Division 3; 1967–70 Division 4; 1970–73 Division 3; 1973–78 Division 4; 1978–79 Division 3; 1979–81 Division 2; 1981–83 Division 1; 1983–84 Division 2; 1984–86 Division 3; 1986–88 Division 4; 1988–92 Division 3; 1992– Division 2.

Honours: *Football League:* Division 1 best season: 6th, 1981–82; Division 2 – Promoted 1980–81 (3rd); Division 3 (S) – Champions 1924–25, 1948–49; Division 3 – Promoted 1978–79 (3rd); Division 4 – Promoted 1969–70 (3rd), 1977–78 (3rd). *FA Cup:* Semi-finals 1926, 1964. *Football League Cup:* best season: 4th rd, 1965, 1977. *Welsh Cup:* Winners 9 times; Runners-up 8 times. *Autoglass Trophy:* Winners 1994. **European Competitions:** *European Cup-Winners' Cup:* 1961–62, 1966–67, 1981–82, 1982–83, 1983–84, 1989–90, 1991–92.

Colours: White shirts with black double pin stripes, black sleeve with red, white shorts with red trim, white stockings with black top. **Change colours:** Black shirts with red stripes, black shorts with red trim, red stockings with black/white hooped tops.

SWANSEA CITY 1994–95 LEAGUE RECORD

Match No.	Date	Venue	Opponents	Result		H/T Score	Lg. Pos.	Goalscorers	Attendance
1	Aug 13	H	Brighton & HA	D	1-1	1-0	—	Penney (pen)	4640
2	20	A	Hull C	W	2-0	0-0	9	Cornforth, Ampadu	3797
3	27	H	Birmingham C	L	0-2	0-0	13		5797
4	Sept 3	A	Cardiff C	D	1-1	1-0	17	Hayes	5523
5	6	A	Shrewsbury T	D	3-3	0-1	—	Hodge, Pascoe, Ford	3534
6	10	H	Bradford C	D	0-0	0-0	16		3445
7	13	H	Bristol R	D	0-0	0-0	—		3226
8	17	A	Cambridge U	W	3-1	2-1	15	Penney 2, Torpey	2795
9	24	H	York C	D	0-0	0-0	16		2875
10	Oct 1	A	Wycombe W	L	0-1	0-1	17		4150
11	8	A	Chester C	D	2-2	1-1	17	Ampadu, Ford	2186
12	15	H	Oxford U	L	1-3	1-3	17	Hendry	3724
13	22	A	Blackpool	L	1-2	0-2	19	Ampadu	4911
14	29	H	Peterborough U	W	2-0	1-0	17	Hendry, Bowen	2733
15	Nov 1	H	Rotherham U	W	1-0	0-0	—	Pascoe	2511
16	5	A	Crewe Alex	W	2-1	1-0	14	Bowen 2	3242
17	19	H	Stockport Co	W	2-0	0-0	14	Ampadu, Cornforth	3019
18	26	A	Wrexham	L	1-4	0-2	15	Ford	3598
19	Dec 10	H	Hull C	W	2-0	1-0	13	Torpey 2	4903
20	17	A	Brighton & HA	D	1-1	1-0	13	Torpey	6817
21	26	H	Plymouth Arg	W	3-0	3-0	12	Hodge, Hayes 2	4859
22	27	A	Leyton Orient	W	1-0	1-0	10	Hayes	3259
23	31	H	Huddersfield T	D	1-1	0-0	11	Torpey	5438
24	Jan 2	A	Bournemouth	L	2-3	1-2	10	Hodge, Penney	3816
25	14	A	Brentford	D	0-0	0-0	14		7211
26	Feb 4	H	Wrexham	D	0-0	0-0	14		4563
27	11	A	Rotherham U	D	3-3	2-3	14	Williams, Pascoe, Hodge	2858
28	17	H	Brentford	L	0-2	0-1	—		3935
29	21	A	Stockport Co	W	1-0	1-0	—	Torpey	3088
30	25	H	Wycombe W	D	1-1	0-0	14	Torpey	3699
31	28	H	Blackpool	W	1-0	0-0	—	Torpey	2308
32	Mar 4	A	York C	W	4-2	1-1	11	Bowen 2, Torpey, Hodge (pen)	2920
33	7	H	Cardiff C	W	4-1	3-0	—	Williams, Penney, Pascoe, Chapple	3943
34	11	A	Birmingham C	W	1-0	1-0	8	Hodge (pen)	16,191
35	17	H	Shrewsbury T	D	0-0	0-0	—		4130
36	21	A	Bradford C	W	3-1	1-0	—	Cornforth, Ampadu 2	4417
37	24	H	Cambridge U	W	1-0	1-0	—	Torpey	4007
38	Apr 1	A	Bristol R	L	0-1	0-0	7		7062
39	4	A	Peterborough U	L	0-1	0-1	—		3764
40	8	A	Huddersfield T	L	0-2	0-1	9		10,105
41	15	H	Leyton Orient	W	2-0	2-0	9	Torpey, Pascoe	3277
42	17	A	Plymouth Arg	L	1-2	1-1	10	Hodge	5890
43	22	H	Bournemouth	W	1-0	0-0	10	Clode	2664
44	25	H	Crewe Alex	L	0-1	0-1	—		2600
45	30	A	Oxford U	W	2-1	2-1	10	Freestone (pen), Chapple	5244
46	May 6	H	Chester C	L	0-1	0-1	10		2065

Final League Position: 10

GOALSCORERS

League (57): Torpey 11, Hodge 7 (2 pens), Ampadu 6, Bowen 5, Pascoe 5, Penney 5 (1 pen), Hayes 4, Cornforth 3, Ford 3, Chapple 2, Hendry 2, Williams 2, Clode 1, Freestone 1 (pen).
Coca-Cola Cup (5): Penney 2 (1 pen), Harris 1, Hodge 1, Pascoe 1.
FA Cup (6): Ford 2, Torpey 2, Ampadu 1, Penney 1.

Freestone R. 44 + 1	Jenkins S.R. 42	Clode M.J. 33	Ford J.S. 46	Harris M.A. 14	Ampadu P.K. 36 + 8	Bowen J.P. 25 + 6	Penney D.M. 29 + 6	Hayes M. 14 + 10	Cornforth J.M. 32 + 1	Hodge J. 38 + 6	Pascoe C.J. 32 + 3	Torpey S.D.J. 37 + 4	Perrett D.J. 3 + 12	Hendry J. 8	Jones L. 2	Basham M. 13	Chapple S.R. 4 + 5	Burns C. 3 + 2	Walker K.C. 28	Barnhouse D.J. 4	McFarlane A.A. 1 + 2	Williams J.N. 6 + 1	Edwards C. 9	Coates J.S. — + 5	Cook A.C. 1	Thomas D.J. 2 + 2	Match No.
1	2	3	4	5	6	7	8	9	10	11	12																1
1	2	3	4	5	6	7	8	9	10	11		12															2
1	2	3	4	5	6		8	7	10	11	12	9	14														3
1	2	3	4	5	6		8	*7*	10	11	12	9	14														4
1	2	3	4	5			8	7	10	11	6	9	12														5
1	2	3	4	5	14	12	8	7	10	*11*	6	9															6
1	2	3	4	5	14	12	8		10	11	6	9	*7*														7
1	2	3	4	5	14	7	8		10	12	6	9	11														8
1	2	3	4	5	12	7	8		10	*11*	6	9	14														9
1	2	3	4	5	12	7	8		10	11	*6*	9	14														10
1	2	3	4	5	7	14	8		10	12	6	*9*		11													11
1	2	3	4	5	7	12	8	14		11	6	*9*		10													12
15	2		3	5	10	7	8			11	6			9	*1*	4	12										13
1	2		3	*5*	14	7	8	12	10	11	6			9		4											14
1	2	3	5		14	7	*8*	12	10	11	6			9		4											15
1	2	3	5		6	7	*8*	12	10	11				9		4	14										16
1	2	3	5		6	7	8		10	*11*		12	14	9		4											17
1	2	3	5		6	7	*8*	12	10	11		14		9		4											18
1	2		5		10	7	8			11		9				4	6	12	3								19
1	*2*		5		10	7	8			11		9	12			4	6	14	3								20
1			5		10		12	7		*11*		9	14			4	6	8	3	2							21
1			5		10		8	7	6	11		9	12			4			3	2							22
1			5		8		12	*7*	10	11		9	14			4		6	3	2							23
1			5		8		12	7	10	11		9	14			4		*6*	3	2							24
1	2		5		6		8	7	10	11		9				4			3		12						25
1	2		5		3	12	8	7	10		6	9							4			11					26
1	2		5		3		8	7	10	12	6	*9*							4		14	11					27
1	2	3	5				8	7	10	12	6	14							4		*9*	11					28
1	2	3	5		10	7				12	6	9							4			11	8				29
1	2	*3*	5		10	7				12	6	9					14		4			11	8				30
1	2	3	5		10	7	8			11	6	9							4								31
1	2	3	5		10	7	12			11	6	9							4			14	8				32
1	2	3	5		10		8			11	6	9					12		4			7					33
1	2	3	5		10	7	12			11	6	9							4				8	14			34
1	2	3	5		10	7	8		12	11	6	9							4					14			35
1	2	3	5		7		12		10	11	6	9							4				8				36
1	2	3	5		7		8		10	11	6	9							4					12			37
1	2		5		7				10	11	*6*	9	8				12		4				3	14			38
1	2	3	5		7				10	11	6	9	12						4				8				39
1	2		5		7	12		14	10	*11*	6	9							4				8		3		40
1	2	3	5		8	7		12	10	11	6	9							4								41
1	2	3	5		*8*	7		12	10	11	6	9							4							14	42
1	2	3	5		8	7		12		11	6	9							4							10	43
	2	3	5		10	7		12		*11*	6	9			1				4				8			14	44
1	2	3	5		11	7			10		6	9					8		4								45
1	2	3	5		12	7			10	11	6	*9*							4					14		8	46

Coca-Cola Cup

First Round	Exeter C (a)	2-2
	(h)	2-0
Second Round	Norwich C (a)	0-3
	(h)	1-0

FA Cup

First Round	Walton & Hersham (a)	2-0
Second Round	Bashley (a)	1-0
Third Round	Middlesbrough (h)	1-1
	(a)	2-1
Fourth Round	Newcastle U (a)	0-3

SWINDON TOWN 1994–95 *Back row (left to right):* Paul Bodin, Luc Nijholt, Brian Kilcline, Fraser Digby, Keith Scott, Nicky Hammond, Shaun Taylor, Andrew Thomson, Edwin Murray.
Third row: Jonathan Trigg (Physio), Ross MacLaren, Mark Robinson, Austin Berkley, Adrian Viveash, Jan Aage Fjortoft, Chris Hamon, Andy Mutch, Marcus Phillips, Ty Gooden, Eddie Buckley (Kit Manager).
Second row: Joey Beauchamp, Martin Ling, Andy Rowland (First Team Coach), Steve McMahon (Player/Manager), John Trollope (Youth Team Manager), Kevin Horlock, Wayne O'Sullivan.
Front row: Ben Worrall, Jamie Pitman, Stuart James, David Elsey.

Division 2 SWINDON TOWN

County Ground, Swindon, Wiltshire SN1 2ED. Telephone: (01793) 430430. Fax: (01793) 536170. Marketing: (01793) 532121. Marketing Fax: (01793) 423771. Superstore: (01793) 423030. Community Office: (01793) 421303. Clubcall: 0891 121640.

Ground capacity: 15,341.

Record attendance: 32,000 v Arsenal, FA Cup 3rd rd, 15 January 1972.

Record receipts: £149,371 v Bolton W, Coca-Cola Cup semi-final 1st leg, 12 February 1995.

Pitch measurements: 114yd × 74yd.

President: C. J. Green.

Chairman: R. V. Hardman. ***Vice-Chairman:*** J. M. Spearman.

Directors: P. T. Archer, Sir Seton Willis Bt, C. J. Puffett, J. R. Hunt (Associate), P. R. Godwin CBE. ***Chief Executive:*** Steve Jones.

Manager: Steve McMahon. ***Assistant Manager:*** Andy Rowland.

Coach: Ross MacLaren. ***Physio:*** Jonathan Trigg.

Secretary: Jon Pollard. ***Youth Team Manager:*** John Trollope.

Marketing Manager: Phil Alexander. ***Community Officer:*** Shane Cook.

Year Formed: 1881 *(*see Foundation*). ***Turned Professional:*** 1894. ***Ltd Co.:*** 1894.

Club Nickname: 'Robins'.

Previous Ground: 1881–96, The Croft.

Foundation: It is generally accepted that Swindon Town came into being in 1881, although there is no firm evidence that the club's founder, Rev. William Pitt, captain of the Spartans (an offshoot of a cricket club) changed his club's name to Swindon Town before 1883, when the Spartans amalgamated with St. Mark's Young Men's Friendly Society.

First Football League game: 28 August, 1920, Division 3, v Luton T (h) W 9-1 – Nash; Kay, Macconachie; Langford, Hawley, Wareing; Jefferson (1), Fleming (4), Rogers, Batty (2), Davies (1). 1 o.g.

Record League Victory: 9–1 v Luton T, Division 3 (S), 28 August 1920 – Nash; Kay, Macconachie; Langford, Hawley, Wareing; Jefferson (1), Fleming (4), Rogers, Batty (2), Davies (1). (1 og).

Record Cup Victory: 10–1 v Farnham U Breweries (away), FA Cup, 1st rd (replay), 28 November 1925 – Nash; Dickenson, Weston, Archer, Bew, Adey; Denyer (2), Wall (1), Richardson (4), Johnson (3), Davies.

Record Defeat: 1–10 v Manchester C, FA Cup 4th rd (replay), 25 January 1930.

Most League Points (2 for a win): 64, Division 3, 1968–69.

Most League Points (3 for a win): 102, Division 4, 1985–86 (League record).

Most League Goals: 100, Division 3 (S), 1926–27.

Highest League Scorer in Season: Harry Morris, 47, Division 3 (S), 1926–27.

Most League Goals in Total Aggregate: Harry Morris, 216, 1926–33.

Most Capped Player: Rod Thomas, 30 (50), Wales.

Most League Appearances: John Trollope, 770, 1960–80.

Record Transfer Fee Received: £1,300,000 from Middlesbrough for Jan-Aage Fjortoft, March 1995.

Record Transfer Fee Paid: £800,000 to West Ham U for Joey Beauchamp, August 1994.

Football League Record: 1920 Original Member of Division 3; 1921–58 Division 3 (S); 1958–63 Division 3; 1963–65 Division 2; 1965–69 Division 3; 1969–74 Division 2; 1974–82 Division 3; 1982–86 Division 4; 1986–87 Division 3; 1987–92 Division 2; 1992–93 Division 1; 1993–94 FA Premier League; 1994–95 Division 1; 1995– Division 2.

Honours: *FA Premier League:* best season: 22nd 1993–94; *Football League* : Division 3 – Runners-up 1962–63, 1968–69; Division 4 – Champions 1985–86 (with record 102 points). *FA Cup:* Semi-finals 1910, 1912. *Football League Cup:* Winners 1969. *Anglo-Italian Cup:* Winners 1970.

Colours: All red. **Change colours:** Black/blue shirts, blue shorts, blue stockings.

SWINDON TOWN 1994–95 LEAGUE RECORD

Match No.	Date		Venue	Opponents	Result		H/T Score	Lg. Pos.	Goalscorers	Attendance
1	Aug	14	H	Port Vale	W	2-0	1-0	—	Fjortoft, Scott	10,431
2		20	A	Tranmere R	L	2-3	2-1	8	Fjortoft 2	8482
3		27	H	Watford	W	1-0	1-0	5	Ling	9781
4		31	H	WBA	D	0-0	0-0	—		11,188
5	Sept	3	A	Notts Co	W	1-0	1-0	2	Fjortoft	6537
6		11	H	Derby Co	D	1-1	1-1	4	Fjortoft	9054
7		14	H	Reading	W	1-0	0-0	—	Scott	11,551
8		17	A	Charlton Ath	L	0-1	0-1	4		9794
9		24	H	Grimsby T	W	3-2	1-1	3	Bodin 2 (1 pen), Scott	8219
10	Oct	1	A	Barnsley	L	1-2	0-1	5	Taylor	3911
11		8	H	Wolverhampton W	W	3-2	2-2	5	Bodin, Scott, Beauchamp	14,036
12		15	A	Portsmouth	L	3-4	1-2	5	Bodin (pen), Fjortoft 2	10,610
13		22	H	Southend U	D	2-2	1-2	5	Fjortoft 2	9909
14		29	A	Middlesbrough	L	1-3	0-1	5	Fjortoft	17,328
15	Nov	1	A	Bolton W	L	0-3	0-1	—		10,046
16		5	H	Millwall	L	1-2	0-0	11	Bodin (pen)	9311
17		20	A	Bristol C	L	2-3	0-0	16	Scott 2	9086
18		23	H	Burnley	D	1-1	1-0	—	Scott	7654
19		26	H	Luton T	L	1-2	1-1	19	Scott	9455
20	Dec	3	A	Southend U	L	0-2	0-1	19		5803
21		10	H	Tranmere R	D	2-2	2-1	20	Bodin, Fjortoft	8608
22		17	A	Port Vale	D	2-2	1-1	19	Taylor, Fjortoft	7747
23		26	A	Stoke C	D	0-0	0-0	19		17,662
24		27	H	Sheffield U	L	1-3	0-1	20	Fjortoft	11,007
25		31	A	Oldham Ath	D	1-1	1-1	20	Ling	8917
26	Jan	15	H	Middlesbrough	W	2-1	1-1	20	Fjortoft, Horlock	8888
27	Feb	4	A	Burnley	W	2-1	1-0	19	Thorne 2	10,960
28		15	H	Bristol C	L	0-3	0-1	—		9881
29		18	A	Luton T	L	0-3	0-1	22		6595
30		25	H	Barnsley	D	0-0	0-0	22		8158
31	Mar	1	A	Millwall	L	1-3	0-0	—	Beauchamp	5950
32		4	A	Grimsby T	D	1-1	0-1	22	Taylor	4934
33		11	A	Watford	L	0-2	0-0	22		7123
34		15	H	Sunderland	W	1-0	1-0	—	Thorne	8233
35		19	A	WBA	W	5-2	0-0	21	Thorne 3, Fjortoft, Gooden	12,960
36		22	A	Derby Co	L	1-3	1-1	—	Fjortoft	16,839
37		25	H	Charlton Ath	L	0-1	0-0	22		9106
38	Apr	1	A	Reading	L	0-3	0-2	22		12,565
39		5	H	Bolton W	L	0-1	0-0	—		8100
40		8	H	Oldham Ath	W	3-1	2-1	21	Viveash, Beauchamp, Taylor	7488
41		15	A	Sheffield U	D	2-2	1-0	21	Gooden, Ling	12,217
42		17	H	Stoke C	L	0-1	0-1	21		10,549
43		22	A	Sunderland	L	0-1	0-1	21		16,874
44		29	H	Portsmouth	L	0-2	0-1	22		9220
45	May	3	H	Notts Co	W	3-0	1-0	—	Hamon, Thorne 2	6553
46		7	A	Wolverhampton W	D	1-1	1-1	21	Thorne	26,245

Final League Position: 21

GOALSCORERS

League (54): Fjortoft 16, Thorne 9, Scott 8, Bodin 6 (3 pens), Taylor 4, Beauchamp 3, Ling 3, Gooden 2, Hamon 1, Horlock 1, Viveash 1.
Coca-Cola Cup (18): Fjortoft 9, Scott 3, Mutch 2, Thorne 2, Thomson 1, own goal 1.
FA Cup (2): Fjortoft 1, Nijholt 1.

Digby F.C. 39	Robinson M. 40	Bodin P. 25	Nijholt L. 35	Whitbread A.R. 1	Taylor S. 37	Ling M. 31 + 5	Fenwick T.W. 2	Fjortoft J.A. 36	Mutch A. 7 + 13	Horlock K. 34 + 4	O'Sullivan W.S. 22 + 8	Scott K. 21 + 3	Kilcline B. 6 + 1	Beauchamp J.D. 38 + 4	Thomson A. 20 + 1	Berkley A.J. — + 1	Webb N.J. 5 + 1	Tiler C. 2	MacLaren R. 3	Murray E.J. 4 + 2	Hamon C. 2 + 3	McMahon S. 16 + 1	Culverhouse I.B. 9	Hammond N.D. 7	Thorne P.L. 20	Gooden T.M. 13 + 3	Todd A.J.J. 13	Viveash A.L. 14	Hooper D. — + 4	Drysdale J. 1	Worrall B.J. 1 + 2	Pitman J.R. 2 + 1	*Match No.*
1	2	3	4	5	6	7	8	9	*10*	11	12	14																					1
1	2	3	5		6	7	8	9	10	11		14	*4*	12																			2
1	2	3	5		6	7		9			11	10		8	4																		3
1	2	3	5		6	7		9	12	14	*11*	10		8	4																		4
1	2		5		6	7		9	12	3	11	10		8	4																		5
1	2	3	5		6	7		9	12	*11*	14	10		8	4																		6
1	2	3	5		6	10		9		11	7	12		8	4																		7
1	2	3	5		6	10		9		11	*7*	8	12		4	14																	8
1	2	3	5		6	7		9	12	*11*	14	10		8	4																		9
1	2	3	5		6	7		9		11		10		8	4																		10
1	2	3	5		6	10		9	12			11		8	4		7																11
1	2	3	4		6	10		9	12	14		11	5	8			7																12
1	2	3	5		6	10		9	12	14		11		*8*	4		7																13
1	2	3	5		*6*	10		9	12	7		11		8	4		14																14
1	2	3	5			12		9	14	7		11	6	*8*	4		10																15
1	2	3	5			12		9	14	7		11	6	8	4		10																16
1	2	3						9	10	7	12	11	*6*	8				5	4	14													17
1	2	3						9	10	12	7	11		8	5			6	4														18
1	2	3						9	10	8	7	11	6	12	5				4		14												19
1	2	3	5			10		9		7		11		8	4							6											20
1	2	3	5					9		7		11		8	4							10	6										21
1		3	5		6	10		9	12	7		11		8	4								2										22
1	2	3	5		6	10		9		7		11		8									4										23
1	2	3	*5*		6	10		9	12	7	14	11		8									4										24
	2	3	5		6	11		9	8	7				12								10	4	1									25
	2	3	5		6	11		9	10	7				8									4	1									26
	2		5		6	11		9		7	8									3			4	1	10	12							27
	2		5			11		9		7	4			8	6					3	12			1	10								28
	2					11		9	12	5	4			8						3		6		1	10	7							29
	2		5		6			9		3	7			8								11	4	1	10								30
					6	12		9		3	7			8						*5*		11	2	1	10	14	4						31
1					6			9		3	2			8								11			10	7	4	5	12				32
1			5		6			9		7	2			12								11			10	*8*	3	4	14				33
1					6			9		5	3			8								11			10	7	2	4					34
1	5				6			9		7	2			8								11			10	12	3	4					35
1	11		5		6	12		9			3			8											10	7	2	4					36
1	5				6	9					12			8								11			10	7	2	4		3			37
1	5				6	7				3				8							12	11			10	9	2	4					38
1	5				6					3	7			8								11			10	9	2	4					39
1	2		5		6	3					7			8								11			10	9		4	12				40
1	3		5		6	7								8								11			10	9	2	4					41
1	3		5		6	7					14			8	12							11			10	9	2	4					42
1	2		5		6	11				8	7										12				10	9	3	4	14				43
1			5		6	11					7			8	3										10	*9*	2	4			12	14	44
1	2		5		6	11				3	12			8							10				9			4			14	*7*	45
1	4		5		6	12				3	2			11						14	*10*				9						8	*7*	46

Coca-Cola Cup

Second Round	Charlton Ath (h)	1-3
	(a)	4-1
Third Round	Brighton & HA (a)	1-1
	(h)	4-1
Fourth Round	Derby Co (h)	2-1
Fifth Round	Millwall (h)	3-1
Semi-final	Bolton W (h)	2-1
	(a)	1-3

FA Cup

Third Round	Marlow (h)	2-0
Fourth Round	Watford (a)	0-1

TORQUAY UNITED 1994–95 *Back row (left to right):* Ellis Laight, Kevin Hodges, Nick Burton, Lee Barrow, Scott Stamps, Duane Darby, Richard Hancox, Paul Buckle.
Centre row: John James, Paul Trollope, Darren Moore, Tim Thornley, Ashley Bayes, Adrian Tucker, Chima Okorie, Adrian Foster, Bruce Stuckey.
Front row: Norman Medhurst, Tom Kelly, Gregory Goodridge, Don O'Riordan, Mike Bateson, Chris Curran, Ian Hathaway, Paul Compton.

Division 3 TORQUAY UNITED

Plainmoor Ground, Torquay, Devon TQ1 3PS. Telephone: (01803) 328666. Fax: (01803) 323976. Clubcall: 0891 121641.

Ground capacity: 6000.

Record attendance: 21,908 v Huddersfield T, FA Cup 4th rd, 29 January 1955.

Record receipts: £26,205 v Exeter C, Division 3, 1 January 1992.

Pitch measurements: 112yd × 74yd.

President: A. J. Boyce.

Chairman/Managing Director: M. Bateson. ***Directors:*** Mrs S. Bateson, M. Beer, M. Benney, I. Hayman, Miss H. Kindeleit, T. Lilley, B. Palk, W. Rogers, D. Turner.

Player-Manager: Don O'Riordan. ***Physio:*** Norman Medhurst.

Company Secretary: Miss H. Kindeleit.

Secretary General Manager: D. F. Turner. ***Lottery Administrators:*** C. Munslow and A. Sandford. ***Commercial Manager:*** D. Turner.

Year Formed: 1898. ***Turned Professional:*** 1921. ***Ltd Co.:*** 1921.

Previous Name: 1910, Torquay Town; 1921, Torquay United.

Nickname: 'The Gulls'.

Previous Grounds: 1898, Teignmouth Road; 1901, Torquay Recreation Ground; 1905, Cricket Field Road; 1907–10, Torquay Cricket Ground.

Foundation: The idea of establishing a Torquay club was agreed by old boys of Torquay College and Torbay College, while sitting in Princess Gardens listening to the band. A proper meeting was subsequently held at Tor Abbey Hotel at which officers were elected. This was in 1898 and the club's first competition was the Eastern League (later known as the East Devon League).

First Football League game: 27 August, 1927, Division 3(S), v Exeter C (h) D 1-1 – Millsom; Cook, Smith; Wellock, Wragg, Connor, Mackey, Turner (1), Jones, McGovern, Thomson.

Record League Victory: 9–0 v Swindon T, Division 3 (S), 8 March 1952 – George Webber; Topping, Ralph Calland; Brown, Eric Webber, Towers; Shaw (1), Marchant (1), Northcott (2), Collins (3), Edds (2).

Record Cup Victory: 7–1 v Northampton T, FA Cup, 1st rd, 14 November 1959 – Gill; Penford, Downs; Bettany, George Northcott, Rawson; Baxter, Cox, Tommy Northcott (1), Bond (3), Pym (3).

Record Defeat: 2–10 v Fulham, Division 3 (S), 7 September 1931 and v Luton T, Division 3 (S), 2 September 1933.

Most League Points (2 for a win): 60, Division 4, 1959–60.

Most League Points (3 for a win): 77, Division 4, 1987–88.

Most League Goals: 89, Division 3 (S), 1956–57.

Highest League Scorer in Season: Sammy Collins, 40, Division 3 (S), 1955–56.

Most League Goals in Total Aggregate: Sammy Collins, 204, 1948–58.

Most Capped Player: None.

Most League Appearances: Dennis Lewis, 443, 1947–59.

Record Transfer Fee Received: £180,000 from Manchester U for Lee Sharpe, May 1988.

Record Transfer Fee Paid: £60,000 to Dundee for Wes Saunders, July 1990.

Football League Record: 1927 Elected to Division 3 (S); 1958–60 Division 4; 1960–62 Division 3; 1962–66 Division 4; 1966–72 Division 3; 1972–91 Division 4; 1991– Division 3.

Honours: *Football League:* Division 3 best season: 4th, 1967–68; Division 3 (S) – Runners-up 1956–57; Division 4 – Promoted 1959–60 (3rd), 1965–66 (3rd), 1990–91 (Play-offs). *FA Cup:* best season: 4th rd, 1949, 1955, 1971, 1983, 1990. *Football League Cup:* never past 3rd rd. *Sherpa Van Trophy:* Runners-up 1989.

Colours: Yellow and navy striped shirts, navy shorts, yellow stockings. **Change colours:** Blue and white striped shirts, white shorts, blue stockings.

TORQUAY UNITED 1994–95 LEAGUE RECORD

Match No.	Date	Venue	Opponents	Result		H/T Score	Lg. Pos.	Goalscorers	Attendance
1	Aug 13	A	Colchester U	W	3-1	2-1	—	Okorie, Buckle, Trollope	3175
2	20	H	Carlisle U	D	1-1	0-0	3	Hancox	3506
3	27	A	Lincoln C	W	2-1	1-1	3	Hancox 2	3154
4	30	H	Northampton T	W	2-1	2-0	—	Okorie 2	3619
5	Sept 3	H	Fulham	W	2-1	2-1	2	Stamps, Okorie	4739
6	10	A	Darlington	L	1-2	1-1	2	Trollope	2161
7	13	A	Hereford U	D	1-1	0-1	—	Goodridge	2153
8	17	H	Colchester U	D	3-3	1-0	4	Trollope, Hancox, Darby	3390
9	24	H	Barnet	L	1-2	0-2	7	Newson (og)	3280
10	Oct 1	A	Chesterfield	L	0-1	0-0	10		2465
11	8	A	Gillingham	L	0-1	0-1	10		2439
12	15	H	Mansfield T	W	2-1	1-1	9	Trollope, Moore	2800
13	22	H	Rochdale	W	4-1	1-0	6	Goodridge 2, Hodges, Hathaway	2547
14	29	A	Doncaster R	L	0-3	0-0	7		2697
15	Nov 5	H	Scunthorpe U	D	1-1	1-0	8	Barrow	3036
16	19	A	Scarborough	D	1-1	0-1	8	Buckle	1241
17	26	H	Wigan Ath	D	0-0	0-0	8		2509
18	Dec 10	A	Carlisle U	L	0-1	0-1	9		5141
19	17	H	Lincoln C	W	2-1	1-0	8	Hancox, Sturridge	2004
20	26	A	Exeter C	W	2-1	0-1	8	Moore, O'Riordan	5538
21	27	H	Hartlepool U	D	2-2	1-1	9	Sturridge, Kelly	3172
22	Jan 2	H	Preston NE	W	1-0	1-0	9	Sturridge	3770
23	7	A	Rochdale	L	0-2	0-0	10		1636
24	14	H	Walsall	W	3-2	0-1	7	Okorie, Hathaway, Sturridge	2976
25	21	A	Scunthorpe U	L	2-3	2-2	9	Curran, Hancox	2229
26	28	H	Doncaster R	L	0-1	0-0	10		2852
27	Feb 4	A	Wigan Ath	D	1-1	1-0	11	Sturridge	1609
28	18	A	Walsall	L	0-1	0-0	12		3708
29	25	H	Chesterfield	D	3-3	1-1	11	Hathaway 2, Darby	3236
30	28	A	Bury	L	1-3	0-1	—	Darby	2241
31	Mar 4	A	Barnet	L	0-2	0-1	14		1816
32	7	H	Scarborough	W	2-1	1-1	—	Barrow, Byng	1492
33	11	H	Darlington	W	1-0	0-0	11	Kelly	2332
34	18	A	Northampton T	L	0-2	0-0	12		3832
35	25	A	Fulham	L	1-2	1-0	12	Hathaway	4941
36	Apr 1	H	Hereford U	L	0-1	0-1	12		2410
37	8	H	Bury	D	2-2	1-1	13	Curran, Moore	1969
38	15	A	Hartlepool U	D	1-1	0-0	14	Hancox	1770
39	18	H	Exeter C	D	0-0	0-0	—		4155
40	22	A	Preston NE	W	1-0	0-0	13	Hancox	9173
41	29	A	Mansfield T	D	2-2	1-1	13	Darby, Barrow	3216
42	May 6	H	Gillingham	W	3-1	1-0	13	Hancox, Kelly, Buckle	2638

Final League Position: 13

GOALSCORERS

League (54): Hancox 9, Hathaway 5, Okorie 5, Sturridge 5, Darby 4, Trollope 4, Barrow 3, Buckle 3, Goodridge 3, Kelly 3, Moore 3, Curran 2, Byng 1, Hodges 1, O'Riordan 1, Stamps 1, own goal 1.
Coca-Cola Cup (4): Hancox 3, Goodridge 1.
FA Cup (3): Hancox 1, Hathaway 1, Okorie 1.

Bayes A.J. 37	Hodges K. 15 + 13	Stamps S. 23 + 2	O'Riordan D.J. 23 + 1	Barrow L.A. 40	Curran C. 27	Trollope P.J. 18	Buckle P.J. 30 + 2	Hancox R. 29 + 7	Okorie C. 26 + 1	Goodridge G.R.S. 27 + 3	Hathaway I.A. 33 + 5	Darby D.A. 13 + 11	Moore D.M. 30	Kelly T.J. 32 + 1	Burton N.J. 7 + 1	Nicholson M. 1	Byng D.G. 6 + 1	Thornley T.J. — + 1	Davis K.G. 2	Winstone S.J. 1 + 1	Laight E.S. 4 + 6	Brass C.P. 7	Sturridge D.C. 10	Pettinger P.A. 3	Povey N.A. 5 + 3	Colcombe S. 10	Morah O. 2	Hawthorne M.D. 1 + 1	*Match No.*
1	2	3	4	5	6	7	8	*9*	10	11	12	14																	1
1	2	3	4	5	6	7	8	9	10	11	12																		2
1		3	4	5	6	7	8	9	10	11		12	2																3
1	2	3		5	6	7	*8*	9	10	11	4	12		14															4
1		3	*4*	5	6	7	8	9	10	11	14	12	2																5
1	12	3		2	6	7	8		10	11		9	5		4														6
1		3		2	6	7	8	*9*	10	11	12		5			4	14	15											7
	2	*3*		6		7	8	9	10	11	4	12	5		14				1										8
	14			2	6	7	8	9	10	11		12	5	3	*4*				1										9
1				2		7	12	8	10	11			5	3	6		*9*			4	14								10
1	12				6	7	8	9	10	*11*	4		5	3	2					14									11
1					6	7		9	10	11	12	8	5	3	4							2							12
1	8	3		6		7		12		11	10		5	4			9					2							13
1	8	3		6		7		12		11	10		5	4			9					2							14
1	12	3	14	6		7		9	8	*11*	10		5	4								2							15
1	9		4	6		7	8		11		10		5	3								2							16
1	9		*4*	6		7	8	11	12	14	10		5	3								2							17
1	12		4	6		7	8	11	9		10		5	3								2							18
1	12		4	6	2			7	8	11	10		5	3									9						19
1	12		4	6	2			7	8	11	10		5	3									9						20
	12		4	6	2			7	8	11	10		5	3									9	1					21
			4	6	2			7	8	11	10		5	3									9	1					22
	12		4	6	2			7	8	11	10		5	3									9	1					23
1	12		4	6	2			7	8	11	10			3									9		5				24
1	12	5		6	2		14	7		11	*10*	8		3									9			4			25
1	5			6	2		4	7		11	*10*	8									12		9		14	3			26
1	5		4	6			11		7	12	10	8		3									9			2			27
1		7	4	6			8		11	12	10			3	5								9			2			28
1	12	7	4	6			5	*9*	8	11	10	14		3												2			29
1		5	4	6			8	12	7		10	9		3	11											2			30
1	7		4	6			8	12		11	10	9	5	3							14					2			31
1			*4*	6			8	12			10	9	5	3			11				14				7	2			32
1		12	4	6			8	14			10	*9*	5	3			11								7	2			33
1		12	4	6	5		8	14			10	9		3			*11*								7	2			34
1		2	4	*6*	5		8				10	12	7	3							11						9	14	35
1		7	4	6	2		8	11			10	12	5	3							14						*9*		36
1	7	2		6	4		8		11		10	12	5	3							9				14				37
1	7	3		6	4		8	11			10		5								9							2	38
1	7	2		6	4		8	5		11	10	12		3							9								39
1		2		6	4		8	7		11	10	9	5	3															40
1	11	2		6	4		8	7			*10*	9	5	3							12				14				41
1	12	2		6	4		8	7			10	9	5	3											11				42

Coca-Cola Cup		
First Round	Cardiff C (a)	0-1
	(h)	4-2
Second Round	Wimbledon (a)	0-2
	(h)	0-1

FA Cup		
First Round	Kidderminster H (a)	1-1
	(h)	1-0
Second Round	Enfield (a)	1-1
	(h)	0-1

TOTTENHAM HOTSPUR 1994–95 *Back row (left to right):* Darren Anderton, Jason Dozzell, Kevin Scott, Ian Walker, Erik Thorstvedt, Chris Day, Sol Campbell, Jason Cundy, Stuart Nethercott.
Centre row: Pat Jennings (Goalkeeping Coach), Danny Hill, Colin Calderwood, Justin Edinburgh, Jurgen Klinsmann, David Howells, Ilie Dumitrescu, Paul Mahorn, Tony Lenaghan (Physio), Roy Reyland (Kit Manager).
Front row: Steve Perryman (Assistant Manager), Micky Hazard, David Kerslake, Nick Barmby, Gary Mabbutt, Ossie Ardiles, Teddy Sheringham, Dean Austin, Steve Carr, Darren Caskey, Chris Hughton (Reserve Team Manager).
(Photograph: Action Images)

FA Premiership **TOTTENHAM HOTSPUR**

748 High Rd, Tottenham, London N17 0AP. Telephone: (0181) 365 5000. Fax: (0181) 365 5005. Commercial Dept: (0181) 365 5010. Ticketline: 0891 100515. Telephone Bookings: (0171) 396 4567. Ticket Office: (0181) 365 5050. Spurs Line: 0891 100500. Members Ticketline: (0181) 365 5100. Additional Recorded Information: (0181) 880 3377.

Ground capacity: 33,147.

Record attendance: 75,038 v Sunderland, FA Cup 6th rd, 5 March 1938.

Record receipts: £336,702 v Manchester U, Division 1, 28 September 1991.

Pitch measurements: 110yd × 73yd.

Directors: A. M. Sugar (Chairman), C. Littner (Chief Executive), C. T. Sandy (Finance). ***Non-Executive:*** A. G. Berry (Deputy Chairman), D. A. Alexiou, I. Yawetz.

President: W. E. Nicholson OBE. ***Vice-President:*** N. Soloman.

Manager: Gerry Francis. ***Assistant Manager:*** Roger Cross. ***Coach:*** Chris Hughton. ***Physio:*** Tony Lenaghan. ***Secretary:*** Peter Barnes. ***Commercial Manager:*** Mike Rollo. ***PRO:*** John Fennelly.

Year Formed: 1882. ***Turned Professional:*** 1895. ***Ltd Co.:*** 1898.

Club Nickname: 'Spurs'.

Previous Name: 1882–85, Hotspur Football Club.

Previous Grounds: 1882, Tottenham Marshes; 1885, Northumberland Park; 1898, White Hart Lane.

Foundation: The Hotspur Football Club was formed from an older cricket club in 1882. Most of the founders were old boys St. John's Presbyterian School and Tottenham Grammar School. The Casey brothers were well to the fore as the family provided the club's first goalposts (painted blue and white) and their first ball. They soon adopted the local YMCA as their meeing place, but after a couple of moves settled at the Red House, which is still their headquarters, although now known simply as 748 High Road.

First Football League game: 1 September, 1908, Division 2, v Wolverhampton W (h) W 3-0 – Hewitson; Coquet, Burton; Morris (1), Steel (D), Darnell; Walton, Woodward (2), Macfarlane, R. Steel, Middlemiss.

Record League Victory: 9–0 v Bristol R, Division 2, 22 October 1977 – Davies; Naylor, Holmes, Hoddle (1), McAllister, Perryman, Pratt, McNab, Morris (3), Lee (4), Taylor (1).

Record Cup Victory: 13–2 v Crewe Alex, FA Cup, 4th rd (replay), 3 February 1960 – Brown; Hills, Henry; Blanchflower, Norman, Mackay; White, Harmer (1), Smith (4), Allen (5), Jones (3 incl. 1p).

Record Defeat: 0–7 v Liverpool, Division 1, 2 September 1978.

Most League Points (2 for a win): 70, Division 2, 1919–20.

Most League Points (3 for a win): 77, Division 1, 1984–85.

Most League Goals: 115, Division 1, 1960–61.

Highest League Scorer in Season: Jimmy Greaves, 37, Division 1, 1962–63.

Most League Goals in Total Aggregate: Jimmy Greaves, 220, 1961–70.

Most Capped Player: Pat Jennings, 74 (119), Northern Ireland.

Most League Appearances: Steve Perryman, 655, 1969–86.

Record Transfer Fee Received: £5,500,000 from Lazio for Paul Gascoigne, May 1992.

Record Transfer Fee Paid: £4,500,000 to Crystal Palace for Chris Armstrong, June 1995.

Football League Record: 1908 Elected to Division 2; 1909–15 Division 1; 1919–20 Division 2; 1920–28 Division 1; 1928–33 Division 2; 1933–35 Division 1; 1935–50 Division 2; 1950–77 Division 1; 1977–78 Division 2; 1978–92 Division 1; 1992– FA Premier League.

Honours: *Football League:* Division 1 – Champions 1950–51, 1960–61; Runners-up 1921–22, 1951–52, 1956–57, 1962–63; Division 2 – Champions 1919–20, 1949–50; Runners-up 1908–09, 1932–33; Promoted 1977–78 (3rd). *FA Cup:* Winners 1901 (as non-League club), 1921, 1961, 1962, 1967, 1981, 1982, 1991 (8 wins stands as the record); Runners-up 1987. *Football League Cup:* Winners 1971, 1973; Runners-up 1982. **European Competitions:** *European Cup:* 1961–62. *European Cup-Winners' Cup:* 1962–63 (winners), 1963–64, 1967–68, 1981–82 (runners-up), 1982–83, 1991–92. *UEFA Cup:* 1971–72 (winners), 1972–73, 1973–74 (runners-up), 1983–84 (winners), 1984–85.

Colours: White shirts, navy blue shorts, white stockings. **Change colours:** Navy/purple.

TOTTENHAM HOTSPUR 1994–95 LEAGUE RECORD

Match No.	Date	Venue	Opponents	Result		H/T Score	Lg. Pos.	Goalscorers	Attendance
1	Aug 20	A	Sheffield W	W	4-3	2-0	—	Sheringham, Anderton, Barmby, Klinsmann	34,051
2	24	H	Everton	W	2-1	2-0	—	Klinsmann 2	24,553
3	27	H	Manchester U	L	0-1	0-0	8		24,502
4	30	A	Ipswich T	W	3-1	3-0	—	Klinsmann 2, Dumitrescu	22,430
5	Sept 12	H	Southampton	L	1-2	1-0	—	Klinsmann	22,387
6	17	A	Leicester C	L	1-3	0-1	9	Klinsmann	21,300
7	24	H	Nottingham F	L	1-4	1-1	12	Dumitrescu	24,558
8	Oct 1	A	Wimbledon	W	2-1	1-1	10	Sheringham, Popescu	16,802
9	8	H	QPR	D	1-1	0-1	10	Barmby	25,799
10	15	A	Leeds U	D	1-1	1-0	12	Sheringham	39,362
11	22	A	Manchester C	L	2-5	1-3	13	Dumitrescu 2 (1 pen)	25,473
12	29	H	West Ham U	W	3-1	1-1	11	Klinsmann, Sheringham, Barmby	26,271
13	Nov 5	A	Blackburn R	L	0-2	0-1	13		26,933
14	19	H	Aston Villa	L	3-4	1-3	15	Sheringham, Klinsmann (pen), Bosnich (og)	26,899
15	23	H	Chelsea	D	0-0	0-0	—		27,037
16	26	A	Liverpool	D	1-1	0-1	14	Ruddock (og)	35,007
17	Dec 3	H	Newcastle U	W	4-2	2-2	11	Sheringham 3, Popescu	28,002
18	10	H	Sheffield W	W	3-1	0-1	10	Barmby, Klinsmann, Calderwood	25,912
19	17	A	Everton	D	0-0	0-0	10		32,813
20	26	A	Norwich C	W	2-0	1-0	8	Barmby, Sheringham	21,814
21	27	H	Crystal Palace	D	0-0	0-0	—		27,730
22	31	A	Coventry C	W	4-0	1-0	6	Darby (og), Barmby, Anderton, Sheringham	19,965
23	Jan 2	H	Arsenal	W	1-0	1-0	6	Popescu	28,747
24	14	A	West Ham U	W	2-1	0-1	6	Sheringham, Klinsmann	24,578
25	25	A	Aston Villa	L	0-1	0-1	—		40,017
26	Feb 5	H	Blackburn R	W	3-1	1-0	6	Klinsmann, Anderton, Barmby	28,124
27	11	A	Chelsea	D	1-1	1-0	6	Sheringham	30,812
28	25	H	Wimbledon	L	1-2	0-1	7	Klinsmann	27,258
29	Mar 4	A	Nottingham F	D	2-2	0-0	6	Sheringham, Calderwood	28,711
30	8	H	Ipswich T	W	3-0	2-0	—	Klinsmann, Barmby, Youds (og)	24,930
31	15	A	Manchester U	D	0-0	0-0	—		43,802
32	18	H	Leicester C	W	1-0	0-0	7	Klinsmann	30,851
33	22	H	Liverpool	D	0-0	0-0	—		31,988
34	Apr 2	A	Southampton	L	3-4	2-2	7	Sheringham 2, Klinsmann	15,105
35	11	H	Manchester C	W	2-1	0-0	—	Howells, Klinsmann	27,410
36	14	A	Crystal Palace	D	1-1	0-1	—	Klinsmann	18,068
37	17	H	Norwich C	W	1-0	1-0	7	Sheringham	32,304
38	29	A	Arsenal	D	1-1	0-0	7	Klinsmann	38,377
39	May 3	A	Newcastle U	D	3-3	3-2	—	Barmby, Klinsmann, Anderton	35,603
40	6	A	QPR	L	1-2	1-0	7	Sheringham	18,637
41	9	H	Coventry C	L	1-3	0-1	—	Anderton	24,930
42	14	H	Leeds U	D	1-1	1-0	7	Sheringham	33,040

Final League Position: 7

GOALSCORERS

League (66): Klinsmann 20 (1 pen), Sheringham 18, Barmby 9, Anderton 5, Dumitrescu 4 (1 pen), Popescu 3, Calderwood 2, Howells 1, own goals 4.
Coca-Cola Cup (8): Klinsmann 4, Anderton 1, Barmby 1, Dumitrescu 1, Sheringham 1.
FA Cup (17): Klinsmann 5 (2 pens), Rosenthal 4, Sheringham 4, Anderton 1, Barmby 1, Nethercott 1, own goal 1.

Walker I.M. 41	Kerslake D. 16 + 2	Edinburgh J.C. 29 + 2	Nethercott S. 8 + 9	Calderwood C. 35 + 1	Campbell S. 29 + 1	Anderton D.R. 37	Barmby N.J. 37 + 1	Klinsmann J. 41	Sheringham E.P. 41 + 1	Dumitrescu I. 11 + 2	Hazard M. 2 + 9	Mabbutt G.V. 33 + 3	Popescu G. 23	Hill D.R.L. 1 + 2	Scott K.W. 4	Dozzell J.A.W. 6 + 1	Austin D.B. 23 + 1	Rosenthal R. 14 + 6	Thorstvedt E. 1	Howells D. 26	Caskey D.M. 1 + 3	McMahon G.J. 2	Turner A.P. 1	Match No.
1	2	3	4	5	*6*	7	8	9	10	11	12	14												1
1	2	3	*4*	5	6	7	8	9	10	11	12	14												2
1	2	3	4	5	6	7	8	9	10	11	12													3
1	2	3	4	5	6	7	8	9	10	11		12												4
1	2	3	4	5	6	7	8	9	10	11	12													5
1	2	3	4	5	6	7	8	9	10	11	12													6
1	2	3			5	7		9	10	11	8	6	4	12										7
1	2					7		9	10	11	12	6	4		5	8	3							8
1	2	3		4	6		8	9	10		12			11	5	7		14						9
1	2	3		12	6		8	9	10	11			4		5	7								10
1	2	3			6		8	9	10	11	12		4		5	7								11
	2	3			5		8	9	12	11	7	6	4	14		10			1					12
1	2	3			5		8	9	10		12	6	4			*11*		14		7				13
1	*2*		14	5	3	7	12	9	10			6	4							11	8			14
1				5	3	7	8	9	10	12		6	4				2			11				15
1				5	3	7	8	9	10	12		6	4				2			11				16
1		12		5	3	7	8	9	10			6	4				2			11				17
1				5	3	7	8	9	10			6					2	11		4				18
1				5	3	7	8		10			6	4				2	9		11				19
1			12	5	3	7	8	9	10			6	4				2			11				20
1			12	5	3	7	*8*	9	10			6	4				2	14		11				21
1			14	5	3	7	8	9	10			6	*4*				2	12		11				22
1			12	5	3	7		9	10			6	4				2	11		8				23
1		12		5	3	7	8	9	10			6	4				2			11				24
1		3		5	11	7	8	9	10			6	4				2				12			25
1		3	12	5	2	7	8	9	10			6	4							11				26
1		3		5	2	7	8	9	10			6	4							11				27
1		3		5	2	7	8	9	10			6	*4*				12	14		11				28
1		3		5		7	8	9	10			6					2	11		4				29
1		3		5		7	8	9	10			6					2	11		4	12			30
1		3		5		7	8	9	10			6					2	11		4				31
1		3		5		7	8	9	10			6					2	11		4				32
1	12	3	4			7	8	9	10			6					2	11		5				33
1	3			5		7	8	9	10			6					2	11		4				34
1		3	12	5		7	8	9	10			6	4				2	14		*11*				35
1		3		5		7	8	9	10			6	4				2	11						36
1		3		5		7	8	9	10			6	4				2	11			12			37
1		3		5		7	8	9	10			6					2	11		4				38
1		3		5	12	7	8	9	10			6					2	11		4				39
1	12	3	14	5	2	7	*8*	9	10			6						11		4				40
1		3	12	5	2	7	8	9	10			6								11		4		41
1	2	3	4	5		7		9	10			6				12						11	8	42

Coca-Cola Cup

Second Round	Watford (a)	6-3
	(h)	2-3
Third Round	Notts Co (a)	0-3

FA Cup

Third Round	Altrincham (h)	3-0
Fourth Round	Sunderland (a)	4-1
Fifth Round	Southampton (h)	1-1
	(a)	6-2
Sixth Round	Liverpool (a)	2-1
Semi-final	Everton at Elland Road	1-4

TRANMERE ROVERS 1994–95 *Back row (left to right):* Kenny Jones (Trainer), Warwick Rimmer (Youth Development Officer), Alan Morgan, Dave Higgins, Dave Rogers, Dave Challinor, Gary Jones, Graham Branch, John McGreal, Ged Brannan, Shaun Garnett, Kenny Irons, John Morrissey, Les Parry (Physio), Ray Mathias (Reserve Team Coach).
Centre row: Harry McNally (Chief Scout), Norman Wilson (Secretary), Ian Moore, Gavin Allen, Chris Malkin, Martin Jones, Eric Nixon, Danny Coyne, Mick Edwards, Jonathan Kenworthy, Ian Nolan, Ronnie Moore (Coach), F. D. Corfe (Chairman).
Front row: Mark Proctor, Tony Thomas, Ian Muir, Steve Mungall, John King (Manager), John Aldridge, Phil Johnson, Liam O'Brien, Pat Nevin.

Division 1 **TRANMERE ROVERS**

Prenton Park, Prenton Road West, Birkenhead L42 9PN. Telephone: (0151) 608 3677. Fax: (0151) 608 4385. Commercial: (0151) 608 0371. Valley Road Training Centre: (0151) 652 2578. Shop: (0151) 608 0438. Ticket Office: (0151) 609 0137.

Ground capacity: 16,789 (all seated).

Record attendance: 24,424 v Stoke C, FA Cup 4th rd, 5 February 1972.

Record receipts: £114,150 v Aston Villa, Coca-Cola Cup semi-final 16 February 1994.

Pitch measurements: 110yd × 70yd.

President: H. B. Thomas.

Chairman and Chief Executive: F. D. Corfe.

Directors: Norman Wilson FAAI, A. J. Adams BDS, G. E. H. Jones LLB, F. J. Williams, J. J. Holsgrove FCA.

Secretary: Norman Wilson FAAI. ***Commercial Manager:*** Janet Ratcliffe.

Manager: John King. ***Trainer:*** Kenny Jones.

Youth Development Officer: Warwick Rimmer.

Coach: Ronnie Moore. ***Physio:*** Les Parry.

Year Formed: 1884. ***Turned Professional:*** 1912. ***Ltd Co.:*** 1920.

Previous Name: Belmont AFC, 1884–85.

Club Nickname: 'The Rovers'.

Previous Grounds: 1884, Steeles Field; 1887, Ravenshaws Field/Old Prenton Park; 1912, Prenton Park.

Foundation: Formed in 1884 as Belmont they adopted their present title the following year and eventually joined their first league, the West Lancashire League in 1889–90, the same year as their first success in the Wirral Challenge Cup. The club almost folded in 1899–1900 when all the players left en bloc to join a rival club, but they survived the crisis and went from strength to strength winning the 'Combination' title in 1907–08 and the Lancashire Combination in 1913–14. They joined the Football League in 1921 from the Central League.

First Football League game: 27 August 1921, Division 3(N), v Crewe Alex (h) W 4-1 – Bradshaw; Grainger, Stuart (1); Campbell, Milnes (1), Heslop; Moreton, Groves (1), Hyam, Ford (1), Hughes.

Record League Victory: 13–4 v Oldham Ath, Division 3 (N), 26 December 1935 – Gray; Platt, Fairhurst; McLaren, Newton, Spencer; Eden, MacDonald (1), Bell (9), Woodward (2), Urmson (1).

Record Cup Victory: 13–0 v Oswestry U, FA Cup 2nd pr rd, 10 October 1914 – Ashcroft; Stevenson, Bullough, Hancock, Taylor, Holden (1), Moreton (1), Cunningham (2), Smith (5), Leck (3), Gould (1).

Record Defeat: 1–9 v Tottenham H, FA Cup 3rd rd (replay), 14 January 1953.

Most League Points (2 for a win): 60, Division 4, 1964–65.

Most League Points (3 for a win): 80, Division 4, 1988–89 and Division 3, 1989–90.

Most League Goals: 111, Division 3 (N), 1930–31.

Highest League Scorer in Season: Bunny Bell, 35, Division 3 (N), 1933–34.

Most League Goals in Total Aggregate: Ian Muir, 141, 1985–95.

Most Capped Player: John Aldridge, 25 (64), Republic of Ireland.

Most League Appearances: Harold Bell, 595, 1946–64 (incl. League record 401 consecutive appearances).

Record Transfer Fee Received: £1,500,000 from Sheffield W for Ian Nolan, August 1994.

Record Transfer Fee Paid: £350,000 to Celtic for Tommy Coyne, March 1993 and £350,000 to Rangers for Gary Stevens, October 1994.

Football League Record: 1921 Original Member of Division 3 (N): 1938–39 Division 2; 1946–58 Division 3 (N); 1958–61 Division 3; 1961–67 Division 4; 1967–75 Division 3; 1975–76 Division 4; 1976–79 Division 3; 1979–89 Division 4; 1989–91 Division 3; 1991–92 Division 2; 1992– Division 1.

Honours: *Football League* Division 1 best season: 4th, 1992–93; Division 3 (N) – Champions 1937–38; Promotion to 3rd Division: 1966–67, 1975–76; Division 4 – Runners-up 1988–89. *FA Cup:* best season: 5th rd, 1968. *Football League Cup:* best season: semi-final 1994. *Welsh Cup:* Winners 1935; Runners-up 1934. *Leyland Daf Cup:* Winners 1990; Runners-up 1991.

Colours: All white. **Change colours:** Yellow and black striped shirts, black shorts, black stockings.

TRANMERE ROVERS 1994–95 LEAGUE RECORD

Match No.	Date		Venue	Opponents	Result		H/T Score	Lg. Pos.	Goalscorers	Attendance
1	Aug	13	A	Stoke C	L	0-1	0-0	—		15,915
2		20	H	Swindon T	W	3-2	1-2	11	Aldridge 2, Nevin	8482
3		27	A	Grimsby T	L	1-3	0-2	16	Aldridge (pen)	4087
4		30	H	Luton T	W	4-2	0-0	—	Aldridge 3 (1 pen), Malkin	5480
5	Sept	3	H	Sheffield U	W	2-1	2-0	4	Malkin, Aldridge	7253
6		10	A	Wolverhampton W	L	0-2	0-1	9		27,030
7		14	A	Portsmouth	D	1-1	0-0	—	O'Brien	6383
8		17	H	Millwall	W	3-1	1-1	5	Malkin 2, Aldridge	6243
9		24	H	Sunderland	W	1-0	0-0	4	Malkin	7500
10	Oct	1	A	Burnley	D	1-1	1-0	4	Aldridge	12,427
11		8	A	Middlesbrough	W	1-0	0-0	4	Aldridge	18,497
12		15	H	WBA	W	3-1	2-1	3	Aldridge 3	7397
13		22	A	Watford	L	0-2	0-1	4		6987
14		29	H	Port Vale	D	1-1	0-0	3	Morrissey	6972
15	Nov	1	H	Barnsley	W	6-1	2-0	—	Aldridge 4, Malkin 2	5592
16		6	A	Oldham Ath	D	0-0	0-0	3		6475
17		19	H	Charlton Ath	D	1-1	0-1	4	Malkin	7567
18		26	A	Reading	W	3-1	2-0	3	Brannan, Muir 2	7887
19	Dec	3	H	Watford	W	2-1	0-0	2	Irons, Malkin	7301
20		6	A	Notts Co	L	0-1	0-0	—		4703
21		10	A	Swindon T	D	2-2	1-2	3	Mungall, Stevens	8608
22		17	H	Stoke C	L	0-1	0-0	4		7601
23		26	H	Derby Co	W	3-1	1-0	2	Malkin 2, Jones	11,581
24		27	A	Bolton W	L	0-1	0-1	3		16,782
25		31	H	Bristol C	W	2-0	2-0	3	Jones, Irons	7439
26	Jan	2	A	Southend U	D	0-0	0-0	3		5195
27		15	A	Port Vale	L	0-2	0-1	4		7944
28		22	H	Oldham Ath	W	3-1	1-1	4	Malkin, Muir, Brannan	5581
29	Feb	4	H	Notts Co	W	3-2	1-0	2	Malkin 2, Morrissey	6105
30		11	A	Barnsley	D	2-2	1-1	3	Jones, Muir	5506
31		18	H	Reading	W	1-0	0-0	2	Muir	8744
32		21	A	Charlton Ath	W	1-0	0-0	—	Nevin	11,860
33		25	H	Burnley	W	4-1	1-0	1	Muir 2, Nevin, Aldridge	9909
34	Mar	5	A	Sunderland	W	1-0	0-0	1	Garnett	12,043
35		7	A	Sheffield U	L	0-2	0-1	—		14,127
36		11	H	Grimsby T	W	2-0	2-0	1	Morrissey, Aldridge (pen)	15,810
37		18	A	Luton T	L	0-2	0-1	1		6660
38		25	A	Millwall	L	1-2	0-0	3	Malkin	7470
39	Apr	1	H	Portsmouth	W	4-2	3-1	2	Malkin, Aldridge 2, Irons	8722
40		8	A	Bristol C	W	1-0	1-0	2	Aldridge (pen)	6723
41		14	H	Bolton W	W	1-0	1-0	—	Nevin	14,959
42		17	A	Derby Co	L	0-5	0-2	3		13,957
43		21	H	Southend U	L	0-2	0-2	—		9971
44		30	A	WBA	L	1-5	0-1	5	Aldridge (pen)	17,486
45	May	3	H	Wolverhampton W	D	1-1	1-0	—	Aldridge	12,306
46		7	H	Middlesbrough	D	1-1	1-0	5	Irons	16,377

Final League Position: 5

GOALSCORERS

League (67): Aldridge 24 (5 pens), Malkin 16, Muir 7, Irons 4, Nevin 4, Jones 3, Morrissey 3, Brannan 2, Garnett 1, Mungall 1, O'Brien 1, Stevens 1.
Coca-Cola Cup (4): Aldridge 1, Brannan 1, Irons 1, Nevin 1.
FA Cup (5): Muir 3, Malkin 1, O'Brien 1.

Coyne D. 5	Higgins D.A. 16	Mungall S.H. 19 + 7	Brannan G.D. 37 + 4	Garnett S.M. 34	O'Brien L.F. 38	Morrissey J.J. 34 + 2	Aldridge J.W. 31 + 2	Irons K. 37 + 1	Nevin P.K.F. 44	Thomas T. 26	Muir I.J. 12 + 7	Malkin C.G. 42 + 1	McGreal J. 42 + 1	Kenworthy J.R. 3 + 3	Jones G.S. 6 + 13	Nixon E.W. 41	Edwards M. 2 + 1	Stevens M.G. 37	Branch G. — + 1	Moore I.R. — + 1	Match No.
1	2	3	4	5	6	7	8	9	10	11	12										1
1	2	14	3	5	6	7	8	4	10	*11*	12	9									2
1	2	11	3	*5*	6	7	8	4	10		12	9	14								3
1	2		3		6	7	8	4	10	11		9	5								4
1		12	3	5	6	7	8	4		11		9	2	10	14						5
			3	5	6	7	8	4	10	11	12	9	2			1					6
		12	3	5	6		8	4	10	11		9	2			1	7				7
		12	3	5	*6*	7	8	4	10	11		9	2		14	1					8
		3	10	5	6	7	8		11			9	4			1		2			9
		3	10	5	6	7	8		11			9	4			1		2			10
		3	10	5	6	7	8		11			9	4			1		2			11
		3	10	5	6	7	8		11			9	4			1		2			12
		3	10	5	6	12	8		11			9	4			1	7	2			13
		3	10	5		7	8	6	11			9	4			1		2			14
	5	3	10			7	8	6	11			9	4			1		2			15
		3	10	5		7		6	11		8	9	4		12	1		2			16
		3	10	5		7		6	11		8	9	4			1		2			17
		3	10	5		7		6	11		8	9	4			1		2			18
		3	10	5		7	8	6	11			9	4			1		2			19
	7	*3*	10	5			8	6	11		12	9	4			1	14	2			20
	4	3	10	5		7	8	6	11		12	9				1		2			21
	5		3		10	7	8	6		11		9	4			1		2	12		22
	5	12			6	7		3	10	11		9	4		8	1		2			23
		5			6	7		3	10	11		9	4		8	1		2			24
	5				6	7		3	10	11		9	4		8	1		2			25
	5	12	3		6	7		10	11			9	4		8	1		2			26
	5		12		6	7		10	11	3	8	9	4			1		2			27
	2	12	5		6	7		10	11	3	8	9	4			1					28
			10	5	6	7			11	3	8	9	4			1		2			29
			10	5	6			7	11	3	8	9	4		12	1		2			30
			10	5	6	7			11	3	8	9	4			1		2			31
			10	5	6	12		7	11	3	8	*9*	4		14	1		2			32
			10	5	6	7	12		11	3	8	9	4			1		2			33
			10	5	6	7	12	14	11	3	8	9	4			1		2			34
			3	5	6	7	8	9	*11*		10	12	4		14	1		2			35
			3	5	6	7	8	10	11		12	9	4			1		2			36
			10	5	6		8	7	11	3		9	4	14	12	1		2			37
	5	3			6		8	10	11			9	4	7	12	1		2			38
	5	3			6	7	8	10	11			*9*	4	12	14	1		2			39
		3	7	5	6		8	10	11				4		9	1		2			40
			12	5	6	7	8	10	11	3		9	4		14	1		2			41
			7	5	6		8	10	11	3		9	4		12	1		2			42
			12	5	6	7	8	10	11	3		*9*	4		14	1		2			43
	5		12		6		8	10	*11*	3			4	7	9	1		2		14	44
			7	5	6		8	10	11	3		9	4			1		2			45
			7	*5*	6		8	10	11	3		9	4	12	14	1		2			46

Coca-Cola Cup

Second Round	Brentford (h)	1-0
	(a)	0-0
Third Round	Norwich C (h)	1-1
	(a)	2-4

FA Cup

Third Round	Bury (a)	2-2
	(h)	3-0
Fourth Round	Wimbledon (h)	0-2

WALSALL 1994–95 *Back row (left to right):* Stuart Watkiss, Dean Peer, Charlie Ntamark, Charlie Palmer, James Walker, Trevor Wood, John Keister, David Mehew, Scott Houghton, Colin Gibson.
Front row: Wayne Evans, Stuart Ryder, Richard Knight, Chris Marsh, Kevin Wilson, Chris Nicholl (Manager), Martin O'Connor, James Rollo, Martin Butler, Kyle Lightbourne, Darren Rogers.

Division 2 **WALSALL**

Bescot Stadium, Bescot Cresent, Walsall WS1 4SA. Telephone: (01922) 22791. Fax: (01922) 613202. Commercial Dept: (01922) 30696. Saddlers Hotline: 0891 555800.

Ground capacity: 9000.

Record attendance: 10,628 B International, England v Switzerland, 20 May 1991.

Record receipts: £98,828 v Leeds U, FA Cup 3rd rd, 7th January 1995.

Pitch measurements: 110yd × 73yd.

Chairman: J. W. Bonsor.

Directors: M. N. Lloyd, K. R. Whalley, C. Welch, R. M. Tisdale.

Manager: Chris Nicholl. ***General Manager:*** Paul Taylor. ***Physio:*** Tom Bradley. ***Coach:*** Kevin Wilson.

Secretary/Commercial Manager: Roy Whalley.

Year Formed: 1888. ***Turned Professional:*** 1888. ***Ltd Co.:*** 1921.

Club Nickname: 'The Saddlers'.

Previous Names: Walsall Swifts (founded 1877) and Walsall Town (founded 1879) amalgamated in 1888 and were known as Walsall Town Swifts until 1895.

Previous Grounds: Fellows Park to 1990.

Foundation: Two of the leading clubs around Walsall in the 1880s were Walsall Swifts (formed 1877) and Walsall Town (formed 1879). The Swifts were winners of the Birmingham Senior Cup in 1881, while the Town reached the 4th round (5th round modern equivalent) of the FA Cup in 1883. These clubs amalgamated as Walsall Town Swifts in 1888, becoming simply Walsall in 1895.

First Football League game: 3 September, 1892, Division 2, v Darwen (h) L 1-2 – Hawkins; Withington, Pinches; Robinson, Whitrick, Forsyth; Marshall, Holmes, Turner, Gray (1), Pangbourn.

Record League Victory: 10–0 v Darwen, Division 2, 4 March 1899 – Tennent; E. Peers (1), Davies; Hickinbotham, Jenkyns, Taggart; Dean (3), Vail (2), Aston (4), Martin, Griffin.

Record Cup Victory: 6–1 v Leytonstone (away), FA Cup, 1st rd, 30 November 1946 – Lewis; Netley, Skidmore; Crutchley, Foulkes, Newman; Maund (1), Talbot, Darby (1), Wilshaw (2), Davies (2). 6–1 v Margate, FA Cup, 1st rd (replay), 24 November 1955 – Davies; Haddington, Vinall; Dorman, McPherson, Crook; Morris, Walsh (3), Richards (2), McLaren (1), Moore.

Record Defeat: 0–12 v Small Heath, 17 December 1892 and v Darwen, 26 December 1896, both Division 2.

Most League Points (2 for a win): 65, Division 4, 1959–60.

Most League Points (3 for a win): 82, Division 3, 1987–88.

Most League Goals: 102, Division 4, 1959–60.

Highest League Scorer in Season: Gilbert Alsop, 40, Division 3 (N), 1933–34 and 1934–35.

Most League Goals in Total Aggregate: Tony Richards, 184, 1954–63, and Colin Taylor, 184, 1958–63, 1964–68, 1969–73.

Most Capped Player: Mick Kearns, 15 (18), Republic of Ireland.

Most League Appearances: Colin Harrison, 467, 1964–82.

Record Transfer Fee Received: £600,000 from West Ham U for David Kelly, July 1988.

Record Transfer Fee Paid: £175,000 to Birmingham C for Alan Buckley, June 1979.

Football League Record: 1892 Elected to Division 2; 1895 Failed re-election; 1896–1901 Division 2; 1901 Failed re-election; 1921 Original Member of Division 3 (N); 1927–31 Division 3 (S); 1931–36 Division 3 (N); 1936–58 Division 3 (S); 1958–60 Division 4; 1960–61 Division 3; 1961–63 Division 2; 1963–79 Division 3; 1979–80 Division 4; 1980–88 Division 3; 1988–89 Division 2; 1989–90 Division 3; 1990–92 Division 4; 1992–95 Division 3; 1995– Division 2.

Honours: *Football League:* Division 2 best season: 6th, 1898–99; Division 3 – Runners-up 1960–61, 1994–95; Division 4 – Champions 1959–60; Runners-up 1979–80. *FA Cup:* best season: 5th rd, 1939, 1975, 1978, and last 16 1889. *Football League Cup:* Semi-final 1984.

Colours: Red shirts, black shorts, red stockings. **Change colours:** Claret and blue shirts, blue shorts, blue stockings.

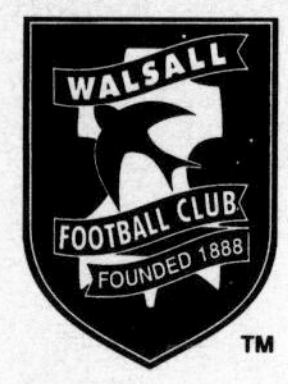

WALSALL 1994–95 LEAGUE RECORD

Match No.	Date		Venue	Opponents	Result		H/T Score	Lg. Pos.	Goalscorers	Attendance
1	Aug	13	A	Fulham	D	1-1	1-0	—	Lightbourne	5308
2		20	H	Lincoln C	W	2-1	1-0	7	O'Connor (pen), Marsh	3813
3		27	A	Hereford U	D	0-0	0-0	10		3004
4		30	H	Carlisle U	L	1-2	1-1	—	Marsh	3610
5	Sept	3	H	Northampton T	D	1-1	1-1	12	Lightbourne	4249
6		10	A	Chesterfield	D	0-0	0-0	13		3027
7		13	A	Colchester U	L	2-3	1-0	—	Lightbourne, Houghton	2239
8		17	H	Fulham	W	5-1	3-0	11	Marsh 2, Lightbourne 3	3378
9		24	H	Gillingham	W	2-1	1-0	10	Wilson, Ryder	3654
10	Oct	1	A	Preston NE	W	2-1	0-1	7	O'Connor, Marsh	7852
11		8	H	Scarborough	W	4-1	1-1	5	O'Connor 2 (2 pens), Ryder, Houghton	3601
12		15	A	Scunthorpe U	W	1-0	1-0	3	Wilson	3609
13		22	A	Hartlepool U	D	1-1	1-1	4	Lightbourne	1704
14		29	H	Bury	L	0-1	0-0	5		5255
15	Nov	5	A	Darlington	D	2-2	0-1	5	Gregan (og), Marsh	2186
16		19	H	Exeter C	W	1-0	1-0	5	O'Connor	3629
17		26	A	Mansfield T	W	3-1	2-0	5	Wilson, O'Connor, Ntamark	2733
18	Dec	10	A	Lincoln	D	1-1	1-1	5	Wilson	2717
19		17	H	Hereford U	W	4-3	1-2	5	Houghton, Lightbourne 2, Ryder	3652
20		26	H	Barnet	W	4-0	2-0	3	Palmer, Wilson, Lightbourne 2	5392
21		27	A	Rochdale	W	2-0	1-0	3	Wilson (pen), Lightbourne	2438
22		31	H	Doncaster R	W	1-0	0-0	2	Marsh	4561
23	Jan	14	A	Torquay U	L	2-3	1-0	2	Houghton, Marsh	2976
24	Feb	4	H	Mansfield T	W	1-0	0-0	2	Wilson	4369
25		18	H	Torquay U	W	1-0	0-0	3	Ryder	3708
26		28	H	Preston NE	D	2-2	1-1	—	Marsh, Wilson	4492
27	Mar	4	A	Gillingham	W	3-1	0-0	3	Lightbourne 2, Houghton	3669
28		7	H	Hartlepool U	W	4-1	1-1	—	O'Connor, Houghton 2, Wilson	3314
29		11	H	Chesterfield	L	1-3	0-1	4	Lightbourne	6219
30		14	H	Darlington	W	2-0	1-0	—	Lightbourne, Wilson	3154
31		18	A	Carlisle U	L	1-2	1-0	3	Wilson	7769
32		25	A	Northampton T	D	2-2	1-1	3	Lightbourne, Wilson	6282
33	Apr	1	H	Colchester U	W	2-0	0-0	3	Lightbourne, O'Connor (pen)	3622
34		4	A	Exeter C	W	3-1	1-0	—	O'Connor, Lightbourne 2	1551
35		8	A	Doncaster R	W	2-0	1-0	3	Wilson 2	2368
36		11	A	Wigan Ath	L	0-1	0-1	—		2176
37		15	H	Rochdale	D	0-0	0-0	3		3766
38		17	A	Barnet	W	3-1	2-1	3	Ryder, Wilson, Lightbourne	2078
39		22	H	Wigan Ath	W	2-0	0-0	3	O'Connor, Lightbourne	3508
40		29	H	Scunthorpe U	W	2-1	0-0	3	Palmer, Lightbourne	4539
41	May	2	A	Scarborough	W	2-1	0-0	—	Houghton, Wilson	2841
42		4	A	Bury	D	0-0	0-0	—		6790

Final League Position: 2

GOALSCORERS

League (75): Lightbourne 23, Wilson 16 (1 pen), O'Connor 10 (4 pens), Marsh 9, Houghton 8, Ryder 5, Palmer 2, Ntamark 1, own goal 1.
Coca-Cola Cup (7): Wilson 3, Lightbourne 1, O'Connor 1, Watkiss 1, own goal 1.
FA Cup (11): Lightbourne 3, Butler 2, Wilson 2, Houghton 1, Marsh 1, O'Connor 1 (pen), own goal 1.

Wood T.J. 39	Evans D.W. 36	Rogers D.J. 20 + 7	Watkiss S.P. 8	Marsh C.J. 36 + 2	Palmer C.A. 39	O'Connor M.J. 39	Ntamark C.B. 31 + 4	Lightbourne K.L. 42	Wilson K.J. 42	Mehew D.S. 6 + 7	Keister J.E.S. 9 + 2	Lillis J.W. — + 1	Butler M.N. 1 + 7	Peer D. 8 + 4	Embleton D.C. — + 1	Houghton S.A. 38	Walker J.B. 3 + 1	Gibson C.J. 31 + 2	Ryder S.H. 34 + 2	Match No.
1	2	3	4	5	6	7	8	9	10	11	12									1
1	2	3	4	5	6	7	8	9	10	*11*	14	12								2
1	2	3		5	6	7	8	9	10	*11*			4	12	15					3
1	2	3	4	5	6	7	8	9	10	11			12							4
1	2	3	4	5	6	7	8	9	10							11				5
	2	3		5	6	7	8	9	10							11	1	4	12	6
		3		5	6		8	9	10					7		11	1	4	2	7
1	2	3		5	6	7	12	9	10					8		11		4		8
1	2	3	4	5		7		9	10					8		11		6	12	9
1		3	4	5		7		9	10					8		11		6	2	10
1	*5*	12	4		6	7		9	10	8			14			11		3	2	11
1		4			6	7	5	9	10	8				12		11		3	2	12
1		4		5	6	7	8	9	10				12			11		3	2	13
1		4		5	6	7	8	9	10	12						11		3	2	14
1		4		5	6	7	8	9	10							11		3	2	15
1	2			5	6	7	8	9	10				12			11		3	4	16
1	2			5	6	7	8	9	10	12				14		11		3	4	17
1	2			5	6	7	8	9	10				12			11		3	4	18
1	2			5	6	7	8	9	10				12			11		3	4	19
1	2	12		5	6	7	8	9	*10*	14						11		3	4	20
1	2	12		5	6		8	9	10		7			14		*11*		3	4	21
1	2			5	6	7	8	9	10							11		3	4	22
1	2			5	6	7	8	9	10							11		3	4	23
1	2	3		5	6	7	8	9	10							11			4	24
1	2	3		5	6	7	8	9	10							11			4	25
1	2			5	6	7	8	9	10							11		3	4	26
1	2			5	6	7	8	9	10							11		3	4	27
1	2			5	6	7	8	9	10	12						11		3	4	28
1	2			5	6	7	8	9	10							11		3	4	29
1	2	12		5	6		8	9	*10*	14	7					11		3	4	30
1	2	3		5	6	7		9	10		8					11			4	31
1	2		6	5		7		9	10	12	8					11		3	4	32
1	2			5	6	7	12	9	10		8					11		3	4	33
1	2			5	6	7		9	10	12	8					11		3	4	34
1	2	12		5	6	7		9	10		8					11		3	4	35
1	2			5	6	7	12	9	10		8					11		3	4	36
1	2			5	6	7	12	9	10		8					11		3	4	37
1	2	12			6	7	8	9	*10*				14	5		11		3	4	38
1	2	12			6	7	8	9	10					5		11		3	4	39
1	2	3		12	6	7	8	9	10					5		11			4	40
1	2	3		12	6	7	8	9	10					5		*11*	15	14	4	41
	2	3		5	6	7	8	9	10							11	1	12	4	42

Coca-Cola Cup

First Round	Plymouth Arg (h)		4-0
		(a)	1-2
Second Round	West Ham U (h)		2-1
		(a)	0-2

FA Cup

First Round	Rochdale (h)		3-0
Second Round	Preston NE (a)		1-1
		(h)	4-0
Third Round	Leeds U (h)		1-1
		(a)	2-5

WATFORD 1994–95 *Back row (left to right):* Ken Brooks (Kit Manager), Alex Inglethorpe, Tommy Mooney, David Holdsworth, Robert Page, Colin Foster, Keith Millen, Jason Soloman, David Barnes, Colin Simpson, Darren Bazeley, Billy Hails (Physio).

Centre row: Stuart Murdoch (Reserve Team Manager), Craig Ramage, Jamie Moralee, Mark Watson, Paul Wilkerson, Perry Digweed, Simon Sheppard, Richard Johnson, Jason Drysdale, Lee Nogan, John McDermott (Youth Development Officer).

Front row: Kenny Jackett (Youth Team Manager), Geoffrey Pitcher, Gerard Lavin, John White, Gary Porter, Glenn Roeder (Manager), Andy Hessenthaler, Matthew Vier, Nigel Gibbs, Derek Payne, Kenny Sansom (Player/Coach).

Division 1 **WATFORD**

Vicarage Road Stadium, Watford WD1 8ER. Telephone: (01923) 230933. Fax: (01923) 239759. Hornet Hotline: 0891 121030. Ticket Office: (01923) 220393. Club Shop: (01923) 220847. Catering: (01923) 221457. Junior Hornets Club/Marketing: (01923) 230933.

Ground capacity: 22,000.

Record attendance: 34,099 v Manchester U, FA Cup 4th rd (replay), 3 February 1969.

Record receipts: £115,000 v Leeds U, Coca Cola Cup 3rd rd, 10 November 1992.

Pitch measurements: 115yd × 75yd.

Life President: Elton John.

Chairman: Dr. S. R. Timperley PHD.

Directors: G. S. Lawson Rogers, C. D. Lissack, J. Petchey, E. Plumley FAAI, M. Winwood.

Chief Executive: Eddie Plumley FAAI. ***Secretary:*** John Alexander.

Team Manager: Glenn Roeder. ***Player-Coach:*** Kenny Sansom.

Reserve Team Coach: Stuart Murdoch. ***Youth Team Coach:*** Kenny Jackett. ***Physio:*** Billy Hails.

Director of Marketing: Brian Blower. ***Public Relations Manager:*** Ed Coan.
Commercial Manager: Paul Biffen.

Year Formed: 1891*(*see Foundation*). ***Turned Professional:*** 1897. ***Ltd Co.:*** 1909.

Club Nickname: 'The Hornets'.

Previous Name: West Herts.

Previous Ground: 1899, Cassio Road; 1922, Vicarage Road.

Foundation: Tracing this club's foundation proves difficult. Nowadays it is suggested that Watford was formed as Watford Rovers in 1891. Another version is that Watford Rovers were not forerunners of the present club whose history began in 1898 with the amalgamation of West Herts and Watford St. Mary's.

First Football League game: 28 August, 1920, Division 3, v QPR (a) W 2-1 – Williams; Horseman, F. Gregory; Bacon, Toone, Wilkinson; Bassett, Ronald (1), Hoddinott, White (1), Waterall.

Record League Victory: 8–0 v Sunderland, Division 1, 25 September 1982 – Sherwood; Rice, Rostron, Taylor, Terry, Bolton, Callaghan (2), Blissett (4), Jenkins (2), Jackett, Barnes.

Record Cup Victory: 10–1 v Lowestoft T, FA Cup, 1st rd, 27 November 1926 – Yates; Prior, Fletcher (1); F. Smith, 'Bert' Smith, Strain; Stephenson, Warner (3), Edmonds (2), Swan (2), Daniels (1). (1 og).

Record Defeat: 0–10 v Wolverhampton W, FA Cup 1st rd (replay), 13 January 1912.

Most League Points (2 for a win): 71, Division 4, 1977–78.

Most League Points (3 for a win): 80, Division 2, 1981–82.

Most League Goals: 92, Division 4, 1959–60.

Highest League Scorer in Season: Cliff Holton, 42, Division 4, 1959–60.

Most League Goals in Total Aggregate: Luther Blissett, 158, 1976–83, 1984–88, 1991–92.

Most Capped Player: John Barnes, 31 (78), England and Kenny Jackett, 31, Wales.

Most League Appearances: Luther Blissett, 415, 1976–83, 1984–88, 1991–92.

Record Transfer Fee Received: £2,300,000 from Chelsea for Paul Furlong, May 1994.

Record Transfer Fee Paid: £550,000 to AC Milan for Luther Blissett, August 1984.

Football League Record: 1920 Original Member of Division 3; 1921–58 Division 3 (S); 1958–60 Division 4; 1960–69 Division 3; 1969–72 Division 2; 1972–75 Division 3; 1975–78 Division 4; 1978–79 Division 3; 1979–82 Division 2; 1982–88 Division 1; 1988–92 Division 2; 1992– Division 1.

Honours: *Football League:* Division 1 – Runners-up 1982–83; Division 2 – Runners-up 1981–82; Division 3 – Champions 1968–69; Runners-up 1978–79; Division 4 – Champions 1977–78; Promoted 1959–60 (4th). *FA Cup:* Runners-up 1984. *Football League Cup:* Semi-final 1979. **European Competitions:** *UEFA Cup:* 1983–84.

Colours: Yellow shirts, black shorts, black stockings. **Change colours:** Burgundy/jade shirts, burgundy shorts, burgundy stockings.

WATFORD 1994–95 LEAGUE RECORD

Match No.	Date	Venue	Opponents	Result		H/T Score	Lg. Pos.	Goalscorers	Attendance
1	Aug 13	A	Sheffield U	L	0-3	0-2	—		16,820
2	20	H	Grimsby T	D	0-0	0-0	22		6324
3	27	A	Swindon T	L	0-1	0-1	24		9781
4	30	H	Wolverhampton W	W	2-1	1-0	—	Foster, Johnson	10,108
5	Sept 3	H	Middlesbrough	D	1-1	0-1	17	Johnson	9478
6	10	A	Barnsley	D	0-0	0-0	19		4251
7	13	A	Oldham Ath	W	2-0	1-0	—	Holdsworth, Porter (pen)	7243
8	17	H	Luton T	L	2-4	2-3	19	Moralee, Mooney	8880
9	24	H	Reading	D	2-2	2-0	18	Johnson, Moralee	8015
10	Oct 1	A	Charlton Ath	L	0-3	0-0	21		8169
11	8	A	Derby Co	D	1-1	1-0	20	Nogan	13,413
12	15	H	Notts Co	W	3-1	2-0	18	Nogan, Moralee, Ramage	7008
13	22	H	Tranmere R	W	2-0	1-0	15	Nogan 2	6987
14	29	A	Bolton W	L	0-3	0-1	17		10,483
15	Nov 1	A	Burnley	D	1-1	1-0	—	Nogan	11,739
16	5	H	WBA	W	1-0	1-0	13	Mooney	8419
17	12	H	Southend U	W	1-0	0-0	7	Nogan	8551
18	19	A	Sunderland	W	3-1	2-0	7	Hessenthaler, Nogan, Mooney (pen)	15,063
19	26	H	Stoke C	D	0-0	0-0	9		9126
20	Dec 3	A	Tranmere R	L	1-2	0-0	10	Moralee	7301
21	10	A	Grimsby T	D	0-0	0-0	13		6288
22	17	H	Sheffield U	D	0-0	0-0	13		8919
23	26	H	Portsmouth	W	2-0	0-0	10	Ramage, Shipperley	9953
24	27	A	Millwall	L	1-2	0-0	14	Ramage	12,289
25	31	H	Port Vale	W	3-2	1-1	10	Foster, Musslewhite (og), Ramage	7794
26	Jan 2	A	Bristol C	D	0-0	0-0	9		9423
27	14	H	Bolton W	D	0-0	0-0	9		9113
28	Feb 1	A	WBA	W	1-0	0-0	—	Ramage (pen)	15,754
29	4	A	Southend U	W	4-0	3-0	7	Bazeley 3, Ramage (pen)	4914
30	11	H	Burnley	W	2-0	0-0	6	Ramage, Bazeley	9297
31	21	H	Sunderland	L	0-1	0-1	—		8189
32	Mar 4	A	Reading	L	1-4	0-1	8	Phillips	9705
33	7	A	Middlesbrough	L	0-2	0-1	—		16,630
34	11	H	Swindon T	W	2-0	0-0	8	Hessenthaler, Phillips	7123
35	18	A	Wolverhampton W	D	1-1	0-1	11	Phillips	24,380
36	21	H	Barnsley	W	3-2	1-0	—	Millen, Porter, Phillips	6883
37	26	A	Luton T	D	1-1	0-1	9	Phillips	7984
38	Apr 1	H	Oldham Ath	L	1-2	1-2	10	Ramage	8090
39	4	A	Stoke C	L	0-1	0-1	—		9576
40	8	A	Port Vale	W	1-0	0-0	10	Porter	7276
41	14	H	Millwall	W	1-0	1-0	—	Pitcher	6907
42	17	A	Portsmouth	L	1-2	0-1	10	Phillips	8396
43	22	H	Bristol C	W	1-0	0-0	10	Phillips	7190
44	29	A	Notts Co	L	0-1	0-1	10		5083
45	May 2	H	Charlton Ath	W	2-0	0-0	—	Beadle, Phillips	6024
46	7	H	Derby Co	W	2-1	1-0	7	Phillips, Ramage (pen)	8492

Final League Position: 7

GOALSCORERS

League (52): Phillips 9, Ramage 9 (3 pens), Nogan 7, Bazeley 4, Moralee 4, Johnson 3, Mooney 3 (1 pen), Porter 3 (1 pen), Foster 2, Hessenthaler 2, Beadle 1, Holdsworth 1, Millen 1, Pitcher 1, Shipperley 1, own goal 1.
Coca-Cola Cup (7): Nogan 2, Ramage 2, Foster 1, Mooney 1, own goal 1.
FA Cup (3): Hessenthaler 2, Holdsworth 1.

Miller K. 44	Bazeley D.S. 22 + 6	Watson M.S. 1	Foster C.J. 34	Holdsworth D.G. 38 + 1	Ramage C.D. 44	Hessenthaler A. 43	Payne D.R. 24	Moralee J.D. 23 + 1	Porter G. 41	Mooney T.J. 29	Soloman J.R. — + 2	Johnson R.M. 27 + 8	Ludden D.J.R. 1	Digweed P.M. 2 + 1	Millen K.D. 31	Sansom K.G. 1	Nogan L.M. 13 + 1	Fitzgerald G.M. 1	Lavin G. 35	Beadle P.C. 9 + 11	Shipperley N.J. 5 + 1	Gibbs N.J. 9 + 2	Jemson N.B. 3 + 1	Connolly D.J. — + 2	Phillips K. 15 + 1	Barnes D. 1	Page R.J. 4 + 1	Quinn M. 4 + 1	Pitcher G. 2 + 2	Match No.
1	2	3	4	5	6	7	8	9	10	11	12																			1
1	2		4	5	6	7	8	9	10	11		3																		2
1	2		4	5	6	7	8	9	10	11		3																		3
1	2		4	5	6	7	8	9	10	11		3																		4
1	2		4	5	6	7		9	10	11		3	*8*	15																5
1	2		4	5	6	7		9		11		3			8	10														6
1	2		4	5	6	7	8	9	10	11		3					12													7
	2			5	6	7	8	9	10	11	12	3		1				4												8
	2		4	5	6	7	8	9				3		1			11		10	12										9
1	3		4	5	6	7		9	10	11		8							2											10
1			4		6	7		9	10	11		3			5		8		2											11
1			4		6	7		9	10	11		3			5		8		2	12										12
1			4		6	7		9	10	11		3			5		8		2											13
1	12		4		6	7			10	11		3			5		8		2	9										14
1	12			4	6	7		9	10	11		3			5		*8*		2	14										15
1				4	6	7		9	10	11		3			5		8		2											16
1			4	5	6	7		9	10	11		3					8		2											17
1			4	5	6	7			10	11		3			9		8		2											18
1			4	5	6	7		12	10	11		3			9		8		2											19
1				5	6	7		9	10	11		3			4		8		2											20
1				5	6	7		9	10	11		3			4		8		2		12									21
1			4	5	6	7			10	11		3					8		2		9									22
1			4	5	6	7		8	10	11		3							2	12	9									23
1	12		4	5	6	7		*8*	10	11		3							2	14	9									24
1	3		4	5	6	7		8	10	11										2	*12*	9	14								25
1	8		4	5	6	7			10	11										2		9	3								26
1	3		4	5	6	7		8	10						11				2				9							27
1	3		4	12	6	7	8		10						5				2			11	*9*	14						28
1	3		4		6	7	8		10						5				2			11	9							29
1	3		4	7	6		8	9	10						5				2			11	12							30
1	3		4	7	6		8		10			12			5				2			11			9					31
1	3		4	8	6	7			*10*	9		12			5							2			14	11				32
1	2			4	6	7	8		10	11		3			*5*							12			9		14			33
1	2			4	6	7	8		10	*11*		12			5					14		3			9					34
1				4	6	7	8		10			12			5				2	14		3			11			*9*		35
1			7	4	6				10	11		3			5				2	12					8			9		36
1			4		6	7	8		10			3			5				2	12					11			9		37
1				4	6	7	8		10			3			5				2	12					11			9		38
1			3	4	6	7	8					12			5				2	9		10			11					39
1			4		6	7	8		10						5				2	9					11		3		12	40
1				4		7	8		10			12			5				2	*9*					11		3	14	6	41
1	12			4		7	8		10			14			5				2	9					11		3		*6*	42
1	12			4	6	7	8		10						5				2	9					11		3			43
1	12		3	4	6	7	8		*10*						5				2	9					11				14	44
1	10		3	4	6	7	8								5				2	9				12	11					45
1	10		3	4	6	7	8					12			5				2	9					11					46

Coca-Cola Cup

First Round	Southend U (a)	0-0
	(h)	1-0
Second Round	Tottenham H (h)	3-6
	(a)	3-2

FA Cup

Third Round	Scarborough (a)	0-0
	(h)	2-0
Fourth Round	Swindon T (h)	1-0
Fifth Round	Crystal Palace (h)	0-0
	(a)	0-1

WEST BROMWICH ALBION 1994–95 *Back row (left to right):* Daryl Burgess, Carl Heggs, Stuart Naylor, Tony Lange, Bob Taylor, Mike Phelan, Steve Lilwall. *Centre row:* Danny Thomas (Physio), Michael Mellon, Ian Hamilton, Paul Raven, Paul Mardon, Darren Bradley, Kieran O'Regan, John Trewick (Reserve Coach). *Front row:* Neil Parsley, Stacy Coldicott, Lee Ashcroft, Alan Buckley (Manager), Arthur Mann (Assistant Manager), Paul Edwards, Bernard McNally, David Smith. (Photograph: Action Images)

Division 1 **WEST BROMWICH ALBION**

The Hawthorns, West Bromwich B71 4LF. Telephone: (0121) 525 8888 (all Depts). Fax: (0121) 553 6634.

Ground capacity: 25,100.

Record attendance: 64,815 v Arsenal, FA Cup 6th rd, 6 March 1937.

Record receipts: £174,235.95 v Stoke C, Div 2, 23 January 1993.

Pitch measurements: 115yd × 74yd.

President: Sir F. A. Millichip. ***Vice-President:*** John G. Silk LL.B (Lond).

Chairman: A. B. Hale.

Directors: C. M. Stapleton, T. J. Summers, J. W. Brandrick, T. K. Guy, B. Hurst.

Manager: Alan Buckley. ***Assistant Manager:*** Arthur Mann. ***Coach:*** John Trewick. ***Physio:*** Danny Thomas.

Secretary: Dr. John J. Evans BA, PHD. (Wales).

Club Statistician: Tony Matthews. ***Commercial Manager:*** Tom Cardall.

Year Formed: 1879. ***Turned Professional:*** 1885. ***Ltd Co.:*** 1892.

Previous Name: 1879–81, West Bromwich Strollers.

Club Nicknames: 'Throstles', 'Baggies', 'Albion'.

Previous Grounds: 1879, Coopers Hill; 1879, Dartmouth Park; 1881, Bunns Field, Walsall Street; 1882, Four Acres (Dartmouth Cricket Club); 1885, Stoney Lane; 1900, The Hawthorns.

Foundation: There is a well known story that when employees of Salter's Spring Works in West Bromwich decided to form a football club in 1879, they had to send someone to the nearby Association Football stronghold of Wednesbury to purchase a football. A weekly subscription of 2d (less than 1p) was imposed and the name of the new club was West Bromwich Strollers.

First Football League game: 8 September, 1888, Football League, v Stoke (a) W 2-0 – Roberts; J. Horton, Green; E. Horton, Perry, Bayliss; Bassett, Woodhall (1), Hendry, Pearson, Wilson (1).

Record League Victory: 12–0 v Darwen, Division 1, 4 April 1892 – Reader; Horton, McCulloch; Reynolds (2), Perry, Groves; Bassett (3), McLeod, Nicholls (1), Pearson (4), Geddes (1). (1 og).

Record Cup Victory: 10–1 v Chatham (away), FA Cup, 3rd rd, 2 March 1889 – Roberts; Horton, Green; Timmins (1), Charles Perry, Horton; Bassett (2), Perry (1), Bayliss (2), Pearson, Wilson (3). (1 og).

Record Defeat: 3–10 v Stoke C, Division 1, 4 February 1937.

Most League Points (2 for a win): 60, Division 1, 1919–20.

Most League Points (3 for a win): 85, Division 2, 1992–93.

Most League Goals: 105, Division 2, 1929–30.

Highest League Scorer in Season: William 'Ginger' Richardson, 39, Division 1, 1935–36.

Most League Goals in Total Aggregate: Tony Brown, 218, 1963–79.

Most Capped Player: Stuart Williams, 33 (43), Wales.

Most League Appearances: Tony Brown, 574, 1963–80.

Record Transfer Fee Received: £1,500,000 from Manchester U for Bryan Robson, October 1981.

Record Transfer Fee Paid: £748,000 to Manchester C for Peter Barnes, July 1979.

Football League Record: 1888 Founder Member of Football League; 1901–02 Division 2; 1902–04 Division 1; 1904–11 Division 2; 1911–27 Division 1; 1927–31 Division 2; 1931–38 Division 1; 1938–49 Division 2; 1949–73 Division 1; 1973–76 Division 2; 1976–86 Division 1; 1986–91 Division 2; 1991–92 Division 3; 1992–93 Division 2; 1933– Division 1.

Honours: *Football League:* Division 1 – Champions 1919–20; Runners-up 1924–25, 1953–54; Division 2 – Champions 1901–02, 1910–11; Runners-up 1930–31, 1948–49; Promoted to Division 1 1975–76 (3rd). *FA Cup:* Winners 1888, 1892, 1931, 1954, 1968; Runners-up 1886, 1887, 1895, 1912, 1935. *Football League Cup:* Winners 1966; Runners-up 1967, 1970. **European Competitions:** *European Cup-Winners' Cup:* 1968–69; *European Fairs Cup:* 1966–67; *UEFA Cup:* 1978–79, 1979–80, 1981–82.

Colours: Navy blue and white striped shirts, white shorts, blue and white stockings. **Change colours:** Yellow shirts with sky blue sleeves, sky blue shorts, yellow stockings.

WEST BROMWICH ALBION 1994–95 LEAGUE RECORD

Match No.	Date		Venue	Opponents	Result		H/T Score	Lg. Pos.	Goalscorers	Attendance
1	Aug	13	A	Luton T	D	1-1	1-0	—	Taylor	8640
2		28	A	Wolverhampton W	L	0-2	0-1	22		27,764
3		31	A	Swindon T	D	0-0	0-0	—		11,188
4	Sept	10	A	Millwall	D	2-2	1-1	24	Taylor 2	8378
5		14	A	Middlesbrough	L	1-2	1-1	—	Ashcroft	14,878
6		17	H	Grimsby T	D	1-1	1-0	24	Ashcroft	14,496
7		24	H	Burnley	W	1-0	0-0	23	Taylor	13,539
8		28	H	Portsmouth	L	0-2	0-1	—		13,545
9	Oct	2	A	Stoke C	L	1-4	1-2	23	Taylor	14,203
10		8	H	Sunderland	L	1-3	0-2	24	Ashcroft	13,717
11		15	A	Tranmere R	L	1-3	1-2	24	Hunt	7397
12		18	H	Sheffield U	W	1-0	0-0	—	Mellon	12,713
13		22	A	Barnsley	L	0-2	0-1	23		5082
14		29	H	Reading	W	2-0	0-0	23	Hunt, Ashcroft	14,313
15	Nov	2	H	Port Vale	D	0-0	0-0	—		14,513
16		5	A	Watford	L	0-1	0-1	23		8419
17		13	A	Charlton Ath	D	1-1	0-1	23	Taylor	10,876
18		19	H	Oldham Ath	W	3-1	2-0	23	Donovan, Ashcroft, Taylor	14,616
19		26	A	Notts Co	L	0-2	0-1	23		10,088
20	Dec	3	H	Barnsley	W	2-1	1-0	21	Heggs, Hamilton	13,921
21		10	A	Sheffield U	L	0-2	0-1	21		13,891
22		18	H	Luton T	W	1-0	1-0	21	Donovan	14,392
23		26	H	Bristol C	W	1-0	0-0	18	Munro (og)	21,071
24		27	A	Southend U	L	1-2	1-1	18	Ashcroft	6856
25		31	H	Bolton W	W	1-0	1-0	18	Hunt	18,184
26	Jan	2	A	Derby Co	D	1-1	1-0	17	Hamilton	16,035
27		14	A	Reading	W	2-0	0-0	16	Hunt, Donovan	9390
28	Feb	1	H	Watford	L	0-1	0-0	—		15,754
29		5	H	Charlton Ath	L	0-1	0-0	17		12,084
30		11	A	Port Vale	L	0-1	0-0	18		10,751
31		18	H	Notts Co	W	3-2	1-0	15	Mardon, Hunt 2	13,748
32		21	A	Oldham Ath	L	0-1	0-1	—		7690
33		25	H	Stoke C	L	1-3	1-1	19	Hamilton	16,591
34	Mar	4	A	Burnley	D	1-1	0-0	19	Hunt	11,885
35		8	A	Portsmouth	W	2-1	1-1	—	Taylor 2	7160
36		15	H	Wolverhampton W	W	2-0	1-0	—	Ashcroft, Taylor	20,661
37		19	H	Swindon T	L	2-5	0-0	16	Hunt, Rees	12,960
38		22	H	Millwall	W	3-0	1-0	—	Hunt 3 (1 pen)	11,782
39		25	A	Grimsby T	W	2-0	1-0	14	Hunt, Donovan	7393
40	Apr	1	H	Middlesbrough	L	1-3	1-0	15	Rees	20,256
41		8	A	Bolton W	L	0-1	0-0	16		16,207
42		15	H	Southend U	W	2-0	1-0	15	Hamilton, Strodder	14,393
43		17	A	Bristol C	L	0-1	0-0	17		8777
44		22	H	Derby Co	D	0-0	0-0	19		15,265
45		30	H	Tranmere R	W	5-1	1-0	19	Donovan, Ashcroft 3 (1 pen), Taylor	17,486
46	May	7	A	Sunderland	D	2-2	0-1	19	Hunt, Agnew	18,232

Final League Position: 19

GOALSCORERS

League (51): Hunt 13 (1 pen), Taylor 11, Ashcroft 10 (1 pen), Donovan 5, Hamilton 4, Rees 2, Agnew 1, Heggs 1, Mardon 1, Mellon 1, Strodder 1, own goal 1.
Coca-Cola Cup (0).
FA Cup (2): Ashcroft 1 (pen), Raven 1.

Naylor S.W. 42	Parsley N. 19 + 4	Edwards P.R. 20	Phelan M.C. 17 + 3	Herbert C.J. 8	Burgess D. 22	Ashcroft L. 36 + 2	Hamilton I.R. 35	Taylor R. 38 + 4	Heggs C.S. 7 + 7	McNally B.A. 16 + 5	Donovan K. 31 + 2	Darton S.R. 7	Mellon M.J. 5 + 2	Strodder G.J. 19	Lilwall S. 14 + 2	Boere J.W.J. 5	Smith D. 16 + 6	Coldicott S. 9 + 2	Mardon P.J. 27 + 1	Hunt A. 33 + 6	O'Regan K. 12 + 8	Raven P.D. 31	Bradley D.M. 11 + 5	Rees A.A. 8 + 6	Lange A.S. 4 + 1	Agnew P. 14	*Match No.*
1	2	3	4	5	6	7	8	9	10	11	12																1
1	2		4	5	6	12	8	9	10	7	11	3	14														2
1	2		4		6		8	9	10		7	3	11	5													3
1			4	6	2	*8*		9		12		3		5	7	10	11	14									4
1				6	2	8		9				3		5	7	10	11	4	12								5
1	12			6		8		9				3		5	7	10	*11*	4	2	14							6
1	2		4	6		*8*		9		12	11	3		5	14	10				7							7
1	2		4	6		8		9		12	11	*3*		5	14	10				7							8
1	2		4	6		8		9		10				5	3		11	12		7							9
1	2		4			8		9	12				11	5	3		10	6		7							10
1	2	6				8		9	12				11	5	3		10		4	7							11
1	2	6				8		9					11		3		10	4	5	7	12						12
1	2	6	12			8		9	14				10	5	3		*11*	4		7							13
1	2	3	4			8	11	9		7									5	10		6					14
1	2	3	4			8	11	9		7			12						5	10		6					15
1	2	3	4			8	11	9	12	7									5	10		6	14				16
1	2	3	*4*			8	11	9	12	7									5	10	14	6					17
1		3				8	11	9	10	7	4								5	12	2	6					18
1	12	3				8	11	9	14	7	4								5		2	6		*10*			19
1		3				8	11	9	10	7	4								5	12	2	6	14				20
1						8	11	9	*10*	7	4				3				5	14	2	6	12				21
1	12					8	11	*9*	14		7				3				5	10	2	6	4				22
1		6				8	11	12	9		7				3				5	10	2		4				23
1	12	6				8	11	9			7				3		14		5	10	*2*		4				24
1	2	3				8	11	9			7						12		5	10		6	4				25
1	2	3				8	11	*9*			7						12		5	10		6	4	14			26
1	2	3				8	11				7						12		5	10	14	6	*4*	9			27
1	*2*	3	12				11	9		14	7						8		5	10	4	6					28
1						14	11	12			7				3		*8*		5	10	2	6	4	9	15		29
		3	11		2	8		9			7								5	10		6	4	12	1		30
		3	12		2	8	11	9			7								5	10		6	4		1		31
		3	4		2	*8*	11	9			12						7		5	10		6		14	1		32
	2				5	8	11	9			*7*									10	12	6	4	14	1	3	33
1			4		2		11							5			8			10	7	6		9		3	34
1			4		2		11	9		12	8								5	10	7	6				3	35
1			4		2	8	11	9			7								5	10	12	6				3	36
1					2	8	11	9		4	7								*5*	10	14	6		12		3	37
1					2	8	11			4	7								5	10		6		9		3	38
1					2		11			4	7			8					5	10	12	6		9		3	39
1					2	8	11	12		*4*	7			5						10	14	6		9		3	40
1					2		11	12		*4*	7			5	8		14			10		6		9		3	41
1					2		11	9			7			5			8			10		6	4			3	42
1					2		11	9			7			5			*12*	3		10	4	6		14		8	43
1					2	8	11	9			7			5			10	4				6				3	44
1					2	8	11	9			7			5			*10*	4		14		6	12			3	45
1					2	8	11	9			7			5			*10*	4		14		6	12			3	46

Coca-Cola Cup		
First Round	Hereford U (a)	0-0
	(h)	0-1

FA Cup		
Third Round	Coventry C (a)	1-1
	(h)	1-2

WEST HAM UNITED 1994–95 *Back row (left to right):* Tim Breacker, Simon Webster, Ludek Miklosko, Jeroen Boere, Ian Feuer, Lee Chapman, Alvin Martin.
Centre row: Joey Beauchamp, Danny Williamson, Steve Jones, Mike Marsh, Dale Gordon, Trevor Morley, Matthew Rush, Kenny Brown, Martin Allen.
Front row: Keith Rowland, Peter Butler, Ian Bishop, Steve Potts, David Burrows, John Moncur, Matty Holmes.

FA Premiership — WEST HAM UNITED

Boleyn Ground, Green Street, Upton Park, London E13 9AZ. Telephone General Office: (0181) 548 2748. Fax: (0181) 548 2758. Membership Office: (0181) 552 7640. Promotions: (0181) 472 5656. Dial-a-seat: (0181) 472 3322. Football in the Community: (0181) 472 2422. Clubcall: 0891 121165.

Ground capacity: 26,014.

Record attendance: 42,322 v Tottenham H, Division 1, 17 October 1970.

Record receipts: £146,074 v Tottenham H, League Cup 5th rd, 27 January 1987.

Pitch measurements: 112yd × 72yd.

Chairman: T. W. Brown FCIS, ATH, FCCA. ***Vice-Chairman:*** M. W. Cearns ACIB.

Directors: C. J. Warner, P. J. Storrie (managing).

Manager: Harry Redknapp. ***Assistant Manager:*** Frank Lampard. ***Coaches:*** Paul Hilton, Tony Carr. ***Physio:*** John Green BSC (hons) MCSP, SRP.

Secretary: Richard Skirrow.

Year Formed: 1895. ***Turned Professional:*** 1900. ***Ltd Co.:*** 1900.

Previous Name: Thames Ironworks FC, 1895–1900.

Club Nickname: 'The Hammers'.

Previous Ground: Memorial Recreation Ground, Canning Town: 1904 Boleyn Ground.

Foundation: Thames Ironworks FC was formed by employees of this shipbuilding yard in 1895 and entered the FA Cup in their initial season at Chatham and the London League in their second. Short of funds, the club was wound up in June 1900 and relaunched a month later as West Ham United. Connection with the Ironworks was not finally broken until four years later.

First Football League game: 30 August, 1919, Division 2, v Lincoln City (h) D 1-1 – Hufton; Cope, Lee; Lane, Fenwick, McCrae; D. Smith, Moyes (1), Puddefoot, Morris, Bradshaw.

Record League Victory: 8–0 v Rotherham U, Division 2, 8 March 1958 – Gregory; Bond, Wright; Malcolm, Brown, Lansdowne; Grice, Smith (2), Keeble (2), Dick (4), Musgrove. 8–0 v Sunderland, Division 1, 19 October 1968 – Ferguson; Bonds, Charles; Peters, Stephenson, Moore (1); Redknapp, Boyce, Brooking (1), Hurst (6), Sissons.

Record Cup Victory: 10–0 v Bury, League Cup, 2nd rd (2nd leg), 25 October 1983 – Parkes; Stewart (1), Walford, Bonds (Orr), Martin (1), Devonshire (2), Allen, Cottee (4), Swindlehurst, Brooking (2), Pike.

Record Defeat: 2–8 v Blackburn R, Division 1, 26 December 1963.

Most League Points (2 for a win): 66, Division 2, 1980–81.

Most League Points (3 for a win): 88, Division 1, 1992–93.

Most League Goals: 101, Division 2, 1957–58.

Highest League Scorer in Season: Vic Watson, 41, Division 1, 1929–30.

Most League Goals in Total Aggregate: Vic Watson, 298, 1920–35.

Most Capped Player: Bobby Moore, 108, England.

Most League Appearances: Billy Bonds, 663, 1967–88.

Record Transfer Fee Received: £2,000,000 from Everton for Tony Cottee, July 1988.

Record Transfer Fee Paid: £1,500,000 to Liverpool for Don Hutchison, August 1994.

Football League Record: 1919 Elected to Division 2; 1923–32 Division 1; 1932–58 Division 2; 1958–78 Division 1; 1978–81 Division 2; 1981–89 Division 1; 1989–91 Division 2; 1991–93 Division 1; 1993– FA Premier League.

Honours: *Football League:* Division 1 best season: 3rd, 1985–86; Division 2 – Champions 1957–58, 1980–81; Runners-up 1922–23, 1990–91. *FA Cup:* Winners 1964, 1975, 1980; Runners-up 1923. *Football League Cup:* Runners-up 1966, 1981. **European Competitions:** *European Cup-Winners' Cup:* 1964–65 (winners), 1965–66, 1975–76 (runners-up), 1980–81.

Colours: Claret shirts, white shorts, white stockings. **Change colours:** All blue.

WEST HAM UNITED 1994–95 LEAGUE RECORD

Match No.	Date	Venue	Opponents	Result	H/T Score	Lg. Pos.	Goalscorers	Attendance
1	Aug 20	H	Leeds U	D 0-0	0-0	—		18,610
2	24	A	Manchester C	L 0-3	0-2	—		19,150
3	27	A	Norwich C	L 0-1	0-0	19		19,110
4	31	H	Newcastle U	L 1-3	0-2	—	Hutchison (pen)	17,375
5	Sept 10	A	Liverpool	D 0-0	0-0	19		30,907
6	17	H	Aston Villa	W 1-0	0-0	17	Cottee	18,326
7	25	H	Arsenal	L 0-2	0-1	19		18,495
8	Oct 2	A	Chelsea	W 2-1	0-0	15	Allen, Moncur	18,696
9	8	H	Crystal Palace	W 1-0	0-0	13	Hutchison	16,959
10	15	A	Manchester U	L 0-1	0-1	15		43,795
11	22	H	Southampton	W 2-0	0-0	12	Allen, Rush	18,853
12	29	A	Tottenham H	L 1-3	1-1	14	Rush	26,271
13	Nov 1	A	Everton	L 0-1	0-0	—		28,353
14	5	H	Leicester C	W 1-0	0-0	14	Dicks (pen)	18,780
15	19	A	Sheffield W	L 0-1	0-1	17		25,300
16	26	H	Coventry C	L 0-1	0-0	17		17,251
17	Dec 4	A	QPR	L 1-2	0-2	18	Boere	12,780
18	10	A	Leeds U	D 2-2	1-2	19	Boere 2	28,987
19	17	H	Manchester C	W 3-0	2-0	17	Cottee 3	17,286
20	26	H	Ipswich T	D 1-1	1-0	18	Cottee	20,562
21	28	A	Wimbledon	L 0-1	0-0	18		11,212
22	31	H	Nottingham F	W 3-1	3-0	16	Cottee, Bishop, Hughes	20,644
23	Jan 2	A	Blackburn R	L 2-4	1-1	16	Cottee, Dicks	25,503
24	14	H	Tottenham H	L 1-2	1-0	19	Boere	24,578
25	23	H	Sheffield W	L 0-2	0-1	—		14,554
26	Feb 4	A	Leicester C	W 2-1	2-1	19	Cottee, Dicks (pen)	20,375
27	13	H	Everton	D 2-2	1-1	—	Cottee 2	21,081
28	18	A	Coventry C	L 0-2	0-1	20		17,563
29	25	H	Chelsea	L 1-2	1-0	20	Hutchison	21,500
30	Mar 5	A	Arsenal	W 1-0	1-0	19	Hutchison	36,295
31	8	A	Newcastle U	L 0-2	0-1	—		34,595
32	11	H	Norwich C	D 2-2	0-1	18	Cottee 2	21,464
33	15	A	Southampton	D 1-1	1-0	—	Hutchison	15,178
34	18	A	Aston Villa	W 2-0	1-0	18	Moncur, Hutchison	28,682
35	Apr 8	A	Nottingham F	D 1-1	0-0	20	Dicks	28,361
36	13	H	Wimbledon	W 3-0	1-0	—	Dicks (pen), Boere, Cottee	21,804
37	17	A	Ipswich T	D 1-1	0-1	18	Boere	18,882
38	30	H	Blackburn R	W 2-0	0-0	16	Reiper, Hutchison	24,202
39	May 3	H	QPR	D 0-0	0-0	—		22,923
40	6	A	Crystal Palace	L 0-1	0-0	16		18,224
41	10	H	Liverpool	W 3-0	1-0	—	Holmes, Hutchison 2	22,446
42	14	H	Manchester U	D 1-1	1-0	14	Hughes	24,783

Final League Position: 14

GOALSCORERS

League (44): Cottee 13, Hutchison 9 (1 pen), Boere 6, Dicks 5 (3 pens), Allen 2, Hughes 2, Moncur 2, Rush 2, Bishop 1, Holmes 1, Rieper 1.
Coca-Cola Cup (5): Hutchison 2, Cottee 1, Moncur 1, own goal 1.
FA Cup (2): Brown 1, Cottee 1.

Miklosko L. 42	Breacker T.S. 33	Burrows D. 4	Potts S.J. 42	Martin A.E. 24	Allen M.J. 26 + 3	Bishop I.W. 31	Butler P.J.F. 5	Morley T.W. 10 + 4	Chapman L.R. 7 + 3	Holmes M.J.E. 24	Whitbread A.R. 3 + 5	Marsh M.A. 13 + 3	Moncur J.F. 30	Jones S.G. 1 + 1	Rowland K. 11 + 1	Hutchison D. 22 + 1	Cottee A.R. 31	Rush M.J. 15 + 8	Dicks J.A. 29	Brown K.J. 8 + 1	Hughes M. 15 + 2	Boere J.W.J. 15 + 5	Reiper M. 17 + 4	Williamson D.A. 4	Webster S.P. — + 5	*Match No.*
1	2	3	4	5	6	7	8	9	10	*11*	12	14														1
1	2	3	4	5	6	7	8	9	*10*	11	12	14														2
1	2	3	4	5	6	7			14		12	10	8	9	*11*											3
1	2	3	4	5	6		8			11		10	7	12		9										4
1	2		4	5	6		8					10	7		3		9	11								5
1	2		4	5	6		8		12			10	7		3		9	11								6
1	2		4	5	6				8	11		10	7		3	9		12								7
1	2		4	5	6				8			10	7		3	9		11								8
1	2		4	5	6				8			10	7		3	11	9	12								9
1	2		4	5	6							10	7		3	8	9	11								10
1	2		4	5	6	7			8			10					9	11	3							11
1			4	5	*6*	7			12		14	10			2	8	9	11	3							12
1			4	5		6			8		2	10				7	9	11	3							13
1			4	5		6		8			2		7			10	9	11	3	12						14
1			4	5	6	8		10				12	7				9	11	3	2						15
1			4			6		8		11	5	10	7				9	12	3	2						16
1			4									6	7		5		9	8	3	2	11	10				17
1			4			6				11					7		9	8	3	2	12	10	5			18
1	2		4	5		6				7							9	10	3		11	8				19
1	2		4	5		6				7							9	8	3		11	10	12			20
1	2		4	5		8				7							9	12	3		11	10	6			21
1	2		4	5		6				7			*8*				9	12	3		11	10	14			22
1	2		4			6				7			8				9	12	3		11	10	5			23
1	2		4	5	12	6		14		7			8				9			3	11	10				24
1	2		4	5	12	6				7			8				9			3	*11*	10	14			25
1	2		4	5	6								7			8	9		3		11	12		10		26
1			4	5	6								7			10	9		3	2	11	12		8		27
1	2		4	*5*	6					11			7			10	9		3			12	14	8		28
1	2		4		6	11		8					7			10	9		3				5			29
1	2		4		6	11		8					7			10	9	12	3				5			30
1	2		4		6	7		12								8	9	10	3		11		5			31
1	2		4			6		8					7			10	9		3		12		5	11		32
1	2		4			6				11			7			10	9	8	3			12	5			33
1	2		4		6	8				11			7		12	*10*	9		3			14	5			34
1			4		6	8				7	12						9		3	2	11	10	5			35
1	2		4		6	8				7							9		3		11	10	5			36
1	2		4		6	8				11			7			12	9		3			10	5			37
1	2		4		6	8				11			7			*9*		12	3			10	5		14	38
1	2		4		6	8		12		11			7			9			3			*10*	5		14	39
1	2		4		*6*	8		12		11			7			9			3			10	5		14	40
1	2		4			6		9		7			8			10			3		11		5		12	41
1	2		4		12	6		9		7			8		3	10					*11*		5		14	42

Coca-Cola Cup

Second Round	Walsall (a)	1-2
	(h)	2-0
Third Round	Chelsea (h)	1-0
Fourth Round	Bolton W (h)	1-3

FA Cup

Third Round	Wycombe W (a)	2-0
Fourth Round	QPR (a)	0-1

WIGAN ATHLETIC 1994–95 *Back row (left to right):* Mark Wright, David Adekola, Chris Duffy, Paul Tait, Neil Ogden.
Centre row: Joe Hinnigan (Coach), Mark Leonard, Ian Patterson, John Robertson, Mark Statham, Simon Farnworth, Greg Strong, David Millar, Ian Kilford, Alex Cribley (Coach/Physio).
Front row: David McKearney, Andy Lyons, Neil Rimmer, John Doolan, Graham Barrow (Manager), Stephen Gage (Chairman), David Crompton (Youth Development Officer), Paul Rennie, Andy Farrell, Matthew Carragher, Joe Jakub.
(Photograph: Derek Davies)

Division 3 WIGAN ATHLETIC

Springfield Park, Wigan WN6 7BA. Telephone: (01942) 244433. Fax: (01942) 494654. Commercial Dept: (01942) 243067. Latics Clubcall: 0891 121655. Football in the Community: (01942) 824599.

Ground capacity: 6674.

Record attendance: 27,500 v Hereford U, 12 December 1953.

Record receipts: £40,577 v Leeds U, FA Cup 6th rd, 15 March 1987.

Pitch measurements: 114yd × 72yd.

President: T. Hitchen.

Chairman: S. Gage

Directors: N. Bitel, S. Jackson, J. Bennett, E. Fryer, C. Ronnie, D. Sharpe, D. Whelan.

Secretary: Mrs Brenda Spencer. ***Assistant Secretary:*** Gordon Allan. ***Marketing Manager:*** B. Eccles. ***Commercial Manager:*** Rod Barry.

Manager: Graham Barrow. ***Coach:*** Joe Hinnigan. ***Physio/Coach:*** Alex Cribley. ***Safety Officer:*** David Johnson. ***Groundsman:*** John Parr.

Year Formed: 1932.

Club Nickname: 'The Latics'.

Foundation: Following the demise of Wigan Borough and their resignation from the Football League in 1931, a public meeting was called in Wigan at the Queen's Hall in May 1932 at which a new club Wigan Athletic, was founded in the hope of carrying on in the Football League. With this in mind, they bought Springfield Park for £2,250, but failed to gain admission to the Football League until 46 years later.

First Football League game: 19 August, 1978, Division 4, v Hereford U (a) D 0-0 – Brown; Hinnigan, Gore, Gillibrand, Ward, Davids, Corrigan, Purdie, Houghton, Wilkie, Wright.

Record League Victory: 7–2 v Scunthorpe U (away), Division 4, 12 March 1982 – Tunks; McMahon, Glenn, Wignall, Cribley, Methven (1), O'Keefe, Barrow (1), Bradd (3), Houghton (2), Evans.

Record Cup Victory: 6–0 v Carlisle U (away), FA Cup, 1st rd, 24 November 1934 – Caunce; Robinson, Talbot; Paterson, Watson, Tufnell; Armes (2), Robson (1), Roberts (2), Felton, Scott (1).

Record Defeat: 1–6 v Bristol R, Division 3, 3 March 1990.

Most League Points (2 for a win): 55, Division 4, 1978–79 and 1979–80.

Most League Points (3 for a win): 91, Division 4, 1981–82.

Most League Goals: 80, Division 4, 1981–82.

Highest League Scorer in Season: Warren Aspinall, 21, Division 3, 1985–86.

Most League Goals in Total Aggregate: Peter Houghton, 62, 1978–84.

Most Capped Player: None.

Most League Appearances: Kevin Langley, 317, 1981–86, 1990–94.

Record Transfer Fee Received: £329,000 from Coventry C for Peter Atherton, August 1991.

Record Transfer Fee Paid: £87,500 to Chester C for Chris Lightfoot, July 1995.

Football League Record: 1978 Elected to Division 4; 1982 –92 Division 3; 1992–93 Division 2; 1993– Division 3.

Honours: *Football League:* Best season in Division 3: 4th, 1985–86, 1986–87; Division 4 – Promoted (3rd) 1981–82. *FA Cup:* 6th rd 1987. *Football League Cup:* best season: 4th rd, 1982. *Freight Rover Trophy:* Winners 1985.

Colours: Blue and white striped shirts, black shorts blue stockings. **Change colours:** Burgundy with gold trim.

WIGAN ATHLETIC 1994–95 LEAGUE RECORD

Match No.	Date	Venue	Opponents	Result	H/T Score	Lg. Pos.	Goalscorers	Attendance
1	Aug 13	A	Carlisle U	L 1-2	0-1	—	Walling (og)	6231
2	20	H	Gillingham	L 0-3	0-1	19		1514
3	27	A	Fulham	L 0-2	0-1	20		4241
4	30	H	Chesterfield	L 2-3	1-2	—	Morton, Gavin	1231
5	Sept 3	H	Barnet	L 1-2	1-1	22	Gavin	1438
6	10	A	Hereford U	W 2-1	0-1	21	Rennie (pen), Rimmer	2771
7	13	A	Lincoln C	L 0-1	0-0	—		2030
8	17	H	Carlisle U	L 0-2	0-0	22		3003
9	24	A	Scunthorpe U	L 1-3	0-1	22	McKearney	2602
10	Oct 1	H	Scarborough	D 1-1	1-1	22	Kilford	1403
11	8	A	Doncaster R	L 3-5	1-3	22	Leonard 2 (1 pen), Benjamin	2060
12	15	H	Rochdale	W 4-0	4-0	22	Kilford 2, Strong, Benjamin	2118
13	22	A	Northampton T	L 0-1	0-1	22		6379
14	29	H	Colchester U	L 1-2	0-2	22	Robertson	1621
15	Nov 5	A	Hartlepool U	W 1-0	1-0	22	McKearney	1683
16	19	H	Darlington	W 4-1	2-1	19	Strong, Lyons 3 (1 pen)	1785
17	26	A	Torquay U	D 0-0	0-0	20		2509
18	Dec 10	A	Gillingham	W 1-0	0-0	18	Leonard	2257
19	17	H	Fulham	D 1-1	1-0	18	Leonard	1791
20	26	A	Bury	D 3-3	2-2	19	Lyons 2, Leonard	3616
21	Jan 7	H	Northampton T	W 2-1	1-0	17	Rimmer, Kilford	1911
22	14	A	Mansfield T	L 3-4	0-1	18	Kilford, Rimmer, Lyons	2618
23	24	H	Preston NE	D 1-1	1-0	—	Lyons	3618
24	28	A	Colchester U	W 1-0	0-0	16	Doolan	3067
25	Feb 4	H	Torquay U	D 1-1	0-1	16	Miller	1609
26	11	A	Darlington	W 3-1	1-0	16	Rodwell, Benjamin, Lyons	1780
27	18	H	Mansfield T	L 0-4	0-2	16		1884
28	21	A	Exeter C	W 4-2	2-1	—	Lyons, McKearney (pen), Benjamin 2	2370
29	25	A	Scarborough	W 1-0	1-0	15	Lyons	1416
30	28	H	Hartlepool U	W 2-0	1-0	—	McKearney, Lyons	1452
31	Mar 18	A	Chesterfield	D 0-0	0-0	14		3808
32	25	A	Barnet	D 1-1	1-1	15	McKearney	2362
33	29	H	Hereford U	D 1-1	0-0	—	Benjamin	1492
34	Apr 1	H	Lincoln C	L 0-1	0-1	15		1696
35	4	H	Scunthorpe U	D 0-0	0-0	—		1307
36	8	H	Exeter C	W 3-1	2-0	12	Miller, Lyons, Rimmer	1417
37	11	H	Walsall	W 1-0	1-0	—	Lyons	2176
38	15	A	Preston NE	L 0-1	0-1	12		10,238
39	18	H	Bury	L 0-3	0-1	—		2531
40	22	A	Walsall	L 0-2	0-0	14		3508
41	29	A	Rochdale	L 0-1	0-1	15		1949
42	May 6	H	Doncaster R	W 3-2	0-0	14	Lyons 2 (1 pen), Miller	1576

Final League Position: 14

GOALSCORERS

League (53): Lyons 15 (2 pens), Benjamin 6, Kilford 5, Leonard 5 (1 pen), McKearney 5 (1 pen), Rimmer 4, Miller 3, Gavin 2, Strong 2, Doolan 1, Morton 1, Rennie 1 (pen), Robertson 1, Rodwell 1, own goal 1.
Coca-Cola Cup (4): Gavin 2, Carragher 1, Rennie 1.
FA Cup (4): Carragher 2, Kilford 1, Leonard 1.

Farnworth S. 41	Rennie P.A. 11 + 3	Wright M.A. 14 + 2	West P.D. 1	Robertson J.N. 39 + 1	Kilford I.A. 35	Campbell D.A. 7	Morton N. 9	Gavin P.J. 9 + 3	Rimmer N. 33	Lyons A. 32	Duffy C.J. — + 4	Strong G. 12 + 5	Carragher M. 41	Ormsby B.T. 2	Harford P. 3	Tait P. 1 + 4	McKearney D.J. 17 + 4	Jakub Y. 16	Leonard M. 28 + 1	Farrell A.J. 30 + 1	Benjamin I.T. 12 + 5	Miller D.B. 31	Adekola D. 1 + 3	Doolan J. 9 + 7	Rodwell A. 5	Furlong C.D. — + 1	Whitney J.D. 12	Black A. 9	Ogden N. — + 1	Statham M. 1 + 1	Millett M.P. 1 + 2	Match No.
1	2	3	*4*	5	6	7	8	9	10	11	12	14																				1
1	4	3		5	6	7	8	9	10	11		12	2																			2
1	2	3		5	6	7	8	9		11	12	4	10																			3
1	2	*3*		5	6	7	8	9		11	12	14	10	4																		4
1	2			5	6		8	9			12	3	10	4	7	11																5
1	2	3		5	6		8	9	10			4	11		7	12																6
1	2	3		5	6		8	9	10			4	11		7		12															7
1	2			5	6		8	9	10			4	11				12	3	7													8
1	2			5	6	7	8	9	10			4	11			14	*12*			3												9
1				5	8	7		12	10			4	2					3	9	6	11											10
1	14				8	7		12		11		4	2					3	9	6	10	5										11
1					7				10	11		4	2			12		3	9	6	8	5										12
1				12	7				10	11		4	*2*					3	9	6	8	5	14									13
1	12			5	7					11		4	2					*3*	9	6	8	10	14									14
1	2			5	7					11			8				10	3	9	6		4										15
1	2			5	7					11		12	8				10	3	9	6		4										16
1				5	7				4	11		2	8				10	3	9	6												17
1				5	7				10	11			2				8	3	9	6		4										18
1				5	7				10	11		12	2				*8*	3	9	6		4	14									19
1		12		5					10	11			2			14		3	9	7		6	*8*	4								20
1				5	7				10	11			8					3	9	6		4		2								21
1	12	3		5	7				10	11			8						9	6	14	4		*2*								22
1		3		5					10	11			2				8		9	6	12	4			7							23
1		3		5						11			2				8		9	6		4		10	7							24
1		3		5					10	11			2				8		9	6	12	4			7							25
1				5					10	11			2				8	3		6	9	4			7							26
1				5					10	11			2				*8*	3		6	9	4		12	7	14						27
1		12		5	7				10	11			2				8	3			9	4		6								28
1		3		5	7				10	11			2				8				9	4		6								29
1		3		5	7				10	11			2				8		12	14	9	4		*6*								30
1		11		5					10				2				8		9	7		4		6			3					31
1		11		5	7				10				2				8		9	6		4		12			3					32
1				5	8				10				2				11		9	6	12	4					3	7				33
1				5	8				10				2						9	6	11	4		12			3	7				34
1				5	8				10	11			2						9	6		4					3	7	12			35
1				5	8				10	11			2				12		9	6		4					3	7				36
1				5	8				10	11			2						9	6		4					3	7				37
1				5	8				10	11			2						9	6		4		12			3	7				38
1				5	8				10	11			2						9	6		4		12			3	7				39
1				5	8				10	11			2				*7*		9	6		4		12			3			15	14	40
				5	8				10	11			2						9		14	4		12			3	7		1	*6*	41
1				5	8			12		11			2							6	10	4		9			3	7			14	42

Coca-Cola Cup

First Round	Crewe Alex (a)	1-2
	(h)	3-0
Second Round	Aston Villa (a)	0-5
	(h)	0-3

FA Cup

First Round	Spennymoor U (h)	4-0
Second Round	Altrincham (a)	0-1

WIMBLEDON 1994–95 *Back row (left to right):* Joe Dillon (Kit Man), Grant Payne, Neal Ardley, Dean Blackwell, Stewart Castledine, Steve Anthrobus, Aidan Newhouse, Brian McAllister, Steve Talboys, Ron Suart (Chief Scout).

Centre row: Syd Neal (Kit Manager), Gavin Fell, John Scales, Gary Blissett, Marcus Gayle, Neil Sullivan, Dean Holdsworth, Hans Segers, Robbie Earle, Vinnie Jones, Scott Fitzgerald, Roger Smith (Youth Development Officer).

Front row: Brian Sparrow (Reserve Team Manager), Gary Elkins, Gerald Dobbs, Chris Perry, Roger Joseph, Warren Barton, Terry Burton (Assistant Manager), Joe Kinnear (Manager), Peter Fear, Andy Clarke, Alan Kimble, Mark Thomas, Paul McGee, Ernie Tippett (Youth Team Manager).

FA Premiership **WIMBLEDON**

Selhurst Park, South Norwood, London SE25 6PY. Telephone: (0181) 771 2233. Fax: (0181) 768 0640. Box Office: (0181) 771 8841.

Ground capacity: 26,500.

Record attendance: 30,115 v Manchester U, FA Premier League, 9 May 1993.

Record receipts: £312,024 v Manchester U, FA Premier League, 16 April 1994.

Pitch measurements: 110yd × 74yd.

Chairman: S. G. Reed. ***Vice-Chairman:*** J. Lelliott.

Managing Director: S. Hammam.

Directors: P. Cork, P. R. Cooper, N. N. Hammam, P. Miller.

Chief Executive: David Barnard.

Manager: Joe Kinnear. ***Assistant Manager:*** Terry Burton. ***Physio:*** Steve Allen.

Secretary: Steve Rooke. ***Marketing Manager:*** Sharon Sillitoe. ***Press Manager:*** Reg Davis.

Year Formed: 1889. ***Turned Professional:*** 1964. ***Ltd Co.:*** 1964.

Previous Name: Wimbledon Old Centrals, 1899–1905.

Previous Ground: Plough Lane.

Club Nickname: 'The Dons'.

Foundation: Old boys from Central School formed this club as Wimbledon Old Centrals in 1889. Their earliest successes were in the Clapham League before switching to the Southern Suburban League in 1902.

First Football League game: 20 August, 1978, Division 4, v Halifax T (h) D 3-3 – Guy; Bryant (1), Galvin, Donaldson, Aitken, Davies, Galliers, Smith, Connell (1), Holmes, Leslie (1).

Record League Victory: 6–0 v Newport C, Division 3, 3 September 1983 – Beasant; Peters, Winterburn, Galliers, Morris, Hatter, Evans (2), Ketteridge (1), Cork (3 incl. 1p), Downes, Hodges (Driver).

Record Cup Victory: 7–2 v Windsor & Eton, FA Cup, 1st rd, 22 November 1980 – Beasant; Jones, Armstrong, Galliers, Mick Smith (2), Cunningham (1), Ketteridge, Hodges, Leslie, Cork (1), Hubbick (3).

Record Defeat: 0–8 v Everton, League Cup 2nd rd, 29 August 1978.

Most League Points (2 for a win): 61, Division 4, 1978–79.

Most League Points (3 for a win): 98, Division 4, 1982–83.

Most League Goals: 97, Division 3, 1983–84.

Highest League Scorer in Season: Alan Cork, 29, 1983–84.

Most League Goals in Total Aggregate: Alan Cork, 145, 1977–92.

Most Capped Player: Terry Phelan, 8 (26), Republic of Ireland.

Most League Appearances: Alan Cork, 430, 1977–92.

Record Transfer Fee Received: £4,000,000 from Newcastle U for Warren Barton, June 1995.

Record Transfer Fee Paid: £920,000 to Norwich C for Efan Ekoku, October 1994.

Football League Record: 1977 Elected to Division 4; 1979–80 Division 3; 1980–81 Division 4; 1981–82 Division 3; 1982–83 Division 4; 1983–84 Division 3; 1984–86 Division 2; 1986–92 Division 1; 1992– FA Premier League.

Honours: *FA Premier League* : best season: 6th, 1993–94; *Football League:* Division 3 – Runners-up 1983–84; Division 4 – Champions 1982–83. *FA Cup:* Winners 1988. *Football League Cup:* best season: 4th rd, 1980, 1984, 1989. *League Group Cup:* Runners-up 1982. *Amateur Cup:* Winners 1963; Runners-up 1935, 1947.

Colours: All navy blue with gold trim. **Change colours:** Red shirts, red shorts, black stockings.

WIMBLEDON 1994–95 LEAGUE RECORD

Match No.	Date	Venue	Opponents	Result		H/T Score	Lg. Pos.	Goalscorers	Attendance
1	Aug 20	A	Coventry C	D	1-1	0-0	—	Castledine	11,005
2	23	H	Ipswich T	D	1-1	1-0	—	Holdsworth	6341
3	27	H	Sheffield W	L	0-1	0-0	16		7453
4	31	A	Manchester U	L	0-3	0-1	—		43,440
5	Sept 10	H	Leicester C	W	2-1	2-1	14	Harford, Willis (og)	7683
6	17	A	Crystal Palace	D	0-0	0-0	13		12,366
7	24	A	QPR	W	1-0	0-0	10	Reeves	11,061
8	Oct 1	H	Tottenham H	L	1-2	1-1	13	Talboys	16,802
9	8	H	Arsenal	L	1-3	0-1	15	Jones	10,842
10	17	A	Nottingham F	L	1-3	0-1	—	Gayle	20,287
11	22	A	Liverpool	L	0-3	0-2	19		31,139
12	30	H	Norwich C	W	1-0	0-0	17	Ekoku	8242
13	Nov 5	A	Leeds U	L	1-3	1-3	18	Ekoku	27,246
14	9	H	Aston Villa	W	4-3	1-2	—	Barton (pen), Ardley, Jones, Leonhardsen	6221
15	19	H	Newcastle U	W	3-2	3-2	14	Clarke, Ekoku, Harford	14,203
16	26	A	Manchester C	L	0-2	0-1	16		21,131
17	Dec 3	H	Blackburn R	L	0-3	0-0	17		12,341
18	10	H	Coventry C	W	2-0	2-0	16	Leonhardsen, Harford	7349
19	16	A	Ipswich T	D	2-2	1-1	—	Holdsworth, Goodman	11,282
20	26	A	Southampton	W	3-2	2-2	13	Holdsworth 2 (1 pen), Harford	14,603
21	28	H	West Ham U	W	1-0	0-0	12	Fear	11,212
22	31	A	Chelsea	D	1-1	0-0	12	Ekoku	16,009
23	Jan 2	H	Everton	W	2-1	2-1	9	Harford 2	9506
24	14	A	Norwich C	W	2-1	1-1	7	Reeves, Ekoku	18,261
25	25	A	Newcastle U	L	1-2	0-1	—	Ekoku	34,374
26	Feb 4	H	Leeds U	D	0-0	0-0	9		10,211
27	11	A	Aston Villa	L	1-7	1-4	9	Barton	23,982
28	22	A	Blackburn R	L	1-2	1-2	—	Ekoku	20,586
29	25	A	Tottenham H	W	2-1	1-0	10	Ekoku 2	27,258
30	Mar 4	H	QPR	L	1-3	1-1	10	Holdsworth	9176
31	7	H	Manchester U	L	0-1	0-0	—		18,224
32	11	A	Sheffield W	W	1-0	0-0	9	Reeves	20,395
33	18	H	Crystal Palace	W	2-0	1-0	8	Jones, Gayle	8835
34	21	H	Manchester C	W	2-0	0-0	—	Thorn, Elkins	5268
35	Apr 1	A	Leicester C	W	4-3	0-1	8	Goodman 2, Leonhardsen 2	15,489
36	10	H	Chelsea	D	1-1	0-1	—	Goodman	7022
37	13	A	West Ham U	L	0-3	0-1	—		21,804
38	17	H	Southampton	L	0-2	0-2	9		10,521
39	29	A	Everton	D	0-0	0-0	9		31,567
40	May 2	H	Liverpool	D	0-0	0-0	—		12,041
41	4	A	Arsenal	D	0-0	0-0	—		32,822
42	13	H	Nottingham F	D	2-2	2-1	9	Holdsworth 2 (1 pen)	15,341

Final League Position: 9

GOALSCORERS

League (48): Ekoku 9, Holdsworth 7 (2 pens), Harford 6, Goodman 4, Leonhardsen 4, Jones 3, Reeves 3, Barton 2 (1 pen), Gayle 2, Ardley 1, Castledine 1, Clarke 1, Elkins 1, Fear 1, Talboys 1, Thorn 1, own goal 1.
Coca-Cola Cup (3): Gayle 1, Harford 1, Holdsworth 1.
FA Cup (4): Clarke 1, Earle 1, Harford 1, Leonhardsen 1.

Segers H. 31 + 1	Barton W.D. 39	Elkins G. 33 + 3	Jones V.P. 33	Scales J.R. 3	Fitzgerald S.B. 14 + 3	Gayle M.A. 22 + 1	Castledine S.M. 5 + 1	Harford M.G. 17 + 10	Holdsworth D.C. 27 + 1	Talboys S. 7	Ardley N.C. 9 + 5	Blissett G.P. 4 + 5	Clarke A.W. 8 + 17	Kimble A.F. 26	Reeves A. 31	Fear P. 8 + 6	Perry C.J. 17 + 5	Thorn A.C. 22 + 1	Ekoku E. 24	Joseph R. 3	Leonhardsen O. 18 + 2	Cunningham K.E. 28	Goodman J. 13 + 6	Earle R.G. 9	Sullivan N. 11	Match No.
1	2	3	4	5	6	7	8	9	10	*11*	12	14														1
1	2	3	4	5	6	7	8		10		11	9	12													2
1	2	3	4	5	6	7	8	9			11	10	12													3
1	2	5	4		6	10	8	9		11	7		12	3												4
1	2	*11*	4		6	8		9	10		7		12	3	5	14										5
1	2	11	4		6	8		9	10		7			3	5											6
1	2	11			6	8		9		4		12	10	3	5	7	14									7
1	2	11			6			9	10	4	7		12	3	*5*	8	14									8
1	2	11	4		6	*8*		9	10		12			3	5	7		14								9
1	2	11	4		6	8	10				12				5	7		3	9							10
1	2	11			6	*8*	14				7	12			5	10	4		9	3						11
1	7	3	4			8				11		10	12		5			6	9	2						12
1	7	3	4			8				11		10	12		5			6	9	2						13
1	2	3	4		14			12		11	7		*9*		5			6	10		8					14
1	2	11	4		12			14					7		5			6	9		10	3	*8*			15
1	7	3	4		12				10				11		5			6	9		8	2				16
1	4	3			5			12	10				11			7		6	9		8	2				17
1	4	11			5			*9*	10				12	3				6	7		8	2	14			18
1	7	12	4		5			14	*10*					3				6	9		11	2	8			19
1	4	11						9	10		12			3			5	6	7			2		8		20
1	7	11	*4*					9	10				12	3		14	5	6	8			2				21
1	7		4					9	10				12	3			5	6	11			2		8		22
1	7		4					9					10	3	5	12	6		11			2		8		23
1	7	12	4						*10*				14	3	5		6		11			2	9	8		24
1	7	12	4									14	*11*	3			5	6	9			2	10	8		25
1	7	3	4					*9*				12			5			6	11		10	2	14	8		26
1	7	3	4					9	*10*						5		12	6	11		8	2	14			27
1	4							12	14		7		*9*	3	5		6		11		10	2		8		28
1	7					10								3	5	11	4	6	9			2		8		29
1	7		4					9	10				12	3	5		6				*11*	2	14	8		30
1	7	11	4			9			10		12			3	5		6					2	8			31
	7	11	4			9		12	*10*					3	5		6				14	2	8		1	32
	7	11	4			*9*		12	10					3	5		6				14	2	8		1	33
		3	4			*9*		12	10						5	14	7	6			11	2	8		1	34
	4	11				9		12	10					3	5		14	6			7	2	8		1	35
	7	11	4			14		12	10					3	5			6			8	2	*9*		1	36
	7	3	4			11		9	10				12		5			6			8	2			1	37
	2		4			9			10				12		5			6	11		8	3	7		1	38
		11	4						10					3	5	7	12	6	*9*		8	2	14		1	39
	7	11	4			*10*							12	3	5	14	6		9			2	8		1	40
	7	11	4						10				12	3	5	14	6				*8*	2	9		1	41
15		*11*	4			7			10				12	3	5		6		9		8	2	14		*1*	42

Coca-Cola Cup

Second Round	Torquay U (h)	2-0
	(a)	1-0
Third Round	Crystal Palace (h)	0-1

FA Cup

Third Round	Colchester U (h)	1-0
Fourth Round	Tranmere R (a)	2-0
Fifth Round	Liverpool (a)	1-1
	(h)	0-2

WOLVERHAMPTON WANDERERS 1994–95 *Back row (left to right):* Andy Thompson, Tony Daley, James Smith, Robbie Dennison, Andy Debont, Tom Bennett, Steven Piearce, Michael Innes, Kevin Keen, James Kelly, Mark Rankine, Paul Birch.

Centre row: Barry Holmes (Physio), Darren Shaw, Chris Marsden, Steve Froggatt, David Kelly, Neil Masters, Mick Stowell, Paul Jones, Neil Emblem, Lee Mills, Paul Cook, Darren Ferguson, Scott Voice, Rob Kelly (Youth Development Officer).

Front row: Andrew Macbeth, Bobby Downes (Assistant Manager), Stuart Gray (Reserve Team Coach), Paul Blades, Steve Bull, Peter Shirtliff, Graham Taylor (Manager), Geoff Thomas, Mark Venus, Darren Simkin, Chris Evans (Youth Team Coach), Steve Harrison (First Team Coach), Jason Barnett.

(Photograph: Action Images)

Division 1 **WOLVERHAMPTON WANDERERS**

Molineux Grounds, Wolverhampton WV1 4QR. Telephone: (01902) 655000; Fax: (01902) 687006.

Ground capacity: 28,525.

Record attendance: 61,315 v Liverpool, FA Cup 5th rd, 11 February 1939.

Record receipts: £236,972 v Leicester C, FA Cup 5th rd, 18 February 1995.

Pitch measurements: 116yd × 74yd.

President: Sir Jack Hayward.

Chairman: Jonathan Hayward.

Directors: Jack Harris, John Harris, Nic Stones, John Richards.

Team Manager: Graham Taylor. ***Assistant Manager:*** Bobby Downes.

Coach: Steve Harrison. ***Physio:*** Barry Holmes.

Secretary: Tom Finn. ***Commercial Director:*** D. Clayton.

Year Formed: 1877*(*see Foundation*). ***Turned Professional:*** 1888. ***Ltd Co.:*** 1982.

Club Nickname: 'Wolves'.

Previous Grounds: 1877, Goldthorn Hill; 1879, John Harper's Field; 1881, Dudley Road; 1889, Molineux.

Previous Names: 1880, St Luke's, Blakenhall combined with Blakenhall Wanderers to become Wolverhampton Wanderers (1923) Ltd until 1982.

Foundation: Another club where precise details of information are confused, due in part to the existence of an earlier Wolverhampton club which played rugby. However, it is now considered likely that it came into being in 1879 when players from St. Luke's (founded 1877) and Goldthorn (founded 1876) broke away to form Wolverhampton Wanderers Association FC.

First Football League game: 8 September, 1888, Football League, v Aston Villa (h) D 1-1 – Baynton; Baugh, Mason; Fletcher, Allen, Lowder; Hunter, Cooper, Anderson, White, Cannon. Scorer – Cox o.g.

Record League Victory: 10–1 v Leicester C, Division 1, 15 April 1938 – Sidlow; Morris, Dowen; Galley, Cullis, Gardiner; Maguire (1), Horace Wright, Westcott (4), Jones (1), Dorsett (4).

Record Cup Victory: 14–0 v Cresswell's Brewery, FA Cup, 2nd rd, 13 November 1886 – I. Griffiths; Baugh, Mason; Pearson, Allen (1), Lowder; Hunter (4), Knight (2), Brodie (4), B. Griffiths (2), Wood. Plus one goal 'scrambled through'.

Record Defeat: 1–10 v Newton Heath, Division 1, 15 October 1892.

Most League Points (2 for a win): 64, Division 1, 1957–58.

Most League Points (3 for a win): 92, Division 4, 1988–89.

Most League Goals: 115, Division 2, 1931–32.

Highest League Scorer in Season: Dennis Westcott, 38, Division 1, 1946–47.

Most League Goals in Total Aggregate: Steve Bull, 202, 1986–95.

Most Capped Player: Billy Wright, 105, England (70 consecutive).

Most League Appearances: Derek Parkin, 501, 1967–82.

Record Transfer Fee Received: £1,150,000 from Manchester C for Steve Daley, September 1979.

Record Transfer Fee Paid: £1,300,000 to Bradford C for Dean Richards, May 1995.

Football League Record: 1888 Founder Member of Football League: 1906–23 Division 2; 1923–24 Division 3 (N); 1924–32 Division 2; 1932–65 Division 1; 1965–67 Division 2; 1967–76 Division 1; 1976–77 Division 2; 1977–82 Division 1; 1982–83 Division 2; 1983–84 Division 1; 1984–85 Division 2; 1985–86 Division 3; 1986–88 Division 4; 1988–89 Division 3; 1989–92 Division 2; 1992– Division 1.

Honours: *Football League:* Division 1 – Champions 1953–54, 1957–58, 1958–59; Runners-up 1937–38, 1938–39, 1949–50, 1954–55, 1959–60; Division 2 – Champions 1931–32, 1976–77; Runners-up 1966–67, 1982–83; Division 3 (N) – Champions 1923–24; Division 3 – Champions 1988–89; Division 4 – Champions 1987–88. *FA Cup:* Winners 1893, 1908, 1949, 1960; Runners-up 1889, 1896, 1921, 1939. *Football League Cup:* Winners 1974, 1980. *Texaco Cup:* 1971. *Sherpa Van Trophy:* Winners 1988. **European Competitions:** *European Cup:* 1958–59, 1959–60. *European Cup-Winners' Cup:* 1960–61. *UEFA Cup:* 1971–72 (runners-up), 1973–74, 1974–75, 1980–81.

Colours: Gold shirts, black shorts, gold stockings. **Change colours:** White shirts, white shorts, white stockings.

WOLVERHAMPTON WANDERERS 1994–95 LEAGUE RECORD

Match No.	Date		Venue	Opponents	Result		H/T Score	Lg. Pos.	Goalscorers	Attendance
1	Aug	13	H	Reading	W	1-0	1-0	—	Froggatt	27,012
2		21	A	Notts Co	D	1-1	0-1	—	Thompson (pen)	8569
3		28	H	WBA	W	2-0	1-0	3	Thompson (pen), Kelly	27,764
4		30	A	Watford	L	1-2	0-1	—	Emblen	10,108
5	Sept	3	A	Sunderland	D	1-1	1-1	7	Venus	15,111
6		10	H	Tranmere R	W	2-0	1-0	3	Stewart, Emblen	27,030
7		13	H	Southend U	W	5-0	3-0	—	Emblen, Kelly, Froggatt, Walters, Bull	23,608
8		17	A	Burnley	W	1-0	0-0	1	Bull	17,766
9		24	A	Portsmouth	W	2-1	1-1	1	Walters, Kelly	13,466
10	Oct	1	H	Port Vale	W	2-1	0-0	1	Thompson 2 (2 pens)	27,469
11		8	A	Swindon T	L	2-3	2-2	1	Kelly 2	14,036
12		15	H	Grimsby T	W	2-1	1-1	1	Thompson (pen), Venus	24,447
13		22	H	Millwall	D	3-3	1-1	1	Bull 2, Venus	25,059
14		30	A	Stoke C	D	1-1	1-1	1	Bull	15,928
15	Nov	1	A	Bristol C	W	5-1	2-1	—	Walters, Thompson (pen), Kelly 3	10,401
16		5	H	Luton T	L	2-3	0-1	1	Stewart, Johnson (og)	26,749
17		20	A	Middlesbrough	L	0-1	0-0	2		19,953
18		23	H	Bolton W	W	3-1	0-1	—	Thompson (pen), Coleman (og), Birch	25,903
19		27	H	Derby Co	L	0-2	0-1	2		22,768
20	Dec	4	A	Millwall	L	0-1	0-0	3		8025
21		10	H	Notts Co	W	1-0	0-0	2	Bull	25,786
22		18	A	Reading	L	2-4	1-2	2	Bull, Quinn (og)	10,136
23		26	A	Oldham Ath	L	1-4	0-1	4	Dennison	11,962
24		28	H	Charlton Ath	W	2-0	2-0	—	Bull, Chapple (og)	26,738
25		31	A	Barnsley	W	3-1	2-1	2	Dennison, Mills, Emblen	9207
26	Jan	2	H	Sheffield U	D	2-2	0-0	2	De Wolf (pen), Emblen	27,809
27		14	H	Stoke C	W	2-0	1-0	2	Kelly, Dennison	28,298
28	Feb	4	A	Bolton W	L	1-5	1-2	4	Goodman	16,964
29		11	H	Bristol C	W	2-0	1-0	2	Dennison, Kelly	25,451
30		21	H	Middlesbrough	L	0-2	0-0	—		27,611
31		25	A	Port Vale	W	4-2	3-1	5	De Wolf 3 (1 pen), Bull	13,676
32	Mar	5	H	Portsmouth	W	1-0	0-0	4	Bull	23,284
33		8	H	Sunderland	W	1-0	0-0	—	Thompson (pen)	25,926
34		15	A	WBA	L	0-2	0-1	—		20,661
35		18	H	Watford	D	1-1	1-0	5	Thomas	24,380
36		24	H	Burnley	W	2-0	1-0	—	Bull, Emblen	25,703
37	Apr	1	A	Southend U	W	1-0	0-0	3	Bull	8522
38		4	A	Luton T	D	3-3	0-2	—	Kelly 2, Emblen	9651
39		8	H	Barnsley	D	0-0	0-0	4		26,385
40		12	A	Derby Co	D	3-3	1-1	—	Goodman, Richards 2	16,040
41		15	A	Charlton Ath	L	2-3	1-1	4	Bull 2	10,922
42		17	H	Oldham Ath	W	2-1	1-1	4	Kelly 2	25,840
43		22	A	Sheffield U	D	3-3	0-1	4	Goodman, Bull, Kelly	16,714
44		29	A	Grimsby T	D	0-0	0-0	4		10,112
45	May	3	A	Tranmere R	D	1-1	0-1	—	Bull	12,306
46		7	H	Swindon T	D	1-1	1-1	4	Thompson (pen)	26,245

Final League Position: 4

GOALSCORERS

League (77): Bull 16, Kelly D 15, Thompson 9 (9 pens), Emblen 7, Dennison 4, De Wolf 4 (2 pens), Goodman 3, Venus 3, Walters 3, Froggatt 2, Richards 2, Stewart 2, Birch 1, Mills 1, Thomas 1, own goals 4.
Coca-Cola Cup (6): Bull 2, Kelly D 2, Birch 1, Froggatt 1.
FA Cup (7): Kelly D 4, Cowans 1, Dennison 1, Mills 1.

Stowell M. 37	Smith J.J.A. 24 + 1	Thompson A.R. 30 + 1	Ferguson D. 22 + 2	Emblen N.R. 23 + 4	Shirtliff P.A. 26 + 2	Keen K.I. 1	Thomas G.R. 13 + 1	Bull S.G. 31	Kelly D.T. 38 + 4	Froggatt S.J. 20	Mills R.L. 6 + 5	Blades P.A. 30 + 2	Venus M. 35 + 4	Rankine S.M. 24 + 3	Birch P. 8 + 2	Stewart P.A. 5 + 3	Walters M.E. 11	Daley A.M. — + 1	Bennett T.M. 4 + 4	De Wolf J. 13	Goodman D.R. 24	Jones P.S. 9	Law B.J. 17	Cowans G.S. 21	Dennison R. 21 + 1	Masters N.B. 3 + 2	Wright J.H. — + 6	Richards D.I. 10	*Match No.*
1	2	3	4	5	6	7	8	9	10	11	12																		1
1	2	3	4		6		8		10	11		5	7	9															2
1	2	3	4	7	6		8		10	11		5	12		9														3
1	2	3	4	7	6		8		*10*	11		5	12	14	9														4
1	2	3	11	4	6				10			5	8	12	7	9													5
1	2	3	8	4	6			9	12	11			5			10	7												6
1	2	3	8	4	6			9	10	11			5				7												7
1	2	3	8	4	6			9	10	11			5				7												8
1	2	3	8		6			9	10	11		5	4				7												9
1	2	3	8		6			9		11		5	4	10			7												10
1	2	3	8		6			9	10			5	4		7		11												11
1	2	3	8		6			9	10	11		5	4	12			7												12
1	2	3	8		6			9	10	11		5	4				7	12											13
1	*2*	3	12	4			8	9	10	11		5	6			14	7												14
1	2	3	4				8	9	10	11		5	6			12	7												15
1	2	3	4	12			8	9	10	11		5	6			14	*7*												16
1		3	4	7			8		10	11		5	6	2	12	9													17
1		3	4	12			8		10	11		5	6	2	7	9													18
1	12	3	4	14			8		10	11		5	6	2	7	*9*													19
1	2		4	7			8	9	10	11	12	5	6						3										20
1	2		4	6				9	12	11		14	3	7					*10*	5	8								21
1	2		10	4				9		11	14	6	3	7	*12*					5	8								22
	2		10	4							9		3	7						5		1	6	8	11	12			23
				4				9			8	2	3						12	5	7	1	6	10	11	14			24
				4					12		9	2	3						8	5	7	1	6	10	11				25
				4					8		9	3	2							5	7	1	6	10	11				26
				4					8		9	2	3		7					5		1	6	10	11				27
		3		*4*			12		8		9	2							14	5	7	1	6	10	11				28
		3		*4*					8		12	2		7					14	5	9	1	6	10	11				29
		3			12		4		8		14		*2*	7						5	9	1	6	10	11				30
		3			6			9	8			2	12	4						5	7	1		10	11				31
1		3			6			9	8			2		4						5	7			10	11				32
1	2	3			6			*9*	8					4					12	5	7			10	11		14		33
1	2	3		12	6			*9*	8					4							7		5	10	11		14		34
1		3			6		8		9			2	12	*7*					4		10		5		11		14		35
1				10	6			9	8			2	3	4							7		5		11				36
1				4				9	8			2	10								7		5		11	3		6	37
1				4				9	12			2	11		7						8		5	10	14	*3*		6	38
1			14	4	12			9	8					2							7		5	10	*11*	3		6	39
1	3				6			9	8				11	4							7		5	10			12	2	40
1	3				*6*			9	8			12	11	4							7		5	10			14	2	41
1					6			9	8				3	4							7		5	10	11			2	42
1		12			6			9	8			2	3	4							7			10	11			5	43
1		2			6			9	8				3	4							7			10	11			5	44
1		2			6			9	8				3	4							7			10	11			5	45
1		2			6			9	8				3	4							7			10	11		12	5	46

Coca-Cola Cup

Second Round	Chesterfield (a)	3-1
	(h)	1-1
Third Round	Nottingham F (h)	2-3

FA Cup

Third Round	Mansfield T (a)	3-2
Fourth Round	Sheffield W (a)	0-0
	(h)	1-1
Fifth Round	Leicester C (h)	1-0
Sixth Round	Crystal Palace (a)	1-1
	(h)	1-4

WREXHAM 1994–95 *Back row (left to right):* Barry Jones, Barry Hunter, Mike Lake, Scott Williams, Karl Connolly, Mark Taylor, Jonathan Cross.
Third row: Kevin Reeves (Assistant Manager), Cliff Sear (Youth Development Officer), Gary Bennett, Mark Cartwright, Bryan Hughes, Andy Marriott, Gareth Owen, Ken Dixon, Phil Hardy, Dudley Hall (Reserve Physio), Steve Wade (Physio).
Second row: Mike Rigg (Community Scheme Organiser), Stephen Pugh, Mel Pejic, David Brammer, Tony Humes, Mr W. P. Griffiths (Chairman), Brian Flynn (Manager), Steve Watkin, Wayne Phillips, Deryn Brace, Mike Buxton (Schoolboy Development Officer).
Front row: Steve Morgan, Tony Merola, Richard Barnes, Kieron Durkan.

Division 2 WREXHAM

Racecourse Ground, Mold Road, Wrexham LL11 2AN. Telephone: (01978) 262129. Fax: (01978) 357821. Commercial Dept: (01978) 352536. Community Office: (01978) 358545. Clubcall: 0891 121642.

Ground capacity: 11,881.

Record attendance: 34,445 v Manchester U, FA Cup 4th rd, 26 January 1957.

Record receipts: £126,012 v West Ham U, FA Cup 4th rd, 4 February 1992.

Pitch measurements: 111yd × 71yd.

Chairman: W. P. Griffiths.

Managing Director: D. L. Rhodes.

Directors: C. Griffiths, S. Mackreth, G. Paletta, B. Williams (vice-chairman), P. Griffiths.

Manager: Brian Flynn. ***Assistant Manager:*** Kevin Reeves.

Secretary: D. L. Rhodes. ***Player-Coach:*** Joey Jones.

Commercial Manager: P. Stokes. ***Physio:*** Steve Wade.

Year Formed: 1873 (oldest club in Wales).

Turned Professional: 1912. ***Ltd Co.:*** 1912.

Previous Ground: Acton Park.

Club Nickname: 'Robins'.

Foundation: The oldest club still in existence in Wales, Wrexham was founded in 1873 by a group of local businessmen initially to play a 17-a-side game against the Provincial Insurance team. By 1875 their team formation was reduced to 11 men and a year later they were among the founders of the Welsh FA.

First Football League game: 27 August, 1921, Division 3(N), v Hartlepools U (h) L 0-2 – Godding; Ellis, Simpson; Matthias, Foster, Griffiths; Burton, Goode, Cotton, Edwards, Lloyd.

Record League Victory: 10–1 v Hartlepools, Division 4, 3 March 1962 – Keelan; Peter Jones, McGavan; Tecwyn Jones, Fox, Ken Barnes; Ron Barnes (3), Bennion (1), Davies (3), Ambler (3), Ron Roberts.

Record Cup Victory: 6–0 v Gateshead, FA Cup, 1st rd, 20 November 1976 – Lloyd; Evans, Whittle, Davis, Roberts, Thomas (Hill), Shinton (3 incl. 1p), Sutton, Ashcroft (2), Lee (1), Griffiths. 6–0 v Charlton Ath, FA Cup, 3rd rd, 5 January 1980 – Davies; Darracott, Kenworthy, Davis, Jones (Hill), Fox, Vinter (3), Sutton, Edwards (1), McNeil (2), Carrodus.

Record Defeat: 0–9 v Brentford, Division 3, 15 October 1963.

Most League Points (2 for a win): 61, Division 4, 1969–70 and Division 3, 1977–78.

Most League Points (3 for a win): 80, Division 3, 1992–93.

Most League Goals: 106, Division 3 (N), 1932–33.

Highest League Scorer in Season: Tom Bamford, 44, Division 3 (N), 1933–34.

Most League Goals in Total Aggregate: Tom Bamford, 175, 1928–34.

Most Capped Player: Dai Davies, 28 (51), Wales.

Most League Appearances: Arfon Griffiths, 592, 1959–61, 1962–79.

Record Transfer Fee Received: £300,000 from Manchester U for Mickey Thomas, November 1978, from Manchester C for Bobby Shinton, July 1979 and from Liverpool for Lee Jones, March 1992.

Record Transfer Fee Paid: £210,000 to Liverpool for Joey Jones, October 1978.

Football League Record: 1921 Original Member of Division 3 (N); 1958–60 Division 3; 1960–62 Division 4; 1962–64 Division 3; 1964–70 Division 4; 1970–78 Division 3; 1978–82 Division 2; 1982–83 Division 3; 1983–92 Division 4; 1992–93 Division 3; 1993– Division 2.

Honours: *Football League:* Division 2 best season: 15th, 1978–79; Division 3 – Champions 1977–78; Division 3 (N) – Runners-up 1932–33; Division 4 – Runners-up 1969–70. *FA Cup:* best season: 6th rd, 1974, 1978. *Football League Cup:* best season: 5th rd, 1961, 1978. *Welsh Cup:* Winners 23 times. Runners-up 22 times. Victories equal record, but record number of final appearances. **European Competition:** *European Cup-Winners' Cup:* 1972–73, 1975–76, 1978–79, 1979–80, 1984–85, 1986–87, 1990–91.

Colours: Red shirts, white shorts, red stockings. **Change colours:** Gold shirts, black shorts, black stockings.

WREXHAM 1994–95 LEAGUE RECORD

Match No.	Date	Venue	Opponents	Result		H/T Score	Lg. Pos.	Goalscorers	Attendance
1	Aug 13	H	Bournemouth	W	2-0	2-0	—	Pejic, Bennett (pen)	3580
2	20	A	Shrewsbury T	D	2-2	2-1	7	Bennett 2 (1 pen)	5748
3	27	H	Brighton & HA	W	2-1	1-0	4	Bennett 2 (1 pen)	3339
4	30	A	Cardiff C	D	0-0	0-0	—		4903
5	Sept 3	A	Brentford	W	2-0	2-0	4	Watkin, Phillips	5820
6	10	H	Crewe Alex	W	1-0	0-0	3	Owen	6399
7	13	H	Bradford C	L	0-1	0-1	—		4179
8	17	A	Bristol R	L	2-4	0-1	8	Brammer, Connolly	4441
9	24	A	Blackpool	L	1-2	0-0	12	Cross	5015
10	Oct 1	H	Birmingham C	D	1-1	1-0	13	Connolly	6002
11	8	A	Cambridge U	W	2-1	0-0	8	Bennett 2 (1 pen)	3221
12	15	H	Hull C	D	2-2	0-1	10	Bennett (pen), Hughes	3418
13	22	H	Oxford U	W	3-2	2-2	10	Richardson 2, Connolly	3925
14	30	A	Chester C	D	1-1	0-1	11	Owen	4974
15	Nov 1	A	Huddersfield T	L	1-2	0-1	—	Connolly	9639
16	5	H	Wycombe W	W	4-1	2-0	8	Bennett 3, Connolly	3747
17	19	A	Plymouth Arg	L	1-4	1-2	9	Durkan	6936
18	26	H	Swansea C	W	4-1	2-0	7	Hughes, Watkin 2, Owen	3598
19	Dec 10	H	Shrewsbury T	L	0-1	0-0	11		5859
20	16	A	Bournemouth	W	3-1	1-1	—	Hughes, Watkin, Bennett	2505
21	26	A	Stockport Co	D	1-1	0-1	9	Bennett (pen)	5636
22	27	H	Peterborough U	D	3-3	0-2	11	Bennett 2 (2 pens), Morris	4689
23	Jan 14	H	Leyton Orient	W	4-1	1-0	13	Bennett 3, Connolly	6616
24	Feb 4	A	Swansea C	D	0-0	0-0	13		4563
25	7	A	York C	W	1-0	1-0	—	Bennett	3140
26	11	H	Huddersfield T	L	1-2	1-0	12	Bennett	5894
27	14	H	Chester C	D	2-2	2-1	—	Connolly, Bennett	5698
28	18	A	Leyton Orient	D	1-1	0-1	12	Hughes	3135
29	21	H	Plymouth Arg	W	3-1	0-1	—	Bennett 2, Hughes	3030
30	25	A	Birmingham C	L	2-5	2-1	12	Bennett 2	18,884
31	Mar 4	H	Blackpool	L	0-1	0-0	13		4251
32	7	H	Brentford	D	0-0	0-0	—		2834
33	11	A	Brighton & HA	L	0-4	0-0	14		7514
34	14	H	Rotherham U	W	3-1	1-1	—	Hughes, Durkan, Bennett	1823
35	18	H	Cardiff C	L	0-3	0-1	14		3023
36	21	A	Crewe Alex	W	3-1	0-0	—	Morris, Connolly, Bennett	3632
37	25	H	Bristol R	D	1-1	0-1	13	Hughes	3170
38	Apr 1	A	Bradford C	D	1-1	1-1	13	Bennett	4461
39	4	A	Oxford U	D	0-0	0-0	—		4729
40	8	H	York C	D	1-1	0-0	14	Connolly	2558
41	11	A	Wycombe W	L	0-3	0-3	—		5115
42	15	A	Peterborough U	L	0-1	0-1	14		4309
43	17	H	Stockport Co	W	1-0	0-0	13	Hughes	3041
44	22	A	Rotherham U	W	1-0	0-0	12	Bennett	2628
45	29	A	Hull C	L	2-3	1-2	13	Connolly, Hughes	3683
46	May 6	H	Cambridge U	L	0-1	0-1	13		3172

Final League Position: 13

GOALSCORERS

League (65): Bennett 29 (8 pens), Connolly 10, Hughes 9, Watkin 4, Owen 3, Durkan 2, Morris 2, Richardson 2, Brammer 1, Cross 1, Pejic 1, Phillips 1.
Coca-Cola Cup (8): Bennett 2 (1 pen), Watkin 2, Connolly 1, Cross 1, Humes 1, Jones 1.
FA Cup (10): Bennett 2 (1 pen), Connolly 2, Durkan 2, Watkin 2, Cross 1, Hughes 1.

Marriott A. 46	Jones B. 44	Hardy P. 44	Lake M.C. 2	Humes A. 28 + 1	Pejic M. 18 + 2	Bennett G.M. 45	Owen G. 24 + 4	Connolly K. 45	Watkin S. 24 + 8	Cross J.N. 18 + 6	Phillips W. 13 + 5	Brammer D. 13 + 1	Taylor P.M.R. 3	Hunter B.V. 35 + 2	Hughes B. 37 + 1	Brace D. 10 + 4	Durkan K.J. 28 + 2	Williams S.J. 8 + 2	Richardson N.J. 4	Morris S. 10 + 2	Pugh S. — + 1	Quigley M.A. 4	Coady L. 2	Barnes R.I. — + 1	McGregor M.D.T. 1	Match No.
1	2	3	4	5	6	7	8	9	10	11	12															1
1	2	3	4	5	*6*	7		9	10		12	8	11	14												2
1	2	3		5		7		9	10		4	8	11	6												3
1	2	3		5		7		9	10		4	8	11	6	12	14										4
1	2	3		5				9	10	7	4	8		6		12	11									5
1	2	3		5		7	8	9	10	12	*4*			6		14	11									6
1	2	3		5		7	8	9		10		4		6			11									7
1	2	3		5		7	8	9	12	10		4		6			11									8
1	*2*	3			6	7	8	9	10	12		4		5		14	11									9
1	2	3			6	7	8	9		10				5	4		11									10
1	2	3		6		7	8	9		10				5	4		11									11
1	2			3	6	7	8	9		10				5	4		11	12								12
1	2	3		6		7	8	9		10				5	11				4							13
1	2	3		6		7	8	9		10				5	11				4							14
1	2	3		6		7	8	9	12	10				5	11				4							15
1	2	3		6		7	8	9	12	10				5	11				4							16
1	2	3		6		7	8	9	10	14	12			5	4		11									17
1	5	3			6	7	8	9	10						4	2	11									18
1	5	3			6	7	8	9	10	12		11			4	2										19
1	2	3		5	6	7	8	9	10	12					4		11									20
1	2	3		5	6	7	8	9							4		11			10						21
1	2	3		5	6	7	8	9						12	4		*11*			10	14					22
1	2	3		6	12	7	8	9		*10*				5	4		11			14						23
1	2	3		6		7		9	10	11	8			5	4											24
1	2	3		6	12	7		9	10					5	4		11	8								25
1	2	3			6	7	12	9	10					5	4		11	8								26
1	2	3			6	7	8	9	10	12				5	4		11									27
1	2	3			6	7		9	10	11				5	4							8				28
1	2	3			6	7		9	10	11				5	4							8				29
1	2	3			6	7		9	10	11				5	4		12					8				30
1	2	3		6		7	12	9	10					5	4		11					8				31
1	2	3		5	6	7	8	9	10		11				4											32
1	2	3		5	6	7	*8*		10	9	11	12			4			14								33
1	6	3		5		7	8	9			4				10	2	11									34
1	2	3		6		7	8	9	10		4			5	11					12						35
1	6	3				7		9						5	4	2	11	8		10						36
1	6	3				7		9	12	10				5	4	2	11	8								37
1	5	3				7		8			12			6	11	2	4	10		9						38
1	6	3				7		9	12					5	4	2	11	8		10						39
1	6	3				7		9	12		2			5	4		11	8		10						40
1	6	3				7		9	12		14			5	4	2	11	*8*		10						41
1	6	3				7	12	9	10		2	8		5	4		11									42
1	6	3		12		7		9	*10*			8		5	4	2	14						11			43
1		3		6		7		9				8		5	4	2				10			11			44
1				3	6	7		9			2	8		5	4		11			10				12		45
1	6	3				7	12	9	14		2	8			4		11			10					5	46

Coca-Cola Cup

First Round	Doncaster R (a)	4-2
	(h)	1-1
Second Round	Coventry C (h)	1-2
	(a)	2-3

FA Cup

First Round	Stockport Co (h)	1-0
Second Round	Rotherham U (h)	5-2
Third Round	Ipswich T (h)	2-1
Fourth Round	Manchester U (a)	2-5

WYCOMBE WANDERERS 1994–95 *Back row (left to right):* Steve Guppy, Simon Stapleton, Glyn Creaser, Terry Evans, Dave Carroll, Simon Garner, Duncan Hocton.
Centre row: Clive Jones, Nicky Smith, Shaun Stevens, Matt Crossley, Keith Ryan, Paul Hyde, Chuck Moussaddik, Lee Turnbull, David Titterton, Jason Cousins, Steve Walford (Youth Team Coach).
Front row: Steve Thompson, Simon Hutchinson, Tony Hemmings, Martin O'Neill (Manager), Paul Franklin (Coach), Steve Brown, Tim Langford, Nicky Reid.

Division 2 WYCOMBE WANDERERS

Adams Park, Hillbottom Road, Sands, High Wycombe HP12 4HJ. Telephone (01494) 472100. Fax: (01494) 527633. Credit Card Hotline: (01494) 441118. Information Line 0891 446855.

Ground Capacity: 9650.

Record attendance: 9002 v West Ham U, FA Cup 3rd rd, 7 January 1995.

Record receipts: £61,221 (net of VAT) v West Ham U, FA Cup 3rd rd, 7 January 1995.

Pitch measurements: 115 × 75yd.

Patron: J. Adams.

President: M. E. Seymour.

Chairman: I. L. Beeks.

Directors: G. Peart (Financial), G. Richards, B. R. Lee, A. Parry, A. Thibault, G. Cox.

Manager: Alan Smith. ***Assistant Manager:*** –. ***Secretary:*** John Reardon. ***Coach:***– . ***Physio:*** David Jones. ***Marketing Manager:*** Mark Austin. ***Promotions Manager:*** Mike Phillips.

Year Formed: 1884. ***Turned professional:*** 1974. ***Club Nicknames:*** 'Chairboys' (after High Wycombe's tradition of furniture making), 'The Blues'.

Previous Ground: 1887 The Rye; 1893 Spring Meadow; 1895 Loakes Park, 1899 Daws Hill Park; 1901 Loakes Park; 1990 Adams Park.

Foundation: In 1884 a group of young furniture trade workers started playing together informally under the name of North Town Wanderers, the area of the town where they lived. They decided to better themselves by entering junior football and in 1887 Jim Ray, secretary, and Datchett Webb, captain, called a meeting at the Steam Engine public house. Wycombe Wanderers FC was formed and probably named after the famous FA Cup winners, The Wanderers, who had visited the town in 1877 for a tie with the original High Wycombe club.

First Football League game: 14 August 1993, Division 3 v Carlisle U (a), D 2-2: Hyde; Cousins, Horton (Langford), Kerr, Crossley, Ryan, Carroll, Stapleton, Thompson, Scott, Guppy (1) (Hutchinson). Wycombe's first goal was an own goal by Chris Curran.

Record League Victory: 4–0 v Scarborough (h), Division 3, 2 November 1993: Hyde; Cousins, Horton, Crossley (1), Evans T, Ryan, Carroll (1), Hayrettin, Thompson (Hemmings), Scott (2), Guppy.

Record Cup Victory: 4–0 v Boston U (h), FA Cup 1st rd replay, 21 November 1990: Granville; Crossley, Walford, Kerr, Creaser (1), Carroll, Blackler, Stapleton (Smith), West (2), Evans N (Ryan (1)), Hutchinson.

Most League points: 70, Division 3, 1993–94.

Most League goals: 66, Division 3, 1993–94.

Highest League goalscorer in season: Keith Scott, 10, 1993–94.

Most League appearances: Paul Hyde 88, 1993–95.

Record Transfer Fee Received: £375,000 from Swindon T for Keith Scott, November 1993.

Record Transfer Fee Paid: £140,000 to Birmingham C for Steve McGavin, March 1995.

Football League Record: Promoted to Division 3 from GMVC in 1993; 1993–94 Division 3; 1994– Division 2.

Honours: *Football League:* Division 2 best season: 6th, 1994–95; *FA Amateur Cup:* Winners 1931; *FA Trophy:* Winners 1991, 1993; *GM Vauxhall Conference:* Winners 1992–93; *FA Cup:* best season: 3rd rd 1975, 1986, 1994, 1995; *Football League Cup:* best season: 2nd rd 1994.

Colours: Light & dark blue quartered shirts, dark blue shorts, dark blue stockings. **Change colours:** First: all yellow. Second: black and red striped shirts.

Founded 1884

WYCOMBE WANDERERS 1994–95 LEAGUE RECORD

Match No.	Date	Venue	Opponents	Result		H/T Score	Lg. Pos.	Goalscorers	Attendance
1	Aug 13	H	Cambridge U	W	3-0	1-0	—	Garner, Hemmings, Cousins (pen)	5782
2	20	A	Huddersfield T	W	1-0	1-0	5	Garner	13,334
3	27	H	Bristol R	D	0-0	0-0	5		5895
4	30	A	Birmingham C	W	1-0	0-0	—	Regis	14,305
5	Sept 3	A	Bradford C	L	1-2	0-1	6	Cousins (pen)	8010
6	10	H	Brentford	W	4-3	1-1	6	Evans, Garner 2, Regis	6847
7	13	H	Hull C	L	1-2	0-1	—	Evans	4626
8	17	A	Crewe Alex	W	2-1	2-0	4	Regis, Carroll	4466
9	24	A	Stockport Co	L	1-4	0-3	5	Turnbull	4607
10	Oct 1	H	Swansea C	W	1-0	1-0	4	Carroll	4150
11	8	H	Leyton Orient	W	2-1	1-0	4	Regis, Thompson	5668
12	15	A	Plymouth Arg	D	2-2	1-2	5	Regis 2	6864
13	22	A	Peterborough U	W	3-1	1-1	3	Regis, Garner, Thompson	5924
14	29	H	York C	D	0-0	0-0	4		7140
15	Nov 1	H	Shrewsbury T	W	1-0	1-0	—	Regis	4620
16	5	A	Wrexham	L	1-4	0-2	5	Ryan	3747
17	19	H	Cardiff C	W	3-1	1-0	4	Ryan 2, Hemmings	5391
18	26	A	Blackpool	W	1-0	0-0	4	Kerr	4846
19	Dec 10	H	Huddersfield T	W	2-1	0-1	3	Booth (og), Garner	6790
20	16	A	Cambridge U	D	2-2	1-1	—	Patterson, Evans	3713
21	26	H	Brighton & HA	D	0-0	0-0	3		7085
22	27	A	Oxford U	W	2-0	1-0	2	Ryan, Garner	9540
23	31	H	Bournemouth	D	1-1	0-1	3	Carroll	5990
24	Jan 14	A	Rotherham U	L	0-2	0-1	6		3537
25	31	A	Chester C	W	2-0	2-0	—	De Souza 2	1524
26	Feb 4	H	Blackpool	D	1-1	1-0	5	De Souza	6380
27	11	A	Shrewsbury T	D	2-2	0-1	5	Stapleton, De Souza (pen)	3945
28	18	H	Rotherham U	W	2-0	0-0	5	De Souza, Stapleton	5153
29	21	A	Cardiff C	L	0-2	0-0	—		3024
30	25	A	Swansea C	D	1-1	0-0	6	De Souza	3699
31	Mar 4	H	Stockport Co	D	1-1	0-1	7	Evans	5275
32	11	A	Bristol R	L	0-1	0-1	9		5118
33	14	A	York C	D	0-0	0-0	—		2800
34	18	H	Birmingham C	L	0-3	0-2	11		7289
35	21	A	Brentford	D	0-0	0-0	—		9530
36	25	H	Crewe Alex	D	0-0	0-0	10		6288
37	28	H	Peterborough U	W	3-1	1-0	—	Garner 2, Brown	4590
38	Apr 1	A	Hull C	D	0-0	0-0	8		5054
39	4	H	Bradford C	W	3-1	3-0	—	Soloman, Hemmings, Carroll	4522
40	8	A	Bournemouth	L	0-2	0-1	7		8615
41	11	H	Wrexham	W	3-0	3-0	—	McGavin, Bell 2	5115
42	15	H	Oxford U	W	1-0	1-0	5	Carroll	7683
43	19	A	Brighton & HA	D	1-1	0-1	—	Carroll	8094
44	22	H	Chester C	W	3-1	2-1	5	Hemmings 2, McGavin	5284
45	29	H	Plymouth Arg	L	1-2	0-1	6	Bell	6850
46	May 6	A	Leyton Orient	W	1-0	0-0	6	Regis	4698

Final League Position: 6

GOALSCORERS

League (60): Garner 9, Regis 9, Carroll 6, De Souza 6 (1 pen), Hemmings 5, Evans 4, Ryan 4, Bell 3, Cousins 2 (2 pens), McGavin 2, Stapleton 2, Thompson 2, Brown 1, Kerr 1, Patterson 1, Soloman 1, Turnbull 1, own goal 1.
Coca-Cola Cup (2): Regis 1, Turnbull 1.
FA Cup (9): Garner 3, Bell 2, Ryan 2, Stapleton 2.

Hyde P.D. 46	Cousins J.M. 41	Titterton D.S.J. 1	Crossley M.J.W. 35 + 1	Evans T.W. 44	Ryan K.J. 24	Carroll D.F. 41	Thompson S. 25 + 10	Regis C. 30 + 5	Garner S. 35 + 6	Stapleton S.J. 24 + 2	Hemmings A.G. 10 + 10	Creaser G.R. 2 + 2	Brown S. 38 + 2	Turner A.P. 3 + 1	Skinner J.J. 4 + 1	Hutchinson S. — + 4	Langford T. 1 + 5	Turnbull L.M. 2 + 3	Bell M. 31	Kerr P.A. — + 1	Patterson G. 9 + 4	De Souza J.M. 6 + 1	Howard T. 20	Skiverton T.J. 8 + 2	Reid N.S. 3	Garland P.J. 5	Soloman J.R. 5 + 1	McGavin S.J. 12	Wallace D.L. — + 1	Clark A.J. 1	*Match No.*
1	2	3	4	5	6	7	8	9	10	*11*	12	14																			1
1	2			5	6	7	8	9	10	11	12	4	3																		2
1	2			5	6	7	8	9	*10*	11	12		3	4	14																3
1	2			5	6	7	8	9	10	11			3	4		12															4
1	2		12	5	6	7	8	9	10	11			*4*		3	14															5
1	2		4	5	6	7	8	9	10	11				12	3																6
1	2		4	5	6	7	8	9	10					11	3		12														7
1	2		4	5	6	7	8	9	10	11					3																8
1	2		4	5	6	7		9	10	11			3				8	12													9
1	2		4	5	6	7	8	9	10	14	12		3					*11*													10
1	2		4	5	6	7	8	9		10	12		3					11													11
1	2		4	5	6	7	8	9	*10*	11			3			12	14														12
1	2			5	6	7	11	9	10	4			3						8												13
1	2			5	6	7	11	9	10	4			3				12		8												14
1	2		4	5	6	7	*12*	9	10	11			3					14	8												15
1	2		4	5	6	7	12	9	10	11			3						8												16
1	2		4	5	6	7	9		10	11	12		3						8												17
1	2		4	5	6	7	9			11	10		3						8	12											18
1	2		4	5	6	7	9		10		11		3					12			8										19
1	2		4	5	6	7	9		10		11		3				12				8										20
1	2		4	5	6	7	8	9	10	11	12		3																		21
1	2		4	5	6	7	12	*9*	10	11			3						8		14										22
1	2		4	5	6	7	12	9	*10*	11			3						8		14										23
1	2		4	5	6	7	11	*9*	10	12			3				14		8												24
1	2		4	5		7	12	9	*10*	11			3						8		14	6									25
1	2		4	5		7	12	9	10	11			3						8			6									26
1	2		4	5				9	10	11		12							8		7	6	3								27
1			4	5			12	9	10	11									8		7	6	3	2							28
1			4	5			12	*9*	10	11			14						8		7	6	3	2							29
1				5			7	9	10				3						8			6	4	2	11						30
1	2			5		7	10	9			12		3						8				4	6	11						31
1	2			5		7	11	9	10				6						8		12		3	4							32
1	2			5		7	12	9	10				4						8		11		3		6						33
1	2			5			7	9	10				*4*			12			8				3	14		6	11				34
1	2		3	5		7		12	10				14						8				4			*6*	11	9			35
1	2		3	5		7		12	10				8						11				4			*6*		9	14		36
1	*2*		3	5		7			10		12		6						8		11		4	14				9			37
1			3	5		7			10		12		6						8		11		4	2				9			38
1	2		3	5		7	12		14		*10*		6						8				4				11	9			39
1	2		3	5		7		12	14		10		6						8				4				*11*	9			40
1	2		4	5		7					10		6						8				3			11		9			41
1	2		4	5		7			12		10		6						8				3			11		9			42
1	2		4			7		12	14		10		6						8				3	5			11	*9*			43
1			4			7	11		12		10	*5*	6						8				3	2			14	9			44
1	2		4	5		7	11		12		10		6						8				3					9			45
1	2		3	5		7		12					6						8		11	14	4					9		*10*	46

Coca-Cola Cup

First Round	Brighton & HA (a)	1-2
	(h)	1-3

FA Cup

First Round	Chelmsford C (h)	4-0
Second Round	Hitchin (a)	5-0
Third Round	West Ham U (h)	0-2

YORK CITY 1994–95 *Back row (left to right):* Paul Mockler, Andy McMillan, Paul Atkin, Paul Stancliffe, Steve Tutill, Tony Barras, Dean Kiely, Andy Warrington, Steve Cooper, Ian Blackstone, Elliott Simpson, Jeff Miller (Physio).

Front row: Scott Jordan, Glenn Naylor, Nigel Pepper, Paul Barnes, Jon McCarthy, Alan Little (Manager), Graeme Murty, Steve Bushell, Tony Canham, Wayne Hall, Tony Barratt.

Division 2 **YORK CITY**

Bootham Crescent, York YO3 7AQ. Telephone: (01904) 624447. Fax: (01904) 631457.

Ground capacity: 9459.

Record attendance: 28,123 v Huddersfield T, FA Cup 6th rd, 5 March 1938.

Record receipts: £38,054 v Liverpool, FA Cup 5th rd, 15 February 1986.

Pitch measurements: 115yd × 74yd.

Chairman: D. M. Craig OBE, JP, BSC, FICE, FI, MUN E, FCI ARB, M CONS E

Directors: B. A. Houghton, C. Webb, E. B. Swallow, J. E. H. Quickfall FCA.

Manager: Alan Little.

Secretary: Keith Usher. ***Commercial Manager:*** Mrs Maureen Leslie.

Physio: Jeff Miller.

Hon. Orthopaedic Surgeon: Mr Peter De Boer MA, FRCS. ***Medical Officer:*** Dr R. Porter.

Year Formed: 1922. ***Turned Professional:*** 1922. ***Ltd Co.:*** 1922.

Club Nickname: 'Minstermen'.

Previous Ground: 1922, Fulfordgate; 1932, Bootham Crescent.

Foundation: Although there was a York City club formed in 1903 by a soccer enthusiast from Darlington, this has no connection with the modern club because it went out of existence during World War I. Unlike many others of that period who restarted in 1919, York City did not re-form until 1922 and the tendency now is to ignore the modern club's pre-1922 existence.

First Football League game: 31 August, 1929, Division 3(N), v Wigan Borough (a) W 2-0 – Farmery; Archibald, Johnson; Beck, Davis, Thompson; Evans, Gardner, Cowie (1), Smailes, Stockhill (1).

Record League Victory: 9–1 v Southport, Division 3 (N), 2 February 1957 – Forgan; Phillips, Howe; Brown (1), Cairney, Mollatt; Hill, Bottom (4 incl. 1p), Wilkinson (2), Wragg (1), Fenton (1).

Record Cup Victory: 6–0 v South Shields (away), FA Cup, 1st rd, 16 November 1968 – Widdowson; Baker (1p), Richardson; Carr, Jackson, Burrows; Taylor, Ross (3), MacDougall (2), Hodgson, Boyer.

Record Defeat: 0–12 v Chester, Division 3 (N), 1 February 1936.

Most League Points (2 for a win): 62, Division 4, 1964–65.

Most League Points (3 for a win): 101, Division 4, 1983–84.

Most League Goals: 96, Division 4, 1983–84.

Highest League Scorer in Season: Bill Fenton, 31, Division 3 (N), 1951–52; Arthur Bottom, 31, Division 3 (N), 1954–55 and 1955–56.

Most League Goals in Total Aggregate: Norman Wilkinson, 125, 1954–66.

Most Capped Player: Peter Scott, 7 (10), Northern Ireland.

Most League Appearances: Barry Jackson, 481, 1958–70.

Record Transfer Fee Received: £100,000 from Carlisle U for Gordon Staniforth, October 1979, and from QPR for John Byrne, October 1985.

Record Transfer Fee Paid: £50,000 to Aldershot for Dale Banton, November 1984 and £50,000 to Stoke C for Paul Barnes, July 1992.

Football League Record: 1929 Elected to Division 3 (N); 1958–59 Division 4; 1959–60 Division 3; 1960–65 Division 4; 1965–66 Division 3; 1966–71 Division 4; 1971–74 Division 3; 1974–76 Division 2; 1976–77 Division 3; 1977–84 Division 4; 1984–88 Division 3; 1988–92 Division 4; 1992–93 Division 3; 1993– Division 2.

Honours: *Football League:* Division 2 best season: 15th, 1974–75; Division 3 – Promoted 1973–74 (3rd); Division 4 – Champions 1983–84. *FA Cup:* Semi-finals 1955, when in Division 3. *Football League Cup:* best season: 5th rd, 1962.

Colours: Red shirts, blue shorts, red stockings. **Change colours:** All blue.

YORK CITY 1994–95 LEAGUE RECORD

Match No.	Date	Venue	Opponents	Result		H/T Score	Lg. Pos.	Goalscorers	Attendance
1	Aug 13	H	Crewe Alex	L	1-2	0-0	—	Cooper	4420
2	20	A	Bristol R	L	1-3	1-1	19	McCarthy	3957
3	27	H	Cardiff C	D	1-1	0-0	18	Barnes	2861
4	31	A	Brighton & HA	L	0-1	0-0	—		6996
5	Sept 3	A	Bournemouth	W	4-1	3-0	18	Barnes 3, McCarthy	3181
6	10	H	Shrewsbury T	W	3-0	1-0	14	Barnes, Pepper, Naylor	3196
7	13	H	Brentford	W	2-1	1-1	—	Pepper, Jordan	2836
8	17	A	Bradford C	D	0-0	0-0	14		8670
9	24	A	Swansea C	D	0-0	0-0	15		2875
10	Oct 1	H	Stockport Co	L	2-4	2-2	16	Barnes (pen), Naylor	3790
11	8	H	Peterborough U	D	1-1	0-0	16	McCarthy	3601
12	15	A	Rotherham U	L	1-2	0-2	16	Pepper	3380
13	22	H	Chester C	W	2-0	1-0	14	McCarthy, Barnes	2820
14	29	A	Wycombe W	D	0-0	0-0	13		7140
15	Nov 1	A	Hull C	L	0-3	0-3	—		6551
16	5	H	Huddersfield T	W	3-0	2-0	15	Baker, Naylor, Barnes	6345
17	19	A	Leyton Orient	W	1-0	0-0	15	Barnes	3532
18	26	H	Plymouth Arg	W	1-0	0-0	14	McCarthy	3185
19	Dec 10	H	Bristol R	L	0-3	0-1	15		3094
20	16	A	Crewe Alex	L	1-2	0-2	—	Barnes (pen)	3432
21	26	H	Blackpool	W	4-0	2-0	14	Barnes 3, Naylor	4542
22	28	A	Cambridge U	L	0-1	0-0	—		3285
23	Jan 2	A	Oxford U	W	2-0	1-0	14	Naylor, Marsh (og)	6386
24	7	A	Chester C	W	4-0	0-0	13	Barnes, Jordan, McCarthy, Alsford (og)	1844
25	14	H	Birmingham C	W	2-0	1-0	12	McCarthy, Canham	6828
26	Feb 4	A	Plymouth Arg	W	2-1	0-1	11	Baker, Naylor	5572
27	7	H	Wrexham	L	0-1	0-1	—		3140
28	18	A	Birmingham C	L	2-4	0-2	13	Baker, McCarthy	14,846
29	21	H	Leyton Orient	W	4-1	2-1	—	Bellamy (og), Baker 2, Naylor	2926
30	25	A	Stockport Co	W	3-2	2-1	10	Baker, Pepper, Dinning (og)	3570
31	28	A	Huddersfield T	L	0-3	0-1	—		10,468
32	Mar 4	H	Swansea C	L	2-4	1-1	12	Canham, Barnes	2920
33	7	H	Bournemouth	W	1-0	0-0	—	Jordan	2301
34	11	A	Cardiff C	W	2-1	2-1	12	Naylor 2	2689
35	14	H	Wycombe W	D	0-0	0-0	—		2800
36	18	H	Brighton & HA	W	1-0	1-0	8	Barnes	2915
37	21	A	Shrewsbury T	L	0-1	0-1	—		2849
38	25	H	Bradford C	D	0-0	0-0	9		5431
39	Apr 1	A	Brentford	L	0-3	0-1	12		6474
40	4	H	Hull C	W	3-1	1-0	—	Baker 2, Murty	4612
41	8	A	Wrexham	D	1-1	0-0	8	Peverell	2558
42	15	H	Cambridge U	W	2-0	1-0	8	Barras, McMillan	3278
43	18	A	Blackpool	W	5-0	3-0	—	Baker 2 (1 pen), Bushell, McCarthy, Murty	3517
44	22	H	Oxford U	L	0-2	0-1	8		3732
45	29	H	Rotherham U	W	2-0	0-0	8	Baker 2 (1 pen)	3183
46	May 6	A	Peterborough U	D	1-1	0-0	9	Baker	4983

Final League Position: 9

GOALSCORERS

League (67): Barnes 16 (2 pens), Baker 13 (2 pens), McCarthy 9, Naylor 9, Pepper 4, Jordan 3, Canham 2, Murty 2, Barras 1, Bushell 1, Cooper 1, McMillan 1, Peverell 1, own goals 4.
Coca-Cola Cup (2): Cooper 1, Pepper 1.
FA Cup (3): Naylor 2, McCarthy 1.

Kiely D.L. 46	McMillan L.A. 39 + 4	Hall W. 33 + 4	Pepper C.N. 35	Tutill S.A. 37 + 2	Stancliffe P.I. 4	McCarthy J.D. 44	Cooper S.B. 9	Barnes P.L. 35 + 1	Bushell S. 10	Canham A. 30 + 5	Naylor G. 21 + 8	Barras A. 27 + 4	Atkin P.A. 30 + 4	Jordan S.D. 33 + 4	Simpson E. 1	Wilson P.A. 21 + 1	Baker D.P. 25 + 5	Murty G.S. 17 + 3	Williams D. — + 1	Peverell N.J. 2 + 7	Barratt A. 7 + 3	Scaife N. — + 1	Match No.
1	2	3	4	5	6	7	8	9	10	11	12												1
1	2	3	4	5		7	8	9	10	11		6	12										2
1	2	3	4	5		7	8	9	10	11		6											3
1	2	3	4	5		7	8	9	10	11		6	12										4
1	2	12	4	5		7	8	9		11		6	3	10									5
1	2	12	4	5		7	*8*	9		11	14	6	3	10									6
1	2		4	5		7	8	9		11		12	6	10	3								7
1	2	3	4	5		7	8	9			12	6	11	10									8
1	2	3	4	5		7	8	9				6	11	10									9
1	2	3	4	5		7		9		12	8	6	11	10									10
1	2		4	5		7		9		11	8	6		10		3							11
1	2		4	5		7		9		11	8	6		10		3	12						12
1	2		4	5		7		9		11	8	6		10		3							13
1	2	12	4	5		7		9		11	8	6		10		3							14
1	2	3	4		5	7		9		11	8	6		10			12						15
1	2	3	4		5	7		9		11	8	6		12			10						16
1	2				5	7		9		11	8	6	4	12		3	10						17
1	2		4			7		9		11	8	6	5	12		3	10						18
1	2	3	4	12		7		9		11	14	6	5	*8*			10						19
1	2	3	4	12		7		9		11		*6*	5	8			10	14					20
1	2	3	4	5		7		9		11	8		6	*10*				12	14				21
1	2	3	4	5		7		9		11	8		6	10									22
1	2	3	4	5		7		9			8		6	10		11							23
1	2	11	4	5		7		*9*			8		6	10		3	12	14					24
1	2	11	4	5		7				12			6	10		3	9	8					25
1	2	11	4	*5*		7				12	14		6	10		3	9	8					26
1	2	11	4	5		7		14		12	8		6	10		3	*9*						27
1	2	12	4	5		7		*9*		11	8		6	10		3	14						28
1	2		4	5		7				11	8		6			3	9	10					29
1	2	10	4	5						11			6	8		3	9			7	12		30
1	2	10	4	5		7		*8*		11		12	6			3	9			14			31
1	2		4	5		7		8		11			6	10		3	9				12		32
1		3		5		7		8		11	12	14	6	10			9	4			2		33
1		3		5		7		8			11	12	6	10			9	4			2		34
1	12	11		5				8			10		6	7		3	9	4			2		35
1	12	11		5		7		9			14		6	4		3	*10*	8			2		36
1	12	11		5		7		9					6	4		3	10	8			2		37
1	12	11	4	5		7		9			*10*	6				3	14	8			2		38
1	2		*4*	5		7		9	8			6	12			3	10	11			14		39
1	2	3		5		7			8		9	6		4			10	11		12			40
1	2	3				7			4	12	*10*	6	5	8			9	11		14			41
1	2	3		5		7			4	11		6		*8*			9	10		12		14	42
1	2	3		5		7			4	11		6		8			9	10		12			43
1		3		*5*		7				11	12	6	14	4			9	10		8	2		44
1	2	3	4			7		*8*		11		6	5	12			9	10		14			45
1	2	3	4			7			8	11		6	5			12	*9*	10		14			46

Coca-Cola Cup

First Round	Burnley (a)	0-1
	(h)	2-2

FA Cup

First Round	Rotherham U (h)	3-3
	(a)	0-3

THE COMMUNITY PROGRAMME IN PROFESSIONAL FOOTBALL

The first Football and Community Capital Schemes established in 1978 attempted to bridge the gap between Professional Football Clubs and their communities and, whilst facilities were successfully established in some areas, it has become clear that there was no attempt made to extend these projects in the long term to help promote football or to cater for local people's needs. During the early 1980's, football experienced a number of difficulties not least of which was the continuing fall in average attendances. The Professional Footballers' Association took the lead in investigating the reasons why football was perceived to be ailing on many fronts. It was evident that supporters had become disenchanted with high admission costs, increased hooliganism and an underlying feeling that their Clubs had lost contact with their community and, particularly, their supporters.

The Professional Footballers' Association decided to bridge the gap that had developed and, with the support of The Football League, launched an experimental "Football and Community Programme Scheme" in 1985. Initially launched on a pilot scheme basis at 6 Clubs in the North West, the project soon expanded further afield with the addition of more Clubs in Lancashire and Cheshire. These early projects, originally funded through the Government's Community Programme Scheme, were so successful that by the end of 1990 a total of 50 Clubs had become involved in locally-based projects.

Club Project	*Telephone Number*	*Club Officer*
AFC Bournemouth	—	—
Arsenal	0171 226 2150	To Be Appointed
Aston Villa	0121 327 2299 ext 256	Ron Wylie
Barnet	0181 441 6932 (Club)	To Be Appointed
Barnsley	01226 731994	Steve Lister
Birmingham City	0121 766 6180	Jason Withe
Blackburn Rovers	01254 698888 ext. 2256	Pete Devine
Blackpool	01253 403268	Craig Madden
Bolton Wanderers	01204 364555	Geoff Lomax
Bradford City	01274 307564	Richard Angus
Brentford	0181 758 9430	Lee Doyle
Brighton & Hove Albion	01273 778855 (Club)	Steve Ford
Bristol City	0117 966 4685	Shaun Parker
Bristol Rovers	0117 986 0809	Terry Connor
Burnley	01282 831456	Bob Oates
Bury	0161 797 5423	Brian Taylor
Cambridge United	01223 416238	Mike Cook
Cardiff City	01222 668325	Glyn Jones
Carlisle United	01228 512266	John Halpin
Charlton Athletic	0181 850 2866	Jason Morgan
Chelsea	0171 385 0710	Shaun Gore
Chester City	01244 377408	John Kerr
Chesterfield	01246 550930	Adrian Shaw
Colchester United	01206 572378	Steve Bradshaw
Coventry City	01203 224093	Barry Powell
Crewe Alexandra	01270 216682	Chris Walters
Crystal Palace	0181 771 5886	Nicky Johns
Darlington	01325 381972	Iain Leckie
Derby County	—	—
Doncaster Rovers	01302 370250	Eric Randerson
Durham County FA	0191 384 8653	Keith Longstaff
Everton	0151 252 0104	Ted Sutton
Exeter City	01395 232784	Steve Neville
Farnborough Town	01252 372640	Geoff Noonan
Fulham	0171 736 6561	Gary Mulcahey
Gillingham	01634 582303	Philip Attfield
Grimsby Town	01472 291776	Ian Knight
Halifax Town	01422 368470	Paddy Roche
Hartlepool United	01429 862595	Terry Bainbridge
Hereford United	01432 341065	Brian Williams
Huddersfield Town	01484 435087	Mark Lillis
Hull City	01482 568088	John Davies
Ipswich Town	—	—
Kent County FA	01634 812032	Darren Hare
Kettering Town	01536 83028 (Club)	Domenico Genovese
Kidderminster Harriers	01562 863821	Nick Griffiths
Leeds United	0113 277 9851	Ces Podd
Leicester City	0116 255 3195	Neville Hamilton
Leyton Orient	0181 556 5973	Neil Watson
Lincoln City	01522 539671	Dean Wheatley
Liverpool	0151 263 2361 (Club)	Brian Hall
Luton Town	01582 411622 (Club)	Colwyn Rowe
Manchester City	0161 226 1782	Alex Williams
Manchester United	0161 930 2903	Dave Ryan
Mansfield Town	01623 25197	Dave Bentley
Merthyr Tydfil	01443 485888	Tommy Hutchison

Middlesbrough	01642 824605	Lawrie Pearson
Millwall	0171 231 0379	Jim Hicks
Newcastle United	0191 261 9715	Ray Hankin
Northampton Town	01604 232101	Russell Lewis
Norwich City	01603 761122	Peter Mendham
Norfolk County FA	01603 761122	Jamie Houchen
Notts County	0115 986 3656	Alan Young
Nottingham Forest	0115 981 0089	Gordon Coleman
Oldham Athletic	0161 678 8464	John Platt
Oxford United	01865 64853	Peter Rhoades-Brown
Peterborough United	—	—
Plymouth Argyle	01752 606710	Steve Rogers
Portsmouth	01705 737391	Gary Holland
Port Vale	01782 575594	Jim Cooper
Preston North End	01772 704275	Ian Johnstone
Queens Park Rangers	0181 743 0262 (Club)	Emlyn Brown
Reading	01734 560898	Chris Whalley
Rochdale	01706 43836	Keith Hicks
Rotherham United	01709 740846	Fraser Foster
Scarborough	01723 367884	Ian Kerr
Scunthorpe United	01724 280716	Richard Passmoor
Sheffield and Hallamshire CFA	0114 267 0068	Jack Detchon
Sheffield United	0114 276 9314	Tony Currie
Sheffield Wednesday	0114 231 3262	Charlie Williamson
Shrewsbury Town	01743 356623	Dick Pratley
Southampton	01703 334172	Alan Smith
Southend United	01702 341351	Frank Banks
Stockport County	0161 477 7560	Neil Mather
Stoke City	01782 744347	To Be Appointed
Sunderland	0191 510 9111	Mick Ferguson
Swansea City	01792 459363	Alan Curtis
Swindon Town	01793 421303	Shane Cook
Torquay United	01803 322551	Frank Prince
Tottenham Hotspur	—	—
Tranmere Rovers	0151 608 2354	Steve Williams
Walsall	01922 644742	Mick Kearns
Watford	01923 440449	Jimmy Gilligan
West Bromwich Albion	0121 525 0226	Mark Ashton
West Ham United	0181 548 2707	Roger Morgan
Wigan Athletic	01942 824599	Frankie Bunn
Wimbledon	0181 771 1772	Jim Lowther
Wolverhampton Wanderers	01902 716348	Tony Evans
Wrexham	01978 358545	Steve Weaver
Wycombe Wanderers	—	—
York City	01904 613017	Gordon Staniforth

Tommy Hutchinson demonstrates to a group of girls at the Llantrisant Leisure Centre.

ENGLISH LEAGUE PLAYERS DIRECTORY

Player	Ht	Wt	Pos	Birth Date	Place	Source	Clubs	League App	Gls
ABBOTT Greg	5 9	10 07	M	14 12 63	Coventry	Apprentice	Coventry C	—	—
							Bradford C	281	38
							Halifax T	28	1
						Guiseley	**Hull C**	93	10
ABLETT Gary	6 2	12 07	D	19 11 65	Liverpool	Apprentice	Liverpool	109	1
							Derby Co (loan)	6	—
							Hull C (loan)	5	—
							Everton	115	5
ABRAHAMS Paul	5 9	11 03	F	31 10 73	Colchester	Trainee	Colchester U	55	8
							Brentford	10	3
ADAMS Darren	5 7	10 07	F	12 1 74	Newham	Danson Furnace	**Cardiff C**	20	1
ADAMS Derek	5 8	11 06	M	25 6 75	Aberdeen	Aberdeen	**Burnley**	—	—
ADAMS Kieran §	5 10	11 06	M	20 10 77	St Ives	Trainee	**Barnet**	4	—
ADAMS Micky	5 8	11 03	M	8 11 61	Sheffield	Apprentice	Gillingham	92	5
							Coventry C	90	9
							Leeds U	73	2
							Southampton	144	7
							Stoke C	10	3
							Fulham	21	7
ADAMS Neil	5 8	10 08	M	23 11 65	Stoke	Local	Stoke C	32	4
							Everton	20	—
							Oldham Ath (loan)	9	—
							Oldham Ath	129	23
							Norwich C	47	3
ADAMS Tony	6 3	13 11	D	10 10 66	London	Apprentice	**Arsenal**	346	23
ADCOCK Tony *	5 10	11 09	F	27 2 63	Bethnal Green	Apprentice	Colchester U	210	98
							Manchester C	15	5
							Northampton T	72	30
							Bradford C	38	6
							Northampton T	35	10
							Peterborough U	111	35
							Luton T	2	—
ADEBOLA Dele	6 3	12 08	F	23 6 75	Lagos	Trainee	**Crewe Alex**	36	8
ADEKOLA David ‡	5 11	12 02	F	19 5 68	Lagos		Bury	35	12
							Exeter C (loan)	3	1
							Bournemouth	—	—
							Wigan Ath	4	—
							Hereford U	—	—
AFFOR Louis ‡	5 4	11 07	F	29 8 72	London	Southend U	**Barnet**	3	—
AGANA Tony	6 0	12 02	F	2 10 63	London	Weymouth	Watford	15	1
							Sheffield U	118	42
							Notts C	13	1
							Leeds U (loan)	2	—
							Notts Co	80	9
AGIADIS Charlie ‡	5 8	10 05	F	18 11 75	Middlesbrough	Trainee	**Middlesbrough**	—	—
AGNEW Paul	5 9	10 07	D	15 8 65	Lisburn	Cliftonville	Grimsby T	241	3
							WBA	14	1
AGNEW Steve	5 10	11 09	M	9 11 65	Shipley	Apprentice	Barnsley	194	29
							Blackburn R	2	—
							Portsmouth (loan)	5	—
							Leicester C	56	4
							Sunderland	16	2
AINSCOUGH Paul ‡	5 11	10 08	M	22 8 75	Blackburn	Trainee	**Blackburn R**	—	—
AINSLEY Jason	6 0	13 01	M	30 7 70	Stockton	Spennymoor	**Hartlepool U**	15	1
AINSWORTH Gareth	5 10	12 05	M	10 5 73	Blackburn	Blackburn R	Preston NE	5	—
							Cambridge U	4	1
							Preston NE	80	12

Player	Ht	Wt	Pos	Birth Date	Birth Place	Source	Clubs	League App	League Gls
AIZLEWOOD Mark *	6 1	13 12	D	1 10 59	Newport	Apprentice	Newport Co	38	1
							Luton T	98	3
							Charlton Ath	152	9
							Leeds U	70	3
							Bradford C	39	1
							Bristol C	101	3
							Cardiff C	39	3
AKINBIYI Adeola	6 1	12 08	F	10 10 74	Hackney	Trainee	**Norwich C**	15	—
							Hereford U (loan)	4	2
							Brighton (loan)	7	4
ALBERT Philippe	6 3	13 00	D	10 8 67	Bouillon	Anderlecht	**Newcastle U**	17	2
ALDOUS Richard	6 0	11 07	G	2 9 76	Sheffield	Trainee	**Sheffield W**	—	—
ALDRIDGE John	5 11	11 04	F	18 9 58	Liverpool	South Liverpool	Newport Co	170	69
							Oxford U	114	72
							Liverpool	83	50
							Real Sociedad	63	33
							Tranmere R	140	88
ALDRIDGE Martin	5 11	12 02	F	6 12 74	Northampton	Trainee	**Northampton T**	70	17
ALEXANDER Graham	5 10	12 07	M	10 10 71	Coventry	Trainee	**Scunthorpe U**	159	18
ALEXANDER Ian ‡	5 8	10 07	D	26 1 63	Glasgow	Leicester J	Rotherham U	11	—
							Motherwell	24	2
							Morton	7	1
						Pezoporikos	**Bristol R**	291	6
ALEXANDER Keith ‡	6 4	13 06	F	14 11 58	Nottingham	Barnet	Grimsby T	83	26
							Stockport Co	11	—
							Lincoln C	45	4
							Mansfield T	2	—
ALEXANDER Tim ‡	6 0	12 00	D	29 3 74	Chertsey	Wimbledon	**Barnet**	36	—
ALLAN Derek	6 0	12 01	D	24 12 74	Irving	Ayr U BC	Ayr U	5	—
							Southampton	1	—
ALLARDYCE Craig	6 3	13 07	D	9 6 75	Bolton	Trainee	Preston NE	1	—
							Blackpool	—	—
ALLEN Bradley	5 7	10 00	F	13 9 71	Harold Wood	School	**QPR**	73	26
ALLEN Chris	5 11	12 02	F	18 11 72	Oxford	Trainee	**Oxford U**	126	9
ALLEN Clive *	5 10	12 03	F	20 5 61	London	Apprentice	QPR	49	32
							Arsenal	—	—
							Crystal Palace	25	9
							QPR	87	40
							Tottenham H	105	60
						Bordeaux	Manchester C	53	16
							Chelsea	16	7
							West Ham U	38	17
							Millwall	12	—
ALLEN Gavin *	5 8	10 05	F	17 6 76	Bangor	Trainee	**Tranmere R**	—	—
ALLEN Graham	6 1	12 00	D	8 4 77	Bolton	Trainee	**Everton**	—	—
ALLEN Leighton ‡	6 0	11 02	F	22 11 73	Brighton	Trainee	Wimbledon	—	—
							Colchester U	2	—
							Gillingham	—	—
ALLEN Malcolm	5 8	11 08	F	21 3 67	Dioniolen	Apprentice	Watford	39	5
							Aston Villa (loan)	4	—
							Norwich C	35	8
							Millwall	81	24
							Newcastle U	10	5
ALLEN Martin	5 10	11 00	M	14 8 65	Reading	School	QPR	136	16
							West Ham U	187	24
ALLEN Paul	5 7	11 03	M	28 8 62	Aveley	Apprentice	West Ham U	152	6
							Tottenham H	292	23
							Southampton	43	1
							Luton T (loan)	4	—
							Stoke C (loan)	17	1
ALLISON Neil	6 2	11 10	D	20 10 73	Hull	Trainee	**Hull C**	60	1

Player	Ht	Wt	Pos	Birth Date	Birth Place	Source	Clubs	League App	League Gls
ALLISON Wayne	6 1	12 06	F	16 10 68	Huddersfield		Halifax T	84	23
							Watford	7	—
							Bristol C	195	48
ALLON Joe	5 11	12 02	F	12 11 66	Gateshead	England Youth	Newcastle U	9	2
							Swansea C	34	11
							Hartlepool U	112	50
							Chelsea	14	2
							Port Vale (loan)	6	—
							Brentford	45	19
							Southend U (loan)	3	—
							Port Vale	23	9
ALLPRESS Tim ‡	6 0	12 10	D	27 1 71	Hitchin	Trainee	Luton T	1	—
							Preston NE (loan)	9	—
						Bayer Uerdingen	**Colchester U**	34	—
ALSFORD Julian	6 2	13 07	D	24 12 72	Poole	Trainee	Watford	13	1
							Chester C	35	—
AMMANN Mike	6 2	14 04	G	8 2 71	California	Cal State Univ	**Charlton Ath**	19	—
AMOKACHI Daniel	5 10	13 00	F	30 12 72	Nigeria	FC Brugge	**Everton**	18	4
AMPADU Kwame	5 10	11 10	F	20 12 70	Bradford	Trainee	Arsenal	2	—
							Plymouth Arg (loan)	6	1
							WBA (loan)	7	1
							WBA	42	3
							Swansea C	57	6
ANDERSON Colin	5 8	10 06	M	26 4 62	Newcastle	Apprentice	Burnley	6	—
							Torquay U	109	11
							QPR (loan)	—	—
							WBA	140	10
							Walsall	26	2
							Hereford U	70	1
							Exeter C	21	1
ANDERSON Ijah			D	30 12 75	Hackney	Tottenham H	**Southend U**	—	—
ANDERSON Lee *	5 7	10 08	D	4 10 73	Manchester	Trainee	**Bury**	29	—
ANDERSON Viv	6 1	13 00	D	29 8 56	Nottingham	Apprentice	Nottingham F	328	15
							Arsenal	120	9
							Manchester U	54	2
							Sheffield W	70	8
							Barnsley	20	3
							Middlesbrough	2	—
ANDERTON Darren	6 1	12 00	F	3 3 72	Southampton	Trainee	Portsmouth	62	7
							Tottenham H	108	17
ANDRADE Jose ‡	5 11	11 07	F	1 6 70	Gaboverde	Academico	**Stoke C**	4	1
ANDREWS Ian	6 2	12 13	G	1 12 64	Nottingham	Apprentice	Leicester C	126	—
							Swindon T (loan)	1	—
							Celtic	5	—
							Leeds U (loan)	1	—
							Southampton	10	—
							Bournemouth	38	—
ANDREWS Nicky ‡	5 10	11 02	D	10 10 75	London	Trainee	**Fulham**	—	—
ANDREWS Philip §	5 11	11 00	F	14 9 76	Andover	Trainee	**Brighton**	10	—
ANGEL Mark *	5 8	11 01	F	23 8 75	Newcastle	Trainee	**Sunderland**	—	—
ANGELL Brett	6 2	13 11	F	20 8 68	Marlborough	Cheltenham T	Derby Co	—	—
							Stockport Co	70	28
							Southend U	115	47
							Everton (loan)	1	—
							Everton	19	1
							Sunderland	8	—
ANGUS Terry	6 0	13 09	D	14 1 66	Coventry	VS Rugby	Northampton T	116	6
							Fulham	59	2
ANNAN Richard ‡	5 8	10 00	D	4 12 68	Leeds	Guiseley	**Crewe Alex**	19	1
ANNON Darren	5 5	10 11	M	17 2 72	London	Carshalton Ath	**Brentford**	19	2
ANSAH Andy	5 9	11 01	F	19 3 69	Lewisham	Crystal Palace	Brentford	8	2
							Southend U	153	33
							Brentford (loan)	3	1

Player	Ht	Wt	Pos	Birth Date	Birth Place	Source	Clubs	League App	League Gls
ANTHONY Graham	5 10	10 08	M	9 8 75	Jarrow	Trainee	**Sheffield U**	1	—
ANTHROBUS Steve	6 0	12 02	F	10 11 68	Lewisham		Millwall	21	4
							Southend U (loan)	—	—
							Wimbledon	28	—
							Peterborough U (loan)	2	—
							Chester C (loan)	7	—
APPLEBY Matty	5 10	11 05	D	16 4 72	Middlesbrough	Trainee	Newcastle U	20	—
							Darlington (loan)	10	1
							Darlington	36	1
APPLEBY Richie	5 8	10 06	M	18 9 75	Middlesbrough	Trainee	**Newcastle U**	—	—
							Darlington (loan)	—	—
APPLETON Michael	5 9	11 13	M	4 12 75	Salford	Trainee	**Manchester U**	—	—
ARCHDEACON Owen	5 7	10 09	M	4 3 66	Glasgow	Gourock U	Celtic	76	7
							Barnsley	195	20
ARCHER Lee	5 6	9 06	M	6 11 72	Bristol	Trainee	**Bristol R**	86	12
ARCHER Paul	5 7	9 04	M	25 4 78	Leicester	Trainee	**Nottingham F**	—	—
ARDLEY Neil	5 9	11 08	M	1 9 72	Epsom	Trainee	**Wimbledon**	65	6
ARMSTRONG Alun	6 0	12 00	F	22 2 75	Gateshead	School	Newcastle U	—	—
							Stockport Co	45	14
ARMSTRONG Chris	6 0	13 03	F	19 6 71	Newcastle	Llay Welfare	Wrexham	60	13
							Millwall	28	5
							Crystal Palace	118	45
ARMSTRONG Craig	5 11	12 04	D	23 5 75	South Shields	Trainee	**Nottingham F**	—	—
							Burnley (loan)	4	—
ARMSTRONG Gordon	6 0	12 11	M	15 7 67	Newcastle	Apprentice	**Sunderland**	348	50
ARNOLD Ian ‡	5 9	11 09	F	4 7 72	Durham City	Trainee	Middlesbrough	3	—
							Carlisle U	47	11
ARNOTT Andy	6 1	12 00	F	18 10 73	Chatham	Trainee	**Gillingham**	72	12
							Manchester U (loan)	—	—
ASABA Carl	6 1	12 12	F	28 1 73	London	Dulwich Hamlet	**Brentford**	—	—
							Colchester U (loan)	12	2
ASHBEE Ian	6 1	12 10	D	6 9 76	Birmingham	Trainee	**Derby Co**	1	—
ASHBY Barry	6 2	12 03	D	21 11 70	London	Trainee	Watford	114	3
							Brentford	48	2
ASHCROFT Lee	5 10	11 00	F	7 9 72	Preston	Trainee	Preston NE	91	13
							WBA	59	13
ASHLEY Kevin	5 7	11 10	D	31 12 68	Birmingham	Apprentice	Birmingham C	57	1
							Wolverhampton W	88	1
							Peterborough U	27	—
ASPIN Neil	6 0	12 06	D	12 4 65	Gateshead	Apprentice	Leeds U	207	5
							Port Vale	237	2
ASPINALL Brendan *	6 0	11 13	D	22 7 75	South Africa	Huddersfield T	**Mansfield T**	20	—
ASPINALL Warren	5 8	10 06	F	13 9 67	Wigan	Apprentice	Wigan Ath	10	1
							Everton	7	—
							Wigan Ath (loan)	41	21
							Aston Villa	44	14
							Portsmouth	132	21
							Swansea C (loan)	5	—
							Bournemouth	33	9
							Carlisle U (loan)	7	1
ATHERTON Peter	5 10	13 12	D	6 4 70	Wigan	Trainee	Wigan Ath	149	1
							Coventry C	114	—
							Sheffield W	41	1
ATKIN Paul	6 0	12 11	D	3 9 69	Nottingham	Trainee	Notts Co	—	—
							Bury	21	1
							York C	112	3

Player	Ht	Wt	Pos	Birth Date	Birth Place	Source	Clubs	League App	League Gls
ATKINS Ian †	6 0	12 03	M	16 1 57	Birmingham	Apprentice	Shrewsbury T	278	58
							Sunderland	77	6
							Everton	7	1
							Ipswich T	77	4
							Birmingham C	93	6
							Colchester U	—	—
							Birmingham C	8	—
							Cambridge U	2	—
							Sunderland	—	—
							Doncaster R	7	—
							Northampton T	—	—
ATKINS Mark	6 1	12 00	D	14 8 68	Doncaster		Scunthorpe U	48	2
							Blackburn R	253	35
ATKINSON Brian	5 9	12 05	M	19 1 71	Darlington	Trainee	**Sunderland**	134	4
ATKINSON Craig	6 0	11 02	M	29 9 77	Rotherham	Trainee	**Nottingham F**	—	—
ATKINSON Dalian	6 0	13 10	F	21 3 68	Shrewsbury		Ipswich T	60	18
							Sheffield W	38	10
							Real Sociedad	26	12
							Aston Villa	87	23
ATKINSON Graeme	5 8	11 07	M	11 11 71	Hull	Trainee	Hull C	149	23
							Preston NE	15	1
AUNGER Geoff ‡	5 8	11 10	F	4 2 68	Red Deer	Vancouver 86ers	Luton T	5	1
							Chester C	5	—
AUSTIN Dean	6 0	11 06	D	26 4 70	Hemel Hempstead	St. Albans C	Southend U	96	2
							Tottenham H	81	—
AUSTIN Kevin	6 1	14 00	D	12 2 73	Hackney	Saffron Walden	**Leyton Orient**	69	2
AWFORD Andy	5 9	11 07	D	14 7 72	Worcester	Worcester C	**Portsmouth**	146	—
BAAH Peter ‡	5 9	10 04	F	1 5 73	Littleborough	Trainee	Blackburn R	1	—
							Fulham	49	4
							Bury	—	—
BABB Phil	6 0	12 03	D	30 11 70	Lambeth	Trainee	Millwall	—	—
							Bradford C	80	14
							Coventry C	77	3
							Liverpool	34	—
BADDELEY Lee	6 1	12 07	D	12 7 74	Cardiff	Trainee	**Cardiff C**	94	1
BAGNALL John ‡	6 0	12 00	G	23 11 73	Southport	Preston NE	Chester C	—	—
							Wigan Ath	—	—
BAILEY Danny *	5 9	12 07	M	21 5 64	Leyton	Apprentice	Bournemouth	2	—
						Local	Torquay U	1	—
						Wealdstone	Exeter C	64	2
							Reading	50	2
							Fulham (loan)	3	—
							Exeter C	75	1
BAILEY Dennis	5 10	11 06	F	13 11 65	Lambeth	Farnborough T	Crystal Palace	5	1
							Bristol R (loan)	17	9
							Birmingham C	75	23
							Bristol R (loan)	6	1
							QPR	39	10
							Charlton Ath (loan)	4	—
							Watford (loan)	8	4
							Brentford (loan)	6	3
BAILEY Gavin	5 8	10 07	F	10 10 76	Chesterfield	Trainee	**Sheffield W**	—	—
BAILEY Mark	5 8	10 12	M	12 8 76	Stoke	Trainee	**Stoke C**	—	—
BAILEY Neil †	5 6	11 04	D	26 9 58	Wigan	Apprentice	Burnley	—	—
							Newport Co	134	7
							Wigan Ath	41	2
							Stockport Co	51	—
							Newport Co (loan)	9	1
						Retired	**Blackpool**	9	—

Player	Ht	Wt	Pos	Birth Date	Birth Place	Source	Clubs	League App	League Gls
BAIRD Ian	6 2	12 12	F	1 4 64	Rotherham	Apprentice	Southampton	22	5
							Cardiff C (loan)	12	6
							Newcastle U (loan)	5	1
							Leeds U	85	33
							Portsmouth	20	1
							Leeds U	77	17
							Middlesbrough	63	19
							Hearts	64	15
							Bristol C	56	11
BAKER Clive	5 9	11 00	G	14 3 59	North Walsham	Amateur	Norwich C	4	—
							Barnsley	291	—
							Coventry C	—	—
							Ipswich T	48	—
BAKER Desmond	5 9	10 12	F	25 8 77	Dublin	Trainee	**Manchester U**	—	—
BAKER Jospeh			M	19 4 77	London	Charlton Ath	**Leyton Orient**	—	—
BAKER Paul	6 1	13 02	F	5 1 63	Newcastle	Bishop Auckland	Southampton	—	—
							Carlisle U	71	11
							Hartlepool U	197	67
							Motherwell	9	1
							Gillingham	62	16
							York C	30	13
BALDRY Simon	5 11	11 00	F	12 2 76	Huddersfield	Trainee	**Huddersfield T**	21	2
BALL Kevin	5 9	12 06	D	12 11 64	Hastings	Apprentice	Portsmouth	105	4
							Sunderland	187	9
BALL Steve	5 11	13 00	M	2 9 69	Colchester	Trainee	Arsenal	—	—
							Colchester U	4	—
							Norwich C	2	—
							Colchester U	56	6
BALMER Stuart	6 1	12 04	D	20 9 69	Falkirk	Celtic BC	Celtic	—	—
							Charlton Ath	147	5
BAMBER Dave *	6 3	13 10	F	1 2 59	St. Helens	Manchester Univ	Blackpool	86	29
							Coventry C	19	3
							Walsall	20	7
							Portsmouth	4	1
							Swindon T	106	31
							Watford	18	3
							Stoke C	43	8
							Hull C	28	5
							Blackpool	113	60
BANGER Nicky	5 9	11 05	F	25 2 71	Southampton	Trainee	Southampton	55	8
							Oldham Ath	28	3
BANKS Ian *	5 10	12 04	M	9 1 61	Mexborough	Apprentice	Barnsley	164	37
							Leicester C	93	14
							Huddersfield T	78	17
							Bradford C	30	3
							WBA	4	—
							Barnsley	96	7
							Rotherham U	76	8
							Darlington	39	1
BANKS Steven	6 0	13 02	G	9 2 72	Hillingdon	Trainee	West Ham U	—	—
							Gillingham	67	—
BANNISTER Andrew *	5 11	11 13	F	23 7 76	Burnley	Trainee	**Burnley**	—	—
BANNISTER Gary *	5 8	11 10	F	22 7 60	Warrington	Apprentice	Coventry C	22	3
							Sheffield W	118	55
							QPR	136	56
							Coventry C	43	11
							WBA	72	18
							Oxford U (loan)	10	2
							Nottingham F	31	8
							Stoke C	15	2
						Hong Kong	**Lincoln C**	29	7
BARACLOUGH Ian	6 1	11 10	M	4 12 70	Leicester	Trainee	Leicester C	—	—
							Wigan Ath (loan)	9	2
							Grimsby T (loan)	4	—
							Grimsby T	1	—
							Lincoln C	73	10
							Mansfield T	36	3

Player	Ht	Wt	Pos	Birth Date	Birth Place	Source	Clubs	League App	League Gls
BARBER Fred	5 10	12 00	G	26 8 63	Ferryhill	Apprentice	Darlington	135	—
							Everton	—	—
							Walsall	153	—
							Peterborough U (loan)	6	—
							Chester (loan)	8	—
							Blackpool (loan)	2	—
							Peterborough U	68	—
							Colchester U (loan)	10	—
							Chesterfield (loan)	—	—
							Luton T (loan)	—	—
BARBER Phil	5 11	12 12	M	10 6 65	Tring	Aylesbury	Crystal Palace	234	35
							Millwall	110	12
							Plymouth Arg (loan)	4	—
BARCLAY Dominic §			F	5 9 76	Bristol	Trainee	**Bristol C**	2	—
BARDSLEY David	5 10	11 00	D	11 9 64	Manchester	Apprentice	Blackpool	45	—
							Watford	100	7
							Oxford U	74	7
							QPR	212	4
BARFOOT Stuart †	5 11	11 00	D	10 12 75	Southampton	Trainee	Bournemouth	2	—
							Torquay U	—	—
BARKER Richard	6 0	11 06	F	30 5 75	Sheffield	Trainee	**Sheffield W**	—	—
BARKER Simon	5 9	11 00	M	4 11 64	Farnworth	Apprentice	Blackburn R	182	35
							QPR	221	21
BARKUS Lea	5 6	9 13	F	7 12 74	Reading	Trainee	**Reading**	15	1
BARLOW Andy *	5 9	11 01	D	24 11 65	Oldham		**Oldham Ath**	261	5
							Bradford C (loan)	2	—
BARLOW Martin	5 7	10 01	M	25 6 71	Barnstable	Trainee	**Plymouth Arg**	152	9
BARLOW Stuart	5 10	11 02	F	16 7 68	Liverpool		**Everton**	68	10
							Rotherham U (loan)	—	—
BARMBY Nick	5 7	11 04	F	11 2 74	Hull	Trainee	**Tottenham H**	87	20
BARNARD Darren	5 10	12 00	D	30 11 71	Rinteln	Wokingham	**Chelsea**	29	2
							Reading (loan)	4	—
BARNARD Mark *	6 0	11 10	D	27 11 75	Sheffield	Trainee	**Rotherham U**	—	—
BARNES David	5 10	11 01	D	16 11 61	London	Apprentice	Coventry C	9	—
							Ipswich T	17	—
							Wolves	88	4
							Aldershot	69	1
							Sheffield U	82	1
							Watford	6	—
BARNES John	5 11	12 07	M	7 11 63	Jamaica	Sudbury Court	Watford	233	65
							Liverpool	243	77
BARNES Paul	5 10	12 09	F	16 11 67	Leicester	Apprentice	Notts Co	53	14
							Stoke C	24	3
							Chesterfield (loan)	1	—
							York C	118	61
BARNES Richard †	5 8	10 00	F	6 9 75	Wrexham	Trainee	**Wrexham**	1	—
BARNESS Anthony	5 10	13 01	D	25 3 72	London	Trainee	Charlton Ath	27	1
							Chelsea	14	—
							Middlesbrough (loan)	—	—
BARNETT Dave	6 0	13 00	D	16 4 67	London	Windsor & Eton	Colchester U	20	—
							WBA	—	—
							Walsall	5	—
						Kidderminster H	Barnet	59	3
							Birmingham C	40	—
BARNETT Gary *	5 6	9 13	M	11 3 63	Stratford upon Avon	Apprentice	Coventry C	—	—
							Huddersfield T	22	1
							Oxford U	45	9
							Wimbledon (loan)	5	1
							Fulham (loan)	2	1
							Fulham	180	30
							Huddersfield T	100	11
							Leyton Orient	63	7
BARNETT Jason	5 9	10 10	F	21 4 76	Shrewsbury	Trainee	**Wolverhampton W**	—	—

Player	Ht	Wt	Pos	Birth Date	Birth Place	Source	Clubs	League App	League Gls
BARNHOUSE David	5 8	10 09	D	19 3 75	Swansea	Trainee	**Swansea C**	8	—
BARNWELL-EDINBORO Jamie	5 10	11 06	F	26 12 75	Hull	Trainee	**Coventry C**	—	—
BARR Billy	5 11	10 08	M	21 1 69	Halifax	Trainee	Halifax T	196	13
						Halifax T	**Crewe Alex**	34	2
BARRAS Tony	6 0	12 09	D	29 3 71	Stockton	Trainee	Hartlepool U	12	—
							Stockport Co	99	5
							Rotherham U (loan)	5	1
							York C	31	1
BARRATT Tony *	5 8	11 00	D	18 10 65	Salford	Billingham T	Grimsby T	22	—
						Billingham T	Hartlepool U	98	4
							York C	147	10
BARRETT Earl	5 11	11 00	D	28 4 67	Rochdale	Apprentice	Manchester C	3	—
							Chester C (loan)	12	—
							Oldham Ath	183	7
							Aston Villa	119	1
							Everton	17	—
BARRETT Michael ‡			G	20 10 63	Exeter	Liskeard	**Exeter C**	4	—
BARRETT Richard	5 0	9 08	D	1 11 77	Sutton Coldfield	Trainee	**Nottingham F**	—	—
BARRETT Scott *	5 11	13 08	G	2 4 63	Derby	Ilkeston T	Wolverhampton W	30	—
							Stoke C	51	—
							Colchester U (loan)	13	—
							Stockport Co (loan)	10	—
							Colchester U	—	—
							Gillingham	51	—
BARRICK Dean	5 7	11 07	D	30 9 69	Hemsworth	Trainee	Sheffield W	11	2
							Rotherham U	99	7
							Cambridge U	88	2
BARRON Michael	5 11	11 09	D	22 12 74	Chester le Street	Trainee	**Middlesbrough**	2	—
BARROW Graham †	6 2	13 07	M	13 6 54	Chorley	Altrincham	Wigan Ath	179	36
							Chester C	248	17
							Wigan Ath	—	—
BARROW Lee	5 11	13 00	D	1 5 73	Worksworth	Trainee	Notts Co	—	—
							Scarborough	11	—
							Torquay U	75	5
BARRY George ‡			D	19 9 67	London		**Leyton Orient**	6	—
BARTLETT Kevin ‡	5 8	11 01	F	12 10 62	Portsmouth	Apprentice	Portsmouth	3	—
						Fareham	Cardiff C	82	25
							WBA	37	10
							Notts Co	99	33
							Port Vale (loan)	5	1
							Cambridge U	8	1
BARTLETT Neal ‡	5 8	12 00	M	7 4 75	Southampton	Trainee	**Southampton**	8	—
BARTLEY Carl §			F	6 10 76	Lambeth	Trainee	**Fulham**	1	—
BARTON Warren	5 11	11 00	D	19 3 69	London	Leytonstone/ Ilford	Maidstone U	42	—
							Wimbledon	180	10
BARTRAM Vince	6 2	13 07	G	7 8 68	Birmingham	Local	Wolverhampton W	5	—
							Blackpool (loan)	9	—
							WBA (loan)	—	—
							Bournemouth	132	—
							Arsenal	11	—
BART-WILLIAMS Chris	5 10	11 11	M	16 6 74	Freetown	Trainee	Leyton Orient	36	2
							Sheffield W	124	16
BASHAM Mike	6 2	12 08	M	27 9 73	Barking	Trainee	West Ham U	—	—
							Colchester U (loan)	1	—
							Swansea C	18	—
BASS David	5 11	12 07	M	29 11 74	Frimley	Trainee	**Reading**	9	—
BASS Jonathan	6 0	12 02	D	1 7 76	Weston Super Mare	Trainee	**Birmingham C**	—	—

Player	Ht	Wt	Pos	Birth Date	Birth Place	Source	Clubs	League App	League Gls
BATES Jamie	6 1	12 12	D	24 2 68	London	Trainee	**Brentford**	279	10
BATTERSBY Tony	6 0	12 09	F	30 8 75	Doncaster	Trainee	**Sheffield U**	—	—
							Southend U (loan)	8	1
BATTY David	5 8	12 00	M	2 12 68	Leeds	Trainee	Leeds U	211	4
							Blackburn R	31	—
BAYES Ashley	6 1	13 05	G	19 4 72	Lincoln	Trainee	Brentford	4	—
							Torquay U	69	—
BAYLISS David §			D	8 6 76	Liverpool	Trainee	**Rochdale**	1	—
BAZELEY Darren	5 10	11 02	F	5 10 72	Northampton	Trainee	**Watford**	102	12
BEADLE Peter	6 0	11 12	F	13 5 72	London	Trainee	Gillingham	67	14
							Tottenham H	—	—
							Bournemouth (loan)	9	2
							Southend U (loan)	8	1
							Watford	20	1
BEAGRIE Peter	5 8	9 10	M	28 11 65	Middlesbrough	Local	Middlesbrough	33	2
							Sheffield U	84	11
							Stoke C	54	7
							Everton	114	11
							Sunderland (loan)	5	1
							Manchester C	46	3
BEARD Mark	5 10	10 12	D	8 10 74	Roehampton	Trainee	**Millwall**	45	2
BEARDSLEY Peter	5 8	11 07	F	18 1 61	Newcastle	Wallsend BC	Carlisle U	102	22
						Vancouver Whitecaps	Manchester U	—	—
						Vancouver Whitecaps	Newcastle U	147	61
							Liverpool	131	46
							Everton	81	25
							Newcastle U	69	33
BEARDSMORE Russell	5 6	8 10	M	28 9 68	Wigan	Apprentice	Manchester U	56	4
							Blackburn R (loan)	2	—
							Bournemouth	67	3
BEASANT Dave	6 4	14 03	G	20 3 59	Ealing	Edgware T	Wimbledon	340	—
							Newcastle U	20	—
							Chelsea	133	—
							Grimsby T (loan)	6	—
							Wolverhampton W (loan)	4	—
							Southampton	38	—
BEASLEY Andy	6 0	13 08	G	5 2 64	Sedgley	Apprentice	Luton T.	—	—
							Mansfield T (loan)	—	—
							Gillingham (loan)	—	—
							Mansfield T	94	—
							Peterborough U (loan)	7	—
							Scarborough (loan)	4	—
							Bristol R (loan)	1	—
							Doncaster R	37	—
							Chesterfield	21	—
BEATTIE James	6 1	12 00	F	27 2 78	Lancaster	Trainee	**Blackburn R**	—	—
BEAUCHAMP Joey	5 10	11 10	M	13 3 71	Oxford	Trainee	Oxford U	124	20
							Swansea C (loan)	5	2
							West Ham U	—	—
							Swindon T	42	3
BEAUMONT Chris	5 11	11 07	F	5 12 65	Sheffield	Denaby	Rochdale	34	7
							Stockport Co	215	39
BECKETT Nathan ‡	6 2	13 00	D	31 5 75	Hertford	Trainee	**Leyton Orient**	—	—
BECKFORD Darren	6 1	11 01	F	12 5 67	Manchester	Apprentice	Manchester C	11	—
							Bury (loan)	12	5
							Port Vale (loan)	11	4
							Port Vale	167	68
							Norwich C	38	8
							Oldham Ath	32	9

Player	Ht	Wt	Pos	Birth Date	Birth Place	Source	Clubs	League App	League Gls
BECKFORD Jason	5 9	12 04	F	14 2 70	Manchester	Trainee	Manchester C	20	1
							Blackburn R (loan)	4	—
							Port Vale (loan)	5	1
							Birmingham C	7	2
							Bury (loan)	3	—
							Stoke C	4	—
							Millwall	9	—
							Northampton T	—	—
BECKHAM David	6 0	11 02	M	2 5 75	Leytonstone	Trainee	**Manchester U**	4	—
							Preston NE (loan)	5	2
BEDROSSIAN Ara ‡	5 9	10 10	M	2 6 67	Cyprus	AP Limassol	**Fulham**	42	1
BEECH Chris	5 10	11 00	M	16 9 74	Blackpool	Trainee	**Blackpool**	64	4
BEECH Chris	5 9	11 00	F	5 11 75	Congleton	Trainee	**Manchester C**	—	—
BEENEY Mark	6 4	14 07	G	30 12 67	Pembury		Gillingham	2	—
							Maidstone U	50	—
							Aldershot (loan)	7	—
							Brighton & HA	69	—
							Leeds U	23	—
BEESLEY Paul	6 1	12 06	D	21 7 65	Liverpool	Marine	Wigan Ath	155	3
							Leyton Orient	32	1
							Sheffield U	168	7
BEESTON Carl	5 10	12 04	M	30 6 67	Stoke	Apprentice	**Stoke C**	202	13
BEINLICH Stefan (To Hansa Rostock)	5 11	11 02	F	13 1 72	Berlin	Bergmann Borsig	**Aston Villa**	16	1
BELL Mike	5 10	11 04	F	15 11 71	Newcastle	Trainee	Northampton T	153	10
							Wycombe W	31	3
BELLAMY Gary	6 2	11 05	D	4 7 62	Worksop	Apprentice	Chesterfield	184	7
							Wolverhampton W	136	9
							Cardiff C (loan)	9	—
							Leyton Orient	100	5
BELLOTTI Ross §			G	15 5 78	Pembury	Trainee	**Exeter C**	2	—
BENALI Francis	5 10	11 01	D	30 12 68	Southampton	Apprentice	**Southampton**	173	—
BENJAMIN Ian	5 11	13 01	F	11 12 61	Nottingham	Apprentice	Sheffield U	5	3
							WBA	2	—
							Notts Co	—	—
							Peterborough U	80	14
							Northampton T	150	59
							Cambridge U	25	2
							Chester C	22	2
							Exeter C	32	4
							Southend U	122	33
							Luton T	13	2
							Brentford	15	2
							Wigan Ath	17	6
BENN Wayne	5 9	11 12	D	7 8 76	Pontefract	Trainee	**Bradford C**	10	—
BENNETT Frankie	5 7	11 12	F	3 1 69	Birmingham	Halesowen T	**Southampton**	8	1
BENNETT Gary	6 0	13 00	D	4 12 61	Manchester	Amateur	Manchester C	—	—
							Cardiff C	87	11
							Sunderland	369	23
BENNETT Gary	5 11	11 00	F	20 9 63	Kirby	Kirby T	Wigan Ath	20	3
							Chester C	126	36
							Southend U	42	6
							Chester C	80	15
							Wrexham	121	77
BENNETT Ian	6 0	12 00	G	10 10 71	Worksop	Newcastle U	Peterborough U	72	—
							Birmingham C	68	—
BENNETT Mickey	5 10	11 11	M	27 7 69	Camberwell	Apprentice	Charlton Ath	35	2
							Wimbledon	18	2
							Brentford	46	4
							Charlton Ath	24	1
							Millwall	—	—
BENNETT Tom	5 11	11 08	D	12 12 69	Falkirk	Trainee	Aston Villa	—	—
							Wolverhampton W	115	2

Player	Ht	Wt	Pos	Birth Date	Birth Place	Source	Clubs	League App	League Gls
BENNETT Troy	5 9	11 13	M	25 12 75	Barnsley	Trainee	**Barnsley**	2	—
BENT Junior	5 5	10 06	F	1 3 70	Huddersfield	Trainee	Huddersfield T	36	6
							Burnley (loan)	9	3
							Bristol C	119	15
							Stoke C (loan)	1	—
BENTLEY Jim	6 1	13 00	D	11 6 76	Liverpool	Trainee	**Manchester C**	—	—
BERESFORD David	5 8	10 09	F	11 11 76	Middlesbrough	Trainee	**Oldham Ath**	3	—
BERESFORD John	5 6	10 12	M	4 9 66	Sheffield	Apprentice	Manchester C	—	—
							Barnsley	88	5
							Portsmouth	107	8
							Newcastle U	109	1
BERESFORD Marlon	6 1	13 01	G	2 9 69	Lincoln	Trainee	Sheffield W	—	—
							Bury (loan)	1	—
							Ipswich T (loan)	—	—
							Northampton T (loan)	13	—
							Crewe Alex (loan)	3	—
							Northampton T (loan)	15	—
							Burnley	130	—
BERG Henning	6 0	12 07	D	1 9 69	Eidsvell	Lillestrom	**Blackburn R**	85	2
BERGKAMP Dennis	6 0	12 05	F	18 5 69	Amsterdam		Ajax	185	103
							Internazionale	52	11
							Arsenal	—	—
BERGSSON Gudni	6 1	12 03	D	21 7 65	Iceland	Valur	Tottenham H	71	2
							Bolton W	8	—
BERKLEY Austin	5 9	10 10	M	28 1 73	Gravesend	Trainee	Gillingham	3	—
							Swindon T	1	—
BERNAL Andy	5 10	12 05	D	16 7 66	Canberra	Sporting Gijon	Ipswich T	9	—
						Sydney Olympic	**Reading**	33	—
BERNARD Paul	5 11	11 08	M	30 12 72	Edinburgh	Trainee	**Oldham Ath**	105	17
BERRY Greg	5 10	12 00	F	5 3 71	Essex	East Thurrock	Leyton Orient	80	14
							Wimbledon	7	1
							Millwall	19	1
BERRY Trevor	5 7	10 08	F	1 8 74	Haslemere	Bournemouth	**Aston Villa**	—	—
BETTS Simon	5 7	11 05	D	3 3 73	Middlesbrough	Trainee	Ipswich T	—	—
							Scarborough	—	—
							Colchester U	91	3
BIBBO Sal	6 2	13 05	G	24 8 74	Basingstoke	Bournemouth	**Sheffield U**	—	—
							Chesterfield (loan)	1	—
BIGGINS Wayne *	5 10	13 00	F	20 11 61	Sheffield	Apprentice	Lincoln C	8	1
						Matlock Town and King's Lynn	Burnley	78	29
							Norwich C	79	16
							Manchester C	32	9
							Stoke C	122	46
							Barnsley	47	16
							Celtic	9	—
							Stoke C	27	6
							Luton T (loan)	7	1
BILLING Peter *	6 2	13 00	D	24 10 64	Liverpool	South Liverpool	Everton	1	—
							Crewe Alex	88	1
							Coventry C	58	1
							Port Vale (loan)	12	—
							Port Vale	14	—
BILLY Chris	6 0	10 09	D	2 1 73	Huddersfield	Trainee	**Huddersfield T**	94	4
BIMSON Stuart	5 11	11 07	D	29 9 69	Liverpool	Macclesfield	**Bury**	19	—
BIRCH Paul	5 6	10 04	M	20 11 62	West Bromwich	Apprentice	Aston Villa	173	16
							Wolverhampton W	135	15
BIRD Anthony	5 10	10 07	F	1 9 74	Cardiff	Trainee	**Cardiff C**	63	10
BISHOP Charlie	5 11	13 07	D	16 2 68	Nottingham	Stoke C	Watford	—	—
							Bury	114	6
							Barnsley	117	1

Player	Ht	Wt	Pos	Birth Date	Birth Place	Source	Clubs	League App	League Gls
BISHOP Eddie *	5 10	12 06	M	28 11 62	Liverpool	Runcorn	Tranmere R	76	19
							Chester C	106	23
							Crewe Alex (loan)	3	—
BISHOP Ian	5 9	10 12	M	29 5 65	Liverpool	Apprentice	Everton	1	—
							Crewe Alex (loan)	4	—
							Carlisle U	132	14
							Bournemouth	44	2
							Manchester C	19	2
							West Ham U	187	10
BISSETT Nicky *	6 2	12 10	D	5 4 64	Fulham	Barnet	**Brighton**	97	9
BJORNEBYE Stig Inge	5 10	11 09	D	11 12 69	Norway	Rosenborg	**Liverpool**	51	—
BLACK Kingsley	5 8	10 11	M	22 6 68	Luton	School	Luton T	127	26
							Nottingham F	96	14
							Sheffield U (loan)	11	2
BLACK Simon	6 1	12 00	F	9 11 75	Marston Green	Trainee	**Birmingham C**	2	—
BLACK Tony	5 8	11 00	F	15 7 69	Barrow	Bamber Bridge	**Wigan Ath**	9	—
BLACKMORE Clayton	5 8	11 12	M	23 9 64	Neath	Apprentice	Manchester U	186	19
							Middlesbrough	30	2
BLACKSTONE Ian	6 0	13 00	F	7 8 64	Harrogate	Harrogate T	York C	129	37
							Scarborough	13	—
BLACKWELL Dean	6 1	12 07	D	5 12 69	London	Trainee	**Wimbledon**	84	1
							Plymouth Arg (loan)	7	—
BLACKWELL Kevin *	5 11	12 10	G	21 12 58	Luton	Barnet	Scarborough	44	—
							Notts Co	—	—
							Torquay U	18	—
							Huddersfield T	5	—
BLADES Paul	6 0	10 12	D	5 1 65	Peterborough	Apprentice	Derby Co	166	1
							Norwich C	47	—
							Wolverhampton W	107	2
BLAIR Scott *	5 10	11 00	D	24 11 75	Nuneaton	Trainee	**Stoke C**	—	—
BLAKE Mark	6 0	12 09	D	17 12 67	Portsmouth	Apprentice	Southampton	18	2
							Colchester U (loan)	4	1
							Shrewsbury T (loan)	10	—
							Shrewsbury T	132	3
							Fulham	35	3
BLAKE Mark	5 11	12 06	M	16 12 70	Nottingham	Trainee	Aston Villa	31	2
							Wolverhampton W (loan)	2	—
							Portsmouth	15	—
							Leicester C	41	4
BLAKE Nathan	5 11	13 12	F	27 1 72	Cardiff	Chelsea	Cardiff C	131	35
							Sheffield U	47	22
BLAKE Robert	5 8	11 00	F	4 3 76	Middlesbrough	Trainee	**Darlington**	9	—
BLAKE Timothy	6 2	13 00	D	25 9 75	Merthyr	Trainee	**Coventry C**	—	—
BLATHERWICK Steve	6 1	12 12	D	20 9 73	Nottingham	Notts Co	**Nottingham F**	3	—
							Wycombe W (loan)	2	—
BLISSETT Gary	6 1	12 02	F	29 6 64	Manchester	Altrincham	Crewe Alex	122	39
							Brentford	233	79
							Wimbledon	27	3
BLOUNT Mark	5 10	12 04	M	5 1 74	Derby	Gresley R	**Sheffield U**	5	—
BLUNT Jason	5 8	10 10	M	16 8 77	Penzance	Trainee	**Leeds U**	—	—
BLYTH Ian ‡	5 10	11 04	D	21 10 74	Coventry	Trainee	**Leicester C**	—	—
BOCHENSKI Simon	5 8	11 13	F	6 12 75	Worksop	Trainee	**Barnsley**	—	—
BODEN Chris	5 9	11 00	D	13 10 73	Wolverhampton	Trainee	Aston Villa	1	—
							Barnsley (loan)	4	—
							Derby Co	6	—

Player	Ht	Wt	Pos	Birth Date	Birth Place	Source	Clubs	League App	League Gls
BODIN Paul	6 0	13 01	D	13 9 64	Cardiff	Chelsea	Newport Co	—	—
							Cardiff C	57	3
						Bath C	Newport Co	6	1
							Swindon T	93	9
							Crystal Palace	9	—
							Newcastle U (loan)	6	—
							Swindon T	113	26
BODLEY Mike	6 1	13 02	D	14 9 67	Hayes	Apprentice	Chelsea	6	1
							Northampton T	20	—
							Barnet	69	3
							Southend U	28	1
							Gillingham (loan)	7	—
							Birmingham C (loan)	3	—
BOERE Jeroen	6 3	13 05	F	18 11 67	Arnheim	Go Ahead	**West Ham U**	24	6
							Portsmouth (loan)	5	—
							WBA (loan)	5	—
BOGIE Ian	5 7	12 00	M	6 12 67	Newcastle	Apprentice	Newcastle U	14	—
							Preston NE	79	12
							Millwall	51	1
							Leyton Orient	65	5
							Port Vale	9	2
BOHINEN Lars	5 11	12 02	M	8 9 66	Vadso	Young Boys	**Nottingham F**	57	7
BOLAND Willie	5 9	11 02	M	6 8 75	Ennis	Trainee	**Coventry C**	40	—
BOLT Danny	5 7	11 08	M	5 2 76	Wandsworth	Trainee	**Fulham**	2	—
BOLTON Nigel *			F	14 1 75	Bishop Auckland	Shildon	**Darlington**	2	—
BONNER Mark	5 10	11 00	M	7 6 74	Ormskirk	Trainee	**Blackpool**	75	7
BOOTH Andy	6 0	11 00	F	17 3 73	Huddersfield	Trainee	**Huddersfield T**	80	38
BOOTHROYD Adrian	5 10	11 04	D	8 2 71	Bradford	Trainee	Huddersfield T	10	—
							Bristol R	16	—
							Hearts	4	—
							Mansfield T	59	1
BOOTY Justin *	5 11	13 12	F	2 6 76	Colchester	Trainee	**Colchester U**	1	—
BOOTY Martyn	5 8	11 02	D	30 5 71	Kirby Muxloe	Trainee	Coventry C	5	—
							Crewe Alex	75	3
BORROWS Brian	5 10	10 12	D	20 12 60	Liverpool	Amateur	Everton	27	—
							Bolton W	95	—
							Coventry C	365	11
							Bristol C (loan)	6	—
BOSNICH Mark	6 1	13 07	G	13 1 72	Fairfield	Croatia Sydney	Manchester U	3	—
							Aston Villa	76	—
BOULD Steve	6 4	14 02	D	16 11 62	Stoke	Apprentice	Stoke C	183	6
							Torquay U (loan)	9	—
							Arsenal	192	5
BOUND Matthew	6 2	14 06	D	9 11 72	Trowbridge	Trainee	Southampton	5	—
							Hull C (loan)	7	1
							Stockport Co	14	—
BOWDEN Jon *	5 10	11 07	F	21 1 63	Stockport	Local	Oldham Ath	82	5
							Port Vale	70	7
							Wrexham	147	20
							Rochdale	106	17
BOWEN Jason	5 6	8 10	M	24 8 72	Merthyr	Trainee	**Swansea C**	124	26
BOWEN Mark	5 8	11 11	D	7 12 63	Neath	Apprentice	Tottenham H	17	2
							Norwich C	289	22
BOWLING Ian *	6 3	13 11	G	27 7 65	Sheffield	Gainsborough T	Lincoln C	59	—
							Hartlepool U (loan)	1	—
							Bradford C (loan)	7	—
							Bradford C	29	—
BOWMAN Robert	6 1	11 12	D	21 11 75	Durham	Trainee	**Leeds U**	4	—
BOWRY Bobby	5 8	10 08	M	19 5 71	Croydon		**Crystal Palace**	50	1
BOWYER Gary *	6 0	12 13	D	26 6 71	Manchester		Hereford U	14	2
							Nottingham F	—	—

Player	Ht	Wt	Pos	Birth Date	Birth Place	Source	Clubs	League App	League Gls
BOWYER Lee	5 9	9 09	M	3 1 77	London	Trainee	**Charlton Ath**	5	—
BOXALL Danny	5 8	10 05	D	24 8 77	Croydon	Trainee	**Crystal Palace**	—	—
BRABIN Gary	5 11	12 00	M	9 12 70	Liverpool	Trainee	Stockport Co	2	—
						Runcorn	**Doncaster R**	28	8
BRACE Deryn	5 9	10 00	D	15 3 75	Haverfordwest	Trainee	Norwich C	—	—
							Wrexham	15	—
BRACEWELL Paul	5 8	10 09	M	19 7 62	Stoke	Apprentice	Stoke C	129	5
							Sunderland	38	4
							Everton	95	7
							Sunderland	113	2
							Newcastle U	73	3
BRACEY Lee	6 0	13 05	G	11 9 68	Ashford	Trainee	West Ham U	—	—
							Swansea C	99	—
							Halifax T	73	—
							Bury	46	—
BRADBURY Shaun ‡	5 10	11 00	F	11 2 74	Birmingham	Trainee	Wolverhampton W	2	2
							Hereford U	—	—
BRADLEY Darren *	5 7	11 12	D	24 11 65	Birmingham	Apprentice	Aston Villa	20	—
							WBA	254	9
BRADLEY Russell	6 2	13 00	D	28 3 66	Birmingham	Dudley T	Nottingham F	—	—
							Hereford U (loan)	12	1
							Hereford U	77	3
							Halifax T	56	3
							Scunthorpe U	59	3
BRADSHAW Carl	5 10	11 06	D	2 10 68	Sheffield	Apprentice	Sheffield W	32	4
							Barnsley (loan)	6	1
							Manchester C	5	—
							Sheffield U	147	8
							Norwich C	26	1
BRADSHAW Darren	5 11	11 04	M	19 3 67	Sheffield	Matlock T	Chesterfield	18	—
							York C	59	3
							Newcastle U	38	—
							Peterborough U	73	1
							Plymouth Arg (loan)	6	1
							Blackpool	26	1
BRADY Gary	5 10	10 02	M	7 9 76	Glasgow	Trainee	**Tottenham H**	—	—
BRADY Matthew §	6 0	10 04	M	27 10 77	London	Trainee	**Barnet**	1	—
BRAMMER David	5 10	11 05	M	28 2 75	Bromborough	Trainee	**Wrexham**	38	3
BRANAGAN Keith	6 0	13 02	G	10 7 66	Fulham		Cambridge U	110	—
							Millwall	46	—
							Brentford (loan)	2	—
							Gillingham (loan)	1	—
							Fulham (loan)	—	—
							Bolton W	99	—
BRANCH Graham	6 2	12 02	F	12 2 72	Liverpool	Heswall Ath	**Tranmere R**	21	—
							Bury (loan)	4	1
BRANNAN Ged	6 0	12 03	D	15 1 72	Liverpool	Trainee	**Tranmere R**	160	14
BRASS Chris	5 9	11 08	D	24 7 75	Easington	Trainee	**Burnley**	5	—
							Torquay U (loan)	7	—
BRAZIER Matthew	5 8	10 07	D	2 7 76	Whipps Cross	Trainee	**QPR**	—	—
BRAZIL Derek	5 11	10 05	D	14 12 68	Dublin	Rivermount BC	Manchester U	2	—
							Oldham Ath (loan)	1	—
							Swansea C (loan)	12	1
							Cardiff C	95	1
BRAZIL Gary	5 11	11 03	F	19 9 62	Tunbridge Wells	Crystal Palace	Sheffield U	62	9
							Port Vale (loan)	6	3
							Preston NE	166	58
							Newcastle U	23	2
							Fulham	195	46
BREACKER Tim	5 11	13 00	D	2 7 65	Bicester		Luton T	210	3
							West Ham U	170	8
BREBNER Grant			M	6 12 77	Edinburgh		**Manchester U**	—	—

Player	Ht	Wt	Pos	Birth Date	Birth Place	Source	Clubs	League App	League Gls
BRECKIN Ian	6 0	11 06	D	24 7 75	Rotherham	Trainee	**Rotherham U**	51	2
BREEN Gary	6 1	12 00	D	12 12 73	London	Charlton Ath	Maidstone U	19	—
							Gillingham	51	—
							Peterborough U	44	1
BREITKREUTZ Matthias (To Hertha Berlin)	5 9	11 03	M	12 5 71	Crivitz	Bergmann Borsig	**Aston Villa**	13	—
BRENNAN Jim	5 9	11 06	M	8 5 77		Sora Lazio	**Bristol C**	—	—
BRENNAN Mark	5 10	10 13	M	4 10 65	Rossendale	Apprentice	Ipswich T	168	19
							Middlesbrough	65	6
							Manchester C	29	6
							Oldham Ath	65	4
BRESSINGTON Graham *	6 0	13 10	D	8 7 66	Eton	Wycombe W	Lincoln C	141	7
							Southend U	48	5
BREVETT Rufus	5 8	11 00	D	24 9 69	Derby	Trainee	Doncaster R	109	3
							QPR	58	—
BRIEN Tony *	6 0	13 00	D	10 2 69	Dublin	Apprentice	Leicester C	16	1
							Chesterfield	204	8
							Rotherham U	43	2
BRIGGS Gary *	6 3	12 10	D	8 5 58	Leeds	Apprentice	Middlesbrough	—	—
							Oxford U	420	18
							Blackpool	137	4
BRIGHT Mark	6 0	12 13	F	6 6 62	Stoke	Leek T	Port Vale	29	10
							Leicester C	42	6
							Crystal Palace	227	92
							Sheffield W	107	41
BRIGHTWELL David	6 1	13 05	D	7 1 71	Lutterworth	Trainee	**Manchester C**	43	1
							Chester C (loan)	6	—
BRIGHTWELL Ian	5 10	11 07	M	9 4 68	Lutterworth	Congleton T	**Manchester C**	234	16
BRISCOE Lee	5 7	10 09	F	30 9 75	Pontefract	Trainee	**Sheffield W**	7	—
BRISSETT Jason	5 11	11 10	M	7 9 74	Redbridge	Arsenal	Peterborough U	35	—
							Bournemouth	25	—
BROCK Kevin ‡	5 9	10 12	M	9 9 62	Middleton Stoney	Apprentice	Oxford U	246	26
							QPR	40	2
							Newcastle U	145	15
							Cardiff C (loan)	14	2
							Stockport Co	—	—
BROCK Stuart			G	26 9 76	Birmingham	Trainee	**Aston Villa**	—	—
BRODIE Stephen	5 6	10 06	F	14 1 73	Sunderland	Trainee	**Sunderland**	12	—
BROOKE David	5 11	11 03	M	23 11 75	Barnsley	Trainee	**Barnsley**	—	—
BROOKES Mark	5 9	10 06	M	19 9 75	Nottingham	Trainee	**Grimsby T**	—	—
BROOKS Matthew ‡	5 11	12 06	M	23 4 75	Warrington	Trainee	**Wigan Ath**	—	—
BROOKS Shaun	5 8	11 00	M	9 10 62	London	Apprentice	Crystal Palace	54	4
							Orient	148	26
							Bournemouth	129	13
							Stockport Co (loan)	—	—
							Leyton Orient	9	—
BROOMES Marlon	6 0	12 07	D	28 11 77	Birmingham	Trainee	**Blackburn R**	—	—
BROUGH John	6 0	12 10	D	8 1 73	Heanor	Trainee	Notts Co	—	—
							Shrewsbury T	16	1
						Telford U	**Hereford U**	18	1
BROWN Andrew	6 3	13 00	F	11 10 76	Edinburgh	Trainee	**Leeds U**	—	—
BROWN Grant	6 0	11 12	D	19 11 69	Sunderland	Trainee	Leicester C	14	—
							Lincoln C	220	11
BROWN Ian *	5 10	13 04	D	2 9 75	Wolverhampton	Trainee	**Aston Villa**	—	—
BROWN Ian *	5 10	11 05	F	11 9 65	Ipswich	Chelmsford C	Bristol C	12	1
							Colchester U (loan)	4	1
							Northampton T	23	4
BROWN Jon *	5 10	11 03	D	8 9 66	Barnsley	Denaby U	**Exeter C**	164	3

Player	Ht	Wt	Pos	Birth Date	Birth Place	Source	Clubs	League App	League Gls
BROWN Kenny	5 8	11 06	D	11 7 67	Barking	Apprentice	Norwich C	25	—
							Plymouth Arg	126	4
							West Ham U	60	5
BROWN Linton	5 9	11 00	F	12 4 68	Driffield	Guiseley	Halifax T	3	—
							Hull C	98	22
BROWN Michael	5 7	10 06	M	25 1 77	Hartlepool	Trainee	**Manchester C**	—	—
BROWN Mickey	5 9	10 12	F	8 2 68	Birmingham	Apprentice	Shrewsbury T	190	9
							Bolton W	33	3
							Shrewsbury T	67	11
							Preston NE	—	—
BROWN Phil	5 11	11 08	D	30 5 59	South Shields	Local	Hartlepool U	217	8
							Halifax T	135	19
							Bolton W	256	14
							Blackpool	31	5
BROWN Richard ‡	5 10	11 02	D	13 1 67	Nottingham	Ilkeston T	Sheffield W	—	—
						Kettering T	Blackburn R	28	—
							Maidstone U (loan)	3	—
							Stockport Co	1	—
BROWN Steve	6 1	13 10	D	13 5 72	Brighton	Trainee	**Charlton Ath**	62	3
BROWN Steve	5 11	12 07	F	6 12 73	Southend	Trainee	Southend U	10	2
							Scunthorpe U	—	—
							Colchester U	62	17
							Gillingham	8	2
BROWN Steve	6 1	10 11	D	6 7 66	Northampton		Northampton T	—	—
						Irthlingborough D	Northampton T	158	19
							Wycombe W	49	3
BROWN Steven ‡	5 9	10 04	M	15 10 74	Sheffield	Trainee	**Sheffield W**	—	—
BROWN Wayne §			G	14 1 77	Southampton	Trainee	**Bristol C**	1	—
BROWNE Paul	6 1	12 00	D	17 2 75	Glasgow	Trainee	**Aston Villa**	—	—
BROWNING Marcus	5 11	13 00	F	22 4 71	Bristol	Trainee	**Bristol R**	103	7
							Hereford U (loan)	7	5
BROWNRIGG Andrew	6 0	11 13	D	2 8 76	Sheffield	Trainee	Hereford U	8	—
							Norwich C	—	—
BRUCE Steve	6 0	13 00	D	31 12 60	Newcastle	Apprentice	Gillingham	205	29
							Norwich C	141	14
							Manchester U	279	35
BRUMWELL Philip *	5 7	11 02	M	8 8 75	Darlington	Trainee	**Sunderland**	—	—
BRUNSKILL Iain	5 10	12 05	D	5 11 76	Ormskirk	Trainee	**Liverpool**	—	—
BRYAN Marvin	6 0	12 02	F	2 8 75	Paddington	Trainee	**QPR**	—	—
							Doncaster R (loan)	5	1
BRYANT Matthew	6 1	12 11	D	21 9 70	Bristol	Trainee	**Bristol C**	171	7
							Walsall (loan)	13	—
BRYDEN Lee	5 11	11 00	D	15 11 74	Stockton	Trainee	**Liverpool**	—	—
BRYSON Ian	5 11	11 11	M	26 11 62	Kilmarnock		Kilmarnock	215	40
							Sheffield U	155	36
							Barnsley	16	3
							Preston NE	66	7
BUCKLE Paul	5 7	10 10	M	16 12 70	Hatfield	Trainee	Brentford	57	1
							Torquay U	48	5
BUCKLEY Simon	5 10	11 02	M	29 2 76	Stafford	Trainee	**Grimsby T**	—	—
BULL Gary	5 9	11 07	F	12 6 66	West Bromwich		Southampton	—	—
							Cambridge U	19	4
						Barnet	Barnet	83	37
							Nottingham F	12	1
							Birmingham C (loan)	10	6
BULL Steve	5 11	11 04	F	28 3 65	Tipton	Apprentice	WBA	4	2
							Wolverhampton W	341	202

Player	Ht	Wt	Pos	Birth Date	Place	Source	Clubs	League App	Gls
BULLIMORE Wayne	5 10	11 07	M	12 9 70	Mansfield	Trainee	Manchester U	—	—
							Barnsley	35	1
							Stockport Co	—	—
							Scunthorpe U	53	9
BULLOCK Darren	5 8	12 06	M	12 2 69	Worcester	Nuneaton	**Huddersfield T**	59	9
BULLOCK Martin	5 4	10 09	M	5 3 75	Derby	Eastwood T	**Barnsley**	29	—
BURCHELL Lee	5 7	10 06	M	12 11 76	Birmingham	Trainee	**Aston Villa**	—	—
BURGESS Daryl	5 11	12 03	D	20 4 71	Birmingham	Trainee	**WBA**	178	5
BURGESS Dave *	5 10	11 02	D	20 1 60	Liverpool.	Local	Tranmere R	218	1
							Grimsby T	69	—
							Blackpool	101	1
							Carlisle U (loan)	6	—
							Carlisle U	40	1
							Hartlepool U (loan)	11	—
BURKE David	5 10	11 06	D	6 8 60	Liverpool	Apprentice	Bolton W	69	1
							Huddersfield T	189	3
							Crystal Palace	81	—
							Bolton W	106	—
							Blackpool	23	—
BURKE Mark *	5 10	11 08	F	12 2 69	Solihull	Apprentice	Aston Villa	7	—
							Middlesbrough	57	6
							Darlington (loan)	5	1
							Ipswich T (loan)	—	—
							Wolverhampton W	68	11
							Luton T (loan)	3	—
							Port Vale	15	2
BURKE Robert ‡	5 11	11 06	M	19 11 75	Burton	Trainee	**Stoke C**	—	—
BURKILL Matthew *	5 10	10 00	F	9 3 76	Doncaster	Trainee	**Sheffield W**	—	—
BURLEY Craig	6 1	11 07	M	24 9 71	Ayr	Trainee	**Chelsea**	60	5
BURLEY George	5 10	11 00	D	3 6 56	Cumnock		Ipswich T	394	5
							Sunderland	54	—
							Gillingham	46	2
							Motherwell	54	—
							Ayr U	67	—
							Falkirk	1	—
							Motherwell	5	—
							Colchester U	7	—
BURNDRED John ‡	5 7	10 00	F	23 3 68	Stoke	Knypersley Vic	**Port Vale**	1	—
BURNETT Wayne	5 11	12 01	M	4 9 71	London	Trainee	Leyton Orient	40	—
							Blackburn R	—	—
							Plymouth Arg	64	3
BURNHAM Jason	5 10	13 03	D	8 5 73	Mansfield	Notts County	Northampton T	88	2
							Chester C	24	—
BURNS Chris	6 0	12 00	M	9 11 67	Manchester	Cheltenham T	Portsmouth	90	9
							Swansea C (loan)	4	—
							Bournemouth (loan)	14	1
							Swansea C	5	—
							Northampton T	17	2
BURNS John	5 8	10 08	M	4 12 77	Dublin	Trainee	**Nottingham F**	—	—

Player	Ht	Wt	Pos	Birth Date	Birth Place	Source	Clubs	League App	League Gls
BURRIDGE John *	5 11	13 03	G	3 12 51	Workington	Apprentice	Workington	27	—
							Blackpool	134	—
							Aston Villa	65	—
							Southend U (loan)	6	—
							Crystal Palace	88	—
							QPR	39	—
							Wolverhampton W	74	—
							Derby Co (loan)	6	—
							Sheffield U	109	—
							Southampton	62	—
							Newcastle U	67	—
							Hibernian	65	—
							Newcastle U	—	—
							Scarborough	3	—
							Lincoln C	4	—
							Aberdeen	3	—
							Newcastle U	—	—
							Dumbarton	3	—
							Falkirk	3	—
							Manchester C	4	—
BURROWS David	5 10	11 08	D	25 10 68	Dudley	Apprentice	WBA	46	1
							Liverpool	146	3
							West Ham U	29	1
							Everton	19	—
							Coventry C	11	—
BURROWS Marc	5 9	10 05	D	20 12 75	Sheffield	Trainee	**Sheffield W**	—	—
BURTON Deon	5 8	10 10	F	25 10 76	Ashford	Trainee	**Portsmouth**	9	2
BURTON Mark	5 7	11 11	M	7 5 73	Barnsley	Trainee	**Barnsley**	5	—
BURTON Nick ‡	5 11	11 12	D	10 2 75	Bury St Edmunds	Portsmouth	**Torquay U**	16	2
BUSHELL Steve	5 9	11 06	M	28 12 72	Manchester	Trainee	**York C**	80	5
BUSST Dave	6 1	12 10	D	30 6 67	Birmingham	Moor Green	**Coventry C**	33	2
BUTLER John	5 11	11 07	D	7 2 62	Liverpool	Prescot Cables	Wigan Ath	245	15
							Stoke C	262	7
BUTLER Lee	6 1	14 04	G	30 5 66	Sheffield	Haworth Colliery	Lincoln C	30	—
							Aston Villa	8	—
							Hull C (loan)	4	—
							Barnsley	117	—
BUTLER Martin	5 11	11 07	F	15 9 74	Dudley	Trainee	**Walsall**	23	3
BUTLER Neal ‡			M	11 9 75	Newport Pagnall	Luton T	**Colchester U**	—	—
BUTLER Paul	6 2	13 00	D	2 11 72	Manchester	Trainee	**Rochdale**	120	7
BUTLER Peter	5 9	11 02	M	27 8 66	Halifax	Apprentice	Huddersfield T	5	—
							Cambridge U (loan)	14	1
							Bury	11	—
							Cambridge U	55	9
							Southend U	142	9
							Huddersfield T (loan)	7	—
							West Ham U	70	3
							Notts Co	20	—
BUTLER Steve	6 2	13 00	F	27 1 62	Birmingham	Wokingham	Brentford	97	44
						Maidstone U (1986)	Watford	62	9
							Bournemouth (loan)	1	—
							Cambridge U	93	41
BUTLER Tony	6 2	11 12	D	28 9 72	Stockport	Trainee	**Gillingham**	112	3
BUTT Nicky	5 10	10 10	M	21 1 75	Manchester	Trainee	**Manchester U**	24	1
BUTTERFIELD Tim *	5 11	11 12	M	18 10 74	Sheffield	Trainee	**Sheffield U**	—	—
BUTTERS Guy	6 3	13 00	D	30 10 69	Hillingdon	Trainee	Tottenham H	35	1
							Southend U (loan)	16	3
							Portsmouth	110	4
							Oxford U (loan)	3	1
BUTTERWORTH Ian ‡	6 1	12 12	D	25 1 64	Crewe	Apprentice	Coventry C	90	—
							Nottingham F	27	—
							Norwich C	235	4

Player	Ht	Wt	Pos	Birth Date	Birth Place	Source	Clubs	League App	League Gls
BYFIELD Darren	5 10	11 00	F	29 9 76	Birmingham	Trainee	**Aston Villa**	—	—
BYNG David §	6 1	13 00	F	9 7 77	Coventry	Trainee	**Torquay U**	10	3
BYRNE John	6 0	12 13	F	1 2 61	Manchester	Apprentice	York C	175	55
							QPR	126	30
						Le Havre	Brighton	51	14
							Sunderland	33	8
							Millwall	17	1
							Brighton (loan)	7	2
							Oxford U	55	18
							Brighton	14	4
BYRNE Paul (on loan from Celtic)	5 11	13 00	M	30 6 72	Dublin		**Brighton**	8	1
BYRNE Ray ‡	6 1	11 02	D	4 7 72	Newry	Newry	Nottingham F	—	—
							Northampton T	2	—
BYRNE Wesley	5 9	11 03	D	9 2 77	Dublin	Trainee	**Middlesbrough**	—	—
CADETTE Richard	5 7	12 00	F	21 3 65	Hammersmith	Wembley	Orient	21	4
							Southend U	90	48
							Sheffield U	28	7
							Brentford	87	20
							Bournemouth (loan)	8	1
							Falkirk	92	32
							Millwall	16	4
CAESAR Gus	6 0	12 09	D	5 3 66	London	Apprentice	Arsenal	44	—
							QPR (loan)	5	—
							Cambridge U	—	—
							Bristol C	10	—
							Airdrieonians	57	1
							Colchester U	39	1
CAHILL Ollie	5 10	11 02	F	29 9 75	Clonmel	Clonmel	**Northampton T**	8	1
CAIG Tony	6 0	13 04	G	11 4 74	Whitehaven	Trainee	**Carlisle U**	61	—
CALDERWOOD Colin	6 0	12 12	D	20 1 65	Stranraer	Amateur	Mansfield T	100	1
							Swindon T	330	20
							Tottenham H	62	2
CALDWELL Peter *	6 1	13 00	G	5 6 72	Dorchester	Trainee	**QPR**	—	—
CALVERT Mark	5 9	11 08	M	11 9 70	Consett	Trainee	Hull C	30	1
							Scarborough	72	5
CAME Mark	6 1	13 00	D	14 9 61	Exeter	Winsford U	Bolton W	195	7
							Chester C	47	1
							Exeter C	32	1
CAMPBELL Corey	5 11	11 06	D	6 3 76	London	Trainee	**Brentford**	—	—
CAMPBELL Dave ‡	5 10	11 02	M	2 6 65	Eglinton	Oxford BC	Nottingham F	41	3
							Notts Co (loan)	18	2
							Charlton Ath	30	1
							Plymouth Arg (loan)	1	—
							Bradford C	35	4
							Shamrock R (loan)	31	5
							WBA	—	—
							Rotherham U	1	—
							Burnley	8	—
							Lincoln C (loan)	4	1
							Wigan Ath	7	—
							Cambridge U	1	—
CAMPBELL Jamie *	6 1	11 03	F	21 10 72	Birmingham	Trainee	**Luton T**	36	1
							Mansfield U (loan)	3	1
							Cambridge U (loan)	12	—
CAMPBELL Kevin	6 1	13 08	F	4 2 70	Lambeth	Trainee	**Arsenal**	166	46
							Leyton Orient (loan)	16	9
							Leicester C (loan)	11	5
CAMPBELL Sol	6 2	14 01	M	18 9 74	Newham	Trainee	**Tottenham H**	65	1
CANHAM Scott	5 7	11 07	M	5 11 74	London	Trainee	**West Ham U**	—	—
CANHAM Tony *	5 8	11 04	M	8 6 60	Leeds	Harrogate Railway	**York C**	347	57

Player	Ht	Wt	Pos	Birth Date	Birth Place	Source	Clubs	League App	League Gls
CANTONA Eric	6 2	14 00	F	24 5 66	Paris		Auxerre	13	2
							Martigues	—	—
							Auxerre	68	21
							Marseille	22	5
							Bordeaux	11	6
							Montpellier	33	10
							Marseille	18	8
							Nimes	17	2
							Leeds U	28	9
							Manchester U	77	39
CAPLETON Mel	5 11	12 00	G	24 10 73	London	Trainee	Southend U	—	—
							Blackpool	10	—
CARBON Matthew	6 2	11 13	D	8 6 75	Nottingham	Trainee	**Lincoln C**	43	7
CARBONE Anthony	5 10	11 06	M	13 10 74	Perth	Perth Italia	**Nottingham F**	—	—
CAREY Alan	5 7	10 10	D	21 8 75	Greenwich	Trainee	**Reading**	3	—
CAREY Brian	6 2	14 04	D	31 5 68	Cork	Cork C	Manchester U	—	—
							Wrexham (loan)	3	—
							Wrexham (loan)	13	1
							Leicester C	39	—
CAREY Shaun	5 9	10 06	M	13 5 76	Kettering	Trainee	**Norwich C**	—	—
CARMICHAEL Matt *	6 0	12 04	F	13 5 64	Singapore	Army	Lincoln C	133	18
							Scunthorpe U	62	20
							Barnet (loan)	3	—
							Preston NE	10	3
CARPENTER Richard	5 10	13 00	M	30 9 72	Sheppey	Trainee	**Gillingham**	109	4
CARR Darren	6 2	13 02	D	4 9 68	Bristol	Trainee	Bristol R	30	—
							Newport Co	9	—
							Sheffield U	13	1
							Crewe Alex	104	5
							Chesterfield	63	3
CARR Franz	5 7	10 12	M	24 9 66	Preston	Apprentice	Blackburn R	—	—
							Nottingham F	131	17
							Sheffield W (loan)	12	—
							West Ham U (loan)	3	—
							Newcastle U	25	3
							Sheffield U	18	4
							Leicester C (loan)	13	1
							Aston Villa	2	—
CARR Steve	5 9	12 02	D	29 8 76	Dublin	Trainee	**Tottenham H**	1	—
CARRAGHER Matthew	5 9	10 07	D	14 1 76	Liverpool	Trainee	**Wigan Ath**	73	—
CARROLL Dave	6 0	11 09	F	20 9 66	Paisley	Ruislip Manor	**Wycombe W**	82	12
CARRUTHERS Martin	5 11	11 10	F	7 8 72	Nottingham	Trainee	Aston Villa	4	—
							Hull C (loan)	13	6
							Stoke C	66	10
CARSLEY Lee	5 11	11 12	D	28 2 74	Birmingham	Trainee	**Derby Co**	23	2
CARSS Anthony *	5 11	12 00	M	31 3 76	Alnwick	Bradford C	**Blackburn R**	—	—
CARTER Danny	5 11	11 12	M	29 6 69	Hackney	Billericay	**Leyton Orient**	188	22
CARTER Jimmy *	5 10	11 01	M	9 11 65	London	Apprentice	Crystal Palace	—	—
							QPR	—	—
							Millwall	110	10
							Liverpool	5	—
							Arsenal	25	2
							Oxford U (loan)	5	—
							Oxford U (loan)	4	—
CARTER Mark	5 10	12 06	F	17 12 60	Liverpool	Runcorn	Barnet	82	30
							Bury	62	34
CARTER Simon *	6 0	11 04	D	8 3 76	Kidderminster	Trainee	**Sheffield W**	—	—

Player	Ht	Wt	Pos	Birth Date	Birth Place	Source	Clubs	League App	League Gls
CARTER Tim *	6 2	13 11	G	5 10 67	Bristol	Apprentice	Bristol R	47	—
							Newport Co (loan)	1	—
							Carlisle U (loan)	4	—
							Sunderland	37	—
							Bristol C (loan)	3	—
							Birmingham C (loan)	2	—
							Hartlepool U	18	—
							Millwall	4	—
CARTWRIGHT Lee	5 10	11 00	M	19 9 72	Rossendale	Trainee	**Preston NE**	156	10
CARTWRIGHT Mark	6 1	12 05	G	13 1 73	Chester	York C	**Wrexham**	—	—
CASE Jimmy *	5 9	12 12	M	18 5 54	Liverpool	South Liverpool	Liverpool	186	23
							Brighton	127	10
							Southampton	215	10
							Bournemouth	40	1
							Halifax T	21	2
							Wrexham	4	—
							Darlington	1	—
						Sittingbourne	**Brighton**	30	—
CASH Stuart ‡	5 10	11 11	D	5 9 65	Tipton	Halesowen	Nottingham F	—	—
							Rotherham U (loan)	8	1
							Brentford (loan)	11	—
							Shrewsbury T (loan)	8	1
							Chesterfield	29	—
							Wycombe W	—	—
CASKEY Darren	5 8	11 09	M	21 8 74	Basildon	Trainee	**Tottenham H**	29	4
CASPER Chris	6 0	11 02	D	28 4 75	Burnley	Trainee	**Manchester U**	—	—
CASS Jamie *	5 4	9 03	M	24 1 76	Hull	Trainee	**Hull C**	—	—
CASSIDY Jamie	5 9	10 07	M	21 11 77	Liverpool	Trainee	**Liverpool**	—	—
CASSIN Graham	5 8	10 07	F	24 3 78	Dublin	Trainee	**Blackburn R**	—	—
CASTLE Steve	5 11	12 10	M	17 5 66	Barkingside	Apprentice	Orient	243	55
							Plymouth Arg	101	35
CASTLEDINE Gary ‡	5 8	11 12	F	27 3 70	Dumfries	Shirebrook	**Mansfield T**	66	3
CASTLEDINE Stewart	6 0	12 00	M	22 1 73	London	Trainee	**Wimbledon**	11	2
CAWLEY Peter	6 3	14 06	D	15 9 65	London	Chertsey	Wimbledon	1	—
							Bristol R (loan)	10	—
							Fulham (loan)	5	—
							Bristol R	3	—
							Southend U	7	1
							Exeter C	7	—
							Barnet	3	—
							Colchester U	83	6
CECERE Michele	6 0	11 04	F	4 1 68	Chester	Apprentice	Oldham Ath	52	8
							Huddersfield T	54	8
							Stockport Co (loan)	1	—
							Walsall	112	32
							Exeter C	30	10
CERAOLO Mark *			F	10 11 75	Birkenhead		**Crewe Alex**	—	—
CHALK Martyn	5 6	10 00	F	30 8 69	Louth	Louth U	Derby Co	7	1
							Stockport Co	33	6
CHALLENDER Greg ‡	6 0	12 08	D	5 2 73	Rochdale	Mossley	**Preston NE**	10	2
CHALLINER Dave	6 1	12 00	D	2 10 75	Chester	Brombrough Pool	**Tranmere R**	—	—
CHALLINOR Paul	6 1	12 02	D	6 4 76	Newcastle under Lyne	Trainee	**Birmingham C**	—	—
CHALLIS Trevor	5 7	10 00	D	23 10 75	Paddington	Trainee	**QPR**	—	—
CHAMBERLAIN Alec	6 2	13 09	G	20 6 64	March	Ramsey T	Ipswich T	—	—
							Colchester U	184	—
							Everton	—	—
							Tranmere R (loan)	15	—
							Luton T	138	—
							Chelsea (loan)	—	—
							Sunderland	61	—
							Liverpool (loan)	—	—

Player	Ht	Wt	Pos	Birth Date	Birth Place	Source	Clubs	League App	League Gls
CHAMBERLAIN Mark *	5 9	10 07	M	19 11 61	Stoke	Apprentice	Port Vale	96	17
							Stoke C	112	17
							Sheffield W	66	8
							Portsmouth	167	20
							Brighton	19	2
CHAMBERS Leroy	5 11	12 00	F	25 10 72	Sheffield	Trainee	Sheffield W	—	—
							Chester C	13	—
CHAMP Paul *	5 10	12 12	D	18 12 75	Colchester	Trainee	**Colchester U**	—	—
CHANDLER Dean	6 1	11 02	D	6 5 76	Ilford	Trainee	**Charlton Ath**	1	1
CHANNING Justin	5 11	11 07	D	19 11 68	Reading	Apprentice	QPR	55	5
							Bristol R	94	10
CHAPMAN Danny *	5 10	11 06	M	21 11 74	Peckham	Trainee	**Millwall**	12	—
CHAPMAN Gary *	5 8	11 07	F	1 5 64	Bradford	Frickley Ath	Bradford C	5	—
							Notts Co	25	4
							Mansfield T (loan)	6	—
							Exeter C	24	5
							Torquay U	8	—
							Darlington	74	9
CHAPMAN Ian	5 9	12 08	M	31 5 70	Brighton	Trainee	**Brighton**	245	11
CHAPMAN Lee	6 2	13 00	F	5 12 59	Lincoln	Amateur	Stoke C	99	34
							Plymouth Arg (loan)	4	—
							Arsenal	23	4
							Sunderland	15	3
							Sheffield W	149	63
						Niort	Nottingham F	48	15
							Leeds U	137	62
							Portsmouth	5	2
							West Ham U	40	7
							Southend U (loan)	1	1
							Ipswich T	16	1
CHAPPLE Phil	6 2	12 07	D	26 11 66	Norwich	Apprentice	Norwich C	—	—
							Cambridge U	187	19
							Charlton Ath	65	7
CHAPPLE Shaun	5 11	12 03	M	14 2 73	Swansea	Trainee	**Swansea C**	63	7
CHARLERY Ken	6 1	13 03	F	28 11 64	Stepney	Beckton U	Maidstone U	59	11
							Peterborough U	51	19
							Watford	48	13
							Peterborough U	70	24
CHARLES Gary	5 9	10 13	D	13 4 70	London	Trainee	Nottingham F	56	1
							Leicester C (loan)	8	—
							Derby Co	61	3
							Aston Villa	16	—
CHARLES Steve *	5 11	11 12	M	10 5 60	Sheffield	Sheffield Univ	Sheffield U	123	10
							Wrexham	113	37
							Mansfield T	237	39
							Scunthorpe U (loan)	4	—
							Scarborough	93	15
CHARLTON Simon	5 8	11 04	D	25 10 71	Huddersfield	Trainee	Huddersfield T	124	1
							Southampton	58	2
CHARNOCK Phil	5 11	11 02	M	14 2 75	Southport	Trainee	**Liverpool**	—	—
CHEESEWRIGHT John *	6 0	13 11	G	12 1 73	Hornchurch	Tottenham H	Southend U	—	—
							Birmingham C	1	—
						Braintree T	**Colchester U**	40	—
CHEETHAM Michael	5 9	12 03	M	30 6 67	Amsterdam	Army	Ipswich T	4	—
							Cambridge U	132	22
							Chesterfield	5	—
							Colchester U	9	1
CHENERY Ben	6 0	12 00	D	28 1 77	Ipswich	Trainee	**Luton T**	—	—
CHERRY Steve *	6 1	13 00	G	5 8 60	Nottingham	Apprentice	Derby Co	77	—
							Port Vale (loan)	4	—
							Walsall	71	—
							Plymouth Arg	73	—
							Chesterfield (loan)	10	—
							Notts Co	266	—

Player	Ht	Wt	Pos	Birth Date	Birth Place	Source	Clubs	League App	League Gls
CHETTLE Steve	6 1	13 03	D	27 9 68	Nottingham	Apprentice	**Nottingham F**	256	7
CHILDS Gary	5 7	10 08	M	19 4 64	Birmingham	Apprentice	WBA	3	—
							Walsall	131	17
							Birmingham C	55	2
							Grimsby T	171	22
CHISHOLM Craig	5 10	10 04	M	21 9 77	Glasgow	Trainee	**Blackburn R**	—	—
CHIVERS Gary ‡	5 11	11 05	D	15 5 60	Stockwell	Apprentice	Chelsea	133	4
							Swansea C	10	—
							QPR	60	—
							Watford	14	—
							Brighton	217	13
							Bournemouth	31	2
CHRISTIE Iyseden			F	14 11 76	Coventry	Trainee	**Coventry C**	—	—
CLAPHAM Jamie	5 9	10 08	M	7 12 75	Lincoln	Trainee	**Tottenham H**	—	—
CLARIDGE Steve	5 11	11 08	F	10 4 66	Portsmouth	Fareham	Bournemouth	7	1
						Weymouth	Crystal Palace	—	—
							Aldershot	62	19
							Cambridge U	79	28
							Luton T	16	2
							Cambridge U	53	18
							Birmingham C	60	27
CLARK Billy	6 0	12 03	D	19 5 67	Christchurch	Trainee	Bournemouth	4	—
							Bristol R	182	11
CLARK Howard *	6 0	12 07	D	19 9 68	Coventry	Apprentice	Coventry C	20	1
							Darlington (loan)	5	—
							Shrewsbury T	56	—
							Hereford U	55	7
CLARK John (To Falkirk)	6 0	13 01	D	22 9 64	Edinburgh	S Form	Dundee U	242	19
							Stoke C	17	—
CLARK Lee	5 7	11 07	M	27 10 72	Wallsend	Trainee	**Newcastle U**	142	19
CLARK Richard	5 11	12 04	G	6 4 77	Nuneaton	Trainee	**Nottingham F**	—	—
CLARK Simon	6 1	12 06	D	12 3 67	London	Stevenage Bor	**Peterborough U**	33	—
CLARK Tony §			F	7 4 77	London		**Wycombe W**	1	—
CLARKE Adrian	5 10	11 00	F	28 9 74	Suffolk	Trainee	**Arsenal**	1	—
CLARKE Andy	5 10	11 07	F	22 7 67	London	Barnet	**Wimbledon**	127	14
CLARKE Chris	6 1	12 10	G	1 5 74	Barnsley	Trainee	Bolton W	—	—
							Rochdale	24	—
CLARKE Dean §	5 9	10 05	F	28 7 77	Hereford	Trainee	**Hereford U**	6	—
CLARKE Matthew	6 3	11 04	G	3 11 73	Sheffield	Trainee	**Rotherham U**	84	—
CLARKE Steve	5 10	10 02	D	29 8 63	Saltcoats	Beith J	St Mirren	151	6
							Chelsea	251	6
CLARKE Tim	6 3	13 07	G	19 9 68	Stourbridge	Halesowen	Coventry C	—	—
							Huddersfield T	70	—
							Rochdale (loan)	2	—
						Halesowen	**Shrewsbury T**	16	—
CLARKE Wayne *	6 0	11 08	F	28 2 61	Wolverhampton	Apprentice	Wolverhampton W	148	30
							Birmingham C	92	38
							Everton	57	18
							Leicester C	11	1
							Manchester C	21	2
							Shrewsbury T (loan)	7	6
							Stoke C (loan)	9	3
							Wolverhampton W (loan)	1	—
							Walsall	39	21
							Shrewsbury T	59	22
CLARKSON Ian	5 10	12 00	D	4 12 70	Birmingham	Trainee	Birmingham C	136	—
							Stoke C	32	—
CLARKSON Phil	5 8	11 02	M	13 11 68	Hambleton	Fleetwood	**Crewe Alex**	93	27

Player	Ht	Wt	Pos	Birth Date	Birth Place	Source	Clubs	League App	League Gls
CLAYTON Gary	5 10	12 03	M	2 2 63	Sheffield	Burton Alb	Doncaster R	35	5
							Cambridge U	179	17
							Peterborough U (loan)	4	—
							Huddersfield T	19	1
CLEGG David			M	23 10 76	Liverpool	Trainee	**Liverpool**	—	—
CLEMENCE Stephen			M	31 3 78	Liverpool	Trainee	**Tottenham H**	—	—
CLIFFORD Mark §			D	11 9 77	Nottingham	Trainee	**Mansfield T**	1	—
CLODE Mark	5 10	10 10	D	24 2 73	Plymouth	Trainee	Plymouth Arg	—	—
							Swansea C	61	2
CLOUGH Nigel	5 9	11 04	M	19 3 66	Sunderland	AC Hunters	Nottingham F	311	101
							Liverpool	37	7
CLYDE Darran	6 4	13 00	D	26 3 76	N Ireland	Trainee	**Barnsley**	—	—
COADY Lewis §	6 1	11 05	F	20 9 76	Liverpool	Trainee	**Wrexham**	2	—
COATES Jonathan	5 8	10 04	F	27 6 75	Swansea	Trainee	**Swansea C**	9	1
COATSWORTH Gary ‡	6 0	13 01	D	7 10 68	Sunderland		Barnsley	6	—
							Darlington	22	2
							Leicester C	32	4
COCKERILL Glenn	5 10	12 06	M	25 8 59	Grimsby	Louth U	Lincoln C	71	10
							Swindon T	26	1
							Lincoln C	115	25
							Sheffield U	62	10
							Southampton	287	32
							Leyton Orient	52	6
CODNER Robert *	5 11	11 08	M	23 1 65	Walthamstow	Barnet	**Brighton**	266	39
COLCOMBE Scott *	5 6	9 13	F	15 12 71	West Bromwich	Trainee	WBA	—	—
							Torquay U	89	1
COLDICOTT Stacy	5 11	11 02	D	29 4 74	Worcester	Trainee	**WBA**	30	—
COLE Andy	5 11	11 02	F	15 10 71	Nottingham	Trainee	Arsenal	1	—
							Fulham (loan)	13	3
							Bristol C (loan)	12	8
							Bristol C	29	12
							Newcastle U	70	55
							Manchester U	18	12
COLEMAN Chris	6 2	14 06	D	10 6 70	Swansea	Apprentice	Swansea C	160	2
							Crystal Palace	137	13
COLEMAN Simon	6 0	10 09	D	13 3 68	Worksop		Mansfield T	96	7
							Middlesbrough	55	2
							Derby Co	70	2
							Sheffield W	16	1
							Bolton W	22	4
COLGAN Nick	6 1	12 00	G	19 9 73	Eire	Drogheda	**Chelsea**	—	—
							Crewe Alex (loan)	—	—
							Grimsby T (loan)	—	—
COLKIN Lee	5 11	12 00	D	15 7 74	Nuneaton	Trainee	**Northampton T**	69	2
COLL Owen	6 1	11 07	D	9 4 76	Donegal	Amateur	**Tottenham H**	—	—
COLLETT Andy	6 0	13 02	G	28 10 73	Middlesbrough	Trainee	Middlesbrough	2	—
							Bristol R	4	—
COLLIER Danny	6 3	12 08	D	15 1 74	Eccles	Trainee	Wolverhampton W	—	—
							Crewe Alex	5	—
COLLIER Darren *	5 11	12 00	G	1 12 67	Stockton	Middlesbrough	Blackburn R	27	—
							Darlington	44	—
COLLINS David *	6 1	12 10	D	30 10 71	Dublin	Trainee	Liverpool	—	—
							Wigan Ath (loan)	9	—
							Oxford U	42	—
COLLINS Sam	6 2	13 05	D	5 6 77	Pontefract	Trainee	**Huddersfield T**	—	—
COLLINS Simon	5 11	13 00	M	16 12 73	Pontefract	Trainee	**Huddersfield T**	6	—
COLLINS Wayne	6 0	12 00	M	4 3 69	Manchester	Winsford U	**Crewe Alex**	75	13

Player	Ht	Wt	Pos	Birth Date	Birth Place	Source	Clubs	League App	League Gls
COLLYMORE Stan	6 2	13 11	F	22 1 71	Stone	Stafford R	Crystal Palace	20	1
							Southend U	30	15
							Nottingham F	65	41
COMYN Andy	6 1	11 13	D	2 6 68	Manchester	Alvechurch	Aston Villa	15	—
							Derby Co	63	1
							Plymouth Arg	76	5
CONNELL Graham *	5 10	11 05	M	31 10 74	Glasgow	Trainee	**Ipswich T**	—	—
CONNELLY Dino ‡	5 9	10 08	M	6 1 70	St. Helier	Celtic BC	Arsenal	—	—
							Barnsley	13	—
							Wigan Ath (loan)	12	2
							Carlisle U (loan)	3	—
							Wigan Ath	20	1
							Stockport Co	—	—
CONNELLY Sean	5 10	11 10	D	26 6 70	Sheffield	Hallam	**Stockport Co**	78	—
CONNOLLY David	5 8	10 09	F	6 6 77	Willesden	Trainee	**Watford**	2	—
CONNOLLY Karl	5 9	11 00	F	9 2 70	Prescot	Napoli (Liverpool Sunday League)	**Wrexham**	162	29
CONNOR James	6 0	13 00	M	22 8 74	Middlesbrough	Trainee	**Millwall**	1	—
CONROY Mike	6 0	12 07	F	31 12 65	Glasgow	Apprentice	Coventry C	—	—
							Clydebank	114	38
							St Mirren	10	1
							Reading	80	7
							Burnley	77	30
							Preston NE	57	22
CONWAY Paul	6 1	12 07	M	17 4 70	London	Oldham Ath	**Carlisle U**	42	10
COOK Andy	5 9	12 00	D	10 8 69	Romsey	Apprentice	Southampton	16	1
							Exeter C	70	1
							Swansea C	29	—
COOK Anthony §			M	17 9 76	Hemel Hempstead	Trainee	**Colchester U**	2	—
COOK Mitch *	6 0	12 00	M	15 10 61	Scarborough	Scarborough	Darlington	34	4
							Middlesbrough	6	—
							Scarborough	81	10
							Halifax T	54	2
							Scarborough (loan)	9	1
							Darlington (loan)	9	—
							Darlington	27	3
							Blackpool	68	—
							Hartlepool U	24	—
COOK Paul	5 11	10 10	M	22 2 67	Liverpool	Marine	Wigan Ath	83	14
							Norwich C	6	—
							Wolverhampton W	193	19
							Coventry C	34	3
COOKE Andrew	6 0	12 00	F	2 1 74	Shrewsbury	Newtown	**Burnley**	—	—
COOKE Terry	5 7	9 09	F	5 8 76	Marston Green	Trainee	**Manchester U**	—	—
COOKSEY Scott	6 3	13 10	G	24 6 72	Birmingham	Bromsgrove R	**Peterborough U**	15	—
COOPER Colin	5 9	11 02	D	28 2 67	Durham		Middlesbrough	188	6
							Millwall	77	6
							Nottingham F	72	8
COOPER David *	6 0	12 00	D	7 3 73	Welwyn	Luton T	**Exeter C**	48	—
COOPER Gary	5 8	11 03	D	20 11 65	Edgware	Fisher Ath	Maidstone U	60	7
							Peterborough U	88	10
							Birmingham C	44	2
COOPER Geoff ‡	5 10	11 00	M	27 12 60	Kingston	Bognor Regis Barnet	Brighton	7	—
							Barnet	31	1
							Wycombe W	—	—
							Barnet	37	3
COOPER Kevin	5 6	10 07	M	8 2 75	Derby	Trainee	**Derby Co**	1	—

Player	Ht	Wt	Pos	Birth Date	Birth Place	Source	Clubs	League App	League Gls
COOPER Mark	6 2	13 04	F	5 4 67	Cambridge	Apprentice	Cambridge U	71	17
							Tottenham H	—	—
							Shrewsbury T	6	2
							Gillingham	49	11
							Leyton Orient	150	45
							Barnet	34	11
COOPER Mark	5 8	11 04	M	18 12 68	Wakefield	Trainee	Bristol C	—	—
							Exeter C	50	12
							Southend U (loan)	5	—
							Birmingham C	39	4
							Fulham	14	—
							Huddersfield T (loan)	10	4
							Wycombe W	2	1
							Exeter C	61	14
COOPER Steve (To Airdrie)	5 11	10 12	F	22 6 64	Birmingham	Moor Green	Birmingham C	—	—
							Halifax T (loan)	7	1
							Mansfield T (loan)	—	—
							Newport Co	38	11
							Plymouth Arg	73	15
							Barnsley	77	13
							Tranmere R	32	3
							Peterborough U (loan)	9	—
							Wigan Ath (loan)	4	—
							York C	38	6
CORAZZIN Carlo	5 9	12 04	F	25 12 71	Canada	Vancouver 86ers	**Cambridge U**	74	29
CORDEN Wayne			M	1 11 75	Leek	Trainee	**Port Vale**	1	—
CORK Alan ‡	6 0	14 01	F	4 3 59	Derby	Amateur	Derby C	—	—
							Lincoln C (loan)	5	—
							Wimbledon	430	145
							Sheffield U	54	7
							Fulham	15	3
CORNFORTH John	6 1	12 11	M	7 10 67	Whitley Bay	Apprentice	Sunderland	32	2
							Doncaster R (loan)	7	3
							Shrewsbury T (loan)	3	—
							Lincoln C (loan)	9	1
							Swansea C	132	14
CORNWELL John ‡	6 4	13 00	M	13 10 64	Bethnal Green	Apprentice	Orient	202	35
							Newcastle U	33	1
							Swindon T	25	—
							Southend U	101	5
							Cardiff C (loan)	5	2
							Brentford (loan)	4	—
							Northampton T (loan)	13	1
COSTELLO Lorcan	5 9	11 02	D	11 11 76	Dublin	Trainee	**Coventry C**	—	—
COTON Tony	6 2	13 07	G	19 5 61	Tamworth	Mile Oak	Birmingham C	94	—
							Hereford U (loan)	—	—
							Watford	233	—
							Manchester C	164	—
COTTEE Tony	5 7	11 03	F	11 7 65	West Ham	Apprentice	West Ham U	212	92
							Everton	184	72
							West Ham U	31	13
COTTERELL Leo	5 9	10 00	D	2 9 74	Cambridge	Trainee	**Ipswich T**	2	—
COTTERILL Steve	6 1	12 05	F	20 7 64	Cheltenham	Burton A	Wimbledon	17	6
							Brighton (loan)	11	4
							Bournemouth	45	15
COUGHLIN Russell *	5 8	11 12	M	15 2 60	Swansea	Apprentice	Manchester C	—	—
							Blackburn R	24	—
							Carlisle U	130	13
							Plymouth Arg	131	18
							Blackpool	102	8
							Shrewsbury T (loan)	5	—
							Swansea C	101	2
							Exeter C	60	—
COUSIN Scott ‡			G	31 1 75	Leeds	Trainee	**Leeds U**	—	—
COUSINS Jason	5 11	12 06	D	14 10 70	Hayes	Trainee	Brentford	21	—
						Wycombe W	**Wycombe W**	78	3
COUZENS Andrew	5 9	11 06	D	4 6 75	Shipley	Trainee	**Leeds U**	4	—

Player	Ht	Wt	Pos	Birth Date	Birth Place	Source	Clubs	League App	League Gls
COWAN Tom	5 8	10 08	D	28 8 69	Bellshill	Netherdale BC	Clyde	16	2
							Rangers	12	—
							Sheffield U	45	—
							Stoke C (loan)	14	—
							Huddersfield T (loan)	10	—
							Huddersfield T	37	2
COWANS Gordon	5 7	9 08	M	27 10 58	Durham	Apprentice	Aston Villa	286	42
							Bari	94	3
							Aston Villa	117	7
							Blackburn R	50	2
							Aston Villa	11	—
							Derby Co	36	—
							Wolverhampton W	21	—
COWE Steven	5 7	10 02	M	29 9 74	Gloucester	Trainee	**Aston Villa**	—	—
COWLING Lee	5 8	9 04	M	22 9 77	Doncaster	Trainee	**Nottingham F**	—	—
COX Ian	6 0	12 00	M	25 3 71	Croydon	Carshalton Ath	**Crystal Palace**	11	—
COX Neil	6 0	13 02	D	8 10 71	Scunthorpe	Trainee	Scunthorpe U	17	1
							Aston Villa	42	3
							Middlesbrough	40	1
COX Paul *	5 11	11 12	D	1 1 72	Nottingham	Trainee	**Notts Co**	44	1
							Hull C (loan)	5	1
COYLE Owen	5 11	10 05	F	14 7 66	Glasgow	Renfrew YM	Dumbarton	103	36
							Clydebank	63	33
							Airdrieonians	123	50
							Bolton W	49	12
COYNE Danny	6 0	12 07	G	27 8 73	Prestatyn	Trainee	**Tranmere R**	11	—
CRADDOCK Jody	6 0	12 04	D	25 7 75	Redditch	Christchurch	**Cambridge U**	58	—
CRAGGS Graham	6 1	13 06	D	5 6 76	Ashington	Trainee	**Blackpool**	—	—
CRANSON Ian	6 0	13 04	D	2 7 64	Easington	Apprentice	Ipswich T	131	5
							Sheffield W	30	—
							Stoke C	193	8
CRAWFORD James	5 11	11 06	M	1 5 73	USA	Bohemians	**Newcastle U**	—	—
CRAWLEY David ‡	6 0	12 00	F	10 6 77	Dundalk	Dundalk	**Manchester C**	—	—
CREANEY Gerry	5 10	10 10	F	13 4 70	Coatbridge	Celtic BC	Celtic	113	36
							Portsmouth	57	29
CREASER Glyn	6 4	14 10	D	1 9 59	London	Barnet	**Wycombe W**	19	2
CRICHTON Paul	6 1	12 05	G	3 10 68	Pontefract	Apprentice	Nottingham F	—	—
							Notts Co (loan)	5	—
							Darlington (loan)	5	—
							Peterborough U (loan)	4	—
							Darlington (loan)	3	—
							Swindon T (loan)	4	—
							Rotherham U (loan)	6	—
							Torquay U (loan)	13	—
							Peterborough U	47	—
							Doncaster R	77	—
							Grimsby T	89	—
CROCKER Marcus *	5 10	12 03	F	8 10 74	Plymouth	Trainee	**Plymouth Arg**	10	—
CROFT Brian *	5 9	10 10	M	27 9 67	Chester	Trainee	Chester C	59	3
							Cambridge U	17	2
							Chester C	114	3
							QPR	—	—
							Shrewsbury T (loan)	4	—
CROFT Gary	5 9	10 08	D	17 2 74	Burton-on-Trent	Trainee	**Grimsby T**	113	2
CROOK Ian	5 8	10 06	M	18 1 63	Romford	Apprentice	Tottenham H	20	1
							Norwich C	276	14
CROOKS Lee	6 1	11 01	M	14 1 78	Wakefield	Trainee	**Manchester C**	—	—
CROSBY Andy	6 2	13 00	D	3 3 73	Rotherham	Leeds U	Doncaster R	51	—
							Darlington	60	—

Player	Ht	Wt	Pos	Birth Date	Birth Place	Source	Clubs	League App	League Gls
CROSBY Gary	5 7	9 11	F	8 5 64	Sleaford	Lincoln U Grantham	Lincoln C Nottingham F Grimsby T (loan) **Huddersfield T**	7 152 3 19	— 12 — 4
CROSS John	5 8	10 10	M	6 4 76	Barking	Trainee	**QPR**	—	—
CROSS Jonathan	5 10	11 05	M	2 3 75	Wallasey	Trainee	**Wrexham**	92	10
CROSS Mark ‡			F	6 5 76	Abergavenny	Trainee	**Hereford U**	1	—
CROSS Nicky	5 9	11 12	F	7 2 61	Birmingham	Apprentice	WBA Walsall Leicester C Port Vale **Hereford U**	105 109 58 144 28	15 45 15 39 6
CROSS Paul *	5 7	10 00	M	31 10 65	Barnsley	Apprentice	Barnsley Preston NE (loan) Hartlepool U **Darlington**	118 5 74 39	— — 1 2
CROSS Ryan	6 0	13 10	D	11 10 72	Plymouth	Trainee	Plymouth Arg Hartlepool U **Bury**	19 50 29	— 2 —
CROSSLEY Mark	6 0	13 09	G	16 6 69	Barnsley	Trainee	**Nottingham F** Manchester U (loan)	200 —	— —
CROSSLEY Matt	6 2	13 04	D	18 3 68	Basingstoke	Overton U	**Wycombe W**	75	2
CRUMPLIN John ‡	5 8	11 10	M	26 5 67	Bath	Bognor Regis	**Brighton**	207	7
CULLING Gary ‡	5 9	11 00	D	6 4 72	Braintree	Braintree	**Colchester U**	2	—
CULVERHOUSE Ian	5 10	11 02	D	22 9 64	Bishop's Stortford	Apprentice	Tottenham H Norwich C **Swindon T**	2 296 9	— 1 —
CUNDY Jason	6 0	13 13	D	12 11 69	Wimbledon	Trainee	Chelsea Tottenham H (loan) **Tottenham H**	41 10 15	1 — 1
CUNNINGHAM Aaron *			F	11 11 73	New Jersey	Trainee	**Portsmouth**	—	—
CUNNINGHAM Ken	6 0	11 08	D	28 6 71	Dublin	Tolka R	Millwall **Wimbledon**	136 28	1 —
CUNNINGTON Shaun	5 10	11 12	M	4 1 66	Bourne	Bourne T	Wrexham Grimsby T **Sunderland**	199 182 58	12 13 8
CURBISHLEY Alan	5 10	11 07	M	8 11 57	Forest Gate	Apprentice	West Ham U Birmingham C Aston Villa Charlton Ath Brighton **Charlton Ath**	85 130 36 63 116 28	5 11 1 6 13 —
CURETON Jamie	5 8	10 07	F	28 8 75	Bristol	Trainee	**Norwich C**	17	4
CURLE Keith	6 0	12 07	D	14 11 63	Bristol	Apprentice	Bristol R Torquay U Bristol C Reading Wimbledon **Manchester C**	32 16 121 40 93 139	4 5 1 — 3 11
CURRAN Chris	5 11	12 04	D	17 9 71	Birmingham	Trainee	**Torquay U**	133	3
CURRIE Darren	5 9	11 07	M	29 11 74	Hampstead	Trainee	**West Ham U** Shrewsbury T (loan)	— 17	— 2
CURRIE David	5 11	12 09	F	27 11 62	Stockton	Local	Middlesbrough Darlington Barnsley Nottingham F Oldham Ath Barnsley Rotherham U (loan) Huddersfield T (loan) **Carlisle U**	113 76 80 8 31 75 5 7 38	31 33 30 1 3 12 2 1 4

Player	Ht	Wt	Pos	Birth Date	Birth Place	Source	Clubs	League App	League Gls
CURTIS Andy ‡	5 8	12 00	F	2 12 72	Doncaster	Trainee	York C	12	—
							Peterborough U	11	1
CURTIS Robbie *	6 0	13 00	D	21 5 72	Mansfield	Boston U	**Northampton T**	13	—
CURTIS Tommy	5 8	11 05	M	1 3 73	Exeter	School	Derby Co	—	—
							Chesterfield	76	5
CUSACK Nick	6 0	11 13	F	24 12 65	Rotherham	Alvechurch	Leicester C	16	1
							Peterborough U	44	10
							Motherwell	77	17
							Darlington	21	6
							Oxford U	61	10
							Wycombe W (loan)	4	—
							Fulham	27	7
CUTLER Neil	6 4	14 00	G	3 9 76	Birmingham	Trainee	**WBA**	—	—
DAISH Liam	6 2	13 05	D	23 9 68	Portsmouth	Apprentice	Portsmouth	1	—
							Cambridge U	139	4
							Birmingham C	56	3
DAKIN Simon	5 9	11 02	D	30 11 74	Nottingham	Derby Co	**Hull C**	30	1
DALE Carl	6 0	12 00	F	29 4 66	Colwyn Bay	Bangor C	Chester C	116	41
							Cardiff C	111	38
DALEY Philip	6 2	12 09	F	12 4 67	Walton	Newton	Wigan Ath	161	39
							Lincoln C	20	4
DALEY Tony	5 8	10 08	F	18 10 67	Birmingham	Apprentice	Aston Villa	233	31
							Wolverhampton W	1	—
DALLI Jean †			D	13 8 76	Enfield		**Colchester U**	1	—
DALTON Paul	5 11	12 07	M	25 4 67	Middlesbrough	Brandon	Manchester U	—	—
							Hartlepool U	151	37
							Plymouth Arg	98	25
DANIEL Ray *	5 8	11 09	D	10 12 64	Luton	Apprentice	Luton T	22	4
							Gillingham (loan)	5	—
							Hull C	58	3
							Cardiff C	56	1
							Portsmouth	100	4
							Notts Co (loan)	5	—
DANIELS Scott *	6 1	11 09	D	22 11 69	Benfleet	Trainee	Colchester U	73	—
							Exeter C	117	7
							Northampton T	8	—
DANZEY Michael †	6 1	12 00	F	8 2 71	Widnes	Trainee	Nottingham F	—	—
							Chester C (loan)	2	—
							Peterborough U	1	—
						St Albans	**Cambridge U**	27	3
							Scunthorpe U (loan)	3	1
DARBY Duane	5 11	12 13	F	17 10 73	Birmingham	Trainee	**Torquay U**	108	26
DARBY Julian	6 0	11 04	D	3 10 67	Bolton	Trainee	Bolton W	270	36
							Coventry C	55	5
DARNBOROUGH Lee			G	15 9 77	Ashton	Trainee	**Oldham Ath**	—	—
DARTON Scott	5 11	11 02	D	27 3 75	Ipswich	Trainee	WBA	15	—
							Blackpool	18	—
DAUGHTRY Paul ‡	5 8	10 07	F	14 2 73	Oldham	Winsford	Stockport Co	—	—
							Hartlepool U	15	—
D'AURIA David	5 9	11 00	M	26 3 70	Swansea	Trainee	Swansea C	45	6
						Barry T	**Scarborough**	34	7
DAVENPORT Peter	5 10	11 06	F	24 3 61	Birkenhead	Everton	Nottingham F	118	54
							Manchester U	92	22
							Middlesbrough	59	7
							Sunderland	99	15
							Airdrie	38	9
							St Johnstone	22	4
							Stockport Co	6	1
DAVEY Simon	5 10	10 05	M	1 10 70	Swansea	Trainee	Swansea C	49	4
							Carlisle U	105	18
							Preston NE	13	3
DAVIDSON Craig *	6 0	12 02	D	2 5 74	Harold Wood	Trainee	**Southend U**	—	—

Player	Ht	Wt	Pos	Birth Date	Birth Place	Source	Clubs	League App	League Gls
DAVIDSON Ross	5 10	12 04	D	13 11 73	Chertsey	Walton & Hersham	**Sheffield U**	1	—
DAVIES Gareth	6 1	11 12	D	11 12 73	Hereford	Trainee	**Hereford U**	95	1
DAVIES Glen	6 1	12 10	D	20 2 76	Brighton	Trainee	**Burnley**	—	—
DAVIES Kevin	6 0	12 12	F	26 3 77	Sheffield	Trainee	**Chesterfield**	65	15
DAVIES Martin ‡	6 2	13 07	G	28 6 74	Swansea	Trainee	**Coventry C**	—	—
DAVIES Michael *	5 8	10 07	D	19 1 66	Stretford	Apprentice	**Blackpool**	310	16
DAVIES Simon	6 0	11 07	M	23 4 74	Middlewich	Trainee	**Manchester U**	5	—
							Exeter C (loan)	6	1
DAVIES Will	6 2	13 04	F	27 9 75	Derby	Trainee	**Derby Co**	2	—
DAVIS Aaron ‡	5 8	11 00	D	11 2 72	London		Torquay U	24	—
							Colchester U	4	—
DAVIS Darren *	6 0	11 00	D	5 2 67	Sutton-in-Ashfield	Apprentice	Notts Co	92	1
							Lincoln C	102	4
							Maidstone U	31	2
						Frickley Ath	**Scarborough**	48	3
DAVIS Kelvin	6 1	13 06	G	29 9 76	Bedford	Trainee	**Luton T**	10	—
							Torquay U (loan)	2	—
DAVIS Mike	6 0	12 00	F	19 10 74	Bristol	Yate T	**Bristol R**	13	1
							Hereford U (loan)	1	1
DAVIS Neil	5 8	11 00	F	15 8 73	Bloxwich	Redditch U	**Aston Villa**	—	—
DAVIS Paul *	5 10	10 13	M	9 12 61	London	Apprentice	**Arsenal**	351	30
DAVIS Steve	5 11	12 12	D	26 7 65	Birmingham	Stoke C	Crewe Alex	145	1
							Burnley	147	11
							Barnsley	56	2
DAVIS Steve	6 2	14 07	D	30 10 68	Hexham	Trainee	Southampton	7	—
							Burnley (loan)	9	—
							Notts Co (loan)	2	—
							Burnley	162	22
DAVISON Aidan	6 1	13 12	G	11 5 68	Sedgefield	Billingham Syn	Notts Co	1	—
							Leyton Orient (loan)	—	—
							Bury	—	—
							Chester C (loan)	—	—
							Blackpool (loan)	—	—
							Millwall	34	—
							Bolton W	35	—
DAVISON Bobby	5 8	11 09	F	17 7 59	South Shields	Seaham CW	Huddersfield T	2	—
							Halifax T	63	29
							Derby Co	206	83
							Leeds U	91	31
							Derby Co (loan)	10	8
							Sheffield U (loan)	11	4
							Leicester C	25	6
							Sheffield U	12	1
							Rotherham U	21	4
DAWE Simon §			M	16 3 77	Plymouth	Trainee	**Plymouth Arg**	4	—
DAWES Ian	5 7	11 10	D	22 2 63	Croydon	Apprentice	QPR	229	3
							Millwall	225	5
DAWS Nick	5 11	13 06	D	15 3 70	Manchester	Altrincham	**Bury**	107	4
DAWS Tony	5 8	11 10	F	10 9 66	Sheffield	Apprentice	Notts Co	8	1
							Sheffield U	11	3
							Scunthorpe U	183	63
							Grimsby T	16	1
							Lincoln C	40	10
DAY Chris	6 3	13 06	G	28 7 75	Whipps Cross	Trainee	**Tottenham H**	—	—

Player	Ht	Wt	Pos	Birth Date	Birth Place	Source	Clubs	League App	League Gls
DAY Mervyn	6 2	14 13	G	26 6 55	Chelmsford	Apprentice	West Ham U	194	—
							Orient	170	—
							Aston Villa	30	—
							Leeds U	227	—
							Coventry C (loan)	—	—
							Luton T (loan)	4	—
							Sheffield U (loan)	1	—
							Carlisle U	16	—
DE FREITAS Fabian	6 1	12 09	F	28 7 72	Paramaribo	Volendam	**Bolton W**	13	2
DE SOUZA Juan	6 1	12 06	F	11 2 70	Newham	Dagenham	Birmingham C	15	—
							Bury (loan)	3	—
							Wycombe W	7	6
DE WOLF John	6 2	14 03	D	10 12 62	Schiedam	Feyenoord	**Wolverhampton W**	13	4
DEAN Craig *	5 10	11 04	M	1 7 75	Nuneaton	Trainee	**Manchester U**	—	—
DEANE Brian	6 3	12 07	F	7 2 68	Leeds	Apprentice	Doncaster R	66	12
							Sheffield U	197	82
							Leeds U	76	20
DEARDEN Kevin	5 11	12 08	G	8 3 70	Luton	Trainee	Tottenham H	1	—
							Cambridge U (loan)	15	—
							Hartlepool U (loan)	10	—
							Oxford U (loan)	—	—
							Swindon T (loan)	1	—
							Peterborough U (loan)	7	—
							Hull C (loan)	3	—
							Rochdale (loan)	2	—
							Birmingham C (loan)	12	—
							Portsmouth (loan)	—	—
							Brentford	78	—
DEARY John	5 9	12 07	M	18 10 62	Ormskirk	Apprentice	Blackpool	303	43
							Burnley	215	23
							Rochdale	17	1
DEBONT Andy	6 2	15 06	G	7 2 74	Wolverhampton	Trainee	**Wolverhampton W**	—	—
DEEGAN Mark *	6 1	11 02	G	12 11 71	Liverpool	Holywell T	**Oxford U**	2	—
DELAP Rory	6 0	11 11	M	6 7 76	Coldfield	Trainee	**Carlisle U**	5	—
DEMPSEY Mark	5 7	11 10	M	10 12 72	Dublin	Trainee	Gillingham	48	2
							Leyton Orient	43	1
DENNIS Tony	5 7	10 02	M	1 12 63	Eton	Slough	Cambridge U	111	10
							Chesterfield	10	—
							Colchester U	33	2
DENNISON Robert	5 7	11 00	F	30 4 63	Banbridge	Glenavon	WBA	16	1
							Wolverhampton W	279	39
DEVLIN Mark	5 10	11 01	M	18 1 73	Irvine	Trainee	**Stoke C**	24	2
DEVLIN Paul	5 8	10 05	F	14 4 72	Birmingham	Stafford R	**Notts Co**	115	19
DEWHURST Rob	6 3	12 00	D	10 9 71	Keighley	Trainee	Blackburn R	13	—
							Darlington R (loan)	11	1
							Huddersfield T (loan)	7	—
							Hull C	68	10
DIBBLE Andy	6 2	13 07	G	8 5 65	Cwmbran	Apprentice	Cardiff C	62	—
							Luton T	30	—
							Sunderland (loan)	12	—
							Huddersfield T (loan)	5	—
							Manchester C	102	—
							Aberdeen (loan)	5	—
							Middlesbrough (loan)	19	—
							Bolton W (loan)	13	—
							WBA (loan)	9	—
							Oldham Ath (loan)	—	—
DICHIO Daniele	6 3	11 00	F	19 10 74	London	Trainee	**QPR**	9	3
							Barnet (loan)	9	2

Player	Ht	Wt	Pos	Birth Date	Birth Place	Source	Clubs	League App	League Gls
DICKINS Matt	6 4	14 00	G	3 9 70	Sheffield	Trainee	Sheffield U	—	—
							Leyton Orient (loan)	—	—
							Lincoln C	27	—
							Blackburn R	1	—
							Blackpool (loan)	19	—
							Lincoln C (loan)	—	—
							Grimsby T (loan)	—	—
							Rochdale (loan)	4	—
							Stockport Co	12	—
DICKOV Paul	5 5	11 09	F	1 11 72	Glasgow	Trainee	**Arsenal**	13	2
							Luton T (loan)	15	1
							Brighton (loan)	8	5
DICKS Julian	5 10	13 00	D	8 8 68	Bristol	Apprentice	Birmingham C	89	1
							West Ham U	159	29
							Liverpool	24	3
							West Ham U	29	5
DIGBY Fraser	6 1	12 12	G	23 4 67	Sheffield	Apprentice	Manchester U	—	—
							Oldham Ath (loan)	—	—
							Swindon T (loan)	—	—
							Swindon T	323	—
							Manchester U (loan)	—	—
DIGWEED Perry *	6 0	11 04	G	26 10 59	London	Apprentice	Fulham	15	—
							Brighton	179	—
							WBA (loan)	—	—
							Charlton Ath (loan)	—	—
							Newcastle U (loan)	—	—
							Chelsea (loan)	3	—
							Wimbledon (loan)	—	—
							Wimbledon	—	—
							Watford	29	—
DINEEN Jack ‡	5 7	10 10	M	29 9 70	Brighton	Torsby	**Scarborough**	2	—
DINNING Tony	5 11	12 00	D	12 4 75	Wallsend	Trainee	Newcastle U	—	—
							Stockport Co	40	1
DIXON Ben	6 1	11 00	F	16 9 74	Lincoln	Trainee	**Lincoln C**	31	—
DIXON Edward ‡	5 9	11 00	M	12 12 75	Gateshead	Trainee	**Crystal Palace**	—	—
DIXON Ken	5 11	11 00	G	24 2 76	Knowsley	Trainee	**Wrexham**	—	—
DIXON Kerry	6 0	13 10	F	24 7 61	Luton	Dunstable	Reading	116	51
							Chelsea	335	147
							Southampton	9	2
							Luton T (loan)	17	3
							Luton T	58	16
							Millwall	9	4
DIXON Lee	5 8	11 08	D	17 3 64	Manchester	Local	Burnley	4	—
							Chester	57	1
							Bury	45	5
							Stoke C	71	5
							Arsenal	254	16
DOBBIN Jim	5 9	10 07	M	17 9 63	Dunfermline	Whitburn BC	Celtic	2	—
							Motherwell (loan)	2	—
							Doncaster R	64	13
							Barnsley	129	12
							Grimsby T	138	18
DOBBS Gerald	5 8	11 07	D	24 1 71	London	Trainee	**Wimbledon**	33	1
DOBSON Tony	6 1	12 10	D	5 2 69	Coventry	Apprentice	Coventry C	54	1
							Blackburn R	41	—
							Portsmouth	38	2
							Oxford U (loan)	5	—
DODD Jason	5 11	12 00	D	2 11 70	Bath	Bath C	**Southampton**	135	3
DOHERTY Kevin ‡	5 9	11 00	F	2 9 75	Londonderry	Trainee	**Southampton**	—	—
DOHERTY Neil	5 8	10 09	M	21 2 69	Barrow	Trainee	Watford	—	—
						Barrow	**Birmingham C**	21	1
DOLAN Paul ‡	6 4	13 05	G	16 4 66	Ottawa	Vancouver W	**Notts Co**	—	—
DOLBY Chris *	5 8	9 12	F	4 9 74	Dewsbury	Trainee	**Rotherham U**	3	—
DOLBY Gavin *	5 9	11 10	F	26 1 76	Peterborough	Trainee	**Ipswich T**	—	—

Player	Ht	Wt	Pos	Birth Date	Birth Place	Source	Clubs	League App	League Gls
DOLBY Tony	5 10	13 00	F	16 4 74	Greenwich	Trainee	**Millwall**	35	1
							Barnet (loan)	16	2
DOLING Stuart	5 6	10 06	M	28 10 72	Newport, IOW	Trainee	**Portsmouth**	37	4
DOMINGUEZ Jose	5 3	10 00	F	16 2 74	Lisbon	Benfica	**Birmingham C**	35	3
DONALDSON O'Neill	6 1	11 08	F	24 11 69	Birmingham	Hinckley	Shrewsbury T	28	4
							Doncaster R	9	2
							Mansfield T (loan)	4	6
							Sheffield W	1	—
DONOVAN Kevin	5 7	10 10	F	17 12 71	Halifax	Trainee	Huddersfield T	20	1
							Halifax T (loan)	6	—
							WBA	102	19
DONOWA Lou	5 9	11 00	F	24 9 64	Ipswich	Apprentice	Norwich C	62	11
							Stoke C (loan)	4	1
						Coruna, Willem II	Ipswich T	23	1
							Bristol C	24	3
							Birmingham C	99	18
							Crystal Palace (loan)	—	—
							Burnley (loan)	4	—
							Shrewsbury T (loan)	4	—
DOOLAN John ‡	6 1	12 10	D	7 5 74	Liverpool	Trainee	Everton	—	—
							Mansfield T	24	1
DOOLAN John	5 10	10 12	M	10 11 68	South Liverpool	Knowsley U	**Wigan Ath**	35	1
DORIGO Tony	5 9	10 10	D	31 12 65	Australia	Apprentice	Aston Villa	111	1
							Chelsea	146	11
							Leeds U	136	4
DOW Andrew	5 9	10 07	M	7 2 73	Dundee	Sporting Club 85	Dundee	18	1
							Chelsea	14	—
							Bradford C (loan)	5	—
DOWELL Wayne	5 10	11 02	D	28 12 73	Co Durham	Trainee	**Burnley**	5	—
DOWIE Iain	6 1	13 11	F	9 1 65	Hatfield	Hendon	Luton T	66	16
							Fulham (loan)	5	1
							West Ham U	12	4
							Southampton	122	30
							Crystal Palace	15	4
DOWNING Keith *	5 8	11 00	M	23 7 65	Oldbury	Mile Oak R	Notts Co	23	1
							Wolverhampton W	191	8
							Birmingham C	1	—
							Stoke C	16	—
DOWNS Greg ‡	5 9	10 07	D	13 12 58	Carlton	Apprentice	Norwich C	169	7
							Torquay U (loan)	1	1
							Coventry C	146	4
							Birmingham C	17	—
							Hereford U	108	2
DOYLE Maurice	5 8	10 07	F	17 10 69	Ellesmere Port	Trainee	Crewe Alex	8	2
							QPR	6	—
							Crewe Alex (loan)	7	2
							Wolverhampton W (loan)	—	—
							Millwall	—	—
DOYLE Steve ‡	5 9	11 01	M	2 6 58	Neath	Apprentice	Preston NE	197	8
							Huddersfield T	161	6
							Sunderland	100	2
							Hull C	47	2
							Rochdale	121	1
DOZZELL Jason	6 1	13 08	M	9 12 67	Ipswich	School	Ipswich T	332	52
							Tottenham H	39	8
DRAPER Mark	5 10	12 00	M	11 11 70	Long Eaton	Trainee	Notts Co	222	40
							Leicester C	39	5
DREYER John	6 1	13 02	D	11 6 63	Alnwick	Wallingford T	Oxford U	60	2
							Torquay U (loan)	5	—
							Fulham (loan)	12	2
							Luton T	214	13
							Stoke C	18	2
							Bolton W (loan)	2	—
DRUCE Mark	6 0	11 11	F	3 3 74	Oxford	Trainee	**Oxford U**	44	4

Player	Ht	Wt	Pos	Birth Date	Birth Place	Source	Clubs	League App	League Gls
DRURY Nathan ‡	6 0	11 02	D	15 1 76	Leeds	Trainee	**Nottingham F**	—	—
DRYDEN Richard	6 0	11 02	D	14 6 69	Stroud	Trainee	Bristol R	13	—
							Exeter C	51	7
							Manchester C (loan)	—	—
							Notts Co	31	1
							Plymouth Arg (loan)	5	—
							Birmingham C	48	—
							Bristol C	19	1
DRYSDALE Jason	5 10	12 00	D	17 11 70	Bristol	Trainee	Watford	145	11
							Swindon T	1	—
DUBERRY Michael	6 1	12 13	D	14 10 75	Enfield	Trainee	**Chelsea**	1	—
DUBLIN Dion	6 0	12 04	F	22 4 69	Leicester		Norwich C	—	—
							Cambridge U	156	52
							Manchester U	12	2
							Coventry C	31	13
DUBLIN Keith	6 0	12 10	D	29 1 66	Wycombe	Apprentice	Chelsea	51	—
							Brighton	132	5
							Watford	168	2
							Southend U	40	2
DUCROS Andrew	5 4	9 08	F	16 9 77	Evesham	Trainee	**Coventry C**	—	—
DUDLEY Derek ‡	6 4	14 00	G	2 2 70	Birmingham	VS Rugby	**WBA**	—	—
DUFFIN Stuart ‡	5 9	11 07	F	27 6 75	Glasgow		**Bristol C**	—	—
DUFFY Chris ‡	5 10	11 11	M	31 10 73	Manchester	Trainee	Crewe Alex	—	—
							Wigan Ath	31	1
DUMITRESCU Ilie ‡	5 9	10 07	M	6 1 69	Bucharest	Steaua	**Tottenham H**	13	4
DUNFORD Neil ‡			G	18 7 67	Rochdale		**Rochdale**	2	—
DUNGEY James §			G	7 2 78	Plymouth	Trainee	**Plymouth Arg**	4	—
DUNN Iain	5 10	11 07	F	1 4 70	Derwent	School	York C	77	11
							Chesterfield	13	1
						Goole T	**Huddersfield T**	101	14
DUNNE Joe	5 8	11 06	D	25 5 73	Dublin	Trainee	**Gillingham**	113	1
DUNPHY Nick	6 0	12 00	D	3 8 74	Birmingham	Hednesford	**Peterborough U**	2	—
DUNPHY Sean ‡	6 3	13 05	D	5 11 70	Rotherham	Trainee	Barnsley	6	—
							Lincoln C	53	2
							Doncaster R (loan)	1	—
							Scarborough (loan)	10	—
DURKAN Kieron	5 10	10 05	M	1 12 73	Chester	Trainee	**Wrexham**	42	3
DURNIN John	5 10	11 04	F	18 8 65	Bootle	Waterloo Dock	Liverpool	—	—
							WBA (loan)	5	2
							Oxford U	161	44
							Portsmouth	44	8
DURRANT Iain (On loan from Rangers)	5 8	9 07	M	29 10 66	Glasgow	Glasgow U	**Rangers**	217	26
							Everton (loan)	5	—
DURRANT Lee	5 10	11 07	M	18 12 73	Gt Yarmouth	Trainee	**Ipswich T**	7	—
DUXBURY Lee	5 8	11 13	M	7 10 69	Keighley	Trainee	Bradford C	209	25
							Rochdale (loan)	10	—
							Huddersfield T	26	2
DYCHE Sean	6 0	13 02	D	28 6 71	Kettering	Trainee	Nottingham F	—	—
							Chesterfield	154	8
DYER Alex	5 11	11 12	M	14 11 65	West Ham	Watford	Blackpool	108	19
							Hull C	60	14
							Crystal Palace	17	2
							Charlton Ath	78	13
							Oxford U	76	6
DYER Bruce	5 11	11 03	F	13 4 75	Ilford	Trainee	Watford	31	6
							Crystal Palace	27	1
DYKSTRA Sieb	6 5	14 07	G	20 10 66	Kerkrade	Roda JC	Motherwell	80	—
							QPR	11	—
DYSON Jon	6 1	12 00	D	18 12 71	Mirfield	School	**Huddersfield T**	65	2

Player	Ht	Wt	Pos	Birth Date	Birth Place	Source	Clubs	League App	League Gls
EADEN Nicky	5 10	11 09	D	12 12 72	Sheffield	Trainee	**Barnsley**	84	3
EADIE Darren	5 7	11 05	F	10 6 75	Chippenham	Trainee	**Norwich C**	41	5
EARLE Robbie	5 9	10 10	F	27 1 65	Newcastle, Staffs.	Stoke C	Port Vale	294	77
							Wimbledon	133	30
EBBRELL John	5 7	9 12	M	1 10 69	Bromborough		**Everton**	185	9
EBDON Marcus	5 8	12 04	M	17 10 70	Pontypool	Trainee	Everton	—	—
							Peterborough U	88	12
ECKHARDT Jeff	6 0	11 07	D	7 10 65	Sheffield		Sheffield U	74	2
							Fulham	249	25
							Stockport Co	27	1
ECKSTEIN Dieter ‡	5 11	11 06	F	12 3 64	Germany	Schalke 04	**West Ham U**	—	—
EDESON Matt *	5 10	11 00	F	11 8 76	Beverley	Trainee	**Hull C**	5	—
EDGHILL Richard	5 9	10 01	D	23 9 74	Oldham	Trainee	**Manchester C**	36	—
EDINBURGH Justin	5 10	11 08	D	18 12 69	Brentwood	Trainee	Southend U	37	—
							Tottenham H (loan)	—	—
							Tottenham H	127	1
EDMONDSON Darren	6 0	12 01	M	4 11 71	Coniston	Trainee	**Carlisle U**	152	7
EDWARDS Alistair	6 1	12 06	F	21 6 68	Wyalla	Selangor	**Millwall**	4	—
EDWARDS Andy	6 3	13 07	D	17 9 71	Epping	Trainee	**Southend U**	147	5
EDWARDS Christian	6 2	11 09	D	23 11 75	Caerphilly	Trainee	**Swansea C**	9	—
EDWARDS David ‡	5 10	10 08	M	13 1 74	Bridgnorth	Trainee	**Walsall**	27	1
EDWARDS Mike	5 11	11 05	M	10 9 74	Bebbington	Trainee	**Tranmere R**	3	—
EDWARDS Neil	5 8	11 02	G	5 12 70	Aberdare	Trainee	Leeds U	—	—
							Huddersfield T (loan)	—	—
							Stockport Co	119	—
EDWARDS Paul	5 11	11 05	G	22 2 65	Liverpool	St. Helens T	Crewe Alex	29	—
							Shrewsbury T	115	—
EDWARDS Paul R	5 11	11 00	D	25 12 63	Birkenhead	Altrincham	Crewe Alex	86	6
							Coventry C	36	—
							Wolverhampton W	46	—
							WBA	35	—
EDWARDS Robert	6 0	11 06	D	1 7 73	Kendal	Trainee	Carlisle U	48	5
							Bristol C	106	3
EDWARDS Robert	5 8	11 07	F	23 2 70	Manchester	Trainee	**Crewe Alex**	123	29
EDWORTHY Mark	5 8	11 10	D	24 12 72	Barnstaple	Trainee	**Plymouth Arg**	69	1
EHIOGU Ugo	6 2	13 03	D	3 11 72	London	Trainee	WBA	2	—
							Aston Villa	68	3
EKELUND Ronnie ‡	5 10	12 06	M	21 8 72	Denmark	Barcelona	**Southampton**	17	5
EKOKU Efan	6 1	12 00	F	8 6 67	Manchester	Sutton U	Bournemouth	62	21
							Norwich C	37	15
							Wimbledon	24	9
ELAD Efon ‡	5 10	12 00	F	5 9 70	Hillingdon	Cologne	Northampton T	10	—
							Cambridge U	3	—
							Mansfield T	2	—
ELI Roger ‡	5 11	11 03	D	11 9 65	Bradford	Apprentice	Leeds U	2	—
							Wolverhampton W	18	—
							Cambridge U	—	—
							Crewe Alex	27	1
							York C	4	1
							Bury	2	—
						Northwich Vic	Burnley	99	11
							Partick T	2	—
							Scunthorpe U	2	—
ELKINS Gary	5 09	11 12	M	4 5 66	Wallingford	Apprentice	Fulham	104	2
							Exeter C (loan)	5	—
							Wimbledon	100	3

				Birth				League	
Player	Ht	Wt	Pos	Date	Place	Source	Clubs	App	Gls
ELLIOTT Matthew	6 3	14 05	D	1 11 68	Epsom	Epsom & Ewell	Charlton Ath	—	—
							Torquay U	124	15
							Scunthorpe U (loan)	8	1
							Scunthorpe U	53	7
							Oxford U	77	9
ELLIOTT Robbie	5 10	10 13	D	25 12 73	Newcastle	Trainee	**Newcastle U**	44	2
ELLIOTT Tony	6 0	13 07	G	30 11 69	Nuneaton		Birmingham C	—	—
							Hereford U	75	—
							Huddersfield T	15	—
							Carlisle U	9	—
ELLIS Kevin §			D	12 5 77	Gt Yarmouth	Trainee	**Ipswich T**	1	—
ELLIS Tony	5 11	11 00	F	20 10 64	Salford	Northwich Vic	Oldham Ath	8	—
							Preston NE	86	26
							Stoke C	77	19
							Preston NE	72	48
							Blackpool	40	17
ELLISON Tony *	5 11	12 03	F	13 1 73	Bishop Auckland	Trainee	Darlington	72	17
							Hartlepool U (loan)	4	1
							Leicester C	—	—
ELSEY David *			D	19 11 75	Swindon	Trainee	**Swindon T**	—	—
EMBERSON Carl	6 1	13 11	G	13 7 73	Epsom	Trainee	Millwall	—	—
							Colchester U (loan)	13	—
							Colchester U	20	—
EMBLEN Neil	6 1	12 07	D	19 6 71	Bromley	Sittingbourne	Millwall	12	—
							Wolverhampton W	27	7
EMBLETON Daniel †	5 11	11 04	G	27 3 75	Liverpool	Trainee	Liverpool	—	—
							Bury	—	—
							Walsall	1	—
EMENALO Michael	5 11	11 04	D	14 7 65	Nigeria	Eintracht Trier	**Notts Co**	7	—
EMERSON Dean ‡	5 11	12 06	M	27 12 62	Salford	Local	Stockport Co	156	7
							Rotherham U	55	8
							Coventry C	114	—
							Hartlepool U	45	1
							Stockport Co	11	—
							Preston NE	2	—
ENGLISH Tony	6 1	12 09	D	19 10 66	Luton	Coventry C	**Colchester U**	330	42
ENQVIST Bjorn	5 10	10 09	M	12 10 77	Lund	Malmo	**Crystal Palace**	—	—
ESTEVES Rui ‡			F	30 1 67	Lisbon	Benfica	**Birmingham C**	—	—
EUSTACE Scott *	6 0	13 12	D	13 6 75	Leicester	Trainee	**Leicester C**	1	—
EVANS Andy	6 1	12 01	F	25 11 75	Aberystwyth	Trainee	**Cardiff C**	13	—
EVANS Darren *	5 10	11 00	D	30 9 74	Wolverhampton	Trainee	**Aston Villa**	—	—
EVANS John ‡	5 10	11 00	M	8 9 74	Liverpool	Trainee	**Tranmere R**	—	—
EVANS Mark ‡	6 0	11 08	G	24 8 70	Leeds	Trainee	Bradford C	12	—
							Scarborough	46	—
EVANS Mike	6 0	13 04	F	1 1 73	Plymouth	Trainee	**Plymouth Arg**	85	14
							Blackburn R (loan)	—	—
EVANS Paul	5 6	10 08	M	1 9 74	Oswestry	Trainee	**Shrewsbury T**	51	5
EVANS Terry	5 8	10 07	D	8 1 76	Pontypridd	Trainee	**Cardiff C**	12	—
EVANS Terry	6 4	15 08	D	12 4 65	Hammersmith	Hillingdon B	Brentford	229	23
							Wycombe W	66	10
EVANS Wayne	5 10	12 02	D	25 8 71	Abermule	Welshpool	**Walsall**	77	—
EVERSHAM Paul *	5 10	11 08	M	28 1 75	Hereford	Trainee	**Hereford U**	13	1
EYRE John	6 1	11 03	F	9 10 74	Humberside	Trainee	**Oldham Ath**	10	1
							Scunthorpe U (loan)	9	8
EYRES David	5 9	11 08	F	26 2 64	Liverpool	Rhyl	Blackpool	158	38
							Burnley	84	27

Player	Ht	Wt	Pos	Birth Date	Birth Place	Source	Clubs	League App	League Gls
FAIRCLOUGH Chris	5 11	11 07	D	12 4 64	Nottingham	Apprentice	Nottingham F	107	1
							Tottenham H	60	5
							Leeds U	193	21
FAIRCLOUGH Wayne	5 10	12 00	D	27 4 68	Nottingham	Apprentice	Notts Co	71	—
							Mansfield T	141	12
							Chesterfield	13	—
FARNWORTH Simon	6 0	11 13	G	28 10 63	Chorley	Apprentice	Bolton W	113	—
							Stockport Co (loan)	10	—
							Tranmere R (loan)	7	—
							Bury	105	—
							Preston NE	81	—
							Wigan Ath	83	—
FARRELL Andy	6 0	11 00	D	7 10 65	Colchester	School	Colchester U	105	5
							Burnley	257	19
							Wigan Ath	31	—
FARRELL David	5 11	11 02	F	11 11 71	Birmingham	Redditch U	**Aston Villa**	6	—
							Scunthorpe U (loan)	5	1
FARRELL Sean	6 0	13 07	F	28 2 69	Watford	Apprentice	Luton T	25	1
							Colchester U (loan)	9	1
							Northampton T (loan)	4	1
							Fulham	94	31
							Peterborough U	33	8
FARRELLY Gareth	6 0	12 07	M	28 8 75	Dublin	Home Farm	**Aston Villa**	—	—
							Rotherham U (loan)	10	2
FARRINGTON Mark ‡	5 10	11 12	F	15 6 65	Liverpool	Everton	Norwich C	14	2
							Cambridge U	10	1
							Cardiff C	31	3
						Feyenoord	Brighton	28	4
							Hereford U	1	—
FASHANU John	6 2	13 07	F	18 9 63	Kensington	Cambridge U	Norwich C	7	1
							Crystal Palace (loan)	1	—
							Lincoln C	36	10
							Millwall	50	12
							Wimbledon	276	107
							Aston Villa	13	3
FAULKNER David	6 0	11 12	D	8 10 75	Sheffield	Trainee	**Sheffield W**	—	—
FEAR Peter	5 10	11 05	D	10 9 73	London	Trainee	**Wimbledon**	41	2
FEARON Dean	6 1	13 12	D	9 1 76	Barnsley	Schoolboy	**Barnsley**	—	—
FEENEY Mark	5 7	11 00	M	26 7 74	Derry	Trainee	**Barnsley**	2	—
FELGATE David	6 1	15 00	G	4 3 60	Blaenau Ffestiniog	Blaenau Ffestiniog	Bolton W	—	—
							Rochdale (loan)	35	—
							Bradford C (loan)	—	—
							Crewe Alex (loan)	14	—
							Rochdale (loan)	12	—
							Lincoln C	198	—
							Cardiff C (loan)	4	—
							Grimsby T (loan)	12	—
							Grimsby T	12	—
							Bolton W	238	—
							Rotherham U (loan)	—	—
							Bury	—	—
							Wolverhampton W	—	—
							Chester C	72	—
FELL Gavin *	5 10	11 10	M	6 6 76	Newcastle	Trainee	**Wimbledon**	—	—
FENSOME Andy	5 8	11 02	D	18 2 69	Northampton	Trainee	Norwich C	—	—
							Newcastle U (loan)	—	—
							Cambridge U	126	1
							Preston NE	73	1
FENTON Graham	5 10	11 03	F	22 5 74	Wallsend	Trainee	**Aston Villa**	29	3
							WBA (loan)	7	3
FENWICK Paul ‡	6 1	12 01	D	25 8 69	London	Winnipeg Fury	**Birmingham C**	19	—

Player	Ht	Wt	Pos	Birth Date	Birth Place	Source	Clubs	League App	League Gls
FENWICK Terry ‡	5 10	11 12	D	17 11 59	Camden, Co. Durham	Apprentice	Crystal Palace QPR Tottenham H Leicester C (loan) **Swindon T**	70 256 93 8 28	— 33 8 1 —
FERDINAND Les	5 11	13 05	F	18 12 66	London	Hayes	**QPR** Brentford (loan) Besiktas (loan)	163 3 —	80 — —
FEREDAY Wayne *	5 9	11 08	M	16 6 63	Warley	Apprentice	QPR Newcastle U Bournemouth WBA **Cardiff C**	197 33 23 48 44	21 — — 3 2
FERGUSON Darren	5 10	10 04	M	9 2 72	Glasgow	Trainee	Manchester U **Wolverhampton W**	27 38	— —
FERGUSON Derek	5 8	11 12	M	31 7 67	Glasgow	Gartcosh U	Rangers Dundee (loan) Hearts **Sunderland**	111 4 103 64	7 — 4 —
FERGUSON Duncan	6 3	13 05	F	27 12 71	Stirling	Carse T	Dundee U Rangers **Everton**	77 14 23	28 2 7
FERNANDES Tamer	6 3	13 07	G	7 12 74	London	Trainee	**Brentford**	5	—
FERNEY Martin *	5 11	12 10	M	8 11 71	Lambeth	Trainee	**Fulham**	60	1
FERRETT Chris §			M	10 2 77	Poole	Trainee	**Bournemouth**	1	—
FETTIS Alan	6 1	11 04	G	1 2 71	Belfast	Ards	**Hull C**	128	2
FEUER Tony	6 7	14 00	G	20 5 71	Las Vegas	Los Angeles Salsa	**West Ham U** Peterborough U (loan)	— 16	— —
FEWINGS Paul §			F	18 2 78	Hull	Trainee	**Hull C**	2	—
FICKLING Ashley	5 10	11 06	D	15 11 72	Sheffield	Trainee	Sheffield U Darlington (loan) **Grimsby T**	— 15 1	— — —
FIELD Darren *	5 8	11 00	M	8 3 73	Barnsley	Local	**Barnsley**	—	—
FILAN John	5 11	13 02	G	8 2 70	Sydney	Budapest St George	Cambridge U Nottingham F (loan) **Coventry C**	68 — 2	— — —
FINLAY Darren ‡	5 4	10 00	F	19 12 73	Belfast	Trainee	QPR **Doncaster R**	— 8	— 1
FINNEY Stephen *	5 10	12 00	F	31 10 73	Hexham	Trainee	Preston NE **Manchester C**	6 —	1 —
FINNIGAN John	5 8	10 05	M	29 3 76	Wakefield	Trainee	**Nottingham F**	—	—
FINNIGAN Tony ‡	5 10	11 09	M	17 10 62	Wimbledon	Crystal Palace	Fulham Crystal Palace Blackburn R Hull C Swindon T Brentford Barnet **Fulham**	— 105 36 18 3 3 6 11	— 10 — 1 — — 1 —
FISHER Neil *	5 10	10 09	M	7 11 70	St Helens	Trainee	**Bolton W**	24	1
FISHLOCK Murray	5 7	11 00	D	23 9 73	Marlborough	Trowbridge T	**Hereford U**	14	—
FITZGERALD Gary	6 1	11 07	D	27 10 76	Hampstead	Trainee	**Watford**	1	—
FITZGERALD Scott	6 0	12 02	D	13 8 69	London	Trainee	**Wimbledon**	102	1
FJORTOFT Jan-Aage	6 3	13 04	F	10 1 67	Aalesund	Rapid Vienna	Swindon T **Middlesbrough**	72 8	28 3
FLAHAVAN Aaron	6 1	12 10	G	15 12 75	Southampton	Trainee	**Portsmouth**	—	—
FLASH Richard *	5 9	11 08	M	8 4 76	Birmingham	Trainee	**Manchester U**	—	—

Player	Ht	Wt	Pos	Birth Date	Place	Source	Clubs	League App	Gls
FLATTS Mark	5 6	9 08	M	14 10 72	Haringey	Trainee	**Arsenal**	16	—
							Cambridge U (loan)	5	1
							Brighton (loan)	10	1
							Bristol C (loan)	6	—
FLECK Robert	5 10	10 03	F	11 8 65	Glasgow	Possil YM	Partick T	2	1
							Rangers	85	29
							Norwich C	143	40
							Chelsea	40	3
							Bolton W (loan)	7	1
							Bristol C (loan)	10	1
FLEMING Craig	6 0	11 07	D	6 10 71	Calder	Trainee	Halifax T	57	—
							Oldham Ath	98	1
FLEMING Curtis	5 10	12 09	D	8 10 68	Manchester	St Patrick's Ath	Swindon T	—	—
						St Patrick's Ath	**Middlesbrough**	113	—
FLEMING Gary	5 9	11 09	D	17 2 67	Derry	Apprentice	Nottingham F	74	—
							Manchester C	14	—
							Notts Co (loan)	3	—
							Barnsley	236	—
FLEMING Paul ‡	5 7	11 08	D	6 9 67	Halifax		Halifax T	139	1
							Mansfield T	68	—
FLEMING Terry	5 9	10 09	D	5 1 73	Marston Green	Trainee	Coventry C	13	—
							Northampton T	31	1
							Preston NE	27	2
FLETCHER Steve	6 2	14 00	F	26 6 72	Hartlepool	Trainee	Hartlepool U	32	4
							Bournemouth	107	16
FLITCROFT David	5 11	13 05	M	14 1 74	Bolton	Trainee	Preston NE	8	2
							Lincoln C (loan)	2	—
							Chester C	40	1
FLITCROFT Garry	6 0	11 08	M	6 11 72	Bolton	Trainee	**Manchester C**	90	13
							Bury (loan)	12	—
FLO Jostein	6 4	13 08	F	3 10 64	Norway	Sogndal	**Sheffield U**	65	15
FLOUNDERS Andy *	5 11	11 06	F	13 12 63	Hull	Apprentice	Hull C	159	54
							Scunthorpe U	196	87
							Rochdale	85	31
							Rotherham U (loan)	6	2
							Carlisle U (loan)	8	1
						Halifax T	**Northampton T**	2	—
FLOWERS Tim	6 2	14 04	G	3 2 67	Kenilworth	Apprentice	Wolverhampton W	63	—
							Southampton (loan)	—	—
							Southampton	192	—
							Swindon T (loan)	2	—
							Swindon T (loan)	5	—
							Blackburn R	68	—
FLYNN Mike	6 0	11 00	D	23 2 69	Oldham	Trainee	Oldham Ath	40	1
							Norwich C	—	—
							Preston NE	136	7
							Stockport Co	99	3
FLYNN Sean	5 8	11 08	M	13 3 68	Birmingham	Halesowen T	**Coventry C**	97	9
FOLEY Steve ‡	5 7	11 03	M	4 10 62	Liverpool	Apprentice	Liverpool	—	—
							Fulham (loan)	3	—
							Grimsby T	31	2
							Sheffield U	66	14
							Swindon T	151	23
							Stoke C	107	10
							Lincoln C	16	—
FOOT Daniel	6 0	11 00	D	6 9 75	Edmonton	Tottenham H	**Southend U**	3	—
FORAN Mark	6 4	13 12	D	30 10 73	Aldershot	Trainee	Millwall	—	—
							Sheffield U	4	1
							Rotherham U (loan)	3	—
FORBES Steven	6 2	12 06	M	24 12 75	London	Sittingbourne	**Millwall**	1	—
FORD Bobby	5 8	10 06	M	22 9 74	Bristol	Trainee	**Oxford U**	37	2
FORD John	6 0	12 00	M	12 4 68	Birmingham	Cradley T	**Swansea C**	160	7
FORD Mark	5 8	10 08	M	10 10 75	Pontefract	Trainee	**Leeds U**	1	—

Player	Ht	Wt	Pos	Birth Date	Birth Place	Source	Clubs	League App	League Gls
FORD Mike	6 0	11 02	D	9 2 66	Bristol	Apprentice	Leicester C	—	—
						Devizes	Cardiff C	145	13
							Oxford U	181	10
FORD Stuart *	5 11	11 13	G	20 7 71	Sheffield	Trainee	Rotherham U	5	—
							Scarborough (loan)	6	—
							Scarborough	22	—
							Bury	—	—
							Doncaster R	6	—
							Scarborough	6	—
FORD Tony	5 9	12 07	D	14 5 59	Grimsby	Apprentice	Grimsby T	354	54
							Sunderland (loan)	9	1
							Stoke C	112	13
							WBA	114	14
							Grimsby T	68	3
							Bradford C (loan)	5	—
							Scunthorpe U	38	2
FOREMAN Darren ‡	5 10	10 08	F	12 2 68	Southampton	Fareham	Barnsley	47	8
							Crewe Alex	23	4
							Scarborough	97	35
FOREMAN Matt ‡	6 0	12 04	D	15 2 75	Gateshead	Trainee	**Sheffield U**	—	—
FORMBY Kevin	5 9	11 04	D	22 7 71	Ormskirk	Burscough	**Rochdale**	33	—
FORREST Craig	6 5	14 00	G	20 9 67	Vancouver	Apprentice	**Ipswich T**	236	—
							Colchester U (loan)	11	—
FORRESTER Jamie	5 7	10 00	F	1 11 74	Bradford	Auxerre	**Leeds U**	9	—
							Southend U (loan)	5	—
							Grimsby T (loan)	9	1
FORSTER Nick	5 9	10 11	F	8 9 73	Oxted	Horley T	Gillingham	67	24
							Brentford	46	24
FORSYTH Mike	5 11	12 05	D	20 3 66	Liverpool	Apprentice	WBA	29	—
							Northampton T (loan)	—	—
							Derby Co	325	8
							Notts Co	7	—
FOSTER Adrian	5 9	11 00	F	19 3 71	Kidderminster	Trainee	WBA	27	2
							Torquay U	75	24
							Gillingham	29	8
FOSTER Colin	6 4	14 01	D	16 7 64	Chislehurst	Apprentice	Orient	174	10
							Nottingham F	72	5
							West Ham U	93	5
							Notts Co (loan)	9	—
							Watford	40	3
FOSTER John	5 10	11 01	D	19 9 73	Manchester	Trainee	**Manchester C**	12	—
FOSTER Martin	5 5	9 10	M	29 10 77	Sheffield	Trainee	**Leeds U**	—	—
FOSTER Steve	6 1	14 00	D	24 9 57	Portsmouth	Apprentice	Portsmouth	109	6
							Brighton	172	6
							Aston Villa	15	3
							Luton T	163	11
							Oxford U	95	9
							Brighton	107	6
FOSTER Wayne (on loan from Partick T)	5 8	11 00	F	11 9 63	Leigh		**Hartlepool U**	4	1
FOWLER Jason	6 1	11 06	M	20 8 74	Bristol	Trainee	**Bristol C**	15	—
FOWLER John	5 10	11 07	M	27 10 74	Preston	Trainee	**Cambridge U**	39	—
							Preston NE (loan)	6	—
FOWLER Robbie	5 11	11 10	F	9 4 75	Liverpool	Trainee	**Liverpool**	70	37
FOX Mark	5 11	10 11	M	17 11 75	Basingstoke	Trainee	**Brighton**	21	1
FOX Peter *	5 10	12 04	G	5 7 57	Scunthorpe	Apprentice	Sheffield W	49	—
							West Ham U (loan)	—	—
							Barnsley (loan)	1	—
							Stoke C	409	—
							Wrexham (loan)	—	—
							Exeter C	57	—

Player	Ht	Wt	Pos	Birth Date	Birth Place	Source	Clubs	League App	League Gls
FOX Ruel	5 6	10 00	M	14 1 68	Ipswich	Apprentice	Norwich C	172	22
							Newcastle U	54	12
FOX Simon §	5 10	10 02	F	28 8 77	Basingstoke	Trainee	**Brighton**	3	—
FOYLE Martin	5 10	11 02	F	2 5 63	Salisbury	Amateur	Southampton	12	1
							Blackburn R (loan)	—	—
							Aldershot	98	35
							Oxford U	126	36
							Port Vale	138	49
FRAIN David ‡	5 8	10 05	F	11 10 62	Sheffield	Rowlinson YC	Sheffield U	44	5
							Rochdale	42	12
							Stockport Co	187	12
							Mansfield T (loan)	6	—
FRAIN John	5 7	11 10	M	8 10 68	Birmingham	Apprentice	**Birmingham C**	250	23
FRANCIS John	5 8	12 13	F	21 11 63	Dewsbury	Emley	Halifax T	4	—
							Sheffield U	42	6
							Burnley	101	26
							Cambridge U	29	3
							Burnley	54	8
FRANCIS Kevin	6 7	15 08	F	6 12 67	Moseley	Mile Oak R	Derby Co	10	—
							Stockport Co	152	88
							Birmingham C	15	8
FRANCIS Steve	6 0	11 05	G	29 5 64	Billericay	Apprentice	Chelsea	71	—
							Reading	216	—
							Huddersfield T	89	—
FREEDMAN Doug	5 9	11 00	F	21 1 74	Glasgow	Trainee	QPR	—	—
							Barnet	42	24
FREEMAN Darren	5 11	13 00	F	22 8 73	Brighton	Horsham T	**Gillingham**	2	—
FREESTONE Chris			F	4 9 71	Nottingham	Arnold T	**Middlesbrough**	1	—
FREESTONE Roger	6 3	14 06	G	19 8 68	Newport	Trainee	Newport Co	13	—
							Chelsea	42	—
							Swansea C (loan)	14	—
							Hereford U (loan)	8	—
							Swansea C	179	1
FROGGATT Steve	5 10	11 00	M	9 3 73	Lincoln	Trainee	Aston Villa	35	2
							Wolverhampton W	20	2
FRY Chris	5 8	10 05	F	23 10 69	Cardiff	Trainee	Cardiff C	55	1
							Hereford U	90	10
							Colchester U	50	8
FUCHS Uwe *	6 0	13 08	F	23 7 66	Germany	Kaiserslautern	**Middlesbrough**	15	9
FUNNELL Simon ‡	6 0	12 08	F	8 8 74	Shoreham	Trainee	**Brighton**	28	2
FURLONG Carl §	5 11	12 06	F	18 10 76	Liverpool	Trainee	**Wigan Ath**	3	1
FURLONG Paul	6 0	12 11	F	1 10 68	London	Enfield	Coventry C	37	4
							Watford	79	37
							Chelsea	36	10
FURNELL Andy	5 10	13 07	F	13 2 77	Peterborough	Trainee	**Peterborough U**	18	1
FUTCHER Andy	5 7	10 07	D	10 2 78	Enfield	Trainee	**Wimbledon**	—	—
FUTCHER Paul ‡	6 0	12 03	D	25 9 56	Chester	Apprentice	Chester	20	—
							Luton T	131	1
							Manchester C	37	—
							Oldham Ath	98	1
							Derby Co	35	—
							Barnsley	230	—
							Halifax T	15	—
							Grimsby T	132	—
GABBIADINI Marco	5 10	13 04	F	20 1 68	Nottingham	Apprentice	York C	60	14
							Sunderland	157	74
							Crystal Palace	15	5
							Derby Co	135	39
GAGE Kevin	5 10	11 02	D	21 4 64	Chiswick	Apprentice	Wimbledon	168	15
							Aston Villa	115	8
							Sheffield U	110	7

Player	Ht	Wt	Pos	Birth Date	Birth Place	Source	Clubs	League App	League Gls
GALE Shaun	6 0	11 06	D	8 10 69	Reading	Trainee	Portsmouth	3	—
							Barnet	27	2
GALE Tony *	6 1	13 07	D	19 11 59	London	Apprentice	Fulham	277	19
							West Ham U	300	5
							Blackburn R	15	—
GALLACHER Kevin	5 8	11 00	F	23 11 66	Clydebank	Duntocher BC	Dundee U	131	27
							Coventry C	100	28
							Blackburn R	40	13
GALLAGHER Tommy	5 10	10 08	D	25 8 74	Nottingham	Trainee	**Notts Co**	20	—
GALLEN Joe *	5 11	11 08	F	2 9 72	Hammersmith	Trainee	Watford	—	—
							Exeter C (loan)	6	—
							Shrewsbury T	6	1
GALLEN Kevin	5 11	12 03	F	21 9 75	Hammersmith	Trainee	**QPR**	37	10
GALLEN Stephen	6 2	13 00	D	21 11 73	Acton	Trainee	QPR	—	—
							Doncaster R	—	—
GALLIMORE Tony	5 10	11 10	D	21 2 72	Crewe	Trainee	Stoke C	11	—
							Carlisle U (loan)	16	—
							Carlisle U (loan)	8	1
							Carlisle U	80	6
GALLOWAY Mick (on loan from Celtic)	5 11	11 07	D	30 5 65	Oswestry		**Leicester C**	5	—
GALLOWAY Mick	5 11	11 05	M	13 10 74	Nottingham	Trainee	**Notts Co**	7	—
GANNON Jim	6 2	13 00	D	7 9 68	London	Dundalk	Sheffield U	—	—
							Halifax T (loan)	2	—
							Stockport Co	217	46
							Notts Co (loan)	2	—
GANNON John	5 9	10 10	M	18 12 66	Wimbledon	Apprentice	Wimbledon	16	2
							Crewe Alex (loan)	15	—
							Sheffield U (loan)	16	1
							Sheffield U	146	5
							Middlesbrough (loan)	7	—
GARDINER Mark *	5 10	10 07	F	25 12 66	Cirencester	Apprentice	Swindon T	10	—
							Torquay U	49	4
							Crewe Alex	193	33
							Chester C (loan)	3	—
GARLAND Peter	5 10	12 00	M	20 1 71	Croydon	Trainee	Tottenham H	1	—
							Newcastle U	2	—
							Charlton Ath	50	2
							Wycombe W (loan)	5	—
GARNER Simon *	5 8	12 07	F	23 11 59	Boston	Apprentice	Blackburn R	484	168
							WBA	33	8
							Wycombe W	53	12
GARNETT Shaun	6 2	13 04	D	22 11 69	Wallasey	Trainee	**Tranmere R**	94	5
							Chester C (loan)	9	—
							Preston NE (loan)	10	2
							Wigan Ath (loan)	13	1
GARRETT Scott ‡	5 10	13 07	D	9 1 74	Gateshead	Trainee	**Hartlepool U**	15	—
GARVEY Steve	5 9	11 01	F	22 11 73	Tameside	Trainee	**Crewe Alex**	50	4
GAUDINO Maurizio	5 11	12 02	M	12 12 66	Brule	Eintracht Frankfurt	**Manchester C**	20	3
GAUGHAN Kevin			D	6 3 78	Glasgow		**Ipswich T**	—	—
GAUGHAN Steve	5 11	11 02	M	14 4 70	Doncaster	Hatfield Main	Doncaster R	67	3
							Sunderland	—	—
							Darlington	130	12

Player	Ht	Wt	Pos	Birth Date	Birth Place	Source	Clubs	League App	League Gls
GAVIN Mark	5 8	10 07	M	10 12 63	Bailleston	Apprentice	Leeds U	30	3
							Hartlepool U (loan)	7	—
							Carlisle U	13	1
							Bolton W	49	3
							Rochdale	23	6
							Hearts	9	—
							Bristol C	69	6
							Watford	13	—
							Bristol C	41	2
							Exeter C	49	2
GAVIN Pat *	6 0	12 00	F	5 6 67	Hammersmith	Hanwell T	Gillingham	13	7
							Leicester C	3	—
							Gillingham (loan)	34	1
							Peterborough U	23	5
							Barnet	—	—
							Northampton T	14	4
							Wigan Ath	42	8
GAYLE Brian	6 2	12 07	D	6 3 65	Kingston		Wimbledon	83	3
							Manchester C	55	3
							Ipswich T	58	4
							Sheffield U	112	9
GAYLE John	6 2	15 04	F	30 7 64	Birmingham	Burton Alb	Wimbledon	20	2
							Birmingham C	44	10
							Walsall (loan)	4	1
							Coventry C	3	—
							Burnley	14	3
							Stoke C	4	—
GAYLE Marcus	6 2	12 13	M	27 9 70	Hammersmith	Trainee	Brentford	156	22
							Wimbledon	33	2
GAYLE Mark	6 0	12 00	G	21 10 69	Bromsgrove	Trainee	Leicester C	—	—
							Blackpool	—	—
						Worcester C	Walsall	75	—
							Crewe Alex	33	—
							Liverpool (loan)	—	—
GEE Phil	5 10	12 03	F	19 12 64	Pelsall	Gresley R	Derby Co	124	26
							Leicester C	51	9
							Plymouth Arg (loan)	6	—
GEMMILL Scot	5 10	10 01	M	2 1 71	Paisley	School	**Nottingham F**	126	18
GENTLE Justin ‡	5 7	10 09	F	6 6 74	Enfield	Trainee	Luton T	—	—
							Colchester U	2	—
GERMAINE Gary	6 2	14 00	G	2 8 76	Birmingham	Trainee	**WBA**	—	—
GERRARD Paul	6 1	12 06	G	22 1 73	Heywood	Trainee	**Oldham Ath**	83	—
GIBB Alistair	5 9	10 08	M	17 2 76	Salisbury	Trainee	**Norwich C**	—	—
GIBBS Nigel	5 7	11 01	D	20 11 65	St Albans	Apprentice	**Watford**	282	3
GIBBS Paul	5 9	11 04	D	26 10 72	Gorleston	Diss T	**Colchester U**	9	—
GIBSON Colin	5 9	11 03	D	6 4 60	Bridport	Apprentice	Aston Villa	185	10
							Manchester U	79	9
							Port Vale (loan)	6	2
							Leicester C	59	4
							Blackpool	2	—
							Walsall	33	—
GIBSON Terry *	5 5	10 00	F	23 12 62	Walthamstow	Apprentice	Tottenham H	18	4
							Coventry C	98	43
							Manchester U	23	1
							Wimbledon	86	22
							Swindon T (loan)	9	1
							Peterborough U	1	—
							Barnet	32	5
GIGGS Ryan	5 11	10 06	F	29 11 73	Cardiff	School	**Manchester U**	148	28
GILBERT David	5 4	10 04	M	22 6 63	Lincoln	Apprentice	Lincoln C	30	1
							Scunthorpe U	1	—
						Boston U	Northampton T	120	21
							Grimsby T	259	41

Player	Ht	Wt	Pos	Birth Date	Birth Place	Source	Clubs	League App	League Gls
GILCHRIST Phil	6 0	12 10	D	25 8 73	Stockton	Trainee	Nottingham F	—	—
							Middlesbrough	—	—
							Hartlepool U	82	—
							Oxford U	18	1
GILKES Michael	5 8	10 10	F	20 7 65	Hackney	Leicester C	**Reading**	317	42
							Chelsea (loan)	1	—
							Southampton (loan)	6	—
GILL Wayne	5 10	11 03	M	28 11 75	Chorley	Trainee	**Blackburn R**	—	—
GILLESPIE Gary	6 2	12 07	D	5 7 60	Stirling	School	Falkirk	22	—
							Coventry C	172	6
							Liverpool	156	14
							Celtic	69	2
							Coventry C	3	—
GILLESPIE Keith	5 10	11 03	F	18 2 75	Larne	Trainee	Manchester U	9	1
							Wigan Ath (loan)	8	4
							Newcastle U	17	2
GILMORE Craig *	5 10	11 00	D	8 12 76	Leeds	Trainee	**Nottingham F**	—	—
GINOLA David	6 0	13 00	F	25 1 67	Gossin		Toulon	81	4
							Racing Paris	61	8
							Brest	50	10
							Paris St Germain	115	32
							Newcastle U	—	—
GINTY Rory	5 9	10 02	F	23 1 77	Galway	Trainee	**Crystal Palace**	—	—
GITTENS Jon	6 0	12 06	D	22 1 64	Moseley	Paget R	Southampton	18	—
							Swindon T	126	6
							Southampton	19	—
							Middlesbrough (loan)	12	1
							Middlesbrough	13	—
							Portsmouth	68	1
GIVEN Shay	6 2	13 04	G	20 4 76	Lifford	Celtic	**Blackburn R**	—	—
							Swindon T (loan)	—	—
GLASS Jimmy	6 1	13 04	G	1 8 73	Epsom	Trainee	**Crystal Palace**	—	—
							Portsmouth (loan)	3	—
GLEGHORN Nigel	6 0	13 02	M	12 8 62	Seaham	Seaham Red Star	Ipswich T	66	11
							Manchester C	34	7
							Birmingham C	142	33
							Stoke C	120	17
GLOVER Dean	5 10	11 13	D	29 12 63	West Bromwich	Apprentice	Aston Villa	23	—
							Sheffield U (loan)	10	—
							Middlesbrough	50	5
							Port Vale	267	12
GLOVER Lee	5 10	12 01	F	24 4 70	Kettering	Trainee	Nottingham F	76	9
							Leicester C (loan)	5	1
							Barnsley (loan)	8	—
							Luton T (loan)	1	—
							Port Vale	28	4
GOATER Shaun	6 1	11 10	F	25 2 70	Bermuda		Manchester U	—	—
							Rotherham U	165	52
							Notts Co (loan)	1	—
GODDARD Paul *	5 7	12 00	F	12 10 59	Harlington	Apprentice	QPR	70	23
							West Ham U	170	54
							Newcastle U	61	19
							Derby Co	49	15
							Millwall	20	1
							Ipswich T	72	13
GONZAQUE Michael ‡	6 1	12 00	D	27 3 75	Canning Town	Trainee	Southend U	—	—
							Hereford U	3	—
GOODACRE Sam *	5 9	10 10	F	1 12 70	Sheffield	School	Sheffield W	—	—
							Scunthorpe U	44	12
GOODALL Danny	5 8	10 04	D	3 9 75	Bury	Trainee	**Blackburn R**	—	—
GOODEN Ty	5 8	12 06	M	23 10 72	Canvey Island	Wycombe W	**Swindon T**	20	2

Player	Ht	Wt	Pos	Birth Date	Birth Place	Source	Clubs	League App	League Gls
GOODING Mick	5 9	10 07	M	12 4 59	Newcastle	Bishop Auckland	Rotherham U	102	10
							Chesterfield	12	—
							Rotherham U	156	33
							Peterborough U	47	21
							Wolverhampton W	44	4
							Reading	231	23
GOODMAN Don	5 10	11 10	F	9 5 66	Leeds	School	Bradford C	70	14
							WBA	158	60
							Sunderland	116	40
							Wolverhampton W	24	3
GOODMAN Jon	5 11	12 11	F	2 6 71	Walthamstow	Bromley	Millwall	109	35
							Wimbledon	19	4
GOODRIDGE Greg	5 6	10 00	F	10 7 71	Barbados	Lambada	**Torquay U**	38	4
GOODWIN Shaun	5 9	10 09	M	14 6 69	Rotherham	Trainee	**Rotherham U**	233	30
GORDON Dale	5 10	11 08	F	9 1 67	Gt Yarmouth	Apprentice	Norwich C	206	31
							Rangers	45	6
							West Ham U	8	1
							Peterborough U (loan)	6	1
GORDON Dean	6 0	13 04	D	10 2 73	Thornton Heath	Trainee	**Crystal Palace**	100	7
GORDON Neville *			F	15 11 75	Greenwich	Trainee	**Millwall**	—	—
GORE Ian *	5 11	12 04	M	10 1 68	Liverpool		Birmingham C	—	—
						Southport	**Blackpool**	200	—
GOSS Jeremy	5 9	11 04	M	11 5 65	Oekolia	Amateur	**Norwich C**	172	13
GOUCK Andy	5 9	11 02	M	8 6 72	Blackpool	Trainee	**Blackpool**	132	11
GOULD Jonathan	6 1	12 07	G	18 7 68	Paddington	Clevedon T	Halifax T	32	—
							WBA	—	—
							Coventry C	25	—
GOURLAY Archie ‡	5 8	10 00	M	29 6 69	Greenock		Morton	2	—
							Newcastle U	3	—
							Morton (loan)	4	—
							Motherwell	3	—
							Hartlepool U	1	—
GOWSHALL Joby	6 1	13 00	D	7 8 75	Louth	Trainee	**Grimsby T**	—	—
GRAHAM Benjamin *			D	23 9 75	Pontypool	Trainee	**Cardiff C**	1	—
GRAHAM Deniol *	5 10	10 05	F	4 10 69	Cannock	Trainee	Manchester U	2	—
							Barnsley	38	2
							Preston NE (loan)	8	—
							Carlisle U (loan)	2	1
							Stockport Co	11	2
GRAHAM Jimmy	6 0	11 08	D	15 11 69	Glasgow	Trainee	Bradford C	7	—
							Rochdale (loan)	11	—
							Rochdale	126	1
							Hull C	39	—
GRAHAM Mark	5 6	10 00	F	24 10 74	Newry	Trainee	**QPR**	—	—
GRAHAM Richard	6 2	12 01	M	28 11 74	Dewsbury	Trainee	**Oldham Ath**	37	3
GRAINGER Martin	5 11	12 00	D	23 8 72	Enfield	Trainee	Colchester U	46	7
							Brentford	68	9
GRANT Kim	5 10	10 12	F	25 9 72	Ghana	Trainee	**Charlton Ath**	93	11
GRANT Tony	5 9	10 00	M	14 11 74	Liverpool	Trainee	**Everton**	5	—
GRANT Tony	5 10	11 08	D	20 8 76	Louth	Trainee	**Leeds U**	—	—
GRANVILLE Danny	6 0	12 00	M	19 1 75	Islington	Trainee	**Cambridge U**	27	7
GRAY Andy	5 6	10 10	F	25 10 73	Southampton	Trainee	Reading	17	3
							Leyton Orient	25	3
GRAY Ian	6 2	12 00	G	25 2 75	Manchester	Trainee	**Oldham Ath**	—	—
							Rochdale (loan)	12	—
GRAY Kevin	6 0	13 00	D	7 1 72	Sheffield	Trainee	Mansfield T	141	3
							Huddersfield T	5	—

Player	Ht	Wt	Pos	Birth Date	Birth Place	Source	Clubs	League App	League Gls
GRAY Martin	5 9	11 04	M	17 8 71	Stockton	Trainee	**Sunderland**	57	1
							Aldershot (loan)	5	—
GRAY Michael	5 8	10 07	D	3 8 74	Sunderland	Trainee	**Sunderland**	65	3
GRAY Phil	5 9	12 05	F	2 10 68	Belfast	Apprentice	Tottenham H	9	—
							Barnsley (loan)	3	—
							Fulham (loan)	3	—
							Luton T	59	22
							Sunderland	83	26
GRAYSON Neil	5 10	12 04	F	1 11 64	York	Rowntree Mackintosh	Doncaster R	29	6
							York C	1	—
							Chesterfield	15	—
						Boston U	**Northampton T**	38	8
GRAYSON Simon	5 11	12 07	D	16 12 69	Ripon	Trainee	Leeds U	2	—
							Leicester C	111	2
GRAYSTON Neil	5 7	10 11	D	25 11 75	Keighley	Trainee	**Bradford C**	5	—
GREEN Matt	5 8	11 04	M	22 10 75	Northampton	Trainee	**Derby Co**	—	—
GREEN Paul *	5 10	10 10	D	25 5 76	Carlisle	Trainee	**Rotherham U**	—	—
GREEN Richard	6 1	13 11	D	22 11 67	Wolverhampton	Apprentice	Shrewsbury T	125	5
							Swindon T	—	—
							Gillingham	127	12
GREEN Scott	5 10	12 05	M	15 1 70	Walsall	Trainee	Derby Co	—	—
							Bolton W	177	21
GREENALL Colin	5 10	11 06	D	30 12 63	Billinge	Apprentice	Blackpool	183	9
							Gillingham	62	4
							Oxford U	67	2
							Bury (loan)	3	—
							Bury	68	5
							Preston NE	29	1
							Chester C	42	1
							Lincoln C	39	3
GREENE David	6 2	13 05	D	26 10 73	Luton	Trainee	**Luton T**	19	—
GREGAN Sean	6 2	13 07	D	29 3 74	Cleveland	Trainee	**Darlington**	82	4
GREGORY David	5 11	11 10	M	23 1 70	Colchester	Trainee	**Ipswich T**	32	2
							Hereford U (loan)	2	—
GREGORY John §			G	16 5 77	Hounslow	Trainee	**Fulham**	1	—
GREGORY Neil	5 11	11 10	F	7 10 72	Zambia	Trainee	**Ipswich T**	3	—
							Chesterfield (loan)	3	1
							Scunthorpe U (loan)	10	7
GRIDELET Phil	5 11	13 00	M	30 4 67	Edgware	Barnet	Barnsley	6	—
							Rotherham U (loan)	9	—
							Southend U	58	5
GRIFFITH Cohen *	5 10	11 07	F	26 12 62	Georgetown	Kettering T	**Cardiff C**	234	39
GRIFFITHS Brian ‡	5 9	11 00	F	26 1 65	Prescot	St Helens T	Wigan Ath	189	44
							Blackpool	57	17
							Scarborough (loan)	5	1
GRIFFITHS Carl	5 9	10 06	F	15 7 71	Oswestry	Trainee	Shrewsbury T	143	54
							Manchester C	18	4
GRIFFITHS Gareth	6 4	14 00	D	10 4 70	Winsford	Rhyl	**Port Vale**	24	2
GRITT Steve	5 9	10 10	D	31 10 57	Bournemouth	Apprentice	Bournemouth	6	3
							Charlton Ath	347	24
							Walsall	20	1
							Charlton Ath	33	1
GROBBELAAR Bruce	6 1	14 02	G	6 10 57	Durban	Vancouver Whitecaps	Crewe Alex	24	1
						Vancouver Whitecaps	Liverpool	440	—
							Stoke C (loan)	4	—
							Southampton	30	—
GROGAN Darren ‡	5 7	10 00	M	16 12 74	Dublin	Trainee	**Tottenham H**	—	—

Player	Ht	Wt	Pos	Birth Date	Birth Place	Source	Clubs	League App	League Gls
GROVES Paul	5 11	11 05	M	28 2 66	Derby	Burton Alb	Leicester C	16	1
							Lincoln C (loan)	8	1
							Blackpool	107	21
							Grimsby T	138	28
GRUGEL Mark	5 8	10 00	M	9 3 76	Liverpool	Local	**Everton**	—	—
GUENTCHEV Bontcho *	5 10	11 07	F	7 7 64	Bulgaria	Sporting Lisbon	**Ipswich T**	61	6
GUEST Mark	5 7	10 00	F	21 1 76	Mexborough	Trainee	**Sheffield W**	—	—
GUINAN Stephen ‡	6 1	12 12	F	24 12 75	Birmingham	Trainee	**Nottingham F**	—	—
GULLIT Ruud	6 0	13 00	F	1 9 62	Surinam	DWS Amsterdam	Haarlem	91	32
							Feyenoord	85	30
							PSV Eindhoven	68	46
							AC Milan	117	35
							Sampdoria	31	15
							AC Milan	8	3
							Sampdoria	22	9
							Chelsea	—	—
GUNN Bryan	6 2	13 13	G	22 12 63	Thurso	Invergordon BC	Aberdeen	15	—
							Norwich C	304	—
GUPPY Steve	5 11	12 00	M	29 3 69	Winchester	Southampton	Wycombe W	41	8
							Newcastle U	—	—
							Port Vale	27	2
GURNEY Andrew	5 7	10 08	D	25 1 74	Bristol	Trainee	**Bristol R**	41	1
GYNN Mick ‡	5 5	11 06	M	19 8 61	Peterborough	Apprentice	Peterborough U	156	33
							Coventry C	241	32
							Stoke C	21	—
							Mansfield T	—	—
HAALAND Alf-Inge	5 10	12 12	M	23 11 72	Stavanger	Bryne	**Nottingham F**	23	1
HACKETT Gary *	5 8	11 06	M	11 10 62	Stourbridge	Bromsgrove R	Shrewsbury T	150	17
							Aberdeen	15	—
							Stoke C	73	7
							WBA	44	3
							Peterborough U	22	1
							Chester C	35	5
HACKETT Warren	6 0	12 05	D	16 12 71	Newham	Tottenham H	Leyton Orient	72	3
							Doncaster R	39	2
HADLEY Stewart	6 1	13 05	F	30 12 73	Dudley	Halesowen	Derby Co	—	—
							Mansfield T	53	19
HAGUE Paul	6 3	13 03	D	16 9 72	Consett	Trainee	Gillingham	9	—
							Leyton Orient	18	1
HAILS Julian	5 10	11 01	F	20 11 67	Lincoln	Hemel Hempstead	Fulham	109	12
							Southend U	26	2
HALL Derek	5 8	11 12	M	5 1 65	Manchester	Apprentice	Coventry C	1	—
							Torquay U (loan)	10	2
							Torquay U	45	4
							Swindon T	10	—
							Southend U	123	15
							Halifax T	49	4
							Hereford U	103	18
							Rochdale	9	1
HALL Gareth	5 8	10 07	D	20 3 69	Croydon	Apprentice	**Chelsea**	133	3
HALL Graeme *			D	22 11 75	Stockton	Trainee	**Arsenal**	—	—
HALL Kevin ‡	5 10	11 00	M	7 2 76	Edinburgh	Trainee	**Crystal Palace**	—	—
HALL Leigh †			F	10 6 75	Hereford		**Hereford U**	1	—
HALL Marcus	6 1	12 02	D	24 3 76	Coventry	Trainee	**Coventry C**	5	—
HALL Mark *	5 6	10 12	M	13 1 73	London	Tottenham H	**Southend U**	12	—
							Barnet (loan)	3	—
HALL Paul	5 9	10 04	F	3 7 72	Manchester	Trainee	Torquay U	93	1
							Portsmouth	71	9

Player	Ht	Wt	Pos	Birth Date	Birth Place	Source	Clubs	League App	League Gls
HALL Richard	6 2	13 11	D	14 3 72	Ipswich	Trainee	Scunthorpe U	22	3
							Southampton	96	11
HALL Wayne	5 9	10 06	D	25 10 68	Rotherham	Darlington	**York C**	236	8
HALLE Gunnar	5 11	11 02	D	11 8 65	Oslo	Lillestrom	**Oldham Ath**	131	11
HALLIDAY Stephen	5 10	11 11	F	3 5 76	Sunderland	Charlton Ath	**Hartlepool U**	39	5
HALLWORTH Jon	6 1	14 03	G	26 10 65	Stockport	School	Ipswich T	45	—
							Swindon T (loan)	—	—
							Fulham (loan)	—	—
							Bristol R (loan)	2	—
							Oldham Ath	159	—
HAMILL Rory	5 8	12 03	F	4 5 76	Coleraine	Portstewart	**Fulham**	23	5
HAMILTON Derrick	5 11	12 09	M	15 8 76	Bradford	Trainee	**Bradford C**	32	2
HAMILTON Ian	5 9	11 03	F	14 12 67	Stevenage	Apprentice	Southampton	—	—
							Cambridge U	24	1
							Scunthorpe U	145	18
							WBA	123	14
HAMLET Alan §	6 0	11 03	D	30 9 77	Watford	Trainee	**Barnet**	3	—
HAMMOND Nicky	6 0	11 13	G	7 9 67	Hornchurch	Apprentice	Arsenal	—	—
							Bristol R (loan)	3	—
							Peterborough U (loan)	—	—
							Aberdeen (loan)	—	—
							Swindon T	67	—
HAMON Chris	6 1	13 07	F	27 4 70	Jersey	St Peter	**Swindon T**	8	1
HANBY Robert	5 10	11 09	D	24 12 74	Pontefract	Trainee	**Barnsley**	—	—
HANCOX Richard	5 10	13 00	F	4 10 70	Stourbridge	Stourbridge S	**Torquay U**	46	9
HANDYSIDE Peter	6 1	12 03	D	31 7 74	Dumfries	Trainee	**Grimsby T**	59	—
HANSEN Vergard	6 2	13 00	D	8 8 69	Drammen	Stromsgodset	**Bristol C**	29	—
HARDING Paul	5 9	12 05	M	6 3 64	Mitcham	Barnet	Notts Co	54	1
							Southend U (loan)	5	—
							Watford (loan)	2	—
							Birmingham C	22	—
HARDWICK Matthew ‡	5 10	11 04	F	12 9 74	Rotherham	School	**Sheffield W**	—	—
HARDY Paul ‡	5 8	10 05	M	29 8 75	Plymouth	Trainee	**Torquay U**	1	—
HARDY Phil	5 8	11 00	D	9 4 73	Chester	Trainee	**Wrexham**	176	—
HARDYMAN Paul *	5 8	11 07	D	11 3 64	Portsmouth	Waterford	Portsmouth	117	3
							Sunderland	106	9
							Bristol R	67	5
HARFORD Mick	6 3	14 05	F	12 2 59	Sunderland	Lambton St BC	Lincoln C	115	41
							Newcastle U	19	4
							Bristol C	30	11
							Birmingham C	92	25
							Luton T	139	57
							Derby Co	58	15
							Luton T	29	12
							Chelsea	28	9
							Sunderland	11	2
							Coventry C	1	1
							Wimbledon	27	6
HARFORD Paul	6 4	13 12	F	21 10 74	Kent	Trainee	**Blackburn R**	—	—
							Wigan Ath (loan)	3	—
							Shrewsbury T (loan)	6	—
HARGREAVES Chris *	5 11	11 00	F	12 5 72	Cleethorpes	Trainee	Grimsby T	51	5
							Scarborough (loan)	3	—
							Hull C	49	—
HARKES John	5 10	11 12	M	8 3 67	New Jersey	USSF	Sheffield W	81	7
							Derby Co	66	2
HARKIN Joe	5 10	11 04	D	9 12 75	Derry	Trainee	**Manchester C**	—	—

Player	Ht	Wt	Pos	Birth Date	Birth Place	Source	Clubs	League App	League Gls
HARKNESS Steve	5 10	11 02	M	27 8 71	Carlisle	Trainee	Carlisle U	13	—
							Liverpool	40	1
							Huddersfield T (loan)	5	—
							Southend U (loan)	6	—
HARLE Mike	5 10	11 12	D	31 10 72	Lewisham	Sittingbourne	**Millwall**	—	—
HARMON Darren	5 5	9 12	M	30 1 73	Northampton	Trainee	Notts Co	—	—
							Shrewsbury T	6	2
							Northampton T	89	12
HARPER Alan	5 9	11 09	M	1 11 60	Liverpool	Apprentice	Liverpool	—	—
							Everton	127	4
							Sheffield W	35	—
							Manchester C	50	1
							Everton	51	—
							Luton T	41	1
							Burnley	27	—
HARPER Lee	6 1	13 00	G	30 10 71	London	Sittingbourne	**Arsenal**	—	—
HARPER Lee	5 11	12 05	D	24 3 75	Bridlington	York C	**Scarborough**	2	—
HARPER Steve	5 10	11 12	F	3 2 69	Stoke	Trainee	Port Vale	28	2
							Preston NE	77	10
							Burnley	69	8
							Doncaster R	64	11
HARPER Steve	6 2	13 00	G	3 2 70	Easington	Seaham Red Star	**Newcastle U**	—	—
HARRINGTON Justin	5 9	10 09	F	18 6 75	Truro	Trainee	**Norwich C**	—	—
HARRIOTT Marvin	5 8	11 06	D	20 4 74	Dulwich	West Ham U	Oldham Ath	—	—
							Barnsley	—	—
							Leyton Orient (loan)	8	—
							Bristol C	36	—
HARRIS Andrew	5 10	11 11	D	26 2 77	Springs	Trainee	**Liverpool**	—	—
HARRIS Mark	6 3	13 11	M	15 7 63	Reading	Wokingham	Crystal Palace	2	—
							Burnley (loan)	4	—
							Swansea C	228	14
HARRISON Gary †	5 9	11 05	F	12 3 75	Northampton	Aston Villa	**Northampton T**	7	—
HARRISON Gerry	5 10	12 12	M	15 4 72	Lambeth	Trainee	Watford	9	—
							Bristol C	38	1
							Cardiff C (loan)	10	1
							Hereford U (loan)	6	—
							Huddersfield T	—	—
							Burnley	19	2
HARRISON Lee	6 2	11 13	G	12 9 71	Billericay	Trainee	Charlton Ath	—	—
							Fulham (loan)	—	—
							Gillingham (loan)	2	—
							Fulham (loan)	—	—
							Fulham	7	—
HART Andy ‡			D	11 3 76	Pontefract		**Carlisle U**	—	—
HARTENBERGER Uwe *	6 1	13 00	F	1 2 68	Lauterecken	Bayer Uerdingen	**Reading**	24	4
HARTFIELD Charles	6 0	12 02	D	4 9 71	London	Trainee	Arsenal	—	—
							Sheffield U	54	1
HARTSON John	5 11	11 13	F	5 4 75	Swansea	Trainee	Luton T	54	11
							Arsenal	15	7
HARVEY Lee	5 11	11 07	M	21 12 66	Harlow	Harrow	Leyton Orient	184	23
							Nottingham F	2	—
							Brentford	51	6
HARVEY Richard	5 10	11 10	D	17 4 69	Letchworth	Apprentice	**Luton T**	117	3
							Blackpool (loan)	5	—
HATHAWAY Ian	5 6	11 00	M	22 8 68	Wordsley	Bedworth U	Mansfield T	44	2
							Rotherham U	13	1
							Torquay U	79	12
HAWORTH Robert *	6 2	13 04	F	21 11 75	Edgware	Trainee	**Fulham**	21	1

Player	Ht	Wt	Pos	Birth Date	Birth Place	Source	Clubs	League App	League Gls
HAWTHORNE Mark ‡	5 9	10 12	M	31 10 73	Glasgow	Trainee	Crystal Palace	—	—
							Sheffield U	—	—
							Walsall	—	—
							Torquay U	2	—
HAY Darran ‡	6 0	13 08	F	17 12 69	Hitchin	Biggleswade	**Cambridge U**	29	3
HAYES Martin *	6 0	12 04	F	21 3 66	Walthamstow	Apprentice	Arsenal	102	26
							Celtic	7	—
							Wimbledon (loan)	2	—
							Swansea C	61	8
HAYNES Junior ‡			M	16 4 76	Croydon		**Barnet**	6	—
HAYRETTIN Hakan *	5 9	11 02	M	4 2 70	London	Trainee	Leyton Orient	—	—
						Barnet	Barnet	6	—
							Torquay U (loan)	4	—
							Wycombe W	19	1
							Cambridge U	17	—
HAYWARD Andy	6 0	11 02	F	21 6 70	Barnsley	Frickley Ath	**Rotherham U**	37	6
HAYWARD Steve	5 10	12 05	M	8 9 71	Walsall	Trainee	Derby Co	26	1
							Carlisle U	9	2
HAYWOOD Paul ‡	5 11	10 02	D	4 10 75	Barnsley	Trainee	**Nottingham F**	—	—
HAZARD Mickey	5 8	11 08	M	5 2 60	Sunderland	Apprentice	Tottenham H	91	13
							Chelsea	81	9
							Portsmouth	8	1
							Swindon T	119	17
							Tottenham H	28	2
HAZEL Des	5 10	11 05	M	15 7 67	Bradford	Apprentice	Sheffield W	6	—
							Grimsby T (loan)	9	2
							Rotherham U	238	30
							Chesterfield	—	—
HEALD Greg	6 1	12 08	D	26 9 71	London	Enfield	**Peterborough U**	29	—
HEALD Oliver *	6 0	12 00	F	13 3 75	Vancouver		**Port Vale**	—	—
HEALD Paul	6 2	14 00	G	20 9 68	Wath-on-Dearne	Trainee	Sheffield U	—	—
							Leyton Orient	176	—
							Coventry C (loan)	2	—
							Crystal Palace (loan)	—	—
							Swindon T (loan)	2	—
HEALY Brett	5 8	10 08	M	6 10 77	Coventry	Trainee	**Coventry C**	—	—
HEANEY Neil	5 9	11 13	F	3 11 71	Middlesbrough	Trainee	Arsenal	7	—
							Hartlepool U (loan)	3	—
							Cambridge U (loan)	13	2
							Southampton	36	2
HEATH Adrian	5 6	11 00	F	11 1 61	Newcastle under Lyne	Apprentice	Stoke C	95	16
							Everton	226	71
						Espanol	Aston Villa	9	—
							Manchester C	75	4
							Stoke C	6	—
							Burnley	111	29
HEATH Michael ‡	5 9	11 00	G	7 2 74	Hull	Trainee	Tottenham H	—	—
							Scunthorpe U	2	—
HEATH Stephen			D	15 11 77	Hull	Trainee	**Leeds U**	—	—
HEATHCOTE Mike	6 2	12 06	D	10 9 65	Durham	Spennymoor U	Sunderland	9	—
							Halifax T (loan)	7	1
							York C (loan)	3	—
							Shrewsbury T	44	6
							Cambridge U	128	13
HEBBERD Trevor *	6 0	11 04	M	19 6 58	Winchester	Apprentice	Southampton	97	7
							Bolton W (loan)	6	—
							Leicester C (loan)	4	1
							Oxford U	260	37
							Derby Co	81	10
							Portsmouth	4	—
							Chesterfield	74	1
							Lincoln C	25	—
HEGGS Carl	6 0	11 08	F	11 10 70	Leicester	Paget R	**WBA**	40	3
							Bristol R (loan)	5	1

Player	Ht	Wt	Pos	Birth Date	Birth Place	Source	Clubs	League App	League Gls
HELDER Glenn	5 11	11 07	F	28 10 68	Leiden		Sparta	93	9
							Vitesse	52	12
							Arsenal	13	—
HELGASON Gudni ‡	5 10	11 10	F	16 7 76	Iceland	Volsungur	**Sunderland**	—	—
HELLIWELL Ian	6 3	14 00	F	7 11 62	Rotherham	Matlock T	York C	160	40
							Scunthorpe U	80	22
							Rotherham U	52	4
							Stockport Co	17	4
HEMMINGS Tony	5 10	12 09	F	21 9 67	Burton	Northwich Vic	**Wycombe W**	46	12
HENDERSON Damian *	6 2	13 10	F	12 5 73	Leeds	Trainee	Leeds U	—	—
							Scarborough	17	5
							Scunthorpe U	37	4
							Hereford U (loan)	5	—
							Hartlepool U (loan)	12	3
HENDERSON Nicky ‡	5 10	11 08	D	11 2 76	Newcastle	Trainee	**Brighton & HA**	—	—
HENDON Ian	6 0	12 10	D	5 12 71	Ilford	Trainee	Tottenham H	4	—
							Portsmouth (loan)	4	—
							Leyton Orient (loan)	6	—
							Barnsley (loan)	6	—
							Leyton Orient	65	2
							Birmingham C (loan)	4	—
HENDRIE John	5 8	12 05	F	24 10 63	Lennoxtown	Apprentice	Coventry C	21	2
							Hereford U (loan)	6	—
							Bradford C	173	46
							Newcastle U	34	4
							Leeds U	27	5
							Middlesbrough	179	43
HENDRIE Lee	5 7	9 00	F	18 5 77	Birmingham	Trainee	**Aston Villa**	—	—
HENDRY Colin	6 1	12 00	D	7 12 65	Keith	Islavale	Dundee	41	2
							Blackburn R	102	22
							Manchester C	63	5
							Blackburn R	132	9
HENDRY John	5 11	10 12	F	6 1 70	Glasgow	Hillington YC	Dundee	2	—
							Forfar Ath (loan)	10	6
							Tottenham H	17	5
							Charlton Ath (loan)	5	1
							Swansea C (loan)	8	2
HENRY Liburd *	5 11	12 12	F	29 8 67	London	Leytonstone/ Ilford	Watford	10	1
							Halifax T (loan)	5	—
							Maidstone U	67	9
							Gillingham	42	2
							Peterborough U	32	7
HENRY Nick	5 6	9 08	M	21 2 69	Liverpool	Trainee	**Oldham Ath**	237	18
HERBERT Craig	6 0	12 00	D	9 11 75	Coventry	Torquay U	**WBA**	8	—
HERRERA Robbie	5 6	10 02	D	12 6 70	Torbay	Trainee	QPR	6	—
							Torquay U (loan)	11	—
							Torquay U (loan)	5	—
							Fulham	50	1
HESKEY Emile §			M	11 1 78	Leicester	Trainee	**Leicester C**	1	—
HESSENTHALER Andy	5 7	11 05	M	17 8 65	Gravesend	Redbridge Forest	**Watford**	165	11
HEWITT Jamie	5 10	11 09	M	17 5 68	Chesterfield	School	Chesterfield	249	14
							Doncaster R	33	—
							Chesterfield	67	6
HEWLETT Matthew	6 2	10 11	M	25 2 76	Bristol	Trainee	**Bristol C**	13	—
HICKS Stuart	6 1	13 00	D	30 5 67	Peterborough	Wisbech	Colchester U	64	—
							Scunthorpe U	67	1
							Doncaster R	36	—
							Huddersfield T	22	1
							Preston NE	12	—
							Scarborough	6	—
HIGGINS Dave	6 0	11 00	D	19 8 61	Liverpool	Eagle	Tranmere R	28	—
						S. Liverpool, Caernarfon	**Tranmere R**	280	10

Player	Ht	Wt	Pos	Birth Date	Birth Place	Source	Clubs	League App	League Gls
HIGGS Shane §	6 2	12 12	G	13 5 77	Oxford	Trainee	**Bristol R**	—	—
HIGNETT Craig	5 9	11 10	M	12 1 70	Whiston	Liverpool	Crewe Alex	121	42
							Middlesbrough	76	17
HILEY Scott	5 9	10 07	M	27 9 68	Plymouth	Trainee	Exeter C	210	12
							Birmingham C	44	—
HILL Andy	5 11	12 00	D	20 1 65	Maltby	Apprentice	Manchester U	—	—
							Bury	264	10
							Manchester C	98	6
HILL Colin	6 0	12 05	D	12 11 63	Hillingdon	Apprentice	Arsenal	46	1
							Brighton (loan)	—	—
						Maritimo	Colchester U	69	—
							Sheffield U	82	1
							Leicester C (loan)	10	—
							Leicester C	101	—
HILL Danny	5 9	11 03	M	1 10 74	Edmonton	Trainee	**Tottenham H**	10	—
HILL David *	5 11	12 04	M	6 6 66	Nottingham	Local	Scunthorpe U	140	10
							Ipswich T	61	—
							Scunthorpe U	65	6
							Lincoln C	58	6
							Chesterfield (loan)	3	—
HILL Keith	6 0	12 06	D	17 5 69	Bolton	Apprentice	Blackburn R	96	3
							Plymouth Arg	99	2
HILLIER David	5 10	12 05	M	19 12 69	Blackheath	Trainee	**Arsenal**	97	2
HILTON Chris ‡	5 9	10 06	D	8 12 75	Barnsley	Trainee	**Rotherham U**	—	—
HILTON David			D	10 11 77	Barnsley	Trainee	**Manchester U**	—	—
HILTON Robert *			D	5 11 75	Warrington	Trainee	**Oldham Ath**	—	—
HIMSWORTH Gary	5 7	9 10	D	19 12 69	Appleton	Trainee	York C	88	8
							Scarborough	92	6
							Darlington	66	5
HINCHCLIFFE Andy	5 10	12 10	D	5 2 69	Manchester	Apprentice	Manchester C	112	8
							Everton	119	4
HINES Leslie			D	7 1 77	Germany	Trainee	**Aston Villa**	—	—
HINSHELWOOD Danny	5 9	10 11	D	4 12 75	Bromley	Trainee	**Nottingham F**	—	—
HIRST David	5 11	13 10	F	7 12 67	Barnsley	Apprentice	Barnsley	28	9
							Sheffield W	233	87
HISLOP Shaka	6 6	12 02	G	22 2 69	London	Howard Univ.	**Reading**	104	—
HITCHCOCK Kevin	6 1	12 02	G	5 10 62	Custom House	Barking	Nottingham F	—	—
							Mansfield T (loan)	14	—
							Mansfield T	168	—
							Chelsea	69	—
							Northampton T (loan)	17	—
							West Ham U (loan)	—	—
HOBSON Gary	6 1	12 10	D	12 11 71	North Ferriby	Trainee	**Hull C**	113	—
HOCKADAY David *	5 9	11 02	D	9 11 57	Billingham	Amateur	Blackpool	147	24
							Swindon T	245	6
							Hull C	72	2
							Stoke C (loan)	7	—
							Shrewsbury T	48	—
HODDLE Carl *	6 4	11 00	M	8 3 67	Harlow	Bishop's Stortford	Leyton Orient	28	2
							Barnet	92	3
HODDLE Glenn	6 0	11 06	M	27 10 57	Hayes	Apprentice	Tottenham	377	88
						Monaco	Chelsea	—	—
							Swindon T	64	1
							Chelsea	31	1
HODGE John	5 7	11 03	F	1 4 69	Ormskirk	Exmouth	Exeter C	65	10
							Swansea C	71	9

Player	Ht	Wt	Pos	Birth Date	Birth Place	Source	Clubs	League App	League Gls
HODGE Martin	6 2	15 03	G	4 2 59	Southport	Apprentice	Plymouth Arg	43	—
							Everton	25	—
							Preston NE (loan)	28	—
							Oldham Ath (loan)	4	—
							Gillingham (loan)	4	—
							Preston NE (loan)	16	—
							Sheffield W	197	—
							Leicester C	75	—
							Hartlepool U	69	—
							Rochdale	42	—
							Plymouth Arg	17	—
HODGE Steve	5 8	9 11	M	25 10 62	Nottingham	Apprentice	Nottingham F	123	30
							Aston Villa	53	12
							Tottenham H	45	7
							Nottingham F	82	20
							Leeds U	54	10
							Derby Co (loan)	10	2
							QPR	15	—
HODGES Glyn	6 1	12 03	M	30 4 63	Streatham	Apprentice	Wimbledon	232	49
							Newcastle U	7	—
							Watford	86	15
							Crystal Palace	7	—
							Sheffield U	125	16
HODGES Kevin *	5 8	10 11	M	12 6 60	Bridport	Apprentice	Plymouth Arg	530	81
							Torquay U (loan)	3	—
							Torquay U	65	4
HODGES Lee	5 9	11 06	F	4 9 73	Epping	Trainee	Tottenham H	4	—
							Plymouth Arg (loan)	7	2
							Wycombe W (loan)	4	—
							Barnet	34	4
HODGES Lee	5 4	9 06	F	2 3 78	Newham	Trainee	**West Ham U**	—	—
HODGSON Doug	6 1	12 05	M	27 2 69	Frankston	Heidelberg	**Sheffield U**	1	—
HOGG Graeme	6 1	13 01	D	17 6 64	Aberdeen	Apprentice	Manchester U	83	1
							WBA (loan)	7	—
							Portsmouth	100	2
							Hearts	58	3
							Notts Co	17	—
HOLCROFT Peter	5 8	10 00	M	3 1 76	Liverpool	Trainee	**Everton**	—	—
HOLDEN Andy	6 1	13 10	D	14 9 62	Flint	Rhyl	Chester C	100	17
							Wigan Ath	49	4
							Oldham Ath	22	4
HOLDEN Mark	5 8	11 00	D	2 4 76	Tamworth	Trainee	**Stoke C**	—	—
HOLDEN Rick	5 11	12 07	M	9 9 64	Skipton		Burnley	1	—
							Halifax T	67	12
							Watford	42	8
							Oldham Ath	129	19
							Manchester C	50	3
							Oldham Ath	60	9
HOLDSWORTH David	6 1	12 04	D	8 11 68	Walthamstow	Trainee	**Watford**	231	9
HOLDSWORTH Dean	5 11	11 13	F	8 11 68	Walthamstow	Trainee	Watford	16	3
							Carlisle U (loan)	4	1
							Port Vale (loan)	6	2
							Swansea C (loan)	5	1
							Brentford (loan)	7	1
							Brentford	110	53
							Wimbledon	106	43
HOLLAND Chris	5 9	11 05	M	11 9 75	Whalley	Trainee	Preston NE	1	—
							Newcastle U	3	—
HOLLAND Matthew	5 9	11 00	M	11 4 74	Bury	Trainee	West Ham U	—	—
							Bournemouth	16	1
HOLLAND Paul	5 11	12 10	M	8 7 73	Lincoln	School	**Mansfield T**	149	25
HOLLIS Steve ‡	6 0	11 00	D	22 8 72	Liverpool	Liverpool	**Wigan Ath**	1	—

Player	Ht	Wt	Pos	Birth Date	Birth Place	Source	Clubs	League App	League Gls
HOLLOWAY Ian	5 8	10 10	M	12 3 63	Kingswood	Apprentice	Bristol R	111	14
							Wimbledon	19	2
							Brentford (loan)	13	2
							Brentford	16	—
							Torquay U (loan)	6	—
							Bristol R	179	26
							QPR	120	3
HOLMES Darren	5 8	11 02	M	30 1 75	Sheffield	Trainee	**Sheffield W**	—	—
HOLMES Matt	5 7	10 07	F	1 8 69	Luton	Trainee	Bournemouth	114	8
							Cardiff C (loan)	1	—
							West Ham U	76	4
HOLMES Paul	5 10	11 03	D	18 2 68	Wortley	Apprentice	Doncaster R	47	1
							Torquay U	138	4
							Birmingham C	12	—
							Everton	20	—
HOLMES Steve	6 2	13 00	D	13 1 72	Middlesbrough	Guisborough T	**Preston NE**	5	1
							Hartlepool U (loan)	5	2
HOLSGROVE Paul	6 1	11 10	F	26 8 69	Wellington	Trainee	Aldershot	3	—
							Wimbledon (loan)	—	—
							WBA (loan)	—	—
						Wokingham	Luton T	2	—
						Heracles	Millwall	11	—
							Reading	24	3
HOLT Gary	6 1	11 11	M	9 3 73	Irvine	Celtic	**Stoke C**	—	—
HOMER Chris §	5 9	11 05	M	16 4 77	Stockton	Trainee	**Hartlepool U**	1	—
HONE Mark	6 1	12 05	D	31 3 68	Croydon	Trainee	Crystal Palace	4	—
						Welling	**Southend U**	40	—
HONOR Chris (on loan from Airdrieonians)	5 9	10 09	D	5 6 68	Bristol		**Cardiff C**	10	—
HONOUR Brian ‡	5 7	12 05	M	16 2 64	Horden	Apprentice	Darlington	74	4
						Peterlee	**Hartlepool U**	319	25
HOOKER Jon	5 7	11 00	M	31 3 72	London	Hertford T	Gillingham	—	—
							Brentford	1	—
HOOPER Dean	5 10	11 06	M	13 4 71	Harefield	Hayes	**Swindon T**	4	—
HOOPER Lyndon ‡	5 4	10 00	M	30 5 66	Guyana	Toronto Blizzard	**Birmingham C**	5	—
HOOPER Michael	6 2	13 05	G	10 2 64	Bristol	Mangotsfield	Bristol C	1	—
							Wrexham (loan)	20	—
							Wrexham	14	—
							Liverpool	51	—
							Leicester C (loan)	14	—
							Newcastle U	25	—
HOPE Chris	6 1	12 07	D	14 11 72	Sheffield	Darlington	Nottingham F	—	—
							Scunthorpe U	65	—
HOPKIN David	5 9	10 03	M	21 8 70	Greenock	Pt Glasgow R BC	Morton	18	—
							Chelsea	40	1
HOPKINS Jeff	6 0	12 11	D	14 4 64	Swansea	Apprentice	Fulham	219	4
							Crystal Palace	70	2
							Plymouth Arg (loan)	8	—
							Bristol R	6	—
							Reading	99	3
HOPPER Neil ‡	6 1	12 08	G	27 1 76	Southampton	Trainee	**Southampton**	—	—
HOPPER Tony	5 11	11 07	M	31 5 76	Carlisle	Trainee	**Carlisle U**	6	—
HORLOCK Kevin	6 0	12 00	D	1 11 72	Plumstead	Trainee	West Ham U	—	—
							Swindon T	90	2
HORNE Barry	5 10	12 02	M	18 5 62	St Asaph	Rhyl	Wrexham	136	17
							Portsmouth	70	7
							Southampton	112	6
							Everton	97	2

Player	Ht	Wt	Pos	Birth Date	Birth Place	Source	Clubs	League App	League Gls
HORNE Brian	5 9	14 06	G	5 10 67	Billericay	Apprentice	Millwall	163	—
							Watford (loan)	—	—
							Middlesbrough (loan)	4	—
							Stoke C (loan)	1	—
							Portsmouth	3	—
							Hartlepool U	41	—
HORNER Philip	6 1	12 07	F	10 11 66	Leeds	Lincoln C	Leicester C	10	—
							Rotherham U (loan)	4	—
							Halifax T	72	4
							Blackpool	187	22
HOTTIGER Marc	5 10	12 09	D	7 11 67	Lausanne	Sion	**Newcastle U**	38	1
HOUCHEN Keith	6 1	13 07	F	25 7 60	Middlesbrough	Chesterfield	Hartlepool U	170	65
							Orient	76	20
							York C	67	19
							Scunthorpe U	9	3
							Coventry C	54	7
							Hibernian	57	11
							Port Vale	49	10
							Hartlepool U	66	21
HOUGHTON Ray	5 7	10 10	M	9 1 62	Glasgow	Amateur	West Ham U	1	—
							Fulham	129	16
							Oxford U	83	10
							Liverpool	153	28
							Aston Villa	95	6
							Crystal Palace	10	2
HOUGHTON Scott	5 7	12 04	F	22 10 71	Hitchin	Trainee	Tottenham H	10	2
							Ipswich T (loan)	8	1
							Cambridge U (loan)	—	—
							Gillingham (loan)	3	—
							Charlton Ath (loan)	6	—
							Luton T	16	1
							Walsall	38	8
HOULT Russell	6 4	14 09	G	22 11 72	Leicester	Trainee	**Leicester C**	10	—
							Lincoln C (loan)	2	—
							Blackpool (loan)	—	—
							Bolton W (loan)	4	—
							Lincoln C (loan)	15	—
							Derby Co (loan)	15	—
HOUSHAM Steven	5 10	11 07	D	24 2 76	Gainsborough T	Trainee	**Scunthorpe U**	4	—
HOVI Tom ‡			D	5 1 72	Norway	Hamkam	**Charlton Ath**	2	—
HOWARD John ‡	6 2	13 02	D	2 4 74	Stafford	Trainee	Wolverhampton W	—	—
							Stockport Co	—	—
HOWARD Jonathan	5 11	12 06	F	7 10 71	Sheffield	Trainee	Rotherham U	36	5
							Chesterfield	12	1
HOWARD Terry	6 1	11 07	D	26 2 66	Stepney	Apprentice	Chelsea	6	—
							C Palace (loan)	4	—
							Chester C (loan)	2	—
							Leyton Orient	328	31
							Wycombe W	20	—
HOWARTH Lee	6 1	13 06	D	3 1 68	Bolton	Chorley	Peterborough U	62	—
							Mansfield T	40	2
HOWE Stephen	5 7	10 04	M	6 11 73	Annitsford	Trainee	**Nottingham F**	4	—
HOWELL David †	6 0	12 00	D	10 10 58	London	Enfield	Barnet	57	3
							Southend U	6	—
							Birmingham C	2	—
HOWELLS David	6 0	12 04	M	15 12 67	Guildford	Trainee	**Tottenham H**	196	17
HOWEY Lee	6 2	13 09	F	1 4 69	Sunderland	AC Hemptinne	**Sunderland**	30	5
HOWEY Steve	6 1	10 05	M	26 10 71	Sunderland	Trainee	**Newcastle U**	118	4
HOY Kristian †			F	27 4 76	Doncaster		**Doncaster R**	1	—
HOYLAND Jamie	6 0	12 08	M	23 1 66	Sheffield	Apprentice	Manchester C	2	—
							Bury	172	35
							Sheffield U	89	6
							Bristol C (loan)	6	—
							Burnley	30	2

Player	Ht	Wt	Pos	Birth Date	Birth Place	Source	Clubs	League App	League Gls
HOYLE Colin	5 11	12 03	F	15 1 72	Derby	Trainee	Arsenal	—	—
							Chesterfield (loan)	3	—
							Barnsley	—	—
							Bradford C	62	1
							Notts Co	3	—
							Mansfield T (loan)	5	—
HUCKERBY Darren	5 9	11 00	M	23 4 76	Nottingham	Trainee	**Lincoln C**	12	3
HUGHES Anthony	6 0	12 05	D	3 10 73	Liverpool	Trainee	**Crewe Alex**	23	1
HUGHES Bryan	5 9	10 00	M	19 6 76	Liverpool	Trainee	**Wrexham**	49	9
HUGHES Ceri	5 10	11 05	M	26 2 71	Pontypridd	Trainee	**Luton T**	116	12
HUGHES Darren ‡	5 11	10 11	D	6 10 65	Prescot	Apprentice	Everton	3	—
							Shrewsbury T	37	1
							Brighton	26	2
							Port Vale	184	4
							Northampton T	13	—
HUGHES David	5 10	11 08	M	30 12 72	St Albans	Trainee	**Southampton**	14	2
HUGHES Ian	5 11	12 00	M	2 8 74	Bangor	Trainee	**Bury**	108	1
HUGHES Luke ‡	5 10	10 04	F	17 9 75	Sunderland	Trainee	**Nottingham F**	—	—
HUGHES Mark	5 10	13 05	F	1 11 63	Wrexham	Apprentice	Manchester U	89	37
							Barcelona	28	4
							Bayern Munich (loan)	18	6
							Manchester U	256	82
HUGHES Mark	6 0	13 00	D	3 2 62	Port Talbot	Apprentice	Bristol R	74	3
							Torquay U (loan)	9	1
							Swansea C	12	—
							Bristol C	22	—
							Tranmere R	266	9
							Shrewsbury T	20	—
HUGHES Michael (on loan from Strasbourg)	5 6	10 08	F	2 8 71	Larne		**West Ham U**	17	2
HUGHES Paul	6 0	11 05	M	19 4 76	Hammersmith	Trainee	**Chelsea**	—	—
HUGHES Steve §			M	18 9 76	Wokingham	Trainee	**Arsenal**	1	—
HULME Kevin	5 10	13 02	F	7 12 67	Farnworth	Radcliffe Borough	Bury	110	21
							Chester C (loan)	4	—
							Doncaster R	34	8
							Bury	28	—
HUMES Tony	5 11	11 05	D	19 3 66	Blyth	Apprentice	Ipswich T	120	10
							Wrexham	102	1
HUMPHREY John *	5 10	11 04	D	31 1 61	Paddington	Apprentice	Wolverhampton W	149	3
							Charlton Ath	194	3
							Crystal Palace	160	2
							Reading (loan)	8	—
HUMPHRIES Mark	5 10	12 12	D	23 12 71	Glasgow	Cove R	Aberdeen	2	—
							Leeds U	—	—
							Bristol C	4	—
HUNT Andy	6 0	11 07	F	9 6 70	Thurrock	Kettering T	Newcastle U	43	11
							WBA (loan)	10	9
							WBA	74	25
HUNT James			M	17 12 76	Derby	Trainee	**Notts Co**	—	—
HUNT Jonathan	5 11	11 10	M	2 11 71	London		Barnet	33	—
							Southend U	49	6
							Birmingham C	20	5
HUNT Kevin	5 10	11 00	M	4 7 75	Chatham		**Gillingham**	—	—
HUNTER Barry	6 4	12 00	D	18 11 68	Coleraine	Crusaders	**Wrexham**	60	1
HUNTER Junior *	5 8	11 00	F	1 2 75	Lambeth	Trainee	**Cambridge U**	40	—
HUNTER Roy *	5 9	11 00	M	29 10 73	Cleveland	Trainee	**WBA**	9	1
HURDLE Gus	5 9	11 01	D	14 10 73	London	Fulham	**Brentford**	9	—

Player	Ht	Wt	Pos	Birth Date	Birth Place	Source	Clubs	League App	League Gls
HURLOCK Terry	5 9	14 01	M	22 9 58	Hackney	Leytonstone/ Ilford	Brentford	220	18
							Reading	29	—
							Millwall	104	8
							Rangers	29	2
							Southampton	61	—
							Millwall	13	—
							Fulham	27	1
HURST Glynn	5 10	11 06	D	17 1 76	Barnsley	Tottenham H	**Barnsley**	2	—
HURST Lee	6 0	11 09	M	21 9 70	Nuneaton	Trainee	**Coventry C**	49	2
HURST Matthew	5 7	10 03	F	3 11 77	Farnborough	Trainee	**Nottingham F**	—	—
HURST Paul	5 7	10 04	D	25 9 74	Sheffield	Trainee	**Rotherham U**	17	—
HURST Richard	6 0	12 00	G	23 12 76	Hammersmith	Trainee	**QPR**	—	—
HUTCHINGS Carl	5 11	11 00	M	24 9 74	London	Trainee	**Brentford**	68	—
HUTCHINSON Simon *	5 10	12 12	F	24 9 69	Sheffield	Eastwood T	**Wycombe W**	12	—
HUTCHISON Don	6 2	11 08	F	9 5 71	Gateshead	Trainee	Hartlepool U	24	2
							Liverpool	45	7
							West Ham U	23	9
HUTCHISON Ian ‡			F	7 11 72	Teeside		**Gillingham**	5	—
HUXFORD Richard	5 10	11 06	D	25 7 69	Scunthorpe	Kettering T	Barnet	33	1
							Millwall	32	—
							Birmingham C (loan)	5	—
							Bradford C	33	1
HYDE Graham	5 7	11 06	M	10 11 70	Doncaster	Trainee	**Sheffield W**	104	7
HYDE Micah	5 10	11 02	M	10 11 74	Newham	Trainee	**Cambridge U**	45	2
HYDE Paul	6 1	15 07	G	7 4 63	Hayes	Hayes	**Wycombe W**	88	—
HYSLOP Christian ‡	5 11	11 13	D	14 6 72	Watford	Trainee	Southend U	19	—
							Northampton T (loan)	8	—
							Colchester U	8	—
HYSON Matty ‡	6 2	12 12	F	2 5 76	Stockton	Trainee	**Hartlepool U**	5	—
IGOE Sammy	5 6	10 08	M	30 9 75	Spelthorne	Trainee	**Portsmouth**	1	—
IMPEY Andrew	5 8	10 06	F	13 9 71	Hammersmith	Yeading	**QPR**	126	8
IMPEY James			M	28 7 77	Bournemouth	Trainee	**Aston Villa**	—	—
INCE Paul	5 10	12 02	M	21 10 67	Ilford	Trainee	West Ham U	72	7
							Manchester U	206	24
INGEBRIGTSEN Kare	5 7	10 03	D	11 11 65	Rosenborg	Rosenborg	**Manchester C**	15	—
INGESSON Klas	6 3	14 00	M	20 8 68	Odeshog	PSV Eindhoven	**Sheffield W**	13	2
INGLETHORPE Alex	5 11	11 04	F	14 11 71	Epsom	School	Watford	12	2
							Barnet (loan)	6	3
							Leyton Orient	—	—
INGRAM Denny	5 10	11 06	D	27 6 76	Sunderland	Trainee	**Hartlepool U**	48	—
INGRAM Rae	5 11	12 02	D	6 12 74	Manchester	Trainee	**Manchester C**	—	—
INNES Lee ‡	6 2	11 10	F	28 2 76	Co Durham	Trainee	**Sheffield U**	—	—
INNES Michael *	6 0	11 00	G	5 11 75	Bangor	Trainee	**Wolverhampton W**	—	—
IORFA Dominic	6 0	12 12	F	1 10 68	Lagos	Antwerp	QPR	8	—
							Peterborough U	60	9
							Southend U	8	1
IRELAND Simon	5 11	10 05	M	23 11 71	Barnstaple	School	Huddersfield T	19	—
							Wrexham (loan)	5	—
							Blackburn R	1	—
							Mansfield T (loan)	9	1
							Mansfield T	40	5
IRONS Kenny	5 9	11 00	M	4 11 70	Liverpool	Trainee	**Tranmere R**	192	27

Player	Ht	Wt	Pos	Birth Date	Place	Source	Clubs	League App	Gls
IRONSIDE Ian	6 2	13 00	G	8 3 64	Sheffield	N. Ferriby U	Scarborough	88	—
							Middlesbrough	13	—
							Scarborough (loan)	7	—
							Stockport Co	19	—
							Scarborough	9	—
IRVING Richard	5 7	10 06	F	10 9 75	Halifax	Trainee	**Manchester U**	—	—
IRWIN Denis	5 8	10 11	D	31 10 65	Cork	Apprentice	Leeds U	72	1
							Oldham Ath	167	4
							Manchester U	194	13
IZZET Mustafa	5 10	10 03	M	31 10 74	Mile End	Trainee	**Chelsea**	—	—
JACKS Danny *	5 6	9 12	M	21 8 76	Worksop	Trainee	**Sheffield W**	—	—
JACKSON Chris	6 0	11 06	F	16 1 76	Barnsley	Trainee	**Barnsley**	15	2
JACKSON Kirk			F	16 10 76	Barnsley	Trainee	**Sheffield W**	—	—
JACKSON Matthew	6 1	12 09	D	19 10 71	Leeds	School	Luton T	9	—
							Preston NE (loan)	4	—
							Everton	124	4
JACKSON Michael	6 0	13 08	D	4 12 73	West Cheshire	Trainee	Crewe Alex	5	—
							Bury	63	2
JACKSON Peter	6 0	13 06	D	6 4 61	Bradford	Apprentice	Bradford C	278	24
							Newcastle U	60	3
							Bradford C	58	5
							Huddersfield T	155	3
							Chester C	32	1
JACOBS Wayne	5 8	11 02	D	3 2 69	Sheffield	Apprentice	Sheffield W	6	—
							Hull C	129	4
							Rotherham U	42	2
							Bradford C	38	1
JAKUB Joe *	5 6	9 06	M	7 12 56	Falkirk	Apprentice	Burnley	42	—
							Bury	265	27
						AZ Alkmaar	Chester C	42	1
							Burnley	163	8
							Chester C	36	—
							Wigan Ath	16	—
JAMES David	6 5	14 02	G	1 8 70	Welwyn	Trainee	Watford	89	—
							Liverpool	85	—
JAMES Julian	5 10	11 10	M	22 3 70	Tring	Trainee	**Luton T**	187	12
							Preston NE (loan)	6	—
JAMES Martin	5 10	11 10	M	18 5 71	Formby	Trainee	Preston NE	98	11
							Stockport Co	32	—
							Rotherham U	40	—
JAMES Stuart *			D	12 9 75	Bristol	Trainee	**Swindon T**	—	—
JAMES Tony	6 3	14 07	D	27 6 67	Sheffield	Gainsborough T	Lincoln C	29	—
							Leicester C	107	11
							Hereford U	18	2
JAQUES Daniel			M	18 1 78	North Ormesby	Trainee	**Leeds U**	—	—
JEFFERS John	5 10	11 10	F	5 10 68	Liverpool	Trainee	Liverpool	—	—
							Port Vale	180	10
							Shrewsbury T (loan)	3	1
JEFFREY Andrew	5 10	12 02	D	15 1 72	Bellshill	Cambridge C	**Cambridge U**	68	2
JEFFREY Mike	5 11	11 06	F	11 8 71	Liverpool	Trainee	Bolton W	15	—
							Doncaster R (loan)	11	6
							Doncaster R	38	13
							Newcastle U	2	—
JEMSON Nigel	5 10	11 10	F	10 8 69	Hutton	Trainee	Preston NE	32	8
							Nottingham F	47	13
							Bolton W (loan)	5	—
							Preston NE (loan)	9	2
							Sheffield W	51	9
							Grimsby T (loan)	6	2
							Notts Co	11	1
							Watford (loan)	4	—
							Coventry C (loan)	—	—

Player	Ht	Wt	Pos	Birth Date	Birth Place	Source	Clubs	League App	League Gls
JENKINS Iain	5 9	11 10	D	24 11 72	Whiston	Trainee	Everton	5	—
							Bradford C (loan)	6	—
							Chester C	74	—
JENKINS Steve	5 10	10 09	D	16 7 72	Merthyr	Trainee	**Swansea C**	150	1
JENKINSON Leigh	6 0	12 02	F	9 7 69	Thorne	Trainee	Hull C	130	13
							Rotherham U (loan)	7	—
							Coventry C	32	1
							Birmingham C (loan)	3	—
JENSEN John	5 10	12 06	M	3 5 65	Denmark	Brondby	**Arsenal**	83	1
JEPSON Ronnie	6 1	13 00	F	12 5 63	Stoke	Nantwich	Port Vale	22	—
							Peterborough U (loan)	18	5
							Preston NE	38	8
							Exeter C	54	21
							Huddersfield T	64	24
JEWELL Paul	5 8	12 01	F	28 9 64	Liverpool	Apprentice	Liverpool	—	—
							Wigan Ath	137	35
							Bradford C	251	53
JOACHIM Julian	5 6	11 11	F	20 9 74	Peterborough	Trainee	**Leicester C**	77	24
JOBLING Kevin	5 9	10 11	M	1 1 68	Sunderland	Apprentice	Leicester C	9	—
							Grimsby T	224	9
							Scunthorpe U (loan)	—	—
JOBSON Richard	6 1	13 05	D	9 5 63	Hull	Burton Alb	Watford	28	4
							Hull C	221	17
							Oldham Ath	177	10
JOHNROSE Lenny	5 11	12 06	F	29 11 69	Preston	Trainee	Blackburn R	42	11
							Preston NE (loan)	3	1
							Hartlepool U	66	11
							Bury	40	4
JOHNSEN Erland	6 0	12 10	D	5 4 67	Fredrikstad (Norway)	Bayern Munich	**Chelsea**	105	1
JOHNSON Alan	5 11	11 12	D	19 2 71	Ince	Trainee	Wigan Ath	180	13
							Lincoln C	41	—
JOHNSON Andy	6 1	12 00	M	2 5 74	Bristol	Trainee	**Norwich C**	13	1
JOHNSON David	6 2	14 03	F	29 10 70	Rother Valley	Trainee	Sheffield W	6	—
							Hartlepool U (loan)	7	2
							Hartlepool U (loan)	3	—
							Lincoln C	65	12
JOHNSON David *	5 6	12 03	F	15 8 76	Kingston	Trainee	**Manchester U**	—	—
JOHNSON Gavin *	5 11	11 12	D	10 10 70	Stowmarket	Trainee	**Ipswich T**	132	11
JOHNSON Ian ‡	5 9	11 08	F	1 9 75	Sunderland	Trainee	Middlesbrough	2	—
							Bradford C	2	—
JOHNSON Marvin	6 0	12 03	D	29 10 68	Wembley	Apprentice	**Luton T**	166	4
JOHNSON Michael	5 11	11 00	D	4 7 73	Nottingham	Trainee	**Notts Co**	107	—
JOHNSON Phil *	5 8	10 06	D	7 4 75	Liverpool	Trainee	**Tranmere R**	—	—
JOHNSON Richard	5 10	11 13	M	27 4 74	Kurri, Kurri	Trainee	**Watford**	65	3
JOHNSON Ross	6 0	12 04	D	2 1 76	Brighton	Trainee	**Brighton**	2	—
JOHNSON Tommy	5 10	11 02	F	15 1 71	Newcastle	Trainee	Notts Co	118	47
							Derby Co	98	30
							Aston Villa	14	4
JONES Barry	6 0	11 07	D	20 6 70	Prescot	Prescot T	Liverpool	—	—
							Wrexham	119	4
JONES Cobi *	5 7	11 04	M	16 6 70	Detroit	USSF	**Coventry C**	21	2
JONES Gary	6 0	12 08	F	6 4 69	Huddersfield	Rossington Main	Doncaster R	20	2
						Boston U	**Southend U**	47	14
							Lincoln C (loan)	4	2
JONES Gary	6 3	14 00	F	10 5 75	Chester	Trainee	**Tranmere R**	25	5
JONES Graeme	6 0	12 12	F	13 3 70	Gateshead	Bridlington T	**Doncaster R**	60	16

Player	Ht	Wt	Pos	Birth Date	Birth Place	Source	Clubs	League App	League Gls
JONES Ian §			D	26 8 76	Germany	Trainee	**Cardiff C**	2	—
JONES Keith	5 9	10 11	M	14 10 65	Dulwich	Apprentice	Chelsea	52	7
							Brentford	169	13
							Southend U	90	11
							Charlton Ath	31	1
JONES Lee	5 8	10 08	F	29 5 73	Wrexham	Trainee	Wrexham	39	10
							Liverpool	1	—
							Crewe Alex (loan)	8	1
JONES Lee	6 3	14 04	G	9 8 70	Pontypridd	Porth	**Swansea C**	2	—
JONES Martin	6 1	12 00	G	27 3 75	Liverpool	Trainee	**Tranmere R**	—	—
JONES Paul	6 3	14 00	G	18 4 67	Chirk	Kidderminster H	**Wolverhampton W**	25	—
JONES Rob	5 8	11 00	D	5 11 71	Wrexham	Trainee	Crewe Alex	75	2
							Liverpool	127	—
JONES Ryan	6 1	12 12	M	23 7 73	Sheffield	Trainee	**Sheffield W**	41	6
JONES Scott	5 10	11 06	D	1 5 75	Sheffield	Trainee	**Barnsley**	—	—
JONES Steve	5 11	12 00	F	17 3 70	Cambridge	Billericay	West Ham U	16	4
							Bournemouth	30	9
JONES Steve	5 11	13 07	G	31 1 74	Teeside	Trainee	**Hartlepool U**	39	—
JONES Tom	5 10	11 07	M	7 10 64	Aldershot	Weymouth	Aberdeen	28	3
							Swindon T	168	12
							Reading	58	2
JONES Vinny	5 11	11 10	M	5 1 65	Watford	Wealdstone	Wimbledon	77	9
							Leeds U	46	5
							Sheffield U	35	2
							Chelsea	42	4
							Wimbledon	93	6
JORDAN Scott	5 10	11 04	M	19 7 75	Newcastle	Trainee	**York C**	38	3
JOSEPH Matthew	5 7	10 00	D	30 9 72	Bethnal Green	Trainee	Arsenal	—	—
							Gillingham	—	—
							Cambridge U	66	4
JOSEPH Roger	5 11	11 10	D	24 12 65	Paddington	Juniors	Brentford	104	2
							Wimbledon	162	—
							Millwall (loan)	5	—
JOYCE Joe	5 10	11 05	D	18 3 61	Consett	School	Barnsley	334	4
							Scunthorpe U	91	2
							Carlisle U	50	—
							Darlington (loan)	4	—
JOYCE Warren	5 8	11 13	M	20 1 65	Oldham	Local	Bolton W	184	17
							Preston NE	177	34
							Plymouth Arg	30	3
							Burnley	27	4
							Hull C (loan)	9	3
JUDGE Alan ‡	5 11	11 06	G	14 5 60	Kingsbury	Amateur	Luton T	11	—
							Reading (loan)	33	—
							Reading	44	—
							Oxford U	80	—
							Lincoln C (loan)	2	—
							Cardiff C (loan)	8	—
							Hereford U	105	—
							Chelsea	—	—
JULES Mark	5 7	11 00	F	5 9 71	Bradford	Trainee	Bradford C	—	—
							Scarborough	77	16
							Chesterfield	56	1
JUPP Duncan	6 0	12 12	D	25 1 75	Guildford	Trainee	**Fulham**	69	2

Player	Ht	Wt	Pos	Birth Date	Birth Place	Source	Clubs	League App	League Gls
JURYEFF Ian ‡	5 11	12 07	F	24 11 62	Gosport	Apprentice	Southampton	—	—
						Sweden	Southampton	2	—
							Mansfield T (loan)	12	5
							Reading (loan)	7	1
							Orient	111	44
							Ipswich T (loan)	2	—
							Halifax T	17	7
							Hereford U	28	4
							Halifax T	72	13
							Darlington	34	6
							Scunthorpe U	44	13
KALOGERACOS Vasili ‡	5 7	10 06	F	21 3 75	Perth	Floreat Athena	**Birmingham C**	—	—
KAMARA Abdul ‡	5 9	11 00	M	10 2 74	Southampton	Southampton	Bristol C	1	—
							Gillingham	—	—
KAMARA Chris †	6 1	12 10	M	25 12 57	Middlesbrough	Apprentice	Portsmouth	63	7
							Swindon T	147	21
							Portsmouth	11	—
							Brentford	152	28
							Swindon T	87	6
							Stoke C	60	5
							Leeds U	20	1
							Luton T	49	—
							Sheffield U (loan)	8	—
							Middlesbrough (loan)	5	—
							Sheffield U	16	—
							Bradford C	23	3
KANCHELSKIS Andrei	5 10	13 03	F	23 1 69	Kirovograd	Donezts	**Manchester U**	123	28
KARL Stefan ‡	5 11	11 12	M	3 2 70	Hohenm-Oelsen	Dortmund	**Manchester C**	6	1
KAVANAGH Graham	5 10	12 08	M	2 12 73	Dublin	Home Farm	**Middlesbrough**	28	2
							Darlington (loan)	5	—
KAVANAGH Jason	5 9	12 04	D	23 11 71	Birmingham	Birmingham C	**Derby Co**	90	1
KAY John	5 9	11 06	D	29 1 64	Sunderland	Apprentice	Arsenal	14	—
							Wimbledon	63	2
							Middlesbrough (loan)	8	—
							Sunderland	199	—
KEANE Roy	5 10	12 05	M	10 8 71	Cork	Cobh Ramblers	Nottingham F	114	22
							Manchester U	62	7
KEARN Stewart *			G	1 12 75	Salisbury		**Sheffield W**	—	—
KEARTON Jason	5 11	12 00	G	9 7 69	Ipswich (Australia)	Brisbane Lions	**Everton**	6	—
							Stoke C (loan)	16	—
							Blackpool (loan)	14	—
							Notts Co (loan)	10	—
KEELEY John ‡	6 1	14 02	G	27 7 61	Plaistow	Apprentice	Southend U	54	—
						Chelmsford C	Brighton	138	—
							Oldham Ath	2	—
							Oxford U (loan)	6	—
							Reading (loan)	6	—
							Chester C (loan)	4	—
							Colchester U	15	—
							Stockport Co	20	—
							Peterborough U	3	—
KEEN Kevin	5 7	10 10	M	25 2 67	Amersham	Apprentice	West Ham U	219	21
							Wolverhampton W	42	7
							Stoke C	21	2
KEISTER John	5 7	10 12	M	11 11 70	Manchester	Fawah FC	**Walsall**	33	1
KELLER Kasey	6 1	13 07	G	27 11 69	Washington	Portland Univ	**Millwall**	134	—
KELLY Alan	6 2	12 05	G	11 8 68	Preston	Trainee	Preston NE	142	—
							Sheffield U	101	—
KELLY David	5 11	11 03	F	25 11 65	Birmingham	Alvechurch	Walsall	147	63
							West Ham U	41	7
							Leicester C	66	22
							Newcastle U	70	35
							Wolverhampton W	78	26

Player	Ht	Wt	Pos	Birth Date	Birth Place	Source	Clubs	League App	League Gls
KELLY Gary	5 11	13 06	G	3 8 66	Fulwood	Apprentice	Newcastle U	53	—
							Blackpool (loan)	5	—
							Bury	211	—
							West Ham U (loan)	—	—
KELLY Gary	5 8	10 12	D	9 7 74	Drogheda	Home Farm	**Leeds U**	86	—
KELLY Gavin	6 0	12 13	G	29 9 68	Beverley	Trainee	Hull C	11	—
							Bristol R (loan)	—	—
							Bristol R	30	—
							Scarborough	24	—
KELLY Jimmy	5 7	11 10	M	14 2 73	Liverpool	Trainee	Wrexham	21	—
							Wolverhampton W	7	—
							Walsall (loan)	10	2
							Wrexham (loan)	9	—
KELLY Ray			F	29 12 76	Athlone	Athlone T	**Manchester C**	—	—
KELLY Tom	5 9	12 07	D	28 3 64	Bellshill	Hibs	Hartlepool U	15	—
							Torquay U	120	—
							York C	35	2
							Exeter C	88	9
							Torquay U	86	8
KELLY Tony	5 11	11 08	F	14 2 66	Meridan		Bristol C	6	1
						St Albans C	Stoke C	58	5
							Hull C (loan)	6	1
							Cardiff C (loan)	5	1
							Bury	57	10
KELLY Tony	5 10	13 10	M	1 10 64	Prescot	Liverpool	Derby Co	—	—
							Wigan Ath	101	15
							Stoke C	36	4
							WBA	26	1
							Chester C (loan)	5	—
							Colchester U (loan)	13	2
							Shrewsbury T	101	15
							Bolton W	106	5
							Port Vale	4	1
							Millwall	2	—
							Wigan Ath	—	—
							Peterborough U	13	2
KENNA Jeff	5 11	12 02	D	27 8 70	Dublin	Trainee	Southampton	114	4
							Blackburn R	9	1
KENNEDY Andy ‡	6 2	13 00	F	8 10 64	Stirling	Sauchie Ath	Rangers	15	3
							Birmingham C	76	18
							Sheffield U (loan)	9	1
							Blackburn R	59	23
							Watford	25	4
							Bolton W (loan)	1	—
							Brighton	42	10
							Gillingham	2	—
KENNEDY Mark	5 11	11 09	F	15 5 76	Dublin	Trainee	Millwall	43	9
							Liverpool	6	—
KENNY Billy	5 07	10 10	M	19 9 73	Liverpool	Trainee	Everton	17	1
							Oldham Ath	4	—
KENT Kevin	5 11	11 00	F	19 3 65	Stoke	Apprentice	WBA	2	—
							Newport Co	33	1
							Mansfield T	229	36
							Port Vale	114	7
KENWORTHY Jon	5 7	10 06	F	18 8 74	St Asaph	Trainee	**Tranmere R**	22	2
KEOWN Martin	6 1	12 04	D	24 7 66	Oxford	Apprentice	Arsenal	22	—
							Brighton (loan)	16	—
							Brighton (loan)	7	1
							Aston Villa	112	3
							Everton	96	—
							Arsenal	80	1
KERNAGHAN Alan	6 2	13 00	D	25 4 67	Otley	Apprentice	Middlesbrough	212	16
							Charlton Ath (loan)	13	—
							Manchester C	46	1
							Bolton W (loan)	11	—
KERR David	5 11	11 00	M	6 9 74	Dumfries	Trainee	**Manchester C**	5	—

Player	Ht	Wt	Pos	Birth Date	Birth Place	Source	Clubs	League App	League Gls
KERR Dylan	5 9	11 04	D	14 1 67	Valetta	Arcadia Shepherds	Leeds U	13	—
							Doncaster R (loan)	7	1
							Blackpool (loan)	12	1
							Reading	81	3
KERR John *	5 8	11 05	F	6 3 65	Toronto	Harrow Borough	Portsmouth	4	—
							Peterborough U (loan)	10	1
						San Diego Sockers	**Millwall**	43	8
KERR Paul ‡	5 8	11 03	F	9 6 64	Portsmouth	Apprentice	Aston Villa	24	3
							Middlesbrough	125	13
							Millwall	44	14
							Port Vale	63	15
							Leicester C (loan)	7	2
							Wycombe W	1	1
KERR Stuart (on loan from Celtic)	6 2	13 00	G	13 11 74	Bellshill		**Brighton**	2	—
KERRY Chris ‡	5 7	10 04	F	15 4 76	Chesterfield	Trainee	**Mansfield T**	2	—
KERSLAKE David	5 9	12 03	D	19 6 66	Stepney	Apprentice	QPR	58	6
							Swindon T	135	1
							Leeds U	8	—
							Tottenham H	35	—
KEY Lance	6 2	14 00	G	13 5 68	Kettering	Histon	**Sheffield W**	—	—
							York C (loan)	—	—
							Oldham Ath (loan)	2	—
							Portsmouth (loan)	—	—
							Oxford U (loan)	6	—
KHARINE Dmitri	6 2	12 04	G	16 8 68	Moscow	CSKA Moscow	**Chelsea**	76	—
KIDD Ryan	6 1	13 00	D	6 10 71	Radcliffe	Trainee	Port Vale	1	—
							Preston NE	83	4
KIELY Dean	6 0	12 13	G	10 10 70	Salford	WBA	Coventry C	—	—
							Ipswich T (loan)	—	—
							York C (loan)	—	—
							York C	170	—
KILBANE Farrell ‡	6 0	13 00	D	21 10 74	Preston	Cambridge U	**Preston NE**	1	—
KILCLINE Brian	6 2	12 00	D	7 5 62	Nottingham	Apprentice	Notts Co	158	9
							Coventry C	173	28
							Oldham Ath	8	—
							Newcastle U	32	—
							Swindon T	17	—
KILFORD Ian	5 10	10 05	M	6 10 73	Bristol	Trainee	Nottingham F	1	—
							Wigan Ath (loan)	8	3
							Wigan Ath	35	5
KIMBLE Alan	5 8	11 00	D	6 8 66	Poole		Charlton Ath	6	—
							Exeter C (loan)	1	—
							Cambridge U	299	24
							Wimbledon	40	—
KING Nathan	6 0	12 06	D	1 8 75	West Bromwich	Trainee	**Shrewsbury T**	—	—
KING Phil	5 8	12 07	D	28 12 67	Bristol	Apprentice	Exeter C	27	—
							Torquay U	24	3
							Swindon T	116	4
							Sheffield W	129	2
							Notts Co (loan)	6	—
							Aston Villa	16	—
KINSELLA Mark	5 9	10 09	M	12 8 72	Dublin	Home Farm	**Colchester U**	128	20
KIRBY Alan			M	8 9 77	Waterford	Johnville	**Aston Villa**	—	—
KIRBY Ryan	6 0	12 00	D	6 9 74	Chingford	Trainee	Arsenal	—	—
							Doncaster R	42	—
KIRKHAM Peter	6 0	11 04	M	28 10 74	Newcastle	Newcastle U	**Darlington**	13	—
KITCHEN Sam ‡	6 0	13 02	D	11 6 67	Rinteln	Frickley Ath	Leyton Orient	43	1
							Doncaster R	22	1

Player	Ht	Wt	Pos	Birth Date	Birth Place	Source	Clubs	League App	League Gls
KITE Phil	6 1	14 07	G	26 10 62	Bristol	Apprentice	Bristol R	96	—
							Tottenham H (loan)	—	—
							Southampton	4	—
							Middlesbrough (loan)	2	—
							Gillingham	70	—
							Bournemouth	7	—
							Sheffield U	11	—
							Mansfield T (loan)	11	—
							Plymouth Arg (loan)	2	—
							Rotherham U (loan)	1	—
							Crewe Alex (loan)	5	—
							Stockport Co (loan)	5	—
							Cardiff C	18	—
							Bristol C	2	—
KITSON Paul	5 11	10 12	F	9 1 71	Co Durham	Trainee	Leicester C	50	6
							Derby Co	105	36
							Newcastle U	26	8
KIWOMYA Andrew †	5 9	10 10	F	1 10 67	Huddersfield	Trainee	Barnsley	1	—
							Sheffield W	—	—
						Retired injury	Dundee	21	1
							Rotherham U	7	—
						Halifax T	**Scunthorpe U**	9	3
KIWOMYA Chris	5 10	10 12	F	2 12 69	Huddersfield	Trainee	Ipswich T	225	51
							Arsenal	14	3
KJELDBJERG Jakob	6 2	13 08	D	21 10 69	Denmark	Silkeborg	**Chelsea**	52	2
KLINSMANN Jurgen	6 2	12 13	F	30 7 64	Goppingen	Gingen	Stuttgart Kickers	61	22
							Stuttgart	156	79
							Internazionale	95	34
							Monaco	65	29
							Tottenham H	41	20
KNIGHT Alan	6 0	13 00	G	3 6 61	Balham	Apprentice	**Portsmouth**	578	—
KNIGHT Richard *	5 9	11 10	D	21 8 74	Burton	Trainee	**Walsall**	29	1
KNILL Alan	6 4	13 00	D	8 10 64	Slough	Apprentice	Southampton	—	—
							Halifax T	118	6
							Swansea C	89	3
							Bury	144	8
							Cardiff C (loan)	4	—
							Scunthorpe U	64	5
KNOTT Gareth	5 11	11 04	F	19 1 76	Blackwood	Trainee	**Tottenham H**	—	—
							Gillingham (loan)	5	—
KNOWLES Darren	5 6	10 06	D	8 10 70	Sheffield	Trainee	Sheffield U	—	—
							Stockport Co	63	—
							Scarborough	81	1
KREFT Stacey	5 9	11 00	D	2 2 76	Southampton	Trainee	**Norwich C**	—	—
KRISTENSEN Bjorn *	6 1	12 05	M	10 10 63	Malling	Aarhus	Newcastle U	80	4
							Bristol C (loan)	4	—
							Portsmouth	71	1
KUBICKI Dariusz	5 11	11 02	D	6 6 63	Warsaw	Legia Warsaw	Aston Villa	25	—
							Sunderland (loan)	15	—
							Sunderland	46	—
KUHL Martin	5 11	11 13	M	10 1 65	Frimley	Apprentice	Birmingham C	111	5
							Sheffield U	38	4
							Watford	4	—
							Portsmouth	157	27
							Derby Co	68	1
							Notts Co (loan)	2	—
							Bristol C	17	1
KYD Michael	5 8	12 00	M	21 5 77	Hackney	Trainee	**Cambridge U**	19	1
KYDD Peter §	5 8	10 00	M	20 1 78	Bournemouth	Trainee	**West Ham U**	—	—
KYTE Jamie	5 7	10 00	M	17 9 77	Erith	Charlton Ath	**Charlton Ath**	—	—
LAIGHT Ellis	5 10	11 02	F	30 6 76	Birmingham	Trainee	**Torquay U**	11	—
LAKE Mike *	6 0	12 05	M	16 11 66	Manchester	Macclesfield T	Sheffield U	35	4
							Wrexham	58	6
LAKE Paul	6 0	12 02	M	28 10 68	Manchester	Trainee	**Manchester C**	110	7

Player	Ht	Wt	Pos	Birth Date	Birth Place	Source	Clubs	League App	League Gls
LAKIN Barry	5 9	12 02	M	19 9 73	Dartford	Trainee	**Leyton Orient**	46	2
LAMBERT Darren *	5 8	10 10	F	15 9 75	Grimsby	Trainee	**Grimsby T**	—	—
LAMBERT James	5 7	10 04	F	14 9 73	Henley	School	**Reading**	44	4
LAMPARD Frank §	5 10	12 04	M	21 6 78	Romford	Trainee	**West Ham U**	—	—
LAMPKIN Kevin	5 10	12 00	M	20 12 72	Liverpool	Trainee	Liverpool	—	—
							Huddersfield T	13	—
							Mansfield T	36	3
LAMPTEY Nii ‡	5 6	10 03	F	10 12 74	Accra	Anderlecht	**Aston Villa**	6	—
LANCASHIRE Graham	5 10	11 12	F	19 10 72	Blackpool	Trainee	Burnley	31	8
							Halifax T (loan)	2	—
							Chester C (loan)	11	7
							Preston NE	17	—
LANCASTER Dave	6 3	14 00	F	8 9 61	Preston	Colne Dynamoes	Blackpool	8	1
							Chesterfield (loan)	12	4
							Chesterfield	69	16
							Rochdale	40	14
						Halifax T	**Bury**	5	1
LANDON Richard	6 3	13 05	F	22 3 70	Barnsley	Bedworth U	**Plymouth Arg**	30	12
LANGE Tony *	6 0	12 09	G	10 12 64	London	Apprentice	Charlton Ath	12	—
							Aldershot (loan)	7	—
							Aldershot	125	—
							Wolverhampton W	8	—
							Aldershot (loan)	2	—
							Torquay U (loan)	1	—
							Portsmouth (loan)	—	—
							WBA	48	—
LANGFORD Tim *	5 6	12 00	F	12 9 65	Kingswinford	Telford U	**Wycombe W**	35	8
LARKIN Andy	6 1	11 09	D	24 9 77	Kent	Trainee	**Charlton Ath**	—	—
LAUNDERS Brian	5 8	11 00	M	8 6 76	Dublin	Trainee	**Crystal Palace**	2	—
LAVIN Gerard	5 9	10 07	M	5 2 74	Corby	Trainee	**Watford**	110	3
LAW Brian	6 2	11 12	D	1 1 70	Merthyr	Apprentice	QPR	20	—
							Wolverhampton W	17	—
LAW Marcus ‡	5 11	11 07	G	28 9 75	Coventry	Trainee	**Bristol R**	2	—
LAW Nicky	6 0	13 07	D	8 9 61	London	Apprentice	Arsenal	—	—
							Barnsley	114	1
							Blackpool	66	1
							Plymouth Arg	38	5
							Notts Co	47	4
							Scarborough (loan)	12	—
							Rotherham U	128	4
							Chesterfield	66	3
LAWFORD Craig	5 10	11 00	M	25 11 72	Dewsbury	Trainee	Bradford C	20	1
							Hull C	31	3
LAWLESS Chris	5 8	10 13	M	4 10 74	Dublin	Home Farm	**Sunderland**	—	—
LAWRENCE Jamie	5 10	12 03	F	8 3 70	Balham	Cowes	Sunderland	4	—
							Doncaster R	25	3
							Leicester C	17	1
LAWS Brian †	5 10	11 05	D	14 10 61	Wallsend	Apprentice	Burnley	125	12
							Huddersfield T	56	1
							Middlesbrough	107	12
							Nottingham F	147	4
							Grimsby T	16	1
LAWSON Ian	5 11	10 05	F	4 11 77	Huddersfield	Trainee	**Huddersfield T**	—	—
LAWTON Craig	5 7	10 03	M	5 1 72	Mancot	Trainee	Manchester U	—	—
							Port Vale	1	—
LE BIHAN Neil	5 11	12 13	M	14 3 76	London	Tottenham H	**Peterborough U**	4	—
LE SAUX Graeme	5 10	11 04	D	17 10 68	Jersey	St Pauls	Chelsea	90	8
							Blackburn R	89	5
LE TISSIER Matthew	6 1	13 08	F	14 10 68	Guernsey	Trainee	**Southampton**	292	119

Player	Ht	Wt	Pos	Birth Date	Birth Place	Source	Clubs	League App	League Gls
LEABURN Carl	6 3	13 00	F	30 3 69	Lewisham	Apprentice	**Charlton Ath**	224	33
							Northampton T (loan)	9	—
LEADBITTER Chris *	5 9	10 07	F	17 10 67	Middlesbrough	Apprentice	Grimsby T	—	—
							Hereford U	36	1
							Cambridge U	176	18
							Bournemouth	54	3
LEANING Andy	6 1	14 07	G	18 5 63	York	Rowntree Mackintosh	York C	69	—
							Sheffield U	21	—
							Bristol C	75	—
							Lincoln C	29	—
LEE Chris	5 10	11 07	M	18 6 71	Halifax	Trainee	Bradford C	—	—
							Rochdale	26	2
							Scarborough	78	3
							Hull C	88	4
LEE Dave	5 7	11 00	M	5 11 67	Whitefield	Schools	Bury	208	35
							Southampton	20	—
							Bolton W	112	14
LEE David	6 3	13 12	D	26 11 69	Kingswood	Trainee	**Chelsea**	118	9
							Reading (loan)	5	5
							Plymouth Arg (loan)	9	1
							Portsmouth (loan)	5	—
LEE Jason	6 3	13 08	F	9 5 71	Newham	Trainee	Charlton Ath	1	—
							Stockport Co (loan)	2	—
							Lincoln C	93	21
							Southend U	24	3
							Nottingham F	35	5
LEE Robert	5 10	11 13	F	1 2 66	West Ham	Hornchurch	Charlton Ath	298	59
							Newcastle U	112	26
LEGG Andy	5 8	10 07	M	28 7 66	Neath	Briton Ferry	Swansea C	163	29
							Notts Co	64	5
LENNON Neil	5 9	11 06	D	25 6 71	Lurgan	Trainee	Manchester C	1	—
							Crewe Alex	122	13
LEONARD Mark	5 11	11 10	F	27 9 62	St Helens	Witton Albion	Everton	—	—
							Tranmere R (loan)	7	—
							Crewe Alex	54	15
							Stockport Co	73	24
							Bradford C	157	29
							Rochdale	9	1
							Preston NE	22	1
							Chester C	32	8
							Wigan Ath	29	5
LEONHARDSEN Oyvind	5 10	11 02	M	17 8 70	Norway	Rosenborg	**Wimbledon**	20	4
LESLIE Steven	5 6	10 00	M	6 2 76	Dumfries	Trainee	**Stoke C**	1	—
LESTER Jack	5 9	11 00	F	8 10 75	Sheffield	Trainee	**Grimsby T**	7	—
LETTS Simon *	5 8	10 10	M	26 2 76	Sheffield	Trainee	**Sheffield U**	—	—
LEVER Mark	6 3	12 08	D	29 3 70	Beverley	Trainee	**Grimsby T**	219	7
LEWIS Mickey	5 8	10 10	M	15 2 65	Birmingham	School	WBA	24	—
							Derby Co	43	1
							Oxford U	281	7
LEWIS Neil	5 7	11 01	M	28 6 74	Wolverhampton	Trainee	**Leicester C**	47	—
LIBURD Richard	5 10	10 12	D	26 9 73	Nottingham	Forest Ath	Middlesbrough	41	1
							Bradford C	9	1
LIDDELL Andrew	5 8	10 09	F	28 6 73	Leeds	Trainee	**Barnsley**	83	16
LIDDLE Craig	5 11	12 03	M	21 10 71	Chester-le-Street	Blythe Spartans	**Middlesbrough**	1	—
LIGHTBOURNE Kyle	6 2	12 02	F	29 9 68	Bermuda		Scarborough	19	3
							Walsall	77	30
LIGHTFOOT Chris	6 2	13 06	M	1 4 70	Penketh	Trainee	**Chester C**	277	32

Player	Ht	Wt	Pos	Birth Date	Birth Place	Source	Clubs	League App	League Gls
LILLIS Jason †	5 11	11 10	M	1 10 69	Chatham	Trainee	Gillingham	29	3
							Maidstone U	75	18
							Carlisle U (loan)	4	1
						Sittingbourne	Walsall	25	6
							Cambridge U	19	4
LILWALL Steve *	5 11	12 00	D	5 2 70	Solihull	Kidderminster H	**WBA**	73	—
LIMBER Nick ‡	5 10	11 12	D	23 1 74	Doncaster	Trainee	Doncaster R	13	1
							Manchester C	—	—
							Peterborough U (loan)	2	—
							Doncaster R	4	—
LIMPAR Anders	5 8	11 07	F	24 9 65	Solna	Cremonese	Arsenal	96	17
							Everton	36	2
LINDSEY Scott	5 9	11 10	D	4 5 72	Walsall	Bridlington T	**Gillingham**	12	—
LING Martin	5 7	10 02	M	15 7 66	West Ham	Apprentice	Exeter C	116	14
							Swindon T	2	—
							Southend U	138	31
							Mansfield T (loan)	3	—
							Swindon T (loan)	1	—
							Swindon T	133	10
LINGER Paul	5 6	10 03	M	20 12 74	Stepney	Trainee	**Charlton Ath**	15	—
LINIGHAN Andy	6 4	13 10	D	18 6 62	Hartlepool	Smiths BC	Hartlepool U	110	4
							Leeds U	66	3
							Oldham Ath	87	6
							Norwich C	86	8
							Arsenal	89	4
LINIGHAN Brian	6 1	11 04	D	2 11 73	Hartlepool	Trainee	**Sheffield W**	1	—
LINIGHAN David	6 2	13 00	D	9 1 65	Hartlepool	Local	Hartlepool U	91	5
							Leeds U (loan)	—	—
							Derby Co	—	—
							Shrewsbury T	65	1
							Ipswich T	275	12
LINTON Des	6 1	13 02	D	5 9 71	Birmingham	Trainee	Leicester C	11	—
							Luton T	66	1
LINYARD Paul §	6 1	12 00	G	18 7 77	Keighley	Trainee	**Hartlepool U**	—	—
LITTLE Glen ‡	6 3	13 00	M	15 10 75	Wimbledon	Trainee	**Crystal Palace**	—	—
LITTLEJOHN Adrian	5 9	10 04	F	26 9 70	Wolverhampton	WBA	Walsall	44	1
							Sheffield U	69	12
LIVETT Simon *	5 10	12 07	M	8 1 69	Newham	Trainee	West Ham U	1	—
							Leyton Orient	24	—
							Cambridge U	12	—
LIVINGSTONE Richard *	5 10	11 06	F	10 4 74	Aberdeen	Trainee	**Burnley**	—	—
LIVINGSTONE Steve	6 1	11 04	F	8 9 69	Middlesbrough	Trainee	Coventry C	31	5
							Blackburn R	30	10
							Chelsea	1	—
							Port Vale (loan)	5	—
							Grimsby T	61	11
LLEWELLYN Andy ‡	5 7	11 00	D	26 2 66	Bristol	Apprentice	Bristol C	301	3
							Exeter C (loan)	15	—
							Hereford U	4	—
LLOYD Kevin	6 0	12 01	D	26 9 70	Llanidloes	Caersws	**Hereford U**	24	3
LOCK Anthony			M	3 9 76	Harlow	Trainee	**Colchester U**	3	1
LOCKE Adam	5 10	12 02	M	20 8 70	Croydon	Trainee	Crystal Palace	—	—
							Southend U	73	4
							Colchester U (loan)	4	—
							Colchester U	22	1
LOCKWOOD Matthew	5 9	10 07	M	17 10 76	Rochford	Trainee	**QPR**	—	—
LOGAN Richard	6 0	13 03	M	24 5 69	Barnsley	Gainsborough T	**Huddersfield T**	43	1
LOMAS Andrew (on loan from Stevenage)			G	26 4 65	Hartlepool		**Cambridge U**	2	—

Player	Ht	Wt	Pos	Birth Date	Birth Place	Source	Clubs	League App	League Gls
LOMAS Steve	6 0	12 08	M	18 1 74	Hanover	Trainee	**Manchester C**	43	2
LONERGAN Darren			D	28 1 74	Cork	Waterford	**Oldham Ath**	—	—
LORMOR Tony	6 0	13 06	F	29 10 70	Ashington	Trainee	Newcastle U	8	3
							Norwich C (loan)	—	—
							Lincoln C	100	30
							Peterborough U	5	—
							Chesterfield	23	10
LOSS Colin *	5 11	11 04	M	15 8 73	Brentwood	Trainee	Norwich C	—	—
							Derby Co	—	—
						Gresley R	**Bristol C**	5	—
LOVELL Stuart	5 10	11 00	M	9 1 72	Sydney	Trainee	**Reading**	151	45
LOVELOCK Andrew	5 9	10 12	F	20 12 76	Swindon	Trainee	**Coventry C**	—	—
LOWE David	5 10	11 06	F	30 8 65	Liverpool	Apprentice	Wigan Ath	188	40
							Ipswich T	134	37
							Port Vale (loan)	9	2
							Leicester C	66	19
							Port Vale (loan)	19	5
LOWE Kenny	6 1	11 04	M	6 11 64	Sedgefield	Apprentice	Hartlepool U	54	3
						Barrow	Scarborough	4	—
						Barrow	Barnet	72	5
							Stoke C	9	—
							Birmingham C	19	3
							Carlisle U (loan)	2	—
LOWNDES Nathan	5 11	10 04	F	2 6 77	Salford	Trainee	**Leeds U**	—	—
LOWTHORPE Adam	5 7	10 06	D	7 8 75	Hull	Trainee	**Hull C**	25	—
LUCAS David			G	23 11 77	Preston	Trainee	**Preston NE**	—	—
LUCAS Richard ‡	5 10	11 04	M	22 9 70	Sheffield	Trainee	Sheffield U	10	—
							Preston NE	50	—
							Lincoln C (loan)	4	—
LUCKETTI Chris	6 0	13 06	D	28 9 71	Littleborough	Trainee	Rochdale	1	—
							Stockport Co	—	—
							Halifax T	78	2
							Bury	66	4
LUDDEN Dominic	5 7	10 09	D	30 3 74	Basildon	Trainee	Leyton Orient	58	1
							Watford	1	—
LUDLAM Craig	5 10	10 04	M	8 11 76	Sheffield	Trainee	**Sheffield W**	—	—
LUDLOW Lee ‡	6 0	11 00	F	14 3 76	Newcastle	Trainee	**Notts Co**	—	—
LUKIC John	6 4	13 12	G	11 12 60	Chesterfield	Apprentice	Leeds U	146	—
							Arsenal	223	—
							Leeds U	181	—
LUND Gary	6 0	11 00	F	13 9 64	Grimsby	School	Grimsby T	60	24
							Lincoln C	44	13
							Notts Co	248	62
							Hull C (loan)	11	3
							Hull C (loan)	11	3
LYDERSEN Pal ‡	6 0	14 01	D	10 9 65	Odense	IK Start.	**Arsenal**	15	—
LYDIATE Jason	5 11	12 04	D	29 10 71	Manchester	Trainee	Manchester U	—	—
							Bolton W	30	—
							Blackpool	11	—
LYNCH Chris	5 10	11 04	F	18 11 74	Middlesbrough	Halifax T	**Hartlepool U**	31	1
LYNCH Tommy	6 0	12 06	D	10 10 64	Limerick	Limerick	Sunderland	4	—
							Shrewsbury T	209	11
LYNE Neil	6 1	12 04	F	4 4 70	Leicester	Leicester U	Nottingham F	—	—
							Walsall (loan)	7	—
							Shrewsbury T (loan)	16	6
							Shrewsbury T	64	11
							Cambridge U	17	—
							Chesterfield (loan)	6	1
							Hereford U	31	1
LYONS Andy	5 10	11 00	M	19 10 66	Blackpool	Fleetwood	Crewe Alex	11	2
							Wigan Ath	65	26

Player	Ht	Wt	Pos	Birth Date	Birth Place	Source	Clubs	League App	League Gls
LYTTLE Des	5 9	12 00	D	24 9 71	Wolverhampton	Worcester C	Swansea C	46	1
							Nottingham F	75	1
MABBUTT Gary	5 10	12 09	D	23 8 61	Bristol	Apprentice	Bristol R	131	10
							Tottenham H	433	27
McALLISTER Brian	5 11	12 05	D	30 11 70	Glasgow	Trainee	**Wimbledon**	53	—
							Plymouth Arg (loan)	8	—
McALLISTER Gary	6 1	10 11	M	25 12 64	Motherwell	Fir Park BC	Motherwell	59	6
							Leicester C	201	47
							Leeds U	195	26
McAREE Rod	5 7	10 02	D	19 8 74	Dungannon	Trainee	Liverpool	—	—
							Bristol C	6	—
MACARI Michael	5 5	10 13	F	4 2 73	Kilwinning	Trainee	West Ham U	—	—
							Stoke C	—	—
MACARI Paul	5 8	11 00	F	23 8 76	Manchester	Trainee	**Stoke C**	—	—
McATEER Jason	5 9	11 05	M	18 6 71	Birkenhead	Marine	**Bolton W**	110	8
MACAULAY Lee ‡	5 9	10 12	D	9 11 75	Harthill	Trainee	**Brighton & HA**	—	—
McAULEY Sean (on loan from St Johnstone)	6 0	11 9	D	23 6 72	Sheffield		**Chesterfield**	1	1
MACAULEY Steve	6 1	12 00	D	4 3 69	Lytham	Fleetwood	**Crewe Alex**	94	11
MACBETH Andy ‡	5 10	10 11	F	9 1 76	Bangor	Trainee	**Wolverhampton W**	—	—
McCALL Steve	5 10	12 06	M	15 10 60	Carlisle	Apprentice	Ipswich T	257	7
							Sheffield W	29	2
							Carlisle U (loan)	6	—
							Plymouth Arg	96	5
McCARTHY Alan	5 11	12 10	D	11 1 72	London	Trainee	**QPR**	11	—
							Watford (loan)	9	—
							Plymouth Arg (loan)	2	—
McCARTHY Jamie ‡	5 10	11 07	M	14 8 73	London	Trainee	**Wimbledon**	—	—
McCARTHY Jon	5 10	11 00	M	18 8 70	Middlesbrough		Hartlepool U	1	—
						Shepshed	**York C**	199	31
McCARTHY Mick	6 2	13 12	D	7 2 59	Barnsley	Apprentice	Barnsley	272	7
							Manchester C	140	2
							Celtic	48	—
						Lyon	**Millwall**	35	2
McCARTHY Paul	6 0	13 06	D	4 8 71	Cork	Trainee	**Brighton**	148	5
McCARTHY Sean	6 0	12 05	F	12 9 67	Bridgend	Bridgend	Swansea C	91	25
							Plymouth Arg	70	19
							Bradford C	131	60
							Oldham Ath	59	22
McCARTHY Tony	6 1	12 03	D	9 11 69	Dublin	Shelbourne	Millwall	21	1
							Crewe Alex (loan)	2	—
							Colchester U	10	1
McCLAIR Brian	5 10	12 09	F	8 12 63	Bellshill	Apprentice	Aston Villa	—	—
							Motherwell	39	15
							Celtic	145	99
							Manchester U	301	85
McCLUSKEY Anthony *	6 0	21 02	M	29 10 75	Hartlepool	Trainee	**Burnley**	—	—
McCREERY David *	5 6	10 07	M	16 9 57	Belfast	Apprentice	Manchester U	87	7
							QPR	57	4
						Tulsa R	Newcastle U	243	2
							Hearts	29	—
							Hartlepool U	30	—
							Carlisle U	35	—
							Hartlepool U	9	—
McCUE James	5 8	10 00	F	29 6 75	Glasgow	Trainee	**WBA**	—	—
McDERMOTT John	5 7	10 00	D	3 2 69	Middlesbrough	Trainee	**Grimsby T**	276	4
McDONALD Alan	6 2	12 07	D	12 10 63	Belfast	Apprentice	**QPR**	337	10
							Charlton Ath (loan)	9	—

Player	Ht	Wt	Pos	Birth Date	Birth Place	Source	Clubs	League App	League Gls
McDONALD Chris *			M	14 10 75	Edinburgh	Trainee	**Arsenal**	—	—
McDONALD David	5 11	11 07	D	2 1 71	Dublin	Trainee	Tottenham H	2	—
							Gillingham (loan)	10	—
							Bradford C (loan)	7	—
							Reading (loan)	11	—
							Peterborough U	29	—
							Barnet	45	—
McDONALD Neil	5 11	11 04	D	2 11 65	Wallsend	Wallsend BC	Newcastle U	180	24
							Everton	90	4
							Oldham Ath	24	1
							Bolton W	4	—
McDONALD Paul	5 6	10 00	F	20 4 68	Motherwell	Merry Street BC	Hamilton Acad	215	26
							Southampton	2	—
McDOUGALD Junior	5 11	12 06	F	12 1 75	Big Spring	Trainee	Tottenham H	—	—
							Brighton	41	10
McELHATTON Michael	6 1	12 11	D	16 4 75	Co.Kerry	Trainee	**Bournemouth**	38	2
McFARLANE Andy	6 3	13 08	F	30 11 66	Wolverhampton	Cradley T	Portsmouth	2	—
							Swansea C	55	8
McGARGLE Stephen			F	24 10 75	Gateshead	Trainee	**Middlesbrough**	—	—
McGARRIGLE Kevin	5 11	11 05	D	9 4 77	Newcastle	Trainee	**Brighton**	18	—
McGAVIN Steve	5 8	11 00	F	24 1 69	North Walsham	Sudbury	Colchester U	58	17
							Birmingham C	23	2
							Wycombe W	12	2
McGEE Paul ‡	5 6	9 10	F	17 5 68	Dublin	Bohemians	Colchester U	3	—
							Wimbledon	60	9
							Peterborough U (loan)	6	—
McGHEE David	5 10	11 04	F	19 6 76	Sussex	Trainee	**Brentford**	7	1
McGIBBON Patrick	6 2	12 11	D	6 9 73	Lurgan	Portadown	**Manchester U**	—	—
McGINLAY John	5 9	11 04	F	8 4 64	Inverness	Elgin C	Shrewsbury T	60	27
							Bury	25	9
							Millwall	34	10
							Bolton W	110	57
McGLASHAN John	6 1	12 00	F	3 6 67	Dundee	Dundee Violet	Montrose	68	11
							Millwall	16	—
							Cambridge U (loan)	1	—
							Fulham (loan)	5	1
							Peterborough U	46	3
							Rotherham U	27	3
McGLEISH Scott *	5 9	10 08	F	10 2 74	London	Edgware T	**Charlton Ath**	6	—
							Leyton Orient (loan)	6	1
McGOLDRICK Eddie	5 10	11 07	F	30 4 65	London	Kettering T	Northampton T	107	9
							Crystal Palace	147	11
							Arsenal	37	—
McGORRY Brian	5 10	12 08	M	16 4 70	Liverpool	Weymouth	Bournemouth	61	11
							Peterborough U	52	6
McGOWAN Gavin	5 11	12 03	M	16 1 76	Blackheath	Trainee	**Arsenal**	3	—
McGRATH Lloyd	5 5	11 06	M	24 2 65	Birmingham	Apprentice	Coventry C	214	4
							Portsmouth	18	—
McGRATH Paul	6 2	14 00	D	4 12 59	Greenford	St Patrick's Ath	Manchester U	163	12
							Aston Villa	223	7
McGREAL John	5 11	10 11	D	2 6 72	Birkenhead	Trainee	**Tranmere R**	61	1
McGREGOR Mark §	5 10	10 05	D	16 2 77	Chester	Trainee	**Wrexham**	1	—
McGREGOR Paul	5 10	10 04	F	17 12 74	Liverpool	Trainee	**Nottingham F**	11	1
McGUCKIN Ian	6 2	14 02	D	24 4 73	Middlesbrough	Trainee	**Hartlepool U**	90	6
McHUGH Michael *	5 9	11 07	F	3 4 71	Donegal		Bradford C	31	4
							Scarborough	3	—
McKAY Andrew	5 10	11 10	D	16 1 75	Bolton	Trainee	**Bolton W**	—	—

Player	Ht	Wt	Pos	Birth Date	Birth Place	Source	Clubs	League App	League Gls
McKEARNEY Dave *	5 10	11 02	M	20 6 68	Crosby	Prescot Cables	Bolton W	—	—
							Crewe Alex	108	12
							Wigan Ath	49	9
MacKENZIE Chris	6 0	12 06	G	14 5 72	Northampton	Corby T	**Hereford U**	22	—
McKINLAY David ‡	6 3	13 11	D	20 11 75	Kinross	Trainee	Middlesbrough	—	—
							Bradford C	—	—
McKOP Henry	5 11	12 00	D	8 7 67	Zimbabwe	Bonner SC	**Bristol C**	5	—
McLAREN Paul	6 0	12 06	D	17 11 76	Wycombe	Trainee	**Luton T**	1	—
MacLAREN Ross	5 10	12 12	M	14 4 62	Edinburgh	Glasgow Rangers	Shrewsbury T	161	18
							Derby Co	122	4
							Swindon T	197	9
McLEAN Ian	6 2	13 02	D	13 8 66	Paisley	Metroford	**Bristol R**	28	2
							Cardiff C (loan)	4	—
McLEARY Alan *	5 10	10 09	D	6 10 64	Lambeth	Apprentice	Millwall	307	5
							Sheffield U (loan)	3	—
							Wimbledon (loan)	4	—
							Charlton Ath	66	3
McLOUGHLIN Alan	5 8	10 02	M	20 4 67	Manchester	Local	Manchester U	—	—
							Swindon T	9	—
							Torquay U	24	4
							Swindon T	97	19
							Southampton	24	1
							Aston Villa (loan)	—	—
							Portsmouth	136	23
McMAHON Gerard	5 11	11 00	F	29 12 73	Belfast	Glenavon	**Tottenham H**	2	—
							Barnet (loan)	10	2
McMAHON Sam	5 9	11 02	M	10 2 76	Newark	Trainee	**Leicester C**	1	—
McMAHON Steve	5 9	11 08	M	20 8 61	Liverpool	Apprentice	Everton	100	11
							Aston Villa	75	7
							Liverpool	204	29
							Manchester C	87	1
							Swindon T	17	—
McMANAMAN Steve	6 0	10 06	F	11 2 72	Liverpool	School	**Liverpool**	133	18
McMILLAN Andy	5 11	11 09	D	22 6 68	Bloemfontein		**York C**	266	3
McMINN Ted	6 0	13 08	F	28 9 62	Castle Douglas	Glenafton Athletic	Queen of the S	62	5
							Rangers	63	4
						Seville	Derby Co	123	9
							Birmingham C	22	—
							Burnley	36	3
McNALLY Bernard *	5 7	10 12	M	17 2 63	Shrewsbury	Apprentice	Shrewsbury T	282	23
							WBA	156	10
McNAMARA Brett *			F	8 7 72	Newark	Stamford	**Northampton T**	1	—
McNIVEN Scott §			D	27 5 78	Leeds	Trainee	**Oldham Ath**	1	—
MacPHAIL John ‡	6 0	12 03	D	7 12 55	Dundee	St. Columba's	Dundee	68	—
							Sheffield U	135	7
							York C	142	24
							Bristol C	26	1
							Sunderland	130	22
							Hartlepool U	163	4
McPHERSON Keith	5 11	11 00	D	11 9 63	Greenwich	Apprentice	West Ham U	1	—
							Cambridge U (loan)	11	1
							Northampton T	182	8
							Reading	177	6
McPHERSON Malcolm	5 10	12 00	F	9 12 74	Glasgow	Yeovil	**West Ham U**	—	—
McROBERT Lee	5 8	10 12	M	4 10 72	Bromley	Sittingbourne	**Millwall**	7	1
McSWEGAN Gary	5 7	10 09	F	24 9 70	Glasgow	Amateur BC	Rangers	18	4
							Notts Co	59	21

Player	Ht	Wt	Pos	Birth Date	Birth Place	Source	Clubs	League App	League Gls
MADDEN Lawrie	5 10	13 00	D	28 9 55	Hackney	Arsenal	Mansfield T	10	—
						Manchester Univ	Charlton Ath	113	7
							Millwall	47	2
							Sheffield W	212	2
							Leicester C (loan)	3	—
							Wolverhampton W	67	1
							Darlington	5	—
							Chesterfield	36	1
MADDISON Lee	5 11	11 00	D	5 10 72	Bristol	Trainee	**Bristol R**	73	—
MADDISON Neil	5 10	11 02	M	2 10 69	Darlington	Trainee	**Southampton**	130	16
MADDIX Danny	5 10	11 07	D	11 10 67	Ashford	Apprentice	Tottenham H	—	—
							Southend U (loan)	2	—
							QPR	166	7
MAGEE Kevin *	5 10	11 03	F	10 4 71	Edinburgh	Armadale Th	Partick T	11	—
							Preston NE	21	1
MAGILTON Jim	6 1	13 12	M	6 5 69	Belfast	Apprentice	Liverpool	—	—
							Oxford U	150	34
							Southampton	57	6
MAGUIRE Gavin	5 10	11 08	M	24 11 67	Hammersmith	Apprentice	QPR	40	—
							Portsmouth	91	—
							Newcastle U (loan)	3	—
							Millwall	12	—
							Scarborough (loan)	2	—
MAHON Alan	5 7	10 00	M	4 4 78	Dublin	Tranmere R	**Tranmere R**	—	—
MAHONEY-JOHNSON Michael	5 10	11 00	F	6 11 76	Paddington	Trainee	**QPR**	—	—
MAHORN Paul	5 10	11 06	F	13 8 73	Whipps Cross	Trainee	**Tottenham H**	1	—
							Fulham (loan)	3	—
MAIL David *	5 11	11 11	D	12 9 62	Bristol	Apprentice	Aston Villa	—	—
							Blackburn R	206	4
							Hull C	150	2
MAKEL Lee	5 11	11 07	M	11 1 73	Sunderland	Trainee	Newcastle U	12	1
							Blackburn R	3	—
MAKIN Chris	5 11	11 00	D	8 5 73	Manchester	Trainee	**Oldham Ath**	55	2
							Wigan Ath (loan)	15	2
MALKIN Chris	6 3	12 00	F	4 6 67	Bebington	Overpool	**Tranmere R**	232	60
MALONE Chris	5 8	10 07	F	29 12 75	Drogheda		**Blackburn R**	—	—
MANN Neil	5 10	12 01	M	19 11 72	Nottingham	Grantham T	**Hull C**	36	2
MANUEL Billy †	5 5	10 00	D	28 6 69	Hackney	Apprentice	Tottenham H	—	—
							Gillingham	87	5
							Brentford	94	1
							Cambridge U	10	—
							Peterborough U	14	1
MARDENBOROUGH Steve ‡	5 8	11 09	F	11 9 64	Birmingham	Apprentice	Coventry C	—	—
							Wolverhampton W	9	1
							Cambridge U (loan)	6	—
							Swansea C	36	7
							Newport Co	64	11
							Cardiff C	32	1
							Hereford U	27	—
							Darlington	106	18
							Lincoln C	21	2
							Scarborough	1	—
MARDON Paul	6 0	11 10	D	14 9 69	Bristol	Trainee	Bristol C	42	—
							Doncaster R (loan)	3	—
							Birmingham C	64	—
							WBA	50	2
MARGETSON Martyn	6 0	13 10	G	8 9 71	West Neath	Trainee	**Manchester C**	6	—
							Bristol R (loan)	3	—
							Bolton W (loan)	—	—
							Luton T (loan)	—	—
MARGINSON Karl *	6 0	11 11	M	11 11 70	Manchester	Ashton U	**Rotherham U**	15	1

Player	Ht	Wt	Pos	Birth Date	Birth Place	Source	Clubs	League App	League Gls
MARKER Nick	6 1	13 00	D	3 5 65	Exeter	Apprentice	Exeter C	202	3
							Plymouth Arg	202	13
							Blackburn R	38	—
MARKS Jamie	5 9	10 13	D	18 3 77	Belfast	Trainee	**Leeds U**	—	—
MARPLES Chris *	5 11	13 06	G	3 8 64	Chesterfield	Goole	Chesterfield	84	—
							Stockport Co	57	—
							York C	138	—
							Scunthorpe U (loan)	1	—
							Chesterfield	57	—
MARQUIS Paul	6 2	14 04	D	29 8 72	Enfield	Trainee	West Ham U	1	—
							Doncaster R	11	—
MARRIOTT Andy	6 0	12 05	G	11 10 70	Nottingham	Trainee	Arsenal	—	—
							Nottingham F	11	—
							WBA (loan)	3	—
							Blackburn R (loan)	2	—
							Colchester U (loan)	10	—
							Burnley (loan)	15	—
							Wrexham	82	—
MARSDEN Chris	5 11	10 12	M	3 1 69	Sheffield	Trainee	Sheffield U	16	1
							Huddersfield T	121	9
							Coventry C (loan)	7	—
							Wolverhampton W	8	—
							Notts Co	7	—
MARSH Chris	6 0	13 02	M	14 1 70	Dudley	Trainee	**Walsall**	195	19
MARSH Mike	5 8	11 00	F	21 7 69	Liverpool	Kirkby T	Liverpool	69	2
							West Ham U	49	1
							Coventry C	15	2
MARSH Simon			D	29 1 77	Ealing	Trainee	**Oxford U**	8	—
MARSHALL Andy	6 2	13 07	G	14 4 75	Bury	Trainee	**Norwich C**	21	—
MARSHALL Daniel *	5 10	11 05	D	18 12 75	Newark	Notts Co	**Chesterfield**	1	—
MARSHALL Dwight	5 7	10 10	F	3 10 65	Jamaica	Grays Ath	Plymouth Arg	99	27
							Middlesbrough (loan)	3	—
							Luton T	45	11
MARSHALL Ian	6 1	12 12	F	20 3 66	Liverpool	Apprentice	Everton	15	1
							Oldham Ath	170	36
							Ipswich T	47	13
MARSHALL John	5 10	12 06	M	18 8 64	Surrey	Apprentice	**Fulham**	395	28
MARSHALL Lee	5 9	9 12	F	1 8 75	Nottingham	Trainee	Nottingham F	—	—
						Grantham	**Stockport Co**	1	—
MARSHALL Scott	6 1	12 05	D	1 5 73	Edinburgh	Trainee	**Arsenal**	2	—
							Rotherham U (loan)	10	1
							Oxford U (loan)	—	—
							Sheffield U (loan)	17	—
MARSTON Marvin	6 5	14 00	D	27 8 76	London	Notts Co	**Sheffield U**	—	—
MARTIN Alvin	6 1	13 07	D	29 7 58	Bootle	Apprentice	**West Ham U**	455	27
MARTIN David	6 1	13 01	M	25 4 63	East Ham	Apprentice	Millwall	140	6
							Wimbledon	35	3
							Southend U	221	19
							Bristol C	38	1
							Northampton T (loan)	7	1
MARTIN Dean ‡	5 11	11 09	M	9 9 67	Halifax	Apprentice	Halifax T	153	7
							Scunthorpe U	106	7
							Rochdale	15	—
MARTIN Eliot	5 6	10 00	D	27 9 72	Plumstead	Trainee	**Gillingham**	60	1
MARTIN Jae *	5 9	11 00	F	5 2 76	London	Trainee	**Southend U**	8	—
							Leyton Orient (loan)	4	—
MARTIN Kevin §			G	22 6 76	Bromsgrove	Trainee	**Scarborough**	3	—
MARTIN Lee	6 0	13 00	G	9 9 68	Huddersfield	Trainee	Huddersfield T	54	—
							Blackpool	98	—
MARTINDALE Dave ‡	5 11	11 10	M	9 4 64	Liverpool	Caernarfon	Tranmere R	166	9
							Doncaster R	—	—

Player	Ht	Wt	Pos	Birth Date	Birth Place	Source	Clubs	League App	League Gls
MARTINDALE Gary *	5 11	11 09	F	24 6 71	Liverpool	Burscough	**Bolton W**	—	—
MARTYN Nigel	6 2	14 07	G	11 8 66	St Austell	St Blazey	Bristol R	101	—
							Crystal Palace	226	—
MASINGA Phil	6 1	12 07	F	28 6 69	South Africa	Mamelodi Sundowns	**Leeds U**	22	5
MASKELL Craig	5 10	11 11	F	10 4 68	Aldershot	Apprentice	Southampton	6	1
							Swindon T (loan)	—	—
							Huddersfield T	87	43
							Reading	72	26
							Swindon T	47	22
							Southampton	16	1
MASON Andrew *	5 11	11 08	F	22 11 74	Bolton	Trainee	**Bolton W**	—	—
MASON Paul	5 9	12 01	M	3 9 63	Liverpool	Groningen	Aberdeen	158	27
							Ipswich T	43	6
MASON Richard	5 9	10 02	D	5 6 77	Sheffield	Trainee	**Sheffield W**	—	—
MASSEY Stuart	5 10	10 10	M	17 11 64	Crawley	Sutton U	Crystal Palace	2	—
							Oxford U	22	—
MASTERS Neil	6 1	10 12	D	25 5 72	Lisburn	Trainee	Bournemouth	38	2
							Wolverhampton W	9	—
MATHIE Alex	5 10	10 07	F	20 12 68	Bathgate	Celtic BC	Celtic	11	—
							Morton	74	31
							Port Vale (loan)	3	—
							Newcastle U	25	4
							Ipswich T	13	2
MATTEO Dominic	6 1	11 10	D	24 4 74	Dumfries	Trainee	**Liverpool**	18	—
							Sunderland (loan)	1	—
MATTHEW Damian	5 11	10 10	M	23 9 70	Islington	Trainee	Chelsea	21	—
							Luton T (loan)	5	—
							Crystal Palace	16	1
MATTHEWS Martin *	5 10	11 03	D	22 12 75	Peterborough	Trainee	**Derby Co**	—	—
MATTHEWS Neil *	6 0	12 12	F	19 9 66	Grimsby	Apprentice	Grimsby T	11	1
							Scunthorpe U (loan)	1	—
							Halifax T (loan)	9	2
							Bolton W (loan)	1	—
							Halifax T	105	29
							Stockport Co	43	15
							Halifax T (loan)	3	—
							Lincoln C	83	20
							Bury (loan)	2	1
MATTHEWS Neil ‡	6 0	11 07	D	3 12 67	Manchester	Apprentice	Blackpool	76	1
							Cardiff C	66	2
							Rochdale	19	—
MATTHEWS Rob	6 0	12 05	F	14 10 70	Slough	Loughborough Univ	Notts Co	43	11
							Luton T	11	—
MATTHEWSON Trevor	6 4	13 06	D	12 2 63	Sheffield	Apprentice	Sheffield W	3	—
							Newport Co	75	—
							Stockport Co	80	—
							Lincoln C	83	8
							Birmingham C	168	12
							Preston NE	12	1
							Bury	18	—
MATTISON Paul	5 8	11 04	M	24 4 73	Wakefield	North Ferriby U	**Darlington**	10	—
MAUGE Ron	5 10	11 10	M	10 3 69	Islington	Trainee	Charlton Ath	—	—
							Fulham	50	2
							Bury	108	10
							Manchester C (loan)	—	—
MAXFIELD Scott	5 8	10 07	D	13 7 76	Doncaster	Trainee	**Doncaster R**	10	—
MAY Andy *	5 8	11 10	M	26 2 64	Bury	Apprentice	Manchester C	150	8
							Huddersfield T	114	5
							Bolton W (loan)	10	2
							Bristol C	90	4
							Millwall	54	1

Player	Ht	Wt	Pos	Birth Date	Birth Place	Source	Clubs	League App	League Gls
MAY David	6 0	12 06	D	24 6 70	Oldham	Trainee	Blackburn R	123	3
							Manchester U	19	2
MEADE Raphael ‡	5 10	11 09	F	22 11 62	Islington	Apprentice	Arsenal	41	14
						Sporting Lisbon	Dundee U	11	4
							Luton T	4	—
							Ipswich T	1	—
						Odense	Plymouth Arg	5	—
							Brighton & HA	40	9
						Dover Ath	**Brighton & HA**	3	—
MEAKER Michael	5 11	11 05	M	18 8 71	Greenford	Trainee	**QPR**	34	1
							Plymouth Arg (loan)	4	—
MEAN Scott	5 11	11 11	M	13 12 73	Crawley	Trainee	**Bournemouth**	60	7
MEARA Jim	5 9	11 02	M	7 10 72	London	Trainee	Watford	2	—
							Doncaster R	15	1
MEASHAM Ian	5 11	11 09	D	14 12 64	Barnsley	Apprentice	Huddersfield T	17	—
							Lincoln C (loan)	6	—
							Rochdale (loan)	12	—
							Cambridge U	46	—
							Burnley	182	2
							Doncaster R	22	—
MEGSON Gary *	5 10	12 00	M	2 5 59	Manchester	Apprentice	Plymouth Arg	78	10
							Everton	22	2
							Sheffield W	123	13
							Nottingham F	—	—
							Newcastle U	24	1
							Sheffield W	110	12
							Manchester C	82	2
							Norwich C	46	1
MEHEW David *	5 10	12 06	M	29 10 67	Camberley	Trainee	Leeds U	—	—
							Bristol R	222	63
							Exeter C (loan)	7	—
							Walsall	13	—
MELLON Michael	5 9	11 03	M	18 3 72	Paisley	Trainee	Bristol C	35	1
							WBA	45	6
							Blackpool	26	4
MELVILLE Andy	6 0	13 03	D	29 11 68	Swansea	School	Swansea C	175	22
							Oxford U	135	13
							Sunderland	80	5
MENDONCA Clive	5 10	10 07	F	9 9 68	Tullington	Apprentice	Sheffield U	13	4
							Doncaster R (loan)	2	—
							Rotherham U	84	27
							Sheffield U	10	1
							Grimsby T (loan)	10	3
							Grimsby T	103	35
MENDUM Craig ‡	5 9	10 08	F	13 4 77	Saltburn	Trainee	**Nottingham F**	—	—
MERCER Billy	6 1	13 07	G	22 5 69	Liverpool	Trainee	Liverpool	—	—
							Rotherham U	104	—
							Sheffield U	3	—
							Nottingham F (loan)	—	—
MEROLA Tony *	5 7	10 07	F	5 10 75	Wrexham	Trainee	**Wrexham**	—	—
MERSON Paul	6 0	13 02	F	20 3 68	London	Apprentice	**Arsenal**	257	67
							Brentford (loan)	7	—
MEYER Adrian	6 0	14 00	D	22 9 70	Bristol	Trainee	**Scarborough**	114	9
MICKLEWHITE Gary	5 7	10 04	M	21 3 61	Southwark	Apprentice	Manchester U	—	—
							QPR	106	11
							Derby Co	240	31
							Gillingham	64	3
MIDDLEMASS Scott *	6 3	12 04	D	17 5 72	Worksop	Morecambe	**Northampton T**	—	—
MIDDLETON Craig	5 9	11 00	M	10 9 70	Nuneaton	Trainee	Coventry C	3	—
							Cambridge U	19	2
MIDDLETON Lee	5 9	11 09	M	10 9 70	Nuneaton	Trainee	Coventry C	2	—
							Swindon T	—	—
MIDDLETON Matthew ‡			D	22 1 75	Lambeth	Trainee	**Millwall**	—	—

Player	Ht	Wt	Pos	Birth Date	Birth Place	Source	Clubs	League App	League Gls
MIDGLEY Craig §			F	24 5 76	Bradford	Trainee	**Bradford C**	3	—
MIDWOOD Michael *			F	19 4 76	Huddersfield	Trainee	**Huddersfield T**	—	—
MIKE Adie	6 0	11 06	F	16 11 73	Manchester	Trainee	**Manchester C**	16	2
							Bury (loan)	7	1
MIKLOSKO Ludek	6 5	14 00	G	9 12 61	Ostrava	Banik Ostrava	**West Ham U**	230	—
MILES Ben	6 1	11 07	G	13 4 76	Middlesex	Trainee	**Swansea C**	—	—
MILLAR Paul	6 2	12 07	F	16 11 66	Belfast	Portadown	Port Vale	40	5
							Hereford U (loan)	5	2
							Cardiff C	120	17
MILLEN Keith	6 2	12 04	D	26 9 66	Croydon	Juniors	Brentford	305	17
							Watford	41	1
MILLER Allan	6 3	14 08	G	29 3 70	Epping	Trainee	Arsenal	8	—
							Plymouth Arg (loan)	13	—
							WBA (loan)	3	—
							Birmingham C (loan)	15	—
							Middlesbrough	41	—
MILLER David	5 11	11 12	M	8 1 64	Burnley	Apprentice	Burnley	32	3
							Crewe Alex (loan)	3	—
							Tranmere R	29	1
							Preston NE	58	2
							Burnley (loan)	4	—
							Carlisle U	109	7
							Stockport Co	81	1
							Wigan Ath	31	3
MILLER Kevin	6 1	13 00	G	15 3 69	Falmouth	Newquay	Exeter C	163	—
							Birmingham C	24	—
							Watford	44	—
MILLER Paul	6 0	11 00	F	31 1 68	Bisley	Trainee	Wimbledon	80	10
							Newport Co (loan)	6	2
							Bristol C (loan)	3	—
							Bristol R	42	16
MILLETT Michael			D	22 9 77	Wigan	Trainee	**Wigan Ath**	3	—
MILLIGAN Mike	5 8	11 00	M	20 2 67	Manchester	Trainee	Oldham Ath	162	17
							Everton	17	1
							Oldham Ath	117	6
							Norwich C	26	2
MILLS Danny ‡	6 0	10 05	M	13 2 75	Sidcup	Trainee	**Charlton Ath**	—	—
MILLS Danny	5 11	11 09	D	18 5 77	Norwich	Trainee	**Norwich C**	—	—
MILLS Gary	5 10	11 10	M	11 11 61	Northampton	Apprentice	Nottingham F	58	8
						Seattle S	Derby Co	18	1
						Seattle S	Nottingham F	79	4
							Notts Co	75	8
							Leicester C	200	15
							Notts Co	34	—
MILLS Lee	6 1	12 11	F	10 7 70	Mexborough	Stocksbridge	Wolverhampton W	25	2
							Derby Co	16	7
MILNER Andy	6 0	11 00	F	10 2 67	Kendal	Netherfield	Manchester C	—	—
							Rochdale	127	25
							Chester C	36	8
MILSOM Paul ‡	6 1	13 03	F	5 10 74	Bristol	Trainee	Bristol C	3	—
							Cardiff C	3	—
MILTON Simon	5 10	11 05	M	23 8 63	Fulham	Bury St Edmunds	**Ipswich T**	201	39
							Exeter C (loan)	2	3
							Torquay U (loan)	4	1
MIMMS Bobby	6 2	12 13	G	12 10 63	York	Halifax T	Rotherham U	83	—
							Everton	29	—
							Notts Co (loan)	2	—
							Sunderland (loan)	4	—
							Blackburn R (loan)	6	—
							Manchester C (loan)	3	—
							Tottenham H	37	—
							Aberdeen (loan)	6	—
							Blackburn R	126	—

Player	Ht	Wt	Pos	Birth Date	Birth Place	Source	Clubs	League App	League Gls
MINETT Jason *	5 10	10 02	M	12 8 71	Peterborough	Trainee	Norwich C	3	—
							Exeter C (loan)	12	—
							Exeter C	76	3
MINTO Scott	5 10	10 00	D	6 8 71	Cheshire	Trainee	Charlton Ath	180	7
							Chelsea	19	—
MINTON Jeffrey	5 6	11 10	M	28 12 73	Hackney	Trainee	Tottenham H	2	1
							Brighton	39	5
MIOTTO Simon ‡			G	5 9 69	Australia	Riverside Olympic	**Blackpool**	—	—
MISON Michael	6 3	13 09	M	8 11 75	London	Trainee	**Fulham**	28	1
MITCHELL Andrew	5 10	11 06	D	12 9 76	Rotherham	Trainee	**Aston Villa**	—	—
MITCHELL Brian *	6 1	13 01	D	30 7 63	Stonehaven	King St	Aberdeen	65	1
							Bradford C	178	9
							Bristol C	16	—
							Hull C	9	—
MITCHELL David ‡	6 1	12 07	F	13 6 62	Glasgow		Rangers	26	6
						Feyenoord	Chelsea	7	—
							Newcastle U (loan)	2	1
							Swindon T	68	16
						Altay Izmir	**Millwall**	55	15
MITCHELL Graham	6 0	11 05	D	16 2 68	Shipley	Apprentice	Huddersfield T	244	2
							Bradford C	26	—
MITCHELL Neil	5 6	10 00	M	7 11 74	Lytham	Trainee	**Blackpool**	67	8
MITCHELL Paul	5 10	12 00	D	20 10 71	Bournemouth	Trainee	Bournemouth	16	—
							West Ham U	1	—
MOCKLER Paul *	6 0	12 13	M	13 2 76	Stockton	Trainee	**York C**	—	—
MOHAN Nicky	6 1	13 01	D	6 10 70	Middlesbrough	Trainee	Middlesbrough	99	4
							Hull C (loan)	5	1
							Leicester C	23	—
MOLBY Jan	6 1	14 07	M	4 7 63	Kolding	Ajax	**Liverpool**	218	44
MONCUR John	5 7	9 10	M	22 9 66	Stepney	Apprentice	Tottenham H	21	1
							Cambridge U (loan)	4	—
							Doncaster R (loan)	4	—
							Portsmouth (loan)	7	—
							Brentford (loan)	5	1
							Ipswich T (loan)	6	—
							Nottingham F (loan)	—	—
							Swindon T	58	5
							West Ham U	30	2
MONINGTON Mark	6 1	14 00	D	21 10 70	Bilsthorpe	Schoolboy	Burnley	84	5
							Rotherham U	25	2
MONKOU Kenneth	6 3	14 04	D	29 11 64	Surinam	Feyenoord	Chelsea	94	2
							Southampton	99	6
MOODY Jimmy	5 10	11 02	D	16 11 77	Hull	Trainee	**Leeds U**	—	—
MOODY Paul	6 3	14 03	F	13 6 67	Portsmouth	Waterlooville	Southampton	12	—
							Reading (loan)	5	1
							Oxford U	56	28
MOONEY Tommy	5 11	12 06	F	11 8 71	Teesside North	Trainee	Aston Villa	—	—
							Scarborough	107	30
							Southend U	14	5
							Watford (loan)	10	2
							Watford	29	3
MOORE Alan	5 9	10 08	F	25 11 74	Dublin	Rivermount	**Middlesbrough**	81	14
MOORE Darren	6 2	15 06	D	22 4 74	Birmingham	Trainee	**Torquay U**	103	8
MOORE David			M	23 11 76	Birmingham	Trainee	**Aston Villa**	—	—
MOORE Ian	5 11	12 00	F	26 8 76	Birkenhead	Trainee	**Tranmere R**	1	—

Player	Ht	Wt	Pos	Birth Date	Birth Place	Source	Clubs	League App	League Gls
MOORE Kevin	5 11	13 02	D	29 4 58	Grimsby	Local	Grimsby T	400	27
							Oldham Ath	13	1
							Southampton	148	10
							Bristol R (loan)	7	—
							Bristol R (loan)	4	1
							Fulham	31	3
MOORE Mike ‡	5 10	11 01	F	7 10 73	Derby	Derby Co	**Swansea C**	1	—
MOORE Neil	6 0	12 00	D	21 9 72	Liverpool	Trainee	**Everton**	5	—
							Blackpool (loan)	7	—
							Oldham Ath (loan)	5	—
MOORE Richard	6 1	12 07	G	2 9 77	Scunthorpe	Trainee	**Everton**	—	—
MORAH Ollie	5 11	13 02	F	3 9 72	Islington	Trainee	Tottenham H	—	—
							Hereford U (loan)	2	—
							Swindon T	—	—
						Sutton U	**Cambridge U**	14	2
							Torquay U (loan)	2	—
MORALEE Jamie	5 11	11 00	F	2 12 71	Wandsworth	Trainee	Crystal Palace	6	—
							Millwall	67	19
							Watford	24	4
MORAN Paul	5 8	11 12	F	22 5 68	Enfield	Trainee	Tottenham H	36	2
							Portsmouth (loan)	3	—
							Leicester C (loan)	10	1
							Newcastle U (loan)	1	—
							Southend U (loan)	1	—
							Cambridge U (loan)	—	—
							Peterborough U	7	—
MORAN Steve *	5 8	11 00	F	10 1 61	Croydon	Amateur	Southampton	180	78
							Leicester C	43	14
							Reading	116	30
							Exeter C	57	27
							Hull C	17	5
MORENO Jaime	5 9	11 09	F	19 1 74	Bolivia	Blooming	**Middlesbrough**	14	1
MORGAN Alan	5 9	10 12	D	2 11 73	Aberystwyth	Trainee	**Tranmere R**	—	—
MORGAN Ian	6 2	12 10	D	11 10 77	Birmingham	Trainee	**Nottingham F**	—	—
MORGAN Jamie *	5 11	11 09	M	1 10 75	Plymouth	Trainee	**Plymouth Arg**	11	—
MORGAN Philip *	6 1	13 00	G	18 12 74	Stoke	Trainee	**Ipswich T**	1	—
MORGAN Simon	5 10	11 13	M	5 9 66	Birmingham	Trainee	Leicester C	160	3
							Fulham	186	28
MORGAN Steve	5 11	13 00	D	19 9 68	Oldham	Apprentice	Blackpool	144	10
							Plymouth Arg	121	6
							Coventry C	68	2
MORGAN Steve ‡	5 8	10 05	F	27 7 76	Wrexham	Trainee	**Wrexham**	—	—
MORGAN Thomas			M	30 3 77	Dublin	Trainee	**Blackburn R**	—	—
MORGAN Trevor ‡	6 2	13 04	F	30 9 56	Forest Gate	Leytonstone	Bournemouth	53	13
							Mansfield T	12	6
							Bournemouth	88	33
							Bristol C	32	8
							Exeter C	30	9
							Bristol R	55	24
							Bristol C	19	8
							Bolton W	77	17
							Colchester U	32	12
							Exeter C	17	3
						Hong Kong	Birmingham C	1	—
							Exeter C	9	1
MORLEY Trevor ‡	5 11	12 01	F	20 3 61	Nottingham	Nuneaton	Northampton T	107	39
							Manchester C	72	18
							West Ham U	178	57
MORRIS Andy	6 5	15 05	F	17 11 67	Sheffield		Rotherham U	7	—
							Chesterfield	218	46
							Exeter C (loan)	7	2
MORRIS Chris	5 11	11 11	D	24 12 63	Newquay		Sheffield W	74	1
							Celtic	163	8
							Middlesbrough	55	1

Player	Ht	Wt	Pos	Birth Date	Birth Place	Source	Clubs	League App	League Gls
MORRIS John *			D	12 12 75	Stone	Trainee	**Port Vale**	—	—
MORRIS Mark	6 1	13 08	D	26 9 62	Morden	Apprentice	Wimbledon	168	9
							Aldershot (loan)	14	—
							Watford	41	1
							Sheffield U	56	3
							Bournemouth	162	7
MORRIS Steve	5 10	11 01	F	13 5 76	Liverpool	Liverpool	**Wrexham**	12	2
MORRISON Andy	5 11	13 10	D	30 7 70	Inverness	Trainee	Plymouth Arg	113	6
							Blackburn R	5	—
							Blackpool	18	—
MORRISON David	5 11	12 05	F	30 11 74	Waltham Forest	Chelmsford C	**Peterborough U**	42	8
MORRISSEY John	5 8	11 09	F	8 3 65	Liverpool	Apprentice	Everton	1	—
							Wolverhampton W	10	1
							Tranmere R	362	47
MORROW Steve	5 11	12 02	D	2 7 70	Belfast	Trainee	**Arsenal**	44	1
							Reading (loan)	10	—
							Watford (loan)	8	—
							Reading (loan)	3	—
							Barnet (loan)	1	—
MORTIMER Paul	5 11	11 03	M	8 5 68	Kensington	Fulham	Charlton Ath	113	17
							Aston Villa	12	1
							Crystal Palace	22	2
							Brentford (loan)	6	—
							Charlton Ath	26	4
MORTLEY Peter ‡	6 0	12 00	D	17 10 75	Gravesend	Trainee	**Ipswich T**	—	—
MORTON Neil ‡	5 9	10 07	F	21 12 68	Congleton	Trainee	Crewe Alex	31	1
						Northwich Vic	Chester C	95	13
							Wigan Ath	48	5
MOSES Adrian	6 1	12 08	D	4 5 75	Doncaster	School	**Barnsley**	4	—
MOSS David	6 0	13 07	F	15 11 68	Doncaster	Boston U	Doncaster R	18	5
							Chesterfield	58	16
MOSS Neil	6 1	12 11	G	10 5 75	New Milton	Trainee	**Bournemouth**	15	—
MOULDEN Paul *	5 8	11 03	F	6 9 67	Farnworth	Apprentice	Manchester C	64	18
							Bournemouth	32	13
							Oldham Ath	38	4
							Brighton (loan)	11	5
							Birmingham C	20	6
							Huddersfield T	2	—
MOUNTFIELD Derek	6 1	13 04	D	2 11 62	Liverpool	Apprentice	Tranmere R	26	1
							Everton	106	19
							Aston Villa	90	9
							Wolverhampton W	83	4
							Carlisle U	31	3
MOUSSADDIK Chuck †	5 11	13 01	G	23 2 70	Morocco	Wimbledon	**Wycombe W**	—	—
MOYES David	6 1	12 10	D	25 4 63	Glasgow	Drumchapel A	Celtic	24	—
							Cambridge U	79	1
							Bristol C	83	6
							Shrewsbury T	96	11
							Dunfermline Ath	105	13
							Hamilton A	5	—
							Preston NE	67	8
MUDD Paul *	5 9	11 04	D	13 11 70	Hull	Trainee	Hull C	1	—
							Scarborough	98	2
							Scunthorpe U	68	4
MUGGLETON Carl	6 2	13 04	G	13 9 68	Leicester	Apprentice	Leicester C	46	—
							Chesterfield (loan)	17	—
							Blackpool (loan)	2	—
							Hartlepool U (loan)	8	—
							Stockport Co (loan)	4	—
							Liverpool (loan)	—	—
							Stoke C (loan)	6	—
							Sheffield U (loan)	—	—
							Celtic	12	—
							Stoke C	24	—

Player	Ht	Wt	Pos	Birth Date	Birth Place	Source	Clubs	League App	League Gls
MUIR Ian	5 8	11 00	F	5 5 63	Coventry	Apprentice	QPR	2	2
							Burnley (loan)	2	1
							Birmingham C	1	—
							Brighton	4	—
							Swindon T (loan)	2	—
							Tranmere R	314	141
MULLIGAN James	5 6	11 07	F	21 4 74	Dublin	Trainee	Stoke C	—	—
							Bury (loan)	3	1
							Bury	15	2
MULLIN John	6 0	11 08	F	11 8 75	Bury	School	**Burnley**	18	2
MULRYNE Philip			M	1 1 78	Belfast	Trainee	**Manchester U**	—	—
MUNDAY Stuart	5 11	10 09	D	28 9 72	Newham	Trainee	**Brighton**	86	4
MUNDEE Denny	5 10	11 07	F	10 10 68	Swindon	Apprentice	QPR	—	—
							Swindon T	—	—
							Bournemouth	100	6
							Torquay U (loan)	9	—
							Brentford	78	16
MUNGALL Steve	5 8	11 05	D	22 5 58	Bellshill		Motherwell	20	—
							Tranmere R	506	13
MUNRO Stuart	5 8	10 05	D	15 9 62	Falkirk	Bo'ness U	St Mirren	1	—
							Alloa	60	6
							Rangers	179	3
							Blackburn R	1	—
							Bristol C	91	—
MURDOCK Colin	6 3	12 09	D	2 7 75	Ballymena	Trainee	**Manchester U**	—	—
MURPHY Brendan	5 11	11 12	G	19 8 75	Wexford	Bradford C	**Wimbledon**	—	—
MURPHY Danny	5 9	10 03	M	18 3 77	Chester	Trainee	**Crewe Alex**	47	7
MURPHY Jamie	6 1	13 00	D	25 2 73	Manchester	Trainee	**Blackpool**	55	1
MURPHY John *	5 9	11 11	D	9 9 75	Cork	Trainee	**Aston Villa**	—	—
MURPHY John §	6 1	14 00	F	18 10 76	Whiston	Trainee	**Chester C**	5	—
MURPHY Matthew	5 10	11 00	F	20 8 71	Northampton	Corby	**Oxford U**	24	7
MURPHY Michael	5 10	11 09	F	5 5 77	Slough	Slough	**Reading**	1	—
MURPHY Shaun	6 0	12 00	D	5 11 70	Sydney	Perth Italia	**Notts Co**	54	2
MURPHY Stephen			M	5 4 78	Dublin	Belvedere	**Huddersfield T**	—	—
MURRAY Edwin	5 11	12 00	D	31 8 73	Redbridge	Trainee	**Swindon T**	7	—
MURRAY Nathan *	6 1	12 07	D	10 9 75	South Shields	Trainee	**Newcastle U**	—	—
MURRAY Paul	5 8	10 00	M	31 8 76	Carlisle	Trainee	**Carlisle U**	13	—
MURRAY Robert	5 11	11 07	F	31 10 74	Hammersmith	Trainee	**Bournemouth**	76	8
MURRAY Scott	5 10	11 00	F	26 5 74	Aberdeen	Fraserburgh	**Aston Villa**	—	—
MURRAY Shaun	5 7	10 10	M	7 2 70	Newcastle	Trainee	Tottenham H	—	—
							Portsmouth	34	1
							Millwall (loan)	—	—
							Scarborough	29	5
							Bradford C	41	5
MURTY Graeme	5 10	11 10	M	13 11 74	Middlesbrough	Trainee	**York C**	21	2
MUSGRAVE Sean *	5 10	12 04	G	27 10 74	Penshaw	Trainee	**Sunderland**	—	—
MUSSELWHITE Paul	6 2	12 07	G	22 12 68	Portsmouth		Portsmouth	—	—
							Scunthorpe U	132	—
							Port Vale	131	—
MUSTOE Robbie	5 10	11 10	M	28 8 68	Oxford		Oxford U	91	10
							Middlesbrough	159	12
MUTCH Andy	5 10	11 00	F	28 12 63	Liverpool	Southport	Wolverhampton W	289	96
							Swindon T	50	6
MUTCHELL Robert ‡	5 10	11 02	D	2 1 74	Solihull	Trainee	Oxford U	—	—
							Barnet	22	—
MYALL Stuart	5 10	12 13	M	12 11 74	Eastbourne	Trainee	**Brighton**	47	2

Player	Ht	Wt	Pos	Birth Date	Birth Place	Source	Clubs	League App	League Gls
MYERS Andy	5 8	9 10	M	3 11 73	Hounslow	Trainee	**Chelsea**	33	1
NARBETT Jon	5 10	10 08	M	21 11 68	Birmingham	Apprentice	Shrewsbury T	26	3
							Hereford U	149	31
							Leicester C (loan)	—	—
							Oxford U	15	—
							Chesterfield	3	—
NAYLOR Dominic	5 9	13 03	D	12 8 70	Watford	Trainee	Watford	—	—
							Halifax T	6	1
						Barnet	Barnet	51	—
							Plymouth Arg	85	—
NAYLOR Glenn	5 11	11 01	F	11 8 72	York	Trainee	**York C**	85	23
NAYLOR Stuart	6 4	12 02	G	6 12 62	Wetherby	Yorkshire A	Lincoln C	49	—
							Peterborough U (loan)	8	—
							Crewe Alex (loan)	38	—
							Crewe Alex (loan)	17	—
							WBA	328	—
NAYLOR Tony	5 8	10 08	F	29 3 67	Manchester	Droylsden	Crewe Alex	122	45
							Port Vale	33	9
NDAH George	6 1	11 04	M	23 12 74	Camberwell	Trainee	**Crystal Palace**	26	1
NDLOVU Peter	5 8	10 02	F	25 2 73	Zimbabwe	Highlanders	**Coventry C**	125	31
NEAL Ashley	6 0	11 10	M	16 12 74	Liverpool	Trainee	**Liverpool**	—	—
NEBBELING Gavin ‡	6 0	12 10	D	15 5 63	Johannesburg	Arcadia Shepherds	Crystal Palace	151	8
							Northampton T (loan)	11	—
							Fulham	88	2
							Hereford U (loan)	3	—
							Preston NE	22	4
NEEDHAM Ben *	5 11	11 00	M	23 10 75	Leicester	Trainee	**Notts Co**	—	—
NEIL James	5 8	10 05	D	28 2 76	Bury St Edmunds	Trainee	**Grimsby T**	—	—
NEILL Warren *	5 9	11 05	M	21 11 62	Acton	Apprentice	QPR	181	3
							Portsmouth	218	2
NEILSON Alan	5 11	11 07	D	26 9 72	Wegburg	Trainee	**Newcastle U**	42	1
NELSON Garry	5 10	11 10	F	16 1 61	Braintree	Amateur	Southend U	129	17
							Swindon T	79	7
							Plymouth Arg	74	20
							Brighton	144	46
							Notts Co (loan)	2	—
							Charlton Ath	155	34
NETHERCOTT Stuart	6 1	13 08	D	21 3 73	Chadwell Heath	Trainee	**Tottenham H**	32	—
							Maidstone U (loan)	13	1
							Barnet (loan)	3	—
NEVILLE Gary	5 11	11 10	D	18 2 75	Bury	Trainee	**Manchester U**	19	—
NEVILLE Philip	5 11	12 00	D	21 1 77	Bury	Trainee	**Manchester U**	2	—
NEVIN Pat	5 6	11 05	F	6 9 63	Glasgow	Gartcosh U	Clyde	73	17
							Chelsea	193	36
							Everton	109	16
							Tranmere R (loan)	8	—
							Tranmere R	132	25
NEWELL Mike	6 1	11 00	F	27 1 65	Liverpool	Liverpool	Crewe Alex	3	—
							Wigan Ath	72	25
							Luton T	63	18
							Leicester C	81	21
							Everton	68	15
							Blackburn R	100	25
NEWELL Paul	6 1	11 05	G	23 2 69	Greenwich	Trainee	Southend U	15	—
							Leyton Orient	61	—
							Colchester U (loan)	14	—
							Barnet	15	—

Player	Ht	Wt	Pos	Birth Date	Birth Place	Source	Clubs	League App	League Gls
NEWHOUSE Aidan	6 2	13 05	M	23 5 72	Wallasey	Trainee	Chester C	44	6
							Wimbledon	23	2
							Tranmere R (loan)	—	—
							Port Vale (loan)	2	—
							Portsmouth (loan)	6	1
NEWLAND Ray	6 3	13 10	G	19 7 71	Liverpool	Everton	Plymouth Arg	26	—
							Chester C	10	—
NEWMAN Ricky	5 10	12 06	M	5 8 70	Guildford	Trainee	**Crystal Palace**	48	3
							Maidstone U (loan)	10	1
NEWMAN Rob	6 2	13 04	D	13 12 63	Bradford-on-Avon	Apprentice	Bristol C	394	52
							Norwich C	123	12
NEWSOME Jon	6 2	13 09	D	6 9 70	Sheffield	Trainee	Sheffield W	7	—
							Leeds U	76	3
							Norwich C	35	3
NEWSON Mark *	5 10	12 06	D	7 12 60	Stepney	Apprentice	Charlton Ath	—	—
						Maidstone U	Bournemouth	177	23
							Fulham	102	4
							Barnet	59	4
NEWTON Eddie	5 11	11 02	F	13 12 71	Hammersmith	Trainee	**Chelsea**	101	7
							Cardiff C (loan)	18	4
NEWTON Shaun	5 8	11 00	M	20 8 75	Camberwell	Trainee	**Charlton Ath**	47	2
NICHOLLS Alan	5 11	14 07	G	28 8 73	Birmingham	Cheltenham T	**Plymouth Arg**	65	—
NICHOLLS Ryan ‡	5 9	12 00	F	10 5 73	Cardiff	Trainee	Leeds U	—	—
							Cardiff C	12	1
NICHOLSON Max †	5 10	12 03	F	3 10 71	Leeds	Trainee	Doncaster R	27	2
							Hereford U	63	7
							Torquay U	1	—
							Scunthorpe U	15	4
NICHOLSON Shane	5 10	12 02	D	3 6 70	Newark	Trainee	Lincoln C	133	6
							Derby Co	54	1
NICOL Steve	5 10	12 00	D	11 12 61	Irvine	Ayr U BC	Ayr U	70	7
							Liverpool	343	36
							Notts Co	19	—
NIELSEN Jimmi	6 2	12 11	G	6 8 77	Aalborg	Aalborg	**Millwall**	—	—
NIJHOLT Luc	5 11	12 01	D	29 7 61	Zaandam	BSC Old Boys Basel	Motherwell	96	5
							Swindon T	67	1
NILSEN Roger	5 9	11 08	D	8 8 69	Norway	Viking St	**Sheffield U**	55	—
NIXON Eric	6 4	15 07	G	4 10 62	Manchester	Curzon Ashton	Manchester C	58	—
							Wolverhampton W (loan)	16	—
							Bradford C (loan)	3	—
							Southampton (loan)	4	—
							Carlisle U (loan)	16	—
							Tranmere R (loan)	8	—
							Tranmere R	308	—
NOGAN Kurt	5 11	12 07	F	9 9 70	Cardiff	Trainee	Luton T	33	3
							Peterborough U	—	—
							Brighton	97	49
							Burnley	15	3
NOGAN Lee	5 10	10 08	F	21 5 69	Cardiff	Apprentice	Oxford U	64	10
							Brentford (loan)	11	2
							Southend U (loan)	6	1
							Watford	105	26
							Southend U (loan)	5	—
							Reading	20	10
NOLAN Ian	6 0	12 01	D	9 7 70	Liverpool	Marine	Tranmere R	88	1
							Sheffield W	42	3
NORBURY Mike	6 1	11 10	F	22 1 69	Hemsworth	Bridlington	Cambridge U	26	3
							Preston NE	42	13
							Doncaster R	22	5
NORFOLK Lee	5 10	11 03	M	17 10 75	Dunedin NZ	Trainee	**Ipswich T**	3	—

Player	Ht	Wt	Pos	Birth Date	Birth Place	Source	Clubs	League App	League Gls
NORMAN Craig	5 10	11 09	D	21 3 75	Perivale	Trainee	**Chelsea**	—	—
NORMAN Tony *	6 2	14 05	G	24 2 58	Mancot	Amateur	Burnley	—	—
							Hull C	372	—
							Sunderland	198	—
NORRIS Steve ‡	5 10	11 00	F	22 9 61	Coventry	Telford	Scarborough	45	13
							Notts Co (loan)	1	—
							Carlisle U	29	5
							Halifax T	56	35
							Chesterfield	97	43
							Scarborough (loan)	8	4
NORTON David	5 7	11 03	M	3 3 65	Cannock	Apprentice	Aston Villa	44	2
							Notts Co	27	1
							Rochdale (loan)	9	—
							Hull C (loan)	15	—
							Hull C	134	5
							Northampton T	38	—
NORTON Paul ‡	5 6	10 08	M	15 10 75	Middlesbrough	Trainee	**Middlesbrough**	—	—
NOTEMAN Kevin *	5 10	12 02	F	15 10 69	Preston	Trainee	Leeds U	1	—
							Doncaster R	106	20
							Mansfield T	95	15
NTAMARK Charlie	5 10	11 10	M	22 7 64	Paddington	Boreham Wood	**Walsall**	196	11
NUGENT Kevin	6 1	13 03	F	10 4 69	Edmonton	Trainee	Leyton Orient	94	20
							Cork C (loan)	—	—
							Plymouth Arg	125	32
NYAMAH Kofi *	5 8	10 07	F	20 6 75	Islington	Trainee	**Cambridge U**	23	2
OAKES Michael	6 1	12 07	G	30 10 73	Northwich	Trainee	**Aston Villa**	—	—
							Scarborough (loan)	1	—
							Tranmere R (loan)	—	—
OAKES Scott	5 11	11 04	F	5 8 72	Leicester	Trainee	Leicester C	3	—
							Luton T	144	24
OAKLEY Matthew §	5 10	11 00	F	17 8 77	Peterborough	Trainee	**Southampton**	1	—
OATWAY Charlie	5 7	10 10	M	28 11 73	Hammersmith	Yeading	**Cardiff C**	30	—
O'BRIEN Liam	6 1	11 10	M	5 9 64	Dublin	Shamrock R	Manchester U	31	2
							Newcastle U	151	19
							Tranmere R	55	2
O'BRIEN Roy	6 1	12 00	D	27 11 74	Cork	Trainee	**Arsenal**	—	—
O'CONNELL Brendan	5 11	12 01	F	12 11 66	London		Portsmouth	—	—
							Exeter C	81	19
							Burnley	64	17
							Huddersfield T (loan)	11	1
							Barnsley	215	34
O'CONNOR Derek			G	9 3 78	Dublin	Crumplin U	**Huddersfield T**	—	—
O'CONNOR Jonathan	5 10	11 03	M	29 10 76	Darlington	Trainee	**Everton**	—	—
O'CONNOR Mark *	5 7	10 02	M	10 3 63	Rochdale	Apprentice	QPR	3	—
							Exeter C (loan)	38	1
							Bristol R	80	10
							Bournemouth	128	12
							Gillingham	116	8
							Bournemouth	58	3
O'CONNOR Martyn	5 9	12 08	M	10 12 67	Walsall	Bromsgrove R	Crystal Palace	2	—
							Walsall (loan)	10	1
							Walsall	53	12
O'DONNELL Paul *	5 10	11 03	M	6 10 75	Limerick	Trainee	**Liverpool**	—	—
O'DRISCOLL Sean *	5 8	11 03	M	1 7 57	Wolverhampton	Alvechurch	Fulham	148	13
							Bournemouth (loan)	19	1
							Bournemouth	404	18
OGDEN Neil	5 10	10 04	M	29 11 75	Billinge	Trainee	**Wigan Ath**	5	—
OGRIZOVIC Steve	6 5	15 00	G	12 9 57	Mansfield	ONRYC	Chesterfield	16	—
							Liverpool	4	—
							Shrewsbury T	84	—
							Coventry C	415	1

Player	Ht	Wt	Pos	Birth Date	Birth Place	Source	Clubs	League App	League Gls
O'HAGAN Danny	6 1	13 08	F	24 4 76	Padstow	Trainee	**Plymouth Arg**	3	1
O'HALLORAN Keith			D	10 11 75	Ireland	Cherry Orchard	**Middlesbrough**	1	—
O'HARA Gary ‡			D	13 12 73	Belfast	Trainee	**Leeds U**	—	—
O'KANE John	5 10	11 09	D	15 11 74	Nottingham	Trainee	**Manchester U**	—	—
OKORIE Chima *	5 10	12 08	F	8 10 68	Izomber		Peterborough U	—	—
							Grimsby T	5	—
							Torquay U	36	6
OLDBURY Marcus *	5 7	10 02	M	29 3 76	Bournemouth	Trainee	**Norwich C**	—	—
OLDFIELD David	6 0	13 04	M	30 5 68	Perth, Australia	Apprentice	Luton T	29	4
							Manchester C	26	6
							Leicester C	188	26
							Millwall (loan)	17	6
O'LEARY David	6 1	13 09	D	2 5 58	London	Apprentice	Arsenal	558	10
							Leeds U	10	—
OLIVER Darren *	5 8	10 05	D	1 11 71	Liverpool	Trainee	Bolton W	3	—
							Peterborough U (loan)	—	—
							Rochdale	28	—
OLIVER Gavin *	5 11	13 10	D	6 9 62	Felling	Apprentice	Sheffield W	20	—
							Tranmere R (loan)	17	1
							Brighton (loan)	16	—
							Bradford C	313	9
OLIVER Keith	5 8	10 09	M	15 1 76	South Shields	Trainee	**Hartlepool U**	19	—
OLIVER Michael	5 10	12 04	M	2 8 75	Cleveland	Trainee	Middlesbrough	—	—
							Stockport Co	13	—
OLNEY Ian	6 1	11 00	F	17 12 69	Luton	Trainee	Aston Villa	88	16
							Oldham Ath	44	13
OLSSON Paul	5 8	10 11	M	24 12 65	Hull	Apprentice	Hull C	—	—
							Exeter C (loan)	8	—
							Exeter C	35	2
							Scarborough	48	5
							Hartlepool U	171	13
							Darlington	42	4
OMIGIE Joe	6 2	13 00	F	13 6 72	Hammersmith	Donna	**Brentford**	—	—
OMOYIMNI Emmanuel ‡	5 8	10 00	M	28 12 77	Nigeria	Trainee	**West Ham U**	—	—
O'NEIL Phil	5 9	11 10	M	22 10 77	Sidcup	Trainee	**Millwall**	—	—
O'NEILL Keith	6 1	11 00	M	16 2 76	Dublin	Trainee	**Norwich C**	1	—
O'NEILL Shane §	5 10	12 00	M	20 6 78	Limavady	Trainee	**Nottingham F**	—	—
ONUORA Iffy	6 2	13 13	F	28 7 67	Glasgow	British Universities	Huddersfield T	165	30
							Mansfield T	14	7
ONWERE Udo	6 0	11 07	M	9 11 71	Hammersmith	Trainee	Fulham	85	7
							Lincoln C	8	—
ORD Richard	6 2	13 05	D	3 3 70	Easington	Trainee	**Sunderland**	154	4
							York C (loan)	3	—
O'REGAN Kieran *	5 8	10 12	M	9 11 63	Cork	Tramore Ath	Brighton	86	2
							Swindon T	26	1
							Huddersfield T	199	25
							WBA	45	2
O'RIORDAN Don	6 0	12 07	D	14 5 57	Dublin	Apprentice	Derby Co	6	1
							Doncaster R (loan)	2	—
						Tulsa	Preston NE	158	8
							Carlisle U	84	18
							Middlesbrough	41	2
							Grimsby T	86	14
							Notts Co	109	5
							Mansfield T (loan)	6	—
							Torquay U	71	3
ORLYGSSON Thorvaldur	5 11	11 03	M	2 8 66	Odense	FC Akureyri	Nottingham F	37	2
							Stoke C	83	16

Player	Ht	Wt	Pos	Birth Date	Birth Place	Source	Clubs	League App	League Gls
ORMEROD Mark	6 0	11 05	G	5 2 76	Bournemouth	Trainee	**Brighton & HA**	—	—
ORMONDROYD Ian	6 5	13 08	F	22 9 64	Bradford	Thackley	Bradford C	87	20
							Oldham Ath (loan)	10	1
							Aston Villa	56	6
							Derby Co	25	8
							Leicester C	77	7
							Hull C (loan)	10	6
ORMSBY Brendan ‡	5 11	11 12	D	1 10 60	Birmingham	Apprentice	Aston Villa	117	4
							Leeds U	46	5
							Shrewsbury T (loan)	1	—
							Doncaster R	78	7
							Scarborough	16	1
						Waterford	**Wigan Ath**	2	—
ORR Stephen	5 7	10 00	F	19 1 78	Belper	Trainee	**Nottingham F**	—	—
OSBORN Simon	5 10	11 04	M	19 1 72	New Addington	Apprentice	Crystal Palace	55	5
							Reading	32	5
O'SHEA Alan	5 10	10 12	D	21 7 77	Dublin	Trainee	**Leeds U**	—	—
O'SHEA Danny	6 0	13 00	D	26 3 63	Kennington	Apprentice	Arsenal	6	—
							Charlton Ath (loan)	9	—
							Exeter C	45	2
							Southend U	118	12
							Cambridge U	203	1
							Northampton T	7	1
OSMAN Russell †	5 11	12 01	D	14 2 59	Repton	Apprentice	Ipswich	294	17
							Leicester C	108	8
							Southampton	96	6
							Bristol C	70	3
							Plymouth Arg	—	—
O'SULLIVAN Wayne	5 8	10 06	D	25 2 74	Akrotiri	Trainee	**Swindon T**	30	—
O'TOOLE Gavin	5 9	11 01	M	19 9 75	Dublin	Trainee	**Coventry C**	—	—
OTTO Ricky	5 10	12 10	M	9 11 67	Hackney	Dartford	Leyton Orient	56	13
							Southend U	64	17
							Birmingham C	24	4
OVENDALE Mark *	6 2	13 02	G	22 11 73	Leicester	Wisbech T	**Northampton T**	6	—
OVERSON Vince	6 2	14 02	D	15 5 62	Kettering	Apprentice	Burnley	211	6
							Birmingham C	182	3
							Stoke C	152	6
OWEN Gareth	5 8	11 08	M	21 10 71	Chester	Trainee	**Wrexham**	172	18
OWEN Philip ‡			M	11 1 75	Bangor	Manchester C	Stockport Co	—	—
							Bradford C	—	—
OWERS Gary	5 10	11 10	M	3 10 68	Newcastle	Apprentice	Sunderland	268	25
							Bristol C	21	2
PAATELAINEN Mixu	6 0	13 11	F	3 2 67	Helsinki	Valkeakosken Haka	Dundee U	133	33
							Aberdeen	75	23
							Bolton W	44	12
PACK Lenny	5 10	12 01	M	27 9 76	Salisbury	Trainee	**Cambridge U**	3	—
PAGE Don *	5 10	11 02	F	18 1 64	Manchester	Runcorn	Wigan Ath	74	15
							Rotherham U	55	13
							Rochdale (loan)	4	1
							Doncaster R	22	4
							Chester C	30	5
PAGE Robert	6 0	11 08	D	3 9 74	Llwynypia	Trainee	**Watford**	9	—
PAINTER Robert	5 11	11 00	M	26 1 71	Ince	Trainee	Chester C	84	8
							Maidstone U	30	5
							Burnley	26	2
							Darlington	74	20
PALLISTER Gary	6 4	14 08	D	30 6 65	Ramsgate	Billingham	Middlesbrough	156	5
							Darlington (loan)	7	—
							Manchester U	236	8

Player	Ht	Wt	Pos	Birth Date	Birth Place	Source	Clubs	League App	League Gls
PALMER Carlton	6 2	12 04	D	5 12 65	West Bromwich	Trainee	WBA	121	4
							Sheffield W	205	14
							Leeds U	39	3
PALMER Charlie	6 0	13 02	D	10 7 63	Aylesbury	Apprentice	Watford	10	1
							Derby Co	51	2
							Hull C	70	1
							Notts Co	182	7
							Walsall	39	2
PALMER Lee *	5 11	13 00	D	19 9 70	Gillingham	Trainee	**Gillingham**	120	5
PALMER Steve	6 1	12 13	M	31 3 68	Brighton	Cambridge University	**Ipswich T**	106	2
PAPAVASILIOU Nicos ‡	5 8	10 02	M	31 8 70	Limassol	Ofi Crete	**Newcastle U**	7	—
PARDEW Alan *	5 11	11 00	M	18 7 61	Wimbledon	Yeovil	Crystal Palace	128	8
							Charlton Ath	104	24
PARKER Garry	5 11	12 05	M	7 9 65	Oxford	Apprentice	Luton T	42	3
							Hull C	84	8
							Nottingham F	103	17
							Aston Villa	95	13
							Leicester C	14	2
PARKER Justin			D	11 11 76	Stoke	Trainee	**Crewe Alex**	—	—
PARKER Paul	5 7	11 11	D	4 4 64	West Ham	Apprentice	Fulham	153	2
							QPR	125	1
							Manchester U	99	1
PARKIN Brian	6 1	12 00	G	12 10 65	Birkenhead	Local	Oldham Ath	6	—
							Crewe Alex (loan)	12	—
							Crewe Alex	86	—
							Crystal Palace (loan)	—	—
							Crystal Palace	20	—
							Bristol R	221	—
PARKIN Steve	5 6	11 03	M	7 11 65	Mansfield	Apprentice	Stoke C	113	5
							WBA	48	2
							Mansfield T	61	2
PARKINSON Gary	5 11	12 08	D	10 1 68	Thornaby	Everton	Middlesbrough	202	5
							Southend U (loan)	6	—
							Bolton W	3	—
							Burnley	63	3
PARKINSON Joe	6 0	13 00	D	11 6 71	Eccles	Trainee	Wigan Ath	119	6
							Bournemouth	30	1
							Everton	34	—
PARKINSON Phil	6 0	11 06	M	1 12 67	Chorley	Apprentice	Southampton	—	—
							Bury	145	5
							Reading	112	7
PARKINSON Steve ‡	5 11	11 11	M	27 8 74	Lincoln	Trainee	**Lincoln C**	5	—
PARKINSON Stuart	5 8	10 12	F	18 2 76	Blackpool	Trainee	**Blackpool**	1	—
PARLOUR Ray	5 10	11 12	M	7 3 73	Romford	Trainee	**Arsenal**	84	4
PARMENTER Steven	5 9	10 07	M	22 1 77	Chelmsford	Trainee	**QPR**	—	—
PARRIS George *	5 9	13 00	D	11 9 64	Ilford	Apprentice	West Ham U	239	12
							Birmingham C	39	1
							Brentford (loan)	5	—
							Bristol C (loan)	6	—
							Brighton (loan)	18	2
PARRISH Sean	5 9	10 00	M	14 3 72	Wrexham	Trainee	Shrewsbury T	3	—
						Telford U	**Doncaster R**	25	3
PARSLEY Neil *	5 10	10 11	D	25 4 66	Liverpool	Witton Alb	Leeds U	—	—
							Chester C (loan)	6	—
							Huddersfield T	57	—
							Doncaster R (loan)	3	—
							WBA	43	—
PARTNER Andy	6 3	13 00	D	21 10 74	Colchester	Trainee	**Colchester U**	2	—
PARTRIDGE Scott	5 9	10 09	F	13 10 74	Leicester	Trainee	Bradford C	5	—
							Bristol C	42	6

Player	Ht	Wt	Pos	Birth Date	Birth Place	Source	Clubs	League App	League Gls
PASCOE Colin	5 10	12 00	F	9 4 65	Port Talbot	Apprentice	Swansea C	174	39
							Sunderland	126	22
							Swansea C (loan)	15	4
							Swansea C	68	10
PASCOE Jason *	5 11	11 11	D	15 2 70	Jarrow	Boston U	**Northampton T**	15	—
PASKIN John	6 1	13 06	F	1 2 62	Capetown	Seiko	WBA	25	5
							Wolverhampton W	34	3
							Stockport Co (loan)	5	1
							Birmingham C (loan)	10	3
							Shrewsbury T (loan)	1	—
							Wrexham	51	11
							Bury	26	8
PASS Steven	5 8	10 10	F	15 9 76	Leigh	Trainee	**Sheffield W**	—	—
PATERSON Scott	5 11	12 00	M	13 5 72	Aberdeen	Cove Rangers	Liverpool	—	—
							Bristol C	3	—
PATES Colin ‡	6 0	13 00	D	10 8 61	Mitcham	Apprentice	Chelsea	281	10
							Charlton Ath	38	—
							Arsenal	21	—
							Brighton (loan)	17	—
							Brighton	50	—
PATMORE Warren ‡			M	14 8 71	Kingsbury		Cambridge U	1	—
							Millwall	1	—
							Northampton T	21	2
PATTERSON Darren	6 2	12 07	D	15 10 69	Belfast	Trainee	WBA	—	—
							Wigan Ath	97	6
							Crystal Palace	22	1
PATTERSON Gary	6 0	12 07	M	27 11 72	Newcastle	Trainee	Notts Co	—	—
							Shrewsbury T	57	2
							Wycombe W	13	1
PATTERSON Ian ‡	6 2	13 00	D	4 4 73	Chatham	Trainee	Sunderland	—	—
							Burnley	1	—
							Wigan Ath	4	—
PATTERSON Mark	5 6	11 04	M	24 5 65	Darwen	Apprentice	Blackburn R	101	20
							Preston NE	55	19
							Bury	42	10
							Bolton W	153	10
PATTERSON Mark	5 10	12 04	D	13 9 68	Leeds	Trainee	Carlisle U	22	—
							Derby Co	51	3
							Plymouth Arg	79	3
PAUL Martin	5 8	9 07	F	2 2 75	Whalley	Trainee	**Bristol R**	9	—
PAYNE Derek	5 6	10 08	M	26 4 67	Edgware	Hayes	Barnet	51	6
							Southend U	35	—
							Watford	24	—
PAYNE Grant	5 9	11 04	F	25 12 75	Woking	Trainee	**Wimbledon**	—	—
PAYNE Ian §			M	19 1 77	Crawley	Trainee	**Plymouth Arg**	1	—
PAYNE Stephen ‡	5 11	12 00	D	1 8 75	Pontefract	Trainee	**Huddersfield T**	—	—
PAYTON Andy	5 9	11 13	F	23 10 67	Burnley	Apprentice	Hull C	144	55
							Middlesbrough	19	3
							Celtic	36	15
							Barnsley	68	24
PAZ Adrian	5 10	11 10	F	9 9 68	Uruguay	Penarol	**Ipswich T**	17	1
PEACOCK Darren	6 2	12 06	D	3 2 68	Bristol	Apprentice	Newport Co	28	—
							Hereford U	59	4
							QPR	126	6
							Newcastle U	44	1
PEACOCK Gavin	5 8	11 08	M	18 11 67	Kent	Apprentice	QPR	17	1
							Gillingham	70	11
							Bournemouth	56	8
							Newcastle U	105	35
							Chelsea	75	12
PEACOCK Lee	6 0	12 05	F	9 10 76	Paisley	Trainee	**Carlisle U**	8	—
PEACOCK Richard	5 10	10 09	F	29 10 72	Sheffield	Sheffield FC	**Hull C**	48	6

Player	Ht	Wt	Pos	Birth Date	Birth Place	Source	Clubs	League App	League Gls
PEAKE Jason	5 11	12 10	M	29 9 71	Leicester	Trainee	Leicester C	8	1
							Hartlepool U (loan)	6	1
							Halifax T	33	1
							Rochdale	49	2
PEAKE Trevor	6 0	12 10	D	10 2 57	Nuneaton	Nuneaton Bor	Lincoln C	171	7
							Coventry C	278	6
							Luton T	160	—
PEARCE Andy	6 4	13 09	D	20 4 66	Bradford on Avon	Halesowen	Coventry C	71	4
							Sheffield W	66	3
PEARCE Dennis *	5 9	11 00	F	10 9 74	Wolverhampton	Trainee	**Aston Villa**	—	—
PEARCE Ian	6 1	12 04	D	7 5 74	Bury St Edmunds	School	Chelsea	4	—
							Blackburn R	33	1
PEARCE Stuart	5 10	12 09	D	24 4 62	London	Wealdstone	Coventry C	51	4
							Nottingham F	337	55
PEARCEY Jason	6 1	13 12	G	23 7 71	Leamington Spa	Trainee	Mansfield T	77	—
							Grimsby T	3	—
PEARS Richard	5 10	11 07	F	16 7 76	Exeter	Trainee	**Exeter C**	30	2
PEARS Steve *	6 0	13 01	G	22 1 62	Brandon	Apprentice	Manchester U	4	—
							Middlesbrough (loan)	12	—
							Middlesbrough	327	—
PEARSON Chris	5 6	10 06	F	5 1 76	Leicester	Trainee	**Notts Co**	—	—
PEARSON John *	6 2	13 05	F	1 9 63	Sheffield	Apprentice	Sheffield W	105	24
							Charlton Ath	61	15
							Leeds U	99	12
							Rotherham U (loan)	11	5
							Barnsley	32	4
							Hull C (loan)	15	—
							Carlisle U	8	—
							Mansfield T	2	—
							Cardiff C	12	—
PEARSON Nigel	6 1	14 03	D	21 8 63	Nottingham	Heanor T	Shrewsbury T	153	5
							Sheffield W	180	14
							Middlesbrough	33	3
PEEL Nathan	6 1	13 03	F	17 5 72	Blackburn	Trainee	Preston NE	10	1
							Sheffield U	1	—
							Halifax T (loan)	3	—
							Burnley	16	2
							Rotherham U (loan)	9	4
PEER Dean *	6 1	12 04	M	8 8 69	Dudley	Trainee	Birmingham C	120	8
							Mansfield T (loan)	10	—
							Walsall	45	8
PEJIC Mel	5 9	11 05	D	27 4 59	Chesterton	Local	Stoke C	1	—
							Hereford U	412	14
							Wrexham	106	3
PEMBERTON John	5 11	12 12	D	18 11 64	Oldham	Chadderton	Rochdale	1	—
							Crewe Alex	121	1
							Crystal Palace	78	2
							Sheffield U	68	—
							Leeds U	36	—
PEMBERTON Martin			M	1 2 76	Bradford	Trainee	**Oldham Ath**	—	—
PEMBRIDGE Mark	5 8	11 12	M	29 11 70	Merthyr Tydfil	Trainee	Luton T	60	6
							Derby Co	110	28
PENDER John	6 0	13 12	D	19 11 63	Luton	Apprentice	Wolverhampton W	117	3
							Charlton Ath	41	—
							Bristol C	83	3
							Burnley	170	8
PENNEY David	5 10	12 00	M	17 8 64	Wakefield	Pontefract	Derby Co	19	—
							Oxford U	110	15
							Swansea C (loan)	12	3
							Swansea C (loan)	11	2
							Swansea C	35	5
PENNOCK Adrian	5 11	12 01	D	27 3 71	Ipswich	Trainee	Norwich C	1	—
							Bournemouth	114	9

Player	Ht	Wt	Pos	Birth Date	Birth Place	Source	Clubs	League App	League Gls
PENNOCK Tony *	6 0	12 06	G	10 4 71	Swansea	School	Stockport Co	—	—
							Wigan Ath (loan)	2	—
							Wigan Ath	8	—
							Hereford U	15	—
PENRICE Gary	5 8	10 06	F	23 3 64	Bristol	Bristol C	Bristol R	188	54
							Watford	43	18
							Aston Villa	20	1
							QPR	79	20
PEPPER Nigel	5 10	11 13	M	25 4 68	Rotherham	Apprentice	Rotherham U	45	1
							York C	166	19
PERIFIMOU Chris §			M	27 11 75	Enfield	Trainee	**Leyton Orient**	4	—
PERKINS Chris	5 11	11 00	M	9 1 74	Nottingham	Trainee	Mansfield T	8	—
							Chesterfield	18	—
PERKINS Declan	5 11	12 04	F	17 10 75	Ilford	Trainee	**Southend U**	6	—
PERRETT Darren	5 8	11 06	F	29 12 69	Cardiff	Cheltenham T	**Swansea C**	26	1
PERRY Chris	5 9	11 01	D	26 4 73	London	Trainee	**Wimbledon**	24	—
PERRY Jason	5 11	10 04	D	2 4 70	Newport	Trainee	**Cardiff C**	232	5
PESCHISOLIDO Paul	5 7	10 12	F	25 5 71	Canada	Toronto Blizzard	Birmingham C	43	16
							Stoke C	40	13
PETERS Mark	6 0	11 03	D	6 7 72	St Asaph	Trainee	Manchester C	—	—
							Norwich C	—	—
							Peterborough U	19	—
							Mansfield T	26	4
PETERS Rob †	5 8	11 02	D	18 5 71	Kensington	Trainee	Brentford	30	1
							Carlisle U	8	—
PETHICK Robbie	5 10	11 07	M	8 9 70	Tavistock	Weymouth	**Portsmouth**	62	1
PETRESCU Dan	5 9	11 09	M	22 12 67	Bucharest	Genoa	**Sheffield W**	29	3
PETTERSON Andy	6 2	14 12	G	26 9 69	Fremantle		Luton T	19	—
							Swindon T (loan)	—	—
							Ipswich T (loan)	—	—
							Ipswich T (loan)	1	—
							Charlton Ath	9	—
							Bradford C (loan)	3	—
PETTINGER Paul	6 0	13 07	G	1 10 75	Sheffield	Barnsley	**Leeds U**	—	—
							Torquay U (loan)	3	—
PETTY Ben			D	22 3 77	Solihull	Trainee	**Aston Villa**	—	—
PEVERELL Nick	5 11	11 10	F	28 4 73	Middlesbrough	Trainee	Middlesbrough	—	—
							Hartlepool U	36	3
							York C	9	1
PEYTON Gerry ‡	6 2	13 09	G	20 5 56	Birmingham	Atherstone T	Burnley	30	—
							Fulham	345	—
							Southend U (loan)	10	—
							Bournemouth	202	—
							Everton	—	—
							Bolton W (loan)	1	—
							Norwich C (loan)	—	—
							Chelsea (loan)	1	—
							Brentford	19	—
							West Ham U	—	—
PHELAN Mike	5 11	11 01	D	24 9 62	Nelson	Apprentice	Burnley	168	9
							Norwich C	156	9
							Manchester U	102	2
							WBA	20	—
PHELAN Terry	5 8	10 00	D	16 3 67	Manchester	Trainee	Leeds U	14	—
							Swansea C	45	—
							Wimbledon	159	1
							Manchester C	94	1
PHILIP Richard ‡	5 11	11 07	D	20 10 74	Surrey	Trainee	**Luton T**	—	—

Player	Ht	Wt	Pos	Birth Date	Birth Place	Source	Clubs	League App	League Gls
PHILLIPS David	5 10	11 02	M	29 7 63	Wegberg	Apprentice	Plymouth Arg	73	15
							Manchester C	81	13
							Coventry C	100	8
							Norwich C	152	18
							Nottingham F	81	5
PHILLIPS Gary	6 0	14 00	G	20 9 61	St Albans		WBA	—	—
						Barnet	Brentford	143	—
							Reading	24	—
							Hereford U	6	—
							Barnet	117	—
PHILLIPS Jimmy	6 0	12 07	D	8 2 66	Bolton	Apprentice	Bolton W	108	2
							Rangers	25	—
							Oxford U	79	8
							Middlesbrough	139	6
							Bolton W	88	1
PHILLIPS Kevin	5 7	11 00	F	25 7 73	Hitchin	Baldock T	**Watford**	16	9
PHILLIPS Marcus ‡	5 11	11 07	M	17 10 73	Bradford on Avon	Trainee	**Swindon T**	—	—
PHILLIPS Martin	5 11	12 08	F	13 3 76	Exeter	Trainee	**Exeter C**	39	2
PHILLIPS Wayne	5 10	10 09	M	15 12 70	Bangor	Trainee	**Wrexham**	117	5
PHILLISKIRK Tony	6 1	13 03	F	10 2 65	Sunderland	Amateur	Sheffield U	80	20
							Rotherham U (loan)	6	1
							Oldham Ath	10	1
							Preston NE	14	6
							Bolton W	141	51
							Peterborough U	43	15
							Burnley	32	8
PHILPOTT Lee	5 10	12 09	F	21 2 70	Hackney	Trainee	Peterborough U	4	—
							Cambridge U	134	17
							Leicester C	69	3
PICK Gary	5 9	11 10	M	9 7 71	Leicester	Leicester U	Stoke C	—	—
							Hereford U	29	2
PICKARD Owen ‡	5 10	11 03	F	18 11 69	Barnstaple	Trainee	Plymouth Arg	16	1
							Hereford U	73	14
							Rochdale	—	—
PICKERING Ally	5 11	11 01	D	22 6 67	Manchester	Buxton	Rotherham U	88	2
							Coventry C	35	—
PIEARCE Stephen	5 11	10 10	F	29 9 74	Sutton Coldfield	Trainee	**Wolverhampton W**	—	—
PIKE Chris	6 2	13 07	F	19 10 61	Cardiff	Barry T	Fulham	42	4
							Cardiff C (loan)	6	2
							Cardiff C	148	65
							Hereford U	38	18
							Gillingham	27	13
PIKE Martin	5 11	12 09	D	21 10 64	South Shields	Apprentice	WBA	—	—
							Peterborough U	126	8
							Sheffield U	129	5
							Tranmere R (loan)	2	—
							Bolton W (loan)	5	1
							Fulham	190	14
							Rotherham U	7	—
PILKINGTON Kevin	6 2	12 10	G	8 3 74	Hitchin	Trainee	**Manchester U**	1	—
PIRIE David *	5 9	11 05	F	15 4 75	Glasgow	Trainee	**Ipswich T**	—	—
PITCHER Darren	5 9	12 02	M	12 10 69	London	Trainee	Charlton Ath	173	8
							Galway (loan)	—	—
							Crystal Palace	25	—
PITCHER Geoffrey	5 6	10 13	M	15 8 75	Sutton	Trainee	Millwall	—	—
							Watford	4	1
PITMAN Jamie	5 9	10 09	M	6 1 76	Warminster	Trainee	**Swindon T**	3	—

Player	Ht	Wt	Pos	Birth Date	Birth Place	Source	Clubs	League App	League Gls
PLATNAUER Nicky *	5 11	12 10	D	10 6 61	Leicester	Bedford T	Bristol R	24	7
							Coventry C	44	6
							Birmingham C	28	2
							Reading (loan)	7	—
							Cardiff C	115	6
							Notts Co	57	1
							Port Vale (loan)	14	—
							Leicester C	35	—
							Scunthorpe U	14	2
							Mansfield T	25	—
							Lincoln C	26	—
PLATT David	5 10	11 12	F	10 6 66	Chadderton	Chadderton	Manchester U	—	—
							Crewe Alex	134	55
							Aston Villa	121	50
							Bari	29	11
							Juventus	16	3
							Sampdoria	55	17
							Arsenal	—	—
PLUMMER Chris	6 3	11 06	D	12 10 76	Isleworth	Trainee	**QPR**	—	—
POINTON Neil	5 10	11 00	D	28 11 64	Church Warsop	Apprentice	Scunthorpe U	159	2
							Everton	102	5
							Manchester C	74	2
							Oldham Ath	90	3
POLLITT Michael	6 4	14 00	G	29 2 72	Bolton	Trainee	Manchester U	—	—
							Oldham Ath (loan)	—	—
							Bury	—	—
							Lincoln C	57	—
							Darlington	40	—
POLLOCK Jamie	5 10	14 01	M	16 2 74	Stockton	Trainee	**Middlesbrough**	124	16
POLSTON John	5 11	11 12	D	10 6 68	Walthamstow	Apprentice	Tottenham H	24	1
							Norwich C	142	6
POOLE Darren	5 8	10 03	F	9 11 77	Northampton	Trainee	**Nottingham F**	—	—
POOLE Gary	6 0	12 04	D	11 9 67	Stratford	Arsenal	Tottenham H	—	—
							Cambridge U	43	—
						Barnet	Barnet	40	2
							Plymouth Arg	39	5
							Southend U	44	2
							Birmingham C	34	—
POOLE Kevin	5 11	12 06	G	21 7 63	Bromsgrove	Apprentice	Aston Villa	28	—
							Northampton T (loan)	3	—
							Middlesbrough	34	—
							Hartlepool U (loan)	12	—
							Leicester C	111	—
POOM Mart	6 4	13 07	G	3 2 72	Tallinn	FC Wil	**Portsmouth**	—	—
POPESCU Gica			M	9 10 67	Calafat	PSV Eindhoven	**Tottenham H**	23	3
PORIC Adem	5 9	11 11	M	22 4 73	London	St George's	**Sheffield W**	10	—
PORTER Andy	5 9	11 02	M	17 9 68	Manchester	Trainee	**Port Vale**	227	7
PORTER Gary	5 6	11 00	M	6 3 66	Sunderland	Apprentice	**Watford**	365	46
POTTER Graham	6 1	11 12	D	20 5 75	Solihull	Trainee	Birmingham C	25	2
							Wycombe W (loan)	3	—
							Stoke C	4	—
POTTS Steve	5 7	10 11	D	7 5 67	Hartford (USA)	Apprentice	**West Ham U**	278	1
POUNDER Tony *	5 10	11 02	M	11 3 66	Yeovil	Weymouth	Bristol R	113	10
						Weymouth	**Hereford U**	28	2
POVEY Neil §	5 8	10 00	M	26 6 77	Birmingham	Trainee	**Torquay U**	8	—
POWELL Chris	5 10	11 07	D	8 9 69	Lambeth	Trainee	Crystal Palace	3	—
							Aldershot (loan)	11	—
							Southend U	221	3
POWELL Darryl	6 0	12 03	F	15 1 71	Lambeth	Trainee	**Portsmouth**	132	16
POWELL Stephen	5 9	11 05	M	14 12 76	Derby	Trainee	**Derby Co**	—	—
POWER Graeme	5 9	12 00	D	7 3 77	Harrow	Trainee	**QPR**	—	—

Player	Ht	Wt	Pos	Birth Date	Birth Place	Source	Clubs	League App	League Gls
POWER Lee	6 0	11 10	F	30 6 72	Lewisham	Trainee	Norwich C	44	10
							Charlton Ath (loan)	5	—
							Sunderland (loan)	3	—
							Portsmouth (loan)	2	—
							Bradford C	30	5
							Millwall (loan)	—	—
PRATT David *	5 8	11 00	F	17 12 74	London		**West Ham U**	—	—
PREECE Andy	6 1	12 00	M	27 3 67	Evesham	Evesham	Northampton T	1	—
						Worcester C.	Wrexham	51	7
							Stockport Co	97	42
							Crystal Palace	20	4
PREECE David	5 6	11 05	M	28 5 63	Bridgnorth	Apprentice	Walsall	111	5
							Luton T	336	21
PREECE David	6 2	11 11	G	28 8 76	Sunderland	Trainee	**Sunderland**	—	—
PREECE Roger	5 8	10 13	M	9 6 69	Much Wenlock	Coventry C	Wrexham	110	12
							Chester C	169	4
PREEDY Phil	5 10	10 07	M	20 11 75	Hereford	Trainee	**Hereford U**	29	1
PRENDERVILLE Barry	6 0	12 08	D	16 10 76	Dublin	Trainee	**Coventry C**	—	—
PRESSLEY Steven	6 0	11 00	D	11 10 73	Elgin	Inverkeithling BC	Rangers	34	1
							Coventry C	19	1
PRESSMAN Kevin	6 1	14 02	G	6 11 67	Fareham	Apprentice	**Sheffield W**	128	—
							Stoke C (loan)	4	—
PRESTON Richard *	5 11	11 02	D	7 5 76	Basildon	Trainee	**Northampton T**	1	—
PRICE Chris	5 9	11 09	M	24 10 75	Liverpool	Trainee	**Everton**	—	—
PRICE Ryan	6 4	14 00	G	13 3 70	Stafford	Stafford R	**Birmingham C**	—	—
PRIEST Chris	5 9	10 10	M	18 10 73	Leigh	Trainee	Everton	—	—
							Chester C	24	1
PRIMUS Linvoy	5 10	12 04	D	14 9 73	Stratford	Trainee	Charlton Ath	4	—
							Barnet	39	—
PRIOR Spencer	6 3	13 00	D	22 4 71	Rochford	Trainee	Southend U	135	3
							Norwich C	30	—
PRITCHARD David	5 7	11 04	D	27 5 72	Wolverhampton	Telford	**Bristol R**	54	—
PROCTOR Mark *	5 10	11 09	M	30 1 61	Middlesbrough	Apprentice	Middlesbrough	109	12
							Nottingham F	64	5
							Sunderland (loan)	5	—
							Sunderland	112	19
							Sheffield W	59	4
							Middlesbrough	120	6
							Tranmere R (loan)	13	1
							Tranmere R	18	—
PROKAS Richard	5 9	11 00	M	22 1 76	Penrith	Trainee	**Carlisle U**	39	1
PRUDHOE Mark	6 0	13 00	G	8 11 63	Washington	Apprentice	Sunderland	7	—
							Hartlepool U (loan)	3	—
							Birmingham C	1	—
							Walsall	26	—
							Doncaster R (loan)	5	—
							Sheffield W (loan)	—	—
							Grimsby T (loan)	8	—
							Hartlepool U (loan)	13	—
							Bristol C (loan)	3	—
							Carlisle U	34	—
							Darlington	146	—
							Stoke C	30	—
							Peterborough U (loan)	6	—
							Liverpool (loan)	—	—
PUGH David	6 2	13 00	F	19 9 64	Liverpool	Runcorn	Chester C	179	23
							Bury	42	16
PUGH Stephen *	5 9	11 00	F	27 11 73	Bangor	Trainee	**Wrexham**	11	—
PURSE Darren	6 2	12 08	D	14 2 77	London	Trainee	**Leyton Orient**	43	3

Player	Ht	Wt	Pos	Birth Date	Birth Place	Source	Clubs	League App	League Gls
PUTNEY Trevor *	5 9	11 08	M	11 2 61	Harold Hill	Brentwood & W	Ipswich T	103	8
							Norwich C	82	9
							Middlesbrough	48	1
							Watford	52	2
							Leyton Orient	22	2
							Colchester U	28	2
PUTTNAM David	5 10	11 09	M	3 2 67	Leicester	Leicester U	Leicester C	7	—
							Lincoln C	172	20
QUIGLEY Jim ‡	5 8	11 02	M	21 9 76	Derry	Trainee	**Everton**	—	—
QUIGLEY Mike *	5 6	9 04	M	2 10 70	Manchester	Trainee	**Manchester C**	12	—
							Wrexham (loan)	4	—
QUINN James	6 1	12 10	F	15 12 74	Coventry	Trainee	Birmingham C	4	—
							Blackpool	55	11
							Stockport Co (loan)	1	—
QUINN Jimmy	6 0	11 06	F	18 11 59	Belfast	Oswestry T	Swindon T	49	10
							Blackburn R	71	17
							Swindon T	64	30
							Leicester C	31	6
							Bradford C	35	14
							West Ham U	47	18
							Bournemouth	43	19
							Reading	123	57
QUINN Mick ‡	5 9	13 00	F	2 5 62	Liverpool	Derby Co	Wigan Ath	69	19
							Stockport Co	63	39
							Oldham Ath	80	34
							Portsmouth	121	54
							Newcastle U	115	59
							Coventry C	64	25
							Plymouth Arg (loan)	3	—
							Portsmouth (loan)	—	—
							Watford (loan)	5	—
QUINN Niall	6 4	13 10	F	6 10 66	Dublin		Arsenal	67	14
							Manchester C	171	58
QUINN Robert	5 11	11 02	D	8 11 76	Sidcup	Trainee	**Crystal Palace**	—	—
QUINN Wayne	5 10	11 07	M	19 11 76	Cornwall		**Sheffield U**	—	—
QUY Andy	6 0	13 01	G	4 7 76	Harlow	Tottenham H	**Derby Co**	—	—
RACHEL Adam			G	10 12 76	Birmingham	Trainee	**Aston Villa**	—	—
RADEBE Lucas	5 11	11 09	M	12 4 69	South Africa	Kaiser Chiefs	**Leeds U**	12	—
RADOSAVLJEVIC Predrag	5 11	12 10	M	24 6 63	Belgrade	St Louis Storms	Everton	46	4
							Portsmouth	40	5
RAE Alex	5 9	11 05	M	30 9 69	Glasgow	Bishopbriggs	Falkirk	83	20
							Millwall	181	50
RAMAGE Andrew *	5 11	12 02	M	3 10 74	Hornchurch	Dagenham	**Gillingham**	13	1
RAMAGE Craig	5 9	11 08	M	30 3 70	Derby	Trainee	Derby Co	42	4
							Wigan Ath (loan)	10	2
							Watford	57	9
RAMMELL Andy	6 0	13 05	F	10 2 67	Nuneaton	Atherstone U	Manchester U	—	—
							Barnsley	165	40
RAMSEY Paul (on loan from St Johnstone)	5 11	13 00	D	3 9 62	Londonderry		**Cardiff C**	11	—
RANDALL Adrian	5 11	12 04	M	10 11 68	Amesbury	Apprentice	Bournemouth	3	—
							Aldershot	107	12
							Burnley	110	8
RANKINE Mark	5 10	11 01	M	30 9 69	Doncaster	Trainee	Doncaster R	164	20
							Wolverhampton W	100	1
RANSON Ray ‡	5 9	11 12	D	12 6 60	St. Helens	Apprentice	Manchester C	183	1
							Birmingham C	137	—
							Newcastle U	83	1
							Manchester C	17	—
							Reading	24	—

Player	Ht	Wt	Pos	Birth Date	Birth Place	Source	Clubs	League App	League Gls
RATCLIFFE Kevin	6 1	13 06	D	12 11 60	Mancot	Apprentice	Everton	359	2
							Dundee	4	—
							Everton	—	—
							Cardiff C	25	1
							Nottingham F	—	—
							Derby Co	6	—
							Chester C	23	—
RATCLIFFE Simon	5 11	11 09	M	8 2 67	Davyhulme	Apprentice	Manchester U	—	—
							Norwich C	9	—
							Brentford	214	14
RATTLE Jon ‡	5 9	11 13	D	22 7 76	Melton	Trainee	**Cambridge U**	6	—
RAVEN Paul	6 0	12 03	D	28 7 70	Salisbury	School	Doncaster R	52	4
							WBA	139	9
							Doncaster R (loan)	7	—
RAVENSCROFT Craig	5 6	9 07	F	20 12 74	London	Trainee	**Brentford**	8	1
RAWLINS Matthew *			F	12 9 75	Bristol	Trainee	**Arsenal**	—	—
RAWLINSON Mark *	5 10	11 00	M	9 6 75	Bolton	Trainee	**Manchester U**	—	—
RAYNOR Paul	6 0	12 11	M	29 4 66	Nottingham	Apprentice	Nottingham F	3	—
							Bristol R (loan)	8	—
							Huddersfield T	50	9
							Swansea C	191	27
							Wrexham (loan)	6	—
							Cambridge U	49	2
							Preston NE	77	9
REA Simon	6 1	13 00	D	20 9 76	Coventry	Trainee	**Birmingham C**	—	—
READ Paul	5 11	12 06	F	25 9 73	Harlow	Trainee	**Arsenal**	—	—
							Leyton Orient (loan)	11	—
READY Karl	6 1	12 00	D	14 8 72	Neath	Trainee	**QPR**	39	2
REDDISH Shane	5 10	11 10	M	5 5 71	Bolsover	Trainee	Doncaster R	60	3
							Carlisle U	37	1
							Chesterfield (loan)	3	—
							Hartlepool	23	—
REDFEARN Neil	5 10	12 08	M	20 6 65	Dewsbury	Nottingham F	Bolton W	35	1
							Lincoln C (loan)	10	1
							Lincoln C	90	12
							Doncaster R	46	14
							Crystal Palace	57	10
							Watford	24	3
							Oldham Ath	62	16
							Barnsley	167	30
REDKNAPP Jamie	6 0	12 00	M	25 6 73	Barton on Sea	Trainee	Bournemouth	13	—
							Liverpool	111	10
REDMOND Steven	5 11	12 13	D	2 11 67	Liverpool	Apprentice	Manchester C	235	7
							Oldham Ath	107	1
REECE Andy	5 10	12 02	M	5 9 62	Shrewsbury	Willenhall	Bristol R	239	17
							Walsall (loan)	9	1
							Walsall (loan)	6	—
							Hereford U	65	5
REECE Paul	5 11	12 07	G	16 7 68	Nottingham	Kettering T	Grimsby T	54	—
							Doncaster R	1	—
							Oxford U	39	—
							Notts Co	11	—
REED Adam	6 0	12 00	D	18 2 75	Bishop Auckland	Trainee	**Darlington**	52	1
REED Ian	5 8	10 09	M	4 9 75	Lichfield	Trainee	**Shrewsbury T**	4	—
REED John	5 6	10 11	F	27 8 72	Rotherham	Trainee	**Sheffield U**	13	2
							Scarborough (loan)	14	6
							Scarborough (loan)	6	—
							Darlington (loan)	10	2
							Mansfield T (loan)	13	2
REES Jason	5 5	9 10	F	22 12 69	Pontypridd	Trainee	Luton T	82	—
							Mansfield T (loan)	15	1
							Portsmouth	19	1

Player	Ht	Wt	Pos	Birth Date	Birth Place	Source	Clubs	League App	League Gls
REES Tony	5 9	11 13	F	1 8 64	Merthyr Tydfil	Apprentice	Aston Villa	—	—
							Birmingham C	95	12
							Peterborough U (loan)	5	2
							Shrewsbury T (loan)	2	—
							Barnsley	31	3
							Grimsby T	141	33
							WBA	14	2
REEVE James *	6 1	11 07	F	26 11 75	Weymouth	Trainee	Bournemouth	7	—
							Hereford U	5	—
REEVES Alan	6 0	12 00	D	19 11 67	Birkenhead	Heswall	Norwich C	—	—
							Gillingham (loan)	18	—
							Chester C	40	2
							Rochdale	121	9
							Wimbledon	31	3
REEVES David	6 0	11 05	F	19 11 67	Birkenhead	Heswall	Sheffield W	17	2
							Scunthorpe U (loan)	4	2
							Scunthorpe U (loan)	6	4
							Burnley (loan)	16	8
							Bolton W	134	29
							Notts Co	13	2
							Carlisle U	76	32
REEVES Steve *	5 11	13 00	G	24 9 74	Dagenham	Trainee	**Everton**	—	—
REGIS Cyrille *	6 0	13 06	F	9 2 58	French Guyana	Hayes	WBA	237	82
							Coventry C	238	47
							Aston Villa	52	12
							Wolverhampton W	19	2
							Wycombe W	35	9
REGIS Dave	6 1	13 08	F	3 3 64	Paddington	Barnet	Notts Co	46	15
							Plymouth Arg	31	4
							Bournemouth (loan)	6	2
							Stoke C	63	15
							Birmingham C	6	2
							Southend U	9	1
REID Nicky *	5 10	12 04	D	30 10 60	Ormston	Apprentice	Manchester C	217	2
							Blackburn R	174	9
							Bristol C (loan)	4	—
							WBA	20	—
							Wycombe W	8	—
REID Paul	5 9	10 08	M	19 1 68	Oldbury	Apprentice	Leicester C	162	21
							Bradford C (loan)	7	—
							Bradford C	82	15
							Huddersfield T	42	6
REID Peter ‡	5 8	12 02	M	20 6 56	Huyton	Apprentice	Bolton W	225	23
							Everton	159	8
							QPR	29	1
							Manchester C	103	1
							Southampton	7	—
							Notts Co	5	—
							Bury	1	—
REID Shaun	5 8	11 10	M	13 10 65	Huyton	Local	Rochdale	133	4
							Preston NE (loan)	3	—
							York C	106	7
							Rochdale	107	10
REINELT Robert	5 10	11 13	M	11 3 74	Epping	Trainee	Aldershot	5	—
							Gillingham	52	5
							Colchester U	5	—
RENNIE David	6 0	12 00	D	29 8 64	Edinburgh	Apprentice	Leicester C	21	1
							Leeds U	101	5
							Bristol C	104	8
							Birmingham C	35	4
							Coventry C	71	1
RENNIE Paul *	5 9	11 04	D	26 10 71	Nantwich	Trainee	Crewe Alex	2	—
							Stoke C	4	—
							Wigan Ath	40	3
RHODES Andy (on loan from St Johnstone)	6 1	13 06	G	23 8 64	Doncaster		**Bolton W**	—	—
RICE Gary *			D	29 9 75	Zambia	Trainee	**Exeter C**	10	—

Player	Ht	Wt	Pos	Birth Date	Birth Place	Source	Clubs	League App	League Gls
RICHARDS Dave			M	31 12 76	Birmingham	Trainee	**Walsall**	—	—
RICHARDS Dean	6 2	13 01	D	9 6 74	Bradford	Trainee	**Bradford C**	86	4
							Wolverhampton W (loan)	10	2
RICHARDSON Barry	6 1	12 01	G	5 8 69	Wallsend	Trainee	Sunderland	—	—
							Scunthorpe U	—	—
							Scarborough	30	—
							Northampton T	96	—
							Preston NE	17	—
RICHARDSON Jon	5 11	12 00	M	29 8 75	Nottingham	Trainee	**Exeter C**	45	1
RICHARDSON Kevin	5 7	11 07	M	4 12 62	Newcastle	Apprentice	Everton	109	16
							Watford	39	2
							Arsenal	96	5
						Real Sociedad	Aston Villa	143	13
							Coventry C	14	—
RICHARDSON Lee	5 11	11 00	M	12 3 69	Halifax		Halifax T	56	2
							Watford	41	1
							Blackburn R	62	3
							Aberdeen	64	6
							Oldham Ath	30	6
RICHARDSON Lloyd			M	7 10 77	Dewsbury	Trainee	**Oldham Ath**	—	—
RICHARDSON Neil	6 0	13 09	D	3 3 68	Sunderland	Brandon U	**Rotherham U**	102	4
RICHARDSON Nick	6 0	12 07	M	11 4 67	Halifax	Local	Halifax T	101	17
							Cardiff C	111	13
							Wrexham (loan)	4	2
							Chester C (loan)	6	1
RICKERS Paul	5 10	11 00	M	9 5 75	Pontefract	Trainee	**Oldham Ath**	4	1
RIDEOUT Paul	5 11	12 01	F	14 8 64	Bournemouth	Apprentice	Swindon T	95	38
							Aston Villa	54	19
							Bari	99	23
							Southampton	75	19
							Swindon T (loan)	9	1
							Notts Co	11	3
							Rangers	12	1
							Everton	77	23
RIDGEWAY Ian	5 8	10 06	M	28 12 75	Nottingham	Trainee	**Notts Co**	1	—
RIEPER Marc	6 4	13 10	D	5 6 68	Denmark	Brondby	**West Ham U**	21	1
RIGBY Malcolm	6 1	12 00	G	13 3 76	Nottingham	Notts Co	**Nottingham F**	—	—
RIGBY Tony	5 10	12 12	M	10 8 72	Ormskirk	Barrow	**Bury**	84	11
RIMMER Neill	5 6	10 03	M	13 11 67	Liverpool	Apprentice	Everton	1	—
							Ipswich T	22	3
							Wigan Ath	160	10
RIMMER Stuart	5 7	11 00	F	12 10 64	Southport	Apprentice	Everton	3	—
							Chester C	114	67
							Watford	10	1
							Notts Co	4	2
							Walsall	88	31
							Barnsley	15	1
							Chester C	147	43
							Rochdale (loan)	3	—
							Preston NE (loan)	2	—
RIOCH Greg *	5 11	10 09	D	24 6 75	Sutton Coldfield	Trainee	**Luton T**	—	—
							Barnet (loan)	3	—
RIPLEY Andrew *	5 8	11 10	M	10 12 75	Middlesbrough	Trainee	**Darlington**	2	—
RIPLEY Stuart	5 11	12 06	F	20 11 67	Middlesbrough	Apprentice	Middlesbrough	249	26
							Bolton W (loan)	5	1
							Blackburn R	117	11
RITCHIE Andy *	5 10	11 11	F	28 11 60	Manchester	Apprentice	Manchester U	33	13
							Brighton	89	23
							Leeds U	136	40
							Oldham Ath	217	82
RITCHIE Paul (on loan from Dundee)	5 11	12 00	F	25 1 69	St Andrews		**Gillingham**	5	1

Player	Ht	Wt	Pos	Birth Date	Birth Place	Source	Clubs	League App	League Gls
RIVERS Mark			D	26 11 75	Crewe	Trainee	**Crewe Alex**	—	—
RIX Graham †	5 9	11 00	F	23 10 57	Doncaster	Apprentice	Arsenal	351	41
							Brentford (loan)	6	—
						Caen, Le Havre	Dundee	14	2
							Chelsea	1	—
ROBERTS Andy	5 10	13 00	M	20 3 74	Dartford	Trainee	**Millwall**	138	5
ROBERTS Ben	6 1	12 11	G	22 6 75	Bishop Auckland	Trainee	**Middlesbrough**	—	—
ROBERTS Danny *	5 8	10 08	D	12 11 75	Chelmsford	Trainee	**Colchester U**	—	—
ROBERTS Darren	5 10	12 01	F	12 10 69	Birmingham	Burton Alb	Wolverhampton W	21	5
							Hereford U (loan)	6	5
							Doncaster R	—	—
							Chesterfield	11	1
ROBERTS Glyn	5 11	12 02	M	19 10 74	Ipswich	Norwich C	**Rotherham U**	16	1
ROBERTS Iwan	6 2	14 02	F	26 6 68	Bangor	Trainee	Watford	63	9
							Huddersfield T	142	50
							Leicester C	63	22
ROBERTS Tony	6 0	12 00	G	4 8 69	Bangor	Trainee	**QPR**	94	—
ROBERTSON John	6 2	13 02	D	8 1 74	Liverpool	Trainee	**Wigan Ath**	98	3
ROBERTSON Sandy	5 9	10 07	M	26 4 71	Edinburgh	S Form	Rangers	26	1
							Coventry C	4	—
ROBINS Mark	5 7	10 06	F	22 12 69	Ashton-under-Lyme	Apprentice	Manchester U	48	11
							Norwich C	67	20
							Leicester C	17	5
ROBINSON David *			D	30 10 74	Wrekin	Liverpool	**Stockport Co**	—	—
ROBINSON Jamie	6 0	12 03	D	22 2 72	Liverpool	Trainee	Liverpool	—	—
							Barnsley	9	—
							Carlisle U	30	2
ROBINSON John	5 10	11 02	M	29 8 71	Bulawayo, Rhodesia	Apprentice	Brighton	62	6
							Charlton Ath	63	6
ROBINSON Les	5 8	11 01	D	1 3 67	Shirerook	Local	Mansfield T	15	—
							Stockport Co	67	3
							Doncaster R	82	12
							Oxford U	169	2
ROBINSON Liam	5 7	12 07	F	29 12 65	Bradford	Nottingham F	Huddersfield T	21	2
							Tranmere R (loan)	4	3
							Bury	262	89
							Bristol C	41	4
							Burnley	39	7
ROBINSON Mark	5 9	11 08	D	21 11 68	Rochdale	Trainee	WBA	2	—
							Barnsley	137	6
							Newcastle U	25	—
							Swindon T	40	—
ROBINSON Matthew	5 10	11 02	M	23 12 74	Exeter	Trainee	**Southampton**	1	—
ROBINSON Phil	5 10	11 07	M	6 1 67	Stafford	Apprentice	Aston Villa	3	1
							Wolverhampton W	71	8
							Notts Co	66	5
							Birmingham C (loan)	9	—
							Huddersfield T	75	5
							Northampton T (loan)	14	—
							Chesterfield	22	8
ROBINSON Ronnie *	5 9	11 05	D	22 10 66	Sunderland	SC Vaux	Ipswich T	—	—
						Vaux Breweries	Leeds U	27	—
							Doncaster R	78	5
							WBA	1	—
							Rotherham U	86	2
							Peterborough U	47	—
							Exeter C	39	1
							Huddersfield T (loan)	2	—
ROBINSON Steve	5 8	10 07	F	10 12 74	Lisburn	Trainee	Tottenham H	2	—
							Leyton Orient (loan)	—	—
							Bournemouth	32	5

Player	Ht	Wt	Pos	Birth Date	Birth Place	Source	Clubs	League App	League Gls
ROBINSON Steven	5 4	10 11	M	17 1 75	Nottingham	Trainee	**Birmingham C**	6	—
ROBSON Bryan	5 9	12 05	M	11 1 57	Witton Gilbert	Apprentice	WBA	197	39
							Manchester U	345	74
							Middlesbrough	22	1
ROBSON Gary	5 8	11 06	M	6 7 65	Durham	Apprentice	WBA	218	28
							Bradford C	69	3
ROBSON Mark	5 7	10 02	M	22 5 69	Newham	Trainee	Exeter C	26	7
							Tottenham H	8	—
							Reading (loan)	7	—
							Watford (loan)	1	—
							Plymouth Arg (loan)	7	—
							Exeter C (loan)	8	1
							West Ham U	47	8
							Charlton Ath	63	5
ROBSON Stewart *	5 11	12 04	M	6 11 64	Billericay	Apprentice	Arsenal	151	16
							West Ham U	69	4
							Coventry C (loan)	4	—
							Coventry C	53	3
ROCASTLE David	5 9	11 12	F	2 5 67	Lewisham	Apprentice	Arsenal	218	24
							Leeds U	25	2
							Manchester C	21	2
							Chelsea	28	—
ROCHE David	6 0	13 02	M	13 12 70	Newcastle	Trainee	Newcastle U	36	—
							Peterborough U (loan)	4	—
							Doncaster R	50	8
							Southend U	4	—
ROCKETT Jason	6 1	13 00	D	26 9 69	London		Rotherham U	—	—
							Scarborough	61	—
RODEN Damien ‡	5 9	11 00	D	17 9 74	Wrexham	Trainee	**Wrexham**	—	—
RODGER Graham	6 2	11 13	D	1 4 67	Glasgow	Apprentice	Wolverhampton W	1	—
							Coventry C	36	2
							Luton T	28	2
							Grimsby T	91	9
RODGER Simon	5 9	11 09	M	3 10 71	Shoreham	Trainee	**Crystal Palace**	91	5
RODGERSON Ian *	5 8	11 06	M	9 4 66	Hereford	Pegasus Juniors	Hereford U	100	6
							Cardiff C	99	4
							Birmingham C	95	13
							Sunderland	10	—
RODWELL Tony	5 11	11 02	F	26 8 62	Southport	Colne Dynamoes	Blackpool	142	17
							Scarborough	8	1
							Wigan Ath (loan)	5	1
ROGAN Anton *	5 11	12 06	D	25 3 66	Belfast	Distillery	Celtic	127	4
							Sunderland	46	1
							Oxford U	58	3
ROGERS Darren	6 0	13 00	D	9 4 70	Birmingham	Trainee	WBA	14	1
							Birmingham C	18	—
							Wycombe W (loan)	1	—
							Walsall	27	—
ROGERS Dave *	6 0	11 01	M	25 8 75	Liverpool	Trainee	**Tranmere R**	—	—
ROGERS Lee	5 11	12 02	D	28 10 66	Doncaster	Doncaster R	**Chesterfield**	293	1
ROGERS Paul	6 0	12 05	M	21 3 65	Portsmouth	Sutton U	**Sheffield U**	109	10
ROOKYARD Carl ‡	5 9	10 05	F	3 9 75	Burton on Trent	Trainee	Nottingham F	—	—
							Walsall	—	—
ROPER Ian	6 4	14 00	D	20 6 77	Nuneaton	Trainee	**Walsall**	—	—
ROSARIO Robert	6 3	12 01	F	4 3 66	Hammersmith	Hillingdon Bor	Norwich C	126	18
							Wolverhampton W (loan)	2	1
							Coventry C	59	8
							Nottingham F	27	3
ROSCOE Andrew	5 9	10 12	M	4 6 73	Liverpool	Trainee	Liverpool	—	—
							Bolton W	3	—
							Rotherham U	31	4

Player	Ht	Wt	Pos	Birth Date	Birth Place	Source	Clubs	League App	League Gls
ROSE Matthew			M	24 9 75	Dartford	Trainee	**Arsenal**	—	—
ROSENIOR Leroy *	6 1	11 10	F	24 3 64	London	School	Fulham	54	16
							QPR	38	7
							Fulham	34	20
							West Ham U	53	15
							Fulham (loan)	11	3
							Charlton Ath (loan)	3	—
							Bristol C	51	12
ROSENTHAL Ronny	5 11	12 13	F	11 10 63	Haifa	Standard Liege	Luton T (loan)	—	—
							Liverpool (loan)	8	7
							Liverpool	66	14
							Tottenham H	35	2
ROSLER Uwe	6 1	12 04	F	15 11 68	Attenburg	Dynamo Dresden	**Manchester C**	43	20
ROSS Mike	5 6	9 13	F	2 9 71	Southampton	Trainee	Portsmouth	4	—
							Exeter C	28	9
							Plymouth Arg	17	—
ROUND Steve	5 10	11 03	D	9 11 70	Buxton	Trainee	**Derby Co**	9	—
ROWBOTHAM Darren *	5 10	11 05	M	22 10 66	Cardiff	Trainee	Plymouth Arg	46	2
							Exeter C	118	47
							Torquay U	14	3
							Birmingham C	36	6
							Hereford U (loan)	8	2
							Mansfield T (loan)	4	—
							Crewe Alex	61	21
ROWE Richard *			M	12 5 76	Plymouth	Southampton	**Bristol C**	—	—
ROWE Rodney	5 8	12 08	F	30 7 75	Huddersfield	Trainee	**Huddersfield T**	13	1
							Scarborough (loan)	14	1
							Bury (loan)	3	—
ROWE Zeke	5 6	9 08	M	30 10 73	Stoke Newington	Trainee	**Chelsea**	—	—
							Barnet (loan)	10	2
ROWETT Gary	6 0	12 10	F	6 3 74	Bromsgrove	Trainee	Cambridge U	63	9
							Everton	4	—
							Blackpool (loan)	17	—
ROWLAND Keith	5 10	10 00	M	1 9 71	Portadown	Trainee	Bournemouth	72	2
							Coventry C (loan)	2	—
							West Ham U	35	—
ROY Bryan	5 10	10 08	M	12 2 69	Amsterdam	Foggia	**Nottingham F**	37	13
ROYCE Simon	6 2	12 08	G	9 9 71	Forest Gate	Heybridge Swifts	**Southend U**	23	—
RUDDOCK Neil	6 2	12 12	D	9 5 68	London	Apprentice	Millwall	—	—
							Tottenham H	9	—
							Millwall	2	1
							Southampton	107	9
							Tottenham H	38	3
							Liverpool	76	5
RUFUS Marvin §			M	11 9 76	Lewisham	Charlton Ath	**Leyton Orient**	7	—
RUFUS Richard	6 1	10 05	D	12 1 75	Lewisham	Trainee	**Charlton Ath**	28	—
RUSH David	5 11	10 10	F	15 5 71	Sunderland	Trainee	Sunderland	59	12
							Hartlepool U (loan)	8	2
							Peterborough U (loan)	4	1
							Cambridge U (loan)	2	—
							Oxford U	34	9
RUSH Ian	6 0	12 06	F	20 10 61	St. Asaph	Apprentice	Chester	34	14
							Liverpool	224	139
							Juventus	29	7
							Liverpool	225	85
RUSH Matthew	5 11	12 10	M	6 8 71	Dalston	Trainee	**West Ham U**	48	5
							Cambridge U (loan)	10	—
							Swansea C (loan)	13	—
RUSSELL Alex	5 8	11 07	M	17 3 73	Crosby	Burscough	**Rochdale**	7	1
RUSSELL Craig	5 10	12 06	F	4 2 74	South Shields	Trainee	**Sunderland**	77	14

Player	Ht	Wt	Pos	Birth Date	Birth Place	Source	Clubs	League App	League Gls
RUSSELL Kevin	5 8	10 12	F	6 12 66	Portsmouth	Brighton	Portsmouth	4	1
							Wrexham	84	43
							Leicester C	43	10
							Peterborough U (loan)	7	3
							Cardiff C (loan)	3	—
							Hereford U (loan)	3	1
							Stoke C (loan)	5	1
							Stoke C	40	5
							Burnley	28	6
							Bournemouth	30	1
							Notts Co	11	—
RUSSELL Lee	5 11	11 04	D	3 9 69	Southampton	Trainee	**Portsmouth**	76	1
							Bournemouth (loan)	3	—
RUSSELL Wayne	6 2	12 13	G	29 11 67	Cardiff	Ebbw Vale	**Burnley**	8	—
RUST Nicky	6 0	13 01	G	25 9 74	Ely	Arsenal	**Brighton**	90	—
RUTHERFORD Paul (To Berwick Rangers)	5 11	12 07	F	23 2 67	Sunderland	Meadowbank T	**Scarborough**	8	1
RYAN Darren	5 9	11 00	M	3 7 72	Oswestry	Trainee	Shrewsbury T	4	—
							Chester C	17	2
							Stockport Co	36	6
							Rochdale	25	2
RYAN John	5 8	11 06	F	7 12 75	Cork	Cork C	**Brighton**	—	—
RYAN Keith	5 11	12 07	M	25 6 70	Northampton	Berkhamsted T	**Wycombe W**	66	5
RYAN Robbie	5 11	11 05	D	11 8 76	Dublin	Belvedere	**Huddersfield T**	—	—
RYAN Tim ‡	5 10	11 00	D	10 12 74	Stockport	Trainee	**Scunthorpe U**	2	—
RYAN Vaughan *	5 9	12 00	M	2 9 68	Westminster		Wimbledon	82	3
							Sheffield U (loan)	3	—
							Leyton Orient	44	—
RYDER Stuart	6 1	12 02	D	6 11 73	Sutton Coldfield	Trainee	**Walsall**	84	5
SADDINGTON James ‡	6 0	11 13	D	12 9 72	Cambridge	Cambridge C	**Millwall**	—	—
SALAKO John	5 9	12 03	F	11 2 69	Nigeria	Trainee	**Crystal Palace**	215	22
							Swansea C (loan)	13	3
SALE Mark	6 5	13 08	F	27 2 72	Burton-on-Trent	Trainee	Stoke C	2	—
							Cambridge U	—	—
							Birmingham C	21	—
							Torquay U	44	8
							Preston NE	13	7
SALMON Mike	6 2	12 12	G	14 7 64	Leyland	Local	Blackburn R	1	—
							Chester C (loan)	16	—
							Stockport Co	118	—
							Bolton W	26	—
							Wrexham (loan)	17	—
							Wrexham	83	—
							Charlton Ath	87	—
SAMPSON Ian	6 2	12 08	D	14 11 68	Wakefield	Goole T	Sunderland	17	1
							Northampton T (loan)	8	—
							Northampton T	42	2
SAMWAYS Mark	6 2	14 00	G	11 11 68	Doncaster	Trainee	Doncaster R	121	—
							Scunthorpe U (loan)	8	—
							Scunthorpe U	114	—
SAMWAYS Vinny	5 8	11 00	M	27 10 68	Bethnal Green	Apprentice	Tottenham H	193	11
							Everton	19	1
SANDEMAN Bradley	5 10	10 08	M	24 2 70	Northampton	Trainee	Northampton T	58	3
							Maidstone U	57	8
							Port Vale	68	1
SANDFORD Lee	6 0	12 12	D	22 4 68	Basingstoke	Apprentice	Portsmouth	72	1
							Stoke C	212	8
SANSAM Christian	6 0	11 07	F	26 12 75	Hull	Trainee	**Scunthorpe U**	16	—

Player	Ht	Wt	Pos	Birth Date	Birth Place	Source	Clubs	League App	League Gls
SANSOM Kenny ‡	5 7	10 04	D	26 9 58	Camberwell	Apprentice	Crystal Palace	172	3
							Arsenal	314	6
							Newcastle U	20	—
							QPR	64	—
							Coventry C	51	—
							Everton	7	1
							Brentford	8	—
						Chertsey	**Watford**	1	—
SANSOME Paul	6 0	13 10	G	6 10 61	N. Addington	Crystal Palace	Millwall	156	—
							Southend U	305	—
SARGENT David			D	22 12 77	Wembley	Watford	**Wycombe W**	—	—
SAUNDERS Dean	5 8	10 06	F	21 6 64	Swansea	Apprentice	Swansea C	49	12
							Cardiff C (loan)	4	—
							Brighton	72	21
							Oxford U	59	22
							Derby Co	106	42
							Liverpool	42	11
							Aston Villa	112	37
SAUNDERS Lee			D	23 3 77	Nuneaton	Trainee	**Doncaster R**	—	—
SAVAGE Dave	6 1	12 07	M	30 7 73	Dublin	Longford T	**Millwall**	37	2
SAVAGE Rob	6 0	10 01	F	18 10 74	Wrexham	Trainee	Manchester U	—	—
							Crewe Alex	6	2
SAVILLE Andrew	6 0	12 06	F	12 12 64	Hull	Local	Hull C	100	18
							Walsall	38	5
							Barnsley	82	21
							Hartlepool U	37	13
							Birmingham C	59	17
							Burnley (loan)	4	1
SCAIFE Nicky	6 0	11 13	M	14 5 75	Middlesbrough	Whitby	**York C**	1	—
SCALES John	6 2	13 05	D	4 7 66	Harrogate		Leeds U	—	—
							Bristol R	72	2
							Wimbledon	240	11
							Liverpool	35	2
SCARGILL Jonathan	6 0	13 10	G	9 4 77	Dewsbury	Trainee	**Sheffield W**	—	—
SCARGILL Wayne ‡	5 11	11 10	D	30 4 68	Barnsley	Frickley Ath	**Bradford C**	1	—
SCHMEICHEL Peter	6 4	16 01	G	18 11 63	Gladsaxe	Brondby	**Manchester U**	154	—
SCHOFIELD Jon	5 11	11 03	M	16 5 65	Barnsley	Gainsborough T	Lincoln C	231	11
							Doncaster R	27	1
SCHOLES Paul	5 7	10 11	F	16 11 74	Salford	Trainee	**Manchester U**	17	5
SCHWARZ Stefan	5 10	12 06	M	18 4 69	Malmo		Malmo	29	—
							Benfica	77	7
							Arsenal	34	2
SCIMECA Riccardo	6 1	12 09	D	13 6 75	Leamington Spa	Trainee	**Aston Villa**	—	—
SCOTT Andrew	6 0	12 11	D	27 6 75	Manchester	Trainee	Blackburn R	—	—
							Cardiff C	13	1
SCOTT Andy	6 1	11 05	F	2 8 72	Epsom	Sutton U	**Sheffield U**	54	5
SCOTT Keith	6 3	14 03	F	9 6 67	London	Leicester U	Lincoln C	16	2
						Wycombe W	Wycombe W	15	10
							Swindon T	51	12
							Stoke C	18	3
SCOTT Kevin	6 4	14 03	D	17 12 66	Easington	Middlesbrough	Newcastle U	227	8
							Tottenham H	16	1
							Port Vale (loan)	17	1
SCOTT Mark *	5 10	11 07	D	21 2 76	Darlington	Trainee	**Norwich C**	—	—
SCOTT Martin	5 10	11 07	M	7 1 68	Sheffield	Apprentice	Rotherham U	94	3
							Nottingham F (loan)	—	—
							Bristol C	171	14
							Sunderland	24	—
SCOTT Peter	5 9	11 12	M	1 10 63	London	Apprentice	Fulham	277	27
							Bournemouth	10	—
							Barnet	58	2

Player	Ht	Wt	Pos	Birth Date	Birth Place	Source	Clubs	League App	League Gls
SCOTT Richard	5 9	10 10	D	29 9 74	Dudley	Trainee	Birmingham C	12	—
							Shrewsbury T	8	1
SCOTT Rob	6 1	11 10	F	15 8 73	Epsom	Sutton U	**Sheffield U**	1	—
							Scarborough (loan)	8	3
SCOTT Ryan *	5 9	11 00	D	20 3 76	Saltburn	Trainee	**Darlington**	1	—
SCOTT Steve ‡	5 7	10 03	M	29 1 76	Edinburgh	Trainee	**Brighton & HA**	—	—
SCOWCROFT James	6 1	12 02	F	15 11 75	Bury St Edmunds	Trainee	**Ipswich T**	—	—
SCULLY Anthony	5 7	11 12	F	12 6 76	Dublin	Trainee	**Crystal Palace**	—	—
							Bournemouth (loan)	10	—
SCULLY Pat	6 1	12 07	D	23 6 70	Dublin	Trainee	Arsenal	—	—
							Preston NE (loan)	13	1
							Northampton T (loan)	15	—
							Southend U	115	6
							Huddersfield T	49	1
SEABURY Kevin	5 9	11 06	D	24 11 73	Shrewsbury	Trainee	**Shrewsbury T**	31	—
SEAGRAVES Mark	6 0	13 04	D	22 10 66	Bootle	Apprentice	Liverpool	—	—
							Norwich C (loan)	3	—
							Manchester C	42	—
							Bolton W	157	7
SEAL David	5 11	12 00	F	26 1 72	Penrith NSW	Aalst	**Bristol C**	9	—
SEALEY Les	6 1	13 06	G	29 9 57	Bethnal Green	Apprentice	Coventry C	158	—
							Luton T	207	—
							Plymouth Arg (loan)	6	—
							Manchester U (loan)	2	—
							Manchester U	31	—
							Aston Villa	18	—
							Coventry C (loan)	2	—
							Birmingham C (loan)	12	—
							Manchester U	—	—
							Blackpool	7	—
							West Ham U	—	—
SEAMAN David	6 4	14 10	G	19 9 63	Rotherham	Apprentice	Leeds U	—	—
							Peterborough U	91	—
							Birmingham C	75	—
							QPR	141	—
							Arsenal	189	—
SEARLE Damon	5 11	10 04	D	26 10 71	Cardiff	Trainee	**Cardiff C**	193	2
SEDGEMORE Ben	5 10	13 11	M	5 8 75	Wolverhampton	Trainee	**Birmingham C**	—	—
							Northampton T (loan)	1	—
SEDGLEY Steve	6 1	13 13	M	26 5 68	Enfield	Apprentice	Coventry C	84	3
							Tottenham H	164	8
							Ipswich T	26	4
SEGERS Hans	5 11	12 12	G	30 10 61	Eindhoven	PSV Eindhoven	Nottingham F	58	—
							Stoke C (loan)	1	—
							Sheffield U (loan)	10	—
							Dunfermline Ath (loan)	4	—
							Wimbledon	263	—
SELLARS Scott	5 7	9 10	M	27 11 65	Sheffield	Apprentice	Leeds U	76	12
							Blackburn R	202	35
							Leeds U	7	—
							Newcastle U	55	5
SELLEY Ian	5 9	10 01	M	14 6 74	Chertsey	Trainee	**Arsenal**	40	—
SEMPLE Ryan §			M	2 7 77	Derry	Trainee	**Peterborough U**	2	—
SERRANT Carl			D	12 9 75	Bradford	Trainee	**Oldham Ath**	—	—
SERTORI Mark	6 2	14 02	M	1 9 67	Manchester		Stockport Co	4	—
							Lincoln C	50	9
							Wrexham	110	3
							Bury	2	—
SHAIL Mark	6 1	13 03	D	15 10 66	Sweden	Yeovil	**Bristol C**	78	4

Player	Ht	Wt	Pos	Birth Date	Birth Place	Source	Clubs	League App	League Gls
SHAKESPEARE Craig	5 10	12 05	M	26 10 63	Birmingham	Apprentice	Walsall	284	45
							Sheffield W	17	—
							WBA	112	12
							Grimsby T	52	6
SHARP Graeme	6 1	11 09	F	16 10 60	Glasgow	Eastercraigs	Dumbarton	40	17
							Everton	322	111
							Oldham Ath	109	30
SHARP Kevin	5 9	11 11	M	19 9 74	Ontario	Auxerre	**Leeds U**	16	—
SHARP Raymond	5 11	12 06	D	16 11 69	Stirling	Gairdoch U	Dunfermline Ath	151	1
							Stenhousemuir (loan)	5	—
							Preston NE	21	—
SHARPE John	5 11	11 06	M	9 8 75	Birmingham	Trainee	**Manchester C**	—	—
SHARPE Lee	6 0	12 07	F	25 7 71	Halesowen	Trainee	Torquay U	14	3
							Manchester U	162	17
SHARPE Richard ‡			F	14 1 67	Wokingham	Coca Expos	**Rochdale**	16	2
SHAW Darren *	6 0	12 02	D	20 12 74	Telford	Trainee	Wolverhampton W	—	—
							Northampton T	—	—
SHAW Graham	5 9	11 05	F	7 6 67	Newcastle under Lyne	Apprentice	Stoke C	99	18
							Preston NE	121	29
							Stoke C	36	5
							Plymouth Arg (loan)	6	—
							Rochdale	4	—
SHAW Paul	5 11	12 02	F	4 9 73	Burnham	Trainee	**Arsenal**	1	—
							Burnley (loan)	9	4
SHAW Richard	5 9	12 08	D	11 9 68	Brentford	Apprentice	**Crystal Palace**	192	3
							Hull C (loan)	4	—
SHAW Simon	6 0	12 00	M	21 9 73	Teeside	Trainee	**Darlington**	66	6
SHEARER Alan	6 0	12 01	F	13 8 70	Newcastle	Trainee	Southampton	118	23
							Blackburn R	103	81
SHEARER Lee §			D	23 10 77	Southend	Trainee	**Leyton Orient**	2	—
SHEARER Peter	6 0	11 06	F	4 2 67	Birmingham	Apprentice	Birmingham C	4	—
							Rochdale	1	—
						Cheltenham T	Bournemouth	85	10
							Birmingham C	25	7
SHEEDY Kevin *	5 9	10 11	M	21 10 59	Builth Wells	Apprentice	Hereford U	51	4
							Liverpool	3	—
							Everton	274	67
							Newcastle U	37	4
							Blackpool	26	1
SHEERIN Paul	5 10	11 10	M	28 8 74	Edinburgh	Whitehill Welfare	Alloa	9	—
							Southampton	—	—
SHEFFIELD Jon	5 11	12 12	G	1 2 69	Bedworth		Norwich C	1	—
							Aldershot (loan)	11	—
							Ipswich T (loan)	—	—
							Aldershot (loan)	15	—
							Cambridge U (loan)	2	—
							Cambridge U	54	—
							Colchester U (loan)	6	—
							Swindon T (loan)	2	—
							Hereford U (loan)	8	—
SHELTON Gary	5 7	11 00	M	21 3 58	Nottingham	Apprentice	Walsall	24	—
							Aston Villa	24	7
							Notts Co (loan)	8	—
							Sheffield W	198	18
							Oxford U	65	1
							Bristol C	150	24
							Rochdale (loan)	3	—
							Chester C	33	2
SHEPPARD James	5 8	10 10	M	18 9 75	Preston	Trainee	**Blackpool**	—	—
SHEPPARD Simon	6 4	14 03	G	7 8 73	Clevedon	Trainee	Watford	23	—
							Scarborough (loan)	9	—
							Reading	—	—
SHERIDAN Darren	5 6	10 12	M	8 12 67	Manchester	Winsford	**Barnsley**	38	2

Player	Ht	Wt	Pos	Birth Date	Birth Place	Source	Clubs	League App	League Gls
SHERIDAN John	5 9	12 00	M	1 10 64	Stretford	Local	Leeds U	230	47
							Nottingham F	—	—
							Sheffield W	178	25
SHERIDAN Tony *	6 0	11 08	F	21 10 74	Dublin		**Coventry C**	9	—
SHERINGHAM Teddy	6 0	12 05	F	2 4 66	Highams Park	Apprentice	Millwall	220	93
							Aldershot (loan)	5	—
							Nottingham F	42	14
							Tottenham H	99	53
SHERLOCK Paul	5 11	11 05	D	17 11 73	Wigan	Trainee	Notts Co	12	1
							Mansfield T	2	—
SHERON Mike	5 9	11 07	F	11 1 72	Liverpool	Trainee	Manchester C	100	24
							Bury (loan)	5	1
							Norwich C	21	1
SHERWOOD Steve ‡	6 4	14 07	G	10 12 53	Selby	Apprentice	Chelsea	16	—
							Brighton (loan)	—	—
							Millwall (loan)	1	—
							Brentford (loan)	16	—
							Brentford (loan)	46	—
							Watford	211	1
							Grimsby T	183	—
							Northampton T	16	—
							Grimsby T	—	—
							Lincoln C	7	—
SHERWOOD Tim	6 0	11 06	M	6 2 69	St Albans	Trainee	Watford	32	2
							Norwich C	71	10
							Blackburn R	126	11
SHILTON Peter	6 1	14 00	G	18 9 49	Leicester	Apprentice	Leicester C	286	1
							Stoke C	110	—
							Nottingham F	202	—
							Southampton	188	—
							Derby Co	175	—
							Plymouth Arg	34	—
							Wimbledon	—	—
							Bolton W	1	—
SHILTON Sam §			M	21 7 78	Nottingham	Schoolboy	**Plymouth Arg**	2	—
SHIPPERLEY Neil	6 1	13 12	F	30 10 74	Chatham	Trainee	Chelsea	37	7
							Watford (loan)	6	1
							Southampton	19	4
SHIRTLIFF Peter	6 0	13 03	D	6 4 61	Barnsley	Apprentice	Sheffield W	188	4
							Charlton Ath	103	7
							Sheffield W	104	4
							Wolverhampton W	67	—
SHORE Jamie	5 9	10 09	M	1 9 77	Bristol	Trainee	**Norwich C**	—	—
SHORT Chris	5 10	12 02	D	9 5 70	Munster	Pickering T	Scarborough	43	1
							Manchester U (loan)	—	—
							Notts Co	92	2
							Huddersfield T (loan)	6	—
SHORT Craig	6 3	13 12	D	25 6 68	Bridlington	Pickering T	Scarborough	63	7
							Notts Co	128	6
							Derby Co	118	9
SHOTTON Malcolm †	6 3	13 12	D	16 2 57	Newcastle	Apprentice	Leicester C	—	—
						Nuneaton	Oxford U	263	12
							Portsmouth	10	—
							Huddersfield T	16	1
							Barnsley	66	6
							Hull C	59	2
							Ayr U	73	3
							Barnsley	8	1
SHOWLER Paul	5 11	11 02	M	10 10 66	Doncaster	Altrincham	Barnet	71	12
							Bradford C	55	7
SHUTT Carl	5 11	10 10	F	10 10 61	Sheffield	Spalding U	Sheffield W	40	16
							Bristol C	46	10
							Leeds U	79	17
							Birmingham C	26	4
							Manchester C (loan)	6	—
							Bradford C	32	4
SIBSON Andrew ‡	5 7	9 06	M	22 11 75	Leeds	Trainee	**Doncaster R**	—	—

Player	Ht	Wt	Pos	Birth Date	Birth Place	Source	Clubs	League App	League Gls
SIDDALL Barry ‡	6 1	14 02	G	12 9 54	Ellesmere Port	Apprentice	Bolton W	137	—
							Sunderland	167	—
							Darlington (loan)	8	—
							Port Vale	81	—
							Blackpool (loan)	7	—
							Stoke C	20	—
							Tranmere R (loan)	12	—
							Manchester C (loan)	6	—
							Blackpool	110	—
							Stockport Co	21	—
							Hartlepool U	11	—
							WBA	—	—
							Carlisle U	24	—
							Chester C	9	—
							Preston NE	1	—
							Bury	—	—
							Burnley	—	—
							Lincoln C	—	—
							Birmingham C	—	—
SIGURDSSON Larus	6 0	12 08	D	4 6 73	Akuveyni	Thor	**Stoke C**	23	1
SIMKIN Darren	6 0	12 00	D	24 3 70	Walsall	Blakenhall	Wolverhampton W	15	—
							Shrewsbury T	12	—
SIMMONDS Danny *	5 11	11 05	M	17 12 74	Eastbourne	Trainee	**Brighton**	18	—
SIMPSON Colin	6 1	11 05	F	30 4 76	Oxford	Trainee	**Watford**	—	—
SIMPSON Elliott *	5 11	11 11	M	1 7 76	York	Trainee	**York C**	1	—
SIMPSON Fitzroy	5 8	10 07	M	26 2 70	Trowbridge	Trainee	Swindon T	105	9
							Manchester C	71	4
							Bristol C (loan)	4	—
SIMPSON Gary	6 2	14 00	D	14 2 76	Ashford	Trainee	**Luton T**	—	—
SIMPSON Jimmy *	5 7	10 12	M	18 9 75	Portsmouth	Trainee	**Norwich C**	—	—
SIMPSON Michael	5 9	10 08	M	28 2 74	Nottingham	Trainee	**Notts Co**	25	3
SIMPSON Paul	5 7	11 12	F	26 7 66	Carlisle	Apprentice	Manchester C	121	18
							Oxford U	144	43
							Derby Co	127	36
SIMPSON Robert	5 10	10 07	F	3 3 76	Luton	Trainee	**Tottenham H**	—	—
SINCLAIR Frank	5 8	11 02	D	3 12 71	Lambeth	Trainee	**Chelsea**	114	4
							WBA (loan)	6	1
SINCLAIR Ron	5 11	12 03	G	19 11 64	Stirling	Apprentice	Nottingham F	—	—
							Wrexham (loan)	11	—
							Derby Co (loan)	—	—
							Sheffield U (loan)	—	—
							Leeds U (loan)	—	—
							Leeds U	8	—
							Halifax T (loan)	4	—
							Halifax T (loan)	10	—
							Bristol C	44	—
							Walsall (loan)	10	—
							Stoke C	79	—
							Bradford C (loan)	—	—
SINCLAIR Trevor	5 10	11 02	M	2 3 73	Dulwich	Trainee	Blackpool	112	15
							QPR	65	8
SINNOTT Lee	6 2	12 13	D	12 7 65	Pelsall	Apprentice	Walsall	40	2
							Watford	78	2
							Bradford C	173	6
							Crystal Palace	55	—
							Bradford C	34	1
							Huddersfield T	25	1
SINTON Andy	5 8	11 00	M	19 3 66	Newcastle	Apprentice	Cambridge U	93	13
							Brentford	149	28
							QPR	160	22
							Sheffield W	50	3
SKEDD Anthony *	5 5	10 01	M	19 5 75	Hartlepool	Trainee	**Hartlepool U**	46	—
SKELLY Richard	5 9	10 06	M	24 3 72	Norwich		Cambridge U	2	—
						Newmarket T	**Northampton T**	3	—

Player	Ht	Wt	Pos	Birth Date	Birth Place	Source	Clubs	League App	League Gls
SKELTON Aaron	5 10	11 05	M	22 11 74	Welwyn Garden	Trainee	**Luton T**	5	—
SKINNER Craig	5 9	11 06	F	21 10 70	Bury	Trainee	Blackburn R	16	—
							Plymouth Arg	53	4
SKINNER Justin	6 0	11 03	M	30 1 69	London	Apprentice	Fulham	135	23
							Bristol R	121	10
SKINNER Justin	5 7	11 00	D	17 9 72	London	Trainee	**Wimbledon**	1	—
							Bournemouth (loan)	16	—
							Wycombe W (loan)	5	—
SKIVERTON Terry	6 0	12 04	D	20 6 75	Mile End	Trainee	**Chelsea**	—	—
							Wycombe W (loan)	10	—
SLADE Steve	5 11	10 10	F	6 10 75	Romford	Trainee	**Tottenham H**	—	—
SLATER Robbie	5 11	13 00	M	26 11 64	Ormskirk	Lens	**Blackburn R**	18	—
SLATER Stuart	5 9	11 06	M	27 3 69	Sudbury	Apprentice	West Ham U	141	11
							Celtic	43	3
							Ipswich T	55	2
SLAVEN Bernie *	5 11	12 00	F	13 11 60	Paisley		Morton	22	1
							Airdrie	2	—
							Queen of the South	2	—
							Albion R	42	27
							Middlesbrough	307	118
							Port Vale	33	9
							Darlington	37	7
SLAWSON Stephen *	6 0	12 06	F	13 11 72	Nottingham	Trainee	**Notts Co**	38	4
							Burnley (loan)	5	2
							Shrewsbury T (loan)	6	—
SLINN Kevin ‡	5 11	11 00	F	2 9 74	Northampton	Trainee	Watford	—	—
							Stockport Co	4	1
SLOAN Scott	5 10	11 13	F	14 12 67	Wallsend	Ponteland	Berwick R	61	20
							Newcastle U	16	1
							Falkirk	64	11
							Cambridge U (loan)	4	1
							Hartlepool U	29	2
SMALL Bryan	5 9	11 09	D	15 11 71	Birmingham	Trainee	**Aston Villa**	36	—
							Birmingham C (loan)	3	—
SMART Allan	6 2	12 07	F	8 7 74	Perth	Caledonian Th	Caledonian Th	4	—
							Preston NE	19	6
SMILLIE Neil	5 6	10 07	F	19 7 58	Barnsley	Apprentice	Crystal Palace	83	7
							Brentford (loan)	3	—
							Brighton	75	2
							Watford	16	3
							Reading	39	—
							Brentford	172	18
							Gillingham	53	3
SMITH Alan	6 3	12 13	F	21 11 62	Birmingham	Alvechurch	Leicester C	191	73
							Leicester C (loan)	9	3
							Arsenal	264	86
SMITH Alex	5 7	9 00	D	15 2 76	Liverpool	Trainee	**Everton**	—	—
SMITH Chris			F	3 1 77	Birmingham	Trainee	**Walsall**	—	—
SMITH David	5 10	11 12	M	26 12 70	Liverpool	Trainee	Norwich C	18	—
							Oxford U	42	—
SMITH David	5 8	10 02	M	29 3 68	Gloucester		Coventry C	154	19
							Bournemouth (loan)	1	—
							Birmingham C	38	3
							WBA	40	—
SMITH Dean	6 1	12 10	D	19 3 71	West Bromwich	Trainee	Walsall	142	2
							Hereford U	35	3
SMITH Eric ‡	6 2	12 08	D	20 10 75	Dublin	Trainee	**Crystal Palace**	—	—

Player	Ht	Wt	Pos	Birth Date	Birth Place	Source	Clubs	League App	League Gls
SMITH Gary *	5 10	12 09	M	3 12 68	Harlow	Apprentice	Fulham	1	—
							Colchester U	11	—
						Enfield, Wycombe W, Welling U	**Barnet**	13	—
SMITH Gavin			F	24 9 77	Sheffield	Trainee	**Sheffield W**	—	—
SMITH Ian			D	28 11 76	Bury	Trainee	**Manchester C**	—	—
SMITH James	5 6	10 08	F	17 9 74	Birmingham	Trainee	**Wolverhampton W**	25	—
SMITH Jason *	6 2	12 04	D	6 9 74	Bromsgrove	Tiverton	**Coventry C**	—	—
SMITH Mark	6 1	13 09	G	2 1 73	Birmingham	Trainee	Nottingham F	—	—
							Crewe Alex	63	—
SMITH Mark *	6 2	13 11	D	21 3 60	Sheffield	Apprentice	Sheffield W	282	16
							Plymouth Arg	82	6
							Barnsley	104	10
							Notts Co	5	—
							Chesterfield (loan)	6	1
							Huddersfield T (loan)	5	—
							Port Vale (loan)	6	—
							Lincoln C	20	1
SMITH Mark *	5 10	12 07	M	19 12 61	Sheffield		Sheffield U	—	—
						Worksop, Gainsborough T	Scunthorpe U	1	—
						Kettering	Rochdale	27	7
							Huddersfield T	96	11
							Grimsby T	77	4
							Scunthorpe U	62	8
SMITH Mark *	5 9	10 04	M	16 12 64	Bellshill	St Mirren BC	Queen's Park	82	7
							Celtic	6	—
							Dunfermline Ath	53	6
							Stoke C (loan)	2	—
							Nottingham F	—	—
							Reading (loan)	3	—
							Shrewsbury T	56	3
SMITH Martin	5 11	12 06	F	13 11 74	Sunderland	Trainee	**Sunderland**	64	18
SMITH Neil	5 9	12 00	M	30 9 71	London	Trainee	Tottenham H	—	—
							Gillingham	133	8
SMITH Nicky ‡	5 7	10 00	M	28 1 69	Berkley		Southend U	60	6
							Colchester U	81	4
							Wycombe W	—	—
						Sudbury	**Northampton T**	6	1
SMITH Paul			M	2 11 71	Lewisham	Horsham	**Barnet**	—	—
SMITH Paul	5 11	13 08	M	18 9 71	Lenham	Trainee	Southend U	20	1
							Brentford	67	6
SMITH Paul	6 0	12 08	F	22 1 76	Easington	Trainee	**Burnley**	1	—
SMITH Paul *	5 10	10 09	F	9 11 64	Rotherham	Apprentice	Sheffield U	36	1
							Stockport Co (loan)	7	5
							Port Vale	44	7
							Lincoln C	232	27
SMITH Paul	5 11	11 03	M	25 1 76	Hastings	Hastings	**Nottingham F**	—	—
SMITH Peter	6 0	12 01	D	12 7 69	Stone	Alma Swanley	**Brighton & HA**	38	1
SMITH Richard	6 0	12 10	D	3 10 70	Leicester	Trainee	**Leicester C**	97	1
							Cambridge U (loan)	4	—
SMITH Richard ‡	5 11	11 10	D	24 1 74	Lichfield	Trainee	**Nottingham F**	—	—
SMITH Scott	5 8	11 06	D	6 3 75	Christchurch	Trainee	**Rotherham U**	11	—
SMITH Shaun	5 10	11 00	D	9 4 71	Leeds	Trainee	Halifax T	7	—
							Crewe Alex	128	19
SMITH Tom			M	25 11 77	Northampton	Trainee	**Manchester U**	—	—
SMITH Tony *	5 11	11 09	D	21 9 71	Sunderland	Trainee	**Sunderland**	20	—
							Hartlepool U (loan)	5	—
SMITHARD Matthew	5 9	10 09	F	13 6 76	Leeds	Trainee	**Leeds U**	—	—
SNEEKES Richard	5 11	12 02	M	30 10 68	Amsterdam	Fortuna Sittard	**Bolton W**	38	6

Player	Ht	Wt	Pos	Birth Date	Birth Place	Source	Clubs	League App	League Gls
SNODIN Glynn *	5 6	11 00	D	14 2 60	Rotherham	Apprentice	Doncaster R	309	61
							Sheffield W	59	1
							Leeds U	94	10
							Oldham Ath (loan)	8	1
							Rotherham U	3	—
							Hearts	34	—
							Barnsley	25	—
SNODIN Ian	5 7	9 01	M	15 8 63	Rotherham	Apprentice	Doncaster R	188	25
							Leeds U	51	6
							Everton	148	3
							Sunderland (loan)	6	—
							Oldham Ath	17	—
SNOOK Eddie ‡	5 7	10 01	M	18 10 68	Washington	Apprentice	**Notts Co**	—	—
SOLOMAN Jason	6 0	12 02	M	6 10 70	Welwyn	Trainee	Watford	100	5
							Peterborough U (loan)	4	—
							Wycombe W	6	1
SOMMER Jurgen	6 4	15 12	G	27 2 64	New York		**Luton T**	80	—
							Brighton (loan)	1	—
							Torquay U (loan)	10	—
SOUTHALL Neville	6 1	12 01	G	16 9 58	Llandudno	Winsford	Bury	39	—
							Everton	494	—
							Port Vale (loan)	9	—
SOUTHALL Nicky	5 10	12 12	F	28 1 72	Teeside	Trainee	**Hartlepool U**	138	24
SOUTHGATE Gareth	5 10	12 03	M	3 9 70	Watford	Trainee	**Crystal Palace**	152	15
SOUTHON Jamie *	5 9	11 09	M	13 10 74	Hornchurch	Trainee	**Southend U**	1	—
SPACKMAN Nigel	6 1	13 02	M	2 12 60	Romsey	Andover	Bournemouth	119	10
							Chelsea	141	12
							Liverpool	51	—
							QPR	29	1
							Rangers	100	1
							Chelsea	51	—
SPARROW Paul	6 0	11 04	D	24 3 75	London	Trainee	**Crystal Palace**	—	—
SPEARING Tony	5 6	11 10	D	7 10 64	Romford	Apprentice	Norwich C	69	—
							Stoke C (loan)	9	—
							Oxford U (loan)	5	—
							Leicester C	73	1
							Plymouth Arg	35	—
							Peterborough U	89	1
SPEED Gary	5 9	12 10	M	8 9 69	Hawarden	Trainee	**Leeds U**	219	37
SPEEDIE David ‡	5 6	11 02	F	20 2 60	Glenrothes	Amateur	Barnsley	23	—
							Darlington	88	21
							Chelsea	162	47
							Coventry C	122	31
							Liverpool	12	6
							Blackburn R	36	23
							Southampton	11	—
							Birmingham C (loan)	10	2
							WBA (loan)	7	2
							West Ham U (loan)	11	4
							Leicester C	37	12
SPENCER John	5 6	10 00	F	11 9 70	Glasgow	Rangers Am BC	Rangers	—	—
							Morton (loan)	4	1
						Lisbung, HK	Rangers	13	2
							Chelsea	71	23
SPINK Dean	5 11	13 08	F	22 1 67	Birmingham	Halesowen	Aston Villa	—	—
							Scarborough (loan)	3	2
							Bury (loan)	6	1
							Shrewsbury T	198	42
SPINK Nigel	6 2	14 08	G	8 8 58	Chelmsford	Chelsmford C	**Aston Villa**	359	—
SPOONER Nicky	5 10	11 09	D	5 6 71	Manchester	Trainee	**Bolton W**	23	2

Player	Ht	Wt	Pos	Birth Date	Birth Place	Source	Clubs	League App	League Gls
SPOONER Steve ‡	5 10	12 00	M	25 1 61	London	Apprentice	Derby Co	8	—
							Halifax T	72	13
							Chesterfield	93	14
							Hereford U	84	19
							York C	72	11
							Rotherham U	19	1
							Mansfield T	58	3
							Blackpool	2	—
							Chesterfield	12	—
SQUIRES Jamie	6 1	12 00	D	15 11 75	Preston	Trainee	**Preston NE**	15	—
SRNICEK Pavel	6 2	14 09	G	10 3 68	Ostrava	Banik Ostrava	**Newcastle U**	111	—
STABB Chris §			D	12 10 76	Bradford	Trainee	**Bradford C**	1	—
STACKMAN Scott ‡	5 11	12 06	D	16 11 75	Arizona	Trainee	**Northampton T**	1	—
STALLARD Mark	6 0	12 04	F	24 10 74	Derby	Trainee	**Derby Co**	24	2
							Fulham (loan)	4	3
STAMP Philip	5 10	12 05	M	12 12 75	Middlesbrough	Trainee	**Middlesbrough**	13	—
STAMPS Scott	5 10	11 02	D	20 3 75	Edgbaston	Trainee	**Torquay U**	33	1
STANCLIFFE Paul *	6 2	13 04	D	5 5 58	Sheffield	Apprentice	Rotherham U	285	8
							Sheffield U	278	12
							Rotherham U (loan)	5	—
							Wolverhampton W	17	—
							York C	91	3
STANISLAUS Roger	5 11	13 02	D	2 11 68	Hammersmith	Trainee	Arsenal	—	—
							Brentford	111	4
							Bury	176	5
STANNARD Jim	6 2	16 06	G	6 10 62	London	Local	Fulham	41	—
							Charlton Ath (loan)	1	—
							Southend U (loan)	17	—
							Southend U	92	—
							Fulham	348	1
STANT Phil	6 1	12 07	F	13 10 62	Bolton	Camberley Army	Reading	4	2
							Hereford U	89	38
							Notts Co	22	6
							Blackpool (loan)	12	5
							Lincoln C (loan)	4	—
							Huddersfield T (loan)	5	1
							Fulham	19	5
							Mansfield T	57	32
							Cardiff C	79	34
							Mansfield T (loan)	4	1
							Bury	20	13
STAPLETON Frank †	6 0	13 01	F	10 7 56	Dublin	Apprentice	Arsenal	225	75
							Manchester U	223	60
							Ajax	4	—
							Derby Co	10	1
						Le Havre	Blackburn R	81	13
							Aldershot	—	—
							Huddersfield T	5	—
							Bradford C	68	2
							Brighton	2	—
STAPLETON Simon	6 0	13 02	M	10 12 68	Oxford	Portsmouth	Bristol R	5	—
						Wycombe W	**Wycombe W**	48	3
STARBUCK Philip	5 10	10 13	F	24 11 68	Nottingham	Apprentice	Nottingham F	36	2
							Birmingham C (loan)	3	—
							Hereford U (loan)	6	—
							Blackburn R (loan)	6	1
							Huddersfield T	137	36
							Sheffield U	23	1
STARK Wayne §			M	14 10 76	Derby	Trainee	**Mansfield T**	1	—
STATHAM Brian	5 11	11 00	D	21 5 69	Zimbabwe	Apprentice	Tottenham H	24	—
							Reading (loan)	8	—
							Bournemouth (loan)	2	—
							Brentford (loan)	18	—
							Brentford	112	1
STATHAM Mark	6 2	12 02	G	11 11 75	Barnsley	Trainee	Nottingham F	—	—
							Wigan Ath	2	—

Player	Ht	Wt	Pos	Birth Date	Birth Place	Source	Clubs	League App	League Gls
STAUNTON Steve	6 0	12 04	D	19 1 69	Drogheda	Dundalk	Liverpool	65	—
							Bradford C (loan)	8	—
							Aston Villa	138	13
STEAD Carl			D	3 9 71	Hull	Doncaster R	**Scarborough**	—	—
STEADMAN Richard *			G	21 10 75	Birmingham	Trainee	**Birmingham C**	—	—
STEELE Tim	5 9	11 07	F	1 12 67	Coventry	Apprentice	Shrewsbury T	61	5
							Wolverhampton W	75	7
							Stoke C (loan)	7	1
							Bradford C	11	—
							Hereford U	25	2
STEIN Mark	5 6	11 02	F	28 1 66	S. Africa		Luton T	54	19
							Aldershot (loan)	2	1
							QPR	33	4
							Oxford U	82	18
							Stoke C	94	50
							Chelsea	42	21
STENSGAARD Michael	6 2	13 04	G	1 9 74	Denmark	Hvidovre	**Liverpool**	—	—
STEPHENSON Paul	5 10	12 02	M	2 1 68	Wallsend	Apprentice	Newcastle U	61	1
							Millwall	98	6
							Gillingham (loan)	12	2
							Brentford	70	2
STERLING Worrell	5 7	10 11	M	8 6 65	Bethnal Green	Apprentice	Watford	94	14
							Peterborough U	193	29
							Bristol R	89	6
STEVENS Gary	5 11	10 11	D	27 3 63	Barrow	Apprentice	Everton	208	8
							Rangers	187	8
							Tranmere R	37	1
STEVENS Ian	5 10	11 07	F	21 10 66	Malta	Trainee	Preston NE	11	2
							Stockport Co	2	—
						Lancaster C	Bolton W	47	7
							Bury	110	38
							Shrewsbury T	38	8
STEVENS Keith	6 0	12 12	D	21 6 64	Merton	Apprentice	**Millwall**	410	7
STEVENS Shaun	5 10	11 05	D	8 3 76	Chertsey		**Wycombe W**	—	—
STEWART Billy *	5 11	11 07	G	1 1 65	Liverpool	Apprentice	Liverpool	—	—
							Wigan Ath	14	—
							Chester C	272	—
							Northampton T	27	—
							Chesterfield (loan)	1	—
STEWART Marcus	5 10	10 06	F	7 11 72	Bristol	Trainee	**Bristol R**	127	36
STEWART Paul	5 11	12 04	M	7 10 64	Manchester	Apprentice	Blackpool	201	56
							Manchester C	51	26
							Tottenham H	131	28
							Liverpool	32	1
							Crystal Palace (loan)	18	3
							Wolverhampton W (loan)	8	2
							Burnley (loan)	6	—
STEWART Simon	6 1	12 08	D	1 11 73	Leeds	Trainee	**Sheffield W**	6	—
STIMSON Mark	5 11	11 00	D	27 12 67	Plaistow	Trainee	Tottenham H	2	—
							Leyton Orient (loan)	10	—
							Gillingham (loan)	18	—
							Newcastle U	86	2
							Portsmouth (loan)	4	—
							Portsmouth	44	1
STOCKWELL Mick	5 9	11 04	M	14 2 65	Chelmsford	Apprentice	**Ipswich T**	315	20
STOKER Gareth	5 9	10 03	M	22 2 73	Bishop Auckland	Leeds U	Hull C	30	2
							Hereford U	10	—
STOKES Dean	5 7	10 07	D	23 5 70	Birmingham	Halesowen	**Port Vale**	24	—
STOKOE Graham †	6 0	11 11	M	17 12 75	Newcastle	Birmingham C	**Stoke C**	—	—
STONE Steven	5 9	11 03	M	20 8 71	Gateshead	Trainee	**Nottingham F**	99	11

Player	Ht	Wt	Pos	Birth Date	Birth Place	Source	Clubs	League App	League Gls
STONEMAN Paul *	6 1	13 06	D	26 2 73	Whitley Bay	Trainee	**Blackpool**	43	—
							Colchester U (loan)	3	1
STORER Stuart	5 11	12 13	F	16 1 67	Harborough	Local	Mansfield T	1	—
							Birmingham C	8	—
							Everton	—	—
							Wigan Ath (loan)	12	—
							Bolton W	123	12
							Exeter C	77	8
							Brighton	2	1
STOWELL Mike	6 2	11 10	G	19 4 65	Preston	Leyland Motors	Preston NE	—	—
							Everton	—	—
							Chester C (loan)	14	—
							York C (loan)	6	—
							Manchester C (loan)	14	—
							Port Vale (loan)	7	—
							Wolverhampton W (loan)	7	—
							Preston NE (loan)	2	—
							Wolverhampton W	194	—
STRACHAN Gordon	5 6	10 06	M	9 2 57	Edinburgh		Dundee	60	13
							Aberdeen	183	55
							Manchester U	160	33
							Leeds U	197	37
							Coventry C	5	—
STRANDLI Frank ‡	5 10	12 07	F	16 5 72	Norway	IK Start	**Leeds U**	14	2
STRANEY Paul ‡	5 11	12 04	G	7 10 75	Downpatrick	Trainee	**Stoke C**	—	—
STRATFORD Lee	5 10	10 08	M	11 11 75	Barnsley	Trainee	**Nottingham F**	—	—
STREET Danny *			D	20 3 76	Cardiff	Trainee	**Cardiff C**	—	—
STRODDER Gary	6 1	12 06	D	1 4 65	Leeds	Apprentice	Lincoln C	132	6
							West Ham U	65	2
							WBA	140	8
STRONG Greg	6 2	11 12	D	5 9 75	Bolton	Trainee	**Wigan Ath**	35	3
STRONG Steve §			F	15 3 78	Watford	Trainee	**Bournemouth**	1	—
STUART Graham	5 9	11 06	F	24 10 70	Tooting, London	Trainee	Chelsea	87	14
							Everton	58	6
STUART Jamie	5 10	11 00	D	15 10 76	Southwark	Trainee	**Charlton Ath**	12	—
STUART Mark	5 10	11 03	D	15 12 66	Hammersmith	QPR	Charlton Ath	107	28
							Plymouth Arg	57	11
							Ipswich T (loan)	5	2
							Bradford C	29	5
							Huddersfield T	15	3
							Rochdale	73	15
STUBBS Alan	6 2	13 10	D	6 10 71	Kirkby	Trainee	**Bolton W**	177	5
STURGESS Paul	5 11	12 05	D	4 8 75	Dartford	Trainee	**Charlton Ath**	35	—
STURRIDGE Dean	5 8	12 01	F	27 7 73	Birmingham	Trainee	**Derby Co**	23	1
							Torquay U (loan)	10	5
STURRIDGE Simon	5 5	10 13	F	9 12 69	Birmingham	Trainee	Birmingham C	150	30
							Stoke C	21	1
SUCKLING Perry	6 2	13 02	G	12 10 65	Leyton	Apprentice	Coventry C	27	—
							Manchester C	39	—
							Crystal Palace	59	—
							West Ham U (loan)	6	—
							Brentford (loan)	8	—
							Watford	39	—
							Doncaster R	9	—
SULLEY Chris *	5 8	10 00	D	3 12 59	Camberwell	Apprentice	Chelsea	—	—
							Bournemouth	206	3
							Dundee U	7	—
							Blackburn R	134	3
							Port Vale	40	1
							Preston NE	21	1
SULLIVAN Neil	6 0	12 01	G	24 2 70	Sutton	Trainee	**Wimbledon**	16	—
							Crystal Palace (loan)	1	—

Player	Ht	Wt	Pos	Birth Date	Birth Place	Source	Clubs	League App	League Gls
SUMMERBEE Nicky	5 11	11 08	F	26 8 71	Altrincham	Trainee	Swindon T	112	6
							Manchester C	41	1
SUMMERFIELD Kevin	5 11	11 00	M	7 1 59	Walsall	Apprentice	WBA	9	4
							Birmingham C	5	1
							Walsall	54	17
							Cardiff C	10	1
							Plymouth Arg	139	26
							Exeter C (loan)	4	—
							Shrewsbury T	162	22
SUNDERLAND Jonathan			M	2 11 75	Newcastle	Trainee	**Blackpool**	2	—
SUNLEY Mark ‡	6 1	12 07	D	13 10 71	Stockton		Middlesbrough	—	—
							Darlington	35	—
							Hartlepool U	2	—
SUSSEX Andy	6 3	13 08	M	23 11 64	Islington	Apprentice	Orient	144	17
							Crewe Alex	102	24
							Southend U	74	14
SUTCH Daryl	6 0	12 00	M	11 9 71	Lowestoft	Trainee	**Norwich C**	68	3
SUTTON Chris	6 3	13 05	F	10 3 73	Nottingham	Trainee	Norwich C	102	35
							Blackburn R	40	15
SUTTON Steve	6 1	14 11	G	16 4 61	Hartington	Apprentice	Nottingham F	199	—
							Mansfield T (loan)	8	—
							Derby Co (loan)	14	—
							Coventry C (loan)	1	—
							Luton T (loan)	14	—
							Derby Co	55	—
SUTTON Wayne	6 0	13 02	D	1 10 75	Derby	Trainee	**Derby Co**	6	—
SWAILES Chris	6 2	12 07	D	19 10 70	Gateshead	Bridlington T	Doncaster R	49	—
							Ipswich T	4	—
SWALES Steve	5 8	10 03	D	26 12 73	Whitby	Trainee	**Scarborough**	54	1
SWAN Peter	6 2	14 12	D	28 9 66	Leeds	Local	Leeds U	49	11
							Hull C	80	24
							Port Vale	111	5
							Plymouth Arg	27	2
SWANN Gary ‡	5 11	11 13	M	11 4 62	York	Apprentice	Hull C	186	9
							Preston NE	199	37
							York C	82	4
							Scarborough	27	3
SWEENEY Paul ‡	5 8	11 5	M	10 1 65	Glasgow	St Kentigern's Acad	Raith R	205	8
							Newcastle U	36	—
							St Johnstone	10	—
							Hartlepool U	1	—
SWEETMAN Nicky ‡	5 8	11 00	M	21 10 74	Herts	Trainee	**Leyton Orient**	—	—
SYKES Paul	6 0	10 05	D	13 1 77	Pontefract	Trainee	**Sheffield W**	—	—
SYMONS Kit	6 1	11 00	D	8 3 71	Basingstoke	Trainee	**Portsmouth**	160	10
SYMONS Paul	5 11	12 00	F	20 4 76	North Shields	Trainee	**Blackpool**	1	—
TAGGART Gerry	6 1	13 12	D	18 10 70	Belfast	Trainee	Manchester C	12	1
							Barnsley	212	16
TAIT Mick	5 11	12 05	M	30 9 56	Wallsend	Apprentice	Oxford U	64	23
							Carlisle U	106	20
							Hull C	33	3
							Portsmouth	240	30
							Reading	99	9
							Darlington	79	2
							Hartlepool U	81	1
TAIT Paul	6 1	10 00	M	31 1 71	Sutton Coldfield	Trainee	**Birmingham C**	117	11
							Millwall (loan)	—	—
TAIT Paul *	5 8	10 10	F	24 10 74	Newcastle	Trainee	Everton	—	—
							Wigan Ath	5	—
TALBOT Stuart			F	14 6 73	Birmingham	Moor Green	**Port Vale**	2	—
TALBOYS Steve	5 11	11 10	M	18 9 66	Bristol	Gloucester C	**Wimbledon**	21	1

Player	Ht	Wt	Pos	Birth Date	Birth Place	Source	Clubs	League App	League Gls
TALIA Frank	6 1	13 06	G	20 7 72	Melbourne	Sunshine George Cross	**Blackburn R**	—	—
							Hartlepool U (loan)	14	—
TALLON Gary	5 11	11 07	F	5 9 73	Drogheda	Trainee	**Blackburn R**	—	—
TANKARD Allen	5 10	11 07	D	21 5 69	Fleet	Trainee	Southampton	5	—
							Wigan Ath	209	4
							Port Vale	65	1
TANNER Adam	6 0	12 01	M	25 10 73	Maldon	Trainee	**Ipswich T**	10	2
TARICCO Mauricio	5 8	11 05	D	10 3 73	Buenos Aires	Argentinos J	**Ipswich T**	—	—
TAYLOR Bob	5 10	11 09	F	3 2 67	Horden	Horden CW	Leeds U	42	9
							Bristol C	106	50
							WBA	149	67
TAYLOR Gareth	6 2	12 05	F	25 2 73	Weston-Super-Mare	Southampton	**Bristol R**	40	12
TAYLOR Ian	6 2	11 06	M	4 6 68	Birmingham	Moor Green	Port Vale	83	28
							Sheffield W	14	1
							Aston Villa	22	1
TAYLOR Jamie	5 6	9 12	F	11 1 77	Bury	Trainee	**Rochdale**	19	1
TAYLOR John	6 3	13 06	F	24 10 64	Norwich	Local	Colchester U	—	—
						Sudbury	Cambridge U	160	46
							Bristol R	95	44
							Bradford C	36	11
							Luton T	9	3
TAYLOR Mark ‡	6 2	13 10	D	8 11 74	Saltburn	Trainee	**Middlesbrough**	—	—
							Darlington (loan)	8	—
TAYLOR Mark	5 8	11 08	M	22 2 66	Walsall	Local	Walsall	113	4
							Sheffield W	9	—
							Shrewsbury T (loan)	19	2
							Shrewsbury T	156	11
TAYLOR Mark ‡	5 7	11 08	M	20 11 64	Hartlepool	Local	Hartlepool U	47	4
							Crewe Alex (loan)	3	—
							Blackpool	100	40
							Cardiff C (loan)	6	3
							Wrexham	61	9
TAYLOR Martin	6 0	13 06	G	9 12 66	Tamworth	Mile Oak R	**Derby Co**	94	—
							Carlisle U (loan)	10	—
							Scunthorpe U (loan)	8	—
TAYLOR Matthew	5 7	11 12	D	6 3 76	Maidstone	Trainee	**Burnley**	—	—
TAYLOR Robert	6 1	13 08	F	30 4 71	Norwich	Trainee	Norwich C	—	—
							Leyton Orient (loan)	3	1
							Birmingham C	—	—
							Leyton Orient	73	20
							Brentford	48	25
TAYLOR Scott	5 10	11 04	F	5 5 76	Chertsey	Staines	**Millwall**	6	—
TAYLOR Scott	5 10	10 00	M	28 11 70	Portsmouth	Trainee	**Reading**	207	24
TAYLOR Shaun	6 1	13 00	D	26 2 63	Plymouth	Bideford	Exeter C	200	16
							Swindon T	167	23
TEALE Shaun	6 0	13 10	D	10 3 64	Southport	Weymouth	Bournemouth	100	4
							Aston Villa	147	2
TEATHER Paul			M	26 12 77	Rotherham	Trainee	**Manchester U**	—	—
TEE Jason *	5 8	11 05	F	28 9 75	Sheffield	Trainee	**Sheffield U**	—	—
TELFER Paul	5 9	11 06	M	21 10 71	Edinburgh	Trainee	**Luton T**	144	19
THACKERAY Andy	5 9	11 00	M	13 2 68	Huddersfield		Manchester C	—	—
							Huddersfield T	2	—
							Newport Co	54	4
							Wrexham	152	14
							Rochdale	119	13
THATCHER Ben	5 10	12 07	D	30 11 75	Swindon	Trainee	**Millwall**	48	1
THEW Lee ‡	5 10	11 05	M	23 10 74	Sunderland	Trainee	**Doncaster R**	32	2

Player	Ht	Wt	Pos	Birth Date	Birth Place	Source	Clubs	League App	League Gls
THIRLBY Anthony	5 9	11 00	M	4 3 76	Germany	Trainee	**Exeter C**	37	2
THOM Stuart	6 2	11 08	D	27 12 76	Dewsbury	Trainee	**Nottingham F**	—	—
THOMAS Brian ‡	5 10	12 00	G	7 6 76	Neath	Trainee	**Hereford U**	3	—
THOMAS David †	5 10	11 07	F	26 9 75	Caerphilly	Trainee	**Swansea C**	4	—
THOMAS Dean *	5 10	11 08	D	19 12 61	Bedworth	Nuneaton Borough	Wimbledon	57	8
						Fortuna Dusseldorf	Northampton T	74	11
							Notts Co	134	8
THOMAS Geoff	5 10	10 07	M	5 8 64	Manchester	Local	Rochdale	11	1
							Crewe Alex	125	20
							Crystal Palace	195	26
							Wolverhampton W	22	5
THOMAS Glen	6 1	12 07	D	6 10 67	Hackney	Apprentice	Fulham	251	6
							Peterborough U	8	—
							Barnet	7	—
THOMAS Mark	5 9	10 10	M	22 11 74	Tooting	Trainee	**Wimbledon**	—	—
THOMAS Martin	5 8	10 08	F	12 9 73	Lyndhurst	Trainee	Southampton	—	—
							Leyton Orient	5	2
							Fulham	23	3
THOMAS Michael	5 9	12 06	M	24 8 67	Lambeth	Apprentice	Arsenal	163	24
							Portsmouth (loan)	3	—
							Liverpool	55	4
THOMAS Mitchell	6 2	12 00	D	2 10 64	Luton	Apprentice	Luton T	107	1
							Tottenham H	157	6
							West Ham U	38	3
							Luton T	56	1
THOMAS Rod	5 7	11 00	F	10 10 70	London	Trainee	Watford	84	9
							Gillingham (loan)	8	1
							Carlisle U	74	15
THOMAS Scott	5 9	10 08	M	30 10 74	Bury	Trainee	**Manchester C**	2	—
THOMAS Tony	5 11	12 05	D	12 7 71	Liverpool	Trainee	**Tranmere R**	196	12
THOMPSON Adrian			G	13 3 77	Sydney		**Walsall**	—	—
THOMPSON Alan	6 0	12 08	M	22 12 73	Newcastle	Trainee	Newcastle U	16	—
							Bolton W	64	13
THOMPSON Andy	5 4	10 06	D	9 11 67	Cannock	Apprentice	WBA	24	1
							Wolverhampton W	299	35
THOMPSON David	6 1	12 07	D	20 11 68	Ashington	Trainee	Millwall	92	6
							Bristol C	17	—
							Brentford	10	1
							Blackpool	17	—
							Cambridge U	7	—
THOMPSON David	5 7	10 00	M	12 9 77	Berkenhead	Trainee	**Liverpool**	—	—
THOMPSON David	5 7	11 12	D	27 5 62	Manchester	Local	Rochdale	155	13
							Manchester U (loan)	—	—
							Notts Co	55	8
							Wigan Ath	108	14
							Preston NE	46	4
							Chester C	80	9
							Rochdale	40	6
THOMPSON Garry	6 1	14 00	F	7 10 59	Birmingham	Apprentice	Coventry C	134	38
							WBA	91	39
							Sheffield W	36	7
							Aston Villa	60	17
							Watford	34	8
							Crystal Palace	20	3
							QPR	19	1
							Cardiff C	43	5
							Northampton T	15	4
THOMPSON Gary ‡	6 0	11 10	F	7 9 72	Ipswich		**Ipswich T**	—	—
THOMPSON Ian *	5 11	12 04	M	17 2 75	Leicester	Trainee	**Leicester C**	—	—

Player	Ht	Wt	Pos	Birth Date	Birth Place	Source	Clubs	League App	League Gls
THOMPSON Neil	5 11	13 08	D	2 10 63	Beverley	Nottingham F	Hull C	31	—
						Scarborough	Scarborough	87	15
							Ipswich T	201	18
THOMPSON Niall *	5 11	11 00	F	16 4 74	Birmingham	Trainee	Crystal Palace	—	—
							Colchester U	13	5
THOMPSON Paul *	5 11	11 13	F	17 4 73	Newcastle	Trainee	**Hartlepool U**	56	9
THOMPSON Simon *	5 9	10 06	D	7 1 68	Sheffield	Trainee	Rotherham U	28	—
							Scarborough	108	6
THOMPSON Steve	5 11	13 00	M	2 11 64	Oldham	Apprentice	Bolton W	335	49
							Luton T	5	—
							Leicester C	127	18
							Burnley	12	—
THOMPSON Steve	5 7	11 09	M	12 1 63	Plymouth	Slough	**Wycombe W**	62	3
THOMPSTONE Ian *	6 0	13 00	F	17 1 71	Manchester	Trainee	Manchester C	1	1
							Oldham Ath	—	—
							Exeter C	15	3
							Halifax T	31	9
							Scunthorpe U	60	8
THOMSEN Claus	6 3	13 06	M	31 5 70	Aarhus	Aarhus	**Ipswich T**	33	5
THOMSON Andrew	6 3	14 12	D	28 3 74	Swindon	Trainee	**Swindon T**	22	—
THOMSON Andy	5 10	10 07	F	1 4 71	Motherwell	Jerviston BC	Q of S	175	93
							Southend U	39	11
THOMSON Martin ‡	5 10	11 08	D	3 10 74	Bradford	Trainee	**Sheffield U**	—	—
THORN Andy	6 0	11 05	D	12 11 66	Carshalton	Apprentice	Wimbledon	107	2
							Newcastle U	36	2
							Crystal Palace	128	3
							Wimbledon	23	1
THORNBER Stephen	5 9	11 08	M	11 10 65	Dewsbury	Local	Halifax T	104	4
							Swansea C	117	6
							Blackpool	24	—
							Scunthorpe U	61	7
THORNE Peter	6 0	12 10	F	21 6 73	Manchester	Trainee	Blackburn R	—	—
							Wigan Ath (loan)	11	—
							Swindon T	20	9
THORNLEY Ben	5 8	11 04	F	21 4 75	Bury	Trainee	**Manchester U**	1	—
THORNLEY Timothy §			G	3 3 77	Leicester	Trainee	**Torquay U**	1	—
THORP Michael			D	5 12 75	Wallington	Trainee	**Reading**	—	—
THORPE Jeff	5 10	12 09	M	17 11 72	Whitehaven	Trainee	**Carlisle U**	97	5
THORPE Lee	6 0	11 06	F	14 12 75	Wolverhampton	Trainee	**Blackpool**	2	—
THORPE Tony	5 9	12 00	F	10 4 74	Leicester	Leicester C	**Luton T**	18	1
THORSTVEDT Erik	6 4	14 03	G	28 10 62	Stavanger	IFK Gothenburg	**Tottenham H**	173	—
TIERNEY Francis	5 10	10 12	M	10 9 75	Liverpool	Trainee	**Crewe Alex**	29	5
TILER Carl	6 2	13 00	D	11 2 70	Sheffield	Trainee	Barnsley	71	3
							Nottingham F	69	1
							Swindon T (loan)	2	—
TILLSON Andy	6 2	12 07	D	30 6 66	Huntingdon	Kettering T	Grimsby T	105	5
							QPR	29	2
							Grimsby T (loan)	4	—
							Bristol R	82	2
TILSON Steve	5 11	12 06	M	27 7 66	Wickford	Burnham	**Southend U**	183	22
							Brentford (loan)	2	—
TIMONS Chris	6 0	12 04	D	8 12 74	Longworth	Clipstone W	**Mansfield T**	22	1
TINKLER Mark	5 11	13 03	M	24 10 74	Bishop Auckland	Trainee	**Leeds U**	13	—
TINNION Brian	5 11	11 05	D	23 2 68	Stanley	Apprentice	Newcastle U	32	2
							Bradford C	145	22
							Bristol C	87	9

Player	Ht	Wt	Pos	Birth Date	Birth Place	Source	Clubs	League App	League Gls
TISDALE Paul	5 9	11 09	M	14 1 73	Malta	School	**Southampton**	7	—
							Northampton T (loan)	5	—
TITTERTON David *	5 11	13 08	D	25 9 71	Hatton	Trainee	Coventry C	2	—
							Hereford U	51	1
							Wycombe W	19	1
TODD Andy	5 10	11 12	D	21 9 74	Derby	Trainee	**Middlesbrough**	8	—
							Swindon T (loan)	13	—
TODD Lee	5 5	10 03	D	7 3 72	Hartlepool	Hartlepool U	**Stockport Co**	142	2
TODD Mark	5 9	10 04	M	4 12 67	Belfast	Trainee	Manchester U	—	—
							Sheffield U	70	5
							Wolverhampton W (loan)	7	—
							Rotherham U	64	7
TOLSON Neil	6 3	11 05	F	25 10 73	Wordley	Trainee	Walsall	9	1
							Oldham Ath	3	—
							Bradford C	32	4
							Chester C (loan)	4	—
TOMAN Andy	5 10	11 07	M	7 3 62	Northallerton	Bishop Auckland	Lincoln C	24	4
							Hartlepool U	112	28
							Darlington	115	10
							Scarborough (loan)	6	—
							Scunthorpe U	15	5
							Scarborough	29	1
TOMLINSON Graeme	5 9	11 05	F	10 12 75	Watford	Trainee	Bradford C	17	6
							Manchester U	—	—
TOMLINSON Michael	5 9	11 00	M	15 9 72	Lambeth	Trainee	Leyton Orient	14	1
							Barnet	38	1
TOMLINSON Paul	6 2	14 04	G	22 2 64	Brierley Hill	Middlewood R	Sheffield U	37	—
							Birmingham C (loan)	11	—
							Bradford C	293	—
TORFASON Gudmundor ‡	6 1	13 02	F	13 12 61	Westann Isles	RSC Genk	St Mirren	76	24
							St Johnstone	39	9
							Doncaster R	4	—
TORPEY Steve	6 3	14 13	F	8 12 70	Islington	Trainee	Millwall	7	—
							Bradford C	96	22
							Swansea C	81	20
TOTTEN Alex	5 8	10 07	M	1 10 76	Southampton	Trainee	**Portsmouth**	4	—
TOVEY Paul	5 8	11 07	M	5 12 73	Wokingham	Trainee	**Bristol R**	1	—
TOWN David			F	9 12 76	Bournemouth	Trainee	**Bournemouth**	6	—
TOWNLEY Leon	6 2	12 09	D	16 2 76	Loughton	Trainee	**Tottenham H**	—	—
TOWNSEND Andy	5 11	12 07	M	23 7 63	Maidstone	Weymouth	Southampton	83	5
							Norwich C	71	8
							Chelsea	110	12
							Aston Villa	64	4
TRACEY Simon	6 0	12 00	G	9 12 67	Woolwich	Apprentice	Wimbledon	1	—
							Sheffield U	143	—
							Manchester C (loan)	3	—
							Norwich C (loan)	1	—
TREBBLE Neil	6 3	13 10	F	16 2 69	Hitchin	Stevenage Bor	Scunthorpe U	14	2
							Preston NE	19	4
							Scarborough	15	3
TRETTON Andrew	6 1	12 07	D	9 10 76	Derby	Trainee	**Derby Co**	—	—
TREVITT Simon	5 11	11 10	D	20 12 67	Dewsbury	Apprentice	**Huddersfield T**	225	3
TRINDER Jason	5 11	14 00	G	3 3 70	Leicester	Grimsby T	**Mansfield T**	7	—
TROLLOPE Paul	6 0	12 05	M	3 6 72	Swindon	Trainee	Swindon T	—	—
							Torquay U (loan)	10	—
							Torquay U	96	16
							Derby Co	24	4
TROTT Dean *	6 2	14 00	F	13 5 67	Barnsley	Boston U	**Northampton T**	22	4
TROTT Robin *	6 1	13 04	D	17 8 74	Orpington	Trainee	**Gillingham**	10	—

Player	Ht	Wt	Pos	Birth Date	Birth Place	Source	Clubs	League App	League Gls
TUCK Stuart	5 11	11 07	D	1 10 74	Brighton	Trainee	**Brighton**	34	—
TURNBULL Lee	6 0	12 08	M	27 9 67	Stockton	Local	Middlesbrough	16	4
							Aston Villa	—	—
							Doncaster R	123	21
							Chesterfield	87	26
							Doncaster R	11	1
							Wycombe W	11	1
							Scunthorpe U (loan)	10	3
TURNER Andy	5 10	11 07	M	23 5 75	Woolwich	Trainee	**Tottenham H**	20	3
							Wycombe W (loan)	4	—
							Doncaster R (loan)	4	1
TURNER Chris *	5 11	11 12	G	15 9 58	Sheffield	Apprentice	Sheffield W	91	—
							Lincoln C (loan)	5	—
							Sunderland	195	—
							Manchester U	64	—
							Sheffield W	75	—
							Leeds U (loan)	2	—
							Leyton Orient	58	—
TURNER Darren	5 3	8 00	M	23 12 77	Derby	Trainee	**Nottingham F**	—	—
TURNER Mark	6 0	11 01	M	4 10 72	Bebbington	Trainee	Wolverhampton W	1	—
							Northampton T	4	—
TURNER Phil	5 9	10 13	M	12 2 62	Sheffield	Apprentice	Lincoln C	241	19
							Grimsby T	62	8
							Leicester C	24	2
							Notts Co	225	15
TURNER Robert	6 3	14 01	M	18 9 66	Durham	Apprentice	Huddersfield T	1	—
							Cardiff C	39	8
							Hartlepool U (loan)	7	1
							Bristol R	26	2
							Wimbledon	10	—
							Bristol C	52	12
							Plymouth Arg	66	17
							Notts Co	8	1
							Shrewsbury T (loan)	9	—
							Exeter C	33	4
TURPIN Simon			D	11 8 75	Blackburn		**Crewe Alex**	—	—
TUTILL Steve	6 1	12 06	D	1 10 69	Derwent	Trainee	**York C**	259	6
TUTTLE David	6 2	12 10	D	6 2 72	Reading	Trainee	Tottenham H	13	—
							Peterborough U (loan)	7	—
							Sheffield U	37	—
TWIDDY Chris	5 11	11 06	M	19 1 76	Pontyridd	Trainee	**Plymouth Arg**	15	1
TWYNHAM Gary ‡	6 0	12 01	M	8 2 76	Manchester	Trainee	**Manchester U**	—	—
TYLER Mark	6 0	12 09	G	2 4 77	Norwich	Trainee	**Peterborough U**	5	—
ULLATHORNE Robert	5 8	10 10	M	11 10 71	Wakefield	Trainee	**Norwich C**	65	7
UNSWORTH David	6 0	14 07	F	16 10 73	Preston	Trainee	**Everton**	51	4
UNSWORTH Lee			D	25 2 73	Eccles	Ashton U	**Crewe Alex**	—	—
VALENTINE Peter	5 10	12 00	D	16 6 63	Huddersfield	Apprentice	Huddersfield T	19	1
							Bolton W	68	1
							Bury	319	16
							Carlisle U	29	2
							Rochdale	27	2
VAN BLERK Jason	6 0	13 00	M	16 3 68	Sydney	Go Ahead Eagles	**Millwall**	27	1
VAN DEN HAUWE Pat ‡	5 11	11 10	D	16 12 60	Dendermonde	Apprentice	Birmingham C	123	1
							Everton	135	2
							Tottenham H	116	—
							Millwall	27	—
VAN DER LAAN Robin	5 11	12 05	F	5 9 68	Schiedam	Wageningen	**Port Vale**	176	24
VAN HEUSDEN Arjan	6 0	12 00	G	11 12 72	Alphen	Noordwijk	**Port Vale**	2	—

Player	Ht	Wt	Pos	Birth Date	Birth Place	Source	Clubs	League App	League Gls
VARADI Imre ‡	5 9	12 03	F	8 7 59	Paddington	Letchworth GC	Sheffield U	10	4
							Everton	26	6
							Newcastle U	81	39
							Sheffield W	76	33
							WBA	32	9
							Manchester C	65	26
							Sheffield W	22	3
							Leeds U	26	5
							Luton T (loan)	6	1
							Oxford U (loan)	5	—
							Rotherham U	67	25
VAUGHAN John	5 10	13 01	G	26 6 64	Isleworth	Apprentice	West Ham U	—	—
							Charlton Ath (loan)	6	—
							Bristol R (loan)	6	—
							Wrexham (loan)	4	—
							Bristol C (loan)	2	—
							Fulham	44	—
							Bristol C (loan)	3	—
							Cambridge U	178	—
							Charlton Ath	6	—
							Preston NE	26	—
VAUGHAN Tony	6 1	11 02	D	11 10 75	Manchester	Trainee	**Ipswich T**	10	—
VEART Carl	5 10	11 05	F	21 5 70	Whyalla	Adelaide C	**Sheffield U**	39	10
VENISON Barry	5 10	11 09	D	16 8 64	Consett	Apprentice	Sunderland	173	2
							Liverpool	110	1
							Newcastle U	109	1
VENUS Mark	6 0	11 08	D	6 4 67	Hartlepool		Hartlepool U	4	—
							Leicester C	61	1
							Wolverhampton W	225	7
VERVEER Etienne ‡	5 11	11 12	M	22 9 67	Surinam	Chur	**Millwall**	56	7
							Bradford C (loan)	9	1
VICK Leigh §			M	8 1 78	Cardiff	Trainee	**Cardiff C**	2	—
VICKERS Steve	6 1	12 12	D	13 10 67	Bishop Auckland	Spennymoor U	Tranmere R	311	11
							Middlesbrough	70	6
VICTORY Jamie *	5 10	12 00	D	14 11 75	London	Trainee	**West Ham U**	—	—
VIER Matthew *	5 10	12 00	M	6 6 76	Welwyn	Trainee	**Watford**	—	—
VINCENT Jamie	5 10	11 09	D	18 6 75	London	Trainee	**Crystal Palace**	—	—
							Bournemouth (loan)	8	—
VINNICOMBE Chris	5 9	10 04	M	20 10 70	Exeter		Exeter C	39	1
							Rangers	23	1
							Burnley	29	1
VIVEASH Adrian	6 1	11 02	D	30 9 69	Swindon	Trainee	**Swindon T**	54	2
							Reading (loan)	5	—
							Reading (loan)	6	—
VOICE Scott *	6 0	11 10	F	12 8 74	Wolverhampton	Trainee	**Wolverhampton W**	—	—
VONK Michael	6 3	13 03	D	28 10 68	Alkmaar	SVV/Dordrecht	**Manchester C**	91	3
VOWDEN Colin	6 0	13 00	D	13 9 71	Newmarket	Cambridge C	**Cambridge U**	—	—
WADDLE Chris	6 2	12 13	F	14 12 60	Hedworth	Tow Law T	Newcastle U	170	46
							Tottenham H	138	33
							Marseille	107	22
							Sheffield W	77	8
WADDOCK Gary	5 10	11 12	M	17 3 62	Alperton	Apprentice	QPR	203	8
						Charleroi	Millwall	58	2
							QPR	—	—
							Swindon T (loan)	6	—
							Bristol R	71	1
							Luton T	40	1
WADE Shaun ‡			F	22 9 69	Stoke	Newcastle T	**Stoke C**	1	—
WALDOCK John *	5 10	11 01	D	27 11 75	North Shields	Trainee	**Sunderland**	—	—

Player	Ht	Wt	Pos	Birth Date	Birth Place	Source	Clubs	League App	League Gls
WALKER Alan ‡	6 2	12 11	D	17 12 59	Mossley	Telford U	Lincoln C	75	4
							Millwall	92	8
							Gillingham	151	7
							Plymouth Arg	2	1
							Mansfield T	22	1
							Barnet	59	2
WALKER Des	5 11	11 09	D	26 11 65	Hackney	Apprentice	Nottingham F	264	1
							Sampdoria	30	—
							Sheffield W	80	—
WALKER Ian	6 2	12 09	G	31 10 71	Watford	Trainee	**Tottenham H**	88	—
							Oxford U (loan)	2	—
							Ipswich T (loan)	—	—
WALKER James	5 11	13 00	G	9 7 73	Sutton-in-Ashfield	Trainee	Notts Co	—	—
							Walsall	35	—
WALKER Justin	5 10	11 08	M	6 9 75	Nottingham	Trainee	**Nottingham F**	—	—
WALKER Keith	6 0	12 08	M	17 4 66	Edinburgh	ICI Juveniles	Stirling Albion	91	17
							St Mirren	43	6
							Swansea C	166	5
WALKER Ray	5 10	11 12	M	28 9 63	North Shields	Apprentice	Aston Villa	23	—
							Port Vale (loan)	15	1
							Port Vale	299	33
WALKER Richard §			M	14 3 77	Cambridge	Trainee	**Cambridge U**	5	—
WALKER Richard	6 0	12 00	D	9 11 71	Derby	Trainee	**Notts Co**	40	4
							Mansfield T (loan)	4	—
WALLACE Danny *	5 4	10 04	F	21 1 64	London	Apprentice	Southampton	255	64
							Manchester U	47	6
							Millwall (loan)	3	—
							Birmingham C	16	2
							Wycombe W	1	—
WALLACE Michael *	5 8	10 02	M	5 10 70	Farnworth	Trainee	Manchester C	—	—
							Stockport Co	70	5
WALLACE Ray	5 6	10 02	D	2 10 69	Lewisham	Trainee	Southampton	35	—
							Leeds U	7	—
							Swansea C (loan)	2	—
							Reading (loan)	3	—
							Stoke C	20	1
							Hull C (loan)	7	—
WALLACE Rodney	5 7	11 03	F	2 10 69	Lewisham	Trainee	Southampton	128	45
							Leeds U	135	39
WALLEY Mark	5 10	10 06	F	17 9 76	Barnsley	Trainee	**Nottingham F**	—	—
WALLING Dean	5 11	11 04	D	17 4 69	Leeds		Leeds U	—	—
							Rochdale	65	8
						Guiseley	**Carlisle U**	141	17
WALLWORK Ronald			D	10 9 77	Manchester	Trainee	**Manchester U**	—	—
WALSH Alan ‡	6 0	12 08	D	9 12 56	Darlington	Horden CW	Middlesbrough	3	—
							Darlington	251	87
							Bristol C	218	77
						Besiktas	Walsall	4	—
						Glenavon	Huddersfield T	4	—
							Shrewsbury T	2	—
							Cardiff C	1	—
							Southampton	—	—
						Taunton	**Hartlepool U**	4	1
WALSH Colin	5 9	11 00	M	22 7 62	Hamilton	Apprentice	Nottingham F	139	32
							Charlton Ath	236	21
							Peterborough U (loan)	5	1
							Middlesbrough (loan)	13	1
WALSH Gary	6 3	15 10	G	21 3 68	Wigan	Apprentice	**Manchester U**	50	—
							Airdrie (loan)	3	—
							Oldham Ath (loan)	6	—
WALSH Michael §			D	5 8 77	Rotherham	Trainee	**Scunthorpe U**	3	—

Player	Ht	Wt	Pos	Birth Date	Birth Place	Source	Clubs	League App	League Gls
WALSH Paul	5 7	10 08	F	1 10 62	Plumstead	Apprentice	Charlton Ath	87	24
							Luton T	80	24
							Liverpool	77	25
							Tottenham H	128	19
							QPR (loan)	2	—
							Portsmouth	73	14
							Manchester C	50	16
WALSH Steve	6 3	14 05	D	3 11 64	Fulwood	Local	Wigan Ath	126	4
							Leicester C	250	41
WALTERS Mark	5 9	11 08	M	2 6 64	Birmingham	Apprentice	Aston Villa	181	39
							Rangers	106	32
							Liverpool	94	14
							Stoke C (loan)	9	2
							Wolverhampton W (loan)	11	3
WALTERS Scott ‡	5 10	11 06	F	23 9 75	Hemel Hempstead	Watford	**Colchester U**	—	—
WALTERS Steve ‡	5 10	11 08	F	9 1 72	Plymouth	Trainee	**Crewe Alex**	146	10
WALTON David	6 2	13 04	D	10 4 73	Bedlingham	Trainee	Sheffield U	—	—
							Shrewsbury T	63	8
WANLESS Paul *	6 0	13 04	M	14 12 73	Banbury	Trainee	**Oxford U**	32	—
WARBURTON Ray	6 0	12 09	D	7 10 67	Rotherham	Apprentice	Rotherham U	4	—
							York C	90	9
							Northampton T (loan)	17	1
							Northampton T	39	3
WARD Ashley	6 1	11 07	F	24 11 70	Manchester	Trainee	Manchester C	1	—
							Wrexham (loan)	4	2
							Leicester C	10	—
							Blackpool (loan)	2	1
							Crewe Alex	61	25
							Norwich C	25	8
WARD Darren	5 11	13 00	G	11 5 74	Worksop	Trainee	**Mansfield T**	81	—
WARD Gavin	6 3	14 12	G	30 6 70	Sutton Coldfield	Aston Villa	Shrewsbury T	—	—
							WBA	—	—
							Cardiff C	59	—
							Leicester C	38	—
WARD Mark	5 6	9 12	M	10 10 62	Prescot	Northwich Vic	Oldham Ath	84	12
							West Ham U	165	12
							Manchester C	55	14
							Everton	83	6
							Birmingham C (loan)	9	1
							Birmingham C	41	3
WARD Mitch	5 8	10 12	M	19 6 71	Sheffield	Trainee	**Sheffield U**	72	5
							Crewe Alex (loan)	4	1
WARD Peter	6 0	11 10	F	15 10 64	Durham	Chester-le-Street	Huddersfield T	37	2
							Rochdale	84	10
							Stockport Co	142	10
WARD Richard ‡	5 8	11 00	M	17 11 73	Scarborough	Trainee	Notts Co	—	—
							Scarborough	—	—
							Huddersfield T	—	—
WARD Richard			M	6 1 77	Middlesbrough	Trainee	**Middlesbrough**	—	—
WARE Paul	5 9	11 05	M	7 11 70	Congleton	Trainee	Stoke C	115	10
							Stockport Co	19	1
WARHURST Paul	6 0	13 00	D	26 9 69	Stockport	Trainee	Manchester C	—	—
							Oldham Ath	67	2
							Sheffield W	66	6
							Blackburn R	36	2
WARK John	5 11	12 12	D	4 8 57	Glasgow	Apprentice	Ipswich T	296	94
							Liverpool	70	28
							Ipswich T	89	23
							Middlesbrough	32	2
							Ipswich T	138	16
WARNER Anthony	6 4	13 09	G	11 5 74	Liverpool	School	**Liverpool**	—	—
WARNER Ashley *	5 10	12 00	F	15 9 71	Leicester	VS Rugby	**Peterborough U**	—	—

Player	Ht	Wt	Pos	Birth Date	Birth Place	Source	Clubs	League App	League Gls
WARNER Robert	5 9	11 07	D	20 4 77	Stratford	Trainee	**Hereford U**	16	—
WARNER Vance	5 11	11 05	D	3 9 74	Leeds	Trainee	**Nottingham F**	2	—
WARREN Christer	5 10	11 03	M	10 10 74	Bournemouth	Cheltenham T	**Southampton**	—	—
WARREN Lee	6 0	12 00	M	28 2 69	Manchester	Trainee	Leeds U	—	—
							Rochdale	31	1
							Hull C	153	1
							Lincoln C (loan)	3	1
							Doncaster R	14	2
WARREN Mark	5 9	10 05	D	12 11 74	Clapton	Trainee	**Leyton Orient**	52	3
							West Ham U (loan)	—	—
WARREN Matt ‡	6 0	12 11	D	14 2 76	Derby	Trainee	**Derby Co**	—	—
WARRINGTON Andrew	6 3	12 13	G	10 6 76	Sheffield	Trainee	**York C**	—	—
WASSALL Darren	5 11	12 10	D	27 6 68	Edgbaston		Nottingham F	27	—
							Hereford U (loan)	5	—
							Bury (loan)	7	1
							Derby Co	81	—
WATKIN Steve	5 10	11 10	F	16 6 71	Wrexham	School	**Wrexham**	142	40
WATKINS Darren ‡	5 11	11 02	D	17 3 77	Middlesbrough	Trainee	**Nottingham F**	—	—
WATKISS Stuart	6 2	13 04	D	8 5 66	Wolverhampton	Apprentice	Wolverhampton W	2	—
						Rushall Olympic	**Walsall**	47	2
WATSON Alex	6 0	11 09	D	5 4 68	Liverpool	Apprentice	Liverpool	4	—
							Derby Co (loan)	5	—
							Bournemouth	151	5
WATSON Andy	5 9	11 02	D	1 4 67	Huddersfield	Harrogate T	Halifax T	83	15
							Swansea C	14	1
							Carlisle U	56	22
							Blackpool	88	37
WATSON Dave	6 0	13 07	D	20 11 61	Liverpool	Amateur	Liverpool	—	—
							Norwich C	212	11
							Everton	306	21
WATSON David	5 11	12 03	G	10 11 73	Barnsley	Trainee	**Barnsley**	51	—
WATSON Gordon	5 10	12 08	F	20 3 71	Sidcup	Trainee	Charlton Ath	31	7
							Sheffield W	66	15
							Southampton	12	3
WATSON Kevin	6 0	12 06	M	3 1 74	Hackney	Trainee	**Tottenham H**	5	—
							Brentford (loan)	3	—
							Bristol C (loan)	2	—
							Barnet (loan)	13	—
WATSON Mark *	6 0	12 06	D	8 9 70	Vancouver		**Watford**	18	—
WATSON Mark			F	28 12 73	Birmingham	Sutton U	**West Ham U**	—	—
WATSON Paul	5 8	10 10	D	4 1 75	Hastings	Trainee	**Gillingham**	54	2
WATSON Steve	6 0	12 07	D	1 4 74	North Shields	Trainee	**Newcastle U**	113	7
WATSON Tommy	5 8	10 10	M	29 9 69	Liverpool	Trainee	**Grimsby T**	170	24
WATTS Grant ‡	6 0	11 02	F	5 11 73	Croydon	Trainee	Crystal Palace	4	—
							Colchester U (loan)	12	2
							Gillingham	3	—
							Sheffield U	—	—
WATTS Julian	6 3	12 08	D	17 3 71	Sheffield	Trainee	Rotherham U	20	1
							Sheffield W	5	—
							Shrewsbury T (loan)	9	—
WDOWCZYK Dariusz	5 11	11 11	D	21 9 62	Warsaw	Legia Warsaw	Celtic	116	4
							Reading	38	—
WEBB Matthew §			M	24 9 76	Bristol	Trainee	**Birmingham C**	1	—
WEBB Neil	6 0	13 07	M	30 7 63	Reading	Apprentice	Reading	72	22
							Portsmouth	123	34
							Nottingham F	146	47
							Manchester U	75	8
							Nottingham F	30	3
							Swindon T (loan)	6	—

Player	Ht	Wt	Pos	Birth Date	Birth Place	Source	Clubs	League App	League Gls
WEBB Simon			M	19 1 78	Castle Bar	Trainee	**Tottenham H**	—	—
WEBBER Damien	6 4	14 00	D	8 10 68	Rustington	Bognor Regis T	**Millwall**	22	2
WEBSTER Kenny ‡	5 7	12 08	D	2 3 73	Hammersmith	Trainee	Arsenal	—	—
							Peterborough U	—	—
WEBSTER Simon	6 0	11 07	D	20 1 64	Earl Shilton	Apprentice	Tottenham H	3	—
							Exeter C (loan)	26	—
							Norwich C (loan)	—	—
							Huddersfield T	118	4
							Sheffield U	37	3
							Charlton Ath	127	7
							West Ham U	5	—
							Oldham Ath (loan)	7	—
WEGERLE Roy	5 11	11 00	F	19 3 64	South Africa	Tampa Bay R	Chelsea	23	3
							Swindon T (loan)	7	1
							Luton T	45	10
							QPR	75	29
							Blackburn R	34	6
							Coventry C	53	9
WELCH Keith	6 0	12 0	G	3 10 68	Bolton	Trainee	Bolton W	—	—
							Rochdale	205	—
							Bristol C	160	—
WELLER Paul	5 8	10 13	F	6 3 75	Brighton	Trainee	**Burnley**	—	—
WELLS David §			G	29 12 77	Portsmouth	Trainee	**Bournemouth**	1	—
WELLS Mark	5 8	10 08	M	17 10 71	Leicester	Trainee	Notts Co	2	—
							Huddersfield T	23	4
							Scarborough	18	1
WELSH Steve (To Partick T)	6 1	12 03	D	19 4 68	Glasgow	Army	Cambridge U	1	—
							Peterborough U	146	2
							Preston NE (loan)	—	—
WEST Colin	6 0	13 11	F	13 11 62	Wallsend	Apprentice	Sunderland	102	21
							Watford	45	20
							Rangers	10	2
							Sheffield W	45	8
							WBA	73	22
							Port Vale (loan)	5	1
							Swansea C	33	12
							Leyton Orient	73	23
WEST Daniel *	5 11	12 07	D	17 4 75	Poole	Christchurch	**Aston Villa**	—	—
WEST Dean	5 10	11 07	D	5 12 72	Wakefield	Leeds U	**Lincoln C**	111	19
WEST Paul *	5 11	11 00	D	22 6 70	Birmingham	Alcester T	Port Vale	—	—
							Bradford C	—	—
							Wigan Ath	3	—
WESTLEY Shane *	6 2	13 08	D	16 6 65	Canterbury	Apprentice	Charlton Ath	8	—
							Southend U	144	10
							Norwich C (loan)	—	—
							Wolverhampton W	50	2
							Brentford	64	1
							Southend U (loan)	5	—
WESTON Kenneth ‡	5 10	11 07	F	5 11 75	Manchester	Trainee	**Ipswich T**	—	—
WESTON Matthew ‡	5 10	11 07	F	5 11 75	Manchester	Trainee	**Ipswich T**	—	—
WESTWOOD Ashley	6 0	11 03	D	31 8 76	Bridgnorth	Trainee	**Manchester U**	—	—
WETHERALL David	6 3	13 12	D	14 3 71	Sheffield	School	Sheffield W	—	—
							Leeds U	84	5
WHALLEY Gareth	5 10	11 00	M	19 12 73	Manchester	Trainee	**Crewe Alex**	80	3
WHALLEY Neil ‡	5 10	11 02	M	29 10 65	Liverpool	Warrington T	**Preston NE**	50	1
WHARTON Paul	5 4	9 09	M	26 6 77	Newcastle	Trainee	**Leeds U**	—	—
WHELAN Noel	6 2	12 03	F	30 12 74	Leeds	Trainee	**Leeds U**	40	7
WHELAN Phil	6 4	14 01	D	7 8 72	Stockport		Ipswich T	82	2
							Middlesbrough	—	—
WHELAN Ronnie	5 9	10 13	M	25 9 61	Dublin	Home Farm	Liverpool	362	46
							Southend U	33	1

Player	Ht	Wt	Pos	Birth Date	Birth Place	Source	Clubs	League App	League Gls
WHELAN Spencer	6 2	13 00	D	17 9 71	Liverpool	Liverpool	**Chester C**	116	1
WHISTON Peter	6 1	12 04	D	4 1 68	Widnes		Plymouth Arg	10	—
							Torquay U (loan)	8	1
							Torquay U	32	—
							Exeter C	85	7
							Southampton	1	—
WHITBREAD Adrian	6 2	11 13	D	22 10 71	Epping	Trainee	Leyton Orient	125	2
							Swindon T	36	1
							West Ham U	8	—
WHITE Alan			D	22 3 76	Darlington		**Middlesbrough**	—	—
WHITE David	6 1	12 09	F	30 10 67	Manchester		Manchester C	285	79
							Leeds U	38	8
WHITE Devon	6 3	14 00	F	2 3 64	Nottingham	Arnold T	Lincoln C	29	4
						Boston U	Bristol R	202	53
							Cambridge U	22	4
							QPR	46	16
WHITE Jason	6 0	12 10	F	19 10 71	Meriden	Derby Co	Scunthorpe U	68	16
							Darlington (loan)	4	1
							Scarborough	63	20
WHITE John	5 8	11 03	M	9 9 74	Honiton	Trainee	**Watford**	—	—
WHITE Steve	5 11	12 02	F	2 1 59	Chipping Sodbury	Mangotsfield U	Bristol R	50	20
							Luton T	72	25
							Charlton Ath	29	12
							Lincoln C (loan)	3	—
							Luton T (loan)	4	—
							Bristol R	101	24
							Swindon T	244	83
							Hereford U	36	15
WHITE Tom	5 11	12 02	D	26 1 76	Bristol	Trainee	**Bristol R**	4	—
WHITEHALL Steve	5 9	11 00	F	8 12 66	Bromborough	Southport	**Rochdale**	157	46
WHITEHEAD Phil	6 3	13 07	G	17 12 69	Halifax	Trainee	Halifax T	42	—
							Barnsley	16	—
							Halifax T (loan)	9	—
							Scunthorpe U (loan)	8	—
							Scunthorpe U (loan)	8	—
							Bradford C (loan)	6	—
							Oxford U	77	—
WHITEHEAD Scot ‡	5 8	11 09	D	13 8 75	Doncaster	Trainee	**Huddersfield T**	—	—
WHITEHOUSE Dane	5 10	10 13	M	14 10 70	Sheffield	Trainee	**Sheffield U**	146	26
WHITINGTON Craig	5 11	12 04	F	3 9 70	Brighton	Crawley T	Scarborough	27	10
							Huddersfield T	1	—
							Rochdale (loan)	1	—
WHITLEY Jim	5 9	11 00	M	14 4 75	Zambia	Trainee	**Manchester C**	—	—
WHITLOW Mike	6 0	12 13	D	13 1 68	Northwich	Witton Alb	Leeds U	77	4
							Leicester C	88	5
WHITNEY Jonathan	5 10	12 00	D	23 12 70	Nantwich	Winsford	**Huddersfield T**	14	—
							Wigan Ath (loan)	12	—
WHITTAKER Stuart	5 7	9 03	M	2 1 75	Liverpool	Liverpool	**Bolton W**	3	—
WHITTAM Philip	5 8	9 08	D	12 8 76	Bolton	Trainee	**Manchester U**	—	—
WHITTINGHAM Guy	5 10	11 12	F	10 11 64	Evesham	Yeovil	Portsmouth	160	88
							Aston Villa	25	5
							Wolverhampton W (loan)	13	8
							Sheffield W	21	9
WHITTLE Justin	6 1	12 12	D	18 3 71	Derby	Celtic	**Stoke C**	—	—
WHITTON Steve	6 0	13 07	M	4 12 60	East Ham	Apprentice	Coventry C	74	21
							West Ham U	39	6
							Birmingham C (loan)	8	2
							Birmingham C	95	28
							Sheffield W	32	4
							Ipswich T	88	15
							Colchester U	44	12

Player	Ht	Wt	Pos	Birth Date	Birth Place	Source	Clubs	League App	League Gls
WHYTE Chris	6 1	11 10	D	2 9 61	London	Amateur	Arsenal	90	8
							Crystal Palace (loan)	13	—
						Los Angeles R	WBA	84	7
							Leeds U	113	5
							Birmingham C	64	1
WHYTE David	5 8	10 07	F	20 4 71	Greenwich	Greenwich Borough	Crystal Palace	27	4
							Charlton Ath (loan)	8	2
							Charlton Ath	38	19
WHYTE Derek	5 11	12 11	D	31 8 68	Glasgow	Celtic BC	Celtic	216	7
							Middlesbrough	113	2
WIDDRINGTON Tommy	5 10	11 12	D	1 10 71	Newcastle	Trainee	**Southampton**	54	1
							Wigan Ath (loan)	6	—
WIETECHA David	6 4	15 00	G	1 11 74	Colchester		**Millwall**	—	—
							Crewe Alex (loan)	—	—
							Rotherham U (loan)	—	—
WIGG Nathan	5 9	10 05	M	27 9 74	Cardiff	Trainee	**Cardiff C**	38	1
WILCOX Jason	5 11	11 10	F	15 7 71	Bolton	Trainee	**Blackburn R**	150	19
WILCOX Russell	6 0	11 10	D	25 3 64	Hemsworth	Apprentice	Doncaster R	1	—
						Cambridge U, Frickley Ath.	Northampton T	138	9
							Hull C	100	7
							Doncaster R	77	6
WILDER Chris	5 11	12 08	D	23 9 67	Wortley	Apprentice	Southampton	—	—
							Sheffield U	93	1
							Walsall (loan)	4	—
							Charlton Ath (loan)	1	—
							Charlton Ath (loan)	2	—
							Leyton Orient (loan)	16	1
							Rotherham U	114	11
WILKERSON Paul	6 3	13 11	G	11 12 74	Hertford		**Watford**	—	—
WILKIE Glen			D	22 1 77	Stepney	Trainee	**Leyton Orient**	11	—
WILKIN Kevin *	5 11	11 07	F	1 10 67	Cambridge	Cambridge C	**Northampton T**	78	11
WILKINS Dean	5 10	12 08	M	12 7 62	Hillingdon	Apprentice	QPR	6	—
							Brighton	2	—
							Orient (loan)	10	—
						PEC Zwolle	**Brighton**	275	22
WILKINS Ray †	5 8	11 02	M	14 9 56	Hillingdon	Apprentice	Chelsea	179	30
							Manchester U	160	7
							AC Milan	73	2
						Paris St Germain	Rangers	70	2
							QPR	154	7
							Crystal Palace	1	—
							QPR	2	—
WILKINS Richard	6 0	12 03	M	28 5 65	Streatham	Haverhill R	Colchester U	152	22
							Cambridge U	81	7
							Hereford U	35	2
WILKINSON Ian	5 11	12 00	G	2 7 73	Warrington	Trainee	Manchester U	—	—
							Stockport Co	—	—
							Crewe Alex	3	—
							Doncaster R (loan)	—	—
WILKINSON Paul	6 1	12 04	F	30 10 64	Louth	Apprentice	Grimsby T	71	27
							Everton	31	7
							Nottingham F	34	5
							Watford	134	52
							Middlesbrough	163	49
WILKINSON Steve	6 0	11 06	F	1 9 68	Lincoln	Apprentice	Leicester C	9	1
							Rochdale (loan)	—	—
							Crewe Alex (loan)	5	2
							Mansfield T	232	83
WILLGRASS Alexandre			M	8 4 76	Scarborough		**Scarborough**	—	—
WILLIAMS Adrian	6 2	12 06	D	16 8 71	Reading	Trainee	**Reading**	165	11

Player	Ht	Wt	Pos	Birth Date	Birth Place	Source	Clubs	League App	League Gls
WILLIAMS Andy *	6 2	12 00	M	29 7 62	Birmingham	Solihull B	Coventry C	9	—
							Rotherham U	87	13
							Leeds U	46	3
							Port Vale (loan)	5	—
							Notts Co	39	2
							Huddersfield T (loan)	6	—
							Rotherham U	51	2
WILLIAMS Chris *	5 9	11 07	F	21 9 76	Neath	Trainee	**Hereford U**	4	—
WILLIAMS Corey *	6 2	12 00	F	22 2 72	Sheffield	Denaby U	**Rotherham U**	2	—
WILLIAMS Darren §			M	28 4 77	Middlesbrough	Trainee	**York C**	1	—
WILLIAMS David	6 0	12 00	G	18 9 68	Liverpool	Trainee	Oldham Ath	—	—
							Burnley	24	—
							Rochdale (loan)	6	—
							Crewe Alex (loan)	—	—
							Cardiff C	40	—
WILLIAMS Dean A ‡	6 1	13 00	F	14 11 70	Hemel Hempstead	Trainee	Cambridge U	1	—
						St Albans	Brentford	3	1
							Doncaster R	1	—
WILLIAMS Dean P	6 1	12 09	G	5 1 72	Lichfield	Tamworth	Brentford	7	—
							Doncaster R	35	—
WILLIAMS Gareth	5 10	11 08	F	12 3 67	Isle of Wight	Gosport Borough	Aston Villa	12	—
							Barnsley	34	6
							Hull C (loan)	4	—
							Hull C (loan)	16	2
							Bournemouth	1	—
							Northampton T	15	—
WILLIAMS Geraint	5 7	12 06	M	5 1 62	Cwmpare	Apprentice	Bristol R	141	8
							Derby Co	277	9
							Ipswich T	109	1
WILLIAMS John *	6 1	13 12	D	3 10 60	Liverpool	Amateur	Tranmere R	173	13
							Port Vale	50	2
							Bournemouth	117	9
							Wigan Ath (loan)	4	—
							Cardiff C	6	—
							Bournemouth	—	—
WILLIAMS John	6 2	12 04	M	11 5 68	Birmingham	Cradley T	Swansea C	39	11
							Coventry C	80	11
							Notts Co (loan)	5	2
							Stoke C (loan)	4	—
							Swansea C (loan)	7	2
WILLIAMS Lee	5 6	11 09	M	3 2 73	Birmingham	Trainee	Aston Villa	—	—
							Shrewsbury T (loan)	3	—
							Peterborough U	58	1
WILLIAMS Mark	6 0	13 00	D	28 9 70	Stalybridge	Newtown	**Shrewsbury T**	102	3
WILLIAMS Mark	5 11	12 00	F	8 2 73	Bangor	Bangor C	**Stockport Co**	1	—
WILLIAMS Martin *	5 9	11 12	F	12 7 73	Luton	Leicester C	**Luton T**	40	2
							Colchester U (loan)	3	—
WILLIAMS Mike ‡			F	3 11 76	Mansfield	Trainee	**Mansfield T**	1	—
WILLIAMS Mike	5 11	11 04	M	21 11 69	Bradford	Maltby	**Sheffield W**	17	1
							Halifax T (loan)	9	1
WILLIAMS Paul	5 7	10 00	F	11 9 69	Leicester	Trainee	Leicester C	—	—
							Stockport Co	70	4
							Coventry C	14	—
							WBA (loan)	5	—
							Huddersfield T (loan)	9	—
WILLIAMS Paul	5 7	10 09	F	16 8 65	London	Woodford T	Charlton Ath	82	23
							Brentford (loan)	7	3
							Sheffield W	93	25
							Crystal Palace	46	7
							Sunderland (loan)	3	—
							Birmingham C (loan)	11	—
WILLIAMS Paul	6 0	14 03	D	26 3 71	Burton	Trainee	**Derby Co**	160	26
							Lincoln C (loan)	3	—

Player	Ht	Wt	Pos	Birth Date	Birth Place	Source	Clubs	League App	League Gls
WILLIAMS Paul	5 11	12 02	D	25 9 70	Liverpool	Trainee	Sunderland	9	—
							Swansea C (loan)	12	1
							Doncaster R	8	—
WILLIAMS Paul A	6 3	14 08	F	8 9 63	Sheffield	Nuneaton	Preston NE	1	—
							Newport Co	26	3
							Sheffield U	8	—
							Hartlepool U	8	—
							Stockport Co	24	14
							WBA	44	5
							Coventry C (loan)	2	—
							Stockport Co	16	3
							Rochdale	25	7
WILLIAMS Scott	6 0	11 00	D	7 8 74	Bangor	Trainee	**Wrexham**	25	—
WILLIAMS Steven	6 3	12 12	G	16 10 74	Aberystwyth	Coventry C	**Cardiff C**	24	—
WILLIAMS Steven	5 11	12 00	F	3 11 75	Sheffield	Trainee	**Lincoln C**	14	2
WILLIAMSON Danny	5 10	11 06	M	5 12 73	London	Trainee	**West Ham U**	7	1
							Doncaster R (loan)	13	1
WILLIS Jimmy	6 0	12 03	D	12 7 68	Liverpool	Blackburn R	Halifax T	—	—
							Stockport Co	10	—
							Darlington	90	6
							Leicester C	48	3
							Bradford C (loan)	9	1
WILLIS Roger	6 1	11 06	D	17 6 67	Sheffield		Grimsby T	9	—
						Barnet	Barnet	44	13
							Watford	36	2
							Birmingham C	19	5
							Southend U	21	4
WILMOT Rhys	6 1	12 00	G	21 2 62	Newport	Apprentice	Arsenal	8	—
							Hereford U (loan)	9	—
							Orient (loan)	46	—
							Swansea C (loan)	16	—
							Plymouth Arg (loan)	17	—
							Plymouth Arg	116	—
							Grimsby T	33	—
							Crystal Palace	6	—
WILSON Clive	5 7	10 00	M	13 11 61	Manchester	Local	Manchester C	98	9
							Chester (loan)	21	2
							Chelsea	81	5
							Manchester C (loan)	11	—
							QPR	172	12
WILSON Danny	5 6	11 00	M	1 1 60	Wigan	Wigan Ath	Bury	90	8
							Chesterfield	100	13
							Nottingham F	10	1
							Scunthorpe U (loan)	6	3
							Brighton	135	33
							Luton T	110	24
							Sheffield W	98	11
							Barnsley	77	2
WILSON Gus *	5 11	12 00	D	11 4 63	Manchester	Runcorn	**Crewe Alex**	115	—
WILSON Kevin	5 7	11 04	F	18 4 61	Banbury	Banbury U	Derby Co	122	30
							Ipswich T	98	34
							Chelsea	152	42
							Notts Co	69	3
							Bradford C (loan)	5	—
							Walsall	42	16
WILSON Paul	5 9	11 04	D	26 9 64	London	Barking	**Barnet**	104	7
WILSON Paul			F	22 2 77	Maidstone	Trainee	**Gillingham**	2	—
WILSON Paul	5 10	11 08	D	2 8 68	Bradford	Trainee	Huddersfield T	15	—
							Norwich C	—	—
							Northampton T	141	6
							Halifax T	45	7
							Burnley	31	—
							York C	22	—
WILSON Ross ‡	5 8	10 00	M	29 9 76	Chatham	Trainee	**Nottingham F**	—	—
WILSON Steve	5 10	10 07	G	24 4 74	Hull	Trainee	**Hull C**	60	—
WINDASS Dean	5 10	12 03	F	1 4 69	Hull	N. Ferriby	**Hull C**	160	53

Player	Ht	Wt	Pos	Birth Date	Birth Place	Source	Clubs	League App	League Gls
WINSTANLEY Mark	6 1	12 07	D	22 1 68	St. Helens	Trainee	Bolton W	220	3
							Burnley	44	2
WINSTONE Simon ‡	5 7	10 00	D	4 10 74	Bristol	Trainee	Stoke C	—	—
							Torquay U	2	—
WINTERBURN Nigel	5 8	11 04	D	11 12 63	Coventry	Local	Birmingham C	—	—
							Oxford U	—	—
							Wimbledon	165	8
							Arsenal	272	5
WISE Dennis	5 6	9 05	F	15 12 66	Kensington	Southampton	Wimbledon	135	27
							Chelsea	152	33
WITHE Chris	5 10	11 12	D	25 9 62	Liverpool	Apprentice	Newcastle U	2	—
							Bradford C	143	2
							Notts Co	80	3
							Bury	31	1
							Chester C (loan)	2	—
							Mansfield T (loan)	11	—
							Mansfield T	65	5
							Shrewsbury T	57	2
WITSCHGE Richard *			F	20 9 69	Amsterdam	Bordeaux	**Blackburn R**	1	—
WITTER Tony	6 1	13 02	D	12 8 65	London	Grays Ath	Crystal Palace	—	—
							QPR	1	—
							Millwall (loan)	—	—
							Plymouth Arg (loan)	3	1
							Reading (loan)	4	—
							Millwall	27	1
WOAN Ian	5 10	11 09	M	14 12 67	Wirrall	Runcorn	**Nottingham F**	122	21
WOOD Paul	5 9	10 05	F	1 11 64	Middlesbrough	Apprentice	Portsmouth	47	6
							Brighton	92	8
							Sheffield U	28	3
							Bournemouth (loan)	21	—
							Bournemouth	78	18
							Portsmouth	17	2
WOOD Simon	5 9	11 08	M	24 9 76	Hull	Trainee	**Coventry C**	—	—
WOOD Steve	6 0	12 04	D	2 2 63	Bracknell	Apprentice	Reading	219	9
							Millwall	110	—
							Southampton	46	—
							Oxford U	2	—
WOOD Trevor	6 0	13 07	G	3 11 68	Jersey	Apprentice	Brighton	—	—
							Port Vale	42	—
							Walsall	39	—
WOODMAN Andy	6 1	12 04	G	11 8 71	Denmark Hill	Apprentice	Crystal Palace	—	—
							Exeter C	6	—
							Northampton T	10	—
WOODS Andrew *			G	15 1 76	Colchester	Trainee	**Oldham Ath**	—	—
WOODS Chris	6 2	14 05	G	14 11 59	Boston	Apprentice	Nottingham F	—	—
							QPR	63	—
							Norwich C (loan)	10	—
							Norwich C	206	—
							Rangers	173	—
							Sheffield W	99	—
WOODS Neil	6 0	12 11	F	30 7 66	York	Apprentice	Doncaster R	65	16
							Rangers	3	—
							Ipswich T	27	5
							Bradford C	14	2
							Grimsby T	159	38
WOODS Ray	5 10	11 09	F	7 6 65	Birkenhead	Apprentice	Tranmere R	7	2
						Colne D.	Wigan Ath	28	3
							Coventry C	21	1
							Wigan Ath (loan)	13	—
							Shrewsbury T (loan)	9	1
							Shrewsbury T	19	—
WOODSFORD Jamie	5 9	11 00	F	9 11 76	Ipswich	Trainee	**Luton T**	7	—
WOODWARD Andy	5 10	10 12	D	23 9 73	Stockport	Trainee	Crewe Alex	20	—
							Bury	8	—
WOOLFORD Stephen ‡	5 10	11 00	F	24 11 76	Leeds	Trainee	**Nottingham F**	—	—

Player	Ht	Wt	Pos	Birth Date	Birth Place	Source	Clubs	League App	League Gls
WOOLGAR Matthew	5 10	11 10	M	5 1 76	Bedford	Trainee	**Luton T**	—	—
WORBOYS Gavin	6 0	11 00	F	14 7 74	Doncaster	Trainee	Doncaster R	7	2
							Notts Co	—	—
							Exeter C (loan)	4	1
							Darlington	27	6
WORRALL Ben	5 8	10 06	M	7 12 75	Swindon	Trainee	**Swindon T**	3	—
WORRELL David	5 9	11 00	D	12 1 78	Dublin	Trainee	**Blackburn R**	—	—
WORTHINGTON Nigel	5 11	12 08	D	4 11 61	Ballymena	Ballymena U	Notts Co	67	4
							Sheffield W	338	12
							Leeds U	27	1
WOTTON Paul §			M	17 8 77	Plymouth	Trainee	**Plymouth Arg**	7	—
WRACK Darren	5 9	11 10	F	5 5 76	Cleethorpes	Trainee	**Derby Co**	16	1
WRATTEN Adam *	6 0	12 00	D	30 11 74	Coventry	Trainee	**Birmingham C**	—	—
WRATTEN Paul ‡	5 7	10 00	M	29 11 70	Middlesbrough	Trainee	Manchester U	2	—
							Hartlepool U	57	1
							York C	—	—
WRIGHT Alan	5 4	9 04	M	28 9 71	Ashton-under-Lyme	Trainee	Blackpool	98	—
							Blackburn R	74	1
							Aston Villa	8	—
WRIGHT Dale	6 00	12 05	D	21 12 74	Middlesbrough	Trainee	**Nottingham F**	—	—
WRIGHT Ian	5 9	11 08	F	3 11 63	Woolwich	Greenwich Borough	Crystal Palace	225	89
							Arsenal	131	80
WRIGHT Ian	6 1	12 08	D	10 3 72	Lichfield	Trainee	Stoke C	6	—
							Bristol R	36	1
WRIGHT Jermaine	5 9	10 03	F	21 10 75	Greenwich	Trainee	Millwall	—	—
							Wolverhampton W	6	—
WRIGHT Johnny	5 8	11 04	D	24 11 75	Belfast	Trainee	**Norwich C**	2	—
WRIGHT Mark	6 2	13 03	D	1 8 63	Dorchester	Amateur	Oxford U	10	—
							Southampton	170	7
							Derby Co	144	10
							Liverpool	91	3
WRIGHT Mark *	5 11	10 12	D	29 1 70	Manchester	Trainee	Everton	1	—
							Blackpool (loan)	3	—
							Huddersfield T (loan)	10	1
							Huddersfield T	22	—
							Wigan Ath	30	1
WRIGHT Nick	5 11	11 02	F	15 10 75	Derby	Trainee	**Derby Co**	—	—
WRIGHT Richard	6 2	13 00	G	5 11 77	Ipswich	Trainee	**Ipswich T**	3	—
WRIGHT Tommy *	5 7	11 05	F	10 1 66	Dunfermline	Apprentice	Leeds U	81	24
							Oldham Ath	112	23
							Leicester C	129	22
							Middlesbrough	53	5
WRIGHT Tommy	6 1	13 05	G	29 8 63	Belfast	Linfield	Newcastle U	73	—
							Hull C (loan)	6	—
							Nottingham F	10	—
WYATT Michael *	5 11	11 03	F	12 9 74	Bristol	Trainee	**Bristol C**	13	—
YALLOP Frank	5 11	12 00	D	4 4 64	Watford	Apprentice	**Ipswich T**	309	7
YATES Dean	6 1	12 00	D	26 10 67	Leicester	Apprentice	Notts Co	314	33
							Derby Co	11	1
YATES Steve	5 11	11 00	D	29 1 70	Bristol	Trainee	Bristol R	197	—
							QPR	52	1
YEBOAH Tony	5 10	13 13	F	6 6 66	Ghana	Okwawu U	Saarbrucken	65	26
							Eintracht Frankfurt	123	68
							Leeds U	18	12
YORKE Dwight	5 11	11 13	F	3 11 71	Tobago	Tobago	**Aston Villa**	128	27

Player	Ht	Wt	Pos	Birth Date	Birth Place	Source	Clubs	League App	League Gls
YOUDS Eddie	6 1	13 03	D	3 5 70	Liverpool	Trainee	Everton	8	—
							Cardiff C (loan)	1	—
							Wrexham (loan)	20	2
							Ipswich T	50	1
							Bradford C (loan)	17	3
YOUNG Eric	6 2	13 05	D	25 3 60	Singapore	Slough T	Brighton	126	10
							Wimbledon	99	9
							Crystal Palace	161	15
YOUNG Neil	5 8	11 03	D	31 8 73	Harlow	Trainee	Tottenham H	—	—
							Bournemouth	32	—
YOUNG Scott			F	14 1 76	Pontypridd	Trainee	**Cardiff C**	28	—
YOUNG Stuart †	5 11	13 00	F	16 12 72	Hull	Arsenal	Hull C	19	2
							Northampton T	8	2
							Scarborough	41	10
							Scunthorpe U	14	2
ZIVKOVIC Lee *	5 11	12 10	M	27 11 75	Doncaster	Trainee	**Sheffield U**	—	—
ZUMRUTEL Soner *	5 6	11 00	F	6 10 74	Islington	Trainee	**Arsenal**	—	—

FA CHARITY SHIELD WINNERS 1908–94

1908	Manchester U v QPR	4-0 after 1-1 draw
1909	Newcastle U v Northampton T	2-0
1910	Brighton v Aston Villa	1-0
1911	Manchester U v Swindon T	8-4
1912	Blackburn R v QPR	2-1
1913	Professionals v Amateurs	7-2
1920	WBA v Tottenham H	2-0
1921	Tottenham H v Burnley	2-0
1922	Huddersfield T v Liverpool	1-0
1923	Professionals v Amateurs	2-0
1924	Professionals v Amateurs	3-1
1925	Amateurs v Professionals	6-1
1926	Amateurs v Professionals	6-3
1927	Cardiff C v Corinthians	2-1
1928	Everton v Blackburn R	2-1
1929	Professionals v Amateurs	3-0
1930	Arsenal v Sheffield W	2-1
1931	Arsenal v WBA	1-0
1932	Everton v Newcastle U	5-3
1933	Arsenal v Everton	3-0
1934	Arsenal v Manchester C	4-0
1935	Sheffield W v Arsenal	1-0
1936	Sunderland v Arsenal	2-1
1937	Manchester C v Sunderland	2-0
1938	Arsenal v Preston NE	2-1
1948	Arsenal v Manchester U	4-3
1949	Portsmouth v Wolverhampton W	1-1*
1950	World Cup Team v Canadian Touring Team	4-2
1951	Tottenham H v Newcastle U	2-1
1952	Manchester U v Newcastle U	4-2
1953	Arsenal v Blackpool	3-1
1954	Wolverhampton W v WBA	4-4*
1955	Chelsea v Newcastle U	3-0
1956	Manchester U v Manchester C	1-0
1957	Manchester U v Aston Villa	4-0
1958	Bolton W v Wolverhampton W	4-1
1959	Wolverhampton W v Nottingham F	3-1
1960	Burnley v Wolverhampton W	2-2*
1961	Tottenham H v FA XI	3-2
1962	Tottenham H v Ipswich T	5-1
1963	Everton v Manchester U	4-0
1964	Liverpool v West Ham U	2-2*
1965	Manchester U v Liverpool	2-2*
1966	Liverpool v Everton	1-0
1967	Manchester U v Tottenham H	3-3*
1968	Manchester C v WBA	6-1
1969	Leeds U v Manchester C	2-1
1970	Everton v Chelsea	2-1
1971	Leicester C v Liverpool	1-0
1972	Manchester C v Aston Villa	1-0
1973	Burnley v Manchester C	1-0
1974	Liverpool† v Leeds U	1-1
1975	Derby Co v West Ham U	2-0
1976	Liverpool v Southampton	1-0
1977	Liverpool v Manchester U	0-0*
1978	Nottingham F v Ipswich T	5-0
1979	Liverpool v Arsenal	3-1
1980	Liverpool v West Ham U	1-0
1981	Aston Villa v Tottenham H	2-2*
1982	Liverpool v Tottenham H	1-0
1983	Manchester U v Liverpool	2-0
1984	Everton v Liverpool	1-0
1985	Everton v Manchester U	2-0
1986	Everton v Liverpool	1-1*
1987	Everton v Coventry C	1-0
1988	Liverpool v Wimbledon	2-1
1989	Liverpool v Arsenal	1-0
1990	Liverpool v Manchester U	1-1*
1991	Arsenal v Tottenham H	0-0*
1992	Leeds U v Liverpool	4-3
1993	Manchester U† v Arsenal	1-1

** Each club retained shield for six months. † Won on penalties.*

FA CHARITY SHIELD 1994

Manchester U (1) 2, Blackburn R (0) 0

At Wembley, 14 August 1994, attendance 60,402

Manchester U: Schmeichel; May, Sharpe, Bruce, Kanchelskis, Pallister, Cantona, Ince, McClair, Hughes, Giggs.

Scorers: Cantona (pen), Ince.

Blackburn R: Flowers; Berg, Le Saux, Atkins (Thorne), Hendry, Gale, Ripley, Sherwood, Pearce, Slater, Wilcox.

LEADING GOALSCORERS 1994–95

FA CARLING PREMIERSHIP	League	FA Cup	Coca-Cola Cup	Other Cups	Total
Alan Shearer (*Blackburn R*)	34	0	2	1	37
Robbie Fowler (*Liverpool*)	25	2	4	0	31
Les Ferdinand (*QPR*)	24	1	1	0	26
Stan Collymore (*Nottingham F*)	22	1	2	0	25
Andy Cole (*Manchester U*)	21	0	2	0	23
(Includes nine League, two Coca-Cola Cup goals for Newcastle U.)					
Jurgen Klinsmann (*Tottenham H*)	20	5	4	0	29
Matt Le Tissier (*Southampton*)	19	5	5	0	29
Ian Wright (*Arsenal*)	18	0	3	9	30
Teddy Sheringham (*Tottenham H*)	18	4	1	0	23
Ashley Ward (*Norwich C*)	16	4	1	0	21
(Includes eight League, four FA Cup and one Coca-Cola Cup goal for Crewe Alex.)					
Uwe Rosler (*Manchester C*)	15	5	2	0	22
Chris Sutton (*Blackburn R*)	15	2	3	1	21
Dean Saunders (*Aston Villa*)	15	1	1	0	17
Paul Rideout (*Everton*)	14	2	0	0	16
Andrei Kanchelskis (*Manchester U*)	14	0	0	0	14
ENDSLEIGH INSURANCE DIVISION 1					
John Aldridge (*Tranmere R*)	24	0	1	1	26
Jan-Aage Fjortoft (*Middlesbrough*)	19	1	9	0	29
(Includes 16 League, one FA Cup and nine Coca-Cola Cup goals for Swindon T.)					
David Whyte (*Charlton Ath*)	19	0	2	0	21
Gerry Creaney (*Portsmouth*)	18	1	3	0	22
Sean McCarthy (*Oldham Ath*)	18	0	0	0	18
Nathan Blake (*Sheffield U*)	17	0	1	0	18
John McGinlay (*Bolton W*)	16	0	4	2	22
Martin Foyle (*Port Vale*)	16	3	1	0	20
Chris Malkin (*Tranmere R*)	16	1	0	2	19
Steve Bull (*Wolverhampton W*)	16	0	2	1	19
David Kelly (*Wolverhampton W*)	15	4	2	1	22
John Hendrie (*Middlesbrough*)	15	1	1	0	17
Neil Woods (*Grimsby T*)	14	0	0	0	14
DIVISION 2					
Gary Bennett (*Wrexham*)	29	2	2	6	39
Andy Booth (*Huddersfield T*)	26	1	0	3	30
Nicky Forster (*Brentford*)	24	0	0	2	26
Robert Taylor (*Brentford*)	23	1	1	0	25
Steve Claridge (*Birmingham C*)	20	0	1	4	25
Paul Moody (*Oxford U*)	20	0	1	2	23
Kevin Francis (*Birmingham C*)	20	0	1	1	22
(Includes 12 League and one Coca-Cola Cup goal for Stockport Co.)					
Shaun Goater (*Rotherham U*)	19	3	0	3	25
Ronnie Jepson (*Huddersfield T*)	19	1	2	1	23
Carlo Corazzin (*Cambridge U*)	19	0	0	2	21
Tony Ellis (*Blackpool*)	17	0	1	0	18
Paul Miller (*Bristol R*)	16	4	0	2	22
Dean Windass (*Hull C*)	16	2	0	0	18
Ken Charlery (*Peterborough U*)	16	2	0	0	18
Paul Barnes (*York C*)	16	0	0	1	17
DIVISION 3					
Phil Stant (*Bury*)	26	0	2	0	28
(Includes 13 League and two Coca-Cola Cup goals for Cardiff C.)					
Doug Freedman (*Barnet*)	24	0	5	0	29
Kyle Lightbourne (*Walsall*)	23	3	1	0	27
Steve Wilkinson (*Mansfield T*)	22	0	3	1	26
David Reeves (*Carlisle U*)	21	2	2	0	25
Kevin Wilson (*Walsall*)	16	2	3	0	21
David Pugh (*Bury*)	16	0	0	1	17
Steve White (*Hereford U*)	15	1	2	1	19
Andy Lyons (*Wigan Ath*)	15	0	0	0	15
Mark Carter (*Bury*)	14	0	1	0	15
Chris Pike (*Gillingham*)	13	4	0	1	18
Keith Houchen (*Hartlepool U*)	13	0	1	0	14
Graeme Jones (*Doncaster R*)	12	1	1	1	15

NB. Players are listed in order of League goals scored. Other cup goals refer to European matches, Auto Windscreens Shield and Anglo-Italian Cup plus play-offs.

Did You Know?

I'm all Wright, Jack
On 23 October 1994, Ian Wright completed 12 goals in 10 successive League and Cup matches, to establish a new **Arsenal** club record. In the 1931-32 season, David Jack had scored in nine consecutive games for 14 goals.

Viva Villa
On 11 February 1995, **Aston Villa** beat Wimbledon 7-1. It was their biggest win for 33 years. Previously they had defeated Leicester City 8-3 on 21 April 1962.

International take-off
Centre-forward George Sparrow was the first **Barnet** player to receive an Amateur International cap when he was chosen for England against Wales in 1925.

Beau legs
At 37 years 3 months, Beau Asquith became the oldest player to appear for **Barnsley** on 19 November 1947. But he still completed two further seasons with Bradford City.

Beau Brummies
In 1994-95, **Birmingham City** completed 20 League matches unbeaten between 3 September 1994 and 2 January 1995 to set a new club record. Previously they had remained undefeated for the last 18 games in 1971-72.

Rovers return
Blackburn Rovers still hold the record for the longest unbeaten run in the FA Cup: 24 matches from November 1883 to November 1886, including one walkover win against Halliwell and two drawn games.

Turn of the century
In 1899-1900, **Blackpool** won the Lancashire Combination. It was their only season out of the Football League after failing to gain re-election.

Red faced army
Bolton Wanderers held their second floodlight friendly match in November 1957 when they beat Soviet Army team CSKA Moscow 3-1 before a crowd of 34,139.

Court's No. 1
Goalkeeper Tom Godwin missed only one match in his first four seasons with **Bournemouth**. He made a then club record 358 League appearances between 1952 and 1962 and won four of his 13 Republic of Ireland caps while at Dean Court.

PT exercises
On 2 November 1994, **Bradford City** goalkeeper Paul Tomlinson set a club record with his 71st clean sheet in eight seasons. His first had been on his debut on 15 August 1987.

Candle power
In the 1973-74 season, **Brentford** general manager Denis Piggott, team manager Mike Everitt and trainer Jess Willard all celebrated their birthdays on 16 January.

Foster's saga
On 24 September 1994, Steve Foster celebrated his 37th birthday and his 250th League game for **Brighton & Hove Albion** in a 2-0 win against Cambridge United.

Seal of approval
In the close season of 1994, **Bristol City** signed Australian-born David Seal from the Belgian club Aalst after he had scored six goals in two trial matches.

Dai is cast
On 14 January 1995, Marcus Stewart's 80th minute goal equalled Dai Ward's 38-year-old record of scoring in eight consecutive League and Cup matches for **Bristol Rovers**.

Vale of nears
When **Burnley** defeated Port Vale 4-3 on 28 March 1995, four of the goals came during an eight minute spell in the second half. Burnley scored in the 60th, 64th and 66th minutes, Port Vale replying in the 68th.

One over the eight
On 15 October 1994, **Bury** had won 9 of their 12 matches, more than any other club in the four English divisions and the three goals they had conceded also represented the best defensive record

Home alone
In 1982-83, **Cambridge United** completed 12 successive home League games without conceding a goal. This is a Football League record.

Not Knighton's day
Cardiff City defeated Knighton Town of the Mid-Wales League 16-0 in a fifth round Welsh Cup tie on 28 January 1961.

Barnet fare
On 24 January 1995, **Carlisle United** completed their 16th successive League game by winning 2-0 at Barnet. Their previous club record had been established in 1950-51 and equalled in 1983-84.

Screen gems
On 5 February 1995, **Charlton Athletic** recorded their first win on live television since their 1-0 FA Cup Final victory over Burnley in 1947. Their victims were West Bromwich Albion in a 1-0 win.

International bridge club
Chelsea had eight internationals in a 5-0 win against Sunderland on 13 December 1930: Tommy Law, Alec Jackson, Alex Cheyne, Hughie Gallacher, Andy Wilson (Scotland), Jack Townrow, Sid Bishop (England), Sam Irving (Ireland).

Thirties something
When still known as **Chester**, the club completed 18 League games without defeat between 27 October 1934 and 16 February 1935 for a club record.

Playing pontoons only
On 18 March 1995, **Chesterfield** set a new club record with their 14th League game without defeat. They went on to increase this sequence to 21 matches.

Only one United?
On 4 February 1995, **Colchester United** were three goals down in eighteen minutes at Scunthorpe United, before eventually winning 4-3. Two of their goals came in the last ten minutes.

Peter the Great
Peter Ndlovu scored in the 21st, 35th (with a penalty) and 85th minutes for **Coventry City** at Liverpool on 14 March 1995 in a 3-2 win. It was the first hat-trick by a visiting player at Anfield for 33 years.

No change at Crewe
In 1938 **Crewe Alexandra** completed 16 home wins in succession. They comprised the last ten in 1937-38, including five in a row in 14 days, and the first six in 1938-39.

Palace gates
In 1969-70, the last season when as many as 29 million spectators attended Football League matches, the opening First Division programme attracted 367,157. The highest was 48,610 at **Crystal Palace** for the 2-2 draw with Manchester United.

Quaker routs
On 23 April 1927, Tom Ruddy scored five goals for **Darlington** in an 8-2 win against South Shields. That season he scored 26 League and Cup goals.

Status Quy
When **Derby County** goalkeeper Steve Sutton was injured in the 86th minute of a third round Coca-Cola Cup tie at Portsmouth on 26 October 1994, substitute goalkeeper Andrew Quy made a four-minute debut as Derby held on to win 1-0.

Workers playtime?
The previous ground record for **Doncaster Rovers** was established at 23,238 against Tranmere Rovers on 11 April 1935 -a Thursday afternoon.

Toffeemen stuck on seven
Everton set a club record of seven League games without conceding a goal in 1994-95. The total time involved was 12 hours 15 minutes.

City slicker
Henry Bartholomew scored for **Exeter City** against Barnet in a first round FA Cup tie at Underhill on 4 December 1948 after just 10 seconds. Exeter won 6-2.

Every second counts
Former Southampton trainee Rory Hamill scored for **Fulham** against Mansfield Town on 2 January 1995 after eight seconds at the beginning of a 4-2 win.

Spring collection
Gillingham assembled a run of unbeaten games at home consisting of 52 League and Cup games from 6 April 1963 to 10 April 1965. During this period, they reached the fourth round of the League Cup in 1963-64.

Watertight Mariners
Grimsby Town had 25 clean sheets in 1955-56 when winning the championship of Division 3 (North). These included the last eight successive matches.

Trading places
On 26 November 1994, **Hartlepool United** player/manager David McCreery, who had taken over from John MacPhail, dropped himself and put in MacPhail against Rochdale. United won 1-0 to move off the bottom.

Fast Eddie
The first Football League victims of a giant-killing act by **Hereford United** were Exeter City beaten 2-0 in a first round replay on 26 November 1953 following a 1-1 draw. Eddie O'Hara scored all three United goals.

Star(buck) struck
Phil Starbuck was a 54th minute substitute for **Huddersfield Town** against Wigan Athletic on Easter Monday 1993. He came on as a corner was about to be taken and scored with a header.

Fettis fetish
Hull City put on reserve goalkeeper Alan Fettis as an 80th minute outfield substitute and he scored after 88 minutes against Oxford United. On 6 May 1995, he played the entire game at Blackpool as a striker scoring in injury time.

Better late than...
On 14 January 1995, **Ipswich Town** won 1-0 at Liverpool. It was the first time they had achieved this feat in 28 visits to Anfield.

Blue was the colour
When **Leeds United** entered the Football League in 1920, their club colours were blue and white vertical stripes and white shorts. In 1934 they changed to blue and gold halved shirts.

Six of the best
In 1956-57 **Leicester City** set up six club records: most wins (35), most away wins (11), fewest defeats (6), most points (61), most goals (109) and the highest individual scorer was Arthur Rowley with 44 goals.

Dutch treat out East
Leyton Orient beat Racing Club Haarlem from Holland 3-1 in their 1951 Festival of Britain match. Jimmy Blair scored one of their goals.

Lincoln's in
The highest attendance recorded in a Vauxhall Conference match was 9432 for **Lincoln City** against Wycombe Wanderers at Sincil Bank on 2 May 1988.

First day clever
When **Liverpool** won 6-1 at Crystal Palace on 20 August 1994, they extended their record having opened a season with more wins than any other first class club -54 out of 92 seasons.

Town twinning
In successive years, **Luton Town** enjoyed runs of 19 matches unbeaten: January to April 1968 and April to October 1969, but in Divisions 3 and 4 respectively.

Under two flags
Manchester City fielded goalkeeper John Burridge against Newcastle United on 29 April 1995. At the time he was employed as part-time goalkeeping coach with Newcastle.

Home alone II
Manchester United conceded their first goal in League matches at Old Trafford on 17 December 1994 after 1135 minutes, when losing 2-1 to Nottingham Forest.

A positive Iffy
On 11 March 1995, **Mansfield Town** beat Lincoln City 6-2. Iffy Onuora scored a seven-minute second-half hat-trick between the 78th and 85th minutes. Mansfield's total of 71 League goals at the time was the highest in the four English Leagues.

Overseas Tees
In 1994-95 **Middlesbrough** fielded Uwe Fuchs (German) and Jaime Moreno (Bolivian), their first foreign duo since Rolando Ugolini (Italian) and Lindy Delapenha (Jamaican), on 28 April 1956.

Forest chopped down
On 30 November 1994, **Millwall** became the first team to win a League Cup tie at Nottingham Forest for 18 years, when they recorded a 2-0 victory.

Geordies' pet plan
Newcastle United equalled their best start to a season in 1994-95 when they remained unbeaten in the opening 11 matches. They had previously set the record in 1950-51.

All Cobblers
Northampton Town had three marksmen with 20 or more goals in 1952-53: Jack English 26, Willie O'Donnell 26 and Freddie Ramscar 22.

Super stiffs
In three successive seasons 1932-33 to 1934-35, Norwich City were Southern League (East) champions, a competition for the club's reserve team at the time.

More shinned against...
Sam Weller Widdowson, inventor of the shin pad, played in 23 FA Cup matches for **Nottingham Forest** between 1878 and 1885 scoring 19 goals. These included four against Sheffield Heeley on 2 December 1882.

Metre made
In August 1994 **Notts County** player Andy Legg, 28, entered the Guiness Book of Records with the longest recorded throw-in with a football: 41 metres.

Borderline case
Centre-forward Tommy Davis is the only **Oldham Athletic** player to have been capped for two different countries at full international level. In 1936-37 he played twice for the Republic of Ireland and once for Northern Ireland.

One over the eight II
In 1994-95, **Oxford United** equalled their best start to a season by remaining unbeaten for nine League games. They were the last English League team to remain undefeated. The club had set their record in 1983-84.

Fast Eddie II
On New Year's Day 1948, Eddie Friedmanis a Latvian International, scored a hat-trick on his debut for **Peterborough United** in a 3-0 Midland League victory over Mansfield Town reserves.

Pilgrim father's son
Sam Shilton was an 89th minute substitute for **Plymouth Argyle** against Bournemouth in a second round FA Cup tie on 3 December 1994, becoming at 16 years 4 months and 12 days, the club's youngest debutant.

Dan, Dan, the very first man
The first **Portsmouth** player to receive full international honours was inside-right Daniel Cunliffe, who was capped for England on 17 March 1900 against Ireland.

Only two can play
When **Port Vale** defeated Fulham 7-1 in a Division 2 match on 2 April 1927, Wilf Kirkham scored four goals and Harry Anstiss the other three.

Your number's up
Jimmy Ross scored 37 FA Cup goals for **Preston North End** between January 1887 and January 1894. These included one 8, two 6's and one 4.

A Royal occasion
The record attendance for any Southern League match is 29,786 for **Queens Park Rangers** v Plymouth Argyle at Park Royal on 25 December 1907. The match ended in a goalless draw.

Graduation Day
A 16th minute substitute for **Reading** against Bristol City on 15 October 1994 was Michael Murphy, 17, just a week after he had been a school student.

Neil downs Rovers
On 1 October 1994, debutant **Rochdale** goalkeeper Neil Dunford, a brickie and pub player, saved a 72nd minute penalty against Doncaster Rovers with the score at 0-0. Rochdale won 2-0.

Bobby's dazzler
On 22 November 1994, Bobby Davison scored a 10 second goal for **Rotherham United** in an FA Cup first round replay against York City. It equalled the second fastest goal in the Cup's history.

Species of eight
Scarborough scored a 1-0 win at Chesterfield on 13 August 1994. This continued their run of not losing the opening match of the season during their eight years in the Football League.

Seventeenth year hitch
Scunthorpe United completed 18 hours unbeaten in 26 home FA Cup matches dating back to 1977, when they lost 2-1 to Birmingham City in a second round replay in 1994-95.

Jock's away
When **Sheffield United** drew 2-2 with Tottenham Hotspur at White Hart Lane on 12 September 1938, Jock Dodds scored his 100th League goal for the club. The player was shortly afterwards transferred to Blackpool for £10,000.

Tied up in Notts
Tom Brandon, captain of **Sheffield Wednesday**, scored their first League goal on 3 September 1892 in a 1-0 win over Notts County. His only other goal that season was in the return match against Notts.

Jack-in-the-box
When **Shrewsbury Town** beat Walsall 5-0 in an FA Cup first round, first leg tie on 17 November 1945, Jackie Maund scored a hat-trick. He joined Walsall a year later.

On the spot
On 1 March 1995, Matt Le Tissier converted a 39th minute penalty in an FA Cup fifth round replay against Tottenham Hotspur. It was his 35th successful spot kick out of 36 attempts in his **Southampton** career.

Paul: on the overhaul
On 2 January 1995, Paul Sansome made his 344th appearance for **Southend United** beating fellow goalkeeper Harry Threadgold's appearances between 1953 and 1963.

Return to victory
A record Edgeley Park crowd of 7000 witnessed Chelsea's first competititve fixture on 2 September 1905. **Stockport County** had just regained their Football League status and won with a George Dodd goal.

The famous five
In the close season of 1895, **Stoke City** signed William Maxwell from Dundee. In six seasons he scored 85 goals in 173 League and Cup games and was leading League scorer for five successive seasons.

Drawn level
Sunderland drew 18 Division Two matches in 1994-95 to equal a club record set up 40 years earlier when they finished fourth in Division Two.

Pembroke(n)!
On 13 March 1995, two days after ending Birmingham City's home run of 22 matches unbeaten, **Swansea City** beat Pembroke Borough 16-0 in the semi-final of the West Wales Senior Cup.

Double with Harry
The career of Harry Cousins began as a 16 year old Chesterfield trialist against Notts County and ended on the same Meadow Lane ground after 24 years with **Swindon Town** in 1947.

Having a Rollerball
On 27 December 1994, 19 year old goalkeeper Paul Pettinger was Rolls-Royce chauffeur driven 300 miles on loan from Leeds United to make his **Torquay United** debut in a 2-2 draw with Hartlepool United.

Teutonic tradition
Jurgen Klinsmann was not the first German player to sign for **Tottenham Hotspur**. Max Seeburg was not only the first German with the club, but also the first foreigner in the Football League in 1907.

Milestone man
Steve Mungall made his 600th League and Cup appearance for **Tranmere Rovers** on 29 October 1994 in a 1-1 draw with Port Vale.

Blazing Saddlers
Walsall recorded their highest FA Cup score outside the competition proper when they beat Warmley 12-0 away in a first qualifying round tie on 27 September 1890.

Clean sheets
On 11 February 1995, **Watford** equalled a 46 year old club record with their eighth successive game without conceding a goal. They beat it the following week in an FA Cup tie against Crystal Palace.

Brave Bob
Bob Taylor, the **West Bromwich Albion** centre-forward was hospitalized on 10 September 1994 for tests on a kidney problem, but left his sick-bed to score twice in the 2-2 draw at Millwall.

Victor Bravo
Vic Watson scored 16 goals in four games for **West Ham United** against Leeds United: six on 9 February 1929, three on 16 November, four in an FA Cup tie on 25 January 1930 and three on 21 March 1931.

Magpies flutter
In the 1953-54 season, **Wigan Athletic**, top of the Lancashire Combination, forced a 2-2 third round FA Cup draw with First Division Newcastle United at St James' Park on 9 January 1954, watched by 52,222. United won the replay 2-2.

Swiftly flowed the Dons
Wimbledon were 3-1 down to Aston Villa on 9 November 1994, before scoring three goals in the last 25 minutes including a last minute winner to edge home 4-3.

Unload of Bull
Steve Bull completed 200 League goals for **Wolverhampton Wanderers** with headed efforts on either side of half-time on 15 April 1995 against Charlton Athletic. He also finished the game as captain.

What it's all about
Right-back Alfie Jones made 503 League and 72 FA Cup appearances between 1923-24 and 1935-36 for **Wrexham**, his only League club.

Barefoot on the park
In August 1956, **Wycombe Wanderers** became the first British team to play a Ugandan touring side, defeating their barefoot visitors 10-1 in front of a 7450 midweek crowd.

Lester's nap
When **York City** beat Horsforth 7-1 in a preliminary round FA Cup tie on 20 September 1924, centre-forward Lester Marshall scored five goals.

ENGLISH LEAGUE MANAGERS

ARSENAL

Managers (and Secretary-Managers)
Sam Hollis 1894–97, Tom Mitchell 1897–98, George Elcoat 1898–99, Harry Bradshaw 1899–1904, Phil Kelso 1904–08, George Morrell 1908–15, Leslie Knighton 1919–25, Herbert Chapman 1925–34, George Allison 1934–47, Tom Whittaker 1947–56, Jack Crayston 1956–58, George Swindin 1958–62, Billy Wright 1962–66, Bertie Mee 1966–76, Terry Neill 1976–83, Don Howe 1984–86, George Graham 1986–95, Bruce Rioch June 1995– .

ASTON VILLA

Managers (and Secretary-Managers)
George Ramsay 1884–1926*, W. J. Smith 1926–34*, Jimmy McMullan 1934–35, Jimmy Hogan 1936–44, Alex Massie 1945–50, George Martin 1950–53, Eric Houghton 1953–58, Joe Mercer 1958–64, Dick Taylor 1965–67, Tommy Cummings 1967–68, Tommy Docherty 1968–70, Vic Crowe 1970–74, Ron Saunders 1974–82, Tony Barton 1982–84, Graham Turner 1984–86, Billy McNeill 1986–87, Graham Taylor 1987–90, Dr. Jozef Venglos 1990–91, Ron Atkinson 1991–94, Brian Little November 1994– .

BARNET

Managers: (since 1946) Lester Finch, George Wheeler, Dexter Adams, Tommy Coleman, Gerry Ward, Gordon Ferry, Brian Kelly, Bill Meadows, Barry Fry, Roger Thompson, Don McAllister, Barry Fry, Edwin Stein, Gary Phillips (player-manager) 1993–94, Ray Clemence January 1994– .

BARNSLEY

Managers (and Secretary-Managers)
Arthur Fairclough 1898–1901*, John McCartney 1901–04*, Arthur Fairclough 1904–12, John Hastie 1912–14, Percy Lewis 1914–19, Peter Sant 1919–26, John Commins 1926–29, Arthur Fairclough 1929–30, Brough Fletcher 1930–37, Angus Seed 1937–53, Tim Ward 1953–60, Johnny Steele 1960–71 (continued as GM), John McSeveney 1971–72, Johnny Steele (GM) 1972–73, Jim Iley 1973–78, Allan Clarke 1978–80, Norman Hunter 1980–84, Bobby Collins 1984–85, Allan Clarke 1985–89, Mel Machin 1989–93, Viv Anderson 1993–94, Danny Wilson June 1994– .

BIRMINGHAM CITY

Managers (and Secretary-Managers)
Alfred Jones 1892–1908*, Alec Watson 1908–1910, Bob McRoberts 1910–15, Frank Richards 1915–23, Billy Beer 1923–27, Leslie Knighton 1928–33, George Liddell 1933–39, Harry Storer 1945–48, Bob Brocklebank 1949–54, Arthur Turner 1954–58, Pat Beasley 1959–60, Gil Merrick 1960–64, Joe Mallett 1965, Stan Cullis 1965–70, Fred Goodwin 1970–75, Willie Bell 1975–77, Jim Smith 1978–82, Ron Saunders 1982–86, John Bond 1986–87, Garry Pendrey 1987–89, Dave Mackay 1989–1991, Lou Macari 1991, Terry Cooper 1991–93, Barry Fry December 1993– .

BLACKBURN ROVERS

Managers (and Secretary-Managers)
Thomas Mitchell 1884–96*, J. Walmsley 1896–1903*, R. B. Middleton 1903–25, Jack Carr 1922–26 (TM under Middleton to 1925), Bob Crompton 1926–30 (Hon. TM), Arthur Barritt 1931–36 (had been Sec. from 1927), Reg Taylor 1936–38, Bob Crompton 1938–41, Eddie Hapgood 1944–47, Will Scott 1947, Jack Bruton 1947–49, Jackie Bestall 1949–53, Johnny Carey 1953–58, Dally Duncan 1958–60, Jack Marshall 1960–67, Eddie Quigley 1967–70, Johnny Carey 1970–71, Ken Furphy 1971–73, Gordon Lee 1974–75, Jim Smith 1975–78, Jim Iley 1978, John Pickering 1978–79, Howard Kendall 1979–81, Bobby Saxton 1981–86, Don Mackay 1987–91, Kenny Dalglish 1991–95, Ray Harford June 1995– .

BLACKPOOL

Managers (and Secretary-Managers)
Tom Barcroft 1903–33* (Hon. Sec.), John Cox 1909–11, Bill Norman 1919–23, Maj. Frank Buckley 1923–27, Sid Beaumont 1927–28, Harry Evans 1928–33 (Hon. TM), Alex "Sandy" Macfarlane 1933–35, Joe Smith 1935–58, Ronnie Suart 1958–67, Stan Mortensen 1967–69, Les Shannon 1969–70, Bob Stokoe 1970–72, Harry Potts 1972–76, Allan Brown 1976–78, Bob Stokoe 1978–79, Stan Ternent 1979–80, Alan Ball 1980–81, Allan Brown 1981–82, Sam Ellis 1982–89, Jimmy Mullen 1989–90, Graham Carr 1990, Bill Ayre 1990–94, Sam Allardyce July 1994– .

BOLTON WANDERERS

Managers (and Secretary-Managers)
Tom Rawthorne 1874–85*, J. J. Bentley 1885–86*, W. G. Struthers 1886–87*, Fitzroy Norris 1887*, J. J. Bentley 1887–95*, Harry Downs 1895–96*, Frank Brettell 1896–98*, John Somerville 1898–1910, Will Settle 1910–15, Tom Mather 1915–19, Charles Foweraker 1919–44, Walter Rowley 1944–50, Bill Ridding 1951–68, Nat Lofthouse 1968–70, Jimmy McIlroy 1970, Jimmy Meadows 1971, Nat Lofthouse 1971 (then admin. man. to 1972), Jimmy Armfield 1971–74, Ian Greaves 1974–80, Stan Anderson 1980–81, George Mulhall 1981–82, John McGovern 1982–85, Charlie Wright 1985, Phil Neal 1985–92, Bruce Rioch 1992–95, Roy McFarland June 1995– .

AFC BOURNEMOUTH

Managers (and Secretary-Managers)
Vincent Kitcher 1914–23*, Harry Kinghorn 1923–25, Leslie Knighton 1925–28, Frank Richards 1928–30, Billy Birrell 1930–35, Bob Crompton 1935–36, Charlie Bell 1936–39, Harry Kinghorn 1939–47, Harry Lowe 1947–50, Jack Bruton 1950–56, Fred Cox 1956–58, Don Welsh 1958–61, Bill McGarry 1961–63, Reg Flewin 1963–65, Fred Cox 1965–70, John Bond 1970–73, Trevor Hartley 1974–78, John Benson 1975–78, Alec Stock 1979–80, David Webb 1980–82, Don Megson 1983, Harry Redknapp 1983–92, Tony Pulis 1992–94, Mel Machin August 1994– .

BRADFORD CITY

Managers (and Secretary-Managers)
Robert Campbell 1903–05, Peter O'Rourke 1905–21, David Menzies 1921–26, Colin Veitch 1926–28, Peter O'Rourke 1928–30, Jack Peart 1930–35, Dick Ray 1935–37, Fred Westgarth 1938–43, Bob Sharp 1943–46, Jack Barker 1946–47, John Milburn 1947–48, David Steele 1948–52, Albert Harris 1952, Ivor Powell 1952–55, Peter Jackson 1955–61, Bob Brocklebank 1961–64, Bill Harris 1965–66, Willie Watson 1966–69, Grenville Hair 1967–68, Jimmy Wheeler 1968–71, Bryan Edwards 1971–75, Bobby Kennedy 1975–78, John Napier 1978, George Mulhall 1978–81, Roy McFarland 1981–82, Trevor Cherry 1982–87, Terry Dolan 1987–89, Terry Yorath 1989–90, John Docherty 1990–91, Frank Stapleton 1991–94, Lennie Lawrence May 1994– .

BRENTFORD

Managers (and Secretary-Managers)
Will Lewis 1900–03*, Dick Molyneux 1903–06, W. G. Brown 1906–08, Fred Halliday 1908–26 (only secretary to 1922), Ephraim Rhodes 1912–15, Archie Mitchell 1921–22, Harry Curtis 1926–49, Jackie Gibbons 1949–52, Jimmy Blain 1952–53, Tommy Lawton 1953, Bill Dodgin Snr 1953–57, Malcolm Macdonald 1957–65, Tommy Cavanagh 1965–66, Billy Gray 1966–67, Jimmy Sirrel 1967–69, Frank Blunstone 1969–73, Mike Everitt 1973–75, John Docherty 1975–76, Bill Dodgin Jnr 1976–80, Fred Callaghan 1980–84, Frank McLintock 1984–87, Steve Perryman 1987–90, Phil Holder 1990–93, David Webb May 1993– .

BRIGHTON & HOVE ALBION

Managers (and Secretary-Managers)
John Jackson 1901–05, Frank Scott-Walford 1905–08, John Robson 1908–14, Charles Webb 1919–47, Tommy Cook 1947, Don Welsh 1947–51, Billy Lane 1951–61, George Curtis 1961–63, Archie Macaulay 1963–68, Fred Goodwin 1968–70, Pat Saward 1970–73, Brian Clough 1973–74, Peter Taylor 1974–76, Alan Mullery 1976–81, Mike Bailey 1981–82, Jimmy Melia 1982–83, Chris Cattlin 1983–86, Alan Mullery 1986–87, Barry Lloyd 1987–93, Liam Brady 1993– .

BRISTOL CITY

Managers (and Secretary-Managers)
Sam Hollis 1897–99, Bob Campbell 1899–1901, Sam Hollis 1901–05, Harry Thickett 1905–10, Sam Hollis 1911–13, George Hedley 1913–15, Jack Hamilton 1915–19, Joe Palmer 1919–21, Alex Raisbeck 1921–29, Joe Bradshaw 1929–32, Bob Hewison 1932–49 (under suspension 1938–39), Bob Wright 1949–50, Pat Beasley 1950–58, Peter Doherty 1958–60, Fred Ford 1960–67, Alan Dicks 1967–80, Bobby Houghton 1980–82, Roy Hodgson 1982, Terry Cooper 1982–88 (Director from 1983), Joe Jordan 1988–90, Jimmy Lumsden 1990–92, Denis Smith 1992–93, Russell Osman 1993–94, Joe Jordan November 1994– .

BRISTOL ROVERS

Managers (and Secretary-Managers)
Alfred Homer 1899–1920 (continued as secretary to 1928), Ben Hall 1920–21, Andy Wilson 1921–26, Joe Palmer 1926–29, Dave McLean 1929–30, Albert Prince-Cox 1930–36, Percy Smith 1936–37, Brough Fletcher 1938–49, Bert Tann 1950–68 (continued as GM to 1972), Fred Ford 1968–69, Bill Dodgin Snr 1969–72, Don Megson 1972–77, Bobby Campbell 1978–79, Harold Jarman 1979–80, Terry Cooper 1980–81, Bobby Gould 1981–83, David Williams 1983–85, Bobby Gould 1985–87, Gerry Francis 1987–91, Martin Dobson 1991, Dennis Rofe 1992, Malcolm Allison 1992–93, John Ward March 1993– .

BURNLEY

Managers (and Secretary-Managers)
Arthur F. Sutcliffe 1893–96*, Harry Bradshaw 1896–99*, Ernest Magnall 1899–1903*, Spen Whittaker 1903–10, R. H. Wadge 1910–11*, John Haworth 1911–25, Albert Pickles 1925–32, Tom Bromilow 1932–35, Alf Boland 1935–39*, Cliff Britton 1945–48, Frank Hill 1948–54, Alan Brown 1954–57, Billy Dougall 1957–58, Harry Potts 1958–70 (GM to 1972), Jimmy Adamson 1970–76, Joe Brown 1976–77, Harry Potts 1977–79, Brian Miller 1979–83, John Bond 1983–84, John Benson 1984–85, Martin Buchan 1985, Tommy Cavanagh 1985–86, Brian Miller 1986–89, Frank Casper 1989–91, Jimmy Mullen October 1991– .

BURY

Managers (and Secretary-Managers)
T. Hargreaves 1887*, H. S. Hamer 1887–1907*, Archie Montgomery 1907–15, William Cameron 1919–23, James Hunter Thompson 1923–27, Percy Smith 1927–30, Arthur Paine 1930–34, Norman Bullock 1934–38, Jim Porter 1944–45, Norman Bullock 1945–49, John McNeil 1950–53, Dave Russell 1953–61, Bob Stokoe 1961–65, Bert Head 1965–66, Les Shannon 1966–69, Jack Marshall 1969, Les Hart 1970, Tommy McAnearney 1970–72, Alan Brown 1972–73, Bobby Smith 1973–77, Bob Stokoe 1977–78, David Hatton 1978–79, Dave Connor 1979–80, Jim Iley 1980–84, Martin Dobson 1984–89, Sam Ellis 1989–90, Mike Walsh December 1990– .

CAMBRIDGE UNITED

Managers (and Secretary-Managers)
Bill Whittaker 1949–55, Gerald Williams 1955, Bert Johnson 1955–59, Bill Craig 1959–60, Alan Moore 1960–63, Roy Kirk 1964–66, Bill Leivers 1967–74, Ron Atkinson 1974–78, John Docherty 1978–83, John Ryan 1984–85, Ken Shellito 1985, Chris Turner 1985–90, John Beck 1990–1992, Ian Atkins 1992–93, Gary Johnson 1993–95, Tommy Taylor May 1995– .

CARDIFF CITY

Managers (and Secretary-Managers)
Davy McDougall 1910–11, Fred Stewart 1911–33, Bartley Wilson 1933–34, B. Watts-Jones 1934–37, Bill Jennings 1937–39, Cyril Spiers 1939–46, Billy McCandless 1946–48, Cyril Spiers 1948–54, Trevor Morris 1954–58, Bill Jones 1958–62, George Swindin 1962–64, Jimmy Scoular 1964–73, Frank O'Farrell 1973–74, Jimmy Andrews 1974–78, Richie Morgan 1978–82, Len Ashurst 1982–84, Jimmy Goodfellow 1984, Alan Durban 1984–86, Frank Burrows 1986–89, Len Ashurst 1989–91, Eddie May 1991–94, Terry Yorath 1994–95, Eddie May March 1995– .

CARLISLE UNITED

Managers (and Secretary-Managers)
H. Kirkbride 1904–05*, McCumiskey 1905–06*, J. Houston 1906–08*, Bert Stansfield 1908–10, J. Houston 1910–12, D. Graham 1912–13, George Bristow 1913–30, Billy Hampson 1930–33, Bill Clarke 1933–35, Robert Kelly 1935–36, Fred Westgarth 1936–38, David Taylor 1938–40, Howard Harkness 1940–45, Bill Clark 1945–46*, Ivor Broadis 1946–49, Bill Shankly 1949–51, Fred Emery 1951–58, Andy Beattie 1958–60, Ivor Powell 1960–63, Alan Ashman 1963–67, Tim Ward 1967–68, Bob Stokoe 1968–70, Ian MacFarlane 1970–72, Alan Ashman 1972–75, Dick Young 1975–76, Bobby Moncur 1976–80, Martin Harvey 1980, Bob Stokoe 1980–85, Bryan "Pop" Robson 1985, Bob Stokoe 1985–86, Harry Gregg 1986–87, Cliff Middlemass 1987–91, Aidan McCaffery 1991–92, David McCreery 1992–93, Mick Wadsworth (Director of Coaching) July 1993– .

CHARLTON ATHLETIC

Managers (and Secretary-Managers)
Bill Rayner 1920–25, Alex McFarlane 1925–27, Albert Lindon 1928, Alex McFarlane 1928–32, Jimmy Seed 1933–56, Jimmy Trotter 1956–61, Frank Hill 1961–65, Bob Stokoe 1965–67, Eddie Firmani 1967–70, Theo Foley 1970–74, Andy Nelson 1974–79, Mike Bailey 1979–81, Alan Mullery 1981–82, Ken Craggs 1982, Lennie Lawrence 1982–91, Steve Gritt/Alan Curbishley 1991–95, Alan Curbishley June 1995– .

CHELSEA

Managers (and Secretary-Managers)
John Tait Robertson 1905–07, David Calderhead 1907–33, A. Leslie Knighton 1933–39, Billy Birrell 1939–52, Ted Drake 1952–61, Tommy Docherty 1962–67, Dave Sexton 1967–74, Ron Suart 1974–75, Eddie McCreadie 1975–77, Ken Shellito 1977–78, Danny Blanchflower 1978–79, Geoff Hurst 1979–81, John Neal 1981–85 (Director to 1986), John Hollins 1985–88, Bobby Campbell 1988–91, Ian Porterfield 1991–93, David Webb 1993, Glenn Hoddle June 1993– .

CHESTER CITY

Managers (and Secretary-Managers)
Charlie Hewitt 1930–36, Alex Raisbeck 1936–38, Frank Brown 1938–53, Louis Page 1953–56, John Harris 1956–59, Stan Pearson 1959–61, Bill Lambton 1962–63, Peter Hauser 1963–68, Ken Roberts 1968–76, Alan Oakes 1976–82, Cliff Sear 1982, John Sainty 1982–83, John McGrath 1984, Harry McNally 1985–92, Graham Barrow 1992–94, Mike Pejic 1994–95, Derek Mann 1995, Kevin Ratcliffe April 1995– .

CHESTERFIELD

Managers (and Secretary-Managers)
E. Russell Timmeus 1891–95*, Gilbert Gillies 1895–1901, E. F. Hind 1901–1902, Jack Hoskin 1902–1906, W. Furness 1906–07, George Swift 1907–10, G. H. Jones 1911–13, R. L. Weston 1913–17, T. Callaghan 1919, J. J. Caffrey 1920–22, Harry Hadley 1922, Harry Parkes 1922–27, Alec Campbell 1927, Ted Davison 1927–32, Bill Harvey 1932–38, Norman Bullock 1938–45, Bob Brocklebank 1945–48, Bobby Marshall 1948–52, Ted Davison 1952–58, Duggie Livingstone 1958–62, Tony McShane 1962–67, Jimmy McGuigan 1967–73, Joe Shaw 1973–76, Arthur Cox 1976–80, Frank Barlow 1980–83, John Duncan 1983–87, Kevin Randall 1987–88, Paul Hart 1988–91, Chris McMenemy 1991–93, John Duncan February 1993– .

COLCHESTER UNITED

Managers (and Secretary-Managers)
Ted Fenton 1946–48, Jimmy Allen 1948–53, Jack Butler 1953–55, Benny Fenton 1955–63, Neil Franklin 1963–68, Dick Graham 1968–72, Jim Smith 1972–75, Bobby Roberts 1975–82, Allan Hunter 1982–83, Cyril Lea 1983–86, Mike Walker 1986–87, Roger Brown 1987–88, Jock Wallace 1989, Mick Mills 1990. Ian Atkins 1990–91, Roy McDonough 1991–94, George Burley 1994, Steve Wignall January 1995– .

COVENTRY CITY

Managers (and Secretary-Managers)
H. R. Buckle 1909–10, Robert Wallace 1910–13*, Frank Scott-Walford 1913–15, William Clayton 1917–19, H. Pollitt 1919–20, Albert Evans 1920–24, Jimmy Kerr 1924–28, James McIntyre 1928–31, Harry Storer 1931–45, Dick Bayliss 1945–47, Billy Frith 1947–48, Harry Storer 1948–53, Jack Fairbrother 1953–54, Charlie Elliott 1954–55, Jesse Carver 1955–56, Harry Warren 1956–57, Billy Frith 1957–61, Jimmy Hill 1961–67, Noel Cantwell 1967–72, Bob Dennison 1972, Joe Mercer 1972–75, Gordon Milne 1972–81, Dave Sexton 1981–83, Bobby Gould 1983–84, Don Mackay 1985–86, George Curtis 1986–87 (became MD), John Sillett 1987–90, Terry Butcher 1990–92, Don Howe 1992, Bobby Gould 1992–93, Phil Neal 1993–95, Ron Atkinson February 1995– .

CREWE ALEXANDRA

Managers (and Secretary-Managers)
W. C. McNeill 1892–94*, J. G. Hall 1895–96*, 1897 R. Roberts* (1st team sec.), J. B. Bromerley 1898–1911* (continued as Hon. Sec. to 1925), Tom Bailey 1925–38, George Lillicrop 1938–44, Frank Hill 1944–48, Arthur Turner 1948–51, Harry Catterick 1951–53, Ralph Ward 1953–55, Maurice Lindley 1955–58, Harry Ware 1958–60, Jimmy McGuigan 1960–64, Ernie Tagg 1964–71 (continued as secretary to 1972), Dennis Viollet 1971, Jimmy Melia 1972–73, Ernie Tagg 1974, Harry Gregg 1975–78, Warwick Rimmer 1978–79, Tony Waddington 1979–81, Arfon Griffiths 1981–82, Peter Morris 1982–83, Dario Gradi June 1983– .

CRYSTAL PALACE

Managers (and Secretary-Managers)
John T. Robson 1905–07, Edmund Goodman 1907–25 (had been secretary since 1905 and afterwards continued in this position to 1933). Alec Maley 1925–27, Fred Maven 1927–30, Jack Tresadern 1930–35, Tom Bromilow 1935–36, R. S. Moyes 1936, Tom Bromilow 1936–39, George Irwin 1939–47, Jack Butler 1947–49, Ronnie Rooke 1949–50, Charlie Slade and Fred Dawes (joint managers) 1950–51, Laurie Scott 1951–54, Cyril Spiers 1954–58, George Smith 1958–60, Arthur Rowe 1960–62, Dick Graham 1962–66, Bert Head 1966–72 (continued as GM to 1973), Malcolm Allison 1973–76, Terry Venables 1976–80, Ernie Walley 1980, Malcolm Allison 1980–81, Dario Gradi 1981, Steve Kember 1981–82, Alan Mullery 1982–84, Steve Coppell 1984–93, Alan Smith 1993–95, Steve Coppell (TD) June 1995– .

DARLINGTON

Managers (and Secretary-Managers)
Tom McIntosh 1902–11, W. L. Lane 1911–12*, Dick Jackson 1912–19, Jack English 1919–28, Jack Fairless 1928–33, George Collins 1933–36, George Brown 1936–38, Jackie Carr 1938–42, Jack Surtees 1942, Jack English 1945–46, Bill Forrest 1946–50, George Irwin 1950–52, Bob Gurney 1952–57, Dick Duckworth 1957–60, Eddie Carr 1960–64, Lol Morgan 1964–66, Jimmy Greenhalgh 1966–68, Ray Yeoman 1968–70, Len Richley 1970–71, Frank Brennan 1971, Ken Hale 1971–72, Allan Jones 1972, Ralph Brand 1972–73, Dick Conner 1973–74, Billy Horner 1974–76, Peter Madden 1976–78, Len Walker 1978–79, Billy Elliott 1979–83, Cyril Knowles 1983–87, Dave Booth 1987–89, Brian Little 1989–91, Frank Gray 1991–92, Ray Hankin 1992, Billy McEwan 1992–93, Alan Murray 1993–95, Paul Futcher 1995, David Hodgson/ Jim Platt (Directors of Coaching) May 1995– .

DERBY COUNTY

Managers (and Secretary-Managers)
Harry Newbould 1896–1906, Jimmy Methven 1906–22, Cecil Potter 1922–25, George Jobey 1925–41, Ted Magner 1944–46, Stuart McMillan 1946–53, Jack Barker 1953–55, Harry Storer 1955–62, Tim Ward 1962–67, Brian Clough 1967–73, Dave Mackay 1973–76, Colin Murphy 1977, Tommy Docherty 1977–79, Colin Addison 1979–82, Johnny Newman 1982, Peter Taylor 1982–84, Roy McFarland 1984, Arthur Cox 1984–93, Roy McFarland 1993–95, Jim Smith June 1995– .

DONCASTER ROVERS

Managers (and Secretary-Managers)
Arthur Porter 1920–21*, Harry Tufnell 1921–22, Arthur Porter 1922–23, Dick Ray 1923–27, David Menzies 1928–36, Fred Emery 1936–40, Bill Marsden 1944–46, Jackie Bestall 1946–49, Peter Doherty 1949–58, Jack Hodgson and Sid Bycroft (joint managers) 1958, Jack Crayston 1958–59 (continued as Sec-Man to 1961), Jackie Bestall (TM) 1959–60, Norman Curtis 1960–61, Danny Malloy 1961–62, Oscar Hold 1962–64, Bill Leivers 1964–66, Keith Kettleborough 1966–67, George Raynor 1967–68, Lawrie McMenemy 1968–71, Maurice Setters 1971–74, Stan Anderson 1975–78, Billy Bremner 1978–85, Dave Cusack 1985–87, Dave Mackay 1987–89, Billy Bremner 1989–91, Steve Beaglehole 1991–93, Ian Atkins 1994, Sammy Chung July 1994– .

EVERTON

Managers (and Secretary-Managers)
W. E. Barclay 1888–89*, Dick Molyneux 1889–1901*, William C. Cuff 1901–18*, W. J. Sawyer 1918–19*, Thomas H. McIntosh 1919–35*, Theo Kelly 1936–48, Cliff Britton 1948–56, Ian Buchan 1956–58, Johnny Carey 1958–61, Harry Catterick 1961–73, Billy Bingham 1973–77, Gordon Lee 1977–81, Howard Kendall 1981–87, Colin Harvey 1987–90, Howard Kendall 1990–93, Mike Walker 1994, Joe Royle November 1994– .

EXETER CITY

Managers (and Secretary-Managers)
Arthur Chadwick 1910–22, Fred Mavin 1923–27, Dave Wilson 1928–29, Billy McDevitt 1929–35, Jack English 1935–39, George Roughton 1945–52, Norman Kirkman 1952–53, Norman Dodgin 1953–57, Bill Thompson 1957–58, Frank Broome 1958–60, Glen Wilson 1960–62, Cyril Spiers 1962–63, Jack Edwards 1963–65, Ellis Stuttard 1965–66, Jock Basford 1966–67, Frank Broome 1967–69, Johnny Newman 1969–76, Bobby Saxton 1977–79, Brian Godfrey 1979–83, Gerry Francis 1983–84, Jim Iley 1984–85, Colin Appleton 1985–87, Terry Cooper 1988–91, Alan Ball 1991–94, Terry Cooper 1994–95, Peter Fox June 1995– .

FULHAM

Managers (and Secretary-Managers)
Harry Bradshaw 1904–09, Phil Kelso 1909–24, Andy Ducat 1924–26, Joe Bradshaw 1926–29, Ned Liddell 1929–31, Jim MacIntyre 1931–34, Jim Hogan 1934–35, Jack Peart 1935–48, Frank Osborne 1948–64 (was secretary-manager or GM for most of this period), Bill Dodgin Snr 1949–53, Duggie Livingstone 1956–58, Bedford Jezzard 1958–64 (GM for last two months), Vic Buckingham 1965–68, Bobby Robson 1968, Bill Dodgin Jnr 1969–72, Alec Stock 1972–76, Bobby Campbell 1976–80, Malcolm Macdonald 1980–84, Ray Harford 1984–86, Ray Lewington 1986–90, Alan Dicks 1990–91, Don Mackay 1991–94, Ian Branfoot June 1994– .

GILLINGHAM

Managers (and Secretary-Managers)
W. Ironside Groombridge 1896–1906* (previously financial secretary), Steve Smith 1906–08, W. I. Groombridge 1908–19*, George Collins 1919–20, John McMillan 1920–23, Harry Curtis 1923–26, Albert Hoskins 1926–29, Dick Hendrie 1929–31, Fred Maven 1932–37, Alan Ure 1937–38, Bill Harvey 1938–39, Archie Clark 1939–58, Harry Barratt 1958–62, Freddie Cox 1962–65, Basil Hayward 1966–71, Andy Nelson 1971–74, Len Ashurst 1974–75, Gerry Summers 1975–81, Keith Peacock 1981–87, Paul Taylor 1988, Keith Burkinshaw 1988–89, Damien Richardson 1989–93, Mike Flanagan 1993–95, Neil Smillie 1995, Tony Pulis June 1995– .

GRIMSBY TOWN

Managers (and Secretary-Managers)
H. N. Hickson 1902–20*, Haydn Price 1920, George Fraser 1921–24, Wilf Gillow 1924–32, Frank Womack 1932–36, Charles Spencer 1937–51, Bill Shankly 1951–53, Billy Walsh 1954–55, Allenby Chilton 1955–59, Tim Ward 1960–62, Tom Johnston 1962–64, Jimmy McGuigan 1964–67, Don McEvoy 1967–68, Bill Harvey 1968–69, Bobby Kennedy 1969–71, Lawrie McMenemy 1971–73, Ron Ashman 1973–75, Tom Casey 1975–76, Johnny Newman 1976–79, George Kerr 1979–82, David Booth 1982–85, Mike Lyons 1985–87, Bobby Roberts 1987–88, Alan Buckley 1988–94, Brian Laws November 1994–

HARTLEPOOL UNITED

Managers (and Secretary-Managers)
Alfred Priest 1908–12, Percy Humphreys 1912–13, Jack Manners 1913–20, Cecil Potter 1920–22, David Gordon 1922–24, Jack Manners 1924–27, Bill Norman 1927–31, Jack Carr 1932–35 (had been player-coach since 1931), Jimmy Hamilton 1935–43, Fred Westgarth 1943–57, Ray Middleton 1957–59, Bill Robinson 1959–62, Allenby Chilton 1962–63, Bob Gurney 1963–64, Alvan Williams 1964–65, Geoff Twentyman 1965, Brian Clough 1965–67, Angus McLean 1967–70, John Simpson 1970–71, Len Ashurst 1971–74, Ken Hale 1974–76, Billy Horner 1976–83, Johnny Duncan 1983, Mike Docherty 1983, Billy Horner 1984–86, John Bird 1986–88, Bobby Moncur 1988–89, Cyril Knowles 1989–91, Alan Murray 1991–93, Viv Busby 1993, John MacPhail 1993–94, David McCreery 1994–95, Keith Houchen April 1995– .

HEREFORD UNITED

Managers (and Secretary-Managers)
Eric Keen 1939, George Tranter 1948–49, Alex Massie 1952, George Tranter 1953–55, Joe Wade 1956–62, Ray Daniels 1962–63, Bob Dennison 1963–67, John Charles 1967–71, Colin Addison 1971–74, John Sillett 1974–78, Mike Bailey 1978–79, Frank Lord 1979–82, Tommy Hughes 1982–83, Johnny Newman 1983–87, Ian Bowyer 1987–90, Colin Addison 1990–91, John Sillett 1991–92, Greg Downs 1992–94, John Layton November 1994– .

HUDDERSFIELD TOWN

Managers (and Secretary-Managers)
Fred Walker 1908–10, Richard Pudan 1910–12, Arthur Fairclough 1912–19, Ambrose Langley 1919–21, Herbert Chapman 1921–25, Cecil Potter 1925–26, Jack Chaplin 1926–29, Clem Stephenson 1929–42, David Steele 1943–47, George Stephenson 1947–52, Andy Beattie 1952–56, Bill Shankly 1956–59, Eddie Boot 1960–64, Tom Johnston 1964–68, Ian Greaves 1968–74, Bobby Collins 1974, Tom Johnston 1975–78 (had been GM since 1975), Mike Buxton 1978–86, Steve Smith 1986–87, Malcolm Macdonald 1987–88, Eoin Hand 1988–92, Ian Ross 1992–93, Neil Warnock 1993–95, Brian Horton June 1995– .

HULL CITY

Managers (and Secretary-Managers)
James Ramster 1904–05*, Ambrose Langley 1905–13, Harry Chapman 1913–14, Fred Stringer 1914–16, David Menzies 1916–21, Percy Lewis 1921–23, Bill McCracken 1923–31, Haydn Green 1931–34, John Hill 1934–36, David Menzies 1936, Ernest Blackburn 1936–46, Major Frank Buckley 1946–48, Raich Carter 1948–51, Bob Jackson 1952–55, Bob Brocklebank 1955–61, Cliff Britton 1961–70 (continued as GM to 1971), Terry Neill 1970–74, John Kaye 1974–77, Bobby Collins 1977–78, Ken Houghton 1978–79, Mike Smith 1979–82, Bobby Brown 1982, Colin Appleton 1982–84, Brian Horton 1984–88, Eddie Gray 1988–89, Colin Appleton 1989, Stan Ternent 1989–91, Terry Dolan February 1991– .

IPSWICH TOWN

Managers (and Secretary-Managers)
Mick O'Brien 1936–37, Scott Duncan 1937–55 (continued as secretary), Alf Ramsey 1955–63, Jackie Milburn 1963–64, Bill McGarry 1964–68, Bobby Robson 1969–82, Bobby Ferguson 1982–87, Johnny Duncan 1987–90, John Lyall 1990–94, George Burley December 1994– .

LEEDS UNITED

Managers (and Secretary-Managers)
Dick Ray 1919–20, Arthur Fairclough 1920–27, Dick Ray 1927–35, Bill Hampson 1935–47, Willis Edwards 1947–48, Major Frank Buckley 1948–53, Raich Carter 1953–58, Bill Lambton 1958–59, Jack Taylor 1959–61, Don Revie 1961–74, Brian Clough 1974, Jimmy Armfield 1974–78, Jock Stein 1978, Jimmy Adamson 1978–80, Allan Clarke 1980–82, Eddie Gray 1982–85, Billy Bremner 1985–88, Howard Wilkinson October 1988– .

LEICESTER CITY

Managers (and Secretary-Managers)
William Clark 1896–97, George Johnson 1898–1907*, James Blessington 1907–09, Andy Aitken 1909–11, J. W. Bartlett 1912–14, Peter Hodge 1919–26, William Orr 1926–32, Peter Hodge 1932–34, Andy Lochhead 1934–36, Frank Womack 1936–39, Tom Bromilow 1939–45, Tom Mather 1945–46, Johnny Duncan 1946–49, Norman Bullock 1949–55, David Halliday 1955–58, Matt Gillies 1959–68, Frank O'Farrell 1968–71, Jimmy Bloomfield 1971–77, Frank McLintock 1977–78, Jock Wallace 1978–82, Gordon Milne 1982–86, Bryan Hamilton 1986–87, David Pleat 1987–91, Brian Little May 1991–94, Mark McGhee December 1994– .

LEYTON ORIENT

Managers (and Secretary-Managers)

Sam Omerod 1905–06, Ike Ivenson 1906, Billy Holmes 1907–22, Peter Proudfoot 1922–29, Arthur Grimsdell 1929–30, Peter Proudfoot 1930–31, Jimmy Seed 1931–33, David Pratt 1933–34, Peter Proudfoot 1935–39, Tom Halsey 1939–39, Billy Wright 1939–45, Billy Hall 1945, Billy Wright 1945–46, Charlie Hewitt 1946–48, Neil McBain 1948–49, Alec Stock 1949–56, 1956–58, 1958–59, Johnny Carey 1961–63, Benny Fenton 1963–64, Dave Sexton 1965, Dick Graham 1966–68, Jimmy Bloomfield 1968–71, George Petchey 1971–77, Jimmy Bloomfield 1977–81, Paul Went 1981, Ken Knighton 1981, Frank Clark 1982--91 (MD), Peter Eustace 1991–94, Chris Turner/John Sitton 1994–95, Pat Holland May 1995– .

LINCOLN CITY

Managers (and Secretary-Managers)

David Calderhead 1900–07, John Henry Strawson 1907–14 (had been secretary), George Fraser 1919–21, David Calderhead Jnr. 1921–24, Horace Henshall 1924–27, Harry Parkes 1927–36, Joe McClelland 1936–46, Bill Anderson 1946–65 (GM to 1966), Roy Chapman 1965–66, Ron Gray 1966–70, Bert Loxley 1970–71, David Herd 1971–72, Graham Taylor 1972–77, George Kerr 1977–78, Willie Bell 1977–78, Colin Murphy 1978–85, John Pickering 1985, George Kerr 1985–87, Peter Daniel 1987, Colin Murphy 1987–90, Allan Clarke 1990, Steve Thompson 1990–93, Keith Alexander 1993–94, Sam Ellis May 1994– .

LIVERPOOL

Managers (and Secretary-Managers)

W. E. Barclay 1892–96, Tom Watson 1896–1915, David Ashworth 1920–22, Matt McQueen 1923–28, George Patterson 1928–36 (continued as secretary), George Kay 1936–51, Don Welsh 1951–56, Phil Taylor 1956–59, Bill Shankly 1959–74, Bob Paisley 1974–83, Joe Fagan 1983–85, Kenny Dalglish 1985–91, Graeme Souness 1991–94, Roy Evans January 1994–

LUTON TOWN

Managers (and Secretary-Managers)

Charlie Green 1901–28*, George Thomson 1925, John McCartney 1927–29, George Kay 1929–31, Harold Wightman 1931–35, Ted Liddell 1936–38, Neil McBain 1938–39, George Martin 1939–47, Dally Duncan 1947–58, Syd Owen 1959–60, Sam Bartram 1960–62, Bill Harvey 1962–64, George Martin 1965–66, Allan Brown 1966–68, Alec Stock 1968–72, Harry Haslam 1972–78, David Pleat 1978–86, John Moore 1986–87, Ray Harford 1987–89, Jim Ryan 1900–91, David Pleat 1991–95, Terry Westley July 1995– .

MANCHESTER CITY

Managers (and Secretary-Managers)

Joshua Parlby 1893–95*, Sam Omerod 1895–1902, Tom Maley 1902–06, Harry Newbould 1906–12, Ernest Magnall 1912–24, David Ashworth 1924–25, Peter Hodge 1926–32, Wilf Wild 1932–46 (continued as secretary to 1950), Sam Cowan 1946–47, John "Jock" Thomson 1947–50, Leslie McDowall 1950–63, George Poyser 1963–65, Joe Mercer 1965–71 (continued as GM to 1972), Malcolm Allison 1972–73, Johnny Hart 1973, Ron Saunders 1973–74, Tony Book 1974–79, Malcolm Allison 1979–80, John Bond 1980–83, John Benson 1983, Billy McNeill 1983–86, Jimmy Frizzell 1986–87 (continued as GM), Mel Machin 1987–89, Howard Kendall 1990, Peter Reid 1990–93, Brian Horton 1993–95, Alan Ball July 1995– .

MANCHESTER UNITED

Managers (and Secretary-Managers)

Ernest Magnall 1900–12, John Robson 1914–21, John Chapman 1921–26, Clarence Hildrith 1926–27, Herbert Bamlett 1927–31, Walter Crickmer 1931–32, Scott Duncan 1932–37, Jimmy Porter 1938–44, Walter Crickmer 1944–45*, Matt Busby 1945–69 (continued as GM then Director), Wilf McGuinness 1969–70, Frank O'Farrell 1971–72, Tommy Docherty 1972–77, Dave Sexton 1977–81, Ron Atkinson 1981–86, Alex Ferguson November 1986– .

MANSFIELD TOWN

Managers (and Secretary-Managers)

John Baynes 1922–25, Ted Davison 1926–28, Jack Hickling 1928–33, Henry Martin 1933–35, Charlie Bell 1935, Harold Wightman 1936, Harold Parkes 1936–38, Jack Poole 1938–44, Lloyd Barke 1944–45, Roy Goodall 1945–49, Freddie Steele 1949–51, George Jobey 1952–53, Stan Mercer 1953–55, Charlie Mitten 1956–58, Sam Weaver 1958–60, Raich Carter 1960–63, Tommy Cummings 1963–67, Tommy Eggleston 1967–70, Jock Basford 1970–71, Danny Williams 1971–74, Dave Smith 1974–76, Peter Morris 1976–78, Billy Bingham 1978–79, Mick Jones 1979–81, Stuart Boam 1981–83, Ian Greaves 1983–89, George Foster 1989–93, Andy King November 1993– .

MIDDLESBROUGH

Managers (and Secretary-Managers)

John Robson 1899–1905, Alex Massie 1905–06, Andy Aitken 1906–09, J. Gunter 1908–10*, Andy Walker 1910–11, Tom McIntosh 1911–19, James Howie 1920–23, Herbert Bamlett 1923–26, Peter McWilliam 1927–34, Wilf Gillow 1934–44, David Jack 1944–52, Walter Rowley 1952–54, Bob Dennison 1954–63, Raich Carter 1963–66, Stan Anderson 1966–73, Jack Charlton 1973–77, John Neal 1977–81, Bobby Murdoch 1981–82, Malcolm Allison 1982–84, Willie Maddren 1984–86, Bruce Rioch 1986–90, Colin Todd 1990–91, Lennie Lawrence 1991–94, Bryan Robson May 1994– .

MILLWALL

Managers (and Secretary-Managers)

William Henderson 1894–99*, E. R. Stopher 1899–1900, George Saunders 1900–11, Herbert Lipsham 1911–19, Robert Hunter 1919–33, Bill McCracken 1933–36, Charlie Hewitt 1936–40, Bill Voisey 1940–44, Jack Cock 1944–48, Charlie Hewitt 1948–56, Ron Gray 1956–57, Jimmy Seed 1958–59, Reg Smith 1959–61, Ron Gray 1961–63, Billy Gray 1963–66, Benny Fenton 1966–74, Gordon Jago 1974–77, George Petchey 1978–80, Peter Anderson 1980–82, George Graham 1982–86, John Docherty 1986–90, Bob Pearson 1990, Bruce Rioch 1990–92, Mick McCarthy March 1992– .

NEWCASTLE UNITED

Managers (and Secretary-Managers)
Frank Watt 1895–32 (continued as secretary to 1932), Andy Cunningham 1930–35, Tom Mather 1935–39, Stan Seymour 1939–47 (Hon-manager), George Martin 1947–50, Stan Seymour 1950–54 (Hon-manager), Duggie Livingstone 1954–56, Stan Seymour (Hon-manager 1956–58), Charlie Mitten 1958–61, Norman Smith 1961–62, Joe Harvey 1962–75, Gordon Lee 1975–77, Richard Dinnis 1977, Bill McGarry 1977–80, Arthur Cox 1980–84, Jack Charlton 1984, Willie McFaul 1985–88, Jim Smith 1988–91, Ossie Ardiles 1991–92, Kevin Keegan February 1992– .

NORTHAMPTON TOWN

Managers (and Secretary-Managers)
Arthur Jones 1897–1907*, Herbert Chapman 1907–12, Walter Bull 1912–13, Fred Lessons 1913–19, Bob Hewison 1920–25, Jack Tresadern 1925–30, Jack English 1931–35, Syd Puddefoot 1935–37, Warney Cresswell 1937–39, Tom Smith 1939–49, Bob Dennison 1949–54, Dave Smith 1954–59, David Bowen 1959–67, Tony Marchi 1967–68, Ron Flowers 1968–69, Dave Bowen 1969–72 (continued as GM and secretary to 1985 when joined the board), Billy Baxter 1972–73, Bill Dodgin Jnr 1973–76, Pat Crerand 1976–77, Bill Dodgin Jnr 1977, John Petts 1977–78, Mike Keen 1978–79, Clive Walker 1979–80, Bill Dodgin Jnr 1980–82, Clive Walker 1982–84, Tony Barton 1984–85, Graham Carr 1985–90, Theo Foley 1990–92, Phil Chard 1992–93, John Barnwell 1993–95, Ian Atkins January 1995– .

NORWICH CITY

Managers (and Secretary-Managers)
John Bowman 1905–07, James McEwen 1907–08, Arthur Turner 1909–10, Bert Stansfield 1910–15, Major Frank Buckley 1919–20, Charles O'Hagan 1920–21, Albert Gosnell 1921–26, Bert Stansfield 1926, Cecil Potter 1926–29, James Kerr 1929–33, Tom Parker 1933–37, Bob Young 1937–39, Jimmy Jewell 1939, Bob Young 1939–45, Cyril Spiers 1946–47, Duggie Lochhead 1947–50, Norman Low 1950–55, Tom Parker 1955–57, Archie Macaulay 1957–61, Willie Reid 1961–62, George Swindin 1962, Ron Ashman 1962–66, Lol Morgan 1966–69, Ron Saunders 1969–73, John Bond 1973–80, Ken Brown 1980–87, Dave Stringer 1987–92, Mike Walker 1992–94, John Deehan 1994–95, Martin O'Neill June 1995– .

NOTTINGHAM FOREST

Managers (and Secretary-Managers)
Harry Radford 1889–97*, Harry Haslam 1897–1909*, Fred Earp 1909–12, Bob Masters 1912–25, John Baynes 1925–29, Stan Hardy 1930–31, Noel Watson 1931–36, Harold Wightman 1936–39, Billy Walker 1939–60, Andy Beattie 1960–63, John Carey 1963–68, Matt Gillies 1969–72, Dave Mackay 1972, Allan Brown 1973–75, Brian Clough 1975–93, Frank Clark May 1993– .

NOTTS COUNTY

Managers (and Secretary-Managers)
Edwin Browne 1883–93*, Tom Featherstone 1893*, Tom Harris 1893–13*, Albert Fisher 1913–27, Horace Henshall 1927–34, Charlie Jones 1934–35, David Pratt 1935, Percy Smith 1935–36, Jimmy McMullan 1936–37, Harry Parkes 1938–39, Tony Towers 1939–42, Frank Womack 1942–43, Major Frank Buckley 1944–46, Arthur Stollery 1946–49, Eric Houghton 1949–53, George Poyser 1953–57, Tommy Lawton 1957–58, Frank Hill 1958–61, Tim Coleman 1961–63, Eddie Lowe 1963–65, Tim Coleman 1965–66, Jack Burkitt 1966–67, Andy Beattie (GM 1967), Billy Gray 1967–68, Jimmy Sirrel 1969–75, Ron Fenton 1975–77, Jimmy Sirrel 1978–82 (continues as GM to 1984), Howard Wilkinson 1982–83, Larry Lloyd 1983–84, Richie Barker 1984–85, Jimmy Sirrel 1985–87, John Barnwell 1987–88, Neil Warnock 1989–93, Mick Walker 1993–94, Russell Slade 1994–95, Howard Kendall 1995, Colin Murphy June 1995– .

OLDHAM ATHLETIC

Managers (and Secretary-Managers)
David Ashworth 1906–14, Herbert Bamlett 1914–21, Charlie Roberts 1921–22, David Ashworth 1923–24, Bob Mellor 1924–27, Andy Wilson 1927–32, Jimmy McMullan 1933–34, Bob Mellor 1934–45 (continued as secretary to 1953), Frank Womack 1945–47, Billy Wootton 1947–50, George Hardwick 1950–56, Ted Goodier 1956–58, Norman Dodgin 1958–60, Jack Rowley 1960–63, Les McDowall 1963–65, Gordon Hurst 1965–66, Jimmy McIlroy 1966–68, Jack Rowley 1968–69, Jimmy Frizzell 1970–82, Joe Royle 1982–94, Graeme Sharp November 1994– .

OXFORD UNITED

Managers (and Secretary-Managers)
Harry Thompson 1949–58 (Player Manager 1949-51), Arthur Turner 1959–69 (continued as GM to 1972), Ron Saunders 1969, George Summers 1969–75, Mike Brown 1975–79, Bill Asprey 1979–80, Ian Greaves 1980–82, Jim Smith 1982–85, Maurice Evans 1985–88, Mark Lawrenson 1988, Brian Horton 1988–93, Denis Smith September 1993– .

PETERBOROUGH UNITED

Managers (and Secretary-Managers)
Jock Porter 1934–36, Fred Taylor 1936–37, Vic Poulter 1937–38, Sam Madden 1938–48, Jack Blood 1948–50, Bob Gurney 1950–52, Jack Fairbrother 1952–54, George Swindin 1954–58, Jimmy Hagan 1958–62, Jack Fairbrother 1962–64, Gordon Clark 1964–67, Norman Rigby 1967–69, Jim Iley 1969–72, Noel Cantwell 1972–77, John Barnwell 1977–78, Billy Hails 1978–79, Peter Morris 1979–82, Martin Wilkinson 1982–83, John Wile 1983–86, Noel Cantwell 1986–88 (continued as GM), Mick Jones 1988–89, Mark Lawrenson 1989–90, Chris Turner 1991–92, Lil Fuccillo 1992–93, John Still June 1994–

PLYMOUTH ARGYLE

Managers (and Secretary-Managers)
Frank Brettell 1903–05, Bob Jack 1905–06, Bill Fullerton 1906–07, Bob Jack 1910–38, Jack Tresadern 1938–47, Jimmy Rae 1948–55, Jack Rowley 1955–60, Neil Dougall 1961, Ellis Stuttard 1961–63, Andy Beattie 1963–64, Malcolm Allison 1964–65, Derek Ufton 1965–68, Billy Bingham 1968–70, Ellis Stuttard 1970–72, Tony Waiters 1972–77, Mike Kelly 1977–78, Malcolm Allison 1978–79, Bobby Saxton 1979–81, Bobby Moncur 1981–83, Johnny Hore 1983–84, Dave Smith 1984–88, Ken Brown 1988–90, David Kemp 1990–92, Peter Shilton 1992–95, Steve McCall 1995, Neil Warnock June 1995– .

PORTSMOUTH

Managers (and Secretary-Managers)
Frank Brettell 1898–1901, Bob Blyth 1901–04, Richard Bonney 1905–08, Bob Brown 1911–20, John McCartney 1920–27, Jack Tinn 1927–47, Bob Jackson 1947–52, Eddie Lever 1952–58, Freddie Cox 1958–61, George Smith 1961–70, Ron Tindall 1970–73 (GM to 1974), John Mortimore 1973–74, Ian St. John 1974–77, Jimmy Dickinson 1977–79, Frank Burrows 1979–82, Bobby Campbell 1982–84, Alan Ball 1984–89, John Gregory 1989–90, Frank Burrows 1990–1991, Jim Smith 1991–95, Terry Fenwick February 1995– .

PORT VALE

Managers (and Secretary-Managers)
Sam Gleaves 1896–1905*, Tom Clare 1905–11, A. S. Walker 1911–12, H. Myatt 1912–14, Tom Holford 1919–24 (continued as trainer), Joe Schofield 1924–30, Tom Morgan 1930–32, Tom Holford 1932–35, Warney Cresswell 1936–37, Tom Morgan 1937–38, Billy Frith 1945–46, Gordon Hodgson 1946–51, Ivor Powell 1951, Freddie Steele 1951–57, Norman Low 1957–62, Freddie Steele 1962–65, Jackie Mudie 1965–67, Sir Stanley Matthews (GM) 1965–68, Gordon Lee 1968–74, Roy Sproson 1974–77, Colin Harper 1977, Bobby Smith 1977–78, Dennis Butler 1978–79, Alan Bloor 1979, John McGrath 1980–83, John Rudge March 1984– .

PRESTON NORTH END

Managers (and Secretary-Managers)
Charlie Parker 1906–15, Vincent Hayes 1919–23, Jim Lawrence 1923–25, Frank Richards 1925–27, Alex Gibson 1927–31, Lincoln Hayes 1931–1932 (run by committee 1932–36), Tommy Muirhead 1936–37, (run by committee 1937–49), Will Scott 1949–53, Scot Symon 1953–54, Frank Hill 1954–56, Cliff Britton 1956–61, Jimmy Milne 1961–68, Bobby Seith 1968–70, Alan Ball Sr 1970–73, Bobby Charlton 1973–75, Harry Catterick 1975–77, Nobby Stiles 1977–81, Tommy Docherty 1981, Gordon Lee 1981–83, Alan Kelly 1983–85, Tommy Booth 1985–86, Brian Kidd 1986, John McGrath 1986–90, Les Chapman 1990–92, John Beck 1992–94, Gary Peters December 1994– .

QUEENS PARK RANGERS

Managers (and Secretary-Managers)
James Cowan 1906–13, James Howie 1913–20, Ted Liddell 1920–24, Will Wood 1924–25 (had been secretary since 1903), Bob Hewison 1925–30, John Bowman 1930–31, Archie Mitchell 1931–33, Mick O'Brien 1933–35, Billy Birrell 1935–39, Ted Vizard 1939–44, Dave Mangnall 1944–52, Jack Taylor 1952–59, Alec Stock 1959–65 (GM to 1968), Jimmy Andrews 1965, Bill Dodgin Jnr 1968, Tommy Docherty 1968, Les Allen 1969–70, Gordon Jago 1971–74, Dave Sexton 1974–77, Frank Sibley 1977–78, Steve Burtenshaw 1978–79, Tommy Docherty 1979–80, Terry Venables 1980–84, Gordon Jago 1984, Alan Mullery 1984, Frank Sibley 1984–85, Jim Smith 1985–88, Trevor Francis 1988–90, Don Howe 1990–91, Gerry Francis 1991–94, Ray Wilkins November 1994– .

READING

Managers (and Secretary-Managers)
Thomas Sefton 1897–1901*, James Sharp 1901–02, Harry Matthews 1902–20, Harry Marshall 1920–22, Arthur Chadwick 1923–25, H. S. Bray 1925–26 (secretary only since 1922 and 26–35), Andrew Wylie 1926–31, Joe Smith 1931–35, Billy Butler 1935–39, John Cochrane 1939, Joe Edelston 1939–47, Ted Drake 1947–52, Jack Smith 1952–55, Harry Johnston 1955–63, Roy Bentley 1963–69, Jack Mansell 1969–71, Charlie Hurley 1972–77, Maurice Evans 1977–84, Ian Branfoot 1984–89, Ian Porterfield 1989–91, Mark McGhee 1991–94, Jimmy Quinn, Mick Gooding December 1994– .

ROCHDALE

Managers (and Secretary-Managers)
Billy Bradshaw 1920, (run by committee 1920–22), Tom Wilson 1922–23, Jack Peart 1923–30, Will Cameron 1930–31, Herbert Hopkinson 1932–34, Billy Smith 1934–35, Ernest Nixon 1935–37, Sam Jennings 1937–38, Ted Goodier 1938–52, Jack Warner 1952–53, Harry Catterick 1953–58, Jack Marshall 1958–60, Tony Collins 1960–68, Bob Stokoe 1967–68, Len Richley 1968–70, Dick Conner 1970–73, Walter Joyce 1973–76, Brian Green 1976–77, Mike Ferguson 1977–78, Doug Collins 1979, Bob Stokoe 1979–80, Peter Madden 1980–83, Jimmy Greenhoff 1983–84, Vic Halom 1984–86, Eddie Gray 1986–88, Danny Bergara 1988–89, Terry Dolan 1989–91, Dave Sutton 1991–94, Mick Docherty January 1995– .

ROTHERHAM UNITED

Managers (and Secretary-Managers)
Billy Heald 1925–29 (secretary only for long spell), Stanley Davies 1929–30, Billy Heald 1930–33, Reg Freeman 1934–52, Andy Smailes 1952–58, Tom Johnston 1958–62, Danny Williams 1962–65, Jack Mansell 1965–67, Tommy Docherty 1967–68, Jimmy McAnearney 1968–73, Jimmy McGuigan 1973–79, Ian Porterfield 1979–81, Emlyn Hughes 1981–83, George Kerr 1983–85, Norman Hunter 1985–87, Dave Cusack 1987–88, Billy McEwan 1988–91, Phil Henson 1991–94, Archie Gemmill/ John McGovern September 1994– .

SCARBOROUGH

Managers (and Secretary-Managers)
B. Chapman 1945–47*, George Hall 1946–47, Harold Taylor 1947–48, Frank Taylor 1948–50, A. C. Bell (Director & Hon. TM) 1950–53, Reg Halton 1953–54, Charles Robson (Hon. TM) 1954–57, George Higgins 1957–58, Andy Smailes 1959–61, Eddie Brown 1961–64, Albert Franks 1964–65, Stuart Myers 1965–66, Graham Shaw 1968–69, Colin Appleton 1969–73, Ken Houghton 1974–75, Colin Appleton 1975–81, Jimmy McAnearney 1981–82, John Cottam 1982–84, Harry Dunn 1984–86, Neil Warnock 1986–88, Colin Morris 1989, Ray McHale 1989–93, Phil Chambers 1993, Steve Wicks 1993–94, Billy Ayre 1994, Ray McHale December 1994– .

SCUNTHORPE UNITED

Managers (and Secretary-Managers)
Harry Allcock 1915–53*, Tom Crilly 1936–37, Bernard Harper 1946–48, Leslie Jones 1950–51, Bill Corkhill 1952–56, Ron Suart 1956–58, Tony McShane 1959, Bill Lambton 1959, Frank Soo 1959–60, Dick Duckworth 1960–64, Fred Goodwin 1964–66, Ron Ashman 1967–73, Ron Bradley 1973–74, Dick Rooks 1974–76, Ron Ashman 1976–81, John Duncan 1981–83, Allan Clarke 1983–84, Frank Barlow 1984–87, Mick Buxton 1987–91, Bill Green 1991–93, Richard Money 1993–94, David Moore June 1994– .

SHEFFIELD UNITED

Managers (and Secretary-Managers)
J. B. Wostinholm 1889–1899*, John Nicholson 1899–1932, Ted Davison 1932–52, Reg Freeman 1952–55, Joe Mercer 1955–58, Johnny Harris 1959–68 (continued as GM to 1970), Arthur Rowley 1968–69, Johnny Harris (GM resumed TM duties) 1969–73, Ken Furphy 1973–75, Jimmy Sirrel 1975–77, Harry Haslam 1978–81, Martin Peters 1981, Ian Porterfield 1981–86, Billy McEwan 1986–88, Dave Bassett January 1988– .

SHEFFIELD WEDNESDAY

Managers (and Secretary-Managers)
Arthur Dickinson 1891–1920*, Robert Brown 1920–33, Billy Walker 1933–37, Jimmy McMullan 1937–42, Eric Taylor 1942–58 (continued as GM to 1974), Harry Catterick 1958–61, Vic Buckingham 1961–64, Alan Brown 1964–68, Jack Marshall 1968–69, Danny Williams 1969–71, Derek Dooley 1971–73, Steve Burtenshaw 1974–75, Len Ashurst 1975–77, Jackie Charlton 1977–83, Howard Wilkinson 1983–88, Peter Eustace 1988–89, Ron Atkinson 1989–91, Trevor Francis 1991–95, David Pleat June 1995– .

SHREWSBURY TOWN

Managers (and Secretary-Managers)
W. Adams 1905–12*, A. Weston 1912–34*, Jack Roscamp 1934–35, Sam Ramsey 1935–36, Ted Bousted 1936–40, Leslie Knighton 1945–49, Harry Chapman 1949–50, Sammy Crooks 1950–54, Walter Rowley 1955–57, Harry Potts 1957–58, Johnny Spuhler 1958, Arthur Rowley 1958–68, Harry Gregg 1968–72, Maurice Evans 1972–73, Alan Durban 1974–78, Richie Barker 1978, Graham Turner 1978–84, Chic Bates 1984–87, Ian McNeill 1987–90, Asa Hartford 1990–91, John Bond 1991–93, Fred Davies February 1994 (previously caretaker-manager from May 1993)– .

SOUTHAMPTON

Managers (and Secretary-Managers)
Cecil Knight 1894–95*, Charles Robson 1895–97, E. Arnfield 1897–1911* (continued as secretary), George Swift 1911–12, E. Arnfield 1912–19, Jimmy McIntyre 1919–24, Arthur Chadwick 1925–31, George Kay 1931–36, George Gross 1936–37, Tom Parker 1937–43, J. R. Sarjantson stepped down from the board to act as secretary-manager 1943–47 with the next two listed being team managers during this period), Arthur Dominy 1943–46, Bill Dodgin Snr 1946–49, Sid Cann 1949–51, George Roughton 1952–55, Ted Bates 1955–73, Lawrie McMenemy 1973–85, Chris Nicholl 1985–91, Ian Branfoot 1991–94, Alan Ball 1994–95, Dave Merrington July 1995–.

SOUTHEND UNITED

Managers (and Secretary-Managers)
Bob Jack 1906–10, George Molyneux 1910–11, O. M. Howard 1911–12, Joe Bradshaw 1912–19, Ned Liddell 1919–20, Tom Mather 1920–21, Ted Birnie 1921–34, David Jack 1934–40, Harry Warren 1946–56, Eddie Perry 1956–60, Frank Broome 1960, Ted Fenton 1961–65, Alvan Williams 1965–67, Ernie Shepherd 1967–69, Geoff Hudson 1969–70, Arthur Rowley 1970–76, Dave Smith 1976–83, Peter Morris 1983–84, Bobby Moore 1984–86, Dave Webb 1986–87, Dick Bate 1987, Paul Clark 1987–88, Dave Webb (GM) 1988–92, Colin Murphy 1992–93, Barry Fry 1993, Peter Taylor 1993–95, Steve Thompson 1995, Ronnie Whelan July 1995– .

STOCKPORT COUNTY

Managers (and Secretary-Managers)
Fred Stewart 1894–1911, Harry Lewis 1911–14, David Ashworth 1914–19, Albert Williams 1919–24, Fred Scotchbrook 1924–26, Lincoln Hyde 1926–31, Andrew Wilson 1932–33, Fred Westgarth 1934–36, Bob Kelly 1936–38, George Hunt 1938–39, Bob Marshall 1939–49, Andy Beattie 1949–52, Dick Duckworth 1952–56, Billy Moir 1956–60, Reg Flewin 1960–63, Trevor Porteous 1963–65, Bert Trautmann (GM) 1965–66, Eddie Quigley (TM) 1965–66, Jimmy Meadows 1966–69, Wally Galbraith 1969–70, Matt Woods 1970–71, Brian Doyle 1972–74, Jimmy Meadows 1974–75, Roy Chapman 1975–76, Eddie Quigley 1976–77, Alan Thompson 1977–78, Mike Summerbee 1978–79, Jimmy McGuigan 1979–82, Eric Webster 1982–85, Colin Murphy 1985, Les Chapman 1985–86, Jimmy Melia 1986, Colin Murphy 1986–87, Asa Hartford 1987–89, Danny Bergara 1989–95, Dave Jones March 1995– .

STOKE CITY

Managers (and Secretary-Managers)
Tom Slaney 1874–83*, Walter Cox 1883–84*, Harry Lockett 1884–90, Joseph Bradshaw 1890–92, Arthur Reeves 1892–95, William Rowley 1895–97, H. D. Austerberry 1897–1908, A. J. Barker 1908–14, Peter Hodge 1914–15, Joe Schofield 1915–19, Arthur Shallcross 1919–23, John "Jock" Rutherford 1923, Tom Mather 1923–35, Bob McGrory 1935–52, Frank Taylor 1952–60, Tony Waddington 1960–77, George Eastham 1977–78, Alan A'Court 1978, Alan Durban 1978–81, Richie Barker 1981–83, Bill Asprey 1984–85, Mick Mills 1985–89, Alan Ball 1989–91, Lou Macari 1991–93, Joe Jordan 1993–94, Lou Macari September 1994– .

SUNDERLAND

Managers (and Secretary-Managers)
Tom Watson 1888–96, Bob Campbell 1896–99, Alex Mackie 1899–1905, Bob Kyle 1905–28, Johnny Cochrane 1928–39, Bill Murray 1939–57, Alan Brown 1957–64, George Hardwick 1964–65, Ian McColl 1965–68, Alan Brown 1968–72, Bob Stokoe 1972–76, Jimmy Adamson 1976–78, Ken Knighton 1979–81, Alan Durban 1981–84, Len Ashurst 1984–85, Lawrie McMenemy 1985–87, Denis Smith 1987–91, Malcolm Crosby 1992–93, Terry Butcher 1993, Mick Buxton 1993–95, Peter Reid March 1995– .

SWANSEA CITY

Managers (and Secretary-Managers)
Walter Whittaker 1912–14, William Bartlett 1914–15, Joe Bradshaw 1919–26, Jimmy Thomson 1927–31, Neil Harris 1934–39, Haydn Green 1939–47, Bill McCandless 1947–55, Ron Burgess 1955–58, Trevor Morris 1958–65, Glyn Davies 1965–66, Billy Lucas 1967–69, Roy Bentley 1969–72, Harry Gregg 1972–75, Harry Griffiths 1975–77, John Toshack 1978–83 (resigned October re-appointed in December) 1983–84, Colin Appleton 1984, John Bond 1984–85, Tommy Hutchison 1985–86, Terry Yorath 1986–89, Ian Evans 1989–90, Terry Yorath 1990–91, Frank Burrows March 1991– .

SWINDON TOWN

Managers (and Secretary-Managers)
Sam Allen 1902–33, Ted Vizard 1933–39, Neil Harris 1939–41, Louis Page 1945–53, Maurice Lindley 1953–55, Bert Head 1956–65, Danny Williams 1965–69, Fred Ford 1969–71, Dave Mackay 1971–72, Les Allen 1972–74, Danny Williams 1974–78, Bobby Smith 1978–80, John Trollope 1980–83, Ken Beamish 1983–84, Lou Macari 1984–89, Ossie Ardiles 1989–91, Glenn Hoddle 1991–93, John Gorman 1993–94, Steve McMahon November 1994– .

TORQUAY UNITED

Managers (and Secretary-Managers)
Percy Mackrill 1927–29, A. H. Hoskins 1929*, Frank Womack 1929–32, Frank Brown 1932–38, Alf Steward 1938–40, Billy Butler 1945–46, Jack Butler 1946–47, John McNeil 1947–50, Bob John 1950, Alex Massie 1950–51, Eric Webber 1951–65, Frank O'Farrell 1965–68, Alan Brown 1969–71, Jack Edwards 1971–73, Malcolm Musgrove 1973–76, Mike Green 1977–81, Frank O'Farrell 1981–82 (continued as GM to 1983), Bruch Rioch 1982–84, Dave Webb 1984–85, John Sims 1985, Stuart Morgan 1985–87, Cyril Knowles 1987–89, Dave Smith 1989–91, John Impey 1991–92, Ivan Golac 1992, Paul Compton 1992–93, Don O'Riordan March 1993– .

TOTTENHAM HOTSPUR

Managers (and Secretary-Managers)
Frank Brettell 1898–99, John Cameron 1899–1906, Fred Kirkham 1907–08, Peter McWilliam 1912–27, Billy Minter 1927–29, Percy Smith 1930–35, Jack Tresadern 1935–38, Peter McWilliam 1938–42, Arthur Turner 1942–46, Joe Hulme 1946–49, Arthur Rowe 1949–55, Jimmy Anderson 1955–58, Bill Nicholson 1958–74, Terry Neill 1974–76, Keith Burkinshaw 1976–84, Peter Shreeves 1984–86, David Pleat 1986–87, Terry Venables 1987–91, Peter Shreeves 1991–92, Ossie Ardiles 1993–94, Gerry Francis November 1994– .

TRANMERE ROVERS

Managers (and Secretary-Managers)
Bert Cooke 1912–35, Jackie Carr 1935–36, Jim Knowles 1936–39, Bill Ridding 1939–45, Ernie Blackburn 1946–55, Noel Kelly 1955–57, Peter Farrell 1957–60, Walter Galbraith 1961, Dave Russell 1961–69, Jackie Wright 1969–72, Ron Yeats 1972–75, John King 1975–80, Bryan Hamilton 1980–85, Frank Worthington 1985–87, Ronnie Moore 1987, John King April 1987– .

WALSALL

Managers (and Secretary-Managers)
H. Smallwood 1888–91*, A. G. Burton 1891–93, J. H. Robinson 1893–95, C. H. Ailso 1895–96*, A. E. Parsloe 1896–97*, L. Ford 1897–98*, G. Hughes 1898–99*, L. Ford 1899–1901*, J. E. Shutt 1908–13*, Haydn Price 1914–20, Joe Burchell 1920–26, David Ashworth 1926–27, Jack Torrance 1927–28, James Kerr 1928–29, S. Scholey 1929–30, Peter O'Rourke 1930–32, G. W. Slade 1932–34, Andy Wilson 1934–37, Tommy Lowes 1937–44, Harry Hibbs 1944–51, Tony McPhee 1951, Brough Fletcher 1952–53, Major Frank Buckley 1953–55, John Love 1955–57, Billy Moore 1957–64, Alf Wood 1964, Reg Shaw 1964–68, Dick Graham 1968, Ron Lewin 1968–69, Billy Moore 1969–72, John Smith 1972–73, Doug Fraser 1973–77, Dave Mackay 1977–78, Alan Ashman 1978, Frank Sibley 1979, Alan Buckley 1979–86, Neil Martin (joint manager with Buckley) 1981–82, Tommy Coakley 1986–88, John Barnwell 1989–90, Kenny Hibbitt 1990–94, Chris Nicholl September 1994– .

WATFORD

Managers (and Secretary-Managers)
John Goodall 1903–10, Harry Kent 1910–26, Fred Pagnam 1926–29, Neil McBain 1929–37, Bill Findlay 1938–47, Jack Bray 1947–48, Eddie Hapgood 1948–50, Ron Gray 1950–51, Haydn Green 1951–52, Len Goulden 1952–55 (GM to 1956), Johnny Paton 1955–56, Neil McBain 1956–59, Ron Burgess 1959–63, Bill McGarry 1963–64, Ken Furphy 1964–71, George Kirby 1971–73, Mike Keen 1973–77, Graham Taylor 1977–87, Dave Bassett 1987–88, Steve Harrison 1988–90, Colin Lee 1990, Steve Perryman 1990–93, Glenn Roeder July 1993– .

WEST BROMWICH ALBION

Managers (and Secretary-Managers)
Louis Ford 1890–92*, Henry Jackson 1892–94*, Edward Stephenson 1894–95*, Clement Keys 1895–96*, Frank Heaven 1896–1902*, Fred Everiss 1902–48, Jack Smith 1948–52, Jesse Carver 1952, Vic Buckingham 1953–59, Gordon Clark 1959–61, Archie Macaulay 1961–63, Jimmy Hagan 1963–67, Alan Ashman 1967–71, Don Howe 1971–75, Johnny Giles 1975–77, Ronnie Allen 1977, Ron Atkinson 1978–81, Ronnie Allen 1981–82, Ron Wylie 1982–84, Johnny Giles 1984–85, Ron Saunders 1986–87, Ron Atkinson 1987–88, Brian Talbot 1988–91, Bobby Gould 1991–92, Ossie Ardiles 1992–93, Keith Burkinshaw 1993–94, Alan Buckley October 1994– .

WEST HAM UNITED

Managers (and Secretary-Managers)
Syd King 1902–32, Charlie Paynter 1932–50, Ted Fenton 1950–61, Ron Greenwood 1961–74 (continued as GM to 1977), John Lyall 1974–89, Lou Macari 1989–90, Billy Bonds 1990–94, Harry Redknapp August 1994– .

WIGAN ATHLETIC

Managers (and Secretary-Managers)
Charlie Spencer 1932–37, Jimmy Milne 1946–47, Bob Pryde 1949–52, Ted Goodier 1952–54, Walter Crook 1954–55, Ron Suart 1955–56, Billy Cooke 1956, Sam Barkas 1957, Trevor Hitchen 1957–58, Malcolm Barrass 1958–59, Jimmy Shirley 1959, Pat Murphy 1959–60, Allenby Chilton 1960, Johnny Ball 1961–63, Allan Brown 1963–66, Alf Craig 1966–67, Harry Leyland 1967–68, Alan Saunders 1968, Ian McNeill 1968–70, Gordon Milne 1970–72, Les Rigby 1972–74, Brian Tiler 1974–76, Ian McNeill 1976–81, Larry Lloyd 1981–83, Harry McNally 1983–85, Bryan Hamilton 1985–86, Ray Mathias 1986–89, Bryan Hamilton 1989–93, Dave Philpotts 1993, Kenny Swain 1993–94, Graham Barrow September 1994– .

WIMBLEDON

Managers (and Secretary-Managers)
Les Henley 1955–71, Mike Everitt 1971–73, Dick Graham 1973–74, Allen Batsford 1974–78, Dario Gradi 1978–81, Dave Bassett 1981–87, Bobby Gould 1987–90, Ray Harford 1990–91, Peter Withe 1991, Joe Kinnear January 1992– .

WOLVERHAMPTON WANDERERS

Managers (and Secretary-Managers)
George Worrall 1877–85*, John Addenbrooke 1885–1922, George Jobey 1922–24, Albert Hoskins 1924–26 (had been secretary since 1922), Fred Scotchbrook 1926–27, Major Frank Buckley 1927–44, Ted Vizard 1944–48, Stan Cullis 1948–64, Andy Beattie 1964–65, Ronnie Allen 1966–68, Bill McGarry 1968–76, Sammy Chung 1976–78, John Barnwell 1978–81, Ian Greaves 1982, Graham Hawkins 1982–84, Tommy Docherty 1984–85, Bill McGarry 1985, Sammy Chapman 1985–86, Brian Little 1986, Graham Turner 1986–94, Graham Taylor March 1994– .

WREXHAM

Managers (and Secretary-Managers)
Ted Robinson 1912–25* (continued as secretary to 1930), Charlie Hewitt 1925–29, Jack Baynes 1929–31, Ernest Blackburn 1932–36, Jimmy Logan 1937–38, Arthur Cowell 1938, Tom Morgan 1938–40, Tom Williams 1940–49, Les McDowall 1949–50, Peter Jackson 1951–54, Cliff Lloyd 1954–57, John Love 1957–59, Billy Morris 1960–61, Ken Barnes 1961–65, Billy Morris 1965, Jack Rowley 1966–67, Alvan Williams 1967–68, John Neal 1968–77, Arfon Griffiths 1977–81, Mel Sutton 1981–82, Bobby Roberts 1982–85, Dixie McNeil 1985–89, Brian Flynn November 1989– .

WYCOMBE WANDERERS

Managers (and Secretary-Managers)
First coach appointed 1951. Prior to Brian Lee's appointment in 1969, the team was selected by a Match Committee which met every Monday evening. James McCormack 1951–52, Sid Cann 1952–61, Graham Adams 1961–62, Don Welsh 1962–64, Barry Darvill 1964–68, Brian Lee 1969–76, Ted Powell 1976–77, John Reardon 1977–78, Andy Williams 1978–80, Mike Keen 1980–84, Paul Bence 1984–86, Alan Gane 1986–87, Peter Suddaby 1987–88, Jim Kelman 1988–90, Martin O'Neill 1990–95, Alan Smith June 1995– .

YORK CITY

Managers (and Secretary-Managers)
Bill Sherrington 1924–60 (was secretary for most of this time but virtually secretary-manager for a long pre-war spell), John Collier 1929–36, Tom Mitchell 1936–50, Dick Duckworth 1950–52, Charlie Spencer 1952–53, Jimmy McCormick 1953–54, Sam Bartram 1956–60, Tom Lockie 1960–67, Joe Shaw 1967–68, Tom Johnston 1968–75, Wilf McGuinness 1975–77, Charlie Wright 1977–80, Barry Lyons 1980–81, Denis Smith 1982–87, Bobby Saxton 1987–88, John Bird 1988–91, John Ward 1991–93, Alan Little March 1993– .

The things they said. . .

FIFA spokesman Guido Tognoni:
"*FIFA encourage players to drink, but they can't do it in the middle of the field.*"

Spurs chairman Alan Sugar, after the FA announced their swingeing punishments:
"*How tempting it will be for other club chairmen or chief executives to say that honesty is not, necessarily, the best policy.*"

Ireland manager Jack Charlton, commenting on Italy, their first World Cup opponents:
"*I've seen them on television on a Sunday morning most days of the week.*"

Spurs chairman Alan Sugar, after arranging the £2.6m transfer of Romanian star Ilie Dumitrescu while manager Ossie Ardiles was away:
"*I don't remember him from the World Cup, but I'm sure he impressed me and will do a great job at Spurs.*"

Spurs new signing Jürgen Klinsmann, pre-empting his reputation at his first press conference on arrival at Tottenham:
"*Is there a diving school in London?*"

Man Utd manager Alex Ferguson on his wayward star Eric Cantona, who got himself sent off against Rangers in the wooden-spoon match of the pre-season Ibrox international tournament:
"*When he feels he has been done an injustice, he's got to prove to the world that he's going to correct it. But he can't control his temper. Love him or hate him, we have to live with it.*"

Eric Cantona, suspended for the start of the Premiership season:
"*It's in my nature to react the way I do. It's an instinct, and to hell with people who are not happy about it.*"

Initial reactions to the trial kick-in law in the Diadora League:
"*Because there's no offside, the opposition can just crowd the 6-yard box and you can't push up. . . If the rule continues, everyone will have a team of giraffes and no midfield.*"

Slough Town manager Graham Roberts:
"*It's an absolute farce, a joke. It will take all the enjoyment out of football and ensure long-ball teams win everything. You need three huge defenders and a 7-ft goalkeeper.*"

PFA chief Gordon Taylor, warning about cheap foreign imports:
"*I think we should bear in mind what happened to English cricket. Not enough attention was given to our own talent. I'm worried that fees like Sutton's [£5m] are forcing clubs to look abroad.*"

Newcastle chairman Sir John Hall, on Gordon Taylor's outburst:
"*The man is an inward-looking islander, and it's his sort of attitude that has led to English football now being in the backwaters.*"

Man Utd chairman Martin Edwards, on the same subject:
"*The more transfer fees and players' wages rise here, the more our clubs are going to look abroad.*"

Wendy Toms, the Football League's first female linesman, on being asked how she found the crowd at Torquay after her first match:
"*No problem at all—abusive as usual.*"

Wimbledon manager Joe Kinnear, bemoaning the new law changes:
"*If football is simply going to be about going forward, then they'll ruin the game.*"

Leicester PRO Alan Birchenall, over the PA system at half-time in the match against Coventry, of the referee Keith Cooper who had sent off a player from each side:
"*The first lad deserved a yellow card and, as for the second, well, I've seen it on the box. It's a bloody joke. We'll end up with four players on each side. It's about contact, for Christ's sake.*"

Sacked Aston Villa manager Ron Atkinson, on remarks made by Tommy Docherty criticising his record:
"*All I do know is that I'll never be able to achieve what Tommy did, and that is take Aston Villa into the Third Division, and better than that, take Manchester United into the Second Division.*"

Opposition leader Tony Blair, speaking at the Scottish Press Fund lunch:
"*Walter Smith [Rangers manager] has done more than the Tory backbenchers to keep Britain out of Europe.*"

FIFA spokesman Guido Tognoni, in an open letter to new Bayern Munich chairman Franz Beckenbauer:
"*Go back to the golf course, breed horses, sail around the world, book a trip to the moon, but leave the rule book of our sport to us.*"

Steve McMahon, after being appointed Swindon player-manager:
"*No more nicey-nicey stuff. . . I don't mind if we pick up a few yellow cards. . . . I'm looking for a team which fights.*" [McMahon picks up two yellow cards himself in his first match, and is sent off.]

Forest manager Frank Clark, after Man Utd boss Alec Ferguson accused Forest of time wasting and fouling following their 2-1 victory over the champions:
"*You get the feeling you are supposed to go to Old Trafford and let them walk all over you.*"

Sheff Utd manager Dave Bassett on Charlie Hartfield's dismissal in the FA Cup against Man Utd:
"*It didn't matter whether Eric Cantona or Mickey Mouse kicked him, he should not have reacted. It cost us the game and will cost him three matches, a week's money and maybe his place in the team. He will look back on that mad moment for the rest of his life.*"

Teenage striker John Hartson, on signing for Arsenal:
"*People think I'm like Alan Smith, but I like the ball played on the floor and Arsenal play that way.*"

Arsenal manager George Graham, hastily intervening:
"*A lot of people, especially those in the media, would disagree.*"

Merthyr chairman John Reddy on the imminent departure of Welsh FA chief executive Alun Evans:
"*Now there could be a six-figure bill over an official who would have cost nothing had he got the sack he deserved. Yes, it's still pantomime time in Wales. . . .*"

Spurs manager Gerry Francis in a radio interview after they came from behind to win at West Ham:
"*What I said to them at half-time would be unprintable on the radio.*"

Beleaguered manager George Graham:
"*I know I have the backing of the Arsenal board.*"

Man Utd manager Alec Ferguson's first reactions to the Eric Cantona affair:
"*I'm devastated. This is a nightmare of the worst kind.*"

A member of the Man Utd Megastore staff the day after Cantona's assault at Selhurst Park, after the player came in to buy a replica United shirt for his 7-year-old son:
"*It was just the normal Eric. He was cool as a cucumber—you would have thought nothing had happened. He walked round as if he did not have a care in the world.*"

Everton chairman Peter Johnson, after referee David Ellery sends two of their players off and books another five at Newcastle:
"*I'm sorry to have to say it, but we do now have a major refereeing problem in this country. I don't believe I'm alone in thinking this way—it's just that many people within the game are scared to speak out and voice an opinion. No one in their right mind is going to hand over hard-earned cash to watch 11 men play against nine men, as happened on Wednesday. This is a physical sport, a man's game.*"

Selhurst Park safety officer George Crawford, quoting a saying of his trade:
"*You can take the supporter out of the terrace, but you can't take the terraces out of the supporter.*"

David Mellor, MP, speaking on BBC 2's *West-minster On-Line*, about the police approach at the Bruges-Chelsea Cup-Winners Cup tie:
"*I think this is what happens when we invite relatively ramshackle countries like Belgium to take part in European competition with a silly little football ground that wasn't really fit. It was an 18,000 maximum for the stadium, with a pitch that Farmer Brown wouldn't let his cows loose on, and mounted police behaved quite outrageously towards perfectly respectable supporters.*"

Wimbledon manager Joe Kinnear's view of Robbie Hart, who refereed their game with Man Utd:
"*He ordered me off the pitch in his normal Hitler fashion. He was a dreadful referee and I know I've got myself into trouble again. He was up for it all night and also threatened to send off [club owner] Sam Hammam. . . . With these refs it depends on what shirt you're wearing.*"

Pseudo philosopher Eric Cantona, at a press conference after his jail sentence was commuted to community service:
"*When seagulls follow the trawler, it is because they think that sardines will be thrown into the sea.*"

The half-time announcement—referring to the dismissal of player-manager Steve McMahon—at the Swindon v Bolton League match that earned PA announcer Pete Lewis the sack:
"*I've seen some crap refereeing decisions, but that's the worst.*"

Gordon Strachan, speaking at the PFA awards:
"*If a Frenchman goes on about seagulls, sardines and trawlers, he's called a philosopher. I'd just be called a short Scottish bum talking crap.*"

Man Utd manager Alex Ferguson, after Eric Cantona decides to stay at the club:
"*I don't think any player in the history of football will get the sentence he got unless they had killed Bert Millichip's dog. . . . When someone is doing well we have to knock him down. We don't do it with horses. Red Rum is more loved than anyone I know. . . . But he must have lost one race.*"

Former Leeds star John Giles, writing in the *Daily Express*:
"*I will always be proud of being part of a Leeds team that was as good as any post-war British club team. But as the years have rolled by, and after talking with Don Revie shortly before his death, I have come to a painful conclusion. It is that at Leeds we got it wrong, as Alex Ferguson is in danger of getting it wrong. . . . We didn't look beyond the business of winning. We didn't grasp that for all our achievements we would always be remembered as a negative influence on football. . . . Ferguson has done wonderfully well in playing terms. . . . But he must still accept that, at some future time, unless the trend is reversed, he will be remembered for giving English football the anarchy of Cantona, Keane and Ince.*"

Graham Souness, rejecting claims in a libel case he brought against a newspaper that he sought to dominate his ex-wife Danielle:
"*A Bengal tiger could not do that.*"

END OF SEASON PLAY-OFFS 1994–95

Semi-finals, First Leg

14 MAY

DIVISION 1

Tranmere R (1) 1 *(Malkin)*

Reading (1) 3 *(Lovell 2, Nogan)* 12,207

Tranmere R: Nixon; Stevens, Thomas (Brannan), McGreal, Garnett, O'Brien, Morrissey, Aldridge, Malkin, Irons, Nevin.

Reading: Hislop; Bernal, Osborn, Wdowczyk, Williams, McPherson, Gilkes, Gooding, Nogan, Lovell, Taylor.

Wolverhampton W (1) 2 *(Bull, Venus)*

Bolton W (0) 1 *(McAteer)* 26,153

Wolverhampton W: Stowell; Thompson, Venus, Rankine, Richards, Shirtliff, Goodman, Kelly D, Bull, Cowans, Dennison.

Bolton W: Shilton; Green, Phillips, McAteer, Bergsson, Stubbs, Dreyer, McDonald, Paatelainen, McGinlay (Coyle), Thompson.

DIVISION 2

Bristol R (0) 0

Crewe Alex (0) 0 8538

Bristol R: Parkin; Pritchard, Gurney, Stewart (Channing), Clark, Tillson, Sterling, Miller, Taylor, Skinner, Archer.

Crewe Alex: Gayle; Booty, Smith S (Wilson), Barr, Macauley, Whalley, Tierney, Collins, Adebola (Clarkson), Lennon, Murphy.

Huddersfield T (1) 1 *(Billy)*

Brentford (1) 1 *(Forster)* 14,160

Huddersfield T: Francis; Trevitt, Cowan, Bullock, Scully, Sinnott, Billy, Duxbury, Booth, Jepson, Crosby (Dunn).

Brentford: Dearden; Statham (Hutchings), Grainger, Bates, Ashby, Smith, Ratcliffe, Mundee, Taylor, Forster, Stephenson.

DIVISION 3

Mansfield T (0) 1 *(Hadley)*

Chesterfield (0) 1 *(Robinson)* 6582

Mansfield T: Ward; Boothroyd, Baraclough, Holland, Howarth, Peters, Ireland, Parkin, Wilkinson, Onuora (Lampkin), Hadley.

Chesterfield: Beasley; Hewitt, Rogers, Curtis, Carr, Law, Robinson, Davies (Howard), Lormor, Moss, Perkins.

Preston NE (0) 0

Bury (1) 1 *(Pugh)* 13,297

Preston NE: Vaughan; Fensome, Fleming, Raynor (Cartwright), Kidd, Moyes, Davey, Bryson, Lancashire, Sale (Conroy), Magee.

Bury: Kelly G; Woodward, Bimson (Hughes), Dawes, Jackson, Lucketti, Kelly T, Carter (Paskin), Stant, Rigby, Pugh.

Semi-finals, Second Leg

17 MAY

DIVISION 1

Bolton W (0) 2 *(McGinlay 2)*

Wolverhampton W (0) 0 *aet* 20,041

Bolton W: Branagan; Green, Phillips, McAteer, Bergsson, Stubbs (Dreyer), Lee (De Freitas), Coyle, Paatelainen, McGinlay, Thompson.

Wolverhampton W: Stowell; Thompson, Venus, Rankine, Richards, Shirtliff, Goodman, Kelly D, Bull, Cowans, Dennison (Wright).

Reading (0) 0

Tranmere R (0) 0 13,245

Reading: Hislop; Bernal, Osborn, Wdowczyk, Williams (Hopkins), McPherson, Gilkes, Gooding, Nogan, Lovell (Quinn), Taylor.

Tranmere R: Coyne; Stevens, Thomas, McGreal, Mungall, Brannan, Morrissey, Aldridge, Malkin (Jones), Irons, Nevin (O'Brien).

Mixu Paatelainen (second left) heads Bolton's third goal past Reading goalkeeper Shaka Hislop. (Colorsport)

Chris Billy dives to head the ball in for Huddersfield Town's final win over Bristol Rovers at 2-1. (Colorsport)

DIVISION 2

Brentford (1) 1 *(Grainger (pen))*
Huddersfield T (1) 1 *(Booth)* 11,161

Brentford: Dearden; Statham, Grainger, Bates, Ashby, Smith, Stephenson, Ratcliffe, Taylor, Forster, Abrahams (Mundee).
Huddersfield T: Francis; Trevitt, Cowan, Bullock, Scully, Sinnott, Billy, Duxbury, Booth, Jepson, Crosby (Dunn).
aet; Huddersfield T won 4-3 on penalties.

Crewe Alex (0) 1 *(Rowbotham)*
Bristol R (0) 1 *(Miller)* 6578

Crewe Alex: Gayle; Booty, Wilson, Barr, Macauley, Whalley, Tierney, Collins (Edwards), Adebola (Rowbotham), Lennon, Murphy.
Bristol R: Parkin; Pritchard, Gurney, Stewart, Clark, Tillson, Sterling, Miller, Taylor, Skinner (Browning), Channing (Archer).
aet; Bristol R won on away goals.

DIVISION 3

Bury (0) 1 *(Rigby)*
Preston NE (0) 0 9094

Bury: Kelly G; Woodward, Stanislaus, Dawes, Lucketti, Jackson, Kelly T, Carter (Paskin), Stant, Rigby, Pugh.
Preston NE: Vaughan; Fensome (Ainsworth), Fleming, Raynor, Kidd, Moyes, Davey, Bryson, Smart, Sale (Conroy), Cartwright.

Chesterfield (1) 5 *(Lormor, Robinson, Law 2 (1 pen), Howard)*
Mansfield T (2) 2 *(Holland, Wilkinson) aet* 8165

Chesterfield: Beasley (Stewart); Hewitt, Rogers, Curtis, Carr, Law, Robinson, Hazel (Perkins), Lormor, Morris, Howard.
Mansfield T: Ward; Boothroyd (Doolan), Baraclough, Holland, Howarth, Peters, Ireland, Parkin, Wilkinson, Hadley (Sherlock), Lampkin.

Finals (at Wembley)

27 MAY
DIVISION 3

Bury (0) 0
Chesterfield (2) 2 *(Lormor, Robinson)* 22,814

Bury: Kelly G; Woodward, Stanislaus, Daws, Lucketti, Jackson, Mulligan (Hughes), Carter (Paskin), Stant, Rigby, Pugh.
Chesterfield: Stewart; Hewitt, Rogers, Curtis, Carr, Law, Robinson, Hazel, Lormor (Davies), Morris, Howard (Perkins).

28 MAY
DIVISION 2

Bristol R (1) 1 *(Stewart)*
Huddersfield T (1) 2 *(Booth, Billy)* 59,175

Bristol R: Parkin; Pritchard, Gurney, Stewart, Clark, Tillson, Sterling, Miller, Taylor (Browning), Skinner, Channing (Archer).
Huddersfield T: Francis; Trevitt (Dyson), Cowan, Bullock, Scully, Sinnott, Billy, Duxbury, Booth, Jepson, Crosby (Dunn).

29 MAY
DIVISION 1

Bolton W (0) 4 *(Coyle, De Freitas 2, Paatelainen)*
Reading (2) 3 *(Nogan, Williams, Quinn) aet* 64,107

Bolton W: Branagan; Green, Phillips, McAteer, Bergsson, Stubbs, McDonald (De Freitas), Coyle, Paatelainen, McGinlay, Thompson.
Reading: Hislop; Bernal (Hopkins), Osborn, Wdowczyk, Williams, McPherson, Gilkes, Goodwin, Nogan (Quinn), Lovell, Taylor.

F.A. Carling Premiership

			Home			Goals		Away			Goals			
		P	W	D	L	F	A	W	D	L	F	A	Pts	GD
1	Blackburn R	42	17	2	2	54	21	10	6	5	26	18	89	+41
2	Manchester U	42	16	4	1	42	4	10	6	5	35	24	88	+49
3	Nottingham F	42	12	6	3	36	18	10	5	6	36	25	77	+29
4	Liverpool	42	13	5	3	38	13	8	6	7	27	24	74	+28
5	Leeds U	42	13	5	3	35	15	7	8	6	24	23	73	+21
6	Newcastle U	42	14	6	1	46	20	6	6	9	21	27	72	+20
7	Tottenham H	42	10	5	6	32	25	6	9	6	34	33	62	+8
8	QPR	42	11	3	7	36	26	6	6	9	25	33	60	+2
9	Wimbledon	42	9	5	7	26	26	6	6	9	22	39	56	-17
10	Southampton	42	8	9	4	33	27	4	9	8	28	36	54	-2
11	Chelsea	42	7	7	7	25	22	6	8	7	25	33	54	-5
12	Arsenal	42	6	9	6	27	21	7	3	11	25	28	51	+3
13	Sheffield W	42	7	7	7	26	26	6	5	10	23	31	51	-8
14	West Ham U	42	9	6	6	28	19	4	5	12	16	29	50	-4
15	Everton	42	8	9	4	31	23	3	8	10	13	28	50	-7
16	Coventry C	42	7	7	7	23	25	5	7	9	21	37	50	-18
17	Manchester C	42	8	7	6	37	28	4	6	11	16	36	49	-11
18	Aston Villa	42	6	9	6	27	24	5	6	10	24	32	48	-5
19	Crystal Palace	42	6	6	9	16	23	5	6	10	18	26	45	-15
20	Norwich C	42	8	8	5	27	21	2	5	14	10	33	43	-17
21	Leicester C	42	5	6	10	28	37	1	5	15	17	43	29	-35
22	Ipswich T	42	5	3	13	24	34	2	3	16	12	59	27	-57

Endsleigh Insurance League Division 1

			Home			Goals		Away			Goals			
		P	W	D	L	F	A	W	D	L	F	A	Pts	GD
1	Middlesbrough	46	15	4	4	41	19	8	9	6	26	21	82	+27
2	Reading	46	12	7	4	34	21	11	3	9	24	23	79	+14
3	Bolton W	46	16	6	1	43	13	5	8	10	24	32	77	+22
4	Wolverhampton W	46	15	5	3	39	18	6	8	9	38	43	76	+16
5	Tranmere R	46	17	4	2	51	23	5	6	12	16	35	76	+9
6	Barnsley	46	15	6	2	42	19	5	6	12	21	33	72	+11
7	Watford	46	14	6	3	33	17	5	7	11	19	29	70	+6
8	Sheffield U	46	12	9	2	41	21	5	8	10	33	34	68	+19
9	Derby Co	46	12	6	5	44	23	6	6	11	22	28	66	+15
10	Grimsby T	46	12	7	4	36	19	5	7	11	26	37	65	+6
11	Stoke C	46	10	7	6	31	21	6	8	9	19	32	63	-3
12	Millwall	46	11	8	4	36	22	5	6	12	24	38	62	+0
13	Southend U	46	13	2	8	33	25	5	6	12	21	48	62	-19
14	Oldham Ath	46	12	7	4	34	21	4	6	13	26	39	61	+0
15	Charlton Ath	46	11	6	6	33	25	5	5	13	25	41	59	-8
16	Luton T	46	8	6	9	35	30	7	7	9	26	34	58	-3
17	Port Vale	46	11	5	7	30	24	4	8	11	28	40	58	-6
18	Portsmouth	46	9	8	6	31	28	6	5	12	22	35	58	-10
19	WBA	46	13	3	7	33	24	3	7	13	18	33	58	-6
20	Sunderland	46	5	12	6	22	22	7	6	10	19	23	54	-4
21	Swindon T	46	9	6	8	28	27	3	6	14	26	46	48	-19
22	Burnley	46	8	7	8	36	33	3	6	14	13	41	46	-25
23	Bristol C	46	8	8	7	26	28	3	4	16	16	35	45	-21
24	Notts Co	46	7	8	8	26	28	2	5	16	19	38	40	-21

Endsleigh Insurance League Division 2

			Home			Goals		Away			Goals			
		P	W	D	L	F	A	W	D	L	F	A	Pts	GD
1	Birmingham C	46	15	6	2	53	18	10	8	5	31	19	89	+47
2	Brentford	46	14	4	5	44	15	11	6	6	37	24	85	+42
3	Crewe Alex	46	14	3	6	46	33	11	5	7	34	35	83	+12
4	Bristol R	46	15	7	1	48	20	7	9	7	22	20	82	+30
5	Huddersfield T	46	14	5	4	45	21	8	10	5	34	28	81	+30
6	Wycombe W	46	13	7	3	36	19	8	8	7	24	27	78	+14
7	Oxford U	46	13	6	4	30	18	8	6	9	36	34	75	+14
8	Hull C	46	13	6	4	40	18	8	5	10	30	39	74	+13
9	York C	46	13	4	6	37	21	8	5	10	30	30	72	+16
10	Swansea C	46	10	8	5	23	13	9	6	8	34	32	71	+12
11	Stockport Co	46	12	3	8	40	29	7	5	11	23	31	65	+3
12	Blackpool	46	11	4	8	40	36	7	6	10	24	34	64	-6
13	Wrexham	46	10	7	6	38	27	6	8	9	27	37	63	+1
14	Bradford C	46	8	6	9	29	32	8	6	9	28	32	60	-7
15	Peterborough U	46	7	11	5	26	29	7	7	9	28	40	60	-15
16	Brighton & H A	46	9	10	4	25	15	5	7	11	29	38	59	+1
17	Rotherham U	46	12	6	5	36	26	2	8	13	21	35	56	-4
18	Shrewsbury T	46	9	9	5	34	27	4	5	14	20	35	53	-8
19	AFC Bournemouth	46	9	4	10	30	34	4	7	12	19	35	50	-20
20	Cambridge U	46	8	9	6	33	28	3	6	14	19	41	48	-17
21	Plymouth Arg	46	7	6	10	22	36	5	4	14	23	47	46	-38
22	Cardiff C	46	5	6	12	25	31	4	5	14	21	43	38	-28
23	Chester C	46	5	6	12	23	42	1	5	17	14	42	29	-47
24	Leyton Orient	46	6	6	11	21	29	0	2	21	9	46	26	-45

Endsleigh Insurance League Division 3

			Home			Goals		Away			Goals			
		P	W	D	L	F	A	W	D	L	F	A	Pts	GD
1	Carlisle U	42	14	5	2	34	14	13	5	3	33	17	91	+36
2	Walsall	42	15	3	3	42	18	9	8	4	33	22	83	+35
3	Chesterfield	42	11	7	3	26	10	12	5	4	36	27	81	+25
4	Bury	42	13	7	1	39	13	10	4	7	34	23	80	+37
5	Preston NE	42	13	3	5	37	17	6	7	8	21	24	67	+17
6	Mansfield T	42	10	5	6	45	27	8	6	7	39	32	65	+25
7	Scunthorpe U	42	12	2	7	40	30	6	6	9	28	33	62	+5
8	Fulham	42	11	5	5	39	22	5	9	7	21	32	62	+6
9	Doncaster R	42	9	5	7	28	20	8	5	8	30	23	61	+15
10	Colchester U	42	8	5	8	29	30	8	5	8	27	34	58	-8
11	Barnet	42	8	7	6	37	27	7	4	10	19	36	56	-7
12	Lincoln C	42	10	7	4	34	22	5	4	12	20	33	56	-1
13	Torquay U	42	10	8	3	35	25	4	5	12	19	32	55	-3
14	Wigan Ath	42	7	6	8	28	30	7	4	10	25	30	52	-7
15	Rochdale	42	8	6	7	25	23	4	8	9	19	44	50	-23
16	Hereford U	42	9	6	6	22	19	3	7	11	23	43	49	-17
17	Northampton T	42	8	5	8	25	29	2	9	10	20	38	44	-22
18	Hartlepool U	42	9	5	7	33	32	2	5	14	10	37	43	-26
19	Gillingham	42	8	7	6	31	25	2	4	15	15	39	41	-18
20	Darlington	42	7	5	9	25	24	4	3	14	18	33	41	-14
21	Scarborough	42	4	7	10	26	31	4	3	14	23	39	34	-21
22	Exeter C	42	5	5	11	25	36	3	5	13	11	34	34	-34

In the Endsleigh Insurance League, goals scored determine League positions where clubs are level on points. If teams still cannot be separated, the team that has conceded fewer goals is placed higher.

FOOTBALL LEAGUE 1888–89 to 1994–95

FA PREMIER LEAGUE

Maximum points: 126

	First	*Pts*	*Second*	*Pts*	*Third*	*Pts*
1992–93	Manchester U	84	Aston Villa	74	Norwich C	72
1993–94	Manchester U	92	Blackburn R	84	Newcastle U	77
1994–95	Blackburn R	89	Manchester U	88	Nottingham F	77

FIRST DIVISION

Maximum points: 138

1992–93	Newcastle U	96	West Ham U	88	Portsmouth††	88
1993–94	Crystal Palace	90	Nottingham F	83	Millwall††	74
1994–95	Middlesbrough	82	Reading††	79	Bolton W	77

SECOND DIVISION

Maximum points: 138

1992–93	Stoke C	93	Bolton W	90	Port Vale††	89
1993–94	Reading	89	Port Vale	88	Plymouth Arg*††	85
1994–95	Birmingham C	89	Brentford††	85	Crewe Alex††	83

THIRD DIVISION

Maximum points: 126

1992–93	Cardiff C	83	Wrexham	80	Barnet	79
1993–94	Shrewsbury T	79	Chester C	74	Crewe Alex	73
1994–95	Carlisle U	91	Walsall	83	Chesterfield	81

††*Not promoted after play-offs.*

FOOTBALL LEAGUE

	First	*Pts*	*Second*	*Pts*	*Third*	*Pts*
1888–89*a*	Preston NE	40	Aston Villa	29	Wolverhampton W	28
1889–90*a*	Preston NE	33	Everton	31	Blackburn R	27
1890–91*a*	Everton	29	Preston NE	27	Notts Co	26
1891–92*b*	Sunderland	42	Preston NE	37	Bolton W	36

FIRST DIVISION to 1991–92

Maximum points: a 44; *b* 52; *c* 60; *d* 68; *e* 76; *f* 84; *g* 126; *h* 120; *k* 114.

1892–93*c*	Sunderland	48	Preston NE	37	Everton	36
1893–94*c*	Aston Villa	44	Sunderland	38	Derby Co	36
1894–95*c*	Sunderland	47	Everton	42	Aston Villa	39
1895–96*c*	Aston Villa	45	Derby Co	41	Everton	39
1896–97*c*	Aston Villa	47	Sheffield U*	36	Derby Co	36
1897–98*c*	Sheffield U	42	Sunderland	37	Wolverhampton W*	35
1898–99*d*	Aston Villa	45	Liverpool	43	Burnley	39
1899–1900*d*	Aston Villa	50	Sheffield U	48	Sunderland	41
1900–01*d*	Liverpool	45	Sunderland	43	Notts Co	40
1901–02*d*	Sunderland	44	Everton	41	Newcastle U	37
1902–03*d*	The Wednesday	42	Aston Villa*	41	Sunderland	41
1903–04*d*	The Wednesday	47	Manchester C	44	Everton	43
1904–05*d*	Newcastle U	48	Everton	47	Manchester C	46
1905–06*e*	Liverpool	51	Preston NE	47	The Wednesday	44
1906–07*e*	Newcastle U	51	Bristol C	48	Everton*	45
1907–08*e*	Manchester U	52	Aston Villa*	43	Manchester C	43
1908–09*e*	Newcastle U	53	Everton	46	Sunderland	44
1909–10*e*	Aston Villa	53	Liverpool	48	Blackburn R*	45
1910–11*e*	Manchester U	52	Aston Villa	51	Sunderland*	45
1911–12*e*	Blackburn R	49	Everton	46	Newcastle U	44
1912–13*e*	Sunderland	54	Aston Villa	50	Sheffield W	49
1913–14*e*	Blackburn R	51	Aston Villa	44	Middlesbrough*	43
1914–15*e*	Everton	46	Oldham Ath	45	Blackburn R*	43
1919–20*f*	WBA	60	Burnley	51	Chelsea	49
1920–21*f*	Burnley	59	Manchester C	54	Bolton W	52
1921–22*f*	Liverpool	57	Tottenham H	51	Burnley	49
1922–23*f*	Liverpool	60	Sunderland	54	Huddersfield T	53
1923–24*f*	Huddersfield T*	57	Cardiff C	57	Sunderland	53
1924–25*f*	Huddersfield T	58	WBA	56	Bolton W	55
1925–26*f*	Huddersfield T	57	Arsenal	52	Sunderland	48
1926–27*f*	Newcastle U	56	Huddersfield T	51	Sunderland	49
1927–28*f*	Everton	53	Huddersfield T	51	Leicester C	48
1928–29*f*	Sheffield W	52	Leicester C	51	Aston Villa	50
1929–30*f*	Sheffield W	60	Derby Co	50	Manchester C*	47
1930–31*f*	Arsenal	66	Aston Villa	59	Sheffield W	52
1931–32*f*	Everton	56	Arsenal	54	Sheffield W	50
1932–33*f*	Arsenal	58	Aston Villa	54	Sheffield W	51
1933–34*f*	Arsenal	59	Huddersfield T	56	Tottenham H	49
1934–35*f*	Arsenal	58	Sunderland	54	Sheffield W	49
1935–36*f*	Sunderland	56	Derby Co*	48	Huddersfield T	48
1936–37*f*	Manchester C	57	Charlton Ath	54	Arsenal	52
1937–38*f*	Arsenal	52	Wolverhampton W	51	Preston NE	49

**Won or placed on goal average, goal difference or most goals scored.*

	First	Pts	Second	Pts	Third	Pts
1938–39*f*	Everton	59	Wolverhampton W	55	Charlton Ath	50
1946–47*f*	Liverpool	57	Manchester U*	56	Wolverhampton W	56
1947–48*f*	Arsenal	59	Manchester U*	52	Burnley	52
1948–49*f*	Portsmouth	58	Manchester U*	53	Derby Co	53
1949–50*f*	Portsmouth*	53	Wolverhampton W	53	Sunderland	52
1950–51*f*	Tottenham H	60	Manchester U	56	Blackpool	50
1951–52*f*	Manchester U	57	Tottenham H*	53	Arsenal	53
1952–53*f*	Arsenal*	54	Preston NE	54	Wolverhampton W	51
1953–54*f*	Wolverhampton W	57	WBA	53	Huddersfield T	51
1954–55*f*	Chelsea	52	Wolverhampton W*	48	Portsmouth*	48
1955–56*f*	Manchester U	60	Blackpool*	49	Wolverhampton W	49
1956–57*f*	Manchester U	64	Tottenham H*	56	Preston NE	56
1957–58*f*	Wolverhampton W	64	Preston NE	59	Tottenham H	51
1958–59*f*	Wolverhampton W	61	Manchester U	55	Arsenal*	50
1959–60*f*	Burnley	55	Wolverhampton W	54	Tottenham H	53
1960–61*f*	Tottenham H	66	Sheffield W	58	Wolverhampton W	57
1961–62*f*	Ipswich T	56	Burnley	53	Tottenham H	52
1962–63*f*	Everton	61	Tottenham H	55	Burnley	54
1963–64*f*	Liverpool	57	Manchester U	53	Everton	52
1964–65*f*	Manchester U*	61	Leeds U	61	Chelsea	56
1965–66*f*	Liverpool	61	Leeds U*	55	Burnley	55
1966–67*f*	Manchester U	60	Nottingham F*	56	Tottenham H	56
1967–68*f*	Manchester C	58	Manchester U	56	Liverpool	55
1968–69*f*	Leeds U	67	Liverpool	61	Everton	57
1969–70*f*	Everton	66	Leeds U	57	Chelsea	55
1970–71*f*	Arsenal	65	Leeds U	64	Tottenham H*	52
1971–72*f*	Derby Co	58	Leeds U*	57	Liverpool*	57
1972–73*f*	Liverpool	60	Arsenal	57	Leeds U	53
1973–74*f*	Leeds U	62	Liverpool	57	Derby Co	48
1974–75*f*	Derby Co	53	Liverpool*	51	Ipswich T	57
1975–76*f*	Liverpool	60	QPR	59	Manchester U	56
1976–77*f*	Liverpool	57	Manchester C	56	Ipswich T	52
1977–78*f*	Nottingham F	64	Liverpool	57	Everton	55
1978–79*f*	Liverpool	68	Nottingham F	60	WBA	59
1979–80*f*	Liverpool	60	Manchester U	58	Ipswich T	53
1980–81*f*	Aston Villa	60	Ipswich T	56	Arsenal	53
1981–82*g*	Liverpool	87	Ipswich T	83	Manchester U	78
1982–83*g*	Liverpool	82	Watford	71	Manchester U	70
1983–84*g*	Liverpool	80	Southampton	77	Nottingham F*	74
1984–85*g*	Everton	90	Liverpool*	77	Tottenham H	77
1985–86*g*	Liverpool	88	Everton	86	West Ham U	84
1986–87*g*	Everton	86	Liverpool	77	Tottenham H	71
1987–88*h*	Liverpool	90	Manchester U	81	Nottingham F	73
1988–89*k*	Arsenal*	76	Liverpool	76	Nottingham F	64
1989–90*k*	Liverpool	79	Aston Villa	70	Tottenham H	63
1990–91*k*	Arsenal†	83	Liverpool	76	Crystal Palace	69
1991–92*g*	Leeds U	82	Manchester U	78	Sheffield W	75

No official competition during 1915–19 and 1939–46.
†2 pts deducted

SECOND DIVISION to 1991–92

Maximum points: a 44; *b* 56; *c* 60; *d* 68; *e* 76; *f* 84; *g* 126; *h* 132; *k* 138.

	First	Pts	Second	Pts	Third	Pts
1892–93*a*	Small Heath	36	Sheffield U	35	Darwen	30
1893–94*b*	Liverpool	50	Small Heath	42	Notts Co	39
1894–95*c*	Bury	48	Notts Co	39	Newton Heath*	38
1895–96*c*	Liverpool*	46	Manchester C	46	Grimsby T*	42
1896–97*c*	Notts Co	42	Newton Heath	39	Grimsby T	38
1897–98*c*	Burnley	48	Newcastle U	45	Manchester C	39
1898–99*d*	Manchester C	52	Glossop NE	46	Leicester Fosse	45
1899–1900*d*	The Wednesday	54	Bolton W	52	Small Heath	46
1900–01*d*	Grimsby T	49	Small Heath	48	Burnley	44
1901–02*d*	WBA	55	Middlesbrough	51	Preston NE*	42
1902–03*d*	Manchester C	54	Small Heath	51	Woolwich A	48
1903–04*d*	Preston NE	50	Woolwich A	49	Manchester U	48
1904–05*d*	Liverpool	58	Bolton W	56	Manchester U	53
1905–06*e*	Bristol C	66	Manchester U	62	Chelsea	53
1906–07*e*	Nottingham F	60	Chelsea	57	Leicester Fosse	48
1907–08*e*	Bradford C	54	Leicester Fosse	52	Oldham Ath	50
1908–09*e*	Bolton W	52	Tottenham H*	51	WBA	51
1909–10*e*	Manchester C	54	Oldham Ath*	53	Hull C*	53
1910–11*e*	WBA	53	Bolton W	51	Chelsea	49
1911–12*e*	Derby Co*	54	Chelsea	54	Burnley	52
1912–13*e*	Preston NE	53	Burnley	50	Birmingham	46
1913–14*e*	Notts Co	53	Bradford PA*	49	Woolwich A	49
1914–15*e*	Derby Co	53	Preston NE	50	Barnsley	47
1919–20*f*	Tottenham H	70	Huddersfield T	64	Birmingham	56
1920–21*f*	Birmingham*	58	Cardiff C	58	Bristol C	51
1921–22*f*	Nottingham F	56	Stoke C*	52	Barnsley	52
1922–23*f*	Notts Co	53	West Ham U*	51	Leicester C	51
1923–24*f*	Leeds U	54	Bury*	51	Derby Co	51
1924–25*f*	Leicester C	59	Manchester U	57	Derby Co	55

* *Won or placed on goal average/goal difference.*

	First	Pts	Second	Pts	Third	Pts
1925–26*f*	Sheffield W	60	Derby Co	57	Chelsea	52
1926–27*f*	Middlesbrough	62	Portsmouth*	54	Manchester C	54
1927–28*f*	Manchester C	59	Leeds U	57	Chelsea	54
1928–29*f*	Middlesbrough	55	Grimsby T	53	Bradford*	48
1929–30*f*	Blackpool	58	Chelsea	55	Oldham Ath	53
1930–31*f*	Everton	61	WBA	54	Tottenham H	51
1931–32*f*	Wolverhampton W	56	Leeds U	54	Stoke C	52
1932–33*f*	Stoke C	56	Tottenham H	55	Fulham	50
1933–34*f*	Grimsby T	59	Preston NE	52	Bolton W*	51
1934–35*f*	Brentford	61	Bolton W*	56	West Ham U	56
1935–36*f*	Manchester U	56	Charlton Ath	55	Sheffield U*	52
1936–37*f*	Leicester C	56	Blackpool	55	Bury	52
1937–38*f*	Aston Villa	57	Manchester U*	53	Sheffield U	53
1938–39*f*	Blackburn R	55	Sheffield U	54	Sheffield W	53
1946–47*f*	Manchester C	62	Burnley	58	Birmingham C	55
1947–48*f*	Birmingham C	59	Newcastle U	56	Southampton	52
1948–49*f*	Fulham	57	WBA	56	Southampton	55
1949–50*f*	Tottenham H	61	Sheffield W*	52	Sheffield U*	52
1950–51*f*	Preston NE	57	Manchester C	52	Cardiff C	50
1951–52*f*	Sheffield W	53	Cardiff C*	51	Birmingham C	51
1952–53*f*	Sheffield U	60	Huddersfield T	58	Luton T	52
1953–54*f*	Leicester C*	56	Everton	56	Blackburn R	55
1954–55*f*	Birmingham C*	54	Luton T*	54	Rotherham U	54
1955–56*f*	Sheffield W	55	Leeds U	52	Liverpool*	48
1956–57*f*	Leicester C	61	Nottingham F	54	Liverpool	53
1957–58*f*	West Ham U	57	Blackburn R	56	Charlton Ath	55
1958–59*f*	Sheffield W	62	Fulham	60	Sheffield U*	53
1959–60*f*	Aston Villa	59	Cardiff C	58	Liverpool*	50
1960–61*f*	Ipswich T	59	Sheffield U	58	Liverpool	52
1961–62*f*	Liverpool	62	Leyton O	54	Sunderland	53
1962–63*f*	Stoke C	53	Chelsea*	52	Sunderland	52
1963–64*f*	Leeds U	63	Sunderland	61	Preston NE	56
1964–65*f*	Newcastle U	57	Northampton T	56	Bolton W	50
1965–66*f*	Manchester C	59	Southampton	54	Coventry C	53
1966–67*f*	Coventry C	59	Wolverhampton W	58	Carlisle U	52
1967–68*f*	Ipswich T	59	QPR*	58	Blackpool	58
1968–69*f*	Derby Co	63	Crystal Palace	56	Charlton Ath	50
1969–70*f*	Huddersfield T	60	Blackpool	53	Leicester C	51
1970–71*f*	Leicester C	59	Sheffield U	56	Cardiff C*	53
1971–72*f*	Norwich C	57	Birmingham C	56	Millwall	55
1972–73*f*	Burnley	62	QPR	61	Aston Villa	50
1973–74*f*	Middlesbrough	65	Luton T	50	Carlisle U	49
1974–75*f*	Manchester U	61	Aston Villa	58	Norwich C	53
1975–76*f*	Sunderland	56	Bristol C*	53	WBA	53
1976–77*f*	Wolverhampton W	57	Chelsea	55	Nottingham F	52
1977–78*f*	Bolton W	58	Southampton	57	Tottenham H*	56
1978–79*f*	Crystal Palace	57	Brighton*	56	Stoke C	56
1979–80*f*	Leicester C	55	Sunderland	54	Birmingham C*	53
1980–81*f*	West Ham U	66	Notts Co	53	Swansea C*	50
1981–82*g*	Luton T	88	Watford	80	Norwich C	71
1982–83*g*	QPR	85	Wolverhampton W	75	Leicester C	70
1983–84*g*	Chelsea*	88	Sheffield W	88	Newcastle U	80
1984–85*g*	Oxford U	84	Birmingham C	82	Manchester C	74
1985–86*g*	Norwich C	84	Charlton Ath	77	Wimbledon	76
1986–87*g*	Derby Co	84	Portsmouth	78	Oldham Ath††	75
1987–88*h*	Millwall	82	Aston Villa*	78	Middlesbrough	78
1988–89*k*	Chelsea	99	Manchester C	82	Crystal Palace	81
1989–90*k*	Leeds U*	85	Sheffield U	85	Newcastle U††	80
1990–91*k*	Oldham Ath	88	West Ham U	87	Sheffield W	82
1991–92*k*	Ipswich T	84	Middlesbrough	80	Derby Co	78

No competition during 1915–19 and 1939–46.
††Not promoted after play-offs.

THIRD DIVISION to 1991–92

Maximum points: 92; 138 from 1981–82.

	First	Pts	Second	Pts	Third	Pts
1958–59	Plymouth Arg	62	Hull C	61	Brentford*	57
1959–60	Southampton	61	Norwich C	59	Shrewsbury T*	52
1960–61	Bury	68	Walsall	62	QPR	60
1961–62	Portsmouth	65	Grimsby T	62	Bournemouth*	59
1962–63	Northampton T	62	Swindon T	58	Port Vale	54
1963–64	Coventry C*	60	Crystal Palace	60	Watford	58
1964–65	Carlisle U	60	Bristol C*	59	Mansfield T	59
1965–66	Hull C	69	Millwall	65	QPR	57
1966–67	QPR	67	Middlesbrough	55	Watford	54
1967–68	Oxford U	57	Bury	56	Shrewsbury T	55
1968–69	Watford*	64	Swindon T	64	Luton T	61
1969–70	Orient	62	Luton T	60	Bristol R	56
1970–71	Preston NE	61	Fulham	60	Halifax T	56
1971–72	Aston Villa	70	Brighton	65	Bournemouth*	62
1972–73	Bolton W	61	Notts Co	57	Blackburn R	55
1973–74	Oldham Ath	62	Bristol R*	61	York C	61
1974–75	Blackburn R	60	Plymouth Arg	59	Charlton Ath	55

**Won or placed on goal average/goal difference.*

	First	Pts	Second	Pts	Third	Pts
1975–76	Hereford U	63	Cardiff C	57	Millwall	56
1976–77	Mansfield T	64	Brighton & HA	61	Crystal Palace*	59
1977–78	Wrexham	61	Cambridge U	58	Preston NE*	56
1978–79	Shrewsbury T	61	Watford*	60	Swansea C	60
1979–80	Grimsby T	62	Blackburn R	59	Sheffield W	58
1980–81	Rotherham U	61	Barnsley*	59	Charlton Ath	59
1981–82	Burnley*	80	Carlisle U	80	Fulham	78
1982–83	Portsmouth	91	Cardiff C	86	Huddersfield T	82
1983–84	Oxford U	95	Wimbledon	87	Sheffield U*	83
1984–85	Bradford C	94	Millwall	90	Hull C	87
1985–86	Reading	94	Plymouth Arg	87	Derby Co	84
1986–87	Bournemouth	97	Middlesbrough	94	Swindon T	87
1987–88	Sunderland	93	Brighton & HA	84	Walsall	82
1988–89	Wolverhampton W	92	Sheffield U	84	Port Vale	84
1989–90	Bristol R	93	Bristol C	91	Notts Co	87
1990–91	Cambridge U	86	Southend U	85	Grimsby T*	83
1991–92	Brentford	82	Birmingham C	81	Huddersfield T	78

FOURTH DIVISION (1958–1992)

Maximum points: 92; 138 from 1981–82.

	First	Pts	Second	Pts	Third	Pts	Fourth	Pts
1958–59	Port Vale	64	Coventry C*	60	York C	60	Shrewsbury T	58
1959–60	Walsall	65	Notts Co*	60	Torquay U	60	Watford	57
1960–61	Peterborough U	66	Crystal Palace	64	Northampton T*	60	Bradford PA	60
1961–62†	Millwall	56	Colchester U	55	Wrexham	53	Carlisle U	52
1962–63	Brentford	62	Oldham Ath*	59	Crewe Alex	59	Mansfield T*	57
1963–64	Gillingham*	60	Carlisle U	60	Workington T	59	Exeter C	58
1964–65	Brighton	63	Millwall*	62	York C	62	Oxford U	61
1965–66	Doncaster R*	59	Darlington	59	Torquay U	58	Colchester U*	56
1966–67	Stockport Co	64	Southport*	59	Barrow	59	Tranmere R	58
1967–68	Luton T	66	Barnsley	61	Hartlepools U	60	Crewe Alex	58
1968–69	Doncaster R	59	Halifax T	57	Rochdale*	56	Bradford C	56
1969–70	Chesterfield	64	Wrexham	61	Swansea C	60	Port Vale	59
1970–71	Notts Co	69	Bournemouth	60	Oldham Ath	59	York C	56
1971–72	Grimsby T	63	Southend U	60	Brentford	59	Scunthorpe U	57
1972–73	Southport	62	Hereford U	58	Cambridge U	57	Aldershot*	56
1973–74	Peterborough U	65	Gillingham	62	Colchester U	60	Bury	59
1974–75	Mansfield T	68	Shrewsbury T	62	Rotherham U	59	Chester*	57
1975–76	Lincoln C	74	Northampton T	68	Reading	60	Tranmere R	58
1976–77	Cambridge U	65	Exeter C	62	Colchester U*	59	Bradford C	59
1977–78	Watford	71	Southend U	60	Swansea C*	56	Brentford	56
1978–79	Reading	65	Grimsby T*	61	Wimbledon*	61	Barnsley	61
1979–80	Huddersfield T	66	Walsall	64	Newport Co	61	Portsmouth*	60
1980–81	Southend U	67	Lincoln C	65	Doncaster R	56	Wimbledon	55
1981–82	Sheffield U	96	Bradford C*	91	Wigan Ath	91	AFC Bournemouth	88
1982–83	Wimbledon	98	Hull C	90	Port Vale	88	Scunthorpe U	83
1983–84	York C	101	Doncaster R	85	Reading*	82	Bristol C	82
1984–85	Chesterfield	91	Blackpool	86	Darlington	85	Bury	84
1985–86	Swindon T	102	Chester C	84	Mansfield T	81	Port Vale	79
1986–87	Northampton T	99	Preston NE	90	Southend U	80	Wolverhampton W††	79
1987–88	Wolverhampton W	90	Cardiff C	85	Bolton W	78	Scunthorpe U††	77
1988–89	Rotherham U	82	Tranmere R	80	Crewe Alex	78	Scunthorpe U††	77
1989–90	Exeter C	89	Grimsby T	79	Southend U	75	Stockport Co††	74
1990–91	Darlington	83	Stockport Co*	82	Hartlepool U	82	Peterborough U	80
1991–92†*	Burnley	80	Rotherham U*	77	Mansfield T	77	Blackpool	76

†*Maximum points:* 88 owing to Accrington Stanley's resignation. ††*Not promoted after play-offs.*
†**Maximum points:* 126 owing to Aldershot being expelled.

THIRD DIVISION—SOUTH (1920–1958)

Maximum points: a 84; *b* 92.

	First	Pts	Second	Pts	Third	Pts
1920–21*a*	Crystal Palace	59	Southampton	54	QPR	53
1921–22*a*	Southampton*	61	Plymouth Arg	61	Portsmouth	53
1922–23*a*	Bristol C	59	Plymouth Arg*	53	Swansea T	53
1923–24*a*	Portsmouth	59	Plymouth Arg	55	Millwall	54
1924–25*a*	Swansea T	57	Plymouth Arg	56	Bristol C	53
1925–26*a*	Reading	57	Plymouth Arg	56	Millwall	53
1926–27*a*	Bristol C	62	Plymouth Arg	60	Millwall	56
1927–28*a*	Millwall	65	Northampton T	55	Plymouth Arg	53
1928–29*a*	Charlton Ath*	54	Crystal Palace	54	Northampton T*	52
1929–30*a*	Plymouth Arg	68	Brentford	61	QPR	51
1930–31*a*	Notts Co	59	Crystal Palace	51	Brentford	50
1931–32*a*	Fulham	57	Reading	55	Southend U	53
1932–33*a*	Brentford	62	Exeter C	58	Norwich C	57
1933–34*a*	Norwich C	61	Coventry C*	54	Reading*	54
1934–35*a*	Charlton Ath	61	Reading	53	Coventry C	51
1935–36*a*	Coventry C	57	Luton T	56	Reading	54
1936–37*a*	Luton T	58	Notts Co	56	Brighton	53
1937–38*a*	Millwall	56	Bristol C	55	QPR*	53
1938–39*a*	Newport Co	55	Crystal Palace	52	Brighton	49
1939–46	Competition cancelled owing to war.					

**Won or placed on goal average/goal difference.*

	First	Pts	Second	Pts	Third	Pts
1946–47*a*	Cardiff C	66	QPR	57	Bristol C	51
1947–48*a*	QPR	61	Bournemouth	57	Walsall	51
1948–49*a*	Swansea T	62	Reading	55	Bournemouth	52
1949–50*a*	Notts Co	58	Northampton T*	51	Southend U	51
1950–51*b*	Nottingham F	70	Norwich C	64	Reading*	57
1951–52*b*	Plymouth Arg	66	Reading*	61	Norwich C	61
1952–53*b*	Bristol R	64	Millwall*	62	Northampton T	62
1953–54*b*	Ipswich T	64	Brighton	61	Bristol C	56
1954–55*b*	Bristol C	70	Leyton O	61	Southampton	59
1955–56*b*	Leyton O	66	Brighton	65	Ipswich T	64
1956–57*b*	Ipswich T*	59	Torquay U	59	Colchester U	58
1957–58*b*	Brighton	60	Brentford*	58	Plymouth Arg	58

THIRD DIVISION—NORTH (1921–1958)

Maximum points: a 76; *b* 84; *c* 80; *d* 92.

	First	Pts	Second	Pts	Third	Pts
1921–22*a*	Stockport Co	56	Darlington*	50	Grimsby T	50
1922–23*a*	Nelson	51	Bradford PA	47	Walsall	46
1923–24*b*	Wolverhampton W	63	Rochdale	62	Chesterfield	54
1924–25*b*	Darlington	58	Nelson*	53	New Brighton	53
1925–26*b*	Grimsby T	61	Bradford PA	60	Rochdale	59
1926–27*b*	Stoke C	63	Rochdale	58	Bradford PA	55
1927–28*b*	Bradford PA	63	Lincoln C	55	Stockport Co	54
1928–29*g*	Bradford C	63	Stockport Co	62	Wrexham	52
1929–30*b*	Port Vale	67	Stockport Co	63	Darlington*	50
1930–31*b*	Chesterfield	58	Lincoln C	57	Wrexham*	54
1931–32*c*	Lincoln C*	57	Gateshead	57	Chester	50
1932–33*b*	Hull C	59	Wrexham	57	Stockport Co	54
1933–34*b*	Barnsley	62	Chesterfield	61	Stockport Co	59
1934–35*b*	Doncaster R	57	Halifax T	55	Chester	54
1935–36*b*	Chesterfield	60	Chester*	55	Tranmere R	55
1936–37*b*	Stockport Co	60	Lincoln C	57	Chester	53
1937–38*b*	Tranmere R	56	Doncaster R	54	Hull C	53
1938–39*b*	Barnsley	67	Doncaster R	56	Bradford C	52
1939–46	Competition cancelled owing to war.					
1946–47*b*	Doncaster R	72	Rotherham U	60	Chester	56
1947–48*b*	Lincoln C	60	Rotherham U	59	Wrexham	50
1948–49*b*	Hull C	65	Rotherham U	62	Doncaster R	50
1949–50*b*	Doncaster R	55	Gateshead	53	Rochdale*	51
1950–51*d*	Rotherham U	71	Mansfield T	64	Carlisle U	62
1951–52*d*	Lincoln C	69	Grimsby T	66	Stockport Co	59
1952–53*d*	Oldham Ath	59	Port Vale	58	Wrexham	56
1953–54*d*	Port Vale	69	Barnsley	58	Scunthorpe U	57
1954–55*d*	Barnsley	65	Accrington S	61	Scunthorpe U*	58
1955–56*d*	Grimsby T	68	Derby Co	63	Accrington S	59
1956–57*d*	Derby Co	63	Hartlepools U	59	Accrington S*	58
1957–58*d*	Scunthorpe U	66	Accrington S	59	Bradford C	57

**Won or placed on goal average.*

PROMOTED AFTER PLAY-OFFS
(Not accounted for in previous section)

1986–87 Aldershot to Division 3.
1987–88 Swansea C to Division 3.
1988–89 Leyton O to Division 3.
1989–90 Cambridge U to Division 3; Notts Co to Division 2; Sunderland to Division 1.
1990–91 Notts Co to Division 1; Tranmere R to Division 2; Torquay U to Division 3.
1991–92 Blackburn R to Premier League; Peterborough U to Division 1.
1992–93 Swindon T to Premier League; WBA to Division 1; York C to Division 2.
1993–94 Leicester C to Premier League; Burnley to Division 1; Wycombe W to Division 2.
1994–95 Huddersfield T to Division 1.

LEAGUE TITLE WINS

FA PREMIER LEAGUE – Manchester U 2, Blackburn R 1.

LEAGUE DIVISION 1 – Liverpool 18, Arsenal 10, Everton 9, Manchester U 7, Aston Villa 7, Sunderland 6, Newcastle U 5, Sheffield W 4, Huddersfield T 3, Leeds U 3, Wolverhampton W 3, Blackburn R 2, Portsmouth 2, Preston NE 2, Burnley 2, Manchester C 2, Tottenham H 2, Derby Co 2, Chelsea 1, Crystal Palace 1, Sheffield U 1, WBA 1, Ipswich T 1, Nottingham F 1, Middlesbrough 1 each.

LEAGUE DIVISION 2 – Leicester C 6, Manchester C 6, Sheffield W 5, Birmingham C (one as Small Heath) 5, Derby Co 4, Liverpool 4, Ipswich T 3, Leeds U 3, Notts Co 3, Preston NE 3, Middlesbrough 3, Stoke C 3, Grimsby T 2, Norwich C 2, Nottingham F 2, Tottenham H 2, WBA 2, Aston Villa 2, Burnley 2, Chelsea 2, Manchester U 2, West Ham U 2, Wolverhampton W 2, Bolton W 2, Huddersfield T, Bristol C, Brentford, Bury, Bradford C, Everton, Fulham, Sheffield U, Newcastle U, Coventry C, Blackpool, Blackburn R, Sunderland, Crystal Palace, Luton T, QPR, Oxford U, Millwall, Oldham Ath, Reading 1 each.

LEAGUE DIVISION 3 – Portsmouth 2, Oxford U 2, Shrewsbury T 2, Carlisle U 2, Plymouth Arg, Southampton, Bury, Northampton T, Coventry C, Hull C, QPR, Watford, Leyton O, Preston NE, Aston Villa, Bolton W, Oldham Ath, Blackburn R, Hereford U, Mansfield T, Wrexham, Grimsby T, Rotherham U, Burnley, Bradford C, Bournemouth, Reading, Sunderland, Wolverhampton W, Bristol R, Cambridge U, Brentford, Cardiff C 1 each.

LEAGUE DIVISION 4 – Chesterfield 2, Doncaster R 2, Peterborough U 2, Port Vale, Walsall, Millwall, Brentford, Gillingham, Brighton, Stockport Co, Luton T, Notts Co, Grimsby T, Southport, Mansfield T, Lincoln C, Cambridge U, Watford, Reading, Huddersfield T, Southend U, Sheffield U, Wimbledon, York C, Swindon T, Northampton T, Wolverhampton W, Rotherham U, Exeter C, Darlington, Burnley 1 each.

To 1957–58

DIVISION 3 (South) – Bristol C 3; Charlton Ath, Ipswich T, Millwall, Notts Co, Plymouth Arg, Swansea T 2 each; Brentford, Bristol R, Cardiff C, Crystal Palace, Coventry C, Fulham, Leyton O, Luton T, Newport Co, Nottingham F, Norwich C, Portsmouth, QPR, Reading, Southampton, Brighton 1 each.

DIVISION 3 (North) – Barnsley, Doncaster R, Lincoln C 3 each; Chesterfield, Grimsby T, Hull C, Port Vale, Stockport Co 2 each; Bradford PA, Bradford C, Darlington, Derby Co, Nelson, Oldham Ath, Rotherham U, Stoke C, Tranmere R, Wolverhampton W, Scunthorpe U 1 each.

RELEGATED CLUBS

1891–92 League extended. Newton Heath, Sheffield W and Nottingham F admitted. *Second Division formed* including Darwen.

1892–93 In Test matches, Sheffield U and Darwen won promotion in place of Notts Co and Accrington S.

1893–94 In Tests, Liverpool and Small Heath won promotion. Newton Heath and Darwen relegated.

1894–95 After Tests, Bury promoted, Liverpool relegated.

1895–96 After Tests, Liverpool promoted, Small Heath relegated.

1896–97 After Tests, Notts Co promoted, Burnley relegated.

1897–98 Test system abolished after success of Stoke C and Burnley. League extended. Blackburn R and Newcastle U elected to First Division. *Automatic promotion and relegation introduced.*

FA PREMIER LEAGUE TO DIVISION 1

1992–93 Crystal Palace, Middlesbrough, Nottingham Forest
1993–94 Sheffield U, Oldham Ath, Swindon T
1994–95 Crystal Palace, Norwich C, Leicester C, Ipswich T

DIVISION 1 TO DIVISION 2

1898–99 Bolton W and Sheffield W
1899–1900 Burnley and Glossop
1900–01 Preston NE and WBA
1901–02 Small Heath and Manchester C
1902–03 Grimsby T and Bolton W
1903–04 Liverpool and WBA
1904–05 League extended. Bury and Notts Co, two bottom clubs in First Division, re-elected.
1905–06 Nottingham F and Wolverhampton W
1906–07 Derby Co and Stoke C
1907–08 Bolton W and Birmingham C
1908–09 Manchester C and Leicester Fosse
1909–10 Bolton W and Chelsea
1910–11 Bristol C and Nottingham F
1911–12 Preston NE and Bury
1912–13 Notts Co and Woolwich Arsenal
1913–14 Preston NE and Derby Co
1914–15 Tottenham H and Chelsea*
1919–20 Notts Co and Sheffield W
1920–21 Derby Co and Bradford PA
1921–22 Bradford C and Manchester U
1922–23 Stoke C and Oldham Ath
1923–24 Chelsea and Middlesbrough
1924–25 Preston NE and Nottingham F
1925–26 Manchester C and Notts Co
1926–27 Leeds U and WBA
1927–28 Tottenham H and Middlesbrough
1928–29 Bury and Cardiff C
1929–30 Burnley and Everton
1930–31 Leeds U and Manchester U
1931–32 Grimsby T and West Ham U
1932–33 Bolton W and Blackpool
1933–34 Newcastle U and Sheffield U
1934–35 Leicester C and Tottenham H
1935–36 Aston Villa and Blackburn R
1936–37 Manchester U and Sheffield W
1937–38 Manchester C and WBA
1938–39 Birmingham C and Leicester C
1946–47 Brentford and Leeds U
1947–48 Blackburn R and Grimsby T
1948–49 Preston NE and Sheffield U
1949–50 Manchester C and Birmingham C
1950–51 Sheffield W and Everton
1951–52 Huddersfield and Fulham
1952–53 Stoke C and Derby Co
1953–54 Middlesbrough and Liverpool
1954–55 Leicester C and Sheffield W
1955–56 Huddersfield and Sheffield U
1956–57 Charlton Ath and Cardiff C
1957–58 Sheffield W and Sunderland
1958–59 Portsmouth and Aston Villa
1959–60 Luton T and Leeds U
1960–61 Preston NE and Newcastle U
1961–62 Chelsea and Cardiff C
1962–63 Majchester C and Leyton O
1963–64 Bolton W and Ipswich T
1964–65 Wolverhampton W and Birmingham C
1965–66 Northampton T and Blackburn R
1966–67 Aston Villa and Blackpool
1967–68 Fulham and Sheffield U
1968–69 Leicester C and QPR
1969–70 Sunderland and Sheffield W
1970–71 Burnley and Blackpool
1971–72 Huddersfield T and Nottingham F
1972–73 Crystal Palace and WBA
1973–74 Southampton, Manchester U, Norwich C
1974–75 Luton T, Chelsea, Carlisle U
1975–76 Wolverhampton W, Burnley, Sheffield U
1976–77 Sunderland, Stoke C, Tottenham H
1977–78 West Ham U, Newcastle U, Leicester C
1978–79 QPR, Birmingham C, Chelsea
1979–80 Bristol C, Derby Co, Bolton W
1980–81 Norwich C, Leicester C, Crystal Palace
1981–82 Leeds U, Wolverhampton W, Middlesbrough
1982–83 Manchester C, Swansea C, Brighton & HA
1983–84 Birmingham C, Notts Co, Wolverhampton W
1984–85 Norwich C, Sunderland, Stoke C
1985–86 Ipswich T, Birmingham C, WBA
1986–87 Leicester C, Manchester C, Aston Villa
1987–88 Chelsea**, Portsmouth, Watford, Oxford U
1988–89 Middlesbrough, West Ham U, Newcastle U
1989–90 Sheffield W, Charlton Ath, Millwall
1990–91 Sunderland and Derby Co
1991–92 Luton T, Notts Co, West Ham U
1992–93 Brentford, Cambridge U, Bristol R
1993–94 Birmingham C, Oxford U, Peterborough U
1994–95 Swindon T, Burnley, Bristol C, Notts Co

***Relegated after play-offs.*
**Subsequently re-elected to Division 1 when League was extended after the War.*

DIVISION 2 TO DIVISION 3

1920–21 Stockport Co
1921–22 Bradford and Bristol C
1922–23 Rotherham C and Wolverhampton W
1923–24 Nelson and Bristol C
1924–25 Crystal Palace and Coventry C
1925–26 Stoke C and Stockport Co
1926–27 Darlington and Bradford C
1927–28 Fulham and South Shields
1928–29 Port Vale and Clapton O
1929–30 Hull C and Notts Co
1930–31 Reading and Cardiff C
1931–32 Barnsley and Bristol C
1932–33 Chesterfield and Charlton Ath
1933–34 Millwall and Lincoln C
1934–35 Oldham Ath and Notts Co
1935–36 Port Vale and Hull C
1936–37 Doncaster R and Bradford C
1937–38 Barnsley and Stockport Co
1938–39 Norwich C and Tranmere R
1946–47 Swansea T and Newport Co
1947–48 Doncaster R and Millwall
1948–49 Nottingham F and Lincoln C
1949–50 Plymouth Arg and Bradford
1950–51 Grimsby T and Chesterfield
1951–52 Coventry C and QPR
1952–53 Southampton and Barnsley
1953–54 Brentford and Oldham Ath
1954–55 Ipswich T and Derby Co

1955–56 Plymouth Arg and Hull C
1956–57 Port Vale and Bury
1957–58 Doncaster R and Notts Co
1958–59 Barnsley and Grimsby T
1959–60 Bristol C and Hull C
1960–61 Lincoln C and Portsmouth
1961–62 Brighton & HA and Bristol R
1962–63 Walsall and Luton T
1963–64 Grimsby T and Scunthorpe U
1964–65 Swindon T and Swansea T
1965–66 Middlesbrough and Leyton O
1966–67 Northampton T and Bury
1967–68 Plymouth Arg and Rotherham U
1968–69 Fulham and Bury
1969–70 Preston NE and Aston Villa
1970–71 Blackburn R and Bolton W
1971–72 Charlton Ath and Watford
1972–73 Huddersfield T and Brighton & HA
1973–74 Crystal Palace, Preston NE, Swindon T
1974–75 Millwall, Cardiff C, Sheffield W
1975–76 Oxford U, York C, Portsmouth
1976–77 Carlisle U, Plymouth Arg, Hereford U
1977–78 Blackpool, Mansfield T, Hull C
1978–79 Sheffield U, Millwall, Blackburn R
1979–80 Fulham, Burnley, Charlton Ath
1980–81 Preston NE, Bristol C, Bristol R
1981–82 Cardiff C, Wrexham, Orient
1982–83 Rotherham U, Burnley, Bolton W
1983–84 Derby Co, Swansea C, Cambridge U
1984–85 Notts Co, Cardiff C, Wolverhampton W
1985–86 Carlisle U, Middlesbrough, Fulham
1986–87 Sunderland**, Grimsby T, Brighton & HA
1987–88 Huddersfield T, Reading, Sheffield U**
1988–89 Shrewsbury T, Birmingham C, Walsall
1989–90 Bournemouth, Bradford, Stoke C
1990–91 WBA and Hull C
1991–92 Plymouth Arg, Brighton & HA, Port Vale
1992–93 Preston NE, Mansfield T, Wigan Ath, Chester C
1993–94 Fulham, Exeter C, Hartlepool U, Barnet
1994–95 Cambridge U, Plymouth Arg, Cardiff C, Chester C, Leyton Orient

DIVISION 3 TO DIVISION 4

1958–59 Rochdale, Notts Co, Doncaster R, Stockport
1959–60 Accrington S, Wrexham, Mansfield T, York C
1960–61 Chesterfield, Colchester U, Bradford C, Tranmere R
1961–62 Newport Co, Brentford, Lincoln C, Torquay U
1962–63 Bradford PA, Brighton, Carlisle U, Halifax T
1963–64 Millwall, Crewe Alex, Wrexham, Notts Co
1964–65 Luton T, Port Vale, Colchester U, Barnsley
1965–66 Southend U, Exeter C, Brentford, York C
1966–67 Doncaster R, Workington, Darlington, Swansea T
1967–68 Scunthorpe U, Colchester U, Grimsby T, Peterborough U (demoted)
1968–69 Oldham Ath, Crewe Alex, Hartlepool, Northampton T
1969–70 Bournemouth, Southport, Barrow, Stockport Co
1970–71 Reading, Bury, Doncaster R, Gillingham
1971–72 Mansfield T, Barnsley, Torquay U, Bradford C
1972–73 Rotherham U, Brentford, Swansea C, Scunthorpe U
1973–74 Cambridge U, Shrewsbury T, Southport, Rochdale
1974–75 AFC Bournemouth, Tranmere R, Watford, Huddersfield T
1975–76 Aldershot, Colchester U, Southend U, Halifax T
1976–77 Reading, Northampton T, Grimsby T, York C
1977–78 Port Vale, Bradford C, Hereford U, Portsmouth
1978–79 Peterborough U, Walsall, Tranmere R, Lincoln C
1979–80 Bury, Southend U, Mansfield T, Wimbledon
1980–81 Sheffield U, Colchester U, Blackpool, Hull C
1981–82 Wimbledon, Swindon T, Bristol C, Chester
1982–83 Reading, Wrexham, Doncaster R, Chesterfield
1983–84 Scunthorpe U, Southend U, Port Vale, Exeter C
1984–85 Burnley, Orient, Preston NE, Cambridge U
1985–86 Lincoln C, Cardiff C, Wolverhampton W, Swansea C
1986–87 Bolton W**, Carlisle U, Darlington, Newport Co
1987–88 Doncaster R, York C, Grimsby T, Rotherham U**
1988–89 Southend U, Chesterfield, Gillingham, Aldershot
1989–90 Cardiff C, Northampton T, Blackpool, Walsall
1990–91 Crewe Alex, Rotherham U, Mansfield T
1991–92 Bury, Shrewsbury T, Torquay U, Darlington

****Relegated after play-offs.*

APPLICATIONS FOR RE-ELECTION

FOURTH DIVISION

Eleven: Hartlepool U.
Seven: Crewe Alex.
Six: Barrow (lost League place to Hereford U 1972), Halifax T, Rochdale, Southport (lost League place to Wigan Ath 1978), York C.
Five: Chester C, Darlington, Lincoln C, Stockport Co, Workington (lost League place to Wimbledon 1977).
Four: Bradford PA (lost League place to Cambridge U 1970), Newport Co, Northampton T.
Three: Doncaster R, Hereford U.
Two: Bradford C, Exeter C, Oldham Ath, Scunthorpe U, Torquay U.
One: Aldershot, Colchester U, Gateshead (lost League place to Peterborough U 1960), Grimsby T, Swansea C, Tranmere R, Wrexham, Blackpool, Cambridge U, Preston NE.
Accrington S resigned and Oxford U were elected 1962.
Port Vale were forced to re-apply following expulsion in 1968.

THIRD DIVISIONS NORTH & SOUTH

Seven: Walsall.
Six: Exeter C, Halifax T, Newport Co.
Five: Accrington S, Barrow, Gillingham, New Brighton, Southport.
Four: Rochdale, Norwich C.
Three: Crystal Palace, Crewe Alex, Darlington, Hartlepool U, Merthyr T, Swindon T.
Two: Aberdare Ath, Aldershot, Ashington, Bournemouth, Brentford, Chester, Colchester U, Durham C, Millwall, Nelson, QPR, Rotherham U, Southend U, Tranmere R, Watford, Workington.
One: Bradford C, Bradford PA, Brighton, Bristol R, Cardiff C, Carlisle U, Charlton Ath, Gateshead, Grimsby T, Mansfield T, Shrewsbury T, Torquay U, York C.

LEAGUE STATUS FROM 1986–87

	RELEGATED FROM LEAGUE	PROMOTED TO LEAGUE
1986–87	Lincoln C	Scarborough
1987–88	Newport Co	Lincoln C
1988–89	Darlington	Maidstone U
1989–90	Colchester U	Darlington
1990–91	—	Barnet
1991–92	—	Colchester U
1992–93	Halifax T	Wycombe W
1993–94	—	—
1994–95	—	—

TRANSFERS 1994–95

	From	To	Fee in £s
June 1994			
21 Abbott, Gary	Welling United	Enfield	undisclosed
16 Appleby, Matthew W.	Newcastle United	Darlington	Free
19 Armstrong, Alun	Newcastle United	Stockport County	35,000
1 Atherton, Peter	Coventry City	Sheffield Wednesday	800,000
21 Beauchamp, Joseph D.	Oxford United	West Ham United	1,000,000
20 Chalk, Martyn P. G.	Derby County	Stockport County	40,000
16 Collier, Daniel	Wolverhampton Wanderers	Crewe Alexandra	Free
3 Daley, Anthony M.	Aston Villa	Wolverhampton Wanderers	1,250,000
17 Forster, Nicholas	Gillingham	Brentford	100,000
30 Frampton, Mark R.	Aldershot Town	Fleet Town	400
6 Gillett, Craig	Kidderminster Harriers	Solihull Borough	undisclosed
27 Milligan, Michael J.	Oldham Athletic	Norwich City	850,000
21 Moncur, John F.	Swindon Town	West Ham United	1,000,000
8 Morah, Olisa H.	Woking	Cambridge United	50,000
30 Newsome, Jon	Leeds United	Norwich City	1,000,000
18 Pape, Andrew M.	Barnet	Enfield	undisclosed
23 Preece, Andrew P.	Stockport County	Crystal Palace	350,000
15 Sedgley, Stephen P.	Tottenham Hotspur	Ipswich Town	1,000,000
14 Smith, Dean	Walsall	Hereford United	80,000
21 Summerbee, Nicholas J.	Swindon Town	Manchester City	1,150,000
24 Warburton, Raymond	York City	Northampton Town	35,000
July 1994			
21 Alford, Carl P.	Macclesfield Town	Kettering Town	25,000
28 Archer, Graeme	Corby Town	Nuneaton Borough	undisclosed
2 Barras, Anthony	Stockport County	York City	25,000
30 Bown, Matthew R.	Poole Town	Trowbridge Town	undisclosed
13 Brabin, Gary	Runcorn	Doncaster Rovers	40,000
13 Collins, Darren	Enfield	Rushden & Diamonds	undisclosed
13 Cowan, Thomas	Sheffield United	Huddersfield Town	150,000
19 Cox, Neil J.	Aston Villa	Middlesbrough	1,000,000
28 Dawber, Mark	Chesham United	Sutton United	undisclosed
20 Diaz, Antonio	Dorchester Town	Clevedon Town	undisclosed
26 Draper, Mark A.	Notts County	Leicester City	1,250,000
22 Dublin, Keith B. L.	Watford	Southend United	exch.
12 Dykstra, Sieb	Motherwell	Queens Park Rangers	250,000
21 Ellis, Anthony	Preston North End	Blackpool	165,000
8 Emberson, Carl W.	Millwall	Colchester United	Free
14 Emblen, Neil R.	Millwall	Wolverhampton Wanderers	600,000 + 400,000
21 Evans, Keith	Curzon Ashton	Ashton United	undisclosed
9 Forbes, Steven D.	Sittingbourne	Millwall	50,000
26 Freedman, Douglas A.	Queens Park Rangers	Barnet	Free
8 Froggatt, Stephen J.	Aston Villa	Wolverhampton Wanderers	1,500,000
19 Gray, Andrew	Reading	Leyton Orient	Free
18 Gray, Kevin J.	Mansfield Town	Huddersfield Town	20,000
9 Heald, Greg J.	Enfield	Peterborough United	35,000
14 Kubicki, Dariusz	Aston Villa	Sunderland	100,000
20 Lancaster, David	Rochdale	Halifax Town	10,000
22 Liburd, Richard	Middlesbrough	Bradford City	200,000
27 Lyne, Neil G. F.	Cambridge United	Hereford United	Free
15 Marshall, Dwight W.	Plymouth Argyle	Luton Town	150,000
1 May, David	Blackburn Rovers	Manchester United	1,400,000
7 Mohan, Nicholas	Middlesbrough	Leicester City	330,000
21 Mooney, Thomas J.	Southend United	Watford	exch. + 95,000
15 Moralee, Jamie D.	Millwall	Watford	450,000 (combined)
21 Muggleton, Carl D.	Celtic	Stoke City	200,000
13 Mulligan, James	Stoke City	Bury	15,000
18 Naylor, Anthony	Crewe Alexandra	Port Vale	150,000
29 Newell, Paul C.	Leyton Orient	Barnet	Free
7 Oliver, Michael	Middlesbrough	Stockport County	15,000
20 Onuora, Ifem	Huddersfield Town	Mansfield Town	undisclosed
21 Payne, Derek R.	Southend United	Watford	exch. + 95,000
19 Pearson, Nigel G.	Sheffield Wednesday	Middlesbrough	500,000 + 250,000
15 Petterson, Andrew K.	Luton Town	Charlton Athletic	35,000
15 Pitcher, Geoffrey	Millwall	Watford	450,000 (combined)
7 Randall, Martin	Northwood	Hayes	undisclosed
26 Redgate, Gary P.	Burton Albion	VS Rugby	undisclosed
25 Richardson, Barry	Northampton Town	Preston North End	20,000
19 Richardson, Lee	Aberdeen	Oldham Athletic	300,000
22 Robinson, Mark	Newcastle United	Swindon Town	600,000
26 Robinson, Spencer L.	Bristol City	Burnley	250,000
26 Sale, Mark D.	Torquay United	Preston North End	20,000
5 Smith, David C.	Norwich City	Oxford United	100,000
13 Sutton, Christopher R.	Norwich City	Blackburn Rovers	5,000,000
23 Swan, Peter H.	Port Vale	Plymouth Argyle	300,000
1 Taylor, Ian K.	Port Vale	Sheffield Wednesday	1,000,000
5 Taylor, John P.	Bristol Rovers	Bradford City	300,000
4 Thomson, Andrew	Queen of the South	Southend United	250,000
1 Walker, Andrew F.	Bolton Wanderers	Celtic	undisclosed
9 Wardle, Paul G.	Bromsgrove Rovers	Gresley Rovers	undisclosed
8 Whyte, David A.	Crystal Palace	Charlton Athletic	exch.
21 Woods, Stephen G.	Preston North End	Motherwell	75,000
4 Worthington, Nigel	Sheffield Wednesday	Leeds United	325,000
Temporary transfers			
26 Kenny, William	Everton	Oldham Athletic	
August 1994			
4 Adcock, Anthony C.	Peterborough United	Luton Town	20,000
11 Alsford, Julian	Watford	Chester City	Free
12 Barber, Frederick	Peterborough United	Luton Town	25,000
10 Bartram, Vincent L.	AFC Bournemouth	Arsenal	250,000 + 150,000
1 Batty, Paul W.	Bath City	Salisbury City	undisclosed
12 Beasley, Andrew	Doncaster Rovers	Chesterfield	nominal
18 Beauchamp, Joseph D.	West Ham United	Swindon Town	800,000
11 Bermingham, Michael J.	Dorchester Town	Bognor Regis Town	undisclosed

	From	To	Fee
12 Blackstone, Ian K.	York City	Scarborough	15,000
4 Bradder, Gary V.	Nuneaton Borough	Hinckley Town	undisclosed
1 Bradshaw, Carl	Sheffield United	Norwich City	500,000
5 Breen, Gary	Gillingham	Peterborough United	50,000
18 Brown, Steven M.	Cheltenham Town	Burton Albion	undisclosed
18 Cook, Paul A.	Wolverhampton Wanderers	Coventry City	600,000
1 Daley, Phillip	Wigan Athletic	Lincoln City	40,000
11 Deighan, Ben	Bognor Regis Town	Basingstoke Town	undisclosed
10 Dennis, John A.	Chesterfield	Colchester United	Free
3 Drysdale, Jason	Watford	Newcastle United	425,000
5 Farrell, Sean P.	Fulham	Peterborough United	80,000
4 Fashanu, John.	Wimbledon	Aston Villa	1,350,000
11 Foster, Adrian M.	Torquay United	Gillingham	60,000
12 Fulton, Stephen	Bolton Wanderers	Falkirk	undisclosed
26 Gayle, John	Coventry City	Burnley	undisclosed
2 Glover, Edward L.	Nottingham Forest	Port Vale	200,000
1 Grainger, Phillip J.	Sutton United	Staines Town	undisclosed
1 Gray, Kevin J.	Mansfield Town	Huddersfield Town	20,000
3 Guppy, Stephen A.	Wycombe Wanderers	Newcastle United	150,000
5 Hall, Derek R.	Hereford United	Rochdale	Free
18 Harford, Michael G.	Coventry City	Wimbledon	70,000
10 Hodge, Martin	Rochdale	Plymouth Argyle	10,000
11 Hone, Mark J.	Welling United	Southend United	50,000
5 Howarth, Lee	Peterborough United	Mansfield Town	15,000
11 Hulme, Kevin	Doncaster Rovers	Bury	42,500
30 Hutchison, Donald	Liverpool	West Ham United	1,500,000
3 Iorfa, Dominic	Peterborough United	Southend United	15,000
12 Ireland, Simon P.	Blackburn Rovers	Mansfield Town	60,000
3 James, Martin J.	Stockport County	Rotherham United	50,000
26 Kenny, William	Everton	Oldham Athletic	Free
3 Kilford, Ian A.	Nottingham Forest	Wigan Athletic	Free
12 Kite, Philip D.	Cardiff City	Bristol City	Free
1 Lovell, Jason P.	Wimborne Town	Salisbury City	undisclosed
7 Ludden, Dominic J.	Leyton Orient	Watford	100,000
12 Miller, Alan J.	Arsenal	Middlesbrough	500,000
7 Miller, Kevin	Birmingham City	Watford	250,000
16 Miller, Paul A.	Wimbledon	Bristol Rovers	100,000
9 Mitchell, Stewart	Marlow	Aldershot Town	Free
11 Murray, Shaun	Scarborough	Bradford City	nominal
17 Nolan, Ian R.	Tranmere Rovers	Sheffield Wednesday	1,500,000
10 O'Neill, Darren S.	Aldershot Town	Kingstonian	2000
12 Osborn, Simon E.	Crystal Palace	Reading	90,000
1 Paatelainen, Mika	Aberdeen	Bolton Wanderers	300,000
1 Peschisolido, Paul P.	Birmingham City	Stoke City	200,000 + exch.
5 Pitcher, Darren E.J.	Charlton Athletic	Crystal Palace	40,000
11 Pollitt, Michael F.	Lincoln City	Darlington	nominal
3 Pugh, David	Chester City	Bury	22,500
2 Reece, Paul J.	Oxford United	Notts County	Free
1 Regis, David	Stoke City	Birmingham City	exch.
1 Richardson, Barry	Northampton Town	Preston North End	20,000
5 Richardson, Stephen J.	Poole Town	Dorchester Town	undisclosed
3 Robinson, Mark J.	Newcastle United	Swindon Town	600,000
12 Rocastle, David C.	Manchester City	Chelsea	1,250,000
13 Russell, Andrew	Kingstonian	Aldershot Town	undisclosed
1 Sale, Mark D.	Torquay United	Preston North End	20,000
5 Sampson, Ian	Sunderland	Northampton Town	30,000
2 Samways, Vincent	Tottenham Hotspur	Everton	2,200,000
9 Scott, Andrew M.	Blackburn Rovers	Cardiff City	Free
26 Sheron, Michael N.	Manchester City	Norwich City	800,000
16 Smith, Malcolm A.	Margate	Ashford Town	undisclosed
11 Stevens, Ian D.	Bury	Shrewsbury Town	20,000
8 Thompson, David S.	Chester City	Rochdale	6000
22 Ullathorne, Simon	Gravesend & Northfleet	Sittingbourne	undisclosed
4 Ward, Mark W.	Everton	Birmingham City	200,000
10 Whiston, Peter M.	Exeter City	Southampton	30,000
17 Whitbread, Adrian R.	Swindon Town	West Ham United	500,000 + exch.
12 Whitington, Craig	Scarborough	Huddersfield Town	nominal
5 Whyte, David A.	Crystal Palace	Charlton Athletic	exch.
3 Williams, Darren P.	Welling United	Dover Athletic	undisclosed
9 Wilmot, Rhys	Grimsby Town	Crystal Palace	80,000
8 Winstanley, Mark A.	Bolton Wanderers	Burnley	150,000

Temporary transfers

	From	To
26 Anthrobus, Stephen A.	Wimbledon	Chester City
23 Ashdjian, John A.	Kettering Town	Corby Town
11 Bass, David	Reading	Aldershot Town
26 Beckett, Nathan J.	Leyton Orient	Leyton
18 Bradshaw, Darren S.	Peterborough United	Plymouth Argyle
20 Cook, Anthony C.	Gloucester City	Dorchester Town
19 Davis, Michael V.	Bristol Rovers	Hereford United
26 Dunphy, Sean	Lincoln City	Scarborough
20 Flemming, David	Enfield	Sittingbourne
26 Foran, Mark J.	Sheffield United	Rotherham United
17 Gayle, John	Coventry City	Burnley
19 Hay, Darren A.	Cambridge United	Woking
22 Hill, David M.	Lincoln City	Chesterfield
30 Hodge, Stephen B.	Leeds United	Derby County
12 Hoult, Russell	Leicester City	Lincoln City
18 Kernaghan, Alan N.	Manchester City	Bolton Wanderers
10 Kilbane, Farrell N.	Preston North End	Barrow
12 Lee, David J.	Chelsea	Portsmouth
25 Marshall, Scott R.	Arsenal	Sheffield United
20 Mitchell, Richard D.	Southport	Hyde United
15 Norton, David W.	Hull City	Northampton Town
8 Parris, George M.	Birmingham City	Brentford
20 Pettinger, Paul A.	Leeds United	Dagenham & Redbridge
25 Powell, Richard	Welling United	Gravesend & Northfleet
26 Putney, Trevor A.	Leyton Orient	Colchester United
11 Rowe, Rodney C.	Huddersfield Town	Scarborough
26 Shaw, Graham P.	Stoke City	Plymouth Argyle
11 Shutt, Carl S.	Birmingham City	Bradford City
26 Sinclair, Ronald M.	Stoke City	Bradford City

	From	To	Fee
26 Skinner, Justin J.	Wimbledon	Wycombe Wanderers	
19 Smith, Andrew	Havant Town	Fareham Town	
26 Turner, Andrew P.	Tottenham Hotspur	Wycombe Wanderers	
24 Voice, Scott	Wolverhampton Wanderers	Shelbourne	
19 Williams, Wayne	Kidderminster Harriers	Bridgnorth Town	
13 Worrall, Rodger	Molesey	Whyteleafe	
September 1994			
5 Andrews, Ian E.	Southampton	AFC Bournemouth	20,000
1 Babb, Philip A.	Coventry City	Liverpool	3,600,000
12 Beadle, Peter C.	Tottenham Hotspur	Watford	undisclosed
6 Burrows, David	West Ham United	Everton	exch.
16 Clark, John B.	Stoke City	Falkirk	100,000
30 Cooper, Stephen	York City	Airdrieonians	undisclosed
7 Cottee, Antony R.	Everton	West Ham United	exch.
27 Crosby, Gary	Nottingham Forest	Huddersfield Town	Free
9 Diaz, Antonio	Clevedon Town	Poole Town	undisclosed
9 Dublin, Dion	Manchester United	Coventry City	1,950,000
22 Farrell, Andrew J.	Burnley	Wigan Athletic	20,000
9 Hague, Paul	Gillingham	Leyton Orient	undisclosed
9 Houghton, Scott A.	Luton Town	Walsall	15,000
16 Hunt, Jonathan R.	Southend United	Birmingham City	exch.
8 Jemson, Nigel B.	Sheffield Wednesday	Notts County	350,000
16 Jones, Keith A.	Southend United	Charlton Athletic	150,000
26 Kitson, Paul	Derby County	Newcastle United	2,250,000
23 McDonald, Rodney	Walsall	Partick Thistle	undisclosed
2 Matthewson, Trevor	Preston North End	Bury	10,000
26 Mills, Gary R.	Leicester City	Notts County	undisclosed
14 O'Hanlon, Kelham	Preston North End	Dundee United	undisclosed
9 Pearson, Neil	Molesey	Crawley Town	undisclosed
30 Peters, Mark	Peterborough United	Mansfield Town	Free
30 Pike, Christopher	Hereford United	Gillingham	15,000
16 Poole, Gary J.	Southend United	Birmingham City	exch.
9 Quail, Simon I.	Sutton United	Wealdstone	undisclosed
7 Reeves, Alan	Rochdale	Wimbledon	300,000
16 Regis, David	Birmingham City	Southend United	exch.
23 Rush, David	Sunderland	Oxford United	100,000
9 Rutherford, Jonathan P.	Meadowbank Thistle	Scarborough	15,000
2 Scales, John R.	Wimbledon	Liverpool	3,500,000
2 Sheppard, Simon	Watford	Reading	undisclosed
28 Shildrick, Andrew	Peppard	Thame United	undisclosed
9 Shutt, Carl S.	Birmingham City	Bradford City	75,000
8 Smith, Adrian	Willenhall Town	Bromsgrove Rovers	undisclosed
8 Teggart, Darren	Witney Town	Salisbury City	undisclosed
8 Ware, Paul D.	Stoke City	Stockport County	15,000
16 Willis, Roger C.	Birmingham City	Southend United	exch.
Temporary transfers			
2 Appleby, Richard D.	Newcastle United	Darlington	
24 Ashdjian, John A.	Kettering Town	Corby Town	
26 Beckett, Nathan J.	Leyton Orient	Leyton	
8 Boere, Jeroen W.J.	West Ham United	West Bromwich Albion	
12 Bull, Gary W.	Nottingham Forest	Birmingham City	
15 Burgess, David J.	Carlisle United	Hartlepool United	
23 Carmichael, Matthew	Scunthorpe United	Barnet	
8 Carr, Franz A.	Sheffield United	Leicester City	
2 Costello, Peter	Dover Athletic	Telford United	
16 Croxford, Stephen	Walton & Hersham	Staines Town	
5 Currie, Darren	West Ham United	Shrewsbury Town	
16 Davis, Kelvin G.	Luton Town	Torquay United	
9 Dickins, Matthew J.	Blackburn Rovers	Grimsby Town	
30 Dunphy, Sean	Lincoln City	Scarborough	
27 Flemming, David	Enfield	Leyton	
1 Forrester, Jamie	Leeds United	Southend United	
2 Frain, David	Stockport County	Mansfield Town	
24 Gallagher, Philip	Hendon	Hampton	
2 Harford, Paul	Blackburn Rovers	Wigan Athletic	
20 Hay, Darren A.	Cambridge United	Woking	
28 Hodge, Stephen B.	Leeds United	Derby County	
2 Houghton, Scott A.	Luton Town	Walsall	
14 Hoult, Russell	Leicester City	Lincoln City	
6 Iddles, Daniel M.	Clevedon Town	Trowbridge Town	
29 Jackson, Peter A.	Huddersfield Town	Chester City	
20 Kalogeracos, Vasili	Birmingham City	Stevenage Borough	
19 Kernaghan, Alan N.	Manchester City	Bolton Wanderers	
8 Kirkham, Paul	Stalybridge Celtic	Witton Albion	
9 Kuhl, Martin	Derby County	Notts County	
23 Le Bihan, Neil R.	Peterborough United	Bishops Stortford	
15 Leonard, Mark A.	Chester City	Wigan Athletic	
22 Lowe, Kenneth	Birmingham City	Carlisle United	
25 Marshall, Scott R.	Arsenal	Sheffield United	
9 McLean, Ian	Bristol Rovers	Cardiff City	
9 Martin, Jae A.	Southend United	Leyton Orient	
30 Mee, Andrew	Stafford Rangers	Bedworth United	
27 Milsom, Paul J.	Bristol City	Clevedon Town	
9 Moore, Neil	Everton	Blackpool	
16 Norton, David W.	Hull City	Northampton Town	
19 Parsons, Mark C.	Kettering Town	Racing Club Warwick	
16 Payne, Stephen J.	Huddersfield Town	Macclesfield Town	
9 Priest, Christopher	Everton	Chester City	
30 Prudhoe, Mark	Stoke City	Peterborough United	
30 Reddish, Shane	Carlisle United	Chesterfield	
2 Rimmer, Stuart A.	Chester City	Rochdale	
9 Ritchie, Paul M.	Dundee	Gillingham	
2 Robinson, Philip J.	Huddersfield Town	Northampton Town	
11 Rowe, Rodney C.	Huddersfield Town	Scarborough	
9 Russell, Lee E.	Portsmouth	AFC Bournemouth	
16 Saddington, James	Millwall	Shelbourne	
21 Shaw, Christopher	Witton Albion	Ashton United	
15 Sheffield, Jonathan	Cambridge United	Hereford United	
16 Simpson, Fitzroy	Manchester City	Bristol City	
8 Skinner, Justin J.	Wimbledon	Wycombe Wanderers	

	From	To	Fee
9 Small, Bryan	Aston Villa	Birmingham City	
23 Stallard, Mark	Derby County	Fulham	
22 Stevens, Michael G.	Rangers	Tranmere Rovers	
2 Stewart, Paul A.	Liverpool	Wolverhampton Wanderers	
30 Sweetman, Nicholas E.	Leyton Orient	Hendon	
12 Symons, Paul	Blackpool	Southport	
9 Thompson, David	Brentford	Blackpool	
9 Waddock, Gary P.	Bristol Rovers	Luton Town	
23 Walker, Raymond	Port Vale	Cambridge United	
9 Walters, Mark E.	Liverpool	Wolverhampton Wanderers	
23 Ward, Richard	Huddersfield Town	Goole Town	
2 Warner, Ashley S.	Peterborough United	Corby Town	
17 Warner, Steven P.	Billericay Town	Collier Row	
16 Whitehead, Scot	Huddersfield Town	Frickley Athletic	
2 Wietecha, David	Millwall	Chesham United	
2 Wilkinson, Ian M.	Crewe Alexandra	Doncaster Rovers	
19 Williams, Wayne	Kidderminster Harriers	Bridgnorth Town	
22 Woodward, Andrew	Crewe Alexandra	Stafford Rangers	
October 1994			
7 Atkinson, Graeme	Hull City	Preston North End	undisclosed
3 Baker, David P.	Gillingham	York City	undisclosed
21 Bell, Michael	Northampton Town	Wycombe Wanderers	nominal
26 Bound, Matthew T.	Southampton	Stockport County	125,000
20 Bradshaw, Darren S.	Peterborough United	Blackpool	undisclosed
4 Butler, Peter J.	West Ham United	Notts County	350,000
11 Carr, Franz A.	Sheffield United	Leicester City	100,000
13 Carty, Paul	Tamworth	Hednesford Town	undisclosed
5 Coleman, Simon	Sheffield Wednesday	Bolton Wanderers	350,000
14 Davison, Robert	Sheffield United	Rotherham United	Free
20 Dicks, Julian A.	Liverpool	West Ham United	2,500,000
14 Ekoku, Efangwu	Norwich City	Wimbledon	920,000
28 Foy, David L.	Stafford Rangers	Tamworth	undisclosed
28 Hodge, Stephen B.	Leeds United	Queens Park Rangers	300,000
5 Humphries, Mark	Leeds United	Bristol City	undisclosed
19 Keen, Kevin I.	Wolverhampton Wanderers	Stoke City	300,000
14 Leonard, Mark A.	Chester City	Wigan Athletic	undisclosed
12 Mercer, William	Rotherham United	Sheffield United	75,000
10 Roberts, Graham P.	Slough Town	Stevenage Borough	undisclosed
20 Robinson, Stephen	Tottenham Hotspur	AFC Bournemouth	Free
4 Sharp, Raymond	Dunfermline Athletic	Preston North End	undisclosed
26 Shaw, Christopher	Witton Albion	Ashton United	undisclosed
14 Stevens, Michael G.	Rangers	Tranmere Rovers	350,000
5 Thorn, Andrew C.	Crystal Palace	Wimbledon	Free
28 Walker, Gary	Buxton	Stafford Rangers	undisclosed
20 Whittle, Justin P.	Celtic	Stoke City	Free
11 Young, Neil A.	Tottenham Hotspur	AFC Bournemouth	Free
Temporary transfers			
28 Alexander, Timothy M.	Barnet	Gravesend & Northfleet	
27 Ashdjian, John A.	Kettering Town	Corby Town	
4 Banger, Nicholas L.	Southampton	Oldham Athletic	
14 Brass, Christopher P.	Burnley	Torquay United	
11 Bull, Gary W.	Nottingham Forest	Birmingham City	
24 Burton, Christopher	Solihull Borough	Tamworth	
13 Cadette, Richard R.	Falkirk	Millwall	
8 Clark, Paul D.	Walton & Hersham	Molesey	
11 Colgan, Nicholas V.	Chelsea	Grimsby Town	
18 Collett, Andrew A.	Middlesbrough	Bristol Rovers	
11 Cooksey, Scott A.	Peterborough United	Welling United	
2 Costello, Peter	Dover Athletic	Telford United	
18 Croxford, Stephen	Walton & Hersham	Staines Town	
4 Currie, Darren	West Ham United	Shrewsbury Town	
28 Daniel, Raymond C.	Portsmouth	Notts County	
14 Dickins, Matthew J.	Blackburn Rovers	Rochdale	
14 Dow, Andrew	Chelsea	Bradford City	
28 Dunphy, Sean	Lincoln City	Scarborough	
3 Durrant, Ian	Rangers	Everton	
25 Eriemo, Soloman	Kingstonian	Hayes	
15 Evans, Richard J	Sutton United	Abingdon Town	
4 Ferguson, Duncan	Rangers	Everton	
1 Fleming, Mark J.	Aylesbury United	Staines Town	
28 Flemming, David	Enfield	Leyton	
14 Foster, Wayne P.	Heart of Midlothian	Hartlepool United	
22 Fowler, Lee	Dagenham & Redbridge	Barking	
24 Gallagher, Phillip	Hendon	Hampton	
28 Hall, Mark	Southend United	Dover Athletic	
7 Hendry, John	Tottenham Hotspur	Swansea City	
15 Hoult, Russell	Leicester City	Lincoln City	
14 Hoyland, Jamie W.	Sheffield United	Burnley	
3 Hoyle, Colin R.	Notts County	Mansfield Town	
7 Huxford, Richard J.	Millwall	Bradford City	
8 Iddles, Daniel M.	Clevedon Town	Trowbridge Town	
31 Jackson, Peter A.	Huddersfield Town	Chester City	
21 Jones, Stephen G.	West Ham United	AFC Bournemouth	
18 Jukes, Andrew	Luton Town	Wealdstone	
23 Le Bihan, Neil E.	Peterborough United	Bishops Stortford	
1 Livett, Simon	Cambridge United	Dagenham & Redbridge	
14 Lucas, Richard	Preston North End	Lincoln City	
7 McKenzie, Christopher	Hereford United	Rushden & Diamonds	
14 McKinlay, David	Middlesbrough	Cork City	
20 McMahon, Gerard J.	Tottenham Hotspur	Barnet	
31 Marshall, Scott R.	Arsenal	Sheffield United	
17 Martin, Dean S.	Scunthorpe United	Halifax Town	
6 Miller, David B.	Stockport County	Wigan Athletic	
12 Moore, Neil	Everton	Blackpool	
28 Morton, Neil	Wigan Athletic	Altrincham	
18 Page, Darrell	Rushden & Diamonds	Wealdstone	
24 Parsons, Mark C.	Kettering Town	Racing Club Warwick	
7 Patterson, Ian D.	Wigan Athletic	Stallybridge Celtic	
17 Payne, Stephen J.	Huddersfield Town	Macclesfield Town	
11 Priest, Christopher	Everton	Chester City	

	From	To	Fee
31 Prudhoe, Mark	Stoke City	Peterborough United	
3 Pugh, Stephen	Wrexham	Runcorn	
13 Putney, Trevor A.	Leyton Orient	Colchester United	
21 Richardson, Nicholas J.	Cardiff City	Wrexham	
4 Robinson, Phillip J.	Huddersfield Town	Northampton Town	
27 Roscoe, Andrew R.	Bolton Wanderers	Rotherham United	
12 Rowe, Rodney C.	Huddersfield Town	Scarborough	
31 Ryan, Tim J.	Scunthorpe United	Buxton	
14 Scully, Anthony D.T.	Crystal Palace	AFC Bournemouth	
15 Sheffield, Jonathon	Cambridge United	Hereford United	
25 Shirtliff, Paul R.	Gateshead	Farsley Celtic	
31 Slawson, Stephen M.	Notts County	Shrewsbury Town	
14 Smith, Paul M.	Lincoln City	Kettering Town	
13 Snodin, Ian	Everton	Sunderland	
1 Stacey, Phillip G.	Aylesbury United	Barton Rovers	
28 Starbuck, Phillip M.	Huddersfield Town	Sheffield United	
4 Stewart, Paul A.	Liverpool	Wolverhampton Wanderers	
5 Sweetman, Nicholas E.	Leyton Orient	Hendon	
28 Taylor, Mark S.	Middlesbrough	Darlington	
12 Thompson, David G.	Brentford	Blackpool	
28 Tracey, Simon P.	Sheffield United	Manchester City	
10 Turner, Andrew P.	Tottenham Hotspur	Doncaster Rovers	
9 Waddock, Gary P.	Bristol Rovers	Luton Town	
11 Walters, Mark E.	Liverpool	Wolverhampton Wanderers	
28 Warner, Ashley S.	Peterborough United	Telford United	
7 Webb, Neil J.	Nottingham Forest	Swindon Town	
7 Webster, Kenneth	Peterborough United	Rushden & Diamonds	
7 Williams, John N.	Coventry City	Notts County	
6 Wilson, Paul A.	Burnley	York City	
14 Witter, Anthony J.	Queens Park Rangers	Millwall	
November 1994			
4 Banger, Nicholas L.	Southampton	Oldham Athletic	250,000
30 Brown, Michael A.	Shrewsbury Town	Preston North End	75,000
3 Cadette, Richard R.	Falkirk	Millwall	135,000
18 Cook, Mitchel C.	Blackpool	Hartlepool United	Free
9 Cunningham, Kenneth	Millwall	Wimbledon	1,300,000*
2 Emerson, Dean	Stockport County	Preston North End	Free
9 Goodman, Jonathan	Millwall	Wimbledon	1,300,000*
25 Guppy, Stephen	Newcastle United	Port Vale	225,000
4 Hoyland, Jamie W.	Sheffield United	Burnley	130,000
22 Jackson, Peter A.	Huddersfield Town	Chester City	Free
8 Jones, Stephen G.	West Ham United	Bournemouth AFC	150,000
15 Marsden, Christopher	Wolverhampton Wanderers	Notts County	250,000
23 Mellon, Michael J.	West Bromwich Albion	Blackpool	50,000
4 Miller, David B.	Stockport County	Wigan Athletic	undisclosed
28 Monington, Mark D.	Burnley	Rotherham United	undisclosed
28 Morton, Neil	Wigan Athletic	Altrincham	Free
21 Norbury, Michael S.	Preston North End	Doncaster Rovers	10,000
4 Norton, David W.	Hull City	Northampton Town	undisclosed
30 Portway, Steven	Gravesend & Northfleet	Gloucester City	undisclosed
18 Reddish, Shane	Carlisle United	Hartlepool United	Free
25 Rees, Anthony A.	Grimsby Town	West Bromwich Albion	50,000
22 Ross, Michael P.	Exeter City	Plymouth Argyle	undisclosed
28 Sealey, Leslie J.	Blackpool	West Ham United	Free
22 Smart, Allan A.C.	Caledonian Thistle	Preston North End	15,000
4 Smith, Brett R.	Chesham United	Slough Town	undisclosed
7 Thompson, David G.	Brentford	Blackpool	undisclosed
18 Valentine, Peter	Carlisle United	Rochdale	15,000
5 Watson, David G.	Thame United	Witney Town	undisclosed
4 Wilson, Paul A.	Burnley	York City	undisclosed
18 Worboys, Gavin A.	Notts County	Darlington	Free
Temporary transfers			
24 Akinbiyi, Adeola P.	Norwich City	Brighton & Hove Albion	
4 Ansah, Andrew	Southend United	Brentford	
18 Barnard, Darren S.	Chelsea	Reading	
4 Benning, Paul M.	Sutton United	Walton & Hersham	
23 Bodley, Michael J.	Southend United	Gillingham	
16 Brass, Christopher P.	Burnley	Torquay United	
4 Butters, Guy	Portsmouth	Oxford United	
25 Campbell, Jamie	Luton Town	Mansfield Town	
18 Cormack, Lee D.	Newport (IW) FC	Fareham Town	
4 Cusack, Nicholas J.	Oxford United	Fulham	
16 Daly, Thomas	Worcester City	Solihull Borough	
25 De Souza, Miguel	Birmingham City	Bury	
29 Dudley, Derek A.	West Bromwich Albion	Halesowen Town	
18 Duffy, Christopher J.	Wigan Athletic	Northwich Victoria	
15 Dunphy, Nicholas O.	Peterborough United	Dagenham & Redbridge	
18 Evans, Richard J.	Sutton United	Abingdon Town	
26 Evans, Richard J.	Sutton United	Marlow	
28 Flemming, David	Enfield	Leyton	
18 Foot, Daniel F.	Southend United	Crawley Town	
29 Fox, Richard	Chelmsford City	Aveley	
4 Gill, Andrew	Chorley	Morecambe	
18 Gray, Ian J.	Oldham Athletic	Rochdale	
28 Hall, Mark A.	Southend United	Dover Athletic	
3 Hoyle, Colin	Notts County	Mansfield Town	
7 Huxford, Richard	Millwall	Bradford City	
9 Innes, Lee M.	Sheffield United	Boston United	
15 Jukes, Andrew	Luton Town	Wealdstone	
1 Kerr, James S.R.	Celtic	Brighton & Hove Albion	
23 Le Bihan, Neil E.	Peterborough United	Bishops Stortford	
4 McAuley, Sean	St. Johnstone	Chesterfield	
26 Magee, Jonathan P.	Kettering Town	Burton Albion	
18 Martin, Dean S.	Scunthorpe United	Halifax Town	
18 Midwood, Michael A.	Huddersfield Town	Macclesfield Town	
28 Milsom, Paul J.	Bristol City	Stafford Rangers	
29 Morrell, Darren	Chelmsford City	Aveley	
5 Morton, Neil	Wigan Athletic	Altrincham	
4 Munden, Maurice	Dover Athletic	Ashford Town	
25 Page, Darrell	Rushden & Diamonds	Wealdstone	

	From	To	Fee
7 Patterson, Ian D.	Wigan Athletic	Stalybridge Celtic	
21 Payne, Stephen J.	Huddersfield Town	Macclesfield Town	
15 Pearcey, Jason	Mansfield Town	Grimsby Town	
29 Prudhoe, Mark	Stoke City	Liverpool	
17 Quinn, Michael	Coventry City	Plymouth Argyle	
4 Ramsey, Paul	St. Johnstone	Cardiff City	
25 Ravenscroft, Craig A.	Brentford	Woking	
4 Robinson, Phillip J.	Huddersfield Town	Northampton Town	
4 Ryan, Tim J.	Scunthorpe United	Buxton	
14 Scully, Anthony D.T.	Crystal Palace	Bournemouth AFC	
3 Slawson, Stephen M.	Notts County	Shrewsbury Town	
28 Smith, Eric	Crystal Palace	Croydon	
13 Smith, Paul M.	Lincoln City	Kettering Town	
28 Starbuck, Philip M.	Huddersfield Town	Sheffield United	
3 Stewart, Paul A.	Liverpool	Wolverhampton Wanderers	
28 Sweetman, Nicholas E.	Leyton Orient	Hendon	
17 Taylor, Colin D.	Telford United	Atherstone United	
28 Taylor, Mark S.	Middlesbrough	Darlington	
18 Tiler, Carl	Nottingham Forest	Swindon Town	
27 Tracey, Simon P.	Sheffield United	Manchester City	
18 Vincent, Jamie R.	Crystal Palace	Bournemouth AFC	
10 Waddock, Gary P.	Bristol Rovers	Luton Town	
28 Warner, Ashley S.	Peterborough United	Telford United	
7 Welsh, Stephen	Peterborough United	Preston North End	
25 Whitington, Craig	Huddersfield Town	Rochdale	
16 Wilkin, Kevin	Northampton Town	Sudbury Town	
17 Williams, Paul R.	Coventry City	Huddersfield Town	
14 Witter, Anthony K.	Queens Park Rangers	Millwall	
1 Worboys, Gavin A.	Notts County	Darlington	
December 1994			
15 Arnold, Ian	Carlisle United	Kettering Town	10,000
30 Bailey, Shane M.	Sudbury Town	Braintree Town	undisclosed
23 Brissett, Jason C.	Peterborough United	Bournemouth AFC	Free
2 Brown, Michael A.	Shrewsbury Town	Preston North End	75,000
13 Burke, Brendon	Witton Albion	Stalybridge Celtic	undisclosed
19 Cowans, Gordon S.	Derby County	Wolverhampton Wanderers	25,000
30 Culverhouse, Ian B.	Norwich City	Swindon Town	250,000
16 Dryden, Richard A.	Birmingham City	Bristol City	200,000
23 Duxbury, Lee E.	Bradford City	Huddersfield Town	250,000
23 Evans, Richard J.	Sutton United	Marlow	undisclosed
13 Ferguson, Duncan	Glasgow Rangers	Everton	4,000,000
21 Flounders, Andrew J.	Halifax Town	Northampton Town	Free
6 Goodman, Donald	Sunderland	Wolverhampton Wanderers	1,100,000
15 Gunn, Brynley C.	Corby Town	Hednesford Town	undisclosed
22 Harlow, David S.	Kingstonian	Farnborough Town	undisclosed
30 Kuhl, Martin	Derby County	Bristol City	330,000
23 Lancashire, Graham	Burnley	Preston North End	55,000
23 Law, Brian J.	Queens Park Rangers	Wolverhampton Wanderers	undisclosed
1 Lay, David	Marlow	Slough Town	undisclosed
23 Lormor, Anthony	Peterborough United	Chesterfield	Free
1 McMahon, Stephen	Manchester City	Swindon Town	undisclosed
23 Mitchell, Graham L.	Huddersfield Town	Bradford City	undisclosed
9 Morrison, Andrew C.	Blackburn Rovers	Blackpool	undisclosed
19 Otto, Ricky	Southend United	Birmingham City	800,000
23 Owers, Gary	Sunderland	Bristol City	exch.
23 Page, Darrell	Rushden & Diamonds	Wealdstone	undisclosed
2 Parnell, Steven P.	Sudbury Town	Halstead Town	undisclosed
9 Patterson, Gary	Shrewsbury Town	Wycombe Wanderers	75,000
14 Pearcey, Jason	Mansfield Town	Grimsby Town	undisclosed
19 Phillips, Kevin	Baldock Town	Watford	undisclosed
9 Robinson, Philip J.	Huddersfield Town	Chesterfield	undisclosed
5 Rodwell, Anthony	Blackpool	Scarborough	10,000
23 Rutherford, Jonathan P.	Scarborough	Berwick Rangers	undisclosed
30 Scott, Keith	Swindon Town	Stoke City	300,000
23 Scott, Martin	Bristol City	Sunderland	450,000
20 Simkin, Darren S.	Wolverhampton Wanderers	Shrewsbury Town	36,000
23 Sinnott, Lee	Bradford City	Huddersfield Town	105,000
21 Taylor, Ian K.	Sheffield Wednesday	Aston Villa	1,000,000
30 Walters, Steven P.	Crewe Alexandra	Northwich Victoria	Free
8 Ward, Ashley S.	Crewe Alexandra	Norwich City	350,000
23 Welsh, Steven G.	Peterborough United	Partick Thistle	undisclosed
23 White, Devon W.	Queens Park Rangers	Notts County	100,000
8 White, Stuart	Welling United	Ashford Town	undisclosed
21 Whittingham, Guy	Aston Villa	Sheffield Wednesday	700,000
12 Witter, Anthony J.	Queens Park Rangers	Millwall	100,000
29 Wright, Jermaine M.	Millwall	Wolverhampton Wanderers	50,000
Temporary transfers			
6 Affor, Louis K.J.	Barnet	Wokingham Town	
23 Akinbiyi, Adeola P.	Norwich City	Brighton & Hove Albion	
23 Allen, Gavin	Tranmere Rovers	Macclesfield Town	
9 Allen, Paul K.	Southampton	Luton Town	
16 Alsop, Julian M.	Tamworth	Racing Club Warwick	
30 Armstrong, Craig	Nottingham Forest	Burnley	
30 Barber, Frederick	Luton Town	Peterborough United	
23 Barber, Philip A.	Millwall	Plymouth Argyle	
7 Barker, Dean E.	Sudbury Town	Braintree Town	
10 Barnett, Benjamin J.	Boreham Wood	Molesey	
13 Berry, Gwynne	Woking	Stafford Rangers	
23 Bodley, Michael J.	Southend United	Gillingham	
23 Brown, Ian	Bristol City	Northampton Town	
8 Bryan, Marvin L.	Queens Park Rangers	Doncaster Rovers	
23 Carter, James W.	Arsenal	Oxford United	
17 Casey, Kim T.	Solihull Borough	Kidderminster Harriers	
9 Chester, Martin G.	Enfield	Purfleet	
19 Conroy, Stephen	Stevenage Borough	Aylesbury United	
16 Cormack, Lee D.	Newport (IW)	Fareham Town	
16 Cox, Paul R.	Notts County	Hull City	
9 Croxford, Stephen	Walton & Hersham	Uxbridge	
9 Culverhouse, Ian B.	Norwich City	Swindon Town	
2 Cusack, Nicholas J.	Oxford United	Fulham	

	From	*To*	*Fee*
9 Cutler, Neil	West Bromwich Albion	Cheltenham Town	
15 Dobson, Anthony J.	Portsmouth	Oxford United	
16 Dolby, Tony C.	Millwall	Chesham United	
23 Donaldson, O'Neill M.	Doncaster Rovers	Mansfield Town	
17 Duffy, Christopher J.	Wigan Athletic	Northwich Victoria	
15 Eyre, John R.	Oldham Athletic	Scunthorpe United	
23 Filan, John R.	Cambridge United	Nottingham Forest	
2 Fleming, Mark J.	Aylesbury United	Staines Town	
20 Foot, Daniel F.	Southend United	Crawley Town	
31 Fowler, Lee	Dagenham & Redbridge	Barking	
18 Gray, Ian J.	Oldham Athletic	Rochdale	
5 Griffiths, Bryan K.	Blackpool	Scarborough	
15 Harford, Paul	Blackburn Rovers	Shrewsbury Town	
23 Harle, Michael J.L.	Millwall	Sittingbourne	
30 Hewlett, Matthew	Bristol City	Bath City	
16 Howe, Stephen R.	Nottingham Forest	Kettering Town	
8 Huxford, Richard	Millwall	Bradford City	
16 Innes, Lee M.	Sheffield United	Boston United	
24 Jones, Stuart J.	Hednesford Town	Bilston Town	
9 Joyce, Paul	Buckingham Town	Bedford Town	
13 Kalogeracos, Vasili	Birmingham City	Waterford United	
6 Kirkham, Paul	Stalybridge Celtic	Hyde United	
30 Loss, Colin P.	Bristol City	Bath City	
23 Lunn, Stephen	Sutton United	Dorking	
2 Lyons, Darren P.	Macclesfield Town	Fleetwood	
25 Magee, Jonathan P.	Kettering Town	Burton Albion	
23 Matthews, Neil	Lincoln City	Bury	
9 McCarthy, Anthony P.	Millwall	Crewe Alexandra	
21 McLean, Ian	Bristol Rovers	Cardiff City	
3 McMamara, Brett	Northampton Town	Corby Town	
2 Moore, Chris T.	Dagenham & Redbridge	Sudbury Town	
30 Morrell, Darren	Chelmsford City	Aveley	
8 Munden, Maurice	Dover Athletic	Ashford Town	
2 Murray, Mark	Macclesfield Town	Fleetwood	
2 Newhouse, Aidan R.	Wimbledon	Portsmouth	
23 Norris, Stephen M.	Chesterfield	Scarborough	
16 Nyamah, Kofi	Cambridge United	Stevenage Borough	
1 Parris, George M.	Birmingham City	Bristol City	
9 Patterson, Ian D.	Wigan Athletic	Stalybridge Celtic	
22 Perkins, Declan O.	Southend United	Chelmsford City	
8 Petterson, Andrew K.	Charlton Athletic	Bradford City	
23 Pettinger, Paul A.	Leeds United	Torquay United	
3 Preston, Richard J.	Northampton Town	Corby Town	
16 Rattle, Jonathan P.	Cambridge United	Stevenage Borough	
16 Richardson, Nicholas J.	Cardiff City	Chester City	
5 Rimmer, Stuart A.	Chester City	Preston North End	
30 Roberts, Darren A.	Chesterfield	Telford United	
16 Roberts, Glyn S.	Rotherham United	Buxton	
22 Roscoe, Andrew R.	Bolton Wanderers	Rotherham United	
30 Saville, Andrew V.	Birmingham City	Burnley	
22 Sedgemore, Benjamin R.	Birmingham City	Northampton Town	
8 Shipperley, Neil J.	Chelsea	Watford	
23 Short, Christian M.	Notts County	Huddersfield Town	
10 Stacey, Philip G.	Aylesbury United	Wokingham Town	
30 Starbuck, Philip M.	Huddersfield Town	Sheffield United	
23 Stoneman, Paul	Blackpool	Colchester United	
16 Sturridge, Dean	Derby County	Torquay United	
2 Taylor, Andrew	Morecambe	Bamber Bridge	
31 Tracey, Simon P.	Sheffield United	Norwich City	
16 Trollope, Paul J.	Torquay United	Derby County	
30 Turpin, Simon J.	Crewe Alexandra	Chorley	
19 Vincent, Jamie R.	Crystal Palace	AFC Bournemouth	
16 Wallace, Raymond G.	Stoke City	Hull City	
7 Wallis, Nigel	Sudbury Town	Braintree Town	
27 Warner, Ashley S.	Peterborough United	Telford United	
2 Watson, Kevin E.	Tottenham Hotspur	Bristol City	
22 Williams, Corey	Rotherham United	Boston United	
23 Williams, John N.	Coventry City	Stoke City	
January 1995			
11 Agnew, Stephen M.	Leicester City	Sunderland	250,000
30 Barrett, Earl D.	Aston Villa	Everton	1,700,000
13 Berry, Gwynne	Woking	Sutton United	undisclosed
19 Chapman, Lee R.	West Ham United	Ipswich Town	70,000
6 Charles, Gary A.	Derby County	Aston Villa	2,900,000**
12 Cole, Andrew	Newcastle United	Manchester United	6,250,000
12 Cormack, Lee D.	Newport (IW)	Fareham Town	undisclosed
6 Cusack, Nicholas J.	Oxford United	Fulham	Free
30 Daniels, Scott	Exeter City	Northampton Town	Free
30 Deary, John S.	Burnley	Rochdale	undisclosed
18 Dennis, Leonard C.	Woking	Sutton United	undisclosed
9 Donaldson, O'Neill M.	Doncaster Rovers	Sheffield Wednesday	50,000
13 Dowie, Iain	Southampton	Crystal Palace	400,000
20 Francis, Kevin M.	Stockport County	Birmingham City	800,000
23 Gayle, John	Burnley	Stoke City	70,000
10 Gillespie, Keith R.	Manchester United	Newcastle United	1,000,000
13 Hartson, John	Luton Town	Arsenal	2,500,000
27 Hogg, Graeme J.	Heart of Midlothian	Notts County	75,000
9 Huxford, Richard	Millwall	Bradford City	50,000
6 Johnson, Thomas	Derby County	Aston Villa	combined fee**
25 Kerton, Neil	Havant Town	Fareham Town	undisclosed
13 Kiwomya, Christopher	Ipswich Town	Arsenal	1,550,000
6 Lawrence, James H.	Doncaster Rovers	Leicester City	175,000
20 Nicol, Stephen	Liverpool	Notts County	Free
12 Nogan, Lee M.	Watford	Reading	250,000
11 Odey, Paul A.	Weymouth	Fareham Town	undisclosed
11 Priest, Christopher	Everton	Chester City	Free
16 Robins, Mark G.	Norwich City	Leicester City	1,000,000
6 Shipperley, Neil J.	Chelsea	Southampton	1,200,000
9 Snodin, Ian	Everton	Oldham Athletic	Free
26 Stant, Philip	Cardiff City	Bury	undisclosed
5 Starbuck, Philip M.	Huddersfield Town	Sheffield United	150,000

	From	*To*	*Fee*
27 Teggart, Darren	Salisbury City	Witney Town	undisclosed
18 Thorne, Peter L.	Blackburn Rovers	Swindon Town	200,000
17 Trollope, Paul J.	Torquay United	Derby County	100,000
26 Yates, Dean R.	Notts County	Derby County	350,000

Temporary transfers

	From	To
20 Allen, Paul K.	Southampton	Stoke City
29 Armstrong, Craig	Nottingham Forest	Burnley
26 Bailey, Dennis L.	Queens Park Rangers	Brentford
12 Barnett, Benjamin J.	Boreham Wood	Molesey
25 Bayliss, Karl	Gloucester City	Forest Green Rovers
20 Biggins, Wayne	Stoke City	Luton Town
28 Black, Simon A.	Birmingham City	Sutton United
23 Bodley, Michael J.	Southend United	Birmingham City
24 Brown, Ian	Bristol City	Northampton Town
7 Brown, John C.	Leek Town	Ashton United
12 Challender, Gregory L.	Preston North End	Southport
13 Chapman, Lee R.	West Ham United	Southend United
14 Cherry, Richard W.	Enfield	Walton & Hersham
13 Chester, Martin G.	Enfield	Purfleet
9 Crawshaw, Gary	Stevenage Borough	Boreham Wood
13 Crocker, Marcus A.	Plymouth Argyle	Bath City
20 Darton, Scott R.	West Bromwich Albion	Blackpool
27 De Souza, Miguel	Birmingham City	Wycombe Wanderers
4 Dudley, Derek A.	West Bromwich Albion	Halesowen Town
22 Duffy, Christopher J.	Wigan Athletic	Northwich Victoria
16 Eyre, John R.	Oldham Athletic	Scunthorpe United
23 Filan, John R.	Cambridge United	Nottingham Forest
12 Fleck, Robert	Chelsea	Bristol City
13 Fleming, Mark J.	Aylesbury United	Wokingham Town
27 Gee, Philip J.	Leicester City	Plymouth Argyle
19 Given, Seamus J.J.	Blackburn Rovers	Swindon Town
15 Gray, Ian J.	Olham Athletic	Rochdale
9 Gregory, David S.	Ipswich Town	Hereford United
17 Harford, Paul	Blackburn Rovers	Shrewsbury Town
26 Haywood, Paul	Nottingham Forest	Grantham Town
27 Heggs, Carl S.	West Bromwich Albion	Bristol Rovers
12 Helliwell, Ian	Rotherham United	Stockport County
27 Henderson, Damien M.	Scunthorpe United	Hereford United
13 Hilton, Robert C.	Oldham Athletic	Northwich Victoria
27 Holland, Matthew R.	West Ham United	Bournemouth AFC
2 Hough, John A.	Sittingbourne	Ashford Town
16 Howe, Stephen R.	Nottingham Forest	Kettering Town
6 Jeffers, John J.	Port Vale	Shrewsbury Town
12 Jemson, Nigel B.	Notts County	Watford
27 Jones, Stuart J.	Hednesford Town	Bilston Town
20 Joyce, Warren G.	Burnley	Hull City
19 Kearton, Jason B.	Everton	Notts County
26 Key, Lance W.	Sheffield Wednesday	Oxford United
27 Livingstone, Richard	Burnley	Stalybridge Celtic
27 Marshall, Lee A.	Nottingham Forest	Grantham Town
13 Martin, Dean S.	Scunthorpe United	Rochdale
6 McNamara, Brett	Northampton Town	Corby Town
27 McPherson, Malcolm	West Ham United	Dagenham & Redbridge
1 Milsom, Paul J.	Bristol City	Stafford Rangers
14 Moore, Chris T.	Dagenham & Redbridge	Bishops Stortford
5 Norris, Stephen M.	Chesterfield	Scarborough
16 Nyamah, Kofi	Cambridge United	Stevenage Borough
27 Ormondroyd, Ian	Leicester City	Hull City
13 Payne, Grant	Wimbledon	Woking
9 Power, Lee M.	Bradford City	Millwall
6 Preston, Richard J.	Northampton Town	Corby Town
16 Rattle, Jonathan P.	Cambridge United	Stevenage Borough
20 Reeve, James M.	Bournemouth AFC	Weymouth
30 Roberts, Darren A.	Chesterfield	Telford United
20 Rodwell, Anthony	Scarborough	Wigan Athletic
23 Rowett, Gary	Everton	Blackpool
13 Scott, Kevin W.	Tottenham Hotspur	Port Vale
23 Short, Christian M.	Notts County	Huddersfield Town
27 Smith, Nicholas L.	Sudbury Town	Northampton Town
20 Smith, Richard	Nottingham Forest	Nuneaton Borough
13 Soloman, Jason R.	Watford	Peterborough United
16 Squires, James A.	Preston North End	Stafford Rangers
13 Stacey, Philip G.	Aylesbury United	Wokingham Town
24 Stoneman, Paul	Blackpool	Colchester United
18 Sturridge, Dean	Derby County	Torquay United
6 Taylor, Andrew	Morecambe	Fleetwood
6 Tolson, Neil	Bradford City	Chester City
31 Tracey, Simon P.	Sheffield United	Norwich City
31 Turpin, Simon J.	Crewe Alexandra	Chorley
20 Viveash, Adrian L.	Swindon Town	Reading
28 Wardle, Paul G.	Gresley Rovers	Tamworth
19 Williams, Paul A.	Crystal Palace	Sunderland
20 Youds, Edward P.	Ipswich Town	Bradford City
2 Young, Roy E.	Poole Town	Stockport County

February 1995

	From	To	Fee
23 Agnew, Paul	Grimsby Town	West Bromwich Albion	65,000
6 Bimson, Stuart J.	Macclesfield Town	Bury	12,500
18 Bradshaw, Mark	Stafford Rangers	Macclesfield Town	undisclosed
13 Brown, Ian	Bristol City	Northampton Town	nominal
24 Byrne, John F.	Oxford United	Brighton & Hove Albion	Free
10 Carr, Franz A.	Leicester City	Aston Villa	250,000
22 Davey, Simon	Carlisle United	Preston North End	75,000
4 De Souza, Juan M.	Birmingham City	Wycombe Wanderers	100,000
23 Forsyth, Michael E.	Derby County	Notts County	undisclosed
22 Gilchrist, Philip A.	Hartlepool United	Oxford United	100,000
8 Helliwell, Ian	Rotherham United	Stockport County	undisclosed
22 Hicks, Stuart J.	Preston North End	Scarborough	undisclosed
10 Lovell, Stephen J.	Hastings Town	Sittingbourne	undisclosed
21 Manson, Gary	Dorchester Town	Salisbury City	undisclosed
24 Mathie, Alexander	Newcastle United	Ipswich Town	500,000

	From	To	Fee
17 McRobert, Lee P.	Sittingbourne	Millwall	35,000
13 Mortimore, Paul J.	Cheltenham Town	Clevedon Town	undisclosed
24 Nogan, Kurt	Brighton & Hove Albion	Burnley	250,000
10 Parker, Garry S.	Aston Villa	Leicester City	550,000
16 Richardson, Kevin	Aston Villa	Coventry City	300,000
2 Roscoe, Andrew R.	Bolton Wanderers	Rotherham United	undisclosed
24 Russell, Kevin J.	AFC Bournemouth	Notts County	60,000
28 Shearer, Michael K.	Gloucester City	Halesowen Town	undisclosed
8 Taylor, Scott	Staines Town	Millwall	15,000
10 Thompson, Garry L.	Cardiff City	Northampton Town	Free
24 Thompson, Steven J.	Leicester City	Burnley	200,000
11 Ullathorne, Simon	Sittingbourne	Gloucester City	undisclosed
21 Young, Roy E.	Poole Town	Aldershot Town	200,000
Temporary transfers			
20 Allen, Paul K.	Southampton	Stoke City	
16 Asaba, Carl	Brentford	Colchester United	
8 Bannister, Andrew	Burnley	Bangor	
11 Barnett, Benjamin J.	Boreham Wood	Molesey	
25 Bayliss, Karl	Gloucester City	Forest Green Rovers	
28 Beckham, David R.	Manchester United	Preston North End	
10 Bibo, Salvatore	Sheffield United	Chesterfield	
20 Biggins, Wayne	Stoke City	Luton Town	
1 Black, Simon	Birmingham City	Sutton United	
10 Blackhurst, James	Southport	Barrow	
4 Brown, John C.	Leek Town	Ashton United	
27 Burns, Philip M.	Aldershot Town	Chesham United	
27 Carruthers, Matthew J.	Dover Athletic	Ashford Town	
24 Clarke, Michael D.	Solihull Borough	Sutton Coldfield Town	
2 Coll, Owen O.	Tottenham Hotspur	Yeovil Town	
17 Cooksey, Scott A.	Peterborough United	Stalybridge Celtic	
21 Cousins, Clifford M.	Buckingham Town	Chesham United	
3 Currie, Darren	West Ham United	Shrewsbury Town	
3 Cutler, Neil	West Bromwich Albion	Cheltenham Town	
19 Darton, Scott R.	West Bromwich Albion	Blackpool	
13 Dickins, Matthew J.	Blackburn Rovers	Stockport County	
13 Donovan, Neil	Worcester City	Racing Club Warwick	
2 Dudley, Derek A.	West Bromwich Albion	Halesowen Town	
10 Dunphy, Nicholas O.	Peterborough United	Hednesford Town	
20 Feuer, Anthony I.	West Ham United	Peterborough United	
13 Fleck, Robert	Chelsea	Bristol City	
11 Fleming, Mark J.	Aylesbury United	Wokingham Town	
1 Fowler, Lee	Dagenham & Redbridge	Barking	
3 Galloway, Michael	Celtic	Leicester City	
17 Gilchrist, Philip A.	Hartlepool United	Oxford United	
10 Glass, James R.	Crystal Palace	Portsmouth	
3 Harkness, Steven	Liverpool	Southend United	
2 Harle, Michael J.	Millwall	Sittingbourne	
27 Holland, Matthew R.	West Ham United	AFC Bournemouth	
3 Honor, Christian R.	Airdrieonians	Cardiff City	
7 Hough, John A.	Sittingbourne	Ashford Town	
17 Hoult, Russell	Leicester City	Derby County	
20 Joyce, Warren G.	Burnley	Hull City	
21 Kearton, Jason B.	Everton	Notts County	
3 Knight, Richard	Walsall	Armitage	
17 Knott, Gareth R.	Tottenham Hotspur	Gillingham	
16 Livett, Simon R.	Cambridge United	Dover Athletic	
1 Livingstone, Richard	Burnley	Stalybridge Celtic	
1 Loss, Colin P.	Bristol City	Bath City	
4 Lunn, Stephen	Sutton United	Dorking	
13 Martin, David	Bristol City	Northampton Town	
3 Middlemass, Scott L.	Northampton Town	Sudbury Town	
24 Midwood, Michael A.	Huddersfield Town	Macclesfield Town	
2 Millen, Andrew F.	Kilmarnock	Ipswich Town	
24 Mills, Lee	Wolverhampton Wanderers	Derby County	
11 Moore, Chris T.	Dagenham & Redbridge	Bishops Stortford	
16 Moore, Neil	Everton	Oldham Athletic	
1 Morrell, Darren	Chelmsford City	Aveley	
3 Musgrave, Sean	Sunderland	Gateshead	
16 Nyamah, Kofi	Cambridge United	Stevenage Borough	
24 Oldfield, David C.	Leicester City	Millwall	
28 Ormondroyd, Ian	Leicester City	Hull City	
9 Parris, George M.	Birmingham City	Brighton & Hove Albion	
14 Payne, Grant	Wimbledon	Woking	
3 Pettinger, Paul A.	Leeds United	Halifax Town	
16 Quigley, Michael A.	Manchester City	Wrexham	
16 Rattle, Jonathan P.	Cambridge United	Stevenage Borough	
18 Reeve, James M.	AFC Bournemouth	Weymouth	
14 Rhodes, Andrew C.	St. Johnstone	Bolton Wanderers	
4 Roberts, Barry J.&	Dagenham & Redbridge	Billericay Town	
27 Roberts, Darren A.	Chesterfield	Telford United	
17 Romasz, Anton	Bognor Regis Town	Worthing	
19 Rowett, Gary	Everton	Blackpool	
13 Scott, Kevin W.	Tottenham Hotspur	Port Vale	
11 Sheppard, James	Blackpool	Horwich RMI	
3 Skelly, Richard B.	Northampton Town	Sudbury Town	
17 Skiverton, Terence J.	Chelsea	Wycombe Wanderers	
16 Squires, James A.	Preston North End	Stafford Rangers	
11 Stacey, Philip G.	Aylesbury United	Wokingham Town	
8 Stewart, Paul A.	Liverpool	Burnley	
3 Taylor, Raymond	Chelmsford City	Purfleet	
11 Thorpe, Lee A.	Blackpool	Horwich RMI	
27 Todd, Andrew	Middlesbrough	Swindon Town	
20 Trebble, Neil D.	Preston North End	Scarborough	
14 Verrall, Damon	Sittingbourne	Ashford Town	
6 Verveer, Etienne	Millwall	Bradford City	
20 Viveash, Adrian L.	Swindon Town	Reading	
10 Watson, David G.	Witney Town	Marlow	
16 Watson, Kevin E.	Tottenham Hotspur	Barnet	
3 Westley, Shane L.M.	Brentford	Southend United	
14 Wilkin, Kevin	Northampton Town	Rushden & Diamonds	
3 Williams, John	Coventry City	Swansea City	

	From	To	Fee
4 Wordsworth, Dean	Dagenham & Redbridge	Billericay Town	
22 Youds, Edward P.	Ipswich Town	Bradford City	
2 Young, Roy E.	Poole Town	Stockport County	

March 1995

9 Abrahams, Paul	Colchester United	Brentford	30,000
23 Angell, Brett A.M.	Everton	Sunderland	600,000
17 Bale, Kevin	Newport (IW)	Whitchurch United	undisclosed
18 Bayliss, Karl	Gloucester City	Forest Green Rovers	undisclosed
2 Blewden, Colin G.	Dover Athletic	Gravesend & Northfleet	undisclosed
24 Boden, Christopher D.	Aston Villa	Derby County	150,000
23 Bogie, Ian	Leyton Orient	Port Vale	50,000
24 Boyce, David J.	Gravesend & Northfleet	Havant Town	undisclosed
22 Brown, Steven R.	Colchester United	Gillingham	exch.
9 Brownrigg, Andrew D.	Hereford United	Norwich City	100,000
2 Burrows, David	Everton	Coventry City	1,100,000
26 Clarke, Kenneth R.	Abingdon Town	Marlow	undisclosed
23 Collett, Andrew A.	Middlesbrough	Bristol Rovers	10,000
22 Darton, Scott R.	West Bromwich Albion	Blackpool	nominal
17 Dickins, Matthew J.	Blackburn Rovers	Stockport County	undisclosed
23 Dickson, Kerry M.	Luton Town	Millwall	5000
23 Drysdale, Jason	Newcastle United	Swindon Town	340,000
23 Fickling, Ashley	Sheffield United	Grimsby Town	Free
17 Filan, John R.	Cambridge United	Coventry City	300,000
31 Fjortoft, Jan-Aage.	Swindon Town	Middlesbrough	1,300,000
30 Hay, Darren A.	Cambridge United	Woking	undisclosed
13 Hayward, Steve L.	Derby County	Carlisle United	100,000
23 Hazel, Desmond L.	Rotherham United	Chesterfield	undisclosed
28 Holmes, David J.	Gresley Rovers	Gloucester City	undisclosed
3 Hooper, Dean R.	Hayes	Swindon Town	undisclosed
23 Houghton, Raymond J.	Aston Villa	Crystal Palace	300,000
23 Ironside, Ian	Stockport County	Scarborough	Free
3 Isaac, Lee	Burgess Hill Town	Hastings Town	undisclosed
15 Kenna, Jeffrey J.	Southampton	Blackburn Rovers	1,500,000
21 Kennedy, Mark	Millwall	Liverpool	2,300,000
12 Lancaster, David	Halifax Town	Bury	Free
31 Lomas, Andrew J.	Stevenage Borough	Rushden & Diamonds	undisclosed
2 Lydiate, Jason L.	Bolton Wanderers	Blackpool	75,000
17 Matthews, Robert	Notts County	Luton Town	80,000
17 McCarthy, Anthony P.	Millwall	Colchester United	Free
20 McGavin, Steven J.	Birmingham City	Wycombe Wanderers	140,000
2 Mills, Lee	Wolverhampton Wanderers	Derby County	400,000
23 O'Shea, Daniel E.	Cambridge United	Northampton Town	Free
6 Rake, Barry D.	Chesham United	Slough Town	undisclosed
23 Reeve, James M.	Bournemouth AFC	Hereford United	undisclosed
10 Reeves, Neil	Clevedon Town	Gloucester City	undisclosed
22 Reinelt, Robert S.	Gillingham	Colchester United	exch.
23 Roche, David	Doncaster Rovers	Southend United	55,000
22 Scott, Richard P.	Birmingham City	Shrewsbury Town	undisclosed
22 Shaw, Darren R.	Wolverhampton Wanderers	Northampton Town	Free
23 Sherlock, Paul G.	Notts County	Mansfield Town	15,000
10 Simpson, Wayne W.	Stafford Rangers	Hednesford Town	undisclosed
17 Soloman, Jason R.	Watford	Wycombe Wanderers	Free
2 Storer, Stuart J.	Exeter City	Brighton & Hove Albion	15,000
22 Strachan, Gordon D.	Leeds United	Coventry City	Free
23 Swailes, Christopher W.	Doncaster Rovers	Ipswich Town	150,000
23 Taylor, John P.	Bradford City	Luton Town	200,000
23 Thompson, David G.	Blackpool	Cambridge United	Free
10 Trebble, Neil D.	Preston North End	Scarborough	undisclosed
17 Watson, Gordon W.	Sheffield Wednesday	Southampton	1,200,000
22 Williams, Richard J.	Atherstone United	Hednesford Town	undisclosed
23 Withers, Peter	Chorley	Morecambe	undisclosed
10 Woodman, Andrew J.	Exeter City	Northampton Town	Free
13 Woodward, Andrew	Crewe Alexandra	Bury	undisclosed
10 Wright, Alan	Blackburn Rovers	Aston Villa	900,000
17 Youds, Edward P.	Ipswich Town	Bradford City	150,000

Temporary transfers

26 Allen, Paul K.	Southampton	Stoke City
19 Asaba, Carl	Brentford	Colchester United
8 Aspinall, Warren	Bournemouth AFC	Carlisle United
31 Banton, Michael	Walton & Hersham	Chertsey Town
28 Barnett, Benjamin J.	Boreham Wood	Leyton
23 Battersby, Tony	Sheffield United	Southend United
10 Bibbo, Salvatore	Sheffield United	Chesterfield
2 Black, Kingsley	Nottingham Forest	Sheffield United
2 Black, Simon A.	Birmingham City	Yeovil Town
29 Bolton, James I.	Kingstonian	Carshalton Athletic
15 Booth, Kevin J.	Stalybridge Celtic	Ashton United
23 Booty, Justin	Colchester United	Wivenhoe Town
31 Brown, Dereck	Walton & Hersham	St Albans City
4 Brown, John C.	Leek Town	Ashton United
9 Byrne, Paul P.	Celtic	Brighton & Hove Albion
10 Campbell, Jamie	Luton Town	Cambridge United
6 Carey, Alan W.	Reading	Weymouth
25 Carruthers, Matthew J.	Dover Athletic	Ashford Town
7 Ceraolo, Mark	Crewe Alexandra	Congleton Town
22 Chamberlain, Alec F.	Sunderland	Liverpool
18 Cooksey, Scott A.	Peterborough United	Stalybridge Celtic
29 Crocker, Marcus A.	Plymouth Argyle	Dorchester Town
19 Darton, Scott R.	West Bromwich Albion	Blackpool
14 Donovan, Neil	Worcester City	Racing Club Warwick
23 Dreyer, John B.	Stoke City	Bolton Wanderers
21 Farrelly, Gareth	Aston Villa	Rotherham United
20 Feuer, Anthony I.	West Ham United	Peterborough United
2 Filan, John R.	Cambridge United	Coventry City
23 Flatts, Mark	Arsenal	Bristol City
16 Fleming, Mark J.	Aylesbury United	Wokingham Town
17 Ford, Stuart T.	Scarborough	Halifax Town
10 Forrester, Jamie	Leeds United	Grimsby Town
7 Galloway, Michael	Celtic	Leicester City
3 Gardiner, Mark C.	Crewe Alexandra	Chester City

	From	To	Fee
18 Garland, Peter J.	Charlton Athletic	Wycombe Wanderers	
10 Germaine, Gary	West Bromwich Albion	Halesowen Town	
28 Gittings, Martin A.	Stevenage Borough	Hendon	
13 Glass, James R.	Crystal Palace	Portsmouth	
23 Gordon, Dale A.	West Ham United	Peterborough United	
24 Gore, Ian G.	Blackpool	Chorley	
3 Gregory, Neil R.	Ipswich Town	Scunthorpe United	
5 Harle, Michael J.	Millwall	Sittingbourne	
4 Harper, Lee J.	Scarborough	Goole Town	
6 Henderson, Damien M.	Scunthorpe United	Hartlepool United	
23 Hendon, Ian M.	Leyton Orient	Birmingham City	
30 Holden, Mark C.	Stoke City	Telford United	
27 Holland, Matthew R.	West Ham United	Bournemouth AFC	
10 Holmes, Steven P.	Preston North End	Hartlepool United	
20 Hoult, Russell	Leicester City	Derby County	
23 Inglethorpe, Alex M.	Watford	Barnet	
23 Jemson, Nigel B.	Notts County	Coventry City	
2 Joseph, Roger A.	Wimbledon	Millwall	
31 Kempton, David H.	Kingstonian	Walton & Hersham	
18 Kirkham, Paul	Stalybridge Celtic	Hyde United	
6 Knight, Richard	Walsall	Armitage	
21 Knott, Gareth R.	Tottenham Hotspur	Gillingham	
10 Langford, Timothy	Wycombe Wanderers	Kidderminster Harriers	
10 Le Bihan, Neil E.	Peterborough United	Yeovil Town	
17 Lomas, Andrew J.	Stevenage Borough	Cambridge United	
23 Lund, Gary J.	Notts County	Hull City	
7 Lunn, Stephen	Sutton United	Dorking	
31 Lyons, Darren P.	Macclesfield Town	Ashton United	
23 Margetson, Martyn W.	Manchester City	Luton Town	
30 Marginson, Karl K.	Rotherham United	Macclesfield Town	
16 Martin, David	Bristol City	Northampton Town	
28 Matteo, Dominic	Liverpool	Sunderland	
10 McGleish, Scott	Charlton Athletic	Leyton Orient	
23 McNamara, Brett	Northampton Town	Kings Lynn	
7 McPherson, Malcolm	West Ham United	Dagenham & Redbridge	
20 Mercer, William	Sheffield United	Nottingham Forest	
27 Midwood, Michael A.	Huddersfield Town	Macclesfield Town	
3 Miles, Benjamin D.	Swansea City	Trowbridge Town	
11 Moore, Chris T.	Dagenham & Redbridge	Bishops Stortford	
23 Morah, Olisa H.	Cambridge United	Torquay United	
5 Musgrave, Sean	Sunderland	Gateshead	
24 Norman, John	Morecambe	Chorley	
28 Norris, Stephen M.	Chesterfield	VS Rugby	
26 Oldfield, David C.	Leicester City	Millwall	
23 O'Neill, Darren S.	Kingstonian	Wealdstone	
20 Owers, Adrian R.	Chelmsford City	Worthing	
29 Palmer, Lee J.	Gillingham	Sittingbourne	
13 Parris, George M.	Birmingham City	Brighton & Hove Albion	
17 Payne, Grant	Wimbledon	Woking	
23 Peel, Nathan J.	Burnley	Rotherham United	
3 Pettinger, Paul A.	Leeds United	Halifax Town	
17 Pettinger, Paul A.	Leeds United	Kettering Town	
9 Price, Gareth	Kettering Town	Gainsborough Trinity	
16 Quinn, Michael	Coventry City	Watford	
10 Read, Paul	Arsenal	Leyton Orient	
14 Rhodes, Andrew C.	Bolton Wanderers	Norwich City	
25 Richards, Dean I.	Bradford City	Wolverhampton Wanderers	
20 Rowe, Rodney C.	Huddersfield Town	Bury	
19 Rowett, Gary	Everton	Blackpool	
15 Scott, Kevin W.	Tottenham Hotspur	Port Vale	
22 Scott, Robert	Sheffield United	Scarborough	
23 Shaw, Paul	Arsenal	Burnley	
24 Shea, Peter	Collier Row	East Thurrock United	
19 Skiverton, Terence J.	Chelsea	Wycombe Wanderers	
17 Stewart, William I.	Northampton Town	Chesterfield	
17 Sugrue, James S.	Kingstonian	Aldershot Town	
3 Taylor, Raymond	Chelmsford City	Purfleet	
18 Timons, Christopher	Mansfield Town	Stafford Rangers	
27 Todd, Andrew	Middlesbrough	Swindon Town	
6 Turnbull, Lee M.	Wycombe Wanderers	Scunthorpe United	
10 Turpin, Simon J.	Crewe Alexandra	Northwich Victoria	
31 Verrall, Damon	Sittingbourne	Erith & Belvedere	
8 Verveer, Etienne	Millwall	Bradford City	
23 Walker, Richard N.	Notts County	Mansfield Town	
28 Warner, Ashley S.	Peterborough United	Bromsgrove Rovers	
31 Warren, Christer	Southampton	Cheltenham Town	
19 Watson, Kevin E.	Tottenham Hotspur	Barnet	
24 Webster, Simon P.	West Ham United	Oldham Athletic	
17 Whitney, John D.	Huddersfield Town	Wigan Athletic	
4 Wild, Robert P.	Aylesbury United	Walton & Hersham	
10 Wilkinson, Ian M.	Crewe Alexandra	Congleton Town	
1 Williams, Christopher	Hereford United	Worcester City	
6 Williams, Darren P.	Dover Athletic	Welling United	
9 Williams, Martin K.	Luton Town	Colchester United	
13 Williams, Paul A.	Crystal Palace	Birmingham City	
17 Williams, Paul R.C.	Coventry City	Huddersfield Town	
13 Wordsworth, Dean	Dagenham & Redbridge	Harlow Town	
2 Wratten, Adam P.	Birmingham City	Yeovil Town	
April 1995			
25 Holland, Matthew R.	West Ham United	AFC Bournemouth	undisclosed
7 Page, Darrell	Wealdstone	Raunds Town	undisclosed
12 Whelan, Philip J.	Ipswich Town	Middlesbrough	undisclosed
May 1995			
15 Beckford, Jason N.	Millwall	Northampton Town	undisclosed
23 Bracewell, Paul W.	Newcastle United	Sunderland	undisclosed
17 Doyle, Maurice	Queens Park Rangers	Millwall	undisclosed
18 Inglethorpe, Alex M.	Watford	Leyton Orient	undisclosed
19 Vowden, Colin D.	Cambridge City	Cambridge United	undisclosed
9 Watson, Mark L.	Sutton United	West Ham United	undisclosed

LEAGUE ATTENDANCES 1994–95

FA CARLING PREMIERSHIP STATISTICS

	Average Gate			Season 1994/95	
	1993/94	1994/95	+/–%	Highest	Lowest
Arsenal	30,563	35,330	+15.6	38,368	27,213
Aston Villa	29,015	29,756	+2.6	40,154	22,241
Blackburn Rovers	17,721	25,272	+42.6	30,545	20,586
Chelsea	19,416	21,057	+8.5	31,139	14,130
Coventry City	13,352	15,980	+19.7	21,858	9,509
Crystal Palace	15,656	14,992	–4.2	18,224	10,964
Everton	22,876	31,291	+36.8	40,011	23,295
Ipswich Town	16,382	16,818	+2.7	22,553	11,282
Leeds United	34,493	32,925	–4.5	39,426	27,246
Leicester City	16,005	19,532	+22.0	21,393	15,248
Liverpool	38,493	34,176	–11.2	40,014	27,183
Manchester City	26,709	22,725	–14.9	27,850	19,150
Manchester United	44,244	43,681	–1.3	43,868	43,120
Newcastle United	33,679	34,690	+3.0	35,626	34,163
Norwich City	18,164	18,625	+2.5	21,843	13,530
Nottingham Forest	23,051	23,633	+2.5	28,882	20,287
Queens Park Rangers	14,228	14,613	+2.7	18,948	10,189
Sheffield Wednesday	27,191	26,572	–2.3	34,051	20,395
Southampton	14,751	14,685	–0.4	15,202	12,876
Tottenham Hotspur	27,160	27,259	+0.4	33,040	22,387
West Ham United	20,572	20,118	–2.2	24,783	16,959
Wimbledon	10,474	10,230	–2.3	18,224	5,268

ENDSLEIGH INSURANCE LEAGUE: DIVISION ONE ATTENDANCES

	Average Gate			Season 1994/95	
	1993/94	1994/95	+/–%	Highest	Lowest
Barnsley	7,610	6,509	–14.5	11,782	3,659
Bolton Wanderers	10,498	13,029	+24.1	18,370	9,519
Bristol City	8,852	8,005	–9.6	11,127	6,030
Burnley	11,317	12,135	+7.2	17,808	9,551
Charlton Athletic	8,056	10,211	+26.8	13,863	8,167
Derby County	15,937	13,589	–14.7	16,839	10,585
Grimsby Town	5,989	5,921	–1.1	10,112	3,216
Luton Town	7,878	7,350	–6.7	9,651	5,764
Middlesbrough	10,400	18,807	+80.8	23,903	14,878
Millwall	9,821	7,685	–21.7	12,412	5,260
Notts County	8,314	7,195	–13.5	11,102	4,703
Oldham Athletic	12,563	8,444	–32.8	11,962	5,465
Port Vale	8,323	9,174	+10.2	19,510	7,141
Portsmouth	11,692	8,269	–29.3	13,466	5,272
Reading	6,932	9,350	+34.9	13,223	6,921
Sheffield United	19,562	14,462	–26.1	20,693	11,568
Southend United	6,105	5,146	–15.7	8,522	3,619
Stoke City	15,931	12,910	–18.9	20,408	9,105
Sunderland	16,934	15,344	–9.4	19,549	11,661
Swindon Town	15,274	9,744	–56.8	14,436	7,658
Tranmere Rovers	8,099	8,906	+10.0	16,377	5,480
Watford	7,907	8,125	+2.8	10,108	6,024
West Bromwich Albion	16,840	15,200	–9.7	21,071	11,782
Wolverhampton Wanderers	22,008	25,940	+17.9	28,298	22,768

ENDSLEIGH INSURANCE LEAGUE: DIVISION TWO ATTENDANCES

	Average Gate			*Season 1994/95*	
	1993/94	1994/95	+/–%	Highest	Lowest
AFC Bournemouth	4,355	4,391	+0.8	10,747	2,505
Birmingham City	14,506	16,983	+17.1	25,581	10,600
Blackpool	4,757	4,771	+0.3	8,333	3,438
Bradford City	6,395	6,152	–3.8	11,300	3,535
Brentford	5,611	6,536	+16.5	10,079	4,031
Brighton & Hove Albion	7,730	7,563	–2.2	11,004	5,316
Bristol Rovers	5,338	5,173	–3.1	8,256	3,694
Cambridge United	3,686	3,443	–6.6	5,828	2,328
Cardiff City	6,072	4,543	–25.2	7,420	2,560
Chester City	3,191	2,388	–25.2	4,974	1,191
Crewe Alexandra	3,991	4,239	+6.2	6,359	3,242
Huddersfield Town	6,372	11,665	+83.1	18,775	8,552
Hull City	5,943	4,721	–20.6	10,220	2,694
Leyton Orient	4,237	3,436	–18.9	7,578	2,338
Oxford United	6,877	6,148	–10.6	9,540	4,594
Peterborough United	7,412	5,055	–31.8	8,796	3,554
Plymouth Argyle	9,003	5,832	–35.2	8,550	3,824
Rotherham United	3,736	3,278	–12.3	6,687	2,208
Shrewsbury Town	4,402	4,013	–8.8	5,949	2,849
Stockport County	5,090	4,525	–11.1	5,652	3,040
Swansea City	3,534	3,582	+1.4	5,807	2,065
Wrexham	3,961	4,071	+2.8	6,472	1,823
Wycombe Wanderers	5,448	5,856	+7.5	7,683	4,388
York City	4,633	3,685	–20.5	6,828	2,301

ENDSLEIGH INSURANCE LEAGUE: DIVISION THREE ATTENDANCES

	Average Gate			*Season 1994/95*	
	1993/94	1994/95	+/–%	Highest	Lowest
Barnet	2,431	2,201	–9.5	3,579	1,325
Bury	2,597	3,223	+24.1	6,790	2,145
Carlisle United	5,524	7,422	+34.4	12,412	5,141
Chesterfield	3,188	3,528	+10.7	7,283	2,136
Colchester United	2,857	3,280	+14.8	6,055	2,231
Darlington	2,276	2,346	+3.1	3,992	1,548
Doncaster Rovers	2,478	2,585	+4.3	4,796	1,611
Exeter City	3,320	2,484	–25.2	5,538	1,551
Fulham	4,655	4,207	–9.6	6,195	2,729
Gillingham	3,148	3,206	+1.8	4,737	2,257
Hartlepool United	2,076	1,953	–5.9	3,854	1,354
Hereford United	2,262	2,367	+4.6	3,135	1,489
Lincoln City	3,179	3,276	+3.1	6,477	1,969
Mansfield Town	2,718	2,946	+8.4	5,197	2,247
Northampton Town	3,454	5,086	+47.2	7,461	2,466
Preston North End	7,377	8,469	+14.8	11,866	5,833
Rochdale	2,657	2,184	–17.8	4,012	1,170
Scarborough	1,681	1,771	+5.4	4,266	1,179
Scunthorpe United	3,182	2,917	–8.3	4,785	2,079
Torquay United	3,437	2,968	–13.7	4,739	1,492
Walsall	4,237	4,071	–3.9	6,219	3,154
Wigan Athletic	1,897	1,748	–7.9	3,618	1,231

LEAGUE ATTENDANCES SINCE 1946–47

Season	*Matches*	*Total*	*Div. 1*	*Div. 2*	*Div. 3 (S)*	*Div. 3 (N)*
1946–47	1848	35,604,606	15,005,316	11,071,572	5,664,004	3,863,714
1947–48	1848	40,259,130	16,732,341	12,286,350	6,653,610	4,586,829
1948–49	1848	41,271,414	17,914,667	11,353,237	6,998,429	5,005,081
1949–50	1848	40,517,865	17,278,625	11,694,158	7,104,155	4,440,927
1950–51	2028	39,584,967	16,679,454	10,780,580	7,367,884	4,757,109
1951–52	2028	39,015,866	16,110,322	11,066,189	6,958,927	4,880,428
1952–53	2028	37,149,966	16,050,278	9,686,654	6,704,299	4,708,735
1953–54	2028	36,174,590	16,154,915	9,510,053	6,311,508	4,198,114
1954–55	2028	34,133,103	15,087,221	8,988,794	5,996,017	4,051,071
1955–56	2028	33,150,809	14,108,961	9,080,002	5,692,479	4,269,367
1956–57	2028	32,744,405	13,803,037	8,718,162	5,622,189	4,601,017
1957–58	2028	33,562,208	14,468,652	8,663,712	6,097,183	4,332,661
					Div. 3	*Div. 4*
1958–59	2028	33,610,985	14,727,691	8,641,997	5,946,600	4,276,697
1959–60	2028	32,538,611	14,391,227	8,399,627	5,739,707	4,008,050
1960–61	2028	28,619,754	12,926,948	7,033,936	4,784,256	3,874,614
1961–62	2015	27,979,902	12,061,194	7,453,089	5,199,106	3,266,513
1962–63	2028	28,885,852	12,490,239	7,792,770	5,341,362	3,261,481
1963–64	2028	28,535,022	12,486,626	7,594,158	5,419,157	3,035,081
1964–65	2028	27,641,168	12,708,752	6,984,104	4,436,245	3,512,067
1965–66	2028	27,206,980	12,480,644	6,914,757	4,779,150	3,032,429
1966–67	2028	28,902,596	14,242,957	7,253,819	4,421,172	2,984,648
1967–68	2028	30,107,298	15,289,410	7,450,410	4,013,087	3,354,391
1968–69	2028	29,382,172	14,584,851	7,382,390	4,339,656	3,075,275
1969–70	2028	29,600,972	14,868,754	7,581,728	4,223,761	2,926,729
1970–71	2028	28,194,146	13,954,337	7,098,265	4,377,213	2,764,331
1971–72	2028	28,700,729	14,484,603	6,769,308	4,697,392	2,749,426
1972–73	2028	25,448,642	13,998,154	5,631,730	3,737,252	2,081,506
1973–74	2027	24,982,203	13,070,991	6,326,108	3,421,624	2,163,480
1974–75	2028	25,577,977	12,613,178	6,955,970	4,086,145	1,992,684
1975–76	2028	24,896,053	13,089,861	5,798,405	3,948,449	2,059,338
1976–77	2028	26,182,800	13,647,585	6,250,597	4,152,218	2,132,400
1977–78	2028	25,392,872	13,255,677	6,474,763	3,332,042	2,330,390
1978–79	2028	24,540,627	12,704,549	6,153,223	3,374,558	2,308,297
1979–80	2028	24,623,975	12,163,002	6,112,025	3,999,328	2,349,620
1980–81	2028	21,907,569	11,392,894	5,175,442	3,637,854	1,701,379
1981–82	2028	20,006,961	10,420,793	4,750,463	2,836,915	1,998,790
1982–83	2028	18,766,158	9,295,613	4,974,937	2,943,568	1,552,040
1983–84	2028	18,358,631	8,711,448	5,359,757	2,729,942	1,557,484
1984–85	2028	17,849,835	9,761,404	4,030,823	2,667,008	1,390,600
1985–86	2028	16,488,577	9,037,854	3,551,968	2,490,481	1,408,274
1986–87	2028	17,379,218	9,144,676	4,168,131	2,350,970	1,715,441
1987–88	2030	17,959,732	8,094,571	5,341,599	2,751,275	1,772,287
1988–89	2036	18,464,192	7,809,993	5,887,805	3,035,327	1,791,067
1989–90	2036	19,445,442	7,883,039	6,867,674	2,803,551	1,891,178
1990–91	2036	19,508,202	8,618,709	6,285,068	2,835,759	1,768,666
1991–92	2064*	20,487,273	9,989,160	5,809,787	2,993,352	1,694,974
			FA Premier	*Div. 1*	*Div. 2*	*Div. 3*
1992–93	2028	20,657,327	9,759,809	5,874,017	3,483,073	1,540,428
1993–94	2028	21,683,381	10,644,551	6,487,104	2,972,702	1,579,024
1994–95	2028	21,856,020	11,213,168	6,044,293	3,037,752	1,560,807

This is the first time since the war that attendances have risen for nine consecutive seasons.

**Figures include matches played by Aldershot.*

LEAGUE CUP FINALISTS 1961–95

Played as a two-leg final until 1966. All subsequent finals at Wembley.

Year	Winners	Runners-up	Score
1961	Aston Villa	Rotherham U	0-2, 3-0 (aet)
1962	Norwich C	Rochdale	3-0, 1-0
1963	Birmingham C	Aston Villa	3-1, 0-0
1964	Leicester C	Stoke C	1-1, 3-2
1965	Chelsea	Leicester C	3-2, 0-0
1966	WBA	West Ham U	1-2, 4-1
1967	QPR	WBA	3-2
1968	Leeds U	Arsenal	1-0
1969	Swindon T	Arsenal	3-1 (aet)
1970	Manchester C	WBA	2-1 (aet)
1971	Tottenham H	Aston Villa	2-0
1972	Stoke C	Chelsea	2-1
1973	Tottenham H	Norwich C	1-0
1974	Wolverhampton W	Manchester C	2-1
1975	Aston Villa	Norwich C	1-0
1976	Manchester C	Newcastle U	2-1
1977	Aston Villa	Everton	0-0, 1-1 (aet), 3-2 (aet)
1978	Nottingham F	Liverpool	0-0 (aet), 1-0
1979	Nottingham F	Southampton	3-2
1980	Wolverhampton W	Nottingham F	1-0
1981	Liverpool	West Ham U	1-1 (aet), 2-1
MILK CUP			
1982	Liverpool	Tottenham H	3-1 (aet)
1983	Liverpool	Manchester U	2-1 (aet)
1984	Liverpool	Everton	0-0 (aet), 1-0
1985	Norwich C	Sunderland	1-0
1986	Oxford U	QPR	3-0
LITTLEWOODS CUP			
1987	Arsenal	Liverpool	2-1
1988	Luton T	Arsenal	3-2
1989	Nottingham F	Luton T	3-1
1990	Nottingham F	Oldham Ath	1-0
RUMBELOWS LEAGUE CUP			
1991	Sheffield W	Manchester U	1-0
1992	Manchester U	Nottingham F	1-0
COCA COLA CUP			
1993	Arsenal	Sheffield W	2-1
1994	Aston Villa	Manchester U	3-1
1995	Liverpool	Bolton W	2-1

LEAGUE CUP WINS
Liverpool 5, Aston Villa 4, Nottingham F 4, Arsenal 2, Manchester C 2, Norwich C 2, Tottenham H 2, Wolverhampton W 2, Birmingham C 1, Chelsea 1, Leeds U 1, Leicester C 1, Luton T 1, Manchester U 1, Oxford U 1, QPR 1, Sheffield W 1, Stoke C 1, Swindon T 1, WBA 1.

APPEARANCES IN FINALS
Liverpool 7, Aston Villa 6, Nottingham F 6, Arsenal 5, Manchester U 4, Norwich C 4, Manchester C 3, Tottenham H 3, WBA 3, Chelsea 2, Everton 2, Leicester C 2, Luton T 2, QPR 2, Sheffield W 2, Stoke C 2, West Ham U 2, Wolverhampton W 2, Birmingham C 1, Bolton W 1, Leeds U 1, Newcastle U 1, Oldham Ath 1, Oxford U 1, Rochdale 1, Rotherham U 1, Southampton 1, Sunderland 1, Swindon T 1.

APPEARANCES IN SEMI-FINALS
Aston Villa 9, Liverpool 9, Tottenham H 8, Arsenal 7, Manchester U 7, West Ham U 7, Nottingham F 6, Chelsea 5, Manchester C 5, Norwich C 5, Leeds U 4, WBA 4, Burnley 3, Everton 3, QPR 3, Sheffield W 3, Swindon T 3, Wolverhampton W 3, Birmingham C 2, Blackburn R 2, Bolton W 2, Bristol C 2, Coventry C 2, Crystal Palace 2, Ipswich T 2, Leicester C 2, Luton T 2, Middlesbrough 2, Oxford U 2, Plymouth Arg 2, Southampton 2, Stoke C 2, Sunderland 2, Blackpool 1, Bury 1, Cardiff C 1, Carlisle U 1, Chester C 1, Derby Co 1, Huddersfield T 1, Newcastle U 1, Oldham Ath 1, Peterborough U 1, Rochdale 1, Rotherham U 1, Shrewsbury T 1, Tranmere R 1, Walsall 1, Watford 1.

COCA-COLA CUP 1994–95

FIRST ROUND FIRST LEG

15 AUG

Doncaster R (1) 2 *(Jones, Torfason)*
Wrexham (0) 4 *(Bennett, Connolly, Humes, Watkin)* 1925
Doncaster R: Suckling; Kitchen, Limber, Brabin, Hackett, Swailes, Lawrence, Thew, Jones (Torfason), Donaldson, Parrish (Finlay).
Wrexham: Marriott; Jones, Hardy, Blake, Humes, Pejic, Bennett, Brammer, Connolly, Watkin, Phillips (Taylor).

16 AUG

Barnet (0) 4 *(Freedman 2, Cooper 2)*
Leyton Orient (0) 0 2187
Barnet: Phillips; McDonald, Gale, Hoddle, Walker, Newson (Primus), Tomlinson (Scott), Freedman, Hodges, Cooper, Wilson.
Leyton Orient: Heald; Warren, Austin, Purse, Hendon, Lakin, Barnett (Gray), Cockerill, Bogie, West, Dempsey.

Blackpool (0) 1 *(Quinn)*
Chesterfield (2) 2 *(Perkins, Cheetham)* 2570
Blackpool: Sealey; Brown, Burke, Horner (Gouck), Briggs, Gore, Rodwell (Quinn), Gibson, Bamber, Ellis, Griffiths.
Chesterfield: Marples; Hewitt, Rogers, Fairclough, Carr, Perkins, Curtis, Norris, Davies, Moss, Cheetham.

Bournemouth (2) 2 *(Russell, Cotterill)*
Northampton T (0) 0 2587
Bournemouth: Moss; O'Driscoll, O'Connor, Morris, Watson, Leadbitter, Beardsmore, Aspinall (Mean), Fletcher, Cotterill, Russell.
Northampton T: Stewart; Pascoe (Wilkin), Curtis, Norton, Warburton, Sampson, Harmon, Byrne, Trott, Grayson, Bell.

Bradford C (0) 2 *(Taylor, Duxbury)*
Grimsby T (0) 1 *(Gilbert)* 5986
Bradford C: Tomlinson; Benn, Jacobs, Robson, Sinnott, Richards, Shutt, Kamara (Duxbury), Taylor, Jewell, Murray (Tolson).
Grimsby T: Crichton; Jobling, Croft, Futcher, Lever, Shakespeare, Watson, Gilbert, Livingstone (Woods), Mendonca, Groves.

Burnley (0) 1 *(Joyce)*
York C (0) 0 6390
Burnley: Beresford; Parkinson, Dowell, Davis, Winstanley, Joyce, Harper, Deary, Heath, Robinson, Lancashire.
York C: Kiely; McMillan, Hall, Pepper, Tutill, Barras, McCarthy, Cooper, Barnes, Bushell, Canham.

Bury (1) 2 *(Carter (pen), Lynch (og))*
Hartlepool U (0) 0 1515
Bury: Kelly G; Cross, Stanislaus, Mauge, Jackson, Lucketti, Mulligan, Carter, Hulme, Hughes (Johnrose), Pugh.
Hartlepool U: Jones; Ingram, Sweeney (Lynch), Gilchrist, McGuckin, Oliver, Ainsley, Sloan, Houchen, Honour (Thompson), Southall.

Cardiff C (0) 1 *(Oatway)*
Torquay U (0) 0 2690
Cardiff C: Williams D; Evans, Brazil, Aizlewood, Perry, Oatway, Griffith, Richardson, Stant, Bird (Dale), Fereday (Millar).
Torquay U: Bayes; Hodges, Stamps, Hathaway, Barrow, Curran, Trollope, Buckle, Hancox, Okorie, Goodridge.

Colchester U (0) 0
Brentford (1) 2 *(Stephenson, Taylor)* 2521
Colchester U: Cheesewright; Culling, English, Allpress, Caesar, Dennis, Fry (Roberts), Brown, Whitton, Kinsella, Abrahams.
Brentford: Dearden; Hurdle, Hutchings, Westley, Bates, Smith, Parris, Harvey, Taylor, Forster (Benjamin), Stephenson.

Crewe Alex (1) 2 *(Garvey, Ward)*
Wigan Ath (0) 1 *(Gavin)* 3054
Crewe Alex: Smith M; Booty, Annan, Wilson (Collier), Macauley, Barr, Tierney, Walters, Ward, Whalley, Garvey (Adebola).
Wigan Ath: Farnworth; Rennie, Wright, Strong, Robertson, Kilford, Campbell, Morton, Gavin (Duffy), Rimmer, Lyons.

Gillingham (0) 0
Reading (0) 1 *(Williams)* 2556
Gillingham: Barrett; Dunne, Palmer, Micklewhite, Green, Butler, Reinelt, Smith, Foster, Baker (Arnott), Watson.
Reading: Hislop; Bernal, Kerr, Hopkins, Williams, Parkinson (Holsgrove), Taylor, Gooding, Quinn, Lovell, Osborn.

Hereford U (0) 0
WBA (0) 0 5425
Hereford U: Pennock; Reece, Preedy (Pick), Davies, Smith, James, Wilkins, Downs, Cross, Williams (Clark), Steele.
WBA: Naylor; Parsley, Edwards, Phelan, Herbert, Raven, Donovan, Hamilton, Taylor, Heggs, McNally (Mellon).

Hull C (1) 2 *(Peacock, Lee)*
Scarborough (0) 1 *(Young)* 2546
Hull C: Fettis; Dakin, Graham, Hobson, Dewhurst, Abbott (Mann), Peacock, Lee, Brown, Windass, Lawford (Atkinson).
Scarborough: Kelly; Knowles, Charles, Calvert, Meyer, Rockett, Rowe, Swann, Young, Thompson, Blackstone.

Lincoln C (1) 2 *(Carbon, Schofield)*
Chester C (0) 0 2531
Lincoln C: Leaning; Schofield, Platnauer, Hebberd, Greenall, Brown, West, Onwere, Daley, Carbon, Johnson D.
Chester C: Felgate; Jenkins, Burnham, Ratcliffe, Whelan, Preece, Flitcroft, Bishop, Milner, Rimmer, Page.

Luton T (0) 1 *(Oakes)*
Fulham (0) 1 *(Moore)* 3287
Luton T: Sommer; James, Johnson, Hughes (Marshall), Greene, Peake, Telfer, Oakes, Dixon, Preece, Houghton (Linton).
Fulham: Stannard; Morgan, Herrera, Mison, Moore, Thomas, Marshall, Jupp, Cork, Brazil, Haworth.

Oxford U (1) 3 *(Moody (pen), Massey, Robinson)*
Peterborough U (1) 1 *(Morrison)* 4185
Oxford U: Whitehead; Robinson, Ford M, Dyer (Druce), Elliott, Rogan, Massey, Smith, Moody, Byrne, Allen.
Peterborough U: Cooksey; Ashley, Clark, Ebdon, Heald, Welsh, Morrison (Williams), Breen, Farrell (McGorry), Charlery, Moran.

Rochdale (1) 1 *(Whitehall)*
Mansfield T (0) 2 *(Wilkinson 2)* 1746
Rochdale: Clarke; Thackeray, Formby, Reid, Reeves, Matthews, Thompson (Ryan), Peake (Hall), Bowden, Whitehall, Stuart.
Mansfield T: Ward; Boothroyd, Baraclough, Holland, Howarth, Aspinall, Ireland, Parkin, Wilkinson, Hadley, Noteman (Castledine).

Rotherham U (0) 1 *(Varadi)*
Carlisle U (0) 0 2055
Rotherham U: Mercer; Wilder, James, Williams A, Brien (Williams C), Richardson, Hazel, Goodwin, Helliwell, Varadi, Goater (Hayward).
Carlisle U: Caig; Joyce, Gallimore, Walling, Mountfield, Edmonson, Thomas, Currie (Thorpe), Reeves, Davey, Reddish.

Scunthorpe U (1) 2 *(Henderson, Bullimore)*
Huddersfield T (0) 1 *(Scully)* 2841
Scunthorpe U: Samways; Ford, Mudd, Thornber, Knill, Bradley, Alexander, Bullimore, Juryeff, Henderson, Smith.
Huddersfield T: Francis; Billy, Cowan, Starbuck, Scully, Dyson, Baldry (Dunn), Bullock, Booth, Jepson, Reid.

Shrewsbury T (1) 2 *(Clarke W, Spink)*
Birmingham C (0) 1 *(Daish)* 5049
Shrewsbury T: Edwards; Hockaday, Lynch, Taylor, Williams, Patterson, Brown (Stevens), Clarke W, Spink, Walton, Woods (Withe).
Birmingham C: Bennett; Hiley, Scott, Shearer, Whyte, Daish, Donowa (Dominguez), Claridge, Regis, Harding, Doherty.

Southend U (0) 0
Watford (0) 0 2859
Southend U: Royce; Poole, Powell, Jones K, Bressington, Dublin, Hunt, Hone, Iorfa, Otto, Thomson (Martin).
Watford: Miller; Bazeley, Johnson, Foster, Holdsworth, Ramage, Hessenthaler, Payne, Moralee, Porter, Mooney.

Walsall (0) 4 *(Wilson 2, Lightbourne, O'Connor)*
Plymouth Arg (0) 0 2810
Walsall: Wood; Evans (Lillis), Rogers, Watkiss, Marsh, Palmer, O'Connor, Ntamark, Lightbourne, Wilson, Mehew.
Plymouth Arg: Hodge; Payne, Edworthy, Comyn, Swan, Hill, Barlow, Burnett, Nugent, Evans, Skinner (Morgan).

17 AUG

Brighton & HA (1) 2 *(McDougald, Nogan)*
Wycombe W (0) 1 *(Regis)* 6884
Brighton & HA: Rust; Munday, Pates, Chapman (Smith), Foster, McCarthy, Minton, McDougald, Nogan, Codner, Wilkins.
Wycombe W: Hyde; Cousins, Titterton (Brown), Creaser, Evans, Ryan, Carroll, Thompson, Regis, Garner (Hemmings), Stapleton.

Bristol R (1) 1 *(Tillson)*
Port Vale (0) 3 *(Foyle, Naylor, Glover L)* 3307
Bristol R: Parkin; Pritchard, Maddison, Channing, Clark, Tillson, Sterling, Miller, Stewart, Skinner, Archer.
Port Vale: Musselwhite; Sandeman, Tankard, Porter, Griffiths, Glover D, Kent, Van der Laan, Foyle, Glover L, Naylor.

Darlington (0) 2 *(Cross, Slaven)*
Barnsley (2) 2 *(Taggart, Redfearn)* 2207
Darlington: Pollitt; Appleby, Cross, Banks, Crosby, Gregan, Slaven, Painter, Gaughan, Olsson, Himsworth (Chapman).
Barnsley: Watson; Eaden, Fleming, Wilson, Taggart, Bishop, O'Connoll, Redfearn, Rammell, Payton, Snodin.

Exeter C (2) 2 *(Turner, Cecere)*
Swansea C (0) 2 *(Harris, Hodge)* 2050
Exeter C: Woodman; Daniels, Anderson (Brown), Bailey, Came, Richardson, Phillips, Thirlby, Turner, Cecere (Pears), Gavin.
Swansea C: Freestone; Jenkins, Clode, Ford, Harris, Ampadu, Bowen, Penney (Pascoe), Hayes, Cornforth, Hodge.

Portsmouth (2) 2 *(Stimson, Powell)* .
Cambridge U (0) 0 3854
Portsmouth: Poom; Gittens, Stimson, McLoughlin, Symons, Dobson, Neill, Pethick, Powell, Daniel, Hall (Rees).
Cambridge U: Filan; Hunter, Barrick, Craddock, Heathcote, O'Shea, Hyde, Rattle, Morah (Butler), Corazzin, Joseph.

Preston NE (0) 1 *(Fensome (pen))*
Stockport Co (1) 1 *(Chalk) (at Bury)* 2385
Preston NE: Richardson; Fensome, Fleming, Whalley, Hicks, Moyes, Cartwright, Kidd, Raynor, Trebble (Sale), Bryson (Conroy).
Stockport Co: Keeley; Miller, Todd, Connelly, Flynn, Gannon, Eckhardt, Ward, Francis, Armstrong, Chalk.

FIRST ROUND SECOND LEG

23 AUG

Barnsley (0) 0
Darlington (0) 0 3263
Barnsley: Watson; Eaden (Liddell), Fleming, Wilson, Taggart, Bishop, O'Connell (Bullock), Redfearn, Rammell, Payton, Snodin.
Darlington: Pollitt; Appleby, Cross, Banks, Crosby, Reed, Slaven, Painter, Gaughan, Olsson, Mattison (Himsworth).
aet; 2-2 on aggregate; Barnsley won on away goals.

Birmingham C (2) 2 *(Saville, Claridge (pen))*
Shrewsbury T (0) 0 9847
Birmingham C: Bennett; Hiley, Scott, Ward, Whyte, Daish, De Souza, Claridge, Saville, Harding, Donowa.
Shrewsbury T: Edwards; Hockaday, Lynch, Taylor, Williams, Patterson, Brown, Clarke W (Summerfield), Spink, Watson, Withe.
Birmingham C won 3-2 on aggregate.

Brentford (1) 2 *(Parris, Smith)*
Colchester U (0) 0 2315
Brentford: Dearden; Hurdle, Hutchings, Bates, Ashby, Smith, Parris, Harvey, Taylor (Mundee), Forster (Ratcliffe), Stephenson.
Colchester U: Emberson; English (Burley), Davis, Allpress, Caesar, Dennis, Roberts, Brown S, Whitton, Kinsella, Abrahams.
Brentford won 4-0 on aggregate.

Cambridge U (1) 2 *(Craddock, Barrick)*
Portsmouth (1) 3 *(Creaney, Powell 2)* 2571
Cambridge U: Filan; Hunter, Barrick, Craddock, Heathcote, O'Shea, Hyde, Granville (Morah), Butler, Corazzin (Elad), Joseph.
Portsmouth: Poom; Gittens, Stimson, McLoughlin, Symons, Dobson, Neill (Daniel), Pethick, Powell, Creaney, Hall (Burton).
Portsmouth won 5-2 on aggregate.

Carlisle U (0) 3 *(Reeves 2, Walling)*
Rotherham U (1) 1 *(Hayward)* 5004
Carlisle U: Caig; Joyce, Gallimore, Walling, Mountfield, Edmondson (Thorpe), Thomas, Currie, Reeves, Davey, Prokas.
Rotherham U: Mercer; Wilder, James, Williams A, Brien, Breckin, Hazel, Goodwin, Hayward, Varadi (Williams C), Todd.
Carlisle U won 3-2 on aggregate.

Chester C (0) 2 *(Whelan, Chambers)*
Lincoln C (3) 3 *(Schofield, West, Johnson D (pen))* 1568
Chester C: Felgate; Jenkins, Burnham, Ratcliffe, Whelan, Preece, Chambers, Bishop, Alsford, Rimmer (Milner), Page.
Lincoln C: Leaning; Schofield, Platnauer, Hebberd, Greenall, Brown, West, Johnson A, Daley, Carbon (Puttnam), Johnson D.
Lincoln C won 5-2 on aggregate.

Chesterfield (3) 4 *(Norris (pen), Davies, Morris, Curtis)*
Blackpool (2) 2 *(Ellis, Brown)* 2516
Chesterfield: Marples; Hewitt, Rogers, Fairclough, Carr, Cheetham, Curtis, Norris, Davies, Spooner, Morris (Jules).
Blackpool: Sealey; Brown, Burke, Horner, Beech, Gore (Gouck), Rodwell, Gibson, Quinn, Ellis, Griffiths (Bamber).
Chesterfield won 6-3 on aggregate.

Fulham (1) 1 *(Haworth)*
Luton T (0) 1 *(Marshall)* 5134
Fulham: Stannard; Morgan, Herrera, Mison, Moore, Thomas G, Marshall (Hails), Jupp, Cork, Brazil, Haworth (Hurlock).
Luton T: Sommer; James, Johnson, Linton (Skelton), Greene (Oakes), Peake, Telfer, Marshall, Dixon, Preece, Hughes.
aet; 2-2 on aggregate; Fulham won 4-3 on penalties.

Grimsby T (1) 1 *(Groves)*
Bradford C (2) 2 *(Murray, Richards)* 3498
Grimsby T: Crichton; Croft, Agnew, Futcher, Lever (Lester), Shakespeare, Childs (Woods), Gilbert, Livingstone, Mendonca, Groves.
Bradford C: Tomlinson; Liburd, Jacobs, Duxbury, Sinnott, Richards, Shutt, Robson (Tolson), Taylor, Jewell, Murray.
Bradford C won 4-2 on aggregate.

Hartlepool U (1) 5 *(Houchen, Southall 2, Jackson (og), Thompson)*
Bury (1) 1 *(Rigby)* 1505
Hartlepool U: Horne; Ingram, Skedd, Gilchrist, McGuckin, Oliver, Thompson, Sloan (Halliday), Houchen, Lynch, Southall.
Bury: Kelly G; Cross, Stanislaus, Mauge, Lucketti, Jackson, Mulligan, Carter, Paskin, Johnrose, Rigby.
aet; Hartlepool U won 5-3 on aggregate.

Huddersfield T (3) 3 *(Jepson 2, Reid)*
Scunthorpe U (0) 0 6455
Huddersfield T: Francis; Billy, Cowan, Logan, Scully, Dyson, Baldry, Bullock, Booth, Jepson, Reid.
Scunthorpe U: Samways; Ford, Mudd, Martin, Knill (Carmichael), Bradley, Alexander, Bullimore, Juryeff, Henderson, Smith (Goodacre).
Huddersfield T won 4-2 on aggregate.

Leyton Orient (0) 1 *(Cockerill)*
Barnet (1) 1 *(Freedman)* 2464
Leyton Orient: Heald; Howard, Austin, Purse, Hendon, Lakin, (Gray), Barnett (Carter), Cockerill, Bogie, West, Dempsey.
Barnet: Phillips; McDonald (Alexander), Gale, Hoddle, Walker, Primus, Tomlinson, Freedman (Scott), Hodges, Cooper, Wilson.
Barnet won 5-1 on aggregate.

Mansfield T (1) 1 *(Wilkinson)*
Rochdale (0) 0 2234
Mansfield T: Ward; Boothroyd, Baraclough (Fleming), Holland, Howarth, Aspinall, Ireland, Parkin, Wilkinson, Hadley, Noteman.
Rochdale: Clarke; Thackeray, Formby, Reid, Reeves, Butler, Thompson, Hall, Williams, Whitehall, Ryan (Stuart).
Mansfield T won 3-1 on aggregate.

Peterborough U (0) 0
Oxford U (1) 1 *(Dyer)* 3351
Peterborough U: Cooksey; Ashley, Clark, Ebdon, Breen, Welsh, Brissett (Henry), Williams, Farrell, Charlery, Moran (McGorry).
Oxford U: Whitehead; Robinson, Ford M, Dyer, Elliott, Rogan, Massey, Smith, Moody, Byrne, Allen (Lewis).
Oxford U won 4-1 on aggregate.

Plymouth Arg (1) 2 *(Swan, Castle)*
Walsall (0) 1 *(Wilson)* 2801
Plymouth Arg: Hodge; Bradshaw, Edworthy, Comyn, Swan, Hill, Barlow, Castle (Twiddy), Nugent, Evans (Landon), Dalton.
Walsall: Wood; Evans, Rogers, Watkiss, Marsh, Palmer, O'Connor, Ntamark, Lightbourne (Butler), Wilson, Mehew.
Walsall won 5-2 on aggregate.

Port Vale (1) 1 *(Glover L)*
Bristol R (0) 1 *(Stewart)* 4728
Port Vale: Musselwhite; Sandeman, Tankard, Porter (Walker), Griffiths, Glover D, Kent, Van der Laan, Foyle, Glover L, Naylor (Burke).
Bristol R: Parkin; Pritchard, Gurney, Channing (Browning), Clark, Tillson, Sterling, Miller, Stewart, Skinner, Archer.
Port Vale won 4-2 on aggregate.

Reading (0) 3 *(Quinn 2, Lovell)*
Gillingham (0) 0 3436
Reading: Hislop; Hopkins, Kerr, Wdowczyk, Williams, Parkinson (Holsgrove), Gilkes, Gooding, Quinn, Lovell, Osborn.
Gillingham: Barrett; Dunne, Palmer, Micklewhite, Green, Butler, Reinelt, Smith, Foster, Baker (Arnott), Watson.
Reading won 4-0 on aggregate.

Scarborough (1) 2 *(Blackstone 2)*
Hull C (0) 0 2287
Scarborough: Kelly; Knowles, Charles, Calvert, Meyer, Rockett, Rowe, Swann, Foreman (Young), White (D'Auria), Blackstone.
Hull C: Fettis; Lowthorpe, Graham, Hobson, Dewhurst, Mann, Peacock, Hargreaves (Dakin), Brown, Windass, Lawford (Atkinson).
Scarborough won 3-2 on aggregate.

Stockport Co (0) 4 *(Emerson, Armstrong, Ward, Beaumont)*
Preston NE (0) 1 *(Moyes)* 5450
Stockport Co: Keeley; Connelly (Wallace), Todd (Beaumont), Eckhardt, Flynn, Gannon, Emerson, Ward, Frain, Armstrong, Chalk.
Preston NE: Richardson; Fensome, Kidd, Whalley, Hicks, Moyes, Ainsworth (Bryson), Cartwright, Sale (Raynor), Conroy, Fleming.
Stockport Co won 5-2 on aggregate.

Swansea C (0) 2 *(Penney 2 (1 pen))*
Exeter C (0) 0 2523
Swansea C: Freestone; Jenkins, Clode, Ford, Harris, Ampadu, Bowen (Hayes), Pascoe, Torpey, Cornforth (Penney), Hodge.
Exeter C: Fox; Minett, Rice, Bailey, Came, Brown, Cooper M, Thirlby, Cecere, Pears, Gavin.
Swansea C won 4-2 on aggregate.

Torquay U (2) 4 *(Goodridge, Hancox 3)*
Cardiff C (2) 2 *(Stant 2)* 2719
Torquay U: Bayes; Hodges, Stamps, Hathaway, Barrow, Curran, Trollope, Buckle, Hancox, Okorie, Goodridge.
Cardiff C: Williams D; Evans, Street (Adams), Young, Brazil, Oatway, Bird, Richardson, Stant, Dale, Millar.
Torquay U won 4-3 on aggregate.

Watford (1) 1 *(Ramage)*
Southend U (0) 0 4582
Watford: Miller; Bazeley, Johnson, Foster, Holdsworth, Ramage, Hessenthaler, Payne, Moralee, Porter, Mooney.
Southend U: Royce; Poole, Powell, Jones K, Edwards, Dublin, Hone, Martin (Hunt), Iorfa (Davidson), Tilson, Sussex.
Watford won 1-0 on aggregate.

Wigan Ath (0) 3 *(Gavin, Rennie, Carragher)*
Crewe Alex (0) 0 1421
Wigan Ath: Farnworth; Rennie, Wright, Strong, Robertson, Kilford, Campbell, Morton, Gavin, Carragher, Lyons.
Crewe Alex: Smith M; Booty, Smith S, Collins, Macauley, Barr, Tierney, Murphy, Ward, Whalley, Rowbotham.
Wigan Ath won 4-2 on aggregate.

Wrexham (1) 1 *(Watkin)*
Doncaster R (0) 1 *(Swailes)* 2215
Wrexham: Marriott; Jones, Hardy, Phillips, Humes, Hunter, Bennett, Brammer, Connolly, Watkin (Cross), Taylor.
Doncaster R: Williams D; Limber (Parrish), Hackett, Brabin, Wilcox, Swailes, Lawrence, Meara, Torfason, Donaldson, Finlay (Kirby).
Wrexham won 5-3 on aggregate.

Wycombe W (0) 1 *(Turnbull)*
Brighton & HA (3) 3 *(Nogan 2, McDougald)* 5281
Wycombe W: Hyde; Cousins, Brown, Creaser (Hemmings), Evans, Ryan, Carroll, Thompson, Regis (Turnbull), Garner, Stapleton.
Brighton & HA: Rust; Bissett, Pates, Case, Foster, McCarthy, Chamberlain (Funnell), McDougald, Nogan, Codner, Wilkins (Simmonds).
Brighton & HA won 5-2 on aggregate.

York C (1) 2 *(Pepper, Cooper)*
Burnley (0) 2 *(Robinson, Gayle)* 3089
York C: Kiely; McMillan, Hall, Pepper, Tutill, Barras, McCarthy, Cooper, Barnes, Bushell, Canham.
Burnley: Beresford; Parkinson, Vinnicombe (Deary), Davis, Winstanley, Joyce (Lancashire), Harper, Gayle, Heath, Robinson, McMinn.
Burnley won 3-2 on aggregate.

6 SEPT

Northampton T (0) 0
Bournemouth (1) 1 *(Cotterill)* 3249
Northampton T: Stewart; Norton, Colkin, Sampson, Warburton, Curtis (Bell), Harmon, Robinson, Trott, Grayson, Aldridge.
Bournemouth: Andrews; O'Driscoll, O'Connor, McElhatton, Watson, Fletcher, Beardsmore, Aspinall (Murray), Russell K, Cotterill (Town), Leadbitter.
Bournemouth won 3-0 on aggregate.

7 SEPT

WBA (0) 0
Hereford U (0) 1 *(White)* 10,604
WBA: Naylor; Burgess, Darton, Phelan, Strodder, Herbert, Mellon, Ashcroft, Heggs, Donovan, Smith.
Hereford U: Pennock; Clark, Preedy (Davies), Pick, Smith, James, Wilkins, Pounder, Cross, White, Pike.
Hereford U won 1-0 on aggregate.

SECOND ROUND FIRST LEG

20 SEPT

Barnet (1) 1 *(Freedman)*
Manchester C (0) 0 3120
Barnet: Phillips; McDonald, Gale, Hoddle, Newson, Primus, Haynes, Freedman, Hodges, Scott, Wilson.
Manchester C: Coton; Edghill, Brightwell I, McMahon, Hill, Vonk (Foster), Summerbee, Walsh, Rosler (Quinn), Lomas, Beagrie.

Blackburn R (0) 2 *(Wilcox, Sutton)*
Birmingham C (0) 0 14,517
Blackburn R: Flowers; Berg, Le Saux, Sherwood, Hendry, Atkins, Ripley, Slater (Pearce), Warhurst, Sutton, Wilcox.
Birmingham C: Bennett; Scott, Frain, Ward, Dryden, Whyte, Harding, Claridge, Cooper (McGavin), Tait, Wallace (Dominguez).

Bristol C (0) 0
Notts Co (0) 1 *(Devlin)* 2546
Bristol C: Welch; Harriott, Scott, Shail, Bryant, Tinnion, McAree, Bent, Partridge, Loss (Brown), Edwards.
Notts Co: Cherry; Sherlock, Turner, Johnson, Murphy, Yates, Devlin, Legg, Lund (Agana), Simpson, McSwegan (Jemson).

Carlisle U (0) 0
QPR (1) 1 *(Ferdinand)* 9570
Carlisle U: Caig; Joyce, Gallimore, Walling, Valentine (Thorpe), Edmondson, Thomas, Currie, Reeves, Davey, Prokas (Mountfield).
QPR: Roberts; Bardsley, Wilson, Barker, Yates, McDonald, Impey, Holloway, Ferdinand, Penrice, Sinclair (Ready).

Chesterfield (1) 1 *(Moss)*
Wolverhampton W (0) 3 *(Bull 2, Kelly D)* 5895
Chesterfield: Marples; Hewitt, Rogers, Madden, Carr, Law, Curtis, Roberts (Jules), Davies (Norris), Moss, Spooner.
Wolverhampton W: Stowell; Smith, Thompson, Emblen (Blades), Venus, Shirtliff, Birch, Ferguson, Bull, Kelly D, Froggatt.

Everton (0) 2 *(Samways, Stuart (pen))*
Portsmouth (2) 3 *(Creaney 2, Kristensen)* 14,043
Everton: Southall; Jackson (Snodin), Burrows, Parkinson, Watson, Unsworth, Samways, Stuart, Amokachi, Rideout (Angell), Hinchcliffe.
Portsmouth: Knight; Gittens, Stimson (Radosavljevic), Symons, Awford, Daniel, Kristensen, McLoughlin, Powell, Creaney, Hall (Pethick).

Fulham (0) 3 *(Moore, Haworth, Blake)*
Stoke C (0) 2 *(Orlygsson (pen), Gleghorn)* 3721
Fulham: Stannard; Morgan, Herrera, Hurlock, Moore, Blake, Marshall, Jupp, Cork, Brazil, Haworth.
Stoke C: Muggleton; Butler, Sandford, Cranson, Dreyer, Orlygsson, Wallace, Downing, Carruthers, Peschisolido, Gleghorn.

Huddersfield T (0) 0
Southampton (0) 1 *(Le Tissier)* 13,814
Huddersfield: Francis; Billy (Jepson), Cowan, Logan, Scully, Dyson, Trevitt, Starbuck, Booth, Dunn, Reid.
Southampton: Grobbelaar; Kenna, Benali, Charlton, Hall, Heaney, Le Tissier, Magilton, Dowie, Maddison (Ekelund), Allen.

Lincoln C (0) 1 *(Johnson D)*
Crystal Palace (0) 0 4310
Lincoln C: Leaning; Schofield, Platnauer, Foley, Greenall, Brown, West, Onwere, Bannister, Puttnam, Johnson D.
Crystal Palace: Martyn; Patterson, Gordon, Southgate, Shaw, Coleman, Ndah, Newman, Armstrong, Dyer (Preece), Salako.

Oxford U (1) 1 *(Ford M)*
Oldham Ath (1) 1 *(Ritchie)* 5070
Oxford U: Whitehead; Robinson, Ford M, Lewis, Elliott, Marsh, Massey, Smith, Moody (Druce), Byrne, Allen.
Oldham Ath: Gerrard; Halle, Makin, Henry, Jobson, Redmond, Richardson, Brennan, Graham, McCarthy, Ritchie (Eyre).

Reading (1) 3 *(Quinn 2, Holsgrove)*
Derby Co (1) 1 *(Gabbiadini)* 6056
Reading: Hislop; Bernal (Hopkins), Kerr, Wdowczyk, Williams, Holsgrove, Gilkes, Gooding, Quinn, Lovell (Taylor), Osborn.
Derby Co: Taylor; Charles, Forsyth, Harkes, Short, Williams, Cowans, Gabbiadini, Johnson, Pembridge, Carsley.

Scarborough (1) 1 *(Rowe)* 4751
Middlesbrough (4) 4 *(Hendrie, Pollock, Moore, Mustoe)*
Scarborough: Kelly; Knowles, Thompson, D'Auria (Young), Dunphy, Meyer, Calvert, Rowe, Charles, Toman (White), Blackstone.
Middlesbrough: Pears; Cox, Fleming, Vickers, Whyte, Hignett, Mustoe, Pollock, Wilkinson, Hendrie, Moore (Wright).

Stockport Co (0) 1 *(Francis)*
Sheffield U (1) 5 *(Whitehouse 3 (1 pen), Flo 2)* 5109
Stockport Co: Keeley; Connelly, Todd, Eckhardt, Flynn, Dinning, Gannon, Ward, Francis, Emerson, Chalk (Ware).
Sheffield U: Kelly; Gage, Nilsen, Rogers, Gayle, Hodgson (Gannon), Ward, Hoyland, Flo, Davison (Blake), Whitehouse.

Tranmere R (1) 1 *(Brannan)*
Brentford (0) 0 3754
Tranmere R: Nixon; Higgins (Jones G), Brannan, Irons (Edwards), Garnett, O'Brien, Morrissey, Aldridge, Malkin, Nevin, Mungall.
Brentford: Dearden; Statham, Grainger, Westley, Ashby, Smith, Hutchings, Harvey, Taylor, Forster, Stephenson.

Walsall (1) 2 *(Watkiss, Potts (og))*
West Ham U (1) 1 *(Ntamark (og))* 5994
Walsall: Wood; Evans, Rogers, Watkiss, Marsh, Palmer (Ryder), O'Connor, Peer, Lightbourne, Wilson, Ntamark (Mehew).
West Ham U: Miklosko; Breacker, Rowland, Potts, Martin, Allen (Whitbread), Moncur, Hutchison, Cottee, Marsh, Rush (Chapman).

Wimbledon (2) 2 *(Gayle, Harford)*
Torquay U (0) 0 2451
Wimbledon: Segers; Barton, Kimble, Jones, Perry, Fitzgerald, Ardley (Fear), Gayle, Harford (Clarke), Holdsworth, Elkins.
Torquay U: Davis; Barrow, Kelly, Burton, Moore, Curran, Trollope, Buckle, Hancox, Okorie, Goodridge.

Wrexham (1) 1 *(Jones)*
Coventry C (0) 2 *(Darby, Flynn)* 5286
Wrexham: Marriott; Jones, Hardy, Brammer, Humes, Hunter, Bennett, Owen, Connolly, Watkin, Durkan.
Coventry C: Ogrizovic; Pickering, Morgan, Cook, Rennie, Busst, Darby, Jones, Dublin, Flynn, Boland.

21 SEPT

Aston Villa (2) 5 *(Yorke, Atkinson 2, Saunders, Lamptey)*
Wigan Ath (0) 0 12,433
Aston Villa: Bosnich; Barrett, King, Teale, Ehiogu, Parker, Lamptey, Townsend (Fenton), Saunders, Atkinson, Yorke.
Wigan Ath: Farnworth; Rennie, Jakub (McKearney), Strong, Robertson, Kilford, Campbell, Morton, Gavin, Rimmer, Carragher.

Brighton & HA (0) 1 *(Nogan)*
Leicester C (0) 0 11,481
Brighton & HA: Rust; Smith, Pates, Wilkins (Munday), Foster, Bissett, Minton, McDougald, Nogan, Codner, Chapman.
Leicester C: Poole; Grayson, Lewis, Mohan, Willis, Draper, Joachim, Blake, Agnew, Roberts (Lowe), Philpott.

Chelsea (1) 1 *(Rocastle)*
Bournemouth (0) 0 8974
Chelsea: Kharine; Clarke, Sinclair, Kjeldbjerg, Johnsen, Newton, Rocastle, Spencer (Shipperley), Furlong, Peacock, Wise.
Bournemouth: Andrews; O'Driscoll (Barfoot), O'Connor, McElhatton, Watson, Fletcher, Beardsmore, Mean, Aspinall (Reeve), Russell K, Leadbitter.

Hartlepool U (0) 0
Arsenal (2) 5 *(Adams, Smith, Wright 2, Merson)* 4421
Hartlepool U: Horne; Burgess, Walsh, Gilchrist, McGuckin, Oliver (Ingram), Thompson, Tait, Houchen, Halliday, Lynch (Hyson).
Arsenal: Seaman; Dixon, Keown, Davis, Linighan, Adams, Selley, Wright, Smith (McGoldrick), Merson, Parlour.

Ipswich T (0) 0
Bolton W (1) 3 *(McAteer, McGinlay, Thompson)* 7787
Ipswich T: Forrest; Yallop, Johnson, Taricco, Wark, Williams, Sedgley, Slater (Kiwomya), Milton, Guentchev, Thomsen (Linighan).
Bolton W: Branagan; Lydiate, Phillips, McAteer, Thompson, Stubbs, Lee, Sneekes, Paatelainen (De Freitas), McGinlay (Coyle), Fisher.

Leeds U (0) 0
Mansfield T (1) 1 *(Ireland)* 7844
Leeds U: Lukic; Kelly, Worthington, Palmer, Fairclough, Strachan (Radebe), Masinga (Deane), Wallace, Whelan, McAllister, Speed.
Mansfield T: Ward; Boothroyd, Baraclough, Holland, Aspinall, Howarth, Ireland, Frain, Wilkinson, Hadley, Noteman (Timons).

Liverpool (1) 2 *(Scales, Fowler)*
Burnley (0) 0 23,359
Liverpool: James, Jones R, Bjornebye, Scales, Molby, Ruddock, McManaman, Redknapp, Rush, Barnes, Fowler.
Burnley: Beresford; Parkinson, Vinnicombe, Davis, Winstanley, Eyres, Harper, Harrison (Deary), Heath, Robinson (Philliskirk), McMinn.

Millwall (2) 2 *(Goodman, Kennedy)*
Sunderland (0) 1 *(Russell)* 5095
Millwall: Keller; Cunningham, Thatcher, Van Den Hauwe, McCarthy, Roberts, Savage, Rae, Mitchell, Goodman, Kennedy (Carter).
Sunderland: Norman; Kubicki, Ord, Bennett, Ferguson (Smith), Melville, Owers, Goodman, Gray P, Russell, Ball.

Newcastle U (1) 2 *(Cole, Fox)*
Barnsley (1) 1 *(Redfearn)* 27,208
Newcastle U: Srnicek; Hottiger, Beresford, Howey, Peacock, Albert (Mathie), Lee, Beardsley, Cole, Fox, Sellars (Watson).
Barnsley: Watson; Snodin, Fleming, Wilson, Taggart, Bishop, O'Connell, Redfearn, Rammell (Liddell), Payton, Davis.

Norwich C (1) 3 *(Sheron, Bradshaw (pen), Adams)*
Swansea C (0) 0 8053
Norwich C: Gunn; Bradshaw, Johnson (Crook), Newsome, Polston (Newman), Goss, Eadie, Ullathorne, Robins, Sheron, Adams.
Swansea C: Freestone; Jenkins, Clode, Ford, Harris, Pascoe (Hodge), Bowen, Penney, Torpey, Cornforth, Perrett (Ampadu).

Nottingham F (0) 2 *(Collymore 2)*
Hereford U (1) 1 *(White)* 10,076
Nottingham F: Crossley; Lyttle, Pearce, Cooper, Chettle, Stone, Phillips, Roy (Woan), Bohinen, Collymore, Black.
Hereford U: Sheffield; Clark, Preedy, Reece, Smith, James, Wilkins, Pick, Cross (Pike), White, Steele (Davies).

Port Vale (1) 1 *(Glover L)*
Manchester U (1) 2 *(Scholes 2)* 18,605
Port Vale: Musselwhite; Sandeman, Tankard, Porter, Griffiths, Glover D, Kent, Van der Laan, Foyle, Glover L, Naylor (Burke).
Manchester U: Walsh; Neville G (O'Kane), Irwin, Butt (Sharpe), May, Keane, Gillespie, Beckham, McClair, Scholes, Davies.

Sheffield W (0) 2 *(Taylor, Hyde)*
Bradford C (0) 1 *(Shutt)* 15,705
Sheffield W: Pressman; Petrescu, Nolan, Atherton, Pearce, Bart-Williams, Ingesson (Taylor), Hyde, Hirst, Bright (Watson), Sheridan.
Bradford C: Tomlinson; Liburd, Jacobs, Duxbury, Benn, Richards, Shutt, Kamara, Taylor, Jewell (Power), Murray.

Swindon T (0) 1 *(Scott)*
Charlton Ath (0) 3 *(Nelson 2, Whyte)* 4932
Swindon T: Digby; Robinson, Bodin, Thomson, Nijholt (Berkley), Kilcline, Ling, Beauchamp, Fjortoft, Scott, O'Sullivan.
Charlton Ath: Petterson; Brown, Sturgess, Garland, Chapple, Balmer, Newton, Nelson, Walsh, Whyte, Robson.

Watford (1) 3 *(Ramage, Mooney, Mabbutt (og))*
Tottenham H (4) 6 *(Anderton, Klinsmann 3, Sheringham, Dumitrescu)* 13,659
Watford: Digweed; Bazeley, Johnson, Millen, Holdsworth, Ramage, Hessenthaler, Payne, Moralee, Porter, Mooney.
Tottenham H: Walker, Kerslake, Edinburgh (Howells), Popescu, Campbell, Mabbutt, Anderton, Hazard (Hill), Klinsmann, Sheringham, Dumitrescu.

Middlesbrough (1) 4 *(Wilkinson 3, Hignett)*
Scarborough (1) 1 *(Charles (pen))* 7739
Middlesbrough: Pears; Morris, Fleming, Vickers (Cox), Whyte, Hignett, Mustoe, Pollock, Wilkinson, Moreno, Wright.
Scarborough: Kelly; Knowles, Thompson (D'Auria), Calvert, Dunphy, Meyer (Davis), Rowe, Charles, White, Foreman, Blackstone.
Middlesbrough won 8-2 on aggregate

Notts Co (1) 3 *(Jemson, Lund 2)*
Bristol C (0) 0 2721
Notts Co: Cherry; Mills, Johnson, Turner, Yates, Murphy, Devlin, Legg, Lund, Jemson (Matthews), Agana.
Bristol C: Welch; Munro, Scott, Shail, Bryant, Paterson, McAree (Fowler), Bent (Brown), Baird, Tinnion, Edwards.
Notts Co won 4-0 on aggregate

Sheffield U (1) 1 *(Scott A)*
Stockport Co (0) 0 5065
Sheffield U: Kelly; Fickling, Scott A, Rogers, Foran, Hoyland, Ward, Gannon, Flo (Littlejohn), Blake, Whitehouse.
Stockport Co: Keeley; Connelly, Todd, Eckhardt (Slinn), Flynn, Dinning, Gannon, Ware, Francis, Armstrong, Brock (Wallace).
Sheffield U won 6-1 on aggregate

Wolverhampton W (1) 1 *(Froggatt)*
Chesterfield (0) 1 *(Jules)* 14,815
Wolverhampton W: Stowell; Smith, Thompson, Venus, Blades, Shirtliff, Birch, Ferguson, Bull (Rankine), Kelly D (Keen), Froggatt.
Chesterfield: Beasley; Hewitt, Rogers, Spooner, Carr, Law, Curtis, Roberts, Morris, Fairclough, Jules.
Wolverhampton W won 4-2 on aggregate

SECOND ROUND, SECOND LEG

27 SEPT

Brentford (0) 0
Tranmere R (0) 0 4076
Brentford: Dearden; Statham, Grainger, Westley, Ashby, Smith, Hutchings, Harvey, Taylor, Forster, Stephenson.
Tranmere R: Nixon; Stevens, Mungall, McGreal, Garnett, O'Brien, Morrissey, Aldridge, Malkin, Brannan, Nevin (Edwards).
Tranmere R won 1-0 on aggregate

Charlton Ath (0) 1 *(Whyte)*
Swindon T (2) 4 *(Fjortoft 3, Petterson (og))* 4932
Charlton Ath: Petterson; Brown, Sturgess, Garland (Bowyer), Chapple, Balmer, Newton (Grant), Nelson, Walsh, Whyte, Robson.
Swindon T: Digby; Robinson, Bodin, Thomson, Nijholt, Taylor, O'Sullivan, Beauchamp, Fjortoft, Ling, Scott (Mutch).
aet; Swindon T won 5-4 on aggregate

28 SEPT

Derby Co (1) 2 *(Gabbiadini, Williams)*
Reading (0) 0 9476
Derby Co: Taylor; Charles, Forsyth, Harkes (Carsley), Short, Williams, Cowans, Gabbiadini, Johnson (Simpson), Pembridge, Wassall.
Reading: Hislop; Bernal (McPherson), Kerr, Hopkins, Williams, Holsgrove, Parkinson (Taylor), Gooding, Quinn, Lovell, Osborn.
aet; 3-3 on aggregate, Derby Co won on away goals

Stoke C (1) 1 *(Peschisolido)*
Fulham (0) 0 7440
Stoke C: Muggleton; Butler, Sandford, Dreyer, Cranson, Orlygsson, Carruthers, Downing, Biggins, Peschisolido, Gleghorn.
Fulham: Stannard; Morgan, Adams, Mison, Moore (Bedrossian), Blake, Marshall, Jupp, Bartley (Haworth), Brazil, Thomas.
aet; 3-3 on aggregate, Stoke C won on away goals

4 OCT

Birmingham C (1) 1 *(McGavin)*
Blackburn R (0) 1 *(Sutton)* 16,275
Birmingham C: Bennett; Bass, Frain, Ward, Barnett, Daish, De Souza (Moulden), Shearer, McGavin, Dominguez, Donowa (Wallace).
Blackburn R: Flowers; Berg, Le Saux, Sherwood, Hendry, Warhurst, Ripley, Atkins, Shearer, Sutton, Wilcox.
Blackburn R won 3-1 on aggregate

Bournemouth (0) 0
Chelsea (0) 1 *(Peacock)* 9784
Bournemouth: Andrews; O'Driscoll (Murray), O'Connor (Adekola), McElhatton, Watson, Fletcher, Beardsmore, Mean, Aspinall, Reeve, Leadbitter.
Chelsea: Kharine; Clarke, Sinclair, Kjeldbjerg, Johnsen, Spackman (Newton), Rocastle, Shipperley, Furlong (Lee), Peacock, Wise.
Chelsea won 2-0 on aggregate

Bradford C (0) 1 *(Taylor)*
Sheffield W (1) 1 *(Bart-Williams)* 13,092
Bradford C: Tomlinson; Benn (Power), Jacobs, Duxbury, Oliver, Robson (Tolson), Shutt, Kamara, Taylor, Jewell, Hamilton.
Sheffield W: Pressman; Atherton, Nolan, Bart-Williams, Pearce, Walker, Sheridan, Hyde, Watson, Bright (Hirst), Sinton (Taylor).
Sheffield W won 3-2 on aggregate

Crystal Palace (0) 3 *(Gordon, Armstrong, Dyer)*
Lincoln C (0) 0 6870
Crystal Palace: Martyn; Patterson (Dyer), Gordon, Southgate, Shaw, Coleman, Bowry, Newman, Armstrong, Ndah (Launders), Salako.
Lincoln C: Leaning; Schofield, Platnauer, Hebberd (Smith), Greenall, Brown, West, Onwere, Bannister, Puttnam (Daley), Johnson D.
aet; Crystal Palace won 3-1 on aggregate

Hereford U (0) 0
Nottingham F (0) 0 8953
Hereford U: Sheffield; Clark, Fishlock, Reece, Smith, James, Wilkins, Pick, Cross, White, Preedy.
Nottingham F: Crossley; Lyttle, Pearce, Cooper, Chettle, Stone, Phillips, Roy, Bohinen, Collymore, Black.
Nottingham F won 2-1 on aggregate

Mansfield T (0) 0
Leeds U (0) 0 7227
Mansfield T: Ward; Boothroyd, Baraclough, Holland, Howarth, Peters, Ireland (Hadley), Hoyle, Wilkinson, Doolan, Noteman.
Leeds U: Lukic; Kelly, Worthington, Palmer, Fairclough (Dorigo), Wetherall, Whelan, Wallace (Pemberton), Deane, McAllister, Speed.
Mansfield T won 1-0 on aggregate

Oldham Ath (0) 1 *(Richardson)*
Oxford U (0) 0 4525
Oldham Ath: Hallworth; Halle, Makin, Henry, Jobson, Redmond, Richardson, Brennan (Holden R), Graham, McCarthy, Ritchie (Sharp).
Oxford U: Whitehead; Robinson, Ford M, Dyer, Elliott, Marsh (Rush), Massey, Smith, Moody, Byrne, Allen.
Oldham Ath won 2-1 on aggregate

Sunderland (0) 1 *(Gray P)*
Millwall (0) 1 *(Goodman)* 9698
Sunderland: Norman; Kubicki, Ord (Michael Gray), Ball, Martin Gray (Howey), Melville, Owers, Goodman, Gray P, Smith, Russell.
Millwall: Keller; Beard, Thatcher, Van Blerk (Chapman), McCarthy, Roberts, Savage, Rae, Kerr, Goodman, Kennedy.
Millwall 3-2 on aggregate

Swansea C (0) 1 *(Pascoe)*
Norwich C (0) 0 3568
Swansea C: Freestone; Jenkins, Clode, Ford, Harris, Pascoe, Ampadu, Penney, Torpey, Cornforth (Bowen), Hodge.
Norwich C: Gunn; Bradshaw, Bowen, Newsome, Prior, Goss, Eadie, Milligan (Crook), Newman, Ekoku (Robins), Adams.
Norwich C won 3-1 on aggregate

Tottenham H (1) 2 *(Barmby, Klinsmann)*
Watford (1) 3 *(Foster, Nogan 2)* 17,798
Tottenham H: Walker; Kerslake, Austin, Howells, Campbell, Mabbutt, Anderton (Hill), Barmby, Klinsmann, Dozzell, Rosenthal.
Watford: Miller; Lavin, Bazeley (Nogan), Foster, Holdsworth, Ramage, Hessenthaler, Johnson, Moralee, Porter, Mooney.
Tottenham H won 8-6 on aggregate

5 OCT

Arsenal (0) 2 *(Campbell, Dickov)*
Hartlepool U (0) 0 20,520
Arsenal: Seaman; Dixon, Winterburn, Hillier, Bould, Keown, McGoldrick, Davis, Campbell, Dickov, Parlour.
Hartlepool U: Horne; Burgess, Walsh, Gilchrist, McGuckin, Oliver, Thompson (Skedd), Ingram, Houchen, Halliday (Sloan), Ainsley.
Arsenal won 7-0 on aggregate

Barnsley (0) 0
Newcastle U (1) 1 *(Cole)* 10,992
Barnsley: Watson; Eaden, Fleming (Liddell), Wilson, Taggart, Davis, O'Connell, Redfearn, Jackson (Rammell), Payton, Bishop.
Newcastle U: Srnicek; Hottiger, Beresford, Howey, Peacock, Albert, Lee, Clark, Cole, Kitson (Mathie), Sellars.
Newcastle U won 3-1 on aggregate

Bolton W (0) 1 *(Sneekes)*
Ipswich T (0) 0 8212
Bolton W: Branagan; Lydiate, Phillips, McAteer (Patterson), Thompson, Spooner, Fisher, Sneekes, Paatelainen (De Freitas), McGinlay, Lee.
Ipswich T: Forrest; Yallop, Johnson, Linighan, Wark (Cotterell), Williams, Sedgley, Slater, Palmer, Guentchev, Thomsen.
Bolton W won 4-0 on aggregate

Burnley (0) 1 *(Robinson)*
Liverpool (1) 4 *(Redknapp 2, Fowler, Clough)* 19,032
Burnley: Beresford; Parkinson, Vinnicombe, Davis, Winstanley, Harper (Harrison), McMinn (Gayle), Philliskirk, Heath, Robinson, Eyres.
Liverpool: James; Jones R, Bjornebye, Nicol, Babb, Ruddock, McManaman (Jones L), Redknapp, Clough, Molby (Thomas), Fowler.
Liverpool won 6-1 on aggregate

Coventry C (1) 3 *(Dublin 2, Wegerle)*
Wrexham (1) 2 *(Cross, Bennett (pen))* 8561
Coventry C: Ogrizovic; Pickering, Morgan, Cook, Gillespie, Busst, Darby, Jones, Dublin, Wegerle, Flynn.
Wrexham: Marriott; Jones, Hardy, Hughes (Watkin), Hunter, Pejic, Bennett, Owen, Connolly, Cross, Durkan.
Coventry C won 5-3 on aggregate

Leicester C (0) 0
Brighton & HA (1) 2 *(Munday, Nogan)* 14,258
Leicester C: Poole; Grayson, Lewis, Mohan, Willis, Whitlow, Draper (Oldfield), Blake (Agnew), Joachim, Roberts, Philpott.
Brighton & HA: Rust; Smith, Tuck, Munday, Foster, Bissett, Case, Minton, Nogan, McDougald (Codner), Chapman.
Brighton & HA won 3-0 on aggregate

Manchester C (0) 4 *(Quinn 2, Walsh, Summerbee)*
Barnet (0) 1 *(Freedman)* 11,545
Manchester C: Dibble; Edghill, Phelan, Flitcroft, Hill, Brightwell I, Summerbee, Walsh (Griffiths), Quinn, Lomas, Beagrie.
Barnet: Phillips; McDonald, Gale (Newell), Hoddle, Newson, Primus, Tomlinson (Haynes), Freedman, Hodges, Scott, Wilson.
Manchester C won 4-2 on aggregate

Manchester U (1) 2 *(McClair, May)*
Port Vale (0) 0 31,615
Manchester U: Walsh; Casper, O'Kane, Butt, May, Pallister, Gillespie (Tomlinson), Beckham, McClair, Scholes, Davies (Neville G).
Port Vale: Musselwhite; Sandeman, Tankard, Porter, Aspin, Glover D, Kelly, Kent (Van der Laan), Foyle, Glover L, Burke (Allon).
Manchester U won 4-1 on aggregate

Portsmouth (0) 1 *(Hall)*
Everton (1) 1 *(Watson)* 13,605
Portsmouth: Knight; Gittens, Stimson, McLoughlin, Symons, Dobson, Radosavljevic (Hall), Kristensen, Powell, Creaney, Pethick.
Everton: Southall; Snodin, Burrows, Parkinson, Watson, Unsworth, Samways, Stuart, Amokachi, Ferguson, Hinchcliffe (Rideout).
Portsmouth won 4-3 on aggregate

QPR (2) 2 *(Allen, Wilson (pen))*
Carlisle U (0) 0 6561
QPR: Roberts; Bardsley, Wilson, Barker, Yates, McDonald, Impey, Holloway, Ferdinand (Gallen), Allen, Sinclair.
Carlisle U: Caig; Joyce (Currie), Gallimore, Walling, Valentine, Mountfield, Thomas (Arnold), Reeves, Davey, Edmondson, Conway.
QPR won 3-0 on aggregate

Southampton (1) 4 *(Le Tissier 4 (1 pen))*
Huddersfield T (0) 0 12,032
Southampton: Grobbelaar; Dodd, Charlton, Magilton, Benali, Monkou, Le Tissier, Ekelund, Dowie (Bennett), Widdrington (Tisdale), Heaney.
Huddersfield T: Francis (Blackwell); Trevitt, Cowan, Logan, Scully, Dyson, Crosby (Billy), Bullock, Booth (Dunn), Jepson, Starbuck.
Southampton won 5-0 on aggregate

Torquay U (0) 0
Wimbledon (1) 1 *(Holdsworth)* 4244
Torquay U: Bayes; Burton, Kelly, Hathaway, Moore, Curran, Trollope, Buckle, Hancox, Okorie, Goodridge.
Wimbledon: Segers; Barton, Kimble, Perry, Clarke (Joseph), Fitzgerald, Fear, Talboys (Ardley), Harford, Holdsworth, Elkins.
Wimbledon won 3-0 on aggregate

West Ham U (0) 2 *(Hutchison, Moncur)*
Walsall (0) 0 13,553
West Ham U: Miklosko; Breacker, Rowland, Potts, Whitbread, Allen, Moncur (Brown), Chapman, Hutchison, Marsh, Bishop.
Walsall: Wood; Ryder, Rogers, Watkiss, Palmer, Marsh (Ntamark), O'Connor (Evans), Peer, Lightbourne, Wilson, Mehew.
aet; West Ham U won 2-1 on aggregate

Wigan Ath (0) 0
Aston Villa (1) 3 *(Lamptey 2, Whittingham)* 2633
Wigan Ath: Farnworth; Carragher (Rennie), Jakub, Strong, Robertson, Farrell, Campbell, Kilford, Gavin, Rimmer, Lyons (Morton).
Aston Villa: Oakes; Staunton, King, Teale, McGrath, Parker, Yorke, Lamptey, Fenton, Whittingham, Farrell.
Aston Villa won 8-0 on aggregate

THIRD ROUND

25 OCT

Liverpool (1) 2 *(Rush 2)*
Stoke C (1) 1 *(Peschisolido)* 32,060
Liverpool: James; Jones R, Bjornebye, Scales, Babb, Ruddock, McManaman, Redknapp, Rush, Barnes, Fowler.
Stoke C: Muggleton; Butler, Sandford, Cranson, Overson, Orlygsson, Beeston, Clarkson, Carruthers (Biggins), Peschisolido, Gleghorn (Potter).

Mansfield T (0) 0
Millwall (1) 2 *(Cadette, Kennedy)* 5359
Mansfield T: Ward; Boothroyd, Baraclough, Holland, Howarth, Peters, Ireland (Hadley), Hoyle, Wilkinson, Doolan, Noteman.
Millwall: Keller; Cunningham, Thatcher, Van Den Hauwe (Beard), McCarthy, Roberts, Savage (Mitchell), Dawes, Cadette, Goodman, Kennedy.

QPR (2) 3 *(Gallen, Sinclair, Penrice)*
Manchester C (1) 4 *(Summerbee, Curle (pen), Beagrie, Lomas)* 11,701
QPR: Dykstra; Bardsley, Wilson, Barker (Penrice), Yates, McDonald, Meaker, Holloway, Dichio, Gallen, Sinclair.
Manchester C: Dibble; Edghill, Phelan, Flitcroft, Curle, Brightwell I, Summerbee, Walsh, Quinn, Lomas, Beagrie.

Notts Co (2) 3 *(Agana, McSwegan 2)*
Tottenham H (0) 0 16,952
Notts Co: Reece; Mills, Walker, Turner, Yates, Johnson (Murphy), Devlin, Butler, Legg, McSwegan (Matthews), Agana.
Tottenham H: Thorstvedt; Edinburgh, Austin, Popescu, Calderwood (Hazard), Campbell, Dozzell, Barmby, Klinsmann, Sheringham, Dumitrescu.

Sheffield U (0) 1 *(Blake)*
Bolton W (1) 2 *(Paatelainen, Scott A (og))* 6939
Sheffield U: Kelly; Gage, Scott A, Hartfield, Gayle, Beesley (Fickling), Reed, Veart, Blake, Littlejohn (Scott R), Whitehouse.
Bolton W: Branagan; Lydiate, Phillips, Patterson, Thompson, Coleman, Green, Sneekes, Paatelainen, McGinlay, Lee (De Freitas).

Oldham Ath (0) 0
Arsenal (0) 0 9303
Oldham Ath: Gerrard; Halle, Pointon, Henry, Jobson, Redmond, Bernard, Banger, Graham, McCarthy, Holden R.
Arsenal: Seaman, Dixon (Keown), Winterburn, Schwarz, Bould, Adams, Selley, Campbell (McGoldrick), Smith, Merson, Parlour.

Wimbledon (0) 0
Crystal Palace (0) 1 *(Armstrong)* 9394
Wimbledon: Segers; Joseph, Elkins, Jones, Thorn, Fitzgerald (Harford), Barton, Gayle (Fear), Clarke, Blissett, Ardley.
Crystal Palace: Martyn; Humphrey, Gordon, Southgate, Shaw, Coleman, Bowry, Newman, Armstrong, Preece, Salako.

Portsmouth (0) 0
Derby Co (0) 1 *(Simpson)* 8568
Portsmouth: Knight; Gittens (Durnin), Stimson, McLoughlin, Symons, McGrath (Kristensen), Pethick, Radosavljevic, Powell, Creaney, Hall.
Derby Co: Sutton (Quy); Charles, Forsyth, Wassall, Short, Williams, Cowans, Carsley, Johnson (Stallard), Gabbiadini, Simpson (Kavanagh).

26 OCT

Aston Villa (1) 1 *(Townsend)*
Middlesbrough (0) 0 19,254
Aston Villa: Bosnich; Barrett, Staunton, Ehiogu, McGrath, Parker, Houghton, Townsend, Saunders, Whittingham (Lamptey), Yorke.
Middlesbrough: Miller; Cox, Fleming, Vickers, Whyte, Blackmore, Todd (Hignett), Pollock, Wilkinson, Hendrie, Moore.

Sheffield W (0) 1 *(Bart-Williams)*
Southampton (0) 0 16,715
Sheffield W: Pressman; Atherton, Nolan, Taylor, Pearce, Walker, Sheridan, Hyde, Wright, Bart-Williams, Sinton.
Southampton: Grobbelar; Kenna, Benali (Charlton), Magilton, Hall, Monkou, Le Tissier, Ekelund (Heaney), Dowie, Maddison, Allen.

Blackburn R (0) 2 *(Shearer 2)*
Coventry C (0) 0 14,538
Blackburn R: Flowers; Berg, Le Saux, Warhurst, Hendry, Gale, Ripley, Atkins, Shearer, Sutton, Wilcox.
Coventry C: Ogrizovic; Borrows, Pickering, Cook, Rennie, Busst, Darby, Ndlovu, Dublin, Wegerle, Flynn (Jones).

Tranmere R (0) 1 *(Aldridge)*
Norwich C (1) 1 *(Polston)* 10,232
Tranmere R: Nixon; Stevens, Mungall, McGreal, Garnett, O'Brien (Irons), Morrissey, Aldridge, Malkin, Brannan, Nevin.
Norwich C: Gunn; Polston, Bowen, Crook, Prior, Newman, Adams (Sutch), Milligan, Robins, Sheron, Eadie (Goss).

Brighton & HA (0) 1 *(McCarthy)*
Swindon T (1) 1 *(Thomson)* 11,382
Brighton & HA: Rust; Bissett, Pates, Smith, Foster, McCarthy, Chamberlain (Codner), McDougald, Nogan, Minton, Chapman.
Swindon T: Digby; Robinson, Bodin, Thomson, Nijholt, Taylor, Horlock, Beauchamp, Fjortoft, Ling, Scott.

West Ham U (1) 1 *(Hutchison)*
Chelsea (0) 0 18,815
West Ham U: Miklosko; Breacker, Dicks, Potts, Martin, Allen, Bishop, Hutchison, Cottee, Marsh, Rush.
Chelsea: Kharine; Hall (Lee), Barness, Kjeldbjerg, Johnsen, Spackman, Rocastle, Newton, Shipperley, Peacock (Hopkin), Wise.

Newcastle U (0) 2 *(Albert, Kitson)*
Manchester U (0) 0 34,178
Newcastle U: Srnicek; Hottiger, Beresford, Howey, Peacock, Albert, Watson, Beardsley, Cole (Guppy), Kitson, Sellars.
Manchester U: Walsh; Neville G, Irwin (Sharpe) (Tomlinson), Bruce, Pallister, Gillespie, Beckham, Scholes, McClair, Davies, Butt.

Wolverhampton W (1) 2 *(Birch, Kelly D)*
Nottingham F (2) 3 *(Pearce, Roy 2)* 28,369
Wolverhampton W: Stowell; Smith, Thompson, Ferguson (Emblen), Blades, Venus, Birch, Thomas, Bull, Kelly D, Froggatt.
Nottingham F: Crossley; Lyttle, Pearce, Cooper, Chettle, Stone, Phillips, Roy, Bohinen, Collymore (Lee), Woan.

THIRD ROUND REPLAYS

9 NOV

Arsenal (2) 2 *(Dickov 2)*
Oldham Ath (0) 0 22,746
Arsenal: Seaman; Keown, Winterburn, Schwarz, Bould, Adams, Selley (Jensen), Campbell, Dickov, Parlour, McGoldrick.
Oldham Ath: Gerrard; Halle, Makin, Henry, Jobson, Redmond, Bernard, Banger, Graham, McCarthy (Ritchie), Brennan (Holden R).

Norwich C (0) 4 *(Prior, McGreal (og), Polston, Newman)*
Tranmere R (1) 2 *(Irons, Nevin)* 13,311
Norwich C: Gunn; Sutch, Bowen, Crook (Goss), Polston, Prior, Eadie, Newman, Robins, Milligan, Adams.
Tranmere R: Nixon; Stevens, Mungall, McGreal, Garnett, Irons, Morrissey, Aldridge, Malkin, Brannan, Nevin.

Swindon T (2) 4 *(Scott 2, Fjortoft 2)*
Brighton & HA (0) 1 *(Chamberlain)* 6482
Swindon T: Digby; Robinson, Bodin, Thomson, Nijholt, Kilcline, Ling, Beauchamp, Fjortoft, Mutch, Scott.
Brighton & HA: Rust; Smith, Tuck, Minton, Pates, McCarthy, Chamberlain, McDougald (Andrews), Nogan, Codner, Chapman.

Norwich C (1) 1 *(Eadie)*
Notts Co (0) 0 14,030
Norwich C: Gunn; Sutch, Bowen, Newsome, Polston, Crook, Milligan, Newman, Eadie (Goss), Sheron (Cureton), Adams.
Notts Co: Cherry; Mills, Legg, Turner, Yates, Johnson, Devlin, Butler, Lund, McSwegan, Agana.

Nottingham F (0) 0
Millwall (2) 2 *(Berry 2)* 12,393
Nottingham F: Crossley; Lyttle, Phillips, Cooper (Haaland), Chettle, Stone, Gemmill, Roy, Bohinen (Lee), Collymore, Woan.
Millwall: Keller; Beard, Thatcher, Roberts, Witter, Stevens, Savage (Dawes), Rae, Berry, Mitchell, Kennedy (Webber).

Swindon T (1) 2 *(Fjortoft 2)*
Derby Co (1) 1 *(Stallard)* 8920
Swindon T: Digby; Robinson, Bodin, Thomson, Nijholt, Kilcline (Ling), O'Sullivan, Horlock, Fjortoft, Mutch (Beauchamp), Scott.
Derby Co: Sutton; Kavanagh, Nicholson, Kuhl, Short, Williams, Harkes (Sturridge), Carsley, Johnson, Stallard, Simpson.

FOURTH ROUND

30 NOV

Arsenal (2) 2 *(Morrow, Wright)*
Sheffield W (0) 0 27,390
Arsenal: Seaman (Bartram); Dixon, Winterburn, Schwarz, Bould, Adams, Morrow (Keown), Wright, Smith, Campbell, McGoldrick (Dickov).
Sheffield W: Pressman; Atherton, Nolan, Petrescu, Pearce, Taylor, Sheridan, Hyde, Watson (Jones), Bart-Williams, Sinton.

Blackburn R (0) 1 *(Sutton)*
Liverpool (1) 3 *(Rush 3)* 30,115
Blackburn R: Flowers; Warhurst, Le Saux, Gale (Newell), Hendry, Berg, Ripley, Sherwood, Shearer, Sutton, Wilcox.
Liverpool: James; Jones R, Bjornebye, Scales, Babb, Ruddock, McManaman, Redknapp, Rush, Thomas, Fowler.

Crystal Palace (0) 4 *(Armstrong 2, Southgate 2)*
Aston Villa (1) 1 *(Atkinson)* 12,653
Crystal Palace: Martyn; Humphrey, Gordon, Southgate, Shaw, Coleman, Bowry, Newman, Armstrong, Preece, Salako.
Aston Villa: Bosnich; Barrett, King, Ehiogu, McGrath, Parker, Houghton, Farrell (Whittingham), Saunders, Atkinson (Fenton), Yorke.

Manchester C (0) 1 *(Rosler)*
Newcastle U (1) 1 *(Jeffrey)* 25,162
Manchester C: Dibble; Hill (Rosler), Brightwell D, Flitcroft, Curle, Brightwell I, Summerbee, Walsh, Quinn, Lomas, Beagrie.
Newcastle U: Srnicek; Hottiger, Beresford, Venison, Neilson, Watson, Mathie, Beardsley, Cole, Clark, Jeffrey.

West Ham U (0) 1 *(Cottee)*
Bolton W (1) 3 *(McGinlay 2, Lee)* 18,190
West Ham U: Miklosko; Brown, Dicks, Potts, Whitbread, Bishop, Moncur, Rush, Cottee, Boere, Holmes (Morley).
Bolton W: Branagan; Green, Phillips, McAteer, Thompson, Stubbs, Coleman, Sneekes, Paatelainen, McGinlay, Lee (Patterson).

FOURTH ROUND REPLAY

21 DEC

Newcastle U (0) 0
Manchester C (1) 2 *(Rosler, Walsh)* 30,156
Newcastle U: Srnicek; Hottiger (Bracewell), Beresford, Venison, Peacock, Albert, Watson, Clark, Cole, Fox, Kitson.
Manchester C: Dibble; Foster, Lomas, Flitcroft, Kernaghan (Vonk), Brightwell I, Summerbee, Walsh, Rosler, Gaudino (Quinn), Beagrie.

FIFTH ROUND

11 JAN

Bolton W (0) 1 *(Lee)*
Norwich C (0) 0 17,029
Bolton W: Branagan; Green, Phillips, McAteer, Coleman, Stubbs, Lee, Sneekes, Paatelainen, McGinlay, Thompson.
Norwich C: Marshall; Sutch, Bowen, Newsome, Polston, Goss, Crook, Newman, Sheron, Eadie (Ullathorne), Adams (Akinbiyi).

Crystal Palace (0) 4 *(Pitcher, Salako, Armstrong, Preece)*
Manchester C (0) 0 16,668
Crystal Palace: Martyn; Humphrey, Gordon, Southgate, Shaw, Coleman, Ndah (Preece), Newman, Armstrong, Pitcher, Salako.
Manchester C: Dibble; Summerbee, Phelan, Lomas (Brightwell D), Curle, Kernaghan, Rosler, Walsh, Quinn (Gaudino), Flitcroft, Beagrie.

Liverpool (0) 1 *(Rush)*
Arsenal (0) 0 35,026
Liverpool: James; Jones R, Bjornebye, Scales, Babb, Ruddock, McManaman, Redknapp, Rush, Barnes (Thomas), Fowler.
Arsenal: Seaman; Dixon, Winterburn, Schwarz, Bould (Morrow), Linighan, Jensen, Wright, Campbell, Hillier, Parlour (Dickov).

Swindon T (2) 3 *(Mutch 2, Fjortoft)*
Millwall (0) 1 *(Mitchell)* 11,772
Swindon T: Hammond; Robinson, Bodin, Culverhouse, Nijholt, Taylor, Horlock, Beauchamp, Fjortoft, Mutch, Ling.
Millwall: Keller; Dawes, Van Blerk, Roberts, Webber, Stevens, Savage, Rae, Cadette, Mitchell, Kennedy.

SEMI-FINALS FIRST LEG

12 FEB

Swindon T (1) 2 *(Thorne 2)*
Bolton W (1) 1 *(Stubbs)* 15,341
Swindon T: Hammond; O'Sullivan, Murray, Robinson, Nijholt, Taylor, Horlock, Beauchamp, Fjortoft, Thorne, Ling.
Bolton W: Branagan; Green, Phillips, McAteer, Coleman, Stubbs, Lee, Sneekes, Paatelainen, Coyle (McGinlay), Thompson.

15 FEB

Liverpool (0) 1 *(Fowler)*
Crystal Palace (0) 0 25,480
Liverpool: James; Jones R, Babb, Redknapp, Scales, Ruddock, McManaman, Walters, Rush, Barnes, Fowler.
Crystal Palace: Martyn; Patterson, Gordon, Southgate, Shaw, Coleman, Humphrey, Pitcher, Matthew, Preece, Salako.

SEMI-FINALS SECOND LEG

8 MAR

Bolton W (0) 3 *(McAteer, Paatelainen, McGinlay)*
Swindon T (0) 1 *(Fjortoft)* 19,851
Bolton W: Branagan; Green, Phillips, McAteer, Seagraves, Stubbs, Lee (Sneekes), Patterson, Coyle (Paatelainen), McGinlay, Thompson.
Swindon T: Digby; O'Sullivan (Hooper), Murray, Viveash, Nijholt, Taylor, Horlock, Beauchamp, Fjortoft, Thorne, Gooden.

Crystal Palace (0) 0
Liverpool (1) 1 *(Fowler)* 18,224
Crystal Palace: Martyn; Patterson, Gordon, Southgate, Shaw, Young, Ndah (Dyer), Pitcher, Coleman, Preece, Salako.
Liverpool: James; Jones R, Bjornebye, Scales, Babb, Ruddock, McManaman, Redknapp, Rush, Barnes, Fowler.

FINAL at Wembley

2 APR

Bolton W (0) 1 *(Thompson)*
Liverpool (1) 2 *(McManaman 2)* 75,595
Bolton W: Branagan; Green (Bergsson), Phillips, McAteer, Seagraves, Stubbs, Lee, Sneekes, Paatelainen, McGinlay, Thompson.
Liverpool: James; Jones R, Bjornebye, Scales, Babb, Ruddock, McManaman, Redknapp, Rush, Barnes, Fowler.
Referee: P. Don (Hanworth Park).

Liverpool's Ian Rush and Robbie Fowler celebrate on the way to Wembley and Coca-Cola Cup success. (Colorsport)

LEAGUE CUP ATTENDANCES

Totals

Season	*Attendances*	*Games*	*Average*
1960/61	1,204,580	112	10,755
1961/62	1,030,534	104	9,909
1962/63	1,029,893	102	10,097
1963/64	945,265	104	9,089
1964/65	962,802	98	9,825
1965/66	1,205,876	106	11,376
1966/67	1,394,553	118	11,818
1967/68	1,671,326	110	15,194
1968/69	2,064,647	118	17,497
1969/70	2,299,819	122	18,851
1970/71	2,035,315	116	17,546
1971/72	2,397,154	123	19,489
1972/73	1,935,474	120	16,129
1973/74	1,722,629	132	13,050
1974/75	1,901,094	127	14,969
1975/76	1,841,735	140	13,155
1976/77	2,236,636	147	15,215
1977/78	2,038,295	148	13,772
1978/79	1,825,643	139	13,134
1979/80	2,322,866	169	13,745
1980/81	2,051,576	161	12,743
1981/82	1,880,682	161	11,681
1982/83	1,679,756	160	10,498
1983/84	1,900,491	168	11,312
1984/85	1,876,429	167	11,236
1985/86	1,579,916	163	9,693
1986/87	1,531,498	157	9,755
1987/88	1,539,253	158	9,742
1988/89	1,552,780	162	9,585
1989/90	1,836,916	168	10,934
1990/91	1,675,496	159	10,538
1991/92	1,622,337	164	9,892
1992/93	1,558,031	161	9,677
1993/94	1,744,120	163	10,700
1994/95	1,500,322	156	9,617

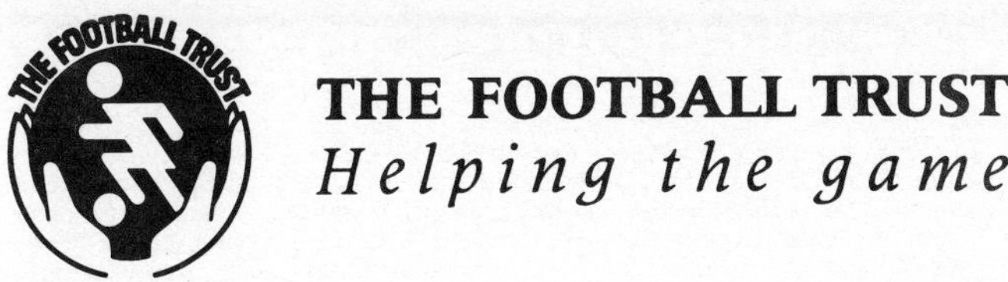

THE FOOTBALL TRUST
Helping the game

Middlesbrough made a return to the Premiership after a one-year break and moved to their new Riverside stadium, which was the chief beneficiary of some £30,000,000 of grants by the Football Trust to clubs.

Top grant for the 1995-96 season was £5,000,000 to Hampden Park in Glasgow for the refurbishment of the South Stand at the mecca of Scottish Football.

The Football Trust, which is jointly financed by the Littlewoods, Vernons and Zetters pools conpanies and the government, has – as its priority task – been helping professional soccer clubs implement the recommendation of the Taylor report. It gives grants for the new stadia, stands, cover and safety work and, since its inception in 1990, has helped fund projects costing a total of £420,000,000 with grants of some £132,000,000.

It also gives financial help to clubs putting in important safety and facility alterations, like facilities for the disabled, family enclosures, toilets and anti-hooligan measures such as closed-circuit television and better stewards' and transport set-ups. In short, better, safer and more comfortable watching of the game in Britain.

TREVOR WILLIAMSON

Schedule of Major Project Grants Offered During 1995-96

Club	Total Project Cost	Trust Grant	Major Project
Barnsley	2,400,000	1,000,000	South Stand
Barnsley	2,400,000	1,050,000	South Stand
Brentford	316,000	222,000	Ealing Road Stand
Bristol City	266,882	186,818	Dolman Stand
Burnley	5,700,000	2,000,000	Redevelopment of ground
Bury	782,570	306,000	East and West Stands
Carlisle United	2,138,000	750,000	East Stand
Celtic	14,900,000	2,000,000	North Stand
Coventry City	1,500,000	200,000	South Stand
Crewe Alexandra	797,042	568,870	West and East Stands
Hampden Park		5,000,000	South Stand
Hibernian	4,200,000	2,000,000	North and South Stands
Leeds United	1,100,000	400,000	North Stand
Lincoln City	1,200,000	692,016	Sincil Bank End
Luton Town	64,647	38,788	Kenilworth Road End
Meadowbank Thistle	6,000,000	500,000	New Stadium
Middlesbrough	10,000,000	2,225,000	Riverside Stadium
Peterborough United	1,400,000	905,000	Glebe Road Stand
Port Vale	1,070,000	663,000	Hamil Road Stand
Preston North End	4,750,000	750,000	West Stand
Queen of the South	523,056	371,228	East Stand
Ross County	92,709	66,000	Jubilee Terrace
Ross County	581,756	407,925	West Stand
Scarborough	474,718	354,484	East Stand
Sheffield Wednesday	4,750,000	756,897	South Stand
Shrewsbury Town	240,524	165,000	Centre Stand
Southend United	630,000	473,569	South Stand
Southend United	145,660	109,245	North Stand
Stockport County	1,200,000	700,000	Cheadle End Stand
Stranraer	43,758	32,819	West Terrace
Tranmere Rovers	2,670,000	2,000,000	Three Stands
Windsor Park	1,800,000	1,500,000	Spion Kop End
Wycombe Wanderers	1,800,000	1,000,000	South Stand
	75,667,322	31,238,733	

INTER-TOTO CUP

The five British teams who entered the UEFA Inter-Toto competition in June/July 1995 were all eliminated before the final stages. In Group 1, Sheffield Wednesday narrowly missed the draw for the Second Round after a spirited improvement. But Tottenham Hotspur fared less well in Group 2, fielding a mixture of young players and those on loan from other clubs. In fact they crashed 8-0 in their last match in Cologne, while the first team were touring Scandinavia. In Group 4, the Welsh League representatives Ton Pentre gave a plucky display considering they were almost out of their depth and improved noticeably towards the end of their matches, though they did not manage to score a goal. In Group 6, Partick Thistle fell away after a promising start, but Wimbledon managed just one goal in four attempts in Group 10, but again turned out a combination of youngsters and loaned players.

Second Round draw: Cologne v Tirol, Bordeaux v Eintracht Frankfurt, Bayer Leverkusen v Odense, Bursaspor v Ofi Crete, Aarau v Karlsruhe, Heerenveen v Farul Constanta, Ceahlaul v Metz, Strasbourg v Steyr.

Tottenham Hotspur, Group 2
v Lucerne, Lost 0-2. 2497 at Brighton.
Day; Newson, Coll, Sampson, Clapham, Byrne (Spencer), Pardew, Watson, McMahon, Slade, Hendry (Wormull).

v Rudar, Won 2-1 away. *Scorers:* Sampson, Hendry.
Day; Newson, Coll, Watson, Clapham, Byrne (Spencer), Pardew, Sampson, McMahon, Hendry, Slade.

v Oysters, Lost 1-2. *Scorer:* McMahon. 2143 at Brighton.
Day; Carr, Newson, Sampson, Clapham, Byrne (Simpson), Watson, Pardew, Hill, Slade, McMahon.

v Cologne, Lost 0-8 away.
Day; Carr, Coll, Newson, Clapham, Byrne (Wormull), Watson, Pardew, Spencer (Simpson), Slade (Mahorn), Turner.

Loan players: Newson (Barnet), Sampson (Northampton T), Byrne (St Mirren), Pardew (Charlton Ath).

Wimbledon, Group 10
v Bursaspor, Lost 0-4. 1879 at Brighton.
Cheesewright; O'Kane, Skinner, Newhouse, O'Shea, Laidlaw (Thomas), Byrne (Euell), Appleton, Dobbs, Piper, Tomlinson.

v Kosice, Drew 1-1 away. *Scorer:* Hodges.
Cheesewright (Murphy); O'Kane, Skinner, O'Shea, Hodges, Thomas, Appleton, Piper, Newhouse, Euell, Tomlinson.

v Beitar, Drew 0-0. 702 at Brighton.
Murphy; O'Kane, Skinner, O'Shea, Hodges, Thomas, Appleton, Piper, Newhouse, Euell (Payne), Tomlinson (Dobbs).

v Charleroi, Lost 0-3 away.
Cheesewright; Appleton, Skinner, O'Shea, Laidlaw, Thomas, Futcher, Piper, Payne (Dobbs), Newhouse (Euell), Tomlinson.

Loan players: Cheesewright (Colchester U), Appleton (Manchester U), O'Shea (Northampton T), Tomlinson (Manchester U), O'Kane (Manchester U).

Sheffield Wednesday, Group 1
v Basle, Lost 1-0.
Bowling; Brien, Williams A, Stewart, Briscoe, German (Faulkner), Williams M, Hyde, Holmes, Pearson, Barker (Bailey).

v Gornik Zabrze, Won 3-2. *Scorers:* Bright, Waddle, Krzetowski (og). 5592 at Rotherham.
Woods; Nolan, Briscoe, Atherton, Walker, Watts, Poric (Whittingham), Hyde, Bright (Barker), Waddle, Sinton.

v Karlsruhe, Drew 1-1 away. *Scorer:* Bright.
Woods; Atherton, Nolan, Walker, Watts, Hyde, Whittingham, Waddle, Hirst (Williams M.), Bright, Sinton.

v Aarhus, Won 3-1. *Scorers:* Bright 2, Petrescu. 6990 at Rotherham
Woods; Petrescu, Nolan (Briscoe), Atherton, Pearce, Walker, Bright, Hyde (Sinton), Hirst (Whittingham), Sheridan, Pembridge.

Ton Pentre, Group 4
v Heerenveen, Lost 7-0; v Bekescsaba, Lost 4-0 away; v Uniao Leiria, Lost 3-0; v Nasteved, Lost 2-0 away.

Loan players: Bowling (Bradford C), German (ex-Halifax) T), Williams A (Rotherham U), Pearson (Cardiff C), Brien (Rotherham U).

Partick Thistle, Group 6
v Linz, Drew 2-2 away; v Keflavik, Won 3-1; v Metz, Lost 1-0 away; v Zagreb, Lost 2-1.

FOOTBALL LEAGUE REPRESENTATIVE MATCH

Italian Serie B Under-21's (1) 2 (*Sala, Amaruso (pen)*) *in Andria*
Football League Under-21's (1) 3 (*Allen, Booth, Stallard*) 3000
Italy: De Sanctis; Nicola, Pierini, Sala, Sussi, Binotto, Cozza, Boscolo (Pavan), Macellari (Micelli), Lemme (Morfeo), Amaruso.
League: Watson (Barnsley); Smith (Wolverhampton W), Rufus (Charlton Ath), Richards (Bradford C), Thatcher (Millwall), Carsley (Derby Co), (Simpson (Notts Co)), Pollock (Middlesbrough), Roberts (Millwall), Allen (Oxford U), Forster (Brentford) (Stallard (Derby Co)), Booth (Huddersfield T).

ANGLO-ITALIAN CUP 1994–95

International Stage

24 AUG

Group A

Ascoli (1) 1 *(Incocciati)*
Notts Co (0) 1 *(Devlin)* 7000
Ascoli: Bizzarri; Fusco, Fiondella (Mancuso), Zanoncelli, Benetti, Zaini, Binotto, Galia, Bierhoff (Spinelli), Menolascina, Incocciati.
Notts Co: Cherry; Hoyle (Cox), Emenalo, Turner, Yates, Murphy, Devlin, Sherlock (Matthews), Lund, Agana, Simpson.

Lecce (0) 0
Wolverhampton W (1) 1 *(Kelly D)* 1795
Lecce: Torchia; Biondo, Fattizzo, Ceramicola, Ricci (Trinchero), Macellari, D'Onofrio (Cazzella), Olive, Monaco, Melchiori, Ayew.
Wolverhampton W: Jones; Smith, Thompson, Ferguson, Blades, Shirtliff, Venus (Emblen), Thomas, Rankine (Birch), Kelly D, Froggatt.

Swindon T (0) 0
Atalanta (0) 2 *(Saurini, Fortunato)* 5167
Swindon T: Digby; Robinson, Bodin, Kilcline, Nijholt, Thomson, Ling, Beauchamp, Fjortoft, Scott (White), Horlock (Gooden).
Atalanta: Ferron; Pavan, Tresoldi, Fortunato, Boselli, Montero, Magoni, Bonacina, Saurini, Scapolo (Zanchi), Vecchiola (Rodriguez).

Tranmere R (2) 2 *(Aldridge, Malkin)*
Venezia (0) 2 *(Cerbone (pen), Bonaldi)* 3012
Tranmere R: Coyne; Higgins, Brannan, Irons, Garnett, O'Brien, Morrissey, Aldridge, Malkin, Nevin, Mungall.
Venezia: Visi; Centurion, Vamoli, Rossi, Servidei, Mariani, Morello (Bonaldi), Fogli, Vieri, Bortolazzi, Cerbone.

Group B

Ancona (2) 2 *(Caccia 2)*
Derby Co (1) 1 *(Pembridge)* 748
Ancona: Pinna; Nicola, Sergio, Sgro, Baroni, Germoni (Cornacchia), Baglieri (Cangini), De Angelis, Caccia, Catanese, Centofanti.
Derby Co: Taylor; Charles (Kavanagh), Forsyth, Kuhl, Nicholson (Cowans), Wassall, Stallard, Hayward, Gabbiadini, Pembridge, Simpson.

Cesena (0) 0
Stoke C (2) 2 *(Carruthers, Clark)* 1065
Cesena: Santarelli; Scugugia, Medri, Romano, Sadotti (Calcaterra), Sussi, Teodorani, Ambrosini (Scarafoni), Zagati, Piangerelli, Hubner.
Stoke C: Muggleton; Clark, Sandford, Dreyer, Cranson, Downing (Clarkson), Butler, Wallace, Biggins (Carruthers), Sturridge, Gleghorn.

Middlesbrough (0) 0
Piacenza (0) 0 5348
Middlesbrough: Miller; Morris, Taylor, Vickers, Todd, Whyte, Stamp (Cox), Pollock (Wilkinson), Hignett, Mustoe, Wright.
Piacenza: Ramon; Polonia (Cesari), Rossini, Suppa, Di Cintio, Lucci, Turrini (Moretti), Brioschi, De Vitis, Iacobelli, Piovani.

Sheffield U (1) 1 *(Littlejohn)*
Udinese (1) 2 *(Marino, Scarchilli)* 7497
Sheffield U: Tracey; Gage, Davidson, Rogers, Hoyland, Hodgson, Veart, Hartfield, Blake, Hodges, Littlejohn.
Udinese: Caniato; Pellegrini, Bertotto, Ametrano, Calori, Pierini, Helveg, Scarchilli, Marino, Pizzi, Kozminski.

6 SEPT

Group A

Atalanta (2) 2 *(Montero, Saurini)*
Tranmere R (0) 0 4000
Atalanta: Ferron; Zanchi, Boselli, Fortunato, Montero, Bonacina, Rotella (Salvatori), Magoni, Saurini (Pavone), Rodriguez, Scapolo.
Tranmere R: Nixon; Higgins, Brannan, Irons, Garnett (Moore), Mungall, Edwards, McGreal, Jones, Branch, Thomas.

Notts Co (0) 1 *(Turner)*
Lecce (0) 0 2495
Notts Co: Reece; Galloway, Emenalo, Turner, Johnson, Yates, Devlin, Legg (Simpson), Agana, McSwegan, Matthews.
Lecce: Torchia; Ricci, Trinchera, Melchiori, Ceramicola, Macellari, Russo (Ayew), Gumprecht, Pittalis, Olive, Cazzella.

Venezia (1) 1 *(Mariani)*
Swindon T (0) 0 1325
Venezia: Visi; Filippini (Centurioni), Ballarin, Rossi, Servidei, Mariani, Morello, Nardini, Bonaldi, Bottazzi, Cerbone (Varriale).
Swindon T: Hammond; Robinson, Horlock, Kilcline, Nijholt, Thomson (Murray), Ling, Beauchamp, Mutch (Digby), Berkley, O'Sullivan (Hamon).

Wolverhampton W (0) 0
Ascoli (0) 1 *(Marcato)* 9599
Wolverhampton W: Jones; Smith, Thompson, Ferguson, Blades, Shirtliff, Emblen, Birch, Stewart, Keen, Venus.
Ascoli: Bizzarri; Fusco, Fiondella (Mancuso), Zanoncelli, Benetti, Marcato, Milana, Bosi, Bierhoff (Spinelli), Menolascina, Pasino.

Group B

Derby Co (5) 6 *(Hodge 2, Kitson 4)*
Cesena (0) 1 *(Ambrosini)* 2010
Derby Co: Taylor; Charles (Kavanagh), Nicholson, Hodge, Short, Wassall, Cowans, Carsley, Kitson, Gabbiadini (Sutton S), Simpson.
Cesena: Santarelli; Scugugia, Calcaterra, Ambrosini, Aloisi, Sussi, Teodorani, Del Bianco (Maenza), Zagati (Piangerelli), Piraccini, Hubner.

Piacenza (1) 2 *(Brioschi, Suppa)*
Sheffield U (1) 2 *(Carr, Gannon)* 4744
Piacenza: Ramon; Di Cintio, Rossini (Manganiello), Suppa (Moretti), Cesari, Lucci, Turrini, Brioschi, De Vitis, Iacobelli, Piovani.
Sheffield U: Tracey; Foreman, Scott A, Blount, Fickling, Hoyland, Scott R, Gannon, Davison, Carr (Battersby), Hawthorne.

Stoke C (0) 1 *(Biggins)*

Ancona (1) 1 *(Caccia)* 3330

Stoke C: Muggleton; Butler, Sandford, Dreyer, Overson, Downing (Leslie), Peschisolido, Wallace, Biggins (Carruthers), Beckford, Gleghorn.
Ancona: Pinna; Cornacchia, Centofanti (Pesaresi), Nicola, Baroni, Sergio, De Angelis, Catanese, Caccia (Cangini), Picasso, Baglieri.

4 OCT

Group A

Tranmere R (0) 0

Ascoli (1) 1 *(Bierhoff (pen)* 4546

Tramere R: Nixon; Stevens, Mungall, McGreal, Garnett, O'Brien, Morrissey, Aldridge, Malkin, Edwards, Nevin.
Ascoli: Bizzarri; Marcato, Mancuso, Zanoncelli, Fusco, Zaini, Milana, Galia, Bierhoff, Bosi, Menolascina.

5 OCT

Atalanta (1) 1 *(Rodriguez)*

Notts Co (0) 1 *(Agana)* 5000

Atalanta: Pinato; Zanchi, Valentini (Bigliardi), Fortunato, Pavan, Montero, Salvatori, Magoni (Rotella), Pisani, Rodriguez, Vecchiola.
Notts Co: Cherry; Mills, Emenalo (Legg), Turner, Yates, Murphy, Matthews, Walker, Lund, Jemson, Agana.

Swindon T (2) 3 *(Mutch 2, Scott)*

Lecce (0) 1 *(Ayew)* 2375

Swindon T: Digby; Robinson, Bodin, Kilcline, Nijholt, Taylor, Horlock, Beauchamp, Mutch, Berkley (Ling), Scott (Fjortoft).
Lecce: Torchia; Biondo, Fattizzo, Trinchera, Melchiori, Frisullo (Ceramicola), Russo (Olive), Gazzani, Ayew, . Pittalis, Monaco.

Venezia (1) 2 *(Rankine (og), Vieri (pen))*

Wolverhampton W (1) 1 *(Venus)* 750

Venezia: Visi; Filippini, Vanoli, Nardini, Servidei, Ballarin, Morello (Bonaldi), Di Gia, Vieri, Bottazzi, Cerboni (Bortoluzzi).
Wolverhampton W: Jones; Rankine, Thompson, Venus, Blades, Bennett, Birch, Ferguson, Bull, Mills, Keen.

Group B

Middlesbrough (0) 1 *(Moreno)*

Cesena (0) 1 *(Hubner)* 3273

Middlesbrough: Pears; Morris, Taylor, Barron, Whyte, Todd, Stamp, Kavanagh, Moreno, Blackmore, Wright.
Cesena: Santarelli; Scugugia, Sussi, Ambrosini, Farabegoli (Confalone), Medri, Del Bianco, Leoni, Maenza (Bombardini), Piraccini, Hubner.

Piacenza (0) 1 *(De Vitis)*

Derby Co (0) 1 *(Williams)* 1710

Piacenza: Ramon; Di Cintio, Manganiello (Moretti), Suppa, Cesari, Lucci, Turrini, Brioschi, De Vitis, Iacobelli, Piovani.
Derby Co: Sutton S; Charles, Nicholson (Kavanagh), Carsley (Davies), Wassall, Williams, Cowans, Sturridge, Harkes, Pembridge, Simpson.

Sheffield U (2) 3 *(Ward, Battersby, Scott A)*

Ancona (1) 3 *(Baglieri, Catanese, De Angelis)* 1827

Sheffield U: Bibbo; Davidson (Scott R), Scott A, Hawthorne, Fickling, Hoyland, Veart, Ward (Foran), Battersby, Anthony, Davison.
Ancona: Berti; Cornacchia (Pesaresi), Cangini, Sgro, Baroni, Sergio, De Angelis, Catanese, Caccia (Arno), Centofanti, Baglieri.

Udinese (1) 1 *(Pizzi)*

Stoke C (0) 3 *(Downing, Biggins, Butler)* 1306

Udinese: Caniato; Bertotto, Compagnon, Pierini, Calori, Ripa, Helveg, Ametrano, Poggi, Pizzi (Zampieri), Bachini (Rossitto).
Stoke C: Muggleton; Wallace, Sandford, Dreyer (Butler), Cranson, Orlygsson, Overson, Downing, Carruthers (Peschisolido), Biggins, Gleghorn.

18 OCT

Udinese (0) 0

Middlesbrough (0) 0 300

Udinese: Camiato; Pellegrini, Bertotto (Compagnon), Ametrano, Calori, Pierini, Lasalandra, Helveg (Ripa), Poggi, Pizzi, Marino.
Middlesbrough: Miller; Fleming, Taylor, Cox (Barron), Vickers, Liddle, Stamp, Kavanagh, Moreno, Todd, Wright.

15 NOV

Group A

Notts Co (1) 3 *(Devlin, Marsden, Murphy)*

Venezia (0) 3 *(Ambrosetti, Barollo 2 (1 pen))* 2861

Notts Co: Reece; Gallagher, Daniel, Turner, Yates, Johnson, Devlin, Butler, Matthews (Murphy), Marsden, Agana.
Venezia: Visi; Accarni, Ballarin, Bortoluzzi, Vanoli, Mariani, Pellegrini, Fogli, Ambrosetti, Di Gia, Cerbone (Barollo).

Wolverhampton W (1) 1 *(Mills)*

Atalanta (1) 1 *(Bonacina)* 7285

Wolverhampton W: Stowell; Emblen, Thompson, Ferguson (Rankine), Blades, Venus, Birch, Thomas, Mills, Stewart, Froggatt.
Atalanta: Pinato; Pavone, Tresoldi, Bonacina, Pavan, Magoni, Rotella (Zauri), Morfeo (Gibellini), Pisani, Rodriguez, Locatelli.

Lecce (0) 0

Tranmere R (0) 0 286

Lecce: Torchia; Biondo, Macellari, Olive, Rossi (Gazzani), Ricci (Frisulio), Melchiori, Pittalis, Russo, Notaristefano, Baldieri.
Tranmere R: Nixon; Stevens, Mungall (Proctor), McGreal, Garnett, Higgins, Morrissey, Muir, Malkin, Irons (Kenworthy), Edwards.

Ascoli (1) 3 *(Bierhoff 3)*

Swindon T (0) 1 *(Hamon)* 3000

Ascoli: Bizzarri; Mancini, Fiondella, Bosi, Pascucci, Marcato, Cavaliere, Favo, Bierhoff, Menolascina (Mancuso), Mirabelli (Incocciati).
Swindon T: Hammond; Robinson, Horlock, MacLaren, Thomson, Kilcline, O'Sullivan (Berkley), Beauchamp, Mutch, Ling (Hamon), Scott.

Group B

Cesena (1) 1 *(Bombardini)*

Sheffield U (1) 4 *(Scott A 2, Hawthorne, Reed)* 3200

Cesena: Santarelli; Farabegoli, Sussi, Del Bianco (Tamburini), Sadotti (Baschetti), Piraccini, Teodorani, Piangerelli, Cagati, Maenza, Bombardini.
Sheffield U: Bibbo; Ward, Scott A, Hawthorne, Fickling, Blount, Scott R, Reed (Foreman), Battersby, Anthony, Gannon.

Derby Co (2) 3 *(Johnson 2, Stallard)*

Udinese (0) 1 *(Berlotto)* 1562

Derby Co: Sutton S; Charles (Kavanagh), Nicholson, Kuhl, Short, Williams, Harkes, Carsley, Johnson (Cooper), Stallard, Sturridge.
Udinese: Battistini; Compagnon, Berlotto, Pierini, Calori, Ripa, Lasalandra, Scarchilli, Banchelli (Prevedini), Pizzi, Poggi.

Stoke C (2) 4 *(Butler, Carruthers 2, Gleghorn)*

Piacenza (0) 0 7240

Stoke C: Muggleton; Butler, Sandford, Cranson, Overson, Clarkson (Shaw), Wallace, Beeston, Carruthers (Biggins), Peschisolido, Gleghorn.
Piacenza: Ramon; Cesari, Rossini, Suppa, Di Cintio, Lucci, Piovani, Brioschi (Colombotti), De Vitis, Moretti, Manganiello (Papais).

Ancona (0) 3 *(Caccia 2, Artistico)*

Middlesbrough (1) 1 *(Morris)* 1500

Ancona: Pinna; Nicola, Cangini (Pasaresi), Tangorra, Tomei, Sergio, Sesia, Catanese, Artistico, Centofanti (Baglieri), Caccia.
Middlesbrough: Roberts; Morris, Byrne, Liddle, Barron, White, Stamp, O'Halloran, Moreno (Richardson), Mustoe (Norton), Wright.

Semi-Final First Leg

8 DEC

Ancona (0) 1 *(Centofanti)*

Ascoli (0) 2 *(Incocciati 2)* 4311

Ancona: Berti; Nicola, Sergio, Tangorra (Centofanti), Cornacchia, Sgro, Cangini, Sesia, Artistico (Baglieri), Catanese, Caccia.
Ascoli: Bizzarri; Mancini, Mancuso (Binotto), Marcato, Pascucci, Zanoncelli, Menolascina, Cavaliere, Mirabelli (Benetti), Favo, Incocciati.

Semi-Final Second Leg

30 DEC

Ascoli (0) 0

Ancona (1) 1 *(Cornacchia)* 3705

Ascoli: Bizzarri; Mancini, Mancuso, Marcato (Spinelli), Fusco, Zanoncelli, Cavaliere, Bosi, Bierhoff, Favo, Mirabelli (Binotto).
Ancona: Berti; Cornacchia, Sergio, Tangorra, Baroni, Sgro, De Angelis, Sesia, Artistico, Cantanese (Cangini), Caccia.

Semi-Final First Leg

24 JAN

Notts Co (0) 0

Stoke C (0) 0 5135

Notts Co: Kearton; Mills, Legg, Turner, Murphy, Johnson (Matthews), Devlin, Butler, Lund (Slawson), Nicol, White.
Stoke C: Sinclair; Clarkson, Sandford, Cranson, Overson, Allen, Butler, Wallace, Carruthers, Gayle, Gleghorn (Downing).

Semi-Final Second Leg

31 JAN

Stoke C (0) 0

Notts Co (0) 0 10,741

Stoke C: Sinclair; Clarkson, Sandford, Cranson, Overson, Allen, Wallace, Peschisolido (Downing), Carruthers, Gayle (Sturridge), Gleghorn.
Notts Co: Kearton; Mills, Legg, Turner, Murphy, Hogg, Simpson, Butler (Johnson), Agana, Nicol, White (Devlin).
aet; Notts Co won 3-2 on penalties.

Final at Wembley

19 MAR

Notts Co (2) 2 *(Agana, White)*

Ascoli (1) 1 *(Mirabelli)* 11,704

Notts Co: Cherry (Reece); Mills, Legg, Turner, Murphy, Johnson (Emenalo), Devlin, Simpson, White, Short, Agana (Gallagher).
Ascoli: Bizzarri; Benetti, Mancuso (Milana), Marcato, Pascucci, Zanoncelli, Binotto (Menolascina), Bosi, Favo, Mirabelli, Bierhoff.
Referee: C. Agius (Malta).

AUTO WINDSCREENS SHIELD 1994–95

First Round

27 SEPT

Darlington (2) 2 *(Himsworth, Olsson)*
Carlisle U (2) 3 *(Currie 2, Gallimore (pen))* 1583
Darlington: Pollitt; Appleby, Cross, Banks, Crosby, Reed (Gregan), Himsworth (Slaven), Painter, Gaughan, Olsson, Chapman.
Carlisle U: Caig; Joyce, Gallimore, Walling, Valentine, Edmondson, Thomas, Currie (Thorpe), Reeves, Davey, Prokas.

Hull C (0) 0
Doncaster R (1) 2 *(Thew, Jones)* 890
Hull C: Wilson; Mail, Graham, Allison, Dewhurst, Abbott, Peacock, Lee, Hargreaves (Mann), Atkinson, Lawford.
Doncaster R: Williams D; Kirby, Hackett, Thew, Wilcox, Swailes, Lawrence, Roche, Jones, Harper, Parrish.

Scunthorpe U (0) 1 *(Alexander)*
Rotherham U (3) 3 *(Helliwell, Goater, Todd)* 1404
Scunthorpe U: Samways; Ford, Mudd, Thornber, Knill, Bradley, Alexander, Bullimore (Martin), Goodacre (Sansam), Henderson, Smith.
Rotherham U: Clarke; Wilder, James, Williams A, Breckin, Brien, Hazel, Goodwin, Helliwell, Goater (Varadi), Todd.

Crewe Alex (0) 0
Wrexham (0) 0 1573
Crewe Alex: Gayle; Booty, Smith S, Murphy, Whalley, Barr, Garvey, Collins, Ward, Gardiner, Rowbotham.
Wrexham: Marriott; Jones, Hardy, Hughes (Williams), Hunter, Pejic, Bennett, Owen, Connolly, Watkin (Cross), Durkan.

Blackpool (1) 1 *(Mitchell)*
Rochdale (0) 2 *(Stuart, Burke (og))* 1817
Blackpool: Martin; Brown, Burke, Horner, Thompson, Moore, Rodwell, Beech, Quinn, Ellis, Mitchell.
Rochdale: Clarke (Ryan); Thackeray, Formby, Russell, Matthews, Butler, Thompson, Peake, Williams, Whitehall, Stuart.

Preston NE (1) 1 *(Trebble)*
Chester C (0) 1 *(Page)* 3242
Preston NE: Richardson; Fensome, Kidd, Whalley (Cartwright), Squires, Moyes, Ainsworth, Bryson, Sale, Trebble (Fleming), Raynor.
Chester C: Newland; Jenkins, Burnham (Ratcliffe), Alsford, Preece, Shelton, Page, Priest, Lightfoot, Chambers (Murphy), Flitcroft.

Cardiff C (0) 2 *(Griffith, Dale)*
Plymouth Arg (0) 0 1299
Cardiff C: Williams D; Perry, Searle, Aizlewood, Baddeley, Oatway, Millar, Griffith, Bird, Dale, Adams (Richardson).
Plymouth Arg: Nicholls; Patterson, Naylor, Hill, Comyn, Burnett (Edworthy), Barlow, Morgan, Evans (Skinner), Landon, Twiddy.

Hereford U (2) 4 *(Smith, Preedy, White, Cross)*
Torquay U (0) 2 *(Laight, Darby)* 1046
Hereford U: Pennock; Clark, Preedy, Reece, Smith, James, Gonzague, Pick, Cross, White, Lyne.
Torquay U: Davis; Hodges (Hathaway), Kelly, Okorie, Moore, Barrow, Trollope, Buckle (Laight), Hancox, Darby, Goodridge.

Oxford U (1) 2 *(Moody 2)*
Bristol R (0) 2 *(Skinner (pen), Clark)* 1518
Oxford U: Deegan; Robinson, Ford M, Lewis, Elliott, Dyer, Massey, Smith, Moody, Byrne (Rush), Allen.
Bristol R: Parkin; Pritchard, Gurney, Browning, Clark, Wright, Paul, Miller, Taylor, Skinner, Archer.

Gillingham (1) 1 *(Carpenter)*
Brighton & HA (1) 1 *(McDougald)* 963
Gillingham: Banks; Dunne, Watson, Carpenter, Green, Butler, Micklewhite, Smith, Reinelt, Ritchie, Smillie (Watts).
Brighton & HA: Rust; Smith, Tuck, Simmonds, McCarthy, Bissett, Munday, McDougald (Andrews), Nogan, Minton, Chapman.

Colchester U (0) 1 *(Abrahams)*
Leyton Orient (0) 0 1486
Colchester U: Cheesewright; Betts, English, Cawley, Caesar, Dennis, Locke, Brown, Whitton, Kinsella, Abrahams.
Leyton Orient: Heald; Warren (Lakin), Austin, Purse, Howard, Hague, Putney, Cockerill, Carter, West, Martin (Barnett).

Barnet (0) 0
Cambridge U (2) 2 *(Lillis, Corazzin)* 995
Barnet: Phillips; McDonald, Gale, Hoddle, Newson, Primus (Alexander) (Tomlinson), Haynes, Freedman, Hodges, Scott, Wilson.
Cambridge U: Filan; Hunter, Barrick, Craddock, O'Shea, Hayrettin (Fowler), Lillis (Morah), Walker, Butler, Corazzin, Joseph.

Peterborough U (2) 3 *(Henry, Brissett, Charlery)*
Birmingham C (3) 5 *(Bull, Dominguez, Hunt 3)* 2044
Peterborough U: Tyler; Webster, Spearing, Ebdon, Heald, Breen, Morrison (Lormor), McGorry, Brissett, Charlery, Henry.
Birmingham C: Price; Scott, Frain, Ward, Barnett, Daish, Hunt, Claridge, Bull (McGavin), Poole, Dominguez (Wallace).

11 OCT

Bradford C (1) 1 *(Kamara)*
Huddersfield T (0) 2 *(Baldry, Booth)* 2772
Bradford C: Tomlinson; Huxford, Grayston, Duxbury, Oliver, Benn, Shutt, Kamara, Taylor, Power, Midgley.
Hudderfield T: Blackwell, Billy, Cowan, Logan, Gray, Mitchell, Crosby (Baldry), Clayton, Booth, Dunn, Starbuck (Collins).

17 OCT

Doncaster R (1) 1 *(Turner)*
Lincoln C (0) 0 1480
Doncaster R: Williams D; Kirby, Hackett, Brabin, Wilcox, Swailes, Lawrence, Roche, Turner (Finlay), Harper, Parrish.
Lincoln C: Hoult; West, Lucas, Foley, Greenall, Brown, Hebberd, Onwere (Daley), Bannister, Carbon, Puttnam (Johnson A).

18 OCT

Carlisle U (0) 2 *(Thomas, Arnold)*
Hartlepool U (0) 0 2563
Carlisle U: Elliott; Edmondson (Murray), Gallimore, Walling, Mountfield, Conway, Thomas (Thorpe), Arnold, Reeves, Davey, Prokas.
Hartlepool U: Horne; Ingram, Walsh, Gilchrist, McGuckin, Ainsley, Sloan, Oliver, Houchen (Thompson), Foster, Southall.

Hudderfield T (1) 3 *(Mitchell, Clayton, Starbuck (pen))*
York C (0) 0 4183
Huddersfield T: Blackwell; Trevitt, Billy, Mitchell, Scully (Dyson), Gray, Crosby, Clayton, Dunn (Baldry), Jepson, Starbuck.
York C: Kiely; McMillan, Wilson, Pepper, Tutill, Barras, McCarthy, Naylor (Baker), Barnes, Jordan (Atkin), Canham.

Rotherham U (0) 1 *(Goater)*
Chesterfield (0) 1 *(Roberts)* 1585
Rotherham U: Clarke; Wilder, James, Williams A, Breckin, Brien, Hayward, Marginson, Davison, Goater, Dolby.
Chesterfield: Beasley; Hewitt, Rogers, Perkins, Madden (Cheetham), Fairclough, Curtis, Davies, Morris (Roberts), Moss, Dyche.

Wrexham (1) 2 *(Bennett 2)*
Mansfield T (0) 0 1002
Wrexham: Marriott; Jones, Hardy, Brammer, Hunter, Humes, Bennett, Owen, Connolly, Cross, Hughes.
Mansfield T: Pearcey; Boothroyd, Aspinall (Marrows), Timons, Howarth, Peters, Ireland, Castledine, Hadley, Doolan, Noteman.

Rochdale (0) 1 *(Taylor)*
Wigan Ath (0) 0 1004
Rochdale: Dickins; Thackeray, Formby, Reid, Doyle, Butler, Thompson (Ryan), Hall, Williams, Whitehall, Sharpe (Taylor).
Wigan Ath: Farnworth; Carragher, Jakub, Strong, Rennie, Farrell, Kilford, Morton (Adekola), Leonard, Rimmer, Lyons.

Chester C (2) 3 *(Shelton 2, Page)*
Bury (0) 1 *(Rigby)* 841
Chester C: Felgate; Jenkins, Burnham, Ratcliffe, Lightfoot, Shelton, Chambers, Priest, Preece, Page, Hackett.
Bury: Kelly G; Jackson (Hughes), Stanislaus, Daws, Lucketti, Matthewson, Paskin (Mulligan), Carter, Rigby, Johnrose, Pugh.

Birmingham C (1) 3 *(Shearer 2, Donowa)*
Walsall (0) 0 10,089
Birmingham C: Bennett; Poole, Donowa, Ward, Barnett, Daish, Hunt, Claridge (Doherty), Bull, De Souza (McGavin), Shearer.
Walsall: Wood; Ryder, Gibson, Rogers, Ntamark, Palmer, Peer, Mehew (Keister), Lightbourne, Wilson, Houghton.

Cambridge U (1) 1 *(Lillis)*
Northampton T (0) 3 *(Warburton, Grayson, Aldridge)* 1497
Cambridge U: Filan; Nyamah (Granville), Barrick, Craddock, O'Shea, Danzey, Lillis (Hay), Walker, Butler, Corazzin, Joseph.
Northampton T: Ovendale; Pascoe (Cahill), Skelly, Sampson, Warburton, Curtis, Harmon, Williams, McNamara (Wilkin), Aldridge, Grayson.

Leyton Orient (4) 5 *(Purse, Dempsey, West 3 (1 pen))*
Fulham (1) 2 *(Mison, Haworth)* 1282
Leyton Orient: Heald; Howard (Warren), Austin, Bellamy, Hendon, Bogie, Lakin, Cockerill, Purse (Carter), West, Dempsey.
Fulham: Stannard; Jupp, Angus, Hurlock, Moore, Blake, Mison, Morgan, Hails (Haworth), Brazil, Thomas M (Bedrossian).

Plymouth Arg (0) 1 *(Naylor)*
Exeter C (1) 3 *(Cecere 2, Cooper)* 1847
Plymouth Arg: Nicholls; Edworthy, Naylor, Hill, Comyn, Burnett, Barlow, Skinner, O'Hagan, Landon (Nugent), Twiddy.
Exeter C: Fox; Minett, Rice, Cooper M, Hare, Brown, Storer, Thirlby (Phillips), Turner, Coughlin, Cecere.

Torquay U (1) 1 *(Moore)*
Swansea C (2) 3 *(Hendry 2, Bowen)* 885
Torquay U: Bayes; Brass, Kelly (Goodridge), Burton, Moore, Curran, Trollope, Darby (Laight), Hancox, Okorie, Hathaway.
Swansea C: Jones; Jenkins, Ford, Basham, Harris, Pascoe, Bowen, Penney, Hendry, Chapple, Hodge (Hayes).

19 OCT

Bristol R (0) 1 *(Stewart (pen))*
Bournemouth (0) 1 *(Murray)* 1725
Bristol R: Collett; Pritchard, Maddison, Channing, Clark, Tillson (Skinner), Sterling, Paul (McLean), Stewart, Browning, Gurney.
Bournemouth: Andrews; Young, Chivers, Morris, Watson (Murray), Pennock, Beardsmore, Mean, Aspinall (Reeve), Fletcher, Scully.

Brighton & HA (0) 0
Brentford (0) 1 *(Forster)* 1104
Brighton & HA: Rust; Munday, Tuck, Simmonds (Pates), McCarthy, Bissett, Chamberlain (Funnell), McDougald, Nogan, Codner, Fox M.
Brentford: Dearden; Statham, Grainger, Westley, Ashby, Ratcliffe, Harvey, Hutchings, Mundee, Forster, Stephenson.

1 NOV

Northampton T (1) 3 *(Aldridge, Harmon, Grayson)*
Barnet (0) 1 *(Cooper)* 2618
Northampton T: Ovendale; Pascoe, Colkin, Sampson, Warburton, Williams, Harmon, Grayson, Aldridge, Robinson, Turner (Cahill).
Barnet: Newell; McDonald (Tomlinson), Walker, Hoddle, Newson, Primus, McMahon, Freedman, Hodges (Wilson), Cooper, Scott.

8 NOV

Bury (0) 1 *(Sertori)*
Preston NE (0) 0 1756
Bury: Kelly G; Jackson, Stanislaus, Daws, Lucketti, Matthewson, Hughes, Sertori, Rigby, Johnrose, Mauge.
Preston NE: Vaughan; Fensome, Sharp, Cartwright, Holmes, Moyes, Trebble, Bryson, Raynor, Sale, Fleming (Whalley).

Chesterfield (0) 1 *(Davies)*
Scunthorpe U (0) 1 *(Bullimore (pen))* 1424
Chesterfield: Beasley; Hewitt, Jules, Perkins, Carr, Fairclough, McAuley, Norris, Roberts (Davies), Moss, Dyche.
Scunthorpe U: Samways; Hope, Bradley, Thompstone, Knill, Thornber (Housham), Alexander, Bullimore, Carmichael, Goodacre (Sansam), Smith.

Lincoln C (0) 1 *(West)*
Hull C (0) 0 1626
Lincoln C: Leaning; West, Johnson A, Schofield, Greenall, Brown, Lucas, Matthews, Daley, Johnson D (Carbon), Hill.
Hull C: Wilson; Dakin, Graham, Hobson, Dewhurst, Mann (Abbott), Peacock, Lee, Hargreaves, Windass, Lawford.

Mansfield T (0) 2 *(Alexander 2)*
Crewe Alex (1) 2 *(Collins, Ward)* 1250
Mansfield T: Ward; Timons, Baraclough, Holland (Alexander), Howarth, Peters, Aspinall, Hoyle, Wilkinson, Stark, Noteman.
Crewe Alex: Gayle; Booty, Smith S, Wilson, Barr, Whalley, Garvey (Collier), Collins, Ward, Lennon, Rowbotham.

Hartlepool U (0) 0
Darlington (0) 2 *(Worboys 2)* 1211
Hartlepool U: Horne; Ingram, Walsh, Gilchrist, McGuckin, Ainsley, Oliver, Halliday, Houchen, Foster, Southall.
Darlington: Pollitt; Appleby, Taylor, Banks, Crosby, Gregan, Worboys, Painter, Gaughan, Casson, Himsworth.

Wigan Ath (1) 1 *(Leonard)*
Blackpool (0) 0 1161
Wigan Ath: Farnworth (Statham); Rennie, Jakub, Miller (Strong), Robertson, Farrell, Kilford, Carragher, Leonard, McKearney, Lyons.
Blackpool: Martin; Brown, Burke, Bradshaw, Thompson, Horner, Mitchell, Gouck (Bonner), Watson, Quinn, Griffiths (Sunderland).

York C (1) 2 *(Barnes, Baker)*
Bradford C (0) 2 *(Murray, Tolson)* 2326
York C: Kiely; McMillan, Hall, Pepper, Atkin, Barras, McCarthy, Naylor, Barnes, Baker, Canham.
Bradford C: Tomlinson; Hamilton, Huxford, Duxbury, Sinnott, Oliver, Murray, Kamara, Taylor, Jewell (Tolson), Showler.

Bournemouth (0) 0
Oxford U (0) 0 1374
Bournemouth: Andrews; Young, Pennock, Morris, Watson (Chivers), Leadbitter, Beardsmore, Mean, Robinson, Jones, Scully (Murray).
Oxford U: Deegan; Robinson, Butters, Lewis, Collins, Marsh, Druce (Murphy), Smith, Wanless, Rush, Ford R.

Brentford (2) 3 *(Annon, Asaba, Ansah)*
Gillingham (0) 1 *(Pike)* 1795
Brentford: Dearden (Fernandes); Hurdle, Grainger, Bates, Ashby, Smith, Hutchings, Asaba (Forster), Taylor (Ravenscroft), Annon, Ansah.
Gillingham: Barrett; Arnott, Palmer, Carpenter, Trott, Butler, Hutchinson, Kamara (Ramage), Pike (Micklewhite), Reinelt, Hooker.

Fulham (1) 3 *(Haworth, Adams, Cusack)*
Colchester U (0) 2 *(Abrahams, Kinsella)* 1451
Fulham: Harrison; Finnigan (Jupp), Herrera, Marshall, Angus, Blake, Mison, Morgan, Cusack, Haworth (Williams), Adams.
Colchester U: Cheeswright; Betts, English, Cawley, Caesar, Dennis, Locke, Brown (Fry), Whitton, Kinsella, Abrahams (Burley).

Swansea C (0) 1 *(Torpey)*
Hereford U (1) 1 *(Reece)* 1215
Swansea C: Freestone; Jenkins, Clode (Torpey), Basham, Ford, Ampadu, Bowen, Penney (Hayes), Hendry, Cornforth, Hodge.
Hereford U: Pennock; Llewellyn, Lloyd, Reece, Davies, James, Steele (Smith), Wilkins, Cross (White), Lyne, Fishlock.

Walsall (1) 2 *(Gibson, Marsh)*
Peterborough U (0) 3 *(Heald, Breen, Henry)* 2104
Walsall: Wood; Evans, Gibson, Rogers, Marsh, Palmer, O'Connor, Ntamark, Butler, Wilson, Houghton.
Peterborough U: Cooksey; Heald, Spearing, Ebdon, Breen, Thomas, Farrell, McGorry, Williams, Morrison, Henry.

15 NOV

Exeter C (0) 1 *(Minett (pen))*
Cardiff C (0) 1 *(Young)* 1203
Exeter C: Fox; Minett, Robinson (Phillips), Cooper M, Came, Richardson, Storer, Bailey, Turner, Brown, Gavin (Ross).
Cardiff C: Williams D; Young, Searle, Aizlewood, Baddeley, Millar, Ramsey, Griffith, Stant, Thompson, Adams (Wigg).
Byes to Second Round: Stockport Co, Scarborough, Wycombe W, Shrewsbury T.

Second Round

28 NOV

Doncaster R (0) 0
Bury (1) 1 *(Pugh)* 2859
Doncaster R: Williams D; Kirby, Hackett, Brabin, Wilcox, Kitchen, Lawrence, Meara (Donaldson), Jones, Norbury, Thew (Warren).
Bury: Kelly G; Jackson, Stanislaus, Johnrose, Lucketti, Matthewson, Kelly T, Hulme (Sertori), Hughes, Reid (Daws), Pugh.

29 NOV

Carlisle U (0) 1 *(Currie)*
Chesterfield (0) 0 3531
Carlisle U: Beasley; Dyche, Rogers, Fairclough, Carr, Law, Hewitt, Davies, Morris, McAuley, Jules.
Chesterfield: Caig; Edmondson, Gallimore, Walling, Mountfield, Conway, Thomas, Currie, Reeves, Davey, Prokas.

Chester C (0) 0 1890
Crewe Alex (3) 6 *(Ward 3 (1 pen), Collins, Whalley, Adebola)*
Chester C: Felgate; Jenkins, Ratcliffe, Alsford, Jackson, Preece, Milner, Flitcroft, Murphy (Bishop), Page, Hackett (Rimmer).
Crewe Alex: Smith M; Booty, Smith S, Wilson, Macauley, Whalley (Gardiner), Garvey (Clarkson), Collins, Ward, Lennon, Adebola.

Rochdale (1) 2 *(Whitehall 2)*
Darlington (2) 2 *(Worboys, Appleby (pen)) aet* 1069
Rochdale: Gray; Thackeray, Formby, Reid, Matthews, Butler, Thompson (Taylor), Doyle (Stuart), Sharpe, Whitehall, Ryan.
Darlington: Pollitt; Appleby, Taylor, Banks, Reed, Gregan, Gaughan, Chapman, Worboys, Olsson, Himsworth (Kirkham).
Rochdale won 4-3 on penalties

Rotherham U (0) 1 *(Goater)*
Wigan Ath (2) 3 *(Rimmer, Leonard, Kilford)* 1587
Rotherham U: Clarke; Wilder, James, Ayrton (Smith), Breckin, Brien, Hayward, Richardson, Davison, Goater, Hurst (Varadi).
Wigan Ath: Farnworth; Strong, Jakub, Miller, Robertson, Farrell, Kilford, Carragher, Leonard, Rimmer, Lyons.

Stockport Co (0) 3 *(Dinning, Bound, Ward)*
Scarborough (0) 1 *(Charles)* 2310
Stockport Co: Edwards; Dinning, Todd, Eckhardt, Flynn, Bound, Gannon, Ward (Wallace), Armstrong, Beaumont, Slinn (Chalk).
Scarborough: Martin; Knowles, Wells, Toman (Thompson), Davis, Rockett, Swann (Calvert), Charles, White, Rutherford, D'Auria.

Wrexham (4) 6 *(Bennett 3, Watkin 2, Owen)*
Bradford C (0) 1 *(Power)* 1407
Wrexham: Marriott; Brace, Hardy, Hughes, Hunter, Jones (Phillips), Bennett, Owen, Connolly, Watkin, Durkan (Cross).
Bradford C: Tomlinson; Huxford, Jacobs, Duxbury, Sinnott, Richards (Power), Shutt (Showler), Oliver, Taylor, Jewell, Murray.

Birmingham C (2) 3 *(McGavin, Poole, Tait)*
Gillingham (0) 0 17,028
Birmingham C: Bennett; Poole, Whyte, Ward (Lowe), Barnett, Daish, Donowa (Cooper), Claridge, McGavin, Dominguez, Tait.
Gillingham: Barrett; Lindsey, Palmer, Carpenter, Arnott, Bodley, Hutchinson, Foster (Ramage), Pike, Reinelt, Watson.

Bristol R (2) 4 *(Skinner, Stewart 2 (1 pen), Miller)*
Cambridge U (2) 2 *(Corazzin, Hay)* 2373
Bristol R: Parkin; Pritchard, Gurney, Browning, Clark, Tillson, Sterling, Miller, Stewart, Skinner, Archer.
Cambridge U: Sheffield; Joseph, Barrick, Craddock, Jeffrey, Hyde, Fowler, Granville, Butler (Lillis), Corazzin (Hunter), Hay.

Exeter C (0) 1 *(Brown)*
Cardiff C (0) 0 1452
Exeter C: Woodman; Minett, Brown, Bailey, Daniels, Richardson, Storer, Coughlin, Cooper M, Cecere (Morgan), Gavin.
Cardiff C: Williams S; Evans (Griffith), Searle, Oatway, Baddeley, Brazil, Ramsey, Richardson, Stant, Thompson, Fereday (Dale).

Hereford U (1) 2 *(James, Reece)*
Peterborough U (0) 0 1301
Hereford U: Pennock; Reece, Lloyd, Smith, Fishlock, James, Pounder, Wilkins, White, Lyne, Pick.
Peterborough U: Tyler; Heald, Spearing, Ebdon (Brissett), Breen, Thomas, Moran, Webster (Clark), Williams, Charlery, Lormor.

Leyton Orient (1) 1 *(West)*
Fulham (0) 0 1575
Leyton Orient: Heald; Hendon, Austin, Bellamy, Howard, Brooks, Barnett, Cockerill, Purse (Bogie), West (Warren), Carter.
Fulham: Stannard; Jupp, Herrera, Hurlock, Moore, Blake, Marshall (Hamill), Morgan, Cusack, Brazil, Adams.

Northampton T (0) 0
Swansea C (1) 1 *(Hendry)* 2706
Northampton T: Stewart; Norton, Skelly, Sampson, Warburton (Curtis), Williams, Harmon, Grayson, Trott (Harrison), Robinson, Cahill.
Swansea C: Freestone; Jenkins, Barnhouse, Basham, Ford, Chapple, Bowen, Penney, Hendry, Cornforth, Hodge (Hayes).

Shrewsbury T (1) 2 *(Williams, Stevens)*
Wycombe W (0) 0 1785
Shrewsbury T: Edwards; Seabury, Lynch, Taylor, Williams, Patterson, Smith, Hughes, Spink (Slawson), Stevens, Evans.
Wycombe W: Hyde; Cousins, Brown, Crossley, Creaser, Ryan, Kerr (Langford), Bell, Turnbull (Hemmings), Reid, Stapleton.

30 NOV

Huddersfield T (0) 3 *(Crosby, Jepson (pen), Dunn)*
Lincoln C (2) 2 *(Daley, Johnson D) aet, sd* 5738
Huddersfield T: Blackwell; Trevitt, Williams, Logan, Gray, Mitchell, Billy, Clayton (Booth), Dunn, Jepson, Collins (Crosby).
Lincoln C: Leaning; West, Johnson A, Foley (Carbon), Dixon, Brown, Johnson D, Hebberd (Matthews), Daley, Daws, Hill.

3 DEC

Brentford (0) 1 *(Grainger (pen))*
Oxford U (0) 2 *(Murphy, Ashby (og))* 2410
Brentford: Dearden; Statham, Grainger, Ashby, Westley (Annon), Harvey, Forster (Hutchings), Taylor, Bates, Mundee, Ansah.
Oxford U: Whitehead; Robinson, Lewis, Dyer, Elliott, Wood (Wanless), Murphy, Smith, Rush, Byrne, Ford R.

Northern Section quarter-final

10 JAN

Carlisle U (1) 2 *(Thomas, Hunter (og))*
Wrexham (0) 1 *(Bennett)* 8771
Carlisle U: Caig; Edmondson, Gallimore, Walling, Robinson, Conway, Thomas (Thorpe), Currie, Reeves (Peters), Davey, Prokas.
Wrexham: Marriott; Jones, Hardy, Hughes, Hunter, Humes, Bennett, Owen, Connolly, Cross (Morris), Durkan.

Southern Section quarter-finals

Birmingham C (1) 3 *(Claridge, Ward (pen), Otto)*
Hereford U (1) 1 *(Lyne)* 22,352
Birmingham C: Bennett; Poole, Cooper, Ward, Barnett, Daish, Donowa, Claridge, Lowe (Dominguez), Otto, Shearer.
Hereford U: McKenzie; Davies, Lloyd, Reece, Smith, Brownrigg, Clark, Gregory (Brough), White, Lyne, Pick.

Leyton Orient (0) 0
Bristol R (0) 0 1381
Leyton Orient: Heald; Howard, Austin, Purse, Hague, Bogie, Carter, Hendon, Warren (Barnett), Brooks, Dempsey.
Bristol R: Parkin; Channing, Gurney, Hardyman, Clark, Tillson, Sterling, Miller, Taylor (Paul), Skinner (Maddison), Archer.
aet; Leyton Orient won 4-3 on penalties

Oxford U (0) 1 *(Ford R)*
Swansea C (1) 2 *(Torpey, Hayes)* 2321
Oxford U: Deegan; Robinson, Marsh, Dyer (Murphy), Elliott, Rogan, Ford R, Smith, Druce, Rush, Allen.
Swansea C: Freestone; Jenkins (Chapple), Walker, Basham, Ford, Ampadu, Hayes, Penney, Torpey, Cornforth, Hodge.

Shrewsbury T (1) 3 *(Spink, Stevens 2)*
Exeter C (0) 1 *(Richardson)* 1960
Shrewsbury T: Edwards; Hockaday, Withe, Taylor (Lynch), Williams, Summerfield, Woods, Clarke W (Stevens), Spink, Walton, Jeffers.
Exeter C: Woodman; Minett, Robinson, Bailey, Daniels, Richardson, Storer, Cooper M, Gavin, Anderson, Cecere.

Northern Section quarter-finals

11 JAN

Rochdale (1) 2 *(Whitehall 2)*
Stockport Co (1) 1 *(Wallace)* 2154
Rochdale: Gray; Thackeray, Formby, Reid (Hall), Matthews, Butler, Thompson, Peake, Sharpe (Russell), Whitehall, Stuart.
Stockport Co: Edwards; Connelly (Gannon), Todd, Dinning (Young), Flynn, Bound, Ware, Wallace, Armstrong, Beaumont, Chalk.

24 JAN

Bury (1) 2 *(Kelly T 2)*
Huddersfield T (0) 1 *(Clayton)* 3311
Bury: Kelly G; Cross, Stanislaus, Mauge (Daws), Lucketti, Hughes, Kelly T, Carter, Paskin, Johnrose, Pugh.
Huddersfield T: Francis; Short (Billy), Cowan, Logan, Scully, Dyson, Dunn, Clayton (Crosby), Booth, Jepson, Reid.

Southern Section semi-finals

31 JAN

Birmingham C (1) 3 *(Claridge, Francis, Tait)*
Swansea C (2) 2 *(Pascoe, Lowe (og)) aet, sd* 20,326
Birmingham C: Bennett; Scott, Cooper, Ward, Barnett, Whyte, Donowa (Dominguez), Claridge, Francis, Otto, Lowe (Tait).
Swansea C: Freestone; Jenkins, Walker, Basham, Ford, Pascoe (McFarlane), Hayes, Penney, Torpey, Cornforth, Hodge (Bowen).

Leyton Orient (1) 2 *(Warren, Brooks)*
Shrewsbury T (0) 1 *(Stevens)* 2913
Leyton Orient: Heald; Hendon, Howard, Bellamy, Purse, Brooks, Carter, Cockerill, Bogie (Gray), Warren, Dempsey.
Shrewsbury T: Edwards; Hockaday, Withe, Taylor, Williams, Lynch, Woods (Seabury), Evans, Spink, Stevens, Jeffers.

Northern Section quarter-final

7 FEB

Wigan Ath (0) 1 *(Farrell)*
Crewe Alex (2) 3 *(Whalley, Macauley, Adebola)* 2063
Wigan Ath: Farnworth; Carragher (Benjamin), Wright (Jakub), Miller, Robertson, Farrell, Doolan, McKearney, Leonard, Rimmer, Lyons.
Crewe Alex: Smith M; Booty, Smith S, Barr, Macauley, Whalley, Murphy, Collins (Collier), Adebola (Tierney), Lennon, Clarkson.

Northern Section semi-finals

Bury (1) 1 *(Paskin)*
Rochdale (2) 2 *(Sharpe, Reid)* 3341
Bury: Kelly G; Daws, Bimson, Mauge, Lucketti, Matthewson (Rigby), Kelly T, Hulme, Paskin (Carter), Johnrose, Pugh.
Rochdale: Gray; Thackeray (Russell), Formby, Reid, Matthews, Butler, Thompson, Peake, Sharpe (Stuart), Whitehall, Deary.

14 FEB

Crewe Alex (0) 0
Carlisle U (1) 1 *(Thomas)* 4046
Crewe Alex: Smith M; Booty, Smith S, Barr, Macauley, Whalley, Murphy, Tierney (Rowbotham), Clarkson, Lennon, Garvey.
Carlisle U: Caig; Edmondson, Gallimore, Walling, Mountfield, Conway, Thomas, Currie (Peters), Reeves, Davey, Murray (Robinson).

Northern Section final, first leg

28 FEB

Carlisle U (3) 4 *(Currie, Thomas 2, Conway)*

Rochdale (0) 1 *(Whitehall (pen))* 8647

Carlisle U: Caig; Edmondson, Gallimore, Walling, Mountfield, Peters, Thomas, Currie (Thorpe), Reeves (Robinson), Conway, Prokas.
Rochdale: Clarke; Thackeray, Formby, Reid, Matthews, Butler, Thompson, Peake, Deary (Hall), Whitehall, Sharpe (Ryan).

Southern Section final, first leg

Birmingham C (0) 1 *(Shearer)*

Leyton Orient (0) 0 24,002

Birmingham C: Bennett; Poole, Cooper, Tait (Whyte), Barnett, Daish, Donowa, Saville (McGavin), Francis, Otto, Shearer.
Leyton Orient: Heald; Hendon, Austin, Bellamy, Purse, Bogie, Carter, Cockerill, Barnett (Warren), West, Dempsey.

Northern Section final, second leg

14 MAR

Rochdale (2) 2 *(Whitehall, Reid)*

Carlisle U (1) 1 *(Mountfield)* 4082

Rochdale: Clarke; Thackeray, Formby (Stuart), Reid (Ryan), Matthews, Butler, Thompson, Peake, Sharpe, Whitehall, Deary.
Carlisle U: Caig; Edmondson, Gallimore, Walling, Mountfield, Hayward, Thorpe (Robinson), Currie, Reeves, Conway, Prokas.

Southern Section final, second leg

Leyton Orient (0) 2 *(Purse, McGleish)*

Birmingham C (1) 3 *(Claridge 2, Williams)* 10,830

Leyton Orient: Heald; Hendon, Austin, Bellamy, Purse, Bogie, McGleish, Cockerill, Read (Hague), West (Warren), Dempsey.
Birmingham C: Bennett; Poole, Whyte, Ward, Barnett, Daish, Esteves (Tait), Claridge, Robinson, Otto (Doherty), Williams.

Final at Wembley

23 APR

Birmingham C (0) 1 *(Tait)*

Carlisle U (0) 0 76,663

Birmingham C: Bennett; Poole, Cooper, Ward, Barnett, Daish, Hunt, Claridge, Francis (Donowa), Otto, Shearer (Tait).
Carlisle U: Caig; Edmondson, Gallimore, Walling, Mountfield (Robinson), Hayward, Thomas, Currie, Reeves, Conway, Prokas (Thorpe).
aet; Birmingham C won on sudden death.
Referee: P. Foakes (Clacton).

David Currie (centre) is carefully watched by two Birmingham defenders as Carlisle lose 1-0 in the Auto Windscreens Shield Final at Wembley. (Colorsport)

FOOTBALL LEAGUE COMPETITION ATTENDANCES

SEASON 1994–1995

ANGLO-ITALIAN CUP

(Games played in England only)

Round	*Aggregate*	*Matches*	*Average*
Inter	67,354	16	4,210
Semi-finals	15,876	2	7,938
Final	11,704	1	11,704
Total	94,934	19	4,997

COCA-COLA CUP

Round	*Aggregate*	*Matches*	*Average*
Round one	195,339	56	3,488
Round two	624,836	64	9,763
Round three	296,298	19	15,595
Round four	148,853	8	18,607
Round five	80,505	4	20,126
Semi-finals	78,896	4	19,724
Final	75,595	1	75,595
Total	1,500,322	156	9,617

AUTO WINDSCREENS SHIELD

Round	*Aggregate*	*Matches*	*Average*
Round one	77,233	42	1,839
Round two	51,203	16	3,200
Area quarter-finals	44,313	8	5,539
Area semi-finals	30,626	4	7,657
Area finals	47,561	4	11,890
Final	76,633	1	76,633
Total	327,569	75	4,368

FA CUP FINALS 1872–1995

1872 and 1874–92	Kennington Oval	1911	Replay at Old Trafford
1873	Lillie Bridge	1912	Replay at Bramall Lane
1886	Replay at Derby (Racecourse Ground)		
1893	Fallowfield, Manchester	1915	Old Trafford, Manchester
1894	Everton	1920–22	Stamford Bridge
1895–1914	Crystal Palace	1923 to date	Wembley
1901	Replay at Bolton	1970	Replay at Old Trafford
1910	Replay at Everton	1981	Replay at Wembley

Year	*Winners*	*Runners-up*	*Score*
1872	Wanderers	Royal Engineers	1-0
1873	Wanderers	Oxford University	2-0
1874	Oxford University	Royal Engineers	2-0
1875	Royal Engineers	Old Etonians	2-0 (after 1-1 draw aet)
1876	Wanderers	Old Etonians	3-0 (after 1-1 draw aet)
1877	Wanderers	Oxford University	2-1 (aet)
1878	Wanderers*	Royal Engineers	3-1
1879	Old Etonians	Clapham R	1-0
1880	Clapham R	Oxford University	1-0
1881	Old Carthusians	Old Etonians	3-0
1882	Old Etonians	Blackburn R	1-0
1883	Blackburn Olympic	Old Etonians	2-1 (aet)
1884	Blackburn R	Queen's Park, Glasgow	2-1
1885	Blackburn R	Queen's Park, Glasgow	2-0
1886	Blackburn R†	WBA	2-0 (after 0-0 draw)
1887	Aston Villa	WBA	2-0
1888	WBA	Preston NE	2-1
1889	Preston NE	Wolverhampton W	3-0
1890	Blackburn R	Sheffield W	6-1
1891	Blackburn R	Notts Co	3-1
1892	WBA	Aston Villa	3-0
1893	Wolverhampton W	Everton	1-0
1894	Notts Co	Bolton W	4-1
1895	Aston Villa	WBA	1-0
1896	Sheffield W	Wolverhampton W	2-1
1897	Aston Villa	Everton	3-2
1898	Nottingham F	Derby Co	3-1
1899	Sheffield U	Derby Co	4-1
1900	Bury	Southampton	4-0
1901	Tottenham H	Sheffield U	3-1 (after 2-2 draw)
1902	Sheffield U	Southampton	2-1 (after 1-1 draw)
1903	Bury	Derby Co	6-0
1904	Manchester C	Bolton W	1-0
1905	Aston Villa	Newcastle U	2-0
1906	Everton	Newcastle U	1-0
1907	Sheffield W	Everton	2-1
1908	Wolverhampton W	Newcastle U	3-1
1909	Manchester U	Bristol C	1-0
1910	Newcastle U	Barnsley	2-0 (after 1-1 draw)
1911	Bradford C	Newcastle U	1-0 (after 0-0 draw)
1912	Barnsley	WBA	1-0 (aet, after 0-0 draw)
1913	Aston Villa	Sunderland	1-0
1914	Burnley	Liverpool	1-0
1915	Sheffield U	Chelsea	3-0
1920	Aston Villa	Huddersfield T	1-0 (aet)
1921	Tottenham H	Wolverhampton W	1-0
1922	Huddersfield T	Preston NE	1-0
1923	Bolton W	West Ham U	2-0
1924	Newcastle U	Aston Villa	2-0
1925	Sheffield U	Cardiff C	1-0
1926	Bolton W	Manchester C	1-0
1927	Cardiff C	Arsenal	1-0
1928	Blackburn R	Huddersfield T	3-1
1929	Bolton W	Portsmouth	2-0
1930	Arsenal	Huddersfield T	2-0
1931	WBA	Birmingham	2-1
1932	Newcastle U	Arsenal	2-1
1933	Everton	Manchester C	3-0
1934	Manchester C	Portsmouth	2-1
1935	Sheffield W	WBA	4-2
1936	Arsenal	Sheffield U	1-0
1937	Sunderland	Preston NE	3-1
1938	Preston NE	Huddersfield T	1-0 (aet)
1939	Portsmouth	Wolverhampton W	4-1
1946	Derby Co	Charlton Ath	4-1 (aet)
1947	Charlton Ath	Burnley	1-0 (aet)
1948	Manchester U	Blackpool	4-2
1949	Wolverhampton W	Leicester C	3-1
1950	Arsenal	Liverpool	2-0
1951	Newcastle U	Blackpool	2-0
1952	Newcastle U	Arsenal	1-0

Year	Winners	Runners-up	Score
1953	Blackpool	Bolton W	4-3
1954	WBA	Preston NE	3-2
1955	Newcastle U	Manchester C	3-1
1956	Manchester C	Birmingham C	3-1
1957	Aston Villa	Manchester U	2-1
1958	Bolton W	Manchester U	2-0
1959	Nottingham F	Luton T	2-1
1960	Wolverhampton W	Blackburn R	3-0
1961	Tottenham H	Leicester C	2-0
1962	Tottenham H	Burnley	3-1
1963	Manchester U	Leicester C	3-1
1964	West Ham U	Preston NE	3-2
1965	Liverpool	Leeds U	2-1 (aet)
1966	Everton	Sheffield W	3-2
1967	Tottenham H	Chelsea	2-1
1968	WBA	Everton	1-0 (aet)
1969	Manchester C	Leicester C	1-0
1970	Chelsea	Leeds U	2-1 (aet)
	(after 2-2 draw, after extra time, at Wembley)		
1971	Arsenal	Liverpool	2-1 (aet)
1972	Leeds U	Arsenal	1-0
1973	Sunderland	Leeds U	1-0
1974	Liverpool	Newcastle U	3-0
1975	West Ham U	Fulham	2-0
1976	Southampton	Manchester U	1-0
1977	Manchester U	Liverpool	2-1
1978	Ipswich	Arsenal	1-0
1979	Arsenal	Manchester U	3-2
1980	West Ham U	Arsenal	1-0
1981	Tottenham H	Manchester C	3-2
	(after 1-1 draw, after extra time, at Wembley)		
1982	Tottenham H	QPR	1-0
	(after 1-1 draw, after extra time, at Wembley)		
1983	Manchester U	Brighton & HA	4-0
	(after 2-2 draw, after extra time, at Wembley)		
1984	Everton	Watford	2-0
1985	Manchester U	Everton	1-0 (aet)
1986	Liverpool	Everton	3-1
1987	Coventry C	Tottenham H	3-2 (aet)
1988	Wimbledon	Liverpool	1-0
1989	Liverpool	Everton	3-2 (aet)
1990	Manchester U	Crystal Palace	1-0
	(after 3-3 draw, after extra time, at Wembley)		
1991	Tottenham H	Nottingham F	2-1 (aet)
1992	Liverpool	Sunderland	2-0
1993	Arsenal	Sheffield W	2-1 (aet)
	(after 1-1 draw, after extra time, at Wembley)		
1994	Manchester U	Chelsea	4-0
1995	Everton	Manchester U	1-0

* *Won outright, but restored to the Football Association.*
† *A special trophy was awarded for third consecutive win.*

FA CUP WINS

Manchester U 8, Tottenham H 8, Aston Villa 7, Arsenal 6, Blackburn R 6, Newcastle U 6, Everton 5, Liverpool 5, The Wanderers 5, WBA 5, Bolton W 4, Manchester C 4, Sheffield U 4, Wolverhampton W 4, Sheffield W 3, West Ham U 3, Bury 2, Nottingham F 2, Old Etonians 2, Preston NE 2, Sunderland 2, Barnsley 1, Blackburn Olympic 1, Blackpool 1, Bradford C 1, Burnley 1, Cardiff C 1, Charlton Ath 1, Chelsea 1, Clapham R 1, Coventry C 1, Derby Co 1, Huddersfield T 1, Ipswich T 1, Leeds U 1, Notts Co 1, Old Carthusians 1, Oxford University 1, Portsmouth 1, Royal Engineers 1, Southampton 1, Wimbledon 1.

APPEARANCES IN FINALS

Manchester U 13, Arsenal 12, Everton 12, Newcastle U 11, WBA 10, Liverpool 10, Aston Villa 9, Tottenham H 9, Blackburn R 8, Manchester C 8, Wolverhampton W 8, Bolton W 7, Preston NE 7, Old Etonians 6, Sheffield U 6, Sheffield W 6, Huddersfield T 5, *The Wanderers 5, Chelsea 4, Derby Co 4, Leeds U 4, Leicester C 4, Oxford University 4, Royal Engineers 4, Sunderland 4, West Ham U 4, Blackpool 3, Burnley 3, Nottingham F 3, Portsmouth 3, Southampton 3, Barnsley 2, Birmingham C 2, *Bury 2, Cardiff C 2, Charlton Ath 2, Clapham R 2, Notts Co 2, Queen's Park (Glasgow) 2, *Blackburn Olympic 1, *Bradford C 1, Brighton & HA 1, Bristol C 1, *Coventry C 1, Crystal Palace 1, Fulham 1, *Ipswich T 1, Luton 4, *Old Carthusians 1, QPR 1, Watford 1, *Wimbledon 1.

* *Denotes undefeated.*

APPEARANCES IN SEMI-FINALS

Everton 23, Manchester U 20, Liverpool 19, WBA 19, Arsenal 18, Aston Villa 17, Blackburn R 16, Sheffield W 16, Tottenham H 15, Derby Co 13, Newcastle U 13, Wolverhampton W 13, Bolton W 12, Nottingham F 12, Chelsea 11, Sheffield U 11, Sunderland 11, Manchester C 10, Preston NE 10, Southampton 10, Birmingham C 9, Burnley 8, Leeds U 8, Huddersfield T 7, Leicester C 7, Old Etonians 6, Oxford University 6, West Ham U 6, Fulham 5, Notts Co 5, Portsmouth 5, The Wanderers 5, Luton T 4, Queen's Park (Glasgow) 4, Royal Engineers 4, Blackpool 3, Cardiff C 3, Clapham R 3, Crystal Palace (professional club) 3, Ipswich T 3, Millwall 3, Norwich C 3, Old Carthusians 3, Oldham Ath 3, Stoke C 3, The Swifts 3, Watford 3, Barnsley 2, Blackburn Olympic 2, Bristol C 2, Bury 2, Charlton Ath 2, Grimsby T 2, Swansea T 2, Swindon T 2, Bradford C 1, Brighton & HA 1, Cambridge University 1, Coventry C 1, Crewe Alex 1, Crystal Palace (amateur club) 1, Darwen 1, Derby Junction 1, Glasgow R 1, Hull C 1, Marlow 1, Old Harrovians 1, Orient 1, Plymouth Arg 1, Port Vale 1, QPR 1, Reading 1, Shropshire W 1, Wimbledon 1, York C 1.

FA CUP 1994–95

SPONSORED BY LITTLEWOODS

PRELIMINARY AND QUALIFYING ROUNDS

Preliminary Round

Dunston Federation Brewery v Darlington Cleveland Social 1-0
Seaham Red Star v Easington Colliery 3-1
Brandon United v Alnwick Town 5-2
Crook Town v Billingham Town 1-1, 2-1
Murton v Hebburn 3-2
Stockton v RTM Newcastle 2-2, 1-6
Guisborough Town v Eppleton CW 2-0
Harrogate Town v Esh Winning 7-0
Penrith v Tow Law Town 2-3
Evenwood Town v Consett 0-3
Ryhope CA v Pickering Town 1-5
South Shields v Prudhoe Town 7-1
Clitheroe v Bamber Bridge 1-0
Farsley Celtic v Great Harwood Town 3-1
Whickham v Willington 1-2
(at Willington)
West Auckland Town v Workington 1-1, 2-1
Yorkshire Amateur v Atherton LR 0-1
Atherton Collieries v Blidworth MW 1-1, 3-1
Belper Town v Blackpool (wren) Rovers 2-1
Alfreton Town v Ashton United 3-1
Chadderton v Armthorpe Welfare 3-2
Arnold Town v Castleton Gabriels 3-2
Caernarfon Town v Darwen 3-1
Congleton Town v Curzon Ashton 4-2
Bradford (Park Avenue) v Burscough 0-3
Hatfield Main v Brigg Town 1-2
Goole Town v Glossop North End 0-2
Denaby United v Hallam 1-1, 0-1
Fleetwood v Eastwood Town 0-3
Glasshoughton Welfare v Eccleshill United 1-0
Maine Road v Louth United 3-1
Bootle v Maltby MW 0-0, 0-1
Immingham Town v Heanor Town 1-2
(at Goole Town)
Liversedge v Ilkeston Town 2-2, 1-4
Prescot AFC v Pontefract Collieries 2-0
Thackley v Radcliffe Borough 0-2
Nantwich Town v Newcastle Town 2-1
Ossett Town v Mossley 0-0, 0-3
Winterton Rangers v Stocksbridge Park Steels 3-0
Ossett Albion v Rossendale United 1-4
Sheffield v Rossington Main 3-1
St Helens Town v Salford City 7-1
Armitage v Brierley Hill Town 1-1, 3-1
Long Buckby v Northampton Spencer 3-3, 1-2
Blakenall v Banbury United 3-2
Bolehall Swifts v Barwell 3-1
Stratford Town v Halesowen Harriers 0-2
Grantham Town v Leicester United 2-0
Hinckley Athletic v Hinckley Town 2-1
Cogenhoe United v Eastwood Hanley 1-1, 0-0, 2-4
Wednesfield v Desborough Town 1-1, 1-2
Lye Town v Racing Club Warwick 2-0
(at Halesowen Harriers)
Bridgnorth Town v Bilston Town 3-1
Oldbury United v Moor Green 1-3
Pelsall Villa v Newport Pagnell Town 2-0
Sutton Coldfield Town v Stourport Swifts 2-3
Dudley Town v Rothwell Town 2-1
Stapenhill v Rushall Olympic 2-1
Stourbridge v Sandwell Borough 1-1, 0-2
Redditch United v Bedworth United 7-0
Evesham United v Tamworth 1-3
Westfields v Wellingborough Town 1-1, 3-1
Hucknall Town v West Midlands Police 0-0, 1-1, 0-1
Cornard United v Chatteris Town 2-0
Lowestoft Town v Diss Town 2-2, 3-3, 0-1
Bourne Town v Billericay Town 1-4
Bury Town v Boston Town 0-4
Holbeach United v Heybridge Swifts 1-2
Burnham Ramblers v Kings Lynn 2-3
Eynesbury Rovers v Gorleston 2-3
Haverhill Rovers v Great Yarmouth Town 2-1
Mirrlees Blackstone v Stamford 2-2, 1-4
Spalding United v March Town United 1-0
Stowmarket Town v Tiptree United 2-2, 1-3
Newmarket Town v Soham Town Rangers 4-2
Hertford Town v Saffron Walden Town 2-5
Kingsbury Town v Kempston Rovers 1-4
Witham Town v Watton United 1-0
Wisbech Town v Fakenham Town 3-0
Brimsdown Rovers v Sudbury Wanderers 1-1, 0-1
Arlesey Town v Brook House 1-2
Aveley v Wootton Blue Cross 1-1, 3-1
Berkhamsted Town v Baldock Town 1-3
Bowers United v Barking 1-4
Chalfont St Peter w.o. v Dunstable removed from competition
Biggleswade Town v Feltham & Hounslow Borough 0-1
(at Feltham & Hounslow Borough)
Collier Row v Cheshunt 2-1
Burnham v Clapton 4-0
(at Flackwell Heath)
Ruislip Manor v Flackwell Heath 5-0
Thamesmead Town v Bedfont 0-3
Harringey Borough v Ford United 1-2
(at Ford United)
Hoddesdon Town v Harefield United 1-1, 0-1
Hillingdon Borough v Royston Town 2-2, 2-1
Romford v Wingate & Finchley 2-0
Southall v Langford 2-1
(at Langford)
Leighton Town v Leyton 2-2, 0-1
Leatherhead v Letchworth Garden City 8-0
Welwyn Garden City v Viking Sports 1-1, 1-0
Tring Town v Wealdstone 0-1
Walthamstow Pennant v Ware 2-2, 0-4
Stotfold v Tower Hamlets 2-1
Slade Green v Tilbury 0-3
Arundel v Burgess Hill Town 1-3
Hampton v Pagham 1-0
Banstead Athletic w.o. v Ash United withdrew
Bracknell Town v Ashford Town 1-3
Tonbridge v Chipstead 1-1, 3-0
Croydon v Three Bridges 7-0
Eastbourne Town v Egham Town 1-7
(at Langney Sports)
Corinthian v Crowborough Athletic 9-0
Uxbridge v Corinthian-Casuals 1-0
Worthing v Horsham 1-0
Herne Bay v Langney Sports 3-0
Horsham YMCA v Lancing 2-1
Folkestone Invicta v Hailsham Town 2-0
Northwood v Godalming & Guildford 2-1
Canterbury City v Newhaven 6-0
Lewes v Fisher 0-1
Oakwood v Peacehaven & Telscombe 0-3
Littlehampton Town v Merstham 2-7
(at Portfield)
Croydon Athletic v Malden Vale 5-2
Ramsgate v Redhill 4-0
Hanwell Town v Whyteleafe 1-2
Shoreham v Ringmer 1-0
Steyning Town v Sheppey United 0-2
Epsom & Ewell v Wembley 1-3
Selsey v Portfield 1-4
Whitstable Town v Tunbridge Wells 2-3

Windsor & Eton v Whitehawk	1-0
Buckingham Town v Brockenhurst	1-0
Abingdon Town v Cove	0-0, 0-1
Bemerton Heath Harlequins v Aldershot Town	0-4
Bournemouth v Basingstoke Town	0-0, 1-3
Fareham Town v Eastleigh	3-1
Fleet Town v Oxford City	3-1
Hungerford Town v Gosport Borough	3-2
Maidenhead United v Havant Town	0-1
Poole Town v Witney Town	3-0
Thame United v Devizes Town	2-0
Ryde v Thatcham Town	3-2
Salisbury City v Totton AFC	5-0
Bridport v Backwell United	1-2
Yate Town v Swanage Town & Herston	2-1
Elmore v Chippenham Town	4-0
Forest Green Rovers v Cinderford Town *(at Gloucester City)*	0-0, 2-3
Odd Down v Newport AFC	0-6
Ilfracombe Town v Paulton Rovers	0-2
Melksham Town v Keynsham Town	4-1
Glastonbury v Frome Town	4-1
Bideford v Falmouth Town	2-1
Taunton Town v Clevedon Town	3-2
Welton Rovers v Saltash United	1-1, 0-4
Calne Town v Torrington	1-3

First Qualifying Round

Barrow v Chester-Le-Street Town	4-1
Seaham Red Star v Billingham Synthonia	2-2, 0-2
Dunston Fed Brewery v Brandon United	2-0
Crook Town v Blyth Spartans	0-2
Bishop Auckland v Harrogate Railway	2-0
RTM Newcastle v Gateshead	0-3
Murton v Guisborough Town	1-1, 4-3
Harrogate Town v Gretna	4-1
Spennymoor United v Shildon	4-1
Consett v Northallerton	1-1, 3-1
Tow Law Town v Pickering Town	4-0
South Shields v Netherfield	0-0, 1-0
Durham City v Peterlee Newtown	5-0
Farsley Celtic v Whitley Bay	3-0
Clitheroe v Willington	1-2
West Auckland Town v Whitby Town	0-2
Chadderton v Winsford United	1-1, 6-5
Atherton Collieries v Buxton	2-0
Atherton LR v Belper Town	1-1, 2-0
Alfreton Town v Guiseley	2-2, 2-4
Brigg Town v Morecambe	0-4
Caernarfon Town v Chorley	2-2, 1-2
Arnold Town v Congleton Town	1-2
Burscough v Horwich RMI	1-0
Colwyn Bay v Flixton	4-0
Hallam v Hyde United	0-3
Glossop North End v Eastwood Town	2-2, 1-1, 3-5
Glasshoughton Welfare v Worksop Town	0-5
Droylsden v Lincoln United	0-3
Maltby MW v Knowsley United	0-4
Maine Road v Heanor Town	1-0
Ilkeston Town v Lancaster City	2-2, 1-3
Emley v Oldham Town	4-1
Radcliffe Borough v North Ferriby United	1-0
Prescot AFC v Nantwich Town	1-3
Mossley v Northwich Victoria	2-4
Frickley Athletic v Skelmersdale United	1-1, 4-1
Rossendale United v Matlock Town	1-2
Winterton Rangers v Sheffield	0-1
St Helens Town v Warrington Town	0-4
Atherstone United v Boldmere St Michaels	1-1, 1-0
Northampton Spencer v Hednesford Town	1-4
Armitage v Blakenall	2-2, 0-2
Bolehall Swifts v Solihull Borough	2-3
Desborough Town v Chasetown	1-0
Grantham Town v Burton Albion	2-4
Halesowen Harriers v Hinckley Athletic	3-3, 1-2
Eastwood Hanley v Rushden & Diamonds	1-0
Corby Town v Paget Rangers	0-5
Bridgnorth Town v Pershore Town	1-1, 2-0
Lye Town v Moor Green	1-5
Pelsall Villa v Raunds Town	0-1
Rocester v Stewarts & Lloyds	1-0
Dudley Town v Leek Town	0-1
Stourport Swifts v Stapenhill	2-1
Sandwell Borough v Gresley Rovers	1-2
Halesowen Town v Willenhall Town	2-1
Tamworth v Telford United	1-1, 1-4
Redditch United v Westfields	1-1, 3-2
West Midlands Police v Gainsborough Trinity	0-0, 0-6
Bishop's Stortford v Braintree Town	1-1, 0-3
Diss Town v Sudbury Town	1-0
Cornard United v Billericay Town	0-4
Boston Town v Basildon United	1-0
Boston United v Harwich & Parkeston	2-0
Kings Lynn v Halstead Town	0-1
Heybridge Swifts v Gorleston	0-0, 2-0
Haverhill Rovers v Felixstowe Town	1-1, 0-2
Saffron Walden Town v Stevenage Borough	1-4
Spalding United v Cambridge City	0-3
Stamford AFC v Tiptree United	2-3
Newmarket Town v Hitchin Town	1-2
Chelmsford City v Barton Rovers	1-0
Witham Town v Wivenhoe Town	2-0
Kempston Rovers v Wisbech Town	2-4
Sudbury Wanderers v Hendon	0-1
Aylesbury United v Boreham Wood	3-1
Aveley v Edgware Town	1-2
Brook House v Baldock Town	0-7
Barking v Canvey Island	3-1
Chesham United v Concord Rangers	4-2
Feltham & Hounslow Boro v Dagenham & Redbridge *(at Dagenham & Redbridge)*	1-3
Chalfont St Peter v Collier Row	2-2, 1-2
Burnham v East Thurrock United *(at East Thurrock United)*	2-0
Enfield v Hemel Hempstead	5-2
Bedfont v Purfleet	0-3
Ruislip Manor v Ford United	2-1
Harefield United v Hornchurch	0-3
Leatherhead v Hayes	1-1, 0-4
Romford v Grays Athletic	4-3
Hillingdon Borough v Southall	2-1
Leyton v St Albans City	1-2
Tilbury v Staines Town	0-1
Wealdstone v Harrow Borough	0-1
Welwyn Garden City v Ware	1-2
Stotfold v Yeading	1-3
Bromley v Bognor Regis Town	3-2
Hampton v Gravesend & Northfleet	1-1, 0-1
Burgess Hill Town v Banstead Athletic	4-3
Ashford Town v Chatham Town	5-0
Uxbridge v Dorking	1-1, 1-3
Croydon v Carshalton Athletic	0-0, 0-5
Tonbridge v Egham Town	3-1
Corinthian v Hastings Town	1-2
Northwood v Erith & Belvedere	3-0
Herne Bay v Dulwich Hamlet	1-3
Worthing v Horsham YMCA	5-3
Folkestone Invicta v Sittingbourne	1-0
Croydon Athletic v Metropolitan Police	2-2, 1-0
Fisher 93 v Kingstonian	2-4
Canterbury City v Peacehaven & Telscombe	1-2
Merstham v Margate	0-2
Molesey v Southwick	1-1, 1-0
Whyteleafe v Dover Athletic	0-0, 0-3
Ramsgate v Shoreham	0-0, 0-2
Sheppey United v Chertsey Town	0-1
Walton & Hersham v Wick	3-0
Portfield v Tooting & Mitcham United	0-3
Wembley v Tunbridge Wells	4-1
Windsor & Eton v Welling United	0-1
Wokingham Town v Bicester Town	5-0
Cove v Andover	0-2
Buckingham Town v Aldershot Town 2-1	
Basingstoke Town v Newport (IW)	2-4
Dorchester Town v Lymington AFC	3-1
Fleet Town v Newbury Town	0-1
Fareham Town v Hungerford Town	1-2
Havant Town v Bashley	1-1, 1-3

Waterlooville v Westbury United 1-0
Thame United v Wimborne Town 0-0, 3-3, 3-1
Poole Town v Ryde 5-1
Salisbury City v Worcester City 2-0
Gloucester City v Exmouth Town 3-0
Yate Town v Merthyr Tydfil 0-3
Backwell United v Elmore 0-6
Cinderford Town v Mangotsfield United 3-2
(at Gloucester City FC)
Trowbridge Town v Minehead 7-0
Paulton Rovers v Moreton Town 2-0
Newport AFC v Melksham Town 4-1
Glastonbury v Barnstaple Town 0-3
Tiverton Town v St Blazey 7-1
Taunton Town v Weston-Super-Mare 2-2, 2-3
Bideford v Saltash United 4-0
Torrington v Weymouth 2-0

Second Qualifying Round
Blyth Spartans v Dunston Federation Brewery 3-2
Barrow v Billingham Synthonia 5-2
Harrogate Town v Murton 1-0
Bishop Auckland v Gateshead 3-1
South Shields v Tow Law Town 2-2, 1-2
Spennymoor United v Consett 3-2
Whitby Town v Willington 6-1
Durham City v Farsley Celtic 1-0
Guiseley v Atherton LR 3-1
Chadderton v Atherton Collieries 1-2
Burscough v Congleton Town 0-0, 3-3, 2-2, 2-5
Morecambe v Chorley 4-2
Worksop Town v Eastwood Town 2-0
Colwyn Bay v Hyde United 2-2, 0-8
Lancaster City v Maine Road 3-2
Lincoln United v Knowsley United 3-2
Northwich Victoria v Nantwich Town 10-0
Emley v Radcliffe Borough 2-0
Warrington Town v Sheffield 2-1
Frickley Athletic v Matlock Town 3-1
Solihull Borough v Blakenall 4-0
Atherstone United v Hednesford Town 3-4
Eastwood Hanley v Hinckley Athletic 2-2, 1-0
Desborough Town v Burton Albion 0-2
Raunds Town v Moor Green 1-2
Paget Rangers v Bridgnorth Town 2-1
Gresley Rovers v Stourport Swifts 4-0
Rocester v Leek Town 0-4
Gainsborough Trinity v Redditch United 3-1
Halesowen Town v Telford United 1-1, 1-3
Boston Town v Billericay Town 1-2
Braintree Town v Diss Town 2-1
Felixstowe Town v Heybridge Swifts 1-5
Boston United v Halstead Town 3-0
Hitchin Town v Tiptee United 3-3, 1-3
Stevenage Borough v Cambridge City 0-2
Hendon v Wisbech Town 2-1
Chelmsford City v Witham Town 1-0
Barking v Baldock Town 2-2, 2-3
Aylesbury United v Edgware Town 2-0
Burnham v Collier Row 0-1
Chesham United v Dagenham & Redbridge 2-0
Hornchurch v Ruislip Manor 0-1
Enfield v Purfleet 3-1
St Albans City v Hillingdon Borough 11-1
Hayes v Romford 1-2
Yeading v Ware 8-0
Staines Town v Harrow Borough 5-3
Ashford Town v Burgess Hill Town 3-2
Bromley v Gravesend & Northfleet 2-2, 1-1, 0-1
Hastings Town v Tonbridge 1-1, 1-0
Dorking v Carshalton Athletic 0-8
Folkestone Invicta v Worthing 1-2
Northwood v Dulwich Hamlet 1-4
Margate v Peacehaven & Telscombe 1-1, 5-3
Croydon Athletic v Kingstonian 1-2
Chertsey Town v Shoreham 1-0
Molesey v Dover Athletic 1-4
Welling United v Wembley 1-4
Walton & Hersham v Tooting & Mitcham United 3-0
Newport (IW) v Buckingham Town 1-0
Wokingham Town v Andover 3-0
Bashley v Hungerford Town 3-0
Dorchester Town v Newbury Town 4-2
Salisbury City v Poole Town 3-2
Waterlooville v Thame United 4-0
Cinderford Town v Elmore 5-4
(at Elmore)
Gloucester City v Merthyr Tydfil 7-1
Barnstaple Town v Newport AFC 1-2
Trowbridge Town v Paulton Rovers 4-1
Torrington v Bideford 1-5
Tiverton Town v Weston-Super-Mare 4-2

Third Qualifying Round
Blyth Spartans v Barrow 3-1
Harrogate Town v Bishop Auckland 0-3
Tow Law Town v Spennymoor United 0-0, 1-2
Whitby Town v Durham City 1-1, 1-3
Guiseley v Atherton Collieries 3-1
Congleton Town v Morecambe 0-3
Eastwood Town v Hyde United 1-1, 0-3
Lancaster City v Lincoln United 5-1
Northwich Victoria v Emley 2-1
Warrington Town v Frickley Athletic 2-0
Solihull Borough v Hednesford Town 3-0
Eastwood Hanley v Burton Albion 0-1
Moor Green v Paget Rangers 4-1
Gresley Rovers v Leek Town 3-1
Gainsborough Trinity v Telford United 0-3
Billericay Town v Braintree Town 1-1, 3-3, 2-3
Heybridge Swifts v Boston United 3-0
Hitchin Town v Cambridge City 3-3, 3-2
Hendon v Chelmsford City 0-1
Baldock Town v Aylesbury United 0-2
Collier Row v Chesham United 0-1
Ruislip Manor v Enfield 0-3
St Albans City v Romford 1-0
Yeading v Staines Town 4-1
Ashford Town v Gravesend & Northfleet 2-1
Hastings Town v Carshalton Athletic 2-2, 2-1
Worthing v Dulwich Hamlet 2-1
Margate v Kingstonian 0-1
Chertsey Town v Dover Athletic 0-0, 0-1
Wembley v Walton & Hersham 0-1
Newport (IW) v Wokingham Town 3-0
Bashley v Dorchester Town 1-1, 2-0
Salisbury City v Waterlooville 3-3, 1-0
Cinderford Town v Gloucester City 0-2
Newport AFC v Trowbridge Town 2-2, 1-1, 1-3
Bideford v Tiverton Town 1-8

Fourth Qualifying Round
Accrington Stanley v Spennymoor United 0-1
Southport v Stalybridge Celtic 2-1
Altrincham v Marine 2-1
Guiseley v Durham City 6-0
Bishop Auckland v Macclesfield Town 2-2, 1-0
Morecambe v Witton Albion 0-1
Northwich Victoria v Blyth Spartans 2-0
Hyde United v Warrington Town 1-1, 2-0
Halifax Town v Lancaster City 3-1
Stafford Rangers v Slough Town 0-4
St Albans City v Enfield 0-0, 2-4
Chesham United v Bromsgrove Rovers 1-1, 1-0
Braintree Town v Gresley Rovers 0-2
Burton Albion v Hitchin Town 0-1
Nuneaton Borough v Heybridge Swifts 2-2, 2-3
VS Rugby v Chelmsford City 0-0, 1-2
Yeading v Telford United 1-0
Moor Green v Aylesbury United 1-1, 1-3
Solihull Borough v Kettering Town 2-4
Gloucester City v Worthing 1-1, 1-2
Marlow v Sutton United 1-0
Tiverton Town v Farnborough Town 4-4, 5-1
Dover Athletic v Kingstonian 1-2
Hastings Town v Crawley Town 1-1, 2-3
Walton & Hersham v Yeovil Town 3-2
Salisbury City v Ashford Town 2-3
Newport (IW) v Trowbridge Town 1-0
Cheltenham Town v Bashley 1-1, 1-2

FA CUP 1994–95

sponsored by Littlewoods Pools

COMPETITION PROPER

FIRST ROUND

11 NOV

Heybridge (0) 0
Gillingham (0) 2 *(Reinelt, Pike) (at Colchester)* 4614
Heybridge: McCutcheon; Bain, Adcock, May, Rolfe, Brush (Sach), Jenkins, Springett, Jones, Hull (Payne), Pollard.
Gillingham: Banks; Dunne, Watson, Carpenter, Green, Butler, Micklewhite, Arnott, Pike, Reinelt, Smillie.

12 NOV

Altrincham (2) 3 *(Green, Morton, France)*
Southport (1) 2 *(Cunningham, McDonald)* 2523
Altrincham: Collings; Cross, Heesom, France, Reid, Morton, Terry, Shaw, Green, Carmody, Sharratt.
Southport: McKenna; Ward, Fuller (Blackhurst), Simms, Goulding, Lodge, Clark (McDonald), Cunningham, Haw, Gamble, Thomas.

Ashford T (1) 2 *(Arter, Dent)*
Fulham (0) 2 *(Adams 2 (2 pens))* 3363
Ashford T: Munden; Morris, Lemoine, Pearson A, Pearson R, Smith, Wheeler, Dent, Arter, Stanton, Ross.
Fulham: Stannard; Finnigan (Jupp), Herrera, Marshall, Moore, Blake, Mison, Morgan, Cork, Haworth, Adams.

Barnet (0) 4 *(McMahon, Cooper 2, Hodges)*
Woking (3) 4 *(Fielder, Dennis, Walker, Steele)* 3114
Barnet: Phillips; McDonald, Walker, Hoddle, Newson (Wilson), Primus, McMahon, Freedman, Hodges (Tomlinson), Cooper, Scott.
Woking: Batty; Tucker, Wye L, Fielder, Brown K, Tierling (Rattray), Wye S, Ellis, Steele (Brown D), Dennis, Walker.

Bath C (0) 0
Bristol R (1) 5 *(Stewart, Miller 4)* 6751
Bath C: Mogg; Gill, Jones, Forbes, Birks, Brooks, Hedges, Mings (Vernon), Adcock, Smart, Dicks.
Bristol R: Parkin; Pritchard, Gurney, Channing (Archer), Clark, Tillson, Sterling, Miller, Stewart, Skinner, Browning.

Bishop Auckland (0) 0
Bury (0) 0 3135
Bishop Auckland: Bishop; West S, Logan (Butler), Waller, Lobb, Adams, Wratten (West C), Todd, Toone, Laws, Parkinson.
Bury: Kelly; Cross, Stanislaus, Daws, Lucketti, Matthewson, Rigby, Johnrose (Mulligan), Sertori, Mauge, Pugh.

Bournemouth (1) 3 *(Morris, Russell, McElhatton)*
Worthing (1) 1 *(Mintram)* 3922
Bournemouth: Andrews; Chivers, Young, Morris, Watson, Leadbitter, Beardsmore (McElhatton), Mean, Robinson (Murray), Pennock, Russell.
Worthing: Penhaligan; Ball, Mintram, Riley, Darnton, Moss (Benson), Quinn, Robson, Brown, Traylen (Dunford), Tiltman.

Bradford C (1) 1 *(Tolson)*
Scunthorpe U (1) 1 *(Hope)* 5481
Bradford C: Tomlinson; Hamilton, Huxford, Duxbury, Sinnott, Oliver, Murray (Shutt), Kamara, Taylor (Power), Tolson, Showler.
Scunthorpe U: Samways; Hope, Mudd, Bullimore, Knill, Bradley, Alexander, Ford, Juryeff, Sansam, Smith.

Burnley (1) 2 *(Heath, Deary)*
Shrewsbury T (1) 1 *(Spink)* 9269
Burnley: Beresford; Parkinson, Dowell, Davis, Winstanley, Randall, Harper, Heath, Deary, Robinson (Francis), Eyres.
Shrewsbury T: Edwards; Hockaday, Withe, Taylor, Williams, Patterson, Woods, Hughes, Spink, Summerfield, Stevens.

Cambridge U (1) 2 *(Lillis, Butler)*
Brentford (1) 2 *(Annon, Taylor)* 3353
Cambridge U: Sheffield; Joseph, Barrick, Craddock, O'Shea, Hyde, Manuel, Lillis (Hunter), Butler, Corazzin, Hay.
Brentford: Dearden; Statham, Grainger, Westley, Ashby, Smith, Annon (Hurdle), Harvey, Taylor, Forster, Hutchings.

Chesham (0) 0
Bashley (0) 1 *(Paskins)* 1302
Chesham: Granville; Cobb, Hyslop, Roberts, Coleman, Kelly, Attrell (Gentle), Rake, Stanley, Dickens (Morgan), Scott.
Bashley: Flower; Ingman, Lisk, Powell, Bye, Sheppard, Stagg, Wilkinson (Stone), Walker, Stickler, Paskins (Sales).

Chester C (2) 2 *(Page, Alsford)*
Witton Alb (0) 0 2666
Chester C: Felgate; Jenkins, Burnham, Alsford, Ratcliffe, Shelton (Rimmer), Milner (Murphy), Flitcroft, Preece, Page, Hackett.
Witton Alb: Mason; Mellor, Macauley, Edey, McNeilis, Brown, Rose, Quirk (O'Callaghan), Higginbotham, Burke, Newton (Quinlan).

Chesterfield (0) 0
Scarborough (0) 0 2902
Chesterfield: Marples; Hewitt, Rogers, Perkins (Jules), Carr, Fairclough, Curtis (Moss), Norris, Morris, McAuley, Dyche.
Scarborough: Martin; Knowles, Swales, Toman, Davis, Rockett, Swann, Charles, White, Rutherford (Young), Wells.

Crewe Alex (1) 7 *(Rowbotham 2, Smith S, Ward 3, Garvey)*
Gresley R (0) 1 *(Devaney)* 4539
Crewe Alex: Smith M; Booty, Smith S, Wilson, Macauley, Whalley, Garvey, Collins, Ward, Lennon, Rowbotham.
Gresley R: Aston; Dick, Harbey, Denby, Evans, Stanborough, Elliot (Wardle), Rigg, Holmes, Garner, Marsden (Devaney).

Doncaster R (0) 1 *(Jones)*

Huddersfield T (2) 4 *(Bullock, Booth, Jepson, Dunn)* 6626

Doncaster R: Williams; Kirby (Jones), Hackett, Brabin, Wilcox, Swailes, Lawrence, Roche, Meara (Thew), Harper, Parrish.
Huddersfield T: Francis; Trevitt, Cowan, Logan (Clayton), Scully, Mitchell, Billy, Bullock, Booth, Jepson (Dunn), Reid.

Enfield (0) 1 *(Abbott)*

Cardiff C (0) 0 2345

Enfield: Pape; Blackford, Carstairs, Turner, Hannigan, Pye, Bailey, Hobson, Abbott, Whale (St Hilaire), Ryan.
Cardiff C: Williams D; Evans, Scott, Oatway, Baddeley, Perry, Ramsey, Griffith (Thompson), Stant, Millar (Aizlewood), Dale.

Exeter C (1) 1 *(Cecere)*

Crawley T (0) 0 3214

Exeter C: Fox; Minett, Robinson, Cooper M, Came, Richardson, Brown, Coughlin, Turner (Storer), Cecere (Morgan), Gavin.
Crawley T: Chatfield; Shepherd, Turner, Smart (Pearson N), O'Shaughnessy, Jeffery, Payne (Pearson M), Lempriere, Fishenden, Vansittart, Dack.

Halifax T (0) 1 *(Kiwomya)*

Runcorn (0) 1 *(Thomas (pen))* 1286

Halifax T: Heyes; German, Prindiville, Jones, Boardman, Fowler, Paterson, Lambert, Lancaster, Worthington (Flounders), Kiwomya.
Runcorn: Morris; Bates, Robertson, Lee (Smith), Hill, Anderson, Thomas, Connor, Hughes, Rutter, McInerney.

Hereford U (0) 2 *(Lyne 2)*

Hitchin T (2) 2 *(Marshall 2)* 3078

Hereford U: Pennock; Llewellyn, Preedy, Smith, Reece, James (Pick), Steele (Pounder), Wilkins, Cross, White, Lyne.
Hitchin T: Sylvester; Bone, Covington, Burke, Price, Scott, Wilson (Ryan), Marshall, Williams, Thompson, Miller.

Hull C (0) 0

Lincoln C (0) 1 *(Bannister)* 5758

Hull C: Wilson; Dakin, Graham, Hobson, Dewhurst, Mann (Abbott), Peacock (Hargreaves), Lee, Brown, Windass, Lawford.
Lincoln C: Leaning; West, Johnson A, Foley, Greenall, Brown, Matthews, Hebberd, Bannister, Hill, Carbon.

Hyde U (1) 1 *(Kimmins)*

Darlington (1) 3 *(Slaven, Worboys 2)* 2315

Hyde U: Williams A; Megram, Switzer, O'Brian, Garton, Little, Kimmins, McMahon, Williams O (Camilleri), Chadwick, Nolan.
Darlington: Pollitt; Appleby, Himsworth, Banks, Crosby, Gregan, Slaven, Painter, Gaughan, Olsson, Worboys.

Kidderminster H (1) 1 *(Humphreys)*

Torquay U (0) 1 *(Hathaway)* 4144

Kidderminster H: Rose, Hodson, Bancroft, Weir, Brindley, Forsyth, Yates (Cartwright), Grainger, Humphreys, Palmer, Hughes.
Torquay U: Bayes; Curran, Stamps (Goodridge), O'Riordan, Moore, Barrow, Trollope, Okorie (Hodges), Hancox, Hathaway, Kelly.

Kingstonian (1) 2 *(Ndah J 2)*

Brighton & HA (1) 1 *(Codner)* 3815

Kingstonian: Root; O'Neill, Barton, Finch, Ndah M (Bird), Okenla (Wingfield), Harlow, Daly, Ndah J, Akuamoah, Kempton.
Brighton & HA: Rust; Smith, Tuck, Minton, Pates, McCarthy, Chamberlain (Munday), McDougald, Nogan, Codner, Chapman (Andrews).

Newport IOW (1) 2 *(Soares 2)*

Aylesbury (1) 3 *(Hercules 2, Pluckrose (pen))* 2217

Newport IOW: Simpkins; Woollen, Wickens, Savage, Phillips, Webb, Rodgers (Cormack), Ritchie, Baldwin, Soares, Fearon (Butler).
Aylesbury: Wild; Harvey, Bashir, Hayward, Barnes, Pluckrose, Hazel, Heard, Hercules, Brayshaw, Murray (Blencowe).

Peterborough U (0) 4 *(Charlery 2 (1 pen), Williams, Henry)*

Northampton T (0) 0 8739

Peterborough U: Cooksey; Ashley, Spearing, Ebdon, Breen, Clark, Farrell (Morrison), McGorry, Williams, Charlery, Henry.
Northampton T: Stewart; Pascoe, Colkin, Sampson, Warburton, Williams, Harmon, Grayson (Aldridge), Trott, Robinson, Norton.

Port Vale (3) 6 *(Griffiths, Allon, Foyle 3, Glover D)*

Hartlepool U (0) 0 6199

Port Vale: Musselwhite; Aspin, Tankard, Porter (Burke), Griffiths, Glover D, Jeffers, Van der Laan, Allon, Foyle (Glover L), Walker.
Hartlepool U: Horne; Ingram, Walsh, Gilchrist, McGuckin, Ainsley (Skedd), Thompson, McCreery (Sloan), Houchen, Halliday, Southall.

Slough (0) 0 13,394

Birmingham C (4) 4 *(Shearer 2, McGavin 2)(at Birmingham)*

Slough: Bunting; Clement, Lee, Richardson (Blackman), Baron, Dell, Catlin, Stone (Bateman), West, Sayer, Bushay.
Birmingham C: Bennett; Poole, Whyte, Ward, Barnett (De Souza), Daish, Hunt, Claridge, McGavin, Donowa, Shearer (Tait).

Tiverton (1) 1 *(Smith)*

Leyton Orient (3) 3 *(Gray, Carter, West)* 3000

Tiverton: Nott; Edwards, Saunders N, Saunders M, Leonard, Steele, Grimshaw, Smith, Everett, Daly, Hynds (Annunziata) (Tragedeon).
Leyton Orient: Heald; Hendon, Austin, Bellamy, Howard, Bogie, Barnett (Lakin), Cockerill, Gray (Dempsey), West, Carter.

Walsall (2) 3 *(Lightbourne, Butler 2)*

Rochdale (0) 0 3619

Walsall: Wood; Evans, Gibson, Rogers, Marsh, Palmer, O'Connor, Ntamark, Butler (Peer), Lightbourne (Mehew), Houghton.
Rochdale: Dunford; Thackeray, Formby (Sharpe), Reid, Matthews, Butler, Doyle, Peake (Ryan), Williams, Whitehall, Stuart.

Wigan Ath (3) 4 *(Leonard, Carragher 2, Kilford)*

Spennymoor (0) 0 2183

Wigan Ath: Farnworth; Rennie, Jakub, Miller, Robertson, Farrell, Kilford, Carragher, Leonard (Adekola), McKearney, Lyons.
Spennymoor: McNary; Tinkler, Petitjean, Watson, Saunders, Mason, Robson, Goodrick, Shaw, Gorman, Veart.

Wrexham (0) 1 *(Watkin)*

Stockport Co (0) 0 4740

Wrexham: Marriott; Jones, Hardy, Phillips (Durkan), Hunter, Humes, Bennett, Owen, Connolly, Cross (Watkin), Hughes.
Stockport Co: Ironside; Connelly, Wallace, Ware (Dinning), Flynn, Bound, Gannon, Ward (Armstrong), Eckhardt, Beaumont, Chalk.

Wycombe W (1) 4 *(Stapleton 2, Bell, Ryan)*

Chelmsford C (0) 0 5654

Wycombe W: Hyde; Cousins, Brown, Crossley, Evans, Ryan, Carroll, Bell, Turnbull (Thompson), Garner (Reid), Stapleton.
Chelmsford C: Shoemake; Hunter, Eliot Martin (Eddie Martin), Clark, Jacques, Keen, Hoddy, Garvey, Rogers, Restarick, Owers (Campbell).

Yeading (1) 2 *(Hippolyte, Graham)*

Colchester U (1) 2 *(Kinsella, Abrahams)* 1715

Yeading: Mackenzie; Dicker, Cuffie, Bunce, McGrath, Hoon-Park, Graham, Bowder, Hippolyte, McKinnon, Cordery.
Colchester U: Emberson; Betts, English, Cawley, Caesar, Dennis, Locke, Brown, Whitton, Kinsella, Abrahams.

York C (1) 3 *(Naylor 2, McCarthy)*

Rotherham U (1) 3 *(Goater 2, Helliwell)* 4020

York C: Kiely; McMillan, Wilson, Atkin, Stancliffe, Barras, McCarthy, Naylor, Barnes, Baker, Canham.
Rotherham U: Clarke; Wilder, James (Helliwell), Williams A, Breckin, Brien, Dolby, Smith, Varadi, Goater, Marginson.

13 NOV

Guiseley (0) 1 *(Brockie) (at Bradford)*

Carlisle U (2) 4 *(Reeves 2, Conway, Mountfield)* 6548

Guiseley: Dickinson; Atkinson, Hogarth, Brockie, Richards, Bottomley, Cawthorns (James), Allen, Colville (Flanagan), Horsfield, Roberts.
Carlisle U: Caig; Edmondson (Joyce), Gallimore, Walling, Mountfield, Conway (Thorpe), Thomas, Currie, Reeves, Davey, Prokas.

Kettering T (0) 0

Plymouth Arg (0) 1 *(Skinner)* 4602

Kettering T: Benstead; Smith, Ashby, Holden, Oxbrow, Taylor (Magee), Martin (Wright), Stringfellow, Alford, Thomas, Brown.
Plymouth Arg: Hodge; Patterson, Naylor, Edworthy, Comyn, Burnett, Barlow, Skinner, Nugent, Evans, Twiddy.

Marlow (0) 2 *(Caesar 2)*

Oxford U (0) 0 3000

Marlow: Mitchell; Nolan, Rhoades-Brown, Ferguson, Muckelberg, Muir, Lay, Phillips (Floyd), Rayson (Holmes), Caesar, McNamara.
Oxford U: Whitehead; Robinson, Collins, Dyer, Elliott, Marsh (Rush), Massey, Smith, Moody, Byrne, Ford R.

14 NOV

Preston NE (1) 1 *(Conroy)*

Blackpool (0) 0 14,036

Preston NE: Richardson; Fensome, Sharp, Cartwright, Holmes, Moyes, Ainsworth (Whalley), Bryson, Raynor, Conroy (Sale), Trebble.
Blackpool: Martin; Brown, Burke, Bradshaw, Thompson, Horner, Mitchell, Beech, Watson, Ellis, Griffiths (Quinn).

21 NOV

Walton & Hersham (0) 0

Swansea C (1) 2 *(Ford, Ampadu)* 2230

Walton & Hersham: McCann; Turner (Joseph), Warmington, Benning, Terry, Gasson, Adams, Wilson, Banton, Price (Davidson), Mitchell.
Swansea C: Freestone; Jenkins, Clode, Basham, Ford, Ampadu, Bowen, Penney, Torpey, Cornforth, Hodge (Hayes).

FIRST ROUND REPLAY

Runcorn (0) 1 *(Pugh)*

Halifax T (0) 3 *(Lancaster 2, Lambert) aet* 728

Runcorn: Morris; Bates, Robertson, Ruffer, Hill, Anderson, Thomas, Connor (Godfrey), Hughes (Pugh), McInerney, Smith.
Halifax T: Heyes; German, Prindiville, Jones, Boardman, Fowler, Paterson, Lambert, Lancaster, Worthington, Flounders.

22 NOV

FIRST ROUND

Mansfield T (1) 3 *(Hadley, Holland 2)*

Northwich V (1) 1 *(Oghani)* 2999

Mansfield T: Ward; Boothroyd, Baraclough, Holland, Howarth, Doolan, Ireland, Parkin, Wilkinson, Hadley, Noteman (Aspinall).
Northwich V: Greygoose; Tinson (Norman), Jones, Abel, Parker, Gallagher (O'Connor), Boyd, Butler, Oghani, Williams, Hardy.

FIRST ROUND REPLAYS

Brentford (1) 1 *(Grainger)*

Cambridge U (2) 2 *(Lillis, Butler (pen))* 4096

Brentford: Dearden; Statham, Grainger, Westley, Ashby, Smith, Bates, Harvey, Taylor, Forster (Hutchings), Mundee.
Cambridge U: Sheffield; Joseph, Barrick, Craddock, O'Shea, Hyde, Fowler, Lillis (Nyamah), Butler, Corazzin (Granville), Hay.

Bury (1) 1 *(Paskin)*

Bishop Auckland (1) 1 *(Todd) aet* 3517

Bury: Kelly G; Cross, Stanislaus, Daws (Hughes), Lucketti, Matthewson, Rigby (Mulligan), Johnrose, Paskin, Mauge, Pugh.
Bishop Auckland: Bishop; Elliott, Logan (Coverdale), Waller, Lobb, Toone, Wratten, Todd, Hyde, Laws, Parkinson.
Bury won 4-2 on penalties.

Colchester U (3) 7 *(Abrahams 2, Whitton 2, Brown 2, Kinsella)*

Yeading (1) 1 *(McKinnon (pen))* 4016

Colchester U: Cheesewright; Betts, English, Cawley, Caesar, Locke (Dennis), Fry, Brown, Whitton (Thompson), Kinsella, Abrahams.
Yeading: MacKenzie; Dicker, Cuffie, Woods, McGrath, Hoon-Park, Graham, Bowder, Hippolyte, McKinnon, Cordery.

Fulham (2) 5 *(Morgan, Adams 2, Blake, Cork)*
Ashford T (1) 3 *(Stanton 2, Dent) aet* 6539
Fulham: Stannard; Jupp, Herrera, Hurlock, Moore, Blake, Mison (Haworth), Morgan, Cork, Marshall, Adams.
Ashford T: Munden; Morris, Lemoine (Ager), Pearson A, Pearson R, Smith, Wheeler, Dent, Arter (Carlton), Stanton, Ross.

Hitchin (1) 4 *(Bone, Williams, Wilson, Marshall)*
Hereford U (2) 2 *(White, Pick)* 3098
Hitchin: Sylvester; Bone, Covington, Burke, Miller, Scott, Wilson, Marshall, Williams, Thompson, Ryan.
Hereford U: Pennock; Reece, Preedy, Smith, Davies, Pick, Pounder (Williams), Wilkins, Cross, White, Lyne.

Rotherham U (3) 3 *(Davison 2, Goater)*
York C (0) 0 4391
Rotherham U: Clarke; Wilder, James, Williams A, Breckin, Brien, Hayward, Richardson, Davison (Varadi), Goater, Hurst.
York C: Kiely; McMillan, Wilson, Atkin, Stancliffe, Barras, McCarthy, Naylor, Barnes, Baker, Canham.

Scarborough (1) 2 *(Toman, White)*
Chesterfield (0) 0 1564
Scarborough: Martin; Knowles, Swales, Toman, Davis, Rockett, Swann, Charles, White, Young (Rutherford), Wells (D'Auria).
Chesterfield: Marples; Dyche, Rogers, Perkins, Carr, Fairclough, Curtis (McAuley), Norris, Davies, Moss, Jules (Morris).

Scunthorpe U (0) 3 *(Carmichael, Alexander, Thompstone)*
Bradford C (0) 2 *(Power, Richards) aet* 4514
Scunthorpe U: Samways; Hope, Mudd, Ford, Knill, Bradley (Carmichael), Alexander, Bullimore, Juryeff, Sansam (Thompstone), Thornber.
Bradford C: Tomlinson; Huxford, Jacobs, Duxbury, Sinnott, Richards, Shutt (Bowling), Kamara, Taylor, Jewell (Power), Murray.

Woking (1) 1 *(Tucker)*
Barnet (0) 0 4859
Woking: Batty; Tucker, Wye L, Fielder, Brown K, Tierling (Rattray), Wye S, Ellis, Steele, Walker, Dennis.
Barnet: Phillips; McDonald, Walker, Hoddle, Newson (Mutchell), Primus, McMahon, Freedman, Wilson, Cooper (Tomlinson), Scott.

23 NOV

Torquay U (0) 1 *(Hancox)*
Kidderminster H (0) 0 3809
Torquay U: Bayes; Curran, Kelly, O'Riordan, Moore, Barrow, Trollope, Buckle, Hodges (Hancox), Hathaway, Okorie.
Kidderminster H: Rose; Hodson, Bancroft, Weir, Brindley, Forsyth, Webb, Grainger, Humphreys, Yates, Hughes.

SECOND ROUND

2 DEC

Birmingham C (0) 0
Scunthorpe U (0) 0 13,832
Birmingham C: Bennett; Poole, Whyte, Ward, Barnett, Daish, Donowa (Lowe), Claridge, McGavin (Cooper), Tait, Dominguez.
Scunthorpe U: Samways; Ford, Mudd, Thornber, Knill, Bradley, Alexander, Bullimore, Juryeff (Thompstone), Henderson, Smith.

3 DEC

Altrincham (1) 1 *(Sharratt)*
Wigan Ath (0) 0 3020
Altrincham: Collings; Cross, Heesom, France, Reid, Morton, Terry, Butler, Green (Shaw), Carmody, Sharratt.
Wigan Ath: Farnworth; Strong (Benjamin), Jakub, Miller, Robertson, Farrell, Kilford, Carragher, Leonard, Rimmer, Lyons.

Crewe Alex (1) 1 *(Ward)*
Bury (0) 2 *(Johnrose, Rigby)* 4875
Crewe Alex: Smith M; Booty, Smith S, Wilson, Macauley, Whalley, Garvey, Collins, Ward, Lennon, Adebola.
Bury: Bracey; Jackson, Stanislaus, Daws, Lucketti, Matthewson, Kelly T, Hughes, Sertori (Rigby), Johnrose, Pugh.

Enfield (1) 1 *(Abbott)*
Torquay U (1) 1 *(Okorie)* 2326
Enfield: Pape; Blackford, Carstairs, Kerr, Hannigan, Pye, Bailey, Hobson, Abbott (Cherry), St Hilaire, Ryan.
Torquay U: Bayes; Brass, Kelly (Hancox), O'Riordan, Moore, Barrow, Trollope, Buckle, Okorie, Hathaway, Goodridge.

Exeter C (1) 1 *(Morgan)*
Colchester U (0) 2 *(Whitton, English)* 3528
Exeter C: Woodman; Minett, Brown, Bailey, Daniels, Richardson, Storer, Coughlin (Robinson), Cooper M (Thirlby), Morgan (Bellotti), Gavin.
Colchester U: Cheesewright; Betts, English, Cawley, Caesar, Locke, Putney (Dennis), Brown (Fry), Whitton, Kinsella, Abrahams.

Gillingham (1) 1 *(Pike)*
Fulham (0) 1 *(Hamill)* 6253
Gillingham: Banks; Carpenter, Watson, Smith, Arnott, Green, Micklewhite, Reinelt, Foster, Pike, Smillie.
Fulham: Harrison; Jupp, Herrera, Hurlock, Moore, Blake, Marshall, Morgan, Cusack (Hamill), Brazil, Cork.

Halifax T (0) 0
Mansfield T (0) 0 2396
Halifax T: Heyes; German, Prindiville, Jones, Boardman, Fowler, Paterson, Lambert, Lancaster, Worthington (Flounders), Kiwomya.
Mansfield T: Ward; Boothroyd, Baraclough, Holland, Howarth, Aspinall, Ireland, Doolan, Wilkinson, Hadley, Campbell.

Hitchin (0) 0
Wycombe W (2) 5 *(Garner 3, Ryan, Bell)* 2765
Hitchin: Sylvester; Bone, Covington, Burke, Miller, Rutherford (McGonagle), Wilson, Marshall (Caines), Williams, Thompson, Ryan.
Wycombe W: Hyde; Cousins, Brown, Crossley, Evans, Ryan, Carroll, Bell, Thompson, Garner (Hemmings), Stapleton (Langford).

Kingstonian (0) 1 *(Akuamoah (pen))*
Aylesbury (2) 4 *(Hercules, Bashir, Pluckrose (pen), Blencowe)* 1891
Kingstonian: Root; O'Neill, Barton, Finch, Ndah M (Bird), Sugrue, Harlow, Daly, Ndah J, Akuamoah, Kempton (Okenla).
Aylesbury: Wild; Harvey, Bashir, Hayward, Brayshaw (Murray), Pluckrose, Hobbs, Heard, Hercules (Ketteridge), Danzey, Blencowe.

Leyton Orient (0) 0
Bristol R (1) 2 *(Stewart 2)* 5071
Leyton Orient: Heald; Howard, Austin, Bellamy (Lakin), Purse, Bogie, Barnett (Brooks), Cockerill, Carter, West, Dempsey.
Bristol R: Parkin; Pritchard, Gurney, Browning, Clark, Tillson, Sterling, Miller, Stewart, Skinner, Archer (Hardyman).

Lincoln C (0) 1 *(Johnson D)*
Huddersfield T (0) 0 4143
Lincoln C: Leaning; West, Johnson A, Carbon, Greenall, Brown, Matthews, Hebberd, Daley, Johnson D (Daws), Hill.
Huddersfield T: Blackwell; Trevitt, Cowan, Crosby, Scully, Mitchell, Billy (Dunn), Bullock, Booth, Jepson, Reid.

Peterborough U (0) 0
Cambridge U (2) 2 *(Barrick, Hay)* 9576
Peterborough U: Cooksey; Ashley, Spearing, Ebdon, Breen, Clark (Thomas), Moran (Brissett), McGorry, Williams, Henry, Lormor.
Cambridge U: Sheffield; Hunter, Barrick, Craddock, Jeffrey, Hyde, Manuel, Joseph, Butler (Fowler), Corazzin, Hay (Lillis).

Plymouth Arg (2) 2 *(Ross 2)*
Bournemouth (0) 1 *(Jones)* 6739
Plymouth Arg: Nicholls; Edworthy, Naylor, Swan, Comyn, Burnett, Barlow, Patterson, Nugent (Landon), Ross, Evans (Shilton S).
Bournemouth: Andrews; Young, Pennock (McElhatton), Morris, Watson, Leadbitter, Beardsmore (Murray), Mean, Robinson, Jones, Russell.

Preston NE (1) 1 *(Smart)*
Walsall (1) 1 *(Wilson)* 9767
Preston NE: Richardson; Fensome, Sharp, Cartwright, Holmes, Moyes, Trebble (Fleming), Bryson, Smart, Conroy, Raynor (Emerson).
Walsall: Wood; Evans, Gibson, Ryder, Marsh, Palmer, O'Connor, Ntamark, Lightbourne, Wilson, Houghton (Butler).

Scarborough (0) 1 *(Swann)*
Port Vale (0) 0 2382
Scarborough: Kelly; Knowles, Wells, Toman (Thompson), Meyer, Rockett, Swann, Charles, White, Rutherford (Blackstone), D'Auria.
Port Vale: Musselwhite; Aspin, Tankard, Porter (Burke), Griffiths, Glover D, Guppy, Van der Laan, Allon (Glover L), Foyle, Walker.

Wrexham (1) 5 *(Connolly 2, Bennett, Hughes, Watkin)*
Rotherham U (1) 2 *(Davison, Hurst)* 4521
Wrexham: Marriott; Brace, Hardy, Hughes, Jones, Pejic, Bennett, Owen, Connolly, Watkin, Cross (Phillips).
Rotherham U: Clarke; Wilder, James, Smith, Breckin, Brien, Hayward (Helliwell), Richardson, Davison, Goater, Hurst.

4 DEC

Bashley (0) 0
Swansea C (0) 1 *(Torpey)* 2047
Bashley: Flower; Ingma (Stone), Lisk, Powell, Bye, Sheppard, Stagg, Wilkinson, Walker, Stickler (Smith P), Paskins.
Swansea C: Freestone; Jenkins, Walker, Basham, Ford, Chapple (Burns), Bowen (Perrett), Penney, Torpey, Cornforth, Hodge.

Carlisle U (0) 2 *(Conway, Currie)*
Darlington (0) 0 8365
Carlisle U: Caig; Edmondson, Gallimore, Walling, Mountfield, Conway, Thomas (Thorpe), Currie (Arnold), Reeves, Davey, Prokas.
Darlington: Pollitt; Gaughan, Himsworth, Banks, Crosby, Reed, Slaven, Painter (Kirkham), Worboys, Olsson, Chapman.

Chester C (0) 1 *(Milner)*
Burnley (0) 2 *(Eyres (pen), Heath)* 4231
Chester C: Felgate; Jenkins, Lightfoot, Alsford, Jackson, Shelton, Flitcroft, Bishop (Milner), Preece, Page, Hackett.
Burnley: Beresford; Parkinson, Dowell (Gayle), Davis, Winstanley, Randall, Harper, Heath, Hoyland, Robinson, Eyres.

Marlow (0) 2 *(Evans R, Evans C)*
Woking (0) 1 *(Tucker)* 2845
Marlow: Mitchell; Regan, Puttnam, Ferguson, Evans C, Rhoades-Brown, Nolan, Phillips (Floyd), McNamara, Rayson (Walton), Evans R.
Woking: Batty; Berry (Brown D), Brown K, Fielder, Tucker, Tierling (Rattray), Wye S, Ellis, Steele, Walker, Dennis.

SECOND ROUND REPLAYS

13 DEC

Fulham (0) 1 *(Hamill)*
Gillingham (1) 2 *(Pike, Reinelt) aet* 6536
Fulham: Stannard; Jupp, Herrera, Mison, Moore, Blake, Marshall, Morgan, Cusack, Brazil, Cork (Hamill).
Gillingham: Banks; Carpenter, Watson, Smith, Arnott, Green, Micklewhite, Butler, Foster (Reinelt), Pike, Smillie.

Mansfield T (0) 2 *(Aspinall, Holland)*
Halifax T (1) 1 *(Lancaster)* 2648
Mansfield T: Ward; Boothroyd, Baraclough, Holland, Aspinall, Peters, Ireland, Campbell, Wilkinson, Pearson, Noteman.
Halifax T: Hayes; German, Prindiville, Jones, Boardman, Fowler (Hall), Martin, Lambert, Lancaster, Flounders, Kiwomya.

Torquay U (0) 0
Enfield (1) 1 *(Kerr)* 3174
Torquay U: Bayes; Brass, Kelly (Okorie), Hodges (Hancox), Moore, Barrow, Trollope, Buckle, Darby, Hathaway, Goodridge (Tucker). *Enfield:* Pape, Blackford, Carstairs, Kerr, Hannigan, Pye, St Hilaire, Hobson, Abbott, Whale (Cherry), Ryan.

Walsall (2) 4 *(Houghton, Wilson, Lightbourne 2)*
Preston NE (0) 0 6468
Walsall: Wood; Evans, Gibson, Ryder, Marsh, Palmer, O'Connor (Peer), Ntamark, Lightbourne, Wilson (Butler), Houghton.
Preston NE: Richardson; Fensome (Emerson), Sharp, Whalley, Holmes, Moyes, Cartwright, Bryson, Smart, Conroy, Raynor (Trebble).

14 DEC

Scunthorpe U (0) 1 *(Bullimore)*
Birmingham C (0) 2 *(McGavin, Cooper)* 6280
Scunthorpe U: Samways; Ford, Mudd (Sansam), Thornber, Knill, Bradley, Alexander, Bullimore, Juryeff, Thompstone (Carmichael), Smith.
Birmingham C: Bennett; Poole, Whyte, Cooper, Barnett, Daish, Donowa, Claridge, McGavin, Dominguez (Doherty), Tait.

THIRD ROUND

7 JAN

Aylesbury (0) 0
QPR (3) 4 *(Maddix, Ferdinand, Gallen, Meaker)* 15,417
Aylesbury: O'Reilly; Harvey, Bashir (Murray), Brayshaw, Barnes, Pluckrose, Hobbs, Heard, Hercules, Danzey (Blencowe), Hazel.
QPR: Roberts; Bardsley, Wilson, Hodge, Maddix, McDonald, Impey, Barker (Holloway), Ferdinand, Gallen (Allen), Meaker.

Barnsley (0) 0
Aston Villa (0) 2 *(Yorke, Saunders)* 11,469
Barnsley: Watson; Eaden, Fleming (Rammell), Wilson (Bullock), Moses, Davis, O'Connell, Redfearn, Payton, Liddell, Sheridan.
Aston Villa: Spink; Barrett, Staunton, Teale, McGrath, Ehiogu, Yorke, Fashanu, Saunders, Taylor, Townsend.

Birmingham C (0) 0
Liverpool (0) 0 25,326
Birmingham C: Bennett; Poole, Cooper, Ward, Barnett, Daish, Donowa, Claridge, Lowe, Otto, Shearer.
Liverpool: James; Jones R, Bjornebye, Scales, Babb, Ruddock, McManaman, Redknapp, Rush, Barnes, Fowler.

Bristol C (0) 0
Stoke C (0) 0 9683
Bristol C: Welch; Hansen, Munro, Shail, Bryant, Tinnion, Kuhl, Bent, Baird (Partridge), Allison, Owers.
Stoke C: Sinclair; Butler, Sandford, Cranson, Overson, Orlygsson, Clarkson, Downing (Sturridge), Scott, Peschisolido, Gleghorn.

Bury (2) 2 *(Lucketti, Stanislaus)*
Tranmere R (0) 2 *(Muir 2)* 5755
Bury: Kelly G; Cross, Stanislaus, Mauge, Lucketti, Matthewson, Hulme (Hughes), Paskin (Rigby), Carter, Johnrose, Pugh.
Tranmere R: Nixon; Stevens, Brannan, Mungall (Muir), Garnett, O'Brien, Morrissey, Jones, Malkin, Irons, Thomas.

Cambridge U (1) 2 *(Butler 2 (1 pen))*
Burnley (2) 4 *(Eyres (pen), Robinson, Randall, Gayle)* 6275
Cambridge U: Sheffield; Joseph, Barrick, Heathcote, Jeffrey, O'Shea, Hyde, Lillis, Butler, Corazzin, Hay (Hunter).
Burnley: Beresford; Parkinson, Eyres, Hoyland, Winstanley, Randall, Harper, Heath, Gayle, Robinson, McMinn (Deary).

Chelsea (2) 3 *(Peacock, Sinclair, Spencer)*
Charlton Ath (0) 0 24,485
Chelsea: Kharine; Clarke, Minto, Kjeldbjerg, Johnsen, Sinclair, Spencer, Furlong, Stein (Newton), Peacock, Spackman.
Charlton Ath: Salmon; Brown, Mortimer, Bennett (Nelson), Chapple, McLeary, Robson, Robinson (Pardew), Leaburn, Whyte, Walsh.

Coventry C (0) 1 *(Wegerle (pen))*
WBA (0) 1 *(Ashcroft (pen))* 16,555
Coventry C: Ogrizovic; Borrows, Morgan, Cook, Pressley, Williams, Flynn, Wegerle (Darby), Dublin, Marsh, Jenkinson.
WBA: Naylor; Parsley, Edwards, Bradley, Mardon, Raven, Donovan, Ashcroft, Hunt, Rees (Smith), Hamilton.

Everton (0) 1 *(Hinchcliffe)*
Derby Co (0) 0 29,406
Everton: Southall; Jackson, Burrows (Limpar), Ebbrell, Watson, Unsworth, Horne, Parkinson, Ferguson, Rideout, Hinchcliffe.
Derby Co: Sutton S; Kavanagh, Nicholson, Sutton W (Forsyth), Short, Williams, Wassall, Carsley, Stallard (Wrack), Gabbiadini, Simpson.

Gillingham (1) 1 *(Pike (pen))*
Sheffield W (2) 2 *(Waddle, Bright)* 10,425
Gillingham: Banks; Arnott, Watson, Carpenter, Butler, Green, Micklewhite, Smith, Foster, Pike, Reinelt.
Sheffield W: Pressman; Atherton, Nolan, Bart-Williams, Pearce, Walker, Hyde, Waddle (Petrescu), Bright, Whittingham (Key), Sheridan.

Grimsby T (0) 0
Norwich C (0) 1 *(Crook)* 11,198
Grimsby T: Crichton; McDermott, Croft, Handyside, Rodger, Groves, Childs (Jobling), Shakespeare, Woods, Mendonca, Gilbert (Lester)
Norwich C: Marshall; Sutch, Ullathorne, Newsome, Polston, Crook, Adams (Cureton), Milligan, Newman, Sheron (Goss), Eadie.

Leicester C (1) 2 *(Oldfield, Roberts)*
Enfield (0) 0 17,351
Leicester C: Poole; Grayson, Whitlow, Hill, Willis, Agnew (Lowe), Oldfield, Thompson, Lewis, Roberts, Philpott.
Enfield: Pape; Blackford, Carstairs, Turner, Hannigan, Pye, Kerr, Hobson, Whale (Bailey), St Hilaire, Ryan (Ridout).

Luton T (1) 1 *(Hartson)*
Bristol R (1) 1 *(Stewart)* 7571
Luton T: Sommer; James, Johnson, Waddock, Thomas, Peake, Telfer, Oakes, Hartson, Preece, Marshall (Adcock).
Bristol R: Parkin; Channing, Gurney, Hardyman, Clark, Tillson, Sterling, Miller (Taylor), Stewart, Skinner, Archer.

Mansfield T (2) 2 *(Donaldson, Ireland)*
Wolverhampton W (0) 3 *(Kelly D, Dennison, Mills)* 6701
Mansfield T: Ward; Boothroyd, Baraclough, Holland, Howarth, Peters, Ireland (Parkin), Donaldson, Wilkinson (Pearson), Hadley, Lampkin.
Wolverhampton W: Jones; Blades, Venus, Emblen, De Wolf (Rankine), Law, Goodman, Kelly D, Mills, Cowans, Dennison.

Millwall (0) 0
Arsenal (0) 0 17,715
Millwall: Keller; Dawes, Thatcher (Kennedy), Roberts, Witter, Stevens, Savage, Rae, Cadette, Mitchell, Van Blerk.
Arsenal: Seaman; Dixon, Winterburn, Schwarz, Bould, Linighan, Jensen (Keown), Wright, Smith (Campbell), Hillier, Parlour.

Nottingham F (2) 2 *(Collymore, Gemmill)*
Plymouth Arg (0) 0 19,821
Nottingham F: Crossley; Lyttle, Pearce, Haaland, Chettle, Stone, Phillips, Gemmill, Roy (Webb), Collymore, Woan.
Plymouth Arg: Nicholls; Patterson, Naylor, Swan, Hill, Edworthy, Barlow, Skinner, Nugent, Burnett, Barber (Evans).

Portsmouth (1) 3 *(Creaney, Radosavljevic 2)*
Bolton W (1) 1 *(Sneekes)* 9721

Portsmouth: Knight; Gittens, Daniel, McGrath, Symons, Butters, Pethick, Radosavljevic, Powell, Creaney, Wood.
Bolton W: Branagan; Green, Phillips, McAteer, Coleman, Stubbs, Paatelainen (Thompson), Sneekes, Coyle, McGinlay, Patterson (Lee).

Reading (1) 1 *(Taylor)*
Oldham Ath (2) 3 *(Sharp, Richardson, Halle)* 8886

Reading: Hislop; Jones, Taylor (Hopkins), Wdowczyk, Bernal, Parkinson, Gilkes, Gooding, Quinn, Lovell (Hartenberger), Holsgrove.
Oldham Ath: Gerrard; Makin, Pointon, Henry, Graham, Redmond, Halle, Sharp, McCarthy (Beckford), Richardson, Brennan.

Scarborough (0) 0
Watford (0) 0 3544

Scarborough: Kelly; Knowles, Charles, D'Auria, Meyer, Davis, Thompson, Rodwell, White, Swann, Swales.
Watford: Digweed; Lavin, Bazeley, Foster, Holdsworth, Ramage, Hessenthaler, Gibbs, Millen, Porter, Mooney.

Southampton (2) 2 *(Heaney, Le Tissier)*
Southend U (0) 0 13,003

Southampton: Grobbelaar; Kenna, Benali, Magilton, Hall, Monkou, Le Tissier, Dodd (Hughes), Maskell, Widdrington, Heaney.
Southend U: Sansome; Hone, Powell, Gridelet, Bressington, Dublin, Ansah, Whelan, Thomson, Willis, Tilson.

Sunderland (0) 1 *(Russell)*
Carlisle U (0) 1 *(Davey)* 15,523

Sunderland: Chamberlain; Kubicki, Scott, Bennett, Ferguson, Ball, Atkinson (Michael Gray), Russell, Gray P, Smith, Armstrong.
Carlisle U: Caig; Edmondson, Gallimore, Walling, Mountfield, Conway, Thomas, Currie, Reeves, Davey, Prokas.

Swansea C (1) 1 *(Ford)*
Middlesbrough (0) 1 *(Moore)* 8407

Swansea C: Freestone; Barnhouse, Walker, Basham, Ford, Ampadu, Hayes (McFarlane), Penney, Torpey, Cornforth, Hodge.
Middlesbrough: Miller; Morris, Fleming, Vickers, Pearson, Whyte (Moore), Mustoe, Pollock, Wilkinson, Hendrie, Hignett.

Swindon T (0) 2 *(Fjortoft, Nijholt)*
Marlow (0) 0 7007

Swindon T: Hammond; Robinson, Bodin, Culverhouse (O'Sullivan), Nijholt, Taylor, Horlock, Beauchamp (Hamon), Fjortoft, Mutch, Ling.
Marlow: Mitchell; Nolan, Rhoades-Brown, Ferguson (Muckelberg), Evans C, McNamara, Mikurenva, Phillips, Evans R (Regan), Caesar, Rayson.

Tottenham H (2) 3 *(Sheringham, Rosenthal, Nethercott)*
Altrincham (0) 0 25,057

Tottenham H: Walker; Austin, Campbell, Howells, Calderwood, Mabbutt, Anderton, Barmby, Klinsmann, Sheringham, Rosenthal (Nethercott).
Altrincham: Collings; Cross, Heesom, France, Reid, Morton (Shaw), Terry, Butler, Green, Carmody, Sharratt (Constable).

Walsall (1) 1 *(Marsh)*
Leeds U (0) 1 *(Wetherall)* 8619

Walsall: Wood; Evans, Gibson (Rogers), Ryder, Marsh, Palmer, O'Connor, Ntamark, Lightbourne, Wilson, Houghton.
Leeds U: Lukic; Kelly, Worthington, Palmer, Wetherall, Pemberton, White (Wallace), Radebe (Masinga), Deane, McAllister, Speed.

Wimbledon (1) 1 *(Harford)*
Colchester U (0) 0 6903

Wimbledon: Segers; Cunningham, Kimble, Jones, Reeves, Thorn, Clarke, Earle, Harford, Holdsworth, Fear.
Colchester U: Cheesewright; Betts, English, Cawley, Caesar, Locke, Putney, Brown, Whitton, Kinsella, Abrahams (Dennis).

Wrexham (0) 2 *(Durkan, Bennett (pen))*
Ipswich T (0) 1 *(Linighan)* 8324

Wrexham: Marriott; Jones, Hardy, Hughes, Hunter, Humes, Bennett, Owen, Connolly, Cross, Durkan.
Ipswich T: Baker; Yallop, Vaughan, Mason (Johnson), Whelan, Linighan, Sedgley, Slater (Paz), Kiwomya, Tanner, Thomsen.

Wycombe W (0) 0
West Ham U (0) 2 *(Cottee, Brown)* 9007

Wycombe W: Hyde; Cousins, Brown, Crossley, Evans, Ryan, Carroll, Bell, Regis (Hemmings), Garner, Thompson (Stapleton).
West Ham U: Miklosko; Breacker, Dicks, Potts, Martin, Bishop, Holmes (Brown), Moncur, Cottee, Boere (Morley), Hughes.

8 JAN

Crystal Palace (3) 5 *(Coleman, Armstrong, Gordon (pen), Salako 2)*
Lincoln C (0) 1 *(Greenall)* 6541

Crystal Palace: Martyn; Humphrey, Gordon, Southgate, Shaw, Coleman, Ndah (Preece), Newman, Armstrong, Pitcher, Salako.
Lincoln C: Leaning; West, Johnson A (Dixon), Hebberd, Greenall, Brown, Hill, Foley (Bannister), Carbon, Daws, Johnson D.

Newcastle U (0) 1 *(Lee)*
Blackburn R (1) 1 *(Sutton)* 31,721

Newcastle U: Srnicek; Venison, Beresford, Elliott (Kitson), Peacock, Howey, Lee, Beardsley, Cole, Fox, Bracewell.
Blackburn R: Flowers; Berg, Le Saux, Sherwood, Hendry, Warhurst, Ripley (Newell), Atkins, Shearer, Sutton, Wilcox.

Notts Co (2) 2 *(Matthews, White)*
Manchester C (1) 2 *(Beagrie, Brightwell D)* 12,376

Notts Co: Cherry; Mills, Legg, Turner, Murphy, Johnson, Devlin, Butler, White, McSwegan, Matthews.
Manchester C: Dibble; Foster (Quinn), Phelan, Lomas, Kernaghan, Brightwell I (Brightwell D), Summerbee, Walsh, Rosler, Flitcroft, Beagrie.

9 JAN

Sheffield U (0) 0
Manchester U (0) 2 *(Hughes, Cantona)* 22,322

Sheffield U: Kelly; Gage, Nilsen, Hartfield, Gayle, Whitehouse (Flo), Rogers, Veart, Blake, Hodges (Starbuck), Scott A.
Manchester U: Schmeichel; O'Kane (Sharpe), Irwin, Bruce, Keane, Pallister, Cantona, Butt, McClair (Scholes), Hughes, Giggs.

THIRD ROUND REPLAYS

17 JAN

Carlisle U (0) 1 *(Walling)*
Sunderland (2) 3 *(Armstrong 2, Gray P)* 12,201
Carlisle U: Caig; Edmondson, Gallimore, Walling, Mountfield, Thorpe (Peters), Thomas, Conway, Reeves, Davey, Robinson.
Sunderland: Chamberlain; Kubicki, Scott, Bennett, Ferguson, Melville, Ball, Russell (Howey), Gray P, Smith, Armstrong.

Leeds U (2) 5 *(Deane, Wetherall, Masinga 3)*
Walsall (1) 2 *(O'Connor (pen), Wetherall (og)) aet* 17,881
Leeds U: Lukic; Kelly, Worthington, Palmer (Radebe), Wetherall, Pemberton, Whelan, Wallace (Masinga), Deane, McAllister, Speed.
Walsall: Wood; Evans, Gibson, Watkiss, Marsh, Palmer, O'Connor (Rogers), Ntamark, Lightbourne, Wilson (Mehew), Houghton.

Middlesbrough (0) 1 *(Hendrie)*
Swansea C (1) 2 *(Torpey, Penney)* 13,940
Middlesbrough: Miller; Morris, Fleming, Vickers, Pearson, Mustoe, Hignett, Pollock, Wilkinson, Hendrie, Moore (Kavanagh).
Swansea C: Freestone; Jenkins, Walker, Basham, Ford, Ampadu, Hayes, Penney, Torpey, Cornforth, Hodge (Chapple).

Watford (0) 2 *(Hessenthaler, Holdsworth)*
Scarborough (0) 0 7047
Watford: Miller; Lavin, Bazeley, Foster, Holdsworth (Page), Ramage, Hessenthaler, Connolly (Watson), Gibbs, Porter, Millen.
Scarborough: Kelly; Knowles, Charles, D'Auria, Meyer, Davis, Thompson (Blackstone), Rodwell, White, Swann (Calvert), Wells.

18 JAN

Arsenal (0) 0
Millwall (1) 2 *(Beard, Kennedy)* 32,319
Arsenal: Seaman; Dixon, Winterburn, Morrow, Keown (Adams), Linighan, Jensen (Flatts), Wright, Campbell, Hillier, Parlour.
Millwall: Keller; Dawes, Van Blerk, Roberts, Witter, Stevens, Beard, Rae, Edwards (Savage), Mitchell (Webber), Kennedy.

Blackburn R (0) 1 *(Sutton)*
Newcastle U (0) 2 *(Hottiger, Clark)* 22,658
Blackburn R: Flowers; Berg, Le Saux, Warhurst, Hendry, Pearce, Slater (Wright), Atkins (Newell), Shearer, Sutton, Wilcox.
Newcastle U: Srnicek; Hottiger, Beresford, Elliott, Peacock, Howey, Lee, Venison, Kitson, Fox, Clark.

Bristol R (0) 0
Luton T (0) 1 *(Marshall)* 8218
Bristol R: Parkin; Pritchard (Hardyman), Clark, Tillson, Gurney, Sterling, Channing, Browning, Taylor, Miller, Archer.
Luton T: Sommer; Chenery, Johnson, Waddock, Thomas, Peake, Telfer, Oakes, Dixon, Preece, Marshall.

Liverpool (1) 1 *(Redknapp)*
Birmingham C (0) 1 *(Otto)* 36,275
Liverpool: James; Jones R, Bjornebye, Scales, Babb, Ruddock, McManaman, Redknapp, Rush, Thomas, Fowler.
Birmingham C: Bennett; Poole, Frain (Dominguez) (McGavin), Ward, Barnett, Daish, Donowa, Claridge, Lowe, Otto, Cooper.
aet; Liverpool won 2-0 on penalties.

Manchester C (3) 5 *(Rosler 4, Gaudino)*
Notts Co (1) 2 *(McSwegan, Matthews)* 14,261
Manchester C: Dibble; Summerbee, Brightwell D, Kernaghan, Curle, Brightwell I, Gaudino, Walsh, Rosler (Quinn), Flitcroft (Simpson), Beagrie.
Notts Co: Cherry; Mills, Legg, Turner, Murphy, Johnson, Devlin, Butler, White, McSwegan (Lund), Matthews.

Stoke C (1) 1 *(Scott)*
Bristol C (0) 3 *(Bent, Baird, Tinnion) aet* 11,579
Stoke C: Sinclair; Clarkson (Carruthers), Sandford, Cranson, Overson, Orlygsson, Butler, Wallace, Scott, Peschisolido, Gleghorn.
Bristol C: Welch; Hansen, Munro, Shail, Bryant, Tinnion, Kuhl (Edwards), Bent, Baird, Allison (Partridge), Owers.

Tranmere R (3) 3 *(O'Brien, Muir, Malkin)*
Bury (0) 0 7921
Tranmere R: Nixon; Stevens (Jones), Thomas, McGreal, Brannan, O'Brien, Morrissey, Muir, Malkin, Irons, Nevin.
Bury: Kelly G; Cross, Stanislaus, Daws, Lucketti, Hughes, Hulme, Carter, Paskin (Kelly T), Johnrose, Rigby.

WBA (0) 1 *(Raven)*
Coventry C (0) 2 *(Dublin, Ndlovu)* 23,230
WBA: Naylor; O'Regan, Edwards, Bradley, Mardon, Raven (Smith), Donovan, Ashcroft, Rees (Taylor), Hunt, Hamilton.
Coventry C: Ogrizovic; Borrows, Morgan, Cook, Rennie, Williams, Darby, Ndlovu, Dublin, Marsh, Jenkinson (Wegerle).

FOURTH ROUND

28 JAN

Burnley (0) 0
Liverpool (0) 0 20,551
Burnley: Russell; Parkinson, Eyres, Davis, Winstanley, Randall, Harper, Hoyland, Mullin, Robinson (McMinn), Saville.
Liverpool: James; Jones R, Matteo, Scales, Babb, Ruddock, McManaman, Redknapp, Rush, Barnes, Fowler.

Coventry C (0) 0
Norwich C (0) 0 15,101
Coventry C: Ogrizovic; Borrows, Morgan (Wegerle), Pickering, Rennie, Pressley, Cook, Ndlovu, Dublin, Marsh, Jenkinson.
Norwich C: Tracey (Marshall); Sutch, Bowen, Newsome, Polston, Ullathorne, Adams, Newman (Akinbiyi), Sheron (Cureton), Milligan, Eadie.

Leeds U (2) 3 *(White, Palmer, Masinga)*
Oldham Ath (0) 2 *(Halle, Palmer (og))* 25,010
Leeds U: Lukic; Kelly, Worthington, Palmer, Wetherall, Pemberton, White, Masinga (Yeboah), Deane, McAllister, Speed.
Oldham Ath: Gerrard; Makin (Holden R), Pointon, Henry, Graham, Redmond, Halle, Ritchie (Beckford), Banger, Richardson, Brennan.

Luton T (0) 1 *(Biggins)*
Southampton (0) 1 *(Shipperley)* 9938
Luton T: Sommer; Oakes, Johnson, Waddock, Thomas, Peake, Telfer, Biggins, Dixon (Williams), Preece, Marshall.
Southampton: Grobbelaar; Kenna, Benali, Charlton (Hughes), Hall, Widdrington, Le Tissier, Magilton, Shipperley, Maddison, Heaney.

Manchester C (1) 1 *(Walsh)*
Aston Villa (0) 0 21,177
Manchester C: Coton; Summerbee, Brightwell D, Brightwell I, Curle, Vonk, Gaudino, Walsh (Quinn), Rosler, Flitcroft, Beagrie.
Aston Villa: Bosnich; Barrett, Staunton, Teale, McGrath, Ehiogu, Yorke (Johnson), Fashanu, Saunders, Taylor, Townsend.

Manchester U (2) 5 *(Irwin 2 (1 pen), Giggs, McClair, Humes (og))*
Wrexham (1) 2 *(Durkan, Cross)* 43,222
Manchester U: Schmeichel; Neville P, Irwin, May, Sharpe, Pallister, Keane (Kanchelskis), Ince, McClair (Beckham), Scholes, Giggs.
Wrexham: Marriott; Jones, Hardy, Hughes (Phillips), Hunter, Humes, Bennett, Owen, Connolly (Cross), Watkin, Durkan.

Millwall (0) 0
Chelsea (0) 0 18,573
Millwall: Keller; Dawes, Van Blerk, Roberts, Witter, Thatcher, Beard, Rae, Edwards, Mitchell, Kennedy.
Chelsea: Kharine; Clarke, Minto, Kjeldbjerg (Burley), Johnsen, Sinclair, Spencer, Spackman, Stein, Peacock, Wise.

Newcastle U (1) 3 *(Kitson 3)*
Swansea C (0) 0 34,372
Newcastle U: Srnicek; Hottiger, Elliott, Venison, Peacock, Howey, Bracewell, Beardsley, Kitson, Fox, Gillespie.
Swansea C: Freestone; Jenkins, Walker, Basham, Ford, Chapple, Hayes (McFarlane), Penney, Torpey, Cornforth, Hodge.

Nottingham F (1) 1 *(Bohinen)*
Crystal Palace (1) 2 *(Armstrong, Dowie)* 16,790
Nottingham F: Crossley; Lyttle, Tiler, Cooper, Chettle, Stone, Phillips, Gemmill (Bull), Bohinen, Collymore, Roy.
Crystal Palace: Martyn; Patterson, Gordon, Southgate, Shaw, Coleman, Dowie, Newman, Armstrong (Preece), Pitcher, Salako.

Portsmouth (0) 0
Leicester C (1) 1 *(Roberts)* 14,928
Portsmouth: Knight; Gittens, Daniel, McGrath (McLoughlin), Russell, Butters, Pethick, Radosavljevic, Powell, Creaney (Flahavan), Kristensen (Rees).
Leicester C: Poole; Smith, Whitlow, Mohan, Hill, Draper, Grayson, Thompson, Robins, Roberts, Philpott.

QPR (1) 1 *(Impey)*
West Ham U (0) 0 17,694
QPR: Roberts; Bardsley, Maddix, Barker, Yates, McDonald, Impey, Holloway, Dichio, Gallen, Sinclair.
West Ham U: Miklosko; Breacker, Dicks, Potts, Martin, Allen, Bishop (Hutchison), Moncur, Cottee, Boere, Hughes.

Watford (1) 1 *(Hessenthaler)*
Swindon T (0) 0 11,202
Watford: Miller; Lavin, Bazeley, Foster, Millen, Ramage, Hessenthaler, Payne, Moralee (Connolly), Porter, Gibbs.
Swindon T: Hammond; Robinson, Murray, Culverhouse, Nijholt (Thorne), Taylor, Horlock, Beauchamp, Fjortoft, Mutch (O'Sullivan), Ling.

29 JAN

Bristol C (0) 0
Everton (0) 1 *(Jackson)* 19,816
Bristol C: Welch; Hansen, Munro, Shail, Bryant (Dryden), Tinnion, Edwards, Bent, Partridge (Seal), Allison, Owers.
Everton: Southall; Jackson, Burrows, Horne, Watson, Unsworth, Limpar, Parkinson, Barlow, Rideout, Hinchcliffe (Stuart).

Sunderland (0) 1 *(Gray P)*
Tottenham H (0) 4 *(Klinsmann 2 (1 pen), Sheringham, Melville (og))* 21,135
Sunderland: Chamberlain; Kubicki, Scott, Bennett, Ferguson, Melville, Howey, Russell, Gray P, Smith, Armstrong (Martin Gray).
Tottenham H: Walker; Campbell, Edinburgh, Popescu, Calderwood, Mabbutt, Anderton, Barmby, Klinsmann, Sheringham, Howells (Nethercott).

Tranmere R (0) 0
Wimbledon (1) 2 *(Leonhardsen, Earle)* 11,637
Tranmere R: Nixon; Stevens, Thomas, McGreal, Garnett, O'Brien (Brannan), Morrissey, Muir (Aldridge), Malkin, Irons, Nevin.
Wimbledon: Segers; Cunningham, Elkins, Jones, Perry, Thorn, Barton, Earle, Harford (Goodman), Leonhardsen, Ekoku (Blissett).

30 JAN

Sheffield W (0) 0
Wolverhampton W (0) 0 21,757
Sheffield W: Pressman; Atherton, Nolan, Bart-Williams, Pearce, Walker, Hyde, Waddle, Bright, Whittingham (Watson), Sheridan (Petrescu).
Wolverhampton W: Jones; Blades, Thompson, Emblen, De Wolf, Law, Birch (Venus), Kelly D, Mills (Goodman), Cowans, Dennison.

FOURTH ROUND REPLAYS

7 FEB

Liverpool (1) 1 *(Barnes)*
Burnley (0) 0 32,109
Liverpool: James; Jones R, Bjornebye (Walters), Scales, Babb, Ruddock, McManaman, Thomas, Rush, Barnes, Fowler.
Burnley: Beresford; Parkinson, Eyres, Davis, Winstanley, Randall, Harper, Hoyland (Peel), Mullin, Robinson, Harrison (McMinn).

8 FEB

Chelsea (0) 1 *(Stein)*
Millwall (0) 1 *(Savage)* 25,515
Chelsea: Kharine; Clarke, Minto, Burley, Lee, Sinclair, Spackman (Newton), Spencer, Stein, Peacock (Furlong), Wise.
Millwall: Keller; Dawes (Webber), Thatcher, Roberts, Witter, Stevens, Beard, Rae, Edwards (Savage), Mitchell, Van Blerk.
aet; Millwall won 5-4 on penalties.

Norwich C (1) 3 *(Sheron 2, Eadie)*
Coventry C (1) 1 *(Ndlovu) aet* 14,673
Norwich C: Marshall; Sutch, Bowen, Newsome, Polston, Ullathorne, Crook (Goss), Milligan, Sheron, Eadie, Adams (Akinbiyi).
Coventry C: Ogrizovic; Borrows, Morgan, Pressley, Rennie, Pickering, Flynn, Ndlovu, Dublin (Darby), Marsh, Wegerle (Jones).

Southampton (4) 6 *(Le Tissier 2 (1 pen), Magilton, Heaney, Monkou, Hughes)*
Luton T (0) 0 15,075

Southampton: Grobbelaar; Kenna, Dodd, Widdrington, Hall, Monkou, Le Tissier (Hughes), Magilton, Shipperley, Maddison (Tisdale), Heaney.
Luton T: Sommer; James (Dixon), Johnson, Waddock, Thomas, Peake, Telfer, Oakes, Biggins (Thorpe), Preece, Marshall.

Wolverhampton W (1) 1 *(Kelly D)*
Sheffield W (0) 1 *(Bright)* 28,136

Wolverhampton W: Jones; Blades (Mills), Thompson, Emblen, De Wolf, Law, Rankine (Bennett), Kelly D, Goodman, Cowans, Dennison.
Sheffield W: Pressman; Atherton, Nolan, Bart-Williams, Pearce, Walker, Hyde, Waddle, Bright, Ingesson (Sheridan), Sinton (Whittingham).
aet; Wolverhampton W won 4-3 on penalties.

FIFTH ROUND

18 FEB

Everton (2) 5 *(Limpar, Parkinson, Rideout, Ferguson, Stuart)*
Norwich C (0) 0 31,616

Everton: Southall; Jackson, Hinchcliffe, Ebbrell, Watson, Ablett, Stuart, Parkinson, Ferguson, Rideout (Barlow), Limpar.
Norwich C: Tracey; Bradshaw, Bowen, Newsome, Newman, Ullathorne (Prior), Sutch, Johnson, Sheron, Eadie, Goss.

QPR (0) 1 *(Wilson (pen))*
Millwall (0) 0 16,457

QPR: Roberts; Bardsley, Wilson, Barker, Maddix, McDonald, Impey, Holloway, Ferdinand, Gallen, Meaker.
Millwall: Keller; Beard, Thatcher, Roberts, Witter, Webber, Savage, May, Mitchell (Edwards), Van Blerk, Kennedy.

Tottenham H (1) 1 *(Klinsmann)*
Southampton (1) 1 *(Le Tissier (pen))* 28,091

Tottenham H: Walker; Campbell, Edinburgh, Popescu, Calderwood, Mabbutt, Anderton, Barmby, Klinsmann (Austin), Sheringham, Howells.
Southampton: Grobbelaar; Kenna, Benali, Widdrington, Hall, Monkou, Le Tissier, Magilton, Shipperley, Maddison, Heaney.

Watford (0) 0
Crystal Palace (0) 0 13,814

Watford: Miller; Lavin, Bazeley, Foster, Millen, Ramage, Holdsworth, Payne, Moralee (Watson), Porter, Gibbs.
Crystal Palace: Martyn; Patterson, Gordon, Southgate, Shaw, Coleman, Humphrey, Pitcher, Armstrong, Preece, Salako.

Wolverhampton W (1) 1 *(Kelly D)*
Leicester C (0) 0 28,544

Wolverhampton W: Jones; Venus, Thompson, Bennett, De Wolf, Law, Rankine, Kelly D, Goodman, Cowans, Dennison.
Leicester C: Poole (Ward); Grayson (Philpott), Whitlow, Hill, Willis, Draper, Galloway, Thompson, Robins, Roberts, Parker.

19 FEB

Liverpool (1) 1 *(Fowler)*
Wimbledon (1) 1 *(Clarke)* 25,124

Liverpool: James; Jones R, Bjornebye, Redknapp, Scales, Ruddock, McManaman, Walters, Rush, Barnes, Fowler.
Wimbledon: Segers; Cunningham, Kimble, Perry, Reeves, Barton, Ardley, Earle, Clarke (Holdsworth), Leonhardsen, Ekoku (Harford).

Manchester U (2) 3 *(Bruce, McClair, Hughes)*
Leeds U (0) 1 *(Yeboah)* 42,744

Manchester U: Schmeichel; Keane, Irwin, Bruce, Sharpe, Pallister, Kanchelskis, Ince, McClair, Hughes, Giggs.
Leeds U: Lukic; Kelly, Dorigo, Whelan, Wetherall, Pemberton, White, Wallace (Worthington), Masinga (Yeboah), McAllister, Speed.

Newcastle U (1) 3 *(Gillespie 2, Beresford)*
Manchester C (1) 1 *(Rosler)* 33,219

Newcastle U: Srnicek; Hottiger, Beresford, Venison, Peacock, Howey, Lee, Beardsley, Kitson, Fox, Gillespie.
Manchester C: Dibble; Summerbee, Brightwell D (Foster), Kernaghan, Curle, Brightwell I, Gaudino, Rosler, Quinn (Mike), Flitcroft, Beagrie.

FIFTH ROUND REPLAYS

28 FEB

Wimbledon (0) 0
Liverpool (2) 2 *(Barnes, Rush)* 12,553

Wimbledon: Segers; Cunningham, Kimble, Barton, Perry, Thorn (Harford), Ardley, Earle, Clarke, Leonhardsen, Ekoku (Holdsworth).
Liverpool: James; Jones R, Bjornebye, Scales, Babb, Ruddock, McManaman, Redknapp, Rush, Barnes, Fowler (Walters).

1 MAR

Crystal Palace (0) 1 *(Ndah)*
Watford (0) 0 aet 10,321

Crystal Palace: Martyn; Humphrey (Preece), Gordon, Southgate, Shaw, Patterson, Dyer (Ndah), Newman, Dowie, Pitcher, Salako.
Watford: Miller; Gibbs, Bazeley (Pitcher), Foster, Millen, Ramage, Holdsworth, Johnson, Moralee (Mooney), Porter, Barnes.

Southampton (2) 2 *(Shipperley, Le Tissier (pen))*
Tottenham H (0) 6 *(Rosenthal 3, Sheringham, Barmby, Anderton) aet* 15,172

Southampton: Grobbelaar; Kenna, Benali, Widdrington (Hughes), Monkou, Dodd, Le Tissier, Magilton, Shipperley, Maddison, Heaney.
Tottenham: Walker; Edinburgh, Austin, Nethercott (Rosenthal), Calderwood, Mabbutt, Anderton, Barmby, Klinsmann, Sheringham, Howells (Caskey).

SIXTH ROUND

11 MAR

Crystal Palace (0) 1 *(Dowie)*
Wolverhampton W (0) 1 *(Cowans)* 14,604

Crystal Palace: Martyn; Southgate, Coleman, Pitcher, Shaw, Young, Matthew (Humphrey), Newman, Dowie (Dyer), Preece, Salako.
Wolverhampton W: Stowell; Smith, Thompson, Law, Rankine, Shirtliff, Goodman, Kelly D, Bull, Cowans, Dennison (Emblen).

Liverpool (1) 1 *(Fowler)*

Tottenham H (1) 2 *(Sheringham, Klinsmann)* 39,592

Liverpool: James; Jones R, Babb, Redknapp, Scales, Ruddock, McManaman, Walters (Bjornebye), Rush, Barnes (Thomas), Fowler.
Tottenham H: Walker; Austin, Edinburgh, Howells, Calderwood, Mabbutt, Anderton, Barmby, Klinsmann, Sheringham, Rosenthal.

12 MAR

Everton (0) 1 *(Watson)*

Newcastle U (0) 0 35,203

Everton: Southall; Jackson, Unsworth, Ebbrell, Watson, Ablett, Horne, Parkinson, Ferguson, Barlow, Limpar (Stuart).
Newcastle: Srnicek; Hottiger (Watson), Beresford (Elliott), Venison, Peacock, Bracewell, Lee, Clark, Kitson, Fox, Gillespie.

Manchester U (1) 2 *(Irwin, Sharpe)*

QPR (0) 0 42,830

Manchester U: Schmeichel; Neville G, Irwin, Bruce, Sharpe, Pallister, Kanchelskis, Ince, McClair, Hughes, Giggs (Keane).
QPR: Roberts; Bardsley, Wilson, Barker, Maddix, McDonald, Impey, Holloway, Ferdinand, Gallen, Brevett (Penrice).

SIXTH ROUND REPLAY

22 MAR

Wolverhampton W (1) 1 *(Kelly D)*

Crystal Palace (3) 4 *(Armstrong 2, Dowie, Pitcher)* 27,548

Wolverhampton W: Stowell; Rankine, Thompson, Bennett (Emblen), Law, Shirtliff, Venus, Goodman, Bull, Kelly D, Dennison.
Crystal Palace: Martyn; Patterson, Coleman, Southgate, Shaw, Young, Dowie, Cox (Newman), Armstrong (Dyer), Pitcher, Salako.

SEMI-FINALS

9 APR

Crystal Palace (1) 2 *(Dowie, Armstrong)* 38,256

Manchester U (0) 2 *(Irwin, Pallister) aet* (at Villa Park)

Crystal Palace: Martyn; Patterson, Coleman (Gordon), Southgate, Shaw, Young, Dowie, Houghton, Armstrong, Pitcher, Salako.
Manchester U: Schmeichel; Neville G, Irwin, Keane, Sharpe, Pallister, Beckham (Butt), Ince, McClair, Hughes, Giggs.

Everton (1) 4 *(Jackson, Stuart, Amokachi 2)* 38,226

Tottenham H (0) 1 *(Klinsmann (pen))* (at Elland Road)

Everton: Southall; Jackson, Ablett, Parkinson, Watson, Unsworth, Limpar, Horne, Stuart, Rideout (Amokachi), Hinchcliffe.
Tottenham H: Walker; Austin, Nethercott (Rosenthal), Popescu, Calderwood, Mabbutt, Anderton, Barmby, Klinsmann, Sheringham, Howells.

SEMI-FINAL REPLAY

12 APR

Manchester U (2) 2 *(Bruce, Pallister)*

Crystal Palace (0) 0 (at Villa Park) 17,987

Manchester U: Schmeichel; Neville G, Irwin, Bruce, Sharpe, Pallister, Butt, Ince, Keane, Hughes, Giggs (McClair).
Crystal Palace: Wilmot; Patterson, Gordon, Southgate, Shaw, Young, Dowie (Cox), Houghton, Armstrong, Pitcher (Newman), Salako.

FINAL at Wembley

20 MAY

Everton (1) 1 *(Rideout)*

Manchester U (0) 0 79,592

Everton: Southall; Jackson, Ablett, Parkinson, Watson, Unsworth, Limpar (Amokachi), Horne, Stuart, Rideout (Ferguson), Hinchcliffe.
Manchester U: Schmeichel; Neville G, Irwin, Bruce (Giggs), Sharpe (Scholes), Pallister, Keane, Ince, McClair, Hughes, Butt.
Referee: G. Ashby (Worcester).

Paul Rideout heads the only goal in the 1995 FA Cup Final to give Everton a 1-0 win over Manchester United. (Colorsport)

FOOTBALL AND THE LAW

Sir Stanley Matthews' 80th birthday on the first day of February crystallised the true dimension of Football and the Law during the 1994-95 season. He was never booked or dismissed from the field and he surfaced as an 18-year-old winger during Stoke City's Football League Second Division Championship-winning team of 1932-33.

Four years later, in a replayed 5th round FA Cup tie at White Hart Lane – won 4-3 by Tottenham after being 3-1 down four minutes from time and described by the losing Everton captain, Joe Mercer, as the greatest game in which he played – his veteran centre-forward, Dixie Dean, was insulted by a fan as he entered the dressing-room tunnel. Retaliation with a punch is alleged in Dean's biography by a former Lord Chancellor's Department Official, Nick Walsh, to have been assisted by a police officer. Yet since no television existed, the occasion has been unrecorded until now, recalled by Cantona's Kung-Fu spectacular counter-attack upon his own abusive spectator.

Correspondingly, Duncan Ferguson's head-butt against a Raith Rovers opponent, which has landed him – subject to appeal – with a prison sentence, was missed by the referee but trapped on television, in the manner that Paul Davis' breakage of Glenn Cockerill's jaw, which resulted in a £3,000 fine and a nine-match suspension, surfaced by disciplinary action. Thus it is not possible to identify the number of criminal or civilly liable offences resulting from deliberately violent foul play which escape unknown and unpunished. In the Peterborough Crown Court, a criminal trial for an alleged assault by a defendant upon an attacker, resulting in a broken chest bone, is in the pipeline; and the ITN London Programme, during a Sunday examination of Park Football, uncovered significant occasions even more serious than the Cantona and Ferguson prosecutions.

Civil actions for damages surface in local county courts more frequently than the two high-profile High Court trials which resulted in Paul Elliott failing to win damages against Dean Saunders and Liverpool, and John O'Neill's settlement out of court against John Fashanu and Wimbledon.

Off the field, the law has been in and out of football's news with George Graham's Arsenal dispute, alleged match throwing and two governing bodies biting the dust. The FA's sanctions on Spurs of ejection from the FA Cup and deduction of Premier League points were overturned on appeal to arbitrators, and the FA of Wales' refusal to allow three Welsh clubs to play in England was twice held in London's High Court as acting in restraint of trade. Finally, yet to come are proceedings in the European Court of Justice by Jean Bosman for breaches of the Treaty of Rome equivalent to restraint of trade that could yet destroy the current transfer system that existed even before Stanley Matthews' day.

Throughout that period when Matthews' Stoke City and Arthur Rowe's Spurs were surviving on £8 per week wages with a £2 bonus for a win and £1 for a draw, British football reigned supreme, and apart from a hiccup when England beat Italy 3-2 in 1934 in what became known as the Battle of Highbury, foul play of the kind which has landed Ferguson in the courts and led to claims for damages in county courts was never prevalent to the degree which is now captured on television. Was the reason discipline in homes, schools and lack of significant financial rewards? Or is there a deeper reason which chroniclers of the future will unravel for those of us unable to do so today?

EDWARD GRAYSON,
Founder President, British Association for Sport and the Law.

THE SCOTTISH SEASON 1994-95

The new system of four divisions in the League caused many comments throughout the season, and a fairly generous slice of self-preservation was apparent in those from the clubs. It could not be said that there was a lack of interest: when it was possible to go from promotion contender to the relegation zone with one loss, there was little chance of boredom. Certainly there was much coming and going, and the only sure fact that established itself early on was that Rangers were going to win the Premier Division title yet again.

The two main contenders for the other honours in this division were Motherwell and Hibernian: two shrewd managers made the best from what they had, and in the end it was the new boy who slipped into the runners-up position. Celtic never quite settled, but promised for the future, whilst Falkirk surprised many with some sound performances. Hearts had a purple patch, but finished in some danger, whilst Kilmarnock had a charge to safety at the right moment; Partick Thistle certainly looked doomed until well into the new year, but they showed real grit and determination in forcing their way from the bottom of the table.

It was left to the unlikely pair of Aberdeen and Dundee United to face the drop: Aberdeen, with a new manager, won the showdown a fortnight from the end of the season, and United sank with hardly a murmur: it was a sad day for Jim McLean who had done so much to create the team and to lead it to a proud position in Europe. Aberdeen were left to play-off for the remaining place with Dunfermline, and they were successful with something to spare.

The First Division was most exciting right to the wire: for some weeks there had been a running battle for the promotion spot, and the lead changed several times. On the last afternoon, all options were still open for Raith Rovers, Dundee and Dunfermline; but Raith achieved the draw they required at Hamilton, whilst a frenzied burst of late goals nearly put Dundee into the play-off place; as it was, Dunfermline finished as runners-up and, as has been noted, they lost the play-off to Aberdeen. It was hugely frustrating for the Pars who thus missed out on promotion for the third time running; whilst Dundee could only look on in despair and regret some throwing away of points in the final weeks of the season. Airdrie never quite maintained the pace with the leaders in the last session, whilst at the foot of the table Stranraer, after enjoying their year in the upper echelons, struggled, and they were joined by Ayr United, who comfortably lost to St Mirren in the race for safety.

Likewise there was a storming finish in the Second Division: here there were four clubs seriously concerned with promotion: Greenock Morton, Dumbarton, Stenhousemuir and Stirling Albion: Stirling had a late run which brought them to the brink of success, whilst Stenhousemuir never quite recovered their form after a magnificent Cup run; Greenock Morton drew clear at the end, but on the last day Dumbarton played Stirling Albion -and won. It was as close as that. At the other end, Brechin and Meadowbank had lifted the relegation spots without much attention from other teams.

There was much interest in the new Third Division, with the two new teams. Ross County were challenging for the top position until very nearly the end of the season, and they quickly adapted to their status. They drew their crowds, too. Caledonian Thistle did not have quite such a comfortable year, but they finished in mid-table. Both these former Highland League teams should soon be looking for promotion.

It was the East coast sides who prospered: Forfar Athletic had a good season throughout, and a series of steady results put them well ahead of the others as they clinched promotion with weeks to go. Montrose were several games behind. and this is not always a healthy position to be in; however, they made no mistakes, and came away strongly in the end to finish as runners-up.

The first year of the Coca-Cola Cup saw the remarkable achievement of Raith Rovers in winning the first final of the year against Celtic at Ibrox. It was a rip-roaring match, with Celtic scoring a late goal which looked to have won them the trophy; but a couple of minutes later, Raith equalized, and extra time led to no further goals: so to the penalty shoot out, and Raith's youngsters kept cool heads, and it was all over. What a season for manager Jimmy Nicholl and the Kirkcaldy club, who went on to clinch promotion to the Premier Division later!

In the earlier stages there were some fine achievements to record: whatever may be the dislike of many for the penalty shoot-out, it certainly breeds excitement, and this form of ending with a result was often in evidence: Falkirk had a real nail-biter against Montrose, but went on to dispose of Rangers at Ibrox -no mean task; Hamilton Accies just failed to oust Dundee United; whilst Airdrie started a remarkable run of cup matches by taking Motherwell in the depths of extra time. Airdrie continued by dismissing Hibs, and then failed to hold Raith Rovers on penalties in the semi-final at McDiarmid Park: it was their only cup failure till the last day of the season.

The B&Q Cup went to Airdrie, who, incidentally, had another penalty duel with Raith, but won this one. The final, in early November, was closely contested, and Dundee lost by the odd goal in five.

The Scottish Cup was notable for two particular performances above all others: Stenhousemuir, who started their campaign in the first round on December 17, won convincing victories over East Stirling and Arbroath before coming against St Johnstone, where they held the home team; at Ochilview a week later they stunned the Perth team, and followed this by disposing of Aberdeen in the fourth round. In the Quarter-finals they took on Hibs (also at Ochilview) and finally met their match in the second half after a 0-0 half time score. Astute instructions to his players, and their whole-hearted enthusiasm meant that Terry Christie made a considerable impact on the competition. Then there was Airdrie -who again came against Raith, and this time defeated them roundly. In the semi-final they won a hard encounter against Hearts, who had themselves had a good run. The final was not a particularly good game, and Celtic beat Airdrie to take their first silverware home for some years: at last the Parkhead fans had something really to cheer, and it was a deserved victory which they had worked hard to achieve.

The club season in Europe was, to say the least, undistinguished, and there was little to give pleasure to Scottish fans. However, Motherwell did well in the two matches with Borussia Dortmund, although in the end lack of experience showed. There has not been much to cheer about in the last year or two, but perhaps next season is the one in which we may make some impact.

On the international front it was encouraging: with the European Championship looming, we still look to have a fair chance of qualifying. This has been done by some workmanlike performances and a good deal of hard graft both by management and players; there have been the usual times when everyone seemed to be injured, but qualification is now in our own hands, and good results in the later stages can ensure success. Craig Brown is to be congratulated, both at the senior level and with the Under 21s who have a batch of young players coming on well.

There was great sadness late in the season when Davie Cooper died suddenly; a very modest and even retiring person, he had not looked for the kind of rewards abroad which his talents could so easily have brought to him. A player of immense ability, he added light to every game he played; after years with Rangers and Motherwell, he had returned to his first club, Clydebank, and was still showing all his old skill, and the ability to beat men and cross to perfection. His death shocked the whole country: it showed the stature of the man that his club asked that his Number 7 jersey should not be used again for the rest of the season -a request willingly granted by the Scottish Football League.

ALAN ELLIOTT

Editor's note: In Match 1, Brechin City v Meadowbank Thistle on 13 August, Meadowbank had three points deducted for fielding an ineligible player. The goals from the game were not counted in the season's totals for either club. Also for Clydebank, the last six appearances by Lansdowne listed as No. 15, are full appearances (see above) and his total should be amended accordingly to 20 + 3.

ABERDEEN — Premier Division

Year Formed: 1903. *Ground & Address:* Pittodrie Stadium, Pittodrie St, Aberdeen AB2 1QH. *Telephone:* 01224 632328.
Ground Capacity: 21,634 seated: All. *Size of Pitch:* 110yd × 72yd.
Chairman: Ian R. Donald. *Secretary:* Ian J. Taggart. *General Manager:* David Johnston.
Manager: Roy Aitken. *Assistant Managers:* Tommy Craig, Drew Jarvie, Neil Cooper. *Physios:* David Wylie, John Sharp.
Managers since 1975: Ally MacLeod; Billy McNeill; Alex Ferguson; Ian Porterfield; Alex Smith and Jocky Scott; Willie Miller. *Club Nicknames(s):* The Dons. *Previous Grounds:* None.
Record Attendance: 45,061 v Hearts, Scottish Cup 4th rd; 13 Mar, 1954.
Record Transfer Fee received: £970,000 for David Robertson to Rangers (July 1991).
Record Transfer Fee paid: £800,000 for Billy Dodds from St Johnstone, 1994.
Record Victory: 13-0 v Peterhead, Scottish Cup; 9 Feb, 1923.
Record Defeat: 0-8 v Celtic, Division 1; 30 Jan, 1965.
Most Capped Players: Alex McLeish, 77, Scotland.
Most League Appearances: 556: Willie Miller, 1973-90.
Most League Goals in Season (Individual): 38: Benny Yorston, Division I; 1929-30.
Most Goals Overall (Individual): 199: Joe Harper.

ABERDEEN 1994–95 LEAGUE RECORD

Match No.	Date	Venue	Opponents	Result		H/T Score	Lg. Pos.	Goalscorers	Attendance
1	Aug 13	H	Hearts	W	3-1	1-0	—	Robertson, Dodds, Booth	14,238
2	20	H	Falkirk	D	2-2	1-1	3	Robertson, Booth	11,143
3	27	A	Dundee U	L	1-2	0-0	5	Grant	9332
4	Sept 10	A	Hibernian	D	2-2	1-2	5	Dodds, Grant	9728
5	17	H	Partick T	D	1-1	0-0	4	Dodds	10,425
6	24	H	Rangers	D	2-2	1-1	4	Booth, Dodds	19,191
7	Oct 1	A	Kilmarnock	L	1-2	1-1	6	Booth	7445
8	8	A	Celtic	D	0-0	0-0	8		29,454
9	15	H	Motherwell	L	1-3	1-0	8	Dodds	12,489
10	22	A	Hearts	L	0-2	0-2	9		10,655
11	29	H	Dundee U	W	3-0	2-0	7	Kane 2, Booth	11,744
12	Nov 5	A	Falkirk	L	1-2	1-1	8	Booth	6185
13	9	H	Hibernian	D	0-0	0-0	—		10,882
14	19	A	Partick T	L	1-2	1-0	8	Dodds	3795
15	25	A	Rangers	L	0-1	0-0	—		45,072
16	Dec 3	H	Kilmarnock	L	0-1	0-1	10		10,345
17	10	A	Motherwell	W	1-0	1-0	9	McCart (og)	7020
18	26	H	Celtic	D	0-0	0-0	—		19,206
19	31	H	Hearts	W	3-1	2-0	9	Shearer 2, Inglis	11,392
20	Jan 2	A	Dundee U	D	0-0	0-0	—		10,560
21	7	H	Falkirk	D	0-0	0-0	7		14,141
22	14	H	Partick T	W	3-1	1-0	6	Dinnie (og), Jess, Shearer	9833
23	21	A	Hibernian	L	2-4	1-3	8	Dodds 2	8076
24	Feb 4	A	Kilmarnock	L	1-3	1-2	9	McKimmie	9384
25	12	H	Rangers	W	2-0	0-0	—	Dodds, Shearer	18,060
26	25	H	Motherwell	L	0-2	0-1	9		10,319
27	Mar 5	A	Celtic	L	0-2	0-1	—		20,621
28	11	A	Partick T	D	2-2	2-0	9	Wright, Dodds	6886
29	18	H	Hibernian	D	0-0	0-0	9		10,384
30	Apr 1	H	Kilmarnock	L	0-1	0-0	9		14,041
31	8	A	Rangers	L	2-3	2-2	10	Dodds, Shearer	44,460
32	15	H	Celtic	W	2-0	2-0	10	Shearer, Irvine	16,668
33	18	A	Motherwell	L	1-2	1-1	—	Dodds	7155
34	29	A	Hearts	W	2-1	0-0	10	Dodds 2	11,466
35	May 6	H	Dundee U	W	2-1	1-0	9	Dodds,Shearer	20,124
36	13	A	Falkirk	W	2-0	1-0	9	Thomson, Glass	12,835

Final League Position: 9

Honours

League Champions: Division I 1954-55. Premier Division 1979-80, 1983-84, 1984-85; *Runners-up:* Division I 1910-11, 1936-37, 1955-56, 1970-71, 1971-72. Premier Division 1977-78, 1980-81, 1981-82, 1988-89, 1989-90, 1990-91, 1992-93, 1993-94.
Scottish Cup Winners: 1947, 1970, 1982, 1983, 1984, 1986, 1990; *Runners-up:* 1937, 1953, 1954, 1959, 1967, 1978, 1993.
League Cup Winners: 1955-56, 1976-77, 1985-86, 1989-90; *Runners-up:* 1946-47, 1978-79, 1979-80, 1987-88, 1988-89, 1992-93.
Drybrough Cup Winners: 1971, 1980.

European: *European Cup* 12 matches (1980-81, 1984-85, 1985-86); *Cup Winners Cup Winners:* 1982-83. Semi-finals 1983-84. 37 matches (1967-68, 1970-71, 1978-79, 1982-83, 1983-84, 1986-87, 1990-91, 1993-94); *UEFA Cup* 36 matches (*Fairs Cup:* 1968-69. *UEFA Cup:* 1971-72, 1972-73, 1973-74, 1977-78, 1979-80, 1981-82, 1987-88, 1988-89, 1989-90, 1991-92, 1994-95).
Club colours: Shirt, Shorts, Stockings: Red with white trim.

Goalscorers: *League (43):* Dodds 15, Shearer 7, Booth 6, Grant 2, Kane 2, Robertson 2, Glass 1, Inglis 1, Irvine 1, Jess 1, McKimmie 1, Thomson 1, Wright 1, own goals 2. *Cup (1):* Jess 1. *League Cup (10):* Shearer 4 (1 pen), Booth 3, Dodds 1, Kane 1, own goal 1.

Snelders T 24	McKimmie S 34	Winnie D 6 + 2	Grant B 32	Irvine B 17	Wright S 33 + 1	Jess E 15 + 10	Shearer D 19 + 4	Kane P 27	Dodds W 35	Robertson H 2 + 1	Hetherston P 13 + 9	Booth S 11 + 1	Miller J 21 + 6	Woodthorpe C 14	McKinnon R 17 + 3	Smith G 31	Watt M 12 + 2	Glass S 11 + 8	Inglis J 16 + 1	Thomson S 6 + 4	Aitken R — + 2	Kpedekpo M — + 1	Match No.
1	2	3	4	5	6	7	*8*	9	10	11	12	14											1
1	2	3	4	*5*	6	14	8	9	10	11		7	12										2
1	2		4	5	6	7	*8*	9	10				14	3	11								3
1	2	11	4		6	7			10			9		3	8	5							4
	2		4	5	6	7			10			*9*	14	3	11	8	1						5
	2		4	5	6	7			*10*		12	9	14	3	11	8	1						6
	2	8	4	5	6				10		7	9	12	3	11		1						7
	2		4	5	6			8	10			9		3	11	7	1						8
	2		4	5	6			8	10		*11*	9	14	3		7	1						9
	2	12	4	5	6			8	10	14	*11*	9		3		7	1						10
1	2	5	4		6			8	10		12	9		3	*11*	7		14					11
1	2	5	4		6		12	8	10			9		*3*	11	7			14				12
1	2	14					*8*	4	10			9		3	11	6			5	7			13
1	2				14	8		4	*10*		12			3	11	6		9	5	7			14
1	*2*		8		6	11		4	10		12			3		7		14	5	9			15
1	2		8		6	7		4	10		12		9	*3*				11	5	14			16
1	2		8		3			4	10		6		9			7		11	5				17
1	2		8		3	14	12	4	10		6		*9*			7		11	5				18
1	2		11		3		8	4	10		7		9		12	6			5				19
1	2		7		3	14	*8*	4	10				9		11	6			5		12		20
1			7		3	14	8	4	10				9		*11*	6		2	5				21
1	2		11		*3*	7	8	4	10				9			6		14	5	12			22
1	2		11			7	8	4	10				*9*		14	6		3	5				23
1	2		8		3		14	4	10				9			6		11	5	7	12		24
1	*2*				3	7	8	4	10				9		11	6		14	5				25
1				5	2	7	*8*	4	10		12		9		*11*	6	15	3		14			26
	2		*4*	5	3	7	12		10		14		9		11	6	1	8					27
1	2		4	5	3	14			10		12		9		*11*	6		8		7			28
1	2		11		3	12	8	4	10		7		*9*			6	15		5	14			29
	2		*11*		3	14	8	4	10		7		9			6	1		5				30
	2		*11*		3	14	8	4	10		7		9			6	1		5				31
	2		11	5	3	12	8	4	10		7		*9*			6	1	14					32
	2		11	5	3	12	8	4	10		7		9			*6*	1	14					33
	2		4	5	3	11	8		10		7		9		12	*6*	1	14					34
1	2		4	5	3	*11*	8		10		7		9			6		14					35
1	2		4	5	3		8						9		10	6		11		*7*		14	36

AIRDRIEONIANS First Division

Year Formed: 1878. *Ground & Address:* Broadwood Stadium, Cumbernauld G68 9NE. Address for all correspondence: 32 Stirling Street, Airdrie, ML6 0AH *Telephone:* 01236 762067.
Ground Capacity: all seated: 6203. *Size of Pitch:* 112yd × 76yd.
Chairman and Secretary: George W. Peat CA. *Commercial Manager:* Dorothy Martin.
Manager: Alex MacDonald. *Assistant Manager:* John McVeigh. *Physio:* Dan Young. *Coach:* John Binnie.
Managers since 1975: I. McMillan; J. Stewart; R. Watson; W. Munro; A. MacLeod; D. Whiteford; G. McQueen; J. Bone.
Club Nickname(s): The Diamonds or The Waysiders. *Previous Grounds:* Mavisbank, Broomfield Park.
Record Attendance: 24,000 v Hearts, Scottish Cup; 8 Mar, 1952.
Record Transfer Fee received: £200,000 for Sandy Clark to West Ham U, May 1982.
Record Transfer Fee paid: £175,000 for Owen Coyle from Clydebank, February 1990.
Record Victory: 15-1 v Dundee Wanderers, Division II; 1 Dec, 1894.
Record Defeat: 1-11 v Hibernian, Division I; 24 Oct, 1959.
Most Capped Player: Jimmy Crapnell, 9, Scotland.
Most League Appearances: 523: Paul Jonquin, 1962-79.
Most League Goals in Season (Individual): 53, Hugh Baird, Division II, 1954-55. *Most Goals Overall (Individual):* —

AIRDRIEONIANS 1994–95 LEAGUE RECORD

Match No.	Date	Venue	Opponents	Result		H/T Score	Lg. Pos.	Goalscorers	Attendance
1	Aug 13	H	Dunfermline Ath	D	0-0	0-0	—		2964
2	20	H	St Johnstone	D	0-0	0-0	8		2161
3	27	A	Hamilton A	W	6-2	3-2	3	Harvey, Lawrence 3, Andrew Smith 2	1180
4	Sept 3	A	Dundee	D	1-1	1-0	3	Lawrence	4020
5	10	H	Ayr U	D	0-0	0-0	3		1620
6	24	H	Clydebank	W	2-0	1-0	2	Andrew Smith, Lawrence	1542
7	Oct 1	A	Stranraer	W	1-0	0-0	2	Lawrence	1001
8	8	H	Raith R	D	0-0	0-0	2		2096
9	15	A	St Mirren	W	1-0	1-0	2	Davies	2930
10	22	A	Dunfermline Ath	D	2-2	1-0	2	Cooper, Andrew Smith	5642
11	29	H	Hamilton A	W	1-0	0-0	2	Andrew Smith	1422
12	Nov 12	A	Ayr U	W	3-0	2-0	2	Cooper 2, Lawrence	2210
13	19	H	Dundee	W	2-1	0-0	2	Anthony Smith, Andrew Smith	2022
14	22	A	St Johnstone	L	0-4	0-1	—		3110
15	26	A	Clydebank	W	1-0	0-0	2	Andrew Smith	1197
16	Dec 3	H	Stranraer	W	8-1	2-1	1	Harvey, Boyle 2 (2 pens), Andrew Smith, Cooper 2, Davies 2	1207
17	26	A	Raith R	L	2-3	1-2	—	Cooper, Boyle	4338
18	31	H	Dunfermline Ath	D	0-0	0-0	3		3252
19	Jan 2	A	Hamilton A	L	0-3	0-2	—		2178
20	7	H	St Johnstone	L	0-2	0-2	3		1957
21	10	H	St Mirren	W	2-0	1-0	—	Cooper, Andrew Smith	1325
22	14	A	Dundee	W	1-0	0-0	2	Andrew Smith	4084
23	24	H	Ayr U	D	2-2	1-1	—	Boyle, Black	1320
24	Feb 4	A	Stranraer	W	4-1	2-0	3	Anthony Smith, Lawrence 2, Hay	945
25	14	H	Clydebank	L	1-2	0-2	—	Black (pen)	1033
26	25	A	St Mirren	W	1-0	0-0	4	Andrew Smith	2564
27	Mar 6	H	Raith R	L	1-2	0-0	—	Cooper	1726
28	18	A	Ayr U	W	2-0	0-0	4	Lawrence 2	1372
29	25	H	Dundee	L	0-3	0-0	4		2528
30	Apr 1	H	Stranraer	W	2-0	0-0	4	Cooper, Andrew Smith	851
31	11	A	Clydebank	D	1-1	0-1	—	Cooper	709
32	15	A	Raith R	W	1-0	1-0	4	Cooper	4494
33	22	H	St Mirren	W	1-0	0-0	4	McIntyre J	2245
34	29	A	Dunfermline Ath	D	0-0	0-0	4		6603
35	May 6	H	Hamilton A	L	0-1	0-0	4		1501
36	13	A	St Johnstone	L	1-2	1-1	4	Stewart	2868

Final League Position: 4

Honours
League Champions: Division II 1902-03, 1954-55, 1973-74; *Runners-up:* Division I 1922-23, 1923-24, 1924-25, 1925-26. First Division 1979-80, 1989-90, 1990-91. Division II 1900-01, 1946-47, 1949-50, 1965-66.
Scottish Cup Winners: 1924; *Runners-up:* 1975, 1992, 1995. *Scottish Spring Cup Winners:* 1976.
League Cup semi-finalists: 1991-92, 1994-95.
B&Q Cup Winners:R: 1994-95.

European: *UEFA Cup* 2 matches (1992-93).
Club colours: Shirt: White with Red diamond. Shorts: White. Stockings: Red.

Goalscorers: *League (50):* Andrew Smith 12, Cooper 11, Lawrence 11, Boyle 4 (2 pens), Davies 3, Black 2 (1 pen), Harvey 2, Tony Smith 2, Hay 1, McIntyre J 1, Stewart 1. *Scottish Cup (9):* Andrew Smith 3, Cooper 2, Harvey 2, Black 1, Davies 1. *League Cup (6):* Boyle 2, Andrew Smith 2, Cooper 1, Lawrence 1. *B&Q Cup (12):* Andrew Smith 3, Boyle 2 (1 pen), Cooper 2, Davies 2, Harvey 1, Lawrence 1, Stewart 1.

Martin J 35	Stewart A 32	Smith Ant 12 + 15	Sandison J 32 + 1	McIntyre T 15 + 1	Black K 31	Boyle J 33 + 1	Wilson M 12 + 3	Smith And 24 + 12	Harvey P 33	Lawrence A 24 + 8	McIntyre J 2 + 11	Hay G 25 + 1	Ferguson I — + 3	Jack P 28	Davies J 25	Honor C 1	Cooper S 26 + 3	McCulloch W 1 + 1	Connelly G 1 + 3	McLelland J 2	Tait S 1	McKenna G — + 1	Match No.
1	2	3	4	5	6	7	8	9	10	11	12												1
1		3	4	5	10	2	8	9	7	11	14	6	12										2
1	8	3	4	5	10	12		9	7	11		6		2									3
1	2	12	4	5	6	7	8	9	10	11			14	3									4
1	2		4	5	6	7		9	10	11			14	3	8								5
1	2				6	7	12	9	10	11	14	5		3	8	4							6
1	2		4			7	6	9	10	11	14	5		3	8		12						7
1	2		4	5	6	7		14	10	11				3	8		9						8
1	2		4	5	6	7		12	10	11		14		3	8		9						9
1	2		4		6	7	12	11	10		14	5		3	8		9						10
1	2	14	4		6	7	8	12		11		5		3	10		9						11
1	3	14	4		10	2		12	7	11		5		6	8		9						12
1	2	11	4		6	7	14	12	10	8		5		3			9	15					13
1		11	4	14	6	2		12	7	10		5		3	8		9						14
1	2	12	4		6	7		14	10	11		5		3	8		9						15
1	2	14	4		6	7		11	10	12		5		3	8		9						16
1	2	14	4		6	7	8	11	10	12		5		3			9						17
1	2	14	4		6	7		12	10	11		5		3	8		9						18
1	2	3	4		6	7		12	10	11		5			8		9						19
1	2	14	4		6	7	8	12		11		5		3	10		9						20
1	2	3	12	5	6	7		11	10					4	8		9		14				21
1	2		4	5	6	7		11	10	14		3			8		9						22
1	2	14	4	5	6	7		11	10	12		3			8		9						23
1	2	3	4		6	7	8	9	10	11	14	5					12						24
1	2	14	4		6	7	8	9	10	11		5		3			12						25
1	2		4	5	6	7		12	10	11	14			3	8		9						26
1	2	12	4	5	6	7		10		11	14			3	8		9						27
1	2	14	4	5	6	7		11	10	12				3	8		9						28
1		2	4		6	7		11	10	12	14	5		3	8		9						29
1		2	4		6	7	8	12	10	11		5		3			9		14				30
1	2	14	4		6	7		11	10	12		5		3	8		9						31
1	2	14	4		6	7		11	10	12		5		3	8		9						32
1	2	3	4			7		6	10	11	14	5			8		9						33
1	2		4			7		6	10	11	12	5		3	8		9						34
1	2	11		4			8	6	10		7			3			9		12	5			35
	2	14		4			6	9	10		11			3				1	7	8	5	12	36

ALBION ROVERS — Third Division

Year Formed: 1882. *Ground & Address:* Cliftonhill Stadium, Main St, Coatbridge ML5 3RB. *Telephone:* 01236 432350.
Ground capacity: total: 1238, seated: 538. *Size of Pitch:* 110yd × 70yd.
Chairman: Robin W Marwick. *Secretary:* D. Forrester CA. *Commercial Manager:* Laurie Cameron. *Manager:* Jim Crease
Coach: Joe McBride. *Physio:* Michael McBride. *Managers since 1975:* G. Caldwell; S. Goodwin; H. Hood; J. Baker; D. Whiteford; M. Ferguson; W. Wilson; B. Rooney; A. Ritchie; T. Gemmell; D. Provan; M. Oliver; B. McLaren; T. Gemmell; T Spence. *Club Nickname(s):* The Wee Rovers. *Previous Grounds:* Cowheath Park, Meadow Park, Whifflet.
Record Attendance: 27,381 v Rangers, Scottish Cup 2nd rd; 8 Feb, 1936.
Record Transfer Fee received: £40,000 from Motherwell for Bruce Cleland.
Record Transfer Fee paid: £7000 for Gerry McTeague to Stirling Albion, September 1989.
Record Victory: 12-0 v Airdriehill, Scottish Cup; 3 Sept, 1887.
Record Defeat: 1-11 v Partick T, League Cup, 11 August 1993.
Most Capped Player: Jock White, 1 (2), Scotland.
Most League Appearances: 399, Murdy Walls, 1921-36.

ALBION ROVERS 1994–95 LEAGUE RECORD

Match No.	Date	Venue	Opponents	Result		H/T Score	Lg. Pos.	Goalscorers	Attendance
1	Aug 13	H	Alloa	L	0-4	0-3	—		310
2	20	H	Montrose	L	2-4	1-2	9	Scott, Seggie	274
3	27	A	Queen's Park	L	1-2	1-0	9	McBride J	443
4	Sept 3	H	Caledonian Th	L	0-1	0-0	10		539
5	10	A	East Stirling	L	0-4	0-2	10		377
6	24	H	Cowdenbeath	L	2-4	1-1	10	Conn, Quinn	314
7	Oct 1	A	Forfar Ath	D	1-1	0-0	10	Deeley	424
8	8	H	Arbroath	L	1-2	0-0	10	Conn	315
9	15	A	Ross C	L	0-3	0-0	10		1017
10	22	A	Alloa	L	0-1	0-0	10		440
11	29	H	Queen's Park	W	3-2	1-1	10	Kerr, McBride J 2	345
12	Nov 5	A	Montrose	L	1-4	0-2	10	McBride J	629
13	12	H	East Stirling	L	0-2	0-1	10		361
14	19	A	Caledonian Th	L	1-2	0-0	10	Scott	954
15	26	A	Cowdenbeath	D	2-2	2-1	10	Scott, Young	380
16	Dec 3	H	Forfar Ath	L	0-1	0-0	10		303
17	24	A	Arbroath	W	1-0	1-0	10	Ryan	467
18	31	H	Ross C	L	0-1	0-0	10		354
19	Jan 2	A	Queen's Park	D	0-0	0-0	—		705
20	14	H	Alloa	L	0-1	0-0	10		400
21	Feb 11	H	Caledonian Th	L	1-2	0-1	10	McBride J	274
22	18	H	Cowdenbeath	W	2-0	0-0	10	Ryan, Scott	273
23	25	A	Forfar Ath	L	0-4	0-3	10		510
24	Mar 4	A	Arbroath	L	0-2	0-0	10		436
25	7	A	East Stirling	L	0-3	0-1	—		312
26	22	H	Montrose	L	1-4	0-2	—	McEwan	187
27	29	A	Ross C	L	1-4	0-1	—	Seggie	967
28	Apr 1	H	Forfar Ath	L	0-3	0-2	10		270
29	5	H	East Stirling	W	3-1	1-0	—	Scott 2, Young	211
30	8	A	Cowdenbeath	L	0-2	0-0	10		186
31	11	A	Caledonian Th	W	2-0	1-0	—	Thompson, Scott	524
32	15	H	Arbroath	L	0-3	0-0	10		214
33	22	H	Ross C	L	1-2	1-1	10	Wilcox	334
34	29	A	Alloa	L	0-5	0-1	10		324
35	May 6	H	Queen's Park	L	0-2	0-1	10		337
36	13	A	Montrose	L	1-4	0-3	10	McEwan	893

Final League Position: 10

Most League Goals in Season (Individual): 41: Jim Renwick, Division II; 1932-33.
Most Goals Overall (Individual): 105: Bunty Weir, 1928-31.

Honours
League Champions: Division II 1933-34, Second Division 1988-89; *Runners-up:* Division II 1913-14, 1937-38, 1947-48.
Scottish Cup Runners-up: 1920. *League Cup:* —.
Club Colours: Shirt: Yellow with red trim. Shorts: Yellow. Stockings: Yellow.

Goalscorers: *League (27):* Scott 7, McBride J 5, Conn 2, McEwan 2, Ryan 2, Seggie 2, Young 2, Deeley 1, Kerr 1, Quinn 1, Thompson 1, Wilcox 1. *Scottish Cup (2):* Docherty 1, McBride J 1. *League Cup (0) B&Q Cup (0)*

Davidson A 21	McDonald D 18 + 1	Beattie J 10 + 1	Conn S 7	Malone P 4	Collins L 16 + 1	McBride M 22 + 4	Docherty A 7 + 3	Thompson D 18 + 2	Quinn K 7 + 4	Gallagher J 26	Seggie D 12 + 7	McBride J 31 + 4	Wight J 15 + 2	Philliben R 4	Riley D 6 + 1	Scott M 33 + 1	Tomnay D 1	Young G 12 + 7	Deeley B 20 + 2	Parry K 3 + 1	Kelly J 14	Ryan M 29	Miller D — + 2	Kerr J 12	Shah S 9	Dolan W 16 + 1	Miller S 1	McEwan A 10 + 2	Brown M 1	Arthur R 2	Wilcox D 9	*Match No.*
1	2	3	4	5	6	7	8	9	*10*	11	12	14	15																			1
1	5	*3*	4		8			11	10	6	12	14		2	7	9																2
1		3	10	4	6		8					11		2	7		5	9	14													3
1	4		5	6	8		7				12	11		2		9		10		3												4
					8		7				12	11	1	2		9		10	6	3	4	5	14									5
1	2		3		8	7			10		12	11				9			6		5			4								6
1			3		8	7			10		*11*	14				9			6		2	5		4								7
1			3		8	7			10		11					9		12	6		2	5		4								8
1	4					7		14	*10*	6	11	12			8	9			3		2	5										9
1				*8*		7	14	10	12	6		11				9			4	3	2	5										10
1						7	6	10				11				9			3		2	5		4	8							11
1					12	7	6	10				*11*				9		14	3		2	5		4	8							12
1					8	7		10				11				9			3		2	5		4	6							13
1					8	7	14	10				9				11		12	3		2	5		*4*	6							14
1	14				8					3		9				11		10			7	5		*4*	6	2						15
1	4					12				3		9	15			11		10	6		2	5			8	7						16
1	2				6	10				3		9				11						5		4	8	7						17
	2				6	11				3		9	1			12		10	14			5		4	*8*	7						18
	2				6					3	12	9	1			11		10				5		4		7	8					19
					6	7				3		9	1			11		12				5		4	8	2		10				20
1	4					7	14			3	11	8			*6*	9										2		10	5			21
1	4					7				3	11	8				9		12			6	5				2		10				22
1		4				7		14		3	11	8				9		12			6	5				2		*10*				23
1	4	*6*				12	10	7		3		8	15			*9*		11				5						14		2		24
	4				10			*7*		3		8	1		6	9						5				14		11		2		25
1	4	5				12		7		3	11	8				9			6							2		10				26
		4						7		3	11	8	1		*6*	9		12		14		5				2		10				27
		6				14		7		3	11	8	1			9						5				2		10			4	28
						11		7		3		8	1			9		10	6			5				2		12			4	29
						11		7		3		8	1			9		10	6			5				2					4	30
		11						7	12	3		8	1			9		10	6			5				2					4	31
		11						7		3	12	8	1			9		10	6			5				2					4	32
	2					11		7	10	3		8	1		12	9			6			5									4	33
	2	14				10		7	12	3	11	8	1			9			6			5									4	34
	2					7			12	3	11	8	1			9			6			5	14					10			4	35
	2					7				3	11	8	1			9			6			5						10			4	36

ALLOA Third Division

Year Formed: 1883. *Ground & Address:* Recreation Park, Clackmannan Rd, Alloa FK10 1RR. *Telephone:* 01259 722695.
Ground Capacity: total: 4100, seated: 424. *Size of Pitch:* 110yd × 75yd.
Chairman: Pat Lawlor. *Secretary:* E. G. Cameron. *Commercial Manager:* William McKie.
Manager: Pat Macaulay. *Assistant Manager:* Jim Dempsey. *Physio:* Alan Anderson.
Managers since 1975: H. Wilson; A. Totten; W. Garner; J. Thomson; D. Sullivan; G. Abel; B. Little; H. McCann; W. Lamont. *Club Nickname(s):* The Wasps. *Previous Grounds:* None.
Record Attendance: 13,000 v Dunfermline Athletic, Scottish Cup 3rd rd replay; 26 Feb, 1939.
Record Transfer Fee received: £60,000 for Paul Sheerin to Southampton (1992).
Record Transfer Fee paid: £10,000 for Douglas Lawrie from Stirling Albion.
Record Victory: 9-2 v Forfar Ath, Division II; 18 Mar, 1933.
Record Defeat: 0-10 v Dundee, Division II; 8 Mar, 1947: v Third Lanark, League Cup, 8 Aug, 1953.
Most Capped Player: Jock Hepburn, 1, Scotland.
Most League Appearances: —.

ALLOA 1994–95 LEAGUE RECORD

Match No.	Date	Venue	Opponents	Result		H/T Score	Lg. Pos.	Goalscorers	Attendance
1	Aug 13	A	Albion R	W	4-0	3-0	—	Nelson, McCormick S, McCulloch, Moffat	310
2	20	A	Forfar Ath	L	2-3	0-2	4	Newbigging, McCulloch	540
3	27	H	East Stirling	L	1-3	0-1	7	Newbigging	404
4	Sept 3	A	Ross C	D	3-3	2-3	7	McAnenay 3	1457
5	10	H	Arbroath	W	3-1	2-0	6	Lamont, McAnenay 2	473
6	24	H	Caledonian Th	D	1-1	1-0	6	Moffat	590
7	Oct 1	A	Cowdenbeath	W	3-1	1-0	5	Moffat, McAnenay, Black (og)	368
8	8	H	Montrose	D	1-1	1-0	6	Lamont	460
9	15	A	Queen's Park	W	1-0	1-0	5	Moffat	520
10	22	H	Albion R	W	1-0	0-0	4	Lamont	440
11	29	A	East Stirling	W	2-1	1-0	3	Moffat, Kemp	570
12	Nov 5	H	Forfar Ath	L	0-1	0-1	4		525
13	12	A	Arbroath	D	0-0	0-0	5		414
14	19	H	Ross C	D	1-1	0-0	6	Lawrie	479
15	26	A	Caledonian Th	D	2-2	0-1	6	Moffat, McAnenay	1039
16	Dec 3	H	Cowdenbeath	W	1-0	0-0	5	McAvoy	462
17	24	A	Montrose	W	2-1	2-0	4	McAvoy, Diver	641
18	31	H	Queen's Park	L	2-3	2-2	4	Lamont, Moffat	541
19	Jan 14	A	Albion R	W	1-0	0-0	5	McCulloch	400
20	24	H	Forfar Ath	L	0-2	0-2	—		498
21	Feb 4	H	Arbroath	W	3-2	1-1	3	Diver 3	384
22	7	H	East Stirling	L	0-1	0-0	—		395
23	11	A	Ross C	L	0-6	0-2	4		1686
24	18	H	Caledonian Th	W	1-0	1-0	4	Lamont	386
25	25	A	Cowdenbeath	W	3-1	2-1	3	Diver, Moffat, Bennett	260
26	Mar 11	A	Queen's Park	L	1-2	0-2	3	Moffat	506
27	18	A	Arbroath	L	1-2	0-1	4	Diver	464
28	25	H	Ross C	D	1-1	1-1	4	McCulloch	535
29	28	H	Montrose	L	0-1	0-0	—		416
30	Apr 1	H	Cowdenbeath	W	2-1	0-1	5	McCulloch, Cadden	367
31	8	A	Caledonian Th	W	1-0	1-0	5	Wylie	912
32	15	A	Montrose	D	0-0	0-0	5		649
33	22	H	Queen's Park	L	0-1	0-0	5		421
34	29	H	Albion R	W	5-0	1-0	5	Moffat 4, Conway	324
35	May 6	A	East Stirling	D	1-1	1-1	5	Diver	418
36	13	A	Forfar Ath	L	0-2	0-2	5		655

Final League Position: 5

Most League Goals in Season (Individual): 49: William 'Wee' Crilley, Division II; 1921-22.
Most Goals Overall (Individual): —.

Honours
League Champions: Division II 1921-22; *Runners-up:* Division II 1938-39. Second Division 1976-77, 1981-82, 1984-85, 1988-89.
Scottish Cup: —.
League Cup: —.
Club colours: Shirt: Gold with black trim. Shorts: Black. Stockings: Gold.

Goalscorers: *League (50):* Moffat 13, Diver 7, McAnenay 7, Lamont 5, McCulloch 5, McAvoy 2, Newbigging 2, Bennett 1, Cadden 1, Conway 1, Kemp 1, Lawrie 1, McCormick S 1, Nelson 1, Wylie 1, own goal 1. *Scottish Cup (2):* Diver 1, Lamont 1. *League Cup (1):* Morrison 1. *B&Q Cup (2):* McAnenay 1, Moffat 1.

Butter J 36	McMillan T 1	Kemp B 20 + 4	Campbell C 3	McCulloch K 28 + 1	Newbigging W 29	Nelson M 17 + 8	McCormack J 34	McCormick S 2	Bennett N 28 + 2	Morrison S 5	McNiven J 1 + 1	Moffat B 28 + 3	Lamont P 21 + 5	Diver D 19 + 8	McAnenay M 17 + 4	McAvoy N 6 + 1	Graham P — + 1	Lawrie D 21 + 2	Cadden S 22	Willock A 3 + 9	Hannah K 13 + 2	Wylie R 11	Whyte M 10 + 4	Conway V 6 + 1	Kirkham D 3 + 4	Cully D 1	Bell D 5	Rixon S 6	Match No.
1	2	3	4	5	6	7	8	9	*10*	11	12	14																	1
1		3	4	12	5	10	6	9	8	11	2	14	*7*																2
1		3	4	5	6	8	2		10	11		14	7	*9*	12														3
1		12		5	6	4	2		3	8			11	9	7	10													4
1		3			5	4	2		6	8		9	11	12	7	*10*	14												5
1		3		5	4	7	2		8			10	14	9	12	*11*		6											6
1		3		5	4	10	2					9	11		7			6	8										7
1		3		5	4	10	2					9	11		7			6	8										8
1		3		5	4	10	2					*9*	11	12	7			6	8	14									9
1		3		5	4	6	2		11			9	*12*	10	7				8	14									10
1		3		5	4	12	2		11			9		10	*7*			6	8	14									11
1		3		5	4	2			11			9	7	10	12			*6*	8	14									12
1		3		5	4	7	2					10	11	9	12			6	*8*	14									13
1		*3*		5	4	8	2		10			9	11	12	7	14		6											14
1		14		5	4		2		11			9	12	10	7			6	8		*3*								15
1					4	6	2		3			9	11	12	7	*10*		5	8		14								16
1		6					4		3				11	9		10		5	8	7	2								17
1		*3*		5			4		14			9	10			7		6	8	11	2								18
1		3		5	6		4		14			10	11	9	7				8	12	*2*								19
1		3		5	4	14	2		10			*9*	11	8	7			6		12									20
1		3		5	4		2		10			9	11	12						14	8	6	*7*						21
1		3		5	4		2		10			9	12	11							8	6	7						22
1		10		5	4	12	2		3			9	*11*	7				6	8	14									23
1		12		5		4	2					10	11	*9*					8		3	6	7	14					24
1		12		5		14	4		3			10	11	9					8		*2*	6	7						25
1				5		10	4		3			9						12	*8*	11	2	6	7		14				26
1				5		14	4		8			9		10				12			2	6	11		7	*3*			27
1				4		12	2		3			9	11	7	10			5				6					8		28
1				5	4		2		3				11	12	7			6			*8*		14				10	9	29
1				5	4		2		3			9			7			*6*	8		12		11		14		10		30
1					4	14	3								7			5	8		2	*6*	9	11	12		10		31
1				5	4		2		11			10	14		7			6				*8*	12	3				9	32
1				5	4		2		10					12				6	7				11	3			8	9	33
1					4	*5*			11			10		12				6	8		2		7	3	14			9	34
1					4		2		11			10		7					8			6	12	3	5			9	35
1					4	14	2		11			10		7					8			*6*	12	3	5			9	36

ARBROATH Third Division

Year Formed: 1878. *Ground & Address:* Gayfield Park, Arbroath DD11 1QB. *Telephone:* 01241 872157.
Ground Capacity: 6488. seated: 715. *Size of Pitch:* 115yd × 71yd.
President: John D. Christison. *Secretary:* Charles Kinnear. *Commercial Manager:* Sandy Watt.
Manager: John Brogan. *Physio:* William Shearer. *Coach:* Jim Kerr.
Managers since 1975: A. Henderson; I. J. Stewart; G. Fleming; J. Bone; J. Young; W. Borthwick; M. Lawson, D. McGrain MBE, J. Scott.
Club Nickname(s): The Red Lichties. *Previous Grounds:* None.
Record Attendance: 13,510 v Rangers, Scottish Cup 3rd rd; 23 Feb, 1952.
Record Transfer Fee received: £120,000 for Paul Tosh to Dundee (Aug 1993).
Record Transfer Fee paid: £20,000 for Douglas Robb from Montrose (1981).
Record Victory: 36-0 v Bon Accord, Scottish Cup 1st rd; 12 Sept, 1885.
Record Defeat: 1-9 v Celtic, League Cup 3rd rd; 25 Aug 1993.
Most Capped Player: Ned Doig, 2 (5), Scotland.
Most League Appearances: 445: Tom Cargill, 1966-81.

ARBROATH 1994–95 LEAGUE RECORD

Match No.	Date	Venue	Opponents	Result		H/T Score	Lg. Pos.	Goalscorers	Attendance
1	Aug 13	A	Caledonian Th	L	2-5	0-3	—	Farnan, Reilly	1855
2	20	A	Cowdenbeath	L	2-6	0-4	10	Reilly, Tosh	315
3	27	H	Forfar Ath	L	0-1	0-0	10		691
4	Sept 3	H	Queen's Park	D	1-1	1-0	9	Tosh	535
5	10	A	Alloa	L	1-3	0-2	9	Downie	473
6	24	A	Ross C	W	4-1	1-0	9	Reid (og), Tosh 3	1320
7	Oct 1	H	Montrose	L	0-3	0-1	9		802
8	8	A	Albion R	W	2-1	0-0	9	Craib, Florence	315
9	15	H	East Stirling	L	0-1	0-0	9		404
10	22	H	Caledonian Th	L	1-2	0-1	9	Elder	542
11	29	A	Forfar Ath	L	0-3	0-0	9		721
12	Nov 5	H	Cowdenbeath	L	0-3	0-3	9		426
13	12	H	Alloa	D	0-0	0-0	9		414
14	19	A	Queen's Park	W	4-0	2-0	9	Murray 2, Scott 2	407
15	26	H	Ross C	L	0-1	0-0	9		568
16	Dec 3	A	Montrose	L	1-3	0-1	9	Craib	1085
17	24	H	Albion R	L	0-1	0-1	9		467
18	31	A	East Stirling	L	0-1	0-0	9		436
19	Jan 14	A	Caledonian Th	D	1-1	0-0	9	Murray	1038
20	21	H	Cowdenbeath	L	0-3	0-1	9		388
21	28	H	Forfar Ath	D	1-1	1-1	9	Shanks	802
22	Feb 4	A	Alloa	L	2-3	1-1	9	Pew, Brock	384
23	15	H	Queen's Park	W	3-1	1-1	—	Porteous 2, Gardner	347
24	18	A	Ross C	W	1-0	1-0	9	Gardner	1648
25	25	H	Montrose	W	4-1	2-1	9	Tosh, Gardner, Scott 2	951
26	Mar 4	H	Albion R	W	2-0	0-0	8	Pew, Scott	436
27	11	H	East Stirling	W	5-2	3-0	8	Scott, Tosh 3, McMillan	596
28	18	H	Alloa	W	2-1	1-0	8	Porteous, Tosh	464
29	25	A	Queen's Park	W	3-2	1-1	8	Tosh, Pew, Gardner	616
30	Apr 1	A	Montrose	L	0-5	0-4	8		1179
31	8	H	Ross C	L	0-1	0-0	8		680
32	15	A	Albion R	W	3-0	0-0	8	McMillan, Pew, Lindsay	214
33	22	A	East Stirling	W	2-0	1-0	7	Porteous, Pew	414
34	29	H	Caledonian Th	W	2-0	0-0	6	Gardner 2	492
35	May 6	A	Forfar Ath	L	1-4	0-3	7	Florence	1069
36	13	A	Cowdenbeath	D	1-1	1-1	7	Farnan	200

Final League Position: 7

Most League Goals in Season (Individual): 45: Dave Easson, Division II; 1958-59.
Most Goals Overall (Individual): 120: Jimmy Jack; 1966-71.

Honours
League Champions Runners-up: Division II 1934-35, 1958-59, 1967-68, 1971-72.
Scottish Cup: Quarter-finals: 1993.
League Cup: —.
Club colours: Shirt: Maroon with sky blue trim. Shorts: White. Stockings: Maroon with sky blue hooped tops.

Goalscorers: *League (51):* Tosh 11, Gardner 6, Scott 6, Pew 5, Porteous 4, Murray 3, Craib 2, Farnan 2, Florence 2, McMillan 2, Reilly 2, Brock 1, Downie 1, Elder 1, Lindsay 1, Shanks 1, own goal 1. *Scottish Cup (0) League Cup (2):* McKinnon 1, Reilly 1. *B&Q Cup (0)*

Jackson D 8 + 1	Mitchell B 2	Dickson A 2	Elder S 18 + 7	Farnan C 31 + 3	Murray M 24	Downie I 6 + 5	Reilly J 3	Brock J 7 + 3	Tosh S 29 + 2	McGovern J 3 + 1	McKinnon C 1 + 2	Elliot D 9 + 10	Middleton A 16 + 4	Shanks D 22 + 1	Craib S 10 + 5	Duncan R 2	Spittal I 25	McGregor S 1 + 1	Florence S 18	Lindsay J 10 + 4	Dunn G 25	McMillan T 27	Benvie G 1	Scott B 14 + 8	Binnie G — + 1	Gardner R 22 + 1	Heggie A 3 + 1	Hendry M 1	Ward J 5	Scott L 1	Martin M 3	Pew D 14	Kerr J 10	Porteous I 14	Martin E 2	Crawford J 7	*Match No.*
1	2	3	4	5	6	7	*8*	9	10	11	12	14																									1
1	3	2	*4*	5	6	7	9	12	10	11	8	14																									2
1			5	2	6		9	12	10	8		7	3	4	11																						3
			8	2	6	7		9	10		12		3	4	11	1	5																				4
			8	2	4	7		9	10	14			3	6	11	1	5	12																			5
1			12	7	4			9	10				3	6	14		5	*11*	2	8																	6
1			14	8	4	12			10			*9*	3	6	11		5		2	7																	7
			11	8	6				*10*			14		4	12		5		3	7	1	2	9														8
			11	6	4	12								8	*10*		5		3	7	1	2		9	14												9
			11		4				7			12	6	8	14		5		3		1	2		*9*		10											10
			9	14	4	12			7				11	*6*	8		5		3		1	2				10											11
			8	4	6				7								5		3		1	2		12		10	9	11									12
15			6		8				7			14					5		3		*1*	2		*9*		11	10		4								13
			6	11	8							9					5		3		1	2		14		7	*10*		4								14
			6	*11*	8				10			9					5		3		1	2		14		7	12		4								15
			6	12	8				10			*11*	3		14		5				1	2				7			4	9							16
				8	6	11			10			7	3		9		4				1	2		12		5											17
				8	5	11			*9*			7	3	14	10		6				1	2				12			4								18
			4	8	6			9	10					7	11		5			12	1	2		14							3						19
			4	7	6			9				12	14	8	11		5			*10*	1	2									3						20
			6	7	4			*9*	11				3	8	14		5				1	2				10											21
1			10	7	4	14		12	11					*8*			5					2				6					3	9					22
				11					12			7		4			5		3		1			2		10						9	6	8			23
				4		14			12			*7*		5					3		1	2		11		10						9	6	8			24
				4					7			12	14	5					*3*		1	2		11		10						9	6	8			25
				4					*7*			12	3	5						14	1	2		11		10							9	6	8		26
				4					*7*			12	3	5						14	1	2		11		10						9	6	8			27
				4					7				3	5							1	2		11		10						9	6	8			28
			14	4	2				7			12	*3*	5										11		10						9	6	8	1		29
1			14	4	3				7					5								2		*11*								9	6	8		10	30
1			12	4					7					5						10		2		11								9	6	8		3	31
				12					7								5		3	4	1	2		14		10						*9*	6	8		11	32
				4					7								5		3	11	1	2		14		10						*9*		8		6	33
			14	4									12				5		3	11	1	2		*7*		10						9		8		6	34
			14	4									12				5		3	*11*	1	2		7		10						9		8		6	35
				4					7				*11*				5		3	12	1	2		14		10						9		8		6	36

AYR UNITED

Second Division

Year Formed: 1910. *Ground & Address:* Somerset Park, Tryfield Place, Ayr KA8 9NB. *Telephone:* 01292 263435.
Ground Capacity: 13,918. seated: 1450. *Size of Pitch:* 110yd × 72yd.
Chairman: D. M. MacIntyre. *Secretary:* J. E. Eyley. *Commercial Manager:* Sandy Kerr.
Manager: Simon Stainrod. *Assistant Manager:* Malcolm Shotton.
Managers since 1975: Alex Stuart; Ally MacLeod; Willie McLean; George Caldwell; Ally MacLeod; George Burley. *Club Nickname(s):* The Honest Men. *Previous Grounds:* None.
Record Attendance: 25,225 v Rangers, Division I; 13 Sept, 1969.
eltic*Record Transfer Fee received:* £300,000 for Steven Nicol to Liverpool (Oct 1981).
Record Transfer Fee paid: £50,000 for Peter Weir from St Mirren, June 1990.
Record Victory: 11-1 v Dumbarton, League Cup; 13 Aug, 1952.
Record Defeat: 0-9 in Division I v Rangers (1929); v Hearts (1931); v Third Lanark (1954).
Most Capped Player: Jim Nisbet, 3, Scotland.
Most League Appearances: 371: Ian McAllister, 1977-90.

AYR UNITED 1994–95 LEAGUE RECORD

Match No.	Date	Venue	Opponents	Result		H/T Score	Lg. Pos.	Goalscorers	Attendance
1	Aug 13	H	Hamilton A	D	1-1	0-1	—	Traynor	2097
2	20	H	St Mirren	D	1-1	0-0	4	Bilsland	2787
3	27	A	Stranraer	L	1-2	1-0	7	McGivern	1653
4	Sept 3	H	St Johnstone	L	3-4	0-2	10	Stainrod, Traynor, Gilzean	2367
5	10	A	Airdrieonians	D	0-0	0-0	10		1620
6	24	H	Dundee	W	3-2	2-1	7	Jackson 2, George	1901
7	Oct 1	A	Raith R	L	0-3	0-1	9		2854
8	8	A	Clydebank	L	0-3	0-1	9		891
9	15	H	Dunfermline Ath	D	0-0	0-0	9		2302
10	22	A	Hamilton A	L	0-2	0-2	9		1066
11	29	H	Stranraer	W	2-1	1-1	8	Burns 2	2073
12	Nov 5	A	St Mirren	L	0-1	0-1	9		2482
13	12	H	Airdrieonians	L	0-3	0-2	9		2210
14	19	A	St Johnstone	L	0-1	0-1	9		2755
15	26	A	Dundee	D	1-1	0-1	9	Hood	2506
16	Dec 3	H	Raith R	D	1-1	1-0	9	Hood	2216
17	10	A	Dunfermline Ath	L	0-6	0-2	9		3197
18	26	H	Clydebank	D	1-1	1-0	—	Gorgues	1969
19	31	H	Hamilton A	L	1-2	1-2	9	Dowe	2079
20	Jan 2	A	Stranraer	L	0-2	0-1	—		1899
21	7	H	St Mirren	W	2-0	1-0	9=	Rolling, Bilsland	2237
22	14	H	St Johnstone	L	1-3	1-0	10	Jackson	1955
23	24	A	Airdrieonians	D	2-2	1-1	—	Gilzean, Rolling	1320
24	Feb 4	A	Raith R	L	1-2	0-1	9	Moore	2799
25	11	H	Dundee	W	1-0	1-0	8	Moore	2042
26	25	H	Dunfermline Ath	L	1-2	0-1	8	McCathie (og)	2183
27	Mar 11	A	Clydebank	D	1-1	0-0	9	Hood	720
28	18	H	Airdrieonians	L	0-2	0-0	9		1372
29	25	A	St Johnstone	D	1-1	0-1	9	Tannock	3551
30	Apr 1	H	Raith R	L	0-1	0-1	9		1995
31	8	A	Dundee	D	1-1	0-1	9	Burns	2765
32	15	H	Clydebank	W	1-0	1-0	9	Gilzean	1798
33	22	A	Dunfermline Ath	L	0-3	0-1	9		4808
34	29	A	Hamilton A	L	0-1	0-0	9		1073
35	May 6	H	Stranraer	W	3-0	1-0	9	Tannock, Jackson, Stainrod	1204
36	13	A	St Mirren	L	1-2	1-1	9	Bilsland	2179

Final League Position: 9

Most League Goals in Season (Individual): 66: Jimmy Smith, 1927-28.
Most Goals Overall (Individual): —.

Honours
League Champions: Division II 1911-12, 1912-13, 1927-28, 1936-37, 1958-59, 1965-66. Second Division 1987-88;
Runners-up: Division II 1910-11, 1955-56, 1968-69.
Scottish Cup: —. *League Cup:* —.
*B&Q Cup: Runners-up:*1990-91, 1991-92.
Club colours: Shirt: White with black sleeves. Shorts: Black. Stockings: White.

Goalscorers: *League (31):* Jackson 4, Bilsland 3, Burns 3, Gilzean 3, Hood 3, Moore 2, Rolling 2, Stainrod 2, Tannock 2, Traynor 2, Dowe 1, George 1, Gorgues 1, McGivern 1, own goal 1. *Scottish Cup (0) League Cup (0) B&Q Cup (5):* Burns 2, George 1, Jackson 1, Paterson 1.

Duncan C 29	Burns H 23	McVicar D 5	Paterson G 10 + 1	Rolling F 33	Sharples J 27	Moore V 13 + 4	McKilligan N 30 + 4	McGivern S 9 + 2	Gilzean I 21 + 2	Bilsland B 11 + 7	Traynor J 9 + 2	Woods T — + 3	Connie C 20 + 1	Stainrod S 15 + 4	McIntosh S 6 + 2	Biggart K 22 + 1	Tannock R 11 + 3	George D 29	Gorgues R 18 + 1	Jackson J 18 + 9	Hood G 15	Spence W 1	Lamont L 1	Nylen N 2	Valetta C 3 + 2	Murray B 1	Fortes J 1 + 1	Dowe J 4 + 3	Grierson G — + 1	Gribben K 4	McFarlane C 3	Agnew S 1 + 1	Okorie K — + 1	Connelly S 1 + 3	*Match No.*
1	2	3	4	5	6	7	8	9	10	*11*	12	14																							1
1	2	3	4	5	6		8	9	*10*	12	7		11	14																					2
1	2	3	4	5		14	6	*9*	10	*8*	7	12	11		15																				3
	2	3	12	5	4		*8*		9	14	6			10	1	7	11																		4
1	2	3	4	5				9	11	12	8			10				6	7																5
1	2		4	5		8					7		3	10				6	11	9															6
1	7		4	5		*8*	10				2	12	3			14		6	11	9															7
1	7		4	5		8	2	14						*10*		3		6	11	9															8
1	7			5		8	14	*9*			2			10		3		6	11	12	4														9
	7		6	5		8	14							10		2		11	3	12	4	1	*9*												10
1	7		9	5		8	2							14		3		6	11	*10*	4														11
1	7		9	5		8	14	12								3		6	11					2	*4*	10									12
1	7			5	4		12	9		14						3		6	11					2	8		*10*								13
1	7			5	6		11	9						*10*		2		8	3		4				12		14								14
1	7			5	6	14	11	9					3			*2*		8		10	4				12										15
1	7			5	6	11	2	*9*					3	14				8		10	4														16
	2			5	6		11		12				3	10	*1*			8		9					4			7	15						17
1	7			5	6		2		9				3					8	11	12	4							10							18
1				5	6		2		9				3			*7*	14	8	11	12	4							10							19
1				5	6	14	2		9				*3*					8	11	12	4							10		7					20
1				5	6	12	2		9	14			3					8	11	*10*	4									7					21
1				5	6		2		9	12			3						11	10	4							14		7	8				22
1				5	4	*8*	2		9	12			3				14		11	10										7	6				23
1				5	4	8	2		9	7			3	14			11			*10*											6				24
1				5	6	8	2		9	7				10		3		11		12	4														25
1				5	6		2		*9*	7			12	10		3	8	11		14	4														26
1				5	6		2		9	7				10		3		11		8	4														27
1				5	6		2		9	7	14			*10*		3	12	11		8	4														28
1	7				6		2		*9*	10	5		11			3	4	8		14												12			29
1	7				6		2		*9*	10	5					3	4	8		14												11	12		30
1	2			5	6		7		9						15	3	8	4	*11*	10															31
	2			5	6		7		9				11		1	3	8	4		10														12	32
	2				6		5		*9*				11		1	3	8	4	12	10								14						7	33
1				5	6		7						3	10		2	4	8	*11*	9								14							34
				5	6		7			11			3	*10*	1	2	8	4		9														14	35
				5	6	11	7		14	9			3	10	1	2	*8*	4																12	36

BERWICK RANGERS Second Division

Year Formed: 1881. *Ground & Address:* Shielfield Park, Tweedmouth, Berwick-upon-Tweed TD15 2EF. *Telephone:* 01289 307424. Club 24 hour hotline 01891 800697. *Ground Capacity:* 4131. seated: 1366. *Size of Pitch:* 112yd × 76yd.
Chairman: Roy McDowell. *Vice-chairman:* Tom Davidson. *Company Secretary:* Colin Walker. *Club Secretary:* Dennis McCleary.
Team Manager: Tom Hendrie. *Assistant Manager:* John Coughlin. *Physio/Coach:* Ian Oliver. *Youth Coaches:* Tom Smith, Warren Hawke
Managers since 1975: H. Melrose; G. Haig; W. Galbraith; D. Smith; F. Connor; J. McSherry; E. Tait; J. Thomson; J. Jefferies; J. Anderson, J. Crease.
Club Nickname(s): The Borderers. *Previous Grounds:* Bull Stob Close, Pier Field, Meadow Field, Union Park, Old Shielfield.
Record Attendance: 13,365 v Rangers, Scottish Cup 1st rd; 28 Jan, 1967.
Record Victory: 8-1 v Forfar Ath. Division II; 25 Dec, 1965; v Vale of Leithen, Scottish Cup; Dec, 1966.
Record Defeat: 1-9 v Hamilton A, First Division; 9 Aug, 1980.
Most Capped Player: —.

BERWICK RANGERS 1994–95 LEAGUE RECORD

Match No.	Date		Venue	Opponents	Result		H/T Score	Lg. Pos.	Goalscorers	Attendance
1	Aug	13	A	Morton	D	1-1	0-0	—	Irvine	1454
2		20	A	Brechin C	W	2-1	2-1	1	Irvine, Fraser	539
3		27	H	Queen of the S	W	1-0	0-0	1	Banks	610
4	Sept	3	A	Clyde	W	4-3	1-0	1	Banks, Forrester, Hawke, Irvine	1141
5		10	H	Dumbarton	W	1-0	0-0	1	Banks	533
6		24	A	Stenhousemuir	D	1-1	0-1	1	Irvine	373
7	Oct	1	H	East Fife	D	1-1	1-1	1	Irvine	573
8		8	H	Meadowbank T	W	2-1	2-1	1	Hawke, Neil	520
9		15	A	Stirling Albion	L	2-3	1-1	2	Hawke, Irvine	863
10		22	H	Morton	W	2-1	1-0	1	Hawke 2	738
11		29	A	Queen of the S	L	4-5	1-3	1	Irvine, Hawke 2, Neil	1298
12	Nov	5	H	Brechin C	W	2-1	1-1	1	Banks 2 (1 pen)	478
13		12	A	Dumbarton	L	2-3	1-0	1	Irvine, Hawke	733
14		19	H	Clyde	W	2-1	2-0	1	Hawke 2	611
15		26	H	Stenhousemuir	D	0-0	0-0	1		703
16	Dec	3	A	East Fife	L	0-3	0-2	1		756
17		10	A	Meadowbank T	L	1-2	1-1	1	Cowan	338
18		31	H	Stirling Albion	W	1-0	1-0	2	Banks (pen)	736
19	Jan	10	H	Queen of the S	W	3-1	1-1	—	Greenwood, Gallacher, Irvine (pen)	448
20		14	A	Morton	L	1-2	0-0	2	Gallacher	1951
21		21	A	Brechin C	L	0-1	0-0	2		387
22	Feb	4	H	Dumbarton	L	1-2	1-0	4	Neil	508
23		11	A	Clyde	W	3-1	2-0	4	Reid, Neil, Hawke	882
24		25	H	East Fife	D	0-0	0-0	4		503
25	Mar	4	H	Meadowbank T	W	1-0	1-0	4	Hawke	455
26		7	A	Stenhousemuir	D	2-2	1-1	—	Neil, Reid	534
27		11	A	Stirling Albion	D	2-2	0-1	3	Irvine, Hawke	582
28		21	A	Dumbarton	L	0-1	0-0	—		1012
29		25	H	Clyde	D	1-1	1-*1	4	Graham	581
30	Apr	1	A	East Fife	W	1-0	1-0	4	Irvine	628
31		8	H	Stenhousemuir	D	0-0	0-0	6		571
32		15	A	Meadowbank T	W	3-0	2-0	5	Fraser, Forrester 2	296
33		22	H	Stirling Albion	D	0-0	0-0	5		601
34		29	H	Morton	L	3-4	3-2	6	Hawke 3	992
35	May	6	A	Queen of the S	L	0-2	0-1	6		1061
36		13	H	Brechin C	W	2-0	1-0	5	Graham, Banks	439

Final League Position: 5

Most League Appearances: 435;: Eric Tait, 1970-87.
Most League Goals in Season (Individual): 38: Ken Bowron, Division II; 1963-64.
Most Goals Overall (Individual): 115: Eric Tait, 1970-87.

Honours
League Champions: Second Division 1978-79. *Runners-up* Second Division 1993-94.
Scottish Cup: —.
League Cup: Semi-final 1963-64.
Club colours: Shirt: Gold with Black seams, shoulders and collar. Shorts: Black, gold trim. Stockings: Black.

Goalscorers: *League (52):* Hawke 16, Irvine 11 (1 pen), Banks 7 (2 pens), Neil 5, Forrester 3, Fraser 2, Gallacher 2, Graham 2, Reid 2, Cowan 1, Greenwood 1. *Scottish Cup (8):* Clegg 1, Fraser 1, Graham 1, Hawke 1, Irvine 1, Neil 1, Valentine 1, own goal 1. *League Cup (0) B&Q Cup (1):* Fraser 1.

Young N 24	Valentine C 36	Banks A 32	Cole A 22	Cowan M 33	Bell D 1 + 1	Forrester P 23 + 9	Neil M 34	Hawke W 35	Irvine W 36	Wilson M 17 + 3	Kane K 15 + 4	Fraser G 20 + 11	Gallacher J 11 + 8	Graham T 23 + 7	Osborne M 12 + 1	Rutherford P 1	Greenwood P 2 + 1	King T 3 + 3	Reid A 14	Robinson A 2	Macaulay L — + 1	Match No.
1	2	*3*	4	5	6	7	8	9	10	11	12	14										1
1	2	3	*4*	5		7	8	9	10	6	11	14	12									2
1	2	3	4	5		7	8	9	10	6			11									3
1	2	3	4	*5*	12	7	8	9	10	6		14	11									4
1	2	3	4			7	6	9	10	8		5	*11*	14								5
1	2	3	4	5		7	8	9	10	6		12	14	11								6
1	2	3	4	5		7	8	9	10	6			14	*11*								7
1	2	3	4	5		7	8	9	10	6			14	*11*								8
1	2	3	4	5		7	8	9	10	6		12	14	11								9
1	2	3	4	5		7	8	*9*	10	6		12	14	11								10
1	2	3	4	5		7	8	9	10	6			14	*11*								11
	2	3	*4*	5		7	8	9	10	6		14	11	12	1							12
	2	3	4	5		8		9	10	6			7	11	1							13
	2	3	4	5		7	8	9	10	6		14	11	12	1							14
	2	3	4	5		*6*	8	9	10	11		14	7	12	1							15
	2	3	*4*	5		7	8	9	10	6		14	12	11	1							16
	2	3	4	5		12	*8*	9	10	6		14	7	11	1							17
	2	3	4	5			8	9	10			6	7		1	11						18
	3		4	5		12	8	9	10			6	7	11	1		2					19
	2	3	4	5			8	9	10		14	6	7	*11*	1		12					20
	3		4	5		7	8	9	10		12	6		11	1		2	14				21
	2	3	*4*	5		7	8	9	10		12	6		11	1			14				22
1	2	3		5		12	8	9	10		7	6		11					4			23
1	4	3				12	8	9	10		7	6		11					5	2		24
1	2	3		5			8	9	10		7	6		11					4			25
1	2	3		5		12	8	9	10		7	6		11					4			26
1	2	3		5		14	8	9	10		11	*7*		12					4	6		27
1	2	*3*		5		12	8	9	10		11	4		7				14	6			28
1	3			5		12	8	9	10		11	6		7				2	4			29
1	3			5		12	8	9	10		11	6		7				2	4			30
1	2	3		5			8	9	10		11	6		7					4			31
1	2	3		5		9	8		10		11	6		7					4			32
1	2	3		5		7	8	9	10		11	6							4			33
1	2	3		5		7	8	9	10	14	11	*6*		12	15				4			34
	2	3		*5*		7	8	9	10	14	11	6		12	1				4			35
1	5	3				*8*		9	10	12	11	6		7				2	4		14	36

BRECHIN CITY — Third Division

Year Formed: 1906. *Ground & Address:* Glebe Park, Trinity Rd, Brechin, Angus DD9 6BJ. *Telephone:* 01356 622856.
Ground Capacity: total: 3980. seated: 1518. *Size of Pitch:* 110yd × 67yd.
Chairman: Hugh Campbell Adamson. *Secretary:* George C. Johnston. *Commercial Manager:* —.
Manager: John Young. *Assistant Manager:* Cammy Evans. *Physio:* Tom Gilmartin.
Managers since 1975: Charlie Dunn; Ian Stewart; Doug Houston; Ian Fleming; John Ritchie, Ian Redford. *Club Nickname(s):* The City. *Previous Grounds:* Nursery Park.
Record Attendance: 8122 v Aberdeen, Scottish Cup 3rd rd; 3 Feb, 1973.
Record Transfer Fee received: £100,000 for Scott Thomson to Aberdeen (1991).
Record Transfer Fee paid: £16,000 for Sandy Ross from Berwick Rangers (1991).
Record Victory: 12-1 v Thornhill, Scottish Cup 1st rd; 28 Jan, 1926.
Record Defeat: 0-10 v Airdrieonians, Albion R and Cowdenbeath, all in Division II; 1937-38.
Most Capped Player: —.
Most League Appearances: 459: David Watt, 1975-89.

BRECHIN CITY 1994–95 LEAGUE RECORD

Match No.	Date		Venue	Opponents	Result		H/T Score	Lg. Pos.	Goalscorers	Attendance
1	Aug	13	H	Meadowbank T	L	1-5	0-0	—	Millar	432
2		20	H	Berwick R	L	1-2	1-2	10	McNeill	539
3		27	A	East Fife	D	1-1	0-0	10	Millar	795
4	Sept	3	H	Stenhousemuir	D	1-1	1-1	10	Vannett	436
5		10	A	Morton	L	0-2	0-0	10		1093
6		24	A	Queen of the S	W	2-0	0-0	9	Smith 2	1032
7	Oct	1	H	Dumbarton	L	1-2	1-1	10	Smith	427
8		8	H	Stirling Albion	L	1-2	0-1	10	Brand	555
9		15	A	Clyde	L	0-4	0-1	10		762
10		22	A	Meadowbank T	L	0-1	0-1	10		149
11		29	H	East Fife	W	2-0	1-0	10	Price, Smith	613
12	Nov	5	A	Berwick R	L	1-2	1-1	10	Smith	478
13		12	H	Morton	L	1-3	0-3	10	Smith	623
14		19	A	Stenhousemuir	L	0-2	0-2	10		342
15		26	H	Queen of the S	L	0-1	0-0	10		406
16	Dec	3	A	Dumbarton	L	0-6	0-3	10		554
17		24	A	Stirling Albion	L	0-2	0-1	10		760
18		31	H	Clyde	L	0-2	0-2	10		484
19	Jan	2	A	East Fife	L	0-4	0-2	—		1155
20		14	H	Meadowbank T	W	3-1	2-0	10	McKellar, Price 2	356
21		21	H	Berwick R	W	1-0	0-0	10	Brand	387
22	Feb	4	A	Morton	L	0-1	0-1	10		1464
23		14	H	Stenhousemuir	L	0-2	0-1	—		345
24		18	A	Queen of the S	W	1-0	0-0	10	Price	1002
25		25	H	Dumbarton	D	0-0	0-0	10		480
26	Mar	4	H	Stirling Albion	W	2-1	1-0	10	Brand, Price	465
27		11	A	Clyde	L	0-1	0-0	10		907
28		18	H	Morton	D	1-1	0-0	10	Brand	481
29		25	A	Stenhousemuir	L	0-3	0-3	10		396
30	Apr	1	A	Dumbarton	L	1-4	0-3	10	McKellar	1103
31		8	H	Queen of the S	L	0-2	0-1	10		389
32		15	A	Stirling Albion	L	0-2	0-1	10		607
33		22	H	Clyde	D	0-0	0-0	10		413
34		29	A	Meadowbank T	L	1-2	0-1	10	McNeill	144
35	May	6	H	East Fife	D	1-1	1-1	10	Price	386
36		13	A	Berwick R	L	0-2	0-1	10		439

Final League Position: 10

Most League Goals in Season (Individual): 26: W. McIntosh, Division II; 1959-60.
Most Goals Overall (Individual): 131: Ian Campbell.

Honours
League Champions: Second Division 1982-83. C Division 1953-54. Second Division 1989-90. *Runners-up:* 1992-93.
Scottish Cup: —.
League Cup: —.
Club colours: Shirt, Shorts, Stockings: Red with white trimmings.

Goalscorers: *League (22):* Price 6, Smith 6, Brand 4, McKellar 2, McNeill 2, Millar 1, Vannett 1. *Scottish Cup (2):* Brand 1, McNeill 1. *League Cup (0) B&Q Cup (0)*

Balfour D 27 + 1	Cairney H 32	Christie G 15	Conway F 33	Nicolson K 9	Scott D 27	Kemlo S 11	Redford I 1	McNeill W 31 + 3	Millar M 8	Vannett R 24 + 3	McKellar J 20 + 7	Bell S 6 + 7	Brown R 21	Brand R 17 + 7	Marr S 14 + 2	Smith R 22 + 3	Mitchell B 27	Feroz C — + 1	Lawrie D 9	Price G 23	Buick G 5 + 2	Mearns G 8 + 1	Baillie R 4	Ferguson S 2	Match No.
1	2	*3*	4	5	6	7	8	9	10	11	12	14													1
1	4	3	2	5	6	11		9	10	8		7													2
1	4	8	2	5	6			11	10	7	12		3	9											3
1	4	3	2	5	6			9	10	8	7	12			11										4
1	4	3	2	5	6			9	10	8	7	12				11									5
1	4		2	5	6			8	10		7	12	3		11	9									6
1	4		2	5	6			8	10			7	3	12	11	9									7
1	4		2	5	6			11	10			7	3	12		9	8								8
1	4		2	5	6	8		11		7			3	9		10		12							9
	4		2		6	3		11			7	14	5	*10*		9	8		1						10
	4		2		6	3		7					5		11	10	8		1	9					11
1	4		2			3		6		12	7		5	14	11	10	8			9					12
			4		6	3		8		2	7		5	12	11	10			1	9					13
			5		6	3		8			14		4	7	11	10	2		1	*9*					14
			4		6			8		14	7		5	12	11	10	3		1	9	2				15
	4		5		6			8					3	12	11	10	2		1	9	7				16
	4		5			3		11		6			2	10		12	8		1	9	7				17
	4		5			3		11		6	14		2			10	8		1	9	*7*				18
15	4		5					14		6	7		3		*11*	10	8		1	9	*2*				19
1	4		5		6			11		8	7		3	10			2			9					20
1	4		5		6			11		8	7		3	10			2			9					21
1	4		5		6			11		8	7		3	10		9	2								22
1	5				6			*11*		2	12	7	3		14	10	4			9		8			23
1	4	5			6			11		8	7	14	*3*			10	2			9					24
1	4	5			6	3		11		8	7					10	2			9					25
1	4	3	5		6			11			7	14		10			2			9		8			26
1	4	3	5		6			*11*		14		7		10		12	2			9		8			27
1	4	3	5		6					8	7			10	11		2			9	14				28
1	4		5							6	7	8		10	*11*	12	2			9	14		3		29
1	5		4					7		6	12			10		11	2			9		8	3		30
1	4	3	5					7		6	12			10		11	2			9		8			31
1	4	3	5					12		11	7			9		10	2					8	6		32
1		5	4					10		11	7			9	14		2					8	*6*	3	33
1	4	3	5		6			10			7				11		2			9		8			34
1	4		5		6			10		8	7		3	12	11		2			9					35
1	4	3	5		6			12		*8*				10		7	2			9		14		11	36

CALEDONIAN THISTLE Third Division

Year Formed: 1994. *Ground & Address:* Telford Street Park, Inverness IV3 5LU. *Telephone:* 01463 230274.
Ground Capacity: 5498, seated 498. *Size of Pitch:* 110 × 70yd.
President: Dugald McGilvray. *Hon. Life President:* John S.McDonald. *Secretary:* Jim Falconer.
Manager: S.W.Paterson.
Record Attendance: 3062, v Ross County, Third Division, 6 May 1995.
Record Victory: 5-2, v Arbroath, Third Division, 13 August 1994.
Record Defeat: 0-4, v Queen's Park, Third Division, 20 August 1994 and v Montrose, Third Division, 14 February 1995.

CALEDONIAN THISTLE 1994–95 LEAGUE RECORD

Match No.	Date		Venue	Opponents	Result		H/T Score	Lg. Pos.	Goalscorers	Attendance
1	Aug	13	H	Arbroath	W	5-2	3-0	—	Hercher 3, MacKenzie, Robertson	1855
2		20	H	Queen's Park	L	0-4	0-2	7		1565
3		27	A	Ross C	W	3-1	1-0	4	Somerville (og), Andrew MacLeod (og), Robertson	3197
4	Sept	3	A	Albion R	W	1-0	0-0	3	MacMillan	539
5		10	H	Forfar Ath	W	3-1	1-1	1	Bennett 2, MacKenzie	1731
6		24	A	Alloa	D	1-1	0-1	1	Scott	590
7	Oct	1	H	East Stirling	D	3-3	1-2	1	Noble (pen), McAllister, Robertson	1229
8		8	H	Cowdenbeath	L	0-3	0-1	4		1273
9		15	A	Montrose	L	1-3	1-0	6	MacMillan	758
10		22	A	Arbroath	W	2-1	1-0	5	McCraw 2	542
11		29	H	Ross C	D	0-0	0-0	5		2866
12	Nov	5	A	Queen's Park	W	2-0	0-0	5	Robertson, MacKenzie (pen)	692
13		12	A	Forfar Ath	L	1-2	1-2	6	McAllister	647
14		19	H	Albion R	W	2-1	0-0	5	Christie 2	954
15		26	H	Alloa	D	2-2	1-0	4	Christie, Andrew (pen)	1039
16	Dec	3	A	East Stirling	L	0-2	0-1	6		508
17		26	A	Cowdenbeath	D	1-1	0-1	—	Andrew	464
18	Jan	2	A	Ross C	L	1-3	1-0	—	Andrew	2749
19		14	H	Arbroath	D	1-1	0-0	7	Brennan	1038
20		21	A	Queen's Park	L	1-4	0-2	7	MacDonald J	456
21	Feb	4	H	Forfar Ath	D	1-1	0-1	7	Scott	793
22		11	A	Albion R	W	2-1	1-0	7	MacMillan, Lisle	274
23		14	H	Montrose	L	0-4	0-0	—		851
24		18	A	Alloa	L	0-1	0-1	7		386
25		25	H	East Stirling	D	3-3	1-1	7	Christie 2, MacKenzie	886
26	Mar	4	H	Cowdenbeath	W	3-1	2-0	7	McAllister, MacMillan, Mitchell	659
27		11	A	Montrose	W	1-0	0-0	6	Robertson	781
28		18	A	Forfar Ath	L	1-4	0-2	6	Scott	538
29	Apr	1	A	East Stirling	L	0-1	0-1	6		391
30		8	H	Alloa	L	0-1	0-1	7		912
31		11	H	Albion R	L	0-2	0-1	—		524
32		15	A	Cowdenbeath	W	3-1	1-0	6	Bennett, Scott, Hercher	183
33		22	H	Montrose	L	0-3	0-2	6		942
34		29	A	Arbroath	L	0-2	0-0	7		492
35	May	6	H	Ross C	W	3-0	1-0	6	MacMillan, Hercher, Christie	3062
36		13	H	Queen's Park	D	1-1	0-1	6	Hercher	782

Final League Position: 6

Most League Appearances: 35, Mark McAllister, 1994-95.
Most League Goals in Season: 6, Charles Christie and Alan Hercher, 1994-95.
Club Colours: Shirts: Blue with White flashes; Shorts: White with Blue flashes; Stockings: Blue.

Goalscorers: *League (48):* Christie 6, Hercher 6, McMillan 5, Robertson 5, MacKenzie 4 (1 pen), Scott 4, Andrew 3 (1 pen), Bennett 3, McAllister 3, McCraw 2, Brennan 1, Lisle 1, MacDonald J 1, Mitchell 1, Noble 1 (pen), own goals 2. *Scottish Cup (1):* McAllister. *League Cup (2):* Robertson 1, own goal 1. *B&Q Cup (1):* MacDonald J 1.

McRitchie M 29	Brennan D 25 + 1	McAllister M 35	Hercher A 13 + 8	Scott J 21 + 2	Andrew M 19	Lisle M 22 + 6	MacKenzie P 20 + 2	Noble M 21	Bennett G 15 + 1	Robertson W 23 + 4	Smart A 2 + 2	MacDonald D 7 + 1	Hastings R 8 + 3	MacMillan N 23 + 4	Christie C 24 + 2	Mitchell C 26 + 2	Baltacha S 9	McCraw B 7 + 8	MacDonald S 10 + 1	Sinclair C 10	Watt G 1 + 1	Calder J 7	Sweeney K 6 + 1	MacDonald J 2	Buchanan D 5 + 1	Sanderson M 3 + 4	Urquhart W 2 + 1	Holmes M 1	Match No.
1	2	3	4	5	6	7	8	9	10	11	12	14																	1
1	2	3	*4*	5	6		8	9	10	11		7	12	14															2
1	2	3	4	5	6		8	9	10	11		7	12																3
1	2	3	4	5			8	9	10	11		7		12	6														4
1	2	3	14	5			8	9	6	11		7		*4*	10														5
1	2	3		5	6		8	9		11		7		4	10														6
1	2	3		14	6	4	8	9	*5*	11	7				10	12													7
1	2	3		5	6	12	8	9		*11*		7		4	10	14													8
1	2	3		12	6	7	8	9				5		11	10	4													9
1	2	3		5	6	8			10					11		7	4	9											10
1	2	3			5	8		6		11				12	10	7	4	*9*	14										11
1	2	3			6	12	8	5	10	11	14			*9*		7	4												12
1	2	3			5	8	11	6	*10*		9					7	4	14											13
1	2	3			5	8	*9*	6	10					11	12	7	4	14											14
1	12	3			6	8	14	*4*						9	10	7		11	2	5									15
1	2	3			5	8	6		12					9	10	7	4	11											16
1		3	4		5	12	9	*8*		11					10	7	6		2		14								17
1	2	3	4		5		9	*8*		11			14		10	7	6												18
	2	3	4			14	9			11			7		10		6	12		5	*8*	1							19
	2	3		8		12	7			11			6	14	10					5		1	4	*9*					20
	5	3		4	6	8				11					10	7		14	2			1		*9*					21
		3	12	4		8				11			5	9	10	7		14	*2*	6		1							22
		3	12	4		8				11			5	9	10	7		14	*2*	6		1							23
			12	4	6	8	14			*11*			3	9	10	7				5		1	2						24
		3		4		8	11			14			6	*9*	10	7				5		1	2						25
1	2	3	12	4		8	11							9	10	7							5		6	14			26
1	2	3		4		8	*11*			14				9	10	7							5		6				27
1	2	3	12	4		8				11				9	*10*	7							5		6	14			28
1	2	3	12	4		8		5		14			6	11	10	7											*9*		29
1		3	12	10	6	*8*		5		11				9		7			2						4	14			30
1		3	4	8				5						11	10	7		14	2				12			*6*	9		31
1		3	4	10				5	8				6	9		7		11	2							12			32
1		3	4			8		5	9	12				10		7		11	2							6			33
1		3	4			8			10	11				9		7			2	5					12	6			34
1	2	*3*	4			12			8	11				9	10	7		14		5					6				35
1	2	3	4			8			6	11					12	7		*9*		5							14	10	36

CELTIC Premier Division

Year Formed: 1888. *Ground & Address:* Celtic Park, 95 Kerrydale St, Glasgow G40 3RE. *Telephone:* 041 556 2611.
Ground Capacity: all seated: 34,000. *Size of Pitch:* 115yd × 75yd.
Managing Director Fergus McCann. *Secretary:* Dominic Keane. *Chief Scout* Davie Hay.
Manager: Tommy Burns. *Assistant Manager:* Billy Stark. *Physio:* Brian Scott. *Coaches:* Frank Connor, Tom McAdam, Willie McStay.
Managers since 1975: Jock Stein, Billy McNeill, David Hay, Billy McNeill, Liam Brady, Lou Macari. *Club Nickname(s):* The Bhoys. *Previous Grounds:* None.
Record Attendance: 92,000 v Rangers, Division I; 1 Jan, 1938.
Record Transfer Fee received: £1,400,000 for Paul Elliott to Chelsea, July 1991.
Record Transfer Fee paid: £1,750,000 for Phil O'Donnell from Motherwell, September 1994.
Record Victory: 11-0 Dundee, Division I; 26 Oct, 1895.
Record Defeat: 0-8 v Motherwell, Division I; 30 Apr, 1937.
Most Capped Player: Paul McStay, 72, Scotland.
Most League Appearances: 486: Billy McNeill 1957-75.
Most League Goals in Season (Individual): 50: James McGrory, Division I; 1935-36.
Most Goals Overall (Individual): 397: James McGrory; 1922-39.

Honours
League Champions: (35 times) Division I 1892-93, 1893-94, 1895-96, 1897-98, 1904-05, 1905-06, 1906-07, 1907-08, 1908-09,

CELTIC 1994–95 LEAGUE RECORD

Match No.	Date	Venue	Opponents	Result		H/T Score	Lg. Pos.	Goalscorers	Attendance
1	Aug 13	A	Falkirk	D	1-1	0-0	—	Walker	12,635
2	20	H	Dundee U	W	2-1	0-0	4	Walker, Mowbray	25,817
3	27	A	Rangers	W	2-0	1-0	2	Collins, McStay	44,607
4	Sept 10	A	Partick T	W	2-1	2-0	1	O'Donnell 2	14,439
5	17	H	Kilmarnock	D	1-1	0-0	2	McGinlay	28,457
6	24	H	Hibernian	W	2-0	1-0	1	O'Donnell, Collins	28,170
7	Oct 1	A	Motherwell	D	1-1	1-0	2	Walker	10,869
8	8	H	Aberdeen	D	0-0	0-0	2		29,454
9	15	A	Hearts	L	0-1	0-1	3		12,086
10	22	H	Falkirk	L	0-2	0-1	4		23,688
11	30	H	Rangers	L	1-3	1-2	—	Byrne	32,171
12	Nov 5	A	Dundee U	D	2-2	2-1	5	Collins 2	10,496
13	9	H	Partick T	D	0-0	0-0	—		21,462
14	19	A	Kilmarnock	D	0-0	0-0	5		13,932
15	30	A	Hibernian	D	1-1	1-0	—	Collins	12,295
16	Dec 3	H	Motherwell	D	2-2	2-1	5	Falconer, Philliben (og)	21,465
17	26	A	Aberdeen	D	0-0	0-0	—		19,206
18	31	H	Falkirk	W	2-0	0-0	4	Grant, Walker	21,294
19	Jan 4	A	Rangers	D	1-1	0-1	—	Byrne	45,794
20	7	H	Dundee U	D	1-1	1-1	4	Collins	21,436
21	11	H	Hearts	D	1-1	1-0	—	Van Hooijdonk	26,491
22	14	H	Kilmarnock	W	2-1	0-0	4	Falconer, Collins	25,342
23	21	A	Partick T	D	0-0	0-0	4		11,904
24	Feb 4	A	Motherwell	L	0-1	0-0	4		10,771
25	11	H	Hibernian	D	2-2	1-1	4	Collins, Falconer	24,284
26	25	A	Hearts	D	1-1	0-0	4	O'Donnell	11,185
27	Mar 5	H	Aberdeen	W	2-0	1-0	—	Van Hooijdonk 2	20,621
28	21	A	Kilmarnock	W	1-0	0-0	—	Walker	10,112
29	Apr 1	H	Motherwell	D	1-1	0-0	4	Walker	24,047
30	15	A	Aberdeen	L	0-2	0-2	6		16,668
31	19	H	Hearts	L	0-1	0-0	—		18,638
32	29	A	Falkirk	W	2-1	1-0	5	O'Donnell, Boyd	9714
33	May 2	H	Partick T	L	1-3	1-1	—	Grant	18,963
34	7	H	Rangers	W	3-0	0-0	—	Van Hooijdonk, Moore (og), Vata	31,025
35	9	A	Hibernian	D	1-1	0-1	—	Falconer	6019
36	13	A	Dundee U	W	1-0	0-0	4	O'Donnell	10,993

Final League Position: 4

1909-10, 1913-14, 1914-15, 1915-16, 1916-17, 1918-19, 1921-22, 1925-26, 1935-36, 1937-38, 1953-54, 1965-66, 1966-67, 1967-68, 1968-69, 1969-70, 1970-71, 1971-72, 1972-73, 1973-74. Premier Division 1976-77, 1978-79, 1980-81, 1981-82, 1985-86, 1987-88. *Runners-up:* 22 times.
Scottish Cup Winners: (30 times) 1892, 1899, 1900, 1904, 1907, 1908, 1911, 1912, 1914, 1923, 1925, 1927, 1931, 1933, 1937, 1951, 1954, 1965, 1967, 1969, 1971, 1972, 1974, 1975, 1977, 1980, 1985, 1988, 1989, 1995; *Runners-up:* 16 times.
League Cup Winners: (9 times) 1956-57, 1957-58, 1965-66, 1966-67, 1967-68, 1968-69, 1969-70, 1974-75, 1982-83; *Runners-up:* 10 times.

European: *European Cup Winners:* 1966-67. 78 matches (1966-67 winners, 1967-68, 1968-69, 1969-70 runners-up, 1970-71, 1971-72 semi-finals, 1972-73, 1973-74 semi-finals, 1974-75, 1977-78, 1979-80, 1981-82, 1982-83, 1986-87, 1988-89); *Cup Winners Cup:* 35 matches (1963-64 semi-finals, 1965-66 semi-finals, 1975-76, 1980-81, 1984-85, 1985-86, 1989-90); *UEFA Cup:* 28 matches (*Fairs Cup:* 1962-63, 1964-65. *UEFA Cup:* 1976-77, 1983-84, 1987-88, 1991-92, 1992-93, 1993-94).
Club colours: Shirt: Green and white hoops. Shorts: White. Stockings: White.

Goalscorers: *League (39):* Collins 8, O'Donnell 6, Walker 6, Falconer 4, Van Hooijdonk 4, Byrne 2, Grant 2, Boyd 1, McGinlay 1, McStay 1, Mowbray 1, Vata 1, own goals 2. *Scottish Cup (10):* Van Hooijdonk 4, Falconer 3, Collins 2, O'Donnell 1. *League Cup (7):* Collins 2, Walker 2, Grant 1, Nicholas 1, O'Neil B 1.

Marshall G 16	Martin L 4	Boyd T 35	McNally M 19 + 1	Mowbray A 15	Grant P 27 + 1	Galloway M 11	McStay P 28 + 1	Falconer W 19 + 7	Walker A 22 + 4	Collins J 33 + 1	Nicholas C 5 + 7	Donnelly S 7 + 10	McGinlay P 7 + 1	O'Neil B 24 + 2	O'Donnell P 25 + 2	McLaughlin B 19 + 2	Smith B 3	Byrne P 6	McKinlay T 17	O'Neill J — + 1	Gray S 8 + 3	Bonner P 20	Hay C 2 + 3	Slavin J 3	Van Hooijdonk P 13 + 1	Vata R 7	Mackay M 1	Match No.
1	2	3	4	5	6	7	8	9	10	11																		1
1	2	3	4	5	6		8	9	10	11	7	12	14															2
1		3	4	5	2	7	8		10	11	12	9	*6*	14														3
1		3	4	5	2	*7*			10	11	12	9	6		8	14												4
1	*2*	3	4	5	6		8		9	11		14	7		10													5
1		3	4	5	6	2			10	11	*9*	12	7	14	8													6
1		3	4		6	2	12	14	10	11	*9*		7	5	8													7
1		3	4			2	8	14	10	11	12	9	7	*5*	6													8
1		3	4		6	2	8	14	10	11	12	*9*			7		5											9
1	2	*3*	4		6			9	12	11	10	14	7	5	8													10
1		3	4				8	14	10	11	12	9		5	6		*2*	7										11
1		2	4		6		8	9	10	11	12	14		5				7	*3*									12
1		2	12	5	6		8			11	10	*9*		4				7	3	14								13
1		2	4		6		8	9	10	11		12		5	7				3									14
1		2	4			6	8	9	10	11				5		7			3		12							15
1		2			6	4	8	9	10			12		5		7			3		11							16
		2		5	6		8		10	11		14		4		9			3			1	7					17
		2			6		8		10	11				4		9	5		*3*		14	1	7					18
		2				5	8		10	11				4	6	9		7			3	1	12					19
		2					8	12	10	11				4	6	9		*7*			3	1	14	5				20
		2				4	8		12	11					6	10		7			3	1		5	9			21
		2	4				8	10		11					6	*7*					3	1	14	5	9			22
		2	5		6			10		11				4	8	7					3	1			9			23
		2	5		6		8	10		11				4	7	14					*3*	1			9			24
		2	5		6			10		11				4	8	7					3	1			9			25
			2	5	6			10	12	11				4	8	7			3			1			9			26
		2		5	6		8	10		12				4	11	7			3			1			9			27
		2		5	12		8	*10*	14	11					6	7			3			1			9	4		28
		2		5			8	12	10	11					6	7			3			1			9	4		29
		2			6		8	9	10	11		12		5	14	7			*3*			1				4		30
		3		5	6			9	10	11		12		4	8	7						1				2		31
		2		5	6		8	9	*10*	11				4	7				3			1			14			32
		2		5	6		8	9		11				4	7				3			1			10			33
		2			6		8	12		11		10		5	14	7			3			1			*9*	4		34
		2			6		8	10						5	11	7			3			1			9	4		35
		2			*6*		8			11	12				10	7			3		14	1			9	4	5	36

CLYDE Second Division

Year Formed: 1878. *Ground & Address:* Broadwood Stadium, Cumbernauld, G68 9NE. *Telephone:* 01236 451511.
Ground Capacity: total: 6103 all seated. *Size of Pitch:* 112yd × 76yd.
Chairman: John F. McBeth FRICS. *Secretary:* John D. Taylor. *Commercial Manager:* John Donnelly.
Manager: Alex Smith. *Assistant Manager:* John Brownlie. *Physio:* J. Watson: *Coach:* Gardner Speirs.
Managers since 1975: S. Anderson; C. Brown; J. Clark. *Club Nickname(s):* The Bully Wee. *Previous Grounds:* Barrowfield & Shawfield Stadium.
Record Attendance: 52,000 v Rangers, Division I; 21 Nov, 1908.
Record Transfer Fee received: £95,000 for Pat Nevin to Chelsea (July 1983).
Record Transfer Fee paid: £14,000 for Harry Hood from Sunderland (1966).
Record Victory: 11-1 v Cowdenbeath, Division II; 6 Oct, 1951.
Record Defeat: 0-11 v Dumbarton, Scottish Cup 4th rd, 22 Nov, 1879; v Rangers, Scottish Cup 4th rd, 13 Nov, 1880.
Most Capped Player: Tommy Ring, 12, Scotland.
Most League Appearances: 428: Brian Ahern.
Most League Goals in Season (Individual): 32: Bill Boyd, 1932-33.
Most Goals Overall (Individual): —.

CLYDE 1994–95 LEAGUE RECORD

Match No.	Date	Venue	Opponents	Result		H/T Score	Lg. Pos.	Goalscorers	Attendance
1	Aug 13	A	Stenhousemuir	L	0-1	0-1	—		680
2	20	A	Queen of the S	W	2-1	1-0	7	Dickson, McConnell	1435
3	27	H	Stirling Albion	L	1-2	0-2	9	Knox	1162
4	Sept 3	H	Berwick R	L	3-4	0-1	9	Parks, MacKenzie, Tennant	1141
5	10	A	East Fife	L	0-2	0-1	9		925
6	24	A	Dumbarton	L	1-2	1-1	10	McGill	776
7	Oct 1	H	Meadowbank T	W	2-1	1-1	8	Knox 2	865
8	8	A	Morton	W	1-0	0-0	7	Knox	1801
9	15	H	Brechin C	W	4-0	1-0	7	McCheyne, Knox, Angus (pen), MacKenzie	762
10	22	H	Stenhousemuir	D	0-0	0-0	6		1072
11	29	A	Stirling Albion	W	1-0	0-0	4	Knox	1118
12	Nov 5	H	Queen of the S	D	2-2	0-2	6	MacKenzie, McAulay	1112
13	12	H	East Fife	D	1-1	0-0	7	McCluskey	1212
14	19	A	Berwick R	L	1-2	0-2	7	Angus	611
15	26	H	Dumbarton	W	3-1	1-1	5	McAulay 2, McCluskey	1102
16	Dec 3	A	Meadowbank T	D	2-2	1-0	7	Dickson, Angus	382
17	26	H	Morton	D	0-0	0-0	—		2023
18	31	A	Brechin C	W	2-0	2-0	6	McCluskey, MacKenzie	484
19	Jan 14	A	Stenhousemuir	D	2-2	0-0	7	Dickson, Parks	669
20	17	H	Stirling Albion	W	2-0	0-0	—	Dickson 2	1345
21	21	H	Queen of the S	L	3-4	1-3	5	Dickson 2, Parks	998
22	Feb 4	A	East Fife	W	3-1	1-1	5	Angus, O'Neill, Parks	885
23	11	H	Berwick R	L	1-3	0-2	5	MacKenzie	882
24	18	A	Dumbarton	D	2-2	1-2	5	Angus, Parks	1183
25	25	H	Meadowbank T	W	4-1	1-0	5	Thomson, Nisbet, O'Neill, McCarron	825
26	Mar 11	H	Brechin C	W	1-0	0-0	5	Dickson	907
27	14	A	Morton	L	1-4	0-4	—	Dickson	1421
28	18	H	East Fife	D	1-1	0-0	5	Nisbet	602
29	25	A	Berwick R	D	1-1	1-1	5	McCluskey	581
30	Apr 1	A	Meadowbank T	W	1-0	1-0	5	Dickson	377
31	8	H	Dumbarton	W	1-0	1-0	4	McCluskey	1189
32	15	H	Morton	L	1-3	0-2	6	Brown	2163
33	22	A	Brechin C	D	0-0	0-0	6		413
34	29	H	Stenhousemuir	W	3-2	0-0	5	McCheyne 2, Muir	1043
35	May 6	A	Stirling Albion	L	0-2	0-0	5		1122
36	13	A	Queen of the S	L	0-1	0-1	6		1502

Final League Position: 6

Honours
League Champions: Division II 1904-05, 1951-52, 1956-57, 1961-62, 1972-73. Second Division 1977-78, 1981-82, 1992-93.
Runners-up: Division II 1903-04, 1905-06, 1925-26, 1963-64.
Scottish Cup Winners: 1939, 1955, 1958; *Runners-up:* 1910, 1912, 1949.
League Cup: —
Club colours: Shirt: White with red and black trim. Shorts: Black. Stockings: Black with red and white tops.

Goalscorers: *League (53):* Dickson 10, Knox 6, Angus 5 (1 pen), McCluskey 5, MacKenzie 5, Parks 5, McAulay 3, McCheyne 3, Nisbet 2, O'Neill 2, Brown 1, McCarron 1, McConnell 1, McGill 1, Muir 1, Tennant 1, Thomson 1. *Scottish Cup (3):* Angus 1, Dickson 1, O'Neill 1. *League Cup (0) B&Q Cup (1):* MacKenzie 1.

Fridge L 25 + 1	Clark M 18	Neill A 10	Knox K 30	Thomson J 30	Watson G 28 + 3	Dickson J 23 + 4	McCheyne G 13	McConnell I 7 + 5	McAulay J 8 + 8	MacKenzie A 22 + 7	Wright A 9	McFarlane R 2	Frater A 2	McCarron J 17 + 5	Wylde G 2	Nisbet I 18 + 7	Angus I 24	Tennant S 1	O'Neill M 20	Parks G 11 + 7	Hillcoat J 11	Brown J 23 + 2	McGill D 2 + 4	Prunty J 11 + 5	Strain B 3 + 3	Falconer M 6 + 4	McCluskey G 18 + 1	Muir J 1 + 1	Fay J 1	*Match No.*
1	2	3	4	5	6	7	8	9	10	11																				1
1	2		4	5	8	7		12			3	6	9	*10*	11	14														2
1	2		4	5	8	7		12				*6*	9	10	11	14	3													3
1		6	5		2	*11*		9	8	14	4						10	3	7	12										4
	2		4	5	*8*		3	9		11						14	10			7	1	6	12							5
12	2		4	5			8	14		*7*				10		6					1		9	3	11					6
1	2		4	5			8			11				10		6			*7*				9	3	14	12				7
1	2		4	5	14		8			11				10		7	3						12		*6*	9				8
1	2		4	5	*6*		8			11				10		7	3						12		14	9				9
1	2		4	5	*6*		8			11				10		7	3						12		14	9				10
1	2		4	5	6	12	8		14	11				*10*		7	3										9			11
1	2		4	5	6		8		14	12				10		*7*	3									11	9			12
1	2		4		6				8	11				*10*		7	3					12		5		14	9			13
1	2		*4*	5	6					12				10		*7*	3			11		14		8			9			14
1		*10*		5	2	7			8	11	4			14			3			12		6					9			15
1		10		5	2	7			*8*	11	4			14			3			12		6					9			16
1	2	10		5	8	7			4	11				12			3			14		6					*9*			17
1		10		5	8	7			12	11				4			3		2	14		6					*9*			18
1		10			8	7		14	12					4			3		2	11		6			5		*9*			19
1		10	5		8	7			14	9				4			3		2	*11*		6		12						20
1		10	5		8	7			11	14				*4*			3		2	9		6		12						21
1.		11	10	5	8	7				12						*4*	3		2	9		6		14						22
1			10	5	8	7			14	12						*4*	3		2	11		6					9			23
1	11		10	5	8	7			12							4	3		2	9		6								24
1	11		10	5	12	7			*8*					14		4	3		2	9		6								25
1	11		10	5	12	7				14				*8*		4	3		2	9		6								26
1	11		10	*5*	8	7				9				12		4	3		2			6					14			27
			10	5		7				11	8					4			2	12	1	6		3			9			28
			10	5	4	7				*11*	8					14			2	12	1	6		3			9			29
			10	5	4	7				11	8					12			2		1	6		3		14	*9*			30
			10	5	8	7				11	*4*					14			2		1	6		3		12	9			31
			10	5	8	7		14		11	4					12			2		1	6		3			9			32
			5		4	14	3	8						10		7			*2*		1	6		12		11	9			33
			10	5		14	11	4		8									2		1	6		3			*9*	7		34
			10	5		7	11	4	12	8									2		1	6		3			*9*	14		35
				5	2	14	3	4								7	10			*8*	1	6		12		9			11	36

CLYDEBANK First Division

Year Formed: 1965. *Ground & Address:* Kilbowie Park, Arran Place, Clydebank G81 2PB. *Telephone:* 0141 952 2887.
Ground Capacity: total: 9950. seated: All. *Size of Pitch:* 110yd × 68yd.
Chairman: C.G.Steedman. *Secretary:* A.Steedman. *Commercial Manager:* David Curwood.
Managing Director: I.C.Steedman. *Physio:* Peter Saula. *Coach:* Brian Wright.
Managers since 1975: William Munro, J.S.Steedman. *Club Nickname(s):* The Bankies. *Previous Grounds:* None.
Record Attendance: 14,900 v Hibernian, Scottish Cup 1st rd; 10 Feb, 1965.
Record Transfer Fee received: £175,000 for Owen Coyle from Airdrieonians, (Feb 1990).
Record Transfer Fee paid: £50,000 for Gerry McCabe from Clyde.
Record Victory: 8-1 Arbroath, First Division; 3 Jan 1977.
Record Defeat: 1-9 v Gala Fairydean, Scottish Cup qual rd; 15 Sept, 1965.
Most Capped Player: —.
Most League Appearances: 620: Jim Fallon; 1968-86.
Most League Goals in Season (Individual): 29: Ken Eadie, First Division, 1990-91.
Most League Goals Overall (Individual): 138, Ken Eadie 1988-95.

CLYDEBANK 1994–95 LEAGUE RECORD

Match No.	Date	Venue	Opponents	Result		H/T Score	Lg. Pos.	Goalscorers	Attendance
1	Aug 13	H	Stranraer	W	2-0	0-0	—	Eadie, Cooper	908
2	20	H	Dunfermline Ath	L	0-1	0-1	3		1597
3	27	A	St Mirren	L	1-2	1-0	5	Currie	2414
4	Sept 3	A	Raith R	D	1-1	0-1	7	Currie	2861
5	10	H	Dundee	W	5-2	2-1	4	Jack, Flannigan 2, Sweeney, Grady	1437
6	24	A	Airdrieonians	L	0-2	0-1	4		1542
7	Oct 1	H	St Johnstone	D	0-0	0-0	5		1025
8	8	H	Ayr U	W	3-0	1-0	4	Grady, Eadie 2	891
9	15	A	Hamilton A	D	0-0	0-0	4		1042
10	22	A	Stranraer	W	1-0	0-0	4	Grady	781
11	29	H	St Mirren	D	1-1	1-0	4	Sweeney	1675
12	Nov 5	A	Dunfermline Ath	L	1-4	0-1	4	Jack	4611
13	12	A	Dundee	L	0-2	0-1	5		2240
14	19	H	Raith R	L	0-3	0-1	6		1002
15	26	H	Airdrieonians	L	0-1	0-0	7		1197
16	Dec 3	A	St Johnstone	D	1-1	0-1	7	Eadie	2724
17	26	A	Ayr U	D	1-1	0-1	—	Currie	1969
18	31	H	Stranraer	L	2-3	0-2	7	Murdoch, Flannigan	652
19	Jan 2	A	St Mirren	D	0-0	0-0	—		3217
20	7	H	Dunfermline Ath	L	1-2	1-0	7	Eadie	1468
21	10	H	Hamilton A	D	0-0	0-0	—		578
22	14	A	Raith R	L	0-1	0-0	7		3129
23	21	H	Dundee	L	0-3	0-2	7		900
24	Feb 4	H	St Johnstone	D	0-0	0-0	7		949
25	14	A	Airdrieonians	W	2-1	2-0	—	Eadie, Grady	1033
26	25	A	Hamilton A	W	1-0	0-0	7	Sherry (og)	1017
27	Mar 11	H	Ayr U	D	1-1	0-0	7	Grady	720
28	18	A	Dundee	L	2-3	1-1	7	Grady, Eadie	1788
29	Apr 1	A	St Johnstone	L	0-1	0-1	7		3337
30	4	H	Raith R	L	1-2	0-0	—	Robertson	1261
31	11	H	Airdrieonians	D	1-1	1-0	—	Grady	709
32	15	A	Ayr U	L	0-1	0-1	8		1798
33	22	H	Hamilton A	L	1-4	1-3	8	Eadie	716
34	29	A	Stranraer	W	1-0	1-0	8	Robertson	582
35	May 6	H	St Mirren	W	2-1	1-0	7	Murdoch, Bowman	1399
36	13	A	Dunfermline Ath	L	1-2	0-2	8	Eadie	7709

Final League Position: 8

Honours

League Champions: Second Division 1975-76; *Runners-up:* First Division 1976-77, 1984-85.
Scottish Cup: Semi-finalists 1990. *League Cup:* —.
Club colours: Shirt: White with Red shoulder band with Black trim. Shorts: White with Red trim. Stockings: White with Red trim.

Goalscorers: *League (33):* Eadie 9, Grady 7, Currie 3, Flannigan 3, Jack 2, Murdoch 2, Robertson 2, Sweeney 2, Bowman 1, Cooper 1, own goal 1. *Scottish Cup (2):* Eadie 2. *League Cup (1):* Grady 1. *B&Q Cup (11):* Grady 4, Cooper 3, Eadie 2, Flannigan 1, Harris 1.

Matthews G 36	Lansdowne A 14 + 9	Bowman G 29 + 2	Murdoch S 28	Sweeney S 27	Currie T 27	Cooper D 19 + 2	Harris C 7 + 1	Eadie K 26 + 3	Grady J 30 + 6	Ferguson G 9 + 3	Flannigan C 11 + 10	Jack S 33 + 2	Kerrigan S 8 + 6	Sutherland S 9	Crawford D 12 + 4	Walker J 14 + 7	Keane G 3	Butcher T 3	Tomlinson C 10	Agnew P 4 + 2	McStay J 19 + 1	Connelly D 1 + 4	Robertson J 6 + 1	Lovering P 3	Dunn R — + 1	*Match No.*
1	2	3	4	5	6	7	8	9	10	11	12															1
1	2	3	4	*5*	6	7	8	9	10	14		11	12													2
1	2	3	4		5	7	8		9	14	10	11	12	*6*												3
1	2		4		5	7			12	*8*	10	11	9	6	3	14										4
1	2		4	5	6	7			9		10	11		3	12	8										5
1	2	*3*	4	5	6	7		12	10		9	11			8	14										6
1	2		4	5	6	7		9	10		12	11			3	8										7
1		3	4	5	6	7	11	9	10		12	2				8										8
1		3	4	5		7	11	9	10		12	2			14	8	*6*									9
1	12	3	4	5		7		9	11		10	2				8	6									10
1	*11*	3	4	5	6	7		9	10		12	2			14	8										11
1	11	3	4		5	7	14	9	10		12	2				*8*		6								12
1		3	4		5	7		12	9		10	11				*8*		6	2	14						13
1		3			5	7	4	9	10			11	12			8		6	*2*	14						14
1		11			5	7		9	10		12	2			3		6		4	8						15
1		11		5	6	12		9	8			14	*10*		3				4	7	2					16
1		11	4	5	6	7		*9*	10		14	12			3					8	2					17
1		3	4	5	6	7	*8*	9	12		10	11				14					2					18
1		*3*	4	5	6	12			14		10	11	9			7				8	2					19
1	14	3	4	5	6			9	8			11	*10*			7					2					20
1		11	4	5	6			9	*10*		14	8			3	7					2					21
1		11	4	5	6	7		9	12		10	8			3	14					*2*					22
1	14	11	*4*	5		7		9	12		10	6			3	8					2					23
1	8	3	4	5	6			9	14		10	11									2	*7*				24
1	7	11	4	5	6			9	*10*	3		8	12								2	14				25
1	7	11		5	6			9	10	3		8				14			4		*2*					26
1	7	11		5	6			9	10	3		8							4		2					27
1	7	11		5	6			9	10	3		8	12	4							2					28
1	15	11		5	6				*10*			8	9	3		12			4		2		14			29
1	15	14	4	5					10			8	9	6	3	12					2		*11*			30
1	15	14	4	5				9	10			8		6	3						2		*11*			31
1	15		4	5				9	10			8	12	6	3						2		11			32
1	15	11	4	5				9	10	12	14	8		*3*		6					2					33
1	15	6			5			9	10	2		8							4			14	*11*	3		34
1		8	6						10	2		5	9						4		12	15	*11*	3	14	35
1			6					12	10	2		5	9		14				4		8	15	*11*	3		36

COWDENBEATH Third Division

Year Formed: 1881. *Ground & Address:* Central Park, Cowdenbeath KY4 9EY. *Telephone:* 01383 610166. *Fax:* 01383 512132.
Ground Capacity: total: 5268. seated: 1622. *Size of Pitch:* 107yd × 66yd.
Chairman: Gordon McDougall. *Secretary:* Tom Ogilvie. *Commercial Manager:* Joe McNamara.
Manager: Thomas Steven.
Managers since 1975: D. McLindon; F. Connor; P. Wilson; A. Rolland; H. Wilson; W. McCulloch; J. Clark; J. Craig; R. Campbell; J. Blackley; J. Brownlie, A. Harrow, J. Reilly, P Dolan. *Previous Grounds:* North End Park, Cowdenbeath.
Record Attendance: 25,586 v Rangers, League Cup quarter-final; 21 Sept, 1949.
Record Transfer Fee received: £30,000 for Nicky Henderson to Falkirk, (March 1994).
Record Transfer Fee paid: —
Record Victory: 12-0 v Johnstone, Scottish Cup 1st rd; 21 Jan, 1928.
Record Defeat: 1-11 v Clyde, Division II; 6 Oct, 1951.
Most Capped Player: Jim Paterson, 3, Scotland.
Most League and Cup Appearances: 491 Ray Allan 1972-75, 1979-89.
Most League Goals in Season (Individual): 53, Rab Walls, Division II, 1938-39.
Most Goals Overall (Individual): 120, Willie Devlin, 1922-26, 1929-30.

COWDENBEATH 1994–95 LEAGUE RECORD

Match No.	Date	Venue	Opponents	Result		H/T Score	Lg. Pos.	Goalscorers	Attendance
1	Aug 13	H	Ross C	L	0-2	0-0	—		678
2	20	H	Arbroath	W	6-2	4-0	6	Yardley 4, Malloy, Soutar	315
3	27	A	Montrose	L	0-2	0-2	8		584
4	Sept 3	H	East Stirling	D	1-1	0-0	8	Winter	258
5	10	A	Queen's Park	W	3-0	0-0	7	Yardley 3	509
6	24	A	Albion R	W	4-2	1-1	4	Malloy, Yardley, Callaghan 2	314
7	Oct 1	H	Alloa	L	1-3	0-1	7	Yardley	368
8	8	A	Caledonian Th	W	3-0	1-0	5	Winter, Yardley 2	1273
9	15	H	Forfar Ath	W	1-0	0-0	3	Callaghan	403
10	22	A	Ross C	L	0-4	0-0	6		1284
11	29	H	Montrose	D	1-1	1-1	6	Yardley	301
12	Nov 5	A	Arbroath	W	3-0	3-0	6	Conn, Yardley, Wardell	426
13	12	H	Queen's Park	W	2-0	0-0	4	Yardley 2	281
14	19	A	East Stirling	W	2-0	0-0	3	Black, Wardell	553
15	26	H	Albion R	D	2-2	1-2	3	Yardley 2	380
16	Dec 3	A	Alloa	L	0-1	0-0	4		462
17	26	H	Caledonian Th	D	1-1	1-0	—	Callaghan	464
18	31	A	Forfar Ath	D	1-1	1-0	5	Yardley	603
19	Jan 2	A	Montrose	W	2-1	2-1	—	Yardley 2	452
20	14	H	Ross C	L	0-3	0-1	6		361
21	21	A	Arbroath	W	3-0	1-0	3	Callaghan, Black, Wardell	388
22	Feb 4	A	Queen's Park	L	0-1	0-0	5		477
23	18	A	Albion R	L	0-2	0-0	6		273
24	25	H	Alloa	L	1-3	1-2	6	Winter	260
25	Mar 4	A	Caledonian Th	L	1-3	0-2	6	De Melo	659
26	11	H	Forfar Ath	L	1-3	1-1	7	Yardley	280
27	18	H	Queen's Park	L	1-3	1-1	7	De Melo	137
28	22	H	East Stirling	L	1-4	0-2	—	Wardell	172
29	25	A	East Stirling	L	0-1	0-1	7		338
30	Apr 1	A	Alloa	L	1-2	1-0	7	Conn	367
31	8	H	Albion R	W	2-0	0-0	6	Black, Yardley	186
32	15	H	Caledonian Th	L	1-3	0-1	7	Yardley	183
33	22	A	Forfar Ath	D	2-2	2-2	8	Black, Wardell	611
34	29	A	Ross C	L	0-2	0-1	8		1356
35	May 6	H	Montrose	L	0-4	0-1	9		379
36	13	H	Arbroath	D	1-1	1-1	9	Soutar	200

Final League Position: 9

Honours

League Champions: Division II 1913-14, 1914-15, 1938-39; *Runners-up:* Division II 1921-22, 1923-24, 1969-70. Second Division 1991-92.
Scottish Cup: Quarter-finals: 1931.
League Cup: Semi-finals: 1959-60, 1970-71.
Club colours: Shirt: Royal Blue 1" vertical stripe with Red piping on sleeve seam. Shorts: White with blue side stripe. Stockings: Royal blue.

Goalscorers: *League (48):* Yardley 23, Callaghan 5, Wardell 5, Black 4, Winter 3, Conn 2, De Melo 2, Malloy 2, Soutar 2. *Scottish Cup (1):* Conn 1. *League Cup (2):* Black 1, Soutar 1. *B&Q Cup (6):* Yardley 4, Soutar 1, Tait 1.

Russell N 31	Scott S 12 + 2	Hamill A 4 + 2	Malloy B 30	Humphreys M 21 + 1	Winter C 23 + 5	Petrie E 12	Black I 31 + 2	Soutar G 16 + 3	Thomson J 1 + 1	Stout D 4	Lynch J 2 + 14	Carr R — + 2	Tait G 22	Yardley M 32	McMahon B 17 + 5	Davidson I 1	Bowmaker K 2	Callaghan W 18 + 2	Murdoch S 17	Hamilton A — + 1	Barclay A 3 + 4	Fellenger D 23 + 1	Maloney J 3	Conn S 19	Wardell S 20 + 3	Weatherston P 8 + 7	Wood G 9	Maratea D 3 + 1	De Melo A 7 + 2	Watson D 2 + 2	Craib S 3	Stewart W — + 2	*Match No.*
1	2	3	4	5	6	7	*8*	9	10	11	12	14																					1
1		3	4	5	7	*2*	8	10	12	11			6	9	14																		2
1		3	4	5	12		8	*10*		11	14		7	9	6	2																	3
1			4	5	6		8	12		*11*	14		7	9	2		3	10															4
1		14	4	5	6	2	*8*	11			12		7	9				10	3														5
1		8	4	5	*6*	2	14	11					7	9	12			10	3														6
1				4	*6*	2	8	11			14		7	9	5			10	3	12													7
1	14		4	5	6	2	8	11					7	9				*10*	3		12												8
1			5	14	7	2	8	*11*						9	4			10	3			6											9
1	12		5	4	6	2	8	*11*			14			9				10	3			7											10
	2		5	4			8				12			9				10	3			6	1	7	11								11
1	2	14		4			*8*				12		6	9				10	3			7		5	11								12
1	2		4		10		8				12		7	9	14				3			*6*		5	11								13
1	2		4		*6*		11				12		7	9				14	3			8		5	10								14
1	2		4		14		8				12		7	9				10	3			6		5	*11*								15
1	2		4		12		8						*6*	9	14			10	3			7		5	11								16
1	2		5		6		12						8	9	4			10	3			7			11								17
1	2		4				8						7	9				10	3			6		5	11	12							18
1	2		4				8	10					7	9	5				3		12	14		*6*	11								19
			4	2			11	9										10	3			8	1	5		6	7	12					20
				4	14		8							9	5			10	3		12		1		11	6	7	*2*					21
1	2			4	14		8	12						9	5			10			*6*				11	3	7						22
1	*2*			7			11				12		3	9	4			10				8		5	6	14							23
1			4	2	7			10					8	9							*11*	6		5	12	3			14				24
1			4		7						14		8	9	2						12	*6*		5	11	3			10	15			25
1			4		7		6						8	9	2			12						5		3			10		11		26
1			5		6		8						7	9	4			10				2			12	3			11	15			27
			6		7		3						8	9								2		4	12		5		10	1	11		28
1			6				3						10	9	4							2		5	7	14	8		12		11		29
1				5		2	8	10						9	14							7		3		12	*6*	4	11				30
1			5	4	6	2	8							9								7			11	14	3		*10*				31
			5	3	6	2	8							9								7			11			4	10	1			32
1			4	*5*	8		9	11				12			3						6	7			10	2						14	33
1			5	2	8		9	11			7				4							6		3	10	12							34
1			5		8		10	12			6			9	3							7		4	11		*2*					14	35
1			5		7	2		11			14			9	6		3							4	*10*	12	8						36

DUMBARTON First Division

Year Formed: 1872. *Ground & Address:* Boghead Park, Miller St, Dumbarton G82 2JA. *Telephone:* 01389 62569/67864.
Ground Capacity: total: 10,700. seated: 303. *Size of Pitch:* 110yd × 68yd.
Chairman: D.Dalglish. *Secretary:* Alistair Paton.
Manager: Murdo MacLeod. *Assistant Manager:* Jim Fallon. *Physio:* D.Stobie. *Coach:* Alistair MacLeod.
Managers since 1975: A. Wright; D. Wilson; S. Fallon; W. Lamont; D. Wilson; D. Whiteford; A. Totten; M. Clougherty; R. Auld; J. George; W. Lamont. *Club Nickname(s):* The Sons. *Previous Grounds:* Broadmeadow, Ropework Lane.
Record Attendance: 18,000 v Raith Rovers, Scottish Cup; 2 Mar, 1957.
Record Transfer Fee received: £125,000 for Graeme Sharp to Everton (March 1982).
Record Transfer Fee paid: £50,000 for Charlie Gibson from Stirling Albion (1989).
Record Victory: 13-1 v Kirkintilloch Cl. 1st Rd; 1 Sept, 1888.
Record Defeat: 1-11 v Albion Rovers, Division II; 30 Jan, 1926: v Ayr United, League Cup; 13 Aug, 1952.
Most Capped Player: John Lindsay, 8, Scotland; James McAulay, 8, Scotland.
Most League Appearances: 297: Andy Jardine, 1957-67.

DUMBARTON 1994–95 LEAGUE RECORD

Match No.	Date	Venue	Opponents	Result		H/T Score	Lg. Pos.	Goalscorers	Attendance
1	Aug 13	A	Queen of the S	L	1-4	0-1	—	Mooney M	1389
2	20	A	Stirling Albion	D	1-1	0-0	9	Mooney M	715
3	27	H	Morton	W	2-1	0-1	6	Mooney M, Ward	1168
4	Sept 3	H	Meadowbank T	L	0-1	0-1	7		644
5	10	A	Berwick R	L	0-1	0-0	8		533
6	24	H	Clyde	W	2-1	1-1	6	Boyd 2	776
7	Oct 1	A	Brechin C	W	2-1	1-1	5	Martin, McGarvey	427
8	8	A	East Fife	W	3-2	1-1	4	Mooney M (pen), Gibson 2	795
9	15	H	Stenhousemuir	L	1-2	0-1	5	Mooney M	601
10	22	H	Queen of the S	D	0-0	0-0	5		725
11	29	A	Morton	L	0-1	0-0	8		1429
12	Nov 5	H	Stirling Albion	W	1-0	1-0	7	McKinnon	778
13	12	H	Berwick R	W	3-2	0-1	4	Mooney M, King, McGarvey	733
14	19	A	Meadowbank T	D	0-0	0-0	5		210
15	26	A	Clyde	L	1-3	1-1	6	Mooney M	1102
16	Dec 3	H	Brechin C	W	6-0	3-0	5	McGarvey 2, McKinnon, Mooney M, King, Campbell	554
17	26	H	East Fife	W	4-0	2-0	—	Mooney M, Ward, McGarvey, Meechan	862
18	31	A	Stenhousemuir	L	0-1	0-0	5		638
19	Jan 14	A	Queen of the S	D	0-0	0-0	6		1066
20	21	H	Stirling Albion	D	2-2	2-0	7	Mooney M, Ward	700
21	24	H	Morton	W	2-1	0-1	—	Ward, Gibson	1307
22	Feb 4	A	Berwick R	W	2-1	0-1	2	Gibson, Meechan	508
23	11	H	Meadowbank T	W	4-0	3-0	2	Mooney M, Ward, Gibson, McGarvey	749
24	18	H	Clyde	D	2-2	2-1	2	Martin, Mooney M	1183
25	25	A	Brechin C	D	0-0	0-0	3		480
26	Mar 4	A	East Fife	W	2-0	1-0	1	Ward 2	662
27	14	H	Stenhousemuir	W	5-1	2-1	—	Mooney M, Ward 3, McKinnon	1132
28	21	H	Berwick R	W	1-0	0-0	—	Ward	1012
29	25	A	Meadowbank T	L	0-1	0-1	1		389
30	Apr 1	H	Brechin C	W	4-1	3-0	1	Mooney M 2, Meechan, Fabiani	1103
31	8	A	Clyde	L	0-1	0-1	1		1189
32	15	H	East Fife	W	2-0	1-0	1	Mooney M, McKinnon	1253
33	22	A	Stenhousemuir	D	0-0	0-0	1		989
34	29	H	Queen of the S	D	2-2	1-1	2	Meechan, Mooney M	1369
35	May 6	A	Morton	L	0-2	0-0	3		6242
36	13	A	Stirling Albion	W	2-0	0-0	2	Ward, Gibson	3003

Final League Position: 2

Most Goals in Season (Individual): 38: Kenny Wilson, Division II; 1971-72.
Most Goals Overall (Individual): 169: Hughie Gallacher, 1954-62 (including C Division 1954-55).

Honours
League Champions: Division I 1890-91 (shared with Rangers), 1891-92. Division II 1910-11, 1971-72. Second Division 1991-92; *Runners-up:* First Division 1983-84. Division II 1907-08.
Scottish Cup Winners: 1883; *Runners-up:* 1881, 1882, 1887, 1891, 1897. *League Cup:* —.
Club colours: Shirt: Gold. Shorts: Gold. Stockings: Gold and black.

Goalscorers: *League (57):* Mooney M 17 (1 pen), Ward 12, Gibson 6, McGarvey 6, McKinnon 4, Meechan 4, Boyd 2, King 2, Martin 2, Campbell 1, Fabiani 1. *Scottish Cup (3):* Ward 2, McKinnon 1. *League Cup (0) B&Q Cup (2):* Campbell 2.

MacFarlane I 33	Marsland J 29	Fabiani R 27 + 1	Melvin M 16	Martin P 28	MacLeod M 24	Mooney M 33 + 3	Meechan J 25 + 3	Gibson C 21 + 5	McGarvey M 23 + 7	Foster A 5	Campbell C 4 + 10	Ward H 24 + 9	Boyd J 10 + 1	Gow S 30 + 1	McKinnon C 25 + 4	Hendry M 1 + 3	Burridge J 3	King T 25 + 1	Mooney S — + 2	McConville R — + 1	Farrell G 1	Hamilton J 9	Dallas S — + 1	Match No.
1	2	3	4	5	6	7	8	9	10	*11*	12	14												1
1	2	3	4		6	7	8	9	10		*11*	14	5											2
1	2	3	4		6	7	8	9	10		*11*	14	5											3
1	2	3	4		6	7	8	9	10		12	11	5											4
1		3	4		6	7	8	9	10		11	12	5	2										5
1		3	4	8	6	7		9	10		11		5	2										6
1	3		4	5	6	7	8	9	10			12		2	*11*	14								7
1	3	*6*	4	5		7	8	9	10			12		2	11	14								8
	3	*6*	4	5		7	8	9	10					2	11	12	1	14						9
	3		4	5	6	7		12					*10*	2	11	9	1	8	14					10
	3		4	5	6	7			8			12	*11*	2	9		1	10	14					11
1		3	4	5	6	14		*9*	12			7	11	2	10			8						12
1		3	4	5	6	12		9	11			7		2	10			8						13
1		3	4		6	7		12	10	5		11	14	2	*9*			8						14
1			4	5		7		*9*	8	3		14	6	2	11			10						15
1			4	5		7	12		8	3	14	11	6	2	9			10						16
1	6	3		5		7	4		10		12	11		2	9			*8*		14				17
1	6	3		5		7	4		10		12	11		2	9			8						18
1	6	3		5		7	4		10			11		2	9			8						19
1	2	3		5	6	7	4		10		14	11		12	*9*			8						20
1	4	3		5	*6*	7	10	9	14			11		2				8						21
1	6	3		5		12	4	9				11		2	10			8			7			22
1	6	3		5		7	4	9	10			11		2	12			8						23
1	6	3		5		7	4		10		12	11		2	9			8						24
1	3			5	6	7	4				12	11		2	9			8				10		25
1	3			5	6	7	4	9	10		14	11		2	12							8		26
1	3	14		5	6	7		9	*10*		12	11		2	8							4		27
1	6	3		5		7	12	9				11		2	10			8				4		28
1	6	3		5		7	12	9	14			*11*		2	10			8				4		29
1	5	3			6	7	10		14			11		2	9			*8*				4	12	30
1	5	3			6	7	10	14	12			11		2	*9*			8				4		31
1	5	3			6	7	10	9	14			11		2	12			8				*4*		32
1	4	3		5	6	7	10		14			*11*		2	9			8						33
1	4	3		5	6	7	10	12				11		2	9			8						34
1	4	3		5	6	7	10	14	11			12		2	*9*			8						35
1	4			5	6	7	10	9		3		11			12			8				2		36

DUNDEE

First Division

Year Formed: 1893. *Ground & Address:* Dens Park, Sandeman St, Dundee DD3 7JY. *Telephone:* 01382 826104. *Fax:* 01382 832284.
Ground Capacity: 16,871. seated: 11,516. *Size of Pitch:* 110yd × 70yd.
Chairman: Ron Dixon. *Vice-chairman:* Malcolm Reid. *Secretary:* Andrew Drummond. *Managing Director:* Nigel Squire.
Manager: Jim Duffy. *Coach:* John McCormack.
Managers since 1975: David White; Tommy Gemmell; Donald Mackay; Archie Knox; Jocky Scott; Dave Smith; Gordon Wallace; Iain Munro, Simon Stainrod. *Club Nickname(s):* The Dark Blues or The Dee. *Previous Grounds:* Carolina Port 1893-98.
Record Attendance: 43,024 v Rangers, Scottish Cup; 1953.
Record Transfer Fee received: £500,000 for Tommy Coyne to Celtic (March 1989).
Record Transfer Fee paid: £200,000 for Jim Leighton (Feb 1992).
Record Victory: 10-0 Division II v Alloa; 9 Mar, 1947 and v Dunfermline Ath; 22 Mar, 1947.
Record Defeat: 0-11 v Celtic, Division I; 26 Oct, 1895.
Most Capped Player: Alex Hamilton, 24, Scotland.
Most League Appearances: 341: Doug Cowie 1945-61.
Most League Goals in Season (Individual): 38: Dave Halliday, Division I; 1923-24.
Most Goals Overall (Individual): 113: Alan Gilzean.

DUNDEE 1994–95 LEAGUE RECORD

Match No.	Date	Venue	Opponents	Result		H/T Score	Lg. Pos.	Goalscorers	Attendance
1	Aug 13	H	St Mirren	W	2-0	1-0	—	Shaw, Britton	4125
2	20	H	Stranraer	W	3-1	2-0	1	Britton 2, McCaffrey (og)	3186
3	27	A	St Johnstone	W	1-0	1-0	1	Pittman	6021
4	Sept 3	H	Airdrieonians	D	1-1	0-1	1	Farningham	4020
5	10	A	Clydebank	L	2-5	1-2	2	Britton 2	1437
6	24	A	Ayr U	L	2-3	1-2	3	Britton, Hamilton	1901
7	Oct 1	H	Dunfermline Ath	D	4-4	1-1	3	Shaw 2, Tosh, Britton	4784
8	8	H	Hamilton A	W	2-0	2-0	3	Hamilton, Britton	2370
9	15	A	Raith R	D	1-1	0-1	3	Anderson	3834
10	22	A	St Mirren	W	2-1	1-0	3	McCann 2	2758
11	29	H	St Johnstone	W	1-0	0-0	3	Shaw	4327
12	Nov 12	H	Clydebank	W	2-0	1-0	3	Bain, Shaw	2240
13	19	A	Airdrieonians	L	1-2	0-0	3	Britton	2022
14	23	A	Stranraer	W	2-0	1-0	—	Tosh, Cargill	765
15	26	H	Ayr U	D	1-1	1-0	3	Tosh	2506
16	Dec 3	A	Dunfermline Ath	W	1-0	0-0	2	Ritchie	6065
17	10	H	Raith R	W	2-1	0-0	1	Hamilton, Wieghorst	3493
18	26	A	Hamilton A	W	1-0	1-0	—	Hamilton	1552
19	31	H	St Mirren	W	4-0	1-0	1	Hamilton, Shaw 3	3715
20	Jan 7	H	Stranraer	W	2-0	1-*0	1	Duffy C, Ritchie	2615
21	11	A	St Johnstone	D	2-2	1-0	—	Hamilton, Britton	5636
22	14	H	Airdrieonians	L	0-1	0-0	1		4084
23	21	A	Clydebank	W	3-0	2-0	1	Jack (og), Duffy C, Hamilton	900
24	Feb 4	H	Dunfermline Ath	L	2-3	1-2	1	Tosh, Britton	5896
25	11	A	Ayr U	L	0-1	0-1	1		2042
26	25	A	Raith R	D	0-0	0-0	2		5885
27	Mar 4	H	Hamilton A	W	2-0	1-0	1	Britton, Teasdale	2342
28	18	H	Clydebank	W	3-2	1-1	1	Shaw 2, Farningham	1788
29	25	A	Airdrieonians	W	3-0	0-0	1	Farningham, Shaw 2	2528
30	Apr 1	A	Dunfermline Ath	D	1-1	1-0	1	Shaw	8341
31	8	H	Ayr U	D	1-1	1-0	3	Duffy C	2765
32	15	A	Hamilton A	W	4-1	4-0	1	Shaw, Hamilton 3	1471
33	22	H	Raith R	L	0-2	0-0	3		7849
34	29	A	St Mirren	L	0-1	0-0	3		2976
35	May 6	H	St Johnstone	W	2-1	0-0	3	Hamilton, Shaw	3906
36	13	A	Stranraer	W	5-0	1-0	3	Hamilton, Wieghorst 2, Shaw, Tosh	1589

Final League Position: 3

Honours
League Champions: Division I 1961-62. First Division 1978-79, 1991-92. Division II 1946-47; *Runners-up:* Division I 1902-03, 1906-07, 1908-09, 1948-49, 1980-81.
Scottish Cup Winners: 1910; *Runners-up:* 1925, 1952, 1964.
League Cup Winners: 1951-52, 1952-53, 1973-74; *Runners-up:* 1967-68, 1980-81.
B&Q (Centenary) Cup: Winners: 1990-91 *Runners-up:* 1994-95.

European: *European Cup:* 1962-63 (semi-final). *Cup Winners:* 1964-65.
UEFA Cup: (*Fairs Cup* 1967-68 semi-final), 1971-72, 1973-74, 1974-75.
Club colours: Shirt: Dark blue with red and white trim. Shorts: White. Stockings: Blue and White.

Goalscorers: *League (65):* Shaw 16, Britton 12, Hamilton 12, Tosh 5, Duffy C 5, Farningham 3, Wieghorst 3, McCann 2, Ritchie 2, Anderson 1, Bain 1, Cargill 1, Pittman 1, Teasdale 1, own goals 2. *Scottish Cup (3):* Shaw 2, Hamilton 1. *League Cup (4):* Tosh 2, Farningham 1, Shaw 1. *B&Q Cup (12):* Britton 6, Wieghorst 2, Bain 1 (pen), McCann 1, Shaw 1, own goal 1.

Pageaud M 35	McQuillan J 30 + 2	Pittman S 3	Duffy C 23 + 1	Blake N 29 + 2	Duffy J 16	Shaw G 33 + 1	Dinnie A 1	Wieghorst M 29	Britton G 23 + 3	McCann N 29 + 3	Tosh P 13 + 14	Farningham R 25 + 2	Anderson I 4 + 6	Vrto D 22	McKeown G — + 1	Teasdale M 13 + 4	Hutchison M 7	Hamilton J 23 + 5	Mathers P 1 + 1	Bain K 20	Cargill A 10 + 4	Dailly M 1	Ritchie P 6 + 9	Match No.
1	2	*3*	4	5	6	7	8	9	10	11	14													1
1	2		6	5		7		9	10	11	14	3	*4*	8	12									2
1	2	3	6	5		7		9	10	*11*	12	4		8		14								3
1	2	3	4	5	6	7		9	10	11	14	*8*												4
1	2		4	5		7		9	10	11	12	6	14	8			3							5
1	2		6	5		7		9	10		*11*	4		8			3	14						6
	3			5	6	7		8	10		9	2				12		11	1	4				7
1	2			5		7		6	10		9			8				11		3	4			8
1	2			5		7		6	10	12	9	4	14	*8*				11		3				9
1	2			14	5			*6*	10	11	12	4	7	8				9		3				10
1	2			12	5	7			*10*	11	9	4					3	14		6	8			11
1	2			5		7		*6*	10	11	12			8		14		9		3	4			12
1	2			5	6	7		9	10	11	12	4		8				14				*3*		13
1	2			5	6	7		8		11	9					3		10			4			14
1	2			5		7		8	10	11	9					3		12		6	4			15
1	2			5		7				*11*	9	4	12			3		10		6	8		14	16
1	2		14	5		7		8		*11*	9	4	12			3		10		6				17
1			2	5		7		6		11	*9*	4		8		3		10			12		14	18
1			2	5		7		*9*	12	11		4		8		3		10		6			14	19
1	14		2	5		7			12	11				8		3		10		6	*4*		9	20
1	14		2	5		7			12	11				8		*3*		10		6	4		9	21
1	2			5		7			10	11		3		8				9		6	4		12	22
1	2		*3*	5		7		4	10	11		12		8				9		6			14	23
1	2		*3*	5				*4*	10	11	7		14	8				9	15	6				24
1	2			5		7		4	10	11	12		*6*	8				9		3			14	25
1			2			7		*9*	10	11		4		8		3		12		6	5		14	26
1			2			14		9	*10*	12		4		8		5	3	11		6			7	27
1	2		5		3	7			10	11	12	4		8				9		6				28
1	2		4		5	7		6		11	14	*10*		8		3							9	29
1	2		4		3	7			10	11		6		8		12				5			9	30
1	2		4	5	6	7		9	11	12	14	8					*3*						10	31
1	2		4	5	6	7		8		11	*9*	12					3	10					14	32
1	2		6	5	4	7		9		11	12	8					3	10						33
1	2		4	5	6	7		9			11	8				*3*		10			14		12	34
1	2		*4*	5	6	7		9		11		8	14			3		10			12			35
1	2		4	5	3	7		9		11	12	*8*	6					10			14			36

DUNDEE UNITED First Division

Year Formed: 1909 (1923). *Ground & Address:* Tannadice Park, Tannadice St, Dundee DD3 7JW. *Telephone:* 01382 833166. *Fax:* 01382 882689. *Ground Capacity:* total: 12,616 all seated: stands: east 2868, west 2104, south 2201, George Fox 5151, executive boxes 292.
Size of Pitch: 110yd × 74yd.
Chairman: James Y. McLean. *Company Secretary:* Miss Priti Trivedi. *Commercial Manager:* Bobby Brown.
Manager: Billy Kirkwood. *Assistant Manager:* Maurice Malpas. *Physio:* David Rankin. *Coach:* Gordon Wallace.
Managers since 1975: J. McLean, I.Golac. *Club Nickname(s):* The Terrors. *Previous Grounds:* None.
Record Attendance: 28,000 v Barcelona, Fairs Cup; 16 Nov, 1966.
Record Transfer Fee received: £4,000,000 for Duncan Ferguson from Rangers (July 1993).
Record Transfer Fee paid: £600,000 for Gordon Petric from Partizan Belgrade (Nov 1993).
Record Victory: 14-0 v Nithsdale Wanderers, Scottish Cup 1st rd; 17 Jan, 1931.
Record Defeat: 1-12 v Motherwell, Division II; 23 Jan, 1954.
Most Capped Player: Maurice Malpas, 55, Scotland.
Most League Appearances: 612, Dave Narey; 1973-94.
Most Appearances in European Matches: 76, Dave Narey (record for Scottish player).
Most League Goals in Season (Individual): 41: John Coyle, Division II; 1955-56.
Most Goals Overall (Individual): 158: Peter McKay.

DUNDEE UNITED 1994–95 LEAGUE RECORD

Match No.	Date	Venue	Opponents	Result		H/T Score	Lg. Pos.	Goalscorers	Attendance
1	Aug 13	A	Hibernian	L	0-5	0-3	—		8838
2	20	A	Celtic	L	1-2	0-0	10	Nixon	25,817
3	27	H	Aberdeen	W	2-1	0-0	8	Welsh, Brewster	9332
4	Sept 10	H	Motherwell	D	1-1	1-0	7	Ristic	7440
5	17	A	Hearts	L	1-2	0-2	9	Nixon	7392
6	24	H	Falkirk	W	1-0	0-0	7	Petric	6899
7	Oct 1	A	Rangers	L	0-2	0-1	8		43,635
8	8	A	Kilmarnock	W	2-0	1-0	6	Welsh, Ristic	7127
9	15	H	Partick T	L	0-1	0-0	7		6687
10	22	H	Hibernian	D	0-0	0-0	7		7983
11	29	A	Aberdeen	L	0-3	0-2	8		11,744
12	Nov 5	H	Celtic	D	2-2	1-2	7	Brewster, Dailly	10,496
13	8	A	Motherwell	D	1-1	0-0	—	Brewster	6145
14	19	H	Hearts	W	5-2	4-1	7	Johnson, Brewster, McKinlay, Dailly 2	7719
15	26	A	Falkirk	W	3-1	0-1	6	Brewster, Nixon, McKinlay	5933
16	Dec 4	H	Rangers	L	0-3	0-1	—		11,187
17	26	H	Kilmarnock	D	2-2	0-1	—	Hannah, Winters	8468
18	31	A	Hibernian	L	0-4	0-3	8		7754
19	Jan 2	H	Aberdeen	D	0-0	0-0	—		10,560
20	7	A	Celtic	D	1-1	1-1	6	Cleland	21,436
21	14	A	Hearts	L	0-2	0-1	8		8656
22	21	H	Motherwell	W	6-1	2-1	7	McKinlay 2, Brewster, Nixon 2, Dailly	7062
23	Feb 4	A	Rangers	D	1-1	1-1	8	Nixon	44,197
24	21	H	Falkirk	W	1-0	0-0	—	Malpas	6457
25	25	H	Partick T	W	2-0	0-0	6	Brewster, Gomes	7227
26	Mar 4	A	Kilmarnock	L	0-2	0-2	7		7630
27	7	A	Partick T	L	0-2	0-0	—		2126
28	18	A	Motherwell	L	1-2	0-0	8	Malpas	4457
29	21	H	Hearts	D	1-1	0-1	—	Gomes	6862
30	Apr 1	H	Rangers	L	0-2	0-2	8		11,035
31	8	A	Falkirk	L	1-3	1-0	9	Gomes	5894
32	15	H	Kilmarnock	L	1-2	1-1	9	Petric	8223
33	18	A	Partick T	W	3-1	1-1	—	Hannah, Welsh 2	4962
34	29	H	Hibernian	L	0-1	0-0	9		8376
35	May 6	A	Aberdeen	L	1-2	0-1	10	Winters	20,124
36	13	H	Celtic	L	0-1	0-0	10		10,993

Final League Position: 10

Honours
League Champions: Premier Division 1982-83. Division II 1924-25, 1928-29; *Runners-up:* Division II 1930-31, 1959-60.
Scottish Cup Winners: 1994; *Runners-up:* 1974, 1981, 1985, 1987, 1988, 1991.
League Cup Winners: 1979-80, 1980-81;*Runners-up:* 1981-82, 1984-85.
Summer Cup Runners-up: 1964-65. *Scottish War Cup Runners-up:* 1939-40.

European: *European Cup:* 8 matches: 1983-84 (semi-finals), 1988-89; *Cup Winners Cup:* 4 matches: 1974-75; *UEFA Cup Runners-up:* 1986-87. *Fairs Cup:* 10 matches: 1966-67, 1969-70, 1970-71. *UEFA Cup:* 70 matches: 1971-72, 1975-76, 1977-78, 1978-79, 1979-80, 1980-81, 1981-82, 1982-83, 1984-85, 1985-86, 1986-87, 1987-88, 1989-90, 1990-91, 1993-94.
Club colours: Tangerine jersey, Black shorts. Change colours: White with two Black hoops with Mauve trim, Black and White with Mauve trim shorts.

Goalscorers: *League (40):* Brewster 7, Nixon 6, Dailly 4, McKinlay 4, Welsh 4, Gomes 3, Hannah 2, Malpas 2, Petric 2, Ristic 2, Winters 2, Cleland 1, Johnson 1. *Scottish Cup (9):* Hannah 2, Bowman 1, Brewster 1, Craig 1, Gomes 1, McKinlay 1, Malpas 1, Nixon 1. *League Cup (3):* Hannah 2, Ristic 1.

Jorgensen H 1 + 1	Cleland A 18	Perry M 9	Hannah D 31 + 1	Petric G 33	Welsh B 26 + 1	Bowman D 31	Connolly P 4 + 2	Ristic D 8 + 2	Brewster C 25 + 2	Nixon J 8 + 20	Bollan G 5 + 2	Main A 6	McInally J 22 + 2	McKinlay W 26 + 1	McLaren A 16 + 4	Dailly C 30 + 3	Malpas M 31	Myers C — + 1	Johnson G 12 + 1	O'Hanlon K 29	Moule A — + 1	Craig D 3 + 3	Winters R 6 + 7	Gomes S 11 + 3	Ferreri J — + 1	Crabbe S 5 + 4	Match No.
1	2	3	4	5	6	7	8	9	10	11	12																1
	2		4	5	6	7		9	10	12		1	3	8	11												2
	2		*4*	5	6	7		9	10	14		1	3	8	11	12											3
	2		4	5	6		*10*	9		14		1	3	8	11	7											4
	2		4	5		*7*		9	10	14		1	6		11	8	3	12									5
	2		4	5	6				10	11		1		8	9	7	3										6
15				5	6	7			10	14	2	*1*	4	8	*9*	11	3		12								7
	2		4	5	6	7		9		11	12		14	8	10		3			1							8
	2		4	5	6	7		*9*		11				8	10	14	3			1							9
	2		4	*5*	6	7		9		14				8		10	3		11	1	12						10
	2		4	5	6	7				14			12	8	9	10	3		*11*	1							11
	2			5	6	7			10	14				8	*9*	11	3		4	1		12					12
	2		14	5	6	7			10					8	*9*	11	3		4	1							13
	2		4	5	6	7			*10*					8	12	9	3		11	1			14				14
			4	5	6	7			10	12	2			8		*9*	3		11	1			14				15
	2		4		6	7			10		5			8		9	3		11	1			14				16
			4	5		7	12		10	14	2			8		6	3		11	1			*9*				17
	2		4	5		7			10	14					*8*	6	3		11	1			9				18
	2		4	5		7	9		*10*	14	6			8		11	3			1			12				19
	2		4	5	6	7	12		10	14			8			11	3			1			*9*				20
	2		4	5	6	7	*9*		10				8	12		11	3			1			14				21
			4	5	6	7			10	14			2	8		11	3			1				*9*	12		22
			4	5		7			10	11			2	8		6	3			1		12	14	*9*			23
			4	5	6	7		12	10	14			*2*	8		11	3			1				9			24
			4	5	6	7			10	14			2	*8*		11	3			1				9		12	25
			4	5	6	7		14	*10*	8			2			11	3			1				9		12	26
			4	5	6	7			14	10			2			11	3			1			8	*9*		12	27
			4	5	6	7			14	12			2	8		11	3			1				*9*		10	28
		4		5		7			10	14			2	8		11	3			1		*6*		9			29
		11	4	5	6	7			*10*				2	8	9	12	3			1				14			30
		4		5	6	7				12			2	8	10	11	3			1				9			31
		2	10	5	12	6				*11*			3	8	14	4				1				9		7	32
		2	10	4	*5*	7							6	8	12	11	3			1				14		9	33
		2	11	4						12			6		*10*	5	3		8	1		14	9			7	34
		2	11						*10*				8		12	4	3		6	1		5	14	9		7	35
		2	10						*9*				6		7	5	3		8	1		4	11	14		12	36

DUNFERMLINE ATHLETIC First Division

Year Formed: 1885. *Ground & Address:* East End Park, Halbeath Rd, Dunfermline KY12 7RB. *Telephone:* 01383 724295. *Fax:* 01383 723468.
Ground Capacity: total: 18,340. seated: 4020. *Size of Pitch:* 114yd × 72yd.
Chairman: C. R. Woodrow. *Secretary:* P. A. M. D'Mello. *Commercial Manager:* Audrey Kelly.
Manager: Bert Paton. *Assistant Manager:* Dick Campbell.
Physio: Philip Yeates, MCSP.
Managers since 1975: G. Miller; H. Melrose; P. Stanton; T. Forsyth; J. Leishman; I. Munro; J. Scott. *Club Nickname(s):* The Pars. *Previous Grounds:* None.
Record Attendance: 27,816 v Celtic, Division I, 30 April, 1968.
Record Transfer Fee received: £200,000 for Ian McCall to Rangers (Aug 1987).
Record Transfer Fee paid: £540,000 for Istvan Kozma from Bordeaux (Sept 1989).
Record Victory: 11-2 v Stenhousemuir, Division II, 27 Sept, 1930.
Record Defeat: 1-11 v Hibernian, Scottish Cup, 3rd rd replay, 26 Oct, 1889.
Most Capped Player: Andy Wilson, 6 (12), Scotland.
Most League Appearances: 360: Bobby Robertson; 1977-88.
Most League Goals in Season (Individual): 55: Bobby Skinner, Division II, 1925-26.
Most Goals Overall (Individual): 154: Charles Dickson.

DUNFERMLINE ATHLETIC 1994–95 LEAGUE RECORD

Match No.	Date	Venue	Opponents	Result		H/T Score	Lg. Pos.	Goalscorers	Attendance
1	Aug 13	A	Airdrieonians	D	0-0	0-0	—		2964
2	20	A	Clydebank	W	1-0	1-0	2	Petrie	1597
3	27	H	Raith R	W	1-0	0-0	2	French (pen)	7373
4	Sept 3	A	St Mirren	D	1-1	0-1	2	French	3895
5	10	H	Hamilton A	W	4-0	3-0	1	McCathie, Petrie 2, French	4029
6	24	H	Stranraer	W	1-0	1-0	1	Petrie	3893
7	Oct 1	A	Dundee	D	4-4	1-1	1	Petrie, Smith, French, McCathie	4784
8	8	H	St Johnstone	W	3-0	2-0	1	Tod, Smith, Petrie	6931
9	15	A	Ayr U	D	0-0	0-0	1		2302
10	22	H	Airdrieonians	D	2-2	0-1	1	French 2	5642
11	29	A	Raith R	W	5-2	2-2	1	Petrie 2, Ward 2, French	5965
12	Nov 5	H	Clydebank	W	4-1	1-0	1	Robertson, Petrie 2, Den Bieman	4611
13	12	A	Hamilton A	L	1-3	1-3	1	Petrie	2103
14	19	H	St Mirren	W	1-0	0-0	1	Smith	4660
15	26	A	Stranraer	D	0-0	0-0	1		1118
16	Dec 3	H	Dundee	L	0-1	0-0	3		6065
17	10	H	Ayr U	W	6-0	2-0	2	French 3 (1 pen), Den Bieman, McNamara, Tod	3197
18	26	A	St Johnstone	L	2-3	2-1	—	Den Bieman 2	6091
19	31	A	Airdrieonians	D	0-0	0-0	2		3252
20	Jan 7	A	Clydebank	W	2-1	0-1	2	Millar, Robertson	1468
21	11	H	Raith R	L	0-1	0-0	—		8457
22	14	A	St Mirren	D	2-2	2-1	3	Petrie 2	2736
23	21	H	Hamilton A	W	2-1	1-0	2	Tod, Petrie	3973
24	Feb 4	A	Dundee	W	3-2	2-1	2	Smith P 2 (1 pen), Fleming	5896
25	14	H	Stranraer	W	3-1	1-0	—	Tod, Ward, McNamara	3528
26	25	A	Ayr U	W	2-1	1-0	1	Ward, Smith P	2183
27	Mar 11	H	St Johnstone	D	1-1	0-0	1	Millar	6522
28	22	A	Hamilton A	W	3-1	1-0	—	Moore, French 2	1343
29	25	H	St Mirren	D	1-1	0-0	2	Tod	5055
30	Apr 1	H	Dundee	D	1-1	0-1	2	Den Bieman	8341
31	8	A	Stranraer	W	1-0	1-0	2	Robertson	988
32	15	A	St Johnstone	D	1-1	0-0	3	Robertson	5039
33	22	H	Ayr U	W	3-0	1-0	2	McCathie, Robertson, Tod	4808
34	29	H	Airdrieonians	D	0-0	0-0	2		6603
35	May 6	A	Raith R	D	0-0	0-0	2		6361
36	13	H	Clydebank	W	2-1	2-0	2	Robertson, McCathie	7709

Final League Position: 2

Honours
League Champions: First Division 1988-89. Division II 1925-26. Second Division 1985-86; *Runners-up:* First Division 1986-87, 1993-94, 1994-95. Division II 1912-13, 1933-34, 1954-55, 1957-58, 1972-73. Second Division 1978-79.
Scottish Cup Winners: 1961, 1968; *Runners-up:* 1965.
League Cup Runners-up: 1949-50, 1991-92.

European: *European Cup:* —. *Cup Winners Cup:* 1961-62, 1968-69 (semi-finals). *UEFA Cup:* 1962-63, 1964-65, 1965-66, 1966-67, 1969-70 (*Fairs Cup*).
Club colours: Shirt: Black and white vertical stripes, stippled with red dots. Shorts: Black with white side panel. Stockings: White with red chevrons.

Goalscorers: *League (63):* Petrie 14, French 12 (2 pens), Robertson 6, Smith 6 (1 pen), Tod 6, Den Bieman 5, McCathie 4, Ward 4, McNamara 2, Millar 2, Fleming 1, Moore 1. *Scottish Cup (4):* Petrie 2, Hawkins 1, Smith 1. *League Cup (4):* Den Bieman 1, McCathie 1, Petrie 1, Ward 1. *B&Q Cup (10):* Petrie 4, French 2 (1 pen), McCathie 1, Robertson 1, Smith 1, Tod 1.

Westwater I 17	Den Bieman I 19 + 12	Bowes M 7	McCathie N 32	Cooper N 14 + 1	Smith P 34	Moore A 11 + 1	Robertson C 35	Petrie S 31 + 2	Laing D 2 + 4	Tod A 30 + 5	McCulloch M 5 + 4	McNamara J 30	Ward K 19 + 4	French H 24 + 1	Will J 5 + 1	McQueen J 1	Sharp R 2	Sinclair C — + 1	Hawkins A 1 + 4	Fleming D 29	Millar M 22 + 2	Higgins G 1 + 1	Paterson G 5	Harrison T 1 + 1	Van De Kamp G 13	Shaw G 6	Fenwick P — + 2	Match No.
1	2	3	4	5	6	7	8	9	*10*	11	14																	1
1	2	3	4	5	6		8	9		11		7	10	12														2
1	2	3	4	5	6		8	10	12	11		7		9	15													3
	2	3	4	5	6		8	10	12	11			7	9	1													4
	7	2	4	5	6		8	10					11	9		1	3											5
1	7	2	4		6		8	10	12	5			*11*	9			3	14										6
1	7	*2*	4		6		8	10	12	5		3	11	9					14									7
1	7		4		6		8	10		5		2	11	9						3								8
1	7		4		6			10		5		2	11	9						3	8							9
1	14				6		8	10	7	5	*4*	2	12	9						3	11							10
1	12		4		6		8	10		5	2		7	*9*						3	11	14						11
1	12		4		6		8	10		5		2	7	9						3	11							12
1	12		4	14	6		8	10		5		2	7	*9*						3	11							13
1	12		4	*5*	6		8	10		14		2	7	9						3	11							14
1	12		4	5	6		8	10		7		2		9						3	11							15
1			4	5	6		8	10		14		2	7	9						3	11							16
1	7		4	5	6		8	*10*		14		2	11	9						3	12							17
1	7			5	6		8	14		*10*		2	11	9						3	12		4					18
	7			5	6		8	10		12		*2*	14	9	1					3	11		4					19
	7		4		6		8	14		12		2		9	1					3	11	*10*	5					20
	14		4		6		8	10		5		2	7	9	1					3	*11*							21
			4	5	6		8	10		9		2	7		1					3	11			14				22
	7			5	6		8	10		9		2	11							3				4	1			23
	7		4		6		8	10		11		2	14	9						3			5		1			24
	14		4		6		8	10		*9*		2	12	7					11	3			5		1			25
	12		4	5	6	7	8	10		2			11							3	9				1			26
			4			7	8			5	6	2	11	9					12	3	10				1			27
	7		4			11	8			5	6	2		9					12	3	10				1			28
1	12		4		6	7	8	10		5		2		9						3	11							29
	14		4		6	7	8	10		5		2								3	11				1	*9*		30
			4		6	7	8	10		5	12	2								3	11				1	9		31
			4		6	9	8	10		5	7	2							12	3	11				1		14	32
	12		4		6	7	8	10		5		2								3	11				1	9		33
	7		4		6	11	8	10		5	14	*2*								3					1	9	12	34
	10		4		6	7	8			5		2								3	11				1	9		35
	7		4		6	12	8	10		5	14	2								3	11				1	*9*		36

EAST FIFE — Second Division

Year Formed: 1903. *Ground & Address:* Bayview Park, Methil, Fife KY8 3AG. *Telephone:* 01333 426323. *Fax:* 01333 426376.
Ground Capacity: total: 5385. seated: 600. *Size of Pitch:* 110yd × 71yd.
Chairman: James Baxter. *General Manager:* David Gorman. *Secretary:* Leona Walker. *Commercial Manager:* James Bonthrone.
Manager: Steve Archibald. *Assistant Manager:* Alan Sneddon. *Physio:* Alex MacQueen. *Coach:* Gordon Rae.
Managers since 1975: Frank Christie; Roy Barry; David Clarke; Gavin Murray, Alex Totten. *Club Nickname(s):* The Fifers.
Previous Grounds: None.
Record Attendance: 22,515 v Raith Rovers, Division I; 2 Jan, 1950.
Record Transfer Fee received: £150,000 for Paul Hunter from Hull C (March 1990).
Record Transfer Fee paid: £70,000 for John Sludden from Kilmarnock (July 1991).
Record Victory: 13-2 v Edinburgh City, Division II; 11 Dec, 1937.
Record Defeat: 0-9 v Hearts, Division I; 5 Oct, 1957.
Most Capped Player: George Aitken, 5 (8), Scotland.
Most League Appearances: 517: David Clarke, 1968-86.

EAST FIFE 1994–95 LEAGUE RECORD

Match No.	Date	Venue	Opponents	Result		H/T Score	Lg. Pos.	Goalscorers	Attendance
1	Aug 13	A	Stirling Albion	W	1-0	0-0	—	Hildersley	808
2	20	A	Stenhousemuir	D	1-1	0-1	2	Hunter	544
3	27	H	Brechin C	D	1-1	0-0	3	Burns	795
4	Sept 3	A	Queen of the S	W	2-0	1-0	2	Andrew, Scott	1412
5	10	H	Clyde	W	2-0	1-0	2	Hunter, Dow	925
6	24	H	Morton	L	1-2	1-1	2	Sneddon	1173
7	Oct 1	A	Berwick R	D	1-1	1-1	4	Scott	573
8	8	H	Dumbarton	L	2-3	1-1	5	Beaton, Scott	795
9	15	A	Meadowbank T	W	1-0	0-0	3	Scott	314
10	22	H	Stirling Albion	W	4-3	1-1	3	Scott, Beaton, Hope, Burns	1039
11	29	A	Brechin C	L	0-2	0-1	3		613
12	Nov 5	H	Stenhousemuir	L	2-3	0-2	4	Hutcheon, Scott	719
13	12	A	Clyde	D	1-1	0-0	5	Archibald	1212
14	19	H	Queen of the S	W	3-1	2-1	3	Hutcheon 2, Scott	699
15	26	A	Morton	L	0-3	0-1	4		1884
16	Dec 3	H	Berwick R	W	3-0	2-0	4	Scott 3	756
17	26	A	Dumbarton	L	0-4	0-2	—		862
18	31	H	Meadowbank T	W	2-1	1-1	4	Scott, Hutcheon	686
19	Jan 2	H	Brechin C	W	4-0	2-0	—	Sneddon, Cusick, Donaghy, Hildersley	1155
20	14	A	Stirling Albion	L	0-3	0-2	4		810
21	21	H	Stenhousemuir	L	0-2	0-2	4		713
22	Feb 4	H	Clyde	L	1-3	1-1	7	Cusick	885
23	14	A	Queen of the S	D	3-3	1-1	—	Hunter 2, Donaghy	890
24	25	A	Berwick R	D	0-0	0-0	7		503
25	28	H	Morton	D	1-1	1-0	—	Hamill	558
26	Mar 4	H	Dumbarton	L	0-2	0-1	7		662
27	11	A	Meadowbank T	W	3-1	1-1	7	Beaton 2, Hope	222
28	18	A	Clyde	D	1-1	0-0	7	Cusick	602
29	25	H	Queen of the S	W	3-1	0-1	7	Scott 2, Hunter	594
30	Apr 1	H	Berwick R	L	0-1	0-1	7		628
31	8	A	Morton	L	1-4	0-1	7	Hamill	1789
32	15	A	Dumbarton	L	0-2	0-1	7		1253
33	22	H	Meadowbank T	D	1-1	0-1	7	Dwarika	355
34	29	H	Stirling Albion	L	1-2	1-0	7	Beaton	510
35	May 6	A	Brechin C	D	1-1	1-1	7	Scott	386
36	13	A	Stenhousemuir	L	1-2	1-2	8	Hutcheon	433

Final League Position: 8

Most League Goals in Season (Individual): 41: Jock Wood, Division II; 1926-27 and Henry Morris, Division II; 1947-48.
Most Goals Overall (Individual): 196: George Dewar (149 in League).

Honours
League Champions: Division II 1947-48; *Runners-up:* Division II 1929-30, 1970-71. Second Division 1983-84.
Scottish Cup Winners: 1938; *Runners-up:* 1927, 1950.
League Cup Winners: 1947-48, 1949-50, 1953-54.
Club colours: Shirt: Amber with black collar and cuffs. Shorts: Amber with black flashes. Stockings: Amber with 3 black stripes on top.

Goalscorers: *League (48):* Scott 14, Beaton 5, Hunter 5, Hutcheon 5, Cusick 3, Burns 2, Donaghy 2, Hamill 2, Hildersley 2, Hope 2, Sneddon 2, Andrew 1, Archibald 1, Dow 1, Dwarika 1. *Scottish Cup (7):* Hutcheon 3, Allan 2, Burns 1 (pen), Donaghy 1. *League Cup (2):* Allan 1, Hope 1. *B&Q Cup (2):* Hunter 1, Scott 1.

Wilson E 23	Bell G 12	Williamson A 1	Barron D 3	Sneddon A 34	Hildersley R 17 + 1	Cusick J 28 + 1	Hope D 31	Scott R 31 + 1	Hunter P 24 + 3	Gibb R 23 + 5	Allan G 18 + 6	Irvine A 1 + 13	Beaton D 29 + 1	Burns W 27 + 1	Andrew B 10 + 7	Dow C 5 + 3	Donaghy M 23 + 3	Hutcheon S 9 + 11	Archibald S 12 + 1	Robertson D 13 + 1	Hamill A 15 + 1	Struthers D 1 + 4	Dwarika A 5 + 1	Balmain K 1	Match No.
1	2	3	4	5	6	7	8	*9*	10	11	12	14													1
1	2		3	4	7	*6*	8	9	10	11	12		5	14											2
1	*2*		6	4	7		11	9	10	3	14		5	8	12										3
1	3			2	8			9	10	11	7	12	5	4	6	14									4
1	3			2	*8*			9	10	11	14	12	5	4	6	7									5
1				2	6	8	3	9	10	11	7	12	5	4		14									6
1	2			3			11	9	10		7	12	5	4	*8*	6	14								7
1				2		12	6	9	10	3	7		5	4		11	*8*	14							8
1	2			3			8	9	10	11			5	4		*6*	7	12	14						9
1	2			3	7		11	9	10				5	4			6		8						10
1				2	7		11	9	10	3			5	4	14		*6*	12	8						11
1				3	*6*	2	11	9					5	4	7	10		14	8						12
1				2		7	11	9		3		12	5	4	14		6	10	8						13
1	3			2		7	6	9		11		14	5	4	12		8	*10*							14
1	3			2	14	7	11	9				12	5	4	8		6	10							15
1				2	6	7	3	9			12	14	5	4			11	*10*	8						16
1				2	3	7	11	9			14	12	5	4			6	10	8						17
1				2	3	6	11	9			7		5	4			10	14	*8*						18
1				2	3	6	11	9		12	7		5	4			10	14	*8*						19
	2				8	6	11	9	12	*3*	7		5	4				10		1	14				20
				2		6	11	9	12	*3*	7		5			14	8	10		1	4				21
	2			4	6	5	*11*	9	10	3	7				12			14		1	8				22
				5		2	11		10	6	*7*			4	12		8	9		1	3				23
				5		2	11		10	6	7	9		4	*8*			14		1	3				24
1				2		5	11		10	3	7			4			6	12	8		9				25
1				2		5	11	9	10	*3*	*7*		12	4			8			15	6				26
				2		6	11	*9*	10	12	7	14	5	4			8			1	3				27
				2		3	11	*9*	10	12	7	14	5	4			8			1	6				28
				2		3	11	9	10				5	4	*7*		8			1	6	12			29
				2		3	11	9	10	14			5	4			8			1	6	*7*	12		30
				2		3		9	12	14	7		5	4			*8*			1	6		10	11	31
				2	*6*	4	11	12	10	7			5		14		8			1	3		9		32
				4	6	5		9	10	3					*2*		12		8	1	11	14	7		33
				2		4		9	10	11	7		5				14	12	8	1	3		*6*		34
1				2		4	11	9		3			5		7		6	14	*8*		10	12			35
1						4	11		7	3	*2*	12	5		10		6	9				14	8		36

EAST STIRLINGSHIRE Third Division

Year Formed: 1880. *Ground & Address:* Firs Park, Firs St, Falkirk FK2 7AY. *Telephone:* 01324 623583.
Ground Capacity: total: 1880. seated: 200. *Size of Pitch:* 112yd × 72yd.
Chairman: William C. White. *Secretary:* Alex Forsyth. *Commercial Manager:* Tom Kirk.
Manager: Billy Little. *Assistant Manager/Coach:* Lenny Reid. *Physio:* Sandra Lawler.
Managers since 1975: I. Ure; D. McLinden; W. P. Lamont; M. Ferguson; W. Little; D. Whiteford; D. Lawson; J. D. Connell; A. Mackin; Dom Sullivan, Bobby McCulley. *Club Nickname(s):* The Shire. *Previous Grounds:* Burnhouse, Randyford Park, Merchiston Park, New Kilbowie Park.
Record Attendance: 12,000 v Partick T, Scottish Cup 3rd rd; 19 Feb 1921.
Record Transfer Fee received: £35,000 for Jim Docherty to Chelsea (1978).
Record Transfer Fee paid: £6,000 for Colin McKinnon from Falkirk (March 1991).
Record Victory: 11-2 v Vale of Bannock, Scottish Cup 2nd rd; 22 Sept, 1888.
Record Defeat: 1-12 v Dundee United, Division II; 13 Apr, 1936.
Most Capped Player: Humphrey Jones, 5 (14), Wales.
Most League Appearances: 379: Gordon Simpson, 1968-80.

EAST STIRLINGSHIRE 1994–95 LEAGUE RECORD

Match No.	Date	Venue	Opponents	Result	H/T Score	Lg. Pos.	Goalscorers	Attendance
1	Aug 13	A	Montrose	L 0-2	0-1	—		537
2	20	H	Ross C	D 2-2	1-1	8	McCallum, Scott	632
3	27	A	Alloa	W 3-1	1-0	5	Millar, Geraghty, Loney	404
4	Sept 3	A	Cowdenbeath	D 1-1	0-0	6	McCallum	258
5	10	H	Albion R	W 4-0	2-0	4	Geraghty 2, Lee I 2	377
6	24	H	Forfar Ath	W 3-1	1-1	3	Russell, Lee I, Cuthbert	419
7	Oct 1	A	Caledonian Th	D 3-3	2-1	4	Sneddon 2, Lee I	1229
8	8	H	Queen's Park	W 3-2	1-1	2	Lee R, Geraghty, McCallum	464
9	15	A	Arbroath	W 1-0	0-0	1	Geraghty	404
10	22	H	Montrose	L 1-2	0-0	3	Russell	631
11	29	H	Alloa	L 1-2	0-1	4	Millar	570
12	Nov 5	A	Ross C	W 4-1	2-0	3	Conroy, Lee I, Yates, Geraghty	1194
13	12	A	Albion R	W 2-0	1-0	3	Lee R, Millar	361
14	19	H	Cowdenbeath	L 0-2	0-0	4		553
15	26	A	Forfar Ath	L 2-3	2-2	5	Dwyer,Lee I	527
16	Dec 3	H	Caledonian Th	W 2-0	1-0	3	Lee I, Geraghty	508
17	26	A	Queen's Park	W 3-2	2-0	—	Russell, Geraghty 2	502
18	31	H	Arbroath	W 1-0	0-0	3	Geraghty	436
19	Jan 21	H	Ross C	L 0-2	0-0	5		459
20	Feb 7	A	Alloa	W 1-0	0-0	—	Dwyer	395
21	18	H	Forfar Ath	L 1-2	0-0	5	McCallum	528
22	25	A	Caledonian Th	D 3-3	1-1	5	Dwyer, Lee R, Geraghty	886
23	Mar 7	H	Albion R	W 3-0	1-0	—	Geraghty, Lee I, Dwyer	312
24	11	A	Arbroath	L 2-5	0-3	4	Dwyer, Cuthbert	596
25	15	H	Montrose	W 1-0	0-0	—	Dwyer	297
26	22	A	Cowdenbeath	W 4-1	2-0	—	Geraghty 2, Lee I, Dwyer	172
27	25	H	Cowdenbeath	W 1-0	1-0	2	Hunter	338
28	Apr 1	H	Caledonian Th	W 1-0	1-0	2	Geraghty	391
29	5	A	Albion R	L 1-3	0-1	—	Dwyer	211
30	8	A	Forfar Ath	L 0-1	0-1	3		623
31	15	A	Queen's Park	L 0-1	0-1	4		480
32	18	H	Queen's Park	W 3-2	2-2	—	Sneddon, Hunter, Watt	382
33	22	H	Arbroath	L 0-2	0-1	4		414
34	29	A	Montrose	L 0-1	0-0	4		858
35	May 6	H	Alloa	D 1-1	1-1	4	Dwyer	418
36	13	A	Ross C	W 3-2	1-2	4	Geraghty, Lee I, Hunter	1005

Final League Position: 4

Most League Goals in Season (Individual): 36: Malcolm Morrison, Division II; 1938-39.
Most Goals Overall (Individual): —.

Honours
League Champions: Division II 1931-32; C Division 1947-48. *Runners-up:* Division II 1962-63. Second Division 1979-80. Division Three 1923-24.
Scottish Cup: —.
League Cup: —.
Club colours: Shirt: Black and white hoops. Shorts: Black. Stockings: Black.

Goalscorers: *League (61):* Garaghty 16, Lee I 10, Dwyer 9, McCallum 4, Hunter 3, Lee R 3, Millar 3, Russell 3, Sneddon 3, Cuthbert 2, Conroy 1, Loney 1, Scott 1, Watt 1, Yates 1. *Scottish Cup (0) League Cup (0) B&Q Cup (1):* Watt 1.

Moffat J 6	Watt D 28 + 3	Cuthbert L 17 + 5	Russell G 22	Yates D 12	Lee R 33	Lee I 36	Millar G 28 + 6	McCallum M 11 + 1	Scott C 16 + 2	Geraghty M 36	Dempsey S — + 1	Stirling D 16 + 5	Scott B 1	Loney J 5 + 5	Sneddon S 32	Ross B 25	Robertson A — + 1	Conroy J 5 + 9	McDougall G 30	Abercromby M 9 + 7	Dwyer P 20	Hunter M 7 + 3	McConville R — + 5	Gilogley W 1	Match No.
1	2	*3*	4	5	6	7	8	9	10	11	12	14													1
1	2		4	5	6	7	8	9	10	11			3	12											2
1	12		4		3	7	8	9	10	11		14		2	*5*	6									3
1	3		2	4		7	8	9	*6*	10		12		11	5		14								4
1	2	3	4			7	8		6	10		9		*11*	5			14							5
1	4	11	2	6	3	7	8	12		10		*9*			5			14							6
	2	11	6	4	3	7	8	9	12	10		14			*5*				1						7
		11	2	4	3	7	8	9	6	10					5			14	1						8
	2	12	11	4	3	7	8	*9*	6	10					5			14	1						9
	2	11	6	4	3	7	8		12	10		*9*		14	5				1						10
			2	4	3	7	8		6	10		9		12	5			11	1						11
		12	2	4	3	7	8		6	10		9		14	5			*11*	1						12
		12	2	4	3	7	8			10		9			5	6		*11*	1	14					13
	4		2		3	7	8			10		*9*			5	6		11	1	14					14
	4		2		3	7	8			10				11	5	6			1	14	9				15
	4		2		3	7	8			10		12			5	6		11	1		9				16
	4		2	5	3	7	8		*11*	10						6		14	1		9				17
	4		2		3	7	*8*		11	10					5	6		14	1		9				18
	2		4		3	7	12	9	10	8					5	6		14	1		11				19
	12		2		3	7	8	9	*4*	10				14	5	6			1		11				20
	14		2		3	7	4	9		8				*11*	5	6			1		10				21
	4	12	2		3	7			10	8					5	6		14	1	*9*	11				22
	2	10			3	7	12		4	8					5	6			1	9	11				23
	2	10			3	7	4			8					5	6		12	1	9	11				24
	2	10			3	7	14			9		*4*			5	6			1		11	8			25
	2	10			3	7	14			9		4			5	6			1	12	11	*8*			26
	2	10			3	7				9		4			5	6			1		11	8			27
	2	*10*			3	7	12			9		4			5	6			1	14	11	8			28
	2	10			3	7	12			9		4			5	6			1	14	11	*8*			29
	2	*10*			3	7	4	9		8					5	6			1	12	11	14			30
	2	*10*			3	7	4			9					5	6			1	8	11	12	14		31
	2				3	7	4			9		10			5	6			1	8		11	12		32
	2	12			3	7	4			*9*					5	6			1	8	11	10	14		33
	2				3	7	4			9		10			5	6			1	8	11		14		34
	2	3				7	4			9		10			5	6			1	8	11		12		35
		3			5	7	4		8	9		10				6			1	11		12		2	36

FALKIRK Premier Division

Year Formed: 1876. *Ground & Address:* Brockville Park, Hope St, Falkirk FK1 5AX. *Telephone:* 01324 624121/632487. *Fax:* 01324 612418.
Ground Capacity: total: 12,800. seated: 2661. *Size of Pitch:* 110yd × 70yd.
Chairman: G. J. Fulston. *Secretary:* A. D. Moffat. *Commercial Executive:* George Miller.
Manager: Jim Jefferies. *Assistant Manager:* Billy Brown. *Physio:* Bob McCallum. *Coach:* Willie Wilson.
Managers since 1975: J. Prentice; G. Miller; W. Little; J. Hagart; A. Totten; G. Abel; W. Lamont; D. Clarke; J. Duffy. *Club Nickname(s):* The Bairns. *Previous Grounds:* Randyford; Blinkbonny Grounds; Hope Street.
Record Attendance: 23,100 v Celtic, Scottish Cup 3rd rd; 21 Feb, 1953.
Record Transfer Fee received: £270,000 for Gordon Marshall to Celtic (Aug 1991).
Record Transfer Fee paid: £225,000 to Chelsea for Kevin McAllister (Aug 1991).
Record Victory: 12-1 v Laurieston, Scottish Cup 2nd rd; 23 Mar, 1893.
Record Defeat: 1-11 v Airdrieonians, Division I; 28 Apr, 1951.
Most Capped Player: Alex Parker, 14 (15), Scotland.
Most League Appearances: (post-war): John Markie, 349.

FALKIRK 1994–95 LEAGUE RECORD

Match No.	Date	Venue	Opponents	Result		H/T Score	Lg. Pos.	Goalscorers	Attendance
1	Aug 13	H	Celtic	D	1-1	0-0	—	McCall	12,635
2	20	A	Aberdeen	D	2-2	1-1	6	Cadette, McDonald	11,143
3	27	H	Partick T	W	2-1	0-1	4	Fulton, Cadette	5402
4	Sept 10	A	Kilmarnock	D	1-1	0-1	3	Cadette	8021
5	17	H	Rangers	L	0-2	0-1	6		12,419
6	24	A	Dundee U	L	0-1	0-0	8		6899
7	Oct 1	H	Hearts	W	2-1	1-1	4	McLaughlin, McAvennie	7589
8	8	A	Motherwell	L	3-5	1-2	7	Clark 2, McAvennie	6239
9	15	H	Hibernian	D	0-0	0-0	6		7388
10	22	A	Celtic	W	2-0	1-0	6	Henderson, Clark	23,688
11	29	A	Partick T	W	2-1	2-1	5	Clark, May	4215
12	Nov 5	H	Aberdeen	W	2-1	1-1	4	Cramb, McGowan	6185
13	8	H	Kilmarnock	D	3-3	0-3	—	Clark 2, Henderson	6134
14	19	A	Rangers	D	1-1	0-1	4	Henderson	44,018
15	26	H	Dundee U	L	1-3	1-0	4	Henderson	5933
16	Dec 3	A	Hearts	D	1-1	1-1	4	McDonald	8960
17	10	A	Hibernian	D	2-2	1-0	4	McDonald, Rice (pen)	7725
18	26	H	Motherwell	L	0-1	0-0	—		7937
19	31	A	Celtic	L	0-2	0-0	5		21,294
20	Jan 7	A	Aberdeen	D	0-0	0-0	5		14,141
21	14	H	Rangers	L	2-3	0-1	7	McDonald, May	12,507
22	17	H	Partick T	L	1-3	0-1	—	MacKenzie	3958
23	21	A	Kilmarnock	L	1-2	1-1	9	Clark	7648
24	Feb 4	H	Hearts	W	2-0	1-0	7	Fulton, Henderson	6028
25	21	A	Dundee U	L	0-1	0-0	—		6457
26	25	H	Hibernian	W	1-0	0-0	7	Kirk	6501
27	Mar 7	A	Motherwell	D	2-2	1-1	—	McLaughlin, Kirk	6100
28	11	A	Rangers	D	2-2	1-1	7	McDonald 2	43,359
29	25	H	Kilmarnock	W	2-0	1-0	6	Kirk, McDonald	5714
30	Apr 1	A	Hearts	W	1-0	1-0	5	McGrillen	9003
31	8	H	Dundee U	W	3-1	0-1	5	Johnston M, Kirk, McDonald	5894
32	15	H	Motherwell	W	3-0	1-0	3	Kirk, Weir, Fulton	5756
33	19	A	Hibernian	W	2-0	1-0	—	Clark, McDonald	5450
34	29	H	Celtic	L	1-2	0-1	3	Rice	9714
35	May 6	A	Partick T	D	0-0	0-0	4		5927
36	13	H	Aberdeen	L	0-2	0-1	5		12,835

Final League Position: 5

Most League Goals in Season (Individual): 43: Evelyn Morrison, Division I; 1928-29.
Most Goals Overall (Individual): Dougie Moran, 86.

Honours
League Champions: Division II 1935-36, 1969-70, 1974-75. First Division 1990-91, 1993-94. Second Division 1979-80; *Runners-up:* Division I 1907-08, 1909-10. First Division 1985-86, 1988-89. Division II 1904-05, 1951-52, 1960-61.
Scottish Cup Winners: 1913, 1957. *League Cup Runners-up:* 1947-48. *B&Q Cup Winners:* 1993-94.
Club colours: Shirt: Dark blue with white flashings. Shorts: White. Stockings: Red.

Goalscorers: *League (48):* McDonald 9, Clark 8. Henderson 5, Kirk 5, Cadette 3, Fulton 3, McAvennie 2, McLaughlin 2, May 2, Rice 2 (1 pen), Cramb 1, Johnston 1, McCall 1, McGowan 1, McGrillen 1, MacKenzie 1, Weir 1. *Scottish Cup (0):* League Cup (4): Cadette 3, McDonald 1.

Parks A 28	Weir D 32	McGowan J 27 + 4	Hughes J 17 + 3	Oliver N 26 + 1	MacKenzie N 36	May E 24	Fulton S 25 + 3	Cadette R 8	McCall I 3 + 2	Johnston F 3	Hamilton G 2 + 1	McDonald C 26 + 5	McLaughlin J 28	Rice B 19 + 7	McStay J — + 1	Henderson N 14 + 7	Cramb C 6 + 2	Lamont W 5 + 3	Clark J 31	McAvennie F 1 + 2	James K 1	Shaw G — + 3	Burridge J 3	Paterson J 1 + 3	McQueen T 3 + 1	Kirk S 11	McGrillen P 6	Johnston M 10	Match No.
1	2	3	4	5	6	7	8	9	*10*	11	12	14																	1
1	2	3		4	6	7	8	9				11	5	*10*	14														2
1	2	3		4	6	7	8	9				11	5			10													3
1	2	3		4	6	7	8	9				11	5			*10*	12	15											4
	2	12		3	6	7	8	9				*11*	5	10				1	4	14									5
1	2			3	*6*	7	8	9				11	5	10		14			4										6
1	2	12		3	6	7	8	9					5	10		14			4	*11*									7
1	2			3	*6*	7	8	9				11		10					4	14	5								8
1	2	3		4	6	7			10				5	*11*		14	9		8			12							9
1	2	3		4	6	7			14			11	5			*10*	9		8										10
1	2	3		4	6	7						11	5			10	9		8										11
1	2	3		4	6	7						11	5			10	9	15	8										12
	2	3		4	6	7			14			11	5	12		10	*9*	1	8										13
	2	3		4	6	7	9					11	5			10			8				1						14
	2	3	12	4	6		9					7	5	11		10	14		*8*				1						15
	2	3	14	4	6	7	9		*10*			11	5						8				1						16
	2	3	14	4	6	7	*9*					11	5	12		10		1	8										17
	2	3	5	4	6	7	9					*11*		12		10		1	8					14					18
	2	14	3	4	*6*	7	9						5	12		10		1	8					11					19
1	2	12	3	4	6	7	10					9	5	*11*					8					14					20
1		3	5	4	11	7	10					9		6		8			2					12					21
1				4	11	7	10				2	8		6		12	9		5						3				22
1		2	5	4	11	7	8					9		12		*10*			6			14			3				23
1	2	8		4	11	7	10					9	5	6		12									3				24
1	2			4	11	7	10			3		*9*	5			8			6			14							25
1	2		4	3	11		10			8			5	12				15	6							7	9		26
1	2	3	4		11		8						5	12					6							7	9	10	27
1		3	4		11						2	9	5	*8*		12			6						14	7		10	28
1	2	3	4		11							8		6					5							7	9	10	29
1	2	3	4	14	11							12	5	*8*					6							7	9	10	30
1	2	3	4		11		14					12	5	*8*					6							7	9	10	31
1	2	3	4		11		12					9	5	8					6							7		10	32
1	2	3	4		11		12					14	5	8					6							7	*9*	10	33
1	2	3	4		11		8					*9*		6		14			5							7		10	34
1	2	3	4		11		8					9	5						6							7		10	35
1	2	3	4		11		9					12	5	8					6							7		10	36

FORFAR ATHLETIC — Second Division

Year Formed: 1885. *Ground & Address:* Station Park, Carseview Road, Forfar. *Telephone:* 01307 463576.
Ground Capacity: total: 8372. seated: 719. *Size of Pitch:* 115yd × 69yd.
Chairman: George Enston. *Secretary:* David McGregor.
Manager: Tommy Campbell. *Assistant Manager:* Brian McLaughlin. *Physio:* Jim Peacock. *Coaches:* Gordon Arthur, Ian McPhee, Tom McCallum, Steven Jackson.
Managers since 1975: Jerry Kerr; Archie Knox; Alex Rae; Doug Houston; Henry Hall; Bobby Glennie; Paul Hegarty. *Club Nickname(s):* Loons. *Previous Grounds:* None.
Record Attendance: 10,780 v Rangers, Scottish Cup 2nd rd; 2 Feb, 1970.
Record Transfer Fee received: £57,000 for Craig Brewster to Raith R (July 1991).
Record Transfer Fee paid: £50,000 for Ian McPhee from Airdrieonians (1991).
Record Victory: 14-1 v Lindertis, Scottish Cup 1st rd; 1 Sept 1988.
Record Defeat: 2-12 v King's Park, Division II; 2 Jan, 1930.
Most Capped Player: —.

FORFAR ATHLETIC 1994–95 LEAGUE RECORD

Match No.	Date	Venue	Opponents	Result		H/T Score	Lg. Pos.	Goalscorers	Attendance
1	Aug 13	A	Queen's Park	W	2-1	1-1	—	Archibald, Lees	457
2	20	H	Alloa	W	3-2	2-0	2	Bingham 2, Kopel	540
3	27	A	Arbroath	W	1-0	0-0	2	McPhee	691
4	Sept 3	H	Montrose	W	1-0	0-0	1	Bingham	1077
5	10	A	Caledonian Th	L	1-3	1-1	2	Heddle	1731
6	24	A	East Stirling	L	1-3	1-1	2	McPhee	419
7	Oct 1	H	Albion R	D	1-1	0-0	3	Bingham	424
8	8	H	Ross C	W	1-0	0-0	1	McPhee	650
9	15	A	Cowdenbeath	L	0-1	0-0	4		403
10	22	H	Queen's Park	W	2-0	1-0	2	Bingham 2	534
11	29	H	Arbroath	W	3-0	0-0	1	Bingham, Ross, McCormick	721
12	Nov 5	A	Alloa	W	1-0	1-0	1	McCormick	525
13	12	H	Caledonian Th	W	2-1	2-1	1	McCormick, Ross	647
14	19	A	Montrose	L	0-2	0-1	2		1259
15	26	H	East Stirling	W	3-2	2-2	2	McCormick 3	527
16	Dec 3	A	Albion R	W	1-0	0-0	2	McCormick	303
17	31	H	Cowdenbeath	D	1-1	0-1	1	Hannigan	603
18	Jan 11	A	Ross C	L	1-2	0-1	—	Ross	1215
19	14	H	Queen's Park	W	3-0	0-0	1	Bingham, Hannigan, Morgan	501
20	24	A	Alloa	W	2-0	2-0	—	McCormick, Bingham	498
21	28	A	Arbroath	D	1-1	1-1	1	Bingham	802
22	Feb 4	A	Caledonian Th	D	1-1	1-0	1	Bingham	793
23	18	A	East Stirling	W	2-1	0-0	1	Morgan, Ross	528
24	25	H	Albion R	W	4-0	3-0	1	Bingham, Ross, Hannigan, Morgan	510
25	Mar 4	H	Ross C	W	4-2	3-2	1	Bingham 2, Hannigan, Ross	880
26	11	A	Cowdenbeath	W	3-1	1-1	1	Ross 3	280
27	18	H	Caledonian Th	W	4-1	2-0	1	Mann, Bingham 3	538
28	25	A	Montrose	W	2-1	1-0	1	McCormick, McPhee	1240
29	Apr 1	A	Albion R	W	3-0	2-0	1	Ross 2, McCormick	270
30	4	H	Montrose	L	1-3	1-2	—	Bingham	1176
31	8	H	East Stirling	W	1-0	1-0	1	Bingham	623
32	15	A	Ross C	W	1-0	1-0	1	Mann	2453
33	22	H	Cowdenbeath	D	2-2	2-2	1	Ross, McVicar	611
34	29	A	Queen's Park	W	2-0	1-0	1	Hannigan 2	557
35	May 6	H	Arbroath	W	4-1	3-0	1	Ross, Morgan, Bingham 2	1069
36	13	H	Alloa	W	2-0	2-0	1	Bingham, Morgan	655

Final League Position: 1

Most League Appearances: 376: Alex Brash, 1974-86.
Most League Goals in Season (Individual): 45: Dave Kilgour, Division II; 1929-30.
Most Goals Overall (Individual): 124, John Clark.

Honours
League Champions: Second Division 1983-84. Third Division 1994-95. C Division 1948-49.
Scottish Cup: Semi-finals 1982.
League Cup: Semi-finals 1977-78.
Club colours: Shirt: Sky Blue with narrow Navy vertical stripe. Shorts: Navy. Stockings: Navy.

Goalscorers: *League (67):* Bingham 22, Ross 13, McCormick 10, Hannigan 6, Morgan 5, McPhee 4, Mann 2, Archibald 1, Heddle 1, Kopel 1, Lees 1, McVicar 1. *Scottish Cup (0) League Cup (0) B&Q Cup (0)*

Arthur G 35	McLaren P 3 + 4	McPhee I 32 + 1	Mann R 26	Archibald E 16	McKillop A 33	O'Neill H 15 + 1	Irvine N 18	Lees G 7 + 7	Bingham D 36	Heddle I 25 + 5	Kopel S 7 + 3	Smith R — + 2	Mearns G 3 + 2	McCormick S 24 + 7	Ross A 28 + 1	Reilly J — + 1	Glennie S 19 + 1	Craig 17 + 5	Hannigan P 12 + 11	Stephen C 1 + 2	Morgan A 20	McVicar D 15 + 1	Loney J 2 + 2	Guthrie D 2	*Match No.*
1	2	3	4	5	6	7	8	*9*	10	11	12	14													1
1		3	4	5	6	7	8	*9*	10	11	2	14													2
1	12	3	4	5	6	7	8	9	10	11	2		14												3
1		3	4	5	6	2	*8*	14	10	11			12	7	9										4
1	2	3	4	5	*6*		8	9	10	11	14			7											5
1	2	3	4	5	6	11			10	8				7	9										6
1		10		5	6	4	7		11	3	2			8	9										7
1		3	4	5	6	11	8		10	12	2			*7*	9	14									8
1		3	4	5	6	11	8	14	10	12	*2*			7	9										9
1		3	4		5	*2*	8	7	11	6				10	9		14								10
1	14	3			5	2	8	7	11	6	12			10	9		4								11
1	14	3			5	2	8	12	11	6	7			*10*	9			4							12
1	12					2	8	7	11	6	3			10	9		5	4							13
1		3	4		5	*2*	8		11	6				*10*	9			7	14	15					14
		3	4	6	5		2	12	11	8			7	10					9	1					15
1			4	6	5		2	12	11	8			7	10				3	9						16
1		3	4	5			2		11	8			6	10					9		7				17
1		3		5	6		4		11	8				10	9		2		14		*7*				18
1		3	4		5		*2*		11	8				10	9		6	14	12		7				19
1		3	4		5	14			11	*8*				10	9		2	6	12		7				20
1		3	4		5	8			11					10	9			6	12		7	2			21
1		3			5	*8*		14	11					10	9		4	6	12		7	2			22
1				4	5				11	8				10	9		2	3	12		7	6			23
1		*3*			5			14	11	8				12	9		2	4	10		7	6			24
1		3		*4*	5				11	8					9		2	14	10		7	6			25
1		3			5				*11*	8				12	9		2	4	10		7	6	14		26
1		3	4		5				11	*8*				12	9		2	14	10		7	6			27
1		3	4		5				11	12				10	*9*		2	8	14		7	6			28
1		3	4		5				*11*	8				10	9		2	14	12		7	6			29
1		3	4		5				11	*8*				10	9		2	14	12		7	6			30
1		3	4		5				11	12				14	9		2	8	*10*		7	6			31
1		3	4		5				11					12	9		2	8	10		7	6			32
1		*3*	4		5				11	14				10	9			8	12		7	6	2		33
1		12	4		5				*11*					14	9		2	3	10		7	6		8	34
1		3	4		5				11					12	9		2	8	10	15	7	*6*	14		35
1		3	4	5					11						14		2	8	10		7	12	*9*	6	36

GREENOCK MORTON First Division

Year Formed: 1874. *Ground & Address:* Cappielow Park, Sinclair St, Greenock. *Telephone:* 01475 723511.
Ground Capacity: total: 14,250. seated: 5150. *Size of Pitch:* 110yd × 71yd.
Chairman: John Wilson. *Secretary:* Mrs Jane Rankin.
Manager: Allan McGraw. *Assistant Manager:* John McMaster. *Physio:* John Tierney. *Coach:* Billy Osborne.
Managers since 1975: Joe Gilroy; Benny Rooney; Alex Miller; Tommy McLean; Willie McLean. *Club Nickname(s):* The Ton. *Previous Grounds:* Grant Street 1874, Garvel Park 1875, Cappielow Park 1879, Ladyburn Park 1882, (Cappielow Park 1883).
Record Attendance: 23,000 v Celtic; 1922.
Record Transfer Fee received: £350,000 for Neil Orr to West Ham U.
Record Transfer Fee paid: £150,000 for Allan Mahood from Nottingham Forest.
Record Victory: 11-0 v Carfin Shamrock, Scottish Cup 1st rd; 13 Nov, 1886.
Record Defeat: 1-10 v Port Glasgow Ath, Division II; 5 May, 1894 and v St Bernards, Division II; 14 Oct, 1933.
Most Capped Player: Jimmy Cowan, 25, Scotland.
Most League Appearances: 358: David Hayes, 1969-84.

GREENOCK MORTON 1994–95 LEAGUE RECORD

Match No.	Date	Venue	Opponents	Result		H/T Score	Lg. Pos.	Goalscorers	Attendance
1	Aug 13	H	Berwick R	D	1-1	0-0	—	Alexander	1454
2	20	A	Meadowbank T	W	1-0	0-0	3	Lilley (pen)	398
3	27	A	Dumbarton	L	1-2	1-0	4	Lilley	1168
4	Sept 3	A	Stirling Albion	L	0-2	0-0	6		1026
5	10	H	Brechin C	W	2-0	0-0	4	McArthur, Alexander	1093
6	24	A	East Fife	W	2-1	1-1	3	Lilley, Alexander	1173
7	Oct 1	H	Stenhousemuir	W	3-2	0-0	3	Anderson, Alexander 2	1280
8	8	H	Clyde	L	0-1	0-0	3		1801
9	15	A	Queen of the S	L	0-3	0-3	6		1126
10	22	A	Berwick R	L	1-2	0-1	7	Lilley	738
11	29	H	Dumbarton	W	1-0	0-0	5	Alexander	1429
12	Nov 5	H	Meadowbank T	W	4-0	1-0	3	Rajamaki 2, Lilley 2	1453
13	12	A	Brechin C	W	3-1	3-0	2	Lindberg, Alexander, McCahill	623
14	22	H	Stirling Albion	D	1-1	0-0	—	Alexander	1941
15	26	H	East Fife	W	3-0	1-0	2	Anderson, Rajamaki 2	1884
16	Dec 3	A	Stenhousemuir	D	0-0	0-0	2		842
17	26	A	Clyde	D	0-0	0-0	—		2023
18	31	H	Queen of the S	D	1-1	0-0	3	Rajamaki	2112
19	Jan 14	H	Berwick R	W	2-1	0-0	3	Rajamaki, Lilley	1951
20	21	A	Meadowbank T	L	0-1	0-0	3		416
21	24	A	Dumbarton	L	1-2	1-0	—	Rajamaki	1307
22	Feb 4	H	Brechin C	W	1-0	1-0	3	Alexander	1464
23	11	A	Stirling Albion	W	3-0	1-0	3	Lilley, McInnes, Mahood	1069
24	25	H	Stenhousemuir	W	1-0	1-0	2	Rajamaki	2754
25	28	A	East Fife	D	1-1	0-1	—	Archibald (og)	558
26	Mar 11	A	Queen of the S	L	0-1	0-1	4		1505
27	14	H	Clyde	W	4-1	4-0	—	Lilley 2, McInnes, Rajamaki	1421
28	18	A	Brechin C	D	1-1	0-0	2	Rajamaki	481
29	25	H	Stirling Albion	D	2-2	1-1	2	Rajamaki 2	2025
30	Apr 1	A	Stenhousemuir	D	1-1	0-0	2	Lilley	1126
31	8	H	East Fife	W	4-1	1-0	2	Anderson, McCahill, Lilley, Laing	1789
32	15	A	Clyde	W	3-1	2-0	2	McArthur, McInnes, Laing	2163
33	22	H	Queen of the S	D	0-0	0-0	2		2395
34	29	A	Berwick R	W	4-3	2-3	1	Lilley 2, Collins, Rajamaki	992
35	May 6	H	Dumbarton	W	2-0	0-0	1	Lilley, Rajamaki	6242
36	13	H	Meadowbank T	W	1-0	1-0	1	Lilley	3165

Final League Position: 1

Most League Goals in Season (Individual): 58: Allan McGraw, Division II; 1963-64.
Most Goals Overall (Individual): —.

Honours
League Champions: First Division 1977-78, 1983-84, 1986-87. Division II 1949-50, 1963-64, 1966-67. Second Division 1994-95. *Runners-up:* Division 1 1916-17, Division II 1899-1900, 1928-29, 1936-37.
Scottish Cup Winners: 1922; *Runners-up:* 1948. *League Cup Runners-up:* 1963-64.
B&Q Cup: Runners-up: 1992-93.

European: *UEFA Cup (Fairs):* 1968-69.
Club colours: Shirt: Royal blue tartan. Shorts: Royal blue. Stockings: Royal blue.

Goalscorers: *League (55):* Lilley 16 (1 pen), Rajamaki 14, Alexander 9, Anderson 3, McInnes 3, Laing 2, McArthur 2, McCahill 2, Collins 1, Lindberg 1, Mahood 1, own goal 1. *Scottish Cup (5):* Anderson 2, Alexander 1, Lilley 1, Rajamaki 1. *League Cup (1):* Lilley 1. *B&Q Cup (5):* Lilley 2, Alexander 1, Anderson 1, Fowler 1.

Wylie D 36	Collins D 33	Cormack P 12	Hunter J 6 + 2	McCahill S 27	Johnstone D 22 + 2	Lilley D 34 + 1	Anderson J 28 + 2	Alexander R 26 + 6	McArthur S 30 + 3	Flannery P 2 + 1	Blair P 8 + 8	Fowler J 9 + 5	Mahood A 18 + 3	Pickering M 6 + 2	Gibson L 3 + 1	McPherson C 9 + 7	McCann M 2	Lindberg J 25	McInnes D 26	Rajamaki M 25	Laing D 9 + 3	Match No.
1	2	3	4	5	6	7	8	9	10	*11*	14											1
1	2	3	4	5	6	7		9	11		14	*8*	10									2
1	2	3	4	5	6	7		9	11		14	*8*	10	12								3
1	2	3	4	5	6	7	14	9	11			8	*10*	12								4
1	2		12	5	6	7		9	11			4	10	3	8							5
1	2	5	4		6	7		9	11			8	10	3								6
1	2	5			6	7	4	9	11	*12*		8	10	3	14							7
1	2	5			6	7	4						10	3	11	8	9					8
1	2	5	6				4		14	7		12	10	3	*11*	8	9					9
1	2	5				7	4	9					8	3				6	10	11		10
1	2	3		5		7	4	9								8		6	10	11		11
1	2	3	12	5	4	7		9	14							*8*		6	10	11		12
1	2			5	4	7		9	3			14				8		*6*	10	11		13
1	2			5	4	7	12	9	3		14	*8*						6	10	11		14
1	2			5		7	4	9	3		8	12						6	10	11		15
1	2			5		7	4	9	3		*8*		14					6	10	11		16
1	2			5		7	4	9	3		8		12					6	10	11		17
1	2			5		7	4	9	3		12		8					6	10	11		18
1	2	*3*		5		7	4	9	12		14		8					6	10	11		19
1	2			5		7	4	12	3		9		8					6	10	11		20
1	2			5		7	4	9	3				8			12		6	10	11		21
1	2			5	14	7	4	9	3		*8*	6				12			10	11		22
1	2				5	7	4	9	3			12	8			14		6	10	*11*		23
1	2				5	7	4	9	3				8					6	10	11	12	24
1	2				5	7	4	9	3				8			14		6	10	11	12	25
1	2				5	12	4	9	3			8				10		6		11	7	26
1	2			5	14	7	4	*9*	3		8					12		6	10	11		27
1	2			5		7	4	*9*	3		8					12		6	10	11	14	28
1	2			5		7	4	9	3		12							6	10	11	8	29
1				5	2	7	4		3				*8*			14		6	10	11	9	30
1				5	2	7	4	12	3			14				8		*6*	10	11	9	31
1	2			5	11	7	4	12	3							8		6	10		9	32
1	2			5	6	7	4	12	3		14					*8*			10	11	9	33
1	8			5	2	7	4		3									6	10	11	9	34
1				5	2	7	4	12	3				8					6	10	11	9	35
1	*8*			5	2	7	4	12	3		11		14					6	10		9	36

HAMILTON ACADEMICAL Division 1

Year Formed: 1874. *Ground:* Firhill Stadium, Glasgow G20 7AL *Telephone (match days only):* 0141 945 4811. *Club Address:* Douglas Park, Douglas Park Lane, Hamilton ML3 0DF. *Telephone:* 01698 286103. *Fax:* 01698 285422.
Ground Capacity: 20,676, seated: 9076. *Size of Pitch:* 110yd × 74yd.
Chairman: David Campbell. *Secretary:* Scott A. Struthers BA. *Commercial Manager:* Sandy Clark.
Manager: Iain Munro. *Physio:* Tom Williamson and Alistair Macfie.
Managers since 1975: J. Eric Smith; Dave McParland; John Blackley; Bertie Auld; John Lambie; Jim Dempsey; John Lambie; Billy McLaren. *Club Nickname(s):* The Accies. *Previous Grounds:* Bent Farm, South Avenue, South Haugh.
Record Attendance: 28,690 v Hearts, Scottish Cup 3rd rd; 3 Mar, 1937.
Record Transfer Fee received: £225,000 for James Weir to Hearts (Aug 1993).
Record Transfer Fee paid: £60,000 for Paul Martin from Kilmarnock (Oct 1988) and for John McQuade from Dumbarton (Aug 1993).
Record Victory: 11-1 v Chryston, Lanarkshire Cup; 28 Nov, 1885.
Record Defeat: 1-11 v Hibernian, Division I; 6 Nov, 1965.
Most Capped Player: Colin Miller, 29 (51), Canada, 1988-95.
Most League Appearances: 447: Rikki Ferguson, 1974-88.

HAMILTON ACADEMICAL 1994–95 LEAGUE RECORD

Match No.	Date	Venue	Opponents	Result		H/T Score	Lg. Pos.	Goalscorers	Attendance
1	Aug 13	A	Ayr U	D	1-1	1-0	—	Lorimer	2097
2	20	A	Raith R	D	1-1	1-1	5	Chalmers	2825
3	27	H	Airdrieonians	L	2-6	2-3	10	McIntosh, Duffield	1180
4	Sept 3	H	Stranraer	W	1-0	1-0	6	Duffield	1083
5	10	A	Dunfermline Ath	L	0-4	0-3	7		4029
6	24	A	St Johnstone	D	1-1	1-0	9	McGill	2790
7	Oct 1	H	St Mirren	D	2-2	1-0	8	Duffield, McQuade	1613
8	8	A	Dundee	L	0-2	0-2	8		2370
9	15	H	Clydebank	D	0-0	0-0	8		1042
10	22	H	Ayr U	W	2-0	2-0	7	Duffield, Renicks	1066
11	29	A	Airdrieonians	L	0-1	0-0	7		1422
12	Nov 5	H	Raith R	L	0-3	0-2	8		1112
13	12	H	Dunfermline Ath	W	3-1	3-1	7	Tighe, Duffield 2 (1 pen)	2103
14	19	A	Stranraer	L	0-2	0-1	7		784
15	26	H	St Johnstone	W	3-1	2-1	6	Duffield 2, McQuade	1445
16	Dec 3	A	St Mirren	W	1-0	0-0	6	Duffield	2273
17	26	H	Dundee	L	0-1	0-1	—		1552
18	31	A	Ayr U	W	2-1	2-1	6	Clark G, McInulty	2079
19	Jan 2	H	Airdrieonians	W	3-0	2-0	—	Duffield, McIntosh, Chalmers	2178
20	7	A	Raith R	L	0-2	0-1	6		3130
21	10	A	Clydebank	D	0-0	0-0	—		578
22	14	H	Stranraer	W	1-0	0-0	6	Duffield	1015
23	21	A	Dunfermline Ath	L	1-2	0-1	6	Clark G	3973
24	Feb 4	H	St Mirren	W	2-0	2-0	6	Clark G, Duffield	1534
25	18	A	St Johnstone	L	0-3	0-1	6		2589
26	25	H	Clydebank	L	0-1	0-0	6		1017
27	Mar 4	A	Dundee	L	0-2	0-1	6		2342
28	22	H	Dunfermline Ath	L	1-3	0-1	—	Duffield	1343
29	25	A	Stranraer	W	5-0	2-0	6	Duffield 2, McCall, McLean, McStay	655
30	Apr 1	A	St Mirren	L	2-3	1-0	6	McCulloch, McEntegart (pen)	2272
31	8	H	St Johnstone	W	1-0	0-0	6	Duffield	858
32	15	H	Dundee	L	1-4	0-4	6	Duffield	1471
33	22	A	Clydebank	W	4-1	3-1	6	McCormick, Duffield 3	716
34	29	H	Ayr U	W	1-0	0-0	6	Lorimer	1073
35	May 6	A	Airdrieonians	W	1-0	0-0	6	Clark G	1501
36	13	H	Raith R	D	0-0	0-0	6		5333

Final League Position: 6

Most League Goals in Season (Individual): 34: David Wilson, Division I; 1936-37.
Most Goals Overall (Individual): 246: David Wilson, 1928-39.

Honours
League Champions: First Division 1985-86, 1987-88. Division II 1903-04; *Runners-up:* Division II 1952-53, 1964-65.
Scottish Cup Runners-up: 1911, 1935. *League Cup:* Semi-finalists three times.
B&Q Cup Winners: 1991-92 and 1992-93.
Club colours: Shirt: Red and white hoops. Shorts: White. Stockings: White.

Goalscorers: *League (42):* Duffield 20 (1 pen), Clark G 4, Chalmers 2, Lorimer 2, McIntosh 2, McQuade 2, McCall 1, McCormick 1, McCulloch 1, McEntegart 1 (pen), McGill 1, McInulty 1, McLean 1, McStay 1, Renicks 1, Tighe 1. *Scottish Cup (1):* Lorimer 1. *League Cup (7):* Baptie 1, Campbell 1, Duffield 1, McEntegart 1, McLean 1, Sherry 1, own goal 1. *B&Q Cup (4):* Duffield 3 (1 pen), McIntosh 1.

Ferguson A 24	McKenzie P 29	McInulty S 29	McEntegart S 30 + 2	Baptie C 24 + 6	McIntosh M 30	McQuade J 27 + 3	Sherry J 12 + 2	Chalmers P 18 + 5	Duffield P 36	Lorimer D 15 + 12	Campbell D — + 2	McLean C 5 + 2	Hartley P 10 + 6	Nicholls D 3	Cormack D 12	Clark P 4	McGill D 4 + 3	McStay J 2	Renicks S 19	Clark G 12 + 5	Tighe M 7 + 3	McCormick S 5 + 3	Hillcoat C 15 + 2	McStay R 9 + 1	Waters M 2 + 1	McCall I 5 + 1	McCulloch S 8	Match No.
1	2	3	4	5	6	7	8	9	10	11	12																	1
1	2	3	4	5	6	7	8	*9*	10	11		14																2
1	2	3	4	5	6	7	8	*9*	10	11		12	14															3
1	2	*3*	4	5	6	12	8	9	10			7	14	11														4
1	2	3	4	5	6	11	8	9	10				7															5
	2	3	4	5	6	7			10					11	1	8	9											6
	2	3	4	5	6	7			10						1	11	9	8										7
	2	3	4	5	6	7	11		10		14				1		*9*	8										8
	2	3	4	5	6	7	14	12	10				11		1				*8*	9								9
	2	3	4	5	6	7		12	10	14			11		1				8	*9*								10
	2	3	4	5	6	7		12	10	9			14		1				*8*		11							11
	2	3	4	5	6	7		12	10	9					1				8		11							12
	5		4	12	6	7	2	9	10	*11*					1		14		3		8							13
	5		4	12	6	7	2	9	10	11					1				3		8							14
	5	3	4		6	8		9	10	11			*7*		1				2		14							15
	5	3	4		6	8		9	10	*11*					1		14		2		7							16
	5	3			6	8		9	10	*11*				4	1		14		2	12	7							17
1	5	3	4	12	6	*8*		9	10	11									2	7	14							18
1	5	3	4	8	6			9	*10*	11									2	7	12	14						19
1	5	3	*4*	8	6			9	10	11			12						2	7			14					20
1		3		8	6			9	10	11			14						2	7			5	4	12			21
1		3		12	6			*9*	10								8		2	14			5	4	7	11		22
1		3	14	9	6	*8*			10	12									2	7			5	4		11		23
1	5		4		6	*11*		9	10	14									2	7			3	8		12		24
1	9		4	5	6	8			10	11			14						*2*	7			3	12				25
1	5		4	6		*9*	2	14	10	12										7			3	8		11		26
1	5	3	4		6	8		9	10										2	7		14	12			*11*		27
1	5	3	4	12				9	10	14									2	*7*	8	11	6					28
1	5	3		6		12			*10*	14		9											2	4	7	8	11	29
1	5	3	14	6		8			10	12		9	7										2	4			*11*	30
1	5		4	12		8			10	14		9	*7*			2							3	6			11	31
1	5		4			8	14		10			9	7			2						12	3	*6*			11	32
1		3	4	5	6		8		10	14			*7*							12		9	2				11	33
1		3	4	5	6	12	8		10	14			7									9	2				*11*	34
1		3	4	5	6	8			10	14			*7*							12		*9*	2				11	35
1		3	4	5	6	8	7		10	14										12		*9*	2				11	36

HEART OF MIDLOTHIAN Premier Division

Year Formed: 1874. *Ground & Address:* Tynecastle Park, Gorgie Rd, Edinburgh EH11 2NL. *Telephone:* 0131 337 6132. *Fax:* 0131 346 0699.
Ground Capacity: variable due to reconstruction. *Size of Pitch:* 108yd × 72yd.
Chairman: Christopher P.Robinson. *Secretary:* L. W. Porteous. *Commercial Managers:* Brian Whittaker, Gary Mackay.
Manager: Tommy McLean. *General Manager:* Sally Robinson.
Physio: Alan Rae. *Coach:* Walter Kidd, Eamonn Bannon, Tom Forsyth.
Managers since 1975: J. Hagart; W. Ormond; R. Moncur; T. Ford; A. MacDonald; A. MacDonald & W. Jardine; A. MacDonald; J. Jordan, S. Clark.
Club Nickname(s): Hearts. *Previous Grounds:* The Meadows 1874, Powderhall 1878, Old Tynecastle 1881, (Tynecastle Park, 1886).
Record Attendance: 53,396 v Rangers, Scottish Cup 3rd rd; 13 Feb, 1932.
Record Transfer Fee received: £2,000,000 for Andy McLaren from Rangers (October 1994).
Record of Transfer paid: £750,000 for Derek Ferguson to Rangers (July 1990).
Record Victory: 21-0 v Anchor, EFA Cup 1880.
Record Defeat: 1-8 v Vale of Leithen, Scottish Cup, 1888.
Most Capped Player: Bobby Walker, 29, Scotland.
Most League Appearances: 482: Henry Smith, 1981-95.

HEART OF MIDLOTHIAN 1994–95 LEAGUE RECORD

Match No.	Date	Venue	Opponents	Result		H/T Score	Lg. Pos.	Goalscorers	Attendance
1	Aug 13	A	Aberdeen	L	1-3	0-1	—	Colquhoun	14,238
2	20	A	Motherwell	D	1-1	0-0	8	Johnston M	8249
3	27	H	Hibernian	L	0-1	0-0	9		12,371
4	Sept 11	A	Rangers	L	0-3	0-0	—		40,653
5	17	H	Dundee U	W	2-1	2-0	8	Thomas, Frail	7392
6	24	H	Kilmarnock	W	3-0	2-0	6	Millar J, McLaren, Mackay	9302
7	Oct 1	A	Falkirk	L	1-2	1-1	7	Robertson	7589
8	8	A	Partick T	W	1-0	1-0	5	Robertson	5076
9	15	H	Celtic	W	1-0	1-0	5	Robertson	12,086
10	22	H	Aberdeen	W	2-0	2-0	5	Frail, Robertson	10,655
11	29	A	Hibernian	L	1-2	0-2	6	Robertson	13,622
12	Nov 5	H	Motherwell	L	1-2	1-1	6	Robertson	8889
13	9	H	Rangers	D	1-1	0-0	—	Colquhoun	12,347
14	19	A	Dundee U	L	2-5	1-4	6	Thomas 2	7719
15	26	A	Kilmarnock	L	1-3	1-0	7	Robertson	8069
16	Dec 3	H	Falkirk	D	1-1	1-1	8	Thomas	8960
17	26	H	Partick T	W	3-0	0-0	—	Hagen, Robertson, Bett	8920
18	31	A	Aberdeen	L	1-3	0-2	6	Thomas	11,392
19	Jan 8	A	Motherwell	W	2-1	1-1	—	Hamilton, Miller C	5117
20	11	A	Celtic	D	1-1	0-1	—	Bett	26,491
21	14	H	Dundee U	W	2-0	1-0	5	Millar J, Jamieson	8656
22	18	H	Hibernian	W	2-0	1-0	—	McPherson, Millar J	12,630
23	21	A	Rangers	L	0-1	0-1	5		44,231
24	Feb 4	A	Falkirk	L	0-2	0-1	5		6028
25	11	H	Kilmarnock	D	2-2	2-2	5	Millar J, Mackay	8374
26	25	H	Celtic	D	1-1	0-0	5	Jamieson	11,185
27	Mar 18	H	Rangers	W	2-1	2-1	5	Robertson, Millar J	9806
28	21	A	Dundee U	D	1-1	1-0	—	Johnston A	6862
29	Apr 1	H	Falkirk	L	0-1	0-1	6		9003
30	4	A	Partick T	L	1-3	1-0	—	Millar J	4526
31	12	A	Kilmarnock	L	2-3	1-2	—	Cramb, Jamieson	7239
32	15	H	Partick T	L	0-1	0-0	7		9007
33	19	A	Celtic	W	1-0	0-0	—	Hagen	18,638
34	29	H	Aberdeen	L	1-2	0-	7	McPherson	11,466
35	May 6	A	Hibernian	L	1-3	1-0	8	Hagen	7122
36	13	H	Motherwell	W	2-0	0-0	6	Hamilton, Robertson (pen)	11,172

Final League Position: 6

Most League Goals in Season (Individual): 44: Barney Battles.
Most Goals Overall (Individual): 206: Jimmy Wardhaugh, 1946-59.

Honours
League Champions: Division I 1894-95, 1896-97, 1957-58, 1959-60. First Division 1979-80; *Runners-up:* Division I 1893-94, 1898-99, 1903-04, 1905-06, 1914-15, 1937-38, 1953-54, 1956-57, 1958-59, 1964-65. Premier Division 1985-86, 1987-88, 1991-92. First Division 1977-78, 1982-83.
Scottish Cup Winners: 1891, 1896, 1901, 1906, 1956; *Runners-up:* 1903, 1907, 1968, 1976, 1986.
League Cup Winners: 1954-55, 1958-59, 1959-60, 1962-63; *Runners-up:* 1961-62.

European: *European Cup* 4 matches (1958-59, 1960-61). *Cup Winners Cup:* 4 matches (1976-77). *UEFA Cup:* 34 matches (*Fairs Cup:* 1961-62, 1963-64, 1965-66. *UEFA Cup:* 1984-85, 1986-87, 1988-89, 1990-91, 1992-93, 1993-94).
Club colours: Shirt: Maroon. Shorts: White. Stockings: Maroon with white tops.

Goalscorers: *League (44):* Robertson 10 (1 pen), Millar J 6, Thomas 5, Hagen 3, Jamieson 3, Bett 2, Colquhoun 2, Frail 2, Hamilton 2, Mackay 2, McPherson 2, Cramb 1, Johnston A 1, Johnston M 1, McLaren 1, Miller C 1. *Scottish Cup (7):* Millar J 2, Robertson 2, McPherson 1, Miller C 1, Thomas 1. *League Cup (6):* Johnston A 2, Colquhoun 1, Locke 1, Millar J 1, Robertson 1.

Smith H 14 + 1	Frail S 25	McKinlay T 11	Locke G 3 + 6	Weir J 2	McLaren A 10	Colquhoun J 23 + 8	Mackay G 21 + 13	Robertson J 27 + 4	Leitch S 18 + 3	Millar J 25 + 3	Johnston A 9 + 12	Thomas K 11 + 7	Walker N 2	Levein C 24	Johnston M 3 + 1	Berry N 29	Hogg G — + 1	Bett J 26	McPherson D 23	Miller C 16	Kidd W 1	Nelson C 20	Jamieson W 13 + 2	Hagen D 16 + 4	Wright G — + 1	Hamilton B 13	Cramb C 3 + 3	Wishart F 8	Match No.
1	2	*3*	4	5	6	7	8	9	10	11	12	14																	1
	2	3		5	6	7	8	*9*	14	11	12		1	4	10														2
	2	*3*			6	7	8	9	11	14	12		1	4	10	5													3
1		3	*2*		6	7		11	8	10	12			4	9	5	14												4
.1	2	3			6	7		9	8	10	14	11		4	12	5													5
1	2	3			6	7	14	9	8	10	12	11		4		5													6
1	2	3			6	7	14	9	8	10	12	11		4		5													7
1	2	3			6	7	12	9		10	14	*11*		4		5		8											8
1	2	3			6	12	7	9	*10*	14		11		4		5		8											9
1	2	3			6	12	*7*	9	14	10	11			4		5		8											10
1	2	3				12	7	9	*10*	14	11			4		5		8	6										11
1	2					7	8	9	10	3	11	12				5		4	6										12
1	2					7	4	9	10	3	11	12				5		8	6										13
1			14			7	4	9	10	3		11				*5*		8	6	2									14
1			*2*			7	4	9	12	10	14	11						8	6	3	5								15
	2					7	12	9		10		*11*				5		8	6	3		1	4	14					16
	2					7	14	9		10		12				5		8	6	*3*		1	4	11					17
	2					7	10	9				12				5		8	6	3		1	*4*	11	14				18
	2						14	12	*10*			9				5		8	6	3		1	4	11		7			19
	2						14	12	*10*			9				5		8	6	3		1	4	11		7			20
	2						12	9		10						5		8	6	3		1	4	11		7			21
	2					14	12	9		10				5				*8*	6	3		1	4	11		7			22
	2					*9*	14	12		10				4				8	6	3		1	5	11		7			23
	2					12	*10*	9			14			4		5		8	6	3		1		11		7			24
	2					7	12	9		10		11		4		*3*		5	6			1		14		8			25
	2					12	8		*3*	10	9	14		4					6			1	5	11		7			26
	2					14	7	*9*	3	10	12					4		8	6			1	5	11					27
	2		14				7		3	10	9			4		6		8				1	5	11			12		28
15							7	9	*10*	3	11			4		5		8	6			*1*		12			14	2	29
1						7	14	9		10		12		4				5	6	*3*				11		8		2	30
			14			7	8			10	11			4		5			6	*3*		1	12				9	2	31
			14			7	8		*3*	10	11			4		6						1	5	12			9	2	32
			14			12	10							4		6		8		3		1	5	*11*		7	9	2	33
						9	10	12						4		5		8	6	3		1	14	11		7		*2*	34
						7	12	9			14			4		5		8	6	*3*		1		11		10		2	35
			14			7	2	9						4		5		*8*	6			1		11		10	12	3	36

HIBERNIAN Premier Division

Year Formed: 1875. *Ground & Address:* Easter Road Stadium, Albion Rd, Edinburgh EH7 5QG. *Telephone:* 0131 661 2159. *Fax:* 0131 659 6488.
Ground Capacity: total: 16,218. *Size of Pitch:* 112yd × 74yd.
Chairman: Douglas Cromb. *Secretary:* Cecil F. Graham, FIFA, MInst CM. *Commercial Manager:* Ian Erskine.
Manager: Alex Miller. *Assistant Manager and Coach:* John Scott.
Physio: Stewart Collie. *Coach Assistant:* Martin Ferguson.
Managers since 1975: Eddie Turnbull; Willie Ormond; Bertie Auld; Pat Stanton; John Blackley. *Club Nickname(s):* Hibees.
Previous Grounds: Meadows 1875-78, Powderhall 1878-79, Mayfield 1879-80, First Easter Road 1880-92, Second Easter Road 1892-.
Record Attendance: 65,860 v Hearts, Division I; 2 Jan, 1950.
Record Transfer Fee received: £1,000,000 for Andy Goram to Rangers (June 1991).
Record Transfer Fee paid: £420,000 for Keith Wright from Dundee.
Record Victory: 22-1 v 42nd Highlanders; 3 Sept, 1881.
Record Defeat: 0-10 v Rangers; 24 Dec, 1898.
Most Capped Player: Lawrie Reilly, 38, Scotland.
Most League Appearances: 446: Arthur Duncan.

HIBERNIAN 1994–95 LEAGUE RECORD

Match No.	Date	Venue	Opponents	Result		H/T Score	Lg. Pos.	Goalscorers	Attendance
1	Aug 13	H	Dundee U	W	5-0	3-0	—	Findlay, Jackson D 2, Harper, O'Neill	8838
2	20	H	Kilmarnock	D	0-0	0-0	2		9107
3	27	A	Hearts	W	1-0	0-0	1	Hunter	12,371
4	Sept 10	H	Aberdeen	D	2-2	2-1	2	Jackson D, O'Neill	9728
5	17	A	Motherwell	D	1-1	0-0	3	O'Neill	7005
6	24	A	Celtic	L	0-2	0-1	3		28,170
7	Oct 1	H	Partick T	W	3-0	2-0	3	Jackson D 2, McGraw	7083
8	8	H	Rangers	W	2-1	0-1	3	Hunter, Harper	12,088
9	15	A	Falkirk	D	0-0	0-0	2		7388
10	22	A	Dundee U	D	0-0	0-0	2		7983
11	29	H	Hearts	W	2-1	2-0	1	Jackson D, O'Neill	13,622
12	Nov 5	A	Kilmarnock	D	0-0	0-0	3		8319
13	9	A	Aberdeen	D	0-0	0-0	—		10,882
14	19	H	Motherwell	D	2-2	2-1	3	McAllister, O'Neill	9160
15	30	H	Celtic	D	1-1	0-1	—	Jackson D	12,295
16	Dec 3	A	Partick T	D	2-2	0-1	3	McGinlay, O'Neill	4667
17	10	H	Falkirk	D	2-2	0-1	3	Jackson D, O'Neill	7725
18	26	A	Rangers	L	0-2	0-2	—		44,892
19	31	H	Dundee U	W	4-0	3-0	3	Wright 3, O'Neill	7754
20	Jan 7	H	Kilmarnock	W	2-1	1-0	2	McGinlay, O'Neill	8918
21	13	A	Motherwell	D	0-0	0-0	—		6724
22	18	A	Hearts	L	0-2	0-1	—		12,630
23	21	H	Aberdeen	W	4-2	3-1	2	McGinlay, Jackson D 2 (1 pen), Wright	8076
24	Feb 4	H	Partick T	L	1-2	1-1	2	McGinlay	7760
25	11	A	Celtic	D	2-2	1-1	2	McGinlay, McGraw	24,284
26	25	A	Falkirk	L	0-1	0-0	3		6501
27	Mar 4	H	Rangers	D	1-1	0-0	3	Wright	11,939
28	18	A	Aberdeen	D	0-0	0-0	3		10,384
29	22	H	Motherwell	W	2-0	1-0	—	Wright 2	5395
30	Apr 1	A	Partick T	D	2-2	1-0	3	Wright, Harper	4041
31	16	A	Rangers	L	1-3	1-1	—	O'Neill	44,193
32	19	H	Falkirk	L	0-2	0-1	—		5450
33	29	A	Dundee U	W	1-0	0-0	4	McGinlay	8376
34	May 6	H	Hearts	W	3-1	0-1	3	Weir, Wright, Harper	7122
35	9	H	Celtic	D	1-1	1-0	—	Harper	6019
36	13	A	Kilmarnock	W	2-1	0-1	3	McGinlay, Wright	11,676

Final League Position: 3

Most League Goals in Season (Individual): 42: Joe Baker.
Most Goals Overall (Individual): 364: Gordon Smith.

Honours
League Champions: Division I 1902-03, 1947-48, 1950-51, 1951-52. First Division 1980-81. Division II 1893-94, 1894-95, 1932-33; *Runners-up:* Division I 1896-97, 1946-47, 1949-50, 1952-53, 1973-74, 1974-75.
Scottish Cup Winners: 1887, 1902; *Runners-up:* 1896, 1914, 1923, 1924, 1947, 1958, 1972, 1979.
League Cup Winners: 1972-73, 1991-92; *Runners-up:* 1950-51, 1968-69, 1974-75, 1993-94.

European: *European Cup:* 6 matches (1955-56 semi-finals). *Cup Winners Cup:* 6 matches (1972-73). *UEFA Cup:* 56 matches (*Fairs Cup:* 1960-61 semi-finals, 1961-62, 1962-63, 1965-66, 1967-68, 1968-69, 1970-71. *UEFA Cup:* 1973-74, 1974-75, 1975-76, 1976-77, 1978-79, 1992-93).
Club colours: Shirt: Green with white sleeves. Shorts: White. Stockings: Green with white trim.

Goalscorers: *League (49):* Jackson D 10 (1 pen), O'Neill 10, Wright 10, McGinlay 7, Harper 5, Hunter 2, McGraw 2, Findlay 1, McAllister 1, Weir 1. *Scottish Cup (9):* Harper 3, McGinlay 2, Jackson D 1, O'Neill 1, Tortolano 1, Wright 1. *League Cup (6):* O'Neill 3, Evans 2, Tweed 1.

Leighton J 36	Miller W 34	Mitchell G 18	Findlay W 12 + 6	Tweed S 33	Hunter G 29	McAllister K 17 + 6	Hamilton B 17 + 1	Evans G 16 + 8	Jackson D 30 + 1	O'Neill M 33	Harper K 15 + 8	Tortolano J 11 + 7	Beaumont D 7	Farrell D 15 + 4	McGraw M 2 + 6	Love G 11 + 1	Weir M 8 + 11	McGinlay P 24	Wright K 19	Millen A 8	Dods D 1	Renwick M — + 1	Match No.
1	2	3	4	5	6	7	8	9	*10*	11	14												1
1	2	3	4	5	6	7	8	*9*	10	11	14	12											2
1	*2*		4	5	6	12	8	9	10	11	7	14	3										3
1			*4*	5		7	8	9	10	11		3	6	2	12	14							4
1	2		7	5	6	12	8	*9*	10	11			4	3			14						5
1	2		7	5	6	12	8	14	10	*11*	9			4		3							6
1	2			5	6		8	9	10	11	*7*			4	14	3	12						7
1	2			5	6		8	9	*10*	11	7			4	14	3	12						8
1	2			5	6		8	9		11	7			4	10	3	12						9
1	2		12	5	*6*		8	9		11	10	14		4		3	7						10
1	2		9	5			8	12	10	11	14	*6*	4			3	7						11
1	2		9	5	6		8	14	10	11	12					3	7	4					12
1	2			5	6	7	8	12	10	11	9					3		4					13
1	2			5	6	7	8		10	11	9					3	12	4					14
1	2		14	5	6	7	*8*		10	11	12					3	9	4					15
1	2		*8*	5	6		14		10	11	9	7	3				12	4					16
1	2		8		6	7		9	10	11			5			3	12	4					17
1	*2*		14	5	6	12	4	8	10	11	7							3	9				18
1		3	12	5	6	7	8	14	10	11				2				4	*9*				19
1	2	3	*8*	5	6	7		12	10	11				14				4	9				20
1	2	3		5	6	7			10	11				8				4	9				21
1	2	3	14	5	6	7			10	11				12			*8*	4	9				22
1	2	3	12	5		7		*8*	10			11		6			14	4	9				23
1	2	3	*11*	5	6	7		8	10		12	14						4	9				24
1	2	3			6				10		8	*11*	5		14		7	4	9				25
1	2	3		5	6				10	11				8	7			4	9				26
1	2	3		5	6	7			10	11		8		4	12				9				27
1	2	3		5	6				10	11	*7*	8		14			12	4	9				28
1	2			5	6				10	11	*7*	8			14		12	4	9	*3*			29
1	2			5	*6*				12	11	7	10		8			14	4	9	3			30
1	2	3		5		14		*7*	10	11		12		8				4	9	6			31
1	2	3		5		7			10	11		14		*8*				4	9	6			32
1	2	3			6	7		8		11	12	10		14				4	9	5			33
1	2	3		5		7		12		11	14	6					10	4	9	8			34
1	2	3		5	6			14		11	*10*	12					7	4	9	8			35
1	2	3		5		12		*7*	10	*11*								4	9	8	6	14	36

KILMARNOCK Premier Division

Year Formed: 1869. *Ground & Address:* Rugby Park, Kilmarnock KA1 2DP. *Telephone:* 01563 525184. *Fax:* 01563 522181.
Ground Capacity: total: 18,168 seated. *Size of Pitch:* 114yd × 72yd.
Chairman: Robert Fleeting. *Secretary:* Kevin Collins. *Commercial Manager:* Denny Martin. *Stadium Manager:* G. Hollas.
Manager: Alex Totten. *Assistant Manager:* Kenny Thomson. *Physio:* Hugh Allan.
Managers since 1975: W. Fernie; D. Sneddon; J. Clunie; E. Morrison; J. Fleeting; T Burns. *Club Nickname(s):* Killie.
Previous Grounds: Rugby Park (Dundonald Road); The Grange; Holm Quarry; Present ground since 1899.
Record Attendance: 35,995 v Rangers, Scottish Cup; 10 March, 1962.
Record Transfer Fee received: £300,000 for Shaun McSkimming to Motherwell,1995.
Record Transfer Fee paid: £300,000 for Paul Wright from St Johnstone, 1995.
Record Victory: 11-1 v Paisley Academical, Scottish Cup; 18 Jan, 1930 (15-0 v Lanemark, Ayrshire Cup; 15 Nov, 1890).
Record Defeat: 1-9 v Celtic, Division I; 13 Aug, 1938.
Most Capped Player: Joe Nibloe, 11, Scotland.
Most League Appearances: 481: Alan Robertson, 1972-88.

KILMARNOCK 1994–95 LEAGUE RECORD

Match No.	Date	Venue	Opponents	Result		H/T Score	Lg. Pos.	Goalscorers	Attendance
1	Aug 13	A	Partick T	L	0-2	0-2	—		6606
2	20	A	Hibernian	D	0-0	0-0	9		9107
3	27	H	Motherwell	L	0-1	0-1	10		7388
4	Sept 10	H	Falkirk	D	1-1	1-0	9	Williamson	8021
5	17	A	Celtic	D	1-1	0-0	10	Williamson	28,457
6	24	A	Hearts	L	0-3	0-2	10		9302
7	Oct 1	H	Aberdeen	W	2-1	1-1	9	Winnie (og), Brown	7445
8	8	H	Dundee U	L	0-2	0-1	9		7127
9	15	A	Rangers	L	0-2	0-0	10		44,099
10	22	H	Partick T	W	2-0	0-0	8	McKee, Brown	7023
11	29	A	Motherwell	L	2-3	2-1	9	Henry, McKee	7436
12	Nov 5	H	Hibernian	D	0-0	0-0	9		8319
13	8	A	Falkirk	D	3-3	3-0	—	Skilling, Black, Henry	6134
14	19	H	Celtic	D	0-0	0-0	9		13,932
15	26	H	Hearts	W	3-1	0-1	8	Mitchell, McKee, Skilling	8069
16	Dec 3	A	Aberdeen	W	1-0	1-0	7	Maskrey	10,345
17	10	H	Rangers	L	1-2	0-1	8	McKee	17,219
18	26	A	Dundee U	D	2-2	1-0	—	Bollan (og), Mitchell	8468
19	31	A	Partick T	D	2-2	1-2	7	Maskrey, MacPherson	5799
20	Jan 7	A	Hibernian	L	1-2	0-1	9	McKee	8918
21	14	A	Celtic	L	1-2	0-0	9	Black (pen)	25,342
22	17	H	Motherwell	W	2-0	2-0	—	Black 2 (1 pen)	7521
23	21	H	Falkirk	W	2-1	1-1	6	Black, McKee	7648
24	Feb 4	H	Aberdeen	W	3-1	2-1	6	Maskrey, Brown, Roberts	9384
25	11	A	Hearts	D	2-2	2-2	6	Maskrey, Brown	8374
26	25	A	Rangers	L	0-3	0-0	8		44,859
27	Mar 4	H	Dundee U	W	2-0	2-0	6	Mitchell 2	7630
28	21	H	Celtic	L	0-1	0-0	—		10,112
29	25	A	Falkirk	L	0-2	0-1	7		5714
30	Apr 1	A	Aberdeen	W	1-0	0-0	7	Skilling	14,041
31	12	H	Hearts	W	3-2	2-1	—	Whitworth 2, Henry	7239
32	15	A	Dundee U	W	2-1	1-1	5	Whitworth, Henry	8223
33	20	H	Rangers	L	0-1	0-1	—		16,532
34	29	H	Partick T	D	0-0	0-0	6		9201
35	May 6	A	Motherwell	L	0-2	0-1	6		7760
36	13	H	Hibernian	L	1-2	1-0	7	Wright	11,676

Final League Position: 7

Most League Goals in Season (Individual): 34: Harry 'Peerie' Cunningham 1927-28 and Andy Kerr 1960-61.
Most Goals Overall (Individual): 148: W. Culley; 1912-23.

Honours
League Champions: Division I 1964-65. Division II 1897-98, 1898-99; *Runners-up:* Division I 1959-60, 1960-61, 1962-63, 1963-64. First Division 1975-76, 1978-79, 1981-82, 1992-93. Division II 1953-54, 1973-74. Second Division 1989-90.
Scottish Cup Winners: 1920, 1929; *Runners-up:* 1898, 1932, 1938, 1957, 1960.
League Cup Runners-up: 1952-53, 1960-61, 1962-63.

European: *European Cup:* 1965-66. *UEFA Cup (Fairs):* 1964-65 (semi-finals), 1969-70, 1970-71.
Club colours: Shirt: Blue and white vertical stripes. Shorts: Blue. Stockings: Blue.

Goalscorers: *League (40):* McKee 6, Black 5 (2 pens), Brown 4, Henry 4, Maskrey 4, Mitchell 4, Skilling 3, Whitworth 3, Williamson 2, MacPherson 1, Roberts 1, Wright 1, own goals 2. *Scottish Cup (6):* Maskrey 4, Black 1, Reilly 1. *League Cup (6):* Maskrey 2, Henry 1, McCluskey 1, Montgomerie 1, Williamson 1.

Geddes R 12	MacPherson A 33	Black T 31 + 1	Montgomerie R 9 + 3	Reilly M 31 + 1	Millen A 13	Mitchell A 33 + 2	Napier C 2 + 1	Williamson R 7 + 8	Connor R 27 + 1	Maskrey S 19 + 11	McCluskey G 2 + 1	Henry J 28 + 2	McSkimming S 8	Brown T 18 + 9	Whitworth N 30	McKee C 22 + 3	Meldrum C 4	Skilling M 13 + 4	Anderson D 20	Ledovic D 20	Roberts M — + 4	Lauchlan J 2	McCarrison D — + 1	Findlay W 5 + 4	Wright P 7	Match No.
1	2	3	4	5	6	7	*8*	9	10	11	14															1
1	2	3	4	5	6	7		14	11	9	*10*	8														2
1	2	3	4	5	6	7		12	10	9	*8*		11	14												3
1	2	3		4	6	7		*9*	10			12	11	14	5	8										4
1	2		12	11	6	7		9	10			4	3		5	8										5
1		12	2	11	6	7		9	10			4	3	14	5	*8*										6
1		3	2	12	6			9	4	14		8	11	10	5	*7*										7
1	2	3	4	11	6	12		9		14		8		10	5	*7*										8
1	2	3		4	6	7		*9*				8	11	10	5	14										9
	2	3		4	6	7						8	11	10	5	9	1									10
	2	3		4	6	7		12		14		8	11	10	5	9	1									11
1	2	3		11	6	7		12		14		8		10	5	9		4								12
1	2	3		11	6	7		12		14		8		10	5	*9*		4								13
	2	3		11		7				12		8		10	5	9	1	4	6							14
	2	3		11		7			12	14		8		10	5	*9*		4	6	1						15
	2			4		7	3	12	10	*11*					5	9		8	6	1	14					16
	2	3		4		7		14	*10*	11		12			5	9		8	6	1						17
	2	3		4		7		14	10	*11*		8			5	9		12	6	1						18
	2	3		4		7			10	*11*		8		14		9		5	6	1						19
	2	3		4		7	12		10	11		*8*		14	5	9			6	1						20
	2	3		4		7			10	14		8		*11*		9		5	6	1						21
	2	3		4		7			10			8		9	5	11			6	1						22
	2	3	4	6		7			10	14		8		*9*		11				1		5				23
	2	3		4		7			10	11		8		*9*	5				6	1	14					24
	2	3		4		7			10	11		8		*9*	5				6	1	14					25
	2	3	12	4		7			10	*11*		8			5	9			6	1	14					26
	2	3		4		7			10	*11*		8			5	9		12	6	1			14			27
	2	3		4		7			10	*11*				9	5	14		8	6	1				12		28
	2	3		4		7			10	11		8		*9*	5	14			6	1				12		29
	2	3		4		7			11	14				10	5			8	6	1				12	*9*	30
	2	3	12			7			10	11		8			5				6	1				4	9	31
	2	3				7			10	11		8		14	5			4	6	1				12	*9*	32
	2	3				7			10	*11*				14	5			4	6	1				8	9	33
	2	3				7			10	11		8		14	5			12	6	1				4	*9*	34
1	2		4	3		7				14		8		12	5	*11*		10						6	9	35
			4	3		14			10	11		*6*		9	5		1	12				2		7	8	36

LIVINGSTON (MEADOWBANK THISTLE)
Third Division

Year Formed: 1974. *Ground:* (at start of season) Meadowbank Stadium, London Rd, Edinburgh EH7 6AE. *Telephone:* 0131 661 5351. Address for correspondence: Preston Farm, Preston Road, Prestonpans, EH32 9LB. *Fax:* 01875 811130.
Ground Capacity: total: 16,500. seated: 16,500. Main stand only used 7500. *Size of Pitch:* 105yd × 72yd.
Chairman: William P Hunter. *Secretary:* J.R.S.Renton. *Vice-chairman:* Hugh Cowan.
Manager: Jim Leishman. *Club Doctor:* Dr M. M. Morrison. *Physio:* Arthur Duncan. *Coach:* Murray McDermott.
Managers since 1975: John Bain; Alec Ness; Willie MacFarlane; Terry Christie; Michael Lawson. *Club Nickname(s):* Thistle; Wee Jags. *Previous Grounds:* None.
Record Attendance: 4000 v Albion Rovers, League Cup 1st rd; 9 Sept, 1974.
Record Transfer Fee received: £115,000 for John Inglis to St Johnstone (1990).
Record Transfer Fee paid: £28,000 for Victor Kasule from Albion Rovers (1987).
Record Victory: 6-0 v Raith R, Second Division; 9 Nov, 1985.
Record Defeat: 0-8 v Hamilton A. Division II; 14 Dec, 1974.
Most Capped Player (under 18): I. Little.

MEADOWBANK THISTLE 1994–95 LEAGUE RECORD

Match No.	Date	Venue	Opponents	Result		H/T Score	Lg. Pos.	Goalscorers	Attendance
1	Aug 13	A	Brechin C	W	5-1	0-0	—	Rutherford, Bailey 3, Sorbie	432
2	20	H	Morton	L	0-1	0-0	5		398
3	27	H	Stenhousemuir	W	3-0	0-0	2	Little, Bailey 2	239
4	Sept 3	A	Dumbarton	W	1-0	1-0	4	Wilson	644
5	10	H	Queen of the S	L	0-1	0-0	6		279
6	24	H	Stirling Albion	L	1-2	0-1	7	Fleming	247
7	Oct 1	A	Clyde	L	1-2	1-1	7	McLeod	865
8	8	A	Berwick R	L	1-2	1-2	9	Little	520
9	15	H	East Fife	L	0-1	0-0	9		314
10	22	H	Brechin C	W	1-0	1-0	9	Williamson S	149
11	29	A	Stenhousemuir	D	1-1	1-0	9	Little	473
12	Nov 5	A	Morton	L	0-4	0-1	9		1453
13	12	A	Queen of the S	D	0-0	0-0	9		1418
14	19	H	Dumbarton	D	0-0	0-0	9		210
15	26	A	Stirling Albion	W	3-2	0-0	9	Samuel 2, Sorbie	518
16	Dec 3	H	Clyde	D	2-2	0-1	9	Bailey, Little	382
17	10	H	Berwick R	W	2-1	1-1	8	Sinclair, Williamson S	338
18	31	A	East Fife	L	1-2	1-1	9	Sorbie	686
19	Jan 10	A	Stenhousemuir	L	1-2	1-0	—	Thorburn	371
20	14	A	Brechin C	L	1-3	0-2	9	Sorbie	356
21	21	H	Morton	W	1-0	0-0	9	Sorbie	416
22	Feb 4	H	Queen of the S	L	1-2	0-1	9	Harris	265
23	11	A	Dumbarton	L	0-4	0-3	9		749
24	25	A	Clyde	L	1-4	0-1	9	Young	825
25	Mar 4	A	Berwick R	L	0-1	0-1	9		455
26	8	H	Stirling Albion	L	0-3	0-0	—		165
27	11	H	East Fife	L	1-3	1-1	9	Bailey	222
28	18	A	Queen of the S	W	3-2	2-0	9	Bailey, Wilson, Williamson S	705
29	25	H	Dumbarton	W	1-0	1-0	9	Young	389
30	Apr 1	H	Clyde	L	0-1	0-1	9		377
31	8	A	Stirling Albion	L	1-2	0-0	9	Callaghan	478
32	15	H	Berwick R	L	0-3	0-2	9		296
33	22	A	East Fife	D	1-1	1-0	9	Sorbie	355
34	29	H	Brechin C	W	2-1	1-0	9	McCartney, Graham	144
35	May 5	H	Stenhousemuir	W	1-0	1-0	—	Bailey	463
36	13	A	Morton	L	0-1	0-1	9		3165

Final League Position: 9

Most League Appearances: 446: Walter Boyd, 1979-89.
Most League Goals in Season (Individual): 21: John McGachie, 1986-87. *(Team):* 69; Second Division, 1986-87.
Most Goals Overall (Individual): 64: David Roseburgh, 1986-93.

Honours
League Champions: Second Division 1986-87; *Runners-up:* Second Division 1982-83. First Division 1987-88.
Scottish Cup: —. *League Cup:* Semi-finals 1984-85. *B&Q Cup:* Semi-finals 1992-93, 1993-94.
Club colours: Shirt: Amber with black trim. Shorts: Black. Stockings: Amber.

Goalscorers: *League (32):* Bailey 6, Sorbie 5, Little 4, Williamson S 3, Samuel 2, Wilson 2, Young 2, Callaghan 1, Fleming 1, Graham 1, Harris 1, McCartney 1, McLeod 1, Sinclair 1, Thorburn 1. *Scottish Cup (5):* Bailey 1, Graham 1, Sinclair 1, Wilson 1, own goal 1. *League Cup (5):* Bailey 1, Hutchison 1, Little 1, McLeod 1, Sorbie 1. *B&Q Cup (1):* Graham 1.

Ellison S 25	Graham T 32	Fleming D 7	Wilson S 32 + 1	Williamson S 28	Hutchison M 2 + 1	Duthie M 13 + 5	McLeod G 31	Little I 27 + 1	Rutherford P 4	Bailey L 24 + 10	Thorburn S 17 + 5	Sorbie S 26 + 6	Coyle M 1 + 7	Price G 2 + 1	Davidson G 26 + 1	Ingram N — + 2	Martin C 16 + 1	Sinclair C 13 + 4	Dallas A 6 + 1	Douglas R 8	Coulston D — + 2	Samuel D 9 + 2	Thomson M 10	Harris C 5 + 1	Young J 10 + 4	Williamson R — + 1	McCartney C 9	Alleyne D 5	Callaghan W 5 + 2	Stoute H 3	Match No.
1	*2*	3	4	5	6	7	8	9	10	11	12	14																			1
1	2	3	4	5	7		8	*9*	6	11		10	12	14																	2
1	2	3	4	*5*	14	7	8	9	6	11		10	12																		3
1	2	3	4	5		7	8	9	6	11		10	12																		4
1	2	3	4	5		7	8	9		11	12	10		6	14																5
1	2	3	4	5			8	9		11	6	10			7																6
1	*2*	3	4	5			8			11	6	10		9	7	12	14														7
1	4		12	5			6	9		*10*	7	8			2		3	11	14												8
	4		7	5		2	6	9		12		8					3	11	*10*	1	14										9
	4		7	5		2	6	9		*10*		8	14				3	11		1	12										10
	4		7	5		14	6	9		12		10			2		3	11	*8*	1											11
	4		8	5		14	6	9		12	7	10			2		3	*11*		1											12
	4		8	5		7	6	9		10	11				2		3			1											13
			8	5		*7*	6	9		10	11		12		2	14	3	4		1											14
	4		8	5			6	9		*10*		12	14		2		3	11		1		7									15
	4		8	5				9		10		6			2		3	11		1		7									16
1	4		8	5		14		9		*10*	3	6	12		2			11				7									17
1	4		8			14	10			9	5	6			2		3	*11*				7									18
1	4		8			14	10	9		12	7	6			2		3	*11*					5								19
1	*4*			7			10	14			12	6			2		3	11				8	5	9							20
1			7	2			11	9		14		6			4		3					10	5	*8*							21
1	4			7			10	11		14	12	6			2		*3*					8	5	9							22
1	5						*10*			11	8	6	7		2		3		9			12	4		14						23
1			7	*5*			10			8	14	6			2		3					11	4	12	9						24
1	2		7	5			10			8	3	11							*6*			14	4	9	12						25
1	2		7	5			10	8		12	3	14							6				4	*9*	11						26
1	2		8	*5*			10	9		11	3	7										6	4		12	14					27
1	5		6	2			10	9		7					3				11						12		4	8			28
1	5		6	2		11		9		*7*		12			3										8		4	10	14		29
1	5		6	2		11		9		*7*		12			3										8		4	10	14		30
1	5		7	*2*				8		12		14			4			11							10		3	6	9		31
1	5		7			2	3	8		12					4			14							10		11	*6*	9		32
1	5		7			*11*	8			12	2	6			4			14							10		3		9		33
	5		7			11	10				2	6			4			12							8		3		9	1	34
	5		10				8			7	2	6			4										11		3		9	1	35
			8				6	9		7	2	10			4			12					5		11		3			1	36

MONTROSE Second Division

Year Formed: 1879. *Ground & Address:* Links Park, Wellington St, Montrose DD10 8QD. *Telephone:* 01674 673200.
Ground Capacity: total: 4338. seated: 1398. *Size of Pitch:* 113yd × 70yd.
Chairman: Bryan Keith. *Secretary:* Malcolm J. Watters.
Manager: Andy Dornan. *Physio:* Bill Ramsay.
Managers since 1975: A. Stuart; K. Cameron; R. Livingstone; S. Murray; D. D'Arcy; I. Stewart; C. McLelland; D. Rougvie; J. Leishman, J Holt.
Club Nickname(s): The Gable Endies. *Previous Grounds:* None.
Record Attendance: 8983 v Dundee, Scottish Cup 3rd rd; 17 Mar, 1973.
Record Transfer Fee received: £50,000 for Gary Murray to Hibernian (Dec 1980).
Record Transfer Fee paid: £17,500 for Jim Smith from Airdrieonians (Feb 1992).
Record Victory: 12-0 v Vale of Leithen, Scottish Cup 2nd rd; 4 Jan, 1975.
Record Defeat: 0-13 v Aberdeen; 17 Mar, 1951.
Most Capped Player: Alexander Keillor, 2 (6), Scotland.
Most League Appearances: 343: Martin Allan, 1983-93.
Most League Goals in Season (Individual): 28: Brian Third, Division II; 1972-73.

MONTROSE 1994–95 LEAGUE RECORD

Match No.	Date	Venue	Opponents	Result		H/T Score	Lg. Pos.	Goalscorers	Attendance
1	Aug 13	H	East Stirling	W	2-0	1-0	—	Grant, Craib	537
2	20	A	Albion R	W	4-2	2-1	1	Masson, Haro, Kennedy 2	274
3	27	H	Cowdenbeath	W	2-0	2-0	1	Robertson, McGlashan	584
4	Sept 3	A	Forfar Ath	L	0-1	0-0	2		1077
5	10	H	Ross C	L	0-2	0-1	3		918
6	24	H	Queen's Park	D	1-1	0-1	5	Grant	575
7	Oct 1	A	Arbroath	W	3-0	1-0	2	McGlashan, Kennedy, Stephen	802
8	8	A	Alloa	D	1-1	0-1	3	MacRonald	460
9	15	H	Caledonian Th	W	3-1	0-1	2	Grant, McGlashan, MacRonald	758
10	22	A	East Stirling	W	2-1	0-0	1	Kennedy 2 (1 pen)	631
11	29	A	Cowdenbeath	D	1-1	1-1	2	Kennedy	301
12	Nov 5	H	Albion R	W	4-1	2-0	2	Tindal, McGlashan 2, Kennedy	629
13	12	A	Ross C	W	1-0	0-0	2	Kennedy	1154
14	19	H	Forfar Ath	W	2-0	1-0	1	Kennedy 2	1259
15	26	A	Queen's Park	D	1-1	0-0	1	Haro	443
16	Dec 3	H	Arbroath	W	3-1	1-0	1	McGlashan 3	1085
17	24	H	Alloa	L	1-2	0-2	1	Haro	637
18	Jan 2	H	Cowdenbeath	L	1-2	1-2	—	Masson	452
19	Feb 4	H	Ross C	D	1-1	0-1	4	McGlashan	882
20	14	A	Caledonian Th	W	4-0	0-0	—	Beedie 2, Milne, Haro	851
21	18	H	Queen's Park	D	2-2	0-0	3	Grant, Kennedy	674
22	25	A	Arbroath	L	1-4	1-2	4	McAvoy	951
23	Mar 11	H	Caledonian Th	L	0-1	0-0	5		781
24	15	A	East Stirling	L	0-1	0-0	—		297
25	22	A	Albion R	W	4-1	2-0	—	McGlashan, Haro, Smith 2	187
26	25	H	Forfar Ath	L	1-2	0-1	5	Kennedy	1240
27	23	A	Alloa	W	1-0	0-0	—	McGlashan	416
28	Apr 1	H	Arbroath	W	5-0	4-0	4	McGlashan 2, McMillan (og), Smith, Cooper	1179
29	4	A	Forfar Ath	W	3-1	2-1	—	Smith, Craib, McGlashan	1176
30	11	A	Queen's Park	L	0-1	0-0	—		367
31	15	H	Alloa	D	0-0	0-0	3		649
32	19	A	Ross C	W	3-0	2-0	—	McAvoy, Cooper, Smith	1702
33	22	A	Caledonian Th	W	3-0	2-0	2	McAvoy, McGlashan (pen), Smith	942
34	29	H	East Stirling	W	1-0	0-0	2	McGlashan	858
35	May 6	A	Cowdenbeath	W	4-0	1-0	2	McGl;ashan, Kennedy 3	379
36	13	H	Albion R	W	4-1	3-0	2	Kennedy 2, McGlashan 2	893

Final League Position: 2

Most Goals Overall (Individual): —.

Honours
League Champions: Second Division 1984-85, *Runners-up:* 1990-91. Third Division, *Runners-up:* 1994-95.
Scottish Cup: Quarter-finals 1973, 1976.
League Cup: Semi-finals 1975-76.
B&Q Cup: Semi-finals: 1992-93.
Club colours: Shirt: Royal Blue with white sleeves. Shorts: White with royal blue and red trim. Stockings: White with royal blue and red tops.

Goalscorers: *League (69):* McGlashan 19 (1 pen), Kennedy 17 (1 pen), Smith 6, Haro 5, Grant 4, McAvoy 3, Beedie 2, Cooper 2, Craib 2, MacRonald 2, Masson 2, Milne 1, Robertson 1, Stephen 1, Tindal 1, own goal 1. *Scottish Cup (10):* Kennedy 3 (1 pen), McGlashan 2, MacRonald 2, Masson 1, Milne 1, Stephen 1. *League Cup (1):* Kennedy 1. *B&Q Cup (6):* McGlashan 3, Cooper 1, Kennedy 1 (pen), Stephen 1.

Larter D 36	Robertson I 32	Tindal K 21	Craib M 22	Grant D 28 + 1	Haro M 34	Garden M 7 + 7	Stephen L 6 + 6	McGlashan C 34	Kennedy A 23 + 10	Masson P 32 + 2	Cooper C 24 + 5	Milne C 2 + 11	Taylor D — + 4	MacDonald I 22 + 1	Brown M — + 3	Tosh J 9	MacRonald C 20 + 1	Beedie S 7	McAvoy N 13 + 4	Mailer C 14	Smith S 10 + 1	Match No.
1	2	3	4	5	6	7	8	9	*10*	11	12	14										1
1	2	3	4	5	6	7	8	*9*	10	11	12		14									2
1	2	3	4	5	6	8		9	*10*	11	7	12	14									3
1	2	3	4	5	6	8		9	10	11	7											4
1	2	3	4	5	6		12	9	*10*	11	7	14		8								5
1	2	3		5	6	8	12	9	*10*	11	7		14	4								6
1	3	2		5	6		11	9	*10*	4	7		12	8	14							7
1	2	3			6		11	9	10	4	7			8	14	*5*	12					8
1	2	3		5	*6*	14	8	9	10	4	12			7			11					9
1	2	3		5	6	12		9	10	4	7			8			11					10
1	2	3		5				9	10	4	7			8		6	11					11
1	2	3	8	5	6			9	10	4				7			11					12
1	2	3	8	5	6	12		9	*10*	4		14		7			11					13
1	2	3	8	5	6			9	10	4				7			11					14
1	2	3	8	5	6	12		9	10	4		14		7			11					15
1	2			5	6	12		9	10	4	7	14		8			11	3				16
1	2			5	6	8		9	10	3	7	12		4			11					17
1	2	3		5	6			9	10	4	7	12		8			11					18
1	2	3		5	6	4	12	9	*10*		14			7			11	8				19
1	2	3		5	6		12			14	7	9		8			*11*	4	10			20
1	2	3		5					14	6	7	9		8			*11*	4	10			21
1	2	3		5	6			9	10	14	7	12		*11*				4	8			22
1		2		5	6		3	9	14	4		12		*11*				8	10	7		23
1			2	5	6			9	*10*	4	7				14			3	11	8		24
1			3		6			9	12	4		14		7		5	11		8	2	*10*	25
1			3		6			9	12	4	14			7		5	11		*8*	2	10	26
1	2		8	5	6			9		*4*	7						11		14	3	10	27
1	2		8	5	6			9	12	*4*	7						11		14	3	10	28
1	2		8	5	6			9	12	4	7						*11*		14	3	10	29
1	2		8	5	6			9	12		7						11		4	3	10	30
1	2		8	5	*6*			9	12	4	7						11		14	3	10	31
1	2		8		6		14	*9*	10	4	7					5			11	3	12	32
1	2		8		6		14	*9*	12	4	7					5			11	3	10	33
1	2		8		6			9		4	7			14		5			11	3	10	34
1	2		8		6	12		9	14	4	7					5			11	3	*10*	35
1	2		*8*	12	6	14		9	10	4				7		5			11	3		36

MOTHERWELL Premier Division

Year Formed: 1886. *Ground & Address:* Fir Park, Motherwell ML1 2QN. *Telephone:* 01698 261437.
Ground Capacity: total: 13,741 all seated. *Size of Pitch:* 110yd × 75yd.
Chairman: John C. Chapman. *Secretary:* Alan C. Dick. *Commercial Manager:* John Swinburne.
Manager: Alex McLeish. *Assistant Manager:* Andy Watson. *Physio:* John Porteous. *Coach:* Jim Griffin.
Managers since 1975: Ian St. John; Willie McLean; Rodger Hynd; Ally MacLeod; David Hay; Jock Wallace; Bobby Watson, Tommy McLean.
Club Nickname(s): The Well. *Previous Grounds:* Roman Road, Dalziel Park.
Record Attendance: 35,632 v Rangers, Scottish Cup 4th rd replay; 12 Mar, 1952.
Record Transfer Fee received: £1,750,000 for Phil O'Donnell to Celtic, September 1994.
Record Transfer Fee paid: £400,000 for Mitchell Van Der Gaag from PSV Eindhoven, March 1995.
Record Victory: 12-1 v Dundee U, Division II; 23 Jan, 1954.
Record Defeat: 0-8 v Aberdeen, Premier Division; 26 Mar, 1979.
Most Capped Player: George Stevenson, 12, Scotland.
Most League Appearances: 626: Bobby Ferrier, 1918-37.

MOTHERWELL 1994–95 LEAGUE RECORD

Match No.	*Date*		*Venue*	*Opponents*	*Result*		*H/T Score*	*Lg. Pos.*	*Goalscorers*	*Attendance*
1	Aug	13	A	Rangers	L	1-2	0-1	—	Coyne (pen)	42,491
2		20	H	Hearts	D	1-1	0-0	7	Coyne	8249
3		27	A	Kilmarnock	W	1-0	1-0	6	Coyne	7388
4	Sept	10	A	Dundee U	D	1-1	0-1	6	Kirk	7440
5		17	H	Hibernian	D	1-1	0-0	5	Shannon	7005
6		24	A	Partick T	D	2-2	0-1	5	Davies, Coyne	4786
7	Oct	1	H	Celtic	D	1-1	0-1	5	Arnott	10,869
8		8	H	Falkirk	W	5-3	2-1	4	Coyne 2, Davies, Arnott 2	6239
9		15	A	Aberdeen	W	3-1	0-1	4	McKinnon, Kirk, Coyne	12,489
10		22	H	Rangers	W	2-1	1-0	3	Arnott 2	11,160
11		29	H	Kilmarnock	W	3-2	1-2	2	Coyne 2, Martin	7436
12	Nov	5	A	Hearts	W	2-1	1-1	2	Shannon, Coyne	8889
13		8	H	Dundee U	D	1-1	0-0	—	Martin	6145
14		19	A	Hibernian	D	2-2	1-2	2	Coyne, Davies	9160
15		26	H	Partick T	W	3-1	3-1	2	Coyne, Davies, Arnott	6893
16	Dec	3	A	Celtic	D	2-2	1-2	2	Coyne 2	21,465
17		10	H	Aberdeen	L	0-1	0-1	2		7020
18		26	A	Falkirk	W	1-0	0-0	—	Shannon	7937
19		31	H	Rangers	L	1-3	0-1	2	McGrillen	11,269
20	Jan	8	H	Hearts	L	1-2	1-1	—	McGrillen	5117
21		13	H	Hibernian	D	0-0	0-0	—		6724
22		17	A	Kilmarnock	L	0-2	0-2	—		7521
23		21	A	Dundee U	L	1-6	1-2	3	Coyne	7062
24	Feb	4	H	Celtic	W	1-0	0-0	3	McKinnon	10,771
25		25	A	Aberdeen	W	2-0	1-0	2	Burns, McKinnon (pen)	10,319
26	Mar	7	H	Falkirk	D	2-2	1-1	—	Lambert, May	6100
27		14	A	Partick T	D	0-0	0-0	—		3525
28		18	H	Dundee U	W	2-1	0-0	2	Burns, Arnott	4457
29		22	A	Hibernian	L	0-2	0-1	—		5395
30	Apr	1	A	Celtic	D	1-1	0-0	2	Coyne	24,047
31		8	H	Partick T	L	1-2	1-1	2	Burns	9631
32		15	A	Falkirk	L	0-3	0-1	2		5756
33		18	H	Aberdeen	W	2-1	1-1	—	McSkimming, Arnott	7155
34		29	A	Rangers	W	2-0	1-0	2	Arnott, McSkimming	43,576
35	May	6	H	Kilmarnock	W	2-0	1-0	2	Arnott, May	7760
36		13	A	Hearts	L	0-2	0-0	2		11,172

Final League Position: 2

Most League Goals in Season (Individual): 52: Willie McFadyen, Division I; 1931-32.
Most Goals Overall (Individual): 283: Hugh Ferguson, 1916-25.

Honours
League Champions: Division I 1931-32. First Division 1981-82, 1984-85. Division II 1953-54, 1968-69; *Runners-up:* Premier Division 1994-95. Division I 1926-27, 1929-30, 1932-33, 1933-34. Division II 1894-95, 1902-03. *Scottish Cup:* 1952, 1991; *Runners-up:* 1931, 1933, 1939, 1951.
League Cup: 1950-51. *Runners-up:* 1954-55 *Scottish Summer Cup:* 1944, 1965.
Club colours: Shirt: Amber with claret hoop and trimmings. Shorts: Claret. Stockings: Amber.

Goalscorers: *League (50):* Coyne 16 (1 pen), Arnott 10, Davies 4, Burns 3, McKinnon 3 (1 pen), Shannon 3, Kirk 2, McGrillen 2, McSkimming 2, Martin 2, May 2, Lambert 1. *Scottish Cup (2):* Burns 2. *League Cup (4):* Burns 1, Coyne 1 (pen), Kirk 1, McCart 1.

Woods S 33	Shannon R 23 + 2	McKinnon R 32	Philliben J 30 + 1	Martin B 32	McCart C 24	Lambert P 36	Davies W 31	Coyne T 30 + 1	O'Donnell P 3	Kirk S 6 + 12	Dolan J 31	Roddie A 4 + 15	Burns A 7 + 7	Arnott D 26 + 1	McGrillen P 2 + 5	McLeish A 2	McSkimming S 10 + 4	Krivokapic M 16	Howie S 3	McMillan S 2 + 1	May E 10	Van Der Gaag M 2	Ritchie I 1	Match No.
1	2	3	4	5	6	7	8	9	10	11														1
1	2		3	5	6	7		9	10	*8*	4	11	14											2
1	2		3	5	6	7	*8*	9	10	12	4	11	14											3
1		3	2	5	6	7	11	9		4	8			*10*	14									4
1	2	3	4	5	6	7	11	9		12	*8*			10	14									5
1	*2*	3	4	5	6	7	11	9		12	8	10		14										6
1	2	3	4	5	6	7	*11*	9		12	8	14		10										7
1	2	3	4	5		7	11	9			8	14		10		6								8
1	2	3	4	5	6	7	11	9		12	*8*	14		10										9
1	2	3	4	5	6	7	*11*	9			8	14		10										10
1	2	3	4	5		7	11	9		12	8			10		6								11
1	2	3	4	5	6	7	11	9		12	*8*	14		10										12
1	2	3	4	5	6	7	*11*	9		12	8	14		10										13
1	2	3	4	5	6	7	11	9		10	8						14							14
1	2	*3*	4	5	6	7	11	9		12	8	14		10										15
1	2	3	4	5	6	7	11	9			8			10										16
1	2	3	4	*5*	6	7	11	9		12	8	14		10										17
1	2	3	4		6	7	11	9						10			8	5						18
1	2	3	4		6	7	11	9		12				*10*	14		8	5						19
1	2	3	4		6	7	11	9				14			10		*8*	5						20
	2	3		5	6	7	10	9		12	8				11			4	1					21
	2	3		5	6	7	*11*	9		10	8						14	4	1					22
	2	3		5		7	11	9		10	8	14			12		6	4	1					23
1		3	2	5	6	7	11	9			8			*10*	12			4		14				24
1	12	3	5		6	7					8	14	*9*	10			11	4			2			25
1		3	*2*	5	6	7					8	14	9	10				4			11			26
1		3		5	6	7	11				8		9	10				4			2			27
1			6	5		7	11				8	12	9	10				4		3	2			28
1	14		6	5		7	11	12			8		9	*10*				4		3	2			29
1		3		5		7	11	9			8		12	10			14	4			*2*	6		30
1		3	14	5		7	11	9			8	2	10				12	4				*6*		31
1	2	3	6	5		7		9			8		12	10			11	4						32
1		3	6	5		7		9			8	14	12	10			11	*4*			2			33
1		3	4	5		7	11	9			8		14	*10*			6				2			34
1		3	4	5		7	11	9			8		14	*10*			6				2			35
1		3	4	5		7	11					12	9	10			6				2		8	36

PARTICK THISTLE Premier Division

Year Formed: 1876. *Ground & Address:* Firhill Park, 80 Firhill Rd, Glasgow G20 7BA. *Telephone:* 0141 945 4811.
Ground Capacity: total: 20,676. seated: 2906. *Size of Pitch:* 110yd × 74yd.
Chairman: James Oliver. *Secretary:* Robert Reid. *Commercial Manager:* Thomas Dickson.
Manager: John Lambie. *Assistant Manager:* Gerry Collins. *Physio:* Frank Ness.
Managers since 1975: R. Auld; P. Cormack; B. Rooney; R. Auld; D. Johnstone; W. Lamont; S. Clark. *Club Nickname(s):* The Jags. *Previous Grounds:* Jordanvale Park; Muirpark; Inchview; Meadowside Park.
Record Attendance: 49,838 v Rangers, Division I; 18 Feb, 1922.
Record Transfer Fee received: £200,000 for Mo Johnston to Watford.
Record Transfer Fee paid: £85,000 for Andy Murdoch from Celtic (Feb 1991).
Record Victory: 16-0 v Royal Albert, Scottish Cup 1st rd; 17 Jan, 1931.
Record Defeat: 0-10 v Queen's Park, Scottish Cup; 3 Dec, 1881.
Most Capped Player: Alan Rough, 51 (53), Scotland.
Most League Appearances: 410: Alan Rough, 1969-82.
Most League Goals in Season (Individual): 41: Alec Hair, Division I; 1926-27.
Most Goals Overall (Individual): —.

PARTICK THISTLE 1994–95 LEAGUE RECORD

Match No.	Date	Venue	Opponents	Result		H/T Score	Lg. Pos.	Goalscorers	Attendance
1	Aug 13	H	Kilmarnock	W	2-0	2-0	—	McWilliams, English	6606
2	20	H	Rangers	L	0-2	0-1	5		14,361
3	27	A	Falkirk	L	1-2	1-0	7	Grant	5402
4	Sept 10	H	Celtic	L	1-2	0-2	8	Grant	14,439
5	17	A	Aberdeen	D	1-1	0-0	7	Charnley	10,425
6	24	H	Motherwell	D	2-2	1-0	9	Grant, McDonald	4786
7	Oct 1	A	Hibernian	L	0-3	0-2	10		7083
8	8	H	Hearts	L	0-1	0-1	10		5076
9	15	A	Dundee U	W	1-0	0-0	9	Cameron	6687
10	22	A	Kilmarnock	L	0-2	0-0	10		7023
11	29	H	Falkirk	L	1-2	1-2	10	Grant	4215
12	Nov 5	A	Rangers	L	0-3	0-0	10		43,696
13	9	A	Celtic	D	0-0	0-0	—		21,462
14	19	H	Aberdeen	W	2-1	0-1	10	Craig, Gibson	3795
15	26	A	Motherwell	L	1-3	1-3	10	Cameron	6893
16	Dec 3	H	Hibernian	D	2-2	1-0	9	Foster, English	4667
17	26	A	Hearts	L	0-3	0-0	—		8920
18	31	H	Kilmarnock	D	2-2	2-1	10	McDonald 2	5799
19	Jan 7	H	Rangers	D	1-1	0-0	10	Taylor	17,298
20	14	A	Aberdeen	L	1-3	0-1	10	Pittman	9833
21	17	A	Falkirk	W	3-1	1-0	—	Dinnie, Foster, McWilliams	3958
22	21	H	Celtic	D	0-0	0-0	10		11,904
23	Feb 4	A	Hibernian	W	2-1	1-1	10	Turner, McDonald	7760
24	25	A	Dundee U	L	0-2	0-0	10		7227
25	Mar 7	H	Dundee U	W	2-0	0-0	—	Smith, Foster	2126
26	11	H	Aberdeen	D	2-2	0-2	10	Pittman, Turner	6886
27	14	H	Motherwell	D	0-0	0-0	—		3525
28	Apr 1	H	Hibernian	D	2-2	0-1	10	Foster 2 (1 pen)	4041
29	4	H	Hearts	W	3-1	0-1	—	Pittman, McDonald, McWilliams	4526
30	8	A	Motherwell	W	2-1	1-1	8	Cameron, Craig	9631
31	15	A	Hearts	W	1-0	0-0	8	Dinnie	9007
32	18	H	Dundee U	L	1-3	1-1	—	Pittman	4962
33	29	A	Kilmarnock	D	0-0	0-0	8		9201
34	May 2	A	Celtic	W	3-1	1-1	—	Grant, Foster 2	18,963
35	6	H	Falkirk	D	0-0	0-0	7		5927
36	13	A	Rangers	D	1-1	0-1	8	Taylor	45,280

Final League Position: 8

Honours
League Champions: First Division 1975-76. Division II 1896-97, 1899-1900, 1970-71; *Runners-up:* First Division 1991-92. Division II 1901-02.
Scottish Cup Winners: 1921; *Runners-up:* 1930.
League Cup Winners: 1971-72; *Runners-up:* 1953-54, 1956-57, 1958-59.

European: *UEFA Cup:* 10 matches (*Fairs Cup:* 1963-64. *UEFA Cup:* 1972-73, 1994-95).
Club colours: Shirt: Red and Yellow broad vertical stripes. Shorts: Black. Stockings: Yellow with Red turnover.

Goalscorers: *League (40):* Foster 7 (1 pen), Grant 5, McDonald 5, Pittman 4, Cameron 3, McWilliams 3, Craig 2, Dinnie 2, English 2, Taylor 2, Turner 2, Charnley 1, Gibson 1, Smith 1. *Scottish Cup (1):* Jamieson 1. *League Cup (5):* Charnley 3 (1 pen), Jamieson 1, Taylor 1.

Nelson C 13	Byrne D 11 + 1	Law R 2 + 3	Jamieson W 15	Tierney G 4 + 1	McWilliams D 27 + 2	Taylor A 17 + 6	Craig A 30	Grant R 14 + 9	English I 6 + 5	Charnley J 19 + 1	Cameron I 27 + 7	Smith T 8 + 6	Dinnie A 23 + 2	Docherty S — + 1	Pittman S 27	Watson G 29	Gibson A 9 + 2	McKee K 16 + 1	McDonald R 22 + 3	Murdoch A 2	Walker N 20	Milne C 3 + 1	Foster W 15	Welsh S 20	Turner T 15	Gray D 1 + 1	Cairns M 1	Eli R — + 2	Ayton S — + 1	Match No.
1	2	3	4	5	6	7	8	9	10	11																				1
1	2	3	4	5	6	7	*8*	9	10	11	12	14																		2
1	2		4	*5*	6	7		9	10	11	8	12	3	14																3
1	2		5		6	11	8	9				12	7		3	4	10													4
1	2		5		6		8	*9*		11	7	12	3			4	10	14												5
1			5		6		8	9		11	14	10	*2*		3	4	12		7											6
	2		5		6		8	12	*10*	11	14	9			3	4			7	1										7
	2		5		6	12		9		11	*10*	8			3	4	14		7	1										8
1	2		5		6	8		14	10		11		12		3	4	9		*7*											9
1	2	14	5					12	*10*		11	6	8		3	4	9		7											10
1		14	5		6	8		9	12		11		10		*3*	4	7	2												11
1			5		11		8		12	14	10		6		3	4	9	*2*	7											12
1			5		6		8	*9*	14	11	7				3	4	10	2												13
1			5		6		8			11	10		3			4	9	2	7											14
1	12		5		6		8		14	11	10		3			4	9	2	*7*											15
	4				6		8		12	11	10		3					2	7		1	5	9							16
		14					8	12		11	10		6			4		2	7		1	3	*9*	5						17
	2					14	8	12			11		6		3	4			7		1		*9*	5	10					18
					9	11	8			10	12		2		3	4			7		1			5	6					19
					9	11	8			*10*	12		2		3	4			7		1			5	6	14				20
					9	11	8			10	12		2		3	4					1		7	5	6					21
					9	11	8			10	12		2		3	4			14		1		7	5	6					22
					14	11	8				10		2		3	4			7		1	12	*9*	5	6					23
				14	12	11	8				*10*		2		3	4			7				9	5	6		1			24
					11		8				10	14			3	4		2	*7*		1		9	5	6					25
					11		8	14			10	12			3	4		2	*7*		1		9	5	6					26
					11		8	7			10				3	4		2	14		1			*9*	5	6				27
					11	12	8				10				3	4		2	7		1		9	5	6			14		28
					11	12	8				10				3	4		2	*7*		1		9	5	6			14		29
					11	12	8	14			10				3	4		2	7		1		9	5	6					30
					9	11	8	12			10		14		3	4		*2*	*7*		1			5	6					31
					9	11	8	7			10		2		3	4			12		1			5	6					32
						6	8	9		11	10	7	2		3			4			1			5						33
						14	8	9		11	10	6	4		3			*2*			1		7	5						34
						6	8	9		11	10	2	4		3						1		7	5						35
				5		11		14			10	8	3			4			7		1	*2*	9	6					12	36

QUEEN OF THE SOUTH Second Division

Year Formed: 1919. *Ground & Address:* Palmerston Park, Terregles St, Dumfries DG2 9BA. *Telephone and Fax:* 01387 254853.
Ground Capacity: total: 8352. seated: 3470. *Size of Pitch:* 112yd × 72yd.
Chairman: Norman Blount. *Secretary:* Mrs Doreen Alcorn. *Commercial Manager:* Robert McKinnel.
Manager: William McLaren. *Physio:* Derek Kelly.
Managers since 1975: M. Jackson; G. Herd; A. Busby; R. Clark; M. Jackson; D. Wilson; W. McLaren; F. McGarvey; A. MacLeod. *Club Nickname(s):* The Doonhamers. *Previous Grounds:* None.
Record Attendance: 24,500 v Hearts, Scottish Cup 3rd rd; 23 Feb, 1952.
Record Transfer Fee received: £100,000 for K. McMinn to Rangers (1985).
Record Transfer Fee paid: —.
Record Victory: 11-1 v Stranraer, Scottish Cup 1st rd; 16 Jan, 1932.
Record Defeat: 2-10 v Dundee, Division I; 1 Dec, 1962.
Most Capped Player: Billy Houliston, 3, Scotland.
Most League Appearances: 619: Allan Ball; 1962-83.
Most League Goals in Season (Individual): 33: Jimmy Gray, Division II; 1927-28.

QUEEN OF THE SOUTH 1994–95 LEAGUE RECORD

Match No.	Date	Venue	Opponents	Result		H/T Score	Lg. Pos.	Goalscorers	Attendance
1	Aug 13	H	Dumbarton	W	4-1	1-0	—	Bryce 2 (1 pen), McGuire, McLaren	1389
2	20	H	Clyde	L	1-2	0-1	6	Bryce	1435
3	27	A	Berwick R	L	0-1	0-0	8		610
4	Sept 3	H	East Fife	L	0-2	0-1	8		1412
5	10	A	Meadowbank T	W	1-0	0-0	7	McLaren	279
6	24	H	Brechin C	L	0-2	0-0	8		1032
7	Oct 1	A	Stirling Albion	L	0-3	0-0	9		697
8	8	A	Stenhousemuir	D	0-0	0-0	8		403
9	15	H	Morton	W	3-0	3-0	8	Mallan 2, Kennedy	1126
10	22	A	Dumbarton	D	0-0	0-0	8		725
11	29	H	Berwick R	W	5-4	3-1	7	Bryce, McFarlane 2, Mallan, Rowe	1298
12	Nov 5	A	Clyde	D	2-2	2-0	8	Mallan, McLaren	1112
13	12	H	Meadowbank T	D	0-0	0-0	8		1418
14	19	A	East Fife	L	1-3	1-2	8	Mallan	699
15	26	A	Brechin C	W	1-0	0-0	8	Bryce	406
16	Dec 3	H	Stirling Albion	L	0-1	0-1	8		1197
17	26	H	Stenhousemuir	L	1-2	0-1	—	McLaren	1437
18	31	A	Morton	D	1-1	0-0	8	Jackson	2112
19	Jan 10	A	Berwick R	L	1-3	1-1	—	Campbell D	448
20	14	H	Dumbarton	D	0-0	0-0	8		1066
21	21	A	Clyde	W	4-3	3-1	8	McFarlane, Mallan, Campbell D, Kennedy	998
22	Feb 4	A	Meadowbank T	W	2-1	1-0	8	Campbell D, Mallan	265
23	14	H	East Fife	D	3-3	1-1	—	Gibb (og), Campbell D, Bryce	890
24	18	H	Brechin C	L	0-1	0-	8		1002
25	25	A	Stirling Albion	D	1-1	1-0	8	Campbell D	528
26	Mar 11	H	Morton	W	1-0	1-0	8	Bryce	1505
27	18	H	Meadowbank T	L	2-3	0-2	8	Mallan, Campbell D	705
28	21	A	Stenhousemuir	D	2-2	1-1	—	Bryce, Hetherington	454
29	25	A	East Fife	L	1-3	1-0	8	Mallan	594
30	Apr 1	H	Stirling Albion	L	1-3	0-1	8	Telfer	1056
31	8	A	Brechin C	W	2-0	1-0	8	Campbell D 2	389
32	15	H	Stenhousemuir	L	1-2	0-2	8	Orr	1230
33	22	A	Morton	D	0-0	0-0	8		2395
34	29	A	Dumbarton	D	2-2	1-*1	8	Marsland (og), McKeown D	1369
35	May 6	H	Berwick R	W	2-0	1-0	8	Ramsay, Campbell D	1061
36	13	H	Clyde	W	1-0	1-0	7	McFarlane	1502

Final League Position: 7

Most Goals Overall (Individual): 109, Andrew Thomson, 1989-94.

Honours
League Champions: Division II 1950-51; *Runners-up:* Division II 1932-33, 1961-62, 1974-75. Second Division 1980-81, 1985-86.
Scottish Cup: —.
League Cup: —.
Club colours: Shirt: Royal blue. Shorts: White. Stockings: Royal blue with white tops.

Goalscorers: *League (46):* Campbell D 9, Mallan 9, Bryce 8 (1 pen), McFarlane 4, McLaren 4, Kennedy 2, Hetherington 1, Jackson 1, McGuire 1, McKeown D 1, Orr 1, Ramsay 1, Rowe 1, Telfer 1, own goals 2. *Scottish Cup (2):* Bell 1, Bryce 1. League Cup (2): Bryce 1, McLaren 1. *B&Q Cup (0)*

Purdie D 24 + 1	Mills D 3	Hetherington K 18 + 3	McKeown D 34	Kennedy D 31 + 1	McFarlane A 28 + 1	McGuire D 5 + 2	Cochrane G 2	McLaren J 15 + 8	Bryce T 32 + 1	Mallan S 34 + 1	Sermanni P 1 + 2	Brown J 16 + 5	McKeown B 30 + 1	Ramsay S 22 + 4	Jackson D 18 + 7	Adams M 1	Leslie S 4 + 2	Campbell C 24	Rowe G 4	McQueen J 12 + 1	Bell A 3 + 6	Campbell D 19	Cook A — + 1	Telfer G 3 + 1	Kane M 1	Orr N 7	Cody S 5 + 1	Match No.
1	2	3	4	5	6	7	8	9	10	11	12																	1
1			2	5	6	7	8	9	10	11	12	3	4															2
1	5	2	3	8	6			9	7	11		12	4	*10*	14													3
1	2	3	4	5	6			*7*	10	12		14		8		9	11											4
1		2	3	5				9	7	11	8		4	6			10											5
1		2	5	7	6	14		*9*	8	11		3	12	10				4										6
1			3	5	6	14		*10*	8	9		12	2	11	7			4										7
1			3	5	8	*11*		14	9	10		12	2	6	7			4										8
1			3	5	6			9	7	10			4	8	11				2									9
1			3	5	8			7	9	10			6		11			4	2									10
1			3	5	8	*11*		14	7	10			6	12	9			4	2									11
1			3	5	6			*10*	7	11			8	12	9		14	4	2									12
1			2	5	8	11		12	7	10		3	4	6	9													13
1		14	2	5	8			10	7	11		3	4	6	9		*12*											14
1		2	3	5	6			10	7	11			4		9		8											15
1		2	3	5	6			11		10		14	8		*9*		7	4		15								16
1		5	3	8	11			7	10				2	14	12			4			*6*	9						17
		5	3	8	6			*10*		11			2	12	7			4		1	14	9						18
			3	6	10					11		5	2	8	7			4		1		9						19
			3	5	8				7	11		2		6	10			4		1	12	9						20
			3	8	7				12	10		5	2	6	11			4		1		9						21
			3	6				12	10	11		5	2		7			4		1	8	9						22
			3	8					7	11		5	*2*	6	10			4		1	12	9	14					23
			3	8				14	7	11		5	2	6	*10*			4		1	12	9						24
1			3	8					7	11		5	2	6				4			12	9		10				25
1		12	3	8					7	11		5	2	6				4				9		10				26
1		12	3	8					7	11		5	2	6	14			4				9		*10*				27
		5	2	7	14				9	11		3	8	6	12			4		1		10						28
		2		5	8				7	11		3			9			4		1	12	10			6			29
		5	3		6			14	9	*11*								4		1	7	10		12		2	8	30
		5	3		6			14	9	11			2					4		1		7				8	*10*	31
15		5	3		10				7	11			2		12			4		*1*		9				8	6	32
1		5	3		4				10	11			2	6								9				8	7	33
1		2	3	12	6				10	11			*7*	5	14							9				4	8	34
1		2	3	8	6				11	9			5	10								7				4	12	35
1		2		5	10			14	9	*11*		3	7	8	12			6								4		36

QUEEN'S PARK Third Division

Year Formed: 1867. *Ground & Address:* Hampden Park, Mount Florida, Glasgow G42 9BA. *Telephone:* 0141 632 1275.
Ground Capacity: total: 38,335 all seated. *Size of Pitch:* 115yd × 75yd.
President: Malcolm D.Mackay. *Secretary:* Alistair Mackay. *Physio:* R.C.Findlay. *Coach:* Hugh McCann.
Coaches since 1975: D.McParland, J.Gilroy, E Hunter. *Club Nickname(s):* The Spiders. *Previous Grounds:* 1st Hampden (Recreation Ground); (Titwood Park was used as an interim measure between 1st & 2nd Hampdens); 2nd Hampden (Cathkin); 3rd Hampden.
Record Attendance: 95,772 v Rangers, Scottish Cup, 18 Jan, 1930.
Record for Ground: 149,547 Scotland v England, 1937.
Record Transfer Fee received: Not applicable due to amateur status.
Record Transfer Fee paid: Not applicable due to amateur status.
Record Victory: 16-0 v St. Peters, Scottish Cup 1st rd; 29 Aug, 1885.
Record Defeat: 0-9 v Motherwell, Division I; 26 Apr, 1930.
Most Capped Player: Walter Arnott, 15, Scotland.
Most League Appearances: 473: J. B. McAlpine.

QUEEN'S PARK 1994–95 LEAGUE RECORD

Match No.	*Date*	*Venue*	*Opponents*	*Result*		*H/T Score*	*Lg. Pos.*	*Goalscorers*	*Attendance*
1	Aug 13	H	Forfar Ath	L	1-2	1-1	—	Orr G	457
2	20	A	Caledonian Th	W	4-0	2-0	5	Orr G, Maxwell 2, Graham	1565
3	27	H	Albion R	W	2-1	0-1	3	Rodden, Graham	443
4	Sept 3	A	Arbroath	D	1-1	0-1	4	Orr G	535
5	10	H	Cowdenbeath	L	0-3	0-0	8		509
6	24	A	Montrose	D	1-1	1-0	7	McPhee	575
7	Oct 1	H	Ross C	W	3-1	2-1	6	McCormick, Orr G, Fitzpatrick	729
8	8	A	East Stirling	L	2-3	1-1	7	Maxwell, McPhee	464
9	15	H	Alloa	L	0-1	0-1	7		520
10	22	A	Forfar Ath	L	0-2	0-1	8		534
11	29	A	Albion R	L	2-3	1-1	8	McGoldrick, Brodie	345
12	Nov 5	H	Caledonian Th	L	0-2	0-0	8		692
13	12	A	Cowdenbeath	L	0-2	0-0	8		281
14	19	H	Arbroath	L	0-4	0-2	8		407
15	26	H	Montrose	D	1-1	0-0	8	Caven	443
16	Dec 3	A	Ross C	L	0-2	0-1	8		1322
17	26	H	East Stirling	L	2-3	0-2	—	McGoldrick 2	502
18	31	A	Alloa	W	3-2	2-2	8	Callan, Edgar, Maxwell	541
19	Jan 2	H	Albion R	D	0-0	0-0	—		705
20	14	A	Forfar Ath	L	0-3	0-0	8		501
21	21	H	Caledonian Th	W	4-1	2-0	8	Maxwell, Orr G, McPhee, Rodden	456
22	Feb 4	H	Cowdenbeath	W	1-0	0-0	8	Caven	477
23	15	A	Arbroath	L	1-3	1-1	—	Orr G	347
24	18	A	Montrose	D	2-2	0-0	8	Callan, Graham	674
25	25	H	Ross C	L	1-2	1-0	8	McCormick	753
26	Mar 11	H	Alloa	W	2-1	2-0	9	McCormick, McPhee	506
27	18	A	Cowdenbeath	W	3-1	1-1	9	McPhee, McCormick 2	137
28	25	H	Arbroath	L	2-3	1-1	9	McPhee, McCormick	616
29	Apr 1	A	Ross C	L	0-1	0-1	9		1469
30	11	H	Montrose	W	1-0	0-0	—	Kerr	367
31	15	H	East Stirling	W	1-0	1-0	9	Sneddon (og)	480
32	18	A	East Stirling	L	2-3	2-2	—	McCormick, Maxwell	382
33	22	A	Alloa	W	1-0	0-0	9	Kerr	421
34	29	H	Forfar Ath	L	0-2	0-1	9		557
35	May 6	A	Albion R	W	2-0	1-0	8	Orr G, McPhee	337
36	13	A	Caledonian Th	D	1-1	1-0	8	McCormick	782

Final League Position: 8

Most League Goals in Season (Individual): 30: William Martin, Division I; 1937-38.
Most Goals Overall (Individual): 163: J. B. McAlpine.

Honours
League Champions: Division II 1922-23. B Division 1955-56. Second Division 1980-81.
Scottish Cup Winners: 1874, 1875, 1876, 1880, 1881, 1882, 1884, 1886, 1890, 1893; *Runners-up:* 1892, 1900.
League Cup: —.
FA Cup runners-up: 1884, 1885.
Club colours: Shirt: White and black hoops. Shorts: White. Stockings: White with black hoops.

Goalscorers: *League (46):* McCormick 8, McPhee 7, Orr G 7, Maxwell 6, Graham 3, McGoldrick 3, Callan 2, Caven 2, Kerr 2, Rodden 2, Brodie 1, Edgar 1, Fitzpatrick 1, own goal 1. *Scottish Cup (3):* Caven 1, Orr G 1, Rodden 1. *League Cup (2):* Maxwell 1, Orr G 1. *B&Q Cup (0)*

Moonie D 15 + 1	Kavanagh J 9	Stevenson C 1	Kerr G 27 + 2	Maxwell I 34	Orr G 28	Brodie D 8 + 3	Fitzpatrick S 15	Edgar S 8 + 7	Rodden J 10 + 7	Graham D 29	Bradley R 4 + 3	McPhee B 22 + 11	Orr J 34	McCormick S 18 + 4	Elder G 19	Lynch M 6 + 1	Caven R 22 + 3	McGoldrick K 16 + 5	Chalmers J 21	Callan D 12 + 3	Ferguson P 10 + 3	Matchett J 7	Campbell S 1	Smith C 2 + 3	McFarlane R 1	Wilson D 10 + 1	Fraser R 7	Match No.
1	2	3	4	5	6	7	8	9	*10*	11	12	14																1
1	3		4	5	6		7	9	10	8	11	12	2															2
1	3		4	5	6	7	8		11	10			2	9														3
1	3		7	5	6		*8*	14	10	9			2	11	4	12												4
1	3		8	5	6	7		14	*10*	11		12	2	9	4													5
1	3		4	5	6	7	8					10	2	9		11												6
1	3		4	5	6	7	8	12		11		10	2	9			14											7
1	3		4	5		7	6		12	11		10	2	9			8											8
1	2			5	8	9	*6*			3		11	4	10			7	14										9
1				5		12	2		9	3	8	10	4			6	7	11										10
				5		14	2		*10*	3	8	9	4			6	7	11	1									11
				3			5		14	*10*		9	2	7	4	6	8	11	1	12								12
				3			5	7				12	2	9	4	8	10	11	1	6								13
				3			5	7	14			9	2	12	4	*8*	10	11	1	6								14
15			4	3			6	*8*		10		9	2	14	5		7	11	*1*	12								15
			4	3			6	8		10		9	2	14	5		7	11	1									16
			14	3	7	*11*		12	9	6	4		2		5		8	10	1									17
			4	3	*7*			11		6		14	2		5		10	9	1	8								18
			4	3	6	12		10	9			11	2		5		8		1	7								19
			4	5	7				12		14	*9*	2				10		1	8	3	6	11					20
			4	5	9				14	6		12	2				10	11	1	7	3			*8*				21
			4	5	7				14	6		12	2				10	*9*	1	8	3			11				22
			4	5	11				12	*8*		9	2	14			10		1	7	3	6						23
			12	5	9				11	6		14	2				8	*10*	1	7	3				4			24
			4	5	9					8	14	12	2	*11*				10	1	7	3	6						25
			3	5	9					6		11	2	10	4		8		1							7		26
			11	6	7					3		10	4	9	5		8	14	1					12		2		27
			11	6	7					3		*10*	4	9	5		8	14	1					12		2		28
			4	6	7			14		3		10			5			*9*	1	2		11				12	8	29
1			8	6	9			12		3		10	4		5						14	11				2	*7*	30
1			8	6	9			12		3		10	4		5						14	*11*				2	7	31
1			11	6	7					3		10	4	9	5						14					2	*8*	32
1			11	6	7							10	4	9	5		14	12			3					2	*8*	33
1			*11*	6	7							10	4	9	5		14	12			3					2	8	34
			5		10					3		14	4	9			8	11	1	12	6					2	*7*	35
					10					3		12	4	9			8	11	1	7	6	*5*		14		2		36

RAITH ROVERS Premier Division

Year Formed: 1883. *Ground & Address:* Stark's Park, Pratt St, Kirkcaldy KY1 1SA. *Telephone & Fax:* 01592 263514.
Ground Capacity: total: 9200. seated: 3040. *Size of Pitch:* 113yd × 67yd.
Chairman: Alex Penman. *Company Secretary:* C.Cant. *General Manager:* W.McPhee.
Manager: Jimmy Nicholl. *Assistant Manager and Coach:* Martin Harvey. *Physio:* Gerry Docherty. *Reserve Coach:* Derek Smith and Jimmy Thomson.
Managers since 1975: R. Paton; A. Matthew; W. McLean; G. Wallace; R. Wilson; F. Connor. *Club Nickname(s):* Rovers.
Previous Grounds: Robbie's Park.
Record Attendance: 31,306 v Hearts, Scottish Cup 2nd rd; 7 Feb, 1953.
Record Transfer Fee received: £250,000 for Craig Brewster to Dundee U (Aug 1993).
Record Transfer Fee paid: £100,000 for Alastair Graham from Motherwell (Sept 1993).
Record Victory: 10-1 v Coldstream, Scottish Cup 2nd rd; 13 Feb, 1954.
Record Defeat: 2-11 v Morton, Division II; 18 Mar, 1936.
Most Capped Player: David Morris, 6, Scotland.
Most League Appearances: 430: Willie McNaught.

RAITH ROVERS 1994–95 LEAGUE RECORD

Match No.	Date	Venue	Opponents	Result		H/T Score	Lg. Pos.	Goalscorers	Attendance
1	Aug 13	H	St Johnstone	D	1-1	0-1	—	Cameron	4374
2	20	H	Hamilton A	D	1-1	1-1	6	Graham	2825
3	27	A	Dunfermline Ath	L	0-1	0-0	8		7373
4	Sept 3	H	Clydebank	D	1-1	1-0	8	Cameron	2861
5	10	A	Stranraer	D	0-0	0-0	8		1078
6	24	A	St Mirren	W	2-1	1-1	6	Crawford, Graham	2967
7	Oct 1	H	Ayr U	W	3-0	1-0	4	Crawford, Dalziel 2 (1 pen)	2854
8	8	A	Airdrieonians	D	0-0	0-0	5		2096
9	15	H	Dundee	D	1-1	1-0	5	Cameron	3834
10	22	A	St Johnstone	L	1-3	0-1	6	Dalziel	3926
11	29	H	Dunfermline Ath	L	2-5	2-2	5	Wilson 2	5965
12	Nov 5	A	Hamilton A	W	3-0	0-0	5	Dalziel, Crawford 2	1112
13	12	H	Stranraer	W	4-2	2-0	4	Dalziel 3, Graham	2556
14	19	A	Clydebank	W	3-0	1-0	4	Dalziel, Graham, Narey	1002
15	Dec 3	A	Ayr U	D	1-1	0-1	4	Dalziel	2216
16	6	H	St Mirren	D	1-1	1-1	—	Dalziel	4084
17	10	A	Dundee	L	1-2	0-0	4	Dalziel	3493
18	26	H	Airdrieonians	W	3-2	2-1	—	Cameron, Dalziel, Sinclair	4338
19	31	H	St Johnstone	W	2-0	1-0	4	Broddle, Dalziel	4973
20	Jan 7	H	Hamilton A	W	2-0	1-0	4	Sinclair, Cameron	3130
21	11	A	Dunfermline Ath	W	1-0	0-0	—	Graham	8457
22	14	H	Clydebank	W	1-0	0-0	4	Dennis	3129
23	24	A	Stranraer	W	4-2	1-1	—	Wilson 2, Crawford, Dalziel	769
24	Feb 4	H	Ayr U	W	2-1	1-0	4	Sinclair, Crawford	2799
25	11	A	St Mirren	W	2-1	2-0	2	Crawford 2	2516
26	25	H	Dundee	D	0-0	0-0	3		5885
27	Mar 6	A	Airdrieonians	W	2-1	0-0	—	Dair, Graham	1726
28	18	H	Stranraer	D	1-1	1-0	2	Dalziel	2197
29	Apr 1	A	Ayr U	W	1-0	1-0	3	Kirkwood	1995
30	4	A	Clydebank	W	2-1	0-0	—	Murdoch (og), Crawford	1261
31	8	H	St Mirren	W	2-1	2-1	1	Cameron 2	3669
32	15	H	Airdrieonians	L	0-1	0-1	2		4494
33	22	A	Dundee	W	2-0	0-0	1	Wilson, Crawford	7849
34	29	A	St Johnstone	W	2-1	0-0	1	Preston (og), Crawford	5124
35	May 6	H	Dunfermline Ath	D	0-0	0-0	1		6361
36	13	A	Hamilton A	D	0-0	0-0	1		5333

Final League Position: 1

Most League Goals in Season (Individual): 38: Norman Haywood, Division II; 1937-38.
Most Goals Overall (Individual): 154: Gordon Dalziel (League), 1987-94.

Honours
League Champions: First Division: 1992-93, 1994-95. Division II 1907-08, 1909-10 (shared), 1937-38, 1948-49; *Runners-up:* Division II 1908-09, 1926-27, 1966-67. Second Division 1975-76, 1977-78, 1986-87.
Scottish Cup Runners-up: 1913. *League Cup Winners: (Coca-Cola Cup):* 1994-95. *Runners-up:* 1948-49.
Club colours: Shirt: Navy blue, white trim. Shorts: White. Stockings: White.

Goalscorers: *League (54):* Dalziel 15 (1 pen), Crawford 11, Cameron 7, Graham 6, Wilson 5, Sinclair 3, Broddle 1, Dair 1, Dennis 1, Kirkwood 1, Narey 1, own goals 2. *Scottish Cup (4):* Cameron 1, Crawford 1, Graham 1, Rowbotham 1. *League Cup (14):* Graham 5, Cameron 4, Dalziel 2, Crawford 1, Dennis 1, Lennon 1. *B&Q Cup (3):* Cameron 1, Crawford 1, Dalziel 1.

Thomson S 35	Rowbotham J 14 + 6	Kirkwood D 9 + 10	Coyle R 9	Dennis S 26	Sinclair D 31 + 1	Lennon D 19 + 1	Dalziel G 25 + 6	Graham A 25 + 2	Cameron C 33 + 2	Dair J 12 + 6	Crawford S 27 + 4	Raeside R 9 + 1	Broddle J 26 + 2	McAnespie S 33 + 1	Redford I 11 + 1	Narey D 21	Wilson B 14 + 12	Nicholl J 13	Allan R 1	McMillan I — + 1	Rougier A 3 + 1	Match No.
1	2	3	4	*5*	6	7	8	9	10	11	12	14										1
1	2		4		6	7	8	9	10	*11*	12	5	3	14								2
1			4		5	7	12	9	8	10	11		3	2	6							3
1	4				6	7	8	9	10		12		3	2	11	5						4
1	*4*	12			6	7	8	9	10				3	2	11	5	14					5
1	4			5		7	12	9	10	*11*	8		3	2	6		14					6
1				5	6	4	12	9	10	11	8		3	2				7				7
1		12		5	6	*4*	8	9	10		11		3	2			14	7				8
1	14			5	6	7	*8*	9	10	12	11		3	2		4						9
1		7		5	4		8	9	10	*11*	12		3	2		6	14					10
		14		5	4	7	12	9	10		8		3	2	*6*		11		1			11
1		12		5	4		*8*	9	10	14	11		3	2		6	7					12
1	14			5		4	8	*9*	10	12	11		3	2		6	7					13
1	4			*5*			8	9	10	12	11		3	2	7	6				14		14
1	12	14		5	4		8		10		9		3	2	7	6	*11*					15
1	12	14		5	4		*8*		10		9		3	2	7	6	11					16
1	4				6		8		10		9		3	2	11	5	12	7				17
1				5	12		8	9	10		11		3	2	6	4		7				18
1		12		5	4		8	9	10		*11*		3	2	7	6	14					19
1		11		5	4		8	9	10				*3*	2		6	14	7				20
1	3	11		5	6		*8*	9	10					2		4	14	7				21
1	3			5		4	*8*		10	14	9			2		6	11	7				22
1		12			4	10	8				9	5	3	2		6	11	7				23
1	14		*4*	5	7	10	8	12	9			6	3	2			11					24
1			4	5	8	11		9	14		10	6	3	2			*7*					25
1	3		4	5	6		12	9	*8*	11	10		14	2			7					26
1	3			5	6	4		9	8	11	10			2			7					27
1	3	2			5		8	9	6		*10*					4	14	7			11	28
1	3	10	4	5	11			14	12	*7*	9	6		2							8	29
1	3	*7*	4	5	6	10		8	11		9			2			14					30
1		3	4	5	6	11		9	7		*10*		14	2			12				8	31
1		3		5	6	4	12	9	8	*11*	10			2	14			7				32
1		12			4		8		10	14	9	5	3	2		6	*11*	7				33
1	12				6		8		10		9	*5*	3	2		4	11	7			14	34
1		14			6	12	*8*		10	11	9	5	3	2		4	7					35
1				5	11		8		10	*9*		6	3	2		4	14	7				36

RANGERS — Premier Division

Year Formed: 1873. *Ground & Address:* Ibrox Stadium, Edminston Drive, Glasgow G51 2XD. *Telephone:* 0141 427 8500. *Fax:* 0141 427 2676.
Ground Capacity: total: 44,500. seated: 36,500. *Size of Pitch:* 115yd × 75yd.
Chairman: David Murray. *Secretary:* R. C. Ogilvie. *Commercial Manager:* Bob Reilly.
Manager: Walter Smith. *Assistant Manager:* Archie Knox. *Physio:* Bill Collins. *Coach:* Davie Dodds. *Reserve team coaches:* John McGregor, Billy Kirkwood.
Managers since 1975: Jock Wallace; John Greig; Jock Wallace; Graeme Souness. *Club Nickname(s):* The Gers. *Previous Grounds:* Burnbank, Kinning Park.
Record Attendance: 118,567 v Celtic, Division I; 2 Jan, 1939.
Record Transfer Fee received: £5,580,000 for Trevor Steven to Marseille (Aug 1991).
Record Transfer Fee paid: £2,500,000 for Alexei Mikhailichenko from Sampdoria (June 1991).
Record Victory: 14-2 v Blairgowrie, Scottish Cup 1st rd; 20 Jan, 1934.
Record Defeat: 2-10 v Airdrieonians; 1886.
Most Capped Player: George Young, 53, Scotland.
Most League Appearances: 496: John Greig, 1962-78.
Most League Goals in Season (Individual): 44: Sam English, Division I; 1931-32.
Most Goals Overall (Individual): 233: Bob McPhail; 1927-39.

Honours
League Champions: (45 times) Division I 1890-91 (shared), 1898-99, 1899-1900, 1900-01, 1901-02, 1910-11, 1911-12, 1912-13, 1917-18, 1919-20, 1920-21, 1922-23, 1923-24, 1924-25, 1926-27, 1927-28, 1928-29, 1929-30, 1930-31, 1932-33, 1933-34, 1934-35, 1936-37, 1938-39, 1946-47, 1948-49, 1949-50, 1952-53, 1955-56, 1956-57, 1958-59, 1960-61, 1962-63,

RANGERS 1994–95 LEAGUE RECORD

Match No.	Date	Venue	Opponents	Result		H/T Score	Lg. Pos.	Goalscorers	Attendance
1	Aug 13	H	Motherwell	W	2-1	1-0	—	Hateley, Ferguson D	42,491
2	20	A	Partick T	W	2-0	1-0	1	Byrne (og), Hateley	14,361
3	27	H	Celtic	L	0-2	0-1	3		44,607
4	Sept 11	H	Hearts	W	3-0	0-0	—	Hateley 2 (1 pen), Durie	40,653
5	17	A	Falkirk	W	2-0	1-0	1	Boli, Laudrup	12,419
6	24	A	Aberdeen	D	2-2	1-1	2	Hateley, Moore	19,191
7	Oct 1	H	Dundee U	W	2-0	1-0	1	Hateley, Laudrup	43,635
8	8	A	Hibernian	L	1-2	1-0	1	Boli	12,088
9	15	H	Kilmarnock	W	2-0	0-0	1	Miller, Robertson D	44,099
10	22	A	Motherwell	L	1-2	0-1	1	Philliben (og)	11,160
11	30	A	Celtic	W	3-1	2-1	—	Hateley 2, Laudrup	32,171
12	Nov 5	H	Partick T	W	3-0	0-0	1	Laudrup, Miller, Hateley	43,696
13	9	A	Hearts	D	1-1	0-0	—	Hateley	12,347
14	19	H	Falkirk	D	1-1	1-0	1	Hateley	44,018
15	25	H	Aberdeen	W	1-0	0-0	—	McCoist	45,072
16	Dec 4	A	Dundee U	W	3-0	1-0	—	Laudrup, Huistra, Durrant	11,187
17	10	A	Kilmarnock	W	2-1	1-0	1	McLaren, Laudrup	17,219
18	26	H	Hibernian	W	2-0	2-0	—	Hateley, Gough	44,892
19	31	A	Motherwell	W	3-1	1-0	1	McCall, Laudrup, Durie	11,269
20	Jan 4	H	Celtic	D	1-1	1-0	—	Ferguson I	45,794
21	7	A	Partick T	D	1-1	0-0	1	Robertson D	17,298
22	14	A	Falkirk	W	3-2	1-0	1	Huistra 2 (1 pen), McCall	12,507
23	21	H	Hearts	W	1-0	1-0	1	Miller	44,231
24	Feb 4	H	Dundee U	D	1-1	1-1	1	Robertson D	44,197
25	12	A	Aberdeen	L	0-2	0-0	—		18,060
26	25	H	Kilmarnock	W	3-0	0-0	1	Durie, Laudrup, Durrant	44,859
27	Mar 4	A	Hibernian	D	1-1	0-0	1	Durie	11,939
28	11	H	Falkirk	D	2-2	1-1	1	Laudrup, Brown	43,359
29	18	A	Hearts	L	1-2	1-2	1	Laudrup	9806
30	Apr 1	A	Dundee U	W	2-0	2-0	1	McLaren, Durie	11,035
31	8	H	Aberdeen	W	3-2	2-2	1	Durrant, Murray, Hateley	44,460
32	16	H	Hibernian	W	3-1	1-1	—	Durie, Durrant, Mikhailichenko	44,193
33	20	A	Kilmarnock	W	1-0	1-0	—	Mikhailichenko	16,532
34	29	H	Motherwell	L	0-2	0-1	1		43,576
35	May 7	A	Celtic	W	0-3	0-0	—		31,025
36	13	H	Partick T	D	1-1	1-0	1	Moore	45,280

Final League Position: 1

1963-64, 1974-75. Premier Division: 1975-76, 1977-78, 1986-87, 1988-89, 1989-90, 1990-91, 1991-92, 1992-93, 1993-94, 1994-95; *Runners-up:* 23 times.
Scottish Cup Winners: (26 times) 1894, 1897, 1898, 1903, 1928, 1930, 1932, 1934, 1935, 1936, 1948, 1949, 1950, 1953, 1960, 1962, 1963, 1964, 1966, 1973, 1976, 1978, 1979, 1981, 1992, 1993; *Runners-up:* 16 times.
League Cup Winners: (19 times) 1946-47, 1948-49, 1960-61, 1961-62, 1963-64, 1964-65, 1970-71, 1975-76, 1977-78, 1978-79, 1981-82, 1983-84, 1984-85, 1986-87, 1987-88, 1988-89, 1990-91, 1992-93, 1993-94; *Runners-up:* 7 times.

European: *European Cup:* 73 matches (1956-57, 1957-58, 1959-60 semi-finals, 1961-62, 1963-64, 1964-65, 1975-76, 1976-77, 1978-79, 1987-88, 1989-90, 1990-91, 1991-92, 1992-93 final pool, 1993-94, 1994-95).
Cup Winners Cup Winners: 1971-72. 50 matches (1960-61 runners-up, 1962-63, 1966-67 runners-up, 1969-70, 1971-72 winners, 1973-74, 1977-78, 1979-80, 1981-82, 1983-84). *UEFA Cup:* 38 matches (*Fairs Cup:* 1967-68, 1968-69 semi-finals, 1970-71 *UEFA Cup*; 1982-83, 1984-85, 1985-86, 1986-87, 1988-89).
Club colours: Shirt: Royal blue with red and white trim. Shorts: White. Stockings: Red.

Goalscorers: *League (60):* Hateley 13 (1 pen), Laudrup 10, Durie 6, Durrant 4, Huistra 3 (1 pen), Miller 3, Robertson D 3, Boli 2, McCall 2, McLaren 2, Mikhailichenko 2, Moore 2, Brown 1, Ferguson D 1, Ferguson I 1, Gough 1, McCoist 1, Murray 1, own goals 2. *Cup (5):* Laudrup 2, Boli 1, Durie 1, Steven 1. *League Cup (7):* Ferguson D 3, Hateley 2, Laudrup 1, McCall 1.

Goram A 18 + 1	Murray N 14 + 6	Robertson D 23	Gough R 25	Boli B 28	McPherson D 9	Durrant I 15 + 10	McCall S 30	McCoist A 4 + 5	Hateley M 23	Laudrup B 33	Ferguson D 1 + 3	Brown J 10 + 3	Moore C 19 + 2	Ferguson I 13 + 3	Pressley S 2	Durie G 17 + 4	Mikhailichenko A 4 + 5	Miller C 21	Huistra P 15	Hagan D — + 2	Wishart F 3 + 1	McLaren A 24	Scott C 3 + 1	McGinty B 1	Maxwell A 10 + 1	Steven T 10 + 1	Bollan G 5 + 1	Cleland A 10	Thomson W 5	Robertson L — + 1	Caldwell N 1	McKnight P — + 1	*Match No.*
1	2	3	4	5	6	7	8	*9*	10	11	14																						1
1			4	5	6		2		10	11	9	3	7	8																			2
1			4	5	6	7	2		10	11	12			8	3	9																	3
1	7	3	4		5	9	2		10	*11*	14		6	8		12																	4
1		3	4	5		7	2		10	11			6	8		9																	5
1	7	3	4	6	5	12	8		10	11			2			9																	6
1	12	3	4	6	5		7	14	10	11			2				8	*9*															7
1	12	3	4	6	*5*		7	14	10	11			2					9	8														8
1	7	3			5		4		10	11			2		6			9	8														9
1	*7*	3		6	5		4		10	11			2					9	8	14													10
1	8	3		6			4	14	10	*11*								9	7	12	2	5											11
1	8	3		6		12	4		10	11								9	7		2	5											12
1	*8*	3		6		9	4	14	10	11			2						7			5											13
1		3		6		12	4	*9*	10	11			2			14		*8*	7			5											14
1		3		6			4	9	*10*	11						14		8	7		2	5											15
1		3	4	6		12	2	9		11						10		8	7			5											16
1	6	3	4			10	2			11				14		9		*8*	7			5											17
		3	4	6			2		10	11			12			9		8	7			5	1										18
		3	4	6			2			11			10	12		9		8	7			5	1										19
		3	4	6		14	2			11		12		8		9		*10*	7			5	1										20
1	11	3				9	4					6	2	8					7			5	15	10									21
	10	3				11	4					6	*2*	8				9	7		14	5			1	12							22
	10		4	6		12	2			11		3	14	8				9				5			1	*7*							23
		3	4	5			6	14	10	11		12	2			*9*		8							1	7							24
		3	4	5		12	8		10	11			2			14		9							1		*6*	7					25
		3	4	6		14	2			11		12				10		9				5			1	*7*		8					26
	8		4	6		12	10					11	*2*	14		9						5			1	7	3						27
			4	6		7	2			11		10		8		9	14					5			1		*3*						28
	14		4	6		12	10			11				8		9						5			1	*7*	*3*	2					29
			4	*6*		10	7			11		3				9	12	8				5					14	2	1				30
	12		4	6					10	*11*		3				9	14	8				5				7		2	1				31
	12		4			6			10	11		3				*9*	14	8				5				7		2	1				32
	6		4			9				11			2	*8*			10					5			1		3	7		14			33
			4	6		9			10	11				8			3					5				7		2	1				34
	14			4		9			10	*11*		*6*	2	8			12					5			15	7		3	1				35
15						9			10	11			4			*8*	6					5			*1*	7		3			2	14	36

ROSS COUNTY Third Division

Year Formed: 1929. *Ground & Address:* Victoria Park, Dingwall IV15 9QW. *Telephone:* 01349 862253. *Fax:* 01349 866277.
Ground Capacity: total 6500, seated 319. *Size of Ground:* 110 × 75yd.
Chairman: Hector Maclennan. *Vice-chairman & Secretary:* Donald MacBean. *Office Secretary:* Mrs Cathie Caird. *Commercial Manager:* Brian Campbell.
Manager: Robert Wilson. *Assistant Manager:* Graeme McKenzie. *Physio:* Douglas Sim. *Record Attendance:* 8000, v Rangers, Scottish Cup, 28 February 1966.
Record Transfer Fee Received: £40,000 for Barry Wilson to Raith R, Sept.1994.
Record Transfer Fee Paid: £25,000 for Barry Wilson from Southampton, Oct.1992.
Record Victory: 11-0 v St Cuthbert Wanderers, Scottish Cup, Dec.1993.

ROSS COUNTY 1994–95 LEAGUE RECORD

Match No.	Date	Venue	Opponents	Result		H/T Score	Lg. Pos.	Goalscorers	Attendance
1	Aug 13	A	Cowdenbeath	W	2-0	0-0	—	MacPherson, Herd	678
2	20	A	East Stirling	D	2-2	1-1	3	MacPherson, Wilson	632
3	27	H	Caledonian Th	L	1-3	0-1	6	Andrew MacLeod	3197
4	Sept 3	H	Alloa	D	3-3	3-2	5	Williamson, Grant, MacPherson	1457
5	10	A	Montrose	W	2-0	1-0	5	Robertson, Duff	918
6	24	H	Arbroath	L	1-4	0-1	8	MacPherson	1320
7	Oct 1	A	Queen's Park	L	1-3	1-2	8	MacPherson	729
8	8	A	Forfar Ath	L	0-1	0-0	8		650
9	15	H	Albion R	W	3-0	0-0	8	Williamson 2, Connelly	1017
10	22	H	Cowdenbeath	W	4-0	0-0	7	Andrew MacLeod 2, Grant 2	1284
11	29	A	Caledonian Th	D	0-0	0-0	7		2866
12	Nov 5	H	East Stirling	L	1-4	0-2	7	Andrew MacLeod	1194
13	12	H	Montrose	L	0-1	0-0	7		1154
14	19	A	Alloa	D	1-1	0-0	7	McKay	479
15	26	A	Arbroath	W	1-0	0-0	7	Bellshaw	568
16	Dec 3	H	Queen's Park	W	2-0	1-0	7	Chalmers (og), Connelly	1322
17	31	A	Albion R	W	1-0	0-0	7	Williamson	354
18	Jan 2	H	Caledonian Th	W	3-1	0-1	—	MacPherson, Grant 2	2749
19	11	H	Forfar Ath	W	2-1	1-0	—	Connelly, MacPherson	1215
20	14	A	Cowdenbeath	W	3-0	1-0	3	Ferries 2, Grant (pen)	361
21	21	A	East Stirling	W	2-0	0-0	2	Connelly, Williamson	459
22	Feb 4	A	Montrose	D	1-1	1-0	2	Grant (pen)	882
23	11	H	Alloa	W	6-0	2-0	2	Andrew MacLeod 2, Grant 2, Connelly, Duff	1686
24	18	H	Arbroath	L	0-1	0-1	2		1648
25	25	A	Queen's Park	W	2-1	0-1	2	Grant, Williamson	753
26	Mar 4	A	Forfar Ath	L	2-4	2-3	2	Grant, Andrew MacLeod	880
27	25	A	Alloa	D	1-1	1-1	3	Wylie (og)	535
28	29	H	Albion R	W	4-1	1-0	—	Duff, Furphy, Connelly, Ferries	967
29	Apr 1	H	Queen's Park	W	1-0	1-0	3	Duff	1469
30	8	A	Arbroath	W	1-0	0-0	2	Duff	680
31	15	H	Forfar Ath	L	0-1	0-1	2		2453
32	19	H	Montrose	L	0-3	0-2	—		1702
33	22	A	Albion R	W	2-1	1-1	3	Andrew MacLeod, Williamson	334
34	29	H	Cowdenbeath	W	2-0	1-0	3	Grant, Andrew MacLeod	1356
35	May 6	A	Caledonian Th	L	0-3	0-1	3		3062
36	13	H	East Stirling	L	2-3	2-1	3	MacPherson, Alex MacLeod	1005

Final League Position: 3

Record Defeat: 1-10 v Inverness Thistle, Highland League.
Most League Appearances: 35, Robbie Williamson, 1994-95.
Most League Goals in Season: 12, Brian Grant, 1994-95.

Goalscorers: *League (59):* Grant 12 (2 pens), Andrew MacLeod 9, MacPherson 8, Williamson 7, Connelly 6, Duff 5, Ferries 3, Bellshaw 1, Furphy 1, Herd 1, McKay 1, Alexander MacLeod 1, Robertson 1, Wilson 1, own goals 2. *Scottish Cup (3):* Connelly 2, MacPherson 1. *League Cup (3):* Grant 2, MacPherson 1. *B&Q Cup (1):* Andrew Macleod 1 (pen).

Hutchison S 29	Somerville C 28	Campbell G 11	Williamson R 35	MacLeod Alex 15 + 3	MacLeod Andy 27 + 3	Ferries K 30 + 2	Grant B 32 + 3	MacPherson J 13 + 4	Herd W 28 + 2	Wilson B 3	Connelly G 28 + 3	Robertson C 6 + 3	Duff A 11 + 14	Reid C 31 + 1	McMillan D 7 + 2	Furphy W 28	McKay D 9 + 6	McFee R 1 + 7	Bellshaw J 24	Stewart R — + 1	Match No.
1	2	3	4	5	6	7	*8*	9	10	11	12	14									1
1	2	3	4	5	6	7	*8*	9	10	11	12		14								2
1	2	3	4	5	6	7	8	9	10	11	12										3
1	2		4	5		7	8	9	6		10	11	12	3							4
	2	6	4	5		7		8	10			11	9	3	1						5
1	2	6	4		11	7	14	10	5				*9*	3		8					6
1	2	6	4	5	7	12	8	*9*	11				14	3	15	10					7
	2	6	4	5	10	7	8					11	9	3	1		12	14			8
	2	3	4	5	11		*8*				10		9	7	1	6		14			9
	2	*3*	4	5	11		8				10		*9*	7	1	6	12	14			10
	2	3	4		11		8				10	5	9	7	1	6		14			11
		3	4		11	14	8				10	5	9	7	1	6		2			12
			4		9	7	8		*11*		10			3	1	6	2	14	5		13
1	2		4		*9*	7	8		12		10			3		6	11	14	5		14
1	2		4		9	7	*8*		12		10		14	3		6	11		5		15
1	2		4		*9*	7	8		6		10		14	3			11	12	5		16
1	2		4			7	8	*9*	6		10	12	14	3			11		5		17
1	2		4			7	8	9	11		10			3		6			5		18
1	2		*4*		14	7	8	9	11		10			3		6			5		19
1	2			14	11	7	8	9	4		10			*3*		6	12		5		20
1	2		4		*9*	7	8		11		10		14	3		6	12		5		21
1			4		14	7	8	*9*	11		10			3		6	2		5		22
1	2		4		11	7	8		9		10		14	*3*		6	12		5		23
1	2		*4*		11	7	8	14	9		10			3		6			5		24
1	2		4		*11*	7	8	14	9		10			3		6			5		25
1	2		4		11	7	8		9		10			3		6			5		26
1			4		*11*	7	8		9		10	12	14	3		6	2		5		27
1			4	12		7	8		11		10		9	3		6	*2*		5	14	28
1			4	3	14	7	*8*		11		10		9	2		6	12		5		29
1	2		4	12	11	7	14		8		10		*9*	3		6			5		30
1	2		4		11	7	14		8		10		*9*	3		6			5		31
1	2		4	3	11	7	8	12	*9*		10		14			6			5		32
1	2		4	3	11	7	*8*		9		10		14	12		6			5		33
1			4	3	11	7	*8*		9		10		14	2		6			5		34
1			4	3	11	7	8	12	9		*10*		14	2		6			5		35
1	2		4	10			8	9				11	12	3	15	6	7		5		36

ST JOHNSTONE First Division

Year Formed: 1884. *Ground & Address:* McDiarmid Park, Crieff Road, Perth PH1 2SJ. *Telephone:* 01738 626961. *Clubcall:* 0898 121559.
Ground Capacity: total: 10,721. seated: 10,721. *Size of Pitch:* 115yd × 75yd.
Chairman: G.S.Brown. *Secretary and Managing Director:* Stewart Duff.
Manager: Paul Sturrock. *Sales Executive:* Stuart Turnbull. *Physio:* David Henderson. *Coach:* John Blackley. *Youth Development Coach:* Alistair Stevenson.
Managers since 1975: J. Stewart; J. Storrie; A. Stuart; A. Rennie; I. Gibson; A. Totten, J. McClelland. *Club Nickname(s):* Saints. *Previous Grounds:* Recreation Grounds, Muirton Park.
Record Attendance: (McDiarmid Park): 10,504 v Rangers, Premier Division; 20 Oct, 1990.
Record Transfer Fee received: £750,000 for Billy Dodds to Aberdeen, 1994.
Record Transfer Fee paid: £300,000 for Billy Dodds from Dundee, 1994.
Record Victory: 9-0 v Albion R, League Cup; 9 March, 1946.
Record Defeat: 1-10 v Third Lanark, Scottish Cup; 24 January, 1903.
Most Capped Player: Sandy McLaren, 5, Scotland.
Most League Appearances: 298: Drew Rutherford.
Most League Goals in Season (Individual): 36: Jimmy Benson, Division II; 1931-32.

St JOHNSTONE 1994–95 LEAGUE RECORD

Match No.	Date	Venue	Opponents	Result		H/T Score	Lg. Pos.	Goalscorers	Attendance
1	Aug 13	A	Raith R	D	1-1	1-0	—	Irons	4374
2	20	A	Airdrieonians	D	0-0	0-0	7		2161
3	27	H	Dundee	L	0-1	0-1	9		6021
4	Sept 3	A	Ayr U	W	4-3	2-0	4	O'Boyle 3, Irons	2367
5	10	H	St Mirren	D	1-1	0-1	5	O'Boyle	3957
6	24	H	Hamilton A	D	1-1	0-1	5	O'Boyle	2790
7	Oct 1	A	Clydebank	D	0-0	0-0	6		1025
8	8	A	Dunfermline Ath	L	0-3	0-2	7		6931
9	15	H	Stranraer	W	3-0	0-0	6	Noren, O'Boyle 2	2678
10	22	H	Raith R	W	3-1	1-0	5	Curran, O'Boyle 2 (1 pen)	3926
11	29	A	Dundee	L	0-1	0-0	5		4327
12	Nov 12	A	St Mirren	D	2-2	1-2	6	Deas, Davenport	2970
13	19	H	Ayr U	W	1-0	1-0	5	Davidson	2755
14	22	H	Airdrieonians	W	4-0	1-0	—	Cherry, O'Boyle, Farquhar, Preston	3110
15	26	A	Hamilton A	L	1-3	1-2	5	McGowne	1445
16	Dec 3	H	Clydebank	D	1-1	1-0	5	Curran	2724
17	10	A	Stranraer	D	2-2	1-1	5	Twaddle, Davenport	780
18	26	H	Dunfermline Ath	W	3-2	1-2	—	McMartin, Davenport, O'Neil	6091
19	31	A	Raith R	L	0-2	0-1	5		4973
20	Jan 7	A	Airdrieonians	W	2-0	2-0	5	Twaddle, Cherry	1957
21	11	H	Dundee	D	2-2	0-1	—	O'Neil, Curran	5636
22	14	A	Ayr U	W	3-1	0-1	5	Curran, Davenport, McMartin	1955
23	21	H	St Mirren	W	5-1	3-0	5	O'Boyle, Dick 2 (2 og), Preston, Cherry	3321
24	Feb 4	A	Clydebank	D	0-0	0-0	5		949
25	18	H	Hamilton A	W	3-0	1-0	5	O'Boyle 2, Cherry	2589
26	25	H	Stranraer	W	3-0	1-0	5	Twaddle, O'Boyle, Wright	2725
27	Mar 11	A	Dunfermline Ath	D	1-1	0-0	5	Twaddle	6522
28	21	A	St Mirren	D	0-0	0-0	—		2169
29	25	H	Ayr U	D	1-1	1-0	5	McKilligan (og)	3551
30	Apr 1	H	Clydebank	W	1-0	1-0	5	O'Boyle	3337
31	8	A	Hamilton A	L	0-1	0-0	5		858
32	15	H	Dunfermline Ath	D	1-1	0-0	5	Farquhar	5039
33	22	A	Stranraer	W	6-2	2-0	5	Cherry, O'Neil, O'Boyle 3, Twaddle	702
34	29	H	Raith R	L	1-2	0-0	5	McMartin	5124
35	May 6	A	Dundee	L	1-2	0-0	5	O'Boyle	3906
36	13	H	Airdrieonians	W	2-1	1-1	5	Scott, Twaddle	2868

Final League Position: 5

Most Goals Overall (Individual): 114: John Brogan, 1977-83.

Honours
League Champions: First Division 1982-83, 1989-90. Division II 1923-24, 1959-60, 1962-63; *Runners-up:* Division II 1931-32. Second Division 1987-88.
Scottish Cup: Semi-finals 1934, 1968, 1989, 1991.
League Cup Runners-up: 1969.

European: *UEFA Cup:* 1971-72.
Club colours: Shirt: Royal blue with white trim. Shorts: White. Stockings: Royal blue, white trim.

Goalscorers: *League (59):* O'Boyle 19 (1 pen), Twaddle 6, Cherry 5, Curran 4, Davenport 4, McMartin 3, O'Neil 3, Farquhar 2, Irons 2, Preston 2, Davidson 1, Deas 1, McGowne 1, Noren 1, Scott 1, Wright 1, own goals 3. *Scottish Cup (1):* own goal 1. *League Cup (7):* O'Boyle 2, O'Neil 2, Irons 1, Miller 1, Scott 1. *B&Q Cup (7):* O'Boyle 5, Davenport 1, Ramsey 1.

Rhodes A 19	Miller C 12	Davidson C 4 + 3	Turner T 10 + 1	McGinnis G 10	McGowne K 30	O'Neil J 26 + 1	Davies J 1 + 2	Davenport P 12 + 10	O'Boyle G 32	Irons D 34	Ramsey P 9 + 2	Scott P 9 + 2	Inglis J 5	Cherry P 27	Preston A 24 + 2	McAuley S 7 + 1	McMartin G 13 + 10	Morgan A — + 2	Curran H 22 + 4	Twaddle K 21 + 4	Farquhar G 10 + 7	Noren P 1	Deas P 7	Walemark J 2	Wright P 5 + 7	Weir J 17	English I 4 + 5	Main A 17	McCluskey S 2	Griffin D 3	Young S 1 + 1	Match No.
1	2	3	4	5	6	7	8	*9*	10	11	12	14																				1
1	3		4	*2*		7	12	9	10	11	8	14	5	6																		2
1	3	*11*	8		6	7	12	9	10	4	14		5	2																		3
1	3		8	6		7		9	10	11	4		5	2	12																	4
1	3		8	6		7		9	10	2	4		5		*11*	12	14															5
1	3		8		2	7		*9*	10	6			5		11	4	12	14														6
1	3			8	5	7		*9*	10	6	4			2	11		12	14														7
1	3				5	7		9	10	6	4			*2*	11		12		8	14												8
1	3	12			6	7		14	10	4				5			2		11		*8*	9										9
1	3				6	7		14	10	4							2		11		8		5	*9*								10
1	3				6	7			10	4					12		2		11		8		5	*9*	14							11
1	3	12	4		6	7		*9*							8		2		11	10	14		5									12
1		7	8		6			*9*	10					5	3		2		11	14						4						13
1			8		6	7			10	4				2	3				11	*9*	12				14	5						14
1			8		6				10	4				2	*3*		12		11	9	7				14	5						15
1			12		6				10	4				2	3		8		11	14	7				*9*	5						16
1					6	7		14		4				2	3		8		11	*10*	12				9	5						17
1					6	7		14		4				2	3		8		11	*10*	12				9	5						18
1					6	7		14		4				2	3		8		11		12				9	5	*10*					19
					6	7			10	4				2	3				8	9			11			5	12	1				20
					6	7		14	*10*	4				2	3				8	9			11			5	12	1				21
					6	7		14	10	4				2	3		12		8	9			*11*			5		1				22
					6	7		14	*10*	4				2	3		12		8	9			11			5		1				23
					6	7		12	*10*	4				2	3	11			8	14					9	5		1				24
					6			14	10	4	8	*7*		2		3			12	9						5	11	1				25
					6			*11*	10	4	8	7		2		3			12	9					14	5		1				26
					6			*11*	10	4	8	7		2		3			12	9					14	5		1				27
									10	4	8	7		2		3	12		6	9					14	5	*11*	1				28
				6		*11*			10	4		7		2		3			12	9					14	5		1	8			29
					6	11			10	4		7			3		2			9	8							1		5		30
		12				*11*			10	4		8			3		2			9	7						14	1	6	5		31
				5	6				10	4		7		2	3		12		8	9	14						11	1				32
				5	6	7			10	4				2	3				11	9	12						14	1			8	33
				5	6	12			10	4				2	3		7		11	9	8							1				34
				5	6	7			10	4				2	3		12		11	9	8							1			14	35
		11			6				10	4		7			3		2			9	8						14	1		*5*		36

ST MIRREN First Division

Year Formed: 1877. *Ground & Address:* St Mirren Park, Love St, Paisley PA3 2EJ. *Telephone:* 0141 889 2558/0141 840 1337. *Fax:* 0141 848 6444.
Ground Capacity: total: 15,410. seated 9395. *Size of Pitch:* 112yd × 73yd.
Chairman/Chief Executive: Bob Earlie. *Secretary and General Manager:* Jack Copland.
Manager: Jimmy Bone. *Physio:* Andrew Binning. *Coaches* Campbell Money and Kenny McDowall.
Managers since 1975: Alex Ferguson; Jim Clunie; Rikki MacFarlane; Alex Miller; Alex Smith; Tony Fitzpatrick; David Hay.
Club Nickname(s): The Buddies. *Previous Grounds:* Short Roods 1877-79, Thistle Park Greenhill 1879-83, Westmarch 1883-94.
Record Attendance: 47,438 v Celtic, League Cup, 20 Aug, 1949.
Record Transfer Fee received: £850,000 for Ian Ferguson to Rangers (1988).
Record Transfer Fee paid: £400,000 for Thomas Stickroth from Bayer Uerdingen (1990).
Record Victory: 15-0 v Glasgow University, Scottish Cup 1st rd; 30 Jan, 1960.
Record Defeat: 0-9 v Rangers, Division I; 4 Dec, 1897.
Most Capped Player: Godmundor Torfason, 29, Iceland.
Most League Appearances: 351: Tony Fitzpatrick, 1973-88.

St MIRREN 1994–95 LEAGUE RECORD

Match No.	Date		Venue	Opponents	Result		H/T Score	Lg. Pos.	Goalscorers	Attendance
1	Aug	13	A	Dundee	L	0-2	0-1	—		4125
2		20	A	Ayr U	D	1-1	0-0	9	Lavety	2787
3		27	H	Clydebank	W	2-1	0-1	4	Gillies R, Lavety	2414
4	Sept	3	H	Dunfermline Ath	D	1-1	1-0	5	Lavety	3895
5		10	A	St Johnstone	D	1-1	1-0	6	Gillies K	3957
6		24	H	Raith R	L	1-2	1-1	8	Lavety	2967
7	Oct	1	A	Hamilton A	D	2-2	0-1	7	Dick, Elliot	1613
8		8	A	Stranraer	D	1-1	0-0	6	Baker	1157
9		15	H	Airdrieonians	L	0-1	0-1	7		2930
10		22	H	Dundee	L	1-2	0-1	8	Elliot	2758
11		29	A	Clydebank	D	1-1	0-1	9	Watson	1675
12	Nov	5	H	Ayr U	W	1-0	1-0	7	Dawson (pen)	2482
13		12	H	St Johnstone	D	2-2	2-1	8	Gillies R, Fullarton	2970
14		19	A	Dunfermline Ath	L	0-1	0-0	8		4660
15	Dec	3	H	Hamilton A	L	0-1	0-0	8		2273
16		6	A	Raith R	D	1-1	1-1	—	Hewitt	4084
17		26	H	Stranraer	W	1-0	0-0	—	Elliot	2505
18		31	A	Dundee	L	0-4	0-1	8		3715
19	Jan	2	H	Clydebank	D	0-0	0-0	—		3217
20		7	A	Ayr U	L	0-2	0-1	8		2237
21		10	A	Airdrieonians	L	0-2	0-1	—		1325
22		14	H	Dunfermline Ath	D	2-2	1-2	8	Taylor, Inglis	2736
23		21	A	St Johnstone	L	1-5	0-3	8	Bone	3321
24	Feb	4	A	Hamilton A	L	0-2	0-2	8		1534
25		11	H	Raith R	L	1-2	0-2	9	McWhirter	2516
26		25	H	Airdrieonians	L	0-1	0-0	9		2564
27	Mar	11	A	Stranraer	W	3-1	1-1	8	Dawson, Watson, Bone	935
28		21	H	St Johnstone	D	0-0	0-0	—		2169
29		25	A	Dunfermline Ath	D	1-1	0-0	8	Lavety	5055
30	Apr	1	H	Hamilton A	W	3-2	0-1	8	Lavety, Baker, Inglis	2272
31		8	A	Raith R	L	1-2	1-2	8	Lavety	3669
32		15	H	Stranraer	W	2-0	2-0	7	Inglis, Dick	2315
33		22	A	Airdrieonians	L	0-1	0-0	7		2245
34		29	H	Dundee	W	1-0	0-0	7	Hewitt	2976
35	May	6	A	Clydebank	L	1-2	0-1	8	Watson	1399
36		13	H	Ayr U	W	2-1	1-1	7	Gillies R, McGrotty	2179

Final League Position: 7

Most League Goals in Season (Individual): 45: Dunky Walker, Division I; 1921-22.
Most Goals Overall (Individual): 221: David McCrae, 1923-24.

Honours
League Champions: First Division 1976-77. Division II 1967-68; *Runners-up:* 1935-36.
Scottish Cup Winners: 1926, 1959, 1987. *Runners-up* 1908, 1934, 1962.
League Cup: Runners-up 1955-56.
B&Q Cup: Runners-up 1993-94 *Victory Cup:* 1919-20. *Summer Cup:* 1943-44. *Anglo-Scottish Cup:* 1979-80.

European: *Cup Winners Cup:* 1987-88. *UEFA Cup:* 1980-81, 1983-84, 1985-86.
Club colours: Shirt: Black and white vertical stripes. Shorts: Black. Stockings: Black with White trim. Change colours: Predominantly red.

Goalscorers: *League (34):* Lavety 7, Elliot 3, Gillies R 3, Inglis 3, Watson 3, Baker 2, Bone 2, Dawson 2 (1 pen), Dick 2, Hewitt 2, Fullarton 1, Gillies K 1, McGrotty 1, McWhirter 1, Taylor 1. *Scottish Cup (0) League Cup (0) B&Q Cup (1):* Watson 1 (pen).

Combe A 20 + 1	Dawson R 29	Watson S 25 + 4	McLaughlin B 31	Taylor S 10 + 3	Archdeacon P 1 + 1	McIntyre P 19 + 1	Bone A 19 + 6	Lavety B 29 + 2	Gardner J 17 + 3	Elliot D 26 + 2	Hick M 2 + 1	Gillies R 13 + 11	Gillies K 5 + 4	Baker M 23 + 3	Dick J 24 + 1	Money C 15	Fullarton J 13 + 4	McWhirter N 23	Scott B — + 1	Orr N 4 + 1	McGrotty G — + 2	McAvennie F 7	Hewitt J 9 + 7	Okorie K 2	Smith B 4 + 1	Boyd J 10 + 2	Hetherston B 1 + 2	Inglis G 7 + 8	Byrne D 6	Galloway G 1	Scrimgeour D 1	*Match No.*
1	2	3	4	5	*6*	7	8	9	10	11	12	14																				1
1		3	4	5		6	8	9	10	11	*2*	14	7	12																		2
1	2	3	4			5	*8*	9	10	11		14	7	12	6																	3
	2	3	4		14	5		9	10	11		8	7		6	1	12															4
	2	3	4			5		9	10	11		8	7	12	6	1	14															5
	2	3	5			6	*7*	9	10	11		14	12		8	1		4														6
	2	3	5			12	*7*	9	10	11				8	6	1		4	14													7
	2		5	12		4	*7*	9	10	11				3	8	1				6	14											8
1	2	12	5			4		9	*10*	11		14		3	7					6		8										9
1	*2*	3	5			8	14		12	11		10			7			4		6		9										10
1		6	5			8		9	14	11	2	12		3	7			4				*10*										11
1	2	6	5			8	14	9		11				3	7		12	4				*10*										12
1	2	*6*	5				14		9	11		7		3			8	4				10	12									13
1	2	6	5					14	*9*	11		7		3			8			4		10	12									14
1		6	5				9	14	7	11		12		3			8					*10*		2	4							15
1	2			5				9		11		*8*	14	3	7					12			10	6	4							16
1	2	12	5					9		11		8		3	7			4					*10*			6	14					17
1	2	8	*5*	12				9		11		14		3	7			4					10			6						18
1	2	5						9		11		8		3	7			4					10			6	12					19
1	2	5						9		11		8	10	3	7			4					14			*6*		12				20
1	2	5	8				14	9		11				3	7			4					12			*6*		10				21
1		5		6			8	9						3	7		11	4					10		*2*	12		14				22
1		5		6			8	9		11		12			2		10	4					14			*3*		7				23
1	2		5	12		*3*	8	9					14		7		6	4					10					11				24
	2	6	5	8		7		9						3	12	1	11	4					*10*					14				25
	2		4			5	14	9	*11*			10		3	8	1	6											12	7			26
	2	6	5	8		9	14			11		*10*		3		1	12	4											7			27
	2		6	5		7	*9*	10	14	11				3		1	8	4										12				28
	2	12	6	5		7	*9*	10	11					3		1	8	4										14				29
	2		6	5		*7*	9	10	11	14				3		1	8	4										12				30
	2	12	6				9	10	*11*	7			14		5	1		4										8	3			31
	2		6				9	*10*	11	7		14			5	1		4								12		8	3			32
15	2	3	6				*9*	10				14			5	*1*		4					11			8		7				33
	2	5	6			7	9	*10*		14						1		4					11			8		12	3			34
1		6	5				9					10		3			4						14		12	8		7	2	*11*		35
		6	5				*9*					10		3	11		4				12		14		2	8	7				1	36

STENHOUSEMUIR Second Division

Year Formed: 1884. *Ground & Address:* Ochilview Park, Gladstone Rd, Stenhousemuir FK5 5QL. *Telephone:* 01324 562992.
Ground Capacity: total: 3480. seated: 340. *Size of Pitch:* 113yd × 78yd.
Chairman: A Terry Bulloch. *Secretary:* David O.Reid. *Commercial Manager:* John Sharp.
Manager: Terry Christie. *Assistant Manager:* Graeme Armstrong. *Physio:* Lee Campbell. *Coach:* Gordon Buchanan.
Managers since 1975: H. Glasgow; J. Black; A. Rose; W. Henderson; A. Rennie; J. Meakin; D. Lawson. *Club Nickname(s):* The Warriors. *Previous Grounds:* Tryst Ground 1884-86, Goschen Park 1886-90.
Record Attendance: 12,500 v East Fife, Scottish Cup 4th rd; 11 Mar, 1950.
Record Transfer Fee received: £30,000 for David Beaton to Falkirk (June 1989).
Record Transfer Fee paid: £7000 to Meadowbank T for Lee Bullen (Nov 1990).
Record Victory: 9-2 v Dundee U, Division II; 19 Apr, 1937.
Record Defeat: 2-11 v Dunfermline Ath. Division II; 27 Sept, 1930.
Most Capped Player: —.

STENHOUSEMUIR 1994–95 LEAGUE RECORD

Match No.	Date	Venue	Opponents	Result		H/T Score	Lg. Pos.	Goalscorers	Attendance
1	Aug 13	H	Clyde	W	1-0	1-0	—	Hutchison	680
2	20	H	East Fife	D	1-1	1-0	4	Sludden	544
3	27	A	Meadowbank T	L	0-3	0-0	7		239
4	Sept 3	A	Brechin C	D	1-1	1-1	5	Steel	436
5	10	H	Stirling Albion	W	3-0	2-0	3	Hutchison, Steel, Christie	555
6	24	H	Berwick R	D	1-1	1-0	5	Hutchison	373
7	Oct 1	A	Morton	L	2-3	0-0	6	Sprott, Hutchison	1280
8	8	H	Queen of the S	D	0-0	0-0	6		403
9	15	A	Dumbarton	W	2-1	1-0	4	Steel, Fisher	601
10	22	A	Clyde	D	0-0	0-0	4		1072
11	29	H	Meadowbank T	D	1-1	0-1	6	Mathieson	473
12	Nov 5	A	East Fife	W	3-2	2-0	5	Mathieson 2, Hutchison	719
13	12	A	Stirling Albion	W	2-0	1-0	3	Steel, Hutchison	696
14	19	H	Brechin C	W	2-0	2-0	2	Steel, Christie	342
15	26	A	Berwick R	D	0-0	0-0	3		703
16	Dec 3	H	Morton	D	0-0	0-0	3		842
17	26	A	Queen of the S	W	2-1	1-0	—	Steel 2	1437
18	31	H	Dumbarton	W	1-0	0-0	1	Steel	638
19	Jan 10	H	Meadowbank T	W	2-1	0-1	—	Donaldson, Mathieson	371
20	14	H	Clyde	D	2-2	0-0	1	Hutchison, Sprott	669
21	21	A	East Fife	W	2-0	2-0	1	Sprott, Mathieson	713
22	Feb 4	H	Stirling Albion	L	0-2	0-1	1		797
23	14	A	Brechin C	W	2-0	1-0	—	Sprott, Hutchison	345
24	25	A	Morton	L	0-1	0-1	1		2754
25	Mar 7	H	Berwick R	D	2-2	1-1	—	Hutchison, Sprott	534
26	14	A	Dumbarton	L	1-5	1-2	—	Donaldson	1132
27	18	A	Stirling Albion	L	1-3	0-1	4	Sprott	431
28	21	H	Queen of the S	D	2-2	1-1	—	Clarke, Christie	454
29	25	H	Brechin C	W	3-0	3-0	3	Fisher, Mathieson 2	396
30	Apr 1	H	Morton	D	1-1	0-0	3	Sprott	1126
31	8	A	Berwick R	D	0-0	0-0	3		571
32	15	A	Queen of the S	W	2-1	2-0	3	Clarke, Steel	1230
33	22	H	Dumbarton	D	0-0	0-00	3		989
34	29	A	Clyde	L	2-3	0-0	4	Haddow, Hutchison	1043
35	May 5	A	Meadowbank T	L	0-1	0-1	—		463
36	13	H	East Fife	W	2-1	2-1	4	Fisher, Mathieson	433

Final League Position: 4

Most League Appearances: 360: Archie Rose.
Most League Goals in Season (Individual): 32: Robert Taylor, Division II; 1925-26.
Most Goals Overall (Individual): —.

Honours
League Champions: —. *Scottish Cup:* Semi-finals 1902-03. Quarter-finals 1994-95 *League Cup:* Quarter-finals 1947-48, 1960-61, 1975-76.
Club colours: Shirt: Maroon with silver stripe. Shorts: White with maroon insert. Stockings: White.

Goalscorers: *League (46):* Hutchison 10, Steel 9, Mathieson 8, Sprott 7, Christie 3, Fisher 3, Clarke 2, Donaldson 2, Haddow 1, Sludden 1. *Scottish Cup (14):* Sprott 4 (1 pen), Mathieson 3, Steel 3, Christie 1, Clarke 1, Donaldson 1, Fisher 1. *League Cup (0) B&Q Cup (0)*

Harkness M 36	Aitken N 2 + 2	Haddow L 18 + 2	Salton K 4	McGeachie G 21 + 1	Christie M 28	Steel T 34 + 1	Swanson D 3	Hutchison G 34	Sludden J 4 + 1	Sprott A 28 + 1	Mathieson M 35	Fisher J 32 + 1	Henderson J 1 + 4	Clarke J 14 + 4	Godfrey P 17 + 3	Irvine J — + 6	Armstrong G 33	McNiven J 19	Roseburgh D 8 + 5	Donaldson E 16 + 1	Russell G 9 + 1	Match No.
1	2	3	4	5	6	7	8	9	10	11												1
1	2	3	4	*5*	6	7	8		10	11	9	12	14									2
1		3	4		6	7	8		10	11	9		12	2	5	14						3
1		3			6	7		10		11	9	8		2	5	12	4					4
1		3			6	7		10		11	9	8		2	5	12	4					5
1		3		6	8	7		*10*	14		9	11		2	5		4					6
1		3		5	6	7		10		11	9	8		2		12	4					7
1		3	2	5	6			10	7	11	9	8				12	4					8
1		3		5	6	7		10		11	9	8			12		4	2				9
1		3			6	7		10		11	9	8		2	5		4					10
1		3		5	6	7		10			9	8			12	14	4	*2*	11			11
1		3			6	7		10			9	8			5		4	2	11			12
1		3			6	7		10		12	9	8			5		4	2	11			13
1		3			6	7		10		11	9	8			5		4	2				14
1		3			6	7		10		11	9	8			5		4	2	12			15
1					6	7		10		11	9	8			5		4	2	3			16
1					6	7		10		11	9	8			5		4	2	3			17
1				12	6	7		10		11	9	*8*		2	5		4		3	14		18
1				6		7		10		11	9	8		12	5		4	2		3		19
1				6		7		10		11	9	8			5		4	2		3		20
1				5	6	*7*		10		11	9	8		14			4	2		3		21
1				5	6	7		10		11	9	*8*					4	2	14	3		22
1				5	6	7		10		11	*9*	8		14			4	2	12	3		23
1				5	6	7		10		11	9	8					4	2	12	3		24
1				5	6	7		10		11	9	8		12			4		3		2	25
1	14				*6*	12		10		11	9	8			5		4		7	3	2	26
1	14				6	7		10		11	9	8			5		4		*12*	3	2	27
1				5	6	7		10		11	9			8	12		4	2		3		28
1					6	7		10			9	8		11	5		4	2		3		29
1				5	6	7		10		11	9	8					4	2		3	12	30
1				5		7		10		11	9	8					4	2		3	6	31
1		14		5		7		10		11	9	8		*6*			4			3	2	32
1		14		5		7		10		*11*	9	8		6			4			3	2	33
1		11		5		7		10			9	8	14	*6*			4			3	2	34
1		11		5		7		10			9	8	14	6			4			3	*2*	35
1		11				7		10			9	8	6	5			4	2			3	36

STIRLING ALBION Second Division

Year Formed: 1945. *Ground & Address:* Forthbank Stadium, Springkerse Industrial Estate, Stirling FK7 7UJ. *Telephone:* 01786 450399.
Chairman: Peter McKenzie. *Secretary:* Marlyn Hallam. *Commercial Manager:* —.
Manager: Kevin Drinkell. *Assistant Manager:* Ray Stewart. *Physio:* George Cameron.
Managers since 1975: A.Smith; G.Peebles; J.Fleeting, J.Brogan. *Club Nickname(s):* The Binos. *Previous Grounds:* Annfield.
Record Attendance: 26,400 v Celtic, Scottish Cup 4th rd; 14 Mar, 1959.
Record Transfer Fee received: £70,000 for John Philliben to Doncaster R (Mar 1984).
Record Transfer Fee paid: £17,000 for Douglas Lawrie from Airdrieonians (Dec 1989).
Record Victory: 20-0 v Selkirk, Scottish Cup 1st rd; 8 Dec, 1984.
Record Defeat: 0-9 v Dundee U, Division I; 30 Dec, 1967.
Most Capped Player: —.
Most League Appearances: 504: Matt McPhee, 1967-81.

STIRLING ALBION 1994–95 LEAGUE RECORD

Match No.	Date	Venue	Opponents	Result		H/T Score	Lg. Pos.	Goalscorers	Attendance
1	Aug 13	H	East Fife	L	0-1	0-0	—		808
2	20	H	Dumbarton	D	1-1	0-0	8	McLeod	715
3	27	A	Clyde	W	2-1	2-0	5	Tait, Watters	1162
4	Sept 3	H	Morton	W	2-0	0-0	3	Gibson, Watters	1026
5	10	A	Stenhousemuir	L	0-3	0-2	5		555
6	24	A	Meadowbank T	W	2-1	1-0	4	Watters, Roberts	247
7	Oct 1	H	Queen of the S	W	3-0	0-0	2	Watters, McLeod, Campbell (og)	697
8	8	A	Brechin C	W	2-1	1-0	2	Watters, Taggart	555
9	15	H	Berwick R	W	3-2	1-1	1	Mitchell, McQuilter, Drinkell	863
10	22	A	East Fife	L	3-4	1-1	2	McInnes, Taggart, Tait	1039
11	29	H	Clyde	L	0-1	0-0	2		1118
12	Nov 5	A	Dumbarton	L	0-1	0-1	2		778
13	12	H	Stenhousemuir	L	0-2	0-1	6		696
14	22	A	Morton	D	1-1	0-0	—	Taggart	1941
15	26	H	Meadowbank T	L	2-3	0-0	7	Taggart, Watters	518
16	Dec 3	A	Queen of the S	W	1-0	1-0	6	Mitchell	1197
17	24	H	Brechin C	W	2-0	1-0	6	Armstrong, McLeod	760
18	31	A	Berwick R	L	0-1	0-1	7		736
19	Jan 14	H	East Fife	W	3-0	2-0	—	McInnes 3	810
20	17	A	Clyde	L	0-2	0-0	5		1345
21	21	A	Dumbarton	D	2-2	0-2	6	Tait, Drinkell	700
22	Feb 4	A	Stenhousemuir	W	2-0	1-0	6	McInnes, Watters	797
23	11	H	Morton	L	0-3	0-1	6		1069
24	25	H	Queen of the S	D	1-1	0-1	6	McInnes	528
25	Mar 4	A	Brechin C	L	1-2	0-1	6	Watters	465
26	8	A	Meadowbank T	W	3-0	0-0	—	Paterson G, Taggart, McInnes	165
27	11	H	Berwick R	D	2-2	1-0	6	McLeod, Farquhar	582
28	18	H	Stenhousemuir	W	3-1	1-0	6	McLeod, Watters 2	431
29	25	A	Morton	D	2-2	1-1	6	Watters, Lilley (og)	2025
30	Apr 1	A	Queen of the S	W	3-1	1-0	6	Watters, Gibson, McLeod	1056
31	8	H	Meadowbank T	W	2-1	0-0	5	Gibson, Watters	478
32	15	H	Brechin C	W	2-0	1-0	4	Watters 2	607
33	22	A	Berwick R	D	0-0	0-0	4		601
34	29	A	East Fife	W	2-1	0-1	3	McLeod, Mitchell	510
35	May 6	H	Clyde	W	2-0	0-0	2	Gibson, McLeod	1122
36	13	H	Dumbarton	L	0-2	0-0	3		3003

Final League Position: 3

Most League Goals in Season (Individual): 27: Joe Hughes, Division II; 1969-70.
Most Goals Overall (Individual): 129: Billy Steele, 1971-83.

Honours
League Champions: Division II 1952-53, 1957-58, 1960-61, 1964-65. Second Division 1976-77, 1990-91; *Runners-up:* Division II 1948-49, 1950-51.
Scottish Cup: —. *League Cup:* —.
Club colours: Shirt: Red with white sleeves. Shorts: White. Stockings: White.

Goalscorers: *League (54):* Watters 15, McLeod 8, McInnes 7, Taggart 5, Gibson 4, Mitchell 3, Tait 3, Drinkell 2, Armstrong 1, Farquhar 1, McQuilter 1, Paterson G 1, Roberts 1, own goals 2. *Scottish Cup (10):* McInnes 3, Taggart 3, McQuilter 1, Mitchell 1 (pen), Tait 1, Watters 1. *League Cup (0) B&Q Cup (4):* Taggart 2, McInnes 1, Watters 1.

McGeown M 29	Hamilton J 3	Tait T 34	Mitchell C 31 + 1	McQuilter R 29 + 1	Reid W 5	McInnes I 34 + 1	Roberts P 3 + 9	Watters W 31 + 3	Taggart C 32 + 2	McLeod J 36	Gibson J 32 + 2	Callaghan T 1 + 3	Armstrong P 18 + 5	Paterson A 28 + 2	Stewart R 1 + 1	Farquhar A 2 + 10	Drinkell K 8 + 2	McAneny P 3 + 1	Kerr R 5 + 3	Monaghan M 7	Watson P 4 + 2	Paterson G 11	Deas P 9 + 1	*Match No.*
1	2	3	4	5	6	7	*8*	9	10	11	12	14												1
1	*2*	6	4	5	7	12	8	9	10	11	14		3											2
1		6	4	5	8	7	12	*9*	10	11	2	14	3											3
1			4	5	8	7		9	10	11	2	6	*3*	12	14									4
1		6	4	5	8	*7*		9	10	11	2	14	3	12										5
1		6	4	5		7	14	9	10	11	3			2		*8*								6
1		6	4	5		7	14	9	10	11	3		12	2			*8*							7
1		6	4	5		7	14	*9*	10	11	3			2			8							8
1		6	4	5		7		9	10	11	3		12	2			8							9
1		6	4	5		7	14	*9*	10	11	3		12	2			8							10
1		6		5		7		14	10	11	3		9	2			*8*	4						11
1		6		5		7	14		10	11	3		9	*2*			8	4						12
1	*2*	6	12	5		*7*		9	10	11	3		8			14		4						13
1		6	4	5		7	12	9	10	*11*	3		8	2					14					14
1		6	4	5		7	12	9	10	*11*	3		8	2					14					15
1		6	4	5		7	14	*9*	10	11	3		12	2	8									16
		6	4			7		*9*	10	11	3		8	2		14				1	5			17
		6	4			7	9		10	11	3		*8*	2		14				1	5			18
			4	5		7		9	10	11	3		8	2					6	1				19
		8	4	5		7		9	10	11	3			2			12		6	1				20
		8	4	5		7		9	10	11	3		14	2			12		*6*	1				21
		6	4	5		7		14	10	11	3		8	2			*9*		12	1				22
		6	4	5		7		14	10	11			3	2			9		*8*	1	12			23
1		6	4	5		7		9	10	11			3	2		14			*8*					24
1		6	*4*	5		7		9	10	11	3		8	2		14								25
1		6	4			7		9	10	*11*	3		8			14		12			2	5		26
1		6	4			7		9	10	11	2		*8*			14					3	5	12	27
1		6		5		7		9	10	11	3			2								4	8	28
1		6		5				9	*10*	11	3			2		7					14	4	8	29
1		6	10	5		7		9		*11*	3			2		14						4	8	30
1		6	5			7		9	*10*	11	3			2		14						4	8	31
1		6	5			7		9	10	11	3			2								4	8	32
1		6	5	12		7		9	10	11	3			2								4	8	33
1		6	5	10		7		9		11	3			2								4	8	34
1		6	5	10		7		9	12	11	3			2								4	8	35
1		6	5	10		7		9	12	11	*3*			2		14						4	8	36

STRANRAER Second Division

Year Formed: 1870. *Ground & Address:* Stair Park, London Rd, Stranraer DG9 8BS. *Telephone:* 01776 703271.
Ground Capacity: total: 5000. seated: 700. *Size of Pitch:* 110yd × 70yd.
Chairman: G. F. Compton. *Secretary:* Graham Rodgers. *Commercial Manager: T. L. Sutherland.*
Manager: Alex McAnespie. *Coach:* Derek McHarg.
Managers since 1975: J. Hughes; N. Hood; G. Hamilton; D. Sneddon; J. Clark; R. Clark; A. McAnespie. *Club Nickname(s):* The Blues. *Previous Grounds:* None.
Record Attendance: 6500 v Rangers, Scottish Cup 1st rd; 24 Jan, 1948.
Record Transfer Fee received: £30,000 for Duncan George to Ayr Utd.
Record Transfer Fee paid: £15,000 for Colin Harkness from Kilmarnock (Aug 1989).
Record Victory: 7-0 v Brechin C, Division II; 6 Feb, 1965.
Record Defeat: 1-11 v Queen of the South, Scottish Cup 1st rd; 16 Jan, 1932.
Most Capped Player: —.
Most League Appearances: 256: Ian McDonald.

STRANRAER 1994–95 LEAGUE RECORD

Match No.	*Date*	*Venue*	*Opponents*	*Result*		*H/T Score*	*Lg. Pos.*	*Goalscorers*	*Attendance*
1	Aug 13	A	Clydebank	L	0-2	0-0	—		908
2	20	A	Dundee	L	1-3	0-2	10	Walker	3186
3	27	H	Ayr U	W	2-1	0-1	6	McCaffrey, Hughes (pen)	1653
4	Sept 3	A	Hamilton A	L	0-1	0-1	9		1083
5	10	H	Raith R	D	0-0	0-0	9		1078
6	24	A	Dunfermline Ath	L	0-1	0-1	10		3893
7	Oct 1	H	Airdrieonians	L	0-1	0-0	10		1001
8	8	H	St Mirren	D	1-1	0-0	10	Walker	1157
9	15	A	St Johnstone	L	0-3	0-0	10		2678
10	22	H	Clydebank	L	0-1	0-0	10		781
11	29	A	Ayr U	L	1-2	1-1	10	Sloan	2073
12	Nov 12	A	Raith R	L	2-4	0-2	10	Ferguson, Walker	2556
13	19	H	Hamilton A	W	2-0	1-0	10	Brannigan, Millar	784
14	23	H	Dundee	L	0-2	0-1	—		765
15	26	H	Dunfermline Ath	D	0-0	0-0	10		1118
16	Dec 3	A	Airdrieonians	L	1-8	1-2	10	Gallagher	1207
17	10	H	St Johnstone	D	2-2	1-1	10	Sloan, Farrell	780
18	26	A	St Mirren	L	0-1	0-0	—		2505
19	31	A	Clydebank	W	3-2	2-0	9=	Grant, Henderson, Ferguson	652
20	Jan 2	H	Ayr U	W	2-0	1-0	—	Gallagher, Grant	1899
21	7	A	Dundee	L	0-2	0-1	9=		2615
22	14	A	Hamilton A	L	0-1	0-0	9		1015
23	24	H	Raith R	L	2-4	1-1	—	Gallagher, Sinclair (og)	769
24	Feb 4	H	Airdrieonians	L	1-4	0-2	10	Sloan	945
25	14	A	Dunfermline Ath	L	1-3	0-1	—	Sloan	3528
26	25	A	St Johnstone	L	0-3	0-1	10		2725
27	Mar 11	H	St Mirren	L	1-3	1-1	10	Henderson	935
28	18	A	Raith R	D	1-1	0-1	10	Reilly	2197
29	25	H	Hamilton A	L	0-5	0-2	10		655
30	Apr 1	A	Airdrieonians	L	0-2	0-0	10		851
31	8	H	Dunfermline Ath	L	0-1	0-1	10		988
32	15	A	St Mirren	L	0-2	0-2	10		2315
33	22	H	St Johnstone	L	2-6	0-2	10	Henderson 2	702
34	29	H	Clydebank	L	0-1	0-1	10		582
35	May 6	A	Ayr U	L	0-3	0-1	10		1204
36	13	H	Dundee	L	0-5	0-1	10		1589

Final League Position: 10

Most League Goals in Season (Individual): 27: Derek Frye, Second Division; 1977-78.
Most Goals Overall (Individual): —.

Honours
League Champions: Second Division 1993-94.
Scottish Cup: —.
League Cup: —.
Qualifying Cup Winners: 1937.
Club colours: Shirt: Royal blue with geometrical design. Shorts: White. Stockings: Royal blue.

Goalscorers: *League (25):* Henderson 4, Sloan 4, Gallagher 3, Walker 3, Ferguson 2, Grant 2, Brannigan 1, Farrell 1, Hughes 1 (pen), McCaffrey 1, Millar 1, Reilly 1, own goal 1. *Scottish Cup (0) League Cup (2):* Cody 1, Ferguson 1. *B&Q Cup (3):* Ferguson 1, Henderson 1, Walker 1.

Ross S 28	Treanor M 4	Hughes J 33	Millar G 28 + 1	Brannigan K 31	McCaffrey J 14 + 3	Reilly R 16 + 9	Cody S 16	Walker T 28 + 3	Duncan G 30 + 1	Henderson D 22	Ferguson W 1 + 13	Gallagher A 23 + 1	McLean P 14 + 12	Grant A 21 + 5	Sloan T 29 + 3	Howard N 16 + 1	McCann J 15 + 1	Farrell S 1 + 3	McAuley I 1	Callaghan T 14 + 2	Duffy B 8 + 1	Robertson J 2 + 1	Fulton B — + 1	McGuire D 1 + 5	Match No.
1	*2*	3	4	5	6	*7*	8	9	10	11	12	14													1
1	2	3	6	5	4		10	9	8	11	12		*7*	14											2
1		3	2	5	4		6	*8*	9	11	12	10		14	7										3
1	10	3	2	*5*	4		6	8		11	12	9	14		7										4
1	4	3	2		5		10	8	9	11		6	12		*7*	14									5
1		3	2		*6*		10	14	9	11		5	12	8	7		4								6
1		3	2	5	4		10			*11*		6	9	8	7			14							7
1		3	2	5	4		10	11	9			6	12	8	*7*			14							8
1		3	2	5	4	*7*		8	9	11		6		12			10								9
1		3		5	*6*	12	10	9	14	11		8		7			4	2							10
1		3	2	5		12		9	6	11			10	8	7		4								11
1		3	2	5		14		9	6		12		10	8	7	4			*11*						12
1		3	2	5		14	*10*	9	11		12				7	6	4			8					13
1		3	*2*	5			10	9	11		12	6	14		7		4			8					14
1		3	2	5		11	*10*	9			12	6	14		7		4			8					15
1		3	2	5		11	10	9				6	14	7	12		*4*			8					16
		3	2	5		*10*			9	11	12	6	8		7	4		14			1				17
1		3	2	5		14			9	11	12	6	10	8	*7*		4								18
1		3	2	5		10			9	11	12	*4*	14	8	7	6									19
1		3		5		10		14	9	*11*	12	4		8	7	6	2								20
1		3		5		10		12	*9*	11		4	14	8	7		2			6					21
1		3		5		2		11	9				12	8	7	4	6			10					22
1		3	2	5	14	11		*10*	9			4	12		7	6				8					23
1		3	2			14	*10*	7				6	11	8	12	5	4			9	15				24
1		3		5	14	*2*		11	9			4	12	8	7	6				10					25
1		2		5	14	12		9	3			4	11	8	7	6				*10*					26
1		3	2	5				10	9	11			7	8	12		4			6					27
1		2	3			11	10	9	6			5		8	7		4			12					28
1			2	5		3	10	8	9	11		*6*			7	4						12	14		29
			4	5		3		8	10	11			7		9	6					1	2		12	30
			4	5		3		7	10				11	8	9	6	14				1	*2*		12	31
		3	2	5		12		9	6	11			*10*	8	7	4					1			14	32
		3	14	5	6			9	2	11				12	8	4				10	1			7	33
		2	*3*	5	4	14			6	11			8	9	7					10	1			12	34
		3	*2*	5	4	8		10	6	11	9			12	7					14	1				35
		2			6			9	11		12	*5*	3	8	7	4				10	1			14	36

Scottish League 1994–95

Premier Division

		Home			*Goals*		*Away*			*Goals*		
	P	W	D	L	F	A	W	D	L	F	A	Pts
Rangers	36	11	5	2	31	14	9	4	5	29	21	69
Motherwell	36	8	6	4	29	23	6	6	6	21	27	54
Hibernian	36	9	7	2	37	19	3	10	5	12	18	53
Celtic	36	6	8	4	23	19	5	10	3	16	14	51
Falkirk	36	8	3	7	26	24	4	9	5	22	23	48
Hearts	36	9	4	5	26	14	3	3	12	18	37	43
Kilmarnock	36	8	4	6	22	16	3	6	9	18	32	43
Partick T	36	4	9	5	23	23	6	4	8	17	27	43
Aberdeen	36	7	7	4	24	16	3	4	11	19	30	41
Dundee U	36	6	6	6	24	20	3	3	12	16	36	36–1

First Division

		Home			*Goals*		*Away*			*Goals*		
	P	W	D	L	F	A	W	D	L	F	A	Pts
Raith R	36	8	8	2	27	18	11	4	3	27	14	69
Dunfermline Ath	36	11	5	2	35	11	7	9	2	28	21	68
Dundee	36	11	4	3	34	18	9	4	5	31	18	68
Airdrieonians	36	7	6	5	22	14	10	4	4	28	19	61
St Johnstone	36	10	6	2	36	15	4	8	6	23	24	56
Hamilton A	36	9	3	6	23	22	5	4	9	19	26	49
St Mirren	36	7	5	6	20	18	1	7	10	14	32	36
Clydebank	36	4	6	8	20	25	4	5	9	13	22	35
Ayr U	36	6	5	7	22	24	0	6	12	9	34	29
Stranraer	36	3	4	11	15	37	1	1	16	10	44	17

Second Division

		Home			*Goals*		*Away*			*Goals*		
	P	W	D	L	F	A	W	D	L	F	A	Pts
Greenock Morton	36	12	5	1	33	11	6	5	7	22	22	64
Dumbarton	36	12	4	2	43	16	5	5	8	14	19	60
Stirling Albion	36	9	3	6	28	20	8	4	6	26	23	58
Stenhousemuir	36	7	10	1	24	14	7	4	7	22	25	56
Berwick R	36	10	6	2	23	13	5	4	9	29	33	55
Clyde	36	8	5	5	33	25	6	5	7	20	23	52
Queen of the S	36	6	3	9	25	26	5	8	5	21	25	44
East Fife	36	7	3	8	31	27	4	7	7	17	29	43
Meadowbank T*	36	7	2	9	16	21	4	3	11	16	33	35
Brechin C	36	4	5	9	15	26	2	1	15	7	34	24

*Meadowbank T had 3 points deducted for fielding an ineligible player

Third Division

		Home			*Goals*		*Away*			*Goals*		
	P	W	D	L	F	A	W	D	L	F	A	Pts
Forfar Ath	36	14	3	1	42	16	11	2	5	25	17	80
Montrose	36	9	4	5	33	17	11	3	4	36	15	67
Ross County	36	9	1	8	35	26	9	5	4	24	18	60
East Stirling	36	10	2	6	28	20	8	3	7	33	30	59
Alloa	36	7	4	7	23	20	8	5	5	27	25	54
Caledonian T	36	5	7	6	27	33	7	2	9	21	28	45
Arbroath	36	6	3	9	21	23	7	2	9	30	39	44
Queen's Park	36	7	2	9	21	27	5	4	9	25	30	42
Cowdenbeath	36	4	5	9	23	36	7	2	9	25	24	40
Albion R	36	3	0	15	16	39	2	3	13	11	43	18

PLAY-OFF: Aberdeen (9th place, Premier Division) v Dunfermline Ath (runners-up, First Division)

21 MAY at Pittodrie
Aberdeen (1) 3 *(Glass, Shearer 2)*
Dunfermline Ath (0) 1 *(Robertson)* 21,000
Aberdeen: Snelders; McKimmie, Wright, Grant, Irvine, Smith, Hetherston, Shearer, Miller, Thomson, Glass.
Dunfermline Ath: Van De Kamp; McNamara, Fleming, McCathie, Tod, Smith, Den Bieman, Robertson, Moore (Shaw), Petrie, McCulloch (Hawkins).

25 MAY at East End Park
Dunfermline Ath (0) 1 *(Smith)*
Aberdeen (0) 3 *(Dodds, Miller, Glass)* 16,000
Dunfermline Ath: Van De Kamp; McNamara, Fleming, McCathie, Tod, Smith, Den Bieman, Robertson, Moore, Petrie, McCulloch (Shaw).
Aberdeen: Snelders; McKimmie, Wright, Grant, Irvine (Inglis), Smith, Hetherston, Shearer, Miller (Kane), Dodds, Glass.

SCOTTISH LEAGUE 1890–91 to 1994–95

*On goal average/difference. †Held jointly after indecisive play-off. ‡Won on deciding match. ††Held jointly. ¶Two points deducted for fielding ineligible player.
Competition suspended 1940–45 during war. ‡‡Two points deducted for registration irregularities.

PREMIER DIVISION

	First	*Pts*	*Second*	*Pts*	*Third*	*Pts*
			Maximum points: 72			
1975–76	Rangers	54	Celtic	48	Hibernian	43
1976–77	Celtic	55	Rangers	46	Aberdeen	43
1977–78	Rangers	55	Aberdeen	53	Dundee U	40
1978–79	Celtic	48	Rangers	45	Dundee U	44
1979–80	Aberdeen	48	Celtic	47	St Mirren	42
1980–81	Celtic	56	Aberdeen	49	Rangers*	44
1981–82	Celtic	55	Aberdeen	53	Rangers	43
1982–83	Dundee U	56	Celtic*	55	Aberdeen	55
1983–84	Aberdeen	57	Celtic	50	Dundee U	47
1984–85	Aberdeen	59	Celtic	52	Dundee U	47
1985–86	Celtic*	50	Hearts	50	Dundee U	47
			Maximum points: 88			
1986–87	Rangers	69	Celtic	63	Dundee U	60
1987–88	Celtic	72	Hearts	62	Rangers	60
			Maximum points: 72			
1988–89	Rangers	56	Aberdeen	50	Celtic	46
1989–90	Rangers	51	Aberdeen*	44	Hearts	44
1990–91	Rangers	55	Aberdeen	53	Celtic*	41
			Maximum points: 88			
1991–92	Rangers	72	Hearts	63	Celtic	62
1992–93	Rangers	73	Aberdeen	64	Celtic	60
1993–94	Rangers	58	Aberdeen	55	Motherwell	54
			Maximum points: 108			
1994–95	Rangers	69	Motherwell	54	Hibernian	53

FIRST DIVISION

	First	*Pts*	*Second*	*Pts*	*Third*	*Pts*
			Maximum points: 52			
1975–76	Partick T	41	Kilmarnock	35	Montrose	30
			Maximum points: 78			
1976–77	St Mirren	62	Clydebank	58	Dundee	51
1977–78	Morton*	58	Hearts	58	Dundee	57
1978–79	Dundee	55	Kilmarnock*	54	Clydebank	54
1979–80	Hearts	53	Airdrieonians	51	Ayr U	44
1980–81	Hibernian	57	Dundee	52	St Johnstone	51
1981–82	Motherwell	61	Kilmarnock	51	Hearts	50
1982–83	St Johnstone	55	Hearts	54	Clydebank	50
1983–84	Morton	54	Dumbarton	51	Partick T	46
1984–85	Motherwell	50	Clydebank	48	Falkirk	45
1985–86	Hamilton A	56	Falkirk	45	Kilmarnock	44
			Maximum points: 88			
1986–87	Morton	57	Dunfermline Ath	56	Dumbarton	53
1987–88	Hamilton A	56	Meadowbank T	52	Clydebank	49
			Maximum points: 78			
1988–89	Dunfermline Ath	54	Falkirk	52	Clydebank	48
1989–90	St Johnstone	58	Airdrieonians	54	Clydebank	44
1990–91	Falkirk	54	Airdrieonians	53	Dundee	52
			Maximum points: 88			
1991–92	Dundee	58	Partick T*	57	Hamilton A	57
1992–93	Raith R	65	Kilmarnock	54	Dunfermline Ath	52
1993–94	Falkirk	66	Dunfermline Ath	65	Airdrieonians	54
			Maximum points: 108			
1994–95	Raith R	69	Dunfermline Ath*	68	Dundee	68

SECOND DIVISION

	First	*Pts*	*Second*	*Pts*	*Third*	*Pts*
			Maximum points: 52			
1975–77	Clydebank*	40	Raith R	40	Alloa	35
			Maximum points: 78			
1976–77	Stirling A	55	Alloa	51	Dunfermline Ath	50
1977–78	Clyde*	53	Raith R	53	Dunfermline Ath	48
1978–79	Berwick R	54	Dunfermline Ath	52	Falkirk	50
1979–80	Falkirk	50	East Stirling	49	Forfar Ath	46
1980–81	Queen's Park	50	Queen of the S	46	Cowdenbeath	45
1981–82	Clyde	59	Alloa*	50	Arbroath	50
1982–83	Brechin C	55	Meadowbank T	54	Arbroath	49

1983–84	Forfar Ath	63	East Fife	47	Berwick R	43
1984–85	Montrose	53	Alloa	50	Dunfermline Ath	49
1985–86	Dunfermline Ath	57	Queen of the S	55	Meadowbank T	49
1986–87	Meadowbank T	55	Raith R*	52	Stirling A	52
1987–88	Ayr U	61	St Johnstone	59	Queen's Park	51
1988–89	Albion R	50	Alloa	45	Brechin C	43
1989–90	Brechin C	49	Kilmarnock	48	Stirling A	47
1990–91	Stirling A	54	Montrose	46	Cowdenbeath	45
			Maximum points: 78			
1991–92	Dumbarton	52	Cowdenbeath	51	Alloa	50
1992–93	Clyde	54	Brechin C*	53	Stranraer	53
1993–94	Stranraer	56	Berwick R	48	Stenhousemuir*	47
			Maximum points: 108			
1994–95	Morton	64	Dumbarton	60	Stirling A	58

THIRD DIVISION

Maximum points: 108

1994–95	Forfar Ath	80	Montrose	67	Ross Co	60

FIRST DIVISION to 1974–75

Maximum points: a 36; b 44; c 40; d 52; e 60; f 68; g 76; h 84.

	First	*Pts*	*Second*	*Pts*	*Third*	*Pts*
1890–91*a*††	Dumbarton	29	Rangers	29	Celtic	24
1891–92*b*	Dumbarton	37	Celtic	35	Hearts	30
1892–93*a*	Celtic	29	Rangers	28	St Mirren	23
1893–94*a*	Celtic	29	Hearts	26	St Bernard's	22
1894–95*a*	Hearts	31	Celtic	26	Rangers	21
1895–96*a*	Celtic	30	Rangers	26	Hibernian	24
1896–97*a*	Hearts	28	Hibernian	26	Rangers	25
1897–98*a*	Celtic	33	Rangers	29	Hibernian	22
1898–99*a*	Rangers	36	Hearts	26	Celtic	24
1899–1900*a*	Rangers	32	Celtic	25	Hibernian	24
1900–01*c*	Rangers	35	Celtic	29	Hibernian	25
1901–02*a*	Rangers	28	Celtic	26	Hearts	22
1902–03*b*	Hibernian	37	Dundee	31	Rangers	29
1903–04*d*	Third Lanark	43	Hearts	39	Rangers*	38
1904–05*d*	Celtic‡	41	Rangers	41	Third Lanark	35
1905–06*e*	Celtic	49	Hearts	43	Airdrieonians	38
1906–07*f*	Celtic	55	Dundee	48	Rangers	45
1907–08*f*	Celtic	55	Falkirk	51	Rangers	50
1908–09*f*	Celtic	51	Dundee	50	Clyde	48
1909–10*f*	Celtic	54	Falkirk	52	Rangers	46
1910–11*f*	Rangers	52	Aberdeen	48	Falkirk	44
1911–12*f*	Rangers	51	Celtic	45	Clyde	42
1912–13*f*	Rangers	53	Celtic	49	Hearts*	41
1913–14*g*	Celtic	65	Rangers	59	Hearts*	54
1914–15*g*	Celtic	65	Hearts	61	Rangers	50
1915–16*g*	Celtic	67	Rangers	56	Morton	51
1916–17*g*	Celtic	64	Morton	54	Rangers	53
1917–18*f*	Rangers	56	Celtic	55	Kilmarnock	43
1918–19*f*	Celtic	58	Rangers	57	Morton	47
1919–20*h*	Rangers	71	Celtic	68	Motherwell	57
1920–21*h*	Rangers	76	Celtic	66	Hearts	56
1921–22*h*	Celtic	67	Rangers	66	Raith R	56
1922–23*g*	Rangers	55	Airdrieonians	50	Celtic	46
1923–24*g*	Rangers	59	Airdrieonians	50	Celtic	41
1924–25*g*	Rangers	60	Airdrieonians	57	Hibernian	52
1925–26*g*	Celtic	58	Airdrieonians*	50	Hearts	50
1926–27*g*	Rangers	56	Motherwell	51	Celtic	49
1927–28*g*	Rangers	60	Celtic*	55	Motherwell	55
1928–29*g*	Rangers	67	Celtic	51	Motherwell	50
1929–30*g*	Rangers	60	Motherwell	55	Aberdeen	53
1930–31*g*	Rangers	60	Celtic	58	Motherwell	56
1931–32*g*	Motherwell	66	Rangers	61	Celtic	48
1932–33*g*	Rangers	62	Motherwell	59	Hearts	50
1933–34*g*	Rangers	66	Motherwell	62	Celtic	47
1934–35*g*	Rangers	55	Celtic	52	Hearts	50
1935–36*g*	Celtic	66	Rangers*	61	Aberdeen	61
1936–37*g*	Rangers	61	Aberdeen	54	Celtic	52
1937–38*g*	Celtic	61	Hearts	58	Rangers	49
1938–39*g*	Rangers	59	Celtic	48	Aberdeen	46
1946–47*e*	Rangers	46	Hibernian	44	Aberdeen	39
1947–48*e*	Hibernian	48	Rangers	46	Partick T	36
1948–49*e*	Rangers	46	Dundee	45	Hibernian	39

1949–50*e*	Rangers	50	Hibernian	49	Hearts	43
1950–51*e*	Hibernian	48	Rangers*	38	Dundee	38
1951–52*e*	Hibernian	45	Rangers	41	East Fife	37
1952–53*e*	Rangers*	43	Hibernian	43	East Fife	39
1953–54*e*	Celtic	43	Hearts	38	Partick T	35
1954–55*e*	Aberdeen	49	Celtic	46	Rangers	41
1955–56*f*	Rangers	52	Aberdeen	46	Hearts*	45
1956–57*f*	Rangers	55	Hearts	53	Kilmarnock	42
1957–58*f*	Hearts	62	Rangers	49	Celtic	46
1958–59*f*	Rangers	50	Hearts	48	Motherwell	44
1959–60*f*	Hearts	54	Kilmarnock	50	Rangers*	42
1960–61*f*	Rangers	51	Kilmarnock	50	Third Lanark	42
1961–62*f*	Dundee	54	Rangers	51	Celtic	46
1962–63*f*	Rangers	57	Kilmarnock	48	Partick T	46
1963–64*f*	Rangers	55	Kilmarnock	49	Celtic*	47
1964–65*f*	Kilmarnock*	50	Hearts	50	Dunfermline Ath	49
1965–66*f*	Celtic	57	Rangers	55	Kilmarnock	45
1966–67*f*	Celtic	58	Rangers	55	Clyde	46
1967–68*f*	Celtic	63	Rangers	61	Hibernian	45
1968–69*f*	Celtic	54	Rangers	49	Dunfermline Ath	45
1969–70*f*	Celtic	57	Rangers	45	Hibernian	44
1970–71*f*	Celtic	56	Aberdeen	54	St Johnstone	44
1971–72*f*	Celtic	60	Aberdeen	50	Rangers	44
1972–73*f*	Celtic	57	Rangers	56	Hibernian	45
1973–74*f*	Celtic	53	Hibernian	49	Rangers	48
1974–75*f*	Rangers	56	Hibernian	49	Celtic	45

SECOND DIVISION to 1974–75

Maximum points: a 76; *b* 72; *c* 68; *d* 52; *e* 60; *f* 36; *g* 44; *h* 52.

1893–94*f*	Hibernian	29	Cowlairs	27	Clyde	24
1894–95*f*	Hibernian	30	Motherwell	22	Port Glasgow	20
1895–96*f*	Abercorn	27	Leith Ath	23	Renton	21
1896–97*f*	Partick T	31	Leith Ath	27	Kilmarnock	21
1897–98*f*	Kilmarnock	29	Port Glasgow	25	Morton	22
1898–99*f*	Kilmarnock	32	Leith Ath	27	Port Glasgow	25
1899–1900*f*	Partick T	29	Morton	26	Port Glasgow	20
1900–01*f*	St Bernard's	26	Airdrieonians	23	Abercorn	21
1901–02*g*	Port Glasgow	32	Partick T	31	Motherwell	26
1902–03*g*	Airdrieonians	35	Motherwell	28	Ayr U	27
1903–04*g*	Hamilton A	37	Clyde	29	Ayr U	28
1904–05*g*	Clyde	32	Falkirk	28	Hamilton A	27
1905–06*g*	Leith Ath	34	Clyde	31	Albion R	27
1906–07*g*	St Bernard's	32	Vale of Leven*	27	Arthurlie	27
1907–08*g*	Raith R	30	Dumbarton	‡‡27	Ayr U	27
1908–09*g*	Abercorn	31	Raith R*	28	Vale of Leven	28
1909–10*g*‡	Leith Ath	33	Raith R	33	St Bernard's	27
1910–11*g*	Dumbarton	31	Ayr U	27	Albion R	25
1911–12*g*	Ayr U	35	Abercorn	30	Dumbarton	27
1912–13*h*	Ayr U	34	Dunfarmline Ath	33	East Stirling	32
1913–14*g*	Cowdenbeath	31	Albion R	27	Dunfermline Ath	26
1914–15*h*	Cowdenbeath*	37	St Bernard's*	37	Leith Ath	37
1921–22*a*	Alloa	60	Cowdenbeath	47	Armadale	45
1922–23*a*	Queen's Park	57	Clydebank	¶50	St Johnstone	¶45
1923–24*a*	St Johnstone	56	Cowdenbeath	55	Bathgate	44
1924–25*a*	Dundee U	50	Clydebank	48	Clyde	47
1925–26*a*	Dunfermline Ath	59	Clyde	53	Ayr U	52
1926–27*a*	Bo'ness	56	Raith R	49	Clydebank	45
1927–28*a*	Ayr U	54	Third Lanark	45	King's Park	44
1928–29*b*	Dundee U	51	Morton	50	Arbroath	47
1929–30*a*	Leith Ath*	57	East Fife	57	Albion R	54
1930–31*a*	Third Lanark	61	Dundee U	50	Dunfermline Ath	47
1931–32*a*	East Stirling*	55	St Johnstone	55	Raith Rovers*	46
1932–33*c*	Hibernian	54	Queen of the S	49	Dunfermline Ath	47
1933–34*c*	Albion R	45	Dunfermline Ath*	44	Arbroath	44
1934–35*c*	Third Lanark	52	Arbroath	50	St Bernard's	47
1935–36*c*	Falkirk	59	St Mirren	52	Morton	48
1936–37*c*	Ayr U	54	Morton	51	St Bernard's	48
1937–38*c*	Raith R	59	Albion R	48	Airdrieonians	47
1938–39*c*	Cowdenbeath	60	Alloa*	48	East Fife	48
1946–47*d*	Dundee	45	Airdrieonians	42	East Fife	31
1947–48*e*	East Fife	53	Albion R	42	Hamilton A	40
1948–49*e*	Raith R*	42	Stirling Albion	42	Airdrieonians*	41
1949–50*e*	Morton	47	Airdrieonians	44	St Johnstone*	36
1950–51*e*	Queen of the S*	45	Stirling Albion	45	Ayr U	36

1951–52*e*	Clyde	44	Falkirk	43	Ayr U	39
1952–53*e*	Stirling Albion	44	Hamilton A	43	Queen's Park	37
1953–54*e*	Motherwell	45	Kilmarnock	42	Third Lanark*	36
1954–55*e*	Airdrieonians	46	Dunfermline Ath	42	Hamilton A	39
1955–56*b*	Queen's Park	54	Ayr U	51	St Johnstone	49
1956–57*b*	Clyde	64	Third Lanark	51	Cowdenbeath	45
1957–58*b*	Stirling Albion	55	Dunfermline Ath	53	Arbroath	47
1958–59*b*	Ayr U	60	Arbroath	51	Stenhousemuir	40
1959–60*b*	St Johnstone	53	Dundee U	50	Queen of the S	49
1960–61*b*	Stirling Albion	55	Falkirk	54	Stenhousemuir	50
1961–62*b*	Clyde	54	Queen of the S	53	Morton	44
1962–63*b*	St Johnstone	55	East Stirling	49	Morton	48
1963–64*b*	Morton	67	Clyde	53	Arbroath	46
1964–65*b*	Stirling Albion	59	Hamilton A	50	Queen of the S	45
1965–66*b*	Ayr U	53	Airdrieonians	50	Queen of the S	49
1966–67*b*	Morton	69	Raith R	58	Arbroath	57
1967–68*b*	St Mirren	62	Arbroath	53	East Fife	40
1968–69*b*	Motherwell	64	Ayr U	53	East Fife*	47
1969–70*b*	Falkirk	56	Cowdenbeath	55	Queen of the S	50
1970–71*b*	Partick T	56	East Fife	51	Arbroath	46
1971–72*b*	Dumbarton*	52	Arbroath	52	Stirling Albion	50
1972–73*b*	Clyde	56	Dumfermline Ath	52	Raith R*	47
1973–74*b*	Airdrieonians	60	Kilmarnock	59	Hamilton A	55
1974–75*a*	Falkirk	54	Queen of the S	53	Montrose	53

Elected to First Division: 1894 Clyde; 1897 Partick T; 1899 Kilmarnock; 1900 Partick T; 1902 Partick T; 1903 Airdrieonians; 1905 Falkirk, Aberdeen and Hamilton A; 1906 Clyde; 1910 Raith R; 1913 Ayr U.

RELEGATED FROM PREMIER DIVISION

1975–76 Dundee, St Johnstone
1976–77 Hearts, Kilmarnock
1977–78 Ayr U, Clydebank
1978–79 Hearts, Motherwell
1979–80 Dundee, Hibernian
1980–81 Kilmarnock, Hearts
1981–82 Partick T, Airdrieonians
1982–83 Morton, Kilmarnock
1983–84 St Johnstone, Motherwell
1984–85 Dumbarton, Morton
1985–86 *No relegation due to League reorganization*
1986–87 Clydebank, Hamilton A
1987–88 Falkirk, Dunfermline Ath, Morton
1988–89 Hamilton A
1989–90 Dundee
1990–91 None
1991–92 St Mirren, Dunfermline Ath
1992–93 Falkirk, Airdrieonians
1993–94 *See footnote*
1994–95 Dundee U

RELEGATED FROM DIVISION 1

1975–76 Dunfermline Ath, Clyde
1976–77 Raith R, Falkirk
1977–78 Alloa Ath, East Fife
1978–79 Montrose, Queen of the S
1979–80 Arbroath, Clyde
1980–81 Stirling A, Berwick R
1981–82 East Stirling, Queen of the S
1982–83 Dunfermline Ath, Queen's Park
1983–84 Raith R, Alloa
1984–85 Meadowbank T, St Johnstone
1985–86 Ayr U, Alloa
1986–87 Brechin C, Montrose
1987–88 East Fife, Dumbarton
1988–89 Kilmarnock, Queen of the S
1989–90 Albion R, Alloa
1990–91 Clyde, Brechin C
1991–92 Montrose, Forfar Ath
1992–93 Meadowbank T, Cowdenbeath
1993–94 *See footnote*
1994–95 Ayr U, Stranraer

RELEGATED FROM DIVISION 2

1994–95 Meadowbank T, Brechin C

RELEGATED FROM DIVISION 1 (TO 1973–74)

1921–22 *Queen's Park, Dumbarton, Clydebank
1922–23 Albion R, Alloa Ath
1923–24 Clyde, Clydebank
1924–25 Third Lanark, Ayr U
1925–26 Raith R, Clydebank
1926–27 Morton, Dundee U
1927–28 Dunfermline Ath, Bo'ness
1928–29 Third Lanark, Raith R
1929–30 St Johnstone, Dundee U
1930–31 Hibernian, East Fife
1931–32 Dundee U, Leith Ath
1932–33 Morton, East Stirling
1933–34 Third Lanark, Cowdenbeath
1934–35 St Mirren, Falkirk
1935–36 Airdrieonians, Ayr U
1936–37 Dunfermline Ath, Albion R
1937–38 Dundee, Morton
1938–39 Queen's Park, Raith R
1946–47 Kilmarnock, Hamilton A
1947–48 Airdrieonians, Queen's Park
1948–49 Morton, Albion R
1949–50 Queen of the S, Stirling Albion
1950–51 Clyde, Falkirk
1951–52 Morton, Stirling Albion
1952–53 Motherwell, Third Lanark
1953–54 Airdrieonians, Hamilton A
1954–55 *No clubs relegated*
1955–56 Stirling Albion, Clyde
1956–57 Dunfermline Ath, Ayr U
1957–58 East Fife, Queen's Park
1958–59 Queen of the S, Falkirk
1959–60 Arbroath, Stirling Albion
1960–61 Ayr U, Clyde
1961–62 St Johnstone, Stirling Albion
1962–63 Clyde, Raith R
1963–64 Queen of the S, East Stirling
1964–65 Airdrieonians, Third Lanark
1965–66 Morton, Hamilton A

1966–67 St Mirren, Ayr U
1967–68 Motherwell, Stirling Albion
1968–69 Falkirk, Arbroath
1969–70 Raith R, Partick T
1970–71 St Mirren, Cowdenbeath
1971–72 Clyde, Dunfermline Ath
1972–73 Kilmarnock, Airdrieonians
1973–74 East Fife, Falkirk

*Season 1921–22 – only 1 club promoted, 3 clubs relegated.

Scottish League championship wins: Rangers 45, Celtic 35, Aberdeen 4, Hearts 4, Hibernian 4, Dumbarton 2, Dundee 1, Dundee United 1, Kilmarnock 1, Motherwell 1, Third Lanark 1.

At the end of the 1993–94 season four divisions were created assisted by the admission of two new clubs Ross County and Caledonian Thistle. Only one club was promoted from Division 1 and Division 2. Three relegated from the Premier joined with teams finishing second to seventh in Division 1 to form the new Division 1. Five relegated from Division 1 combined with those who finished second to sixth to form a new Division 2 and the bottom eight in Division 2 linked with the two newcomers to form a new Division 3.

Rangers Brian Laudrup is tackled by Mick Galloway of Celtic. (Action Images)

SCOTTISH LEAGUE CUP FINALS 1946–95

Season	*Winners*	*Runners-up*	*Score*
1946–47	Rangers	Aberdeen	4-0
1947–48	East Fife	Falkirk	4-1 after 0-0 draw
1948–49	Rangers	Raith R	2-0
1949–50	East Fife	Dunfermline Ath	3-0
1950–51	Motherwell	Hibernian	3-0
1951–52	Dundee	Rangers	3-2
1952–53	Dundee	Kilmarnock	2-0
1953–54	East Fife	Partick T	3-2
1954–55	Hearts	Motherwell	4-2
1955–56	Aberdeen	St Mirren	2-1
1956–57	Celtic	Partick T	3-0 after 0-0 draw
1957–58	Celtic	Rangers	7-1
1958–59	Hearts	Partick T	5-1
1959–60	Hearts	Third Lanark	2-1
1960–61	Rangers	Kilmarnock	2-0
1961–62	Rangers	Hearts	3-1 after 1-1 draw
1962–63	Hearts	Kilmarnock	1-0
1963–64	Rangers	Morton	5-0
1964–65	Rangers	Celtic	2-1
1965–66	Celtic	Rangers	2-1
1966–67	Celtic	Rangers	1-0
1967–68	Celtic	Dundee	5-3
1968–69	Celtic	Hibernian	6-2
1969–70	Celtic	St Johnstone	1-0
1970–71	Rangers	Celtic	1-0
1971–72	Partick T	Celtic	4-1
1972–73	Hibernian	Celtic	2-1
1973–74	Dundee	Celtic	1-0
1974–75	Celtic	Hibernian	6-3
1975–76	Rangers	Celtic	1-0
1976–77	Aberdeen	Celtic	2-1
1977–78	Rangers	Celtic	2-1
1978–79	Rangers	Aberdeen	2-1
1979–80	Dundee U	Aberdeen	3-0 after 0-0 draw
1980–81	Dundee U	Dundee	3-0
1981–82	Rangers	Dundee U	2-1
1982–83	Celtic	Rangers	2-1
1983–84	Rangers	Celtic	3-2
1984–85	Rangers	Dundee U	1-0
1985–86	Aberdeen	Hibernian	3-0
1986–87	Rangers	Celtic	2-1
1987–88	Rangers	Aberdeen	3-3
		(Rangers won 5-3 on penalties)	
1988–89	Rangers	Aberdeen	3-2
1989–90	Aberdeen	Rangers	2-1
1990–91	Rangers	Celtic	2-1
1991–92	Hibernian	Dunfermline Ath	2-0
1992–93	Rangers	Aberdeen	2-1
1993–94	Rangers	Hibernian	2-1
1994–95	Raith R	Celtic	2-2
		(Raith R won 6-5 on penalties)	

SCOTTISH LEAGUE CUP WINS

Rangers 19, Celtic 9, Hearts 4, Aberdeen 4, Dundee 3, East Fife 3, Dundee U 2, Hibernian 2, Motherwell 1, Partick T 1, Raith R 1.

APPEARANCES IN FINALS

Rangers 25, Celtic 21, Aberdeen 10, Hibernian 7, Dundee 5, Hearts 5, Dundee U 4, Partick T 4, East Fife 3, Kilmarnock 3, Dunfermline Ath 2, Motherwell 2, Raith R 2, Falkirk 1, Morton 1, St Johnstone 1, St Mirren 1, Third Lanark 1.

COCA-COLA CUP 1994–95

FIRST ROUND

9 AUG

Berwick R (0) 0
Montrose (0) 0 *aet* 515

Berwick R: Young N; Bell, Banks, Valentine, Cole (Fraser), Wilson, Forrester, Neil, Hawke, Irvine, Kane.
Montrose: Larter; Robertson, Tindal, Craib, Grant, Haro, Garden, Stephen, McGlashan, Kennedy, Masson.
(Montrose won 3-2 on penalties)

East Fife (0) 1 *(Allan)*
Forfar Ath (0) 0 797

East Fife: Wilson; Bell, Williamson, Barron, Sneddon, Hildersley, Cusick (Allan), Hope, Scott (Irvine), Hunter, Gibb.
Forfar Ath: Arthur; McLaren, McPhee, Mann, Archibald, McKillop, O'Neill, Irvine, Lees, Bingham, Heddle.

East Stirling (0) 0
Caledonian T (2) 2 *(Robertson, Lee I (og))* 899

East Stirling: Moffat; Watt, Cuthbert, Russell, Yates, Lee R, Lee I, Millar, McCallum, Scott (Stirling), Geraghty.
Caledonian T: McRitchie; Brennan, McAllister, Hercher, Scott, Andrew, MacDonald, MacKenzie (Smart), Noble, Bennett, Robertson.

Stenhousemuir (0) 0 396
Meadowbank T (1) 4 *(Bailey, McLeod, Hutchison, Little)*

Stenhousemuir: Harkness; Aitken, Hallford, Clarke (Hutchison), McGeachie, Christie, Steel, Haddow, Mathieson, Sludden (Henderson), Sprott.
Meadowbank T: Ellison; Graham, Fleming, Wilson, Williamson, Hutchison, Duthie, McLeod, Little, Rutherford (Price), Bailey (Thorburn).

10 AUG

Arbroath (0) 1 *(Reilly)*
Alloa (1) 1 *(Morrison) aet* 750

Arbroath: Jackson; Mitchell, McKinnon, Murray, Elder, McGovern, Downie, Reilly (Elliot), Brock, Tosh, Finlay.
Alloa: Butter; McNiven (Nelson), Kemp, Campbell, McCulloch, McCormack J, Morrison, Cadden, McCormick S, Bennett, Willock (McAvoy).
(Arbroath won 5-4 on penalties)

Queen of the S (0) 2 *(McLaren, Bryce)*
Albion R (0) 0 1304

Queen of the S: Purdie; Hetherington, Rowe (Sermanni), McKeown D, Mills, Kennedy, McGuire, Bryce, McLaren, McFarlane, Mallan.
Albion R: Davidson; Riley, Conn, McDonald, Malone, Collins, Walker (McBride M), Docherty, Thompson, Quinn, Gallagher.

Ross Co (1) 3 *(Grant 2, MacPherson)*
Queen's Park (0) 2 *(Orr G, Maxwell)* 1924

Ross Co: Hutchison; Somerville, Campbell, Williamson, Alex MacLeod, Andrew MacLeod, Ferries, Grant, MacPherson, Herd, Wilson (Robertson).
Queen's Park: Moonie; Fitzpatrick, Kavanagh, Kerr, Maxwell, Orr G, Campbell (Bradley), Graham, Brodie, McCormick (Edgar), Rodden.

Stranraer (1) 2 *(Cody, Ferguson)*
Cowdenbeath (1) 2 *(Black, Soutar) aet* 776

Stranraer: Ross; Millar, Hughes, Cody, Brannigan, Howard (McLean), Reilly, Grant, Walker (Ferguson), Duncan, Henderson.
Cowdenbeath: Russell; Scott, Hamill, Malloy, Humphreys, Davidson, Carr (Winter), Black, Soutar (Lynch), Thomson, Stout.
(Stranraer won 4-2 on penalties)

SECOND ROUND

16 AUG

Ayr U (0) 0
Celtic (1) 1 *(Grant)* 8182

Ayr U: Duncan; Burns, McVicar, Paterson, Rolling, Sharples, Traynor (Moore), McKilligan, McGivern, Gilzean (Woods), Connie.
Celtic: Marshall; Martin, Boyd, McNally, Mowbray, Grant, Galloway, McStay, Falconer, Walker (Donnelly), Collins.

Dumbarton (0) 0
Hearts (2) 4 *(Millar, Robertson, Johnston A 2)* 1412

Dumbarton: MacFarlane; Marsland, Boyd, Melvin, Martin, MacLeod, Mooney M, Meechan, Gibson, McGarvey, Ward (Campbell).
Hearts: Walker; Frail, McKinlay (Leitch), Levein, MacKay (Weir), McLaren, Colquhoun, Johnston A, Robertson, Johnston M, Millar.

Falkirk (0) 1 *(Cadette)*
Montrose (0) 1 *(Kennedy) aet* 2467

Falkirk: Parks; Hamilton, Weir (James), Oliver, McLaughlin, McKenzie, May, Fulton, Cadette, McCall, Johnston (McDonald).
Montrose: Larter; Robertson, Tindal, Craib, Grant, Haro, Garden (Cooper), Stephen, McGlashan, Kennedy, Masson.
(Falkirk won 5-4 on penalties)

Greenock Morton (1) 1 *(Lilley)*
Airdrieonians (1) 1 *(Andrew Smith) aet* 1417

Greenock Morton: Wylie; Collins, Pickering (Anderson), Hunter, McCahill, Johnstone, Lilley, Fowler, Alexander, McArthur, Cormack.
Airdrieonians: Martin; Stewart, Tony Smith, Sandison, McIntyre T, Hay (Boyle), Harvey (Ferguson), Wilson, Andrew Smith, Black, Lawrence.
(Airdrieonians won 5-3 on penalties)

Motherwell (1) 3 *(Burns, Coyne (pen), Kirk)*
Clydebank (0) 1 *(Grady)* 4172

Motherwell: Woods; Philliben, McKinnon, Davies (Ritchie), McLeish, Martin, Lambert, Burns, Coyne, O'Donnell, Arnott (Kirk).
Clydebank: Matthews; Lansdowne (Kerrigan), Bowman, Murdoch, Sweeney, Currie, Cooper, Harris, Eadie (Sutherland), Grady, Jack.

Partick T (3) 5 *(Taylor, Jamieson, Charnley 3 (1 pen))*
Brechin C (0) 0 1970

Partick T: Nelson; Byrne, Law, Jamieson, Tierney, McWilliams (Cameron), Taylor, Smith, Grant, English, Charnley.
Brechin C: Balfour; Conway, Christie, Cairney, Nicolson, Scott, Bell, Vannett, McNeill (McKellar), Millar, Kemlo.

St Mirren (0) 0

Dundee U (0) 1 *(Ristic) aet* 3002

St Mirren: Combe; Hick (Gillies R), Watson, McLaughlin, Taylor, McIntyre, Gillies K (Hetherston), Bone, Lavety, Gardner, Elliot.
Dundee U: Jorgensen; McInally (Craig), Bollan, Hannah, Petric, Welsh, Bowman, Perry, Ristic, Brewster, Nixon (Connolly).

17 AUG

Aberdeen (0) 1 *(Shearer)*

Stranraer (0) 0 8158

Aberdeen: Snelders; McKimmie, Winnie, Grant, Irvine, Wright, Jess (Miller), Shearer (Booth), Kane, Dodds, Robertson.
Stranraer: Ross; Treanor, Hughes, McCaffrey (Ferguson), Brannigan, Millar, McLean, Duncan (Brown), Walker, Cody, Henderson.

Arbroath (1) 1 *(McKinnon)*

Rangers (3) 6 *(Hateley 2, Ferguson D 3, McCall)* 4556

Arbroath: Jackson; Mitchell, Rae, Farnan, Elder, Murray, Downie (Finlay), McKinnon, Reilly (Brock), Tosh, McGovern.
Rangers: Maxwell; McCall, Brown, Gough, Boli, McPherson, Moore, Ferguson I, Ferguson D, Hateley, Durrant (Murray).

Dundee (1) 3 *(Shaw, Tosh 2)*

Caledonian T (0) 0 3112

Dundee: Pageaud; McQuillan, Pittman, McKeown, Blake, Dinnie, Shaw, Anderson (Tosh), Duffy C, Britton (Farningham), McCann.
Caledonian T: McRitchie; Brennan, McAllister, Hercher, Scott, Andrew, Smart, MacKenzie (MacDonald), Noble, Bennett, Robertson.

Dunfermline Ath (2) 4 *(McCathie, Den Bieman, Petrie, Ward)*

Meadowbank T (0) 1 *(Sorbie)* 3230

Dunfermline Ath: Westwater; Den Bieman, Bowes, McCathie, Cooper, Smith, McNamara, Robertson, Tod (Laing), Petrie, Moore (Ward).
Meadowbank T: Ellison; Graham, Fleming, Wilson, Williamson, Hutchison (Thorburn), Duthie, McLeod, Little (Coyle), Sorbie, Bailey.

Hamilton A (1) 5 *(McEntegart, Baptie, McLean, Campbell, Sherry)*

Clyde (0) 0 942

Hamilton A: Ferguson; McKenzie, McInulty, McEntegart, Baptie, McIntosh, McQuade, Sherry, Chalmers (McLean), Duffield, Lorimer (Campbell).
Clyde: Fridge; Clark (O'Neill), Neil (Frater), Knox, Thomson, Strain, Watson, Wright, McConnell, McAulay, Parks.

Kilmarnock (2) 4 *(Henry, McCluskey, Maskrey 2)*

East Fife (0) 1 *(Hope)* 4243

Kilmarnock: Geddes; MacPherson, Black, Montgomerie, Reilly, Millen, Mitchell, Henry, Maskrey, McCluskey (Williamson), Connor (McSkimming).
East Fife: Wilson; Bell, Williamson, Barron, Sneddon, Hildersley (Cusick), Allan, Hope, Scott (Irvine), Hunter, Gibb.

Queen of the S (0) 0

Hibernian (2) 3 *(Evans, Tweed, O'Neill)* 5022

Queen of the S: Purdie; Hetherington, McKeown D, McKeown B (Adams), Mills, McFarlane, McGuire, Kennedy, McLaren (Sermanni), Bryce, Mallan.
Hibernian: Leighton; Miller, Mitchell, Findlay, Tweed, Hunter (Beaumont), McAllister, Hamilton, Evans, Jackson D, O'Neill (Harper).

Ross Co (0) 0

Raith R (0) 5 *(Cameron, Graham 3, Dalziel)* 2288

Ross Co: Hutchison; Somerville, Campbell, Williamson, Alex MacLeod, Andrew MacLeod, Ferries, Grant (Duff), MacPherson, Herd, Wilson.
Raith R: Thomson; Rowbotham, Kirkwood (Broddle), Coyle, Raeside, Sinclair, Lennon, Dalziel, Graham, Cameron (Crawford), Dair.

Stirling Albion (0) 0

St Johnstone (1) 2 *(O'Boyle, Scott)* 1512

Stirling Albion: McGeown; Hamilton, Armstrong, Mitchell, McQuilter, Tait, Reid (McInnes), Roberts, Watters, Taggart, McLeod.
St Johnstone: Rhodes; McGinnis, Miller, Turner, Inglis, McGowne (Scott), O'Neil, Ramsey, Davenport, O'Boyle, Irons.

THIRD ROUND

30 AUG

Hibernian (1) 2 *(O'Neill 2)*

Dunfermline Ath (0) 0 9305

Hibernian: Leighton; Beaumont, Tortolano, Findlay (Farrell), Tweed, Hunter (Harper), McAllister, Hamilton, Evans, Jackson D, O'Neill.
Dunfermline Ath: Will; Den Bieman, Bowes, McCathie, Cooper, Smith, Ward, Robertson, French, Petrie, Tod (Laing).

Partick T (0) 0

Aberdeen (2) 5 *(Shearer 3 (1 pen), Kane, Dodds)* 5046

Partick T: Nelson; Byrne, Law, Jamieson, Tierney, McWilliams, Taylor, Cameron, Grant (Smith), English, Charnley.
Aberdeen: Snelders; McKimmie, Woodthorpe, Grant, Irvine (Winnie), Wright, Jess, Shearer, Kane, Dodds, McKinnon (Booth).

31 AUG

Dundee (1) 1 *(Farningham)*

Celtic (1) 2 *(Collins, Walker)* 11,431

Dundee: Pageaud; McQuillan, Duffy J, Duffy C, Blake (Teasdale), Farningham, Shaw, Vrto, Wieghorst (Tosh), Britton, McCann.
Celtic: Marshall; Grant, Boyd, McNally, Mowbray, McGinlay, Galloway, McStay, Donnelly (Nicholas), Walker, Collins.

Hamilton A (0) 2 *(Cleland (og), Duffield)*

Dundee U (1) 2 *(Hannah 2) aet* 2180

Hamilton A: Ferguson; McKenzie, McInulty, McEntegart, Baptie, McIntosh, McLean (McQuade), Sherry, Chalmers (Hartley), Duffield, Nicholls.
Dundee U: Main; Cleland, McInally, Hannah, Petric, Dailly, Bowman, McKinlay, Ristic (Myers), Brewster (Nixon), McLaren.
(Dundee U won 5-3 on penalties)

Hearts (2) 2 *(Locke, Colquhoun)*

St Johnstone (0) 4 *(O'Neil, Miller, O'Boyle, Irons)* 8467

Hearts: Walker; Frail, Weir, Levein, Berry, McLaren, Colquhoun, Locke, Robertson, Johnston A (Foster) (Harrison), Millar.
St Johnstone: Rhodes; Cherry, Miller, Ramsey, McGinnis, Deas (Preston), O'Neil, Davies, Davenport, O'Boyle, Irons.

Motherwell (0) 1 *(McCart)*
Airdrieonians (1) 2 *(Boyle 2) aet* 6010

Motherwell: Woods; Shannon, Philliben, Dolan (Davies), Martin, McCart, Lambert, Burns (Kirk), Coyne, O'Donnell, Roddie.
Airdrieonians: Martin; Boyle, Stewart, Sandison, McIntyre T, Black, Lawrence (McIntyre J), Harvey, Smith (Ferguson), Wilson, Jack.

Raith R (2) 3 *(Cameron 3)*
Kilmarnock (1) 2 *(Montgomerie, Williamson)* 4181

Raith R: Thomson; McAnespie, Broddle, Rowbotham, Narey, Sinclair, Lennon, Dalziel (Crawford), Graham, Cameron, Redford (Coyle).
Kilmarnock: Geddes; MacPherson, Black, Montgomerie, Reilly, Millen, Mitchell, Napier (Williamson), Brown, Connor, Maskrey.

Rangers (0) 1 *(Laudrup)*
Falkirk (1) 2 *(Cadette 2)* 40,741

Rangers: Goram; McCall, Robertson, Gough, McPherson (Ferguson D), Moore, Durrant, Ferguson I, Durie, Hateley, Laudrup.
Falkirk: Parks; Weir, McGowan, Oliver, McLaughlin, McKenzie, May, Fulton, Cadette, Henderson (Cramb), McDonald.

QUARTER-FINALS

20 SEPT

St Johnstone (0) 1 *(O'Neil)*
Raith R (2) 3 *(Dennis, Graham, Lennon)* 6287

St Johnstone: Rhodes; Cherry, Miller, Ramsey (Preston), McGinnis, McGowne, O'Neil, Turner (McMartin), Davenport, O'Boyle, Irons.
Raith R: Thomson; McAnespie, Broddle, Rowbotham, Dennis, Sinclair, Nicholl, Crawford (Dair), Graham, Cameron, Lennon.

21 SEPT

Celtic (0) 1 *(Collins)*
Dundee U (0) 0 28,859

Celtic: Marshall; Galloway, Boyd, McNally, Mowbray, Grant, McGinlay, McStay (O'Neil B), Donnelly (Nicholas), Walker, Collins.
Dundee U: Main; Cleland, Malpas, Hannah, Petric, Welsh, McInally (Myers), McKinlay, Ristic, Connolly (Brewster), Nixon.

Falkirk (1) 1 *(McDonald)*
Aberdeen (2) 4 *(Booth 3, Rice (og))* 9450

Falkirk: Parks; McGowan, McQueen, Clark, McLaughlin, McKenzie, May, Henderson (McAvennie), Cadette, Rice, McDonald.
Aberdeen: Watt; McKimmie, Woodthorpe, Grant, Winnie, Wright, Jess, Smith, Booth, Dodds (Miller), McKinnon.

Hibernian (0) 1 *(Evans)*
Airdrieonians (2) 2 *(Andrew Smith, Lawrence)* 9578

Hibernian: Leighton; Miller, Farrell, Jackson C (Harper), Tweed, Hunter, McAllister, Hamilton, Evans, Jackson D, O'Neill.
Airdrieonians: Martin; Boyle, Jack, Sandison, McIntyre T, Stewart, Harvey (Hay), Wilson, Andrew Smith, Black, Lawrence (McIntyre J).

SEMI-FINALS

25 OCT at McDiarmid Park

Airdrieonians (0) 1 *(Cooper)*
Raith R (1) 1 *(Graham) aet* 7260

Airdrieonians: Martin; Stewart, Jack, Sandison, Hay, Black, Boyle, Wilson (McIntyre T), Cooper, Harvey (Andrew Smith), Lawrence.
Raith R: Thomson; McAnespie, Broddle (Rowbotham), Sinclair, Dennis, Narey, Lennon, Dalziel (Crawford), Graham, Cameron, Kirkwood (Potter).
(Raith R won 5-4 on penalties)

26 OCT at Ibrox Stadium

Celtic (0) 1 *(O'Neil B)*
Aberdeen (0) 0 44,000

Celtic: Marshall; Smith, Boyd, McNally, O'Neil B, Grant, Byrne (McGinlay), McStay, Donnelly, Walker (Nicholas), Collins.
Aberdeen: Snelders; McKimmie, Woodthorpe, Grant, Winnie, Wright, Smith, Kane (Robertson), Booth, Dodds, McKinnon (Hetherston).

FINAL at Ibrox Stadium

27 NOV

Raith R (1) 2 *(Crawford, Dalziel)*
Celtic (1) 2 *(Walker, Nicholas) aet* 45,384

Raith R: Thomson; McAnespie, Broddle (Rowbotham), Narey, Dennis, Sinclair, Crawford, Dalziel (Redford), Graham, Cameron, Dair.
Celtic: Marshall; Galloway, Boyd, McNally, Mowbray, O'Neil B, Donnelly (Falconer), McStay, Nicholas (Byrne), Walker, Collins.
(Raith R won 6-5 on penalties)
Referee: J McCluskey (Stewarton).

SCOTTISH CUP FINALS 1874–1995

Year	*Winners*	*Runners-up*	*Score*
1874	Queen's Park	Clydesdale	2-0
1875	Queen's Park	Renton	3-0
1876	Queen's Park	Third Lanark	2-0 after 1-1 draw
1877	Vale of Leven	Rangers	3-2 after 0-0 and 1-1 draws
1878	Vale of Leven	Third Lanark	1-0
1879	Vale of Leven*	Rangers	
1880	Queen's Park	Thornlibank	3-0
1881	Queen's Park†	Dumbarton	3-1
1882	Queen's Park	Dumbarton	4-1 after 2-2 draw
1883	Dumbarton	Vale of Leven	2-1 after 2-2 draw
1884	Queen's Park‡	Vale of Leven	
1885	Renton	Vale of Leven	3-1 after 0-0 draw
1886	Queen's Park	Renton	3-1
1887	Hibernian	Dumbarton	2-1
1888	Renton	Cambuslang	6-1
1889	Third Lanark§	Celtic	2-1
1890	Queen's Park	Vale of Leven	2-1 after 1-1 draw
1891	Hearts	Dumbarton	1-0
1892	Celtic¶	Queen's Park	5-1
1893	Queen's Park	Celtic	2-1
1894	Rangers	Celtic	3-1
1895	St Bernard's	Renton	2-1
1896	Hearts	Hibernian	3-1
1897	Rangers	Dumbarton	5-1
1898	Rangers	Kilmarnock	2-0
1899	Celtic	Rangers	2-0
1900	Celtic	Queen's Park	4-3
1901	Hearts	Celtic	4-3
1902	Hibernian	Celtic	1-0
1903	Rangers	Hearts	2-0 after 1-1 and 0-0 draws
1904	Celtic	Rangers	3-2
1905	Third Lanark	Rangers	3-1 after 0-0 draw
1906	Hearts	Third Lanark	1-0
1907	Celtic	Hearts	3-0
1908	Celtic	St Mirren	5-1
1909	●●		
1910	Dundee	Clyde	2-1 after 2-2 and 0-0 draws
1911	Celtic	Hamilton A	2-0 after 0-0 draw
1912	Celtic	Clyde	2-0
1913	Falkirk	Raith R	2-0
1914	Celtic	Hibernian	4-1 after 0-0 draw
1920	Kilmarnock	Albion R	3-2
1921	Partick T	Rangers	1-0
1922	Morton	Rangers	1-0
1923	Celtic	Hibernian	1-0
1924	Airdrieonians	Hibernian	2-0
1925	Celtic	Dundee	2-1
1926	St Mirren	Celtic	2-0
1927	Celtic	East Fife	3-1
1928	Rangers	Celtic	4-0
1929	Kilmarnock	Rangers	2-0
1930	Rangers	Partick T	2-1 after 0-0 draw
1931	Celtic	Motherwell	4-2 after 2-2 draw
1932	Rangers	Kilmarnock	3-0 after 1-1 draw
1933	Celtic	Motherwell	1-0
1934	Rangers	St Mirren	5-0
1935	Rangers	Hamilton A	2-1
1936	Rangers	Third Lanark	1-0
1937	Celtic	Aberdeen	2-1
1938	East Fife	Kilmarnock	4-2 after 1-1 draw
1939	Clyde	Motherwell	4-0
1947	Aberdeen	Hibernian	2-1
1948	Rangers	Morton	1-0 after 1-1 draw
1949	Rangers	Clyde	4-1
1950	Rangers	East Fife	3-0
1951	Celtic	Motherwell	1-0
1952	Motherwell	Dundee	4-0
1953	Rangers	Aberdeen	1-0 after 1-1 draw
1954	Celtic	Aberdeen	2-1
1955	Clyde	Celtic	1-0 after 1-1 draw
1956	Hearts	Celtic	3-1
1957	Falkirk	Kilmarnock	2-1 after 1-1 draw
1958	Clyde	Hibernian	1-0
1959	St Mirren	Aberdeen	3-1
1960	Rangers	Kilmarnock	2-0
1961	Dunfermline Ath	Celtic	2-0 after 0-0 draw
1962	Rangers	St Mirren	2-0
1963	Rangers	Celtic	3-0 after 1-1 draw
1964	Rangers	Dundee	3-1

Year	Winners	Runners-up	Score
1965	Celtic	Dunfermline Ath	3-2
1966	Rangers	Celtic	1-0 after 0-0 draw
1967	Celtic	Aberdeen	2-0
1968	Dunfermline Ath	Hearts	3-1
1969	Celtic	Rangers	4-0
1970	Aberdeen	Celtic	3-1
1971	Celtic	Rangers	2-1 after 1-1 draw
1972	Celtic	Hibernian	6-1
1973	Rangers	Celtic	3-2
1974	Celtic	Dundee U	3-0
1975	Celtic	Airdrieonians	3-1
1976	Rangers	Hearts	3-1
1977	Celtic	Rangers	1-0
1978	Rangers	Aberdeen	2-1
1979	Rangers	Hibernian	3-2 after 0-0 and 0-0 draws
1980	Celtic	Rangers	1-0
1981	Rangers	Dundee U	4-1 after 0-0 draw
1982	Aberdeen	Rangers	4-1 (aet)
1983	Aberdeen	Rangers	1-0 (aet)
1984	Aberdeen	Celtic	2-1 (aet)
1985	Celtic	Dundee U	2-1
1986	Aberdeen	Hearts	3-0
1987	St Mirren	Dundee U	1-0 (aet)
1988	Celtic	Dundee U	2-1
1989	Celtic	Rangers	1-0
1990	Aberdeen	Celtic	0-0 (aet)
		(Aberdeen won 9-8 on penalties)	
1991	Motherwell	Dundee U	4-3 (aet)
1992	Rangers	Airdrieonians	2-1
1993	Rangers	Aberdeen	2-1
1994	Dundee U	Rangers	1-0
1995	Celtic	Airdrieonians	1-0

*Vale of Leven awarded cup, Rangers failing to appear for replay after 1-1 draw.
†After Dumbarton protested the first game, which Queen's Park won 2-1.
‡Queen's Park awarded cup, Vale of Leven failing to appear.
§Replay by order of Scottish FA because of playing conditions in first match, won 3-0 by Third Lanark.
¶After mutually protested game which Celtic won 1-0.
●●Owing to riot, the cup was withheld after two drawn games – Celtic 2-1, Rangers 2-1.

SCOTTISH CUP WINS

Celtic 30, Rangers 26, Queen's Park 10, Aberdeen 7, Hearts 5, Clyde 3, St Mirren 3, Vale of Leven 3, Dunfermline Ath 2, Falkirk 2, Hibernian 2, Kilmarnock 2, Motherwell 2, Renton 2, Third Lanark 2, Airdrieonians 1, Dumbarton 1, Dundee 1, Dundee U 1, East Fife 1, Morton 1, Partick Th 1, St Bernard's 1.

APPEARANCES IN FINAL

Celtic 47, Rangers 43, Aberdeen 14, Queen's Park 12, Hearts 10, Hibernian 10, Kilmarnock 7, Vale of Leven 7, Clyde 6, Dumbarton 6, St Mirren 6, Third Lanark 6, Dundee U 7, Motherwell 6, Renton 5, Airdrieonians 4, Dundee 4, Dunfermline Ath 3, East Fife 3, Falkirk 2, Hamilton A 2, Morton 2, Partick Th 2, Albion R 1, Cambuslang 1, Clydesdale 1, Raith R 1, St Bernard's 1, Thornlibank 1.

SCOTTISH CUP 1995

FIRST ROUND

17 DEC

Caledonian T (0) 1 *(McAllister)*
Queen of the S (0) 2 *(Bell, Bryce)* 1112
Caledonian T: McRitchie; Brennan, McAllister, Hercher, Andrew, Baltacha, MacDonald, Noble, MacMillan (MacKenzie), Christie, Robertson.
Queen of the S: Purdie; McKeown B, McKeown D, Campbell C, Hetherington, McFarlane, Bryce, Bell, McLaren (Brown), Kennedy, Jackson.

Dumbarton (1) 3 *(Ward 2, McKinnon)*
Stirling Albion (1) 3 *(Watters, Mitchell (pen), Tait)* 794
Dumbarton: MacFarlane; Gow, Foster, Melvin, Fabiani, MacLeod (Meechan), Mooney M (Campbell), King, McKinnon, McGarvey, Ward.
Stirling Albion: Monaghan; Paterson, Gibson, Mitchell, Watson, Tait, McInnes, Stewart (Armstrong), Watters (Farquhar), Taggart, McLeod.

Stenhousemuir (1) 3 *(Mathieson, Sprott (pen), Christie)*
East Stirling (0) 0 745
Stenhousemuir: Harkness; McNiven, Donaldson, Armstrong, Godfrey, Christie, Steel, Fisher, Mathieson, Hutchison, Sprott.
East Stirling: McDougall; Russell, Lee R, Watt (Stirling), Millar, Ross, Lee I, Scott, Dwyer, Geraghty, Conroy.

26 DEC

Albion R (1) 2 *(McBride J, Docherty)*
Montrose (2) 5 *(MacRonald 2, Milne, Kennedy (pen), McGlashan)* 356
Albion R: Davidson; McDonald, Gallagher, Kerr, Ryan, Collins, Dolan, Shah (Docherty), McBride J, McBride M (Quinn), Scott.
Montrose: Larter; Robertson, Tindal, Garden, Masson, Haro, Cooper (Milne), Stephen, McGlashan, Kennedy, MacRonald.

FIRST ROUND REPLAYS

19 DEC

Stirling Albion (1) 3 *(Taggart 2, McInnes)*
Dumbarton (0) 0 727
Stirling Albion: Monaghan; Paterson (Kerr), Gibson, Mitchell, Watson, Tait, McInnes, Armstrong, Watters, Taggart, McLeod.
Dumbarton: MacFarlane; Gow, Fabiani, Melvin, Marsland, Campbell, Mooney (Gibson), King, McKinnon, McGarvey, Ward.

SECOND ROUND

7 JAN

Alloa (1) 2 *(Lamont, Diver)*
Ross Co (2) 3 *(Connelly 2, McPherson)* 1364
Alloa: Butter; Hannah (Willock), Bennett (McAnenay), Kemp, McCulloch, Lawrie, McAvoy, Cadden, Diver, Moffat, Lamont.
Ross Co: Hutchison; Somerville, Reid, Williamson, Bellshaw, Furphy, Ferries (McKay), Grant, McPherson (Duff), Connelly, Herd.

Brechin C (0) 2 *(McNeill, Brand)*
Stirling Albion (2) 3 *(McInnes 2, Taggart)* 503
Brechin C: Balfour; Buick, Marr, Cairney, Conway, Vannett (Bell), McKellar, Mitchell, Price, Smith (Brand), McNeill.
Stirling Albion: Monaghan; Paterson, Gibson, Mitchell, McQuilter, Kerr, McInnes, Armstrong, Watters (Drinkell), Taggart, McLeod.

Buckie T (1) 1 *(Robertson)*
Berwick R (2) 4 *(Hawke, Graham, Mann (og), Valentine)* 907
Buckie T: Innes; Girling, Bruce I, Mathieson, Henderson, Mann, Gibson, Robertson, Begg (Galbraith), McPherson, Smith.
Berwick R: Osborne; Fraser, Valentine, Cole, Cowan, Irvine, Gallagher, Forrester (Kane), Hawke, Rutherford, Graham (Clegg).

Burntisland Shipyards (5) 6 *(Matthew 3, Taylor, Paton, Drummond)*
St Cuthbert W (0) 2 *(Tweedie, Baker)* 654
Burntisland Shipyards: Shanahan; Parnell, Taylor (Lewis), Lawrie, Bray, McIlvean, Matthew, Horsburgh (Murray), Campbell, Paton, Drummond.
St Cuthbert W: McHenry; Johnston, Kirkpatrick, Christie, McCulloch, Crosbie (Murray), Niven, Durham (Maxwell), Tweedie, Simpson, Baker.

Cove R (1) 2 *(Caldwell 2)*
Cowdenbeath (1) 1 *(Conn)* 490
Cove R: MacLean; Morrison, Whyte, Morland, Paterson, Baxter, Megginson, Park (Walker), Caldwell, Lorimer, Beattie (Buchan).
Cowdenbeath: Russell; Scott (Barclay), Murdoch, Humphreys, Conn, Tait (Callaghan), Fellenger, Black, Yardley, Soutar (Maloney), Wardell.

Forfar Ath (0) 0
Meadowbank T (0) 1 *(Sinclair)* 656
Forfar Ath: Arthur; Irvine, McPhee, Mann, Archibald, Glennie, Mearns (Hannigan), Heddle, Ross, McCormick, Bingham.
Meadowbank T: Ellison; Davidson, Martin, Graham (Thorburn), Thomson, Sorbie, Samuel, Wilson, Little, McLeod, Bailey (Sinclair).

Gala Fairydean (1) 2 *(Cockburn, Hunter)*
East Fife (3) 6 *(Burns (pen), Hutcheon 3, Allan, Donaghy)* 789
Gala Fairydean: Brown; Catterson, Henry, Potts (Dixon), Rae, Wilson (Campbell), Hunter, Sinclair, De Melo, Cockburn, Ritchie.
East Fife: Wilson; Sneddon (Gibb), Hildersley, Burns, Beaton, Cusick, Allan, Donaghy, Scott, Hutcheon (Hunter), Hope.

Keith (0) 2 *(Rougvie (og), Thomson)*
Huntly (2) 2 *(Whyte, Thomson)* 1370
Keith: Thain (Marr); Thow, Tosh, Allan, Collie, Gibson, Maver, Thomson, Lavelle, Will, Wilson (McPherson).
Huntly: Gardiner; Murphy, Dunsire, Mone, Rougvie, De Barros, Gray, Stewart (Grant), Thomson (Yeats), Whyte, Lennox.

Queen of the S (0) 0
Clyde (0) 2 *(Dickson, O'Neill)* 1803
Queen of the S: McQueen; McKeown B, McKeown D, Campbell C, Hetherington, Bell (McLaren), Kennedy (Jackson), Ramsay, Campbell D, Bryce, Mallan.

Clyde: Fridge; O'Neill, Angus, McCarron (McAulay), Thomson, Brown, Dickson, Watson, McCluskey (McConnell), Neill, Parks.

Stenhousemuir (3) 4 *(Fisher, Mathieson 2, Steel)*
Arbroath (0) 0 685
Stenhousemuir: Harkness; McNiven, Roseburgh (McGeachie), Armstrong, Godfrey, Christie, Steel, Fisher (Donaldson), Mathieson, Hutchison, Sprott.
Arbroath: Dunn; McMillan (Shanks), Elder, Ward, Murray, Spittal, Elliot, Farnan, Gardner, Tosh (Craib), Downie.

Whitehill Welfare (0) 0
Montrose (0) 0 853
Whitehill Welfare: Elen; Richford, Gowrie, Hunter, Steel, Millar, O'Rourke (Smith R), Bird (Blackie), Sneddon, Purves, Smith D.
Montrose: Larter; Robertson, Tindal, Stephen, Masson, Haro, Cooper, MacDonald (Milne), McGlashan, Kennedy, MacRonald.

9 JAN

Queen's Park (0) 2 *(Orr G, Rodden)*
Greenock Morton (2) 2 *(Alexander, Anderson)* 1516
Queen's Park: Chalmers; Orr J (Campbell), Maxwell, Kerr, Elder, Graham, Callan, Orr G, McPhee, Caven, Edgar (Rodden).
Greenock Morton: Wylie; Collins, Cormack, Anderson, McCahill, Lindberg, McArthur, Mahood, Alexander, McInnes, Rajamaki.

SECOND ROUND REPLAYS

14 JAN

Huntly (1) 3 *(Rougvie, Stewart, Whyte)*
Keith (1) 1 *(Lavelle)* 1777
Huntly: Gardiner; Grant, Dunsire, Mone, Rougvie, De Barros, Gray, Stewart (Yeats), Thomson, Whyte (Copland), Lennox.
Keith: Cathcart; Thow (Leddie), Tosh, Allan, Collie, Gibson, Maver, Thomson, Lavelle, Will, Wilson (McPherson).

Montrose (2) 5 *(Kennedy 2, Masson, McGlashan, Stephen)*
Whitehill Welfare (1) 2 *(Millar, Steel)* 807
Montrose: Larter; Robertson, Tindal, Masson, Grant, Haro, MacDonald (Cooper), Stephen, McGlashan, Kennedy, MacRonald.
Whitehill Welfare: Elen; Purves, Gowrie, Hunter, Steel, Millar, O'Rourke (McCulloch), Smith R, Sneddon, Brown, Smith D (Bird).

17 JAN

Greenock Morton (0) 2 *(Rajamaki, Lilley)*
Queen's Park (1) 1 *(Caven) aet* 2127
Greenock Morton: Wylie; Collins, McArthur, Anderson, McCahill, Lindberg, Lilley, Mahood, Alexander, Blair (McPherson), Rajamaki.
Queen's Park: Chalmers; Orr J, Ferguson, Kerr, Maxwell, Matchett, Callan, Smith (Bradley), Orr G, Caven, McGoldrick (Rodden).

THIRD ROUND

28 JAN

Aberdeen (1) 1 *(Jess)*
Stranraer (0) 0 9183
Aberdeen: Snelders; Wright, Glass, Kane, Inglis, Smith, Jess, Shearer (Thomson), Miller, Dodds, Grant.
Stranraer: Ross; McLean, Hughes, Gallagher, Howard, Millar, Sloan, Walker, Duncan, Callaghan (Cody), Reilly.

Celtic (0) 2 *(Falconer, Van Hooijdonk)*
St Mirren (0) 0 28,449
Celtic: Bonner; Boyd, Gray, O'Neil B, McNally, Grant, McLaughlin, O'Donnell, Van Hooijdonk (Walker), Falconer, Collins.
St Mirren: Money; Dawson, McIntyre, McWhirter, McLaughlin, Fullarton, Dick, Bone (Inglis), Lavety, Gillies R (Hewitt), Elliot.

Cove R (0) 0
Dunfermline Ath (4) 4 *(Petrie 2, Smith, Hawkins)* 2200
Cove R: Charles; Morrison, Whyte, Walker, Paterson, Buchan, Megginson (Gibson), Park, Caldwell (Leslie), Lorimer, Beattie.
Dunfermline Ath: Van De Kamp; McNamara, Fleming, McCathie, Cooper, Smith, French, Robertson, Tod, Petrie, Hawkins (Ward).

Dundee U (0) 0
Clyde (0) 0 7413
Dundee U: O'Hanlon; Perry, Malpas, Hannah, Petric, Welsh, Bowman, McInally, Nixon, Brewster, Dailly.
Clyde: Fridge; O'Neill, Angus, Nisbet, Knox, Brown, Dickson, Watson, McCluskey (MacKenzie), Neill, Parks.

Huntly (4) 7 *(Stewart 3, Whyte, Lawrie (og), Thornton, De Barros)*
Burntisland Shipyards (0) 0 1420
Huntly: Gardiner; Yeats, Dunsire (Copland), Mone, Grant, De Barros, Gray, Stewart, Thomson, Whyte, Lennox (Robertson).
Burntisland Shipyards: Shanahan (Kelly); Parnell, Taylor, Lawrie (Lewis), Bray, McIlvean, Matthew, Horsburgh, Campbell, Paton (Murray), Drummond.

Kilmarnock (0) 0
Greenock Morton (0) 0 8271
Kilmarnock: Lekovic; MacPherson, Black, Montgomerie, Anderson, Reilly, Mitchell (Maskrey), Henry, Brown, Connor, McKee (Williamson).
Greenock Morton: Wylie; Collins, McArthur, Anderson, McCahill, Lindberg, Lilley, Blair (Fowler), Alexander, McInnes, Rajamaki.

Montrose (0) 0
Hibernian (0) 2 *(McGinlay, Jackson D)* 3812
Montrose: Larter; Robertson, Tindal, Masson (Cooper), Grant, Haro (Stephen), Garden, Beedie, McGlashan, Kennedy, MacRonald.
Hibernian: Leighton; Miller, Mitchell, McGinlay, Tweed, Farrell, McAllister (Findlay), Evans, Wright, Jackson D, Tortolano.

Raith R (1) 1 *(Crawford)*
Ayr U (0) 0 4156
Raith R: Thomson; McAnespie, Broddle, Coyle, Raeside, Sinclair, Nicoll, Dalziel, Crawford (Graham), Lennon, Wilson.
Ayr U: Duncan; McKilligan, Connie, Sharples, Rolling, MacFarlane, Gribben (Bilsland), Moore, Gilzean, Jackson, Gorgues (Tannock).

29 JAN

Dundee (1) 2 *(Shaw, Hamilton)*
Partick T (0) 1 *(Craig)* 6320
Dundee: Pageaud; McQuillan, Duffy C, Wieghorst (Ritchie), Duffy J, Bain, Shaw, Vrto, Hanilton, Britton, McCann.

Partick T: Walker; Dinnie, Pittman, Watson, Welsh, Turner, McDonald (Gibson), Craig, Foster, McWilliams, Taylor.

31 JAN

St Johnstone (1) 1 *(McNiven (og))*
Stenhousemuir (0) 1 *(Sprott)* 3173
St Johnstone: Main; Cherry, Preston, Irons, Weir, McGowne, O'Neil, Curran, Twaddle (Davenport), O'Boyle, Deas.
Stenhousemuir: Harkness; McNiven, Donaldson, Armstrong, McGeachie, Christie, Steel, Fisher, Mathieson, Hutchison, Sprott.

1 FEB

Clydebank (1) 1 *(Eadie)*
Hearts (1) 1 *(Robertson)* 3427
*Clydebank:*Matthews; McStay, Crawford, Murdoch, Sweeney, Currie, Cooper, Lansdowne, Eadie, Flannigan, Jack.
Hearts: Nelson; Frail, Miller C, Levein, Mackay, McPherson, Hamilton, Bett (Colquhoun), Thomas (Jamieson), Robertson, Hagen.

East Fife (0) 1 *(Allan)*
Ross Co (0) 0 2106
East Fife: Robertson; Bell, Hamill, Sneddon, Cusick, Donaghy, Allan, Hildersley, Scott, Hunter (Hutcheon), Hope.
Ross CO: Hutchison; Somerville, Reid, Williamson, Bellshaw, Furphy, Ferries, Grant, Herd, Connelly, Andrew MacLeod (MacPherson).

Stirling Albion (1) 1 *(McQuilter)*
Airdrieonians (2) 2 *(Andrew Smith 2)* 1699
Stirling Albion: Monaghan; Paterson, Gibson, Mitchell, McQuilter, Kerr (Drinkell), McInnes, Tait, Watters, Taggart, McLeod.
Airdrieonians: Martin; Stewart, Tony Smith, Sandison, Hay, Black, Boyle, Lawrence, Cooper (McIntyre J), Harvey (Wilson), Andrew Smith.

6 FEB

Falkirk (0) 0
Motherwell (1) 2 *(Burns 2)* 7552
Falkirk: Parks; Weir, McQueen (James), Oliver, McLaughlin, Rice, May, McGowan, McDonald (Henderson), Fulton, MacKenzie.
Motherwell: Woods; Philliben, McKinnon, Krivokapic (McMillan), Martin, McCart, Lambert, Dolan, Burns, McGrillen (Roddie), Davies.

Hamilton A (0) 1 *(Lorimer)*
Rangers (2) 3 *(Steven, Boli, Laudrup)* 18,379
Hamilton A: Ferguson; Renicks, Hillcoat, McEntegart, McCall, McIntosh, Clark, McStay (Lorimer), Chalmers, Duffield, McQuade (Baptie).
Rangers: Maxwell; Moore, Robertson, Gough, Boli, McCall, Steven, Miller, Durie (Brown), Hateley, Laudrup.

Meadowbank T (0) 1 *(Cowan (og))*
Berwick R (0) 1 *(Fraser)* 858
Meadowbank T: Ellison; Davidson, Martin, Williamson, Thomson, Sorbie (Little), Wilson, Bailey, Harris, McLeod, Sinclair (Samuel).
Berwick R: Osborne; Greenwood, Banks, Valentine, Cowan, Fraser, Forrester (Kane), Neil, Hawke, Irvine, Graham.

THIRD ROUND REPLAYS

31 JAN

Greenock Morton (1) 1 *(Anderson)*
Kilmarnock (0) 2 *(Maskrey 2) aet* 6533
Greenock Morton: Wylie; Collins, McArthur, Anderson, McCahill, Lindberg, Lilley (Fowler), Mahood, Alexander (McPherson), McInnes, Rajamaki.
Kilmarnock: Lekovic; MacPherson, Black, Montgomerie, Whitworth, Anderson (Maskrey), Mitchell, Henry, Brown, Reilly, Williamson (Napier).

7 FEB

Berwick R (0) 3 *(Irvine, Neil, Clegg)*
Meadowbank T (1) 3 *(Graham, Bailey, Wilson) aet* 991
Berwick R: Osborne; Greenwood, Banks, Valentine, Cowan (Clegg), Fraser, Forrester (Graham), Neil, Hawke, Irvine, Kane.
Meadowbank T: Ellison; Davidson, Martin, Williamson, Graham, Samuel, Wilson, Little, Harris (Bailey), McLeod, Sinclair (Sorbie).
(Meadowbank T won 7-6 on penalties)

Clyde (1) 1 *(Angus)*
Dundee U (3) 5 *(McKinlay, Craig, Hannah, Bowman, Nixon)* 5387
Clyde: Fridge; O'Neill, Angus, Nisbet (Neill), Thomson, Brown, Dickson, Watson, Parks, Knox, MacKenzie (Prunty).
Dundee U: O'Hanlon; McInally (Welsh), Malpas, Hannah, Petric, Dailly, Bowman, McKinlay (Nixon), Brewster, Ristic, Craig.

Hearts (1) 2 *(Robertson, Thomas)*
Clydebank (0) 1 *(Eadie)* 8503
Hearts: Nelson; Frail, Berry, Levein, Bett, McPherson, Colquhoun (Mackay), Hamilton, Thomas (Miller C), Robertson, Hagen.
Clydebank: Matthews; McStay, Crawford (Bowman), Murdoch, Sweeney, Currie, Cooper, Lansdowne, Eadie, Flannigan (Grady), Jack.

Stenhousemuir (2) 4 *(Sprott 2, Clarke, Donaldson)*
St Johnstone (0) 0 2340
Stenhousemuir: Harkness; McNiven, Donaldson, Armstrong, McGeachie, Christie, Steel (Clarke), Fisher, Mathieson, Hutchison (Roseburgh), Sprott.
St Johnstone: Main; Cherry, Preston (O'Boyle), Irons, Weir, McGowne, O'Neil, Curran, Wright, Twaddle (English), Farquhar.

FOURTH ROUND

18 FEB

Airdrieonians (1) 2 *(Cooper, Andrew Smith)*
Dunfermline Ath (0) 0 4397
Airdrieonians: Martin; Stewart, Jack, Sandison, McIntyre T, Black, Boyle, Davies, Cooper, Harvey (Andrew Smith), Lawrence.
Dunfermline Ath: Van De Kamp; Den Bieman, Fleming, McCathie, Paterson, Smith, French, Robertson, Tod (Moore), Petrie, Ward.

Celtic (3) 3 *(Van Hooijdonk 2, Falconer)*
Meadowbank T (0) 0 23,710
Celtic: Marshall; McNally, McKinlay, O'Neil, Mowbray, Grant, McLaughlin (Walker), O'Donnell (Craig), Van Hooijdonk, Falconer, Collins.
Meadowbank T: Ellison; Davidson, Martin, Graham, Williamson, Sorbie, Wilson, Bailey (Thorburn), Harris (Little), McLeod, Samuel.

Dundee (1) 1 *(Shaw)*
Raith R (0) 2 *(Graham, Rowbotham)* 7622

Dundee: Pageaud; Farningham, Duffy J (Hamilton), Duffy C, Blake (Tosh), Bain, Shaw, Vrto, Wieghorst, Britton, McCann.
Raith R: Thomson; McAnespie, Broddle (Rowbotham), Coyle, Dennis, Raeside (Wilson), Sinclair, Cameron, Graham, Lennon, Crawford.

Hibernian (1) 2 *(Harper, McGinlay)*
Motherwell (0) 0 10,639

Hibernian: Leighton; Miller, Mitchell, McGinlay, Tweed, Hunter (Tortolano), Weir, Harper, Wright, Jackson D (McGraw), Jackson C.
Motherwell: Woods; Shannon, McKinnon, Krivokapic, Martin, Philliben, Lambert (McGrillen), Dolan (Kirk), Burns, Arnott, Davies.

Huntly (0) 1 *(Stewart)*
Dundee U (2) 3 *(Brewster, Malpas, Hannah)* 4524

Huntly: Gardiner; Murphy, Dunsire, Mone, Rougvie, De Barros, Gray (Copland), Stewart, Thomson, Whyte (Yeats), Lennox.
Dundee U: O'Hanlon; McInally, Malpas, Hannah, Petric, Welsh, Bowman, McKinlay, Gomes (Nixon), Brewster (Ristic), Dailly.

Kilmarnock (2) 4 *(Maskrey 2, Reilly, Black)*
East Fife (0) 0 7003

Kilmarnock: Lekovic; MacPherson (McKee), Black, Reilly, Whitworth, Anderson, Mitchell, Henry, Brown, Connor, Maskrey.
East Fife: Robertson; Bell, Hamill, Burns, Sneddon, Gibb, Allan, Archibald, Andrews, Hunter, Hope (Hutcheon).

Stenhousemuir (0) 2 *(Steel 2)*
Aberdeen (0) 0 3452

Stenhousemuir: Harkness; Clarke, Donaldson, Armstrong, McGeachie, Christie, Steel, Fisher, Mathieson, Hutchison, Sprott.
Aberdeen: Snelders; Wright, Glass, Kane, Inglis (Irvine), Smith, Jess, Shearer, Miller (Hetherston), Dodds, McKinnon.

20 FEB

Hearts (2) 4 *(Miller C, McPherson, Robertson, Thomas)*
Rangers (0) 2 *(Laudrup, Durie)* 12,375

*Hearts:*Nelson; Frail, Miller C (Colquhoun), Levein, Bett, McPherson, Hamilton, Mackay, Robertson (Thomas), Millar J, Hagen.
Rangers: Maxwell; Moore, Robertson (Durrant), Gough, McLaren, Cleland (Brown), Steven, McCall, Miller, Durie, Laudrup.

QUARTER-FINALS

10 MAR

Celtic (1) 1 *(Collins)*
Kilmarnock (0) 0 30,881

Celtic: Bonner; Boyd, McKinlay, O'Neil, Mowbray, O'Donnell (Grant), McLaughlin, McStay, Van Hooijdonk, Falconer, Collins.
Kilmarnock: Lekovic; MacPherson, Black, Reilly, Whitworth, Anderson, Mitchell, Henry, McKee (Skilling), Connor (McCarrison), Maskrey.

11 MAR

Raith R (0) 1 *(Cameron)*
Airdrieonians (2) 4 *(Harvey 2, Davies, Black)* 7130

Raith R: Thomson; McAnespie, Rowbotham, Cameron, Dennis, Sinclair, Wilson (Dalziel), Crawford, Graham, Lennon (Broddle), Dair.
Airdrieonians: Martin; Stewart, Jack, Sandison, Hay, Black, Boyle, Davies, Cooper, Harvey (Lawrence), Andrew Smith.

Stenhousemuir (0) 0
Hibernian (0) 4 *(Harper 2, Tortolano, O'Neill)* 3520

Stenhousemuir: Harkness; Clarke (Roseburgh), Donaldson, Armstrong, McGeachie (McNiven), Christie, Steel, Fisher, Mathieson, Hutchison, Sprott.
Hibernian: Leighton; Miller, Mitchell, Farrell, Tweed, Hunter, Harper, Tortolano, Wright, Jackson D, O'Neill.

12 MAR

Hearts (2) 2 *(Millar J 2)*
Dundee U (1) 1 *(Gomes)* 12,515

*Hearts:*Nelson; Frail, Millar J, Berry, Jamieson, McPherson, Colquhoun (Thomas), Hamilton, Robertson, Mackay, Hagen (Leitch).
Dundee U: O'Hanlon; McInally, Malpas, Hannah (Brewster), Petric, Welsh, Bowman, McKinlay, Gomes, Crabbe (Nixon), Dailly.

SEMI-FINALS

7 APR at Ibrox Stadium

Celtic (0) 0
Hibernian (0) 0 40,950

Celtic: Bonner; Boyd, McKinlay, Vata, O'Neil, Grant, McLaughlin, McStay, Van Hooijdonk (Falconer), Walker, Collins
Hibernian: Leighton; Miller, Mitchell, McGinlay, Tweed, Millen, Harper, Farrell, Wright, Jackson D, O'Neill.

8 APR at Hampden Park

Airdrieonians (1) 1 *(Cooper)*
Hearts (0) 0 22,538

Airdrieonians: Martin; Stewart, Jack, Sandison, Andrew Smith (Hay), Black, Boyle, Davies, Cooper, Harvey (Tony Smith), Lawrence.
Hearts: Nelson; Mackay, Miller C, Levein, Jamieson (Thomas), McPherson, Hamilton (Colquhoun), Bett, Robertson, Millar J, Hagen.

SEMI-FINAL REPLAY at Ibrox Stadium

11 APR

Celtic (2) 3 *(Falconer, Collins, O'Donnell)*
Hibernian (0) 1 *(Wright)* 32,410

Celtic: Bonner; Boyd, McKinlay, Vata, O'Neil, Grant (O'Donnell), McLaughlin, McStay, Falconer, Walker (Donnelly), Collins.
Hibernian: Leighton; Miller, Mitchell, McGinlay, Tweed, Millen, Harper (Tortolano), McGraw (Evans), Wright, Jackson D, O'Neill.

FINAL at Hampden Park

27 MAY

Celtic (1) 1 *(Van Hooijdonk)*
Airdrieonians (0) 0 36,915

Celtic: Bonner; Boyd, McKinlay, Vata, McNally, Grant, McLaughlin, McStay, Van Hooijdonk (Falconer), Donnelly (O'Donnell), Collins.
Airdrieonians: Martin; Stewart, Jack, Sandison, Hay (McIntyre J), Black, Boyle, Andrew Smith, Cooper, Harvey (Tony Smith), Lawrence.

B & Q CUP 1994–95

FIRST ROUND

17 SEPT

Airdrieonians (2) 3 *(Davies, Andrew Smith 2)*
Berwick R (0) 1 *(Fraser)* 985

Airdrieonians: Martin; Boyle, Stewart, Sandison, McIntyre T, Jack, Harvey, Davies, Andrew Smith, Black (Honor), Lawrence.
Berwick R: Young N; Valentine, Banks, Cole, Fraser, Wilson (King), Forrester, Neil, Hawke, Irvine, Gallacher (Graham).

Brechin C (0) 0
Dunfermline Ath (2) 2 *(Petrie, McCathie)* 857

Brechin C: Balfour; Conway, Brown, Cairney, Nicolson, Scott, Bell, McNeill, Smith (Feroz), Millar, Christie.
Dunfermline Ath: McQueen; Bowes, Sharp, McCathie, Tod, Smith, Den Bieman, Robertson, French (Laing), Petrie, Ward (Sinclair).

Cowdenbeath (0) 2 *(Soutar, Tait)*
Clyde (0) 1 *(MacKenzie)* 454

Cowdenbeath: Russell; Petrie, Murdoch, Malloy, Humphreys, Winter, Tait, Hamill, Yardley, Callaghan, Black (Soutar).
Clyde: Hillcoat; Prunty, McCheyne, Knox, Thomson, Watson (O'Neill), Dickson, McAulay, MacKenzie, McCarron, Nisbet.

Dumbarton (0) 2 *(Campbell 2)*
St Johnstone (2) 4 *(Ramsey, O'Boyle 2, Davenport)* 961

Dumbarton: MacFarlane (Dennison); Marsland (Farrell), Fabiani, Melvin, Boyd, MacLeod, Mooney M, Meechan (Campbell), Gibson, McGarvey, Ward.
St Johnstone: Rhodes; Cherry, Miller, Ramsey (McGinnis), Inglis, McGowne, O'Neil, Irons, Davenport, O'Boyle, Davidson (McMartin).

Dundee (2) 5 *(Britton 4, Shaw)*
Arbroath (0) 0 2205

Dundee: Pageaud; McQuillan, Hutchison, Teasdale, Blake, Duffy J, Shaw, Farningham, Tosh, Britton (Hamilton), Anderson (Vrto).
Arbroath: Jackson; Mitchell, Middleton, Murray, Spittal, Shanks, McGovern, Elder, McGregor, Tosh, Downie (Finlay).

East Fife (0) 2 *(Hunter, Scott)*
Ross Co (0) 1 *(Andrew MacLeod (pen))* 1031

East Fife: Wilson; Bell (Irvine), Sneddon, Burns, Beaton, Dow, Allan, Hildersley (Cusick), Scott, Hunter, Gibb.
Ross Co: McMillan; Somerville, Reid, Williamson, Herd, Campbell, Ferries, Grant, Duff, McPherson, Andrew MacLeod.

Forfar Ath (0) 0
Alloa (0) 1 *(Moffat)* 516

Forfar Ath: Arthur; Mearns, McPhee, Mann, Archibald, McKillop (Heddle), O'Neill, Irvine (Kopel), McCormick, Bingham, Lees.
Alloa: Graham; McCormack J, Kemp, Nelson, McCulloch, Lawrie, McAnenay, Moffat, Diver, Bennett, Lamont.

Hamilton A (2) 2 *(Duffield 2 (1 pen))*
Stenhousemuir (0) 0 738

Hamilton A: Cormack; McKenzie, McInulty, McEntegart, Baptie, Nicholls, McQuade (Hartley), Sherry, Campbell, Duffield, Lorimer.
Stenhousemuir: Harkness; Clarke, Roseburgh (Hallford), Armstrong, Godfrey, Christie, Steel, Fisher, Irvine (Sludden), Hutchison, Sprott.

Meadowbank T (1) 1 *(Graham)*
Montrose (1) 2 *(McGlashan, Cooper) aet* 171

Meadowbank T: Ellison; Graham, Fleming, Wilson, Williamson, Martin (Duthie), Davidson (Price), McLeod, Little, Sorbie, Bailey.
Montrose: Larter; Robertson, Craib (Garden), Beedie, Grant, Haro, MacDonald, Stephen (Cooper), McGlashan, Milne, Masson.

Queen of the S (0) 0
Raith R (2) 2 *(Cameron, Crawford)* 1376

Queen of the S: Purdie; Kennedy, McKeown D, McKeown B, McFarlane, Ramsay, Sermanni, Bryce, McLaren (Cochrane), Leslie (McGuire), Mallan.
Raith R: Thomson; McAnespie, Rowbotham, Lennon, Narey, Sinclair, Nicholl, Crawford, Graham, Cameron, Wilson (Dair).

Queen's Park (0) 0
Clydebank (3) 5 *(Grady 3, Cooper, Eadie)* 894

Queen's Park: Moonie; Orr J, Kavanagh, Kerr, Maxwell, Orr G, Fitzpatrick, Lynch, McCormick (Edgar), McPhee, Graham (Williamson).
Clydebank: Matthews; Lansdowne, Crawford, Murdoch, Sweeney, Currie, Walker (Agnew), Jack, Eadie, Grady (Kerrigan), Cooper.

Stirling Albion (3) 4 *(McInnes, Taggart 2, Watters)*
Albion R (0) 0 517

Stirling Albion: McGeown; Paterson, Gibson, Mitchell (Kerr), McQuilter, Tait, McInnes, Farquhar, Watters, Taggart, McLeod.
Albion R: Davidson; Philliben, Parry, McDonald, Conn, Kelly, Scott, Docherty (Seggie), Young, Quinn (McBride), Deeley.

Stranraer (0) 1 *(Ferguson)*
St Mirren (0) 1 *(Watson (pen)) aet* 1220

Stranraer: Ross; Millar, Hughes, McCann (Grant), McCaffrey, Gallagher, Sloan, McLean (Ferguson), Duncan, Cody, Henderson.
St Mirren: Money; Dawson, Watson, McLaughlin, McIntyre, Dick, Gillies K (Gillies R), Baker, Lavety, Gardner (Fullarton), Elliot.
(Stranraer won 5-4 on penalties)

18 SEPT

East Stirling (1) 1 *(Watt)*
Ayr U (0) 1 *(Burns) aet* 768

East Stirling: Moffat; Russell, Cuthbert, Yates, Sneddon, Watt, Lee I, Millar, Geraghty (Conroy), Scott, Stirling (McCallum).
Ayr U: Duncan; Burns, Connie, Paterson, Rolling, George, Gorgues, Moore, McGivern (Sharples), Stainrod, Bilsland (Gilzean).
(Ayr U won 4-2 on penalties)

SECOND ROUND

27 SEPT

Airdrieonians (1) 1 *(Lawrence)*
Raith R (1) 1 *(Dalziel) aet* 1360

Airdrieonians: Martin; Stewart, Jack (Wilson), Sandison, Hay, Black, Boyle, Davies, Andrew Smith, Harvey, Lawrence.
Raith R: Thomson; McAnespie, Redford (Broddle), Lennon, Dennis, Narey, Wilson, Dalziel (Sinclair), Crawford, Cameron, Dair.
(Airdrieonians won 5-3 on penalties)

Alloa (1) 1 *(McAnenay)*
Clydebank (2) 3 *(Grady, Eadie, Harris)* 452
Alloa: Graham; McCormack J, Kemp (Bennett), Newbigging, McCulloch, Lawrie, McAvoy (Diver), Nelson, Moffat, McAnenay, Lamont.
Clydebank: Matthews; Lansdowne, Crawford, Murdoch, Currie, Harris (Flannigan), Cooper, Agnew, Eadie (Walker), Grady, Jack.

Ayr U (2) 4 *(Burns, Jackson, Paterson, George)*
Stranraer (2) 2 *(Walker, Henderson)* 2489
Ayr U: Duncan; Burns, Connie, Paterson, Rolling, George, Traynor, Moore, Jackson, Stainrod (Gilzean) (McKilligan), Gorgues.
Stranraer: Ross; Millar, Hughes, McLean, Gallagher, McCaffrey, Sloan, Walker (Grant), Duncan, Cody (McCann), Henderson.

Dunfermline Ath (2) 4 *(French (pen), Robertson, Petrie 2)*
Hamilton A (1) 2 *(McIntosh, Duffield)* 2884
Dunfermline Ath: Westwater; Bowes, McNamara, McCathie, Tod, Smith, Den Bieman, Robertson, French, Petrie, Ward.
Hamilton A: Cormack; McKenzie, McNulty, McEntegart, Baptie, McIntosh, McQuade, Sherry (Clark), McGill, Duffield, Nicholls.

East Fife (0) 0
Cowdenbeath (1) 3 *(Yardley 3)* 949
East Fife: Wilson; Sneddon, Hope, Burns, Beaton, Hildersley, Allan (Dow), Irvine, Scott, Hunter, Gibb.
Cowdenbeath: Russell; Petrie, Murdoch, Malloy, McMahon, Winter, Tait, Hamill (Black), Yardley, Callaghan, Soutar (Humphreys).

Greenock Morton (2) 4 *(Lilley 2, Alexander, Fowler)*
St Johnstone (2) 3 *(O'Boyle 3) aet* 1446
Greenock Morton: Wylie; Collins, Pickering, Anderson, Cormack, Johnstone, Lilley, Fowler, Alexander, Mahood, McArthur (Gibson).
St Johnstone: Rhodes; Cherry (Turner), McAuley, McGinnis, Inglis, McGowne, O'Neil, McMartin (Ramsey), Davenport, O'Boyle, Irons.

Montrose (1) 3 *(Stephen, McGlashan 2)*
Stirling Albion (0) 0 561
Montrose: Larter; Robertson, Tindal, Masson, Grant, Haro, Cooper (Brown), MacDonald, McGlashan, Kennedy (Milne), Stephen.
Stirling Albion: McGeown; Paterson, Gibson, Mitchell, McQuilter, Tait, McInnes, Farquhar (Roberts), Watters, Taggart, McLeod.

28 SEPT

Caledonian T (1) 1 *(MacDonald)*
Dundee (0) 1 *(Wieghorst) aet* 1336
Caledonian T: McRitchie; Brennan, McAllister, Sinclair, Scott (Lisle), Andrew, MacDonald (Smart), MacKenzie, MacMillan, Christie, Robertson.
Dundee: Mathers; Farningham, Hutchison, Duffy C, Blake, Duffy J, Shaw, Dailly (Hamilton), Wieghorst (Teasdale), Britton, Bain.
(Dundee won 4-3 on penalties)

QUARTER-FINALS

4 OCT

Airdrieonians (1) 2 *(Cooper, Davies)*
Ayr U (0) 0 1500
Airdrieonians: Martin; Stewart, Jack, Sandison, McIntyre T, Black, Boyle, Davies, Cooper, Harvey (Honor), Lawrence.
Ayr U: Duncan; Biggart, McVicar (Bilsland), Sharples, Rolling, McKilligan, Burns, Moore (Connie), Paterson, Jackson, Gorgues.

Cowdenbeath (0) 1 *(Yardley)*
Dunfermline Ath (2) 3 *(Smith, French, Petrie)* 3163
Cowdenbeath: Russell; Petrie, Murdoch, Malloy, McMahon, Winter, Lynch (Humphreys), Black, Yardley, Callaghan, Soutar (Barclay).
Dunfermline Ath: Westwater; McNamara, Hawkins, McCathie, Tod, Smith, Den Bieman, Robertson, French, Petrie (Laing), Ward.

Dundee (1) 2 *(Britton, Wieghorst)*
Greenock Morton (0) 1 *(Anderson)* 2199
Dundee: Pageaud; McQuillan, Bain, Farningham, Blake, Duffy J (Hutchison), Shaw, Wieghorst, Tosh, Britton, Hamilton.
Greenock Morton: Wylie; Collins, Pickering, Anderson, Cormack, Johnstone, McCann, Fowler (Hunter), Alexander (Gibson), Mahood, McArthur.

5 OCT

Montrose (0) 1 *(Kennedy (pen))*
Clydebank (0) 2 *(Flannigan, Cooper) aet* 825
Montrose: Larter; Robertson, Tindal, Masson, Tosh, Haro, Cooper (Brown), MacDonald, McGlashan, Kennedy, Stephen (MacRonald).
Clydebank: Matthews; Lansdowne, Crawford, Murdoch, Currie, Bowman, Cooper, Walker, Eadie, Grady (Flannigan), Jack (Harris).

SEMI-FINALS

18 OCT

Airdrieonians (0) 3 *(Boyle, Stewart, Cooper)*
Clydebank (0) 1 *(Cooper)* 1737
Airdrieonians: Martin; Stewart, Jack, Sandison, Hay, Black, Boyle, Davies, Cooper, Harvey (Wilson), Andrew Smith (McIntyre J).
Clydebank: Matthews; Jack, Crawford, Murdoch, Sweeney, Bowman (Grady), Cooper, Walker, Eadie, Flannigan, Harris (Lansdowne).

Dunfermline Ath (0) 1 *(Tod)*
Dundee (1) 2 *(Bain (pen), McCann)* 7154
Dunfermline Ath: Westwater; McNamara, Bowes, McCathie, Tod, Smith, Den Bieman, Robertson, French, Petrie, Ward (Hawkins).
Dundee: Pageaud; McQuillan, Bain, Farningham, Duffy J, Wieghorst, Shaw, Vrto, Tosh, Britton, McCann.

FINAL

6 NOV at McDiarmid Park, Perth

Airdrieonians (1) 3 *(Harvey, Boyle (pen), Andrew Smith)*
Dundee (1) 2 *(Hay (og), Britton) aet* 8844
Airdrieonians: Martin; Stewart (Tony Smith), Jack, Sandison, Hay, Black, Boyle, Davies, Cooper, Harvey, Lawrence (Andrew Smith).
Dundee: Pageaud; McQuillan, Bain, Farningham, Duffy J, Wieghorst, Shaw, Vrto, Tosh (Hamilton), Britton, McCann.
Referee: H F Williamson (Renfrew).

KONICA LEAGUE OF WALES 1994–95

		Home			*Goals*		*Away*			*Goals*		
	P	*W*	*D*	*L*	*F*	*A*	*W*	*D*	*L*	*F*	*A*	*Pts*
Bangor City	38	14	4	1	58	17	13	3	3	38	9	88
Afan Lido	38	12	4	3	31	19	12	3	4	29	17	79
Ton Pentre	38	12	4	3	34	19	11	4	4	50	31	77
Newtown	38	12	4	3	50	20	8	4	7	28	27	68
Cwmbran Town	38	10	3	6	37	26	10	4	5	32	23	67
Flint Town United	38	10	3	6	44	23	10	0	9	33	37	63
Barry Town	38	10	5	4	38	25	6	6	7	33	32	59
Holywell United	38	10	3	6	35	27	6	7	6	27	28	58
Llansantffraid	38	7	7	5	33	27	8	3	8	24	30	55
Inter Cardiff	38	8	2	9	34	20	6	9	4	24	23	53
Rhyl	38	8	3	8	40	36	8	2	9	34	33	53
Conwy United	38	9	3	7	36	30	5	4	10	24	35	49
Ebbw Vale	38	8	4	7	30	27	4	5	10	21	30	45
Caersws	38	6	5	8	27	31	5	6	8	30	33	44
Connah's Quay Nomads	38	7	3	9	24	37	5	4	10	33	42	43
Porthmadog	38	3	5	11	25	33	8	2	9	32	40	40
Aberystwyth Town	38	5	8	6	31	29	4	4	11	26	46	39
Llanelli	38	6	2	11	37	52	4	4	11	27	52	36
Mold Alexandra	38	6	2	11	29	36	4	2	13	28	54	34
Maesteg Park Athletic	38	2	4	13	15	47	0	2	17	8	66	12

KONICA LEAGUE OF WALES

	Aberystwyth Town	Afan Lido	Bangor City	Barry Town	Caersws	Connah's Quay	Conwy Utd	Cwmbran Town	Ebbw Vale	Flint Town U	Holywell Town	Inter Cardiff	Llanelli	Llansantffraid	Maesteg Park Ath	Mold Alexandra	Newtown	Porthmadog	Rhyl	Ton Pentre
Aberystwyth Town	—	1-1	1-2	2-2	1-1	1-2	1-1	0-2	4-1	1-3	1-1	1-1	2-2	1-2	2-0	1-0	2-2	5-1	1-4	3-1
Afan Lido	2-2	—	0-1	2-0	1-0	2-0	3-2	2-1	1-1	0-2	3-2	2-1	2-1	2-1	2-2	3-1	1-0	0-1	2-0	1-1
Bangor City	7-2	2-3	—	2-0	3-1	2-2	4-1	3-2	2-0	6-3	1-1	1-1	3-0	2-1	7-0	4-0	3-0	4-0	2-0	0-0
Barry Town	3-1	0-2	1-0	—	1-1	1-1	2-1	2-3	1-1	3-0	2-1	2-2	6-3	2-2	3-0	3-0	3-0	2-3	2-1	0-3
Caersws	2-1	0-1	0-5	0-1	—	2-2	4-1	2-2	2-4	2-3	1-1	0-0	0-2	0-1	2-0	5-2	0-0	0-1	3-1	2-1
Connah's Quay Nomads	3-2	1-2	0-8	2-2	2-1	—	0-0	0-1	1-0	2-1	2-2	0-1	1-2	1-2	1-0	1-3	1-4	4-1	0-4	2-1
Conwy United	3-2	1-0	1-4	3-1	0-3	4-5	—	0-1	3-0	4-1	0-1	1-1	0-0	2-0	3-0	3-3	4-2	2-0	1-2	2-4
Cwmbran Town	2-2	2-0	0-2	2-3	1-1	3-0	1-1	—	1-0	2-0	2-0	4-0	3-1	5-2	2-0	4-3	1-2	1-4	1-4	0-1
Ebbw Vale	2-2	0-3	2-2	2-2	0-3	2-0	3-2	0-0	—	1-2	1-0	1-0	1-2	2-0	3-0	6-1	0-2	1-0	1-3	2-3
Flint Town United	3-0	1-2	1-0	1-3	4-1	1-0	1-3	0-1	2-2	—	1-1	0-0	8-0	4-0	5-1	3-1	5-0	3-2	0-3	1-3
Holywell Town	1-2	1-2	0-2	1-0	2-0	2-0	2-0	1-4	1-0	2-3	—	1-1	4-2	0-2	2-0	3-1	1-0	5-2	3-3	3-3
Inter Cardiff	1-2	0-2	0-0	2-3	3-0	5-0	4-0	0-1	1-1	3-1	1-2	—	3-0	1-2	5-0	3-2	0-1	0-1	1-0	1-2
Llanelli	0-2	1-3	1-0	3-2	2-2	0-9	2-4	2-3	1-3	4-1	2-3	0-3	—	3-3	6-0	2-1	2-4	1-4	5-2	0-2
Llansantffraid	3-0	0-0	1-1	1-1	2-3	4-3	3-0	0-2	0-0	0-3	2-0	1-3	4-2	—	1-1	5-3	0-0	1-2	3-1	2-2
Maesteg Park Athletic	0-1	2-1	0-2	2-1	1-1	1-1	0-4	0-4	1-5	0-4	0-1	0-1	2-6	0-3	—	1-2	1-1	2-2	1-2	1-5
Mold Alexandra	4-2	1-2	1-2	0-2	2-1	1-3	0-2	3-1	2-1	0-2	2-3	1-2	5-1	0-0	2-0	—	0-2	1-1	1-2	3-7
Newtown	1-1	1-1	0-2	2-2	3-3	3-0	2-0	2-1	1-0	2-1	4-1	3-4	4-0	0-1	9-0	4-0	—	3-1	3-0	3-2
Porthmadog	4-0	1-2	0-1	1-4	1-3	2-0	0-1	2-2	0-1	1-4	1-1	1-1	1-1	0-1	5-0	1-2	0-4	—	2-2	2-3
Rhyl	3-2	0-1	0-1	3-1	4-3	2-3	1-1	1-1	3-0	1-2	1-2	3-1	2-2	3-1	3-1	1-2	3-2	3-4	—	3-6
Ton Pentre	2-0	2-1	0-3	1-1	0-2	4-2	2-0	3-0	3-1	3-0	1-1	1-1	2-0	2-0	3-2	1-1	0-2	3-2	1-0	—

ALLBRIGHT BITTER WELSH CUP 1994–95

Preliminary Round

Abercynon Athletic v Chepstow Town	1-2
Albion Rovers v Fields Park/Pontllanfraith	3-2
Bala Town v Llay Welfare	2-3
British Steel v BP Llandarcy	0-2
Cardiff Corinthians v Cardiff Institute	3-1
Felinheli v Llanrwst United	0-0, 4-3
Goytre United v Seven Sisters	6-1
Newport YMCA v Pontlottyn Blast Furnace	4-4, 0-7
Panteg v Trelewis Welfare	2-1
Pontyclun v Risca United	2-2, 3-4
Porthcawl Town v Newcastle Emlyn	6-0
Presteigne St Andrews v Penparcau	7-2
Rhyl Delta v British Aerospace	2-1
Skewen Athletic v Pontardawe Athletic	1-2
Tondu Robins v South Wales Constabulary	4-0

First Round

Abergavenny Thursdays v Panteg	1-1, 2-1
AFC Porth v Pontardawe Athletic	3-0
Albion Rovers v Tondu Robins	0-3
BP Llandarcy v Morrison Town	2-0
Brecon Corinthians v Goytre United	1-1, 1-2
Briton Ferry Athletic v Carmarthen Town	0-0, 1-2
Brymbo v Llanfairfech	2-2, 2-2, 2-0
Buckley Town v Penycae	3-5
Cardiff Corinthians v Caerau	2-1
Cardiff Civil Services v Caldicot Town	3-1
Carno v Llanidloes Town	7-1
Chepstow Town v Bridgend Town	3-0
Ferndale Athletic v Ammanford Town	0-1
Lex XI v Camaesbay AFC	1-2
Llandrindod Wells v Welshpool Town	0-3
Llandudno v Llay Welfare	7-1
Locomotive Llanberis v Gresford Athletic	0-2
Mostyn v Llanfairpwll	2-2, 1-6
Nantlle Vale v Llangefni Town	2-6
Nefyn United v Knighton Town	3-0
New Broughton v Cefn Druids	0-2
Oswestry Town v New Brighton	1-0
Pembroke Borough v Haverfordwest County	0-5
Pontlottyn Blast Furnace v Caerleon	2-0
Pontypridd Town v Porthcawl Town	3-1
Port Talbot Athletic v Aberaman Athletic	0-1
Presteigne St Andrews v Penrhyncoch	2-1
Rhos Aelwyd v Chirk AAA	2-2, 3-1
Rhyl Delta v Rhayader Town	1-2
Risca United v Llanwern	2-2, 4-1
Ruthin Town v Llandyrnog United	0-3
Treowen Stars v Taffs Well	1-3
Felinheli v Prestatyn Town	0-5

Second Round

Ebbw Vale v Aberaman Athletic	3-0
Cardiff Corinthians v Llanelli	2-0
Cardiff Civil Services v Cwmbran Town	0-3
Carmarthen Town v Haverfordwest County	3-0
Cefn Druids v Llansantffraid	1-0
Connah's Quay Nomads v Mold Alexandra	3-2
Flint Town United v Brymbo	2-2, 1-3
Gresford Athletic v Aberystwyth Town	1-2
Llandyrnog United v Rhos Aelwyd	0-3
Llangefni Town v Welshpool Town	3-0
Maesteg Park Athletic v BP Llandarcy	2-1
Merthyr Tydfil v Goytre United	5-0
Nefyn United v Llandudno	1-2
Newtown v Penycae	6-0
Oswestry Town v Caersws	1-1, 1-3
Pontlottyn Blast Furnace v Afan Lido	1-1, 0-5
Pontypridd Town v AFC Porth	3-2
Porthmadog v Conwy United	3-0
Prestatyn Town v Cemaes Bay	0-4
Presteigne St Andrews v Carno	3-3, 1-6
Rhayader Town v Holywell Town	0-2
Rhyl v Llanfairpwll	3-0
Risca United v Ammanford Town	3-0
Taffs Well v Chepstow Town	2-0
Tondu Robins v Abergavenny Thursdays	0-2

Third Round

Taffs Well v Swansea City	0-7
Bangor City v Carno	2-0
Brymbo v Aberystwyth Town	1-3
Caersws v Rhos Aelwyd	4-0
Cardiff Corinthians v Afan Lido	0-1
Carmarthen Town v Barry Town	2-3
Cefn Druids v Connah's Quay Nomads	0-2
Holywell Town v Porthmadog	1-3
Llandudno v Llangefni Town	3-0
Maesteg Park Athletic v Inter Cardiff	1-0
Merthyr Tydfil v Cwmbran Town	5-0
Rhyl v Cemaes Bay	3-0
Risca United v Pontypridd Town	2-0
Ton Pentre v Abergavenny Thursdays	2-1
Ebbw Vale v Cardiff City	1-1, 0-7
Newtown v Wrexham	1-1, 0-2

Fourth Round

Swansea City v Rhyl	5-1
Afan Lido v Ton Pentre	0-3
Bangor City v Maesteg Park Athletic	12-1
Barry Town v Llandudno	1-1, 1-3
Merthyr Tydfil v Aberystwyth Town	1-0
Porthmadog v Caersws	0-0, 2-1
Wrexham v Connah's Quay Nomads	4-0
Cardiff City v Risca United	4-0

Fifth Round

Bangor City v Wrexham	2-2, 0-1
Merthyr Tydfil v Ton Pentre	2-0
Swansea City v Porthmadog	8-0
Llandudno v Cardiff City	0-1

Semi-finals (two legs)

Wrexham v Merthyr Tydfil	3-1
Merthyr Tydfil v Wrexham	0-1
Swansea City v Cardiff City	0-1
Cardiff City v Swansea City	0-0

Final: Cardiff City 1, Wrexham 2

(At National Stadium, Cardiff, 21 May 1995) Att: 12,810

Cardiff City: Williams S; Brazil, Searle, Richardson, Baddeley, Perry, Wigg, Bird (Young), Millar (Oatway), Dale, Griffith. *Scorer:* Dale.

Wrexham: Marriott; Brace, Hardy, Hunter, Jones, Hughes, Bennett, Owen, Connolly, Morris (Watkin), Durkan. *Scorer:* Bennett 2 (1 pen).

Referee: V. Reed.

NORTHERN IRISH FOOTBALL 1994–95

"Northern Ireland soccer is at the crossroads" was the message hammered out by Jim Boyce following his election as President of the Irish FA in succession to Sammy Walker (Coleraine). He is the first Cliftonville delegate to occupy the office.

His sentiments aptly summed up the situation at both international and domestic level after a season of dramatic change – a season of frenzy and fear.

The introduction of promotion and relegation from this new campaign generated an astonishing battle between clubs attempting to finish in the top eight.

Huge sums were spent on English, Scottish and South of Ireland players in an attempt to prevent the dreaded drop into a lower division. Some succeeded but others failed and now wonder just what fate will befall them in the financially stringent days ahead.

P and R was generally accepted with the consensus that eight was too small a number. This and other aspects of the system, however, will be examined over the next few months and a report issued before next April's annual general meeting.

This is how the new set-up is composed based on accumulated placings over two seasons: Premier Division—Glenavon, Crusaders, Portadown, Linfield, Ards, Cliftonville, Glentoran, Bangor; First Division—Coleraine, Distillery, Ballymena United, Omagh Town, Ballyclare Comrades, Carrick Rangers, Newry Town, Larne.

There was a spread of the trophies with Crusaders, always the pacemakers, winning the Irish League Championship for the first time in 19 years and Linfield, who had an indifferent season, ensuring qualification for Europe by winning the Irish Cup.

Glenavon, as runners-up, took the second UEFA Cup representation but, unless there is an improvement in the Irish League clubs co-efficient over the next two years, this place could be in jeopardy.

Sponsorship continues with virtually every tournament commercially backed although there were several changes in companies involved. "We are happy with the outcome of all our discussions. Football is generally well supported by the Ulster business community but it is an on-going process and we must be continually searching for new outlets" said League president Morton McKnight.

Internationally it was a peculiar nine months. Manager Bryan Hamilton, who has worked prodigiously in the development of the game from schoolboys to the senior squad, had a sweet and sour experience.

There were excellent European Championship results against Austria in Vienna (2-1), Latvia in Rigo (1-0) and the Republic in Dublin (1-1). Then came a disastrous 2-0 defeat by Canada in Edmonton, then 2-1 by Chile but with a much improved performance before the 2-1 humiliation by Latvia at Windsor Park.

What a catastrophe that proved to be in view of the Republic being held to a scoreless draw in Liechtenstein and then losing 2-1 to Austria at Lansdowne Road. Those three points would have put Northern Ireland back into qualification reckoning for next summer's finals in England. All hope has gone and now the build-up must be for the France 98 World Cup preliminary series.

There is a long hard road ahead but the Irish FA general secretary David Bowen in his annual report stresed there was a "feel good" climate in the game with the advent of a youth development programme, appointment of special staff to deal with this and the introduction of mini-soccer.

The basis of long-term strategy has been laid but it is essential to have teams competing in every category especially under-21 to bridge that all important gap between under-18 and the senior side.

And, as Hamilton stressed, young players with English clubs must figure regularly in the first eleven. "The more we have in the Premier Division the better it will be for us. Languishing in the reserves or on the substitutes bench is not the preparation for international football" he said. Nobody would disagree.

MALCOLM BRODIE

BUDWEISER CUP 1994-95

First Round

Glentoran v Distillery	2-3
Glenavon v Cliftonville	1-2
Omagh Town v Linfield	0-2
Ards v Bangor	1-2
Crusaders v Newry Town	0-0
(Newry won 3-2 on penalties)	
Ballymena United v Ballyclare Comrades	0-1
Portadown v Carrick Rangers	3-1
Larne v Coleraine	1-2

Quarter-finals

Linfield v Distillery	1-2
Ballyclare Comrades v Newry Town	1-0
Bangor v Coleraine	3-2
Portadown v Cliftonville	1-0

Semi-finals

Distillery v Ballyclare Comrades	
Bangor v Portadown	1-3

Final

Portadown 4 Distillery 2 *(at Windsor Park, 6 December 1994)*

Portadown: Hamilton; Major, Murray, Casey, Strain, Tlemo, Cunningham, Shepherd, Ferguson (Doolin), Candlish (Fraser), Russell.

Distillery: O'Neill; Drake, Kennedy B, Kennedy J, Brady, Allen, Totten, Armstrong (Trainor), Hall (Small), Mitchell, Dykes.

Scorers: Portadown–Strain, Cunningham, Russell, Doolin; Distillery–Totten, Dykes.

Referee: L. Irvine (Limavady).

Previous Winners: 1988: Glentoran, 1989: Glenavon, 1990: Glentoran, 1991: Portadown, 1992: Omagh Town, 1993: Portadown, 1994: Linfield.

WILKINSON SWORD LEAGUE CUP FINAL 1994-95

Ards 0 Cliftonville 0 *(at Windsor Park, Belfast, 25 April 1995)*

(Aet; Ards won 2-0 on penalties)

Ards: Kee; McBride, Murphy, Brady, Mooney, O'Sullivan, Cullen C, McCann M, Patmore (Erskine), Cullen P, Morrison (Heaney).

Cliftonville: Rice; Hill, Loughran (Gill), McDonald, Kerr, Strang, McCann T, Sliney (O'Neill), Manley, McAllister, Donnelly.

Referee: N. Cowie (Belfast).

Attendance: 4500

Previous Winners: 1992: Linfoeld, 1993: Bangor, 1994: Linfield.

SMIRNOFF IRISH LEAGUE CHAMPIONSHIP FINAL TABLE

	P	*W*	*D*	*L*	*F*	*A*	*Pts*
Crusaders	30	20	7	3	58	25	67
Glenavon	30	18	6	6	76	40	60
Portadown	30	15	5	10	59	41	50
Ards	30	15	5	10	55	42	50
Glentoran	30	14	8	8	53	41	50
Cliftonville	30	13	11	6	44	32	50
Coleraine	30	12	13	5	52	39	49
Linfield	30	11	11	8	48	34	44
Omagh Town	30	10	12	8	42	38	42
Distillery	30	12	6	12	45	47	42
Bangor	30	8	14	8	42	38	38
Ballymena United	30	7	8	15	43	53	29
Carrick Rangers	30	7	7	16	46	75	28
Ballyclare Comrades	30	5	6	19	39	66	21
Newry Town	30	4	9	17	34	74	21
Larne	30	3	4	23	18	69	13

IRISH LEAGUE CHAMPIONSHIP WINNERS

1891 Linfield
1892 Linfield
1893 Linfield
1894 Glentoran
1895 Linfield
1896 Distillery
1897 Glentoran
1898 Linfield
1899 Distillery
1900 Belfast Celtic
1901 Distillery
1902 Linfield
1903 Distillery
1904 Linfield
1905 Glentoran
1906 Cliftonville/ Distillery
1907 Linfield
1908 Linfield
1909 Linfield
1910 Cliftonville
1911 Linfield
1912 Glentoran
1913 Glentoran
1914 Linfield
1915 Belfast Celtic
1920 Belfast Celtic
1921 Glentoran
1922 Linfield
1923 Linfield
1924 Queen's Island
1925 Glentoran
1926 Belfast Celtic
1927 Belfast Celtic
1928 Belfast Celtic
1929 Belfast Celtic
1930 Linfield
1931 Glentoran
1932 Linfield
1933 Belfast Celtic
1934 Linfield
1935 Linfield
1936 Belfast Celtic
1937 Belfast Celtic
1938 Belfast Celtic
1939 Belfast Celtic
1940 Belfast Celtic
1948 Belfast Celtic
1949 Linfield
1950 Linfield
1951 Glentoran
1952 Glenavon
1953 Glentoran
1954 Linfield
1955 Linfield
1956 Linfield
1957 Glentoran
1958 Ards
1959 Linfield
1960 Glenavon
1961 Linfield
1962 Linfield
1963 Distillery
1964 Glentoran
1965 Derry City
1966 Linfield
1967 Glentoran
1968 Glentoran
1969 Linfield
1970 Glentoran
1971 Linfield
1972 Glentoran
1973 Crusaders
1974 Coleraine
1975 Linfield
1976 Crusaders
1977 Glentoran
1978 Linfield
1979 Linfield
1980 Linfield
1981 Glentoran
1982 Linfield
1983 Linfield
1984 Linfield
1985 Linfield
1986 Linfield
1987 Linfield
1988 Glentoran
1989 Linfield
1990 Portadown
1991 Portadown
1992 Glentoran
1993 Linfield
1994 Linfield
1995 Crusaders

ULSTER CUP

SECTIONAL TABLES

Section A	*P*	*W*	*D*	*L*	*F*	*A*	*Pts*
Bangor	3	2	1	0	6	2	7
Linfield	3	2	0	1	4	3	6
Carrick Rangers	3	1	0	2	7	7	3
Glentoran	3	0	1	2	2	7	1
Section B	*P*	*W*	*D*	*L*	*F*	*A*	*Pts*
Portadown	3	2	1	0	9	4	7
Newry Town	3	2	0	1	5	6	6
Coleraine	3	1	1	1	4	4	4
Ards	3	0	0	3	2	6	0
Section C	*P*	*W*	*D*	*L*	*F*	*A*	*Pts*
Glenavon	3	3	0	0	10	1	9
Distillery	3	2	0	1	4	3	6
Ballymena United	3	0	1	1	1	7	1
Larne	3	0	1	2	2	6	1
Section D	*P*	*W*	*D*	*L*	*F*	*A*	*Pts*
Ballyclare Comrades	3	3	0	0	7	3	9
Crusaders	3	2	0	1	8	3	6
Cliftonville	3	0	1	2	2	4	1
Omagh Town	3	0	1	2	1	8	1

ULSTER CUP FINAL 1994–95

Quarter-finals

Glenavon v Crusaders 4-1
Ballyclare Comrades v Distillery 1-2
Portadown v Linfield 0-3
Bangor v Newry Town 1-0

Semi-finals

Bangor v Glenavon *(New Grosvesnor Stadium)* 3-2 (aet)
Linfield v Distillery *(The Oval)* 3-1

Final

Bangor 2 Linfield 1 *(at The Oval, Belfast 4 October 1994)*
Bangor: Currie; Dornan R, Glendenning, McCaffrey, Brown, Melly, Surgeon, Kenny, Collins, Hill, Batey.
Linfield: Lamont; Dornan A, Easton, Peebles, McConnell, Beatty, Campbell, Gorman, Haylock, Fenlon, Bailie.
Scorers: Bangor–Brown, Kenny; Linfield–Campbell.
Referee: A. Snoddy (Carryduff).
Attendance: 4200

Winners

1949 Linfield
1950 Larne
1951 Glentoran
1952
1953 Glentoran
1954 Crusaders
1955 Glenavon
1956 Linfield
1957 Linfield
1958 Distillery
1959 Glenavon
1960 Linfield
1961 Ballymena U
1962 Linfield
1963 Crusaders
1964 Linfield
1965 Coleraine
1966 Glentoran
1967 Linfield
1968 Coleraine
1969 Coleraine
1970 Linfield
1971 Linfield
1972 Coleraine
1973 Ards
1974 Linfield
1975 Coleraine
1976 Glentoran
1977 Linfield
1978 Linfield
1979 Linfield
1980 Ballymena U
1981 Glentoran
1982 Glentoran
1983 Glentoran
1984 Linfield
1985 Coleraine
1986 Coleraine
1987 Larne
1988 Glentoran
1989 Glentoran
1990 Portadown
1991 Bangor
1992 Linfield
1993 Crusaders
1994 Bangor

TNT GOLD CUP

SECTIONAL TABLES

Section A	*P*	*W*	*D*	*L*	*F*	*A*	*Pts*
Linfield	3	3	0	0	9	1	9
Coleraine	3	2	0	1	5	4	6
Distillery	3	1	0	2	5	8	3
Larne	3	0	0	3	2	8	0
Section B	*P*	*W*	*D*	*L*	*F*	*A*	*Pts*
Ballymena United	3	2	0	1	5	3	6
Portadown	3	2	0	1	3	2	6
Bangor	3	2	0	1	3	3	6
Omagh Town	3	0	0	3	2	5	0
Section C	*P*	*W*	*D*	*L*	*F*	*A*	*Pts*
Glenavon	3	2	1	0	12	2	7
Cliftonville	3	2	0	1	6	7	6
Ballyclare Comrades	3	1	0	2	4	7	3
Newry Town	3	0	1	2	5	11	1
Section D	*P*	*W*	*D*	*L*	*F*	*A*	*Pts*
Glentoran	3	3	0	0	10	3	9
Crusaders	3	1	1	1	6	7	4
Carrick Rangers	3	1	1	1	3	5	4
Ards	3	1	1	3	2	6	1

TNT GOLD CUP FINAL 1994-95

Quarter-finals

Linfield v Portadown 2-2 (aet)
(Linfield won 4-2 on penalties)
Ballymena United v Coleraine 0-1
Glentoran v Cliftonville 2-1 (aet)
Glenavon v Crusaders 0-1

Semi-finals

Linfield v Crusaders *(The Oval)* 1-2
Coleraine v Glentoran *(Windsor Park)* 2-0

Final

Crusaders 1 Glentoran 1 *(at Windsor Park, Belfast, 25 October 1994)*
(aet; 90 mins 1-1; Glentoran won 3-0 on penalties)
Crusaders: McKeown; Lawlor, Stewart, Dunlop, Callaghan, Hunter K, McCartney, Murray (Carroll), Baxter (Livingstone), Hunter G, Burrows.
Glentoran: Armstrong; Neill, Smyth M, Parker, Smyth G, Mathieson (Kelly) D), Kelly N, Martindale (Nixon), Campbell, Cunnington, McBride.
Scorers: Crusaders–Murray; Glentoran–Campbell.
Referee: D. Magill (Belfast).
Attendance: 2000

Club Records: Linfield 30, Glentoran 11, Belfast Celtic 10, Portadown 6, Coleraine 4, Distillery 5, Cliftonville 3, Glenavon 3, Ards 2, Ballymena United 1, Crusaders 1, Derry City 1, Shelbourne 1.

IRISH CUP FINALS (from 1946–47)

1946–47 Belfast Celtic 1, Glentoran 0
1947–48 Linfield 3, Coleraine 0
1948–49 Derry City 3, Glentoran 1
1949–50 Linfield 2, Distillery 1
1950–51 Glentoran 3, Ballymena U 1
1951–52 Ards 1, Glentoran 0
1952–53 Linfield 5, Coleraine 0
1953–54 Derry City 1, Glentoran 0
1954–55 Dundela 3, Glenavon 0
1955–56 Distillery 1, Glentoran 0
1956–57 Glenavon 2, Derry City 0
1957–58 Ballymena U 2, Linfield 0
1958–59 Glenavon 2, Ballymena U 0
1959–60 Linfield 5, Ards 1
1960–61 Glenavon 5, Linfield 1
1961–62 Linfield 4, Portadown 0
1962–63 Linfield 2, Distillery 1
1963–64 Derry City 2, Glentoran 0
1964–65 Coleraine 2, Glenavon 1
1965–66 Glentoran 2, Linfield 0
1966–67 Crusaders 3, Glentoran 1
1967–68 Crusaders 2, Linfield 0
1968–69 Ards 4, Distillery 2
1969–70 Linfield 2, Ballymena U 1
1970–71 Distillery 3, Derry City 0
1971–72 Coleraine 2, Portadown 1
1972–73 Glentoran 3, Linfield 2
1973–74 Ards 2, Ballymena U 1
1974–75 Coleraine 1:0:1, Linfield 1:0:0
1975–76 Carrick Rangers 2, Linfield 1
1976–77 Coleraine 4, Linfield 1
1977–78 Linfield 3, Ballymena U 1
1978–79 Cliftonville 3, Portadown 2
1979–80 Linfield 2, Crusaders 0
1980–81 Ballymena U 1, Glenavon 0
1981–82 Linfield 2, Coleraine 1
1982–83 Glentoran 1:2, Linfield 1:1
1983–84 Ballymena U 4, Carrick Rangers 1
1984–85 Glentoran 1:1, Linfield 1:0
1985–86 Glentoran 2, Coleraine 1
1986–87 Glentoran 1, Larne 0
1987–88 Glentoran 1, Glenavon 0
1988–89 Ballymena U 1, Larne 0
1989–90 Glentoran 3, Portadown 0
1990–91 Portadown 2, Glenavon 1
1991–92 Glenavon 2, Linfield 1
1992–93 Bangor 1:1:1, Ards 1:1:0
1993–94 Linfield 2, Bangor 0
1994-95 Linfield 3, Carrick Rangers 1

WHERE THE TROPHIES WENT

	Winners	*Runners-up*
Smirnoff Irish League	Crusaders	Glenavon
Bass Irish Cup	Linfield	Carrick Rangers
TNT Gold Cup	Glentoran	Crusaders
Budweiser Cup	Portadown	Distillery
Wilkinson Sword League Cup	Ards	Cliftonville
Ulster Cup	Bangor	Linfield
Cawoods Co Antrim Shield	Linfield	Glenavon

Wilkinson Sword B Division

Section One	Loughall	Dungannon Swifts
Section Two	Bangor Res	Glentoran II
Coca Cola Irish Youth Cup	Glentoran Colts	Lurgan Town Boys
Intermediate Cup	Ballinamallard Utd	Park
Cawood Co Antrim Junior Shield	Immaculata	
Wilkinson Sword George Wilson Cup	Bangor Res	Crusaders Res
Ted Clark Mid Ulster Cup	Portadown	Newry Town
Mid Ulster Shield	Oxford Utd	Sparta
Cawoods Steel and Sons Cup	Bangor Res	Linfield Swifts
North West Senior Cup	Coleraine	Limavady Utd
North West Junior Cup	Ardmore	Tullyally Colts
McEwans Sixes	Cliftonville	Ballyclare Comrades
Bob Radcliffe Memorial Cup	Dungannon Swifts	Loughgall
McEwans Charity Shield	Linfield	Bangor
Ormo Irish Junior Cup	Oxford Utd	Dergview
Smirnoff Knock Out Cup	Dundela	Loughgall
Irish Youth League	Linfield Rangers	Glentoran Colts
Irish Youth League Cup	Ballyclare Colts	Linfield Rangers

BASS IRISH CUP 1994–95

Fifth Round (First Round Proper)

Ards v Chimney Corner	3-1
Newry Town v Larne	3-0
Omagh Town v Ballymena United	0-0, 1-0
Ballyclare Comrades v Glenavon	2-3
Dundela v Crumlin United	3-1
Linfield v Crusaders	2-0
Glentoran v Coleraine	1-1, 1-2
Portadown v Donegall Celtic	4-0
Brantwood v Moyola Park	2-2, 3-2
Distillery v Bangor	1-5
Carrick Rangers v Ballinamallard United	2-0
Crewe United v Cliftonville	0-2
Limavady United v Dungiven	1-2
Dungannon Swifts v Cookstown United	1-0
Loughgall v Kilmore Rec	2-1
Banbridge Town v Dunmurry Rec	7-0

(For the first time in the history of the competition, all matches were postponed on Saturday, January 22 because of flooded pitches. They were staged throughout the following week).

Sixth Round

Ards v Brantwood	4-1
Carrick Rangers v Dundela	2-1
Cliftonville v Banbridge	4-0
Coleraine v Portadown	0-0, 1-3
Loughgall v Dungiven	2-1
Newry Town v Bangor	1-1, 1-2
Omagh Town v Glenavon	1-1, 1-3
Dungannon Swifts v Linfield	3-5

Quarter-finals

Ards v Glenavon	3-2
Carrick Rangers v Bangor	2-1
Linfield v Loughgall	1-1, 1-0
Portadown v Cliftonville	0-1

Semi-finals

Ards v Linfield *(The Oval)*	0-0, 1-2
Carrick Rangers v Portadown *(Windsor Park)*	1-0

Final

Carrick Rangers 1 Linfield 3 *(at The Oval, Belfast, 7 May 1995)*

Carrick Rangers: Miskelly; Wilson, Gilmore, Muldoon, Gordon, Coulter, Kirk, McDermott, Donaghy (Doherty), Ferris, McAuley (Crawford).

Linfield: Lamont; Dornan, Easton, Peebles (McCoosh), Spiers, Beatty, Campbell, Gorman, Haylock, Fenlon, Bailie.

Scorers: Carrick Rangers–Gilmore; Linfield–Haylock (2), McCoosh.

Referee: G. Keatley (Bangor).

Attendance: 6000.

INTERNATIONAL DIRECTORY

The latest available information has been given regarding numbers of clubs and players registered with FIFA, the world governing body. Where known, official colours are listed. With European countries, League tables show a number of signs. * indicates relegated teams, + play-offs, *+ relegated after play-offs, + + promoted.
When provisional members are added there will be 190 FIFA countries. The four home countries, England, Scotland, Northern Ireland and Wales, are dealt with elsewhere in the Yearbook; but basic details appear in this directory.

EUROPE

ALBANIA

Federation Albanaise De Football, Rruga Dervish Hima Nr. 31, Tirana.
Founded: 1930; *Number of Clubs:* 49; *Number of Players:* 5,192; *National Colours:* Red shirts, black shorts, red stockings.
Telephone: 00–355–42 27 877; *Cable:* ALBSPORT TIRANA; *Telex:* 2228 bfssh ab. *Fax:* 00 355–42 27 877.

International matches 1994
Macedonia (a) 1-5, Wales (a) 0-2, Germany (h) 1-2, Georgia (h) 0-1, Germany (a) 1-2.

League Championship wins (1945–95)
Dinamo Tirana 15; Partizani Tirana 15; 17 Nentori 8; Vllaznia 7; Flamurtari 1; Labinoti 1; Teuta 1, SK Tirana 1.

Cup wins (1948–95)
Partizani Tirana 13; Dinamo Tirana 12; 17 Nentori 6; Vllaznia 5; Flamurtari 2; Labinoti 1; Elbasan 1; SK Tirana 1, Teuta 1.

Final League Table 1994–95

	P	*W*	*D*	*L*	*F*	*A*	Pts
SK Tirana	30	19	6	5	57	27	44
Teuta	30	13	6	11	37	27	32
Partizani	30	12	8	10	36	30	32
Flamurtari	30	11	10	9	34	29	32
Shqiponia	30	11	9	10	38	33	31
Albpetrol	30	13	5	12	37	43	31
Shkumbini	30	11	8	11	32	20	30
Dinamo	30	10	10	10	37	27	30
Tomori	30	12	6	12	21	25	30
Apolonia	30	12	6	12	33	38	30
Vllaznia	30	12	5	13	31	29	29
Elbasan	30	10	9	11	22	20	29
Beselidhja	30	11	7	12	29	34	29
Laci*	30	13	3	14	30	40	29
Beca*	30	12	2	16	30	40	26
Iliria*	30	7	2	21	22	64	16

Top scorer: Shehu (Shqiponia) 21.
Cup Final: Teuta 0, SK Tirana 0.
Teuta won 4-3 on penalties.

ARMENIA

Football Federation of Armenia, 9, Abovian Str. 375001 Erevan, Armenia.
Number of Clubs: 956; *Number of Players:* 12,055.
Telephone: 007 8852 52 98 62; *Telex:* 885–52 3376. *Fax:* 007 8852 15 15 73.

International matches 1994
USA (a) 0-1, Belgium (1) 0-2, Cyprus (h) 0-0, Cyprus (a) 0-2.

League Championship wins 1992–94
Shirak Gyumri 2; Ararat Erevan 1.

Cup winners 1992–94
Ararat Erevan 2.

Final League Table 1994

	P	*W*	*D*	*L*	*F*	*A*	Pts
Shirak Gyumri	28	24	4	0	83	19	52
Homenetmen	28	23	1	4	113	24	47
Ararat Erevan	28	21	5	2	109	21	47
Homenmen	28	15	6	7	65	45	36
Banants	28	17	1	10	95	56	35
Tsement	28	11	6	11	54	49	28
Kotaik	28	12	3	13	73	53	27
Aznavour	28	11	3	14	43	72	25
Yerazank	28	9	5	14	29	50	23
Van	28	9	4	15	34	72	22
Zankezour	28	9	4	15	25	77	22
Nayrit*	28	7	6	15	22	43	18
Armee Arayi*	28	6	5	17	39	79	17
Lori*	28	5	6	17	22	65	16
Kanaz*	28	1	3	24	15	89	5

Top scorers: Avetissian A (Homenetmen) 39.
Cup Final: Ararat Erevan 4, Kotaik 2.

AUSTRIA

Oesterreichischer Fussball-Bund, Wiener Stadion, Sektor A/F, Meierestrasse, A-1020 Wien.
Founded: 1904; *Number of Clubs:* 2,081; *Number of Players:* 253,576; *National Colours:* White shirts, black shorts, black stockings.
Telephone: 0043 1 727 18; *Cable:* FOOTBALL WIEN; *Telex:* 111919 oefb a; *Fax:* 0043 1 728 1632.

International matches 1994
Hungary (h) 1-1, Scotland (h) 1-2, Poland (a) 4-3, Germany (h) 1-5, Russia (h) 0-3, Liechtenstein (a) 4-0, Northern Ireland (h) 1-2, Portugal (a) 0-1.

League Championship wins (1912–95)
Rapid Vienna 29; FK Austria 22; Admira-Energie-Wacker (prev. Sportklub Admira & Admira-Energie) 8; First Vienna 6; Tirol-Svarowski-Innsbruck (prev. Wacker Innsbruck) 7; Wiener Sportklub 3; Austria Salzburg 2; FAC 1; Hakoah 1; Linz ASK 1; Wacker Vienna 1; WAF 1; Voest Linz 1.

Cup wins (1919–95)
FK Austria 25; Rapid Vienna 14; TS Innsbruck (prev. Wacker Innsbruck) 7; Admira-Energie-Wacker (prev. Sportklub Admira & Admira-Energie) 5; First Vienna 3; Linz ASK 1; Wacker Vienna 1; WAF 1; Wiener Sportklub 1; Graz 1; Stockerau 1.

Final table 1994–95

	P	*W*	*D*	*L*	*F*	*A*	Pts
Austria Salzburg	36	15	17	4	48	24	47
Sturm Graz	36	18	11	7	58	41	47
Rapid	36	18	9	9	61	50	44
FK Austria	36	16	11	9	58	38	43
Innsbruck	36	15	10	11	61	44	40
Linz ASK	36	14	11	11	51	44	39
Admira Wacker	36	11	12	13	48	53	34
Vorwaerts	36	9	11	16.	40	49	29
Linz*+	36	5	10	21	33	81	20
Modling*	36	4	8	24	28	62	16

Top scorer: Sane (Innsbruck) 20.
Cup Final: Rapid 1, Leoben 0.

AZERBAIJAN

Azerbaijan Football Association, G.Gadjiev Street 42, 370009 Baku, Azerbaijan.
Number of Clubs: 2,200. *Number of Players:* 131,000.
Telephone: 00994 12 94 05 42; *Fax:* 00994 12 98 93 93; *Telex:* 142349 affa su.

International matches 1994
Malta (a) 0-5, Moldovo (a) 1-2, Romania (a) 0-3, Poland (a) 0-1, Israel (h) 0-2, France (h) 0-2.

BELARUS

Football Federation of Belarus, 8–2 Kyrov Str. 220600 Minsk, Belarus.
Founded: 1992; Number of Players: 120,000.
Telephone: 007 0172 27 29 20; *Telex:*252175 athlet su; *Fax:* 007 0172 27 29 20.

International matches 1994
Ukraine (a) 1-3, Poland (a) 1-1, Norway (a) 0-1, Luxembourg (h) 2-0, Norway (h) 0-4.

League Championship wins 1992–95
Dynamo Minsk 4.

Cup wins 1992–94
Dynamo Minsk 2; Neman 1.

Final League Table 1994–95

	P	*W*	*D*	*L*	*F*	*A*	Pts
Dynamo Minsk	30	20	8	2	83	24	48
Dvina	30	17	12	1	46	13	46
Dynamo 93	30	16	10	4	52	22	42
Molodechno	30	12	11	7	48	30	35
Dnepr	30	12	9	9	43	33	33
Torpedo Minsk	30	11	10	9	36	29	32
Neman	30	10	10	10	24	27	30
Obuvshchik	30	10	10	10	32	36	30
Dynamo Brest	30	9	10	11	33	33	28
Torpedo Mogilev	30	8	12	10	28	32	28
Traktor	30	8	12	10	31	36	28
Vedrich	30	10	8	12	22	33	28
Shnnik	30	7	9	14	31	50	23
Shakhtjor	30	6	9	15	24	41	21
Gomselmash	30	6	6	18	26	59	18
Lokomotiv	30	3	4	23	14	75	10

BELGIUM

Union Royale Belge Des Societes De Football; Eturl, Association, Rue De La Loi 43, Boite 1, B-1040 Bruxelles.
Founded: 1895; *Number of Clubs:* 2,120; *Number of Players:* 390,468; *National Colours:* Red shirts with tri-coloured trim, red shorts, red stockings with trim.
Telephone: 0032 2 477 12 11; *Cable:* UBSFA BRUXELLES; *Telex:* 23257 bvbfbf b; *Fax:* 0032 2 478 23 91.

International matches 1994
Malta (a) 0-1, Zambia (h) 9-0, Hungary (h) 3-1, Morocco (n) 1-0, Holland (n) 1-0, Saudi Arabia (n) 0-1, Germany (n) 2-3, Armenia (h) 2-0,.Denmark (a) 1-3, Macedonia (h) 1-1, Spain (h) 1-4.

League Championship wins (1896–1995)
Anderlecht 24; Union St Gilloise 11; FC Brugge 9; Standard Liege 8; Beerschot 7; RC Brussels 6; FC Liège 5; Daring Brussels 5; Antwerp 4; Mechelen 4; Lierse SK 3; SV Brugge 3; Beveren 2; RWD Molenbeek 1.

Cup wins (1954–95)
Anderlecht 8; FC Brugge 6; Standard Liege 5; Beerschot 2; Waterschei 2; Beveren 2; Gent 2; Antwerp 2; Lierse SK 1; Racing Doornik 1; Waregem 1; SV Brugge 1; Mechelen 1; FC Liège 1.

Final League Table 1994–95

	P	*W*	*D*	*L*	*F*	*A*	Pts
Anderlecht	34	23	6	5	80	31	52
Standard Liege	34	21	9	4	53	23	51
FC Brugge	34	21	7	6	68	32	49
Aalst	34	14	11	9	58	56	39
Ekeren	34	12	13	9	57	39	37
Lierse	34	14	9	11	52	52	37
Lommel	34	13	9	12	44	40	35
St Truiden	34	11	13	10	34	35	35
Seraing	34	12	10	12	53	45	34
Beveren	34	10	12	12	40	46	32
RWD Molenbeek	34	10	11	13	34	41	31
Charleroi	34	10	11	13	33	43	31
Gent	34	11	8	15	41	53	30
Mechelen	34	10	9	15	40	47	29
CS Brugge	34	9	10	15	43	52	28
Antwerp	34	8	8	18	40	56	24
Liege*	34	6	7	21	36	71	19
Ostend*	34	5	9	20	32	76	19

Top scorer: Vidmar (Standard) 22.
Cup Final: FC Brugge 3, Ekeren 1.

BULGARIA

Bulgarian Football Union, Gotcho Gopin 19, 1000 Sofia.
Founded: 1923; *Number of Clubs:* 376; *Number of Players:* 48,240; *National Colours:* White shirts, green shorts, red stockings.
Telephone: 00359 2 87 74 90; *Cable:* BULFUTBOL; *Telex:* 23145 bfs bg; *Fax:* 00359 2 80 32 37.

International matches 1994
Mexico (h) 1-1, Oman (a) 1-1, Kuwait (a) 2-2, Ukraine (h) 1-1, Nigeria (n) 0-3, Greece (n) 4-0, Argentina (n) 2-0, Mexico (n) 1-1, Germany (n) 2-1, Italy (n) 1-2, Sweden (n) 0-4, Georgia (h) 2-0, Moldovo (h) 4-1, Wales (a) 3-0.

League Championship wins (1925–95)
CSKA Sofia 27; Levski Sofia 19; Slavia Sofia 6; Vladislav Varna 3; Lokomotiv Sofia 3; Trakia Plovdiv 2; AS 23 Sofia 1; Botev Plovdiv 1; SC Sofia 1; Sokol Varna 1; Spartak Plovdiv 1; Tichka Varna 1; ZSZ Sofia 1; Beroe Stara Zagora 1; Etur 1.

Cup wins (1946–95)
Levski Sofia 18; CSKA Sofia 14; Slavia Sofia 6; Lokomotiv Sofia 4; Botev Plovdiv 1; Spartak Plovdiv 1; Spartak Sofia 1; Marek Stanke 1; Trakia Plovdiv 1; Spartak Varna 1; Sliven 1.

Final League Table 1994–95

	P	*W*	*D*	*L*	*F*	*A*	Pts
Levski Sofia	30	26	1	3	84	15	79
Lokomotiv Sofia	30	21	5	4	59	30	68
Botev Plovdiv	30	18	6	6	66	31	60
Slavia Sofia	30	16	5	9	63	35	53
CSKA Sofia	30	13	7	10	51	46	46
Spartak Plovdiv	30	12	7	11	33	34	43
Lokomotiv Plovdiv	30	13	3	14	48	38	42
Neftochimik	30	12	3	15	41	50	39
Chumen	30	10	6	14	33	50	36
Lovetch Lex	30	10	6	14	25	46	36
Etur	30	10	6	14	31	54	36
Dobroudja	30	10	5	15	32	43	35
Montana	30	9	7	14	31	41	34
Lokomotiv Gorna*	30	10	3	17	35	53	33
Pirin*	30	9	3	18	30	46	30
Beroe*	30	3	3	24	27	77	12

Top scorer: Mihtarski (CSKA Sofia) 23.
Cup Final: Lokomotiv Sofia 4, Botev Plovdiv 2.

CROATIA

Croatian Football Federation, Illica 21/11, CRO-41000 Zagreb, Croatia.
Telephone: 00385 41 45 41 00. *Fax:* 00385 41 42 46 39.

International matches 1994
Spain (a) 2-0, Slovakia (a) 1-4, Hungary (a) 2-2, Argentina (h) 0-0, Israel (a) 4-0, Estonia (a) 2-0, Lithuania (h) 2-0, Italy (a) 2-1.

League Championship wins 1993–95
Hajduk Split 2; Croatia Zagreb 1.

Cup wins 1993–95
Hajduk Split 2, Croatia Zagreb 1.

Final League Table 1994–95

	P	*W*	*D*	*L*	*F*	*A*	Pts
Hajduk Split	30	19	8	3	68	25	65
Croatia Zagreb	30	19	7	4	53	26	64
Osijek	30	16	11	3	65	30	59
Zagreb	30	14	11	5	41	26	53
Marsonia	30	13	8	9	42	32	47
Varteks	30	11	10	9	35	27	43
Inker	30	11	6	13	41	41	39
Segesta	30	10	7	13	32	31	37
Sibenik	30	9	10	11	44	46	37
Vinkovci	30	9	10	11	20	31	37
Rijeka	30	8	10	12	28	34	34
Istra Pola	30	8	8	14	30	46	32
Zadar*	30	7	10	13	33	47	31
Promarac*	30	7	10	13	27	49	31
Neretva*	30	4	11	15	20	44	23
Belisce*	30	4	4	22	26	69	16

Top scorer: Spehar (Osijek) 23.
Cup Final: Hajduk Split 3, 1, Croatia Zagreb 2, 0.

CYPRUS

Cyprus Football Association, Stasinos Str. 1, Engomi 152, P.O. Box 5071, Nicosia.
Founded: 1934; *Number of Clubs:* 85; *Number of Players:* 6,000; *National Colours:* Sky blue shirts, white shorts, blue and white stockings.
Telephone: 00357 2 44 53 41; *Cable:* FOOTBALL NICOSIA; *Telex:* 3880 football cy; *Fax:* 00357 2 47 25 44.

International matches 1994
Estonia (h) 2-0, Slovenia (a) 0-3, Spain (h) 1-2, Armenia (a) 0-0, Armenia (h) 2-0, Macedonia (a) 0-3.

League Championship wins (1935–95)
Omonia 17; Apoel 15; Anorthosis 7; AEL 5; EPA 3; Olympiakos 3; Apollon 2; Pezoporikos 2; Chetin Kayal 1; Trast 1.

Cup wins (1935–95)
Apoel 14; Omonia 10; AEL 6; EPA 5; Anorthosis 4; Apollon 4; Trast 3; Chetin Kayal 2; Olympiakos 1; Pezoporikos 1; Salamina 1.

Final League Table 1993–95

	P	*W*	*D*	*L*	*F*	*A*	Pts
Anorthosis	33	22	7	4	71	25	73
Omonia	33	20	7	6	82	32	67
Salamina	33	17	6	10	59	50	57
Ethnikos	33	14	5	14	52	59	47
Apoel	33	13	7	13	43	43	46
Apollon	33	13	6	14	50	46	45
Paralimni	33	12	9	12	44	49	45
Olympiakos	33	13	5	15	41	65	44
AEK	33	12	6	15	50	48	42
AEL	33	12	5	16	44	57	41
Aris*	33	10	7	16	44	49	37
Aradippu*	33	3	4	26	37	94	13

Top scorer: Androu (Salmina) 25.
Cup Final: Apoel 4, Apollon 2.

CZECH REPUBLIC

Football Association of Czech Republic, Diskarska 100, 169 00 Prague 6, Czech Republic.
Number of Clubs: 3,562; *Number of Players:* 237,200; *National Colours:* Red shirts, white shorts, blue stockings.
Telephone: 0042 2 35 69 13; *Fax:* 0042 2 35 27 84.

International matches 1994
Turkey (a) 4-1, Switzerland (a) 0-3, Lithuania (h) 5-3, Republic of Ireland (a) 3-1, France (a) 2-2, Malta (h) 6-1, Malta (a) 0-0, Holland (a) 0-0.

League Championship wins (1926–93)
Sparta Prague 20; Slavia Prague 12; Dukla Prague (prev. UDA) 11; Slovan Bratislava 7; Spartak Trnava 5; Banik Ostrava 3; Inter-Bratislava 1; Spartak Hradec Kralove 1; Viktoria Zizkov 1; Zbrojovka Brno 1; Bohemians 1; Vitkovice 1.

Cup wins (1961–93)
Dukla Prague 8; Sparta Prague 8; Slovan Bratislava 5; Spartak Trnava 4; Banik Ostrava 3; Lokomotiv Kosice 3; TJ Gottwaldov 1; Dunajska Streda 1.
From 1993–94, there were two separate countries: the Czech Republic and Slovakia.

League Championship wins (1994–95)
Sparta Prague 2.

Cup wins (1994–95)
Viktoria Zizkov 1; Spartak Hradec Kralove 1.

Final League Table 1994–95

	P	*W*	*D*	*L*	*F*	*A*	Pts
Sparta Prague	30	22	4	4	67	17	70
Slavia Prague	30	19	7	4	52	20	64
Boby Brno	30	15	9	6	52	27	54
Slovan Liberec	30	16	3	11	49	46	51
Viktoria Zizkov	30	15	4	11	61	38	49
Petra Drnovice	30	15	3	12	46	44	48
Ceske Budejovice	30	12	10	8	29	28	46
Sigma Olomouc	30	12	7	11	31	31	43
Viktoria Plzen	30	12	4	14	32	37	40
Jablonek	30	11	6	13	37	33	39
Banik Ostrava	30	10	8	12	36	41	38
Hradec Kralove	30	10	6	14	35	45	36
Union Cheb	30	8	7	15	29	45	31
Svit Zlin	30	8	6	16	21	40	30
Bohemians*	30	6	5	19	35	62	23
Svarc Benesov*	30	3	3	24	23	78	12

Top scorer: Drulak (Petra Drnovice) 15.
Cup Final: Hradec Kralove 0, Viktoria Zizkov 0.
Hradec Kralove won 3-1 on penalties.

DENMARK

Dansk Boldspil Union, Ved Amagerbanen 15, DK-2300, Copenhagen S.
Founded: 1889; *Number of Clubs:* 1,555; *Number of Players:* 268,517; *National Colours:* Red shirts, white shorts, red stockings.
Telephone: 0045 31 95 05 11; *Cable:* DANSKBOLDSPIL COPENHAGEN; *Telex:* 15545 dbu dk; *Fax:* 0045 31 95 05 88.

International matches 1994
England (a) 0-1, Hungary (h) 3-1, Sweden (h) 1-0, Norway (a) 1-2, Finland (h) 2-1, Macedonia (a) 1-1, Belgium (h) 3-1, Spain (a) 0-3.

League Championship wins (1913–95)
KB Copenhagen 15; B 93 Copenhagen 9; AB (Akademisk) 9; B 1903 Copenhagen 7; Frem 6; Esbjerg BK 5; Vejle BK 5; AGF Aarhus 5; Brondby 4; Hvidovre 3; Odense BK 3; B 1909 Odense 2; Koge BK 2; Lyngby 2; FC Copenhagen 1; Silkeborg 1, AaB Aalborg 1.

Cup wins (1955–95)
Aarhus GF 8; Vejle BK 6; Randers Freja 3; Lyngby 3; OB Odense 3; B1909 Odense 2; Aalborg BK 2; Esbjerg BK 2; Frem 2; B 1903 Copenhagen 2; Brondby 2; B 93 Copenhagen 1; KB Copenhagen 1; Vanlose 1; Hvidovre 1; B1913 Odense 1, FC Copenhagen 1.

Qualifying Table 1994

	P	*W*	*D*	*L*	*F*	*A*	Pts
Brondby	18	12	3	3	41	19	27
Aalborg	18	12	2	4	44	25	26
Odense	18	10	4	4	31	21	24
Lynby	18	6	7	5	34	27	19
Silkeborg	18	5	7	6	21	23	17
Naestved	18	5	7		26	31	17
FC Copenhagen	18	6	4	8	30	34	16
Aarhus	18	5	5	8	21	35	15
Ikast	18	3	5	10	22	29	11
Fremad	18	4	0	14	21	47	8

Final League Table 1994–95

	P	*W*	*D*	*L*	*F*	*A*	Pts
Aalborg	14	7	4	3	30	13	31
Brondby	14	6	3	5	21	18	29
Silkeborg	14	6	3	5	23	16	24
Aarhus	14	7	2	5	21	23	24
Naestved	14	5	4	5	21	22	23
FC Copenhagen	14	5	4	5	21	28	22
Lyngby	14	5	1	8	20	28	21
Odense	14	3	3	8	17	26	21

Top scorer: Andersen (Aalborg) 24.
Cup Final: FC Copenhagen 5, AB Copenhagen 0.

ENGLAND

The Football Association, 16 Lancaster Gate, London W2 3LW*Founded:* 1863; *Number of Clubs:* 42,000; *Number of Players:* 2,250,000; *National Colours:* White shirts, navy blue shorts, white stockings.
Telephone: 0171 262 4542; *Cable:* FOOTBALL ASSOCIATION LONDON W2; *Telex:* 261110; *Fax:* 0171 402 0486.

ESTONIA

Estonian Football Association, Refati PST 1-376, 20 0103 Tallinn.
Number of Clubs: 40; *Number of Players:* 12,000.
Telephone: 00372 2 23 77 58; *Telex:* 173236 sport su; *Fax:* 00372 2 23 77 58.

International matches 1994
Cyprus (a) 0-2, USA (a) 0-4, Wales (h) 1-2, Macedonia (a) 0-2, Lithuania (a) 0-3, Latvia (a) 0-2, Iceland (a) 0-4, Croatia (h) 0-2, Italy (h) 0-2, Finland (h) 0-7, Latvia (a) 0-0, Ukraine (a) 0-3

League Championship wins (1992–95)
Norma Tallinn 2; Flora Tallinn 2.

Cup Wins (1992–95)
VMV Tallinn 1; Nikol Tallinn 1; Norma Tallinn 1; Lantana 1.

Final Pool Table 1994–95

	P	*W*	*D*	*L*	*F*	*A*	Pts
Flora	10	7	3	0	27	6	41
Lantana	10	7	2	1	26	9	40
Trans	10	4	1	5	9	15	26
Sadam	10	4	0	6	11	14	25
Johvi	10	4	0	6	17	24	21
Norma	10	1	0	9	6	28	8

Top Scorer: Morozov (Lantana) 25.
Cup Final: Lantana 5, Trans Narva 3 aet.

FAEROE ISLANDS

Fotboltssamband Foroya, The Faeroes' Football Assn., Gundalur, P.O. Box 1028, FR-110, Torshavn.
Founded: 1979; *Number of Clubs:* 16; *Number of Players:* 1,014.
Telephone: 00298 16 707; *Telex:* 81332 itrott FA; *Fax:* 00298 19 079.

International matches 1994
Greece (h) 1-5, Scotland (a) 1-5, Finland (a) 0-5.

League Championship wins 1942–94
KI Klaksvik 15; HB Torshavn 14; TB Tvoroyri 7; B36 Torshavn 5; GI Gotu 5; B68 Toftir 3; SI Sorvag 1; IF Fuglafjordur 1; B71 Sandur 1.

Cup wins 1955–94
HB Torshavn 23; TB Tvoroyri 5; KI Klaksvik 4; B36 Torshavn 2; GI Gotu 2; B71 Sandur 1, VB Vagur 1; NSI Runavik 1.

Final League Table 1994

	P	*W*	*D*	*L*	*F*	*A*	Pts
GI	18	14	2	2	59	16	30
HB	18	14	2	2	47	14	30
B71	18	10	4	4	31	12	24
KI	18	8	4	6	40	26	20
B68	18	5	7	6	22	30	17
NSI	18	6	3	9	28	29	16
B36	18	5	5	8	24	34	15
TB	18	6	2	10	32	49	14
IF*	18	3	2	13	17	44	8
EB*	18	2	3	13	15	61	7

Cup Final: KI 2, B71 1.

FINLAND

Suomen Palloliitto Finlands Bollfoerbund, Kuparitie 1, P.O. Box 29, SF-00441 Helsinki.
Founded: 1907; *Number of Clubs:* 1,135; *Number of Players:* 66,100; *National Colours:* White shirts, blue shorts, white stockings.
Telephone: 00358 0 701 01 01; *Cable:* SUOMIFOTBOLL HELSINKI; *Telex :* 126033 spl sf; *Fax:* 00358 0 701 01 099.

International matches 1994
Qatar (a) 0-1, Oman (a) 2-0, Oman (a) 1-1, Morocco (a) 0-0, Italy (a) 0-2, Spain (h) 1-2, Denmark (a) 1-2, Scotland (h) 0-2, Greece (a) 0-4, Estonia (a) 7-0, Faeroes (h) 5-0, San Marino (h) 4-1.

League Championship wins (1949–94)
Helsinki JK 9; Turun Palloseura 5; Kuopion Palloseura 5; Valkeakosken Haka 4; Kuusysi 4; Lahden Reipas 3; Ilves-Kissat 2; IF Kamraterna 2; Kotkan TP 2; OPS Oulu 2; Torun Pyrkivä 1; IF Kronohagens 1; Helsinki PS 1; Kokkolan PV 1; IF Kamraterna 1; Vasa 1; Jazz Pori 1; TPV Tampere 1.

Cup wins (1955–94)
Valkeakosken Haka 9; Lahden Reipas 7; Kotkan TP 4; Helsinki JK 4; Mikkelin 2; Kuusysi 2; Kuopion Palloseura 2; Ilves Tampere 2; TPS Turku 2; IFK Abo 1; Drott 1; Helsinki PS 1; Pallo-Peikot 1; Rovaniemi PS 1; MyPa 1.

Final League Table 1994

	P	*W*	*D*	*L*	*F*	*A*	Pts
TPV Tampere	26	16	4	6	46	27	52
MyPa	26	15	5	6	49	21	50
HJK Helsinki	26	12	7	7	40	29	43
Jazz Pori	26	13	3	10	49	36	42
Haka	26	12	4	10	38	29	40
RoPS Rovaniemi	26	10	8	8	32	32	38
Jaro	26	10	7	9	35	39	37
TPS Turku	26	9	7	10	38	34	34
Finn Pa	26	8	9	9	25	35	33
Kuusysi	26	9	4	13	41	50	31
Mikkeli	26	7	8	11	25	31	29
Ilves	26	7	7	12	35	45	28
Oulu*	26	6	9	11	32	42	27
KuPS Kuopio*	26	6	2	18	24	59	20

Top scorer: Dionisio (TPV Tampere) 17.
Cup Final: HJK Helsinki 2, Jazz Pori 0.

FRANCE

Federation Francaise De Football, 60 Bis A venue D'Iena, F-75783 Paris, Cedex 16.
Founded: 1919; *Number of Clubs:* 21,629; *Number of Players:* 1,692,205; *National Colours:* Blue shirts, white shorts, red stockings.
Telephone: 0033 1 44 31 73 00; *Cable:* CEFI PARIS 034; *Telex:* 640000 fedfoot f; *Fax:* 0033 1 47 20 82 96.

International matches 1994
Italy (a) 1-0, Chile (h) 3-1, Australia (h) 1-0, Japan (a) 4-1, Czech Republic (h) 2-2, Slovakia (a) 0-0, Romania (h) 0-0, Poland (a) 0-0, Azerbaijan (a) 2-0.

League Championship wins (1933–95)
Saint Etienne 10; Olympique Marseille 8; Nantes 7; Stade de Reims 6; AS Monaco 5; OGC Nice 4; Girondins Bordeaux 4; Lille OSC 3; Paris St Germain 2; FC Sete 2; Sochaux 2; Racing Club Paris 1 Roubaix-Tourcoing 1; Strasbourg 1.

Cup wins (1918–95)
Olympique Marseille 10; Saint Etienne 6; Lille OSC 5; Racing Club Paris 5; Red Star 5; AS Monaco 5; Olympique Lyon 4; Girondins Bordeaux 3; Paris St Germain 3; CAS Genereaux 2; Nancy 2; OGC Nice 2; Racing Club Strasbourg 2; Sedan 2; FC Sete 2; Stade de Reims 2; SO Montpellier 2; Stade Rennes 2; AS Cannes 1; Club Français 1; Excelsior Roubaix 1; Le Havre 1; Olympique de Pantin 1; CA Paris 1; Sochaux 1; Toulouse 1; Bastia 1; Nantes 1; Metz 1; Auxerre 1.

Final League Table 1994–95

	P	*W*	*D*	*L*	*F*	*A*	Pts
Nantes	38	21	16	1	71	34	79
Lyon	38	19	12	7	56	38	69
Paris St Germain	38	20	7	11	58	41	67
Auxerre	38	15	17	6	59	34	62
Lens	38	15	14	9	48	44	59
Monaco	38	15	12	11	60	39	57
Bordeaux	38	16	9	13	52	47	57
Metz	38	16	8	14	50	44	56
Cannes	38	15	8	15	56	48	53
Strasbourg	38	13	12	13	43	43	51
Martigues	38	13	12	13	37	49	51
Le Havre	38	12	13	13	46	49	49
Rennes	38	12	12	14	53	55	48
Lille	38	13	9	16	29	44	48
Bastia	38	11	11	16	44	56	44
Nice	38	11	10	17	39	52	43
Montpellier	38	9	14	15	38	53	41
St Etienne	38	9	11	18	45	55	38
Caen*	38	10	6	22	38	58	36
Sochaux*	38	6	5	27	29	68	23

Top scorer: Loko (Nantes) 22.
Cup Final: Paris St Germain 1, Strasbourg 0.

GEORGIA

Football Federation of Georgia, 5 Shota Iamanidze Str, Tbillisi 380012, Georgia.
Founded: 1992; Number of Clubs: 4050. *Number of Players:* 115,000.
Telephone: 007 8832 96 07 10; *Telex:* 340744. *Fax:* 0049 5151 86 33 (satellite-fax).

International matches 1994
Slovenia (h) 0-1, Malta (a) 1-0, Tunisia (a) 2-0, Israel (a) 0-2, Nigeria (a) 1-5, Latvia (a) 3-1, Moldovo (h) 0-1, Bulgaria (a) 0-2, Wales (h) 5-0, Albania (a) 1-0.

League Championship wins (1991–95)
Dynamo Tbilisi 5.

Cup wins (1991–95)
Dynamo Tbilisi 5.
Although Dynamo Tbilisi won the championship with 78 points from 30 matches four teams were deducted points on the last day of the season. After Kolcheti had beaten Samgurali 10-5 and Torpedo had defeated Sapovnela 11-4, the teams involved were accused of arranging for both winners to have their top scorers credited with 9 goals each!
Cup Final: Dynamo Tbilisi 1, Batumi 0.

GERMANY

Deutsche Fussball-Bund, Otto-Fleck-Schneise 6, Postfach 710265, D-6000, Frankfurt (Main) 71.
Founded: 1900; *Number of Clubs:* 26,760; *Number of Players:* 5,260,320; *National Colours:* White shirts, black shorts, white stockings.
Telephone: 0049 69 678 80; *Cable:* FUSSBALL FRANKFURT; *Telex:* 416815 dfb d; *Fax:* 0049 69 678 82 66.

International matches 1994
Italy (h) 2-1, UAR (a) 2-0, Republic of Ireland (h) 0-2, Austria (a) 5-1, Canada (a) 2-0, Bolivia (n) 1-0, Spain (n) 1-1, South Korea (n) 3-2, Belgium (n) 3-2, Bulgaria (n) 1-2, Russia (a) 1-0,.Hungary (a) 0-0, Albania (a) 2-1, Moldovo (a) 3-0, Albania (h) 2-1.

League Championship wins (1903–95)
Bayern Munich 13; IFC Nuremberg 9; Schalke 04 7; SV Hamburg 6; Borussia Moenchengladbach 5; VfB Stuttgart 4; Borussia Dortmund 4; VfB Leipzig 3; Sp Vgg Furth 3; IFC Cologne 3; IFC Kaiserslautern 3; Werder Bremen 3; Viktoria Berlin 2; Hertha Berlin 2; Hanover 96 2; Dresden SC 2; Munich 1860 1; Union Berlin 1; FC Freiburg 1; Phoenix Karlsruhe 1; Karlsruher FV 1; Holsten Kiel 1; Fortuna Dusseldorf 1; Rapid Vienna 1; VfB Mannheim 1; Rot-Weiss Essen 1; Eintracht Frankfurt 1; Eintracht Brunswick 1.

Cup wins (1935–95)
Bayern Munich 8; IFC Cologne 4; Eintracht Frankfurt 4; IFC Nuremberg 3; SV Hamburg 3; Werder Bremen 3; Moenchengladbach 3; Dresden SC 2; Fortuna Dusseldorf 2; Karlsruhe SC 2; Munich 1860 2; Schalke 04 2; VfB Stuttgart 2; Borussia Borussia Dortmund 2; First Vienna 1; VfB Leipzig 1; Kickers Offenbach 1; Rapid Vienna 1; Rot-Weiss Essen 1; SW Essen 1; Bayer Uerdingen 1; IFC Kaiserslautern 1; Hannover 96 1; Leverkusen 1.

Final League Table 1994–95

	P	*W*	*D*	*L*	*F*	*A*	Pts
Borussia Dortmund	34	20	9	5	67	33	49
Werder Bremen	34	20	8	6	70	39	48
Freiburg	34	20	6	8	66	44	46
Kaiserslautern	34	17	12	5	58	41	46
Moenchengladbach	34	17	9	8	66	41	43
Bayern Munich	34	15	13	6	55	41	43
Leverkusen	34	13	10	11	62	51	36
Karlsruhe	34	11	14	9	51	47	36
Eintracht Frankfurt	34	12	9	13	41	49	33
Cologne	34	11	10	13	54	54	32
Schalke	34	10	11	13	48	54	31
Stuttgart	34	10	10	14	52	66	30
Hamburg	34	10	9	15	43	50	29
Munich 1860	34	8	11	15	41	57	27
Uerdingen	34	7	11	16	37	52	25
Bochum*	34	9	4	21	43	67	22
Duisburg*	34	6	8	20	31	64	20
Dynamo Dresden*	34	4	8	22	33	68	16

Top scorers: Basler (Werder Bremen), Herrlich (Moenchengladbach) 20.
Cup Final: Moenchengladbach 3, Wolfsburg 0.

GREECE

Federation Hellenique De Football, Singrou Avenue 137, Athens.
Founded: 1926; *Number of Clubs:* 4,050; *Number of Players:* 180,000; *National Colours:* White shirts, blue shorts, white stockings.
Telephone: 0030 1 933 88 50; *Cable:* FOOTBALL ATHENES; *Telex:* 215328 epo gr; *Fax:* 0030 1 935 96 66.

International matches 1994
Poland (h) 0-0, Saudi Arabia (h) 5-1, Cameroon (h) 0-3, Bolivia (h) 0-0, England (a) 0-5, USA (a) 1-1, Colombia (a) 0-2,.Argentina (n) 0-4, Bulgaria (n) 0-4, Nigeria (n) 0-2, Faeroes (a) 5-1, Finland (h) 4-0, San Marino (h) 2-0, Scotland (h) 1-0.

League Championship wins (1928–95)
Olympiakos 25; Panathinaikos 17; AEK Athens 11; Aris Salonika 3; PAOK Salonika 2; Larissa 1.

Cup wins (1932–95)
Olympiakos 20; Panathinaikos 16; AEK Athens 9; PAOK Salonika 2; Aris Salonika 1; Ethnikos 1; Iraklis 1; Panionios 1; Kastoria 1; Larissa 1; Ofi Crete 1.

Final League Table 1994–95

	P	*W*	*D*	*L*	*F*	*A*	Pts
Panathinaikos	34	26	5	3	83	21	83
Olympiakos	34	20	7	7	69	31	67
PAOK Salonika	34	20	5	9	55	29	65
Apollon	34	20	3	11	61	37	63
AEK Athens	34	17	11	6	61	33	62
Aris Salonika	34	19	5	10	46	34	62
Iraklis	34	17	8	9	62	40	59
Xanthi	34	14	8	12	52	54	50
Ofi Crete	34	15	4	15	40	38	49
Ethnikos	34	11	9	14	40	48	42
Edessiakos	34	13	3	18	45	54	42
Larissa	34	11	7	16	41	46	40
Athinaikos	34	10	10	14	29	35	40
Panionios	34	10	6	18	36	58	36
Ionikos	34	9	7	18	27	53	34
Doxa Drama*	34	8	5	21	27	71	29
Levadiakos*	34	5	5	24	23	67	20
Kavala*	34	5	4	25	27	75	19

Top scorers: R. Warzycha (Panathinaikos) 29.
Cup Final: Panathinaikos 1, AEK Athens 0 aet.

HOLLAND

Koninklijke Nederlandsche Voetbalbond, Woudenbergseweg 56, Postbus 515, NL-3700 AM, Zeist.
Founded: 1889; *Number of Clubs:* 3,097; *Number of Players:* 962,397; *National Colours:* Orange shirts, white shorts, orange stockings.
Telephone: 0031 3439 92 11; *Cable:* VOETBAL ZEIST; *Telex:* 40497 knvb nl; *Fax:* 0031 3439 1397.

International matches 1994
Tunisia (a) 2-2, Scotland (a) 1-0, Republic of Ireland (h) 0-1, Scotland (h) 3-1, Hungary (h) 7-1, Canada (a) 3-0, Saudi Arabia (n) 2-1,.Belgium (n) 0-1, Morocco (n) 2-1, Republic of Ireland (n) 2-0, Brazil (n) 2-3, Luxembourg (a) 4-0, Norway (a) 1-1, Czech Republic (h) 0-0, Luxembourg (h) 5-0.

League Championship wins (1898–95)
Ajax Amsterdam 25; Feyenoord 14; PSV Eindhoven 13; HVV The Hague 8; Sparta Rotterdam 6; Go Ahead Deventer 4; HBS The Hague 3; Willem II Tilburg 3; RCH Haarlem 2; RAP 2; Heracles 2; ADO The Hague 2; Quick The Hague 1; BVV Schiedam 1; NAC Breda 1; Eindhoven 1; Enschede 1; Volewijckers Amsterdam 1; Limburgia 1; Rapid JC Haarlem 1; DOS Utrecht 1; DWS Amsterdam 1; Haarlem 1; Be Quick Groningen 1; SVV Schiedam 1; AZ 67 Alkmaar 1.

Cup wins (1899–95)
Ajax Amsterdam 12; Feyenoord 10; PSV Eindhoven 7; Quick The Hague 4; AZ 67 Alkemaar 3; Rotterdam 3; DFC 2; Fortuna Geleen 2; Haarlem 2; HBS The Hague 2; RCH 2; VOC 2; Wageningen 2; Willem II Tilburg 2; FC Den Haag 2; Concordia Rotterdam 1; CVV 1; Eindhoven 1; HVV The Hague 1; Longa 1; Quick Nijmegen 1; RAP 1; Roermond 1; Schoten 1; Velocitas Breda 1; Velocitas Gr oningen 1; VSV 1; VUC 1; VVV Groningen 1; ZFC 1; NAC Breda 1; Twente Enschede 1; Utrecht 1.

Final League Table 1994–95

	P	*W*	*D*	*L*	*F*	*A*	Pts
Ajax	34	27	7	0	106	28	61
Roda	34	22	10	2	70	28	54
PSV Eindhoven	34	20	7	7	85	46	47
Feyenoord	34	19	5	10	66	56	43
Twente	34	17	8	9	66	50	42
Vitesse	34	14	12	8	53	44	40
Willem II	34	13	8	13	44	48	34
RKC Waalwijk	34	11	11	12	46	49	33
Heerenveen	34	12	6	16	48	60	30
NAC Breda	34	11	7	16	54	60	29
Volendam	34	8	13	13	37	55	29
Utrecht	34	8	11	15	43	60	27
Groningen	34	8	10	16	47	63	26
Sparta	34	8	10	16	42	58	26
NEC Nijmegen	34	9	7	18	48	60	25
Maastricht* +	34	7	9	18	41	71	23
Go Ahead +	34	7	9	18	41	74	23
Dordrecht*	34	5	10	19	40	67	20

Top scorer: Ronaldo (PSV Eindhoven) 30.
Cup Final: Feyenoord 2, Volendam 1.

HUNGARY

Magyar Labdarugo Szovetseg, Hungarian Football Federation, Nepkoztarsasag Utja 47, H-1061 Budapest VI.
Founded: 1901; *Number of Clubs:* 1944; *Number of Players* 95,986; *National Colours:* Red shirts, white shorts, green stockings.
Telephone: 0036 1 252 92 96; *Cable:* MLSZ BUDAPEST; *Telex:* 225782 misz h; *Fax:* 0036 1 252 99 86.

International matches 1994
Switzerland (h) 1-2, Austria (a) 1-1, Slovenia (h) 0-1, Denmark (a) 1-3, Poland (a) 2-3, Croatia (h) 2-2, Holland (a) 1-7, Belgium (a) 1-3, Turkey (h) 2-2, Germany (h) 0-0, Sweden (a) 0-2, Mexico (a) 1-5.

League Championship wins (1901–95)
Ferencvaros (prev. FRC) 25; MTK-VM Budapest (prev. Hungaria, Bastay and Vörös Lobogo) 19; Ujpest Dozsa 19; Honved 13; Vasas Budapest 6; Csepel 3; Raba Györ (prev. Vasas Györ) 3; BTC 2; Nagyvarad 1; Vac 1.

Cup wins (1910–95)
Ferencvaros (prev. FRC)17; MTK-VM Budapest (prev. Hungaria, Bastay and Vörös Lobogo) 9; Ujpest Dozsa 8; Raba Györ (prev. Vasas Györ) 4; Vasas Budapest 3; Honved 3; Diösgyör 2; Bocskai 1; III Ker 1; Kispesti AC 1; Soroksar 1; Szolnoki MAV 1; Siofok Banyasz 1; Bekescsaba 1; Pecs 1.
Cup not regularly held until 1964

Final League Table 1994–95

	P	*W*	*D*	*L*	*F*	*A*	Pts
Ferencvaros	30	17	8	5	62	41	59
Ujpest	30	15	7	8	57	34	52
Debrecen	30	14	7	9	45	37	49
Kispest Honved	30	14	6	10	60	42	48
Bekescsaba	30	11	15	4	48	33	48
BVSC	30	14	4	12	51	46	46
Zalaegerszeg	30	12	6	12	49	55	42
PMSC	30	12	6	12	37	43	42
Stadler	30	9	10	11	31	35	37
Vasas	30	10	7	13	38	45	37
Gyori	30	11	5	14	42	40	35
Csepel	30	8	11	11	23	26	35
Vac +	30	8	11	11	39	46	35
Parmalat +	30	9	7	14	44	50	34
Nagykanizsa*	30	7	6	17	24	57	27
Sopron*	30	6	10	14	36	56	25

Top scorer: Preisinger (Zalaegerszeg) 21.
Cup Final: Ferencvaros 2, 4, Vac 0, 3.

ICELAND

Knattspyrnusamband Island, P.O. Box 8511, 128 Reykjavik.
Founded: 1929; *Number of Clubs:* 73; *Number of Players:* 23,673; *National Colours;* Blue shirts, white shorts, blue stockings.
Telephone: 00354 1 81 44 44; *Cable* KSI REYKJAVIK; *Telex:* 2314 isi is; *Fax:* 00354 1 68 97 93.

International matches 1994
Saudia Arabia (a) 0-2, USA (a) 2-1, Brazil (a) 0-3, Bolivia (h) 1-0, Estonia (h) 4-0, Sweden (h) 0-1, Turkey (a) 0-5, Kuwait (a) 1-0, Switzerland (a) 0-1.

League Championship wins (1912–94)
KR 20; Valur 19; Fram 18; IA Akranes 15; Vikingur 5; IBK Keflavik 3; IBV Vestmann 2; KA Akureyri 1.

Cup wins (1960–94)
Valur 8; KR 7; Fram 7; IA Akranes 5; IBV Vestmann 3; IBA Akureyri 1; Vikingur 1; IBK Keflavik 1, KR Reykjavik 1.

Final League Table 1994

	P	*W*	*D*	*L*	*F*	*A*	Pts
IA Akranes	18	12	3	3	35	11	39
FH	18	10	3	5	25	17	33
IBK	18	8	7	3	36	24	31
KR	18	8	6	4	29	19	30
Valur	18	8	4	6	25	25	28
Fram	18	4	8	6	27	30	20
UBK	18	6	2	10	23	35	20
IBV	18	4	7	7	22	29	19
Thor*	18	3	5	10	27	38	14
Starjnan*	18	2	5	11	18	39	11

Top scorer: Bibercic (IA Akranes) 14.
Cup Final: KR Reykjavik 2, UMF Grindavik 0.

REPUBLIC OF IRELAND

The Football Association of Ireland, (Cumann Peile Na H-Eireann), 80 Merrion Square, South Dublin 2.
Founded: 1921; *Number of Clubs:* 3,190; *Number of Players:* 124,615; *National Colours:* Green shirts, white shorts, green stockings.
Telephone: 00353 1 676 68 64; *Cable:* SOCCER DUBLIN; *Telex:* 91397 fai ei; *Fax:* 00353 1 661 09 31.

League Championship wins (1922–95)
Shamrock Rovers 15; Dundalk 9; Shelbourne 8; Bohemians 7; Waterford 6; Cork United 5; Drumcondra 5; St Patrick's Athletic 4; St James's Gate 2; Cork Athletic 2; Sligo Rovers 2; Limerick 2; Athlone Town 2; Dolphin 1; Cork Hibernians 1; Cork Celtic 1; Derry City 1, Cork City 1.

Cup wins (1922–95)
Shamrock Rovers 24; Dundalk 8; Drumcondra 5; Bohemians 5; Shelbourne 3; Cork Athletic 2; Cork United 2; St James's Gate 2; St Patrick's Athletic 2; Cork Hibernians 2; Limerick 2; Waterford 2; Derry City 2; Alton United 1; Athlone Town 2; Sligo 2; Cork 1; Fordsons 1; Transport 1; Finn Harps 1; Home Farm 1; UCD 1; Bray Wanderers 1; Galway United 1.

Final League Table 1994–95

	P	*W*	*D*	*L*	*F*	*A*	Pts
Dundalk	33	17	8	8	41	25	51
Shelbourne	33	16	9	8	45	32	49
Derry City	33	16	10	7	45	30	46
Bohemians	33	14	11	8	48	31	45
St Patricks Ath	33	13	14	6	53	36	41
Cork City	33	15	4	14	54	42	39
Shamrock Rovers	33	14	9	10	46	36	39
Sligo Rovers	33	12	7	14	43	41	35
Galway U	33	10	9	14	39	53	31
Athlone T +	33	6	14	13	31	44	30
Cobh Ramblers*	33	5	11	17	29	51	26
Monaghan U*	33	5	4	24	22	75	25

Top scorer: Caufield (Cork City) 16. *Cup Final:* Derry City 2, Shelbourne 1.

ISRAEL

Israel Football Association, 12 Carlibach Street, P.O. Box 20188, Tel Aviv 61201.
Founded: 1928; *Number of Clubs:* 544; *Number of Players:* 30,449; *National Colours:* White shirts, blue shorts, white stockings.
Telephone: 00972 3 570 90 59; *Cable:* CADUREGEL TEL AVIV; *Fax:* 00972 3 570 20 44.

International matches 1994
Georgia (h) 2-0, Ukraine (h) 1-0, Lithuania (a) 1-1, Croatia (h) 0-4, Poland (h) 2-1, Slovakia (h) 2-2, Azerbaijan (a) 2-0, Romania (h) 1-1.

League Championship wins (1932–95)
Maccabi Tel Aviv 17; Hapoel Tel Aviv 12; Hapoel Petah Tikva 6; Maccabi Haifa 5; Maccabi Netanya 5; Beitar Jerusalem 2; Hakoah Ramat Gan 2; Hapoel Beersheba 2; Bnei Yehouda 1; British Police 1; Hapoel Kfar Sava 1; Hapoel Ramat Gan 1.

Cup wins (1928–95)
Maccabi Tel Aviv 18; Hapoel Tel Aviv 9; Beitar Jerusalem 5; Maccabi Haifa 4; Hapoel Haifa 3; Hapoel Kfar Sava 3; Beitar Tel Aviv 2; Bnei Yehouda 2; Hakoah Ramat Gan 2; Hapoel Petah Tikva 2; Maccabi Petah Tikva 2; British Police 1; Hapoel Jerusalem 1; Hapoel Lod 1; Maccabi Netanya 1.

Final League Table 1994–95

	P	*W*	*D*	*L*	*F*	*A*	Pts
Maccabi Tel Aviv	30	19	6	5	59	27	63
Maccabi Haifa	30	17	7	6	68	34	58
Hapoel Beersheba	30	14	8	8	53	35	50
Hapoel Tel Aviv	30	10	15	5	40	32	45
Hapoel Petah Tikva	30	12	8	10	42	36	44
Beitar Jerusalem	30	12	8	10	42	36	44
Zafirim Holon	30	13	5	12	56	56	44
Maccabi Petah Tikva	30	7	14	9	40	41	35
Ironi Rishon	30	7	13	10	39	44	34
Bnei Yehuda	30	8	10	12	43	49	34
Beitar Tel Aviv	30	10	4	16	43	60	34
Hapoel Beit Shean	30	8	10	12	30	50	34
Hapoel Haifa	30	8	9	13	45	51	33
Maccabi Herzliya	30	8	9	13	30	49	33
Ironi Ashdod*	30	7	11	12	42	52	32
Maccabi Netanya*	30	7	9	14	33	50	30

Top scorers: Revivo (Maccabi Haifa), Turjeman (Ironi) 17.
Cup Final: Maccabi Haifa 2, Hapoel Haifa 0.

ITALY

Federazione Italiana Giuoco Calcio, Via Gregorio Allegri 14, C.P. 2450, 1-00198, Roma.
Founded: 1898; *Number of Clubs:* 20,961; *Number of Players:* 1,420,160; *National Colours:* Blue shirts, white shorts, blue stockings, white trim.
Telephone: 0039 6 849 11 11; *Cable:* FEDERCALCIO ROMA; *Telex:* 611483 calcio i; *Fax:* 0039 6 849 12 239.

International matches 1994
France (h) 0-1, Germany (a) 1-2, Finland (h) 2-0, Switzerland (h) 1-0, Costa Rica (h) 1-0, Republic of Ireland (n) 0-1, Norway (n) 1-0, Mexico (n) 1-1, Nigeria (n) 2-1, Spain (n) 2-1, Bulgaria (n) 2-1, Brazil (n) 0-0, Slovenia (a) 1-1, Estonia (a) 2-0, Croatia (h) 1-2, Turkey (h) 3-1.

League Championship wins (1898–1995)
Juventus 23; AC Milan 14; Inter-Milan 13; Genoa 9; Torino 8; Pro Vercelli 7; Bologna 7; Fiorentina 2; Napoli 2; AS Roma 2; Casale 1; Novese 1; Cagliari 1; Lazio 1; Verona 1; Sampdoria 1.

Cup wins (1922–95)
Juventus 9; AS Roma 8; Torino 4; Fiorentina 4; AC Milan 4; Sampdoria 4; Inter-Milan 3; Napoli 3; Bologna 2; Atalanta 1; Genoa 1; Lazio 1; Vado 1; Venezia 1; Parma 1.

Final League Table 1994–95

	P	*W*	*D*	*L*	*F*	*A*	Pts
Juventus	34	23	4	7	59	32	73
Lazio	34	19	6	9	69	34	63
Parma	34	18	9	7	51	30	63
AC Milan	34	17	9	8	53	32	60
Roma	34	16	11	7	46	25	59
Internazionale	34	14	10	10	39	34	52
Napoli	34	13	12	9	40	45	51
Sampdoria	34	13	11	10	51	37	50
Cagliari	34	13	10	11	40	39	49
Fiorentina	34	12	11	11	61	57	47
Torino	34	12	9	13	44	48	45
Bari	34	12	8	14	40	43	44
Cremonese	34	11	8	15	35	38	41
Genoa	34	10	10	14	34	49	40
Padova +	34	12	4	18	37	58	40
Foggia*	34	8	10	16	32	50	34
Reggiana*	34	4	6	24	23	56	18
Brescia*	34	2	6	26	18	65	12

Top scorer: Batistuta (Fiorentina) 26.
Cup Final: Juventus 1, 2, Parma 0, 0.

LATVIA

Latvian Football Federation, Augsiela, 1, LV-1009, Riga.
Founded: 1921; *Number of Clubs:* 50; *Number of Players:* 12,000.
National Colours: Carmine red shirts, white shorts, carmine red stockings.
Telephone: 00371 2 29 29 88; *Telex:* 161183 ritm su; *Fax:* 00371 8 82 83 31.
Cable: Augsiela 1, LV–1009, Riga.

International matches 1994
Malta (h) 2-0, Georgia (h) 1-3, Estonia (h) 2-0, Lithuania (a) 0-1, Republic of Ireland (h) 0-3, Portugal (h) 1-3, Estonia (h) 0-0, Liechtenstein (a) 1-0.

League Championship wins (1922–94)
ASK Riga 9; RFK Riga 8; Olympia Liepaya 7; Sarkanais Metalurgs Liepaya 7; VEF Riga 6; Energija Riga 4; Skonto Riga 4; Elektrons Riga 3; Torpedo Riga 3; Daugava Liepaya 2; ODO Riga 2; Khimikis Daugavpils 2; RAF Yelgava 2; Keisermezhs Riga 2; Dinamo Riga 1; Zhmilyeva Team 1; Darba Rezervi 1; REZ Riga 1; Start Brotseni 1; Venta Ventspils 1; Yurnieks Riga 1; Alfa Riga 1; Gauya Valmiera 1.

Cup wins (1937–94)
Elektrons Riga 7; Sarkanais Metalurgs Liepaya 5; ODO Riga 3; VEF Riga 3; ASK Riga 3; Tseltnieks Riga 3; RFK Riga 2; Daugava Liepaya 2; Start Brotseni 2; Selmash Liepaya 2; Yurnieks Riga 2; Khimikis Daugavpils 2; RAF Yelgava 2; Rigas Vilki 1; Dinamo Liepaya 1; Dinamo Riga 1; REZ Riga 1; Voulkan Kouldiga 1; Baltija Liepaya 1; Venta Ventspils 1; Pilot Riga 1; Lielupe Yurmala 1; Energija Riga 1; Torpedo Riga 1; Daugava SKIF Riga 1; Tseltnieks Daugavpils 1; Skonto Riga 1, Olympia Riga 1.

Final League Table 1994

	P	*W*	*D*	*L*	*F*	*A*	Pts
Skonto Riga	22	20	2	0	65	9	42
RAF Yelgava	22	13	7	2	38	11	33
DAG Riga	22	11	7	4	35	17	29
Olympia Riga	22	10	8	4	32	19	28
Vairogs Rezekne	22	9	6	7	29	28	24
Pardaugava Riga	22	6	10	6	24	24	22
Vidus Riga	22	8	5	9	22	31	21
Auseklis Daugavplis	22	5	7	10	26	29	16
Interskonto Riga	22	5	7	10	17	27	16
Gemma Riga	22	4	6	12	17	46	14
FK Liepaja*	22	2	5	15	16	46	9
Kimikis Daugavplis*	22	1	6	15	10	44	8

Top scorer: Zuyev (RAF Yelgava) 13.
Cup Final: Olympia 2, DAG 0.

LIECHTENSTEIN

Liechtensteiner Fussball-Verband, Am schragen Weg 17, Postfach 165, 9490 Vaduz.
Founded: 1933; *Number of Clubs:* 7; *Number of Players:* 1,247; *National Colours:* Blue & red shirts, red shorts, blue stockings.
Telephone: 004175 233 24 28; *Cable:* FUSSBALLVERBAND VADUZ; *Fax:* 004175 233 24 30.

International matches 1994
Northern Ireland (a) 1-4, Switzerland (a) 0-2, Austria (h) 0-4, Republic of Ireland (a) 0-4, Latvia (h) 0-1, Portugal (a) 0-8.
Liechtenstein has no national league. Teams compete in Swiss regional leagues.
Cup wins (1946–94)
Vaduz 25; Balzers 10; Triesen 8; Eschen/Mauren 4; Schaan 2.

LITHUANIA

Lithuanian Football Federation, 6, Zemaites Street, 232675 Vilnius. Championship of 14 teams.
Number of Clubs: 20; *Number of Players:* 16,600.
Telephone: 00370 2 35 36 54; *Telex:* 261118 lsk su; *Fax:* 00370 2 35 36 51.
International matches 1994
Israel (h) 1-1, Czech Republic (a) 3-5, Estonia (h) 3-0, Latvia (h) 1-0, Sweden (a) 2-4, Ukraine (a) 2-0, Croatia (a) 0-2, Slovenia (a) 2-1.
League Championship wins (1922–95)
Kovas Kaunas 6; KSS Klaipeda 6; LFLS Kaunas 4; Zalgiris Vilnius 3; LGSF Kaunas 2; MSK Kaunas 1; Ekranas Panevezys 1; Romar Mazeikiai 1.
Cup wins 1992–95

Zalgiris Vilnius 3; Inkaras 1.

Final League Table 1994–95

	P	*W*	*D*	*L*	*F*	*A*	Pts
Zalgiris	22	17	2	3	61	14	36
Inkaras	22	16	4	2	50	12	36
Romar	22	15	4	3	49	12	34
Panerys	22	11	6	5	35	25	28
Aras	22	13	1	8	41	28	27
FBK	22	8	8	6	23	20	24
Siauliai	22	9	4	9	37	23	22
Ekranas	22	7	8	7	21	18	22
Banga	22	3	6	13	19	56	12
Musa*	22	3	5	14	12	58	11
Sirius*	22	2	3	17	12	39	7
Interas*	22	1	3	18	8	63	5

Top scorer; Poderis (Inkaras) 24.
Cup Final: Inkaras 2, Zalgiris 1.

LUXEMBOURG

Federation Luxembourgeoise De Football, (F.L.F.), 50, Rue De Strasbourg, L-2560, Luxembourg.
Founded: 1908; *Number of Clubs:* 126; *Number of Players:* 21,684; *National Colours:* Red shirts, white shorts, blue stockings.
Telephone: 00352 48 86 65; *Cable:* FOOTBALL LUXEMBOURG; *Telex:* 2426 flf lu; *Fax:* 00352 40 02 01.
International matches 1994
Morocco (h) 1-2, Holland (h) 0-4, Belarus (a) 0-2,.Holland (a) 0-5.
League Championship wins (1910–95)
Jeunesse Esch 22; Spora Luxembourg 11; Stade Dudelange 10; Avenir Beggen 7; Red Boys Differdange 6; US Hollerich-Bonnevoie 5; Fola Esch 5; US Luxembourg 5; Aris Bonnevoie 3; Progres Niedercor 3.
Cup wins (1922–95)
Red Boys Differdange 16; Jeunesse Esch 9; US Luxembourg 9; Spora Luxembourg 8; Avenir Beggen 6; Stade Dudelange 4; Progres Niedercorn 4; Fola Esch 3; Alliance Dudelange 2; US Rumelange 2; Aris Bonnevoie 1; US Dudelange 1; Jeunesse Hautchar age 1; National Schiffige 1; Racing Luxembourg 1; SC Tetange 1; Hesperange 1, Grevenmacher 1.
Final Table 1994–95

	P	*W*	*D*	*L*	*F*	*A*	Pts
Jeunesse Esch	22	15	5	2	63	17	35
Grevenmacher	22	15	5	2	35	12	35
Avenir Beggen	22	13	4	5	64	31	30
F91 Dudelange	22	10	3	9	41	37	23
Union	22	8	6	8	40	30	22
FC Wiltz 71	22	7	8	7	36	40	22
Spora	22	7	6	9	38	36	20
Aris	22	7	5	10	39	45	19
Petange	22	7	5	10	30	43	19
Red Boys	22	6	5	11	44	60	17
Swift*	22	6	4	12	33	58	16
Wormeldange*	22	1	4	17	13	68	6

Top scorer: Heinen (Red Boys) 22.
Cup Final: Grevenmacher 3, Jeunesse Esch 2.
After a 1-1 draw.

MACEDONIA

Football Association of the Former Yugoslav Republic of Macedonia, VIII-ma Udarna Brigada 31A, MAC-91000Skopje.
Telephone: 00389 1 22 90 42; *Fax:* 00389 1 23 54 48.

International matches 1994
Slovenia (h) 2-0, Albania (h) 5-1, Estonia (h) 2-0, Turkey (h) 0-2, Denmark (h) 1-1, Spain (h) 0-2, Belgium (a) 1-1, Cyprus (h) 3-0.

League Championship wins (1994–95)
Vardar 2.

Cup wins (1994)
Sileks 1.

Final League Table 1994–95

	P	*W*	*D*	*L*	*F*	*A*	Pts
Vardar	30	23	7	0	79	17	76
Sileks	30	18	6	6	66	28	60
Sloga	30	17	7	6	43	26	58
Pobeda	30	16	5	9	55	35	53
Pelister	30	15	6	9	57	40	51
Osogovo	30	11	9	10	53	34	42
Sasa	30	11	8	11	39	30	41
FK Ohrid	30	11	5	14	45	43	38
Balkan Bisi	30	11	5	14	48	51	38
Belasica	30	11	4	15	48	62	37
Tikves	30	11	4	15	35	53	37
Rudar	30	10	4	16	32	45	34
Ljuboten	30	10	4	16	37	54	34
FCU 55	30	9	6	15	31	40	33
Borec*	30	9	6	15	28	57	33
Kozuv*	30	2	4	24	18	99	7

Kozuv had three points deducted.
Cup Final: Vardar 2, Sileks 1.

MALTA

Malta Football Association, 280 St. Paul Street, Valletta.
Founded: 1900; *Number of Clubs:* 252; *Number of Players:* 5,544; *National Colours:* Red shirts, white shorts, red stockings.
Telephone: 00356 22 26 97; *Cable:* FOOTBALL MALTA VALLETTA; *Telex:* 1752 malfa mw; *Fax:* 00356 24 51 36.

International matches 1994
Tunisia (h) 1-1, Georgia (h) 0-1, Slovenia (h) 0-1, Belgium (h) 1-0, Slovakia (h) 1-2, Azerbaijan (h) 5-0, Latvia (a) 0-2, Slovakia (a) 1-1, Czech Republic (a) 1-6, Czech Republic (h) 0-0, Norway (h) 0-1.

League Championship wins (1910–95)
Floriana 25; Sliema Wanderers 22; Valletta 15; Hibernians 8; Hamrun Spartans 6; Rabat Ajax 2; St George's 1; KOMR 1.

Cup wins (1935–95)
Floriana 18; Sliema Wanderers 17; Valletta 7; Hamrun Spartans 6; Hibernians 5; Gzira United 1; Melita 1; Zurrieq 1; Rabat Ajax 1.

Final League Table 1994–95

	P	*W*	*D*	*L*	*F*	*A*	Pts
Hibernians	18	13	4	1	42	10	43
Sliema Wanderers	18	12	3	3	55	22	39
Valletta	18	11	4	3	45	12	37
Floriana	18	10	5	3	33	13	35
Hamrun Spartans	18	10	2	6	33	23	32
Birkirkara	18	5	6	7	17	24	21
Zurrieq	18	6	2	10	18	36	20
Naxxar Lions	18	4	3	11	15	37	15
Pieta Hotspurs*	18	2	3	13	11	40	9
St George's*	18	0	2	16	4	56	2

Top scorer: Saunders (Sliema) 18.
Cup Final: Valletta 1, Hamrun Spartans 0.

MOLDOVA

Moldavian Football Federation, Bd Stefan cel Mare 73, 277001 Chisinau, Moldavia.
Number of Clubs: 143; *Number of Players:* 75,000.
Telephone: 00373 2 22 12 95. *Fax:* 00373 2 22 22 44. *Telex:* 64163218.

International matches 1994
USA (a) 0-3, Azerbaijan (h) 2-1, Georgia (a) 1-0, Wales (h) 3-2, Bulgaria (a) 1-4, Germany (h) 0-3.

League Championship wins (1994–95)
Zimbru Chisinau 2.

Cup wins (1994–95)
Tiligul Tiraspol 2.

Final League Table 1994–95

	P	*W*	*D*	*L*	*F*	*A*	Pts
Zimbru Chisinau	26	21	4	1	71	10	67
Tiligul Tiraspol	26	21	3	2	78	18	66
Balti	26	17	6	3	54	24	57
Bender	26	18	2	6	43	18	56
Otaci	26	15	4	7	55	25	49
MHM 93	26	10	6	10	28	30	36
Comrat	26	10	1	15	29	56	31
Agro	26	8	6	12	24	37	30
Calarasi	26	8	5	13	28	38	29
Torentul	26	6	5	15	24	46	23
Sportul	26	7	2	17	23	46	23
Briceni	26	7	2	17	22	56	23
Cioburciu	26	5	5	16	27	46	20
Falesti	26	2	3	21	15	71	9

Top scorer: Gavriliuc (Zimbru Chisinau) 20.
Cup Final: Tiligul Tiraspol 1, Zimbru Chisinau 0.

NORTHERN IRELAND

Irish Football Association Ltd, 20 Windsor Avenue, Belfast BT9 6EG.
Founded: 1880; *Number of Clubs:* 1,555; *Number of Players:* 24,558; *National Colours:* Green shirts, white shorts, green stockings.
Telephone: 01232 66 94 58/59; *Cable:* FOOTBALL BELFAST; *Telex:* 747317 ifa ni g; *Fax:* 01232 66 76 20.

NORWAY

Norges Fotballforbund Ullevaal Stadion, Postboks 3823, Ulleval Hageby, 0805 Oslo 8.
Founded: 1902; *Number of Clubs:* 1,810; *Number of Players:* 300,000; *National Colours:* Red shirts, white shorts, blue & white stockings.
Telephone: 0047 22 95 10 00; *Cable* FOTBALLFORBUND OSLO; *Telex:* 71722 nff n; *Fax:* 0047 22 95 10 10.

International matches 1994
USA (a) 1-2, Costa Rica (a) 0-0, Wales (a) 3-1, Portugal (h) 0-0, England (a) 0-0, Denmark (h) 2-1, Sweden (a) 0-2, Mexico(n)1-0,.Italy(n)0-1,RepublicofIreland(n)0-0,Belarus (h) 1-0, Holland (h) 1-1, Belarus (a) 4-0, Malta (a) 1-0.

League Championship wins (1938–94)
Fredrikstad 9; Viking Stavanger 8; Rosenborg Trondheim 8; Lillestroem 6; Valerengen 4; Larvik Turn 3; Brann Bergen 2; Lyn Oslo 2; IK Start 2; Friedig 1; Fram 1; Skeid Oslo 1; Strömsgodset Drammen 1; Moss 1.

Cup wins (1902–94)
Odds Bk, Skien 11; Fredrikstad 10; Lyn Oslo 8; Skeid Oslo 8; Sarpsborg FK 6; Brann Bergen 5; Rosenborg Trondheim 5; Orn F Horten 4; Lillestroem 4; Viking Stavanger 4; Strömsgodset Drammen 4; Frigg 3; Mjondalens F 3; Bodo Glimt 2; Mercantile 2; Grane Nordstrand 1; Kvik Halden 1; Sparta 1; Gjovik 1; Valerengen 1; Moss 1; Tromso 1; Byrne 1, Molde 1.
(Until 1937 the cup-winners were regarded as champions.)

Final League Table 1994

	P	*W*	*D*	*L*	*F*	*A*	Pts
Rosenborg	22	15	4	3	70	23	49
Lillestrom	22	12	5	5	42	23	41
Viking	22	11	6	5	41	26	39
Start	22	9	8	5	42	22	35
Kongsvinger	22	11	2	9	38	35	35
Brann	22	9	4	9	38	46	31
Tromso	22	7	7	8	22	28	28
Hamark	22	7	5	10	34	46	26
Valerengen	22	5	7	10	32	40	22
Bodo-Glimt	22	5	7	10	30	46	22
Sogndal*	22	6	4	12	19	40	22
Stromsgodset*	22	4	3	15	22	55	15

Top scorer: Brattbakk (Rosenborg) 17.
Cup Final: Molde 3, Lyn 2.

POLAND

Federation Polonaise De Foot-Ball, Al. Ujazdowskie 22, 00-478 Warszawa.
Founded: 1923; *Number of Clubs:* 5,881; *Number of Players:* 317,442; *National Colours:* White shirts, red shorts, white & red stockings.
Telephone: 0048 2 621 91 75; *Cable:* PEZETPEEN WARSZAWA; *Telex:* 815320 pzpn pl; *Fax:* 0048 2 229 24 89.

International matches 1994
Spain (a) 1-1, Greece (a) 0-0,.Saudi Arabia (h) 1-0, Hungary (h) 3-2, Austria (h) 3-4, Belarus (h) 1-1, Israel (a) 1-2, Azerbaijan (h) 1-0, France (h) 0-0, Saudi Arabia (a) 2-0,.Saudi Arabia (a) 2-1.

League Championship wins (1921–95)
Gornik Zabrze 14; Ruch Chorzow 13; Wisla Krakow 6; Legia Warsaw 6; Lech Poznan 5; Pogon Lwow 4; Cracovia 3; Warta Poznan 2; Polonia Bytom 2; Stal Mielec 2; Widzew Lodz 2; Garbarnia Krakow 1; Polonia Warsaw 1; LKS Lodz 1; Slask Wroclaw 1; Szombierki Bytom 1; Zaglebie Lubin 1.

Cup wins (1951–95)
Legia Warsaw 11; Gornik Zabrze 6; Zaglebie Sosnowiec 4; Lech Poznan 3; GKS Katowice 3: Ruch Chorzow 2; Slask Wroclaw 2; Gwardia Warsaw 1; LKS Lodz 1; Polonia Warsaw 1; Wisla Krakow 1; Stal Rzeszow 1; Arka Gdynia 1; Lechia Gdansk 1; Widzew Lodz 1; Miedz Legnica 1.

Final League Table 1994–95

	P	*W*	*D*	*L*	*F*	*A*	Pts
Legia	34	23	5	6	58	20	51
Widzew	34	17	11	6	47	25	45
Katowice	34	16	10	8	45	27	42
Zaglebie Lubin	34	16	10	8	48	41	42
Gornik Zabrze	34	12	13	9	48	39	37
Lech	34	13	8	13	46	40	34
LKS Lodz	34	10	14	10	39	41	34
Pogon	34	10	13	11	33	34	33
Sokol	34	9	14	11	33	43	32
Olimpia	34	9	13	12	46	41	31
Hutnik	33	9	13	11	36	38	31
Rakow	34	9	13	12	31	43	31
Stomil	34	7	16	11	35	40	30
Stal	33	8	14	11	43	49	30
Petrochemia*	34	8	14	12	35	42	30
Ruch*	34	7	15	12	39	46	29
Wola*	34	10	9	15	34	47	29
Warta*	34	7	5	22	35	75	19

Top scorers: Cygan (Stal) 16.
Cup Final: Legia 2, Katowice 0.

PORTUGAL

Federacao Portuguesa De Futebol, Praca De Alegria N.25, Apartado 21.100, P-1128, Lisboa Codex.
Founded: 1914; *Number of Clubs:* 204; *Number of Players:* 79,235; *National Colours:* Red shirts, white shorts, red stockings.
Telephone: 00351 1 347 59 34; *Cable:* FUTEBOL LISBOA; *Telex:* 13489 fpf p; *Fax:* 00351 1 346 72 31.

International matches 1994
Spain (a) 2-2, Norway (a) 0-0, Northern Ireland (a) 2-1, Latvia (a) 3-1, Austria (h) 1-0, Liechtenstein (h) 8-0.

League Championship wins (1935–95)
Benfica 30; Sporting Lisbon 16; FC Porto 14; Belenenses 1.

Cup wins (1939–95)
Benfica 22; Sporting Lisbon 12; FC Porto 8; Boavista 4; Belenenses 3; Vitoria Setubal 2; Academica Coimbra 1; Leixoes Porto 1; Sporting Braga 1; Amadora 1.

Final League Table 1994–95

	P	*W*	*D*	*L*	*F*	*A*	Pts
Porto	34	29	4	1	73	15	62
Sporting Lisbon	34	22	9	3	57	22	53
Benfica	34	22	5	7	61	28	49
Guimaraes	34	16	10	8	54	43	42
Farense	34	16	5	13	44	38	37
Leiria	34	13	10	11	41	44	36
Maritimo	34	12	11	11	41	45	35
Tirsense	34	14	6	14	35	34	34
Braga	34	11	10	13	34	42	32
Boavista	34	12	8	14	40	49	32
Salgueiros	34	11	7	16	43	50	29
Belenenses	34	10	7	17	30	39	27
Gil Vicente	34	7	13	14	30	40	27
Chaves	34	10	7	17	33	49	27
Amadora	34	6	14	14	27	40	26
Madeira*	34	7	10	17	30	54	24
Beira Mar*	34	8	5	21	33	54	21
Setubal*	34	3	13	18	25	45	19

Top scorer: Hassan Nader (Farense) 21.
Cup Final: Sporting Lisbon 2, Maritimo 0.

ROMANIA

Federatia Romana De Fotbal, Vasile Conta 16, Bucharest 70130.
Founded: 1908; *Number of Clubs:* 414; *Number of Players:* 22,920; *National Colours:* Yellow shirts, blue shorts, red stockings.
Telephone: 0040 1 617 33 43; *Cable:* SPORTROM BUCURESTI-FOTBAL; *Telex:* 10097 frf r; *Fax:* 0040 1 312 83 24

International matches 1994
Hong Kong (a) 1-1, USA (h) 2-1, South Korea (a) 2-1, Northern Ireland (a) 0-2, Bolivia (h) 3-0,.Nigeria (h) 2-0, Slovenia (h) 0-0, Sweden (h) 1-1, Colombia (n) 3-1, Switzerland (n) 1-4, USA (n) 1-0, Argentina (n) 3-2, Sweden (n) 2-2, Azerbaijan (h) 3-0, France (a) 0-0, England (a) 1-1, Slovakia (h) 3-2, Israel (a) 1-1.

League Championship wins (1910–95)
Steaua Bucharest (prev. CCA) 17; Dinamo Bucharest 14; Venus Bucharest 8, Chinezul Timisoara 6; UT Arad 6; Ripensia Temesvar 4; Uni Craiova 4; Petrolul Ploesti 3; Olimpia Bucharest 2; Colentina Bucharest 2; Arges Pitesti 2; ICO Oradea 2; Soc RA Bucharest 1; Prahova Ploesti 1; Coltea Brasov 1; Juventus Bucharest 1; Metalochimia Resita1; Ploesti United 1; Unirea Tricolor 1; Rapid Bucharest 1.

Cup wins (1934–95)
Steaua Bucharest (prev. CCA) 17; Rapid Bucharest 9; Dinamo Bucharest 7; Uni Craiova 6; UT Arad 2; Ripensia Temesvar 2; Politehnica Timisoara 2; Petrolul Ploesti 2; ICO Oradeo 1; Metalochimia Resita 1; Stinta Cluj 1; CFR Turnu Severin 1; Chimia Rannicu Vilcea 1; Jiul Petroseni 1; Progresul Bucharest 1; Progresul Oradea 1; Gloria Bistrita 1.

Final League Table 1994–95

	P	*W*	*D*	*L*	*F*	*A*	Pts
Steaua	34	23	8	3	72	25	77
Uni Craiova	34	21	5	8	84	41	68
Dinamo	34	20	5	9	61	35	65
Rapid Bucharest	34	16	6	12	55	42	54
Ceahlaul	34	16	5	13	56	54	53
Gloria	34	16	4	14	66	59	52
National	34	16	4	14	66	60	52
Arges	34	16	4	14	47	54	52
Inter Sibiu	34	16	3	15	53	52	51
Petrolul	34	14	7	13	44	41	49
Farul	34	13	6	15	43	50	45
Uni Cluj	34	13	4	17	39	42	43
Otelul	34	11	9	14	47	51	42
Brasov	34	10	9	15	40	54	39
Elect. Craiova	34	11	5	18	42	53	38
Sportul	34	8	10	16	26	44	34
Maramures*	34	6	9	19	34	69	27
UT Arad*	34	4	9	21	28	77	21

Top scorer: Craioveanu (Uni Craiova) 25.
Cup Final: Rapid Bucharest 1, Petrolul 1.
Petrolul won 5-3 on penalties.

RUSSIA

Football Union of Russia; Luzhnetskaya Naberezyhnaja, 8. SU-119270 Moscow. Telephone: 0070 95 248 08 34; *Telex:* 411287 priz su; *Fax:* 0070 502 220 20 37;
Founded: 1992; *Number of Clubs:* 43,700; *Number of Players:* 2,170,000.

International matches 1994
USA (a) 1-1, Mexico (a) 4-1, Republic of Ireland (a) 0-0, Turkey (a) 1-0, Slovakia (h) 2-1, Brazil (h) 0-2, Sweden (h) 1-3, Cameroon (h) 6-1, Austria (a) 3-0, Germany (h) 0-1, San Marino (h) 4-0, Scotland (a) 1-1.

League Championship wins (1945–95)
Spartak Moscow 14; Dynamo Kiev 13; Dynamo Moscow 11; CSKA Moscow 7; Torpedo Moscow 3; Dynamo Tbilisi 2; Dnepr Dnepropetrovsk 2; Saria Voroshilovgrad 1; Ararat Erevan 1; Dynamo Minsk 1; Zenit Leningrad 1.

Cup wins (1936–95)
Spartak Moscow 11; Dynamo Kiev 10; Torpedo Moscow 7; Dynamo Moscow 7; CSKA Moscow 5; Donetsk Shaktyor 4; Lokomotiv Moscow 2; Dynamo Tbilisi 2; Ararat Erevan 2; Karpaty Lvov 1; SKA Rostov 1; Zenit Leningrad 1; Metallist Kharkov 1; Dnepr 1.

Final League Table 1994–95

	P	*W*	*D*	*L*	*F*	*A*	Pts
Spartak Moscow	30	21	8	1	73	21	50
Dynamo Moscow	30	13	13	4	55	35	39
Lokomotiv Moscow	30	12	12	6	49	28	36
Volgograd	30	10	16	4	39	23	36
Vladikavkaz	30	11	11	8	32	34	33
Novgorod	30	11	9	10	36	34	31
Kamaz	30	11	9	10	38	37	31
Tekstilchik Kamychin	30	11	7	12	30	37	29
Sotchi	30	8	11	11	44	48	27
CSKA Moscow	30	8	10	12	30	32	25
Torpedo Moscow	30	7	12	11	28	37	25
Krylia Sovekov	30	6	12	12	30	51	24
Toumen	30	7	10	13	24	49	24
Ekaterinbourg	30	7	9	14	33	49	23
Stavropol*	30	6	11	13	25	34	23
Lada*	30	6	10	14	24	41	22

Top scorer: Simoutenkov (Dynamo Moscow) 21.
Cup Final: Dynamo Moscow 0, Volgograd 0.
Dynamo Moscow won 8-7 on penalties.

SAN MARINO

Federazione Sammarinese Giuoco Calcio, Viale Campo dei Giudei, 14; 47031-Rep. San Marino.
Founded: 1931; *Number of Clubs:* 17; *Number of Players:* 1,033; *Colours:* Blue and white.
Telephone: 0039549 99 05 15; *Cable:*FEDERCALCIO SAN MARINO; *Telex:* 0505284 cogmar;*Fax:* 0039549 99 23 48.

International matches 1994
Russia (a) 0-4, Greece (a) 0-2, Finland (a) 1-4.

League Championship wins (1986–95)
Tre Fiori 4; Fiorita 2; Faetano 2; Domagnano 1; Montevito 1.

Cup wins (1986–94)
Domagnano 3; Libertas 3; Faetano 1, Fiorita 1, Tre Fiori 1.

Final League Table 1994–95

	P	*W*	*D*	*L*	*F*	*A*	Pts
Tre Fiori+*	18	12	2	4	36	15	26
Cosmos+*	18	9	6	3	29	20	24
Domagnano+*	18	9	5	4	29	7	23
La Fiorita+*	18	10	3	5	24	25	23
Murata	18	8	6	4	22	16	22
Cailungo	18	4	6	8	18	26	14
Virtus	18	3	8	7	12	20	14
Faetano	18	5	3	10	26	24	13
Libertas*	18	4	5	9	25	32	13
Juvenes*	18	2	4	12	18	34	8

Play-Offs
San Giovanni 0, Domagnano 3; Cosmos 2, La Fiorita 3; San Giovanni 0, Cosmos 1; Domagnano 0, La Fiorita 2; Domagnano 2, Cosmos 4; Tre Fiori 0, La Fiorita 0 (Tre Fiori won 6-5 on penalties); La Fiorita 1, Cosmos 0.

Final
Tre Fiori 1, La Fiorita 0.
Top scorer: Ugolini (Tre Fiori) 16.

SCOTLAND

The Scottish Football Association Ltd, 6 Park Gardens, Glasgow G3 7YF.
Founded: 1873; *Number of Clubs:* 6,148; *Number of Players:* 135,474; *National Colours:* Dark blue shirts, white shorts, red stockings.
Telephone: 0141 332 6372; *Cable:* EXECUTIVE GLASGOW; *Telex:* 778904 sfa g; *Fax:* 0141 332 7559.

SLOVAKIA

Slovak Football Association, Junacka 6, 83280 Bratislava, Slovakia.
Number of Clubs: 2,140; *Number of Players:* 141,000.
Telephone: 0042 7 279 01 51; *Fax:* 0042 7 279 05 54.

International matches 1994
UAR (a) 1-0, Egypt (a) 0-1, Morocco (a) 1-2, Malta (a) 2-1, Croatia (h) 4-1, Russia (a) 1-2, Malta (h) 1-1, France (h) 0-0, Israel (a) 2-2, Romania (a) 2-3.

League Championship wins (1994–95)
Slovan Bratislava 2.

Cup wins (1994–95)
Tatran Presov 1, Inter 1.

Final League Table 1994–95

	P	*W*	*D*	*L*	*F*	*A*	Pts
Slovan Bratislava	32	21	9	2	63	25	72
Kosice	32	15	7	10	54	42	52
Inter	32	14	8	10	47	45	50
Dunajska Streda	32	13	7	12	41	42	46
Dukla Bystrica	32	12	8	12	53	44	44
Spartak Trnava	32	12	8	12	43	35	44

Promotion/Relegation Table 1994–95

	P	*W*	*D*	*L*	*F*	*A*	Pts
Bardejov + +	32	12	7	13	46	46	43
Prievidza + +	32	12	6	14	35	50	42
Lokomotiv Kosice + +	32	13	3	16	55	60	39
Tatran Presov + +	32	9	10	13	42	49	37
Humenne*	32	8	8	16	32	57	32
Zilina*	32	9	3	20	37	53	30

Top scorer: Semenik (Dukla Bystrica) 18.
Cup Final: Inter 1, Dunajska Streda 1.
Inter won 3-1 on penalties.

SLOVENIA

Nogometna Zveza Slovenije, dunajska 47/V, P.P. 90, 61109 Ljubljana, Slovenia.
Founded: 1992; *Number of Clubs:* 232; *Number of Players:* 15,048.
Telephone: 00386 61 133 40 63; *Fax:* 00386 61 30 23 37.

International matches 1994
Georgia (a) 1-0, Tunisia (h) 2-2, Malta (a) 1-0, Macedonia (a) 0-2, Hungary (a) 1-0, Cyprus (h) 3-0, Romania (a) 0-0, Italy (h) 1-1, Ukraine (a) 0-0, Lithuania (h) 1-2.

League Championship wins 1992–95
SCT Olimpija 4.

Cup wins 1992–95
Branik Maribor 2; SCT Olimpija 1; Mura 1.

Final League Table 1994–95

	P	*W*	*D*	*L*	*F*	*A*	Pts
Olimpija	30	20	4	6	78	30	44
Branik Maribor	30	17	8	5	60	24	42
Gorica	30	18	5	7	66	30	41
Mura	30	17	6	7	46	24	40
Beltinci	30	15	8	7	74	32	38
Publikum	30	16	6	8	50	27	38
Rudar	30	16	6	8	55	33	38
Korotan	30	14	4	12	53	36	32
Primorje +	30	12	8	10	50	45	32
Oscar +	30	13	4	13	49	43	30
Istrabenz +	30	9	8	18	24	34	26
Donit +	30	8	4	18	36	58	20
Isola*	30	7	6	17	30	73	20
Zivila*	30	5	9	16	34	48	19
Kocevje*	30	4	9	17	24	91	16
Jadran*	30	0	3	27	12	113	3

Top scorer: Skaper (Beltinci) 25.
Cup Final: Mura 1, 1, Publikum 1, 0.

SPAIN

Real Federacion Espanola De Futbol, Calle Alberto Bosch 13, Apartado Postal 347, E-28014 Madrid.
Founded: 1913; *Number of Clubs:* 10,240; *Number of Players:* 408,135; *National Colours:* Red shirts, dark blue shorts, black stockings, yellow trim.
Telephone: 0034 1 420 13 62; *Cable:* FUTBOL MADRID; *Telex:* 42420 rfef e; *Fax:* 0034 1 420 20 94.

International matches 1994
Portugal (h) 2-2, Poland (h) 1-1, Croatia (h) 0-2, Finland (a) 2-1, Canada (a) 2-0, South Korea (n) 2-2, Germany (n) 1-1, Bolivia (n) 3-1, Switzerland (n) 3-0, Italy (n) 1-2, Cyprus (a) 2-1, Macedonia (a) 2-0, Denmark (h) 3-0, Belgium (a) 4-1.

League Championship wins (1945–95)
Real Madrid 26; Barcelona 14; Atletico Madrid 8; Athletic Bilbao 8; Valencia 4; Real Sociedad 2; Real Betis 1; Seville 1.

Cup wins (1902–95)
Athletic Bilbao 23; Barcelona 22; Real Madrid 17; Atletico Madrid 8; Valencia 5; Real Zaragoza 4; Real Union de Irun 3; Seville 3; Espanol 2; Arenas 1; Ciclista Sebastian 1; Racing de Irun 1; Vizcaya Bilbao 1; Real Betis 1; Real Sociedad 1, La Coruna 1.

Final League Table 1994–95

	P	*W*	*D*	*L*	*F*	*A*	Pts
Real Madrid	38	23	9	6	76	29	55
La Coruna	38	20	11	7	68	32	51
Betis	38	15	16	7	46	25	46
Barcelona	38	18	10	10	60	45	46
Espanol	38	14	15	9	51	35	43
Sevilla	38	16	11	11	55	41	43
Zaragoza	38	18	7	13	56	51	43
Athletic Bilbao	38	16	10	12	39	42	42
Oviedo	38	13	13	12	45	42	39
Real Sociedad	38	12	14	12	56	44	38
Valencia	38	13	12	13	53	48	38
Santander	38	13	10	15	42	47	36
Celta	38	11	14	13	36	48	36
Atletico Madrid	38	13	9	16	56	54	35
Tenerife	38	13	9	16	57	57	35
Compostela	38	11	12	15	44	56	34
Albacete* +	38	10	14	14	44	61	34
Sporting Gijon +	38	8	12	18	42	67	28
Valladolid*	38	8	9	21	25	63	25
Logrones*	38	2	9	27	15	79	13

Top scorer: Zamorano (Real Madrid) 28.
Cup Final: La Coruna 2, Valencia 1.
Match abandoned 79 minutes waterlogged pitch, score at 1-1. Last 11 minutes replayed.

SWEDEN

Svenska Fotbollfoerbundet, Box 1216, S-17123 Solna.
Founded: 1904; *Number of Clubs:* 3,250; *Number of Players:* 485,000; *National Colours:* Yellow shirts, blue shorts, yellow and blue stockings.
Telephone: 0046 8 735 09 00; *Cable:* FOOTBALL-S; *Telex:* 17711 fotboll s; *Fax:* 0046 8 27 51 47.

International matches 1994
Colombia (a) 0-0, USA (a) 3-1, Mexico (a) 1-2, Wales (a) 2-0, Nigeria (h) 3-1, Denmark (a) 0-1, Norway (h) 2-0, Romania (a) 1-1, Cameroon (n) 2-2, Russia (n) 3-1, Brazil (n) 1-1, Saudi Arabia (n) 3-1, Romania (n) 2-2, Brazil (n) 0-1, Bulgaria (n) 4-0, Lithuania (h) 4-2, Iceland (a) 1-0, Switzerland (a) 2-4, Hungary (h) 2-0.

League Championship wins (1896–1994)
IFK Gothenburg 15; Oergryte IS Gothenburg 14; Malmo FF 14; IFK Norrköping 12; AIK Stockholm 9; Djurgaarden 8; GAIS Gothenburg 6; IF Helsingborg 5; Boras IF Elfsborg 4; Oster Vaxjo 4; Halmstad 2; Atvidaberg 2; IFK Ekilstune 1; IF Gavic Brynas 1; IF Gothenburg 1; Fassbergs 1; Norrköping IK Sleipner 1.

Cup wins (1941–94)
Malmo FF 13; IFK Norrköping 6; AIK Stockholm 4; IFK Gothenburg 4; Atvidaberg 2; Kalmar 2; GAIS Gothenburg 1; IF Helsingborg 1; Raa 1; Landskrona 1; Oster Vaxjo 1; Djurgaarden 1; Degerfors 1, Halmstad 1.

Final League Table 1994

	P	W	D	L	F	A	Pts
IFK Gothenburg	26	16	6	4	54	28	54
Orebro	26	15	7	4	61	30	52
Malmo	26	14	7	5	51	33	49
Norrkoping	26	13	8	5	52	21	47
Osters	26	13	6	7	48	30	45
AIK	26	11	6	9	42	41	39
Halmstad	26	10	8	8	41	39	38
Degerfors	26	8	8	10	28	37	32
Helsingborg	26	9	5	12	30	46	32
Trelleborg	26	7	9	10	25	40	30
Frolunda	26	7	6	13	30	33	27
Hammarby	26	4	8	14	25	44	20
Landskrona*	26	4	6	16	22	56	18
Hacken*	26	2	8	16	27	58	14

Top scorer: Kindvall (Norrkoping) 23.
Cup Final: Halmstad 3, AIK 1.

SWITZERLAND

Schweizerisher Fussballverband. Haus des Schweizer Fussballs, Worbstrasse 48, 3074 Muri/BE. Mailing Address: PO Box 3000 Bern 15.
Founded: 1895; *Number of Clubs:* 1,473; *Number of Players:* 185,286; *National Colours:* Red shirts, white shorts, red stockings.
Telephone: 0041 31 950 81 11; *Cable:* SWISSFOOT BERNE; *Telex:* 912910 sfv ch; *Fax:* 0041 31 950 81 81.

International matches 1994
USA (a) 1-1, Mexico (a) 5-1, Hungary (a) 2-1, Czech Republic (h) 3-0, Liechtenstein (h) 2-0, Italy (a) 0-1, Bolivia (a) 0-0, USA (n) 1-1, Romania (n) 4-1, Colombia (n) 0-2, Spain (n) 0-3, UAR (h) 1-0, Sweden (h) 4-2, Iceland (h) 1-0, Turkey (a) 2-1.

League Championship wins (1898–1995)
Grasshoppers 23; Servette 16; Young Boys Berne 11; FC Zurich 9; FC Basle 8; Lausanne 7; La Chaux-de-Fonds 3; FC Lugano 3; Winterthur 3; FX Aarau 3; Neuchatel Xamax 2; FC Anglo-American 1; St Gallen 1; FC Brühl 1; Cantonal-Neuchatel 1; Biel 1; Bellinzona 1; FC Etoile Le Chaux-de-Fonds 1; Lucerne 1; Sion 1.

Cup wins (1926–95)
Grasshoppers 18; Lausanne 7; FC Sion 7; La Chaux-de-Fonds 6; Young Boys Berne 6; Servette 6; FC Basle 5; FC Zurich 5; Lucerne 2; FC Lugano 2; FC Granges 1; St Gallen 1; Urania Geneva 1; Young Fellows Zurich 1; Aarau.

Qualifying Table 1994–95

	P	W	D	L	F	A	Pts
Grasshoppers	22	13	5	4	36	21	31
Lugano	22	8	9	5	30	17	25
Aarau	22	8	9	5	34	22	25
Neuchatel Xamax	22	9	6	7	33	31	24
Lausanne	22	8	8	6	34	34	24
Sion	22	10	3	9	32	37	23
Basle	22	6	8	8	18	15	20
Lucerne	22	7	6	9	22	31	20
Zurich	22	4	11	7	23	27	19
Servette	22	6	6	10	26	31	18
St Gallen	22	4	10	8	20	28	18
Young Boys Berne	22	6	5	11	23	37	17

Final Table 1995

	P	W	D	L	F	A	Pts
Grasshoppers	14	9	3	2	25	13	37
Lugano	14	6	5	3	25	17	30
Neuchatel Xamax	14	6	4	4	27	20	28
Aarau	14	5	4	5	17	16	27
Lucerne	14	5	5	4	14	18	25
Basle	14	7	0	7	20	19	24
Sion	14	5	2	7	24	25	24
Lausanne	14	1	1	12	11	35	15

Promotion/Relegation 1995

	P	W	D	L	F	A	Pts
Young Boys Berne + +	14	7	3	4	22	14	17
St Gallen + +	14	5	6	3	20	13	16
Zurich + +	14	5	6	3	19	16	16
Servette + +	14	5	6	3	15	13	16
Kriens*	14	4	7	3	18	14	15
Yverdon*	14	6	3	5	18	15	15
Winterthur*	14	3	7	4	13	13	13
Soleure*	14	0	4	10	4	31	4

Top scorer: Aleksandrov (Neuchatel Xamax) 24.
Cup Final: Sion 4, Grasshoppers 2.

TURKEY

Federation Turque De Football, Konur Sokak No. 10, Ankara Kizilay.
Founded: 1923; *Number of Clubs:* 230; *Number of Players:* 64,521; *National Colours:* White shirts, white shorts, red and white stockings.
Telephone: 0090 212 282 70 10; *Cable:* FUTBOLSPOR ANKARA; *Fax:* 0090 212 282 70 15.

International matches 1994
Czech Republic (h) 1-4, Russia (h) 0-1, Macedonia (a) 2-0, Hungary (a) 2-2, Iceland (h) 5-0, Switzerland (h) 1-2, Italy (a) 1-3.

League Championship wins (1960–95)
Fenerbahce 12; Galatasaray 10; Besiktas 10; Trabzonspor 6.

Cup wins (1963–95)
Galatasaray 10; Besiktas 5; Trabzonspor 5; Fenerbahce 4; Goztepe Izmir 2; Atay Ismir 2; Ankaragucu 2; Eskisehirspor 1; Bursapor 1; Genclerbirligi 1; Sakaryaspor 1.

Final League Table 1994–95

	P	W	D	L	F	A	Pts
Besiktas	34	24	7	3	80	26	79
Trabzonspor	34	23	7	4	79	28	76
Galatasaray	34	21	6	7	76	38	69
Fenerbahce	34	20	7	7	78	35	67
Genclerbirligi	34	17	8	9	61	45	59
Bursa	34	13	12	9	47	39	51
Gaziantep	34	14	6	14	50	51	48
Samsun	34	12	9	13	54	60	45
Kocaeli	34	12	8	14	57	60	44
Altay	34	11	11	12	42	55	44
Kayseri	34	12	6	16	62	69	42
Van	34	11	6	17	36	48	39
Antalya	34	10	8	16	39	46	38
Ankaragucu	34	10	8	16	39	57	38
Denizli	34	8	11	15	42	55	35
Zeytinburnu*	34	7	9	18	35	74	30
Petrolofisi*	34	8	5	21	38	73	29
Adanademir*	34	3	6	25	25	81	15

Top scorer: Aykut (Fenerbahce) 27.
Cup Final: Galatasaray 2, 0, Trabzonspor 3, 1.

UKRAINE

Football Federation of Ukraine, 42, Kuybysheva Street, 252023 Kiev 23, Ukraine.
Founded: 1992; *Number of Teams:* 30,460; *Number of Players:* 757,758.
Telephone: 0070 44 264 72 98; *Fax:* 0070 44 264 75 64.

International matches 1994
Israel (a) 0-1, Belarus (h) 3-1, Bulgaria (a) 1-1, Lithuania (h) 0-2, Slovenia (h) 0-0, Estonia (h) 3-0.

League Championship wins (1992–95)
Dynamo Kiev 3, Tavria Simferopol 1.

Cup wins (1992–95)
Chernomorets 2, Dynamo Kiev 1, Shakhtjor Donetsk 1.

Final League Table 1994–95

	P	W	D	L	F	A	Pts
Dynamo Kiev	34	25	8	1	87	25	83
Dnepr	34	21	8	5	62	29	71
Chernomorets	34	21	7	6	60	31	70
Donetsk	34	18	8	8	54	29	62
Tavria	34	17	8	9	61	37	59
Krivbass	34	13	9	12	36	31	48
Torpedo	34	14	3	17	47	49	45
Karpaty	34	12	9	13	32	36	45
Kremen	34	12	6	16	42	54	42
Ternopol	34	12	5	17	40	39	41
Prekarpate	34	11	8	15	40	52	41
Metallurg	34	10	10	14	41	42	40
Nikolaev	34	11	5	18	33	59	38
Vinnitsa	34	10	7	17	38	52	37
Volyn	34	11	3	20	29	58	36
Zarja	34	10	5	19	36	70	35
Temp	34	10	4	20	31	41	34
Veres	34	8	7	19	28	63	31

Cup Final: Donetsk 1, Dnepr 1.
Donetsk won 8-7 on penalties.

WALES

The Football Association of Wales Limited, Plymouth Chambers, 3 Westgate Street, Cardiff.
Founded: 1876; *Number of Clubs:* 2,326; *Number of Players:* 53,926; *National Colours:* All red. *Telephone:* 01222 372325; *Telex:* 497 363 faw g; *Fax:* 01222 343961.

YUGOSLAVIA

Yugoslav Football Association, P.O. Box 263, Terazije 35, 11000 Beograd.
Founded: 1919; *Number of Clubs:* 6,532; *Number of Players:* 229,024; *National Colours:* Blue shirts, white shorts, red stockings.
*Telephone:*00381 11 33 34 47; *Cable:* JUGOFUDBAL BEOGRAD; *Telex:* 11666 sfj yu; *Fax:* 00381 11 33 34 33.

International matches 1994
Brazil (a) 0-2, Argentina (a) 0-1.

League Championship wins (1923–95)
Red Star Belgrade 20; Partizan Belgrade 13; Hajduk Split 9; Gradjanski Zagreb; BSK Belgrade 5; Dynamo Zagreb 4; Jugoslavija Belgrade 2; Concordia Zagreb 2; FC Sarajevo 2; Vojvodina Novi Sad 2; HASK Zagreb 1; Zeljeznicar 1.

Cup wins (1947–95)
Red Star Belgrade 14; Hajduk Split 9; Dynamo Zagreb 8; Partizan Belgrade 7; BSK Belgrade 2; OFK Belgrade 2; Rejeka 2; Velez Mostar 2; Vardar Skopje 1; Borac Banjaluka 1.

Final League Table 1994–95
Group A

	P	*W*	*D*	*L*	*F*	*A*	Pts
Red Star Belgrade	18	14	3	1	63	17	42
Partizan Belgrade	18	13	2	3	43	20	38
Vojvodina	18	10	4	4	37	26	37
Becej	18	7	4	7	17	27	26
Zemun	18	7	4	7	25	25	25
OFK Belgrade	18	7	3	8	21	26	24
Rad*	18	4	6	8	24	38	20
Borac*	18	3	5	10	15	29	18
Radnicki Belgrade*	18	3	3	12	21	39	17
Hajduk Kula*	18	4	2	12	15	32	15

Group B

	P	*W*	*D*	*L*	*F*	*A*	Pts
Buducnost + +	18	9	4	5	31	23	30
Radnicki Nis + +	18	8	5	5	27	13	29
Proleter + +	18	8	4	6	30	27	24
Napredak + +	18	8	2	8	19	21	23
Obilic	18	7	3	8	25	27	22
Sloboda	18	7	5	6	16	18	21
Loznica	18	7	3	8	26	29	21
Spartak +	18	7	3	8	15	18	20
Sutjeska*	18	7	2	9	23	25	17
Rudar*	18	5	3	10	17	28	16

Top scorer: Milosevic (Partizan Belgrade) 30.
Cup Final: Red Star Belgrade 4, 0, Obilic 0, 0.

SOUTH AMERICA

ARGENTINA

Asociacion Del Futbol Argentina, Viamonte 1366/76, 1053 Buenos Aires.
Founded: 1893; *Number of Clubs:* 3,035; *Number of Players:* 306,365; *National Colours:* Blue & white shirts, black shorts, white stockings.
Telephone: 00541 404 276; *Cable:* FUTBOL BUENOS AIRES; *Telex:* 17848 AFA AR; *Fax:* 54-1 3754410.
League Champions 1994: Independiente.

BOLIVIA

Edificio Federacion Boliviana De Futbol, Av. Libertador Bolivar No. 1148, Casilla de Correo 484, Cochabamba, Bolivia.
Founded: 1925; *Number of Clubs:* 305; *Number of Players:* 15,290; *National Colours:* Green shirts, white shorts, green stockings.
Telephone: 0059142 45889; *Cable:* FEDFUTBOL COCHABAMBA; *Telex:* 6239 FEDBOL; *Fax:* 0059142 82132.
League Champions 1994: Bolivar.

BRAZIL

Confederacao Brasileira De Futebol, Rua Da Alfandega, 70, P.O. Box 1078, 20.070 Rio De Janeiro.
Founded: 1914; *Number of Clubs:* 12,987; *Number of Players:* 551,358; *National Colours:* Yellow shirts, blue shorts, white stockings, green trim.
Telephone: 005521 221 5937; *Cable:* DESPORTOS RIO DE JANEIRO; *Telex:* 2121509 CBDS BR; *Fax:* 005521 252 9294.
League Champions 1994: Palmeiras.

CHILE

Federacion De Futbol De Chile, Avda. Quillin No. 5635, Casilla postal 3733, Correo Central, Santiago de Chile.
Founded: 1895; *Number of Clubs:* 4,598; *Number of Players:* 609,724; *National Colours:* Red shirts, blue shorts, white stockings.
Telephone: 00562 2849000; *Cable:* FEDFUTBOL SANTIAGO DE CHILE; *Telex:* 440474 FEBOL CZ; *Fax:* 00562 2843510.
League Champions 1994: Uni de Chile.

COLOMBIA

Presidencia: Federacion Colombiana De Futbol, Avenida 32, No. 16-22 Apartado Aereo No. 17.602, Bogota D.E.
Founded: 1925; *Number of Clubs:* 3,685; *Number of Players:* 188,050; *National Colours:* Red shirts, blue shorts, tricolour stockings.
Telephone: 00571 2455370; *Telex:* 45598 COLFU CO; *Fax:* 00571 2854340.
League Champions 1994: Atletico Nacional.

ECUADOR

Federacion Ecuatoriana De Futbol, Calle Jose Mascote 1.103 (Piso 2), Luque, Casilla 7447, Guayaquil.
Founded: 1925; *Number of Clubs:* 170; *Number of Players:* 15,700; *National Colours:* Yellow shirts, blue shorts, red stockings.
Telephone: 005934 371674; *Cable:* ECUAFUTBOL GUAYAQUIL; *Telex:* 42970 FEECFU ED; *Fax:* 005934 373320.
League Champions 1994: Emelec.

PARAGUAY

Liga Paraguaya De Futbol, Estadio De Sajonia, Calles Mayor Martinez Y Alejo Garcia, Asuncion.
Founded: 1906; *Number of Clubs:* 1,500; *Number of Players:* 140,000; *National Colours:* Red & white shirts, blue shorts, blue stockings.
Telephone: 0059521 81743; *Telex:* 627 PY FUTBOL; *Fax:* 0059521 81743.
League Champions 1994: Cerro Porteno.

PERU

Federacion Peruana De Futbol, Estadio Nacional, Puerto No. 4, Calle Jose Diaz, Lima.
Founded: 1922; *Number of Clubs:* 10,000; *Number of Players:* 325,650; *National Colours:* White shirts, red trim, white shorts, white stockings.
Telephone: 005114 337070; *Cable* FEPEFUTBOL LIMA; *Fax:* 005114 335552; *Telex:* 20066 FEPEFUT PE.
League Champions 1994: Sporting Cristal.

URUGUAY

Asociacion Uruguaya De Futbol, Guayabo 1531, Montevideo.
Founded: 1900; *Number of Clubs:* 1,091; *Number of Players:* 134,310; *National Colours:* Light blue shirts, black shorts, black stockings.
Telephone: 00598442 407101; *Cable:* FUTBOL MONTEVIDEO; *Fax:* 00598442 407873; *Telex:* AUF UY 22607.
League Champions 1994: Penarol.

VENEZUELA

Federacion Venezolana De Futbol, Avda Este Estadio Nacional, El Paraiso Apdo. Postal 14160, Candelaria, Caracas.
Founded: 1926; *Number of Clubs:* 1,753; *Number of Players:* 63,175; *National Colours:* Magenta shirts, white shorts, white stockings.
Telephone/Fax: 00582 4618010; *Cable:* FEVEFUTBOL CARACAS; *Telex:* 26140 FVFCS VC.
League Champions 1994: Caracas.

ASIA

AFGHANISTAN

The Football Federation of National Olympic Committee, Kabul.
Founded: 1922; *Number of Clubs:* 30; *Number of Players:* 3,300; *National Colours:* White shirts, white shorts, white stockings.
Telephone: 0093 20579; *Cable:* OLYMPIC KABUL.

BAHRAIN

Bahrain Football Association, P.O. Box 5464, Bahrain.
Founded: 1951; *Number of Clubs:* 25; *Number of Players:* 2,030; *National Colours:* White shirts, red shorts, white stockings.
Telephone: 00973 728218; *Cable:* BAHKORA BAHRAIN; *Telex:* 9040 FAB BN; *Fax:* 00973 729361.

BANGLADESH

Bangladesh Football Federation, Stadium, Dhaka 2.
Founded: 1972; *Number of Clubs:* 1,265; *Number of Players:* 30,385; *National Colours:* Orange shirts, white shorts, green stockings.
Telephone: 008802 236072; *Cable:* FOOTBALFED DHAKA; *Telex:* 642460 BHL BJ. *Fax:* 00880–2 863191.

BRUNEI

Brunei Amateur Football Association, P.O. Box 2010, Bandar Seri Begawan 1920, Brunei Darussalam.
Founded: 1959; *Number of Clubs:* 22; *Number of Players:* 830; *National Colours:* Gold shirts, black shorts, gold stockings.
Telephone: 006732 242283; *Cable:* BAFA BRUNEI; *Telex:* BU 2575 Attn: BAFA; *Fax:* 006732 242300.

BURMA (now Myanmar)

Myanmar Football Federation, Aung San Memorial Stadium, Kandawgalay Post Office, Yangon.
Founded: 1947; *Number of Clubs:* 600; *Number of Players:* 21,000; *National Colours:* Red shirts, white shorts, red stockings.
Telephone: 00951 75249; *Cable:* YANGON MYANMAR; *Telex:* 21218 BRCROS BRN.

CAMBODIA

Federation Khmere De Football Association, C.P. 101, Complex Sportif National, Phnom-Penh.
Founded: 1933; *Number of Clubs:* 30; *Number of Players:* 650; *National Colours:* Red shirts, white shorts, red stockings.
Telephone: 0085523 22469; *Cable:* FKFA PHNOMPENH.

CHINA PR

Football Association of The People's Republic of China, 9 Tiyuguan Road, Beijing.
Founded: 1924; *Number of Clubs:* 1,045; *Number of Players:* 2,250,000; *National Colours:* Red shirts, white shorts, red stockings.
Telephone: 00861 7017018; *Cable:* SPORTSCHINE BEIJING; *Telex:* 22034 ACSF CN; *Fax:* 00861 5112533.

HONG KONG

The Hong Kong Football Association Ltd, 55 Fat Kwong Street, Homantin, Kowloon, Hong Kong.
Founded: 1914; *Number of Clubs:* 69; *Number of Players:* 3,274; *National Colours:* Red shirts, white shorts, red stockings.
Telephone: 00852 7129122; *Cable:* FOOTBALL HONG KONG; *Telex:* 40518 FAHKG HX; *Fax:* 00852 7604303.

INDIA

All India Football Federation Green Lawns, Talap, P.O. Box 429, Cannanore 670 002/ Kerala.
Founded: 1937; *Number of Clubs:* 2,000; *Number of Players:* 56,000; *National Colours:* Light blue shirts, white shorts, dark blue stockings.
Telephone: 0091497 500199; *Cable:* SOCCER CALCUTTA; *Telex:* 212216 MCPL IN; *Fax:* 0091 497500923.

INDONESIA

All Indonesia Football Federation, Main Stadium Senayan, Gate VII, P.O. Box 2305, Jakarta.
Founded: 1930; *Number of Clubs:* 2,880; *Number of Players:* 97,000; *National Colours:* Red shirts, white shorts, red stockings.
Telephone: 006221 581541; *Cable:* PSSI JAKARTA; *Telex:* 65739 as; *Fax:* 006221 584386.

IRAN

Football Federation of The Islamic Republic of Iran, Ave Varzandeh No. 10, P.O. Box 11/1642, Tehran.
Founded: 1920; *Number of Clubs:* 6,326; *Number of Players:* 306,000; *National Colours:* Green shirts, white shorts, red stockings.
Telephone: 009821 825534; *Cable:* FOOTBALL IRAN TEHRAN; *Fax:* 009821 8835672; *Telex:* 212691 VARZ IR.

IRAQ

Iraqi Football Association, Olympic Committee Building, Palestine Street, Baghdad.
Founded: 1948; *Number of Clubs:* 155; *Number of Players:* 4,400; *National Colours:* White shirts, white shorts, white stockings.
Telephone: 009641 774 8261; *Cable:* BALL BAGHDAD; *Telex:* 214074 IRFA IK; *Fax:* 009641 7728424.

JAPAN

The Football Association of Japan, 2nd Floor, Gotoh Ikueikai Bldg, 1-10-7 Dogenzaka, Shibuya-Ku, Tokyo 150, Japan.
Founded: 1921; *Number of Clubs:* 13,047; *Number of Players:* 358,989; *National Colours:* Blue shirts, white shorts, blue stockings.
Telephone: 00813 3476211; *Cable:* SOCCERJAPAN TOKYO; *Telex:* 2422975 FOTJPN J; *Fax:* 00813 34762291.

JORDAN

Jordan Football Association, P.O. Box 1054, Amman.
Founded: 1949; *Number of Clubs:* 98; *Number of Players:* 4,305; *National Colours:* White shirts, white shorts, white stockings.
Telephone: 009626 624481; *Cable:* JORDAN FOOTBALL ASSOCIATION AM; *Telex:* 22415 FOBALL JO. *Fax:* 009626 624454.

KAZAKHSTAN

Football Association of the Republic of Kazakhstan, 44 Abai Street, 480072 Almaty, Kazakhstan.
Number of Clubs: 5,793; *Number of Players:* 260,000.
Telephone: 0073272 674492; *Fax:* 0073272 671885; *Telex:* 251347 TREK SU.

KOREA, NORTH

Football Association of The Democratic People's Rep. of Korea, Munsin-Dong 2, Dongdaewon Distr, Pyongyang.
Founded: 1928; *Number of Clubs:* 90; *Number of Players:* 3,420; *National Colours:* Red shirts, white shorts, red stockings.
Telephone: 008502 3998; *Cable:* DPR KOREA FOOTBALL PYONGYANG; *Telex:* 5472 KP; *Fax:* 008502 814403.

KOREA, SOUTH

Korea Football Association, 110-39, Kyeonji-Dong, Chongro-Ku, Seoul.
Founded: 1928; *Number of Clubs:* 476; *Number of Players:* 2,047; *National Colours:* Red shirts, red shorts, red stockings.
Telephone: 00822 7336764; *Cable:* FOOTBALLKOREA SEOUL; *Telex:* KFASEL K 25373; *Fax:* 00822 7352755.

KUWAIT

Kuwait Football Association, Udailiyya, BL. 4, Al-Ittihad St, P.O. Box 2029 (Safat), 13021 Safat.
Founded: 1952; *Number of Clubs:* 14 (senior); *Number of Players:* 1,526; *National Colours:* Blue shirts, white shorts, blue stockings.
Telephone: 00965 2555851; *Cable:* FOOTKUWAIT; *Telex:* FOOTKUW 22600 KT; *Fax:* 00965 2563737.

KYRGYZSTAN

Football Association of Kyrgyzstan, 17 Togolok Moldo Street, 720033 Bishkek, Kyrgyzstan.
Number of Players: 20,000.
Telephone: 0073312 225492; *Fax:* 0073312 267004; *Telex:* 251239 SALAM SU.

LAOS

Federation De Foot-Ball Lao, c/o Dir. Des Sports, Education, Physique Et Artistique, Vientiane.
Founded: 1951; *Number of Clubs:* 76; *Number of Players:* 2,060; *National Colours:* Red shirts, white shorts, blue stockings.
Telephone: 0085621 2741; *Cable:* FOOTBALL VIENTIANE.

LEBANON

Federation Libanaise De Football Association, P.O. Box 4732, Verdun Street, Bristol, Radwan Centre Building, Beirut.
Founded: 1933; *Number of Clubs:* 105; *Number of Players:* 8,125; *National Colours:* Red shirts, white shorts, red stockings.
Telephone/Fax: 009611 868099; *Cable:* FOOTBALL BEIRUT; *Telex:* 21404 LIBALL.

MACAO

Associacao De Futebol De Macau (AFM), P.O. Box 920, Macau.
Founded: 1939; *Number of Clubs:* 52; *Number of Players:* 800; *National Colours:* Green shirts, white shorts, green and white stockings.
Telephone: 00853 71996; *Fax:* 00853 260148; *Cable:* FOOTBALL MACAU.

MALDIVES REPUBLIC

Football Association of Maldives, Attn. Mr. Bandhu Ahamed Saleem, Sports Division, G. Banafsa Magu 20-04, Male.
Founded: 1986; *Number of Clubs: Number of Players: National Colours:* Green shirts, white shorts, green and white stockings.
Telephone: 0096032 5758; *Telex:* 77039 MINHOM MF; *Fax:* 0096032 4739.

MALAYSIA

Football Association of Malaysia, Wisma Fam, Tingkat 4, Jalan SS5A/9, Kelana Jaya, 47301 Petaling, Jaya Selangor.
Founded: 1933; *Number of Clubs:* 450; *Number of Players:* 11,250; *National Colours:* Black and gold shirts, white shorts, black and gold stockings.
Telephone: 00603 7763766; *Cable:* FOOTBALL PETALING JAYA SELANGO; *Telex:* FAM PJ MA 35701; *Fax:* 00603 7757984.

NEPAL

All-Nepal Football Association, Dasharath Rangashala, Tripureshwor, Kathmandu.
Founded: 1951; *Number of Clubs:* 85; *Number of Players:* 2,550; *National Colours:* Red shirts, blue shorts, blue and white stockings.
Telephone: 009771 15703; *Cable:* ANFA KATHMANDU; *Telex:* 2390 NSC NP.

OMAN

Oman Football Association, P.O. Box 6462, Ruwi-Muscat.
Founded: 1978; *Number of Clubs:* 47; *Number of Players:* 2,340; *National Colours:* White shirts, red shorts, white stockings.
Telephone: 00968 593840; *Cable:* FOOTBALL MUSCAT; *Telex:* 5320 FOOTBALL ON; *Fax:* 00968 593736.

PAKISTAN

Pakistan Football Federation, Mr. Hafiz Salman Butt, General Secretary, Punjab University Ground, Lahore 54000, Pakistan.
Founded: 1948; *Number of Clubs:* 882; *Number of Players:* 21,000; *National Colours:* Green shirts, white shorts, green stockings.
Telephone: 009242 5832786; *Cable:* FOOTBALL QUETTA; *Telex:* 47643 PFF PK; *Fax:* 009242 7281541.

PHILIPPINES

Philippine Football Federation, Room 207, Administration Building, Rizal Memorial Sports Complex, Vito Cruz, Metro Manila.
Founded: 1907; *Number of Clubs:* 650; *Number of Players:* 45,000; *National Colours:* Blue shirts, white shorts, blue stockings.
Telephone: 00632 594655; *Cable:* FOOTBALL MANILA; *Telex:* 65014 POC PACA PN; *Fax:* 00632 588317.

QATAR

Qatar Football Association, P.O. Box 5333, Doha.
Founded: 1960; *Number of Clubs:* 8 (senior); *Number of Players:* 1,380; *National Colours:* White shirts, maroon shorts, white stockings.
Telephone: 00974 351641, 454444; *Cable:* FOOTQATAR DOHA; *Telex:* 4749 QATFOT DH; *Fax:* 00974 411660.

SAUDI ARABIA

Saudi Arabian Football Federation, Al Mather Quarter (Olympic Complex), P.O. Box 5844, Riyadh 11432.
Founded: 1959; *Number of Clubs:* 120; *Number of Players:* 9,600; *National Colours:* White shirts, white shorts, white stockings.
Telephone: 009661 4022699; *Cable:* KORA RIYADH; *Telex:* 404300 SAFOTB SJ; *Fax:* 009661 4921276.

SINGAPORE

Football Association of Singapore, Jalan Besar Stadium, Tyrwhitt Road, Singapore 0820.
Founded: 1892; *Number of Clubs:* 250; *Number of Players:* 8,000; *National Colours:* Sky blue shirts, sky blue shorts, sky blue stockings.
Telephone: 0065 2931477; *Cable:* SOCCER SINGAPORE; *Fax:* 0065 2933728; *Telex:* SINFA RS 37683.

SRI LANKA

Football Federation of Sri Lanka, No. 2, Old Grand Stand, Race Course, Reid Avenue, Colombo 7.
Founded: 1939; *Number of Clubs:* 600; *Number of Players:* 18,825; *National Colours:* Maroon shirts, white shorts, white stockings.
Telephone: 00941 696179; *Cable:* SOCCER COLOMBO; *Telex:* 21537 METALIX CE; *Fax:* 00941 580721.

SYRIA

Association Arabe Syrienne De Football, General Sport Fed. Building, October Stadium, Damascus _ Baremke.
Founded: 1936; *Number of Clubs:* 102; *Number of Players:* 30,600; *National Colours:* White shirts, white shorts, white stockings.
Telephone: 0096311 335866; *Cable:* FOOTBALL DAMASCUS; *Telex:* HOTECH 411935.

TAJIKISTAN

Football Federation of Tajikistan, 44, Rudaki Ave., PB 26, 734012 Dushanbe, Tajikistan.
Number of Clubs: 1,804; *Number of Players:* 71,400.
Telephone: 0073772 223603; *Fax:* 0073772 230996; *Telex:* 116119 SAWDO SU.

THAILAND

The Football Association of Thailand, c/o National Stadium, Rama I Road, Bangkok.
Founded: 1916; *Number of Clubs:* 168; *Number of Players:* 15,000; *National Colours:* Crimson shirts, white shorts, crimson stockings.
Telephone: 00662 2141058; *Cable:* FOOTBALL BANGKOK; *Telex:* 20211 FAT TH; *Fax:* 00662 2154494.

TURKMENISTAN

Football Federation of Turkmenistan, 44 Engels Street, 744000 Ashkabad, Turkmenistan.
Number of Players: 75,000.
Telephone: 0073632 253844; *Fax:* 0073632 290646; *Telex:* 116175 TINTO SU.

UNITED ARAB EMIRATES

United Arab Emirates Football Association, P.O. Box 5458, Dubai.
Founded: 1971; *Number of Clubs:* 23 (senior); *Number of Players:* 1,787; *National Colours:* White shirts, white shorts, white stockings.
Telephone: 009714 245636; *Cable:* FOOTBALL EMIRATES DUBAI; *Telex:* 47623 UAEFA EM; *Fax:* 009714 245559.

UZBEKISTAN

Football Federation of Uzbekistan, Karl Marx Street 32, 700047 Tashkent, Uzbekistan.
Number of Clubs: 15,000; *Number of Players:* 217,000.
Telephone: 0073712 322854; *Fax:* 0073712 443183; *Telex:* 116108 PTB SU.

VIETNAM

Association De Football De La Republique Du Viet-Nam, No. 36, Boulevard Tran-Phu, Hanoi. *Founded:* 1962; *Number of Clubs:* 55 (senior); *Number of Players:* 16,000; *National Colours:* Red shirts, white shorts, red stockings.
Telephone: 00844 4867; *Cable:* AFBVN, 36, TRAN-PHU-HANOI.

YEMEN

Yemen Football Association, P.O. Box 908, Sana'a.
Founded: 1962; *Number of Clubs:* 26; *Number of Players:* 1750; *National Colours:* Green.
Telephone: 009672 215720. *Telex:* 2710 YOUTH YE

CONCACAF

ANTIGUA

The Antigua Football Association, P.O. Box 773, St. Johns.
Founded: 1928; *Number of Clubs:* 60; *Number of Players:* 1,008; *National Colours:* Gold shirts, black shorts, black stockings.
Telephone: 001809 4623945; *Cable:* AFA ANTIGUA; *Telex:* 2177 SIDAN AK; *Fax:* 001809 4622649.

ARUBA

Arubaanse Voetbal Bond, Schoenerstraat 2, PO Box 376, Oranjestad, Aruba.
Founded: 1932; *Number of Clubs:* 50; *Number of Players:* 1,000; *National Colours:* Yellow shirts, blue shorts, yellow stockings.
Telephone: 00297 828016; *Fax:* 00297 838438.

BAHAMAS

Bahamas Football Association, P.O. Box N 8434, Nassau, N.P.
Founded: 1967; *Number of Clubs:* 14; *Number of Players:* 700; *National Colours:* Yellow shirts, black shorts, yellow stockings.
Telephone: 001809 3247099; *Cable:* BAHSOCA NASSAU; *Fax:* 001809 3246484.

BARBADOS

Barbados Football Association, P.O. Box 833E, Bridgetown.
Founded: 1910; *Number of Clubs:* 92; *Number of Players:* 1,100; *National Colours;* Royal blue shirts, gold shorts, royal blue stockings.
Telphone: 001809 426 1170; *Cable:* FOOTBALL BRIDGETOWN; *Telex:* 2306 SHAMROCK WB; *Fax:* 001809 4360363.

BELIZE

Belize National Football Association, P.O. Box 1742, Belize City.
Founded: 1986; *National Colours:* Blue shirts, red & white trim, white shorts, blue stockings.
Telephone: 005012 82609 or 82637; *Telex:* 102 FOREIGN BZ.

BERMUDA

The Bermuda Football Association, P.O. Box HM 745, Hamilton 5 HM CX.
Founded: 1928; *Number of Clubs:* 30; *Number of Players:* 1,947; *National Colours:* Blue shirts, white shorts, white stockings.
Telephone: 001809 2952199; *Cable:* FOOTBALL BERMUDA; *Telex:* 3441 BFA BA; *Fax:* 001809 2959773.

CANADA

The Canadian Soccer Association, 1600 James Naismith Drive, Gloucester, Ont. K1B 5N4.
Founded: 1912; *Number of Clubs:* 1,600; *Number of Players:* 224,290; *National Colours:* R ed shirts, red shorts, red stockings.
Telephone: 001613 7485667; *Cable:* SOCCANADA OTTAWA; *Telex:* 0533350; *Fax:* 001613 7451938.

CAYMAN ISLANDS

Cayman Islands Football Association, PO Box 178, Georgetown, Grand Cayman, Cayman Islands W1.
Number of Clubs: 25; *Number of Players:* 875.
Telephone: 001809 9494733, 809–949 8228. *Fax:* 001809 9498738.

COSTA RICA

Federacion Costarricense De Futbol, Apartado 670-1000, Calle 40, Avda CTL I, San Jose.
Founded: 1921; *Number of Clubs:* 431; *Number of Players:* 12,429; *National Colours:* Red shirts, blue shorts, white stockings.
Telephone: 00506 2221544; *Cable:* FEDEFUTBOL SAN JOSE; *Telex:* 3394 DIDER CR; *Fax:* 00506 2552674.

CUBA

Asociacion De Futbol De Cuba, c/o Comite Olimpico Cubano, Calle 13 No. 601, Esq. C. Vedado, La Habana, ZP4.
Founded: 1924; *Number of Clubs:* 70; *Number of Players:* 12,900; *National Colours:* White shirts, blue shorts, white stockings.
Telephone: 00537 403581; *Cable:* FOOTBALL HABANA; *Telex:* 511332 INDER CU.

DOMINICA

Dominica Football Association, P.O. Box 372, Roseau, Commonwealth of Dominica.
Number of Clubs: 30; *Number of Players:* 500.
Telephone: 00180944 87545; *Fax:* 00180944 81111.

DOMINICAN REPUBLIC

Federacion Dominicana de Futbol, Apartado De Correos No. 1953, Santo Domingo.
Founded: 1953; *Number of Clubs:* 128; *Number of Players:* 10,706; *National Colours:* Blue shirts, white shorts, red stockings.
Telephone: 001809542 6923. *Cable:* FEDOFUTBOL SANTO DOMINGO.

EL SALVADOR

Federacion Salvadorena De Futbol, Av. J.M. Delgado, Col. Escalon, Centro Espanol, Apartado 1029, San Salvador.
Founded: 1936; *Number of Clubs:* 944; *Number of Players:* 21,294; *National Colours:* Blue shirts, blue shorts, blue stockings.
Telephone: 00503 237362; *Cable:* FESFUT SAN SALVADOR; *Fax:* 00503 235893; *Telex:* 20484 FESFUT SAL.

GRENADA

Grenada Football Association, St. Juilles Street, P.O. Box 326, Grenada, West Indies.
Founded: 1924; *Number of Clubs:* 15; *Number of Players:* 200; *National Colours:* Green & yellow shirts, red shorts, green & yellow stockings.
Telephone: 001809 4401986; *Cable:* GRENBALL GRENADA; *Telex:* 3431 CW BUR; *Fax:* 001809 4401986.

GUATEMALA

Federacion Nacional De Futbol De Guatemala C.A., Palacio de los Deportes, Segundo Nivel, Zona 4, Ciudad de Guatemala.
Founded: 1933; *Number of Clubs:* 1,611; *Number of Players:* 43,516; *National Colours:* White/blue diagonal striped shirts, blue shorts, white stockings.
Telephone: 005022 362211; *Fax:* 005022 367268; *Cable:* FEDFUTBOL GUATEMALA.

GUYANA

Guyana Football Association, P.O. Box 10727 Georgetown.
Founded: 1902; *Number of Clubs:* 103; *Number of Players:* 1,665; *National Colours:* Green & yellow shirts, black shorts, white & green stockings.
Telephone: 005922 59458/9; *Cable:* FOOTBALL GUYANA; *Telex:* 2266 RICEBRD GY; *Fax:* 005922 52169.

HAITI

Federation Haitienne De Football, B.P. 2258, Stade Sylvio-Cator, Port-Au-Prince.
Founded: 1904; *Number of Clubs:* 40; *Number of Players:* 4,000; *National Colours:* Red shirts, black shorts, red stockings.
Telephone: 00509 223237; *Cable:* FEDHAFOOB PORT-AU-PRINCE.

HONDURAS

Federacion Nacional Autonoma De Futbol De Honduras, Apartado Postal 827, Costa Oeste Del Est. Nac, Tegucigalpa, De. C.
Founded: 1951; *Number of Clubs:* 1,050; *Number of Players:* 15,300; *National Colours:* Blue shirts, blue shorts, blue stockings.
Telephone: 00504 321897; *Cable* FENAFUTH TEGUCIGALPA; *Telex:* 1209 FENEFUTH; *Fax:* 00504 311428.

JAMAICA

Jamaica Football Federation, Attn. Anthony James, President, Room 8 INSPORTS, Independence Park, Kingston 6.
Founded: 1910; *Number of Clubs:* 266; *Number of Players:* 45,200; *National Colours:* Green shirts, black shorts, green & gold stockings.
Telephone: 001809 9290483; *Fax:* 001809 9622858; *Telex:* 2224 FEDLASCO JA; *Cable:* FOOTBALL JAMAICA KINGSTON.

MEXICO

Federacion Mexicana De Futbol Asociacion, A.C., Abraham Gonzales 74, C.P. 06600, Col. Juarez, Mexico 6, D.F.
Founded: 1927; *Number of Clubs:* 77 (senior); *Number of Players:* 1,402,270; *National Colours:* Green shirts, white shorts, green stockings.
Telephone: 00525 5662155; *Cable:* MEXFUTBOL MEXICO; *Telex:* 1771678 MSUTME; *Fax:* 00525 5667580.

NETHERLANDS ANTILLES

Nederlands Antiliaanse Voetbal Unie, P.O. Box 341, Curacao, N.A.
Founded: 1921; *Number of Clubs:* 85; *Number of Players:* 4,500; *National Colours:* white shirts, white shorts, red stockings.
Telephone:Cable: NAVU CURACAO; *Telex:* 1046 ENNIA NA; *Fax:* 005999 611173.

NICARAGUA

Federacion Nicaraguense De Futbol, Inst. Nicaraguense De Deportes, Apartado Postal 976 6 383, Managua.
Founded: 1968; *Number of Clubs:* 31; *Number of Players:* 160 (senior); *National Colours:* Blue shirts, blue shorts, blue stockings.
Telephone/Fax: 005052 664134; *Cable:* FEDEFOOT MANAGUA; *Telex:* 2156 IND NK.

PANAMA

Federacion Nacional De Futbol De Panama, Estadio Revolucion, Apartado Postal 1523, Panama 1.
Founded: 1937; *Number of Clubs:* 65; *Number of Players:* 4,225; *National Colours:* Red & white shirts, blue shorts, red stockings.
Telephone: 00507 335726; *Cable:* PANAOLIMPIC PANAMA; *Telex:* 2534 INDE PG; *Fax:* 00507 620289.

PUERTO RICO

Federacion Puertorriquena De Futbol, Coliseo Roberto Clemente, P.O. Box 4355, Hato Rey, 00919-4355.
Founded: 1940; *Number of Clubs:* 175; *Number of Players:* 4,200; *National Colurs:* White & red shirts, blue shorts, white & blue stockings.
Telephone/Fax: 001809 7642025; *Cable:* BORIKENFPF; *Telex:* 3450296.

SAINT LUCIA

St Lucia National Football Union, PO Box 255, Castries, St Lucia.
Number of Clubs: 100; *Number of Players:* 4,000; *National Colours:* Blue and white striped shirts, black shorts, blue stockings.
Telephone: 001809 31519; *Fax:* 001809 4524127; *Telex:* 6394 FOR AFF LC.

SAINT KITTS AND NEVIS

St Kitts and Nevis Football Association, P.O. Box 465, Basseterre, St Kitts, West Indies.
Number of Clubs: 36; *Number of Players:* 600.
Telephone: 001809 4652521/ 4654086; *Fax:* 001809 4655501/ 4651042.

SAINT VINCENT & THE GRENADINES

St Vincent & The Grenadines Football Federation, PO Box 1278, Kingstown, St Vincent.
Number of Clubs: 500; *Number of Players:* 5,000.
Telephone: 001809 4561525; *Fax:* 001809 4572970.

SURINAM

Surinaamse Voetbal Bond, Cultuuruinlaan 7, P.O. Box 1223, Paramaribo.
Founded: 1920; *Number of Clubs:* 168; *Number of Players:* 4,430; *National Colours:* Red shirts, white shorts, white stockings.
Telephone: 00597 473112; *Fax:* 00597 479718; *Cable:* SVB Paramaribo.

TRINIDAD AND TOBAGO

Trinidad & Tobago Football Association, Cor. Duke & Scott-Bushe Street, Port of Spain, Trinidad, P.O. Box 400.
Founded: 1906; *Number of Clubs:* 124; *Number of Players:* 5,050; *National Colours:* Red shirts, black shorts, red stockings.
Telephone: 001809 6245183. *Cable:* TRAFA PORT OF SPAIN; *Telex:* 22652 TRAFA WG; *Fax:* 001809 6277661.

USA

United States Soccer Federation, U.S. Soccer House, 1801-1811 S. Prairie Avenue, Chicago, Illinois 60616.
Founded: 1913; *Number of Clubs:* 7,000; *Number of Players:* 1,411,500; *National Colours:* White shirts, blue shorts, red stockings.
Telephone: 001312 5784678; *Telex:* 450024 US SOCCER FED; *Fax:* 001312 5784636.

OCEANIA

AUSTRALIA

Australian Soccer Federation, First Floor, 23-25 Frederick Street, Rockdale, NSW 2216.
Founded: 1961; *Number of Clubs:* 6,816; *Number of Players:* 433,957; *National Colours:* Gold shirts, green shorts, white stockings.
Telephone: 00612 5976611; *Cable:* FOOTBALL SYDNEY; *Telex:* AA 170512; *Fax:* 00612 5993593.

COOK ISLANDS

Cook Islands Football Federation, PO Box 473, Rarotonga, Cook Islands.
Number of Clubs: 9; *Number of Players:* -.
Telephone: 00682 29363; *Fax:* 00682 22095.

FIJI

Fiji Football Association, Mr. J.D. Maharaj, Hon. Secretary, Government Bldgs, P.O.Box 2514, Suva.
Founded: 1946; *Number of Clubs;* 140: *Number of Players:* 21,300; *National Colours:* White shirts, black shorts, black stockings.
Telephone: 00679 300453; *Cable:* FOOTSOCCER SUVA; *Telex:* 2366 FJ; *Fax:* 00679 304642.

NEW ZEALAND

New Zealand Football Association, Inc., P.O. Box 62-532, Central Park, Green Lane, Auckland 6.
Founded: 1891; *Number of Clubs:* 312; *Number of Players:* 52,969; *National Colours:* White shirts, black shorts, white stockings.
Telephone: 00649 5256120; *Fax:* 00649 5256123; *Telex:* NZ 63007 NZFAOFC.

PAPUA NEW GUINEA

Papua New Guinea Football (Soccer) Association Inc., c/o National Sports Institute, P.O. Box 337, Goroka, EHP.
Founded: 1962; *Number of Clubs:* 350; *Number of Players:* 8,250; *National Colours:* Red shirts, black shorts, red stockings.
Telephone: 00675 722391; *Telex:* TOTOTRA NE 23436; *Fax:* 00675 721941.

SOLOMAN ISLANDS

Soloman Islands Football Federation, PO Box 532, Honiara, Soloman Islands.
Number of Players: 4,000; *National Colours:* Blue shirts, white shorts, white stockings.
Telephone: 00677 23553; *Fax:* 00677 20391; *Telex:* HQ 66349.

TAHITI

Federation Tahitienne de Football, Attn. Napoleon Spitz, B.P. 650, Papeete, Tahiti, French Polynesia.
Founded: 1938; *National Colours:* Red shirts, white shorts, white stockings.
Telephone: 00689 420410; *Fax:* 00689 421479; *Telex:* 454 FP.

TONGA

Tonga Football Association, PO Box 36, Nuku'alofa, Kingdom of Tonga.
Number of Clubs: 23; *Number of Players:* 350.
Telephone: 00676 24417; *Fax:* 00676 23555.

VANUATU

Vanuatu Football Federation, P.O. Box 226, Port Vila, Vanuatu.
Founded: 1934; *National Colours:* Gold shirts, black shorts, gold stockings.
Telephone: 00678 22009; *Fax:* 00678 23579.

WESTERN SAMOA

Western Samoa Football (Soccer) Association, Min. of Youth, Sports Culture, Private Bag, Apia.
Founded: 1986; *National Colours:* Blue shirts, white shorts, blue and white stockings.
Telephone: 00685 21420; *Fax:* 00685 24166; *Telex:* 230 SAMGAMES SX.

AFRICA

ALGERIA

Federation Algerienne De Futbol, Route Ahmed Ouaked, Boite Postale No. 39, Alger _ Dely Ibrahim.
Founded: 1962; *Number of Clubs:* 780; *Number of Players:* 58,567; *National Colours:* Green shirts, white shorts, red stockings.
Telephone: 00213 799943; *Cable:* FAFOOT ALGER; *Telex:* 61378. *Fax:* 00213 366181.

ANGOLA

Federation Angolaise De Football, B.P. 3449, Luanda.
Founded: 1977; *Number of Clubs:* 276; *Number of Players:* 4,269; *National Colours:* Red shirts, black shorts, red stockings.
Telephone: 002442 338635/338233; *Cable:* FUTANGOLA; *Telex:* 4072 CIAM AN.

BENIN

Federation Beninoise De Football, B.P. 965, Cotonou.
Founded: 1968; *Number of Clubs:* 117; *Number of Players:* 6,700; *National Colours:* Green shirts, green shorts, green stockings.
Telephone: 00229 330537; *Cable:* FEBEFOOT COTONOU K; *Telex:* 5033 BIMEX COTONOU; *Fax:* 00229 312485.

BOTSWANA

Botswana Football Association, P.O. Box 1396, Gabarone.
Founded: 1976; *National Colours:* Sky blue shirts, white shorts, sky blue stockings.
Telephone: 00267 300279; *Cable:* BOTSBALL GABARONE; *Telex:* 2977 BD; *Fax:* 00267 372911.

BURKINA FASO

Federation Burkinabe De Foot-Ball, B.P. 57, Ouagadougou.

Founded: 1960; *Number of Clubs:* 57; *Number of Players:* 4,672; *National Colours:* Black shirts, white shorts, red stockings.
Telephone: 00226 302850; *Cable:* FEDEFOOT OUAGADOUGOU.

BURUNDI

Federation De Football Du Burundi, B.P. 3426, Bujumbura.
Founded: 1948; *Number of Clubs:* 132; *Number of Players:* 3,930; *National Colours:* Red shirts, white shorts, green stockings.
Telephone: 00257 225160; *Fax:* 00257 228283; *Cable:* FFB BUJA.

CAMEROON

Federation Camerounaise De Football, B.P. 1116, Yaounde.
Founded: 1960; *Number of Clubs:* 200; *Number of Players:* 9,328; *National Colours:* Green shirts, red shorts, yellow stockings.
Telephone: 00237 202538; *Cable:* FECAFOOT YAOUNDE; *Telex:* 8568 JEUNESPO KN.

CAPE VERDE ISLANDS

Federacao Cabo-Verdiana De Futebol, P.O. Box 234, Praia.
Founded: 1986; *National Colours:* Green shirts, green shorts, green stockings.
Telephone: 00238 611362; *Cable:* FCF-CV; *Telex:* 6030 MICDE CV.

CENTRAL AFRICAN REPUBLIC

Federation Centrafricaine De Football, B.P. 344, Bangui.
Founded: 1937; *Number of Clubs:* 256; *Number of Players:* 7,200; *National Colours:* Grey & blue shirts, white shorts, red stockings.
Telephone: 00236 2141; *Cable:* FOOTBANGUI BANGUI.

CONGO

Federation Congolaise De Football, B.P. 4041, Brazzaville.
Founded: 1962; *Number of Clubs:* 250; *Number of Players:* 5,940; *National Colours:* Red shirts, red shorts, white stockings.
Telephone: 00242 815101; *Cable:* FECOFOOT BRAZZAVILLE; *Telex:* 5210 KG.

DJIBOUTI

Federation Djiboutienne de Football, B.P. 1916, Djibouti.
Number of Players: 2,000.
Fax: 00253 356830.

EGYPT

Egyptian Football Association, 5, Shareh Gabalaya, Guezira, Al Borg Post Office, Cairo.
Founded: 1921; *Number of Clubs:* 247; *Number of Players:* 19,735; *National Colours:* Red shirts, white shorts, black stockings.
Telephone: 00202 3401793; *Cable:* KORA CAIRO; *Fax:* 00202 3417817; *Telex:* 23504 KORA.

ETHIOPIA

Ethiopia Football Federation, Addis Ababa Stadium, P.O. Box 1080, Addis Ababa.
Founded: 1943; *Number of Clubs:* 767; *Number of Players:* 20,594; *National Colours:* Green shirts, yellow shorts, red stockings.
Telephone: 002511 514453/514321. *Cable:* FOOTBALL ADDIS ABABA; *Fax:* 002511 513345; *Telex:* 21377 NESCO ET.

GABON

Federation Gabonaise De Football, B.P. 181, Libreville.
Founded: 1962; *Number of Clubs:* 320; *Number of Players:* 10,000; *National Colours:* Blue shirts, white shorts, white stockings.
Telephone: 00241 744747; *Cable:* FEGAFOOT LIBREVILLE; *Telex:* 5642 GO.

GAMBIA

Gambia Football Association, Independence Stadium, Bakau, P.O. Box 523, Banjul.
Founded: 1952; *Number of Clubs:* 30; *Number of Players:* 860; *National Colours:* White & red shirts, white shorts, white stockings.
Telephone: 00220 95834; *Cable:* SPORTS GAMBIA BANJUL; *Fax:* 00220 29837; *Telex:* 2262 FISCO GV.

GHANA

Ghana Football Association, P.O. Box 1272, Accra.
Founded: 1957; *Number of Clubs:* 347; *Number of Players:* 11,275; *National Colours:* White shirts, white shorts, white stockings.
Telephone: 0023321 663924; *Cable:* GFA, ACCRA; *Fax:* 0023321 21662; *Telex:* 2519 SPORTS GH.

GUINEA

Federation Guineenne De Football, P.O. Box 3645, Conakry.
Founded: 1959; *Number of Clubs:* 351; *Number of Players:* 10,000; *National Colours:* Red shirts, yellow shorts, green stockings.
Telephone: 00224 445041; *Cable:* GUINEFOOT CONAKRY; *Telex:* 22302 MJ GE; Fax: 00224 442781.

GUINEA-BISSAU

Federacao De Football Da Guinea-Bissau, Rua4 No. 10-C, Apartado 375, 1035 Bissau Codex.
Founded: 1986; *National Colours: Green shirts, green shorts, green stockings.*
Telephone: 00245 201918; *Cable:* FUTEBOL BISSAU; *Telex:* 205 PUBLICO BI.

GUINEA, EQUATORIAL

Federacion Ecuatoguineana De Futbol, Malabo.
Founded: 1986; *National Colours:* All red.
Telephone: 00240 26523; *Telex:* 9991111 EG; *Cable:* FEGUIFUT/MALABO.

IVORY COAST

Federation Ivoirienne De Football, Stade Felix Houphouet Boigny, B.P. 1202, Abidjan.
Founded: 1960; *Number of Clubs:* 84 (senior); *Number of Players:* 3,655; *National Colours:* Orange shirts, white shorts, green stockings.
Telephone: 00225 240027; *Cable:* FIF ABIDJAN; *Telex:* 42344 FIF CI.

KENYA

Kenya Football Federation, Nyayo National Stadium, P.O. Box 40234, Nairobi.
Founded: 1960; *Number of Clubs:* 351; *Number of Players:* 8,880; *National Colours:* Red shirts, red shorts, red stockings.
Telephone: 002542 501853; *Cable:* KEFF NAIROBI; *Fax:* 002542 501120; *Telex:* 25784 KFF.

LESOTHO

Lesotho Sports Council, P.O. Box 138, Maseru 100, Lesotho.
Founded: 1932; *Number of Clubs:* 88; *Number of Players:* 2,076; *National Colours:* Blue shirts, green shorts, white stockings.
Telephone: 00266 311291; *Cable:* LIPAPALI MASERU; *Fax:* 00266 310914; *Telex:* 4493.

LIBERIA

The Liberia Football Association, P.O. Box 1066, Monrovia 10.
Founded: 1962; *National Colours:* Blue & white shirts, white shorts, blue & white stockings.
Telephone: 00231 222177; *Cable:* LIBFOTASS MONROVIA; *Telex:* 44508 IFA LI. *Fax:* 00231 735003.

LIBYA

Libyan Arab Jamahiriya Football Federation, P.O. Box 5137, Tripoli.
Founded: 1963; *Number of Clubs:* 89; *Number of Players:* 2,941; *National Colours:* Green shirts, white shorts, green stockings.
Telephone: 0021821 46610; *Telex:* 20896 KURATP LY. *Fax:* 0021821 607016.

MADAGASCAR

Federation Malagasy De Football, c/o Comite Nat. De Coordination De Football, B.P. 4409, Antananarivo 101.
Founded: 1961; *Number of Clubs:* 775; *Number of Players:* 23,536; *National Colours:* Red shirts, white shorts, green stockings.
Telephone: 002612 28051; *Telex:* 22393 MOTEL MG.

MALAWI

Football Association of Malawi, P.O. Box 865, Blantyre.
Founded: 1966; *Number of Clubs:* 465; *Number of Players:* 12,500; *National Colours:* Red shirts, red shorts, red stockings.
Telephone: 00265 636686; *Cable:* FOOTBALL BLANTYRE; *Telex:* 4526 SPORTS MI. *Fax:* 00265 636941.

MALI

Federation Malienne De Football, Stade Mamdou Konate, B.P. 1020, Bamako.
Founded: 1960; *Number of Clubs:* 128; *Number of Players:* 5,480; *National Colours:* Green shirts, yellow shorts, red stockings.
Telephone: 00223 224152; *Cable:* MALIFOOT BAMAKO; Telex: 1200/1202.

MAURITANIA

Federation De Foot-Ball De La Rep. Isl. De Mauritanie, B.P. 566, Nouakshott.
Founded: 1961; *Number of Clubs:* 59; *Number of Players:* 1,930; *National Colours:* Green and yellow shirts, blue shorts, green stockings.
Telephone/Fax: 00222 259057; *Telex:* 577 MTN NKTT RIM; *Cable:* FOOTRIM NOUAKSHOTT.

MAURITIUS

Mauritius Football Association, Chancery House, 14 Lislet Geoffroy Street, (2nd Floor, Nos. 303.305), Port Louis.
Founded: 1952; *Number of Clubs:* 397; *Number of Players:* 29,375; *National Colours:* Red shirts, white shorts, red stockings.
Telephone: 00230 2121418, 2125771; *Cable:* MFA PORT LOUIS; *Telex:* 4427 MSA IW; *Fax:* 00230 2084100.

MOROCCO

Federation Royale Marocaine De Football, Av. Ibn Sina, C.N.S. Bellevue, B.P. 51, Rabat.
Founded: 1955; *Number of Clubs:* 350; *Number of Players:* 19,768; *National Colours:* Red shirts, green shorts, red stockings.
Telephone: 002127 672706/08 or 67 26 07; *Cable:* FERMAFOOT RABAT; *Telex:* 32940 FERMFOOT M. *Fax:* 002127 671070

MOZAMBIQUE

Federacao Mocambicana De Futebol, Av. Samora Machel, 11-2, Caixa Postal 1467, Maputo.
Founded: 1978; *Number of Clubs:* 144; *National Colours:* Red shirts, red shorts, red stockings.
Telephone: 002581 26475; *Cable:* MOCAMBOLA MAPUTO; *Telex:* 6575 PERCO MO.

NAMIBIA

Namibia Football Federation, 18 Curt von Francois Str. PO Box 1345, Windhoek 2000; Namibia.
Number of Clubs: 244; *Number of Players:* 7320.
Fax: 0026461 224454.

NIGER

Federation Nigerienne De Football, Stade du 29 Juillet, B.P. 10299, Niamey.
Founded: 1967; *Number of Clubs:* 64; *Number of Players:* 1,525; *National Colours:* Orange shirts, white shorts, green stockings.
Telephone: 00227 734705; *Fax:* 00227 735512; *Telex:* 5527 or 5349; *Cable:* FEDERFOOT NIGER NIAMEY.

NIGERIA

Nigeria Football Association National Sports Commission, National Stadium, P.O. Box 466, Lagos.
Founded: 1945; *Number of Clubs:* 326; *Number of Players:* 80,190; *National Colours:* Green shirts, white shorts, green stockings.
Telephone: 002341 835265; *Cable:* FOOTBALL LAGOS; *Telex:* 26570 NFA NG; *Fax:* 002341 2630810.

RWANDA

Federation Rwandaise De Foot-Ball Amateur, B.P. 2000, Kigali.
Founded: 1972; *Number of Clubs:* 167; *National Colours:* Red shirts, red shorts, red stockings.
Telephone: 00250 82605; *Cable:* MIJENCOOP KIGALI; *Telex:* 22504 PUBLIC RW; *Fax:* 00250 76574.

SENEGAL

Federation Senegalaise De Football, Stade De L'Amitie, Route De L'Aeroport De Yoff, B.P. 130 21, Dakar.
Founded: 1960; *Number of Clubs:* 75 (senior); *Number of Players:* 3,977; *National Colours:* Green shirts, yellow shorts, red stockings.
Telephone: 00221 243524; *Fax:* 00221 220241; *Telex:* 21741; *Cable:* SENEFOOT DAKAR.

SEYCHELLES

Seychelles Football Federation, P.O. Box 580, Mont Fleuri, Victoria.
Founded: 1986; *National Colours:* Green shirts, yellow shorts, red stockings.
Telephone: 00248 24126; *Telex:* 2240 CULSPT SZ; *Fax:* 00248 23518.

ST. THOMAS AND PRINCIPE

Federation Santomense De Fut., P.O. Box 42, Sao Tome.
Founded: 1986; *National Colours:* Green shirts, green shorts, green stockings.
Telephone: 0023912 22311; *Telex:* 213 PUBLICO STP.

SIERRA LEONE

Sierra Leone Amateur Football Association, Siaka Stevens Stadium, Brookfields, P.O. Box 672, Freetown.
Founded: 1967; *Number of Clubs:* 104; *Number of Players:* 8,120; *National Colours:* Green shirts, white shorts, blue stockings.
Telephone: 0023222 41872; *Cable:* SLAFA FREETOWN; *Telex:* 3210 BOOTH SL.

SOMALIA

Somali Football Federation, Ministry of Sports, P.O. Box 247, Mogadishu.
Founded: 1951; *Number of Clubs:* 46 (senior); *Number of Players:* 1,150; *National Colours:* Sky blue shirts, white shorts, white stockings.
Telephone: 002521 20501; *Cable:* SOMALIA FOOTBALL MOGADISHU; *Telex:* 3061 SONOC SM.

SOUTH AFRICA

South African Football Association, First National Bank Stadium, Nasrec; PO Box 910, Johannesburg 2000; South Africa.
Number of Teams: 51,944; *Number of Players:* 1,039,880.
Telephone: 002711 4943522; Fax: 002711 4943447.

SUDAN

Sudan Football Association, P.O. Box 437, Khartoum.
Founded: 1936; *Number of Clubs:* 750; *Number of Players:* 42,200; *National Colours:* White shirts, white shorts, white stockings.
Telephone: 0024911 76633; *Cable:* ALKOURA, KHARTOUM; *Telex:* 23007 KORA SD.

SWAZILAND

National Football Association of Swaziland, P.O. Box 641, Mbabane.
Founded: 1976; *Number of Clubs:* 136; *National Colours:* Blue and gold shirts, white shorts, blue and gold stockings.
Telephone: 00268 46852; *Telex:* 2245 EXP WD.

TANZANIA

Football Association of Tanzania, P.O. Box 1574, Dar Es Salaam.
Founded: 1930; *Number of Clubs:* 51; *National Colours:* Yellow shirts, yellow shorts, yellow stockings.
Telephone: 0025551 32334; *Telex:* 41873 TZ; *Cable:* FAT DAR ES SALAAM.

TOGO

Federation Togolaise De Football, C.P. 5, Lome.
Founded: 1960; *Number of Clubs:* 144; *Number of Players:* 4,346; *National Colours:* Red shirts, white shorts, red stockings.
Telephone: 00228 212698; *Cable:* TOGOFOOT LOME; *Telex:* 5015 CNOT TG. *Fax:* 00228 221314.

TUNISIA

Federation Tunisienne De Football, 2 rue Hamza Abderlmottaleb, El-Menzah VI, Tunis 1004.
Founded: 1957; *Number of Clubs:* 215; *Number of Players:* 18,300; *National Colours:* Red shirts, white shorts, red stockings.
Telephone: 002161 233303, 233544; *Cable:* FOOTBALL TUNIS; *Fax:* 002161 767929; *Telex:* 14783 FTFOOT TN.

UGANDA

Federation of Uganda Football Associations, P.O. Box 20077, Kampala, Uganda.
Founded: 1924; *Number of Clubs:* 400; *Number of Players:* 1,518; *National Colours:* Yellow shirts, black shorts, yellow stockings.
Telephone: 0025641 254477; *Cable:* FUFA KAMPALA; *Telex:* 61272; *Fax:* 0025641 245580; *Telegrams:* fufa lugogo stadium.

ZAIRE

Federation Zairoise De Football-Association, P.O. Box 1284, rue Dima No. 10, Kinshasa 1.
Founded: 1919; *Number of Clubs:* 3,800; *Number of Players:* 64,627; *National Colours:* Green shirts, yellow shorts, yellow stockings. *Cable:* FEZAFA KINSHASA; *Telex:* 63915. *Fax:* 0024312 506555.

ZAMBIA

Football Association of Zambia, P.O. Box 347 51, Lusaka.
Founded: 1929; *Number of Clubs:* 20 (senior); *Number of Players:* 4,100; *National Colours:* Green shirts, white shorts, black stockings.
Telephone: 002601 221145; *Cable:* FOOTBALL LUSAKA; *Telex:* 40204 FAZ ZA; *Fax:* 002601 225046.

ZIMBABWE

Zimbabwe Football Association, P.O. Box 8343, Causeway, Harare.
Founded: 1965; *National Colours:* White shirts, black shorts, black stockings.
Telephone: 002634 791275; *Cable:* SOCCER HARARE; *Telex:* 22299 SOCCER ZW; *Fax:* 002634 793320.
Other addition: CHAD (readmitted).

OTHER INTERNATIONAL TOURNAMENTS

BALTIC CUP

Latvia 2, Estonia 0
Lithuania 7, Estonia 0
Latvia 2, Lithuania 0

	P	*W*	*D*	*L*	*F*	*A*	Pts
Latvia	2	2	0	0	4	0	4
Lithuania	2	1	0	1	7	2	2
Estonia	2	0	0	2	0	9	0

US CUP

USA 3, Nigeria 2
Colombia 1, Nigeria 0
USA 4, Mexico 0
Mexico 0, Colombia 0
Mexico 2, Nigeria 1
USA 0, Colombia 0

	P	*W*	*D*	*L*	*F*	*A*	Pts
USA	3	2	1	0	7	2	7
Colombia	3	1	2	0	1	0	5
Mexico	3	1	1	1	2	5	4
Nigeria	3	0	0	3	3	6	0

COPA CENTENARIO (in Chile)

Paraguay 0, Turkey 0
Chile 3, New Zealand 1
Chile 0, Paraguay 1
Chile 0, Turkey 0
Paraguay 3, New Zealand 2
Turkey 2, New Zealand 1

	P	*W*	*D*	*L*	*F*	*A*	Pts
Paraguay	3	2	1	0	4	2	7
Turkey	3	1	2	0	2	1	5
Chile	3	1	1	1	3	2	4
New Zealand	3	0	0	3	4	8	0

CENTENARY TOURNAMENT (in Switzerland)

Switzerland 0, Italy 1
Italy 0, Germany 2
Switzerland 1, Germany 2

	P	*W*	*D*	*L*	*F*	*A*	Pts
Germany	2	2	0	0	4	1	6
Italy	2	1	0	1	1	2	3
Switzerland	2	0	0	2	1	3	0

EUROPEAN FOOTBALL CHAMPIONSHIP
(formerly EUROPEAN NATIONS' CUP)

Year	*Winners*		*Runners-up*		*Venue*	*Attendance*
1960	USSR	2	Yugoslavia	1	Paris	17,966
1964	Spain	2	USSR	1	Madrid	120,000
1968	Italy	2	Yugoslavia	0	Rome	60,000
	After 1-1 draw					75,000
1972	West Germany	3	USSR	0	Brussels	43,437
1976	Czechoslovakia	2	West Germany	2	Belgrade	45,000
	(Czechoslovakia won on penalties)					
1980	West Germany	2	Belgium	1	Rome	47,864
1984	France	2	Spain	0	Paris	48,000
1988	Holland	2	USSR	0	Munich	72,308
1992	Denmark	2	Germany	0	Gothenburg	37,800

EUROPEAN CHAMPIONSHIP 1994–96
Qualifying Tournament

Qualifying tournament

Group 1

Tel Aviv, 4 September 1994, 3500

Israel (1) 2 *(Harazi R 43, 58)*

Poland (0) 1 *(Kosecki 80)*

Israel: Ginzburg; Harazi A, Klinger, Balbul, Glam, Hazan, Berkovitch (Levi 86), Banin, Revivo, Rosenthal (Atar 89), Harazi R.
Poland: Wandzik; Bak, Szewczyk, Waldoch, Maciejewski, Lapinski, Jalocha (Chenik 46), Mielcarski (Gesior 58), Brzeczek, Kosecki, Kowalczyk.
Referee: Van den Wijngaert (Belgium).

Bratislava, 7 September 1994, 14,238

Slovakia (0) 0

France (0) 0

Slovakia: Molnar; Glonek, Stupala, Zeman, Tittel, Kinder, Tomaschek, Kristofik, Zvara (Penska 63), Rusnak (Weiss 80), Moravcik.
France: Lama; Angloma, Blanc, Roche, Di Meco, Deschamps, Le Guen, Ginola, Djorkaeff (Lizarazu 82), Cantona, Pedros (Dugarry 63).
Referee: Mikkelsen (Denmark).

Bucharest, 7 September 1994, 10,000

Romania (1) 3 *(Belodedici 43, Petrescu 58, Raducioiu 88)*

Azerbaijan (0) 0

Romania: Stelea (Stangaciu 85); Petrescu, Prodan, Belodedici, Selymes (Carstea 82), Lupescu (Timofte D 75), Popescu, Munteanu, Lacatus, Raducioiu, Dumitrescu.
Azerbaijan: Jidkov; Alazerdiev, Asadov, Achmedov T, Drozdov, Abusev, Diniev, Guseynov (Agalev 80), Alekperov, Suleimanov (Ryzalev 59), Kasumov.
Referee: Sedlacek (Austria).

St Etienne, 8 October 1994, 31,744

France (0) 0

Romania (0) 0

France: Lama; Blanc, Angloma, Roche, Lizarazu, Karembeu, Desailly, Loko (Dugarry 83), Pedros, Cantona, Ouedec (Zidane 71).
Romania: Stelea; Belodedici, Prodan, Petrescu, Lupescu, Timofte (Lacatus 71), Popescu, Hagi, Selymes, Dumitrescu, Raducioiu (Panduru 80).
Referee: Sundell (Sweden).

Tel Aviv, 12 October 1994, 10,000

Israel (2) 2 *(Harazi R 23, Banin 32 (pen))*

Slovakia (2) 2 *(Rusnak 5, Moravcik 14)*

Israel: Ginzburg; Balbul, Glam, Klinger (Shelach 67), Harazi A, Hazan, Berkovitch, Banin (Nimni 60), Revivo, Harazi R, Rosenthal.
Slovakia: Molnar; Stupala, Tittel, Glonek, Kinder, Zeman, Kristofik, Dubovsky, Weiss (Kozak 75), Moravcik, Rusnak (Zvara 76).
Referee: Blankenstein (Holland).

Mielec, 12 October 1994, 10,000

Poland (1) 1 *(Juskowiak 44)*

Azerbaijan (0) 0

Poland: Wandzik; Waldoch, Jaskulski, Lapinski (Maciejewski 79), Kozminski (Fedoruk 70), Swierczewski P, Czereszewski, Brzeczek, Kosecki, Warzycha, Juskowiak.
Azerbaijan: Jidkov; Alazerdiev, Kerimov, Achmedov T, Asadov, Abusev (Kurbanov 89), Guseynov, Diniev, Mardanov, Kasumov, Alekperov.
Referee: Koho (Finland).

Bucharest, 12 November 1994, 15,000

Romania (1) 3 *(Popescu 7, Hagi 46, Prodan 80)*

Slovakia (0) 2 *(Dubovsky 56, Chvila 78)*

Romania: Stelea; Petrescu, Belodedici, Prodan, Munteanu, Lacatus (Timofte 75), Popescu, Lupescu, Hagi, Raducioiu (Vladoiu 83), Dumitrescu.
Slovakia: Molnar; Stupala, Chvila, Tittel, Glonek, Kinder, Tomaschek, Kristofik, Moravcik, Penska (Timko 46), Dubovsky.
Referee: Zhuk (Russia).

Zabrze, 16 November 1994, 20,000

Poland (0) 0

France (0) 0

Poland: Wandzik; Jakulski, Czereszewski, Swierczewski M, Waldoch, Swierczewski P, Baluszynski (Gesior 80), Kozminski (Bak 28), Juskowiak, Kosecki, Warzycha.

France: Lama; Angloma, Blanc, Roche, Di Meco, Karembeu, Desailly, Le Guen, Ouedec (Dugarry 76), Cantona, Pedros (Djorkaeff 25).
Referee: Amendolia (Italy).

Trabzon, 16 November 1994, 3000

Azerbaijan (0) 0

Israel (1) 2 *(Harazi R 30, Rosenthal 51)*

Azerbaijan: Jidkov; Alazerdiev, Achmedov T, Mayorov (Adjaiev 46), Gadirov, Asadov, Guseynov (Ryzalev 77), Diniev, Kasumov, Suleimanov, Alekperov.
Israel: Ginzburg; Balbul, Harazi A, Klinger, Glam, Hazan, Banin, Berkovitch (Nimni 66), Revivo, Harazi R (Shelah 83), Rosenthal.
Referee: Vagner (Hungary).

Tel Aviv, 14 December 1994, 40,000

Israel (0) 1 *(Rosenthal 84)*

Romania (0) 1 *(Lacatus 70)*

Israel: Ginzburg; Balbul, Klinger, Harazi A, Glam, Hazan, Berkovitch, Levi R (Zohar 75), Revivo, Harazi R (Shelach 90), Rosenthal.
Romania: Stelea; Petrescu, Belodedici, Prodan, Selymes, Hagi, Popescu, Lupescu, Munteanu (Vladoiu 52), Lacatus, Dumitrescu (Galca 74).
Referee: Navarrete (Spain).

Trabzon, 14 December 1994, 4000

Azerbaijan (0) 0

France (1) 2 *(Papin 25, Loko 56)*

Azerbaijan: Jidkov (Gasanov 41); Alazerdiev, Varapzade, Abusev, Agalev, Jabarov, Asadov (Kerinov 78), Kasumov, Diniev (Ryzalev 78), Guseynov, Alekperov.
France: Lama; Angloma, Roche, Blanc, Di Meco, Desailly (Ferri 71), Le Guen, Cantona, Loko, Papin, Pedros (Martins 76).
Referee: Pedersen (Norway).

Bucharest, 29 March 1995, 22,000

Romania (1) 2 *(Raducioiu 45, Wandzik 55 (og))*

Poland (1) 1 *(Juskowiak 43 (pen))*

Romania: Stelea; Petrescu, Prodan, Belodedici, Selymes, Hagi (Vladoiu 88), Dumitrescu, Popescu, Munteanu, Lacatus (Lupu 46), Raducioiu.
Poland: Wandzik; Jaskulski, Swierczewski M, Waldoch, Swierczewski P, Novak (Wieszczycki 58), Czereszewski (Sokolowski 73), Baluszynski, Warzycha K, Juskowiak, Kosecki.
Referee: Rothlisberger (Switzerland).

Kosice, 29 March 1995, 12,400

Slovakia (3) 4 *(Tittel 35, Timko 40, 50, Dubovsky 45 (pen))*

Azerbaijan (0) 1 *(Suleimanov 80 (pen))*

Slovakia: Molnar; Stupala, Glonek, Zeman, Kinder, Kristofik, Tittel, Moravcik (Prazenica 73), Dubovsky, Timko, Penska.
Azerbaijan: Gasanov; Aliev (Kapirov 65), Varapzade, Abusev, Jabarov, Asadov, Guseynov, Agalev, Diniev, Suleimanov, Kasumov (Alekperov 56).
Referee: Nikakis (Greece).

Tel Aviv, 29 March 1995, 45,000

Israel (0) 0

France (0) 0

Israel: Ginzburg; Halfon, Klinger, Harazi A, Glam, Hazan, Banin, Revivo, Berkovitch (Zohar 64), Rosenthal, Harazi R.
France: Lama; Angloma, Roche, Blanc, Di Meco, Desailly, Le Guen, Martins (Djorkaeff 78), Pedros, Loko, Ouedec (Ginola 66).
Referee: McCluskey (Scotland).

Zabrze, 25 April 1995, 5500

Poland (1) 4 *(Nowak 1, Juskowiak 50, Kowalczyk 55, Kosecki 62)*

Israel (2) 3 *(Rosenthal 37, Revivo 42, Zohar 77)*

Poland: Wandzik; Lapinski, Swierczewski M, Waldoch, Swierczewski P, Nowak (Bukalski 46), Kozminski, Baluszynski (Wieszczycki 46), Juskowiak, Kowalczyk, Kosecki.
Israel: Ginzburg; Halfon, Harazi A, Klinger, Glam, Hazan, Banin, Revivo, Berkovitch, Mizrahi (Zohar 73), Rosenthal.
Referee: Anders (Sweden).

Trabzon, 26 April 1995, 500

Azerbaijan (1) 1 *(Suleimanov 4)*

Romania (2) 4 *(Raducioiu 1 (pen), 68, 76, Dumitrescu 38)*

Azerbaijan: Gasanov; Asadov, Ghesmam, Akhmedov (Varapzade 21), Jabarov (Kapirov 75), Abusev, Guseynov, Diniev, Lukin, Suleimanov, Alekperov.
Romania: Stelea; Petrescu, Prodan, Belodedici, Selymes, Popescu (Timofte D 81), Munteanu, Lupescu, Dumitrescu, Lacatus (Lupu 69), Raducioiu.
Referee: Momirov (Bulgaria).

Nantes, 26 April 1995, 26,000

France (2) 4 *(Kristofik 27 (og), Ginola 42, Blanc 57, Guerin 62)*

Slovakia (0) 0

France: Lama; Angloma, Blanc, Roche, Di Meco, Deschamps, Desailly, Guerin, Zidane (Djorkaeff 73), Loko, Ginola.
Slovakia: Molnar; Stupala, Zeman, Glonek, Kinder, Kristofik, Tittel, Tomaschek (Timko 46), Moravcik, Penska (Maixner 73), Dubovsky.
Referee: Heynemann (Germany).

Zabrze, 7 June 1995, 20,000

Poland (1) 5 *(Juskowiak 10, 70, Wieszczycki 58, Kosecki 63, Nowak 70)*

Slovakia (0) 0

Poland: Szczesny; Jaskulski (Czereszewski 76), Zielinski, Bukalski, Waldoch, Kozminski, Swierczewski P, Nowak, Kosecki, Juskowiak, Kowalczyk, (Wieszczycki 46).
Slovakia: Vencel; Kozak (Penska 60), Zeman, Glonek, Prazenica, Tomaschek, Solar, Kristofik (Weiss 71), Timko, Dubovsky, Moravcik.
Referee: Sedlacek (Austria).

Bucharest, 7 June 1995, 20,000

Romania (1) 2 *(Lacatus 16, Munteanu 65)*

Israel (0) 1 *(Berkovitch 50)*

Romania: Stelea; Petrescu, Prodan, Belodedici, Selymes, Munteanu, Lupescu, Lupu (Panduru 87), Dumitrescu (Vladoiu 63), Lacatus, Raducioiu.

Israel: Cohen; Halfon, Shelah (Balbul 65) (Zohar 74), Bruner, Amsalem, Hazan, Klinger, Mizrahi, Banin, Berkovitch, Dricks.
Referee: Pedersen (Norway).

	P	*W*	*D*	*L*	*F*	*A*	*Pts*
Romania	7	5	2	0	15	6	17
France	6	2	4	0	6	0	10
Poland	6	3	1	2	12	7	10
Israel	7	2	3	2	11	10	9
Slovakia	6	1	2	3	8	15	5
Azerbaijan	6	0	0	6	2	16	0

Group 2

Brussels, 7 September 1994, 11,000

Belgium (1) 2 *(Oliveira 3, Degryse 73)*

Armenia (0) 0

Belgium: Preud'homme; Genaux, De Wolf, Albert, Smidts, Staelens (Emmers 75), Van der Elst F, Van der Heyden (Boffin 67), Degryse, Oliveira, Weber.
Armenia: Arm. Petrossian; Art. Petrossian, Kerpasian, Tonoian, Ovsepian, Khatchatrian, Soukiassian, Oganesian, Shakhgeldian (Avetissian 46), Grigorian (Mikhitarian 75), Michitarian.
Referee: Ferry (Northern Ireland).

Limassol, 7 September 1994, 12,000

Cyprus (1) 1 *(Sotiriou 35)*

Spain (2) 2 *(Higuera 18, 26)*

Cyprus: Panayiotou; Costa, Constandinou, Christophi M, Charalambous M, Pittas, Ioannou D, Phasouliotis (Malekos 62), Savvides (Andreou 77), Gogic, Sotiriou.
Spain: Zubizarreta; Voro, Nadal, Camarasa, Sergi, Goicoechea, Hierro, Guerrero, Guardiola (Caminero 63), Higuera, Amavisca (Ciganda 78).
Referee: Batta (France).

Skopje, 7 September 1994, 22,000

Macedonia (1) 1 *(Stojkovski 4)*

Denmark (0) 1 *(Povlsen 87)*

Macedonia: Traciev; Stanojkovic, Najdoski, Markovski, Jovanovski, Stojkovski, Boskovski (Serafimovski 82), Djurovski B, Babunski (Kanatlarovski 65), Pancev, Micevski.
Denmark: Schmeichel; Helveg, Rieper, Olsen, Friis-Hansen, Steen-Nielsen, Jensen J (Larsen 65), Vilfort (Povlsen 50), Christensen B, Laudrup M, Laudrup B.
Referee: Van der Ende (Holland).

Erevan, 8 October 1994, 6000

Armenia (0) 0

Cyprus (0) 0

Armenia: Abramian; Soukissian, Hatslatian (Kerpasian 46), Donodjian, Ovsepian, Vardanian, Bedrossian, Grigorian, Adamian, Abedasian A, Mikhitarian (Abedasian B 79).
Cyprus: Christophi M; Kalotheou, Pittas, Ioannou D, Stephani, Zembashis, Charalambous, Sotiriou, Gogic, Phasouliotis (Malekos 70), Savvides.
Referee: Bremisla (Poland).

Copenhagen, 12 October 1994, 40,000

Denmark (1) 3 *(Vilfort 35, Jensen J 72, Strudal 86)*

Belgium (1) 1 *(Degryse 31)*

Denmark: Schmeichel; Helveg, Olsen, Rieper, Friis-Hansen, Risager (Kjeldbjerg 78), Vilfort (Jensen J 72), Laudrup M, Steen-Nielsen, Laudrup B, Strudal.
Belgium: Bodart; Genaux, Van Meir, Albert, Smidts, Borkelmans (Oliveira 77), Verheyen, Van der Elst, Staelens, Degryse, Weber.
Referee: Pairetto (Italy).

Skopje, 12 October 1994, 30,000

Macedonia (0) 0

Spain (2) 2 *(Julio Salinas 16, 25)*

Macedonia: Traciev (Micevski 50); Stanojkovic, Stojkovski, Djurovski B, Najdoski, Jovanovski, Boskovski, Savevski, Babunski (Markovski 39), Djurovski M (Serafimovski 70), Micevski.
Spain: Zubizarreta; Ferrer, Abelardo, Alkorta, Caminero, Nadal, Hierro (Amavisca 76), Sergi, Luis Enrique, Higuera, Julio Salinas (Loggi 65).
Referee: Grabner (Austria).

Brussels, 16 November 1994, 17,000

Belgium (1) 1 *(Verheyen 31)*

Macedonia (0) 1 *(Boskovski 54)*

Belgium: Preud'homme; Genaux, Crasson, Smidts, Boffin, Staelens, Van der Elst, Walem (De Bilde 72), Verheyen, Degryse, Nilis.
Macedonia: Celeski; Stanojkovic, Djurovski B, Najdoski, Janevski, Jovanovski, Boskovski (Kanatlarovski 87), Markovski, Djurovski M (Serafimovski 80), Stojkovski, Micevski T.
Referee: Kusainov (Russia).

Limassol, 16 November 1994, 8000

Cyprus (1) 2 *(Sotiriou 7, Phasouliotis 87)*

Armenia (0) 0

Cyprus: Christophi M; Andreou, Ioannou, Evagoras, Stephani, Zembashis (Elia 89), Malekos (Phasouliotis 68), Savvides, Pittas, Gogic, Sotiriou.
Armenia: Abramian; Tonoian, Oganesian, Vardanian, Kerpasian, Petrossian Art, Grigorian, Mikhitarian (Abedasian B 85), Obsenpian, Soukiassian, Egspegian (Abedasian A 69).
Referee: Ashby (England).

Seville, 16 November 1994, 38,000

Spain (1) 3 *(Nadal 41, Donato 57, Luis Enrique 87)*

Denmark (0) 0

Spain: Zubizarreta; Ferrer, Belsue, Alkorta, Abelardo, Nadal, Luis Enrique, Caminero (Bakero 72), Sergi, Donato, Julio Salinas (Higuera 57).
Denmark: Schmeichel; Helveg, Rieper, Olsen, Risager, Friis Hansen (Christensen B 65), Steen-Nielsen (Jensen J 46), Vilfort, Strudal, Laudrup B, Laudrup M.
Referee: McCluskey (Scotland).

Skopje, 17 December 1994, 12,000

Macedonia (2) 3 *(Djurovski B 15, 36, 89)*

Cyprus (0) 0

Macedonia: Celeski; Stanojkovic, Janevski, Najdoski, Stojkovski, Markovski, Babunski (Jovanovski 72), Djurovski B, Boskovski (Serafimovski 86), Djurovski M, Micevski.
Cyprus: Christophi M; Kalotheou, Charalambous M, Ioannou, Christophi E, Stephani, Charalambous C, Phasouliotis, Savvides (Malekos 67), Gogic, Sotiriou (Andreou 78).
Referee: Strampe (Germany).

Brussels, 17 December 1994, 25,000

Belgium (1) 1 *(Degryse 6)*

Spain (1) 4 *(Hierro 28, Donato 55 (pen), Julio Salinas 68, Luis Enrique 89)*

Belgium: Preud'homme; Genaux, Crasson, Albert, Smidts, Bettagno, Van der Elst F, Staelens, Boffin, Degryse, De Bilde.
Spain: Zubizaretta; Belsue, Abelardo, Nadal, Alkorta, Hierro, Sergi, Donato, Guerrero (Voro 57), Luis Enrique, Julio Salinas (Goicoechea 70).
Referee: Cakar (Turkey).

Seville, 29 March 1995, 27,000

Spain (1) 1 *(Guerrero 24)*

Belgium (1) 1 *(Degryse 25)*

Spain: Zubizaretta; Belsue, Abelardo, Nadal, Sergi, Hierro, Luis Enrique, Guerrero (Higuera 37), Donato, Julio Salinas (Pizzi 63), Amavisca.
Belgium: Bodart; Genaux, Medved, Renier, Smidts, Walem (Verheyen 68), Karagiannis (Crasson 83), Staelens, Degryse, De Bilde, Schepens.
Referee: Harrel (France).

Limassol, 29 March 1995, 15,000

Cyprus (1) 1 *(Agathocleous 45)*

Denmark (1) 1 *(Schjonberg 2)*

Cyprus: Panayiotou; Costa, Pittas, Ioannou D, Charalambous, Christodolou, Engomitis, Andreou A, Hadjilukas (Constandinou C 89), Gogic, Agathocleous.
Denmark: Schmeichel; Laursen, Rieper, Friis-Hansen (Helveg 46), Hogh, Schjonberg, Steen-Nielsen, Nielsen P, Laudrup M, Rasmussen, Laudrup B.
Referee: Shorte (Eire).

Erevan, 26 April 1995, 40,000

Armenia (0) 0

Spain (0) 2 *(Amavisca 49, Goicoechea 63)*

Armenia: Abramian; Soukissian, Hovsepian, Tonoian, Hovanesian, Vardanian, Petrossian, Grigorian (Takhmazian 65), Mikhitarian, Shakhgeldian, Adamian (Avetissian 55).
Spain: Zubizarreta; Belsue, Alkorta, Karanka, Otero, Nadal, Donato (Camarasa 69), Luis Enrique, Goicoechea, Pizzi (Julio Salinas 58), Amavisca.
Referee: Porumboiu (Romania).

Copenhagen, 26 April 1995, 38,888

Denmark (0) 1 *(Nielsen P 70)*

Macedonia (0) 0

Denmark: Schmeichel; Laursen, Rieper, Hogh, Schjonberg, Thomsen, Steen-Nielsen, Rasmussen (Andersen 46), Laudrup M, Nielsen P (Helveg 78), Laudrup B.
Macedonia: Celeski; Stanojkovic, Stojkovski, Najdoski, Markovski (Nedzmedine 26), Jovanovski, Boskovski, Djurovski, Micevski, Pancev, Serafimovski (Stojkoski 77).
Referee: Ihring (Slovakia).

Brussels, 26 April 1995, 13,000

Belgium (1) 2 *(Karagiannis 20, Schepens 47)*

Cyprus (0) 0

Belgium: Bodart; Renier, Medved, Grun, Smidts, Staelens, Karagiannis, Degryse, Schepens, Nilis, De Bilde (Goossens 81).
Cyprus: Panayiotou; Kalotheou, Charalambous M, Ioannou D, Pittas, Christodolou, Larkou, Andreou A, Engomitis, Agathocleous (Larkou 62), Papavassiliou (Sotiriou 85).
Referee: Elleray (England).

Erevan, 10 May 1995, 12,500

Armenia (1) 2 *(Grigorian 21, 51)*

Macedonia (0) 2 *(Hristov 59, Markovski 70)*

Armenia: Abramian; Soukissian, Hovsepian, Tonoian, Hovanesian, Vardanian, Petrossian, Grigorian, Mikhitarian (Gspeyan), Shakhgeldian, Avetissian (Takhmazian).
Macedonia: Celeski; Stanojkovic, Stojkovski, Najdoski, Markovski, Jovanovski (Kanatlarovski), Hristov, Babunski, Micevski (Nedzmedine), Pancev, Serafimovski.
Referee: Fajilstrom (Sweden).

Copenhagen, 7 June 1995, 40,199

Denmark (1) 4 *(Vilfort 45, 50, Laudrup B 58, Laudrup M 75)*

Cyprus (0) 0

Denmark: Schmeichel; Laursen, Rieper, Hogh, Schjonberg, Steen-Nielsen (Rasmussen P 46), Jensen, Vilfort (Andersen E 87), Beck, Laudrup M, Laudrup B.
Cyprus: Petrides; Costa, Pittas, Christodolou, Charalambous, Andreou A, Engomitis, Larkou, Hadjilucas (Phasouliotis 60), Gogic, Sotiriou (Andreou P 68).
Referee: Muller (Switzerland).

Seville, 7 June 1995, 20,000

Spain (0) 1 *(Hierro 64 (pen))*

Armenia (0) 0

Spain: Zubizarreta; Belsue, Aranzabal, Alkorta, Abelardo, Hierro, Goicoechea (Julio Salinas 46), Guerrero (Caminero 78), Nadal, Luis Enrique, Amavisca.
Armenia: Abrahamian; Sosoukiassian, Haousepian, Tonoyan, Nighoyan (Ter-petrossian 71), Valdanian, Petrossian (Avetissian V 76), Tahmazian, Mekhitarian, Shahgheldian, Avetissian A.
Referee: Philippi (Luxembourg).

Skopje, 7 June 1995, *

Macedonia (0) 0

Belgium (4) 5 *(Grun 15, Scifo 18, 60, Schepens 28, Versavel 43)*

Macedonia: Celeski; Stanojkovic, Najdovski, Stojkoviski, Boskovski, Djurovski (Hristov 61), Janevski, Bubunski, Micevski, Pancev, Serafimovski.
Belgium: Bodart; Genaux, Renier, Grun, Smidts, Staelens, Karagiannis, Schepens (Leonard 83), Scifo, Versavel, De Bilde.
Referee: Wojciki (Poland).
**Match played behind closed doors as disciplinary punishment.*

	P	*W*	*D*	*L*	*F*	*A*	*Pts*
Spain	7	6	1	0	15	3	19
Belgium	7	3	2	2	13	9	11
Denmark	6	3	2	1	10	6	11
Macedonia	7	1	3	3	7	12	6
Cyprus	7	1	2	4	4	12	5
Armenia	6	0	2	4	2	9	2

Group 3

Reykjavik, 7 September 1994, 15,000

Iceland (0) 0

Sweden (1) 1 *(Ingesson 37)*

Iceland: Kristinsson B; Kristinsson R, Jonsson K, Bergsson, Gislason, Gudjohnsen, Orlygsson (Gunnlaugsson B 60), Jonsson S, Stefansson, Gunnlaugsson A, Sverrisson.
Sweden: Ravelli; Nilsson, Andersson P, Bjorklund, Ljung, Brolin, Mild, Schwarz, Ingesson, Dahlin (Larsson 67), Andersson K.
Referee: Mottram (Scotland).

Budapest, 7 September 1994, 10,000

Hungary (2) 2 *(Kiprich 4, Halmai 45)*

Turkey (0) 2 *(Hakan 66, Bulent 70)*

Hungary: Petry; Telek, Meszoly, Lipcsei, Kozma, Halmai, Detari, Urban, Duro (Banfi 62), Kiprich (Wukovics 67), Kovacs.
Turkey: Engin; Gokhan (Arif 46), Recep, Bulent, Ilker, Ogun, Oguz, Tugay, Orhan, Ertugrul (Abdullah 87), Hakan.
Referee: Pairetto (Italy).

Istanbul, 12 October 1994, 20,000

Turkey (3) 5 *(Saffet 11, 28, Hakan 30, 62, Yalcin 65)*

Iceland (0) 0

Turkey: Engin; Gokhan, Recep, Bulent, Orhan (Mutlu 3), Arif, Oguz, Ogun, Abdullah, Saffet, Hakan (Yalcin 64).
Iceland: Kristinsson B (Finnbogasen 5), Jonsson S, Kristinsson R, Bergsson, Gislason, Gudjohnsen, Orlygsson, Jonsson K, Stefansson, Sverisson, Gunnlaugsson A.
Referee: Levnikov (Russia).

Berne, 12 October 1994, 24,000

Switzerland (1) 4 *(Ohrel 36, Blomqvist 64 (og), Sforza 79, Turkyilmaz 81)*

Sweden (1) 2 *(Andersson K 6, Dahlin 61)*

Switzerland: Pascolo; Hottiger, Herr, Geiger, Thuler, Ohrel, Yakin (Henchoz 83), Sforza, Sutter, Grassi (Turkyilmaz 69), Chapuisat.
Sweden: Ravelli; Nilsson, Andersson P, Bjorklund, Kamark, Brolin, Thern (Mild 49), Schwarz, Blomqvist (Larsson 82), Dahlin, Andersson K.
Referee: Elleray (England).

Stockholm, 16 November 1994, 27,571

Sweden (1) 2 *(Brolin 44, Dahlin 70)*

Hungary (0) 0

Sweden: Ravelli; Nilsson, Andersson P, Bjorklund, Kamark, Brolin (Rehn 70), Schwarz, Thern, Andersson K, Dahlin, Larsson.
Hungary: Petry; Banfi, Meszoly, Lorincz, Kozma, Lipcsei (Halmai 58), Urban, Detari, Duro (Kovacs 75), Kiprich, Klausz.
Referee: Van der Ende (Holland).

Lausanne, 16 November 1994, 15,800

Switzerland (1) 1 *(Bickel 45)*

Iceland (0) 0

Switzerland: Pascolo; Hottiger, Henchoz, Geiger, Thuler, Ohrel, Sforza, Bickel, Sutter, Grassi (Turkyilmaz 68), Chapuisat.
Iceland: Kristinsson B; Kristinsson R, Bergsson, Gislason (Ingolfsson 84), Jonsson K, Dervic, Gretarsson A (Gunnlaugsson B 64), Orlygsson, Stefansson, Sverrisson, Gunnlaugsson A.
Referee: Kelly (Northern Ireland).

Istanbul, 14 December 1994, 25,000

Turkey (1) 1 *(Recep 39)*

Switzerland (2) 2 *(Koller 7, Bickel 16)*

Turkey: Rustu; Recep, Bulent, Gokhan K, Abdullah, Ogun, Oguz, Cengiz (Ilker 46), Arif (Sergen 75), Hakan, Saffet.
Switzerland: Pascolo; Hottiger, Herr, Geiger, Thuler, Ohrel, Sforza, Koller, Sutter A, Bickel (Bonvin 65), Subiat (Grassi 80).
Referee: Craciunescu (Romania).

Budapest, 29 March 1995, 13,000

Hungary (0) 2 *(Kiprich 50, Illes 72)*

Switzerland (0) 2 *(Subiat 73, 85)*

Hungary: Petry; Mracsko, Lorincz, Meszoly, Kovacs, Kozma, Halmai, Salloi, Illes, Kiprich (Marton 69), Vincze (Klausz 82).
Switzerland: Pascolo; Hottiger, Herr, Geiger, Fernandez, Koller, Ohrel, Sforza, Bickel (Grassi 65), Sutter A, Subiat (Henchoz 89).
Referee: Wieser (Austria).

Istanbul, 29 March 1995, 20,000

Turkey (0) 2 *(Emre 64, Sergen 75)*

Sweden (1) 1 *(Andersson K 23 (pen))*

Turkey: Engin; Recep, Bulent, Emre, Alpay, Abdullah, Metin, Tolunay, Sergen (Mutlu 77), Hakan, Ertugrul (Oguz 46).
Sweden: Ravelli; Nilsson, Andersson P, Bjorklund, Ljung, Schwarz, Zetterberg (Rehn 81), Thern, Larsson (Blomqvist 75), Dahlin, Andersson K.
Referee: Trentalange (Italy).

Budapest, 26 April 1995, 10,000

Hungary (1) 1 *(Halmai 2)*

Sweden (0) 0

Hungary: Vegh; Csabi, Meszoly, Mracsko, Kozma, Halmai, Lipcsei, Illes, Salloi, Csertoi (Szlezak 86), Vincze (Urban 68).
Sweden: Ravelli; Nilsson, Andersson P, Kamark, Ljung, Schwarz, Zetterberg, Mild (Andersson R 62), Ingesson, Alexandersson (Gudmundsson 82), Andersson K.
Referee: Lopez Nieto (Spain).

Berne, 26 April 1995, 24,000

Switzerland (1) 1 *(Hottiger 38)*

Turkey (1) 2 *(Hakan 17, Ogun 56)*

Switzerland: Pascolo; Hottiger, Herr, Geiger, Fernandez (Walker 75), Ohrel, Sforza, Bickel, Sutter A, Grassi, Bonvin (Zuffi 70).
Turkey: Engin; Emre, Bulent, Alpay, Recep, Ogun, Oguz (Ertugrul 83), Tolunay, Sergen (Suat 79), Abdullah, Hakan.
Referee: Van den Wijngaert (Belgium).

Stockholm, 1 June 1995, 25,676

Sweden (1) 1 *(Brolin 16 (pen))*

Iceland (1) 1 *(Gunnlaugsson A 2)*

Sweden: Ravelli; Sundgren, Andersson P, Mattsson, Kamark, Brolin, Schwarz, Thern, Limpar (Larsson 51), Dahlin, Andersson K.
Iceland: Kristinsson B; Orlygsson, Bergsson, Adolfsson, Jonsson K, Gudjohnsen (Thordarsson 90), Stefansson, Jonsson S, Kristinsson R, Sverrisson, Gunnlaugsson A (Gunnlaugsson B 78).
Referee: Ouzounov (Bulgaria).

Reykjavik, 11 June 1995, 4500

Iceland (0) 2 *(Bergsson 63, Jonsson S 69)*

Hungary (1) 1 *(Vincze 20)*

Iceland: Kristinsson B; Bergsson, Adolfsson, Jonsson K, Jonsson S, Kristinsson R, Gretarsson, Gunnlaugsson A, Thordarsson (Gunnlaugsson B 68), Gudjohnsen, Sverrisson.
Hungary: Petry; Csabi, Meszoly, Lipcsei, Mracsko, Halmai, Illes (Marton 68), Salloi, Kozma, Csertoi, Vincze (Hamar 70).
Referee: Sars (France).

	P	*W*	*D*	*L*	*F*	*A*	*Pts*
Turkey	5	3	1	1	12	6	10
Switzerland	5	3	1	1	10	7	10
Sweden	6	2	1	3	7	8	7
Hungary	5	1	2	2	6	8	5
Iceland	5	1	1	3	3	9	4

Group 4

Tallinn, 4 September 1994, 1500

Estonia (0) 0

Croatia (1) 2 *(Suker 45, 72)*

Estonia: Poom; Lemsalu, Prins, Kaljend, Kallaste T, Alonen, Olumets (Reim 46), Klavan, Kristal, Kirs (Krom 75), Linnumae.

Croatia: Ladic; Turkovic, Bilic, Stimac, Jarni, Jerkan, Asanovic (Cvitanovic 90), Prosinecki, Boban, Suker, Boksic.
Referee: Krondl (Czech Republic).

Maribor, 7 September 1994, 18,000

Slovenia (1) 1 *(Udovic 13)*

Italy (1) 1 *(Costacurta 15)*

Slovenia: Simeunovic; Jermanis, Novak, Milanic, Galic, Englaro, Katanec (Binkovski 58), Zidan (Krizan 90), Ceh, Udovic, Gliha.
Italy: Pagliuca; Mussi, Baresi, Costacurta, Panucci, Donadoni, Dino Baggio (Evani 55), Albertini, Signori, Casiraghi, Zola (Berti 55).
Referee: Heynemann (Germany).

Kiev, 7 September 1994, 25,000

Ukraine (0) 0

Lithuania (0) 2 *(Ivanauskas 55, Skarbelius 61)*

Ukraine: Tiapushkin; Skripnik, Sak (Kovalets 8), Yevtushok, Popov, Petrov I, Pokhlebaev (Nagornyak 59), Maksimov, Finkel, Protassov, Konovalov.
Lithuania: Stauce; Ziukas, Sukristovas, Tereskinas, Vainoras, Vaineikas (Stonkas 81), Gudaitis, Stumbrys, Suika (Zuta 54), Ivanauskas, Skarbelius.
Referee: Karlsson (Sweden).

Tallinn, 8 October 1994, 4000

Estonia (0) 0

Italy (1) 2 *(Panucci 19, Casiraghi 77)*

Estonia: Poom; Lemsalu, Kallaste T, Alonen, Klavan (Kallaste R 75), Kaljend, Kristal, Reim, Krom (Olumets 67), Linnumae, Kirs.
Italy: Pagliuca; Panucci, Favalli (Apolloni 87), Evani (Albertini 83), Costacurta, Maldini, Rambaudi, Dino Baggio, Casiraghi, Zola, Signori.
Referee: Muller (Switzerland).

Zagreb, 9 October 1994, 12,000

Croatia (0) 2 *(Jerkan 56, Kozniku 61)*

Lithuania (0) 0

Croatia: Ladic; Mladenovic, Jarni, Bilic, Jerkan, Stimac (Brajkovic 88), Jurcevic, Asanovic, Suker, Boban, Boksic (Kozniku 78).
Lithuania: Stauce; Ziukas, Mazeikis, Gudaitis, Tereskinas, Vainoras, Sukristovas, Stumbrys, Suika (Poderis 76), Skarbelius, Vaineikas (Korsakovas 59).
Referee: Wieser (Austria).

Kiev, 12 October 1994, 12,000

Ukraine (0) 0

Slovenia (0) 0

Ukraine: Tiapushkin; Loujni, Dyriavka, Kuznetsov O, Shmatovalenko, Lezhentsev, Mikhailichenko (Petrov I 70), Mikhailenko, Konovalov (Guseynov 61), Kovalets, Leonenko.
Slovenia: Boskovic, Galic, Krizan, Milanic, Jermanis, Ceh, Novak (Kokol 75), Zidan, Benedejcic, Udovic (Gliha 65), Florjancic.
Referee: Oezenov (Bulgaria).

Kiev, 13 November 1994, 500

Ukraine (2) 3 *(Konovalov 31, Kirs 45 (og), Guseynov 76)*

Estonia (0) 0

Ukraine: Chovkovski (Suslov 83); Loujni, Kuznetsov O, Lezhentsev, Popov, Bezhenar, Kovalets (Petrov 75), Litovtchenko, Orbu, Skachenko (Guseynov 46), Konovalov.
Estonia: Vessenberg; Lemsalu, Kirs, Linnumae, Kallaste R, Alonen, Olumets, Lindmaa, Pari, Kristal, Zelinski.
Referee: Schellings (Belgium).

Palermo, 16 November 1994, 33,570

Italy (0) 1 *(Dino Baggio 90)*

Croatia (1) 2 *(Suker 32, 60)*

Italy: Pagliuca; Negro, Costacurta, Maldini, Panucci, Lombardo, Albertini (Di Matteo 65), Dino Baggio, Rambaudi (Donadoni 46), Casiraghi, Roberto Baggio.
Croatia: Ladic; Brajkovic, Jarni, Bilic, Stimac, Asanovic, Jerkan, Prosinecki (Mladenovic 57), Boban, Suker, Jurcevic (Kozniku 90).
Referee: Quiniou (France).

Maribor, 16 November 1994, 2500

Slovenia (0) 1 *(Zahovic 55)*

Lithuania (0) 2 *(Sukristovas 64, Zuta 87)*

Slovenia: Boskovic; Galic, Krizan, Englaro (Polisak 46), Jermanis, Ceh, Zidan, Benedejcic (Binkovski 46), Zahovic, Florjancic, Gliha.
Lithuania: Stauce; Suika (Zuta 76), Sukristovas, Mazeikis, Tereskinas, Vainoras, Gudaitis, Stumbrys, Narbekovas, Ivanauskas, Apanavicius.
Referee: Ihring (Slovakia).

Zagreb, 25 March 1995, 30,000

Croatia (2) 4 *(Boban 13, Suker 21, 79, Prosinecki 71)*

Ukraine (0) 0

Croatia: Ladic; Jerkan, Bilic, Pavlicic, Jarni, Prosinecki, Boban, Asanovic, Jurcevic (Vlaovic 79), Boksic (Turkovic 75), Suker.
Ukraine: Tiapushkin; Loujni, Shmatovalenko, Mizine, Telesnenko, Martynov (Orbu 46), Boukel, Kalitvintsev, Shevchenko, Leonenko, Konovalov.
Referee: Weber (Germany).

Salerno, 25 March 1995, 35,000

Italy (1) 4 *(Zola 45, 65, Albertini 58, Ravanelli 82)*

Estonia (0) 1 *(Reim 74)*

Italy: Peruzzi; Negro, Maldini, Minotti, Carboni, Albertini, Eranio (Lombardo 57), Dino Baggio, Del Piero (Berti 69), Zola, Ravanelli.
Estonia: Poom; Lemsalu, Kallaste T, Kirs, Kallaste R, Olumets, Lindmaa, Linnumae, Kristal, Lelle (Pari 76), Krom (Reim 72).
Referee: Philippi (Luxembourg).

Vilnus, 29 March 1995, 9500

Lithuania (0) 0

Croatia (0) 0

Lithuania: Stauce; Ziukas, Sukristovas, Stonkas, Vainoras, Suika, Gudaitis, Zdancius (Zuta 70), Narbekovas (Pocius 69), Ivanauskas, Skarbelius.
Croatia: Ladic; Pavlicic (Mladenovic 46), Stimac, Bilic, Jarni, Soldo, Prosinecki, Brajkovic, Asanovic, Suker, Boksic.
Referee: Burge (Wales).

Kiev, 29 March 1995, 10,000

Ukraine (0) 0

Italy (2) 2 *(Lombardo 11, Zola 37)*

Ukraine: Tiapushkin; Loujni (Boukel 60), Telesnenko, Khomin, Yevtushok, Orbu, Mizine, Kalitvintsev, Leonenko, Shevchenko, Konovalov (Pokhlebaev 76).
Italy: Peruzzi; Benarrivo, Apolloni, Minotti, Maldini, Albertini, Di Matteo, Zola, Berti, Lombardo (Conte 73), Casiraghi (Ravanelli 65).
Referee: Puhl (Hungary).

Maribor, 29 March 1995, 6000

Slovenia (1) 3 *(Zahovic 40, Gliha 53, Kokol 90)*

Estonia (0) 0

Slovenia: Boskovic; Galic, Milanic, Jermanis (Skaper 70), Englaro, Ceh, Novak, Zahovic (Kokol 68), Zidan, Florjancic, Gliha.

Estonia: Poom; Kallaste R, Kallaste T, Olesk, Arbeiter (Lelle 77), Olumets, Linnumae, Lindmaa, Lepik, Reim, Kirs.
Referee: Mendes (Portugal).

Tallinn, 26 April 1995, 500

Estonia (0) 0

Ukraine (1) 1 *(Guseynov 17)*

Estonia: Poom; Lemsalu, Kirs, Kallaste T, Kallaste R, Alonen, Olumets, Reim (Pari 68), Krom (Lepa 46), Lelle, Kristal.
Ukraine: Suslov; Loujni, Shmatovalenko, Dyriavka, Golovko, Orbu, Jabchenko, Maksimov, Nadouda (Yevtushok 85), Nagornyak (Konovalov 46), Guseynov.
Referee: Hollung (Norway).

Vilnius, 26 April 1995, 15,000

Lithuania (0) 0

Italy (1) 1 *(Zola 12)*

Lithuania: Stauce; Ziukas, Sukristovas, Vainoras, Tereskinas, Suika, Gudaitis (Poderis 70), Skarbelius, Apanavicius (Preiksaitis 46), Ivanauskas, Slekys.
Italy: Pagliuca; Benarrivo, Costacurta, Minotti, Maldini, Conte (Dino Baggio 24), Di Matteo, Crippa (Berti 85), Lombardo, Casiraghi, Zola.
Referee: McCluskey (Scotland).

Zagreb, 26 April 1995, 25,000

Croatia (1) 2 *(Prosinecki 17, Suker 90)*

Slovenia (0) 0

Croatia: Ladic; Jerkan, Bilic, Stimac, Jarni, Prosinecki, Boban, Asanovic, Jurcevic (Gabric 13), Suker, Boksic.
Slovenia: Boskovic; Galic, Englaro, Milanic (Skaper 89), Binkovski, Jermanis, Novak, Zidan, Zahovic (Kokol 71), Florjancic, Gliha.
Referee: Saravan (Turkey).

Vilnius, 7 June 1995, 6000

Lithuania (0) 2 *(Stonkas 47, Suika 69)*

Slovenia (0) 1 *(Gliha 82)*

Lithuania: Stauce; Ziukas, Sukristovas, Tereskinas, Vainoras, Stonkas, Maciulevicius (Baltusniskas 75), Preiksaitis (Suika 68), Skarbelius, Slekys, Ivanauskas.
Slovenia: Boskovic; Galic (Krizan 78), Englaro, Milanic, Jermanis, Ceh, Novak (Skaper 58), Kokol, Zahovic, Florjancic, Gliha.
Referee: Vagner (Hungary).

Tallinn, 11 June 1995, 2000

Estonia (1) 1 *(Reim 27)*

Slovenia (1) 3 *(Novak 37, 68, Zahovic 78)*

Estonia: Poom; Lepa (Klavan 46), Kirs, Kallaste T, Olumets, Alonen, Pari, Linnumae, Kristal, Reim, Arbeiter (Rajala 59).
Slovenia: Boskovic; Galic, Englaro, Milanic, Novak, Jermanis (Cviki 64), Kokol (Krizan 46), Ceh, Zahovic, Florjancic, Gliha.
Referee: Durkin (England).

Kiev, 11 June 1995, 8500

Ukraine (1) 1 *(Kalitvintsev 13)*

Croatia (0) 0

Ukraine: Suslov; Jabchenko, Skripnik, Golovko, Maksimov, Orbu, Pokhlebaev, Kalitvintsev, Palyanitsa (Nagornyak 77), Gorily, Guseynov (Chkapenko 46).

Croatia: Gabric; Pavlicic (Mrlic 28), Jarni, Soldo, Jerkan, Bilic, Asanovic (Pralija 48), Mladenovic, Suker, Boban (Butorovic 38), Boksic.
Referee: Rothlisberger (Switzerland).

	P	*W*	*D*	*L*	*F*	*A*	*Pts*
Croatia	7	5	1	1	12	2	16
Italy	6	4	1	1	11	4	13
Lithuania	6	3	1	2	6	5	10
Ukraine	7	3	1	3	5	8	10
Slovenia	7	2	2	3	9	8	8
Estonia	7	0	0	7	2	18	0

Group 5

Prague, 6 September 1994, 10,226

Czech Republic (3) 6 *(Smejkal 6 (pen), Kubik 33, Siegl 35, 49, 81, Berger P 89)*

Malta (0) 1 *(Laferla 75)*

Czech Republic: Kouba; Suchoparek, Kubik, Novotny J, Latal (Vesely 87), Nemecek, Frydek (Berger P 83), Nemec, Smejkal, Kuka, Siegl.
Malta: Cluett; Vella S, Galea, Buttigieg, Buhagiar, Camilleri J, Gregory (Camilleri E 83), Brincat, Saliba, Laferla, Busuttil.
Referee: Loizou (Cyprus).

Luxembourg, 7 September 1994, 8200

Luxembourg (0) 0

Holland (1) 4 *(Roy 22, Ronald de Boer 62, 64, Jonk 90)*

Luxembourg: Koch; Ferron, Weis, Strasser, Birsens, Wolf, Holtz, Saibene, Groff, Cardoni (Morocutti 80), Langers (Theis 89).
Holland: De Goey; Valckx, Blind, Frank de Boer, Winter, Jonk, Witschge, Overmars, Bosman, Ronald de Boer, Roy (Van Vossen 75).
Referee: Snoddy (Northern Ireland).

Oslo, 7 September 1994, 16,739

Norway (0) 1 *(Frigaard 88)*

Belarus (0) 0

Norway: Grodaas; Lydersen, Pedersen T, Berg H, Bjornebye, Flo (Frigaard 70), Mykland, Rekdal, Bohinen (Leonhardsen 46), Jakobsen, Fjortoft.
Belarus: Shantolosov; Gurenko, Sosnitski, Zygmantovich, Khatskevich, Yakhimovich, Gerasimets, Metlitsky, Kulanin (Kachuro 46), Antonovitch, Markhel.
Referee: Goethals (Belgium).

Valletta, 12 October 1994, 4000

Malta (0) 0

Czech Republic (0) 0

Malta: Cluett; Buttigieg, Galea, Vella S, Camilleri J, Saliba (Sant-fournier 77), Brincat, Carabott (Camilleri E 90), Gregory, Busuttil, Laferla.
Czech Republic: Srnicek; Suchoparek, Kubik, Novotny J, Latal, Nemecek (Kadlec 44), Hasek, Nemec, Smejkal (Frydek 70), Skuhravy, Kuka.
Referee: Coroado (Portugal).

Oslo, 12 October 1994, 22,293

Norway (0) 1 *(Rekdal 52 (pen))*

Holland (1) 1 *(Roy 22)*

Norway: Thorstvedt; Lydersen, Berg, Pedersen, Bjornebye, Rushfeldt (Flo 63), Bohinen, Rekdal, Mykland, Leonhardsen, Fjortoft (Frigaard 77).
Holland: De Goey; Blind, Reiziger (Van Gobbel 77), Valckx, Frank de Boer, Winter, Jonk, Witschge, Overmars, Bergkamp (Ronald de Boer 71), Roy.
Referee: McCluskey (Scotland).

Minsk, 12 October 1994, 5000

Belarus (0) 2 *(Romashchenko 67, Gerasimets 76)*

Luxembourg (0) 0

Belarus: Shantolosov; Gurenko, Rodnionok (Sosnitski 80), Jakhimovic, Zygmantovich, Gerasimets, Markhel (Antonovitch 65), Aleinikov, Romashchenko, Shukanov, Metlitsky.
Luxembourg: Koch; Ferron (Vanek 83), Strasser, Birsens, Wolf, Cardoni, Hellers, Weis, Holtz (Morocutti 58), Saibene, Fanelli.
Referee: O'Hanlon (Republic of Ireland).

Minsk, 16 November 1994, 8000

Belarus (0) 0

Norway (2) 4 *(Berg 34, Leonhardsen 39, Bohinen 52, Rekdal 83)*

Belarus: Shantalosov; Yaskovich, Zygmantovich, Rodnionok, Yakhimovich, Metlitsky, Markhel (Youssipets 82), Antonovitch, Romashchenko (Gurinovich 82), Gerasimets, Shukanov.
Norway: Grodaas; Halle, Berg, Johnsen (Jakobsen 80), Bjornebye (Lydersen 42), Mykland, Leonhardsen, Bohinen, Rekdal, Rushfeldt, Fjortoft.
Referee: Spassov (Bulgaria).

Rotterdam, 16 November 1994, 40,000

Holland (0) 0

Czech Republic (0) 0

Holland: De Goey; Valckx, Blind, Frank de Boer, Witschge (Numan 78), Winter, Roy, Jonk, Van Vossen, Mulder (Kluivert 70), Taument.
Czech Republic: Srnieck; Latal, Kadlec, Suchoparek, Hapal, Kubik, Nemec, Bilek, Kuka (Samec 90), Siegl, Poborsky (Berger 75).
Referee: Puhl (Hungary).

Rotterdam, 14 December 1994, 26,000

Holland (3) 5 *(Mulder 6, Roy 17, Jonk 40, Ronald de Boer 52, Seedorf 90)*

Luxembourg (0) 0

Holland: De Goey; Valckx, Blind, Frank de Boer, Winter (Van Hooydonk 75), Jonk, Numan, Overmars, Ronald de Boer, Mulder (Seedorf 46), Roy.
Luxembourg: Koch; Ferron, Weis, Wolf, Birsens, Strasser, Holtz, Hellers, Cardoni, Groff, Langers (Theis 61).
Referee: Roduit (Switzerland).

Ta Qali, 14 December 1994, 9000

Malta (0) 0

Norway (1) 1 *(Fjortoft 10)*

Malta: Cluett; Vella S, Woods, Buttigieg, Camilleri J, Brincat, Busuttil, Saliba (Scerri 82), Carabott (Buhagiar 60), Gregory, Laferla.
Norway: Grodaas; Halle, Berg, Johnsen, Bjornebye, Mykland, Rekdal, Ruschfeldt (Jakobsen 82), Flo, Bohinen, Fjortoft.
Referee: Beschin (Italy).

Valletta, 22 February 1995, 6000

Malta (0) 0

Luxembourg (0) 1 *(Cardoni 54)*

Malta: Cluett; Vella S, Brincat, Buttigieg, Buhagiar, Camilleri J, Busuttil, Suda (Sciberras 60), Carabott (Saliba 78), Gregory, Laferla.
Luxembourg: Koch; Vanek, Weis, Wolf, Deville, Saibene, Hellers, Birsens, Groff, Langers (Schneider 89), Cardoni (Holtz 87).
Referee: Berusan (Croatia).

Luxembourg, 29 March 1995, 3000

Luxembourg (0) 0

Norway (1) 2 *(Leonhardsen 35, Aase 80)*

Luxembourg: Rohmann; Ferron, Vanek, Birsens (Schneider 85), Strasser, Deville, Saibene (Feyder 78), Weis, Groff, Langers, Cardoni.
Norway: Thorstvedt; Haaland, Johnsen, Berg, Bjornebye, Flo (Aase 46), Leonhardsen, Rekdal, Bohinen, Fjortoft (Mykland 25), Jakobsen.
Referee: Levnikov (Russia).

Rotterdam, 29 March 1995, 34,000

Holland (1) 4 *(Seedorf 39, Bergkamp 77 (pen), Winter 80, Kluivert 85)*

Malta (0) 0

Holland: De Goey; Valckx, Blind, Frank de Boer, Jonk, Winter, Seedorf, Overmars, Ronald de Boer (Kluivert 76), Bergkamp, Roy (Van de Luer 58).
Malta: Cluett; Vella S (Gregory 90), Buhigiar, Galea, Woods, Camilleri J, Busuttil (Agius 88), Saliba, Sant Fournier, Camilleri E, Laferla.
Referee: Orrason (Iceland).

Ostrava, 29 March 1995, 5549

Czech Republic (2) 4 *(Kadlec 5, Berger 18, 63, Kuka 69)*

Belarus (1) 2 *(Gerasimets 44 (pen), Gurinovich 88)*

Czech Republic: Srnicek; Repka, Kadlec, Latal, Frydek (Bilek 86), Nemecek, Berger, Hapal, Smejkal, Kuka, Siegl (Samec 89).
Belarus: Shantolosov; Yakhimovich (Rodnionok 77), Gurenko, Zygmantovich, Sosnitski, Juravel (Kachentsev 81), Taikov, Metlitsky, Youssipets, Gerasimets, Gurinovich.
Referee: Veissiere (France).

Minsk, 26 April 1995, 13,000

Belarus (0) 1 *(Taikov 53)*

Malta (0) 1 *(Carabott 72)*

Belarus: Marchoukel; Gurenko, Zygmantovich, Taikov, Juravel, Metlitsky (Rodiokov 70), Youssipets (Romashchenko 75), Shukanov, Gerasimets, Gurinovich, Antonovitch.
Malta: Cluett; Vella S, Buttigieg, Camilleri E, Woods, Saliba, Gregory (Agius 24), Laferla, Sant Fournier, Carabott, Busuttil (Attard 88).
Referee: Gadosi (Slovakia).

Prague, 26 April 1995, 20,000

Czech Republic (0) 3 *(Skuhravy 49, Nemecek 57, Berger 62)*

Holland (1) 1 *(Jonk 7)*

Czech Republic: Kouba; Repka, Kadlec, Suchoparek, Berger, Hapal, Nemecek, Nemec, Frydek (Latal 46), Kuka (Siegl 89), Skuhravy.
Holland: De Goey; Valckx, Blind, Frank de Boer, Winter (Kluivert 65), Jonk, Seedorf, Numan, Overmars, Ronald de Boer, Van Vossen (Bosz 46).
Referee: Krug (Germany).

Oslo, 26 April 1995, 15,124

Norway (3) 5 *(Jakobsen 11, Fjortoft 12, Brattbakk 24, Berg 46, Rekdal 49)*

Luxembourg (0) 0

Norway: Grodaas; Berg (Haaland 76), Johnsen, Nielsen, Halle, Bohinen (Solbakken 35), Rekdal, Leonhardsen, Jakobsen, Brattbakk, Fjortoft.
Luxembourg: Koch; Feyder, Vanek, Holtz (Theis 34), Strasser, Deville, Hellers, Saibene (Lambourelle 75), Langers, Cardoni, Groff.
Referee: Ferry (Northern Ireland).

Luxembourg, 7 June 1995, 1500

Luxembourg (0) 1 *(Hellers 90)*

Czech Republic (0) 0

Luxembourg: Koch; Vanek, Strasser, Weis, Birsens, Ganser (Cardoni 87), Hellers, Groff, Deville, Langers, Theis (Saibene 75).
Czech Republic: Kouba; Suchoparek, Repka (Frydek 69), Kadlec, Hapal, Latal, Nemec, Nemecek, Berger, Kuka, Skuhravy (Drulak 60).
Referee: Ashman (Wales).

Oslo, 7 June 1995, 15,000

Norway (1) 2 *(Fjortoft 43, Flo 88)*

Malta (0) 0

Norway: Thorstvedt; Haaland (Brattbakk 69), Johnsen, Berg, Nilsen, Flo, Mykland, Solbakken, Rekdal (Ingebrigtsen 83), Fjortoft, Jakobsen.
Malta: Cluett; Vella S, Buhagiar (Saliba 76), Attard, Woods, Buttigieg (Camilleri E 28), Busuttil, Agius, Laferla, Sant Fournier, Carabott.
Referee: Przesmycki (Poland).

Minsk, 7 June 1995, 12,000

Belarus (1) 1 *(Gerasimets 27)*

Holland (0) 0

Belarus: Shantolosov; Dovnar (Kachentsev 86), Taikov, Gurenko, Rodnionok, Zygmantovitch, Juravel, Youssipets, Romashchenko (Antonovitch 54), Kachuro, Gerasimets.
Holland: Van der Sar; De Kock, Blind (Winter 69), Valckx (Numan 64), Seedorf, Jonk, Van't Schip, Davids, Ronald de Boer, Kluivert, Overmars.
Referee: Porumboiu (Romania).

	P	*W*	*D*	*L*	*F*	*A*	*Pts*
Norway	7	6	1	0	16	1	19
Holland	7	3	2	2	15	5	11
Czech Republic	6	3	2	1	13	5	11
Belarus	6	2	1	3	6	10	7
Luxembourg	7	2	0	5	2	18	6
Malta	7	0	2	5	2	15	2

Group 6

Windsor Park, 20 April 1994, 7000

Northern Ireland (3) 4 *(Quinn 5, 33, Lomas 25, Dowie 48)*

Liechtenstein (0) 1 *(Hasler 84)*

Northern Ireland: Wright; Fleming, Taggart, Donaghy, Worthington, Magilton (O'Neill 81), Wilson, Lomas, Hughes, Quinn, Dowie (Gray 78).
Liechtenstein: Oehry; Stocker, Frick C, Ospelt J, Moser, Quaderer, Ritter, Zech, Telser, Matt (Hasler 70), Frick M.
Referee: Luinge (Holland).

Riga, 7 September 1994, 2200

Latvia (0) 0

Republic of Ireland (2) 3 *(Aldridge 16, 75 (pen), Sheridan 29)*

Latvia: Karavayev; Troicki, Sevliakovs, Lobanev, Zemlinsky, Astafyev, Mikutsky (Yeliseyev 62), Milevskis (Stepanov 46), Sharando, Bulders, Babichev.
Republic of Ireland: Kelly A; Kelly G, Babb, McGrath, Irwin, McAteer (McGoldrick 80), Sheridan, Townsend, Staunton, Aldridge, Quinn (Cascarino 70).
Referee: Frisk (Sweden).

Eschen, 7 September 1994, 5800

Liechtenstein (0) 0

Austria (3) 4 *(Polster 18, 45, 79, Aigner 22)*

Liechtenstein: Heeb; Moser, Hefti, Ospelt J, Quaderer, Telser, Zech (Matt 68), Klaunzer, Ospelt W (Hanselmann 28), Frick M, Hasler.
Austria: Wohlfahrt; Schottel, Werner, Kogler, Prosenik, Stoger, Pfeifenberger (Flogel 74), Feiersinger, Aigner, Ogris (Cerny 63), Polster.
Referee: Ziller (Germany).

Windsor Park, 7 September 1994, 6000

Northern Ireland (0) 1 *(Quinn 58 (pen))*

Portugal (1) 2 *(Rui Costa 8, Oliveira 81)*

Northern Ireland: Fettis; Fleming, Morrow (Taggart 81), McDonald, Worthington, Gillespie (O'Boyle 81), Magilton, Lomas, Hughes, Quinn, Gray.
Portugal: Vitor Baia; Joao Pinto I, Paulo Madeira, Paulinho Santos, Helder, Tavares, Paulo Sousa, Vitor Paneira (Folha 63), Figo, Rui Costa, Sa Pinto (Oliveira 80).
Referee: Pedersen (Norway).

Riga, 9 October 1994, 2000

Latvia (0) 1 *(Monyak 88)*

Portugal (1) 3 *(Joao Pinto II 33, 72, Vigo 73)*

Latvia: Karavayev; Troicki, Astafyev, Zemlinsky, Sevliakovs, Sprogis (Monyak 69), Stepanov, Ivanov, Babichev, Glazov (Milevskis 46), Semenov.
Portugal: Vitor Baia; Joao Pinto I, Cristovao, Paulo Madeira, Nelo, Paulo Sousa, Vitor Paneira (Alves 60), Joao Pinto II, Figo (Tavares 81), Rui Costa, Domingos.
Referee: Blareau (Belgium).

Vienna, 12 October 1994, 20,000

Austria (1) 1 *(Polster 24 (pen))*

Northern Ireland (2) 2 *(Gillespie 3, Gray 36)*

Austria: Wohlfahrt; Kogler, Schottel, Werner, Artner, Prosenik (Pfeifenberger 65), Stoger, Feiersinger, Hutter, Ogris (Hasenhuttl 45), Polster.
Northern Ireland: Kee; Fleming, Worthington, Taggart, McDonald, Lomas, Gillespie (O'Neill 66), Magilton, Dowie (Quinn 74), Gray, Hughes.
Referee: Nieto (Spain).

Dublin, 12 October 1994, 32,980

Republic of Ireland (3) 4 *(Coyne 2, 4, Quinn 30, 82)*

Liechtenstein (0) 0

Republic of Ireland: Bonner; Kelly G, Irwin (McLoughlin 46), McAteer, Kernaghan, Babb, McGoldrick, Coyne, Quinn, Sheridan, Staunton.
Liechtenstein: Heeb; Hefti, Telser, Ritter, Moser, Ospelt J, Hanselmann, Zech, Modestus (Klaunzer 77), Frick M, Heidegger (Matt 71).
Referee: Bergmann (Iceland).

Lisbon, 13 November 1994, 50,000

Portugal (1) 1 *(Figo 36)*

Austria (0) 0

Portugal: Vitor Baia; Joao Pinto I, Paulo Madeira, Helder, Paulinho Santos, Paulo Sousa, Figo, Oceano, Rui Costa (Domingos 84), Joao Pinto II, Sa Pinto (Paneira 70).
Austria: Konrad; Schottel, Furstaller, Kogler, Feiersinger, Artner, Stoger, Winklhofer, Kuhbauer (Prosenik 46), Cerny (Hutter 70), Polster.
Referee: Mikkelsen (Denmark).

Eschen-Mauren, 15 November 1994, 1300

Liechtenstein (0) 0

Latvia (1) 1 *(Babichev 14)*

Liechtenstein: Heeb; Moser, Telser, Hefti, Ritter, Hilti, Zech (Klaunzer 60), Ospelt J, Frick M, Heidegger (Oehri 59), Hasler.
Latvia: Karavayev; Troicki, Astafyev, Zemlinsky, Sevliakovs, Sprogis, Blagonadiejny (Mikutsky 46), Ivanov, Semenov, Milevskis, Babichev (Sharando 71).
Referee: Werner (Poland).

Windsor Park, 16 November 1994, 10,336

Northern Ireland (0) 0

Republic of Ireland (3) 4 *(Aldridge 6, Keane 11, Sheridan 38, Townsend 54)*

Northern Ireland: Kee; Fleming, Worthington, Morrow, Taggart, O'Neill (Patterson 46), Gillespie (Wilson 62), Magilton, Dowie, Gray, Hughes.
Republic of Ireland: Kelly A; Kelly G, Irwin, Keane (McAteer 44), McGrath, Babb, Sheridan, Aldridge (Coyne 46), Quinn, Townsend, Staunton.
Referee: Muhmenthaler (Switzerland).

Lisbon, 18 December 1994, 30,000

Portugal (3) 8 *(Domingos 2, 11, Oceano 45, Joao Pinto II 56, Fernando Couto 72, Folha 74, Paulo Alves 75, 79)*

Liechtenstein (0) 0

Portugal: Vitor Baia; Joao Pinto I, Fernando Couto, Oceano, Paulinho Santos, Figo, Vitor Paneira (Paulo Alves 57), Rui Costa, Joao Pinto II (Secretario 70), Domingos, Folha.
Liechtenstein: Heeb; Telser, Hefti, Ospelt W (Oehri R 44), Moser, Hilti, Ritter, Zech, Hasler (Matt 58), Frick M, Heidegger.
Referee: Pucek (Czech Republic).

Dublin, 29 March 1995, 32,200

Republic of Ireland (0) 1 *(Quinn 47)*

Northern Ireland (0) 1 *(Dowie 72)*

Republic of Ireland: Kelly A; Kelly G, Irwin, Keane, McGrath, Babb, Sheridan, Kelly D (McAteer 75), Quinn (Cascarino 82), Townsend, Staunton.
Northern Ireland: Fettis; Patterson, Worthington, Hill, Taggart, McDonald, Morrow, Magilton, Dowie, Hughes, Gillespie.
Referee: Van der Ende (Holland).

Salzburg, 29 March 1995, 5500

Austria (2) 5 *(Herzog 18, 58, Pfeifenberger 41, Polster 69 (pen), 90)*

Latvia (0) 0

Austria: Konrad; Furstaller, Kogler, Feiersinger, Pfeifenberger, Marasek, Artner (Hutter 76), Kuhbauer, Herzog, Ogris (Ramusch 46), Polster.
Latvia: Laizan; Sevliakovs, Sprogis, Lobanev, Troicki, Astafyev, Zemlinsky (Mikutsky 66), Blagonadezhdin, Teplov, Monyak, Babichev (Shtolcers 74).
Referee: Agius (Malta).

Riga, 26 April 1995, 1560

Latvia (0) 0

Northern Ireland (0) 1 *(Dowie 69 (pen))*

Latvia: Laizan; Troicki, Astafyev, Zemlinsky, Sevliakovs, Sprogis, Stepanov, Blagonadezhdin (Butkus 30), Teplov, Babichev, Yeliseyev.
Northern Ireland: Fettis; Patterson, Worthington, Hunter, McDonald, Hill, Gillespie (O'Boyle 78), Wilson K, Dowie (Quinn 80), Horlock, Hughes.
Referee: Lambek (Denmark).

Salzburg, 26 April 1995, 5700

Austria (3) 7 *(Kuhbauer 8, Polster 11, 53, Sabitzer 17, Purk 84, Hutter 87, 90)*

Liechtenstein (0) 0

Austria: Konrad; Feiersinger, Kogler, Furstaller (Hutter A 71), Ramusch, Artner, Herzog, Kuhbauer, Marasek, Sabitzer (Purk 69), Polster.
Liechtenstein: Oehry; Moser, Stocker, Ospelt J, Ritter (Matt 66), Hilti, Telser, Zech H, Hasler, Oehri (Marxer 46), Burgmaier.
Referee: Melnitschuk (Ukraine).

Dublin, 26 April 1995, 33,000

Republic of Ireland (1) 1 *(Vitor Baia 45 (og))*

Portugal (0) 0

Republic of Ireland: Kelly A; Kelly G, Irwin, Townsend, McGrath, Babb, Sheridan, Houghton (Kenna 84), Aldridge (Cascarino 84), Quinn, Staunton.
Portugal: Vitor Baia; Joao Pinto I, Fernando Couto, Helder (Folha 64), Paulinho Santos, Jorge Costa, Paulo Sousa, Figo (Pedro Barbosa 76), Rui Costa, Joao Pinto II, Domingos.
Referee: Amendolia (Italy).

Porto, 3 June, 1995, 40,000

Portugal (3) 3 *(Figo 5, Secretario 19, Domingos 21)*

Latvia (0) 2 *(Rimkus 49, 83)*

Portugal: Vitor Baia; Nelson (Pedro Barbosa 79), Fernando Couto, Jorge Costa, Paulinho Santos, Figo, Secretario, Domingos, Folha, Paulo Sousa (Futre 46), Rui Costa.
Latvia: Laizan; Troicki, Sevliakovs, Teplov (Sprogis 59), Astafyev, Zemlinsky, Monyak, Valeriy, Zeiberlins, Rimkus, Bleidelis (Babichev 37).
Referee: Petrovic (Yugoslavia).

Eschen, 3 June 1995, 4500

Liechtenstein (0) 0

Republic of Ireland (0) 0

Liechtenstein: Heeb; Hasler, Hanselmann, Ospelt J (Zech J 32), Ritter, Zech H, Hilti, Telser, Ospelt W (Marxer 64), Burgmaier, Frick M.
Republic of Ireland: Kelly A; Kelly G, Irwin, McAteer (Kenna 73), McGrath, Babb, Sheridan, Aldridge, Quinn (Cascarino 60), Whelan, Staunton.
Referee: Agius (Malta).

Windsor Park, 7 June 1995, 6000

Northern Ireland (1) 1 *(Dowie 44)*

Latvia (0) 2 *(Zeiberlins 58, Astafyev 62)*

Northern Ireland: Fettis; McGibbon (Patterson 46), Worthington, Morrow, Taggart, McDonald, McMahon, Magilton, Dowie, Hughes, Rowland (Gillespie 64).
Latvia: Laizan; Monyak, Sprogis, Zakresevskis, Bleidelis, Troicki, Astafyev, Zeiberlins, Ivanov, Rimkus (Yeliseyev 69), Babichev (Teplov 82).
Referee: Roca (Spain).

Dublin, 11 June 1995, 33,000

Republic of Ireland (0) 1 *(Houghton 65)*

Austria (0) 3 *(Polster 69, 78, Ogris 72)*

Republic of Ireland: Kelly A; Kelly G, Irwin, Houghton, McGrath, Babb, Sheridan, Coyne, Quinn (Cascarino 57), Whelan, Staunton (Kenna 46).
Austria: Konsel; Pfeffer, Schottel, Furstaller, Kogler, Prosenik, Kuhbauer, Pfeifenberger (Hutter 83), Masarek, Ramusch (Ogris 71), Polster.
Referee: Merk (Germany).

	P	*W*	*D*	*L*	*F*	*A*	*Pts*
Portugal	6	5	0	1	17	5	15
Republic of Ireland	7	4	2	1	14	4	14
Austria	6	4	0	2	20	4	12
Northern Ireland	7	3	1	3	10	11	10
Latvia	7	2	0	5	6	16	6
Liechtenstein	7	0	1	6	1	28	1

Group 7

Tbilisi, 7 September 1994, 40,000

Georgia (0) 0

Moldova (1) 1 *(Oprea 40)*

Georgia: Zidze; Nemsadze, Tskhadadze, Shelia, Kavelashvili, Arveladze R (Revishvili 70), Arveladze A, Camarauli, Arveladze S, Guruli (Inalishvili 46), Kinkladze.

Moldova: Coshelev; Secu, Belous, Pogorelov, Stroenco A, Stroenco S (Rebeja 55), Curtianu, Nani, Clescenko, Oprea, Spiridon (Kosse 82).
Referee: Sakari (Turkey).

Cardiff Arms Park, 7 September 1994, 15,791

Wales (1) 2 *(Coleman 9, Giggs 67)*

Albania (0) 0

Wales: Southall; Williams, Melville, Coleman, Bodin, Goss (Pembridge 74), Phillips, Speed, Giggs, Rush, Blake (Roberts I 80).
Albania: Strakosha; Shulku, Xhumba, Vata, Kacaj, Kola A (Fortuzi 53), Bellai, Kola B, Demollari, Bano, Shehu (Dosti 81).
Referee: Beschin (Italy).

Kishinev, 12 October 1994, 12,000

Moldova (2) 3 *(Belous 9, Secu 29, Pogorelov 79)*

Wales (1) 2 *(Speed 6, Blake 70)*

Moldova: Coshelev; Secu, Stroenco S, Nani, Pogorelov, Rebeja, Belous, Oprea, Curtianu, Spiridon, Miterev (Kosse 46).
Wales: Southall; Bowen M, Coleman, Symons, Williams, Horne, Phillips, Blake (Melville 87), Roberts, Pembridge, Speed.
Referee: Vad (Hungary).

Sofia, 12 October 1994, 45,000

Bulgaria (0) 2 *(Kostadinov 55, 62)*

Georgia (0) 0

Bulgaria: Popov; Kiriakov, Ivanov, Houbchev, Tzvetanov, Yankov, Borimirov (Kostadinov 55), Lechkov, Balakov, Sirakov (Penev 70), Stoichkov.
Georgia: Devadze; Revishvili, Tskhadadze, Shelia, Chikhradze, Koudinov, Nemsadze (Inalishvili 71), Gogichaivshvili, Ketsbaia, Kinkladze, Arveladze S (Guruli 76).
Referee: Gadosi (Slovakia).

Tirana, 16 November 1994, 20,000

Albania (1) 1 *(Zmijani 32)*

Germany (1) 2 *(Klinsmann 18, Kirsten 46)*

Albania: Strakosha; Vata, Kacaj, Xhumba, Zmijani (Bano 65), Lekbello, Demollari (Kola 55), Millo, Bellai, Kushta, Rraklli.
Germany: Kopke; Matthaus, Kohler, Berthold, Reuter, Eilts, Sammer (Strunz 46), Weber (Schuster 83), Moller, Kirsten, Klinsmann.
Referee: Melnitschuk (Ukraine).

Sofia, 16 November 1994, 50,000

Bulgaria (1) 4 *(Stoichkov 45, 85, Balakov 65, Kostadinov 88)*

Moldova (0) 1 *(Clescenko 60)*

Bulgaria: Mikhailov; Houbchev, Kiriakov, Ivanov, Tsvetanov, Penev (Sirakov 80), Yordanov, Lechkov (Stoilov 86), Balakov, Stoichkov, Kostadinov.
Moldova: Coshelev; Stroenco S, Secu, Pogorelov, Nani, Rebeja, Belous, Curtianu (Kosse 86), Spiridon, Oprea, Clescenko.
Referee: McArdle (Northern Ireland).

Tbilisi, 16 November 1994, 45,000

Georgia (2) 5 *(Ketsbaia 31, 49, Kinkladze 41, Gogrichiani 59, Arveladze S 67)*

Wales (0) 0

Georgia: Devadze; Gogichaivshvili, Tskhadadze, Shelia, Chikhradze, Revishvili, Kinkladze, Nehsadze (Inalishvili 41), Ketsbaia (Kavelashvili 75), Gogrishiani, Arveladze S.
Wales: Southall; Neilson (Symons 46), Bowen, Horne, Melville, Coleman, Phillips, Saunders, Rush, Hughes, Speed.
Referee: Sars (France).

Chisinau, 14 December 1994, 20,000

Moldova (0) 0

Germany (2) 3 *(Kirsten 7, Klinnsman 38, Matthaus 73)*

Moldova: Coshelev; Secu, Stroenco S, Nani, Pogorelov, Rebeja (Testimitanu 81), Spiridon, Curtianu, Belous, Oprea (Gaidamasciuk 58), Clescenko.
Germany: Kopke; Berthold, Matthaus, Helmer, Reuter, Hassler, Sammer, Moller (Kuntz 79), Weber, Kirsten (Strunz 69), Klinsmann.
Referee: Van Vliet (Holland).

Cardiff, 14 December 1994, 20,000

Wales (0) 0

Bulgaria (2) 3 *(Ivanov 5, Kostadinov 15, Stoichkov 51)*

Wales: Southall; Phillips, Bowen, Aizlewood, Coleman, Melville, Jones, Saunders, Rush, Hughes, Speed.
Bulgaria: Mikhailov; Kremenliev, Ivanov, Tzvetanov, Yankov, Yordanov, Lechkov, Balakov, Kostadinov (Siriakov 73), Penev (Kiriakov 73), Stoichkov.
Referee: Sundell (Sweden).

Tirana, 14 December 1994, 15,000

Albania (0) 0

Georgia (1) 1 *(Arveladze S 17)*

Albania: Strakosha; Dema, Vata (Shulku 30), Xhumba, Kacaj, Lekbello (Malko 46), Bellai, Rraklli, Demollari, Fortuzi, Kola.
Georgia: Devadze; Revishvili, Shelia, Koudinov, Chikhradze, Gogichaivshvili (Djishkaran 62), Inalishvili, Gogrishiani, Ketsbaia, Kinkladze, Arveladze S (Djamarauli 30).
Referee: Molnar (Hungary).

Kaiserslautern, 18 December 1995, 20,310

Germany (2) 2 *(Matthaus 8 (pen), Klinsmann 17)*

Albania (0) 1 *(Rraklli 58)*

Germany: Kopke; Matthaus, Berthold, Helmer, Weber, Reuter, Sammer, Hassler (Strunz 77), Moller, Kirsten (Kuntz 59), Klinsmann.
Albania: Strakosha; Xhumba, Dema, Kajac, Shulka, Zmijani, Demollari, Malki, Bellai, Rraklli, Fortuzi (Zalla 62).
Referee: Christensen (Denmark).

Tbilisi, 29 March 1995, 75,000

Georgia (0) 0

Germany (2) 2 *(Klinsmann 24, 45)*

Georgia: Devadze; Revishvili, Tskhadadze, Shelia, Chikhradze, Gogichaivshvili, Koudinov, Kinkladze, Djamarauli (Gogrishiani 70), Arveladze R (Kavelashvili 75), Arveladze S.
Germany: Kopke; Reuter, Kohler, Helmer, Babbel, Weber (Freund 46), Eilts, Basler, Moller, Klinsmann, Herrlich.
Referee: Bodenham (England).

Sofia, 29 March 1995, 60,000

Bulgaria (1) 3 *(Balakov 37, Penev 70, 82)*

Wales (0) 1 *(Saunders 83)*

Bulgaria: Mikhailov; Ivanov, Houbchev, Tsvetanov (Kiriakov 85), Balakov, Yankov, Kremenliev, Lechkov, Stoichkov, Penev, Kostadinov.
Wales: Southall; Phillips, Bowen, Jones (Cornforth 78), Symons, Coleman, Speed, Horne, Saunders, Hartson, Giggs.
Referee: Piraux (Belgium).

Tirana, 29 March 1995, 20,000

Albania (2) 3 *(Kushta 32, 78, Kacaj 73)*

Moldova (0) 0

Albania: Strakosha (Nallbani 80); Malko, Xhumba (Fortuzi 66), Vata, Shulku, Kacaj, Bellai, Rraklli, Abazi, Kushta (Dalipi 88), Demollari.
Moldova: Coshelev; Secu, Pogorelov, Belous, Gaidamasciuk (Stroenco A 66), Stroenco S, Oprea, Curtianu (Caras 72), Spiridon, Nani, Clescenko.
Referee: Meier (Switzerland).

Tbilisi, 26 April 1995, 20,000

Georgia (2) 2 *(Arveladze S 3, Ketsbaia 43)*

Albania (0) 0

Georgia: Devadze; Revishvili, Tskhadadze, Koudinov, Shelia, Ketsbaia, Gogichaivshvili, Djamaramauli, Kinkladze, Arveladze S, Gogrishiani.
Albania: Strakosha; Nema, Vata, Xhumba, Kacaj, Fortuzi (Prenga 46), Malko, Dalipi, Demollari, Rraklli, Kushta (Dosti 87).
Referee: Luinge (Holland).

Chisinau, 26 April 1995, 17,000

Moldova (0) 0

Bulgaria (1) 3 *(Balakov 29, Stoichkov 54, 68)*

Moldova: Coshelev; Secu, Fistican, Nani, Pogorelov, Caras (Gaidamasciuk 65), Rebeja, Oprea (Cibotaru 72), Belous, Curtianu, Clescenko.
Bulgaria: Mikhailov; Kremenliev (Kiriakov 82), Houbchev, Ivanov, Tsvetanov, Yankov, Lechkov, Balakov, Yordanov, Penev, Stoichkov (Mihtarski 79).
Referee: Ulrich (Czech Republic).

Dusseldorf, 26 April 1995, 45,000

Germany (1) 1 *(Herrlich 42)*

Wales (1) 1 *(Saunders 7)*

Germany: Kopke; Reuter, Freund, Babbel, Eilts, Basler (Scholl 76), Hassler, Weber (Kuntz 86), Ziege, Herrlich, Klinsmann.
Wales: Southall; Phillips, Bowen, Jones, Symons, Coleman (Williams 45), Horne, Hughes (Hartson 90), Rush, Saunders, Speed.
Referee: Encinar (Spain).

Sofia, 7 June 1995, 50,000

Bulgaria (1) 3 *(Stoichkov 45 (pen), 66 (pen), Kostadinov 69)*

Germany (2) 2 *(Klinsmann 18, Strunz 44)*

Bulgaria: Mikhailov; Kremenliev, Houbchev, Ivanov, Tsvetanov, Yankov, Lechkov (Sirakov 80), Balakov, Yordanov (Kostadinov 65), Penev, Stoichkov.
Germany: Kopke; Helmer, Sammer, Babbel, Reuter, Eilts, Basler (Moller 80), Hassler, Strunz (Kirsten 89), Klinsmann, Herrlich.
Referee: Pairetto (Italy).

Cardiff, 7 June 1995, 6500

Wales (0) 0

Georgia (0) 1 *(Kinkladze 73)*

Wales: Southall; Phillips, Bowen, Jones, Williams, Symons, Horne, Saunders (Pembridge 84), Rush, Cornforth, Hughes (Hartson 84).
Georgia: Devadze; Beradze, Tskhadadze, Shelia, Chikhradze, Inalishvili, Gogichaivsili, Kinkladze, Ketsbaia, Kavelashvili (Tskitishvili 74), Arveladze S (Kilasonia 88).
Referee: Koho (Finland).

Chisinau, 7 June 1995, 7000

Moldova (2) 2 *(Curtianu 10, Cleschenko 15)*

Albania (2) 3 *(Kushta 7, Bellai 25, Vata 71)*

Moldova: Ivanov; Secu, Fistican, Pogorelov, Rebeja (Kosse 74), Stroenko S, Stroenko A, Belous (Miterev 55), Nani, Curtianu, Clescenko.
Albania: Strakosha; Bano, Shulku, Malko, Vata, Kacaj, Kushta, Bellai, Kola, Rraklli (Prenga 87), Demollari (Bano 79).
Referee: Schelings (Belgium).

	P	*W*	*D*	*L*	*F*	*A*	*Pts*
Bulgaria	6	6	0	0	18	4	18
Germany	6	4	1	1	12	6	13
Georgia	7	4	0	3	9	5	12
Albania	7	2	0	5	8	11	6
Moldova	7	2	0	5	7	18	6
Wales	7	1	1	5	6	16	4

Group 8

Toftir, 7 September 1994, 2412

Faeroes (0) 1 *(Apostolakis (og) 89)*

Greece (2) 5 *(Saravakos 12, Tsalouhidis 18, 85, Alexandris 54, 60)*

Faeroes: Knudsen; Hansen T, Hansen A, Johannesen O, Jarnskor M, Hansen J, Morkore A (Rasmussen 85), Dam J, Muller, Jonsson, Hansen O (Jarnskor H 56).
Greece: Karkamanis; Apostolakis, Pavlopoulos, Kallitzakis, Karataidis, Hantzidis (Zagorakis 82), Tsalouhidis, Tsartas, Kostis (Markos 77), Alexandris, Saravakos.
Referee: Piraux (Belgium).

Helsinki, 7 September 1994, 12,845

Finland (0) 0

Scotland (1) 2 *(Shearer 29, Collins 66)*

Finland: Jakonen; Makela, Hyrylainen, Kanerva, Heinola (Holmgren 28), Suominen, Litmanen, Lindberg, Rantanen (Jarvinen 41), Paatelainen, Hjelm.
Scotland: Goram; McKimmie, Hendry, Levein (McCall 78), Boyd, McLaren, McStay, McAllister, Collins, Walker (Jess 65), Shearer.
Referee: Wocjik (Poland).

Hampden Park, 12 October 1994, 20,885

Scotland (3) 5 *(McGinlay 4, Booth 34, Collins 40, 72, McKinlay 61)*

Faeroes (0) 1 *(Muller 75)*

Scotland: Goram; McLaren, McKimmie, Levein, Hendry (McKinlay 58), McStay, Boyd, Nevin, Booth (Walker 69), McGinlay, Collins.
Faeroes: Knudsen; Dam J (Joensen 53), Hansen T, Johannesen O, Hansen J, Hansen O (Rasmussen 73), Jarnskor H, Morkore K, Jarnskor M, Muller, Jonsson.
Referee: Hauge (Norway).

Salonika, 12 October 1994, 30,000

Greece (1) 4 *(Markos 23, Batista 70, Mahlas 76, 90)*

Finland (0) 0

Greece: Atmatzidis; Apostolakis, Kassapis, Dabizas, Kallitzakis, Tsalouhidis, Zagorakis, Markos (Toursounidis 65), Mahlas, Tsartas, Vrizas (Batista 43).
Finland: Jakonen; Makela, Kanerva, Hyrylainen, Heinola (Holmgren 30), Suominen, Jarvinen, Lindberg, Hjelm, Litmanen, Paatelainen.
Referee: Leduc (France).

Moscow, 12 October 1994, 20,000

Russia (1) 4 *(Karpin 43, Kolyvanov 64, Nikiforov 65, Radchenko 67)*

San Marino (0) 0

Russia: Cherchesov; Kulkov (Tetradze 65), Nikiforov, Tsymbalar (Kolyvanov 55), Shalimov, Karpin, Onopko, Kanchelskis, Pyatnitski, Radchenko, Kiryakov.
San Marino: Benedettini; Gobbi, Gennari, Mazza M, Valentini, Guerra (Della Valle 23), Manzaroli, Matteoni, Bacciocchi, Bonini, Francini (Canti 67).
Referee: Hamer (Luxembourg).

Helsinki, 16 November 1994, 2240

Finland (1) 5 *(Sumiala 37, Litmanen 51 (pen), 71, Paatelainen 75, 85)*

Faeroes (0) 0

Finland: Laukkanen; Makela, Kanerva, Eriksson, Helin, Litmanen, Ukkonen, Lindberg (Rajamaki 78), Sumiala (Ruhanen 90), Hjelm, Paatelainen.
Faeroes: Knudsen; Johannesen, Rasmussen, Hansen O (Rasmussen J E 80), Hansen T, Morkore K, Jarnskor M, Jarnskor H, Joensen, Muller, Jonsson.
Referee: Orrason (Iceland).

Athens, 16 November 1994, 15,000

Greece (1) 2 *(Mahlas 21, Frantzeskos 84)*

San Marino (0) 0

Greece: Atmatzidis; Apostolakis, Dabizas, Kallitzakis, Kassapis, Maragos (Frantzeskos 46), Zagorakis, Toursounidis, Tsartas, Mahlas, Vrizas (Batista 70).
San Marino: Benedettini; Gobbi, Valentini, Guerra, Gennari (Canti 46), Manzaroli, Della Valle (Gasperoni 75), Francini, Bonini, Bacciocchi, Gualtieri.
Referee: Lipkovitch (Israel).

Hampden Park, 16 November 1994, 31,254

Scotland (1) 1 *(Booth 19)*

Russia (1) 1 *(Radchenko 25)*

Scotland: Goram; McKimmie, Boyd, McCall, Levein, McLaren, McKinlay (Nevin 83), McAllister, Booth, McGinlay (Spencer 63), Collins.
Russia: Cherchesov; Gorlukovich, Nikiforov, Kulkov, Shalimov, Kanchelskis, Karpin, Pyatniski (Tetradze), Onopko, Radimov, Radchenko.
Referee: Karlsson (Sweden).

Helsinki, 14 December 1994, 3140

Finland (2) 4 *(Paatelainen 24, 30, 85, 90)*

San Marino (1) 1 *(Della Valle 34)*

Finland: Laukkanen; Makela, Kanerva, Eriksson, Lindberg, Helin (Myyry 74), Ukkonen, Sumiala, Litmanen, Hjelm, Paatelainen.
San Marino: Benedettini; Canti, Gasperoni, Gobbi, Gennari, Bonini, Guerra, Manzaroli, Della Valle, Bacciocchi (Peverani 15), Mularoni (Gualtieri 60).
Referee: Albrecht (Germany).

Athens, 18 December 1994, 20,310

Greece (1) 1 *(Apostolakis 18 (pen))*

Scotland (0) 0

Greece: Atmatzidis; Apostolakis, Vlahos, Kallitzakis, Kassapis, Tsalouhidis, Zagorakis, Nioblias (Karassavidis 88), Toursounidis, Mahlas, Alexandris (Maragos 72).
Scotland: Goram (Leighton 78); McKimmie, Hendry, McLaren, Boyd, McCall, McAllister, Collins, McGinlay, McKinlay (Spencer 46), Ferguson.
Referee: Blankenstein (Holland).

Moscow, 29 March 1995, 25,000

Russia (0) 0

Scotland (0) 0

Russia: Kharine; Khlestov, Nikiforov, Kovtoun, Karpin, Onopko, Dobrovolski, Shalimov (Radimov 69), Kanchelskis, Kiryakov, Radchenko (Pisarev 57).
Scotland: Leighton; McKimmie, Calderwood, Hendry, McLaren, McStay, Boyd, Collins, McAllister, McGinlay (McKinlay 84), Jackson (Shearer 78).
Referee: Strampe (Germany).

San Marino, 29 March 1995, 1000

San Marino (0) 0

Finland (1) 2 *(Litmanen 45, Sumiala 65)*

San Marino: Benedettini; Gobbi, Valentini, Guerra, Gennari, Mazza (Matteoni 70), Manzaroli, Francini, Bonini, Montagna (Gualtieri 75), Mularoni.
Finland: Laukkanen; Makela (Hyypia 74), Ukkonen, Helin, Lindberg, Eriksson, Sumiala, Myyry, Litmanen, Hjelm, Jarvinen (Rajamaki 69).
Referee: Suheli (Israel).

Serrevalle, 26 April 1995, 2738

San Marino (0) 0

Scotland (1) 2 *(Collins 19, Calderwood 85)*

San Marino: Benedettini; Manzaroli, Canti, Guerra, Gobbi, Gennari, Mazza M, Delia, Bonini (Matteoni 46), Mularoni (Gualtieri 72), Bacciocchi.
Scotland: Leighton; McLaren, Boyd, Calderwood, Hendry, Jackson, Collins, McGinlay, Shearer (Spencer 67), McAllister, Nevin (McKinlay 78).
Referee: Loizou (Cyprus).

Salonika, 26 April 1995, 30,000

Greece (0) 0

Russia (1) 3 *(Nikiforov 36, Zagorakis 78 (og), Bestchastnikh 79)*

Greece: Atmatzidis; Apostolakis, Kallitzakis, Dabizas, Zagorakis, Tsalouhidis, Kassapis, Nioplias (Tsartas 46), Toursounidis, Mahlas (Nikolaidis 60), Donis.
Russia: Kharine; Kovtoun, Nikiforov, Kulkov, Khlestov, Karpin, Onopko, Dobrovolski, Piatnitski (Kiryakov 46), Radchenko (Mostovoi 77), Bestchastnikh.
Referee: Stafoggia (Italy).

Toftir, 26 April 1995, 1000

Faeroes (0) 0

Finland (0) 4 *(Hjelm 55, Paatelainen 75, Lindberg 78, Helin 83)*

Faeroes: Knudsen; Morkore A, Rasmussen J, Johannesen O, Hansen J, Hansen O, Johnsson, Morkore K, Jonsen A, Jarnskor M (Jarnskor H 80), Jonsson.
Finland: Laukkanen; Makela, Ukkonen, Eriksson, Helin, Hyypia, Litmanen, Lindberg (Suominen 82), Sumiala (Kolkka 61), Hjelm, Paatelainen.
Referee: Howells (Wales).

Moscow, 6 May 1995, 9500

Russia (0) 3 *(Ketschinov 52, Pisarev 73, Moukhamadiev 80)*

Faeroes (0) 0

Russia: Cherchesov; Khlestov, Nikiforov, Kovtoun, Tetradze, Ketschinov, Onopko, Cherichev, Piatnitski (Lebed 22), Pisarev, Moukhamadiev.
Faeroes: Knudsen; Johannesen O, Hansen J, Rasmussen J, Morkore K, Jonsen A, Jarnskor M, Hansen E, Jarnskor H (Jonsen D 69), Jonsson, Rasmussen J E.
Referee: Kvartskelia (Georgia).

Toftir, 25 May 1995, 3452

Faeroes (2) 3 *(Hansen J 7, Rasmussen J E 9, Johnsson 62)*

San Marino (0) 0

Faeroes: Knudsen; Jarnskor H, Hansen J, Johannesen O, Rasmussen J, Hansen O, Johnsson, Morkore K, Jarnskor M, Jonsson, Rasmussen J E.
San Marino: Benedettini; Gasperoni, Gobbi, Valentini, Gennari, Canti, Manzaroli, Bonini (Ugolini 57), Francini, Bacciocchi, Mularoni.

Serravalle, 7 June 1995, 1400

San Marino (0) 0

Russia (2) 7 *(Dobrovolski 30 (pen), Gobbi 35 (og), Kiryakov 49, Shalimov 50, Bestchastnikh 59, Kolyvanov 65, Tcherychev 88)*

San Marino: Benedettini; Gobbi, Gennari, Mazza, Valentini, Guerra, Manzaroli, Della Valle (Canti 64), Francini, Montagna (Bonini 78), Bacciocchi.

Russia: Cherchesov; Kulkov, Tetradze, Kovtoun, Karpin, Onopko, Shalimov, Dobrovolski (Radchenko 60), Kiryakov, Kolyvanov, Bestchastnikh (Cherichev 84).
Referee: Bohunek (Czech Republic).

Toftir, 7 June 1995, 3881

Faeroes (0) 0

Scotland (2) 2 *(McKinlay 25, McGinlay 29)*

Faeroes: Knudsen; Jarnskor H, Hansen T, Johannesen O, Rasmussen J, Hansen J, Johnsson, Jarnskor M (Jonsen A 56), Hansen O, Rasmussen J E (Muller 75), Jonsson.
Scotland: Leighton; McKimmie, McLaren, Burley, Calderwood, McKinnon, McKinlay, Jackson, Shearer (Robertson 86), McGinlay (Gemmill 75), Collins.
Referee: Hrinak (Slovakia).

Helsinki, 11 June 1995, 7000

Finland (1) 2 *(Litmanen 45 (pen), Hjelm 55)*

Greece (1) 1 *(Nikolaidis 6)*

Finland: Laukkanen; Makela, Tuomela, Holmgren, Helin, Lindberg, Sumiala (Jarvinen 63), Myyry, Hjelm, Litmanen, Paatelainen (Tiainen 85).
Greece: Michopoulos; Apostolakis, Kassapis, Dabizas, Alexiou, Tsalouhidis, Nikolaidis, Markos (Batista 57), Zagorakis, Tsartas (Mahlas 70), Donis.
Referee: Krug (Germany).

	P	*W*	*D*	*L*	*F*	*A*	*Pts*
Finland	7	5	0	2	17	8	15
Russia	6	4	2	0	18	1	14
Scotland	7	4	2	1	12	3	14
Greece	6	4	0	2	13	6	12
Faeroes	7	1	0	6	5	24	3
San Marino	7	0	0	7	1	24	0

EUROPEAN CHAMPIONSHIP 1996

Remaining fixtures

Group 1
(France, Romania, Poland, Israel, Slovakia, Azerbaijan)

16. 8.95 France–Poland
16. 8.95 Azerbaijan–Slovakia
6. 9.95 France–Azerbaijan
6. 9.95 Slovakia–Israel
6. 9.95 Poland–Romania
11.10.95 Romania–France
11.10.95 Israel–Azerbaijan
11.10.95 Slovakia–Poland
15.11.95 Slovakia–Romania
15.11.95 Azerbaijan–Poland
15.11.95 France–Israel

Group 2
(Denmark, Spain, Belgium, F.Y.R. Macedonia, Cyprus, Armenia)

16. 8.95 Armenia–Denmark
6. 9.95 Belgium–Denmark
6. 9.95 Spain–Cyprus
6. 9.95 F.Y.R. Macedonia–Armenia
7.10.95 Armenia–Belgium
11.10.95 Denmark–Spain
11.10.95 Cyprus–F.Y.R. Macedonia
15.11.95 Spain–F.Y.R. Macedonia
15.11.95 Cyprus–Belgium
15.11.95 Denmark–Armenia

Group 3
(Sweden, Switzerland, Hungary, Iceland, Turkey)

16. 8.95 Iceland–Switzerland
6. 9.95 Sweden–Switzerland
6. 9.95 Turkey–Hungary
11.10.95 Switzerland–Hungary
11.10.95 Iceland–Turkey
11.11.95 Hungary–Iceland
15.11.95 Sweden–YTurkey

Group 4
(Italy, Ukraine, Croatia, Lithuania, Estonia, Slovenia)

16. 8.95 Estonia–Lithuania
3. 9.95 Croatia–Estonia
6. 9.95 Italy–Slovenia
6. 9.95 Lithuania–Ukraine
8.10.95 Croatia–Italy
11.10.95 Slovenia–Ukraine
11.10.95 Lithuania–Estonia
11.11.95 Italy–Ukraine
15.11.95 Slovenia–Croatia
15.11.95 Italy–Lithuania

Group 5
(Netherlands, Norway, Czech Republic, Belarus, Malta, Luxembourg)

16. 8.95 Norway–Czech Republic
6. 9.95 Czech Republic–Norway
6. 9.95 Luxembourg–Malta
6. 9.95 Netherlands–Belarus
7.10.95 Belarus–Czech Republic
8.10.95 Malta–Netherlands
11.10.95 Luxembourg–Belarus
12.11.95 Malta–Belarus
15.11.95 Czech Republic–Luxembourg
15.11.95 Netherlands–Norway

Group 6
(Rep. of Ireland, Portugal, Northern Ireland, Austria, Latvia, Liechtenstein)

15. 8.95 Liechtenstein–Portugal
16. 8.95 Latvia–Austria
3. 9.95 Portugal–Northern Ireland
6. 9.95 Austria–Rep. of Ireland
6. 9.95 Latvia–Liechtenstein
11.10.95 Rep. of Ireland–Latvia
11.10.95 Austria–Portugal
11.10.95 Liechtenstein–Northern Ireland
15.11.95 Portugal–Rep. of Ireland
15.11.95 Northern Ireland–Austria

Group 7
(Germany, Wales, Bulgaria, Georgia, Albania, Moldova)

6. 9.95 Germany–Georgia
6. 9.95 Wales–Moldova
6. 9.95 Albania–Bulgaria
7.10.95 Bulgaria–Albania
8.10.95 Germany–Moldova
11.10.95 Wales–Germany
11.10.95 Georgia–Bulgaria
15.11.95 Germany–Bulgaria
15.11.95 Albania–Wales
15.11.95 Moldova–Georgia

Group 8
(Russia, Greece, Scotland, Finland, Faroe Islands, San Marino)

16. 8.95 Scotland–Greece
16. 8.95 Finland–Russia
16. 8.95 Faroe Islands–San Marino
6. 9.95 Scotland–Finland
6. 9.95 Faroe Islands–Russia
6. 9.95 San Marino–Greece
11.10.95 Russia–Greece
11.10.95 Scotland–Faroe Islands
15.11.95 Scotland–San Marino
15.11.95 Russia–Finland
15.11.95 Greece–Faroe Islands

THE WORLD CUP 1930–94

Year	Winners	Runners-up	Venue	Attendance	Referee
1930	Uruguay 4	Argentina 2	Montevideo	90,000	Langenus (B)
1934	Italy 2 (after extra time)	Czechoslovakia 1	Rome	50,000	Eklind (Se)
1938	Italy 4	Hungary 2	Paris	45,000	Capdeville (F)
1950	Uruguay 2	Brazil 1	Rio de Janeiro	199,854	Reader (E)
1954	West Germany 3	Hungary 2	Berne	60,000	Ling (E)
1958	Brazil 5	Sweden 2	Stockholm	49,737	Guigue (F)
1962	Brazil 3	Czechoslovakia 1	Santiago	68,679	Latychev (USSR)
1966	England 4 (after extra time)	West Germany 2	Wembley	93,802	Dienst (Sw)
1970	Brazil 4	Italy 1	Mexico City	107,412	Glockner (EG)
1974	West Germany 2	Holland 1	Munich	77,833	Taylor (E)
1978	Argentina 3 (after extra time)	Holland 1	Buenos Aires	77,000	Gonella (1)
1982	Italy 3	West Germany 1	Madrid	90,080	Coelho (Br)
1986	Argentina 3	West Germany 2	Mexico City	114,580	Filho (Br)
1990	West Germany 1	Argentina 0	Rome	73,603	Codesal (Mex)
1994	Brazil 0	Italy 0	Los Angeles	94,194	Puhl (Hungary)

(*Brazil won 3-2 on penalties act*)

GOALSCORING AND ATTENDANCES IN WORLD CUP FINAL ROUNDS

Venue	*Matches*	*Goals (avge)*	*Attendance (avge)*
1930, Uruguay	18	70 (3.9)	434,500 (24,138)
1934, Italy	17	70 (4.1)	395,000 (23,235)
1938, France	18	84 (4.6)	483,000 (26,833)
1950, Brazil	22	88 (4.0)	1,337,000 (60,772)
1954, Switzerland	26	140 (5.4)	943,000 (36,270)
1958, Sweden	35	126 (3.6)	868,000 (24,800)
1962, Chile	32	89 (2.8)	776,000 (24,250)
1966, England	32	89 (2.8)	1,614,677 (50,458)
1970, Mexico	32	95 (2.9)	1,673,975 (52,311)
1974, West Germany	38	97 (2.5)	1,774,022 (46,684)
1978, Argentina	38	102 (2.7)	1,610,215 (42,374)
1982, Spain	52	146 (2.8)	2,064,364 (38,816)
1986, Mexico	52	132 (2.5)	2,441,731 (46,956)
1990, Italy	52	115 (2.2)	2,515,168 (48,368)
1994, USA	52	141 (2.71)	3,567,415 (68,604)

LEADING GOALSCORERS

Year	*Player*	*Goals*
1930	Guillermo Stabile (Argentina)	8
1934	Angelo Schiavio (Italy)	
	Oldrich Nejedly (Czechoslovakia)	
	Edmund Conen (Germany)	4
1938	Leonidas da Silva (Brazil)	8
1950	Ademir (Brazil)	9
1954	Sandor Kocsis (Hungary)	11
1958	Just Fontaine (France)	13
1962	Drazen Jerkovic (Yugoslavia)	5
1966	Eusebio (Portugal)	9
1970	Gerd Muller (West Germany)	10
1974	Grzegorz Lato (Poland)	7
1978	Mario Kempes (Argentina)	6
1982	Paolo Rossi (Italy)	6
1986	Gary Lineker (England)	6
1990	Salvatore Schillaci (Italy)	6
1994	Oleg Salenko (Russia)	
	Hristo Stoichkov (Bulgaria)	6

BRITISH AND IRISH INTERNATIONAL RESULTS 1872–1995

Note: In the results that follow, WC = World Cup, EC = European Championship, UI = Umbro International Trophy. For Ireland, read Northern Ireland from 1921.

ENGLAND v SCOTLAND

Played: 107; England won 43, Scotland won 40, Drawn 24. *Goals:* England 188, Scotland 168.

			E	*S*
1872	30 Nov	Glasgow	0	0
1873	8 Mar	Kennington Oval	4	2
1874	7 Mar	Glasgow	1	2
1875	6 Mar	Kennington Oval	2	2
1876	4 Mar	Glasgow	0	3
1877	3 Mar	Kennington Oval	1	3
1878	2 Mar	Glasgow	2	7
1879	5 Apr	Kennington Oval	5	4
1880	13 Mar	Glasgow	4	5
1881	12 Mar	Kennington Oval	1	6
1882	11 Mar	Glasgow	1	5
1883	10 Mar	Sheffield	2	3
1884	15 Mar	Glasgow	0	1
1885	21 Mar	Kennington Oval	1	1
1886	31 Mar	Glasgow	1	1
1887	19 Mar	Blackburn	2	3
1888	17 Mar	Glasgow	5	0
1889	13 Apr	Kennington Oval	2	3
1890	5 Apr	Glasgow	1	1
1891	6 Apr	Blackburn	2	1
1892	2 Apr	Glasgow	4	1
1893	1 Apr	Richmond	5	2
1894	7 Apr	Glasgow	2	2
1895	6 Apr	Everton	3	0
1896	4 Apr	Glasgow	1	2
1897	3 Apr	Crystal Palace	1	2
1898	2 Apr	Glasgow	3	1
1899	8 Apr	Birmingham	2	1
1900	7 Apr	Glasgow	1	4
1901	30 Mar	Crystal Palace	2	2
1902	3 Mar	Birmingham	2	2
1903	4 Apr	Sheffield	1	2
1904	9 Apr	Glasgow	1	0
1905	1 Apr	Crystal Palace	1	0
1906	7 Apr	Glasgow	1	2
1907	6 Apr	Newcastle	1	1
1908	4 Apr	Glasgow	1	1
1909	3 Apr	Crystal Palace	2	0
1910	2 Apr	Glasgow	0	2
1911	1 Apr	Everton	1	1
1912	23 Mar	Glasgow	1	1
1913	5 Apr	Chelsea	1	0
1914	14 Apr	Glasgow	1	3
1920	10 Apr	Sheffield	5	4
1921	9 Apr	Glasgow	0	3
1922	8 Apr	Aston Villa	0	1
1923	14 Apr	Glasgow	2	2
1924	12 Apr	Wembley	1	1
1925	4 Apr	Glasgow	0	2
1926	17 Apr	Manchester	0	1
1927	2 Apr	Glasgow	2	1
1928	31 Mar	Wembley	1	5
1929	13 Apr	Glasgow	0	1
1930	5 Apr	Wembley	5	2
1931	28 Mar	Glasgow	0	2
1932	9 Apr	Wembley	3	0
1933	1 Apr	Glasgow	1	2
1934	14 Apr	Wembley	3	0
1935	6 Apr	Glasgow	0	2
1936	4 Apr	Wembley	1	1
1937	17 Apr	Glasgow	1	3
1938	9 Apr	Wembley	0	1
1939	15 Apr	Glasgow	2	1
1947	12 Apr	Wembley	1	1
1948	10 Apr	Glasgow	2	0
1949	9 Apr	Wembley	1	3
WC1950	15 Apr	Glasgow	1	0
1951	14 Apr	Wembley	2	3
1952	5 Apr	Glasgow	2	1
1953	18 Apr	Wembley	2	2
WC1954	3 Apr	Glasgow	4	2
1955	2 Apr	Wembley	7	2
1956	14 Apr	Glasgow	1	1
1957	6 Apr	Wembley	2	1
1958	19 Apr	Glasgow	4	0
1959	11 Apr	Wembley	1	0
1960	19 Apr	Glasgow	1	1
1961	15 Apr	Wembley	9	3
1962	14 Apr	Glasgow	0	2
1963	6 Apr	Wembley	1	2
1964	11 Apr	Glasgow	0	1
1965	10 Apr	Wembley	2	2
1966	2 Apr	Glasgow	4	3
EC1967	15 Apr	Wembley	2	3
EC1968	24 Jan	Glasgow	1	1
1969	10 May	Wembley	4	1
1970	25 Apr	Glasgow	0	0
1971	22 May	Wembley	3	1
1972	27 May	Glasgow	1	0
1973	14 Feb	Glasgow	5	0
1973	19 May	Wembley	1	0
1974	18 May	Wembley	0	2
1975	24 May	Wembley	5	1
1976	15 May	Glasgow	1	2
1977	4 June	Wembley	1	2
1978	20 May	Glasgow	1	0
1979	26 May	Wembley	3	1
1980	24 May	Glasgow	2	0
1981	23 May	Wembley	0	1
1982	29 May	Glasgow	1	0
1983	1 June	Wembley	2	0
1984	26 May	Glasgow	1	1
1985	25 May	Glasgow	0	1
1986	23 Apr	Wembley	2	1
1987	23 May	Glasgow	0	0
1988	21 May	Wembley	1	0
1989	27 May	Glasgow	2	0

ENGLAND v WALES

Played: 97; England won 62, Wales won 14, Drawn 21. *Goals:* England 239, Scotland 90.

			E	*W*
1879	18 Jan	Kennington Oval	2	1
1880	15 Mar	Wrexham	3	2
1881	26 Feb	Blackburn	0	1
1882	13 Mar	Wrexham	3	5
1883	3 Feb	Kennington Oval	5	0
1884	17 Mar	Wrexham	4	0

			E	W
1885	14 Mar	Blackburn	1	1
1886	29 Mar	Wrexham	3	1
1887	26 Feb	Kennington Oval	4	0
1888	4 Feb	Crewe	5	1
1889	23 Feb	Stoke	4	1
1890	15 Mar	Wrexham	3	1
1891	7 May	Sunderland	4	1
1892	5 Mar	Wrexham	2	0
1893	13 Mar	Stoke	6	0
1894	12 Mar	Wrexham	5	1
1895	18 Mar	Queen's Club, Kensington	1	1
1896	16 Mar	Cardiff	9	1
1897	29 Mar	Sheffield	4	0
1898	28 Mar	Wrexham	3	0
1899	20 Mar	Bristol	4	0
1900	26 Mar	Cardiff	1	1
1901	18 Mar	Newcastle	6	0
1902	3 Mar	Wrexham	0	0
1903	2 Mar	Portsmouth	2	1
1904	29 Mar	Wrexham	2	2
1905	27 Mar	Liverpool	3	1
1906	19 Mar	Cardiff	1	0
1907	18 Mar	Fulham	1	1
1908	16 Mar	Wrexham	7	1
1909	15 Mar	Nottingham	2	0
1910	14 Mar	Cardiff	1	0
1911	13 Mar	Millwall	3	0
1912	11 Mar	Wrexham	2	0
1913	17 Mar	Bristol	4	3
1914	16 Mar	Cardiff	2	0
1920	15 Mar	Highbury	1	2
1921	14 Mar	Cardiff	0	0
1922	13 Mar	Liverpool	1	0
1923	5 Mar	Cardiff	2	2
1924	3 Mar	Blackburn	1	2
1925	28 Feb	Swansea	2	1
1926	1 Mar	Crystal Palace	1	3
1927	12 Feb	Wrexham	3	3
1927	28 Nov	Burnley	1	2
1928	17 Nov	Swansea	3	2
1929	20 Nov	Chelsea	6	0
1930	22 Nov	Wrexham	4	0
1931	18 Nov	Liverpool	3	1
1932	16 Nov	Wrexham	0	0
1933	15 Nov	Newcastle	1	2
1934	29 Sept	Cardiff	4	0
1936	5 Feb	Wolverhampton	1	2
1936	17 Oct	Cardiff	1	2
1937	17 Nov	Middlesbrough	2	1
1938	22 Oct	Cardiff	2	4
1946	13 Nov	Manchester	3	0
1947	18 Oct	Cardiff	3	0
1948	10 Nov	Aston Villa	1	0
WC1949	15 Oct	Cardiff	4	1
1950	15 Nov	Sunderland	4	2
1951	20 Oct	Cardiff	1	1
1952	12 Nov	Wembley	5	2
WC1953	10 Oct	Cardiff	4	1
1954	10 Nov	Wembley	3	2
1955	27 Oct	Cardiff	1	2
1956	14 Nov	Wembley	3	1
1957	19 Oct	Cardiff	4	0
1958	26 Nov	Aston Villa	2	2
1959	17 Oct	Cardiff	1	1
1960	23 Nov	Wembley	5	1
1961	14 Oct	Cardiff	1	1
1962	21 Oct	Wembley	4	0
1963	12 Oct	Cardiff	4	0
1964	18 Nov	Wembley	2	1
1965	2 Oct	Cardiff	0	0
EC1966	16 Nov	Wembley	5	1
EC1967	21 Oct	Cardiff	3	0
1969	7 May	Wembley	2	1
1970	18 Apr	Cardiff	1	1
1971	19 May	Wembley	0	0
1972	20 May	Cardiff	3	0
WC1972	15 Nov	Cardiff	1	0
WC1973	24 Jan	Wembley	1	1
1973	15 May	Wembley	3	0
1974	11 May	Cardiff	2	0
1975	21 May	Wembley	2	2
1976	24 Mar	Wrexham	2	1
1976	8 May	Cardiff	1	0
1977	31 May	Wembley	0	1
1978	3 May	Cardiff	3	1
1979	23 May	Wembley	0	0
1980	17 May	Wrexham	1	4
1981	20 May	Wembley	0	0
1982	27 Apr	Cardiff	1	0
1983	23 Feb	Wembley	2	1
1984	2 May	Wrexham	0	1

ENGLAND v IRELAND

Played: 96; England won 74, Ireland won 6, Drawn 16. *Goals:* England 319, Ireland 80.

			E	I
1882	18 Feb	Belfast	13	0
1883	24 Feb	Liverpool	7	0
1884	23 Feb	Belfast	8	1
1885	28 Feb	Manchester	4	0
1886	13 Mar	Belfast	6	1
1887	5 Feb	Sheffield	7	0
1888	31 Mar	Belfast	5	1
1889	2 Mar	Everton	6	1
1890	15 Mar	Belfast	9	1
1891	7 Mar	Wolverhampton	6	1
1892	5 Mar	Belfast	2	0
1893	25 Feb	Birmingham	6	1
1894	3 Mar	Belfast	2	2
1895	9 Mar	Derby	9	0
1896	7 Mar	Belfast	2	0
1897	20 Feb	Nottingham	6	0
1898	5 Mar	Belfast	3	2
1899	18 Feb	Sunderland	13	2
1900	17 Mar	Dublin	2	0
1901	9 Mar	Southampton	3	0
1902	22 Mar	Belfast	1	0
1903	14 Feb	Wolverhampton	4	0
1904	12 Mar	Belfast	3	1
1905	25 Feb	Middlesbrough	1	1
1906	17 Feb	Belfast	5	0
1907	16 Feb	Everton	1	0
1908	15 Feb	Belfast	3	1
1909	13 Feb	Bradford	4	0
1910	12 Feb	Belfast	1	1
1911	11 Feb	Derby	2	1
1912	10 Feb	Dublin	6	1
1913	15 Feb	Belfast	1	2
1914	14 Feb	Middlesbrough	0	3
1919	25 Oct	Belfast	1	1
1920	23 Oct	Sunderland	2	0
1921	22 Oct	Belfast	1	1
1922	21 Oct	West Bromwich	2	0
1923	20 Oct	Belfast	1	2
1924	22 Oct	Everton	3	1
1925	24 Oct	Belfast	0	0
1926	20 Oct	Liverpool	3	3
1927	22 Oct	Belfast	0	2

			E	I				E	I
1928	22 Oct	Everton	2	1	1962	20 Oct	Belfast	3	1
1929	19 Oct	Belfast	3	0	1963	20 Nov	Wembley	8	3
1930	20 Oct	Sheffield	5	1	1964	3 Oct	Belfast	4	3
1931	17 Oct	Belfast	6	2	1965	10 Nov	Wembley	2	1
1932	17 Oct	Blackpool	1	0	EC1966	20 Oct	Belfast	2	0
1933	14 Oct	Belfast	3	0	EC1967	22 Nov	Wembley	2	0
1935	6 Feb	Everton	2	1	1969	3 May	Belfast	3	1
1935	19 Oct	Belfast	3	1	1970	21 Apr	Wembley	3	1
1936	18 Nov	Stoke	3	1	1971	15 May	Belfast	1	0
1937	23 Oct	Belfast	5	1	1972	23 May	Wembley	0	1
1938	16 Nov	Manchester	7	0	1973	12 May	Everton	2	1
1946	28 Sept	Belfast	7	2	1974	15 May	Wembley	1	0
1947	5 Nov	Everton	2	2	1975	17 May	Belfast	0	0
1948	9 Oct	Belfast	6	2	1976	11 May	Wembley	4	0
WC1949	16 Nov	Manchester	9	2	1977	28 May	Belfast	2	1
1950	7 Oct	Belfast	4	1	1978	16 May	Wembley	1	0
1951	14 Nov	Aston Villa	2	0	EC1979	7 Feb	Wembley	4	0
1952	4 Oct	Belfast	2	2	1979	19 May	Belfast	2	0
WC1953	11 Nov	Everton	3	1	EC1979	17 Oct	Belfast	5	1
1954	2 Oct	Belfast	2	0	1980	20 May	Wembley	1	1
1955	2 Nov	Wembley	3	0	1982	23 Feb	Wembley	4	0
1956	10 Oct	Belfast	1	1	1983	28 May	Belfast	0	0
1957	6 Nov	Wembley	2	3	1984	24 Apr	Wembley	1	0
1958	4 Oct	Belfast	3	3	WC1985	27 Feb	Belfast	1	0
1959	18 Nov	Wembley	2	1	WC1985	13 Nov	Wembley	0	0
1960	8 Oct	Belfast	5	2	EC1986	15 Oct	Wembley	3	0
1961	22 Nov	Wembley	1	1	EC1987	1 Apr	Belfast	2	0

SCOTLAND v WALES

Played: 101; Scotland won 60, Wales won 18, Drawn 23. *Goals:* Scotland 238, Wales 111.

			S	W				S	W
1876	25 Mar	Glasgow	4	0	1921	12 Feb	Aberdeen	2	1
1877	5 Mar	Wrexham	2	0	1922	4 Feb	Wrexham	1	2
1878	23 Mar	Glasgow	9	0	1923	17 Mar	Paisley	2	0
1879	7 Apr	Wrexham	3	0	1924	16 Feb	Cardiff	0	2
1880	3 Apr	Glasgow	5	1	1925	14 Feb	Tynecastle	3	1
1881	14 Mar	Wrexham	5	1	1925	31 Oct	Cardiff	3	0
1882	25 Mar	Glasgow	5	0	1926	30 Oct	Glasgow	3	0
1883	12 Mar	Wrexham	4	1	1927	29 Oct	Wrexham	2	2
1884	29 Mar	Glasgow	4	1	1928	27 Oct	Glasgow	4	2
1885	23 Mar	Wrexham	8	1	1929	26 Oct	Cardiff	4	2
1886	10 Apr	Glasgow	4	1	1930	25 Oct	Glasgow	1	1
1887	21 Mar	Wrexham	2	0	1931	31 Oct	Wrexham	3	2
1888	10 Mar	Edinburgh	5	1	1932	26 Oct	Edinburgh	2	5
1889	15 Apr	Wrexham	0	0	1933	4 Oct	Cardiff	2	3
1890	22 Mar	Paisley	5	0	1934	21 Nov	Aberdeen	3	2
1891	21 Mar	Wrexham	4	3	1935	5 Oct	Cardiff	1	1
1892	26 Mar	Edinburgh	6	1	1936	2 Dec	Dundee	1	2
1893	18 Mar	Wrexham	8	0	1937	30 Oct	Cardiff	1	2
1894	24 Mar	Kilmarnock	5	2	1938	9 Nov	Edinburgh	3	2
1895	23 Mar	Wrexham	2	2	1946	19 Oct	Wrexham	1	3
1896	21 Mar	Dundee	4	0	1947	12 Nov	Glasgow	1	2
1897	20 Mar	Wrexham	2	2	WC1948	23 Oct	Cardiff	3	1
1898	19 Mar	Motherwell	5	2	1949	9 Nov	Glasgow	2	0
1899	18 Mar	Wrexham	6	0	1950	21 Oct	Cardiff	3	1
1900	3 Feb	Aberdeen	5	2	1951	14 Nov	Glasgow	0	1
1901	2 Mar	Wrexham	1	1	WC1952	18 Oct	Cardiff	2	1
1902	15 Mar	Greenock	5	1	1953	4 Nov	Glasgow	3	3
1903	9 Mar	Cardiff	1	0	1954	16 Oct	Cardiff	1	0
1904	12 Mar	Dundee	1	1	1955	9 Nov	Glasgow	2	0
1905	6 Mar	Wrexham	1	3	1956	20 Oct	Cardiff	2	2
1906	3 Mar	Edinburgh	0	2	1957	13 Nov	Glasgow	1	1
1907	4 Mar	Wrexham	0	1	1958	18 Oct	Cardiff	3	0
1908	7 Mar	Dundee	2	1	1959	4 Nov	Glasgow	1	1
1909	1 Mar	Wrexham	2	3	1960	20 Oct	Cardiff	0	2
1910	5 Mar	Kilmarnock	1	0	1961	8 Nov	Glasgow	2	0
1911	6 Mar	Cardiff	2	2	1962	20 Oct	Cardiff	3	2
1912	2 Mar	Tynecastle	1	0	1963	20 Nov	Glasgow	2	1
1913	3 Mar	Wrexham	0	0	1964	3 Oct	Cardiff	2	3
1914	28 Feb	Glasgow	0	0	EC1965	24 Nov	Glasgow	4	1
1920	26 Feb	Cardiff	1	1	EC1966	22 Oct	Cardiff	1	1

			S	W				S	W
1967	22 Nov	Glasgow	3	2	wc1977	12 Oct	Liverpool	2	0
1969	3 May	Wrexham	5	3	1978	17 May	Glasgow	1	1
1970	22 Apr	Glasgow	0	0	1979	19 May	Cardiff	0	3
1971	15 May	Cardiff	0	0	1980	21 May	Glasgow	1	0
1972	24 May	Glasgow	1	0	1981	16 May	Swansea	0	2
1973	12 May	Wrexham	2	0	1982	24 May	Glasgow	1	0
1974	14 May	Glasgow	2	0	1983	28 May	Cardiff	2	0
1975	17 May	Cardiff	2	2	1984	28 Feb	Glasgow	2	1
1976	6 May	Glasgow	3	1	wc1985	27 Mar	Glasgow	0	1
wc1976	17 Nov	Glasgow	1	0	wc1985	10 Sept	Cardiff	1	1
1977	28 May	Wrexham	0	0					

SCOTLAND v IRELAND

Played: 91; Scotland won 60, Ireland won 15, Drawn 16. *Goals:* Scotland 253, Ireland 81.

			S	I				S	I
1884	26 Jan	Belfast	5	0	1934	20 Oct	Belfast	1	2
1885	14 Mar	Glasgow	8	2	1935	13 Nov	Edinburgh	2	1
1886	20 Mar	Belfast	7	2	1936	31 Oct	Belfast	3	1
1887	19 Feb	Glasgow	4	1	1937	10 Nov	Aberdeen	1	1
1888	24 Mar	Belfast	10	2	1938	8 Oct	Belfast	2	0
1889	9 Mar	Glasgow	7	0	1946	27 Nov	Glasgow	0	0
1890	29 Mar	Belfast	4	1	1947	4 Oct	Belfast	0	2
1891	28 Mar	Glasgow	2	1	1948	17 Nov	Glasgow	3	2
1892	19 Mar	Belfast	3	2	1949	1 Oct	Belfast	8	2
1893	25 Mar	Glasgow	6	1	1950	1 Nov	Glasgow	6	1
1894	31 Mar	Belfast	2	1	1951	6 Oct	Belfast	3	0
1895	30 Mar	Glasgow	3	1	1952	5 Nov	Glasgow	1	1
1896	28 Mar	Belfast	3	3	1953	3 Oct	Belfast	3	1
1897	27 Mar	Glasgow	5	1	1954	3 Nov	Glasgow	2	2
1898	26 Mar	Belfast	3	0	1955	8 Oct	Belfast	1	2
1899	25 Mar	Glasgow	9	1	1956	7 Nov	Glasgow	1	0
1900	3 Mar	Belfast	3	0	1957	5 Oct	Belfast	1	1
1901	23 Feb	Glasgow	11	0	1958	5 Nov	Glasgow	2	2
1902	1 Mar	Belfast	5	1	1959	3 Oct	Belfast	4	0
1903	21 Mar	Glasgow	0	2	1960	9 Nov	Glasgow	5	2
1904	26 Mar	Dublin	1	1	1961	7 Oct	Belfast	6	1
1905	18 Mar	Glasgow	4	0	1962	7 Nov	Glasgow	5	1
1906	17 Mar	Dublin	1	0	1963	12 Oct	Belfast	1	2
1907	16 Mar	Glasgow	3	0	1964	25 Nov	Glasgow	3	2
1908	14 Mar	Dublin	5	0	1965	2 Oct	Belfast	2	3
1909	15 Mar	Glasgow	5	0	1966	16 Nov	Glasgow	2	1
1910	19 Mar	Belfast	0	1	1967	21 Oct	Belfast	0	1
1911	18 Mar	Glasgow	2	0	1969	6 May	Glasgow	1	1
1912	16 Mar	Belfast	4	1	1970	18 Apr	Belfast	1	0
1913	15 Mar	Dublin	2	1	1971	18 May	Glasgow	0	1
1914	14 Mar	Belfast	1	1	1972	20 May	Glasgow	2	0
1920	13 Mar	Glasgow	3	0	1973	16 May	Glasgow	1	2
1921	26 Feb	Belfast	2	0	1974	11 May	Glasgow	0	1
1922	4 Mar	Glasgow	2	1	1975	20 May	Glasgow	3	0
1923	3 Mar	Belfast	1	0	1976	8 May	Glasgow	3	0
1924	1 Mar	Glasgow	2	0	1977	1 June	Glasgow	3	0
1925	28 Feb	Belfast	3	0	1978	13 May	Glasgow	1	1
1926	27 Feb	Glasgow	4	0	1979	22 May	Glasgow	1	0
1927	26 Feb	Belfast	2	0	1980	17 May	Belfast	0	1
1928	25 Feb	Glasgow	0	1	wc1981	25 Mar	Glasgow	1	1
1929	23 Feb	Belfast	7	3	1981	19 May	Glasgow	2	0
1930	22 Feb	Glasgow	3	1	wc1981	14 Oct	Belfast	0	0
1931	21 Feb	Belfast	0	0	1982	28 Apr	Belfast	1	1
1931	19 Sept	Glasgow	3	1	1983	24 May	Glasgow	0	0
1932	12 Sept	Belfast	4	0	1983	13 Dec	Belfast	0	2
1933	16 Sept	Glasgow	1	2	1992	19 Feb	Glasgow	1	0

WALES v IRELAND

Played: 90; Wales won 42, Ireland won 27, Drawn 21. *Goals:* Wales 181, Ireland 126.

			W	I				W	I
1882	25 Feb	Wrexham	7	1	1886	27 Feb	Wrexham	5	0
1883	17 Mar	Belfast	1	1	1887	12 Mar	Belfast	1	4
1884	9 Feb	Wrexham	6	0	1888	3 Mar	Wrexham	11	0
1885	11 Apr	Belfast	8	2	1889	27 Apr	Belfast	3	1

Year	Date	Venue	W	I
1890	8 Feb	Shrewsbury	5	2
1891	7 Feb	Belfast	2	7
1892	27 Feb	Bangor	1	1
1893	8 Apr	Belfast	3	4
1894	24 Feb	Swansea	4	1
1895	16 Mar	Belfast	2	2
1896	29 Feb	Wrexham	6	1
1897	6 Mar	Belfast	3	4
1898	19 Feb	Llandudno	0	1
1899	4 Mar	Belfast	0	1
1900	24 Feb	Llandudno	2	0
1901	23 Mar	Belfast	1	0
1902	22 Mar	Cardiff	0	3
1903	28 Mar	Belfast	0	2
1904	21 Mar	Bangor	0	1
1905	18 Apr	Belfast	2	2
1906	2 Apr	Wrexham	4	4
1907	23 Feb	Belfast	3	2
1908	11 Apr	Aberdare	0	1
1909	20 Mar	Belfast	3	2
1910	11 Apr	Wrexham	4	1
1911	28 Jan	Belfast	2	1
1912	13 Apr	Cardiff	2	3
1913	18 Jan	Belfast	1	0
1914	19 Jan	Wrexham	1	2
1920	14 Feb	Belfast	2	2
1921	9 Apr	Swansea	2	1
1922	4 Apr	Belfast	1	1
1923	14 Apr	Wrexham	0	3
1924	15 Mar	Belfast	1	0
1925	18 Apr	Wrexham	0	0
1926	13 Feb	Belfast	0	3
1927	9 Apr	Cardiff	2	2
1928	4 Feb	Belfast	2	1
1929	2 Feb	Wrexham	2	2
1930	1 Feb	Belfast	0	7
1931	22 Apr	Wrexham	3	2
1931	5 Dec	Belfast	0	4
1932	7 Dec	Wrexham	4	1
1933	4 Nov	Belfast	1	1
1935	27 Mar	Wrexham	3	1
1936	11 Mar	Belfast	2	3
1937	17 Mar	Wrexham	4	1
1938	16 Mar	Belfast	0	1
1939	15 Mar	Wrexham	3	1
1947	16 Apr	Belfast	1	2
1948	10 Mar	Wrexham	2	0
1949	9 Mar	Belfast	2	0
WC1950	8 Mar	Wrexham	0	0
1951	7 Mar	Belfast	2	1
1952	19 Mar	Swansea	3	0
1953	15 Apr	Belfast	3	2
WC1954	31 Mar	Wrexham	1	2
1955	20 Apr	Belfast	3	2
1956	11 Apr	Cardiff	1	1
1957	10 Apr	Belfast	0	0
1958	16 Apr	Cardiff	1	1
1959	22 Apr	Belfast	1	4
1960	6 Apr	Wrexham	3	2
1961	12 Apr	Belfast	5	1
1962	11 Apr	Cardiff	4	0
1963	3 Apr	Belfast	4	1
1964	15 Apr	Cardiff	2	3
1965	31 Mar	Belfast	5	0
1966	30 Mar	Cardiff	1	4
EC1967	12 Apr	Belfast	0	0
EC1968	28 Feb	Wrexham	2	0
1969	10 May	Belfast	0	0
1970	25 Apr	Swansea	1	0
1971	22 May	Belfast	0	1
1972	27 May	Wrexham	0	0
1973	19 May	Everton	0	1
1974	18 May	Wrexham	1	0
1975	23 May	Belfast	0	1
1976	14 May	Swansea	1	0
1977	3 June	Belfast	1	1
1978	19 May	Wrexham	1	0
1979	25 May	Belfast	1	1
1980	23 May	Cardiff	0	1
1982	27 May	Wrexham	3	0
1983	31 May	Belfast	1	0
1984	22 May	Swansea	1	1

OTHER BRITISH INTERNATIONAL RESULTS 1908–1995

ENGLAND

v ALBANIA

Year	Date	Venue	E	A
WC1989	8 Mar	Tirana	2	0
WC1989	26 Apr	Wembley	5	0

v ARGENTINA

Year	Date	Venue	E	A
1951	9 May	Wembley	2	1
1953	17 May	Buenos Aires	0	0
(abandoned after 21 mins)				
WC1962	2 June	Rancagua	3	1
1964	6 June	Rio de Janeiro	0	1
WC1966	23 July	Wembley	1	0
1974	22 May	Wembley	2	2
1977	12 June	Buenos Aires	1	1
1980	13 May	Wembley	3	1
WC1986	22 June	Mexico City	1	2
1991	25 May	Wembley	2	2

v AUSTRALIA

Year	Date	Venue	E	A
1980	31 May	Sydney	2	1
1983	11 June	Sydney	0	0
1983	15 June	Brisbane	1	0
1983	18 June	Melbourne	1	1
1991	1 June	Sydney	1	0

v AUSTRIA

Year	Date	Venue	E	A
1908	6 June	Vienna	6	1
1908	8 June	Vienna	11	1
1909	1 June	Vienna	8	1
1930	14 May	Vienna	0	0
1932	7 Dec	Chelsea	4	3
1936	6 May	Vienna	1	2
1951	28 Nov	Wembley	2	2
1952	25 May	Vienna	3	2
WC1958	15 June	Boras	2	2
1961	27 May	Vienna	1	3
1962	4 Apr	Wembley	3	1
1965	20 Oct	Wembley	2	3
1967	27 May	Vienna	1	0
1973	26 Sept	Wembley	7	0
1979	13 June	Vienna	3	4

v BELGIUM

Year	Date	Venue	E	B
1921	21 May	Brussels	2	0
1923	19 Mar	Highbury	6	1
1923	1 Nov	Antwerp	2	2
1924	8 Dec	West Bromwich	4	0
1926	24 May	Antwerp	5	3
1927	11 May	Brussels	9	1
1928	19 May	Antwerp	3	1
1929	11 May	Brussels	5	1
1931	16 May	Brussels	4	1
1936	9 May	Brussels	2	3

			E	B
1947	21 Sept	Brussels	5	2
1950	18 May	Brussels	4	1
1952	26 Nov	Wembley	5	0
WC1954	17 June	Basle	4	4*
1964	21 Oct	Wembley	2	2
1970	25 Feb	Brussels	3	1
EC1980	12 June	Turin	1	1
WC1990	27 June	Bologna	1	0*

*After extra time

		v BOHEMIA	E	B
1908	13 June	Prague	4	0

		v BRAZIL	E	B
1956	9 May	Wembley	4	2
WC1958	11 June	Gothenburg	0	0
1959	13 May	Rio de Janeiro	0	2
WC1962	10 June	Vina del Mar	1	3
1963	8 May	Wembley	1	1
1964	30 May	Rio de Janeiro	1	5
1969	12 June	Rio de Janeiro	1	2
WC1970	7 June	Guadalajara	0	1
1976	23 May	Los Angeles	0	1
1977	8 June	Rio de Janeiro	0	0
1978	19 Apr	Wembley	1	1
1981	12 May	Wembley	0	1
1984	10 June	Rio de Janeiro	2	0
1987	19 May	Wembley	1	1
1990	28 Mar	Wembley	1	0
1992	17 May	Wembley	1	1
1993	13 June	Washington	1	1
UI1995	11 June	Wembley	1	3

		v BULGARIA	E	B
WC1962	7 June	Rancagua	0	0
1968	11 Dec	Wembley	1	1
1974	1 June	Sofia	1	0
EC1979	6 June	Sofia	3	0
EC1979	22 Nov	Wembley	2	0

		v CAMEROON	E	C
WC1990	1 July	Naples	3	2*
1991	6 Feb	Wembley	2	0

		v CANADA	E	C
1986	24 May	Burnaby	1	0

		v CHILE	E	C
WC1950	25 June	Rio de Janeiro	2	0
1953	24 May	Santiago	2	1
1984	17 June	Santiago	0	0
1989	23 May	Wembley	0	0

		v CIS	E	C
1992	29 Apr	Moscow	2	2

		v COLOMBIA	E	C
1970	20 May	Bogota	4	0
1988	24 May	Wembley	1	1

		v CYPRUS	E	C
EC1975	16 Apr	Wembley	5	0
EC1975	11 May	Limassol	1	0

		v CZECHOSLOVAKIA	E	C
1934	16 May	Prague	1	2
1937	1 Dec	Tottenham	5	4
1963	29 May	Bratislava	4	2
1966	2 Nov	Wembley	0	0
WC1970	11 June	Guadalajara	1	0
1973	27 May	Prague	1	1
EC1974	30 Oct	Wembley	3	0
EC1975	30 Oct	Bratislava	1	2
1978	29 Nov	Wembley	1	0
WC1982	20 June	Bilbao	2	0
1990	25 Apr	Wembley	4	2
1992	25 Mar	Prague	2	2

		v DENMARK	E	D
1948	26 Sept	Copenhagen	0	0
1955	2 Oct	Copenhagen	5	1
WC1956	5 Dec	Wolverhampton	5	2
WC1957	15 May	Copenhagen	4	1
1966	3 July	Copenhagen	2	0
EC1978	20 Sept	Copenhagen	4	3
EC1979	12 Sept	Wembley	1	0
EC1982	22 Sept	Copenhagen	2	2
EC1983	21 Sept	Wembley	0	1
1988	14 Sept	Wembley	1	0
1989	7 June	Copenhagen	1	1
1990	15 May	Wembley	1	0
EC1992	11 June	Malmo	0	0
1994	9 Mar	Wembley	1	0

		v ECUADOR	E	Ec
1970	24 May	Quito	2	0

		v EGYPT	E	Eg
1986	29 Jan	Cairo	4	0
WC1990	21 June	Cagliari	1	0

		v FIFA	E	FIFA
1938	26 Oct	Highbury	3	0
1953	21 Oct	Wembley	4	4
1963	23 Oct	Wembley	2	1

		v FINLAND	E	F
1937	20 May	Helsinki	8	0
1956	20 May	Helsinki	5	1
1966	26 June	Helsinki	3	0
WC1976	13 Juje	Helsinki	4	1
WC1976	13 Oct	Wembley	2	1
1982	3 June	Helsinki	4	1
WC1984	17 Oct	Wembley	5	0
WC1985	22 May	Helsinki	1	1
1992	3 June	Helsinki	2	1

		v FRANCE	E	F
1923	10 May	Paris	4	1
1924	17 May	Paris	3	1
1925	21 May	Paris	3	2
1927	26 May	Paris	6	0
1928	17 May	Paris	5	1
1929	9 May	Paris	4	1
1931	14 May	Paris	2	5
1933	6 Dec	Tottenham	4	1
1938	26 May	Paris	4	2
1947	3 May	Highbury	3	0
1949	22 May	Paris	3	1
1951	3 Oct	Highbury	2	2
1955	15 May	Paris	0	1
1957	27 Nov	Wembley	4	0
EC1962	3 Oct	Sheffield	1	1
EC1963	27 Feb	Paris	2	5
WC1966	20 July	Wembley	2	0
1969	12 Mar	Wembley	5	0
WC1982	16 June	Bilbao	3	1
1984	29 Feb	Paris	0	2
1992	19 Feb	Wembley	2	0
EC1992	14 June	Malmo	0	0

		v GERMANY	E	G
1930	10 May	Berlin	3	3
1935	4 Dec	Tottenham	3	0

			E	G
	1938	14 May	Berlin	6	3
	1991	11 Sept	Wembley	0	1
	1993	19 June	Detroit	1	2

v EAST GERMANY

				E	EG
	1963	2 June	Leipzig	2	1
	1970	25 Nov	Wembley	3	1
	1974	29 May	Leipzig	1	1
	1984	12 Sept	Wembley	1	0

v WEST GERMANY

				E	WG
	1954	1 Dec	Wembley	3	1
	1956	26 May	Berlin	3	1
	1965	12 May	Nuremberg	1	0
	1966	23 Feb	Wembley	1	0
WC	1966	30 July	Wembley	4	2*
	1968	1 June	Hanover	0	1
WC	1970	14 June	Leon	2	3*
EC	1972	29 Apr	Wembley	1	3
EC	1972	13 May	Berlin	0	0
	1975	12 Mar	Wembley	2	0
	1978	22 Feb	Munich	1	2
WC	1982	29 June	Madrid	0	0
	1982	13 Oct	Wembley	1	2
	1985	12 June	Mexico City	3	0
	1987	9 Sept	Dusseldorf	1	3
WC	1990	4 July	Turin	1	1*

**After extra time*

v GREECE

				E	G
EC	1971	21 Apr	Wembley	3	0
EC	1971	1 Dec	Athens	2	0
EC	1982	17 Nov	Athens	3	0
EC	1983	30 Mar	Wembley	0	0
	1989	8 Feb	Athens	2	1
	1994	17 May	Wembley	5	0

v HOLLAND

				E	H
	1935	18 May	Amsterdam	1	0
	1946	27 Nov	Huddersfield	8	2
	1964	9 Dec	Amsterdam	1	1
	1969	5 Nov	Amsterdam	1	0
	1970	14 Jun	Wembley	0	0
	1977	9 Feb	Wembley	0	2
	1982	25 May	Wembley	2	0
	1988	23 Mar	Wembley	2	2
EC	1988	15 June	Dusseldorf	1	3
WC	1990	16 June	Cagliari	0	0
WC	1993	28 Apr	Wembley	2	2
WC	1993	13 Oct	Rotterdam	0	2

v HUNGARY

				E	H
	1908	10 June	Budapest	7	0
	1909	29 May	Budapest	4	2
	1909	31 May	Budapest	8	2
	1934	10 May	Budapest	1	2
	1936	2 Dec	Highbury	6	2
	1953	25 Nov	Wembley	3	6
	1954	23 May	Budapest	1	7
	1960	22 May	Budapest	0	2
WC	1962	31 May	Rancagua	1	2
	1965	5 May	Wembley	1	0
	1978	24 May	Wembley	4	1
WC	1981	6 June	Budapest	3	1
WC	1982	18 Nov	Wembley	1	0
EC	1983	27 Apr	Wembley	2	0
EC	1983	12 Oct	Budapest	3	0
	1988	27 Apr	Budapest	0	0
	1990	12 Sept	Wembley	1	0
	1992	12 May	Budapest	1	0

v ICELAND

				E	I
	1982	2 June	Reykjavik	1	1

v REPUBLIC OF IRELAND

				E	RI
	1946	30 Sept	Dublin	1	0
	1949	21 Sept	Everton	0	2
WC	1957	8 May	Wembley	5	1
WC	1957	19 May	Dublin	1	1
	1964	24 May	Dublin	3	1
	1976	8 Sept	Wembley	1	1
EC	1978	25 Oct	Dublin	1	1
EC	1980	6 Feb	Wembley	2	0
	1985	26 Mar	Wembley	2	1
EC	1988	12 June	Stuttgart	0	1
WC	1990	11 June	Cagliari	1	1
EC	1990	14 Nov	Dublin	1	1
EC	1991	27 Mar	Wembley	1	1
	1995	15 Feb	Dublin	0	1

(abandoned after 27 mins)

v ISRAEL

				E	I
	1986	26 Feb	Ramat Gan	2	1
	1988	17 Feb	Tel Aviv	0	0

v ITALY

				E	I
	1933	13 May	Rome	1	1
	1934	14 Nov	Highbury	3	2
	1939	13 May	Milan	2	2
	1948	16 May	Turin	4	0
	1949	30 Nov	Tottenham	2	0
	1952	18 May	Florence	1	1
	1959	6 May	Wembley	2	2
	1961	24 May	Rome	3	2
	1973	14 June	Turin	0	2
	1973	14 Nov	Wembley	0	1
	1976	28 May	New York	3	2
WC	1976	17 Nov	Rome	0	2
WC	1977	16 Nov	Wembley	2	0
EC	1980	15 June	Turin	0	1
	1985	6 June	Mexico City	1	2
	1989	15 Nov	Wembley	0	0
WC	1990	7 July	Bari	1	2

v JAPAN

				E	J
UI	1995	3 June	Wembley	2	1

v KUWAIT

				E	K
WC	1982	25 June	Bilbao	1	0

v LUXEMBOURG

				E	L
	1927	21 May	Luxembourg	5	2
WC	1960	19 Oct	Luxembourg	9	0
WC	1961	28 Sept	Highbury	4	1
WC	1977	30 Mar	Wembley	5	0
WC	1977	12 Oct	Luxembourg	2	0
EC	1982	15 Dec	Wembley	9	0
EC	1983	16 Nov	Luxembourg	4	0

v MALAYSIA

				E	M
	1991	12 June	Kuala Lumpur	4	2

v MALTA

				E	M
EC	1971	3 Feb	Valletta	1	0
EC	1971	12 May	Wembley	5	0

v MEXICO

				E	M
	1959	24 May	Mexico City	1	2
	1961	10 May	Wembley	8	0
WC	1966	16 July	Wembley	2	0
	1969	1 June	Mexico City	0	0
	1985	9 June	Mexico City	0	1
	1986	17 May	Los Angeles	3	0

v MOROCCO

				E	M
WC	1986	6 June	Monterrey	0	0

		v NEW ZEALAND	E	NZ
1991	3 June	Auckland	1	0
1991	8 June	Wellington	2	0

		v NIGERIA	E	N
1994	16 Nov	Wembley	1	0

		v NORWAY	E	N
1937	14 May	Oslo	6	0
1938	9 Nov	Newcastle	4	0
1949	18 May	Oslo	4	1
1966	29 June	Oslo	6	1
WC1980	10 Sept	Wembley	4	0
WC1981	9 Sept	Oslo	1	2
WC1992	14 Oct	Wembley	1	1
WC1993	2 June	Oslo	0	2
1994	22 May	Wembley	0	0

		v PARAGUAY	E	P
WC1986	18 June	Mexico City	3	0

		v PERU	E	P
1959	17 May	Lima	1	4
1962	20 May	Lima	4	0

		v POLAND	E	P
1966	5 Jan	Everton	1	1
1966	5 July	Chorzow	1	0
WC1973	6 June	Chorzow	0	2
WC1973	17 Oct	Wembley	1	1
WC1986	11 June	Monterrey	3	0
WC1989	3 June	Wembley	3	0
WC1989	11 Oct	Katowice	0	0
EC1990	17 Oct	Wembley	2	0
EC1991	13 Nov	Poznan	1	1
WC1993	29 May	Katowice	1	1
WC1993	8 Sept	Wembley	3	0

		v PORTUGAL	E	P
1947	25 May	Lisbon	10	0
1950	14 May	Lisbon	5	3
1951	19 May	Everton	5	2
1955	22 May	Oporto	1	3
1958	7 May	Wembley	2	1
WC1961	21 May	Lisbon	1	1
WC1961	25 Oct	Wembley	2	0
1964	17 May	Lisbon	4	3
1964	4 June	São Paulo	1	1
WC1966	26 July	Wembley	2	1
1969	10 Dec	Wembley	1	0
1974	3 Apr	Lisbon	0	0
EC1974	20 Nov	Wembley	0	0
EC1975	19 Nov	Lisbon	1	1
WC1986	3 June	Monterrey	0	1

		v ROMANIA	E	R
1939	24 May	Bucharest	2	0
1968	6 Nov	Bucharest	0	0
1969	15 Jan	Wembley	1	1
WC1970	2 June	Guadalajara	1	0
WC1980	15 Oct	Bucharest	1	2
WC1981	29 April	Wembley	0	0
WC1985	1 May	Bucharest	0	0
WC1985	11 Sept	Wembley	1	1
1994	12 Oct	Wembley	1	1

		v SAN MARINO	E	SM
WC1992	17 Feb	Wembley	6	0
WC1993	17 Nov	Bologna	7	1

		v SAUDI ARABIA	E	SA
1988	16 Nov	Riyadh	1	1

		v SPAIN	E	S
1929	15 May	Madrid	3	4
1931	9 Dec	Highbury	7	1
WC1950	2 July	Rio de Janeiro	0	1
1955	18 May	Madrid	1	1
1955	30 Nov	Wembley	4	1
1960	15 May	Madrid	0	3
1960	26 Oct	Wembley	4	2
1965	8 Dec	Madrid	2	0
1967	24 May	Wembley	2	0
EC1968	3 Apr	Wembley	1	0
EC1968	8 May	Madrid	2	1
1980	26 Mar	Barcelona	2	0
EC1980	18 June	Naples	2	1
1981	25 Mar	Wembley	1	2
WC1982	5 July	Madrid	0	0
1987	18 Feb	Madrid	4	2
1992	9 Sept	Santander	0	1

		v SWEDEN	E	S
1923	21 May	Stockholm	4	2
1923	24 May	Stockholm	3	1
1937	17 May	Stockholm	4	0
1947	19 Nov	Highbury	4	2
1949	13 May	Stockholm	1	3
1956	16 May	Stockholm	0	0
1959	28 Oct	Wembley	2	3
1965	16 May	Gothenburg	2	1
1968	22 May	Wembley	3	1
1979	10 June	Stockholm	0	0
1986	10 Sept	Stockholm	0	1
WC1988	19 Oct	Wembley	0	0
WC1989	6 Sept	Stockholm	0	0
EC1992	17 June	Stockholm	1	2
UI1995	8 June	Leeds	3	3

		v SWITZERLAND	E	S
1933	20 May	Berne	4	0
1938	21 May	Zurich	1	2
1947	18 May	Zurich	0	1
1948	2 Dec	Highbury	6	0
1952	28 May	Zurich	3	0
WC1954	20 June	Berne	2	0
1962	9 May	Wembley	3	1
1963	5 June	Basle	8	1
EC1971	13 Oct	Basle	3	2
EC1971	10 Nov	Wembley	1	1
1975	3 Sept	Basle	2	1
1977	7 Sept	Wembley	0	0
WC1980	19 Nov	Wembley	2	1
WC1981	30 May	Basle	1	2
1988	28 May	Lausanne	1	0

		v TUNISIA	E	T
1990	2 June	Tunis	1	1

		v TURKEY	E	T
WC1984	14 Nov	Istanbul	8	0
WC1985	16 Oct	Wembley	5	0
EC1987	29 Apr	Izmir	0	0
EC1987	14 Oct	Wembley	8	0
EC1991	1 May	Izmir	1	0
EC1991	16 Oct	Wembley	1	0
WC1992	18 Nov	Wembley	4	0
WC1993	31 Mar	Izmir	2	0

		v URUGUAY	E	U
1953	31 May	Montevideo	1	2
WC1954	26 June	Basle	2	4
1964	6 May	Wembley	2	1
WC1966	11 July	Wembley	0	0
1969	8 June	Montevideo	2	1
1977	15 June	Montevideo	0	0

			E	U
1984	13 June	Montevideo	0	2
1990	22 May	Wembley	1	2
1995	29 Mar	Wembley	0	0

		v USA	*E*	*USA*
WC1950	29 June	Belo Horizonte	0	1
1953	8 June	New York	6	3
1959	28 May	Los Angeles	8	1
1964	27 May	New York	10	0
1985	16 June	Los Angeles	5	0
1993	9 June	Foxboro	0	2
1994	7 Sept	Wembley	2	0

		v USSR	*E*	*USSR*
1958	18 May	Moscow	1	1
WC1958	8 June	Gothenburg	2	2
WC1958	17 June	Gothenburg	0	1
1958	22 Oct	Wembley	5	0
1967	6 Dec	Wembley	2	2
EC1968	8 June	Rome	2	0
1973	10 June	Moscow	2	1
1984	2 June	Wembley	0	2
1986	26 Mar	Tbilisi	1	0
EC1988	18 June	Frankfurt	1	3
1991	21 May	Wembley	3	1

		v YUGOSLAVIA	*E*	*Y*
1939	18 May	Belgrade	1	2
1950	22 Nov	Highbury	2	2
1954	16 May	Belgrade	0	1
1956	28 Nov	Wembley	3	0
1958	11 May	Belgrade	0	5
1960	11 May	Wembley	3	3
1965	9 May	Belgrade	1	1
1966	4 May	Wembley	2	0
EC1968	5 June	Florence	0	1
1972	11 Oct	Wembley	1	1
1974	5 June	Belgrade	2	2
EC1986	12 Nov	Wembley	2	0
EC1987	11 Nov	Belgrade	4	1
1989	13 Dec	Wembley	2	1

SCOTLAND

		v ARGENTINA	*S*	*A*
1977	18 June	Buenos Aires	1	1
1979	2 June	Glasgow	1	3
1990	28 Mar	Glasgow	1	0

		v AUSTRALIA	*S*	*A*
WC1985	20 Nov	Glasgow	2	0
WC1985	4 Dec	Melbourne	0	0

		v AUSTRIA	*S*	*A*
1931	16 May	Vienna	0	5
1933	29 Nov	Glasgow	2	2
1937	9 May	Vienna	1	1
1950	13 Dec	Glasgow	0	1
1951	27 May	Vienna	0	4
WC1954	16 June	Zurich	0	1
1955	19 May	Vienna	4	1
1956	2 May	Glasgow	1	1
1960	29 May	Vienna	1	4
1963	8 May	Glasgow	4	1
(*abandoned after 79 mins*)				
WC1968	6 Nov	Glasgow	2	1
WC1969	5 Nov	Vienna	0	2
EC1978	20 Sept	Vienna	2	3
EC1979	17 Oct	Glasgow	1	1
1994	20 Apr	Vienna	2	1

		v BELGIUM	*S*	*B*
1947	18 May	Brussels	1	2
1948	28 Apr	Glasgow	2	0
1951	20 May	Brussels	5	0
EC1971	3 Feb	Liège	0	3
EC1971	10 Nov	Aberdeen	1	0
1974	2 June	Brussels	1	2
EC1979	21 Nov	Brussels	0	2
EC1979	19 Dec	Glasgow	1	3
EC1982	15 Dec	Brussels	2	3
EC1983	12 Oct	Glasgow	1	1
EC1987	1 Apr	Brussels	1	4
EC1987	14 Oct	Glasgow	2	0

		v BRAZIL	*S*	*B*
1966	25 June	Glasgow	1	1
1972	5 July	Rio de Janeiro	0	1
1973	30 June	Glasgow	0	1
WC1974	18 June	Frankfurt	0	0
1977	23 June	Rio de Janeiro	0	2
WC1982	18 June	Seville	1	4
1987	26 May	Glasgow	0	2
WC1990	20 June	Turin	0	1

		v BULGARIA	*S*	*B*
1978	22 Feb	Glasgow	2	1
EC1986	10 Sept	Glasgow	0	0
EC1987	11 Nov	Sofia	1	0
EC1990	14 Nov	Sofia	1	1
EC1991	27 Mar	Glasgow	1	1

		v CANADA	*S*	*C*
1983	12 June	Vancouver	2	0
1983	16 June	Edmonton	3	0
1983	20 June	Toronto	2	0
1992	21 May	Toronto	3	1

		v CHILE	*S*	*C*
1977	15 June	Santiago	4	2
1989	30 May	Glasgow	2	0

		v CIS	*S*	*C*
EC1992	18 June	Norrkoping	3	0

		v COLOMBIA	*S*	*C*
1988	17 May	Glasgow	0	0

		v COSTA RICA	*S*	*CR*
WC1990	11 June	Genoa	0	1

		v CYPRUS	*S*	*C*
WC1968	17 Dec	Nicosia	5	0
WC1969	11 May	Glasgow	8	0
WC1989	8 Feb	Limassol	3	2
WC1989	26 Apr	Glasgow	2	1

		v CZECHOSLOVAKIA	*S*	*C*
1937	22 May	Prague	3	1
1937	8 Dec	Glasgow	5	0
WC1961	14 May	Bratislava	0	4
WC1961	26 Sept	Glasgow	3	2
WC1961	29 Nov	Brussels	2	4*
1972	2 July	Porto Alegre	0	0
WC1973	26 Sept	Glasgow	2	1
WC1973	17 Oct	Prague	0	1
WC1976	13 Oct	Prague	0	2
WC1977	21 Sept	Glasgow	3	1

*After extra time

		v DENMARK	S	D
1951	12 May	Glasgow	3	1
1952	25 May	Copenhagen	2	1
1968	16 Oct	Copenhagen	1	0
EC1970	11 Nov	Glasgow	1	0
EC1971	9 June	Copenhagen	0	1
WC1972	18 Oct	Copenhagen	4	1
WC1972	15 Nov	Glasgow	2	0
EC1975	3 Sept	Copenhagen	1	0
EC1975	29 Oct	Glasgow	3	1
WC1986	4 June	Nezahualcayotl	0	1

		v ECUADOR	S	E
1995	24 May	Toyama	2	1

		v EGYPT	S	E
1990	16 May	Aberdeen	1	3

		v ESTONIA	S	E
WC1993	19 May	Tallinn	3	0
WC1993	2 June	Aberdeen	3	1

		v FAEROES	S	F
EC1994	12 Oct	Glasgow	5	1
EC1995	7 June	Toftir	2	0

		v FINLAND	S	F
1954	25 May	Helsinki	2	1
WC1964	21 Oct	Glasgow	3	1
WC1965	27 May	Helsinki	2	1
1976	8 Sept	Glasgow	6	0
1992	25 Mar	Glasgow	1	1
EC1994	7 Sept	Helsinki	2	0

		v FRANCE	S	F
1930	18 May	Paris	2	0
1932	8 May	Paris	3	1
1948	23 May	Paris	0	3
1949	27 Apr	Glasgow	2	0
1950	27 May	Paris	1	0
1951	16 May	Glasgow	1	0
WC1958	15 June	Orebro	1	2
1984	1 June	Marseilles	0	2
WC1989	8 Mar	Glasgow	2	0
WC1989	11 Oct	Paris	0	3

		v GERMANY	S	G
1929	1 June	Berlin	1	1
1936	14 Oct	Glasgow	2	0
EC1992	15 June	Norrkoping	0	2
1993	24 Mar	Glasgow	0	1

		v EAST GERMANY	S	EG
1974	30 Oct	Glasgow	3	0
1977	7 Sept	East Berlin	0	1
EC1982	13 Oct	Glasgow	2	0
EC1983	16 Nov	Halle	1	2
1985	16 Oct	Glasgow	0	0
1990	25 Apr	Glasgow	0	1

		v WEST GERMANY	S	WG
1957	22 May	Stuttgart	3	1
1959	6 May	Glasgow	3	2
1964	12 May	Hanover	2	2
WC1969	16 Apr	Glasgow	1	1
WC1969	22 Oct	Hamburg	2	3
1973	14 Nov	Glasgow	1	1
1974	27 Mar	Frankfurt	1	2
WC1986	8 June	Queretaro	1	2

		v GREECE	S	G
EC1994	18 Dec	Athens	0	1

		v HOLLAND	S	H
1929	4 June	Amsterdam	2	0
1938	21 May	Amsterdam	3	1
1959	27 May	Amsterdam	2	1
1966	11 May	Glasgow	0	3
1968	30 May	Amsterdam	0	0
1971	1 Dec	Rotterdam	1	2
WC1978	11 June	Mendoza	3	2
1982	23 Mar	Glasgow	2	1
1986	29 Apr	Eindhoven	0	0
EC1992	12 June	Gothenburg	0	1
1994	23 Mar	Glasgow	0	1
1994	27 May	Utrecht	1	3

		v HUNGARY	S	H
1938	7 Dec	Glasgow	3	1
1954	8 Dec	Glasgow	2	4
1955	29 May	Budapest	1	3
1958	7 May	Glasgow	1	1
1960	5 June	Budapest	3	3
1980	31 May	Budapest	1	3
1987	9 Sept	Glasgow	2	0

		v ICELAND	S	I
WC1984	17 Oct	Glasgow	3	0
WC1985	28 May	Reykjavik	1	0

		v IRAN	S	I
WC1978	7 June	Cordoba	1	1

		v REPUBLIC OF IRELAND	S	RI
WC1961	3 May	Glasgow	4	1
WC1961	7 May	Dublin	3	0
1963	9 June	Dublin	0	1
1969	21 Sept	Dublin	1	1
EC1986	15 Oct	Dublin	0	0
EC1987	18 Feb	Glasgow	0	1

		v ISRAEL	S	I
WC1981	25 Feb	Tel Aviv	1	0
WC1981	28 Apr	Glasgow	3	1
1986	28 Jan	Tel Aviv	1	0

		v ITALY	S	I
1931	20 May	Rome	0	3
WC1965	9 Nov	Glasgow	1	0
WC1965	7 Dec	Naples	0	3
1988	22 Dec	Perugia	0	2
WC1992	18 Nov	Glasgow	0	0
WC1993	13 Oct	Rome	1	3

		v JAPAN	S	J
1995	21 May	Hiroshima	0	0

		v LUXEMBOURG	S	L
1947	24 May	Luxembourg	6	0
EC1986	12 Nov	Glasgow	3	0
EC1987	2 Dec	Esch	0	0

		v MALTA	S	M
1988	22 Mar	Valletta	1	1
1990	28 May	Valletta	2	1
WC1993	17 Feb	Glasgow	3	0
WC1993	17 Nov	Valletta	2	0

		NEW ZEALAND	S	NZ
WC1982	15 June	Malaga	5	2

		v NORWAY	S	N
1929	28 May	Oslo	7	3
1954	5 May	Glasgow	1	0
1954	19 May	Oslo	1	1
1963	4 June	Bergen	3	4
1963	7 Nov	Glasgow	6	1

			S	N
1974	6 June	Oslo	2	1
EC1978	25 Oct	Glasgow	3	2
EC1979	7 June	Oslo	4	0
WC1988	14 Sept	Oslo	2	1
WC1989	15 Nov	Glasgow	1	1
1992	3 June	Oslo	0	0

		v PARAGUAY	S	P
WC1958	11 June	Norrkoping	2	3

		v PERU	S	P
1972	26 Apr	Glasgow	2	0
WC1978	3 June	Cordoba	1	3
1979	12 Sept	Glasgow	1	1

		v POLAND	S	P
1958	1 June	Warsaw	2	1
1960	4 June	Glasgow	2	3
WC1965	23 May	Chorzow	1	1
WC1965	13 Oct	Glasgow	1	2
1980	28 May	Poznan	0	1
1990	19 May	Glasgow	1	1

		v PORTUGAL	S	P
1950	21 May	Lisbon	2	2
1955	4 May	Glasgow	3	0
1959	3 June	Lisbon	0	1
1966	18 June	Glasgow	0	1
EC1971	21 Apr	Lisbon	0	2
EC1971	13 Oct	Glasgow	2	1
1975	13 May	Glasgow	1	0
EC1978	29 Nov	Lisbon	0	1
EC1980	26 Mar	Glasgow	4	1
WC1980	15 Oct	Glasgow	0	0
WC1981	18 Nov	Lisbon	1	2
WC1992	14 Oct	Glasgow	0	0
WC1993	28 Apr	Lisbon	0	5

		v ROMANIA	S	R
EC1975	1 June	Bucharest	1	1
EC1975	17 Dec	Glasgow	1	1
1986	26 Mar	Glasgow	3	0
EC1990	12 Sept	Glasgow	2	1
EC1991	16 Oct	Bucharest	0	1

		v RUSSIA	S	R
EC1994	16 Nov	Glasgow	1	1
EC1995	29 Mar	Moscow	0	0

		v SAN MARINO	S	SM
EC1991	1 May	Serravalle	2	0
EC1991	13 Nov	Glasgow	4	0
EC1995	26 Apr	Serravalle	2	0

		v SAUDI ARABIA	S	SA
1988	17 Feb	Riyadh	2	2

		v SPAIN	S	Sp
WC1957	8 May	Glasgow	4	2
WC1957	26 May	Madrid	1	4
1963	13 June	Madrid	6	2
1965	8 May	Glasgow	0	0
EC1974	20 Nov	Glasgow	1	2
EC1975	5 Feb	Valencia	1	1
1982	24 Feb	Valencia	0	3
WC1984	14 Nov	Glasgow	3	1
WC1985	27 Feb	Seville	0	1
1988	27 Apr	Madrid	0	0

		v SWEDEN	S	Sw
1952	30 May	Stockholm	1	3
1953	6 May	Glasgow	1	2
1975	16 Apr	Gothenburg	1	1
1977	27 Apr	Glasgow	3	1
WC1980	10 Sept	Stockholm	1	0
WC1981	9 Sept	Glasgow	2	0
WC1990	16 June	Genoa	2	1

		v SWITZERLAND	S	Sw
1931	24 May	Geneva	3	2
1948	17 May	Berne	1	2
1950	26 Apr	Glasgow	3	1
WC1957	19 May	Basle	2	1
WC1957	6 Nov	Glasgow	3	2
1973	22 June	Berne	0	1
1976	7 Apr	Glasgow	1	0
EC1982	17 Nov	Berne	0	2
EC1983	30 May	Glasgow	2	2
EC1990	17 Oct	Glasgow	2	1
EC1991	11 Sept	Berne	2	2
WC1992	9 Sept	Berne	1	3
WC1993	8 Sept	Aberdeen	1	1

		v TURKEY	S	T
1960	8 June	Ankara	2	4

		v URUGUAY	S	U
WC1954	19 June	Basle	0	7
1962	2 May	Glasgow	2	3
1983	21 Sept	Glasgow	2	0
WC1986	13 June	Nezahualcoyotl	0	0

		v USA	S	USA
1952	30 Apr	Glasgow	6	0
1992	17 May	Denver	1	0

		v USSR	S	USSR
1967	10 May	Glasgow	0	2
1971	14 June	Moscow	0	1
WC1982	22 June	Malaga	2	2
1991	6 Feb	Glasgow	0	1

		v YUGOSLAVIA	S	Y
1955	15 May	Belgrade	2	2
1956	21 Nov	Glasgow	2	0
WC1958	8 June	Vasteras	1	1
1972	29 June	Belo Horizonte	2	2
WC1974	22 June	Frankfurt	1	1
1984	12 Sept	Glasgow	6	1
WC1988	19 Oct	Glasgow	1	1
WC1989	6 Sept	Zagreb	1	3

		v ZAIRE	S	Z
WC1974	14 June	Dortmund	2	0

WALES

		v ALBANIA	W	A
EC1994	7 Sept	Cardiff	2	0

		v ARGENTINA	W	A
1992	3 June	Tokyo	0	1

		v AUSTRIA	W	A
1954	9 May	Vienna	0	2
EC1955	23 Nov	Wrexham	1	2
EC1974	4 Sept	Vienna	1	2
1975	19 Nov	Wrexham	1	0
1992	29 Apr	Vienna	1	1

		v BELGIUM	W	B
1949	22 May	Liège	1	3
1949	23 Nov	Cardiff	5	1
EC1990	17 Oct	Cardiff	3	1
EC1991	27 Mar	Brussels	1	1
WC1992	18 Nov	Brussels	0	2
WC1993	31 Mar	Cardiff	2	0

		v BRAZIL	W	B
WC1958	19 June	Gothenburg	0	1
1962	12 May	Rio de Janeiro	1	3
1962	16 May	São Paulo	1	3
1966	14 May	Rio de Janeiro	1	3
1966	18 May	Belo Horizonte	0	1
1983	12 June	Cardiff	1	1
1991	11 Sept	Cardiff	1	0

		v BULGARIA	W	B
EC1983	27 Apr	Wrexham	1	0
EC1983	16 Nov	Sofia	0	1
EC1994	14 Dec	Cardiff	0	3
EC1995	29 Mar	Sofia	1	3

		v CANADA	W	C
1986	10 May	Toronto	0	2
1986	20 May	Vancouver	3	0

		v CHILE	W	C
1966	22 May	Santiago	0	2

		v COSTA RICA	W	CR
1990	20 May	Cardiff	1	0

		v CYPRUS	W	C
WC1992	14 Oct	Limassol	1	0
WC1993	13 Oct	Cardiff	2	0

		v CZECHOSLOVAKIA	W	C
WC1957	1 May	Cardiff	1	0
WC1957	26 May	Prague	0	2
EC1971	21 Apr	Swansea	1	3
EC1971	27 Oct	Prague	0	1
WC1977	30 Mar	Wrexham	3	0
WC1977	16 Nov	Prague	0	1
WC1980	19 Nov	Cardiff	1	0
WC1981	9 Sept	Prague	0	2
EC1987	29 Apr	Wrexham	1	1
EC1987	11 Nov	Prague	0	2
WC1993	28 Apr	Ostrava†	1	1
WC1993	8 Sept	Cardiff†	2	2

		v DENMARK	W	D
WC1964	21 Oct	Copenhagen	0	1
WC1965	1 Dec	Wrexham	4	2
EC1987	9 Sept	Cardiff	1	0
EC1987	14 Oct	Copenhagen	0	1
1990	11 Sept	Copenhagen	0	1

		v ESTONIA	W	E
1994	23 May	Tallinn	2	1

		v FINLAND	W	F
EC1971	26 May	Helsinki	1	0
EC1971	13 Oct	Swansea	3	0
EC1987	10 Sept	Helsinki	1	1
EC1987	1 Apr	Wrexham	4	0
WC1988	19 Oct	Swansea	2	2
WC1989	6 Sept	Helsinki	0	1

		v FAEROES	W	F
WC1992	9 Sept	Cardiff	6	0
WC1993	6 June	Toftir	3	0

		v FRANCE	W	F
1933	25 May	Paris	1	1
1939	20 May	Paris	1	2
1953	14 May	Paris	1	6
1982	2 June	Toulouse	1	0

		v GEORGIA	W	G
EC1994	16 Nov	Tbilisi	0	5
EC1995	7 June	Cardiff	0	1

		v GERMANY	W	G
EC1995	26 Apr	Dusseldorf	1	1

		v EAST GERMANY	W	EG
WC1957	19 May	Leipzig	1	2
WC1957	25 Sept	Cardiff	4	1
WC1969	16 Apr	Dresden	1	2
WC1969	22 Oct	Cardiff	1	3

		v WEST GERMANY	W	WG
1968	8 May	Cardiff	1	1
1969	26 Mar	Frankfurt	1	1
1976	6 Oct	Cardiff	0	2
1977	14 Dec	Dortmund	1	1
EC1979	2 May	Wrexham	0	2
EC1979	17 Oct	Cologne	1	5
WC1989	31 May	Cardiff	0	0
WC1989	15 Nov	Cologne	1	2
EC1991	5 June	Cardiff	1	0
EC1991	16 Oct	Nuremberg	1	4

		v GREECE	W	G
WC1964	9 Dec	Athens	0	2
WC1965	17 Mar	Cardiff	4	1

		v HOLLAND	W	H
WC1988	14 Sept	Amsterdam	0	1
WC1989	11 Oct	Wrexham	1	2
1992	30 May	Utrecht	0	4

		v HUNGARY	W	H
WC1958	8 June	Sanviken	1	1
WC1958	17 June	Stockholm	2	1
1961	28 May	Budapest	2	3
EC1962	7 Nov	Budapest	1	3
EC1963	20 Mar	Cardiff	1	1
EC1974	30 Oct	Cardiff	2	0
EC1975	16 Apr	Budapest	2	1
1985	16 Oct	Cardiff	0	3

		v ICELAND	W	I
WC1980	2 June	Reykjavik	4	0
WC1981	14 Oct	Swansea	2	2
WC1984	12 Sept	Reykjavik	0	1
WC1984	14 Nov	Cardiff	2	1
1991	1 May	Cardiff	1	0

		v IRAN	W	I
1978	18 Apr	Teheran	1	0

		v REPUBLIC OF IRELAND	W	RI
1960	28 Sept	Dublin	3	2
1979	11 Sept	Swansea	2	1
1981	24 Feb	Dublin	3	1
1986	26 Mar	Dublin	1	0
1990	28 Mar	Dublin	0	1
1991	6 Feb	Wrexham	0	3
1992	19 Feb	Dublin	1	0
1993	17 Feb	Dublin	1	2

		v ISRAEL	W	I
WC1958	15 Jan	Tel Aviv	2	0
WC1958	5 Feb	Cardiff	2	0

			W	I
1984	10 June	Tel Aviv	0	0
1989	8 Feb	Tel Aviv	3	3

		v ITALY	W	I
1965	1 May	Florence	1	4
wc1968	23 Oct	Cardiff	0	1
wc1969	4 Nov	Rome	1	4
1988	4 June	Brescia	1	0

		v JAPAN	W	J
1992	7 June	Matsuyama	1	0

		v KUWAIT	W	K
1977	6 Sept	Wrexham	0	0
1977	20 Sept	Kuwait	0	0

		v LUXEMBOURG	W	L
EC1974	20 Nov	Swansea	5	0
EC1975	1 May	Luxembourg	3	1
EC1990	14 Nov	Luxembourg	1	0
EC1991	13 Nov	Cardiff	1	0

		v MALTA	W	M
EC1978	25 Oct	Wrexham	7	0
EC1979	2 June	Valletta	2	0
1988	1 June	Valletta	3	2

		v MEXICO	W	M
wc1958	11 June	Stockholm	1	1
1962	22 May	Mexico City	1	2

		v MOLDOVA	W	M
EC1994	12 Oct	Kishinev	2	3

		v NORWAY	W	N
EC1982	22 Sept	Swansea	1	0
EC1983	21 Sept	Oslo	0	0
1984	6 June	Trondheim	0	1
1985	26 Feb	Wrexham	1	1
1985	5 June	Bergen	2	4
1994	9 Mar	Cardiff	1	3

		v POLAND	W	P
wc1973	28 Mar	Cardiff	2	0
wc1973	26 Sept	Katowice	0	3
1991	29 May	Radom	0	0

		v PORTUGAL	W	P
1949	15 May	Lisbon	2	3
1951	12 May	Cardiff	2	1

		v ROMANIA	W	R
EC1970	11 Nov	Cardiff	0	0
EC1971	24 Nov	Bucharest	0	2
1983	12 Oct	Wrexham	5	0
wc1992	20 May	Bucharest	1	5
wc1993	17 Nov	Cardiff	1	2

		v SAUDI ARABIA	W	SA
1986	25 Feb	Dahran	2	1

		v SPAIN	W	S
wc1961	19 Apr	Cardiff	1	2
wc1961	18 May	Madrid	1	1
1982	24 Mar	Valencia	1	1
wc1984	17 Oct	Seville	0	3
wc1985	30 Apr	Wrexham	3	0

		v SWEDEN	W	S
wc1958	15 June	Stockholm	0	0
1988	27 Apr	Stockholm	1	4
1989	26 Apr	Wrexham	0	2
1990	25 Apr	Stockholm	2	4
1994	20 Apr	Wrexham	0	2

		v SWITZERLAND	W	S
1949	26 May	Berne	0	4
1951	16 May	Wrexham	3	2

		v TURKEY	W	T
EC1978	29 Nov	Wrexham	1	0
EC1979	21 Nov	Izmir	0	1
wc1980	15 Oct	Cardiff	4	0
wc1981	25 Mar	Ankara	1	0

		v REST OF UNITED KINGDOM	W	UK
1951	5 Dec	Cardiff	3	2
1969	28 July	Cardiff	0	1

		v URUGUAY	W	U
1986	21 Apr	Wrexham	0	0

		v USSR	W	USSR
wc1965	30 May	Moscow	1	2
wc1965	27 Oct	Cardiff	2	1
wc1981	30 May	Wrexham	0	0
wc1981	18 Nov	Tbilisi	0	3
1987	18 Feb	Swansea	0	0

		v YUGOSLAVIA	W	Y
1953	21 May	Belgrade	2	5
1954	22 Nov	Cardiff	1	3
EC1976	24 Apr	Zagreb	0	2
EC1976	22 May	Cardiff	1	1
EC1982	15 Dec	Titograd	4	4
EC1983	14 Dec	Cardiff	1	1
1988	23 Mar	Swansea	1	2

NORTHERN IRELAND

		v ALBANIA	NI	A
wc1965	7 May	Belfast	4	1
wc1965	24 Nov	Tirana	1	1
EC1982	15 Dec	Tirana	0	0
EC1983	27 Apr	Belfast	1	0
wc1992	9 Sept	Belfast	3	0
wc1993	17 Feb	Tirana	2	1

		v ALGERIA	NI	A
wc1986	3 June	Guadalajara	1	1

		v ARGENTINA	NI	A
wc1958	11 June	Halmstad	1	3

		v AUSTRALIA	NI	A
1980	11 June	Sydney	2	1
1980	15 June	Melbourne	1	1
1980	18 June	Adelaide	2	1

		v AUSTRIA	NI	A
wc1982	1 July	Madrid	2	2
EC1982	13 Oct	Vienna	0	2
EC1983	21 Sept	Belfast	3	1
EC1990	14 Nov	Vienna	0	0
EC1991	16 Oct	Belfast	2	1
EC1994	12 Oct	Vienna	2	1

		v BELGIUM	NI	B
WC1976	10 Nov	Liège	0	2
WC1977	16 Nov	Belfast	3	0

		v BRAZIL	NI	B
WC1986	12 June	Guadalajara	0	3

		v BULGARIA	NI	B
WC1972	18 Oct	Sofia	0	3
WC1973	26 Sept	Sheffield	0	0
EC1978	29 Nov	Sofia	2	0
EC1979	2 May	Belfast	2	0

		v CANADA	NI	C
1995	22 May	Edmonton	0	2

		v CHILE	NI	C
1989	26 May	Belfast	0	1
1995	25 May	Edmonton	1	2

		v COLOMBIA	NI	C
1994	4 June	Boston	0	2

		v CYPRUS	NI	C
EC1971	3 Feb	Nicosia	3	0
EC1971	21 Apr	Belfast	5	0
WC1973	14 Feb	Nicosia	0	1
WC1973	8 May	London	3	0

		v CZECHOSLOVAKIA	NI	C
WC1958	8 June	Halmstad	1	0
WC1958	17 June	Malmo	2	1*

**After extra time*

		v DENMARK	NI	D
EC1978	25 Oct	Belfast	2	1
EC1979	6 June	Copenhagen	0	4
1986	26 Mar	Belfast	1	1
EC1990	17 Oct	Belfast	1	1
EC1991	13 Nov	Odense	1	2
WC1992	18 Nov	Belfast	0	1
WC1993	13 Oct	Copenhagen	0	1

		v FAEROES	NI	F
EC1991	1 May	Belfast	1	1
EC1991	11 Sept	Landskrona	5	0

		v FINLAND	NI	F
WC1984	27 May	Pori	0	1
WC1984	14 Nov	Belfast	2	1

		v FRANCE	NI	F
1951	12 May	Belfast	2	2
1952	11 Nov	Paris	1	3
WC1958	19 June	Norrkoping	0	4
1982	24 Mar	Paris	0	4
WC1982	4 July	Madrid	1	4
1986	26 Feb	Paris	0	0
1988	27 Apr	Belfast	0	0

		v GERMANY	NI	G
1992	2 June	Bremen	1	1

		v WEST GERMANY	NI	WG
WC1918	15 June	Malmo	2	2
WC1960	26 Oct	Belfast	3	4
WC1961	10 May	Hamburg	1	2
1966	7 May	Belfast	0	2
1977	27 Apr	Cologne	0	5
EC1982	17 Nov	Belfast	1	0
EC1983	16 Nov	Hamburg	1	0

		v GREECE	NI	G
WC1961	3 May	Athens	1	2
WC1961	17 Oct	Belfast	2	0
1988	17 Feb	Athens	2	3

		v HOLLAND	NI	H
1962	9 May	Rotterdam	0	4
WC1965	17 Mar	Belfast	2	1
WC1965	7 Apr	Rotterdam	0	0
WC1976	13 Oct	Rotterdam	2	2
WC1977	12 Oct	Belfast	0	1

		v HONDURAS	NI	H
WC1982	21 June	Zaragoza	1	1

		v HUNGARY	NI	H
WC1988	19 Oct	Budapest	0	1
WC1989	6 Sept	Belfast	1	2

		v ICELAND	NI	I
WC1977	11 June	Reykjavik	0	1
WC1977	21 Sept	Belfast	2	0

		v REPUBLIC OF IRELAND	NI	RI
EC1978	20 Sept	Dublin	0	0
EC1979	21 Nov	Belfast	1	0
WC1988	14 Sept	Belfast	0	0
WC1989	11 Oct	Dublin	0	3
WC1993	31 Mar	Dublin	0	3
WC1993	17 Nov	Belfast	1	1
EC1994	16 Nov	Belfast	0	4
EC1995	29 Mar	Dublin	1	1

		v ISRAEL	NI	I
1968	10 Sept	Jaffa	3	2
1976	3 Mar	Tel Aviv	1	1
WC1980	26 Mar	Tel Aviv	0	0
WC1981	18 Nov	Belfast	1	0
1984	16 Oct	Belfast	3	0
1987	18 Feb	Tel Aviv	1	1

		v ITALY	NI	I
WC1957	25 Apr	Rome	0	1
1957	4 Dec	Belfast	2	2
WC1958	15 Jan	Belfast	2	1
1961	25 Apr	Bologna	2	3

		v LATVIA	NI	L
WC1993	2 June	Riga	2	1
WC1993	8 Sept	Belfast	2	0
EC1995	26 Apr	Riga	1	0
EC1995	7 June	Belfast	1	2

		v LIECHTENSTEIN	NI	L
EC1994	20 Apr	Belfast	4	1

		v LITHUANIA	NI	L
WC1992	28 Apr	Belfast	2	2
WC1993	25 May	Vilnius	1	0

		v MALTA	NI	M
1988	21 May	Belfast	3	0
WC1989	26 Apr	Valletta	2	0

		v MEXICO	NI	M
1966	22 June	Belfast	4	1
1994	11 June	Miami	0	3

		v MOROCCO	NI	M
1986	23 Apr	Belfast	2	1

		v NORWAY	NI	N
EC1974	4 Sept	Oslo	1	2
EC1975	29 Oct	Belfast	3	0
1990	27 Mar	Belfast	2	3

		v POLAND	NI	P
EC1962	10 Oct	Katowice	2	0
EC1962	28 Nov	Belfast	2	0
1988	23 Mar	Belfast	1	1
1991	5 Feb	Belfast	3	1

		v PORTUGAL	NI	P
WC1957	16 Jan	Lisbon	1	1
WC1957	1 May	Belfast	3	0
WC1973	28 Mar	Coventry	1	1
WC1973	14 Nov	Lisbon	1	1
WC1980	19 Nov	Lisbon	0	1
WC1981	29 Apr	Belfast	1	0
EC1994	7 Sept	Belfast	1	2

		v ROMANIA	NI	R
WC1984	12 Sept	Belfast	3	2
WC1985	16 Oct	Bucharest	1	0
1994	23 Mar	Belfast	2	0

		v SPAIN	NI	S
1958	15 Oct	Madrid	2	6
1963	30 May	Bilbao	1	1
1963	30 Oct	Belfast	0	1
EC1970	11 Nov	Seville	0	3
EC1972	16 Feb	Hull	1	1
WC1982	25 June	Valencia	1	0
1985	27 Mar	Palma	0	0
WC1986	7 June	Guadalajara	1	2
WC1988	21 Dec	Seville	0	4
WC1989	8 Feb	Belfast	0	2
WC1992	14 Oct	Belfast	0	0
WC1993	28 Apr	Seville	1	3

		v SWEDEN	NI	S
EC1974	30 Oct	Solna	2	0
EC1975	3 Sept	Belfast	1	2
WC1980	15 Oct	Belfast	3	0
WC1981	3 June	Solna	0	1

		v SWITZERLAND	NI	S
WC1964	14 Oct	Belfast	1	0
WC1964	14 Nov	Lausanne	1	2

		v TURKEY	NI	T
WC1968	23 Oct	Belfast	4	1
WC1968	11 Dec	Istanbul	3	0
EC1983	30 Mar	Belfast	2	1
EC1983	12 Oct	Ankara	0	1
WC1985	1 May	Belfast	2	0
WC1985	11 Sept	Izmir	0	0
EC1986	12 Nov	Izmir	0	0
EC1987	11 Nov	Belfast	1	0

		v URUGUAY	NI	U
1964	29 Apr	Belfast	3	0
1990	18 May	Belfast	1	0

		v USSR	NI	USSR
WC1969	19 Sept	Belfast	0	0
WC1969	22 Oct	Moscow	0	2
EC1971	22 Sept	Moscow	0	1
EC1971	13 Oct	Belfast	1	1

		v YUGOSLAVIA	NI	Y
EC1975	16 Mar	Belfast	1	0
EC1975	19 Nov	Belgrade	0	1
WC1982	17 June	Zaragoza	0	0
EC1987	29 Apr	Belfast	1	2
EC1987	14 Oct	Sarajevo	0	3
EC1990	12 Sept	Belfast	0	2
EC1991	27 Mar	Belgrade	1	4

REPUBLIC OF IRELAND

		v ALBANIA	RI	A
WC1992	26 May	Dublin	2	0
WC1993	26 May	Tirana	2	1

		v ALGERIA	RI	A
1982	28 Apr	Algiers	0	2

		v ARGENTINA	RI	A
1951	13 May	Dublin	0	1
1979	29 May	Dublin	0	0*
1980	16 May	Dublin	0	1

* Not considered a full international

		v AUSTRIA	RI	A
1952	7 May	Vienna	0	6
1953	25 Mar	Dublin	4	0
1958	14 Mar	Vienna	1	3
1962	8 Apr	Dublin	2	3
EC1963	25 Sept	Vienna	0	0
EC1963	13 Oct	Dublin	3	2
1966	22 May	Vienna	0	1
1968	10 Nov	Dublin	2	2
EC1971	30 May	Dublin	1	4
EC1971	10 Oct	Linz	0	6
EC1995	11 June	Dublin	1	3

		v BELGIUM	RI	B
1928	12 Feb	Liège	4	2
1929	30 Apr	Dublin	4	0
1930	11 May	Brussels	3	1
WC1934	25 Feb	Dublin	4	4
1949	24 Apr	Dublin	0	2
1950	10 May	Brussels	1	5
1965	24 Mar	Dublin	0	2
1966	25 May	Liège	3	2
WC1980	15 Oct	Dublin	1	1
WC1981	25 Mar	Brussels	0	1
EC1986	10 Sept	Brussels	2	2
EC1987	29 Apr	Dublin	0	0

		v BOLIVIA	RI	B
1994	24 May	Dublin	1	0

		v BRAZIL	RI	B
1974	5 May	Rio de Janeiro	1	2
1982	27 May	Uberlandia	0	7
1987	23 May	Dublin	1	0

		v BULGARIA	RI	B
WC1977	1 June	Sofia	1	2
WC1977	12 Oct	Dublin	0	0
EC1979	19 May	Sofia	0	1
EC1979	17 Oct	Dublin	3	0
WC1987	1 Apr	Sofia	1	2
WC1987	14 Oct	Dublin	2	0

		v CHILE	*RI*	*C*
1960	30 Mar	Dublin	2	0
1972	21 June	Recife	1	2
1974	12 May	Santiago	2	1
1982	22 May	Santiago	0	1
1991	22 May	Dublin	1	1

		v CHINA	*RI*	*C*
1984	3 June	Sapporo	1	0

		v CYPRUS	*RI*	*C*
WC1980	26 Mar	Nicosia	3	2
WC1980	19 Nov	Dublin	6	0

		v CZECHOSLOVAKIA	*RI*	*C*
1938	18 May	Prague	2	2
EC1959	5 Apr	Dublin	2	0
EC1959	10 May	Bratislava	0	4
WC1961	8 Oct	Dublin	1	3
WC1961	29 Oct	Prague	1	7
EC1967	21 May	Dublin	0	2
EC1967	22 Nov	Prague	2	1
WC1969	4 May	Dublin	1	2
WC1969	7 Oct	Prague	0	3
1979	26 Sept	Prague	1	4
1981	29 Apr	Dublin	3	1
1986	27 May	Reykjavik	1	0

		v CZECH REPUBLIC	*RI*	*C*
1994	5 June	Dublin	1	3

		v DENMARK	*RI*	*D*
WC1956	3 Oct	Dublin	2	1
WC1957	2 Oct	Copenhagen	2	0
WC1968	4 Dec	Dublin	1	1
(*abandoned after 51 mins*)				
WC1969	27 May	Copenhagen	0	2
WC1969	15 Oct	Dublin	1	1
EC1978	24 May	Copenhagen	3	3
EC1979	2 May	Dublin	2	0
WC1984	14 Nov	Copenhagen	0	3
WC1985	13 Nov	Dublin	1	4
WC1992	14 Oct	Copenhagen	0	0
WC1993	28 Apr	Dublin	1	1

		v ECUADOR	*RI*	*E*
1972	19 June	Natal	3	2

		v EGYPT	*RI*	*E*
WC1990	17 June	Palermo	0	0

		v ENGLAND	*RI*	*E*
1946	30 Sept	Dublin	0	1
1949	21 Sept	Everton	2	0
WC1957	8 May	Wembley	1	5
WC1957	19 May	Dublin	1	1
1964	24 May	Dublin	1	3
1976	8 Sept	Wembley	1	1
EC1978	25 Oct	Dublin	1	1
EC1980	6 Feb	Wembley	0	2
1985	26 Mar	Wembley	1	2
EC1988	12 June	Stuttgart	1	0
WC1990	11 June	Cagliari	1	1
EC1990	14 Nov	Dublin	1	1
EC1991	27 Mar	Wembley	1	1
1995	15 Feb	Dublin	1	0
(*abandoned after 27 mins*)				

		v FINLAND	RI	F
WC1949	8 Sept	Dublin	3	0
WC1949	9 Oct	Helsinki	1	1
1990	16 May	Dublin	1	1

		v FRANCE	*RI*	*F*
1937	23 May	Paris	2	0
1952	16 Nov	Dublin	1	1
WC1953	4 Oct	Dublin	3	5
WC1953	25 Nov	Paris	0	1
WC1972	15 Nov	Dublin	2	1
WC1973	19 May	Paris	1	1
WC1976	17 Nov	Paris	0	2
WC1977	30 Mar	Dublin	1	0
WC1980	28 Oct	Paris	0	2
WC1981	14 Oct	Dublin	3	2
1989	7 Feb	Dublin	0	0

		v GERMANY	*RI*	*G*
1935	8 May	Dortmund	1	3
1936	17 Oct	Dublin	5	2
1939	23 May	Bremen	1	1
1994	29 May	Hanover	2	0

		v WEST GERMANY	*RI*	*WG*
1951	17 Oct	Dublin	3	2
1952	4 May	Cologne	0	3
1955	28 May	Hamburg	1	2
1956	25 Nov	Dublin	3	0
1960	11 May	Dusseldorf	1	0
1966	4 May	Dublin	0	4
1970	9 May	Berlin	1	2
1975	1 Mar	Dublin	1	0†
1979	22 May	Dublin	1	3
1981	21 May	Bremen	0	3†
1989	6 Sept	Dublin	1	1

†v West Germany 'B'

		v HOLLAND	*RI*	*H*
1932	8 May	Amsterdam	2	0
1934	8 Apr	Amsterdam	2	5
1935	8 Dec	Dublin	3	5
1955	1 May	Dublin	1	0
1956	10 May	Rotterdam	4	1
WC1980	10 Sept	Dublin	2	1
WC1981	9 Sept	Rotterdam	2	2
EC1982	22 Sept	Rotterdam	1	2
EC1983	12 Oct	Dublin	2	3
EC1988	18 June	Gelsenkirchen	0	1
WC1990	21 June	Palermo	1	1
1994	20 Apr	Tilburg	1	0
WC1994	4 July	Orlando	0	2

		v HUNGARY	*RI*	*H*
1934	15 Dec	Dublin	2	4
1936	3 May	Budapest	3	3
1936	6 Dec	Dublin	2	3
1939	19 Mar	Cork	2	2
1939	18 May	Budapest	2	2
WC1969	8 June	Dublin	1	2
WC1969	5 Nov	Budapest	0	4
WC1989	8 Mar	Budapest	0	2
WC1989	4 June	Dublin	2	0
1991	11 Sept	Gyor	2	1

		v ICELAND	*RI*	*I*
EC1962	12 Aug	Dublin	4	2
EC1962	2 Sept	Reykjavik	1	1
EC1982	13 Oct	Dublin	2	0
EC1983	21 Sept	Reykjavik	3	0
1986	25 May	Reykjavik	2	1

		v IRAN	*RI*	*I*
1972	18 June	Recife	2	1

		v N. IRELAND	*RI*	*NI*
EC1978	20 Sept	Dublin	0	0
EC1979	21 Nov	Belfast	0	1

			RI	NI
WC1988	14 Sept	Belfast	0	0
WC1989	11 Oct	Dublin	3	0
WC1993	31 Mar	Dublin	3	0
WC1993	17 Nov	Belfast	1	1
EC1994	16 Nov	Belfast	4	0
EC1995	29 Mar	Dublin	1	1

		v ISRAEL	*RI*	*I*
1984	4 Apr	Tel Aviv	0	3
1985	27 May	Tel Aviv	0	0
1987	10 Nov	Dublin	5	0

		v ITALY	*RI*	*I*
1926	21 Mar	Turin	0	3
1927	23 Apr	Dublin	1	2
EC1970	8 Dec	Rome	0	3
EC1971	10 May	Dublin	1	2
1985	5 Feb	Dublin	1	2
WC1990	30 June	Rome	0	1
1992	4 June	Foxboro	0	2
WC1994	18 June	New York	1	0

		v LATVIA	*RI*	*L*
WC1992	9 Sept	Dublin	4	0
WC1993	2 June	Riga	2	1
EC1994	7 Sept	Riga	3	0

		v LIECHTENSTEIN	*RI*	*L*
EC1994	12 Oct	Dublin	4	0
EC1995	3 June	Eschen	0	0

		v LITHUANIA	*RI*	*L*
WC1993	16 June	Vilnius	1	0
WC1993	8 Sept	Dublin	2	0

		v LUXEMBOURG	*RI*	*L*
1936	9 May	Luxembourg	5	1
WC1953	28 Oct	Dublin	4	0
WC1954	7 Mar	Luxembourg	1	0
EC1987	28 May	Luxembourg	2	0
EC1987	9 Sept	Dublin	2	1

		v MALTA	*RI*	*M*
EC1983	30 Mar	Valletta	1	0
EC1983	16 Nov	Dublin	8	0
WC1989	28 May	Dublin	2	0
WC1989	15 Nov	Valletta	2	0
1990	2 June	Valletta	3	0

		v MEXICO	*RI*	*M*
1984	8 Aug	Dublin	0	0
WC1994	24 June	Orlando	1	2

		v MOROCCO	*RI*	*M*
1990	12 Sept	Dublin	1	0

		v NORWAY	*RI*	*N*
WC1937	10 Oct	Oslo	2	3
WC1937	7 Nov	Dublin	3	3
1950	26 Nov	Dublin	2	2
1951	30 May	Oslo	3	2
1954	8 Nov	Dublin	2	1
1955	25 May	Oslo	3	1
1960	6 Nov	Dublin	3	1
1964	13 May	Oslo	4	1
1973	6 June	Oslo	1	1
1976	24 Mar	Dublin	3	0
1978	21 May	Oslo	0	0
WC1984	17 Oct	Oslo	0	1
WC1985	1 May	Dublin	0	0
1988	1 June	Oslo	0	0
WC1994	28 June	New York	0	0

		v POLAND	*RI*	*P*
1938	22 May	Warsaw	0	6
1938	13 Nov	Dublin	3	2
1958	11 May	Katowice	2	2
1958	5 Oct	Dublin	2	2
1964	10 May	Cracow	1	3
1964	25 Oct	Dublin	3	2
1968	15 May	Dublin	2	2
1968	30 Oct	Katowice	0	1
1970	6 May	Dublin	1	2
1970	23 Sept	Dublin	0	2
1973	16 May	Wroclaw	0	2
1973	21 Oct	Dublin	1	0
1976	26 May	Poznan	2	0
1977	24 Apr	Dublin	0	0
1978	12 Apr	Lodz	0	3
1981	23 May	Bydgoszcz	0	3
1984	23 May	Dublin	0	0
1986	12 Nov	Warsaw	0	1
1988	22 May	Dublin	3	1
EC1991	1 May	Dublin	0	0
EC1991	16 Oct	Poznan	3	3

		v PORTUGAL	*RI*	*P*
1946	16 June	Lisbon	1	3
1947	4 May	Dublin	0	2
1948	23 May	Lisbon	0	2
1949	22 May	Dublin	1	0
1972	25 June	Recife	1	2
1992	7 June	Boston	2	0
EC1995	26 Apr	Dublin	1	0

		v ROMANIA	*RI*	*R*
1988	23 Mar	Dublin	2	0
WC1990	25 June	Genoa	0	0*

**After extra time*

		v RUSSIA	*RI*	*R*
1994	23 Mar	Dublin	0	0

		v SCOTLAND	*RI*	*S*
WC1961	3 May	Glasgow	1	4
WC1961	7 May	Dublin	0	3
1963	9 June	Dublin	1	0
1969	21 Sept	Dublin	1	1
EC1986	15 Oct	Dublin	0	0
EC1987	18 Feb	Glasgow	1	0

		v SPAIN	*RI*	*S*
1931	26 Apr	Barcelona	1	1
1931	13 Dec	Dublin	0	5
1946	23 June	Madrid	1	0
1947	2 Mar	Dublin	3	2
1948	30 May	Barcelona	1	2
1949	12 June	Dublin	1	4
1952	1 June	Madrid	0	6
1955	27 Nov	Dublin	2	2
EC1964	11 Mar	Seville	1	5
EC1964	8 Apr	Dublin	0	2
WC1965	5 May	Dublin	1	0
WC1965	27 Oct	Seville	1	4
WC1965	10 Nov	Paris	0	1
EC1966	23 Oct	Dublin	0	0
EC1966	7 Dec	Valencia	0	2
1977	9 Feb	Dublin	0	1
EC1982	17 Nov	Dublin	3	3
EC1983	27 Apr	Zaragoza	0	2
1985	26 May	Cork	0	0
WC1988	16 Nov	Seville	0	2
WC1989	26 Apr	Dublin	1	0
WC1992	18 Nov	Seville	0	0
WC1993	13 Oct	Dublin	1	3

		v SWEDEN	RI	S
WC1949	2 June	Stockholm	1	3
WC1949	13 Nov	Dublin	1	3
1959	1 Nov	Dublin	3	2
1960	18 May	Malmo	1	4
EC1970	14 Oct	Dublin	1	1
EC1970	28 Oct	Malmo	0	1

		v SWITZERLAND	RI	S
1935	5 May	Basle	0	1
1936	17 Mar	Dublin	1	0
1937	17 May	Berne	1	0
1938	18 Sept	Dublin	4	0
1948	5 Dec	Dublin	0	1
EC1975	11 May	Dublin	2	1
EC1975	21 May	Berne	0	1
1980	30 Apr	Dublin	2	0
WC1985	2 June	Dublin	3	0
WC1985	11 Sept	Berne	0	0
1992	25 Mar	Dublin	2	1

		v TRINIDAD & TOBAGO	RI	TT
1982	30 May	Port of Spain	1	2

		v TUNISIA	RI	T
1988	19 Oct	Dublin	4	0

		v TURKEY	RI	T
EC1966	16 Nov	Dublin	2	1
EC1967	22 Feb	Ankara	1	2
EC1974	20 Nov	Izmir	1	1
EC1975	29 Oct	Dublin	4	0
1976	13 Oct	Ankara	3	3
1978	5 Apr	Dublin	4	2
1990	26 May	Izmir	0	0
EC1990	17 Oct	Dublin	5	0
EC1991	13 Nov	Istanbul	3	1

		v URUGUAY	RI	U
1974	8 May	Montevideo	0	2
1986	23 Apr	Dublin	1	1

		v USA	RI	USA
1979	29 Oct	Dublin	3	2
1991	1 June	Boston	1	1
1992	29 Apr	Dublin	4	1
1992	30 May	Washington	1	3

		v USSR	RI	USSR
WC1972	18 Oct	Dublin	1	2
WC1973	13 May	Moscow	0	1
EC1974	30 Oct	Dublin	3	0
EC1975	18 May	Kiev	1	2
WC1984	12 Sept	Dublin	1	0
WC1985	16 Oct	Moscow	0	2
EC1988	15 June	Hanover	1	1
1990	25 Apr	Dublin	1	0

		v WALES	RI	W
1960	28 Sept	Dublin	2	3
1979	11 Sept	Swansea	1	2
1981	24 Feb	Dublin	1	3
1986	26 Mar	Dublin	0	1
1990	28 Mar	Dublin	1	0
1991	6 Feb	Wrexham	3	0
1992	19 Feb	Dublin	0	1
1993	17 Feb	Dublin	2	1

		v YUGOSLAVIA	RI	Y
1955	19 Sept	Dublin	1	4
1988	27 Apr	Dublin	2	0

OTHER BRITISH AND IRISH INTERNATIONAL MATCHES 1994–95

Wembley, 7 September 1994, 38,629

England (2) 2 *(Shearer 2)*

USA (0) 0

England: Seaman; Jones, Le Saux, Venison, Adams, Pallister, Anderton, Platt, Shearer (Wright), Sheringham (Ferdinand), Barnes.
USA: Friedel (Sommer); Caligiuri, Lalas, Balboa, Agoos (Lapper), Perez (Wynalda), Dooley, Reyna (Moore), Sorber, Jones, Stewart (Klopas).

Wembley, 12 October 1994, 48,754

England (1) 1 *(Lee)*

Romania (1) 1 *(Dumitrescu)*

England: Seaman; Jones (Pearce), Le Saux, Lee (Wise), Adams, Pallister, Le Tissier, Wright (Sheringham), Shearer, Ince, Barnes.
Romania: Stelea (Prunea); Belodedico, Petrescu, Prodan, Munteanu, Popescu, Lupescu, Dumitrescu, Hagi (Selymes), Lacatus (Cirstea), Raducioiu (Timofte).

Wembley, 16 November 1994, 37,196

England (1) 1 *(Platt)*

Nigeria (0) 0

England: Flowers; Jones, Le Saux, Lee (McManaman), Howey, Ruddock, Platt, Beardsley (Le Tissier), Shearer (Sheringham), Barnes, Wise.
Nigeria: Rufai; Okafor, Eguavon, Okechukwu, Iroha, George, Adepoju (Kanu), Okocha, Amunike, Amokachi (Ikpeba), Yekini (Ekoku).

Dublin, 15 February 1995, 46,000

Republic of Ireland (1) 1 *(Kelly D)*

England (0) 0

Republic of Ireland: Kelly A; Irwin, Phelan, Kernaghan, McGrath, Staunton, Sheridan, Kelly D, Quinn, Townsend, McGoldrick.
England: Seaman; Barton, Le Saux, Platt, Adams, Pallister, Beardsley, Ince, Shearer, Le Tissier, Anderton.
Match abandoned after 27 minutes.

Wembley, 29 March 1994, 34,849

England (0) 0

Uruguay (0) 0

England: Flowers; Jones, Le Saux (McManaman), Venison, Adams, Pallister, Anderton, Beardsley (Barmby), Sheringham (Cole), Platt, Barnes.
Uruguay: Ferro; Lopez, Aguirregaray, Gutierrez, Montero, Cedras, Dorta, Bengoechea, Francescoli (Debray), Poyet, Fonseca.

INTERNATIONAL APPEARANCES

This is a list of full international appearances by Englishmen, Irishmen, Scotsmen and Welshmen in matches against the Home Countries and against foreign nations. It does not include unofficial matches against Commonwealth and Empire countries. The year indicated refers to the season; ie 1994 is the 1993-94 season. Explanatory code for matches played by all five countries: A represents Austria; Alb, Albania; Alg, Algeria; Arg, Argentina; Aus, Australia; B, Bohemia; Bel, Belgium; Bol, Bolivia; Br, Brazil; Bul, Bulgaria; C, CIS; Ca, Canada; Cam, Cameroon; Ch, Chile; Chn, China; Co, Colombia; Cr, Costa Rica; Cy, Cyprus; Cz, Czechoslovakia; CzR, Czech Republic; D, Denmark; E, England; Ec, Ecuador; Ei, Republic of Ireland; EG, East Germany; Eg, Egypt; Es, Estonia; F, France; Fa, Faeroes; Fi, Finland; G, Germany; Ge, Georgia; Gr, Greece; H, Hungary; Ho, Holland; Hon, Honduras; I, Italy; Ic, Iceland; Ir, Iran; Is, Israel; J,Japan; K, Kuwait; L, Luxembourg; La, Latvia; Li, Lithuania; Lie, Liechtenstein; M, Mexico; Ma, Malta; Mal, Malaysia; Mol, Moldova; Mor, Morocco; N, Norway; Ni, Ng, Nigeria; Northern Ireland; Nz, New Zealand; P, Portugal; Para, Paraguay; Pe, Peru; Pol, Poland; R, Romania; RCS, Republic of Czechs and Slovaks; R of E, Rest of Europe; R of UK, Rest of United Kingdom; R of W, Rest of World; Ru, Russia; S.Ar, Saudi Arabia; S, Scotland; Se, Sweden; Sm, San Marino; Sp, Spain; Sw, Switzerland; T, Turkey; Tr, Trinidad & Tobago; Tun, Tunisia; U, Uruguay; US, United States of America; USSR, Soviet Union; W, Wales; WG, West Germany; Y, Yugoslavia; Z, Zaire.

As at June 1995.

ENGLAND

Abbott, W. (Everton), 1902 v W (1)

A'Court, A. (Liverpool), 1958 v Ni, Br, A, USSR; 1959 v W (5)

Adams, T. A. (Arsenal), 1987 v Sp, T, Br; 1988 v WG, T, Y, Ho, H, S, Co, Sw, Ei, Ho, USSR; 1989 v D, Se, S.Ar.; 1991 v Ei (2); 1993 v N, T, Sm, T, Ho, Pol, N; 1994 v Pol, Ho, D, Gr, N; 1995 v US, R, Ei, U (35)

Adcock, H. (Leicester C), 1929 v F, Bel, Sp; 1930 v Ni, W (5)

Alcock, C. W. (Wanderers), 1875 v S (1)

Alderson, J. T. (C Palace), 1923 v F (1)

Aldridge, A. (WBA), 1888 v Ni; (with Walsall Town Swifts), 1889 v Ni (2)

Allen, A. (Stoke C) 1960 v Se, W, Ni (3)

Allen, A. (Aston Villa), 1888 v Ni (1)

Allen, C. (QPR), 1984 v Br (sub), U, Ch; (with Tottenham H), 1987 v T; 1988 v Is (5)

Allen, H. (Wolverhampton W), 1888 v S, W, Ni; 1889 v S; 1890 v S (5)

Allen, J. P. (Portsmouth), 1934 v Ni, W (2)

Allen, R. (WBA), 1952 v Sw; 1954 v Y, S; 1955 v WG, W (5)

Alsford, W. J. (Tottenham H), 1935 v S (1)

Amos, A. (Old Carthusians), 1885 v S; 1886 v W (2)

Anderson, R. D. (Old Etonians), 1879 v W (1)

Anderson, S. (Sunderland), 1962 v A, S (2)

Anderson, V. (Nottingham F), 1979 v Cz, Se; 1980 v Bul, Sp; 1981 v N, R, W, S; 1982 v Ni, Ic; 1984 v Ni; (with Arsenal), 1985 v T, Ni, Ei, R, Fi, S, M, US; 1986 v USSR, M; 1987 v Se, Ni (2), Y, Sp, T; (with Manchester U), 1988 v WG, H, Co (30)

Anderton, D. R. (Tottenham H), 1994 v D, Gr, N; 1995 v US, Ei, U, J, Se, Br (9)

Angus, J. (Burnley), 1961 v A (1)

Armfield, J. C. (Blackpool), 1959 v Br, Pe, M, US; 1960 v Y, Sp, H, S; 1961 v L, P, Sp, M, I, A, W, Ni, S; 1962 v A, Sw, Pe, W, Ni, S, L, P, H, Arg, Bul, Br; 1963 v F (2), Br, EG, Sw, Ni, W, S; 1964 v R of W, W, Ni, S; 1966 v Y, Fi (43)

Armitage, G. H. (Charlton Ath), 1926 v Ni (1)

Armstrong, D. (Middlesbrough), 1980 v Aus; (with Southampton), 1983 v WG; 1984 v W (3)

Armstrong, K. (Chelsea), 1955 v S (1)

Arnold, J. (Fulham), 1933 v S (1)

Arthur, J. W. H. (Blackburn R), 1885 v S, W, Ni; 1886 v S, W; 1887 v W, Ni (7)

Ashcroft, J. (Woolwich Arsenal), 1906 v Ni, W, S (3)

Ashmore, G. S. (WBA), 1926 v Bel (1)

Ashton, C. T. (Corinthians), 1926 v Ni (1)

Ashurst, W. (Notts Co), 1923 v Se (2); 1925 v S, W, Bel (5)

Astall, G. (Birmingham C), 1956 v Fi, WG (2)

Astle, J. (WBA), 1969 v W; 1970 v S, P, Br (sub), Cz (5)

Aston, J. (Manchester U), 1949 v S, W, D, Sw, Se, N, F; 1950 v S, W, Ni, Ei, I, P, Bel, Ch, US; 1951 v Ni (17)

Athersmith, W. C. (Aston Villa), 1892 v Ni, 1897 v S, W, Ni; 1898 v S, W, Ni; 1899 v S, W, Ni; 1900 v S, W (12)

Atyeo, P. J. W. (Bristol C), 1956 v Br, Se, Sp; 1957 v D, Ei (2) (6)

Austin, S. W. (Manchester C), 1926 v Ni (1)

Bach, P. (Sunderland), 1899 v Ni (1)

Bache, J. W. (Aston Villa), 1903 v W; 1904 v W, Ni; 1905 v S; 1907 v Ni; 1910 v Ni; 1911 v S (7)

Baddeley, T. (Wolverhampton W), 1903 v S, Ni; 1904 v S, W, Ni (5)

Bagshaw, J. J. (Derby Co), 1920 v Ni (1)

Bailey, G. R. (Manchester U), 1985 v Ei, M (2)

Bailey, H. P. (Leicester Fosse), 1908 v W, A (2), H, B (5)

Bailey, M. A. (Charlton Ath), 1964 v US; 1965 v W (2)

Bailey, N. C. (Clapham Rovers), 1878 v S; 1879 v S, W; 1880 v S; 1881 v S; 1882 v S, W; 1883 v S, W; 1884 v S, W, Ni; 1885 v S, W, Ni; 1886 v S, W; 1887 v S, W (19)

Baily, E. F. (Tottenham H), 1950 v Sp; 1951 v Y, Ni, W; 1952 v A (2), Sw, W; 1953 v Ni (9)

Bain, J. (Oxford University), 1887 v S (1)

Baker, A. (Arsenal), 1928 v W (1)

Baker, B. H. (Everton), 1921 v Bel; (with Chelsea), 1926 v Ni (2)

Baker, J. H. (Hibernian), 1960 v Y, Sp, H, Ni, S; (with Arsenal) 1966 v Sp, Pol, Ni (8)

Ball, A. J. (Blackpool), 1965 v Y, WG, Se; 1966 v S, Sp, Fi, D, U, Arg, P, WG (2), Pol (2); (with Everton), 1967 v W, S, Ni, A, Cz, Sp; 1968 v W, S, USSR, Sp (2), Y, WG; 1969 v Ni, W, S, R (2), M, Br, U; 1970 v P, Co, Ec, R, Br, Cz (sub), WG, W, S, Bel; 1971 v Ma, EG, Gr, Ma (sub), Ni, S; 1972 v Sw, Gr; (with Arsenal) WG (2), S; 1973 v W (3), Y, S (2), Cz, Ni, Pol; 1974 v P (sub); 1975 v WG, Cy (2), Ni, W, S (72)

Ball, J. (Bury), 1928 v Ni (1)

Balmer, W. (Everton), 1905 v Ni (1)

Bamber, J. (Liverpool), 1921 v W (1)

Bambridge, A. L. (Swifts), 1881 v W; 1883 v W; 1884 v Ni (3)

Bambridge, E. C. (Swifts), 1879 v S; 1880 v S; 1881 v S; 1882 v S, W, Ni; 1883 v W; 1884 v S, W, Ni; 1885 v S, W, Ni; 1886 v S, W; 1887 v S, W, Ni (18)

Bambridge, E. H. (Swifts), 1876 v S (1)

Banks, G. (Leicester C), 1963 v S, Br, Cz, EG; 1964 v W, Ni, S, R of W, U, P (2), US, Arg; 1965 v Ni, S, H, Y, WG, Se; 1966 v Ni, S, Sp, Pol (2), WG (2), Y, Fi, U, M, F, Arg, P; 1967 v Ni, W, S, Cz; (with Stoke C), 1968 v W, Ni, S, USSR (2), Sp, WG, Y; 1969 v Ni, S, R (2), F, U, Br; 1970 v W, Ni, S, Ho, Bel, Co, Ec, R, Br, Cz; 1971 v Gr, Ma (2), Ni, S; 1972 v Sw, Gr, WG (2), W, S (73)

Banks, H. E. (Millwall), 1901 v Ni (1)

Banks, T. (Bolton W), 1958 v USSR (3), Br, A; 1959 v Ni (6)

Bannister, W. (Burnley), 1901 v W; (with Bolton W), 1902 v Ni (2)

Barclay, R. (Sheffield U), 1932 v S; 1933 v Ni; 1936 v S (3)

Bardsley, D. J. (QPR), 1993 v Sp (sub), Pol (2)

Barham, M. (Norwich C), 1983 v Aus (2) (2)

Barkas, S. (Manchester C), 1936 v Bel; 1937 v S; 1938 v W, Ni, Cz (5)

Barker, J. (Derby Co), 1935 v I, Ho, S, W, Ni; 1936 v G, A, S, W, Ni; 1937 v W (11)

Barker, R. (Herts Rangers), 1872 v S (1)

Barker, R. R. (Casuals), 1895 v W (1)

Barlow, R. J. (WBA), 1955 v Ni (1)

Barmby, N.J. (Tottenham H), 1995 v U (sub), Se (sub) (2)

Barnes, J. (Watford), 1983 v Ni (sub), Aus (sub), Aus (2); 1984 v D, L (sub), F (sub), S, USSR, Br, U, Ch; 1985 v EG, Fi, T, Ni, R, Fi, S, I (sub), M, WG (sub), US (sub); 1986 v R (sub), Is (sub), M (sub), Ca (sub), Arg (sub); 1987 v Se, T (sub), Br; (with Liverpool), 1988 v WG, T, Y, Is, Ho, S, Co, Sw, Ei, Ho, USSR; 1989 v Se, Gr, Alb, Pol, D; 1990 v Se, I, Br, D, U, Tun, Ei, Ho, Eg, Bel, Cam; 1991 v H, Pol, Cam, Ei, T, USSR, Arg; 1992 v Cz, Fi; 1993 v Sm, T, Ho, Pol, US, G; 1995 v US, R, Ng, U, Se (78)

Barnes, P. S. (Manchester C), 1978 v I, WG, Br, W, S, H; 1979 v D, Ei, Cz, Ni (2), S, Bul, A; (with WBA), 1980 v D, W; 1981 v Sp (sub), Br, W, Sw (sub); (with Leeds U), 1982 v N (sub), Ho (sub) (22)

Barnet, H. H. (Royal Engineers), 1882 v Ni (1)

Barrass, M. W. (Bolton W), 1952 v W, Ni; 1953 v S (3)

Barrett, A. F. (Fulham), 1930 v Ni (1)

Barrett, E. D. (Oldham Ath), 1991 v Nz; 1993 v Br, G (3)

Barrett, J. W. (West Ham U), 1929 v Ni (1)

Barry, L. (Leicester C), 1928 v F, Bel; 1929 v F, Bel, Sp (5)

Barson, F. (Aston Villa), 1920 v W (1)

Barton, J. (Blackburn R), 1890 v Ni (1)

Barton, P. H. (Birmingham), 1921 v Bel; 1922 v Ni; 1923 v F; 1924 v Bel, S, W; 1925 v Ni (7)

Barton, W. D. (Wimbledon), 1995 v Ei; (with Newcastle U), Se, Br (sub) (3)

Bassett, W. I. (WBA), 1888 v Ni, 1889 v S, W; 1890 v S, W; 1891 v S, Ni; 1892 v S; 1893 v S, W; 1894 v S; 1895 v S, Ni; 1896 v S, W, Ni (16)

Bastard, S. R. (Upton Park), 1880 v S (1)

Bastin, C. S. (Arsenal), 1932 v W; 1933 v I, Sw; 1934 v S, Ni, W, H, Cz; 1935 v S, Ni, I; 1936 v S, W, G, A; 1937 v W, Ni; 1938 v S, G, Sw, F (21)

Batty, D. (Leeds U), 1991 v USSR (sub), Arg, Aus, Nz, Mal; 1992 v G, T, H (sub), F, Se; 1993 v N, Sm, US, Br; (with Blackburn R), 1994 v D (sub); 1995 v J, Br (17)

Baugh, R. (Stafford Road), 1886 v Ni; (with Wolverhampton W) 1890 v Ni (2)

Bayliss, A. E. J. M. (WBA), 1891 v Ni (1)

Baynham, R. L. (Luton T), 1956 v Ni, D, Sp (3)

Beardsley, P. A. (Newcastle U), 1986 v Eg (sub), Is, USSR, M, Ca (sub), P (sub), Pol, Para, Arg; 1987 v Ni (2), Y, Sp, Br, S; (with Liverpool), 1988 v WG, T, Y, Is, Ho, H, S, Co, Sw, Ei, Ho; 1989 v D, Se, S.Ar, Gr (sub), Alb (sub+1), Pol, D; 1990 v Se, Pol, I, Br, U (sub), Tun (sub), Ei, Eg (sub), Cam (sub), WG, I; 1991 v Pol (sub), Ei (2), USSR (sub); (with Newcastle U), 1994 v D, Gr, N; 1995 v Ng, Ei, U, J, Se (57)

Beasant, D. J. (Chelsea), 1990 v I (sub), Y (sub) (2)

Beasley, A. (Huddersfield T), 1939 v S (1)

Beats, W. E. (Wolverhampton W), 1901 v W; 1902 v S (2)

Beattie, T. K. (Ipswich T), 1975 v Cy (2), S; 1976 v Sw, P; 1977 v Fi, I (sub), Ho; 1978 v L (sub) (9)

Becton, F. (Preston NE), 1895 v Ni; (with Liverpool), 1897 v W (2)

Bedford, H. (Blackpool), 1923 v Se; 1925 v Ni (2)

Bell, C. (Manchester C), 1968 v Se, WG; 1969 v W, Bul, F, U, Br; 1970 v Ni (sub), Ho (2), P, Br (sub), Cz, WG (sub); 1972 v Gr, WG (2), W, Ni, S; 1973 v W (3), Y, S (2), Ni, Cz, Pol; 1974 v A, Pol, I, W, Ni, S, Arg, EG, Bul, Y; 1975 v Cz, P, WG, Cy (2), Ni, S; 1976 v Sw, Cy (48)

Bennett, W. (Sheffield U), 1901 v S, W (2)

Benson, R. W. (Sheffield U), 1913 v Ni (1)

Bentley, R. T. F. (Chelsea), 1949 v Se; 1950 v S, P, Bel, Ch, USA; 1953 v W, Bel; 1955 v W, WG, Sp, P (12)

Beresford, J. (Aston Villa), 1934 v Cz (1)

Berry, A. (Oxford University), 190[illegible] Ni (1)

Berry, J. J. (Manchester U), 1953 v Arg, Ch, U; 1956 v Se (4)

Bestall, J. G. (Grimsby T), 1935 v Ni (1)

Betmead, H. A. (Grimsby T), 1937 v Fi (1)

Betts, M. P. (Old Harrovians), 1877 v S (1)

Betts, W. (Sheffield W), 1889 v W (1)

Beverley, J. (Blackburn R), 1884 v S, W, Ni (3)

Birkett, R. H. (Clapham Rovers), 1879 v S (1)

Birkett, R. J. E. (Middlesbrough), 1936 v Ni (1)

Birley, F. H. (Oxford University), 1874 v S; (with Wanderers), 1875 v S (2)

Birtles, G. (Nottingham F), 1980 v Arg (sub), I; 1981 v R (3)

Bishop, S. M. (Leicester C), 1927 v S, Bel, L, F (4)

Blackburn, F. (Blackburn R), 1901 v S; 1902 v Ni; 1904 v S (3)

Blackburn, G. F. (Aston Villa), 1924 v F (1)

Blenkinsop, E. (Sheffield W), 1928 v F, Bel; 1929 v S, W, Ni, F, Bel, Sp; 1930 v S, W, Ni, G, A; 1931 v S, W, Ni, F, Bel; 1932 v S, W, Ni, Sp; 1933 v S, W, Ni, A (26)

Bliss, H. (Tottenham H), 1921 v S (1)

Blissett, L. (Watford), 1983 v WG (sub), L, W, Gr (sub), H, Ni, S (sub), Aus (1+1 sub); (with AC Milan), 1984 v D (sub), H, W (sub), S, USSR (14)

Blockley, J. P. (Arsenal), 1973 v Y (1)

Bloomer, S. (Derby Co), 1895 v S, Ni; 1896 v W, Ni; 1897 v S, W, Ni; 1898 v S; 1899 v S, W, Ni; 1900 v S; 1901 v S, W; 1902 v S, W, Ni; 1904 v S; 1905 v S, W, Ni; (with Middlesbrough), 1907 v S, W (23)

Blunstone, F. (Chelsea), 1955 v W, S, F, P; 1957 v Y (5)

Bond, R. (Preston NE), 1905 v Ni, W; 1906 v S, W, Ni; (with Bradford C), 1910 v S, W, Ni (8)

Bonetti, P. P. (Chelsea), 1966 v D; 1967 v Sp, A; 1968 v Sp; 1970 v Ho, P, WG (7)

Bonsor, A. G. (Wanderers), 1873 v S; 1875 v S (2)

Booth, F. (Manchester C), 1905 v Ni (1)

Booth, T. (Blackburn R), 1898 v W; (with Everton), 1903 v S (2)

Bould, S. A. (Arsenal), 1994 v Gr, N (2)

Bowden, E. R. (Arsenal), 1935 v W, I; 1936 v W, Ni, A; 1937 v H (6)

Bower, A. G. (Corinthians), 1924 v Ni, Bel; 1925 v W, Bel; 1927 v W (5)

Bowers, J. W. (Derby Co), 1934 v S, Ni, W (3)

Bowles, S. (QPR), 1974 v P, W, Ni; 1977 v I, Ho (5)

Bowser, S. (WBA), 1920 v Ni (1)

Boyer, P. J. (Norwich C), 1976 v W (1)

Boyes, W. (WBA), 1935 v Ho; (with Everton), 1939 v W, R of E (3)

Boyle, T. W. (Burnley), 1913 v Ni (1)

Brabrook, P. (Chelsea), 1958 v USSR; 1959 v Ni; 1960 v Sp (3)

Bracewell, P. W. (Everton), 1985 v WG (sub), US; 1986 v Ni (3)

Bradford, G. R. W. (Bristol R), 1956 v D (1)

Bradford, J. (Birmingham), 1924 v Ni; 1925 v Bel; 1928 v S; 1929 v Ni, W, F, Sp; 1930 v S, Ni, G, A; 1931 v W (12)

Bradley, W. (Manchester U), 1959 v I, US, M (sub) (3)

Bradshaw, F. (Sheffield W), 1908 v A (1)
Bradshaw, T. H. (Liverpool), 1897 v Ni (1)
Bradshaw, W. (Blackburn R), 1910 v W, Ni; 1912 v Ni; 1913 v W (4)
Brann, G. (Swifts), 1886 v S, W; 1891 v W (3)
Brawn, W. F. (Aston Villa), 1904 v W, Ni (2)
Bray, J. (Manchester C), 1935 v W; 1936 v S, W, Ni, G; 1937 v S (6)
Brayshaw, E. (Sheffield W), 1887 v Ni (1)
Bridges, B. J. (Chelsea), 1965 v S, H, Y; 1966 v A (4)
Bridgett, A. (Sunderland), 1905 v S; 1908 v S, A (2), H, B; 1909 v Ni, W, H (2), A (11)
Brindle, T. (Darwen), 1880 v S, W (2)
Brittleton, J. T. (Sheffield W), 1912 v S, W, Ni; 1913 v S; 1914 v W (5)
Britton, C. S. (Everton), 1935 v S, W, Ni, I; 1937 v S, Ni, H, N, Se (9)
Broadbent, P. F. (Wolverhampton W), 1958 v USSR; 1959 v S, W, Ni, I, Br; 1960 v S (7)
Broadis, I. A. (Manchester C), 1952 v S, A, I; 1953 v S, Arg, Ch, U, US; (with Newcastle U), 1954 v S, H, Y, Bel, Sw, U (14)
Brockbank, J. (Cambridge University), 1872 v S (1)
Brodie, J. B. (Wolverhampton W), 1889 v S, Ni; 1891 v Ni (3)
Bromilow, T. G. (Liverpool), 1921 v W; 1922 v S, W; 1923 v Bel; 1926 v Ni (5)
Bromley-Davenport, W. E. (Oxford University), 1884 v S, W (2)
Brook, E. F. (Manchester C), 1930 v Ni; 1933 v Sw: 1934 v S, W, Ni, F, H, Cz; 1935 v S, W, Ni, I; 1936 v S, W, Ni; 1937 v H; 1938 v W, Ni (18)
Brooking, T. D. (West Ham U), 1974 v P, Arg, EG, Bul, Y; 1975 v Cz (sub), P; 1976 v P, W, Br, I, Fi; 1977 v Ei, Fi, I, Ho, Ni, W; 1978 v I, WG, W, S (sub), H; 1979 v D, Ei, Ni, W (sub), S, Bul, Se (sub), A; 1980 v D, Ni, Arg (sub), W, Ni, S, Bel, Sp; 1981 v Sw, Sp, R, H; 1982 v H, S, Fi, Sp (sub) (47)
Brooks, J. (Tottenham H), 1957 v W, Y, D (3)
Broome, F. H. (Aston Villa), 1938 v G, Sw, F; 1939 v N, I, R, Y (7)
Brown, A. (Aston Villa), 1882 v S, W, Ni (3)
Brown, A. S. (Sheffield U), 1904 v W; 1906 v Ni (2)
Brown, A. (WBA), 1971 v W (1)
Brown, G. (Huddersfield T), 1927 v S, W, Ni, Bel, L, F; 1928 v W; 1929 v S; (with Aston Villa), 1933 v W (9)
Brown, J. (Blackburn R), 1881 v W; 1882 v Ni; 1885 v S, W, Ni (5)
Brown, J. H. (Sheffield W), 1927 v S, W, Bel, L, F; 1930 v Ni (6)
Brown, K. (West Ham U), 1960 v Ni (1)
Brown, W. (West Ham U), 1924 v Bel (1)
Bruton, J. (Burnley), 1928 v F, Bel; 1929 v S (3)
Bryant, W. I. (Clapton), 1925 v F (1)
Buchan, C. M. (Sunderland), 1913 v Ni; 1920 v W; 1921 v W, Bel; 1923 v F; 1924 v S (6)
Buchanan, W. S. (Clapham R), 1876 v S (1)
Buckley, F. C. (Derby Co), 1914 v Ni (1)
Bull, S. G. (Wolverhampton W), 1989 v S (sub), D (sub); 1990 v Y, Cz, D (sub), U (sub), Tun (sub), Ei (sub), Ho (sub), Eg, Bel (sub); 1991 v H, Pol (13)
Bullock, F. E. (Huddersfield T), 1921 v Ni (1)
Bullock, N. (Bury), 1923 v Bel; 1926 v W; 1927 v Ni (3)
Burgess, H. (Manchester C), 1904 v S, W, Ni; 1906 v S (4)
Burgess, H. (Sheffield W), 1931 v S, Ni, F, Bel (4)
Burnup, C. J. (Cambridge University), 1896 v S (1)
Burrows, H. (Sheffield W), 1934 v H, Cz; 1935 v Ho (3)
Burton, F. E. (Nottingham F), 1889 v Ni (1)
Bury, L. (Cambridge University), 1877 v S; (with Old Etonians), 1879 v W (2)
Butcher, T. (Ipswich T), 1980 v Aus; 1981 v Sp; 1982 v W, S, F, Cz, WG, Sp; 1983 v D, WG, L, W, Gr, H, Ni, S, Aus (3); 1984 v D, H, L, F, Ni; 1985 v EG, Fi, T, Ni, Ei, R, Fi, S, I, WG, US; 1986 v Is, USSR, S, M, Ca, P, Mor, Pol, Para, Arg; (with Rangers), 1987 v Se, Ni (2), Y, Sp, Br, S; 1988 v T, Y; 1989 v D, Se, Gr, Alb (2), Ch, S, Pol, D; 1990 v Se, Pol, I, Y, Br, Cz, D, U, Tun, Ei, Ho, Bel, Cam, WG (77)
Butler, J. D. (Arsenal), 1925 v Bel (1)
Butler, W. (Bolton W), 1924 v S (1)
Byrne, G. (Liverpool), 1963 v S; 1966 v N (2)
Byrne, J. J. (C Palace), 1962 v Ni; (with West Ham U), 1963 v Sw; 1964 v S, U, P (2), Ei, Br, Arg; 1965 v W, S (11)
Byrne, R. W. (Manchester U), 1954 v S, H, Y, Bel, Sw, U; 1955 v S, W, Ni, WG, F, Sp, P; 1956 v S, W, Ni, Br, Se, Fi, WG, D, Sp; 1957 v S, W, Ni, Y, D (2), Ei (2); 1958 v W, Ni, F (33)

Callaghan, I. R. (Liverpool), 1966 v Fi, F; 1978 v Sw, L (4)
Calvey, J. (Nottingham F), 1902 v Ni (1)
Campbell, A. F. (Blackburn R), 1929 v W, Ni; (with Huddersfield T), 1931 v W, S, Ni; 1932 v W, Ni, Sp (8)
Camsell, G. H. (Middlesbrough), 1929 v F, Bel; 1930 v Ni, W; 1934 v F; 1936 v S, G, A, Bel (9)
Capes, A. J. (Stoke C), 1903 v S (1)
Carr, J. (Middlesbrough), 1920 v Ni; 1923 v W (2)
Carr, J. (Newcastle U), 1905 v Ni; 1907 v Ni (2)
Carr, W. H. (Owlerton, Sheffield), 1875 v S (1)
Carter, H. S. (Sunderland), 1934 v S, H; 1936 v G; 1937 v S, Ni, H; (with Derby Co), 1947 v S, W, Ni, Ei, Ho, F, Sw (13)
Carter, J. H. (WBA), 1926 v Bel; 1929 v Bel, Sp (3)
Catlin, A. E. (Sheffield W), 1937 v W, Ni, H, N, Se (5)
Chadwick, A. (Southampton), 1900 v S, W (2)
Chadwick, E. (Everton), 1891 v S, W; 1892 v S; 1893 v S; 1894 v S; 1896 v Ni; 1897 v S (7)
Chamberlain, M (Stoke C), 1983 v L (sub); 1984 v D (sub), S, USSR, Br, U, Ch; 1985 v Fi (sub) (8)
Chambers, H. (Liverpool), 1921 v S, W, Bel; 1923 v S, W, Ni, Bel; 1924 v Ni (8)
Channon, M. R. (Southampton), 1973 v Y, S (2), Ni, W, Cz, USSR, I; 1974 v A, Pol, I, P, W, Ni, S, Arg, EG, Bul, Y; 1975 v Cz, P, WG, Cy (2), Ni (sub), W, S; 1976 v Sw, Cz, P, W, Ni, S, Br, I, Fi; 1977 v Fi, I, L, Ni, W, S, Br (sub), Arg, U; (with Manchester C), 1978 v Sw (46)
Charles, G. A. (Nottingham F), 1991 v Nz, Mal (2)
Charlton, J. (Leeds U), 1965 v S, H, Y, WG, Se; 1966 v W, Ni, S, A, Sp, Pol (2), WG (2), Y, Fi, D, U, M, F, Arg, P; 1967 v W, S, Ni, Cz; 1968 v W, Sp; 1969 v W, R, F; 1970 v Ho (2), P, Cz (35)
Charlton, R. (Manchester U), 1958 v S, P, Y; 1959 v S, W, Ni, USSR, I, Br, Pe, M, US; 1960 v W, S, Se, Y, Sp, H; 1961 v Ni, W, S, L, P, Sp, M, I, A; 1962 v W, Ni, S, A, Sw, Pe, L, P, H, Arg, Bul, Br; 1963 v S, F, Br, Cz, EG, Sw; 1964 v S, W, Ni, R of W, U, P, Ei, Br, Arg, US (sub); 1965 v Ni, S, Ho; 1966 v W, Ni, S, A, Sp, WG (2), Y, Fi, N, Pol, U, M, F, Arg, P; 1967 v Ni, W, S, Cz; 1968 v W, Ni, S, USSR (2), Sp (2), Se, Y; 1969 v S, W, Ni, R (2), Bul, M, Br; 1970 v W, Ni, Ho (2), P, Co, Ec, Cz, R, Br, WG (106)
Charnley, R. O. (Blackpool), 1963 v F (1)
Charsley, C. C. (Small Heath), 1893 v Ni (1)
Chedgzoy, S. (Everton), 1920 v W; 1921 v W, S, Ni; 1922 v Ni; 1923 v S; 1924 v W; 1925 v Ni (8)
Chenery, C. J. (C Palace), 1872 v S; 1873 v S; 1874 v S (3)
Cherry, T. J. (Leeds U), 1976 v W, S (sub), Br, Fi; 1977 v Ei, I, L, Ni, S (sub), Br, Arg, U; 1978 v Sw, L, I, Br, W; 1979 v Cz, W, Se; 1980 v Ei, Arg (sub), W, Ni, S, Aus, Sp (sub) (27)
Chilton, A. (Manchester U), 1951 v Ni; 1952 v F (2)
Chippendale, H. (Blackburn R), 1894 v Ni (1)

Chivers, M. (Tottenham H), 1971 v Ma (2), Gr, Ni, S; 1972 v Sw (1 + 1 sub), Gr, WG (2), Ni (sub), S; 1973 v W (3), S (2), Ni, Cz, Pol, USSR, I; 1974 v A, Pol (24)
Christian, E. (Old Etonians), 1879 v S (1)
Clamp, E. (Wolverhampton W), 1958 v USSR (2), Br, A (4)
Clapton, D. R. (Arsenal), 1959 v W (1)
Clare, T. (Stoke C), 1889 v Ni; 1892 v Ni; 1893 v W; 1894 v S (4)
Clarke, A. J. (Leeds U), 1970 v Cz; 1971 v EG, Ma, Ni, W (sub), S (sub); 1973 v S (2), W, Cz, Pol, USSR, I; 1974 v A, Pol, I; 1975 v P; 1976 v Cz, P (sub) (19)
Clarke, H. A. (Tottenham H), 1954 v S (1)
Clay, T. (Tottenham H), 1920 v W; 1922 v W, S, Ni (4)
Clayton, R. (Blackburn R), 1956 v Ni, Br, Se, Fi, WG, Sp; 1957 v S, W, Ni, Y, D (2), Ei (2); 1958 v S, W, Ni, F, P, Y, USSR; 1959 v S, W, Ni, USSR, I, Br, Pe, M, US; 1960 v W, Ni, S, Se, Y (35)
Clegg, J. C. (Sheffield W), 1872 v S (1)
Clegg, W. E. (Sheffield W), 1873 v S; (with Sheffield Albion), 1879 v W (2)
Clemence, R. N. (Liverpool), 1973 v W (2); 1974 v EG, Bul, Y; 1975 v Cz, P, WG, Cy, Ni, W, S; 1976 v Sw, Cz, P, W (2), Ni, S, Br, Fi; 1977 v Ei, Fi, I, Ho, L, S, Br, Arg, U; 1978 v Sw, L, I, WG, Ni, S; 1979 v D, Ei, Ni (2), S, Bul, A (sub); 1980 v D, Bul, Ei, Arg, W, S, Bel, Sp; 1981 v R, Sp, Br, Sw, H; (with Tottenham H), 1982 v N, Ni, Fi; 1983 v L; 1984 v L (61)
Clement, D. T. (QPR), 1976 v W (sub + 1), I; 1977 v I, Ho (5)
Clough, B. H. (Middlesbrough), 1960 v W, Se (2)
Clough, N. H. (Nottingham F), 1989 v Ch; 1991 v Arg (sub), Aus, Mal; 1992 v F, Cz, C; 1993 v Sp, T (sub), Pol (sub), N (sub), US, Br, G (14)
Coates, R. (Burnley), 1970 v Ni; 1971 v Gr (sub); (with Tottenham H), Ma, W (4)
Cobbold, W. N. (Cambridge University), 1883 v S, Ni; 1885 v S, Ni; 1886 v S, W; (with Old Carthusians), 1887 v S, W, Ni (9)
Cock, J. G. (Huddersfield T), 1920 v Ni; (with Chelsea), v S (2)
Cockburn, H. (Manchester U), 1947 v W, Ni, Ei; 1948 v S, I; 1949 v S, Ni, D, Sw, Se; 1951 v Arg, P; 1952 v F (13)
Cohen, G. R. (Fulham), 1964 v U, P, Ei, US, Br; 1965 v W, S, Ni, Bel, H, Ho, Y, WG, Se; 1966 v W, S, Ni, A, Sp, Pol (2), WG (2), N, D, U, M, F, Arg, P; 1967 v W, S, Ni, Cz, Sp; 1968 v W, Ni (37)
Cole, A. (Manchester U), 1995 v U (sub) (1)
Coleclough, H. (C Palace), 1914 v W (1)
Coleman, E. H. (Dulwich Hamlet), 1921 v W (1)
Coleman, J. (Woolwich Arsenal), 1907 v Ni (1)
Collymore, S. V. (Nottingham F), 1995 v J, Br (sub) (2)
Common, A. (Sheffield U), 1904 v W, Ni; (with Middlesbrough), 1906 v W (3)
Compton, L. H. (Arsenal), 1951 v W, Y (2)
Conlin, J. (Bradford C), 1906 v S (1)
Connelly, J. M. (Burnley), 1960 v W, N, S, Se; 1962 v W, A, Sw, P; 1963 v W, F; (with Manchester U), 1965 v H, Y, Se; 1966 v W, Ni, S, A, N, D, U (20)
Cook, T. E. R. (Brighton), 1925 v W (1)
Cooper, C. T. (Nottingham F), 1995 v Se, Br (2)
Cooper, N. C. (Cambridge University), 1893 v Ni (1)
Cooper, T. (Derby Co), 1928 v Ni; 1929 v W, Ni, S, F, Bel, Sp; 1931 v F; 1932 v W, Sp; 1933 v S; 1934 v S, H, Cz; 1935 v W (15)
Cooper, T. (Leeds U), 1969 v W, S, F, M; 1970 v Ho, Bel, Co, Ec, R, Cz, Br, WG; 1971 v EG, Ma, Ni, W, S; 1972 v Sw (2); 1975 v P (20)
Coppell, S. J. (Manchester U), 1978 v I, WG, Br, W, Ni, S, H; 1979 v D, Ei, Cz, Ni (2), W (sub), S, Bul, A; 1980 v D, Ni, Ei (sub), Sp, Arg, W, S, Bel, I; 1981 v R (sub), Sw, R, Br, W, S, Sw, H; 1982 v H, S, Fi, F, Cz, K, WG; 1983 v L, Gr (42)
Copping, W. (Leeds U), 1933 v I, Sw; 1934 v S, Ni, W, F; (with Arsenal), 1935 v Ni, I; 1936 v A, Bel; 1937 v N, Se, Fi; 1938 v S, W, Ni, Cz; 1939 v W, R of E; (with Leeds U), R (20)
Corbett, B. O. (Corinthians), 1901 v W (1)
Corbett, R. (Old Malvernians), 1903 v W (1)
Corbett, W. S. (Birmingham), 1908 v A, H, B (3)
Corrigan, J. T. (Manchester C), 1978 v I (sub), Br; 1979 v W; 1980 v Ni, Aus; 1981 v W, S; 1982 v W, Ic (9)
Cottee, A. R. (West Ham U), 1987 v Se (sub), Ni (sub); 1988 v H (sub); (with Everton) 1989 v D (sub), Se (sub), Ch (sub), S (7)
Cotterill, G. H. (Cambridge University), 1891 v Ni; (with Old Brightonians), 1892 v W; 1893 v S, Ni (4)
Cottle, J. R. (Bristol C), 1909 v Ni (1)
Cowan, S. (Manchester C), 1926 v Bel; 1930 v A; 1931 v Bel (3)
Cowans, G. (Aston Villa), 1983 v W, H, Ni, S, Aus (3); (with Bari), 1986 v Eg, USSR; (with Aston Villa), 1991 v Ei (10)
Cowell, A. (Blackburn R), 1910 v Ni (1)
Cox, J. (Liverpool), 1901 v Ni; 1902 v S; 1903 v S (3)
Cox, J. D. (Derby Co), 1892 v Ni (1)
Crabtree, J. W. (Burnley), 1894 v Ni; 1895 v Ni, S; (with Aston Villa), 1896 v W, S, Ni; 1899 v S, W, Ni; 1900 v S, W, Ni; 1901 v W; 1902 v W (14)
Crawford, J. F. (Chelsea), 1931 v S (1)
Crawford, R. (Ipswich T), 1962 v Ni, A (2)
Crawshaw, T. H. (Sheffield W), 1895 v Ni; 1896 v S, W, Ni; 1897 v S, W, Ni; 1901 v Ni; 1904 v W, Ni (10)
Crayston, W. J. (Arsenal), 1936 v S, W, G, A, Bel; 1938 v W, Ni, Cz (8)
Creek, F. N. S. (Corinthians), 1923 v F (1)
Cresswell, W. (South Shields), 1921 v W; (with Sunderland), 1923 v F; 1924 v Bel; 1925 v Ni; 1926 v W; 1927 v Ni; (with Everton), 1930 v Ni (7)
Crompton, R. (Blackburn R), 1902 v S, W, Ni; 1903 v S, W; 1904 v S, W, Ni; 1906 v S, W, Ni; 1907 v S, W, Ni; 1908 v S, W, Ni, A (2), H, B; 1909 v S, W, Ni, H (2), A; 1910 v S, W; 1911 v S, W, Ni; 1912 v S, W, Ni; 1913 v S, W, Ni; 1914 v S, W, Ni (41)
Crooks, S. D. (Derby Co), 1930 v S, G, A; 1931 v S, W, Ni, F, Bel; 1932 v S, W, Ni, Sp; 1933 v Ni, W, A; 1934 v S, Ni, W, F, H, Cz; 1935 v Ni; 1936 v S, W; 1937 v W, H (26)
Crowe, C. (Wolverhampton W), 1963 v F (1)
Cuggy, F. (Sunderland), 1913 v Ni; 1914 v Ni (2)
Cullis, S. (Wolverhampton W), 1938 v S, W, Ni, F, Cz; 1939 v S, Ni, R of E, N, I, R, Y (12)
Cunliffe, A. (Blackburn R), 1933 v Ni, W (2)
Cunliffe, D. (Portsmouth), 1900 v Ni (1)
Cunliffe, J. N. (Everton), 1936 v Bel (1)
Cunningham, L. (WBA), 1979 v W, Se, A (sub); (with Real Madrid), 1980 v Ei, Sp (sub); 1981 v R (sub) (6)
Curle, K. (Manchester C), 1992 v C (sub), H, D (3)
Currey, E. S. (Oxford University), 1890 v S, W (2)
Currie, A. W. (Sheffield U), 1972 v Ni; 1973 v USSR, I; 1974 v A, Pol, I; 1976 v Sw; (with Leeds U), 1978 v Br, W (sub), Ni, S, H (sub); 1979 v Cz, Ni (2), W, Se (17)
Cursham, A. W. (Notts Co), 1876 v S; 1877 v S; 1878 v S; 1879 v W; 1883 v S, W (6)
Cursham, H. A. (Notts Co), 1880 v W; 1882 v S, W, Ni; 1883 v S, W, Ni; 1884 v Ni (8)

Daft, H. B. (Notts Co), 1889 v Ni; 1890 v S, W; 1891 v Ni; 1892 v Ni (5)
Daley, A. M. (Aston Villa), 1992 v Pol (sub), C, H, Br, Fi (sub), D (sub), Se (7)
Danks, T. (Nottingham F), 1885 v S (1)
Davenport, P. (Nottingham F), 1985 v Ei (sub) (1)
Davenport, J. K. (Bolton W), 1885 v W; 1890 v Ni (2)
Davis, G. (Derby Co), 1904 v W, Ni (2)

Davis, H. (Sheffield W), 1903 v S, W, Ni (3)
Davison, J. E. (Sheffield W), 1922 v W (1)
Dawson, J. (Burnley), 1922 v S, Ni (2)
Day, S. H. (Old Malvernians), 1906 v Ni, W, S (3)
Dean, W. R. (Everton), 1927 v S, W, F, Bel, L; 1928 v S, W, Ni, F, Bel; 1929 v S, W, Ni; 1931 v S; 1932 v Sp; 1933 v Ni (16)
Deane, B. C. (Sheffield U), 1991 v Nz (sub + 1); 1993 v Sp (sub) (3)
Deeley, N. V. (Wolverhampton W), 1959 v Br, Pe (2)
Devey, J. H. G. (Aston Villa), 1892 v Ni; 1894 v Ni (2)
Devonshire, A. (West Ham U), 1980 v Aus (sub), Ni; 1982 v Ho, Ic; 1983 v WG, W, Gr; 1984 v L (8)
Dewhurst, F. (Preston NE), 1886 v W, Ni; 1887 v S, W, Ni; 1888 v S, W, Ni; 1889 v W (9)
Dewhurst, G. P. (Liverpool Ramblers), 1895 v W (1)
Dickinson, J. W. (Portsmouth), 1949 v N, F; 1950 v S, W, Ei, P, Bel, Ch, US, Sp; 1951 v Ni, W, Y; 1952 v W, Ni, S, A (2), I, Sw; 1953 v W, Ni, S, Bel, Arg, Ch, U, US; 1954 v W, Ni, S, R of E, H (2), Y, Bel, Sw, U; 1955 v Sp, P; 1956 v W, Ni, S, D, Sp; 1957 v W, Y, D (48)
Dimmock, J. H. (Tottenham H), 1921 v S; 1926 v W, Bel (3)
Ditchburn, E. G. (Tottenham H), 1949 v Sw, Se; 1953 v US; 1957 v W, Y, D (6)
Dix, R. W. (Derby Co), 1939 v N (1)
Dixon, J. A. (Notts Co), 1885 v W (1)
Dixon, K. M. (Chelsea), 1985 v M (sub), WG, US; 1986 v Ni, Is, M (sub), Pol (sub); 1987 v Se (8)
Dixon, L. M. (Arsenal), 1990 v Cz; 1991 v H, Pol, Ei (2), Cam, T, Arg; 1992 v G, T, Pol, Cz (sub); 1993 v Sp, N, T, Sm, T, Ho, N, US; 1994 v Sm (21)
Dobson, A. T. C. (Notts Co), 1882 v Ni; 1884 v S, W, Ni (4)
Dobson, C. F. (Notts Co), 1886 v Ni (1)
Dobson, J. M. (Burnley), 1974 v P, EG, Bul, Y; (with Everton), 1975 v Cz (5)
Doggart, A. G. (Corinthians), 1924 v Bel (1)
Dorigo, A. R. (Chelsea), 1990 v Y (sub), Cz (sub), D (sub), I; 1991 v H (sub), USSR; (with Leeds U), 1992 v G, Cz (sub), H, Br; 1993 v Sm, Pol, US, Br; 1994 v H (15)
Dorrell, A. R. (Aston Villa), 1925 v W, Bel, F; 1926 v Ni (4)
Douglas, B. (Blackburn R), 1958 v S, W, Ni, F, P, Y, USSR (2), Br, A; 1959 v S, USSR; 1960 v Y, H; 1961 v Ni, W, S, L, P, Sp, M, I, A; 1962 v W, Ni, S, Pe, L, P, H, Arg, Bul, Br; 1963 v S, Br, Sw (36)
Downs, R. W. (Everton), 1921 v Ni (1)
Doyle, M. (Manchester C), 1976 v W, S (sub), Br, I; 1977 v Ho (5)
Drake, E. J. (Arsenal), 1935 v Ni, I; 1936 v W; 1937 v H; 1938 v F (5)
Ducat, A. (Woolwich Arsenal), 1910 v S, W, Ni; (with Aston Villa), 1920 v S, W; 1921 v Ni (6)
Dunn, A. T. B. (Cambridge University), 1883 v Ni; 1884 v Ni; (with Old Etonians), 1892 v S, W (4)
Duxbury, M. (Manchester U), 1984 v L, F, W, S, USSR, Br, U, Ch; 1985 v EG, Fi (10)

Earle, S. G. J. (Clapton), 1924 v F; (with West Ham U), 1928 v Ni (2)
Eastham, G. (Arsenal), 1963 v Br, Cz, EG; 1964 v W, Ni, S, R of W, U, P, Ei, US, Br, Arg; 1965 v H, WG, Se; 1966 v Sp, Pol, D (19)
Eastham, G. R. (Bolton W), 1935 v Ho (1)
Eckersley, W. (Blackburn R), 1950 v Sp; 1951 v S, Y, Arg, P; 1952 v A (2), Sw; 1953 v Ni, Arg, Ch, U, US; 1954 v W, Ni, R of E, H (17)
Edwards, D. (Manchester U), 1955 v S, F, Sp, P; 1956 v S, Br, Se, Fi, WG; 1957 v S, Ni, Ei (2), D (2); 1958 v W, Ni, F (18)
Edwards, J. H. (Shropshire Wanderers), 1874 v S (1)
Edwards, W. (Leeds U), 1926 v S, W; 1927 v W, Ni, S, F, Bel, L; 1928 v S, F, Bel; 1929 v S, W, Ni; 1930 v W, Ni (16)
Ellerington, W. (Southampton), 1949 v N, F (2)
Elliott, G. W. (Middlesbrough), 1913 v Ni; 1914 v Ni; 1920 v W (3)
Elliott, W. H. (Burnley), 1952 v I, A; 1953 v Ni, W, Bel (5)
Evans, R. E. (Sheffield U), 1911 v S, W, Ni; 1912 v W (4)
Ewer, F. H. (Casuals), 1924 v F; 1925 v Bel (2)

Fairclough, P. (Old Foresters), 1878 v S (1)
Fairhurst, D. (Newcastle U), 1934 v F (1)
Fantham, J. (Sheffield W), 1962 v L (1)
Fashanu, J. (Wimbledon), 1989 v Ch, S (2)
Felton, W. (Sheffield W), 1925 v F (1)
Fenton, M. (Middlesbrough), 1938 v S (1)
Fenwick, T. (QPR), 1984 v W (sub), S, USSR, Br, U, Ch; 1985 v Fi, S, M, US; 1986 v R, T, Ni, Eg, M, P, Mor, Pol, Arg; (with Tottenham H), 1988 v Is (sub) (20)
Ferdinand, L. (QPR), 1993 v Sm, Ho, N, US; 1994 v Pol, Sm; 1995 v US (sub) (7)
Field, E. (Clapham Rovers), 1876 v S; 1881 v S (2)
Finney, T. (Preston NE), 1947 v W, Ni, Ei, Ho, F, P; 1948 v S, W, Ni, Bel, Se, I; 1949 v S, W, Ni, Se, N, F; 1950 v S, W, Ni, Ei, I, P, Bel, Ch, US, Sp; 1951 v W, S, Arg, P; 1952 v W, Ni, S, F, I, Sw, A; 1953 v W, Ni, S, Bel, Arg, Ch, U, US; 1954 v W, S, Bel, Sw, U, H, Y; 1955 v WG; 1956 v S, W, Ni, D, Sp; 1957 v S, W, Y, D (2), Ei (2); 1958 v W, S, F, P, Y, USSR (2); 1959 v Ni, USSR (76)
Fleming, H. J. (Swindon T), 1909 v S, H (2); 1910 v W, Ni; 1911 v W, Ni; 1912 v Ni; 1913 v S, W; 1914 v S (11)
Fletcher, A. (Wolverhampton W), 1889 v W; 1890 v W (2)
Flowers, R. (Wolverhampton W), 1955 v F; 1959 v S, W, I, Br, Pe, US, M (sub); 1960 v W, Ni, S, Se, Y, Sp, H; 1961 v Ni, W, S, L, P, Sp, M, I, A; 1962 v W, Ni, S, A, Sw, Pe, L, P, H, Arg, Bul, Br; 1963 v Ni, W, S, F (2), Sw; 1964 v Ei, US, P; 1965 v W, Ho, WG; 1966 v N (49)
Flowers, T. D. (Southampton), 1993 v Br; (with Blackburn R), 1994 v Gr; 1995 v Ng, U, J, Se, Br (7)
Forman, Frank (Nottingham F), 1898 v S, Ni; 1899 v S, W, Ni; 1901 v S; 1902 v S, Ni; 1903 v W (9)
Forman, F. R. (Nottingham F), 1899 v S, W, Ni (3)
Forrest, J. H. (Blackburn R), 1884 v W; 1885 v S, W, Ni; 1886 v S, W; 1887 v S, W, Ni; 1889 v S; 1890 v Ni (11)
Fort, J. (Millwall), 1921 v Bel (1)
Foster, R. E. (Oxford University), 1900 v W; (with Corinthians), 1901 v W, Ni, S; 1902 v W (5)
Foster, S. (Brighton & HA), 1982 v Ni, Ho, K (3)
Foulke, W. J. (Sheffield U), 1897 v W (1)
Foulkes, W. A. (Manchester U), 1955 v Ni (1)
Fox, F. S. (Millwall), 1925 v F (1)
Francis, G. C. J. (QPR), 1975 v Cz, P, W, S; 1976 v Sw, Cz, P, W, Ni, S, Br, Fi (12)
Francis, T. (Birmingham C), 1977 v Ho, L, S, Br; 1978 v Sw, L, I (sub), WG (sub), Br, W, S, H; (with Nottingham F), 1979 v Bul (sub), Se, A (sub); 1980 v Ni, Bul, Sp; 1981 v Sp, R, S (sub), Sw; (with Manchester C), 1982 v N, Ni, W, S (sub), Fi (sub), F, Cz, K, WG, Sp; (with Sampdoria), 1983 v D, Gr, H, Ni, S, Aus (3); 1984 v D, Ni, USSR; 1985 v EG (sub), T (sub), Ni (sub), R, Fi, S, I, M; 1986 v S (52)
Franklin, C. F. (Stoke C), 1947 v S, W, Ni, Ei, Ho, F, Sw, P; 1948 v S, W, Ni, Bel, Se, I; 1949 v S, W, Ni, D, Sw, N, F, Se; 1950 v W, S, Ni, Ei, I (27)
Freeman, B. C. (Everton), 1909 v S, W; (with Burnley), 1912 v S, W, Ni (5)
Froggatt, J. (Portsmouth), 1950 v Ni, I; 1951 v S; 1952 v S, A (2), I, Sw; 1953 v Ni, W, S, Bel, US (13)
Froggatt, R. (Sheffield W), 1953 v W, S, Bel, US (4)
Fry, C. B. (Corinthians), 1901 v Ni (1)
Furness, W. I. (Leeds U), 1933 v I (1)

Galley, T. (Wolverhampton W), 1937 v N, Se (2)
Gardner, T. (Aston Villa), 1934 v Cz; 1935 v Ho (2)
Garfield, B. (WBA), 1898 v Ni (1)
Garratty, W. (Aston Villa), 1903 v W (1)
Garrett, T. (Blackpool), 1952 v S, I; 1954 v W (3)
Gascoigne, P. J. (Tottenham H), 1989 v D (sub), S.Ar (sub), Alb (sub), Ch, S (sub); 1990 v Se (sub), Br (sub), Cz, D, U, Tun, Ei, Ho, Eg, Bel, Cam, WG; 1991 v H, Pol, Cam; (with Lazio), 1993 v N, T, Sm, T, Ho, Pol, N; 1994 v Pol, D; 1995 v J (sub), Se (sub), Br (sub) (32)
Gates, E. (Ipswich T), 1981 v N, R (2)
Gay, L. H. (Cambridge University), 1893 v S; (with Old Brightonians), 1894 v S, W (3)
Geary, F. (Everton), 1890 v Ni; 1891 v S (2)
Geaves, R. L. (Clapham Rovers), 1875 v S (1)
Gee, C. W. (Everton), 1932 v W, Sp; 1937 v Ni (3)
Geldard, A. (Everton), 1933 v I, Sw; 1935 v S; 1938 v Ni (4)
George, C. (Derby Co), 1977 v Ei (1)
George, W. (Aston Villa), 1902 v S, W, Ni (3)
Gibbins, W. V. T. (Clapton), 1924 v F; 1925 v F (2)
Gidman, J. (Aston Villa), 1977 v L (1)
Gillard, I. T. (QPR), 1975 v WG, W; 1976 v Cz (3)
Gilliat, W. E. (Old Carthusians), 1893 v Ni (1)
Goddard, P. (West Ham U), 1982 v Ic (sub) (1)
Goodall, F. R. (Huddersfield T), 1926 v S; 1927 v S, F, Bel, L; 1928 v S, W, F, Bel; 1930 v S, G, A; 1931 v S, W, Ni, Bel; 1932 v Ni; 1933 v W, Ni, A, I, Sw; 1934 v W, Ni, F (25)
Goodall, J. (Preston NE), 1888 v S, W; 1889 v S, W; (with Derby Co), 1891 v S, W; 1892 v S; 1893 v W; 1894 v S; 1895 v S, Ni; 1896 v S, W; 1898 v W (14)
Goodhart, H. C. (Old Etonians), 1883 v S, W, Ni (3)
Goodwyn, A. G. (Royal Engineers), 1873 v S (1)
Goodyer, A. C. (Nottingham F), 1879 v S (1)
Gosling, R. C. (Old Etonians), 1892 v W; 1893 v S; 1894 v W; 1895 v W, S (5)
Gosnell, A. A. (Newcastle U), 1906 v Ni (1)
Gough, H. C. (Sheffield U), 1921 v S (1)
Goulden, L. A. (West Ham U), 1937 v Se, N; 1938 v W, Ni, Cz, G, Sw, F; 1939 v S, W, R of E, I, R, Y (14)
Graham, L. (Millwall), 1925 v S, W (2)
Graham, T. (Nottingham F), 1931 v F; 1932 v Ni (2)
Grainger, C. (Sheffield U), 1956 v Br, Se, Fi, WG; 1957 v W, Ni; (with Sunderland), 1957 v S (7)
Gray, A. A. (C Palace), 1992 v Pol (1)
Greaves, J. (Chelsea), 1959 v Pe, M, US; 1960 v W, Se, Y, Sp; 1961 v Ni, W, S, L, P, Sp, I, A; (with Tottenham H), 1962 v S, Sw, Pe, H, Arg, Bul, Br; 1963 v Ni, W, S, F (2), Br, Cz, Sw; 1964 v W, Ni, R of W, P (2), Ei, Br, U, Arg; 1965 v Ni, S, Bel, Ho, H, Y; 1966 v W, A, Y, N, D, Pol, U, M, F; 1967 v S, Sp, A (57)
Green, F. T. (Wanderers), 1876 v S (1)
Green, G. H. (Sheffield U), 1925 v F; 1926 v S, Bel, W; 1927 v W, Ni; 1928 v F, Bel (8)
Greenhalgh, E. H. (Notts Co), 1872 v S; 1873 v S (2)
Greenhoff, B. (Manchester U), 1976 v W, Ni; 1977 v Ei, Fi, I, Ho, Ni, W, S, Br, Arg, U; 1978 v Br, W, Ni, S (sub), H (sub); (with Leeds U), 1980 v Aus (sub) (18)
Greenwood, D. H. (Blackburn R), 1882 v S, Ni (2)
Gregory, J. (QPR), 1983 v Aus (3); 1984 v D, H, W (6)
Grimsdell, A. (Tottenham H), 1920 v S, W; 1921 v S, Ni; 1923 v W, Ni (6)
Grosvenor, A. T. (Birmingham), 1934 v Ni, W, F (3)
Gunn, W. (Notts Co), 1884 v S, W (2)
Gurney, R. (Sunderland), 1935 v S (1)

Hacking, J. (Oldham Ath), 1929 v S, W, Ni (3)
Hadley, N. (WBA), 1903 v Ni (1)
Hagan, J. (Sheffield U), 1949 v D (1)
Haines, J. T. W. (WBA), 1949 v Sw (1)
Hall, A. E. (Aston Villa), 1910 v Ni (1)
Hall, G. W. (Tottenham H), 1934 v F; 1938 v S, W, Ni, Cz; 1939 v S, Ni, R of E, I, Y (10)
Hall, J. (Birmingham C), 1956 v S, W, Ni, Br, Se, Fi, WG, D, Sp; 1957 v S, W, Ni, Y, D (2), Ei (2) (17)
Halse, H. J. (Manchester U), 1909 v A (1)
Hammond, H. E. D. (Oxford University), 1889 v S (1)
Hampson, J. (Blackpool), 1931 v Ni, W; 1933 v A (3)
Hampton, H. (Aston Villa), 1913 v S, W; 1914 v S, W (4)
Hancocks, J. (Wolverhampton W), 1949 v Sw; 1950 v W; 1951 v Y (3)
Hapgood, E. (Arsenal), 1933 v I, Sw; 1934 v S, Ni, W, H, Cz; 1935 v S, Ni, W, I, Ho; 1936 v S, Ni, W, G, A, Bel; 1937 v Fi; 1938 v S, G, Sw, F; 1939 v S, W, Ni, R of E, N, I, Y (30)
Hardinge, H. T. W. (Sheffield U), 1910 v S (1)
Hardman, H. P. (Everton), 1905 v W; 1907 v S, Ni; 1908 v W (4)
Hardwick, G. F. M. (Middlesbrough), 1947 v S, W, Ni, Ei, Ho, F, Sw, P; 1948 v S, W, Ni, Bel, Se (13)
Hardy, H. (Stockport Co), 1925 v Bel (1)
Hardy, S. (Liverpool), 1907 v S, W, Ni; 1908 v S; 1909 v S, W, Ni, H (2), A; 1910 v S, W, Ni; 1912 v Ni; (with Aston Villa), 1913 v S; 1914 v Ni, W, S; 1920 v S, W, Ni (21)
Harford, M. G. (Luton T), 1988 v Is (sub); 1989 v D (2)
Hargreaves, F. W. (Blackburn R), 1880 v W; 1881 v W; 1882 v Ni (3)
Hargreaves, J. (Blackburn R), 1881 v S, W (2)
Harper, E. C. (Blackburn R), 1926 v S (1)
Harris, G. (Burnley), 1966 v Pol (1)
Harris, P. P. (Portsmouth), 1950 v Ei; 1954 v H (2)
Harris, S. S. (Cambridge University), 1904 v S; (with Old Westminsters), 1905 v Ni, W; 1906 v S, W, Ni (6)
Harrison, A. H. (Old Westminsters), 1893 v S, Ni (2)
Harrison, G. (Everton), 1921 v Bel; 1922 v Ni (2)
Harrow, J. H. (Chelsea), 1923 v Ni, Se (2)
Hart, E. (Leeds U), 1929 v W; 1930 v W, Ni; 1933 v S, A; 1934 v S, H, Cz (8)
Hartley, F. (Oxford C), 1923 v F (1)
Harvey, A. (Wednesbury Strollers), 1881 v W (1)
Harvey, J. C. (Everton), 1971 v Ma (1)
Hassall, H. W. (Huddersfield T), 1951 v S, Arg, P; 1952 v F; (with Bolton W), 1954 v Ni (5)
Hateley, M. (Portsmouth), 1984 v USSR (sub), Br, U, Ch; (with AC Milan), 1985 v EG (sub), Fi, Ni, Ei, Fi, S, I, M; 1986 v R, T, Eg, S, M, Ca, P, Mor, Para (sub); 1987 v T (sub), Br (sub), S; (with Monaco), 1988 v WG (sub), Ho (sub), H (sub), Co (sub), Ei (sub), Ho (sub), USSR (sub); (with Rangers), 1992 v Cz (32)
Haworth, G. (Accrington), 1887 v Ni, W, S; 1888 v S; 1890 v S (5)
Hawtrey, J. P. (Old Etonians), 1881 v S, W (2)
Hawkes, R. M. (Luton T), 1907 v Ni; 1908 v A (2), H, B (5)
Haygarth, E. B. (Swifts), 1875 v S (1)
Haynes, J. N. (Fulham), 1955 v Ni; 1956 v S, Ni, Br, Se, Fi, WG, Sp; 1957 v W, Y, D, Ei (2); 1958 v W, Ni, S, F, P, Y, USSR (3), Br, A; 1959 v S, Ni, USSR, I, Br, Pe, M, US; 1960 v Ni, Y, Sp, H; 1961 v Ni, W, S, L, P, Sp, M, I, A; 1962 v W, Ni, S, A, Sw, Pe, P, H, Arg, Bul, Br (56)
Healless, H. (Blackburn R), 1925 v Ni; 1928 v S (2)
Hector, K. J. (Derby Co), 1974 v Pol (sub), I (sub) (2)
Hedley, G. A. (Sheffield U), 1901 v Ni (1)
Hegan, K. E. (Corinthians), 1923 v Bel, F; 1924 v Ni, Bel (4)
Hellawell, M. S. (Birmingham C), 1963 v Ni, F (2)
Henfrey, A. G. (Cambridge University), 1891 v Ni; (with Corinthians), 1892 v W; 1895 v W; 1896 v S, W (5)
Henry, R. P. (Tottenham H), 1963 v F (1)
Heron, F. (Wanderers), 1876 v S (1)
Heron, G. H. H. (Uxbridge), 1873 v S; 1874 v S; (with Wanderers), 1875 v S; 1876 v S; 1878 v S (5)
Hibbert, W. (Bury), 1910 v S (1)

Hibbs, H. E. (Birmingham), 1930 v S, W, A, G; 1931 v S, W, Ni; 1932 v W, Ni, Sp; 1933 v S, W, Ni, A, I, Sw; 1934 v Ni, W, F; 1935 v S, W, Ni, Ho; 1936 v G, W (25)
Hill, F. (Bolton W), 1963 v Ni, W (2)
Hill, G. A. (Manchester U), 1976 v I; 1977 v Ei (sub), Fi (sub), L; 1978 v Sw (sub), L (6)
Hill, J. H. (Burnley), 1925 v W; 1926 v S; 1927 v S, Ni, Bel, F; 1928 v Ni, W; (with Newcastle U), 1929 v F, Bel, Sp (11)
Hill, R. (Luton T), 1983 v D (sub), WG; 1986 v Eg (sub) (3)
Hill, R. H. (Millwall), 1926 v Bel (1)
Hillman, J. (Burnley), 1899 v Ni (1)
Hills, A. F. (Old Harrovians), 1879 v S (1)
Hilsdon, G. R. (Chelsea), 1907 v Ni; 1908 v S, W, Ni, A, H, B; 1909 v Ni (8)
Hine, E. W. (Leicester C), 1929 v W, Ni; 1930 v W, Ni; 1932 v W, Ni (6)
Hinton, A. T. (Wolverhampton W), 1963 v F; (with Nottingham F), 1965 v W, Bel (3)
Hirst, D. E. (Sheffield W), 1991 v Aus, Nz (sub); 1992 v F (3)
Hitchens, G. A. (Aston Villa), 1961 v M, I, A; (with Inter-Milan), 1962 v Sw, Pe, H, Br (7)
Hobbis, H. H. F. (Charlton Ath), 1936 v A, Bel (2)
Hoddle, G. (Tottenham H), 1980 v Bul, W, Aus, Sp; 1981 v Sp, W, S; 1982 v N, Ni, W, Ic, Cz (sub), K; 1983 v L (sub), Ni, S; 1984 v H, L, F; 1985 v Ei (sub), S, I (sub), M, WG, US; 1986 v R, T, Ni, Is, USSR, S, M, Ca, P, Mor, Pol, Para, Arg; 1987 v Se, Ni, Y, Sp, T, S; (with Monaco), 1988 v WG, T (sub), Y (sub), Ho (sub), H (sub), Co (sub), Ei (sub), Ho, USSR (53)
Hodge, S. B. (Aston Villa), 1986 v USSR (sub), S, Ca, P (sub), Mor (sub), Pol, Para, Arg; 1987 v Se, Ni, Y; (with Tottenham H), Sp. Ni, T, S; (with Nottingham F), 1989 v D; 1990 v I (sub), Y (sub), Cz, D, U, Tun; 1991 v Cam (sub), T (sub) (24)
Hodgetts, D. (Aston Villa), 1888 v S, W, Ni; 1892 v S, Ni; 1894 v Ni (6)
Hodgkinson, A. (Sheffield U), 1957 v S, Ei (2), D; 1961 v W (5)
Hodgson, G. (Liverpool), 1931 v S, Ni, W (3)
Hodkinson, J. (Blackburn R), 1913 v W, S; 1920 v Ni (3)
Hogg, W. (Sunderland), 1902 v S, W, Ni (3)
Holdcroft, G. H. (Preston NE), 1937 v W, Ni (2)
Holden, A. D. (Bolton W), 1959 v S, I, Br, Pe, M (5)
Holden, G. H. (Wednesbury OA), 1881 v S; 1884 v S, W, Ni (4)
Holden-White, C. (Corinthians), 1888 v W, S (2)
Holford, T. (Stoke), 1903 v Ni (1)
Holley, G. H. (Sunderland), 1909 v S, W, H (2), A; 1910 v W; 1912 v S, W, NI; 1913 v S (10)
Holliday, E. (Middlesbrough), 1960 v W, Ni, Se (3)
Hollins, J. W. (Chelsea), 1967 v Sp (1)
Holmes, R. (Preston NE), 1888 v Ni; 1891 v S; 1892 v S; 1893 v S, W; 1894 v Ni; 1895 v Ni (7)
Holt, J. (Everton), 1890 v W; 1891 v S, W; 1892 v S, Ni; 1893 v S; 1894 v S, Ni; 1895 v S; (with Reading), 1900 v Ni (10)
Hopkinson, E. (Bolton W), 1958 v W, Ni, S, F, P, Y; 1959 v S, I, Br, Pe, M, US; 1960 v W, Se (14)
Hossack, A. H. (Corinthians), 1892 v W; 1894 v W (2)
Houghton, W. E. (Aston Villa), 1931 v Ni, W, F, Bel; 1932 v S, Ni; 1933 v A (7)
Houlker, A. E. (Blackburn R), 1902 v S; (with Portsmouth), 1903 v S, W; (with Southampton), 1906 v W, Ni (5)
Howarth, R. H. (Preston NE), 1887 v Ni; 1888 v S, W; 1891 v S; (with Everton), 1894 v Ni (5)
Howe, D. (WBA), 1958 v S, W, Ni, F, P, Y, USSR (3), Br, A; 1959 v S, W, Ni, USSR, I, Br, Pe, M, US; 1960 v W, Ni, Se (23)
Howe, J. R. (Derby Co), 1948 v I; 1949 v S, Ni (3)
Howell, L. S. (Wanderers), 1873 v S (1)
Howell, R. (Sheffield U), 1895 v Ni; (with Liverpool) 1899 v S (2)
Howey, S. N. (Newcastle U), 1995 v Ng (1)
Hudson, A. A. (Stoke C), 1975 v WG, Cy (2)
Hudson, J. (Sheffield), 1883 v Ni (1)
Hudspeth, F. C. (Newcastle U), 1926 v Ni (1)
Hufton, A. E. (West Ham U), 1924 v Bel; 1928 v S, Ni; 1929 v F, Bel, Sp (6)
Hughes, E. W. (Liverpool), 1970 v W, Ni, S, Ho, P, Bel; 1971 v EG, Ma (2), Gr, W; 1972 v Sw, Gr, WG (2), W, Ni, S; 1973 v W (3), S (2), Pol, USSR, I; 1974 v A, Pol, I, W, Ni, S, Arg, EG, Bul, Y; 1975 v Cz, P, Cy (sub), Ni; 1977 v I, L, W, S, Br, Arg, U; 1978 v Sw, L, I, WG, Ni, S, H; 1979 v D, Ei, Ni, W, Se; (with Wolverhampton W), 1980 v Sp (sub), Ni, S (sub) (62)
Hughes, L. (Liverpool), 1950 v Ch, US, Sp (3)
Hulme, J. H. A. (Arsenal), 1927 v S, Bel, F; 1928 v S, Ni, W; 1929 v Ni, W; 1933 v S (9)
Humphreys, P. (Notts Co), 1903 v S (1)
Hunt, G. S. (Tottenham H), 1933 v I, Sw, S (3)
Hunt, Rev K. R. G. (Leyton), 1911 v S, W (2)
Hunt, R. (Liverpool), 1962 v A; 1963 v EG; 1964 v S, US, P; 1965 v W; 1966 v S, Sp, Pol (2), WG (2), Fi, N, U, M, F, Arg, P; 1967 v Ni, W, Cz, Sp, A; 1968 v W, Ni, USSR (2), Sp (2), Se, Y; 1969 v R (2) (34)
Hunt, S. (WBA), 1984 v S (sub), USSR (sub) (2)
Hunter, J. (Sheffield Heeley), 1878 v S; 1880 v S, W; 1881 v S, W; 1882 v S, W (7)
Hunter, N. (Leeds U), 1966 v WG, Y, Fi, Sp (sub); 1967 v A; 1968 v Sp, Se, Y, WG, USSR; 1969 v R, W; 1970 v Ho, WG (sub); 1971 v Ma; 1972 v WG (2), W, Ni, S; 1973 v W (2) USSR (sub); 1974 v A, Pol, Ni (sub), S; 1975 v Cz (28)
Hurst, G. C. (West Ham U), 1966 v S, WG (2), Y, Fi, D, Arg, P; 1967 v Ni, W, S, Cz, Sp, A; 1968 v W, Ni, S, Se (sub), WG, USSR (2); 1969 v Ni, S, R (2), Bul, F, M, U, Br; 1970 v W, Ni, S, Ho (1+1 sub), Bel, Co, Ec, R, Br, WG; 1971 v EG, Gr, W, S; 1972 v Sw (2), Gr, WG (49)

Ince, P. E. C. (Manchester U), 1993 v Sp, N, T (2), Ho, Pol, US, Br, G; 1994 v Pol, Ho, Sm, D, N; 1995 v R, Ei (16)
Iremonger, J. (Nottingham F), 1901 v S; 1902 v Ni (2)

Jack, D. N. B. (Bolton W), 1924 v S, W; 1928 v F, Bel; (with Arsenal), 1930 v S, G, A; 1933 v W, A (9)
Jackson, E. (Oxford University), 1891 v W (1)
Jarrett, B. G. (Cambridge University), 1876 v S; 1877 v S; 1878 v S (3)
Jefferis, F. (Everton), 1912 v S, W (2)
Jezzard, B. A. G. (Fulham), 1954 v H; 1956 v Ni (2)
Johnson, D. E. (Ipswich T), 1975 v W, S; 1976 v Sw; (with Liverpool), 1980 v Ei, Arg, Ni, S, Bel (8)
Johnson, E. (Saltley College), 1880 v W; (with Stoke C), 1884 v Ni (2)
Johnson, J. A. (Stoke C), 1937 v N, Se, Fi, S, Ni (5)
Johnson, T. C. F. (Manchester C), 1926 v Bel; 1930 v W; (with Everton), 1932 v S, Sp; 1933 v Ni (5)
Johnson, W. H. (Sheffield U), 1900 v S, W, Ni; 1903 v S, W, Ni (6)
Johnston, H. (Blackpool), 1947 v S, Ho; 1951 v S; 1953 v Arg, Ch, U, US; 1954 v W, Ni, H (10)
Jones, A. (Walsall Swifts), 1882 v S, W; (with Great Lever), 1883 v S (3)
Jones, H. (Blackburn R), 1927 v S, Bel, L, F; 1928 v S, Ni (6)
Jones, H. (Nottingham F), 1923 v F (1)
Jones, M. D. (Sheffield U), 1965 v WG, Se; (with Leeds U), 1970 v Ho (3)
Jones, R. (Liverpool), 1992 v F; 1994 v Pol, Gr, N; 1995 v US, R, Ng, U (8)

Jones, W. (Bristol C), 1901 v Ni (1)
Jones, W. H. (Liverpool), 1950 v P, Bel (2)
Joy, B. (Casuals), 1936 v Bel (1)

Kail, E. I. L. (Dulwich Hamlet), 1929 v F, Bel, Sp (3)
Kay, A. H. (Everton), 1963 v Sw (1)
Kean, F. W. (Sheffield W), 1923 v S, Bel; 1924 v W; 1925 v Ni; 1926 v Ni, Bel; 1927 v L; (with Bolton W), 1929 v F, Sp (9)
Keegan, J. K. (Liverpool), 1973 v W (2); 1974 v W, Ni, Arg, EG, Bul, Y; 1975 v Cz, WG, Cy (2), Ni, S; 1976 v Sw, Cz, P, W (2), Ni, S, Br, Fi; 1977 v Ei, Fi, I, Ho, L; (with SV Hamburg), W, Br, Arg, U; 1978 v Sw, I, WG, Br, H; 1979 v D, Ei, Cz, Ni, W, S, Bul, Se, A; 1980 v D, Ni, Ei, Sp (2), Arg, Bel, I; (with Southampton), 1981 v Sp, Sw, H; 1982 v N, H, Ni, S, Fi, Sp (sub) (63)
Keen, E. R. L. (Derby Co), 1933 v A; 1937 v W, Ni, H (4)
Kelly, R. (Burnley), 1920 v S; 1921 v S, W, Ni; 1922 v S, W; 1923 v S; 1924 v Ni; 1925 v W, Ni, S; (with Sunderland), 1926 v W; (with Huddersfield T), 1927 v L; 1928 v S (14)
Kennedy, A. (Liverpool), 1984 v Ni, W (2)
Kennedy, R. (Liverpool), 1976 v W (2), Ni, S; 1977 v L, W, S, Br (sub), Arg (sub); 1978 v Sw, L; 1980 v Bul, Sp, Arg, W, Bel (sub), I (17)
Kenyon-Slaney, W. S. (Wanderers), 1873 v S (1)
Keown, M. R. (Everton), 1992 v F, Cz, C, H, Br, Fi, D, Fe, Se; (with Arsenal), 1993 v Ho, G (sub) (11)
Kevan, D. T. (WBA), 1957 v S; 1958 v W, Ni, S, P. Y, USSR (3), Br, A; 1959 v M, US; 1961 v M (14)
Kidd, B. (Manchester U), 1970 v Ni, Ec (sub) (2)
King, R. S. (Oxford University), 1882 v Ni (1)
Kingsford, R. K. (Wanderers), 1874 v S (1)
Kingsley, M. (Newcastle U), 1901 v W (1)
Kinsey, G. (Wolverhampton W), 1892 v W; 1893 v S; (with Derby Co), 1896 v W, Ni (4)
Kirchen, A. J. (Arsenal), 1937 v N, Se, Fi (3)
Kirton, W. J. (Aston Villa), 1922 v Ni (1)
Knight, A. E. (Portsmouth), 1920 v Ni (1)
Knowles, C. (Tottenham H), 1968 v USSR, Sp, Se, WG (4)

Labone, B. L. (Everton), 1963 v Ni, W, F; 1967 v Sp, A; 1968 v S, Sp, Se, Y, USSR, WG; 1969 v Ni, S, R, Bul, M, U, Br; 1970 v S, W, Bel, Co, Ec, R, Br, WG (26)
Lampard, F. R. G. (West Ham U), 1973 v Y; 1980 v Aus (2)
Langley, E. J. (Fulham), 1958 v S, P, Y (3)
Langton, R. (Blackburn R), 1947 v W, Ni, Ei, Ho, F, Sw; 1948 v Se; (with Preston NE), 1949 v D, Se; (with Bolton W), 1950 v S; 1951 v Ni (11)
Latchford, R. D. (Everton), 1978 v I, Br, W; 1979 v D, Ei, Cz (sub), Ni (2), W, S, Bul, A (12)
Latheron, E. G. (Blackburn R), 1913 v W; 1914 v Ni (2)
Lawler, C. (Liverpool), 1971 v Ma, W, S; 1972 v Sw (4)
Lawton, T. (Everton), 1939 v S, W, Ni, R of E, N, I, R, Y; (with Chelsea), 1947 v S, W, Ni, Ei, Ho, F, Sw, P; 1948 v W, Ni, Bel; (with Notts Co), 1948 v S, Se, I; 1949 v D (23)
Leach, T. (Sheffield W), 1931 v W, Ni (2)
Leake, A. (Aston Villa), 1904 v S, Ni; 1905 v S, W, Ni (5)
Lee, E. A. (Southampton), 1904 v W (1)
Lee, F. H. (Manchester C), 1969 v Ni, W, S, Bul, F, M, U; 1970 v W, Ho (2), P, Bel, Co, Ec, R, Br, WG; 1971 v EG, Gr, Ma, Ni, W, S; 1972 v Sw (2), Gr, WG (27)
Lee, J. (Derby Co), 1951 v Ni (1)
Lee, R. M. (Newcastle U), 1995 v R, Ng (2)
Lee, S. (Liverpool), 1983 v Gr, L, W, Gr, H, S, Aus; 1984 v D, H, L, F, Ni, W, Ch (sub) (14)
Leighton, J. E. (Nottingham F), 1886 v Ni (1)
Le Saux, G. P. (Blackburn R), 1994 v D, Gr, N; 1995 v US, R, Ng, Ei, U, Se, Br (10)
Le Tissier, M. P. (Southampton), 1994 v D (sub), Gr (sub), N (sub); 1995 v R, Ng (sub), Ei (6)
Lilley, H. E. (Sheffield U), 1892 v W (1)
Linacre, H. J. (Nottingham F), 1905 v W, S (2)
Lindley, T. (Cambridge University), 1886 v S, W, Ni; 1887 v S, W, Ni; 1888 v S, W, Ni; (with Nottingham F), 1889 v S; 1890 v S, W; 1891 v Ni (13)
Lindsay, A. (Liverpool), 1974 v Arg, EG, Bul, Y (4)
Lindsay, W. (Wanderers), 1877 v S (1)
Lineker, G. (Leicester C), 1984 v S (sub); 1985 v Ei, R (sub), S (sub), I (sub), WG, US; (with Everton), 1986 v R, T, Ni, Eg, USSR, Ca, P, Mor, Pol, Para, Arg; (with Barcelona), 1987 v Ni (2), Y, Sp, T, Br; 1988 v WG, T, Y, Ho, H, S, Co, Sw, Ei, Ho, USSR; 1989 v Se, S.Ar, Gr, Alb (2), Pol, D; (with Tottenham H) 1990 v Se, Pol, I, Y, Br, Cz, D, U, Tun, Ei, Ho, Eg, Bel, Cam, WG, I; 1991 v H, Pol, Ei (2), Cam, T, Arg, Aus, Nz, Mal; 1992 v G, T, Pol, F (sub), Cz (sub), C, H, Br, Fi, D, F, Se (80)
Lintott, E. H. (QPR), 1908 v S, W, Ni; (with Bradford C), 1909 v S, Ni, H (2) (7)
Lipsham, H. B. (Sheffield U), 1902 v W (1)
Little, B. (Aston Villa), 1975 v W (sub) (1)
Lloyd, L. V. (Liverpool), 1971 v W; 1972 v Sw, Ni; (with Nottingham F), 1980 v W (4)
Lockett, A. (Stoke C), 1903 v Ni (1)
Lodge, L. V. (Cambridge University), 1894 v W; 1895 v S, W; (with Corinthians), 1896 v S, Ni (5)
Lofthouse, J. M. (Blackburn R), 1885 v S, W, Ni; 1887 v S, W; (with Accrington), 1889 v Ni; (with Blackburn R), 1890 v Ni (7)
Lofthouse, N. (Bolton W), 1951 v Y; 1952 v W, Ni, S, A (2), I, Sw; 1953 v W, Ni, S, Bel, Arg, Ch, U, US; 1954 v W, Ni, R of E, Bel, U; 1955 v Ni, S, F, Sp, P; 1956 v W, S, Sp, D, Fi (sub); 1959 v W, USSR (33)
Longworth, E. (Liverpool), 1920 v S; 1921 v Bel; 1923 v S, W, Bel (5)
Lowder, A. (Wolverhampton W), 1889 v W (1)
Lowe, E. (Aston Villa), 1947 v F, Sw, P (3)
Lucas, T. (Liverpool), 1922 v Ni; 1924 v F; 1926 v Bel (3)
Luntley, E. (Nottingham F), 1880 v S, W (2)
Lyttelton, Hon. A. (Cambridge University), 1877 v S (1)
Lyttelton, Hon. E. (Cambridge University), 1878 v S (1)

McCall, J. (Preston NE), 1913 v S, W; 1914 v S; 1920 v S; 1921 v Ni (5)
McDermott, T. (Liverpool), 1978 v Sw, L; 1979 v Ni, W, Se; 1980 v D, Ni (sub), Ei, Ni, S, Bel (sub), Sp; 1981 v N, R, Sw, R (sub), Br, Sw (sub), H; 1982 v N, H, W (sub), Ho, S (sub), Ic (25)
McDonald, C. A. (Burnley), 1958 v USSR (3), Br, A; 1959 v W, Ni, USSR (8)
McFarland, R. L. (Derby Co), 1971 v Gr, Ma (2), Ni, S; 1972 v Sw, Gr, WG, W, S; 1973 v W (3), Ni, S, Cz, Pol, USSR, I; 1974 v A, Pol, I, W, Ni; 1976 v Cz, S; 1977 v Ei, I (28)
McGarry, W. H. (Huddersfield T), 1954 v Sw, U; 1956 v W, D (4)
McGuinness, W. (Manchester U), 1959 v Ni, M (2)
McInroy, A. (Sunderland), 1927 v Ni (1)
McMahon, S. (Liverpool), 1988 v Is, H, Co, USSR; 1989 v D (sub); 1990 v Se, Pol, I, Y (sub), Br, Cz (sub), D, Ei (sub), Eg, Bel, I; 1991 v Ei (17)
McManaman, S. (Liverpool), 1995 v Ng (sub), U (sub), J (sub) (3)
McNab, R. (Arsenal), 1969 v Ni, Bul, R (1 + 1 sub) (4)
McNeal, R. (WBA), 1914 v S, W (2)
McNeil, M. (Middlesbrough), 1961 v W, Ni, S, L, P, Sp, M, I; 1962 v L (9)
Mabbutt, G. (Tottenham H), 1983 v WG, Gr, L, W, Gr, H, Ni, S (sub); 1984 v H; 1987 v Y, Ni, T; 1988 v WG; 1992 v T, Pol, Cz (16)
Macaulay, R. H. (Cambridge University), 1881 v S (1)

Macdonald, M. (Newcastle U), 1972 v W, Ni, S (sub); 1973 v USSR (sub); 1974 v P, S (sub), Y (sub); 1975 v WG, Cy (2), Ni; 1976 v Sw (sub), Cz, P (14)
Macrae, S. (Notts Co), 1883 v S, W, Ni; 1884 v S, W, Ni (6)
Maddison, F. B. (Oxford University), 1872 v S (1)
Madeley, P. E. (Leeds U), 1971 v Ni; 1972 v Sw (2), Gr, WG (2), W, S; 1973 v S, Cz, Pol, USSR, I; 1974 v A, Pol, I; 1975 v Cz, P, Cy; 1976 v Cz, P, Fi; 1977 v Ei, Ho (24)
Magee, T. P. (WBA), 1923 v W, Se; 1925 v S, Bel, F (5)
Makepeace, H. (Everton), 1906 v S; 1910 v S; 1912 v S, W (4)
Male, C. G. (Arsenal), 1935 v S, Ni, I, Ho; 1936 v S, W, Ni, G, A, Bel; 1937 v S, Ni, H, N, Se, Fi; 1939 v I, R, Y (19)
Mannion, W. J. (Middlesbrough), 1947 v S, W, Ni, Ei, Ho, F, Sw, P; 1948 v W, Ni, Bel, Se, I; 1949 v N, F; 1950 v S, Ei, P, Bel, Ch, US; 1951 v Ni, W, S, Y; 1952 v F (26)
Mariner, P. (Ipswich T), 1977 v L (sub), Ni; 1978 v L, W (sub), S; 1980 v W, Ni (sub), S, Aus, I (sub), Sp (sub); 1981 v N, Sw, Sp, Sw, H; 1982 v N, H, Ho, S, Fi, F, Cz, K, WG, Sp; 1983 v D, WG, Gr, W; 1984 v D, H, L; (with Arsenal), 1985 v EG, R (35)
Marsden, J. T. (Darwen), 1891 v Ni (1)
Marsden, W. (Sheffield W), 1930 v W, S, G (3)
Marsh, R. W. (QPR), 1972 v Sw (sub); (with Manchester C), WG (sub+1), W, Ni, S; 1973 v W (2), Y (9)
Marshall, T. (Darwen), 1880 v W; 1881 v W (2)
Martin, A. (West Ham U), 1981 v Br, S (sub); 1982 v H, Fi; 1983 v Gr, L, W, Gr, H; 1984 v H, L, W; 1985 v Ni; 1986 v Is, Ca, Para; 1987 v Se (17)
Martin, H. (Sunderland), 1914 v Ni (1)
Martyn, A. N. (C Palace), 1992 v C (sub), H; 1993 v G (3)
Marwood, B. (Arsenal), 1989 v S.Ar (sub) (1)
Maskrey, H. M. (Derby Co), 1908 v Ni (1)
Mason, C. (Wolverhampton W), 1887 v Ni; 1888 v W; 1890 v Ni (3)
Matthews, R. D. (Coventry C), 1956 v S, Br, Se, WG; 1957 v Ni (5)
Matthews, S. (Stoke C), 1935 v W, I; 1936 v G; 1937 v S; 1938 v S, W, Cz, G, Sw, F; 1939 v S, W, Ni, R of E, N, I, Y; 1947 v S; (with Blackpool), 1947 v Sw, P; 1948 v S, W, Ni, Bel, I; 1949 v S, W, Ni, D, Sw; 1950 v Sp; 1951 v Ni, S; 1954 v Ni, R of E, H, Bel, U; 1955 v Ni, W, S, F, WG, Sp, P; 1956 v W, Br; 1957 v S, W, Ni, Y, D (2), Ei (54)
Matthews, V. (Sheffield U), 1928 v F, Bel (2)
Maynard, W. J. (1st Surrey Rifles), 1872 v S; 1876 v S (2)
Meadows, J. (Manchester C), 1955 v S (1)
Medley, L. D. (Tottenham H), 1951 v Y, W; 1952 v F, A, W, Ni (6)
Meehan, T. (Chelsea), 1924 v Ni (1)
Melia, J. (Liverpool), 1963 v S, Sw (2)
Mercer, D. W. (Sheffield U), 1923 v Ni, Bel (2)
Mercer, J. (Everton), 1939 v S, Ni, I, R, Y (5)
Merrick, G. H. (Birmingham C), 1952 v Ni, S, A (2), I, Sw; 1953 v Ni, W, S, Bel, Arg, Ch, U; 1954 v W, Ni, S, R of E, H (2), Y, Bel, Sw, U (23)
Merson, P. C. (Arsenal), 1992 v G (sub), Cz, H, Br (sub), Fi (sub), D, Se (sub); 1993 v Sp (sub), N (sub), Ho (sub), Br (sub), G; 1994 v Ho, Gr (14)
Metcalfe, V. (Huddersfield T), 1951 v Arg, P (2)
Mew, J. W. (Manchester U), 1921 v Ni (1)
Middleditch, B. (Corinthians), 1897 v Ni (1)
Milburn, J. E. T. (Newcastle U), 1949 v S, W, Ni, Sw; 1950 v W, P, Bel, Sp; 1951 v W, Arg, P; 1952 v F; 1956 v D (13)
Miller, B. G. (Burnley), 1961 v A (1)
Miller, H. S. (Charlton Ath), 1923 v Se (1)
Mills, G. R. (Chelsea), 1938 v W, Ni, Cz (3)
Mills, M. D. (Ipswich T), 1973 v Y; 1976 v W (2), Ni, S, Br, I (sub), Fi; 1977 v Fi (sub), I, Ni, W, S; 1978 v WG, Br, W, Ni, S, H; 1979 v D, Ei, Ni (2), S, Bul, A; 1980 v D, Ni, Sp (2); 1981 v Sw (2), H; 1982 v N, H, S, Fi, F, Cz, K, WG, Sp (42)
Milne, G. (Liverpool), 1963 v Br, Cz, EG; 1964 v W, Ni, S, R of W, U, P, Ei, Br, Arg; 1965 v Ni, Bel (14)
Milton, C. A. (Arsenal), 1952 v A (1)
Milward, A. (Everton), 1891 v S, W; 1897 v S, W (4)
Mitchell, C. (Upton Park), 1880 v W; 1881 v S; 1883 v S, W; 1885 v W (5)
Mitchell, J. F. (Manchester C), 1925 v Ni (1)
Moffat, H. (Oldham Ath), 1913 v W (1)
Molyneux, G. (Southampton), 1902 v S; 1903 v S, W, Ni (4)
Moon, W. R. (Old Westminsters), 1888 v S, W; 1889 v S, W; 1890 v S, W; 1891 v S (7)
Moore, H. T. (Notts Co), 1883 v Ni; 1885 v W (2)
Moore, J. (Derby Co), 1923 v Se (1)
Moore, R. F. (West Ham U), 1962 v Pe, H, Arg, Bul, Br; 1963 v W, Ni, S, F (2), Br, Cz, EG, Sw; 1964 v W, Ni, S, R of W, U, P (2), Ei, Br, Arg; 1965 v Ni, S, Bel, H, Y, WG, Se; 1966 v W, Ni, S, A, Sp, Pol (2), WG (2), N, D, U, M, F, Arg, P; 1967 v W, Ni, S, Cz, Sp, A; 1968 v W, Ni, S, USSR (2), Sp (2), Se, Y, WG; 1969 v Ni, W, S, R, Bul, F, M, U, Br; 1970 v W, Ni, S, Ho, P, Bel, Co, Ec, R, Br, Cz, WG; 1971 v EG, Gr, Ma, Ni, S; 1972 v Sw (2), Gr, WG (2), W, S; 1973 v W (3), Y, S (2), Ni, Cz, Pol, USSR, I; 1974 v I (108)
Moore, W. G. B. (West Ham U), 1923 v Se (1)
Mordue, J. (Sunderland), 1912 v Ni; 1913 v Ni (2)
Morice, C. J. (Barnes), 1872 v S (1)
Morley, A. (Aston Villa), 1982 v H (sub), Ni, W, Ic; 1983 v D, Gr (6)
Morley, H. (Notts Co), 1910 v Ni (1)
Morren, T. (Sheffield U), 1898 v Ni (1)
Morris, F. (WBA), 1920 v S; 1921 v Ni (2)
Morris, J. (Derby Co), 1949 v N, F; 1950 v Ei (3)
Morris, W. W. (Wolverhampton W), 1939 v S, Ni, R (3)
Morse, H. (Notts Co), 1879 v S (1)
Mort, T. (Aston Villa), 1924 v W, F; 1926 v S (3)
Morten, A. (C Palace), 1873 v S (1)
Mortensen, S. H. (Blackpool), 1947 v P; 1948 v W, S, Ni, Bel, Se, I; 1949 v S, W, Ni, Se, N; 1950 v S, W, Ni, I, P, Bel, Ch, US, Sp; 1951 v S, Arg; 1954 v R of E, H (25)
Morton, J. R. (West Ham U), 1938 v Cz (1)
Mosforth, W. (Sheffield W), 1877 v S; (with Sheffield Albion), 1878 v S; 1879 v S, W; 1880 v S, W; (with Sheffield W), 1881 v W; 1882 v S, W (9)
Moss, F. (Arsenal), 1934 v S, H, Cz; 1935 v I (4)
Moss, F. (Aston Villa), 1922 v S, Ni; 1923 v Ni; 1924 v S, Bel (5)
Mosscrop, E. (Burnley), 1914 v S, W (2)
Mozley, B. (Derby Co), 1950 v W, Ni, Ei (3)
Mullen, J. (Wolverhampton W), 1947 v S; 1949 v N, F; 1950 v Bel (sub), Ch, US; 1954 v W, Ni, S, R of E, Y, Sw (12)
Mullery, A. P. (Tottenham H), 1965 v Ho; 1967 v Sp, A; 1968 v W, Ni, S, USSR, Sp (2), Se, Y; 1969 v Ni, S, R, Bul, F, M, U, Br; 1970 v W, Ni, S (sub), Ho (sub), Bel, P, Co, Ec, R, Cz, WG, Br; 1971 v Ma, EG, Gr; 1972 v Sw (35)

Neal, P. G. (Liverpool), 1976 v W, I; 1977 v W, S, Br, Arg, U; 1978 v Sw, I, WG, Ni, S, H; 1979 v D, Ei, Ni (2), S, Bul, A; 1980 v D, Ni, Sp, Arg, W, Bel, I; 1981 v R, Sw, Sp, Br, H; 1982 v N, H, W, Ho, Ic, F (sub), K; 1983 v D, Gr, L, W, Gr, H, Ni, S, Aus (2); 1984 v D (50)
Needham, E. (Sheffield U), 1894 v S; 1895 v S; 1897 v S, W, Ni; 1898 v S, W; 1899 v S, W, Ni; 1900 v S, Ni; 1901 v S, W, Ni; 1902 v W (16)
Neville, G. A. (Manchester U), 1995 v J, Br (2)
Newton, K. R. (Blackburn R), 1966 v S, WG; 1967 v Sp, A; 1968 v W, S, Sp, Se, Y, WG; 1969 v Ni, W, S, R, Bul, M, U, Br, F; (with Everton), 1970 v Ni, S, Ho, Co, Ec, R, Cz, WG (27)

Nicholls, J. (WBA), 1954 v S, Y (2)
Nicholson, W. E. (Tottenham H), 1951 v P (1)
Nish, D. J. (Derby Co), 1973 v Ni; 1974 v P, W, Ni, S (5)
Norman, M. (Tottenham H), 1962 v Pe, H, Arg, Bul, Br; 1963 v S, F, Br, Cz, EG; 1964 v W, Ni, S, R of W, U, P (2), US, Br, Arg; 1965 v Ni, Bel, Ho (23)
Nuttall, H. (Bolton W), 1928 v W, Ni; 1929 v S (3)

Oakley, W. J. (Oxford University), 1895 v W; 1896 v S, W, Ni; (with Corinthians), 1897 v S, W, Ni; 1898 v S, W, Ni; 1900 v S, W, Ni; 1901 v S, W, Ni (16)
O'Dowd, J. P. (Chelsea), 1932 v S; 1933 v Ni, Sw (3)
O'Grady, M. (Huddersfield T), 1963 v Ni; (with Leeds U), 1969 v F (2)
Ogilvie, R. A. M. M. (Clapham R), 1874 v S (1)
Oliver, L. F. (Fulham), 1929 v Bel (1)
Olney, B. A. (Aston Villa), 1928 v F, Bel (2)
Osborne, F. R. (Fulham), 1923 v Ni, F; (with Tottenham H), 1925 v Bel; 1926 v Bel (4)
Osborne, R. (Leicester C), 1928 v W (1)
Osgood, P. L. (Chelsea), 1970 v Bel, R (sub), Cz (sub); 1974 v I (4)
Osman, R. (Ipswich T), 1980 v Aus; 1981 v Sp, R, Sw; 1982 v N, Ic; 1983 v D, Aus (3); 1984 v D (11)
Ottaway, C. J. (Oxford University), 1872 v S; 1874 v S (2)
Owen, J. R. B. (Sheffield), 1874 v S (1)
Owen, S. W. (Luton T), 1954 v H, Y, Bel (3)

Page, L. A. (Burnley), 1927 v S, W, Bel, L, F; 1928 v W, Ni (7)
Paine, T. L. (Southampton), 1963 v Cz, EG; 1964 v W, Ni, S, R of W, U, US, P; 1965 v Ni, H, Y, WG, Se; 1966 v W, A, Y, N, M (19)
Pallister, G. A. (Middlesbrough), 1988 v H; 1989 v S.Ar; (with Manchester U), 1991 v Cam (sub), T; 1992 v G; 1993 v N, US, Br, G; 1994 v Pol, Ho, Sm, D; 1995 v US, R, Ei, U, Se (18)
Palmer, C. L. (Sheffield W), 1992 v C, H, Br, Fi (sub), D, F, Se; 1993 v Sp (sub), N (sub), T, Sm, T, Ho, Pol, N, US, Br (sub); 1994 v Ho (18)
Pantling, H. H. (Sheffield U), 1924 v Ni (1)
Paravacini, P. J. de (Cambridge University), 1883 v S, W, Ni (3)
Parker, P. A. (QPR), 1989 v Alb (sub), Ch, D; 1990 v Y, U, Ho, Eg, Bel, Cam, WG, I; 1991 v H, Pol, USSR, Aus, Nz; (with Manchester U), 1992 v G; 1994 v Ho, D (19)
Parker, T. R. (Southampton), 1925 v F (1)
Parkes, P. B. (QPR), 1974 v P (1)
Parkinson, J. (Liverpool), 1910 v S, W (2)
Parr, P. C. (Oxford University), 1882 v W (1)
Parry, E. H. (Old Carthusians), 1879 v W; 1882 v W, S (3)
Parry, R. A. (Bolton W), 1960 v Ni, S (2)
Patchitt, B. C. A. (Corinthians), 1923 v Se (2) (2)
Pawson, F. W. (Cambridge University), 1883 v Ni; (with Swifts), 1885 v Ni (2)
Payne, J. (Luton T), 1937 v Fi (1)
Peacock, A. (Middlesbrough), 1962 v Arg, Bul; 1963 v Ni, W; (with Leeds U), 1966 v W, Ni (6)
Peacock, J. (Middlesbrough), 1929 v F, Bel, Sp (3)
Pearce, S. (Nottingham F), 1987 v Br, S; 1988 v WG (sub), Is, H; 1989 v D, Se, S.Ar, Gr, Alb (2), Ch, S, Pol, D; 1990 v Pol, I, Y, Br, Cz, D, U, Tun, Ei, Ho, Eg, Bel, Cam, WG; 1991 v H, Pol, Ei (2), Cam, T, Arg, Aus, Nz (2), Mal; 1992 v T, Pol, F, Cz, Br (sub), Fi, D, F, Se; 1993 v Sp, N, T; 1994 v Pol, Sm, Gr (sub); 1995 v R (sub), J, Br (59)
Pearson, H. F. (WBA), 1932 v S (1)
Pearson, J. H. (Crewe Alex), 1892 v Ni (1)
Pearson, J. S. (Manchester U), 1976 v W, Ni, S, Br, Fi; 1977 v Ei, Ho (sub), W, S, Br, Arg, U; 1978 v I (sub), WG, Ni (15)
Pearson, S. C. (Manchester U), 1948 v S; 1949 v S, Ni; 1950 v Ni, I; 1951 v P; 1952 v S, I (8)
Pease, W. H. (Middlesbrough), 1927 v W (1)
Pegg, D. (Manchester U), 1957 v Ei (1)
Pejic, M. (Stoke C), 1974 v P, W, Ni, S (4)
Pelly, F. R. (Old Foresters), 1893 v Ni; 1894 v S, W (3)
Pennington, J. (WBA), 1907 v S, W; 1908 v S, W, Ni, A; 1909 v S, W, H (2), A; 1910 v S, W; 1911 v S, W, Ni; 1912 v S, W, Ni; 1913 v S, W; 1914 v S, Ni; 1920 v S, W (25)
Pentland, F. B. (Middlesbrough), 1909 v S, W, H (2), A (5)
Perry, C. (WBA), 1890 v Ni; 1891 v Ni; 1893 v W (3)
Perry, T. (WBA), 1898 v W (1)
Perry, W. (Blackpool), 1956 v Ni, S, Sp (3)
Perryman, S. (Tottenham H), 1982 v Ic (sub) (1)
Peters, M. (West Ham U), 1966 v Y, Fi, Pol, M, F, Arg, P, WG; 1967 v Ni, W, S, Cz; 1968 v W, Ni, S, USSR (2), Sp (2), Se, Y; 1969 v Ni, S, R, Bul, F, M, U, Br; 1970 v Ho (2), P (sub), Bel; (with Tottenham H), W, Ni, S, Co, Ec, R, Br, Cz, WG; 1971 v EG, Gr, Ma (2), Ni, W, S; 1972 v Sw, Gr, WG (1 + 1 sub), Ni (sub); 1973 v S (2), Ni, W, Cz, Pol, USSR, I; 1974 v A, Pol, I, P, S (67)
Phelan, M. C. (Manchester U), 1990 v I (sub) (1)
Phillips, L. H. (Portsmouth), 1952 v Ni; 1955 v W, WG (3)
Pickering, F. (Everton), 1964 v US; 1965 v Ni, Bel (3)
Pickering, J. (Sheffield U), 1933 v S (1)
Pickering, N. (Sunderland), 1983 v Aus (1)
Pike, T. M. (Cambridge University), 1886 v Ni (1)
Pilkington, B. (Burnley), 1955 v Ni (1)
Plant, J. (Bury), 1900 v S (1)
Platt, D. (Aston Villa), 1990 v I (sub), Y (sub), Br, D (sub), Tun (sub), Ho (sub), Eg (sub), Bel (sub), Cam, WG, I; 1991 v H, Pol, Ei (2), T, USSR, Arg, Aus, Nz (2), Mal; (with Bari), 1992 v G, T, Pol, Cz, C, Br, Fi, D, F, Se; (with Juventus), 1993 v Sp, N, T, Sm, T, Ho, Pol, N, Br (sub), G; (with Sampdoria), 1994 v Pol, Ho, Sm, D, Gr, N; 1995 v US, Ng, Ei, U, J, Se, Br (55)
Plum, S. L. (Charlton Ath), 1923 v F (1)
Pointer, R. (Burnley), 1962 v W, L, P (3)
Porteous, T. S. (Sunderland), 1891 v W (1)
Priest, A. E. (Sheffield U), 1900 v Ni (1)
Prinsep, J. F. M. (Clapham Rovers), 1879 v S (1)
Puddefoot, S. C. (Blackburn R), 1926 v S, Ni (2)
Pye, J. (Wolverhampton W), 1950 v Ei (1)
Pym, R. H. (Bolton W), 1925 v S, W; 1926 v W (3)

Quantrill, A. (Derby Co), 1920 v S, W; 1921 v W, Ni (4)
Quixall, A. (Sheffield W), 1954 v W, Ni, R of E; 1955 v Sp, P (sub) (5)

Radford, J. (Arsenal), 1969 v R; 1972 v Sw (sub) (2)
Raikes, G. B. (Oxford University), 1895 v W; 1896 v W, Ni, S (4)
Ramsey, A. E. (Southampton), 1949 v Sw; (with Tottenham H), 1950 v S, I, P, Bel, Ch, US, Sp; 1951 v S, Ni, W, Y, Arg, P; 1952 v S, W, Ni, F, A (2), I, Sw; 1953 v Ni, W, S, Bel, Arg, Ch, U, US; 1954 v R of E, H (32)
Rawlings, A. (Preston NE), 1921 v Bel (1)
Rawlings, W. E. (Southampton), 1922 v S, W (2)
Rawlinson, J. F. P. (Cambridge University), 1882 v Ni (1)
Rawson, H. E. (Royal Engineers), 1875 v S (1)
Rawson, W. S. (Oxford University), 1875 v S; 1877 v S (2)
Read, A. (Tufnell Park), 1921 v Bel (1)
Reader, J. (WBA), 1894 v Ni (1)
Reaney, P. (Leeds U), 1969 v Bul (sub); 1970 v P; 1971 v Ma (3)
Reeves, K. (Norwich C), 1980 v Bul; (with Manchester C), Ni (2)
Regis, C. (WBA), 1982 v Ni (sub), W (sub), Ic; 1983 v WG; (with Coventry C), 1988 v T (sub) (5)

Reid, P. (Everton), 1985 v M (sub), WG, US (sub); 1986 v R, S (sub), Ca (sub), Pol, Para, Arg; 1987 v Br; 1988 v WG, Y (sub), Sw (sub) (13)
Revie, D. G. (Manchester C), 1955 v Ni, S, F; 1956 v W, D; 1957 v Ni (6)
Reynolds, J. (WBA), 1892 v S; 1893 v S, W; (with Aston Villa), 1894 v S, Ni; 1895 v S; 1897 v S, W (8)
Richards, C. H. (Nottingham F), 1898 v Ni (1)
Richards, G. H. (Derby Co), 1909 v A (1)
Richards, J. P. (Wolverhampton W), 1973 v Ni (1)
Richardson, J. R. (Newcastle U), 1933 v I, Sw (2)
Richardson, K. (Aston Villa), 1994 v Gr (1)
Richardson, W. G. (WBA), 1935 v Ho (1)
Rickaby, S. (WBA), 1954 v Ni (1)
Rigby, A. (Blackburn R), 1927 v S, Bel, L, F; 1928 v W (5)
Rimmer, E. J. (Sheffield W), 1930 v S, G, A; 1932 v Sp (4)
Rimmer, J. J. (Arsenal), 1976 v I (1)
Ripley, S. E. (Blackburn R), 1994 v Sm (1)
Rix, G. (Arsenal), 1981 v N, R, Sw (sub), Br, W, S; 1982 v Ho (sub), Fi (sub), F, Cz, K, WG, Sp; 1983 v D, WG (sub), Gr (sub); 1984 v Ni (17)
Robb, G. (Tottenham H), 1954 v H (1)
Roberts, C. (Manchester U), 1905 v Ni, W, S (3)
Roberts, F. (Manchester C), 1925 v S, W, Bel, F (4)
Roberts, G. (Tottenham H), 1983 v Ni, S; 1984 v F, Ni, S, USSR (6)
Roberts, H. (Arsenal), 1931 v S (1)
Roberts, H. (Millwall), 1931 v Bel (1)
Roberts, R. (WBA), 1887 v S; 1888 v Ni; 1890 v Ni (3)
Roberts, W. T. (Preston NE), 1924 v W, Bel (2)
Robinson, J. (Sheffield W), 1937 v Fi; 1938 v G, Sw; 1939 v W (4)
Robinson, J. W. (Derby Co), 1897 v S, Ni; (with New Brighton Tower), 1898 v S, W, Ni; (with Southampton), 1899 v W, S; 1900 v S, W, Ni; 1901 v Ni (11)
Robson, B. (WBA), 1980 v Ei, Aus; 1981 v N, R, Sw, Sp, R, Br, W, S, Sw, H; 1982 v N; (with Manchester U), H, Ni, W, Ho, S, Fi, F, Cz, WG, Sp; 1983 v D, Gr, L, S; 1984 v H, L, F, Ni, S, USSR, Br, U, Ch; 1985 v EG, Fi, T, Ei, R, Fi, S, M, I, WG, US; 1986 v R, T, Is, M, P, Mor; 1987 v Ni (2), Sp, T, Br, S; 1988 v T, Y, Ho, H, S, Co, Sw, Ei, Ho, USSR; 1989 v S, Se, S.Ar, Gr, Alb (2), Ch, S, Pol, D; 1990 v Pol, I, Y, Cz, U, Tun, Ei, Ho; 1991 v Cam, Ei; 1992 v T (90)
Robson, R. (WBA), 1958 v F, USSR (2), Br, A; 1960 v Sp, H; 1961 v Ni, W, S, L, P, Sp, M, I; 1962 v W, Ni, Sw, L, P (20)
Rocastle, D. (Arsenal), 1989 v D, S.Ar, Gr, Alb (2), Pol (sub), D; 1990 v Se (sub), Pol, Y, D (sub); 1992 v Pol, Cz, Br (sub) (14)
Rose, W. C. (Wolverhampton W), 1884 v S, W, Ni; (with Preston NE), 1886 v Ni; (with Wolverhampton W), 1891 v Ni (5)
Rostron, T. (Darwen), 1881 v S, W (2)
Rowe, A. (Tottenham H), 1934 v F (1)
Rowley, J. F. (Manchester U), 1949 v Sw, Se, F; 1950 v Ni, I; 1952 v S (6)
Rowley, W. (Stoke C), 1889 v Ni; 1892 v Ni (2)
Royle, J. (Everton), 1971 v Ma; 1973 v Y; (with Manchester C), 1976 v Ni (sub), I; 1977 v Fi, L (6)
Ruddlesdin, H. (Sheffield W), 1904 v W, Ni; 1905 v S (3)
Ruddock, N. (Liverpool), 1995 v Ng (1)
Ruffell, J. W. (West Ham U), 1926 v S; 1927 v Ni; 1929 v S, W, Ni; 1930 v W (6)
Russell, B. B. (Royal Engineers), 1883 v W (1)
Rutherford, J. (Newcastle U), 1904 v S; 1907 v S, Ni, W; 1908 v S, Ni, W, A (2), H, B (11)

Sadler, D. (Manchester U), 1968 v Ni, USSR; 1970 v Ec (sub); 1971 v EG (4)
Sagar, C. (Bury), 1900 v Ni; 1902 v W (2)
Sagar, E. (Everton), 1936 v S, Ni, A, Bel (4)
Salako, J. A. (C Palace), 1991 v Aus (sub), Nz (sub + 1), Mal; 1992 v G (5)
Sandford, E. A. (WBA), 1933 v W (1)
Sandilands, R. R. (Old Westminsters), 1892 v W; 1893 v Ni; 1894 v W; 1895 v W; 1896 v W (5)
Sands, J. (Nottingham F), 1880 v W (1)
Sansom, K. (C Palace), 1979 v W; 1980 v Bul, Ei, Arg, W (sub), Ni, S, Bel, I; (with Arsenal), 1981 v N, R, Sw, Sp, R, Br, W, S, Sw; 1982 v Ni, W, Ho, S, Fi, F, Cz, WG, Sp; 1983 v D, WG, Gr, L, Gr, H, Ni, S; 1984 v D, H, L, F, S, USSR, Br, U, Ch; 1985 v EG, Fi, T, Ni, Ei, R, Fi, S, I, M, WG, US; 1986 v R, T, Ni, Eg, Is, USSR, S, M, Ca, P, Mor, Pol, Para, Arg; 1987 v Se, Ni (2), Y, Sp, T; 1988 v WG, T, Y, Ho, S, Co, Sw, Ei, Ho, USSR (86)
Saunders, F. E. (Swifts), 1888 v W (1)
Savage, A. H. (C Palace), 1876 v S (1)
Sayer, J. (Stoke C), 1887 v Ni (1)
Scales, J. R. (Liverpool), 1995 v J, Se (sub), Br (3)
Scattergood, E. (Derby Co), 1913 v W (1)
Schofield, J. (Stoke C), 1892 v W; 1893 v W; 1895 v Ni (3)
Scott, L. (Arsenal), 1947 v S, W, Ni, Ei, Ho, F, Sw, P; 1948 v S, W, Ni, Bel, Se, I; 1949 v W, Ni, D (17)
Scott, W. R. (Brentford), 1937 v W (1)
Seaman, D. A. (QPR), 1989 v S.Ar, D (sub); 1990 v Cz (sub); (with Arsenal), 1991 v Cam, Ei, T, Arg; 1992 v Cz, H (sub); 1994 v Pol, Ho, Sm, D, N; 1995 v US, R, Ei (17)
Seddon, J. (Bolton W), 1923 v F, Se (2); 1924 v Bel; 1927 v W; 1929 v S (6)
Seed, J. M. (Tottenham H), 1921 v Bel: 1923 v W, Ni, Bel; 1925 v S (5)
Settle, J. (Bury), 1899 v S, W, Ni; (with Everton), 1902 v S, Ni; 1903 v Ni (6)
Sewell, J. (Sheffield W), 1952 v Ni, A, Sw; 1953 v Ni; 1954 v H (2) (6)
Sewell, W. R. (Blackburn R), 1924 v W (1)
Shackleton, L. F. (Sunderland), 1949 v W, D; 1950 v W; 1955 v W, WG (5)
Sharp, J. (Everton), 1903 v Ni; 1905 v S (2)
Sharpe, L. S. (Manchester U), 1991 v Ei (sub); 1993 v T (sub), N, US, Br, G; 1994 v Pol, Ho (8)
Shaw, G. E. (WBA), 1932 v S (1)
Shaw, G. L. (Sheffield U), 1959 v S, W, USSR, I; 1963 v W (5)
Shea, D. (Blackburn R), 1914 v W, Ni (2)
Shearer, A. (Southampton), 1992 v F, C, F; (with Blackburn R), 1993 v Sp, N, T; 1994 v Ho, D, Gr, N; 1995 v US, R, Ng, Ei, J, Se, Br (17)
Shellito, K. J. (Chelsea), 1963 v Cz (1)
Shelton A. (Notts Co), 1889 v Ni; 1890 v S, W; 1891 v S, W; 1892 v S (6)
Shelton, C. (Notts Rangers), 1888 v Ni (1)
Shepherd, A. (Bolton W), 1906 v S; (with Newcastle U), 1911 v Ni (2)
Sheringham, E. P. (Tottenham H), 1993 v Pol, N; 1995 v US, R (sub), Ng (sub), U, J (sub), Se, Br (9)
Shilton, P. L. (Leicester C), 1971 v EG, W; 1972 v Sw, Ni; 1973 v Y, S (2), Ni, W, Cz, Pol, USSR, I; 1974 v A, Pol, I, W, Ni, S, Arg; (with Stoke C), 1975 v Cy; 1977 v Ni, W; (with Nottingham F), 1978 v W, H; 1979 v Cz, Se, A; 1980 v Ni, Sp, I; 1981 v N, Sw, R; 1982 v H, Ho, S, F, Cz, K, WG, Sp; (with Southampton), 1983 v D, WG, Gr, W, Gr, H, Ni, S, Aus (3); 1984 v D, H, F, Ni, W, S, USSR, Br, U, Ch; 1985 v EG, Fi, T, Ni, R, Fi, S, I, WG; 1986 v R, T, Ni, Eg, Is, USSR, S, M, Ca, P, Mor, Pol, Para, Arg; 1987 v Se, Ni (2), Sp, Br; (with Derby Co), 1988 v WG, T, Y, Ho, S, Co, Sw, Ei, Ho; 1989 v D, Se, Gr, Alb (2), Ch, S, Pol, D; 1990 v Se, Pol, I, Y, Br, Cz, D, U, Tun, Ei, Ho, Eg, Bel, Cam, WG, I (125)
Shimwell, E. (Blackpool), 1949 v Se (1)
Shutt, G. (Stoke C), 1886 v Ni (1)

Silcock, J. (Manchester U), 1921 v S, W; 1923 v Se (3)
Sillett, R. P. (Chelsea), 1955 v F, Sp, P (3)
Simms, E. (Luton T), 1922 v Ni (1)
Simpson, J. (Blackburn R), 1911 v S, W, Ni; 1912 v S, W, Ni; 1913 v S; 1914 v W (8)
Sinton, A. (QPR), 1992 v Pol, C, H (sub), Br, F, Se; 1993 v Sp, T, Br, G; (with Sheffield W), 1994 v Ho (sub), Sm (12)
Slater, W. J. (Wolverhampton W), 1955 v W, WG; 1958 v S, P, Y, USSR (3), Br, A; 1959 v USSR; 1960 v S (12)
Smalley, T. (Wolverhampton W), 1937 v W (1)
Smart, T. (Aston Villa), 1921 v S; 1924 v S, W; 1926 v Ni; 1930 v W (5)
Smith, A. (Nottingham F), 1891 v S, W; 1893 v Ni (3)
Smith, A. K. (Oxford University), 1872 v S (1)
Smith, A. M. (Arsenal), 1989 v S.Ar (sub), Gr, Alb (sub), Pol (sub); 1991 v T, USSR, Arg; 1992 v G, T, Pol (sub), H (sub), D, Se (sub) (13)
Smith, B. (Tottenham H), 1921 v S; 1922 v W (2)
Smith, C. E. (C Palace), 1876 v S (1)
Smith, G. O. (Oxford University), 1893 v Ni; 1894 v W, S; 1895 v W; 1896 v Ni, W, S; (with Old Carthusians), 1897 v Ni, W, S; 1898 v Ni, W, S; (with Corinthians), 1899 v Ni, W, S; 1899 v Ni, W, S; 1901 v S (20)
Smith, H. (Reading), 1905 v W, S; 1906 v W, Ni (4)
Smith, J. (WBA), 1920 v Ni; 1923 v Ni (2)
Smith, Joe (Bolton W), 1913 v Ni; 1914 v S, W; 1920 v W, Ni (5)
Smith, J. C. R. (Millwall), 1939 v Ni, N (2)
Smith, J. W. (Portsmouth), 1932 v Ni, W, Sp (3)
Smith, Leslie (Brentford), 1939 v R (1)
Smith, Lionel (Arsenal), 1951 v W; 1952 v W, Ni; 1953 v W, S, Bel (6)
Smith, R. A. (Tottenham H), 1961 v Ni, W, S, L, P, Sp; 1962 v S; 1963 v S, F, Br, Cz, EG; 1964 v W, Ni, R of W (15)
Smith, S. (Aston Villa), 1895 v S (1)
Smith, S. C. (Leicester C), 1936 v Ni (1)
Smith, T. (Birmingham C), 1960 v W, Se (2)
Smith, T. (Liverpool), 1971 v W (1)
Smith, W. H. (Huddersfield T), 1922 v W, S; 1928 v S (3)
Sorby, T. H. (Thursday Wanderers, Sheffield), 1879 v W (1)
Southworth, J. (Blackburn R), 1889 v W; 1891 v W; 1892 v S (3)
Sparks, F. J. (Herts Rangers), 1879 v S; (with Clapham Rovers), 1880 v S, W (3)
Spence, J. W. (Manchester U), 1926 v Bel; 1927 v Ni (2)
Spence, R. (Chelsea), 1936 v A, Bel (2)
Spencer, C. W. (Newcastle U), 1924 v S; 1925 v W (2)
Spencer, H. (Aston Villa), 1897 v S, W; 1900 v W; 1903 v Ni; 1905 v W, S (6)
Spiksley, F. (Sheffield W), 1893 v S, W; 1894 v S, Ni; 1896 v Ni; 1898 v S, W (7)
Spilsbury, B. W. (Cambridge University), 1885 v Ni; 1886 v Ni, S (3)
Spink, N. (Aston Villa), 1983 v Aus (sub) (1)
Spouncer, W. A. (Nottingham F), 1900 v W (1)
Springett, R. D. G. (Sheffield W), 1960 v Ni, S, Y, Sp, H; 1961 v Ni, S, L, P, Sp, M, I, A; 1962 v W, Ni, S, A, Sw, Pe, L, P, H, Arg, Bul, Br; 1963 v Ni, W, F (2), Sw; 1966 v W, A, N (33)
Sproston, B. (Leeds U), 1937 v W; 1938 v S, W, Ni, Cz, G, Sw, F; (with Tottenham H), 1939 v W, R of E; (with Manchester C), N (11)
Squire, R. T. (Cambridge University), 1886 v S, W, Ni (3)
Stanbrough, M. H. (Old Carthusians), 1895 v W (1)
Staniforth, R. (Huddersfield T), 1954 v S, H, Y, Bel, Sw, U; 1955 v W, WG (8)
Starling, R. W. (Sheffield W), 1933 v S; (with Aston Villa), 1937 v S (2)
Statham, D. (WBA), 1983 v W, Aus (2) (3)
Steele, F. C. (Stoke C), 1937 v S, W, Ni, N, Se, Fi (6)
Stein, B. (Luton T), 1984 v F (1)
Stephenson, C. (Huddersfield T), 1924 v W (1)
Stephenson, G. T. (Derby Co), 1928 v F, Bel; (with Sheffield W), 1931 v F (3)
Stephenson, J. E. (Leeds U), 1938 v S; 1939 v Ni (2)
Stepney, A. C. (Manchester U), 1968 v Se (1)
Sterland, M. (Sheffield W), 1989 v S.Ar (1)
Steven, T. M. (Everton), 1985 v Ni, Ei, R, Fi, I, US (sub); 1986 v T (sub), Eg, USSR (sub), M (sub), Pol, Para, Arg; 1987 v Se, Y (sub), Sp (sub); 1988 v T, Y, Ho, H, S, Sw, Ho, USSR; 1989 v S; (with Rangers), 1990 v Cz, Cam (sub), WG (sub), I; 1991 v Cam; (with Marseille), 1992 v G, C, Br, Fi, D, F (36)
Stevens, G. A. (Tottenham H), 1985 v Fi (sub), T (sub), Ni; 1986 v S (sub), M (sub), Mor (sub), Para (sub) (7)
Stevens, M. G. (Everton), 1985 v I, WG; 1986 v R, T, Ni, Eg, Is, S, Ca, P, Mor, Pol, Para, Arg; 1987 v Br, S; 1988 v T, Y, Is, Ho, H (sub), S, Sw, Ei, Ho, USSR; (with Rangers), 1989 v D, Se, Gr, Alb (2), S, Pol; 1990 v Se, Pol, I, Br, D, Tun, Ei, I; 1991 v USSR; 1992 v C, H, Br, Fi (46)
Stewart, J. (Sheffield W), 1907 v S, W; (with Newcastle U), 1911 v S (3)
Stewart, P. A. (Tottenham H), 1992 v G (sub), Cz (sub), C (sub) (3)
Stiles, N. P. (Manchester U), 1965 v S, H, Y, Se; 1966 v W, Ni, S, A, Sp, Pol (2), WG (2), N, D, U, M, F, Arg, P; 1967 v Ni, W, S, Cz; 1968 v USSR; 1969 v R; 1970 v Ni, S (28)
Stoker, J. (Birmingham), 1933 v W; 1934 v S, H (3)
Storer, H. (Derby Co), 1924 v F; 1928 v Ni (2)
Storey, P. E. (Arsenal), 1971 v Gr, Ni, S; 1972 v Sw, WG, W, Ni, S; 1973 v W (3), Y, S (2), Ni, Cz, Pol, USSR, I (19)
Storey-Moore, I. (Nottingham F), 1970 v Ho (1)
Strange, A. H. (Sheffield W), 1930 v S, A, G; 1931 v S, W, Ni, F, Bel; 1932 v S, W, Ni, Sp; 1933 v S, Ni, A, I, Sw; 1934 v Ni, W, F (20)
Stratford, A. H. (Wanderers), 1874 v S (1)
Streten, B. (Luton T), 1950 v Ni (1)
Sturgess, A. (Sheffield U), 1911 v Ni; 1914 v S (2)
Summerbee, M. G. (Manchester C), 1968 v S, Sp, WG; 1972 v Sw, WG (sub), W, Ni; 1973 v USSR (sub) (8)
Sunderland, A. (Arsenal), 1980 v Aus (1)
Sutcliffe, J. W. (Bolton W), 1893 v W; 1895 v S, Ni; 1901 v S; (with Millwall), 1903 v W (5)
Swan, P. (Sheffield W), 1960 v Y, Sp, H; 1961 v Ni, W, S, L, P, Sp, M, I, A; 1962 v W, Ni, S, A, Sw, L, P (19)
Swepstone, H. A. (Pilgrims), 1880 v S; 1882 v S, W; 1883 v S, W, Ni (6)
Swift, F. V. (Manchester C), 1947 v S, W, Ni, Ei, Ho, F, Sw, P; 1948 v S, W, Ni, Bel, Se, I; 1949 v S, W, Ni, D, N (19)

Tait, G. (Birmingham Excelsior), 1881 v W (1)
Talbot, B. (Ipswich T), 1977 v Ni (sub), S, Br, Arg, U; (with Arsenal), 1980 v Aus (6)
Tambling, R. V. (Chelsea), 1963 v W, F; 1966 v Y (3)
Tate, J. T. (Aston Villa), 1931 v F, Bel; 1933 v W (3)
Taylor, E. (Blackpool), 1954 v H (1)
Taylor, E. H. (Huddersfield T), 1923 v S, W, Ni, Bel; 1924 v S, Ni, F; 1926 v S (8)
Taylor, J. G. (Fulham), 1951 v Arg, P (2)
Taylor, P. H. (Liverpool), 1948 v W, Ni, Se (3)
Taylor, P. J. (C Palace), 1976 v W (sub + 1), Ni, S (4)
Taylor, T. (Manchester U), 1953 v Arg, Ch, U; 1954 v Bel, Sw; 1956 v S, Br, Se, Fi, WG; 1957 v Ni, Y (sub), D (2), Ei (2); 1958 v W, Ni, F (19)
Temple, D. W. (Everton), 1965 v WG (1)
Thickett, H. (Sheffield U), 1899 v S, W (2)
Thomas, D. (Coventry C), 1983 v Aus (1 + 1 sub) (2)
Thomas, D. (QPR), 1975 v Cz (sub), P, Cy (sub + 1), W, S (sub); 1976 v Cz (sub), P (sub) (8)

Thomas, G. R. (C Palace), 1991 v T, USSR, Arg, Aus, Nz (2), Mal; 1992 v Pol, F (9)
Thomas, M. L. (Arsenal), 1989 v S.Ar; 1990 v Y (2)
Thompson, P. (Liverpool), 1964 v P (2), Ei, US, Br, Arg; 1965 v Ni, W, S, Bel, Ho; 1966 v Ni; 1968 v Ni, WG; 1970 v S, Ho (sub) (16)
Thompson, P. B. (Liverpool), 1976 v W (2), Ni, S, Br, I, Fi; 1977 v Fi; 1979 v Ei (sub), Cz, Ni, S, Bul, Se (sub), A; 1980 v D, Ni, Bul, Ei, Sp (2), Arg, W, S, Bel, I; 1981 v N, R, H; 1982 v N, H, W, Ho, S, Fi, F, Cz, K, WG, Sp; 1983 v WG, Gr (42)
Thompson T. (Aston Villa), 1952 v W; (with Preston NE), 1957 v S (2)
Thomson, R. A. (Wolverhampton W), 1964 v Ni, US, P, Arg; 1965 v Bel, Ho, Ni, W (8)
Thornewell, G. (Derby Co), 1923 v Se (2); 1924 v F; 1925 v F (4)
Thornley, I. (Manchester C), 1907 v W (1)
Tilson, S. F. (Manchester C), 1934 v H, Cz; 1935 v W; 1936 v Ni (4)
Titmuss, F. (Southampton), 1922 v W; 1923 v W (2)
Todd, C. (Derby Co), 1972 v Ni; 1974 v P, W, Ni, S, Arg, EG, Bul, Y; 1975 v P (sub), WG, Cy (2), Ni, W, S; 1976 v Sw, Cz, P, Ni, S, Br, Fi; 1977 v Ei, Fi, Ho (sub), Ni (27)
Toone, G. (Notts Co), 1892 v S, W (2)
Topham, A. G. (Casuals), 1894 v W (1)
Topham, R. (Wolverhampton W), 1893 v Ni; (with Casuals) 1894 v W (2)
Towers, M. A. (Sunderland), 1976 v W, Ni (sub), I (3)
Townley, W. J. (Blackburn R), 1889 v W; 1890 v Ni (2)
Townrow, J. E. (Clapton Orient), 1925 v S; 1926 v W (2)
Tremelling, D. R. (Birmingham), 1928 v W (1)
Tresadern, J. (West Ham U), 1923 v S, Se (2)
Tueart, D. (Manchester C), 1975 v Cy (sub), Ni; 1977 v Fi, Ni, W (sub), S (sub) (6)
Tunstall, F. E. (Sheffield U), 1923 v S; 1924 v S, W, Ni, F; 1925 v Ni, S (7)
Turnbull, R. J. (Bradford), 1920 v Ni (1)
Turner, A. (Southampton), 1900 v Ni; 1901 v Ni (2)
Turner, H. (Huddersfield T), 1931 v F, Bel (2)
Turner, J. A. (Bolton W), 1893 v W; (with Stoke C) 1895 v Ni; (with Derby Co) 1898 v Ni (3)
Tweedy, G. J. (Grimsby T), 1937 v H (1)

Ufton, D. G. (Charlton Ath), 1954 v R of E (1)
Underwood A. (Stoke C), 1891 v Ni; 1892 v Ni (2)
Unsworth, D. G. (Everton), 1995 v J (1)
Urwin, T. (Middlesbrough), 1923 v Se (2); 1924 v Bel; (with Newcastle U), 1926 v W (4)
Utley, G. (Barnsley), 1913 v Ni (1)

Vaughton, O. H. (Aston Villa), 1882 v S, W, Ni; 1884 v S, W (5)
Veitch, C. C. M. (Newcastle U), 1906 v S, W, Ni; 1907 v S, W; 1909 v W (6)
Veitch, J. G. (Old Westminsters), 1894 v W (1)
Venables, T. F. (Chelsea), 1965 v Ho, Bel (2)
Venison, B. (Newcastle U), 1995 v US, U (2)
Vidal, R. W. S. (Oxford University), 1873 v S (1)
Viljoen, C. (Ipswich T), 1975 v Ni, W (2)
Viollet, D. S. (Manchester U), 1960 v H; 1962 v L (2)
Von Donop (Royal Engineers), 1873 v S; 1875 v S (2)

Wace, H. (Wanderers), 1878 v S; 1879 v S, W (3)
Waddle, C. R. (Newcastle U), 1985 v Ei, R (sub), Fi (sub), S (sub), I, M (sub), WG, US; (with Tottenham H), 1986 v R, T, Ni, Is, USSR, S, M, Ca, P, Mor, Pol (sub), Arg (sub); 1987 v Se (sub), Ni (2), Y, Sp, T, Br, S; 1988 v WG, Is, H, S (sub), Co, Sw (sub), Ei, Ho (sub); 1989 v Se, S.Ar, Alb (2), Ch, S, Pol, D (sub); (with Marseille), 1990 v Se, Pol, I, Y, Br, D, U, Tun, Ei, Ho, Eg, Bel, Cam, WG, I (sub); 1991 v H (sub), Pol (sub); 1992 v T (62)
Wadsworth, S. J. (Huddersfield T), 1922 v S; 1923 v S, Bel; 1924 v S, Ni; 1925 v S, Ni; 1926 v W; 1927 v Ni (9)
Wainscoat, W. R. (Leeds U), 1929 v S (1)
Waiters, A. K. (Blackpool), 1964 v Ei, Br; 1965 v W, Bel, Ho (5)
Walker, D. S. (Nottingham F), 1989 v D (sub), Se (sub), Gr, Alb (2), Ch, S, Pol, D; 1990 v Se, Pol, I, Y, Br, Cz, D, U, Tun, Ei, Ho, Eg, Bel, Cam, WG, I; 1991 v H, Pol, Ei (2), Cam, T, Arg, Aus, Nz (2), Mal; 1992 v T, Pol, F, Cz, C, H, Br, Fi, D, F, Se; (with Sampdoria), 1993 v Sp, N, T, Sm, T, Ho, Pol, N, US (sub), Br, G; (with Sheffield W), 1994 v Sm (59)
Walden, F. I. (Tottenham H), 1914 v S; 1922 v W (2)
Walker, W. H. (Aston Villa), 1921 v Ni; 1922 v Ni, W, S; 1923 v Se (2); 1924 v S; 1925 v Ni, W, S, Bel, F; 1926 v Ni, W, S; 1927 v Ni, W; 1933 v A (18)
Wall, G. (Manchester U), 1907 v W; 1908 v Ni; 1909 v S; 1910 v W, S; 1912 v S; 1913 v Ni (7)
Wallace, C. W. (Aston Villa), 1913 v W; 1914 v Ni; 1920 v S (3)
Wallace, D. L. (Southampton), 1986 v Eg (1)
Walsh, P. (Luton T), 1983 v Aus (2 + 1 sub); 1984 v F, W (5)
Walters, A. M. (Cambridge University), 1885 v S, N; 1886 v S; 1887 v S, W; (with Old Carthusians), 1889 v S, W; 1890 v S, W (9)
Walters, K. M. (Rangers), 1991 v Nz (1)
Walters, P. M. (Oxford University), 1885 v S, Ni; (with Old Carthusians), 1886 v S, W, Ni; 1887 v S, W; 1888 v S, Ni; 1889 v S, W; 1890 v S, W (13)
Walton, N. (Blackburn R), 1890 v Ni (1)
Ward, J. T. (Blackburn Olympic), 1885 v W (1)
Ward, P. (Brighton & HA), 1980 v Aus (sub) (1)
Ward, T. V. (Derby Co), 1948 v Bel; 1949 v W (2)
Waring, T. (Aston Villa), 1931 v F, Bel; 1932 v S, W, Ni (5)
Warner, C. (Upton Park), 1878 v S (1)
Warren, B. (Derby Co), 1906 v S, W, Ni; 1907 v S, W, Ni; 1908 v S, W, Ni, A (2), H, B; (with Chelsea), 1909 v S, Ni, W, H (2), A; 1911 v S, Ni, W (22)
Waterfield, G. S. (Burnley), 1927 v W (1)
Watson, D. (Norwich C), 1984 v Br, U, Ch; 1985 v M, US (sub); 1986 v S; (with Everton), 1987 v Ni; 1988 v Is, Ho, S, Sw (sub), USSR (12)
Watson, D. V. (Sunderland), 1974 v P, S (sub), Arg, EG, Bul, Y; 1975 v Cz, P, WG, Cy (2), Ni, W, S; (with Manchester C), 1976 v Sw, Cz (sub), P; 1977 v Ho, L, Ni, W, S, Br, Arg, U; 1978 v Sw, L, I, WG, Br, W, Ni, S, H; 1979 v D, Ei, Cz, Ni (2), W, S, Bul, Se, A; (with Werder Bremen), 1980 v D; (with Southampton), Ni, Bul, Ei, Sp (2), Arg, Ni, S, Bel, I; 1981 v N, R, Sw, R, W, S, Sw, H; (with Stoke C), 1982 v Ni, Ic (65)
Watson, V. M. (West Ham U), 1923 v W, S; 1930 v S, G, A (5)
Watson, W. (Burnley), 1913 v S; 1914 v Ni; 1920 v Ni (3)
Watson, W. (Sunderland), 1950 v Ni, I; 1951 v W, Y (4)
Weaver, S. (Newcastle U), 1932 v S, 1933 v S, Ni (3)
Webb, G. W. (West Ham U), 1911 v S, W (2)
Webb, N. J. (Nottingham F), 1988 v WG (sub), T, Y, Is, Ho, S, Sw, Ei, USSR (sub); 1989 v D, Se, Gr, Alb (2), Ch, S, Pol, D; (with Manchester U), 1990 v Se, I (sub); 1992 v F, H, Br (sub), Fi, D (sub), Se (26)
Webster, M. (Middlesbrough), 1930 v S, A, G (3)
Wedlock, W. J. (Bristol C), 1907 v S, Ni, W; 1908 v S, Ni, W, A (2), H, B; 1909 v S, W, Ni, H (2), A; 1910 v S, W, Ni; 1911 v S, W, Ni; 1912 v S, W, Ni; 1914 v W (26)
Weir, D. (Bolton W), 1889 v S, Ni (2)
Welch, R. de C. (Wanderers), 1872 v S; (with Harrow Chequers), 1874 v S (2)
Weller, K. (Leicester C), 1974 v W, Ni, S, Arg (4)
Welsh, D. (Charlton Ath), 1938 v G, Sw; 1939 v R (3)

West, G. (Everton), 1969 v W, Bul, M (3)
Westwood, R. W. (Bolton W), 1935 v S, W, Ho; 1936 v Ni, G; 1937 v W (6)
Whateley, O. (Aston Villa), 1883 v S, Ni (2)
Wheeler, J. E. (Bolton W), 1955 v Ni (1)
Wheldon, G. F. (Aston Villa), 1897 v Ni; 1898 v S, W, Ni (4)
White, D. (Manchester C), 1993 v Sp (1)
White, T. A. (Everton), 1933 v I (1)
Whitehead, J. (Accrington), 1893 v W; (with Blackburn R), 1894 v Ni (2)
Whitfeld, H. (Old Etonians), 1879 v W (1)
Whitham, M. (Sheffield U), 1892 v Ni (1)
Whitworth, S. (Leicester C), 1975 v WG, Cy, Ni, W, S; 1976 v Sw, P (7)
Whymark, T. J. (Ipswich T), 1978 v L (sub) (1)
Widdowson, S. W. (Nottingham F), 1880 v S (1)
Wignall, F. (Nottingham F), 1965 v W, Ho (2)
Wilkes, A. (Aston Villa), 1901 v S, W; 1902 v S, W, Ni (5)
Wilkins, R. G. (Chelsea), 1976 v I; 1977 v Ei, Fi, Ni, Br, Arg, U; 1978 v Sw (sub), L, I, WG, W, Ni, S, H; 1979 v D, Ei, Cz, Ni, W, S, Bul, Se (sub), A; (with Manchester U), 1980 v D, Ni, Bul, Sp (2), Arg, W (sub), Ni, S, Bel, I; 1981 v Sp (sub), R, Br, W, S, Sw, H (sub); 1982 v Ni, W, Ho, S, Fi, F, Cz, K, WG, Sp; 1983 v D, WG; 1984 v D, Ni, W, S, USSR, Br, U, Ch; (with AC Milan), 1985 v EG, Fi, T, Ni, Ei, R, Fi, S, I, M; 1986 v T, Ni, Is, Eg, USSR, S, M, Ca, P, Mor; 1987 v Se, Y (sub) (84)
Wilkinson, B. (Sheffield U), 1904 v S (1)
Wilkinson, L. R. (Oxford University), 1891 v W (1)
Williams, B. F. (Wolverhampton W), 1949 v F; 1950 v S, W, Ei, I, P, Bel, Ch, US, Sp; 1951 v Ni, W, S, Y, Arg, P; 1952 v W, F; 1955 v S, WG, F, Sp, P; 1956 v W (24)
Williams, O. (Clapton Orient), 1923 v W, Ni (2)
Williams, S. (Southampton), 1983 v Aus (1 + 1 sub); 1984 v F; 1985 v EG, Fi, T (6)
Williams, W. (WBA), 1897 v Ni; 1898 v W, Ni, S; 1899 v W, Ni (6)
Williamson, E. C. (Arsenal), 1923 v Se (2) (2)
Williamson, R. G. (Middlesbrough), 1905 v Ni; 1911 v Ni, S, W; 1912 v S, W; 1913 v Ni (7)
Willingham, C. K. (Huddersfield T), 1937 v Fi; 1938 v S, G, Sw, F; 1939 v S, W, Ni, R of E, N, I, Y (12)
Willis, A. (Tottenham H), 1952 v F (1)
Wilshaw, D. J. (Wolverhampton W), 1954 v W, Sw, U; 1955 v S, F, Sp, P; 1956 v W, Ni, Fi, WG; 1957 v Ni (12)
Wilson, C. P. (Hendon), 1884 v S, W (2)
Wilson, C. W. (Oxford University), 1879 v W; 1881 v S (2)
Wilson, G. (Sheffield W), 1921 v S, W, Bel; 1922 v S, Ni; 1923 v S, W, Ni, Bel; 1924 v W, Ni, F (12)
Wilson, G. P. (Corinthians), 1900 v S, W (2)
Wilson, R. (Huddersfield T), 1960 v S, Y, Sp, H; 1962 v W, Ni, S, A, Sw, Pe, P, H, Arg, Bul, Br; 1963 v Ni, F, Br, Cz, EG, Sw; 1964 v W, S, R of W, U, P (2), Ei, Br, Arg; (with Everton), 1965 v S, H, Y, WG, Se; 1966 v WG (sub), W, Ni, A, Sp, Pol (2), Y, Fi, D, U, M, F, Arg, P, WG; 1967 v Ni, W, S, Cz, A; 1968 v Ni, S, USSR (2), Sp (2), Y (63)
Wilson, T. (Huddersfield T), 1928 v S (1)
Winckworth, W. N. (Old Westminsters), 1892 v W; 1893 v Ni (2)
Windridge, J. E. (Chelsea), 1908 v S, W, Ni, A (2), H, B; 1909 v Ni (8)
Wingfield-Stratford, C. V. (Royal Engineers), 1877 v S (1)
Winterburn, N. (Arsenal), 1990 v I (sub); 1993 v G (sub) (2)
Wise, D. F. (Chelsea), 1991 v T, USSR, Aus (sub), Nz (2); 1994 v N; 1995 v R (sub), Ng (8)
Withe, P. (Aston Villa), 1981 v Br, W, S; 1982 v N (sub), W, Ic; 1983 v H, Ni, S; 1984 v H (sub); 1985 v T (11)
Wollaston, C. H. R. (Wanderers), 1874 v S; 1875 v S; 1877 v S; 1880 v S (4)
Wolstenholme, S. (Everton), 1904 v S; (with Blackburn R), 1905 v W, Ni (3)
Wood, H. (Wolverhampton W), 1890 v S, W; 1896 v S (3)
Wood, R. E. (Manchester U), 1955 v Ni, W; 1956 v Fi (3)
Woodcock, A. S. (Nottingham F), 1978 v Ni; 1979 v Ei (sub), Cz, Bul (sub), Se; 1980 v Ni; (with Cologne), Bul, Ei, Sp (2), Arg, Bel, I; 1981 v N, R, Sw, R, W (sub), S; 1982 v Ni (sub), Ho, Fi (sub), WG (sub), Sp; (with Arsenal), 1983 v WG (sub), Gr, L, Gr; 1984 v L, F (sub), Ni, W, S, Br, U (sub); 1985 v EG, Fi, T, Ni; 1986 v R (sub), T (sub), Is (sub) (42)
Woodger, G. (Oldham Ath), 1911 v Ni (1)
Woodhall, G. (WBA), 1888 v S, W (2)
Woodley, V. R. (Chelsea), 1937 v S, N, Se, Fi; 1938 v S, W, Ni, Cz, G, Sw, F; 1939 v S, W, Ni, R of E, N, I, R, Y (19)
Woods, C. C. E. (Norwich C), 1985 v US; 1986 v Eg (sub), Is (sub), Ca (sub); (with Rangers), 1987 v Y, Sp (sub), Ni (sub), T, S; 1988 v Is, H, Sw (sub), USSR; 1989 v D (sub); 1990 v Br (sub), D (sub); 1991 v H, Pol, Ei, USSR, Aus, Nz (2), Mal; (with Sheffield W), 1992 v G, T, Pol, F, C, Br, Fi, D, F, Se; 1993 v Sp, N, T, Sm, T, Ho, Pol, N, US (43)
Woodward, V. J. (Tottenham H), 1903 v S, W, Ni; 1904 v S, Ni; 1905 v S, W, Ni; 1907 v S; 1908 v S, W, Ni, A (2), H, B; 1909 v W, Ni, H (2), A; (with Chelsea), 1910 v Ni; 1911 v W (23)
Woosnam, M. (Manchester C), 1922 v W (1)
Worrall, F. (Portsmouth), 1935 v Ho; 1937 v Ni (2)
Worthington, F. S. (Leicester C), 1974 v Ni (sub), S, Arg, EG, Bul, Y; 1975 v Cz, P (sub) (8)
Wreford-Brown, C. (Oxford University), 1889 v Ni; (with Old Carthusians), 1894 v W; 1895 v W; 1898 v S (4)
Wright, E, G. D. (Cambridge University), 1906 v W (1)
Wright, I. E. (C Palace), 1991 v Cam, Ei (sub), USSR, Nz; (with Arsenal), 1992 v H (sub); 1993 v N, T (2), Pol (sub), N (sub), US (sub), Br, G (sub); 1994 v Pol, Ho (sub), Sm, Gr (sub), N (sub); 1995 v US (sub), R (20)
Wright, J. D. (Newcastle U), 1939 v N (1)
Wright, M. (Southampton), 1984 v W; 1985 v EG, Fi, T, Ei, R, I, WG; 1986 v R, T, Ni, Eg, USSR; 1987 v Y, Ni, S; (with Derby Co), 1988 v Is, Ho (sub), Co, Sw, Ei, Ho; 1990 v Cz (sub), Tun (sub), Ho, Eg, Bel, Cam, WG, I; 1991 v H, Pol, Ei (2), Cam, USSR, Arg, Aus, Nz, Mal; (with Liverpool), 1992 v F, Fi; 1993 v Sp (43)
Wright, T. J. (Everton), 1968 v USSR; 1969 v R (2), M (sub), U, Br; 1970 v W, Ho, Bel, R (sub), Br (11)
Wright, W. A. (Wolverhampton W), 1947 v S, W, Ni, Ei, Ho, F, Sw, P; 1948 v S, W, Ni, Bel, Se, I; 1949 v S, W, Ni, D, Sw, Se, N, F; 1950 v S, W, Ni, Ei, I, P, Bel, Ch, US, Sp; 1951 v Ni, S, Arg; 1952 v W, Ni, S, F, A (2), I, Sw; 1953 v Ni, W, S, Bel, Arg, Ch, U, US; 1954 v W, Ni, S, R of E, H (2), Y, Bel, Sw, U; 1955 v W, Ni, S, WG, F, Sp, P; 1956 v Ni, W, S, Br, Se, Fi, WG, D, Sp; 1957 v S, W, Ni, Y, D (2), Ei (2); 1958 v W, Ni, S, P, Y, USSR (3), Br, A, F; 1959 v W, Ni, S, USSR, I, Br, Pe, M, US (105)
Wylie, J. G. (Wanderers), 1878 v S (1)

Yates, J. (Burnley), 1889 v Ni (1)
York, R. E. (Aston Villa), 1922 v S; 1926 v S (2)
Young, A. (Huddersfield T), 1933 v W; 1937 v S, H, N, Se; 1938 v G, Sw, F; 1939 v W (9)
Young, G. M. (Sheffield W), 1965 v W (1)

R. E. Evans also played for Wales against E, Ni, S; J. Reynolds also played for Ireland against E, W, S.

NORTHERN IRELAND

Aherne, T. (Belfast C), 1947 v E; 1948 v S; 1949 v W; (with Luton T), 1950 v W (4)
Alexander, A. (Cliftonville), 1895 v S (1)
Allen, C. A. (Cliftonville), 1936 v E (1)
Allen, J. (Limavady), 1887 v E (1)
Anderson, T. (Manchester U), 1973 v Cy, E, S, W; 1974 v Bul, P; (with Swindon T), 1975 v S (sub); 1976 v Is; 1977 v Ho, Bel, WG, E, S, W, Ic; 1978 v Ic, Ho, Bel; (with Peterborough U), S, E, W; 1979 v D (sub) (22)
Anderson, W. (Linfield), 1898 v W, E, S; 1899 v S (4)
Andrews, W. (Glentoran), 1908 v S; (with Grimsby T), 1913 v E, S (3)
Armstrong, G. (Tottenham H), 1977 v WG, E, W (sub), Ic (sub); 1978 v Bel, S, E, W; 1979 v Ei, D, Bul, E, Bul, E, S, W, D; 1980 v E, Ei, Is, S, E, W, Aus (3); 1981 v Se; (with Watford), P, S, P, S, Se; 1982 v S, Is, E, F, W, Y, Hon, Sp, A, F; 1983 v A, T, Alb, S, E, W; (with Real Mallorca), 1984 v A, WG, E, W, Fi; 1985 v R, Fi, E, Sp; (with WBA), 1986 v T, R (sub), E (sub), F (sub); (with Chesterfield), D (sub), Br (sub) (63)

Baird, G. (Distillery), 1896 v S, E, W (3)
Baird, H. (Huddersfield T), 1939 v E (1)
Balfe, J. (Shelbourne), 1909 v E; 1910 v W (2)
Bambrick, J. (Linfield), 1929 v W, S, E; 1930 v W, S, E; 1932 v W; (with Chelsea), 1935 v W; 1936 v E, S; 1938 v W (11)
Banks, S. J. (Cliftonville), 1937 v W (1)
Barr, H. H. (Linfield), 1962 v E; (with Coventry C), 1963 v E, Pol (3)
Barron, H. (Cliftonville), 1894 v E, W, S; 1895 v S; 1896 v S; 1897 v E, W (7)
Barry, H. (Bohemians), 1900 v S (1)
Baxter, R. A. (Cliftonville), 1887 v S, W (2)
Bennett, L. V. (Dublin University), 1889 v W (1)
Berry, J. (Cliftonville), 1888 v S, W; 1889 v E (3)
Best, G. (Manchester U), 1964 v W, U; 1965 v E, Ho (2), S, Sw (2), Alb; 1966 v S, E, Alb; 1967 v E; 1968 v S; 1969 v E, S, W, T; 1970 v S, E, W, USSR; 1971 v Cy (2), Sp, E, S, W; 1972 v USSR, Sp; 1973 v Bul; 1974 v P; (with Fulham), 1977 v Ho, Bel, WG; 1978 v Ic, Ho (37)
Bingham, W. L. (Sunderland), 1951 v F; 1952 v E, S, W; 1953 v E, S, F, W; 1954 v E, S, W; 1955 v E, S, W; 1956 v E, S, W; 1957 v E, S, W, P (2), I; 1958 v S, E, W, I (2), Arg, Cz (2), WG, F; (with Luton T), 1959 v E, S, W, Sp; 1960 v S, E, W; (with Everton), 1961 v E, S, WG (2), Gr, I; 1962 v E, Gr; 1963 v E, S, Pol (2), Sp; (with Port Vale), 1964 v S, E, Sp (56)
Black, J. (Glentoran), 1901 v E (1)
Black, K. (Luton T), 1988 v Fr (sub), Ma (sub); 1989 v Ei, H, Sp (2), Ch (sub); 1990 v H, N, U; 1991 v Y (2), D, A, Pol, Fa; (with Nottingham F), 1992 v Fa, A, D, S, Li, G; 1993 v Sp, D (sub), Alb, Ei (sub), Sp; 1994 v D (sub), Ei (sub), R (sub) (30)
Blair, H. (Portadown), 1931 v S; 1932 v S; (with Swansea), 1934 v S (3)
Blair, J. (Cliftonville), 1907 v W, E, S; 1908 v E, S (5)
Blair, R. V. (Oldham Ath), 1975 v Se (sub), S (sub), W; 1976 v Se, Is (5)
Blanchflower, R. D. (Barnsley), 1950 v S, W; 1951 v E, S; (with Aston Villa), F; 1952 v W; 1953 v E, S, W, F; 1954 v E, S, W; 1955 v E, S (with Tottenham H), W; 1956 v E, S, W; 1957 v E, S, W, I, P (2); 1958 v E, S, W, I (2), Cz (2), Arg, F, WG; 1959 v E, S, W, Sp; 1960 v E, S, W; 1961 v E, S, W, WG (2); 1962 v E, S, W, Gr, Ho; 1963 v E, S, Pol (2) (56)
Blanchflower, J. (Manchester U), 1954 v W; 1955 v E, S; 1956 v S, W; 1957 v S, E, P; 1958 v S, E, I (2) (12)
Bookman, L. O. (Bradford C), 1914 v W; (with Luton T), 1921 v S, W; 1922 v E (4)
Bothwell, A. W. (Ards), 1926 v S, E, W; 1927 v E, W (5)
Bowler, G. C. (Hull C), 1950 v E, S, W (3)
Boyle, P. (Sheffield U), 1901 v E; 1902 v E; 1903 v S, W; 1904 v E (5)
Braithwaite, R. S. (Linfield), 1962 v W; 1963 v P, Sp; (with Middlesbrough), 1964 v W, U; 1965 v E, S, Sw (2), Ho (10)
Breen, T. (Belfast C), 1935 v E, W; 1937 v E, S; (with Manchester U), 1937 v W; 1938 v E, S; 1939 v W, S (9)
Brennan, B. (Bohemians), 1912 v W (1)
Brennan, R. A. (Luton T), 1949 v W; (with Birmingham C), 1950 v E, S, W; (with Fulham), 1951 v E (5)
Briggs, W. R. (Manchester U), 1962 v W; (with Swansea T), 1965 v Ho (2)
Brisby, D. (Distillery), 1891 v S (1)
Brolly, T. (Millwall), 1937 v W; 1938 v W; 1939 v E, W (4)
Brookes, E. A. (Shelbourne), 1920 v S (1)
Brotherston, N. (Blackburn R), 1980 v S, E, W, Aus (3); 1981 v Se, P; 1982 v S, Is, E, F, S, W, Hon (sub), A (sub); 1983 v A (sub), WG, Alb, T, Alb, S (sub), E (sub), W; 1984 v T; 1985 v Is (sub), T (27)
Brown, J. (Glenavon), 1921 v W; (with Tranmere R), 1924 v E, W (3)
Brown, J. (Wolverhampton W), 1935 v E, W; 1936 v E; (with Coventry C), 1937 v E, W; 1938 v S, W; (with Birmingham C), 1939 v E, S, W (10)
Brown, W. G. (Glenavon), 1926 v W (1)
Brown, W. M. (Limavady), 1887 v E (1)
Browne, F. (Cliftonville), 1887 v E, S, W; 1888 v E, S (5)
Browne, R. J. (Leeds U), 1936 v E, W; 1938 v E, W; 1939 v E, S (6)
Bruce, W. (Glentoran), 1961 v S; 1967 v W (2)
Buckle, H. (Cliftonville), 1882 v E (1)
Buckle, H. R. (Sunderland), 1904 v E; (with Bristol R), 1908 v W (2)
Burnett, J. (Distillery), 1894 v E, W, S; (with Glentoran), 1895 v E, W (5)
Burnison, J. (Distillery), 1901 v E, W (2)
Burnison, S. (Distillery), 1908 v E; 1910 v E, S; (with Bradford), 1911 v E, S, W; (with Distillery), 1912 v E; 1913 v W (8)
Burns, J. (Glenavon), 1923 v E (1)
Butler, M. P. (Blackpool), 1939 v W (1)

Campbell, A. C. (Crusaders), 1963 v W; 1965 v Sw (2)
Campbell, D. A. (Nottingham F), 1986 v Mor (sub), Br; 1987 v E (2), T, Y; (with Charlton Ath), 1988 v Y, T (sub), Gr (sub), Pol (sub) (10)
Campbell, J. (Cliftonville), 1896 v W; 1897 v E, S, W; (with Distillery), 1898 v E, S, W; (with Cliftonville), 1899 v E; 1900 v E, S; 1901 v S, W; 1902 v S; 1903 v E; 1904 v S (15)
Campbell, J. P. (Fulham), 1951 v E, S (2)
Campbell, R. (Bradford C), 1982 v S, W (sub) (2)
Campbell, W. G. (Dundee), 1968 v S, E; 1969 v T; 1970 v S, W, USSR (6)
Carey, J. J. (Manchester U), 1947 v E, S, W; 1948 v E; 1949 v E, S, W (7)
Carroll, E. (Glenavon), 1925 v S (1)
Casey, T. (Newcastle U), 1955 v W; 1956 v W; 1957 v E, S, W, I, P (2); 1958 v WG, F; (with Portsmouth), 1959 v E, Sp (12)
Cashin, M. (Cliftonville), 1898 v S (1)
Caskey, W. (Derby Co), 1979 v Bul, E, Bul, E, D (sub); 1980 v E (sub); (with Tulsa R), 1982 v F (sub) (7)
Cassidy, T. (Newcastle U), 1971 v E (sub); 1972 v USSR (sub); 1974 v Bul (sub), S, E, W; 1975 v N; 1976 v S, E, W; 1977 v WG (sub); 1980 v E, Ei (sub), Is, S, E, W, Aus

(3); (with Burnley), 1981 v Se, P; 1982 v Is, Sp (sub) (24)

Caughey, M. (Linfield), 1986 v F (sub), D (sub) (2)

Chambers, J. (Distillery), 1921 v W; (with Bury), 1928 v E, S, W; 1929 v E, S, W; 1930 v S, W; (with Nottingham F), 1932 v E, S, W (12)

Chatton, H. A. (Partick T), 1925 v E, S; 1926 v E (3)

Christian, J. (Linfield), 1889 v S (1)

Clarke, C. J. (Bournemouth), 1986 v F, D, Mor, Alg (sub), Sp, Br; (with Southampton), 1987 v E, T, Y; 1988 v Y, T, Gr, Pol, F, Ma; 1989 v Ei, H, Sp (1 + 1 sub); (with QPR), Ma, Ch; 1990 v H, Ei, N; (with Portsmouth), 1991 v Y (sub), D, A, Pol, Y (sub), Fa; 1992 v Fa, D, S, G; 1993 v Alb, Sp, D (38)

Clarke, R. (Belfast C), 1901 v E, S (2)

Cleary, J. (Glentoran), 1982 v S, W; 1983 v W (sub); 1984 v T (sub); 1985 v Is (5)

Clements, D. (Coventry C), 1965 v W, Ho; 1966 v M; 1967 v S, W; 1968 v S, E; 1969 v T (2), S, W; 1970 v S, E, W, USSR (2); 1971 v Sp, E, S, W, Cy; (with Sheffield W), 1972 v USSR (2), Sp, E, S, W; 1973 v Bul, Cy (2), P, E, S, W; (with Everton), 1974 v Bul, P, S, E, W; 1975 v N, Y, E, S, W; 1976 v Se, Y; (with New York Cosmos), E, W (48)

Clugston, J. (Cliftonville), 1888 v W; 1889 v W, S, E; 1890 v E, S; 1891 v E, W; 1892 v E, S, W; 1893 v E, S, W (14)

Cochrane, D. (Leeds U), 1939 v E, W; 1947 v E, S, W; 1948 v E, S, W; 1949 v S, W; 1950 v S, E (12)

Cochrane, M. (Distillery), 1898 v S, W, E; 1899 v E; 1900 v E, S, W; (with Leicester Fosse), 1901 v S (8)

Cochrane, T. (Coleraine), 1976 v N (sub); (with Burnley), 1978 v S (sub), E (sub), W (sub); 1979 v Ei (sub); (with Middlesbrough), D, Bul, E, Bul, E; 1980 v Is, E (sub), W (sub), Aus (1 + 2 sub); 1981 v Se (sub), P (sub), S, P, S, Se; 1982 v E (sub), F; (with Gillingham), 1984 v S, Fi (sub) (26)

Collins, F. (Celtic), 1922 v S (1)

Condy, J. (Distillery), 1882 v W; 1886 v E, S (3)

Connell, T. (Coleraine), 1978 v W (sub) (1)

Connor, J. (Glentoran), 1901 v S, E; (with Belfast C), 1905 v E, S, W; 1907 v E, S; 1908 v E, S; 1909 v W; 1911 v S, E, W (13)

Connor, M. J. (Brentford), 1903 v S, W; (with Fulham), 1904 v E (3)

Cook, W. (Celtic), 1933 v E, W, S; (with Everton), 1935 v E; 1936 v S, W; 1937 v E, S, W; 1938 v E, S, W; 1939 v E, S, W (15)

Cooke, S. (Belfast YMCA), 1889 v E; (with Cliftonville), 1890 v E, S (3)

Coulter, J. (Belfast C), 1934 v E, S, W; (with Everton), 1935 v E, S, W; 1937 v S, W; (with Grimsby T), 1938 v S, W; (with Chelmsford C), 1939 v S (11)

Cowan, J. (Newcastle U), 1970 v E (sub) (1)

Cowan, T. S. (Queen's Island), 1925 v W (1)

Coyle, F. (Coleraine), 1956 v E, S; 1957 v P; (with Nottingham F), 1958 v Arg (4)

Coyle, L. (Derry C), 1989 v Ch (sub) (1)

Coyle, R. I. (Sheffield W), 1973 v P, Cy (sub), W (sub); 1974 v Bul (sub), P (sub) (5)

Craig, A. B. (Rangers), 1908 v E, S, W; 1909 v S; (with Morton), 1912 v S, W; 1914 v E, S, W (9)

Craig, D. J. (Newcastle U), 1967 v W; 1968 v W; 1969 v T (2), E, S, W; 1970 v E, S, W, USSR; 1971 v Cy (2), Sp, S (sub); 1972 v USSR, S (sub); 1973 v Cy (2), E, S, W; 1974 v Bul, P; 1975 v N (25)

Crawford, S. (Distillery), 1889 v E, W; (with Cliftonville), 1891 v E, S, W; 1893 v E, W (7)

Croft, T. (Queen's Island), 1924 v E (1)

Crone, R. (Distillery), 1889 v S; 1890 v E, S, W (4)

Crone, W. (Distillery), 1882 v W; 1884 v E, S, W; 1886 v E, S, W; 1887 v E; 1888 v E, W; 1889 v S; 1890 v W (12)

Crooks, W. (Manchester U), 1922 v W (1)

Crossan, E. (Blackburn R), 1950 v S; 1951 v E; 1955 v W (3)

Crossan, J. A. (Sparta-Rotterdam), 1960 v E; (with Sunderland), 1963 v W, P, Sp; 1964 v E, S, W, U, Sp; 1965 v E, S, Sw (2); (with Manchester C), W, Ho (2), Alb; 1966 v S, E, Alb, WG; 1967 v E, S; (with Middlesbrough), 1968 v S (24)

Crothers, C. (Distillery), 1907 v W (1)

Cumming, L. (Huddersfield T), 1929 v W, S; (with Oldham Ath), 1930 v E (3)

Cunningham, R. (Ulster), 1892 v S, E, W; 1893 v E (4)

Cunningham, W. E. (St Mirren), 1951 v W; 1953 v E; 1954 v S; 1955 v S; (with Leicester C), 1956 v E, S, W; 1957 v E, S, W, I, P (2); 1958 v S, W, I, Cz (2), Arg, WG, F; 1959 v E, S, W; 1960 v E, S, W; (with Dunfermline Ath), 1961 v W; 1962 v W, Ho (30)

Curran, S. (Belfast C), 1926 v S, W; 1928 v S (3)

Curran, J. J. (Glenavon), 1922 v W; (with Pontypridd), 1923 v E, S; (with Glenavon), 1924 v E (4)

Cush, W. W. (Glenavon), 1951 v E, S; 1954 v S, E; 1957 v W, I, P (2); (with Leeds U), 1958 v I (2), W, Cz (2), Arg, WG, F; 1959 v E, S, W, Sp; 1960 v E, S, W; (with Portadown), 1961 v WG, Gr; 1962 v Gr (26)

Dalton, W. (YMCA), 1888 v S; (with Linfield), 1890 v S, W; 1891 v S, W; 1892 v E, S, W; 1894 v E, S, W (11)

D'Arcy, S. D. (Chelsea), 1952 v W; 1953 v E; (with Brentford), 1953 v S, W, F (5)

Darling, J. (Linfield), 1897 v E, S; 1900 v S; 1902 v E, S, W; 1903 v E, S, W; 1905 v E, S, W; 1906 v E, S, W; 1908 v W; 1909 v E; 1910 v E, S, W; 1912 v S (21)

Davey, H. H. (Reading), 1926 v E; 1927 v E, S; 1928 v E; (with Portsmouth), 1928 v W (5)

Davis, T. L. (Oldham Ath), 1937 v E (1)

Davison, J. R. (Cliftonville), 1882 v E, W; 1883 v E, W; 1884 v E, W, S; 1885 v E (8)

Dennison, R. (Wolverhampton W), 1988 v F, Ma; 1989 v H, Sp Ch (sub); 1990 v Ei, U; 1991 v Y (2), A. Pol, Fa (sub); 1992 v Fa, A, D (sub); 1993 v Sp (sub); 1994 v Co (sub) (17)

Devine, J. (Glentoran), 1990 v U (sub) (1)

Devine, W. (Limavady), 1886 v E, W; 1887 v W; 1888 v W (4)

Dickson, D. (Coleraine), 1970 v S (sub), W; 1973 v Cy, P (4)

Dickson, T. A. (Linfield), 1957 v S (1)

Dickson, W. (Chelsea), 1951 v W, F; 1952 v E, S, W; 1953 v E, S, W, F; (with Arsenal), 1954 v E, W; 1955 v E (12)

Diffin, W. (Belfast C), 1931 v W (1)

Dill, A. H. (Knock and Down Ath), 1882 v E, W; (with Cliftonville), 1883 v W; 1884 v E, S, W; 1885 v E, S, W (9)

Doherty, I. (Belfast C), 1901 v E (1)

Doherty, J. (Cliftonville), 1933 v E, W (2)

Doherty, L. (Linfield), 1985 v Is; 1988 v T (sub) (2)

Doherty, M. (Derry C), 1938 v S (1)

Doherty, P. D. (Blackpool), 1935 v E, W; 1936 v E, S; (with Manchester C), 1937 v E, W; 1938 v E, S; 1939 v E, W; (with Derby Co), 1947 v E; (with Huddersfield T), 1947 v W; 1948 v E, W; 1949 v S; (with Doncaster R), 1951 v S (16)

Donaghy, M. (Luton T), 1980 v S, E, W; 1981 v Se, P, S (sub); 1982 v S, Is, E, F, S, W, Y, Hon, Sp, F; 1983 v A, WG, Alb, T, Alb, S, E, W; 1984 v A, T, WG, S, E, W, Fi; 1985 v R, Fi, E, Sp, T; 1986 v T, R, E, F, D, Mor, Alg, Sp, Br; 1987 v E (2), T, Is, Y; 1988 v Y, T, Gr, Pol, F, Ma; 1989 v Ei, H; (with Manchester U), Sp (2), Ma, Ch; 1990 v Ei, N; 1991 v Y (2), D, A, Pol, Fa; 1992 v Fa, A, D, S, Li, G; (with Chelsea), 1993 v Alb, Sp, D, Alb, Ei, Sp, Li, La; 1994 v La, D, Ei, R, Lie, Co, M (91)

Donnelly, L. (Distillery), 1913 v W (1)

Doran, J. F. (Brighton), 1921 v E; 1922 v E, W (3)

Dougan, A. D. (Portsmouth), 1958 v Cz; (with Blackburn R), 1960 v S; 1961 v E, W, I, Gr; (with Aston Villa), 1963 v S, Pol (2); (with Leicester C), 1966 v S, E, W, M, Alb, WG; 1967 v E, S; (with Wolverhampton W), 1967 v W; 1968 v S, W, Is; 1969 v T (2), E, S, W; 1970 v S, E, USSR (2); 1971 v Cy (2), Sp, E, S, W; 1972 v USSR (2), E, S, W; 1973 v Bul, Cy (43)
Douglas, J. P. (Belfast C), 1947 v E (1)
Dowd, H. O. (Glenavon), 1974 v W; (with Sheffield W), 1975 v N (sub), Se (3)
Dowie, I. (Luton T), 1990 v N (sub), U; 1991 v Y, D, A (sub), (with West Ham U), Y, Fa; (with Southampton) 1992 v Fa, A, D (sub), S (sub), Li; 1993 v Alb (2), Ei, Sp (sub), Li, La; La, D, Ei (sub), R (sub), Lie, Co, M (sub); 1995 v A, Ei; (with C Palace) Ei, La, Ca, Ch, La (32)
Duggan, H. A. (Leeds U), 1930 v E; 1931 v E, W; 1933 v E; 1934 v E; 1935 v S, W; 1936 v S (8)
Dunlop, G. (Linfield), 1985 v Is; 1987 v E, Y; 1990 v Ei (4)
Dunne, J. (Sheffield U), 1928 v W; 1931 v W, E; 1932 v E, S; 1933 v E, W (7)

Eames, W. L. E. (Dublin U), 1885 v E, S, W (3)
Eglington, T. J. (Everton), 1947 v S, W; 1948 v E, S, W; 1949 v E (6)
Elder, A. R. (Burnley), 1960 v W; 1961 v S, E, W, WG (2), Gr; 1962 v E, S, Gr; 1963 v E, S, W, P (2), Sp; 1964 v W, U; 1965 v E, S, W, Sw (2), Ho (2), Alb; 1966 v E, S, W, M, Alb; 1967 v E, S, W; (with Stoke C), 1968 v E, W; 1969 v E (sub), S, W; 1970 v USSR (40)
Elleman, A. R. (Cliftonville), 1889 v W; 1890 v E (2)
Elwood, J. H. (Bradford), 1929 v W; 1930 v E (2)
Emerson, W. (Glentoran), 1920 v E, S, W; 1921 v E; 1922 v E, S; (with Burnley), 1922 v W; 1923 v E, S, W; 1924 v E (11)
English, S. (Rangers), 1933 v W, S (2)
Enright, J. (Leeds C), 1912 v S (1)

Falloon, E. (Aberdeen), 1931 v S; 1933 v S (2)
Farquharson, T. G. (Cardiff C), 1923 v S, W; 1924 v E, S, W; 1925 v E, S (7)
Farrell, P. (Distillery), 1901 v S, W (2)
Farrell, P. (Hibernian), 1938 v W (1)
Farrell, P. D. (Everton), 1947 v S, W; 1948 v E, S, W; 1949 v E, W (7)
Feeney, J. M. (Linfield), 1947 v S; (with Swansea T), 1950 v E (2)
Feeney, W. (Glentoran), 1976 v Is (1)
Ferguson, W. (Linfield), 1966 v M; 1967 v E (2)
Ferris, J. (Belfast C), 1920 v E, W; (with Chelsea), 1921 v S, E; (with Belfast C), 1928 v S (5)
Ferris, R. O. (Birmingham C), 1950 v S; 1951 v F; 1952 v S (3)
Fettis, A. (Hull C), 1992 v D, Li; 1993 v D; 1994 v M; 1995 v P, Ei, La, Ca, Ch, La (10)
Finney, T. (Sunderland), 1975 v N, E (sub), S, W; 1976 v N, Y, S; (with Cambridge U), 1980 v E, Is, S, E, W, Aus (2) (14)
Fitzpatrick, J. C. (Bohemians), 1896 v E, S (2)
Flack, H. (Burnley), 1929 v S (1)
Fleming, J. G. (Nottingham F), 1987 v E (2), Is, Y; 1988 v T, Gr, Pol; 1989 v Ma, Ch; (with Manchester C), 1990 v H, Ei; (with Barnsley), 1991 v Y; 1992 v Li (sub), G; 1993 v Alb, Sp, D, Alb, Sp, Li, La; 1994 v La, D, Ei, R, Lie, Co, M; 1995 v P, A, Ei (31)
Forbes, G. (Limavady), 1888 v W; (with Distillery), 1891 v E, S (3)
Forde, J. T. (Ards), 1959 v Sp; 1961 v E, S, WG (4)
Foreman, T. A. (Cliftonville), 1899 v S (1)
Forsyth, J. (YMCA), 1888 v E, S (2)
Fox, W. (Ulster), 1887 v E, S (2)
Fulton, R. P. (Belfast C), 1930 v W; 1931 v E, S, W; 1932 v W, E; 1933 v E, S; 1934 v E, W, S; 1935 v E, W, S; 1936 v S, W; 1937 v E, S, W; 1938 v W (20)

Gaffikin, J. (Linfield Ath), 1890 v S, W; 1891 v S, W; 1892 v E, S, W; 1893 v E, S, W; 1894 v E, S, W; 1895 v E, W (15)
Galbraith, W. (Distillery), 1890 v W (1)
Gallagher, P. (Celtic), 1920 v E, S; 1922 v S; 1923 v S, W; 1924 v S, W; 1925 v S, W, E; (with Falkirk), 1927 v S (11)
Gallogly, C. (Huddersfield T), 1951 v E, S (2)
Gara, A. (Preston NE), 1902 v E, S, W (3)
Gardiner, A. (Cliftonville), 1930 v S, W; 1931 v S; 1932 v E, S (5)
Garrett, J. (Distillery), 1925 v W (1)
Gaston, R. (Oxford U), 1969 v Is (sub) (1)
Gaukrodger, G. (Linfield), 1895 v W (1)
Gaussen, A. W. (Moyola Park), 1884 v E, S; 1888 v E, W; 1889 v E, W (6)
Geary, J. (Glentoran), 1931 v S; 1932 v S (2)
Gibb, J. T. (Wellington Park) 1884 v S, W; 1885 v S, E, W; 1886 v S; 1887 v S, E, W; 1889 v S (10)
Gibb, T. J. (Cliftonville), 1936 v W (1)
Gibson W. K. (Cliftonville), 1894 v S, W, E; 1895 v S; 1897 v W; 1898 v S, W, E; 1901 v S, W, E; 1902 v S, W (13)
Gillespie, K.R. (Manchester U), 1995 v P, A, Ei; (with Newcastle U) Ei, La, Ca, Ch (sub), La (sub) (8)
Gillespie, R. (Hertford), 1886 v E, S, W; 1887 v E, S, W (6)
Gillespie, W. (Sheffield U), 1913 v E, S; 1914 v E, W; 1920 v S, W; 1921 v E; 1922 v E, S, W; 1923 v E, S, W; 1924 v E, S, W; 1925 v E, S; 1926 v S, W; 1927 v E, W; 1928 v E; 1929 v E; 1931 v E (25)
Gillespie, W. (West Down), 1889 v W (1)
Goodall, A. L. (Derby Co), 1899 v S, W; 1900 v E, W; 1901 v E; 1902 v S; 1903 v E, W; (with Glossop), 1904 v E, W (10)
Goodbody, M. F. (Dublin University), 1889 v E; 1891 v W (2)
Gordon, H. (Linfield), 1891 v S; 1892 v E, S, W; 1893 v E, S, W; 1895 v E, W; 1896 v E, S (11)
Gordon, T. (Linfield), 1894 v W; 1895 v E (2)
Gorman, W. C. (Brentford), 1947 v E, S, W; 1948 v W (4)
Gowdy, J. (Glentoran), 1920 v E; (with Queen's Island), 1924 v W; (with Falkirk), 1926 v E, S; 1927 v E, S (6)
Gowdy, W. A. (Hull C), 1932 v S; (with Sheffield W), 1933 v S; (with Linfield), 1935 v E, S, W; (with Hibernian), 1936 v W (6)
Graham, W. G. L. (Doncaster R), 1951 v W, F; 1952 v E, S, W; 1953 v S, F; 1954 v E, W; 1955 v S, W; 1956 v E, S; 1959 v E (14)
Gray, P. (Luton T), 1993 v D (sub), Alb, Ei, Sp; (with Sunderland), 1994 v La, D, Ei, R, Lie (sub); 1995 v P, A, Ei, Ca, Ch (sub) (14)
Greer, W. (QPR), 1909 v E, S, W (3)
Gregg, H. (Doncaster R), 1954 v W; 1957 v E, S, W, I, P (2); 1958 v E, I; (with Manchester U), 1958 v Cz, Arg, WG, F, W; 1959 v E, W; 1960 v S, E, W; 1961 v E, S; 1962 v S, Gr; 1964 v S, E (25)

Hall, G. (Distillery), 1897 v E (1)
Halligan, W. (Derby Co), 1911 v W; (with Wolverhampton W), 1912 v E (2)
Hamill, M. (Manchester U), 1912 v E; 1914 v E, S; (with Belfast C), 1920 v E, S, W; (with Manchester C), 1921 v S (7)
Hamilton, B. (Linfield), 1969 v T; 1971 v Cy (2), E, S, W; (with Ipswich T), 1972 v USSR (1+1 sub), Sp; 1973 v Bul, Cy (2), P, E, S, W; 1974 v Bul, S, E, W; 1975 v N, Se, Y, E; 1976 v Se, N, Y; (with Everton), Is, S, E, W; 1977 v

Ho, Bel, WG, E, S, W, Ic; (with Millwall), 1978 v S, E, W; 1979 v Ei (sub); (with Swindon T), Bul (2), E, S, W, D; 1980 v Aus (2 sub) (50)
Hamilton, J. (Knock), 1882 v E, W (2)
Hamilton, R. (Distillery), 1908 v W (1)
Hamilton, R. (Rangers), 1928 v S; 1929 v E; 1930 v S, E; 1932 v S (5)
Hamilton, W. (QPR), 1978 v S (sub); (with Burnley), 1980 v S, E, W, Aus (2); 1981 v Se, P, S, P, S, Se; 1982 v S, Is, E, W, Y, Hon, Sp, A, F; 1983 v A, WG, Alb (2), S, E, W; 1984 v A, T, WG, S, E, W, Fi; (with Oxford U), 1985 v R, Sp; 1986 v Mor (sub), Alg, Sp (sub), Br (sub) (41)
Hamilton, W. D. (Dublin Association), 1885 v W (1)
Hamilton, W. J. (Dublin Association), 1885 v W (1)
Hampton, H. (Bradford C), 1911 v E, S, W; 1912 v E, W; 1913 v E, S, W; 1914 v E (9)
Hanna, D. R. A. (Portsmouth), 1899 v W (1)
Hanna, J. (Nottingham F), 1912 v S, W (2)
Hannon, D. J. (Bohemians), 1908 v E, S; 1911 v E, S; 1912 v W; 1913 v E (6)
Harkin, J. T. (Southport), 1968 v W; 1969 v T; (with Shrewsbury T), W (sub); 1970 v USSR; 1971 v Sp (5)
Harland, A. I. (Linfield), 1923 v E (1)
Harris, J. (Cliftonville), 1921 v W (1)
Harris, V. (Shelbourne), 1906 v E; 1907 v E, W; 1908 v E, W, S; (with Everton), 1909 v E, W, S; 1910 v E, S, W; 1911 v E, S, W; 1912 v E; 1913 v E, S; 1914 v S, W (20)
Harvey, M. (Sunderland), 1961 v I; 1962 v Ho; 1963 v W, Sp; 1964 v S, E, W, U, Sp; 1965 v E, S, W, Sw (2), Ho (2), Alb; 1966 v S, E, W, M, Alb, WG; 1967 v E, S; 1968 v E, W; 1969 v Is, T (2), E; 1970 v USSR; 1971 v Cy, W (sub) (34)
Hastings, J. (Knock), 1882 v E, W; (with Ulster), 1883 v W; 1884 v E, S; 1886 v E, S (7)
Hatton, S. (Linfield), 1963 v S, Pol (2)
Hayes, W. E. (Huddersfield T), 1938 v E, S; 1939 v E, S (4)
Healy, F. (Coleraine), 1982 v S, W, Hon (sub); (with Glentoran), 1983 v A (sub) (4)
Hegan, D. (WBA), 1970 v USSR; (with Wolverhampton W), 1972 v USSR, E, S, W; 1973 v Bul, Cy (7)
Hehir, J. C. (Bohemians), 1910 v W (1)
Henderson, A. W. (Ulster), 1885 v E, S, W (3)
Hewison, G. (Moyola Park), 1885 v E, S (2)
Hill, C. F. (Sheffield U), 1990 v N, U; 1991 v Pol, Y; 1992 v A, D; (with Leicester C) 1995 v Ei, La (8)
Hill, M. J. (Norwich C), 1959 v W; 1960 v W; 1961 v WG; 1962 v S; (with Everton), 1964 v S, E, Sp (7)
Hinton, E. (Fulham), 1947 v S, W; 1948 v S, E, W; (with Millwall), 1951 v W, F (7)
Hopkins, J. (Brighton), 1926 v E (1)
Horlock, K. (Swindon T), 1995 v La, Ca (2)
Houston, J. (Linfield), 1912 v S, W; 1913 v W; (with Everton), 1913 v E, S; 1914 v S (6)
Houston, W. (Linfield), 1933 v W (1)
Houston, W. G. (Moyola Park), 1885 v E, S (2)
Hughes, M. E. (Manchester C), 1992 v D, S, Li, G; (with Strasbourg), 1993 v Alb, Sp, D, Ei, Sp, Li, La; 1994 v La, D, Ei, R, Lie, Co, M; 1995 v P, A, Ei (2) La, Ca, Ch, La (26)
Hughes, P. (Bury), 1987 v E, T, Is (3)
Hughes, W. (Bolton W), 1951 v W (1)
Humphries, W. (Ards), 1962 v W; (with Coventry C), 1962 v Ho; 1963 v E, S, W, Pol, Sp; 1964 v S, E, Sp; 1965 v S; (with Swansea T), 1965 v W, Ho, Alb (14)
Hunter, A. (Distillery), 1905 v W; 1906 v W, E, S; (with Belfast C), 1908 v W; 1909 v W, E, S (8)
Hunter, A. (Blackburn R), 1970 v USSR; 1971 v Cy (2), E, S, W; (with Ipswich T), 1972 v USSR (2), Sp, E, S, W; 1973 v Bul, Cy (2), P, E, S, W; 1974 v Bul, S, E, W; 1975 v N, Se, Y, E, S, W; 1976 v Se, N, Y, Is, S, E, W; 1977 v Ho, Bel, WG, E, S, W, Ic; 1978 v Ic, Ho, Bel; 1979 v Ei, D, S, W, D; 1980 v E, Ei (53)
Hunter, B. V. (Wrexham), 1995 v La (1)
Hunter, R. J. (Cliftonville), 1884 v E, S, W (3)
Hunter, V. (Coleraine), 1962 v E; 1964 v Sp (2)

Irvine, R. J. (Linfield), 1962 v Ho; 1963 v E, S, W, Pol (2), Sp; (with Stoke C), 1965 v W (8)
Irvine, R. W. (Everton), 1922 v S; 1923 v E, W; 1924 v E, S; 1925 v E; 1926 v E; 1927 v E, W; 1928 v E, S; (with Portsmouth), 1929 v E; 1930 v S; (with Connah's Quay), 1931 v E; (with Derry C), 1932 v W (15)
Irvine, W. J. (Burnley), 1963 v W, Sp; 1965 v S, W, Sw, Ho (2), Alb; 1966 v S, E, W, M, Alb; 1967 v E, S; 1968 v E, W; (with Preston NE), 1969 v Is, T, E; (with Brighton), 1972 v E, S, W (23)
Irving, S. J. (Dundee), 1923 v S, W; 1924 v S, E, W; 1925 v S, E, W; 1926 v S, W; (with Cardiff C), 1927 v S, E, W; 1928 v S, E, W; (with Chelsea), 1929 v E; 1931 v W (18)

Jackson, T. (Everton), 1969 v Is, E, S, W; 1970 v USSR (1 + 1 sub); (with Nottingham F), 1971 v Sp; 1972 v E, S, W; 1973 v Cy, E, S, W; 1974 v Bul, P, S (sub), E (sub), W (sub); 1975 v N (sub), Se, Y, E, S, W; (with Manchester U); 1976 v Se, N, Y; 1977 v Ho, Bel, WG, E, S, W, Ic (35)
Jamison, J. (Glentoran), 1976 v N (1)
Jennings, P. A. (Watford), 1964 v W, U; (with Tottenham H), 1965 v E, S, Sw (2), Ho, Alb; 1966 v S, E, W, Alb, WG; 1967 v E, S; 1968 v S, E, W; 1969 v Is, T (2), E, S, W; 1970 v S, E, USSR (2); 1971 v Cy (2), E, S, W; 1972 v USSR, Sp, S, E, W; 1973 v Bul, Cy, P, E, S, W; 1974 v P, S, E, W; 1975 v N, Se, Y, E, S, W; 1976 v Se, N, Y, Is, S, E, W; 1977 v Ho, Bel, WG, E, S, W, Ic; (with Arsenal), 1978 v Ic, Ho, Bel; 1979 v Ei, D, Bul, E, Bul, E, S, W, D; 1980 v E, Ei, Is; 1981 v S, P, S, Se; 1982 v S, Is, E, W, Y, Hon, Sp, F; 1983 v Alb, S, E, W; 1984 v A, T, WG, S, W, Fi; 1985 v R, Fi, E, Sp, T; (with Tottenham H), 1986 v T, R, E, F, D, Mor; (with Tottenham H), Alg, Sp, Br (119)
Johnston, H. (Portadown), 1927 v W (1)
Johnston, R. (Old Park), 1885 v S, W (2)
Johnston, S. (Distillery), 1882 v W; 1884 v E; 1886 v E, S (4)
Johnston, S. (Linfield), 1890 v W; 1893 v S, W; 1894 v E (4)
Johnston, S. (Distillery), 1905 v W (1)
Johnston, W. C. (Glenavon), 1962 v W; (with Oldham Ath), 1966 v M (sub) (2)
Jones, J. (Linfield), 1930 v S, W; 1931 v S, W, E; 1932 v S, E; 1933 v S, E, W; 1934 v S, E, W; 1935 v S, E, W; 1936 v E, S; (with Hibernian), 1936 v W; 1937 v E, W, S; (with Glenavon), 1938 v E (23)
Jones, J. (Glenavon), 1956 v W; 1957 v E, W (3)
Jones, S. (Distillery), 1934 v E; (with Blackpool), 1934 v W (2)
Jordan, T. (Linfield), 1895 v E, W (2)

Kavanagh, P. J. (Celtic), 1930 v E (1)
Keane, T. R. (Swansea T), 1949 v S (1)
Kearns, A. (Distillery), 1900 v E, S, W; 1902 v E, S, W (6)
Kee, P. V. (Oxford U), 1990 v N; 1991 v Y (2), D, A, Pol, Fa; (with Ards), 1995 v A, Ei (9)
Keith, R. M. (Newcastle U), 1958 v E, W, Cz (2), Arg, I, WG, F; 1959 v E, S, W, Sp; 1960 v S, E; 1961 v S, E, W, I, WG (2), Gr; 1962 v W, Ho (23)
Kelly, H. R. (Fulham), 1950 v E, W; (with Southampton), 1951 v E, S (4)
Kelly, J. (Glentoran), 1896 v E (1)

Kelly, J. (Derry C), 1932 v E, W; 1933 v E, W, S; 1934 v W; 1936 v E, S, W; 1937 v S, E (11)
Kelly, P. (Manchester C), 1921 v E (1)
Kelly, P. M. (Barnsley), 1950 v S (1)
Kennedy, A. L. (Arsenal), 1923 v W; 1925 v E (2)
Kernaghan, N. (Belfast C), 1936 v W; 1937 v S; 1938 v E (3)
Kirkwood, H. (Cliftonville), 1904 v W (1)
Kirwan, J. (Tottenham H), 1900 v W; 1902 v E, W; 1903 v E, S, W; 1904 v E, S, W; 1905 v E, S, W; (with Chelsea), 1906 v E, S, W; 1907 v W; (with Clyde), 1909 v S (17)

Lacey, W. (Everton), 1909 v E, S, W; 1910 v E, S, W; 1911 v E, S, W; 1912 v E; (with Liverpool), 1913 v W; 1914 v E, S, W; 1920 v E, S, W; 1921 v E, S, W; 1922 v E, S; (with New Brighton), 1925 v E (23)
Lawther, W. I. (Sunderland), 1960 v W; 1961 v I; (with Blackburn R), 1962 v S, Ho (4)
Leatham, J. (Belfast C), 1939 v W (1)
Ledwidge, J. J. (Shelbourne), 1906 v S, W (2)
Lemon, J. (Glentoran), 1886 v W; 1888 v S; (with Belfast YMCA), 1889 v W (3)
Lennon, N. F. (Crewe Alex), 1994 v M (sub); 1995 v Ch (2)
Leslie, W. (YMCA), 1887 v E (1)
Lewis, J. (Glentoran), 1899 v S, E, W; (with Distillery), 1900 v S (4)
Little, J. (Glentoran), 1898 v W (1)
Lockhart, H. (Rossall School), 1884 v W (1)
Lockhart, N. (Linfield), 1947 v E; (with Coventry C), 1950 v W; 1951 v W; 1952 v W; (with Aston Villa), 1954 v S, E; 1955 v W; 1956 v W (8)
Lomas, S. M. (Manchester C), 1994 v R, Lie, Co (sub), M (sub); 1995 v P, A (6)
Lowther, R. (Glentoran), 1888 v E, S (2)
Loyal, J. (Clarence), 1891 v S (1)
Lutton, R. J. (Wolverhampton W), 1970 v S, E; (with West Ham U), 1973 v Cy (sub), S (sub), W (sub); 1974 v P (6)
Lyner, D. (Glentoran), 1920 v E, W; 1922 v S, W; (with Manchester U), 1923 v E; (with Kilmarnock), 1923 v W (6)

McAdams, W. J. (Manchester C), 1954 v W; 1955 v S; 1957 v E; 1958 v S, I; (with Bolton W), 1961 v E, S, W, I, WG (2), Gr; 1962 v E, Gr; (with Leeds U), Ho (15)
McAlery, J. M. (Cliftonville), 1882 v E, W (2)
McAlinden, J. (Belfast C), 1938 v S; 1939 v S; (with Portsmouth), 1947 v E; (with Southend U), 1949 v E (4)
McAllen, J. (Linfield), 1898 v E; 1899 v E, S, W; 1900 v E, S, W; 1901 v W; 1902 v S (9)
McAlpine, W. J. (Cliftonville), 1901 v S (1)
McArthur, A. (Distillery), 1886 v W (1)
McAuley, J. L. (Huddersfield T), 1911 v E, W; 1912 v E, S; 1913 v E, S (6)
McAuley, P. (Belfast C), 1900 v S (1)
McBride, S. (Glenavon), 1991 v D (sub), Pol (sub); 1992 v Fa (sub), D (4)
McCabe, J. J. (Leeds U), 1949 v S, W; 1950 v E; 1951 v W; 1953 v W; 1954 v S (6)
McCabe, W. (Ulster), 1891 v E (1)
McCambridge, J. (Ballymena), 1930 v S, W; (with Cardiff C), 1931 v W; 1932 v E (4)
McCandless, J. (Bradford), 1912 v W; 1913 v W; 1920 v W, S; 1921 v E (5)
McCandless, W. (Linfield), 1920 v E, W; 1921 v E; (with Rangers), 1921 v W; 1922 v S; 1924 v W, S; 1925 v S; 1929 v W (9)
McCann, P. (Belfast C), 1910 v E, S, W; 1911 v E; (with Glentoran), 1911 v S; 1912 v E; 1913 v W (7)
McCashin, J. (Cliftonville), 1896 v W; 1898 v S, W; 1899 v S (4)
McCavana, W. T. (Coleraine), 1955 v S; 1956 v E, S (3)
McCaw, D. (Distillery), 1882 v E (1)
McCaw, J. H. (Linfield), 1927 v W; 1930 v S; 1931 v E, S, W (5)
McClatchey, J. (Distillery), 1886 v E, S, W (3)
McClatchey, R. (Distillery), 1895 v S (1)
McCleary, J. W. (Cliftonville), 1955 v W (1)
McCleery, W. (Linfield), 1930 v E, W; 1931 v E, S, W; 1932 v S, W; 1933 v E, W (9)
McClelland, J. (Arsenal), 1961 v W, I, WG (2), Gr; (with Fulham), 1966 v M (6)
McClelland, J. (Mansfield T), 1980 v S (sub), Aus (3); 1981 v Se, S; (with Rangers), S, Se (sub); 1982 v S, W, Y, Hon, Sp, A, F; 1983 v A, WG, Alb, T, Alb, S, E, W; 1984 v A, T, WG, S, E, W, Fi; 1985 v R, Is; (with Watford), Fi, E, Sp, T; 1986 v T, F (sub); 1987 v E (2), T, Is, Y; 1988 v T, Gr, F, Ma; 1989 v Ei, H, Sp (2), Ma; (with Leeds U), 1990 v N (53)
McCluggage, A. (Bradford), 1924 v E; (with Burnley), 1927 v S, W; 1928 v S, E, W; 1929 v S, E, W; 1930 v W; 1931 v E, W (12)
McClure, G. (Cliftonville), 1907 v S, W; 1908 v E; (with Distillery), 1909 v E (4)
McConnell, E. (Cliftonville), 1904 v S, W; (with Glentoran), 1905 v S; (with Sunderland), 1906 v E; 1907 v E; 1908 v S, W; (with Sheffield W), 1909 v S, W; 1910 v S, W, E (12)
McConnell, P. (Doncaster R), 1928 v W; (with Southport), 1932 v E (2)
McConnell, W. G. (Bohemians), 1912 v W; 1913 v E, S; 1914 v E, S, W (6)
McConnell, W. H. (Reading), 1925 v W; 1926 v E, W; 1927 v E, S, W; 1928 v E, W (8)
McCourt, F. J. (Manchester C), 1952 v E, W; 1953 v E, S, W, F (6)
McCoy, J. (Distillery), 1896 v W (1)
McCoy, R. (Coleraine), 1987 v Y (sub) (1)
McCracken, R. (C Palace), 1921 v E; 1922 v E, S, W (4)
McCracken, W. (Distillery), 1902 v E, W; 1903 v E; 1904 v E, S, W; (with Newcastle U), 1905 v E, S, W; 1907 v E; 1920 v E; 1922 v E, S, W; (with Hull C), 1923 v S (15)
McCreery, D. (Manchester U), 1976 v S (sub), E, W; 1977 v Ho, Bel, WG, E, S, W, Ic; 1978 v Ic, Ho, Bel, S, E, W; 1979 v Ei, D, Bul, E, Bul, W, D; (with QPR), 1980 v E, Ei, S (sub), E (sub), W (sub), Aus (1 + 1 sub); 1981 v Se (sub), P (sub); (with Tulsa R), S, P, Se; 1982 v S, Is, E (sub), F, Y, Hon, Sp, A, F; (with Newcastle U), 1983 v A; 1984 v T (sub); 1985 v R, Sp (sub); 1986 v T (sub), R, E, F, D, Alg, Sp, Br; 1987 v T, E, Y; 1988 v Y; 1989 v Sp, Ma, Ch; (with Hearts), 1990 v H, Ei, N, U (sub) (67)
McCrory, S. (Southend U), 1958 v E (1)
McCullough, K. (Belfast C), 1935 v W; 1936 v E; (with Manchester C), 1936 v S; 1937 v E, S (5)
McCullough, W. J. (Arsenal), 1961 v I; 1963 v Sp; 1964 v S, E, W, U, Sp; 1965 v E, Sw; (with Millwall), 1967 v E (10)
McCurdy, C. (Linfield), 1980 v Aus (sub) (1)
McDonald, A. (QPR), 1986 v R, E, F, D, Mor, Alg, Sp, Br; 1987 v E (2), T, Is, Y; 1988 v Y, T, Pol, F, Ma; 1989 v Ei, H, Sp, Ch; 1990 v H, Ei, U; 1991 v Y, D, A, Fa; 1992 v Fa, S, Li, G; 1993 v Alb, Sp, D, Alb, Ei, Sp, Li, La; 1994 v D, Ei; 1995 v P, A, Ei, La, Ca, Ch, La (50)
McDonald, R. (Rangers), 1930 v S; 1932 v E (2)
McDonnell, J. (Bohemians), 1911 v E, S; 1912 v W; 1913 v W (4)
McElhinney, G. (Bolton W), 1984 v WG, S, E, W, Fi; 1985 v R (6)
McFaul, W. S. (Linfield), 1967 v E (sub); (with Newcastle U), 1970 v W; 1971 v Sp; 1972 v USSR; 1973 v Cy; 1974 v Bul (6)
McGarry, J. K. (Cliftonville), 1951 v W, F, S (3)
McGaughey, M. (Linfield), 1985 v Is (sub) (1)
McGee, G. (Wellington Park), 1885 v E, S, W (3)

McGibbon, P. C. G. (Manchester U), 1995 v Ca (sub), Ch, La (3)
McGrath, R. C. (Tottenham H), 1974 v S, E, W; 1975 v N; 1976 v Is (sub); 1977 v Ho; (with Manchester U), Bel, WG, E, S, W, Ic; 1978 v Ic, Ho, Bel, S, E, W; 1979 v Bul (sub), E (2 sub) (21)
McGregor, S. (Glentoran), 1921 v S (1)
McGrillen, J. (Clyde), 1924 v S; (with Belfast C), 1927 v S (2)
McGuire, E. (Distillery), 1907 v S (1)
McIlroy, H. (Cliftonville), 1906 v E (1)
McIlroy, J. (Burnley), 1952 v E, S, W; 1953 v E, S, W; 1954 v E, S, W; 1955 v E, S, W; 1956 v E, S, W; 1957 v E, S, W, I, P (2); 1958 v E, S, W, I (2), Cz (2), Arg, WG, F; 1959 v E, S, W, Sp; 1960 v E, S, W; 1961 v E, W, WG (2), Gr; 1962 v E, S, Gr, Ho; 1963 v E, S, Pol (2); (with Stoke C), 1963 v W; 1966 v S, E, Alb (55)
McIlroy, S. B. (Manchester U), 1972 v Sp, S (sub); 1974 v S, E, W; 1975 v N, Se, Y, E, S, W; 1976 v Se, N, Y, S, E, W; 1977 v Ho, Bel, E, S, W, Ic; 1978 v Ic, Ho, Bel, S, E, W; 1979 v Ei, D, Bul, E, Bul, E, S, W, D; 1980 v E, Ei, Is, S, E, W; 1981 v Se, P, S, P, S, Se; 1982 v S, Is; (with Stoke C), E, F, S, W, Y, Hon, Sp, A, F; 1983 v A, WG, Alb, T, Alb, S, E, W; 1984 v A, T, S, E, W, Fi; 1985 v Fi, E, T; (with Manchester C), 1986 v T, R, E, F, D, Mor, Alg, Sp, Br; 1987 v E (sub) (88)
McIlvenny, J. (Distillery), 1890 v E; 1891 v E (2)
McIlvenny, P. (Distillery), 1924 v W (1)
McKeag, W. (Glentoran), 1968 v S, W (2)
McKee, F. W. (Cliftonville), 1906 v S, W; (with Belfast C), 1914 v E, S, W (5)
McKelvie, H. (Glentoran), 1901 v W (1)
McKenna, J. (Huddersfield), 1950 v E, S, W; 1951 v E, S, F; 1952 v E (7)
McKenzie, H. (Distillery), 1923 v S (1)
McKenzie, R. (Airdrie), 1967 v W (1)
McKeown, H. (Linfield), 1892 v E, S, W; 1893 v S, W; 1894 v S, W (7)
McKie, H. (Cliftonville), 1895 v E, S, W (3)
McKinney, D. (Hull C), 1921 v S; (with Bradford C), 1924 v S (2)
McKinney, V. J. (Falkirk), 1966 v WG (1)
McKnight, A. (Celtic), 1988 v Y, T, Gr, Pol, F, Ma; (with West Ham U) 1989 v Ei, H, Sp (2) (10)
McKnight, J. (Preston NE), 1912 v S; (with Glentoran), 1913 v S (2)
McLaughlin, J. C. (Shrewsbury T), 1962 v E, S, W, Gr; 1963 v W; (with Swansea T), 1964 v W, U; 1965 v E, W, Sw (2); 1966 v W (12)
McLean, T. (Limavady), 1885 v S (1)
McMahon, G. J. (Tottenham H), 1995 v Ca (sub), Ch, La (3)
McMahon, J. (Bohemians), 1934 v S (1)
McMaster, G. (Glentoran), 1897 v E, S, W (3)
McMichael, A. (Newcastle U), 1950 v E, S; 1951 v E, S, F; 1952 v E, S, W; 1953 v E, S, W, F; 1954 v E, S, W; 1955 v E, W; 1956 v W; 1957 v E, S, W, I, P (2); 1958 v E, S, W, I (2), Cz (2), Arg, WG, F; 1959 v S, W, Sp; 1960 v E, S, W (40)
McMillan, G. (Distillery), 1903 v E; 1905 v W (2)
McMillan, S. (Manchester U), 1963 v E, S (2)
McMillen, W. S. (Manchester U), 1934 v E; 1935 v S; 1937 v S; (with Chesterfield), 1938 v S, W; 1939 v E, S (7)
McMordie, A. S. (Middlesbrough), 1969 v Is, T (2), E, S, W; 1970 v E, S, W, USSR; 1971 v Cy (2), E, S, W; 1972 v USSR, Sp, E, S, W; 1973 v Bul (21)
McMorran, E. J. (Belfast C), 1947 v E; (with Barnsley), 1951 v E, S, W; 1952 v E, S, W; 1953 v E, S, F; (with Doncaster R), 1953 v W; 1954 v E; 1956 v W; 1957 v I, P (15)
McMullan, D. (Liverpool), 1926 v E, W; 1927 v S (3)
McNally, B. A. (Shrewsbury T), 1986 v Mor; 1987 v T (sub); 1988 v Y, Gr, Ma (sub) (5)
McNinch, J. (Ballymena), 1931 v S; 1932 v S, W (3)
McParland, P. J. (Aston Villa), 1954 v W; 1955 v E, S; 1956 v E, S; 1957 v E, S, W, P; 1958 v E, S, W, I (2), Cz (2), Arg, WG, F; 1959 v E, S, W, Sp; 1960 v E, S, W; 1961 v E, S, W, I, WG (2), Gr; (with Wolverhampton W), 1962 v Ho (34)
McShane, J. (Cliftonville), 1899 v S; 1900 v E, S, W (4)
McVickers, J. (Glentoran), 1888 v E; 1889 v S (2)
McWha, W. B. R. (Knock), 1882 v E, W; (with Cliftonville), 1883 v E, W; 1884 v E; 1885 v E, W (7)
Macartney, A. (Ulster), 1903 v S, W; (with Linfield), 1904 v S, W; (with Everton), 1905 v E, S; (with Belfast C), 1907 v E, S, W; 1908 v E, S, W; (with Glentoran), 1909 v E, S, W (15)
Mackie, J. (Arsenal), 1923 v W; (with Portsmouth), 1935 v S, W (3)
Madden, O. (Norwich C), 1938 v E (1)
Magill, E. J. (Arsenal), 1962 v E, S, Gr; 1963 v E, S, W, Pol (2), Sp; 1964 v E, S, W, U, Sp; 1965 v E, S, Sw (2), Ho, Alb; 1966 v S, (with Brighton), E, Alb, W, WG, M (26)
Magilton, J. (Oxford U), 1991 v Pol, Y, Fa; 1992 v Fa, A, D, S, Li, G; 1993 v Alb, D, Alb, Ei, Li, La; 1994 v La, D, Ei; (with Southampton), R, Lie, Co, M; 1995 v P, A, Ei (2), Ca, Ch, La (29)
Maginnis, H. (Linfield), 1900 v E, S, W; 1903 v S, W; 1904 v E, S, W (8)
Maguire, E. (Distillery), 1907 v S (1)
Mahood, J. (Belfast C), 1926 v S; 1928 v E, S, W; 1929 v E, S, W; 1930 v W; (with Ballymena), 1934 v S (9)
Manderson, R. (Rangers), 1920 v W, S; 1925 v S, E; 1926 v S (5)
Mansfield, J. (Dublin Freebooters), 1901 v E (1)
Martin, C. J. (Glentoran), 1947 v S; (with Leeds U), 1948 v E, S, W; (with Aston Villa), 1949 v E; 1950 v W (6)
Martin, D. (Bo'ness), 1925 v S (1)
Martin, D. C. (Cliftonville), 1882 v E, W; 1883 v E (3)
Martin, D. K. (Belfast C), 1934 v E, S, W; 1935 v S; (with Wolverhampton W), 1935 v E; 1936 v W; (with Nottingham F), 1937 v S; 1938 v E, S; 1939 v S (10)
Mathieson, A. (Luton T), 1921 v W; 1922 v E (2)
Maxwell, J. (Linfield), 1902 v W; 1903 v W, E; (with Glentoran), 1905 v W, S; (with Belfast C), 1906 v W; 1907 v S (7)
Meek, H. L. (Glentoran), 1925 v W (1)
Mehaffy, J. A. C. (Queen's Island), 1922 v W (1)
Meldon, P. A. (Dublin Freebooters), 1899 v S, W (2)
Mercer, H. V. A. (Linfield), 1908 v E (1)
Mercer, J. T. (Distillery), 1898 v E, S, W; 1899 v E; (with Linfield), 1902 v E, W; (with Distillery), 1903 v S, W; (with Derby Co), 1904 v E, W; 1905 v S (11)
Millar, W. (Barrow), 1932 v W; 1933 v S (2)
Miller, J. (Middlesbrough), 1929 v W, S; 1930 v E (3)
Milligan, D. (Chesterfield), 1939 v W (1)
Milne, R. G. (Linfield), 1894 v E, S, W; 1895 v E, W; 1896 v E, S, W; 1897 v E, S; 1898 v E, S, W; 1899 v E, W; 1901 v W; 1902 v E, S, W; 1903 v E, S; 1904 v E, S, W; 1906 v E, S, W (27)
Mitchell, E. J. (Cliftonville), 1933 v S; (with Glentoran), 1934 v W (2)
Mitchell, W. (Distillery), 1932 v E, W; 1933 v E, W; (with Chelsea), 1934 v W, S; 1935 v S, E; 1936 v S, E; 1937 v E, S, W; 1938 v E, S (15)
Molyneux, T. B. (Ligoniel), 1883 v E, W; (with Cliftonville), 1884 v E, W, S; 1885 v E, W; 1886 v E, W, S; 1888 v S (11)
Montgomery, F. J. (Coleraine), 1955 v E (1)
Moore, C. (Glentoran), 1949 v W (1)
Moore, J. (Linfield Ath), 1891 v E, S, W (3)
Moore, P. (Aberdeen), 1933 v E (1)
Moore, T. (Ulster), 1887 v S, W (2)
Moore, W. (Falkirk), 1923 v S (1)
Moorhead, F. W. (Dublin University), 1885 v E (1)
Moorhead, G. (Linfield), 1923 v S; 1928 v S; 1929 v S (3)

Moran, J. (Leeds C), 1912 v S (1)
Moreland, V. (Derby Co), 1979 v Bul (2 sub), E, S; 1980 v E, Ei (6)
Morgan, F. G. (Linfield), 1923 v E; (with Nottingham F), 1924 v S; 1927 v E; 1928 v E, S, W; 1929 v E (7)
Morgan, S. (Port Vale), 1972 v Sp; 1973 v Bul (sub), P, Cy, E, S, W; (with Aston Villa), 1974 v Bul, P, S, E; 1975 v Se; 1976 v Se (sub), N, Y; (with Brighton & HA), S, W (sub); (with Sparta Rotterdam), 1979 v D (18)
Morrison, J. (Linfield Ath), 1891 v E, W (2)
Morrison, T. (Glentoran), 1895 v E, S, W; (with Burnley), 1899 v W; 1900 v W; 1902 v E, S (7)
Morrogh, E. (Bohemians), 1896 v S (1)
Morrow, S. J. (Arsenal), 1990 v U (sub); 1991 v A (sub), Pol, Y; 1992 v Fa, S (sub), G (sub); 1993 v Sp (sub), Alb, Ei; 1994 v R, Co, M (sub); 1995 v P, Ei (2), La (17)
Morrow, W. J. (Moyola Park), 1883 v E, W; 1884 v S (3)
Muir, R. (Oldpark), 1885 v S, W (2)
Mullan, G. (Glentoran), 1983 v S, E, W, Alb (sub) (4)
Mulholland, S. (Celtic), 1906 v S, E (2)
Mulligan, J. (Manchester C), 1921 v S (1)
Murphy, J. (Bradford C), 1910 v E, S, W (3)
Murphy, N. (QPR), 1905 v E, S, W (3)
Murray, J. M. (Motherwell), 1910 v E, S; (with Sheffield W), 1910 v W (3)

Napier, R. J. (Bolton W), 1966 v WG (1)
Neill, W. J. T. (Arsenal), 1961 v I, Gr, WG; 1962 v E, S, W, Gr; 1963 v E, W, Pol, Sp; 1964 v S, E, W, U, Sp; 1965 v E, S, W, Sw, Ho (2), Alb; 1966 v S, E, W, Alb, WG, M; 1967 v S, W; 1968 v S, E; 1969 v E, S, W, Is, T (2); 1970 v S, E, W, USSR (2); (with Hull C), 1971 v Cy, Sp; 1972 v USSR (2), Sp, S, E, W; 1973 v Bul, Cy (2), P, E, S, W (59)
Nelis, P. (Nottingham F), 1923 v E (1)
Nelson, S. (Arsenal), 1970 v W, E (sub); 1971 v Cy, Sp, E, S, W; 1972 v USSR (2), Sp, E, S, W; 1973 v Bul, Cy, P; 1974 v S, E; 1975 v Se, Y; 1976 v Se, N, Is, E; 1977 v Bel (sub), WG, W, Ic; 1978 v Ic, Ho, Bel; 1979 v Ei, D, Bul, E, Bul, E, S, W, D; 1980 v E, Ei, Is; 1981 v S, P, S, Se; (with Brighton & HA), 1982 v E, S, Sp (sub), A (51)
Nicholl, C. J. (Aston Villa), 1975 v Se, Y, E, S, W; 1976 v Se, N, Y, S, E, W; 1977 v W; (with Southampton), 1978 v Bel (sub), S, E, W; 1979 v Ei, Bul, E, Bul, E, W; 1980 v Ei, Is, S, E, W, Aus (3); 1981 v Se, P, S, P, S, Se; 1982 v S, Is, E, F, W, Y, Hon, Sp, A, F; 1983 v S (sub), E, W; (with Grimsby T), 1984 v A, T (51)
Nicholl, H. (Belfast C), 1902 v E, W; 1905 v E (3)
Nicholl, J. M. (Manchester U), 1976 v Is, W (sub); 1977 v Ho, Bel, E, S, W, Ic; 1978 v Ic, Ho, Bel, S, E, W; 1979 v Ei, D, Bul, E, Bul, E, S, W, D; 1980 v E, Ei, Is, S, E, W, Aus (3); 1981 v Se, P, S, P, S, Se; 1982 v S, Is, E; (with Toronto B), F, W, Y, Hon, Sp, A, F; (with Sunderland), 1983 v A, WG, Alb, T, Alb; (with Toronto B), S, E, W; 1984 v T; (with Rangers), WG, S, E; (with Toronto B), Fi; 1985 v R; (with WBA), Fi, E, Sp, T; 1986 v T, R, E, F, Alg, Sp, Br (73)
Nicholson, J. J. (Manchester U), 1961 v S, W; 1962 v E, W, Gr, Ho; 1963 v E, S, Pol (2); (with Huddersfield T), 1965 v W, Ho (2), Alb; 1966 v S, E, W, Alb, M; 1967 v S, W; 1968 v S, E, W; 1969 v S, E, W, T (2); 1970 v S, E, W, USSR (2); 1971 v Cy (2), E, S, W; 1972 v USSR (2) (41)
Nixon, R. (Linfield), 1914 v S (1)
Nolan-Whelan, J. V. (Dublin Freebooters), 1901 v E, W; 1902 v S, W (4)

O'Boyle, G. (Dunfermline Ath), 1994 v Co (sub), M; (with St Johnstone), 1995 v P (sub), La (sub), Ca (sub), Ch (sub) (6)
O'Brien, M. T. (QPR), 1921 v S; (with Leicester C), 1922 v S, W; 1924 v S, W; (with Hull C), 1925 v S, E, W; 1926 v W; (with Derby Co), 1927 v W (10)
O'Connell, P. (Sheffield W), 1912 v E, S; (with Hull C), 1914 v E, S, W (5)
O'Doherty, A. (Coleraine), 1970 v E, W (sub) (2)
O'Driscoll, J. F. (Swansea T), 1949 v E, S, W (3)
O'Hagan, C. (Tottenham H), 1905 v S, W; 1906 v S, W, E; (with Aberdeen), 1907 v E, S, W; 1908 v S, W; 1909 v E (11)
O'Hagan, W. (St Mirren), 1920 v E, W (2)
O'Kane, W. J. (Nottingham F), 1970 v E, W, S (sub); 1971 v Sp, E, S, W; 1972 v USSR (2); 1973 v P, Cy; 1974 v Bul, P, S, E, W; 1975 v N, Se, E, S (20)
O'Mahoney, M. T. (Bristol R), 1939 v S (1)
O'Neill, C. (Motherwell), 1989 v Ch (sub); 1990 v Ei (sub); 1991 v D (3)
O'Neill, J. (Leicester C), 1980 v Is, S, E, W, Aus (3); 1981 v P, S, P, S, Se; 1982 v S, Is, E, F, S, F (sub); 1983 v A, WG, Alb, T, Alb, S; 1984 v S (sub); 1985 v Is, Fi, E, Sp, T; 1986 v T, R, E, F, D, Mor, Alg, Sp, Br (39)
O'Neill, J. (Sunderland), 1962 v W (1)
O'Neill, M. A. (Newcastle U), 1988 v Gr, Pol, F, Ma; 1989 v Ei, H, Sp (sub), Sp (sub), Ma (sub), Ch; (with Dundee U), 1990 v H (sub), Ei; 1991 v Pol; 1992 v Fa (sub), S (sub), G (sub); 1993 v Alb (sub + 1), Ei, Sp, Li, La; (with Hibernian), 1994 v Lie (sub); 1995 v A (sub), Ei (25)
O'Neill, M. H. (Distillery), 1972 v USSR (sub), (with Nottingham F), Sp (sub), W (sub); 1973 v P, Cy, E, S, W; 1974 v Bul, P, E (sub), W; 1975 v Se, Y, E, S; 1976 v Y (sub); 1977 v E (sub), S; 1978 v Ic, Ho, S, E, W; 1979 v Ei, D, Bul, E, Bul, D; 1980 v Ei, Is, Aus (3); 1981 v Se, P; (with Norwich C), P, S, Se; (with Manchester C), 1982 v S; (with Norwich C), E, F, S, Y, Hon, Sp, A, F; 1983 v A, WG, Alb, T, Alb, S, E; (with Notts Co), 1984 v A, T, WG, E, W, Fi; 1985 v R, Fi (64)
O'Reilly, H. (Dublin Freebooters), 1901 v S, W; 1904 v S (3)

Parke, J. (Linfield), 1964 v S; (with Hibernian), 1964 v E, Sp; (with Sunderland), 1965 v Sw, S, W, Ho (2), Alb; 1966 v WG; 1967 v E, S; 1968 v S, E (14)
Patterson, D. J. (C Palace), 1994 v Co (sub), M (sub); 1995 v Ei (sub+1), La, Ca, Ch (sub), La (sub) (8)
Peacock, R. (Celtic), 1952 v S; 1953 v F; 1954 v W; 1955 v E, S; 1956 v E, S; 1957 v W, I, P; 1958 v S, E, W, I (2), Arg, Cz (2), WG; 1959 v E, S, W; 1960 v S, E; 1961 v E, S, I, WG (2), Gr; (with Coleraine), 1962 v S (31)
Peden, J. (Linfield), 1887 v S, W; 1888 v W, E; 1889 v S, E; 1890 v W, S; 1891 v W, E; 1892 v W, E; 1893 v E, S, W; (with Distillery), 1896 v W, E, S; 1897 v W, S; 1898 v W, E, S; (with Linfield), 1899 v W (24)
Penney, S. (Brighton & HA), 1985 v Is; 1986 v T, R, E, F, D, Mor, Alg, Sp; 1987 v E, T, Is; 1988 v Pol, F, Ma; 1989 v Ei, Sp (17)
Percy, J. C. (Belfast YMCA), 1889 v W (1)
Platt, J. A. (Middlesbrough), 1976 v Is (sub); 1978 v S, E, W; 1980 v S, E, W, Aus (3); 1981 v Se, P; 1982 v F, S, W (sub), A; 1983 v A, WG, Alb, T; (with Ballymena U), 1984 v E, W (sub); (with Coleraine), 1986 v Mor (sub) (23)
Ponsonby, J. (Distillery), 1895 v S; 1896 v E, S, W; 1897 v E, S, W; 1899 v E (8)
Potts, R. M. C. (Cliftonville), 1883 v E, W (2)
Priestley, T. J. (Coleraine), 1933 v S; (with Chelsea), 1934 v E (2)
Pyper, Jas. (Cliftonville), 1897 v S, W; 1898 v S, E, W; 1899 v S; 1900 v E (7)
Pyper, John (Cliftonville), 1897 v E, S, W; 1899 v E, W; 1900 v E, W, S; 1902 v S (9)
Pyper, M. (Linfield), 1932 v W (1)

Quinn, J. M. (Blackburn R), 1985 v Is, Fi, E, Sp, T; 1986 v T, R, E, F, D (sub), Mor (sub); 1987 v E (sub), T; (with Swindon T), 1988 v Y (sub), T, Gr, Pol, F (sub), Ma;

(with Leicester C), 1989 v Ei, H (sub), Sp (sub + 1); (with Bradford C), Ma, Ch; 1990 v H, (with West Ham U), N; 1991 v Y (sub); (with Bournemouth), 1992 v Li; (with Reading), 1993 v Sp, D, Alb (sub), Ei (sub), La (sub); 1994 v La, D (sub), Ei, R, Lie, Co, M; 1995 v P, A (sub), La (sub) (44)

Rafferty, P. (Linfield), 1980 v E (sub) (1)
Ramsey, P. (Leicester C), 1984 v A, WG, S; 1985 v Is, E, Sp, T; 1986 v T, Mor; 1987 v Is, E, Y (sub); 1988 v Y; 1989 v Sp (14)
Rankine, J. (Alexander), 1883 v E, W (2)
Raper, E. O. (Dublin University), 1886 v W (1)
Rattray, D. (Avoniel), 1882 v E; 1883 v E, W (3)
Rea, B. (Glentoran), 1901 v E (1)
Redmond, J. (Cliftonville), 1884 v W (1)
Reid, G. H. (Cardiff C), 1923 v S (1)
Reid, J. (Ulster), 1883 v E; 1884 v W; 1887 v S; 1889 v W; 1890 v S, W (6)
Reid, S. E. (Derby Co), 1934 v E, W; 1936 v E (3)
Reid, W. (Hearts), 1931 v E (1)
Reilly, M. M. (Portsmouth), 1900 v E; 1902 v E (2)
Renneville, W. T. (Leyton), 1910 v S, E, W; (with Aston Villa), 1911 v W (4)
Reynolds, J. (Distillery), 1890 v E, W; (with Ulster), 1891 v E, S, W (5)
Reynolds, R. (Bohemians), 1905 v W (1)
Rice, P. J. (Arsenal), 1969 v Is; 1970 v USSR; 1971 v E, S, W; 1972 v USSR, Sp, E, S, W; 1973 v Bul, Cy, E, S, W; 1974 v Bul, P, S, E, W; 1975 v N, Y, E, S, W; 1976 v Se, N, Y, Is, S, E, W; 1977 v Ho, Bel, WG, E, S, Ic; 1978 v Ic, Ho, Bel; 1979 v Ei, D, E (2), S, W, D; 1980 v E (49)
Roberts, F. C. (Glentoran), 1931 v S (1)
Robinson, P. (Distillery), 1920 v S; (with Blackburn R), 1921 v W (2)
Rogan, A. (Celtic), 1988 v Y (sub), Gr, Pol (sub); 1989 v Ei (sub), H, Sp (2), Ma (sub), Ch; 1990 v H, N (sub), U; 1991 v Y (2), D, A; (with Sunderland), 1992 v Li (sub) (17)
Rollo, D. (Linfield), 1912 v W; 1913 v W; 1914 v W, E; (with Blackburn R), 1920 v S, W; 1921 v E, S, W; 1922 v E; 1923 v E; 1924 v S, W; 1925 v W; 1926 v E; 1927 v E (16)
Rosbotham, A. (Cliftonville), 1887 v E, S, W; 1888 v E, S, W; 1889 v E (7)
Ross, W. E. (Newcastle U), 1969 v Is (1)
Rowland, K. (West Ham U), 1995 v Ca, Ch, La (3)
Rowley, R. W. M. (Southampton), 1929 v S, W; 1930 v W, E; (with Tottenham H), 1931 v W; 1932 v S (6)
Russell, A. (Linfield), 1947 v E (1)
Russell, S. R. (Bradford C), 1930 v E, S; (with Derry C), 1932 v E (3)
Ryan, R. A. (WBA), 1950 v W (1)

Sanchez, L. P. (Wimbledon), 1987 v T (sub); 1989 v Sp, Ma (3)
Scott, E. (Liverpool), 1920 v S; 1921 v E, S, W; 1922 v E; 1925 v W; 1926 v E, S, W; 1927 v E, S, W; 1928 v E, S, W; 1929 v E, S, W; 1930 v E; 1931 v E; 1932 v W; 1933 v E, S, W; 1934 v E, S, W; (with Belfast C), 1935 v S; 1936 v E, S, W (31)
Scott, J. (Grimsby), 1958 v Cz, F (2)
Scott, J. E. (Cliftonville), 1901 v S (1)
Scott, L. J. (Dublin University), 1895 v S, W (2)
Scott, P. W. (Everton), 1975 v W; 1976 v Y; (with York C), Is, S, E (sub), W; 1978 v S, E, W; (with Aldershot), 1979 v S (sub) (10)
Scott, T. (Cliftonville), 1894 v E, S; 1895 v S, W; 1896 v S, E, W; 1897 v E, W; 1898 v E, S, W; 1900 v W (13)
Scott, W. (Linfield), 1903 v E, S, W; 1904 v E, S, W; (with Everton), 1905 v E, S; 1907 v E, S; 1908 v E, S, W; 1909 v E, S, W; 1910 v E, S; 1911 v E, S, W; 1912 v E; (with Leeds City), 1913 v E, S, W (25)
Scraggs, M. J. (Glentoran), 1921 v W; 1922 v E (2)
Seymour, H. C. (Bohemians), 1914 v W (1)
Seymour, J. (Cliftonville), 1907 v W; 1909 v W (2)
Shanks, T. (Woolwich Arsenal), 1903 v S; 1904 v W; (with Brentford), 1905 v E (3)
Sharkey, P. (Ipswich T), 1976 v S (1)
Sheehan, Dr G. (Bohemians), 1899 v S; 1900 v E, W (3)
Sheridan, J. (Everton), 1903 v W, E, S; 1904 v E, S; (with Stoke C), 1905 v E (6)
Sherrard, J. (Limavady), 1885 v S; 1887 v W; 1888 v W (3)
Sherrard, W. (Cliftonville), 1895 v E, W, S (3)
Sherry, J. J. (Bohemians), 1906 v E; 1907 v W (2)
Shields, J. (Southampton), 1957 v S (1)
Silo, M. (Belfast YMCA), 1888 v E (1)
Simpson, W. J. (Rangers), 1951 v W, F; 1954 v E, S; 1955 v E; 1957 v I, P; 1958 v S, E, W, I; 1959 v S (12)
Sinclair, J. (Knock), 1882 v E, W (2)
Slemin, J. C. (Bohemians), 1909 v W (1)
Sloan, A. S. (London Caledonians), 1925 v W (1)
Sloan, D. (Oxford U), 1969 v Is; 1971 v Sp (2)
Sloan, H. A. de B. (Bohemians), 1903 v E; 1904 v S; 1905 v E; 1906 v W; 1907 v E, W; 1908 v W; 1909 v S (8)
Sloan, J. W. (Arsenal), 1947 v W (1)
Sloan, T. (Cardiff C), 1926 v S, W, E; 1927 v W, S; 1928 v E, W; 1929 v E; (with Linfield), 1930 v W, S; 1931 v S (11)
Sloan, T. (Manchester U), 1979 v S, W (sub), D (sub) (3)
Small, J. (Clarence), 1887 v E (1)
Small, J. M. (Cliftonville), 1893 v E, S, W (3)
Smith, E. E. (Cardiff C), 1921 v S; 1923 v W, E; 1924 v E (4)
Smith, J. (Distillery), 1901 v S, W (2)
Smyth, R. H. (Dublin University), 1886 v W (1)
Smyth, S. (Wolverhampton W), 1948 v E, S, W; 1949 v S, W; 1950 v E, S, W; (with Stoke C), 1952 v E (9)
Smyth, W. (Distillery), 1949 v E, S; 1954 v S, E (4)
Snape, A. (Airdrie), 1920 v E (1)
Spence, D. W. (Bury), 1975 v Y, E, S, W; 1976 v Se, Is, E, W, S (sub); (with Blackpool), 1977 v Ho (sub), WG (sub), E (sub), S (sub), W (sub), Ic (sub); 1979 v Ei, D (sub), E (sub), Bul (sub), E (sub), S, W, D; 1980 v Ei; (with Southend U), Is (sub), Aus (sub); 1981 v S (sub), Se (sub); 1982 v F (sub) (29)
Spencer, S. (Distillery), 1890 v E, S; 1892 v E, S, W; 1893 v E (6)
Spiller, E. A. (Cliftonville), 1883 v E, W; 1884 v E, W, S (5)
Stanfield, O. M. (Distillery), 1887 v E, S, W; 1888 v E, S, W; 1889 v E, S, W; 1890 v E, S; 1891 v E, S, W; 1892 v E, S, W; 1893 v E, W; 1894 v E, S, W; 1895 v E, S; 1896 v E, S, W; 1897 v E, S, W (30)
Steele, A. (Charlton Ath), 1926 v W, S; (with Fulham), 1929 v W, S (4)
Stevenson, A. E. (Rangers), 1934 v E, S, W; (with Everton), 1935 v E, S; 1936 v S, W; 1937 v E, W; 1938 v E, W; 1939 v E, S, W; 1947 v S, W; 1948 v S (17)
Stewart, A. (Glentoran), 1967 v W; 1968 v S, E; (with Derby Co), 1968 v W; 1969 v Is, T (1 + 1 sub) (7)
Stewart, D. C. (Hull C), 1978 v Bel (1)
Stewart, I. (QPR), 1982 v F (sub); 1983 v A, WG, Alb, T, Alb, S, E, W; 1984 v A, T, WG, S, E, W, Fi; 1985 v R, Fi, Is, E, Sp, T; (with Newcastle U), 1986 v R, E, D, Mor, Alg (sub), Sp (sub), Br; 1987 v E, Is (sub) (31)
Stewart, R. H. (St Columb's Court), 1890 v E, S, W; (with Cliftonville), 1892 v E, S, W; 1893 v E, W; 1894 v E, S, W (11)
Stewart, T. C. (Linfield), 1961 v W (1)
Swan, S. (Linfield), 1899 v S (1)

Taggart, G. P. (Barnsley), 1990 v N, U; 1991 v Y, D, A, Pol, Fa; 1992 v Fa, A, D, S, Li, G; 1993 v Alb, Sp, D, Alb, Ei,

Sp, Li, La; 1994 v La, D, Ei, R, Lie, Co, M; 1995 v P (sub), A, Ei (2), Ca, Ch, La (35)
Taggart, J. (Walsall), 1899 v W (1)
Thompson, F. W. (Cliftonville), 1910 v E, S, W; (with Bradford C), 1911 v E; (with Linfield), v W; 1912 v E, W; 1913 v E, S, W; (with Clyde), 1914 v E, S (12)
Thompson, J. (Belfast Ath), 1889 v S (1)
Thompson, J. (Distillery), 1897 v S (1)
Thunder, P. J. (Bohemians), 1911 v W (1)
Todd, S. J. (Burnley), 1966 v M (sub); 1967 v E; 1968 v W; 1969 v E, S, W; 1970 v S, USSR; (with Sheffield W), 1971 v Cy (2), Sp (sub) (11)
Toner, J. (Arsenal), 1922 v W; 1923 v W; 1924 v W, E; 1925 v E, S; (with St Johnstone), 1927 v E, S (8)
Torrans, R. (Linfield), 1893 v S (1)
Torrans, S. (Linfield), 1889 v S; 1890 v S, W; 1891 v S, W; 1892 v E, S, W; 1893 v E, S; 1894 v E, S, W; 1895 v E; 1896 v E, S, W; 1897 v E, S, W; 1898 v E, S; 1899 v E, W; 1901 v S, W (26)
Trainor, D. (Crusaders), 1967 v W (1)
Tully, C. P. (Celtic), 1949 v E; 1950 v E; 1952 v S; 1953 v E, S, W, F; 1954 v S; 1956 v E; 1959 v Sp (10)
Turner, E. (Cliftonville), 1896 v E, W (2)
Turner, W. (Cliftonville), 1886 v E; 1886 v S; 1888 v S (3)
Twoomey, J. F. (Leeds U), 1938 v W; 1939 v E (2)

Uprichard, W. N. M. C. (Swindon T), 1952 v E, S, W; 1953 v E, S; (with Portsmouth), 1953 v W, F; 1955 v E, S, W; 1956 v E, S, W; 1958 v S, I, Cz; 1959 v S, Sp (18)

Vernon, J. (Belfast C), 1947 v E, S; (with WBA), 1947 v W; 1948 v E, S, W; 1949 v E, S, W; 1950 v E, S; 1951 v E, S, W, F; 1952 v S, E (17)

Waddell, T. M. R. (Cliftonville), 1906 v S (1)
Walker, J. (Doncaster R), 1955 v W (1)
Walker, T. (Bury), 1911 v S (1)
Walsh, D. J. (WBA), 1947 v S, W; 1948 v E, S, W; 1949 v E, S, W; 1950 v W (9)
Walsh, W. (Manchester C), 1948 v E, S, W; 1949 v E, S (5)
Waring, R. (Distillery), 1899 v E (1)
Warren, P. (Shelbourne), 1913 v E, S (2)
Watson, J. (Ulster), 1883 v E, W; 1886 v E, S, W; 1887 v S, W; 1889 v E, W (9)
Watson, P. (Distillery), 1971 v Cy (sub) (1)
Watson, T. (Cardiff C), 1926 v S (1)
Wattle, J. (Distillery), 1899 v E (1)
Webb, C. G. (Brighton), 1909 v S, W; 1911 v S (3)
Weir, E. (Clyde), 1939 v W (1)
Welsh, E. (Carlisle U), 1966 v W, WG, M; 1967 v W (4)
Whiteside, N. (Manchester U), 1982 v Y, Hon, Sp, A, F; 1983 v WG, Alb, T; 1984 v A, T, WG, S, E, W, Fi; 1985 v R, Fi, Is, E, Sp, T; 1986 v R, E, F, D, Mor, Alg, Sp, Br; 1987 v E (2), Is, Y; 1988 v T, Pol, F; (with Everton), 1990 v H, Ei (38)
Whiteside, T. (Distillery), 1891 v E (1)
Whitfield, E. R. (Dublin University), 1886 v W (1)
Williams, J. R. (Ulster), 1886 v E, S (2)
Williams, P. A. (WBA), 1991 v Fa (sub) (1)
Williamson, J. (Cliftonville), 1890 v E; 1892 v S; 1893 v S (3)
Willigham, T. (Burnley), 1933 v W; 1934 v S (2)
Willis, G. (Linfield), 1906 v S, W; 1907 v S; 1912 v S (4)
Wilson, D. J. (Brighton & HA), 1987 v T, Is, E (sub); (with Luton T), 1988 v Y, T, Gr, Pol, F, Ma; 1989 v Ei, H, Sp, Ma, Ch; 1990 v H, Ei, N, U; (with Sheffield W), 1991 v Y, D, A, Fa; 1992 v A (sub), S (24)
Wilson, H. (Linfield), 1925 v W (1)
Wilson, K. J. (Ipswich T), 1987 v Is, E, Y; (with Chelsea), 1988 v Y, T, Gr (sub), Pol (sub), F (sub); 1989 v H (sub), Sp (2), Ma, Ch; 1990 v Ei (sub), N, U; 1991 v Y (2), A, Pol, Fa; 1992 v Fa, A, D, S; (with Notts Co), Li, G; 1993 v Alb, Sp, D, Sp, Li, La; 1994 v La, D, Ei, R, Lie, Co, M; (with Walsall), 1995 v Ei (sub), La (42)
Wilson, M. (Distillery), 1884 v E, S, W (3)
Wilson, R. (Cliftonville), 1888 v S (1)
Wilson, S. J. (Glenavon), 1962 v S; 1964 v S; (with Falkirk), 1964 v E, W, U, Sp; 1965 v E, Sw; (with Dundee), 1966 v W, WG; 1967 v S; 1968 v E (12)
Wilton, J. M. (St Columb's Court), 1888 v E, W; 1889 v S, E; (with Cliftonville), 1890 v E; (with St Columb's Court), 1892 v W; 1893 v S (7)
Worthington, N. (Sheffield W), 1984 v W, Fi (sub); 1985 v Is, Sp (sub); 1986 v T, R (sub), E (sub), D, Alg, Sp; 1987 v E (2), T, Is, Y; 1988 v Y, T, Gr, Pol, F, Ma; 1989 v Ei, H, Sp, Ma; 1990 v H, Ei, U; 1991 v Y, D, A, Fa; 1992 v A, D, S, Li, G; 1993 v Alb, Sp, D, Ei, Sp, Li, La; 1994 v La, D, Ei, Lie, Co, M; (with Leeds U), 1995 v P, A, Ei (2), La, Ca (sub), Ch, La (58)
Wright, J. (Cliftonville), 1906 v E, S, W; 1907 v E, S, W (6)
Wright, T. J. (Newcastle U), 1989 v Ma, Ch; 1990 v H, U; 1992 v Fa, A, S, G; 1993 v Alb, Sp, Alb, Ei, Sp, Li, La; 1994 v La; (with Nottingham F), D, Ei, R, Lie, Co, M (sub) (22)
Young, S. (Linfield), 1907 v E, S; 1908 v E, S; (with Airdrie), 1909 v E; 1912 v S; (with Linfield), 1914 v E, S, W (9)

SCOTLAND

Adams, J. (Hearts), 1889 v Ni; 1892 v W; 1893 v Ni (3)
Agnew, W. B. (Kilmarnock), 1907 v Ni; 1908 v W, Ni (3)
Aird, J. (Burnley), 1954 v N (2), A, U (4)
Aitken, A. (Newcastle U), 1901 v E; 1902 v E; 1903 v E, W; 1904 v E; 1905 v E, W; 1906 v E; (with Middlesbrough), 1907 v E, W; 1908 v E; (with Leicester Fosse), 1910 v E; 1911 v E, Ni (14)
Aitken, G. G. (East Fife), 1949 v E, F; 1950 v W, Ni, Sw; (with Sunderland), 1953 v W, Ni; 1954 v E (8)
Aitken, R. (Dumbarton), 1886 v E; 1888 v Ni (2)
Aitken, R. (Celtic), 1980 v Pe (sub), Bel, W (sub), E, Pol; 1983 v Bel, Ca (1 + 1 sub); 1984 v Bel (sub), Ni, W (sub); 1985 v E, Ic; 1986 v W, EG, Aus (2), Is, R, E, D, WG, U; 1987 v Bul, Ei (2), L, Bel, E, Br; 1988 v H, Bel, Bul, L, S.Ar, Ma, Sp, Co, E; 1989 v N, Y, I, Cy, F, Cy, E, Ch; 1990 v Y, F, N; (with Newcastle U), Arg (sub), Pol, Ma, Cr, Se, Br; (with St Mirren), 1992 v R (sub) (57)
Aitkenhead, W. A. C. (Blackburn R), 1912 v Ni (1)
Albiston, A. (Manchester U), 1982 v Ni; 1984 v U, Bel, EG, W, E; 1985 v Y, Ic, Sp (2), W; 1986 v EG, Ho, U (14)
Alexander, D. (East Stirlingshire), 1894 v W, Ni (2)
Allan, D. S. (Queen's Park), 1885 v E, W; 1886 v W (3)
Allan, G. (Liverpool), 1897 v E (1)
Allan, H. (Hearts), 1902 v W (1)
Allan, J. (Queen's Park), 1887 v E, W (2)
Allan, T. (Dundee), 1974 v WG, N (2)
Ancell, R. F. D. (Newcastle U), 1937 v W, Ni (2)
Anderson, A. (Hearts), 1933 v E; 1934 v A, E, W, Ni; 1935 v E, W, Ni; 1936 v E, W, Ni; 1937 v G, E, W, Ni, A; 1938 v E, W, Ni, Cz, Ho; 1939 v W, H (23)
Anderson, F. (Clydesdale), 1874 v E (1)
Anderson, G. (Kilmarnock), 1901 v Ni (1)
Anderson, H. A. (Raith R), 1914 v W (1)
Anderson, J. (Leicester C), 1954 v Fi (1)

Anderson, K. (Queen's Park), 1896 v Ni; 1898 v E, Ni (3)
Anderson, W. (Queen's Park), 1882 v E; 1883 v E, W; 1884 v E; 1885 v E, W (6)
Andrews, P. (Eastern), 1875 v E (1)
Archibald, A. (Rangers), 1921 v W; 1922 v W, E; 1923 v Ni; 1924 v E, W; 1931 v E; 1932 v E (8)
Archibald, S. (Aberdeen), 1980 v P (sub); (with Tottenham H), Ni, Pol, H; 1981 v Se (sub), Is, Ni, Is, Ni, E; 1982 v Ni, P, Sp (sub), Ho, Nz (sub), Br, USSR; 1983 v EG, Sw (sub), Bel; 1984 v EG, E, F; (with Barcelona), 1985 v Sp, E, Ic (sub); 1986 v WG (27)
Armstrong, M. W. (Aberdeen), 1936 v W, Ni; 1937 v G (3)
Arnott, W. (Queen's Park), 1883 v W; 1884 v E, Ni; 1885 v E, W; 1886 v E; 1887 v E, W; 1888 v E; 1889 v E; 1890 v E; 1891 v E; 1892 v E; 1893 v E (14)
Auld, J. R. (Third Lanark), 1887 v E, W; 1889 v W (3)
Auld, R. (Celtic), 1959 v H, P; 1960 v W (3)

Baird, A. (Queen's Park), 1892 v Ni; 1894 v W (2)
Baird, D. (Hearts), 1890 v Ni; 1891 v E; 1892 v W (3)
Baird, H. (Airdrieonians), 1956 v A (1)
Baird, J. C. (Vale of Leven), 1876 v E; 1878 v W; 1880 v E (3)
Baird, S. (Rangers), 1957 v Y, Sp (2), Sw, WG; 1958 v F, Ni (7)
Baird, W. U. (St Bernard), 1897 v Ni (1)
Bannon, E. (Dundee U), 1980 v Bel; 1983 v Ni, W, E, Ca; 1984 v EG; 1986 v Is, R, E, D (sub), WG (11)
Barbour, A. (Renton), 1885 v Ni (1)
Barker, J. B. (Rangers), 1893 v W; 1894 v W (2)
Barrett, F. (Dundee), 1894 v Ni; 1895 v W (2)
Battles, B. (Celtic), 1901 v E, W, Ni (3)
Battles, B. jun. (Hearts), 1931 v W (1)
Bauld, W. (Hearts), 1950 v E, Sw, P (3)
Baxter, J. C. (Rangers), 1961 v Ni, Ei (2), Cz; 1962 v Ni, W, E, Cz (2), U; 1963 v W, Ni, E, A, N, Ei, Sp; 1964 v W, E, N, WG; 1965 v W, Ni, Fi; (with Sunderland), 1966 v P, Br, Ni, W, E, I; 1967 v W, E, USSR; 1968 v W (34)
Baxter, R. D. (Middlesbrough), 1939 v E, W, H (3)
Beattie, A. (Preston NE), 1937 v E, A, Cz; 1938 v E; 1939 v W, Ni, H (7)
Beattie, R. (Preston NE), 1939 v W (1)
Begbie, I. (Hearts), 1890 v Ni; 1891 v E; 1892 v W; 1894 v E (4)
Bell, A. (Manchester U), 1912 v Ni (1)
Bell, J. (Dumbarton), 1890 v Ni; 1892 v E; (with Everton), 1896 v E; 1897 v E; 1898 v E; (with Celtic), 1899 v E, W, Ni; 1900 v E, W (10)
Bell, M. (Hearts), 1901 v W (1)
Bell, W. J. (Leeds U), 1966 v P, Br (2)
Bennett, A. (Celtic), 1904 v W; 1907 v Ni; 1908 v W; (with Rangers), 1909 v W, Ni, E; 1910 v E, W; 1911 v E, W; 1913 v Ni (11)
Bennie, R. (Airdrieonians), 1925 v W, Ni; 1926 v Ni (3)
Bernard, P. R. J. (Oldham Ath), 1995 v J (sub), Ec (2)
Berry, D. (Queen's Park), 1894 v W; 1899 v W, Ni (3)
Berry, W. H. (Queen's Park), 1888 v E; 1889 v E; 1890 v E; 1891 v E (4)
Bett, J. (Rangers), 1982 v Ho; 1983 v Bel; (with Lokeren), 1984 v Bel, W, E, F; 1985 v Y, Ic, Sp (2), W, E, Ic; (with Aberdeen), 1986 v W, Is, Ho; 1987 v Bel; 1988 v H (sub); 1989 v Y; 1990 v F (sub), N, Arg, Eg, Ma, Cr (25)
Beveridge, W. W. (Glasgow University), 1879 v E, W; 1880 v W (3)
Black, A. (Hearts), 1938 v Cz, Ho; 1939 v H (3)
Black, D. (Hurlford), 1889 v Ni (1)
Black, E. (Metz), 1988 v H (sub), L (sub) (2)
Black, I. H. (Southampton), 1948 v E (1)
Blackburn, J. E. (Royal Engineers), 1873 v E (1)
Blacklaw, A. S. (Burnley), 1963 v N, Sp; 1966 v I (3)
Blackley, J. (Hibernian), 1974 v Cz, E, Bel, Z; 1976 v Sw; 1977 v W, Se (7)
Blair, D. (Clyde), 1929 v W, Ni; 1931 v E, A, I; 1932 v W, Ni; (with Aston Villa), 1933 v W (8)
Blair, J. (Sheffield W), 1920 v E, Ni; (with Cardiff C), 1921 v E; 1922 v E; 1923 v E, W, Ni; 1924 v W (8)
Blair, J. (Motherwell), 1934 v W (1)
Blair, J. A. (Blackpool), 1947 v W (1)
Blair, W. (Third Lanark), 1896 v W (1)
Blessington, J. (Celtic), 1894 v E, Ni; 1896 v E, Ni (4)
Blyth, J. A. (Coventry C), 1978 v Bul, W (2)
Bone, J. (Norwich C), 1972 v Y (sub); 1973 v D (2)
Booth, S. (Aberdeen), 1993 v G (sub), Es (2 subs); 1994 v Sw, Ma (sub); 1995 v Fa, Ru (7)
Bowie, J. (Rangers), 1920 v E, Ni (2)
Bowie, W. (Linthouse), 1891 v Ni (1)
Bowman, D. (Dundee U), 1992 v Fi, US (sub); 1993 v G, Es; 1994 v Sw, I (6)
Bowman, G. A. (Montrose), 1892 v Ni (1)
Boyd, J. M. (Newcastle U), 1934 v Ni (1)
Boyd, R. (Mossend Swifts), 1889 v Ni; 1891 v W (2)
Boyd, T. (Motherwell), 1991 v R (sub), Sw, Bul, USSR; (with Chelsea), 1992 v Sw, R; (with Celtic), Fi, Ca, N, C; 1993 v Sw, P, I, Ma, G, Es (2); 1994 v I, Ma (sub), Ho (sub), A; 1995 v Fi, Fa, Ru, Gr, Ru, Sm (27)
Boyd, W. G. (Clyde), 1931 v I, Sw (2)
Brackenbridge, T. (Hearts), 1888 v Ni (1)
Bradshaw, T. (Bury), 1928 v E (1)
Brand, R. (Rangers), 1961 v Ni, Cz, Ei (2); 1962 v Ni, W, Cz, U (8)
Branden, T. (Blackburn R), 1896 v E (1)
Brazil, A. (Ipswich T), 1980 v Pol (sub), H; 1982 v Sp, Ho (sub), Ni, W, E, Nz, USSR (sub); 1983 v EG, Sw (with Tottenham H), W, E (sub) (13)
Bremner, D. (Hibernian), 1976 v Sw (sub) (1)
Bremner, W. J. (Leeds U), 1965 v Sp; 1966 v E, Pol, P, Br, I (2); 1967 v W, Ni, E; 1968 v W, E; 1969 v W, E, Ni, D, A, WG, Cy (2); 1970 v Ei, WG, A; 1971 v W, E; 1972 v P, Bel, Ho, Ni, W, E, Y, Cz, Br; 1973 v D (2), E (2), Ni (sub), Sw, Br; 1974 v Cz, WG, Ni, W, E, Bel, N, Z, Br, Y; 1975 v Sp (2); 1976 v D (54)
Brennan, F. (Newcastle U), 1947 v W, Ni; 1953 v W, Ni, E; 1954 v Ni, E (7)
Breslin, B. (Hibernian), 1897 v W (1)
Brewster, G. (Everton), 1921 v E (1)
Brogan, J. (Celtic), 1971 v W, Ni, P, E (4)
Brown, A. (Middlesbrough), 1904 v E (1)
Brown, A. (St Mirren), 1890 v W; 1891 v W (2)
Brown, A. D. (East Fife), 1950 v Sw, P, F; (with Blackpool), 1952 v USA, D, Se; 1953 v W; 1954 v W, E, N (2), Fi, A, U (14)
Brown, G. C. P. (Rangers), 1931 v W; 1932 v E, W, Ni; 1933 v E; 1934 v A; 1935 v E, W; 1936 v E, W; 1937 v G, E, W, Ni, Cz; 1938 v E, W, Cz, Ho (19)
Brown, H. (Partick T), 1947 v W, Bel, L (3)
Brown, J. (Cambuslang), 1890 v W (1)
Brown, J. B. (Clyde), 1939 v W (1)
Brown, J. G. (Sheffield U), 1975 v R (1)
Brown, R. (Dumbarton), 1884 v W, Ni (2)
Brown, R. (Rangers), 1947 v Ni; 1949 v Ni; 1952 v E (3)
Brown, R. jun. (Dumbarton), 1885 v W (1)
Brown, W. D. F. (Dundee), 1958 v F; 1959 v E, W, Ni; (with Tottenham H), 1960 v W, Ni, Pol, A, H, T; 1962 v Ni, W, E, Cz; 1963 v W, Ni, E, A; 1964 v Ni, W, N; 1965 v E, Fi, Pol, Sp; 1966 v Ni, Pol, I (28)
Browning, J. (Celtic), 1914 v W (1)
Brownlie, J. (Hibernian), 1971 v USSR; 1972 v Pe, Ni, E; 1973 v D (2); 1976 v R (7)
Brownlie, J. (Third Lanark), 1909 v E, Ni; 1910 v E, W, Ni; 1911 v W, Ni; 1912 v W, Ni, E; 1913 v W, Ni, E; 1914 v W, Ni, E (16)
Bruce, D. (Vale of Leven), 1890 v W (1)
Bruce, R. F. (Middlesbrough), 1934 v A (1)

Buchan, M. M. (Aberdeen), 1972 v P (sub), Bel; (with Manchester U), W, Y, Cz, Br; 1973 v D (2), E; 1974 v WG, Ni, W, N, Br, Y; 1975 v EG, Sp, P; 1976 v D, R; 1977 v Fi, Cz, Ch, Arg, Br; 1978 v EG, W (sub), Ni, Pe, Ir, Ho; 1979 v A, N, P (34)
Buchanan, J. (Cambuslang), 1889 v Ni (1)
Buchanan, J. (Rangers), 1929 v E; 1930 v E (2)
Buchanan, P. S. (Chelsea), 1938 v Cz (1)
Buchanan, R. (Abercorn), 1891 v W (1)
Buckley, P. (Aberdeen), 1954 v N; 1955 v W, Ni (3)
Buick, A. (Hearts), 1902 v W, Ni (2)
Burley, C. W. (Chelsea), 1995 v J, Ec, Fa (3)
Burley, G. (Ipswich T), 1979 v W, Ni, E, Arg, N; 1980 v P, Ni, E (sub), Pol; 1982 v W (sub), E (11)
Burns, F. (Manchester U), 1970 v A (1)
Burns, K. (Birmingham C), 1974 v WG; 1975 v EG (sub), Sp (2); 1977 v Cz (sub), W, Se, W (sub); (with Nottingham F), 1978 v Ni (sub), W, E, Pe, Ir; 1979 v N; 1980 v Pe, A, Bel; 1981 v Is, Ni, W (20)
Burns, T. (Celtic), 1981 v Ni; 1982 v Ho (sub), W; 1983 v Bel (sub), Ni, Ca (1 + 1 sub); 1988 v E (sub) (8)
Busby, M. W. (Manchester C), 1934 v W (1)

Cairns, T. (Rangers), 1920 v W; 1922 v E; 1923 v E, W; 1924 v Ni; 1925 v W, E, Ni (8)
Calderhead, D. (Queen of the South), 1889 v Ni (1)
Calderwood, C. (Tottenham H), 1995 v Ru, Sm, J, Ec, Fa (5)
Calderwood, R. (Cartvale), 1885 v Ni, E, W (3)
Caldow, E. (Rangers), 1957 v Sp (2), Sw, WG, E; 1958 v Ni, W, Sw, Par, H, Pol, Y, F; 1959 v E, W, Ni, WG, Ho, P; 1960 v E, W, Ni, A, H, T; 1961 v E, W, Ni, Ei (2), Cz; 1962 v Ni, W, E, Cz (2), U; 1963 v W, Ni, E (40)
Callaghan, P. (Hibernian), 1900 v Ni (1)
Callaghan, W. (Dunfermline Ath), 1970 v Ei (sub), W (2)
Cameron, J. (Rangers), 1886 v Ni (1)
Cameron, J. (Queen's Park), 1896 v Ni (1)
Cameron, J. (St Mirren), 1904 v Ni; (with Chelsea), 1909 v E (2)
Campbell, C. (Queen's Park), 1874 v E; 1876 v W; 1877 v E, W; 1878 v E; 1879 v E; 1880 v E; 1881 v E; 1882 v E, W; 1884 v E; 1885 v E; 1886 v E (13)
Campbell, H. (Renton), 1889 v W (1)
Campbell, Jas (Sheffield W), 1913 v W (1)
Campbell, J. (South Western), 1880 v W (1)
Campbell, J. (Kilmarnock), 1891 v Ni; 1892 v W (2)
Campbell, John (Celtic), 1893 v E, Ni; 1898 v E, Ni; 1900 v E, Ni; 1901 v E, W, Ni; 1902 v W, Ni; 1903 v W (12)
Campbell, John (Rangers), 1899 v E, W, Ni; 1901 v Ni (4)
Campbell, K. (Liverpool), 1920 v E, W, Ni; (with Partick T), 1921 v W, Ni; 1922 v W, Ni, E (8)
Campbell, P. (Rangers), 1878 v W; 1879 v W (2)
Campbell, P. (Morton), 1898 v W (1)
Campbell, R. (Falkirk), 1947 v Bel, L; (with Chelsea), 1950 v Sw, P, F (5)
Campbell, W. (Morton), 1947 v Ni; 1948 v E, Bel, Sw, F (5)
Carabine, J. (Third Lanark), 1938 v Ho; 1939 v E, Ni (3)
Carr, W. M. (Coventry C), 1970 v Ni, W, E; 1971 v D; 1972 v Pe; 1973 v D (sub) (6)
Cassidy, J. (Celtic), 1921 v W, Ni; 1923 v Ni; 1924 v W (4)
Chalmers, S. (Celtic), 1965 v W, Fi; 1966 v P (sub), Br; 1967 v Ni (5)
Chalmers, W. (Rangers), 1885 v Ni (1)
Chalmers, W. S. (Queen's Park), 1929 v Ni (1)
Chambers, T. (Hearts), 1894 v W (1)
Chaplin, G. D. (Dundee), 1908 v W (1)
Cheyne, A. G. (Aberdeen), 1929 v E, N, G, Ho; 1930 v F (5)
Christie, A. J. (Queen's Park), 1898 v W; 1899 v E, Ni (3)
Christie, R. M. (Queen's Park), 1884 v E (1)
Clark, J. (Celtic), 1966 v Br; 1967 v W, Ni, USSR (4)
Clark, R. B. (Aberdeen), 1968 v W, Ho; 1970 v Ni; 1971 v W, Ni, E, D, P, USSR; 1972 v Bel, Ni, W, E, Cz, Br; 1973 v D, E (17)
Clarke, S. (Chelsea), 1988 v H, Bel, Bul, S.Ar, Ma; 1994 v Ho (6)
Cleland, J. (Royal Albert), 1891 v Ni (1)
Clements, R. (Leith Ath), 1891 v Ni (1)
Clunas, W. L. (Sunderland), 1924 v E; 1926 v W (2)
Collier, W. (Raith R), 1922 v W (1)
Collins, J. (Hibernian), 1988 v S.Ar; 1990 v EG, Pol (sub), Ma (sub); (with Celtic), 1991 v Sw (sub), Bul (sub); 1992 v Ni (sub), Fi; 1993 v P, Ma, G, P, Es (2); 1994 v Sw, Ho (sub), A, Ho; 1995 v Fi, Fa, Ru, Gr, Ru, Sm, Fa (25)
Collins, R. Y. (Celtic), 1951 v W, Ni, A; 1955 v Y, A, H; 1956 v Ni, W; 1957 v E, W, Sp (2), Sw, WG; 1958 v Ni, W, Sw, H, Pol, Y, F, Par; (with Everton), 1959 v E, W, Ni, WG, Ho, P; (with Leeds U), 1965 v E, Pol, Sp (31)
Collins, T. (Hearts), 1909 v W (1)
Colman, D. (Aberdeen), 1911 v E, W, Ni; 1913 v Ni (4)
Colquhoun, E. P. (Sheffield U), 1972 v P, Ho, Pe, Y, Cz, Br; 1973 v D (2), E (9)
Colquhoun, J. (Hearts), 1988 v S.Ar (sub) (1)
Combe, J. R. (Hibernian), 1948 v E, Bel, Sw (3)
Conn, A. (Hearts), 1956 v A (1)
Conn, A. (Tottenham H), 1975 v Ni (sub), E (2)
Connachan, E. D. (Dunfermline Ath), 1962 v Cz, U (2)
Connelly, G. (Celtic), 1974 v Cz, WG (2)
Connolly, J. (Everton), 1973 v Sw (1)
Connor, J. (Airdrieonians), 1886 v Ni (1)
Connor, J. (Sunderland), 1930 v F; 1932 v Ni; 1934 v E; 1935 v Ni (4)
Connor, R. (Dundee), 1986 v Ho; (with Aberdeen), 1988 v S.Ar (sub); 1989 v E; 1991 v R (4)
Cook, W. L. (Bolton W), 1934 v E; 1935 v W, Ni (3)
Cooke, C. (Dundee), 1966 v W, I; (with Chelsea), P, Br; 1968 v E, Ho; 1969 v W, Ni, A, WG (sub), Cy (2); 1970 v A; 1971 v Bel; 1975 v Sp, P (16)
Cooper, D. (Rangers), 1980 v Pe, A (sub); 1984 v W, E; 1985 v Y, Ic, Sp (2), W; 1986 v W (sub), EG, Aus (2), Ho, WG (sub), U (sub); 1987 v Bul, L, Ei, Br; (with Motherwell), 1990 v N, Eg (22)
Cormack, P. B. (Hibernian), 1966 v Br; 1969 v D (sub); 1970 v Ei, WG; (with Nottingham F), 1971 v D (sub), W, P, E; 1972 v Ho (sub) (9)
Cowan, J. (Aston Villa), 1896 v E; 1897 v E; 1898 v E (3)
Cowan, J. (Morton), 1948 v Bel, Sw; F; 1949 v E, W, F; 1950 v E, W, Ni, Sw, P, F; 1951 v E, W, Ni, A (2), D, F, Bel; 1952 v Ni, W, USA, D, Se (25)
Cowan, W. D. (Newcastle U), 1924 v E (1)
Cowie, D. (Dundee), 1953 v E, Se; 1954 v Ni, W, Fi, N, A, U; 1955 v W, Ni, A, H; 1956 v W, A; 1957 v Ni, W; 1958 v H, Pol, Y, Par (20)
Cox, C. J. (Hearts), 1948 v F (1)
Cox, S. (Rangers), 1949 v E, F; 1950 v E, F, W, Ni, Sw, P; 1951 v E, D, F, Bel, A; 1952 v Ni, W, USA, D, Se; 1953 v W, Ni, E; 1954 v W, Ni, E (24)
Craig, A. (Motherwell), 1929 v N, Ho; 1932 v E (3)
Craig, J. (Celtic), 1977 v Se (sub) (1)
Craig, J. P. (Celtic), 1968 v W (1)
Craig, T. (Rangers), 1927 v Ni; 1928 v Ni; 1929 v N, G, Ho; 1930 v Ni, E, W (8)
Craig, T. B. (Newcastle U), 1976 v Sw (1)
Crapnell, J. (Airdrieonians), 1929 v E, N, G; 1930 v F; 1931 v Ni, Sw; 1932 v E, F; 1933 v Ni (9)
Crawford, D. (St Mirren), 1894 v W, Ni; 1900 v W (3)
Crawford, J. (Queen's Park), 1932 v F, Ni; 1933 v E, W, Ni (5)
Crawford, S. (Raith R), 1995 v Ec (sub) (1)
Crerand, P. T. (Celtic), 1961 v Ei (2), Cz; 1962 v Ni, W, E, Cz (2), U; 1963 v W, Ni; (with Manchester U), 1964 v Ni; 1965 v E, Pol, Fi; 1966 v Pol (16)

Cringan, W. (Celtic), 1920 v W; 1922 v E, Ni; 1923 v W, E (5)
Crosbie, J. A. (Ayr U), 1920 v W; (with Birmingham), 1922 v E (2)
Croal, J. A. (Falkirk), 1913 v Ni; 1914 v E, W (3)
Cropley, A. J. (Hibernian), 1972 v P, Bel (2)
Cross, J. H. (Third Lanark), 1903 v Ni (1)
Cruickshank, J. (Hearts), 1964 v WG; 1970 v W, E; 1971 v D, Bel; 1976 v R (6)
Crum, J. (Celtic), 1936 v E; 1939 v Ni (2)
Cullen, M. J. (Luton T), 1956 v A (1)
Cumming, D. S. (Middlesbrough), 1938 v E (1)
Cumming, J. (Hearts), 1955 v E, H, P, Y; 1960 v E, Pol, A, H, T (9)
Cummings, G. (Partick T), 1935 v E; 1936 v W, Ni; (with Aston Villa), E; 1937 v G; 1938 v W, Ni, Cz; 1939 v E (9)
Cunningham, A. N. (Rangers), 1920 v Ni; 1921 v W, E; 1922 v Ni; 1923 v E, W; 1924 v E, Ni; 1926 v E, Ni; 1927 v E, W (12)
Cunningham, W. C. (Preston NE), 1954 v N (2), U, Fi, A; 1955 v W, E, H (8)
Curran, H. P. (Wolverhampton W), 1970 v A; 1971 v Ni, E, D, USSR (sub) (5)

Dalglish, K. (Celtic), 1972 v Bel (sub), Ho; 1973 v D (1+1 sub), E (2), W, Ni, Sw, Br; 1974 v Cz (2), WG (2), Ni, W, E, Bel, N (sub), Z, Br, Y; 1975 v EG, Sp (sub+1), Se, P, W, Ni, E, R; 1976 v D (2), R, Sw, Ni, E; 1977 v Fi, Cz, W (2), Se, Ni, E, Ch, Arg, Br; (with Liverpool), 1978 v EG, Cz, W, Bul, Ni (sub), W, E, Pe, Ir, Ho; 1979 v A, N, P, W, Ni, E, Arg, N; 1980 v Pe, A, Bel (2), P, Ni, W, E, Pol, H; 1981 v Se, P, Is; 1982 v Se, Ni, P (sub), Sp, Ho, Ni, W, E, Nz, Br (sub); 1983 v Bel, Sw; 1984 v U, Bel, EG; 1985 v Y, Ic, Sp, W; 1986 v EG, Aus, R; 1987 v Bul (sub), L (102)
Davidson, D. (Queen's Park), 1878 v W; 1879 v W; 1880 v W; 1881 v E, W (5)
Davidson, J. A. (Partick T), 1954 v N (2), A, U; 1955 v W, Ni, E, H (8)
Davidson, S. (Middlesbrough), 1921 v E (1)
Dawson, A. (Rangers), 1980 v Pol (sub), H; 1983 v Ni, Ca (2) (5)
Dawson, J. (Rangers), 1935 v Ni; 1936 v E; 1937 v G, E, W, Ni, A, Cz; 1938 v W, Ho, Ni; 1939 v E, Ni, H (14)
Deans, J. (Celtic), 1975 v EG, Sp (2)
Delaney, J. (Celtic), 1936 v W, Ni; 1937 v G, E, A, Cz; 1938 v Ni; 1939 v W, Ni; (with Manchester U), 1947 v E; 1948 v E, W, Ni (13)
Devine, A. (Falkirk), 1910 v W (1)
Dewar, G. (Dumbarton), 1888 v Ni; 1889 v E (2)
Dewar, N. (Third Lanark), 1932 v E, F; 1933 v W (3)
Dick, J. (West Ham U), 1959 v E (1)
Dickie, M. (Rangers), 1897 v Ni; 1899 v Ni; 1900 v W (3)
Dickson, W. (Dumbarton), 1888 v Ni (1)
Dickson, W. (Kilmarnock), 1970 v Ni, W, E; 1971 v D, USSR (5)
Divers, J. (Celtic), 1895 v W (1)
Divers, J. (Celtic), 1939 v Ni (1)
Docherty, T. H, (Preston NE), 1952 v W; 1953 v E, Se; 1954 v N (2), A, U; 1955 v W, E, H (2), A; 1957 v E, Y, Sp (2), Sw, WG; 1958 v Ni, W, E, Sw; (with Arsenal), 1959 v W, E, Ni (25)
Dodds, D. (Dundee U), 1984 v U (sub), Ni (2)
Dodds, J. (Celtic), 1914 v E, W, Ni (3)
Doig, J. E. (Arbroath), 1887 v Ni; 1889 v Ni; (with Sunderland), 1896 v E; 1899 v E; 1903 v E (5)
Donachie, W. (Manchester C), 1972 v Pe, Ni, E, Y, Cz, Br; 1973 v D, E, W, Ni; 1974 v Ni; 1976 v R, Ni, W, E; 1977 v Fi, Cz, W (2), Se, Ni, E, Ch, Arg, Br; 1978 v EG, W, Bul, W, E, Ir, Ho; 1979 v A, N, P (sub) (35)
Donaldson, A. (Bolton W), 1914 v E, Ni, W; 1920 v E, Ni; 1922 v Ni (6)
Donnachie, J. (Oldham Ath), 1913 v E; 1914 v E, Ni (3)
Dougall, C. (Birmingham C), 1947 v W (1)
Dougall, J. (Preston NE), 1939 v E (1)
Dougan, R. (Hearts), 1950 v Sw (1)
Douglas, A. (Chelsea), 1911 v Ni (1)
Douglas, J. (Renfrew), 1880 v W (1)
Dowds, P. (Celtic), 1892 v Ni (1)
Downie, R. (Third Lanark), 1892 v W (1)
Doyle, D. (Celtic), 1892 v E; 1893 v W; 1894 v E; 1895 v E, Ni; 1897 v E; 1898 v E, Ni (8)
Doyle, J. (Ayr U), 1976 v R (1)
Drummond, J. (Falkirk), 1892 v Ni; (with Rangers), 1894 v Ni; 1895 v Ni, E; 1896 v E, Ni; 1897 v Ni; 1898 v E; 1900 v E; 1901 v E; 1902 v E, W, Ni; 1903 v Ni (14)
Dunbar, M. (Cartvale), 1886 v Ni (1)
Duncan, A. (Hibernian), 1975 v P (sub), W, Ni, E, R; 1976 v D (sub) (6)
Duncan, D. (Derby Co), 1933 v E, W; 1934 v A, W; 1935 v E, W; 1936 v E, W, Ni; 1937 v G, E, W, Ni; 1938 v W (14)
Duncan, D. M. (East Fife), 1948 v Bel, Sw, F (3)
Duncan, J. (Alexandra Ath), 1878 v W; 1882 v W (2)
Duncan, J. (Leicester C), 1926 v W (1)
Duncanson, J. (Rangers), 1947 v Ni (1)
Dunlop, J. (St Mirren), 1890 v W (1)
Dunlop, W. (Liverpool), 1906 v E (1)
Dunn, J. (Hibernian), 1925 v W, Ni; 1927 v Ni; 1928 v Ni, E; (with Everton), 1929 v W (6)
Durie, G. S. (Chelsea), 1988 v Bul (sub); 1989 v I (sub), Cy; 1990 v Y, EG, Eg, Se; 1991 v Sw (sub), Bul (2), USSR (sub), Sm; (with Tottenham H), 1992 v Sw, R, Sm, Ni (sub), Fi, Ca, N (sub), Ho, G; 1993 v Sw, I; 1994 v Sw, I; (with Rangers), Ho (2) (27)
Durrant, I. (Rangers), 1988 v H, Bel, Ma, Sp; 1989 v N (sub); 1993 v Sw (sub), P (sub), I, P (sub); 1994 v I (sub), Ma (11)
Dykes, J. (Hearts), 1938 v Ho; 1939 v Ni (2)

Easson, J. F. (Portsmouth), 1931 v A, Sw; 1934 v W (3)
Ellis, J. (Mossend Swifts), 1892 v Ni (1)
Evans, A. (Aston Villa), 1982 v Ho, Ni, E, Nz (4)
Evans, R. (Celtic), 1949 v E, W, Ni, F; 1950 v W, Ni, Sw, P; 1951 v E, A; 1952 v Ni; 1953 v Se; 1954 v Ni, W, E, N, Fi; 1955 v Ni, P, Y, A, H; 1956 v E, Ni, W, A; 1957 v WG, Sp; 1958 v Ni, W, E, Sw, H, Pol, Y, Par, F; 1959 v E, WG, Ho, P; 1960 v E, Ni, W, Pol; (with Chelsea), 1960 v A, H, T (48)
Ewart, J. (Bradford C), 1921 v E (1)
Ewing, T. (Partick T), 1958 v W, E (2)

Farm, G. N. (Blackpool), 1953 v W, Ni, E, Se; 1954 v Ni, W, E; 1959 v WG, Ho, P (10)
Ferguson, D. (Rangers), 1988 v Ma, Co (sub) (2)
Ferguson, D. (Dundee U), 1992 v US (sub), Ca, Ho (sub); 1993 v G; (with Rangers) 1995 v Gr (5)
Ferguson, I. (Rangers), 1989 v I, Cy (sub), F; 1993 v Ma (sub), Es; 1994 v Ma, A (sub), Ho (sub) (8)
Ferguson, J. (Vale of Leven), 1874 v E; 1876 v E, W; 1877 v E, W; 1878 v W (6)
Ferguson, R. (Kilmarnock), 1966 v W, E, Ho, P, Br; 1967 v W, Ni (7)
Fernie, W. (Celtic), 1954 v Fi, A, U; 1955 v W, Ni; 1957 v E, Ni, W, Y; 1958 v W, Sw, Par (12)
Findlay, R. (Kilmarnock), 1898 v W (1)
Fitchie, T. T. (Woolwich Arsenal), 1905 v W; 1906 v W, Ni; (with Queen's Park), 1907 v W (4)
Flavell, R. (Airdrieonians), 1947 v Bel, L (2)
Fleck, R. (Norwich C), 1990 v Arg, Se, Br (sub); 1991 v USSR (4)
Fleming, C. (East Fife), 1954 v Ni (1)

Fleming, J. W. (Rangers), 1929 v G, Ho; 1930 v E (3)
Fleming, R. (Morton), 1886 v Ni (1)
Forbes, A. R. (Sheffield U), 1947 v Bel, L, E; 1948 v W, Ni; (with Arsenal), 1950 v E, P, F; 1951 v W, Ni, A; 1952 v W, D, Se (14)
Forbes, J. (Vale of Leven), 1884 v E, W, Ni; 1887 v W, E (5)
Ford, D. (Hearts), 1974 v Cz (sub), WG (sub), W (3)
Forrest, J. (Rangers), 1966 v W, I; (with Aberdeen), 1971 v Bel (sub), D, USSR (5)
Forrest, J. (Motherwell), 1958 v E (1)
Forsyth, A. (Partick T), 1972 v Y, Cz, Br; 1973 v D; (with Manchester U), E; 1975 v Sp, Ni (sub), R, EG; 1976 v D (10)
Forsyth, C. (Kilmarnock), 1964 v E; 1965 v W, Ni, Fi (4)
Forsyth, T. (Motherwell), 1971 v D; (with Rangers), 1974 v Cz; 1976 v Sw, Ni, W, E; 1977 v Fi, Se, W, Ni, E, Ch, Arg, Br; 1978 v Cz, W, Ni, W (sub), E, Pe, Ir (sub), Ho (22)
Foyers, R. (St Bernards), 1893 v W; 1894 v W (2)
Fraser, D. M. (WBA), 1968 v Ho; 1969 v Cy (2)
Fraser, J. (Moffat), 1891 v Ni (1)
Fraser, M. J. E. (Queen's Park), 1880 v W; 1882 v W, E; 1883 v W, E (5)
Fraser, J. (Dundee), 1907 v Ni (1)
Fraser, W. (Sunderland), 1955 v W, Ni (2)
Fulton, W. (Abercorn), 1884 v Ni (1)
Fyfe, J. H. (Third Lanark), 1895 v W (1)

Gabriel, J. (Everton), 1961 v W; 1964 v N (sub) (2)
Gallacher, H. K. (Airdrieonians), 1924 v Ni; 1925 v E, W, Ni; 1926 v W; (with Newcastle U), 1926 v E, Ni; 1927 v E, W, Ni; 1928 v E, W; 1929 v E, W, Ni; 1930 v W, Ni, F; (with Chelsea), 1934 v E; (with Derby Co), 1935 v E (20)
Gallacher, K. W. (Dundee U), 1988 v Co, E (sub); 1989 v N, I; (with Coventry C), 1991 v Sm; 1992 v R (sub), Sm (sub), Ni (sub), N (sub), Ho (sub), G (sub), C; 1993 v Sw (sub), P; (with Blackburn R), P, Es (2); 1994 v I, Ma (19)
Gallacher, P. (Sunderland), 1935 v Ni (1)
Galloway, M. (Celtic), 1992 v R (1)
Galt, J. H. (Rangers), 1908 v W, Ni (2)
Gardiner, I. (Motherwell), 1958 v W (1)
Gardner, D. R. (Third Lanark), 1897 v W (1)
Gardner, R. (Queen's Park), 1872 v E; 1873 v E; (with Clydesdale), 1874 v E; 1875 v E; 1878 v E (5)
Gemmell, T. (St Mirren), 1955 v P, Y (2)
Gemmell, T. (Celtic), 1966 v E; 1967 v W, Ni, E, USSR; 1968 v Ni, E; 1969 v W, Ni, E, D, A, WG, Cy; 1970 v E, Ei, WG; 1971 v Bel (18)
Gemmill, A. (Derby Co), 1971 v Bel; 1972 v P, Ho, Pe, Ni, W, E; 1976 v D, R, Ni, W, E; 1977 v Fi, Cz, W (2), Ni (sub), E (sub), Ch (sub), Arg, Br; 1978 v EG (sub); (with Nottingham F), Bul, Ni, W, E (sub), Pe (sub), Ir, Ho; 1979 v A, N, P, N; (with Birmingham C), 1980 v A, P, Ni, W, E, H; 1981 v Se, P, Is, Ni (43)
Gemmill, S. (Nottingham F), 1995 v J, Ec, Fa (sub) (3)
Gibb, W. (Clydesdale), 1873 v E (1)
Gibson, D. W. (Leicester C), 1963 v A, N, Ei, Sp; 1964 v Ni; 1965 v W, Fi (7)
Gibson, J. D. (Partick T), 1926 v E; 1927 v E, W, Ni; (with Aston Villa), 1928 v E, W; 1930 v W, Ni (8)
Gibson, N. (Rangers), 1895 v E, Ni; 1896 v E, Ni; 1897 v E, Ni; 1898 v E; 1899 v E, W, Ni; 1900 v E, Ni; 1901 v W; (with Partick T), 1905 v Ni (14)
Gilchrist, J. E. (Celtic), 1922 v E (1)
Gilhooley, M. (Hull C), 1922 v W (1)
Gillespie, G. (Rangers), 1880 v W; 1881 v E, W; 1882 v E; (with Queen's Park), 1886 v W; 1890 v W; 1891 v Ni (7)
Gillespie, G. T. (Liverpool), 1988 v Bel, Bul, Sp; 1989 v N, F, Ch; 1990 v Y, EG, Eg, Pol, Ma, Br (sub); 1991 v Bul (13)
Gillespie, Jas (Third Lanark), 1898 v W (1)
Gillespie, John (Queen's Park), 1896 v W (1)
Gillespie, R. (Queen's Park), 1927 v W; 1931 v W; 1932 v F; 1933 v E (4)
Gillick, T. (Everton), 1937 v A, Cz; 1939 v W, Ni, H (5)
Gilmour, J. (Dundee), 1931 v W (1)
Gilzean, A. J. (Dundee), 1964 v W, E, N, WG; 1965 v Ni, (with Tottenham H), Sp; 1966 v Ni, W, Pol, I; 1968 v W; 1969 v W, E, WG, Cy (2), A (sub); 1970 v Ni, E (sub), WG, A; 1971 v P (22)
Glavin, R. (Celtic), 1977 v Se (1)
Glen, A. (Aberdeen), 1956 v E, Ni (2)
Glen, R. (Renton), 1895 v W; 1896 v W; (with Hibernian), 1900 v Ni (3)
Goram, A. L. (Oldham Ath), 1986 v EG (sub), R, Ho; 1987 v Br; (with Hibernian) 1989 v Y, I; 1990 v EG, Pol, Ma; 1991 v R, Sw, Bul (2), USSR, Sm; (with Rangers), 1992 v Sw, R, Sm, Fi, N, Ho, G, C; 1993 v Sw, P, I, Ma, P; 1994 v Ho; 1995 v Fi, Fa, Ru, Gr (33)
Gordon, J. E. (Rangers), 1912 v E, Ni; 1913 v E, Ni, W; 1914 v E, Ni; 1920 v W, E, Ni (10)
Gossland, J. (Rangers), 1884 v Ni (1)
Goudle, J. (Abercorn), 1884 v Ni (1)
Gough, C. R. (Dundee U), 1983 v Sw, Ni, W, E, Ca (3); 1984 v U, Bel, EG, Ni, W, E, F; 1985 v Sp, E, Ic; 1986 v W, EG, Aus, Is, R, E, D, WG, U; (with Tottenham H), 1987 v Bul, L, Ei (2), Bel, E, Br; 1988 v H; (with Rangers), S.Ar, Sp, Co, E; 1989 v Y, I, Cy, F, Cy; 1990 v F, Arg, EG, Eg, Pol, Ma, Cr; 1991 v USSR, Bul; 1992 v Sm, Ni, Ca, N, Ho, G, C; 1993 v Sw, P (61)
Gourlay, J. (Cambuslang), 1886 v Ni; 1888 v W (2)
Govan, J. (Hibernian), 1948 v E, W, Bel, Sw, F; 1949 v Ni (6)
Gow, D. R. (Rangers), 1888 v E (1)
Gow, J. J. (Queen's Park), 1885 v E (1)
Gow, J. R. (Rangers), 1888 v Ni (1)
Graham, A. (Leeds U), 1978 v EG (sub); 1979 v A (sub), N, W, Ni, E, Arg, N; 1980 v A; 1981 v W (10)
Graham, G. (Arsenal), 1972 v P, Ho, Ni, Y, Cz, Br; 1973 v D (2); (with Manchester U), E, W, Ni, Br (sub) (12)
Graham, J. (Annbank), 1884 v Ni (1)
Graham, J. A. (Arsenal), 1921 v Ni (1)
Grant, J. (Hibernian), 1959 v W, Ni (2)
Grant, P. (Celtic), 1989 v E (sub), Ch (2)
Gray, A. (Hibernian), 1903 v Ni (1)
Gray, A. M. (Aston Villa), 1976 v R, Sw; 1977 v Fi, Cz; 1979 v A, N; (with Wolverhampton W), 1980 v P, E (sub); 1981 v Se, P, Is (sub), Ni; 1982 v Se (sub), Ni (sub); 1983 v Ni, W, E, Ca (1 + 1 sub); (with Everton), 1985 v Ic (20)
Gray, D. (Rangers), 1929 v W, Ni, G, Ho; 1930 v W, E, Ni; 1931 v W; 1933 v W, Ni (10)
Gray, E. (Leeds U), 1969 v E, Cy; 1970 v WG, A; 1971 v W, Ni; 1972 v Bel, Ho; 1976 v W, E; 1977 v Fi, W (12)
Gray, F. T. (Leeds U), 1976 v Sw; 1979 v N, P, W, Ni, E, Arg (sub); (with Nottingham F), 1980 v Bel (sub); 1981 v Se, P, Is, Ni, Is, W; (with Leeds U), Ni, E; 1982 v Se, Ni, P, Sp, Ho, W, Nz, Br, USSR; 1983 v EG, Sw, Bel, Sw, W, E, Ca (32)
Gray, W. (Pollokshields Ath), 1886 v E (1)
Green, A. (Blackpool), 1971 v Bel (sub), P (sub), Ni, E; (with Newcastle U), 1972 v W, E (sub) (6)
Greig, J. (Rangers), 1964 v E, WG; 1965 v W, Ni, E, Fi (2), Sp, Pol; 1966 v Ni, W, E, Pol, I (2), P, Ho, Br; 1967 v W, Ni, E; 1968 v Ni, W, E, Ho; 1969 v W, Ni, E, D, A, WG, Cy (2); 1970 v W, E, Ei, WG, A; 1971 v D, Bel, W (sub), Ni, E; 1976 v D (44)
Groves, W. (Hibernian), 1888 v W; (with Celtic), 1889 v Ni; 1890 v E (3)
Guilliland, W. (Queen's Park), 1891 v W; 1892 v Ni; 1894 v E; 1895 v E (4)
Gunn, B. (Norwich C), 1990 v Eg; 1993 v Es (2); 1994 v Sw, I, Ho (sub) (6)

Haddock, H. (Clyde), 1955 v E, H (2), P, Y; 1958 v E (6)
Haddow, D. (Rangers), 1894 v E (1)
Haffey, F. (Celtic), 1960 v E; 1961 v E (2)
Hamilton, A. (Queen's Park), 1885 v E, W; 1886 v E; 1888 v E (4)
Hamilton, A. W. (Dundee), 1962 v Cz, U, W, E; 1963 v W, Ni, E, A, N, Ei; 1964 v Ni, W, E, N, WG; 1965 v Ni, W, E, Fi (2), Pol, Sp; 1966 v Pol, Ni (24)
Hamilton, G. (Aberdeen), 1947 v Ni; 1951 v Bel, A; 1954 v N (2) (5)
Hamilton, G. (Port Glasgow Ath), 1906 v Ni (1)
Hamilton, J. (Queen's Park), 1892 v W; 1893 v E, Ni (3)
Hamilton, J. (St Mirren), 1924 v Ni (1)
Hamilton, R. C. (Rangers), 1899 v E, W, Ni; 1900 v W; 1901 v E, Ni; 1902 v W, Ni; 1903 v E; 1904 v Ni; (with Dundee), 1911 v W (11)
Hamilton, T. (Hurlford), 1891 v Ni (1)
Hamilton, T. (Rangers), 1932 v E (1)
Hamilton, W. M. (Hibernian), 1965 v Fi (1)
Hannah, A. B. (Renton), 1888 v W (1)
Hannah, J. (Third Lanark), 1889 v W (1)
Hansen, A. D. (Liverpool), 1979 v W, Arg; 1980 v Bel, P; 1981 v Se, P, Is; 1982 v Se, Ni, P, Sp, Ni (sub), W, E, Nz, Br, USSR; 1983 v EG, Sw, Bel, Sw; 1985 v W (sub); 1986 v R (sub); 1987 v Ei (2), L (26)
Hansen, J. (Partick T), 1972 v Bel (sub), Y (sub) (2)
Harkness, J. D. (Queen's Park), 1927 v E, Ni; 1928 v E; (with Hearts), 1929 v W, E, Ni; 1930 v E, W; 1932 v W, F; 1934 v Ni, W (12)
Harper, J. M. (Aberdeen), 1973 v D (1+1 sub); (with Hibernian), 1976 v D; (with Aberdeen), 1978 v Ir (sub) (4)
Harper, W. (Hibernian), 1923 v E, Ni, W; 1924 v E, Ni, W; 1925 v E, Ni, W; (with Arsenal), 1926 v E, Ni (11)
Harris, J. (Partick T), 1921 v W, Ni (2)
Harris, N. (Newcastle U), 1924 v E (1)
Harrower, W. (Queen's Park), 1882 v E; 1884 v Ni; 1886 v W (3)
Hartford, R. A. (WBA), 1972 v Pe, W (sub), E, Y, Cz, Br; (with Manchester C), 1976 v D, R, Ni (sub); 1977 v Cz (sub), W (sub), Se, W, Ni, E, Ch, Arg, Br; 1978 v EG, Cz, W, Bul, W, E, Pe, Ir, Ho; 1979 v A, N, P, W, Ni, E, Arg, N; (with Everton), 1980 v Pe, Bel; 1981 v Ni (sub), Is, W, Ni, E; 1982 v Se; (with Manchester C), Ni, P, Sp, Ni, W, E, Br (50)
Harvey, D. (Leeds U), 1973 v D; 1974 v Cz, WG, Ni, W, E, Bel, Z, Br, Y; 1975 v EG, Sp (2); 1976 v D (2); 1977 v Fi (sub) (16)
Hastings, A. C. (Sunderland), 1936 v Ni; 1938 v Ni (2)
Haughney, M. (Celtic), 1954 v E (1)
Hay, D. (Celtic), 1970 v Ni, W, E; 1971 v D, Bel, W, P, Ni; 1972 v P, Bel, Ho; 1973 v W, Ni, E, Sw, Br; 1974 v Cz (2), WG, Ni, W, E, Bel, N, Z, Br, Y (27)
Hay, J. (Celtic), 1905 v Ni; 1909 v Ni; 1910 v W, Ni, E; 1911 v Ni, E; (with Newcastle U), 1912 v E, W; 1914 v E, Ni (11)
Hegarty, P. (Dundee U), 1979 v W, Ni, E, Arg, N (sub); 1980 v W, E; 1983 v Ni (8)
Heggie, C. (Rangers), 1886 v Ni (1)
Henderson, G. H. (Rangers), 1904 v Ni (1)
Henderson, J. G. (Portsmouth), 1953 v Se; 1954 v Ni, E, N; 1956 v W; (with Arsenal), 1959 v W, Ni (7)
Henderson, W. (Rangers), 1963 v W, Ni, E, A, N, Ei, Sp; 1964 v W, Ni, E, N, WG; 1965 v Fi, Pol, E, Sp; 1966 v Ni, W, Pol, I, Ho; 1967 v W, Ni; 1968 v Ho; 1969 v Ni, E, Cy; 1970 v Ei; 1971 v P (29)
Hendry, E. C. J. (Blackburn R), 1993 v Es (2); 1994 v Ma, Ho, A, Ho; 1995 v Fi, Fa, Gr, Ru, Sm (11)
Hepburn, J. (Alloa Ath), 1891 v W (1)
Hepburn, R. (Ayr U), 1932 v Ni (1)
Herd, A. C. (Hearts), 1935 v Ni (1)
Herd, D. G. (Arsenal), 1959 v E, W, Ni; 1961 v E, Cz (5)
Herd, G. (Clyde), 1958 v E; 1960 v H, T; 1961 v W, Ni (5)
Herriot, J. (Birmingham C), 1969 v Ni, E, D, Cy (2), W (sub); 1970 v Ei (sub), WG (8)
Hewie, J. D. (Charlton Ath), 1956 v E, A; 1957 v E, Ni, W, Y, Sp (2), Sw, WG; 1958 v H, Pol, Y, F; 1959 v Ho, P; 1960 v Ni, W, Pol (19)
Higgins, A. (Kilmarnock), 1885 v Ni (1)
Higgins, A. (Newcastle U), 1910 v E, Ni; 1911 v E, Ni (4)
Highet, T. C. (Queen's Park), 1875 v E; 1876 v E, W; 1878 v E (4)
Hill, D. (Rangers), 1881 v E, W; 1882 v W (3)
Hill, D. A. (Third Lanark), 1906 v Ni (1)
Hill, F. R. (Aberdeen), 1930 v F; 1931 v W, Ni (3)
Hill, J. (Hearts), 1891 v E; 1892 v W (2)
Hogg, G (Hearts), 1896 v E, Ni (2)
Hogg, J. (Ayr U), 1922 v Ni (1)
Hogg, R. M. (Celtic), 1937 v Cz (1)
Holm, A. H. (Queen's Park), 1882 v W; 1883 v E, W (3)
Holt, D. D. (Hearts), 1963 v A, N, Ei, Sp; 1964 v WG (sub) (5)
Holton, J. A. (Manchester U), 1973 v W, Ni, E, Sw, Br; 1974 v Cz, WG, Ni, W, E, N, Z, Br, Y; 1975 v EG (15)
Hope, R. (WBA), 1968 v Ho; 1969 v D (2)
Houliston, W. (Queen of the South), 1949 v E, Ni, F (3)
Houston, S. M. (Manchester U), 1976 v D (1)
Howden, W. (Partick T), 1905 v Ni (1)
Howe, R. (Hamilton A), 1929 v N, Ho (2)
Howie, J. (Newcastle U), 1905 v E; 1906 v E; 1908 v E (3)
Howie, H. (Hibernian), 1949 v W (1)
Howieson, J. (St Mirren), 1927 v Ni (1)
Hughes, J. (Celtic), 1965 v Pol, Sp; 1966 v Ni, I (2); 1968 v E; 1969 v A; 1970 v Ei (8)
Hughes, W. (Sunderland), 1975 v Se (sub) (1)
Humphries, W. (Motherwell), 1952 v Se (1)
Hunter, A. (Kilmarnock), 1972 v Pe, Y; (with Celtic), 1973 v E; 1974 v Cz (4)
Hunter, J. (Dundee), 1909 v W (1)
Hunter, J. (Third Lanark), 1874 v E; (with Eastern), 1875 v E; (with Third Lanark), 1876 v E; 1877 v W (4)
Hunter, R. (St Mirren), 1890 v Ni (1)
Hunter, W. (Motherwell), 1960 v H, T; 1961 v W (3)
Husband, J. (Partick T), 1947 v W (1)
Hutchison, T. (Coventry C), 1974 v Cz (2), WG (2), Ni, W, Bel (sub), N, Z (sub), Y (sub); 1975 v EG, Sp (2), P, E (sub), R (sub); 1976 v D (17)
Hutton, J. (Aberdeen), 1923 v E, W, Ni; 1924 v Ni; 1926 v W, E, Ni; (with Blackburn R), 1927 v Ni; 1928 v W, Ni (10)
Hutton, J. (St Bernards), 1887 v Ni (1)
Hyslop, T. (Stoke C), 1896 v E; (with Rangers), 1897 v E (2)

Imlach, J. J. S. (Nottingham F), 1958 v H, Pol, Y, F (4)
Imrie, W. N. (St Johnstone), 1929 v N, G (2)
Inglis, J. (Kilmarnock Ath), 1884 v Ni (1)
Inglis, J. (Rangers), 1883 v E, W (2)
Irons, J. H. (Queen's Park), 1900 v W (1)
Irvine, B. (Aberdeen), 1991 v R; 1993 v G, Es (2); 1994 v Sw, I, Ma, A, Ho (9)

Jackson, A. (Cambuslang), 1886 v W; 1888 v Ni (2)
Jackson, A. (Aberdeen), 1925 v E, W, Ni; (with Huddersfield T), 1926 v E, W, Ni; 1927 v W, Ni; 1928 v E, W; 1929 v E, W, Ni; 1930 v E, W, Ni, F (17)
Jackson, C. (Rangers), 1975 v Se, P (sub), W; 1976 v D, R, Ni, W, E (8)
Jackson, D. (Hibernian), 1995 v Ru, Sm, J, Ec, Fa (5)
Jackson, J. (Partick T), 1931 v A, I, Sw; 1933 v E; (with Chelsea), 1934 v E; 1935 v E; 1936 v W, Ni (8)

Jackson, T. A. (St Mirren), 1904 v W, E, Ni; 1905 v W; 1907 v W, Ni (6)
James, A. W. (Preston NE), 1926 v W; 1928 v E; 1929 v E, Ni; (with Arsenal), 1930 v E, W, Ni; 1933 v W (8)
Jardine, A. (Rangers), 1971 v D (sub); 1972 v P, Bel, Ho; 1973 v E, Sw, Br; 1974 v Cz (2), WG (2), Ni, W, E, Bel, N, Z, Br, Y; 1975 v EG, Sp (2), Se, P, W, Ni, E; 1977 v Se (sub), Ch (sub), Br (sub); 1978 v Cz, W, Ni, Ir; 1980 v Pe, A, Bel (2) (38)
Jarvie, A. (Airdrieonians), 1971 v P (sub), Ni (sub), E (sub) (3)
Jenkinson, T. (Hearts), 1887 v Ni (1)
Jess, E. (Aberdeen), 1993 v I (sub), Ma; 1994 v Sw (sub), I, Ho (sub), A, Ho (sub); 1995 v Fi (sub) (8)
Johnston, L. H. (Clyde), 1948 v Bel, Sw (2)
Johnston, M. (Watford), 1984 v W (sub), E (sub), F; 1985 v Y; (with Celtic), Ic, Sp (2), W; 1986 v EG; 1987 v Bul, Ei (2), L; (with Nantes), 1988 v H, Bel, L, S.Ar, Sp, Co, E; 1989 v N, Y, I, Cy, F, Cy, E, Ch (sub); (with Rangers), 1990 v F, N, EG, Pol, Ma, Cr, Se, Br; 1992 v Sw, Sm (sub) (38)
Johnston, R. (Sunderland), 1938 v Cz (1)
Johnston, W. (Rangers), 1966 v W, E, Pol, Ho; 1968 v W, E; 1969 v Ni (sub); 1970 v Ni; 1971 v D; (with WBA), 1977 v Se, W (sub), Ni, E, Ch, Arg, Br; 1978 v EG, Cz, W (2), E, Pe (22)
Johnstone, D. (Rangers), 1973 v W, Ni, E, Sw, Br; 1975 v EG (sub), Se (sub); 1976 v Sw, Ni (sub), E (sub); 1978 v Bul (sub), Ni, W; 1980 v Bel (14)
Johnstone, J. (Abercorn), 1888 v W (1)
Johnstone, J. (Celtic), 1965 v W, Fi; 1966 v E; 1967 v W, USSR; 1968 v W; 1969 v A, WG; 1970 v E, WG; 1971 v D, E; 1972 v P, Bel, Ho, Ni, E (sub); 1974 v W, E, Bel, N; 1975 v EG, Sp (23)
Johnstone, Jas (Kilmarnock), 1894 v W (1)
Johnstone, J. A. (Hearts), 1930 v W; 1933 v W, Ni (3)
Johnstone, R. (Hibernian), 1951 v E, D, F; 1952 v Ni, E; 1953 v E, Se; 1954 v W, E, N, Fi; 1955 v Ni, H; (with Manchester C), 1955 v E; 1956 v E, Ni, W (17)
Johnstone, W. (Third Lanark), 1887 v Ni; 1889 v W; 1890 v E (3)
Jordan, J. (Leeds U), 1973 v E (sub), Sw (sub), Br; 1974 v Cz (sub + 1), WG (sub), Ni (sub), W, E, Bel, N, Z, Br, Y; 1975 v EG, Sp (2); 1976 v Ni, W, E; 1977 v Cz, W, Ni, E; 1978 v EG, Cz, W; (with Manchester U), Bul, Ni, E, Pe, Ir, Ho; 1979 v A, P, W (sub), Ni, E, N; 1980 v Bel, Ni (sub), W, E, Pol; 1981 v Is, W, E; (with AC Milan), 1982 v Se, Ho, W, E, USSR (52)

Kay, J. L. (Queen's Park), 1880 v E; 1882 v E, W; 1883 v E, W; 1884 v W (6)
Keillor, A. (Montrose), 1891 v W; 1892 v Ni; (with Dundee), 1894 v Ni; 1895 v W; 1896 v W; 1897 v W (6)
Keir, L. (Dumbarton), 1885 v W; 1886 v Ni; 1887 v E, W; 1888 v E (5)
Kelly, H. T. (Blackpool), 1952 v USA (1)
Kelly, J. (Renton), 1888 v E; (with Celtic), 1889 v E; 1890 v E; 1892 v E; 1893 v E, Ni; 1894 v W; 1896 v Ni (8)
Kelly, J. C. (Barnsley), 1949 v W, Ni (2)
Kelso, R. (Renton), 1885 v W, Ni; 1886 v W; 1887 v E, W; 1888 v E, Ni; (with Dundee), 1898 v Ni (8)
Kelso, T. (Dundee), 1914 v W (1)
Kennaway, J. (Celtic), 1934 v A (1)
Kennedy, A. (Eastern), 1875 v E; 1876 v E, W; (with Third Lanark), 1878 v E; 1882 v W; 1884 v W (6)
Kennedy, J. (Celtic), 1964 v W, E, WG; 1965 v W, Ni, Fi (6)
Kennedy, J. (Hibernian), 1897 v W (1)
Kennedy, S. (Aberdeen), 1978 v Bul, W, E, Pe, Ho; 1979 v A, P; 1982 v P (sub) (8)
Kennedy, S. (Partick T), 1905 v W (1)
Kennedy, S. (Rangers), 1975 v Se, P, W, Ni, E (5)
Ker, G. (Queen's Park), 1880 v E; 1881 v E, W; 1882 v W, E (5)
Ker, W. (Granville), 1872 v E; (with Queen's Park), 1873 v E (2)
Kerr, A. (Partick T), 1955 v A, H (2)
Kerr, P. (Hibernian), 1924 v Ni (1)
Key, G. (Hearts), 1902 v Ni (1)
Key, W. (Queen's Park), 1907 v Ni (1)
King, A. (Hearts), 1896 v E, W; (with Celtic), 1897 v Ni; 1898 v Ni; 1899 v Ni, W (6)
King, J. (Hamilton A), 1933 v Ni; 1934 v Ni (2)
King, W. S. (Queen's Park), 1929 v W (1)
Kinloch, J. D. (Partick T), 1922 v Ni (1)
Kinnaird, A. F. (Wanderers), 1873 v E (1)
Kinnear, D. (Rangers), 1938 v Cz (1)

Lambert, P. (Motherwell), 1995 v J, Ec (sub) (2)
Lambie, J. A. (Queen's Park), 1886 v Ni; 1887 v Ni; 1888 v E (3)
Lambie, W. A. (Queen's Park), 1892 v Ni; 1893 v W; 1894 v E; 1895 v E, Ni; 1896 v E, Ni; 1897 v E, Ni (9)
Lamont, D. (Pilgrims), 1885 v Ni (1)
Lang, A. (Dumbarton), 1880 v W (1)
Lang, J. J. (Clydesdale), 1876 v W; (with Third Lanark), 1878 v W (2)
Latta, A. (Dumbarton), 1888 v W; 1889 v E (2)
Law, D. (Huddersfield T), 1959 v W, Ni, Ho, P; 1960 v Ni, W; (with Manchester C), 1960 v E, Pol, A; 1961 v E, Ni; (with Torino), 1962 v Cz (2), E; (with Manchester U), 1963 v W, Ni, E, A, N, Ei, Sp; 1964 v W, E, N, WG; 1965 v W, Ni, E, Fi (2), Pol, Sp; 1966 v Ni, E, Pol; 1967 v W, E, USSR; 1968 v Ni; 1969 v Ni, A, WG; 1972 v Pe, Ni, W, E, Y, Cz, Br; (with Manchester C), 1974 v Cz (2), WG (2), Ni, Z (55)
Law, G. (Rangers), 1910 v E, Ni, W (3)
Law, T. (Chelsea), 1928 v E; 1930 v E (2)
Lawrence, J. (Newcastle U), 1911 v E (1)
Lawrence, T. (Liverpool), 1963 v Ei; 1969 v W, WG (3)
Lawson, D. (St Mirren), 1923 v E (1)
Leckie, R. (Queen's Park), 1872 v E (1)
Leggat, G. (Aberdeen), 1956 v E; 1957 v W; 1958 v Ni, H, Pol, Y, Par; (with Fulham), 1959 v E, W, Ni, WG, Ho; 1960 v E, Ni, W, Pol, A, H (18)
Leighton, J. (Aberdeen), 1983 v EG, Sw, Bel, Sw, W, E, Ca (2); 1984 v U, Bel, Ni, W, E, F; 1985 v Y, Ic, Sp (2), W, E, Ic; 1986 v W, EG, Aus (2), Is, D, WG, U; 1987 v Bul, Ei (2), L, Bel, E; 1988 v H, Bel, Bul, L, S.Ar, Ma, Sp; (with Manchester U), Co, E; 1989 v N, Cy, F, Cy, E, Ch; 1990 v Y, F, N, Arg, Ma (sub, Cr, Se, Br; (with Hibernian), 1994 v Ma, A, Ho; 1995 v Gr (sub), Ru, Sm, J, Ec, Fa (67)
Lennie, W. (Aberdeen), 1908 v W, Ni (2)
Lennox, R. (Celtic), 1967 v Ni, E, USSR; 1968 v W, L; 1969 v D, A, WG, Cy (sub); 1970 v W (sub) (10)
Leslie, L. G. (Airdrieonians), 1961 v W, Ni, Ei (2), Cz (5)
Levein, C. (Hearts), 1990 v Arg, EG, Eg (sub), Pol, Ma (sub), Se; 1992 v R, Sm; 1993 v P, G, P; 1994 v Sw, Ho; 1995 v Fi, Fa, Ru (16)
Liddell, W. (Liverpool), 1947 v W, Ni; 1948 v E, W, Ni; 1950 v E, W, P, F; 1951 v W, Ni, E, A; 1952 v W, Ni, E, USA, D, Se; 1953 v W, Ni, E; 1954 v W; 1955 v P, Y, A, H; 1956 v Ni (28)
Liddle, D. (East Fife), 1931 v A, I, Sw (3)
Lindsay, D. (St Mirren), 1903 v Ni (1)
Lindsay, J. (Dumbarton), 1880 v W; 1881 v W, E; 1884 v W, E; 1885 v W, E; 1886 v E (8)
Lindsay, J. (Renton), 1888 v E; 1893 v E, Ni (3)
Linwood, A. B. (Clyde), 1950 v W (1)
Little, R. J. (Rangers), 1953 v Se (1)
Livingstone, G. T. (Manchester C), 1906 v E; (with Rangers), 1907 v W (2)
Lochhead, A. (Third Lanark), 1889 v W (1)
Logan, J. (Ayr U), 1891 v W (1)

Logan, T. (Falkirk), 1913 v Ni (1)
Logie, J. T. (Arsenal), 1953 v Ni (1)
Loney, W. (Celtic), 1910 v W, Ni (2)
Long, H. (Clyde), 1947 v Ni (1)
Longair, W. (Dundee), 1894 v Ni (1)
Lorimer, P. (Leeds U), 1970 v A (sub); 1971 v W, Ni; 1972 v Ni (sub), W, E; 1973 v D (2), E (2); 1974 v WG (sub), E, Bel, N, Z, Br, Y; 1975 v Sp (sub); 1976 v D (2), R (sub) (21)
Love, A. (Aberdeen), 1931 v A, I, Sw (3)
Low, A. (Falkirk), 1934 v Ni (1)
Low, T. P. (Rangers), 1897 v Ni (1)
Low, W. L. (Newcastle U), 1911 v E, W; 1912 v Ni; 1920 v E, Ni (5)
Lowe, J. (Cambuslang), 1891 v Ni (1)
Lowe, J. (St Bernards), 1887 v Ni (1)
Lundie, J. (Hibernian), 1886 v W (1)
Lyall, J. (Sheffield W), 1905 v E (1)

McAdam, J. (Third Lanark), 1880 v W (1)
McAllister, G. (Leicester C), 1990 v EG, Pol, Ma (sub); (with Leeds U), 1991 v R, Sw, Bul, USSR (sub), Sm; 1992 v Sw (sub), Sm, Ni, Fi (sub), US, Ca, N, Ho, G, C; 1993 v Sw, P, I, Ma; 1994 v Sw, I, Ma, Ho, A, Ho; 1995 v Fi, Ru, Gr, Ru, Sm (33)
McArthur, D. (Celtic), 1895 v E, Ni; 1899 v W (3)
McAtee, A. (Celtic), 1913 v W (1)
McAulay, J. (Dumbarton), 1882 v W; (with Arthurlie), 1884 v Ni (2)
McAulay, J. (Dumbarton), 1883 v E, W; 1884 v E; 1885 v E, W; 1886 v E; 1887 v E, W (8)
McAuley, R. (Rangers), 1932 v Ni, W (2)
McAvennie, F. (West Ham U), 1986 v Aus (2), D (sub), WG (sub); (with Celtic), 1988 v S.Ar (5)
McBain, E. (St Mirren), 1894 v W (1)
McBain, N. (Manchester U), 1922 v E; (with Everton), 1923 v Ni; 1924 v W (3)
McBride, J. (Celtic), 1967 v W, Ni (2)
McBride, P. (Preston NE), 1904 v E; 1906 v E; 1907 v E, W; 1908 v E; 1909 v W (6)
McCall, J. (Renton), 1886 v W; 1887 v E, W; 1888 v E; 1890 v E (5)
McCall, S. M. (Everton), 1990 v Arg, EG, Eg (sub), Pol, Ma, Cr, Se, Br; 1991 v Sw, USSR, Sm; (with Rangers), 1992 v Sw, R, Sm, US, Ca, N, Ho, G, C; 1993 v Sw, P (2); 1994 v I, Ho, A (sub), Ho; 1995 v Fi (sub), Ru, Gr (30)
McCalliog, J. (Sheffield W), 1967 v E, USSR; 1968 v Ni; 1969 v D; (with Wolverhampton W), 1971 v P (5)
McCallum, N. (Renton), 1888 v Ni (1)
McCann, R. J. (Motherwell), 1959 v WG; 1960 v E, Ni, W; 1961 v E (5)
McCartney, W. (Hibernian), 1902 v Ni (1)
McClair, B. (Celtic), 1987 v L, Ei, E, Br (sub); (with Manchester U), 1988 v Bul, Ma (sub), Sp (sub); 1989 v N, Y, I (sub), Cy, F (sub); 1990 v N (sub), Arg (sub); 1991 v Bul (2), Sm; 1992 v Sw (sub), R, Ni, US, Ca (sub), N, Ho, G, C; 1993 v Sw, P (sub), Es (2) (30)
McClory, A. (Motherwell), 1927 v W; 1928 v Ni; 1935 v W (3)
McCloy, P. (Ayr U), 1924 v E; 1925 v E (2)
McCloy, P. (Rangers), 1973 v W, Ni, Sw, Br (4)
McCoist, A. (Rangers), 1986 v Ho; 1987 v L (sub), Ei (sub), Bel, E, Br; 1988 v H, Bel, Ma, Sp, Co, E; 1989 v Y (sub), F, Cy, E; 1990 v Y, F, N, EG (sub), Eg, Pol, Ma (sub), Cr (sub), Se (sub), Br; 1991 v R, Sw, Bul (2), USSR; 1992 v Sw, Sm, Ni, Fi (sub), US, Ca, N, Ho, G, C; 1993 v Sw, P, I, Ma, P (46)
McColl, A. (Renton), 1888 v Ni (1)
McColl, I. M. (Rangers), 1950 v E, F; 1951 v W, Ni, Bel; 1957 v E, Ni, W, Y, Sp, Sw, WG; 1958 v Ni, E (14)
McColl, R. S. (Queen's Park), 1896 v W, Ni; 1897 v Ni; 1898 v Ni; 1899 v Ni, E, W; 1900 v E, W; 1901 v E, W; (with Newcastle U), 1902 v E; (with Queen's Park), 1908 v Ni (13)
McColl, W. (Renton), 1895 v W (1)
McCombie, A. (Sunderland), 1903 v E, W; (with Newcastle U), 1905 v E, W (4)
McCorkindale, J. (Partick T), 1891 v W (1)
McCormick, R. (Abercorn), 1886 v W (1)
McCrae, D. (St Mirren), 1929 v N, G (2)
McCreadie, A. (Rangers), 1893 v W; 1894 v E (2)
McCreadie, E. G. (Chelsea), 1965 v E, Sp, Fi, Pol; 1966 v P, Ni, W, Pol, I; 1967 v E, USSR; 1968 v Ni, W, E, Ho; 1969 v W, Ni, E, D, A, WG, Cy (2) (23)
McCulloch, D. (Hearts), 1935 v W; (with Brentford), 1936 v E; 1937 v W, Ni; 1938 v Cz; (with Derby Co), 1939 v H, W (7)
MacDonald, A. (Rangers), 1976 v Sw (1)
McDonald, J. (Edinburgh University), 1886 v E (1)
McDonald, J. (Sunderland), 1956 v W, Ni (2)
MacDougall, E. J. (Norwich C) 1975 v Se, P, W, Ni, E; 1976 v D, R (sub) (7)
McDougall, J. (Liverpool), 1931 v I, A (2)
McDougall, J. (Airdrieonians), 1926 v Ni (1)
McDougall, J. (Vale of Leven), 1877 v E, W; 1878 v E; 1879 v E, W (5)
McFadyen, W. (Motherwell), 1934 v A, W (2)
Macfarlane, A. (Dundee), 1904 v W; 1906 v W; 1908 v W; 1909 v Ni; 1911 v W (5)
McFarlane, R. (Greenock Morton), 1896 v W (1)
Macfarlane, W. (Hearts), 1947 v L (1)
McGarr, E. (Aberdeen), 1970 v Ei, A (2)
McGarvey, F. P. (Liverpool), 1979 v Ni (sub), Arg; (with Celtic), 1984 v U, Bel (sub), EG (sub), Ni, W (7)
McGeoch, A. (Dumbreck), 1876 v E, W; 1877 v E, W (4)
McGhee, J. (Hibernian), 1886 v W (1)
McGhee, M. (Aberdeen), 1983 v Ca (1 + 1 sub); 1984 v Ni (sub), E (4)
McGinlay, J. (Bolton W), 1994 v A, Ho; 1995 v Fa, Ru, Gr, Ru, Sm, Fa (8)
McGonagle, W. (Celtic), 1933 v E; 1934 v A, E, Ni; 1935 v Ni, W (6)
McGrain, D. (Celtic), 1973 v W, Ni, E, Sw, Br; 1974 v Cz (2), WG, W (sub), E, Bel, N, Z, Br, Y; 1975 v Sp, Se, P, W, Ni, E, R; 1976 v D (2), Sw, Ni, W, E; 1977 v Fi, Cz, W (2), Se, Ni, E, Ch, Arg, Br; 1978 v EG, Cz; 1980 v Bel, P, Ni, W, E, Pol, H; 1981 v Se, P, Is, Ni, Is, W (sub), Ni, E; 1982 v Se, Sp, Ho, Ni, E, Nz, USSR (sub) (62)
McGregor, J. C. (Vale of Leven), 1877 v E, W; 1878 v E; 1880 v E (4)
McGrory, J. E. (Kilmarnock), 1965 v Ni, Fi; 1966 v P (3)
McGrory, J. (Celtic), 1928 v Ni; 1931 v E; 1932 v Ni, W; 1933 v E, Ni; 1934 v Ni (7)
McGuire, W. (Beith), 1881 v E, W (2)
McGurk, F. (Birmingham), 1934 v W (1)
McHardy, H. (Rangers), 1885 v Ni (1)
McInally, A. (Aston Villa), 1989 v Cy (sub), Ch; (with Bayern Munich), 1990 v Y (sub), F (sub), Arg, Pol (sub), Ma, Cr (8)
McInally, J. (Dundee U), 1987 v Bel, Br; 1988 v Ma (sub); 1991 v Bul (2); 1992 v US (sub), N (sub), C (sub); 1993 v G, P (10)
McInally, T. B. (Celtic), 1926 v Ni; 1927 v W (2)
McInnes, T. (Cowlairs), 1889 v Ni (1)
McIntosh, W. (Third Lanark), 1905 v Ni (1)
McIntyre, A. (Vale of Leven), 1878 v E; 1882 v E (2)
McIntyre, H. (Rangers), 1880 v W (1)
McIntyre, J. (Rangers), 1884 v W (1)
McKay, D. (Celtic), 1959 v E, WG, Ho, P; 1960 v E, Pol, A, H, T; 1961 v W, Ni; 1962 v Ni, Cz, U (sub) (14)
Mackay, D. C. (Hearts), 1957 v Sp; 1958 v F; 1959 v W, Ni; (with Tottenham H), 1959 v WG, E; 1960 v W, Ni, A, Pol, H, T; 1961 v W, Ni, E; 1963 v E, A, N; 1964 v Ni, W, N; 1966 v Ni (22)

Mackay, G. (Hearts), 1988 v Bul (sub), L (sub), S.Ar (sub), Ma (4)
McKay, J. (Blackburn R), 1924 v W (1)
McKay, R. (Newcastle U), 1928 v W (1)
McKean, R. (Rangers), 1976 v Sw (sub) (1)
McKenzie, D. (Brentford), 1938 v Ni (1)
Mackenzie, J. A. (Partick T), 1954 v W, E, N, Fi, A, U; 1955 v E, H; 1956 v A (9)
McKeown, M. (Celtic), 1889 v Ni; 1890 v E (2)
McKie, J. (East Stirling), 1898 v W (1)
McKillop, T. R. (Rangers), 1938 v Ho (1)
McKimmie, S. (Aberdeen), 1989 v E, Ch; 1990 v Arg, Eg, Cr (sub), Br; 1991 v R, Sw, Bul, Sm; 1992 v Sw, R, Ni, Fi, US, Ca (sub), N (sub), Ho, G, C; 1993 v P, Es (sub); 1994 v Sw, I, Ho, A, Ho; 1995 v Fi, Fa, Ru, Gr, Ru, Fa (33)
McKinlay, D. (Liverpool), 1922 v W, Ni (2)
McKinlay, W. (Dundee U), 1994 v Ma, Ho (sub), A, Ho; 1995 v Fa (sub), Ru, Gr, Ru (sub), Sm (sub), J, Ec, Fa (12)
McKinnon, A. (Queen's Park), 1874 v E (1)
McKinnon, R. (Rangers), 1966 v W, E, I (2), Ho, Br; 1967 v W, Ni, E; 1968 v Ni, W, E, Ho; 1969 v D, A, WG, Cy; 1970 v Ni, W, E, Ei, WG, A; 1971 v D, Bel, P, USSR, D (28)
McKinnon, R. (Motherwell), 1994 v Ma; 1995 v J, Fa (3)
MacKinnon, W. (Dumbarton), 1883 v E, W; 1884 v E, W (4)
McKinnon, W. W. (Queen's Park), 1872 v E; 1873 v E; 1874 v E; 1875 v E; 1876 v E, W; 1877 v E; 1878 v E; 1879 v E (9)
McLaren, A. (St Johnstone), 1929 v N, G, Ho; 1933 v W, Ni (5)
McLaren, A. (Preston NE), 1947 v E, Bel, L; 1948 v W (4)
McLaren, A. (Hearts), 1992 v US, Ca, N; 1993 v I, Ma, G, Es (sub + 1); 1994 v I, Ma, Ho, A; 1995 v Fi, Fa; (with Rangers), Ru, Gr, Ru, Sm, J, Ec, Fa (21)
McLaren, J. (Hibernian), 1888 v W; (with Celtic), 1889 v E; 1890 v E (3)
McLean, A. (Celtic), 1926 v W, Ni; 1927 v W, E (4)
McLean, D. (St Bernards), 1896 v W; 1897 v Ni (2)
McLean, D. (Sheffield W), 1912 v E (1)
McLean, G. (Dundee), 1968 v Ho (1)
McLean, T. (Kilmarnock), 1969 v D, Cy, W; 1970 v Ni, W; 1971 v D (6)
McLeish, A. (Aberdeen), 1980 v F, Ni, W, E, Pol, H; 1981 v Se, Is, Ni, Is, Ni, E; 1982 v Se, Sp, Ni, Br (sub); 1983 v Bel, Sw (sub), W, E, Ca (3); 1984 v U, Bel, EG, Ni, W, E, F; 1985 v Y, Ic, Sp (2), W, E, Ic; 1986 v W, EG, Aus (2), E, Ho, D; 1987 v Bel, E, Br; 1988 v Bel, Bul, L, S.Ar (sub), Ma, Sp, Co, E; 1989 v N, Y, I, Cy, F, Cy, E, Ch; 1990 v Y, F, N, Arg, EG, Eg, Cr, Se, Br; 1991 v R, Sw, USSR, Bul; 1993 v Ma (77)
McLeod, D. (Celtic), 1905 v Ni; 1906 v E, W, Ni (4)
McLeod, J. (Dumbarton), 1888 v Ni; 1889 v W; 1890 v Ni; 1892 v E; 1893 v W (5)
MacLeod, J. M. (Hibernian), 1961 v E, Ei (2), Cz (4)
MacLeod, M. (Celtic), 1985 v E (sub); 1987 v Ei, L, E, Br; (with Borussia Dortmund), 1988 v Co, E; 1989 v I, Ch; 1990 v Y, F, N (sub), Arg, EG, Pol, Se Br; (with Hibernian), 1991 v R, Sw, USSR (sub) (20)
McLeod, W. (Cowlairs), 1886 v Ni (1)
McLintock, A. (Vale of Leven), 1875 v E; 1876 v E; 1880 v E (3)
McLintock, F. (Leicester C), 1963 v N (sub), Ei, Sp; (with Arsenal), 1965 v Ni; 1967 v USSR; 1970 v Ni; 1971 v W, Ni, E (9)
McLuckie, J. S. (Manchester C), 1934 v W (1)
McMahon, A. (Celtic), 1892 v E; 1893 v E, Ni; 1894 v E; 1901 v Ni; 1902 v W (6)
McMenemy, J. (Celtic), 1905 v Ni; 1909 v Ni; 1910 v E, W; 1911 v Ni, W, E; 1912 v W; 1914 v W, Ni, E; 1920 v Ni (12)
McMenemy, J. (Motherwell), 1934 v W (1)
McMillan, J. (St Bernards), 1897 v W (1)
McMillan, I. L. (Airdrieonians), 1952 v E, USA, D; 1955 v E; 1956 v E; (with Rangers), 1961 v Cz (6)
McMillan, T. (Dumbarton), 1887 v Ni (1)
McMullan, J. (Partick T), 1920 v W; 1921 v W, Ni, E; 1924 v E, Ni; 1925 v E; 1926 v W; (with Manchester C), 1926 v E; 1927 v E, W; 1928 v E, W; 1929 v W, E, Ni (16)
McNab, A. (Morton), 1921 v E, Ni (2)
McNab, A. (Sunderland), 1937 v A; (with WBA), 1939 v E (2)
McNab, C. D. (Dundee), 1931 v E, W, A, I, Sw; 1932 v E (6)
McNab, J. S. (Liverpool), 1923 v W (1)
McNair, A. (Celtic), 1906 v W; 1907 v Ni; 1908 v E, W; 1909 v E; 1910 v W; 1912 v E, W, Ni; 1913 v E; 1914 v E, Ni; 1920 v E, W, Ni (15)
McNaught, W. (Raith R), 1951 v A, W, Ni; 1952 v E; 1955 v Ni (5)
McNeil, H. (Queen's Park), 1874 v E; 1875 v E; 1876 v E, W; 1877 v W; 1878 v E; 1879 v E, W; 1881 v E, W (10)
McNeil, M. (Rangers), 1876 v W; 1880 v E (2)
McNeill, W. (Celtic), 1961 v E, Ei (2), Cz; 1962 v Ni, E, Cz, U; 1963 v Ei, Sp; 1964 v W, E, WG; 1965 v E, Fi, Pol, Sp; 1966 v Ni, Pol; 1967 v USSR; 1968 v E; 1969 v Cy, W, E, Cy (sub); 1970 v WG; 1972 v Ni, W, E (29)
McPhail, J. (Celtic), 1950 v W; 1951 v W, Ni, A; 1954 v Ni (5)
McPhail, R. (Airdrieonians), 1927 v E; (with Rangers), 1929 v W; 1931 v E, Ni; 1932 v W, Ni, F; 1933 v E, Ni; 1934 v A, Ni; 1935 v E; 1937 v G, E, Cz; 1938 v W, Ni (17)
McPherson, D. (Kilmarnock), 1892 v Ni (1)
McPherson, D. (Hearts), 1989 v Cy, E; 1990 v N, Ma, Cr, Se, Br; 1991 v Sw, Bul (2), USSR (sub), Sm; 1992 v Sw, R, Sm, Ni, Fi, US, Ca, N, Ho, G, C; (with Rangers), 1993 v Sw, I, Ma, P (27)
McPherson, J. (Clydesdale), 1875 v E (1)
McPherson, J. (Vale of Leven), 1879 v E, W; 1880 v E; 1881 v W; 1883 v E, W; 1884 v E; 1885 v Ni (8)
McPherson, J. (Kilmarnock), 1888 v W; (with Cowlairs), 1889 v E; 1890 v Ni, E; (with Rangers), 1892 v W; 1894 v E; 1895 v E, Ni; 1897 v Ni (9)
McPherson, J. (Hearts), 1891 v E (1)
McPherson, R. (Arthurlie), 1882 v E (1)
McQueen, G. (Leeds U), 1974 v Bel; 1975 v Sp (2), P, W, Ni, E, R; 1976 v D; 1977 v Cz, W (2), Ni, E; 1978 v EG, Cz, W; (with Manchester U), Bul, Ni, W; 1979 v A, N, P, Ni, E, N; 1980 v Pe, A, Bel; 1981 v W (30)
McQueen, M. (Leith Ath), 1890 v W; 1891 v W (2)
McRorie, D. M. (Morton), 1931 v W (1)
McSpadyen, A. (Partick T), 1939 v E, H (2)
McStay, P. (Celtic), 1984 v U, Bel, EG, Ni, W, E (sub); 1985 v Y, Ic, Sp (2), W; 1986 v EG (sub), Aus, Is, U; 1987 v Bul, Ei (1 + 1 sub), L (sub), Bel, E, Br; 1988 v H, Bel, Bul, L, S.Ar, Sp, Co, E; 1989 v N, Y, I, Cy, F, Cy, E, Ch; 1990 v Y, F, N, Arg, EG (sub), Eg, Pol (sub), Ma, Cr, Se (sub), Br; 1991 v R, USSR, Bul; 1992 v Sm, Fi, US, Ca, N, Ho, G, C; 1993 v Sw, P, I, Ma, P, Es (2); 1994 v I (sub), Ho; 1995 v Fi, Fa, Ru (72)
McStay, W. (Celtic), 1921 v W, Ni; 1925 v E, Ni, W; 1926 v E, Ni, W; 1927 v E, Ni, W; 1928 v W, Ni (13)
McTavish, J. (Falkirk), 1910 v Ni (1)
McWhattie, G. C. (Queen's Park), 1901 v W, Ni (2)
McWilliam, P. (Newcastle U), 1905 v E; 1906 v E; 1907 v E, W; 1909 v E, W; 1910 v E; 1911 v W (8)
Macari, L. (Celtic), 1972 v W (sub), E, Y, Cz, Br; 1973 v D; (with Manchester U), E (2), W (sub), Ni (sub); 1975 v Se, P (sub), W, E (sub), R; 1977 v Ni (sub), E (sub), Ch, Arg; 1978 v EG, W, Bul, Pe (sub), Ir (24)
Macauley, A. R. (Brentford), 1947 v E; (with Arsenal), 1948 v E, W, Ni, Bel, Sw, F (7)

Madden, J. (Celtic), 1893 v W; 1895 v W (2)
Main, F. R. (Rangers), 1938 v W (1)
Main, J. (Hibernian), 1909 v Ni (1)
Maley, W. (Celtic), 1893 v E, Ni (2)
Malpas, M. (Dundee U), 1984 v F; 1985 v E, Ic; 1986 v W, Aus (2), Is, R, E, Ho, D, WG; 1987 v Bul, Ei, Bel; 1988 v Bel, Bul, L, S.Ar, Ma; 1989 v N, Y, I, Cy, F, Cy, E, Ch; 1990 v Y, F, N, Eg, Pol, Ma, Cr, Se, Br; 1991 v R, Bul (2), USSR, Sm; 1992 v Sw, R, Sm, Ni, Fi, US, Ca (sub), N, Ho, G; 1993 v Sw, P, I (55)
Marshall, G. (Celtic), 1992 v US (1)
Marshall, H. (Celtic), 1899 v W; 1900 v Ni (2)
Marshall, J. (Middlesbrough), 1921 v E, W, Ni; 1922 v E, W, Ni; (with Llanelly), 1924 v W (7)
Marshall, J. (Third Lanark), 1885 v Ni; 1886 v W; 1887 v E, W (4)
Marshall, J. (Rangers), 1932 v E; 1933 v E; 1934 v E (3)
Marshall, R. W. (Rangers), 1892 v Ni; 1894 v Ni (2)
Martin, B. (Motherwell), 1995 v J, Ec (2)
Martin, F. (Aberdeen), 1954 v N (2), A, U; 1955 v E, H (6)
Martin, N. (Hibernian), 1965 v Fi, Pol; (with Sunderland), 1966 v I (3)
Martis, J. (Motherwell), 1961 v W (1)
Mason, J. (Third Lanark), 1949 v E, W, Ni; 1950 v Ni; 1951 v Ni, Bel, A (7)
Massie, A. (Hearts), 1932 v Ni, W, F; 1933 v Ni; 1934 v E, Ni; 1935 v E, Ni, W; 1936 v W, Ni; (with Aston Villa), 1936 v E; 1937 v G, E, W, Ni, A; 1938 v W (18)
Masson, D. S. (QPR), 1976 v Ni, W, E; 1977 v Fi, Cz, W, Ni, E, Ch, Arg, Br; 1978 v EG, Cz, W; (with Derby Co), Ni, E, Pe (17)
Mathers, D. (Partick T), 1954 v Fi (1)
Maxwell, W. S. (Stoke C), 1898 v E (1)
May, J. (Rangers), 1906 v W, Ni; 1908 v E, Ni; 1909 v W (5)
Meechan, P. (Celtic), 1896 v Ni (1)
Meiklejohn, D. D. (Rangers), 1922 v W; 1924 v W; 1925 v W, Ni, E; 1928 v W, Ni; 1929 v E, Ni; 1930 v E, Ni; 1931 v E; 1932 v W, Ni; 1934 v A (15)
Menzies, A. (Hearts), 1906 v E (1)
Mercer, R. (Hearts), 1912 v W; 1913 v Ni (2)
Middleton, R. (Cowdenbeath), 1930 v Ni (1)
Millar, A. (Hearts), 1939 v W (1)
Millar, J. (Rangers), 1897 v E; 1898 v E, W (3)
Millar, J. (Rangers), 1963 v A, Ei (2)
Miller, J. (St Mirren), 1931 v E, I, Sw; 1932 v F; 1934 v E (5)
Miller, P. (Dumbarton), 1882 v E; 1883 v E, W (3)
Miller, T. (Liverpool), 1920 v E; (with Manchester U), 1921 v E, Ni (3)
Miller, W. (Third Lanark), 1876 v E (1)
Miller, W. (Celtic), 1947 v E, W, Bel, L; 1948 v W, Ni (6)
Miller, W. (Aberdeen), 1975 v R; 1978 v Bul; 1980 v Bel, W, E, Pol, H; 1981 v Se, P, Is (sub), Ni, W, Ni, E; 1982 v Ni, P, Ho, Br, USSR; 1983 v EG, Sw (2), W, E, Ca (3); 1984 v U, Bel, EG, W, E, F; 1985 v Y, Ic, Sp (2), W, E, Ic; 1986 v W, EG, Aus (2), Is, R, E, Ho, D, WG, U; 1987 v Bul, E, Br; 1988 v H, L, S.Ar, Ma, Sp, Co, E; 1989 v N, Y; 1990 v Y, N (65)
Mills, W. (Aberdeen), 1936 v W, Ni; 1937 v W (3)
Milne, J. V. (Middlesbrough), 1938 v E; 1939 v E (2)
Mitchell, D. (Rangers), 1890 v Ni; 1892 v E; 1893 v E, Ni; 1894 v E (5)
Mitchell, J. (Kilmarnock), 1908 v Ni; 1910 v Ni, W (3)
Mitchell, R. C. (Newcastle U), 1951 v D, F (2)
Mochan, N. (Celtic), 1954 v N, A, U (3)
Moir, W. (Bolton W), 1950 v E (1)
Moncur, R. (Newcastle U), 1968 v Ho; 1970 v Ni, W, E, Ei; 1971 v D, Bel, W, P, Ni, E, D; 1972 v Pe, Ni, W, E (16)
Morgan, H. (St Mirren), 1898 v W; (with Liverpool), 1899 v E (2)
Morgan, W. (Burnley), 1968 v Ni; (with Manchester U), 1972 v Pe, Y, Cz, Br; 1973 v D (2), E (2), W, Ni, Sw, Br; 1974 v Cz (2), WG (2), Ni, Bel (sub), Br, Y (21)
Morris, D. (Raith R), 1923 v Ni; 1924 v E, Ni; 1925 v E, W, Ni (6)
Morris, H. (East Fife), 1950 v Ni (1)
Morrison, T. (St Mirren), 1927 v E (1)
Morton, A. L. (Queen's Park), 1920 v W, Ni; (with Rangers), 1921 v E; 1922 v E, W; 1923 v E, W, Ni; 1924 v E, W, Ni; 1925 v E, W, Ni; 1927 v E, Ni; 1928 v E, W, Ni; 1929 v E, W, Ni; 1930 v E, W, Ni; 1931 v E, W, Ni; 1932 v E, W, F (31)
Morton, H. A. (Kilmarnock), 1929 v G, Ho (2)
Mudie, J. K. (Blackpool), 1957 v W, Ni, E, Y, Sw, Sp (2), WG; 1958 v Ni, E, W, Sw, H, Pol, Y, Par, F (17)
Muir, W. (Dundee), 1907 v Ni (1)
Muirhead, T. A. (Rangers), 1922 v Ni; 1923 v E; 1924 v W; 1927 v Ni; 1928 v Ni; 1929 v W, Ni; 1930 v W (8)
Mulhall, G. (Aberdeen), 1960 v Ni; (with Sunderland), 1963 v Ni; 1964 v Ni (3)
Munro, A. D. (Hearts), 1937 v W, Ni; (with Blackpool), 1938 v Ho (3)
Munro, F. M. (Wolverhampton W), 1971 v Ni (sub), E (sub), D, USSR; 1975 v Se, W (sub), Ni, E, R (9)
Munro, I. (St Mirren), 1979 v Arg, N; 1980 v Pe, A, Bel, W, E (7)
Munro, N. (Abercorn), 1888 v W; 1889 v E (2)
Murdoch, J. (Motherwell), 1931 v Ni (1)
Murdoch, R. (Celtic), 1966 v W, E, I (2); 1967 v Ni; 1968 v Ni; 1969 v W, Ni, E, WG, Cy; 1970 v A (12)
Murphy, F. (Celtic), 1938 v Ho (1)
Murray, J. (Renton), 1895 v W (1)
Murray, J. (Hearts), 1958 v E, H, Pol, Y, F (5)
Murray, J. W. (Vale of Leven), 1890 v W (1)
Murray, P. (Hibernian), 1896 v Ni; 1897 v W (2)
Murray, S. (Aberdeen), 1972 v Bel (1)
Mutch, G. (Preston NE), 1938 v E (1)

Napier, C. E. (Celtic), 1932 v E; 1935 v E, W; (with Derby Co), 1937 v Ni, A (5)
Narey, D. (Dundee U), 1977 v Se (sub); 1979 v P, Ni (sub), Arg; 1980 v P, Ni, Pol, H; 1981 v W, E (sub); 1982 v Ho, W, E, Nz (sub), Br, USSR; 1983 v EG, Sw, Bel, Ni, W, E, Ca (3); 1986 v Is, R, Ho, WG, U; 1987 v Bul, E, Bel; 1989 v I, Cy (35)
Neil, R. G. (Hibernian), 1896 v W; (with Rangers), 1900 v W (2)
Neill, R. W. (Queen's Park), 1876 v W; 1877 v E, W; 1878 v W; 1880 v E (5)
Neilles, P. (Hearts), 1914 v W, Ni (2)
Nelson, J. (Cardiff C), 1925 v W, Ni; 1928 v E; 1930 v F (4)
Nevin, P. K. F. (Chelsea), 1986 v R (sub), E (sub); 1987 v L, Ei, Bel (sub); 1988 v L; (with Everton), 1989 v Cy, E; 1991 v R (sub), Bul (sub), Sm (sub); 1992 v US, G (sub), C (sub); (with Tranmere R), 1993 v Ma, P (sub), Es; 1994 v Sw, Ma, Ho, A (sub), Ho; 1995 v Fa, Ru (sub), Sm (25)
Niblo, T. D. (Aston Villa), 1904 v E (1)
Nibloe, J. (Kilmarnock), 1929 v E, N, Ho; 1930 v W; 1931 v E, Ni, A, I, Sw; 1932 v E, F (11)
Nicholas, C. (Celtic), 1983 v Sw, Ni, E, Ca (3); (with Arsenal), 1984 v Bel, F (sub); 1985 v Y (sub), Ic (sub), Sp (sub), W (sub); 1986 v Is, R (sub), E, D, U (sub); 1987 v Bul, E (sub); (with Aberdeen), 1989 v Cy (sub) (20)
Nicol, S. (Liverpool), 1985 v Y, Ic, Sp, W; 1986 v W, EG, Aus, E, D, WG, U; 1988 v H, Bul, S.Ar, Sp, Co, E; 1989 v N, Y, Cy, F; 1990 v Y, F; 1991 v Sw, USSR, Sm; 1992 v Sw (27)
Nisbet, J. (Ayr U), 1929 v N, G, Ho (3)
Niven, J. B. (Moffatt), 1885 v Ni (1)

O'Donnell, F. (Preston NE), 1937 v E, A, Cz; 1938 v W; (with Blackpool), E, Ho (6)
O'Donnell, P. (Motherwell), 1994 v Sw (sub) (1)
Ogilvie, D. H. (Motherwell), 1934 v A (1)
O'Hare, J. (Derby Co), 1970 v W, Ni, E; 1971 v D, Bel, W, Ni; 1972 v P, Bel, Ho (sub), Pe, Ni, W (13)
Ormond, W. E. (Hibernian), 1954 v E, N, Fi, A, U; 1959 v E (6)
O'Rourke, F. (Airdrieonians), 1907 v Ni (1)
Orr, J. (Kilmarnock), 1892 v W (1)
Orr, R. (Newcastle U), 1902 v E; 1904 v E (2)
Orr, T. (Morton), 1952 v Ni, W (2)
Orr, W. (Celtic), 1900 v Ni; 1903 v Ni; 1904 v W (3)
Orrock, R. (Falkirk), 1913 v W (1)
Oswald, J. (Third Lanark), 1889 v E; (with St Bernards), 1895 v E; (with Rangers), 1897 v W (3)

Parker, A. H. (Falkirk), 1955 v P, Y, A; 1956 v E, Ni, W, A; 1957 v Ni, W, Y; 1958 v Ni, W, E, Sw; (with Everton), Par (15)
Parlane, D. (Rangers), 1973 v W, Sw, Br; 1975 v Sp (sub), Se, P, W, Ni, E, R; 1976 v D (sub); 1977 v W (12)
Parlane, R. (Vale of Leven), 1878 v W; 1879 v E, W (3)
Paterson, G. D. (Celtic), 1939 v Ni (1)
Paterson, J. (Leicester C), 1920 v E (1)
Paterson, J. (Cowdenbeath), 1931 v A, I, Sw (3)
Paton, A. (Motherwell), 1952 v D, Se (2)
Paton, D. (St Bernards), 1896 v W (1)
Paton, M. (Dumbarton), 1883 v E; 1884 v W; 1885 v W, E; 1886 v E (5)
Paton, R. (Vale of Leven), 1879 v E, W (2)
Patrick, J. (St Mirren), 1897 v E, W (2)
Paul, H. McD. (Queen's Park), 1909 v E, W, Ni (3)
Paul, W. (Partick T), 1888 v W; 1889 v W; 1890 v W (3)
Paul, W. (Dykebar), 1891 v Ni (1)
Pearson, T. (Newcastle U), 1947 v E, Bel (2)
Penman, A. (Dundee), 1966 v Ho (1)
Pettigrew, W. (Motherwell), 1976 v Sw, Ni, W; 1977 v W (sub), Se (5)
Phillips, J. (Queen's Park), 1877 v E, W; 1878 v W (3)
Plenderleith, J. B. (Manchester C), 1961 v Ni (1)
Porteous, W. (Hearts), 1903 v Ni (1)
Pringle, C. (St Mirren), 1921 v W (1)
Provan, D. (Rangers), 1964 v Ni, N; 1966 v I (2), Ho (5)
Provan, D. (Celtic), 1980 v Bel (2 sub), P (sub), Ni (sub); 1981 v Is, W, E; 1982 v Se, P, Ni (10)
Pursell, P. (Queen's Park), 1914 v W (1)

Quinn, J. (Celtic), 1905 v Ni; 1906 v Ni, W; 1908 v Ni, E; 1909 v E; 1910 v E, Ni, W; 1912 v E, W (11)
Quinn, P. (Motherwell), 1961 v E, Ei (2); 1962 v U (4)

Rae, J. (Third Lanark), 1889 v W; 1890 v Ni (2)
Raeside, J. S. (Third Lanark), 1906 v W (1)
Raisbeck, A. G. (Liverpool), 1900 v E; 1901 v E; 1902 v E; 1903 v E, W; 1904 v E; 1906 v E; 1907 v E (8)
Rankin, G. (Vale of Leven), 1890 v Ni; 1891 v E (2)
Rankin, R. (St Mirren), 1929 v N, G, Ho (3)
Redpath, W. (Motherwell), 1949 v W, Ni; 1951 v E, D, F, Bel, A; 1952 v Ni, E (9)
Reid, J. G. (Airdrieonians), 1914 v W; 1920 v W; 1924 v Ni (3)
Reid, R. (Brentford), 1938 v E, Ni (2)
Reid, W. (Rangers), 1911 v E, W, Ni; 1912 v Ni; 1913 v E, W, Ni; 1914 v E, Ni (9)
Reilly, L. (Hibernian), 1949 v E, W, F; 1950 v W, Ni, Sw, F; 1951 v W, E, D, F, Bel, A; 1952 v Ni, W, E, USA, D, Se; 1953 v Ni, W, E, Se; 1954 v W; 1955 v H (2), P, Y, A, E; 1956 v E, W, Ni, A; 1957 v E, Ni, W, Y (38)
Rennie, H. G. (Hearts), 1900 v E, Ni; (with Hibernian), 1901 v E; 1902 v E, Ni, W; 1903 v Ni, W; 1904 v Ni; 1905 v W; 1906 v Ni; 1908 v Ni, W (13)
Renny-Tailyour, H. W. (Royal Engineers), 1873 v E (1)
Rhind, A. (Queen's Park), 1872 v E (1)
Richmond, A. (Queen's Park), 1906 v W (1)
Richmond, J. T. (Clydesdale), 1877 v E; (with Queen's Park), 1878 v E; 1882 v W (3)
Ring, T. (Clyde), 1953 v Se; 1955 v W, Ni, E, H; 1957 v E, Sp (2), Sw, WG; 1958 v Ni, Sw (12)
Rioch, B. D. (Derby Co), 1975 v P, W, Ni, E, R; 1976 v D (2), R, Ni, W, E; 1977 v Fi, Cz, W; (with Everton), W, Ni, E, Ch, Br; 1978 v Cz; (with Derby Co), Ni, E, Pe, Ho (24)
Ritchie, A. (East Stirlingshire), 1891 v W (1)
Ritchie, H. (Hibernian), 1923 v W; 1928 v Ni (2)
Ritchie, J. (Queen's Park), 1897 v W (1)
Ritchie, W. (Rangers), 1962 v U (sub) (1)
Robb, D. T. (Aberdeen), 1971 v W, E, P, D (sub), USSR (5)
Robb, W. (Rangers), 1926 v W; (with Hibernian), 1928 v W (2)
Robertson, A. (Clyde), 1955 v P, A, H; 1958 v Sw, Par (5)
Robertson, D. (Rangers), 1992 v Ni; 1994 v Sw, Ho (3)
Robertson, G. (Motherwell), 1910 v W; (with Sheffield W), 1912 v W; 1913 v E, Ni (4)
Robertson, G. (Kilmarnock), 1938 v Cz (1)
Robertson, H. (Dundee), 1962 v Cz (1)
Robertson, J. (Dundee), 1931 v A, I (2)
Robertson, J. (Hearts), 1991 v R, Sw, Bul (sub), Sm (sub); 1992 v Sm, Ni (sub), Fi; 1993 v I (sub), Ma (sub), G, Es; 1995 v J (sub), Ec, Fa (sub) (14)
Robertson, J. N. (Nottingham F), 1978 v Ni, W (sub), Ir; 1979 v P, N; 1980 v Pe, A, Bel (2), P; 1981 v Se, P, Is, Ni, Is, Ni, E; 1982 v Se, Ni (2), E (sub), Nz, Br, USSR; 1983 v EG, Sw; (with Derby Co), 1984 v U, Bel (28)
Robertson, J. G. (Tottenham H), 1965 v W (1)
Robertson, J. T. (Everton), 1898 v E; (with Southampton), 1899 v E; (with Rangers), 1900 v E, W; 1901 v W, Ni, E; 1902 v W, Ni, E; 1903 v E, W; 1904 v E, W, Ni; 1905 v W (16)
Robertson, P. (Dundee), 1903 v Ni (1)
Robertson, T. (Queen's Park), 1889 v Ni; 1890 v E; 1891 v W; 1892 v Ni (4)
Robertson, T. (Hearts), 1898 v Ni (1)
Robertson, W. (Dumbarton), 1887 v E, W (2)
Robinson, R. (Dundee), 1974 v WG (sub); 1975 v Se, Ni, R (sub) (4)
Rough, A. (Partick T), 1976 v Sw, Ni, W, E; 1977 v Fi, Cz, W (2), Se, Ni, E, Ch, Arg, Br; 1978 v Cz, W, Ni, E, Pe, Ir, Ho; 1979 v A, P, W, Arg, N; 1980 v Pe, A, Bel (2), P, W, E, Pol, H; 1981 v Se, P, Is, Ni, Is, W, E; 1982 v Se, Ni, Sp, Ho, W, E, Nz, Br, USSR; (with Hibernian), 1986 v W (sub), E (53)
Rougvie, D. (Aberdeen), 1984 v Ni (1)
Rowan, A. (Caledonian), 1880 v E; (with Queen's Park), 1882 v W (2)
Russell, D. (Hearts), 1895 v E, Ni; (with Celtic), 1897 v W; 1898 v Ni; 1901 v W, Ni (6)
Russell, J. (Cambuslang), 1890 v Ni (1)
Russell, W. F. (Airdrieonians), 1924 v W; 1925 v E (2)
Rutherford, E. (Rangers), 1948 v F (1)

St John, I. (Motherwell), 1959 v WG; 1960 v E, Ni, W, Pol, A; 1961 v E; (with Liverpool), 1962 v Ni, W, E, Cz (2), U; 1963 v W, Ni, E, N, Ei (sub), Sp; 1964 v Ni; 1965 v E (21)
Sawers, W. (Dundee), 1895 v W (1)
Scarff, P. (Celtic), 1931 v Ni (1)
Schaedler, E. (Hibernian), 1974 v WG (1)
Scott, A. S. (Rangers), 1957 v Ni, Y, WG; 1958 v W, Sw; 1959 v P; 1962 v Ni, W, E, Cz, U; (with Everton), 1964 v W, N; 1965 v Fi; 1966 v P, Br (16)
Scott, J. (Hibernian), 1966 v Ho (1)
Scott, J. (Dundee), 1971 v D (sub), USSR (2)

Scott, M. (Airdrieonians), 1898 v W (1)
Scott, R. (Airdrieonians), 1894 v Ni (1)
Scoular, J. (Portsmouth), 1951 v D, F, A; 1952 v E, USA, D, Se; 1953 v W, Ni (9)
Sellar, W. (Battlefield), 1885 v E; 1886 v E; 1887 v E, W; 1888 v E; (with Queen's Park), 1891 v E; 1892 v E; 1893 v E, Ni (9)
Semple, W. (Cambuslang), 1886 v W (1)
Shankly, W. (Preston NE), 1938 v E; 1939 v E, W, Ni, H (5)
Sharp, G. M. (Everton), 1985 v Ic; 1986 v W, Aus (2 sub), Is, R, U; 1987 v Ei; 1988 v Bel (sub), Bul, L, Ma (12)
Sharp, J. (Dundee), 1904 v W; (with Woolwich Arsenal), 1907 v W, E; 1908 v E; (with Fulham), 1909 v W (5)
Shaw, D. (Hibernian), 1947 v W, Ni; 1948 v E, Bel, Sw, F; 1949 v W, Ni (8)
Shaw, F. W. (Pollokshields Ath), 1884 v E, W (2)
Shaw, J. (Rangers), 1947 v E, Bel, L; 1948 v Ni (4)
Shearer, D. (Aberdeen), 1994 v A (sub), Ho (sub); 1995 v Fi, Ru (sub), Sm, Fa (6)
Shearer, R. (Rangers), 1961 v E, Ei (2), Cz (4)
Sillars, D. C. (Queen's Park), 1891 v Ni; 1892 v E; 1893 v W; 1894 v E; 1895 v W (5)
Simpson, J. (Third Lanark), 1895 v E, W, Ni (3)
Simpson, J. (Rangers), 1935 v E, W, Ni; 1936 v E, W, Ni; 1937 v G, E, W, Ni, A, Cz; 1938 v W, Ni (14)
Simpson, N. (Aberdeen), 1983 v Ni; 1984 v F (sub); 1987 v E; 1988 v E (4)
Simpson, R. C. (Celtic), 1967 v E, USSR; 1968 v Ni, E; 1969 v A (5)
Sinclair, G. L. (Hearts), 1910 v Ni; 1912 v W, Ni (3)
Sinclair, J. W. E. (Leicester C), 1966 v P (1)
Skene, L. H. (Queen's Park), 1904 v W (1)
Sloan, T. (Third Lanark), 1904 v W (1)
Smellie, R. (Queen's Park), 1887 v Ni; 1888 v W; 1889 v E; 1891 v E; 1893 v E, Ni (6)
Smith, A. (Rangers), 1898 v E; 1900 v E, Ni, W; 1901 v E, Ni, W; 1902 v E, Ni, W; 1903 v E, Ni, W; 1904 v Ni; 1905 v W; 1906 v E, Ni; 1907 v W; 1911 v E, Ni (20)
Smith, D. (Aberdeen), 1966 v Ho; (with Rangers), 1968 v Ho (2)
Smith, G. (Hibernian), 1947 v E, Ni; 1948 v W, Bel, Sw, F; 1952 v E, USA; 1955 v P, Y, A, H; 1956 v E, Ni, W; 1957 v Sp (2), Sw (18)
Smith, H. G. (Hearts), 1988 v S.Ar (sub); 1992 v Ni, Ca (3)
Smith, J. (Rangers), 1935 v Ni; 1938 v Ni (2)
Smith, J. (Ayr U), 1924 v E (1)
Smith, J. (Aberdeen), 1968 v Ho (sub); (with Newcastle U), 1974 v WG, Ni (sub), W (sub) (4)
Smith, J. E. (Celtic), 1959 v H, P (2)
Smith, Jas (Queen's Park), 1872 v E (1)
Smith, John (Mauchline), 1877 v E, W; 1879 v E, W; (with Edinburgh University), 1880 v E; (with Queen's Park), 1881 v W, E; 1883 v E, W; 1884 v E (10)
Smith, N. (Rangers), 1897 v E; 1898 v W; 1899 v E, W, Ni; 1900 v E, W, Ni; 1901 v Ni, W; 1902 v E, Ni (12)
Smith, R. (Queen's Park), 1872 v E; 1873 v E (2)
Smith, T. M. (Kilmarnock), 1934 v E; (with Preston NE), 1938 v E (2)
Somers, P. (Celtic), 1905 v E, Ni; 1907 v Ni; 1909 v W (4)
Somers, W. S. (Third Lanark), 1879 v E, W; (with Queen's Park), 1880 v W (3)
Somerville, G. (Queen's Park), 1886 v E (1)
Souness, G. J. (Middlesbrough), 1975 v EG, Sp, Se; (with Liverpool), 1978 v Bul, W, E (sub), Ho; 1979 v A, N, W, Ni, E; 1980 v Pe, A, Bel, P, Ni; 1981 v P, Is (2); 1982 v Ni, P, Sp, W, E, Nz, Br, USSR; 1983 v EG, Sw, Bel, Sw, W, E, Ca (2 + 1 sub); 1984 v U, Ni, W; (with Sampdoria), 1985 v Y, Ic, Sp (2), W, E, Ic; 1986 v EG, Aus (2), R, E, D, WG (54)

Speedie, D. R. (Chelsea), 1985 v E; 1986 v W, EG (sub), Aus, E; (with Coventry C), 1989 v Y (sub), I (sub), Cy (1 + 1 sub), Ch (10)
Speedie, F. (Rangers), 1903 v E, W, Ni (3)
Speirs, J. H. (Rangers), 1908 v W (1)
Spencer, J. (Chelsea), 1995 v Ru (sub), Gr (sub), Sm (sub), J (4)
Stanton, P. (Hibernian), 1966 v Ho; 1969 v Ni; 1970 v Ei, A; 1971 v D, Bel, P, USSR, D; 1972 v P, Bel, Ho, W; 1973 v W, Ni; 1974 v WG (16)
Stark, J. (Rangers), 1909 v E, Ni (2)
Steel, W. (Morton), 1947 v E, Bel, L; (with Derby Co), 1948 v F, E, W, Ni; 1949 v E, W, Ni, F; 1950 v E, W, Ni, Sw, P, F; (with Dundee), 1951 v W, Ni, E, A (2), D, F, Bel; 1952 v W; 1953 v W, E, Ni, Se (30)
Steele, D. M. (Huddersfield), 1923 v E, W, Ni (3)
Stein, C. (Rangers), 1969 v W, Ni, D, E, Cy (2); 1970 v A (sub), Ni (sub), W, E, Ei, WG; 1971 v D, USSR, Bel, D; 1972 v Cz (sub); (with Coventry C), 1973 v E (2 sub), W (sub), Ni (21)
Stephen, J. F. (Bradford), 1947 v W; 1948 v W (2)
Stevenson, G. (Motherwell), 1928 v W, Ni; 1930 v Ni, E, F; 1931 v E, W; 1932 v W, Ni; 1933 v Ni; 1934 v E; 1935 v Ni (12)
Stewart, A. (Queen's Park), 1888 v Ni; 1889 v W (2)
Stewart, A. (Third Lanark), 1894 v W (1)
Stewart, D. (Dumbarton), 1888 v Ni (1)
Stewart, D. (Queen's Park), 1893 v W; 1894 v Ni; 1897 v Ni (3)
Stewart, D. S. (Leeds U), 1978 v EG (1)
Stewart, G. (Hibernian), 1906 v W, E; (with Manchester C), 1907 v E, W (4)
Stewart, J. (Kilmarnock), 1977 v Ch (sub); (with Middlesbrough), 1979 v N (2)
Stewart, R. (West Ham U), 1981 v W, Ni, E; 1982 v Ni, P, W; 1984 v F; 1987 v Ei (2), L (10)
Stewart, W. E. (Queen's Park), 1898 v Ni; 1900 v Ni (2)
Storrier, D. (Celtic), 1899 v E, W, Ni (3)
Strachan, G. (Aberdeen), 1980 v Ni, W, E, Pol, H (sub); 1981 v Se, P; 1982 v Ni, P, Sp, Ho (sub), Nz, Br, USSR; 1983 v EG, Sw, Bel, Sw, Ni (sub), W, E, Ca (2 + 1 sub); 1984 v EG, Ni, E, F; (with Manchester U), 1985 v Sp (sub), E, Ic; 1986 v W, Aus, R, D, WG, U; 1987 v Bul, Ei (2); 1988 v H; 1989 v F (sub); (with Leeds U), 1990 v F; 1991 v USSR, Bul, Sm; 1992 v Sw, R, Ni, Fi (50)
Sturrock, P. (Dundee U), 1981 v W (sub), Ni, E (sub); 1982 v P, Ni (sub), W (sub), E (sub); 1983 v EG (sub), Sw, Bel (sub), Ca (3); 1984 v W; 1985 v Y (sub); 1986 v Is (sub), Ho, D, U; 1987 v Bel (20)
Summers, W. (St Mirren), 1926 v E (1)
Symon, J. S. (Rangers), 1939 v H (1)

Tait, T. S. (Sunderland), 1911 v W (1)
Taylor, J. (Queen's Park), 1872 v E; 1873 v E; 1874 v E; 1875 v E; 1876 v E, W (6)
Taylor, J. D. (Dumbarton), 1892 v W; 1893 v W; 1894 v Ni; (with St Mirren), 1895 v Ni (4)
Taylor, W. (Hearts), 1892 v E (1)
Telfer, W. (Motherwell), 1933 v Ni; 1934 v Ni (2)
Telfer, W. D. (St Mirren), 1954 v W (1)
Templeton, R. (Aston Villa), 1902 v E; (with Newcastle U), 1903 v E, W; 1904 v E; (with Woolwich Arsenal), 1905 v W; (with Kilmarnock), 1908 v Ni; 1910 v E, Ni; 1912 v E, Ni; 1913 v W (11)
Thomson, A. (Arthurlie), 1886 v Ni (1)
Thomson, A. (Third Lanark), 1889 v W (1)
Thomson, A. (Airdrieonians), 1909 v Ni (1)
Thomson, A. (Celtic), 1926 v E; 1932 v F; 1933 v W (3)
Thomson, C. (Hearts), 1904 v Ni; 1905 v E, Ni, W; 1906 v W, Ni; 1907 v E, W, Ni; 1908 v E, W, Ni; (with Sunderland), 1909 v W; 1910 v E; 1911 v Ni; 1912 v E, W; 1913 v E, W; 1914 v E, Ni (21)
Thomson, C. (Sunderland), 1937 v Cz (1)

Thomson, D. (Dundee), 1920 v W (1)
Thomson, J. (Celtic), 1930 v F; 1931 v E, W, Ni (4)
Thomson, J. J. (Queen's Park), 1872 v E; 1873 v E; 1874 v E (3)
Thomson, J. R. (Everton), 1933 v W (1)
Thomson, R. (Celtic), 1932 v W (1)
Thomson, R. W. (Falkirk), 1927 v E (1)
Thomson, S. (Rangers), 1884 v W, Ni (2)
Thomson, W. (Dumbarton), 1892 v W; 1893 v W; 1898 v Ni, W (4)
Thomson, W. (Dundee), 1896 v W (1)
Thornton, W. (Rangers), 1947 v W, Ni; 1948 v E, Ni; 1949 v F; 1952 v D, Se (7)
Thomson, W. (St Mirren), 1980 v Ni; 1981 v Ni (sub+1) 1982 v P; 1983 v Ni, Ca; 1984 v EG (7)
Toner, W. (Kilmarnock), 1959 v W, Ni (2)
Townsley, T. (Falkirk), 1926 v W (1)
Troup, A. (Dundee), 1920 v E; 1921 v W, Ni; 1922 v Ni; (with Everton), 1926 v E (5)
Turnbull, E. (Hibernian), 1948 v Bel, Sw; 1951 v A; 1958 v H, Pol, Y, Par, F (8)
Turner, T. (Arthurlie), 1884 v W (1)
Turner, W. (Pollokshields Ath), 1885 v Ni; 1886 v Ni (2)

Ure, J. F. (Dundee), 1962 v W, Cz; 1963 v W, Ni, E, A, N, Sp; (with Arsenal), 1964 v Ni, N; 1968 v Ni (11)
Urquhart, D. (Hibernian), 1934 v W (1)

Vallance, T. (Rangers), 1877 v E, W; 1878 v E; 1879 v E, W; 1881 v E, W (7)
Venters, A. (Cowdenbeath), 1934 v Ni; (with Rangers), 1936 v E; 1939 v E (3)

Waddell, T. S. (Queen's Park), 1891 v Ni; 1892 v E; 1893 v E, Ni; 1895 v E, Ni (6)
Waddell, W. (Rangers), 1947 v W; 1949 v E, W, Ni, F; 1950 v E, Ni; 1951 v E, D, F, Bel, A; 1952 v Ni, W; 1954 v Ni; 1955 v W, Ni (17)
Wales, H. M. (Motherwell), 1933 v W (1)
Walker, A. (Celtic), 1988 v Co (sub); 1995 v Fi, Fa (sub) (3)
Walker, F. (Third Lanark), 1922 v W (1)
Walker, G. (St Mirren), 1930 v F; 1931 v Ni, A, Sw (4)
Walker, J. (Hearts), 1895 v Ni; 1897 v W; 1898 v Ni; (with Rangers), 1904 v W, Ni (5)
Walker, J. (Swindon T), 1911 v E, W, Ni; 1912 v E, W, Ni; 1913 v E, W, Ni (9)
Walker, N. (Hearts), 1993 v G (1)
Walker, R. (Hearts), 1900 v E, Ni; 1901 v E, W; 1902 v E, W, Ni; 1903 v E, W, Ni; 1904 v E, W, Ni; 1905 v E, W, Ni; 1906 v Ni; 1907 v E, Ni; 1908 v E, W, Ni; 1909 v E, W; 1912 v E, W, Ni; 1913 v E, W (29)
Walker, T. (Hearts), 1935 v E, W; 1936 v E, W, Ni; 1937 v G, E, W, Ni, A, Cz; 1938 v E, W, Ni, Cz, Ho; 1939 v E, W, Ni, H (20)
Walker, W. (Clyde), 1909 v Ni; 1910 v Ni (2)
Wallace, I. A. (Coventry C), 1978 v Bul (sub); 1979 v P (sub), W (3)
Wallace, W. S. B. (Hearts), 1965 v Ni; 1966 v E, Ho; (with Celtic), 1967 v E, USSR (sub); 1968 v Ni; 1969 v E (sub) (7)
Wardhaugh, J. (Hearts), 1955 v H; 1957 v Ni (2)
Wark, J. (Ipswich T), 1979 v W, Ni, E, Arg, N (sub); 1980 v Pe, A, Bel (2); 1981 v Is, Ni; 1982 v Se, Sp, Ho, Ni, Nz, Br, USSR; 1983 v EG, Sw (2), Ni, E (sub); 1984 v U, Bel, EG; (with Liverpool), E, F; 1985 v Y (29)
Watson, A. (Queen's Park), 1881 v E, W; 1882 v E (3)
Watson, J. (Sunderland), 1903 v E, W; 1904 v E; 1905 v E; (with Middlesbrough), 1909 v E, Ni (6)
Watson, J. (Motherwell), 1948 v Ni; (with Huddersfield T), 1954 v Ni (2)
Watson, J. A. K. (Rangers), 1878 v W (1)
Watson, P. R. (Blackpool), 1934 v A (1)
Watson, R. (Motherwell), 1971 v USSR (1)
Watson, W. (Falkirk), 1898 v W (1)
Watt, F. (Kilbirnie), 1889 v W, Ni; 1890 v W; 1891 v E (4)
Watt, W. W. (Queen's Park), 1887 v Ni (1)
Waugh, W. (Hearts), 1938 v Cz (1)
Weir, A. (Motherwell), 1959 v WG; 1960 v E, P, A, H, T (6)
Weir, J. (Third Lanark), 1887 v Ni (1)
Weir, J. B. (Queen's Park), 1872 v E; 1874 v E; 1875 v E; 1878 v W (4)
Weir, P. (St Mirren), 1980 v Ni, W, Pol (sub), H; (with Aberdeen), 1983 v Sw; 1984 v Ni (6)
White, John (Albion R), 1922 v W; (with Hearts), 1923 v Ni (2)
White, J. A. (Falkirk), 1959 v WG, Ho, P; 1960 v Ni; (with Tottenham H), 1960 v W, Pol, A, T; 1961 v W; 1962 v Ni, W, E, Cz (2); 1963 v W, Ni, E; 1964 v Ni, W, E, N, WG (22)
White, W. (Bolton W), 1907 v E; 1908 v E (2)
Whitelaw, A. (Vale of Leven), 1887 v Ni; 1890 v W (2)
Whyte, D. (Celtic), 1988 v Bel (sub), L; 1989 v Ch (sub); 1992 v US (sub); (with Middlesbrough), 1993 v P, I; 1995 v J (sub), Ec (8)
Wilson, A. (Sheffield W), 1907 v E; 1908 v E; 1912 v E; 1913 v E, W; 1914 v Ni (6)
Wilson, A. (Portsmouth), 1954 v Fi (1)
Wilson, A. N. (Dunfermline), 1920 v E, W, Ni; 1921 v E, W, Ni; (with Middlesbrough), 1922 v E, W, Ni; 1923 v E, W, Ni (12)
Wilson, D. (Queen's Park), 1900 v W (1)
Wilson, D. (Oldham Ath), 1913 v E (1)
Wilson, D. (Rangers), 1961 v E, W, Ni, Ei (2), Cz; 1962 v Ni, W, E, Cz, U; 1963 v W, E, A, N, Ei, Sp; 1964 v E, WG; 1965 v Ni, E, Fi (22)
Wilson, G. W. (Hearts), 1904 v W; 1905 v E, Ni; 1906 v W; (with Everton), 1907 v E; (with Newcastle U), 1909 v E (6)
Wilson, Hugh, (Newmilns), 1890 v W; (with Sunderland), 1897 v E; (with Third Lanark), 1902 v W; 1904 v Ni (4)
Wilson, I. A. (Leicester C), 1987 v E, Br; (with Everton), 1988 v Bel, Bul, L (5)
Wilson, J. (Vale of Leven), 1888 v W; 1889 v E; 1890 v E; 1891 v E (4)
Wilson, P. (Celtic), 1926 v Ni; 1930 v F; 1931 v Ni; 1933 v E (4)
Wilson, P. (Celtic), 1975 v Sp (sub) (1)
Wilson, R. P. (Arsenal), 1972 v P, Ho (2)
Wiseman, W. (Queen's Park), 1927 v W; 1930 v Ni (2)
Wood, G. (Everton), 1979 v Ni, E, Arg (sub); (with Arsenal), 1982 v Ni (4)
Woodburn, W. A. (Rangers), 1947 v E, Bel, L; 1948 v W, Ni; 1949 v E, F; 1950 v E, W, Ni, P, F; 1951 v E, W, Ni, A (2), D, F, Bel; 1952 v E, W, Ni, USA (24)
Wotherspoon, D. N. (Queen's Park), 1872 v E; 1873 v E (2)
Wright, K. (Hibernian), 1992 v Ni (1)
Wright, S. (Aberdeen), 1993 v G, Es (2)
Wright, T. (Sunderland), 1953 v W, Ni, E (3)
Wylie, T. G. (Rangers), 1890 v Ni (1)

Yeats, R. (Liverpool), 1965 v W; 1966 v I (2)
Yorston, B. C. (Aberdeen), 1931 v Ni (1)
Yorston, H. (Aberdeen), 1955 v W (1)
Young, A. (Hearts), 1960 v E, A (sub), H, T; 1961 v W, Ni; (with Everton), Ei; 1966 v P (8)
Young, A. (Everton), 1905 v E; 1907 v W (2)
Young, G. L. (Rangers), 1947 v E, Ni, Bel, L; 1948 v E, Ni, Bel, Sw, F; 1949 v E, W, Ni, F; 1950 v E, W, Ni, Sw, P,

F; 1951 v E, W, Ni, A (2), D, F, Bel; 1952 v E, W, Ni, USA, D, Se; 1953 v W, E, Ni, Se; 1954 v Ni, W; 1955 v W, Ni, P, Y; 1956 v Ni, W, E, A; 1957 v E, Ni, W, Y, Sp, Sw (53)

Young, J. (Celtic), 1906 v Ni (1)

Younger, T. (Hibernian), 1955 v P, Y, A, H; 1956 v E, Ni, W, A; (with Liverpool), 1957 v E, Ni, W, Y, Sp (2), Sw, WG; 1958 v Ni, W, E, Sw, H, Pol, Y, Par (24)

WALES

Adams, H. (Berwyn R), 1882 v Ni, E; (with Druids), 1883 v Ni, E (4)

Aizlewood, M. (Charlton Ath), 1986 v S.Ar, Ca (2); 1987 v Fi; (with Leeds U), USSR, Fi (sub); 1988 v D (sub), Se, Ma, I; 1989 v Ho, Se (sub), WG; (with Bradford C), 1990 v Fi, WG, Ei, Cr; (with Bristol C), 1991 v D, Bel (2), L, Ei, Ic, Pol, WG; 1992 v Br, L, Ei, A, R, Ho, Arg, J; 1993 v Ei, Bel, Fa; 1994 v RCS, Cy; (with Cardiff C) 1995 v Bul (39)

Allchurch, I. J. (Swansea T), 1951 v E, Ni, P, Sw; 1952 v E, S, Ni, R of UK; 1953 v S, E, Ni, F, Y; 1954 v S, E, Ni, A; 1955 v S, E, Ni, Y; 1956 v E, S, Ni, A; 1957 v E, S; 1958 v Ni, Is (2), H (2), M, Sw, Br; (with Newcastle U), 1959 v E, S, Ni; 1960 v E, S; 1961 v Ni, H, Sp (2); 1962 v E, S, Br (2), M; (with Cardiff C), 1963 v S, E, Ni, H (2); 1964 v E; 1965 v S, E, Ni, Gr, I, USSR; (with Swansea T), 1966 v USSR, E, S, D, Br (2), Ch (68)

Allchurch, L. (Swansea T), 1955 v Ni; 1956 v A; 1958 v S, Ni, EG, Is; 1959 v S; (with Sheffield U), 1962 v S, Ni, Br; 1964 v E (11)

Allen, B. W. (Coventry C), 1951 v S, E (2)

Allen, M. (Watford), 1986 v S.Ar (sub), Ca (1 + 1 sub); (with Norwich C), 1989 v Is (sub); 1990 v Ho, WG; (with Millwall), Ei, Se, Cr (sub); 1991 v L (sub), Ei (sub); 1992 v A; 1993 v Ei (sub); (with Newcastle U), 1994 v R (sub) (14)

Arridge, S. (Bootle), 1892 v S, Ni; (with Everton), 1894 v Ni; 1895 v Ni; 1896 v E; (with New Brighton Tower), 1898 v E, Ni; 1899 v E (8)

Astley, D. J. (Charlton Ath), 1931 v Ni; (with Aston Villa), 1932 v E; 1933 v E, S, Ni; 1934 v E, S; 1935 v S; 1936 v E, Ni; (with Derby Co), 1939 v E, S; (with Blackpool), F (13)

Atherton, R. W. (Hibernian), 1899 v E, Ni; 1903 v E, S, Ni; (with Middlesbrough), 1904 v E, S, Ni; 1905 v Ni (9)

Bailiff, W. E. (Llanelly), 1913 v E, S, Ni; 1920 v Ni (4)

Baker, C. W. (Cardiff C), 1958 v M; 1960 v S, Ni; 1961 v S, E, Ei; 1962 v S (7)

Baker, W. G. (Cardiff C), 1948 v Ni (1)

Bamford, T. (Wrexham), 1931 v E, S, Ni; 1932 v Ni; 1933 v F (5)

Barnes, W. (Arsenal), 1948 v E, S, Ni; 1949 v E, S, Ni; 1950 v E, S, Ni, Bel; 1951 v E, S, Ni, P; 1952 v E, S, Ni, R of UK; 1954 v E, S; 1955 v S, Y (22)

Bartley, T. (Glossop NE), 1898 v E (1)

Bastock, A. M. (Shrewsbury), 1892 v Ni (1)

Beadles, G. H. (Cardiff C), 1925 v E, S (2)

Bell, W. S. (Shrewsbury Engineers), 1881 v E, S; (with Crewe Alex), 1886 v E, S, Ni (5)

Bennion, S. R. (Manchester U), 1926 v S; 1927 v S; 1928 v S, E, Ni; 1929 v S, E, Ni; 1930 v S; 1932 v Ni (10)

Berry, G. F. (Wolverhampton W), 1979 v WG; 1980 v Ei, WG (sub), T; (with Stoke C), 1983 v E (sub) (5)

Blackmore, C. G. (Manchester U), 1985 v N (sub); 1986 v S (sub), H (sub), S.Ar, Ei, U; 1987 v Fi (2), USSR, Cz; 1988 v D (2), Cz, Y, Se, Ma, I; 1989 v Ho, Fi, Is, WG; 1990 v F; Ho, WG, Cr; 1991 v Bel, L; 1992 v Ei (sub), A, R (sub), Ho, Arg, J; 1993 v Fa, Cy, Bel, RCS; 1994 v Se (sub) (38)

Blake, N. A. (Sheffield U), 1994 v N, Se (sub); 1995 v Alb, Mol (4)

Blew, H. (Wrexham), 1899 v E, S, Ni; 1902 v S, Ni; 1903 v E, S; 1904 v E, S, Ni; 1905 v S, Ni; 1906 v E, S, Ni; 1907 v S; 1908 v E, S, Ni; 1909 v E, S; 1910 v E (22)

Boden, T. (Wrexham), 1880 v E (1)

Bodin, P. J. (Swindon T), 1990 v Cr; 1991 v D, Bel, L, Ei; (with C Palace), Bel, Ic, Pol, WG; 1992 v Br, G, L (sub); (with Swindon T), Ei (sub), Ho, Arg; 1993 v Ei, Bel, RCS, Fa; 1994 v R, Se, Es (sub); 1995 v Alb (23)

Boulter, L. M. (Brentford), 1939 v Ni (1)

Bowdler, H. E. (Shrewsbury), 1893 v S (1)

Bowdler, J. C. H. (Shrewsbury), 1890 v Ni; (with Wolverhampton W), 1891 v S; 1892 v Ni; (with Shrewsbury), 1894 v E (4)

Bowen, D. L. (Arsenal), 1955 v S, Y; 1957 v Ni, Cz, EG; 1958 v E, S, Ni, EG, Is (2), H (2), M, Se, Br; 1959 v E, S, Ni (19)

Bowen, E. (Druids), 1880 v S; 1883 v S (2)

Bowen, J. P. (Swansea C), 1994 v Es (1)

Bowen, M. R. (Tottenham H), 1986 v Ca (2 sub); (with Norwich C), 1988 v Y (sub); 1989 v Fi (sub), Is, Se, WG (sub); 1990 v Fi (sub), Ho, WG, Se; 1992 v Br (sub), G, L, Ei, A, R, Ho (sub), J; 1993 v Fa, Cy, Bel (1 + sub), RCS (sub); 1994 v RCS, Se; 1995 v Mol, Ge, Bul (2), G, Ge (32)

Bowsher, S. J. (Burnley), 1929 v Ni (1)

Boyle, T. (C Palace), 1981 v Ei, S (sub) (2)

Britten, T. J. (Parkgrove), 1878 v S; (with Presteigne), 1880 v S (2)

Brookes, S. J. (Llandudno), 1900 v E, Ni (2)

Brown, A. I. (Aberdare Ath), 1926 v Ni (1)

Bryan, T. (Oswestry), 1886 v E, Ni (2)

Buckland, T. (Bangor), 1899 v E (1)

Burgess, W. A. R. (Tottenham H), 1947 v E, S, Ni; 1948 v E, S; 1949 v E, S, Ni, P, Bel, Sw; 1950 v E, S, Ni, Bel; 1951 v S, Ni, P, Sw; 1952 v E, S, Ni, R of UK; 1953 v S, E, Ni, F, Y; 1954 v S, E, Ni, A (32)

Burke, T. (Wrexham), 1883 v E; 1884 v S; 1885 v E, S, Ni; (with Newton Heath), 1887 v E, S; 1888 v S (8)

Burnett, T. B. (Ruabon), 1877 v S (1)

Burton, A. D. (Norwich C), 1963 v Ni, H; (with Newcastle U), 1964 v E; 1969 v S, E, Ni, I, EG; 1972 v Cz (9)

Butler, J. (Chirk), 1893 v E, S, Ni (3)

Butler, W. T. (Druids), 1900 v S, Ni (2)

Cartwright, L. (Coventry C), 1974 v E (sub), S, Ni; 1976 v S (sub); 1977 v WG (sub); (with Wrexham), 1978 v Ir (sub); 1979 v Ma (7)

Carty, T. – See McCarthy – (Wrexham).

Challen, J. B. (Corinthians), 1887 v E, S; 1888 v E; (with Wellingborough GS), 1890 v E (4)

Chapman, T. (Newtown), 1894 v E, S, Ni; 1895 v S, Ni; (with Manchester C), 1896 v E; 1897 v E (7)

Charles, J. M. (Swansea C), 1981 v Cz, T (sub), S (sub), USSR (sub); 1982 v Ic; 1983 v N (sub), Y (sub), Bul (sub), S, Ni, Br; 1984 v Bul (sub); (with QPR), Y (sub), S; (with Oxford U), 1985 v Ic (sub), Sp, Ic; 1986 v Ei; 1987 v Fi (19)

Charles, M. (Swansea T), 1955 v Ni; 1956 v E, S, A; 1957 v E, Ni, Cz (2), EG; 1958 v E, S, EG, Is (2), H (2), M, Se, Br; 1959 v E, S; (with Arsenal), 1961 v Ni, H, Sp (2); 1962 v E, S; (with Cardiff C), 1962 v Br, Ni; 1963 v S, H (31)

Charles, W. J. (Leeds U), 1950 v Ni; 1951 v Sw; 1953 v Ni, F, Y; 1954 v E, S, Ni, A; 1955 v S, E, Ni, Y; 1956 v E, S,

A, Ni; 1957 v E, S, Ni, Cz (2), EG; (with Juventus), 1958 v Is (2), H (2) M, Se; 1960 v S; 1962 v E, Br (2), M; (with Leeds U), 1963 v S; (with Cardiff C), 1964 v S; 1965 v S, USSR (38)

Clarke, R. J. (Manchester C), 1949 v E; 1950 v S, Ni, Bel; 1951 v E, S, Ni, P, Sw; 1952 v S, E, Ni, R of UK; 1953 v S, E; 1954 v E, S, Ni; 1955 v Y, S, E; 1956 v Ni (22)

Coleman, C. (C Palace), 1992 v A (sub); 1993 v Ei (sub); 1994 v N, Es; 1995 v Alb, Mol, Ge, Bul (2), G (10)

Collier, D. J. (Grimsby T), 1921 v S (1)

Collins, W. S. (Llanelly), 1931 v S (1)

Conde, C. (Chirk), 1884 v E, S, Ni (3)

Cook, F. C. (Newport Co), 1925 v E, S; (with Portsmouth), 1928 v E, S; 1930 v E, S, Ni; 1932 v E (8)

Cornforth, J.M. (Swansea C), 1995 v Bul (sub), Ge (2)

Crompton, W. (Wrexham), 1931 v E, S, Ni (3)

Cross, E. A. (Wrexham), 1876 v S; 1877 v S (2)

Cross, K. (Druids), 1879 v S; 1881 v E, S (3)

Crowe, V. H. (Aston Villa), 1959 v E, Ni; 1960 v E, Ni; 1961 v S, E, Ni, Ei, H, Sp (2); 1962 v E, S, Br, M; 1963 v H (16)

Cumner, R. H. (Arsenal), 1939 v E, S, Ni (3)

Curtis, A. (Swansea C), 1976 v E, Y (sub), S, Ni, Y (sub), E; 1977 v WG, S (sub), Ni (sub); 1978 v WG, E, S; 1979 v WG, S; (with Leeds U), E, Ni, Ma; 1980 v Ei, WG, T; (with Swansea C), 1982 v Cz, Ic, USSR, Sp, E, S, Ni; 1983 v N; 1984 v R (sub); (with Southampton), S; 1985 v Sp, N (1 + 1 sub); 1986 v H; (with Cardiff C), 1987 v USSR (35)

Curtis, E. R. (Cardiff C), 1928 v S; (with Birmingham), 1932 v S; 1934 v Ni (3)

Daniel, R. W. (Arsenal), 1951 v E, Ni, P; 1952 v E, S, Ni, R of UK; 1953 v S, E, Ni, F, Y; (with Sunderland), 1954 v E, S, Ni; 1955 v E, Ni; 1957 v S, E, Ni, Cz (21)

Darvell, S. (Oxford University), 1897 v S, Ni (2)

Davies, A. (Manchester U), 1983 v Ni, Br; 1984 v E, Ni; 1985 v Ic; (with Newcastle U), 1986 v H; (with Swansea C), 1988 v Ma, I; 1989 v Ho; (with Bradford C), 1990 v Fi, Ei (11)

Davies, A. (Wrexham), 1876 v S; 1877 v S (2)

Davies, A. (Druids), 1904 v S; (with Middlesbrough), 1905 v S (2)

Davies, A. O. (Barmouth), 1885 v Ni; 1886 v E, S; (with Swifts), 1887 v E, S; 1888 v E, Ni; (with Wrexham), 1889 v S; (with Crewe Alex), 1890 v E (9)

Davies, A. T. (Shrewsbury), 1891 v Ni (1)

Davies, C. (Brecon), 1899 v Ni; (with Hereford), 1900 v Ni (2)

Davies, C. (Charlton Ath), 1972 v R (sub) (1)

Davies, D. (Bolton W), 1904 v S, Ni; 1908 v E (sub) (3)

Davies, D. C. (Brecon), 1899 v Ni; (with Hereford); 1900 v Ni (2)

Davies, D. W. (Treharris), 1912 v Ni; (with Oldham Ath), 1913 v Ni (2)

Davies, E. Lloyd (Stoke C), 1904 v E; 1907 v E, S, Ni; (with Northampton T), 1908 v S; 1909 v Ni; 1910 v Ni; 1911 v E, S; 1912 v E, S; 1913 v E, S; 1914 v Ni, E, S (16)

Davies, E. R. (Newcastle U), 1953 v S, E; 1954 v E, S; 1958 v E, EG (6)

Davies, G. (Fulham), 1980 v T, Ic; 1982 v Sp (sub), F (sub); 1983 v E, Bul, S, Ni, Br; 1984 v R (sub), S (sub), E, Ni; 1985 v Ic; (with Manchester C), 1986 v S.Ar, Ei (16)

Davies, Rev. H. (Wrexham), 1928 v Ni (1)

Davies, Idwal (Liverpool Marine), 1923 v S (1)

Davies, J. E. (Oswestry), 1885 v E (1)

Davies, Jas (Wrexham), 1878 v S (1)

Davies, John (Wrexham), 1879 v S (1)

Davies, Jos (Newton Heath), 1888 v E, S, Ni; 1889 v S; 1890 v E; (with Wolverhampton W), 1892 v E; 1893 v E (7)

Davies, Jos (Everton), 1889 v S, Ni; (with Chirk), 1891 v Ni; (with Ardwick), v E, S; (with Sheffield U), 1895 v E, S, Ni; (with Manchester C), 1896 v E; (with Millwall), 1897 v E; (with Reading), 1900 v E (11)

Davies, J. P. (Druids), 1883 v E, Ni (2)

Davies, Ll. (Wrexham), 1907 v Ni; 1910 v Ni, S, E; (with Everton), 1911 v S, Ni; (with Wrexham), 1912 v Ni, S, E; 1913 v Ni, S, E; 1914 v Ni (13)

Davies, L. S. (Cardiff C), 1922 v E, S, Ni; 1923 v E, S, Ni; 1924 v E, S, Ni; 1925 v S, Ni; 1926 v E, Ni; 1927 v E, Ni; 1928 v S, Ni, E; 1929 v S, Ni, E; 1930 v E, S (23)

Davies, O. (Wrexham), 1890 v S (1)

Davies, R. (Wrexham), 1883 v Ni; 1884 v Ni; 1885 v Ni (3)

Davies, R. (Druids), 1885 v E (1)

Davies, R. O. (Wrexham), 1892 v Ni, E (2)

Davies, R. T. (Norwich C), 1964 v Ni; 1965 v E; 1966 v Br (2), Ch; (with Southampton), 1967 v S, E, Ni; 1968 v S, Ni, WG; 1969 v S, E, Ni, I, WG, R of UK; 1970 v E, S, Ni; 1971 v Cz, S, E, Ni; 1972 v R, E, S, N; (with Portsmouth), 1974 v E (29)

Davies, R. W. (Bolton W), 1964 v E; 1965 v E, S, Ni, D, Gr, USSR; 1966 v E, S, Ni, USSR, D, Br (2), Ch (sub); 1967 v S; (with Newcastle U), E; 1968 v S, Ni, WG; 1969 v S, E, Ni, I; 1970 v EG; 1971 v R, Cz; (with Manchester C), 1972 v E, S, Ni; (with Manchester U), 1973 v E, S (sub), Ni; (with Blackpool), 1974 v Pol (34)

Davies, Stanley (Preston NE), 1920 v E, S, Ni; (with Everton), 1921 v E, S, Ni; (with WBA), 1922 v E, S, Ni; 1923 v S; 1925 v S, Ni; 1926 v S, E, Ni; 1927 v S; 1928 v S; (with Rotherham U), 1930 v Ni (18)

Davies, T. (Oswestry), 1886 v E (1)

Davies, T. (Druids), 1903 v E, Ni, S; 1904 v S (4)

Davies, W. (Wrexham), 1884 v Ni (1)

Davies, W. (Swansea T), 1924 v E, S, Ni; (with Cardiff C), 1925 v E, S, Ni; 1926 v E, S, Ni; 1927 v S; 1928 v Ni; (with Notts Co), 1929 v E, S, Ni; 1930 v E, S, Ni (17)

Davies, William (Wrexham), 1903 v Ni; 1905 v Ni; (with Blackburn R), 1908 v E, S; 1909 v E, S, Ni; 1911 v E, S, Ni; 1912 v Ni (11)

Davies, W. C. (C Palace), 1908 v S; (with WBA), 1909 v E; 1910 v S; (with C Palace), 1914 v E (4)

Davies, W. D. (Everton), 1975 v H, L, S, E, Ni; 1976 v Y (2), E, Ni; 1977 v WG, S (2), Cz, E, Ni; 1978 v K; (with Wrexham), S, Cz, WG, Ir, E, S, Ni; 1979 v Ma, T, WG, S, E, Ni, Ma; 1980 v Ei, WG, T, E, S, Ni, Ic; 1981 v T, Cz, Ei, T, S, E, USSR; (with Swansea C), 1982 v Cz, Ic, USSR, Sp, E, S, F; 1983 v Y (52)

Davies, W. H. (Oswestry), 1876 v S; 1877 v S; 1879 v E; 1880 v E (4)

Davies, W. O. (Millwall Ath), 1913 v E, S, Ni; 1914 v S, Ni (5)

Davis, G. (Wrexham), 1978 v Ir, E (sub), Ni (3)

Day, A. (Tottenham H), 1934 v Ni (1)

Deacy, N. (PSV Eindhoven), 1977 v Cz, S, E, Ni; 1978 v K (sub), S (sub), Cz (sub), WG, Ir, S (sub), Ni; (with Beringen), 1979 v T (12)

Dearson, D. J. (Birmingham), 1939 v S, Ni, F (3)

Derrett, S. C. (Cardiff C), 1969 v S, WG; 1970 v I; 1971 v Fi (4)

Dewey, F. T. (Cardiff Corinthians), 1931 v E, S (2)

Dibble, A. (Luton T), 1986 v Ca (1+1 sub); (with Manchester C), 1989 v Is (3)

Doughty, J. (Druids), 1886 v S; (with Newton Heath), 1887 v S, Ni; 1888 v E, S, Ni; 1889 v S; 1890 v E (8)

Doughty, R. (Newton Heath and Druids), 1888 v S, Ni (2)

Durban, A. (Derby Co), 1966 v Br (sub); 1967 v Ni; 1968 v E, S, Ni, WG; 1969 v EG, S, E, Ni, WG; 1970 v E, S, Ni, EG, I; 1971 v R, S, E, Ni, Cz, Fi; 1972 v Fi, Cz, E, S, Ni (27)

Dwyer, P. (Cardiff C), 1978 v Ir, E, S, Ni; 1979 v T, S, E, Ni, Ma (sub); 1980 v WG (10)

Edwards, C. (Wrexham), 1878 v S (1)
Edwards, G. (Birmingham C), 1947 v E, S, Ni; 1948 v E, S, Ni; (with Cardiff C), 1949 v Ni, P, Bel, Sw; 1950 v E, S (12)
Edwards, H. (Wrexham Civil Service), 1878 v S; 1880 v E; 1882 v E, S; 1883 v S; 1884 v Ni; 1887 v Ni (7)
Edwards, J. H. (Wanderers), 1876 v S (1)
Edwards, J. H. (Oswestry), 1895 v Ni; 1897 v E, Ni (3)
Edwards, J. H. (Aberystwyth), 1898 v Ni (1)
Edwards, L. T. (Charlton Ath), 1957 v Ni, EG (2)
Edwards, R. I. (Chester), 1978 v K (sub); 1979 v Ma, WG; (with Wrexham), 1980 v T (sub) (4)
Edwards, T. (Linfield), 1932 v S (1)
Egan, W. (Chirk), 1892 v S (1)
Ellis, B. (Motherwell), 1932 v E; 1933 v E, S; 1934 v S; 1936 v E; 1937 v S (6)
Ellis, E. (Nunhead), 1931 v S; (with Oswestry), E; 1932 v Ni (3)
Emanuel, W. J. (Bristol C), 1973 v E (sub), Ni (sub) (2)
England, H. M. (Blackburn R), 1962 v Ni, Br, M; 1963 v Ni, H; 1964 v E, S, Ni; 1965 v E, D, Gr (2), USSR, Ni, I; 1966 v E, S, Ni, USSR, D; (with Tottenham H), 1967 v S, E; 1968 v E, Ni, WG; 1969 v EG; 1970 v R of UK, EG, E, S, Ni, I; 1971 v R; 1972 v Fi, E, S, Ni; 1973 v E (3), S; 1974 v Pol; 1975 v H, L (44)
Evans, B. C. (Swansea C), 1972 v Fi, Cz; 1973 v E (2), Pol, S; (with Hereford U), 1974 v Pol (7)
Evans, D. G. (Reading), 1926 v Ni; 1927 v Ni, E; (with Huddersfield T), 1929 v S (4)
Evans, H. P. (Cardiff C), 1922 v E, S, Ni; 1924 v E, S, Ni (6)
Evans, I. (C Palace), 1976 v A, E, Y (2), E, Ni; 1977 v WG, S (2), Cz, E, Ni; 1978 v K (13)
Evans, J. (Oswestry), 1893 v Ni; 1894 v E, Ni (3)
Evans, J. (Cardiff C), 1912 v Ni; 1913 v Ni; 1914 v S; 1920 v S, Ni; 1922 v Ni; 1923 v E, Ni (8)
Evans, J. H. (Southend U), 1922 v E, S, Ni; 1923 v S (4)
Evans, Len (Aberdare Ath), 1927 v Ni; (with Cardiff C), 1931 v E, S; (with Birmingham), 1934 v Ni (4)
Evans, M. (Oswestry), 1884 v E (1)
Evans, R. (Clapton), 1902 v Ni (1)
Evans, R. E. (Wrexham), 1906 v E, S; (with Aston Villa), Ni; 1907 v E; 1908 v E, S; (with Sheffield U), 1909 v S; 1910 v E, S, Ni (10)
Evans, R. O. (Wrexham), 1902 v Ni; 1903 v E, S, Ni; (with Blackburn R), 1908 v Ni; (with Coventry C), 1911 v E, Ni; 1912 v E, S, Ni (10)
Evans, R. S. (Swansea T), 1964 v Ni (1)
Evans, T. J. (Clapton Orient), 1927 v S; 1928 v E, S; (with Newcastle U), Ni (4)
Evans, W. (Tottenham H), 1933 v Ni; 1934 v E, S; 1935 v E; 1936 v E, Ni (6)
Evans, W. A. W. (Oxford University), 1876 v S; 1877 v S (2)
Evans, W. G. (Bootle), 1890 v E; 1891 v E; (with Aston Villa), 1892 v E (3)
Evelyn, E. C. (Crusaders), 1887 v E (1)
Eyton-Jones, J. A. (Wrexham), 1883 v Ni; 1884 v Ni, E, S (4)

Farmer, G. (Oswestry), 1885 v E, S (2)
Felgate, D. (Lincoln C), 1984 v R (sub) (1)
Finnigan, R. J. (Wrexham), 1930 v Ni (1)
Flynn, B. (Burnley), 1975 v L (2 sub), H (sub), S, E, Ni; 1976 v A, E, Y (2), E, Ni; 1977 v WG (sub), S (2), Cz, E, Ni; 1978 v K (2), S; (with Leeds U), Cz, WG, Ir (sub), E, S, Ni; 1979 v Ma, T, S, E, Ni, Ma; 1980 v Ei, WG, E, S, Ni, Ic; 1981 v T, Cz, Ei, T, S, E, USSR; 1982 v Cz, USSR, E, S, Ni, F; 1983 v N; (with Burnley), Y, E, Bul, S, Ni, Br; 1984 v N, R, Bul, Y, S, N, Is (66)
Ford, T. (Swansea T), 1947 v S; (with Aston Villa), 1947 v Ni; 1948 v S, Ni; 1949 v E, S, Ni, P, Bel, Sw; 1950 v E, S, Ni, Bel; 1951 v S; (with Sunderland), 1951 v E, Ni, P, Sw; 1952 v E, S, Ni, R of UK; 1953 v S, E, Ni, F, Y; (with Cardiff C), 1954 v A; 1955 v S, E, Ni, Y; 1956 v S, Ni, E, A; 1957 v S (38)
Foulkes, H. E. (WBA), 1932 v Ni (1)
Foulkes, W. I. (Newcastle U), 1952 v E, S, Ni, R of UK; 1953 v E, S, F, Y; 1954 v E, S, Ni (11)
Foulkes, W. T. (Oswestry), 1884 v Ni; 1885 v S (2)
Fowler, J. (Swansea T), 1925 v E; 1926 v E, Ni; 1927 v S; 1928 v S; 1929 v E (6)

Garner, J. (Aberystwyth), 1896 v S (1)
Giggs, R. J. (Manchester U), 1992 v G (sub), L (sub), R (sub); 1993 v Fa (sub), Bel (sub + 1), RCS, Fa; 1994 v RCS, Cy, R; 1995 v Alb, Bul (13)
Giles, D. (Swansea C), 1980 v E, S, Ni, Ic; 1981 v T, Cz, T (sub), E (sub), USSR (sub); (with C Palace), 1982 v Sp (sub); 1983 v Ni (sub), Br (12)
Gillam, S. G. (Wrexham), 1889 v S (sub), Ni; (with Shrewsbury), 1890 v E, Ni; (with Clapton), 1894 v S (5)
Glascodine, G. (Wrexham), 1879 v E (1)
Glover, E. M. (Grimsby T), 1932 v S; 1934 v Ni; 1936 v S; 1937 v E, S, Ni; 1939 v Ni (7)
Godding, G. (Wrexham), 1923 v S, Ni (2)
Godfrey, B. C. (Preston NE), 1964 v Ni; 1965 v D, I (3)
Goodwin, U. (Ruthin), 1881 v E (1)
Goss, J. (Norwich C), 1991 v Ic, Pol (sub); 1992 v A; 1994 v Cy (sub), R (sub), Se; 1995 v Alb (7)
Gough, R. T. (Oswestry White Star), 1883 v S (1)
Gray, A. (Oldham Ath), 1924 v E, S, Ni; 1925 v E, S, Ni; 1926 v E, S; 1927 v S; (with Manchester C), 1928 v E, S; 1929 v E, S, Ni; (with Manchester Central), 1930 v S; (with Tranmere R), 1932 v E, S, Ni; (with Chester), 1937 v E, S, Ni; 1938 v E, S, Ni (24)
Green, A. W. (Aston Villa), 1901 v Ni; (with Notts Co), 1903 v E; 1904 v S, Ni; 1906 v Ni, E; (with Nottingham F), 1907 v E; 1908 v S (8)
Green, C. R. (Birmingham C), 1965 v USSR, I; 1966 v E, S, USSR, Br (2); 1967 v E; 1968 v E, S, Ni, WG; 1969 v S, I, Ni (sub) (15)
Green, G. H. (Charlton Ath), 1938 v Ni; 1939 v E, Ni, F (4)
Grey, Dr W. (Druids), 1876 v S; 1878 v S (2)
Griffiths, A. T. (Wrexham), 1971 v Cz (sub); 1975 v A, H (2), L (2), E, Ni; 1976 v A, E, S, E (sub), Ni, Y (2); 1977 v WG, S (17)
Griffiths, F. J. (Blackpool), 1900 v E, S (2)
Griffiths, G. (Chirk), 1887 v Ni (1)
Griffiths, J. H. (Swansea T), 1953 v Ni (1)
Griffiths, L. (Wrexham), 1902 v S (1)
Griffiths, M. W. (Leicester C), 1947 v Ni; 1949 v P, Bel; 1950 v E, S, Bel; 1951 v E, Ni, P, Sw; 1954 v A (11)
Griffiths, P. (Chirk), 1884 v E, Ni; 1888 v E; 1890 v S, Ni; 1891 v Ni (6)
Griffiths, P. H. (Everton), 1932 v S (1)
Griffiths, S. (Wrexham), 1902 v S (1)
Griffiths, T. P. (Everton), 1927 v E, Ni; 1929 v E; 1930 v E; 1931 v Ni; 1932 v Ni, S, E; (with Bolton W), 1933 v E, S, Ni; (with Middlesbrough), F; 1934 v E, S; 1935 v E, Ni; 1936 v S; (with Aston Villa), Ni; 1937 v E, S, Ni (21)

Hall, G. D. (Chelsea), 1988 v Y (sub), Ma, I; 1989 v Ho, Fi, Is; 1990 v Ei; 1991 v Ei; 1992 v A (sub) (9)
Hallam, J. (Oswestry), 1889 v E (1)
Hanford, H. (Swansea T), 1934 v Ni; 1935 v S; 1936 v E; (with Sheffield W), 1936 v Ni; 1938 v E, S; 1939 v F (7)
Harrington, A. C. (Cardiff C), 1956 v Ni; 1957 v E, S; 1958 v S, Ni, Is (2); 1961 v S, E; 1962 v E, S (11)
Harris, C. S. (Leeds U), 1976 v E, S; 1978 v WG, Ir, E, S, Ni; 1979 v Ma, T, WG, E (sub), Ma; 1980 v Ni (sub), Ic (sub); 1981 v T, Cz (sub), Ei, T, S, E, USSR; 1982 v Cz, Ic, E (sub) (24)

Harris, W. C. (Middlesbrough), 1954 v A; 1957 v EG, Cz; 1958 v E, S, EG (6)
Harrison, W. C. (Wrexham), 1899 v E; 1900 v E, S, Ni; 1901 v Ni (5)
Hartson, J. (Arsenal), 1995 v Bul, G (sub), Ge (sub) (3)
Hayes, A. (Wrexham), 1890 v Ni; 1894 v Ni (2)
Hennessey, W. T. (Birmingham C), 1962 v Ni, Br (2); 1963 v S, E, H (2); 1964 v E, S; 1965 v S, E, D, Gr, USSR; 1966 v E, USSR; (with Nottingham F), 1966 v S, Ni, D, Br (2), Ch; 1967 v S, E; 1968 v E, S, Ni; 1969 v WG, EG, R of UK; 1970 v EG; (with Derby Co), E, S, Ni; 1972 v Fi, Cz, E, S; 1973 v E (39)
Hersee, A. M. (Bangor), 1886 v S, Ni (2)
Hersee, R. (Llandudno), 1886 v Ni (1)
Hewitt, R. (Cardiff C), 1958 v Ni, Is, Se, H, Br (5)
Hewitt, T. J. (Wrexham), 1911 v E, S, Ni; (with Chelsea), 1913 v E, S, Ni; (with South Liverpool), 1914 v E, S (8)
Heywood, D. (Druids), 1879 v E (1)
Hibbott, H. (Newtown Excelsior), 1880 v E, S; (with Newtown), 1885 v S (3)
Higham, G. G. (Oswestry), 1878 v S; 1879 v E (2)
Hill, M. R. (Ipswich T), 1972 v Cz, R (2)
Hockey, T. (Sheffield U), 1972 v Fi, R; 1973 v E (2); (with Norwich C), Pol, S, E, Ni; (with Aston Villa), 1974 v Pol (9)
Hoddinott, T. F. (Watford), 1921 v E, S (2)
Hodges, G. (Wimbledon), 1984 v N (sub), Is (sub); 1987 v USSR, Fi, Cz; (with Newcastle U), 1988 v D; (with Watford), D (sub), Cz (sub), Se, Ma (sub), I (sub); 1990 v Se, Cr; (with Sheffield U), 1992 v Br (sub), Ei (sub), A (16)
Hodgkinson, A. V. (Southampton), 1908 v Ni (1)
Holden, A. (Chester C), 1984 v Is (sub) (1)
Hole, B. G. (Cardiff C), 1963 v Ni; 1964 v Ni; 1965 v S, E, Ni, D, Gr (2), USSR, I; 1966 v E, S, Ni, USSR, D, Br (2), Ch; (with Blackburn R), 1967 v S, E, Ni; 1968 v E, S, Ni, WG; (with Aston Villa), 1969 v I, WG, EG; 1970 v I; (with Swansea C), 1971 v R (30)
Hole, W. J. (Swansea T), 1921 v Ni; 1922 v E; 1923 v E, Ni; 1928 v E, S, Ni; 1929 v E, S (9)
Hollins, D. M. (Newcastle U), 1962 v Br (sub), M; 1963 v Ni, H; 1964 v E; 1965 v Ni, Gr, I; 1966 v S, D, Br (11)
Hopkins, I. J. (Brentford), 1935 v S, Ni; 1936 v E, Ni; 1937 v E, S, Ni; 1938 v E, Ni; 1939 v E, S, Ni (12)
Hopkins, J. (Fulham), 1983 v Ni, Br; 1984 v N, R, Bul, Y, S, E, Ni, N, Is; 1985 v Ic (1 + 1 sub), N; (with C Palace), 1990 v Ho, Cr (16)
Hopkins, M. (Tottenham H), 1956 v Ni; 1957 v Ni, S, E, Cz (2), EG; 1958 v E, S, Ni, EG, Is (2), H (2), M, Se, Br; 1959 v E, S, Ni; 1960 v E, S; 1961 v Ni, H, Sp (2); 1962 v Ni, Br (2), M; 1963 v S, Ni, H (34)
Horne, B. (Portsmouth), 1988 v D (sub), Y, Se (sub), Ma, I; 1989 v Ho, Fi, Is; (with Southampton), Se, WG; 1990 v WG (sub), Ei, Se, Cr; 1991 v D, Bel (2), L, Ei, Ic, Pol, WG; 1992 v Br, G, L, Ei, A, R, Ho, Arg, J; (with Everton), 1993 v Fa, Cy, Bel, Ei, Bel, RCS, Fa; 1994 v RCS, Cy, R, N, Se, Es; 1995 v Mol, Ge, Bul, G, Ge (49)
Howell, E. G. (Builth), 1888 v Ni; 1890 v E; 1891 v E (3)
Howells, R. G. (Cardiff C), 1954 v E, S (2)
Hugh, A. R. (Newport Co), 1930 v Ni (1)
Hughes, A. (Rhos), 1894 v E, S (2)
Hughes, A. (Chirk), 1907 v Ni (1)
Hughes, C. M. (Luton T), 1992 v Ho (sub); 1994 v N (sub), Se (sub), Es (4)
Hughes, E. (Everton), 1899 v S, Ni; (with Tottenham H), 1901 v E, S; 1902 v Ni; 1904 v E, Ni, S; 1905 v E, Ni, S; 1906 v E, Ni; 1907 v E (14)
Hughes, E. (Wrexham), 1906 v S; (with Nottingham F), 1906 v Ni; 1908 v S, E; 1910 v Ni, E, S; 1911 v Ni, E, S; (with Wrexham), 1912 v Ni, E, S; (with Manchester C), 1913 v E, S; 1914 v N (16)
Hughes, F. W. (Northwich Victoria), 1882 v E, Ni; 1883 v E, Ni, S; 1884 v S (6)
Hughes, I. (Luton T), 1951 v E, Ni, P, Sw (4)
Hughes, J. (Cambridge University), 1877 v S; (with Aberystwyth), 1879 v S (2)
Hughes, J. (Liverpool), 1905 v E, S, Ni (3)
Hughes, J. I. (Blackburn R), 1935 v Ni (1)
Hughes, L. M. (Manchester U), 1984 v E, Ni; 1985 v Ic, Sp, Ic, N, S, Sp, N; 1986 v S, H, U; (with Barcelona), 1987 v USSR, Cz; 1988 v D (2), Cz, Se, Ma, I; (with Manchester U), 1989 v Ho, Fi, Is, Se, WG; 1990 v Fi, WG, Cr; 1991 v D, Bel (2), L, Ic, Pol, WG; 1992 v Br, G, L, Ei, R, Ho, Arg, J; 1993 v Fa, Cy, Bel, Ei, Bel, RCS, Fa; 1994 v RCS, Cy, N; 1995 v Ge, Bul, G, Ge (57)
Hughes, P. W. (Bangor), 1887 v Ni; 1889 v Ni, E (3)
Hughes, W. (Bootle), 1891 v E; 1892 v S, Ni (3)
Hughes, W. A. (Blackburn R), 1949 v E, Ni, P, Bel, Sw (5)
Hughes, W. M. (Birmingham), 1938 v E, Ni, S; 1939 v E, Ni, S, F; 1947 v E, S, Ni (10)
Humphreys, J. V. (Everton), 1947 v Ni (1)
Humphreys, R. (Druids), 1888 v Ni (1)
Hunter, A. H. (FA of Wales Secretary), 1887 v Ni (1)

Jackett, K. (Watford), 1983 v N, Y, E, Bul, S; 1984 v N, R, Y, S, Ni, N, Is; 1985 v Ic, Sp, Ic, N, S, Sp, N; 1986 v S, H, S.Ar, Ei, Ca (2); 1987 v Fi (2); 1988 v D, Cz, Y, Se (31)
Jackson, W. (St Helens Rec), 1899 v Ni (1)
James, E. (Chirk), 1893 v E, Ni; 1894 v E, S, Ni; 1898 v S, E; 1899 v Ni (8)
James, E. G. (Blackpool), 1966 v Br (2), Ch; 1967 v Ni; 1968 v S; 1971 v Cz, S, E, Ni (9)
James, L. (Burnley), 1972 v Cz, R, S (sub); 1973 v E (3), Pol, S, Ni; 1974 v Pol, E, S, Ni; 1975 v A, H (2), L (2), S, E, Ni; 1976 v A; (with Derby Co), S, E, Y (2), Ni; 1977 v WG, S (2), Cz, E, Ni; 1978 v K (2); (with QPR), WG; (with Burnley), 1979 v T; (with Swansea C), 1980 v E, S, Ni, Ic; 1981 v T, Ei, T, S, E; 1982 v Cz, Ic, USSR, E (sub), S, Ni, F; (with Sunderland), 1983 v E (sub) (54)
James, R. M. (Swansea C), 1979 v Ma, WG (sub), S, E, Ni, Ma; 1980 v WG; 1982 v Cz (sub), Ic, Sp, E, S, Ni, F; 1983 v N, Y, E, Bul; (with Stoke C), 1984 v N, R, Bul, Y, S, E, Ni, N, Is; 1985 v Ic, Sp, Ic; (with QPR), N, S, Sp, N; 1986 v S, S.Ar, Ei, U, Ca (2); 1987 v Fi (2), USSR, Cz; (with Leicester C), 1988 v D (2); (with Swansea C), Y (47)
James, W. (West Ham U), 1931 v Ni; 1932 v Ni (2)
Jarrett, R. H. (Ruthin), 1889 v Ni; 1890 v S (2)
Jarvis, A. L. (Hull C), 1967 v S, E, Ni (3)
Jenkins, E. (Lovell's Ath), 1925 v E (1)
Jenkins, J. (Brighton), 1924 v Ni, E, S; 1925 v S, Ni; 1926 v E, S; 1927 v S (8)
Jenkins, R. W. (Rhyl), 1902 v Ni (1)
Jenkyns, C. A. L. (Small Heath), 1892 v E, S, Ni; 1895 v E; (with Woolwich Arsenal), 1896 v S; (with Newton Heath), 1897 v Ni; (with Walsall), 1898 v S, E (8)
Jennings, W. (Bolton W), 1914 v E, S; 1920 v S; 1923 v Ni, E; 1924 v E, S, Ni; 1927 v S, Ni; 1929 v S (11)
John, R. F. (Arsenal), 1923 v S, Ni; 1925 v Ni; 1926 v E; 1927 v E; 1928 v E, Ni; 1930 v E, S; 1932 v E; 1933 v F, Ni; 1935 v Ni; 1936 v S; 1937 v E (15)
John, W. R. (Walsall), 1931 v Ni; (with Stoke C), 1933 v E, S, Ni, F; 1934 v E, S; (with Preston NE), 1935 v E, S; (with Sheffield U), 1936 v E, S, Ni; (with Swansea T), 1939 v E, S (14)
Johnson, M. G. (Swansea T), 1964 v Ni (1)
Jones, A. (Port Vale), 1987 v Fi, Cz (sub); 1988 v D, (with Charlton Ath), D (sub), Cz (sub); 1990 v Hol (sub) (6)
Jones, A. F. (Oxford University), 1877 v S (1)
Jones, A. T. (Nottingham F), 1905 v E; (with Notts Co), 1906 v E (2)

Jones, Bryn (Wolverhampton W), 1935 v Ni; 1936 v E, S, Ni; 1937 v E, S, Ni; 1938 v E, S, Ni; (with Arsenal), 1939 v E, S, Ni; 1947 v S, Ni; 1948 v E; 1949 v S (17)
Jones, B. S. (Swansea T), 1963 v S, E, Ni, H (2); 1964 v S, Ni; (with Plymouth Arg), 1965 v D; (with Cardiff C), 1969 v S, E, Ni, I (sub), WG, EG, R of UK (15)
Jones, Charlie (Nottingham F), 1926 v E; 1927 v S, Ni; 1928 v E; (with Arsenal), 1930 v E, S; 1932 v E; 1933 v F (8)
Jones, Cliff (Swansea T), 1954 v A; 1956 v E, Ni, S, A; 1957 v E, S, Ni, Cz (2), EG; 1958 v EG, E, S, Is (2); (with Tottenham H), 1958 v Ni, H (2), M, Se, Br; 1959 v Ni; 1960 v E, S, Ni; 1961 v S, E, Ni, Sp, H, Ei; 1962 v E, Ni, S, Br (2), M; 1963 v S, Ni, H; 1964 v E, S, Ni; 1965 v E, S, Ni, D, Gr (2), USSR, I; 1967 v S, E; 1968 v E, S, WG; (with Fulham), 1969 v I, R of UK (59)
Jones, C. W. (Birmingham), 1935 v Ni; 1939 v F (2)
Jones, D. (Chirk), 1888 v S, Ni; (with Bolton W), 1889 v E, S, Ni; 1890 v E; 1891 v S; 1892 v Ni; 1893 v E; 1894 v E; 1895 v E; 1898 v S; (with Manchester C), 1900 v E, Ni (14)
Jones, D. E. (Norwich C), 1976 v S, E (sub); 1978 v S, Cz, WG, Ir, E; 1980 v E (8)
Jones, D. O. (Leicester C), 1934 v E, Ni; 1935 v E, S; 1936 v E, Ni; 1937 v Ni (7)
Jones, Evan (Chelsea), 1910 v S, Ni; (with Oldham Ath), 1911 v E, S; 1912 v E, S; (with Bolton W), 1914 v Ni (7)
Jones, F. R. (Bangor), 1885 v E, Ni; 1886 v S (3)
Jones, F. W. (Small Heath), 1893 v S (1)
Jones, G. P. (Wrexham), 1907 v S, Ni (2)
Jones, H. (Aberaman), 1902 v Ni (1)
Jones, Humphrey (Bangor), 1885 v E, Ni, S; 1886 v E, Ni, S; (with Queen's Park), 1887 v E; (with East Stirlingshire), 1889 v E, Ni; 1890 v E, S, Ni; (with Queen's Park), 1891 v E, S (14)
Jones, Ivor (Swansea T), 1920 v S, Ni; 1921 v Ni, E; 1922 v S, Ni; (with WBA), 1923 v E, Ni; 1924 v S; 1926 v Ni (10)
Jones, Jeffrey (Llandrindod Wells), 1908 v Ni; 1909 v Ni; 1910 v S (3)
Jones, J. (Druids), 1876 v S (1)
Jones, J. (Berwyn Rangers), 1883 v S, Ni; 1884 v S (3)
Jones, J. (Wrexham), 1925 v Ni (1)
Jones, J. L. (Sheffield U), 1895 v E, S, Ni; 1896 v Ni, S, E; 1897 v Ni, S, E; (with Tottenham H), 1898 v Ni, E, S; 1899 v S, Ni; 1900 v S; 1902 v E, S, Ni; 1904 v E, S, Ni (21)
Jones, J. Love (Stoke C), 1906 v S; (with Middlesbrough), 1910 v Ni (2)
Jones, J. O. (Bangor), 1901 v S, Ni (2)
Jones, J. P. (Liverpool), 1976 v A, E, S; 1977 v WG, S (2), Cz, E, Ni; 1978 v K (2), S, Cz, WG, Ir, E, S, Ni; (with Wrexham), 1979 v Ma, T, WG, S, E, Ni, Ma; 1980 v Ei, WG, T, E, S, Ni, Ic; 1981 v T, Ei, T, S, E, USSR; 1982 v Cz, Ic, USSR, Sp, E, S, Ni, F; 1983 v N; (with Chelsea), Y, E, Bul, S, Ni, Br; 1984 v N, R, Bul, Y, S, E, Ni, N, Is; 1985 v Ic, N, S, N; (with Huddersfield T), 1986 v S, H, Ei, U, Ca (2) (72)
Jones, J. T. (Stoke C), 1912 v E, S, Ni; 1913 v E, Ni; 1914 v S, Ni; 1920 v E, S, Ni; (with C Palace), 1921 v E, S; 1922 v E, S, Ni (15)
Jones, K. (Aston Villa), 1950 v S (1)
Jones, Leslie J. (Cardiff C), 1933 v F; (with Coventry C), 1935 v Ni; 1936 v S; 1937 v E, S, Ni; (with Arsenal), 1938 v E, S, Ni; 1939 v E, S (11)
Jones, P. W. (Bristol R), 1971 v Fi (1)
Jones, R. (Bangor), 1887 v S; 1889 v E; (with Crewe Alex), 1890 v E (3)
Jones, R. (Leicester Fosse), 1898 v S (1)
Jones, R. (Druids), 1899 v S (1)
Jones, R. (Bangor), 1900 v S, Ni (2)
Jones, R. (Millwall), 1906 v S, Ni (2)
Jones, R. A. (Druids), 1884 v E, Ni, S; 1885 v S (4)
Jones, R. A. (Sheffield W), 1994 v Es (1)
Jones, R. S. (Everton), 1894 v Ni (1)
Jones, S. (Wrexham), 1887 v Ni; (with Chester), 1890 v S (2)
Jones, S. (Wrexham), 1893 v S, Ni; (with Burton Swifts), 1895 v S; 1896 v E, Ni; (with Druids), 1899 v E (6)
Jones, T. (Manchester U), 1926 v Ni; 1927 v E, Ni; 1930 v Ni (4)
Jones, T. D. (Aberdare), 1908 v Ni (1)
Jones, T. G. (Everton), 1938 v Ni; 1939 v E, S, Ni; 1947 v E, S; 1948 v E, S, Ni; 1949 v E, Ni, P, Bel, Sw; 1950 v E, S, Bel (17)
Jones, T. J. (Sheffield W), 1932 v Ni; 1933 v F (2)
Jones, V. P. (Wimbledon), 1995 v Bul (2), G, Ge (4)
Jones, W. E. A. (Swansea T), 1947 v E, S; (with Tottenham H), 1949 v E, S (4)
Jones, W. J. (Aberdare), 1901 v E, S; (with West Ham U), 1902 v E, S (4)
Jones, W. Lot (Manchester C), 1905 v E, Ni; 1906 v E, S, Ni; 1907 v E, S, Ni; 1908 v S; 1909 v E, S, Ni; 1910 v E; 1911 v E; 1913 v E, S; 1914 v S, Ni; (with Southend U), 1920 v E, Ni (20)
Jones, W. P. (Druids), 1889 v E, Ni; (with Wynstay), 1890 v S, Ni (4)
Jones, W. R. (Aberystwyth), 1897 v S (1)

Keenor, F. C. (Cardiff C), 1920 v E, Ni; 1921 v E, Ni, S; 1922 v Ni; 1923 v E, Ni, S; 1924 v E, Ni, S; 1925 v E, Ni, S; 1926 v S; 1927 v E, Ni, S; 1928 v E, Ni, S; 1929 v E, Ni, S; 1930 v E, Ni, S; 1931 v E, Ni, S; (with Crewe Alex), 1933 v S (32)
Kelly, F. C. (Wrexham), 1899 v S, Ni; (with Druids), 1902 v Ni (3)
Kelsey, A. J. (Arsenal), 1954 v Ni, A; 1955 v S, Ni, Y; 1956 v E, Ni, S, A; 1957 v E, Ni, S, Cz (2), EG; 1958 v E, S, Ni, Is (2), H (2), M, Se, Br; 1959 v E, S; 1960 v E, Ni, S; 1961 v E, Ni, S, H, Sp (2); 1962 v E, S, Ni, Br (2) (41)
Kenrick, S. L. (Druids), 1876 v S; 1877 v S; (with Oswestry), 1879 v E, S; (with Shropshire Wanderers), 1881 v E (5)
Ketley, C. F. (Druids), 1882 v Ni (1)
King, J. (Swansea T), 1955 v E (1)
Kinsey, N. (Norwich C), 1951 v Ni, P, Sw; 1952 v E; (with Birmingham C), 1954 v Ni; 1956 v E, S (7)
Knill, A. R. (Swansea C), 1989 v Ho (1)
Krzywicki, R. L. (WBA), 1970 v EG, I; (with Huddersfield T), Ni, E, S; 1971 v R, Fi; 1972 v Cz (sub) (8)

Lambert, R. (Liverpool), 1947 v S; 1948 v E; 1949 v P, Bel, Sw (5)
Latham, G. (Liverpool), 1905 v E, S; 1906 v S; 1907 v E, S, Ni; 1908 v E; 1909 v Ni; (with Southport Central), 1910 v E; (with Cardiff C), 1913 v Ni (10)
Law, B. J. (QPR), 1990 v Se (1)
Lawrence, E. (Clapton Orient), 1930 v Ni; (with Notts Co), 1932 v S (2)
Lawrence, S. (Swansea T), 1932 v Ni; 1933 v F; 1934 v S, E, Ni; 1935 v E, S; 1936 v S (8)
Lea, A. (Wrexham), 1889 v E; 1891 v S, Ni; 1893 v Ni (4)
Lea, C. (Ipswich T), 1965 v Ni, I (2)
Leary, P. (Bangor), 1889 v Ni (1)
Leek, K. (Leicester C), 1961 v S, E, Ni, H, Sp (2); (with Newcastle U), 1962 v S; (with Birmingham C), v Br (sub), M; 1963 v E; 1965 v S, Gr; (with Northampton T), 1965 v Gr (13)
Lever, A. R. (Leicester C), 1953 v S (1)
Lewis, B. (Chester), 1891 v Ni; (with Wrexham), 1892 v S, E, Ni; (with Middlesbrough), 1893 v S, E; (with Wrexham), 1894 v S, E, Ni; 1895 v S (10)
Lewis, D. (Arsenal), 1927 v E; 1928 v Ni; 1930 v E (3)

Lewis, D. (Swansea C), 1983 v Br (sub) (1)
Lewis, D. J. (Swansea T), 1933 v E, S (2)
Lewis, D. M. (Bangor), 1890 v Ni, S (2)
Lewis, J. (Bristol R), 1906 v E (1)
Lewis, J. (Cardiff C), 1926 v S (1)
Lewis, T. (Wrexham), 1881 v E, S (2)
Lewis, W. (Bangor), 1885 v E; 1886 v E, S; 1887 v E, S; 1888 v E; 1889 v E, Ni, S; (with Crewe Alex), 1890 v E; 1891 v E, S; 1892 v E, S, Ni; 1894 v E, S, Ni; (with Chester), 1895 v S, Ni, E; 1896 v E, S, Ni; (with Manchester C), 1897 v E, S; (with Chester), 1898 v Ni (27)
Lewis, W. L. (Swansea T), 1927 v E, Ni; 1928 v E, Ni; 1929 v S; (with Huddersfield T), 1930 v E (6)
Lloyd, B. W. (Wrexham), 1976 v A, E, S (3)
Lloyd, J. W. (Wrexham), 1879 v S; (with Newtown), 1885 v S (2)
Lloyd, R. A. (Ruthin), 1891 v Ni; 1895 v S (2)
Lockley, A. (Chirk), 1898 v Ni (1)
Lovell, S. (C Palace), 1982 v USSR (sub); (with Millwall), 1985 v N; 1986 v S (sub), H (sub), Ca (1+1 sub) (6)
Lowrie, G. (Coventry C), 1948 v E, S, Ni; (with Newcastle U), 1949 v P (4)
Lowndes, S. (Newport Co), 1983 v S (sub), Br (sub); (with Millwall), 1985 v N (sub); 1986 v S.Ar (sub), Ei, U, Ca (2); (with Barnsley), 1987 v Fi (sub); 1988 v Se (sub) (10)
Lucas, P. M. (Leyton Orient), 1962 v Ni, M; 1963 v S, E (4)
Lucas, W. H. (Swansea T), 1949 v S, Ni, P, Bel, Sw; 1950 v E; 1951 v E (7)
Lumberg, A. (Wrexham), 1929 v Ni; 1930 v E, S; (with Wolverhampton W), 1932 v S (4)

McCarthy, T. P. (Wrexham), 1899 v Ni (1)
McMillan, R. (Shrewsbury Engineers), 1881 v E, S (2)
Maguire, G. T. (Portsmouth), 1990 v Fi (sub), Ho, WG, Ei, Se; 1992 v Br (sub), G (7)
Mahoney, J. F. (Stoke C), 1968 v E; 1969 v EG; 1971 v Cz; 1973 v E (3), Pol, S, Ni; 1974 v Pol, E, S, Ni; 1975 v A, H (2), L (2), S, E, Ni; 1976 v A, Y (2), E, Ni; 1977 v WG, Cz, S, E, Ni; (with Middlesbrough), 1978 v K (2), S, Cz, Ir, E (sub), S, Ni; 1979 v WG, S, E, Ni, Ma; (with Swansea C), 1980 v Ei, WG, T (sub); 1982 v Ic, USSR; 1983 v Y, E (51)
Martin, T. J. (Newport Co), 1930 v Ni (1)
Marustik, C. (Swansea C), 1982 v Sp, E, S, Ni, F; 1983 v N (6)
Mates, J. (Chirk), 1891 v Ni; 1897 v E, S (3)
Mathews, R. W. (Liverpool), 1921 v Ni; (with Bristol C), 1923 v E; (with Bradford), 1926 v Ni (3)
Matthews, W. (Chester), 1905 v Ni; 1908 v E (2)
Matthias, J. S. (Brymbo), 1896 v S, Ni; (with Shrewsbury), 1897 v E, S; (with Wolverhampton W), 1899 v S (5)
Matthias, T. J. (Wrexham), 1914 v S, E; 1920 v Ni, S, E; 1921 v S, E, Ni; 1922 v S, E, Ni; 1923 v S (12)
Mays, A. W. (Wrexham), 1929 v Ni (1)
Medwin, T. C. (Swansea T), 1953 v Ni, F, Y; (with Tottenham H), 1957 v E, S, Ni, Cz (2), EG; 1958 v E, S, Ni, Is (2), H (2), M, Br; 1959 v E, S, Ni; 1960 v E, S, Ni; 1961 v S, Ei, E, Sp; 1963 v E, H (30)
Melville, A. K. (Swansea C), 1990 v WG, Ei, Se, Cr (sub); (with Oxford U), 1991 v Ic, Pol, WG; 1992 v Br, G, L, R, Ho, J (sub); 1993 v RCS, Fa (sub); (with Sunderland), 1994 v RCS (sub), R, N, Se, Es; 1995 v Alb, Mol (sub), Ge, Bul (24)
Meredith, S. (Chirk), 1900 v S; 1901 v S, E, Ni; (with Stoke C), 1902 v E; 1903 v Ni; 1904 v E; (with Leyton), 1907 v E (8)
Meredith, W. H. (Manchester C), 1895 v E, Ni; 1896 v E, Ni; 1897 v E, Ni, S; 1898 v E, Ni; 1899 v E; 1900 v E, Ni; 1901 v E, Ni; 1902 v E, S; 1903 v E, S, Ni; 1904 v E; 1905 v E, S; (with Manchester U), 1907 v E, S, Ni; 1908 v E, Ni; 1909 v E, S, Ni; 1910 v E, S, Ni; 1911 v E, S, Ni; 1912 v E, S, Ni; 1913 v E, S, Ni; 1914 v E, S, Ni; 1920 v E, S, Ni (48)
Mielczarek, R. (Rotherham U), 1971 v Fi (1)
Millership, H. (Rotherham Co), 1920 v E, S, Ni; 1921 v E, S, Ni (6)
Millington, A. H. (WBA), 1963 v S, E, H; (with C Palace), 1965 v E, USSR; (with Peterborough U), 1966 v Ch, Br; 1967 v E, Ni; 1968 v Ni, WG; 1969 v I, EG; (with Swansea T), 1970 v E, S, Ni; 1971 v Cz, Fi; 1972 v Fi (sub), Cz, R (21)
Mills, T. J. (Clapton Orient), 1934 v E, Ni; (with Leicester C), 1935 v E, S (4)
Mills-Roberts, R. H. (St Thomas' Hospital), 1885 v E, S, Ni; 1886 v E; 1887 v E; (with Preston NE), 1888 v E, Ni; (with Llanberis), 1892 v E (8)
Moore, G. (Cardiff C), 1960 v E, S, Ni; 1961 v Ei, Sp; (with Chelsea), 1962 v Br; 1963 v Ni, H; (with Manchester U), 1964 v S, Ni; (with Northampton T), 1966 v Ni, Ch; (with Charlton Ath), 1969 v S, E, Ni, R of UK; 1970 v E, S, Ni, I; 1971 v R (21)
Morgan, J. R. (Cambridge University), 1877 v S; (with Swansea T), 1879 v S; (with Derby School Staff), 1880 v E, S; 1881 v E, S; 1882 v E, S, Ni; (with Swansea T), 1883 v E (10)
Morgan, J. T. (Wrexham), 1905 v Ni (1)
Morgan-Owen, H. (Oxford University), 1901 v E; 1902 v S; 1906 v E, Ni; (with Welshpool), 1907 v S (5)
Morgan-Owen, M. M. (Oxford University), 1897 v S, Ni; 1898 v E, S; 1899 v S; 1900 v E, S; (with Corinthians), 1903 v S; 1906 v S, E, Ni; 1907 v E (12)
Morley, E. J. (Swansea T), 1925 v E; (with Clapton Orient), 1929 v E, S, Ni (4)
Morris, A. G. (Aberystwyth), 1896 v E, Ni, S; (with Swindon T), 1897 v E; 1898 v S; (with Nottingham F), 1899 v E, S; 1903 v E, S; 1905 v E, S; 1907 v E, S; 1908 v E; 1910 v E, S, Ni; 1911 v E, S, Ni; 1912 v E (21)
Morris, C. (Chirk), 1900 v E, S, Ni; (with Derby Co), 1901 v E, S, Ni; 1902 v E, S; 1903 v E, S, Ni; 1904 v Ni; 1905 v E, S, Ni; 1906 v S; 1907 v S; 1908 v E, S; 1909 v E, S, Ni; 1910 v E, S, Ni; (with Huddersfield T), 1911 v E, S, Ni (28)
Morris, E. (Chirk), 1893 v E, S, Ni (3)
Morris, H. (Sheffield U), 1894 v S; (with Manchester C), 1896 v E; (with Grimsby T), 1897 v E (3)
Morris, J. (Oswestry), 1887 v S (1)
Morris, J. (Chirk), 1898 v Ni (1)
Morris, R. (Chirk), 1900 v E, Ni; 1901 v Ni; 1902 v S; (with Shrewsbury T), 1903 v E, Ni (6)
Morris, R. (Druids), 1902 v E, S; (with Newtown), Ni; (with Liverpool), 1903 v S, Ni; 1904 v E, S, Ni; (with Leeds C), 1906 v S; (with Grimsby T), 1907 v Ni; (with Plymouth Arg), 1908 v Ni (11)
Morris, S. (Birmingham), 1937 v E, S; 1938 v E, S; 1939 v F (5)
Morris, W. (Burnley), 1947 v Ni; 1949 v E; 1952 v S, Ni, R of UK (5)
Moulsdale, J. R. B. (Corinthians), 1925 v Ni (1)
Murphy, J. P. (WBA), 1933 v F, E, Ni; 1934 v E, S; 1935 v E, S, Ni; 1936 v E, S, Ni; 1937 v S, Ni; 1938 v E, S (15)

Nardiello, D. (Coventry C), 1978 v Cz, WG (sub) (2)
Neal, J. E. (Colwyn Bay), 1931 v E, S (2)
Neilson, A. B. (Newcastle U), 1992 v Ei; 1994 v Se, Es; 1995 v Ge (4)
Newnes, J. (Nelson), 1926 v Ni (1)
Newton, L. F. (Cardiff Corinthians), 1912 v Ni (1)
Nicholas, D. S. (Stoke C), 1923 v S; (with Swansea T), 1927 v E, Ni (3)
Nicholas, P. (C Palace), 1979 v S (sub), Ni (sub), Ma; 1980 v Ei, WG, T, E, S, Ni, Ic; 1981 v T, Cz, E; (with Arsenal), T, S, E, USSR; 1982 v Cz, Ic, USSR, Sp, E, S, Ni, F; 1983 v Y, Bul, S, Ni; 1984 v N, Bul, N, Is; (with C Palace),

1985 v Sp; (with Luton T), N, S, Sp, N; 1986 v S, H, S.Ar, Ei, U, Ca (2); 1987 v Fi (2) USSR, Cz; (with Aberdeen), 1988 v D (2), Cz, Y, Se; (with Chelsea), 1989 v Ho, Fi, Is, Se, WG; 1990 v Fi, Ho, WG, Ei, Se, Cr; 1991 v D (sub), Bel, L, Ei; (with Watford), Bel, Pol, WG; 1992 v L (73)
Nicholls, J. (Newport Co), 1924 v E, Ni; (with Cardiff C), 1925 v E, S (4)
Niedzwiecki, E. A. (Chelsea), 1985 v N (sub); 1988 v D (2)
Nock, W. (Newtown), 1897 v Ni (1)
Nogan, L. M. (Watford), 1992 v A (sub) (1)
Norman, A. J. (Hull C), 1986 v Ei (sub), U, Ca; 1988 v Ma, I (5)
Nurse, M. T. G. (Swansea T), 1960 v E, Ni; 1961 v S, E, H, Ni, Ei, Sp (2); (with Middlesbrough), 1963 v E, H; 1964 v S (12)

O'Callaghan, E. (Tottenham H), 1929 v Ni; 1930 v S; 1932 v S, E; 1933 v Ni, S, E; 1934 v Ni, S, E; 1935 v E (11)
Oliver, A. (Blackburn R), 1905 v E; (with Bangor), S (2)
O'Sullivan, P. A. (Brighton), 1973 v S (sub); 1976 v S; 1979 v Ma (sub) (3)
Owen, D. (Oswestry), 1879 v E (1)
Owen, E. (Ruthin Grammar School), 1884 v E, Ni, S (3)
Owen, G. (Chirk), 1888 v S; (with Newton Heath), 1889 v S, Ni; 1893 v Ni (4)
Owen, J. (Newton Heath), 1892 v E (1)
Owen, Trevor (Crewe Alex), 1899 v E, S (2)
Owen, T. (Oswestry), 1879 v E (1)
Owen, W. (Chirk), 1884 v E; 1885 v Ni; 1887 v E; 1888 v E; 1889 v E, Ni, S; 1890 v S, Ni; 1891 v E, S, Ni; 1892 v E, S; 1893 v S, Ni (16)
Owen, W. P. (Ruthin), 1880 v E, S; 1881 v E, S; 1882 v E, S, Ni; 1883 v E, S; 1884 v E, S, Ni (12)
Owens, J. (Wrexham), 1902 v S (1)

Page, M. E. (Birmingham C), 1971 v Fi; 1972 v S, Ni; 1973 v E (1+1 sub), Ni; 1974 v S, Ni; 1975 v H, L, S, E, Ni; 1976 v E, Y (2), E, Ni; 1977 v WG, S; 1978 v K (sub+1), WG, Ir, E, S; 1979 v Ma, WG (28)
Palmer, D. (Swansea T), 1957 v Cz; 1958 v E, EG (3)
Parris, J. E. (Bradford), 1932 v Ni (1)
Parry, B. J. (Swansea T), 1951 v S (1)
Parry, C. (Everton), 1891 v E, S; 1893 v E; 1894 v E; 1895 v E, S; (with Newtown), 1896 v E, S, Ni; 1897 v Ni; 1898 v E, S, Ni (13)
Parry, E. (Liverpool), 1922 v S; 1923 v E, Ni; 1925 v Ni; 1926 v Ni (5)
Parry, M. (Liverpool), 1901 v E, S, Ni; 1902 v E, S, Ni; 1903 v E, S; 1904 v E, Ni; 1906 v E; 1908 v E, S, Ni; 1909 v E, S (16)
Parry, T. D. (Oswestry), 1900 v E, S, Ni; 1901 v E, S, Ni; 1902 v E (7)
Parry, W. (Newtown), 1895 v Ni (1)
Pascoe, C. (Swansea C), 1984 v N, Is; (with Sunderland), 1989 v Fi, Is, WG (sub); 1990 v Ho (sub), WG (sub); 1991 v Ei, Ic (sub); 1992 v Br (10)
Paul, R. (Swansea T), 1949 v E, S, Ni, P, Sw; 1950 v E, S, Ni, Bel; (with Manchester C), 1951 v S, E, Ni, P, Sw; 1952 v E, S, Ni, R of UK; 1953 v S, E, Ni, F, Y; 1954 v E, S, Ni; 1955 v S, E, Y; 1956 v E, Ni, S, A (33)
Peake, E. (Aberystwyth), 1908 v Ni; (with Liverpool), 1909 v Ni, S, E; 1910 v S, Ni; 1911 v Ni; 1912 v E; 1913 v E, Ni; 1914 v Ni (11)
Peers, E. J. (Wolverhampton W), 1914 v Ni, S, E; 1920 v E, S; 1921 v S, Ni, E; (with Port Vale), 1922 v E, S, Ni; 1923 v E (12)
Pembridge, M. A. (Luton T), 1992 v Br, Ei, R (with Derby Co), Ho, J (sub); 1993 v Bel (sub), Ei; 1994 v N (sub); 1995 v Alb (sub), Mol, Ge (sub) (11)
Perry, E. (Doncaster R), 1938 v E, S, Ni (3)
Perry, J. (Cardiff C), 1994 v N (1)
Phennah, E. (Civil Service), 1878 v S (1)
Phillips, C. (Wolverhampton W), 1931 v Ni; 1932 v E; 1933 v S; 1934 v E, S, Ni; 1935 v E, S, Ni; 1936 v S; (with Aston Villa), 1936 v E, Ni; 1938 v S (13)
Phillips, D. (Plymouth Arg), 1984 v E, Ni, N; (with Manchester C), 1985 v Sp, Ic, S, Sp, N; 1986 v S, H, S.Ar, Ei, U; (with Coventry C), 1987 v Fi, Cz; 1988 v D (2), Cz, Y, Se; 1989 v Se, WG; (with Norwich C), 1990 v Fi, Ho, WG, Ei, Se; 1991 v D, Bel, Ic, Pol, WG; 1992 v L, Ei, A, R, Ho (sub), Arg, J; 1993 v Fa, Cy, Bel, Ei, Bel, RCS, Fa; (with Nottingham F), 1994 v RCS, Cy, R, N, Se, Es; 1995 v Alb, Mol, Ge, Bul (2), G, Ge (59)
Phillips, L. (Cardiff C), 1971 v Cz, S, E, Ni; 1972 v Cz, R, S, Ni; 1973 v E; 1974 v Pol (sub), Ni; 1975 v A; (with Aston Villa), H (2), L (2), S, E, Ni; 1976 v A, E, Y (2), E, Ni; 1977 v WG, S (2), Cz, E; 1978 v K (2), S, Cz, WG, E, S; 1979 v Ma; (with Swansea C), T, WG, S, E, Ni, Ma; 1980 v Ei, WG, T, S (sub), Ni, Ic; 1981 v T, Cz, T, S, E, USSR; (with Charlton Ath), 1982 v Cz, USSR (58)
Phillips, T. J. S. (Chelsea), 1973 v E; 1974 v E; 1975 v H (sub); 1978 v K (4)
Phoenix, H. (Wrexham), 1882 v S (1)
Poland, G. (Wrexham), 1939 v Ni, F (2)
Pontin, K. (Cardiff C), 1980 v E (sub), S (2)
Powell, A. (Leeds U), 1947 v E, S; 1948 v E, S, Ni; (with Everton), 1949 v E; 1950 v Bel; (with Birmingham C), 1951 v S (8)
Powell, D. (Wrexham), 1968 v WG; (with Sheffield U), 1969 v S, E, Ni, I, WG; 1970 v E, S, Ni, EG; 1971 v R (11)
Powell, I. V. (QPR), 1947 v E; 1948 v E, S, Ni; (with Aston Villa), 1949 v Bel; 1950 v S, Bel; 1951 v S (8)
Powell, J. (Druids), 1878 v S; 1880 v E, S; 1882 v E, S, Ni; 1883 v E, S, Ni; (with Bolton W), 1884 v E; (with Newton Heath), 1887 v E, S; 1888 v E, S, Ni (15)
Powell, Seth (WBA), 1885 v S; 1886 v E, Ni; 1891 v E, S; 1892 v E, S (7)
Price, H. (Aston Villa), 1907 v S; (with Burton U), 1908 v Ni; (with Wrexham), 1909 v S, E, Ni (5)
Price, J. (Wrexham), 1877 v S; 1878 v S; 1879 v E; 1880 v E, S; 1881 v E, S; (with Druids), 1882 v S, E, Ni; 1883 v S, Ni (12)
Price, P. (Luton T), 1980 v E, S, Ni, Ic; 1981 v T, Cz, Ei, T, S, E, USSR; (with Tottenham H), 1982 v USSR, Sp, F; 1983 v N, Y, E, Bul, S, Ni; 1984 v N, R, Bul, Y, S (sub) (25)
Pring, K. D. (Rotherham U), 1966 v Ch, D; 1967 v Ni (3)
Pritchard, H. K. (Bristol C), 1985 v N (sub) (1)
Pryce-Jones, A. W. (Newtown), 1895 v E (1)
Pryce-Jones, W. E. (Cambridge University), 1887 v S; 1888 v S, E, Ni; 1890 v Ni (5)
Pugh, A. (Rhostyllen), 1889 v S (1)
Pugh, D. H. (Wrexham), 1896 v S, Ni; 1897 v S, Ni; (with Lincoln C), 1900 v S; 1901 v S, E (7)
Pugsley, J. (Charlton Ath), 1930 v Ni (1)
Pullen, W. J. (Plymouth Arg), 1926 v E (1)

Rankmore, F. E. J. (Peterborough), 1966 v Ch (sub) (1)
Ratcliffe, K. (Everton), 1981 v Cz, Ei, T, S, E, USSR; 1982 v Cz, Ic, USSR, Sp, E; 1983 v Y, E, Bul, S, Ni, Br; 1984 v N, R, Bul, Y, S, E, Ni, N, Is; 1985 v Ic, Sp, Ic, N, S, Sp; 1986 v S, H, S.Ar, U; 1987 v Fi (2), USSR, Cz; 1988 v D (2), Cz; 1989 v Fi, Is, Se, WG; 1990 v Fi; 1991 v D, Bel (2), L, Ei, Ic, Pol, WG; 1992 v Br, G; (with Cardiff C), 1993 v Bel (59)
Rea, J. C. (Aberystwyth), 1894 v Ni, S, E; 1895 v S; 1896 v S, Ni; 1897 v S, Ni; 1898 v Ni (9)
Reece, G. I. (Sheffield U), 1966 v E, S, Ni, USSR; 1967 v S; 1969 v R of UK (sub); 1970 v I (sub); 1971 v S, E, Ni, Fi; 1972 v Fi, R, E (sub), S, Ni; (with Cardiff C), 1973 v E (sub), Ni; 1974 v Pol (sub), E, S, Ni; 1975 v A, H (2), L (2), S, Ni (29)
Reed, W. G. (Ipswich T), 1955 v S, Y (2)

Rees, A. (Birmingham C), 1984 v N (sub) (1)
Rees, J. M. (Luton T), 1992 v A (sub) (1)
Rees, R. R. (Coventry C), 1965 v S, E, Ni, D, Gr (2), I, R; 1966 v E, S, Ni, R, D, Br (2), Ch; 1967 v E, Ni; 1968 v E, S, Ni; (with WBA), WG; 1969 v I; (with Nottingham F), 1969 v WG, EG, S (sub), R of UK; 1970 v E, S, Ni, EG, I; 1971 v Cz, R, E (sub), Ni (sub), Fi; 1972 v Cz (sub), R (39)
Rees, W. (Cardiff C), 1949 v Ni, Bel, Sw; (with Tottenham H), 1950 v Ni (4)
Richards, A. (Barnsley), 1932 v S (1)
Richards, D. (Wolverhampton W), 1931 v Ni; 1933 v E, S, Ni; 1934 v E, S, Ni; 1935 v E, S, Ni; 1936 v S; (with Brentford), 1936 v E, Ni; 1937 v S, E; (with Birmingham), Ni; 1938 v E, S, Ni; 1939 v E, S (21)
Richards, G. (Druids), 1899 v E, S, Ni; (with Oswestry), 1903 v Ni; (with Shrewsbury), 1904 v S; 1905 v Ni (6)
Richards, R. W. (Wolverhampton W), 1920 v E, S; 1921 v Ni; 1922 v E, S; (with West Ham U), 1924 v E, S, Ni; (with Mold), 1926 v S (9)
Richards, S. V. (Cardiff C), 1947 v E (1)
Richards, W. E. (Fulham), 1933 v Ni (1)
Roach, J. (Oswestry), 1885 v Ni (1)
Robbins, W. W. (Cardiff C), 1931 v E, S; 1932 v Ni, E, S; (with WBA), 1933 v F, E, S, Ni; 1934 v S; 1936 v S (11)
Roberts, A. M. (QPR), 1993 v Ei (sub) (1)
Roberts, D. F. (Oxford U), 1973 v Pol, E (sub), Ni; 1974 v E, S; 1975 v A; (with Hull C), L, Ni; 1976 v S, Ni, Y; 1977 v E (sub), Ni; 1978 v K (1+1 sub), S, Ni (17)
Roberts, I. W. (Watford), 1990 v Ho; (with Huddersfield T), 1992 v A, Arg, J; (with Leicester C), 1994 v Se; 1995 v Alb (sub), Mol (7)
Roberts, Jas (Chirk), 1898 v S (1)
Roberts, Jas (Wrexham), 1913 v S, Ni (2)
Roberts, J. (Corwen), 1879 v S; 1880 v E, S; 1882 v E, S, Ni; (with Berwyn R), 1883 v E (7)
Roberts, J. (Ruthin), 1881 v S; 1882 v S (2)
Roberts, J. (Bradford C), 1906 v Ni; 1907 v Ni (2)
Roberts, J. G. (Arsenal), 1971 v S, E, Ni, Fi; 1972 v Fi, E, Ni; (with Birmingham C), 1973 v E (2), Pol, S, Ni; 1974 v Pol, E, S, Ni; 1975 v A, H, S, E; 1976 v E, S (22)
Roberts, J. H. (Bolton), 1949 v Bel (1)
Roberts, P. S. (Portsmouth), 1974 v E; 1975 v A, H, L (4)
Roberts, R. (Druids), 1884 v S; (with Bolton W), 1887 v S; 1888 v S, E; 1889 v S, E; 1890 v S; 1892 v Ni; (with Preston NE), S (9)
Roberts, R. (Wrexham), 1886 v Ni; 1887 v Ni (2)
Roberts, R. (Rhos), 1891 v Ni; (with Crewe Alex), 1893 v E (2)
Roberts, W. (Llangollen), 1879 v E, S; 1880 v E, S; (with Berwyn R), 1881 v S; 1883 v S (6)
Roberts, W. (Wrexham), 1886 v E, S, Ni; 1887 v Ni (4)
Roberts, W. H. (Ruthin), 1882 v E, S; 1883 v E, S, Ni; (with Rhyl), 1884 v S (6)
Rodrigues, P. J. (Cardiff C), 1965 v Ni, Gr (2); 1966 v USSR, E, S, D; (with Leicester C), Ni, Br (2), Ch; 1967 v S; 1968 v E, S, Ni; 1969 v E, Ni, EG, R of UK; 1970 v E, S, Ni, EG; (with Sheffield W), 1971 v R, E, S, Cz, Ni; 1972 v Fi, Cz, R, E, Ni (sub); 1973 v E (3), Pol, S, Ni; 1974 v Pol (40)
Rogers, J. P. (Wrexham), 1896 v E, S, Ni (3)
Rogers, W. (Wrexham), 1931 v E, S (2)
Roose, L. R. (Aberystwyth), 1900 v Ni; (with London Welsh), 1901 v E, S, Ni; (with Stoke C), 1902 v E, S; 1904 v E; (with Everton), 1905 v S, E; (with Stoke C), 1906 v E, S, Ni; 1907 v E, S, Ni; (with Sunderland), 1908 v E, S; 1909 v E, S, Ni; 1910 v E, S, Ni; 1911 v S (24)
Rouse, R. V. (C Palace), 1959 v Ni (1)
Rowlands, A. C. (Tranmere R), 1914 v E (1)
Rowley, T. (Tranmere R), 1959 v Ni (1)
Rush, I. (Liverpool), 1980 v S (sub), Ni; 1981 v E (sub); 1982 v Ic (sub), USSR, E, S, Ni, F; 1983 v N, Y, E, Bul; 1984 v N, R, Bul, Y, S, E, Ni; 1985 v Ic, N, S, Sp; 1986 v S, S.Ar, Ei, U; 1987 v Fi (2), USSR, Cz; (with Juventus), 1988 v D, Cz, Y, Se, Ma, I; (with Liverpool), 1989 v Ho, Fi, Se, WG; 1990 v Fi, Ei; 1991 v D, Bel (2), L, Ei, Pol, WG; 1992 v G, L, R; 1993 v Fa, Cy, Bel (2), RCS, Fa; 1994 v RCS, Cy, R, N, Se, Es; 1995 v Alb, Ge, Bul, G, Ge (71)
Russell, M. R. (Merthyr T), 1912 v S, Ni; 1914 v E; (with Plymouth Arg), 1920 v E, S, Ni; 1921 v E, S, Ni; 1922 v E, Ni; 1923 v E, S, Ni; 1924 v E, S, Ni; 1925 v E, S; 1926 v E, S; 1928 v S; 1929 v E (23)

Sabine, H. W. (Oswestry), 1887 v Ni (1)
Saunders, D. (Brighton & HA), 1986 v Ei (sub), Ca (2); 1987 v Fi, USSR (sub); (with Oxford U), 1988 v Y, Se, Ma, I (sub); 1989 v Ho (sub), Fi; (with Derby Co), Is, Se, WG; 1990 v Fi, Ho, WG, Se, Cr; 1991 v D, Bel (2), L, Ei, Ic, Pol, WG; (with Liverpool), 1992 v Br, G, Ei, R, Ho, Arg, J; 1993 v Fa; (with Aston Villa), Cy, Bel (2), RCS, Fa; 1994 v RCS, Cy, R, N (sub); 1995 v Ge, Bul (2), G, Ge (49)
Savin, G. (Oswestry), 1878 v S (1)
Sayer, P. (Cardiff C), 1977 v Cz, S, E, Ni; 1978 v K (2), S (7)
Scrine, F. H. (Swansea T), 1950 v E, Ni (2)
Sear, C. R. (Manchester C), 1963 v E (1)
Shaw, E. G. (Oswestry), 1882 v Ni; 1884 v S, Ni (3)
Sherwood, A. T. (Cardiff C), 1947 v E, Ni; 1948 v S, Ni; 1949 v E, S, Ni, P, Sw; 1950 v E, S, Ni, Bel; 1951 v E, S, Ni, P, Sw; 1952 v E, S, Ni, R of UK; 1953 v S, E, Ni, F, Y; 1954 v E, S, Ni, A; 1955 v S, E, Y, Ni; 1956 v E, S, Ni, A; (with Newport Co), 1957 v E, S (41)
Shone, W. W. (Oswestry), 1879 v E (1)
Shortt, W. W. (Plymouth Arg), 1947 v Ni; 1950 v Ni, Bel; 1952 v E, S, Ni, R of UK; 1953 v S, E, Ni, F, Y (12)
Showers, D. (Cardiff C), 1975 v E (sub), Ni (2)
Sidlow, C. (Liverpool), 1947 v E, S; 1948 v E, S, Ni; 1949 v S; 1950 v E (7)
Sisson, H. (Wrexham Olympic), 1885 v Ni; 1886 v S, Ni (3)
Slatter, N. (Bristol R), 1983 v S; 1984 v N (sub), Is; 1985 v Ic, Sp, Ic, N, S, Sp, N; (with Oxford U), 1986 v H (sub), S.Ar, Ca (2); 1987 v Fi (sub), Cz; 1988 v D (2), Cz, Ma, I; 1989 v Is (sub) (22)
Smallman, D. P. (Wrexham), 1974 v E (sub), S (sub), Ni; (with Everton), 1975 v H (sub), E, Ni (sub); 1976 v A (7)
Southall, N. (Everton), 1982 v Ni; 1983 v N, E, Bul, S, Ni, Br; 1984 v N, R, Bul, Y, S, E, Ni, N, Is; 1985 v Ic, Sp, Ic, N, S, Sp, N; 1986 v S, H, S.Ar, Ei; 1987 v USSR, Fi, Cz; 1988 v D, Cz, Y, Se; 1989 v Ho, Fi, Se, WG; 1990 v Fi, Ho, WG, Ei, Se, Cr; 1991 v D, Bel (2), L, Ei, Ic, Pol, WG; 1992 v Br, G, L, Ei, A, R, Ho, Arg, J; 1993 v Fa, Cy, Bel, Ei, Bel, RCS, Fa; 1994 v RCS, Cy, R, N, Se, Es; 1995 v Alb, Mol, Ge, Bul (2), G, Ge (81)
Speed, G. A. (Leeds U), 1990 v Cr (sub); 1991 v D, L (sub), Ei (sub), Ic, WG (sub); 1992 v Br, G (sub), L, Ei, R, Ho, Arg, J; 1993 v Fa, Cy, Bel, Ei, Bel, Fa (sub); 1994 v RCS (sub), Cy, R, N, Se; 1995 v Alb, Mol, Ge, Bul (2), G (31)
Sprake, G. (Leeds U), 1964 v S, Ni; 1965 v S, D, Gr; 1966 v E, Ni, USSR; 1967 v S; 1968 v E, S; 1969 v S, E, Ni, WG, R of UK; 1970 v EG, I; 1971 v R, S, E, Ni; 1972 v Fi, E, S, Ni; 1973 v E (2), Pol, S, Ni; 1974 v Pol; (with Birmingham C), S, Ni; 1975 v A, H, L (37)
Stansfield, F. (Cardiff C), 1949 v S (1)
Stevenson, B. (Leeds U), 1978 v Ni; 1979 v Ma, T, S, E, Ni, Ma; 1980 v WG, T, Ic (sub); 1982 v Cz; (with Birmingham C), Sp, S, Ni, F (15)
Stevenson, N. (Swansea C), 1982 v E, S, Ni; 1983 v N (4)
Stitfall, R. F. (Cardiff C), 1953 v E; 1957 v Cz (2)

Sullivan, D. (Cardiff C), 1953 v Ni, F, Y; 1954 v Ni; 1955 v E, Ni; 1957 v E, S; 1958 v Ni, H (2), Se, Br; 1959 v S, Ni; 1960 v E, S (17)

Symons, C. J. (Portsmouth), 1992 v Ei, Ho, Arg, J; 1993 v Fa, Cy, Bel, Ei, RCS, Fa; 1994 v RCS, Cy, R; 1995 v Mol, Ge (sub), Bul, G, Ge (18)

Tapscott, D. R. (Arsenal), 1954 v A; 1955 v S, E, Ni, Y; 1956 v E, Ni, S, A; 1957 v Ni, Cz, EG; (with Cardiff C), 1959 v E, Ni (14)

Taylor, J. (Wrexham), 1898 v E (1)

Taylor, O. D. S. (Newtown), 1893 v S, Ni; 1894 v S, Ni (4)

Thomas, C. (Druids), 1899 v Ni; 1900 v S (2)

Thomas, D. A. (Swansea T), 1957 v Cz; 1958 v EG (2)

Thomas, D. S. (Fulham), 1948 v E, S, Ni; 1949 v S (4)

Thomas, E. (Cardiff Corinthians), 1925 v E (1)

Thomas, G. (Wrexham), 1885 v E, S (2)

Thomas, H. (Manchester U), 1927 v E (1)

Thomas, M. (Wrexham), 1977 v WG, S (1+1 sub), Ni (sub); 1978 v K (sub), S, Cz, Ir, E, Ni (sub); 1979 v Ma; (with Manchester U), T, WG, Ma (sub); 1980 v Ei, WG (sub), T, E, S, Ni; 1981 v Cz, S, E, USSR; (with Everton), 1982 v Cz; (with Brighton & HA), USSR (sub), Sp, E, S (sub), Ni (sub); 1983 (with Stoke C), v N, Y, E, Bul, S, Ni, Br; 1984 v R, Bul, Y; (with Chelsea), S, E; 1985 v Ic, Sp, Ic, S, Sp, N; 1986 v S; (with WBA), H, S.Ar (sub) (51)

Thomas, M. R. (Newcastle U), 1987 v Fi (1)

Thomas, R. J. (Swindon T), 1967 v Ni; 1968 v WG; 1969 v E, Ni, I, WG, R of UK; 1970 v E, S, Ni, EG, I; 1971 v S, E, Ni, R, Cz; 1972 v Fi, Cz, R, E, S, Ni; 1973 v E (3), Pol, S, Ni; 1974 v Pol; (with Derby Co), E, S, Ni; 1975 v H (2), L (2), S, E, Ni; 1976 v A, Y, E; 1977 v Cz, S, E, Ni; 1978 v K, S; (with Cardiff C), Cz (50)

Thomas, T. (Bangor), 1898 v S, Ni (2)

Thomas, W. R. (Newport Co), 1931 v E, S (2)

Thomson, D. (Druids), 1876 v S (1)

Thomson, G. F. (Druids), 1876 v S; 1877 v S (2)

Toshack, J. B. (Cardiff C), 1969 v S, E, Ni, WG, EG, R of UK; 1970 v EG, I; (with Liverpool), 1971 v S, E, Ni, Fi; 1972 v Fi, E; 1973 v E (3), Pol, S; 1975 v A, H (2), L (2), S, E; 1976 v Y (2), E; 1977 v S; 1978 v K (2), S, Cz; (with Swansea C), 1979 v WG (sub), S, E, Ni, Ma; 1980 v WG (40)

Townsend, W. (Newtown), 1887 v Ni; 1893 v Ni (2)

Trainer, H. (Wrexham), 1895 v E, S, Ni (3)

Trainer, J. (Bolton W), 1887 v S; (with Preston NE), 1888 v S; 1889 v E; 1890 v S; 1891 v S; 1892 v Ni, S; 1893 v E; 1894 v Ni, E; 1895 v Ni, E; 1896 v S; 1897 v Ni, S, E; 1898 v S, E; 1899 v Ni, S (20)

Turner, H. G. (Charlton Ath), 1937 v E, S, Ni; 1938 v E, S, Ni; 1939 v Ni, F (8)

Turner, J. (Wrexham), 1892 v E (1)

Turner, R. E. (Wrexham), 1891 v E, Ni (2)

Turner, W. H. (Wrexham), 1887 v E, Ni; 1890 v S; 1891 v E, S (5)

Van Den Hauwe, P. W. R. (Everton), 1985 v Sp; 1986 v S, H; 1987 v USSR, Fi, Cz; 1988 v D (2), Cz, Y, I; 1989 v Fi, Se (13)

Vaughan, Jas (Druids), 1893 v E, S, Ni; 1899 v E (4)

Vaughan, John (Oswestry), 1879 v S; 1880 v S; 1881 v E, S; 1882 v E, S, Ni; 1883 v E, S, Ni; (with Bolton W), 1884 v E (11)

Vaughan, J. O. (Rhyl), 1885 v Ni; 1886 v Ni, E, S (4)

Vaughan, N. (Newport Co), 1983 v Y (sub), Br; 1984 v N; (with Cardiff C), R, Bul, Y, Ni (sub), N, Is; 1985 v Sp (sub) (10)

Vaughan, T. (Rhyl), 1885 v E (1)

Vearncombe, G. (Cardiff C), 1958 v EG; 1961 v Ei (2)

Vernon, T. R. (Blackburn R), 1957 v Ni, Cz (2), EG; 1958 v E, S, EG, Se; 1959 v S; (with Everton), 1960 v Ni; 1961 v S, E, Ei; 1962 v Ni, Br (2), M; 1963 v S, E, H; 1964 v E, S; (with Stoke C), 1965 v Ni, Gr, I; 1966 v E, S, Ni, USSR, D; 1967 v Ni; 1968 v E (32)

Villars, A. K. (Cardiff C), 1974 v E, S, Ni (sub) (3)

Vizard, E. T. (Bolton W), 1911 v E, S, Ni; 1912 v E, S; 1913 v S; 1914 v E, Ni; 1920 v E; 1921 v E, S, Ni; 1922 v E, S; 1923 v E, Ni; 1924 v E, S, Ni; 1926 v E, S; 1927 v S (22)

Walley, J. T. (Watford), 1971 v Cz (1)

Walsh, I. (C Palace), 1980 v Ei, T, E, S, Ic; 1981 v T, Cz, Ei, T, S, E, USSR; 1982 v Cz (sub), Ic; (with Swansea C), Sp, S (sub), Ni (sub), F (18)

Ward, D. (Bristol R), 1959 v E; (with Cardiff C), 1962 v E (2)

Warner, J. (Swansea T), 1937 v E; (with Manchester U), 1939 v F (2)

Warren, F. W. (Cardiff C), 1929 v Ni; (with Middlesbrough), 1931 v Ni; 1933 v F, E; (with Hearts), 1937 v Ni; 1938 v Ni (6)

Watkins, A. E. (Leicester Fosse), 1898 v E, S; (with Aston Villa), 1900 v E, S; (with Millwall), 1904 v Ni (5)

Watkins, W. M. (Stoke C), 1902 v E; 1903 v E, S; (with Aston Villa); 1904 v E, S, Ni; (with Sunderland), 1905 v E, S, Ni; (with Stoke C), 1908 v Ni (10)

Webster, C (Manchester U), 1957 v Cz; 1958 v H, M, Br (4)

Whatley, W. J. (Tottenham H), 1939 v E, S (2)

White, P. F. (London Welsh), 1896 v Ni (1)

Wilcocks, A. R. (Oswestry), 1890 v Ni (1)

Wilding, J. (Wrexham Olympians), 1885 v E, S, Ni; 1886 v E, Ni; (with Bootle), 1887 v E; 1888 v S, Ni; (with Wrexham), 1892 v S (9)

Williams, A. (Reading), 1994 v Es; 1995 v Alb, Mol, G (sub), Ge (5)

Williams, A. L. (Wrexham), 1931 v E (1)

Williams, B. (Bristol C), 1930 v Ni (1)

Williams, B. D. (Swansea T), 1928 v Ni, E; 1930 v E, S; (with Everton), 1931 v Ni; 1932 v E; 1933 v E, S, Ni; 1935 v Ni (10)

Williams, D. G. (Derby Co), 1988 v Cz, Y, Se, Ma, I; 1989 v Ho, Is, Se, WG; 1990 v Fi, Ho; (with Ipswich T), 1993 v Ei (12)

Williams, D. M. (Norwich C), 1986 v S.Ar (sub), U, Ca (2); 1987 v Fi (5)

Williams, D. R. (Merthyr T), 1921 v E, S; (with Sheffield W), 1923 v S; 1926 v S; 1927 v E, Ni; (with Manchester U), 1929 v E, S (8)

Williams, E. (Crewe Alex), 1893 v E, S (2)

Williams, E. (Druids), 1901 v E, Ni, S; 1902 v E, Ni (5)

Williams, G. (Chirk), 1893 v S; 1894 v S; 1895 v E, S, Ni; 1898 v Ni (6)

Williams, G. E. (WBA), 1960 v Ni; 1961 v S, E, Ei; 1963 v Ni, H; 1964 v E, S, Ni; 1965 v S, E, Ni, D, Gr (2), USSR, I; 1966 v Ni, Br (2), Ch; 1967 v S, E, Ni; 1968 v Ni; 1969 v I (26)

Williams, G. G. (Swansea T), 1961 v Ni, H, Sp (2); 1962 v E (5)

Williams, G. J. J. (Cardiff C), 1951 v Sw (1)

Williams, G. O. (Wrexham), 1907 v Ni (1)

Williams, H. J. (Swansea), 1965 v Gr (2); 1972 v R (3)

Williams, H. T. (Newport Co), 1949 v Ni, Sw; (with Leeds U), 1950 v Ni; 1951 v S (4)

Williams, J. H. (Oswestry), 1884 v E (1)

Williams, J. J. (Wrexham), 1939 v F (1)

Williams, J. T. (Middlesbrough), 1925 v Ni (1)

Williams, J. W. (C Palace), 1912 v S, Ni (2)

Williams, R. (Newcastle U), 1935 v S, E (2)

Williams, R. P. (Caernarvon), 1886 v S (1)

Williams, S. G. (WBA), 1954 v A; 1955 v E, Ni; 1956 v E, S, A; 1958 v E, S, Ni, Is (2), H (2), M, Se, Br; 1959 v E, S, Ni; 1960 v E, S, Ni; 1961 v Ni, Ei, H, Sp (2); 1962 v E,

S, Ni, Br (2), M; (with Southampton), 1963 v S, E, H (2); 1964 v E, S; 1965 v S, E, D; 1966 v D (43)

Williams, W. (Druids), 1876 v S; 1878 v S; (with Oswestry), 1879 v E, S; (with Druids), 1880 v E; 1881 v E, S; 1882 v E, S, Ni; 1883 v Ni (11)

Williams, W. (Northampton T), 1925 v S (1)

Witcomb, D. F. (WBA), 1947 v E, S; (with Sheffield W), 1947 v Ni (3)

Woosnam, A. P. (Leyton Orient), 1959 v S; (with West Ham U), E; 1960 v E, S, Ni; 1961 v S, E, Ni, Ei, Sp, H; 1962 v E, S, Ni, Br; (with Aston Villa), 1963 v Ni, H (17)

Woosnam, G. (Newton White Star), 1879 v S (1)

Worthington, T. (Newtown), 1894 v S (1)

Wynn, G. A. (Wrexham), 1909 v E, S, Ni; (with Manchester C), 1910 v E; 1911 v Ni; 1912 v E, S; 1913 v E, S; 1914 v E, S (11)

Wynn, W. (Chirk), 1903 v Ni (1)

Yorath, T. C. (Leeds U), 1970 v I; 1971 v S, E, Ni; 1972 v Cz, E, S, Ni; 1973 v E, Pol, S; 1974 v Pol, E, S, Ni; 1975 v A, H (2), L (2), S; 1976 v A, E, S, Y (2), E, Ni; (with Coventry C), 1977 v WG, S (2), Cz, E, Ni; 1978 v K (2), S, Cz, WG, Ir, E, S, Ni; 1979 v T, WG, S, E, Ni; (with Tottenham H), 1980 v Ei, T, E, S, Ni, Ic; 1981 v T, Cz; (with Vancouver W), Ei, T, USSR (59)

Young, E. (Wimbledon), 1990 v Cr; (with C Palace), 1991 v D, Bel (2), L, Ei; 1992 v G, L, Ei, A; 1993 v Fa, Cy, Bel, Ei, Bel, Fa; 1994 v RCS, Cy, R, N (20)

REPUBLIC OF IRELAND

Aherne, T. (Belfast C), 1946 v P, Sp; (with Luton T), 1950 v Fi, E, Fi, Se, Bel; 1951 v N, Arg, N; 1952 v WG (2), A, Sp; 1953 v F; 1954 v F (16)

Aldridge, J. W. (Oxford U), 1986 v W, U, Ic, Cz; 1987 v Bel, S, Pol; (with Liverpool), S, Bul, Bel, Br, L; 1988 v Bul, Pol, N, E, USSR, Ho; 1989 v Ni, Tun, Sp, F (sub), H, Ma (sub), H; 1990 v WG; (with Real Sociedad), Ni, Ma, Fi (sub), T, E, Eg, Ho, R, I; 1991 v T, E (2), Pol; (with Tranmere R), 1992 v H (sub), T, W (sub), Sw (sub), US (sub), Alb, I, P (sub); 1993 v La, D, Sp, D, Alb, La, Li; 1994 v Li, Ni, CzR, I (sub), M (sub), N; 1995 v La, Ni, P, Lie (64)

Ambrose, P. (Shamrock R), 1955 v N, Ho; 1964 v Pol, N, E (5)

Anderson, J. (Preston NE), 1980 v Cz (sub), US (sub); 1982 v Ch, Br, Tr; (with Newcastle U), 1984 v Chn; 1986 v W, Ic, Cz; 1987 v Bul, Bel, Br, L; 1988 v R (sub), Y (sub); 1989 v Tun (16)

Andrews, P. (Bohemians), 1936 v Ho (1)

Arrigan, T. (Waterford), 1938 v N (1)

Babb, P. A. (Coventry C), 1994 v Ru, Ho, Bol, G, CzR (sub), I, M, N, Ho; (with Liverpool), 1995 v La, Lie, Ni (2), P, Lie, A (16)

Bailham, E. (Shamrock R), 1964 v E (1)

Barber, E. (Shelbourne), 1966 v Sp; (with Birmingham C), 1966 v Bel (2)

Barry, P. (Fordsons), 1928 v Bel; 1929 v Bel (2)

Beglin, J. (Liverpool), 1984 v Chn; 1985 v M, D, I, Is, E, N, Sw; 1986 v Sw, USSR, D, W; 1987 v Bel (sub), S, Pol (15)

Bermingham, J. (Bohemians), 1929 v Bel (1)

Bermingham, P. (St James' Gate), 1935 v H (1)

Braddish, S. (Dundalk), 1978 v T (sub), Pol (2)

Bonner, P. (Celtic), 1981 v Pol; 1982 v Alg; 1984 v Ma, Is, Chn; 1985 v I, Is, E, N; 1986 v U, Ic; 1987 v Bel (2), S (2), Pol, Bul, Br, L; 1988 v Bul, R, Y, N, E, USSR, Ho; 1989 v Sp, F, H, Sp, Ma, H; 1990 v WG, Ni, Ma, W, Fi, T, E, Eg, Ho, R, I; 1991 v Mor, T, E (2), W, Pol, US; 1992 v H, Pol, T, W, Sw, Alb, I; 1993 v La, D, Sp, W, Ni, D, Alb, La, Li; 1994 v Li, Sp, Ni, Ru, Ho, Bol, CzR, I, M, N, Ho; 1995 v Lie (78)

Bradshaw, P. (St James' Gate), 1939 v Sw, Pol, H (2), G (5)

Brady, F. (Fordsons), 1926 v I; 1927 v I (2)

Brady, T. R. (QPR), 1964 v A (2), Sp (2), Pol, N (6)

Brady, W. L. (Arsenal), 1975 v USSR, T, Sw, USSR, Sw, WG; 1976 v T, N, Pol; 1977 v E, T, F (2), Sp, Bul; 1978 v Bul, N; 1979 v Ni, E, D, Bul, WG; 1980 v W, Bul, E, Cy; (with Juventus), 1981 v Ho, Bel, F, Cy, Bel; 1982 v Ho, F, Ch, Br, Tr; (with Sampdoria), 1983 v Ho, Sp, Ic, Ma; 1984 v Ic, Ho, Ma, Pol, Is; (with Internazionale), 1985 v USSR, N, D, I, E, N, Sp, Sw; 1986 v Sw, USSR, D, W; (with Ascoli), 1987 v Bel, S (2), Pol; (with West Ham U), Bul, Bel, Br, L; 1988 v L, Bul; 1989 v F, H (sub), H (sub); 1990 v WG, Fi (72)

Breen, T. (Manchester U), 1937 v Sw, F; (with Shamrock R), 1947 v E, Sp, P (5)

Brennan, F. (Drumcondra), 1965 v Bel (1)

Brennan, S. A. (Manchester U), 1965 v Sp; 1966 v Sp, A, Bel; 1967 v Sp, T, Sp; 1969 v Cz, D, H; 1970 v S, Cz, D, H, Pol (sub), WG; (with Waterford), 1971 v Pol, Se, I (19)

Brown, J. (Coventry C), 1937 v Sw, F (2)

Browne, W. (Bohemians), 1964 v A, Sp, E (3)

Buckley, L. (Shamrock R), 1984 v Pol (sub); (with Waregem), 1985 v M (2)

Burke, F. (Cork Ath), 1952 v WG (1)

Burke, J. (Cork), 1934 v Bel (1)

Burke, J. (Shamrock R), 1929 v Bel (1)

Byrne, A. B. (Southampton), 1970 v D, Pol, WG; 1971 v Pol, Se (2), I (2), A; 1973 v F, USSR (sub), F, N; 1974 v Pol (14)

Byrne, D. (Shelbourne), 1929 v Bel; (with Shamrock R), 1932 v Sp; (with Coleraine), 1934 v Bel (3)

Byrne, J. (Bray Unknowns), 1928 v Bel (1)

Byrne, J. (QPR), 1985 v I, Is (sub), E (sub), Sp (sub); 1987 v S (sub), Bel (sub), Br, L (sub); 1988 v L, Bul (sub), Is, R, Y (sub), Pol (sub); (with Le Havre), 1990 v WG (sub), W, Fi, T (sub), Ma; (with Brighton & HA), 1991 v W; (with Sunderland), 1992 v T, W; (with Millwall), 1993 v W (23)

Byrne, P. (Shamrock R), 1984 v Pol, Chn; 1985 v M; 1986 v D (sub), W (sub), U (sub), Ic (sub), Cz (8)

Byrne, P. (Dolphin), 1931 v Sp; 1932 v Ho; (with Drumcondra), 1934 v Ho (3)

Byrne, S. (Bohemians), 1931 v Sp (1)

Campbell, A. (Santander), 1985 v I (sub), Is, Sp (3)

Campbell, N. (St Patrick's Ath), 1971 v A (sub); (with Fortuna, Cologne), 1972 v Ir, Ec, Ch, P; 1973 v USSR, F (sub); 1975 v WG; 1976 v N; 1977 v Sp, Bul (sub) (11)

Cannon, H. (Bohemians), 1926 v I; 1928 v Bel (2)

Cantwell, N. (West Ham U), 1954 v L; 1956 v Sp, Ho; 1957 v D, WG, E (2); 1958 v D, Pol, A; 1959 v Pol, Cz (2); 1960 v Se, Ch, Se; 1961 v N; (with Manchester U), S (2); 1962 v Cz (2), A; 1963 v Ic (2), S; 1964 v A, Sp, E; 1965 v Pol, Sp; 1966 v Sp (2), A, Bel; 1967 v Sp, T (36)

Carey, B. P. (Manchester U), 1992 v US (sub); 1993 v W; (with Leicester C), 1994 v Ru (3)

Carey, J. J. (Manchester U), 1938 v N, Cz, Pol; 1939 v Sw, Pol, H (2), G; 1946 v P, Sp; 1947 v E, Sp, P; 1948 v P, Sp; 1949 v Sw, Bel, P, Se, Sp; 1950 v Fi, E, Fi, Se; 1951 v N, Arg, N; 1953 v F, A (29)

Carolan, J. (Manchester U), 1960 v Se, Ch (2)
Carroll, B. (Shelbourne), 1949 v Bel; 1950 v Fi (2)
Carroll, T. R. (Ipswich T), 1968 v Pol; 1969 v Pol, A, D; 1970 v Cz, Pol, WG; 1971 v Se; (with Birmingham C), 1972 v Ir, Ec, Ch, P; 1973 v USSR (2), Pol, F, N (17)
Cascarino, A. G. (Gillingham), 1986 v Sw, USSR, D; (with Millwall), 1988 v Pol, N (sub), USSR (sub), Ho (sub); 1989 v Ni, Tun, Sp, F, H, Sp, Ma, H; 1990 v WG (sub), Ni, Ma; (with Aston Villa), W, Fi, T, E, Eg, Ho (sub), R (sub), I (sub); 1991 v Mor (sub), T (sub), E (2 sub), Pol (sub), Ch (sub), US; (with Celtic), 1992 v Pol, T; (with Chelsea), W, Sw, US (sub); 1993 v W, Ni (sub), D (sub), Alb (sub), La (sub); 1994 v Li (sub), Sp (sub), Ni (sub), Ru, Bol (sub), G, CzR, Ho (sub); (with Marseille), 1995 v La (sub), Ni (sub), P (sub), Lie (sub), A (sub) (56)
Chandler, J. (Leeds U), 1980 v Cz (sub), US (2)
Chatton, H. A. (Shelbourne), 1931 v Sp; (with Dumbarton), 1932 v Sp; (with Cork), 1934 v Ho (3)
Clarke, J. (Drogheda U), 1978 v Pol (sub) (1)
Clarke, K. (Drumcondra), 1948 v P, Sp (2)
Clarke, M. (Shamrock R), 1950 v Bel (1)
Clinton, T. J. (Everton), 1951 v N; 1954 v F, L (3)
Coad, P. (Shamrock R), 1947 v E, Sp, P; 1948 v P, Sp; 1949 v Sw, Bel, P, Se; 1951 v N (sub); 1952 v Sp (11)
Coffey, T. (Drumcondra), 1950 v Fi (1)
Colfer, M. D. (Shelbourne), 1950 v Bel; 1951 v N (2)
Collins, F. (Jacobs), 1927 v I (1)
Conmy, O. M. (Peterborough U), 1965 v Bel; 1967 v Cz; 1968 v Cz, Pol; 1970 v Cz (5)
Connolly, H. (Cork), 1937 v G (1)
Connolly, J. (Fordsons), 1926 v I (1)
Conroy, G. A. (Stoke C), 1970 v Cz, D, H, Pol, WG; 1971 v Pol, Se (2), I; 1973 v USSR, F, USSR, N; 1974 v Pol, Br, U, Ch; 1975 v T, Sw, USSR, Sw, WG (sub); 1976 v T (sub), Pol; 1977 v E, T, Pol (27)
Conway, J. P. (Fulham), 1967 v Sp, T, Sp; 1968 v Cz; 1969 v A (sub), H; 1970 v S, Cz, D, H, Pol, WG; 1971 v I, A; 1974 v U, Ch; 1975 v WG (sub); 1976 v N, Pol; (with Manchester C), 1977 v Pol (20)
Corr, P. J. (Everton), 1949 v P, Sp; 1950 v E, Se (4)
Courtney, E. (Cork U), 1946 v P (1)
Coyle, O. C. (Bolton W), 1994 v Ho (sub) (1)
Coyne, T. (Celtic), 1992 v Sw, US, Alb (sub), US (sub), I (sub), P (sub); 1993 v W (sub), La (sub); (with Tranmere R), Ni; (with Motherwell), 1994 v Ru (sub), Ho, Bol, G (sub), CzR (sub), I, M, Ho; 1995 v Lie, Ni (sub), A (20)
Cummins, G. P. (Luton T), 1954 v L (2); 1955 v N (2), WG; 1956 v Y, Sp; 1958 v D, Pol, A; 1959 v Pol, Cz (2); 1960 v Se, Ch, WG, Se; 1961 v S (2) (19)
Cuneen, T. (Limerick), 1951 v N (1)
Curtis, D. P. (Shelbourne), 1957 v D, WG; (with Bristol C), 1957 v E (2); 1958 v D, Pol, A; (with Ipswich T), 1959 v Pol; 1960 v Se, Ch, WG, Se; 1961 v N, S; 1962 v A; 1963 v Ic; (with Exeter C), 1964 v A (17)
Cusack, S. (Limerick), 1953 v F (1)

Daish, L. S. (Cambridge U), 1992 v W, Sw (sub) (2)
Daly, G. A. (Manchester U), 1973 v Pol (sub), N; 1974 v Br (sub), U (sub); 1975 v Sw (sub), WG; 1977 v E, T, F; (with Derby Co), F, Bul; 1978 v Bul, T, D; 1979 v Ni, E, D, Bul; 1980 v Ni, E, Cy, Sw, Arg; (with Coventry C), 1981 v WG'B', Ho, Bel, Cy, W, Bel, Cz, Pol (sub); 1982 v Alg, Ch, Br, Tr; 1983 v Ho, Sp (sub), Ma (sub); 1984 v Is (sub), Ma; (with Birmingham C), 1985 v M (sub), N, Sp, Sw; 1986 v Sw; (with Shrewsbury T), U, Ic (sub), Cz (sub); 1987 v S (sub) (48)
Daly, J. (Shamrock R), 1932 v Ho; 1935 v Sw (2)
Daly, M. (Wolverhampton W), 1978 v T, Pol (2)
Daly, P. (Shamrock R), 1950 v Fi (sub) (1)
Davis, T. L. (Oldham Ath), 1937 v G, H; (with Tranmere R), 1938 v Cz, Pol (4)
Deacy, E. (Aston Villa), 1982 v Alg (sub), Ch, Br, Tr (4)
De Mange, K. J. P. P. (Liverpool), 1987 v Br (sub); (with Hull C), 1989 v Tun (sub) (2)
Dempsey, J. T. (Fulham), 1967 v Sp, Cz; 1968 v Cz, Pol; 1969 v Pol, A, D; (with Chelsea), 1969 v Cz, D; 1970 v H, WG; 1971 v Pol, Se (2), I; 1972 v Ir, Ec, Ch, P (19)
Dennehy, J. (Cork Hibernians), 1972 v Ec (sub), Ch; (with Nottingham F), 1973 v USSR (sub), Pol, F, N; 1974 v Pol (sub); 1975 v T (sub), WG (sub); (with Walsall), 1976 v Pol (sub); 1977 v Pol (sub) (11)
Desmond, P. (Middlesbrough), 1950 v Fi, E, Fi, Se (4)
Devine, J. (Arsenal), 1980 v Cz, Ni; 1981 v WG'B', Cz; 1982 v Ho, Alg; 1983 v Sp, Ma; (with Norwich C), 1984 v Ic, Ho, Is; 1985 v USSR, N (13)
Donnelly, J. (Dundalk), 1935 v H, Sw, G; 1936 v Ho, Sw, H, L; 1937 v G, H; 1938 v N (10)
Donnelly, T. (Drumcondra), 1938 v N; (Shamrock R), 1939 v Sw (2)
Donovan, D. C. (Everton), 1955 v N, Ho, N, WG; 1957 v E (5)
Donovan, T. (Aston Villa), 1980 v Cz; 1981 v WG'B'(sub) (2)
Dowdall, C. (Fordsons), 1928 v Bel; (with Barnsley), 1929 v Bel; (with Cork), 1931 v Sp (3)
Doyle, C. (Shelbourne), 1959 v Cz (1)
Doyle, D. (Shamrock R), 1926 v I (1)
Doyle, L. (Dolphin), 1932 v Sp (1)
Duffy, B. (Shamrock R), 1950 v Bel (1)
Duggan, H. A. (Leeds U), 1927 v I; 1930 v Bel; 1936 v H, L; (with Newport Co), 1938 v N (5)
Dunne, A. P. (Manchester U), 1962 v A; 1963 v Ic, S; 1964 v A, Sp, Pol, N, E; 1965 v Pol, Sp; 1966 v Sp (2), A, Bel; 1967 v Sp, T, Sp; 1969 v Pol, D, H; 1970 v H; 1971 v Se, I, A; (with Bolton W), 1974 v Br (sub), U, Ch; 1975 v T, Sw, USSR, Sw, WG; 1976 v T (33)
Dunne, J. (Sheffield U), 1930 v Bel; (with Arsenal), 1936 v Sw, H, L; (with Southampton), 1937 v Sw, F; (with Shamrock R), 1938 v N (2), Cz, Pol; 1939 v Sw, Pol, H (2), G (15)
Dunne, J. C. (Fulham), 1971 v A (1)
Dunne, L. (Manchester C), 1935 v Sw, G (2)
Dunne, P. A. J. (Manchester U), 1965 v Sp; 1966 v Sp (2), WG; 1967 v T (5)
Dunne, S. (Luton T), 1953 v F, A; 1954 v F, L; 1956 v Sp, Ho; 1957 v D, WG, E; 1958 v D, Pol, A; 1959 v Pol; 1960 v WG, Se (15)
Dunne, T. (St Patrick's Ath), 1956 v Ho; 1957 v D, WG (3)
Dunning, P. (Shelbourne), 1971 v Se, I (2)
Dunphy, E. M. (York C), 1966 v Sp; (with Millwall), 1966 v WG; 1967 v T, Sp, T, Cz; 1968 v Cz, Pol; 1969 v Pol, A, D (2), H; 1970 v D, H, Pol, WG (sub); 1971 v Pol, Se (2), I (2), A (23)
Dwyer, N. M. (West Ham U), 1960 v Se, Ch, WG, Se; (with Swansea T), 1961 v W, N, S (2); 1962 v Cz (2); 1964 v Pol (sub), N, E; 1965 v Pol (14)

Eccles, P. (Shamrock R), 1986 v U (sub) (1)
Egan, R. (Dundalk), 1929 v Bel (1)
Eglington, T. J. (Shamrock R), 1946 v P, Sp; (with Everton), 1947 v E, Sp, P; 1948 v P; 1949 v Sw, P, Se; 1951 v N, Arg; 1952 v WG (2), A, Sp; 1953 v F, A; 1954 v F, L, F; 1955 v N, Ho, WG; 1956 v Sp (24)
Ellis, P. (Bohemians), 1935 v Sw, G; 1936 v Ho, Sw, L; 1937 v G, H (7)

Fagan, E. (Shamrock R), 1973 v N (sub) (1)
Fagan, F. (Manchester C), 1955 v N; 1960 v Se; (with Derby Co), 1960 v Ch, WG, Se; 1961 v W, N, S (8)
Fagan, J. (Shamrock R), 1926 v I (1)
Fairclough, M. (Dundalk), 1982 v Ch (sub), Tr (sub) (2)
Fallon, S. (Celtic), 1951 v N; 1952 v WG (2), A, Sp; 1953 v F; 1955 v N, WG (8)

Fallon, W. J. (Notts Co), 1935 v H; 1936 v H; 1937 v H, Sw, F; 1939 v Sw, Pol; (with Sheffield W), 1939 v H, G (9)
Farquharson, T. G. (Cardiff C), 1929 v Bel; 1930 v Bel; 1931 v Sp; 1932 v Sp (4)
Farrell, P. (Hibernian), 1937 v Sw, F (2)
Farrell, P. D. (Shamrock R), 1946 v P, Sp; (with Everton), 1947 v Sp, P; 1948 v P, Sp; 1949 v Sw, P (sub), Sp; 1950 v E, Fi, Se; 1951 v Arg, N; 1952 v WG (2), A, Sp; 1953 v F, A; 1954 v F (2); 1955 v N, Ho, WG; 1956 v Y, Sp; 1957 v E (28)
Feenan, J. J. (Sunderland), 1937 v Sw, F (2)
Finucane, A. (Limerick), 1967 v T, Cz; 1969 v Cz, D, H; 1970 v S, Cz; 1971 v Se, I (1+1 sub); 1972 v A (11)
Fitzgerald, F. J. (Waterford), 1955 v Ho; 1956 v Ho (2)
Fitzgerald, P. J. (Leeds U), 1961 v W, N, S; (with Chester), 1962 v Cz (2) (5)
Fitzpatrick, K. (Limerick), 1970 v Cz (1)
Fitzsimons, A. G. (Middlesbrough), 1950 v Fi, Bel; 1952 v WG (2), A, Sp; 1953 v F, A; 1954 v F, L, F; 1955 v Ho, N, WG; 1956 v Y, Sp, Ho; 1957 v D, WG, E (2); 1958 v D, Pol, A; 1959 v Pol; (with Lincoln C), 1959 v Cz (26)
Flood, J. J. (Shamrock R), 1926 v I; 1929 v Bel; 1930 v Bel; 1931 v Sp; 1932 v Sp (5)
Fogarty, A. (Sunderland), 1960 v WG, Se; 1961 v S; 1962 v Cz (2); 1963 v Ic (2), S (sub); 1964 v A (2); (with Hartlepools U), Sp (11)
Foley, J. (Cork), 1934 v Bel, Ho; (with Celtic), 1935 v H, Sw, G; 1937 v G, H (7)
Foley, M. (Shelbourne), 1926 v I (1)
Foley, T. C. (Northampton T), 1964 v Sp, Pol, N; 1965 v Pol, Bel; 1966 v Sp (2), WG; 1967 v Cz (9)
Foy, T. (Shamrock R), 1938 v N; 1939 v H (2)
Fullam, J. (Preston NE), 1961 v N; (with Shamrock R), 1964 v Sp, Pol, N; 1966 v A, Bel; 1968 v Pol; 1969 v Pol, A, D; 1970 v Cz (sub) (11)
Fullam, R. (Shamrock R), 1926 v I; 1927 v I (2)

Gallagher, C. (Celtic), 1967 v T, Cz (2)
Gallagher, M. (Hibernian), 1954 v L (1)
Gallagher, P. (Falkirk), 1932 v Sp (1)
Galvin, A. (Tottenham H), 1983 v Ho, Ma; 1984 v Ho (sub), Is (sub); 1985 v M, USSR, N, D, I, N, Sp; 1986 v U, Ic, Cz; 1987 v Bel (2), S, Bul, L; (with Sheffield W), 1988 v L, Bul, R, Pol, N, E, USSR, Ho; 1989 v Sp; (with Swindon T), 1990 v WG (29)
Gannon, E. (Notts Co), 1949 v Sw; (with Sheffield W), 1949 v Bel, P, Se, Sp; 1950 v Fi; 1951 v N; 1952 v WG, A; 1954 v L, F; 1955 v N; (with Shelbourne), 1955 v N, WG (14)
Gannon, M. (Shelbourne), 1972 v A (1)
Gaskins, P. (Shamrock R), 1934 v Bel, Ho; 1935 v H, Sw, G; (with St James' Gate), 1938 v Cz, Pol (7)
Gavin, J. T. (Norwich C), 1950 v Fi (2); 1953 v F; 1954 v L; (with Tottenham H), 1955 v Ho, WG; (with Norwich C), 1957 v D (7)
Geoghegan, M. (St James' Gate), 1937 v G; 1938 v N (2)
Gibbons, A. (St Patrick's Ath), 1952 v WG; 1954 v L; 1956 v Y, Sp (4)
Gilbert, R. (Shamrock R), 1966 v WG (1)
Giles, C. (Doncaster R), 1951 v N (1)
Giles, M. J. (Manchester U), 1960 v Se, Ch; 1961 v W, N, S (2); 1962 v Cz (2), A; 1963 v Ic, S; (with Leeds U), 1964 v A (2), Sp (2), Pol, N, E; 1965 v Sp; 1966 v Sp (2), A, Bel; 1967 v Sp, T (2); 1969 v A, D, Cz; 1970 v S, Pol, WG; 1971 v I; 1973 v F, USSR; 1974 v Br, U, Ch; 1975 v USSR, T, Sw, USSR, Sw; (with WBA), 1976 v T; 1977 v E, T, F (2), Pol, Bul; (with Shamrock R), 1978 v Bul, T, Pol, N, D; 1979 v Ni, D, Bul, WG (59)
Givens, D. J. (Manchester U), 1969 v D, H; 1970 v S, Cz, D, H; (with Luton T), 1970 v Pol, WG; 1971 v Se, I (2), A; 1972 v Ir, Ec, P; (with QPR), 1973 v F, USSR, Pol, F, N; 1974 v Pol, Br, U, Ch; 1975 v USSR, T, Sw, USSR, Sw, WG; 1976 v T, N, Pol; 1977 v E, T, F (2), Sp, Bul; 1978 v Bul, N, D; (with Birmingham C), 1979 v Ni (sub), E, D, Bul, WG; 1980 v US (sub), Ni (sub), Sw, Arg; 1981 v Ho, Bel, Cy (sub), W; (with Neuchatel X), 1982 v F (sub) (56)
Glen, W. (Shamrock R), 1927 v I; 1929 v Bel; 1930 v Bel; 1932 v Sp; 1936 v Ho, Sw, H, L (8)
Glynn, D. (Drumcondra), 1952 v WG; 1955 v N (2)
Godwin, T. F. (Shamrock R), 1949 v P, Se, Sp; 1950 v Fi, E; (with Leicester C), 1950 v Fi, Se, Bel; 1951 v N; (with Bournemouth), 1956 v Ho; 1957 v E; 1958 v D, Pol (13)
Golding, J. (Shamrock R), 1928 v Bel; 1930 v Bel (2)
Gorman, W. C. (Bury), 1936 v Sw, H, L; 1937 v G, H; 1938 v N, Cz, Pol; 1939 v Sw, Pol (with Brentford) H; 1947 v E, P (13)
Grace, J. (Drumcondra), 1926 v I (1)
Grealish, A. (Orient), 1976 v N, Pol; 1978 v N, D; 1979 v Ni, E, WG; (with Luton T), 1980 v W, Cz, Bul, US, Ni, E, Cy, Sw, Arg; 1981 v WG'B', Ho, Bel, F, Cy, W, Bel, Pol; (with Brighton & HA), 1982 v Ho, Alg, Ch, Br, Tr; 1983 v Ho, Sp, Ic, Sp; 1984 v Ic, Ho; (with WBA), Pol, Chn; 1985 v M, USSR, N, D, Sp (sub), Sw; 1986 v USSR, D (45)
Gregg, E. (Bohemians), 1978 v Pol, D (sub); 1979 v E (sub), D, Bul, WG; 1980 v W, Cz (8)
Griffith, R. (Walsall), 1935 v H (1)
Grimes, A. A. (Manchester U), 1978 v T, Pol, N (sub); 1980 v Bul, US, Ni, E, Cy; 1981 v WG'B' (sub), Cz, Pol; 1982 v Alg; 1983 v Sp (2); (with Coventry C), 1984 v Pol, Is; (with Luton T), 1988 v L, R (18)

Hale, A. (Aston Villa), 1962 v A; (with Doncaster R), 1963 v Ic; 1964 v Sp (2); (with Waterford), 1967 v Sp; 1968 v Pol (sub); 1969 v Pol, A, D; 1970 v S, Cz; 1971 v Pol (sub); 1972 v A (sub) (13)
Hamilton, T. (Shamrock R), 1959 v Cz (2) (2)
Hand, E. K. (Portsmouth), 1969 v Cz (sub); 1970 v Pol, WG; 1971 v Pol, A; 1973 v USSR, F, USSR, Pol, F; 1974 v Pol, Br, U, Ch; 1975 v T, Sw, USSR, Sw, WG; 1976 v T (20)
Harrington, W. (Cork), 1936 v Ho, Sw, H, L; 1938 v Pol (sub) (5)
Hartnett, J. B. (Middlesbrough), 1949 v Sp; 1954 v L (2)
Haverty, J. (Arsenal), 1956 v Ho; 1957 v D, WG, E (2); 1958 v D, Pol, A; 1959 v Pol; 1960 v Se, Ch; 1961 v W, N, S (2); (with Blackburn R), 1962 v Cz (2); (with Millwall), 1963 v S; 1964 v A, Sp, Pol, N, E; (with Celtic), 1965 v Pol; (with Bristol R), 1965 v Sp; (with Shelbourne), 1966 v Sp (2), WG, A, Bel; 1967 v T, Sp (32)
Hayes, A. W. P. (Southampton), 1979 v D (1)
Hayes, W. E. (Huddersfield T), 1947 v E, P (2)
Hayes, W. J. (Limerick), 1949 v Bel (1)
Healey, R. (Cardiff C), 1977 v Pol; 1980 v E (sub) (2)
Heighway, S. D. (Liverpool), 1971 v Pol, Se (2), I, A; 1973 v USSR; 1975 v USSR, T, USSR, WG; 1976 v T, N; 1977 v E, F (2), Sp, Bul; 1978 v Bul, N, D; 1979 v Ni, Bul; 1980 v Bul, US, Ni, E, Cy, Arg; 1981 v Bel, F, Cy, W, Bel; (with Minnesota K), 1982 v Ho (34)
Henderson, B. (Drumcondra), 1948 v P, Sp (2)
Hennessy, J. (Shelbourne), 1965 v Pol, Bel, Sp; 1966 v WG; (with St Patrick's Ath), 1969 v A (5)
Herrick, J. (Cork Hibernians), 1972 v A, Ch (sub); (with Shamrock R), 1973 v F (sub) (3)
Higgins, J. (Birmingham C), 1951 v Arg (1)
Holmes, J. (Coventry C), 1971 v A (sub); 1973 v F, USSR, Pol, F, N; 1974 v Pol, Br; 1975 v USSR, Sw; 1976 v T, N, Pol; 1977 v E, T, F, Sp; (with Tottenham H), F, Pol, Bul; 1978 v Bul, T, Pol, N, D; 1979 v Ni, E, D, Bul; (with Vancouver W), 1981 v W (30)
Horlacher, A. F. (Bohemians), 1930 v Bel; 1932 v Sp, Ho; 1934 v Ho (sub); 1935 v H; 1936 v Ho, Sw (7)

Houghton, R. J. (Oxford U), 1986 v W, U, Ic, Cz; 1987 v Bel (2), S (2), Pol, L; 1988 v L, Bul; (with Liverpool), Is, Y, N, E, USSR, Ho; 1989 v Ni, Tun, Sp, F, H, Sp, Ma, H; 1990 v Ni, Ma, Fi, E, Eg, Ho, R, I; 1991 v Mor, T, E (2), Pol, Ch, US; 1992 v H, Alb, US, I, P; (with Aston Villa), 1993 v D, Sp, Ni, D, Alb, La, Li; 1994 v Li, Sp, Ni, Bol, G (sub), I, M, N, Ho; (with C Palace), 1995 v P, A (64)

Howlett, G. (Brighton & HA), 1984 v Chn (sub) (1)

Hoy, M. (Dundalk), 1938 v N; 1939 v Sw, Pol, H (2), G (6)

Hughton, C. (Tottenham H), 1980 v US, E, Sw, Arg; 1981 v Ho, Bel, F, Cy, W, Bel, Pol; 1982 v F; 1983 v Ho, Sp, Ma, Sp; 1984 v Ic, Ho, Ma; 1985 v M (sub), USSR, N, I, Is, E, Sp; 1986 v Sw, USSR, U, Ic; 1987 v Bel, Bul; 1988 v Is, Y, Pol, N, E, USSR, Ho; 1989 v Ni, F, H, Sp, Ma, H; 1990 v W (sub), USSR (sub), Fi, T (sub), Ma; 1991 v T; (with West Ham U), Ch; 1992 v T (53)

Hurley, C. J. (Millwall), 1957 v E; (with Sunderland), 1958 v D, Pol, A; 1959 v Cz (2); 1960 v Se, Ch, WG, Se; 1961 v W, N, S (2); 1962 v Cz (2), A; 1963 v Ic (2), S; 1964 v A (2), Sp (2), Pol, N; 1965 v Sp; 1966 v WG, A, Bel; 1967 v T, Sp, T, Cz; 1968 v Cz, Pol; 1969 v Pol, D, Cz, (with Bolton W), H (40)

Hutchinson, F. (Drumcondra), 1935 v Sw, G (2)

Irwin, D. J. (Manchester U), 1991 v Mor, T, W, E, Pol, US; 1992 v H, Pol, W, US, Alb, US (sub), I; 1993 v La, D, Sp, Ni, D, Alb, La, Li; 1994 v Li, Sp, Ni, Bol, G, I, M; 1995 v La, Lie, Ni, E, Ni, P, Lie, A (36)

Jordan, D. (Wolverhampton W), 1937 v Sw, F (2)

Jordan, W. (Bohemians), 1934 v Ho; 1938 v N (2)

Kavanagh, P. J. (Celtic), 1931 v Sp; 1932 v Sp (2)

Keane, R. M. (Nottingham F), 1991 v Ch; 1992 v H, Pol, W, Sw, Alb, US; 1993 v La, D, Sp, W, Ni, D, Alb, La, Li; (with Manchester U), 1994 v Li, Sp, Ni, Bol, G, CzR (sub), I, M, N, Ho; 1995 v Ni (2) (28)

Keane, T. R. (Swansea T), 1949 v Sw, P, Se, Sp (4)

Kearin, M. (Shamrock R), 1972 v A (1)

Kearns, F. T. (West Ham U), 1954 v L (1)

Kearns, M. (Oxford U), 1971 v Pol (sub); (with Walsall), 1974 v Pol (sub), U, Ch; 1976 v N, Pol; 1977 v E, T, F (2), Sp, Bul; 1978 v N, D; 1979 v Ni, E; (with Wolverhampton W), 1980 v US, Ni (18)

Kelly, A. T. (Sheffield U), 1993 v W (sub); 1994 v Ru (sub), G; 1995 v La, Ni, E, Ni, P, Lie, A (10)

Kelly, D. T. (Walsall), 1988 v Is, R, Y; (with West Ham U), 1989 v Tun (sub); (with Leicester C), 1990 v USSR, Ma; 1991 v Mor, W (sub), Ch, US; 1992 v H; (with Newcastle U), I (sub), P; 1993 v Sp (sub), Ni; (with Wolverhampton W), 1994 v Ru, N (sub); 1995 v E, Ni (19)

Kelly, G. (Leeds U), 1994 v Ru, Ho, Bol (sub), G (sub), CzR, N, Ho; 1995 v La, Lie, Ni (2), P, Lie, A (14)

Kelly, J. (Derry C), 1932 v Ho; 1934 v Bel; 1936 v Sw, L (4)

Kelly, J. A. (Drumcondra), 1957 v WG, E; (with Preston NE), 1962 v A; 1963 v Ic (2), S; 1964 v A (2), Sp (2), Pol; 1965 v Bel; 1966 v A, Bel; 1967 v Sp (2), T, Cz; 1968 v Pol, Cz; 1969 v Pol, A, D, Cz, D, H; 1970 v S, D, H, Pol, WG; 1971 v Pol, Se (2), I (2), A; 1972 v Ir, Ec, Ch, P; 1973 v USSR, F, USSR, Pol, F, N (47)

Kelly, J. P. V. (Wolverhampton W), 1961 v W, N, S; 1962 v Cz (2) (5)

Kelly, M. J. (Portsmouth), 1988 v Y, Pol (sub); 1989 v Tun; 1991 v Mor (4)

Kelly, N. (Nottingham F), 1954 v L (1)

Kendrick, J. (Everton), 1927 v I; (with Dolphin) 1934 v Bel, Ho; 1936 v Ho (4)

Kenna, J. J. (Blackburn R), 1995 v P (sub), Lie (sub), A (sub) (3)

Kennedy, M. F. (Portsmouth), 1986 v Ic, Cz (sub) (2)

Kennedy, W. (St James' Gate), 1932 v Ho; 1934 v Bel, Ho (3)

Keogh, J. (Shamrock R), 1966 v WG (sub) (1)

Keogh, S. (Shamrock R), 1959 v Pol (1)

Kernaghan, A. N. (Middlesbrough), 1993 v La, D (2), Alb, La, Li; 1994 v Li; (with Manchester C), Sp, Ni, Bol (sub), CzR; 1995 v Lie, E (13)

Kiernan, F. W. (Shamrock R), 1951 v Arg, N; (with Southampton), 1952 v WG (2), A (5)

Kinnear, J. P. (Tottenham H), 1967 v T; 1968 v Cz, Pol; 1969 v A; 1970 v Cz, D, H, Pol; 1971 v Se (sub), I; 1972 v Ir, Ec, Ch, P; 1973 v USSR, F; 1974 v Pol, Br, U, Ch; 1975 v USSR, T, Sw, USSR, WG; (with Brighton & HA), 1976 v T (sub) (26)

Kinsella, J. (Shelbourne), 1928 v Bel (1)

Kinsella, O. (Shamrock R), 1932 v Ho; 1938 v N (2)

Kirkland, A. (Shamrock R), 1927 v I (1)

Lacey, W. (Shelbourne), 1927 v I; 1928 v Bel; 1930 v Bel (3)

Langan, D. (Derby Co), 1978 v T, N; 1980 v Sw, Arg; (with Birmingham C), 1981 v WG'B', Ho, Bel, F, Cy, W, Bel, Cz, Pol; 1982 v Ho, F; (with Oxford U), 1985 v N, Sp, Sw; 1986 v W, U; 1987 v Bel, S, Pol, Br (sub), L (sub); 1988 v L (26)

Lawler, J. F. (Fulham), 1953 v A; 1954 v L, F; 1955 v N, H, N, WG; 1956 v Y (8)

Lawlor, J. C. (Drumcondra), 1949 v Bel; (with Doncaster R), 1951 v N, Arg (3)

Lawlor, M. (Shamrock R), 1971 v Pol, Se (2), I (sub); 1973 v Pol (5)

Lawrenson, M. (Preston NE), 1977 v Pol; (with Brighton), 1978 v Bul, Pol, N (sub); 1979 v Ni, E; 1980 v E, Cy, Sw; 1981 v Ho, Bel, F, Cy, Pol; (with Liverpool), 1982 v Ho, F; 1983 v Ho, Sp, Ic, Ma, Sp; 1984 v Ic, Ho, Ma, Is; 1985 v USSR, N, D, I, E, N; 1986 v Sw, USSR, D; 1987 v Bel, S; 1988 v Bul, Is (38)

Leech, M. (Shamrock R), 1969 v Cz, D, H; 1972 v A, Ir, Ec, P; 1973 v USSR (sub) (8)

Lennon, C. (St James' Gate), 1935 v H, Sw, G (3)

Lennox, G. (Dolphin), 1931 v Sp; 1932 v Sp (2)

Lowry, D. (St Patrick's Ath), 1962 v A (sub) (1)

Lunn, R. (Dundalk), 1939 v Sw, Pol (2)

Lynch, J. (Cork Bohemians), 1934 v Bel (1)

McAlinden, J. (Portsmouth), 1946 v P, Sp (2)

McAteer, J. W. (Bolton W), 1994 v Ru, Ho (sub), Bol (sub), G, CzR (sub), I (sub), M (sub), N, Ho (sub); 1995 v La, Lie, Ni (2 sub), Lie (14)

McCann, J. (Shamrock R), 1957 v WG (1)

McCarthy, J. (Bohemians), 1926 v I; 1928 v Bel; 1930 v Bel (3)

McCarthy, M. (Manchester C), 1984 v Pol, Chn; 1985 v M, D, I, Is, E, Sp, Sw; 1986 v Sw, USSR, W (sub), U, Ic, Cz; 1987 v S (2), Pol, Bul, Bel (with Celtic), Br, L; 1988 v Bul, Is, R, Y, N, E, USSR, Ho; 1989 v Ni, Tun, Sp, F, H, Sp; (with Lyon), 1990 v WG, Ni (with Millwall), W, USSR, Fi, T, E, Eg, Ho, R, I; 1991 v Mor, T, E, US; 1992 v H, T, Alb (sub), US, I, P (57)

McCarthy, M. (Shamrock R), 1932 v Ho (1)

McConville, T. (Dundalk), 1972 v A; (with Waterford), 1973 v USSR, F, USSR, Pol, F (6)

McDonagh, Joe (Shamrock R), 1984 v Pol (sub), Ma (sub); 1985 v M (sub) (3)

McDonagh, J. (Everton), 1981 v WG'B', W, Bel, Cz; (with Bolton W), 1982 v Ho, F, Ch, Br; 1983 v Ho, Sp, Ic, Ma, Sp; (with Notts Co), 1984 v Ic, Ho, Pol; 1985 v M, USSR, N, D, Sp, Sw; 1986 v Sw, USSR (with Wichita Wings) D (25)

McEvoy, M. A. (Blackburn R), 1961 v S (2); 1963 v S; 1964 v A, Sp (2), Pol, N, E; 1965 v Pol, Bel, Sp; 1966 v Sp (2); 1967 v Sp, T, Cz (17)

McGee, P. (QPR), 1978 v T, N (sub), D (sub); 1979 v Ni, E, D (sub), Bul (sub); 1980 v Cz, Bul; (with Preston NE), US, Ni, Cy, Sw, Arg; 1981 v Bel (sub) (15)
McGoldrick, E. J. (C Palace), 1992 v Sw, US, I, P (sub); 1993 v D, W, Ni (sub), D; (with Arsenal), 1994 v Ni, Ru, Ho, CzR; 1995 v La (sub), Lie, E (15)
McGowan, D. (West Ham U), 1949 v P, Se, Sp (3)
McGowan, J. (Cork U), 1947 v Sp (1)
McGrath, M. (Blackburn R), 1958 v A; 1959 v Pol, Cz (2); 1960 v Se, WG, Se; 1961 v W; 1962 v Cz (2); 1963 v S; 1964 v A (2), E; 1965 v Pol, Bel, Sp; 1966 v Sp; (with Bradford), 1966 v WG, A, Bel; 1967 v T (22)
McGrath, P. (Manchester U), 1985 v I (sub), Is, E, N (sub), Sw (sub); 1986 v Sw (sub), D, W, Ic, Cz; 1987 v Bel (2), S (2), Pol, Bul, Br, L; 1988 v L, Bul, Y, Pol, N, E, Ho; 1989 v Ni, F, H, Sp, Ma, H; (with Aston Villa), 1990 v WG, Ma, USSR, Fi, T, E, Eg, Ho, R, I; 1991 v E (2), W, Pol, Ch (sub), US; 1992 v Pol, T, Sw, US, Alb, US, I, P; 1993 v La, Sp, Ni, D, La, Li; 1994 v Sp, Ni, G, CzR, I, M, N, Ho; 1995 v La, Ni, E, Ni, P, Lie, A (76)
McGuire, W. (Bohemians), 1936 v Ho (1)
McKenzie, G. (Southend U), 1938 v N (2), Cz, Pol; 1939 v Sw, Pol, H (2), G (9)
Mackey, G. (Shamrock R), 1957 v D, WG, E (3)
McLoughlin, A. F. (Swindon T), 1990 v Ma, E (sub), Eg (sub); 1991 v Mor (sub), E (sub); (with Southampton), W, Ch (sub); 1992 v H (sub), W (sub); (with Portsmouth), US, I (sub), P; 1993 v W; 1994 v Ni (sub), Ru, Ho (sub); 1995 v Lie (sub) (17)
McLoughlin, F. (Fordsons), 1930 v Bel; (with Cork), 1932 v Sp (2)
McMillan, W. (Belfast Celtic), 1946 v P, Sp (2)
McNally, J. B. (Luton T), 1959 v Cz; 1961 v S; 1963 v Ic (3)
Macken, A. (Derby Co), 1977 v Sp (1)
Madden, O. (Cork), 1936 v H (1)
Maguire, J. (Shamrock R), 1929 v Bel (1)
Malone, G. (Shelbourne), 1949 v Bel (1)
Mancini, T. J. (QPR), 1974 v Pol, Br, U, Ch; (with Arsenal), 1975 v USSR (5)
Martin, C. (Bo'ness), 1927 v I (1)
Martin, C. J. (Glentoran), 1946 v P (sub), Sp; 1947 v E; (with Leeds U), 1947 v Sp; 1948 v P, Sp; (with Aston Villa), 1949 v Sw, Bel, P, Se, Sp; 1950 v Fi, E, Fi, Se, Bel; 1951 v Arg; 1952 v WG, A, Sp; 1954 v F (2), L; 1955 v N, Ho, N, WG; 1956 v Y, Sp, Ho (30)
Martin, M. P. (Bohemians), 1972 v A, Ir, Ec, Ch, P; 1973 v USSR; (with Manchester U), 1973 v USSR, Pol, F, N; 1974 v Pol, Br, U, Ch; 1975 v USSR, T, Sw, USSR, Sw, WG; (with WBA), 1976 v T, N, Pol; 1977 v E, T, F (2), Sp, Pol, Bul; (with Newcastle U), 1979 v D, Bul, WG; 1980 v W, Cz, Bul, US, Ni; 1981 v WG'B', F, Bel, Cz; 1982 v Ho, F, Alg, Ch, Br, Tr; 1983 v Ho, Sp, Ma, Sp (52)
Meagan, M. K. (Everton), 1961 v S; 1962 v A; 1963 v Ic; 1964 v Sp; (with Huddersfield T), 1965 v Bel; 1966 v Sp (2), A, Bel; 1967 v Sp, T, Sp, T, Cz; 1968 v Cz, Pol; (with Drogheda), 1970 v S (17)
Meehan, P. (Drumcondra), 1934 v Ho (1)
Milligan, M. J. (Oldham Ath), 1992 v US (sub) (1)
Monahan, P. (Sligo R), 1935 v Sw, G (2)
Mooney, J. (Shamrock R), 1965 v Pol, Bel (2)
Moore, P. (Shamrock R), 1931 v Sp; 1932 v Ho; (with Aberdeen), 1934 v Bel, Ho; 1935 v H, G; (with Shamrock R), 1936 v Ho; 1937 v G, H (9)
Moran, K. (Manchester U), 1980 v Sw, Arg; 1981 v WG'B', Bel, F, Cy, W (sub), Bel, Cz, Pol; 1982 v F, Alg; 1983 v Ic; 1984 v Ic, Ho, Ma, Is; 1985 v M; 1986 v D, Ic, Cz; 1987 v Bel (2), S (2), Pol, Bul, Br, L; 1988 v L, Bul, Is, R, Y, Pol, N, E, USSR, Ho; (with Sporting Gijon), 1989 v Ni, Sp, H, Sp, Ma, H; 1990 v Ni, Ma; (with Blackburn R), W, USSR (sub), Ma, E, Eg, Ho, R, I; 1991 v T (sub), W, E, Pol, Ch, US; 1992 v Pol, US; 1993 v D, Sp, Ni, Alb; 1994 v Li, Sp, Ho, Bol (71)
Moroney, T. (West Ham U), 1948 v Sp; 1949 v P, Se, Sp; 1950 v Fi, E, Fi, Bel; 1951 v N (2); 1952 v WG; (with Evergreen U), 1954 v F (12)
Morris, C. B. (Celtic), 1988 v Is, R, Y, Pol, N, E, USSR, Ho; 1989 v Ni, Tun, Sp, F, H (1 + 1 sub); 1990 v WG, Ni, Ma (sub), W, USSR, Fi (sub), T, E, Eg, Ho, R, I; 1991 v E; 1992 v H (sub), Pol, W, Sw, US (2), P; (with Middlesbrough), 1993 v W (35)
Moulson, C. (Lincoln C), 1936 v H, L; (with Notts Co), 1937 v H, Sw, F (5)
Moulson, G. B. (Lincoln C), 1948 v P, Sp; 1949 v Sw (3)
Mucklan, C. (Drogheda U), 1978 v Pol (1)
Muldoon, T. (Aston Villa), 1927 v I (1)
Mulligan, P. M. (Shamrock R), 1969 v Cz, D, H; 1970 v S, Cz, D; (with Chelsea), 1970 v H, Pol, WG; 1971 v Pol, Se, I; 1972 v A, Ir, Ec, Ch, P; (with C Palace), 1973 v F, USSR, Pol, F, N; 1974 v Pol, Br, U, Ch; 1975 v USSR, T, Sw, USSR, Sw; (with WBA), 1976 v T, Pol; 1977 v E, T, F (2), Pol, Bul; 1978 v Bul, N, D; 1979 v E, D, Bul (sub), WG; (with Shamrock R), 1980 v W, Cz, Bul, US (sub) (50)
Munroe, L. (Shamrock R), 1954 v L (1)
Murphy, A. (Clyde), 1956 v Y (1)
Murphy, B. (Bohemians), 1986 v U (1)
Murphy, J. (C Palace), 1980 v W, US, Cy (3)
Murray, T. (Dundalk), 1950 v Bel (1)

Newman, W. (Shelbourne), 1969 v D (1)
Nolan, R. (Shamrock R), 1957 v D, WG, E; 1958 v Pol; 1960 v Ch, WG, Se; 1962 v Cz (2); 1963 v Ic (10)

O'Brien, F. (Philadelphia F), 1980 v Cz, E, Cy (sub) (3)
O'Brien, L. (Shamrock R), 1986 v U; (with Manchester U), 1987 v Br; 1988 v Is (sub), R (sub), Y (sub), Pol (sub); 1989 v Tun; (with Newcastle U), Sp (sub); 1992 v Sw (sub); 1993 v W; (with Tranmere R), 1994 v Ru (11)
O'Brien, M. T. (Derby Co), 1927 v I; (with Walsall), 1929 v Bel; (with Norwich C), 1930 v Bel; (with Watford), 1932 v Ho (4)
O'Brien, R. (Notts Co), 1976 v N, Pol; 1977 v Sp, Pol; 1980 v Arg (sub) (5)
O'Byrne, L. B. (Shamrock R), 1949 v Bel (1)
O'Callaghan, B. R. (Stoke C), 1979 v WG (sub); 1980 v W, US; 1981 v W; 1982 v Br, Tr (6)
O'Callaghan, K. (Ipswich T), 1981 v WG'B', Cz, Pol; 1982 v Alg, Ch, Br, Tr (sub); 1983 v Sp, Ic (sub), Ma (sub), Sp (sub); 1984 v Ic, Ho, Ma; 1985 v M (sub), N (sub), D (sub), (with Portsmouth) E (sub); 1986 v Sw (sub), USSR (sub); 1987 v Br (21)
O'Connell, A. (Dundalk), 1967 v Sp; (with Bohemians), 1971 v Pol (sub) (2)
O'Connor, T. (Shamrock R), 1950 v Fi, E, Fi, Se (4)
O'Connor, T. (Fulham), 1968 v Cz; (with Dundalk), 1972 v A, Ir (sub), Ec (sub), Ch; (with Bohemians), 1973 v F (sub), Pol (sub) (7)
O'Driscoll, J. F. (Swansea T), 1949 v Sw, Bel, Se (3)
O'Driscoll, S. (Fulham), 1982 v Ch, Br, Tr (sub) (3)
O'Farrell, F. (West Ham U), 1952 v A; 1953 v A; 1954 v F; 1955 v Ho, N; 1956 v Y, Ho; (with Preston NE), 1958 v D; 1959 v Cz (9)
O'Flanagan, K. P. (Bohemians), 1938 v N, Cz, Pol; 1939 v Pol, H (2), G; (with Arsenal), 1947 v E, Sp, P (10)
O'Flanagan, M. (Bohemians), 1947 v E (1)
O'Hanlon, K. G. (Rotherham U), 1988 v Is (1)
O'Kane, P. (Bohemians), 1935 v H, Sw, G (3)
O'Keefe, E. (Everton), 1981 v W; (with Port Vale), 1984 v Chn; 1985 v M, USSR (sub), E (5)
O'Keefe, T. (Cork), 1934 v Bel; (with Waterford), 1938 v Cz, Pol (3)
O'Leary, D. (Arsenal), 1977 v E, F (2), Sp, Bul; 1978 v Bul, N, D; 1979 v E, Bul, WG; 1980 v W, Bul, Ni, E, Cy; 1981

v WG'B', Ho, Cz, Pol; 1982 v Ho, F; 1983 v Ho, Ic, Sp; 1984 v Pol, Is, Chn; 1985 v USSR, N, D, Is, E (sub), N, Sp, Sw; 1986 v Sw, USSR, D, W; 1989 v Sp, Ma, H; 1990 v WG, Ni (sub), Ma, W (sub), USSR, Fi, T, Ma, R (sub); 1991 v Mor, T, E (2), Pol, Ch; 1992 v H, Pol, T, W, Sw, US, Alb, I, P; 1993 v W (68)

O'Leary, P. (Shamrock R), 1980 v Bul, US, Ni, E (sub), Cz, Arg; 1981 v Ho (7)

O'Mahoney, M. T. (Bristol R), 1938 v Cz, Pol; 1939 v Sw, Pol, H, G (6)

O'Neill, F. S. (Shamrock R), 1962 v Cz (2); 1965 v Pol, Bel, Sp; 1966 v Sp (2), WG, A; 1967 v Sp, T, Sp, T; 1969 v Pol, A, D, Cz, D (sub), H (sub); 1972 v A (20)

O'Neill, J. (Everton), 1952 v Sp; 1953 v F, A; 1954 v F, L, F; 1955 v N, Ho, N, WG; 1956 v Y, Sp; 1957 v D; 1958 v A; 1959 v Pol, Cz (2) (17)

O'Neill, J. (Preston NE), 1961 v W (1)

O'Neill, W. (Dundalk), 1936 v Ho, Sw, H, L; 1937 v G, H, Sw, F; 1938 v N; 1939 v H, G (11)

O'Regan, K. (Brighton & HA), 1984 v Ma, Pol; 1985 v M, Sp (sub) (4)

O'Reilly, J. (Brideville), 1932 v Ho; (with Aberdeen), 1934 v Bel, Ho; (with Brideville), 1936 v Ho; Sw, H, L; (with St James' Gate), 1937 v G, H, Sw, F; 1938 v N (2), Cz, Pol; 1939 v Sw, Pol, H (2), G (20)

O'Reilly, J. (Cork U), 1946 v P, Sp (2)

Peyton, G. (Fulham), 1977 v Sp (sub); 1978 v Bul, T, Pol; 1979 v D, Bul, WG; 1980 v W, Cz, Bul, E, Cy, Sw, Arg; 1981 v Ho, Bel, F, Cy; 1982 v Tr; 1985 v M (sub); 1986 v W, Cz; (with Bournemouth), 1988 v L, Pol; 1989 v Ni, Tun; 1990 v USSR, Ma; 1991 v Ch; (with Everton) 1992 v US (2), I (sub), P (33)

Peyton, N. (Shamrock R), 1957 v WG; (with Leeds U), 1960 v WG, Se (sub); 1961 v W; 1963 v Ic, S (6)

Phelan, T. (Wimbledon), 1992 v H, Pol (sub), T, W, Sw, US, I (sub), P; (with Manchester C), 1993 v La (sub), D, Sp, Ni, Alb, La, Li; 1994 v Li, Sp, Ni, Ho, Bol, G, CzR, I, M, Ho; 1995 v E (26)

Quinn, N. J. (Arsenal), 1986 v Ic (sub), Cz; 1987 v Bul (sub), Br (sub); 1988 v L (sub), Bul (sub), Is, R (sub), Pol (sub), E (sub); 1989 v Tun (sub), Sp (sub), H (sub); (with Manchester C), 1990 v USSR, Ma, Eg (sub), Ho, R, I; 1991 v Mor, T, E (2) W, Pol; 1992 v H, W (sub), US, Alb, US, I (sub), P; 1993 v La, D, Sp, Ni, D, Alb, La, Li; 1994 v Li, Sp, Ni; 1995 v La, Lie, Ni, E, Ni, P, Lie, A (51)

Reid, C. (Brideville), 1931 v Sp (1)

Richardson, D. J. (Shamrock R), 1972 v A (sub); (with Gillingham), 1973 v N (sub); 1980 v Cz (3)

Rigby, A. (St James' Gate), 1935 v H, Sw, G (3)

Ringstead, A. (Sheffield U), 1951 v Arg, N; 1952 v WG (2), A, Sp; 1953 v A; 1954 v F; 1955 v N; 1956 v Y, Sp, Ho; 1957 v E (2); 1958 v D, Pol, A; 1959 v Pol, Cz (2) (20)

Robinson, J. (Bohemians), 1928 v Bel; (with Dolphin), 1931 v Sp (2)

Robinson, M. (Brighton & HA), 1981 v WG'B', F, Cy, Bel, Pol; 1982 v Ho, F, Alg, Ch; 1983 v Ho, Sp, Ic, Ma; (with Liverpool), 1984 v Ic, Ho, Is; 1985 v USSR, N; (with QPR), N, Sp, Sw; 1986 v D (sub), W, Cz (24)

Roche, P. J. (Shelbourne), 1972 v A; (with Manchester U), 1975 v USSR, T, Sw, USSR, Sw, WG; 1976 v T (8)

Rogers, E. (Blackburn R), 1968 v Cz, Pol; 1969 v Pol, A, D, Cz, D, H; 1970 v S, D, H; 1971 v I (2), A; (with Charlton Ath), 1972 v Ir, Ec, Ch, P; 1973 v USSR (19)

Ryan, G. (Derby Co), 1978 v T; (with Brighton & HA), 1979 v E, WG; 1980 v W, Cy (sub), Sw, Arg (sub); 1981 v WG'B', F (sub), Pol (sub); 1982 v Br (sub), Ho (sub), Alg (sub), Ch (sub), Tr; 1984 v Pol, Chn; 1985 v M (18)

Ryan, R. A. (WBA), 1950 v Se, Bel; 1951 v N, Arg, N; 1952 v WG (2), A, Sp; 1953 v F, A; 1954 v F, L, F; 1955 v N; (with Derby Co), 1956 v Sp (16)

Saward, P. (Millwall), 1954 v L; (with Aston Villa), 1957 v E (2); 1958 v D, Pol, A; 1959 v Pol, Cz; 1960 v Se, Ch, WG, Se; 1961 v W, N; (with Huddersfield T), 1961 v S; 1962 v A; 1963 v Ic (2) (18)

Scannell, T. (Southend U), 1954 v L (1)

Scully, P. J. (Arsenal), 1989 v Tun (sub) (1)

Sheedy, K. (Everton), 1984 v Ho (sub), Ma; 1985 v D, I, Is, Sw; 1986 v Sw, D; 1987 v S, Pol; 1988 v Is, R, Pol, E (sub), USSR; 1989 v Ni, Tun, H, Sp, Ma, H; 1990 v Ni, Ma, W (sub), USSR, Fi (sub), T, E, Eg, Ho, R, I; 1991 v W, E, Pol, Ch, US; 1992 v H, Pol, T, W; (with Newcastle U), Sw (sub), Alb; 1993 v La, W (sub) (45)

Sheridan, J. J. (Leeds U), 1988 v R, Y, Pol, N (sub); 1989 v Sp; (with Sheffield W), 1990 v W, T (sub), Ma, I (sub); 1991 v Mor (sub), T, Ch, US (sub); 1992 v H; 1993 v La; 1994 v Sp (sub), Ho, Bol, G, CzR, I, M, N, Ho; 1995 v La, Lie, Ni, E, Ni, P, Lie, A (32)

Slaven, B. (Middlesbrough), 1990 v W, Fi, T (sub), Ma; 1991 v W, Pol (sub); 1993 v W (7)

Sloan, J. W. (Arsenal), 1946 v P, Sp (2)

Smyth, M. (Shamrock R), 1969 v Pol (sub) (1)

Squires, J. (Shelbourne), 1934 v Ho (1)

Stapleton, F. (Arsenal), 1977 v T, F, Sp, Bul; 1978 v Bul, N, D; 1979 v Ni, E (sub), D, WG; 1980 v W, Bul, Ni, E, Cy; 1981 v WG'B', Ho, Bel, F, Cy, Bel, Cz, Pol; (with Manchester U), 1982 v Ho, F, Alg; 1983 v Ho, Sp, Ic, Ma, Sp; 1984 v Ic, Ho, Ma, Pol, Is, Chn; 1985 v N, D, I, Is, E, N, Sw; 1986 v Sw, USSR, D, U, Ic, Cz (sub); 1987 v Bel (2), S (2), Pol, Bul, L; (with Ajax), 1988 v L, Bul; (with Derby Co), R, Y, N, E, USSR, Ho; (with Le Havre), 1989 v F, Sp, Ma; (with Blackburn R), 1990 v WG, Ma (sub) (71)

Staunton, S. (Liverpool), 1989 v Tun, Sp (2), Ma, H; 1990 v WG, Ni, Ma, W, USSR, Fi, T, Ma, E, Eg, Ho, R, I; 1991 v Mor, T, E (2), W, Pol, Ch, US; (with Aston Villa), 1992 v Pol, T, Sw, US, Alb, US, I, P; 1993 v La, Sp, Ni, D, Alb, La, Li; 1994 v Li, Sp, Ho, Bol, G, CzR, I, M, N, Ho; 1995 v La, Lie, Ni, E, Ni, P, Lie, A (59)

Stevenson, A. E. (Dolphin), 1932 v Ho; (with Everton), 1947 v E, Sp, P; 1948 v P, Sp; 1949 v Sw (7)

Strahan, F. (Shelbourne), 1964 v Pol, N, E; 1965 v Pol; 1966 v WG (5)

Sullivan, J. (Fordsons), 1928 v Bel (1)

Swan, M. M. G. (Drumcondra), 1960 v Se (sub) (1)

Synnott, N. (Shamrock R), 1978 v T, Pol; 1979 v Ni (3)

Taylor, T. (Waterford), 1959 v Pol (sub) (1)

Thomas, P. (Waterford), 1974 v Pol, Br (2)

Townsend, A. D. (Norwich C), 1989 v F, Sp (sub), Ma (sub), H; 1990 v WG (sub), Ni, Ma, W, USSR, Fi (sub), T, Ma (sub), E, Eg, Ho, R, I; (with Chelsea), 1991 v Mor, T, E (2), W, Pol, Ch, US; 1992 v Pol, W, US, Alb, US, I; 1993 v La, D, Sp, Ni, D, Alb, La, Li; (with Aston Villa), 1994 v Li, Ni, Ho, Bol, G, CzR, I, M, N, Ho; 1995 v La, Ni, E, Ni, P (54)

Traynor, T. J. (Southampton), 1954 v L; 1962 v A; 1963 v Ic (2), S; 1964 v A (2), Sp (8)

Treacy, R. C. P. (WBA), 1966 v WG; 1967 v Sp, Cz; 1968 v Cz; (with Charlton Ath), 1968 v Pol; 1969 v Pol, Cz, D; 1970 v S, D, H (sub), Pol (sub), WG (sub); 1971 v Pol, Se (sub+1), I, A; (with Swindon T), 1972 v Ir, Ec, Ch, P; 1973 v USSR, F, USSR, Pol, F, N; 1974 v Pol; (with Preston NE), Br; 1975 v USSR, Sw (2), WG; 1976 v T, N (sub), Pol (sub); (with WBA), 1977 v F, Pol; (with Shamrock R), 1978 v T, Pol; 1980 v Cz (sub) (42)

Tuohy, L. (Shamrock R), 1956 v Y; 1959 v Cz (2); (with Newcastle U), 1962 v A; 1963 v Ic (2); (with Shamrock R), 1964 v A; 1965 v Bel (8)

Turner, C. J. (Southend U), 1936 v Sw; 1937 v G, H, Sw, F; 1938 v N (2), (with West Ham U) Cz, Pol; 1939 v H (10)
Turner, P. (Celtic), 1963 v S; 1964 v Sp (2)

Vernon, J. (Belfast C), 1946 v P, Sp (2)

Waddock, G. (QPR), 1980 v Sw, Arg; 1981 v W, Pol (sub); 1982 v Alg; 1983 v Ic, Ma, Sp, Ho (sub); 1984 v Ma (sub), Ic, Ho, Is; 1985 v I, Is, E, N, Sp; 1986 v USSR; (with Millwall), 1990 v USSR, T (21)
Walsh, D. J. (Linfield), 1946 v P, Sp; (with WBA), 1947 v Sp, P; 1948 v P, Sp; 1949 v Sw, P, Se, Sp; 1950 v E, Fi, Se; 1951 v N; (with Aston Villa), Arg, N; 1952 v Sp; 1953 v A; 1954 v F (2) (20)
Walsh, J. (Limerick), 1982 v Tr (1)
Walsh, M. (Blackpool), 1976 v N, Pol; 1977 v F (sub), Pol; (with Everton), 1979 v Ni (sub); (with QPR), D (sub), Bul, WG (sub); (with Porto), 1981 v Bel (sub), Cz; 1982 v Alg (sub); 1983 v Sp, Ho (sub), Sp (sub); 1984 v Ic (sub), Ma, Pol, Chn; 1985 v USSR, N (sub), D (21)
Walsh, M. (Everton), 1982 v Ch, Br, Tr; 1983 v Ic (4)
Walsh, W. (Manchester C), 1947 v E, Sp, P; 1948 v P, Sp; 1949 v Bel; 1950 v E, Se, Bel (9)
Waters, J. (Grimsby T), 1977 v T; 1980 v Ni (sub) (2)
Watters, F. (Shelbourne), 1926 v I (1)
Weir, E. (Clyde), 1939 v H (2), G (3)
Whelan, R. (St Patrick's Ath), 1964 v A, E (sub) (2)
Whelan, R. (Liverpool), 1981 v Cz (sub); 1982 v Ho (sub), F; 1983 v Ic, Ma, Sp; 1984 v Is; 1985 v USSR, N, I (sub), Is, E, N (sub), Sw (sub); 1986 v USSR (sub), W; 1987 v Bel (sub), S, Bul, Bel, Br, L; 1988 v L, Bul, Pol, N, E, USSR, Ho; 1989 v Ni, F, H, Sp, Ma; 1990 v WG, Ni, Ma, W, Ho (sub); 1991 v Mor, E; 1992 v Sw; 1993 v La, W (sub), Li (sub); 1994 v Li (sub), Sp, Ru, Ho, G (sub), N (sub); (with Southend U), 1995 v Lie, A (53)
Whelan, W. (Manchester U), 1956 v Ho; 1957 v D, E (2) (4)
White, J. J. (Bohemians), 1928 v Bel (1)
Whittaker, R. (Chelsea), 1959 v Cz (1)
Williams, J. (Shamrock R), 1938 v N (1)

UMBRO INTERNATIONAL TROPHY

Wembley, 3 June 1995, 21,142

England (0) 2 *(Anderton, Platt (pen))*
Japan (0) 1 *(Ihara)*

England: Flowers; Neville G, Pearce, Batty (Gascoigne), Scales, Unsworth, Anderton, Beardsley (McManaman), Shearer, Collymore (Sheringham), Platt.
Japan: Maekawa; Tasaka, Hashiratani, Ihara, Narahashi, Morishama (Fukuda), Yamaguchi, Kitazawa, Soma (Yanagimoto), Miura, Nakayama (Kurosaki).

Villa Park, 4 June 1995, 20,131

Brazil (1) 1 *(Edmundo)*
Sweden (0) 0

Brazil: Zetti; Jorginho, Roberto Carlos, Ronaldao, Aldair, Cesar Sampaio (Cruz), Zinho, Dunga, Ronaldo, Edmundo, Juninho.
Sweden: Andersson B; Kamark, Ljung, Alexandersson, Lucic, Bjorklund, Mild, Erlingmark, Dahlin (Lidman), Andersson K (Larsson), Thern (Gudmundsson).

Goodison Park, 6 June 1995, 29,327

Japan (0) 0
Brazil (1) 3 *(Roberto Carlos, Zinho 2)*

Japan: Kojima; Ihara, Narahashi, Tasaka (Moriyasu), Omura, Souma, Morishima (Kurosaki), Kitazawa, Yamaguchi, Miura, Nakayama (Fukuda).
Brazil: Zetti; Jorginho, Roberto Carlos, Marcio Santos, Aldair, Doriva, Zinho (Rivaldo), Dunga, Ronaldo, Edmundo, Juninho (Leonardo).

Elland Road, 8 June 1995, 32,008

England (1) 3 *(Sheringham, Platt, Anderton)*
Sweden (2) 3 *(Mild 2, Andersson K)*

England: Flowers; Barton, Le Saux, Platt, Cooper, Pallister (Scales), Anderton, Beardsley (Barmby), Shearer, Barnes (Gascoigne), Sheringham.
Sweden: Ravelli; Sundgren, Kamark, Alexandersson, Lucic, Bjorklund, Mild, Erlingmark (Andersson O), Gudmundsson, Andersson K (Lidman), Larsson.

City Ground, 10 June 1995, 5591

Sweden (0) 2 *(Andersson K 2)*
Japan (1) 2 *(Fujita, Kurosaki)*

Sweden: Ravelli; Sundgren, Kamark, Alexandersson, Lucic, Bjorklund, Wibran, Andersson O, Gudmundsson (Nilsson), Andersson K, Larsson.
Japan: Shimokawa; Narahashi (Yangaimoto), Ihara, Hashiratani, Omura, Fujita (Moriyasu), Yamaguchi, Kitazawa (Fukuda), Soma, Miura, Kurosaki.

Wembley, 11 June 1995, 67,318

England (1) 1 *(Le Saux)*
Brazil (0) 3 *(Juninho, Ronaldo, Edmundo)*

England: Flowers; Neville G, Pearce, Batty (Gascoigne), Scales (Barton), Cooper, Anderton, Platt, Shearer (Collymore), Sheringham, Le Saux.
Brazil: Zetti; Jorginho, Roberto Carlos, Marcio Santos, Aldair (Ronaldao), Cesar Sampaio, Zinho, Dunga, Ronaldo (Giovanni), Edmundo, Juninho (Leonardo).

	P	*W*	*D*	*L*	*F*	*A*	*Pts*
Brazil	3	3	0	0	7	1	9
England	3	1	1	1	6	7	4
Sweden	3	0	2	1	5	6	2
Japan	3	0	1	2	3	7	1

BRITISH AND IRISH INTERNATIONAL GOALSCORERS SINCE 1872

Where two players with the same surname and initials have appeared for the same country, and one or both have scored, they have been distinguished by reference to the club which appears *first* against their name in the international appearances section (pages 780–830). Unfortunately, four of the scorers in Scotland's 10-2 victory v Ireland in 1888 are unknown, as is the scorer of one of their nine goals v Wales in March 1878.

ENGLAND

A'Court, A. 1
Adams, T. A. 4
Adcock, H. 1
Alcock, C. W. 1
Allen, A. 3
Allen, R. 2
Anderson, V. 2
Anderton, D. R. 3
Astall, G. 1
Athersmith, W. C. 3
Atyeo, P. J. W. 5

Bache, J. W. 4
Bailey, N. C. 2
Baily, E. F. 5
Baker, J. H. 3
Ball, A. J. 8
Bambridge, A. L. 1
Bambridge, E. C. 12
Barclay, R. 2
Barnes, J. 11
Barnes, P. S. 4
Barton, J. 1
Bassett, W. I. 7
Bastin, C. S. 12
Beardsley, P. A. 9
Beasley, A. 1
Beattie, T. K. 1
Becton, F. 2
Bedford, H. 1
Bell, C. 9
Bentley, R. T. F. 9
Bishop, S. M. 1
Blackburn, F. 1
Blissett, L. 3
Bloomer, S. 28
Bond, R. 2
Bonsor, A. G. 1
Bowden, E. R. 1
Bowers, J. W. 2
Bowles, S. 1
Bradford, G. R. W. 1
Bradford, J. 7
Bradley, W. 2
Bradshaw, F. 3
Bridges, B. J. 1
Bridgett, A. 3
Brindle, T. 1
Britton, C. S. 1
Broadbent, P. F. 2
Broadis, I. A. 8
Brodie, J. B. 1
Bromley-Davenport, W. 2
Brook, E. F. 10
Brooking, T. D. 5
Brooks, J. 2
Broome, F. H. 3
Brown, A. 4
Brown, A. S. 1
Brown, G. 5
Brown, J. 3
Brown, W. 1
Buchan, C. M. 4
Bull, S. G. 4
Bullock, N. 2
Burgess, H. 4
Butcher, T. 3
Byrne, J. J. 8

Camsell, G. H. 18
Carter, H. S. 7
Carter, J. H. 4
Chadwick, E. 3
Chamberlain, M. 1
Chambers, H. 5
Channon, M. R. 21
Charlton, J. 6
Charlton, R. 49
Chenery, C. J. 1
Chivers, M. 13
Clarke, A. J. 10
Cobbold, W. N. 7
Cock, J. G. 2
Common, A. 2
Connelly, J. M. 7
Coppell, S. J. 7
Cotterill, G. H. 2
Cowans, G. 2
Crawford, R. 1
Crawshaw, T. H. 1
Crayston, W. J. 1
Creek, F. N. S. 1
Crooks, S. D. 7
Currey, E. S. 2
Currie, A. W. 3
Cursham, A. W. 2
Cursham, H. A. 5

Daft, H. B. 3
Davenport, J. K. 2
Davis, G. 1
Davis, H. 1
Day, S. H. 2
Dean, W. R. 18
Devey, J. H. G. 1
Dewhurst, F. 11
Dix, W. R. 1
Dixon, K. M. 4
Dixon, L. M. 1
Douglas, B. 11
Drake, E. J. 6
Ducat, A. 1
Dunn, A. T. B. 2

Eastham, G. 2
Edwards, D. 5
Elliott, W. H. 3
Evans, R. E. 1

Ferdinand, L. 3
Finney, T. 30
Fleming, H. J. 9
Flowers, R. 10
Forman, Frank 1
Forman, Fred 3
Foster, R. E. 3
Francis, G. C. J. 3
Francis, T. 12
Freeman, B. C. 3
Froggatt, J. 2
Froggatt, R. 2

Galley, T. 1
Gascoigne, P. J. 6
Geary, F. 3
Gibbins, W. V. T. 3
Gilliatt, W. E. 3
Goddard, P. 1
Goodall, J. 12
Goodyer, A. C. 1
Gosling, R. C. 2
Goulden, L. A. 4
Grainger, C. 3
Greaves, J. 44
Grovesnor, A. T. 2
Gunn, W. 1

Haines, J. T. W. 2
Hall, G. W. 9
Halse, H. J. 2
Hampson, J. 5
Hampton, H. 2
Hancocks, J. 2
Hardman, H. P. 1
Harris, S. S. 2
Hassall, H. W. 4
Hateley, M. 9
Haynes, J. N. 18
Hegan, K. E. 4
Henfrey, A. G. 2
Hilsdon, G. R. 14
Hine, E. W. 4
Hirst, D. E. 1
Hitchens, G. A. 5
Hobbis, H. H. F. 1
Hoddle, G. 8
Hodgetts, D. 1
Hodgson, G. 1
Holley, G. H. 8
Houghton, W. E. 5
Howell, R. 1
Hughes, E. W. 1
Hulme, J. H. A. 4
Hunt, G. S. 1
Hunt, R. 18
Hunter, N. 2
Hurst, G. C. 24

Ince, P. E. C. 2

Jack, D. N. B. 3
Johnson, D. E. 6
Johnson, E. 2
Johnson, J. A. 2
Johnson, T. C. F. 5
Johnson, W. H. 1

Kail, E. I. L. 2
Kay, A. H. 1
Keegan, J. K. 21
Kelly, R. 8
Kennedy, R. 3
Kenyon-Slaney, W. S. 2
Keown, M. R. 3
Kevan, D. T. 8
Kidd, B. 1
Kingsford, R. K. 1
Kirchen, A. J. 2
Kirton, W. J. 1

Langton, R. 1
Latchford, R. D. 5
Latherton, E. G. 1
Lawler, C. 1
Lawton, T. 22
Lee, F. 10
Lee, J. 1
Lee, R. M. 1
Lee, S. 2
Le Saux, G. P. 1
Lindley, T. 15
Lineker, G. 48
Lofthouse, J. M. 3
Lofthouse, N. 30
Hon. A. Lyttelton 1

Mabbutt, G. 1
Macdonald, M. 6
Mannion, W. J. 11
Mariner, P. 13
Marsh, R. W. 1
Matthews, S. 11
Matthews, V. 1
McCall, J. 1
McDermott, T. 3
Medley, L. D. 1
Melia, J. 1
Mercer, D. W. 1
Metson, P. C. 1
Milburn, J. E. T. 10
Miller, H. S. 1
Mills, G. R. 3
Milward, A. 3
Mitchell, C. 5
Moore, J. 1
Moore, R. F. 2
Moore, W. G. B. 2
Morren, T. 1
Morris, F. 1
Morris, J. 3
Mortensen, S. H. 23
Morton, J. R. 1
Mosforth, W. 3
Mullen, J. 6
Mullery, A. P. 1

Neal, P. G. 5
Needham, E. 3
Nicholls, J. 1
Nicholson, W. E. 1

O'Grady, M. 3
Osborne, F. R. 3
Own goals 22

Page, L. A. 1
Paine, T. L. 7
Palmer, C. L. 1
Parry, E. H. 1
Parry, R. A. 1
Pawson, F. W. 1
Payne, J. 2
Peacock, A. 3
Pearce, S. 4
Pearson, J. S. 5
Pearson, S. C. 5
Perry, W. 2
Peters, M. 20
Pickering, F. 5
Platt, D. 26
Pointer, R. 2

Quantrill, A. 1

Ramsay, A. E. 3
Revie, D. G. 4
Reynolds, J. 3
Richardson, J. R. 2
Rigby, A. 3
Rimmer, E. J. 2
Roberts, H. 1
Roberts, W. T. 4
Robinson, J. 3

Player	Goals
Robson, B.	26
Robson, R.	4
Rowley, J. F.	6
Royle, J.	2
Rutherford, J.	3
Sagar, C.	1
Sandilands, R. R.	2
Sansom, K.	1
Schofield, J.	1
Seed, J. M.	1
Settle, J.	6
Sewell, J.	3
Shackleton, L. F.	1
Sharp, J.	1
Shearer, A.	5
Shepherd, A.	2
Sheringham, E. P.	1
Simpson, J.	1
Smith, A. M.	2
Smith, G. O.	12
Smith, Joe	1
Smith, J. R.	2
Smith, J. W.	4
Smith, R.	13
Smith, S.	1
Sorby, T. H.	1
Southworth, J.	3
Sparks, F. J.	3
Spence, J. W.	1
Spiksley, F.	5
Spilsbury, B. W.	5
Steele, F. C.	8
Stephenson, G. T.	2
Steven, T. M.	4
Stewart, J.	2
Stiles, N. P.	1
Storer, H.	1
Summerbee, M. G.	1
Tambling, R. V.	1
Taylor, P. J.	2
Taylor, T.	16
Thompson, P. B.	1
Thornewell, G.	1
Tilson, S. F.	6
Townley, W. J.	2
Tueart, D.	2
Vaughton, O. H.	6
Veitch, J. G.	3
Violett, D. S.	1
Waddle, C. R.	6
Walker, W. H.	9
Wall, G.	2
Wallace, D.	1
Walsh, P.	1
Waring, T.	4
Warren, B.	2
Watson, D. V.	4
Watson, V. M.	4
Webb, G. W.	1
Webb, N.	4
Wedlock, W. J.	2
Weir, D.	2
Weller, K.	1
Welsh, D.	1
Whateley, O.	2
Wheldon, G. F.	6
Whitfield, H.	1
Wignall, F.	2
Wilkes, A.	1
Wilkins, R. G.	3
Willingham, C. K.	1
Wilshaw, D. J.	10
Wilson, D.	1
Wilson, G. P.	1
Winckworth, W. N.	1
Windridge, J. E.	7
Wise, D. F.	1
Withe, P.	1
Wollaston, C. H. R.	1
Wood, H.	1
Woodcock, T.	16
Woodhall, G.	1
Woodward, V. J.	29
Worrall, F.	2
Worthington, F. S.	2
Wright, I. E.	5
Wright, M.	1
Wright, W. A.	3
Wylie, J. G.	1
Yates, J.	3

NORTHERN IRELAND

Player	Goals
Anderson, T.	4
Armstrong, G.	12
Bambrick, J.	12
Barr, H. H.	1
Barron, H.	3
Best, G.	9
Bingham, W. L.	10
Black, K.	1
Blanchflower, D.	2
Blanchflower, J.	1
Brennan, B.	1
Brennan, R. A.	1
Brotherston, N.	3
Brown, J.	1
Browne, F.	2
Campbell, J.	1
Campbell, W. G.	1
Casey, T.	2
Caskey, W.	1
Cassidy, T.	1
Chambers, J.	3
Clarke, C. J.	13
Clements, D.	2
Cochrane, T.	1
Condy, J.	1
Connor, M. J.	1
Coulter, J.	1
Croft, T.	1
Crone, W.	1
Crossan, E.	1
Crossan, J. A.	10
Curran, S.	2
Cush, W. W.	5
Dalton, W.	6
D'Arcy, S. D.	1
Darling, J.	1
Davey, H. H.	1
Davis, T. L.	1
Dill, A. H.	1
Doherty, L.	1
Doherty, P. D.	3
Dougan, A. D.	8
Dowie, I.	7
Dunne, J.	4
Elder, A. R.	1
Emerson, W.	1
English, S.	1
Ferguson, W.	1
Ferris, J.	1
Ferris, R. O.	1
Finney, T.	2
Gaffkin, J.	5
Gara, A.	3
Gawkrodger, G.	1
Gibb, J. T.	2
Gibb, T. J.	1
Gibson, W. K.	1
Gillespie, K. R.	1
Gillespie, W.	12
Goodall, A. L.	2
Gray, P.	3
Halligan, W.	1
Hamill, M.	1
Hamilton, B.	4
Hamilton, W.	5
Hannon, D. J.	1
Harkin, J. T.	2
Harvey, M.	3
Hill, C. F.	1
Hughes, M.	1
Humphries, W.	1
Hunter, A. (*Distillery*)	1
Hunter, A. (*Blackburn R*)	1
Irvine, R. W.	3
Irvine, W. J.	8
Johnston, H.	2
Johnston, S.	2
Johnston, W. C.	1
Jones, S.	1
Jones, J.	1
Kelly, J.	4
Kernaghan, N.	2
Kirwan, J.	2
Lacey, W.	3
Lemon, J.	2
Lockhart, N.	3
Lomas, S. M.	1
Magilton, J.	4
Mahood, J.	2
Martin, D. K.	3
Maxwell, J.	7
McAdams, W. J.	7
McAllen, J.	1
McAuley, J. L.	1
McCandless, J.	3
McCaw, J. H.	1
McClelland, J.	1
McCluggage, A.	2
McCracken, W.	1
McCrory, S.	1
McCurdy, C.	1
McDonald, A.	3
McGarry, J. K.	1
McGrath, R. C.	4
McIlroy, J.	10
McIlroy, S. B.	5
McKnight, J.	2
McLaughlin, J. C.	6
McMordie, A. S.	3
McMorran, E. J.	4
McParland, P. J.	10
McWha, W. B. R.	1
Meldon, J.	1
Mercar, J.	1
Mercer, J. T.	1
Millar, W.	1
Milligan, D.	1
Milne, R. G.	2
Molyneux, T. B.	1
Moreland, V.	1
Morgan, S.	3
Morrow, S. J.	1
Morrow, W. J.	1
Murphy, N.	1
Neill, W. J. T.	2
Nelson, S.	1
Nicholl, C. J.	3
Nicholl, J. M.	2
Nicholson, J. J.	6
O'Hagan, C.	2
O'Kane, W. J.	1
O'Neill, J.	1
O'Neill, M. A.	1
O'Neill, M. H.	8
Own goals	5
Peacock, R.	2
Peden, J.	7
Penney, S.	2
Pyper, James	2
Pyper, John	1
Quinn, J. M.	11
Reynolds, J.	1
Rowley, R. W. M.	2
Sheridan, J.	2
Sherrard, J.	1
Simpson, W. J.	5
Sloan, H. A. de B.	4
Smyth, S.	5
Spence, D. W.	3
Stanfield, O. M.	9
Stevenson, A. E.	5
Stewart, I.	2
Taggart, G. P.	5
Thompson, F. W.	2
Tully, C. P.	3
Turner, E.	1
Walker, J.	1
Walsh, D. J.	5
Welsh, E.	1
Whiteside, N.	9
Whiteside, T.	1
Williams, J. R.	1
Williamson, J.	1
Wilson, D. J.	1
Wilson, K. J.	6
Wilson, S. J.	7
Wilton, J. M.	2
Young, S.	2

SCOTLAND

Player	Goals
Aitken, R.	1
Aitkenhead, W. A. C.	2
Alexander, D.	1
Allan, D. S.	4
Allan, J.	2
Anderson, F.	1
Anderson, W.	4
Andrews, P.	1
Archibald, A.	1
Archibald, S.	4
Baird, D.	2
Baird, J. C.	2
Baird, S.	2
Bannon, E.	1
Barbour, A.	1
Barker, J. B.	4
Battles, B. Jr	1
Bauld, W.	2
Baxter, J. C.	3
Bell, J.	5
Bennett, A.	2
Berry, D.	1
Bett, J.	1
Beveridge, W. W.	1
Black, A.	3
Black, D.	1
Bone, J.	1
Booth, S.	3
Boyd, R.	2
Boyd, W. G.	1
Brackenridge, T.	1
Brand, R.	8
Brazil, A.	1
Bremner, W. J.	3
Brown, A. D.	6
Buchanan, P. S.	1
Buchanan, R.	1
Buckley, P.	1
Buick, A.	2
Burns, K.	1
Cairns, T.	1
Calderwood, C.	1
Calderwood, R.	2
Caldow, E.	4
Campbell, C.	1
Campbell, John (*Celtic*)	5
Campbell, John (*Rangers*)	4
Campbell, P.	2
Campbell, R.	1
Cassidy, J.	1
Chalmers, S.	3
Chambers, T.	1

Player	Goals
Cheyne, A. G.	4
Christie, A. J.	1
Clunas, W. L.	1
Collins, J.	8
Collins, R. Y.	10
Combe, J. R.	1
Conn, A.	1
Cooper, D.	6
Craig, J.	1
Craig, T.	1
Crawford, S.	1
Cunningham, A. N.	5
Curran, H. P.	1
Dalglish, K.	30
Davidson, D.	1
Davidson, J. A.	1
Delaney, J.	3
Devine, A.	1
Dewar, G.	1
Dewar, N.	4
Dickson, W.	4
Divers, J.	1
Docherty, T. H.	1
Dodds, D.	1
Donaldson, A.	1
Donnachie, J.	1
Dougall, J.	1
Drummond, J.	2
Dunbar, M.	1
Duncan, D.	7
Duncan, D. M.	1
Duncan, J.	1
Dunn, J.	2
Durie, G. S.	4
Easson, J. F.	1
Ellis, J.	1
Ferguson, J.	6
Fernie, W.	1
Fitchie, T. T.	1
Flavell, R.	2
Fleming, C.	2
Fleming, J. W.	3
Fraser, M. J. E.	4
Gallacher, H. K.	23
Gallacher, K. W.	2
Gallacher, P.	1
Galt, J. H.	1
Gemmell, T. (*St Mirren*)	1
Gemmell, T. (*Celtic*)	1
Gemmill, A.	8
Gibb, W.	1
Gibson, D. W.	3
Gibson, J. D.	2
Gibson, N.	1
Gillespie, Jas.	3
Gillick, T.	3
Gilzean, A. J.	12
Gossland, J.	2
Goudie, J.	1
Gough, C. R.	6
Gourlay, J.	1
Graham, A.	2
Graham, G.	3
Gray, A.	7
Gray, E.	3
Gray, F.	1
Greig, J.	3
Groves, W.	5
Hamilton, G.	4
Hamilton, J. (*Queen's Park*)	3
Hamilton, R. C.	14
Harper, J. M.	2
Harrower, W.	5
Hartford, R. A.	4
Heggie, C.	5
Henderson, J. G.	1
Henderson, W.	5
Hendry, E. C. J.	1
Herd, D. G.	4
Hewie, J. D.	2
Higgins, A. (*Newcastle U*)	1
Higgins, A. (*Kilmarnock*)	4
Highet, T. C.	1
Holton, J. A.	2
Houliston, W.	2
Howie, H.	1
Howie, J.	2
Hughes, J.	1
Hunter, W.	1
Hutchison, T.	1
Hutton, J.	1
Hyslop, T.	1
Imrie, W. N.	1
Jackson, A.	8
Jackson, C.	1
James, A. W.	3
Jardine, A.	1
Jenkinson, T.	1
Johnston, L. H.	1
Johnston, M.	14
Johnstone, D.	2
Johnstone, J.	4
Johnstone, Jas.	1
Johnstone, R.	9
Johnstone, W.	1
Jordan, J.	11
Kay, J. L.	5
Keillor, A.	3
Kelly, J.	1
Kelso, J.	1
Ker, G.	10
King, A.	1
King, J.	1
Kinnear, D.	1
Lambie, W. A.	5
Lang, J. J.	1
Law, D.	30
Leggat, G.	8
Lennie, W.	1
Lennox, R.	3
Liddell, W.	6
Lindsay, J.	6
Linwood, A. B.	1
Logan, J.	1
Lorimer, P.	4
Love, A.	1
Lowe, J. (*Cambuslang*)	1
Lowe, J. (*St Bernards*)	1
Macari, L.	5
MacDougall, E. J.	3
MacLeod, M.	1
Mackay, D. C.	4
Mackay, G.	1
MacKenzie, J. A.	1
Madden, J.	5
Marshall, H.	1
Marshall, J.	1
Mason, J.	4
Massie, A.	1
Masson, D. S.	5
McAdam, J.	1
McAllister, G.	4
McAulay, J.	1
McAvennie, F.	1
McCall, J.	1
McCall, S. M.	1
McCalliog, J.	1
McCallum, N.	1
McClair, B. J.	2
McCoist, A.	15
McColl, R. S.	13
McCulloch, D.	3
McDougall, J.	4
McFarlane, A.	1
McFadyen, W.	2
McGhee, M.	2
McGinlay, J.	3
McGregor, J. C.	1
McGrory, J.	6
McGuire, W.	1
McInally, A.	3
McInnes, T.	2
McKie, J.	2
McKimmie, S.	1
McKinlay, W.	4
McKinnon, A.	1
McKinnon, R.	1
McKinnon, W. W.	5
McLaren, A.	4
McLaren, J.	1
McLean, A.	1
McLean, T.	1
McLintock, F.	1
McMahon, A.	6
McMenemy, J.	5
McMillan, I. L.	2
McNeil, H.	5
McNeill, W.	3
McPhail, J.	3
McPhail, R.	7
McPherson, J.	8
McPherson, R.	1
McQueen, G.	5
McStay, P.	9
Meiklejohn, D. D.	3
Millar, J.	2
Miller, T.	2
Miller, W.	1
Mitchell, R. C.	1
Morgan, W.	1
Morris, D.	1
Morris, H.	3
Morton, A. L.	5
Mudie, J. K.	9
Mulhall, G.	1
Munro, A. D.	1
Munro, N.	1
Murdoch, R.	5
Murphy, F.	1
Murray, J.	1
Napier, C. E.	3
Narey, D.	1
Neil, R. G.	2
Nevin, P. K. F.	4
Nicholas, C.	5
Nisbet, J.	2
O'Donnell, F.	2
O'Hare, J.	5
Ormond, W. E.	1
O'Rourke, F.	1
Orr, R.	1
Orr, T.	1
Oswald, J.	1
Own goals	14
Parlane, D.	1
Paul, H. McD.	2
Paul, W.	6
Pettigrew, W.	2
Provan, D.	1
Quinn, J.	7
Quinn, P.	1
Rankin, G.	2
Rankin, R.	2
Reid, W.	4
Reilly, L.	22
Renny-Tailyour, H. W.	1
Richmond, J. T.	1
Ring, T.	2
Rioch, B. D.	6
Ritchie, J.	1
Robertson, A.	2
Robertson, J.	2
Robertson, J. N.	9
Robertson, J. T.	2
Robertson, T.	1
Robertson, W.	1
Russell, D.	1
Scott, A. S.	5
Sellar, W.	4
Sharp, G.	1
Shaw, F. W.	1
Shearer, D.	2
Simpson, J.	1
Smith, A.	5
Smith, G.	4
Smith, J.	1
Smith, John	12
Somerville, G.	1
Souness, G. J.	3
Speedie, F.	2
St John, I.	9
Steel, W.	12
Stein, C.	10
Stevenson, G.	4
Stewart, R.	1
Stewart, W. E.	1
Strachan, G.	5
Sturrock, P.	3
Taylor, J. D.	1
Templeton, R.	1
Thomson, A.	1
Thomson, C.	4
Thomson, R.	1
Thomson, W.	1
Thornton, W.	1
Waddell, T. S.	1
Waddell, W.	6
Walker, J.	2
Walker, R.	7
Walker, T.	9
Wallace, I. A.	1
Wark, J.	7
Watson, J. A. K.	1
Watt, F.	2
Watt, W. W.	1
Weir, A.	1
Weir, J. B.	2
White, J. A.	3
Wilson, A.	2
Wilson, A. N.	13
Wilson, D. (*Queen's Park*)	2
Wilson, D. (*Rangers*)	9
Wilson, H.	1
Wylie, T. G.	1
Young, A.	5

WALES

Player	Goals
Allchurch, I. J.	23
Allen, M.	3
Astley, D. J.	12
Atherton, R. W.	2
Bamford, T.	1
Barnes, W.	1
Blackmore, C. G.	1
Blake, N. A.	1
Bodin, P. J.	3
Boulter, L. M.	1
Bowdler, J. C. H.	3
Bowen, D. L.	1
Bowen, M.	3
Boyle, T.	1
Bryan, T.	1
Burgess, W. A. R.	1
Burke, T.	1
Butler, A.	1
Chapman, T.	2
Charles, J.	1
Charles, M.	6
Charles, W. J.	15
Clarke, R. J.	5
Coleman, C.	3
Collier, D. J.	1
Cross, K.	1
Cumner, R. H.	1
Curtis, A.	6
Curtis, E. R.	3
Davies, D. W.	1
Davies, E. Lloyd	1

Davies, G. 2
Davies, L. S. 6
Davies, R. T. 8
Davies, R. W. 7
Davies, S. 5
Davies, W. 6
Davies, W. H. 1
Davies, William 5
Davies, W. O. 1
Deacy, N. 4
Doughty, J. 6
Doughty, R. 2
Durban, A. 2
Dwyer, P. 2

Edwards, G. 2
Edwards, R. I. 4
England, H. M. 3
Evans, I. 1
Evans, J. 1
Evans, R. E. 2
Evans, W. 1
Eyton-Jones, J. A. 1

Flynn, B. 7
Ford, T. 23
Foulkes, W. I. 1
Fowler, J. 3

Giles, D. 2
Giggs, R. J. 3
Glover, E. M. 7
Godfrey, B. C. 2
Green, A. W. 3
Griffiths, A. T. 6
Griffiths, M. W. 2
Griffiths, T. P. 3

Harris, C. S. 1
Hersee, R. 1
Hewitt, R. 1
Hockey, T. 1
Hodges, G. 2
Hole, W. J. 1
Hopkins, I. J. 2
Horne, B. 2
Howell, E. G. 3
Hughes, L. M. 12

James, E. 2
James, L. 10
James, R. 8
Jarrett, R. H. 3
Jenkyns, C. A. 1
Jones, A. 1
Jones, Bryn 6
Jones, B. S. 2
Jones, Cliff 15
Jones, C. W. 1
Jones, D. E. 1
Jones, Evan 1
Jones, H. 1
Jones, I. 1
Jones, J. O. 1
Jones, J. P. 1
Jones, Leslie J. 1
Jones, R. A. 2
Jones, W. L. 6

Keenor, F. C. 2
Krzywicki, R. L. 1

Leek, K. 5
Lewis, B. 3
Lewis, J. 1
Lewis, W. 10
Lewis, W. L. 2
Lovell, S. 1
Lowrie, G. 2

Mahoney, J. F. 1
Mays, A. W. 1
Medwin, T. C. 6
Meredith, W. H. 11
Mills, T. J. 1
Moore, G. 1
Morgan, J. R. 2
Morgan-Owen, H. 1
Morgan-Owen, M. M. 2
Morris, A. G. 9
Morris, H. 2
Morris, R. 1

Nicholas, P. 2

O'Callaghan, E. 3
O'Sullivan, P. A. 1
Owen, G. 2
Owen, W. 4
Owen, W. P. 6
Own goals 12

Palmer, D. 3
Parry, T. D. 3
Paul, R. 1
Peake, E. 1
Pembridge, M. 1
Perry, E. 1
Phillips, C. 5
Phillips, D. 2
Powell, A. 1
Powell, D. 1
Price, J. 4
Price, P. 1
Pryce-Jones, W. E. 3
Pugh, D. H. 2

Reece, G. I. 2
Rees, R. R. 3
Richards, R. W. 1
Roach, J. 2
Robbins, W. W. 4
Roberts, J. (*Corwen*) 1
Roberts, Jas. 1
Roberts, P. S. 1
Roberts, R. (*Druids*) 1
Roberts, W. (*Llangollen*) 2
Roberts, W. (*Wrexham*) 1
Roberts, W. H. 1
Rush, I. 28
Russell, M. R. 1

Sabine, H. W. 1
Saunders, D. 16
Shaw, E. G. 2
Sisson, H. 4
Slatter, N. 2
Smallman, D. P. 1
Speed, G. A. 1

Tapscott, D. R. 4
Thomas, M. 4
Thomas, T. 1
Toshack, J. B. 13
Trainer, H. 2

Vaughan, John 2
Vernon, T. R. 8
Vizard, E. T. 1

Walsh, I. 7
Warren, F. W. 3
Watkins, W. M. 4
Wilding, J. 4
Williams, G. E. 1
Williams, G. G. 1
Williams, W. 1
Woosnam, A. P. 4
Wynn, G. A. 1

Yorath, T. C. 2
Young, E. 1

EIRE

Aldridge, J. 17
Ambrose, P. 1
Anderson, J. 1

Bermingham, P. 1
Bradshaw, P. 4
Brady, L. 9
Brown, D. 1
Byrne, J. (*Bray*) 1
Byrne, J. (*QPR*) 4

Cantwell, J. 14
Carey, J. 3
Carroll, T. 1
Cascarino, A. 12
Coad, P. 3
Conroy, T. 2
Conway, J. 3
Coyne, T. 6
Cummings, G. 5
Curtis, D. 8

Daly, G. 13
Davis, T. 4
Dempsey, J. 1
Dennehy, M. 2
Donnelly, J. 3
Donnelly, T. 1
Duffy, B. 1
Duggan, H. 1
Dunne, J. 12
Dunne, L. 1

Eglington, T. 2
Ellis, P. 1

Fagan, F. 5
Fallon, S. 2
Fallon, W. 2
Farrell, P. 3
Fitzgerald, P. 2
Fitzgerald, J. 1
Fitzsimmons, A. 7
Flood, J. J. 4
Fogarty, A. 3
Fullam, J. 1
Fullam, R. 1

Galvin, A. 1
Gavin, J. 2
Geoghegan, M. 2
Giles, J. 5
Givens, D. 19
Glynn, D. 1
Grealish, T. 8
Grimes, A. A. 1

Hale, A. 2
Hand, E. 2
Haverty, J. 3
Holmes, J. 1
Horlacher, A. 2
Houghton, R. 5
Hughton, C. 1
Hurley, C. 2

Irwin, D. 1

Jordan, D. 1

Keane, R. M. 1
Kelly, D. 8
Kelly, G. 1
Kelly, J. 2
Kernaghan, A. N. 1

Lacey, W. 1
Lawrenson, M. 5
Leech, M. 2

McCann, J. 1
McCarthy, M. 2
McEvoy, A. 6
McGee, P. 4
McGrath, P. 7
McLoughlin, A. F. 1
Madden, O. 1
Mancini, T. 1
Martin, C. 6
Martin, M. 4
Mooney, J. 1
Moore, P. 7
Moran, K. 6
Moroney, T. 1
Mulligan, P. 1

O'Callaghan, K. 1
O'Connor, T. 2
O'Farrell, F. 2
O'Flanagan, K. 3
O'Keefe, E. 1
O'Leary, D. A. 1
O'Neill, F. 1
O'Reilly, J. 2
O'Reilly, J. 1
Own goals 7

Quinn, N. 13

Ringstead, A. 7
Robinson, M. 4
Rogers, E. 5
Ryan, G. 1
Ryan, R. 3

Sheedy, K. 9
Sheridan, J. 5
Slaven, B. 1
Sloan, W. 1
Squires, J. 1
Stapleton, F. 20
Staunton, S. 5
Strahan, J. 1
Sullivan, J. 1

Townsend, A. D. 6
Treacy, R. 5
Touhy, L. 4

Waddock, G. 3
Walsh, D. 5
Walsh, M. 3
Waters, J. 1
White, J. J. 2
Whelan, R. 3

KIRIN CUP AND CANADA CUP

Kirin Cup

Hiroshima, 21 May 1995, 24,566

Japan (0) 0

Scotland (0) 0

Japan: Maekawa, Hashiratanai, Ihara, Omura, Narahashi, Yanagimoto, Ramos (Fukuda), Yamagaguchi, Miura, Nakayama, Morishima (Kitazawa).
Scotland: Leighton; McLaren, McKinnon, Martin, Calderwood (Whyte), Lambert (Robertson), McKinlay, Spencer, Gemmill (Bernard), Jackson, Burley.

Kirin Cup

Toyama, 24 May 1995, 5669

Ecuador (0) 1 *(Hurtado I (pen))*

Scotland (0) 2 *(Robertson, Crawford)*

Ecuador: Cevallos; Capurro, Nonega, Hurtado I, Verduga, Guaman, Carcelen, Garay (Delgado), Zambrano, Herrera (Mora), Hurtado E.
Scotland: Leighton; McLaren, Martin, Calderwood, Bernard, McKinlay, Gemmill, Jackson (Crawford), Whyte (Lambert), Robertson, Burley.

Canada Cup

Edmonton, 22 May 1995, 12,112

Canada (2) 2 *(Peschisolido 2)*

Northern Ireland (0) 0

Canada: Dolan; Yallop, Fraser, Samuel, Watson, Dasovic (Rizi), Miller, Hooper, Aunger (Holness), Peschisolido, Corazzin.
Northern Ireland: Fettis; Patterson, Taggart, McDonald (McGibbon), Rowland, Horlock (Worthington), Gillespie (McMahon), Magilton, Hughes, Dowie (O'Boyle), Gray.

Canada Cup

Edmonton, 26 May 1995, 6124

Chile (1) 2 *(Valencia, Mardones)*

Northern Ireland (0) 1 *(Dowie)*

Chile: Cornez; Acuna, Fuentes, Ramirez, Mendoza, Mussri (Fabian), Mardones, Guevara, Perez (Valencia), Goldberg (Rozental), Salas.
Northern Ireland: Fettis; Worthington, Taggart, McDonald, McGibbon (Patterson), Hughes, Lennon, Rowland, McMahon (Gillespie), Magilton (O'Boyle), Dowie (Gray).

INTERNATIONAL MANAGERS

England

Walter Winterbottom 1946–1962 (after period as coach); Alf Ramsey 1963–1974; Joe Mercer (caretaker) 1974; Don Revie 1974–1977; Ron Greenwood 1977–1982; Bobby Robson 1982–1990; Graham Taylor 1990–1993; Terry Venables (coach) from January 1994.

Northern Ireland

Billy Bingham 1967–1971; Terry Neill 1971–1975; Dave Clements (player-manager)1975–76; Danny Blanchflower 1976–1979; Billy Bingham 1980–1993; Bryan Hamilton from February 1994.

Scotland

Bobby Brown 1967–1971; Tommy Docherty 1971–1972; Willie Ormond 1973–1977; Ally MacLeod 1977–1978; Jock Stein 1978–1985; Alex Ferguson (caretaker) 1985–1986; Andy Roxburgh (coach) 1986–1993; Craig Brown from September 1993.

Wales

Mike Smith 1974–1979; Mike England 1980–1988; David Williams (caretaker) 1988; Terry Yorath 1988–1993; John Toshack 1994 for one match; Mike Smith 1994–1995.

Republic of Ireland

Liam Tuohy 1971–1972; Johnny Giles 1973–1980 (after period as player-manager); Eoin Hand 1980–1985; Jack Charlton from February 1986.

OTHER FOREIGN INTERNATIONAL MATCHES 1994

(For European Matches—see International Directory)

January
Barbados 0, Grenada 0
Ghana 2, Egypt 1
Mali 1, Burkina Faso 1
Mauritania 1, Mali 3
Barbados 0, Puerto Rico 1
Guyana 0, Surinam 2
Mali 1, Senegal 0
Saudi Arabia 1, China 0
Puerto Rico 0, Grenada 1
Saudi Arabia 1, China 1
Barbados 3, Grenada 2
Burkina Faso 5, Guinea 4
Burkina Faso 0, Ivory Coast 1
Niger 3, Guinea 1
Senegal 0, Mali 0

February
Morocco 1, Egypt 1
Oman 1, Kenya 0
UEA 1, Morocco 1
Oman 2, Kenya 0
Saudi Arabia 1, Colombia 1
UEA 0, Egypt 1
Saudi Arabia 0, Colombia 1
Malawi 0, Zambia 3
Malawi 0, Zambia 2
USA 1, Bolivia 1
Colombia 2, Bolivia 0
Mali 0, Ghana 0
Colombia 2, South Korea 2
Zimbabwe 2, Zambia 2
Gabon 0, Senegal 0

March
Mexico 0, Colombia 0
USA 1, South Korea 0
Cayman Islands 3, Jamaica 2
Nigeria 0, Ghana 0
Dominican Republic 0, Haiti 1
USA 1, South Korea 1
Zambia 2, Zimbabwe 1
Egypt 0, Cameroon 0
Tunisia 4, Niger 2
Brazil 2, Argentina 0
Saudi Arabia 0, Chile 2
USA 2, Bolivia 2
Barbados 2, St Vincent/Grenadines 0
Saudi Arabia 2, Chile 2

April
Cayman Islands 2, Haiti 3
Colombia 0, Bolivia 1
Surinam 2, Cayman Islands 0
Surinam 1, Haiti 1
Trinidad & Tobago 2, Barbados 0
Trinidad & Tobago 3, Surinam 2
Colombia 1, Nigeria 0
Argentina 3, Morocco 1
Swaziland 0, Mozambique 1
South Africa 1, Zimbabwe 0
USA 0, Chile 2

May
South Korea 2, Cameroon 2
Colombia 1, Peru 0
Honduras 1, El Salvador 3
South Korea 2, Cameroon 1
Saudi Arabia 0, Bolivia 1
Colombia 3, El Salvador 0
Honduras 2, Peru 1
South Africa 1, Zambia 0
Cameroon 1, Bolivia 1
Chile 3, Argentina 3
Japan 1, Australia 1
Fiji 2, Tahiti 2
Chile 2, Peru 1
Fiji 2, Tahiti 0

June
Canada 1, Morocco 1
Trinidad & Tobago 2, Saudi Arabia 3
USA 1, Mexico 0
Canada 1, Brazil 1
Ivory Coast 4, Liberia 1
South Korea 1, Ecuador 2
Australia 1, South Africa 0
Bolivia 0, Peru 0
Brazil 8, Honduras 2
South Korea 3, Honduras 0
Australia 1, South Africa 0
Brazil 4, El Salvador 0

July
Botswana 0, Namibia 1
Japan 3, Ghana 2
Japan 2, Ghana 1

August
Ivory Coast 2, Mali 1
Niger 0, Togo 0
Niger 3, Togo 2
Peru 2, Ecuador 0
Egypt 2, Ghana 0

September
Liberia 1, Togo 1
India 4, Bangladesh 2
Oman 2, Qatar 0
Bangladesh 1, Yemen 0
Qatar 2, Sudan 0
India 0, Yemen 2
South Korea 0, UAE 0
Sudan 1, Oman 1
Chile 1, Bolivia 2
Ecuador 0, Peru 0
Oman 4, India 1
Yemen 0, Qatar 2
India 0, Yemen 2
Qatar 1, Oman 2
Kuwait 0, Australia 0
Zambia 3, Ghana 0
Japan 0, Australia 0

October
Senegal 3, Niger 1
Zambia 2, Malawi 1
Peru 0, Uruguay 1
Saudi Arabia 2, USA 1
Oman 0, Senegal 1
Oman 2, Senegal 1
UAE 3, Senegal 2

November
UAE 2, Qatar 0
Bahrain 2, Kuwait 1
Oman 1, Saudi Arabia 2
Bahrain 1, Oman 1
UAE 1, Saudi Arabia 1
Kuwait 1, Qatar 0
Morocco 1, Cameroon 1
Tunisia 2, Ivory Coast 0
Qatar 4, Oman 2
UAE 2, Kuwait 0
Saudi Arabia 3, Bahrain 1
Qatar 1, Saudi Arabia 2
UAE 0, Bahrain 0
Oman 0, Kuwait 0
Bahrain 1, Qatar 1
Chile 0, Argentina 3
Kuwait 0, Saudi Arabia 2
Oman 0, UAE 2
Trinidad & Tobago 1, USA 0
Jamaica 0, USA 3
Ivory Coast 2, Cameroon 1
Kenya 3, Somalia 1
South Africa 2, Ghana 1
Kenya 4, Djibouti 1
Tanzania 4, Somalia 0
Ghana 1, Cameroon 0
South Africa 0, Ivory Coast 0

December
Somalia 2, Djibouti 1
Tanzania 1, Kenya 0
Uganda 2, Seychelles 0
Tanzania 3, Djibouti 0
Ghana 1, Ivory Coast 1
South Africa 1, Cameroon 1
Togo 2, Burkina Faso 0
Namibia 2, Ivory Coast 1
USA 1, Honduras 1
Tunisia 1, Algeria 0
Saudi Arabia 3, Costa Rica 1
Cameroon 1, Togo 1
Saudi Arabia 0, South Korea 1
Mali 0, Mauritania 0
Saudi Arabia 1, Zambia 0
Mali 0, Mauritania 0

UEFA UNDER-21 CHAMPIONSHIP 1994–96

(Also used as qualification for Olympics)

Group 1
Israel 2, Poland 2
Romania 5, Azerbaijan 2
Slovakia 0, France 3
France 0, Romania 0
Israel 2, Slovakia 0
Poland 5, Azerbaijan 0
Romania 0, Slovakia 0
Poland 0, France 4
Azerbaijan 1, Israel 2
Israel 0, Romania 1
Azerbaijan 0, France 5
Israel 1, France 1
Romania 1, Poland 2
Slovakia 3, Azerbaijan 0
Poland 1, Israel 0
Azerbaijan 0, Romania 5
France 0, Slovakia 1
Poland 1, Slovakia 0
Romania 1, Israel 0

Group 2
Belgium 7, Armenia 0
Cyprus 0, Spain 6
Macedonia 5, Denmark 3
Armenia 1, Cyprus 2
Denmark 0, Belgium 1
Macedonia 0, Spain 1
Belgium 7, Macedonia 0
Spain 1, Denmark 0
Cyprus 2, Armenia 1
Belgium 3, Spain 3
Macedonia 1, Cyprus 0
Spain 1, Belgium 1
Cyprus 1, Denmark 5
Belgium 1, Cyprus 0
Denmark 5, Macedonia 2
Armenia 0, Spain 3
Armenia 2, Macedonia 0
Denmark 4, Cyprus 0
Spain 4, Armenia 0
Macedonia 3, Belgium 0

Group 3
Hungary 2, Turkey 1
Iceland 0, Sweden 1
Switzerland 0, Sweden 5
Turkey 3, Iceland 0
Sweden 0, Hungary 1
Switzerland 2, Iceland 1
Turkey 1, Switzerland 1
Hungary 1, Switzerland 0
Turkey 0, Sweden 0
Hungary 2, Sweden 1
Switzerland 0, Turkey 2
Sweden 1, Iceland 0
Iceland 1, Hungary 2

Group 4
Estonia 1, Croatia 2
Ukraine 3, Lithuania 2
Slovenia 1, Italy 1
Estonia 1, Italy 4
Croatia 2, Lithuania 0
Ukraine 1, Slovenia 0
Ukraine 3, Estonia 0
Slovenia 3, Lithuania 0
Italy 2, Croatia 1
Italy 7, Estonia 0
Croatia 1, Ukraine 0
Lithuania 0, Croatia 1
Slovenia 5, Estonia 0
Ukraine 2, Italy 1
Croatia 0, Slovenia 2
Estonia 2, Ukraine 5
Lithuania 0, Italy 2
Lithuania 1, Slovenia 2
Estonia 1, Slovenia 2
Ukraine 1, Croatia 1

Group 5
Czech Republic 1, Malta 0
Luxembourg 0, Holland 4
Norway 4, Belarus 0
Malta 0, Czech Republic 7
Norway 1, Holland 0
Belarus 3, Luxembourg 0
Holland 2, Czech Republic 2
Malta 2, Norway 3
Holland 3, Luxembourg 0
Malta 1, Luxembourg 0
Luxembourg 0, Norway 8
Holland 4, Malta 0
Czech Republic 2, Belarus 0
Norway 5, Luxembourg 0
Belarus 4, Malta 0
Czech Republic 2, Holland 2
Belarus 4, Norway 2
Luxembourg 0, Czech Republic 7
Norway 3, Malta 0
Belarus 3, Holland 1

Group 6
England 0, Portugal 0
Latvia 1, Republic of Ireland 1
Latvia 0, Portugal 1
Austria 1, England 3
Portugal 2, Austria 0
England 1, Republic of Ireland 0
Republic of Ireland 0, England 2
Austria 0, Latvia 0
Republic of Ireland 1, Portugal 1
Latvia 0, England 1
Portugal 4, Latvia 0
Republic of Ireland 3, Austria 0

Group 7
Georgia 3, Moldova 0
Bulgaria 1, Georgia 0
Moldova 1, Wales 0
Bulgaria 2, Moldova 0
Georgia 1, Wales 2
Wales 1, Bulgaria 1
Moldova 1, Germany 1
Bulgaria 3, Wales 1
Georgia 0, Germany 2
Germany 1, Wales 0
Moldova 0, Bulgaria 0
Bulgaria 2, Germany 0
Wales 5, Georgia 1

Group 8
Finland 1, Scotland 0
Greece 3, Finland 4
Russia 3, San Marino 0
Greece 4, San Marino 0
Scotland 2, Russia 1
Finland 4, San Marino 0
Greece 1, Scotland 2
San Marino 0, Finland 6
Russia 1, Scotland 2
Greece 0, Russia 1
San Marino 0, Scotland 1
San Marino 0, Russia 7
Finland 1, Greece 0

OLYMPIC FOOTBALL

Previous medallists

1896 Athens*	1 Denmark 2 Greece
1990 Paris*	1 Great Britain 2 France
1904 St Louis**	1 Canada 2 USA
1908 London	1 Great Britain 2 Denmark 3 Holland
1912 Stockholm	1 England 2 Denmark 3 Holland
1920 Antwerp	1 Belgium 2 Spain 3 Holland
1924 Paris	1 Uruguay 2 Switzerland 3 Sweden
1928 Amsterdam	1 Uruguay 2 Argentina 3 Italy
1932 Los Angeles	no tournament
1936 Berlin	1 Italy 2 Austria 3 Norway
1948 London	1 Sweden 2 Yugoslavia 3 Denmark
1952 Helsinki	1 Hungary 2 Yugoslavia 3 Sweden
1956 Melbourne	1 USSR 2 Yugoslavia 3 Bulgaria
1960 Rome	1 Yugoslavia 2 Denmark 3 Hungary
1964 Tokyo	1 Hungary 2 Czechoslovakia 3 East Germany
1968 Mexico City	1 Hungary 2 Bulgaria 3 Japan
1972 Munich	1 Poland 2 Hungary 3 E Germany/USSR
1976 Montreal	1 East Germany 2 Poland 3 USSR
1980 Moscow	1 Czechoslovakia 2 East Germany 3 USSR
1984 Los Angeles	1 France 2 Brazil 3 Yugoslavia
1988 Seoul	1 USSR 2 Brazil 3 West Germany
1992 Barcelona	1 Spain 2 Poland 3 Ghana

* No official tournament
** No official tournament but gold medal later awarded by IOC

10th UEFA UNDER-18 CHAMPIONSHIP 1993–94

Final tournament in Spain, July 1994

Group 1
France 1, Portugal 3
Holland 1, Sweden 1
France 2, Holland 3
Portugal 2, Sweden 0
Portugal 1, Holland 0
Sweden 1, France 3

Group 2
Spain 4, Russia 2
Belarus 0, Germany 3
Germany 1, Russia 2
Belarus 1, Spain 4
Germany 3, Spain 1
Russia 3, Belarus 2

Fifth place
France 0, Russia 2

Third place
Holland 2, Spain 5

Final
Portugal 1, Germany 1
(*Portugal won 5-2 on penalties*)
(*Portugal, Germany, Holland, Spain and Russia qualified for the FIFA Under-20 World Championship*)

8th WORLD YOUTH CHAMPIONSHIP

(in Qatar, April 1995)

Group A
Qatar 1, Russia 1
Syria 0, Brazil 6
Qatar 0, Syria 1
Russia 0, Brazil 0
Qatar 0, Brazil 2
Russia 2, Syria 0

Group B
Burundi 1, Spain 5
Chile 2, Japan 2
Burundi 1, Chile 1
Spain 2, Japan 1
Burundi 0, Japan 2
Spain 6, Chile 3

Group C
Holland 0, Argentina 1
Honduras 2, Portugal 3
Holland 7, Honduras 1*
Argentina 0, Portugal 1
Holland 0, Portugal 3
Argentina 4, Honduras 2
**match abandoned after 80 mins; Honduras reduced to six players.*

Group D
Australia 2, Costa Rica 0
Cameroon 1, Germany 1
Australia 2, Cameroon 3
Costa Rica 2, Germany 1
Australia 1, Germany 1
Costa Rica 1, Cameroon 3

Quarter-finals
Brazil 2, Japan 1
Spain 4, Russia 1
Portugal 2, Australia 1 *in sudden death*
Cameroon 0, Argentina 2

Semi-finals
Brazil 1, Portugal 0
Spain 0, Argentina 3

Third place
Portugal 3, Spain 2

Final
Brazil 0, Argentina 2

13th UEFA UNDER-16 CHAMPIONSHIP 1995

Group 1
Luxembourg 0, France 1
Northern Ireland 1, Luxembourg 0
France 4, Northern Ireland 0

Group 2
Sweden 2, Denmark 0
Republic of Ireland 0, Sweden 2
Denmark 2, Republic of Ireland 1

Group 3
Iceland 0, Finland 2
Finland 0, Scotland 1
Iceland 0, Scotland 0
Finland 1, Iceland 0
Scotland 3, Finland 2
Scotland 4, Iceland 0

Group 4
Latvia 0, Spain 2
Croatia 3, Latvia 0
Spain 1, Croatia 0

Group 5
Czech Republic 6, Malta 0
Malta 2, Estonia 0
Estonia 0, Czech Republic 10

Group 6
Poland 2, Switzerland 0
Switzerland 3, Poland 1

Group 7
Moldova 1, Austria 1
Albania 0, Moldova 3
Austria 4, Albania 0

Group 8
Slovakia, Cyprus, Azerbaijan

Group 9
Georgia 5, Armenia 2
Armenia 0, Slovenia 4
Slovenia 2, Georgia 1

Group 10
Israel 3, Ukraine 0
Germany 4, Ukraine 2
Israel 1, Germany 3

Group 11
Liechtenstein 0, Lithuania 1
Norway 6, Liechtenstein 0
Lithuania 0, Norway 1

Group 12
England, Greece, Romania

Group 13
Holland 8, Belarus 1
Turkey 3, Belarus 0
Belarus 0, Turkey 1
Belarus 0, Holland 2
Holland 4, Turkey 3
Turkey v Holland

Group 14
Wales, Bulgaria, Portugal

Group 15
Hungary 4, Russia 1
Russia 3, Hungary 1
Russia 0, Italy 1
Italy 2, Hungary 1
Italy v Russia
Hungary v Italy

Final tournament in Belgium, April 1995

Group A
Poland 1, Czech Republic 2
Sweden 1, Italy 1
Poland 0, Sweden 1
Czech Republic 1, Italy 0
Italy 0, Poland 0
Czech Republic 4, Sweden 1

Group B
Belgium 4, France 1
Norway 0, Austria 1
Belgium 3, Norway 0
France 1, Austria 0
Austria 0, Belgium 0
France 4, Norway 0

Group C
Germany 0, Spain 3
Slovenia 0, Turkey 2
Turkey 0, Spain 2
Slovenia 0, Germany 3
Spain 3, Slovenia 1
Turkey 1, Germany 4

Group D
Portugal 4, Slovakia 0
Scotland 1, England 1
England 2, Slovakia 1
Scotland 1, Portugal 3
England 3, Portugal 1
Slovakia 2, Scotland 1

Quarter-finals
Czech Republic 0, Germany 2
Spain 1, Sweden 0
Belgium 0, Portugal 1
England 0, France 1 *aet*

Semi-finals
France 0, Spain 2
Germany 1, Portugal 3

Third place
Germany 2, France 1 *in sudden death*

Final
Portugal 2, Spain 0

ENGLAND UNDER-21 RESULTS 1976–95

EC UEFA Competition for Under-21 Teams

v ALBANIA

Year	Date		Venue	Eng	Alb
EC1989	Mar	7	Shkroda	2	1
EC1989	April	25	Ipswich	2	0

v ANGOLA

Year	Date		Venue	Eng	Ang
1995	June	10	Toulon	1	0

v AUSTRIA

Year	Date		Venue	Eng	Aus
1994	Oct	11	Kapfenberg	3	1

v BELGIUM

Year	Date		Venue	Eng	Bel
1994	June	5	Marseille	2	1

v BRAZIL

Year	Date		Venue	Eng	B
1993	June	11	Toulon	0	0
1995	June	6	Toulon	0	2

v BULGARIA

Year	Date		Venue	Eng	Bulg
EC1979	June	5	Pernik	3	1
EC1979	Nov	20	Leicester	5	0
1989	June	5	Toulon	2	3

v CZECHOSLOVAKIA

Year	Date		Venue	Eng	Cz
1990	May	28	Toulon	2	1
1992	May	26	Toulon	1	2
1993	June	9	Toulon	1	1

v DENMARK

Year	Date		Venue	Eng	Den
EC1978	Sept	19	Hvidovre	2	1
EC1979	Sept	11	Watford	1	0
EC1982	Sept	21	Hvidovre	4	1
EC1983	Sept	20	Norwich	4	1
EC1986	Mar	12	Copenhagen	1	0
EC1986	Mar	26	Manchester	1	1
1988	Sept	13	Watford	0	0
1994	Mar	8	Brentford	1	0

v EAST GERMANY

Year	Date		Venue	Eng	EG
EC1980	April	16	Sheffield	1	2
EC1980	April	23	Jena	0	1

v FINLAND

Year	Date		Venue	Eng	Fin
EC1977	May	26	Helsinki	1	0
EC1977	Oct	12	Hull	8	1
EC1984	Oct	16	Southampton	2	0
EC1985	May	21	Mikkeli	1	3

v FRANCE

Year	Date		Venue	Eng	Fra
EC1984	Feb	28	Sheffield	6	1
EC1984	Mar	28	Rouen	1	0
1987	June	11	Toulon	0	2
EC1988	April	13	Besancon	2	4
EC1988	April	27	Highbury	2	2
1988	June	12	Toulon	2	4
1990	May	23	Toulon	7	3
1991	June	3	Toulon	1	0
1992	May	28	Toulon	0	0
1993	June	15	Toulon	1	0
1994	May	31	Aubagne	0	3
1994	Sept	6	Leicester	0	0
1995	June	10	Toulon	0	2

v GERMANY

Year	Date		Venue	Eng	G
1991	Sept	10	Scunthorpe	2	1

v GREECE

Year	Date		Venue	Eng	Gre
EC1982	Nov	16	Piraeus	0	1
EC1983	Mar	29	Portsmouth	2	1
1989	Feb	7	Patras	0	1

v HOLLAND

Year	Date		Venue	Eng	H
EC1993	Apr	27	Portsmouth	3	0
EC1993	Oct	12	Utrecht	1	1

v HUNGARY

Year	Date		Venue	Eng	Hun
EC1981	June	5	Keszthely	2	1
EC1981	Nov	17	Nottingham	2	0
EC1983	April	26	Newcastle	1	0
EC1983	Oct	11	Nyiregyhaza	2	0
1990	Sept	11	Southampton	3	1
1992	May	12	Budapest	2	2

v ITALY

Year	Date		Venue	Eng	Italy
EC1978	Mar	8	Manchester	2	1
EC1978	April	5	Rome	0	0
EC1984	April	18	Manchester	3	1
EC1984	May	2	Florence	0	1
EC1986	April	9	Pisa	0	2
EC1986	April	23	Swindon	1	1

v ISRAEL

Year	Date		Venue	Eng	Isr
1985	Feb	27	Tel Aviv	2	1

v LATVIA

Year	Date		Venue	Eng	Lat
1995	April	25	Riga	1	0
1995	June	7	Burnley	4	0

v MALAYSIA

Year	Date		Venue	Eng	Mal
1995	June	8	Toulon	2	0

v MEXICO

Year	Date		Venue	Eng	Mex
1988	June	5	Toulon	2	1
1991	May	29	Toulon	6	0
1992	May	25	Toulon	1	1

v MOROCCO

Year	Date		Venue	Eng	Mor
1987	June	7	Toulon	2	0
1988	June	9	Toulon	1	0

v NORWAY

Year	Date		Venue	Eng	Nor
EC1977	June	1	Bergen	2	1
EC1977	Sept	6	Brighton	6	0
1980	Sept	9	Southampton	3	0
1981	Sept	8	Drammen	0	0
EC1992	Oct	13	Peterborough	0	2
EC1993	June	1	Stavanger	1	1

v POLAND

Year	Date		Venue	Eng	Pol
EC1982	Mar	17	Warsaw	2	1
EC1982	April	7	West Ham	2	2
EC1989	June	2	Plymouth	2	1
EC1989	Oct	10	Jastrzebie	3	1
EC1990	Oct	16	Tottenham	0	1
EC1993	May	28	Zdroj	4	1
EC1993	Sept	7	Millwall	1	2

v PORTUGAL

Year	Date		Venue	Eng	Por
1987	June	13	Toulon	0	0
1990	May	21	Toulon	0	1
1993	June	7	Toulon	2	0
1994	June	7	Toulon	2	0

v REPUBLIC OF IRELAND

Year	Date		Venue	Eng	Rep Ire
1981	Feb	25	Liverpool	1	0
1985	Mar	25	Portsmouth	3	2
1989	June	9	Toulon	0	0
EC1990	Nov	13	Cork	3	0
EC1991	Mar	26	Brentford	3	0
1994	Nov	15	Newcastle	1	0
1995	Mar	27	Dublin	2	0

v ROMANIA

Year	Date		Venue	Eng	Rom
EC1980	Oct	14	Ploesti	0	4
EC1981	April	28	Swindon	3	0
EC1985	April	30	Brasov	0	0
EC1985	Sept	10	Ipswich	3	0

v RUSSIA

Year	Date		Venue	Eng	Rus
1994	May	30	Bandol	2	0

v SAN MARINO

Year	Date		Venue	Eng	SM
EC1993	Feb	16	Luton	6	0
EC1993	Nov	17	San Marino	4	0

v SENEGAL

Year	Date		Venue	Eng	Sen
1989	June	7	Toulon	6	1
1991	May	27	Toulon	2	1

v SCOTLAND

Year	Date		Venue	Eng	Scot
1977	April	27	Sheffield	1	0
EC1980	Feb	12	Coventry	2	1
EC1980	Mar	4	Aberdeen	0	0
EC1982	April	19	Glasgow	1	0
EC1982	April	28	Manchester	1	1
EC1988	Feb	16	Aberdeen	1	0
EC1988	Mar	22	Nottingham	1	0
1993	June	13	Toulon	1	0

			v SPAIN	Eng	Spa
EC1984	May	17	Seville	1	0
EC1984	May	24	Sheffield	2	0
1987	Feb	18	Burgos	2	1
1992	Sept	8	Burgos	1	0
			v SWEDEN	Eng	Swe
1979	June	9	Vasteras	2	1
1986	Sept	9	Ostersund	1	1
EC1988	Oct	18	Coventry	1	1
EC1989	Sept	5	Uppsala	0	1
			v SWITZERLAND	Eng	Swit
EC1980	Nov	18	Ipswich	5	0
EC1981	May	31	Neuenburg	0	0
1988	May	28	Lausanne	1	1
			v USA	Eng	USA
1989	June	11	Toulon	0	2
1994	June	2	Toulon	3	0
			v TURKEY	Eng	Tur
EC1984	Nov	13	Bursa	0	0
EC1985	Oct	15	Bristol	3	0
EC1987	April	28	Izmir	0	0
EC1987	Oct	13	Sheffield	1	1
				Eng	Tur
EC1991	April	30	Izmir	2	2
1991	Oct	15	Reading	2	0
EC1992	Nov	17	Orient	0	1
EC1993	Mar	30	Izmir	0	0
			v USSR	Eng	USSR
1987	June	9	Toulon	0	0
1988	June	7	Toulon	1	0
1990	May	25	Toulon	2	1
1991	May	31	Toulon	2	1
			v WALES	Eng	Wales
1976	Dec	15	Wolverhampton	0	0
1979	Feb	6	Swansea	1	0
1990	Dec	5	Tranmere	0	0
			v WEST GERMANY	Eng	WG
EC1982	Sept	21	Sheffield	3	1
EC1982	Oct	12	Bremen	2	3
1987	Sept	8	Ludenscheid	0	2
			v YUGOSLAVIA	Eng	Yugo
EC1978	April	19	Novi Sad	1	2
EC1978	May	2	Manchester	1	1
EC1986	Nov	11	Peterborough	1	1
EC1987	Nov	10	Zemun	5	1

ENGLAND B RESULTS 1949–95

Year	*Date*		*Venue*		
			v ALGERIA	Eng	Alg
1990	Dec	11	Algiers	0	0
			v AUSTRALIA	Eng	Aust
1980	Nov	17	Birmingham	1	0
			v CIS	Eng	CIS
1992	April	28	Moscow	1	1
			v CZECHOSLOVAKIA	Eng	Cz
1978	Nov	28	Prague	1	0
1990	April	24	Sunderland	2	0
1992	Mar	24	Budejovice	1	0
			v FINLAND	Eng	Fin
1949	May	15	Helsinki	4	0
			v FRANCE	Eng	Fra
1952	May	22	Le Havre	1	7
1992	Feb	18	Loftus Road	3	0
			v WEST GERMANY	Eng	WG
1954	Mar	24	Gelsenkirchen	4	0
1955	Mar	23	Sheffield	1	1
1978	Feb	21	Augsburg	2	1
			v HOLLAND	Eng	Hol
1949	May	18	Amsterdam	4	0
1950	Feb	22	Newcastle	1	0
1952	Mar	26	Amsterdam	1	0
			v ICELAND	Eng	Ice
1989	may	19	reykjavik	2	0
1991	April	27	Watford	1	0
			v ITALY	Eng	It
1950	May	11	Milan	0	5
1989	Nov	14	Brighton	1	1
			v LUXEMBOURG	Eng	Lux
1950	May	21	Luxembourg	2	1
			v MALAYSIA	Eng	Mal
1978	May	30	Kuala Lumpur	1	1
			v MALTA	Eng	Mal
1987	Oct	14	Ta'Qali	2	0
			v NEW ZEALAND	Eng	NZ
1978	June	7	Christchurch	4	0
1978	June	11	WEllington	3	1
1978	June	14	Auckland	4	0
1979	Oct	15	Leyton	4	1
1984	Nov	13	Nottingham	2	0
			v NORTHERN IRELAND	Eng	NI
1994	May	10	Sheffield	4	2
			v NORWAY	Eng	Nor
1989	May	22	Stavanger	1	0
			v REPUBLIC OF IRELAND	Eng	RoI
1990	Mar	27	Cork	1	4
1994	Dec	13	Liverpool	2	0
			v SCOTLAND	Eng	Scot
1953	Mar	11	Edinburgh	2	2
1954	Mar	3	Sunderland	1	1
1956	Feb	29	Dundee	2	2
1957	Feb	6	Birmingham	4	1
			v SINGAPORE	Eng	Sin
1978	June	18	Singapore	8	0
			v SPAIN	Eng	Sp
1980	Mar	26	Sunderland	1	0
1981	Mar	25	Granada	2	3
1991*	Dec	18	Castellon	1	0
			v SWITZERLAND	Eng	SW
1950	Jan	18	Sheffield	5	0
1954	May	22	Basle	0	2
1956	Mar	21	Southampton	4	1
1989	May	16	Winterthur	2	0
1991	May	20	Walsall	2	1
			v USA	Eng	USA
1980	Oct	14	Manchester	1	0
			v WALES	Eng	Wal
1991	Feb	5	Swansea	1	0
			v YUGOSLAVIA	Eng	Yug
1954	May	16	Ljubljana	1	2
1955	Oct	19	Manchester	5	1
1989	Dec	12	Millwall	2	1

*Spanish Olympic IX

BRITISH AND IRISH UNDER-21 TEAMS 1994-95

England Under-21 internationals

6 Sept

England (0) 0
France (0) 0 6487
England: Gerrard; Watson S, Gordon, Sinclair, Campbell, Unsworth, Redknapp, Barmby (Dyer), Fowler, Bart-Williams, Joachim.

11 Oct

Austria (1) 1 *(Haas)*
England (2) 3 *(Redknapp 3)* 2800
England: Gerrard; Edghill, Gordon, Watson S, Campbell, Unsworth, Redknapp, Parlour, Fowler, Bart-Williams (Whelan), Joachim (Barmby).

15 Nov

England (1) 1 *(Whelan)*
Republic of Ireland (0) 0 25,863
England: Gerrard; Watson S, Gordon, Butt, Campbell, Unsworth, Fenton, Sinclair, Whelan (Pollock), Bart-Williams (Smith M), Joachim.
Republic of Ireland: Given; Carr, Woods, Greene, Breen, Boland, Kavanagh, Moore (Scully), Perkins (Launders), Kennedy, Turner.

27 Mar

Republic of Ireland (0) 0
England (0) 2 *(Sinclair, Shipperley)* 6000
Republic of Ireland: Given; Carr, Hardy, Greene, Breen, Woods, Boland (Farrelly), Savage, Durkan, Kennedy, Turner (Launders).
England: Gerrard; Watson S, Pearce, Gordon, Unsworth, Roberts, Butt, Gallen, Shipperley, Bart-Williams, Sinclair.

25 Apr

Latvia (0) 0
England (0) 1 *(Sinclair)* 300
England: Gerrard; Watson S, Gordon, Nethercott, Unsworth, Roberts, Butt, Gallen (Booth), Shipperley, Bart-Williams, Sinclair.

6 June

England (0) 0
Brazil (1) 2 *(Leonardo, Leandro)* 3000
England: Watson D; Neville P, Croft, Hill, Richards, Ryder, Beckham, Holland P, Joachim, Forster, Myers (Allen).

7 June

England (2) 4 *(Bart-Williams, Shipperley, Watson S, Booth)*
Latvia (0) 0 7288
England: Gerrard; Watson S, Gordon, Pearce, Nethercott, Roberts, Holland C, Gallen (Booth), Shipperley, Bart-Williams, Thompson.

8 June

England (2) 2 *(Joachim, Myers)*
Malaysia (0) 0 700
England: Marshall; Neville P, Croft, Hill (Couzens), Richards, Casper, Beckham, Holland P, Joachim, Forster, Myers.

10 June

England (1) 1 *(Forster)*
Angola (0) 0 250
England: Davis; Neville P, Croft, Hill, Richards, Ryder, Beckham, Holland P, Joachim, Forster, Couzens (Myers).

12 June

England (0) 0
France (0) 2 *(Corridon, Histilloles)* 650
England: Watson D; Neville P, Croft, Hill, Richards, Ryder (Allen), Beckham, Holland P (Couzens), Joachim, Forster, Myers.

Scotland Under-21 internationals

6 Sept

Finland (1) 1 *(Ristilla (pen))*
Scotland (0) 0 2321
Scotland: Kerr; Jupp, Robertson, Murray, Pressley, Dailly, Lock, Hannah, Crawford (Lavety), Donnelly (McDonald), McCann.

15 Nov

Scotland (0) 2 *(Crawford, Varlamov (og))*
Russia (0) 1 *(Simoutenkov)* 6350
Scotland: Stille; Jupp, Love, Handyside, Pressley, Marshall (Freedman), Johnston, Murray, Crawford, Dailly, McDonald (Hannah).

17 Dec

Greece (0) 1 *(Gianakopoulos)*
Scotland (0) 2 *(Crawford 2)* 1000
Scotland: Kerr; McNamara, Baker, Murray, Marshall, Dailly, Thomas (McCann), Hannah, Crawford, Miller (Donnelly), Bollan.

28 Mar

Russia (1) 1 *(Lebed)*
Scotland (1) 2 *(Miller, Freedman)* 2464
Scotland: Stille; Jupp, Bollan, Dailly, Pressley, Hannah (Harper), McNamara (O'Neill), Miller, Crawford, Freedman, McLaughlin.

25 Apr

San Marino (0) 0
Scotland (0) 1 *(Pressley)* 930
Scotland: Stille; Jupp, Murray, Dailly, McLaughlin, McNamara, Crawford, Freedman (Hamilton), McCann (Liddell).

5 June

Scotland (1) 1 *(Freedman)*
Mexico (1) 2 *(Luna 2)* 400
Scotland: Stille; Jupp, Dailly, Pressley, Baker, Hannah, Fullarton, Glass, McLaughlin (McDonald), Freedman (Liddell), Crawford.

7 June

France (1) 1 *(Histilloles)*
Scotland (1) 2 *(Glass, Gray)* 1500
Scotland: Stille; Jupp (Crawford), Pressley, Dailly, Gray, Hannah (Baker), Fullarton, Glass, O'Neill (McDonald), Liddell, Freedman.

9 June

South Korea (0) 0

Scotland (0) 1 *(Hannah)* 500
Scotland: Stille; Jupp (Crawford), Pressley, Dailly, Gray, O'Neill (Baker), Hannah, Fullarton, Glass (McLaughlin), Freedman, Liddell.

12 June

Brazil (2) 4 *(Caico, Juninho, Leonardo, Jupp (og))*

Scotland (0) 0 1100
Scotland: Stille; Jupp, Pressley, Dailly, Gray (Crawford), Hannah, Fullarton (McLaughlin), Glass, O'Neill, Freedman (McDonald), Hamilton.

Wales Under-21 internationals

11 Oct

Moldovo (1) 1 *(Khizilov)*

Wales (0) 0 5000
Wales: Coyne; Barnhouse, Williams, Twiddy, Page, Hughes, Bird, Morgan, Hartson, Jones L, Kenworthy (Davies).

15 Nov

Georgia (0) 1 *(Anchabadze)*

Wales (1) 2 *(Twiddy, Jones (pen))* 10,000

Wales: Coyne; Williams, Brace, Page, Edwards, Hughes, Jones L, Davies, Hartson, Taylor, Twiddy (Bird).

13 Dec

Wales (0) 1 *(Hartson)*

Bulgaria (0) 1 *(Ionkov)* 630
Wales: Coyne; Williams, Brace, Davies (Evans), Hughes, Chapple, Morgan, Bird, Hartson, Taylor, Jones R.

28 Mar

Bulgaria (2) 3 *(Ivanov, Pramatarov, Hristo)*

Wales (1) 1 *(Savage)* 25,000
Wales: Coyne; Williams, Brace, Davies, Page, Edwards, Savage, Chapple, Taylor, Jones R, Kenworthy.

Republic of Ireland Under-21 internationals

6 Sept

Latvia (1) 1 *(Bleidelis)*

Republic of Ireland (0) 1 *(Moore)* 500
Republic of Ireland: Given; Gallen, Hardy, Greene, Breen, Boland, Sheridan, Kavanagh, Moore, Launders (Perkins), Kennedy.

25 Apr

Republic of Ireland (0) 1 *(Kennedy)*

Portugal (0) 1 *(Kenedy)* 2300
Republic of Ireland: Colgan; Carr, Hardy (Woods), Greene, Breen, Savage, Scully, Kavanagh, Moore, Launders, Kennedy.

10 June

Republic of Ireland (2) 3 *(Durkan, Perkins 2)*

Austria (0) 0 1654
Republic of Ireland: Colgan; Carr, Hardy, Greene, Breen, Woods, Boland, Farrelly, Durkan, Perkins, Launders (Sherlock).

B INTERNATIONALS

13 Dec

England B (1) 2 *(Cole, Fowler)*

Republic of Ireland B (0) 0 7431
England B: Pressman (James); Barton, Beresford, Sherwood, Scales (Ehiogu), Ruddock, Campbell (Redknapp), Sutton (Barmby), Cole (Fowler), Fox, Wilcox.
Republic of Ireland B: Branagan; Cunningham, Kenna, McAteer, Babb, Daish, Whelan (Milligan), McLoughlin, Kelly D (Coyle), Coyne, Townsend.

21 Feb

Scotland B (1) 3 *(Tweed, Jackson, Wright)*

Northern Ireland B (0) 0 5067
Scotland B: Walker (Woods); Wright, McKinnon, Tweed, Martin, O'Neil, Lambert (Cameron), Rae, Brown (Dodds), Jackson, McGinlay
Northern Ireland B: Fettis; Wright, Rowland, Dunlop, McGibbon, Matthews, Morrow, Sonner, O'Boyle, Lennon, Finlay.

SEMI-PROFESSIONAL INTERNATIONALS

28 Feb

England (0) 1 *(Hine)*

Wales (0) 0 703
England: Batty (Woking); Webb (Kidderminster Harriers), Hogarth (Guiseley), Reid (Altrincham), Brown (Woking), Stott (Bromsgrove Rovers), Terry (Altrincham), Forsyth (Kidderminster Harriers) [Hine (Gateshead)], Ross (Marine), Humphreys (Kidderminster Harriers), Watson (Marine) [Arnold (Kettering Town)].

11 Apr

Holland (0) 0

England (0) 0 500
England: Batty (Woking) [Farrelly (Macclesfield Town)]; Webb (Kidderminster Harriers), Hogarth (Guiseley), Brown (Woking), Holden (Kettering Town) [Howarth (Macclesfield Town)], Forsyth (Kidderminster Harriers), Venables (Stevenage Borough), Hine (Gateshead) [Stott (Bromsgrove Rovers)], Ross (Marine), Arnold (Kettering Town) [Browne (Dover Athletic)], Humphreys (Kidderminster Harriers) [Watson (Marine)].

31 May

Gibraltar (1) 2

England (2) 3 *(Taylor, Bolton, Venables)* 800
England: Batty (Woking) [Farrelly (Macclesfield Town)]; Webb (Kidderminster Harriers), Ashby (Kettering Town), Brown (Woking), Holden (Kettering Town), Stott (Bromsgrove Rovers) [McDonald (Macclesfield Town)], Venables (Stevenage Borough), Forsyth (Kidderminster Harriers), Bolton (Kingstonian), Taylor (Bromsgrove Rovers), Richardson (Dagenham & Redbridge) [May (Stafford Rangers)].

UNDER-21 APPEARANCES 1976–1995

ENGLAND

Ablett, G. (Liverpool), 1988 v F (1)
Adams, A. (Arsenal). 1985 v Ei, Fi; 1986 v D; 1987 v Se, Y (5)
Adams, N. (Everton), 1987 v Se (1)
Allen, B. (QPR), 1992 v H, M, Cz, F; 1993 v N (sub), T, P, Cz (sub) (8)
Allen, C. A. (Oxford U), 1995 v Br (sub), F (sub) (2)
Allen, C. (QPR), 1980 v EG (sub); (with C Palace), 1981 v N, R (3)
Allen, M. (QPR), 1987 v Se (sub); 1988 v Y (sub) (2)
Allen, P. (West Ham U), 1985 v Ei, R; (with Tottenham H, 1986 v R (3)
Anderson, V. A. (Nottingham F), 1978 v I (1)
Anderton, D. R. (Tottenham H), 1993 v Sp, Sm, Ho, Pol, N, P, Cz, Br, S, F; 1994 v Pol, Sm (12)
Andrews, I. (Leicester C), 1987 v Se (1)
Ardley, N. C. (Wimbledon), 1993 v Pol, N, P, Cz, Br, S, F, 1994 v Pol (sub), Ho, Sm (10)
Ashcroft, L. (Preston NE), 1992 v H (sub) (1)
Atherton, P. (Coventry C), 1992 v T (1)
Atkinson, B. (Sunderland), 1991 v W (sub), Sen, M, USSR (sub), F; 1992 v Pol (sub) (6)
Awford, A. T. (Portsmouth), 1993 v Sp, N, T, P, Cz, Br, S, F; 1994 v Ho (9)

Bailey, G. R. (Manchester U), 1979 v W, Bul; 1980 v D, S (2), EG; 1982 v N; 1983 v D, Gr; 1984 v H, F (2), I, Sp (14)
Baker, G. E. (Southampton), 1981 v N, R (2)
Barker, S. (Blackburn R), 1985 v Is (sub), Ei, R; 1986 v I (4)
Barmby, N. J. (Tottenham H), 1994 v D; 1995 v P, A (sub) (3)
Bannister, G. (Sheffield W), 1982 v Pol (1)
Barnes, J. (Watford), 1983 v D, Gr (2)
Barnes, P. S. (Manchester C), 1977 v W (sub), S, Fi, N; 1978 v N, Fi, I (2), Y (9)
Barrett, E. D. (Oldham Ath), 1990 v P, F, USSR, Cz (4)
Bart-Williams, C. G. (Sheffield W), 1993 v Sp, N, T; 1994 v D, Ru, F, Bel, P; 1995 v P, A, Ei (2), La (2) (14)
Batty, D. (Leeds U), 1988 v Sw (sub); 1989 v Gr (sub), Bul, Sen, Ei, US; 1990 v Pol (7)
Bazeley, D. S. (Watford), 1992 v H (sub) (1)
Beagrie, P. (Sheffield U), 1988 v WG, T (2)
Beardsmore, R. (Manchester U), 1989 v Gr, Alb (sub), Pol, Bul, USA (5)
Beckham, D. R. J. (Manchester U), 1995 v Br, Mal, An, F (4)
Beeston, C (Stoke C), 1988 v USSR (1)
Bertschin, K. E. (Birmingham C), 1977 v S; 1978 v Y (2) (3)
Birtles, G. (Nottingham F), 1980 v Bul, EG (sub) (2)
Blackwell, D. R. (Wimbledon), 1991 v W, T, Sen (sub), M, USSR, F (6)
Blake, M. A. (Aston Villa), 1990 v F (sub), Cz (sub); 1991 v H, Pol, Ei (2), W; 1992 v Pol (8)
Blissett, L. L. (Watford), 1979 v W, Bul (sub), Se; 1980 v D (4)
Booth, A. D. (Huddersfield T), 1995 v La (2 subs) (2)
Bracewell, P. (Stoke C), 1983 v D, Gr (1 + 1 sub), H; 1984 v D, H, F (2), I (2), Sp (2); 1985 v T (13)
Bradshaw, P. W. (Wolverhampton W), 1977 v W, S; 1978 v Fi, Y (4)
Breacker, T. (Luton T), 1986 v I (2) (2)
Brennan, M. (Ipswich T), 1987 v Y, Sp, T, Mor, F (5)
Brightwell, I. (Manchester C), 1989 v D, Alb; 1990 v Se (sub), Pol (4)
Brock, K. (Oxford U), 1984 v I, Sp (2); 1986 v I (4)
Bull, S. G. (Wolverhampton W), 1989 v Alb (2) Pol; 1990 v Se, Pol (5)
Burrows, D. (WBA), 1989 v Se (sub); (with Liverpool), Gr, Alb (2), Pol; 1990 v Se, Pol (7)
Butcher, T. I. (Ipswich T), 1979 v Se; 1980 v D, Bul, S (2), EG (2) (7)
Butt, N. (Manchester U), 1995 v Ei (2), La (3)
Butters, G. (Tottenham H), 1989 v Bul, Sen (sub), Ei (sub) (3)
Butterworth, I. (Coventry C), 1985 v T, R; (with Nottingham F), 1986 v R, T, D (2), I (2) (8)

Caesar, G. (Arsenal), 1987 v Mor, USSR (sub), F (3)
Callaghan, N. (Watford), 1983 v D, Gr (sub), H (sub); 1984 v D, H, F (2), I, Sp (9)
Campbell, K. J. (Arsenal), 1991 v H, T (sub); 1992 v G, T (4)
Campbell, S. (Tottenham), 1994 v D, Ru, F, US, Bel, P; 1995 v P, A, Ei (9)
Carr, C. (Fulham), 1985 v Ei (sub) (1)
Carr, F. (Nottingham F), 1987 v Se, Y, Sp (sub), Mor, USSR; 1988 v WG (sub), T, Y, F (9)
Casper, C. M. (Manchester U), 1995 v Mal (1)
Caton, T. (Manchester C), 1982 v N, H (sub), Pol (2), S; 1983 v WG (2), Gr; 1984 v D, H, F (2), I (2) (14)
Chamberlain, M. (Stoke C), 1983 v Gr; 1984 v F (sub), I, Sp (4)
Chapman, L. (Stoke C), 1981 v Ei (1)
Charles, G. A. (Nottingham F), 1991 v H, W (sub), Ei; 1992 v T (4)
Chettle, S. (Nottingham F), 1988 v M, USSR, Mor, F; 1989 v D, Se, Gr, Alb (2), Bul; 1990 v Se, Pol (12)
Clark, L. R. (Newcastle U), 1992 v Cz, F; 1993 v Sp, N, T, Ho (sub), Pol (sub), Cz, Br, S; 1994 v Ho (11)
Clough, N. (Nottingham F), 1986 v D (sub); 1987 v Se, Y, T, USSR, F (sub), P; 1988 v WG, T, Y, S (2), M, Mor, F (15)
Cole, A. A. (Arsenal), 1992 v H, Cz (sub), F (sub); (with Bristol C), 1993 v Sm; (with Newcastle U), Pol, N; 1994 v Pol, Ho (8)
Coney, D. (Fulham), 1985 v T (sub); 1986 v R; 1988 v T, WG (4)
Connor, T. (Brighton & HA), 1987 v Y (1)
Cooke, R. (Tottenham H), 1986 v D (sub) (1)
Cooper, C. (Middlesbrough), 1988 v F (2), M, USSR, Mor; 1989 v D, Se, Gr (8)
Corrigan, J. T. (Manchester C), 1978 v I (2), Y (3)
Cottee, A. (West Ham U), 1985 v Fi (sub), Is (sub), Ei, R, Fi; 1987 v Sp, P; 1988 v WG (8)
Couzens, A. J. (Leeds U), 1995 v Mal (sub), An, F (sub) (3)
Cowans, G. S. (Aston Villa), 1979 v W, Se; 1980 v Bul, EG; 1981 v R (5)
Cox, N. J. (Aston Villa), 1993 v T, Ho, Pol, N; 1994 v Pol, Sm (6)
Cranson, I. (Ipswich T), 1985 v Fi, Is, R; 1986 v R, I (5)
Croft, G. (Grimsby T), 1995 v Br, Mal, An, F (4)
Crooks, G. (Stoke C), 1980 v Bul, S (2), EG (sub) (4)
Crossley, M. G. (Nottingham F), 1990 v P, USSR, Cz (3)
Cundy, J. V. (Chelsea), 1991 v Ei (2); 1992 v Pol (3)
Cunningham, L. (WBA), 1977 v S, Fi, N (sub); 1978 v N, Fi, I (6)
Curbishley, L. C. (Birmingham C), 1981 v Sw (1)

Daniel, P. W. (Hull C), 1977 v S, Fi, N; 1978 v Fi, I, Y (2) (7)
Davis, K. G. (Luton T), 1995 v An (1)
Davis, P. (Arsenal), 1982 v Pol, S; 1983 v D, Gr (1 + 1 sub), H (sub); 1987 v T; 1988 v WG, T, Y, Fr (11)
D'Avray, M. (Ipswich T), 1984 v I, Sp (sub) (2)

Deehan, J. M. (Aston Villa), 1977 v N; 1978 v N, Fi, I; 1979 v Bul, Se (sub); 1980 v D (7)
Dennis, M. E. (Birmingham C), 1980 v Bul; 1981 v N, R (3)
Dickens, A. (West Ham U), 1985 v Fi (sub) (1)
Dicks, J. (West Ham U), 1988 v Sw (sub), M, Mor, F (4)
Digby, F. (Swindon T), 1987 v Sp (sub), USSR, P; 1988 v T; 1990 v Pol (5)
Dillon, K. P. (Birmingham C), 1981 v R (1)
Dixon, K. (Chelsea), 1985 v Fi (1)
Dobson, A. (Coventry C), 1989 v Bul, Sen, Ei, US (4)
Dodd, J. R. (Southampton), 1991 v Pol, Ei, T, Sen, M, F; 1992 v G, Pol (8)
Donowa, L. (Norwich C), 1985 v Is, R (sub), Fi (sub) (3)
Dorigo, A. (Aston Villa), 1987 v Se, Sp, T, Mor, USSR, F, P; 1988 v WG, Y, S (2) (11)
Dozzell, J. (Ipswich T), 1987 v Se, Y (sub), Sp, USSR, F, P; 1989 v Se, Gr (sub); 1990 v Se (sub) (9)
Draper, M. A. (Notts Co), 1991 v Ei (sub); 1992 v G, Pol (3)
Duxbury, M. (Manchester U), 1981 v Sw (sub), Ei (sub), R (sub), Sw; 1982 v N; 1983 v WG (2) (7)
Dyer, B. A. (Crystal Palace), 1994 v Ru, F, US, Bel, P; 1995 v P (sub) (6)
Dyson, P. I. (Coventry C), 1981 v N, R, Sw, Ei (4)

Eadie, D. M. (Norwich C), 1994 v F (sub), US (2)
Ebbrell, J. (Everton), 1989 v Sen, Ei, US (sub); 1990 v P, F, USSR, Cz; 1991 v H, Pol, Ei, W, T; 1992 v G, T (14)
Edghill, R. A. (Manchester C), 1994 v D, Ru; 1995 v A (3)
Ehiogu, U. (Aston Villa), 1992 v H, M, Cz, F; 1993 v Sp, N, T, Sm, T, Ho, Pol, N; 1994 v Pol, Ho, Sm (15)
Elliott, P. (Luton T), 1985 v Fi; 1986 v T, D (3)

Fairclough, C. (Nottingham F), 1985 v T, Is, Ei; 1987 v Sp, T; (with Tottenham H), 1988 v Y, F (7)
Fairclough, D. (Liverpool), 1977 v W (1)
Fashanu, J. (Norwich C), 1980 v EG; 1981 v N (sub), R, Sw, Ei (sub), H; (with Nottingham F), 1982 v N, H, Pol, S; 1983 v WG (sub) (11)
Fear, P. (Wimbledon), 1994 v Ru, F, US (sub) (3)
Fenton, G. A. (Aston Villa), 1995 v Ei (1)
Fenwick, T. W. (C Palace), 1981 v N, R, Sw, Ei; (with QPR), R; 1982 v N, H, S (2); 1983 v WG (2) (11)
Fereday, W. (QPR), 1985 v T, Ei (sub). Fi; 1986 v T (sub), I (5)
Flitcroft, G. W. (Manchester C), 1993 v Sm, Hol, N, P, Cz, Br, S, F; 1994 v Pol, Ho (10)
Flowers, T. (Southampton), 1987 v Mor, F; 1988 v WG (sub) (3)
Forster, N. M. (Brentford), 1995 v Br, Mal, An, F (4)
Forsyth, M. (Derby Co), 1988 v Sw (1)
Foster, S. (Brighton & HA), 1980 v EG (sub) (1)
Fowler, R. B. (Liverpool), 1994 v Sm, Ru (sub), F, US; 1995 v P, A (6)
Froggatt, S. J. (Aston Villa), 1993 v Sp, Sm (sub) (2)
Futcher, P. (Luton T), 1977 v W, S, Fi, N; (with Manchester C), 1978 v N, Fi, I (2), Y (2); 1979 v D (11)

Gabbiadini, M. (Sunderland), 1989 v Bul, USA (2)
Gale, A. (Fulham), 1982 v Pol (1)
Gallen, K. A. (QPR), 1995 v Ei, La (2) (3)
Gascoigne, P. (Newcastle U), 1987 v Mo, USSR, P; 1988 v WG, Y, S (2), F (2), Sw, M, USSR (sub), Mor (13)
Gayle, H. (Birmingham C), 1984 v I, Sp (2) (3)
Gernon, T. (Ipswich T), 1983 v Gr (1)
Gerrard, P. W. (Oldham Ath), 1993 v T, Ho, Pol, N, P, Cz, Br, S, F; 1994 v D, Ru; 1995 v P, A, Ei (2), La (2) (17)
Gibbs, N. (Watford), 1987 v Mor, USSR, F, P; 1988 v T (5)
Gibson, C. (Aston Villa), 1982 v N (1)
Gilbert, W. A. (C Palace), 1979 v W, Bul; 1980 v Bul; 1981 v N, R, Sw, R, Sw, H; 1982 v N (sub), H (11)

Goddard, P. (West Ham U), 1981 v N, Sw, Ei (sub); 1982 v N (sub), Pol, S; 1983 v WG (2) (8)
Gordon, D. (Norwich C), 1987 v T (sub), Mor (sub), F, P (4)
Gordon, D. D. (Crystal Palace), 1994 v Ru, F, US, Bel, P; 1995 v P, A, Ei (2), La (2) (11)
Gray, A. (Aston Villa), 1988 v S, F (2)

Haigh, P. (Hull C), 1977 v N (sub) (1)
Hall, R. A. (Southampton), 1992 v H (sub), F; 1993 v Sm, T, Ho, Pol, P, Cz, Br, S, F (11)
Hardyman, P. (Portsmouth), 1985 v Ei; 1986 v D (2)
Hateley, M. (Coventry C), 1982 v Pol, S; 1983 v Gr (2), H; (with Portsmouth), 1984 v F (2), I, Sp (2) (10)
Hayes, M. (Arsenal), 1987 v Sp, T; 1988 v F (sub) (3)
Hazell, R. J. (Wolverhampton W), 1979 v D (1)
Heaney, N. A. (Arsenal), 1992 v H, M, Cz, F; 1993 v N, T (6)
Heath, A. (Stoke C), 1981 v R, Sw, H; 1982 v N, H; (with Everton), Pol, S; 1983 v WG (8)
Hendon, I. M. (Tottenham H), 1992 v H, M, Cz, F; 1993 v Sp, N, T (7)
Hesford, I. (Blackpool), 1981 v Ei (sub), Pol (2), S (2); 1983 v WG (2) (7)
Hilaire, V. (C Palace), 1980 v Bul, S (1+1 sub), EG (2); 1981 v N, R, Sw (sub); 1982 v Pol (sub) (9)
Hill, D. R. L. (Tottenham H), 1995 v Br, Mal, An, F (4)
Hillier, D. (Arsenal), 1991 v T (1)
Hinchcliffe, A. (Manchester C), 1989 v D (1)
Hinshelwood, P. A. (C Palace), 1978 v N; 1980 v EG (2)
Hirst, D. (Sheffield W), 1988 v USSR, F; 1989 v D, Bul (sub), Sen, Ei, US (7)
Hoddle, G. (Tottenham H), 1977 v W (sub); 1978 v Fi (sub), I (2), Y; 1979 v D, W, Bul; 1980 v S (2), EG (2) (12)
Hodge, S. (Nottingham F), 1983 v Gr (sub); 1984 v D, F, I, Sp (2); (with Aston Villa), 1986 v R, T (8)
Hodgson, D. J. (Middlesbrough), 1981 v N, R (sub), Sw, Ei; 1982 v Pol; 1983 v WG (6)
Holdsworth, D. (Watford), 1989 v Gr (sub) (1)
Holland, C. J. (Newcastle U), 1995 v La (1)
Holland, P. (Mansfield T), 1995 v Br, Mal, An, F (4)
Horne, B. (Millwall), 1989 v Gr (sub), Pol, Bul, Ei, US (5)
Hucker, P. (QPR), 1984 v I, Sp (2)

Impey, A. R. (QPR), 1993 v T (1)
Ince, P. (West Ham U), 1989 v Alb; 1990 v Se (2)

Jackson, M. A. (Everton), 1992 v H, M, Cz, F; 1993 v Sm (sub), T, Ho, Pol, N; 1994 v Pol (10)
James, D. (Watford), 1991 v Ei (2), T, Sen, M, USSR, F; 1992 v G, T, Pol (10)
James, J. C. (Luton T), 1990 v F, USSR (2)
Jemson, N. B. (Nottingham F), 1991 v W (1)
Joachim, J. K. (Leicester C), 1994 v D (sub); 1995 v P, A, Ei, Br, Mal, An, F (8)
Johnson, T. (Notts Co), 1991 v H (sub), Ei (sub); 1992 v G, T, Pol; (with Derby Co), M, Cz (sub) (7)
Johnston, C. P. (Middlesbrough), 1981 v N, Ei (2)
Jones, D. R. (Everton), 1977 v W (1)
Jones, C. H. (Tottenham H), 1978 v Y (sub) (1)
Jones, R. (Liverpool), 1993 v Sm, Ho (2)

Keegan, G. A. (Manchester C), 1977 v W (1)
Kenny, W. (Everton), 1993 v T (1)
Keown, M. (Aston Villa), 1987 v Sp, Mor, USSR, P; 1988 v T, S, F (2) (8)
Kerslake, D. (QPR), 1986 v T (1)
Kilcline, B. (Notts C), 1983 v D, Gr (2)
King, A. E. (Everton), 1977 v W; 1978 v Y (2)
Kitson, P. (Leicester C), 1991 v Sen (sub), M, F; 1992 v Pol; (with Derby Co), M, Cz, F (7)
Knight, A. (Portsmouth), 1983 v Gr, H (2)
Knight, I. (Sheffield W), 1987 v Se (sub), Y (2)

Lake, P. (Manchester C), 1989 v D, Alb (2), Pol; 1990 v Pol (5)
Langley, T. W. (Chelsea), 1978 v I (sub) (1)
Lee, D. J. (Chelsea), 1990 v F; 1991 v H, Pol, Ei (2), T, Sen, USSR, F; 1992 v Pol (10)
Lee, R. (Charlton Ath), 1986 v I (sub); 1987 v Se (sub) (2)
Lee, S. (Liverpool), 1981 v R, Sw, H; 1982 v S; 1983 v WG (2) (6)
Le Saux, G. (Chelsea), 1990 v P, F, USSR, Cz (4)
Lowe, D. (Ipswich T), 1988 v F, Sw (sub) (2)
Lukic, J. (Leeds U), 1981 v N, R, Ei, R, Sw, H; 1982 v H (7)
Lund, G. (Grimsby T), 1985 v T; 1986 v R, T (3)

McCall, S. H. (Ipswich T), 1981 v Sw, H; 1982 v H, S; 1983 v WG (2) (6)
McDonald, N. (Newcastle U), 1987 v Se (sub), Sp, T; 1988 v WG, Y (sub) (5)
McGrath, L. (Coventry C), 1986 v D (1)
MacKenzie, S. (WBA), 1982 v N, S (2) (3)
McLeary, A. (Millwall), 1988 v Sw (1)
McMahon, S. (Everton), 1981 v Ei; 1982 v Pol; 1983 v D, Gr (2); (with Aston Villa), 1984 v H (6)
McManaman, S. (Liverpool), 1991 v W, M (sub); 1993 v N, T, Sm, T; 1994 v Pol (7)
Mabbutt, G. (Bristol R), 1982 v Pol (2), S; (with Tottenham H), 1983 v D; 1984 v F; 1986 v D, I (7)
Makin, C. (Oldham Ath), 1994 v Ru (sub), F, US, Bel, P (5)
Marriott, A. (Nottingham F), 1992 v M (1)
Marshall, A. J. (Norwich C), 1995 v Mal (1)
Martin, L. (Manchester U), 1989 v Gr (sub), Alb (sub) (2)
Martyn, N. (Bristol R), 1988 v S (sub), M, USSR, Mor, F; 1989 v D, Se, Gr, Alb (2); 1990 v Se (11)
Matteo, D. (Liverpool), 1994 v F (sub), Bel, P (3)
Matthew, D. (Chelsea), 1990 v P, USSR (sub), Cz; 1991 v Ei, M, USSR, F; 1992 v G (sub), T (9)
May, A. (Manchester C), 1986 v I (sub) (1)
Merson, P. (Arsenal), 1989 v D, Gr, Pol (sub); 1990 v Pol (4)
Middleton, J. (Nottingham F), 1977 v Fi, N; (with Derby Co), 1978 v N (3)
Miller, A. (Arsenal), 1988 v Mor (sub); 1989 v Sen; 1991 v H, Pol (4)
Mills, G. R. (Nottingham F), 1981 v R; 1982 v N (2)
Mimms, R. (Rotherham U), 1985 v Is (sub), Ei (sub); (with Everton), 1986 v I (3)
Minto, S. C. (Charlton Ath), 1991 v W; 1992 v H, M, Cz; 1993 v T; 1994 v Ho (6)
Moran, S. (Southampton), 1982 v N (sub); 1984 v F (2)
Morgan, S. (Leicester C), 1987 v Se, Y (2)
Mortimer, P. (Charlton Ath), 1989 v Sen, Ei (2)
Moses, R. M. (WBA), 1981 v N (sub), Sw, Ei, R, Sw, H; 1982 v N (sub); (with Manchester U), H (8)
Mountfield, D. (Everton), 1984 v Sp (1)
Muggleton, C. D. (Leicester C), 1990 v F (1)
Mutch, A. (Wolverhampton W), 1989 v Pol (1)
Myers. A. (Chelsea), 1995 v Br, Mal, An (sub), F (4)

Nethercott, S. (Tottenham), 1994 v D, Ru, F, US, Bel, P; 1995 v La (2) (8)
Neville, P. J. (Manchester U), 1995 v Br, Mal, An, F (4)
Newell, M. (Luton T), 1986 v D (1 + 1 sub), I (1 + 1 sub) (4)
Newton, E. J. I. (Chelsea), 1993 v T (sub); 1994 v Sm (2)
Nicholls, A. (Plymouth Arg), 1994 v F (1)

Oakes, M. C. (Aston Villa), 1994 v D (sub), F (sub), US, Bel, P (5)
Oakes, S. J. (Luton T), 1993 v Br (sub) (1)
Oldfield, D. (Luton T), 1989 v Se (1)
Olney, I. A. (Aston Villa), 1990 v P, F, USSR, Cz; 1991 v H, Pol, Ei (2), T; 1992 v Pol (sub) (10)
Ord, R. J. (Sunderland), 1991 v W, M, USSR (3)
Osman, R. C. (Ipswich T), 1979 v W (sub), Se; 1980 v D, S (2), EG (2) (7)
Owen, G. A. (Manchester C), 1977 v S, Fi, N; 1978 v N, Fi, I (2), Y; 1979 v D, W; (with WBA), Bul, Se (sub); 1980 v D, S (2), EG; 1981 v Sw, R; 1982 v N (sub), H; 1983 v WG (2) (22)

Painter, I. (Stoke C), 1986 v I (1)
Palmer, C. (Sheffield W), 1989 v Bul, Sen, Ei, US (4)
Parker, G. (Hull C), 1986 v I (2); (with Nottingham F), F; 1987 v Se, Y (sub), Sp (6)
Parker, P. (Fulham), 1985 v Fi, T, Is (sub), Ei, R, Fi; 1986 v T, D (8)
Parkes, P. B. F. (QPR), 1979 v D (1)
Parkin, S. (Stoke C), 1987 v Sp (sub); 1988 v WG (sub), T, S (sub), F (5)
Parlour, R. (Arsenal), 1992 v H, M, Cz, F; 1993 v Sp, N, T; 1994 v D, Ru, Bel, P; 1995 v A (12)
Peach, D. S. (Southampton), 1977 v S, Fi, N; 1978 v N, I (2) (6)
Peake, A. (Leicester C), 1982 v Pol (1)
Pearce, I. A. (Blackburn R), 1995 v Ei, La (2)
Pearce, S. (Nottingham F), 1987 v Y (1)
Pickering N. (Sunderland), 1983 v D (sub), Gr, H; 1984 v F (sub + 1), I (2), Sp; 1985 v Is, R, Fi; 1986 v R, T; (with Coventry C), D, I (15)
Platt, D. (Aston Villa), 1988 v M, Mor, F (3)
Pollock, J. (Middlesbrough), 1995 v Ei (sub) (1)
Porter, G. (Watford), 1987 v Sp (sub), T, Mor, USSR, F, P (sub); 1988 v T (sub), Y, S (2), F, Sw (12)
Pressman, K. (Sheffield W), 1989 v D (sub) (1)
Proctor, M. (Middlesbrough), 1981 v Ei (sub), Sw; (with Nottingham F) 1982 v N, Pol (4)

Ramage, C. D. (Derby Co), 1991 v Pol (sub), W; 1992 v Fr (sub) (3)
Ranson, R. (Manchester C), 1980 v Bul, EG; 1981 v R (sub), R, Sw (1 + 1 sub), H, Pol (2), S (10)
Redknapp, J. F. (Liverpool), 1993 v Sm, Pol, N, P, Cz, Br, S, F; 1994 v Pol, Ho (sub), D, Ru, F, US, Bel, P; 1995 v P, A (18)
Redmond, S. (Manchester C), 1988 v F (2), M, USSR, Mor, F; 1989 v D, Se, Gr, Alb (2), Pol; 1990 v Se, Pol (14)
Reeves, K. P. (Norwich C), 1978 v I, Y (2); 1979 v N, W, Bul, Sw; 1980 v D, S; (with Manchester C), EG (10)
Regis, C. (WBA), 1979 v D, Bul, Se; 1980 v S, EG; 1983 v D (6)
Reid, N. S. (Manchester C), 1981 v H (sub); 1982 v H, Pol (2), S (2) (6)
Reid, P. (Bolton W), 1977 v S, Fi, N; 1978 v Fi, I, Y (6)
Richards, D. I. (Wolverhampton W), 1995 v Br, Mal, An, F (4)
Richards, J. P. (Wolverhampton W), 1977 v Fi, N (2)
Rideout, P. (Aston Villa), 1985 v Fi, Is, Ei (sub), R; (with Bari), 1986 v D (5)
Ripley, S. (Middlesbrough), 1988 v USSR, F (sub); 1989 v D (sub), Se, Gr, Alb (2); 1990 v Se (8)
Ritchie, A. (Brighton & HA), 1982 v Pol (1)
Rix, G. (Arsenal), 1978 v Fi (sub), Y; 1979 v D, Se; 1980 v D (sub), Bul, S (7)
Roberts, A. J. (Millwall), 1995 v Ei, La (2) (3)
Robins, M. G. (Manchester U), 1990 v P, F, USSR, Cz; 1991 v H (sub), Pol (6)
Robson, B. (WBA), 1979 v W, Bul (sub), Se; 1980 v D, Bul, S (2) (7)
Robson, S. (Arsenal), 1984 v I; 1985 v Fi, Is, Fi; 1986 v R, I (with West Ham U); 1988 v S, Sw (8)
Rocastle, D. (Arsenal), 1987 v Se, Y, Sp, T; 1988 v WG, T, Y, S (2), F (2 subs), M, USSR, Mor (14)
Rodger, G. (Coventry C), 1987 v USSR, F, P; 1988 v WG (4)
Rosario, R. (Norwich C), 1987 v T (sub), Mor, F, P (sub) (4)

Rowell, G. (Sunderland), 1977 v Fi (1)
Ruddock, N. (Southampton), 1989 v Bul (sub), Sen, Ei, US (4)
Ryan, J. (Oldham Ath), 1983 v H (1)
Ryder, S.H. (Walsall), 1995 v Br, An, F (3)

Samways, V. (Tottenham H), 1988 v Sw (sub), USSR, F; 1989 v D, Se (5)
Sansom, K. G. (C Palace), 1979 v D, W, Bul, Se; 1980 v S (2), EG (2) (8)
Seaman, D. (Birmingham C), 1985 v Fi, T, Is, Ei, R, Fi; 1986 v R, F, D, I (10)
Sedgley, S. (Coventry C), 1987 v USSR, F (sub), P; 1988 v F; 1989 v D (sub), Se, Gr, Alb (2), Pol; (with Tottenham H), 1990 v Se (11)
Sellars, S. (Blackburn R), 1988 v S (sub), F, Sw (3)
Selley, I. (Arsenal), 1994 v Ru (sub), F (sub), US (3)
Sharpe, L. (Manchester U), 1989 v Gr; 1990 v P (sub), F, USSR, Cz; 1991 v H, Pol (sub), Ei (8)
Shaw, G. R. (Aston Villa), 1981 v Ei, Sw, H; 1982 v H, S; 1983 v WG (2) (7)
Shearer, A. (Southampton), 1991 v Ei (2), W, T, Sen, M, USSR, F; 1992 v G, T, Pol (11)
Shelton, G. (Sheffield W), 1985 v Fi (1)
Sheringham, T. (Millwall), 1988 v Sw (1)
Sheron, M. N. (Manchester C), 1992 v H, F; 1993 v N (sub), T (sub), Sm, Ho, Pol, N, P, Cz, Br, S, F; 1994 v Pol (sub), Ho, Sm (16)
Sherwood, T. A. (Norwich C), 1990 v P, F, USSR, Cz (4)
Shipperley, N. J. (Chelsea), 1994 v Sm (sub); (with Southampton) 1995 v Ei, La (2) (4)
Simpson, P. (Manchester C), 1986 v D (sub); 1987 v Y, Mor, F, P (5)
Sims, S. (Leicester C), 1977 v W, S, Fi, N; 1978 v N, Fi, I (2), Y (2) (10)
Sinclair, F. M. (Chelsea), 1994 v Ho, Sm, D, Ru, F, US, Bel, P (8)
Sinclair, T. (QPR), 1995 v P, Ei (2), La (4)
Sinnott, L. (Watford), 1985 v Is (sub) (1)
Slater, S. I. (West Ham U), 1990 v P, USSR (sub), Cz (sub) (3)
Small, B. (Aston Villa), 1993 v Sm, T, Ho, Pol, N, P, Cz, Br, S, F; 1994 v Pol, Sm (12)
Smith, D. (Coventry C), 1988 v M, USSR (sub), Mor; 1989 v D, Se, Alb (2), Pol; 1990 v Se, Pol (10)
Smith, M. (Sheffield W), 1981 v Ei, R, Sw, H; 1982 v Pol (sub) (5)
Smith, M. (Sunderland), 1995 v Ei (sub) (1)
Snodin, I. (Doncaster R), 1985 v T, Is, R, Fi (4)
Statham, B. (Tottenham H), 1988 v Sw; 1989 v D (sub), Se (3)
Statham, D. J. (WBA), 1978 v Fi, 1979 v W, Bul, Se; 1980 v D; 1983 v D (6)
Stein, B. (Luton T), 1984 v D, H, I (3)
Sterland, M. (Sheffield W), 1984 v D, H, F (2), I, Sp (2) (7)
Steven, T. (Everton), 1985 v Fi, T (2)
Stevens, G. (Brighton & HA), 1983 v H; (with Tottenham H), 1984 v H, F (1+1 sub), I (sub), Sp (1+1 sub); 1986 v I (8)
Stewart, P. (Manchester C), 1988 v F (1)
Stuart, G. C. (Chelsea), 1990 v P (sub), F, USSR, Cz; 1991 v T (sub) (5)
Suckling, P. (Coventry C), 1986 v D; (with Manchester C), 1987 v Se (sub), Y, Sp, T; (with C Palace), 1988 v S (2), F (2), Sw (10)
Summerbee, N.J. (Swindon T), 1993 v P (sub), S (sub), F (3)
Sunderland, A. (Wolverhampton W), 1977 v W (1)
Sutton, C. R. (Norwich), 1993 v Sp (sub), T (sub + 1), Ho, P (sub), Cz, Br, S, F; 1994 v Pol, Ho, Sm, D (13)
Swindlehurst, D. (C Palace), 1977 v W (1)
Sutch, D. (Norwich C), 1992 v H, M, Cz; 1993 v T (4)

Talbot, B. (Ipswich T), 1977 v W (1)
Thomas, D. (Coventry C), 1981 v Ei; 1983 v WG (2), Gr, H; (with Tottenham H), I, Sp (7)
Thomas, M. (Luton T), 1986 v T, D, I (3)
Thomas, M. (Arsenal), 1988 v Y, S, F (2), M, USSR, Mor; 1989 v Gr, Alb (2), Pol; 1990 v Se (12)
Thomas, R. E. (Watford), 1990 v P (1)
Thompson, A. (Bolton W), 1995 v La (1)
Thompson, G. L. (Coventry C), 1981 v R, Sw, H; 1982 v N, H, S (6)
Thorn, A. (Wimbledon), 1988 v WG (sub). Y, S, F, Sw (5)
Tiler, C. (Barnsley), 1990 v P, USSR, Cz; 1991 v H, Pol, Ei (2), T, Sen, USSR, F; (with Nottingham F), 1992 v G, T (13)

Unsworth, D. G. (Everton), 1995 v A, Ei (2), La (4)

Venison, B. (Sunderland), 1983 v D, Gr; 1985 v Fi, T, Is, Fi; 1986 v R, T, D (2) (10)
Vinnicombe, C. (Rangers), 1991 v H (sub), Pol, Ei (2), T, Sen, M, USSR (sub), F; 1992 v G, T, Pol (12)

Waddle, C. (Newcastle U), 1985 v Fi (1)
Wallace, D. (Southampton), 1983 v Gr, H; 1984 v D, H, F (2), I, Sp (sub); 1985 v Fi, T, Is; 1986 v R, D, I (14)
Wallace, Ray (Southampton), 1989 v Bul, Sen (sub), Ei; 1990 v Se (4)
Wallace, Rod (Southampton), 1989 v Bul, Ei (sub), US; 1991 v H, Pol, Ei, T, Sen, M, USSR, F (11)
Walker, D. (Nottingham F), 1985 v Fi; 1987 v Se, T; 1988 v WG, T, S (2) (7)
Walker, I. M. (Tottenham H), 1991 v W; 1992 v H, Cz, F; 1993 v Sp, N, T, Sm; 1994 v Pol (9)
Walsh, G. (Manchester U), 1988 v WG, Y (2)
Walsh, P. M. (Luton T), 1983 v D (sub), Gr (2), H (4)
Walters, K. (Aston Villa), 1984 v D (sub), H (sub); 1985 v Is, Ei, R; 1986 v R, T, D, I (sub) (9)
Ward, P. D. (Brighton & HA), 1978 v N; 1980 v EG (2)
Warhurst, P. (Oldham Ath), 1991 v H, Pol, W, Sen, M (sub), USSR, F (sub); (with Sheffield W), 1992 v G (8)
Watson, D. (Norwich C), 1984 v D, F (2), I (2), Sp (2) (7)
Watson, D. N. (Barnsley), 1994 v Ho, Sm; 1995 v Br, F (4)
Watson, G. (Sheffield W), 1991 v Sen, USSR (2)
Watson, S. C. (Newcastle U), 1993 v Sp (sub), N; 1994 v Sm (sub), D; 1995 v P, A, Ei (2), La (2) (10)
Webb, N. (Portsmouth), 1985 v Ei; (with Nottingham F), 1986 v D (2) (3)
Whelan, P. J. (Ipswich T), 1993 v Sp, T (sub), P (3)
Whelan, N. (Leeds U), 1995 v A (sub), Ei (2)
White, D. (Manchester C), 1988 v S (2), F, USSR; 1989 v Se; 1990 v Pol (6)
Whyte, C. (Arsenal), 1982 v S (1+1 sub); 1983 v D, Gr (4)
Wicks, S. (QPR), 1982 v S (1)
Wilkins, R. C. (Chelsea), 1977 v W (1)
Wilkinson, P. (Grimsby T), 1985 v Ei, R (sub); (with Everton), 1986 v R (sub), I (4)
Williams, P. (Charlton Ath), 1989 v Bul, Sen, Ei, US (sub) (4)
Williams, P. D. (Derby Co), 1991 v Sen, M, USSR; 1992 v G, T, Pol (6)
Williams, S. C. (Southampton), 1977 v S, Fi, N; 1978 v N, I (1 + 1 sub), Y (2); 1979 v D, Bul, Se (sub); 1980 v D, EG (2) (14)
Winterburn, N. (Wimbledon), 1986 v I (1)
Wise, D. (Wimbledon), 1988 v Sw (1)
Woodcook, A. S. (Nottingham F), 1978 v Fi, I (2)
Woods, C. C. E. (Nottingham F), 1979 v W (sub), Se; (with QPR), 1980 v Bul, EG; 1981 v Sw; (with Norwich C), 1984 v D (6)
Wright, A. G. (Blackburn), 1993 v Sp, N (2)
Wright, M. (Southampton), 1983 v Gr, H; 1984 v D, H (4)

Wright, W. (Everton), 1979 v D, W, Bul; 1980 v D, S (2) (6)

Yates, D. (Notts Co), 1989 v D (sub), Bul, Sen, Ei, US (5)

SCOTLAND

Aitken, R. (Celtic), 1977 v Cz, W, Sw; 1978 v Cz, W; 1979 v P, N (2); 1980 v Bel, E; 1984 v EG, Y (2); 1985 v WG, Ic, Sp (16)
Albiston, A. (Manchester U), 1977 v Cz, W, Sw; 1978 v Sw, Cz (5)
Archdeacon, O. (Celtic), 1987 v WG (sub) (1)
Archibald, S. (Aberdeen), 1980 v B, E (2), WG; (with Tottenham H), 1981 v D (5)

Bain, K. (Dundee), 1993 v P, I, Ma, P (4)
Baker, M. (St. Mirren), 1993 v F, M, E; 1994 v Ma, A; 1995 v Gr, M, F (sub), Sk (sub) (9)
Bannon, E. J. P. (Hearts), 1979 v US; (with Chelsea), P, N (2); (with Dundee U), 1980 v Bel, WG, E (7)
Beattie, J. (St Mirren), 1992 v D, US, P, Y (4)
Beaumont, D. (Dundee U), 1985 v Ic (1)
Bell, D. (Aberdeen), 1981 v D; 1984 v Y (2)
Bernard, P. R. J. (Oldham Ath), 1992 v R (sub), D, Se (sub), US; 1993 v Sw, P, I, Ma, P, F, Bul, M, E; 1994 v I, Ma (15)
Bett, J. (Rangers), 1981 v Se, D; 1982 v Se, D, I, E (2) (7)
Black, E. (Aberdeen), 1983 v EG, Sw (2), Bel; 1985 v Ic, Sp (2), Ic (8)
Blair, A. (Coventry C), 1980 v E; 1981 v Se; (with Aston Villa), 1982 v Se, D, I (5)
Bollan, G. (Dundee U), 1992 v D, G (sub), US, P, Y; 1993 v Sw, P, I, P, F, Bul, M, E; 1994 v Sw; 1995 v Gr; (with Rangers) v Ru, Sm (17)
Booth, S. (Aberdeen), 1991 v R (sub), Bul (sub + 1), Pol, F (sub); 1992 v Sw, R, D, Se, US, P, Y; 1993 v Ma, P (14)
Bowes, M. J. (Dunfermline Ath), 1992 v D (sub) (1)
Bowman, D. (Hearts), 1985 v WG (sub) (1)
Boyd, T. (Motherwell), 1987 v WG, Ei (2), Bel; 1988 v Bel (5)
Brazil, A. (Hibernian), 1978 v W (1)
Brazil, A. (Ipswich T), 1979 v N; 1980 v Bel (2), E (2), WG; 1981 v Se; 1982 v Se (8)
Brough, J. (Hearts), 1981 v D (1)
Burley, G. E. (Ipswich T), 1977 v Cz, W, Sw; 1978 v Sw, Cz (5)
Burley, C. (Chelsea), 1992 v D; 1993 v Sw, P, I, P; 1994 v Sw, I (sub) (7)
Burns, H. (Rangers), 1985 v Sp, Ic (sub) (2)
Burns, T. (Celtic), 1977 v Cz, W, E; 1978 v Sw; 1982 v E (5)

Campbell, S. (Dundee), 1989 v N (sub), Y, F (3)
Casey, J. (Celtic), 1978 v W (1)
Christie, M. (Dundee), 1992 v D, P (sub), Y (3)
Clark, R. (Aberdeen), 1977 v Cz, W, Sw (3)
Clarke, S. (St Mirren), 1984 v Bel, EG, Y; 1985 v WG, Ic, Sp (2), Ic (8)
Cleland, A. (Dundee U), 1990 v F, N (2); 1991 v R, Sw, Bul; 1992 v Sw, R, G, Se (2) (11)
Collins, J. (Hibernian), 1988 v Bel, E; 1989 v N, Y, F; 1990 v Y, F, N (8)
Connolly, P. (Dundee U), 1991 v R (sub), Sw, Bul (3)
Connor, R. (Ayr U), 1981 v Se; 1982 v Se (2)
Cooper, D. (Clydebank), 1977 v Cz, W, Sw, E; (with Rangers), 1978 v Sw, Cz (6)
Cooper, N. (Aberdeen), 1982 v D, E (2); 1983 v Bel, EG, Sw (2); 1984 v Bel, EG, Y; 1985 v Ic, Sp, Ic (13)
Crabbe, S. (Hearts), 1990 v Y (sub), F (2)
Craig, T. (Newcastle U), 1977 v E (1)
Crainie, D. (Celtic), 1983 v Sw (sub) (1)
Crawford, S. (Raith R), 1994 v A, Eg, P, Bel; 1995 v Fi, Ru, Gr, Ru, Sm, M, F (sub), Sk (sub), Br (sub) (13)
Creaney, G. (Celtic), 1991 v Sw, Bul (2), Pol, F; 1992 v Sw, R, G (2), Se (2) (11)

Dailly, C. (Dundee U), 1991 v R; 1992 v US, R; 1993 v Sw, P, I, Ic, P, F, Bul, M, E; 1994 v Sw, I, Ma, A, Eg, P, Bel; 1995 v Fi, Ru, Gr, Ru, Sm, M, F, Sk, Br (28)
Dawson, A. (Rangers), 1979 v P, N (2); 1980 v B (2), E (2), WG (8)
Deas, P. A. (St Johnstone), 1992 v D (sub); 1993 v Ma (2)
Dennis, S. (Raith R), 1992 v Sw (1)
Dickov, P. (Arsenal), 1992 v Y; 1993 v F, M, E (4)
Dodds, D. (Dundee U), 1978 v W (1)
Donald, G. S. (Hibernian), 1992 v US (sub), P, Y (sub) (3)
Donnelly, S. (Celtic), 1994 v Eg, P, Bel; 1995 v Fi, Gr (sub) (5)
Dow, A. (Dundee), 1993 v Ma (sub), Ic; (with Chelsea) 1994 v I (3)
Duffy, J. (Dundee), 1987 v Ei (1)
Durie, G. S. (Chelsea), 1987 v WG, Ei, Bel; 1988 v Bel (4)
Durrant, I. (Rangers), 1987 v WG, Ei, Bel; 1988 v E (4)
Doyle, J. (Partick Th), 1981 v D, I (sub) (2)

Ferguson, D. (Rangers), 1987 v WG, Ei, Bel; 1988 v E; 1990 v Y (5)
Ferguson, D. (Dundee U), 1992 v D, G, Se (2); 1993 v Sw, I, Ma (7)
Ferguson, D. (Manchester U), 1992 v US, P (sub), Y; 1993 v Sw, Ma (5)
Ferguson, I. (Dundee), 1983 v EG (sub), Sw (sub); 1984 v Bel (sub), EG (4)
Ferguson, I. (Clyde), 1987 v WG (sub), Ei; (with St Mirren), Ei, Bel; 1988 v Bel; (with Rangers), E (sub) (6)
Ferguson, R. (Hamilton A), 1977 v E (1)
Findlay, W. (Hibernian), 1991 v R, Pol, Bul (2), Pol (5)
Fitzpatrick, A. (St Mirren), 1977 v W (sub), Sw (sub), E; 1978 v Sw, Cz (5)
Flannigan, C. (Clydebank), 1993 v Ic (sub) (1)
Fleck, R. (Rangers), 1987 v WG (sub), Ei, Bel; (with Norwich C), 1988 v E (2); 1989 v Y (6)
Freedman, D. A. (Barnet), 1995 v Ru (sub + 1), Sm, M, F, Sk, Br (7)
Fridge, L. (St Mirren), 1989 v F; 1990 v Y (2)
Fullarton, J. (St. Mirren), 1993 v F, Bul; 1994 v Ma, A, Eg, P, Bel; 1995 v M, F, Sk, Br (11)
Fulton, M. (St Mirren), 1980 v Bel, WG, E; 1981 v Se, D (sub) (5)
Fulton, S. (Celtic), 1991 v R, Sw, Bul, Pol, F; 1992 v G (2) (7)

Gallacher, K. (Dundee U), 1987 v WG, Ei (2), Bel (sub); 1988 v E (2); 1990 v Y (7)
Galloway, M. (Hearts), 1989 v F; (with Celtic), 1990 v N (2)
Gardiner, J. (Hibernian), 1993 v F (1)
Geddes, R. (Dundee), 1982 v Se, D, E (2); 1988 v E (5)
Gemmill, S. (Nottingham F), 1992 v Sw, R (sub), G (sub), Se (sub) (4)
Gillespie, G. (Coventry C), 1979 v US; 1980 v E; 1981 v D; 1982 v Se, D, I (2), E (8)
Glass, S. (Aberdeen), 1995 v M, F, Sk, Br (4)
Glover, L. (Nottingham F), 1988 v Bel (sub); 1989 v N; 1990 v Y (3)
Goram, A. (Oldham Ath), 1987 v Ei (1)
Gough, C. R. (Dundee U), 1983 v EG, Sw, Bel; 1984 v Y (2) (5)
Grant, P. (Celtic), 1985 v WG, Ic, Sp; 1987 v WG, Ei (2), Bel; 1988 v Bel, E (2) (10)
Gray S. (Celtic), 1995 v F, Sk, Br (3)
Gray, S. (Aberdeen), 1987 v WG (1)
Gunn, B. (Aberdeen), 1984 v EG, Y (2); 1985 v WG, Ic, Sp (2), Ic; 1990 v F (9)

Hagen, D. (Rangers), 1992 v D (sub), US (sub), P, Y; 1993 v Sw (sub), P, Ic, P (8)
Hamilton, B. (St Mirren), 1989 v Y, F (sub); 1990 v F, N (4)
Hamilton, J. (Dundee) 1995 v Sm (sub), Br (2)
Handyside, P. (Grimsby T), 1993 v Ic (sub), Bul, M, E; 1995 v Ru (5)
Hannah, D. (Dundee U), 1993 v F (sub), Bul, M; 1994 v A, Eg, P, Bel; 1995 v Fi, Ru (sub), Gr, Ru, M, F, Sk, Br (15)
Harper, K. (Hibernian), 1995 v Ru (sub) (1)
Hartford, R. A. (Manchester C), 1977 v Sw (1)
Hegarty, P. (Dundee U), 1987 v WG, Bel; 1988 v E (2); 1990 v F, N (6)
Hendry, J. (Tottenham H), 1992 v D (sub) (1)
Hewitt, J. (Aberdeen), 1982 v I; 1983 v EG, Sw (2); 1984 v Bel, Y (sub) (6)
Hogg, G. (Manchester U), 1984 v Y; 1985 v WG, Ic, Sp (4)
Hood, G. (Ayr U), 1993 v F, E (sub); 1994 v A (3)
Howie, S. (Cowdenbeath), 1993 v Ma, Ic, P; 1994 v Sw, I (5)
Hunter, G. (Hibernian), 1987 v Ei (sub); 1988 v Bel, E (3)
Hunter, P. (East Fife), 1989 v N (sub), F (sub); 1990 v F (sub) (3)

Jardine, I. (Kilmarnock), 1979 v US (1)
Jess, E. (Aberdeen), 1990 v F (sub), N (sub); 1991 v R, Sw, Bul (2), Pol, F; 1992 v Sw, R, G (2), Se (1 + 1 sub) (14)
Johnson, G. I. (Dundee U), 1992 v US, P, Y; 1993 v Sw, P, Ma (6)
Johnston, A. (Hearts), 1994 v Bel; 1995 v Ru (2)
Johnston, F. (Falkirk), 1993 v Ic (1)
Johnston, M. (Partick Th), 1984 v EG (sub); (with Watford), Y (2) (3)
Jupp, D. A. (Fulham), 1995 v Fi, Ru (2), Sm, M, F, Sk, Br (8)

Kirkwood, D. (Hearts), 1990 v Y (1)
Kerr, S. (Celtic), 1993 v Bul, M, E; 1994 v Ma, A, Eg, P, Bel; 1995 v Fi, Gr (10)

Lambert, P. (St Mirren), 1991 v R, Sw, Bul (2), Pol, F; 1992 v Sw, R, G (2), Se (11)
Lavety, B. (St. Mirren), 1993 v Ic, Bul (sub), M (sub), E; 1994 v Ma, A (sub), Eg (sub), Bel (sub); 1995 v Fi (sub) (9)
Lavin, G. (Watford), 1993 v F, Bul, M; 1994 v Ma, Eg, P, Bel (7)
Leighton, J. (Aberdeen), 1982 v I (1)
Levein, C. (Hearts), 1985 v Sp, Ic (2)
Liddell, A. M. (Barnsley), 1994 v Ma (sub); 1995 v Sm (sub), M (sub), F, Sk (5)
Lindsey, J. (Motherwell), 1979 v US (1)
Locke, G. (Hearts), 1994 v Ma, A, Eg, P; 1995 v Fi (5)
Love, G. (Hibernian), 1995 v Ru (1)

McAllister, G. (Leicester C), 1990 v N (1)
McAlpine, H. (Dundee U), 1983 v EG, Sw (2), Bel; 1984 v Bel (5)
McAuley, S. (St. Johnstone), 1993 v P (sub) (1)
McAvennie, F. (St Mirren), 1982 v I, E; 1985 v Is, Ei, R (5)
McBride, J. (Everton), 1981 v D (1)
McCall, S. (Bradford C), 1988 v E; (with Everton), 1990 v F (2)
McCann, N. (Dundee), 1994 v A, Eg, P, Bel; 1995 v Fi, Gr (sub), Sm, (7)
McClair, B. (Celtic), 1984 v Bel (sub), EG, Y (1 + 1 sub); 1985 v WG, Ic, Sp, Ic (8)
McCluskey, G. (Celtic), 1979 v US, P; 1980 v Bel (2); 1982 v D, I (6)
McCoist, A. (Rangers), 1984 v Bel (1)
McCulloch, A. (Kilmarnock); 1981 v Se (1)
McCulloch, I. (Notts Co), 1982 v E (2)
MacDonald, J. (Rangers), 1980 v WG (sub); 1981 v Se; 1982 v Se (sub), L, I (2), E (2 sub) (8)
McDonald, C. (Falkirk), 1995 v Fi (sub), Ru, M (sub), F (sub), Br (sub) (5)
McGarvey, F. (St Mirren), 1977 v E; 1978 v Cz; (with Celtic), 1982 v D (3)
McGarvey, S. (Manchester U), 1982 v E (sub); 1983 v Bel, Sw; 1984 v Bel (4)
McGhee, M. (Aberdeen), 1981 v D (1)
McGinnis, G. (Dundee U), 1985 v Sp (1)
McGrillen, P. (Motherwell), 1994 v Sw (sub), I (2)
McInally, J. (Dundee U), 1989 v F (1)
McKimmie, S. (Aberdeen), 1985 v WG, Ic (2) (3)
McKinlay, T. (Dundee), 1984 v EG (sub); 1985 v WG, Ic, Sp (2), Ic (6)
McKinlay, W. (Dundee U), 1989 v N, Y (sub), F; 1990 v Y, F, N (6)
McKinnon, R. (Dundee U), 1991 v R, Pol (sub); 1992 v G (2), Se (2) (6)
McLaren, A, (Hearts), 1989 v F; 1990 v Y, N; 1991 v Sw, Bul, Pol, F; 1992 v R, G, Se (2) (11)
McLaren, A. (Dundee U), 1993 v I, Ma (sub); 1994 v Sw, I (sub) (4)
McLaughlin, B. (Celtic), 1995 v Ru, Sm, M, Sk (sub), Br (sub) (5)
McLaughlin, J. (Morton), 1981 v D; 1982 v Se, D, I, E (2); 1983 v EG, Sw (2), Bel (10)
McLeish, A. (Aberdeen), 1978 v W; 1979 v US; 1980 v Bel, E (2); 1987 v Ei (6)
MacLeod, A. (Hibernian), 1979 v P, N (2) (3)
McLeod, J. (Dundee U), 1989 v N; 1990 v F (2)
MacLeod, M. (Dumbarton), 1979 v US; (with Celtic), P (sub), N (2); 1980 v Bel (5)
McNab, N. (Tottenham H), 1978 v W (1)
McNally, M. (Celtic), 1991 v Bul; 1993 v Ic (2)
McNamara, J. (Dunfermline Ath), 1994 v A, Bel; 1995 v Gr, Ru, Sm (5)
McNichol, J. (Brentford), 1979 v P, N (2); 1980 v Bel (2), WG, E (7)
McNiven, D. (Leeds U), 1977 v Cz, W (sub), Sw (sub) (3)
McPherson, D. (Rangers), 1984 v Bel; 1985 v Sp; (with Hearts), 1989 v N, Y (4)
McQuilken, J. (Celtic), 1993 v Bul, E (2)
McStay, P. (Celtic), 1983 v EG, Sw (2); 1984 v Y (2) (5)
McWhirter, N. (St Mirren), 1991 v Bul (sub) (1)
Main, A. (Dundee U), 1988 v E; 1989 v Y; 1990 v N (3)
Malpas, M. (Dundee U), 1983 v Bel, Sw (1 + 1 sub); 1984 v Bel, EG, Y (2); 1985 v Sp (8)
Marshall, S. R. (Arsenal), 1995 v Ru, Gr (2)
May, E. (Hibernian), 1989 v Y (sub), F (2)
Melrose, J. (Partick Th), 1977 v Sw; 1979 v US, P, N (2); 1980 v Bel (sub), WG, E (8)
Miller, C. (Rangers), 1995 v Gr, Ru (2)
Miller, J. (Aberdeen), 1987 v Ei (sub); 1988 v Bel; (with Celtic), E; 1989 v N, Y; 1990 v F, N (7)
Miller, W. (Aberdeen), 1978 v Sw, Cz (2)
Miller, W. (Hibernian), 1991 v R, Sw, Bul, Pol, F; 1992 v R, G (sub) (7)
Milne, R. (Dundee U), 1982 v Se (sub); 1984 v Bel, EG (3)
Money, I. C. (St Mirren), 1987 v Ei; 1988 v Bel; 1989 v N (3)
Muir, L. (Hibernian), 1977 v Cz (sub) (1)
Murray, N. (Rangers), 1993 v P (sub), Ma, Ic, P; 1994 v Sw, I; 1995 v Fi, Ru, Gr, Sm (10)
Murray, R. (Bournemouth), 1993 v Ic (sub) (1)

Narey, D. (Dundee U), 1977 v Cz, Sw; 1978 v Sw, Cz (4)
Nevin, P. (Chelsea), 1985 v WG, Ic, Sp (2), Ic (5)
Nicholas, C. (Celtic), 1981 v Se; 1982 v Se; 1983 v EG, Sw, Bel; (with Arsenal), 1984 v Y (6)

Nicol, S. (Ayr U), 1981 v Se; 1982 v Se, D; (with Liverpool), I (2), E (2); 1983 v EG, Sw (2), Bel; 1984 v Bel, EG, Y (14)
Nisbet, S. (Rangers), 1989 v N, Y, F; 1990 v Y, F (5)

O'Donnell, P. (Motherwell), 1992 v Sw (sub), R, D, G (2), Se (1 + 1 sub); 1993 v P (8)
O'Neil, B. (Celtic), 1992 v D, G, Se (2); 1993 v Sw, P, I (7)
O'Neil, J. (Dundee U), 1991 v Bul (sub) (1)
O'Neill, M. (Clyde), 1995 v Ru (sub), F, Sk, Br (4)
Orr, N. (Morton), 1978 v W (sub); 1979 v US, P, N (2); 1980 v Bel, E (7)

Parlane, D. (Rangers), 1977 v W (1)
Paterson, C. (Hibernian), 1981 v Se; 1982 v I (2)
Payne, G. (Dundee U), 1978 v Sw, Cz, W (3)
Pressley, S. (Rangers), 1993 v Ic, F, Bul, M, E; 1994 v Sw, I, M, A, Eg, P, Bel; 1995 v Fi; (with Coventry C), Ru (2), Sm, M, F, Sk, Br (20)
Provan, D. (Kilmarnock), 1977 v Cz (sub) (1)

Rae, A. (Millwall), 1991 v Bul (sub + 1), F (sub); 1992 v Sw, R, G (sub), Se (2) (8)
Redford, I. (Rangers), 1981 v Se (sub); 1982 v Se, D, I (2), E (6)
Reid, B. (Rangers), 1991 v F; 1992 v D, US, P (4)
Reid, C. (Hibernian), 1993 v Sw, P, I (3)
Reid, M. (Celtic), 1982 v E; 1984 v Y (2)
Reid, R. (St Mirren), 1977 v W, Sw, E (3)
Rice, B. (Hibernian), 1985 v WG (1)
Richardson, L. (St Mirren), 1980 v WG, E (sub) (2)
Ritchie, A. (Morton), 1980 v Bel (1)
Robertson, A. (Rangers) 1991 v F (1)
Robertson, C. (Rangers), 1977 v E (sub) (1)
Robertson, D. (Aberdeen), 1987 v Ei (sub); 1988 v E (2); 1989 v N, Y; 1990 v Y, N (7)
Robertson, H. (Aberdeen), 1994 v Eg; 1995 v Fi (2)
Robertson, J. (Hearts), 1985 v WG, Ic (sub) (2)
Robertson, L. (Rangers), 1993 v F, M (sub), E (sub) (3)
Roddie, A. (Aberdeen), 1992 v US, P; 1993 v Sw (sub), P, Ic (5)
Ross, T. W. (Arsenal), 1977 v W (1)
Russell, R. (Rangers), 1978 v W; 1980 v Bel; 1984 v Y (3)

Salton, D. B. (Luton T), 1992 v D, US, P, Y; 1993 v Sw, I (6)
Scott, P. (St Johnstone), 1994 v A (sub), Eg (sub), P, Bel (4)
Shannon, R. (Dundee), 1987 v WG, Ei (2), Bel; 1988 v Bel, E (2) (7)
Sharp, G. (Everton), 1982 v E (1)
Sharp, R. (Dunfermline Ath), 1990 v N (sub); 1991 v R, Sw, Bul (4)
Simpson, N. (Aberdeen), 1982 v I (2), E; 1983 v EG, Sw (2), Bel; 1984 v Bel, EG, Y; 1985 v Sp (11)
Sinclair, G. (Dumbarton), 1977 v E (1)
Skilling, M. (Kilmarnock), 1993 v Ic (sub); 1994 v I (2)
Smith, B. M. (Celtic), 1992 v G (2), US, P, Y (5)
Smith, G. (Rangers), 1978 v W (1)
Smith, H. G. (Hearts), 1987 v WG, Bel (2)
Sneddon, A. (Celtic), 1979 v US (1)
Speedie, D. (Chelsea), 1985 v Sp (1)
Spencer, J. (Rangers), 1991 v Sw (sub), F; 1992 v Sw (3)
Stanton, P. (Hibernian), 1977 v Cz (1)
Stark, W. (Aberdeen), 1985 v Ic (1)
Stephen, R. (Dundee), 1983 v Bel (sub) (1)
Stevens, G. (Motherwell), 1977 v E (1)
Stewart, J. (Kilmarnock), 1978 v Sw, Cz; (with Middlesbrough), 1979 v P (3)
Stewart, R. (Dundee U), 1979 v P, N (2); (with West Ham U), 1980 v Bel (2), E (2), WG; 1981 v D; 1982 v I (2), E (12)
Stille, D. (Aberdeen), 1995 v Ru (2), Sm, M, F, Sk, Br (7)
Strachan, G. (Aberdeen), 1980 v Bel (1)
Sturrock, P. (Dundee U), 1977 v Cz, W, Sw, E; 1978 v Sw, Cz; 1982 v Se, I, E (9)
Sweeney, S. (Clydebank), 1991 v R, Sw (sub), Bul (2), Pol; 1992 v Sw, R (7)

Telfer, P. (Luton T), 1993 v Ma, P; 1994 v Sw (3)
Thomas, K. (Hearts), 1993 v F (sub), Bul, M, E; 1994 v Sw, Ma; 1995 v Gr (7)
Thomson, W. (Partick Th), 1977 v E (sub); 1978 v W; (with St Mirren), 1979 v US, N (2); 1980 v Bel (2), E (2), WG (10)
Tolmie, J. (Morton), 1980 v Bel (sub) (1)
Tortolano, J. (Hibernian), 1987 v WG, Ei (2)
Tweed, S. (Hibernian), 1993 v Ic; 1994 v Sw, I (3)

Walker, A. (Celtic), 1988 v Bel (1)
Wallace, I. (Coventry C), 1978 v Sw (1)
Walsh, C. (Nottingham F), 1984 v EG, Sw (2), Bel; 1984 v EG (5)
Wark, J. (Ipswich T), 1977 v Cz, W, Sw; 1978 v W; 1979 v P; 1980 v E (2), WG (8)
Watson, A. (Aberdeen), 1981 v Se, D; 1982 v D, I (sub) (4)
Watson, K. (Rangers), 1977 v E; 1978 v Sw (sub) (2)
Watt, M. (Aberdeen), 1991 v R, Sw, Bul (2), Pol, F; 1992 v Sw, R, G (2), Se (2) (12)
Whyte, D. (Celtic), 1987 v Ei (2), Bel; 1988 v E (2); 1989 v N, Y; 1990 v Y, N (9)
Will, J. A. (Arsenal), 1992 v D (sub), Y; 1993 v Ic (sub) (3)
Wilson, T. (St Mirren), 1983 v Sw (sub) (1)
Wilson, T. (Nottingham F), 1988 v E; 1989 v N, Y; 1990 v F (4)
Winnie, D. (St Mirren), 1988 v Bel (1)
Wright, P. (Aberdeen), 1989 v Y, F; (with QPR), 1990 v Y (sub) (3)
Wright, S. (Aberdeen), 1991 v Bul, Pol, F; 1992 v Sw, G (2), Se (2); 1993 v Sw, P, I, Ma; 1994 v I, Ma (14)
Wright, T. (Oldham Ath), 1987 v Bel (sub) (1)

WALES

Aizlewood, M. (Luton T), 1979 v E; 1981 v Ho (2)

Balcombe, S. (Leeds U), 1982 v F (sub) (1)
Barnhouse, D. J. (Swansea), 1995 v Mol (1)
Bater, P. T. (Bristol R), 1977 v E, S (2)
Bird, A. (Cardiff C), 1993 v Cy (sub); 1994 v Cy (sub); 1995 v Mol, Ge (sub), Bul (5)
Blackmore, C. (Manchester U), 1984 v N, Bul, Y (3)
Blake, N. (Cardiff C), 1991 v Pol (sub); 1993 v Cy, Bel, RCS; 1994 v RCS (5)
Bodin, P. (Cardiff C), 1983 v Y (1)
Bowen, J. P. (Swansea C), 1993 v Cy, Bel (2); 1994 v RCS, R (sub) (5)
Bowen, M. (Tottenham H), 1983 v N; 1984 v Bul, Y (3)
Boyle, T. (C Palace), 1982 v F (1)
Brace, D. P. (Wrexham), 1995 v Ge, Bul (2) (3)

Cegielski, W. (Wrexham), 1977 v E (sub), S (2)
Chapple, S. R. (Swansea C), 1992 v R; 1993 v Cy, Bel (2), RCS; 1994 v RCS; Bul (2) (8)
Charles, J. M. (Swansea C), 1979 v E; 1981 v Ho (2)
Clark, J. (Manchester U), 1978 v S; (with Derby Co), 1979 v E (2)
Coleman, C. (Swansea C); 1990 v Pol; 1991 v E, Pol (3)
Coyne, D. (Tranmere R), 1992 v R; 1994 v Cy (sub), R; 1995 v Mol, Ge, Bul (2) (7)
Curtis, A. T. (Swansea C), 1977 v E (1)

Davies, A. (Manchester U), 1982 v F (2), Ho; 1983 v N, Y, Bul (6)
Davies, G. M. (Hereford U), 1993 v Bel, RCS; 1995 v Mol (sub), Ge, Bul (2) (6)
Davies, I. C. (Norwich C), 1978 v S (sub) (1)
Deacy, N. (PSV Eindhoven), 1977 v S (1)
Dibble, A. (Cardiff C), 1983 v Bul; 1984 v N, Bul (3)

Doyle, S. C. (Preston NE), 1979 v E (sub); (with Huddersfield T), 1984 v N (2)
Dwyer, P. J. (Cardiff C), 1979 v E (1)

Ebdon, M. (Everton), 1990 v Pol; 1991 v E (2)
Edwards, R. (Bristol C), 1991 v Pol; 1992 v R; 1995 v Ge, Bul (4)
Edwards, R. I. (Chester), 1977 v S; 1978 v W (2)
Edwards, R. W. (Bristol C), 1993 v Cy, Bel (2), RCS; 1994 v RCS, Cy, R (7)
Evans, A. (Bristol R), 1977 v E (1)
Evans, T. (Cardiff C), 1995 v Bul (sub) (1)

Foster, M. G. (Tranmere R), 1993 v RCS (1)
Freestone, R. (Chelsea), 1990 v Pol (1)

Gale, D. (Swansea C), 1983 v Bul; 1984 v N (sub) (2)
Giggs, R. (Manchester U), 1991 v Pol (1)
Giles, D. C. (Cardiff C), 1977 v S; 1978 v S; (with Swansea C), 1981 v Ho; (with C Palace), 1983 v Y (4)
Giles, P. (Cardiff C), 1982 v F (2), Ho (3)
Graham, D. (Manchester U), 1991 v E (1)
Griffith, C. (Cardiff C), 1990 v Pol (1)
Griffiths, C. (Shrewsbury T), 1991 v Pol (sub) (1)

Hall, G. D. (Chelsea), 1990 v Pol (1)
Hartson, J. (Luton T), 1994 v Cy, R; 1995 v Mol, Ge, Bul (5)
Hodges, G. (Wimbledon), 1983 v Y (sub), Bul (sub); 1984 v N, Bul, Y (5)
Holden, A. (Chester C), 1984 v Y (sub) (1)
Hopkins, J. (Fulham), 1982 v F (sub), Ho; 1983 v N, Y, Bul (5)
Hughes, D. R. (Southampton), 1994 v R (1)
Hughes, I. (Bury), 1992 v R; 1993 v Cy, Bel (sub), RCS; 1994 v Cy, R; 1995 v Mol, Ge, Bul (9)
Hughes, L. M. (Manchester U), 1983 v N, Y; 1984 v N, Bul, Y (5)
Hughes, W. (WBA), 1977 v E, S; 1978 v S (3)

Jackett, K. (Watford), 1981 v Ho; 1982 v F (2)
James, R. M. (Swansea C), 1977 v E, S; 1978 v S (3)
Jenkins, S. R. (Swansea C), 1993 v Cy (sub), Bel (2)
Jones, F. (Wrexham), 1981 v Ho (1)
Jones, L. (Cardiff C), 1982 v F (2), Ho (3)
Jones, P. L. (Liverpool), 1992 v R; 1993 v Cy, Bel (2), RCS; 1994 v RCS (sub), Cy, R; 1995 v Mol, Ge (10)
Jones, R. (Sheffield W), 1994 v R; 1995 v Bul (2) (3)
Jones, V. (Bristol R), 1979 v E; 1981 v Ho (2)

Kendall, M. (Tottenham H), 1978 v S (1)
Kenworthy, J. R. (Tranmere R), 1994 v Cy; 1995 v Mol, Bul (3)

Law, B. J. (QPR), 1990 v Pol; 1991 v E (2)
Letheran, G. (Leeds U), 1977 v E, S (2)
Lewis, D. (Swansea C), 1982 v F (2), Ho; 1983 v N, Y, Bul; 1984 v N, Bul, Y (9)
Lewis, J. (Cardiff C), 1983 v N (1)
Loveridge, J. (Swansea C), 1982 v Ho; 1983 v N, Bul (3)
Lowndes, S. R. (Newport Co), 1979 v E; 1981 v Ho; (with Millwall), 1984 v Bul, Y (4)

McCarthy, A. J. (QPR), 1994 v RCS, Cy, R (3)
Maddy, P. (Cardiff C), 1982 v Ho; 1983 v N (sub) (2)
Margetson, M. W. (Manchester C), 1992 v R; 1993 v Cy, Bel (2), RCS; 1994 v RCS, Cy (7)
Marustik, C. (Swansea C), 1982 v F (2); 1983 v Y, Bul; 1984 v N, Bul, Y (7)
Meaker, M. J. (QPR), 1994 v RCS (sub), R (sub) (2)
Melville, A. K. (Swansea C), 1990 v Pol; (with Oxford U), 1991 v E (2)
Micallef, C. (Cardiff C), 1982 v F, Ho; 1983 v N (3)
Morgan, A. M. (Tranmere R), 1995 v Mol, Bul (2)

Nardiello, D. (Coventry C), 1978 v S (1)
Neilson, A. B. (Newcastle U), 1993 v Cy, Bel (2), RCS; 1994 v RCS, Cy, R (7)
Nicholas, P. (C Palace), 1978 v S; 1979 v E; (with Arsenal), 1982 v F (3)
Nogan, K. (Luton T), 1990 v Pol; 1991 v E (2)
Nogan, L. (Oxford U) 1991 v E (1)

Owen, G. (Wrexham), 1991 v E (sub), Pol; 1992 v R; 1993 v Cy, Bel (2); 1994 v Cy, R (8)

Page, R. J. (Watford), 1995 v Mol, Ge, Bul (3)
Pascoe, C. (Swansea C), 1983 v Bul (sub); 1984 v N (sub), Bul, Y (4)
Pembridge, M. (Luton T), 1991 v Pol (1)
Perry, J. (Cardiff C), 1990 v Pol; 1991 v E, Pol (3)
Peters, M. (Manchester C), 1992 v R; (with Norwich C), 1993 v Cy, RCS (3)
Phillips, D. (Plymouth Arg), 1984 v N, Bul, Y (3)
Phillips, L. (Swansea C), 1979 v E; (with Charlton Ath), 1983 v N (2)
Pontin, K. (Cardiff C), 1978 v S (1)
Powell, L. (Southampton), 1991 v Pol (sub); 1992 v R (sub); 1993 v Bel (sub); 1994 v RCS (4)
Price, P. (Luton T), 1981 v Ho (1)
Pugh, D. (Doncaster R), 1982 v F (2) (2)
Pugh, S. (Wrexham), 1993 v Bel (2 subs) (2)

Ratcliffe, K. (Everton), 1981 v Ho; 1982 v F (2)
Ready, K. (QPR), 1992 v R; 1993 v Bel (2); 1994 v RCS, Cy (5)
Rees, A. (Birmingham C), 1984 v N (1)
Rees, J. (Luton T), 1990 v Pol; 1991 v E, Pol (3)
Roberts, A. (QPR), 1991 v E, Pol (2)
Roberts, G. (Hull C), 1983 v Bul (1)
Roberts, J. G. (Wrexham), 1977 v E (1)
Robinson, J. (Brighton & HA), 1992 v R; (with Charlton Ath), 1993 v Bel; 1994 v RCS, Cy, R (5)
Rush, I. (Liverpool), 1981 v Ho; 1982 v F (2)

Savage, R. W. (Crewe Alex), 1995 v Bul (1)
Sayer, P. A. (Cardiff C), 1977 v E, S (2)
Searle, D. (Cardiff C), 1991 v Pol (sub); 1992 v R; 1993 v Cy, Bel (2), RCS; 1994 v RCS (6)
Slatter, N. (Bristol R), 1983 v N, Y, Bul; 1984 v N, Bul, Y (6)
Speed, G. A. (Leeds U), 1990 v Pol; 1991 v E, Pol (3)
Stevenson, N. (Swansea C), 1982 v F, Ho (2)
Stevenson, W. B. (Leeds U), 1977 v E, S; 1978 v S (3)
Symons, K. (Portsmouth), 1991 v E, Pol (2)

Taylor, G. K. (Bristol R), 1995 v Ge, Bul (2) (3)
Thomas, Martin R. (Bristol R), 1979 v E; 1981 v Ho (2)
Thomas, Mickey R. (Wrexham), 1977 v E; 1978 v S (2)
Thomas, D. G. (Leeds U), 1977 v E; 1979 v E; 1984 v N (3)
Tibbott, L. (Ipswich T), 1977 v E, S (2)
Twiddy, C. (Plymouth Arg), 1995 v Mol, Ge (2)

Vaughan, N. (Newport Co), 1982 v F, Ho (2)

Walsh, I. P. (C Palace), 1979 v E; (with Swansea C), 1983 v Bul (2)
Walton, M. (Norwich C.), 1991 v Pol (sub) (1)
Williams, D. (Bristol R), 1983 v Y (1)
Williams, G. (Bristol R), 1983 v Y, Bul (2)
Williams, S. J. (Wrexham), 1995 v Mol, Ge, Bul (2) (4)
Wilmot, R. (Arsenal), 1982 v F (2), Ho; 1983 v N, Y; 1984 v Y (6)

International Records

MOST GOALS IN AN INTERNATIONAL

England	Malcolm Macdonald (Newcastle U) 5 goals v Cyprus, at Wembley	16.4.1975
	Willie Hall (Tottenham H) 5 goals v Ireland, at Old Trafford	16.11.1938
	G. O. Smith (Corinthians) 5 goals v Ireland, at Sunderland	18.2.1899
	Steve Bloomer (Derby Co) 5 goals* v Wales, at Cardiff	16.3.1896
	Oliver Vaughton (Aston Villa) 5 goals v Ireland, at Belfast	18.2.82
Scotland	Charles Heggie (Rangers) 5 goals v Ireland, at Belfast	20.3.1886
Ireland	Joe Bambrick (Linfield) 6 goals v Wales, at Belfast	1.2.1930
Wales	James Price (Wrexham) 4 goals v Ireland, at Wrexham	25.2.1882
	Mel Charles (Cardiff C) 4 goals v Ireland, at Cardiff	11.4.1962
	Ian Edwards (Chester) 4 goals v Malta, at Wrexham	25.10.1978

* There are conflicting reports which make it uncertain whether Bloomer scored four or five goals in this game.

MOST GOALS IN AN INTERNATIONAL CAREER

		Goals	Games
England	Bobby Charlton (Manchester U)	49	106
Scotland	Denis Law (Huddersfield T, Manchester C, Torino, Manchester U)	30	55
	Kenny Dalglish (Celtic, Liverpool)	30	102
Ireland	Colin Clarke (Bournemouth, Southampton, QPR, Portsmouth	13	38
Wales	Ian Rush (Liverpool, Juventus)	28	71
	Ivor Allchurch (Swansea T, Newcastle U, Cardiff C)	23	68
Republic of Ireland	Frank Stapleton (Arsenal, Manchester U, Ajax, Derby Co, Le Havre, Blackburn R)	20	70

HIGHEST SCORES

World Cup Match	New Zealand	13	Fiji	0	1981
European Championship	Spain	12	Malta	1	1983
Olympic Games	Denmark	17	France	1	1908
	Germany	16	USSR	0	1912
International Match	Germany	13	Finland	0	1940
	Spain	13	Bulgaria	0	1933
European Cup	Feyenoord	12	K R Reykjavik	2	1969
European Cup-Winners' Cup	Sporting Lisbon	16	Apoel Nicosia	1	1963
Fairs & UEFA Cups	Ajax	14	Red Boys	0	1984

GOALSCORING RECORDS

World Cup Final	Geoff Hurst (England) 3 goals v West Germany	1966
World Cup Final tournament	Just Fontaine (France) 13 goals	1958
Major European Cup game	Lothar Emmerich (Borussia Dortmund) v Floriana in Cup-Winners' Cup – 6 goals	1965
Career	Arthur Friedenreich (Brazil) 1329 goals	1910–30
	Pelé (Brazil) 1281 goals	*1956–78
	Franz 'Bimbo' Binder (Austria, Germany) 1006 goals	1930–50

**Pelé subsequently scored two goals in Testimonial matches making his total 1283.*

MOST CAPPED INTERNATIONALS IN BRITISH ISLES

England	Peter Shilton	125 appearances	1970–90
Northern Ireland	Pat Jennings	119 appearances	1964–86
Scotland	Kenny Dalglish	102 appearances	1971–86
Wales	Neville Southall	81 appearances	1982–95
Republic of Ireland	Paddy Bonner	78 appearances	1981–95

TRANSFERS

Record British moves (UK only)

£8,500,000 Stan Collymore, Nottingham F to Liverpool, June 1995
£6,250,000 Andy Cole, Newcastle U to Manchester U, January 1995
£6,000,000 Les Ferdinand, QPR to Newcastle U, June 1995
£5,000,000 Chris Sutton, Norwich to Blackburn R, July 1994
£5,000,000 Andrei Kanchelskis, Manchester U to Everton, July 1995
£4,500,000 Chris Armstrong, Crystal Palace to Tottenham H, June 1995
£4,000,000 Duncan Ferguson, Dundee U to Rangers, July 1993
£4,000,000 Duncan Ferguson, Rangers to Everton, December 1994
£4,000,000 Warren Barton, Wimbledon to Newcastle U, June 1995
£3,750,000 Roy Keane, Nottingham F to Manchester U, July 1993

Other British moves

£7,000,000 Paul Ince, Manchester U to Internazionale, June 1995
£6,500,000 David Platt, Bari to Juventus, May 1992
£5,500,000 David Platt, Aston Villa to Bari, July 1991
£5,500,000 Paul Gascoigne, Tottenham H to Lazio, May 1992
£5,200,000 David Platt, Juventus to Sampdoria, July 1993
£5,000,000 Trevor Steven, Rangers to Marseille, August 1991
£4,750,000 David Platt, Sampdoria to Arsenal, July 1995
£4,500,000 Chris Waddle, Tottenham H to Marseille, July 1989
£4,300,000 Paul Gascoigne, Lazio to Rangers, July 1995
£3,200,000 Ian Rush, Liverpool to Juventus, June 1987
£2,800,000 Ian Rush, Juventus to Liverpool, August 1988
£2,750,000 Gary Lineker, Everton to Barcelona, June 1986

World records

£13,000,000 Gianluigi Lentini, Torino to AC Milan, June 1992
£12,000,000 Gianluca Vialli, Sampdoria to Juventus, June 1992
£10,000,000 Jean-Pierre Papin, Marseille to AC Milan, June 1992

INTERCONTINENTAL CUP

Group A
Saudi Arabia 0, Mexico 2
Saudi Arabia 0, Denmark 2
Denmark 1, Mexico 1

Group B
Japan 0, Nigeria 3
Argentina 5, Japan 1
Argentina 0, Nigeria 0

Third Place
Mexico 1, Nigeria 1
(*Mexico won 5-4 on penalties*)

Final
Denmark 2, Argentina 0

FA SCHOOLS AND YOUTH GAMES 1994–95

ENGLAND UNDER-16

26 Feb

Greece 0

England 4 *(Morris, Wright, Ormerod, Wicks)*

England: Heritage (Sheffield U); Dickman (Manchester U), Crowe (Arsenal), Curtis (Manchester U), Wicks (Arsenal), Gower (Tottenham H), O'Connor (Wimbledon) [Brightwell (Manchester U)], Staton (Blackburn R) [Ormerod (Middlesbrough)], Branch (Everton), Morris (Chelsea), Wright (Leeds U).

28 Feb

Romania 2

England 3 *(Branch 3)*

England: Heritage (Sheffield U); Dickman (Manchester U), Crowe (Arsenal), Curtis (Manchester U), Wicks (Arsenal), Gower (Tottenham H), Brightwell (Manchester U) [O'Connor (Wimbledon)], Staton (Blackburn R), Branch (Everton), Morris (Chelsea), Wright (Leeds U) [Clement (Chelsea)].

17 Sept

Holland 1

England 1 *(Wilson)*

England: Weaver (Leyton Orient) [Heritage (Sheffield U)]; Dickman (Manchester U), Clement (Chelsea), Curtis (Manchester U) [Wicks (Arsenal)], Perry (QPR), Morris (Chelsea), Brightwell (Manchester U), Gower (Tottenham H), Bunn (Tottenham H) [Smith (Crewe Alex)], Wilson (Manchester U) [Ormerod (Middlesbrough)], Platts (Sheffield W) [Wright (Leeds U)].

19 Nov

Turkey 3

England 2 *(Morris 2 (1 pen))*

England: Heritage (Sheffield U); [Weaver (Leyton Orient)]; Dickman (Manchester U), Clement (Chelsea) [Wicks (Manchester U)], Curtis (Manchester U), Perry (QPR), Gower (Tottenham H), Brightwell (Manchester U) [Ormerod (Middlesbrough)], Morris (Chelsea), Branch (Everton), Platts (Sheffield W) [Wilson (Manchester U)], Wright (Leeds U) [Smith (Crewe Alex)].

21 Jan

Portugal 0

England 0

England: Heritage (Sheffield U); Dickman (Manchester U), Crowe (Arsenal), Curtis (Manchester U), Wicks (Manchester U), Gower (Tottenham H), O'Connor (Wimbledon) [Brightwell (Manchester U)], Morris (Chelsea), Branch (Everton) [Burgess (Aston Villa)], Staton (Blackburn R) [Ormerod (Middlesbrough)], Wright (Leeds U) [Platts (Middlesbrough)].

24 Apr

England 1 *(Branch)*

Scotland 1

England: Heritage (Sheffield U); Dickman (Manchester U), Crowe (Arsenal) [Clement (Chelsea)], Curtis (Manchester U), Wicks (Manchester U), Morris (Chelsea), Brightwell (Manchester U), Gower (Tottenham H) [Ormerod (Middlesbrough)], Branch (Everton), Staton (Blackburn R), Wright (Leeds U).

26 Apr

England 2 *(Wicks, Curtis)*

Slovakia 1

England: O'Toole (Everton); Dickman (Manchester U), Crowe (Arsenal), Curtis (Manchester U), Wicks (Manchester U) [Clement (Chelsea)], Morris (Chelsea), Ormerod (Middlesbrough), Bunn (Tottenham H), Branch (Everton), Staton (Blackburn R), Wright (Leeds U).

28 Apr

England 3 *(Morris, Clement, Wright)*

Portugal 1

England: O'Toole (Everton); Dickman (Manchester U), Crowe (Arsenal), Curtis (Manchester U), Clement (Chelsea), Morris (Chelsea), Ormerod (Middlesbrough) [Wright (Leeds U)], Gower (Tottenham H), Branch (Everton), Staton (Blackburn R), Bunn (Tottenham H) [Smith (Crewe Alex)].

1 May

England 0

France 1

England: Heritage (Sheffield U); Dickman (Manchester U), Crowe (Arsenal), Curtis (Manchester U), Clement (Chelsea), Morris (Chelsea), Ormerod (Middlesbrough) [Brightwell (Manchester U)], Gower (Tottenham H), Branch (Everton), Staton (Blackburn R), Wright (Leeds U) [Bunn (Tottenham H)].

23 May

England 2 *(Branch, Clement)*
Oman 3
England: O'Toole (Everton) [Heritage (Sheffield U)]; Culshaw (Liverpool), Clement (Chelsea), Curtis (Manchester U), Gower (Tottenham H), Morris (Chelsea), Brightwell (Manchester U), Marshall (Everton) [Smith (Crewe Alex)], Branch (Everton), Wilson (Manchester U), Wright (Leeds U) [Johnson (Crewe Alex)].

26 May

England 1 *(Wright)*
Oman 1
England: Heritage (Sheffield U) [O'Toole (Everton)]; Brightwell (Manchester U), Clement (Chelsea), Curtis (Manchester U), Culshaw (Liverpool) [Brown (Manchester U)], Morris (Chelsea), Gower (Tottenham H), Marshall (Everton) [Haslam (Sheffield W)], Branch (Everton), Wilson (Manchester U) [Wright (Leeds U)], Smith (Crewe Alex) [Owen (Liverpool)].

ENGLAND UNDER-18

22 Feb

England 5 *(Bowyer, Moore 3, Davies)*
Denmark 6
England: Cutler (WBA); Allen (Everton), Aljofrey (Bolton W) [Millett (Wigan Ath)], Ashbee (Derby Co) [Hendrie (Aston Villa)], Mills (Norwich C), O'Connor (Everton), Thompson (Liverpool), Bowyer (Charlton Ath), Cooke (Manchester U), Davies (Chesterfield [Beresford (Oldham Ath)], Moore (Tranmere R).

24 July

Norway 3
England 3 *(Cooke 2, Murphy)*
England: Cutler (WBA); Neville (Manchester U), Power (QPR), Howell (Arsenal) [Murphy (Crewe Alex)], O'Connor (Everton), Mills (Norwich C), Bowyer (Charlton Ath), Beresford (Oldham Ath) [Spencer (Tottenham H)], Davies (Chesterfield), Hughes (Arsenal), Cooke (Manchester U).

26 July

Norway 2
England 3 *(Hughes, Davies, Bowyer)*
England: Tyler (Peterborough U); Neville (Manchester U), Power (QPR) [Mills (Norwich C)], Bowyer (Charlton Ath), O'Connor (Everton), Allen (Everton), Murphy (Crewe Alex) [Howell (Arsenal)], Spencer (Tottenham H), Davies (Chesterfield) [Cooke (Manchester U)], Hughes (Arsenal), Walley (Nottingham F).

6 Sept

England 2 *(Murphy 2)*
France 3
England: Cutler (WBA); Neville (Manchester U), Taylor (Arsenal) [Power (QPR)], Thompson (Liverpool) [Beresford (Oldham Ath)], Plummer (QPR), Allen (Everton) [O'Connor (Everton)], Bowyer (Charlton Ath), Hughes (Arsenal), Murphy (Crewe Alex), Davies (Chesterfield) [Furnell (Peterborough U)], Cooke (Manchester U).

13 Nov

England 3 *(Murphy 2, Beresford)*
Slovenia 0
England: Cutler (WBA); Murray (Carlisle U) [Allen (Everton)], Taylor (Arsenal), Thompson (Liverpool), Hodges (Wimbledon), O'Connor (Everton), Beresford (Oldham Ath) [Hendrie (Aston Villa)], Bowyer (Charlton Ath), Davies (Chesterfield), Murphy (Crewe Alex), Cooke (Manchester U).

17 Nov

England 0
Latvia 0
England: Cutler (WBA); Allen (Everton), Taylor (Arsenal), Thompson (Liverpool), Hodges (Wimbledon), O'Connor (Everton), Cooke (Manchester U), Bowyer (Charlton Ath), Davies (Chesterfield) [Woodsford (Luton T)], Murphy (Crewe Alex), Hendrie (Aston Villa) [Hughes (Arsenal)].

29 Mar

Hungary 0
England 1 *(Moore)*
England: Davis (Luton T); Neville (Manchester U), Stuart (Charlton Ath), O'Connor (Everton), Westwood (Manchester U), Beresford (Oldham Ath) [Ducros (Coventry C)], Murphy (Crewe Alex), Clemence (Tottenham H), Cooke (Manchester U), Davies (Chesterfield), Moore (Tranmere R).

25 Apr

England 0
Hungary 2 *(aet)*
England: Davis (Luton T); Neville (Manchester U), Westwood (Manchester U), O'Connor (Everton), Stuart (Charlton Ath) [Broomes (Blackburn R)], Piper (Wimbledon), Beresford (Oldham Ath) [Ducros (Coventry C)], Clemence (Tottenham H), Moore (Tranmere R), Murphy (Crewe Alex), Cooke (Manchester U).

FA WOMEN'S PREMIER LEAGUE

National Division

	P	*W*	*D*	*L*	*F*	*A*	*Pts*
Arsenal	18	17	1	0	60	8	52
Liverpool	18	12	3	3	58	17	39
Doncaster Belles	18	12	2	4	56	24	38
Croydon	18	9	2	7	42	24	29
Wembley	18	8	3	7	34	17	27
Leasowe Pacific	18	5	3	10	36	47	18
Ilkeston Town Rangers	18	4	3	11	20	49	15
Millwall Lionesses	18	4	3	11	25	60	15
Wolverhampton Wanderers	18	4	1	13	23	66	13
Red Star Southampton	18	3	3	12	23	65	12

Northern Division

	P	*W*	*D*	*L*	*F*	*A*	*Pts*
Villa Aztecs	18	11	4	3	59	22	37
Cowgate Kestrels	18	11	3	4	63	30	36
St Helens/Garswood	18	11	3	4	44	26	36
Sheffield Wednesday	18	9	4	5	38	27	31
Ipswich Town	18	8	4	6	33	29	28
Bronte	18	8	3	7	42	28	27
Langford	18	8	0	10	30	40	24
Kidderminster Harriers	18	4	2	12	24	57	14
Nottingham Argyle	18	3	2	13	22	66	11
Solihull Borough	18	4	1	13	22	52	10*

*3 points deducted

Southern Division

	P	*W*	*D*	*L*	*F*	*A*	*Pts*
Maidstone Tigresses	14	10	2	2	34	10	32
Berkhamsted & Hemel	14	8	4	2	28	13	28
Oxford United	14	7	3	4	28	28	24
Wimbledon	14	6	2	6	28	20	20
Brighton & Hove Albion	14	6	1	7	20	30	19
Town & Country	14	5	3	6	22	25	18
Brentford	14	3	4	7	29	41	13
Horsham	14	0	3	11	16	38	3

FA WOMEN'S CHALLENGE CUP 1994–95

First Round

Blackburn Rovers v Brighouse 3-0
Middlesbrough v Wakefield 3-0
Huddersfield Town v Newcastle 12-0
Wigginton Grasshoppers v Oakland Rangers 2-3
Grimsby withdrew v Bradford City w.o.
City Roses v Barnsley 2-5
Preston Rangers v Kilnhurst 6-1
South Lakes v South Shields 0-6
Sheffield Hallam United v Vernon-Carus 5-0
Amble Town v Cleveland 0-1
Manchester Belle Vue v Manchester City 4-1
Bolton v Manchester United 1-4
Rochdale v Wigan 1-7
Stockport v Tranmere Rovers 1-5
Liverpool Feds v Warrington Town 2-5
Stockport County v Colls 7-0
Oldham Athletic v Port Vale 7-2
Bangor City Girls v Leek Town 1-3
Radcliffe Borough v Chester City 7-0
Haslingden v Wrexham 5-1
Leicester City v Birmingham City 3-4
Derby City v Chesterfield 4-5
Derby County v Rugby 3-1
Pye v Calverton MW 0-2
Nettleham v Sparta Nottingham 5-0
Rainworth Miners Welfare v Notts County 0-2
Peterborough Diamonds v Highfield Rangers 0-11
Milton Keynes Athletic v Leyton Orient 0-7
Enfield v St Germaine 3-3, 3-2
Charlton v Milton Keynes United 11-1
Dunstable v Mill Hill United 4-6
Queens Park Rangers v Redbridge Wanderers 8-1
Fulham v Leighton Linsdale 7-1
Clapton Orient v Slough Town 3-4
Barnet v Bedford Bells 1-5
Harlow Town v Clacton 3-1
Watford v Wycombe Wanderers 6-0
Collier Row v Colchester 5-1
Farnborough v Teynham Gunners 9-1
Havant v St Georges 2-6
Abbey Rangers v Binfield 0-7
Pagham v Hassocks 4-3
Carterton Town v Crowborough Athletic 0-2

Gosport Borough v Sutton Athletic 7-2
Comets v Eastleigh 0-9
Sittingbourne v Reading Royals 3-3, 3-3
(Reading Royals won 4-2 on penalties)
Isle of Wight v Surbiton Town 0-6
Chailey Mavericks w.o. v Chislehurst United amalgamated with Charlton
Edenbridge Town v Newbury 0-7
Whitehawk v Palace Eagles 5-0
Worthing v Portsmouth 0-4
Gillingham Girls v Lambeth 1-6
Plymouth Pilgrims v Cheltenham YMCA 4-2
Swindon Town Spitfires v Bournemouth 3-1
Yate Town v Torquay United 0-6
Worcester City v Exeter Rangers 8-2
Clevedon Town v Gloucester Greyhounds 8-1
Dorchester withdrew v Truro City w.o.
Brislington v Southampton 1-6
Frome v Sturminster Newton 10-1
Bristol Rovers withdrew v Bristol City w.o.
Swindon Town v Weymouth 8-0
Cardiff Institute v Tongwynlais 1-3

Second Round
Huddersfield Town v Barnsley 16-0
Haslingden v Bronte 0-5
Wigan v Bradford City 2-0
Preston Rangers v Middlesbrough 5-2
Oaklands Rangers v Radcliffe Borough 1-7
Oldham Athletic v Blackburn Rovers 5-1
South Shields v Manchester Belle Vue 0-11
Sheffield Hallam United v Cowgate Kestrels 2-6
Newsham v St Helens/Garswood 3-4
Tranmere Rovers v Cleveland 8-0
Warrington Town v Manchester United 3-4
Wilford withdrew v Birmingham City w.o.
Stockport County v Calverton MW 1-2
Leek Town v Nottingham Argyle 1-4
Bedford Bells v Sheffield Wednesday 0-2
Highfield Rangers v Solihull Borough 2-3
Chesterfield v Villa Aztecs 2-5
Nettleham v Kidderminster Harriers 1-6
Notts County v Derby County 7-0
Brighton & Hove Albion v Reading 14-0
St Georges v Surbiton Town 1-2
Colchester Royals v Pagham 3-1
Whitehawk v Queens Park Rangers 7-0
Harlow Town v Watford 2-0
Berkhamsted & Hemel v Epsom & Ewell 9-1
Reading Royals v Langford 2-4
Leyton Orient v Slough Town 25-0
Town & Country v Chailey Mavericks 22-0
Lambeth v Binfield 1-0
Collier Row v Enfield 0-2
Crowborough Athletic v Wimbledon 0-7
Mill Hill United v Horsham 0-1
Fulham v Ipswich Town 2-5
Maidstone Tigresses v Charlton 2-1
Brentford v Farnborough 6-3
Bristol disbanded v Tongwynlais w.o.
Clevedon Town v Oxford United 0-9
Inter Cardiff v Plymouth Pilgrims 2-4
Swindon Town v Southampton 2-1
Portsmouth v Newbury 2-3
Worcester City v Frome 4-3
Gosport Borough v Bristol City 1-8
Swindon Town Spitfires v Truro City 3-4
Torquay United v Eastleigh 4-1

Third Round
Villa Aztecs v Huddersfield Town 4-4, 0-4
(Replay ordered; Huddersfield Town fielded an ineligible player), 0-2
Preston Rangers v Cowgate Kestrels 1-4
Notts County v Nottingham Argyle 4-2
Oldham Athletic v Birmingham City 2-1
Wigan v Manchester United 4-1
Tranmere Rovers v Sheffield Wednesday 5-5, 5-2
St Helens/Garswood v Bronte 4-2
Radcliffe Borough v Calverton MW 3-6
Manchester Belle Vue v Solihull Borough 3-1
Berkhamsted & Hemel v Wimbledon 3-4
Maidstone Tigresses v Langford 2-0
Town & Country v Brentford 3-4
Brighton & Hove Albion v Whitehawk 5-1
Leyton Orient v Lambeth 6-1
Enfield v Colchester Royals 6-1
Harlow Town v Surbiton Town 0-1
Ipswich Town v Horsham 0-0, 5-0
Plymouth Pilgrims v Tongwynlais 3-1
Oxford United v Torquay United 8-1
Bristol City v Kidderminster Harriers 7-1
Truro City v Worcester City 2-2, 5-2
Swindon Town v Newbury 3-4

Fourth Round
Brentford v Red Star Southampton 2-2, 1-2
Huddersfield Town v Ipswich Town 7-3
Tranmere Rovers v Leasowe Pacific 1-3
Newbury v Notts County 1-2
St Helens/Garswood v Oxford United 2-1
Leyton Orient v Enfield 7-0
Wolverhampton Wanderers v Millwall Lionesses 0-2
Doncaster Belles v Truro City 6-0
Liverpool v Surbiton Town 8-0
Wimbledon v Cowgate Kestrels 2-0
Ilkeston Town Rangers v Brighton & Hove Albion 5-1
Oldham Athletic v Croydon 1-7
Manchester Belle Vue v Wigan 2-3
Bristol City v Plymouth Pilgrims 6-2
Arsenal v Maidstone Tigresses 3-0
Calverton MW v Wembley 0-12

Fifth Round
Arsenal v Leasowe Pacific 3-1
Liverpool v Notts County 5-0
Huddersfield Town v Ilkeston Town Rangers 3-1
Leyton Orient v Red Star Southampton 3-1
Bristol City v Millwall Lionesses 3-2
Wimbledon v Croydon 0-5
Wembley v Doncaster Belles 3-3, 1-2
Wigan v St Helens/Garswood 1-3

Sixth Round
Liverpool v Croydon 3-0
Leyton Orient v Arsenal 1-8
Bristol City v Huddersfield Town 4-3
Doncaster Belles v St Helens/Garswood 4-0

Semi-finals
Doncaster Belles v Arsenal 1-3
Bristol City v Liverpool 0-5

Final at Tranmere Rovers FC

Arsenal (1) 3 *(Lonergan 2, Spacey)*

Liverpool (2) 2 *(Burke 2)* 3000

Arsenal: Cope; Pealing, Slee, Wylie, Spry, Churchman (Ball), Williams, Spacey, Kurley (Few), Lonergan, Britton. *Scorers: Lonergan 2, Spacey.*
Liverpool: Davidson; Taylor, Ryde, Thomas (Griffiths), Oldham, Burke, Easton, Murray, Gallimore, Harper, Hewitt (McQuiggan). *Scorer:* Burke 2.
Referee: J. Winter.

2ND WOMEN'S WORLD CHAMPIONSHIP

Group A
Germany 1, Japan 0
Brazil 1, Sweden 0
Japan 2, Brazil 1
Sweden 3, Germany 2
Sweden 2, Japan 0
Germany 6, Brazil 1

	P	*W*	*D*	*L*	*F*	*A*	*Pts*
Germany	3	2	0	1	9	4	6
Sweden	3	2	0	1	5	3	6
Japan	3	1	0	2	2	4	3
Brazil	3	1	0	2	3	8	3

Group B
Norway 8, Nigeria 0
England 3, Canada 2
Nigeria 3, Canada 3
Norway 2, England 0
Norway 7, Canada 0
England 3, Nigeria 2

	P	*W*	*D*	*L*	*F*	*A*	*Pts*
Norway	3	3	0	0	17	0	9
England	3	2	0	1	6	6	6
Canada	3	0	1	2	5	12	1
Nigeria	3	0	1	2	5	14	1

Group C
USA 3, China 3
Denmark 5, Australia 0
USA 2, Denmark 0
China 4, Australia 2
USA 4, Australia 1
China 3, Denmark 1

	P	*W*	*D*	*L*	*F*	*A*	*Pts*
USA	3	2	1	0	9	4	7
China	3	2	1	0	10	6	7
Denmark	3	1	0	2	6	5	3
Australia	3	0	0	3	3	13	0

Quarter-finals
USA 4, Japan 0
Norway 3, Denmark 1
China 1, Sweden 1
(*aet; China won 4-3 on penalties*)
Germany 3, England 0

Semi-finals
Norway 1, USA 0
Germany 1, China 0

Third Place
USA 2, China 0

Final: Stockholm, 18 June 1995, 17,158
Norway (2) 2 (*Riise, Pettersen*)
Germany (0) 0
Norway: Nordby; Svensson, Andersen N, Espeseth, Myklebust, Riise, Haugen, Andersen A, Pettersen, Aarones, Medalen.
Germany: Goller; Bernhard, Austermuhl, Lohn, Mohr, Neid, Wiegmann, Voss, Pohlman (Wunderlich), Meinert (Smisek), Prinz.

EUROPEAN CUP

EUROPEAN CUP FINALS 1956–95

Year	Winners	Runners-up	Venue	Attendance	Referee
1956	Real Madrid 4	Reims 3	Paris	38,000	Ellis (E)
1957	Real Madrid 2	Fiorentina 0	Madrid	124,000	Horn (Ho)
1958	Real Madrid 3	AC Milan 2 *(aet)*	Brussels	67,000	Alsteen (Bel)
1959	Real Madrid 2	Reims 0	Stuttgart	80,000	Dutsch (WG)
1960	Real Madrid 7	Eintracht Frankfurt 3	Glasgow	135,000	Mowat (S)
1961	Benfica 3	Barcelona 2	Berne	28,000	Dienst (Sw)
1962	Benfica 5	Real Madrid 3	Amsterdam	65,000	Horn (Ho)
1963	AC Milan 2	Benfica 1	Wembley	45,000	Holland (E)
1964	Internazionale 3	Real Madrid 1	Vienna	74,000	Stoll (A)
1965	Internazionale 1	Benfica 0	Milan	80,000	Dienst (Sw)
1966	Real Madrid 2	Partizan Belgrade 1	Brussels	55,000	Kreitlein (WG)
1967	Celtic 2	Internazionale 1	Lisbon	56,000	Tschenscher (WG)
1968	Manchester U 4	Benfica 1 *(aet)*	Wembley	100,000	Lo Bello (I)
1969	AC Milan 4	Ajax 1	Madrid	50,000	Ortiz (Sp)
1970	Feyenoord 2	Celtic 1 *(aet)*	Milan	50,000	Lo Bello (I)
1971	Ajax 2	Panathinaikos 0	Wembley	90,000	Taylor (E)
1972	Ajax 2	Internazionale 0	Rotterdam	67,000	Helies (F)
1973	Ajax 1	Juventus 0	Belgrade	93,500	Guglovic (Y)
1974	Bayern Munich 1	Atletico Madrid 1	Brussels	65,000	Loraux (Bel)
Replay	Bayern Munich 4	Atletico Madrid 0	Brussels	65,000	Delcourt (Bel)
1975	Bayern Munich 2	Leeds U 0	Paris	50,000	Kitabdjian (F)
1976	Bayern Munich 1	St Etienne 0	Glasgow	54,864	Palotai (H)
1977	Liverpool 3	Moenchengladbach 1	Rome	57,000	Wurtz (F)
1978	Liverpool 1	FC Brugge 0	Wembley	92,000	Corver (Ho)
1979	Nottingham F 1	Malmo 0	Munich	57,500	Linemayr (A)
1980	Nottingham F 1	Hamburg 0	Madrid	50,000	Garrido (P)
1981	Liverpool 1	Real Madrid 0	Paris	48,360	Palotai (H)
1982	Aston Villa 1	Bayern Munich 0	Rotterdam	46,000	Konrath (F)
1983	Hamburg 1	Juventus 0	Athens	75,000	Rainea (R)
1984	Liverpool 1	Roma 1	Rome	69,693	Fredriksson (Se)
	(aet; Liverpool won 4–2 on penalties)				
1985	Juventus 1	Liverpool 0	Brussels	58,000	Daina (Sw)
1986	Steaua Bucharest 0	Barcelona 0	Seville	70,000	Vautrot (F)
	(aet; Steaua won 2–0 on penalties)				
1987	Porto 2	Bayern Munich 1	Vienna	59,000	Ponnet (Bel)
1988	PSV Eindhoven 0	Benfica 0	Stuttgart	70,000	Agnolin (I)
	(aet; PSV won 6–5 on penalties)				
1989	AC Milan 4	Steaua Bucharest 0	Barcelona	97,000	Tritschler (WG)
1990	AC Milan 1	Benfica 0	Vienna	57,500	Kohl (A)
1991	Red Star Belgrade 0	Marseille 0	Bari	56,000	Lanese (I)
	(aet; Red Star won 5–3 on penalties)				
1992	Barcelona 1	Sampdoria 0 *(aet)*	Wembley	70,827	Schmidhuber (G)
1993	Marseille* 1	AC Milan 0	Munich	64,400	Rothlisberger (Sw)
1994	AC Milan 4	Barcelona 0	Athens	70,000	Don (E)
1995	Ajax 1	AC Milan 0	Vienna	49,730	Craciunescu (Ro)

**Subsequently stripped of title.*

EUROPEAN CUP 1994–95

Preliminary Round, First Leg

AEK Athens (1) 2 *(Saravakos 44, 70)*, Rangers (0) 0 35,000

Avenir Beggen (0) 1 *(Zaritski 50)*, Galatasaray (2) 5 *(Turkyilmaz 30, Saffet 35, Hakan 69, Arif 76, 89)* 6200

Legia Warsaw (0) 0, Hajduk Split (1) 1 *(Rapajic 22)* 18,000

Maccabi Haifa (0) 1 *(Revivo 47 (pen))*, Salzburg (0) 2 *(Hutter 82, Mladenovic 88 (pen))* 10,000

Paris St Germain (1) 3 *(Ricardo 30, Weah 48, Roche 82)*, Vac (0) 0 25,000

Silkeborg (0) 0, Dynamo Kiev (0) 0 4298

Sparta Prague (0) 1 *(Budka 89)*, IFK Gothenburg (0) 0 9600 *(in Jablonec)*

Steaua (3) 4 *(Ilie 1, Stan 17 (pen), Parvu 26, Lacatus 51)*, Servette (0) 1 *(Neuville 72)* 15,000

Preliminary Round, Second Leg

Dynamo Kiev (2) 3 *(Skatchenko 21, Kovalets 28, Kossovski 90)*, Silkeborg (0) 1 *(Fernandez 74)* 24,000

Galatasaray (0) 4 *(Hakan Sukur 52, 70, 83 (pen), Saffet 63)*, Avenir Beggen (0) 0 20,000

IFK Gothenburg (1) 2 *(Blomqvist 22, Lindqvist 63)*, Sparta Prague (0) 0 8000

Hajduk Split (0) 4 *(Asanovic 50, Vulic 64, Rapajic 80, Erceg 89)*, Legia Warsaw (0) 0 7500

Rangers (0) 0, AEK Athens (0) 1 *(Savevski 43)* 44,789

Salzburg (0) 3 *(Mladenovic 49, 53, Jurcevic 78)* Maccabi Haifa (0) 1 *(Hazan 89)* 9000

Servette (1) 1 *(Schepull 15)*, Steaua (0) 1 *(Parvu 62)* 7250

Vac (1) 1 *(Fule 31)*, Paris St Germain (1) 2 *(Mboma 19, 66)* 1800

CHAMPIONS LEAGUE

Group A

Manchester U (1) 4 *(Giggs 33, 65, Kanchelskis 48, Sharpe 70)*, IFK Gothenburg (1) 2 *(Petterson 27, Rehn 50)* 33,625

Barcelona (1) 2 *(Koeman 30, Amor 50)*, Galatasaray (1) 1 *(Turkyilmaz 14)* 76,000

IFK Gothenburg (0) 2 *(Erlingmark 74, Blomqvist 89)*, Barcelona (1) 1 *(Stoichkov 10)* 32,215

Galatasaray (0) 0, Manchester U (0) 0 35,000

Manchester U (1) 2 *(Hughes 18, Sharpe 80)*, Barcelona (1) 2 *(Romario 34, Bakero 49)* 40,064

IFK Gothenburg (0) 1 *(Erlingmark 76)*, Galatasaray (0) 0 26,412

Barcelona (2) 4 *(Pallister 9 (og), Romario 45, Stoichkov 52, Ferrer 88)*, Manchester U (0) 0 114,432

Galatasaray (0) 0, IFK Gothenburg (0) 1 *(Nilsson 86)* 30,000

IFK Gothenburg (1) 3 *(Blomqvist 10, Erlingmark 64, Kamark 71 (pen))*, Manchester U (0) 1 *(Hughes 64)* 36,350

Galatasaray (0) 2 *(Hakan 72 (pen), Arif 88)*, Barcelona (1) 1 *(Romario 15)* 30,000

Manchester U (2) 4 *(Davies 2, Beckham 37, Keane 48, Bulent (og))*, Galatasaray (0) 0 39,220

Barcelona (0) 1 *(Bakero 81)*, IFK Gothenburg (0) 1 *(Rehn 90)* 75,000

Final table

	P	*W*	*D*	*L*	*F*	*A*	*Pts*
IFK Gothenburg	6	4	1	1	10	7	9
Barcelona	6	2	2	2	11	8	6
Manchester United	6	2	2	2	11	11	6
Galatasaray	6	1	1	4	3	9	3

Group B

Dynamo Kiev (0) 3 *(Leonenko 48, 76, Rebrov 86)*, Spartak Moscow (2) 2 *(Pisarev 12, Tichonov 39)* 93,000

Paris St Germain (1) 2 *(Weah 41, Bravo 83)*, Bayern Munich (0) 0 36,924

Bayern Munich (1) 1 *(Scholl 9)*, Dynamo Kiev (0) 0 26,000

Spartak Moscow (1) 1 *(Rachimov 38)*, Paris St Germain (0) 2 *(Le Guen 56, Valdo 60)* 30,000

Spartak Moscow (0) 1 *(Pisarev 78)*, Bayern Munich (0) 1 *(Babbel 90)* 25,000

Dynamo Kiev (1) 1 *(Leonenko 32 (pen))*, Paris St Germain (1) 2 *(Guerin 26, Weah 76)* 60,000

Bayern Munich (2) 2 *(Nerlinger 29, Kuffour 36)*, Spartak Moscow (2) 2 *(Tikhonov 4, Alenichev 32)* 25,000

Paris St Germain (0) 1 *(Weah 68)*, Dynamo Kiev (0) 0 33,741

Spartak Moscow (0) 1 *(Mukhamadiyev 52)*, Dynamo Kiev (0) 0 40,000

Bayern Munich (0) 0, Paris St Germain (0) 1 *(Weah 81)* 35,000

Dynamo Kiev (1) 1 *(Shevchenko 35)*, Bayern Munich (1) 4 *(Nerlinger 45, Papin 56, 82, Scholl 87)* 60,000

Paris St Germain (2) 4 *(Weah 28, 52, Ginola 42, Rai 59)*, Spartak Moscow (0) 1 *(Rodionov 66)* 31,461

Final table

	P	*W*	*D*	*L*	*F*	*A*	*Pts*
Paris St Germain	6	6	0	0	12	3	12
Bayern Munich	6	2	2	2	8	7	6
Spartak Moscow	6	1	2	3	8	12	4
Dynamo Kiev	6	1	0	5	5	11	2

Group C

Hajduk Split (0) 0, Benfica (0) 0 38,000

Anderlecht (0) 0, Steaua (0) 0 16,000

Steaua (0) 0, Hajduk Split (0) 1 *(Asanovic 88)* 24,000

Benfica (2) 3 *(Caniggia 27, 40, Tavares 72)*, Anderlecht (0) 1 *(Madeira 85 (og))* 32,000

Benfica (1) 2 *(Caniggia 44 (pen), Joao Pinto II 60)*, Steaua (0) 1 *(Militaru 89)* 18,100

Hajduk Split (1) 2 *(Pralija 34, Butorovic 86)*, Anderlecht (0) 1 *(Weber 88)* 38,000

Steaua (1) 1 *(Panduru 27)*, Benfica (0) 1 *(Helder 64)* 22,000

Anderlecht (0) 0, Hajduk Split (0) 0 21,000

Benfica (1) 2 *(Isaias 33, Joao Pinto 76)*, Hajduk Split (0) 1 *(Andrijasevic 72)* 45,000

Steaua (0) 1 *(Dobos 52)*, Anderlecht (1) 1 *(Bosman 42)* 12,000

Hajduk Split (0) 1 *(Andrijasevic 48)*, Steaua (3) 4 *(Ille 11, 32, Lacatus 21, Galca 90)* 15,000

Anderlecht (0) 1 *(Rutjes 49)*, Benfica (0) 1 *(Edilson 83)* 22,000

Final table

	P	*W*	*D*	*L*	*F*	*A*	*Pts*
Benfica	6	3	3	0	9	5	9
Hajduk Split	6	2	2	2	5	7	6
Steaua	6	1	3	2	7	6	5
Anderlecht	6	0	4	2	4	7	4

Group D

Salzburg (0) 0, AEK Athens (0) 0 *in Vienna* 22,500

Ajax (0) 2 *(Ronald de Boer 51, Litmanen 65)*, AC Milan (0) 0 42,000

AC Milan (1) 3 *(Stroppa 39, Simone 59, 63)*, Salzburg (0) 0 22,475
AEK Athens (1) 1 *(Savevski 30)*, Ajax (1) 2 *(Litmanen 29, Kluivert 63)* 30,000
AEK Athens (0) 0, AC Milan (0) 0 30,000
Salzburg (0) 0, Ajax (0) 0 18,200
AC Milan (0) 2 *(Panucci 68, 74)*, AEK Athens (1) 1 *(Savevski 16)* 17,264
Ajax (0) 1 *(Litmanen 85)*, Salzburg (0) 1 *(Kocljan 62)* 40,000
AEK Athens (1) 1 *(Vlachos 29)*, Salzburg (2) 3 *(Pfeifenberger 6, 8, Hasenhuttl 76)* 20,000
AC Milan (0) 0, Ajax (1) 2 *(Litmanen 2, Baresi 65 (og))* *in Trieste* 29,764
Salzburg (0) 0, AC Milan (1) 1 *(Massaro 29)* 47,500
Ajax (1) 2 *(Oulida 7, 78)*, AEK Athens (0) 0 42,000

Final table

	P	*W*	*D*	*L*	*F*	*A*	*Pts*
Ajax	6	4	2	0	9	2	10
AC Milan	6	3	1	2	6	5	5
Salzburg	6	1	3	2	4	6	5
AEK Athens	6	0	2	4	3	9	2

AC Milan deducted 2 pts for crowd trouble.

Quarter-finals, first leg

Bayern Munich (0) 0, IFK Gothenburg (0) 0 45,000
Hajduk Split (0) 0, Ajax (0) 0 35,000
AC Milan (0) 2 *(Simone 63, 75)*, Benfica (0) 0 48,858
Barcelona (0) 1 *(Korneev 48)*, Paris St Germain (0) 1 *(Weah 54)* 114,700

Quarter-finals, second leg

Ajax (2) 3 *(Kanu 39, Frank De Boer 43, 68)*, Hajduk Split (0) 0 42,000
Benfica (0) 0, AC Milan (0) 0 70,000
IFK Gothenburg (0) 2 *(Lilienberg 75, Martinsson 90)*; Bayern Munich (0) 2 *(Zickler 63, Nerlinger 71)* 36,525
Paris St Germain (0) 2 *(Rai 73, Guerin 83)*, Barcelona (0) 1 *(Bakero 49)* 45,700

Semi-finals, first leg

Bayern Munich (0) 0, Ajax (0) 0 60,000
Paris St Germain (0) 0, AC Milan (0) 1 *(Boban 90)* 45,000

Semi-finals, second leg

Ajax (3) 5 *(Litmanen 10, 46, George 40, Ronald de Boer 43, Overmars 88)*, Bayern Munich (1) 2 *(Witeczek 36, Scholl 76)* 41,000
AC Milan (1) 2 *(Savicevic 21, 68)*, Paris St Germain (0) 0 79,855

Final: Ajax (0) 1, AC Milan (0) 0

(in Vienna, 24 May 1995, 49,730)

Ajax: Van der Sar; Reiziger, Blind, Frank de Boer, Rijkaard, Seedorf (Kanu 53), Davids, Litmanen (Kluivert 68), George, Ronald de Boer, Overmars.

Scorer: Kluivert 85.

AC Milan: Rossi; Panucci, Baresi, Costacurta, Maldini, Desailly, Donadoni, Albertini, Boban (Lentini 85), Massaro (Eranio 90), Simone.

Referee: Craciunescu (Romania).

Patrick Kluivert (No. 15) scores the only goal of the European Cup Final for Ajax against AC Milan. (Colorsport)

EUROPEAN CUP 1994–95 – BRITISH AND IRISH

Manchester United's Steve Bruce is challenged by Galatasaray No. 2 Ergun at Old Trafford. (Action Images)

Preliminary Round, First Leg

10 AUG

AEK Athens (1) 2 *(Saravakos 2)*

Rangers (0) 0 35,000

AEK Athens: Atmatsidis; Vlachos, Manolas, Papadopoulos, Kostis, Sabanadzovic, Savevski, Kassapis, Tsartas, Saravakos, Ketspajia (Dimitriades) (Agorogiannis).
Rangers: Goram; Pressley, Gough, Stevens, Murray, Ferguson, Durie (Durrant), McCall, Robertson, Hateley, Laudrup.

Preliminary Round, Second Leg

24 AUG

Rangers (0) 0

AEK Athens (1) 1 *(Savevski)* 44,789

Rangers: Goram; Boli, Gough, McPherson, Robertson, Durie (Durrant), Ferguson I, McCall, Laudrup, Hateley, Ferguson D.
AEK Athens: Atmatsidis; Agorogiannis, Vlachos, Manolas, Papadopoulos, Kassapis, Saravakos, Sabanadzovic, Savevski (Stamatis), Kostis, Tsartas (Kopitsis).

Group A

14 SEPT

Manchester U (1) 4 *(Giggs 2, Kanchelskis, Sharpe)*

IFK Gothenburg (1) 2 *(Pettersson, Rehn)* 33,625

Manchester U: Schmeichel; May, Irwin, Bruce, Sharpe, Pallister, Kanchelskis, Ince, Butt, Hughes, Giggs.
IFK Gothenburg: Ravelli; Kaamark, Johansson, Olsson (Rehn), Bjorklund, Nilsson, Martinsson, Lindqvist, Erlingmark, Blomqvist, Pettersson.

28 SEPT

Galatasaray (0) 0

Manchester U (0) 0 35,000

Galatasaray: Stauce; Mert, Bulent, Sedat, Yusuf, Tugay (Arif), Mapeza, Hamza, Turkyilmaz, Saffet (Osman), Hakan.
Manchester U: Schmeichel; May, Bruce, Pallister, Sharpe, Kanchelskis, Butt, Keane, Ince, Giggs (Parker), Hughes.

19 OCT

Manchester U (1) 2 *(Hughes, Sharpe)*

Barcelona (1) 2 *(Romario, Bakero)* 40,064

Manchester U: Schmeichel; May (Bruce), Irwin, Parker, Sharpe, Pallister, Kanchelskis, Ince, Keane, Hughes, Butt (Scholes).
Barcelona: Busquets; Abelardo, Koeman, Sergi, Guardiola, Nadal, Luis (Uesebio), Bakero, Beguristain (Jordi), Stoichkov, Romario.

2 NOV

Barcelona (2) 4 *(Pallister (og), Romario, Stoichkov, Ferrer)*

Manchester U (0) 0 114,432

Barcelona: Busquets; Abelardo, Koeman, Sergi, Ferrer, Amor, Guardiola, Bakero (Sanchez Jara), Stoichkov, Romario, Jordi (Iglesias).
Manchester U: Walsh; Parker, Irwin, Bruce, Kanchelskis, Pallister, Butt, Ince, Keane, Hughes, Giggs (Scholes).

23 NOV

IFK Gothenburg (1) 3 *(Blomqvist, Erlingmark, Kamark (pen))*

Manchester U (0) 1 *(Hughes)* 36,350

IFK Gothenburg: Ravelli; Kamark, Johansson, Bjorklund, Nilsson, Martinsson (Wahlstedt), Rehn, Lindqvist, Blomqvist, Erlingmark, Pettersson (Andersson).
Manchester U: Walsh; May (Neville), Irwin, Bruce, Kanchelskis, Pallister, Cantona, Ince, McClair, Hughes, Davies (Butt).

7 DEC

Manchester U (2) 4 *(Davies, Beckham, Keane, Bulent (og))*

Galatasaray (0) 0 39,220

Manchester U: Walsh; Neville, Irwin, Bruce, Keane, Pallister, Cantona, Beckham, McClair, Butt, Davies.
Galatasaray: Stauce; Sedat, Bulent, Mert, Suat, Tugay (Yusuf), Hamza (Ugar), Ergun, Arif, Turkyilmaz, Hakan.

EUROPEAN CUP-WINNERS' CUP

EUROPEAN CUP-WINNERS' CUP FINALS 1961–95

Year	Winners	Runners-up	Venue	Attendance	Referee
1961	Fiorentina 2	Rangers 0 *(1st Leg)*	Glasgow	80,000	Steiner (A)
	Fiorentina 2	Rangers 1 *(2nd Leg)*	Florence	50,000	Hernadi (H)
1962	Atletico Madrid 1	Fiorentina 1	Glasgow	27,389	Wharton (S)
Replay	Atletico Madrid 3	Fiorentina 0	Stuttgart	45,000	Tschenscher (WG)
1963	Tottenham Hotspur 5	Atletico Madrid 1	Rotterdam	25,000	Van Leuwen (Ho)
1964	Sporting Lisbon 3	MTK Budapest 3 *(aet)*	Brussels	9000	Van Nuffel (Bel)
Replay	Sporting Lisbon 1	MTK Budapest 0	Antwerp	18,000	Versyp (Bel)
1965	West Ham U 2	Munich 1860 0	Wembley	100,000	Szolt (H)
1966	Borussia Dortmund 2	Liverpool 1 *(aet)*	Glasgow	41,657	Schwinte (F)
1967	Bayern Munich 1	Rangers 0 *(aet)*	Nuremberg	69,480	Lo Bello (I)
1968	AC Milan 2	Hamburg 0	Rotterdam	60,000	Ortiz (Sp)
1969	Slovan Bratislava 3	Barcelona 2	Basle	40,000	Van Ravens (Ho)
1970	Manchester C 2	Gornik Zabrze 1	Vienna	10,000	Schiller (A)
1971	Chelsea 1	Real Madrid 1 *(aet)*	Athens	42,000	Scheurer (Sw)
Replay	Chelsea 2	Real Madrid 1 *(aet)*	Athens	24,000	Bucheli (Sw)
1972	Rangers 3	Moscow Dynamo 2	Barcelona	35,000	Ortiz (Sp)
1973	AC Milan 1	Leeds U 0	Salonika	45,000	Mihas (Gr)
1974	Magdeburg 2	AC Milan 0	Rotterdam	5000	Van Gemert (Ho)
1975	Dynamo Kiev 3	Ferencvaros 0	Basle	13,000	Davidson (S)
1976	Anderlecht 4	West Ham U 2	Brussels	58,000	Wurtz (F)
1977	Hamburg 2	Anderlecht 0	Amsterdam	65,000	Partridge (E)
1978	Anderlecht 4	Austria/WAC 0	Paris	48,679	Adlinger (WG)
1979	Barcelona 4	Fortuna Dusseldorf 3 *(aet)*	Basle	58,000	Palotai (H)
1980	Valencia 0	Arsenal 0	Brussels	40,000	Christov (Cz)
	(aet; Valencia won 5-4 on penalties)				
1981	Dynamo Tbilisi 2	Carl Zeiss Jena 1	Dusseldorf	9000	Lattanzi (I)
1982	Barcelona 2	Standard Liege 1	Barcelona	100,000	Eschweiler (WG)
1983	Aberdeen 2	Real Madrid 1 *(aet)*	Gothenburg	17,804	Menegali (I)
1984	Juventus 2	Porto 1	Basle	60,000	Prokop (EG)
1985	Everton 3	Rapid Vienna 1	Rotterdam	30,000	Casarin (I)
1986	Dynamo Kiev 3	Atletico Madrid 0	Lyon	39,300	Wohrer (A)
1987	Ajax 1	Lokomotiv Leipzig 0	Athens	35,000	Agnolin (I)
1988	Mechelen 1	Ajax 0	Strasbourg	39,446	Pauly (WG)
1989	Barcelona 2	Sampdoria 0	Berne	45,000	Courtney (E)
1990	Sampdoria 2	Anderlecht 0	Gothenburg	20,103	Galler (Sw)
1991	Manchester U 2	Barcelona 1	Rotterdam	45,000	Karlsson (Se)
1992	Werder Bremen 2	Monaco 0	Lisbon	16,000	D'Elia (I)
1993	Parma 3	Antwerp 1	Wembley	37,393	Assenmacher (G)
1994	Arsenal 1	Parma 0	Copenhagen	33,765	Krondl (Czr)
1995	Zaragoza 2	Arsenal 1	Paris	42,424	Ceccarini (I)

EUROPEAN CUP-WINNERS' CUP 1994–95

Preliminary Round, First Leg

Pirin (2) 3 *(Orachev 18, Yanev 28, Petrov 60 (pen))*, Schaen (0) 0 2000
Norma Tallinn (0) 1 *(Rychkov 83)*, Branik Maribor (0) 4 *(Galic 54, Milevski 63, Djurovski 78, Simundza 90)* 1000
Fandok (2) 4 *(Yeryomko 1, 5, Khripach 65, Savostikov 72)*, SK Tirana (0) 1 *(Prenga 90)* 5000
Tiligul (0) 0, Omonia (1) 1 *(Gogrichiani 16)* 3000
Ferencvaros (3) 6 *(Neagoe 3, Szekeres 17, 76, Paling 45, Lipcsei 57, Albert 78)*, Dudelange (0) 1 *(Fanelli 82)* 10,000
Floriana (0) 2 *(Stefanovic 53, 90)*, Sligo Rovers (2) 2 *(Moran 12, Reid 31)* 1500
Barry Town (0) 0, Zalgiris Vilnius (0) 1 *(Vencevicius 77)* 1914
Bodo Glimt (2) 6 *(Berstad 5, Berg 53, 89, Bjorkan 70, Johnsen 35, 82)*, Olimpija (0) 0 2290
Viktoria Zizkov (0) 1 *(Poborsky 72)*, Norrkoping (0) 0 1905
B71 Sandur (0) 0, HJK Helsinki (2) 5 *(Yanitalu 3, 86, Lius 20, 68, Heinola 80)* 462
Bangor (0) 0, Tatran Presov (0) 1 *(Nenadic 72)* 1100
IB Keflavik (0) 1 *(Tanasic 75)*, Maccabi Tel Aviv (1) 2 *(Klinger 36, Nimny 83)* 500

Preliminary Round, Second Leg

Branik Maribor (8) 10 *(Djurovski 5, 8, Gutalj 20, 45, Bozgo 22, 24, 42, 82, Simundza 40, 86)*, Norma Tallinn (0) 0 4500
Dudelange (1) 1 *(Morgante 21)*, Ferencvaros (3) 6 *(Lisztes 5, Paling 18, Lipcsei 38, 68, Kristiansen 55, Zavadszky 88)* 750
HJK Helsinki (1) 2 *(Kottila 1, Suokonautio 80)*, B71 Sandur (0) 0 2000
Maccabi Tel Aviv (3) 4 *(Brumer A 13, Brumer G 16 (pen), Klinger 25, Kriks 68)*, IB Keflavik (1) 1 *(Tanasic 36)* 8125
Norrkoping (1) 3 *(Hansson 41, 71, Vaattovaara 90 (pen))*, Viktoria Zizkov (0) 3 *(Trval 54, Kordule 57, Vrabec 88 (pen))* 6500
Olimpija (0) 0, Bodo Glimt (0) 0 2500
Omonia (2) 3 *(Kantilos 5 (pen), Tutic 45, Savvides 89)*, Tiligul (0) 1 *(Belous 51)* 6500
Schaen (0) 0, Pirin (1) 1 *(Jankov 2)* 800
Sligo Rovers (0) 1 *(Brennan 72)*, Floriana (0) 0 6000
SK Tirana (1) 3 *(Fortuzi 45, 75, 90)*, Fandok (0) 0 6000
Tatran Presov (2) 4 *(Kocis 13, 48, Matta 42, Hoger 52)*, Bangor (0) 0 5450
Zalgiris Vilnius (2) 6 *(Karvelis 18, 50, Baltusnikas 40, Poderis 48, Maciulevicius 68, Jankauskas 89)*, Barry Town (0) 0 2900

First Round, First Leg

Besiktas (2) 2 *(Oktay 28, Ertugrul 36)*, HJK Helsinki (0) 0 37,500
Bodo Glimt (2) 3 *(Staurvik 3, Johnsen 33, 58)*, Sampdoria (0) 2 *(Bertarelli 47, Platt 69)* 2015
Branik Maribor (0) 1 *(Bozgo 46 (pen))*, FK Austria (1) 1 *(Prosenik 23)* 4000
Brondby (1) 3 *(Jensen 19 (pen), Hansen B 56, Bjur 66)*, SK Tirana (0) 0 6035
Chelsea 2) 4 *(Furlong 2, Sinclair 4, Rocastle 52, Wise 69)*, Viktoria Zizkov (2) 2 *(Majoros 35, 41)* 22,036
Croatia Zagreb (2) 3 *(Jelicic 1, Soldo 40, Pamic 65)*, Auxerre (1) 1 *(Diomede 20)* 18,000
CSKA Moscow (0) 2 *(Mamchur 50, Sergeyev 73)*, Ferencvaros (0) 1 *(Christiansen 58)* 6000
Dundee U (1) 3 *(Petric 16, Nixon 66, Hannah 69)*, Tatran Presov (2) 2 *(Skalka 10, Zvara 41 (pen))* 9454
Gloria Bistrita (0) 2 *(Raduta 51, Lungu 54)*, Zaragoza (1) 1 *(Esnaider 43)* 13,000
Grasshoppers (1) 3 *(Bickel 41, Koller 52, Subiat 85)*, Odessa (0) 0 3600
Maccabi Tel Aviv (0) 0, Werder Bremen (0) 0 10,000
Omonia (0) 1 *(Malekos 72)*, Arsenal (1) 3 *(Merson 37, 80, Wright 50)* 14,500
Pirin (0) 0, Panathinaikos (0) 2 *(Nioblias 70, Alexoudis 83)* 25,000
Porto (0) 2 *(Domingos 72, Rui Barros 77)*, LKS Lodz (0) 0 25,000
Sligo Rovers (1) 1 *(Kenny 44)*, FC Brugge (1) 2 *(Vermant 10, Verheyen 63)* 6000
Zalgiris Vilnius (0) 1 *(Tereskinas 88 (pen)*, Feyenoord (1) 1 *(Larsson 9)* 7000

First Round, Second Leg

Arsenal (2) 3 *(Wright 9, 70, Schwarz 31)*, Omonia (0) 0 24,265
FK Austria (1) 3 *(Flogel 21, Kubica 53, 56)*, Branik Maribor (0) 0 10,000
Auxerre (1) 3 *(Diomede 41, Mahe 75, Lamouchi 90)*, Croatia Zagreb (0) 0 20,000
FC Brugge (2) 3 *(Staelens 4, 45 (pen), Eykelkamp 58)*, Sligo Rovers (1) 1 *(Rooney 7)* 5500
Ferencvaros (2) 2 *(Sinov 36 (og), Neagoe 45)*, CSKA Moscow (1) 1 *(Radimov 15)* 20,000 *Ferencvaros won 7-6 on penalties*
Feyenoord (0) 2 *(Larsson 54, Heus 66 (pen)*, Zalgiris Vilnius (0) 1 *(Vencevicius 89)* 17,500
HJK Helsinki (0) 1 *(Rantanen 67)*, Besiktas (0) 1 *(Derelioglu 86)* 3000
LKS Lodz (0) 0, Porto (1) 1 *(Drulovic 45)* 7000
Odessa (1) 1 *(Guseynov 9)*, Grasshoppers (0) 0 12,000
Panathinaikos (3) 6 *(Alexoudis 6, 17, Warzycha 30, 87, 90, Borelli 64)*, Pirin (1) 1 *(Orachev 44)* 21,000
Sampdoria (2) 2 *(Platt 13, Lombardo 37)*, Bodo Glimt (0) 0 35,000
Tatran Presov (2) 3 *(Zvara 10, 71, Kocis 18)*, Dundee U (1) 1 *(Nixon 2)* 8184
SK Tirana (0) 0, Brondby (1) 1 *(Strudal 31)* 3500
Viktoria Zizkov (0) 0, Chelsea (0) 0 *in Jablonec* 6000
Werder Bremen (0) 2 *(Bode 55, Basler 80)*, Maccabi Tel Aviv (0) 0 22,431
Zaragoza (2) 4 *(Pardeza 11, Aguado 42, Poyet 49, 55)*, Gloria Bistrita (0) 0 *in Valencia* 5000

Second Round, First Leg

Besiktas (2) 2 *(Mehmet 42, Ertugrul 44)*, Auxerre (0) 2 *(Saib 50, Martins 56)* 20,900
Brondby (0) 1 *(Strudal 53)*, Arsenal (2) 2 *(Wright 16, Smith 18)* 13,406
FC Brugge (1) 1 *(Staelens 4 (pen))*, Panathinaikos (0) 0 18,000
Chelsea (0) 0, FK Austria (0) 0 22,560
Feyenoord (0) 1 *(Larsson 65)*, Werder Bremen (0) 0 39,000
Porto (3) 6 *(Jorge Costa 17, Rui Barros 19, Drulovic 40, 58, Domingos 86, Aloisio 89)*, Ferencvaros (0) 0 16,000
Sampdoria (1) 3 *(Melli 45, Mihajlovic 76, Maspero 83)*, Grasshoppers (0) 0 25,000
Tatran Presov (0) 0, Zaragoza (2) 4 *(Poyet 26, Varga 44 (og), Esnaider 49, 88)* 12,105

Second Round, Second Leg

Arsenal (1) 2 *(Wright 25 (pen), Selley 46)*, Brondby (1) 2 *(Hansen B 2, Eggen 69)* 32,290
FK Austria (0) 1 *(Narbekovas 73)*, Chelsea (1) 1 *(Spencer 40)* 25,000
Auxerre (1) 2 *(Lamouchi 45, 49)*, Besiktas (0) 0 20,000

Ferencvaros (1) 2 *(Zavatsky 26, Neagoe 59)*, Porto (0) 0 15,000
Grasshoppers (1) 3 *(Willems 12, Bickel 51, Koller 55)*, Sampdoria (2) 2 *(Melli 17, Lombardo 40)* 12,100
Panathinaikos (0) 0, FC Brugge (0) 0 70,000
Werder Bremen (1) 3 *(Bestchastnich 12, 60, Basler 90)*, Feyenoord (2) 4 *(Larsson 20, 34, 66 (pen), Heus 56 (pen))* 31,118
Zaragoza (1) 2 *(Esnaider 5, Celada 56)*, Tatran Presov (1) 1 *(Kocis 38)* 9000 *In Valencia*

Quarter-finals, First Leg

FC Brugge (0) 1 *(Verheyen 83)*, Chelsea (0) 0 18,021
Arsenal (0) 1 *(Wright 59 (pen))*, Auxerre (0) 1 *(Verlaat 62)* 35,508
Feyenoord (0) 1 *(Larsson 62)*, Zaragoza (0) 0 47,000
Sampdoria (0) 0, Porto (0) 1 *(Yuran 64)* 31,000

Quarter-finals, Second Leg

Auxerre (0) 0, Arsenal (1) 1 *(Wright 16)* 22,000
Chelsea (2) 2 *(Stein 16, Furlong 38)*, FC Brugge (0) 0 28,661
Porto (0) 0, Sampdoria (0) 1 *(Mancini 48)* 43,000 *Sampdoria won 5-3 on penalties.*
Zaragoza (0) 2 *(Pardeza 58, Esnaider 72)*, Feyenoord (0) 0 36,800

Semi-finals, First Leg

Arsenal (2) 3 *(Bould 34, 36, Wright 68)*, Sampdoria (0) 2 *(Jugovic 51, 77)* 38,809
Zaragoza (2) 3 *(Pardeza 8, Esnaider 26, 57)*, Chelsea (0) 0 35,000

Semi-finals, Second Leg

Chelsea (1) 3 *(Furlong 30, Sinclair 62, Stein 86)*, Zaragoza (0) 1 *(Aragon 54)* 26,456
Sampdoria (1) 3 *(Mancini 13, Bellucci 82, 84)*, Arsenal (0) 2 *(Wright 60, Schwarz 87)* 35,000 *Arsenal won 3-2 on penalties.*

Final: Arsenal (0) 1, Zaragoza (0) 2 aet

(in Paris, 10 May 1995, 42,424)

Arsenal: Seaman; Dixon, Winterburn (Morrow 47), Schwarz, Linighan, Adams, Keown (Hillier 46), Wright, Hartson, Merson, Parlour.

Scorer: Hartson 76.

Zaragoza: Cedrun; Belsue, Aguado, Caceres, Solana, Poyet, Aragon, Nayim, Higuera (Sanjuan 67) (Geli 114), Pardeza, Esnaider.

Scorers: Esnaider 68, Nayim 120. *Referee:* Ceccarini (Italy).

Zaragoza players celebrated after the Cup-Winners' Cup Final victory over Arsenal. (Action Images)

EUROPEAN CUP-WINNERS' CUP 1994–95 – BRITISH AND IRISH

Preliminary Round, First Leg

11 AUG

Barry Town (0) 0

Zalgiris Vilnius (0) 1 *(Vencevicius)* 1914

Barry Town: Livingstone; Griffiths, Williams, Boyle, Davies (Leask), Ellis, Giles, Wright (Mitchell), D'Auria, Jones, Scott.
Zalgiris Vilnius: Spetyla; Suliauskas, Maciulevicius, Baltusnikas, Stonkus, Novikovas, Karvelis (Vencevicius), Tereskinas, Preiksaitis, Jankauskas, Poderis (Rimkus).

Bangor (0) 0

Tatran Presov (0) 1 *(Nenadic)* 1100

Bangor: Dalton; Glendining, Ferguson (Dornan), McCaffrey, Brown, Melly, Hill, Batey, McCallan, Magee (Wilkinson), McEvoy.
Tatran Presov: Jakubech; Bajtos, Kocis, Varga, Nenadic, Hlusko, Skalka, Hoger, Kantos, Zvara, Matta.

Floriana (0) 2 *(Stefanovic 2)*

Sligo Rovers (2) 2 *(Moran, Reid)* 1500

Floriana: Cluett; Cauchi, Wright (Marlow), Delia, Farrugia, Buttigieg, Busuttil, Stefanovic, Scriberras, Carvana, Buhagiar R.
Sligo Rovers: McLean; Reid D, Brunton, Boyle, Dykes, Kenny, Hastie, Carr, Brennan, Reid M, Moran (McDonnell).

Preliminary Round, Second Leg

25 AUG

Sligo Rovers (0) 1 *(Brennan)*

Floriana (0) 0 6000

Sligo Rovers: McLean; Reid D, Boyle, Dykes, McDonnell, Hastie, Kenny (Rooney), Moran, Brennan, Reid M, Brunton.
Floriana: Cluett; Cauchi, Farrugia (Carvana), Delia, Brincat, Buttigieg, Busuttil, Stefanovic, Scriberras, Marlow (Buhagiar J), Buhagiar R.

Tatran Presov (2) 4 *(Kocis 2, Matta, Hoger)*

Bangor (0) 0 4972

Tatran Presov: Jakubech; Bajtos, Kantos, Varga, Hlusko, Matta, Zvara, Shulka (Chihuri), Hoger, Kocis, Nenadic.
Bangor: Dalton; Glendinning, Ferguson, McCaffrey, Brown (Spiers), Melly, Hill, Wilkinson (Surgeon), McCallan, Magee, McEvoy.

Zalgiris Vilnius (2) 6 *(Karvelis 2, Baltusnikas, Poderis, Maciulevicius, Jankauskas)*

Barry Town (0) 0 2900

Zalgiris Vilnius: Spetyla (Koncevicius), Novikovas, Maciulevicius, Baltusnikas, Stonkus, Vencevicius, Suliauskas, Tereskinas, Preiksaitis (Urbonas), Karvelis (Jankauskas), Poderis.
Barry Town: Livingstone; Threlfall (Scott), Griffiths, Leask, Boyle, Ellis, Curtis, Sanderson, Mitchell, Jones, Giles.

First Round, First Leg

15 SEPT

Chelsea (2) 4 *(Furlong, Sinclair, Rocastle, Wise)*

Viktoria Zizkov (2) 2 *(Majoros 2)* 22,036

Chelsea: Kharine; Minto, Sinclair, Newton, Johnsen, Spackman, Rocastle (Rix), Spencer, Furlong, Peacock, Wise.
Viktoria Zizkov: Zitka; Kordule, Casko, Gabriel, Petrous, Poborsky, Bilek, Majoros, Vrabec, Jancula (Masek), Trval (Krejcik).

Dundee U (1) 3 *(Petric, Nixon, Hannah)*

Tatran Presov (2) 2 *(Skalka, Zvara (pen))* 9454

Dundee U: Main; McInally, Malpas, Hannah, Petric, Welsh, Bowman, McKinlay, Ristic (McLaren), Brewster (Dailly), Nixon.
Tatran Presov: Jakubech; Bajtos, Chihuri (Kocis), Varga, Menadic, Hlusko, Skalka, Hoger, Kentos (Pertus), Zvara, Matta.

Omonia (0) 1 *(Malekos)*

Arsenal (1) 3 *(Merson 2, Wright)* 14,500

Omonia: Christou; Constantinou, Panagiotou, Christophi, Christodoulou, Malekos, Savvides, Xiourouppas (Kaifas), Kantilos (Kizilasvili), Andreou, Gogritsiani.
Arsenal: Seaman; Dixon, Winterburn, Schwarz (Morrow), Keown, Linighan, Jensen, Wright, Smith, Merson, Parlour.

Sligo Rovers (1) 1 *(Kenny)*

FC Brugge (1) 2 *(Vermant, Verheyen)* 6000

Sligo Rovers: McLean; Kelly, Brunton, Boyle, Dykes, Kenny, Hastie, Carr, Houlihan, Annand, Moran.
FC Brugge: Verlinden; Medved, Van der Elst, Verheyen, Borkelmans, Van der Heyden, Okon, Vermant, Staelens, Eykelkamp, Plovie.

First Round, Second Leg

29 SEPT

Arsenal (2) 3 *(Wright 2, Schwarz)*

Omonia (0) 0 24,265

Arsenal: Seaman; Dixon, Winterburn, Schwarz, Linighan, Adams, Jensen (Hillier), Wright, Smith, Merson (Campbell), Parlour.
Omonia: Christou; Christodoulou, Christophi, Constantinou, Panagiotou, Savvides, Kalotheou, Andreou, Kantilos (Kaiafas), Malekos, Xiourouppas (Tutic).

Viktoria Zizkov (0) 0

Chelsea (0) 0 6000

Viktoria Zizkov: Silhavy; Notin, Kordule, Gabriel, Bileck, Petrous, Poborsky, Majoros (Trval), Vrabec (Masek), Casko, Jancula.
Chelsea: Kharine; Clarke, Johnsen, Sinclair, Barness, Wise, Rocastle, Newton, Rix, Peacock, Furlong.

Tatran Presov (2) 3 *(Zvara 2, Kocis)*

Dundee U (1) 1 *(Nixon)* 8184

Tatran Presov: Jakubech; Bajtos, Kentos, Lukac, Ptreus, Hlusko, Skalka, Hoger, Kocis (Lesko), Zvara, Matta (Pukah).
Dundee U: Main; Cleland (Craig), Malpas, Hannah, Petric, Welsh, Dailly, McKinlay, McLaren (Brewster), McInally, Nixon.

FC Brugge (2) 3 *(Staelens 2 (1 pen), Eykelkamp)*

Sligo Rovers (1) 1 *(Rooney)* 5500

FC Brugge: Belpaire; Medved, Van der Elst, Verheyen, Borkelmans, Van der Heyden, Okon, Vermant (Vrul), Staelens, Eykelkamp, Plovie.
Sligo Rovers: McLean; Kelly, Lynch, Boyle, Dykes, Kenny, Hastie, Carr, Houlihan (Annand), Rooney, McDonnell (Moran).

Second Round, First Leg

20 OCT

Brondby (0) 1 *(Strudal)*

Arsenal (2) 2 *(Wright, Smith)* 13,406

Brondby: Krogh; Colding (Hogh), Rieper, Eggen, Risager, Bjur, Vilfort, Jensen (Kristensen), Thogersen, Strudal, Hansen.
Arsenal: Seaman; Dixon, Winterburn, Schwarz, Bould, Adams, Jensen, Wright, Smith, Campbell, Parlour.

Chelsea (0) 0

FK Austria (0) 0 22,560

Chelsea: Kharine; Newton, Sinclair (Barness) (Rix), Kjeldbjerg, Johnsen, Spackman, Rocastle, Shipperley, Furlong, Peacock, Wise.
FK Austria: Wohlfahrt; Belaic, Kogler, Pfeffer, Sekerlioglu, Zsak, Schmid, Prosenik, Flogel, Mjelde (Zechner), Ogris (Kubica).

Quarter Finals, First Leg

28 FEB

FC Brugge (0) 1 *(Verheyen)*

Chelsea (0) 0 18,000

FC Brugge: Verlinden; Medved, Okon, Van der Elst (De Broule), Renier, Borkelmans, Verheyen, Vernant, Staelens, Buelinckx, Eijkelkamp.
Chelsea: Hitchcock; Clarke, Minto, Spackman, Johnsen, Sinclair, Newton, Spencer, Furlong, Peacock, Wise (Rocastle).

2 MAR

Arsenal (0) 1 *(Wright (pen))*

Auxerre (0) 1 *(Verlaat)* 35,508

Arsenal: Seaman; Dixon, Winterburn, Schwarz, Bould, Adams, Jensen, Wright, Kiwomya (Parlour), Merson, McGoldrick (Hartson).
Auxerre: Cool; Verlaat, Goma, West, Mahe, Rabarivony (Remy), Lamouchi, Violeau, Martins, Vahirua (Baticle), Laslandes.

Quarter Finals, Second Leg

14 MAR

Chelsea (2) 2 *(Stein, Furlong)*

FC Brugge (0) 0 28,661

Chelsea: Hitchcock; Clarke, Minto (Hall), Spackman, Johnsen, Sinclair, Rocastle (Lee), Furlong, Stein, Peacock, Burley.
FC Brugge: Verlinden (Belpaire); Medved (Vermant), Okon, Renier, Verheyen, Van Der Elst, Borkelmans, De Brul, Staelens, Buelinckx (Van Der Hayden), Eykelkamp.

16 MAR

Auxerre (0) 0

Arsenal (1) 1 *(Wright)* 22,000

Auxerre: Cool; Goma, Verlaat, Silvestre, Mahe, Saib, Martins, Rabarivony (Cocard), Lamouchi, Vahirua (Baticle), Laslandes.
Arsenal: Seaman; Dixon, Winterburn, Schwarz, Bould, Adams, Keown, Wright, Hartson (Morrow), Merson, Parlour.

Semi-Finals, First Leg

6 APR

Arsenal (2) 3 *(Bould 2, Wright)*

Sampdoria (0) 2 *(Jugovic 2)* 38,809

Arsenal: Seaman; Dixon, Winterburn, Schwarz, Bould, Adams, Hillier, Wright (Kiwomya), Hartson, Merson (Morrow), Parlour.
Sampdoria: Zenga; Sacchetti, Rossi, Mannini, Invernizzi (Maspero), Evani, Jugovic, Serena, Mancini, Salsano, Lombardo.

Zaragoza (2) 3 *(Pardeza, Esnaider 2)*

Chelsea (0) 0 35,000

Zaragoza: Juanmi; Belsue, Aguado, Caceres, Solana, Aragon (Sanjuan), Poyet, Nayim, Higuera, Esnaider, Pardeza (Oscar).
Chelsea: Hitchcock; Clarke, Minto, Myers, Johnsen, Sinclair, Rocastle (Hoddle), Spencer (Stein), Furlong, Peacock, Spackman.

Semi-Finals, Second Leg

20 APR

Chelsea (1) 3 *(Furlong, Sinclair, Stein)*

Zaragoza (0) 1 *(Aragon)* 26,456

Chelsea: Hitchcock; Clarke, Minto, Lee, Johnsen (Hoddle), Sinclair, Rocastle (Spencer), Furlong, Stein, Peacock, Spackman.
Zaragoza: Juanmi; Belsue, Caceres, Solana, Cafu, Higuera (Jeli), Aragon, Oscar, Nayim, Esnaider (Rodriguez), Pardeza.

Sampdoria (1) 3 *(Mancini, Bellucci 2)*

Arsenal (0) 2 *(Wright, Schwarz)* 35,000

Sampdoria: Zenga; Mannini, Ferri (Bellucci), Vierchowod, Serena, Evani (Invernizzi), Jugovic, Maspero, Lombardo, Mihajlovic, Mancini.
Arsenal: Seaman; Dixon, Winterburn, Schwarz, Bould, Adams, Keown, Wright (Kiwomya), Hartson, Merson, Hillier (McGoldrick).

Final

10 MAY

Arsenal (0) 1 *(Hartson)*

Zaragoza (0) 2 *(Esnaider, Nayim) aet* 42,424

Arsenal: Seaman; Dixon, Winterburn (Morrow), Schwarz, Linighan, Adams, Keown (Hillier), Wright, Hartson, Merson, Parlour.
Zaragoza: Cedrun; Belsue, Aguado, Caceres, Solana, Poyet, Aragon, Nayim, Higuera (Sanjuan) (Geli), Pardeza, Esnaider.

INTER-CITIES FAIRS & UEFA CUP

FAIRS CUP FINALS 1958–71

(Winners in italics)

Year	First Leg	Attendance	Second Leg	Attendance
1958	London 2 Barcelona 2	45,466	*Barcelona* 6 London 0	62,000
1960	Birmingham C 0 Barcelona 0	40,500	*Barcelona* 4 Birmingham C 1	70,000
1961	Birmingham C 2 Roma 2	21,005	*Roma* 2 Birmingham C 0	60,000
1962	Valencia 6 Barcelona 2	65,000	Barcelona 1 *Valencia* 1	60,000
1963	Dynamo Zagreb 1 Valencia 2	40,000	*Valencia* 2 Dynamo Zagreb 0	55,000
1964	*Zaragoza* 2 Valencia 1	50,000	(in Barcelona)	
1965	*Ferencvaros* 1 Juventus 0	25,000	(in Turin)	
1966	Barcelona 0 Zaragoza 1	70,000	Zaragoza 2 *Barcelona* 4	70,000
1967	Dynamo Zagreb 2 Leeds U 0	40,000	Leeds U 0 *Dynamo Zagreb* 0	35,604
1968	Leeds U 1 Ferencvaros 0	25,368	Ferencvaros 0 *Leeds U* 0	70,000
1969	Newcastle U 3 Ujpest Dozsa 0	60,000	Ujpest Dozsa 2 *Newcastle U* 3	37,000
1970	Anderlecht 3 Arsenal 1	37,000	*Arsenal* 3 Anderlecht 0	51,612
1971	Juventus 0 Leed U 0 *(abandoned 51 minutes)*	42,000		
	Juventus 2 Leeds U 2	42,000	*Leeds U* 1* Juventus 1	42,483

UEFA CUP FINALS 1972–95

(Winners in italics)

Year	First Leg	Attendance	Second Leg	Attendance
1972	Wolverhampton W 1 Tottenham H 2	45,000	*Tottenham H* 1 Wolverhampton W 1	48,000
1973	Liverpool 0 Moenchengladbach 0 *(abandoned 27 minutes)*	44,967		
	Liverpool 3 Moenchengladbach 0	41,169	Moenchengladbach 2 *Liverpool* 0	35,000
1974	Tottenham H 2 Feyenoord 2	46,281	*Feyenoord* 2 Tottenham 0	68,000
1975	Moenchengladbach 0 Twente 0	45,000	Twente 1 *Moenchengladbach* 5	24,500
1976	Liverpool 3 FC Brugge 2	56,000	FC Brugge 1 *Liverpool* 1	32,000
1977	Juventus 1 Athletic Bilbao 0	75,000	Athletic Bilbao 2 *Juventus* 1*	43,000
1978	Bastia 0 PSV Eindhoven 0	15,000	*PSV Eindhoven* 3 Bastia 0	27,000
1979	Red Star Belgrade 1 Moenchengladbach 1	87,500	*Moenchengladbach* 1 Red Star Belgrade 0	45,000
1980	Moenchengladbach 3 Eintracht Frankfurt 2	25,000	*Eintracht Frankfurt* 1* Moenchengladbach 0	60,000
1981	Ipswich T 3 AZ 67 Alkmaar 0	27,532	AZ 67 Alkmaar 4 *Ipswich T* 2	28,500
1982	Gothenburg 1 Hamburg 0	42,548	Hamburg 0 *Gothenburg* 3	60,000
1983	Anderlecht 1 Benfica 0	45,000	Benfica 1 *Anderlecht* 1	80,000
1984	Anderlecht 1 Tottenham H 1	40,000	*Tottenham H* 1[1] Anderlecht 1	46,258
1985	Videoton 0 Real Madrid 3	30,000	*Real Madrid* 0 Videoton 1	98,300
1986	Real Madrid 5 Cologne 1	80,000	Cologne 2 *Real Madrid* 0	15,000
1987	Gothenburg 1 Dundee U 0	50,023	Dundee U 1 *Gothenburg* 1	20,911
1988	Espanol 3 Bayer Leverkusen 0	42,000	*Bayer Leverkusen* 3[2] Espanol 0	22,000
1989	Napoli 2 Stuttgart 1	83,000	Stuttgart 3 *Napoli* 3	67,000
1990	Juventus 3 Fiorentina 1	45,000	Fiorentina 0 *Juventus* 0	32,000
1991	Internazionale 2 Roma 0	68,887	Roma 1 *Internazionale* 0	70,901
1992	Torino 2 Ajax 2	65,377	*Ajax** 0 Torino 0	40,000
1993	Borussia Dortmund 1 Juventus 3	37,000	*Juventus* 3 Borussia Dortmund 0	62,781
1994	Salzburg 0 Internazionale 1	47,500	*Internazionale* 1 Salzburg 0	80,326
1995	Parma 1 Juventus 0	23,000	Juventus 1 *Parma* 1	80,750

**won on away goals* [1]*Tottenham H won 4-3 on penalties aet* [2]*Bayer Leverkusen won 3-2 on penalties aet*

UEFA CUP 1994–95

Preliminary Round, First Leg

Slavia Prague (1) 2 *(Smicer 37, Suchoparek 68)*, Cork City (0) 0 3690
Motherwell (2) 3 *(Coyne 20, McGrillen 34, Kirk 83)*, Havnar (0) 0 7517
FC Copenhagen (0) 0, Jazz (1) 1 *(Ruhanen 33)* 4390
Portadown (0) 0, Slovan Bratislava (0) 2 *(Timko 58, Rosnak 75)* 2000
Bangor City (1) 1 *(Mottram 23)*, IA Akranes (1) 2 *(Reynisson 42, Jonsson 47)* 3426
Inter Bratislava (0) 0, MyPa (2) 3 *(Kolkka 11, 30, Rajamaki 49)* 2007
Odense (1) 3 *(Thorup 13, Schonberg 58, Madsen 89)*, Flora Tallinn (0) 0 2834
Lillestrom (2) 4 *(Hedman 2, Johnsen 42, Gulbrandsen 49, Pedersen 68)*, Donetsk (0) 1 *(Petrov 58)* 2779
GI Gotu (0) 0, Trelleborgs (1) 1 *(Karlsson 44)* 814
Gornik Zabrze (2) 7 *(Szemonski 30, 83, Baluszynski 35 (pen), Kosela 52, Kubik 61, 80, Orzeszek 78)*, Shamrock Rovers (0) 0 7001
Romar (0) 0, AIK Stockholm (1) 2 *(Johansson 26, Simpson 60)* 4000
Inter Cardiff (0) 0, Katowice (0) 2 *(Sermak 84 (pen), 89)* 1115
Aarau (0) 1 *(Kucharski 71)*, Mura Sobota (0) 0 4800
Anorthosis (2) 2 *(Charalambous 19, Nicolic 40)*, Shumen (0) 0 6000
Dynamo Tbilisi (1) 2 *(Kinkladze 27, Arveladze S 59)*, Uni Craiova (0) 0 45,000
Vardar Skopje (1) 1 *(Milosevski 38)*, Bekescsaba (1) 1 *(Nracko 44)* 20,000
Fenerbahce (2) 5 *(Uygun 15, Aykut 44, 66, 88, Nielsen 81)*, Turan Tauz (0) 0 30,000
Valletta (1) 2 *(Agius 16, Zerafa 68)*, Rapid Bucharest (2) 6 *(Chebac 5, Vladoiu 14, 46, Kira 74, Chirita 78, Voinea 84)* 3000
Kispest Honved (1) 4 *(Illes 27, 68, Pisont 60, Hamar 76)*, Zimbru (0) 1 *(Timbur 58)* 5000
CSKA Sofia (2) 3 *(Tanev 21 (pen), Koilov 44, 74)*, Ararat Erevan (0) 0 4000
Dynamo Minsk (0) 3 *(Kashentsev 69, Kachuro 78, Yaskovich 85)*, Hibernians (1) 1 *(Lawrence 6)* 7000
Teuta (1) 1 *(Fraholli 12)*, Apollon (0) 4 *(Spoliaric 57, Krcmarevic 80, 84, Cepovic 82)* 14,000
Aris Salonika (1) 3 *(Sapountzis 8, 64, (pen) Ivan 89)*, Hapoel Beer Sheba (1) 1 *(Guseyev 14)* 19,000
Hafnafjordur (0) 1 *(Magnusson 74)*, Linfield (0) 0 700
Skonto Riga (0) 0, Aberdeen (0) 0 2300
Grevenmacher (0) 1 *(Silva 83)*, Rosenborg (1) 2 *(Leonhardsen 4, Loken 89 (pen))* 500
Olimpija Ljubljana (2) 3 *(Dosti 35, 37, 73)*, Levski Sofia (0) 2 *(Sirakov 57, 72)* 4000

Preliminary Round, Second Leg

Aberdeen (0) 1 *(Kane 90)*, Skonto Riga (0) 1 *(Semenov 55)* 8500
AIK Stockholm (1) 2 *(Lidman 21, 63)*, Romar (0) 0 4000
IA Akranes (2) 2 *(Ingolfsson 8, Thordarson 21)*, Bangor City (0) 0 800
Apollon (2) 4 *(Cepovic 24, 29, Hadjiloizou 60, Pittas 89)*, Teuta (0) 2 *(Citsa 73, Ampazi 78)* 5000
Ararat Erevan (0) 0, CSKA Sofia (0) 0 7000
Bekescsaba (0) 1 *(Csato 61)*, Vardar Skopje (0) 0 3500
Cork City (0) 0, Sparta Prague (1) 4 *(Hogen 33, 50, Vaura 49, Berger 90)* 3200
Flora Tallinn (0) 0, Odense (1) 3 *(Hemmingsen 19, 49, Tchami 68)* 1000
Havnar Boltfelag (0) 1 *(Hansen 59)*, Motherwell (1) 4 *(Kirk 13, 69, Davies 20, Burns 88)* 750
Hibernians (1) 4 *(Ostrovsky 55 (og), Xerri 71, Spiteri 90, Miller 109)*, Dynamo Minsk (1) 3 *(Yuravin 44 (pen), Plaskevic 94, Spiteri 105 (og))* 2400
Hapoel Beer Sheba (0) 1 *(Madar 46)*, Aris Salonika (1) 2 *(Bouyouklis 30, Milojevic 55)* 6800
Jazz (0) 0, FC Copenhagen (0) 4 *(Johansen 54, Nielsen M. 81, Frandsen 83, Nielsen A. 87)* 1800
Katowice (3) 6 *(Walcsak 25, 83, Maciejewski 33, 45 (pen), Jojko 75 (pen), Wolny 89)*, Inter Cardiff (0) 0 4500
Linfield (3) 3 *(Beatty 15, Gorman 31, Peebles 36)*, Hafnarfjordur (1) 1 *(Podunavac 21)* 3201
Levski Sofia (1) 1 *(Stoilov 2)*, Olimpija Ljubljana (1) 2 *(Novak 24, Paulin 89)* 6800
MyPa (0) 0, Inter Bratislava (1) 1 *(Rupec 3)* 800
Mura Sobota (0) 0, Aarau (1) 1 *(Skrzypczak 17)* 1800
Rosenborg (2) 6 *(Strand 37, 87, Bergersen 45, Jakobsen 62, Brattbakk 77, 84)*, Grevenmacher (0) 0 11,000
Rapid Bucharest (1) 1 *(Tira 32)*, Valletta (1) 1 *(Agius 22)* 5000
Donetsk (0) 2 *(Orbu 49, Petrov 58)*, Lillestrom (0) 0 14,000
Shamrock Rovers (0) 0, Gornik Zabrze (0) 1 *(Baluszynski 49)* 5000
Shumen (1) 1 *(Iskrenov 43 (pen))*, Anorthosis (0) 2 *(Ashiotis 61, Kokich 82)* 4750
Slovan Bratislava (2) 3 *(Faktor 15, Tittel 33, Rusnak 65)*, Portadown (0) 0 6500
Turan Tauz (0) 0, Fenerbahce (0) 2 *(Ali 83 (pen), Bulent 87)* 1000
Trelleborg (2) 3 *(Karlsson 6 (pen), Eriksson 12, Rasmusson 48)*, GI Goto (0) 2 *(Jarnskor H. 55, Jarnskor M. 83)* 5500
Uni Craiova (0) 1 *(Pigulea 59)*, Dynamo Tbilisi (1) 2 *(Kavelasvili 3, Kinkladze 83)* 13,000
Zimbru (0) 0, Kispest Honved (0) 1 *(Orosz 83)* 3000

First Round, First Leg

Aarau (0) 0, Maritimo (0) 0 5400
Admira Wacker (2) 5 *(Gager 7 (pen), 60 (pen), Schiener 18, Klausz 66, Waldoch 90 (og))*, Gornik Zabrze (2) 2 *(Szemonski 26, Orzeszek 35)* 1500
AIK Stockholm (0) 0, Slavia Prague (0) 0 3190
IA Akranes (0) 0, Kaiserslautern (2) 4 *(Hamann 33, Anders 44, Kuntz 53, Kuka 59)* 4000
Anorthosis (2) 2 *(Gogic 6, Tamboris 41)*, Athletic Bilbao (0) 0 3000
Antwerp (0) 0, Newcastle U (3) 5 *(Lee 1, 9, 51, Sellars 40, Watson 78)* 15,000
Apollon (1) 1 *(Krcmarevic 36)*, Sion (0) 3 *(Bonvin 70, Marin 82, 85)* 4000
Bayer Leverkusen (4) 5 *(Kirsten 6, 16, 41, Dooley 14, Schuster 73)*, PSV Eindhoven (2) 4 *(Ronaldo 11 (pen), 45, 61, Nilis 87)* 16,000
Blackburn R (0) 0, Trelleborg (0) 1 *(Sandell 71)* 13,775
Boavista (1) 2 *(Artur 2, Gomes 62)*, MyPa (1) 1 *(Laaksonen 42)* 2000
Bordeaux (2) 3 *(Dugarry 4, Johnsen 38 (og), Witschge 85)*, Lillestrom (1) 1 *(Huard 6 (og))* 15,000
Borussia Dortmund (0) 1 *(Moller 57)*, Motherwell (0) 0 35,420
Cannes (0) 4 *(Durix 49 (pen), Kozniku 56, 80, Horlaville 67)*, Fenerbahce (0) 0 7500
CSKA Sofia (1) 3 *(Mihtarski 44, 82, Radukanov 70)*, Juventus (1) 2 *(Porrini 39, Del Piero 76)* 22,000
Dynamo Minsk (0) 0, Lazio (0) 0 20,000
Dynamo Tbilisi (1) 1 *(Arveladze 40 (pen)*, Tirol Innsbruck (0) 0 45,000
Internazionale (0) 1 *(Bergkamp 75 (pen)*, Aston Villa (0) 0 22,639
Kamyshin (1) 6 *(Goessakov 38, Polstyanov 55, 90, Volgin 58, Filipov 80, 90)*, Bekescsaba (1) 1 *(Szarvas 14)* 1500

Katowice (1) 1 *(Maciejewski 20 (pen))*, Aris Salonika (0) 0 8000
Linfield (0) 1 *(Anderson 86)*, Odense (0) 1 *(Schjonberg 46)* 3585
Napoli (1) 2 *(Carbone 30 (pen), 49)*, Skonto Riga (0) 0 12,000
Olimpija Ljubljana (1) 1 *(Siljak 3)*, Eintracht Frankfurt (0) 1 *(Legat 84)* 3500
Olympiakos (0) 1 *(Ivic 57)*, Marseille (1) 2 *(Ferrer 31, Marquet 79)* 40,000
Rapid Bucharest (1) 2 *(Chirita 18, Vladoiu 73)*, Charleroi (0) 0 7000
Real Madrid (1) 1 *(Vazquez 11)*, Sporting Lisbon (0) 0 80,000
Rosenborg (0) 1 *(Loken 52)*, La Coruna (0) 0 5281
Seraing (0) 3 *(Wamberto 67, Schaessens 75, Edmilson 90)*, Dynamo Moscow (3) 4 *(Smirnov 17, Tsjerisjev 26, 61, Simutenkov 44)* 3750
Slovan Bratislava (0) 1 *(Tomaschek 76)*, FC Copenhagen (0) 0 7570
Trabzonspor (2) 2 *(Orhan K 7, Soner 19)*, Dynamo Bucharest (1) 1 *(Ivan 29)* 20,000
Twente (1) 1 *(Mols 38)*, Kispest Honved (1) 4 *(Kovacs 19, 52, 75, Hamar 88)* 6000
Vitesse (0) 1 *(Gillhaus 51)*, Parma (0) 0 9200
Volgograd (1) 3 *(Gerasimenko 42, Nechayev 63, Veretennikov 75)*, Nantes (1) 2 *(Ouedec 28, N'Doram 81)* 19,000

First Round, Second Leg

Aris Salonika (1) 1 *(Sapountzis 47)*, Katowice (0) 0 8000 *Katowice won 4-3 on penalties*
Aston Villa (1) 1 *(Houghton 41)*, Internazionale (0) 0 30,533 *Villa won 4-3 on penalties*
Athletic Bilbao (2) 3 *(Guerrero 17, Panayiotou 24 (og), Andrinua 89)*, Anorthosis (0) 0 29,000
Bekescsaba (0) 1 *(Csato 77 (pen))*, Kamyshin (0) 0 2000
Charleroi (0) 2 *(Balog 89, Misse 90)*, Rapid Bucharest (0) 1 *(Tira 48)* 7000
FC Copenhagen (1) 1 *(Nielsen 45 (pen))*, Slovan Bratislava (1) 1 *(Negro 24)* 4232
Dynamo Bucharest (1) 3 *(Ceausila 6, Niculescu 51, Lica 82)*, Trabzonspor (2) 3 *(Orhan K 21, Orhan B 23, Soner 78)* 7000
Dynamo Moscow (0) 0, Seraing (0) 1 *(Schaessens 87)* 7000
Eintracht Frankfurt (1) 2 *(Dickhaut 9, Yeboah 84)*, Olimpija Ljubljana (0) 0 11,500
Fenerbahce (0) 1 *(Bulent 58)*, Cannes (2) 5 *(Tayfur 21 (og), Horlaville 25, 62, Micoud 50, Vieira 77)* 31,000
Gornik Zabrze (1) 1 *(Baluszynski 30)*, Admira Wacker (1) 1 *(Litovchenko 45)* 8500
Juventus (1) 5 *(Ravanelli 9, 75, 79, 81, 86)*, CSKA Sofia (0) 1 *(Mihtarski 90)* 22,000
Kaiserslautern (0) 4 *(Kuka 56, 84, Wagner 59, Haber 81)*, IA Akranes (0) 1 *(Gislason 88)* 23,070
Kispest Honved (0) 1 *(Illes 58 (pen))*, Twente (1) 3 *(Vurens 34, Ellerman 67, Boerebach 87)* 7000
Lazio (1) 4 *(Ostrovski 45 (og), Favalli 61, Boksic 74, Fuser 84)* Dynamo Minsk (1) 1 *(Kachuro 9)* 37,000
La Coruna (0) 4 *(Bebeto 81, 98, 114, Donato 107 (pen))*, Rosenborg (0) 1 *(Brattbakk 92)* 21,000
Lillestrom (0) 0, Bordeaux (2) 2 *(Zidane 2, Fournier 15)* 2003
Maritimo (0) 1 *(Paulo Alves 63)*, Aarau (0) 0 8500
Marseille (0) 3 *(Cascarino 53, 89, Ferreri 85)*, Olympiakos (0) 0 40,000
Motherwell (0) 0, Borussia Dortmund (0) 2 *(Riedle 54, 64)* 9362
MyPa (0) 1 *(Gronholm 75)*, Boavista (0) 1 *(Artur 89 (pen))* 3616
Nantes (1) 3 *(Ouedec 29, 61, Loko 75)*, Volgograd (0) 0 26,000
Newcastle U (4) 5 *(Lee 11, Cole 26, 39, 88, Beardsley 38 (pen)*, Antwerp (0) 2 *(Kiekens 75, Severeyns 77)* 29,737

Odense (4) 5 *(Nedergaard 5, 85, Schjonberg 25, 42 (pen), Thorup 40)*, Linfield (0) 0 4518
Parma (1) 2 *(Zola 23, 73)*, Vitesse (0) 0 9081
PSV Eindhoven (0) 0, Bayer Leverkusen (0) 0 21,500
Sion (0) 2 *(Marin 89, Orlando 101)*, Apollon (0) 3 *(Krcmarevic 49, Spoljaric 66, Cepovic 77)* 5000
Slavia Prague (1) 2 *(Suchoparek 26, Bejbl 57)*, AIK Stockholm (1) 2 *(Lidman 35, Sundgren 81)* 6329
Skonto Riga (0) 0, Napoli (1) 1 *(Buso 31)* 2589
Sporting Lisbon (2) 2 *(Joao Pinto 3, Oceano 31)*, Real Madrid (1) 1 *(Laudrup 14)* 58,000
Tirol Innsbruck (3) 5 *(Cerny 4, Stoger 32, Danek 35, 56, Janeschitz 89)*, Dynamo Tbilisi (1) 1 *(Arveladze S 38)* 7000
Trelleborg (0) 2 *(Karlsson J 50, 85)*, Blackburn R (1) 2 *(Sutton 18, Shearer 84)* 6730

Second Round, First Leg

Admira Wacker (1) 1 *(Gager 36 (pen))*, Cannes (0) 1 *(Bedrossian 66)* 4000
AIK Stockholm (0) 0, Parma (0) 1 *(Crippa 72)* 18,146
Boavista (1) 1 *(Sanchez 26)*, Napoli (0) 1 *(Carbone 57)* 7000
Dynamo Moscow (0) 2 *(Simutenkov 65, Cheryshev 69)*, Real Madrid (1) 2 *(Sandro 21, Zamorano 73)* 7000
Kaiserslautern (0) 1 *(Sforza 75)*, Odense (0) 1 *(Hemmingsen C 71)* 19,872
Katowice (0) 1 *(Strojek 88)*, Bordeaux (0) 0 6000
Kispest Honved (0) 0, Bayer Leverkusen (1) 2 *(Munch 16, Sergio 80)* 8500
Maritimo (0) 0, Juventus (0) 1 *(Ravanelli 78)* 15,500
Nantes (1) 2 *(Ouedec 32 (pen), 61)*, Kamyshin (0) 0 34,000
Newcastle U (2) 3 *(Fox 9, Beardsley 34 (pen), Cole 56)*, Athletic Bilbao (0) 2 *(Ziganda 71, Suances 79)* 32,140
Rapid Bucharest (0) 2 *(Vladoiu 67, Voinea 74)*, Eintracht Frankfurt (0) 1 *(Furtok 64)* 10,000
Sion (2) 2 *(Wicky 25, Kunz 41)*, Marseille (0) 0 15,500
Slovan Bratislava (0) 2 *(Rusnak 49, 60)*, Borussia Dortmund (1) 1 *(Tomacek 18 (og))* 18,060
Tirol Innsbruck (1) 2 *(Sane 30, Stoger 56)*, La Coruna (0) 0 11,800
Trabzonspor (0) 1 *(Orhan K 78)*, Aston Villa (0) 0 27,500
Trelleborg (0) 0, Lazio (0) 0 7303

Second Round, Second Leg

Aston Villa (0) 2 *(Atkinson 77, Ehiogu 90)*, Trabzonspor (0) 1 *(Orhan K 90)* 23,858
Athletic Bilbao (0) 1 *(Ziganda 67)*, Newcastle U (0) 0 47,000
Bayer Leverkussen (2) 5 *(Kirsten 28, 65, 68, Hapal 32, Tolkmitt 60)*, Kispest Honved (0) 0 14,900
Bordeaux (1) 1 *(Histilloes 18)*, Katowice (0) 1 *(Walczak 70 (pen))* 20,000
Borussia Dortmund (1) 3 *(Moller 15, Riedle 46, 68)*, Slovan Bratislava (0) 0 32,534
Cannes (0) 2 *(Kozniku 48, Charvel 87)*, Admira Wacker (3) 4 *(Mayrieb 7, Klausz 16, 56, Schiener 23)* 9000
Eintracht Frankfurt (3) 5 *(Bommer 10, Yeboah 13, 17, Furtok 65, 67)*, Rapid Bucharest (0) 0 12,000
Juventus (1) 2 *(Ravanelli 33, 51)*, Maritimo (0) 1 *(Paulo Alves 79)* 4254
Kamyshin (0) 1 *(Polstyanov 67)*, Nantes (0) 2 *Ouedec 47, 63) in Moscow* 1000
La Coruna (3) 4 *(Claudio 35, 37, Donato 40 (pen), Manjarin 71)*, Tirol Innsbruck (0) 0 25,000
Lazio (0) 1 *(Boksic 90)*, Trelleborg (0) 0 45,000
Napoli (2) 2 *(Agostini 18, 36)*, Boavista (0) 1 *(Luciano 76)* 45,000
Marseille (0) 3 *(Libbra 47, 65, Ferreri 73)*, Sion (1) 1 *(Kunz 5)* 40,000
Odense (0) 0, Kaiserslautern (0) 0 14,192
Parma (2) 2 *(Minotti 4, 16)*, AIK Stockholm (0) 0 5301
Real Madrid (0) 4 *(Zamorano 48, Redondo 76, Dani 89, 90)*, Dynamo Moscow (0) 0 60,000

Third Round, First Leg

Admira Wacker (0) 1 *(Binder 56)*, Juventus (3) 3 *(Conte 9, Roberto Baggio 14, 43)* 8000
Athletic Bilbao (0) 1 *(Ziganda 48)*, Parma (0) 0 45,000
Eintracht Frankfurt (0) 1 *(Buso 55 (og))*, Napoli (0) 0 42,000
Katowice (0) 1 *(Nikodem 54)*, Bayer Leverkusen (3) 4 *(Kirsten 29, 44, Lehnhoff 41, 64)* 8000
La Coruna (1) 1 *(Bebeto 23)*, Borussia Dortmund (0) 0 25,000
Nantes (2) 4 *(Loko 16, Ferri 33, N'Doram 54, Makelele 79)*, Sion (0) 0 34,000
Odense (1) 2 *(Schjonberg 45, Hjorth 79)*, Real Madrid (0) 3 *(Zamorano 66, Amavisca 69, Laudrup 90)* 15,000
Trabzonspor (0) 1 *(Unal 67)*, Lazio (0) 2 *(Rambaudi 59, Negri 61)* 25,000

Third Round, Second Leg

Bayer Leverkusen (4) 4 *(Schuster 11, Thom 13, Scholz 15, Hapal 28)*, Katowice (0) 0 24,000
Borussia Dortmund (0) 3 *(Zorc 50, Riedle 115, Ricken 118)*, La Coruna (0) 1 *(Alfredo 102) aet* 35,800
Juventus (1) 2 *(Ferrara 17, Vialli 86)*, Admira Wacker (0) 1 *(Wimmer 73)* 5732
Lazio (1) 2 *(Cravero 27, Di Valo 75)*, Trabzonspor (0) 1 *(Soner 73)* 24,000
Napoli (0) 0, Eintracht Frankfurt (0) 1 *(Falkenmayer 56)* 25,000
Parma (2) 4 *(Zola 20, Dino Baggio 38, 47, Fernando Couto 64)*, Athletic Bilbao (0) 2 *(Vales 65, Guerrero 75)* 14,600
Real Madrid (0) 0, Odense (0) 2 *(Pedersen 71, Bisgaard 92) aet* 50,000
Sion (0) 2 *(Herr 76, Marin 82)*, Nantes (2) 2 *(Loko 30, N'Doram 31)* 12,000

Quarter-finals, First Leg

Eintracht Frankfurt (0) 1 *(Furtok 73)*, Juventus (1) 1 *(Marocchi 36)* 42,000
Bayer Leverkusen (2) 5 *(Lehnhoff 9, Kirsten 18, 89, Sergio 79, 84)*, Nantes (0) 1 *(Ouedec 64 (pen))* 21,400
Lazio (0) 1 *(Freund 69 (og))*, Borussia Dortmund (0) 0 50,000
Parma (0) 1 *(Zola 49 (pen))*, Odense (0) 0 6300

Quarter-finals, Second Leg

Borussia Dortmund (1) 2 *(Chapuisat 11 (pen), Riedle 90)*, Lazio (0) 0 35,400
Juventus (0) 3 *(Conte 77, Ravanelli 88, Del Piero 89)*, Eintracht Frankfurt (0) 0 20,000
Nantes (0) 0, Bayer Leverkusen (0) 0 34,210
Odense (0) 0, Parma (0) 0 13,000

Semi-finals, First Leg

Bayer Leverkusen (1) 1 *(Sergio 20)*, Parma (0) 2 *(Dino Baggio 48, Asprilla 53)* 21,500
Juventus (1) 2 *(Roberto Baggio 25 (pen), Kohler 88)*, Borussia Dortmund (1) 2 *(Reuter 7, Moller 70)* 80,000

Semi-finals, Second Leg

Borussia Dortmund (1) 1 *(Cesar 10)*, Juventus (2) 2 *(Porrini 7, Roberto Baggio 31)* 35,400
Parma (1) 3 *(Asprilla 3, 55, Zola 67)*, Bayer Leverkusen (0) 0 16,000

Final, First Leg: Parma (1) 1, Juventus (0) 0

(in Parma, 3 May 1995, 22,062)

Parma: Bucci; Benarrivo (Mussi 9), Minotti, Apolloni, Fernando Couto, Di Chiara, Pin, Dino Baggio, Sensini, Zola (Fiore 89), Asprilla. *Scorer:* Dino Baggio 5.
Juventus: Rampulla; Fusi (Del Piero 72), Tacchinardi, Carrera (Marocchi 46), Jarni, Paulo Sousa, Di Livio, Deschamps, Vialli, Roberto Baggio, Ravanelli. *Referee:* Lopez Nieto (Spain).

Final, Second Leg: Juventus (1) 1, Parma (0) 1

(in Milan, 17 May 1995, 80,750)

Juventus: Peruzzi; Ferrara, Torricelli, Porrini, Jarni, Paulo Sousa, Di Livio (Carrera 82), Marocchi (Del Piero 75), Roberto Baggio, Vialli, Ravanelli. *Scorer:* Vialli 33.
Parma: Bucci; Benarrivo (Mussi 46), Minotti, Susic, Fernando Couto, Di Chiara (Castellini 81), Dino Baggio, Fiore, Crippa, Zola, Asprilla. *Scorer:* Dino Baggio 53. *Referee:* Van den Wijngaert (Belgium).

Gianluca Vialli (striped shirt) eludes several Parma defenders as Juventus are held by their Italian opponents. (Action Images)

UEFA CUP 1994–95 – BRITISH AND IRISH

Preliminary Round, First Leg

9 AUG

Bangor City (1) 1 *(Mottram)*
IA Akranes (1) 2 *(Reynisson, Jonsson)* 3426

Bangor City: Adkins; Jones, Rutter, Wiggins, Middleton, Humphries, Evans, Noble, Mottram, Lloyd-Williams (McClelland), Barnett.
IA Akranes: Thordarsson T; Adolfsson, Miljhovic, Hervasson, Haraldsson S, Haraldsson P, Jonsson, Thordarsson O, Ingolfsson, Reynisson (Tordarsson), Bibercic (Petursson).

Gornik Zabrze (2) 7 *(Szemonski 2, Baluszynski 1 (pen), Kosela, Orzeszek, Kubik 2)*
Shamrock Rovers (0) 0 7001

Gornik Zabrze: Klak; Jegor, Waldoch, Brzoza, Zadylak, Grembocki (Orzeszek), Kosela, Brzeczek, Kubik, Szemonski, Baluszynski (Jarosz).
Shamrock Rovers: O'Neill; Burke, Brazil, Whelan, Nolan, McGrath, Mullen, Dodd, Toal, Bacon (Gannon), Eviston (Giles).

Hafnafjordur (0) 1 *(Magnusson)*
Linfield (0) 0 700

Hafnafjordur: Arnarson S; Racnarsson, Podunavic, Vikingsson, Mrazek, Jonsson, Helgason, Marteinsson, Magnusson, Arnarson H, Kirstjansson K.
Linfield: Lamont; Dornan, Easton, Peebles, Spires, Beatty, Campbell, McCoosh (McIlroy), Haylock, Fenlon, Bailie.

Inter Cardiff (0) 0
Katowice (0) 2 *(Sermak 2 (1 pen))* 1115

Inter Cardiff: Wood; Knight, Batchelor, Lewis, John, Jones L, Beattie, Thomas, O'Brien, Evans P (Williams), Taylor (Burrows).
Katowice: Jojko; Wegrzyn, Swierczewski, Maciejewski, Strojek, Widuch, Sermak, Borawski, Wolny, Janoszka (Walczak), Kucz (Nikodem).

Motherwell (2) 3 *(Coyne, McGrillen, Kirk)*
Havnar Boltfelag (0) 0 7517

Motherwell: Woods; Shannon, McKinnon, Philliben, Martin, McCart, Lambert, Dolan, McGrillen (Kirk), O'Donnell (Davies), Coyne.
Havnar Boltfelag: Johannesen; Jakobsen, Dahl, Hansen, Wang, Dam J, Nolsoe, Thomasson, Johnsson, Mohr, Dam J H (Eydun).

Portadown (0) 0
Slovan Bratislava (0) 2 *(Timpko, Rosnak)* 2000

Portadown: Keenan; Major, Murray, Mills, Sloan, Stewart, Cunningham, Shepherd, Casey, Smith, Russell.
Slovan Bratislava: Molnar; Seman, Chvila, Tomaschek, Kinder, Tittel, Pecko, Lancz, Faktor, Maixner (Rusnaik), Timko (Klinovsky).

Skonto Riga (0) 0
Aberdeen (0) 0 2300

Skonto Riga: Laizans; Troytsky, Zemlinsky, Mikutsky, Shevlykakov, Monyak, Semenov, Blagomadezhdin, Stepanov, Babichev, Yeliseyez.
Aberdeen: Snelders; McKimmie, Woodthorpe, Grant, Irvine, Wright, Robertson, Shearer (Booth), McKinnon, Dodds, Winnie.

Slavia Prague (1) 2 *(Smicer, Suchoparek)*
Cork City (0) 0 3690

Slavia Prague: Stejskal; Vaura, Suchoparek, Bejbl, Smejkal, Korel, Smicer, Penicka, Kristofik, Berger, Knoflicek (Hogen).
Cork City: Harrington; Daly, Smith, O'Donoghue (Cotter), Napier, Caulfield (Woods), Barry, Hyde, Murphy, Gaynor, Morley.

Preliminary Round, Second Leg

23 AUG

Aberdeen (0) 1 *(Kane)*
Skonto Riga (0) 1 *(Semenov)* 8500

Aberdeen: Snelders; Irvine (Miller), McKimmie, Winnie, Wright, McKinnon, Kane, Hetherston (Shearer), Woodthorpe, Dodds, Booth.
Skonto Riga: Laizan; Troitski, Monyak, Shevlyakov, Mikutsky, Lobanev, Stepanov, Babichev, Blagonadazhdin, Yeliseyev, Semenov.

Cork City (0) 0
Slavia Prague (1) 4 *(Hogen 2, Vaura, Berger)* 3200

Cork City: Harrington; Daly, Smith, O'Donoghue, Napier, Murphy, Barry, Hyde (Cotter), Caulfield, Gaynor, Morley.
Slavia Prague: Stejskal; Vaura, Suchoparek, Bejbl, Smejkal, Kozel, Hogen, Penicka, Kristofik (Vesely), Berger, Knoflicek (Lerch).

Katowice (3) 6 *(Walczak 2, Maziejewski 2 (1 pen), Jojko (pen), Wolny)*
Inter Cardiff (0) 0 4000

Katowice: Jojko; Maciejewski, Borawski, Wegrzyn, Nikodem (Szala), Wolny, Kucz (Szczygiel), Strojek, Walczak, Swierczewski, Sermak.
Inter Cardiff: Wood (Fisher); Knight, Jones V, Batchelor, O'Brien, Lyons, Burrows, Jones D, Hunter, Beattie, Taylor (Jones W).

Havnar Boltfelag (0) 1 *(Hansen)*
Motherwell (1) 4 *(Kirk 2, Davies, Burns)* 750

Havnar Boltfelag: Johannesen K; Jakobsen, Dahl, Hansen, Johannesen N, Dam, Nolsoe, Wang, Jonsson, Mohr, Clementsen.
Motherwell: Woods; Shannon, Philliben, Martin, McLeish, McCart, Burns, Dolan, Kirk, Davies, McGrillen.

Linfield (3) 3 *(Beatty, Gorman, Peebles)*
Hafnafjordur (1) 1 *(Podunavac)* 3201

Linfield: Lamont; Dornan, Easton, Peebles, Spires, Beatty, Knell, Gorman (McCoosh), Anderson, Fenlon, Bailie.
Hafnafjordur: Arnarson S; Podunavic, Halldorsson (Einarsson), Vikingsson, Mrazek, Arnarson H, Helgason, Marteinsson, Magnusson, Jonsson (Ragnarsson), Kristjansson H.

Shamrock R (0) 0
Gornik Zabrze (0) 1 *(Baluszynski)* 5000

Shamrock R: O'Neill; Burke (Giles), O'Duchon, Brazil, Whelan, Toal, McCormack, McGrath, Gannon (Greene), Bacon, Mullen.
Gornik Zabrze: Klytta; Zadylak, Brzoza, Jegor, Waldoch, Agafon, Kubik (Grembocki), Kosela, Orzeszek (Jarosz), Brzeczek, Baluszynski.

Slovan Bratislava (2) 3 *(Faktor, Tittel, Rusnak)*
Portadown (0) 0 6500

Slovan Bratislava: Molnar (Kakas); Seman (Pecko), Tittel, Chvila, Kinder, Faktor, Tomaschek (Demo), Negro, Lancz, Maixnor, Rusnak.
Portadown: Keenan; Major, Strain (Evans), Stewart, Mills (Gray), Cunningham, Shepherd, Casey, Russell, Murray, Frazer.

24 AUG

IA Akranes (2) 2 *(Ingolfsson, Thordarson O)*
Bangor City (0) 0 1200

IA Akranes: Thordarson T; Haraldsson S (Thordarson S), Haraldsson P, Jonsson, Hervarsson, Miljkovic, Hognason, Gislason, Bibercic (Petursson), Thordarson O, Ingolfsson.
Bangor City: Adkins; Jones, Middleton, Evans, Rutter, Humphries (Hughes), Wiggins, Barnett, Mottram, Williams (Barry), Noble.

First Round, First Leg

13 SEPT

Antwerp (0) 0
Newcastle U (3) 5 *(Lee 3, Sellars, Watson)* 19,700

Antwerp: Svilar; Broeckaert, Kulcsar, Emmerechts, Smidts, Porte, Kiekens, Godfroid, Zohar (Monteiro), Severeyns, Vangompel.
Newcastle U: Srnicek; Hottiger, Beresford, Venison, Peacock, Albert, Lee, Beardsley (Watson), Cole (Jeffrey), Fox, Sellars.

Blackburn R (0) 0
Trelleborg (0) 1 *(Sandell)* 13,775

Blackburn R: Flowers; Berg, Le Saux, Slater (Atkins), Hendry, Gale, Ripley, Sherwood (Makel), Shearer, Sutton, Wilcox.
Trelleborg: Jankowski; Brorsson, Andersson, Karlsson C, Mattsson, Hansson, Engqvist, Severin, Blixt (Larsson), Sandell, Karlsson J.

Borussia Dortmund (0) 1 *(Moller)*
Motherwell (0) 0 35,420

Borussia Dortmund: Klos; Schmidt, Julio Cesar, Kree (Povlsen), Reuter, Zorc, Sammer, Reinhardt, Moller, Chapuisat, Riedle (Ricken).
Motherwell: Woods; Shannon, McCart, Philliben, Martin, McKinnon, Lambert, Dolan, Davies (McGrillen), Coyne, Arnott (Kirk).

Linfield (0) 1 *(Anderson)*
Odense (0) 1 *(Schjonberg)* 3585

Linfield: Lamont; Dornan, Easton, Peebles, McConnell, Beatty, Campbell, Knell (Anderson), Haylock, Fenlon, Bailie.
Odense: Hogh; Nedergaard, Hemmingsen M, Hansen, Schjonberg, Hemmingsen C, Melvang, Dethefsen, Bisgaard (Petterson), Tchami (Madson), Thorup.

15 SEPT

Internazionale (0) 1 *(Bergkamp (pen))*
Aston Villa (0) 0 22,639

Internazionale: Pagliuca; Bergomi, Festa, Bia (Paganin), Conte, Bianchi, Berti, Seno, Jonk, Bergkamp, Sosa (Del Vecchio).
Aston Villa: Spink; Barrett, King, Ehiogu, McGrath, Richardson, Townsend, Fashanu (Houghton), Saunders, Atkinson, Staunton.

First Round, Second Leg

27 SEPT

Newcastle U (4) 5 *(Lee, Cole 3, Beardsley (pen))*
Antwerp (0) 2 *(Kiekens, Severeyns)* 29,737

Newcastle U: Srnieck; Hottiger, Beresford, Howey, Peacock, Albert, Lee (Watson), Beardsley (Clark), Cole, Fox, Sellars.
Antwerp: Van der Straeten; Emmerechts (Moukram), Smidts, Taeymans, Godfroid, Kiekens, Porte, Kulcsar, Vangompel (Nilson), Zohar, Severeyns.

Odense (4) 5 *(Nedergaard 2, Schjonberg 2 (1 pen), Thorup)*
Linfield (0) 0 4518

Odense: Hogh; Nedergaard, Hemmingsen M, Hansen, Schjonberg, Hemmingsen C, Melvang, Dethlefsen, Bisgaard (Pederson), Tchami, Thorup (Madsen).
Linfield: Lamont; Dornan, Easton, Peebles, McConnell, Beatty, Campbell, Gorman, Haylock, McCoosh, Bailie.

Trelleborg (0) 2 *(Karlsson 2)*
Blackburn R (1) 2 *(Sutton, Shearer)* 6730

Trelleborg: Jankowski; Mattasson, Karlsson C, Brorsson M, Andersson M, Severin, Palmer (Eriksson), Engqvist, Karlsson J, Hansson, Sandell.
Blackburn R: Flowers; Berg, Le Saux, Sherwood, Hendry, Gale (Pearce), Ripley, Atkins (Warhurst), Shearer, Sutton, Wilcox.

28 SEPT

Motherwell (0) 0
Borussia Dortmund (0) 2 *(Riedle 2)* 9362

Motherwell: Woods; Shannon, McKinnon, Philliben, Martin, McCart, Lambert (Kirk), Dolan, Coyne, Arnott, Davies (Burns).
Borussia Dortmund: Klos; Reinhardt (Tanko), Julio Cesar, Sammer, Schmidt, Reuter, Freund, Moller, Zorc, Chapuisat, Riedle (Ricken).

29 SEPT

Aston Villa (1) 1 *(Houghton)*
Internazionale (0) 0 30,533

Aston Villa: Spink; Barrett, King, Ehiogu, McGrath, Richardson (Parker), Houghton, Townsend, Saunders (Whittingham), Atkinson, Staunton.
Internazionale: Pagliuca; Bergomi, Festa, Paganin, Bia, Conte (Orlandini), Berti, Bergkamp, Seno, Pancev (Fontolan), Sosa.

Second Round, First Leg

18 OCT

Newcastle U (2) 3 *(Fox, Beardsley (pen), Cole)*
Athletic Bilbao (0) 2 *(Ziganda, Suances)* 32,140

Newcastle U: Srnicek; Hottiger, Beresford, Howey, Peacock, Albert, Clark, Beardsley, Cole, Fox, Sellars.
Athletic Bilbao: Valencia; Trabuenca (Suances), Adrinua, Karanka, Larrazabal, Estibariz (Konno), Vales, Alkiza, Garitano, Mendiguren, Ziganda.

Trabzonspor (0) 1 *(Orhan)*
Aston Villa (0) 0 27,500

Trabzonspor: Grishko; Ogon, Lemi, Kernal, Chengiz, Abdullah, Soner, Tolunay, Unal, Hami (Hamdi), Orhan (Katcharava).
Aston Villa: Spink; Barrett, King, Ehiogu, McGrath, Richardson, Houghton, Townsend, Saunders, Whittingham, Staunton.

Second Round, Second Leg

1 NOV

Aston Villa (0) 2 *(Atkinson, Ehiogu)*
Trabzonspor (0) 1 *(Orhan)* 23,858

Aston Villa: Spink; Barrett, King, Ehiogu, McGrath, Richardson (Parker), Houghton, Townsend, Saunders, Atkinson, Staunton.
Trabzonspor: Grisco; Ogun, Cengiz, Kemal, Hamdi, Soner, Tolunay, Unal, Abdullah, Hami (Katcharava), Orhan (Osman).

Athletic Bilbao (0) 1 *(Ziganda)*
Newcastle U (0) 0 47,000

Athletic Bilbao: Valencia; Tabuenka, Andrinua, Karanka, Larrazabal, Larrainzar (Urrutia), Garitano, Mendiguren (Kortina), Alkiza, Suances, Ziganda.
Newcastle U: Srnicek; Hottiger, Beresford, Howey, Peacock, Albert, Watson, Beardsley, Lee, Fox (Jeffrey), Sellars (Clark).

EUROPEAN CUP DRAWS 1995–96

EUROPEAN CUP

Preliminary Round

Grasshoppers Zurich v Maccabi Tel Aviv, Rangers v Famagusta (Cyprus), Legia Warsaw v IFK Gothenburg, Salzburg (Austria) v Steaua Bucharest, Dynamo Kiev (Ukraine) v Aalborg (Denmark), Rosenborg (Norway) v Besiktas (Turkey), Anderlecht v Ferencvaros (Hungary), Panathinaikos (Greece) v Hajduk Split (Croatia).

EUROPEAN CUP-WINNERS' CUP

Preliminary Round

Tiligul Tiraspol (Moldova) v Sion (Switzerland), VAC Samsung (Hungary) v FC Sileks (Macedonia), Turku (Finland) v FC Teuta (Albania), FC Vaduz (Liechtenstein) v Hradec Kralove (Czech Republic), Hapoel Nicosia (Cyprus) v Nefski Baku (Azerbaijan), Wrexham v Petrolul Ploesti (Romania), Valletta (Malta) v Inter Bratislava (Slovakia), Shakytyor (Ukraine) v Linfield, Zalgiris Vilnius (Lithuania) v NK Mura (Slovenia), Katowice (Poland) v Ararat Erevan (Armenia), FC Obilic (Yugoslavia) v Dinamo Batumi (Georgia), Lokomotiv Sofia (Bulgaria) v Derry City, Maccabi Haifa (Israel) v Klakksvikar (Faeroes), Dinamo-93 Minsk (Belarus) v Molde FK (Norway), Grevenmacher (Luxembourg) v Reykjavik (Iceland), Dag-Liepaja (Latvia) v FC Lantana (Estonia).

UEFA CUP

Preliminary Round

Orebro SK (Sweden) v Beggen (Luxembourg), Tampere (Finland) v Viking FK (Norway), Bangor City (Wales) v Widzew Lodz (Poland), Shelbourne v Akranes (Iceland), Glenavon v FC Hafnarfjordur (Iceland), Brondby (Denmark) v Inkaras-Grifas (Lithuania), Lillestroem (Norway) v Flora Tallinn (Estonia), Motherwell v MyPa-47 (Finland), Skonto Riga (Latvia) v Maribor Branik (Slovenia), Sturm Graz (Austria) v Slavia Prague (Czech Republic), Jeunesse d'Esch (Luxembourg) v FC Lugano (Switzerland), Slovan Bratislava (Slovakia) v NK Osijek (Croatia), Dundalk v Malmo (Sweden), Crusaders v Silkeborg (Denmark), Afan Lido v RAF Riga (Latvia), Raith Rovers v Gotu Itrottarfelag (Faeroes), Slavia Sofia (Bulgaria) v Olympiakos (Greece), Zimbru Chisinau (Moldova) v Hapoel Tel Aviv (Israel), Sparta Prague (Czech Republic) v Galatasaray (Turkey), Omonia Nicosia (Cyprus) v Sliema Wanderers (Malta), FC Kosice (Slovakia) v Ujpest Egylet (Hungary), Universitatea Craiova (Romania) v Dinamo Minsk (Belarus), Fenerbahce (Turkey) v FC Partizan (Albania), FC Varda (Macedonia) v FC Samtredia (Georgia), Botev Plovdiv (Bulgaria) v Dinamo Tbilisi (Georgia), Apollon Athens (Greece) v Olimpija Ljublijana (Slovenia), Red Star Belgrade (Yugoslavia) v Neuchatel Xamax (Switzerland), Hibernians FC (Malta) v Chernomorets (Ukraine), Kapaz Ganja (Azerbaijan) v FK Austria Memphis, FC Tirana (Albania) v Hapoel Beer Sheva (Israel), Levski Sofia (Bulgaria) v Dinamo Bucharest (Romania), Zaglebie Lubin (Poland) v Shirak Erevan (Armenia).

Summary of Appearances

EUROPEAN CUP (1955–95)

English clubs
12 Liverpool
7 Manchester U
3 Nottingham F, Leeds U
2 Derby Co, Wolverhampton W, Everton, Aston Villa, Arsenal
1 Burnley, Tottenham H, Ipswich T, Manchester C

Scottish clubs
16 Rangers
15 Celtic
3 Aberdeen
2 Hearts
1 Dundee, Dundee U, Kilmarnock, Hibernian

Welsh clubs
1 Cwmbran

Clubs for Northern Ireland
18 Linfield
8 Glentoran
2 Crusaders, Portadown
1 Glenavon, Ards, Distillery, Derry C, Coleraine

Clubs for Eire
7 Shamrock R, Dundalk
6 Waterford
3 Drumcondra
2 Bohemians, Limerick, Athlone T, Shelbourne
1 Cork Hibs, Cork Celtic, Cork City, Derry C*, Sligo Rovers, St Patrick's Ath

Winners: Celtic 1966–67; Manchester U 1967–68; Liverpool 1976–77, 1977–78, 1980–81, 1983–84; Nottingham F 1978–79, 1979–80; Aston Villa 1981–82

Finalists: Celtic 1969–70; Leeds U 1974–75; Liverpool 1984–85

EUROPEAN CUP-WINNERS' CUP (1960–95)

English clubs
6 Tottenham H
5 Manchester U
4 West Ham U, Liverpool
3 Arsenal, Chelsea
2 Everton, Manchester C
1 Wolverhampton W, Leicester C, WBA, Leeds U, Sunderland, Southampton, Ipswich T

Scottish clubs
10 Rangers
8 Aberdeen
7 Celtic
3 Dundee U
2 Dunfermline Ath
1 Dundee, Hibernian, Hearts, St Mirren, Motherwell, Airdrie

Welsh clubs
14 Cardiff C
7 Wrexham, Swansea C
2 Bangor C
1 Borough U, Newport Co, Merthyr Tydfil, Barry T

Clubs from Northern Ireland
7 Glentoran
4 Ballymena U, Coleraine, Glenavon
3 Crusaders
2 Ards, Bangor, Linfield
1 Derry C, Distillery, Portadown, Carrick Rangers, Cliftonville

Clubs from Eire
6 Shamrock R
3 Limerick, Waterford, Dundalk, Bohemians
2 Cork Hibs, Galway U, Shelbourne, Sligo Rovers
1 Cork Celtic, St Patrick's Ath, Finn Harps, Home Farm, University College Dublin, Derry C*, Cork City, Bray Wanderers

Winners: Tottenham H 1962–63; West Ham U 1964–65; Manchester C 1969–70; Chelsea 1970–71; Rangers 1971–72; Aberdeen 1982–83; Everton 1984–85; Manchester U 1990-91; Arsenal 1993–94

Finalists: Rangers 1960–61, 1966–67; Liverpool 1965–66; Leeds U 1972–73; West Ham U 1975–76; Arsenal 1979–80, 1994–95

EUROPEAN FAIRS CUP & UEFA CUP (1955–95)

English clubs
8 Leeds U, Ipswich T
7 Liverpool
6 Everton, Arsenal, Manchester U, Aston Villa
5 Southampton, Tottenham H, Newcastle U
4 Manchester C, Birmingham C, Nottingham F, Wolverhampton W, WBA
3 Chelsea, Sheffield W
2 Stoke C, Derby Co, QPR
1 Burnley, Coventry C, Norwich C, London Rep XI, Watford, Blackburn R

Scottish clubs
17 Dundee U
14 Hibernian
11 Aberdeen
9 Celtic, Hearts
8 Rangers
5 Dunfermline Ath
4 Dundee
3 St Mirren, Kilmarnock
2 Partick Th
1 Morton, St Johnstone, Motherwell

Welsh Clubs
1 Inter Cardiff, Bangor C

Clubs from Northern Ireland
11 Glentoran
6 Coleraine
5 Linfield
3 Glenavon, Portadown
1 Ards, Ballymena U, Bangor, Crusaders

Clubs from Eire
8 Bohemians
4 Dundalk, Shamrock R
3 Finn Harps
2 Shelbourne, Drumcondra, St Patrick's Ath, Derry C*, Cork City
1 Cork Hibs, Athlone T, Limerick, Drogheda U, Galway U

Winners: Leeds U 1967–68, 1970–71; Newcastle U 1968–69; Arsenal 1969–70; Tottenham H 1971–72, 1983–84; Liverpool 1972–73, 1975–76; Ipswich T 1980–81

Finalists: London 1955–58, Birmingham C 1958–60, 1960–61; Leeds U 1966–67; Wolverhampton W 1971–72; Tottenham H 1973–74; Dundee U 1986–87

* *Now play in League of Ireland.*

WORLD CLUB CHAMPIONSHIP

Played annually up to 1974 and intermittently since then between the winners of the European Cup and the winners of the South American Champions Cup — known as the Copa Libertadores. In 1980 the winners were decided by one match arranged in Tokyo in February 1981 and the venue has been the same since. AC Milan replaced Marseille who had been stripped of their European Cup title in 1993.

1960 Real Madrid beat Penarol 0-0, 5-1
1961 Penarol beat Benfica 0-1, 5-0, 2-1
1962 Santos beat Benfica 3-2, 5-2
1963 Santos beat AC Milan 2-4, 4-2, 1-0
1964 Inter-Milan beat Independiente 0-1, 2-0, 1-0
1965 Inter-Milan beat Independiente 3-0, 0-0
1966 Penarol beat Real Madrid 2-0, 2-0
1967 Racing Club beat Celtic 0-1, 2-1, 1-0
1968 Estudiantes beat Manchester United 1-0, 1-1
1969 AC Milan beat Estudiantes 3-0, 1-2
1970 Feyenoord beat Estudiantes 2-2, 1-0
1971 Nacional beat Panathinaikos* 1-1, 2-1
1972 Ajax beat Independiente 1-1, 3-0
1973 Independiente beat Juventus* 1-0
1974 Atlético Madrid* beat Independiente 0-1, 2-0
1975 Independiente and Bayern Munich could not agree dates; no matches.
1976 Bayern Munich beat Cruzeiro 2-0, 0-0
1977 Boca Juniors beat Borussia Moenchengladbach* 2-2, 3-0
1978 Not contested
1979 Olimpia beat Malmö* 1-0, 2-1
1980 Nacional beat Nottingham Forest 1-0
1981 Flamengo beat Liverpool 3-0
1982 Penarol beat Aston Villa 2-0
1983 Gremio Porto Alegre beat SV Hamburg 2-1
1984 Independiente beat Liverpool 1-0
1985 Juventus beat Argentinos Juniors 4-2 on penalties after a 2-2 draw
1986 River Plate beat Steaua Bucharest 1-0
1987 FC Porto beat Penarol 2-1 after extra time
1988 Nacional (Uru) beat PSV Eindhoven 7-6 on penalties after 1-1 draw
1989 AC Milan beat Atletico Nacional (Col) 1-0 after extra time
1990 AC Milan beat Olimpia 3-0
1991 Red Star Belgrade beat Colo Colo 3-0
1992 Sao Paulo beat Barcelona 2-1
1993 Sao Paulo beat AC Milan 3-2

*European Cup runners-up; winners declined to take part.

1994

1 December in Tokyo

Velez Sarsfield (0) 2 *(Trotta 50 (pen), Asad 57)*

AC Milan (0) 0 55,860

Velez Sarsfield: Chilavert; Trotta, Cardozo, Almandoz, Gomez, Sotomayor, Bassedas, Basualdo, Asad, Pompei, Flores.

AC Milan: Rossi; Tassotti, Maldini, Albertini, Costacurta, Baresi, Bonadoni, Desailly, Boban, Savicevic (Simone 60), Massaro (Panucci 86).
Referee: Torres (Colombia).

EUROPEAN SUPER CUP

Played annually between the winners of the European Champions' Cup and the European Cup-Winners' Cup. AC Milan replaced Marseille in 1993–94.

Previous Matches

1972 Ajax beat Rangers 3-1, 3-2
1973 Ajax beat AC Milan 0-1, 6-0
1974 Not contested
1975 Dynamo Kiev beat Bayern Munich 1-0, 2-0
1976 Anderlecht beat Bayern Munich 4-1, 1-2
1977 Liverpool beat Hamburg 1-1, 6-0
1978 Anderlecht beat Liverpool 3-1, 1-2
1979 Nottingham F beat Barcelona 1-0, 1-1
1980 Valencia beat Nottingham F 1-0, 1-2
1981 Not contested
1982 Aston Villa beat Barcelona 0-1, 3-0
1983 Aberdeen beat Hamburg 0-0, 2-0
1984 Juventus beat Liverpool 2-0
1985 Juventus v Everton not contested due to UEFA ban on English clubs
1986 Steaua Bucharest beat Dynamo Kiev 1-0
1987 FC Porto beat Ajax 1-0, 1-0
1988 KV Mechelen beat PSV Eindhoven 3-0, 0-1
1989 AC Milan beat Barcelona 1-1, 1-0
1990 AC Milan beat Sampdoria 1-1, 2-0
1991 Manchester U beat Red Star Belgrade 1-0
1992 Barcelona beat Werder Bremen 1-1, 2-1
1993 Parma beat AC Milan 0-1, 2-0

1994-95

First Leg, 1 February 1995, Highbury

Arsenal (0) 0

AC Milan (0) 0 38,044

Arsenal: Seaman; Dixon, Winterburn, Schwarz, Bould, Adams, Jensen, (Hillier 85), Wright, Hartson, Selley, Campbell (Merson 74).
AC Milan: Rossi; Tassotti, Maldini, Albertini, Costacurta, Baresi, Donadoni, Desailly, Simone, Savicevic (Dir Canio 89), Massaro.
Referee: Van der Ende (Holland).

Second Leg, 8 February 1995, Milan

AC Milan (1) 2 *(Boban 41, Massaro 67)*

Arsenal (0) 0 23,953

AC Milan: Rossi; Tassotti, Albertini, Costacurta, Baresi, Donadoni, Desailly, Savicevic (Eranio 89), Boban, Massaro (Di Canio 80).
Arsenal: Seaman; Dixon (Keown 66), Winterburn, Schwarz, Bould, Adams, Campbell (Parlour 76), Wright, Hartson, Merson, Selley.
Referee: Krug (Germany).

SOUTH AMERICA

COPA LIBERTADORES 1994
(*Results continued from last edition*)

Quarter-Finals, First Leg
Olimpia 1, Bolivar 0
Indep. Medellin 0, Junior 2
Minerven 0, Velez Sarsfield 0
Union Espanola 1, Sao Paulo 1

Quarter-Finals, Second Leg
Bolivar 0, Olimpia 2
Junior 0, Indep. Medellin 0
Velez Sarsfield 2, Minerven 0
Sao Paulo 4, Union Espanola 3

Semi-Finals, First Leg
Junior 2, Velez Sarsfield 1
Sao Paulo 2, Olimpia 1

Semi-Finals, Second Leg
Velez Sarsfield 2, Junior 1
(*aggregate 3-3; Velez Sarsfield won 5-4 on penalties*)
Olimpia 1, Sao Paulo 0
(*aggregate 2-2; Sao Paulo won 4-3 on penalties*)

Final First Leg
Velez Sarsfield 1, Sao Paulo 0

Final Second Leg
Sao Paulo 1, Velez Sarsfield 0
(*aggregate 1-1; Velez Sarsfield won 5-3 on penalties*)

SOUTH AMERICAN SUPER CUP

First Round, First Leg
Flamengo 0, Estudiantes 0
River Plate 2, Nacional (U) 2
Santos 1, Independiente 0
Olimpia 2, Cruzeiro 0
Penarol 1, Boca Juniors 0
Gremio 1, Racing Club 1
Colo Colo 4, Argentinos Juniors 1
At. Nacional 0, Sao Paulo 2

First Round, Second Leg
Cruzeiro 4, Olimpia 0
Nacional (U) 0, River Plate 1
Independiente 4, Santos 0
Estudiantes 2, Flamengo 0
Sao Paulo 1, At. Nacional 1
Argentinos Juniors 1, Colo Colo 1
Boca Juniors 4, Penarol 1
Racing Club 1, Gremio 2

Quarter Finals, First Leg
Colo Colo 2, Sao Paulo 1
Estudiantes 1, Cruzeiro 0
Gremio 1, Independiente 1
River Plate 0, Boca Juniors 0

Quarter Finals, Second Leg
Independiente 2, Gremio 0
Cruzeiro 3, Estudiantes 0
Sao Paulo 4, Colo Colo 1
Boca Juniors 1, River Plate 1
(*aggregate 1-1; Boca Juniors won 5-4 on penalties*)

Semi-finals, First Leg
Boca Juniors 2, Sao Paulo 0
Cruzeiro 1, Independiente 0

Semi-Finals, Second Leg
Independiente 4, Cruzeiro 0
Sao Paulo 1, Boca Juniors 0

Final First Leg
Boca Juniors 1, Independiente 1

Final Second Leg
Independiente 1, Boca Juniors 0

COPA LIBERTADORES 1995

First Round

Group 1

	P	*W*	*D*	*L*	*F*	*A*	*Pts*
River Plate	6	3	3	0	11	3	12
Penarol	6	2	3	1	9	7	9
Independiente	6	2	1	3	5	7	7
Cerro	6	1	1	4	5	13	4

Group 2

	P	*W*	*D*	*L*	*F*	*A*	*Pts*
Cerro Porteno	6	4	2	0	16	6	14
Olimpia	6	3	3	0	16	7	12
Caracas	6	2	0	4	8	18	6
Trujillanos	6	0	1	5	8	17	1

Group 3

	P	*W*	*D*	*L*	*F*	*A*	*Pts*
Millonarios	6	3	1	2	11	8	10
At. Nacional	6	2	3	1	5	4	9
Univ de Chile	6	2	1	3	7	7	7
Univ Catolica	6	2	1	3	10	14	7

(*Play-off: Univ Catolica 4, Univ de Chile 1*)

Group 4

	P	*W*	*D*	*L*	*F*	*A*	*Pts*
Palmeiras	6	4	1	1	15	5	13
Gremio	6	3	2	1	12	7	11
Emelec	6	1	2	3	8	12	5
Nacional	6	1	1	4	3	14	4

Group 5

	P	*W*	*D*	*L*	*F*	*A*	*Pts*
Sporting Cristal	6	3	3	0	15	4	12
Bolivar	6	2	3	1	8	5	9
Alianza	6	1	2	3	10	11	5
Wilsterman	6	1	2	3	6	19	5

Second Round, First Leg
Olimpia 0, Gremio 3
Emelec 2, Cerro Porteno 0
Alianza 1, Millonarios 1
Bolivar 1, Palmeiras 0
Caracas 2, Sporting Cristal 2
At. Nacional 3, Penarol 1
Velez Sarsfield 3, Independiente 0
Univ Catolica 2, River Plate 1

Second Round, Second Leg
River Plate 3, Univ Catolica 1
Cerro Porteno 2, Emelec 0
(*aggregate 2-2; Emelec won 5-4 on penalties*)
Millonarios 2, Alianza 0
Palmeiros 3, Bolivar 0
Penarol 1, At. Nacional 3
Gremio 2, Olimpia 0
Velez Sarsfield 2, Independiente 2
Sporting Cristal 6, Caracas 3
Tournament still being completed

COPA AMERICA 1995

Uruguay won the Copa America for the South American Championship, the oldest international competition still being played in the world. Their record of never having lost a tournament played on their own territory held good, though they needed an immaculate series of penalties after the normal 90 minutes, to defeat World Cup holders Brazil.

Group A
Uruguay 4, Venezuela 1
Mexico 1, Paraguay 2
Uruguay 1, Paraguay 0
Mexico 3, Venezuela 1
Paraguay 3, Venezuela 2
Uruguay 1, Mexico 1

Group B
Colombia 1, Peru 1
Brazil 1, Ecuador 0
Colombia 1, Ecuador 0
Peru 0, Brazil 2
Peru 1, Ecuador 2
Brazil 3, Colombia 0

Group C
USA 2, Chile 1
Argentina 2, Bolivia 1
USA 0, Bolivia 1
Chile 0, Argentina 4
Bolivia 2, Chile 2
Argentina 0, USA 3

Quarter-finals
Paraguay 1, Colombia 1
Colombia won 5-4 on penalties.
Uruguay 2, Bolivia 1
USA 0, Mexico 0
USA won 4-1 on penalties.
Brazil 2, Argentina 2
Brazil won 4-2 on penalties.

Semi-finals
Uruguay 2, Colombia 0
USA 0, Brazil 1

Third place
Colombia 4, USA 1

Uruguay (0) 1 *(Bengoechea)*
Brazil (1) 1 *(Tulio) in Montevideo* 70,000
Uruguay: Alvez; Mendez, Moas, Herrera, Silva (Adinolfi), Dorta (Bengoechea), Gutierrez, Poyet, Francescoli, Otero, Fonseca (Martinez).
Brazil: Taffarel; Jorghino, Aldair, Cruz, Roberto Carlos, Sempao, Dunga, Juninho (Beto), Zinho, Edmundo, Tulio.
Referee: Brizio (Mexico).
Uruguay won 5-3 on penalties.

Conmebol Cup
Final first leg
Sao Paulo 6, Penarol 1

Final second leg
Penarol 3, Sao Paulo 0

Masters Cup (for super Cup Winners)
Final first leg
Olimpia 0, Cruzeiro 0

Final second leg
Cruzeiro 1, Olimpia 0

PANAMERICAN GAMES
Final
Argentina 0, Mexico 0
(*Argentina won 5-4 on penalties*)

American Airlines Cup 1994
Final
Cartagines (Costa Rica) 3, Atlante (Mexico) 2

AFRICA

East and Central African Cup
Final
Tanzania 2, Uganda 2
(*Tanzania won 4-3 on penalties*)

East and Central African Club Championship
Final
SC Simba 1, Express 1
(*Simba won 4-2 on penalties*)

Four Nations Cup

	P	*W*	*D*	*L*	*F*	*A*	*Pts*
Ivory Coast	3	1	2	0	3	2	5
South Africa	3	1	2	0	3	2	5
Ghana	3	1	1	1	3	3	4
Cameroon	3	0	1	2	2	4	1

ASIA

Gulf Cup

	P	*W*	*D*	*L*	*F*	*A*	*Pts*
Saudi Arabia	5	4	1	0	10	4	9
UAE	5	3	2	0	7	1	8
Bahrain	5	1	3	1	5	6	5
Qatar	5	1	1	3	6	8	3
Kuwait	5	1	1	3	2	6	3
Oman	5	0	2	3	4	9	2

ASIAN GAMES
Final
Uzbekistan 4, China 2

South Asian Gold Cup
Final
Sri Lanka 1, India 0
(*sudden-death extra time*)

Dynasty Cup
Final
Japan 2, South Korea 2
(*Japan won 5-3 on penalties*)

VAUXHALL CONFERENCE 1994-95

VAUXHALL CONFERENCE TABLE 1994–95

		Home			Goals			Away		Goals		
	P	W	D	L	F	A	W	D	L	F	A	Pts
Macclesfield Town	42	14	3	4	39	18	10	5	6	31	22	80
Woking	42	11	8	2	46	23	10	4	7	30	31	75
Southport	42	13	4	4	46	21	8	5	8	22	29	72
Altrincham	42	10	3	8	34	27	10	5	6	43	33	68
Stevenage Borough	42	10	4	7	40	27	10	3	8	28	22	67
Kettering Town	42	12	5	4	40	25	7	5	9	33	31	67
Gateshead	42	12	4	5	28	13	7	6	8	33	40	67
Halifax Town	42	11	6	4	46	20	6	6	9	22	34	63
Runcorn	42	11	7	3	39	28	5	3	13	20	43	58
Northwich Victoria	42	7	8	6	39	30	7	7	7	38	36	57
Kidderminster Harriers	46	6	5	10	28	29	10	4	7	35	32	57
Bath City	42	10	6	5	35	26	5	6	10	20	30	57
Bromsgrove Rovers	42	9	7	5	42	35	5	6	10	24	34	55
Farnborough Town	42	8	5	8	23	31	7	5	9	22	33	55
Dagenham & Redbridge	42	8	5	8	28	32	5	8	8	28	37	52
Dover Athletic	42	6	10	5	28	25	5	6	10	20	30	49
Welling United	42	9	3	9	31	33	4	7	10	26	41	49
Stalybridge Celtic	42	9	6	6	29	27	2	8	11	23	45	47
Telford United	42	9	9	3	30	20	1	7	13	23	42	46
Merthyr Tydfil	42	10	4	7	37	27	1	7	13	16	36	44
Stafford Rangers	42	5	5	11	29	34	4	6	11	24	45	38
Yeovil Town	42	5	8	8	29	31	3	6	12	21	40	37

Note: Yeovil Town deducted 1 point

ATTENDANCES BY CLUB 1994–95

	Aggregate Attendance 1994–95	Average Attendance 1994–95	Average Attendance 1993–94	% Change
Altrincham	21,050	1002	751	+33
Bath City	13,579	647	683	–5
Bromsgrove Rovers	23,738	1130	1139	0
Dagenham & Redbridge	19,935	949	952	0
Dover Athletic	23,119	1101	1347	–18
Farnborough Town	16,766	798	513	+55
Gateshead	14,548	693	477	+45
Halifax Town	20,455	974	1035	–6
Kettering Town	38,584	1837	2025	–9
Kidderminster Harriers	41,129	1959	2250	–13
Macclesfield Town	26,458	1260	853	+48
Merthyr Tydfil	12,621	601	581	+3
Northwich Victoria	19,821	944	933	+1
Runcorn	9,818	468	594	–21
Southport	22,649	1079	1293	–17
Stafford Rangers	14,953	712	949	–25
Stalybridge Celtic	14,916	710	615	+15
Stevenage Borough	29,909	1424	1064	+34
Telford United	17,029	811	929	–13
Welling United	15,525	739	967	–24
Woking	38,122	1815	1712	+6
Yeovil Town	36,659	1746	2495	–30

HIGHEST ATTENDANCES 1994–95

4347	Kidderminster Harriers v Bromsgrove Rovers	26.12.94
3267	Bromsgrove Rovers v Kidderminster Harriers	2.1.95
3049	Kettering Town v Kidderminster Harriers	23.8.94
2734	Gateshead v Yeovil Town	3.9.94
2650	Kettering Town v Runcorn	5.11.94
2532	Kettering Town v Stevenage Borough	26.12.94
2406	Woking v Dagenham & Redbridge	26.12.94
2386	Macclesfield Town v Altrincham	25.2.95
2368	Woking v Kidderminster Harriers	5.11.94
2351	Yeovil Town v Bath City	6.9.94
2340	Kettering Town v Woking	19.11.94
2325	Woking v Macclesfield Town	25.4.95

VAUXHALL CONFERENCE LEADING GOALSCORERS 1994–95

Conf.			FAC	BLT	FAT
25	Paul Dobson *(Gateshead)*	+	2	2	3
23	Carl Alford *(Kettering Town)*	+	1	3	—
21	Leroy May *(Stafford Rangers)*	+	—	1	—
19	Andy Green *(Altrincham)*	+	2	—	—
	Clive Walker *(Woking)*	+	1	—	5
18	Recky Carter *(Bromsgrove Rovers)*	+	—	12	—
	David Leworthy *(Dover Athletic)*	+	5	2	—
	Phil Power *(Macclesfield Town)*	+	—	2	3
	Malcolm O'Connor *(Northwich Victoria)*	+	4	—	1
17	Darran Hay *(Woking)*	+	—	—	—
16	Dean Birkby *(Bath City)*	+	—	2	—
	Mark Hughes *(Runcorn)*	+	—	1	2
15	Paul Wilson *(Yeovil Town)*	+	—	—	—

CLUB REVIEW

	VC	FAT	BLT	FAC
Altrincham	4	QF	QF	3
1993–94	10	1	1	4q
Bath City	12	2	2	1
	12	2	2	3
Bromsgrove Rovers	13	1	W	4q
	18	3	SF	3
Dagenham & Red.	15	1	SF	2q
	6	2	QF	4q
Dover Athletic	16	1	QF	4q
	8	3	2	1q
Farnborough Town	14	2	2	4q
	21	2	2	1
Gateshead	7	3	1	2q
	11	QF	3	3q
Halifax Town	8	1	1	2
	13	3	QF	2
Kettering Town	6	2	F	1
	2	2	1	1
Kidderminster H.	11	F	2	1
	1	1	QF	5
Macclesfield Town	1	QF	SF	4q
	7	3	W	2
Merthyr Tydfil	20	3	1	2q
	20	3	1	4q
Northwich Victoria	10	1	2	1
	15	1	SF	1q
Runcorn	9	3	2	1
	5	F	2	1
Southport	3	1	2	1
	4	3	1	4q
Stafford Rangers	21	1	2	4q
	9	2	2	4q
Stalybridge Celtic	18	1	QF	4q
	14	1	2	2
Stevenage Borough	5	3	1	2q
	22	1	1	1
Telford United	19	2	1	4q
	17	2	1	1
Welling United	17	2	1	2q
	16	2	QF	1q
Woking	2	W	QF	2
	3	W	2	2
Yeovil Town	22	2	2	4q
	19	1	F	2

HIGHEST SCORERS

4 David Leworthy *DOVER ATHLETIC* v Molesey (FA Cup 24.9.94)
4 Terry Robbins *WELLING UNITED* v Marlow (FA Trophy 30.1.95)

HIGHEST AGGREGATE SCORES

Bromsgrove Rovers 5–5 Woking 14.1.95
Dagenham & Redbridge 5–3 Woking 26.12.94
Farnborough Town 5–3 Telford United 1.4.95
Yeovil Town 4–4 Northwich Victoria 6.5.95
Bath City 3–5 Kidderminster Harriers 24.9.94

LARGEST HOME WINS

Halifax Town 6–0 Stafford Rangers 5.11.94
Bromsgrove Rovers 5–0 Yeovil Town 27.9.94
Northwich Victoria 5–0 Dagenham & Redbridge 3.9.94
Southport 5–0 Gateshead 23.8.94
Southport 5–0 Runcorn 26.12.94
Stevenage Borough 5–0 Yeovil Town 17.12.94

LARGEST AWAY WINS

Welling United 1–5 Northwich Victoria 19.11.94
Welling United 1–5 Bath City 28.1.95
Dagenham & Redbridge 0–4 Altrincham 4.2.95
Dagenham & Redbridge 0–4 Macclesfield Town 19.11.94
Telford United 0–4 Dagenham & Redbridge 18.2.95
Farnborough Town 0–4 Runcorn 24.9.94

MATCHES WITHOUT DEFEAT

13 Macclesfield Town
11 Woking
10 Southport
9 Northwich Victoria, Southport

MATCHES WITHOUT SUCCESS

11 Dover Athletic
10 Telford United
9 Bath City, Stafford Rangers, Stalybridge Celtic, Yeovil Town (twice)
8 Northwich Victoria, Stafford Rangers, Stalybridge Celtic, Stevenage Borough

CONSECUTIVE CONFERENCE VICTORIES

10 Macclesfield Town (Conference Record)
5 Woking
4 Altrincham, Farnborough Town, Halifax Town, Northwich Victoria, Southport, Stevenage Borough

CONSECUTIVE CONFERENCE DEFEATS

6 Stafford Rangers, Yeovil Town
5 Bath City, Farnborough Town, Stalybridge Celtic
4 Kidderminster Harriers, Merthyr Tydfil, Northwich Victoria, Stafford Rangers, Welling United, Yeovil Town

VAUXHALL CONFERENCE 1994–95

APPEARANCES AND GOALSCORERS

Altrincham
Vauxhall Appearances: Bolland, P. 0(1); Butler, B. 25(7); Carmody, M. 36; Cockram, D. 2(4); Collings, P. 42; Constable, S. 5(14); Cox, P. 0(2); Cross, S. 42; France, P. 41; Green, A. 35(1); Harris, R. 16; Hatton, B. 0(3); Heesom, D. 41; Martindale, D. 2; Morton, N. 27(1); O'Neill, S. 18(7); Ramoon, L. 0(2); Reid, A. 34(1); Sharratt, C. 39; Shaw, N. 10(5); Terry, S. 34; Whalley, N. 8
Goals (77): Green 19, Terry 12, Morton 10, Sharratt 6, France 6, Harris 5, O'Neill 4, Constable 3, Reid 3, Shaw 3, Cross 2, Butler 1, Cockram 1, Heesom 1, Ramoon 1.

Bath City
Vauxhall Appearances: Adcock, P. 26; Adekola, D. 7; Baldwin, D. 5; Birkby, D. 37; Birks, S. 22; Brooks, N. 25; Chenoweth, P. 34; Clements, S. 1; Cousins, R. 36; Crocker, M. 3; Crowley, R. 14; Dicks, G. 27; Forbes, D. 16; Gill, J. 40; Hedges, I. 32; Hervin, M. 4; Hewlett, M. 3; Jackson, D. 8; James, L. 3; Jones, V. 7; Loss, C. 5; Lucas, J. 4; McLoughlin, P. 14; Mings, A. 22; Mogg, D. 38; Ricketts, A. 12; Smart, G. 30; Spencer, M. 7; Taylor, C. 13; Tilley, D. 3; Vernon, D. 18; Walsh, A. 8.
Goals (55): Birkby 16, Adcock 10, Smart 7, Brooks 4, Chenoweth 3, Mings 3, Adekola 2, Crocker 2, McLoughlin 2, Birks 1, Cousins 1, Crowley 1, Dicks 1, Vernon 1, og 1.

Bromsgrove Rovers
Vauxhall Appearances: Bayliss, S. 0(1); Booth, S. 0(2); Boston, K. 1(3); Brain, S. 1(1); Brighton, S. 1(3); Burgher, S. 11; Carter, R. 33; Clarke, N. 34; Crane, S. 0(2); Daly, T. 0(2); Devery, B. 17(5); Gaunt, C. 41; Glasser, N. 17(3); Gray, A. (1); Gray, B. 18(8); Gray, M. 12(3); Grealish, T. 3(1); Green, R. 21(20); Greenman, C. 2(1); Humphrey, P. 4(3); Judge, A. 21(9); Marlowe, A. 10(4); Morley, T. 0(1); Pearce, C. 7(4); Power, A. 29(4); Radburn, C. 1; Richardson, K. 27; Shilvock, R. 12(17); Skelding, J. 38; Smith, A. 16(7); Stott, S. 39; Taylor, C. 0(2); Taylor, S. 30(1); Walker, R. 0(3); Warner, A. 4(1); Whitehead, S. 0(3); Young, L. 2(3).
Goals (66): Carter 18, Stott 9, Taylor 9, Skelding 6, Gray B 5, Pearce 4, Devery 2, Gaunt 2, Gray M 2, Brain 1, Brighton 1, Clarke 1, Marlow 1, Power 1, Shilvock 1, Smith 1, Warner 1, Young 1.

Dagenham & Redbridge
Vauxhall Appearances: Bennett, G. 8; Bolder, B. 29(3); Boyle, G. 2; Broom, J. 31; Cavell, P. 14(3); Conner, S. 26(1); Cook, J. 19; Cooper, W. 0(5); Culverhouse, D. 23(7); Devereux, J. 6(7); Dunphy, N. 6; Emery, N. 0(2); Forbes, R. 7(3); Fowler, L. 5(2); Gammons, R. 3(12); Gothard, P. 4(17); Greene, D. 33(6); Groves, P. 6; Haag, K. 12(1); Jones, D. 6(1); Kalogeracos, V. 1; Kimble, G. 2(4); Livett, S. 6; Martin, D. 3(4); McDonough, R. 23; McPherson, M. 4(1); Moore, C. 10(1); Moore, M. 0(2); O'Sullivan, J. 0(3); Oliver, S. 2(10); Pettinger, P. 7; Philip, R. (1); Richardson, I. 36; Risley, M. 2(3); Roberts, B. 7(12); Shipp, D. 9; Sinclair, R. 0(1); Sorrell, T. 15(1); Steam, M. 0(5); Stebbing, G. 41; Tomlinson, D. 1; Wallace, A. 9(1); Watts, P. 33; Wordsworth, D. 10(3).
Goals (56): Richardson 10, McDonough 7, Haag 6, Shipp 6, Greene 5, Wordsworth 4, Bennett 3, Broom 3, Cavell 3, Conner 2, Stebbing 2, Cook 1, Cooper 1, Jones 1, Martin 1, Sorrell 1.

Dover Athletic
Vauxhall Appearances: Barlett, J. 7; Blewden, C. 18(7); Bond, K. 7; Browne, C. 26(2); Budden, J. 38; Carruthers, M. 0(12); Carter, I. 17; Chambers, P. 5(7); Costello, P. 3(5); Darlington, J. 9(14); Dixon, A. 35; Donn, N. 25(11); Ebbli, E. 13; Eeles, A. 10(8); Embery, J. 0(3); Fox, L. 0(2); Hall, M. 10; Lewis, J. 30(7); Leworthy, D. 35(2); Lillis, J. 4; Livett, S. 4; Milton, R. 31; Munden, M. 6(4); O'Brien, P. 13(10); O'Connell, I. 15(2); Omogbehin, C. 1(2); Partner, L. 0(1); Restarick, S. 9(1); Scott, D. 26; Strouts,J. 5(1); Walker, D. 37(3); Williams, D. 23(3); Wilks, M. 0(9).
Goals (48): Leworthy 18, Lewis 5, Chambers 4, Blewden 3, Budden 2, Browne 2, Darlington 2, Eeles 2, Hall 2, Restarick 2, Carruthers 1, Carter 1, Costello 1, Lillis 1, Scott 1, og 1.

Farnborough Town
Vauxhall Appearances: Baker, K. 10; Baker, S. 37; Boothe, C. 39; Coney, D. 30; Day, K. 34(1); Denny, R. 12(8); Dobson, R. 3(1); Harlow, D. 20; Hayward, D. 0(1); Horton, J. 16(4); Jones, Mark 26; Jones, Murray 17(2); Juryeff, I. 3; Pratt, B. 36; Read, S. 11(3); Rowe, A. 6; Rowe, D. 1(1); Savage, I. 3(5); Steadman, C. 2; Stemp, W. 30; Stevens, G. 1(2); Taylor, M. 36; Terry, P. 26(5); Thompson, N. 11(2); Turkington, M. 29(1); Underwood, J. 11(5); Walters, D. 12(1).
Goals (45): Boothe 14, Denny 9, Read 5, Turkington 5, Harlow 3, Jones Murray 2, Baker S 1, Day 1, Horton 1, Pratt 1, Terry 1, Thompson 1, og 1.

Gateshead
Vauxhall Appearances: Cavell, P. 15(2); Copeland, L. 2; Corner, D. 5(1); Cramman, K. 38(2); Dobson, P. 39; Dowson, A. 37; Farrey, M. 30(3); Hine, M. 37(1); Lacey, N. 9; Lamb, A. 12(18); Musgrave, S. 9; Nobbs, K. 28(5); Parkinson, G. 39; Proudlock, P. 21(11); Robinson, D. 6(12); Rowe, B. 31(3); Rowntree, P. 0(1); Smith, S. 1; Stephenson, N. 0(2); Sweeney, P. 0(4); Taylor, I. 31; Watson, J. 31(3); Wrightson, J. 40(2).
Goals (61): Dobson 25, Cramman 6, Lamb 6, Hine 5, Proudlock 4, Cavell 3, Dowson 2, Farrey 2, Robinson 2, Corner 1, Lacey 1, Watson 1, og 3.

Halifax Town
Vauxhall Appearances: Beddard, E. 6(10); Boardman, C. 32(1); Circuit, S. 1; Dunphy, S. 2(2); Flemming, P. 23; Flounders, A. 9(8); Ford, S. 5(7); Fowler, L. 12(7); German, D. 22(6); Gray, R. 0(2); Hall, D. 4(5); Hanson, D. 26(5); Heyes, D. 28(14); Horner, N. 1(2); Johnson, S. 3; Jones, A. 39; Kiwomya, A. 29(1); Lambert, C. 38(1); Lancaster, D. 21(3); Langley, K. 13(1); Leitch, G. 11(6); Martin, D. 5(1); Patterson, J. 13(3); Pettinger, P. 7(1); Prindiville, S. 39; Rathbone, M. 5(1); Sunley, M. 7(2); Trotter, M. 18(4); Wilmot, R. 2(21); Worthington, G. 29(8).
Goals (68): Kiwomya 13, Hanson 11, Worthington 9, Lancaster 7, Patterson 5, Prindiville 5, German 3, Lambert 3, Beddard 2, Jones 2, Flemming 1, Flounders 1, Ford 1, Johnson 1, Leitch 1, Rathbone 1, Wilmot, og 1.

Kettering Town
Vauxhall Appearances: Alford, C. 38(2); Arnold, I. 22; Ashby, N. 34; Ashdjian, J. 0(2); Barnes, R. 4(5); Benstead, G. 22; Brown, P. 40(1); Chard, P. 6(1); Clarke, S. 29(5); Donald, W. 19(2); Dunphy, S. 1; Gleasure, P. 15(10); Graham, J. 8(13); Holden, S. 32; Howe, S. 6; Magee, J. 0(2); Martin, D. 9(4); Oxbrow, D. 12; Pettinger, P. 5; Price, G. 12(4); Reed, G. 18; Saddington, J. 25; Smith, P. 8; Stringfellow, I. 31(2); Taylor, R. 27(1); Thomas, A. 30(6); Wright, O. 8(6).
Goals (73): Alford 23, Arnold 11, Brown 10, Thomas 8, Stringfellow 6, Graham 4, Taylor 4, Holden 3, Clarke 2, Howe 1, og 1.

Kidderminster Harriers
Vauxhall Appearances: Bancroft, P. 20; Brindley, C. 26; Cartwright, N. 26; Casey, K. 7; Davies, D. 1; Davies, P. 6; Deakin, J. 16; Dearlove, M. 5; Eades, G. 2; Forsyth, R. 42; Grainger, P. 19; Hodson, S. 42; Hughes, L. 35; Humphreys, D. 34; Langford, T. 3; Palmer, L. 16; Phillips, R. 2; Powell, J. 19; Purdie, J. 18; Rose, K. 28; Steadman, D. 16; Webb, P. 42; Weir, M. 21; Yates, M. 42
Goals (63): Forsyth 13, Davies Paul 11, Yates 10, Hughes 9, Humphreys 8, Brindley 2, Casey 2, Webb 2, Dearlove 1, Palmer 1, Phillips 1, Weir 1, og 2.

Macclesfield Town
Vauxhall Appearances: Allen, G. 2(1); Askey, J. 30; Bimson, S. 21; Bradshaw, M. 15; Crisp, M. 4(4); Farrelly, S. 42; Howarth, N. 39; Kendall, P. 11(2); Lillis, M. 0(1); Locke, S. 16(2); Lyons, D. 20(8); McDonald, M. 38; Marginson, K. 7; Midwood, M. 7; Monk, I. 16(7); Murray, M. 20; Norman, D. 13(1); Payne, S. 33; Power, P. 37; Shepherd, G. 12; Sorvel, N. 38(2); Tobin, S. 14(10); Wright, P. 4(4); Wood, S. 35(2).
Goals (70): Power 18, Howarth 11, Askey 9, Wood 9, Sorvel 5, Lyons 4, McDonald 3, Monk 3, Midwood 2, Tobin 2, Marginson 1, Payne 1, Shepherd 1, Wright 1.

Merthyr Tydfil
Vauxhall Appearances: Abraham, G. 24(1); Adebowle, A. 10; Beattie, A. 8(1); Boyle, T. 7(1); Costa, L. 3(2); David, R. 2(1); Davies, M. 13(1); Downs, G. 8; Dyer, S. 29(6); French, I. 11(5); Holtam, M. 29(6); Hopkins, A. 13(1); Hunter, P. 2; James, Rob1; James, Ryan4; Jenkins, A. 20(7); Jones, Lee2(3); Jones, Nathan36(2); Loss, C. 11; Mitchell, I. 20(7); Morris, S. 1; Narbett, J. 1; Needs, A. 7(2); O'Brien, N. 13; Popham, P. 3(2); Rogers, K. 38(1); Sanderson, P. 4(1); Scott, M. 15(5); Threlfall, D. 0(2); Vowles, P. 3(1); Wager, G. 41; Walton, M. 0(1); Webley, D. 28(4); Williams, M. 19; Woolgar, M. 3; York, A. 33.
Goals (53): Webley 12, Dyer 9, Mitchell 6, Rogers 6, Jones N 4, Jenkins 3, Abraham 2, Holtam 2, Hunter 2, Scott 2, Adebowle 1, French 1, York 1, og 2.

Northwich Victoria
Vauxhall Appearances: Abel, G. 33(1); Adams, C. 0(4); Baab, P. 5; Boyd, C. 30(1); Bullock, A. 0(1); Butler, B. 37(1); Cooke, I. 25(9); Deeley, N. 0(1); Duffy, C. 28; Gallagher, J. 22(4); Greygoose, D. 42; Hardy, N. 11(9); Hilton, R. 2; Jones, M. 33(2); Mitten, P. 0(2); Nesbitt, C. 2; Norman, D. 9(1); O'Connor, M. 31(7); Oghani, G. 29(8); Parker, J. 31; Radcliffe, R. 0(4); Snowden, T. 9(1); Tinson, D. 34(2); Turpin, S. 3; Vicary, D. 10(1); Walters, S. 16; Williams, C. 24(5).
Goals (77): O'Connor 18, Cooke 13, Oghani 12, Williams 11, Butler 7, Vicary 4, Hardy 3, Abel 2, Boyd 1, Duffy 1, Norman 1, Parker 1, Snowden 1, Turpin 1, Walters 1.

Runcorn
Vauxhall Appearances: Anderson, G. 30; Bates, J. 39; Brady, I. 16(1); Byrne, P. 34; Connor, J. 31; Curtis, R. 2(1); Doherty, N. 10(11); Ellis, P. 6; Finley, A. 25; Godfrey, W. 0(2); Hill, G. 26; Hughes, M. 39(1); Lee, A. 13(1); McInerney, I. 30(5); Morris, M. 40; Murphy, C. 2; Pugh, S. 4(3); Robertson, P. 35; Ruffer, C. 16(5); Shaw, N. 6; Smith, M. 24(15); Taylor, C. 0(3); Thomas, K. 34(1).
Goals (59): Hughes 16, Thomas 11, Anderson 6, Brady 4, Connor 4, McInerney 4, Smith 3, Shaw 3, Bates 2, Byrne 1, Doherty 1, Finley 1, Hill 1, Pugh 1, og 1.

Southport
Vauxhall Appearances: Blackhurst, J. 15(11); Challender, G. 5(1); Clark, M. 37; Comstive, P. 24(5); Cooper, L. 0(1); Cunningham, H. 27(6); Dove, L. 36; Edwards, E. 5; Fuller, D. 30; Gamble, D. 31(6); Goulding, D. 38; Haw, S. 30(5); Lodge, P. 38; McDonald, A. 17(7); McKenna, J. 42; McNally, J. 1; Penman, J. 9(11); Pritchard, B. 8; Quinlan, P. 0(1); Simms, M. 11; Sloan, M. 0(2); Symons, P. 1; Thomas, G. 24(5); Ward, D. 33.
Goals (68): Gamble 12, Haw 12, Comstive 9, Blackhurst 6, Thomas 6, Cunningham 5, Clark 3, Dove 3, Goulding 3, McDonald 3, Penman 2, Ward 2, Challender 1, Lodge 1.

Stafford Rangers
Vauxhall Appearances: Abbishaw, D. 2(1); Berry, George6(6); Berry, Gwynne4; Boughey, D. 34(2); Bradshaw, M. 27; Brown, G. 6(2); Cooke, J. 1(1); Corbett, S. 1(1); Crisp, M. 6; Crowley, D. 8(2); Davies, M. 13; Dawson, D. 7(1); Drewitt, I. 29; Duffin, S. 13; Edensor, J. 1; Foy, D. 10; Griffiths, A. 17(6); Hassall, J. 23(4); Harrison, M. 2; Hawkins, R. 0(2); Hicks, N. 1(2); Kilbane, F. 13; Law, M. 5; Leeming, D. 8; Luby, S. 1; Mackenzie, S. 16(2); Mardenborough, S. 10; May, L. 35(1); Mee, A. 2(4); Milson, P. 6; Molloy, P. 8(1); O'Toole, P. 14; Penny, A. 10(1); Rees, M. 3(2); Shepstone, P. 3; Simpson, W. 29; Smith, Mark2; Smith, Robert9(1); Squires, J. 8; Timons, C. 5; Walker, G. 19; Williams, D. 31(3); Woodward, A. 2(1); Wright, E. 1(1).
Goals (53): May 21, Duffin 6, Mardenborough 5, Drewitt 4, Kilbane 3, Crisp 2, Milsom 2, Williams 2, Berry George 1, Bradshaw 1, Griffiths 1, Mackenzie 1, Shepstone 1, Simpson 1, og 2.

Stalybridge Celtic
Vauxhall Appearances: Anderson, S. 26(8); Bauress, G. 33(6); Bennett, P. 9(4); Booth, K. 6(7); Burke, B. (21); Clayton, P. 34(2); Coathup, L. 38(1); Cooksey, S. 13; Dixon, P. 11; Edmonds, N. 28(3); Ellis, N. 2(3); Frain, D. 7; Hall, D. 12; Hughes, R. 26; Jackson R. 11; Leicester, S. 1(2); Livingstone, R. 2(1); Megson, K. 25(6); Ogley, M. 35; O'Shaughnessy, S. 11; Patterson, I. 19; Robinson, P. 22; Ryan, J. 31; Shaughnessy, S. 29(9); Sunley, M. 2; Wheeler, P. 27(13); Zelem, A. 1.
Goals (52): Shaughnessy 7, Wheeler 7, Clayton 6, Jackson 6, Bauress 5, Ryan 4, Burke 3, Megson 3, Anderson 2, Dixon 2, Edmonds 2, Frain 2, Hall 1, Leicester 1, og 1.

Stevenage Borough
Vauxhall Appearances: Allinson, K. 0(3); Bates, M. 0(3); Bedrossian, A. 5; Beevor, S. 24(4); Brock, K. 5(2); Case, S. 5; Conroy, S. 3(2); Crawshaw, G. 5; Cretton, S. 0(3); Dillon, K. 12; Fortune-West, L. 13(4); Gallagher, D. 29(13); Gittings, M. 10(3); Hayles, B. 35;Hedman, R. 31(3); Joyce, T. 2; Kalogeracos, V. 2(1); Lomas, A. 12(12); Luque, M. 4(12); Lynch, A. 28(10); Manual, W. 2; Neville, C. 0(11); Nugent, R. 27(2); Nyamah, K. 6; Omogbehin, C. 1(1); Parker, A. 7(11); Pennyfather, G. 3(1); Phillips, M. 1(1); Rattle, J. 20; Roberts, G. 11; Rudgley, S. 1(3); Simpson, P. 22(1); Sodje, P. 22(9); Smart, G. 18(2); Smith, M. 41; Venables, D. 37; Webster, K. 13(1); Whitmarsh,P. 0(5); Williams, D. 4(3).
Goals (68): Hayles 13, Lynch 8, Venables 8, Fortune-West 7, Smith 4, Beevor 3, Williams 3, Dillon 2, Gittings 2, Hedman 2, Nugent 2, Simpson 2, Bates 1, Brock 1, Conroy 1, Crawshaw 1, Kalogeracos 1, Nyamah 1, Omogbehin 1, Rattle 1, Roberts 1, Sodje 1, Smart 1, og 1.

Telford United
Vauxhall Appearances: Adams, C. 13(6); Bignot, M. 37; Brough, J. 6(1); Carr, D. 17(2); Castledine, G. 3(3); Costello, P. 4(1); Crisp, R. 27(4); Crookes, D. 24(10); Davidson, J. 15(2); Donnelly, S. 3(1); Dougherty, P. 2; Ford, G. 13; Foster, S. 34(2); Fowler, L. 8(1); Goodwin, N. 39; Griffiths, B. 16(1); Holden, M. 5(1); Howell, P. 9(5); Hughes, K. 3; Kearney, M. 38; Myers, M. 35(1); Niblett, N. 24; Roberts, D. 10; Taylor, C. 4; Treharne, J. 1(2); Warner, A. 11(3); Wilcox, B. 25(3); Wilson, L. 33(4); Winstone, S. 3; Wood, J. 0(2).
Goals (53): Wilson 9, Myers 6, Warner 6, Roberts 5, Kearney 4, Bignot 3, Crookes 2, Donnelly 2, Griffiths 2, Howell 2, Niblett 2, Brough 1, Costello 1, Ford 1, Foster 1, Fowler 1, Holden 1, Taylor 1, og 1.

Welling United
Vauxhall Appearances: Barnes, S. 24(11); Barrett, C. 14(1); Brown, W. 38; Burgess, R. 0(1); Cleevely, L. 10; Collins, P. 2(3); Copley, P. 28; Cooksey, S. 5; Farley,J. 26(2); Finnan, S. 14(5); Gamble, B. 0(1); Gorman, P. 17; Hales, K. 28(2); Hancock, D. 5(1); Hopping, A. 12; Horton, D. 25(1); Kimble, G. 11; Martin, D. 3; Napier, M. 1; Quamina, M. 31(4); Ransom, N. 34; Reynolds, A. 2; Robinson, S. 32; Robbins, T. 42; Rutherford, M. 23; Smith, D. 5(12); Wastell, J. 3; White, S. 15; Williams, D. 12.
Goals (57): Gorman 13, Robbins 10, Copley 6, Barnes 5, Ransom 5, Brown 3, Farley 3, Robinson 3, Quamina 2, Smith 2, White 2, Finnan 1, Reynolds 1, og 1.

Woking
Vauxhall Appearances: Alexander, T. 7(1); Batty, L. 38; Benton, J. 2; Berry, G. 5(1); Brooks, S. 0(1); Brown,D. 12(3); Brown, K. 37; Crumplin, J. 11(1); DeGaris, P. 1; Dennis, L. 14(9); Ellis, A. 26(1); Fielder, C. 41; Girdler, 1(1); Greene, D. 4(1), Hay, D. 25; Newberry, R. 3(4); Payne, G. 6(1); Rattray, K. 21(9); Ravenscroft, C. 1(2); Read, T. 3(1); Steele, S. 37(2); Tierling, L. 21(2); Timothy, D. 1(1); Tucker, M. 42; Wye, L. 40; Wye, S. 28.
Goals (76): Walker 19, Hay 17, Dennis 8, Steele 6, Rattray 5, Payne 4, Ellis 3, Fielder 3, Greene 3, Tucker 2, Crumplin 1, Newberry 1, Wye L 1, Wye S 1, og 2.

Yeovil Town
Vauxhall Appearances: Benbow, I. 13(8); Black, S. 10(1); Brock, K. 16(1); Burwood, D. 0(2); Cleeveley, L. 1; Coates, M. 11(13); Coll, O. 2; Conning, P. 26(2); Cooper, R. 18(3); Cordice, N. 34(1); Dillon, K. 13; Dobbins, W. 8(5); Evans, R. 21(9); Ferns, P. 18; Flory, A. 4(2); Groves, L. 3(4); Hornby, L. 12; LeBihan, N. 6; Leonard, M. 0(1); Lowe, T. 1; Llewellyn, A. 13; Mason, P. 41; McClelland, J. 20(1); Morris, D. 16(3); Powell, L. 3(8); Sherwood, J. 16; Spencer, M. 20(5); Wallace, A. 21; Whale, L. 10(1); White, C. 29; Williams, N. 7(1); Wilson, P33(1); Wratten, A. 0(1).
Goals (50): Wilson 15, Coates 5, Black 4, Spencer 4, Evans 3, Groves 3, Brock 2, Dillon 2, Morris 2, Wallace 2, Whale 2, Cooper 1, Dobbins 1, McClelland 1, White 1, og 2.

VAUXHALL CONFERENCE: MEMBERS CLUBS SEASON 1995–96

Club: ALTRINCHAM
Colours: Red and white striped shirts, black shorts
Ground: Moss Lane, Altrincham, Cheshire WA15 8AP
Tel: 0161-928 1045
Year Formed: 1903
Record Gate: 10,275 (1925 v Sunderland Boys) Nickname: The Robins
Manager: John King
Secretary: Graham Heathcote

Club: BATH CITY
Colours: Black and white striped shirts, black shorts
Ground: Twerton Park, Bath BA2 1DB
Tel: 01225 423087 and 313247
Year Formed: 1889
Record Gate: 18,020 (1960 v Brighton)
Nickname: City
Manager: Tony Ricketts
Secretary: Bob Twyford

Club: BROMSGROVE ROVERS
Colours: Green and white striped shirts, black shorts
Ground: Victoria Ground, Birmingham Road, Bromsgrove, Worcs. B61 0DR
Tel: 01527 876949
Year Formed: 1885
Record Gate: 7563 (1957–58 v Worcester City)
Nickname: Rovers
Manager: Brian Kenning
Secretary: Brian Hewings

Club: DAGENHAM & REDBRIDGE
Colours: Red shirts, red shorts
Ground: Victoria Road Ground, Victoria Road, Dagenham, Essex RM10 7XL
Tel: 0181-592 7194
Year Formed: 1992
Record Gate: 5300 v Leyton Orient (1992)
Nickname: The Daggers
Manager: David Cusack
Secretary: Derek Almond

Club: DOVER ATHLETIC
Colours: White shirts, black shorts
Ground: Crabble Athletic Ground, Lewisham Road, River, Dover, Kent CT17 0PB
Tel: 01304 822373
Year Formed: 1983
Record Gate: 4035 versus Bromsgrove Rovers (1992)
Nickname: The Lilywhites
Manager: John Ryan
Secretary: John Durrant

Club: FARNBOROUGH TOWN
Colours: Yellow and royal blue shirts, yellow shorts
Ground: Cherrywood Road, Farnborough, Hampshire GU14 8UD
Tel: 01252 541469
Year Formed: 1967
Record Gate: 3069 (1991 v Colchester U)
Nickname: Boro
Manager: Alan Taylor
Secretary: Terry Parr

Club: GATESHEAD
Colours: Black and white halved shirts, black shorts
Ground: International Stadium, Neilson Road, Gateshead NE10 0EF
Tel: 0191-478 3883
Year Formed: 1977 (Reformed)
Record Gate: 20,752 (1937 v Lincoln C)
Nickname: Tynesiders
Manager: Colin Richardson
Secretary: Mark Donnelly

Club: HALIFAX TOWN
Colours: Blue and white shirts, white shorts
Ground: Shay Ground, Halifax HX1 2YS
Tel: 01422 345543 (330383 Match Days Only)
Year Formed: 1911
Record Gate: 36,885 versus Tottenham Hotspur (1953)
Nickname: The Shaymen
Manager: John Bird
Secretary: Derek Newiss

Club: HEDNESFORD TOWN
Colours: White and black shirts with red trim, black shorts with red and white trim
Ground: Keys Park, Hill Street, Hednesford, Staffordshire
Tel: tba
Year Formed: 1880
Record Gate: 10,000 (1927 v Walsall)
Nickname: The Pitmen
Manager: John Baldwin
Secretary: Richard Murning

Club: KETTERING TOWN
Colours: Red and white striped shirts, red shorts
Ground: Rockingham Road, Kettering, Northants NN16 9AW
Tel: 01536 83028/410815
Year Formed: 1875
Record Gate: 11,536 (1947 v Peterborough)
Nickname: The Poppies
Manager: Gary Johnson
Secretary: Gerry Knowles

Club: KIDDERMINSTER HARRIERS
Colours: Red and white shirts, red shorts
Ground: Aggborough, Hoo Road, Kidderminster DY10 1NB
Tel: 01562 823931
Year Formed: 1886
Record Gate: 9155 (1948 v Hereford)
Nickname: The Harriers
Manager: Graham Allner
Secretary: Ray Mercer

Club: MACCLESFIELD TOWN
Colours: Royal blue shirts, white shorts
Ground: Moss Rose Ground, London Road, Macclesfield, Cheshire SK10 3JH
Tel: 01625 424324/511113
Year Formed: 1875
Record Gate: 8900 (1968 v Stockport Co)
Nickname: The Silkmen
Manager: Sammy McIlroy
Secretary: Colin Garlick

Club: MORECAMBE
Colours: Red and white striped shirts, black shorts
Ground: Christie Park, Lancaster Road, Morecambe, Lancashire LA4 5TJ
Tel: 01524 411797
Year Formed: 1920
Record Gate: 9326 (1962 FA Cup Third Round Proper v Weymouth)
Nickname: The Shrimps
Manager: Jim Harvey
Secretary: Neil Marsdin

Club: NORTHWICH VICTORIA
Colours: Green and white shirts, white shorts with green trim
Ground: The Drill Field, Northwich, Cheshire CW9 5HN
Tel: 01606 41450
Year Formed: 1874
Record Gate: 11,290 (1949 v Witton A) 12,000 (1977 v Watford FAC4)
Nickname: The Vics
Manager: Brian Kettle
Secretary: Derek Nuttall

Club: RUNCORN
Colours: Yellow shirts, green shorts
Ground: Canal Street, Runcorn, Cheshire WA7 1RZ
Tel: 01928 560076
Year Formed: 1919
Record Gate: 10,011 (1939 v Preston NE)
Nickname: The Linnets
Manager: John Carroll
Secretary: Graham Ost

Club: SLOUGH TOWN
Colours: Amber shirts, navy blue shorts
Ground: Wexham Park Stadium, Wexham Road, Slough, Berkshire SL2 5QR
Tel: 01753 523358
Year Formed: 1980
Record Gate: 5000 (1982 v Millwall at Wexham Park Stadium)
Nickname: The Rebels
Manager: David Russell
Secretary: David Stanley

Club: SOUTHPORT
Colours: Old gold shirts, black shorts
Ground: Haig Avenue, Southport PR8 6JZ
Tel: 01704 533422
Year Formed: 1881
Record Gate: 20,010 (1932 v Newcastle United)
Nickname: The Sandgrounders
Manager: Billy Ayre
Secretary: Roy Morris

Club: STALYBRIDGE CELTIC
Colours: Blue shirts, blue shorts
Ground: Bower Ford, Mottram Road, Stalybridge, Cheshire SK15 2RT
Tel: 0161-338 2828
Year Formed: 1911
Record Gate: 9753 (1992–23 v West Bromwich Albion)
Nickname: Celtic
Manager: Peter Wragg
Secretary: Martyn Torr

Club: STEVENAGE BOROUGH
Colours: Red and white shirts, white shorts
Ground: Broadhall Way, Stevenage, Herts SG2 8RH
Tel: 01438 743322
Year Formed: 1976
Record Gate: 3005 (1994 v Harrow Borough)
Nickname: The Boro
Manager: Paul Fairclough
Secretary: Janice Hutchings

Club: TELFORD UNITED
Colours: White shirts, white shorts
Ground: Bucks Head, Watling Street, Telford TF1 2NJ
Tel: 01952 223838
Year Formed: 1877
Record Gate: 13,000 (1935 v Shrewsbury)
Nickname: The Lillywhites
Manager: Wayne Clarke
Secretary: Mike Ferriday

Club: WELLING UNITED
Colours: Red shirts, red shorts
Ground: Park View Road Ground, Welling, Kent DA16 1SY
Tel: 0181-301 1196
Year Formed: 1963
Record Gate: 4020 (1989 v Gillingham)
Nickname: The Wings
Manager: Kevin Hales
Secretary: Barrie Hobbins

Club: WOKING
Colours: Red and white halved shirts, black shorts
Ground: Kingfield Sports Ground, Kingfield, Woking, Surrey GU22 9AA
Tel: 01483 772470
Year Formed: 1889
Record Gate: 6000 (1978–79 v Swansea)
Nickname: The Cardinals
Manager: Geoff Chapple
Secretary: Phil Ledger, JP

VAUXHALL CONFERENCE RESULTS 1994–95

	Altrincham	Bath City	Bromsgrove Rovers	Dagenham & Redbridge	Dover Athletic	Farnborough Town	Gateshead	Halifax Town	Kettering Town	Kidderminster Harriers	Macclesfield Town	Merthyr Tydfil	Northwich Victoria	Runcorn	Southport	Stafford Rangers	Stalybridge Celtic	Stevenage Borough	Telford United	Welling United	Woking	Yeovil Town
Altrincham	—	1-0	1-1	0-1	3-0	2-0	1-3	3-1	2-4	2-0	1-2	1-0	1-3	3-2	0-0	5-1	1-0	1-2	3-1	1-1	1-2	1-3
Bath City	0-3	—	1-1	3-0	0-0	2-0	0-2	0-0	2-0	3-5	1-0	1-0	2-2	4-3	1-2	3-3	2-3	2-1	1-1	2-0	2-0	3-0
Bromsgrove Rovers	0-3	1-1	—	2-2	2-0	2-2	2-2	0-1	2-4	4-3	2-2	2-0	1-4	1-0	1-1	2-1	2-1	2-1	0-1	4-1	5-5	5-0
Dagenham & Redbridge	0-4	1-0	2-0	—	2-0	0-1	0-0	1-4	2-1	1-2	0-4	2-1	1-2	3-2	5-1	3-3	2-2	0-1	3-2	0-0	0-2	0-0
Dover Athletic	1-3	3-0	0-2	1-1	—	1-1	2-2	1-1	0-2	1-0	0-0	2-2	3-1	1-1	1-2	3-2	0-0	2-0	2-0	1-1	2-3	1-1
Farnborough Town	2-3	0-0	0-3	1-3	1-0	—	3-1	2-0	0-0	1-0	1-0	2-1	2-1	0-4	1-4	0-0	0-0	1-1	5-3	1-2	0-2	0-3
Gateshead	1-0	0-1	2-1	2-1	1-0	2-0	—	1-2	0-0	1-0	2-1	2-0	4-0	4-0	0-1	1-1	0-0	1-2	0-0	2-0	2-0	0-3
Halifax Town	1-1	4-2	4-2	1-1	4-0	0-1	3-2	—	2-1	1-2	0-1	2-2	0-0	4-0	2-0	6-0	1-1	0-2	1-1	4-0	4-0	2-1
Kettering Town	2-2	0-0	0-1	2-2	1-0	4-1	2-4	5-1	—	0-0	1-0	4-1	3-3	3-0	1-0	1-0	1-0	0-2	3-2	4-3	0-1	3-2
Kidderminster Harriers	2-2	2-1	0-1	1-1	0-0	0-1	2-3	3-0	1-3	—	1-2	2-0	1-2	1-1	0-1	1-2	3-2	0-3	1-1	3-0	1-3	3-0
Macclesfield Town	4-2	1-0	2-2	2-0	3-0	4-1	2-1	1-1	1-0	1-3	—	0-0	3-1	0-1	3-0	1-2	3-0	0-3	2-0	3-1	2-0	1-0
Merthyr Tydfil	2-5	2-0	2-1	2-0	2-3	1-1	1-2	2-0	2-1	0-1	1-2	—	2-0	3-0	1-2	4-1	4-2	2-2	3-1	0-2	1-1	0-0
Northwich Victoria	1-1	1-1	3-1	5-0	1-3	1-2	1-1	3-0	3-2	3-4	1-3	2-0	—	4-1	2-1	0-1	2-2	0-1	1-1	1-1	2-2	2-2
Runcorn	3-0	1-1	3-1	0-0	3-3	1-0	3-2	0-3	1-2	2-2	2-2	0-0	2-2	—	2-1	3-1	0-3	3-1	4-1	3-2	1-0	2-1
Southport	1-4	3-1	2-1	1-1	2-2	0-1	5-0	4-0	1-1	4-1	2-3	3-1	0-2	5-0	—	3-0	3-1	2-1	2-1	1-0	2-0	0-0
Stafford Rangers	0-1	0-2	1-1	1-2	1-0	1-1	3-1	0-1	2-3	1-2	0-3	2-1	1-3	1-2	1-1	—	5-0	0-3	2-2	1-1	2-3	4-1
Stalybridge Celtic	2-1	0-1	1-1	1-0	2-1	4-1	0-1	1-0	1-4	1-3	2-2	1-1	2-1	0-0	1-1	2-3	—	1-0	1-0	1-3	2-1	3-1
Stevenage Borough	4-2	3-0	1-0	3-1	0-3	3-1	2-3	1-0	2-2	2-3	1-1	0-0	1-1	0-1	1-2	1-0	5-1	—	4-3	1-2	0-1	5-0
Telford United	2-3	3-0	2-2	0-4	1-1	1-1	3-1	1-1	1-0	3-1	2-0	1-1	1-0	2-0	0-0	0-0	1-1	1-2	—	4-2	0-0	1-0
Welling United	0-0	1-5	1-2	4-1	0-1	1-3	3-0	1-1	2-1	0-2	0-1	2-1	1-5	1-2	3-1	3-1	3-3	1-0	1-0	—	1-2	2-1
Woking	4-0	2-2	4-0	3-5	0-0	3-2	1-1	1-3	3-1	0-0	1-0	4-1	1-1	2-0	3-0	2-2	4-1	3-0	2-1	1-1	—	2-2
Yeovil Town	1-3	1-2	2-0	2-2	1-3	0-1	1-1	3-1	1-1	1-1	1-2	1-3	4-4	1-0	0-1	1-0	3-0	0-0	1-1	3-3	1-2	—

BOB LORD TROPHY 1994–95

First Round (*two legs*)
Altrincham 1(*O'Neill*)
Telford 1 (*Brough*) 671

Telford 0
Altrincham 3 (*Terry, Carmody, O'Neill*) 604

Bath City 3 (*Vernon, Smart, Adcock*)
Welling United 1 (*Gorman*) 323

Welling United 2 (*Rutherford, og*)
Bath City 6 (*Mings, Smart, McLoughlin, Adcock, Birkby 2*) 226

Gateshead 2 (*Dobson 2*)
Stalybridge Celtic 3 (*Clayton, Wheeler 2*) 296

Stalybridge Celtic 3 (*Shaughnessy 2, Edmonds*)
Gateshead 2 (*Lamb, Robinson*) 261

Halifax Town 0
Northwich Victoria 1 (*Butler*) 476

Northwich Victoria 1 (*Williams*)
Halifax Town 1 (*Lambert*) 780

Merthyr Tydfil 2 (*Rogers, Williams*)
Bromsgrove Rovers 1 (*B Gray*) 306

Bromsgrove Rovers 4 (*Glasser, Carter, Stott, Burgher*)
Merthyr Tydfil 1 (*Scott*) 941

Stevenage Borough 1 (*Whitmarsh*)
Farnborough Town 2 (*Baker, Boothe*) 673

Farnborough Town 3 (*Boothe 2, Baker*)
Stevenage Borough 1 (*Gittings*) 504

Byes to Second Round
Dagenham & Redbridge, Dover Athletic, Kettering Town, Kidderminster Harriers, Macclesfield Town, Runcorn, Southport, Stafford Rangers, Woking, Yeovil Town

Second Round
Altrincham 3 (*Terry 2, Morton*)
Northwich Victoria 2 (*Williams, Oghani*) 811

Bath City 0
Dover Athletic 1 (*Hall*) 276

Kidderminster Harriers 1 (*Humphreys*)
Kettering Town 5 (*og, Stringfellow, Magee, Martin, Brown*) 914

Macclesfield Town 4 (*Power, McDonald, Askey, Tobin*)
Runcorn 2 (*Anderson, Hughes*) 441

Stalybridge Celtic 3 (*Clayton 2, Ryan*)
Southport 1 (*Blackhurst*) 326

Stafford Rangers 1 (*May*)
Bromsgrove Rovers 4 (*Carter 3, Taylor*) 356

Woking 0
Farnborough Town 0 1375

Farnborough Town 0
Woking 1 (*Rattray*) 935

Yeovil Town 2 (*Cooper, Ferns*)
Dagenham & Redbridge 4 (*Bennett 3, Wordsworth*) 719

Quarter-Finals
Dagenham & Redbridge 4 (*Greene, Bennett 2, Conner*)
Dover Athletic 3 (Scott, Leworthy 2) 399

Kettering Town 2 (*Arnold, Alford*)
Woking 1 (*Rattray*) 964

Macclesfield Town 2 (*Sorvel, Midwood*)
Altrincham 1 (*Sharratt*) 853

Stalybridge Celtic 3 (*Ryan, Jackson, Coathup*)
Bromsgrove Rovers 3 (*Gaunt, Carter, Taylor*) 427

Bromsgrove Rovers 2 (*Taylor, Stott*)
Stalybridge Celtic 0 765

Semi-Finals (*two legs*)
Kettering Town 0
Dagenham & Redbridge 2 (*Richardson, Haag*) 1033

Dagenham & Redbridge 2 (*McPherson, Haag*)
Kettering Town 4 (*Alford, Brown, Arnold, Thomas*) 750

Macclesfield Town 2 (*Lyons, Power*)
Bromsgrove Rovers 1 (*Carter*) 660

Bromsgrove Rovers 4 (*Carter 2, Taylor, Burgher*)
Macclesfield Town 1 (*Midwood*) 1118

Final (*two legs*)
Bromsgrove Rovers 4 (*Carter 2, Taylor, og*)
Kettering Town 1 (*Clarke*) 1393

Kettering Town 1 (*Alford*)
Bromsgrove Rovers 6 (*Stott, Taylor 3, Carter 2*) 1311

UNIBOND LEAGUE

PREMIER DIVISION

		Home					*Away*					*Total*
	P	W	D	L	F	A	W	D	L	F	A	Pts
Marine	42	17	3	1	43	15	12	8	1	40	12	98
Morecambe	42	14	5	2	56	20	14	5	2	43	14	94
Guiseley	42	16	4	1	54	22	12	5	4	42	28	93
Hyde United	42	14	2	5	57	30	8	8	5	32	29	76
Boston United	42	11	5	5	50	25	9	6	6	30	18	71
Spennymoor United	42	12	6	3	41	24	8	5	8	25	28	71
Buxton	42	9	5	7	34	27	9	4	8	31	35	63
Gainsborough Trinity	42	9	8	4	34	25	7	5	9	35	36	61
Bishop Auckland (3)	42	6	8	7	26	26	10	4	7	42	29	57
Witton Albion	42	6	7	8	27	31	8	7	6	27	25	56
Barrow	42	10	4	7	37	29	7	1	13	31	42	56
Colwyn Bay	42	8	5	8	33	32	8	3	10	38	48	56
Emley	42	9	7	5	32	26	5	6	10	30	42	55
Matlock Town	42	7	4	10	34	31	8	1	12	28	41	50
Accrington Stanley	42	6	5	10	29	42	6	8	7	26	35	49
Knowsley United	42	7	6	8	32	36	4	8	9	32	47	47
Winsford United	42	6	5	10	34	37	4	6	11	22	38	41
Chorley	42	5	1	15	28	45	6	6	9	36	42	40
Frickley Athletic	42	4	7	10	29	38	6	3	12	24	41	40
Droylsden	42	7	3	11	30	43	3	5	13	26	50	38
Whitley Bay	42	4	5	12	20	39	4	3	14	26	58	32
Horwich RMI	42	4	3	14	25	47	5	1	15	24	47	31

FIRST DIVISION

		Home					*Away*					*Total*
	P	W	D	L	F	A	W	D	L	F	A	Pts
Blyth Spartans	42	14	5	2	54	27	12	4	5	41	28	87
Bamber Bridge	42	14	5	2	56	19	11	5	5	45	32	85
Warrington Town	42	14	5	2	42	19	11	4	6	32	21	84
Alfreton Town	42	15	3	3	53	24	10	4	7	41	25	82
Lancaster City	42	13	4	4	44	18	10	6	5	37	26	79
Worksop Town	42	15	2	4	63	29	4	12	5	32	39	71
Radcliffe Borough	42	8	5	8	37	37	10	5	6	39	33	64
Ashton United	42	12	4	5	44	25	6	4	11	36	45	62
Netherfield	42	9	5	7	33	30	8	2	11	21	26	58
Eastwood Town	42	9	7	5	40	26	5	6	10	27	35	55
Gretna	42	6	8	7	36	36	8	5	8	28	30	55
Atherton LR	42	8	5	8	33	27	6	3	12	27	40	50
Harrogate Town	42	10	1	10	35	40	4	7	10	22	38	50
Caernarfon Town	42	6	6	9	26	29	7	4	10	32	33	49
Curzon Ashton	42	8	8	5	39	33	2	8	11	25	47	46
Great Harwood Town	42	7	6	8	37	50	4	7	10	29	37	46
Congleton Town	42	3	7	11	22	38	8	6	7	30	37	46
Fleetwood (3)	42	9	5	7	27	21	3	6	12	24	53	44
Farsley Celtic	42	7	5	9	36	38	5	2	14	30	62	43
Workington	42	6	3	12	31	41	6	3	12	30	50	42
Goole Town	42	7	5	9	30	36	4	2	15	16	45	40
Mossley (1)	42	7	3	11	25	29	4	2	15	27	61	37

(-) points deducted for breach of rule

Leading goalscorers

Premier Division

Lge	*Cup*	*Tot*	
31	15	46	John Coleman (Morecambe)
31	5	36	Andy Whittaker (Barrow)
29	10	39	Jim McCluskie (Morecambe)
24	9	33	Ged Kimmins (Hyde United)
23	7	30	Brian Ross (Marine)
22	10	32	Geoff Horsfield (Guiseley)
21	14	35	David Laws (Bishop Auckland)
20	15	35	Colin Little (Hyde United)
20	6	26	Tony McDonald (Chorley)
19	4	23	Darren Hunton (Boston United)
17	5	22	David Nolan (Hyde United)
17	4	21	Paul Beck (Accrington Stanley)
16	4	20	Colin Bishop (Gainsborough Trinity)
16	1	17	Grant Morrow (Gainsborough Trinity)

First Division

Lge	*Cup*	*Tot*	
36	21	57	Kenny Clark (Worksop Town)
30	6	36	Keith Evans (Ashton United)
24	10	34	Robbie Whellans (Farsley Celtic)
23	6	29	Tony Carroll (Barber Bridge–12 + 1 for Radcliffe Borough)
21	11	32	Stephen Pyle (Blyth Spartans)
21	8	29	Richie Bond (Blyth Spartans)
20	4	24	Mark Edwards (Bamber Bridge–15 + 2 for Horwich RMI/Ashton Utd)
20	1	21	Martin Henderson (Workington)
20	1	21	John McFadzean (Alfreton Town)
18	15	33	Stuart Diggle (Lancaster City)
17	7	24	Chris Shaw (Ashton United)
17	5	22	Ian Lunt (Radcliffe Borough)
17	4	21	Paul Heavey (Warrington Town)

UNIBOND LEAGUE—PREMIER DIVISION RESULTS 1994–95

	Accrington Stanley	Barrow	Bishop Auckland	Boston United	Buxton	Chorley	Colwyn Bay	Droylsden	Emley	Frickley Athletic	Gainsborough Trinity	Guiseley	Horwich RMI	Hyde United	Knowsley United	Marine	Matlock Town	Morecambe	Spennymoor United	Whitley Bay	Winsford United	Witton United
Accrington Stanley	—	5-2	1-4	0-4	1-0	1-1	1-3	2-1	1-1	1-1	1-2	1-4	3-0	1-0	2-2	1-5	0-2	0-4	0-1	4-1	2-2	1-2
Barrow	2-2	—	2-1	2-5	4-2	2-1	5-0	1-1	1-0	1-2	1-0	2-3	1-0	1-1	2-3	0-3	3-1	0-1	1-1	4-0	2-1	0-1
Bishop Auckland	2-0	3-0	—	0-0	2-2	2-2	3-3	0-1	2-2	2-0	1-1	0-1	2-1	0-2	0-2	0-1	3-1	0-3	0-0	2-2	2-1	0-1
Boston United	4-2	3-1	1-2	—	0-1	2-0	5-2	5-1	1-2	5-0	2-2	2-2	4-0	2-1	6-1	1-1	2-0	0-2	2-3	2-1	0-0	1-1
Buxton	0-1	1-0	2-2	0-0	—	1-2	4-2	2-2	0-1	3-2	0-4	3-2	4-0	1-2	1-0	0-2	4-0	1-2	3-0	2-1	1-1	1-1
Chorley	1-2	3-1	1-1	0-1	0-1	—	3-2	2-4	2-3	2-3	0-2	2-4	2-3	1-0	3-1	1-4	0-1	1-4	1-2	1-4	2-0	0-2
Colwyn Bay	3-3	1-2	1-3	0-1	1-2	3-2	—	3-2	3-0	1-2	0-0	2-4	3-1	1-0	1-1	0-1	0-4	0-0	2-1	5-1	1-0	2-2
Droylsden	1-3	1-0	1-4	1-0	1-2	0-0	1-3	—	0-0	2-1	2-6	1-3	2-1	3-3	1-3	1-4	3-2	3-2	1-2	0-1	5-1	0-2
Emley	0-0	2-1	1-4	1-4	2-0	1-4	1-0	3-1	—	2-0	3-2	1-0	1-1	1-3	3-3	0-0	0-1	0-0	5-1	4-0	1-1	0-0
Frickley Athletic	1-1	1-2	2-2	1-1	1-1	3-3	1-2	2-0	3-2	—	1-2	2-1	1-2	1-2	2-2	0-1	0-1	1-4	0-2	1-5	3-0	2-2
Gainsborough Trinity	0-1	4-3	2-2	2-0	0-2	3-2	6-1	2-2	3-0	1-1	—	0-1	1-0	1-1	2-1	0-0	3-2	0-0	0-3	2-2	1-1	1-0
Guiseley	4-0	2-1	2-1	2-1	3-1	2-1	3-2	2-0	2-0	2-1	1-0	—	1-2	3-3	5-0	2-1	3-0	2-2	1-1	6-3	5-1	1-1
Horwich RMI	1-5	1-6	0-2	0-4	4-1	6-0	0-1	2-2	4-4	0-3	2-1	0-2	—	0-1	1-2	1-4	0-3	0-2	0-0	2-3	1-0	0-1
Hyde United	4-1	3-1	1-0	1-0	4-2	2-3	4-3	5-2	1-1	6-0	5-1	1-2	2-1	—	3-0	1-2	6-3	1-4	1-1	3-0	1-2	2-1
Knowsley United	0-0	0-2	2-3	2-2	1-3	1-2	2-2	3-0	4-2	0-3	4-2	2-1	2-1	1-2	—	1-1	0-0	1-1	2-0	3-0	0-5	1-4
Marine	2-1	4-0	2-0	2-1	1-1	3-1	1-0	4-1	2-1	2-0	1-4	1-1	2-0	1-1	1-0	—	3-0	2-1	1-0	2-0	2-1	4-1
Matlock Town	0-1	1-1	4-0	0-1	2-1	2-2	1-2	3-2	5-1	0-2	2-1	2-3	3-2	0-1	3-3	0-0	—	0-2	1-2	5-1	0-2	0-1
Morecambe	3-0	1-3	1-0	2-1	1-1	2-0	1-1	4-0	2-1	3-1	4-0	2-2	7-1	1-3	1-1	0-0	5-0	—	3-2	2-0	6-1	5-2
Spennymoor United	5-1	0-1	1-0	1-1	4-1	2-2	5-2	2-1	2-1	2-0	1-1	1-1	2-1	1-1	2-1	0-3	2-1	1-3	—	4-0	1-1	2-1
Whitley Bay	0-0	3-1	1-4	0-1	1-3	2-1	0-2	0-1	0-3	2-2	2-2	0-1	0-3	2-2	5-3	0-4	0-2	0-2	1-0	—	0-1	1-1
Winsford United	2-2	3-0	0-4	1-2	1-2	1-3	0-1	2-1	2-3	2-0	2-0	2-2	2-3	5-1	2-2	2-2	2-4	0-2	1-2	1-1	—	1-0
Witton Albion	0-0	0-3	1-3	0-0	1-2	1-4	1-4	1-1	2-2	2-0	1-2	1-2	2-1	2-2	1-1	1-1	2-0	1-2	2-1	3-0	2-0	—

UNIBOND CHALLENGE CUP

First Round
Alfreton Town 0, Worksop Town 0
(*after 2-2 draw; aet, Worksop won 4-3 on penalties*)
Ashton United 1, Congleton Town 2
Atherton LR 3, Radcliffe Borough 0
Blyth Spartans 1, Bamber Bridge 2
Caernarfon Town 3, Mossley 0
Eastwood Town 3, Harrogate Town 0
Goole Town 1, Farsley Celtic 2
Great Harwood Town 5, Horwich RMI 2
Guiseley 2, Fleetwood 1
Lancaster City 4, Gretna 0 (*after 2-2 draw*)
Warrington Town 3, Curzon Ashton 0
Workington 4, Netherfield 1

Second Round
Accrington Stanley 2, Hyde United 0
Atherton LR 0, Barrow 1 (*after 2-2 draw*)
Bamber Bridge 2, Whitley Bay 1
Bishop Auckland 5, Frickley Athletic 2
Boston United 2, Matlock Town 1
Buxton 1, Droylsden 0
Caernarfon Town 0, Warrington Town 1 (*aet and a 1-1 draw*)
Chorley 3, Guiseley 2
Colwyn Bay 2, Congleton Town 1
Emley 3, Spennymoor United 0
Farsley Celtic 1, Gainsborough Trinity 0
Great Harwood Town 0, Marine 1
Knowsley United 3, Morecambe 1
Lancaster City 3, Workington 0
Witton Albion 3, Winsford United 1
Worksop Town 2, Eastwood Town 1

Third Round
Accrington Stanley 4, Farsley Celtic 2
Bamber Bridge 2, Marine 1 (*after 2-2 draw*)
Chorley 1, Lancaster City 0
Colwyn Bay 1, Knowsley United 4
Emley 2, Bishop Auckland 3 (*after 2-2 draw*)
Matlock Town 3, Worksop Town 2
Warrington Town 2, Barrow 1
Witton Albion 2, Buxton 3

Fourth Round
Accrington Stanley 3, Bishop Auckland 5 (*aet and a 1-1 draw*)
Bamber Bridge 3, Knowsley United 2
Buxton 0, Matlock Town 4
Chorley 2, Warrington Town 0 (*after 0-0 draw*)

Semi-finals (two legs)
Bamber Bridge 7, Chorley 2
Chorley 2, Bamber Bridge 0
(*Bamber Bridge won 7-4 on aggregate*)
Bishop Auckland 0, Matlock Town 2
Matlock Town 1, Bishop Auckland 4

Final
Bamber Bridge 2, Bishop Auckland 1 (*at Bolton Wanderers*)

UNIBOND PRESIDENT'S CUP

First Round
Barrow 1, Lancaster City 3
Bishop Auckland 0, Ashton United 2
Frickley Athletic 1, Boston United 2
Hyde United 3, Alfreton Town 0 (*after 2-2 draw*)
Marine 3, Warrington Town 0
Morecambe 3, Netherfield 2
Spennymoor United 3, Guiseley 1
Witton Albion 8, Colwyn Bay 1

Second Round
Boston United 3, Hyde United 0
Marine 0, Lancaster City 1
Morecambe 3, Witton Albion 5
Spennymoor United 2, Ashton United 1

Semi-finals
Boston United 1, Witton Albion 1
Witton Albion 2, Boston United 1
Lancaster City 3, Spennymoor United 1
Spennymoor United 2, Lancaster City 1
(*Lancaster City won 4-3 on aggregate*)

Final (two legs)
Witton Albion 0, Lancaster City 0
Lancaster City 3, Witton Albion 2
(*aet; Lancaster City won 3-2 on aggregate*)

UNIFILLA FIRST DIVISION CUP

First Round
Blyth Spartans 2, Workington 0
Congleton Town 0, Caernarfon Town 3
Harrogate Town 0, Farsley Celtic 1
Mossley 0, Curzon Ashton 2 (*after 2-2 draw*)
Radcliffe Borough 2, Gretna 0 (*after 2-2 draw*)
Worksop Town 5, Goole Town 1

Second Round
Bamber Bridge 1, Great Harwood Town 3
Blyth Spartans 3, Radcliffe Borough 2
Caernarfon Town 2, Warrington Town 0 (*after 0-0 draw*)
Curzon Ashton 0, Ashton United 3 (*after 1-1 draw*)
Eastwood Town 1, Alfreton Town 2
Fleetwood Town 3, Atherton LR 2
Lancaster City 2, Netherfield 4
Worksop Town 6, Farsley Celtic 1

Third Round
Blyth Spartans 2, Ashton United 0
Caernarfon Town 4, Netherfield 3
Great Harwood Town 4, Fleetwood 0
Worksop Town 2, Alfreton Town 5 (*after 2-2 draw*)

Semi-finals (two legs)
Great Harwood Town 3, Caernarfon Town 4
Caernarfon Town 0, Great Harwood Town 3
(*Great Harwood Town won 6-4 on aggregate*)
Blyth Spartans 3, Alfreton Town 3
Alfreton Town 1, Blyth Spartans 3
(*Blyth Spartans won 6-4 on aggregate*)

Final (two legs)
Great Harwood Town 0, Blyth Spartans 1
Blyth Spartans 4, Great Harwood Town 2
(*Blyth Spartans won 5-2 on aggregate*)

BEAZER HOMES LEAGUE 1994–95

Premier Division

	P	W	D	L	F	A	Pts
Hednesford Town	42	28	9	5	99	49	93
Cheltenham Town	42	25	11	6	87	39	86
Burton Albion	42	20	15	7	55	39	75
Gloucester City	42	22	8	12	76	48	74
Rushden & Diamonds	42	19	11	12	99	65	68
Dorchester Town	42	19	10	13	84	61	67
Leek Town	42	19	10	13	72	60	67
Gresley Rovers	42	17	12	13	70	63	63
Cambridge City	42	18	8	16	60	55	62
Worcester City	42	14	15	13	46	34	57
Crawley Town	42	15	10	17	64	71	55
Hastings Town	42	13	14	15	55	57	53
Halesowen Town	42	14	10	18	81	80	52
Gravesend & Northfleet	42	13	13	16	38	55	52
Chelmsford City	42	14	6	22	56	60	48
Atherstone United	42	12	12	18	51	67	48
VS Rugby	42	11	14	17	49	61	47
Sudbury Town	42	12	10	20	50	77	46
Solihull Borough	42	10	15	17	39	65	45
Sittingbourne	42	11	10	21	51	73	43
Trowbridge Town	42	9	13	20	43	69	40
Corby Town*	42	4	10	28	36	113	21

(*Corby Town—one point deducted—ineligible player[s])

Midland Division

	P	W	D	L	F	A	Pts
Newport AFC	42	29	8	5	106	39	95
Ilkeston Town	42	25	6	11	101	75	81
Tamworth	42	24	8	10	98	70	80
Moor Green	42	23	8	11	105	63	77
Bridgnorth Town	42	22	10	10	75	49	76
Buckingham Town	42	20	14	8	55	37	74
Nuneaton Borough	42	19	11	12	76	55	68
Rothwell Town	42	19	7	16	71	71	64
King's Lynn	42	18	8	16	76	64	62
Racing Club Warwick	42	17	11	14	68	63	62
Dudley Town	42	17	10	15	65	69	61
Bilston Town	42	17	8	17	73	64	59
Bedworth United	42	17	7	18	64	68	58
Evesham United	42	14	10	18	57	56	52
Hinckley Town	42	14	10	18	61	76	52
Stourbridge	42	15	7	20	59	77	52
Sutton Coldfield Town	42	12	10	20	62	72	46
Forest Green Rovers	42	11	13	18	56	76	46
Redditch United	42	8	14	20	47	64	38
Leicester United	42	10	8	24	51	99	38
Grantham Town	42	8	9	25	55	93	33
Armitage	42	2	5	35	35	116	11

Southern Division

	P	W	D	L	F	A	Pts
Salisbury City	42	30	7	5	88	37	97
Baldock Town	42	28	10	4	92	44	94
Havant Town	42	25	10	7	81	34	85
Waterlooville	42	24	8	10	77	36	80
Ashford Town	42	21	12	9	106	72	75
Weston-Super-Mare	42	18	13	11	82	54	67
Bashley	42	18	11	13	62	49	65
Weymouth	42	16	13	13	60	55	61
Newport IOW	42	17	10	15	67	67	61
Witney Town	42	14	14	14	57	57	56
Clevedon Town	42	14	13	15	73	64	55
Tonbridge Angels	42	14	12	16	74	87	54
Margate	42	15	7	20	60	72	52
Braintree Town	42	12	13	17	64	71	49
Wealdstone	42	13	8	21	76	94	47
Yate Town	42	11	13	18	57	75	46
Fisher 93	42	9	16	17	54	70	43
Bury Town	42	11	8	23	59	86	41
Erith & Belvedere	42	10	9	23	49	94	39
Poole Town	42	10	8	24	53	79	38
Fareham Town	42	10	8	24	46	91	38
Burnham	42	7	7	28	40	89	28

LEADING GOALSCORERS

(LEAGUE AND CUP)

Premier Division

J. O'Connor (Hednesford Town)	35
O. Pickard (Dorchester Town)	29
I. Wheaton (Leek Town)	27
D. Watkins (Rushden & Diamonds)	26
S. Lovell (Sittingbourne)	21
J. Smith (Cheltenham Town)	21

Midland Division

P. Davies (Moor Green)	38
D. Taylor (Ilkeston Town)	35
C. Williams (Newport AFC)	33
G. Piggott (Dudley Town)	29
R. Straw (Nuneaton Borough)	26
J. Symonds (Bedworth United)	24

Southern Division

D. Arter (Ashford Town)	37
S. Cuggy (Margate)	36
S. Devine (Fisher 93)	30
S. Lovell (Salisbury City)	26
S. Penny (Clevedon Town)	26
M. Stanton (Ashford Town)	25
E. Fearon (Newport IOW)	23
N. Selby (Waterlooville)	23

ATTENDANCES

Premier Division

Aggregate: 293,435
Highest individual: Rushden & Diamonds 1521.

Midland Division

Aggregate: 146,951
Highest individual: Newport AFC 1191.

Southern Division

Aggregate: 116,731
Highest individual: Weymouth 796.

BEAZER HOMES PREMIER DIVISION RESULTS 1994–95

	Atherstone United	Burton Albion	Cambridge City	Chelmsford City	Cheltenham Town	Corby Town	Crawley Town	Dorchester Town	Gloucester City	Gravesend & Northfleet	Gresley Rovers	Halesowen Town	Hastings Town	Hednesford Town	Leek Town	Rushden & Diamonds	Sittingbourne	Solihull Borough	Sudbury Town	Trowbridge Town	VS Rugby	Worcester City
Atherstone United	—	1-2	0-2	1-1	2-4	4-0	0-0	0-1	1-0	3-0	1-2	1-1	1-3	1-3	1-1	1-7	3-1	2-0	3-0	1-2	1-1	0-0
Burton Albion	1-1	—	0-0	2-1	2-0	3-2	1-0	1-1	0-1	2-1	2-1	0-0	1-1	2-4	1-1	2-2	1-0	2-0	1-1	2-0	3-1	0-1
Cambridge City	0-2	2-0	—	1-0	0-1	2-1	2-1	2-1	0-1	1-0	0-1	2-2	1-0	1-1	5-1	2-3	4-1	2-4	1-1	4-0	2-0	0-2
Chelmsford City	4-1	0-4	2-0	—	1-2	5-0	1-2	3-1	0-2	1-2	2-4	4-3	0-0	1-2	2-2	2-2	2-1	3-1	1-0	0-1	3-2	1-0
Cheltenham Town	2-2	1-2	1-1	1-0	—	8-0	1-2	1-1	1-1	2-0	1-1	3-0	6-0	2-0	1-0	3-0	2-1	2-0	3-0	3-2	1-0	1-1
Corby Town	0-0	1-1	1-2	1-4	2-2	—	1-1	2-4	0-6	0-2	1-2	0-2	1-1	3-1	0-1	0-4	2-1	1-2	3-4	1-1	1-0	2-1
Crawley Town	2-1	3-4	1-0	1-0	1-1	2-2	—	2-1	0-1	1-2	1-1	5-1	5-2	2-4	0-1	2-4	2-0	0-1	2-0	4-2	1-0	1-0
Dorchester Town	2-3	0-1	0-1	1-0	1-4	5-0	5-2	—	4-2	4-5	1-1	3-1	3-1	0-0	2-1	4-2	3-1	1-1	3-0	1-3	3-1	1-1
Gloucester City	4-0	1-0	5-1	2-0	1-2	2-2	4-1	0-3	—	3-3	3-3	1-2	1-0	2-2	2-0	1-0	0-0	1-2	3-0	2-0	3-0	1-2
Gravesend & Northfleet	2-1	0-1	1-1	1-0	0-1	1-0	0-2	2-1	1-0	—	1-0	1-1	0-0	0-0	1-1	0-1	1-1	0-0	3-0	0-0	0-0	0-0
Gresley Rovers	1-2	1-1	3-1	1-0	1-4	1-0	2-4	1-3	3-2	0-0	—	3-2	3-2	1-2	2-1	4-3	1-1	5-1	0-1	5-1	2-2	0-0
Halesowen Town	3-0	0-1	1-0	3-2	1-1	4-1	2-2	2-5	1-1	4-1	1-4	—	1-2	1-2	4-5	2-4	3-0	4-2	5-1	2-0	5-0	0-3
Hastings Town	3-1	1-1	4-3	0-1	3-1	1-1	2-2	2-1	2-1	1-2	2-0	3-1	—	0-0	1-2	0-2	1-1	3-0	4-1	1-0	1-1	1-1
Hednesford Town	6-1	5-1	2-1	2-1	3-1	4-1	2-1	0-0	1-3	5-1	2-1	3-2	2-1	—	3-0	5-2	2-1	5-0	1-1	4-1	2-0	1-1
Leek Town	2-1	0-1	4-1	0-3	1-3	6-1	3-0	4-5	3-1	2-0	1-1	3-0	1-0	1-3	—	3-3	2-0	0-1	4-1	3-0	0-0	0-0
Rushden & Diamonds	2-2	2-2	2-1	3-1	0-2	6-1	5-0	2-1	1-2	6-2	0-1	1-1	3-1	2-3	5-0	—	5-0	3-1	2-2	2-1	4-1	1-1
Sittingbourne	1-0	0-2	1-1	2-3	0-3	4-0	3-1	1-2	2-1	4-0	0-0	3-2	2-1	3-2	0-0	3-1	—	2-1	0-4	4-1	1-1	1-2
Solihull Borough	0-1	1-1	0-2	1-1	0-0	0-0	1-1	2-4	1-2	0-0	0-0	2-2	1-3	2-2	1-2	0-0	2-1	—	1-1	1-0	0-3	1-0
Sudbury Town	0-2	0-1	1-2	1-0	1-5	5-1	0-0	1-1	0-1	2-0	2-1	0-4	1-0	3-2	1-3	1-0	2-2	0-1	—	2-4	3-1	0-0
Trowbridge Town	0-0	0-0	1-2	1-0	1-2	2-0	1-1	1-1	1-2	2-0	3-2	2-2	0-0	1-2	1-1	1-1	1-1	0-0	4-3	—	1-3	0-1
VS Rugby	1-1	0-0	1-1	0-0	2-0	3-0	3-1	1-0	3-3	0-2	6-3	0-2	0-0	0-3	1-3	2-0	2-0	2-3	2-2	0-0	—	2-0
Worcester City	0-1	1-0	1-3	3-0	2-2	3-0	4-2	0-0	0-1	1-0	0-1	3-1	1-1	0-1	1-3	1-1	4-0	1-1	0-1	3-0	0-1	—

DR. MARTENS CUP

Preliminary Round First Leg
Tonbridge 1, Margate 4
Armitage 1, Racing Club Warwick 1

Preliminary Round Second Leg
Margate 3, Tonbridge 1
Racing Club Warwick 2, Armitage 1

First Round First Leg
Hastings Town 2, Gravesend & Northfleet 1
Ashford Town 2, Erith & Belvedere 1
Fisher 93 1, Margate 5
Sittingbourne 0, Crawley Town 1
Cambridge City 2, Grantham Town 1
Sudbury Town 3, Wealdstone 3
Chelmsford City 3, Buckingham Town 1
King's Lynn 3, Corby Town 1
Newport AFC 0, Forest Green 2
Yate Town 0, Cheltenham Town 1
Salisbury City 2, Bashley 2
Dorchester Town 2, Newport IOW 0
Tamworth 2, Witney Town 1
Poole Town 0, Waterlooville 3
Fareham Town 2, Havant Town 0
Trowbridge 0, Weymouth 2
Dudley Town 1, Redditch United 1
Nuneaton Borough 3, VS Rugby 3
Weston-Super-Mare 0, Worcester City 2
Clevedon Town 0, Gloucester City 1
Rushden & Diamonds 0, Rothwell Town 0
Halesowen Town 1, Bedworth United 2
Burnham 0, Baldock Town 3
Bury Town 1, Braintree Town 1
Bilston Town 1, Ilkeston Town 0
Atherstone United 2, Hednesford Town 0
Solihull Borough 1, Burton Albion 1
Stourbridge 0, Bridgnorth Town 0
Hinckley Town 1, Gresley Rovers 0
Moor Green 0, Evesham United 1
Leicester United 3, Sutton Coldfield Town 3
Racing Club Warwick 1, Leek Town 2

First Round Second Leg
Gravesend & Northfleet 2, Hastings Town 2
Erith & Belvedere 1, Ashford Town 6
Margate 2, Fisher 93 2
Crawley Town 1, Sittingbourne 2
Grantham Town 1, Cambridge City 3
Wealdstone 1, Sudbury Town 2
Buckingham Town 2, Chelmsford City 1
Corby Town 0, King's Lynn 3
Forest Green 0, Newport AFC 3
Cheltenham Town 2, Yate Town 0
Bashley 2, Salisbury City 0
Newport IOW 2, Dorchester Town 1
Witney Town 3, Tamworth 1
Waterlooville 4, Poole Town 0
Havant Town 4, Fareham Town 0
Weymouth 1, Trowbridge 2
Redditch United 1, Dudley Town 5
VS Rugby 0, Nuneaton Borough 0
Worcester City 2, Weston-Super-Mare 1
Gloucester City 2, Clevedon Town 1
Rothwell Town 1, Rushden & Diamonds 2
Bedworth United 1, Halesowen Town 1
Baldock Town 0, Burnham 0
Braintree Town 3, Bury Town 1
Ilkeston Town 2, Bilston Town 3
Hednesford Town 1, Atherstone United 1
Burton Albion 1, Solihull Borough 2
Bridgnorth Town 3, Stourbridge 1
Gresley Rovers 1, Hinckley Town 3
Evesham United 1, Moor Green 0
Sutton Coldfield Town 1, Leicester United 2
Leek Town 4, Racing Club Warwick 0

Second Round
Hastings Town 3, Ashford Town 0
Margate 1, Sittingbourne 0
Cambridge City 2, Sudbury Town 3
Chelmsford City 3, King's Lynn 1
Newport AFC 2, Cheltenham Town 3
Bashley 2, Dorchester Town 2
Replay: Dorchester Town 2, Bashley 0
Witney Town 0, Waterlooville 1
Havant Town 2, Weymouth 2
Replay: Weymouth 2, Havant Town 1
Dudley Town 1, VS Rugby 1
Replay: VS Rugby 3, Dudley Town 0
Worcester City 2, Gloucester City 1
Rushden & Diamonds 4, Bedworth United 2
Baldock Town 3, Braintree Town 1
Bilston Town 0, Atherstone United 0
Replay: Atherstone United 3, Bilston Town 1
Solihull Borough 3, Bridgnorth Town 1
Hinckley Town 3, Evesham United 0
Leicester United 1, Leek Town 4

Third Round
Hastings Town 0, Margate 0
Replay: Margate 1, Hastings Town 3
Sudbury Town 1, Chelmsford City 2
Cheltenham Town 1, Dorchester Town 1
Replay: Dorchester Town 1, Cheltenham Town 2
Waterlooville 5, Weymouth 1
VS Rugby 1, Worcester City 3
Rushden & Diamonds 3, Baldock Town 0
Atherstone United 4, Solihull Borough 0
Hinckley Town 0, Leek Town 2

Fourth Round
Hastings Town 2, Chelmsford City 0
Cheltenham Town 0, Waterlooville 1
Worcester City 0, Rushden & Diamonds 0
Replay: Rushden & Diamonds 3, Worcester City 1
Atherstone United 0, Leek Town 1

Semi-final First Leg
Hastings Town 7, Waterlooville 2
Rushden & Diamonds 0, Leek Town 4

Semi-final Second Leg
Waterlooville 0, Hastings Town 1
Leek Town 0, Rushden & Diamonds 2

Final First Leg
Hastings Town 1, Leek Town 0

Final Second Leg
Leek Town 1, Hastings Town 2

DIADORA FOOTBALL LEAGUE 1994–95

Premier Division

		Home			*Away*			*Totals*			*Goals*		
	P	*W*	*D*	*L*	*W*	*D*	*L*	*W*	*D*	*L*	*F*	*A*	*Pts*
Enfield	42	14	5	2	14	4	3	28	9	5	106	43	93
Slough Town	42	13	6	2	9	7	5	22	13	7	82	56	79
Hayes	42	12	6	3	8	8	5	20	14	8	66	47	74
Aylesbury United	42	14	5	2	7	1	13	21	6	15	86	59	69
Hitchin Town	42	9	7	5	9	5	7	18	12	12	68	59	66
Bromley	42	10	5	6	8	6	7	18	11	13	76	67	65
St Albans City	42	13	5	3	4	8	9	17	13	12	96	81	64
Molesey	42	9	5	7	9	3	9	18	8	16	65	61	62
Yeading	42	7	8	6	7	7	7	14	15	13	60	59	57
Harrow Borough	42	10	2	9	7	4	10	17	6	19	64	67	57
Dulwich Hamlet	42	9	4	8	7	5	9	16	9	17	70	82	57
Carshalton Athletic	42	7	6	8	9	3	9	16	9	17	69	84	57
Kingstonian	42	10	2	9	6	6	9	16	8	18	62	57	56
Walton & Hersham	42	9	5	7	5	6	10	14	11	17	75	73	53
Sutton United	42	8	5	8	5	7	9	13	12	17	74	69	51
Purfleet	42	6	6	9	7	6	8	13	12	17	76	90	51
Hendon	42	8	7	6	4	7	10	12	14	16	57	65	50
Grays Athletic	42	4	8	9	7	8	6	11	16	15	57	61	49
Bishop's Stortford	42	8	5	8	4	6	11	12	11	19	53	76	47
Chesham United	42	7	5	9	5	4	12	12	9	21	60	87	45
Marlow	42	7	6	8	3	3	15	10	9	23	52	84	39
Wokingham Town	42	4	5	12	2	4	15	6	9	27	39	86	27

Division One

		Home			*Away*			*Totals*			*Goals*		
	P	*W*	*D*	*L*	*W*	*D*	*L*	*W*	*D*	*L*	*F*	*A*	*Pts*
Boreham Wood	42	17	3	1	14	2	5	31	5	6	90	38	98
Worthing	42	13	6	2	8	7	6	21	13	8	93	49	76
Chertsey Town	42	12	4	5	9	7	5	21	11	10	109	57	74
Aldershot Town	42	14	2	5	9	3	9	23	5	14	80	53	74
Billericay Town	42	9	5	7	11	4	6	20	9	13	68	52	69
Staines Town	42	8	6	7	9	6	6	17	12	13	83	65	63
Basingstoke Town	42	7	8	6	10	2	9	17	10	15	81	71	61
Tooting & Mitcham United	42	6	10	5	9	4	8	15	14	13	58	48	59
Wembley	42	8	4	9	8	7	6	16	11	15	70	61	59
Abingdon Town	42	10	6	5	6	5	10	16	11	15	67	69	59
Whyteleafe	42	11	4	6	6	3	12	17	7	18	70	78	58
Maidenhead United	42	11	3	7	4	9	8	15	12	15	73	76	57
Uxbridge	42	9	4	8	6	7	8	15	11	16	54	62	56
Leyton	42	8	6	7	7	4	10	15	10	17	67	66	55
Barking	42	8	4	9	8	3	10	16	7	19	74	77	55
Heybridge Swifts	42	9	4	8	7	2	12	16	6	20	73	78	54
Ruislip Manor	42	10	5	6	4	6	11	14	11	17	70	75	53
Bognor Regis Town	42	8	6	7	5	8	8	13	14	15	57	63	53
Berkhamsted Town	42	8	5	8	6	5	10	14	10	18	54	70	52
Newbury Town	42	7	6	8	5	9	7	12	15	15	58	71	51
Wivenhoe Town	42	6	4	11	2	3	16	8	7	27	47	94	31
Dorking	42	1	2	18	2	1	18	3	3	36	40	163	12

Division Two

		Home			*Away*			*Totals*			*Goals*		
	P	*W*	*D*	*L*	*W*	*D*	*L*	*W*	*D*	*L*	*F*	*A*	*Pts*
Thame United	42	17	1	3	13	2	6	30	3	9	97	49	93
Barton Rovers	42	13	4	4	12	3	6	25	7	10	93	51	82
Oxford City	42	10	6	5	14	2	5	24	8	10	86	47	80
Bracknell Town	42	10	4	7	13	5	3	23	9	10	86	47	78
Metropolitan Police	42	12	3	6	7	9	5	19	12	11	81	65	69
Hampton	42	11	3	7	9	6	6	20	9	13	79	74	69
Croydon	42	13	3	5	7	2	12	20	5	17	85	65	65
Banstead Athletic	42	10	4	7	8	6	7	18	10	14	73	59	64
Saffron Walden Town	42	12	6	3	5	7	9	17	13	12	64	59	64
Chalfont St Peter	42	8	6	7	9	6	6	17	12	13	67	54	63
Witham Town	42	10	4	7	8	5	8	18	9	15	75	64	63
Leatherhead	42	12	4	5	4	8	9	16	12	14	71	75	60
Edgware Town	42	8	5	8	8	5	8	16	10	16	70	66	58
Tilbury	42	10	8	3	5	1	15	15	9	18	62	82	54
Cheshunt	42	7	8	6	6	5	10	13	13	16	66	81	52
Ware	42	10	2	9	4	5	12	14	7	21	61	81	49
Egham Town	42	7	6	8	4	8	9	11	14	17	60	65	47
Hemel Hempstead	42	6	7	8	4	4	13	10	11	21	45	76	41
Hungerford Town	42	8	2	11	3	5	13	11	7	24	55	81	40
Windsor & Eton	42	6	5	10	4	3	14	10	8	24	58	84	38
Aveley	42	4	5	12	5	0	16	9	5	28	48	95	32
Maiden Vale	42	3	5	13	2	4	15	5	9	28	46	108	24

Division Three

		Home			Away			Totals			Goals		
	P	*W*	*D*	*L*	*W*	*D*	*L*	*W*	*D*	*L*	*F*	*A*	*Pts*
Collier Row	40	15	4	1	15	1	4	30	5	5	86	23	95
Canvey Island	40	14	4	2	14	0	6	28	4	8	88	42	88
Bedford Town	40	9	7	4	13	4	3	22	11	7	90	50	77
Northwood	40	12	4	4	10	4	6	22	8	10	80	47	74
Horsham	40	11	3	6	11	3	6	22	6	12	84	61	72
Southall	40	10	5	5	11	3	6	21	8	11	87	59	71
Leighton Town	40	9	4	7	11	4	5	20	8	12	66	43	68
Camberley Town	40	9	5	6	10	3	7	19	8	13	59	39	65
Kingsbury Town	40	10	4	6	8	7	5	18	11	11	72	54	65
Hornchurch	40	8	3	9	9	5	6	17	8	15	64	63	59
Clapton	40	8	6	6	6	5	9	14	11	15	69	61	53
Tring Town	40	9	4	7	4	8	8	13	12	15	68	69	51
East Thurrock United	40	8	2	10	6	6	8	14	8	18	60	79	50
Epsom & Ewell	40	5	6	9	8	4	8	13	10	17	58	62	49
Harlow Town	40	7	2	11	6	6	8	13	8	19	53	83	47
Harefield United	40	6	4	10	6	4	10	12	8	20	51	79	44
Hertford Town	40	8	3	9	3	7	10	11	10	19	56	78	43
Feltham & Hounslow	40	6	3	11	7	1	12	13	4	23	64	87	43
Flackwell Heath	40	6	2	12	2	2	16	8	4	28	50	99	28
Lewes	40	4	3	13	2	2	16	6	5	29	34	104	23
Cove	40	3	3	14	0	2	18	3	5	32	37	94	14

LEADING GOALSCORERS

Premier Division		*Lge*	*Lge Cup*	*Carlsberg*
34	Gary Abbott (Enfield)	34		
32	Shaun Marshall (Hitchin Town)	27	1	4
31	Mark West (Slough Town)	21	8	2
30	Steve Clark (St Albans City)	28	2	
29	David Crown (Purfleet)	28	1	
	Jim Bolton (Carshalton Athletic)	19	8	2
28	Neil Fraser (Harrow Borough)	25	1	2
	Brian Stein (Enfield)	22	2	4
	(*Includes 16 League, 2 League Cup & 4 Carlsberg Cup for St Albans City*)			
27	Dean Williams (Aylesbury United)	21	5	1
25	Ansil Bushay (Slough Town)	17	6	2
Division One				
34	Lee Charles (Chertsey Town)	30		4
26	Paul Coombs (Basingstoke Town)	23	1	2
25	Jeff Wood (Barking)	24	1	
	Mark Butler (Aldershot Town)	21	3	1
24	Mark Hynes (Whyteleafe)	23	1	
23	Steve Darlington (Staines Town)	16	2	5
20	Paul Battram (Billericay Town)	19		1
	Tony Samuels (Boreham Wood)	18		2
	(*Includes 1 League for Leyton*)			
Division Two				
32	Damon Miles (Ware)	31		1
28	Gordon Guile (Barton Rovers)	28		
24	Nigel Mott (Thame United)	24		
	Andy Shildrick (Thame United)	22		2
	Justin Day (Bracknell Town)	21		3
23	Micky Waite (Witham Town)	21	2	
Division Three				
36	Steve Fraser (Southall)	29	1	6
26	Andy Jones (Canvey Island)	23	2	1
25	Gary Sealey (Tring Town)	25		
24	Jason Reed (Bedford Town)	23	1	
23	Marc Salmon (Harlow Town)	21	1	1
21	Mark Ivers (Kingsbury Town)	21		

ATTENDANCES

Premier Division
Aggregate: 207,869
Highest Individual average: Enfield 894
Division One
Aggregate: 132,201
Highest Individual average: Aldershot Town 1853
Division Two
Aggregate: 46,113
Highest Individual average: Oxford City 194
Division Three
Aggregate: 47,520
Highest Individual average: Bedford Town 390

DIADORA FOOTBALL LEAGUE PREMIER DIVISION 1994–95

	Aylesbury United	Bishop's Stortford	Bromley	Carshalton Athletic	Chesham United	Dulwich Hamlet	Enfield	Grays Athletic	Harrow Borough	Hayes	Hendon	Hitchin Town	Kingstonian	Marlow	Molesey	Purfleet	St Albans City	Slough Town	Sutton United	Walton & Hersham	Wokingham Town	Yeading
Aylesbury United	—	3-0	3-2	5-0	5-1	5-3	3-3	2-0	3-0	2-0	1-0	2-1	2-0	0-0	2-4	1-1	0-0	3-3	3-0	4-0	4-1	1-2
Bishop's Stortford	2-1	—	2-1	3-4	0-3	3-3	1-1	0-1	0-2	2-2	1-2	1-0	2-1	2-0	3-1	2-5	1-2	2-2	1-1	0-2	5-1	2-0
Bromley	3-2	0-1	—	0-1	1-3	0-2	2-0	2-1	1-0	2-0	1-1	0-2	3-1	0-6	4-3	2-2	2-2	1-1	4-4	5-0	3-1	3-1
Carshalton Athletic	1-3	1-2	0-3	—	1-1	2-1	1-3	0-1	3-4	0-0	3-0	2-4	0-0	3-1	2-0	2-2	2-0	1-3	2-1	1-0	2-2	1-1
Chesham United	0-2	1-1	0-3	6-2	—	2-1	0-3	1-1	2-0	2-3	3-1	2-2	0-5	1-0	0-3	1-1	1-6	0-1	1-3	1-0	5-1	1-1
Dulwich Hamlet	4-3	0-2	2-2	1-2	1-0	—	1-2	1-1	2-3	4-2	1-0	0-1	1-5	3-2	3-2	2-2	4-1	0-2	4-2	4-3	1-1	1-3
Enfield	2-2	1-0	3-1	2-1	1-1	8-1	—	2-1	3-0	0-1	5-1	4-1	1-1	5-0	1-1	3-1	3-1	0-1	2-1	1-1	6-0	3-0
Grays Athletic	0-2	2-3	0-3	3-4	5-0	0-0	2-3	—	1-1	0-3	2-1	1-3	0-0	2-1	0-0	1-2	2-2	3-3	2-2	1-1	2-0	1-3
Harrow Borough	3-0	2-0	2-0	2-1	1-0	1-2	0-1	1-2	—	0-1	2-4	2-4	1-1	3-1	5-2	3-5	2-1	0-3	1-3	4-2	3-0	1-1
Hayes	2-0	1-0	2-2	5-0	2-0	1-1	1-4	1-2	1-1	—	1-1	0-0	1-0	2-0	3-2	4-1	1-1	3-1	2-1	2-0	1-0	1-3
Hendon	2-1	1-1	1-1	0-1	2-1	4-0	1-3	3-3	1-2	0-0	—	4-1	0-0	3-0	3-1	1-0	1-1	1-2	0-1	1-6	2-0	2-2
Hitchin Town	3-1	1-1	3-3	0-1	4-3	0-1	0-3	0-0	0-0	0-0	2-0	—	1-1	4-2	1-3	3-2	2-0	1-0	1-1	3-1	1-0	1-3
Kingstonian	2-0	1-0	1-0	0-1	5-1	0-1	3-2	1-0	3-1	1-1	1-2	3-1	—	2-1	0-1	0-1	3-5	0-3	1-1	2-5	5-0	0-1
Marlow	3-2	3-1	1-2	1-1	1-4	0-4	2-2	1-4	2-0	1-3	0-0	0-4	1-0	—	3-0	1-0	4-4	0-2	1-3	2-2	1-1	1-0
Molesey	1-3	4-0	1-1	4-1	1-2	1-0	0-2	1-1	2-0	0-2	1-1	0-0	1-2	2-1	—	1-2	3-2	0-2	1-1	2-1	1-0	1-0
Purfleet	0-3	3-3	2-1	4-4	3-1	1-2	2-2	0-3	4-2	1-2	3-3	1-3	0-3	3-1	0-1	—	0-4	3-0	2-2	2-5	4-3	2-2
St Albans City	2-1	5-0	1-2	3-1	4-2	3-2	1-2	1-1	1-0	1-1	3-2	3-3	8-3	3-2	0-2	2-0	—	3-1	3-2	2-2	6-2	1-1
Slough Town	1-0	1-0	4-1	3-3	5-2	1-1	1-4	2-0	1-1	3-1	2-2	3-2	2-1	4-0	3-1	2-4	1-1	—	3-2	0-0	1-0	5-3
Sutton United	1-3	5-0	1-2	3-2	1-2	4-2	0-2	2-2	2-1	3-3	3-1	0-0	4-1	1-2	2-3	1-2	5-1	1-1	—	0-0	0-2	2-0
Walton & Hersham	2-0	5-2	2-3	2-4	1-1	4-1	1-3	2-1	1-2	3-1	2-0	4-1	0-2	1-1	1-2	2-2	3-2	3-3	1-0	—	0-1	1-1
Wokingham Town	0-1	0-0	1-1	2-3	2-1	0-1	0-3	0-1	0-2	1-2	1-1	1-3	0-1	1-2	1-1	5-1	2-2	2-0	0-1	3-2	—	0-3
Yeading	4-2	1-1	1-3	3-2	1-1	1-1	4-2	1-1	0-3	1-1	0-1	0-1	1-0	0-0	0-4	1-0	7-2	0-0	2-1	0-1	1-1	—

DIADORA FOOTBALL LEAGUE CUP 1994–95

Preliminary Round
Aldershot Town 3, Bracknell Town 1
Barton Rovers 2, Egham Town 4
Chalfont St Peter 4, Kingsbury Town 1
Chertsey Town 2, Oxford City 3
Cheshunt 0, Ware 1
Clapton 2, Hemel Hempstead 3 *aet*
East Thurrock United 2, Banstead Athletic 0 *aet*
Epsom & Ewell 0, Hornchurch 0 *aet*
Feltham & Hounslow Borough 0 Leighton Town 0 *aet*
Hampton 1, Edgware Town 3
Harefield United 1, Hungerford Town 2
Hertford Town 1, Camberley Town 3
Horsham 2, Cove 0
Leatherhead 1, Canvey Island 2 *aet*
Lewes 1, Aveley 1 *aet*
Malden Vale 2, Harlow Town 4
Newbury Town 3, Metropolitan Police 0
Northwood 0, Bedford Town 1
Southall 2, Saffron Walden Town 6
Tilbury 1, Flackwell Heath 1 *aet*
Tring Town 1, Collier Row 3 *aet*
Windsor & Eton 3, Croydon 1
Witham Town 5, Thame United 4 *aet*

Replays
Aveley 1, Lewes 1 *aet*
(*Lewes won 5-4 on penalties*)
**Lewes removed from competition for playing an ineligible player.*
Flackwell Heath 3, Tilbury 0
Hornchurch 3, Epsom & Ewell 0
Leighton Town 1, Feltham & Hounslow Borough 1 *aet*
(*Leighton Town won 3-2 on penalties*)

First Round
Aldershot Town 4, Basingstoke 2
Aylesbury United 4, Whyteleafe 2
Barking 2, Wokingham Town 0
Bedford Town 2, Dulwich Hamlet 3 *aet*
Billericay Town 1, Purfleet 2
Bishop's Stortford 2, Marlow 6
Bognor Regis Town 4, Hemel Hempstead 1
Bromley 0, Oxford City 1
Carshalton Athletic 6, Flackwell Heath 0
Chalfont St Peter 2, Saffron Walden Town 3
Chesham United 2, Aveley 1 *aet*
Collier Row 2, Yeading 0
Dorking 1, Ware 0
East Thurrock United 2, Uxbridge 0
Edgware Town 3, Enfield 4
Egham Town 1, Wembley 2
Grays Athletic 2, Harlow Town 1
Hayes 0, Slough Town 1
Heybridge Swifts 2, Boreham Wood 0
Hitchin Town 3, Berkhamsted Town 1
Kingstonian 1, Abingdon Town 2
Leighton Town 0, Staines Town 2
Leyton 4, Camberley Town 0
Maidenhead United 0, Walton & Hersham 2
Molesey 1, Newbury Town 2
Ruislip Manor 2, Horsham 1 *aet*
St Albans City 2, Harrow Borough 1
Sutton United 1, Canvey Island 1 *aet*
Tooting & Mitcham United v Hornchurch
Witham Town 3, Windsor & Eton 1
Wivenhoe Town 0, Hungerford Town 2
Worthing 3, Hendon 3 *aet*

Replays
Canvey Island 2, Sutton United 4 *aet*
Hendon 2, Worthing 2 *aet*
(*Hendon won 3-1 on penalties*)

Second Round
Abingdon Town 2, St Albans City 3
Aldershot Town 2, Walton & Hersham 1 *aet*
Carshalton Athletic 7, Dorking 0
Grays Athletic 5, Saffron Walden Town 1
Heybridge Swifts 1, Aylesbury United 2
Hungerford Town 0, Dulwich Hamlet 6
Leyton 2, Hendon 1 *aet*
Marlow 2, Newbury Town 1 *aet*
Oxford City 2, Chesham United 1
Purfleet 2, East Thurrock United 0
Ruislip Manor 1, Sutton United 3
Slough Town 4, Collier Row 0
Staines Town 4, Barking 1
Tooting & Mitcham United 1, Hitchin Town 2
Wembley 2, Bognor Regis Town 1
Witham Town 0, Enfield 5

Third Round
Aldershot Town 3, Staines Town 2
Aylesbury United 2, Grays Athletic 0
Carshalton Athletic 3, Enfield 1
Dulwich Hamlet 3, Wembley 2
Leyton 1, Marlow 2
Oxford City 1, St Albans City 2
Purfleet 1, Hitchin Town 2 *aet*
Slough Town 5, Sutton United 1

Fourth Round
Aldershot Town 1, Aylesbury United 2
Carshalton Athletic 1, Dulwich Hamlet 1 *aet*
Marlow 2, Hitchin Town 0
St Albans City 3, Slough Town 4

Replay
Dulwich Hamlet 5, Carshalton Athletic 1

Semi-finals First Leg
Aylesbury United 4, Marlow 0
Slough Town 3, Dulwich Hamlet 1

Semi-finals Second Leg
Dulwich Hamlet 1, Slough Town 2
(*Slough Town won 5-2 on aggregate*)
Marlow 2, Aylesbury United 2
(*Aylesbury United won 6-2 on aggregate*)

Final
Aylesbury United 1, Slough Town 1 *aet*
(*Aylesbury United won 7-6 on penalties*)
(*at Marlow FC*)

CARLSBERG CUP 1994–95

First Round
Billericay Town 2, Barking 0
Bognor Regis Town 1, Aldershot Town 2
Boreham Wood 2, Wivenhoe Town 1
Chertsey Town 1, Newbury Town 0
Chesham United 3, Grays Athletic 1
Dorking 3, Dulwich Hamlet 1
Hitchin Town 2, Enfield 1
Maidenhead United 1, Tooting & Mitcham United 3
Uxbridge 1, St Albans City 5
Walton & Hersham 5, Marlow 1
Whyteleafe 0, Basingstoke Town 3
Yeading 2, Wembley 1

Second Round
Berkhamsted Town 1, Bishop's Stortford 1 *aet*
(*Berkhamsted Town won 6-5 on penalties*)
Billericay Town 2, Heybridge Swifts 1 *aet*
Boreham Wood 3, Purfleet 1
Carshalton Athletic 2, Tooting & Mitcham United 0
Chertsey Town 2, Aldershot Town 0
Chesham United 1, Harrow Borough 5
Hendon 5, Aylesbury United 1
Hitchin Town 3, Leyton 1
Kingstonian 1, Sutton United 3
Molesey 3, Bromley 3 *aet*
(*Molesey won 4-3 on penalties*)

St Albans City 1, Ruislip Manor 1 *aet*
(*Ruislip Manor won 4-2 on penalties*)
Staines Town 6, Dorking 0
Walton & Hersham 5, Abingdon Town 4 *aet*
Wokingham Town 1, Basingstoke Town 4
Worthing 3, Slough Town 6
Yeading 2, Hayes 3

Third Round
Basingstoke Town 3, Sutton United 5 *aet*
Berkhamsted Town 1, Billericay Town 1 *aet*
(*Berkhamsted Town won 5-4 on penalties*)
Chertsey Town 3, Slough Town 2 *aet*
Hendon 0, Boreham Wood 2
Hitchin Town 3, Harrow Borough 1
Molesey 1, Walton & Hersham 0
Ruislip Manor 1, Hayes 4
Staines Town 5, Carshalton Athletic 1

Fourth Round
Berkhamsted Town 0, Boreham Wood 1
Hitchin Town 2, Hayes 2 *aet*
(*Hayes won 4-3 on penalties*)
Staines Town 3, Molesey 0
Sutton United 2, Chertsey Town 1

Semi-finals
Hayes 1, Boreham Wood 2
Sutton United 2, Staines Town 3 *aet*

Final
Staines Town 3, Boreham Wood 3 *aet*
(*Staines Town won 4-2 on penalties*)
(*at Harrow Borough FC*)

CARLSBERG TROPHY 1994–95

First Round
Cheshunt 1, East Thurrock United 1 *aet*
(*East Thurrock United won 3-2 on penalties*)
Croydon 3, Leatherhead 1
Hampton 2, Metropolitan Police 3
Hertford Town 2, Barton Rovers 1
Horsham 1, Bracknell Town 2
Leighton Town 2, Tring Town 1
Lewes 5, Banstead Athletic 2 *aet*
Oxford City 4, Epsom & Ewell 1
Saffron Walden Town 1, Collier Row 3
Southall 4, Clapton 2
Windsor & Eton 0, Camberley Town 2

Second Round
Canvey Island 2, Witham Town 2 *aet*
Chalfont St Peter 1, Hungerford Town 1 *aet*
(*Hungerford Town won 3-1 on penalties*)
Croydon 3, Oxford City 1
(*Croydon removed from competition for playing an ineligible player*)
Edgware Town 3, Collier Row 5 *aet*
Feltham & Hounslow Borough 1, Bracknell Town 3
Flackwell Heath 6, Cove 1
Harefield United 1, Egham Town 3
Harlow Town 3, Hertford Town 1
Hemel Hempstead 1, Kingsbury Town 1 *aet*
(*Hemel Hempstead won 5-4 on penalties*)
Leighton Town 1, Bedford Town 1 *aet*
(*Leighton Town wn 4-1 on penalties*)
Lewes 3, Malden Vale 1
Northwood 0, Metropolitan Police 1
Southall 3, East Thurrock United 0
Thame United 4, Camberley Town 1
Tilbury 3, Aveley 0
Ware 2, Hornchurch 5 *aet*

Replay
Witham Town 4, Canvey Island 2 *aet*

Third Round
Flackwell Heath 1, Egham Town 0
Harlow Town 1, Leighton Town 3
Hornchurch 0, Collier Row 2
Hungerford Town 1, Bracknell Town 0
Metropolitan Police 5, Lewes 3
Southall 0, Witham Town 0 *aet*
(*Southall won 6-5 on penalties*)
Thame United 2, Oxford City 1
Tilbury 1, Hemel Hempstead 4

Fourth Round
Flackwell Heath 2, Hungerford Town 2 *aet*
(*Hungerford Town won 3-2 on penalties*)
Hemel Hempstead 1, Collier Row 2
Leighton Town 1, Southall 3
Thame United 1, Metropolitan Police 2 *aet*

Semi-finals
Hungerford Town 0, Collier Row 3
Metropolitan Police 2, Southall 2 *aet*

Replay
Southall 1, Metropolitan Police 2

Final
Metropolitan Police 1, Collier Row 1 *aet*
(*Metropolitan Police won 4-3 on penalties*)
(*at Boreham Wood FC*)

NEW SPONSOR FOR ISTHMIAN LEAGUE

ICIS (pronounced 'eye-siss'), which manufactures football strips, takes over from Diadora as sponsor of the Isthmian Football League.

ICIS Sportswear Limited is based on the fringe of the Lake District. In addition to football clothing they make leisurewear for the sport and corporate markets. They are a subsidiary of one of the UK's leading sales promotion companies—ICIS Limited—Innovative Consumer Incentive Services—who have a variety of 'blue chip' clients.

Although ICIS acquired the sportswear company less than 12 months ago, it has a 20 year history of manufacturing football clothing under the name of New Olympic.

The new management has restructured the business to cater for larger clubs and the corporate sector. They sell direct to football clubs—providing both 'off-the-shelf' and 'bespoke' designs.

For 1995/96 the company has introduced new fabrics and shirt designs—from traditional to modern.

FA UMBRO TROPHY 1994–95

Preliminary Round
Chester-le-Street Town v Tow Law Town 2-4
Fisher 93 v Whyteleafe 1-1, 0-1
Poole Town v Havant Town 1-2
(at Havant Town)

First Qualifying Round
Whitley Bay v Bamber Bridge 0-4
Bedlington Terriers v Peterlee Newtown 2-1
West Auckland Town v Shildon 5-0
Harrogate Town v Eppleton CW 4-0
Tow Law Town v Lancaster City 2-3
Consett v RTM Newcastle 0-0, 0-2
Guisborough Town v Murton 2-0
Hebburn v Prudhoe Town 2-1
Accrington Stanley v Emley 1-0
Workington v Great Harwood Town 2-2, 2-4
Dunston Federation Brewery v Netherfield 2-0
Bridgnorth Town v Sutton Coldfield Town 2-0
Leicester United v Caernarfon Town 2-2, 2-1
Goole Town v Knowsley United 1-1, 2-6
Gresley Rovers v Congleton Town 3-1
Chorley v Bilston Town 2-0
Redditch United v Eastwood Town 0-1
Mossley v Dudley Town 2-2, 5-4
Farsley Celtic v Droylsden 1-1, 3-6
Fleetwood v Radcliffe Borough 3-0
Horwich RMI v Nuneaton Borough 0-3
Hinckley Town v Ilkeston Town 3-3, 0-1
Matlock Town v Buxton 2-1
Armitage v Curzon Ashton 1-4
Stourbridge v Gainsborough Trinity 3-6
Solihull Borough v Atherton LR 1-0
Burton Albion v Ashton United 1-1, 0-3
Moor Green v Worksop Town 8-4
Alfreton Town v Bedworth United 2-4
Kings Lynn v Burnham 3-3, 0-2
Leyton v Purfleet 0-1
Berkhamsted Town v Boreham Wood 0-2
Wivenhoe Town v Rothwell Town 1-2
Hayes v Tamworth 1-0
Racing Club Warwick v Harrow Borough 1-3
(Harrow Borough played ineligible player; match replayed: 2-5)
Heybridge Swifts v Billericay Town 2-0
Rushden & Diamonds v Hendon 0-0, 4-1
Wembley v Bury Town 5-2
Aylesbury United v Barking 5-0
Cambridge City v Bishops Stortford 6-1
Ruislip Manor v Baldock Town 0-3
Sudbury Town v Corby Town 5-0
VS Rugby v Braintree Town 4-3
Hastings Town v Gravesend & Northfleet 0-2
Chertsey Town v Tonbridge 3-1
Whyteleafe v Uxbridge 1-2
Dulwich Hamlet v Dorking 3-1
Ashford Town v Bognor Regis Town 3-4
Molesey v Sittingbourne 1-0
Wealdstone v Bromley 3-0
Tooting & Mitcham United v Walton & Hersham 0-2
Margate v Yeading 0-2
Erith & Belvedere v Staines Town 0-1
Gloucester City v Weymouth 1-0
Newbury Town v Buckingham Town 0-0, 1-1, 2-0
Maidenhead United v Fareham Town 0-1
Yate Town v Forest Green Rovers 0-2
Havant Town v Waterlooville 3-0
Evesham United v Basingstoke Town 0-1
Newport AFC v Aldershot Town 1-3
Abingdon Town v Witney Town 1-1, 0-1
Dorchester Town v Wokingham Town 2-0
Newport (IW) v Salisbury City 2-4
Clevedon Town v Bashley 1-1, 0-1

Second Qualifying Round
Droylsden v Hebburn 2-2, 4-0
RTM Newcastle v Dunston Federation Brewery 0-2
Curzon Ashton v Harrogate Town 4-2
Guisborough Town v Bedlington Terriers 2-1
Chorley v Bamber Bridge 1-2
Lancaster City v Knowsley United 1-1, 1-2
Great Harwood Town v Fleetwood 1-2
Accrington Stanley v West Auckland Town 2-2, 1-3
Baldock Town v Matlock Town 2-0
Nuneaton Borough v Ashton United 1-2
Rothwell Town v Eastwood Town 5-4
Ilkeston Town v Leicester United 6-1
Bedworth United v Bridgnorth Town 2-0
Mossley v Moor Green 1-3
Solihull Borough v VS Rugby 0-1
Gainsborough Trinity v Gresley Rovers 1-1, 0-1
Yeading v Burnham 0-0, 4-0
Heybridge Swifts v Chertsey Town 1-1, 1-3
Sudbury Town v Hayes 2-0
Dulwich Hamlet v Aylesbury United 1-2
Walton & Hersham v Cambridge City 2-1
Wealdstone v Purfleet 0-3
Boreham Wood v Uxbridge 1-1, 2-1
Rushden & Diamonds v Wembley 2-1
Molesey v Staines Town 4-2
Gravesend & Northfleet v Harrow Borough 1-1, 1-5
Basingstoke Town v Aldershot Town 0-1
Havant Town v Dorchester Town 1-3
Salisbury City v Bognor Regis Town 0-0, 2-4
Forest Green Rovers v Newbury Town 1-1, 1-2
Witney Town v Bashley 1-2
Gloucester City v Fareham Town 3-0

Third Qualifying Round
Northallerton v Blyth Spartans 0-2
Warrington Town v Colwyn Bay 1-1, 0-3
Knowsley United v Ashton United 1-4
Fleetwood v Spennymoor United 1-1, 0-3
Curzon Ashton v Gresley Rovers 0-1
Barrow v Winsford United 1-1, 2-4
Frickley Athletic v Whitby Town 1-2
Guisborough Town v West Auckland Town 1-2
Hyde United v Boston United 1-0
Dunston Federation Brewery v Ilkeston Town 2-3
Bamber Bridge v Grantham Town 3-1
Droylsden v Leek Town 0-1
Gretna v Seaham Red Star 2-1
Rushden & Diamonds v Crawley Town 2-1
Cheltenham Town v Worthing 4-0
Aldershot Town v Rothwell Town 1-1
(tie awarded to Rothwell Town; Aldershot included an ineligible player)
Sudbury Town v Carshalton Athletic 6-1
Gloucester City v Chelmsford City 0-2
Grays Athletic v Chertsey Town 0-0, 1-1, 3-1
Hednesford Town v Trowbridge Town 2-1
Bedworth United v Boreham Wood 0-1
Worcester City v Molesey 2-2, 0-2
Moor Green v Marlow 0-0, 0-1
Bashley v Yeading 1-1, 0-1
St Albans City v Purfleet 4-3
Baldock Town v Walton & Hersham 1-1, 1-2
Halesowen Town v Hitchin Town 4-0
Aylesbury United v Dorchester Town 2-1
Weston-Super-Mare v Chesham United 1-3
Kingstonian v Harrow Borough 3-1
VS Rugby v Bognor Regis Town 2-1
Atherstone United v Newbury Town 1-2

First Round
Runcorn v Northwich Victoria 2-1
Leek Town v Durham City 2-1
Gretna v Halesowen Town 1-1, 1-4
Telford United v Southport 2-0
Witton Albion v Guiseley 0-0, 2-2, 1-2
Gresley Rovers v Stafford Rangers 2-0

Bamber Bridge v Halifax Town	1-0
Hednesford Town v Altrincham	1-2
Stalybridge Celtic v Hyde United	3-3, 1-3
Billingham Synthonia v Ashton United	1-2
Bishop Auckland v Gateshead	0-1
West Auckland Town v Macclesfield Town *(at Macclesfield)*	1-2
Colwyn Bay v Blyth Spartans	1-1, 2-2, 2-1
Marine v Whitby Town	3-1
Spennymoor United v Morecambe	0-3
Ilkeston Town v Winsford United	4-2
Newbury Town v Rothwell Town	1-2
Boreham Wood v Grays Athletic	1-0
VS Rugby v Aylesbury United	2-1
Woking v Chesham United	3-0
Molesey v Cheltenham Town	0-2
Chelmsford City v Yeovil Town	2-4
Merthyr Tydfil v Slough Town	3-2
Rushden & Diamonds v Sudbury Town	3-1
Stevenage Borough v Dagenham & Redbridge	2-1
St Albans City v Kidderminster Harriers	2-3
Kingstonian v Yeading	3-2
Welling United v Marlow	2-2, 5-1
Farnborough Town v Dover Athletic	1-0
Sutton United v Bath City	1-1, 0-1
Bromsgrove Rovers v Enfield	1-3
Walton & Hersham v Kettering Town	2-2, 0-1

Second Round

Farnborough Town v Rushden & Diamonds	0-1
Halesowen Town v Guiseley	2-1
Bath City v Marine	1-2
Runcorn v Leek Town	4-2
Ashton United v Macclesfield Town	0-5
Altrincham v VS Rugby	1-1, 2-1
Colwyn Bay v Enfield	1-2
Gresley Rovers v Morecambe	2-3
Merthyr Tydfil v Bamber Bridge	2-1
Gateshead v Rothwell Town	6-1
Hyde United v Telford United	2-0
Woking v Cheltenham Town	3-1
Welling United v Ilkeston Town	1-1, 0-3
Yeovil Town v Stevenage Borough	1-1, 0-2
Kingstonian v Kidderminster Harriers	0-0, 0-1
Boreham Wood v Kettering Town	2-1

Third Round

Marine v Boreham Wood	2-0
Runcorn v Hyde United	0-0, 0-4
Gateshead v Macclesfield Town	0-1
Rushden & Diamonds v Halesowen Town	6-1
Ilkeston Town v Kidderminster Harriers	2-2, 1-2
Stevenage Borough v Woking	0-3
Morecambe v Altrincham	2-3
Enfield v Merthyr Tydfil	1-1, 1-1 (abandoned), 1-0

Fourth Round

Marine v Hyde United	1-3
Enfield v Rushden & Diamonds	1-1, 3-4
Kidderminster Harriers v Altrincham	5-0
Macclesfield Town v Woking	0-1

Semi-finals (two legs)

Kidderminster Harriers v Hyde United	2-0, 0-1
Rushden & Diamonds v Woking	1-0, 0-2

FA Umbro Trophy Final at Wembley

14 May

Kidderminster Harriers (0) 1 *(Davies)*

Woking (1) 2 *(Steele, Fielder) aet* 17,815

Kidderminster Harriers: Rose; Hodson, Bancroft, Webb, Brindley (Cartwright), Forsyth, Deakin, Yates, Humphreys (Hughes), Davies, Purdie.
Woking: Batty; Tucker, Wye L, Fielder, Brown, Crumplin (Rattray), Wye S, Ellis, Steele, Hay (Newbery), Walker.
Referee: D. Gallagher (Oxfordshire).

Woking captain Colin Fielder (left) with the FA Umbro Trophy at Wembley following the team's success against Kidderminster Harriers. (Action Images).

FA CARLSBERG VASE 1994–95

Extra Preliminary Round

Cleator Moor Celtic v Norton & Stockton Ancients 1-2
Morpeth Town v Horden CW 4-3
Langley Park S & S United v Shotton Comrades 3-1
Marske United v Seaton Delaval Amateurs 4-3
Ponteland United v North Shields 8-1
Sunderland Kennek Roker v Annfield Plain 4-1
Waterloo Dock v Kimberley Town 3-0
Maghull v Merseyside Police 1-2
South Normanton Athletic v Long Eaton United 3-0
Staveley MW v Daisy Hill 3-1
Rainworth MW v Wythenshawe Amateur 3-1
Heswall v Cheadle Town 2-1
Borrowash Victoria v Nuthall 2-2, 1-1, 2-2, 1-0
Shirebrook Town v Grove United 1-2
Vauxhall v Lucas Sports 6-3
Nettleham v Glapwell 0-2
Garforth Town v Oakham United 0-1
Harworth CI v Castleton Gabriels 4-3
Ashville v Hall Road Rangers 0-1
Clipstone Welfare v Poulton Victoria 1-3
Holwell Sports v Birstall United 4-3
Friar Lane OB v St Andrews 1-2
Cradley Town v Westfields 1-1, 1-5
Knowle v Pegasus Juniors 4-0
Northfield Town v Darlaston 4-1
Kings Heath v Meir KA 0-1
Lutterworth Town v Bloxwich Town 0-0, 0-0, 0-2
Gedling Town v Coleshill Town 4-2
Brantham Athletic v Mildenhall Town 4-1
Great Wakering Rovers v Clacton Town 2-0
Swaffham Town v Somersham Town 1-1, 2-1
Downham Town v Stanway Rovers 4-1
(at Long Sutton Athletic)
Warboys Town v Hullbridge Sports 5-1
Southend Manor v Maldon Town 1-2
Milton Keynes v Shillington 0-5
Stansted v Potters Bar Town 0-1
East Ham United v Leverstock Green 0-3
Rayners Lane v Eton Wick 0-3
St Margaretsbury v Cockfosters 1-2
(at Hertford Town)
Harpenden Town v Brentwood 1-0
Beaconsfield SYCOB v Eton Manor 4-1
London Colney v Waltham Abbey 4-0
Tower Hamlets v Totternhoe 9-1
West Wickham v Cobham 0-4
Worthing United v East Grinstead 2-1
Stamco v Furness 2-1
Thamesmead Town v Eastbourne United 2-1
Cranleigh v Broadbridge Heath 0-2
Greenwich Borough v Mile Oak 3-4
Sherborne Town v North Leigh 0-3
Flight Refuelling v Peppard 2-1
Petersfield Town v Hamworthy United 6-0
Sandhurst Town v Carterton Town 1-2
Bridgwater Town v Dawlish Town 4-1
Chard Town v Bishop Sutton 1-2
Cadbury Heath v Brislington 1-5
Cirencester Town v DRG AFC 3-2
Bristol Manor Farm v Almondsbury Town 1-3
(at Almondsbury Town)
Crediton United v Clyst Rovers 0-1
Wotton Rovers v Old Georgians 2-2, 2-0

Preliminary Round

Alnwick Town v Esh Winning 3-0
Ponteland United v West Allotment Celtic 2-2, 1-0
Penrith v Billingham Town 7-0
Walker v Washington 3-4
Morpeth Town v Ryhope CA 1-0
Crook Town v Langley Park S & S United 9-0
Pickering Town v Harrogate Railway 4-0
Darlington Cleveland Soc v Wolviston 3-5
Marske United v Willington 3-4
Easington Colliery v Evenwood Town 1-2
Norton & Stockton Ancients v Sunderland Kennek Roker 4-2
Armthorpe Welfare v North Ferriby United 2-3
Salford City v Skelmersdale United 1-1, 1-1, 2-0
Hucknall Town v Formby 5-1
Chadderton v Sheffield 4-1
Maltby MW v Blackpool (Wren) Rovers 1-4
Borrowash Victoria v Blidworth MW 3-1
Heanor Town v Kidsgrove Athletic 2-1
Rossendale United v St Helens Town 1-2
Tadcaster Albion v Glapwell 3-1
Ashfield United v Harworth CI 3-0
Heswall v Darwen 1-0
Ossett Town v Grove United 1-1, 0-1
Oakham United v Merseyside Police 2-1
Worsbro Bridge MW v Prescot AFC 3-2
Priory (Eastwood) v Trafford 0-7
Louth United v Hallam 2-1
Bradford (Park Avenue) v South Normanton Ath 6-4
Clitheroe v Waterloo Dock 3-4
Winterton Rangers v Newcastle Town 0-1
Lincoln United v Poulton Victoria 4-5
RES Parkgate v Denaby United 2-0
Staveley MW v Bootle 0-2
Maine Road v Immingham Town 1-0
Bacup Borough v Glasshoughton Welfare 2-4
Yorkshire Amateur v Rainworth MW 0-2
Atherton Collieries v Hatfield Main 0-1
Liversedge v Hall Road Rangers 2-4
Pontefract Collieries v Ossett Albion 1-5
Oldham Town v Rossington Main 1-1, 4-0
Vauxhall v Eccleshill United 3-2
Knowle v Willenhall Town 0-2
Stourport Swifts v Bolehall Swifts 3-2
Highgate United v St Andrews 1-5
Brierley Hill Town v Barwell 0-1
Meir KA v Chasetown 4-2
Shepshed Dynamo v Holwell Sports 2-3
Halesowen Harriers v Stewarts & Lloyds 1-2
Stapenhill v Gedling Town 2-3
Oldbury United v Shifnal Town 4-2
Knypersley Victoria v Westfields 4-1
Blakenall v Rocester 2-1
Lye Town v Stratford Town 3-1
Paget Rangers v Boldmere St Michaels 2-1
Long Buckby v Wellingborough Town 3-0
Sandwell Borough v Northampton Spencer 0-1
Northfield Town v Bloxwich Town 0-1
Rushall Olympic v Newport Pagnell Town 1-2
Desborough Town v Wednesfield 1-5
Brantham Athletic v Cornard United 2-0
Harwich & Parkeston v Stowmarket Town 0-2
Holbeach United v Eynesbury Rovers 0-4
Sudbury Wanderers v Haverhill Rovers 2-2, 2-2, 0-1
Swaffham Town v Long Sutton Athletic 4-1
Burnham Ramblers v Gorleston 1-1, 0-5
Watton United v Wroxham 0-4
Warboys Town v Downham Town 1-0
Ipswich Wanderers v Felixstowe Town 0-2
Norwich United v Newmarket Town 0-3
Stamford AFC v Sawbridgeworth Town 1-0
Bowers United v Great Yarmouth Town 1-0
Woodbridge Town v Maldon Town 0-1
Hadleigh United v March Town United 4-3
Chatteris Town v Witham Town 1-6
Great Wakering Rovers v Fakenham Town 2-2, 4-2
Ely City v Tiptree United 1-4
Histon v Spalding United 2-3
Bourne Town v Mirrlees Blackstone 2-1
Ashford Town (Middx) v Stotfold 1-2
Harlow Town v Hanwell Town 0-0, 2-0
Haringey Borough v Wootton Blue Cross 1-1, 3-1
Hampton v Viking Sports 0-1
Northwood v Ford United 2-0
East Thurrock United v Leverstock Green 5-2
London Colney v Harpenden Town 1-0
Harefield United v Langford 6-1

Kingsbury Town v Royston Town	0-2
Cockfosters v Edgware Town	3-0
Southall v Eton Wick	3-4
Brook House v Biggleswade Town	7-5
Potton United v Hemel Hempstead	1-3
Kempston Rovers v Concord Rangers	1-2
Beaconsfield SYCOB v Tower Hamlets	1-2
Tilbury v Shillington	3-1
Welwyn Garden City v Wingate & Finchley	3-5
Leighton Town v Bedford Town	2-1
Letchworth Garden City w.o. v Dunstable removed from competition	
Ware v Hertford Town	1-2
Hornchurch v Flackwell Heath	5-0
Clapton v Hillingdon Borough	0-1
Cheshunt v Romford	0-3
Potters Bar Town v Feltham & Hounslow Borough	2-1
Croydon Athletic v Whitstable Town	2-7
Southwick v Chichester City	8-0
Sheppey United v Stamco	2-4
Burgess Hill Town v Chipstead	1-0
Corinthian v Canterbury City	4-3
Camberley Town v Ramsgate	3-2
Cobham v Epsom & Ewell	0-0, 1-0
Newhaven v Chatham Town	1-4
Three Bridges v Slade Green	2-1
Wick v Eastbourne Town	3-0
Deal Town v Arundel	5-2
Selsey v Broadbridge Heath	2-0
Redhill v Leatherhead	3-4
Mile Oak v Thamesmead Town	1-4
Corinthian-Casuals v Bracknell Town	1-4
Steyning Town v Dartford	1-3
Worthing United v Horsham	0-4
Langney Sports v Ash United	3-0
Ringmer v Shoreham	0-3
Bedfont v Beckenham Town	1-3
Folkestone Invicta v Horsham YMCA	5-1
Cray Wanderers v Merstham	1-1, 1-2
Crowborough Athletic v Pagham	2-1
Portfield v Oakwood	2-0
Lancing v Egham Town	0-3
Godalming & Guildford v Littlehampton Town	3-4
Bemerton Heath Harlequins v Eastleigh	2-2, 0-3
Gosport Borough v Hungerford Town	2-3
Thatcham Town v First Tower United	2-5
Totton AFC v Abingdon United	1-3
Swanage Town & Herston v Westbury United	0-4
Cove v Carterton Town	4-3
Flight Refuelling v Lymington AFC	1-2
Swindon Supermarine v Brockenhurst	1-2
Wantage Town v Fleet Town	2-1
Kintbury Rangers v Bournemouth	2-3
Bicester Town v Milton United	1-2
Christchurch v Petersfield Town	2-3
North Leigh v Calne Town	3-3, 3-0
Banbury United v Ryde	3-0
Cirencester Town v Tuffley Rovers	1-3
Porthleven v Fairford Town	6-1
Cinderford Town v Bishop Sutton *(at Bishop Sutton)*	3-1
Frome Town v Devizes Town	2-2, 1-2
Clyst Rovers v Glastonbury	3-2
Torrington v Bridgwater Town	3-1
Ilfracombe Town v Odd Down	3-2
Bridport v Backwell United	2-1
Melksham Town v Barnstaple Town	1-2
Chippenham Town v Brislington	3-1
Elmore v Warminster Town	5-1
Larkhall Athletic v Saltash United	1-3
Minehead v Exmouth Town	0-4
Keynsham Town v St Blazey	5-3
Newquay v Mangotsfield United	1-3
Almondsbury Town v Wotton Rovers	1-2
Wellington Town v Liskeard Athletic	1-3
Hallen v Shortwood United	1-2

First Round

Ponteland United v Washington	1-2
Crook Town v Willington	0-1
Ossett Albion v Wolviston	8-0
Whickham v Norton & Stockton Ancients	3-1
Pickering Town v Evenwood Town	1-0
Thackley v Morpeth Town	4-0
Blackpool (Wren) Rovers v Waterloo Dock	0-2
Alnwick Town v South Shields	1-4
North Ferriby United v Penrith	2-1
Oldham Town v Tadcaster Albion	3-0
Bootle v Newcastle Town	7-6
Hall Road Rangers v Trafford	0-1
Grove United v Hatfield Main	1-1, 2-4
Borrowash Victoria v Chadderton	3-1
Poulton Victoria v Parkgate	4-1
Bradford (Park Avenue) v St Helens Town	3-0
Ashfield United v Stocksbridge Park Steels	1-2
Rainworth MW v Vauxhall	1-0
Hucknall Town v Nantwich Town	2-1
Oakham United v Louth United	2-0
Worsbro Bridge MW v Glossop North End	2-4
Heanor Town v Salford City	2-1
Maine Road v Glasshoughton Welfare	5-2
Flixton v Heswall	8-1
St Andrews v Bloxwich Town	2-0
Paget Rangers v Barwell	2-3
Lye Town v Wednesfield	1-3
Meir KA v Gedling Town	1-1, 4-2
Arnold Town v Long Buckby	2-0
Knypersley Victoria v Oldbury United	0-1
Stewarts & Lloyds v Raunds Town	1-5
Cogenhoe United v Bourne Town	4-1
Holwell Sports v West Midlands Police	1-1, 0-2
Pershore Town v Willenhall Town	0-2
Northampton Spencer v Blakenall	1-2
Spalding United v Stamford	2-1
Stourport Swifts v Newport Pagnell Town	0-2
Northwood v Tiptree United	6-3
Potters Bar Town v Hadleigh United	3-4
Harefield United v Tring Town	0-2
Hertford Town v Swaffham Town	2-0
Newmarket Town v Brimsdown Rovers	2-0
Maldon Town v Haringey Borough	5-1
Letchworth Garden City v Aveley *(Aveley included ineligible player; Letchworth Garden City re-instated)*	1-2
Barton Rovers v Felixstowe Town	2-1
Collier Row v Concord Rangers	3-1
Cockfosters v Halstead Town	0-1
Stotfold v Witham Town	0-0, 2-0
Viking Sports v Tower Hamlets	3-4
Gorleston v Harlow Town	5-1
Hornchurch v East Thurrock United	1-2
Great Wakering Rovers v Tilbury	4-2
Wroxham v Brantham Athletic	2-2, 1-0
Royston Town v Brook House	1-1, 2-2, 2-0
Eynesbury Rovers v Hemel Hempstead	1-0
Hillingdon Borough v Stowmarket Town	4-2
Basildon United v Haverhill Rovers	3-0
Bowers United v Wingate & Finchley	2-5
Leighton Town v Soham Town Rangers	2-0
Warboys Town v London Colney	3-2
Lowestoft Town v Romford	5-0
Littlehampton Town v Camberley Town	2-2, 0-4
Cobham v Horsham	2-3
North Leigh v Lewes	3-2
Shoreham v Bracknell Town	2-1
Wantage Town v Hailsham Town	1-4
Crowborough Athletic v Cove	1-5
Milton United v Langney Sports	6-2
Eton Wick v Andover	6-4
Hungerford Town v Portfield	4-1
Bournemouth v Beckenham Town	5-0
Stamco v Whitstable Town	4-2
Burgess Hill Town v Wick	0-3
Oxford City v Herne Bay	4-1
Abingdon United v Selsey	0-2
Thame United v Leatherhead	1-2
Deal Town v Dartford	3-2
Three Bridges v Thamesmead Town	1-3

Eastleigh v Banbury United 2-1
Egham Town v Brockenhurst 6-2
Chatham Town v Merstham 4-0
Southwick v Petersfield Town 1-2
Folkestone Invicta v Corinthian 1-2
First Tower United v Lymington AFC 3-4
Mangotsfield United v Moreton Town 2-0
Torrington v Welton Rovers 3-0
Elmore v Clyst Rovers 4-0
Ilfracombe Town v Falmouth Town 1-9
Tuffley Rovers v Wotton Rovers 2-1
Bridport v Shortwood United 6-0
Chippenham Town v Cinderford Town 3-4
Westbury United v Devizes Town 0-0, 2-1
Barnstaple Town v Keynsham Town 3-1
Liskeard Athletic v Bideford 2-1
Torpoint Athletic v Exmouth Town 4-1
Saltash United v Porthleven 6-3

Second Round
Heanor Town v Hatfield Main 2-4
South Shields v Flixton 3-2
Cammell Laird v Meir KA 2-2, 2-0
Whickham v Pickering Town 0-0, 2-3
Brandon United v Dunkirk 2-1
Arnold Town v Trafford 2-1
North Ferriby United v Thackley 0-3
Waterloo Dock v Hucknall Town 1-2
Burscough v Brigg Town 2-0
Rainworth MW v Poulton Victoria 0-4
Stocksbridge Park Steels v Oakham United 2-1
Glossop North End v Bootle 2-0
Eastwood Hanley v Bradford (Park Avenue) 3-1
Ossett Albion v Stockton 2-0
Maine Road v Borrowash Victoria 2-1
Belper Town v Washington 5-0
Oldham Town v Willington 1-2
Great Wakering Rovers v Raunds Town 1-2
Diss Town v Cogenhoe United 3-2
Hoddesdon Town v Arlesey Town 0-2
Boston Town v Walthamstow Pennant 1-0
Tower Hamlets v West Midlands Police 2-2, 0-1
Letchworth Garden City v Hadleigh United 0-3
Stotfold v Warboys Town 3-1
St Andrews v Willenhall Town 3-1
Oadby Town v Wednesfield 5-4
Collier Row v Newport Pagnell Town 7-0
Wisbech Town v Blakenall 3-1
Halstead Town v Saffron Walden Town 4-2
East Thurrock United v Canvey Island 0-2
Wroxham v Pelsall Villa 0-1
Royston Town v Basildon United 0-1
Eynesbury Rovers v Spalding United 2-0
Newmarket Town v Tring Town 2-1
Lowestoft Town v Maldon Town 3-1
Gorleston v Barton Rovers 0-4
Leighton Town v Wingate & Finchley 0-3
Barwell v Hertford Town 2-1
Oldbury United v Hinckley Athletic 1-2
Wick v Chalfont St Peter 2-1
Horsham v Malden Vale 1-1, 3-1
Cove v Hailsham Town 2-3
Hillingdon Borough v Northwood 0-1
Stamco v Leatherhead 4-0
Corinthian v Egham Town 4-3
Windsor & Eton v Shoreham 2-3
Metropolitan Police v Eton Wick 3-1
Camberley Town v Banstead Athletic 0-2
Thamesmead Town v Croydon 1-6
Peacehaven & Telscombe v Deal Town 3-0
Whitehawk v Chatham Town 1-0
Selsey v Tunbridge Wells 0-1
Eastleigh v Lymington AFC 6-3
Milton United v Oxford City 1-4
Bridport v Falmouth Town 1-3
Liskeard Athletic v Cinderford Town 3-1
Petersfield Town v Taunton Town 0-7
Bournemouth v Torpoint Athletic 4-3
North Leigh v Elmore 0-4
Tiverton Town v Saltash United 9-0
Westbury United v Tuffley Rovers 4-1
Wimborne Town v Torrington 4-2
Barnstaple Town v Hungerford Town 3-1
Mangotsfield United v Paulton Rovers 3-2

Third Round
Oadby Town v Ossett Albion 0-6
Hatfield Main v Maine Road 0-1
Barwell v Brandon United 0-1
Thackley v Cammell Laird 1-1, 1-1, 1-2
Eastwood Hanley v Pickering Town 3-1
Poulton Victoria v St Andrews 2-3
Arnold Town v Burscough 2-3
Glossop North End v Stocksbridge Park Steels 0-5
South Shields v Hucknall Town 3-1
Belper Town v Willington 6-4
Wisbech Town v Stotfold 3-4
Hadleigh United v Corinthian 3-1
Newmarket Town v Canvey Island 0-5
Wingate & Finchley v Basildon United 1-2
Diss Town v Barton Rovers 3-1
Lowestoft Town v Raunds Town 1-3
Metropolitan Police v Collier Row 2-1
Eynesbury Rovers v Halstead Town 2-3
Hinckley Athletic v Pelsall Villa 1-2
Boston Town v Arlesey Town 1-2
West Midlands Police v Northwood 3-2
Bournemouth v Croydon 1-2
Hailsham Town v Eastleigh 0-4
Taunton Town v Westbury United 4-2
Wick v Elmore 4-4, 1-4
Tiverton Town v Horsham 4-1
Banstead Athletic v Falmouth Town 3-5
Mangotsfield United v Whitehawk 4-0
Stamco v Shoreham 5-3
Oxford City v Peacehaven & Telscombe 1-0
Wimborne Town v Barnstaple Town 1-4
Tunbridge Wells v Liskeard Athletic 1-1, 0-2

Fourth Round
Burscough v Brandon United 3-0
Stocksbridge Park Steels v Eastwood Hanley 1-1, 1-3
Pelsall Villa v Cammell Laird 1-2
Halstead Town v Hadleigh United 5-5, 2-3
West Midlands Police v Raunds Town 0-2
Ossett Albion v Diss Town 1-1, 1-1, 0-3
St Andrews v Maine Road 2-1
Belper Town v South Shields 4-0
Liskeard Athletic v Falmouth Town 0-2
Stotfold v Basildon United 0-4
Mangotsfield United v Canvey Island 1-5
Barnstaple Town v Arlesey Town 0-2
Croydon v Oxford City 1-2
Taunton Town v Elmore 2-1
Eastleigh v Metropolitan Police 1-3
Stamco v Tiverton Town 4-3

Fifth Round
Raunds Town v St Andrews 3-0
Arlesey Town v Diss Town 1-0
Falmouth Town v Belper Town 1-5
Taunton Town v Oxford City 0-3
Canvey Island v Stamco 3-0
Cammell Laird v Burscough 4-2
Metropolitan Police v Hadleigh United 4-1
Eastwood Hanley v Basildon United 2-3

Sixth Round

Arlesey Town v Cammell Laird	3-0
Oxford City v Canvey Island	2-0
Metropolitan Police v Belper Town	0-1
Basildon United v Raunds Town	0-2

Semi-finals (two legs)

Raunds Town v Arlesey Town	3-0, 0-5
Belper Town v Oxford City	1-0, 1-3

Vase Final at Wembley

13 May

Arlesey Town (1) 2 *(Palma, Gyalog)*
Oxford City (0) 1 *(Fontaine S)* 13,670

Arlesey Town: Young; Cardines, Hull, Gonsalves, Bambrick, Gyalog, Cox, O'Keefe, Marshall (Nicholls), Palma (Ward), Kane.
Oxford City: Fleet; Brown (Fisher), Hume, Shepherd, Muttock, Hamilton (Kemp), Thomas, Spittle, Fontaine C, Sherwood, Fontaine S.
Referee: G. Willard (Worthing).

FA COUNTY YOUTH CHALLENGE CUP 1994–95

First Round

Lancashire v East Riding	0-3
Westmorland v Sheffield & Hallamshire	1-2
Liverpool v Nottinghamshire	3-2
North Riding v Lincolnshire	0-3
Herefordshire v Northamptonshire	0-2
Leicestershire & Rutland v Worcestershire	3-3, 3-1
Hertfordshire v Cambridgeshire	4-1
Bedfordshire v London	2-1
Berks & Bucks v Surrey	0-1
Dorset v Devon	2-3
Wiltshire v Somerset & Avon	3-3, 1-3
Hampshire v Army	3-1

Second Round

Shropshire v West Riding	1-3
Cumberland v East Riding	1-1, 1-0
Northumberland v Sheffield & Hallamshire	3-1
Durham v Liverpool	0-1
Manchester v Lincolnshire	4-1
Derbyshire v Northamptonshire	6-0
Cheshire v Leicestershire & Rutland	2-1
Birmingham v Hertfordshire	1-4
Huntingdonshire v Staffordshire	3-2
Norfolk v Bedfordshire	3-2
Suffolk v Surrey	1-2
Gloucestershire v Sussex	3-1
Kent v Essex	3-4
Oxfordshire v Devon	4-2
Middlesex v Somerset & Avon (South)	1-3
Cornwall v Hampshire	5-0

Third Round

Derbyshire v Liverpool	2-4
West Riding v Cheshire	4-2
Hertfordshire v Northumberland	1-1, 1-2
Manchester v Cumberland	2-1
Oxfordshire v Essex	1-2
Huntingdonshire v Somerset & Avon (South)	2-4
Cornwall v Surrey	3-2
Gloucestershire v Norfolk	2-3

Fourth Round

Liverpool v Norfolk	2-2, 1-0
Somerset & Avon (South) v Essex	1-3
Manchester v Northumberland	0-1
West Riding v Cornwall	1-2

Semi-finals

Liverpool v Cornwall	2-2, 3-0
Northumberland v Essex	0-2

Final

Liverpool v Essex	3-2

FA XI MATCHES

18 Oct

FA XI 1 *(Genovese)*
Huntingdonshire FA 1 120
FA XI: Ladley (Holbeach United) [Crane (Rushden & Diamonds)]; Mountain (Spalding United), Fuff (Rushden & Diamonds), Quow (Sudbury Town) [Genovese (Holbeach United)], Gray (Holbeach United), Rhule (Stamford), Crunkhorn (Holbeach United), Carr (Raunds Town), Keeble (Raunds Town), Boon (Stotfold), Fortune (Holbeach United).

15 Nov

FA XI 2 *(Connor, Green)*
Northern Premier League 2 137
FA XI: Farrelly (Macclesfield Town); Cross (Altrincham), Bimson (Macclesfield Town), France (Altrincham), Reid (Altrincham), Connor (Runcorn) [Anderson (Stalybridge Celtic)], Thomas (Runcorn) [Terry (Altrincham)], McDonald (Macclesfield Town) [Sorvel (Macclesfield Town)], Green (Altrincham), Carmody (Altrincham), Shrratt (Altrincham).

7 Dec

FA XI 1 *(Rattray)*
Isthmian League 0 250
FA XI: Williams (Dover Athletic) [Batty (Woking)]; Tucker (Woking), Brown (Welling United), Brown K (Woking), Wye (Woking), Brown D (Woking), Browne (Dover Athletic) [Boothe (Farnborough Town)], Leworthy (Dover Athletic), Robbins (Welling United) [Rattray (Woking)], Broom (Dagenham & Redbridge).

10 Jan

FA XI 4 *(Carter, Stott, May, Forsyth)*
British Students 0 140
FA XI: Goodwin (Telford United) [Steadman (Kidderminster Harriers); Bignot (Telford United) [Skelding (Bromsgrove Rovers)], Bancroft (Kidderminster Harriers), Yates (Kidderminster Harriers), Foster (Telford United) [Weir (Kidderminster Harriers)], Forsyth (Kidderminster Harriers), Snape (Halesowen Town), Stott (Bromsgrove Rovers), May (Stafford Rangers) [Burton (Westfields)], Carter (Bromsgrove Rovers) [O'Connor (Hednesford Town)], Coogan (Solihull Borough).

17 Jan

FA XI 2 *(Terry, Dove)*
Combined Services 0 100
FA XI: Morris (Runcorn); Norman (Macclesfield Town), Robertson (Runcorn), Ruffer (Runcorn), Howarth (Macclesfield Town)], Bimson (Macclesfield Town), Bimson (Macclesfield Town), Terry (Altrincham), Dove (Southport), Burke (Stalybridge Celtic), Power (Macclesfield Town), Sorvel (Macclesfield Town).

19 May

FA XI 3 *(Richardson I, May, Hayles)*
Highland League 4 450
FA XI: Williams (Dover Athletic) [Mogg (Bath City)]; Webb (Kidderminster Harriers), Ashby (Kettering Town), Brown K (Woking), Reid (Altrincham) [Richardson (Bromsgrove Rovers)], Richardson I (Dagenham & Redbridge), Venables (Stevenage Borough) [Pye (Enfield)], Forsyth (Kidderminster Harriers), Stott (Bromsgrove Rovers), Bolton (Kingstonian) [Hayles (Stevenage Borough)], May (Stafford Rangers) [Taylor (Bromsgrove Rovers)].

FA SUNDAY CUP 1994–95

First Round

Dock v Newfield 1-3
Croxteth & Gilmoss RBL v Humbledon Plains Farm 1-3
BRNESC v Albion Sports 2-2, 3-1
A3 v Dudley & Weetslade 1-0
Lobster v Nenthead 4-1
Baildon Athletic v Mode Force Boulevard 1-1, 0-1
Northwood v SDV 5-0
Clubmoor Nalgo v Etnaward 0-0, 0-3
East Bowling Unity v Mitre 1-2
Boundary w.o. v Iron Bridge withdrew
Sandon v Hartlepool Staincliffe Hotel 3-2
Waterloo Social Club Blyth v Littlewoods Athletic 2-3
Seaton Sluice SC v Britannia 1-1, 2-3
Queens Park v Stockton Roseworth Social 3-2
Salerno v Fiddlers Horse 93 7-2
Townley v Bolton Woods 5-0
Cork & Bottle v Walford Maritime 3-1
Almithak v Poets Corner 2-0
Egerton Boys v Norwich Busmen 1-1, 3-0
Slade Celtic v Clifton Albion 2-1
Elliott Bull & Tiger v Poringland Wanderers 5-1
Capel Plough v Grosvenor Park 2-1
Greyhound 83 v Hammer 0-4
Dereham Hobbies v Brookvale Athletic 0-1
Leavesden Sports & Social v Melton Youth Old Boys 2-2, 0-2
Hundred Acre v Leicester City Bus 0-1
Sawston Keys v Continental 2-1
St Joseph's (Sth Oxhey) v Altone Steels 0-2
Collier Row Supporters withdrew v London Boys w.o.
Sandwell v Kenwick Dynamo 0-3
Forest Athletic v Oakwood Sports 0-2
Fryerns Community v Caversham Park 10-0
Courage v BRSC Aidan 0-4
Olympic Star v Erdington Cosmos 0-2
Sheerness Steel United v Charlton Royal 89 3-0
Inter Royale v Shell Club 2-3
Somersett Ambury V&E v Oxford Road Social 4-1
Hartley Wintney Sunday v Hanham Sunday 0-4
Biddestone (Sun) v Evergreen 3-4
Chequers (Herts) v Pitsea 2-3
Poole Town Social v British Rail SA 2-3
Park Royals v St Joseph's AFC (Bristol) 1-1, 1-0
Coach & Horses v Gracelands 4-4, 4-3
Vosper Sunday v Watford Labour Club 2-3

Second Round

Allerton v Cork & Bottle 4-2
Newfield v Boundary 2-1
Littlewoods Athletic v B&A Scaffolding 0-1
Mode Force Boulevard v A3 2-1
Sandon v Mitre 5-4
Hartlepool Lion Hotel v Salerno 2-0
Nicosia v Townley 3-4
Northwood v Queens Park AFC 2-4
Lobster v BRNESC 1-0
Etnaward v Humbledon Plains Farm 1-2
Britannia v Lion Hotel 0-3
Almithak v Oakenshaw 2-4
Seymour v Manfast Kirkby 3-2
Leicester City Bus v Hammer 0-2
Brookvale Athletic v Egerton Boys 2-0
Heathfield v London Boys 2-3
Ouzavich v Sacred Heart 0-4
Lodge Cottrell v Fryerns Community 4-0
Marston Sports v Slade Celtic 1-3
St Clements Hospital v Capel Plough 1-1, 2-4
Melton Youth Old Boys v St Josephs (Luton) 2-3
Erdington Cosmos v Kenwick Dynamo 1-4
Sawston Keys v Altone Steels 1-3
Oakwood Sports v Elliott Bull & Tiger 2-3
BRSC Aidan v Pitsea 0-0, 1-0
Shell Club v Park Royals 2-0
British Rail SA v Lebeq Tavern 1-3
Coach & Horses v Bedfont Sunday 2-1
Evergreen v Watford Labour Club 2-0
Theale Sunday v Hanham Sunday 3-0
Reading Borough v Somersett Ambury V&E 6-2
bye: Sheerness Steel United

Third Round

Allerton v Townley 4-0
Oakenshaw v Altone Steels 2-4
B&A Scaffolding v Slade Celtic 3-1
Brookvale Athletic v Humbledon Plains Farm 0-4
Lion Hotel v Newfield 0-2
Seymour v Mode Force Boulevard 1-3
Lobster v Hartlepool Lion Hotel 0-2
Sandon v Queens Park AFC 0-2
Hammer v Kenwick Dynamo 3-0
Coach & Horses v Reading Borough 7-0
Sacred Heart v Theale Sunday 3-0
Sheerness Steel United v Shell Club 1-0
Lebeq Tavern v London Boys 4-1
Evergreen v Lodge Cottrell 0-2
BRSC Aidan v St Josephs (Luton) 1-2
Capel Plough v Elliott Bull & Tiger 3-0

Fourth Round

Hartlepool Lion Hotel v Allerton 0-1
Newfield v Altone Steels 6-1
Queens Park AFC v Humbledon Plains Farm 1-2
B&A Scaffolding v Mode Force Boulevard 4-2
Sheerness Steel United v Coach & Horses 2-0
Lebeq Tavern v Lodge Cottrell 1-0
Hammer v Capel Plough 1-2
Sacred Heart v St Josephs (Luton) 0-1

Fifth Round

Allerton v Newfield 3-1
B&A Scaffolding v Humbledon Plains Farm 4-0
Lebeq Tavern v St Josephs (Luton) 1-3
Capel Plough v Sheerness Steel United 3-2

Semi-finals

Allerton v B&A Scaffolding 0-2
Capel Plough v St Josephs (Luton) 0-0, 1-1
(St Josephs (Luton) won 4-2 on penalties)

Final

St Josephs (Luton) v B&A Scaffolding 2-1

FA YOUTH CHALLENGE CUP 1994–95

Extra Preliminary Round

Atherton LR withdrew v Warrington Town w.o.
Mansfield Town v Wrexham 1-4
Worksop Town v Redditch United 1-2
Bedworth United v Stourport Swifts 3-1
Corby Town v Wednesfield 2-1
Barkingside v Stevenage Borough 0-4
Eaton Manor v Hemel Hempstead 1-2
(at Hemel Hempstead)
Ruislip Manor v Wingate & Finchley 2-4
Bromley v Sittingbourne 1-2
Bracknell Town v Kingstonian 0-2
Farnborough Town v Windsor & Eton 3-2
Newhaven withdrew v Basingstoke Town w.o.

Preliminary Round

Harrogate Town v Darlington 4-2
Hartlepool United v Lancaster City 1-0
Chorley v Carlisle United 0-7
Morecambe v Guisborough Town 2-0
Chadderton v Bolton Wanderers 1-1, 2-4
Chesterfield v Huddersfield Town 0-2
Lincoln City v Warrington Town 7-5
Wigan Athletic v Bury 0-1
Port Vale v Marine 3-1
Rochdale v Southport 2-1
Stalybridge Celtic v Wrexham 1-10
Stockport County v Oldham Town 3-1
Hinckley Athletic v Burton Albion 1-2
Hinckley Town v Lutterworth Town 2-1
Hednesford Town v Redditch United 2-0
Pelsall Villa v Birstall United 2-3
Bridgnorth Town v Bilston Town 1-4
Brierley Hill Town v Chasetown 0-1
Nuneaton Borough v Bedworth United 1-1, 1-0
Oldbury United v Boldmere St Michaels 2-4
Lye Town v Daventry Town 2-2, 4-0
Northampton Spencer v Rushden & Diamonds 0-6
Stratford Town v Corby Town 1-0
VS Rugby v Kettering Town 3-3, 1-7
Halstead Town v Braintree Town 1-5
March Town United v Saffron Walden Town 1-2
Wivenhoe Town v Bishops Stortford 0-0, 0-2
Concord Rangers v Chatteris Town 4-4, 5-2
Enfield v Baldock Town 6-1
Barnet v Royston Town 12-1
St Albans City v Canvey Island 0-1
Letchworth Garden City v East Thurrock United 1-8
Edgware Town v Brook House 4-4, 1-6
Hillingdon Borough v Kempston Rovers 4-0
Kingsbury Town v Stevenage Borough 3-3, 2-5
Leighton Town v Clapton 1-0
Hampton v Feltham & Hounslow Borough 1-4
Hanwell Town withdrew v Harefield United w.o.
Harlow Town v Hemel Hempstead 2-6
Hayes v Flackwell Heath 1-1, 2-1
Viking Sports did not enter v Staines Town w.o.
Waltham Abbey v Welwyn Garden City 1-3
Wembley v Wingate & Finchley 1-2
Bedfont v Uxbridge 1-0
Corinthian v Ashford Town 2-0
(match abandoned 50 minutes; floodlit failure) 4-1
Dover Athletic v Gillingham 0-3
Herne Bay v Sittingbourne 0-4
Dartford v Chatham Town 6-1
Crawley Town v Chertsey Town 4-2
Marlow v Croydon Athletic 1-2
Dorking v Kingstonian 1-3
Egham Town withdrew v Chipstead w.o.
Thamesmead Town v Welling United 1-1, 1-3
Tonbridge v Malden Vale 0-1
Redhill v Farnborough Town 0-3
Whyteleafe v Whitstable Town 3-6
Three Bridges v Ringmer 6-1
Whitehawk v Woking 2-2, 1-3
Aldershot Town v Basingstoke Town 3-0
Fleet Town v Southwick 4-0
Wokingham Town v Newbury Town 1-1, 0-2
Oxford City v Maidenhead United 4-4, 6-0
Thatcham Town v Banbury United 1-2
Chippenham Town v Abingdon Town 1-4
Dorchester Town v Bashley 2-2, 0-1
Weymouth v Weston-Super-Mare 1-2
Yeovil Town v Romsey Town 7-0
Clevedon Town withdrew v Eastleigh w.o.
Cheltenham Town v Yate Town 4-0
Forest Green Rovers v Gloucester City 3-3, 4-5
Hereford United v Worcester City 6-0
Mangotsfield United v Bristol Rovers 0-3

First Qualifying Round

Morecambe v Harrogate Town 6-0
Carlisle United v Hartlepool United 7-2
Bury v Bolton Wanderers 4-0
Lincoln City v Huddersfield Town 1-10
Stockport County v Port Vale 0-1
Wrexham v Rochdale 2-1
Birstall United v Burton Albion 2-2, 0-1
Hednesford Town v Hinckley Town 0-4
Boldmere St Michaels v Bilston Town 3-0
Nuneaton Borough v Chasetown 3-1
Kettering Town v Lye Town 1-1, 1-1
(Kettering Town won 5-4 on penalties)
Stratford Town v Rushden & Diamonds 1-1, 2-3
Concord Rangers v Braintree Town 0-7
Bishops Stortford v Saffron Walden Town 3-2
East Thurrock United v Enfield 2-2, 0-1
Canvey Island v Barnet 0-3
Leighton Town v Brook House 8-0
Stevenage Borough v Hillingdon Borough 2-3
Hayes v Feltham & Hounslow Borough 1-5
Hemel Hempstead v Harefield United 1-2
Bedfont v Staines Town 3-4
Wingate & Finchley v Welwyn Garden City 2-4
Dartford v Corinthian 3-1
Sittingbourne v Gillingham 2-2, 1-2
Chipstead v Crawley Town 1-3
Kingstonian v Croydon Athletic 0-0, 1-4
Whitstable Town v Welling United 1-3
Farnborough Town v Malden Vale 2-0
Fleet Town v Three Bridges 1-2
Aldershot Town v Woking 2-3
Abingdon Town v Newbury Town 2-5
Banbury United v Oxford City 2-3
Eastley v Bashley 0-1
Yeovil Town v Weston-Super-Mare 8-2
Bristol Rovers v Cheltenham Town 3-0
Hereford United v Gloucester City 2-0

Second Qualifying Round

Morecambe v Carlisle United 1-8
Bury v Huddersfield Town 2-0
Port Vale v Wrexham 0-5
Burton Albion v Hinckley Town 1-0
Boldmere St Michaels v Nuneaton Borough 2-1
Kettering Town v Rushden & Diamonds 3-4
Braintree Town v Bishops Stortford 2-4
Enfield v Barnet 0-3
Leighton Town v Hillingdon Borough 1-0
Feltham & Hounslow Borough v Harefield United 4-1
Staines Town v Welwyn Garden City 2-1
Dartford v Gillingham 0-3
Crawley Town v Croydon Athletic 2-2, 2-2
(Croydon Athletic won 4-3 on penalties)
Welling United v Farnborough Town 3-0
Three Bridges v Woking 1-2
Newbury Town v Oxford City 1-2
(at Oxford City)
Bashley v Yeovil Town 2-3
Bristol Rovers v Hereford United 2-2, 3-1

First Round

Doncaster Rovers v Scunthorpe United 2-0
Hull City v Blackburn Rovers 0-3
Carlisle United v Sunderland 0-2
Preston North End v Rotherham United 4-1
Newcastle United v Everton 0-2
Oldham Athletic v Bury 3-0
Grimsby Town v Sheffield Wednesday 1-3
Tranmere Rovers v Burnley 5-0
Barnsley v Blackpool 1-3
Leicester City v Kidderminster Harriers 4-1
Northampton Town v Walsall 1-2
Peterborough United v Rushden & Diamonds 7-1
Shrewsbury Town v Birmingham City 1-2
Aston Villa v Derby County 1-1, 3-0
Boldmere St Michaels v Cambridge City 2-1
Wrexham v Burton Albion 8-0
Wolverhampton Wanderers v Cambridge United 1-1, 6-2
Woking v Charlton Athletic 0-8
Bishops Stortford v Ipswich Town 0-2
Wycombe Wanderers v Gillingham 2-1
Luton Town v Staines Town 5-0
Lewes v Croydon Athletic 0-2
Enfield v Fulham 1-2
Leighton Town v Sutton United 4-2
Watford v Welling United 0-0, 1-2
Witney Town v Boreham Wood 1-3
Dulwich Hamlet v Feltham & Hounslow Borough 4-1
Cardiff City v Torquay United 3-1
Exeter City v Plymouth Argyle 0-2
Bournemouth AFC v Swansea City 5-0
Bristol Rovers v Oxford United 0-2
Oxford City v Yeovil Town 0-2
Southampton v Reading 1-0
Colchester United w.o. v Epsom & Ewell withdrew

Second Round

Peterborough United v Everton 0-1
Liverpool v Tranmere Rovers 1-2
Stoke City v Notts County 1-0
Crewe Alexandra v Blackburn Rovers 3-0
Nottingham Forest v Leicester City 2-1
Aston Villa v Leeds United 1-0
Manchester United v Wrexham 4-1
Sunderland v Sheffield Wednesday 1-1, 1-0
York City v Birmingham City 0-0, 2-0
Middlesbrough v Oldham Athletic 4-3
Manchester City v Walsall 1-1, 1-1
(Manchester City won 4-1 on penalties)
West Bromwich Albion v Doncaster Rovers 0-1
Preston North End v Blackpool 1-2
Bradford City v Sheffield United 1-1, 0-3
Arsenal v Brighton & Hove Albion 5-0
West Ham United v Wimbledon 2-2, 2-4
Wycombe Wanderers v Luton Town 1-0
Leyton Orient v Chelsea 0-0, 2-0
Tottenham Hotspur v Boldmere St Michaels 10-0
Norwich City v Millwall 2-1
Ipswich Town v Croydon Athletic 3-0
Wolverhampton Wanderers v Brentford 2-0
Bournemouth AFC v Bristol City 0-0, 1-3
Colchester United v Yeovil Town 3-0
Dulwich Hamlet v Welling United 1-1, 3-1
Oxford United v Leighton Town 6-0
Fulham v Boreham Wood 5-0
Portsmouth v Swindon Town 0-0, 1-1
(Portsmouth won 11-10 on penalties)
Charlton Athletic v Cardiff City 2-1
Southend United v Crystal Palace 2-1
Queens Park Rangers v Plymouth Argyle 3-1
Southampton v Coventry City 0-5

Third Round

Bristol City v Nottingham Forest 0-0, 1-0
Crewe Alexandra v Oxford United 1-0
Sheffield United v York City 1-0
Wycombe Wanderers v Colchester United 0-5
Sunderland v Doncaster Rovers 0-0, 2-0
Stoke City v Norwich City 0-0, 1-0
Dulwich Hamlet v Fulham 0-2
(Tie awarded to Dulwich Hamlet; Fulham included an ineligible player)
Manchester City v Portsmouth 2-2, 1-0
Aston Villa v Leyton Orient 1-0
Tottenham Hotspur v Wolverhampton Wanderers 4-2
Southend United v Tranmere Rovers 4-3
Queens Park Rangers v Arsenal 0-2
Wimbledon v Ipswich Town 4-0
Everton v Blackpool 6-5
Manchester United v Charlton Athletic 1-1, 5-2
Coventry City v Middlesbrough 2-2, 6-2

Fourth Round

Aston Villa v Colchester United 4-0
Tottenham Hotspur v Southend United 1-1, 2-1
Dulwich Hamlet v Bristol City 2-3
Manchester United v Arsenal 2-1
Sunderland v Crewe Alexandra 3-1
Everton v Sheffield United 1-3
Coventry City v Manchester City 2-3
Stoke City v Wimbledon 1-2

Fifth Round

Sunderland v Manchester City 2-2, 1-3
Bristol City v Tottenham Hotspur 1-2
Aston Villa v Manchester United 2-3
Wimbledon v Sheffield United 3-3, 3-2

Semi-finals (two legs)

Manchester City v Tottenham Hotspur 0-5, 1-2
Manchester United v Wimbledon 2-1, 3-0

FA Youth Cup Final, first leg

11 May

Tottenham H (1) 2 *(Wormull, Allen)*

Manchester U (0) 1 *(Cooke)* 8213

Tottenham H: Brown; Carr, Maher, Darcy, Arber, Wormull, Clemence, Spencer, Gain, Allen (Bunn), Fenn.
Manchester U: Gibson; Neville P, Westwood, Clegg, Wallwork, Mulryne (Gordon), Mustoe, Hall, Baker (Curtis), Johnson, Cooke.
Referee: P. Vanes (Birmingham).

FA Youth Cup Final, second leg

15 May

Manchester U (0) 1 *(Cooke)*

Tottenham H (0) 0 20,190

Manchester U: Gibson; Neville P, Westwood, Curtis, Wallwork, Mulryne (Hilton), Mustoe, Hall (Gardner), Baker, Brebner, Cooke.
Tottenham H: Brown; Carr, Maher, Darcy, Arber, Wormull (Clemence), Brady, Spencer, Gain, Allen (Winston), Fenn.
aet; Manchester U won 4-3 on penalties.
Referee: P. Vanes (Birmingham).

SCHOOLS FOOTBALL 1994–95

ESFA FUJI FILM TROPHY

SEMI-FINALS:
South Tyneside v Manchester 2-0
Newport v Islington & Camden 1-2

FINAL: 1ST LEG
South Tyneside v Islington & Camden 1-1
Played at Sunderland FC on 4 May

FINAL: 2ND LEG
Islington & Camden v South Tyneside 3-0
Played at Arsenal FC on 12 May

ESFA SNICKERS U.16 COMPETITION

SEMI-FINALS
Mount St Marys, Leeds v Cardinal Heenan, Liverpool 0-0, 1-2
Denefield, Reading v St. Michaels, Watford 2-2, 0-3

FINAL
Cardinal Heenan, Liverpool v St Michaels, Watford 0-0
Played at Tranmere Rovers FC on 18 May

ESFA SNICKERS U.19 COMPETITION

SEMI-FINALS
Swindon College v Northgate High, Ipswich 3-3, 1-2
Winstanley College, Manchester v Preston College* 0-0, 3-3
**Preston College won on penalties*

FINAL
Northgate High, Ipswich v Preston College 1-2
Played at Ipswich Town FC on 10 May

ESFA ADIDAS U.16 INTER COUNTY COMPETITION

SEMI-FINALS
Staffordshire v Greater Manchester 1-3
Avon v Kent 1-2

FINAL
Greater Manchester v Kent 2-1
Played at Rochdale FC on 21 October

ESFA PREMIER LEAGUE U.16 COUNTY COMPETITION

SEMI-FINALS
Greater Manchester v West Midlands 0-0, 2-2, 2-1
Essex v Sussex 3-5

FINAL
Greater Manchester v Sussex 0-1
Played at Ashton United FC on 27 May

ESFA PREMIER LEAGUE U.19 INTER COUNTY COMPETITION

SEMI-FINALS
Humberside v Hampshire 1-1, 2-4
West Yorkshire v Essex 3-2

FINAL
West Yorkshire v Hampshire 0-0
Played at Bradford City FC on 15 May

ESFA PREDATOR PREMIER 7-A-SIDE TROPHY

SEMI-FINALS
Swindon* v Stevenage 0-0
Wirral* v Telford 0-0
**Won on corners gained*

THIRD PLACE
Telford v Stevenage 1-0

FINAL
Wirral v Swindon 2-0
Played at Wembley Stadium on 11 March

ESFA PREDATOR 6-A-SIDE TROPHY

SEMI-FINALS
Priestmead Middle School, Harrow v Broadstone Middle School, Poole 2-1
Ling Moor Primary School, Lincoln* v St Aidan's Primary, Hartlepool 0-0
**Won on corners gained*

THIRD PLACE
Broadstone v St. Aidan's 3-2

FINAL
Priestmead v Ling Moor 0-0
Played at Wembley Stadium on 10 June

BOODLE & DUNTHORNE INDEPENDENT SCHOOLS FA CUP 1994–95

FIRST ROUND
Bye–Wellingborough
Latymer Upper 1, Manchester GS 5
Bradfield 3, Aldenham 1
QEGS, Blackburn 3, Kimbolton 1
Wolverhampton GS 2, Lancing 0
Bury GS 0, Hampton 1
Ardingly 2, Bolton 1
St Bede's 4, Charterhouse 0
Malvern 1, King's School, Chester 4
Shrewsbury 1, Eton 2
KES, Witley 0, Chigwell 1
Hulme GS 0, Forest 0 *aet* (*Forest won 3-1 on penalties*)
Alleyn's 2, Repton 2 *aet* (*Alleyn's won 5-4 on penalties*)
Batley GS 5, Oswestry 1
Westminster 1, Brentwood 4
John Lyon 7, Highgate 1

SECOND ROUND
Chigwell 2, Forest 1
Brentwood 2, King's School, Chester 0
Ardingly 6, John Lyon 2
St Bede's 3, Alleyn's 0
Eton 1, Batley GS 3 *aet*
QEGS, Blackburn 2, Hampton 1
Bradfield 5, Wellingborough 0
Wolverhampton GS 3, Manchester GS 2

THIRD ROUND
Wolverhampton GS 7, Bradfield 1
Ardingly 4, Brentwood 0
QEGS, Blackburn 3, St Bede's 3 *aet* (*St Bede's won 5-3 on penalties*)
Batley GS 2, Chigwell 1 *aet*

SEMI-FINALS
Wolverhampton GS 1, St Bede's 2
Ardingly 3, Batley GS 0

FINAL
St Bede's 3, Ardingly 2 *aet* (*at Craven Cottage*)

INTERNATIONAL PROGRAMME 1994–95

UNDER 15
England 2, Wales 2–Newport, 10 February
England 7, Belgium 0–Plymouth, 3 March
England 1, Brazil 0–Wembley, 11 March
England 1, N. Ireland 0–Newtownards, 24 March
England 2, Scotland 1–Newcastle, 28 April
England 5, Austria 0–Salzburg, 10 May
England 0, Eire 2–Dublin, 23 May
England 2, Germany 4–Wembley, 10 June
Overall Record....Played 8, Won 5, Drawn 1, Lost 2, Goals For 20 Goals Against 9
Goals: Owen (12), Hibburt (2), Jones (2), Ball, Burt, Kell, O'Brien

UNDER 18
England 0, France 5–Armenttieres, 15 February
England 1, Holland 3–Bodegraven, 28 February
England 4, Wales 4–Mansfield, 27 March
England 0, Switzerland 0–Nottingham, 31 March
England 0, Eire 0–Huddersfield, 10 April
Overall Record....Played 5, Won 0, Drawn 3, Lost 2, Goals For 5 Goals Against 12
Goals: Miles (3), Pierson, Ward

VICTORY SHIELD 1994–95

Wales 2, England 2–Newport, 10 February
N. Ireland 1, Wales 3–Belfast, 24 February
Scotland 5, N. Ireland 1–East Fife, 10 March
Scotland 7, Wales 3–Dumbarton, 16 March
N. Ireland 0, England 1–Newtownards, 24 March
England 2, Scotland 1–Newcastle, 28 April

	P	W	D	L	F	A	Pts
England	3	2	1	0	5	3	5
Scotland	3	2	0	1	13	6—	4
Wales	3	1	1	1	8	10	3
N. Ireland	3	0	0	0	2	9	0

CENTENARY SHIELD 1994–95

England 4, Wales 4–Mansfield, 27 March
Wales 0, Switzerland 1–Nottingham, 29 March
England 0, Switzerland 0–Nottingham, 31 March

	P	W	D	L	F	A	Pts
Switzerland	2	1	1	0	1	0	3
England	2	0	2	0	4	4	2
Wales	2	0	1	1	4	5	1

England photographed before a coaching weekend at Lilleshall National Sports Centre
Back Row (left to right): Ian Foster, Sufyan Ghazghazi, Richard Ward, Nicholas Miles, Richard Cort, David Gee, Graham Knight
Centre Row: Paul Bracknell (Team Manager), David Cook (Assistant Manager), Andrew Fotiadis, Lee Bray, David Diggle, Christopher Jones, Dr Daniel Baron (Team Doctor), Frank Melia (Physiotherapist)
Front Row: Dean Tallentire, Richard Fidler (Captain), David Willacy (Chairman), Gregg Dalley, Christopher Pedrick

THE AVON INSURANCE COMBINATION

Division One

	P	W	D	L	F	A	Pts
Tottenham Hotspur	38	19	13	6	67	34	70
Southampton	38	21	7	10	78	54	70
Charlton	38	20	9	9	71	46	69
QPR	38	19	9	10	68	34	66
Chelsea	38	17	13	8	76	53	64
Ipswich Town	38	14	13	11	65	50	55
Crystal Palace	38	15	10	13	50	40	55
West Ham United	38	16	6	16	49	39	54
Watford	38	15	9	14	48	49	54
Norwich City	38	13	12	13	62	58	51
Luton Town	38	14	7	17	57	66	49
Millwall	38	14	6	18	51	62	48
Wimbledon	38	11	14	13	55	56	47
Arsenal	38	11	14	13	61	69	47
Bristol City	38	12	10	16	61	65	46
Bristol Rovers	38	10	10	18	50	81	40
Swindon Town	38	9	12	17	34	60	39
Brighton & HA	38	10	9	19	54	84	39
Portsmouth	38	11	6	21	31	72	39
Oxford United	38	9	11	18	50	66	38

Division Two

	P	W	D	L	F	A	Pts
Swansea City	20	12	6	2	42	27	42
Birmingham City	20	11	5	4	42	20	38
Cardiff City	20	12	1	7	47	27	37
Torquay United	20	11	2	7	49	37	35
Exeter City	20	10	4	6	40	36	34
Plymouth Argyle	20	10	1	9	33	26	31
AFC Bournemouth	20	8	4	8	36	33	28
Bath City	20	7	2	11	32	47	23
Cheltenham Town	20	4	5	11	22	46	17
Hereford United	20	3	4	13	27	45	13
Yeovil Town	20	3	4	13	27	53	13

League Cup Tables

Group A

	P	W	D	L	F	A	Pts
Torquay United	8	4	3	1	22	15	15
AFC Bournemouth	8	4	2	2	22	19	14
Plymouth Argyle	8	2	4	2	19	16	10
Exeter City	8	2	4	2	11	13	10
Yeovil Town	8	1	1	6	9	20	4

Group B

	P	W	D	L	F	A	Pts
Swansea City	10	8	1	1	36	7	25
Birmingham City	10	5	3	2	29	15	18
Cardiff City	10	4	1	5	18	18	13
Hereford United	10	3	3	4	13	18	12
Cheltenham Town	10	3	1	6	13	35	10
Bath City	10	1	3	6	8	24	6

THE CENTRAL LEAGUE

Division One

	P	W	D	L	F	A	Pts
Bolton Wanderers	34	22	5	7	69	46	71
Everton	34	17	10	7	63	32	61
Leeds United	34	19	4	11	53	37	61
Sheffield United	34	17	8	9	49	36	59
Tranmere Rovers	34	16	9	9	65	53	57
Derby County	34	15	7	12	51	52	52
Notts County	34	15	6	13	46	48	51
West Bromwich Albion	34	13	8	13	53	54	47
Wolverhampton Wanderers	34	12	11	11	40	52	47
Manchester United	34	12	9	13	45	45	45
Stoke City	34	12	7	15	46	44	43
Blackburn Rovers	34	10	12	12	31	37	42
Liverpool	34	11	9	14	41	48	42
Nottingham Forest	34	9	11	14	45	46	38
Sunderland	34	10	8	16	49	56	38
Aston Villa	34	11	4	19	41	53	37
Coventry City	34	8	7	19	30	45	31
Rotherham United	34	7	5	22	34	67	26

Division Two

	P	W	D	L	F	A	Pts
Newcastle United	34	22	4	8	68	38	70
Birmingham City	34	21	5	8	74	39	68
Sheffield Wednesday	34	20	6	8	74	40	66
Oldham Athletic	34	20	6	8	73	51	66
Leicester City	34	20	4	10	72	42	64
Middlesbrough	34	17	7	10	84	48	58
Barnsley	34	17	7	10	68	45	58
Manchester City	34	17	5	12	52	40	56
Burnley	34	15	6	13	67	68	51
Port Vale	34	12	11	11	58	52	47
Preston North End	34	10	12	12	51	57	42
Grimsby Town	34	10	7	17	47	62	37
York City	34	10	7	17	39	53	37
Blackpool	34	10	3	21	41	59	33
Mansfield Town	34	8	5	21	42	87	29
Huddersfield Town	34	7	7	20	38	67	28
Hull City	34	7	5	22	26	80	26
Bradford City	34	6	7	21	32	78	25

THE FEDERATION BREWERY NORTHERN LEAGUE

Division One

	P	W	D	L	F	A	Pts
Tow Law Town	38	28	6	4	105	39	90
Billingham Synthonia	38	23	7	8	99	35	76
Whitby Town	38	22	10	6	88	45	76
Bedlington Terriers	38	21	12	5	72	35	75
RTM Newcastle	38	21	9	8	93	42	72
Guisborough Town	38	19	11	8	79	48	68
Durham City	38	17	12	9	75	45	63
Dunston FB	38	16	12	10	70	62	60
Consett	38	15	11	12	74	55	56
Shildon	38	12	13	13	57	63	49
Hebburn*	38	14	9	15	57	68	48
West Auckland	38	13	8	17	47	61	47
Seaham Red Star*	38	14	6	18	72	72	45
Peterlee Newtown	38	12	9	17	62	80	45
Murton	38	10	5	23	48	89	35
Chester Le Street	38	8	7	23	57	99	31
Ferryhill Athletic*	38	9	6	23	34	80	30
Eppleton CW	38	8	4	26	38	97	28
Northallerton*	38	9	3	26	35	93	27
Prudhoe Town	38	6	6	26	39	93	24

Division Two

	P	W	D	L	F	A	Pts
Whickham	38	26	10	2	103	37	88
Crook Town	38	26	6	6	102	40	84
Stockton**	38	26	5	7	116	49	77
Brandon United	38	21	9	8	77	39	72
Billingham Town*	38	23	4	11	95	50	70
Hartlepool Town**	38	22	9	7	91	50	69
Ashington	38	19	2	17	77	66	59
Evenwood Town	38	17	8	13	72	63	59
Washington*	38	17	9	12	74	55	57
Easington Colliery	38	15	10	13	55	51	55
Willington	38	17	3	10	62	61	54
Shotton Comrades	38	15	8	15	86	83	53
Esh Winning	38	15	7	16	78	88	52
Morpeth Town	38	13	6	19	69	67	45
Ryhope CA	38	12	9	17	55	62	45
Norton	38	13	4	21	71	83	43
Alnwick Town	38	10	6	22	60	87	33
Darlington CS	38	4	5	29	37	140	17
Hordern CW	38	3	3	32	42	151	12
Langley Park*	38	3	3	32	40	140	9

*Three points deducted

**Six points deducted

SKOL MIDLAND FOOTBALL COMBINATION

Premier Division

	P	W	D	L	F	A	Pts
Northfield Town	33	27	3	3	96	37	84
Bloxwich Town	32	21	8	3	103	36	71
Wellesbourne	32	20	4	8	60	40	64
Alvechurch Villa	32	14	11	7	64	37	53
Handrahan Timbers	32	14	9	9	60	43	51
Olton Royale	31	15	5	11	62	66	50
Meir KA	30	13	8	9	68	52	47
Shirley Town	33	13	6	14	56	64	45
Studley BKL	31	12	8	11	59	48	44
West Midland Fire	33	11	10	12	38	44	43
Chelmsley Town	32	9	10	13	49	60	37
Knowle	33	9	10	14	40	60	37
Coleshill Town	33	9	9	15	45	59	36
Kings Heath	32	8	7	17	44	67	31
Ansells	31	9	4	18	35	58	31
Sherwood Celtic	31	8	5	18	46	71	29
Upton Town	34	7	7	20	45	68	28
Highgate United	33	6	4	23	34	94	22

Division One

	P	W	D	L	F	A	Pts
Southam United	31	20	3	8	71	42	63
Sphinx	28	19	5	4	68	24	62
Bilston Community College	32	19	4	9	86	40	61
Massey Ferguson	26	17	7	2	62	22	58
GPT (Coventry)	30	18	3	9	86	53	57
Jaguar-Daimler	30	16	5	9	54	39	53
Kenilworth Town	30	11	9	10	55	46	42
Hams Hall	29	11	5	13	38	48	38
Polesworth North Warwick	31	11	5	15	65	78	38
Dudley Sports	29	10	7	12	50	57	37
Colletts Green	32	10	7	15	54	65	37
Monica Star	31	8	12	11	39	49	36
Wilmcote	31	9	5	17	45	79	32
Badsey Rangers	29	8	6	15	42	58	30
Kings Norton Ex Service	31	7	7	17	44	73	28
Barlestone St Giles	32	7	7	18	48	82	28
Thimblemill REC	32	6	3	23	40	92	21

Division Two

	P	W	D	L	F	A	Pts
Richmond Swifts	28	23	2	3	91	22	71
Alveston	28	17	5	6	56	27	56
Fairfield Villa	30	15	8	7	58	43	53
Holly Lane 92	30	16	4	10	81	47	52
Albright & Wilson	30	14	9	7	65	46	51
Rugby Town	30	14	6	10	61	57	48
Continental Star	30	14	4	12	57	47	46
Alvis SGL	29	14	3	12	43	35	45
Earlswood Town	30	11	10	9	54	40	43
Enville Athletic	30	12	6	12	53	56	42
Blackheath Electrodrives	30	10	8	12	43	49	38
Ledbury Town '84	30	9	3	18	54	73	30
Coleshill Town Res	30	8	6	16	38	85	30
Archdale '73	30	8	4	18	42	66	28
Burntwood	30	6	3	21	28	80	21
Studley BKL Res	29	2	7	20	26	77	13

LANCASHIRE LEAGUE

Division One

	P	W	D	L	F	A	Pts
Manchester United A	22	15	5	2	65	24	50
Crewe Alexandra Reserve	22	13	5	4	65	40	44
Burnley A	22	14	2	6	52	33	44
Everton A	22	12	0	10	49	34	36
Blackburn Rovers A	22	11	3	8	38	35	36
Tranmere Rovers A	22	10	5	7	46	33	35
Liverpool A	22	10	4	8	41	28	34
Oldham Athletic A	22	8	4	10	34	40	28
Bury A	22	7	5	10	28	44	26
Blackpool A	22	6	3	13	36	50	21
Marine Reserve	22	4	1	17	29	64	13
Morecambe Reserves	22	2	3	17	14	72	9

Division Two

	P	W	D	L	F	A	Pts
Manchester City A	36	25	5	6	89	34	80
Blackburn Rovers B	36	24	6	6	84	33	78
Manchester United B	36	21	6	9	93	47	69
Preston North End B	36	20	7	9	90	54	67
Liverpool B	36	21	4	11	80	52	67
Crewe Alexandra A	36	17	5	14	73	62	56
Tranmere Rovers B	36	16	7	13	64	49	55
Everton B	36	15	9	12	67	61	54
Burnley B	36	16	6	14	61	66	54
Wigan Athletic A	36	16	6	14	65	73	54
Oldham Athletic B	36	15	5	16	54	54	50
Bolton Wanderers A	36	13	10	13	43	45	49
Blackpool B	36	15	3	18	70	66	48
Carlisle United A	36	12	8	16	61	63	44
Stockport County A	36	10	6	20	66	94	36
Chester City A	36	9	6	21	49	95	33
Rochdale A	36	8	6	22	44	94	30
Bury B	36	7	6	23	47	92	27
Marine Youth	36	4	5	27	25	91	17

CARLING NORTH WEST COUNTIES LEAGUE

Division One

	P	W	D	L	F	A	Pts
Bradford Park Avenue	42	30	4	8	98	43	94
Clitheroe	42	27	9	6	104	49	90
St Helens Town	42	27	8	7	86	42	89
Trafford	42	27	5	10	98	52	86
Newcastle Town	42	24	7	11	75	57	79
Glossop North End	42	23	8	11	88	59	77
Blackpool Rovers	42	22	7	13	81	64	73
Burscough	42	19	15	8	102	65	72
Prescot	42	16	8	18	47	47	56
Penrith	42	16	7	18	72	71	55
Chadderton	42	15	7	20	56	70	52
Maine Road	42	14	9	19	68	83	51
Holker Old Boys	42	13	11	18	61	69	50
Kidsgrove Athletic	42	14	8	20	66	78	50
Eastwood Hanley	42	14	8	20	74	81	50
Nantwich Town	42	14	6	21	84	82	49
Darwen	42	14	5	19	65	82	47
Rossendale United	42	12	11	19	60	82	47
Bootle	42	11	9	21	45	67	43
Skelmersdale United	42	10	7	25	67	118	37
Salford City	42	9	9	24	45	85	36
Bacup	42	3	6	33	35	132	15

Division Two

	P	W	D	L	F	A	Pts
Flixton	30	21	6	3	98	32	69
Oldham Town	30	20	6	4	83	34	66
Tetley Walker	30	18	5	7	75	46	59
Atherton Collieries	30	18	4	8	67	41	58
Stantondale	30	18	3	9	58	43	57
Nelson	30	13	8	9	64	44	47
Haslingden	30	14	4	12	76	64	46
Blackpool Mechanics	30	12	8	10	72	57	44
Maghull	30	11	8	11	58	46	41
Formby	30	11	6	13	57	53	39
Cheadle Town	30	10	7	13	48	52	37
Castleton Gabriels	30	9	9	12	56	75	36
Daisy Hill	30	6	8	16	53	73	26
Ashton Town	30	6	2	22	39	92	20
Irlam Town	30	5	3	22	30	98	18
Squires Gate	30	2	5	23	30	114	11

VAUX WEARSIDE LEAGUE

Division One

	P	W	D	L	F	A	Pts
South Shields	34	28	2	4	116	44	86
Marske United	34	24	8	2	109	44	80
Jarrow Roofing	34	21	5	8	104	40	68
Nissan	34	20	6	8	84	36	66
Annfield Plain	34	20	6	8	81	63	66
Windscale	34	17	8	9	89	58	59
Kennek Roker*	34	19	4	11	71	52	58
Ryhope CW	34	15	7	12	67	56	52
Boldon CA	34	15	5	14	66	53	50
North Shields	34	14	6	14	52	60	48
Cleadon SC	34	14	5	15	53	52	47
Jarrow*	34	13	4	17	66	71	40
Wolviston	34	10	6	18	65	90	36
Herrington CW	34	8	8	18	44	76	32
Hartlepool BWOB*	34	7	6	21	48	70	24
North Ormesby	34	6	4	24	47	99	22
Cleator Moor	34	4	7	23	28	118	19
Silksworth	34	0	5	29	31	129	5

Division Two

	P	W	D	L	F	A	Pts
Birtley Town	24	18	2	4	84	29	56
Brinkburn CA	24	14	4	6	71	40	46
SC Fulwell	24	12	9	3	47	22	45
Murton Inter	24	13	5	6	61	42	44
Whitehaven Ams*	24	13	6	5	69	43	42
Harton & Westoe CW	24	12	4	8	56	47	40
Stanley United	24	10	8	6	65	44	38
Wingate	24	7	7	10	53	48	28
Guisborough Priory	24	7	7	10	42	49	28
Chilton Moor	24	8	2	14	41	64	26
Northallerton TS*	24	4	4	16	37	76	16
Washington Glebe	24	3	5	16	34	82	14
Prudhoe Swinton	24	1	3	20	24	96	6

*3 points deducted

THE JEWSON SOUTH-WESTERN FOOTBALL LEAGUE

	P	W	D	L	F	A	Pts
Launceston	34	26	8	2	115	24	84
Bodmin Town	34	25	4	5	89	36	79
Truro City	34	23	4	7	93	45	73
Falmouth Town	34	22	5	7	106	45	71
Torpoint Athletic	34	21	5	8	79	40	68
Porthleven	34	16	9	9	84	54	57
Millbrook	34	14	11	9	68	58	53
Holsworthy	34	14	9	11	44	44	51
Wadebridge Town	34	14	7	13	66	75	49
Tavistock*	34	12	8	14	46	71	43
Appledore/BAAC	34	10	4	20	55	79	34
Mullion	34	8	10	16	46	77	34
Newquay	34	9	6	19	66	86	33
St Blazey	34	9	6	19	60	70	33
Okehampton Argyle	34	8	4	22	49	102	28
Devon/Cornwall Police	34	8	3	23	52	93	27
Penzance	34	6	7	21	35	79	25
St Austell	34	4	6	24	31	96	18

*One point deducted

NORTHERN ALLIANCE LEAGUE

Premier Division

	P	W	D	L	F	A	Pts
Benfield Park	28	20	4	4	76	32	64
West Allotment Celtic	28	20	2	6	78	34	62
Gillford Park	28	19	4	5	74	30	61
Seaton Delaval Amateurs	28	18	6	4	72	38	60
Carlisle City	28	18	5	5	93	39	59
Ponteland United	28	15	6	7	64	43	51
Westerhope	28	11	9	8	61	53	42
Winlaton*	28	13	5	10	69	55	41
Blyth Seahorse	28	9	7	12	53	60	34
Spittal Rovers	28	9	6	13	54	47	33
Heaton Stannington	28	7	2	19	46	80	23
Walker**	28	8	3	17	57	72	21
Longbenton*	28	5	4	19	40	92	16
Haltwhistle Crown Paints	28	2	3	23	21	102	9
Wark	28	2	2	24	20	101	8

Division One

	P	W	D	L	F	A	Pts
Amble Town*	30	25	0	5	108	46	72
North Shields St Columbas	30	19	4	7	77	46	61
Hexham Swinton	30	16	8	6	59	40	56
Orwin Rosehill*	30	18	4	8	96	51	55
Ashington Hirst	30	16	4	10	98	64	52
Percy Main Amateurs	30	13	9	8	60	37	48
Hebburn Reyrolle	30	13	6	11	90	64	45
Newbiggin Central Welfare*	30	14	4	12	70	72	43
Dudley Welfare	30	13	4	13	64	75	43
Forest Hall	30	12	6	12	49	52	42
Gosforth Bohemians	30	10	5	15	55	68	35
Swalwell*	30	8	10	12	63	76	31
Procter and Gamble	30	8	2	20	54	90	26
Ryton	30	6	6	18	51	86	24
Northern Counties	30	5	5	20	46	122	20
Wylam	30	4	3	23	53	104	15

Division Two

	P	W	D	L	F	A	Pts
Walker Ledwood	30	24	2	4	118	43	74
Shankhouse	30	21	1	8	108	44	64
Rutherford	30	20	3	7	98	42	63
Newcastle University	30	18	5	7	77	57	59
Monkseaton Kosa	30	13	6	11	66	65	45
Otterburn	30	12	8	10	51	43	44
Highfields United	30	13	2	15	71	65	41
Heddon Institute	30	11	7	12	67	68	40
Wheelcroft	30	11	5	14	56	71	38
Throckley†	30	16	1	13	82	65	37
Stobswood Welfare	30	11	4	15	55	71	37
Hexham Border Counties*	30	12	4	14	66	91	37
Marden Athletic	30	10	4	16	66	78	34
Aydon Forest	30	9	4	17	63	83	31
Shilbottle Col/Welfare	30	7	5	18	52	87	26
Norgas United*	30	0	3	27	29	152	0

*Three points deducted
**Six points deducted
†Twelve points deducted

INTERLINK EXPRESS MIDLAND FOOTBALL ALLIANCE

	P	W	D	L	F	A	Pts
Paget Rangers	38	24	9	5	65	32	81
Hinckley Athletic	38	20	9	9	76	49	69
Stratford Town	38	19	9	10	69	46	66
Shepshed Dynamo	38	18	10	10	63	51	64
Halesowen Harriers	38	19	6	13	87	55	63
Shifnal Town	38	16	14	8	65	45	62
Boldmere St Michael	38	18	8	12	65	48	62
Oldbury United	38	18	8	12	58	47	62
Knypersley Victoria	38	15	12	11	82	54	57
Willenhall Town	38	15	7	16	55	58	52
West Midlands Police	38	14	8	16	53	51	50
Stapenhill	38	15	5	18	60	80	50
Rocester	38	12	12	14	48	50	48
Sandwell Borough	38	12	12	14	62	69	48
Barwell	38	12	9	17	58	69	45
Pershore Town	38	12	9	17	49	71	45
Chasetown	38	8	13	17	52	72	37
Rushall Olympic	38	9	10	19	60	85	37
Bolehall Swifts	38	9	9	20	45	60	36
Brierley Hill Town	38	3	5	30	27	107	14

MANCHESTER LEAGUE

Premier Division

	P	*W*	*D*	*L*	*F*	*A*	*Pts*
Abbey Hey	30	20	5	5	79	39	65
Mitchell Shackleton	30	17	5	8	72	45	56
East Manchester	30	17	4	9	56	49	55
Wythenshawe Town	30	16	6	8	55	40	54
Woodley SC	30	16	5	9	73	53	53
Wythenshawe Amateurs	30	14	7	9	56	37	49
Ramsbottom United	30	12	8	10	55	48	44
Atherton Town	30	14	1	15	71	62	43
BTCL	30	11	8	11	47	49	41
Dukinfield Town	30	11	7	12	50	56	40
Prestwich Heys	30	10	5	15	56	61	35
Stockport Georgians	30	10	4	16	43	62	34
Little Hulton United	30	9	6	15	41	53	33
Springhead	30	9	5	16	47	60	32
Sacred Heart	30	8	5	17	39	71	29
Monton	30	4	3	23	40	95	15

Division One

	P	*W*	*D*	*L*	*F*	*A*	*Pts*
Highfield United	30	23	4	3	102	31	73
Avro	30	19	9	2	73	28	66
Hollinwood	30	17	9	4	77	38	60
Stand Athletic	30	17	5	8	73	42	56
Milton	30	15	5	10	63	45	50
Manchester Royal	30	15	3	12	56	62	48
Breightmet United	30	12	9	9	54	48	45
Whitworth Valley	30	11	10	9	60	51	43
Pennington	30	11	8	11	62	53	41
Coldhurst United	30	12	2	16	61	81	38
Old Alts	30	10	5	15	65	80	35
Whalley Range	30	10	1	19	46	73	31
New Mills	30	8	6	16	49	82	30
Zeneca	30	7	3	20	34	79	24
GMP	30	7	2	21	54	80	23
Ashton Athletic	30	4	3	23	32	88	15

WINSTONLEAD KENT LEAGUE

Division One

	P	*W*	*D*	*L*	*F*	*A*	*Pts*
Sheppey United	40	29	9	2	118	32	96
Chatham Town	40	26	10	4	117	41	88
Furness	40	24	9	7	81	33	81
Folkestone Invicta	40	21	11	8	107	51	74
Ramsgate	40	21	11	8	91	45	74
Thamesmead Town	40	21	10	9	87	52	73
Herne Bay	40	19	13	8	68	35	70
Deal Town	40	18	10	12	87	62	64
Whitstable Town	40	17	11	12	83	61	62
Beckenham Town	40	15	11	14	61	61	56
Dartford	40	14	11	15	61	51	53
Corinthian	40	15	8	17	50	63	53
Canterbury City	40	14	6	20	66	80	48
Tunbridge Wells	40	12	11	17	48	66	47
Greenwich Borough	40	13	6	21	71	94	45
Crockenhill	40	10	12	18	45	62	42
Slade Green	40	10	12	18	49	73	42
Faversham Town	40	9	8	23	49	118	35
Cray Wanderers	40	6	14	20	45	76	32
Darenth Heathside	40	3	4	33	32	137	13
Kent Police	40	4	1	35	30	153	13

Division Two

	P	*W*	*D*	*L*	*F*	*A*	*Pts*
Thamesmead Town	28	19	5	4	74	31	62
Dover Athletic	28	18	5	5	73	44	59
Tonbridge FC	28	16	4	8	67	40	52
Herne Bay	28	15	2	11	69	47	47
Ramsgate	28	13	8	7	46	39	47
Hastings Town	28	11	9	8	59	42	42
Chatham Town*	28	12	5	11	57	54	40
Furness	28	11	7	10	40	37	40
Folkestone Invicta	28	11	6	11	60	54	39
Beckenham Town	28	8	8	12	48	56	32
Corinthian	28	8	6	14	37	56	30
Whitstable Town	28	6	9	13	49	56	27
Faversham Town**	28	7	5	16	31	61	23
Deal Town	28	6	4	18	40	78	22
Canterbury City	28	5	5	18	26	81	20

*One point deducted

**Three points deducted

GREAT MILLS LEAGUE

Premier Division

	P	*W*	*D*	*L*	*F*	*A*	*Pts*
Tiverton Town	34	28	3	3	128	23	87
Elmore	34	27	5	2	94	39	86
Taunton Town	34	15	12	7	59	28	57
Barnstaple Town	34	16	8	10	58	48	56
Westbury United	34	16	6	12	71	53	54
Mangotsfield United	34	16	6	12	51	50	54
Paulton Rovers	34	15	7	12	62	71	52
Chippenham Town	34	14	9	11	54	54	51
Bristol Manor Farm	34	14	6	14	51	48	48
Liskeard Athletic	34	12	9	13	59	55	45
Saltash United	34	12	9	13	38	43	45
Odd Down	34	11	9	14	47	53	42
Bridport	34	11	6	17	44	59	39
Calne Town	34	11	3	20	36	68	36
Bideford	34	10	5	19	48	69	35
Crediton United	34	8	6	20	43	77	30
Torrington	34	6	10	18	49	89	28
Frome Town	34	3	3	28	36	101	12

First Division

	P	*W*	*D*	*L*	*F*	*A*	*Pts*
Brislington	40	30	7	3	113	25	97
Glastonbury	40	26	8	6	91	35	86
Backwell UnitEd	40	26	8	6	75	33	86
Warminster Town	40	26	7	7	93	42	85
Chard Town	40	25	10	5	74	35	85
Bridgwater Town	40	18	13	9	62	47	67
Keynsham Town	40	17	11	12	73	62	62
Bishop Sutton	40	17	7	16	61	61	58
Exmouth Town	40	16	6	18	55	63	54
Melksham Town	40	14	10	16	62	61	52
Clyst Rovers	40	15	5	20	60	84	50
Amesbury Town	40	14	7	19	67	61	49
Wellington	40	14	7	18	55	59	49
Ilfracombe Town	40	13	8	19	64	58	47
Heavitree United	40	12	7	21	52	94	43
Welton Rovers	40	11	9	20	50	62	42
Devizes Town	40	11	7	22	57	82	40
Pewsey Vale	40	10	8	22	52	77	38
Larkhall Athletic	40	8	8	24	39	89	32
Dawlish Town	40	8	8	24	41	92	32
Minehead	40	5	7	28	24	98	22

JEWSON (EAST COUNTIES) LEAGUE

Premier Division

	P	*W*	*D*	*L*	*F*	*A*	*Pts*
Halstead Town	42	31	8	3	129	35	101
Wroxham	42	29	7	6	96	44	94
Wisbech Town	42	28	7	7	108	46	91
Diss Town	42	27	6	9	114	49	87
Harwich & Parkeston	42	24	8	10	130	77	80
Fakenham Town	42	22	7	13	80	53	73
Lowestoft Town	42	20	12	10	77	56	72
Newmarket Town	42	20	8	14	69	57	68
Sudbury Wanderers	42	19	10	13	77	63	67
Woodbridge Town	42	17	11	14	66	58	62
Stowmarket Town	42	15	11	16	77	72	56
Tiptree United	42	17	5	20	76	86	56
Felixstowe Town	42	17	4	21	54	70	55
March Town United	42	13	14	15	51	56	53
Hadleigh United	42	12	10	20	64	80	46
Great Yarmouth Town	42	11	8	23	44	69	41
Haverhill Rovers	42	11	7	24	52	82	40
Soham Town Rangers	42	9	11	22	60	99	38
Watton United	42	10	6	26	44	87	36
Cornard United	42	8	10	24	46	99	34
Histon	42	10	3	29	54	127	33
Chatteris Town	42	2	7	33	30	133	13

Division One

	P	W	D	L	F	A	Pts
Clacton Town	36	25	5	6	86	39	80
Sudbury Town Reserves	36	23	6	7	102	49	75
Warboys Town	36	23	5	8	82	45	74
Gorleston	36	21	10	5	101	44	73
Downham Town	36	20	9	7	99	43	69
Ely City	36	21	5	10	87	45	68
Brightlingsea United	36	20	5	11	69	46	65
Ipswich Wanderers	36	18	8	10	85	62	62
Somersham Town	36	16	5	15	61	61	53
Swaffham Town	36	15	7	14	69	59	52
Mildenhall Town	36	15	5	16	57	60	50
King's Lynn Reserves	36	14	6	16	66	67	48
Norwich United	36	8	13	15	48	59	37
Stanway Rovers	36	11	4	21	60	89	37
Thetford Town	36	9	7	20	38	76	34
Long Sutton Athletic	36	9	3	24	47	91	30
Cambridge City Res	36	7	9	20	37	83	30
Brantham Athletic	36	6	5	25	45	82	23
Bury Town Reserves	36	2	1	33	33	172	7

JOHN SMITH'S BITTER CENTRAL MIDLANDS LEAGUE

Supreme Division

	P	W	D	L	F	A	Pts
Heanor Town	32	26	1	5	92	34	79
Oakham United	32	23	2	6	84	36	71
Priory (Eastwood)	32	21	6	5	73	32	69
Kimberley Town	32	15	9	8	60	48	54
Glapwell	32	15	8	9	63	45	53
Borrowash Victoria	32	13	13	6	43	27	52
Kiveton Park	32	15	5	12	60	45	50
Harworth CI	32	12	9	11	55	56	45
Sandiacre Town	32	11	10	11	58	61	43
Gedling Town	32	12	5	15	62	54	41
Shirebrook Town	32	11	5	16	43	68	38
Staveley MW	32	8	7	17	40	64	31
Sheffield Aurora	32	7	8	17	47	88	29
South Normanton Ath	32	7	7	18	45	72	28
Nettleham	32	5	10	17	31	57	25
Long Eaton United	32	6	7	19	43	71	25
Rossington	32	4	10	18	45	86	22

Premier Division

	P	W	D	L	F	A	Pts
Clipstone Welfare	32	23	4	5	88	28	73
Case Sports	32	21	7	4	97	37	70
Thorne Colliery	32	20	7	5	82	30	67
Mickleover Sports	32	20	4	8	84	51	64
Nuthall	32	18	7	7	62	34	61
Derby C&WR	32	18	3	11	73	44	57
Radford	32	16	6	10	57	43	54
Shardlow St. James	32	14	7	11	46	43	49
Askern Welfare	32	13	7	12	80	57	46
Derby Rolls Royce	32	13	4	15	51	69	43
Holbrook MW	32	9	8	15	47	65	35
Newhall United	32	9	7	16	56	82	34
Mexborough Athletic	32	9	5	18	59	80	32
Killamarsh Athletic	32	7	6	19	52	82	27
Stanton Ilkeston	32	5	10	17	42	74	25
Mickleover RBL	32	4	9	19	33	82	21
Blackwell MW	32	1	3	28	22	130	6

LONDON SPARTAN FOOTBALL LEAGUE

Premier Division

	P	W	D	L	F	A	Pts
Croydon	30	23	3	4	87	31	72
St Margaretsbury	30	21	5	4	77	38	68
Barkingside	30	18	4	8	58	47	58
Brimsdown Rovers	30	17	5	8	56	39	56
Corinthian Casuals	30	16	4	10	70	45	52
Willesden	30	12	9	9	55	36	45
Brook House	30	13	5	12	69	52	44
Cockfosters	30	10	11	9	52	45	41
Hillingdon Borough	30	10	7	13	43	66	37
Tower Hamlets*	30	11	4	15	58	67	34
Beaconsfield	30	9	6	15	31	51	33
Waltham Abbey	30	8	7	15	39	59	31
Harringey Borough*	30	10	3	17	37	49	30
Hanwell Town	30	6	12	12	37	60	30
Walthamstow Pennant	30	8	5	17	43	56	29
Amersham Town	30	2	2	25	46	84	8

*Three points deducted – ineligible player

ESSEX SENIOR LEAGUE

Premier Division

	P	W	D	L	F	A	Pts
Great Wakering Rovers	28	23	2	3	82	14	71
Sawbridgeworth Town	28	23	2	3	73	20	71
Romford	28	18	7	3	54	30	61
Maldon Town	28	16	6	6	58	33	54
Ford United	28	13	6	9	48	30	45
Bowers United	28	12	3	13	41	45	39
Burnham Ramblers	28	12	3	13	42	47	39
Basildon United	28	10	8	10	57	35	38
East Ham United	28	9	9	10	28	32	36
Brentwood	28	7	11	10	39	37	32
Concord Rangers	28	9	5	14	32	42	32
Stansted	28	8	7	13	40	57	31
Southend Manor	28	3	8	17	32	80	17
Hullbridge Sports	28	4	1	23	17	67	13
Eton Manor	28	2	4	22	19	93	10

NORTHERN COUNTIES EAST LEAGUE

Premier Division

	P	W	D	L	F	A	Pts
Lincoln United	38	29	5	4	116	49	92
Arnold Town	38	25	7	6	98	46	82
Stockbridge PS	38	21	6	11	74	46	69
Belper Town	38	19	8	11	78	44	65
Ashfield United	38	18	11	9	65	48	65
Pickering Town	38	19	7	12	89	63	64
North Ferriby United	38	18	8	12	68	60	62
Armthorpe Welfare	38	13	18	7	56	41	57
Thackley	38	15	11	12	76	56	56
Ossett Albion	38	15	9	14	48	57	54
Brigg Town	38	14	10	14	49	57	52
Ossett Town	38	12	10	16	50	56	46
Maltby MW	38	13	7	18	59	71	46
Denaby United	38	12	9	17	48	77	45
Hucknall Town	38	9	13	16	47	60	40
Glasshoughton Welfare	38	10	9	19	60	68	39
Hallam	38	9	8	21	46	76	35
Sheffield	38	6	12	20	45	87	30
Liversedge	38	7	8	23	48	81	29
Pontefract Collieries	38	3	10	25	30	107	19

Division 1

	P	W	D	L	F	A	Pts
Hatfield Main	30	25	2	3	88	32	77
Worsborough Bridge	30	19	4	7	66	40	61
Immingham Town	30	18	4	8	66	43	58
Selby Town	30	16	9	5	62	38	57
Yorkshire Amateurs	30	15	8	7	53	29	53
Hall Road Rangers	30	15	7	8	57	44	52
Harrogate Railway	30	16	4	10	64	52	52
Eccleshill United	30	13	5	12	62	47	44
Garforth Town	30	11	8	11	58	49	41
Louth United	30	9	8	13	39	50	35
Rossington Main	30	9	7	14	48	63	34
Tadcaster Albion	30	6	8	16	36	59	26
Blidworth Welfare	30	7	5	18	39	63	26
Winterton Rangers	30	7	3	20	44	72	24
Parkgate*	30	5	5	20	47	84	18
Brodsworth MW	30	2	7	21	15	79	13

*Two points deducted

SOUTH EAST COUNTIES LEAGUE

Division One

	P	W	D	L	F	A	Pts
Tottenham Hotspur	30	21	4	5	67	32	46
Chelsea	30	17	6	7	66	45	40
Arsenal	30	18	3	9	72	39	39
Watford	30	16	5	9	53	48	37
Fulham	30	15	5	10	59	44	35
Norwich City	30	15	5	10	56	44	35
West Ham United	30	11	10	9	57	48	32
Gillingham	30	11	8	11	35	40	30
Millwall	30	11	7	12	44	55	29
Cambridge United	30	11	4	15	53	54	26
Charlton Athletic	30	7	12	11	39	46	26
Queens Park Rangers	30	9	7	14	44	57	25
Ipswich Town	30	8	8	14	31	43	24
Leyton Orient	30	6	9	15	26	40	21
Southend United	30	7	7	16	35	54	21
Portsmouth	30	5	4	21	32	80	14

Division Two

	P	W	D	L	F	A	Pts
Crystal Palace	28	20	5	3	68	26	45
Wimbledon	28	19	5	4	97	45	43
Bristol City	28	16	5	7	64	29	37
Swindon Town	28	16	3	9	57	35	35
Oxford United	28	12	11	5	49	33	35
AFC Bournemouth	28	13	7	8	57	57	33
Brentford	28	12	8	8	40	38	32
Tottenham Hotspur	28	12	4	12	58	59	28
Southampton	28	9	8	11	39	40	26
Brighton & Hove Albion	28	11	4	13	51	67	26
Luton Town	28	9	4	15	49	47	22
Colchester United	28	8	6	14	43	59	22
Reading	28	5	6	17	30	73	16
Bristol Rovers	28	1	11	16	28	54	13
Wycombe Wanderers	28	2	3	23	24	92	7

HELLENIC LEAGUE

Premier Division

	P	W	D	L	F	A	Pts
Cinderford Town	30	23	4	3	118	24	73
Fairford Town	30	21	4	5	73	25	67
Swindon Supermarine	30	16	4	10	76	44	52
North Leigh	30	15	7	8	55	39	52
Shortwood United	30	16	3	11	60	53	51
Cirencester Town	30	15	5	10	56	43	50
Tuffley Rovers	30	14	7	9	65	44	49
Banbury United	30	12	7	11	44	44	43
Pegasus Juniors	30	11	9	10	49	43	42
Bicester Town*	30	12	6	12	70	60	40
Abingdon United	30	11	5	14	55	58	38
Almondsbury Town	30	10	7	13	49	53	37
Carterton Town	30	7	9	14	36	60	30
Brackley Town	30	7	5	18	42	80	26
Highworth Town	30	2	6	22	30	93	12
Kintbury Rangers*	30	3	2	25	30	145	9

*Two points deducted

THE WASHINGTON AND DISTRICT LEAGUE

	P	W	D	L	F	A	Pts
Cabplant	26	19	3	4	55	30	60
Deneside	26	19	2	5	102	34	59
Belford House	26	18	3	5	84	46	57
Jig Net	26	17	2	7	73	47	53
Springwell	26	14	3	9	63	50	45
Easington Mechanics*	26	12	8	6	78	42	41
Throston	26	11	8	7	67	40	41
Dawdon	26	10	7	9	61	59	37
Simonside	26	8	6	12	49	62	30
Westwood	26	6	6	14	43	78	24
Mallard	26	6	4	16	43	72	22
Boldon Rossi	26	6	2	18	45	73	21
Whitehill	26	6	2	18	49	77	20
Wearmouth	26	1	1	24	27	165	4

**Points deducted*

MINERVA FOOTBALLS SOUTH MIDLANDS LEAGUE

Premier Division

	P	W	D	L	F	A	Pts
Arlesey Town	45	34	5	6	90	32	107
Wingate & Finchley	45	25	13	7	97	49	88
Brache Sparta	45	23	15	7	85	61	84
Royston Town	45	24	11	10	77	42	83
Shillington	45	22	11	12	64	38	77
Potters Bar Town	45	19	7	19	75	70	64
Biggleswade Town	45	17	10	18	65	71	61
Langford	45	15	15	15	61	64	60
Milton Keynes	45	15	14	16	71	77	59
Hoddesdon Town	45	15	11	19	56	57	56
Hatfield Town	45	14	12	19	66	80	54
Welwyn Garden City	45	11	13	21	53	72	46
Buckingham Athletic	45	10	13	22	51	88	43
Dunstable United	45	11	10	24	39	77	43
Harpenden Town	45	9	12	24	60	72	39
Letchworth Garden City	45	5	10	30	58	118	25

Senior Division

	P	W	D	L	F	A	Pts
London Colney	26	22	2	2	87	20	68
Toddington Rovers	26	16	4	6	80	30	52
New Bradwell St Peter	26	15	6	5	90	32	51
Leverstock Green	26	14	8	4	50	21	50
Stony Stratford Town	26	16	1	9	60	37	49
ACD FC	26	14	3	9	56	39	45
Tring Athletic	26	10	6	10	44	38	36
Bedford United	26	9	7	10	30	47	34
Ampthill Town	26	7	7	12	57	66	28
Winslow United	26	7	6	13	45	65	27
Totternhoe	26	8	2	16	40	64	26
Risborough Gardens	26	6	6	14	47	68	24
The 61 FC (Luton)	26	6	4	16	33	69	22
Pitstone & Ivinghoe	26	0	2	24	22	145	2

Division One

	P	W	D	L	F	A	Pts
Houghton Town	26	20	3	3	82	17	63
Kent Athletic	26	16	7	3	68	31	55
Walden Rangers	26	17	4	5	57	37	55
Eaton Bray	26	16	3	7	48	25	51
De Havilland	26	10	10	6	44	30	40
Bow Brickhill	26	10	7	9	47	44	37
Scot	26	9	6	11	42	52	33
Cranfield United	26	9	5	12	42	64	32
Caddington	26	8	7	11	50	45	31
Flamstead	26	9	2	15	27	48	29
Abbey National (MK)	26	6	5	15	32	65	23
Mercedes Benz	26	4	10	12	27	46	22
Emberton	26	5	7	14	31	52	22
Clifton Old Boys	26	2	6	18	20	61	12

TYNE WEAR THORPE LEAGUE

	P	W	D	L	F	A	Pts
Freeman	24	21	2	1	100	33	65
Grange Athletic	24	18	3	3	97	41	57
Fort	24	18	2	4	88	41	56
Crown Photo	24	17	1	6	94	64	52
Dunsfords	24	12	2	10	82	54	38
Rolls Royce*	24	11	3	10	74	54	36
Chowdene	24	10	2	12	57	73	32
Weardale*	24	10	4	10	63	69	28
Low Fell	24	8	1	15	47	78	25
New Ship	24	4	4	16	45	88	16
East North	24	5	1	18	42	87	13
251 Field*	24	5	3	16	32	89	12
Ivy House	24	8	2	14	29	96	11

**Points deducted*

HEREWARD SPORTS UNITED COUNTIES FOOTBALL LEAGUE

Premier Division

	P	W	D	L	F	A	Pts
Boston	36	25	5	6	92	36	80
Raunds	36	23	11	2	82	42	80
Cogenhoe	36	24	5	7	90	37	77
Holbeach	36	18	9	9	56	39	63
Northampton Spencer	36	17	8	11	69	47	59
Eynesbury	36	15	11	10	53	41	56
Mirrless Blackstone	36	14	10	12	53	52	52
Bourne	36	14	9	13	53	68	51
Stotfold	36	12	13	11	50	41	49
Spalding	36	11	12	13	57	54	45
Desborough	36	11	12	13	53	60	45
Long Buckby	36	9	16	11	58	61	43
Wootton	36	10	10	16	47	59	40
Potton	36	11	6	19	46	69	39
Stamford	36	9	9	18	50	69	36
Newport Pagnell	36	8	12	16	31	54	36
S & L Corby	36	8	10	18	40	65	34
Wellingborough	36	5	10	21	40	84	25
Kempston	36	4	10	22	46	88	22

Division One

	P	W	D	L	F	A	Pts
St Neots	36	28	3	5	119	41	87
Higham	36	27	4	5	92	31	85
Thrapston	36	25	7	4	107	44	82
Northampton Vanaid	36	24	4	8	132	51	76
Whitworths	36	23	5	8	115	45	74
Bugbrooke	36	22	6	8	84	43	72
St Ives	36	17	10	9	92	53	61
Olney	36	16	8	12	75	60	56
O N Chenecks	36	15	9	12	76	57	54
Blisworth	36	13	7	16	74	81	46
Ford Sports	36	13	6	17	86	81	45
Ramsey	36	12	7	17	66	76	43
Burton P W	36	12	4	20	59	91	40
Sharnbrook	36	11	6	19	46	79	39
British Timken	36	7	8	21	38	92	29
Irchester	36	6	9	21	40	86	27
Cottingham	36	5	6	25	44	84	21
Harrowby	36	5	2	29	24	171	17
Daventry	36	3	5	28	34	137	14

JEWSON WESSEX FOOTBALL LEAGUE

	P	W	D	L	F	A	Pts
Fleet Town	42	32	4	6	116	43	100
Bournemouth	42	31	5	6	109	33	98
Thatcham Town	42	29	9	4	104	44	96
Wimborne Town	42	22	14	6	102	52	80
Bemerton Heath Har	42	24	8	10	75	48	80
Brockenhurst	42	24	4	14	87	59	76
Andover	42	23	5	14	122	69	74
AFC Lymington	42	17	10	15	85	67	61
AFC Totton	42	18	6	18	69	70	60
Gosport Borough	42	17	6	19	83	66	57
Portsmouth RN	42	16	8	18	65	64	56
Ryde	42	16	6	20	81	88	54
BAT	42	15	8	19	62	82	53
Eastleigh	42	14	9	19	66	73	51
Cowes Sports	42	14	8	20	61	87	50
East Cowes Vics	42	13	10	19	65	72	49
Aerostructures S&S	42	12	10	20	60	77	46
Christchurch	42	12	8	22	58	95	44
Swanage & Herston	42	11	6	25	49	112	39
Downton	42	7	11	24	45	86	32
Petersfield Town	42	7	5	30	56	161	26
Horndean	42	6	4	32	49	121	22

HIGHLAND LEAGUE

	P	W	D	L	F	A	Pts
Huntly	30	24	2	4	102	30	74
Cove Rangers	30	18	3	9	69	38	57
Lossiemouth	30	17	3	10	75	53	54
Keith	30	16	5	9	59	32	53
Brora Rangers	30	15	7	8	63	41	52
Peterhead	30	15	7	8	64	43	52
Fraserburgh	30	16	4	10	56	43	52
Elgin City	30	15	3	12	52	42	48
Deveronvale	30	14	5	11	58	49	47
Buckie Thistle	30	12	8	10	50	52	44
Forres Mechanics	30	12	5	13	46	56	41
Fort William	30	11	4	15	46	57	37
Clachnacuddin	30	7	5	18	37	61	26
Wick Academy	30	7	4	19	32	77	25
Rothes	30	2	5	23	27	77	11
Nairn County	30	3	2	25	20	105	11

MIDLAND AMATEUR ALLIANCE

Division One	P	W	D	L	F	A	Pts
Sherwood Amateurs	20	17	3	0	77	20	37
Magdala Amateurs	20	13	3	4	81	28	29
Lady Bay	20	13	3	4	72	35	29
Old Elizabethans	20	8	7	5	47	37	23
Peoples College	20	7	6	7	44	39	20
Old Bemrosians	20	8	4	8	37	44	20
Bassingfield	20	7	4	9	57	55	18
F.C. Toton	20	6	2	12	39	67	14
Brunts Old Boys	20	3	6	11	17	54	12
Derbyshire Amateurs	20	2	7	11	31	66	11
Kirton B. W.	20	2	3	15	26	83	7
Division Two							
Old Elizabethans Res.	22	13	7	2	67	46	33
Magdala Amateurs Res.	22	10	8	4	47	32	28
Sherwood Amateurs Res.	22	10	7	5	63	33	27
County Nalgo	22	10	4	8	66	49	24
Chilwell	22	9	6	7	48	41	24
Bassingfield Res.	22	8	8	6	46	48	24
Nottingham Univ. Postgraduates	22	9	5	8	62	62	23
Nottinghamshire	22	10	2	10	49	43	22
Keyworth A.F.C.	22	8	3	11	36	54	19
Woodborough United	22	6	5	11	33	63	17
Ilkeston Electric	22		4	14	32	49	12
Tibshelf Old Boys	22	3	5	14	32	68	11
Division Three							
Beeston Old Boys Assn.	18	13	4	1	64	25	30
Ilkeston Rangers	18	12	4	2	62	30	28
Lady Bay Res.	18	9	4	5	48	37	22
Old Elizabethans 3rd	18	9	3	6	55	33	21
West-Clif	18	7	5	6	45	47	19
Peoples College Res.	18	7	1	10	43	41	15
Derbyshire Amateurs Res.	18	5	3	10	42	51	13
Nottingham Res.	18	4	4	10	27	53	12
Old Bemrosians Res.	18	3	5	10	19	48	11
Tibshelf Old Boys Res.	18	1	7	10	24	65	9
Division Four							
Brunts Old Boys Res.	20	18	0	2	85	24	36
South Forest	20	17	0	3	95	27	34
Magdala Amateurs 3rd	20	15	2	3	80	35	32
Beeston O.B. Assn. Res.	20	9	3	8	55	45	21
Derbyshire Amateurs 3rd	20	8	4	8	47	37	20
Peoples College 3rd	20	6	4	10	37	70	16
Old Elizabethans 4th	20	6	2	12	37	82	14
Ilkeston Rangers Res.	20	6	1	13	45	69	13
Nottinghamshire 3rd	20	5	2	13	32	63	12
Old Bemrosians 3rd	20	5	2	13	29	63	12
West-Clif Res.	20	5	0	15	39	66	10

Senior Cup–won by Sherwood Amateurs
Intermediate Cup–won by Sherwood Amateurs Res.
Minor Cup–won by A.C. College 3rd
Challenge Trophy–won by Magdala Amateurs
Division Two Challenge Cup–won by Old Elizabethans Res.
Division Three Challenge Cup–won by Derbyshire Amateurs Res.
Division Four Challenge Cup–Brunts Old Boys Res.
Division Three Supplementary Cup–Beeston O.B.A.
Division Four Supplementary Cup–South Forest
H.B. Poole Trophy–won by Sherwood Amateurs

AMATEUR FOOTBALL ALLIANCE 1994–95

AFA SENIOR CUP

1st Round Proper
Witan 2, Carshalton 3
Hale End Athletic 1, West Wickham 2
Old Owens 1, Civil Service 3
Old Suttonians 2, City of London 1
Old Danes 0, Old Salvatorians 2
Old Lyonian 0, Old Ignatians 3
Old Dorkinian 1*:0, Norsemen 1*:4
Old Esthameians 4, Old Aloysians 1
Old Parkonians 0, Old Chigwellians 1
Old Malvernian 3, Wandsworth Borough 2
Old Wokingians 1, South Bank 3
UCL Academicals 0, Old Salesians 6
Alexandra Park 1, Old Foresters 4
Ealing Association 3, Old Woodhouseians 2
Winchmore Hill 1, Old Latymerians 2
Bank of England 1, Old Kingsburians 3
Old Camdenians 0, Cuaco 7
Merton 1, Cardinal Manning OB 4
Old Hamptonians 4, Polytechnic 0
Old Grocers 1*:0, Old Isleworthians 1*:1
Westerns 3, Midland Bank 2
William Fitt 0, Duncombe Sports 5
Old Wilsonians 0, Crouch End Vampires 1
Old Michendenians 1, Old Manorians 3
Old Reptonian 3*:1, Wake Green 3*:3
Mill Hill Village 0, Glyn Old Boys 2
Broomfield 4, Old Westhamians 0
St Mary's College 1*:5, Southgate County 1*:1
E. Barnet Old Grammarians 2, Old Stationers 1
Nottsborough 1*:2, Old Meadonians 1*:4
Kew Association 3, Old Grammarians 4
National Westminster Bank 3, Old Tenisonians 0

2nd Round Proper
Carshalton 2, West Wickham 1
Civil Service 3, Old Suttonians 1
Old Salvatorians 2:0, Old Ignatians 2:3
Norsemen 1, Old Esthameians 5
Old Chigwellians 5, Wandsworth Borough 0
South Bank 8, Old Salesians 0
Old Foresters 3, Ealing Association 1
Old Latymerians 5, Old Kingsburians 0
Cuaco 4, Cardinal Manning OB 3
Old Hamptonians 0, Old Isleworthians 2
Westerns 5, Duncombe Sports 4
Crouch End Vampires 2, Old Manorians 1
Wake Green 3, Glyn Old Boys 1
Broomfield 2, St Mary's College 3
E. Barnet Old Grammarian 2, Old Meadonians 1
Old Grammarians 1, National Westminster Bank 3

3rd Round Proper
Carshalton 2, Civil Service 5
Old Ignatians 4, Old Esthameians 2
Old Chigwellians 1, South Bank 3
Old Foresters 2*:1, Old Latymerians 2*:0
Cuaco 0*:0, Old Isleworthians 0*:1
Westerns 2, Crouch End Vampires 1
Wake Green 2, St Mary's College 3
E. Barnet Old Grammarians 3, National Westminster Bank 4

4th Round Proper
Civil Service 2, Old Ignatians 1
South Bank 2, Old Foresters 1
Old Isleworthians 4, Westerns 1
St Mary's College 3, National Westminster Bank 4

Semi-finals
Civil Service 2, South Bank 1
Old Isleworthians 1, National Westminster Bank 2
**after extra time*

Final
National Westminster Bank 3, Civil Service 1

ARTHUR DUNN CUP

Final
Old Salopians (1) 2 (*Honychurch 2*)
Old Foresters (1) 1 (*Pratt*)
Old Salopians: J. Skelton; A. Pollock, T. Cooke, P. Deans, H. Raven, M. Lascelles, R. Cooke, S. Ellis, D. Honychurch, D. Arthur, P. Dyke.
Old Foresters: M. Butler; C. Hossain, A. Heyes, J. Banks, M. Sheppard, D. Pratt, R. Harnack, L. Douris, B. Barnet, N. Francis, C. Elliott.
Referee: B. Harvey (Surrey).

OTHER AFA CUP RESULTS 1994–95

Intermediate
Polytechnic Res. 3*:1, Civil Service Res. 3*:2
Junior
Norsemen 3rd 1*, National Westminster Bank 3rd 2*
Minor
Norsemen 4th 3, Kew Association 4th 0
Senior Novets
Cardinal Manning OB 5th 2*, Old Finchleians 5th 1*
Intermediate Novets
Civil Service 6th 1, Polytechnic 6th 0
Junior Novets
Old Parmiterians 8th 0, Old Parmiterians 11th 1
Veterans
Old Chigwellian Veterans 8, Broomfield Veterans 2
Open Veterans
Toby Veterans 0, Port of London Authority Veterans 2
Essex Senior
Old Foresters 2, Old Parmiterians 0

Middlesex Senior
Old Actonians Association 2, St Mary's College 1

Surrey Senior
National Westminster Bank 3*, South Bank 4*

Essex Intermediate
Old Buckwellians 1st 2, Old Parmiterians Res. 3

Kent Intermediate
Cuaco Res. 4*:1, Old Sedcopians 1st 4*:2

Middlesex Intermediate
Old Latymerians Res. 2, Latymer Old Boys Res. 1

Surrey Intermediate
National Westminster Bank Res. 3, Nottsborough Res. 1

W E Greenland Memorial
South Bank 3, Old Ignatians 1
**after extra time*

LONDON OLD BOYS' CUPS

Senior
Old Parmiterians 3*, Old Meadonians 1*

Intermediate
Old Danes Res. 4, Phoenix Old Boys Res. 2

Junior
Old Tollingtonians 3rd 2, Clapham O. Xaverians 3rd 1

Minor
Old Actonians 4th 2, Old Southallians 4th 0

Novets
Old Actonians 5th 1, Old Salvatorians 5th 0
Drummond Cup
Old Salesians 6th 3, Old Suttonians 6th 2
Nemean Cup
Latymer Old Boys 7th 2, Old Parmiterians 11th 4
Veterans' Cup
Old Kingsburians Veterans 2, City of London Veterans 4
**after extra time*

OLD BOYS' INVITATION CUPS

Senior
Old Esthameians 3, Old Tenisonians 0
Junior
Old Tenisonians Res 1, Old Lyonians 2
Minor
Old Latymerians 3rd 2, Glyn Old Boys 3rd 3
4th XI
Old Stationers 4th 6, Old Finchleians 4th 2
5th XI
Old Finchleians 5th 3, Old Stationers 5th 2
6th XI
Old Suttonians 6th 2, Old Stationers 6th 1
7th XI
Old Latymerians 7th 3, Old Stationers 7th 2
Veterans' XI
Old Stationers Veterans 3, Old Esthameians Veterans 1

SOUTHERN OLYMPIAN LEAGUE

Senior Section

Division One	*P*	*W*	*D*	*L*	*F*	*A*	*Pts*
Witan	18	14	0	4	53	26	28
Old Owens	18	12	3	3	47	23	27
Nottsborough	18	10	4	4	52	24	24
Ulysses	18	7	7	4	33	25	21
Old Grammarians	18	7	4	7	29	44	18
St Mary's College	18	5	6	7	31	29	16
Parkfield	18	5	5	8	33	42	15
Southgate County	18	4	6	8	22	28	14
Wandsworth Borough	18	2	4	12	22	49	8
Mill Hill Village	18	4	1	13	21	53	7*

Division Two	*P*	*W*	*D*	*L*	*F*	*A*	*Pts*
Hale End Athletic	20	14	3	3	66	25	31
Albanian	19	13	3	3	46	17	29
Ealing Association	20	10	6	4	38	30	26
Honourable Artillery Company	19	11	2	6	39	21	24
UCL Academicals	20	9	4	7	34	29	22
Old Bealonians	20	6	7	7	43	42	19
Corinthians-Casuals "A"	20	6	5	9	21	37	17
Old Finchleians	20	8	0	12	46	59	16
Hadley	20	5	5	10	20	30	15
Old Fairlopians	20	3	4	13	26	54	10
Duncombe Sports	20	3	3	14	20	55	8*

Division Three	*P*	*W*	*D*	*L*	*F*	*A*	*Pts*
City of London	20	14	2	4	58	29	29*
Old Woodhouseians	20	13	3	4	66	38	29
BBC	20	13	1	6	74	43	27
Fulham Compton Old Boys	20	12	3	5	60	33	27
Pollygons	20	9	2	9	46	62	20
Old Monovians	20	9	1	10	45	71	19
Westerns	20	9	0	11	46	54	18
London Welsh	20	7	3	10	43	46	17
Birkbeck College	20	6	4	10	36	50	16
Old Colfeians	20	3	5	12	30	52	11
Brent	20	2	2	16	23	49	6

Division Four	*P*	*W*	*D*	*L*	*F*	*A*	*Pts*
Broadfields United	20	17	1	2	95	23	35
Old Simmarobians	20	14	4	2	73	23	32
Hampstead Heathens	20	13	3	4	44	28	29
Cardinal Pole Old Boys	20	11	4	5	52	44	26
Inland Revenue	20	9	3	8	49	35	21
London Airways	20	10	1	9	45	45	21
Pegasus (Inner Temple)	20	7	5	8	43	40	19
Centymca	20	7	2	11	37	55	16
Economicals	20	3	2	15	32	74	8
Mayfield Athletic	20	3	2	15	29	59	6*
Bourneside	20	1	3	16	21	94	5

**points deducted for breach of rule*

Intermediate Section
Division One:–10 Teams–won by Old Owens Res.
Division Two:–10 Teams–won by Hampstead Heathens Res.
Division Three:–11 Teams–won by St Mary's College Res.
Division Four:–11 Teams–won by Centymca Res.

Junior Section
Division One:–10 Teams–won by Albanian 3rd
Division Two:–10 Teams–won by Old Owens 3rd
Division Three:–9 Teams–won by Old Finchleians 5th
Division Four:–10 Teams–won by City of London 5th

Minor Section
Division "A":–10 Teams–won by Ealing Association 4th
Division "B":–10 Teams–won by Broadfields United 4th
Division "C":–10 Teams–won by Broadfields United 5th
Division "D":–10 Teams–won by Broadfields United 6th
Division "E":–10 Teams–won by Old Owens 6th
Division "F":– 8 Teams–won by Broadfields United 8th
Senior Challenge Bowl:–won by Nottsborough
Senior Challenge Shield:–won by Old Owens
Intermediate Challenge Cup:–won by Old Owens Res.
Intermediate Challenge Shield:–won by Nottsborough Res.
Junior Challenge Cup:–won by Old Owens 3rd
Junior Challenge Shield:–won by Old Woodhouseians 3rd
Mander Cup:–won by City of London 4th
Mander Shield:–won by Broadfields 4th
Burntwood Trophy:–won by Albanian 5th
Burntwood Shield:–won by Old Finchleians 5th
Thomas Parmiter Cup:–won by Albanian 6th
Thomas Parmiter Shield:–won by Broadfields 7th
Veterans' Challenge Cup:–won by City of London Veterans
Veterans' Challenge Shield:–won by Parkfield Veterans

ARTHURIAN LEAGUE

Premier Division	*P*	*W*	*D*	*L*	*F*	*A*	*Pts*
Old Chigwellians	16	14	2	0	51	7	30
Lancing Old Boys	16	9	2	5	30	18	20
Old Carthusians	16	8	3	5	29	19	19
Old Reptonians	16	6	4	6	21	35	16
Old Aldenhamians	16	7	1	8	26	35	15
Old Etonians	16	5	4	7	28	31	14
Old Malvernians	16	4	5	7	20	30	13
Old Brentwoods	16	3	4	9	28	32	10
Old Wellingburians	16	1	5	10	15	41	7

Division One	*P*	*W*	*D*	*L*	*F*	*A*	*Pts*
Old Foresters	18	18	0	0	78	19	36
Old Cholmeleians	18	14	1	3	61	22	29
Old Harrovians	18	9	3	6	43	32	21
Old Wykehamists	18	9	3	6	43	46	21
Old Salopians	18	8	4	6	50	38	20
Old Bradfieldians	18	5	4	9	41	58	14
Old Haileyburians	18	4	3	11	39	54	11
Old Witleians	18	4	3	11	34	54	11
Old Westminsters	18	3	4	11	30	49	10
Old Ardinians	18	1	5	12	22	69	5*

Division Two	*P*	*W*	*D*	*L*	*F*	*A*	*Pts*
Old Haberdashers	18	13	1	4	55	35	27
Old Carthusians Res.	18	10	4	4	46	26	24
Old Cholmeleians Res.	18	10	4	4	32	27	24
Old Chigwellians Res.	18	9	3	6	56	30	21
Old Chigwellians 3rd	18	9	2	7	43	33	20
Old Etonians Res.	18	6	5	7	47	38	17
Lancing Old Boys Res.	18	6	3	9	35	44	15
Old Foresters Res.	18	5	3	10	34	45	13
Old Aldenhamians Res.	18	3	1	11	34	64	13
Old Reptonians Res.	18	2	2	14	23	63	6

Division Three	*P*	*W*	*D*	*L*	*F*	*A*	*Pts*
Old Cholmeleians 3rd	16	10	5	1	50	24	25
Old Salopians Res.	16	9	1	6	36	31	19
Old Brentwoods Res.	16	6	5	5	45	41	17
Old Harrovians Res.	16	6	3	7	39	36	15
Old Westminsters Res.	16	5	5	6	34	36	15
Old Malvernians Res.	16	4	6	6	38	41	14
Old Etonians 3rd	16	4	6	6	32	41	14
Old Wellingburians Res.	16	6	1	9	30	37	13
Old Bradfieldians Res.	16	4	4	8	31	48	12

**2 points deducted breach of rule*

Division Four–won by Old Haberdashers Res.
Division Five–won by Old Cholmeleians 5th
Junior League Cup: Old Chigwellians Res. 0*:4p, Old Cholmeleians Res. 0*:1p
Derrik Moore Veterans' Cup: Old Chigwellians Vets 0, Old Carthusians Vets 3
(**p–after extra time & penalties*)

LONDON LEGAL LEAGUE

Division One	P	W	D	L	F	A	Pts
Grays Inn	18	15	0	3	63	25	30
Wilde Sapte	18	13	2	3	78	26	28
Nabarro Nathanson	18	9	2	7	43	32	20
Linklaters & Paines	18	9	2	7	42	43	20
Pegasus (Inner Temple)	18	6	5	7	38	39	17
Slaughter & May	18	7	2	9	41	43	16
D. J. Freeman & Co	18	4	6	8	33	41	14
Cameron Markby Hewitt	18	5	3	10	37	66	13
Freshfields	18	4	4	10	35	56	12
Herbert Smith	18	4	2	12	24	63	10

Division Two	P	W	D	L	F	A	Pts
Clifford Chance	18	14	1	3	54	17	29
Gouldens	18	12	3	3	53	28	27
Norton Rose	18	12	3	3	52	33	27
Lovell White Durrant	18	8	4	6	47	38	20
Stephenson Harwood	18	9	1	8	50	51	19
S. J. Berwin	18	8	3	7	32	38	19
Watson Farley & Williams	18	6	4	8	33	39	16
Allen & Overy	18	4	3	11	21	41	11
Taylor Joynson Garrett	18	3	1	14	23	47	7
Simmons & Simmons	18	1	3	14	13	52	5

Division Three	P	W	D	L	F	A	Pts
Macfarlanes	14	12	0	2	62	20	24
Rosling King	14	9	3	2	47	22	21
Denton Hall	14	9	1	4	48	25	19
McKenna & Co	14	8	1	5	27	32	17
Oyez	14	6	2	6	40	33	14
Baker & McKenzie	14	3	2	9	34	40	8
Richards Butler	14	1	3	10	17	42	5
Rowe & Maw	14	2	0	12	13	74	4

League Challenge Cup:–Gray's Inn 1, Nabarro Nathanson 3
Weavers Arms Cup:–Gouldens 2, Freshfields 4
Invitation Cup:–Norton Rose 5, Stephenson Harwood 3
Division 3 Cup:–Macfarlanes 2, Baker & McKenzie 5

LONDON FINANCIAL FA

Senior Section

Division One	P	W	D	L	F	A	Pts
Coutts	16	9	3	4	43	23	21
Royal Bank of Scotland	16	10	1	5	43	32	21
Bank America	16	9	2	5	52	23	20
Temple Bar	16	7	4	5	31	42	18
Sun Alliance	16	6	4	6	34	33	16
Liverpool Victoria	16	6	2	8	31	42	14
Hong Kong Bank	16	7	1	8	50	43	13*
Kleinwort Benson	16	4	2	10	33	46	10
Chemical Bank	16	4	1	11	31	64	9

Division Two	P	W	D	L	F	A	Pts
Citibank	18	15	2	1	48	18	32
Morgan Stanley International	18	12	2	4	53	28	26
Allied Irish Bank	18	9	3	6	34	27	21
Sedgwick	18	8	3	7	40	27	18*
Bardhill	18	7	3	8	23	34	17
Granby	18	6	4	8	32	36	16
Invesco	18	6	2	10	38	40	14
Eagle Star	18	4	5	9	37	52	13
Salomon Brothers	18	6	1	11	28	49	13
Royal Bank of Scotland Res.	18	3	3	12	18	40	9

Division Three	P	W	D	L	F	A	Pts
Morgan Guaranty	18	12	5	1	71	21	29
Churchill Insurance	18	12	5	1	60	27	29
Union Bank of Switzerland	18	11	1	6	51	24	23
Bowring	18	10	3	5	58	40	23
Direct Line Insurance	18	8	4	6	38	41	20
Coutts Res.	18	7	3	8	43	45	17
Sedgwick Noble Lowndes	18	2	10	6	27	37	14
United Bank of Kuwait	18	4	3	11	47	56	11
Temple Bar Res.	18	3	3	12	25	69	9
Gaflac	18	1	3	14	23	83	5

Division Four	P	W	D	L	F	A	Pts
Chase Manhattan Bank	18	13	4	1	63	25	30
ANZ Banking Group	18	8	5	5	38	26	21
Lincoln National	18	8	5	5	40	35	21
Granby Res.	18	6	7	5	41	38	19
Asphalia	18	9	0	9	41	48	18
U C B Bank	18	7	3	8	43	39	17
Royal Bank of Scotland 3rd	18	7	3	8	26	34	17
Citibank Res.	18	6	4	8	36	44	16
Sun Alliance Res.	18	3	5	10	37	55	11
Liverpool Victoria Res.	18	4	2	12	34	55	10

**points deduction breach of rule*

Division Five:–11 Teams–won by Bank America Res.
Division Six:–10 Teams–won by Credit Suisse Financial Res.
Sportsmanship Trophy:–won by Asphalia

OLD BOYS' LEAGUE

Premier Division	P	W	D	L	F	A	Pts
Old Ignatians	20	14	3	3	52	27	31
Old Meadonians	20	13	5	2	46	22	31
Glyn Old Boys	20	13	3	4	49	20	29
Cardinal Manning Old Boys	20	11	2	7	46	29	24
Old Tenisonians	20	10	3	7	44	35	23
Old Hamptonians	20	8	3	9	31	45	19
Old Aloysians	20	8	1	11	29	32	17
Clapham Old Xaverians	20	5	5	10	37	65	15
Old Danes	20	4	6	10	38	54	14
Old Wilsonians	20	4	3	13	28	43	11
Chertsey Old Salesians	20	2	2	16	31	59	6

Senior Division One	P	W	D	L	F	A	Pts
Latymer Old Boys	20	15	2	3	61	22	32
Old Isleworthians	20	12	1	7	47	36	25
Phoenix Old Boys	20	9	6	6	42	42	22
Old Tiffinians	20	9	3	8	61	37	21
Shene Old Grammarians	20	9	3	8	35	31	21
Old Tenisonians Res.	20	9	3	8	29	48	21
Old Suttonians	20	9	2	9	52	38	20
Old Kingsburians	20	9	1	10	53	44	19
Old Salvatorians	19	7	4	8	35	32	18
Old Wokingians	20	7	3	10	38	50	17
Old Edmontonians	19	0	2	17	26	99	0*

Senior Division Two	P	W	D	L	F	A	Pts
Old Manorians	22	16	4	2	82	20	36
Old Vaughanians	22	17	2	3	56	27	36
Old Michendenians	22	13	2	7	61	31	28
Old Meadonians Res.	22	13	2	7	66	53	28
Old Tollingtonians	22	11	2	9	55	45	24
Enfield Old Grammarians	22	11	0	11	76	49	22
Old Westhamians	22	10	2	10	51	48	22
Mill Hill County Old Boys	22	8	4	10	49	59	20
Old Southallians	22	7	3	12	49	62	17
Old Camdenians	22	8	1	13	40	66	17
John Fisher Old Boys	22	5	1	16	29	85	11
Old Ignatians Res.	22	1	1	20	21	90	3

Senior Division Three	P	W	D	L	F	A	Pts
Latymer Old Boys Res.	20	15	2	3	66	25	32
Phoenix Old Boys Res.	20	11	4	5	58	33	26
Old Grocers	20	10	6	4	54	38	26
Old Salvatorians Res.	20	9	3	8	30	35	21
Old Vaughanians Res.	20	8	4	8	45	37	20
Glyn Old Boys Res.	20	8	4	8	40	51	20
Old Hamptonians Res.	20	8	4	8	36	47	20
Chorley Wood Danes Old Boys	20	6	6	8	35	41	18
Leyton County Old Boys	20	5	6	9	32	48	16
Old Greenfordians	20	3	8	9	31	49	14
Old Alpertonians	20	2	3	15	28	51	7

**–points deducted for breach of rule*

Intermediate Division North:–12 Teams–won by Old Buckwellians
Intermediate Division South:–12 Teams–won by Old Dorkinians
Division One North:–11 Teams–won by Queen Mary College Old Boys
Division One South:–12 Teams–won by Old St Mary's

Division One West:–11 Teams–won by Old Kingsburians Res.
Division Two North:–10 Teams–won by Wood Green Old Boys Res.
Division Two South:–11 Teams–won by Glyn Old Boys 3rd
Division Two West:–10 Teams–won by Old Manorians 3rd
Division Three North:–11 Teams–won by Old Grocers Res.
Division Three South:–12 Teams–won by Chertsey Old Salesians 3rd
Division Three West:–10 Teams won by Old Manorians 4th
Division Four North:–11 Teams–won by Davenant Wanderers
Division Four South:–11 Teams–won by Old Meadonians 5th
Division Four West:–9 Teams–won by Shene Old Grammarians 4th
Division Five North:–9 Teams–won by Old Camdenians 5th
Division Five South:–10 Teams–won by Old Reigatians 4th
Division Five West:–10 Teams–won by Cardinal Manning OB 4th
Division Six North:–9 Teams–won by Old Tollingtonians 6th
Division Six South:–9 Teams–won by Old Wilsonians 5th
Division Six West:–9 Teams–won by Phoenix Old Boys 5th
Division Seven North:–8 Teams–won by Ravenscroft Old Boys 3rd
Division Seven South:–10 Teams–won by Old Sinjuns 4th
Division Seven West:–11 Teams–won by Cardinal Manning O.B. 5th
Division Eight South:–9 Teams–won by Old Suttonians 8th
Division Eight West:–11 Teams–won by Old Southallians 5th
Division Nine South:–8 Teams–won by Old Sedcopians 5th

SOUTHERN AMATEUR LEAGUE

Senior Section

First Division	*P*	*W*	*D*	*L*	*F*	*A*	*Pts*
South Bank Polytechnic	22	17	3	2	48	17	37
Old Esthameians	22	13	3	6	47	30	29
East Barnet Old Grammarians	22	11	4	7	47	42	26
Old Actonians Association	22	9	6	7	39	37	24
Civil Service	22	10	3	9	32	35	23
Norsemen	22	7	6	9	26	26	20
Crouch End Vampires	22	6	8	8	34	35	20
West Wickham	22	7	6	9	26	30	20
Winchmore Hill	22	4	10	8	29	38	17*
National Westminster Bank	22	7	3	12	32	43	17
Midland Bank	22	5	5	12	28	38	15
Old Latymerians	22	6	3	13	33	49	15

Second Division	*P*	*W*	*D*	*L*	*F*	*A*	*Pts*
Carshalton	22	15	2	5	47	29	32
Kew Association	22	14	3	5	55	26	31
Polytechnic	22	13	4	5	49	31	30
Lloyds Bank	22	13	3	6	48	34	29
Old Parkonians	22	9	7	6	35	27	25
Old Parmiterians	22	9	4	9	40	34	22
Alexandra Park	22	6	10	6	38	39	22
Old Bromleians	22	7	4	11	33	36	18
Lensbury	22	7	3	12	34	45	17
Old Stationers	22	7	1	14	26	43	15
Broomfield	22	5	4	13	33	50	14
Old Westminster Citizens	22	4	1	17	27	71	9

Third Division	*P*	*W*	*D*	*L*	*F*	*A*	*Pts*
Old Lyonians	20	15	4	1	62	21	34
Barclays Bank	20	15	3	2	73	22	33
Southgate Olympic	20	9	6	5	39	31	24
Old Salesians	20	10	3	7	46	32	23
Cuaco	20	10	3	7	39	36	23
Brentham	20	10	0	10	64	51	20
Bank of England	20	8	3	9	31	28	19
Alleyn Old Boys	20	7	5	8	41	44	19
Ibis	20	5	2	13	31	56	12
Merton	20	4	3	13	29	65	11
Reigate Priory	20	0	2	18	17	86	2

**1 point deducted–breach of rule*

Reserve Teams Section
First Division:–12 Teams–won by Polytechnic Res.
Second Division:–12 Teams–won by Old Latymerians Res.
Third Division:–11 Teams–won by Cuaco Res.
3rd Teams Section:
First Division:–12 Teams–won by Civil Service 3rd
Second Division:–12 Teams–won by Crouch End Vampires 3rd
Third Division:–11 Teams–won by Cuaco 3rd
4th Teams Section:
First Division:–12 Teams–won by Winchmore Hill 4th
Second Division:–12 Teams–won by Barclays Bank 4th
Third Division:–11 Teams–won by Merton 4th
5th Teams Section:
First Division:–10 Teams–won by Polytechnic 5th
Second Division:–10 Teams–won by Civil Service 5th
Third Division:–10 Teams–won by Old Salesians 5th
6th Teams Section:
First Division:–9 Teams–won by Civil Service 6th
Second Division:–9 Teams–won by Old Parmiterians 6th
Third Division:–9 Teams–won by Carshalton 6th
7th Teams Section:
First Division:–8 Teams–won by National Westminster Bank 7th
Second Division:–9 Teams–won by Old Actonians Association 7th
8th Teams Section:
First Division:–9 Teams–won by Old Parmiterians 8th
9th, 10th & 11th Teams Sections:
First Division:–9 Teams–won by Old Parmiterians 9th
Second Division:–8 Teams–won by Old Parmiterians 11th

UNIVERSITY FOOTBALL 1994–95

111TH UNIVERSITY MATCH

(at Craven Cottage, Fulham)

Oxford 1, Cambridge 0

Oxford: Novy; Prest, Campbell, Washington, Smith A, Smith M, Mills, Worthington, Kraft, Hanssen (D'Andrea), Seymour (Cotton). *Scorer:* Washington.
Cambridge: Park; Budd (Batstone), Bullmore, White, Thompson, Collins, Pett, Luke, Millar, Smart, Morrow (McMurray).
Referee: M. Halsey (Herts).
Cambridge have not won the fixture for seven years, but still lead Oxford by 45 wins to 41 with 25 drawn.

UNIVERSITY OF LONDON INTER-COLLEGIATE LEAGUE

Premier Division

	P	*W*	*D*	*L*	*F*	*A*	*Pts*
Royal Holloway College	14	12	1	1	63	14	25
Imperial College	14	11	2	1	47	20	24
London School of Economics	14	7	2	5	35	28	16
Goldsmiths' College	14	5	1	8	28	40	11
University College	14	5	1	8	23	37	11
Queen Mary Westfield College	14	4	2	8	25	34	10
King's College	14	3	2	9	19	42	8
R. Free Hospital Sch. of Medicine	14	2	3	9	18	43	7

Division One

	P	*W*	*D*	*L*	*F*	*A*	*Pts*
Ch. Cross & W'min. Hosp. Med. Sch.	18	13	3	2	45	19	29
Royal Holloway College Res.	18	11	4	3	54	25	26
University College Res.	18	8	8	2	41	22	24
Queen Mary Westfield College Res.	18	10	1	7	41	38	21
St. Bartholomew's Hosp. Med. Sch.	18	7	2	9	42	43	16
London Sch. Economics Res.	18	6	4	8	31	40	16
Univ. Coll. & Middx. Hosp. Med. Sch.	18	6	3	9	29	28	15
St George's Hospital Med. Sch.	18	4	6	8	31	40	14
U.M.D.S.	18	5	4	9	19	40	14
King's College Hosp. Med. Sch.	18	2	1	15	22	60	5

Division Two

	P	*W*	*D*	*L*	*F*	*A*	*Pts*
Royal London Hosp. Med. College	18	13	3	2	83	32	29
Royal Holloway College 3rd	18	13	1	4	65	31	27
Imperial College Res.	18	11	3	4	64	39	25
St Mary's Hospital Med. Sch.	18	8	2	8	49	41	18
King's College Res.	18	8	2	8	38	43	18
Sch. Slavonic & East European Studies	18	7	3	8	32	42	17
University College 3rd	18	6	1	11	47	46	13
Imperial College 3rd	18	5	3	10	40	52	13
Royal School of Mines (IC)	18	5	0	12	25	71	10
Goldsmiths' College Res.	18	4	0	13	17	63	8

Division Three

	P	*W*	*D*	*L*	*F*	*A*	*Pts*
Royal Holloway College 4th	16	10	4	2	42	26	24
London Sch. Economics 3rd.	16	9	4	3	45	28	22
Royal Veterinary College	16	9	3	4	61	26	21
King's College 3rd	16	9	2	5	43	34	20
University College 4th	16	6	2	8	47	51	14
Queen Mary Westfield College 3rd	16	6	1	9	59	42	13
Goldsmiths' College 3rd	16	5	2	9	40	61	12
Ch. Cross & W'min Hosp. Med. Sch. Res.	16	5	1	10	28	54	11
St George's Hospital Medical School Res.	16	2	3	11	26	69	7

Division Four—10 Teams–won by London School of Economics 4th.
Division Five—10 Teams–won by Royal Holloway College 5th.
Division Six— 8 Teams–won by Royal London Hospital Med. College Res.
Challenge Cup: R. Holloway College 3, Goldsmiths' College 1
Upper Reserves Cup: R. Holloway Res. 4, University College Res. 0

Lower Reserves Cup: King's College 4th 2*, UC & Middx. Hosp. M.S. 5th 4*
(**–after extra time & penalties*)
United Hospitals:
Senior Cup: Charing Cross & Westminster Hospital Medical School 3, University College & Middlesex Hospital Medical School 2
Junior Cup: Royal Free Hospital Sch. of Medicine Res. 1, St. Georges's Hospital Medical School Res. 0 *aet*

BRITISH UNIVERSITIES SPORTS ASSOCIATION CHAMPIONSHIP

First XI Final
Greenwich 2, Crewe 2 (*at Walsall FC*)
(*Greenwich won 5-4 on penalties*)

Second XI Final
Leeds 1, Loughborough (*at Crewe & Alsager*)

Third XI Final
Nottingham Trent 3, West Sussex 4 (*at Birmingham*)

Fourth XI Final
Loughborough 3, De Montfort (Beds) 2 *aet* (*at Warwick*)

Women's Final
De Montfort (Beds) 3, Crewe & Alsager 2 *aet* (*at Loughborough*)

ENGLISH UNIVERSITIES FOOTBALL (MEN)

English Universities 2, Stoke City 2
English Universities 2, Royal Navy 2
English Universities 1, Bradford City 1
English Universities 0, Irish Universities 0

HOME NATIONS TOURNAMENT

English Universities 2, N. Ireland 2
English Universities 2, Scottish Universities 0
English Universities 4, Welsh Universities 0
N. Ireland 3, Scottish Universities 1
N. Ireland 2, Welsh Universities 0
Scottish Universities 5, Welsh Universities 1

Positions
1. English Universities
2. N. Irish Universities
3. Scottish Universities
4. Welsh Universities

ENGLISH UNIVERSITIES (WOMEN)

English Universities 3, Welsh Universities 0
English Universities 4, Scottish Universities 2

CAMBRIDGE UNIVERSITY 1994–95

Amateur Football Alliance	Lost	0-2
Old Blues	Won	5-3
Army Crusaders	Lost	0-2
U.C.W. College Cardiff	Lost	0-2
Ipswich Town XI	Lost	1-12
Royal Navy F.A.	Won	2-1
Tottenham Hotspur XI	Lost	0-6
Royal Air Force U-21	Lost	0-3
Luton Town XI	Lost	1-5
Loughborough University	Drawn	0-0
Lloyds Select XI	Won	3-2
Arthurian League	Drawn	0-0
London Legal League	Won	5-1
Leicester University	Won	4-2
Southern Amateur League	Drawn	0-0
London University	Won	3-2
C.U. "Falcons"	Lost	2-3
Territorial Army	Won	3-2
Honourable Artillery Company	Won	2-1
Lloyds Select XI	Won	3-2
London Legal League	Won	2-1
Oxford University	Lost	0-1

LONDON UNIVERSITY 1994–95

United Hospitals	Won	3-1
Ulysses	Won	2-1
Old Boys' League	Won	4-0
Barnet XI	Won	4-2
Southern Amateur League	Lost	3-4
Royal Navy	Lost	2-4
Fulham XI	Lost	2-3
Charlton XI	Won	5-1
Arthurian League	Won	3-2
Royal Air Force U-21	Won	1-0
London Legal League	Won	3-2
Army Crusaders	Won	5-1
Metropolitan Police	Lost	1-2
Oxford University	Won	2-0
Cambridge University	Lost	2-3
Amateur Football Alliance	Drawn	1-1
Crystal Palace XI	Lost	0-1
Millwall XI	Won	3-1

RECORDS

Major British Records

HIGHEST WINS

First-Class Match		Arbroath (*Scottish Cup 1st Round*)	36	Bon Accord	0	12 Sept 1885
International Match		England	13	Ireland	0	18 Feb 1882
FA Cup		Preston NE (*1st Round*)	26	Hyde U	0	15 Oct 1887
League Cup		West Ham U (*2nd Round, 2nd Leg*)	10	Bury	0	25 Oct 1983
		Liverpool (*2nd Round, 1st Leg*)	10	Fulham	0	23 Sept 1986
FA PREMIER LEAGUE						
	(*Home*)	Manchester U	9	Ipswich T	0	4 March 1995
FOOTBALL LEAGUE						
Division 1	(*Home*)	WBA	12	Darwen	0	4 April 1892
		Nottingham F	12	Leicester Fosse	0	21 April 1909
	(*Away*)	Newcastle U	1	Sunderland	9	5 Dec 1908
		Cardiff C	1	Wolverhampton W	9	3 Sept 1955
Division 2	(*Home*)	Newcastle U	13	Newport Co	0	5 Oct 1946
	(*Away*)	Burslem PV	0	Sheffield U	10	10 Dec 1892
Division 3	(*Home*)	Gillingham	10	Chesterfield	0	5 Sept 1987
	(*Away*)	Halifax T	0	Fulham	8	16 Sept 1969
Division 3(S)	(*Home*)	Luton T	12	Bristol R	0	13 April 1936
	(*Away*)	Northampton T	0	Walsall	8	2 Feb 1947
Division 3(N)	(*Home*)	Stockport Co	13	Halifax T	0	6 Jan 1934
	(*Away*)	Accrington S	0	Barnsley	9	3 Feb 1934
Division 4	(*Home*)	Oldham Ath	11	Southport	0	26 Dec 1962
	(*Away*)	Crewe Alex	1	Rotherham U	8	8 Sept 1973
Aggregate Division 3(N)		Tranmere R	13	Oldham Ath	4	26 Dec 1935
SCOTTISH LEAGUE						
Premier Division	(*Home*)	Aberdeen	8	Motherwell	0	26 March 1979
	(*Away*)	Hamilton A	0	Celtic	8	5 Nov 1988
Division 1	(*Home*)	Celtic	11	Dundee	0	26 Oct 1895
	(*Away*)	Airdrieonians	1	Hibernian	11	24 Oct 1950
Division 2	(*Home*)	Airdrieonians	15	Dundee Wanderers	1	1 Dec 1894
	(*Away*)	Alloa Ath	0	Dundee	10	8 March 1947

LEAGUE CHAMPIONSHIP HAT-TRICKS

Huddersfield T	1923–24 to 1925–26
Arsenal	1932–33 to 1934–35
Liverpool	1981–82 to 1983–84

MOST GOALS FOR IN A SEASON

		Goals	Games	Season
FA PREMIER LEAGUE				
	Newcastle U	82	42	1993–94
FOOTBALL LEAGUE				
Division 1	Aston V	128	42	1930–31
Division 2	Middlesbrough	122	42	1926–27
Division 3(S)	Millwall	127	42	1927–28
Division 3(N)	Bradford C	128	42	1928–29
Division 3	QPR	111	46	1961–62
Division 4	Peterborough U	134	46	1960–61
SCOTTISH LEAGUE				
Premier Division	Rangers	101	44	1991–92
	Dundee U	90	36	1982–83
	Celtic	90	36	1982–83
	Celtic	90	44	1986–87
Division 1	Hearts	132	34	1957–58
Division 2	Raith R	142	34	1937–38
New Division 1	Dunfermline Ath	93	44	1993–94
	Motherwell	92	39	1981–82
New Division 2	Ayr U	95	39	1987–88
New Division 3	Montrose	69	36	1994–95

FEWEST GOALS FOR IN A SEASON

		Goals	Games	Season
FA PREMIER LEAGUE				
	Crystal Palace	34	42	1994–95
FOOTBALL LEAGUE	(minimum 42 games)			
Division 1	Stoke C	24	42	1984–85
Division 2	Watford	24	42	1971–72
	Leyton Orient	30	46	1994–95
Division 3(S)	Crystal Palace	33	42	1950–51
Division 3(N)	Crewe Alex	32	42	1923–24
Division 3	Stockport Co	27	46	1969–70
Division 4	Crewe Alex	29	46	1981–82
SCOTTISH LEAGUE	(minimum 30 games)			
Premier Division	Hamilton A	19	36	1988–89
	Dunfermline Ath	22	44	1991–92
Division 1	Brechin C	30	44	1993–94
	Ayr U	20	34	1966–67
Division 2	Lochgelly U	20	38	1923–24
New Division 1	Stirling Alb	18	39	1980–81
New Division 2	Berwick R	22	36	1994–95
New Division 3	Albion R	27	36	1994–95
	Berwick R	32	39	1987–88

MOST GOALS AGAINST IN A SEASON

		Goals	Games	*Season*
FA PREMIER LEAGUE				
	Swindon T	100	42	1993–94
FOOTBALL LEAGUE				
Division 1	Blackpool	125	42	1930–31
Division 2	Darwen	141	34	1898–99
Division 3(S)	Merthyr T	135	42	1929–30
Division 3(N)	Nelson	136	42	1927–28
Division 3	Accrington S	123	46	1959–60
Division 4	Hartlepools U	109	46	1959–60
SCOTTISH LEAGUE				
Premier Division	Morton	100	36	1984–85
	Morton	100	44	1987–88
Division 1	Leith Ath	137	38	1931–32
Division 2	Edinburgh C	146	38	1931–32
New Division 1	Queen of the S	99	39	1988–89
	Cowdenbeath	109	44	1992–93
New Division 2	Meadowbank T	89	39	1977–78
New Division 3	Albion R	82	36	1994–95

FEWEST GOALS AGAINST IN A SEASON

		Goals	Games	*Season*
FA PREMIER LEAGUE				
	Arsenal	28	42	1993–94
	Manchester U	28	42	1994–95
FOOTBALL LEAGUE	(minimum 42 games)			
Division 1	Liverpool	16	42	1978–79
Division 2	Manchester U	23	42	1924–25
	West Ham U	34	46	1990–91
Division 3(S)	Southampton	21	42	1921–22
Division 3(N)	Port Vale	21	46	1953–54
Division 3	Middlesbrough	30	46	1986–87
Division 4	Lincoln C	25	46	1980–81
SCOTTISH LEAGUE	(minimum 30 games)			
Premier Division	Rangers	19	36	1989–90
	Rangers	23	44	1986–87
	Celtic	23	44	1987–88
Division 1	Celtic	14	38	1913–14
Division 2	Morton	20	38	1966–67
New Division 1	Hibernian	24	39	1980–81
	Falkirk	32	44	1993–94
New Division 2	St Johnstone	24	39	1987–88
	Stirling Alb	24	39	1990–91
New Division 3	Montrose	32	36	1994–95

MOST POINTS IN A SEASON

FOOTBALL LEAGUE	(under old system of two points for a win)	*Points*	Games	*Season*
Division 1	Liverpool	68	42	1978–79
Division 2	Tottenham H	70	42	1919–20
Division 3	Aston V	70	46	1971–72
Division 3(S)	Nottingham F	70	46	1950–51
	Bristol C	70	46	1954–55
Division 3(N)	Doncaster R	72	42	1946–47
Division 4	Lincoln C	74	46	1975–76
SCOTTISH LEAGUE				
Premier Division	Aberdeen	59	36	1984–85
	Rangers	73	44	1992–93
Division 1	Rangers	76	42	1920–21
Division 2	Morton	69	38	1966–67
New Division 1	St Mirren	62	39	1976–77
	Falkirk	66	44	1993–94
New Division 2	Forfar Ath	63	39	1983–84
FA PREMIER LEAGUE	(three points for a win)			
	Manchester U	92	42	1993–94
FOOTBALL LEAGUE				
Division 1	Everton	90	42	1984–85
	Liverpool	90	40	1987–88
Division 2	Chelsea	99	46	1988–89
Division 3	Bournemouth	97	46	1986–87
Division 4	Swindon T	102	46	1985–86
SCOTTISH LEAGUE				
Premier Division	Rangers	69	36	1994–95
New Division 1	Raith R	69	36	1994–95
New Division 2	Morton	64	36	1994–95
New Division 3	Forfar Ath	80	36	1994–95

FEWEST POINTS IN A SEASON

FA PREMIER LEAGUE		*Points*	Games	Season
	Ipswich T	27	42	1994–95
FOOTBALL LEAGUE	(minimum 34 games)			
Division 1	Stoke C	17	42	1984–85
Division 2	Doncaster R	8	34	1904–05
	Loughborough T	8	34	1899–1900
	Walsall	31	46	1988–89
Division 3	Rochdale	21	46	1973–74
	Cambridge U	21	46	1984–85
Division 3(S)	Merthyr T	21	42	1924–25 & 1929–30
	QPR	21	42	1925–26
Division 3(N)	Rochdale	11	40	1931–32
Division 4	Workington	19	46	1976–77
SCOTTISH LEAGUE	(minimum 30 games)			
Premier Division	St Johnstone	11	36	1975–76
	Morton	16	44	1987–88
Division 1	Stirling Alb	6	30	1954–55
Division 2	Edinburgh C	7	34	1936–37
New Division 1	Queen of the S	10	39	1988–89
	Cowdenbeath	13	44	1992–93
New Division 2	Berwick R	16	39	1987–88
	Stranraer	16	39	1987–88

MOST WINS IN A SEASON

FA PREMIER LEAGUE		*Wins*	Games	Season
	Manchester U	27	42	1993–94
	Blackburn R	27	42	1994–95
FOOTBALL LEAGUE				
Division 1	Tottenham H	31	42	1960–61
Division 2	Tottenham H	32	42	1919–20
Division 3(S)	Millwall	30	42	1927–28
	Plymouth Arg	30	42	1929–30
	Cardiff C	30	42	1946–47
	Nottingham F	30	46	1950–51
	Bristol C	30	46	1954–55

Division 3(N)	Doncaster R	33	42	1946–47
Division 3	Aston Villa	32	46	1971–72
Division 4	Lincoln C	32	46	1975–76
	Swindon T	32	46	1985–86
SCOTTISH LEAGUE				
Premier Division	Aberdeen	27	36	1984–85
	Rangers	33	44	1991–92
	Rangers	33	44	1992–93
Division 1	Rangers	35	42	1920–21
Division 2	Morton	33	38	1966–67
New Division 1	Motherwell	26	39	1981–82
New Division 2	Forfar Ath	27	39	1983–84
	Ayr U	27	39	1987–88
New Division 3	Forfar Ath	25	36	1994–95

RECORD HOME WINS IN A SEASON

Brentford won all 21 games in Division 3(S), 1929–30

UNDEFEATED AT HOME

Liverpool 85 games (63 League, 9 League Cup, 7 European, 6 FA Cup), Jan 1978–Jan 1981

RECORD AWAY WINS IN A SEASON

Doncaster R won 18 of 21 games in Division 3(N), 1946–47

FEWEST WINS IN A SEASON

FA PREMIER LEAGUE		*Wins*	Games	*Season*
	Swindon T	5	42	1993–94
FOOTBALL LEAGUE				
Division 1	Stoke C	3	22	1889–90
	Woolwich Arsenal	3	38	1912–13
	Stoke C	3	42	1984–85
Division 2	Loughborough T	1	34	1899–1900
	Walsall	5	46	1988–89
Division 3(S)	Merthyr T	6	42	1929–30
	QPR	6	42	1925–26
Division 3(N)	Rochdale	4	40	1931–32
Division 3	Rochdale	2	46	1973–74
Division 4	Southport	3	46	1976–77
SCOTTISH LEAGUE				
Premier Division	St Johnstone	3	36	1975–76
	Kilmarnock	3	36	1982–83
	Morton	3	44	1987–88
Division 1	Vale of Leven	0	22	1891–92
Division 2	East Stirlingshire	1	22	1905–06
	Forfar Ath	1	38	1974–75
New Division 1	Queen of the S	2	39	1988–89
	Cowdenbeath	3	44	1992–93
New Division 2	Forfar Ath	4	26	1975–76
	Stranraer	4	39	1987–88
New Division 3	Albion R	5	36	1994–95

MOST DEFEATS IN A SEASON

FA PREMIER LEAGUE		*Defeats*	Games	*Season*
	Ipswich T	29	42	1994–95
FOOTBALL LEAGUE				
Division 1	Stoke C	31	42	1984–85
Division 2	Tranmere R	31	42	1938–39
	Chester C	33	46	1992–93
Division 3	Cambridge U	33	46	1984–85
Division 3(S)	Merthyr T	29	42	1924–25
	Walsall	29	46	1952–53
	Walsall	29	46	1953–54

Division 3(N)	Rochdale	33	40	1931–32
Division 4	Newport Co	33	46	1987–88

SCOTTISH LEAGUE

Premier Division	Morton	29	36	1984–85
Division 1	St Mirren	31	42	1920–21
Division 2	Brechin C	30	36	1962–63
	Lochgelly	30	38	1923–24
New Division 1	Queen of the S	29	39	1988–89
	Cowdenbeath	34	44	1992–93
New Division 2	Berwick R	29	39	1987–88
New Division 3	Albion R	28	36	1994–95

HAT-TRICKS

Career 34 Dixie Dean (Tranmere R, Everton, Notts Co, England)
Division 1 (one season post-war) 6 Jimmy Greaves (Chelsea), 1960–61
Three for one team one match
West, Spouncer, Hooper, Nottingham F v Leicester Fosse, Division 1, 21 April 1909
Barnes, Ambler, Davies, Wrexham v Hartlepools U, Division 4, 3 March 1962
Adcock, Stewart, White, Manchester C v Huddersfield T, Division 2, 7 Nov 1987
Loasby, Smith, Wells, Northampton T v Walsall, Division 3S, 5 Nov 1927
Bowater, Hoyland, Readman, Mansfield T v Rotherham U, Division 3N, 27 Dec 1932

FEWEST DEFEATS IN A SEASON

(Minimum 20 games)

FA PREMIER LEAGUE		*Defeats*	Games	*Season*
	Manchester U	4	42	1993–94
FOOTBALL LEAGUE				
Division 1	Preston NE	0	22	1888–89
	Arsenal	1	38	1990–91
	Liverpool	2	40	1987–88
	Leeds U	2	42	1968–69
Division 2	Liverpool	0	28	1893–94
	Burnley	2	30	1897–98
	Bristol C	2	38	1905–06
	Leeds U	3	42	1963–64
	Chelsea	5	46	1988–89
Division 3	QPR	5	46	1966–67
	Bristol R	5	46	1989–90
Division 3(S)	Southampton	4	42	1921–22
	Plymouth Arg	4	42	1929–30
Division 3(N)	Port Vale	3	46	1953–54
	Doncaster R	3	42	1946–47
	Wolverhampton W	3	42	1923–24
Division 4	Lincoln C	4	46	1975–76
	Sheffield U	4	46	1981–82
	Bournemouth	4	46	1981–82
SCOTTISH LEAGUE				
Premier Division	Celtic	3	44	1987–88
Division 1	Rangers	0	18	1898–99
	Rangers	1	42	1920–21
Division 2	Clyde	1	36	1956–57
	Morton	1	36	1962–63
	St Mirren	1	36	1967–68
New Division 1	Partick T	2	26	1975–76
	St Mirren	2	39	1976–77
	Raith R	4	44	1992–93
	Falkirk	4	44	1993–94
New Division 2	Raith R	1	26	1975–76
	Clydebank	3	26	1975–76
	Forfar Ath	3	39	1983–84
	Raith R	3	39	1986–87
New Division 3	Forfar Ath	6	36	1994–95

MOST DRAWN GAMES IN A SEASON

FA PREMIER LEAGUE		*Draws*	Games	*Season*
	Manchester C	18	42	1993–94
	Sheffield U	18	42	1993–94
	Southampton	18	42	1994–95
FOOTBALL LEAGUE				
Division 1	Norwich C	23	42	1978–79
Division 4	Exeter C	23	46	1986–87
SCOTTISH LEAGUE				
Premier Division	Aberdeen	21	44	1993–94
New Division 1	East Fife	21	44	1986–87

MOST GOALS IN A GAME

FA PREMIER LEAGUE	Andy Cole (Manchester U) 5 goals v Ipswich T	4 Mar 1995
FOOTBALL LEAGUE		
Division 1	Ted Drake (Arsenal) 7 goals v Aston Villa	14 Dec 1935
	James Ross (Preston NE) 7 goals v Stoke	6 Oct 1888
Division 2	Tommy Briggs (Blackburn R) 7 goals v Bristol R	5 Feb 1955
	Neville Coleman (Stoke C) 7 goals v Lincoln C (away)	23 Feb 1957
Division 3(S)	Joe Payne (Luton T) 10 goals v Bristol R	13 April 1936
Division 3(N)	Bunny Bell (Tranmere R) 9 goals v Oldham Ath	26 Dec 1935
Division 3	Steve Earle (Fulham) 5 goals v Halifax T	16 Sept 1969
	Barrie Thomas (Scunthorpe U) 5 goals v Luton T	24 April 1965
	Keith East (Swindon T) 5 goals v Mansfield T	20 Nov 1965
	Alf Wood (Shrewsbury T) 5 goals v Blackburn R	2 Oct 1971
	Tony Caldwell (Bolton W) 5 goals v Walsall	10 Sept 1983
	Andy Jones (Port Vale) 5 goals v Newport Co	4 May 1987
	Steve Wilkinson (Mansfield T) 5 goals v Birmingham C	3 April 1990
Division 4	Bert Lister (Oldham Ath) 6 goals v Southport	26 Dec 1962
FA CUP	Ted MacDougall (Bournemouth) 9 goals v Margate (*1st Round*)	20 Nov 1971
LEAGUE CUP	Frankie Bunn (Oldham Ath) 6 goals v Scarborough	25 Oct 1989
SCOTTISH LEAGUE CUP	Jim Fraser (Ayr U) 5 goals v Dumbarton	13 Aug 1952
SCOTTISH LEAGUE		
Premier Division	Paul Sturrock (Dundee U) 5 goals v Morton	17 Nov 1984
Division 1	Jimmy McGrory (Celtic) 8 goals v Dunfermline Ath	14 Sept 1928
Division 2	Owen McNally (Arthurlie) 8 goals v Armadale	1 Oct 1927
	Jim Dyet (King's Park) 8 goals v Forfar Ath	2 Jan 1930
	John Calder (Morton) 8 goals v Raith R	18 April 1936
	Norman Hayward (Raith R) 8 goals v Brechin C	20 Aug 1937
SCOTTISH CUP	John Petrie (Arbroath) 13 goals v Bon Accord (*1st Round*)	12 Sept 1885

MOST LEAGUE GOALS IN A SEASON

		Goals	Games	*Season*
FA PREMIER LEAGUE	Andy Cole (Newcastle U)	34	40	1993–94
	Alan Shearer (Blackburn R)	34	42	1994–95
Division 1	Dixie Dean (Everton)	60	39	1927–28
Division 2	George Camsell (Middlesbrough)	59	37	1926–27
Division 3(S)	Joe Payne (Luton T)	55	39	1936–37
Division 3(N)	Ted Harston (Mansfield T)	55	41	1936–37
Division 3	Derek Reeves (Southampton)	39	46	1959–60
Division 4	Terry Bly (Peterborough U)	52	46	1960–61
FA CUP	Sandy Brown (Tottenham H)	15	8	1900–01
LEAGUE CUP	Clive Allen (Tottenham H)	12	9	1986–87
SCOTTISH LEAGUE				
Division 1	William McFadyen (Motherwell)	52	34	1931–32
Division 2	Jim Smith (Ayr U)	66	38	1927–28

MOST LEAGUE GOALS IN A CAREER

FOOTBALL LEAGUE		*Goals*	Games	*Season*
Arthur Rowley	WBA	4	24	1946–48
	Fulham	27	56	1948–50
	Leicester C	251	303	1950–58
	Shrewsbury T	152	236	1958–65
		434	619	
SCOTTISH LEAGUE				
Jimmy McGrory	Celtic	1	3	1922–23
	Clydebank	13	30	1923–24
	Celtic	396	375	1924–38
		410	408	

MOST CUP GOALS IN A CAREER

FA CUP (post-war)

Denis Law 41 (Huddersfield T, Manchester C, Manchester U)
Ian Rush 41 (Chester, Liverpool)
Pre-war: Henry Cursham 48 (Notts Co)

A CENTURY OF LEAGUE AND CUP GOALS IN CONSECUTIVE SEASONS

George Camsell	Middlesbrough	59 Lge	5 Cup	1926–27
(101 goals)		33	4	1927–28
Steve Bull	Wolverhampton W	34 Lge	18 Cup	1987–88
(102 goals)		37	13	1988–89

(Camsell's cup goals were all scored in the FA Cup; Bull had 12 in the Sherpa Van Trophy, 3 Littlewoods Cup, 3 FA Cup in 1987–88; 11 Sherpa Van Trophy, 2 Littlewoods Cup in 1988–89.)

LONGEST SEQUENCE OF CONSECUTIVE SCORING (Individual)

FA PREMIER LEAGUE

Mark Stein (Chelsea)	9 in 7 games	1993–94

FOOTBALL LEAGUE RECORD

Dixie Dean (Everton)	23 in 12 games	1930–31

LONGEST WINNING SEQUENCE

FOOTBALL LEAGUE		*Games*	*Season*
Division 1	Everton	12	1893–94 (4) and 1894–95 (8)
Division 2	Manchester U	14	1904–05
	Bristol C	14	1905–06
	Preston NE	14	1950–51
Division 3	Reading	13	1985–86
From *Season's start*			
Division 1	Tottenham H	11	1960–61
Division 3	Reading	13	1985–86

LONGEST WINNING SEQUENCE IN A SEASON

FOOTBALL LEAGUE		*Games*	*Season*
Division 1	Tottenham H	11	1960–61
Division 2	Manchester U	14	1904–05
Division 2	Bristol C	14	1905–06
Division 2	Preston NE	14	1950–51
SCOTTISH LEAGUE			
Division 2	Morton	23	1963–64

LONGEST UNBEATEN SEQUENCE

FOOTBALL LEAGUE		Games	*Seasons*
Division 1	Nottingham F	42	Nov 1977–Dec 1978

LONGEST UNBEATEN CUP SEQUENCE

Liverpool 25 rounds League/Milk Cup 1980–84

LONGEST UNBEATEN SEQUENCE IN A SEASON

FOOTBALL LEAGUE		*Games*	*Season*
Division 1	Burnley	30	1920–21

LONGEST UNBEATEN START TO A SEASON

FOOTBALL LEAGUE		Games	*Season*
Division 1	Leeds U	29	1973–74
Division 1	Liverpool	29	1987–88

LONGEST SEQUENCE WITHOUT A WIN IN A SEASON

FOOTBALL LEAGUE		Games	*Season*
Division 2	Cambridge U	31	1983–84

LONGEST SEQUENCE WITHOUT A WIN FROM SEASON'S START

Division 1	Manchester U	12	1930–31

LONGEST SEQUENCE OF CONSECUTIVE DEFEATS

FOOTBALL LEAGUE		Games	*Season*
Division 2	Darwen	18	1898–99

GOALKEEPING RECORDS (without conceding a goal)

British record (all competitive games)
Chris Woods, Rangers, in 1196 minutes from 26 November 1986 to 31 January 1987.

Football League
Steve Death, Reading, 1103 minutes from 24 March to 18 August 1979.

PENALTIES

Most in a *Season (individual)*		*Goals*	*Season*
Division 1	Francis Lee (Manchester C)	13	1971–72
Most awarded in one game			
Five	Crystal Palace (4 – 1 scored, 3 missed) v Brighton & HA (1 scored), Div 2		1988–89
Most saved in a *Season*			
Division 1	Paul Cooper (Ipswich T)	8 (of 10)	1979–80

MOST LEAGUE APPEARANCES

996 Peter Shilton (286 Leicester City, 110 Stoke City, 202 Nottingham Forest, 188 Southampton, 175 Derby County, 34 Plymouth Argyle, Bolton Wanderers) 1966–95
824 Terry Paine (713 Southampton, 111 Hereford United) 1957–77
795 Tommy Hutchison (165 Blackpool, 314 Coventry City, 46 Manchester City, 92 Burnley 178 Swansea City, also 68 Alloa 1965–68) 1968–91
777 Alan Oakes (565 Manchester City, 211 Chester City, 1 Port Vale) 1959–84
770 John Trollope (all for Swindon Town) 1960–80†
764 Jimmy Dickinson (all for Portsmouth) 1946–65
762 John Burridge (27 Workington, 134 Blackpool, 65 Aston Villa, 6 Southend U (loan), 88 Crystal Palace, 39 QPR, 74 Wolverhampton W, 6 Derby Co (loan), 109 Sheffield U, 62 Southampton, 67 Newcastle U, 65 Hibernian, 3 Scarborough, 4 Lincoln C, 3 Aberdeen, 3 Dumbarton, 3 Falkirk, 4 Manchester C) 1968–96
761 Roy Sproson (all for Port Vale) 1950–72
758 Ray Clemence (48 Scunthorpe United, 470 Liverpool, 240 Tottenham Hotspur) 1966–87
757 Pat Jennings (48 Watford, 472 Tottenham Hotspur, 237 Arsenal) 1963–86
† record for one club

Consecutive
401 Harold Bell (401 Tranmere R; 459 in all games) 1946–55

FA CUP
88 Ian Callaghan (79 Liverpool, 7 Swansea C, 2 Crewe Alex)

Most Senior Matches
1379 Peter Shilton (996 League, 86 FA Cup, 102 League Cup, 125 Internationals, 13 Under-23, 4 Football League XI, 53 others including European Cup, UEFA Cup, World Club Championship, various domestic cup competitions)

MOST FA CUP FINAL GOALS

Ian Rush (Liverpool) 5: 1986(2), 1989(2), 1992(1)

MOST LEAGUE MEDALS

Phil Neal (Liverpool) 8: 1976, 1977, 1979, 1980, 1982, 1983, 1984, 1986

OTHER RECORDS

YOUNGEST PLAYERS
FA Premier League Andy Turner, 17 years 145 days, Tottenham H v Southampton, 15.8.92
FA Premier League Scorer Andy Turner, 17 years 166 days, Tottenham H v Everton, 5.9.92.
Football League Albert Geldard, 15 years 158 days, Bradford Park Avenue v Millwall, Division 2, 16.9.29; and Ken Roberts, 15 years 158 days, Wrexham v Bradford Park Avenue, Division 3N, 1.9.51
Football League scorer
Ronnie Dix, 15 years 180 days, Bristol Rovers v Norwich City, Division 3S, 3.3.28.
Division 1
Derek Forster, 15 years 185 days, Sunderland v Leicester City, 22.8.84.
Division 1 scorer
Jason Dozzell, 16 years 57 days as substitute Ipswich Town v Coventry City, 4.2.84
Division 1 hat-tricks
Alan Shearer, 17 years 240 days, Southampton v Arsenal, 9.4.88
Jimmy Greaves, 17 years 10 months, Chelsea v Portsmouth, 25.12.57
FA Cup (any round)
Andy Awford, 15 years 88 days as substitute Worcester City v Borehamwood, 3rd Qual. rd, 10.10.87
FA Cup proper
Scott Endersby, 15 years 288 days, Kettering v Tilbury, 1st rd, 26.11.77
FA Cup Final
James Prinsep, 17 years 245 days, Clapham Rovers v Old Etonians, 1879
FA Cup Final scorer
Norman Whiteside, 18 years 18 days, Manchester United v Brighton & Hove Albion, 1983
FA Cup Final captain
David Nish, 21 years 212 days, Leicester City v Manchester City, 1969
League Cup Final scorer
Norman Whiteside, 17 years 324 days, Manchester United v Liverpool, 1983
League Cup Final captain
Barry Venison, 20 years 7 months 8 days, Sunderland v Norwich City, 1985

OLDEST PLAYERS

Football League

Neil McBain, 52 years 4 months, New Brighton v Hartlepools United, Div 3N, 15.3.47 (McBain was New Brighton's manager and had to play in an emergency)

Division 1

Stanley Matthews, 50 years 5 days, Stoke City v Fulham, 6.2.65

FA Cup Final

Walter Hampson, 41 years 8 months, Newcastle United v Aston Villa, 1924

FA Cup

Billy Meredith, 49 years 8 months, Manchester City v Newcastle United, 29.3.24

International debutant

Leslie Compton, 38 years 2 months, England v Wales, 15.11.50

International

Billy Meredith, 45 years 229 days, Wales v England, 15.3 20

SENDINGS-OFF

Season	314 (League alone)	1994–95
Day	15 (3 League, 12 FA Cup*) **worst overall FA Cup total*	20 Nov 1982
League	13	14 Dec 1985
Weekend	15	22/23 Dec 1990
FA Cup Final	Kevin Moran, Manchester U v Everton	1985
Wembley	Boris Stankovic, Yugoslavia v Sweden (Olympics)	1948
	Antonio Rattin, Argentina v England (World Cup)	1966
	Billy Bremner (Leeds U) and Kevin Keegan (Liverpool), Charity Shield	1974
	Gilbert Dresch, Luxembourg v England (World Cup)	1977
	Mike Henry, Sudbury T v Tamworth (FA Vase)	1989
	Lee Dixon, Arsenal v Tottenham H (FA Cup semi-final)	1993
	Peter Swan, Port Vale v WBA (play-offs)	1993
	Michael Wallace and Chris Beaumont (both Stockport Co) v Burnley (play-offs)	1994
Quickest	Mark Smith, Crewe Alex v Darlington (away) Div 3: 19 secs	12 March 1994
Division 1	Liam O'Brien, Manchester U v Southampton (away): 85 secs	3 Jan 1987
World Cup	Jose Batista, Uruguay v Scotland, Neza, Mexico (World Cup): 55 secs	13 June 1986
Most one game	Four: Northampton T (0) v Hereford U (4) Div 3	11 Nov 1992
	Four: Crewe Alex (2) v Bradford PA (2) Div 3N	8 Jan 1955
	Four: Sheffield U (1) v Portsmouth (3) Div 2	13 Dec 1986
	Four: Port Vale (2) v Northampton T (2) Littlewoods Cup	18 Aug 1987
	Four: Brentford (2) v Mansfield T (2) Div 3	12 Dec 1987

RECORD ATTENDANCES

FA Premier League	45,347	Aston Villa v Liverpool, Villa Park	7.5.1994
Football League	83,260	Manchester U v Arsenal, Maine Road	17.1.1948
Scottish League	118,567	Rangers v Celtic, Ibrox Stadium	2.1.1939
FA Cup Final	126,047*	Bolton W v West Ham U, Wembley	28.4.1923
European Cup	135,826	Celtic v Leeds U, semi-final at Hampden Park	15.4.1970
Scottish Cup	146,433	Celtic v Aberdeen, Hampden Park	24.4.37
World Cup	199,854†	Brazil v Uruguay, Maracana, Rio	16.7.50

* It has been estimated that as many as 70,000 more broke in without paying.

† 173,830 paid.

ADDRESSES

The Football Association: R. H. G. Kelly, F.C.I.S., 16 Lancaster Gate, London W2 3LW

Scotland: J. Farry, 6 Park Gardens, Glasgow G3 7YE. *0141-332 6372*
Northern Ireland (Irish FA): D. I. Bowen, 20 Windsor Avenue, Belfast BT9 6EG. *01232 669458*
Wales: A. Evans, 3 Westgate Street, Cardiff, South Glamorgan CF1 1JF. *01222 372325*
Republic of Ireland (FA of Ireland): S. Connolly, 80 Merrion Square South, Dublin 2. *003531 766864*
International Federation (FIFA): S. Blatter, FIFA House, Hitzigweg 11, CH-8032 Zurich, Switzerland. *00 411 384 9595. Fax: 00 411 384 9696*
Union of European Football Associations: G. Aigner, Chermin de la Redoute 54, Case Postale 303 CH-1260 Nyon, Switzerland. *0041 22 994 44 44. Fax: 0041 22 994 44 88*

THE LEAGUES

The Premier League: R. N. Parry, 16 Lancaster Gate, London W2 3LW. *0171-262 4542.*
The Football League: J. D. Dent, F.C.I.S., The Football League, Lytham St Annes, Lancs FY8 1JG. *01253-729421. Telex 67675*
The Scottish League: P. Donald, 188 West Regent Street, Glasgow G2 4RY. *0141-248 384415*
The Irish League: H. Wallace, 87 University Street, Belfast BT7 1HP. *01232 242888*
Football League of Ireland: E. Morris, 80 Merrion Square South, Dublin 2. *003531 765120*
Vauxhall Conference: J. A. Moules, 24 Barnehurst Road, Bexleyheath, Kent DA7 6EZ. *01322 521116*
Central League: A. Williamson, The Football League, Lytham St Annes, Lancs FY8 1JG. *01253 729421*
North West Counties League: M. Darby, 87 Hillary Road, Hyde, Cheshire SK14 4EB.
Eastern Counties League: C. Lamb, 26 Dunthorpe Road, Clacton, Essex CO12 8UJ. *01255 436398*
Football Combination: N. Chamberlain, 2 Vicarage Close, Old Costessey, Norwich NR8 5DL. *01603 743998*
Hellenic League: M. J. Jenkins, 3 Leamington Drive, Faringdon, Oxon SN7 7JZ. *01367 240042*
Kent League: R. Vinter, The Thatched Barn, Lower Hardres, Canterbury, Kent CT4 5PG
Lancashire Amateur League: R. G. Bowker, 13 Shores Green Drive, Wincham, Northwich, Cheshire CW9 6EE. *0161-480 7723*
Lancashire Football League: J. W. Howarth, 465 Whalley Road, Clapton-le-Moors, Accrington, Lancs BB5 5RP. *01254 398957*
Leicestershire Senior League: D. Jamieson, 48 King Georges Road, Loughborough, Leics LE11 2PA. *01509 263411*
London Spartan: D. Cordell, 44 Greenleas, Waltham Abbey, Essex EN9 1SZ. *01992 712428*
Manchester League: F. J. Fitzpatrick, 102 Victoria Road, Stretford, Manchester M32 0AD. *0161-865 2726*
Midland Combination: N. Harvey, 115 Millfield Road, Handsworth Wood, Birmingham B20 1ED.
Mid-Week Football League: N. A. S. Matthews, Cedar Court, Steeple Aston, Oxford. *01869 40347*
Northern Premier: R. D. Bayley, 22 Woburn Drive, Hale, Altrincham, Cheshire WA15 8LZ. *0161-980 7007*
Northern Intermediate League: G. Thompson, Clegg House, 253 Pitsmoor Road, Sheffield S3 9AQ. *01742 27817*
Northern League: T. Golightly, 85 Park Road North, Chester-le-Street, Co Durham DH3 3SA. *0191-388 2056*
North Midlands League: G. Thompson, 7 Wren Park Close, Ridgway, Sheffield.
Peterborough and District League: M. J. Croson, 44 Storrington Way, Werrington, Peterborough, Cambs PE4 6QP.
Isthmian League: N. Robinson, 226 Rye Lane, Peckham SE15 4NL. *0181-653 3903*
Southern Amateur League: S. J. Lucas, 23 Beaufort Close, North Weald Bassett, Epping, Essex CM16 6JZ. *0137882 3932*
South-East Counties League: A. Leather, 66 Green Acres, Chichester Road, Croydon, Surrey CR0 5UX. *0181-681 7100*
Southern League: D. J. Strudwick, 11 Welland Close, Durrington, Worthing, West Sussex BN13 3NR. *01903 67788*
South Midlands League: M. Mitchell, 26 Leighton Court, Dunstable, Beds LU6 1EW. *01582 67291*
South Western League: M. Goodenough, Rose Cottage, Horrels Ford, Milton Damerel, Holsworthy, Devon EX22 7NJ. *01409 261402*
United Counties League: R. Gamble, 8 Bostock Avenue, Northampton. *01604 37766*
Wearside League: B. Robson, 12 Deneside, Howden-le-Wear, Crook, Co. Durham DL15 8JR. *01388 762034*
Western League: M. E. Washer, 16 Heathfield Road, Nailsea, Bristol BS19 1EB.
The Welsh League: K. J. Tucker, 16 The Parade, Merthyr Tydfil, Mid Glamorgan CF47 0ET. *01685 723884*
West Midlands Regional League: N. R. Juggins, 14 Badger Way, Blackwell, Bromsgrove, Worcs B60 1EX.
West Yorkshire League: W. Keyworth, 2 Hill Court Grove, Bramley, Yorks L13 2AP. *0113 74465*
Northern Counties (East): B. Wood, 6 Restmore Avenue, Guiseley, Nr Leeds LS20 9DG. *01943 874558 (home); 01274 29595 (9 a.m. to 5 p.m.)*

COUNTY FOOTBALL ASSOCIATIONS

Bedfordshire: P. D. Brown, Century House, Skimpot Road, Dunstable, LU5 4JU. *01582 565111*
Berks and Bucks: W. S. Gosling, 15a London Street, Faringdon, Oxon SN7 8AG. *01367 242099*
Birmingham County: M. Pennick, County FA Offices, Rayhall Lane, Great Barr, Birmingham B43 6JE. *0121-357 4278*
Cambridgeshire: A. K. Pawley, 3 Signet Court, Swanns Road, Cambridge CB5 8LA. *01223 277290*
Cheshire: A. Collins, The Cottage, Hartford Moss Rec Centre, Winnington, Northwich CW8 4BG.
Cornwall: J. M. Ryder, Penare, 16 Gloweth View, Truro, Cornwall TR1 3JZ.
Cumberland: R. Johnson, 72 Victoria Road, Workington, Cumbria CA14 2QT. *01900 3979*
Derbyshire: K. Compton, The Grandstand, Moorways Stadium, Moor Lane, Derby DE2 8FB. *01332 361422*
Devon County: C. Squirrel, County HQ, Coach Road, Newton Abbot, Devon TQ12 1EJ. *01626 332077*
Dorset County: P. Hough, County Ground, Blandford Close, Hamsworthy, Poole, Dorset BH15 4BF. *01202 682375*
Durham: J. R. Walsh, 'Codeslaw', Ferens Park, Durham DH1 1JZ. *01385 48653*
East Riding County: D. R. Johnson, 52 Bethune Ave, Hull HU4 7EJ. *01482 641458*
Essex County: T. Alexander, 31 Mildmay Road, Chelmsford, Essex CM2 0DN. *01245 357727*
Gloucestershire: P. Britton, Fernleigh House, South Road, Kingswood, Bristol BS15 2JL. *0117 940 7700*
Guernsey: D. Dorey, Haut Regard, St. Clair Hill, St. Sampson's, Guernsey, GY2 4DT, CI. *01481 46231*
Hampshire: R. G. Barnes, 8 Ashwood Gardens, off Winchester Road, Southampton SO9 2UA. *01703 766884*
Herefordshire: E. R. Prescott, 7 Kirkland Close, Hampton Park, Hereford HR1 1XP. *01432 51134*

Hertfordshire: R. G. Kibble, Marquis House, 68 Great North Road, Hatfield, Herts AL9 5ER.

Huntingdonshire: M. M. Armstrong, 1 Chapel End, Great Giddings, Huntingdon, Cambs PE17 5NP. *018323 262*

Isle of Man: Mrs A. Garrett, 60 Ballagarey Road, Glen Vine, IOM. *01624 676349*

Jersey: D. G. Speed, 93 Les Cinq Chenes, Five Oaks, St. Saviour, Jersey JE2 7UE.

Kent County: K. T. Masters, 69 Maidstone Road, Chatham, Kent ME4 6DT. *01634 43824*

Lancashire: J. Kenyon, 31a Wellington St, St John's, Blackburn, Lancs BB1 8AU. *01254 64333*

Leicestershire and Rutland: R. E. Barston, Holmes Park, Dog and Gun Lane, Whetstone, Leicester LE8 3LJ. *01533 867828*

Lincolnshire: F. S. Richardson, PO Box 26, 12 Dean Road, Lincoln LN2 4DP. *01522 24917*

Liverpool County: F. L. J. Hunter, 23 Greenfield Road, Old Swann, Liverpool L13 3EN. *0151-526 9515*

London: R. S. Ashford, Aldworth Grove, London SE13 6HY. *0181-690 9626*

Manchester County: F. Brocklehurst, Sports Complex, Brantingham Road, Chorlton, Manchester M21 1TG. *0161-881 0299*

Middlesex County: P. J. Clayton, 39 Roxborough Road, Harrow, Middx HA1 1NS. *0181-424 8524*

Norfolk County: R. Kiddell, 153 Middleton Lane, Hellesdon, Norwich, Norfolk NR6 5SF. *01603 488222*

Northamptonshire: B. Walden, 2 Duncan Close, Red House Road, Moulton Park, Northampton NN3 1WL. *01604 670741*

North Riding County: P. Kirby, 284 Linthorpe Road, Middlesbrough TS1 3QU. *01642 224585*

Northumberland: R. E. Maughan, Seymour House, 10 Brenkley Way, Blezard Bus Park, Seaton Burn, Newcastle upon Tyne NE13 6DT. *0191-297 0101*

Nottinghamshire: W. T. Annable, 7 Clarendon Street, Nottingham NG1 5HS. *01602 418954*

Oxfordshire: P. J. Ladbrook, 3 Wilkins Road, Cowley, Oxford OX4 2HY. *01865 775432*

Sheffield and Hallamshire: G. Thompson, Clegg House, 5 Onslow Road, Sheffield S11 7AF. *01142 670068*

Shropshire: A. W. Brett, 5 Ebnal Road, Shrewsbury SY2 6PW. *01743 56066*

Somerset & Avon (South): Mrs H. Marchment, 30 North Road, Midsomer Norton, Bath BA3 2QQ. *01761 413176*

Staffordshire: G. S. Brookes, County Showground, Weston Road, Stafford ST18 0DB. *01785 56994*

Suffolk County: W. M. Steward, 2 Millfields, Haughley, Suffolk IP14 3PU. *01449 673481*

Surrey County: A. P. Adams, 321 Kingston Road, Leatherhead, Surrey KT22 7TU. *01372 373543*

Sussex County: D. M. Worsfold, County Office, Culver Road, Lancing, Sussex BN15 9AX. *01903 753547*

Westmorland: J. B. Fleming, 101 Burneside Road, Kendal, Cumbria LA9 4RZ. *01539 730946*

West Riding County: R. Carter, Fleet Lane, Woodlesford, Leeds LS26 8NX. *0113 2821222*

Wiltshire: E. M. Parry, 44 Kennet Avenue, Swindon SN2 3LG. *01793 29036*

Worcestershire: M. R. Leggett Fermain, 12 Worcester Road, Eyesham, Worcs WR11 4JV. *01905 612336*

OTHER USEFUL ADDRESSES

Amateur Football Alliance: W. P. Goss, 55 Islington Park Street, London N1 1QB. *0171-359 3493*

English Schools FA: M. R. Berry, 1/2 Eastgate Street, Stafford ST16 2NN. *01785 51142*

Oxford University: M. H. Matthews, University College, Oxford OX1 4BH.

Cambridge University: Dr A. J. Little, St Catherine's College, Cambridge CB2 1RL.

Army: Major T. C. Knight, Clayton Barracks, Aldershot, Hants GU11 2BG. *01252 24431 Ext 3571*

Royal Air Force: Group Capt P. W. Hilton, 15 Western Court, Western Road, Cheltenham, Glos GL50 3RH. *01242 255215*

Royal Navy: Lt-Cdr J. Danks, R.N. Sports Office, H.M.S. Temeraire, Portsmouth, Hants PO1 4QS. *01705 822351 Ext 2271*

British Universities Sports Association: G. Gregory-Jones, Chief Executive: BUSA, 8 Union Street, London SE1 1SZ. *0171-357 8555*

Central Council of Physical Recreation: General Secretary, 70 Brompton Road, London SW3 1HE. *0171-584 6651*

British Olympic Association: 6 John Prince's Street, London W1M 0DH. *0171-408 2029*

National Federation of Football Supporters' Clubs: Chairman: Tony Kershaw, 87 Brookfield Avenue, Loughborough, Leicestershire LE11 3LN. *01509 267643 (and fax)*. National Secretary: Mark Agate, "The Stadium", 14 Coombe Close, Lordswood, Chatham, Kent ME5 8NU. *01634 863520 (and fax)*

National Playing Fields Association: Col R. Satterthwaite, O.B.E., 578b Catherine Place, London, SW1.

The Scottish Football Commercial Managers Association: J. E. Hillier (Chairman), c/o Keith FC Promotions Office, 60 Union Street, Keith, Banffshire, Scotland.

Professional Footballers' Association: G. Taylor, 2 Oxford Court, Bishopsgate, Off Lower Mosley Street, Manchester M2 3W2. *0161-236 0575*

Referees' Association: W. J. Taylor, Cross Offices, Summerhill, Kingswinford, West Midlands DY6 9JE. *01384 288386*

Women's Football Alliance: Miss H. Jeavons, 9 Wyllyotts Place, Potters Bar, Herts EN6 2JB. *01707 651840*

The Association of Football League Commercial Managers: G. H. Dimbleby, Secretary WBA FC, The Hawthorns, Halford Lane, West Bromwich B71 4LF.

The Association of Football Statisticians: R. J. Spiller, 22 Bretons, Basildon, Essex SS15 5BY. *01268 416020*

The Football Programme Directory: David Stacey, 'The Beeches', 66 Southend Road, Wickford, Essex SS11 8EN.

England Football Supporters Association: Publicity Officer, David Stacey, 66 Southend Road, Wickford, Essex SS11 8EN.

The Football League Executive Staffs Association: PO Box 52, Leamington Spa, Warwickshire.

The Ninety-Two Club: 104 Gilda Crescent, Whitchurch, Bristol BS14 9LD.

Scottish 38 Club: Mark Byatt, 6 Greenfields Close, Loughton, Essex IG10 3HG. *0181-508 6088*

The Football Trust: Second Floor, Walkden House, 10 Melton Street, London NW1 2EJ. *0171-388 4504*

The Football Supporters Association: PO Box 11, Liverpool L26 1XP. *0151-709 2594*

Association of Provincial Football Supporters' Clubs in London: Tina A. Robertson, 45 Durham Avenue, Heston, Middlesex TW5 0HG. *0181-843 9854*

World Association of Friends of English Football: New St 25A, Dk 6330 Pattburg, Denmark. *0045 467 4911*

Football Postcard Collectors Club: PRO: Bryan Horsnell, 275 Overdown Road, Tilehurst, Reading RG3 6NX. *01734 424448*

OTHER AWARDS 1994–95

FOOTBALLER OF THE YEAR

The Football Writers' Association Award for the Footballer of the Year went to Jurgen Klinsmann of Tottenham Hotspur and Germany.

Past Winners

1947–48 Stanley Matthews (Blackpool), 1948–49 Johnny Carey (Manchester U), 1949–50 Joe Mercer (Arsenal), 1950–51 Harry Johnston (Blackpool), 1951–52 Billy Wright (Wolverhampton W), 1952–53 Nat Lofthouse (Bolton W), 1953–54 Tom Finney (Preston NE), 1954–55 Don Revie (Manchester C), 1955–56 Bert Trautmann (Manchester C), 1956–57 Tom Finney (Preston NE), 1957–58 Danny Blanchflower (Tottenham H), 1958–59 Syd Owen (Luton T), 1959–60 Bill Slater (Wolverhampton W), 1960–61 Danny Blanchflower (Tottenham H), 1961–62 Jimmy Adamson (Burnley), 1962–63 Stanley Matthews (Stoke C), 1963–64 Bobby Moore (West Ham U), 1964–65 Bobby Collins (Leeds U), 1965–66 Bobby Charlton (Manchester U), 1966–67 Jackie Charlton (Leeds U), 1967–68 George Best (Manchester U), 1968–69 Dave Mackay (Derby Co) shared with Tony Book (Manchester C), 1969–70 Billy Bremner (Leeds U), 1970–71 Frank McLintock (Arsenal), 1971–72 Gordon Banks (Stoke C), 1972–73 Pat Jennings (Tottenham H), 1973–74 Ian Callaghan (Liverpool), 1974–75 Alan Mullery (Fulham), 1975–76 Kevin Keegan (Liverpool), 1976–77 Emlyn Hughes (Liverpool), 1977–78 Kenny Burns (Nottingham F), 1978–79 Kenny Dalglish (Liverpool), 1979–80 Terry McDermott (Liverpool), 1980–81 Frans Thijssen (Ipswich T), 1981–82 Steve Perryman (Tottenham H), 1982–83 Kenny Dalglish (Liverpool), 1983–84 Ian Rush (Liverpool), 1984–85 Neville Southall (Everton), 1985–86 Gary Lineker (Everton), 1986–87 Clive Allen (Tottenham H), 1987–88 John Barnes (Liverpool), 1988–89 Steve Nicol (Liverpool), 1989–90 John Barnes (Liverpool), 1990–91 Gordon Strachan (Leeds U), 1991–92 Gary Lineker (Tottenham H), 1992–93 Chris Waddle (Sheffield W), 1993–94 Alan Shearer (Blackburn R).

THE PFA AWARDS 1995

Player of the Year: Alan Shearer (Blackburn R).

Previous Winners: 1974 Norman Hunter (Leeds U); 1975 Colin Todd (Derby Co); 1976 Pat Jennings (Tottenham H); 1977 Andy Gray (Aston Villa); 1978 Peter Shilton (Nottingham F); 1979 Liam Brady (Arsenal); 1980 Terry McDermott (Liverpool); 1981 John Wark (Ipswich T); 1982 Kevin Keegan (Southampton); 1983 Kenny Dalglish (Liverpool); 1984 Ian Rush (Liverpool); 1985 Peter Reid (Everton); 1986 Gary Lineker (Everton); 1987 Clive Allen (Tottenham H); 1988 John Barnes (Liverpool); 1989 Mark Hughes (Manchester U); 1990 David Platt (Aston Villa); 1991 Mark Hughes (Manchester U); 1992 Gary Pallister (Manchester U); 1993 Paul McGrath (Aston Villa); 1994 Eric Cantona (Manchester U).

Young Player of the Year: Robbie Fowler (Liverpool).

Previous Winners: 1974 Kevin Beattie (Ipswich T); 1975 Mervyn Day (West Ham U); 1976 Peter Barnes (Manchester C); 1977 Andy Gray (Aston Villa); 1978 Tony Woodcock (Nottingham F); 1979 Cyrille Regis (WBA); 1980 Glenn Hoddle (Tottenham H); 1981 Gary Shaw (Aston Villa); 1982 Steve Moran (Southampton); 1983 Ian Rush (Liverpool); 1984 Paul Walsh (Luton T); 1985 Mark Hughes (Manchester U); 1986 Tony Cottee (West Ham U); 1987 Tony Adams (Arsenal); 1988 Paul Gascoigne (Tottenham H); 1989 Paul Merson (Arsenal); 1990 Matthew Le Tissier (Southampton); 1991 Lee Sharpe (Manchester U); 1992 Ryan Giggs (Manchester U); 1993 Ryan Giggs (Manchester U); 1994 Andy Cole (Newcastle U).

Merit Award: Gordon Strachan.

Previous Winners: 1974 Bobby Charlton CBE, Cliff Lloyd OBE; 1975 Denis Law; 1976 George Eastham OBE; 1977 Jack Taylor OBE; 1978 Bill Shankly OBE; 1979 Tom Finney OBE; 1980 Sir Matt Busby CBE; 1981 John Trollope MBE; 1982 Joe Mercer OBE; 1983 Bob Paisley OBE; 1984 Bill Nicholson; 1985 Ron Greenwood; 1986 The 1966 England World Cup team, Sir Alf Ramsey, Harold Shepherdson; 1987 Sir Stanley Matthews; 1988 Billy Bonds MBE; 1989 Nat Lofthouse; 1990 Peter Shilton; 1991 Tommy Hutchison; 1992 Brian Clough; 1993 the 1968 Manchester United team; 1994 Billy Bingham.

THE SCOTTISH PFA AWARDS 1995

Player of the Year: Brian Laudrup (Rangers).

Previous Winners: 1978 Derek Johnstone (Rangers); 1979 Paul Hegarty (Dundee U); 1980 Davie Provan (Celtic); 1981 Sandy Clark (Airdrieonians); 1982 Mark McGhee (Aberdeen); 1983 Charlie Nicholas (Celtic); 1984 Willie Miller (Aberdeen); 1985 Jim Duffy (Morton); 1986 Richard Gough (Dundee U); 1987 Brian McClair (Celtic); 1988 Paul McStay (Celtic); 1989 Theo Snelders (Aberdeen); 1990 Jim Bett (Aberdeen); 1991 Paul Elliott (Celtic); 1993 Ally McCoist (Rangers); 1993 Andy Goram (Rangers); 1994 Mark Hateley (Rangers).

Young Player of the Year: Charlie Miller (Rangers).

Previous Winners: 1978 Graeme Payne (Dundee U); 1979 Graham Stewart (Dundee U); 1980 John MacDonald (Rangers); 1981 Francis McAvennie (St Mirren); 1982 Charlie Nicholas (Celtic); 1983 Pat Nevin (Clyde); 1984 John Robertson (Hearts); 1985 Craig Levein (Hearts); 1986 Craig Levein (Hearts); 1987 Robert Fleck (Rangers); 1988 John Collins (Hibernian); 1989 Bill McKinlay (Dundee U); 1990 Scott Crabbe (Hearts); 1991 Eoin Jess (Aberdeen); 1992 Phil O'Donnell (Motherwell); 1993 Eoin Jess (Aberdeen); 1994 Phil O'Donnell (Motherwell).

SCOTTISH FOOTBALL WRITERS' ASSOCIATION

Player of the Year 1995 – Brian Laudrup (Rangers)

1965 Billy McNeill (Celtic)
1966 John Greig (Rangers)
1967 Ronnie Simpson (Celtic)
1968 Gordon Wallace (Raith R)
1969 Bobby Murdoch (Celtic)
1970 Pat Stanton (Hibernian)
1971 Martin Buchan (Aberdeen)
1972 Dave Smith (Rangers)
1973 George Connelly (Celtic)
1974 Scotland's World Cup Squad
1975 Sandy Jardine (Rangers)
1976 John Greig (Rangers)
1977 Danny McGrain (Celtic)
1978 Derek Johnstone (Rangers)
1979 Andy Ritchie (Morton)
1980 Gordon Strachan (Aberdeen)
1981 Alan Rough (Partick Th)
1982 Paul Sturrock (Dundee U)
1983 Charlie Nicholas (Celtic)
1984 Willie Miller (Aberdeen)
1985 Hamish McAlpine (Dundee U)
1986 Sandy Jardine (Hearts)
1987 Brian McClair (Celtic)
1988 Paul McStay (Celtic)
1989 Richard Gough (Rangers)
1990 Alex McLeish (Aberdeen)
1991 Maurice Malpas (Dundee U)
1992 Ally McCoist (Rangers)
1993 Andy Goram (Rangers)
1994 Mark Hateley (Rangers)

EUROPEAN FOOTBALLER OF THE YEAR 1994

Hristo Stoichkov (Barcelona) became the first Bulgarian to be honoured as European Footballer of the Year in the annual *France Football* award. He was also runner-up in FIFA's World Player of the Year for 1994 behind the winner Romario of Brazil.

Past winners

1956 **Stanley Matthews** (Blackpool
1957 **Alfredo Di Stefano** (Real Madrid)
1958 **Raymond Kopa** (Real Madrid)
1959 **Alfredo Di Stefano** (Real Madrid)
1960 **Luis Suarez** (Barcelona)
1961 **Omar Sivori** (Juventus)
1962 **Josef Masopust** (Dukla Prague)
1963 **Lev Yashin** (Moscow Dynamo)
1964 **Denis Law** (Manchester United)
1965 **Eusebio** (Benfica)
1966 **Bobby Charlton** (Manchester United)
1967 **Florian Albert** (Ferencvaros)
1968 **George Best** (Manchester United)
1969 **Gianni Rivera** (AC Milan)
1970 **Gerd Muller** (Bayern Munich)
1971 **Johan Cruyff** (Ajax)
1972 **Franz Beckenbauer** (Bayern Munich)
1973 **Johan Cruyff** (Barcelona)
1974 **Johan Cruyff** (Barcelona)
1975 **Oleg Blokhin** (Dynamo Kiev)
1976 **Franz Beckenbauer** (Bayern Munich)
1977 **Allan Simonsen** (Borussia Moenchengladbach)
1978 **Kevin Keegan** (SV Hamburg)
1979 **Kevin Keegan** (SV Hamburg)
1980 **Karl-Heinz Rummenigge** (Bayern Munich)
1981 **Karl-Heinz Rummenigge** (Bayern Munich)
1982 **Paolo Rossi** (Juventus)
1983 **Michel Platini** (Juventus)
1984 **Michel Platini** (Juventus)
1985 **Michel Platini** (Juventus)
1986 **Igor Belanov** (Dynamo Kiev)
1987 **Ruud Gullit** (AC Milan)
1988 **Marco Van Basten** (AC Milan)
1989 **Marco Van Basten** (AC Milan)
1990 **Lothar Matthaus** (Inter-Milan)
1991 **Jean-Pierre Papin** (Marseille)
1992 **Marco Van Basten** (AC Milan)
1993 **Roberto Baggio** (Juventus)

THE CARLING AWARDS WINNERS 1994–95

Carling is the first football sponsor to include fans on its Awards panel which judges the Carling Manager of the Month, Carling Player of the Month and Carling No.1 Awards. The Carling Panel represents all sides of the game. **Gordon Taylor** Chief Executive, Professional Footballers Association; **Jim Smith** Chief Executive, League Managers Association; **Rick Parry** Chief Executive, The FA Premier League; **Graham Kelly** Chief Executive, The Football Association; **Neil Midgley** President, Referees Association; **Brian Barwick** Editor, Sportsnight/Match of the Day BBC TV; **Vic Wakeling** Head of Sport, BSkyB; **Trevor East** Deputy Controller, ITV Sport; **Alex Montgomery** Chairman, Football Writers Association; **Terry Venables** England Coach; **Tim Crabbe** Chairman, Football Supporters Association; **Tony Kershaw** Chairman, The National Federation of Supporters Clubs; **Paul Hughes** Sponsorship Director, Bass Brewers Ltd.

Carling Manager of the Month

August	Kevin Keegan	Newcastle United
September	Frank Clark	Nottingham Forest
October	Alex Ferguson	Manchester United
November	Kenny Dalglish	Blackburn Rovers
December	Gerry Francis	Tottenham Hotspur
January	Brian Little	Aston Villa
February	Kevin Keegan	Newcastle United
March	Ron Atkinson	Coventry City
April	Howard Wilkinson	Leeds United

Each winner receives a Carling Manager of the Month trophy, a cheque for £750 and a magnum of champagne.

Carling Manager of the Season	**Kenny Dalglish**	**Blackburn Rovers**
Carling No.1 of the Season	**Frank Clark**	**Nottingham Forest**

Carling Player of the Month

August	**Jürgen Klinsmann**	Tottenham Hotspur
September	**Robert Lee**	Newcastle United
October	**Paul Ince**	Manchester United
November	**Alan Shearer/Chris Sutton**	Blackburn Rovers
December	**Matthew Le Tissier**	Southampton
January	**Chris Waddle**	Sheffield Wednesday
February	**Duncan Ferguson**	Everton
March	**Anthony Yeboah**	Leeds United
April	**David Seaman**	Arsenal
Carling Player of the Season	**Alan Shearer**	**Blackburn Rovers**

Carling No.1 Awards

The Carling No.1 Award goes to the person or people who make the most outstanding contribution to the domestic game.

August 1994	**Match of the Day** As a salute to its 30 years on the air.
September 1994	**Chelsea Independent Supporters Association** Organising a trip of a lifetime for a seriously ill young fan from Canada to see his heroes at Stamford Bridge.
January 1995	**Sir Stanley Matthews** The 80th birthday of an English football legend.

November was clearly a good month for Blackburn Rovers. Left to right: Alan Shearer, Manager Kenny Dalglish and Chris Sutton.

FROM THE CHAPLAIN

There are perhaps seven questions often asked about football club chaplaincy. This article raises these questions, and tries to answer them.

1. *What is a football chaplain?*
He is similar to a chaplain in industry, education or the armed forces—in other words, he is a clergyman working in a secular situation. Usually he is a minister or vicar in a local church who, as part of his ministry, gives time to working with his local football club. This involvement varies from usually between 3–4 hours up to a whole day or more per week in certain situations.

2. *What does he do?*
The club and chaplain together agree on the precise nature of the chaplain's involvement, but essentially he is available as a pastoral and spiritual safety-net at the club. He visits the club regularly and tries to get to know its employees—players and non-playing staff alike. With all of them he tries to build friendship, offer his availability and support, functions as a listening ear, a counsellor, a source of advice when asked and is generally a confidential and trustworthy source of care and spiritual input.

3. *Why do clubs need chaplains?*
Football clubs need chaplains because the chaplain's role is to help people, and at clubs there are many sorts of people. He is available to all at the club: directors and cleaners, YTS trainees and superstars, office workers and management. He offers his unique input when crises arise: when people face hospitalisation, major surgery, serious family illness or bereavement. He is a trusted listener when personal problems or family difficulties arise. He can be available to listen and offer counsel when there may be difficulties over money, relationships, the police, drugs or a career. He doesn't impose himself on folk; he must be absolutely confidential, and must always remain 'neutral'. He is part of the club, but is not there to represent the club line—or indeed, any other line. Sometimes he is required for the more formal side of his professional services: taking wedding, funeral, christening or thanksgiving services, or being involved on behalf of the club in a memorial service, a centenary or other anniversary service or a service of remembrance.

4. *Do chaplains pray for success?*
Chaplains pray for people but they aren't witch-doctors! They are not involved in offering up incantations to ensure the club will be successful, or will win crucial matches. It is players, managers and coaches who deserve credit for success, and I hope no chaplain ever claims he or his prayers are the reason for his club's victories.

However, some players and managers have used the chaplain as a source of help and inspiration at times of stress and significance. More than once, a chaplain has been asked by a player before a big match, 'Rev, can we find a quiet corner—I need you to pray for me. This is a big game, and I've got responsibilities—I need God's help today', or some such.

So in specific situations, and as part of their routine prayer commitment, chaplains pray for their clubs. It is not so that God will bring instant success—we can't really pray for the opposing defence to open up *à la* Red Sea before Moses—but so that people will know the reality of God's love, His help, His strength, His closeness.

5. *Do chaplains preach to their clubs?*
The chaplain's role is different from that of a minister in his church. There, he has every freedom to preach from the pulpit. His job in football is not that of a preacher. He doesn't go around threatening people with sermons or imposing his beliefs on unwilling listeners. The chaplain must have the freedom to speak about spiritual matters and, if asked, would be expected to explain his faith. However, such input is broadly reactive, not proactive. He responds to questions and discussions, but is not there to impose such debate on an audience which does not wish to hear or listen.

People have to feel 'safe' with the chaplain about. They have to feel they can introduce spiritual issues into a conversation, and that these will be taken seriously. Equally, they may seek to discuss other issues, or just simply have a normal, friendly conversation, without being 'Bible-bashed'.

6. *Do all clubs have chaplains?*
No—but chaplaincy in football is a relatively recent development. In the mid-1970s there were perhaps half a dozen with chaplains; now, throughout the league, there are around 45. So this is a growing movement. Yet, if a club decides it doesn't want a chaplain, it is quite entitled to that opinion. Obviously, we believe that a right understanding of football chaplaincy, combined with the right man for the job, will bring real benefits to a club and its staff.

7. *How do we find out more about chaplaincy?*
The chaplains, contactable at their clubs, will explain their individual involvements. Otherwise contact with the following organisations may be helpful:

SCORE (Sports Chaplaincy Offering Resources and Encouragement), PO Box 123, Sale, Manchester M33 4ZA

Christians in Sport, PO Box 93, Oxford OX2 7YP

Continued on Page 936

STOP PRESS

George Graham banned for a year... Graham Kelly becomes FA's 'El Supremo'... PFA to help ex-players become referees... Peter Beardsley MBE, Harry Gregg MBE... Bruce Grobbelaar, John Fashanu and Hans Segers to face charges in October... Peter Shilton joins Coventry at 45... Italian exiles David Platt and Paul Gascoigne come back... Foreign imports soar... transfer spending continues and tops £100 million.

June moves: Warren Barton, Wimbledon to Newcastle U £4 million (Dons record); Tom Bennett, Wolverhampton W to Stockport Co; John Butler, Stoke C to Wigan Ath; Darren Carter, Leyton Orient to Peterborough U; Marc Edworthy, Plymouth Arg to Crystal Palace; Les Ferdinand, QPR to Newcastle U, £6 million (record fees for both clubs); Steve Finney, Manchester C to Swindon T; Neil Fisher, Bolton W to Chester C; Paul Holland, Mansfield T to Sheffield U; Mike Jeffrey, Newcastle U to Rotherham U; Ian Muir, Tranmere R to Birmingham C; Alan Neilson, Newcastle U to Southampton; Dean Richards, Bradford C to Wolverhampton W; Mark Seagraves, Bolton W to Swindon T; Lee Turnbull, Wycombe W to Scunthorpe U; Jason White, Scarborough to Northampton T; Steve Wilkinson, Mansfield T to Preston NE; Clive Wilson, QPR to Tottenham H.

Major Moves

Stan Collymore, Nottingham F to Liverpool, £8.5m; **Dennis Bergkamp,** Inter to Arsenal, £7.5m; **Les Ferdinand,** QPR to Newcastle U; **Paul Ince,** Manchester U to Inter, £7m; **Andrei Kanchelskis,** Manchester U to Everton, £5m; **David Platt,** Sampdoria to Arsenal, £4.7m (taking his total to £22.15m); **Chris Armstrong,** Crystal Palace to Tottenham H, £4.5m; **Warren Barton,** Wimbledon to Newcastle U, £4m; **Savo Milosevic,** Partizan Belgrade to Aston Villa, £3.5m; **Mark Draper,** Leicester C to Aston Villa, £3.25m; **Gica Popescu,** Tottenham H to Barcelona, £3m; **David Ginola,** Paris St Germain to Newcastle U, £2.5m; **Stefan Schwarz,** Arsenal to Fiorentina, £2.5m; **Gareth Southgate,** Crystal Palace to Aston Villa, £2.5m; **Craig Short,** Derby Co to Everton, £2.4m; **Georgi Kinkladze,** Dynamo Tbilisi to Manchester C, £2m; **Dean Richards,** Bradford C to Wolverhampton W, £1.85m; **Andy Roberts,** Millwall to Crystal Palace, £1.8m; **Andrea Silenzi,** Torino to Nottingham F, £1.8m; **Jurgen Klinsmann,** Tottenham H to Bayern Munich, £1.7m; **Marc Degryse,** Anderlecht to Sheffield W, £1.5m; **Mark Hughes,** Manchester U to Chelsea, £1.5m; **Dean Saunders,** Aston Villa to Galatasaray, £1.5m; **Simon Osborn,** Reading to QPR, £1.1m; **Marco Boogers,** Sparta Rotterdam to West Ham U, £1m; **Ruud Gullit,** Sampdoria to Chelsea – free!

OFFICIAL CHAPLAINS TO FA PREMIERSHIP AND FOOTBALL LEAGUE CLUBS

Rev John Bingham—Chesterfield
Rev Richard Chewter—Exeter C
Rev Michael Lowe—Bournemouth
Rev Andrew Taggart—Torquay U
Rev David Jeans—Sheffield W
Rev Nigel Sands—Crystal Palace
Rev Graham Spencer—Leicester C
Rev Phillip Miller—Ipswich T
Rev Allen Bagshawe—Hull C
Rev David Tully—Newcastle U
Rev Derek Cleave—Bristol C
Rev Brian Rice—Hartlepool U
Rev Ken Sykes—Watford
Rev Michael Chantry—Oxford U
Rev Michael Futens—Derby C
Very Rev Brandon Jackson—Lincoln C
Rev Paul Bennett—Swindon T
Rev Ken Hawkins—Birmingham C
Rev Simon Stevenette—Bristol R
Rev Michael Hunter—Grimsby T
Rev Dick Syms—York City
Rev Dennis Hall—Wigan Ath
Rev William Hall—Middlesbrough
Rev Canon John Hestor—Brighton & HA
Rev Mervyn Terrett—Luton T
Rev Jim Rushton—Carlisle U
Rev Robert de Berry—Queen's Park Rangers
Rev Gary Piper—Fulham
Rev Charlie Mackenzie—Barnsley
Rev Barry Kirk—Reading
Rev Martin Short—Bradford C
Rev John Boyers—Manchester U
Rev Martin Butt—Walsall
Rev Steve Riley—Leeds U
Revs Alan Poulter and Gerald Courell—Tranmere R
Rev Mark Kichenside—Charlton Ath
Rev Owen Beament—Millwall
Rev Elwin Cockett—West Ham U
Rev Mike Woodhead—Sheffield U
Rev Jim Pearce—Southampton
Rev Alan Comfort—Leyton Orient
Rev John Hall-Matthews—Wolverhampton Wanderers
Rev Mark Cockayne—Doncaster Rovers

The chaplains hope that those who read this article will see the value and benefit of chaplaincy work in sport, and will take appropriate steps to spread the word where this is possible. They would also like to thank the editor of the Rothmans Yearbook for his continued support for this specialist and growing area of work.

OBITUARIES

Adie, John 'Jock' (b. 1925; d. 1995). A full-back with Hearts who joined East Fife in the mid-fifties, making 49 appearances.

Anders, Harry (b. St Helens 26.11.26; d. 10.94). A diminutive winger who, with his younger brother Jimmy, signed for Preston North End in 1945 and made 69 League appearances, often as an understudy to Tom Finney. Joined Manchester City in March, 1953, and had 32 outings before a move to Port Vale in July, 1956. After only three League matches he was signed by Accrington Stanley, where he linked up once more with his brother. There he hit 18 goals in 114 games before completing his career with Workington in the 1960–61 season.

Anderson, John (b. Newcastle 9.11.24; d. 14.11.94). Goalkeeper who joined Middlesbrough in November, 1945, but only made one League appearance. Had a spell with Blackhall Colliery before returning to League football with Crystal Palace in 1951. After 38 games, he moved to Bristol Rovers where he won a Third Division (South) Championship medal in 1954 and repeated the feat a year later following a transfer to neighbours Bristol City.

Armstrong, William (b. Newcastle 3.7.12; d. 9.1.95). A half-back, he signed for Rochdale in 1931 from Brockley and then had spells with Aston Villa and Swindon Town before skippering Gillingham in the late thirties.

Auld, Robert (b. Aberdeen 1923 d. 4.95). Played League football with Dundee in the 1940s before moving on to Fraserburgh.

Bacuzzi, Joe (b. London 25.9.16; d. 1.2.95). A fine Fulham full-back who made 70 pre-war League appearances before the Second World War, then a further 213 games for the Cottagers until the mid-fifties. He won a Second Division Championship medal in 1949 and represented England on 13 occasions during war-time internationals.

Baxter, Jim C. (b. Hill of Beath 8.11.25; d. 5.94). Joined Barnsley from Dunfermline for £3000 in 1945 and went on to make 224 League appearances for the Tykes, scoring 56 goals. A talented inside-forward, Jim was snapped up by Preston North End in 1952 and had 245 outings (65 goals) before returning to Barnsley in 1959 where he completed his League career.

Bell, Harold (b. Liverpool 22.11.24; d. 7.94). Began as a centre-forward, but converted to a centre-half by Tranmere Rovers, for whom he signed professionally in 1941. Harold went on to make 401 consecutive League appearances for Rovers between 1946 and 1955—a record which is likely to stand forever. He retired at the end of the 1959–60 season after giving sterling service to his one and only club and amassing 595 League games in the process.

Berry, Johnny (b. Aldershot 1.6.26; d. 9.94). A skilful winger who began with Birmingham City in 1944 and played 103 League games between 1946 and 1951 before joining Manchester United for £25,000. With the Red Devils he won Championship medals in 1952, 1956 and 1957 and won an FA Cup runners-up medal in 1957. He was injured in the Munich air disaster of 1958, which forced a premature retirement at 31. In a wonderful career, Johnny made 247 League appearances for United and scored 37 times. He also represented England on four occasions.

Bicknell, Charlie (b. New Tupton 6.11.05; d. 6.9.94). A full-back who signed for local club Chesterfield in 1927, he had 79 League outings before joining Bradford City in 1930. At City he didn't miss a match for 5½ years and amassed 240 League games, eventually becoming skipper. In 1936 he departed for West Ham United and combined playing for the Hammers during war time (210 games) with his job as a policeman. Was captain when the Hammers beat Blackburn in the Football League War Cup at Wembley. He was still skipper at 41 and continued playing after hostilities, making a further 19 League appearances in 1946–47.

Blakeman, Alec (b. Headington 11.6.18; d. 12.94). An inside-forward who started out with local club Oxford City in 1945 and moved to Brentford the following year. Scored seven goals in 42 League outings for the Bees before joining Sheffield United in November, 1948. Five games later he was transferred to Bournemouth in February, 1949, where he hit eight goals in 25 games.

Bradford, Geoff (b. Bristol 18.7.27; d. 31.12.94). A one club man with Bristol Rovers, who made 461 League appearances and scored a phenomenal 245 goals, which included many hat-tricks. Geoff holds both club records for total aggregate goals, plus the highest number of League goals in a season. In 1952–53 when Rovers won the Third Division (South) Championship, he hit the target 33 times. An England cap was celebrated in 1955, with a goal in the 5-1 win over Denmark.

Frank Broome (left) and Raich Carter

Broome, Frank (b. Berkhamsted 11.6.15; d. 9.94). A versatile forward who joined Aston Villa in 1934. Four years later he won a Second Division championship medal and made his England debut, scoring against Germany. It was one of seven international appearances before the Second World War when he hit 77 goals in 132 League appearances. During hostilities Frank scored 68 goals in 112 games as well as making guest appearances for Birmingham, Northampton, Chesterfield, Nottingham Forest, Notts County, Watford and Wolves. He left Villa for Derby after just one League game following the war and at the Baseball Ground he hit 45 goals in 112 games. In 1949 he moved to Notts County, where he scored a further 35 goals in 105 matches. Frank had a short spell with Brentford in 1953 before completing his playing career with Crewe (16 goals in 36 games). Managerial appointments followed with Notts County, Exeter City and Southend United.

Brown, Hugh (b. Carmyle 7.12.21; d. 7.94). Scotland international half-back with three caps who was signed by Torquay United in November 1950 from Partick Thistle. He made 55 League appearances for the Plainmoor Club before leaving the game in 1952.

Brown, James (b. Kilmarnock 31.12.08; d. 9.1.94). Moved to America as a teenager, where he took up soccer, and was a member of the 1930 United States World Cup side. John came to England following the Wall Street crash and joined Manchester United as a forward, for whom he played 40 matches between 1932 and 1934, scoring 17 goals. He had short spells with Brentford and Tottenham, but returned to the States following the war.

Burgon, Archie (b. 29.3.12; d. 9.94). A forward, Archie signed for Notts County in 1932, but was snapped up by Spurs three years later. After only four matches, he joined Wrexham in October, 1935, where he enjoyed great success as a winger. He left the Racecourse Ground for Carlisle United in the summer of 1939, but his only two appearances for the Cumbrians were deleted at the outbreak of war and he never played League soccer again.

Cabrielli, Peter (b. 1909; d. 14.12.94). Of Italian extraction, Peter had trials with Inter Milan and Genoa, before playing for Dundee United, Forfar Athletic, Falkirk, Raith Rovers and Montrose.

Campbell, William (b. 26.7.20; d. 7.12.94). A fine half-back who signed for Morton in 1942 and won a Scottish Cup runners-up medal in 1948. Billy also won five full caps for Scotland before retiring through ill health in 1949.

Cape, Jackie (b. Carlisle 16.11.10; d. 6.6.94). John joined his local club, Carlisle United, in 1929, but after 15 League games, he left for Newcastle. At United the winger scored 18 goals in 51 games and, on 3rd September, 1930, he played in front of Newcastle's record attendance—68,386—and scored the only goal against Chelsea. He also scored twice n the Magpies' record Cup victory—a 9-0 win over Southport in 1932. Jackie signed for Manchester United in 1934 and won a Second Division Championship medal in 1936. A year later he moved on to QPR and played in the club's record Cup win over Bristol Rovers. In 1939, he returned to Air Ministry work in Carlisle and after the war rejoined his local club.

Carter, Raich (b. Sunderland 21.12.13; d. 9.10.94). A wonderfully accomplished inside-forward whose career was unfortunately interrupted by the war, but he still managed to win England caps either side of hostilities (only Tommy Lawton and Stanley Matthews achieved a similar feat). Was overlooked by Leicester in 1930 and joined Sunderland the following year. He skippered the Rokerites to the First Division Championship in 1936 and to victory in the 1937 FA Cup final. Raich hit a remarkable 118 goals in 246 League games for the club before joining Derby, whom he helped win the Cup in 1946. He scored 34 goals in 63 games for the Rams and then moved on to Hull City in April, 1948, as player-manager. He led the Tigers to the Third Division (North) Championship the following year and scored 56 goals in 136 League matches. Two years later he resigned as player-manager but continued playing for Hull until 1952. Managerial posts with Leeds (1953–58), Mansfield (1960–63) and Middlesbrough (1963–66) followed. He also played first-class cricket for Derbyshire in 1946.

Chadder, Alwyn (b. 1903; d. 23.12.94). A centre-half with Corinthians, he won six England amateur caps. He was also a founder of Pegasus, the joint Oxford-Cambridge amateur club.

Cooper, Davie (b. Hamilton 25.2.56; d. 2.95). A supremely skilful winger who joined Clydebank in 1974 and won the first of six Scotland Under-21 caps in 1977. That same year he moved to Rangers after hitting 28 goals in 90 League games. A year later he was part of the side who won the Championship, Scottish Cup and League Cup, scoring in the final of the latter against Celtic. In 1979, Davie won the first of his 22 full caps and won another Scottish Cup medal. Two years later he scored in the replayed Scottish Cup Final against Dundee United and hit another goal against United the following year as Rangers won the League Cup. Further League Cup success came in 1986 when he scored a penalty in a 2-1 win over Celtic. That summer he was in the Scotland World Cup party for Mexico. He won further titles with Rangers in 1987 and 1989 and in between helped the club beat Aberdeen on penalties in the League Cup. Following 377 games he moved to Motherwell in 1989 and won a Scottish Cup medal in 1991 after a thrilling 4-3 win over Dundee United. In 1993, he rejoined Clydebank.

Cooper, George (b. Kingswinford 1.10.32; d. 5.94). Industrious inside-forward signed by Crystal Palace from Brierly Hill in 1955. Top scorer in 1957-58 with 17 goals from 25 appearances. Subsequently had two seasons with Rochdale.

Cooper, William (b. 1910; d. 5.94). Willie signed for Aberdeen in 1927, having represented Scotland at schoolboy level. A consistent right-back throughout the thirties, he continued playing after the war and scored the goal that put the Dons into the 1947 Scottish Cup Final, which he unfortunately missed through injury. Set a club record between 1932 and 1936 of 162 consecutive appearances. Twenty-nine years after signing for Aberdeen, he left Pittodrie to become player-manager of Huntly.

Dare, Billy (b. Willesden 14.2.27; d. 8.5.94). Billy began at Brentford in 1948 and scored 61 goals in 208 games as a centre-forward. He joined West Ham in January, 1955, and became the first player to be filmed for television signing a contract. In 1958, he won a Second Division Championship medal and scored 44 times in 111 League games for the Hammers.

Drake, Ted (b. Southampton 16.8.12; d. 31.5.95). A life president of Fulham, Ted Drake was a brave, uncompromising centre-forward, who scored 150 goals for Arsenal before the war and also played cricket for Hampshire between 1931 and 1936. Ted started out at Southampton, whom he joined from Winchester City in 1931. He scored 48 goals in 72 League games for the Saints, but in 1934, a £6500 fee took him to Arsenal, where he won League Championship medals in 1935 and 1938. He hit the winner for Arsenal in the 1936 FA Cup final against Sheffield United and he holds two records from the thirties; on 14th December, 1935, he scored the most goals ever in an away game—all seven at Aston Villa and an Arsenal club record of 42 goals in 41 appearances, also during 1934–35. Added to that Ted hit six goals in as many international appearances for England, but in 1944 was forced to retire from playing through injury. From 1947 to 1952, he took charge of Reading, then in the summer of 1952 he became boss at Chelsea. He became the first man to play in, and manage a title-winning side (1955). The likes of Jimmy Greaves, Peter Bonetti, Bobby Tambling and Terry Venables came through his youth scheme. He left Stamford Bridge in 1961, joined the Fulham backroom staff in 1965, then became assistant manager of Barcelona in 1970. He returned to Craven Cottage as reserve team manager, before a Chief Scout post followed in 1975 and then, on retirement, Ted joined the board at Fulham.

Dyson, Barry (b. Oldham 6.9.42; d. 26.2.95). Barry started out with Bury in 1960, but left two years later to join Tranmere Rovers. He was a great success at Prenton Park, scoring 99 goals in 174 League games. In 1966, the talented inside-forward moved to Crystal Palace, but a couple of years later he was on his travels again—to Watford. There he notched 19 goals in 38 games and was snapped up by Orient in December, 1968, as a consequence. There he was involved in a more midfield role and had great success, helping the O's to the Third Division title in 1970. After 160 games and 28 goals, he moved to Colchester where he ended his first class career.

Edwards, Don (b. Wrexham 2.8.30; d. 3.95). Signed for Norwich City in September, 1947 and became their youngest ever goalkeeper when he played against Torquay United that same month as a 17-year-old. He made two appearances for the club before being transferred to Gorleston in 1953.

Ted Drake (left) and Len Goulden

Feehan, Ignatius 'Sonny' (b. Dublin 17.9.26; d. 11.3.95). A goalkeeper who joined Manchester United from Waterford in 1948 and helped them finish fourth in the League. But after making 12 League appearances he signed for Northampton Town in 1950, where he had 39 outings. Four years later, he was off to Brentford where he completed his career, retiring in 1959.

Frodsham, Ian (b. 27.12.75; d. 2.1.95). Signed for Liverpool as a junior aged 14 and joined the professional ranks three years later. A regular in the Reds' reserve team, he played for the England Youth team, making his debut in 1993. Ian fought bravely against cancer.

Garrett, Archie (b. Lesmahagow 17.6.19; d. 10.4.94). A forward who joined Preston North End from Hearts in 1938, but played for Bristol City during hostilities. After the war he signed for Northampton Town and hit 35 goals in only 51 League games, prompting interest from Birmingham. But after only 18 games he went back to Northampton where he completed his playing career in 1950.

Gilbert, Tim (b. South Shields 28.8.58; d. 31.5.95). A defender who signed for Sunderland in August, 1976 and went on to make 36 appearances for the Rokerites, scoring three times. In February, 1981, Tim moved on to Cardiff City where he had 33 League outings, scoring once. August, 1982, saw him transferred to Darlington, for whom he made 65 League appearances, with three goals to his credit.

Greenwood, John (b. Manchester 22.1.21; d. 25.11.94). Signed for Manchester City in September, 1946, but only made one League appearance before moving to Exeter City three years later. A half-back, John had 31 League outings for the Grecians, then in 1951 he was transferred to Aldershot. After 12 League matches, he joined Halifax Town later that year.

Goulden, Len (b. West Ham 16.7.12; d. 14.2.95). Cultured inside-forward with West Ham and Chelsea, his career spanning the war years in which he guested for Chelsea. A former schoolboy international he later won 14 full caps, another five in wartime internationals and played for the Football League. Subsequently coach at Chelsea and manager at Watford in 1952, where ironically he had made his professional debut for the Hammers in a London Combination game.

Guest, William (b. Birmingham 26.6.17; d. 11.94). A winger who joined the Birmingham City groundstaff in 1928 and scored 15 goals in 76 League appearances for the Blues. Signed for Blackburn Rovers in 1937 and played against West Ham in the 1940 Wartime Cup final. Bill hit 30 goals in only 88 League games for the Rovers and continued playing for them until August, 1947 when he joined Walsall, where he saw out his first-class career.

Hair, George (b. Ryton 28.4.25; d. 24.10.94). George was an outside-left who signed for Newcastle United during the war and played 23 games (7 goals) when League football resumed after hostilities. He joined Grimsby Town in February, 1949, for £6000 and hit a further 9 goals in 68 League games for the Mariners. Left for Peterborough United in 1951 when the Posh were in the Midland League.

Hall, Almerick (b. Hove 12.11.12; d. 11.94); An inside-forward, he joined his local side, Brighton and Hove Albion in 1931, but moved on to Spurs two years later for whom he scored three goals in 10 outings. Signed for Southend in 1937 and hit 10 goals in 37 games before a transfer to Bradford City in June, 1939. After hostilities Almer moved to West Ham where he scored 11 goals in 50 appearances. He became manager of Margate Town on retiring from first-class football and spent 30 years at the helm of the Kent club.

Harkness, Willie CBE (b. Dumfries 1919; d. 14.1.95). Played for his local club, Queen of the South, for whom he later became a scout, Director and chairman. He was appointed president of the Scottish Football Association in 1978 and stayed to lead Scotland to the 1982 World Cup finals.

Heaton, Mick (b. Sheffield 15.1.47; d. 11.4.95). A full-back who began with Sheffield United, signing in November, 1964. Then, after 33 games, he joined Blackburn Rovers for £7000 and played 171 matches for the Rovers between 1971 and 1975, when he was forced to retire through injury. After a spell out of the game, he returned to Rovers as first-team coach in 1978. When manager Howard Kendall went to Everton, Mick joined him and enjoyed Championship, FA Cup and Cup-Winners' Cup success at Goodison. When Kendall left for Athletic Bilbao, Mick managed Workington before the pair reunited at Manchester City in 1990. Mick's untimely death earlier this year occurred in a road accident.

Hibbitt, Terry (b. Bradford 1.12.47; d. 5.8.94). Terry signed for Leeds United in 1964 and played 47 League games, scoring nine times from midfield. In 1968, he won a European Inter-Cities Cup medal. Three years later he was off to Newcastle United, where he stayed until 1975, making 138 League appearances. In August of that year a move to Birmingham ensued, but following 110 outings and 11 goals he was back at Newcastle, where he finished his first-class career with a further 90 League matches and five goals.

Hill, Frank (b. Forfar 21.5.06; d. 1994). Originally a half-back with Forfar Athletic in 1924, Frank was transferred to Aberdeen where he won the first of three Scotland caps in 1930–31. Transferred to Arsenal in 1932, he won Championship medals in 1933 and again in 1934, but only had nine outings in the title winning team of 1935. Joined Blackpool in 1936, but left for Southampton a year later. Frank departed The Dell in 1938–39 to become assistant-trainer at Preston, but in 1944 he went to Crewe as player-manager. He continued playing after the war, finally hanging up his boots in his 41st year. In 1948, he took over at Burnley where he remained until 1954, laying great foundations. A spell at Preston followed, then in 1958 he became boss at Notts County and discovered Tony Hateley. He later managed Charlton Athletic in the 1960s.

Hindmarsh, Billy (b. Crook 26.12.19; d. 28.11.94). Signed by Portsmouth in 1939, he had to wait until 1946 to make his debut. Billy was a full-back in the Pompey side who won the Championship in 1948–49, but his 10 League appearances at the end of the campaign did not constitute a medal. When Pompey repeated the feat the following season, he amassed 34, coming in for the fourth match of the season and being a consistent member of a reaguard which only conceded 38 goals. He was transferred to Swindon in 1951, but after 11 matches he left the professional game.

Holt, Arthur (b. Southampton 8.4.11; d. 28.7.94). Arthur joined his local club, Southampton, in 1932 and made his debut at Manchester United the following year, deputizing for Ted Drake. An inside-forward, he scored 206 goals in 206 League matches and also played cricket for Hampshire between 1935 and 1948.

Hopkins, Idris 'Dai' (b. Merthyr Tydfil 11.10.07; d. 9.10.94). Idris had spells for Sheffield Wednesday and Crystal Palace before he signed for Brentford in 1932 and was a key member of the side who lifted the Third Division Championship a year later. He won 12 caps on the wing for Wales and played in nine wartime internationals. In 1942, he was a member of the Brentford side that defeated Pompey 1-0 to win the London Cup at Wembley. He made 290 League appearances for the Bees and scored 75 goals. A move to Bristol City came in May, 1947, where he made 24 appearances, scoring once.

Houghton, Frank (b. Preston 15.2.26; d. 19.8.94). Joined his local club, North End, as an amateur in 1942–43. He was then transferred to Ballymena, before signing for Newcastle for a club record fee of £5500. A half-back, Frank scored 10 goals in 55 League games. After injury and illness which appeared to have ended his career, he bravely came back with Exeter City in 1954. He hit 11 goals in 28 games to complete his first-class career.

Houldsworth, Freddie (b. Henley-on-Thames 29.5.11; d. 1994). A goalkeeper who played for Stoke City, Swindon Town, Ipswich Town and Reading.

Jarvis, Syd (b. 1905; d. 24.6.94). Syd signed for Middlesbrough as a full-back in 1927 and made his debut the following year. He won a Second Division Championship medal in 1929 and played 86 League games, scoring once. He finished his professional career at Darlington.

Jessop, William (b. Preston 2.4.22; d. 5.94). Outside-left Billy signed for his local club, North End, in 1940, and played 25 war-time games. Following hostilities, he made a further four League apearances before joining Stockport County in April, 1947. There he had 17 outings and scored four times. The following year he moved on to Oldham, where in 94 games, he hit the target 16 times. He completed his first-class career at Wrexham, for whom he scored twice in 14 matches.

Jones, John (b. Bromborough 3.7.13; d. 26.1.95). A full-back who joined Everton in 1932 and made 90 League appearances. After the war, he signed for Sunderland, where he had 24 League outings.

Lattimer, Frank (b. Durham 3.10.23; d. 11.94). A half-back for Brentford between 1945 and 1956. He made 171 League appearances for the Bees, scoring three times.

Liddle, Jimmy (b. Felling 7.12; d. 7.10.94). Jimmy played on the right wing for Reading and Crystal Palace in the thirties, amassing 34 goals in 66 League appearances for the Elm Park club. At Palace he had 13 League outings, scoring once.

Little, Barry (b. Greenwich 25.8.64; d. 9.94). An England Youth international who signed for Charlton in July, 1982, following his apprenticeship with the Valiants. He scored on his debut against Queens Park Rangers, but made only one further League appearance for Charlton. A talented midfielder, Barry went on to have spells with Dagenham, Barnet and Fisher Athletic, before helping Dover Athletic to win the Beazer Homes League Championship in 1993.

Loughran, Joe (b. Consett 12.8.15; d. 23.8.94). Joe joined Birmingham City in 1935, but after 35 League games and two goals he left for Luton two years later. On the eve of the Second World War he was transferred to Burnley, following 25 games for the Hatters. Joe then had to wait until September, 1946, before he was able to make his League debut at full-back. He made 65 League appearances for the Clarets before he moved to Southend United, where he had 147 outings, scoring once.

Low, Norman (b. Newcastle 23.3.14; d. 1994). A centre-half who began his career with Liverpool in 1933. Norman moved on to Newport County three years later, whom he helped win the Third Division (South) title in 1939. He resumed playing for County after the war, but Norwich City ended his 112 match association by signing him for £750. He made 150 League appearances before becoming manager at Carrow Road in 1950. He stayed until 1955, before taking further posts at Workington and Port Vale.

Malkin, John (b. Stoke 9.11.25; d. 19.5.94). A small, but effective winger, John signed for his local club in July, 1947, and took over from Stanley Matthews when the great man left for Blackpool. He went on to make 175 League appearances for the Potters and scored 23 goals. In 1956, he received a serious knee injury, which forced his early retirement.

March, Zechariah (b. Chichester 25.10.1892; d. 9.94). Zechariah died in Bognor Regis just weeks before his 102nd birthday. He started out at Brighton in 1913, but his career was disrupted by the First World War. He made 29 appearances in the Southern League for Brighton and a further 56 League games before a move along the coast to Pompey, then in the Third Division. In 1922–23, he made four appearances, three in the No. 7 shirt and once wearing No. 11. Before his death, he was believed to have been Britain's oldest surviving professional footballer.

McBennett, James (Seamus) (b. Newcastle, Northern Ireland 16.11.25; d. 23.2.95). Joined Cardiff City from Belfast Celtic in September, 1947. Scored twice in four League games for City and then in November, 1948, he moved to Tranmere. At Rovers, the right-winger had 12 outings and scored once.

McDonald, Gordon (b. Hampstead 7.2.32 d. 2.1995). Full-back with Crystal Palaceand later Swindon Town. After making 13 League appearances with Palace he was transferred in July 1957 and added a further ten matches at the County Ground.

Millar, Gordon (b. 1948; d. 9.6.94). A goalkeeper who saw service with Hearts, Morton and Stirling Albion. He also played in South Africa but returned to coach Cowdenbeath, Montrose and Rossyth.

Mochan, Neil (b. 6.4.27; 28.8.94). A centre-forward, Neil started out with Morton in 1944, before moving to Middlesbrough in 1951 for £14,000 and scored 14 times in 38 League games. Two years later he was on his way to Celtic for £8000. There he helped the club win the League and Cup double (1954) and League Cup in 1958. Won a Scotland 'B' cap in March, 1954, then went on to win three full internationals. He joined Dundee United in 1960 and ended his first class playing career with Raith Rovers. Neil, nicknamed 'Smiler', became head trainer at Celtic, being with the side throughout the late 1960s until his death last August.

Morgan, Billy (b. Burnley 16.12.1896; d. 4.11.93). Billy began at his local club in 1920, making his League debut the following year. A wing-half, his career came to a sad end when he was badly injured in 1924, enforcing his retirement from first-class football with 28 League appearances to his name.

Moulson, George (b. Clogheen 6.8.14; d. 11.11.94). A goalkeeper, George was bought out of the Army to sign for Grimsby Town in 1936, but did not make his League debut until 1947. It was his only League appearance before a move to Lincoln City in June, 1947. He proved a great success, helping the club to win the Third Division (North) Championship and was selected for the Republic of Ireland on three occasions by virtue of many superb performances. After 60 League outings, he left to join Peterborough United.

Moyse, Alec (b. Mitcham 5.8.35; d. 1994). Alec played on the wing, signing for Crystal Palace in 1956, and scored once in four League games. In August, 1958, he joined Swindon, but after only a month and four matches he signed for Millwall. There he scored three times in 22 League games. Cambridge City then benefited from his talent and he was converted to a defender during a five-year stay.

Mullett, Joe (b. Birmingham 2.10.36; d. 3.94). A full-back who joined Norwich City in February, 1959, having spent four years at Birmingham City, where he made three League appearances. At Norwich he had 213 League outings and scored twice before bringing his professional playing career to a close in 1968.

Munnings, Charles (b. 1907; d. 10.3.95). Began as a winger at Boston United and moved on to Grimsby, but he was unable to make a first team appearance for the Mariners. He had subsequent moves to Swindon Town and Hull City in 1930 and 1931 respectively. Returned to Swindon in 1932 and completed his first-class career with Mansfield Town in 1934.

Nicholls, Johnny (b. Wolverhampton 3.4.31; d. 1.4.95). An inside-forward, Johnny signed for West Bromwich Albion in 1950 and went on to make 131 League appearances for the Baggies, scoring 58 goals. He won an FA Cup medal in 1954 and two full caps, scoring against Scotland on his debut. In 1957, he joined Cardiff City, but after only eight games and two goals he was off to Exeter City, which made him one of the first to play in all four Divisions of the Football League. At Exeter, he hit an impressive 23 goals in 56 League matches but, in 1959, four seasons after playing in the top Division, he found himself in the Southern League with Worcester City.

Nicholls, Ron (b. Sharpness 4.12.33; d. 7.94). A goalkeeper who began as an amateur with Fulham before signing for Bristol Rovers in November, 1954. He made 71 League appearances for the then Eastville club before a move to Cardiff City in 1958. At Ninian Park he had 51 League outings and then saw out his first-class football career with Bristol City, playing 39 League games. An opening batsman for Gloucestershire, Ron played 534 Championship matches in his 24-year county career.

Oliver, Ken (b. Loughborough 10.8.24; d. 13.5.94). A dominating centre-half, who began as a forward. Ken started out with Sunderland in 1946, but after nine League games and one goal he left for Derby County three years later. At the Baseball Ground he made 184 League appearances, before completing his playing career with Exeter City in 1960 following 92 League matches.

Page, Albert (b. Walthamstow 18.3.16; d. 10.1.95). Joined Spurs from Leyton as an amateur in 1935 and turned professional the following year. He played 56 League matches for Tottenham as a half-back before signing for Colchester United in 1947.

Parker, Stan (b. Worksop 31.7.20; d. 14.11.94). An inside-forward, Stan signed for Ipswich Town in May, 1946 and hit 48 goals in 126 League games. Joined Norwich in August, 1951, but did not play any first team matches for the Canaries.

Pearson, Harold (b. Tamworth 5.08; d. 2.11.94). A reliable goalkeeper, he began with WBA in 1925 and eventually made 281 League appearances for the Baggies. In 1932 he won an England cap (replacing his cousin Harry Hibbs between the posts). In 1937, he moved to Millwall and collected a Third Division (South) Championship medal in his first season. He went on to have 39 League outings before retiring.

Penman, Andy (b. . . . ; d.20.7.94). A wonderfully gifted inside-forward who starred for Dundee in the 1960s, having signed, originally as an amateur in 1959. He was capped at youth and four times for Scotland Under-23's. Andy's one full cap came in May, 1966. He won a Championship medal with Dundee in 1962 and moved to Rangers five years later for £35,000. He completed his professional career with Arbroath in the 1970s.

Reeves, Derek (b. Parkstone 27.8.34; d. 25.5.95). Centre-forward Derek was holder of the Third Division post-war goalscoring record—39 goals in only 46 games for Southampton in 1959–60. He signed for the Saints in December, 1962, and in 273 League outings he hit a remarkable 145 goals. Moved on to Bournemouth in 1962, where he managed 11 goals in 35 games before completing his professional career.

Russell, Sid (b. Feltham 4.10.37; d. 6.94). Played cricket for both Middlesex and Gloucestershire, winning his county cap for the latter. A full-back with Brentford, whom he joined in 1956. Sid made 54 League appearances for the Bees, but quit to concentrate on cricket. In all he hit 5,464 first class runs.

Rutherford, Joe (b. Chester-le-Street 20.9.14; d. 12.94). Joe was a former blacksmith who had an unsuccessful trial with West Ham, but went on to join Southport where he made 88 League appearances between 1936 and 1939. In March, 1939, he signed for Aston Villa for £2500 and played eleven games in goal before the outbreak of war and a further 137 matches following hostilities.

Seed, Trevance (b. Preston 3.9.23; d. 12.94). A centre-half who signed for his local club, North End, in July, 1946, but before he had made a League debut he moved to Carlisle at the end of the year. Trevance made 81 League games for the Cumbrians and in 1950 he joined Accrington Stanley. Unfortunately, he was only able to play one League match, injury curtailing his career.

Stokes, Bobby (b. Portsmouth 30.1.51; d. 31.5.95). Bobby joined Southampton in February, 1968, playing in 218 League games for the Saints, and scoring 40 goals in a hard grafting inside-forward role. But the goal he will always be remembered for was the stunning solo effort that beat Alex Stepney and Manchester United in the 1976 FA Cup final. The Saints were then in the Second Division and produced one of the great Cup upsets. In August, 1977, Bobby joined his home town club, Pompey, where he made 24 appearances, scoring twice, before seeing out his career with Washington Diplomats.

Streten, Bernard (b. Gillingham 14.1.21; d. 5.94). An excellent goalkeeper who had spells with Notts County and Shrewsbury Town before settling at Luton Town, whom he joined in January, 1948. In all Bernard played 276 League games for the Hatters and played for England in their 9-2 victory over Northern Ireland in November, 1949. A wonderful character who had a great rapport with fans behind his goal. Bernard retired from the first-class game in 1957.

Sykes, Albert (b. 1900; d. 12.94). A left-half with Brighton in the Third Division (South) between 1926 and 1928, making 16 League outings.

Tadman, George (b. Rainham, Kent 5.5.14; d. 29.9.94). Started out with Gillingham in 1932, but joined Bristol Rovers a year later without making a League debut for the Gills. George scored on his debut in April, 1934, but after two goals in five League games, he rejoined Gillingham and finished top scorer with 18 goals in 40 League outings. George then signed for Charlton Athletic for £1000 in 1936 where he led the Valiants' goalscoring three seasons in succession to finish with 46 League goals in 87 games. Unfortunately, the Second World War terminated a fine career.

Tadman, Maurice (b. Rainham, Kent 28.6.21; d. 11.94). The younger brother of George who started his professional career with Charlton Athletic, but after only three League games he was sold to Plymouth Argyle for £4000. At Home Park, he became a real favourite, scoring 107 goals in 240 League matches and helped the club win the Third Division (South) in 1951–52. That season he amassed 27 goals which is still Argyle's post-war scoring record. He was the club's top marksman on five occasions before leaving in 1955.

Taylor, Richard (b. Wolverhampton 9.4.18; d. 28.1.95). A centre-half who began with Grimsby Town in 1935, making his debut three years later. After 38 League games (four prior to the war), he joined Scunthorpe in May, 1948. Then in the Midland League, Dick made 131 appearances, scoring twice, before becoming trainer-coach at the club. He later assisted Joe Mercer at Sheffield United and Aston Villa, then took over the helm at Villa Park in 1964, staying until 1967.

Timmins, Arnold (b. Whitehaven 29.1.40; d. 14.5.94). Scored on his League debut for Workington in the 1960–61 season and in total he made 44 League appearances, scoring 10 goals. An inside-forward, he left the club in August, 1964, to play non-league football.

Walter, Joe (b. 1896; d. 24.5.95). One of the Huddersfield Town Legends who helped the club to win the First Division Championship in 1923, 1924 and 1925 died in his 99th year. An outside-right, he made 55 League appearances and scored five goals.

White, Len (b. Skellow 23.3.30; d. 6.94). A goalscoring inside-forward and one of four brothers who played League football. Len began with Rotherham United in May, 1948 and hit 14 goals in 43 League games for the Millers. In February, 1953, came a big move to Newcastle United, where he was a great success, scoring 142 goals in 243 League games. It made him the Magpies' second highest goalscorer of all time, behind Jackie Milburn, whom he succeeded at St. James' Park. In the 1955 FA Cup final, he provided the corner-kick from which Milburn scored after 45 seconds, to eventually beat Manchester City 3-1. After nearly ten years at the club, he left for Huddersfield in February, 1962, where he scored another 39 goals in 105 League games. A superb career in the top flight was completed with 22 goals in 53 games for Stockport between 1965 and May 1966.

White, Ron (b. Bethnal Green 9.11.31; d. 12.8.94). A forward with Charlton Athletic who joined the club in March, 1954 and played 165 League games, scoring eight times. He completed his career at The Valley in 1962.

Wright, Ken DFC (b. Lode 16.5.22; d. 6.6.94). Ken was a bomber pilot who won the Distinguished Flying Cross for his heroism during the Second World War. On leave from the RAF in 1943, he guested for West Ham and in 1945–46 scored five goals in five games. After the war the Flight-Lieutenant hit a further 20 goals in 51 League games for the Hammers, but retired from first-class football in 1950, then saw active service in Korea. Ken passed away on the 50th anniversary of D-Day 1994.

Wright, Billy CBE (b. Ironbridge 6.2.24; d. 3.9.94). A pillar of the Wolves and England defence, he was the inspirational skipper of both in the immediate post-war years. Billy captained Wolves to three Championships in 1954, 1958 and 1959 and FA Cup success in 1949. He began on the groundstaff at Molineux, but was originally sent home for being too small! He made his international debut against Belgium and went on to make 105 appearances for England, 90 as captain, a record he shares with Bobby Moore. He was footballer of the Year in 1952 and amassed 491 League games for his beloved Wolves, scoring 13 times. On his retirement he was awarded the CBE and appointed manager of the England Youth side, eventually taking over the Under-23 team. He also had a spell as manager of Arsenal in 1962 and left four years later to enjoy a successful career in television with ATV. A player to whom so many football-mad children of the day wished to aspire, he was an astute passer of the ball, a solid, but fair tackler, and a thorough gentleman, on and off the pitch. In 1990, he became a director of Wolverhampton Wanderers and a superb, new stand at Molineux was appropriately named in his honour.

Billy Wright (white shirt) leading out Wolverhampton Wanderers against Honved in 1954, with Ferenc Puskas on his left.

THE FA CARLING PREMIERSHIP and ENDSLEIGH INSURANCE LEAGUE FIXTURES 1995–96

Saturday 12 August 1995

Endsleigh League Division 1
Birmingham C v Ipswich T
Crystal Palace v Barnsley
Millwall v Grimsby T
Oldham Ath v Huddersfield T
Portsmouth v Southend U
Stoke C v Reading
Sunderland v Leicester C
Tranmere R v Wolverhampton W
Watford v Sheffield U
WBA v Charlton Ath

Endsleigh League Division 2
Bradford C v AFC Bournemouth
Bristol C v Blackpool
Burnley v Rotherham U
Carlisle U v Bristol R
Hull C v Swindon T
Oxford U v Chesterfield
Peterborough U v Brighton & HA
Swansea C v Shrewsbury T
Walsall v Stockport Co
Wrexham v Notts Co
Wycombe W v Crewe Alex
York C v Brentford

Endsleigh League Division 3
Chester C v Hartlepool U
Colchester U v Plymouth Arg
Doncaster R v Scarborough
Exeter C v Darlington
Fulham v Mansfield T
Gillingham v Wigan Ath
Hereford U v Barnet
Leyton Orient v Torquay U
Northampton T v Bury
Preston NE v Lincoln C
Rochdale v Cardiff C
Scunthorpe U v Cambridge U

Sunday 13 August 1995

Endsleigh League Division 1
Derby Co v Port Vale
Luton T v Norwich C

Saturday 19 August 1995

FA Carling Premiership
Aston Villa v Manchester U
Blackburn R v QPR
Chelsea v Everton
Liverpool v Sheffield W
Manchester C v Tottenham H
Newcastle U v Coventry C
Southampton v Nottingham F
West Ham U v Leeds U
Wimbledon v Bolton W

Endsleigh League Division 1
Barnsley v Oldham Ath
Charlton Ath v Birmingham C
Grimsby T v Portsmouth
Huddersfield T v Watford
Ipswich T v Crystal Palace
Leicester C v Stoke C
Norwich C v Sunderland
Port Vale v Millwall
Reading v Derby Co
Sheffield U v Tranmere R
Southend U v Luton T

Endsleigh League Division 2
AFC Bournemouth v Peterborough U
Blackpool v Wrexham
Brentford v Oxford U
Brighton & HA v Bradford C
Bristol R v Swansea C
Chesterfield v Carlisle U
Notts Co v Wycombe W
Rotherham U v Hull C
Shrewsbury T v Walsall
Stockport Co v Burnley
Swindon T v York C

Endsleigh League Division 3
Barnet v Colchester U
Bury v Chester C
Cambridge U v Hereford U
Cardiff C v Northampton T
Darlington v Rochdale
Hartlepool U v Exeter C
Lincoln C v Gillingham
Mansfield T v Leyton Orient
Plymouth Arg v Preston NE
Scarborough v Fulham
Torquay U v Doncaster R
Wigan Ath v Scunthorpe U

Sunday 20 August 1995

FA Carling Premiership
Arsenal v Middlesbrough

Endsleigh League Division 1
Wolverhampton W v WBA

Monday 21 August 1995

FA Carling Premiership
Leeds U v Liverpool

Tuesday 22 August 1995

FA Carling Premiership
Bolton W v Newcastle U

Wednesday 23 August 1995

FA Carling Premiership
Coventry C v Manchester C
Everton v Arsenal
Manchester U v West Ham U
Nottingham F v Chelsea
QPR v Wimbledon
Sheffield W v Blackburn R
Tottenham H v Aston Villa

Saturday 26 August 1995

FA Carling Premiership
Bolton W v Blackburn R
Coventry C v Arsenal
Everton v Southampton
Leeds U v Aston Villa
Manchester U v Wimbledon
Middlesbrough v Chelsea
Nottingham F v West Ham U
QPR v Manchester C
Tottenham H v Liverpool

Endsleigh League Division 1
Birmingham C v Norwich C
Crystal Palace v Charlton Ath
Derby Co v Grimsby T
Luton T v Leicester C
Millwall v Southend U
Oldham Ath v Sheffield U
Portsmouth v Reading
Stoke C v Port Vale
Sunderland v Wolverhampton W
Tranmere R v Huddersfield T
Watford v Barnsley
WBA v Ipswich T

Endsleigh League Division 2
Bradford C v Shrewsbury T
Bristol C v Stockport Co
Burnley v Brentford
Carlisle U v Swindon T
Hull C v Blackpool
Oxford U v Rotherham U
Peterborough U v Notts Co
Swansea C v Chesterfield
Walsall v Bristol R
Wrexham v Brighton & HA
Wycombe W v AFC Bournemouth
York C v Crewe Alex

Endsleigh League Division 3
Chester C v Plymouth Arg
Colchester U v Lincoln C
Doncaster R v Cardiff C
Exeter C v Scarborough
Fulham v Torquay U
Gillingham v Cambridge U
Hereford U v Bury
Leyton Orient v Darlington
Northampton T v Mansfield T
Preston NE v Wigan Ath
Rochdale v Hartlepool U
Scunthorpe U v Barnet

Sunday 27 August 1995

FA Carling Premiership
Sheffield W v Newcastle U

Monday 28 August 1995

FA Carling Premiership
Blackburn R v Manchester U

Endsleigh League Division 3
Lincoln C v Scunthorpe U

Tuesday 29 August 1995

FA Carling Premiership
Arsenal v Nottingham F

Endsleigh League Division 1
Barnsley v Tranmere R
Charlton Ath v Watford
Grimsby T v Luton T
Ipswich T v Stoke C
Port Vale v Sunderland
Reading v Millwall
Sheffield U v Crystal Palace
Southend U v WBA

Endsleigh League Division 2
AFC Bournemouth v Wrexham
Blackpool v Peterborough U
Brentford v Hull C
Brighton & HA v Wycombe W
Bristol R v Burnley
Chesterfield v York C
Crewe Alex v Walsall
Notts Co v Bradford C
Rotherham U v Carlisle U
Shrewsbury T v Bristol C
Stockport Co v Swansea C

Endsleigh League Division 3
Barnet v Gillingham
Bury v Preston NE
Cambridge U v Colchester U
Cardiff C v Exeter C
Darlington v Fulham
Hartlepool U v Northampton T
Mansfield T v Doncaster R
Plymouth Arg v Hereford U
Torquay U v Rochdale
Wigan Ath v Chester C

Wednesday 30 August 1995

FA Carling Premiership
Aston Villa v Bolton W
Chelsea v Coventry C
Liverpool v QPR
Manchester C v Everton
Newcastle U v Middlesbrough
Southampton v Leeds U
West Ham U v Tottenham H
Wimbledon v Sheffield W

Endsleigh League Division 1
Huddersfield T v Birmingham C
Leicester C v Portsmouth
Norwich C v Oldham Ath
Wolverhampton W v Derby Co

Endsleigh League Division 2
Swindon T v Oxford U

Endsleigh League Division 3
Scarborough v Leyton Orient

Saturday 2 September 1995

Endsleigh League Division 1
Barnsley v Birmingham C
Charlton Ath v Huddersfield T
Crystal Palace v Tranmere R
Grimsby T v Watford
Ipswich T v Sunderland
Leicester C v Wolverhampton W
Luton T v Derby Co
Norwich C v Port Vale
Portsmouth v Millwall
Southend U v Reading
Stoke C v Oldham Ath
WBA v Sheffield U

Endsleigh League Division 2
AFC Bournemouth v Rotherham U
Bradford C v Wycombe W
Brentford v Swindon T
Brighton & HA v Notts Co
Bristol R v Wrexham
Burnley v Walsall
Chesterfield v Hull C
Oxford U v York C
Peterborough U v Bristol C
Shrewsbury T v Blackpool
Stockport Co v Crewe Alex
Swansea C v Carlisle U

Endsleigh League Division 3
Barnet v Lincoln C
Bury v Plymouth Arg
Chester C v Hereford U
Darlington v Cardiff C
Doncaster R v Hartlepool U
Exeter C v Scunthorpe U
Gillingham v Colchester U
Leyton Orient v Fulham
Preston NE v Cambridge U
Rochdale v Northampton T
Scarborough v Wigan Ath
Torquay U v Mansfield T

Saturday 9 September 1995

FA Carling Premiership
Blackburn R v Aston Villa
Bolton W v Middlesbrough
Coventry C v Nottingham F
Everton v Manchester U
QPR v Sheffield W
Southampton v Newcastle U
Tottenham H v Leeds U
Wimbledon v Liverpool

Endsleigh League Division 1
Birmingham C v Crystal Palace
Derby Co v Leicester C
Huddersfield T v Ipswich T
Millwall v Barnsley
Oldham Ath v WBA
Port Vale v Portsmouth
Reading v Luton T
Sheffield U v Norwich C
Sunderland v Southend U
Tranmere R v Charlton Ath
Watford v Stoke C
Wolverhampton W v Grimsby T

Endsleigh League Division 2
Blackpool v Stockport Co
Bristol C v Brighton & HA
Carlisle U v Burnley
Crewe Alex v Shrewsbury T
Hull C v Oxford U
Notts Co v AFC Bournemouth
Rotherham U v Brentford
Swindon T v Chesterfield
Walsall v Swansea C
Wrexham v Bradford C
Wycombe W v Peterborough U
York C v Bristol R

Endsleigh League Division 3
Cambridge U v Barnet
Cardiff C v Torquay U
Colchester U v Chester C
Fulham v Doncaster R
Hartlepool U v Darlington
Hereford U v Preston NE
Lincoln C v Rochdale
Mansfield T v Scarborough
Northampton T v Exeter C
Plymouth Arg v Leyton Orient
Scunthorpe U v Gillingham
Wigan Ath v Bury

Sunday 10 September 1995

FA Carling Premiership
Manchester C v Arsenal

Monday 11 September 1995

FA Carling Premiership
West Ham U v Chelsea

Tuesday 12 September 1995

FA Carling Premiership
Middlesbrough v Southampton

Endsleigh League Division 1
Birmingham C v Stoke C
Huddersfield T v Barnsley
Oldham Ath v Ipswich T
Port Vale v Leicester C
Reading v Grimsby T
Sheffield U v Charlton Ath
Sunderland v Portsmouth
Tranmere R v WBA
Watford v Crystal Palace

Endsleigh League Division 2
Blackpool v AFC Bournemouth
Bristol C v Brentford
Carlisle U v Peterborough U
Crewe Alex v Brighton & HA
Hull C v Swansea C
Notts Co v Stockport Co
Rotherham U v Bristol R
Walsall v Oxford U
Wrexham v Shrewsbury T
Wycombe W v Chesterfield
York C v Burnley

Endsleigh League Division 3
Cambridge U v Exeter C
Cardiff C v Scarborough
Colchester U v Preston NE
Fulham v Rochdale
Hartlepool U v Torquay U
Hereford U v Gillingham
Lincoln C v Bury
Mansfield T v Darlington
Northampton T v Leyton Orient
Plymouth Arg v Doncaster R
Scunthorpe U v Chester C
Wigan Ath v Barnet

Wednesday 13 September 1995

Endsleigh League Division 1
Derby Co v Southend U
Millwall v Luton T
Wolverhampton W v Norwich C

Endsleigh League Division 2
Swindon T v Bradford C

Saturday 16 September 1995

FA Carling Premiership
Arsenal v West Ham U
Aston Villa v Wimbledon
Chelsea v Southampton
Leeds U v QPR
Liverpool v Blackburn R
Manchester U v Bolton W
Middlesbrough v Coventry C
Newcastle U v Manchester C
Sheffield W v Tottenham H

Endsleigh League Division 1
Barnsley v Sheffield U
Charlton Ath v Oldham Ath
Crystal Palace v Huddersfield Town
Grimsby T v Port Vale
Ipswich T v Watford
Leicester C v Reading
Luton T v Sunderland
Norwich C v Millwall
Portsmouth v Derby Co
Southend U v Wolverhampton W
Stoke C v Tranmere R
WBA v Birmingham C

Endsleigh League Division 2
AFC Bournemouth v Crewe Alex
Bradford C v Bristol C
Brentford v Walsall
Brighton & HA v Blackpool
Bristol R v Swindon T
Burnley v Hull City
Chesterfield v Rotherham U
Oxford U v Carlisle U
Peterborough U v Wrexham
Shrewsbury T v Notts Co
Stockport Co v Wycombe W
Swansea C v York C

Endsleigh League Division 3
Barnet v Plymouth Arg
Bury v Cambridge U
Chester C v Lincoln C
Darlington v Colchester U
Doncaster R v Northampton T
Exeter C v Fulham
Gillingham v Cardiff C
Leyton Orient v Hartlepool U
Preston NE v Scunthorpe U
Rochdale v Mansfield T
Scarborough v Hereford U
Torquay U v Wigan Ath

Sunday 17 September 1995

FA Carling Premiership
Nottingham F v Everton

Saturday 23 September 1995

FA Carling Premiership
Arsenal v Southampton

Aston Villa v Nottingham F
Blackburn R v Coventry C
Liverpool v Bolton W
Manchester C v Middlesbrough
Sheffield W v Manchester U
West Ham U v Everton
Wimbledon v Leeds U

Endsleigh League Division 1
Barnsley v Derby Co
Grimsby T v Norwich C
Huddersfield T v Sheffield U
Ipswich T v Charlton Ath
Leicester C v Southend U
Millwall v Sunderland
Oldham Ath v Crystal Palace
Portsmouth v Tranmere R
Reading v Port Vale
Stoke C v WBA
Watford v Birmingham C
Wolverhampton W v Luton T

Endsleigh League Division 2
AFC Bournemouth v Brighton & HA
Blackpool v Crewe Alex
Bristol R v Brentford
Carlisle U v Hull C
Chesterfield v Burnley
Notts Co v Bristol C
Peterborough U v Bradford C
Shrewsbury T v Stockport Co
Swansea C v Oxford U
Swindon T v Rotherham U
Wycombe W v Wrexham
York C v Walsall

Endsleigh League Division 3
Bury v Barnet
Chester C v Gillingham
Colchester U v Hereford U
Darlington v Scarborough
Doncaster R v Rochdale
Exeter C v Leyton Orient
Fulham v Preston NE
Hartlepool U v Cardiff C
Lincoln C v Cambridge U
Mansfield T v Scunthorpe U
Torquay U v Northampton T
Wigan Ath v Plymouth Arg

Sunday 24 September 1995

FA Carling Premiership
Newcastle U v Chelsea

Monday 25 September 1995

FA Carling Premiership
QPR v Tottenham H

Saturday 30 September 1995

FA Carling Premiership
Bolton W v QPR
Chelsea v Arsenal
Coventry C v Aston Villa
Leeds U v Sheffield W
Middlesbrough v Blackburn R
Nottingham F v Manchester C
Southampton v West Ham U
Tottenham H v Wimbledon

Endsleigh League Division 1
Birmingham C v Oldham Ath
Charlton Ath v Barnsley
Crystal Palace v Stoke C
Derby Co v Millwall
Luton T v Portsmouth
Norwich C v Leicester C
Port Vale v Wolverhampton W
Sheffield U v Ipswich T
Southend U v Grimsby T
Sunderland v Reading
Tranmere R v Watford
WBA v Huddersfield T

Endsleigh League Division 2
Bradford C v Blackpool
Brentford v Chesterfield
Brighton & HA v Shrewsbury T
Bristol C v Wycombe W
Burnley v Swansea C
Crewe Alex v Notts Co
Hull C v York C
Oxford U v Bristol R
Rotherham U v Peterborough U
Stockport Co v AFC Bournemouth
Walsall v Carlisle U
Wrexham v Swindon T

Endsleigh League Division 3
Barnet v Darlington
Cambridge U v Hartlepool U
Cardiff C v Mansfield T
Gillingham v Bury
Hereford U v Wigan Ath
Leyton Orient v Doncaster R
Northampton T v Fulham
Plymouth Arg v Lincoln C
Preston NE v Chester C
Rochdale v Exeter C
Scarborough v Torquay U
Scunthorpe U v Colchester U

Sunday 1 October 1995

FA Carling Premiership
Everton v Newcastle U
Manchester U v Liverpool

Saturday 7 October 1995

Endsleigh League Division 1
Barnsley v Leicester C
Birmingham C v Southend U
Charlton Ath v Grimsby T
Crystal Palace v Sunderland
Huddersfield T v Port Vale
Ipswich T v Wolverhampton W
Oldham Ath v Portsmouth
Sheffield U v Derby Co
Stoke C v Norwich C
Tranmere R v Luton T
Watford v Millwall
WBA v Reading

Endsleigh League Division 2
Brentford v Blackpool
Bristol R v AFC Bournemouth
Burnley v Wycombe W
Carlisle U v Notts Co
Chesterfield v Crewe Alex
Hull C v Shrewsbury T
Oxford U v Stockport Co
Rotherham U v Brighton & HA
Swansea C v Bradford C
Swindon T v Bristol C
Walsall v Peterborough U
York C v Wrexham

Endsleigh League Division 3
Barnet v Exeter C
Bury v Leyton Orient
Cambridge U v Cardiff C
Chester C v Doncaster R
Colchester U v Hartlepool U
Gillingham v Rochdale
Hereford U v Torquay U
Lincoln C v Darlington
Plymouth Arg v Fulham
Preston NE v Scarborough
Scunthorpe U v Northampton T
Wigan Ath v Mansfield T

Tuesday 10 October 1995

Endsleigh League Division 2
Crewe Alex v Bristol C

Saturday 14 October 1995

FA Carling Premiership
Aston Villa v Chelsea
Blackburn R v Southampton
Bolton W v Everton
Leeds U v Arsenal
Liverpool v Coventry C
Manchester U v Manchester C
QPR v Newcastle U
Tottenham H v Nottingham F

Endsleigh League Division 1
Derby Co v Ipswich T
Grimsby T v Oldham Ath
Leicester C v Charlton Ath
Luton T v WBA
Millwall v Tranmere R
Norwich C v Barnsley
Port Vale v Crystal Palace
Portsmouth v Birmingham C
Reading v Huddersfield T
Southend U v Sheffield U
Sunderland v Watford
Wolverhampton W v Stoke C

Endsleigh League Division 2
AFC Bournemouth v Burnley
Blackpool v Chesterfield
Bradford City v Bristol R
Brighton & HA v Swindon T
Bristol C v Hull C
Crewe Alex v Carlisle U
Notts Co v Rotherham U
Peterborough U v Swansea C
Shrewsbury T v York C
Stockport Co v Brentford
Wrexham v Oxford U
Wycombe W v Walsall

Endsleigh League Division 3
Cardiff C v Barnet
Darlington v Gillingham
Doncaster R v Hereford U
Exeter C v Wigan Ath
Fulham v Bury
Hartlepool U v Scunthorpe U
Leyton Orient v Chester C
Mansfield T v Plymouth Arg
Northampton T v Cambridge U
Rochdale v Colchester U
Scarborough v Lincoln C
Torquay U v Preston NE

Sunday 15 October 1995

FA Carling Premiership
Sheffield W v Middlesbrough

Monday 16 October 1995

FA Carling Premiership
Wimbledon v West Ham U

Saturday 21 October 1995

FA Carling Premiership
Arsenal v Aston Villa
Chelsea v Manchester U
Coventry C v Sheffield W
Everton v Tottenham H
Manchester C v Leeds U
Middlesbrough v QPR
Newcastle U v Wimbledon
Nottingham F v Bolton W
West Ham U v Blackburn R

Endsleigh League Division 1
Barnsley v Port Vale
Birmingham C v Grimsby T
Charlton Ath v Norwich C
Crystal Palace v Millwall
Huddersfield T v Sunderland
Ipswich T v Luton T
Oldham Ath v Reading
Sheffield U v Leicester C
Stoke C v Derby Co
Tranmere R v Southend U
Watford v Wolverhampton W
WBA v Portsmouth

Endsleigh League Division 2
Brentford v Peterborough U
Bristol R v Notts Co
Burnley v Brighton & HA
Carlisle U v Bradford C
Chesterfield v Shrewsbury T
Hull C v Stockport Co
Oxford U v Wycombe W
Rotherham U v Blackpool
Swansea C v AFC Bournemouth
Swindon T v Crewe Alex
Walsall v Wrexham
York C v Bristol C

Endsleigh League Division 3
Barnet v Rochdale
Bury v Scarborough
Cambridge U v Darlington
Chester C v Fulham
Colchester U v Northampton T
Gillingham v Doncaster R
Hereford U v Exeter C
Lincoln C v Cardiff C
Plymouth Arg v Torquay U
Preston NE v Mansfield T
Scunthorpe U v Leyton Orient
Wigan Ath v Hartlepool U

Sunday 22 October 1995

FA Carling Premiership
Southampton v Liverpool

Saturday 28 October 1995

FA Carling Premiership
Aston Villa v Everton
Blackburn R v Chelsea
Leeds U v Coventry C
Liverpool v Manchester C
Manchester U v Middlesbrough
QPR v Nottingham F
Sheffield W v West Ham U
Wimbledon v Southampton

Endsleigh League Division 1
Derby Co v Oldham Ath
Grimsby T v Stoke C
Leicester C v Crystal Palace
Luton T v Charlton Ath
Millwall v WBA
Norwich C v Tranmere R
Port Vale v Birmingham C
Portsmouth v Watford
Reading v Ipswich T
Southend U v Huddersfield T
Sunderland v Barnsley
Wolverhampton W v Sheffield U

Endsleigh League Division 2
AFC Bournemouth v Carlisle U
Blackpool v Oxford U
Bradford C v Burnley
Brighton & HA v Bristol R
Bristol C v Walsall
Crewe Alex v Brentford
Notts Co v Swindon T
Peterborough U v York C
Shrewsbury T v Rotherham U
Stockport Co v Chesterfield
Wrexham v Swansea C
Wycombe W v Hull C

Endsleigh League Division 3
Cardiff C v Colchester U
Darlington v Plymouth Arg
Doncaster R v Preston NE
Exeter C v Lincoln C
Fulham v Hereford U
Hartlepool U v Gillingham
Leyton Orient v Wigan Ath
Mansfield T v Bury
Northampton T v Barnet
Rochdale v Cambridge U
Scarborough v Chester C
Torquay U v Scunthorpe U

Sunday 29 October 1995

FA Carling Premiership
Tottenham H v Newcastle U

Monday 30 October 1995

FA Carling Premiership
Bolton W v Arsenal

Endsleigh League Division 3
Doncaster R v Cambridge U

Tuesday 31 October 1995

Endsleigh League Division 2
AFC Bournemouth v Swindon T
Blackpool v Bristol R
Bradford C v Walsall
Brighton & HA v Swansea C
Bristol C v Chesterfield
Crewe Alex v Hull C
Notts Co v Brentford
Peterborough U v Burnley
Shrewsbury T v Oxford U
Stockport Co v Rotherham U
Wrexham v Carlisle U
Wycombe W v York C

Endsleigh League Division 3
Cardiff C v Scunthorpe U
Darlington v Wigan Ath
Exeter C v Gillingham
Fulham v Colchester U
Hartlepool U v Barnet
Leyton Orient v Hereford U
Mansfield T v Lincoln C
Northampton T v Preston NE
Rochdale v Chester C
Scarborough v Plymouth Arg
Torquay U v Bury

Saturday 4 November 1995

FA Carling Premiership
Arsenal v Manchester U
Chelsea v Sheffield W
Coventry C v Tottenham H
Manchester C v Bolton W
Middlesbrough v Leeds U
Newcastle U v Liverpool
Nottingham F v Wimbledon
Southampton v QPR
West Ham U v Aston Villa

Endsleigh League Division 1
Barnsley v Wolverhampton W
Birmingham C v Millwall
Charlton Ath v Sunderland
Crystal Palace v Reading
Huddersfield T v Norwich C
Ipswich T v Grimsby T
Oldham Ath v Port Vale
Sheffield U v Portsmouth
Stoke C v Luton T
Tranmere R v Derby Co
Watford v Southend U
WBA v Leicester C

Endsleigh League Division 2
Brentford v Shrewsbury T
Bristol R v Peterborough U
Burnley v Notts Co
Carlisle U v Brighton & HA
Chesterfield v Bradford C
Hull C v Wrexham
Oxford U v Bristol C
Rotherham U v Crewe Alex
Swansea C v Wycombe W
Swindon T v Blackpool
Walsall v AFC Bournemouth
York C v Stockport Co

Endsleigh League Division 3
Barnet v Doncaster R
Bury v Darlington
Cambridge U v Scarborough
Chester C v Torquay U
Colchester U v Exeter C
Gillingham v Northampton T
Hereford U v Mansfield T
Lincoln C v Hartlepool U
Plymouth Arg v Cardiff C
Preston NE v Leyton Orient
Scunthorpe U v Rochdale
Wigan Ath v Fulham

Sunday 5 November 1995

FA Carling Premiership
Everton v Blackburn R

Wednesday 8 November 1995

FA Carling Premiership
Newcastle U v Blackburn R

Saturday 11 November 1995

Endsleigh League Division 1
Derby Co v WBA
Grimsby T v Barnsley
Leicester C v Watford
Luton T v Oldham Ath
Millwall v Ipswich T
Norwich C v Crystal Palace
Port Vale v Sheffield U
Portsmouth v Huddersfield T
Reading v Birmingham C
Southend U v Stoke C
Sunderland v Tranmere R
Wolverhampton W v Charlton Ath

Saturday 18 November 1995

FA Carling Premiership
Aston Villa v Newcastle U
Blackburn R v Nottingham F
Bolton W v West Ham U
Leeds U v Chelsea
Liverpool v Everton
Manchester U v Southampton
Sheffield W v Manchester C
Tottenham H v Arsenal
Wimbledon v Middlesbrough

Endsleigh League Division 1
Derby Co v Charlton Ath
Grimsby T v WBA
Leicester C v Tranmere R
Luton T v Birmingham C
Millwall v Huddersfield T
Norwich C v Ipswich T
Port Vale v Watford
Portsmouth v Stoke C
Reading v Barnsley
Southend U v Crystal Palace
Sunderland v Sheffield U
Wolverhampton W v Oldham Ath

Endsleigh League Division 2
AFC Bournemouth v Brentford
Blackpool v York C
Bradford C v Hull C
Brighton & HA v Walsall
Bristol C v Carlisle U
Crewe Alex v Swansea C
Notts Co v Chesterfield
Peterborough U v Oxford U
Shrewsbury T v Burnley
Stockport Co v Swindon T
Wrexham v Rotherham U
Wycombe W v Bristol R

Endsleigh League Division 3
Cardiff C v Bury
Darlington v Scunthorpe U
Doncaster R v Colchester U
Exeter C v Preston NE
Fulham v Barnet
Hartlepool U v Plymouth Arg
Leyton Orient v Cambridge U
Mansfield T v Chester C
Northampton T v Wigan Ath

Rochdale v Hereford U
Scarborough v Gillingham
Torquay U v Lincoln C

Sunday 19 November 1995

FA Carling Premiership
QPR v Coventry C

Monday 20 November 1995

FA Carling Premiership
Southampton v Aston Villa

Tuesday 21 November 1995

FA Carling Premiership
Arsenal v Sheffield W
Middlesbrough v Tottenham H

Endsleigh League Division 1
Barnsley v Portsmouth
Birmingham C v Derby Co
Charlton Ath v Reading
Crystal Palace v Wolverhampton W
Huddersfield T v Leicester C
Ipswich T v Southend U
Oldham Ath v Millwall
Sheffield U v Grimsby T
Tranmere R v Port Vale
Watford v Luton T
WBA v Norwich C

Wednesday 22 November 1995

FA Carling Premiership
Chelsea v Bolton W
Coventry C v Manchester U
Everton v QPR
Manchester C v Wimbledon
Nottingham F v Leeds U
West Ham U v Liverpool

Endsleigh League Division 1
Stoke C v Sunderland

Saturday 25 November 1995

FA Carling Premiership
Chelsea v Tottenham H
Coventry C v Wimbledon
Everton v Sheffield W
Manchester C v Aston Villa
Middlesbrough v Liverpool
Newcastle U v Leeds U
Nottingham F v Manchester U
Southampton v Bolton W
West Ham U v QPR

Endsleigh League Division 1
Barnsley v Luton T
Birmingham C v Leicester C
Charlton Ath v Port Vale
Crystal Palace v Derby Co
Huddersfield T v Wolverhampton W
Ipswich T v Portsmouth
Oldham Ath v Southend U
Sheffield U v Reading
Stoke C v Millwall
Tranmere R v Grimsby T
Watford v Norwich C
WBA v Sunderland

Endsleigh League Division 2
Brentford v Bradford C
Bristol R v Stockport Co
Burnley v Wrexham
Carlisle U v Wycombe W
Chesterfield v AFC Bournemouth
Hull C v Peterborough U
Oxford U v Crewe Alex
Rotherham U v Bristol C
Swansea C v Notts Co
Swindon T v Shrewsbury T
Walsall v Blackpool
York C v Brighton & HA

Endsleigh League Division 3
Barnet v Leyton Orient
Bury v Exeter C
Cambridge U v Torquay U
Chester C v Darlington
Colchester U v Mansfield T
Gillingham v Fulham
Lincoln C v Northampton T
Plymouth Arg v Rochdale
Preston NE v Hartlepool U
Scunthorpe U v Scarborough
Wigan Ath v Doncaster R

Sunday 26 November 1995

FA Carling Premiership
Arsenal v Blackburn R

Endsleigh League Division 3
Hereford U v Cardiff C

Saturday 2 December 1995

FA Carling Premiership
Aston Villa v Arsenal
Blackburn R v West Ham U
Bolton W v Nottingham F
Leeds U v Manchester C
Liverpool v Southampton
Manchester U v Chelsea
QPR v Middlesbrough
Tottenham H v Everton

Endsleigh League Division 1
Derby Co v Sheffield U
Grimsby T v Charlton Ath
Leicester C v Barnsley
Luton T v Tranmere R
Millwall v Watford
Norwich C v Stoke C
Port Vale v Huddersfield T
Portsmouth v Oldham Ath
Reading v WBA
Southend U v Birmingham C
Sunderland v Crystal Palace
Wolverhampton W v Ipswich T

Sunday 3 December 1995

FA Carling Premiership
Wimbledon v Newcastle U

Monday 4 December 1995

FA Carling Premiership
Sheffield W v Coventry C

Tuesday 5 December 1995

Endsleigh League Division 1
Millwall v Charlton Ath

Saturday 9 December 1995

FA Carling Premiership
Bolton W v Liverpool
Chelsea v Newcastle U
Coventry C v Blackburn R
Everton v West Ham U
Leeds U v Wimbledon
Manchester U v Sheffield W
Middlesbrough v Manchester C
Southampton v Arsenal
Tottenham H v QPR

Endsleigh League Division 1
Birmingham C v Watford
Charlton Ath v Ipswich T
Crystal Palace v Oldham Ath
Derby Co v Barnsley
Luton T v Wolverhampton W
Norwich C v Grimsby T
Port Vale v Reading
Sheffield U v Huddersfield T
Southend U v Leicester C
Sunderland v Millwall
Tranmere R v Portsmouth
WBA v Stoke C

Endsleigh League Division 2
Bradford C v Peterborough U
Brentford v Bristol R
Brighton & HA v AFC Bournemouth
Bristol C v Notts Co
Burnley v Chesterfield
Crewe Alex v Blackpool
Hull C v Carlisle U
Oxford U v Swansea C
Rotherham U v Swindon T
Stockport Co v Shrewsbury T
Walsall v York C
Wrexham v Wycombe W

Endsleigh League Division 3
Barnet v Bury
Cambridge U v Lincoln C
Cardiff C v Hartlepool U
Gillingham v Chester C
Hereford U v Colchester U
Leyton Orient v Exeter C
Northampton T v Torquay U
Plymouth Arg v Wigan Ath
Preston NE v Fulham
Rochdale v Doncaster R
Scarborough v Darlington
Scunthorpe U v Mansfield T

Sunday 10 December 1995

FA Carling Premiership
Nottingham F v Aston Villa

Saturday 16 December 1995

FA Carling Premiership
Arsenal v Chelsea
Aston Villa v Coventry C
Blackburn R v Middlesbrough
Manchester C v Nottingham F
Newcastle U v Everton
QPR v Bolton W
Sheffield W v Leeds U
West Ham U v Southampton
Wimbledon v Tottenham H

Endsleigh League Division 1
Barnsley v Charlton Ath
Grimsby T v Southend U
Huddersfield T v WBA
Ipswich T v Sheffield U
Leicester C v Norwich C
Millwall v Derby Co
Oldham Ath v Birmingham C
Portsmouth v Luton T
Reading v Sunderland
Stoke C v Crystal Palace
Watford v Tranmere R
Wolverhampton W v Port Vale

Endsleigh League Division 2
AFC Bournemouth v Stockport Co
Blackpool v Bradford C
Bristol R v Oxford U
Carlisle U v Walsall
Chesterfield v Brentford
Notts Co v Crewe Alex
Peterborough U v Rotherham U
Shrewsbury T v Brighton & HA
Swansea C v Burnley
Swindon T v Wrexham
Wycombe W v Bristol C
York C v Hull C

Endsleigh League Division 3
Bury v Gillingham
Chester C v Preston NE
Colchester U v Scunthorpe U
Darlington v Barnet
Doncaster R v Leyton Orient
Exeter C v Rochdale
Fulham v Northampton T
Hartlepool U v Cambridge U
Lincoln C v Plymouth Arg
Mansfield T v Cardiff C

Torquay U v Scarborough
Wigan Ath v Hereford U

Sunday 17 December 1995

FA Carling Premiership
Liverpool v Manchester U

Tuesday 19 December 1995

Endsleigh League Division 2
Peterborough U v Stockport Co

Endsleigh League Division 3
Hereford U v Scunthorpe U

Wednesday 20 December 1995

Endsleigh League Division 1
Southend U v Port Vale
Stoke C v Sheffield U

Friday 22 December 1995

Endsleigh League Division 1
Ipswich T v Barnsley

Endsleigh League Division 2
Brighton & HA v Chesterfield
Carlisle U v York C
Notts Co v Blackpool
Wrexham v Brentford

Endsleigh League Division 3
Doncaster R v Exeter C
Leyton Orient v Rochdale

Saturday 23 December 1995

FA Carling Premiership
Coventry C v Everton
Liverpool v Arsenal
Manchester C v Chelsea
Middlesbrough v West Ham U
Newcastle U v Nottingham F
QPR v Aston Villa
Sheffield W v Southampton
Tottenham H v Bolton W
Wimbledon v Blackburn R

Endsleigh League Division 1
Birmingham C v Tranmere R
Derby Co v Sunderland
Grimsby T v Leicester C
Luton T v Huddersfield T
Oldham Ath v Watford
Portsmouth v Norwich C
Reading v Wolverhampton W
WBA v Crystal Palace

Endsleigh League Division 2
AFC Bournemouth v Hull C
Bradford C v Oxford U
Bristol R v Crewe Alex
Burnley v Bristol C
Swansea C v Rotherham U
Walsall v Swindon T
Wycombe W v Shrewsbury T

Endsleigh League Division 3
Bury v Colchester U
Chester C v Barnet
Fulham v Cardiff C
Mansfield T v Hartlepool U
Plymouth Arg v Cambridge U
Preston NE v Gillingham
Scarborough v Northampton T
Torquay U v Darlington
Wigan Ath v Lincoln C

Sunday 24 December 1995

FA Carling Premiership
Leeds U v Manchester U

Tuesday 26 December 1995

FA Carling Premiership
Arsenal v QPR
Aston Villa v Liverpool
Blackburn R v Manchester C
Chelsea v Wimbledon
Everton v Middlesbrough
Manchester U v Newcastle U
Nottingham F v Sheffield W
Southampton v Tottenham H
West Ham U v Coventry C

Endsleigh League Division 1
Barnsley v Stoke C
Charlton Ath v Portsmouth
Crystal Palace v Luton T
Huddersfield T v Derby Co
Leicester C v Ipswich T
Norwich C v Southend U
Port Vale v WBA
Sheffield U v Birmingham C
Sunderland v Grimsby T
Tranmere R v Oldham Ath
Watford v Reading
Wolverhampton W v Millwall

Endsleigh League Division 2
Blackpool v Burnley
Brentford v Brighton & HA
Bristol C v Swansea C
Chesterfield v Peterborough U
Crewe Alex v Wrexham
Hull C v Notts Co
Oxford U v AFC Bournemouth
Rotherham U v Walsall
Shrewsbury T v Bristol R
Stockport Co v Carlisle U
Swindon T v Wycombe W
York C v Bradford C

Endsleigh League Division 3
Barnet v Mansfield T
Cambridge U v Wigan Ath
Cardiff C v Chester C
Colchester U v Leyton Orient
Darlington v Doncaster R
Exeter C v Torquay U
Gillingham v Plymouth Arg
Hartlepool U v Scarborough
Lincoln C v Fulham
Northampton T v Hereford U
Rochdale v Preston NE
Scunthorpe U v Bury

Wednesday 27 December 1995

FA Carling Premiership
Bolton W v Leeds U

Saturday 30 December 1995

FA Carling Premiership
Arsenal v Wimbledon
Aston Villa v Sheffield W
Blackburn R v Tottenham H
Bolton W v Coventry C
Chelsea v Liverpool
Everton v Leeds U
Manchester U v QPR
Nottingham F v Middlesbrough
Southampton v Manchester C
West Ham U v Newcastle U

Endsleigh League Division 1
Barnsley v WBA
Charlton Ath v Southend U
Crystal Palace v Grimsby T
Huddersfield T v Stoke C
Leicester C v Oldham Ath
Norwich C v Reading
Port Vale v Luton T
Sheffield U v Millwall
Sunderland v Birmingham C
Tranmere R v Ipswich T
Watford v Derby Co
Wolverhampton W v Portsmouth

Endsleigh League Division 2
Blackpool v Swansea C
Brentford v Wycombe W
Bristol C v Bristol R
Chesterfield v Walsall
Crewe Alex v Peterborough U
Hull C v Brighton & HA
Oxford U v Notts Co
Rotherham U v Bradford C
Shrewsbury T v Carlisle U
Stockport Co v Wrexham
Swindon T v Burnley
York C v AFC Bournemouth

Endsleigh League Division 3
Barnet v Torquay U
Cambridge U v Fulham
Cardiff C v Wigan Ath
Colchester U v Scarborough
Darlington v Preston NE
Exeter C v Chester C
Gillingham v Mansfield T
Hartlepool U v Hereford U
Lincoln C v Leyton Orient
Northampton T v Plymouth Arg
Rochdale v Bury
Scunthorpe U v Doncaster R

Monday 1 January 1996

FA Carling Premiership
Coventry C v Southampton
Leeds U v Blackburn R
Liverpool v Nottingham F
Manchester C v West Ham U
Middlesbrough v Aston Villa
Sheffield W v Bolton W
Tottenham H v Manchester U
Wimbledon v Everton

Endsleigh League Division 1
Birmingham C v Wolverhampton W
Derby Co v Norwich C
Grimsby T v Huddersfield T
Ipswich T v Port Vale
Luton T v Sheffield U
Millwall v Leicester C
Oldham Ath v Sunderland
Portsmouth v Crystal Palace
Reading v Tranmere R
Southend U v Barnsley
Stoke C v Charlton Ath
WBA v Watford

Endsleigh League Division 2
AFC Bournemouth v Shrewsbury T
Bradford C v Crewe Alex
Brighton & HA v Stockport Co
Bristol R v Chesterfield
Burnley v Oxford U
Carlisle U v Blackpool
Notts Co v York C
Peterborough U v Swindon T
Swansea C v Brentford
Walsall v Hull C
Wrexham v Bristol C
Wycombe W v Rotherham U

Endsleigh League Division 3
Bury v Hartlepool U
Chester C v Northampton T
Darlington v Hereford U
Doncaster R v Lincoln C
Fulham v Scunthorpe U
Hereford U v Darlington (*postponed*)
Leyton Orient v Gillingham
Mansfield T v Cambridge U
Plymouth Arg v Exeter C
Preston NE v Cardiff C
Scarborough v Barnet
Torquay U v Colchester U

Tuesday 2 January 1996

FA Carling Premiership
Newcastle U v Arsenal

QPR v Chelsea

Endsleigh League Division 3
Wigan Ath v Rochdale

Saturday 6 January 1996

Endsleigh League Division 2
AFC Bournemouth v Bristol C
Blackpool v Wycombe W
Brentford v Carlisle U
Brighton & HA v Oxford U
Bristol R v Hull C
Chesterfield v Wrexham
Crewe Alex v Burnley
Notts Co v Walsall
Rotherham U v York C
Shrewsbury T v Peterborough U
Stockport Co v Bradford C
Swindon T v Swansea C

Endsleigh League Division 3
Barnet v Preston NE
Bury v Doncaster R
Cambridge U v Chester C
Cardiff C v Leyton Orient
Darlington v Northampton T
Hartlepool U v Fulham
Lincoln C v Hereford U
Mansfield T v Exeter C
Plymouth Arg v Scunthorpe U
Scarborough v Rochdale
Torquay U v Gillingham
Wigan Ath v Colchester U

Saturday 13 January 1996

FA Carling Premiership
Bolton W v Wimbledon
Coventry C v Newcastle U
Everton v Chelsea
Leeds U v West Ham U
Manchester U v Aston Villa
Middlesbrough v Arsenal
Nottingham F v Southampton
QPR v Blackburn R
Sheffield W v Liverpool
Tottenham H v Manchester C

Endsleigh League Division 1
Birmingham C v Charlton Ath
Crystal Palace v Ipswich T
Derby Co v Reading
Luton T v Southend U
Millwall v Port Vale
Oldham Ath v Barnsley
Portsmouth v Grimsby T
Stoke C v Leicester C
Sunderland v Norwich C
Tranmere R v Sheffield U
Watford v Huddersfield T
WBA v Wolverhampton W

Endsleigh League Division 2
Bradford C v Brighton & HA
Bristol C v Crewe Alex
Burnley v Stockport Co
Carlisle U v Chesterfield
Hull C v Rotherham U
Oxford U v Brentford
Peterborough U v AFC Bournemouth
Swansea C v Bristol R
Walsall v Shrewsbury T
Wrexham v Blackpool
Wycombe W v Notts Co
York C v Swindon T

Endsleigh League Division 3
Chester C v Bury
Colchester U v Barnet
Doncaster R v Torquay U
Exeter C v Hartlepool U
Fulham v Scarborough
Gillingham v Lincoln C
Hereford U v Cambridge U
Leyton Orient v Mansfield T
Northampton T v Cardiff C
Preston NE v Plymouth Arg
Rochdale v Darlington
Scunthorpe U v Wigan Ath

Saturday 20 January 1996

FA Carling Premiership
Arsenal v Everton
Aston Villa v Tottenham H
Blackburn R v Sheffield W
Chelsea v Nottingham F
Liverpool v Leeds U
Manchester C v Coventry C
Newcastle U v Bolton W
Southampton v Middlesbrough
West Ham U v Manchester U
Wimbledon v QPR

Endsleigh League Division 1
Barnsley v Crystal Palace
Charlton Ath v WBA
Grimsby T v Millwall
Huddersfield T v Oldham Ath
Ipswich T v Birmingham C
Leicester C v Sunderland
Norwich C v Luton T
Port Vale v Derby Co
Reading v Stoke C
Sheffield U v Watford
Southend U v Portsmouth
Wolverhampton W v Tranmere R

Endsleigh League Division 2
AFC Bournemouth v Bradford C
Blackpool v Bristol C
Brentford v York C
Brighton & HA v Peterborough U
Bristol R v Carlisle U
Chesterfield v Oxford U
Crewe Alex v Wycombe W
Notts Co v Wrexham
Rotherham U v Burnley
Shrewsbury T v Swansea C
Stockport Co v Walsall
Swindon T v Hull C

Endsleigh League Division 3
Barnet v Hereford U
Bury v Northampton T
Cambridge U v Scunthorpe U
Cardiff C v Rochdale
Darlington v Exeter C
Hartlepool U v Chester C
Lincoln C v Preston NE
Mansfield T v Fulham
Plymouth Arg v Colchester U
Scarborough v Doncaster R
Torquay U v Leyton Orient
Wigan Ath v Gillingham

Saturday 27 January 1996

Endsleigh League Division 2
Bradford C v Notts Co
Bristol C v Shrewsbury T
Burnley v Bristol R
Carlisle U v Rotherham U
Hull C v Brentford
Oxford U v Swindon T
Peterborough U v Blackpool
Swansea C v Stockport Co
Walsall v Crewe Alex
Wrexham v AFC Bournemouth
Wycombe W v Brighton & HA
York C v Chesterfield

Endsleigh League Division 3
Chester C v Wigan Ath
Colchester U v Cambridge U
Doncaster R v Mansfield T
Exeter C v Cardiff C
Fulham v Darlington
Gillingham v Barnet
Hereford U v Plymouth Arg
Leyton Orient v Scarborough
Northampton T v Hartlepool U
Preston NE v Bury
Rochdale v Torquay U
Scunthorpe U v Lincoln C

Saturday 3 February 1996

FA Carling Premiership
Arsenal v Coventry C
Aston Villa v Leeds U
Blackburn R v Bolton W
Chelsea v Middlesbrough
Liverpool v Tottenham H
Manchester C v QPR
Newcastle U v Sheffield W
Southampton v Everton
West Ham U v Nottingham F
Wimbledon v Manchester U

Endsleigh League Division 1
Barnsley v Watford
Charlton Ath v Crystal Palace
Grimsby T v Derby Co
Huddersfield T v Tranmere R
Ipswich T v WBA
Leicester C v Luton T
Norwich C v Birmingham C
Port Vale v Stoke C
Reading v Portsmouth
Sheffield U v Oldham Ath
Southend U v Millwall
Wolverhampton W v Sunderland

Endsleigh League Division 2
AFC Bournemouth v Wycombe W
Blackpool v Hull C
Brentford v Burnley
Brighton & HA v Wrexham
Bristol R v Walsall
Chesterfield v Swansea C
Crewe Alex v York C
Notts Co v Peterborough U
Rotherham U v Oxford U
Shrewsbury T v Bradford C
Stockport Co v Bristol C
Swindon T v Carlisle U

Endsleigh League Division 3
Barnet v Scunthorpe U
Bury v Hereford U
Cambridge U v Gillingham
Cardiff C v Doncaster R
Darlington v Leyton Orient
Hartlepool U v Rochdale
Lincoln C v Colchester U
Mansfield T v Northampton T
Plymouth Arg v Chester C
Scarborough v Exeter C
Torquay U v Fulham
Wigan Ath v Preston NE

Saturday 10 February 1996

FA Carling Premiership
Bolton W v Aston Villa
Coventry C v Chelsea
Everton v Manchester C
Leeds U v Southampton
Manchester U v Blackburn R
Middlesbrough v Newcastle U
Nottingham F v Arsenal
QPR v Liverpool
Sheffield W v Wimbledon
Tottenham H v West Ham U

Endsleigh League Division 1
Birmingham C v Huddersfield T
Crystal Palace v Sheffield U
Derby Co v Wolverhampton W
Luton T v Grimsby T
Millwall v Reading
Oldham Ath v Norwich C
Portsmouth v Leicester C
Stoke C v Ipswich T
Sunderland v Port Vale
Tranmere R v Barnsley

Watford v Charlton Ath
WBA v Southend U

Endsleigh League Division 2
Bradford C v Stockport Co
Bristol C v AFC Bournemouth
Burnley v Crewe Alex
Carlisle U v Brentford
Hull C v Bristol R
Oxford U v Brighton & HA
Peterborough U v Shrewsbury T
Swansea C v Swindon T
Walsall v Notts Co
Wrexham v Chesterfield
Wycombe W v Blackpool
York C v Rotherham U

Endsleigh League Division 3
Chester C v Cambridge U
Colchester U v Wigan Ath
Doncaster R v Bury
Exeter C v Mansfield T
Fulham v Hartlepool U
Gillingham v Torquay U
Hereford U v Lincoln C
Leyton Orient v Cardiff C
Northampton T v Darlington
Preston NE v Barnet
Rochdale v Scarborough
Scunthorpe U v Plymouth Arg

Saturday 17 February 1996

FA Carling Premiership
Arsenal v Manchester C
Aston Villa v Blackburn R
Chelsea v West Ham U
Leeds U v Tottenham H
Liverpool v Wimbledon
Manchester U v Everton
Middlesbrough v Bolton W
Newcastle U v Southampton
Nottingham F v Coventry C
Sheffield W v QPR

Endsleigh League Division 1
Barnsley v Huddersfield T
Charlton Ath v Sheffield U
Crystal Palace v Watford
Grimsby T v Reading
Ipswich T v Oldham Ath
Leicester C v Port Vale
Luton T v Millwall
Norwich C v Wolverhampton W
Portsmouth v Sunderland
Southend U v Derby Co
Stoke C v Birmingham C
WBA v Tranmere R

Endsleigh League Division 2
AFC Bournemouth v Blackpool
Bradford C v Swindon T
Brentford v Bristol C
Brighton & HA v Crewe Alex
Bristol R v Rotherham U
Burnley v York C
Chesterfield v Wycombe W
Oxford U v Walsall
Peterborough U v Carlisle U
Shrewsbury T v Wrexham
Stockport Co v Notts Co
Swansea C v Hull C

Endsleigh League Division 3
Barnet v Wigan Ath
Bury v Lincoln C
Chester C v Scunthorpe U
Darlington v Mansfield T
Doncaster R v Plymouth Arg
Exeter C v Cambridge U
Gillingham v Hereford U
Leyton Orient v Northampton T
Preston NE v Colchester U
Rochdale v Fulham
Scarborough v Cardiff C

Torquay U v Hartlepool U

Tuesday 20 February 1996

Endsleigh League Division 1
Birmingham C v Barnsley
Huddersfield T v Charlton Ath
Oldham Ath v Stoke C
Port Vale v Norwich C
Reading v Southend U
Sheffield U v WBA
Sunderland v Ipswich T
Tranmere R v Crystal Palace
Watford v Grimsby T

Endsleigh League Division 2
Blackpool v Shrewsbury T
Bristol C v Peterborough U
Carlisle U v Swansea C
Crewe Alex v Stockport Co
Hull C v Chesterfield
Notts Co v Brighton & HA
Rotherham U v AFC Bournemouth
Walsall v Burnley
Wrexham v Bristol R
Wycombe W v Bradford C
York C v Oxford U

Endsleigh League Division 3
Cambridge U v Preston NE
Cardiff C v Darlington
Colchester U v Gillingham
Fulham v Leyton Orient
Hartlepool U v Doncaster R
Hereford U v Chester C
Lincoln C v Barnet
Mansfield T v Torquay U
Northampton T v Rochdale
Plymouth Arg v Bury
Scunthorpe U v Exeter C
Wigan Ath v Scarborough

Wednesday 21 February 1996

Endsleigh League Division 1
Derby Co v Luton T
Millwall v Portsmouth
Wolverhampton W v Leicester C

Endsleigh League Division 2
Swindon T v Brentford

Saturday 24 February 1996

FA Carling Premiership
Blackburn R v Liverpool
Bolton W v Manchester U
Coventry C v Middlesbrough
Everton v Nottingham F
Manchester C v Newcastle U
QPR v Leeds U
Southampton v Chelsea
Tottenham H v Sheffield W
West Ham U v Arsenal
Wimbledon v Aston Villa

Endsleigh League Division 1
Birmingham C v WBA
Derby Co v Portsmouth
Huddersfield T v Crystal Palace
Millwall v Norwich C
Oldham Ath v Charlton Ath
Port Vale v Grimsby T
Reading v Leicester C
Sheffield U v Barnsley
Sunderland v Luton T
Tranmere R v Stoke C
Watford v Ipswich T
Wolverhampton W v Southend U

Endsleigh League Division 2
Blackpool v Brighton & HA
Bristol C v Bradford C
Carlisle U v Oxford U
Crewe Alex v AFC Bournemouth
Hull C v Burnley

Notts Co v Shrewsbury T
Rotherham U v Chesterfield
Swindon T v Bristol R
Walsall v Brentford
Wrexham v Peterborough U
Wycombe W v Stockport Co
York C v Swansea C

Endsleigh League Division 3
Cambridge U v Bury
Cardiff C v Gillingham
Colchester U v Darlington
Fulham v Exeter C
Hartlepool U v Leyton Orient
Hereford U v Scarborough
Lincoln C v Chester C
Mansfield T v Rochdale
Northampton T v Doncaster R
Plymouth Arg v Barnet
Scunthorpe U v Preston NE
Wigan Ath v Torquay U

Monday 26 February 1996

Endsleigh League Division 3
Doncaster R v Fulham

Tuesday 27 February 1996

Endsleigh League Division 1
Barnsley v Millwall
Charlton Ath v Tranmere R
Crystal Palace v Birmingham C
Grimsby T v Wolverhampton W
Ipswich T v Huddersfield T
Luton T v Reading
Southend U v Sunderland
WBA v Oldham Ath

Endsleigh League Division 2
AFC Bournemouth v Notts Co
Bradford C v Wrexham
Brentford v Rotherham U
Brighton & HA v Bristol C
Bristol R v York C
Burnley v Carlisle U
Chesterfield v Swindon T
Oxford U v Hull C
Peterborough U v Wycombe W
Shrewsbury T v Crewe Alex
Stockport Co v Blackpool
Swansea C v Walsall

Endsleigh League Division 3
Barnet v Cambridge U
Bury v Wigan Ath
Chester C v Colchester U
Darlington v Hartlepool U
Exeter C v Northampton T
Gillingham v Scunthorpe U
Leyton Orient v Plymouth Arg
Preston NE v Hereford U
Rochdale v Lincoln C
Scarborough v Mansfield T
Torquay U v Cardiff C

Wednesday 28 February 1996

Endsleigh League Division 1
Leicester City v Derby Co
Norwich C v Sheffield U
Portsmouth v Port Vale
Stoke C v Watford

Saturday 2 March 1996

FA Carling Premiership
Coventry C v West Ham U
Leeds U v Bolton W
Liverpool v Aston Villa
Manchester C v Blackburn R
Middlesbrough v Everton
Newcastle U v Manchester U
QPR v Arsenal
Sheffield W v Nottingham F
Tottenham H v Southampton
Wimbledon v Chelsea

Endsleigh League Division 1
Birmingham C v Sheffield U
Derby Co v Huddersfield T
Grimsby T v Sunderland
Ipswich T v Leicester C
Luton T v Crystal Palace
Millwall v Wolverhampton W
Oldham Ath v Tranmere R
Portsmouth v Charlton Ath
Reading v Watford
Southend U v Norwich C
Stoke C v Barnsley
WBA v Port Vale

Endsleigh League Division 2
AFC Bournemouth v Oxford U
Bradford C v York C
Brighton & HA v Brentford
Bristol R v Shrewsbury T
Burnley v Blackpool
Carlisle U v Stockport Co
Notts Co v Hull C
Peterborough U v Chesterfield
Swansea C v Bristol C
Walsall v Rotherham U
Wrexham v Crewe Alex
Wycombe W v Swindon T

Endsleigh League Division 3
Bury v Scunthorpe U
Chester C v Cardiff C
Doncaster R v Darlington
Fulham v Lincoln C
Hereford U v Northampton T
Leyton Orient v Colchester U
Mansfield T v Barnet
Plymouth Arg v Gillingham
Preston NE v Rochdale
Scarborough v Hartlepool U
Torquay U v Exeter C
Wigan Ath v Cambridge U

Saturday 9 March 1996

FA Carling Premiership
Arsenal v Liverpool
Aston Villa v QPR
Blackburn R v Wimbledon
Bolton W v Tottenham H
Chelsea v Manchester C
Everton v Coventry C
Manchester U v Leeds U
Nottingham F v Newcastle U
Southampton v Sheffield W
West Ham U v Middlesbrough

Endsleigh League Division 1
Barnsley v Ipswich T
Charlton Ath v Millwall
Crystal Palace v WBA
Huddersfield T v Luton T
Leicester C v Grimsby T
Norwich C v Portsmouth
Port Vale v Southend U
Sheffield U v Stoke C
Sunderland v Derby Co
Tranmere R v Birmingham C
Watford v Oldham Ath
Wolverhampton W v Reading

Endsleigh League Division 2
Blackpool v Notts Co
Brentford v Wrexham
Bristol C v Burnley
Chesterfield v Brighton & HA
Crewe Alex v Bristol R
Hull C v AFC Bournemouth
Oxford U v Bradford C
Rotherham U v Swansea C
Shrewsbury T v Wycombe W
Stockport Co v Peterborough U
Swindon T v Walsall
York C v Carlisle U

Endsleigh League Division 3
Barnet v Chester C
Cambridge U v Plymouth Arg
Cardiff C v Fulham
Colchester U v Bury
Darlington v Torquay U
Exeter C v Doncaster R
Gillingham v Preston NE
Hartlepool U v Mansfield T
Lincoln C v Wigan Ath
Northampton T v Scarborough
Rochdale v Leyton Orient
Scunthorpe U v Hereford U

Saturday 16 March 1996

FA Carling Premiership
Coventry C v Bolton W
Leeds U v Everton
Liverpool v Chelsea
Manchester C v Southampton
Middlesbrough v Nottingham F
Newcastle U v West Ham U
QPR v Manchester U
Sheffield W v Aston Villa
Tottenham H v Blackburn R
Wimbledon v Arsenal

Endsleigh League Division 1
Birmingham C v Sunderland
Derby Co v Watford
Grimsby T v Crystal Palace
Ipswich T v Tranmere R
Luton T v Port Vale
Millwall v Sheffield U
Oldham Ath v Leicester C
Portsmouth v Wolverhampton W
Reading v Norwich C
Southend U v Charlton Ath
Stoke C v Huddersfield T
WBA v Barnsley

Endsleigh League Division 2
AFC Bournemouth v York C
Bradford C v Rotherham U
Brighton & HA v Hull C
Bristol R v Bristol C
Burnley v Swindon T
Carlisle U v Shrewsbury T
Notts Co v Oxford U
Peterborough U v Crewe Alex
Swansea C v Blackpool
Walsall v Chesterfield
Wrexham v Stockport Co
Wycombe W v Brentford

Endsleigh League Division 3
Bury v Rochdale
Chester C v Exeter C
Doncaster R v Scunthorpe U
Fulham v Cambridge U
Hereford U v Hartlepool U
Leyton Orient v Lincoln C
Mansfield T v Gillingham
Plymouth Arg v Northampton T
Preston NE v Darlington
Scarborough v Colchester U
Torquay U v Barnet
Wigan Ath v Cardiff C

Saturday 23 March 1996

FA Carling Premiership
Arsenal v Newcastle U
Aston Villa v Middlesbrough
Blackburn R v Leeds U
Bolton W v Sheffield W
Chelsea v QPR
Everton v Wimbledon
Manchester U v Tottenham H
Nottingham F v Liverpool
Southampton v Coventry C
West Ham U v Manchester C

Endsleigh League Division 1
Barnsley v Southend U
Charlton Ath v Stoke C
Crystal Palace v Portsmouth
Huddersfield T v Grimsby T
Leicester C v Millwall
Norwich C v Derby Co
Port Vale v Ipswich T
Sheffield U v Luton T
Sunderland v Oldham Ath
Tranmere R v Reading
Watford v WBA
Wolverhampton W v Birmingham C

Endsleigh League Division 2
Blackpool v Carlisle U
Brentford v Swansea C
Bristol C v Wrexham
Chesterfield v Bristol R
Crewe Alex v Bradford C
Hull C v Walsall
Oxford U v Burnley
Rotherham U v Wycombe W
Shrewsbury T v AFC Bournemouth
Stockport Co v Brighton & HA
Swindon T v Peterborough U
York C v Notts Co

Endsleigh League Division 3
Barnet v Scarborough
Cambridge U v Mansfield T
Cardiff C v Preston NE
Colchester U v Torquay U
Darlington v Hereford U (*postponed*)
Exeter C v Plymouth Arg
Gillingham v Leyton Orient
Hartlepool U v Bury
Hereford U v Darlington
Lincoln C v Doncaster R
Northampton T v Chester C
Rochdale v Wigan Ath
Scunthorpe U v Fulham

Saturday 30 March 1996

FA Carling Premiership
Aston Villa v West Ham U
Blackburn R v Everton
Bolton W v Manchester C
Leeds U v Middlesbrough
Liverpool v Newcastle U
Manchester U v Arsenal
QPR v Southampton
Sheffield W v Chelsea
Tottenham H v Coventry C
Wimbledon v Nottingham F

Endsleigh League Division 1
Derby Co v Stoke C
Grimsby T v Birmingham C
Leicester C v Sheffield U
Luton T v Ipswich T
Millwall v Crystal Palace
Norwich C v Charlton Ath
Port Vale v Barnsley
Portsmouth v WBA
Reading v Oldham Ath
Southend U v Tranmere R
Sunderland v Huddersfield T
Wolverhampton W v Watford

Endsleigh League Division 2
AFC Bournemouth v Bristol R
Blackpool v Brentford
Bradford C v Swansea C
Brighton & HA v Rotherham U
Bristol C v Swindon T
Crewe Alex v Chesterfield
Notts Co v Carlisle U
Peterborough U v Walsall
Shrewsbury T v Hull C
Stockport Co v Oxford U
Wrexham v York C
Wycombe W v Burnley

Endsleigh League Division 3
Cardiff C v Cambridge U
Darlington v Lincoln C
Doncaster R v Chester C
Exeter C v Barnet
Fulham v Plymouth Arg
Hartlepool U v Colchester U
Leyton Orient v Bury
Mansfield T v Wigan Ath
Northampton T v Scunthorpe U
Rochdale v Gillingham
Scarborough v Preston NE
Torquay U v Hereford U

Tuesday 2 April 1996

Endsleigh League Division 1
Barnsley v Norwich C
Birmingham C v Portsmouth
Charlton Ath v Leicester C
Crystal Palace v Port Vale
Huddersfield T v Reading
Ipswich T v Derby Co
Oldham Ath v Grimsby T
Sheffield U v Southend U
Tranmere R v Millwall
Watford v Sunderland
WBA v Luton T

Endsleigh League Division 2
Brentford v Stockport Co
Bristol R v Bradford C
Burnley v AFC Bournemouth
Carlisle U v Crewe Alex
Chesterfield v Blackpool
Hull C v Bristol C
Oxford U v Wrexham
Rotherham U v Notts Co
Swansea C v Peterborough U
Walsall v Wycombe W
York C v Shrewsbury T

Endsleigh League Division 3
Barnet v Cardiff C
Bury v Fulham
Cambridge U v Northampton T
Chester C v Leyton Orient
Colchester U v Rochdale
Gillingham v Darlington
Hereford U v Doncaster R
Lincoln C v Scarborough
Plymouth Arg v Mansfield T
Preston NE v Torquay U
Scunthorpe U v Hartlepool U
Wigan Ath v Exeter C

Wednesday 3 April 1996

Endsleigh League Division 1
Stoke C v Wolverhampton W

Endsleigh League Division 2
Swindon T v Brighton & HA

Saturday 6 April 1996

FA Carling Premiership
Arsenal v Leeds U
Chelsea v Aston Villa
Coventry C v Liverpool
Everton v Bolton W
Manchester C v Manchester U
Middlesbrough v Sheffield W
Newcastle U v QPR
Nottingham F v Tottenham H
Southampton v Blackburn R
West Ham U v Wimbledon

Endsleigh League Division 1
Barnsley v Sunderland
Birmingham C v Port Vale
Charlton Ath v Luton T
Crystal Palace v Leicester C
Huddersfield T v Southend U
Ipswich T v Reading
Oldham Ath v Derby Co
Sheffield U v Wolverhampton W
Stoke C v Grimsby T
Tranmere R v Norwich C
Watford v Portsmouth
WBA v Millwall

Endsleigh League Division 2
Brentford v Crewe Alex
Bristol R v Brighton & HA
Burnley v Bradford C
Carlisle U v AFC Bournemouth
Chesterfield v Stockport Co
Hull C v Wycombe W
Oxford U v Blackpool
Rotherham U v Shrewsbury T
Swansea C v Wrexham
Swindon T v Notts Co
Walsall v Bristol C
York C v Peterborough U

Endsleigh League Division 3
Barnet v Northampton T
Bury v Mansfield T
Cambridge U v Rochdale
Chester C v Scarborough
Colchester U v Cardiff C
Gillingham v Hartlepool U
Hereford U v Fulham
Lincoln C v Exeter C
Plymouth Arg v Darlington
Preston NE v Doncaster R
Scunthorpe U v Torquay U
Wigan Ath v Leyton Orient

Monday 8 April 1996

FA Carling Premiership
Aston Villa v Southampton
Blackburn R v Newcastle U
Bolton W v Chelsea
Leeds U v Nottingham F
Liverpool v West Ham U
Manchester U v Coventry C
QPR v Everton
Sheffield W v Arsenal
Tottenham H v Middlesbrough
Wimbledon v Manchester C

Endsleigh League Division 1
Derby Co v Tranmere R
Grimsby T v Ipswich T
Norwich C v Huddersfield T
Port Vale v Oldham Ath
Portsmouth v Sheffield U
Reading v Crystal Palace
Southend U v Watford
Sunderland v Charlton Ath
Wolverhampton W v Barnsley

Endsleigh League Division 2
Blackpool v Rotherham U
Bradford C v Carlisle U
Bristol C v York C
Crewe Alex v Swindon T
Peterborough U v Brentford
Stockport Co v Hull C
Wrexham v Walsall
Wycombe W v Oxford U

Endsleigh League Division 3
Cardiff C v Lincoln C
Darlington v Cambridge U
Doncaster R v Gillingham
Exeter C v Hereford U
Fulham v Chester C
Hartlepool U v Wigan Ath
Leyton Orient v Scunthorpe U
Mansfield T v Preston NE
Northampton T v Colchester U
Rochdale v Barnet
Torquay U v Plymouth Arg

Tuesday 9 April 1996

Endsleigh League Division 1
Leicester C v WBA
Luton T v Stoke C

Endsleigh League Division 2
AFC Bournemouth v Swansea C
Brighton & HA v Burnley
Notts Co v Bristol R
Shrewsbury T v Chesterfield

Endsleigh League Division 3
Scarborough v Bury

Wednesday 10 April 1996

Endsleigh League Division 1
Millwall v Birmingham C

Saturday 13 April 1996

FA Carling Premiership
Arsenal v Tottenham H
Chelsea v Leeds U
Coventry C v QPR
Everton v Liverpool
Manchester C v Sheffield W
Middlesbrough v Wimbledon
Newcastle U v Aston Villa
Nottingham F v Blackburn R
Southampton v Manchester U
West Ham U v Bolton W

Endsleigh League Division 1
Barnsley v Reading
Birmingham C v Luton T
Charlton Ath v Derby Co
Crystal Palace v Southend U
Huddersfield T v Millwall
Ipswich T v Norwich C
Oldham Ath v Wolverhampton W
Sheffield U v Sunderland
Stoke C v Portsmouth
Tranmere R v Leicester C
Watford v Port Vale
WBA v Grimsby T

Endsleigh League Division 2
Brentford v Notts Co
Bristol R v Blackpool
Burnley v Peterborough U
Carlisle U v Wrexham
Chesterfield v Bristol C
Hull C v Crewe Alex
Oxford U v Shrewsbury T
Rotherham U v Stockport Co
Swansea C v Brighton & HA
Swindon T v AFC Bournemouth
Walsall v Bradford C
York C v Wycombe W

Endsleigh League Division 3
Barnet v Hartlepool U
Bury v Torquay U
Cambridge U v Doncaster R
Chester C v Rochdale
Colchester U v Fulham
Gillingham v Exeter C
Hereford U v Leyton Orient
Lincoln C v Mansfield T
Plymouth Arg v Scarborough
Preston NE v Northampton T
Scunthorpe U v Cardiff C
Wigan Ath v Darlington

Saturday 20 April 1996

Endsleigh League Division 1
Derby Co v Birmingham C
Grimsby T v Sheffield U
Leicester C v Huddersfield T
Luton T v Watford
Millwall v Oldham Ath
Norwich C v WBA
Port Vale v Tranmere R
Portsmouth v Barnsley
Reading v Charlton Ath
Southend U v Ipswich T
Sunderland v Stoke C

Wolverhampton W v Crystal Palace

Endsleigh League Division 2
AFC Bournemouth v Walsall
Blackpool v Swindon T
Bradford C v Chesterfield
Brighton & HA v Carlisle U
Bristol C v Oxford U
Crewe Alex v Rotherham U
Notts Co v Burnley
Peterborough U v Bristol R
Shrewsbury T v Brentford
Stockport Co v York C
Wrexham v Hull C
Wycombe W v Swansea C

Endsleigh League Division 3
Cardiff C v Plymouth Arg
Darlington v Bury
Doncaster R v Barnet
Exeter C v Colchester U
Fulham v Wigan Ath
Hartlepool U v Lincoln C
Leyton Orient v Preston NE
Mansfield T v Hereford U
Northampton T v Gillingham
Rochdale v Scunthorpe U
Scarborough v Cambridge U
Torquay U v Chester C

Saturday 27 April 1996

FA Carling Premiership
Aston Villa v Manchester C
Blackburn R v Arsenal
Bolton W v Southampton
Leeds U v Newcastle U
Liverpool v Middlesbrough
Manchester U v Nottingham F
QPR v West Ham U
Sheffield W v Everton
Tottenham H v Chelsea
Wimbledon v Coventry C

Endsleigh League Division 1
Derby Co v Crystal Palace
Grimsby T v Tranmere R
Leicester C v Birmingham C
Luton T v Barnsley
Millwall v Stoke C
Norwich C v Watford
Port Vale v Charlton Ath
Portsmouth v Ipswich T
Reading v Sheffield U
Southend U v Oldham Ath
Sunderland v WBA
Wolverhampton W v Huddersfield T

Endsleigh League Division 2
AFC Bournemouth v Chesterfield
Blackpool v Walsall
Bradford C v Brentford
Brighton & HA v York C
Bristol C v Rotherham U
Crewe Alex v Oxford U
Notts Co v Swansea C
Peterborough U v Hull C
Shrewsbury T v Swindon T
Stockport Co v Bristol R
Wrexham v Burnley
Wycombe W v Carlisle U

Endsleigh League Division 3
Cardiff C v Hereford U
Darlington v Chester C
Doncaster R v Wigan Ath
Exeter C v Bury
Fulham v Gillingham
Hartlepool U v Preston NE
Leyton Orient v Barnet
Mansfield T v Colchester U
Northampton T v Lincoln C
Rochdale v Plymouth Arg
Scarborough v Scunthorpe U
Torquay U v Cambridge U

Saturday 4 May 1996

FA Carling Premiership
Arsenal v Bolton W
Chelsea v Blackburn R
Coventry C v Leeds U
Everton v Aston Villa
Manchester C v Liverpool
Middlesbrough v Manchester U
Newcastle U v Tottenham H
Nottingham F v QPR
Southampton v Wimbledon
West Ham U v Sheffield W

Endsleigh League Division 1
Barnsley v Grimsby T
Birmingham C v Reading
Charlton Ath v Wolverhampton W
Crystal Palace v Norwich C
Huddersfield T v Portsmouth
Ipswich T v Millwall
Oldham Ath v Luton T
Sheffield U v Port Vale
Stoke C v Southend U
Tranmere R v Sunderland
Watford v Leicester C
WBA v Derby Co

Endsleigh League Division 2
Brentford v AFC Bournemouth
Bristol R v Wycombe W
Burnley v Shrewsbury T
Carlisle U v Bristol C
Chesterfield v Notts Co
Hull C v Bradford C
Oxford U v Peterborough U
Rotherham U v Wrexham
Swansea C v Crewe Alex
Swindon T v Stockport Co
Walsall v Brighton & HA
York C v Blackpool

Endsleigh League Division 3
Barnet v Fulham
Bury v Cardiff C
Cambridge U v Leyton Orient
Chester C v Mansfield T
Colchester U v Doncaster R
Gillingham v Scarborough
Hereford U v Rochdale
Lincoln C v Torquay U
Plymouth Arg v Hartlepool U
Preston NE v Exeter C
Scunthorpe U v Darlington
Wigan Ath v Northampton T

FA CARLING PREMIERSHIP FIXTURES 1995–96

	Arsenal	Aston Villa	Blackburn R	Bolton W	Chelsea	Coventry C	Everton	Leeds U	Liverpool	Manchester C	Manchester U	Middlesbrough	Newcastle U	Nottingham F	QPR	Sheffield W	Southampton	Tottenham H	West Ham U	Wimbledon
Arsenal	—	21.10	26.11	4.5	16.12	3.2	20.1	6.4	9.3	17.2	4.11	20.8	23.3	29.8	26.12	21.11	23.9	13.4	16.9	20.12
Aston Villa	2.12	—	17.2	30.8	14.10	16.12	28.10	3.2	26.12	27.4	19.8	23.3	18.11	23.9	9.3	30.12	8.4	20.1	30.3	16.9
Blackburn R	27.4	9.9	—	3.2	28.10	23.9	30.3	23.3	24.2	26.12	28.8	16.12	8.4	18.11	19.8	20.1	14.10	30.12	2.12	9.3
Bolton W	30.10	10.2	26.8	—	8.4	30.12	14.10	27.12	9.12	30.3	24.2	9.9	22.8	2.12	30.9	23.3	27.4	9.3	18.11	13.1
Chelsea	30.9	6.4	4.5	22.11	—	30.8	19.8	13.4	30.12	9.3	21.10	3.2	9.12	20.1	23.3	4.11	16.9	25.11	17.2	26.12
Coventry C	26.8	30.9	9.12	16.3	10.2	—	23.12	4.5	6.4	23.8	22.11	24.2	13.1	9.9	13.4	21.10	1.1	4.11	2.3	25.11
Everton	23.8	4.5	5.11	6.4	13.1	9.3	—	30.12	13.4	10.2	9.9	26.12	1.10	24.2	22.11	25.11	26.8	21.10	9.12	23.3
Leeds U	14.10	26.8	1.1	2.3	18.11	28.10	16.3	—	21.8	2.12	24.12	30.3	27.4	8.4	16.9	30.9	10.2	17.2	13.1	9.12
Liverpool	23.12	2.3	16.9	23.9	16.3	14.10	18.11	20.1	—	28.10	17.12	27.4	30.3	1.1	30.8	19.8	2.12	3.2	8.4	17.2
Manchester C	10.9	25.11	2.3	4.11	23.12	20.1	30.8	21.10	4.5	—	6.4	23.9	24.2	16.12	3.2	13.4	16.3	19.8	1.1	22.11
Manchester U	30.3	13.1	10.2	16.9	2.12	8.4	17.2	9.3	1.10	14.10	—	28.10	26.12	27.4	30.12	9.12	18.11	23.3	23.8	26.8
Middlesbrough	13.1	1.1	30.9	17.2	26.8	16.9	2.3	4.11	25.11	9.12	4.5	—	10.2	16.3	21.10	6.4	12.9	21.11	23.12	13.4
Newcastle U	2.1	13.4	8.11	20.1	24.9	19.8	16.12	25.11	4.11	16.9	2.3	30.8	—	23.12	6.4	3.2	17.2	4.5	16.3	21.10
Nottingham F	10.2	10.12	13.4	21.10	23.8	17.2	17.9	22.11	23.3	30.9	25.11	30.12	9.3	—	4.5	26.12	13.1	6.4	26.8	4.11
QPR	2.3	23.12	13.1	16.12	2.1	19.11	8.4	24.2	10.2	26.8	16.3	2.12	14.10	28.10	—	9.9	30.3	25.9	27.4	23.8
Sheffield W	8.4	16.3	23.8	1.1	30.3	4.12	27.4	16.12	13.1	18.11	23.9	15.10	27.8	2.3	17.2	—	23.12	16.9	28.10	10.2
Southampton	9.12	20.11	6.4	25.11	24.2	23.3	3.2	30.8	22.10	30.12	13.4	20.1	9.9	19.8	4.11	9.3	—	26.12	30.9	4.5
Tottenham H	18.11	23.8	16.3	23.12	27.4	30.3	2.12	9.9	26.8	13.1	1.1	8.4	29.10	14.10	9.12	24.2	2.3	—	10.2	30.9
West Ham U	24.2	4.11	21.10	13.4	11.9	26.12	23.9	19.8	22.11	23.3	20.1	9.3	30.12	3.2	25.11	4.5	16.12	30.8	—	6.4
Wimbledon	16.3	24.2	23.12	19.8	2.3	27.4	1.1	23.9	9.9	8.4	3.2	18.11	3.12	30.3	20.1	30.8	28.10	16.12	16.10	—

ENDSLEIGH INSURANCE FIXTURES 1995–96

DIVISION ONE

	Barnsley	Birmingham C	Charlton Ath	Crystal Palace	Derby Co	Grimsby T	Huddersfield T	Ipswich T	Leicester C	Luton T	Millwall	Norwich C	Oldham Ath	Port Vale	Portsmouth	Reading	Sheffield U	Southend U	Stoke C	Sunderland	Tranmere R	Watford	WBA	Wolverhampton
Barnsley	—	2.9	16.12	20.1	23.9	4.5	17.2	9.3	7.10	25.11	27.2	2.4	19.8	21.10	21.11	13.4	16.9	23.3	26.12	6.4	29.8	3.2	30.12	4.11
Birmingham C	20.2	—	13.1	9.9	21.11	21.10	10.2	12.8	25.11	13.4	4.11	26.8	30.9	6.4	2.4	4.5	2.3	7.10	12.9	16.3	23.12	9.12	24.2	1.1
Charlton Ath	30.9	19.8	—	3.2	13.4	7.10	2.9	9.12	2.4	6.4	9.3	21.10	16.9	25.11	26.12	21.11	17.2	30.12	23.3	4.11	27.2	29.8	20.1	4.5
Crystal Palace	12.8	27.2	26.8	—	25.11	30.12	16.9	13.1	6.4	26.12	21.10	4.5	9.12	2.4	23.3	4.11	10.2	13.4	30.9	7.10	2.9	17.2	9.3	21.11
Derby Co	9.12	20.4	18.11	27.4	—	26.8	2.3	14.10	9.9	21.2	30.9	1.1	28.10	13.8	24.2	13.1	2.12	13.9	30.3	23.12	8.4	16.3	11.11	10.2
Grimsby T	11.11	30.3	2.12	16.3	3.2	—	1.1	8.4	23.12	29.8	20.1	23.9	14.10	16.9	19.8	17.2	20.4	16.12	23.10	2.3	27.4	2.9	18.11	27.2
Huddersfield T	12.9	30.8	20.2	24.2	26.12	23.3	—	9.9	21.11	9.3	13.4	4.11	20.1	7.10	4.5	2.4	23.9	6.4	30.12	21.10	3.2	19.8	16.12	25.11
Ipswich T	22.12	20.1	23.9	19.8	2.4	4.11	27.2	—	2.3	21.10	4.5	13.4	17.2	1.1	25.11	6.4	16.12	21.11	29.8	2.9	16.3	16.9	3.2	7.10
Leicester C	2.12	27.4	14.10	28.10	28.2	9.3	20.4	26.12	—	3.2	23.3	16.12	30.12	17.2	30.8	16.9	30.3	23.9	19.8	20.1	18.11	11.11	9.4	2.9
Luton T	27.4	18.11	28.10	2.3	2.9	10.2	23.12	30.3	26.8	—	17.2	13.8	11.11	16.3	30.9	27.2	1.1	13.1	9.4	16.9	2.12	20.4	14.10	9.12
Millwall	9.9	10.4	5.12	30.3	16.12	12.8	18.11	11.11	1.1	13.9	—	24.2	20.4	13.1	21.2	10.2	16.3	26.8	27.4	23.9	14.10	2.12	28.10	2.3
Norwich C	14.10	3.2	30.3	11.11	23.3	9.12	8.4	18.11	30.9	20.1	16.9	—	30.8	2.9	9.3	30.12	28.2	26.12	2.12	19.8	28.10	27.4	20.4	17.2
Oldham Ath	13.1	16.12	24.2	23.9	6.4	2.4	12.8	12.9	16.3	4.5	21.11	10.2	—	4.11	7.10	21.10	26.8	25.11	20.2	1.1	2.3	23.12	9.9	13.4
Port Vale	30.3	28.10	27.4	14.10	20.1	24.2	2.12	23.3	12.9	30.12	19.8	20.2	8.4	—	9.9	9.12	11.11	9.3	3.2	29.8	20.4	18.11	26.12	30.9
Portsmouth	20.4	14.10	2.3	1.1	16.9	13.1	11.11	27.4	10.2	16.12	2.9	23.12	2.12	28.2	—	26.8	8.4	12.8	18.11	17.2	23.9	28.10	30.3	16.3
Reading	18.11	11.11	20.4	8.4	19.8	12.9	14.10	28.10	24.2	9.9	29.8	16.3	30.3	23.9	3.2	—	27.4	20.2	20.1	16.12	1.1	2.3	2.12	23.12
Sheffield U	24.2	26.12	12.9	29.8	7.10	21.11	9.12	30.9	21.10	23.3	30.12	9.9	3.2	4.5	4.11	25.11	—	2.4	9.3	13.4	19.8	20.1	20.2	6.4
Southend U	1.1	2.12	16.3	18.11	17.2	30.9	28.10	20.4	9.12	19.8	3.2	2.3	27.4	20.12	20.1	2.9	14.10	—	11.11	27.2	30.3	8.4	29.8	16.9
Stoke C	2.3	17.2	1.1	16.12	21.10	6.4	16.3	10.2	13.1	4.11	25.11	7.10	2.9	26.8	13.4	12.8	20.12	4.5	—	22.11	16.9	28.2	23.9	3.4
Sunderland	28.10	30.12	8.4	2.12	9.3	26.12	30.3	20.2	12.8	24.2	9.12	13.1	23.3	10.2	12.9	30.9	18.11	9.9	20.4	—	11.11	14.10	27.4	26.8
Tranmere R	10.2	9.3	9.9	20.2	4.11	25.11	26.8	30.12	13.4	7.10	2.4	6.4	26.12	21.11	9.12	23.3	13.1	21.10	24.2	4.5	—	30.9	12.9	12.8
Watford	26.8	23.9	10.2	12.9	30.12	20.2	13.1	24.2	4.5	21.11	7.10	25.11	9.3	13.4	6.4	26.12	12.8	4.11	9.9	2.4	16.12	—	23.3	21.10
WBA	16.3	16.9	12.8	23.12	4.5	13.4	30.9	26.8	4.11	2.4	6.4	21.11	27.2	2.3	21.10	7.10	2.9	10.2	9.12	25.11	17.2	1.1	—	13.1
Wolverhampton	8.4	23.3	11.11	20.4	30.8	9.9	27.4	2.12	21.2	23.9	26.12	13.9	18.11	16.12	30.12	9.3	28.10	24.2	14.10	3.2	20.1	30.3	20.8	—

ENDSLEIGH INSURANCE FIXTURES 1995–96

DIVISION TWO

	Blackpool	Bournemouth	Bradford C	Brentford	Brighton & HA	Bristol C	Bristol R	Burnley	Carlisle U	Chesterfield	Crewe Alex	Hull C	Notts Co	Oxford U	Peterborough U	Rotherham U	Shrewsbury T	Stockport Co	Swansea C	Swindon T	Walsall	Wrexham	Wycombe W	York C
Blackpool	—	12.9	16.12	30.3	24.2	20.1	31.10	26.12	23.3	14.10	23.9	3.2	9.3	28.10	29.8	8.4	20.2	9.9	30.12	20.4	27.4	19.8	6.1	18.11
Bournemouth	17.2	—	20.1	18.11	23.9	6.1	30.3	14.10	28.10	27.4	16.9	23.12	27.2	2.3	19.8	2.9	1.1	16.12	9.4	31.10	20.4	29.8	3.2	16.3
Bradford C	30.9	12.8	—	27.4	13.1	16.9	14.10	28.10	8.4	20.4	1.1	18.11	27.1	23.12	9.12	16.3	26.8	10.2	30.3	17.2	31.10	27.2	2.9	2.3
Brentford	7.10	4.5	25.11	—	26.12	17.2	9.12	3.2	6.1	30.9	6.4	29.8	13.4	19.8	21.10	27.2	4.11	2.4	23.3	2.9	16.9	9.3	30.12	20.1
Brighton & HA	16.9	9.12	19.8	2.3	—	27.2	28.10	9.4	20.4	22.12	17.2	16.3	2.9	6.1	20.1	30.3	30.9	1.1	31.10	14.10	18.11	3.2	29.8	27.4
Bristol C	12.8	10.2	24.2	12.9	9.9	—	30.12	9.3	18.11	31.10	13.1	14.10	9.12	20.4	20.2	27.4	27.1	26.8	26.12	30.3	28.10	23.3	30.9	8.4
Bristol R	13.4	7.10	2.4	23.9	6.4	16.3	—	29.8	20.1	1.1	23.12	6.1	21.10	16.12	4.11	17.2	2.3	25.11	19.8	16.9	3.2	2.9	4.5	27.2
Burnley	2.3	2.4	6.4	26.8	21.10	23.12	27.1	—	27.2	9.12	10.2	16.9	4.11	1.1	13.4	12.8	4.5	13.1	30.9	16.3	2.9	25.11	7.10	17.2
Carlisle U	1.1	6.4	21.10	10.2	4.11	4.5	12.8	9.9	—	13.1	2.4	23.9	7.10	24.2	12.9	27.1	16.3	2.3	20.2	26.8	16.12	13.4	25.11	22.12
Chesterfield	2.4	25.11	4.11	16.12	9.3	13.4	23.3	23.9	19.8	—	7.10	2.9	4.5	20.1	26.12	16.9	21.10	6.4	3.2	27.2	30.12	6.1	17.2	29.8
Crewe Alex	9.12	24.2	23.3	28.10	12.9	10.10	9.3	6.1	14.10	30.3	—	31.10	30.9	27.4	30.12	20.4	9.9	20.2	18.11	8.4	29.8	26.12	20.1	3.2
Hull C	26.8	9.3	4.5	27.1	30.12	2.4	10.2	24.2	9.12	20.2	13.4	—	26.12	9.9	25.11	13.1	7.10	21.10	12.9	12.8	23.3	4.11	6.4	30.9
Notts Co	22.12	9.9	29.8	31.10	20.2	23.9	9.4	20.4	30.3	18.11	16.12	2.3	—	16.3	3.2	14.10	24.2	12.9	27.4	28.10	6.1	20.1	19.8	1.1
Oxford U	6.4	26.12	9.3	13.1	10.2	4.11	30.9	23.3	16.9	12.8	25.11	27.2	30.12	—	4.5	26.8	13.4	7.10	9.12	27.1	17.2	2.4	21.10	2.9
Peterborough U	27.1	13.1	23.9	8.4	12.8	2.9	20.4	31.10	17.2	2.3	16.3	27.4	26.8	18.11	—	16.12	10.2	19.12	14.10	1.1	30.3	16.9	27.2	28.10
Rotherham U	21.10	20.2	30.12	9.9	7.10	25.11	12.9	20.1	29.8	24.2	4.11	19.8	2.4	3.2	30.9	—	6.4	13.4	9.3	9.12	26.12	4.5	23.3	6.1
Shrewsbury T	2.9	23.3	3.2	20.4	16.12	29.8	26.12	18.11	30.12	9.4	27.2	30.3	16.9	31.10	6.1	28.10	—	23.9	20.1	27.4	19.8	17.2	9.3	14.10
Stockport Co	27.2	30.9	6.1	14.10	23.3	3.2	27.4	19.8	26.12	28.10	2.9	8.4	17.2	30.3	9.3	31.10	9.12	—	29.8	18.11	20.1	30.12	16.9	20.4
Swansea C	16.3	21.10	7.10	1.1	13.4	2.3	13.1	16.12	2.9	26.8	4.5	17.2	25.11	23.9	2.4	23.12	12.8	27.1	—	10.2	27.2	6.4	4.11	16.9
Swindon T	4.11	13.4	13.9	21.2	3.4	7.10	24.2	30.12	3.2	9.9	21.10	20.1	6.4	30.8	23.3	23.9	25.11	4.5	6.1	—	9.3	16.12	26.12	19.8
Walsall	25.11	4.11	13.4	24.2	4.5	6.4	26.8	20.2	30.9	16.3	27.1	1.1	10.2	12.9	7.10	2.3	13.1	12.8	9.9	23.12	—	21.10	2.4	9.12
Wrexham	13.1	27.1	9.9	22.12	26.8	1.1	20.2	27.4	31.10	10.2	2.3	20.4	12.8	14.10	24.2	18.11	12.9	16.3	28.10	30.9	8.4	—	9.12	30.3
Wycombe W	10.2	26.8	20.2	16.3	27.1	16.12	18.11	30.3	27.4	12.9	12.8	28.10	13.1	8.4	9.9	1.1	23.12	24.2	20.4	2.3	14.10	23.9	—	31.10
York C	4.5	30.12	26.12	12.8	25.11	21.10	9.9	12.9	9.3	27.1	26.8	16.12	23.3	20.2	6.4	10.2	2.4	4.11	24.2	13.1	23.9	7.10	13.4	—

ENDSLEIGH INSURANCE FIXTURES 1995–96

DIVISION THREE

	Barnet	Bury	Cambridge U	Cardiff C	Chester C	Colchester U	Darlington	Doncaster R	Exeter C	Fulham	Gillingham	Hartlepool U	Hereford U	Leyton O	Lincoln C	Mansfield T	Northampton T	Plymouth Arg	Preston NE	Rochdale	Scarborough	Scunthorpe U	Torquay U	Wigan Ath
Barnet	—	9.12	27.2	2.4	9.3	19.8	30.9	4.11	7.10	4.5	29.8	13.4	20.1	25.11	2.9	26.12	6.4	16.9	6.1	21.10	23.3	3.2	30.12	17.2
Bury	23.9	—	16.9	4.5	19.8	23.12	4.11	6.1	25.11	2.4	16.12	1.1	3.2	7.10	17.2	6.4	20.1	2.9	29.8	16.3	21.10	2.3	13.4	27.2
Cambridge U	9.9	24.2	—	7.10	6.1	29.8	21.10	13.4	12.9	30.12	3.2	30.9	19.8	4.5	9.12	23.3	2.4	9.3	20.2	6.4	4.11	20.1	25.11	26.12
Cardiff C	14.10	18.11	30.3	—	26.12	28.10	20.2	3.2	29.8	9.3	24.2	9.12	27.4	6.1	8.4	30.9	19.8	20.4	23.3	20.1	12.9	31.10	9.9	30.12
Chester C	23.12	13.1	10.2	2.3	—	27.2	25.11	7.10	16.3	21.10	23.9	12.8	2.9	2.4	16.9	4.5	1.1	26.8	16.12	13.4	6.4	17.2	4.11	27.1
Colchester U	13.1	9.3	27.1	6.4	9.9	—	24.2	4.5	4.11	13.4	20.2	7.10	23.9	26.12	26.8	25.11	21.10	12.8	12.9	2.4	30.12	16.12	23.3	10.2
Darlington	16.12	20.4	8.4	2.9	27.4	16.9	—	26.12	20.1	29.8	14.10	27.2	1.1	3.2	30.3	17.2	6.1	28.10	30.12	19.8	23.9	18.11	9.3	31.10
Doncaster R	20.4	10.2	30.10	26.8	30.3	18.11	2.3	—	22.12	26.2	8.4	2.9	14.10	16.12	1.1	27.1	16.9	17.2	28.10	23.9	12.8	16.3	13.1	27.4
Exeter C	30.3	27.4	17.2	27.1	30.12	20.4	12.8	9.3	—	16.9	31.10	13.1	8.4	23.9	28.10	10.2	27.2	23.3	18.11	16.12	26.8	2.9	26.12	14.10
Fulham	18.11	14.10	16.3	23.12	8.4	31.10	27.1	9.9	24.2	—	27.4	10.2	28.10	20.2	2.3	12.8	16.12	30.3	23.9	12.9	13.1	1.1	26.8	20.4
Gillingham	27.1	30.9	26.8	16.9	9.12	2.9	2.4	21.10	13.4	25.11	—	6.4	17.2	23.3	13.1	30.12	4.11	26.12	9.3	7.10	4.5	27.2	10.2	12.8
Hartlepool U	31.10	23.3	16.12	23.9	20.1	30.3	9.9	20.2	19.8	6.1	28.10	—	30.12	24.2	20.4	9.3	29.8	18.11	27.4	3.2	26.12	14.10	12.9	8.4
Hereford U	12.8	26.8	13.1	26.11	20.2	9.12	23.3	2.4	21.10	6.4	12.9	16.3	—	13.4	10.2	4.11	2.3	27.1	9.9	4.5	24.2	19.12	7.10	30.9
Leyton O	27.4	30.3	18.11	10.2	14.10	2.3	26.8	30.9	9.12	2.9	1.1	16.9	31.10	—	16.3	13.1	17.2	27.2	20.4	22.12	27.1	8.4	12.8	28.10
Lincoln C	20.2	12.9	23.9	21.10	24.2	3.2	7.10	23.3	6.4	26.12	19.8	4.11	6.1	30.12	—	13.4	25.11	16.12	20.1	9.9	2.4	28.8	4.5	9.3
Mansfield T	2.3	28.10	1.1	16.12	18.11	27.4	12.9	29.8	6.1	20.1	16.3	23.12	20.4	19.8	31.10	—	3.2	14.10	8.4	24.2	9.9	23.9	20.2	30.3
Northampton T	28.10	12.8	14.10	13.1	23.3	8.4	10.2	24.2	9.9	30.9	20.4	27.1	26.12	12.9	27.4	26.8	—	30.12	31.10	20.2	9.3	30.3	9.12	18.11
Plymouth Arg	24.2	20.2	23.12	4.11	3.2	20.1	6.4	12.9	1.1	7.10	2.3	4.5	29.8	9.9	30.9	2.4	16.3	—	19.8	25.11	13.4	6.1	21.10	9.12
Preston NE	10.2	27.1	2.9	1.1	30.9	17.2	16.3	6.4	4.5	9.12	23.12	25.11	27.2	4.11	12.8	21.10	13.4	13.1	—	2.3	7.10	16.9	2.4	26.8
Rochdale	8.4	30.12	28.10	12.8	31.10	14.10	13.1	9.12	30.9	17.2	30.3	26.8	18.11	9.3	27.2	16.9	2.9	27.4	26.12	—	10.2	20.4	27.1	23.3
Scarborough	1.1	9.4	20.4	17.2	28.10	16.3	9.12	20.1	3.2	19.8	18.11	2.3	16.9	30.8	14.10	27.2	23.12	31.10	30.3	6.1	—	27.4	30.9	2.9
Scunthorpe U	26.8	26.12	12.8	13.4	12.9	30.9	4.5	30.12	20.2	23.3	9.9	2.4	9.3	21.10	27.1	9.12	7.10	10.2	24.2	4.11	25.11	—	6.4	13.1
Torquay U	16.3	31.10	27.4	27.2	20.4	1.1	23.12	19.8	2.3	3.2	6.1	17.2	30.3	20.1	18.11	2.9	23.9	8.4	14.10	29.8	16.12	28.10	—	16.9
Wigan Ath	12.9	9.9	2.3	16.3	29.8	6.1	13.4	25.11	2.4	4.11	20.1	21.10	16.12	6.4	23.12	7.10	4.5	23.9	3.2	2.1	20.2	19.8	24.2	—

OTHER FIXTURES—SEASON 1995–96

August
9 Wed Euro Comps Prel Rd–1st Leg
12 Sat Commencement of Football League season
13 Sun Littlewoods Pools FA Charity Shield—Wembley Stadium
16 Wed International Date
FL Coca-Cola Cup—1st Rd–1st Leg
19 Sat Commencement of FA Premier League season
23 Wed Euro Comps Prel Rd–2nd Leg
FL Coca-Cola Cup—1st Rd–2nd Leg
26 Sat FA Cup Sponsored by Littlewoods Pools—Prel Rd

September
2 Sat+ FA Carlsberg Vase—1st Rd Qual (*ex-Extra Prel Rd*)
Portugal v England (U21)
6 Wed International Date England v Croatia (F)
9 Sat FA Cup Sponsored by Littlewoods Pools—1st Rd Qual
FA Youth Cup—Extra Prel Rd*
13 Wed Euro Comps 1st Rd–1st Leg
16 Sat FA Umbro Trophy—Prel Rd (*if required*)
FA Youth Cup—Prel Rd
17 Sun FA Women's Cup—1st Rd
20 Wed FL Coca-Cola Cup—2nd Rd–1st Leg
23 Sat FA Cup Sponsored by Littlewoods Pools—2nd Rd Qual
24 Sun FA Sunday Cup—Prel Rd (*if required*)
27 Wed Euro Comps 1st Rd–2nd Leg
FL Auto Windscreens Shield—1st Rd–1st Leg
30 Sat FA Carlsberg Vase—2nd Rd Qual (*ex-Prel Rd*)

October
4 Wed FL Coca-Cola Cup—2nd Rd–2nd Leg
7 Sat+ FA Cup Sponsored by Littlewoods—3rd Rd Qual
FA Youth Cup—1st Rd Qual
10 Tue Norway v England (U21)
11 Wed Norway v England (F)
14 Sat FA Umbro Trophy—1st Rd Qual
FA County Youth Cup—1st Rd*
15 Sun FA Women's Cup—2nd Rd
18 Wed Euro Comps 2nd Rd–1st Leg
FL Auto Windscreens Shield–1st Rd–2nd Leg
21 Sat FA Cup Sponsored by Littlewoods Pools—4th Rd
FA Youth Cup—2nd Rd Qual*
25 Wed FL Coca-Cola Cup—3rd Rd
28 Sat FA Carlsberg Vase—1st Rd Proper
29 Sun FA Sunday Cup—1st Rd

November
1 Wed Euro Comps 2nd Rd–2nd Leg
4 Sat FA Umbro Trophy—2nd Rd Qual
8 Wed FL Coca-Cola Cup—3rd Rd Poss Replays
FL Auto Windscreens Shield—1st Rd–3rd Leg
11 Sat+ FA Cup Sponsored by Littlewoods Pools—1st Rd Proper
12 Sun FA Women's Cup—3rd Rd
14 Tue England v Austria (U21)
FA XI v Northern Premier League
15 Wed England v Switzerland (F)
18 Sat FA Carlsberg Vase—2nd Rd Proper
FA Youth Cup—1st Rd Proper*
19 Sun FA Sunday Cup—2nd Rd
22 Wed Euro Comps 3rd Rd–1st Leg
FA Cup Sponsored by Littlewoods Pools—1st Rd Poss Replays
25 Sat FA Umbro Trophy—3rd Rd Qual
FA County Youth Cup—2nd Rd*
29 Wed FL Coca-Cola Cup—4th Rd
FL Auto Windscreens Shield–2nd Rd

December
2 Sat FA Cup Sponsored by Littlewoods Pools—2nd Rd Proper
3 Sun FA Women's Cup—4th Rd
5 Tue FA XI v Isthmian League
6 Wed Euro Comps 3rd Rd–2nd Leg
9 Sat FA Carlsberg Vase—3rd Rd Proper
FA Youth Cup—2nd Rd Proper*
10 Sun FA Sunday Cup—3rd Rd
12 Tue Draw for Qualifying Competition of 1998 World Cup
13 Wed International Date
FA Cup Sponsored by Littlewoods Pools—2nd Rd Poss Replays
17 Sun Euro '96 Draw
20 Wed FL Coca-Cola Cup—4th Rd Replays

January 1996
6 Sat FA Cup Sponsored by Littlewoods Pools—3rd Rd Proper
9 Tues FA XI v British Students
10 Wed FL Coca-Cola Cup—5th Rd
FL Auto Windscreens Shield—Area Quarter Finals
13 Sat FA Carlsberg Vase—4th Rd Proper
FA Youth Cup—3rd Rd Proper*
FA County Youth Cup—3rd Rd*
14 Sun FA Sunday Cup—4th Rd
16 Tue FA XI v Combined Services
17 Wed FA Cup Sponsored by Littlewoods Pools—3rd Rd Poss Replays
20 Sat FA Umbro Trophy—1st Rd Proper
21 Sun FA Women's Cup—5th Rd
24 Wed International Date (*not UEFA*)
FL Coca-Cola Cup—5th Rd Poss Replays
27 Sat FA Cup Sponsored by Littlewoods Pools—4th Rd Proper
31 Wed FL Auto Windscreens Shield—Area Semi-Finals

February
3 Sat FA Carlsberg Vase—5th Rd Proper
7 Wed International Date (*not UEFA*)
FA Cup Sponsored by Littlewoods Pools—4th Rd Poss Replays
10 Sat FA Umbro Trophy—2nd Rd Proper
11 Sun FA Sunday Cup—5th Rd
FL Coca-Cola Cup—Semi-Final–1st Leg
14 Wed FL Coca-Cola Cup—Semi-Final–1st Leg
17 Sat FA Cup Sponsored by Littlewoods Pools—5th Rd Proper
FA Youth Cup—4th Round Proper*
FA County Youth Cup—4th Rd*
18 Sun FA Women's Cup—6th Rd
21 Wed FL Coca-Cola Cup—Semi Final–2nd Leg
24 Sat FA Carlsberg Vase—6th Rd Proper
25 Sun FL Coca-Cola Cup—Semi Final–2nd Leg
28 Wed FA Cup Sponsored by Littlewoods Pools—5th Rd Poss Replays

March
2 Sat FA Umbro Trophy—3rd Rd Proper
6 Wed Euro Comps Quarter Finals–1st Leg
FL Auto Windscreen Shield—Area Final–1st Leg
9 Sat FA Cup Sponsored by Littlewoods Pools—6th Rd Proper
FA Youth Cup—5th Rd Proper*
13 Wed FL Auto Windscreens Shield—Area Final–2nd Leg
16 Sat FA Carlsberg Vase—Semi-Final–1st Leg
FA County Youth Cup—Semi-Final*
17 Sun FA Sunday Cup—Semi-Finals
20 Wed Euro Comps Quarter Finals–2nd Leg
FA Cup Sponsored by Littlewoods Pools—6th Rd Poss Replays
23 Sat FA Umbro Trophy—4th Rd Proper
FA Carlsberg Vase—Semi-Final–2nd Leg
24 Sun FL Coca-Cola Cup—Final Tie—Wembley Stadium
FA Women's Cup—Semi-Finals
27 Wed International Date
FA Carlsberg Vase—Semi-Final Poss Replays (*prov*)
31 Sun FA Cup Sponsored by Littlewoods Pools—Semi-Finals

April
3 Wed Euro Comps Semi-Finals–1st Leg
FA Cup Sponsored by Littlewoods Pools—Semi-Finals Poss Replays
6 Sat FA Youth Cup—Semi-Final*
13 Sat FA Umbro Trophy—Semi-Final–1st Leg
14 Sun FL Auto Windscreens Shield—Final Tie—Wembley Stadium
17 Wed Euro Comps Semi Finals–2nd Leg
20 Sat+ FA Umbro Trophy—Semi-Final–2nd Leg
24 Wed International Date
FA Umbro Trophy—Semi-Final Poss Replays (*prov*)
27 Sat FA County Youth Cup Final (*fixed date*)
28 Sun FA Women's Cup—Final Tie (*venue to be decided*)

May
1 Wed UEFA Cup–1st Leg
4 Sat Final matches in FA Premier & Football League
5 Sun FA Sunday Cup—Final Tie (*venue to be decided*)
8 Wed European Cup Winners Cup Final (*venue to be decided*)
11 Sat FA Cup Sponsored by Littlewoods Pools—Final Tie—Wembley Stadium
FA Youth Cup—Final*
12 Sun FA Carlsberg Vase—Final Tie—Wembley Stadium
FL Play-Off Semi-Final–1st Leg
14 Tue FA Carlsberg Vase—Final Tie Poss Replay
15 Wed UEFA Cup Final–2nd Leg
FL Play-Off Semi-Final–2nd Leg
16 Thu FA Cup Sponsored by Littlewoods Pools—Final Tie Poss Replay
18 Sat Possible England International
19 Sun FA Umbro Trophy—Final Tie—Wembley Stadium
22 Wed European Champion Clubs' Cup Final
23 Thu FA Umbro Trophy—Final Tie Poss Replay
25 Sat FL Third Division Play-Off Final–Wembley Stadium
26 Sun FL Second Division Play-Off Final–Wembley Stadium
27 Mon FL First Division Play-Off Final–Wembley Stadium

REFEREEING AND THE REFEREES

The most fundamental change in the Laws of the Game for the 1995/96 Season is to alter the number of players allowed to take part in a match. Instead of two substitutes plus a goalkeeper (at any time) being available there is to be a switch to a fourteen man game with any three named substitutes taking part. This means that a team can choose in their absolute discretion either three outfield players or two outfield players and a goalkeeper. All competitions must now stipulate whether 3, 4, or 5 substitutes may be nominated.

As far as the field of play is concerned, a new mark *may* be made off the field of play eleven yards from the corner flag to ensure that distance is observed at the taking of a corner. Publicity may not be allowed on the field especially advertising on nets, corner flags, or goal posts. Finally it is recommended that actual markings be used to define the "Technical Area" when it is desired to incorporate such an area.

For the first time spitting has become a separate section under Fouls and Misconduct. There are now 10 penal offences rather than nine and at the taking of a penalty kick all players must now stand behind the penalty spot at a distance of 10 yards rather than merely standing 10 yards away from the penalty spot which has caused problems in the past.

Finally two existing practical situations are now officially incorporated into the Laws. Following on from last season's change in the Off-side Law a player will only be penalised for being in an off-side position if in the referee's opinion he is "involved in active play". The second inclusion is that the fourth match referee becomes officially recognised as it is now stated "the fourth official will assist the referee at all times".

The National List of Referees for the forthcoming Season consists of 67 men of whom the most senior is Mr David Allison of Lancaster. In all 15 officials left the List last Season of whom perhaps the most notable were FIFA referee Phil Don (retired through work commitments) ex-FIFA men Joe Worrall and Brian Hill and such stalwarts as Terry Holbrook, Kelvin Morton, Peter Fowkes and last season's Coca-Cola Cup Final fourth official Jim Parker.

The new men on the List are Messrs. Baines, Bennett, Fletcher, Frankland, Knight, Laws, Leake, Pearson, Stretton, Taylor and Wiley.

KEN GOLDMAN

The full List is as follows:

NATIONAL LIST OF REFEREES FOR SEASON 1995–96

Paul Alcock, (Redhill, Surrey)
David Allison, (Lancaster)
Gerald Ashby, (Worcester)
Mick Bailey, (Impington, Cambs.)
Steve Baines, (Chesterfield)
Graham Barber, (Warwick)
Neale Barry, (Scunthorpe)
Steve Bennett, (Dartford)
Martin Bodenham, (Looe, Cornwall)
John Brandwood, (Lichfield, Staffs.)
Kevin Breen, (Liverpool)
Keith Burge, (Tonypandy)
Bill Burns, (Scarborough)
Alan Butler, (Sutton-in-Ashfield)
George Cain, (Bootle)
Keith Cooper, (Pontypridd)
Keith A. Cooper, (Swindon)
Ian Cruikshanks, (Hartlepool)
Paul Danson, (Leicester)
Roger Dilkes, (Mossley, Lancs.)
Stephen Dunn, (Bristol)
Paul Durkin, (Portland, Dorset)
Andy D'Urso, (Billericay, Essex)
David Elleray, (Harrow-on-the-Hill)
Mick Fletcher, (Warley, West Midlands)
Graham Frankland, (Middlesbrough)
Roger Furnandiz, (Doncaster)
Dermot Gallagher, (Banbury, Oxon.)
Rodger Gifford, (Llanbradach, Mid. Glam.)
Bob Harris, (Oxford)
Robbie Hart, (Darlington)
Terry Heilbron, (Newton Aycliffe)
Ian Hemley, (Ampthill, Beds.)
Peter Jones, (Loughborough)
John Kirkby, (Sheffield)
Barry Knight, (Orpington)
David Laws, (Whitley Bay)
Ken Leach, (Brewood, Staffs.)
Tony Leake, (Darwen, Lancs.)
John Lloyd, (Wrexham)
Steve Lodge, (Barnsley)
Eddie Lomas, (Manchester)
Terry Lunt, (Ashton-in-Makerfield, Lancs.)
Kevin Lynch, (Knaresborough)
Scott Mathieson, (Stockport)
David Orr, (Iver, Bucks.)
Roy Pearson, (Peterlee, Durham)
Mick Pierce, (Portsmouth)
Graham Poll, (Tring, Hertfordshire)
Graham Pooley, (Bishops Stortford)
Richard Poulain, (Huddersfield)
Mike Reed, (Birmingham)
Paul Rejer, (Tipton, West Midlands)
Uriah Rennie, (Sheffield)
Phil Richards, (Preston)
Mike Riley, (Leeds)
Jim Rushton, (Stoke-on-Trent)
Gurnam Singh, (Wolverhampton)
Frazer Stretton, (Nottingham)
Paul Taylor, (Cheshunt, Hertfordshire)
Trever West, (Hull)
Alan Wiley, (Walsall)
Clive Wilkes, (Gloucester)
Alan Wilkie, (Chester-le-Street)
Gary Willard, (Worthing, W. Sussex)
Jeff Winter, (Stockton-on-Tees)
Eddie Wolstenholme, (Blackburn)

of horizontal equity: equal treatment of equals. When horizontal equity exists, two individuals who are identical in every relevant economic aspect achieve the same level of utility or satisfaction.

4. A widely embraced principle of process equity is equality of opportunity, that people should have equal access to whatever economic opportunities they are willing and able to pursue.
5. Process equity and end-results equity are linked by the principles of equality of opportunity and horizontal equity because equality of opportunity tends to produce horizontal equity.

The second section of the chapter described the use of models in economic analysis.

6. A model is a simplified description of reality that tries to capture the essential features of real-world issues and events. Economic models are conceptual versions of the natural scientist's controlled laboratory experiment. Like controlled experiments, economic models are useful for discovering cause-and-effect relationships because they allow the economist to study the effects of changing one economic variable while holding all other variables constant.
7. Economists always ask: What is true on the margin? The margin refers to the effects of small changes in an economic variable. Looking at the margin is important because it points the way to efficient solutions of the economic problem.

The third section of the chapter described the distinction between normative and positive economic analysis.

8. Normative analysis studies what ought to be. It develops the norms or criteria for judging the solutions to economic problems and the results of economic exchanges. The two norms in economic analysis are efficiency and equity. Normative analysis also determines the objectives of an economic problem. All normative statements are based on value judgments; they cannot be proved or disproved.
9. Positive analysis studies what is. It describes the alternatives and constraints of the economic problem and indicates how the alternatives relate to both the objectives and the constraints. Positive analysis also describes how the conditions under which economic exchanges take place determine the results of the exchanges. Positive statements can be tested with real-world data; in principle, they can be shown to be true or false.

The final section of Chapter 2 discussed the distinction between microeconomics and macroeconomics.

10. Microeconomics studies the economy "in the small." It focuses on the economic problems of individual consumers, business firms, and government agencies; the incentives that motivate them to engage in economic exchanges with one another, and the results of their economic exchanges for particular products and factors of production.
11. Macroeconomics studies the economy "in the large." It focuses on the overall level of economic activity. Economists use four objectives to judge the performance of an economy: full employment, price stability, long-run economic growth, and stability in a nation's international economic relations.

of choices lets the brightest students reach their full academic potential, but leaves the average students behind. Another set of choices improves the education of all students to some extent, but leaves the brightest students far short of achieving their full academic potential. The town will have to appeal to its sense of what is fair to determine which set of choices is better (assuming they cost the same).

Analyzing Economic Exchange

Regarding economic exchange, normative analysis establishes the norms for judging the effectiveness of economic exchanges. Economists judge economic exchanges using the norms of efficiency and equity, the same norms used to judge the solutions to economic problems.

The positive analysis of exchange describes the actual conditions under which exchange takes place and determines the implications of those conditions. Exchange occurs in a number of different environments. Wheat is produced by thousands of farmers and turned into a wide variety of products that reach hundreds of millions of consumers each day. The consumers and farmers never actually meet. Airplanes, in contrast, are produced by a handful of business firms and sold to a small number of other firms and to governments. The buyers and sellers are in close contact with each other. What results can be expected in each of these environments? What will the prices be? The quantities exchanged? Will the exchanges be orderly? The norms of efficiency and equity complete the analysis. Will the exchanges generate an efficient allocation of resources? Will they be even-handed and fair to all parties.

Positive analysis also describes how economic exchanges respond to government policy initiatives. How will individuals and business firms react to a 1 percent increase in a state's sales tax? If the federal government adds $5 billion to its educational grant-in-aid programs for state and local governments, will state and local spending for education increase by $5 billion? By more than $5 billion? By less than $5 billion? Positive analysis of this kind is obviously central to the conduct of effective government policy. The best of intentions can easily go awry if governments misjudge the responses to their policies.

MICROECONOMICS AND MACROECONOMICS

The study of economics is traditionally divided into microeconomics and macroeconomics. This text follows that tradition.

Microeconomics

As the name suggests, **microeconomics** studies the economy "in the small." Microeconomics takes snapshots of tiny sections of the economy and magnifies them. It focuses on (1) the economic problems of individual consumers, business firms, and government agencies; (2) the incentives that motivate them to engage in economic exchanges with one another; and (3) the results of their economic exchanges for particular products and factors of production, such as automobiles or labor. The vast majority of economic exchanges take place in

MICROECONOMICS
The study of the economy "in the small"; analyzes the economic problems of individual economic agents and the exchanges between them.

organized markets in the U.S. economy. Therefore, our study of microeconomics will concentrate on how markets work in the United States.

Microeconomics attempts to answer the following kinds of questions: Why do markets form so easily? What causes the prices of individual products to rise and fall? Should the government give poor families food stamps as well as cash? Is good weather necessarily good for farmers? Does minimum wage legislation prevent teen-agers from finding jobs? Why do 30 million Americans live in poverty? How do large corporations use their market power to increase their profits? To what extent does discrimination explain the fact that women receive lower wages than men? Are U.S. markets generally efficient or inefficient? Will the job prospects of college graduates improve over the next five years? Do taxes destroy people's incentives to work?

You will be better able to answer these questions when you have completed the microeconomic chapters.

Macroeconomics

MACROECONOMICS
The study of the economy "in the large"; analyzes the overall performance of the economy.

FULL EMPLOYMENT
The condition when all people who want to work have a job.

UNEMPLOYMENT
The condition when people are actively looking for work, but are unable to find a suitable job.

PRICE STABILITY
Prices in general are neither rising nor falling.

PRICE INFLATION
A persistent increase in the prices of most goods and services.

LONG-RUN ECONOMIC GROWTH
A continuing process in which the economy is able to produce ever-increasing amounts of goods and services year after year.

STABLE DOLLAR
The value of the dollar remains constant relative to the currencies of other nations.

Macroeconomics studies the economy "in the large," that is, the overall performance of the economy. It focuses on aggregate data such as the total consumption by all consumers, the total investment in plant and equipment by all business firms, the combined spending of all government agencies, the entirety of U.S. economic interactions with the other nations of the world, the total employment in all labor markets, and the total income earned and output produced by all factors of production.

Economists judge the overall performance of an economy on the basis of four broad objectives called the macroeconomic policy goals: full employment, price stability, long-run economic growth, and stability in a nation's international economic relations.

- **Full employment** exists whenever there is a job for all people who want to work. **Unemployment** exists whenever people are actively looking for work, but are unable to find a suitable job.
- **Price stability** occurs whenever prices in general are neither rising nor falling. Most nations today wrestle with the problem of **price inflation,** which is a persistent increase in the prices of most goods and services.
- **Long-run economic growth** is taking place whenever the economy is able to produce ever-increasing amounts of goods and services year after year.
- **Stability in international economic relations** has two dimensions. One is achieving an equality between the value of the nation's imports from other countries and the value of its exports to other countries. The other is achieving a stable dollar. A **stable dollar** exists whenever the value of the dollar remains constant relative to the currencies of other nations, such as the Japanese yen or French franc.

Pursuing the first three macroeconomic policy goals is a matter or law in the United States. Both the Employment Act of 1946 and the Humphrey-Hawkins Act of 1978 require the federal government to formulate economic policies that promote maximum employment, production (growth), and purchasing power (stable prices). No U.S. laws require an equality between imports and exports or a stable dollar, but even the most casual observer of economic events knows that the United States is deeply concerned about each of these issues.

The United States does not usually attempt to achieve the macroeconomic policy goals directly. National, state, and local governments do not routinely employ all the unemployed. Governments directly control only a very few prices. No government can dictate the rate of economic growth. The federal government does place some direct controls on international trade and makes some attempts to influence the value of the dollar, but by and large trade is free, and the value of the dollar is set in the marketplace. The federal government's macroeconomic policies are directed instead toward the overall level of economic activity. The idea is to try to achieve the macroeconomic policy goals indirectly by influencing the performance of the entire economy.

The macroeconomic policy record over the past twenty years has not been especially impressive. Unemployment averaged 6.1 percent of the labor force in the 1970s, 7.2 percent in the 1980s, and 6.5 percent in the first three years of the 1990s. These percentages are higher than the American public, and many economists, are willing to accept. Prices have not been stable. They rose an average of 7.1 percent per year in the 1970s, 5.6 percent per year in the 1980s, and 4.1 percent in the first three years of the 1990s. Since 1973 the rate of economic growth has been far below its trend for the entire twentieth century. The United States has not been able to achieve equality between its imports and exports. The value of imports has greatly exceeded the value of exports since 1981. Finally, the dollar has been very unstable. The value of the dollar fell steadily relative to most foreign currencies throughout most of the 1970s, rose sharply in the early and mid-1980s, and then fell again in the late 1980s and into the 1990s.

REFLECTION: Whic macroeconomic policy Clinton administration concerned about? The about?

The macroeconomic chapters will explain how the government's macroeconomic policies attempt to achieve the macroeconomic policy goals and why they often do not succeed.

SUMMARY

The first section of Chapter 2 discussed the two criteria that economists use to judge the solutions to economic problems, efficiency and equity.

1. The meaning of efficiency depends on whether the economic problem has one or more objectives.
   a. If the economic problem has a single objective, then efficiency means coming as close to the objective as possible. If the objective has no natural limit, then efficiency means maximizing the objective. For example, a firm is efficient if it is maximizing its profit.
   b. If the economic problem has more than one objective, then efficiency means that the Law of Substitution holds: A solution is efficient if moving closer to one objective requires moving farther away from at least one other objective.
2. Equity has two dimensions, end-results equity and process equity. End-results equity judges whether economic outcomes are fair. Process equity judges whether the rules under which the economy operates are fair.
3. Economic events and policies invariably help some people and harm others. The fundamental question of end-results equity is how to evaluate and compare the benefits of those who gain against the losses of those who lose. The only consensus that has emerged on this question is the principle

KEY TERMS

consumer sovereignty
efficiency
end-results equity
equality of opportunity
full employment
horizontal equity
Law of Substitution
long-run economic growth
macroeconomics
the margin
microeconomics
model
normative economic analysis
positive economic analysis
price inflation
process equity
stable dollar

QUESTIONS

1. Economists are often criticized because their economic models do not fully and accurately describe the "real world." How might economists defend themselves against this charge?
2. a. What is the distinction between end-results and process equity?
   b. President Clinton has expressed concern that the wealthiest people in the United States gained relative to everyone else during the 1980s. Is his concern one of end-results equity or process equity?
3. What is the main difference between microeconomics and macroeconomics?
4. Many firms in the United States today are "downsizing," reducing the number of employees to lower their production costs. Why does the downsizing phenomenon fall within the realm of both microeconomics and macroeconomics?
5. What is the Law of Substitution, and how does it relate to the concept of efficiency?
6. Suppose that a farmer can grow either corn or wheat on his land. He thinks about different ways of planting the land and comes up with the following possible combinations of corn and wheat output. The numbers are in thousands of bushels.

CORN	WHEAT
100	0
75	60
50	50
45	75
35	60
0	95

   Are any of these possibilities clearly inefficient? Why?
7. Which of the following statements are normative, and which are positive?
   a. Baseball players make too much money.
   b. The price of computer equipment usually starts to fall after it has been on the market for a long time.
   c. A 50-cent-a-gallon gasoline tax will cause some commuters to shift from using automobiles to public transportation.
   d. Charging a toll on the turnpike is fair because those who use the turnpike pay for its construction and maintenance.
8. Suppose Brenda knows the exact value that she derives from eating "buffalo wings" (chicken wings) in terms of money.

NUMBER OF WINGS EATEN	BRENDA'S TOTAL VALUE
1	$1.00
2	2.00
3	2.90
4	3.70
5	4.30
6	4.60
7	4.55

   a. What is the marginal value to Brenda of eating the fourth buffalo wing? Of eating the sixth buffalo wing?
   b. *Extra credit:* If buffalo wings cost $.50 each, how many will Brenda buy? How many will she eat if they are free?

CHAPTER

3

Society's Economic Problem

LEARNING OBJECTIVES

CONCEPTS TO LEARN

Society's economic problem

The four fundamental economic questions

1. The what or output question
2. The how or input question
3. The for whom or distribution question
4. The now versus the future question

The production possibilities frontier

Long-run economic growth

The elements of an economic system

Pure market capitalism

Centrally planned socialism

CONCEPTS TO RECALL

The three-part economic problem [1]

Interdependence [1]

Opportunity cost [1]

Efficiency [2]

Equity [2]

In 1989 the seven Eastern European countries of Bulgaria, Czechoslovakia, East Germany, Hungary, Poland, Romania, and Yugoslavia quite literally stunned the world. They declared their freedom from decades of Soviet political and economic domination, completely rejected communism, and announced that they were going to abandon their current economic systems in favor of a completely different type of system. The only modern example of such an abrupt and total transformation of such large economies occurred in the former Soviet Union following the Russian Revolution in 1917. The Soviet example does not offer much of a guideline for the Eastern European countries, however, because the Soviets adopted an economic system that was tightly controlled by the national government. The Eastern European countries chose to go in the opposite direction. They cast off the tight reigns of centrally planned socialism in favor of a decentralized market economy.

Events since 1989 have shown that the transformation to capitalism will not come easily. West Germany immediately offered to serve as a benefactor to the East Germans as part of the reunification of Germany. The other countries were not so lucky. The tragic war among Croats, Serbs, and Muslims tore apart the former Yugoslavia, and Czechoslovakia split in two. The world watches anxiously as the great social and economic experiments in Eastern Europe unfold.

The economic problem is not limited to individuals, business firms, and government agencies. Society as a whole faces the standard economic problem with its objectives, alternatives, and constraints. Chapter 3 describes society's economic problem and the difficult choices that all societies have to make as they try to find the best solution to their respective economic problems.

Each of the seven Eastern European countries named above concluded in 1989 that market capitalism would do a far better job of solving its economic problem than centrally planned socialism had done. We will return to their prospects for success in transforming their economies after describing society's economic problem.

SOCIETY'S ECONOMIC PROBLEM

Modern economies are incredibly complex. Billions of exchanges of goods and services and factors of production take place every day, themselves the results of billions of economic decisions by individuals, business firms, and government agencies. No one can possibly comprehend the workings of an entire economy. The best we can do is gain a broad perspective on what is taking place within the economy and what is being accomplished. An excellent way to gain this perspective is to think of society as facing a giant economic problem consisting of objectives, alternatives, and constraints. Then we can view all economic activity as an attempt to solve society's economic problem, for better or worse. Using the economic problem to organize your thinking about an economy is especially helpful in understanding what a society expects from its economy. It is also helpful in judging whether an economy is performing anywhere near to its potential.

What is the structure of society's economic problem? What are the principal economic objectives, alternatives, and constraints for society as a whole?

Objectives

Humanism, the intellectual and philosophical movement that swept through Europe during the Middle Ages and gave rise to the Renaissance, stressed the interests of individuals over religion or the natural world. Those of us living in the Western Hemisphere have been raised in the humanist tradition. We take for granted that the primary goal of a nation's economy is to improve the economic well-being of its citizens. What exactly does this goal mean, however?

A humanistic society would undoubtedly like to make each of its members as well off as possible, or at least try to ensure that all people can develop their full economic potential. Uplifting as these goals may be, neither can serve as an economic objective for society, nor even as an ideal to strive for. These objectives are not merely unattainable; they are meaningless.

An overall economy is subject to the Law of Scarcity, just as are all its individual consumers, business firms, and government agencies. The Law of Substitution must eventually apply, no matter what choices are made among the various alternatives, simply because resources are limited. Giving more resources to some people so they can be better off necessarily means that other people must sacrifice—they are made worse off. Resources used to help me achieve my full economic potential are not available to help you achieve your full economic potential.

If societies cannot maximize each person's economic well-being or potential, then what economic objectives can they pursue? The answers are the two objectives discussed in Chapter 2, efficiency and equity.

Although a humanistic society cannot try to make everyone as well off as possible, it can strive to be efficient, to ensure that the Law of Substitution does hold. A society would not want to waste its scarce resources by being able to improve the economic well-being of some of its members without sacrifice to any other members. Economic efficiency is a fundamental objective of all humanistic societies.

Most economies generate fairly wide disparities in income. Some people are poor, and others are quite rich, with the remainder filling up the middle. A humanistic society will be moved to ask whether this situation is fair and, if not, what should be done about it. A society can never be content unless it perceives that people are being treated fairly in economic matters. Equity is also a fundamental economic objective of all humanistic societies.

Alternatives

A society is confronted with innumerable economic choices in its pursuit of efficiency and equity. Economists divide these choices into four broad categories, posed as the four fundamental questions that every society must answer: What? How? For Whom? Now versus the Future? These questions incorporate the two objectives of efficiency and equity along with the alternatives.

WHAT OR OUTPUT QUESTION

Asks what goods and services the economy will produce and in what quantities; one of the four fundamental economic questions that every society must answer.

THE *WHAT* OR *OUTPUT* QUESTION What goods and services will the economy produce, and in what quantities? The output question refines the efficiency and equity objectives by recognizing that people's economic well-being ultimately depends on what goods and services they consume. Different people have different tastes. A teen-ager and an elderly person with the same incomes undoubtedly want to consume different kinds of goods and services. Tastes also change over time. For instance, American consumers as a whole are now spending a much higher percentage of their incomes on health care and a much lower percentage on food than they did in 1950. To be fully efficient and equitable, therefore, an economy must be responsive to individual preferences.

Consumers ultimately answer the What question in a market economy such as the United States, even though business firms produce the goods and services. The pursuit of profits leads firms to respond to consumers' desires as they decide what, and how much, to produce. Firms try to guess what consumers want to buy. If they guess right, they do well; if not, they lose. Business firms do try to influence consumers' purchases through advertising and related sales techniques, and they no doubt succeed to some extent. For the most part, however, firms respond to the demands of consumers. Consumers in the United States buy what they want within the limitations of their budgets.

HOW OR INPUT QUESTION

Asks how the economy produces its goods and services; one of the four fundamental economic questions that every society must answer.

THE *HOW* OR *INPUT* QUESTION Once business firms decide what goods and services to provide, how will they produce each one of them? There are usually many different ways to produce any one good or service, and, in fact, similar products tend to be produced very differently throughout the world, even in different regions within a country. The Japanese use robotics in manufacturing their automobiles far more than the U.S. auto makers do. Textiles are produced very differently worldwide, the techniques varying from hand weaving to the use of extremely sophisticated machinery. Methods of farming also vary considerably throughout the world. There are nearly as many examples as there are products.

PRODUCTION TECHNOLOGY

A blueprint or method for transforming inputs into outputs.

Answering the How question involves choosing a **production technology,** which is a blueprint or method for transforming inputs into outputs. The inputs are the factors of production: labor, land and natural resources, capital, and semi-finished material inputs. The outputs are the goods and services. Technologies are products of people's minds. Scientists, engineers, and other people directly involved in production processes are continually inventing new materials, different machinery, and more effective ways of utilizing already existing resources. Most production technologies become widely known soon after they have been invented; keeping ideas a secret is very difficult.

Even so, the choice of technology is an economic problem, not just a scientific or an engineering problem of using the latest technologies hot off the drawing board. The reason for this is that different technologies require different kinds of resources, and similar kinds of resources are not at all equally available worldwide. Some countries have lots of capital and a highly skilled labor force. Other countries have relatively little capital and mostly unskilled labor. If the resources that are readily available are not particularly well suited to the latest technology, then using an older technology that the resources are suited for makes good *economic* sense. All societies have an economic interest in producing each unit of output with the least expenditure of their scarce resources. They have no particular interest in using the latest technologies.

THE *FOR WHOM* OR *DISTRIBUTION* QUESTION The For Whom question asks: Who will receive the various goods and services produced in answer to the What question? As such, it recognizes the fundamental importance of equity in the presence of scarce resources and is therefore as much one of the objectives as it is one of the alternatives.

FOR WHOM OR DISTRIBUTION QUESTION
Asks who will receive the various goods and services that are produced; one of the four fundamental economic questions that every society must answer.

The For Whom question is determined primarily by the quantity and quality of the resources that each individual owns in a market economy. Labor, land, and funds supplied to firms for purchasing capital are the sources of income, and people's incomes determine in large part what they are able to consume. Are you willing to work long hours? Are you highly educated or relatively unskilled? Is there much demand for whatever skills you do possess? Do you own land that is valuable to farmers or mining companies or developers? Have you inherited vast amounts of wealth that can be lent to business firms for them to buy plant and equipment? The answers to such questions determine whether you number among the haves or have-nots in a market economy.

The For Whom question is not just a matter of equity. It also has an important efficiency dimension to it in a market economy. The incomes people earn for their labor, land, and capital reflect how scarce their resources are relative to the demand for them. People have an incentive to supply more of the resources that are relatively scarce and thus earn high incomes. At the same time, high incomes translate into high input prices from the point of view of the business firms, so firms have an incentive to use less of the resources that are relatively scarce. The opposite incentives apply when resources earn low incomes. We shall discover in later chapters why both of these incentives are crucial to the efficient operation of a market economy.

The What, How, and For Whom questions are closely interrelated in a market economy. For example, large numbers of people decided during the 1980s that they would rather rent movies and watch them at home on their VCRs than attend movie theaters. This choice was made possible, of course, through the introduction of new technologies associated with the video cassette and the VCR, an example of a change in answering the How question. Firms responded to the consumers' desires as expected. VCR and video cassette production expanded rapidly, as did the number of stores that rent video cassette movies. At the same time, a number of movie theaters closed. A decided change occurred in answering the What question. Finally, resources specific to video cassette production and distribution found their incomes increasing, whereas resources specific to the movie theaters lost income. Some of the answers to the For Whom question changed as well.

THE *NOW* VERSUS THE *FUTURE* QUESTION Should society favor the current generation at the expense of future generations, or the reverse? At issue here is long-run economic growth, the rate of growth of income or output over time. As a general rule, faster rates of growth favor future generations over the current generation and slower rates of growth favor the current generation over future generations. We will consider the economic issues associated with the growth question in the next section of this chapter.

NOW VERSUS THE FUTURE QUESTION
Asks whether society will favor the current generation over future generations, or the reverse; one of the four fundamental economic questions that every society must answer.

Constraints

PRODUCTION POSSIBILITIES
The economy's capacity for producing goods and services, assuming that it produces them efficiently.

The level of economic well-being that a nation can enjoy is ultimately limited by its **production possibilities,** defined as its capacity for producing goods and services. The production possibilities, in turn, depend on (1) the quantity and quality of a nation's primary factors of production and (2) the technologies available for turning these resources into goods and services.

Regarding the factors of production, larger countries can produce more than smaller countries can simply because they are larger, other things equal. Their business firms have access to more labor and more funds to purchase capital. Larger quantities of land, other things equal, support more agricultural activity and supply more natural resources. But other things might not be equal. The quality of a nation's resources matters as well. Are workers literate and well educated? Are they healthy? Are they industrious, inventive, and interested in self-improvement? Is the plant and equipment modern? Is much of the land suitable for farming—level, well drained, rich in nutrients, and located in temperate climates? Does the land contain high-grade natural resources that are easily accessible? Nations that can answer yes to most of these questions invariably rank among the world's richest countries. Particularly important are the quality of the labor force and the total amount of capital in place for the labor to work with. Size alone is not enough for economic well-being.

For instance, China and India are the two most populous nations and rank second and eighth in land area. Because they are so large, their economies produce large quantities of goods and services, but they are both among the world's poorest countries in terms of income *per person,* the most commonly used measure of economic well-being. China and India are held back by the quality of their labor. Their workers are generally poorly educated and unskilled, not at all well suited to work with modern production technologies. Also, neither China nor India has been able to provide their workers with enough capital to make them highly productive.

Japan is a relatively small country compared with China or India. It ranks seventh among the world's countries in population and is only one-tenth the size of India and one-thirtieth the size of China in land area. It also has relatively few natural resources. But Japan ranks fourth among the world's countries in income per person. In contrast to China and India, its workers are highly skilled and able to adapt to modern technologies, and the Japanese economy has provided relatively large amounts of capital to each worker.

The production technologies that are available to business firms clearly affect a nation's production possibilities. Innovations such as the steam engine in the early 1800s, electricity in the late 1800s and early 1900s, and the modern, high-speed computer over the past 30 years each had obvious and dramatic effects on production possibilities worldwide. As noted above, however, technology and the quality of a nation's resources are closely interrelated. The latest advances in technology may be well known to a nation's business firms, but they will have little actual impact on production if the nation's resources are unsuited for them.

PRODUCTION POSSIBILITIES FRONTIER
A graphical representation of the economy's capacity for producing goods and services, assuming that it produces them efficiently.

THE PRODUCTION POSSIBILITIES FRONTIER The notion that a society is constrained by its production possibilities can be represented by a simple diagram

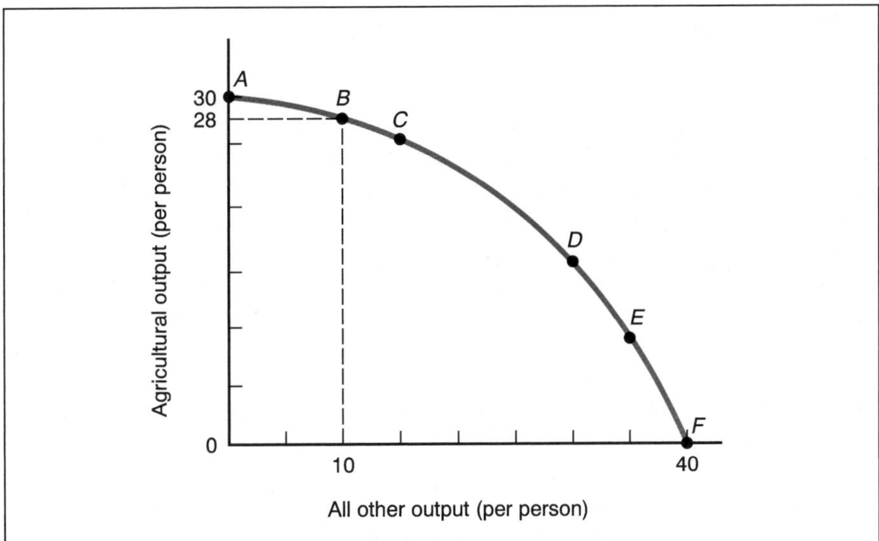

FIGURE 3.1

The Production Possibilities Frontier

The solid line is the production possibilities frontier for the hypothetical data in Table 3.1. The frontier shows the combinations of agricultural output and all other output, per person, that the economy is able to produce, assuming that production is efficient. At point *A*, society puts all its resources into agriculture and is able to produce 30 units of agricultural output. At point *F*, society puts all its resources into all other goods and services and is able to produce 40 units of all other output. Points *B*, *C*, *D*, and *E* show different combinations of agricultural output and all other output that the economy is able to produce as it transfers some resources from agriculture to all other goods and services, or vice-versa.

known as the **production possibilities frontier.** To construct the frontier, everything that is produced must be placed into one of two categories so that production can be represented in two dimensions. Let's begin by dividing all production into agricultural output and all other output of goods and services. Represent the quantity of agricultural output per person on the vertical axis and the quantity of all other output per person on the horizontal axis, as in Figure 3.1. The figure corresponds with the data in Table 3.1. These data are completely hypothetical and are only meant to illustrate some of the properties of the production possibilities frontier. The data do not even have well-defined

TABLE 3.1 **Production Possibilities for a Hypothetical Economy**

POINTS	AGRICULTURAL OUTPUT PER PERSON	ALL OTHER OUTPUT PER PERSON
A	30	0
B	28	10
C	25	15
D	17	30
E	9	35
F	0	40

units because they represent combinations of many different kinds of goods and services.

Suppose, first, that society devotes all its resources to the production of agricultural output, using the farming technologies best suited to its resources. There would be some maximum amount of agricultural output attainable, 30 units according to our hypothetical data, represented by distance 0*A* in Figure 3.1. Alternatively, imagine that society devotes all its resources to the production of all other non-agricultural output, choosing the most suitable technology in each instance. There would be some maximum amount of all other output attainable, 40 units according to our hypothetical data, represented by distance 0*F* in Figure 3.1. Notice that the end points of the production possibilities frontier have different values. There is no necessary relationship between the distances 0*A* and 0*F*, since different kinds of goods (and services) are being produced at each point.

To determine the other points on the frontier, return to point *A*. Imagine taking a few resources out of agricultural production and using them to produce all other output. Do so in a manner that provides the best possible answer to the How question. That is, take the resources that are best suited to all other production and least suited to farming. Also, combine the resources now available to each category of output such that they can produce the maximum possible agricultural and all other output. Suppose that production moves to point *B*, with agricultural production dropping to 28 units and all other production increasing from zero to 10 units. The 28 units of agricultural output and 10 units of all other output at point *B* represent the maximum possible production of agricultural and all other output, given the resources allocated to each category. Continuing to transfer resources from agriculture to all other goods and services in like manner, always providing the best possible answer to the How question, we locate points *C, D, E,* and so forth. When we have transferred all resources to all other output, production again takes place at point *F*. The curve *ABCDEF* is society's *production possibilities frontier*. A number of its properties are worth noting.

THE PRODUCTION POSSIBILITIES FRONTIER AND THE CONSTRAINTS The distance of the frontier from the origin is the most direct representation of the underlying constraints that limit how well off a society can be. Figure 3.2 depicts the relative positions of the production possibilities frontiers for a resource-rich country and a resource-poor country. The resource-rich country is endowed with large quantities of high-quality resources that can be adapted to the very latest production technologies. Its frontier is relatively far from the origin. The resource-poor country is less fortunate. Its production choices lie well inside those of the resource-rich country, and its frontier is relatively close to the origin.

INCREASING OPPORTUNITY COSTS ALONG THE FRONTIER Notice that the production possibilities frontiers depicted in Figures 3.1 and 3.2 are bowed outward from the origin. As such, they are said to represent *increasing cost* production, in the sense of *increasing opportunity cost.* To see why a bowed-out frontier represents increasing opportunity cost, refer to Figure 3.3, which reproduces Figure 3.1.

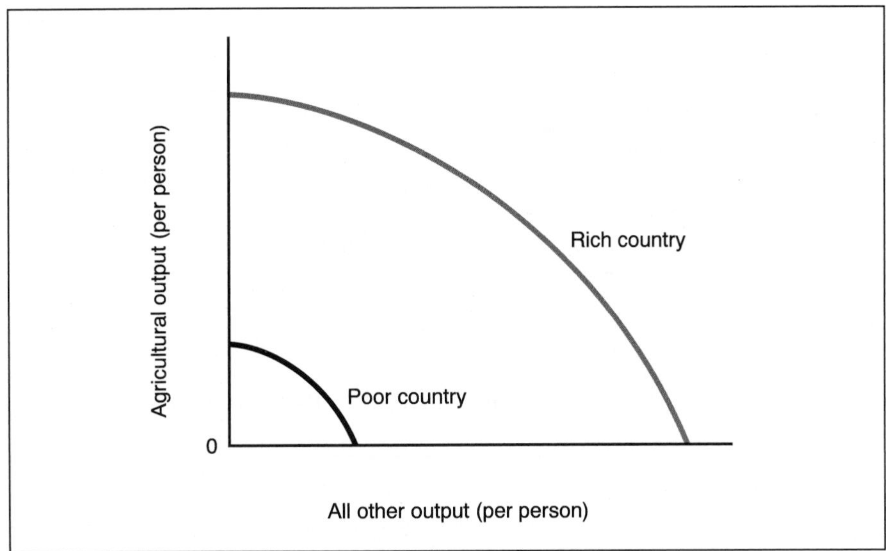

FIGURE 3.2

Production Possibilities Frontiers: Rich versus Poor Countries

The production possibilities frontier of a rich country is much farther away from the origin than the production possibilities frontier of a poor country. The rich country can produce many more goods and services per person than the poor country can because it has more high-quality resources and can use more productive technologies.

Note, first, that the Law of Substitution holds at all points along the frontier. Increasing production of all other output can occur only by reducing agricultural output, and vice versa. Since both goods are desirable, the cost of producing additional amounts of all other output is defined as the quantity of agricultural output that must be foregone. In other words, the cost of increasing all other output is an opportunity cost. In Figure 3.3 the opportunity cost of increasing all other output from 10 units at point *B* to 15 units at point *C* is the 3 units of agricultural output sacrificed in moving from *B* to *C* (3 = 28 − 25).

When the frontier is bowed outward from the origin, the opportunity cost of producing all other output increases as resources continue to be transferred out of agriculture into all other output. To see this, compare the move from points *D* to *E* with the move from points *B* to *C*. All other output increases by 5 units in each instance [5 = (15 − 10) = (35 − 30)]. But the opportunity cost in terms of lost agricultural output is 8 units in moving from *D* to *E* (8 = 17 − 9), whereas it was only 3 units in moving from *B* to *C*. The opportunity costs of increasing all other output have increased from point *B* to point *D*.

Increasing opportunity cost almost certainly applies to actual economies because some resources are better suited to certain activities than to others. At point *B* in Figure 3.3 most of society's resources are being used to farm. No doubt many of those resources are not very productive in farming—perhaps because of hilly terrain, infertile soil, or people who have neither the talent nor taste for farming. Much of this land and many of these people would be far more productive in producing other goods and services. If these resources are transferred in order to increase all other output from *B* (10 units) to *C* (15 units), it is possible to increase all other output with very little cost at all in terms of lost agricultural output. At point *D*, however, many of society's scarce resources are already producing all other output. Presumably only those resources better suited to agricultural production remain in the agricultural sector. Now, if society wishes to increase the production of all other goods and services, it can do so only at relatively great sacrifice of agricultural production.

FIGURE 3.3

The Increasing Cost Production Possibilities Frontier

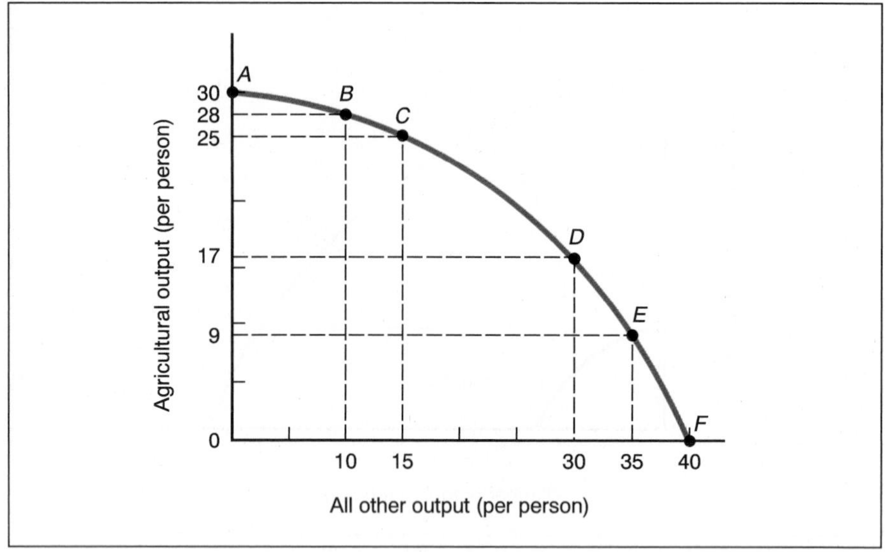

The production possibilities frontier is bowed outward from the origin because of increasing opportunity costs of production. Society must sacrifice ever increasing amounts of agricultural output for each additional unit of all other output that it produces as it increases production of all other output. The opportunity costs increase along the frontier because some resources are better suited to certain activities than to other activities.

This example is hardly unrealistic. History long ago taught us that farmers often have great difficulty leaving the farm to work in factories in a more urban environment. The slogan "women and children first" did not originate on a sinking ship. It was the hiring policy of the English textile mills at the beginning of the Industrial Revolution. Mill operators discovered very quickly that men did not take well to the long hours and dull routine of the factories. They became restless, irritable, and destructive. Women and children had fewer alternatives for work and were relatively more docile and productive as factory workers. Many of them had previously been domestics of various kinds in the feudal society of pre-Industrial England, if they had worked outside the home at all. Many farmers who left their farms in England journeyed to the New World to continue farming, rather than work in the English mills.

THE PRODUCTION POSSIBILITIES FRONTIER AND EFFICIENCY All points along the production possibilities frontier represent efficient combinations of agricultural outputs and all other outputs. Society would like to produce more of each kind of output than it is able to. In a production context, therefore, efficiency requires that in order to have more of one kind of output, society must sacrifice some of the other output. But this is always true along the frontier, where the Law of Substitution holds.

Which is most efficient among points *A*, *B*, *C*, *D*, *E*, and *F* in Figure 3.1? The question has no meaning. These points each satisfy the requirements of production efficiency; they each represent the best possible resolution of the How question, given the resources allocated to each output. Nothing more can be said. Only if we bring in the desires of consumers for each product can a

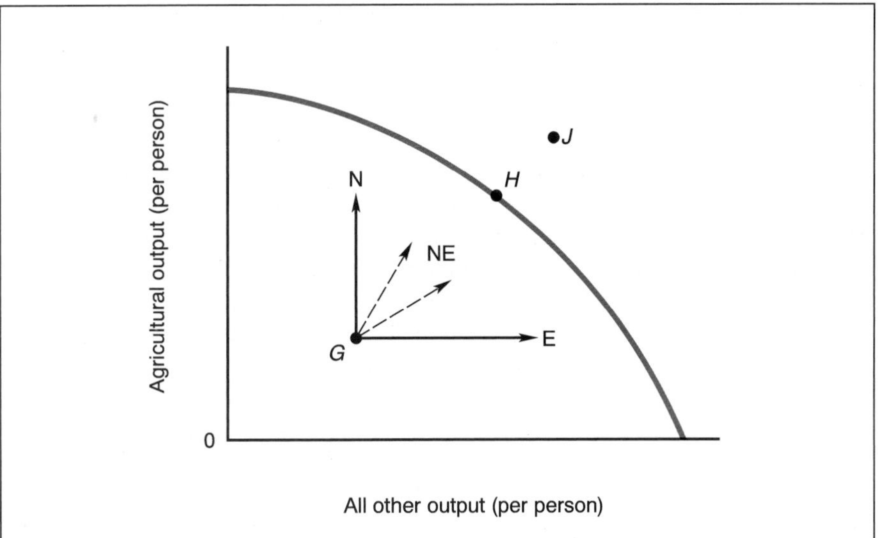

FIGURE 3.4

Efficient, Inefficient, and Unattainable Production Points

All points such as point *H* on the production possibilities frontier are efficient because the Law of Substitution holds: To produce more of all other output society must reduce its production of agricultural output, and vice-versa. All points such as *G* that lie inside the frontier are possible but inefficient. By reallocating its scarce resources, society can move north, east, or northeast of *G*, producing more of one kind of good without reducing its production of the other kind of good, or producing more of both kinds of goods. Points such as *J* beyond the frontier are unattainable given the quantity and quality of the nation's resources and the available production technologies.

best point be determined. But this would be decided on the basis of efficiency defined in terms of individuals' well-being, not simply in terms of production.

All points inside the production possibilities frontier are inefficient, however. Consider point *G* in Figure 3.4. Since *G* lies inside the frontier, it is possible to move north, east, or northeast of *G* on the graph by reallocating resources to better answer the How question. A move to the north brings more agricultural output without sacrificing any output of all other goods and services. Similarly, a move to the east increases all other output without sacrificing any agricultural output. A move to the northeast brings more output of both goods. Since both goods are desirable, presumably any of these reallocations would be preferred to *G*. If possible, society should keep reallocating resources until it hits the frontier. Only then are these free gains of output exhausted. In other words, there is always some point on the frontier that dominates a given point under the frontier.

Why might an economy be producing beneath its production possibilities frontier? There are two possible causes. Either society is not using all of its scarce resources, or it is not allocating the scarce resources it is using in the best possible manner. The latter problem always exists to some extent, since no society can hope to allocate every last resource exactly as required for production efficiency. But when market economies produce far below their potential, as the U.S. economy did in the early 1980s, the primary culprit is unused resources. In the depths of the 1981–82 recession, industrial production sank to 75 percent of its capacity, and over 10.6 million workers were unemployed, representing 9.5 percent of the labor force. During the Great Depression of the 1930s, unemployment in the United States exceeded 14 percent every year from 1931 through 1940 and exceeded 20 percent annually from 1932 through 1936. Unused resources of these magnitudes clearly dominate any inefficiencies caused by misallocating the resources that are being used.

Economists are fond of counseling: "There is no such thing as a free lunch." They are referring to the principle of opportunity cost, that a decision to do something implies some other opportunity foregone. But the comparison between efficient and inefficient production points illustrates that this advice is somewhat misleading. There is no free lunch only if decisions are made efficiently. There are, for example, no free lunches along the production possibilities frontier. Free lunches abound, however, whenever decisions are made inefficiently. We saw that production increases can be made from point *G* in Figure 3.4 in any number of ways without any cost whatsoever. Indeed, an economist's particular expertise lies in discovering free lunches by advising people how to allocate their resources more effectively. Without free lunches economists would go hungry!

Here is a final thought along these same lines. Employing a worker who would otherwise be unemployed at a point such as *G* is costless from a social perspective, a "free lunch," *even if the worker draws a salary*. The output produced by the worker "pays" for the salary, and nothing has been sacrificed in the process.

PRICE INFLATION AND THE FRONTIER Finally, what can be said about points beyond the frontier, such as *J* in Figure 3.4? A society would certainly prefer *J* to a point on the frontier such as *H* because it would mean an increase in both kinds of output. But *J* is unattainable, given current resources and technologies. The frontier defines the limits of what is possible.

Countries do occasionally try to reach beyond their means, however. When a market economy such as the United States attempts to do this, it suffers price inflation. The typical scenario is as follows. The government prints more money and places it in the economy so that consumers, business firms, and the government itself can spend more on goods and services. Once the economy reaches its production possibilities frontier, however, all the extra money does is drive up prices. The economy cannot produce any more goods and services. The *dollar value* of the goods and services continues to rise, but only because their prices, not the quantities themselves, are rising. Economists call this **demand pull inflation,** inflation resulting from the attempt to purchase more goods and services than the economy is capable of producing.

DEMAND PULL INFLATION

Price inflation resulting from the attempt to purchase more goods and services than the economy is capable of producing.

HISTORICAL NOTE: The last time the United States consciously tried to live beyond its means was in 1966 as a result of the Vietnam War. President Johnson increased the defense budget by $30 billion (over $120 billion in today's dollars) to fight the war without increasing taxes at a time when the economy was already operating on its production possibilities frontier. The predictable result was a significant increase in inflation over the next few years.

A more interesting problem for market economies is that prices can rise even if the economy is operating well below its production possibilities frontier. We will have to wait until the macroeconomics section of this text to understand how this can happen. The production possibilities frontier cannot explain why an economy can experience inflation with lots of unemployed resources. This is not a knock against the production possibilities frontier; it merely underscores the uses and limitations of economic models. The production possibilities frontier is a highly simplified description or model of an economy that yields many useful insights. We have seen how it helps us understand the concepts of production efficiency, full employment, and demand pull inflation. We will see in the next section how it helps us understand the process of economic growth. But it definitely has its limitations as a model of the economy; it is not at all helpful in understanding why inflation and unemployed resources can exist at the same time. We need a different model to understand this problem.

LONG-RUN ECONOMIC GROWTH

The production possibilities frontier is an extremely useful device for illustrating the Now versus the Future question that all societies must address, the question of long-run economic growth. The frontier pictures the constraints on production in a given year. But societies do not have to accept the same frontier year after year. They can undertake policies to push the frontier out over time so that they can produce, and consume, ever-increasing amounts of all goods and services.

Long-run economic growth is defined as a *persistent* increase in the economy's *potential* for producing goods and services, with emphasis on the words *potential* and *persistent.* Potential refers to production possibilities, to the maximum possible quantities of goods and services that the economy can produce each year. The potential for producing goods and services must be distinguished from the actual production of goods and services, which may or may not be on the frontier. The increases in the economy's potential must also persist. Long-run economic growth is a continuing process. In terms of the production possibilities frontier, long-run economic growth refers to a persistent march of the frontier away from the origin.

LONG-RUN ECONOMIC GROWTH
A persistent increase in the economy's potential for producing goods and services.

Interest in economic growth is a fairly recent phenomenon in the broad sweep of history, dating back no further than the late 1700s. Until that time poverty, hunger, and disease were simply accepted as the fate of humankind. People had no hint of the vast improvement in living standards that would occur in a few countries over the next hundred years, made possible by sustained economic growth. Once these few countries showed the way, however, all countries wanted to follow. Long-run economic growth is a principal objective of all the world's nations.

The Growth Scorecard

Unfortunately, most countries have not been very successful. The World Bank divides the world's countries into four categories on the basis of their annual income per person in 1990: (1) low-income countries ($610 or less per person), (2) lower middle income countries (between $611 and $2,465 per person), (3) upper middle income countries (between $2,466 and $7,619 per person), and (4) high-income countries ($7,620 or more per person). Table 3.2 lists the number of countries in each category and the average dollar value of income per capita for each category as of 1990. As the table shows, living standards in most of the world's countries are very low. Citizens of the United States would have trouble imagining how anyone could survive on an average income of $610 per year or less, and even the $7,619 maximum income per person of the upper middle income countries is just about at the poverty level in the United

HISTORICAL NOTE: The United States, Japan, and (West) Germany have become the true giants among the world's economies. Together they account for 50 percent of all output produced for markets worldwide. In 1988 the United States was far and away the largest economy, producing 27 percent of the world's output, followed by Japan at 16 percent and West Germany at 7 percent.

TABLE 3.2 **Classification of Countries by Stage of Development**

COUNTRY CLASSIFICATION	NUMBER OF COUNTRIES	AVERAGE INCOME PER PERSON (1990)
Low Income	51	$610 or less
Lower Middle Income	56	Between $611 and $2,465
Upper Middle Income	39	Between $2,466 and $7,619
High Income[1]	40	$7,620 or more

[1]Includes the 21 large developed market economies of Asia, the Pacific, Western Europe, and North America, which are members of the Organization for Economic Cooperation and Development (OECD), and nineteen smaller, non-OECD countries. Among the smaller countries are many of the oil-exporting countries.

SOURCE: The World Bank, *Social Indicators of Development, 1991/92* (Washington, DC: Johns Hopkins University Press, 1992), Table B.1, pp. 378–379.

States. Economic growth has clearly proved to be an elusive target for all but a relatively few countries.

Achieving vigorous long-run economic growth is a complex process requiring just the right blend of social, cultural, demographic, political, and economic factors. At this point we want to concentrate on the most important economic determinants of growth.

Strategies for Economic Growth

The general strategies for achieving long-run economic growth are easily described in terms of the production possibilities frontier. The position of the frontier in any one year depends on the quantity and quality of a nation's primary factors of production and on the set of technologies available. These are the fundamental constraints underlying the frontier. Therefore, expanding the frontier necessarily involves (1) increasing the quantity of the primary factors of production, (2) improving the quality of these resources, or (3) inventing and employing new production technologies. Sustained economic growth is impossible without these changes.

Of the three primary factors of production—labor, capital, and land—labor and capital are far more important to the process of growth than is land. The total amount of land in a country is essentially fixed. Moreover, exploiting the resources contained in the land, through either farming or mining, requires applications of both labor and capital. So we can safely restrict our attention to increases in the quantity and quality of labor and capital when considering the role of resources in the process of growth.

INCREASING THE LABOR SUPPLY Growth in the supply of labor is the single most important contributor to growth in a nation's *total* income or output for the simple reason that labor is by far the most important primary factor of production. In the United States, labor receives nearly 80 percent of all income paid by firms to primary factors of production. But increasing the supply of labor does not usually contribute very much to the growth of income or output *per person,* the key to improving a nation's economic standard of living. The problem is that increases in the labor supply typically result from increases in the overall population. When both output and population increase, the ratio of output to population, or output per person, does not increase very much.

Vigorous growth in output per person is possible if a country experiences an increase in **labor force participation,** the percentage of population that joins the labor force. Labor force participation has been increasing rapidly in the United States over the past 40 years, as ever more women have decided to work outside the home. In 1950 only 34 percent of all women were part of the labor force; by 1992 the percentage had grown to 57.8 percent. But such dramatic changes in labor force participation are unusual—they were unprecedented in the United States. And increases in labor force participation cannot continue indefinitely. Over the long run, increases in labor supply and increases in population tend to go hand in hand.

LABOR FORCE PARTICIPATION
The percentage of the population that joins the labor force.

INCREASING THE AMOUNT OF CAPITAL Increasing the amount of capital is the key to increasing output per person. The single most important *economic* difference between the developed and the developing countries is that the former have been able to amass a large amount of capital per person, whereas the latter have not. Table 3.3 presents a recent estimate of the value of capital per person in 1980 for a sample of 10 countries that range from very low to very high income. With the exception of Korea (and Keyna, to a minor extent), there is a very high correlation between national output per person and capital per person: The more capital available per person, the higher the output produced per person. The table also indicates that increasing the amount of capital remains essential to economic growth long after a country passes through the early stages of development. These data are exactly what economists would expect, for a number of reasons. Some definitions are in order, however, before developing the point.

TABLE 3.3 Output and Stock of Capital per Person for Selected Countries (1980 $)

COUNTRY	OUTPUT PER PERSON	STOCK OF CAPITAL PER PERSON
INDIA	$ 244	$ 242
KENYA	412	1,272
INDONESIA	473	1,162
KOREA	1,607	4,028
BRAZIL	1,996	1,990
PORTUGAL	2,431	3,233
MEXICO	2,612	3,904
GREECE	4,302	5,653
SPAIN	5,616	5,133
UNITED STATES	11,998	29,741

SOURCE: K. M. Dadkhab and F. Zahedi, "Simultaneous Estimation of Production Functions and Capital Stocks for Developing Countries," *Review of Economics and Statistics* 3 (August 1986). Data were converted to dollars using exchange rates for 1980 reported in the *International Financial Statistics Yearbook, 1986* (Washington, D.C.: International Monetary Fund, 1986).

INVESTMENT

A flow variable that refers to the increase in the stock of capital during the year.

FLOW VARIABLE

A variable that can be measured only with reference to a period of time.

STOCK VARIABLE

A variable that can be measured at a given point in time.

LABOR PRODUCTIVITY

The amount of output produced per worker.

Capital refers to the amount of plant and equipment in place at any given time in private businesses and government-run enterprises, plus buildings used as residences. The nonresidential capital is most directly relevant to economic growth. **Investment** refers to increases in the amount of capital. It is a **flow variable,** meaning that it can only be measured with reference to a period of time, usually a year. In contrast, capital is a **stock variable;** it can be measured at a given point in time. For example, investment in plant and equipment in the United States in 1992 totaled $770.4 billion, meaning that firms added $770.4 billion to the nation's stock of plant and equipment during 1992. By December 1992 the U.S. Department of Commerce estimated that the United States had a stock of capital totaling $8.8 trillion of nonresidential capital and $14.0 trillion including residences. Thus, saying that continued increases in the stock of capital are the key to economic growth is equivalent to saying that sustaining a high level of investment is the key to economic growth.

Investment promotes economic growth because it simultaneously pursues all the possible strategies for growth. First, capital is one of the primary factors of production. Increasing the stock of capital directly increases a nation's productive capacity. Moreover, the gains in output are per-person gains because no corresponding increase in population occurs.

The increased quantity of capital in and of itself is only a small part of investment's contribution to growth, however. Far more important is the quality dimension of the new capital. New plant and equipment is improved plant and equipment. Growth in output per person could not continue if the new capital were not different from the capital already in place. To see why, imagine a farming situation in which three workers share one shovel. The shovel is the capital in this example. Adding new shovels should increase output, but only to the point at which each worker has a shovel. Adding more than three shovels cannot increase output because a worker can only use one shovel at a time. For growth to continue the shovels have to be replaced with better hand tools or machines such as tractors that increase **labor productivity,** defined as the output produced per worker.

What improved capital can do for labor productivity it can do for all other factors of production. New, and better, equipment in farming and mining improves the productivity of land. New and better equipment also improves the productivity of other capital, such as existing factories. In other words, investment acts to improve the *quality* of all factors of production by making them more productive.

NEW TECHNOLOGIES We noted earlier that developing new technologies is essential for long-run economic growth. New technologies are only ideas or blueprints, however. To increase production they must actually be incorporated into production processes. Here, again, investment is a key because new technologies typically become incorporated into production through new capital. New machines are better machines precisely because they embody scientific and engineering advances.

HUMAN CAPITAL Finally, investment has a direct effect on the quality of labor in addition to providing workers with new and better machinery. Economists distinguish between investments in physical and human capital. Investment in physical capital is the purchase of new plant and equipment that we have been referring to so far. **Investment in human capital** refers to investment in education, both the general education received in primary and secondary schools and in colleges and the more specialized forms of education such as graduate education and on-the-job training within businesses. The value of **human capital** is the market value of all accumulated knowledge and skills. Human capital is extremely difficult to evaluate, but economists believe that the value of human capital is about twice as large as the value of physical capital in the United States.

INVESTMENT IN HUMAN CAPITAL
Expenditures on education, both formal education received in school and on-the-job training provided by business firms.

HUMAN CAPITAL
The market value of all accumulated knowledge and skills.

Investment in human capital may well be the single most important determinant of long-run economic growth. It contributes to growth in a number of ways. Scientific and engineering knowledge is essential for the development of new technologies. A high level of general education is also extremely important to sustaining economic growth. Only a highly literate, well-educated labor force can adapt itself easily to working with new equipment that embodies the latest technologies. For instance, learning the skills necessary to function in a modern computerized working environment is extremely difficult without a good general education. Finally, production processes and business organizations become ever larger and more complex as an economy grows. The managerial skills learned in a nation's business schools are needed to manage large-scale businesses effectively. Human capital contributes to growth in so many ways that it is virtually impossible to imagine a modern industrial economy arising without the benefit of a highly educated, highly skilled labor force.

The Sources of Economic Growth

Empirical studies of the sources of economic growth confirm that both physical and human capital are very important to the growth process. Table 3.4 reports the factors contributing to growth in total output for the United States from 1929 to 1982. The estimates come from Edward Denison, long considered one of the foremost authorities on U.S. economic growth.

Notice that the growth in the labor supply is the largest single contributor to growth in total output, which reflects the importance of labor in the production process. But remember that some of the growth in labor supply resulted from the natural growth in population, so that 32 percent overstates labor's contribution to growth in output per person. The direct and indirect

TABLE 3.4 Factors Contributing to U.S. Growth of Output, 1929–82

FACTOR	CONTRIBUTION
GROWTH IN LABOR SUPPLY	32%
TECHNOLOGICAL ADVANCE	28
GROWTH IN CAPITAL STOCK	19
EDUCATION AND TRAINING	14
ALL OTHER	7

SOURCE: E. F. Denison, *Trends in American Economic Growth, 1929–1982* (Washington D.C.: Brookings Institution, 1985), 300.

TABLE 3.5 **Investment and Growth in Labor Productivity in Six High-Income Market Economies, 1971–80**

COUNTRY	AVERAGE ANNUAL INVESTMENT/OUTPUT RATIO	AVERAGE ANNUAL GROWTH IN OUTPUT PER MAN-HOUR
JAPAN	34.0%	7.4%
FRANCE	24.2	4.8
GERMANY	23.7	4.9
ITALY	22.4	4.9
UNITED KINGDOM	19.2	2.9
UNITED STATES	19.2	2.5

SOURCE: *Economic Report of the President, 1983* (Washington, D.C.: U.S. Government Printing Office, February 1983).

effects of growth in the nation's capital stock account for 61 percent, or nearly all, of the remaining contributions to U.S. economic growth. Moreover, these percentages apply to growth in output per person as well as to growth in total output. Denison's estimates also underscore the importance of investment in human capital. Technological advance and education and training, both aspects of human capital, accounted for 42 percent of U.S. output growth. In contrast, growth in the stock of physical capital in and of itself contributed only 19 percent of the growth in output.

The data in Table 3.5 provide another indication of the close connection between increases in capital and economic growth. The table compares rates of growth in output per man-hour in manufacturing, a common measure of labor productivity, with investment as a percentage of domestically produced output for six of the high-income market economies for the period 1971–80. Japan's growth in labor productivity was by far the highest during the 1970s; so was its percentage of output devoted to investment goods. In contrast, both the United States and Great Britain lagged well behind the other countries in labor productivity growth, and they also had the lowest investment/output ratios.

The Opportunity Costs of Growth

If investment is the key to long-run economic growth, why don't the low- and middle-income developing countries simply increase the percentage of their resources devoted to investment? The problem is one of opportunity cost. Providing more resources for the production of investment goods means that fewer resources will be available for the production of consumer goods. When *total* output produced per person is only $1,500 per year (and in many countries it is far less than that), sacrificing consumption for investment can be very costly indeed. It can mean widespread starvation. Moreover, those who sacrifice, and survive, may not enjoy the benefits of their sacrifice. The returns to investing may not occur for a generation or more.

The necessary trade-off between investment and consumption can be explained in one of two ways. The production possibilities frontier provides the

FIGURE 3.5

The Opportunity Cost of Economic Growth

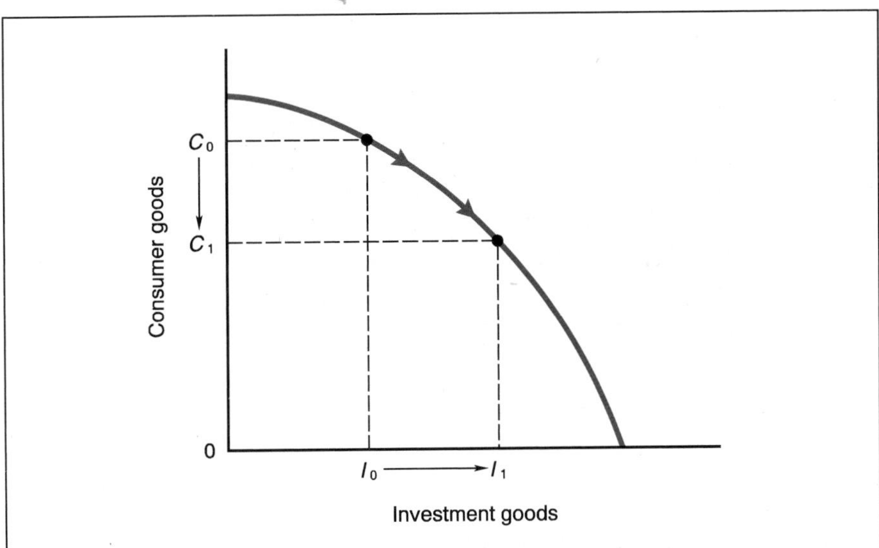

An economy can produce only two kinds of final goods and services, consumer goods and investment goods. The figure illustrates the production possibilities frontier for consumer goods and investment goods. In order to increase investment from I_0 to I_1 to promote long-run economic growth, society must sacrifice, $(C_0 - C_1)$ of consumer goods. The sacrifice of consumer goods today is the opportunity cost of economic growth.

most direct approach. This time we will divide all output produced into consumer goods and investment goods. Referring to Figure 3.5, the vertical axis represents the quantity of consumer goods (C) produced, and the horizontal axis represents the quantity of investment goods (I) produced. This is a legitimate two-way division of total output because all final goods produced are either consumer goods or new capital sold to businesses (and government enterprises). All other produced goods are semi-finished products that are sold to other businesses as material inputs for further processing.

The trade-off between investment and consumption is immediately apparent in Figure 3.5. An increase in investment from I_0 to I_1 involves a sacrifice of consumption from C_0 to C_1. If C_0 is barely enough for survival, the increase in investment may well not be forthcoming.

The investment-consumption trade-off can also be explained by looking at how income flows through factor markets. Individuals receive the total income that flows through the factor markets in one of three forms: as wages and salaries for offering labor services to firms, as interest payments and profits in return for offering firms the funds for investment, and as rents in return for the use of their land. Once individuals receive income, they can use it in only one of two ways: They can either save it or use it to purchase consumer goods and services. The savings in turn become the source of funds that firms use to buy new plant and equipment. For example, people save by purchasing corporate bonds or stocks that firms offer as a means of raising funds. Or they deposit some of their income in bank accounts, and banks then loan the funds to business firms to be used for investment. Whatever the channels, the amount of income that individuals save in any one year must exactly equal the

FIGURE 3.6

The Strategy for Long-run Economic Growth

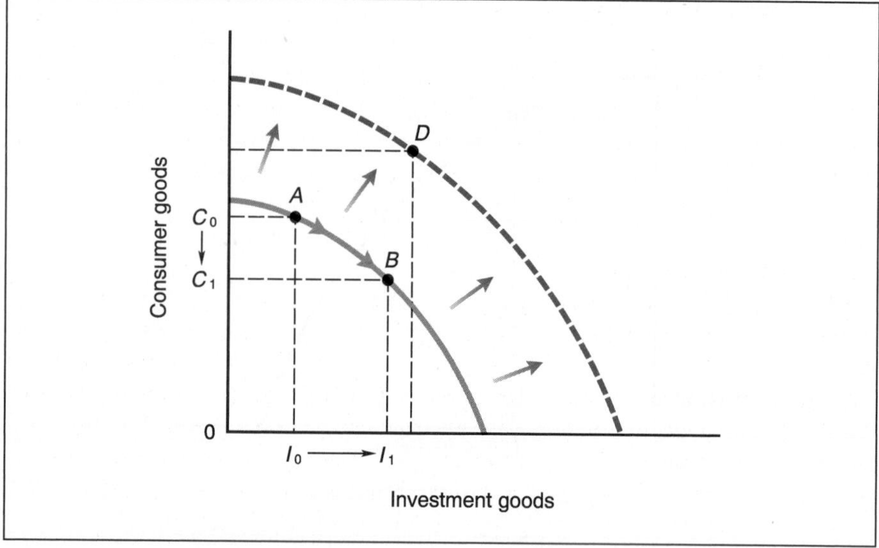

An economy is initially at point A on its production possibilities frontier, producing C_0 of consumer goods and I_0 of investment goods. In order to grow, society moves from point A to point B, increasing production of investment goods to I_1 and decreasing production of consumer goods to C_1. If growth takes, the production possibilities frontier moves out over time. Society can eventually move to a point such as D, producing more investment goods *and* more consumer goods than was possible before economic growth occurred.

amount of investment by firms because total income must match total spending on final output, consumer goods plus investment goods. So, in order to invest more, individuals must be willing to save more, which necessarily leaves less income available for purchasing consumer goods.

Every country must sacrifice some consumption for investment if only to maintain the existing stock of capital. All capital goods wear out over time. If there were no investment at all, the stock of capital would diminish and, with it, the nation's production capacity. The production possibilities frontier would march steadily inward to the origin. A level of investment just sufficient to maintain the existing stock of capital keeps the frontier more or less constant. Sustained economic growth is possible only by increasing investment beyond the replacement level, both now and in the future.

The strategy for economic growth, then, is depicted in Figure 3.6. An economy begins at point A, investing I_0 and consuming C_0. I_0 is just sufficient to maintain the capital stock and the economy's production possibilities. Growth is made possible by an initial move to point B, with investment increasing to I_1 at the cost of reducing current consumption to C_1. The idea is not to remain at point B, however. If growth occurs, the production possibilities frontier begins to move outward. Eventually, as it moves out far enough, the economy will be able to produce at points such as D, consuming more *and* investing more than when it began. Continued growth becomes ever less painful; the opportunity costs decrease. The problem for the low-income developing countries, though, is starting the process of economic growth. They may well need help from the developed nations in order to avoid the extreme sacrifices of consumption that would otherwise be necessary.

The Economic Health of a Nation

Our discussion of the production possibility frontier has revealed the two key determinants of the overall economic health of a nation: long-run economic growth and full employment of a nation's resources. In order to prosper, a nation must first increase its potential or capacity for producing goods and services. Its factors of production must become increasingly productive, which requires a high level of investment in both physical and human capital. Countries that are able to push their production possibilities frontiers out rapidly and continuously over time enjoy a high standard of living. Countries that cannot extend their production possibilities frontiers suffer low standards of living.

A nation must also realize its increased potential in order to prosper. Actual production must occur on or very near the production possibilities frontier, which requires efficient answers to the How question. A nation must use all its scarce resources and use them well. With reference to Figure 3.6, the increase in potential well-being created by moving the frontier out from the solid line to the dotted line does no good at all if the economy actually remains at point *B*. Societies must chase their frontiers as they move out over time.

CHOOSING AN ECONOMIC SYSTEM

Our discussion of society's economic problem has ignored one essential decision that must be made prior to addressing the four fundamental economic questions: What economic system will society choose to structure its economic activities? An **economic system** is the set of decision-making mechanisms, organizational arrangements, and rules for allocating society's scarce resources and determining the appropriate distribution of income. In short, it is the institutional setting in which society pursues the four economic questions.

ECONOMIC SYSTEM

The set of decision-making mechanisms, organizational arrangements, and rules for allocating society's scarce resources and determining the appropriate distribution of income.

Societies usually do not consciously choose an economic system. Rather, economic systems tend to evolve slowly over a long period of time in a manner consistent with a nation's cultural, social, and political mores. This is why the seven Eastern European nations stunned the world in 1989 with their intention to completely transform their economies in short order. History offers no precedent for what they are attempting. Let's take a closer look at what constitutes an economic system before discussing the prospects of the Eastern European economies.

People have a tendency to label economic systems with various forms of "isms"—capitalism, socialism, communism, and the like. Such labels are possible, but not especially helpful, because no actual economic system meets all the attributes of any one "ism" in its pure form. Economists want to understand how different economic systems affect the performance of the economy. For this purpose they have found it far more useful to identify the characteristics of economic systems that are most likely to differ from country to country and that have a direct bearing on how the economy performs. Four such characteristics stand out above all others: who has the decision-making authority within the economy, what methods are used to process and coordinate economic information, who owns the capital and land, and what incentives are used to motivate economic behavior.

Characteristics of Economic Systems

CENTRALIZED ECONOMY

An economic system in which an agency of the national government has authority over all economic decisions and full access to all relevant economic information.

FULLY DECENTRALIZED ECONOMY

An economic system in which individuals and business firms make all economic decisions and are responsible for generating and processing all relevant economic information.

DECISION-MAKING AUTHORITY Who makes the economic decisions? The answer to this question turns on the delegation of authority throughout the economy and how economic information is obtained and utilized. The spectrum runs from a completely centralized economy to a fully decentralized economy. In a **centralized economy** an agency of the national government has authority over all economic decisions and full access to all relevant economic information. Lower-level decision-making units, including consumers and business firms, receive only limited information, just enough to carry out the wishes of the central authority. In a **fully decentralized economy** individuals and business firms make all economic decisions and are responsible for generating and processing all relevant economic information.

No actual economic system is completely centralized or decentralized. Individuals, business firms, and government agencies always have some decision-making authority and share economic information. But nations do exhibit definite tendencies toward centralization or decentralization. Cuba and the People's Republic of China have chosen a centralized approach to their major economic decisions. So did the countries of Eastern Europe and the Soviet Union prior to 1989. The high-income market economies of Western Europe, the United States, Canada, and Japan, among others, lean just as heavily toward a decentralized approach.

NATIONAL ECONOMIC PLAN

A plan developed by the central authority that sets national economic objectives regarding the four fundamental economic questions and instructs lower-level decision-making units on how to carry out the plan.

INFORMATION PROCESSING AND COORDINATION How does the economy process and coordinate economic information? Two mutually exclusive options are available for processing and coordinating information: the national economic plan and the market. A **national economic plan** goes hand in hand with centralized decision making. The central authority develops a plan that sets national economic objectives regarding the four fundamental economic questions and simply instructs lower-level decision-making units on how to carry out the plan. The plan also provides an incentive structure to ensure that lower-level units, especially individuals and business firms, follow the central agency's directives. The plan carries the force of law.

MARKET

Any institutional arrangement through which buyers and sellers engage in the free exchange of goods, services, and factors of production.

A market system is the opposite of central planning and goes hand in hand with a decentralized decision-making strategy. A **market** is any institutional arrangement through which buyers and sellers engage in the free exchange of goods, services, and factors of production. "Free" exchange does not mean that goods and services are traded free of charge. Rather, it implies that buyers and sellers enter into exchanges voluntarily and in pursuit of their own self-interests. Markets, in other words, honor the principle of consumer (and producer) sovereignty.

Prices process and coordinate all economic information in a market economy. The interaction of buyers and sellers in markets determines the prices at which the goods, services, and factors of production are exchanged. The prices established by their interaction incorporate all relevant economic information, such as which resources are abundant and which are scarce, which goods are costly to produce, and which goods and services consumers want to buy. We will take a closer look at markets and prices in Chapter 4.

A national economic plan is also an institutional arrangement for exchanging goods and services, but, in contrast with the market, it honors the preferences of the central authority, not of individuals and business firms. This is why the market and the plan are mutually exclusive.

PROPERTY RIGHTS: THE OWNERSHIP OF FACTORS OF PRODUCTION Who owns the factors of production, and how is the income associated with them to be distributed? The assignment of **property rights,** that is, deciding who owns the factors of production, is one of the more important issues that a society must resolve. It far transcends narrow economic concerns. The determination of property rights has a direct effect on all social interactions, including the amount of freedom that people enjoy.

PROPERTY RIGHTS
The ownership of the factors of production.

Virtually all societies believe that people should own their own labor services and are entitled to the income derived from them. Therefore, the question of property rights applies to capital and land, not to labor.

The property rights to capital and land may be private, or public, or cooperative (collective). Private ownership means that individuals are granted all rights associated with ownership, including the right to transfer the property and the rights to receive all income generated by the property. Private ownership of capital and land, "private property," is a hallmark of capitalism. Public ownership means that the government owns the capital and land and receives all the income earned by these factors. Therefore, the government decides how to dispose of the income from capital and land. The income is often earmarked for investment, but not always. Public ownership is the defining characteristic of **socialism.** Collective ownership is a variant of public ownership under which the property rights to capital and land are held collectively by the citizens. They vote on how to use and distribute the earnings from these factors.

SOCIALISM
An economic system with public ownership of capital and land.

The assignment of property rights to capital and land has its most direct impact on the For Whom or Distribution question, but it can be expected to affect the allocation of these resources as well. In answering the How question, private owners offer their capital and land to whoever pays them the highest return. Although capital and land may be allocated on the same basis under public (or collective) ownership, broader social concerns are likely to come into play.

INCENTIVES What incentive mechanisms will be used to encourage individuals and firms to engage in economic activity consistent with society's objectives? Economic systems may operate with either moral or material incentives. **Moral incentives** encourage behavior for the good of society and may be enforced with legal sanctions if such behavior is not forthcoming. **Material incentives,** in contrast, appeal to economic self-interest by allowing individuals and business firms to keep the gains from their exchanges. Material incentives are necessarily the primary incentive in a market economy because markets operate on the principle that individuals and business firms enter into market exchanges to pursue their own economic objectives. They must be allowed to keep the gains from their exchanges for the system to work.

MORAL INCENTIVES
Incentives that encourage behavior for the good of society and may be enforced with legal sanctions.

MATERIAL INCENTIVES
Incentives that appeal to economic self-interest by allowing individuals and business firms to keep the gains from their exchanges.

Material incentives are also used in centrally planned economies. Since people own the rights to their own labor, material incentives are a natural way of encouraging lower-level managers and workers to meet the plan's directives and to match labor supplies to the requirements of the plan. They may also use material incentives to reward and punish political behavior, as when the central planners reserve the highest paid jobs for those who are loyal to the ruling political party. Nonetheless, centrally planned economies are likely to rely heavily on moral incentives as well.

Pure Market Capitalism and Centrally Planned Socialism

The choices that a society makes regarding these four characteristics essentially define its economic system. Many different economic systems are possible. They can be thought of as lying along a spectrum whose endpoints are two stylized economic systems, pure market capitalism and centrally planned socialism. All of the world's economies are mixtures of these two paradigms.

PURE MARKET CAPITALISM

An economic system characterized by fully decentralized decision making, the use of markets to process economic information and coordinate exchange, private ownership of capital and land, and the use of material incentives.

CENTRALLY PLANNED SOCIALISM

An economic system characterized by centralized decision making, the use of a national economic plan to process information and coordinate exchange, public ownership of capital and land, and the use of both moral and material incentives.

The four principal characteristics of **pure market capitalism** are (1) decentralized decision making, (2) the use of markets and prices for processing and coordinating all economic information, (3) private ownership of capital and land, and (4) the exclusive use of material incentives. The government has only one necessary economic function to perform. It must ensure that market exchanges proceed in a free and even-handed manner. Beyond this, government economic activity may be justified if markets perform sufficiently badly in some areas. For example, markets cannot be relied on to provide for the national security; this is a task for the government. But the citizens, not the government, determine when government involvement in the economy is justified.

The four principal characteristics of **centrally planned socialism** are (1) centralized decision making within an agency of the national government, which sets all national objectives; (2) the use of a national economic plan designed by the central authority to process and coordinate all economic information and binding on all lower-level units, including all individuals and business firms; (3) public ownership of capital and land, with the central planning authority determining the disposition of all returns to the capital and land; and (4) the use of both moral and material incentives to implement the national plan. In its purest form, centrally planned socialism leaves no role at all for a free market system.

Pure market capitalism and centrally planned socialism each have their advantages relative to the other. The foremost advantage of pure market capitalism is the freedom it gives to its citizens to pursue their own economic self-interests. One immediate consequence of this freedom is that pure market capitalism is highly responsive to the wishes of individual consumers. Business firms respond to consumers' desires, so that consumers are able to buy what they want within the limits of their resources. Freedom and responsiveness to consumers are very big advantages in a humanistic society, since the whole purpose of an economic system is to promote individual well-being. Centrally planned socialism, in contrast, severely limits the personal freedom of its citizens and creates a privileged class of managers and government bureaucrats.

Pure market capitalism also has a decided advantage in promoting economic efficiency. Nothing comes close to matching the market as an efficient allocator of society's scarce resources. The market generally does a fine job of processing and coordinating economic information so that resources are directed to their most productive and valued uses. In the 1960s central planners in the former Soviet Union and the other socialist economies had hoped that the advent of powerful computers would allow them to model the economy in great detail and thereby allocate resources more efficiently. Their hopes were never realized, however. A modern economy has proved much too complex for even the most powerful computers to model effectively. The result is that national plans remain very poor processors and coordinators of economic information. Also, individuals without property rights to capital and land or the freedom to pursue their own self-interests have little incentive to conserve scarce resources and use them efficiently. Moral incentives that urge people to follow the dictates of the national plan for the good of society have not been very effective substitutes for self-interested material incentives. Centrally planned socialism proved to be grossly inefficient.

Centrally planned socialism is not without its advantages relative to pure market capitalism, however. It is better able to formulate and pursue national objectives simply because of the top-down nature of the decision-making authority. To cite one example, following the Russian Revolution the Soviet planners wanted to direct the nation's saving and investment toward the heavy manufacturing industries such as steel and were able to do so. In contrast, both political parties in the United States have been urging higher levels of saving and investment to promote economic growth for the past 20 years without any effect whatsoever. One can argue that centrally planned socialism's advantage in promoting national objectives is not worth much if the objectives do not reflect the will of the people. Perhaps U.S. citizens just do not want to save more. In any event, the market has been generating low levels of saving and investment in the United States, and the government has not been able to override this result despite the apparent political will to do so.

Centrally planned socialism also has a decided advantage in resolving the For Whom or Distribution question if society's preferences lean toward equality. The centrally planned socialist economies generally have a much more equal distribution of economic well-being than do the market economies. One reason relates to the income from capital. The government receives all income from capital under centrally planned socialism, whereas individuals receive the income from capital under pure market capitalism. The ownership of capital tends to become highly concentrated in the hands of a few in pure market economies. For instance, 70 percent of the capital in the United States is held by less than 10 percent of the population. Consequently, nearly all the income from capital is earned by a small percentage of the population, which is one reason why the distribution of income is far from equal in the United States. Also, central planners dictate the wages for different occupations, so they can avoid large disparities in wage income if they want to. Wage income is generally much more evenly distributed in the centrally planned socialist economies. Finally, the centrally planned socialist economies can, and typically do, ensure that everyone is provided with the basic necessities—food, clothing, shelter, medical care, even education. These items are either heavily subsidized or provided directly through government agencies. For example, energy in Poland was virtually free to consumers from 1960 to 1989. In contrast, many of the poor who are left behind in the market economies cannot afford even the most basic necessities.

A final advantage of centrally planned socialism is its ability to avoid having resources lie idle. The national plan dictates the allocation of all resources, so it can virtually guarantee that labor is fully employed and that capital and land are fully utilized. Pure market capitalism, in contrast, often experiences periods of high unemployment and underutilized capital and land.

Both economic systems, then, are prone to inefficiencies and are destined to operate below their production possibilities frontiers. The chief problem under centrally planned socialism is that scarce resources are badly misallocated. The chief problem under market capitalism is that resources lie idle at times. Overall, though, the efficiency advantage lies with pure market capitalism, as noted above. Resources are not always idle in the market economies, whereas resources are almost always badly misallocated in the centrally planned socialist economies.

The Eastern European Economies

The economic transitions under way in Eastern Europe are all the more remarkable because these countries are not just seeking small adjustments in their economic systems. Instead, they are trying to jump the entire length of the economic spectrum, replacing economies that were close to the ideal of centrally planned socialism with economies that are close to the ideal of pure market capitalism. When these countries began to transform their economies in 1989 fully 80 to 90 percent of their businesses were owned and operated by the government. They intend to make all these businesses private in short order and to dismantle the central planning bureaucracy. The world has never witnessed economic reforms quite like these.

What are their prospects of succeeding? In truth, they each face a formidable set of obstacles in trying to transform their economies.[1] Foremost among them are the crushing inefficiencies inherited from the old centrally planned system. Western economists estimated in 1989 that 30 to 40 percent of their businesses were not competitive in the world's marketplace. For this reason alone the move to market capitalism must proceed slowly, or these countries will face massive bankruptcies and unemployment that they simply cannot cope with.

Given the existing inefficiencies, another difficult problem is how to turn over their businesses from public to private ownership. Here the countries face a nasty Catch 22. Private investors will want to know the extent to which the businesses are competitive before they buy them, in other words, how much they should pay to become the owners. The competitiveness and value of the government-owned businesses are difficult to determine, however, because they had been buying their inputs and selling their products at completely artificial prices set by the central planners. The true value of the businesses cannot be determined until they become private and are forced to buy their inputs and sell their products at established market prices. But private investors will not buy the businesses and open them up to competition until they know their true values. Hence, the Catch 22. Furthermore, even if the businesses'

---

[1]The former East Germany is obviously something of an exception, since it has unified with West Germany, and the West Germans have agreed to help ease the transition. Nonetheless, the economy and citizens of East Germany face many of the obstacles listed below. The transformation of the East German economy will not be painless.

true values were known, the citizens of these countries do not have anywhere near enough wealth to buy the businesses themselves. The government could allow foreign investors to buy the businesses, but countries are always leery of foreign ownership. A final option is simply to give the businesses away to the citizens. This is likely to be viewed as very unfair, however. One family could receive stock in a viable, highly competitive business and become rich. Another family could receive stock in one of the noncompetitive businesses that quickly goes under, and so the family would remain poor. People are unlikely to tolerate such uneven outcomes generated simply by the luck of the draw. The question of how to privatize the government-owned businesses has economists stumped. No one is quite sure how best to do it.

The example of the luck of the draw points to a more general problem. These countries began the transformation of their economies with a fairly even distribution of income, and their citizens have an ingrained belief in equality. Also, they are accustomed to a system of government-owned capital and land in which no one profits directly from these resources, and they have been taught to distrust the profit motive. As the market economy evolves, one can only wonder how people will react to entrepreneurial citizens who own and manage profitable businesses and become well-to-do from the receipt of profits. Income from capital (and land) will almost certainly become highly concentrated, just as it is in the existing market economies. Wide disparities in income arising from profits could generate enormous social tensions throughout Eastern Europe.

An equally difficult problem will occur at the other end of the income distribution. Many firms will fail if the government-owned businesses are as inefficient as Western economists estimate. Unemployment will be high, and the governments will have to provide a huge safety net of public transfers to prevent widespread poverty. Will these countries be able to afford the safety net? This is an open question for all but the East Germans who have been promised support from the West Germans. The other countries will undoubtedly require aid from abroad to provide an adequate safety net for the unemployed and their families.

The final major obstacle in changing to a market economy is a legal one. The Eastern European countries do not have legal systems in place that can support a market economy. These countries must draft new laws that, at a minimum, clearly define the property rights to capital and land, are able to enforce private contracts, and can adequately resolve the inevitable rash of bankruptcies that will occur. The transformation to a market economy cannot proceed until these laws are passed and are being enforced.

Can the Eastern European countries overcome these obstacles? Economists are divided on this question. The pessimists believe that the obstacles are simply too great to permit anything approaching a smooth transition to a market economy. They doubt that the United States, Japan, and Western Europe will provide the aid required to avoid widespread poverty and deep social unrest. They see the distinct possibility of a populist counterrevolution to retain centrally planned socialism, driven by the belief in equality and the distrust of the profit motive. They also fear that deep-seated enmities among ethnic groups will resurface as the central governments lose their grips, a fear that was realized so immediately and tragically in Yugoslavia. Finally, the pessimists see the entrenched managers of the government enterprises as fighting the move to privatization at every turn so they can maintain their privileged positions.

Worse yet, few people besides the public managers have any managerial training or experience. The current managers will be difficult to replace if they resist privatization.

The optimists point to three factors that they believe will facilitate the transformation to a market economy. The first is simply a very strong will to succeed within some of the countries. Hungary, Poland, and the former Czechoslovakia are determined to join the European Economic Community in the near future, and they know they must achieve viable market economies to do so. The jury is still out on the will to succeed within Bulgaria and Romania and, of course, among the Croats, Serbs, and Muslims in the war-torn former Yugoslavia. Second, the countries all rely heavily on international trade. The optimists see this as a plus because trading in international markets forces businesses to set proper prices for inputs and outputs in order to compete at all. They argue that the resulting price discipline will cause their businesses to become competitive more quickly. Finally, the optimists believe that the Western market economies will provide the necessary financial assistance during the transition period. They point out that the West very much wants market capitalism to succeed in Eastern Europe. Also, the Eastern European countries have size working in their favor. The combined national output of the original seven countries (including the former East Germany) is only one-quarter as large as the national output of West Germany alone. The West can easily provide the aid required during the transition. The optimists concede that the obstacles listed above are serious and that the Eastern Europeans will need to be patient. Even the most optimistic economists believe that the transformation will take at least 15 years to complete.

REFLECTION: Do the news reports from Eastern Europe suggest that any of the original seven countries are well on their way to transforming their economies into successful market economies?

We should note in closing that many of the economists who are optimistic about the prospects of the Eastern European countries are quite pessimistic about the more modest market reforms being undertaken in the countries of the former Soviet Union. The will to succeed does not appear to be very strong. The former Communist bureaucracy was much larger and far more entrenched there than in any of the Eastern European countries, and the popular support for market reforms is still very shaky. The countries of the former Soviet Union are also much less dependent on international trade than are the economies of Eastern Europe, so the disciplining force of the international marketplace is missing. In summary, the former Soviet countries face the same obstacles as the Eastern Europeans in trying to move to a more market-oriented economy, but they seem less well positioned to overcome them.

SUMMARY

Chapter 3 began with a discussion of society's economic problem, consisting of objectives, alternatives, and constraints.

1. The economic objectives of a humanistic society are efficiency and equity.
2. Economists express the alternatives as four fundamental economic questions that all societies must answer. These questions also incorporate the objectives of efficiency and equity.
   a. The What or Output question: What goods and services should society produce and in what amounts?

b. The How or Input question: How should firms produce each of the goods and services, and what factors of production and production technologies should they use?
c. The For Whom or Distribution question: Who will receive the goods and services?
d. The Now versus the Future question: Should society favor the current generation at the expense of future generations, or vice versa? This is the question of long-run economic growth.

3. The constraints that ultimately limit how well off a society can be consist of the quantity and quality of the nation's resources and the production technologies available for turning inputs into outputs.
4. The production possibilities frontier is a two-dimensional diagram representing the constraints of society's economic problem. The frontier shows the combinations of goods and services that the society is potentially able to produce, assuming that production is efficient.
5. An economy operates under its production possibilities frontier if its resources are either misallocated or unused. No society can operate beyond its frontier.
6. The production possibilities frontier exhibits increasing opportunity cost because some resources are better suited to produce particular goods and services. Increasing opportunity cost means that producing more of one output requires ever-increasing sacrifices of the other output.

The second section of the chapter described the process of long-run economic growth.

7. Long-run economic growth refers to persistent increases in the potential of an economy to produce goods and services. It is represented as a continuing shift of the production possibilities frontier away from the origin.
8. Long-run economic growth requires a change in the quantity or quality of a nation's resources or the introduction of new production technologies.
9. Investment in physical and human capital (education) is the key to economic growth because it meets all three requirements for growth. Capital is an important factor of production, new capital tends to make all factors of production more productive, and new production technologies are usually embodied in new capital.
10. The opportunity cost of growth is that more investment comes at the expense of consumption. The sacrifice of consumption is very costly for poor countries, making the growth process difficult to start.

The final section of Chapter 3 discussed society's choice of an economic system to solve the economic problem.

11. The four principal characteristics of an economic system that determine how an economy performs are the delegation of the decision-making authority, the way in which economic information is processed and coordinated, the ownership of capital and land, and the incentives used to encourage consumers and producers to pursue society's objectives.
12. Pure market capitalism and centrally planned socialism are stylized economic systems that lie at the endpoints of the spectrum of economic systems. All real-world economies are blends of these two systems.

13. Pure market capitalism decentralizes the decision-making authority to individuals and business firms, uses markets and prices to process and coordinate economic information, allows private ownership of capital and land, and relies entirely on material incentives. Its principal strengths are individual freedom, responsiveness to consumers' desires, and efficiency in the allocation of scarce resources.
14. Centrally planned socialism centralizes the decision-making authority in an agency of the national government, uses a national plan to process and coordinate economic information, has public ownership of capital and land, and relies on both material and moral incentives. Its principal strengths are the ability to formulate and pursue national objectives, a fairly equal distribution of income, and a virtual guarantee of full employment.
15. In 1989 seven Eastern European countries (Bulgaria, Czechoslovakia, East Germany, Hungary, Poland, Romania, and Yugoslavia) announced that they were going to transform their economic systems. They would replace systems designed along the lines of centrally planned socialism with systems designed along the lines of pure market capitalism. They face a number of obstacles in transforming their economies. Foremost among them is the fact that 30 to 40 percent of their companies were not competitive in 1989. The transformations of their economies will probably take at least 15 years under the best of circumstances.

KEY TERMS

centrally planned socialism
economic system
for whom or distribution question
how or input question
human capital
investment
long-run economic growth
market
national economic plan
now versus the future question
production possibilities frontier
pure market capitalism
what or output question

QUESTIONS

1. What is the production possibilities frontier, and which components of society's economic problem does it illustrate?
2. Suppose that an economy produces only two goods, *X* and *Y*.
   a. Draw a reasonable production possibilities frontier for the economy. Why did you draw it as you did?
   b. Suppose that a new technological advance makes the economy much more productive in producing good *Y*. Show how this discovery might affect the production possibilities frontier that you drew. Explain.
   c. Does this technological change permit society to consume more of good *X*?
   d. Pick a point on the original production possibilities frontier and label it *A*. After the technological change occurs, is *A* an efficient production point? Why or why not?
   e. Explain what the opportunity cost of producing more *X* is at point *A* before and after the technological change occurs.
3. How do the four fundamental questions that any society must answer relate to the components of society's economic problem?
4. Explain why the following statement is true: The *production possibilities frontier* illustrates the concepts of the *Law of Scarcity*, *efficiency*, and *opportunity cost*.
5. Suppose that an economy produces only two goods: baseball bats and 2 × 4s. Also, the only input needed to make these goods is trees. Here 1 tree makes 10 baseball bats, and 1 tree makes 20 2 × 4s. If there are 50 trees in the economy, draw the production possibilities frontier for this economy. Does this frontier illustrate the principle of increasing opportunity cost?

6. a. Why do economists believe that investment is the key to long-run economic growth?
   b. The poorer nations of the world understand that investment is the key to long-run economic growth, yet they are often reluctant or unable to increase investment significantly. Why is this?
7. President Clinton argues that the United States needs to improve formal education and also train workers who lack basic skills if it hopes to have a rapidly growing economy. Does this argument make sense?
8. What are the four principal characteristics that determine how an economic system operates? Describe the features of pure market capitalism and centrally planned socialism in terms of these characteristics.
9. Discuss the relative strengths and weaknesses of pure market capitalism and centrally planned socialism.
10. Describe some of the problems that the Eastern European countries will face as they attempt to convert from centrally planned economies to market-based economies.

CHAPTER

4

Markets, Prices, and the U.S. Economy

LEARNING OBJECTIVES

CONCEPTS TO LEARN

A market
The economic function of prices
The principle of comparative advantage
The circular flow of economic activity
Highlights of the U.S. economy

CONCEPTS TO RECALL

Economic exchange [1]
Interdependence [1]
Pure market capitalism [3]

The U.S. economy is incomprehensibly large. Over 250 million individuals, 18 million business firms, and 89,000 government agencies engage in billions of market exchanges every day. The annual value of final goods and services produced in the United States passed the $6 trillion mark in 1993. How large is $6 trillion? Imagine the following exercise. Take 100 one-dollar bills, and tie them into a bundle one inch high. Keep doing this until you have bundled $6 trillion worth of dollar bills. Then pile all the one-inch, $100 bundles one on top of another. How tall would the stack be? The answer is tall enough to reach the moon and return to earth—twice!

The miracle of a modern decentralized market economy is that it works at all because capitalism would appear to be a recipe for chaos. The millions of individuals and business firms interact in thousands of markets without any direction whatsoever. Moreover, the market system says to each of them, in effect, "Do your own thing. Pursue your own self-interest as much as you possibly can. Forget about anyone else. Let others look out for themselves." Yet market exchanges are nearly always orderly, not chaotic, and markets are the most effective mechanism yet devised for promoting economic efficiency. One of the main goals of a first course in economics is to understand how this can be.

The two main themes in economic analysis are the economic problem and the exchange of goods and services and factors of production. Chapters 1 through 3 discussed the economic problem as it relates to individual economic agents and to society as a whole. Chapter 4 completes the introductory part of the text with a discussion of some fundamental issues related to exchange in a modern market economy. It provides the background information that we will need for our study of how markets operate in the U.S. economy. The natural place to begin is with a description of what a market is.

MARKETS

The thousands of markets in which buyers and sellers exchange products and factors of production are the heart and soul of a capitalist economy. What exactly is a market? In Chapter 3 we defined a market in a very general way as any institutional arrangement that permits the voluntary exchange of a good, service, or factor of production between buyers and sellers. Defining the concept of a market more precisely than this is difficult because markets take many different forms. Market exchanges occur in a variety of institutional settings, and markets have distinctive product and geographic dimensions that vary considerably from market to market.

The Institutional Setting

Think for a moment about the many different ways in which exchanges of consumer goods and services take place. The majority of transactions involving consumer goods occur in retail outlets, both large and small. But agricultural produce is often sold at roadside stands and open air markets. Other goods are sold through the mail or door to door. Many financial securities are traded electronically over phone lines. The dollar amounts of these telephone exchanges are transferred from one computer's memory to another without anything tangible changing hands. Some exchanges involve direct contact between the buyer and the seller. This is particularly true of services such as those provided by electricians, hairdressers, and restaurants. In contrast, manufactured goods are more often exchanged indirectly through intermediaries. For instance, retail outlets are usually intermediaries between the consumers and the producers. Retailers buy the goods from the manufacturers and then resell them to the consumers.

The same variety of institutional settings exists in factor markets. Many professional and skilled blue-collar labor services are exchanged by means of a formal contract that stipulates the salary and the requirements of the job. People can negotiate their own contracts, or they can be represented by intermediaries such as agents or union negotiators. Other occupations do not use formal contacts. Many white-collar jobs operate under implicit contracts in which the salary and the job requirements are well understood, even though nothing is put in writing. Exchanges involving unskilled labor are sometimes even more casual and intermittent. On some construction jobs laborers are hired daily on a first come–first hired basis and paid at the end of the day. Whether workers show up for work on any one day does not affect their chances of being hired on any subsequent day.

Transactions involving land can also occur in a variety of ways. Parcels of land can be sold directly from buyer to seller or through intermediaries such as real estate agents. Two wealthy doctors in Los Angeles may exchange 1,000 acres of Iowa farmland that neither has ever seen.

These examples illustrate why you cannot associate the concept of a market with any one particular institutional setting.

Market Boundaries

Markets have both product and geographic dimensions. Economists define individual markets by product or factor of production, as in the market for orange juice, or four-year liberal arts colleges, or computer scientists, or professional baseball players. But the boundaries between individual products and factors of production are not often clear-cut from either the buyers' or the suppliers' perspective. Consider product markets by way of example.

Economists first attempt to distinguish individual products from the buyers' perspective. Do buyers view the product as reasonably distinct? Are close substitutes available? How "close" is a close substitute? These are sometimes difficult questions to answer. Consider various writing implements as an example. Do consumers view felt-tipped pens as substitutes for ball point pens? Are pens and pencils substitutes for each other? Are they two products or one essentially interchangeable product? Consumers undoubtedly think of pens and electronic typewriters as reasonably distinct products, but do they consider electronic typewriters and word processors to be distinct products?

INDUSTRY
The collection of all firms producing the same product.

The supplier's perspective enters into the determination of individual product markets as well. Products are produced by business firms, and an **industry** is the collection of all firms producing the same product. Particular industries may not be clearly defined, however. For example, even if consumers view felt-tipped and ball point pens as distinct products, business firms might see them as virtually identical because they can easily switch production from one to the other as demand dictates. If so, then a firm producing only felt-tipped pens at the moment is still very much in the market for ball point pens. The felt-tipped pen and ball point pen *industries* are not distinct. But are there distinct *markets* for the two kinds of pens? The buyers and sellers may reach different conclusions in this case.

Geography is yet another factor that determines what constitutes a distinct market. Economists do not typically use the term *market* as market researchers do when they speak of the Minneapolis–St. Paul "market." Market researchers use a geographic definition of a market because they are primarily interested in the sales potential of a particular geographic area. Economists define a market in terms of an individual product or factor of production because they are primarily interested in the exchanges of particular products and factors between buyers and sellers. Nonetheless, geography can create distinct local markets for otherwise identical products or factors of production because of the transportation costs between different regions of the country.

A blue-collar construction worker in Miami is in a market distinct from that of a blue-collar construction worker in Atlanta because it is costly to transport workers between the two cities. A construction worker in Miami cannot replace a construction worker in Atlanta, even if the workers have identical abilities and are performing the same tasks. Cement is bought and sold nationwide, but the exchanges occur in numerous distinct local markets, again because of the high costs of transporting cement over long distances.

At the other extreme, the markets for a large number of financial securities are virtually worldwide, with exchanges occurring 24 hours a day. National boundaries create no important transaction costs for electronic exchanges, and financial markets are always open in some time zones around the clock. Money managers can easily move funds from Tokyo to New York to London. Similarly, the markets for ever more manufactured products are becoming international in scope, as large multinational corporations set up offices and factories throughout the world. For example, there may no longer be a separate U.S. market for automobiles, given that nearly 40 percent of all new cars sold in the United States are produced by foreign firms. Some of the foreign auto makers operate factories in the United States. At the same time, Chrysler, General Motors, and Ford each produce cars in Europe. In sum, the geographic dimension makes it difficult to determine the proper extent of a market from an economic perspective, that is, the numbers of buyers and sellers to include when analyzing a market.

REFLECTION: How would you describe the institutional arrangements of the market that brought you to your college or university? Is this market national or international in scope?

These difficulties notwithstanding, defining and analyzing individual product and factor markets is a useful way to understand how a market economy operates. We will analyze individual markets throughout the text on the assumption that the markets are well defined, and in many cases they are reasonably well defined.

CHARACTERISTICS OF MODERN MARKET ECONOMIES

Analyzing the behavior of prices is a central focus of economics because markets function by means of prices. Economists think about prices somewhat differently than most people do. Whenever people stop to think about prices, their typical concern is that prices are too high or too low, for instance, that their salaries are too low or that the price of medical care is too high. Economists also describe instances in which prices can be said to be too high or too low. But their main interest in prices is how they process economic information and coordinate economic decisions. The fundamental economic question about market exchange is this: How do prices coordinate market exchanges and thereby allocate society's scarce resources?

Why are market exchanges orderly rather than chaotic, and why are markets such an effective mechanism for promoting economic efficiency? The answers must lie in how prices work. We have seen that individuals and business firms enter into market exchanges with completely different economic problems: They have different objectives, different alternatives, and different constraints. They share only one piece of information in common, the price to be paid for a good or service or a factor of production. Therefore, prices act as the signals that bring buyers and sellers together, and they must incorporate all the economic information that is necessary for exchange to take place. As such, prices bear the burden of making a market economy function smoothly and efficiently—nothing else can do this. Markets and prices are so closely tied together that a market economy is sometimes referred to interchangeably as a price system.

Subsequent chapters will describe how prices coordinate market exchanges in various market settings. In this introductory chapter we simply want to gain an appreciation for the enormous amount of work that prices are required to do in a modern, highly developed market economy such as that of the United States.

Three characteristics of the modern market economy place special burdens on prices. The first is that production is highly specialized. Specialization in production separates economic agents from one another and increases the number of market exchanges they must engage in. The second is that market exchanges do not occur in isolation. An economy is essentially a giant closed circle in which all markets are necessarily interrelated. As a result, prices must do more than bring buyers and sellers together in each individual market. The smooth and efficient functioning of a market economy requires that prices in different interrelated markets bear particular relationships to one another. The third characteristic is simply the sheer size and diversity of a developed market economy. Prices have to coordinate a huge number and variety of exchanges. Let's take a look at each of these characteristics.

Specialization

Each of us consumes a wide variety of goods and services. But we are typically involved in the production of only a very few goods and services, perhaps only one, or perhaps none at all. Indeed, most of us have no idea how to produce many of the products that we consume. This disparity between consumption and production is true in all but the most primitive economies. As economies develop, people become generalists in consumption and specialists in production.

DIVISION OF LABOR

As an economy grows and as business firms become larger, the process by which factors of production tend to become ever more specialized, performing highly specific tasks associated with only one small part of the production process.

ECONOMIES OF SCALE

A characteristic of production in which production costs rise proportionately less than output as production increases, so that costs per unit of output fall.

HISTORICAL NOTE: In the early 1900s Henry Ford ran ads claiming that his cars were cheaper to purchase and maintain than good ol' Dobbin the horse.

Specialization in production and economic development go hand in hand: Neither can proceed without the other. Once an economy begins to grow and business firms become larger, factors of production tend to become ever more specialized, performing highly specific tasks associated with only one small part of the production process. The process of specialization is called the **division of labor,** but it applies to capital as well. Workers performing specific tasks use capital that is also designed just for those tasks. The automobile assembly line is a classic example. One worker bolts the right-hand side of the engine block to the chassis. Farther down the line another worker mounts the left front tire, and all the workers along the assembly line have their own sets of tools and machines.

The division of labor is profitable because it generates a phenomenon called **economies of scale,** which describes the relationship between the cost of production and the output as the scale of an operation is increased. Economies of scale arise whenever production costs rise proportionally less than output as output increases, so that the costs of producing each individual unit of output fall. Once again the automobile assembly line is a perfect example. Before Henry Ford introduced the assembly line to automobile manufacturing, cars were assembled in small garages by a few mechanics performing a large number of different tasks. Ford discovered that he could produce cars much more cheaply if they were manufactured in huge quantities on a highly specialized assembly line. The largest assembly lines today produce hundreds of thousands of cars each year.

The division of labor and resulting economies of scale in turn promote further economic growth. With lower unit costs, firms can sell their products at lower prices, which encourages people to buy more of the products. As firms sell more output, they employ more factors of production and generate more income that can be used to buy even more products. The economy develops and creates new possibilities for cost-cutting economies of scale through ever greater division of labor. With still greater specialization comes further economic growth, and the interaction of specialization and economic growth continues onward. At the level of the firm the process of specialization and economic growth culminates in the giant corporation, in which production occurs on a massive scale and uses large amounts of sophisticated capital. All functions within the corporation, including production, marketing, finance, and management, are highly specialized.

With specialization comes separation of consumers and producers. People have to engage in market exchanges with producers for almost all the goods and services that they consume. Separation also occurs within production. More and more firms produce intermediate, semi-finished products, which they sell to other firms for further processing in a hierarchical chain of production. This necessitates the development of still other markets to facilitate exchanges between the firms. Market exchanges, and prices, become ever more important to the operation of the economy as it continues to grow.

The use of money, such as dollar bills and checks written against checking accounts, is an essential ingredient of the process of specialization and economic growth. This is why all but the most primitive societies use money to facilitate exchange. Without money all exchanges would be **barter** arrangements in which goods exchange directly for other goods. Two people would only engage in exchange if they each had something that the other wanted. For instance, economists who want new suits would have to find tailors who want economic advice; both are likely to go wanting. Barter is no longer necessary with the use of money. Economists can offer economic advice to people who want it, accept money in return, and exchange the money for suits. Tailors will accept the money, knowing that they, too, can exchange it for the things they want. So the use of money permits the specialization and the separation required for economic growth. At the same time the use of money requires the existence of prices so that people know how much money they must exchange for any good or service.

BARTER

An exchange of goods directly for other goods.

INTERNATIONAL SPECIALIZATION AND TRADE: THE PRINCIPLE OF COMPARATIVE ADVANTAGE

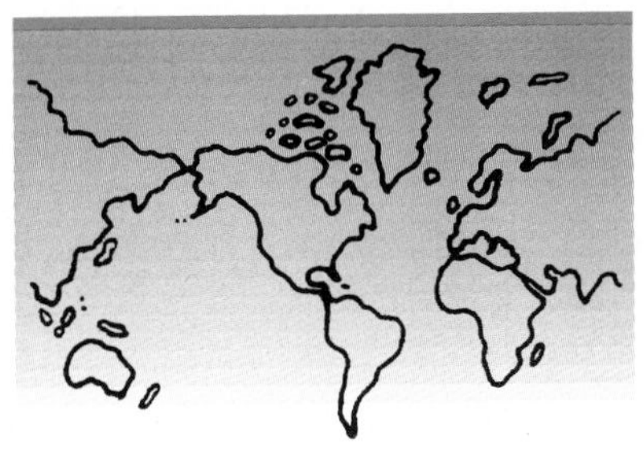

The gains from the division of labor and specialization in production extend well beyond national borders. Entire nations can gain by specializing their production in some goods and trading them for the goods that other nations specialize in producing. Moreover, a nation does not necessarily have to be the best at producing anything to benefit from international trade. The gains from specialization and international trade result from differences among nations in their opportunity costs of producing goods and services, and not necessarily from any absolute productivity advantages they may have.

David Ricardo, a London stockbroker who dabbled in economics and became the leading English economist of the early 1800s, was the first to demonstrate the potential gains from international trade on the basis of differences in opportunity costs. He was a staunch advocate of international trade among nations, and his argument in support of free trade became known as the principle of comparative advantage.

One country is said to have a **comparative advantage** over another in the production of a good if it can produce it with lower opportunity costs. Ricardo showed that two countries can *each* gain from trade if they specialize their production in the goods in which they have a comparative advantage and trade them for the goods in which they have a comparative disadvantage. Since every country is virtually certain to have a comparative advantage is something, specialization and international trade can benefit all countries.

COMPARATIVE ADVANTAGE

The principle that a country should specialize its production in those goods that it can produce with lower opportunity costs than can other countries and trade for those goods that other countries can produce with lower opportunity costs.

The following simple example illustrates Ricardo's principle of comparative advantage. Suppose that the United States and England each use only labor to produce two goods, food (F) and clothing (C). In the United States 1 unit of labor can produce either 4 units of food or 3 units of clothing. In England 1 unit of labor can produce either 2 units of food or 2 units of clothing. The following summarizes the productivity of 1 unit of labor in each country:

United States:	4F	3C
England:	2F	2C

Notice that labor in the United States is more productive than is labor in England in producing both goods; the United States has an absolute productivity advantage in both food and clothing. Nonetheless, both the United States and England can gain from specialization and trade because the opportunity costs of producing food and clothing differ in each country.

The opportunity costs of food. Producing 4 more units of food in the United States entails an opportunity cost of 3 units of clothing. Producing 4 more units of food in England entails an opportunity cost of 4 units of clothing. Therefore, the opportunity cost of producing food is lower in the United States than in England; the United States has a comparative advantage in producing food.

The opportunity costs of clothing. Producing 3 more units of clothing in the United States entails an opportunity cost of 4 units of food. Producing 3 more units of clothing in England entails an opportunity cost of only 3 units of food. Therefore, the opportunity cost of producing clothing is lower in England than in the United States; England has a comparative advantage in producing clothing.

Both countries can increase their consumption possibilities if the United States specializes in the production of food, England specializes in the production of clothing, and they trade U.S. food for English clothing. They both gain so long as they trade food for clothing somewhere between the ratios of 4F for 3C and 1F for 1C. Receiving more than 3C for 4F reduces the opportunity cost of clothing in the United States. At the same time, receiving more than 1F for 1C reduces the opportunity cost of food in England. The simultaneous reduction of opportunity costs is what allows both countries to increase their consumption possibilities through trade.

Here is one example illustrating the possibility of mutual gains through specialization and trade. Suppose that each country has 100 units of labor, and without trade they produce (and consume) the following:

- The United States allocates 55 units of labor to food and 45 units of labor to clothing, producing 220F and 135C (220 = 55 * 4; 135 = 45 * 3).
- England allocates 72 units of labor to food and 28 units of labor to clothing, producing 144F and 56C (144 = 72 * 2; 56 = 28 * 2).

The countries understand Ricardo's principle of comparative advantage, so they specialize and trade. The United States puts all its labor into food, producing 400F (400 = 100 * 4). England puts all its labor into clothing, producing 200C (200 = 100 * 2). They then trade 175 U.S. food units for 140 English clothing units, a trading ratio of 5F for 4C (175F/140C = 5F/4C). Thus, the trading ratio 5F for 4C is between the U.S. ratio of 4F for 3C and the English ratio of 1F for 1C, as required.

The United States consumes the remaining 225F (225F = 400F − 175F) and the 140C received in trade.

England consumes the 175F received in trade and the remaining 60C (60C = 200C − 140C).

Both countries have increased their consumption through specialization and trade:

United States: (225F, 140C) versus (220F, 135C)
England: (175F, 60C) versus (144F, 56C)

Ricardo's principle of comparative advantage is one of the more important principles in economics. It shows that *relative* cost advantages/disadvantages motivate people and countries to exchange goods and services. In our example the superior productivity of the United States does not prevent England from enjoying the benefits of exchange. The principle of comparative advantage is also a powerful argument against tariffs, quotas, and other means of "protecting" nations from foreign competition. Free trade, not protection from trade, increases a nation's economic well-being.

The Circular Flow of Economic Activity

The principle of interdependence that we described in Chapter 1 does not apply just to the economic problem. Interdependence is also a fundamental principle of market exchange. The entire economy of a nation is essentially a closed, interdependent circle along which all markets are interrelated. This principle is fundamental to economics and will appear again and again throughout the text.

Recall that individuals and business firms each have two economic roles to play. Individuals purchase goods and services from firms and supply them with the three primary factors of production, labor, land, and the funds to buy capital. Business firms purchase the factors of production to produce the goods and services that they then sell to individuals. Hence, individuals and business firms meet each other twice—and in such a way as to create a closed circle.

The flow of goods and services and factors of production throughout the economy from their interactions is called the **circular flow of economic activity** and is illustrated by the **circular flow diagram** in Figure 4.1. At the top of the circle are the markets for goods and services, in which the individuals are the buyers and the business firms are the suppliers. At the bottom of the circle are the markets for the factors of production: labor, land, and capital. Here the roles are reversed; the individuals are the suppliers, and the business firms are the buyers. The reversal of roles in each set of markets makes the flow of economic activity circular. The solid inner line indicates the direction of the flow of physical, or real, quantities of goods, services, and factors (for example, physical units of labor supplied to firms in the labor markets and actual units of goods and services going from firms to consumers in the product markets). The dotted outer line indicates the flow of dollars in a market economy. Consumers offer dollars to firms in exchange for goods and services, and they receive dollars from firms in exchange for their factors of production. The total dollar value of the flow of activity in the product markets defines the **national product** of a country. Similarly, the total dollar value of the flow of activity through the factor markets defines the **national income** of a country.

CIRCULAR FLOW OF ECONOMIC ACTIVITY

The flow of goods and services and factors of production through the product and the factor markets of the economy that results from the interactions of individuals and business firms; the flow is circular because firms sell products to individuals in the product markets and individuals sell factors of production to firms in the factor markets.

CIRCULAR FLOW DIAGRAM

A graphical representation of the circular flow of economic activity through the nation's product and factor markets.

NATIONAL PRODUCT

The total dollar value of the flow of economic activity through the product markets of a nation.

NATIONAL INCOME

The total dollar value of the flow of economic activity through the factor markets of a nation.

FIGURE 4.1

The Circular Flow of Economic Activity

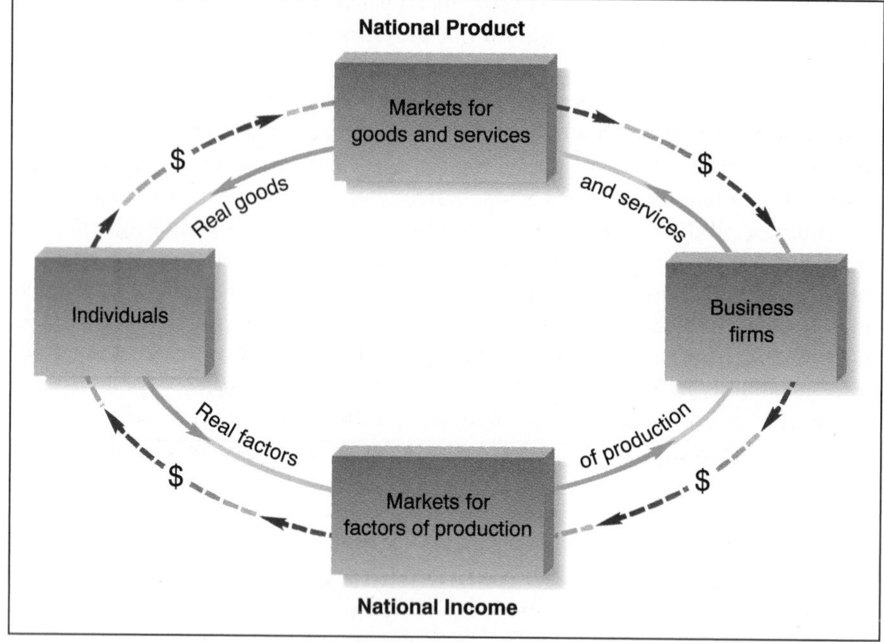

Economic activity is circular because individuals and business firms meet each other twice, in the markets for goods and services and in the factor markets, with their roles reversed. In the markets for goods and services, individuals are the buyers and the business firms are the suppliers. In the factor markets, individuals are the suppliers and the business firms are the buyers. The inner circle shows the flow of real goods and services and factors of production through the two sets of markets. The outer circle shows the flow of dollars through the two sets of markets. The government plays both roles of consumer and producer. The only breaks in the circular flow of economic activity are the exports to other countries and the imports from other countries.

Figure 4.1 appears to ignore a key player in the economy, the government. Where do the national, state, and local governments fit into the circular flow of economic activity? The answer is that governments play both roles of buyer and supplier. When the Department of Defense orders military aircraft from Boeing to provide for the national security, the government is acting as a consumer on behalf of the citizens. When the national government delivers our mail and hires men and women to operate military bases or when local governments educate our children, these governments are acting as business firms, producing public goods and services on behalf of the citizens. So the presence of governments does not change the nature of the circular flow of economic activity.

IMPORTS

Goods and services, and factors of production, purchased from foreign individuals and business firms for domestic use.

EXPORTS

Domestically produced goods and services, and factors of production, sold to foreign individuals, businesses, and governments.

There is only one exception to the concept of an economy as a giant, closed circle, the imports from and exports to foreign countries. Individuals, businesses, and governments purchase some of their goods and services and factors of production from foreign individuals and business firms. These purchases are **imports** from foreign countries. Similarly, individuals, businesses, and governments in foreign countries purchase goods and services and factors of production from domestic individuals and business firms. These purchases are **exports** to other countries. Because imported goods and services are not produced domestically, they represent a flow through the product markets for which there is no corresponding flow through the domestic factor markets. Imports appear as part of the flow of national income through other countries' factor markets. Similarly, when firms produce goods for export, they increase individuals' incomes because they purchase domestic factors of production to produce the goods. But the corresponding purchases of the exports appear as part of the flow of national product through other countries' product markets. Notice, though, that the circular flow of economic activity is maintained for the world's economy taken as a whole. The total amount of imports from other countries worldwide must equal the total amount of exports to other countries worldwide.

Imports and exports are important for virtually all countries, but thinking about economic activity as a circular flow is often a reasonable approximation. For most countries the value of imports approximately equals the value of exports, which means that the dollar values of domestic national product and national income are equal as well. The United States is an exception to this rule. Recently, U.S. imports have exceeded exports by a wide margin. Even so, the difference between U.S. imports and U.S. exports has only been about 1 percent of national product in recent years, so that the notion of the U.S. economy as a closed circle is not too far wide of the mark.

Interdependence of Economic Events

Markets are naturally interrelated because the flow of economic activity is circular. The effects of an important economic event always spread beyond the immediate impact of the event.

For instance, OPEC (Organization of Petroleum Exporting Countries) lost its control over the price of oil in the early 1980s, with the result that the price of a barrel of crude oil plummeted from $34 in 1981 to $10 by mid-decade. The market for oil felt the immediate consequence of the oil price decrease. On the one hand, factors of production associated with the oil industry suffered. People who worked in the oil industry either lost their jobs or were forced to take cuts in pay, and the returns to capital and land in the oil industry also declined. On the other hand, consumers of oil and oil-related products gained because of the price cuts.

The consequences spread far beyond the market for oil, however. States such as Texas that rely heavily on the income from oil suffered widespread economic losses. Because many of the citizens of Texas had less income, they could not spend as much as before on goods and services. Retailers soon felt the pinch as their businesses suffered. The real estate market also collapsed as more people were unable to afford houses and businesses did not need as much office and factory space, given their declining sales. As business suffered generally, people who had no direct connection with the oil industry also lost their jobs or received lower incomes, which contributed even further to the downward spiraling of the Texas economy. What started as a collapse in one market spread quickly throughout the entire Texas economy.

The experience was just the opposite in Massachusetts, an oil-consuming state. The Massachusetts economy was booming throughout the 1980s. The decline in the price of oil certainly helped to sustain the boom, as both consumers and businesses were able to buy fuel at lower prices. Massachusetts consumers could spend more of their incomes on other goods and services.

The oil price decrease had still further implications. One of the more notable was the comeback of the larger, heavier luxury automobiles. Large, gas-guzzling cars had fallen out of favor in the 1970s following oil price increases that were just as dramatic as the oil price declines of the 1980s.

The repercussions of major economic events are virtually endless as they work their way through the circular flow of activity. This must be so because as market events cause different people to have different incomes or cause different goods to be more or less expensive, people want to buy different kinds and amounts of goods and services. Businesses adjust their production accordingly to meet the new demands, which causes prices and incomes to adjust again, leading to still further changes in demands and in production. Prices and incomes continue to change indefinitely. These interdependent repercussions are part of what makes economic events so interesting—and often quite unpredictable.

The Size and Diversity of Modern Economies

The process of specialization and economic growth culminates in the modern, highly developed market economy such as that of the United States. Modern economies generate vast amounts of economic information, and innumerable economic decisions must be coordinated. Furthermore, modern economies are forever changing—they move through periods of expansion and contraction; new technologies and new products appear, while old technologies and old products disappear; clever new arrangements for exchanging goods and services evolve over time; and so on, endlessly. Prices must continually update economic information, and markets must be flexible enough to accommodate ever more and different kinds of economic decisions.

How many markets are there in the United States? No one knows. The annual Census of Manufacturers undertaken by the U.S. Department of Commerce identifies approximately 11,000 products within the manufacturing sector alone. But 11,000 far understates the number of manufactured goods that consumers would identify as distinct products. For example, under the product class "grape wines" the census lists only three products: red wine, white wine, and rose wine. Ernest and Julio Gallo would certainly hope that consumers distinguish between their varietal red jug wines and their limited reserve Zinfandels, and, of course, consumers do. How many service markets are there? How many markets for factors of production? So far as we know, no one has ever tried to count either of them.

THE U.S. ECONOMY

The U.S. economy provides a good example of the enormous size and diversity of modern developed market economies and of how much modern economies change over time. Let's look briefly at some of its highlights. This will give us some useful background information for our study of how markets operate in the U.S. economy.[1]

Size and Diversity

Thinking about a $6 trillion economy becomes somewhat more manageable if it is divided into its four major subsectors suggested by the circular flow of economic activity: the household sector, the business sector, the government sector, and the rest-of-the world sector. Figure 4.2 indicates the relative importance of each sector as a user and a producer of the final goods and services that pass through the nation's product markets.

THE HOUSEHOLD SECTOR The **household sector** consists of all individuals in their dual roles as consumers of final goods and services and as suppliers of factors of production to business firms. It is by far the largest user of the final goods and services produced by the economy, accounting for 69 percent of all purchases.

HOUSEHOLD SECTOR
The sector of the economy that consists of individuals in their dual roles as consumers of final goods and services and as suppliers of factors of production to business firms.

This sector derives its name from the fact that individuals are organized into residences, or households, consisting of one or more people. In fact, when a government or private agency collects data on individuals, it often surveys by residence, so that many economic data are available only for households or families, not for individuals. (A family refers to related individuals, whereas a household may consist of unrelated individuals.) Grouping data by household or family is entirely appropriate, however, if the household or family is the relevant decision-making unit.

No matter how they are counted, an enormous number of decision-making units comprise the household sector. In 1992 the total population of the United States was 255.4 million people. In 1990, when the population was 251.4 million, they were organized into 94.3 million households, of which 66.3 million were family households and 65 million consisted of a single person.

INCOME People earn income primarily through their labor. Approximately 80 percent of all income received in factor markets is wage and salary income. In 1992, 66.3 percent of all people aged 16 and older were in the civilian (nonmilitary) labor force, meaning that a total of 127 million people were working

---

[1]The data in this section come from three sets of sources that economists keep close at hand for information on the U.S. economy:

1. *The Economic Report of the President* (annual), prepared by the President's Council of Economic Advisers. The place to start, it includes data on all sectors of the economy. Also *Economic Indicators*, a monthly.
2. Three publications of the U.S. Department of Commerce:
   a. *The Statistical Abstract of the United States* (annual). The next place to turn, it is a compendium of economic, social, and demographic data.
   b. *Current Population Reports, Series P 60, Consumer Income* (approximately annual). A number of reports with detailed data on earnings and poverty are issued each year.
   c. The *Survey of Current Business.* Contains voluminous monthly data on the U.S. economy.
3. Two publications of the Board of Governors of the Federal Reserve Banking System, the nation's central bank:
   a. *Balance Sheets for the U.S. Economy (Publication C.9)* (annual). This publication provides data on U.S. wealth holdings, including capital and land.
   b. *Flow of Funds Accounts (Publication Z1)* (quarterly). This publication traces the flow of funds through the nation's financial markets.

FIGURE 4.2

The Composition of Final Output by Sector in the United States in 1992.

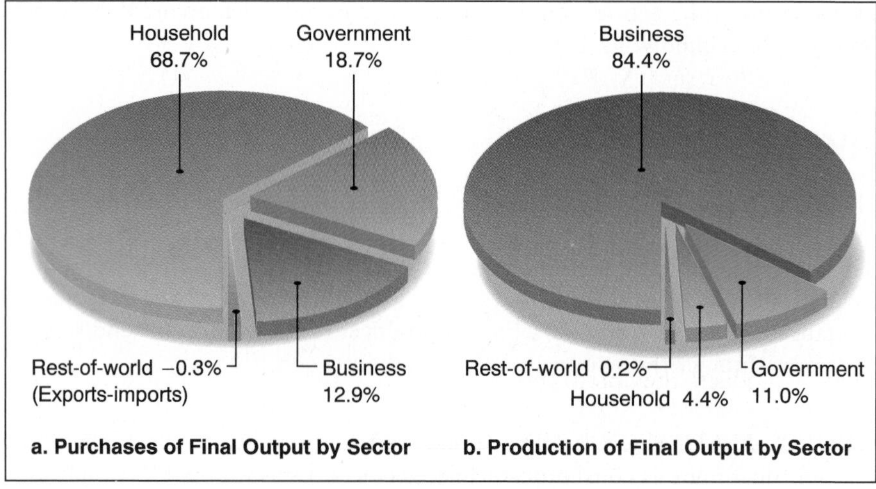

The pie-charts show the purchases and production of final output in the United States during 1992, by each of the four sectors of the economy—the household sector, the business sector, the government sector, and the rest-of-world (foreign) sector. The household sector is by far the largest purchaser of goods and services and the business sector is by far the largest producer of goods and services.

or actively seeking employment. That year 75.6 percent of all males and 57.8 percent of all females were in the labor force. Most of the remaining income represents income from saving, to be discussed below.

Not all the income received by households in the factor markets is available for their own consumption and saving. For instance, some income is taken by governments through taxation. Households consume the vast majority of income that is available to them, between 90 and 95 percent in most years. The remaining 5 to 10 percent of available income is saved.

CONSUMER DURABLES

Manufactured goods that typically last more than one year.

CONSUMER NONDURABLES

Manufactured goods that typically last less than one year.

SERVICES

Purchases by consumers that are not manufactured, but that provide them with something useful.

WEALTH

For a household, the accumulation of all savings over time; also called *net worth*.

REFLECTION: Would you say that your own pattern of consumption during the past year was roughly in line with the national average: 12 percent consumer durables, 31 percent nondurables, and 57 percent services?

CONSUMPTION Economists distinguish three kinds of consumer goods and services: consumer durables, consumer nondurables, and services. **Consumer durables** are manufactured goods that typically last more than one year, primarily motor vehicles, furniture, and household appliances. In 1992 they represented 12 percent of all consumption expenditures. **Consumer nondurables** are the remaining manufactured goods and include such items as food, clothing, gasoline, and heating fuels. They accounted for 31 percent of total consumption in 1992. The purchase of **services,** as from plumbers and electricians, airlines and rental car companies, and physicians and hospitals, accounted for the majority of consumer expenditures, 57 percent of total consumption in 1992.

SAVING AND WEALTH The act of saving is a decision to postpone consumption to some future date. Households hope to earn a return on their savings that will allow them to consume more goods and services in the future than they have sacrificed by not consuming today. Saving occurs in one of two forms. Households can purchase real, or tangible, assets such as a home or a parcel of land. They can also purchase financial assets such as corporate stocks and bonds, insurance of various kinds, pensions that will provide an income during retirement, and a variety of bank accounts and deposits. A household's **wealth,** or net worth, is the accumulation of all its saving over time. Despite fairly low savings rates, U.S. households have accumulated on enormous amount of wealth. In 1992 the net worth of the United States totaled $17.7 trillion, an average net worth of $69,000 per person.

THE BUSINESS SECTOR The **business sector** consists of all the private business firms. In 1988, the last year for which data are available, there were 18.9 million business firms in the United States (excluding over 2 million farms). The business sector is the major producer of final goods and services in the United States, accounting for over 87 percent of total production in 1992.

BUSINESS SECTOR
The sector of an economy that consists of all the private business firms and is the major producer of final goods and services.

Business firms are distinguished by their size, their legal structure, and the kinds of products they produce.

FIRM SIZE Most businesses in the United States are small businesses. In 1988, 78.8 percent of the 18.9 million firms had total receipts of less than $100,000. A relatively few large firms dominate in terms of value goods and services produced, however. Only 3.8 percent of the firms, about 730,000, had receipts greater than $1 million, but these firms accounted for 88.4 percent of total business receipts in 1988.

LEGAL STRUCTURE Nearly all businesses in the United States are structured as single proprietorships, partnerships, or corporations. Table 4.1 shows the percentage of firms that have each kind of legal structure.

The **single proprietorship** is the simplest form of business. It has a single owner, or proprietor, who has complete freedom to transfer funds into and out of the business and total control over the operation of the business. Proprietorships are often service-oriented, individual- or family-run businesses such as family restaurants, neighborhood variety stores, carpenters, and dry cleaners. The proprietorship structure is appropriate only for relatively small businesses, since it is limited by the owner's ability to raise funds. Also, proprietorships are quite risky, since the business's assets are not legally distinct from the owner's personal assets. Therefore, owners must be prepared to cover any business losses out of their personal wealth. As indicated in Table 4.1, although

SINGLE PROPRIETORSHIP
A form of business in which a single owner has total control over the operation of the business and has complete freedom to transfer funds into and out of the business.

TABLE 4.1 Comparison of U.S. Business Firms by Legal Type of Organization, 1988

TYPE OF FIRM	NUMBER OF FIRMS (THOUSANDS) (PERCENTAGE OF TOTAL)	VALUE OF RECEIPTS (MILLIONS) (PERCENTAGE OF TOTAL)
Proprietorships	13,679 (72.4)	$672 (6.1)
Partnerships	1,654 (8.8)	464 (4.2)
Corporations	3,563 (18.8)	9,804 (89.6)
Totals	18,896	10,940

SOURCE: U.S. Department of Commerce, Bureau of the Census, *Statistical Abstract of the United States, 1992* (Washington, D.C.: U.S. Government Printing Office, 1993).

most businesses are proprietorships, they generate only a small percentage of total business receipts.

PARTNERSHIP

A form of business with two or more owners who have total control over the operation of the business and who jointly determine how to transfer funds into and out of the business.

A **partnership** is the next step up in complexity. It has two or more owners, or partners, who jointly determine how to transfer funds into and out of the business and who have total control over the operation of the business. Law firms and investment banks are commonly organized as partnerships. Overall, though, relatively few business firms are structured as partnerships, and they generate an even smaller percentage of total business receipts. Partnerships suffer the same two handicaps that proprietorships do as a legal structure suitable for large businesses. The partners' ability to raise funds is somewhat limited, and their own personal wealth is at risk in the business.

CORPORATION

A form of business that is a recognized legal entity distinct from the owners of the firm, allows owners to transfer their shares of stock, allows owners to delegate authority and responsibility to a group of managers, has a potentially unlimited life, and has limited liability for business losses.

Corporations generate the overwhelming percentage of total receipts, as indicated in Table 4.1. The dominance of corporations is hardly surprising because the principles underlying the corporate structure are virtually essential to the efficient operation of any large-scale enterprise over a long period of time. There are five main principles of incorporation: (1) The corporation is recognized as a legal entity distinct from the owners of the firm; (2) owners have the right to transfer their shares of stock, which are their certificates of ownership; (3) the owners (stockholders) may delegate authority and responsibility to a group of managers; (4) the corporation has a potentially unlimited life; and (5) corporations enjoy limited liability for business losses, meaning that the financial liability of the owners is limited to the assets of the corporation. It does not extend to their personal assets.

These five principles give the corporate structure many advantages over the other two forms of business structure. People can easily supply funds to a corporation by purchasing stock without becoming involved with the firm in any essential manner and without risking personal bankruptcy. If they wish, owners can easily sever their financial ties to the firm by selling their stock. Funds for capital can therefore be raised easily and in great quantities. Furthermore, the life of the corporation continues beyond the lives of any of its owners. The corporate structure permits the separation of ownership from management, so that the terms of ownership and the identities of the owners need not have any effect on the operation of the business.

The main disadvantage of the corporate structure is that U.S. tax laws recognize the corporation as a separate identity subject to its own set of taxes. As a result, income earned by corporations is taxed twice, first by corporation income taxes and then by personal income taxes when the owners receive income from the profits of the corporation. Without this tax treatment, many more businesses would be likely to incorporate.

TYPE OF PRODUCT The third characteristic that distinguishes business firms from one another is the type of product or service they produce. The U.S. Department of Commerce divides all final goods and services produced into 10 major product, or industry, subgroups. Table 4.2 lists each subgroup, along with the percentage of total final output accounted for by each in 1988. The business sector includes all product categories except agriculture, government and government enterprises, and rest-of-world.

The table suggests the diversity of the U.S. economy; no one industry is dominant. Agriculture, mining, construction, and rest-of-world are all relatively minor; each produces less than 5 percent of the total output. The other in-

TABLE 4.2 **Production of U.S. Final Output by Major Industry Group, 1988**

INDUSTRY	PERCENTAGE OF TOTAL
Agriculture	2.3%
Mining	3.2
Construction	4.4
Manufacturing	23.0
Transportation	9.7
Wholesale and Retail Trade	17.2
Finance, Insurance, Real Estate	14.5
Services	15.3
Government, Government Enterprises	10.5
Rest of World	1.0

NOTE: Totals add to slightly more than 100 percent because of rounding error.

SOURCE: *Economic Report of the President, 1991* (data series discontinued after the 1991 *Report*) (Washington, D.C.: U.S. Government Printing Office, February 1991).

dustries produce from 9.7 percent (transportation) to 23.0 percent (manufacturing) of total output.

A final point relates to the economists' traditional division of final output into goods and services. The two components are roughly equal, with services having a slight edge. In 1992, 46 percent of total U.S. output consisted of manufactured goods (including structures) and 54 percent consisted of services. The service component has been steadily increasing throughout the post–World War II period. Services were only about 40 percent of final output in 1950.

GOVERNMENT SECTOR

In the United States, the economic activities of the federal government, the state governments, and all local governments.

THE GOVERNMENT SECTOR The **government sector** in the United States includes the economic activities of the federal government, the 50 state governments, and over 89,000 local governmental jurisdictions. These governments are significant purchasers and producers of final goods and services. In 1992 they accounted for about 19 percent of total purchases and over 11 percent of total production of final output. One-sixth of all workers are employed in the government sector.

When people refer to "the government," they usually mean the federal government. But the state and local governments are important components of the government sector as well. They are actually more important than the federal government as purchasers of final goods and services, and they are far more important as producers of final output. The federal government accounted for only 40 percent of all government purchases in 1992, and roughly 75 percent of these goods and services were purchased for defense or defense-related activities. No one category of expenditures is nearly so dominant at the state and local level. State and local governments purchase, and produce, a variety of public goods and services, including primary, secondary, and higher education; highways and public transportation; health and hospitals; and public safety. They produce 70 percent of all government output and account for 84 percent of all government employment. The state and local portion of the government sector clearly has a great impact on the daily lives of many U.S. citizens.

Although governments have the power to raise funds through taxation, government decision making is an integral part of the market system. With rare exceptions such as an occasional military draft, governments do not commandeer inputs for public production. They purchase factors of production in the marketplace and are therefore in direct competition with the business sector for these resources. Military personnel and teachers for local school systems must be paid a high enough wage to bid them away from alternative employment in the private sector. Similarly, governments purchase many goods and services from the private sector, including military hardware and supplies of all types. As with employees, the prices for these goods and services must be high enough to make it profitable for firms to sell to the government. In competing with the business sector for goods and services and for factors of production, the governments add to the information that must be processed and coordinated by the market economy.

The data on government purchases and production in Figure 4.2 significantly understate the overall impact of the federal, state, and local governments on the U.S. economy. Government spending far exceeds government purchases of final output. In 1992 government expenditures totaled $2.1 trillion, whereas government spending on goods and services and on factors of production was only $1.1 trillion. The difference, approximately $1 trillion, was **transfer payments.** Unlike government expenditures on goods and services, transfer payments do not use up scarce resources. A government transfer payment is simply a transfer of existing income to another economic agent. Therefore, transfer payments are not included as part of the purchases or production of the government sector.

TRANSFER PAYMENT

The redistribution of existing income from one economic agent to another.

Transfer payments fall into one of three categories. The largest category is transfers to individuals as part of a legislated government program. These transfers are based on who the people are rather than on any services they have provided to the government. The two largest transfers to individuals are transfers to the aged under the Social Security System in the form of retirement pensions and medical insurance (Medicare) and transfers to individuals and families with low incomes through public assistance programs (Medicaid, Aid to Families with Dependent Children, Food Stamps, and numerous other programs). Interest payments on the government debt (discussed below) make up the second largest category of transfer payments. Grants-in-aid from one government to another comprise the third important category of transfer payments. Examples include federal transportation grants to states to help them pay for highway construction and maintenance and for public transit and state grants to their localities to help pay for local school systems. These transfers obviously have an important impact on many peoples' lives. In fact, in 1992 approximately two-thirds of the federal government's expenditures were transfer payments, and these federal transfer payments accounted for almost 90 percent of all government transfer payments.

A final characteristic of the government sector to consider is taxes. Governments collect an enormous amount of revenue, just over $1.8 trillion in 1992. The federal government relies primarily on a personal income tax and a payroll tax on wage income that is earmarked for the Social Security System. Sales taxes and personal income taxes are the chief revenue raisers at the state level, and the property tax is the most important source of tax revenue for local governments.

The revenues from all these taxes have not been sufficient to cover government expenditures in recent years. Recall that government expenditures were $2.1 trillion in 1992, nearly $300 billion more than tax revenues. When expenditures exceed revenues, government budgets are in **deficit** and governments finance their deficits by borrowing from the other sectors. The federal government was responsible for the revenue shortfall in 1992. It ran a $298 billion deficit, while the state and local governments ran a $16 billion **surplus** of revenues over expenditures. This has been typical of most years since 1981, when the federal government began to run annual deficits at levels unprecedented in U.S. history during times of peace. The federal debt was just under $1 trillion in 1980; by 1990 the federal debt exceeded $3.2 trillion, and by 1993 it exceeded $4 trillion. The continuing federal budget deficits are one of the leading economic issues of the 1990s, and reducing these deficits is one of President Clinton's top priorities.

BUDGET DEFICIT
A situation in which a government's expenditures exceed its revenues.

BUDGET SURPLUS
A situation in which a government's revenues exceed its expenditures.

THE REST-OF-WORLD SECTOR The **rest-of-world sector** summarizes a nation's economic relationships with other countries. The purchase of final output by the rest-of-world sector is the difference between a nation's exports to other countries and its imports from other countries. This difference vastly understates the extent of a nation's international economic relationships, however. For example, the data in Figure 4.2 appear to suggest that economic relations with other countries are unimportant for the United States, but this is simply not true. The United States is an integral part of the world economy; U.S. exports and imports are each very important to the United States and to many other nations, and the United States has a major influence on capital markets throughout the world.

REST-OF-WORLD SECTOR
The sector of an economy that consists of a country's economic relations with foreign countries.

In 1992, 11 percent of all final goods and services purchased by the other three sectors were purchased as imports from other countries. Similarly, 11 percent of all final output produced that year was exported to other countries. The majority of U.S. exports and imports, 60 to 65 percent, are exchanged with the high-income capitalist countries such as Canada, Japan, and the Western European nations. Also, U.S. trade is concentrated in three product categories: industrial supplies and materials, capital goods, and automobiles. These three categories accounted for 74 percent of all exports and 68 percent of all imports in 1992. Trade in industrial and capital goods suggests that a substantial portion of U.S. trade consists of U.S. producers and foreign producers in the developed market countries exchanging factors of production with one another. The automobile trade is primarily with these same countries as well.

Only two other products are of any great significance in U.S. trade. The United States is the world's largest exporter of agricultural products. In 1992 agricultural products accounted for 9 percent of U.S. exports. The United States is also a major importer of petroleum and petroleum products. They accounted for 10 percent of all U.S. imports in 1992.

Today U.S. and foreign capital markets are also highly integrated, and funds for capital move easily across national borders. In 1992 U.S. asset holdings abroad totaled $2.2 trillion, of which $1.9 trillion were held by private U.S. citizens and businesses. Foreign asset holdings in the United States were even larger, $2.6 trillion, of which $2.2 trillion were held by foreign private citizens and businesses.

Thirty years ago domestic policy issues could safely be analyzed without paying much attention to international repercussions, but this is no longer true. Economic conditions in the United States have long had a significant impact on many other countries. The difference today is that economic conditions and policies in other countries now have a significant impact on the U.S. economy.

Changes in the U.S. Economy

The U.S. economy is hardly a static entity; it changes continually, sometimes even dramatically. The changes throughout the economy greatly increase the amount of information that prices must process and coordinate if they are to allocate resources properly. Here is a brief sampling of the more important changes over the past 40 to 50 years.

ECONOMIC CHANGES Economic growth has been the rule rather than the exception for the United States throughout its history, and the same has been true in the last half of the twentieth century. The circular flow of real goods and services through U.S. markets increased in every decade since 1950. As a result, the flow of real goods and services was roughly 3.5 times larger in 1992 than in 1950, which generated a significant increase in overall economic well-being. Consumption per person of goods and services more than doubled, despite a 66 percent increase in the U.S. population.

The leading growth sectors in the period from 1950 to 1992 were the government and rest-of-world sectors. Government expenditures on final goods and services increased by 260 percent, and transfer payments increased by 840 percent (correcting for price changes). The growth in exports and imports was even more dramatic. Exports grew by 1100 percent and imports by 1240 percent, which underscores the substantial internationalization of the U.S. economy since World War II.

Economic growth is never constant in market economies. At times the economy is booming, and the circular flow of economic activity grows vigorously; at other times the economy is mired in a recession, and the circular flow of economic activity actually declines. For example, the U.S. economy grew at an average rate of 3.1 percent per year from 1950 to 1992. But the actual annual rates of growth varied considerably during this period, from a high of 10.3 percent in 1951 to a low of −2.5 percent in 1982. Why market economies experience periods of boom and bust is one of the outstanding puzzles in macroeconomics.

A final indication of the amount of economic change in the U.S. economy relates to the business sector. Each year large numbers of new firms come into being, while others fail and pass from the scene. In 1990, for example, Dun and Bradstreet estimated that there were 647,000 new incorporations and 60,432 business failures. These numbers are typical of recent years.

DEMOGRAPHIC CHANGES The United States has undergone tremendous demographic changes since World War II. Significant demographic changes always have important economic consequences.

There was an unprecedented baby boom that lasted from 1947 through 1964, followed by an equally unprecedented baby bust from 1965 through the 1970s. Consequently, during the first half of the post-World War II period the average age of the population declined, and the proportion of youth swelled, despite continuing increases in the life expectancy of elder Americans. Since 1970, however, the population has been aging, and it will continue to age well into the twenty-first century. In 1970, 38 percent of the population was 20 and under, and 9.8 percent was 65 and older. By 1990 the percentage of youth declined to 28.8 percent, while the percentage of elderly rose to 12.4 percent. The average age of the population has increased by more than four years since 1970.

Demographic changes of this magnitude have an enormous impact on the composition and productivity of the labor force, on savings behavior, on the type of goods and services demanded, and on government transfer programs such as public assistance and Social Security. In short, these changes have an impact on virtually every aspect of the economy. The aging of the population as it continues into the next century may well be the single most important determinant of how the U.S. economy will perform.

The work experiences of American women have changed radically since 1950. Recall that 57.8 percent of all women aged 16 and older were in the labor force in 1992. The percentage was 33.9 in 1950. Throughout this period record numbers of women began trading hours of work in the home for hours of work in the market. Meanwhile, men began moving out of the market and into the home. The percentage of men in the labor force has dropped by 10 points since 1950. The American stereotype of the traditional two-parent family—husband working, wife staying at home—has been a myth for some time now.

Entry into the labor force has not been easy for women. They have had difficulty obtaining good, high-paying jobs, and they still shoulder most of the responsibility for managing the household. The economic status of working women is one of the leading concerns in the United States today.

Along with the increase in women working, the number of female-head-of-family households with no male present has increase substantially, especially among blacks. From 1970 to 1990 the number of such families grew from 7.2 percent to 17 percent of all families. For black families the percentages increased from 21.8 percent to 45.9 percent. Single-parent families headed by females are particularly vulnerable to poverty. They are three to four times more likely to be impoverished than are two-parent families.

The number of single-person households has increased even more dramatically—from 13.1 percent of all households in 1960 to 25 percent of all households by 1990. If the household is the relevant decision-making unit, then the number of such units in the household sector has been increasing much more rapidly than the growth in population would suggest.

The U.S. population is becoming ever more urbanized and concentrated. The percentage of the population living in urban areas increased from 69.9 percent in 1960 to 77.5 percent in 1990. The decline in the farming population has been especially dramatic. One of every eight workers was employed in agriculture in 1950. The ratio had declined to 1 in 40 workers by 1992. The influx of population to the cities has created some very difficult social and economic problems. Most of the nation's major cities are suffering from a lack of affordable housing, high crime rates, severely strained social services, deteriorating public school systems, and dangerously high levels of pollution.

Our survey of the economy concludes with two themes that have long been at the forefront of U.S. economic policy concerns: the concentration of wealth and power, and economic discrimination against nonwhites and women.

Concentrations of Income, Wealth, and Power

Many people worry that concentrations of income, wealth, and power in the U.S. economy undermine equality of economic opportunity. There is evidence of significant concentration in both the household and the business sectors. Income is highly concentrated: Over 46 percent of all income is earned by 20 percent of the families. Wealth is even more concentrated. According to the federal government's 1983 survey of wealth, 72 percent of all the nation's wealth is held by 10 percent of the nation's families. The richest 0.5 percent of families holds 35 percent of all wealth.

Within the business sector, the largest 100 corporations accounted for 75 percent of total manufacturing assets in 1991. The largest of these corporations are truly enormous. In 1982 Exxon's sales exceeded the total production of final goods and services of all but 19 *nations*.

To what extent do size and wealth confer unfair advantages in the marketplace and in the political arena? Should the government attempt to break down concentrations of income and wealth? Americans have struggled with these questions throughout the twentieth century.

Economic Discrimination

Racial and sexual discrimination appear to be serious problems in the United States, perhaps more so than in any of the other high-income market economies. A brief look at the data certainly suggests that nonwhites and whites, and men and women, have very different economic opportunities.

Whites fare much better economically than do blacks. For example, in 1990:

MEDIAN INCOME

The income of the family in the middle of the income distribution (half the families have incomes higher than the median and half have incomes lower than the median).

- The median income of white families was $36,915; the median income of black families was $21,423, only 58 percent of white family income. (The **median income** is the income of the family in the middle of the income distribution. Half of the families have incomes higher than the median income, and half of the families have incomes lower than the median income.)
- Only 10.7 percent of all whites lived in poverty compared with 31.9 percent of all blacks.
- The unemployment rate for whites was 4.7 percent; the black unemployment rate was 11.3 percent.
- Of all white families, 68.2 percent owned their own homes; only 43.4 percent of black families owned their homes.
- Of white children 18 years old and younger, 79 percent lived with both parents, and 17 percent lived with their mother only; 38 percent of black children lived with both parents, and 51 percent lived with their mother only.

Women who work fare much worse than do men in the labor market. In 1990, for example:

- Women earned two-thirds as much as men, on average, a ratio that has not changed much since 1939. As one consequence of their lower wages, women are more vulnerable to poverty than are men.
- The average earnings of female *college* graduates were less than the average earnings of male *high school* graduates.
- Of all women who work, 70 percent were nurses and health technicians, elementary and secondary school teachers, retail sales clerks, clerical workers, apparel and textile workers, or service workers.
- To make matters worse, when both husband and wife work, the wife bore two-thirds of the responsibility for the household chores on average.

Not all of the economic differences between nonwhites and whites, and between men and women, are due to discrimination. Other factors such as differences in educational background and job experience partially explain these differences. Economic research has left little doubt, however, that economic discrimination against nonwhites and women is partly responsible for their economic disadvantages. The only area of disagreement among economists is what proportion of their disadvantages is due to discrimination.

Looking Ahead

Having completed our overview of the U.S. economy in these first few chapters, we are now prepared to see how markets operate in the United States. We will make our first pass at understanding market exchanges. The pages just ahead describe how markets function when they are highly competitive and operate according to the Laws of Supply and Demand.

SUMMARY

Chapter 4 began by discussing the nature of markets in a highly developed market economy.

1. A market is an institutional arrangement that permits the voluntary exchange of goods and services and factors of production between buyers and sellers.
2. Markets take on many different forms because market exchanges occur in many different institutional settings. Markets also have distinct product and geographic dimensions. Economists define markets by product or factor of production. A market for a single product becomes more distinct the fewer substitutes the product has in consumption and the less easily firms can switch their production from the product to another product. The transaction costs of engaging in exchange help determine the geographic extent of a market, from local to worldwide.

Markets function by means of prices. The second section of Chapter 4 discussed three characteristics of highly developed market economies that place a special burden on the work that prices have to perform: specialization in production, the circular flow of economic activity, and the size and diversity of modern market economies.

3. As an economy grows, firms engage in a division of labor in which factors of production are assigned ever more specialized tasks. The division of labor is profitable because it generates economies of scale, which lower the costs of producing each unit of output as the business expands. Lower costs and lower prices encourage more expansion and growth, which in turn lead to even more specialization and further economies of scale. Growth and specialization go hand in hand and are made possible by the use of money. Without money, all market exchanges would have to be barter arrangements. The number of market exchanges increases with the degree of specialization and economic growth.
4. Entire nations can gain from specialization and international trade by following Ricardo's principle of comparative advantage, which is based on differences among nations in the opportunity costs of production. Two countries can *each* gain from trade if they specialize their production in the goods in which they have a comparative advantage and trade them for the goods in which they have a comparative disadvantage. Since every country is virtually certain to have a comparative advantage in something, specialization and international trade can benefit all countries.
5. Individuals and business firms meet each other twice, in both the product and the factor markets. Individuals supply firms with factors of production and buy the products that firms produce. Firms buy the factors of production and use them to produce the products that they sell to consumers. The result of their interactions is a circular flow of economic activity through the product and the factor markets. Governments act as both consumers and producers of goods and services. The only exceptions to the circular flow are exports to other countries and imports from other countries. Because economic activity is circular, all markets are interrelated.
6. The final burden on prices is the sheer size and diversity of modern market economies. Prices have to coordinate billions of market exchanges in these economies.

The third section presented an overview of the U.S. economy, which emphasized the size and diversity of the economy and discussed some of the more important economic and demographic changes that have occurred since 1950.

7. The economies have four main subsectors: the household sector, the business sector, the government sector, and the rest-of-world sector. The household sector consists of individuals in their dual roles as consumers of goods and services and as suppliers of factors of production. The business sector consists of the more than 18 million private business firms in the United States. The government sector includes the economic activities of the federal government, the 50 state governments, and over 89,000 local governmental jurisdictions. The rest-of-world sector consists of the nation's economic relationships with other countries.

KEY TERMS

barter
business sector
circular flow of economic activity
comparative advantage
division of labor
economies of scale
government sector
household sector
industry
national income
national product
rest-of-world sector

QUESTIONS

1. State whether each of the following is a good or service. If the commodity is a good, state whether it is a durable or a nondurable good.
   a. Ford Taurus
   b. rare bottle of wine
   c. children's clothing
   d. four-bedroom house
   e. haircut
   f. Principles of Economics course
   g. toaster oven
2. a. List the principal characteristics of a corporation.
   b. What are the advantages and disadvantages of the corporate form of business?
   c. How does a corporation differ from a partnership? Give examples of each.
3. Group the following products by industry. (*Hint:* Products may belong to more than one group)
   a. wooden baseball bat
   b. tennis racquet
   c. two-person tent
   d. down parka
   e. fur coat
   f. Harley-Davidson motorcycle
   g. mountain bike
   h. Lincoln Town car
   i. Honda Accord
   j. catcher's mitt
4. Consider the following seven-person economy. The data are for 1994.

PERSON	INCOME	CONSUMPTION
1	$ 20,000	$ 19,000
2	18,000	18,000
3	45,000	43,000
4	5,000	5,000
5	70,000	53,000
6	30,000	20,000
7	150,000	145,000

   a. What is the median income in the economy?
   b. How much did each person add to net worth (wealth) during 1994?
5. Describe the circular flow of economic activity. What role do prices play in the circular flow?
6. a. List and discuss three characteristics of modern market economies.
   b. Discuss the roles that the four sectors of the economy play in modern market economies.
7. Define *national product* and *national income.* How do they differ?
8. List some of the economic areas in which the U.S. government is an active participant. What social objectives might the government be trying to fulfill in each of these areas?
9. Two countries, A and B, use only labor to produce food and clothing. In country A, 1 unit of labor can produce 2 units of food and 3 units of clothing. In country B, 1 unit of labor can produce 1 unit of food and 2 units of clothing.
   a. Which country has the comparative advantage in the production of food? Which country has the comparative advantage in the production of clothing?
   b. Suppose that each country has 100 workers. Without trade, A devotes 50 workers to the production of food and 50 workers to the production of clothing. Without trade, B devotes 80 workers to the production of food and 20 workers to the production of clothing. Show with an example how both countries can gain by specializing their production in one of the goods and trading for the other.
   c. How would your answer to part a change if, in country B, 1 unit of labor can produce 4 units of food and 6 units of clothing?

CASE

Growth Through International Trade

A number of the major oil exporting countries—Bahrain, Brunei, Kuwait, Libyan Arab Republic, Oman, Qatar, Saudi Arabia, and United Arab Emirates—are a decided exception to some of the general principles of economic growth discussed in Chapter 3. They have fairly limited production possibilities for most goods and services, yet their incomes per person are among the highest in the world. Moreover, they achieved their lofty positions relatively painlessly, with low opportunity costs. They were able to play the growth game by different rules because they are blessed with large supplies of oil, a natural resource in very great demand, and they were able to exploit this advantage through international trade. By trading oil for goods and services, these countries created a set of **consumption possibilities** that greatly exceeded their production possibilities. The result was instant riches and the possibility of relatively painless sustained economic growth. They played David Ricardo's principle of comparative advantage to the hilt.

Their strategy of growth through international trade is depicted in Figure CS1.1. The two goods this time are oil (horizontal axis) and all other goods and services (vertical axis). The production possibilities frontier, represented by the solid inner line, shows that these countries are particularly good at producing oil and not so good at producing all other goods and services. Without trade they would be forced to produce along their frontier at a point very close to the maximum of all other goods and services. They need very little oil for themselves and would simply do the best they could in producing everything else.

International trade offers them the opportunity of exporting oil and in return importing all other goods and services produced elsewhere. They *produce* mostly oil and relatively few of all other goods and services. The production point is represented by point B in Figure CS1.1, with oil production equal to $0B_1$ and all other production equal to $0B_2$. They still need very little oil for themselves—say, an amount equal to $0D_1$. The remainder, D_1B_1, is exported to other countries, which trade all other goods and services for the oil. In 1980, for example, oil production in Saudi Arabia was nearly 78 percent of total output produced, and over 95 percent of the oil produced was exported.

The price of oil on the world oil market determines how many of all other goods and services the oil-exporting coun-

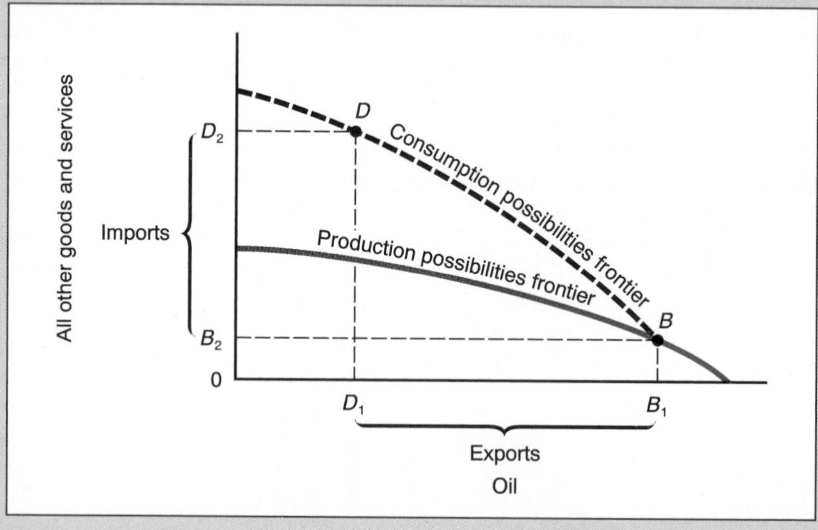

FIGURE CS1.1
Growth Through Trade

The oil exporting countries produce at point B on their production possibilities frontier. They then trade D_1B_1 barrels of oil for B_2D_2 of all other goods and services that they are not so good at producing themselves. Trading oil for other goods and services allows them to expand their consumption possibilities far beyond their production possibilities; they consume at point D on their consumption possibilities frontier. The price of oil determines how many other goods and services they can receive in trade for their oil. Some of the other goods and services that they trade for are investment goods, which help them expand their production possibilities frontier over time.

tries will be able to buy in exhange for their exported oil. Figure CS1.1 assumes that they can trade D_1B_1 of oil for B_2D_2 of all other goods and services. Hence, they end up *consuming* $0D_1$ of oil and $0D_2$ of all other goods and services, point D in the figure. D is a point on the **consumption possibilities frontier,** the dotted line in Fig. CS1.1, which shows how much oil and all other goods and services these countries are able to consume after trade has occurred. The consumption possibilities frontier pictured in the figure represents every consumption combination of oil and all other goods and services attainable by producing $0B_1$ of oil and trading increasing quantities of it for all other goods and services.

The ability to expand a nation's consumption possibilities beyond its production possibilities through international trade is available to all countries, although to a far lesser extent than is the case for the oil-exporting countries. It pays all countries to specialize their production in those things they produce relatively more effectively than others and to trade for those goods that other countries produce more effectively. For most countries, however, the constraints underlying their production possibilities are truly binding. International trade can expand consumption possibilities somewhat beyond the production possibilities frontier, but it cannot transform a poor country into a rich country by itself. The oil-exporting countries are truly exceptions in this respect.

Nevertheless, the oil-exporting countries have to increase their production possibilities if they hope to enjoy continued prosperity because the ability to trade oil for goods must eventually come to an end. The supply of oil is finite, and, in any event, new technologies will probably reduce the world's dependence on oil long before the supply of oil is exhausted.

Furthermore, instant riches do not produce a modern economy overnight. The oil-exporting countries will have to invest in both physical and human capital, just like all other developing nations, in order to increase their production possibilities. Their incomes may be high, but they still exhibit many of the same social and economic characteristics that the middle- and low-income developing countries do. For example, compare the following indicators of social well-being for Saudi Arabia with those of the United States in 1988 as estimated by the World Bank. The U.S. figures are in parentheses.

- Adult literacy: 51.1 percent (96 percent)
- Life expectancy: Male—62 (72); female—65 (79)
- Infant mortality per 1,000 births: 70 (10)

Achieving the U.S. social indicator rates will take the Saudis a generation or two, just as it would all developing countries.

The oil-exporting countries still have an enormous opportunity cost advantage over the other developing countries of the world, however, because they do not have to sacrifice nearly as much to achieve economic growth. By purchasing a mix of consumption and investment goods with their oil exports, they can build the capital base necessary for growth while enjoying a high level of consumption. The price of crude oil will determine how painless growth will be for them. The 1980s and 1990s have not been as kind in that regard as the 1970s were.

ECONOMIC ADVISOR'S REPORT

Suppose you are hired as an economic advisor to the government of Saudi Arabia. Answer the following questions.

1. The leaders ask you what Saudi Arabia should buy from other countries with its oil money. Would you advise the Saudis to buy only consumer goods, only capital goods, or a mixture of consumer goods and capital goods?
2. The leaders tell you that they would like to expand their country's production possibilities frontier to match their consumption possibilities frontier and to do this very rapidly, within five years. They ask you how they can do this. What would you say to them?

PART

II

The Laws of Supply and Demand

CHAPTER

5

Demand and Elasticity

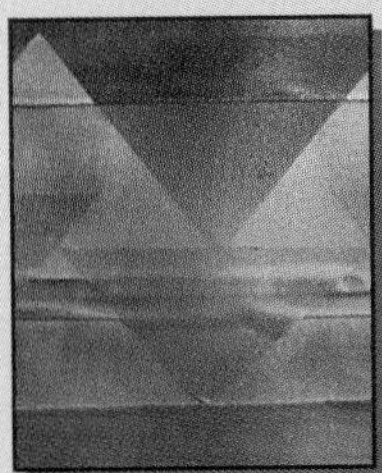

LEARNING OBJECTIVES

CONCEPTS TO LEARN

The factors that determine the demand for goods and services

The individual and market demand curves

The Law of Demand

The substitution and income effects of a price change

The elasticity of demand

CONCEPTS TO RECALL

The consumer's three-part economic problem [1]

The margin in economic analysis [2]

Chapters 5 through 9 describe how markets function when they operate according to the Laws of Supply and Demand. Supply and demand analysis is one of the more useful models for understanding market exchanges. It is very simple, yet it does an excellent job of explaining and predicting the pattern of prices and quantities in the vast majority of markets. What will be the price of compact discs next year, and how many will be sold? What will the job market be like for this year's graduating seniors? When health conscious Americans began eating fish and chicken instead of beef, the price of fish skyrocketed, but the price of chicken hardly increased at all. Why is this? Technological change has driven down the price of personal computers and driven up the price of medical care. Why has price responded so differently to technological change in these two markets? The Laws of Supply and Demand help us answer these questions.

The study of supply and demand also helps us judge how well our economy is performing. Markets that operate according to the Laws of Supply and Demand perform as well as markets possibly can. They allocate resources efficiently, and they are equitable in the sense of promoting equality of opportunity and horizontal equity. As such, the Laws of Supply and Demand are the benchmark for judging the performance of all market exchanges.

DEMAND

The amount of a product that individuals are willing and able to buy over a certain period of time.

Chapter 5 begins our study of supply and demand with an analysis of the demand for goods and services. Demand refers to the buyers' side of the marketplace. The **demand** for a product is the amount that individuals are willing and able to buy over a certain period of time. As such, demand is a statement of desires, of what individuals want to buy rather than what they actually buy. We will see that the amount consumers demand is not always equal to the amount they actually buy.

What determines the demand for each of the goods and services that we buy? This is the principal question that Chapter 5 addresses.

INDIVIDUAL DEMAND AND THE CONSUMER'S ECONOMIC PROBLEM

The demand for any product arises from the three-part economic problem that we all face in our role as consumers, consisting of objectives, alternatives, and constraints. To keep the consumer's economic problem as simple as possible, suppose that all decisions have been made with respect to how income is earned and that all income is spent on goods and services. There is no saving. Recall from Chapter 1 the structure of the individual's three-part economic problem under these assumptions.

The *objective* is to achieve the greatest possible utility, or satisfaction, from consuming goods and services.

The *alternatives* are the various goods and services that provide utility. Particular characteristics further distinguish one good or service from another. Consider, for example, all the attributes that distinguish one house from another or the numerous options that are available to you when you buy a new car.

The *constraints* are a combination of limited income and the prices of the various goods and services. The constraints assure that we cannot buy endless quantities of goods and services. We always want more than we can have.

The structure of the consumer's economic problem indicates that the demand for any one product depends on tastes or preferences, income, and prices.

Tastes or *preferences* determine how much satisfaction is achieved from consuming different amounts of each product. Does consuming some product make you feel good? Does it advance your knowledge? Does it cause your friends to look up to you? Do you prefer Pepsi or Coke? Tastes or preferences serve as a catch-all for every possible motive underlying consumption and for all the quality distinctions, real or imagined, that people perceive among various products.

Income is the scarce resource in this problem. What we want to buy depends on our resources as well as our preferences. The income that is relevant is the income actually available to us for consumption. Taxes reduce the income available to spend on goods and services. Conversely, transfers received from governments or other family members increase available income. Therefore, taxes and transfers should be included in the list of factors that affect demand, along with income earned in the factor markets.

Prices include not only the price of the product itself, but prices of other products as well. For example, music lovers can satisfy their passion by purchasing cassette tapes or compact discs or by attending concerts. Since these products all provide a similar kind of satisfaction, the demand for any one of them depends on the prices of all the other options.

The Individual Demand Curve

Economists have a special interest in the effect of the price of a product on its quantity demanded because prices are the centerpiece of a free market system. As noted in Chapter 4, prices incorporate all relevant economic information and coordinate market exchanges between buyers and sellers. In order to understand how prices perform these functions, we need to isolate the effect of price on the quantity that buyers demand (and the quantity that sellers supply). However, tastes, income, and all the other factors are continually changing, and these changes simultaneously affect quantity demanded. Therefore, if we want to isolate the influence of price on quantity demanded, we must assume that all the factors influencing quantity demanded *except price* are held constant. Holding all other things equal, or constant, how do changes in the price of the product affect the quantity demanded? (In economics the other things equal assumption is often stated in its Latin version, *ceteris paribus*. We will use the English version, other things equal, throughout this text.)

For most people and most products, most of the time, price and quantity demanded are inversely related, other things equal. The higher the price of a product, the smaller the quantity demanded; the lower the price of a product, the larger the quantity demanded. The inverse relationship between price and quantity demanded is illustrated by the hypothetical demand schedule for compact discs in Table 5.1. The **demand schedule** indicates, at different prices, how many compact discs a consumer wants to buy during the course of the year, other things equal. At the relatively high price of $24 the consumer wants to buy only 3 discs. As the price decreases to $16, the quantity of discs de-

INDIVIDUAL DEMAND SCHEDULE

The quantity of a good that an individual is willing and able to buy at each price, other things equal.

TABLE 5.1 **A Consumer's One-Year Demand Schedule for Compact Discs (Hypothetical Data)**

PRICE OF COMPACT DISCS	QUANTITY DEMANDED OF COMPACT DISCS
$24	3
20	5
16	6
12	7
8	8
4	10

manded increases to 6. A further decrease in price to $8 leads to a further increase in quantity demanded to 8 discs; and so on. Price and quantity demanded are inversely related.

A demand curve is the graph of a demand schedule. The line labeled *d* in Figure 5.1 is the **individual demand curve** for compact discs associated with the consumer's demand schedule in Table 5.1. Price is on the vertical axis, and quantity demanded is on the horizontal axis. The demand curve is drawn as a solid line to allow for all possible combinations of price and quantity demanded, not just the few price-quantity combinations shown in Table 5.1. Notice how the line slopes downward and to the right, indicating that price and quantity demanded are inversely related.

INDIVIDUAL DEMAND CURVE

A graphical representation of the individual demand schedule, showing the quantity of a good that an individual is willing and able to buy at each price, other things equal.

The Law of Demand

The inverse relationship between price and quantity demanded holds with such regularity that it is elevated to the status of a law of human behavior, the Law of Demand. The **Law of Demand** says, *other things equal,* the lower the price of a product, the larger the quantity demanded; the higher the price of a product, the smaller the quantity demanded. In terms of the demand curve, the Law of Demand says that individuals' demand curves slope downward to the right, just like the individual demand curve for compact discs does in Figure 5.1.

Laws of human behavior never hold as universally as physical laws such as the Law of Gravity. Situations arise for which the Law of Demand is violated. However, the force of the law is that these situations are quite rare, truly exceptional. We always *expect* price and quantity demanded to be inversely related. The same notion of expectation applies to any law of human behavior.

LAW OF DEMAND

Other things equal, the lower the price of a product, the larger the quantity demanded; the higher the price of a product, the smaller the quantity demanded.

REFLECTION: Can you think of any product for which your demand curve is upward sloping? That is, you are willing to buy more of the product the higher its price, other things equal?

The Substitution and Income Effects

What lies behind the Law of Demand? Why are the individual demand curves for most products downward sloping? Economists have identified two separate effects of a change in price—the substitution effect and the income effect—to explain the Law of Demand.

The substitution effect of a price change is a relative price effect. It is based on the idea that consumers compare the prices of all products when deciding

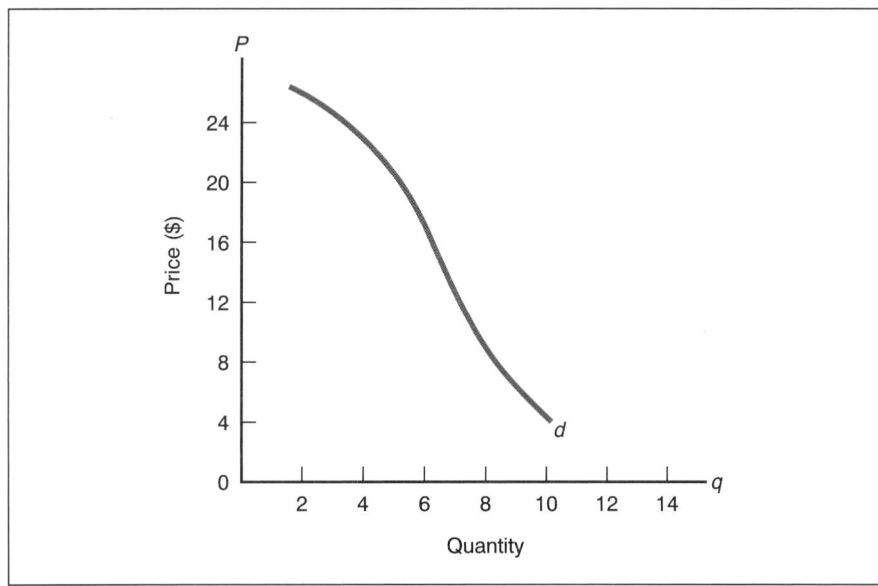

FIGURE 5.1

The Individual Demand Curve for Compact Discs

The individual demand curve for compact discs, *d*, is a graph of the hypothetical individual demand schedule for compact discs in Table 5.1. The demand curve is downward sloping in accordance with the Law of Demand; price and quantity demanded are inversely related. The higher the price, the lower the quantity demanded, and the lower the price, the higher the quantity demanded, other things equal.

how much of each product they want to buy. As a result of the **substitution effect,** when prices change, consumers tend to purchase more of those products that have become relatively cheaper and fewer of those products that have become relatively more expensive.

SUBSTITUTION EFFECT (OF A PRICE CHANGE)

The tendency to purchase more of those products that have become relatively cheaper and fewer of those products that have become relatively more expensive when relative prices change.

Points along a demand curve are drawn on the assumption that only the price of the product is changing. The prices of all other products remain constant. Therefore, referring to Figure 5.1, when the price of compact discs declines from $16 to $8, compact discs have become cheaper relative to all other products. According to the substitution effect, the individual responds by substituting in favor of compact discs and against other products. The quantity of compact discs demanded increases. Therefore, when price decreases from $16 to $8, the substitution effect helps explain why quantity demanded increases from 6 to 8 discs.

The income effect of a change in price is an absolute price, or purchasing power effect. **Purchasing power** refers to the amount of goods and services consumers are able to buy with their limited incomes. Economists also refer to purchasing power as *real income.* Real income implicitly compares the dollar value of income with the prices of the goods and services that the income will be used to purchase.

PURCHASING POWER

The amount of goods and services that consumers are able to buy with their limited incomes, given prices; also called *real income.*

Purchasing power increases when the price of any product decreases, other things equal, because consumers can buy more goods and services with their limited incomes. Conversely, purchasing power decreases when the price of any product increases, other things equal. Refer again to Figure 5.1. The individual purchases 6 compact discs when the price is $16. The total expenditure on discs is $96 ($96 = $16 · 6). If the price of discs decreases to $8, the individual can purchase 6 discs for a total expenditure of only $48 ($48 = $8 · 6). The decrease in price has freed up $48 that can be used to buy more goods and services. The individual's purchasing power has increased.

INCOME EFFECT (OF A PRICE CHANGE)

The change in the quantity demanded of a good due to the effect that the change in its price has on an individual's purchasing power or real income.

As a result of the **income effect**, consumers tend to buy more of most goods and services when their purchasing power increases. Therefore, when the price of compact discs decreases from $16 to $8, the consumer responds by using some of the increased purchasing power to purchase more compact discs (and other products as well). The income effect of the price decrease helps explain why the quantity of discs demanded increases from 6 to 8.

In conclusion, when the price of a product decreases, other things equal, both the substitution and the income effects lead to an increase in quantity demanded. In our example, the combination of the two effects explains why the quantity of discs demanded increases from 6 to 8 when the price decreases from $16 to $8.

THE MARKET DEMAND CURVE

MARKET DEMAND SCHEDULE
The total amount demanded of a good by all the consumers at each price, other things equal; the summation of the individual demand schedules.

Analyzing market events requires knowledge of market demand. The *market demand curve* for a product registers the *total* quantity demanded at each price by *all* consumers, other things equal. Table 5.2 and Figure 5.2 show how to construct the market demand curve for compact discs from the individual demand curves. For purposes of illustration the example assumes that the entire demand for compact discs comes from two individuals, persons 1 and person 2.

Table 5.2 shows the individual demand schedules of the two people and the market demand schedule. Person 1 has the demand schedule for compact discs from Table 5.1, reproduced in the second column of the table. Person 2 has a different demand schedule for compact discs, shown in the third column of the table. Individual demand schedules for compact discs, or any other product, are likely to differ because people have different tastes and different incomes. The fourth column of the table records the **market demand schedule**, the total quantity demanded by all consumers at each price.

The market demand schedule is the sum of the individual demand schedules. (column 4 = column 2 + column 3). For example, at a price of $24 person 1 wants to buy 3 discs, but person 2 finds the price is too high and does not want to buy any discs at that price. Therefore, the total quantity demanded at $24 is 3 discs (3 = 3 + 0), as shown in the fourth column. Similarly, at a price of $16 person 1 wants to buy 6 discs and person 2 wants

FIGURE 5.2

The Market Demand Curve for Compact Discs

The individual and market demand curves for compact discs are graphs of the hypothetical demand schedules in Table 5.2. The market demand curve, *D*, in Figure 5.2(c) indicates the total quantity demanded at each price, other things equal. It is the horizontal summation of the two individual demand curves, assuming that Person 1 and Person 2 are the only two buyers in the market. The market demand curve is downward sloping, in accordance with the Law of Demand. Price and quantity demanded are inversely related, other things equal.

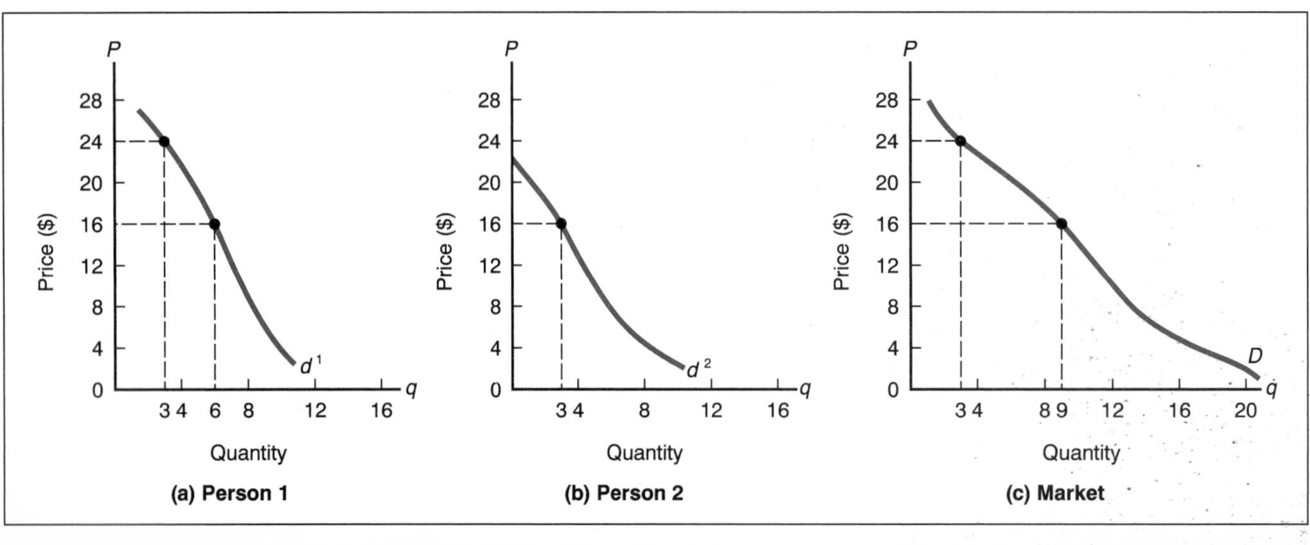

TABLE 5.2 One-Year Individual Demand and Market Demand Schedules for Compact Discs (Hypothetical Data)

PRICE OF COMPACT DISCS	QUANTITY DEMANDED OF COMPACT DISCS	QUANTITY DEMANDED OF COMPACT DISCS	QUANTITY DEMANDED OF COMPACT DISCS
	Consumer 1	**Consumer 2**	**Total Market**
$24	3	0	3
20	5	1	6
16	6	3	9
12	7	4	11
8	8	5	13
4	10	9	19

to buy 3 discs. The total quantity demanded at $16 is 9 discs (9 = 6 + 3). The construction of the market demand schedule is the same whether the market consists of two or two million individual consumers. In either case the total (market) quantity demanded at each price is the sum of the quantities demanded by all the individuals.

The **market demand curve** is the graph of the market demand schedule, with price on the vertical axis and quantity on the horizontal axis. Figure 5.2 pictures the individual and market demand curves corresponding to the individual and market demand schedules in Table 5.2. The demand curve of person 1 is shown in Figure 5.2(a), and the demand curve of person 2 is shown in Figure 5.2(b). The market demand curve is shown in Figure 5.2(c).

MARKET DEMAND CURVE

A graphical representation of the market demand schedule, showing the total quantity demanded of a good by all consumers at each price, other things equal; the horizontal summation of the individual demand curves.

As illustrated in Figure 5.2, the market demand curve is derived by adding the individual demand curves horizontally at each price. For example, at a price of $16, the quantity on the market demand curve (9) is equal to the sum of the quantities on the two individual demand curves (6 + 3). Notice that the market demand curve is downward sloping. This must be so, since the market demand curve is just the horizontal summation of the individual demand curves, each of which is downward sloping. Thus, the Law of Demand applies to the market demand curve.

In actual market situations total quantities demanded at any given price are enormously larger than each individual quantity demanded. For example, in the United States the market demand for compact discs is millions of times larger at every price than the average individual demand. Therefore, to distinguish between individual and market demands we will use D to represent market demand curves and d to represent individual demand curves, as in Figure 5.2. Similarly, we will use Q on the horizontal axis to represent market quantity demanded and q to represent individual quantity demanded when we are not using actual numbers as in this example. Q is understood to be many times larger than q. Note, however, that prices are the same on the market and the individual demand curves. In both cases, price is measured as dollars per unit of the product. In our example price is the cost to each consumer of a single compact disc.

Change in Quantity Demanded versus Change in Demand

The analysis of market events requires a very subtle distinction in terminology between a change in quantity demanded and a change in demand. A **change**

CHANGE IN QUANTITY DEMANDED

A movement along the demand curve as price changes, other things equal.

in quantity demanded refers to movements along the demand curve as price changes, other things equal. Along the market demand curve in Figure 5.2(c), an increase in price from $16 to $20 causes a *decrease* in quantity demanded from 9 compact discs to 6 compact discs. Conversely, a decrease in price from $16 to $8 causes an *increase* in quantity demanded from 9 discs to 13 discs.

CHANGE IN DEMAND

A shift in the entire demand curve.

A **change in demand** refers to a shift in the entire demand curve. A change in demand occurs when one of the "other things" influencing demand, such as incomes, tastes, or the price of a related product, changes. These factors are not shown on the horizontal or vertical axis for the graph of a demand curve. They lie behind the demand curve, determining the position and slope of the curve. If one, or more, of these factors changes, the entire demand curve shifts to a new position.

In Figure 5.3 the shift in the demand curve upward and to the right from D to D' is an *increase* in demand. The quantity demanded increases at every price. The shift in the demand curve downward and to the left from D to D'' is a *decrease* in demand. The quantity demanded decreases at every price. Let's take a brief look at some of the more important factors that cause the demand curve to shift.

INCOME When consumers have more income, their ability to purchase goods and services increases. Therefore, an increase in consumers' incomes leads to an increase in demand for a wide range of products. Their demand curves shift up and to the right, as from D to D' in Figure 5.3. Conversely, a decrease in consumers' incomes leads to a decrease in demand for most products. Their demand curves shift down and to the left, as from D to D'' in Figure 5.3. Products whose demands respond to income in this way are called **normal goods** because this is how we expect changes in income to shift their demand curves.

NORMAL GOOD

A good whose consumption rises as income rises, other things equal.

For some products, however, changes in income shift the demand curve in the opposite direction. An increase in income decreases demand, and a de-

FIGURE 5.3

Shifts in the Market Demand Curve

The entire market demand curve shifts when one of the factors that influences demand, other than the price of the product, changes. For example, an increase in consumers' incomes causes an increase in the demand for most products; the market demand curve shifts up and to the right, from D to D'. Conversely, a decrease in consumers' incomes causes a decrease in the demand for most products; the market demand curve shifts down and to the left, from D to D''.

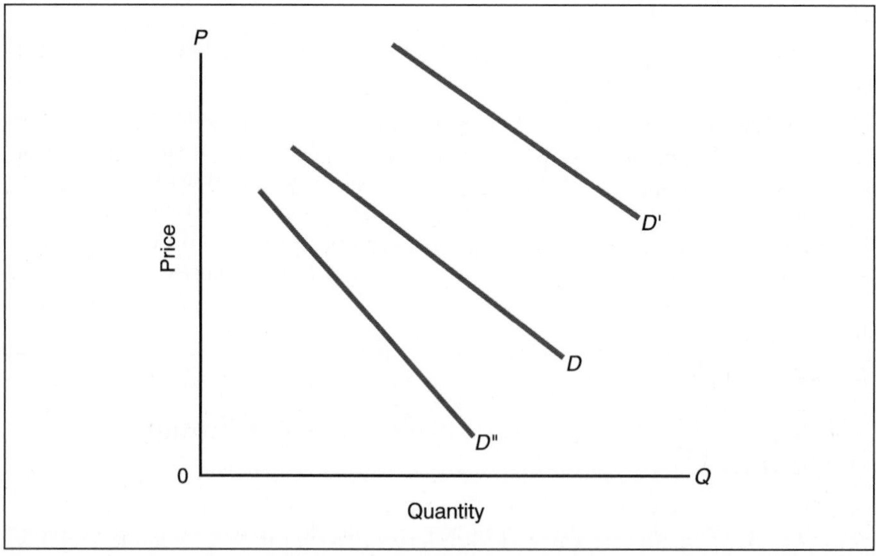

crease in income increases demand. An example is a less tender cut of beef such as chuck steak. As people's incomes increase, they tend to buy less chuck steak and more of the tender cuts of beef such as sirloin. Products such as chuck steak are called *inferior goods* because consumers clearly prefer other products. Families with very low incomes buy chuck steak only because they cannot afford to buy sirloin. If their incomes were to increase so that they could afford to buy sirloin, they would switch from chuck steak to sirloin.

TASTES OR PREFERENCES Changes in consumers' tastes shift demand curves as well. We see this very clearly with the coming and going of fads. You may remember the Cabbage Patch doll craze when you were a youngster. Demand increased so rapidly that it outpaced the ability of producers to supply dolls. At the height of the craze anxious parents were willing to pay $100 or more to anyone who could supply them with a doll. The Cabbage Patch fad lasted for about two years, after which the demand curve shifted back down. The price of the dolls returned to a normal level for dolls of that type.

REFLECTION: Is any product currently a fad among college students? If so, has the price of the product been rising?

POPULATION An increasing population tends to increase demand for all products simply because more and more individual demand curves are being added to the market demand curve. The market demand curve shifts to the right. Conversely, a decreasing population tends to decrease demand for all products. The market demand curve shifts to the left.

PRICES OF RELATED PRODUCTS: SUBSTITUTES AND COMPLEMENTS Two products are said to be related if a change in the price of one of them changes the demand for the other. Related products can be either substitutes or complements. Two products are unrelated if a change in the price of either one of them has no effect on the demand for the other.

Substitutes are products that provide the same general kind of service. Compact discs and cassette tapes are substitute products because each one provides a means of listening to recorded music. When two products are **substitutes**, a decrease in the price of one of them decreases the demand for the other. Conversely, an increase in the price of one increases the demand for the other. For example, if the price of compact discs decreases, they become more attractive to consumers relative to cassette tapes. The demand for cassette tapes decreases.

SUBSTITUTES

Products that provide the same general kind of services; specifically, two goods whose relationship is such that a decrease in the price of one good decreases the demand for the other good.

Complements are products that are used together to provide a service. Compact discs and compact disc players are complements. When two products are complements, a decrease in the price of one of them increases the demand for the other. Conversely, an increase in the price of one decreases the demand for the other. For example, if the price of compact discs decreases, they become more attractive to consumers, and the demand for compact disc players increases.

COMPLEMENTS

Products that are used together to provide a service; specifically, two goods whose relationship is such that a decrease in the price of one good increases the demand for the other.

A final example involving compact discs, cassette tapes, and compact disc players will highlight the important distinction between a change in quantity demanded and a change in demand. Figure 5.4 pictures the demand curves for the three products.

Suppose that the price of compact discs decreases. Figure 5.4(a) shows the demand curve for compact discs. The decrease in the price of compact discs from P_0 to P_1 results in an increase in the *quantity demanded* from Q_0 to Q_1.

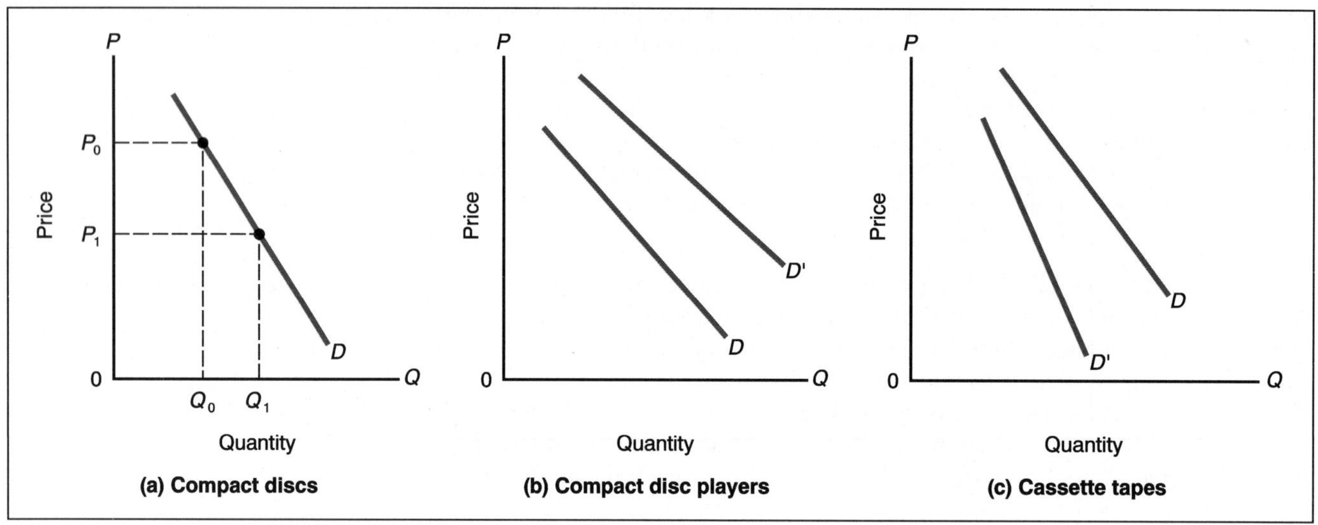

FIGURE 5.4

Complements and Substitutes

Compact discs and compact disc players are complements. Compact discs and cassette tapes are substitutes. Therefore, a decrease in the price of compact discs from P_0 to P_1 causes: a). an increase in the quantity demanded of compact discs from Q_0 to Q_1 in Figure 5.4(a); b). an increase in the demand for compact disc players—the demand curve shifts up and to the right from D to D' in Figure 5.4(b), and c). a decrease in the demand for cassette tapes—the demand curve shifts down and to the left from D to D' in Figure 5.4(c).

The decrease in price results in a movement along the demand curve for compact discs.

Figure 5.4(a) and 5.4(b) picture the demand curves for compact disc players and cassette tapes, respectively. The decrease in the price of compact discs shifts the demand curves in these markets because the price of compact discs does not appear in either panel. It is one of the factors in the background being held constant. Since compact discs and compact disc players are complements, the fall in the price of compact discs makes compact disc players more attractive to consumers. The *demand* for compact disc players increases from D to D', as shown in the middle graph. Since compact discs and cassette tapes are substitutes, the fall in the price of compact discs makes cassette tapes less attractive to consumers. The *demand* for cassette tapes decreases from D to D', as shown in the right-hand graph.

Take care in distinguishing between a change in quantity demanded and a change in demand. They refer to very different phenomena.

Graphing Other Demand Relationships

A demand curve selects price, one of the many factors determining quantity demanded, and graphs it against quantity demanded, holding all other factors constant. As we have just seen, changes in these other factors are represented as shifts in the demand curve. Economists put price on the axis and draw a demand curve because they have a special interest in the separate or independent effect of price on quantity demanded. However, the separate effects of the other factors are also of interest in many applications. Any one of them could be selected and graphed against quantity demanded, holding all other factors constant *including price.* The resulting graph would picture the separate effect of that factor on quantity demanded, other things equal.

INCOME AND QUANTITY DEMANDED For instance, suppose that we are interested in the other things equal relationship between a representative con-

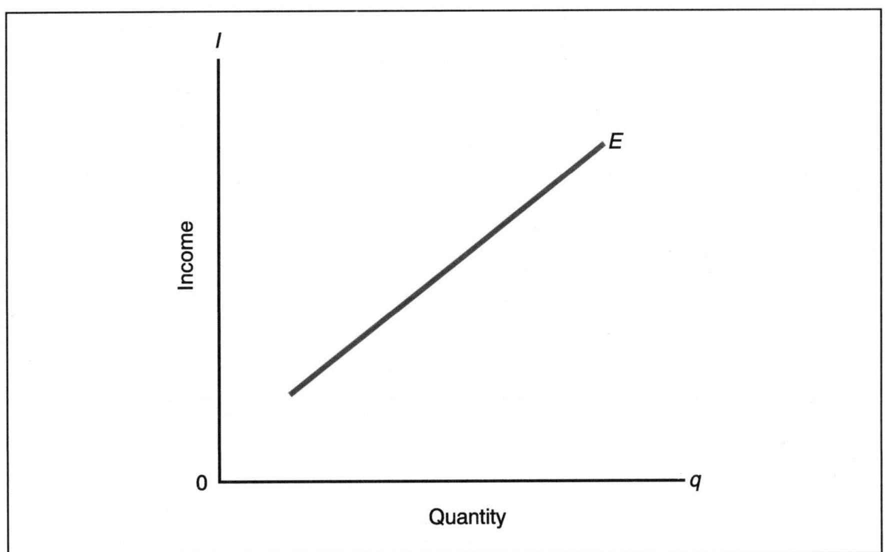

FIGURE 5.5
Engel's Curve

The Engel's curve for a product, *E*, shows the relationship between income and quantity demanded, other things equal. The Engel's curve for normal goods is upward sloping. An increase in income increases quantity demanded and a decrease in income decreases quantity demanded.

sumer's income and quantity demanded for some product. To graph this relationship, we place income on the vertical axis and quantity demanded on the horizontal axis, as shown in Figure 5.5. The graph of income against quantity demanded is called an **Engel's curve**, after the Prussian statistician Ernst Engel. Engel's nineteenth-century study of the effect of income on quantity demanded for a wide range of products is a landmark of economic analysis. For normal goods the relationship is upward sloping, as pictured in Figure 5.5. An increase in income increases quantity demanded, other things equal.

ENGEL'S CURVE
A graphical representation of the relationship between income and quantity demanded, other things equal.

Engel's curves can apply to individual consumers or the entire market. A market Engel's curve shows the other things equal relationship between the total income available to consumers and the total quantity demanded for all consumers. The market Engel's curve is not the horizontal summation of each individual Engel's curve, however, because both income and quantity demanded are added when deriving the market curve from the individual curves. The relationship between total consumer income and total demand for all products, the aggregation of all market Engel's curves, is central to the study of the macroeconomics.

ELASTICITY

The Law of Demand tells us the *direction* that quantity demanded changes as price changes. For instance, it tells us that an increase in price, other things equal, can be expected to decrease quantity demanded. We would like to know more than that, however, when analyzing market events. We would also like to have some idea how much the quantity demanded can be expected to decrease: A lot? A little? Hardly at all? The concept of elasticity tells us this.

(PRICE) ELASTICITY OF DEMAND
A measure of the responsiveness of quantity demanded to changes in the price of a product along a demand curve; specifically, the percentage change in quantity demanded divided by the percentage change in price in absolute value.

Elasticity of demand measures the responsiveness of quantity demanded to changes in the factors that determine quantity demanded. The **price elasticity of demand** refers to the responsiveness of quantity demanded to changes in the price of the product along a demand curve. We will refer to the price elasticity of demand simply as the elasticity of demand, or demand elasticity, throughout the text. This is standard practice in economics. Elasticity always refers to price elasticity unless otherwise modified.

The elasticity of demand is a crucial piece of information in the analysis of almost any market event. Here is one example to illustrate that hits fairly close to home for students. The costs of providing a college education increased rapidly during the 1970s and 1980s. Colleges responded by increasing tuitions equally rapidly to bring in the revenues needed to cover the cost increases. During those two decades college tuitions increased much more than did prices generally. The strategy of raising tuitions to increase revenues worked, in large part because the colleges faced a very favorable demand situation throughout the 1970s and 1980s. The post–World War II baby boomers reached college age and wanted a college education. Consequently, the demand curve for a college education shifted out rapidly, and colleges were able to increase tuitions and still enjoy higher enrollments.

The days of rapidly increasing demand for a college education are over, however. The baby bust generation of the 1970s has now reached college age, with the result that the market demand curve will remain essentially constant throughout most of the 1990s. If college costs continue to increase, colleges may no longer enjoy the luxury of simply raising tuitions to bring in more revenue. Now the response to an increase in tuition is essentially a change in quantity demanded along a single, unshifting market demand curve. What effect raising tuition will have on revenues is uncertain in this new environment. Raising tuition increases total revenue in and of itself because higher tuitions increase the revenue received from each student. But raising tuition also lowers quantity demanded according to the Law of Demand. At higher tuitions fewer students want to attend college. The decrease in enrollments decreases total revenue in and of itself because colleges collect tuition revenues from fewer students. Whether total revenue increases or decreases depends on the responsiveness of enrollments to tuition increases. In other words, it depends on the elasticity of demand.

FIGURE 5.6

College Tuition Revenues and the Elasticity of Demand for College

The figure shows what happens to college tuition revenues when colleges increase tuition and the demand curve for college, D, is not shifting. The increase in tuitions from P_0 to P_1 decreases the number of students enrolled in college from Q_0 to Q_1. Tuition revenues change from $P_0 \cdot Q_0$, the rectangular area $0P_0aQ_0$, to $P_1 \cdot Q_1$, the rectangular area $0P_1bQ_1$. Tuition revenues decrease if the demand for college is elastic, stay the same if the demand for college is unit-elastic, and increase if the demand for college is inelastic.

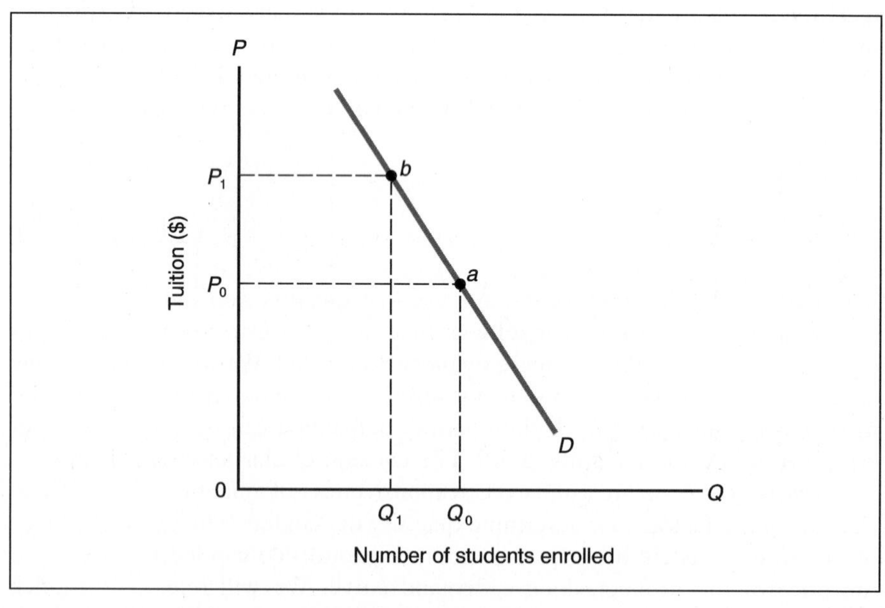

Figure 5.6 shows graphically the effect of a tuition increase on total revenue along a constant market demand curve. D is the market demand curve for a college education. Suppose that the average tuition at all colleges is P_0 and that total college enrollments are Q_0. The total revenue received by the colleges (TR_0) is price times quantity, the average tuition per student (P_0) times the total college enrollments (Q_0). That is, $TR_0 = P_0 \cdot Q_0$.

The picture of total revenue (or total expenditure) at a point on a demand curve is the area of the rectangle formed by the price and the quantity under the demand curve. The height of the rectangle is the price; the base of the rectangle is the quantity; and the area of the rectangle is height times base, or price times quantity, which equals total revenue. In Figure 5.6, $TR_0 = P_0 \cdot Q_0$ is the area of rectangle $0P_0\,aQ_0$.

Increasing average tuition to P_1 decreases total enrollments to Q_1. The new total revenue is $TR_1 = P_1 \cdot Q_1$, equal to the area of rectangle $0P_1b\,Q_1$. Which rectangle is larger? The answer depends on how much college enrollments respond to the increase in tuitions. The effect of the tuition increase on total revenue defines whether demand is elastic or inelastic.

The Total Revenue Measure of Elasticity

When price increases from P_0 to P_1, total revenue can increase, remain the same, or decrease. Figure 5.7 illustrates the three possibilities.

1. If total revenue decreases, $TR_1 < TR_0$, demand is said to be *elastic* between the two prices. Figure 5.7(a) represents the case of elastic demand. The area of rectangle $0P_1bQ_1$ is less than the area of rectangle $0P_0aQ_0$. Quantity demanded is relatively responsive to a change in price. The quantity effect on total revenue dominates the price effect.
2. If total revenue stays the same, $TR_1 = TR_0$, demand is said to be *unit-elastic* between the two prices. Figure 5.7(b) represents the case of unit-elastic demand. The area of rectangle $0P_1bQ_1$ equals the area of rectangle $0P_0aQ_0$. The quantity and price effects on total revenue exactly cancel one another.

FIGURE 5.7

Elastic, Unit-Elastic, and Inelastic Demand

Demand is elastic along the relatively flat demand curve in Figure 5.7(a). An increase in price from P_0 to P_1 reduces total expenditures (total revenues). $P_1 \cdot Q_1 < P_0 \cdot Q_0$. Demand is unit-elastic along the demand curve in Figure 5.7(b). An increase in price from P_0 to P_1 leaves total expenditures (total revenues) unchanged. $P_1 \cdot Q_1 = P_0 \cdot Q_0$. Demand is inelastic along the relatively steep demand curve in Figure 5.7(c). An increase in price from P_0 to P_1 increases total expenditures (total revenues). $P_1 \cdot Q_1 > P_0 \cdot Q_0$.

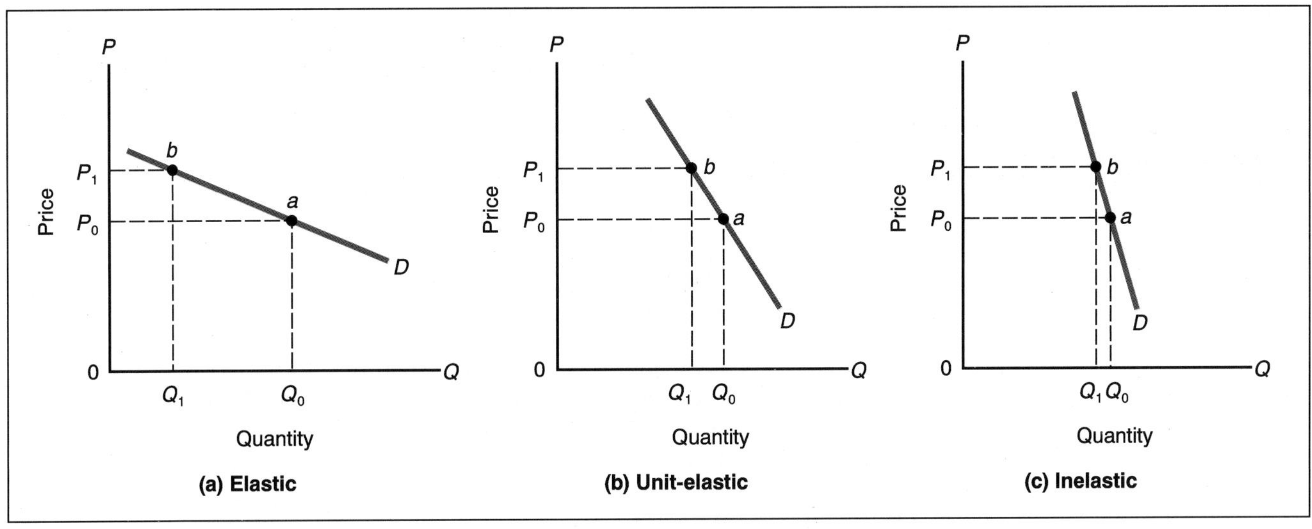

3. If total revenue increases, $TR_1 > TR_0$, demand is said to be *inelastic* between the two prices. Figure 5.7(c), represents the case of inelastic demand. The area of rectangle $0P_1bQ_1$ is greater than the area of rectangle $0P_0aQ_0$. Quantity demanded is relatively unresponsive to a change in price. The price effect on total revenue dominates the quantity effect.

The total revenue definition of elasticity applies to a price decrease as well, but the direction of the inequalities is reversed. A decrease in price increases quantity demanded according to the Law of Demand. If demand is *elastic* between the two prices, the quantity effect on total revenue dominates the price effect, and total revenue *increases.* If demand is *inelastic* between the two prices, the price effect on total revenue dominates the quantity effect, and total revenue *decreases.*

Returning to the example of college tuitions, we see that the colleges' tuition strategy for the 1990s depends on the elasticity of demand for a college education. If demand is inelastic, colleges can continue to raise revenues by raising tuitions. If demand is elastic, colleges will have to lower tuitions and attract more students in order to increase revenues. The possibility of elastic demand is not particularly attractive to colleges, though, because educating more students raises costs even higher. The colleges are hoping that the demand for a college education is inelastic.

The Percentage Change Measure of Elasticity

A second measure of the price elasticity of demand compares the percentage change in quantity demanded with the percentage change in price. The percentage change comparison has the advantage that it applies symmetrically to price increases or decreases. It is also the most commonly used measure of elasticity.

The percentage change measure of elasticity is the ratio of the percentage change in quantity demanded to the percentage change in price. The elasticity ratio is defined as an absolute number. Plus and minus signs are ignored when computing the percentage changes. In algebraic terms, the price elasticity of demand is

$$E_D = |\% \text{ change in quantity demanded } | \,/\, | \text{ \% change in price}|$$

where E_D is the price elasticity of demand. Demand is said to be elastic, unit-elastic, or inelastic depending on whether E_D is greater than, equal to, or less than 1.

1. If $E_D > 1$, demand is *elastic* between the prices. The percentage change in quantity exceeds the percentage change in price. Quantity demanded is relatively responsive to a change in price in percentage terms.
2. If $E_D = 1$, demand is *unit-elastic* between the prices.
3. If $E_D < 1$, demand is *inelastic* between the prices. The percentage change in quantity is less than the percentage change in price. Quantity demanded is relatively unresponsive to a change in price in percentage terms.

CALCULATING PERCENTAGE CHANGES The following example illustrates how to compute the percentage change measure. Suppose that the quantity demanded of some product decreases from 600 to 300 units when the price of the product increases from \$1 to \$3. Is the demand for that product elastic, unit-elastic, or inelastic between \$1 and \$3?

Calculating the elasticity of demand runs into an immediate problem because percentage changes are arbitrary numbers. A percentage change of any variable is the amount the variable changes divided by a base amount and multiplied by 100 to convert decimals to percentages. In our example quantity demanded decreases from 600 to 300 units. The change in the quantity demanded is 300 units (300 = 600 − 300). But what base quantity should we use in the denominator to divide into the change? In everyday practice the initial quantity of 600 is usually chosen as the base. Using this convention, the percentage change in quantity demanded is

$$\begin{aligned}|(\text{Change in quantity/base quantity})\cdot 100| &= |(300/600)\cdot 100| \\ &= 50\%\end{aligned}$$

The decrease in quantity demanded from 600 to 300 units is commonly represented as a 50 percent decrease.

Suppose, however, that the price returns to \$1 and the quantity demanded to 600 units. By how much has the quantity demanded increased in percentage terms? Following the standard practice, 300 units would now be used as the initial base quantity. The 300-unit increase in quantity demanded would be represented as a 100 percent increase:

$$\begin{aligned}|(\text{Change in quantity/base quantity})\cdot 100| &= |(300/300)\cdot 100| \\ &= 100\%\end{aligned}$$

The two percentage changes are not symmetric, even though the actual change in quantity demanded is the same in each case.

To make increases and decreases symmetric, economists define the base quantity as halfway between the original and the new quantities. In our example the base would be 450 units (450 = (300 + 600)/2 = 900/2), and both the increase and the decrease in quantity demanded would be represented as a 67 percent change in quantity demanded.

$$\begin{aligned}|(\text{Change in quantity/base quantity})\cdot 100| &= |(300/450)\cdot 100| \\ &= 67\%\end{aligned}$$

The percentage change in price is calculated the same way. When the price increases from \$1 to \$3, the change in price is \$2 (\$2 = \$3 − \$1). The halfway point between the original and the new prices is \$2 (\$2 = (\$1 + \$3)/2 = \$4/2). Therefore, \$2 increase in price is represented as a 100 percent increase:

$$\begin{aligned}|(\text{Change in price/base price})\cdot 100| &= |(\$2/\$2)\cdot 100| \\ &= 100\%\end{aligned}$$

The elasticity of demand between the two prices is the ratio of the percentage change in quantity to the percentage in change in price:

$$E_D = 67\%/100\% = .67$$

Since the elasticity is less than 1, demand for the product is inelastic between \$1 and \$3. Notice that the total revenue measure of elasticity reaches the same conclusion. Total revenue increases as a result of the price increase, indicating that demand is inelastic between the prices ($TR_{\$3}$ = \$3 · 300 = \$900; $TR_{\$1}$ = \$1 · 600 = \$600).[1]

PROPERTIES OF THE PERCENTAGE CHANGE MEASURE A number of comments on the percentage change measure of elasticity are in order.

1. Absolute values are used to make all elasticity numbers positive. Otherwise, price elasticity calculations along demand curves would be negative numbers. When price increases (+), quantity demanded decreases (−). When prices decreases (−), quantity demanded increases (+). Comparing negative numbers is confusing.
2. The comparison between a change in price and the resulting change in quantity demanded must be made in percentage terms to avoid an "apples versus oranges" comparison between prices and quantities. Prices and quantities are measured in different units. Comparing actual changes in dollars with actual changes in units, or tons, or bushels is meaningless. For example, suppose that a \$2.50 decrease in the price of compact discs increases the quantity demanded for the entire market by 60,000 discs per month. How can \$2.50 be compared directly with 60,000 compact discs?

   Percentage changes are pure, unit-free numbers. In computing the percentage change in quantity, the units in which the quantity is measured appear in both the numerator and the denominator. Therefore, the units cancel in the calculation. Similarly, in computing the percentage change in price, dollars appear in both the numerator and the denominator. Therefore, dollars also cancel in the calculation. Since elasticity is the ratio of the two pure, unit-free numbers, elasticity is also a pure, unit-free number.
3. Students with a knowledge of calculus can demonstrate the relationship between the percentage change and the total revenue measures of elasticity. The basis of the relationship is that the quantity effect on total revenue dominates the price effect whenever the *percentage* change in quantity exceeds the *percentage* change in price. This is the case when demand is elastic. The opposite applies to inelastic demand.
4. Finally, the price elasticity of demand is an other things equal concept because it measures responsiveness of quantity demanded to price along a demand curve. All other factors that might influence quantity demanded are assumed to be constant.

Determinants of Elasticity

So far the discussion of price elasticity has focused on how elasticity is measured and its relationship to the demand curve. These mechanics need to be

---

[1]Elasticity calculated between two points on a demand curve is called the arc elasticity of demand. Elasticity can also be measured at a point along a demand curve on the assumption that price changes by only a small amount. Write the ratio of the percentage change in output to the percentage change in price as $E_D = [(\Delta Q/Q)/\Delta P/P)]$. The Greek symbol Δ, called "delta", stands for "change in." Rearranging terms, $E_D = [(\Delta Q/\Delta P) \cdot (P/Q)]$. The term $(\Delta Q/\Delta P)$ is the inverse of the slope of the demand curve at the given price and quantity P and Q. E_D expressed this way is called the point elasticity of demand. Notice that E_D varies along a straight line demand curve. The slope is constant along a straight line demand curve so that $(\Delta Q/\Delta P)$, the inverse of the slope, is constant. But (P/Q) varies along the demand curve, falling as P decreases and Q increases. Therefore, E_D also falls along a straight line demand curve as P decreases and Q increases.

mastered, but the question of primary economic interest is this: What properties of goods and services determine whether their demands are price elastic or inelastic? Four principal factors determine the price elasticity of demand: whether the product is considered to be essential or inessential, whether it is expensive or inexpensive, the availability of substitute products, and the passage of time.

ESSENTIAL/INESSENTIAL Do consumers consider the product essential or something of a luxury? The more essential the product, the more inelastic its demand; the less essential the product, the more elastic its demand. For example, we would expect the demand for food consumed at home to be far more inelastic than the demand for food purchased in restaurants. Similarly, consumers' demand for automobiles is likely to be more inelastic than is their demand for air travel. Most people living in the suburbs consider the automobile a virtual necessity. In contrast, most people use air travel for vacations and visits to friends and relatives. If air fares increase significantly, this type of leisure travel can be postponed easily.

Empirical studies of demand elasticities support these conjectures. One study estimates that the elasticity of demand for food purchased for use at home is .21, extremely inelastic. A separate study of restaurant demand estimates its elasticity to be 2.27, highly elastic. A number of studies have estimated automobile demand elasticity, and the results are generally close to 1, unit-elastic. Consumers' demand for air travel is apparently highly elastic: One estimate sets its elasticity at 2.4.

EXPENSIVE/INEXPENSIVE As a general rule the less expensive a product, the more inelastic its demand; the more expensive a product, the more elastic its demand. Consumers are likely to be price sensitive to more expensive products for the simple reason that these products use more of their scarce incomes. The opportunity costs of consuming more expensive products are higher.

A pound of table salt costs about $.30 and seems to last for years. It is so cheap that most people probably do not know its price when they buy it. Even fairly large percentage increases or decreases in the price of table salt are unlikely to have much effect on quantity demanded. In comparison, an automobile is one of the more expensive items that consumers purchase. This factor alone tends to increase its price elasticity, which partially offsets the fact that so many people consider the automobile essential. The high cost of automobiles also helps explain why manufacturer incentives such as cash rebates and low-interest car loans succeed in increasing new car sales.

THE AVAILABILITY OF SUBSTITUTES Price elasticity is extremely sensitive to the availability of substitute products. The more readily available substitute products are, the more elastic the demand is; the less readily available substitute products are, the less elastic the demand is.

For example, the more narrowly a product is defined, the higher the elasticity is, in general, because the availability of substitutes increases. The study of the price elasticity for food mentioned above reported much higher price elasticities for beef (.50), pork (.45) and butter (.70) than for all food (.21). A study of Colorado students' demands for 15 skiing sites in the state estimated price elasticities at each site in excess of 2.0. Sensitivity to price changes increases when products have competitors for consumers' scarce dollars.[2] Our example of college tuitions is a final illustration of this principle. Even if the overall market demand for a college education is inelastic, the demand for any one college may be highly elastic. Colleges are natural substitutes for one another. If one college raises its tuition much more than other colleges do, it may suffer a huge decline in enrollment. The strategy of raising tuition to increase revenues can work only if all colleges raise tuitions together.

Sometimes the three factors we have examined thus far combine to create a strong presumption that demand is either elastic or inelastic. At other times they give mixed signals. For example, the demand for table salt is presumably highly inelastic. Salt is considered essential by most people, it is inexpensive, and it does not have many close substitutes. Conversely, the demand for a Zenith 25-inch color television is presumably highly elastic. Owning a 25-inch color television is hardly one of life's essentials; a 25-inch color television costs hundreds of dollars; and a Zenith 25-inch color television has may close substitutes, the 25-inch color televisions of the other manufacturers. The characteristics of automobiles give mixed signals. The automobile is a necessity for many people, which tends to make its demand inelastic, but it is also very expensive, which tends to make its demand elastic. Public transportation and air and rail travel are substitutes in some uses, but in other uses the automobile has no reasonable substitutes. Because the signals are mixed, we cannot presume that the demand for automobiles is elastic or inelastic. As indicated above, the conflicting influences on the demand elasticitiy for automobiles are equally strong in the sense that the estimated elasticities are approximately unit-elastic.

THE PASSAGE OF TIME The final determinant of demand elasticity is the passage of time. It differs from the other determinants because it applies to all products regardless of their characteristics. Demand becomes more elastic with the passage of time following a change in price simply because people need time to adjust to price changes. We are all creatures of habit to some extent and tend to resist change for any reason. Also, people may react to price changes by demanding different kinds of products. Business firms need time to change production to meet the new demands.

The effect of the passage of time on demand elasticity is depicted in Figure 5.8. Suppose that price rises unexpectedly from P_0 to P_1. At first, consumers cling to their old habits. Curve D_{MR}, the *momentary demand curve,* applies. It is highly inelastic. Quantity demanded decreases only slightly from Q_0 to Q_{MR}, and total expenditures increase substantially from $P_0 \cdot Q_0$ to $P_1 \cdot Q_{MR}$. After some time passes, consumers begin to adjust to the higher prices and find ways of conserving on their use of the product. They begin to turn to substitutes. Curve D_{SR}, the *short-run demand curve,* now applies. Quantity demanded declines from Q_{MR} to Q_{SR}, and total expenditures decrease from $P_1 \cdot Q_{MR}$ to $P_1 \cdot Q_{SR}$. More adjustments appear over time as firms develop new substitute products and as consumers continue to shake old habits. Curve D_{LR}, the *long-run demand curve,* now applies. Quantity demanded declines still further from Q_{SR} to Q_{LR}, and total expenditures decrease from $P_1 \cdot Q_{SR}$ to $P_1 \cdot Q_{LR}$. Demand

[2]The ski site estimates are from E. Morey, "The Choice of Ski Areas: Estimates of a Generalized CES Preference Ordering with Characteristics," *Review of Economics and Statistics* LXVI, No. 4 (November, 1984): 584–590. References for the other elasticities mentioned above can be found in Tables 5.4 through 5.6.

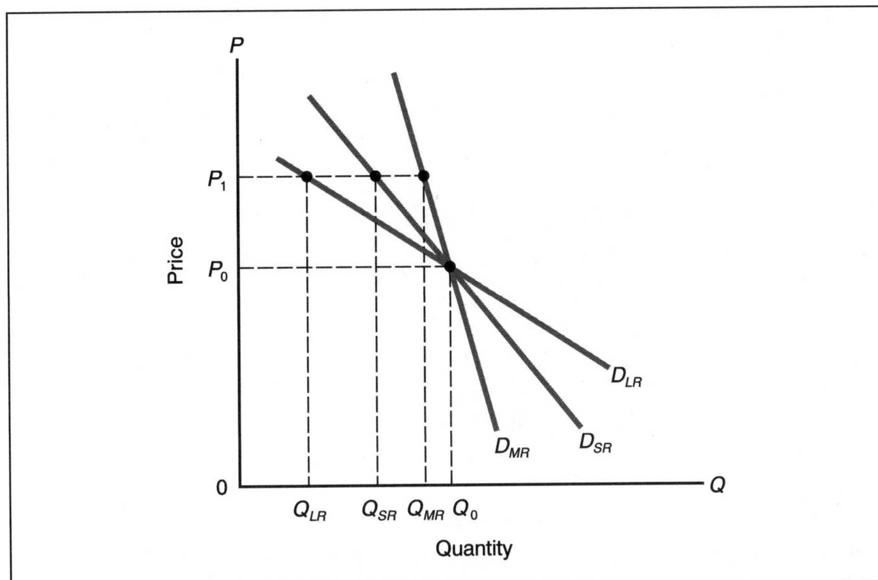

FIGURE 5.8

Demand Elasticity and the Passage of Time

Demand becomes more elastic with the passage of time following a change in price. Immediately after an increase in price from P_0 to P_1, in the momentary run, the demand curve D_{MR} applies. Quantity demanded decreases only slightly from Q_0 to Q_{MR} and total expenditures on the product are likely to rise. As more time passes the short-run demand curve D_{SR} applies. Quantity demanded decreases further to Q_{SR}. As still more time passes the long-run demand curve, D_{LR}, applies. Quantity demanded decreases further to its final value of Q_{LR}. Demand in the long-run may be quite elastic, and total expenditures may decrease despite the increase in price.

that appeared to be quite inelastic immediately after the price increase could turn out to be fairly elastic after consumers have completely adjusted. While $P_1 \cdot Q_{MR}$ is greater than $P_0 \cdot Q_0$, $P_1 \cdot Q_{LR}$ may be less than $P_0 \cdot Q_0$.

This pattern of adjustment over time occurred when OPEC quadrupled the price of oil in 1974. At first, consumers were stuck and allocated a much higher share of their incomes to oil derivatives such as gasoline and home heating oil. Americans were used to cheap energy. They drove large cars, often commuted to work alone by car, and heated their homes to 70° and more. The demand for oil-related products appeared to be highly inelastic, but slowly they began to adjust. They lowered their thermostats and added insulation to their houses. They also changed their driving habits. Car pooling became more common, and driving for pleasure diminished. Consumers bought smaller, more fuel efficient cars and clamored for more. As more time passed, Detroit and the foreign automobile manufacturers were able to satisfy the demand for smaller cars. People who used to drive 10-mpg gas guzzlers were driving 20-, 30-, and 40-mpg fuel-efficient automobiles by the end of the decade. Many consumers were not spending any more on gasoline than they had before the oil price increase.

Table 5.3 reports economist Robert Pindyck's estimates of the elasticity of demand for gasoline following the 1974 oil price increase. Pindyck's estimates show the pattern of increasing adjustment to the price increases over time. In

TABLE 5.3 Price Elasticity of Demand for Gasoline

TIME PERIOD	ELASTICITY
IMMEDIATE	0.10
2–3 YEARS	0.25
5 YEARS	0.49
10 YEARS	0.82
15 YEARS	1.03

SOURCE: R. S. Pindyck, *The Structure of World Energy Demand* (Cambridge: MIT Press, 1979).

the very long run (15 years) the demand for gasoline is approximately unit-elastic.

The following Concept Summary table summarizes the various determinants of demand elasticity.

CONCEPT SUMMARY

DETERMINANTS OF DEMAND ELASTICITY

FACTOR	MORE ELASTIC	LESS ELASTIC
ESSENTIAL/ INESSENTIAL	Product considered inessential	Product considered essential
EXPENSIVE/ INEXPENSIVE	The more expensive the product	The cheaper the product
AVAILABILITY OF SUBSTITUTES	Substitute products readily available	Substitute products not readily available
PASSAGE OF TIME	The longer the time from a price change	The shorter the time from a price change

The Limiting Cases: Perfectly Inelastic and Perfectly Elastic Demand

How small can demand elasticity be over a range of prices? How large can demand elasticity be? The reasonable limits are presented in Figure 5.9.

In Figure 5.9(a) the demand curve is vertical. The vertical line indicates that quantity demanded is totally unresponsive to changes in price: No matter what the price, quantity demanded remains at Q_0. When the demand curve is vertical, demand is *perfectly inelastic.* The percentage change measure of elasticity is zero.

People often talk about their demands for products as if they were perfectly inelastic. They speak of needs, as in "I need three pairs of jeans," which implies that they will buy three pairs of jeans no matter what the price. On closer inspection, however, demands are almost never perfectly inelastic. People would reassess their "needs" if the price of jeans were to triple. They may decide that they can get by with one or two pairs of jeans or with corduroys instead of jeans. Drug addicts may have "needs," but most people, most of the time, have downward sloping demand curves. The demand for most products obeys the Law of Demand. Higher prices and the availability of substitutes can be counted on to generate some elasticity of demand.

The horizontal demand curve in Figure 5.9(b) represents the opposite extreme. Quantity demanded is as responsive to price changes as it can possibly be. Suppose that the quantity demanded is originally at Q_0. Any increase in price above P_0 causes quantity demanded to go to zero. Any decrease in price below P_0 causes quantity demanded to grow without bound. When the demand curve is horizontal, demand is *perfectly elastic.* The percentage change measure of elasticity is infinitely large.

Consumers' demand curves are unlikely to approach perfect elasticity. There is probably no product for which tiny increases or decreases in price would cause wide swings in quantity demanded. Yet the limiting case of perfectly

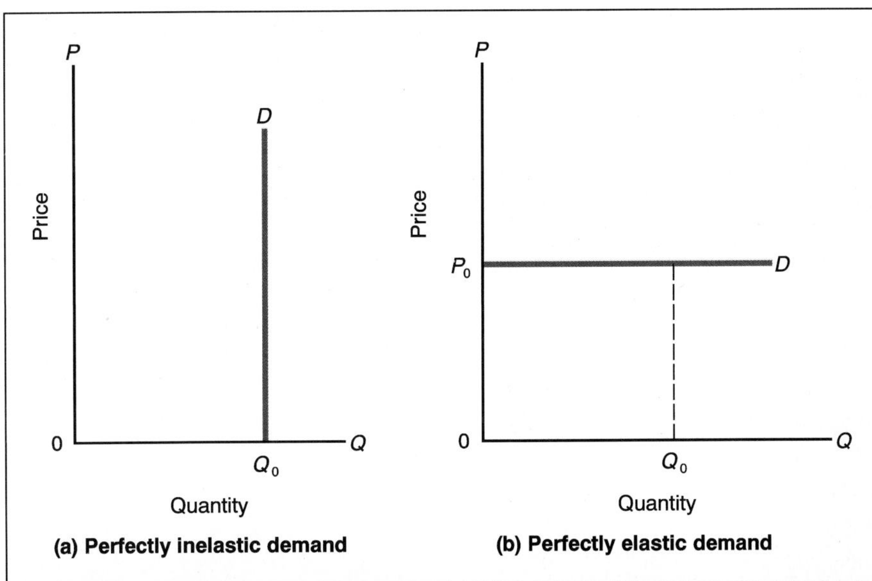

FIGURE 5.9

Perfectly Inelastic and Perfectly Elastic Demand

The extreme cases of demand elasticity are perfectly inelastic demand and perfectly elastic demand. The demand curve is vertical when demand is perfectly inelastic (Figure 5.9(a)). The quantity demanded is Q_0 no matter what the price. A change in price causes no change in quantity demanded. The demand curve is horizontal when demand is perfectly elastic (Figure 5.9(b)). The slightest increase in price above P_0 causes quantity demanded to fall to zero. The slightest decrease in price below P_0 causes quantity demanded to increase without limit.

elasic demand is very important to economic analysis. As we will see later on in the text, it *is* a good approximation of the demand curve facing an individual business firm selling in a highly competitive market environment. The reason why is that the firm's customers can buy virtually the same product from a number of other firms. The other firms' products are very close substitutes.

Elasticity Estimates

Table 5.4 presents estimated price elasticities for a selection of products that students might purchase. The items are grouped into three categories: inelastic, approximately unit-elastic, and elastic. Perhaps the most striking aspect of the table is the wide range of the estimates. Consumers react very differently to changes in price for different kinds of products.

REFLECTION: For which of the goods and services that you buy is your demand highly elastic? Highly inelastic? Why?

Income Elasticity of Demand

Elasticity can also be defined with respect to income (or any other factor determining quantity demanded), analogously to the percentage change definition of price elasticity. The **income elasticity of demand,** E_I, is the ratio of the percentage change in quantity demanded to the percentage change in income, other things equal.

INCOME ELASTICITY OF DEMAND
A measure of the responsiveness of quantity demanded to change in income; specifically, the percentage change in quantity demanded divided by the percentage change in income.

$$E_I = \text{(percentage change in quantity demanded)}/\text{(percentage change in income)}$$

Income elasticity measures the responsiveness of quantity demanded to changes in income along an Engel's curve. Note that we do not use absolute values when computing income elasticities because the positive and the negative signs give important information. Income elasticity is positive for normal

TABLE 5.4 Price Elasticities of Demand for Selected Products

PRODUCT	PRICE ELASTICITY
INELASTIC	
Water	0.14
Food	0.21
Lively arts (theater, etc.)	(0.07, 0.29)
Cigarettes	(0.3, 0.4)
Legal services	0.50
Stationery	0.57
Jewelry, watches	0.67
APPROXIMATELY UNIT-ELASTIC (0.80–1.20)	
Beer	1.13
Electricity	1.14
Mass transit, bus	1.20
New cars	1.20
ELASTIC	
Charitable giving	1.29
Marijuana	1.50
Air travel	2.40
Toilet articles, preparations	3.04
Motion pictures	3.70

SOURCES: The two classic studies on price elasticities, which contain many of these estimates, are H. Houthakker and L. Taylor, *Consumer Demand in the United States: Analysis and Projections* (Cambridge: Harvard University Press, 1970), and H Wold, *Demand Analysis: A Study in Econometrics*, (New York: Wiley, 1953). Also: H. F. Gallash, Jr., "Price Elasticities of Demand at Retail and Wholesale Levels: An Automotive Example," *Business Economics* XIX, No. 1 (January 1984): 61–62; J. Gapinski, "The Lively Arts as Substitutes for the Lively Arts," *AEA Papers and Proceedings* 76, No. 2 (May 1986): 20–25; E. Morey, "The Choice of Ski Areas: Estimation of a Generalized CES Preference Ordering with Characteristics," *Review of Economics and Statistics* LXVI, No. 4 (1985): 584–590.

goods because quantity demanded and income move in the same direction. Income elasticity is negative for inferior goods because quantity demanded and income move in opposite direction.

Economists distinguish between luxuries and necessities on the basis of products' income elasticities. A *luxury* good or service has an income elasticity greater than 1. As income increases, the good becomes an increasingly important part of a consumer's purchases. A *necessity* has an income elasticity of less than 1 (but greater than or equal to zero). It becomes relatively more important as the consumer's income decreases. For example, a well-known study of consumer demand found that food purchased for home consumption is a necessity, as expected. Its demand is fairly income inelastic, .5. However, food purchased in restaurants is a luxury; it has an income elasticity of 1.4. Another well-known study found physicians to be a necessity, but found dentists to be a luxury. The estimated income elasticities were .75 for physicians and 1.42 for dentists.[3]

---

[3]The food-restaurant elasticities are from H. Wold, *Demand Analysis: A Study in Econometrics* (New York: Wiley, 1953). The physicians-dentists elasticities are from H. Houthakker and L. Taylor, *Consumer Demand in the United States: Analysis and Projections* (Cambridge: Harvard University Press, 1970).

TABLE 5.5 **Income Elasticities of Demand for Selected Products**

PRODUCT	INCOME ELASTICITY
INFERIOR	
Flour	−0.36
Margarine	−0.20
NECESSITIES	
Lively arts (theater, etc.)	(0.06, 0.26)
Electricity	(0.07, 0.74)
Physicians	0.75
APPROXIMATELY UNIT-ELASTIC	
Liquors	1.00
Tobacco	1.02
Clothing	1.02
LUXURIES	
Books	1.44
New cars	2.45
Private education	2.46
Durable goods (appliances, etc.)	2.90

SOURCES: H. Houthakker and L. Taylor, *Consumer Demand in the United States: Analysis and Projections* (Cambridge: Harvard University Press, 1970); H. Wold, *Demand Analysis: A Study in Econometrics* (New York: Wiley, 1953). Also: J. Gapinski, "The Lively Arts as Substitutes for the Lively Arts," *AEA Papers and Proceedings* 76, No. 2 (May 1986): 20–25. C. Hsiao and D. Mountain, "Estimating the Short-Run Income Elasticity of Demand for Electricity by Using Cross-Sectional Categorized Data," *Journal of the American Statistical Association* 80, No. 390 (June 1985): 259–265.

Table 5.5 lists the income elasticities for a selection of products purchased by college students. Once again the variation in elasticities is striking. Note, too, that margarine and flour are inferior products. The table also highlights the other things equal nature of all elasticity estimates. While these are products purchased by students, their elasticities were estimated using data taken from a more general population. The actual income elasticities of students may well differ. Books are an obvious example. The student demand for required textbooks may be highly income inelastic because required textbooks are necessities.

Cross-Price Elasticities

A final elasticity measure that is often used in economic analysis is the cross-price elasticity between two related goods, either substitutes and complements. The **cross-price elasticity** measures the responsiveness of the demand for one good to a change in the price of the other good in terms of percentage changes.

CROSS-PRICE ELASTICITY OF DEMAND
The percentage change in the demand for one good divided by the percentage change in the price of a related good.

$$E_{\text{cross-price}} = \frac{\text{(percentage change in the demand for good A)}}{\text{(percentage change in the price of good B)}}$$

The cross-price elasticity is positive for substitutes because an increase in the price of good B increases the demand for substitute product A. Conversely,

TABLE 5.6 Cross-Price Elasticities of Substitutes for Selected Products

PRODUCT	SUBSTITUTE PRODUCT	CROSS-PRICE ELASTICITY
BEEF	Pork	0.28
BUTTER	Margarine	0.67
ELECTRICITY	Natural gas	0.20
NATURAL GAS	Fuel oil	0.44
THEATER	All other lively arts	0.12
SYMPHONY	All other lively arts	0.53

SOURCES: H. Wold, *Demand Analysis: A Study in Econometrics* (New York: Wiley, 1953). Also: J. Gapinski, "The Lively Arts as Substitutes for the Lively Arts," *AEA Papers and Proceedings* 76, No. 2 (May 1986): pp. 20–25. C. Hsiao and D. Mountain "Estimating the Short-Run Income Elasticity of Demand for Electricity by Using Cross-Sectional Categorized Data," *Journal of the American Statistical Association* 80, No. 390 (June 1985): pp. 259–265.

the cross-price elasticity is negative for complements because an increase in the price of good B decreases the demand for complement product A.

Table 5.6 lists the estimated cross-price elasticities for a selection of products presumed to be substitutes. The entries are all positive, as expected.

The Elasticity Measures Summarized

The Concept Summary table on page 123 summarizes the price, income, and cross-price elasticity measures developed above.

SUMMARY

The first section of Chapter 5 showed how the individual's demand for a product arises from the consumer's economic problem and discussed the properties of the individual demand curve.

1. The demand for a product is that amount that consumers are willing and able to buy over a certain period of time. The structure of the consumer's economic problem indicates that the demand for a product is determined by the price of the product, the prices of related products, income, and tastes or preferences.
2. A demand schedule shows the quantity demanded at different prices, other things equal. A demand curve is a graph of a demand schedule. Demand schedules and demand curves obey the Law of Demand: The higher the price, the lower the quantity demanded, and vice versa.
3. The Law of Demand results from the substitution and the income effects of a price change. As a result of the substitution effect, consumers tend to substitute toward products that have become relatively cheaper. The income effect is a purchasing power effect that arises because a decrease in price increases purchasing power and therefore quantity demanded, and vice versa.

The second section of the chapter discussed the market demand curve.

CONCEPT SUMMARY

THE PRICE, INCOME, AND CROSS-PRICE ELASTICITIES

I. PRICE ELASTICITY OF DEMAND

A. Percentage Change Measure

$$E_D = \frac{|(\text{percentage change in quantity demanded})|}{|(\text{percentage change in price})|}$$

$E_D > 1$ elastic
$E_D = 1$ unit-elastic
$E_D < 1$ inelastic

B. Total Revenue (Expenditure) Measure

Elastic: price decrease increases total revenue
price increase decreases total revenue
The quantity effect on total revenue dominates the price effect.

Unit-elastic: price decrease or increase leaves total revenue unchanged
The quantity and price effects on total revenue exactly offset one another.

Inelastic: price decrease decreases total revenue
price increase increases total revenue
The price effect on total revenue dominates the quantity effect.

II. INCOME ELASTICITY OF DEMAND

$$E_I = \frac{(\text{percentage change in quantity demanded})}{(\text{percentage change in income})}$$

$E_I > 1$ luxury
$E_I < 1$ necessity
$E_I < 0$ inferior good

III. CROSS-PRICE ELASTICITY OF DEMAND

$$E_{\text{cross-price}} = \frac{(\text{percentage change in the demand for one good})}{(\text{percentage change in the price of the other good})}$$

$E_{\text{cross-price}} > 0$ substitutes
$E_{\text{cross-price}} < 0$ complements
$E_{\text{cross-price}} = 0$ unrelated goods (measured in both directions)

4. The market demand schedule is the sum of the individual consumers' demand schedules. Demand curves are graphical representations of these demand schedules. Thus, the market demand curve is the horizontal summation of the individual demand curves.
5. Market demand curves shift when one of the other variables influencing demand changes. The principal demand shifters are changes in income, population, tastes, and the prices of substitutes and complements.
6. An Engel's curve is the graph of the relationship between income and quantity demanded, other things equal, including the price of the product. Engel's curves are upward sloping for most goods.

The final section of Chapter 5 discussed the concept of elasticity.

7. Demand elasticity is defined by the change in total revenue (expenditure) as price changes, other things equal. When price increases, demand is inelastic if total revenue increases, unit-elastic if total revenue remains the same, and elastic if total revenue decreases.

8. A second measure of elasticity computes the absolute value of the ratio of the percentage change in quantity demanded to the percentage change in price. Demand is elastic if the ratio is greater than 1, unit-elastic if the ratio equals 1, and inelastic if the ratio is less than 1. The percentage change measure is also used to measure the income elasticity of demand and the price elasticity of supply.
9. The principal determinants of demand elasticity are whether the product is considered to be essential or inessential, whether it is expensive or inexpensive, the availability of substitutes, and the passage of time.
10. The income elasticity of demand is the ratio of the percentage change in quantity demanded to the percentage change in income. Luxuries are goods whose income elasticities are greater than 1. Necessities are goods whose income elasticities are less than 1 (and greater than or equal to zero). Inferior goods have negative income elasticities.
11. The cross-price elasticity between related goods A and B is the ratio of the percentage change in the demand for good A to the percentage change in the price of good B. The cross-price elasticity is positive for substitutes and negative for complements.

KEY TERMS

change in demand
change in quantity demanded
complements
cross-price elasticity of demand
demand
(price) elasticity of demand
Engel's curve
income effect (of a price change)
income elasticity of demand
individual demand curve
law of demand
market demand curve
purchasing power
substitutes
substitution effect (of a price change)

QUESTIONS

1. a. What is the Law of Demand?
   b. How is it supported by the substitution and the income effects of a price change?
   c. What are the "other things equal" with respect to the demand curve?
2. Suppose that a consumer buys only one good, X. The consumer has income of $200 to spend on X, and the price of X is $5. How would you define his/her purchasing power (real income)? What happens to the consumer's purchasing power (real income) if the price of X rises to $10?
3. Are the following pairs of goods likely to be complements, substitutes, or unrelated?
   a. baseball; California Angels ticket
   b. haircut; shampoo
   c. cream cheese; bagel
   d. golf clubs; tennis racquet
   e. Ford Taurus; Harley-Davidson motorcycle
4. The sale of greeting cards increases enormously around Valentine's Day. Is this an example of a change in quantity demanded or a change in demand?
5. Would the following tend to increase or decrease the demand for American automobiles?
   a. A popular automotive magazine claims that American automobiles consume far more gasoline than do comparable foreign automobiles.
   b. Consumer incomes decrease by 5 percent.
   c. The price of foreign automobiles decreases by 10 percent.
   d. New technologies decrease the annual cost of maintenance on American cars by 20 percent.
   e. The cost of producing American automobiles decreases by 20 percent.
6. Three people have the following individual demand schedules for product A.

PRICE	PERSON 1	PERSON 2	PERSON 3
$1	5	8	7
2	4	8	7
3	3	8	2
4	2	6	0
5	1	6	0

The numbers in columns two through four are the quantities demanded at each price in the first column.

a. What is the market demand schedule for this product? (Assume that these three people are the only buyers.) Draw the market demand curve.
b. Why might the three people have different demand schedules?
c. Is person 1's demand elastic or inelastic between the prices of $1 and $2. Between the prices of $4 and $5? Answer the same questions for person 2.

7. Rank the following items from least elastic to most elastic, and explain your ranking.
   a. table salt
   b. Ford Taurus
   c. dental care (assume no dental insurance)
8. Are the following goods likely to be inferior goods or normal goods and, if normal goods, luxuries or necessities?
   a. potatoes
   b. polyester suit
   c. Lincoln Town car
   d. butter
   e. compact discs
9. a. Is the cross-price elasticity of demand between cream cheese and bagels likely to be positive, negative, or zero? Between golf clubs and a tennis racket?
   b. Is the income elasticity of demand for a polyester suit likely to be positive, negative, or zero? For a Lincoln Towne car?
10. Draw a reasonable Engel's curve for a normal good.
    a. What factors that influence the demand for the good are being held constant in the diagram?
    b. Suppose that the price of the good increases. How might this affect the Engel's curve?
11. *Extra credit:* Prove that the price elasticity of demand varies along a straight line demand curve from elastic at higher prices to inelastic at lower prices.

CHAPTER

6

Supply and Marginal Cost

LEARNING OBJECTIVES

CONCEPTS TO LEARN

The conditions for a competitive market

The factors that determine the competitive firm's supply of goods and services

The individual and the market supply curves

The Law of Supply

Marginal cost

The marginal benefit equals marginal cost decision rule

The profit-maximizing supply rule

The Law of Diminishing Returns

The marginal product of labor

The elasticity of supply

CONCEPTS TO RECALL

Opportunity cost [1]

The firm's three-part economic problem [1]

Efficiency [2]

The margin in economic analysis [2]

The production possibilities frontier [3]

We saw in Chapter 3 that consumers dictate the answer to the What or Output question in a market economy. They tell businesses what they want more of and what they want less of, and the businesses follow their desires. The prices and profits determined by the Laws of Supply and Demand are the signals that indicate to businesses what they should do. High prices and profits are a clear signal that investors should bring more resources into an industry and expand production. Low prices and losses are an equally clear signal that an industry should contract. The resources are better used elsewhere.

Never underestimate the power of the profit motive in driving businesses to supply the goods and services that consumers want. For example, part of the American dream for many people is owning their own business, and a remarkably large number of people actually pursue this dream. We saw in Chapter 4 that over 600,000 new businesses appear each year in the United States, the majority of them small, privately held firms. The investors who start these businesses are convinced that they have a product or service that consumers will want to buy at prices high enough to bring them a handsome profit. By the same token, over 50,000 businesses fail each year. The market has told these investors that consumers were not interested in what they were producing. They will have to follow their dreams elsewhere in the pursuit of profit.

SUPPLY

The amount of a product that a firm is willing and able to sell over a certain period of time.

Chapter 6 turns to the factors that influence the supply of goods and services. Supply refers to the sellers' side of the marketplace. The **supply** of a product is the amount that business firms are willing and able to sell over a given period of time. Notice that supply, like demand, is a statement of desires, of what firms want to sell rather than what they actually sell. The actual quantities bought and sold in the marketplace depend on the interaction of market supply and market demand.

What determines the supply for each of the goods and services that firms sell? This is the principal question that Chapter 6 addresses.

WHICH FIRMS HAVE SUPPLY CURVES?

Nearly all consumers make their demand decisions in the same way. This is why, in Chapter 5, we could think about ourselves as representative consumers desiring some common, everyday product when developing the concept of an individual's demand for a product. The notion of a "representative firm" does not carry over to the supply of a product, however. Different firms make their decisions about how much output they will supply to a market in very different ways. Our intuition tells us, correctly, that the supply decisions of giant corporations such as General Motors and IBM are fundamentally different from the supply decisions of the corner grocery store or the small clothing store in the middle of town. They are very different kinds of firms.

COMPETITIVE MARKET

A market in which a large number of firms sell very similar or identical products, consumers are well informed about the price that each firm charges for its product, and resources move easily into and out of the market in response to profits and losses.

One important difference between them is that small, localized firms tend to operate in more competitive markets than do the giant corporations, which sell their products nationwide (and even internationally). A **competitive market** is one in which a large number of firms sell very similar or even identical products and consumers are well informed about the price that each firm charges for its product. In other words, consumers have many options of where to shop and are concerned primarily about price. They search for the firm that charges the lowest price. One further characteristic of a competitive market is that resources move easily into or out of the market in response to profits and losses. If investors see a market is profitable, they can enter the market, compete with the existing firms, and try to share in the profits.

The market environment in which the giant corporations operate is often not very competitive in two respects. First, a few large firms sometimes dominate the market and limit the options of consumers. Kodak in photography and AT&T, Sprint, and MCI in telecommunications are examples. In contrast, the corner grocery store usually faces stiff competition from many other grocery stores in the area. Second, resources do not always move easily into and out of markets dominated by large corporations. Starting an automobile company to take on the Japanese and Detroit manufacturers is a formidable undertaking. Starting a small clothing store is much easier.

The market environment in which firms operate affects the nature of their economic problems. The giant corporations have somewhat different objectives than do the small, local firms. They also tend to have more control over the prices of their products. These differences have a profound effect on the supply decision because a firm's decision about how much output to supply results directly from the solution to its economic problem. Firms with different economic problems approach the supply decision differently.

Firms' Objectives

As noted in Chapter 1, the pursuit of profit is the objective usually associated with business firms in a free market system. But the assumption that firms strive to *maximize* profit applies much more accurately to the small, localized firms than to the giant corporations. Profits come more easily to the large national firms, on average, because they are more protected from competition. The giant corporations are interested in making a profit for their stockholders, to be sure, but they also have the luxury of being able to pursue other goals. In contrast, life for the small firms is generally more of a struggle. They often have to squeeze every last opportunity for profit out of the marketplace in order to provide a satisfactory return to their investors. The assumption that the small firms try to maximize profit is reasonably accurate.

The Ability to Control Price

The giant corporations and the small, local firms also differ in their abilities to control the prices of their products. For the most part, the giant corporations determine the prices that they will charge for their products. They are price setters. For example, IBM sets the prices on its entire line of computers. In contrast, small, local firms generally have far less latitude in setting the prices of their products. They tend to be price takers. Price is more nearly determined for them by the combined interaction of all consumers and all firms in the marketplace.

For example, suppose that you operate a small clothing store and sell a standard white cotton tee shirt. The market for tee shirts is highly competitive

ELABORATION: Businesses compete against one another in many different ways, through price, advertising, changes in product quality, and so forth. In its purest form, a competitive market is one in which the only form of competition is through price and all firms end up charging the same price. We will study other ways that firms compete in later chapters.

because many stores in your town and in neighboring towns sell the same tee shirt. If the merchants in your area are charging $5.00 for a tee shirt, you will also sell the tee shirts for $5.00. If you sell the shirt for $5.50, your sales are likely to decline substantially because your customers know they can buy the same shirt from your competitors for $5.00. Conversely, if you sell the shirt for $4.50, customers who normally shop at your competitors' stores will flock to your store, but then you are simply throwing away $.50 per shirt. Therefore, you are essentially a **price taker**, locked into charging the going market price of $5.00.

PRICE TAKER

A firm or individual who has no influence over the market price.

The Law of Supply that we will develop in Chapter 6 applies only to price-taking firms whose objective is to maximize profit. Therefore, despite the fact that the giant corporations capture the headlines and the attention of the American public, Chapter 6 concentrates on the smaller, price-taking firms. Only highly competitive markets operate according to the Laws of Supply and Demand. The analysis of the giant corporations such as General Motors and IBM will have to wait until later chapters in the microeconomics section of the text.

REFLECTION: Which industries whose products you buy appear to have become more competitive over the past few years? Less competitive?

CURRENT ISSUE: The former Communist nations have found another advantage of small businesses as they try to convert their economies to capitalism: The small businesses are the easiest to privatize. For example, Russia began its conversion by privatizing retail shops, restaurants, and other small businesses, and was able to proceed at a fairly rapid pace. By the end of 1992, approximately 20 percent of the Russian labor force worked in the private sector. But Russia did not succeed in privatizing any of its large manufacturing firms until 1993, and then only a few. (*The Economist*, November 28, 1992, p. 17.)

Be assured, though, that the Laws of Supply and Demand are very relevant to the U.S. economy. Product markets in the United States are fairly competitive for the most part. Somewhere between 60 and 80 percent of all products are sold in markets that are competitive enough to be reasonably well modeled by the Laws of Supply and Demand. Supply and demand analysis is a very useful model for predicting price and quantity in these markets.

In addition, competitive markets that operate according to the Laws of Supply and Demand best satisfy society's twin goals of efficiency and equity. As such, the competitive markets that the small, local firms operate in set the standards that economists use to judge the markets dominated by the giant corporations.

SUPPLY AND THE FIRM'S ECONOMIC PROBLEM

The supply of any product arises from the three-part economic problem that all firms must solve, consisting of objectives, alternatives, and constraints. A competitive, price-taking firm's economic problem has the following structure.

The firm's *objective* is to achieve the maximum amount of profit, the difference between total revenue and total cost.

The firm faces two sets of *alternatives*:

1. what products to produce, and in what amounts; and
2. how to produce each product. (Recall from Chapter 1 that the How question involves the choice of a production technology along with the associated factors of production for that technology.)

The firm's *constraints* are threefold:

1. the production technologies available to the firm for producing each product;
2. the prices of the various factors of production associated with each technology; and
3. the demand for each product, which determines the price at which the firm can sell each product.

The structure of the firm's economic problem indicates that its willingness to supply any one product depends on available production technologies, factor prices, the price of the product, and the prices of other products that the firm is able to produce.

The *production technologies* establish the physical link between the firm's inputs and outputs. They indicate the amounts of various factors of production needed to produce the quantities of each product supplied.

The *factor prices* include the prices of various kinds of labor; the material inputs purchased from other firms, including energy; land and raw materials; and capital. The factor prices, along with the chosen production technology, determine the total cost of producing whatever quantity of product the firm chooses to supply.

The *price of the product* determines the total revenue received for whatever quantity of the product the firm chooses to supply. Total revenue is just price times quantity supplied.

The *prices of all other products* the firm is capable of supplying determine the total revenue from supplying those products. Therefore, these prices help determine whether supplying the product is more profitable than supplying other products.

Taxes on firms also influence the supply decision because they add to the firm's costs. For example, a sales tax causes firms to raise the prices of their products.

The Individual Firm's Supply Curve

As with demand, we are interested in the relationship between the price of the product and the quantity supplied, holding constant all variables that influence quantity supplied except price. Other things equal, how do changes in the price of the product affect the quantity supplied?

For most firms and most products, most of the time, price and quantity supplied are directly related. The lower the price of a product, the smaller the quantity supplied; the higher the price of a product, the larger the quantity supplied. The direct relationship between price and quantity supplied is illustrated by the hypothetical supply schedule of a firm selling compact discs in Table 6.1.

INDIVIDUAL FIRM'S SUPPLY SCHEDULE

The quantity that the firm is willing and able to supply at each price, other things equal.

The **supply schedule** shows, at different prices, how many compact discs a firm is willing to supply throughout the course of a year, other things equal.

TABLE 6.1 One-Year Supply Schedule of an Individual Compact Disc Firm (Hypothetical Data)

PRICE OF COMPACT DISCS	QUANTITY SUPPLIED OF COMPACT DISCS (THOUSANDS)
$28	125
24	120
20	110
16	90
12	60
8	40
4	10

FIGURE 6.1

The Individual Firm's Supply Curve for Compact Discs

The individual firm's supply curve for compact discs, *s*, is a graph of the hypothetical supply schedule for compact discs in Table 6.1. The supply curve is upward sloping in accordance with the Law of Supply; price and quantity supplied are directly related. The lower the price the lower the quantity supplied, and the higher the price the higher the quantity supplied, other things equal.

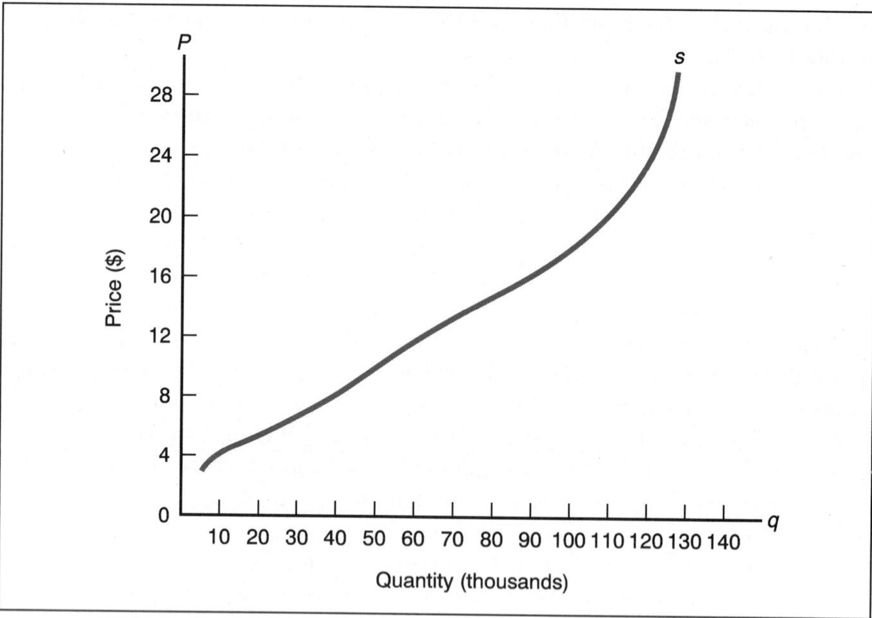

At the relatively low price of $4 the quantity supplied is also relatively low. The compact disc firm is willing to supply only 10,000 discs each year. As the price rises to $16, the quantity the firm is willing to supply rises to 90,000 discs. As the price increases further to $24, the quantity supplied increases to 120,000 discs. Price and quantity supplied are directly related.

INDIVIDUAL FIRM'S SUPPLY CURVE

A graphical representation of the individual firm's supply schedule, showing the quantity that the firm is willing and able to supply at each price, other things equal.

A **firm's supply curve** is the graph of its supply schedule. The line labeled *s* in Figure 6.1 is the compact disc firm's supply curve associated with the firm's supply schedule in Table 6.1. Price is on the vertical axis, and quantity supplied is on the horizontal axis. The supply curve is drawn as a solid line to allow for all possible combinations of price and quantity supplied, not just the few price-quantity combinations shown in Table 6.1. Notice how the supply curve slopes up and to the right, indicating that price and quantity supplied are directly related.

The Law of Supply

LAW OF SUPPLY

Other things equal, the lower the price of a product, the smaller the quantity supplied; the higher the price of a product, the larger the quantity supplied.

The direct relationship between price and quantity supplied occurs with such regularity that it is called the Law of Supply. The **Law of Supply** says, *other things equal*, the lower the price of a product, the smaller the quantity supplied; the higher the price of a product, the larger the quantity supplied.

MARGINAL COST

The addition to total cost of producing an additional unit of output; in general, the change in total cost divided by the change in output.

Why are supply curves upward sloping? Why must price rise in order to induce firms to supply more of a product? The answer lies in the pattern of the typical firm's cost of production, in particular, marginal cost. Recall from Chapter 2 that the margin in economics refers to the effects of small changes in economic activity. **Marginal cost** is the addition to total cost of producing an additional unit of output. At any given quantity it is the increase in total cost incurred by producing the last unit of output. For example, if a firm produces 50,000 compact discs, the marginal cost at 50,000 discs is the cost of producing the 50,000th disc. Notice that the concept of marginal cost is analogous to the concept of the marginal grade from the study example in Chapter 2. The marginal grade in that example referred to the increase in the student's test score for each additional hour of study.

Marginal cost is directly relevant to the supply decision because firms compare price with marginal cost when deciding whether to increase output. Price is the additional revenue a competitive firm receives from supplying one more unit of output. Marginal cost is the additional cost to the firm of supplying one more unit of output. A firm will increase quantity supplied only if the price (additional revenue) is greater than the marginal cost (additional cost), so that the firm's profit increases.

Supply curves are upward sloping because the cost of producing *additional* output, the marginal cost, increases for most firms the more output the firm is already producing. Therefore, they have to charge higher prices to cover the higher costs. Refer again to the supply schedule in Table 6.1. The table indicates that the compact disc firm requires a price of $8 to increase its rate of production by 30,000 discs from 10,000 to 40,000 and a price of $16 to increase its rate of production by 30,000 discs from 60,000 to 90,000. The underlying reason for requiring a higher price in the second instance is that the cost to the firm of producing an *additional* 30,000 discs is much higher starting from 60,000 discs than starting from 10,000 discs. For example, the firm might have to run a second shift in its factory to increase production from 60,000 discs to 90,000 discs, whereas the day shift alone can increase production from 10,000 to 40,000 discs. The second shift is unlikely to be as productive as the first shift because workers are less alert at night. Also, running two shifts works the machines harder, and they are likely to break down more often. Whatever the reason, most firms do find that the cost of producing additional output, the marginal cost, rises as the rate of production increases.

The intuition behind the phenomenon of rising marginal cost comes from the production possibilities frontier of Chapter 3. Recall that the frontier bows outward because the opportunity cost of producing any one product increases as more and more of that product is produced. Business firms experience these rising opportunity costs directly in their costs of production. When they try to expand their own production, they find that the additional units of output are ever the more costly to produce. Therefore, firms are willing to increase production only if they receive a higher price for their products to offset the higher marginal cost. Their supply curves are upward sloping.

BEHIND THE LAW OF SUPPLY: SOLVING THE FIRM'S ECONOMIC PROBLEM

Our intuitive discussion of the Law of Supply is sufficient for understanding how competitive markets operate. But economists are also interested in evaluating market outcomes. Do markets generate an efficient allocation of society's scarce resources? Are the market results fair according to accepted standards of equity? Why are markets that operate according the the Laws of Supply and Demand the standard against which all other markets are judged? Answering these questions requires a deeper understanding of how a firm's supply curve is related to its cost of production and, in particular, to its marginal cost.

Two fundamental propositions on supply underlie the intuitive discussion above:

- Proposition 1: A competitive, price-taking firm's supply curve is its marginal cost curve.
- Proposition 2: A competitive firm's supply curve is expected to be upward sloping in the short run.

The second proposition is the Law of Supply. Since it follows from the first proposition, we will consider the two propositions in order.

Proposition 1: Supply Curves and Marginal Cost

That a competitive firm's supply decision is closely related to its production costs is hardly surprising. The firm's objective is to maximize profit, the difference between its total revenue and its total cost. As indicated above, firms operating in a highly competitive market environment are essentially price takers. They have no choice but to sell at the going market price, and the market price sets the revenue side of the profit relationship for any quantity the firm chooses to supply. To see why, return to our example of the clothing store selling white cotton tee shirts for \$5.00. The firm is essentially locked into selling its tee shirts for that price. Therefore, the clothier faces a perfectly elastic, horizontal demand for its tee shirts at the established market price of \$5.00, as pictured in Figure 6.2. It can sell as many tee shirts as it wants at \$5.00 a shirt.

Total revenue is price times quantity. The total revenue from selling 10 tee shirts is \$50 (\$50 = \$5 · 10); the total revenue from selling 11 tee shirts is \$55 (\$55 = \$5 · 11); and similarly at all other quantities. The firm knows what its total revenue is for every quantity that it chooses to sell. The only remaining question, then, relates to the cost side of the profit relationship.

AN INDIVIDUAL FIRM'S DEMAND CURVE A comment is in order before moving on to the cost of producing the tee shirts. Notice that the demand curve pic-

FIGURE 6.2

The Demand Curve Facing a Competitive Firm Selling Tee Shirts

The demand curve, *d*, facing a clothing firm selling tee shirts is essentially horizontal, perfectly elastic, at the going market price for tee shirts, assumed to be \$5.00 in the figure. If the clothing store prices its tee shirts above \$5.00, its customers will buy tee shirts at other stores. If the clothing store prices its tee shirts below \$5.00, everyone will want to buy its tee shirts. Competitive firms are price takers; they can sell as much or as little as they want at the going market price.

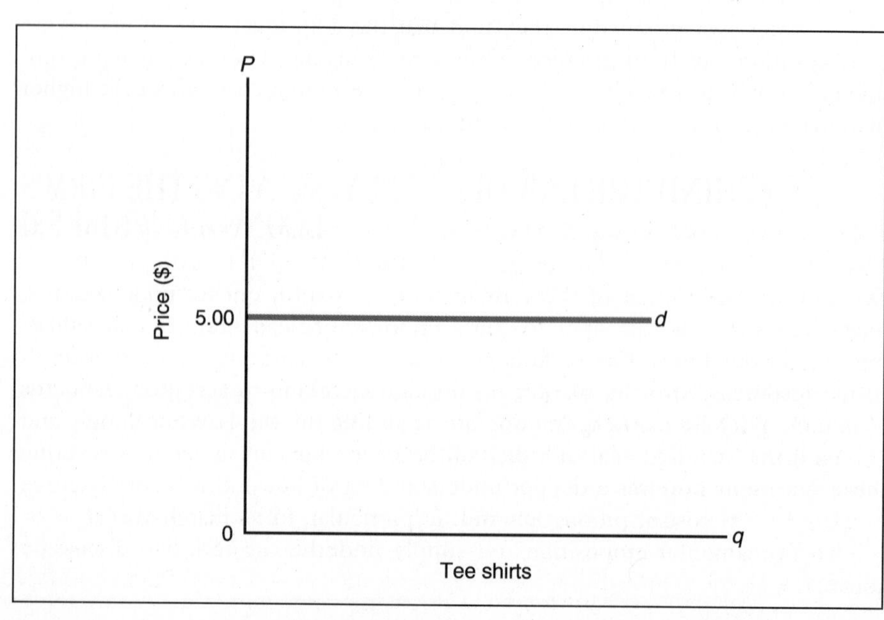

tured in Figure 6.2 differs from both the individual consumer's demand curve and the market demand curve described in Chapter 5. It is a demand curve from the perspective of an individual business firm.

Every business firm faces a demand curve for each product it sells. The firm's demand curve indicates, at every price, the total quantity demanded by all the firm's customers. As such, it lies somewhere between an individual consumer's demand curve and the market demand curve.

Since the firm's demand curve derives from the demands of its customers, it is similar to the individual consumer's demand curve in certain respects. It is an other things equal relationship between the price of the product and the quantity demanded, and it tends to be downward sloping. But because the demand curve is defined from the viewpoint of the individual firm, its slope depends as much on the nature of the firm's competition as it does on its customers obeying the Law of Demand. Quantity demanded decreases for two reasons when a single firm raises its price. First, each of its customers wants to buy less. Second, the firm loses customers, and sales, to competing firms. Similarly, a decrease in price induces new purchases by the firm's regular customers and brings in new customers from other firms.

So two meanings of an individual demand curve will be carried throughout this text, one from the point of view of an individual consumer and one from the point of view of an individual business firm. There is only one market demand curve, however, consisting of the sum of the individual consumer's demand curves, as described in Chapter 5. This market demand curve is the *industry* demand curve from the business perspective, the total demand for the product experienced by all firms combined in the industry.

MARGINAL COST Returning to the cost side of the profit relationship, the *total* cost of production certainly increases as the quantity supplied increases. The firm wants to know this: What quantity maximizes profit, the difference between total revenue and total cost? The answer depends on exactly how cost increases as quantity increases. Proposition 1 says that the key to the supply decision lies on the margin. The firm's *marginal* cost of production determines its willingness to supply at any given price.

As noted above, marginal cost is the cost of producing an additional unit of output. In general, marginal cost (MC) is defined as the change in total cost (TC) divided by the change in output (q), written as

$$MC = \Delta TC/\Delta q$$

The Greek symbol Δ, called *delta*, refers to the change in both total cost and quantity. We will use Δ to represent the change in a variable throughout this text. The general expression for marginal cost indicates that marginal cost is expressed on a per unit basis if a firm cannot produce single units of output. For example, suppose that a firm can only change its production by 50 units at a time. If increasing production by 50 units increases total cost by \$200, the marginal cost is \$4 ($\Delta TC/\Delta q$ = \$200/50 = \$4). Whenever production increases by just one unit, $\Delta q = 1$ and MC is just the change in total cost, consistent with the original definition.

To see why a competitive, price-taking firm's supply decision is based on its marginal cost, let's continue with our example of the clothing store selling white cotton tee shirts for \$5.00. The price of the shirts is \$5.00 at every

TABLE 6.2 Marginal Cost of Producing Tee Shirts

QUANTITY OF TEE SHIRTS	MARGINAL COST	QUANTITY OF TEE SHIRTS	MARGINAL COST
1–100	$ .10	130th	$3.00
101st	.10	⋮	⋮
102nd	.20	135th	3.50
103rd	.30	⋮	⋮
104th	.40	140th	4.00
⋮	⋮	⋮	⋮
109th	.90	149th	4.90
110th	1.00	150th	5.00
⋮	⋮	151st	5.10
116th	1.60	⋮	⋮
⋮	⋮	159th	5.90
120th	2.00	160th	6.00
⋮	⋮	161st	6.10
127th	2.70	⋮	⋮
⋮	⋮	180th	8.00
		⋮	⋮

quantity. To demonstrate proposition 1, we need to know the marginal cost of producing shirts at every quantity. Assume that the tee shirts can be manufactured one at a time and that the pattern of marginal costs is as given in Table 6.2. The numbers in the table are hypothetical; they do not represent the actual costs of producing tee shirts.

The first 100 shirts cost $.10 each to produce (and sell). Therefore, the marginal cost of producing shirts is $.10 at all quantities from 0 through 100. The total cost of producing the first 100 shirts is $10.00.

The 101st shirt also costs $.10 to produce. Beyond 101 shirts, the marginal cost of producing additional shirts rises according to the simple pattern indicted in Table 6.2. (Proposition 2 will demonstrate why increasing marginal cost is a reasonable assumption.)

The 102nd shirt costs an additional $.20 to produce; the 103rd shirt costs an additional $.30 to produce; and so on. In other words, *marginal cost* increases by $.10 for each shirt beyond 101. The pattern is assumed to continue indefinitely. For example, the 110th shirt costs an additional $1.00 to produce, the 130th an additional $3.00, the 147th an additional $4.70, and the 160th an additional $6.00. To be sure you understand that the numbers in the table refer to marginal cost, you should verify that the *total* cost of producing 103 shirts is $10.60 ($10.00 for the first 100, plus $.10 for the 101st, $.20 for the 102nd, and $.30 for the 103rd = $10.60 total).

Figure 6.3 provides a graph of the hypothetical entries in Table 6.2, with marginal cost on the vertical axis and quantity on the horizontal axis. The graph represents the firm's **marginal cost curve**. It is horizontal at a value of $.10 for quantities 1 through 101 and then rises in constant increments of $.10 for each unit in excess of 101. The graph displays a few of the (q, MC) combinations listed in Table 6.2 for quantities in excess of 101.

MARGINAL COST CURVE

A graphical representation of marginal cost, showing at each output the addition to total cost of producing an additional unit of output.

If the firm can sell as many shirts as it wants at $5.00, how many should it produce and sell *to maximize its profit*? This is the supply question. We emphasize the goal of profit maximization because it is central to the development of the supply curve.

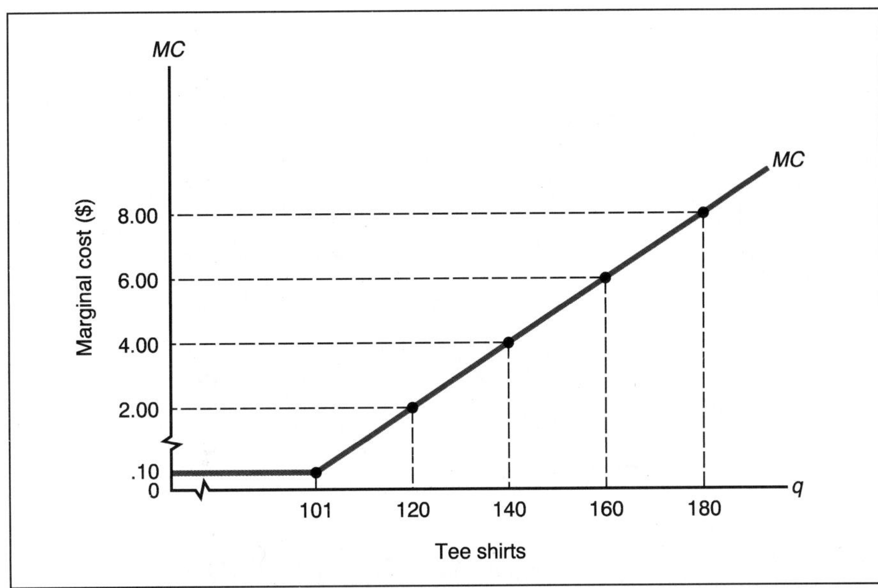

FIGURE 6.3

The Marginal Cost Curve for Tee Shirts

The marginal cost curve, *MC*, is a graph of the hypothetical marginal cost data for producing and selling tee shirts from Table 6.2. The first 101 tee shirts cost $.10 each to produce and sell. Starting with the 102nd tee shirt, the marginal costs increase by $.10 for each additional tee shirt.

THE FIRM'S BEST-PROFIT SUPPLY RULE To see why marginal cost holds the key to the supply question, think of the profitability of supplying tee shirts one shirt at a time. Figure 6.4 provides a picture of the decision-making process by combining the firm's horizontal demand curve from Figure 6.2 with the graph of its marginal costs from Figure 6.3.

Should the firm supply 1 shirt? The answer is yes. The cost of producing the first shirt is only $.10, but the firm can sell the shirt for $5.00. Therefore, producing and selling the first shirt brings a profit of $4.90. In Figure 6.4, the $4.90 of profit is the vertical distance between the horizontal demand curve ($5.00) and the marginal cost curve ($.10) above the first unit of output. Move on to the 2nd shirt. It, too, brings a profit of $4.90. The same is true of shirts 3 through 101. Producing and selling each of them increases profit by $4.90. The vertical distance between the two curves remains the same for the first 101 shirts.

Should the firm supply the 102nd shirt? Yes, it should. The marginal cost of producing the 102nd shirt increases to $.20, but it can still be sold for $5.00. Therefore, if the firm produces and sells the 102nd shirt, it increases profit by $4.80, the vertical distance between the demand and marginal cost curves above the 102nd shirt. The addition to profit declines by $.10 for each shirt beyond the 102nd (as does the vertical distance between the two curves). Nonetheless, so long as the market price of $5.00 exceeds the marginal cost of producing the next shirt, the firm should produce that shirt. Profits continue to increase. For instance, producing the 130th shirt costs an additional $3.00. But since the shirt can be sold for $5.00, producing and selling the unit adds $2.00 to the firm's profit.

Continuing along shirt by shirt, profits continue to increase through the first 149 shirts. The 149th shirt has a marginal cost of $4.90. But since it sells for $5.00, producing and selling it increases profit by $.10. The demand curve is still above the marginal cost curve. The two curves intersect at the 150th shirt. The 150th shirt costs an additional $5.00 to produce, exactly as much as the

FIGURE 6.4

The Competitive Firm's Best-Profit Supply Rule

The figure combines the demand curve for tee shirts, *d*, from Figure 6.2 and the marginal cost curve for producing and selling tee shirts, *MC*, from Figure 6.3. The clothing store maximizes profit by producing and selling 150 tee shirts each period, at the intersection of *d* and *MC*. Producing and selling fewer than 150 shirts sacrifices profit because price exceeds marginal cost. Producing and selling more than 150 tee shirts sacrifices profit because marginal cost exceeds price. A competitive firm's best-profit output is the quantity at which price equals marginal cost.

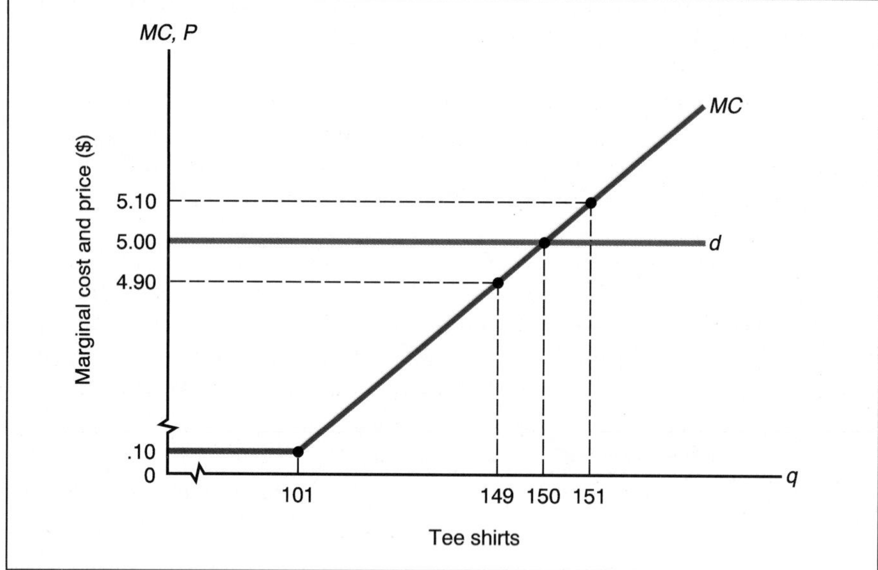

sales price. Therefore, producing and selling the 150th shirt neither increases nor decreases the firm's profit.

The firm will certainly not produce and sell more than 150 shirts because all shirts above 150 subtract from profits. The marginal cost curve lies above the demand curve beyond 150. For instance, the 151st shirt costs \$5.10 to produce. Selling it for \$5.00 subtracts \$.10 from the firm's total profit. All shirts above 151 would continue to subtract from profit in ever-increasing amounts. The vertical distance between the demand and the marginal cost curves is increasingly negative.

In conclusion, to maximize its profit the firm should produce and sell either 149 or 150 shirts during each time period, whatever the relevant period of time happens to be. Notice that the firm does not even have to compute total profit to determine that 149 or 150 is its best-profit output. As it considers increasing output shirt by shirt, all the firm needs to ask is this: What is true on the margin?

SUPPLY RULE FOR MAXIMIZING PROFIT

A competitive firm should produce the output at which price (marginal revenue) equals marginal cost.

A simple **supply rule for maximizing profit** results from this analysis: A competitive, price-taking firm should produce the output at which price equals marginal cost. In terms of the diagram, the best-profit output occurs at the intersection of the demand and the marginal cost curves. According to the diagram, the best-profit output is 150 shirts.

In fact, we know that producing and selling either 149 or 150 shirts generates the same amount of profit. That happens because of the discrete nature of the example—the firm cannot produce a fraction of a shirt. However, the smooth marginal cost curve in Figure 6.4 implicitly assumes that producing a fraction of a shirt is possible. If fractional units were possible, the firm would produce an output infinitesimally close to the intersection of the demand and the marginal cost curves. Therefore, the price = marginal cost version of the supply rule covers both the discrete and the fractional units cases.

THE MARGINAL BENEFIT = MARGINAL COST PRINCIPLE The price = marginal cost supply rule for a competitive, price-taking firm is a specific application of a fundamental general principle of economic analysis that applies in any context involving the economic problem. The general decision rule for solving the economic problem is this: *An activity should be continued to the point at which the marginal benefit of the activity equals the marginal cost of the activity.* **Marginal benefit** is defined as the additional benefit, in terms of the objectives, of the next unit of activity. The units in which marginal benefit and marginal cost are measured depend on the context in which the economic problem arises.

MARGINAL BENEFIT

The additional benefit, in terms of the objectives, of the next unit of an activity.

Recall that cost refers to opportunity cost in economic analysis. With that in mind, the intuition behind the rule is that if the benefit of the next unit of activity exceeds its cost, then the scarce resources employed in the next unit of the activity are better used in that activity than elsewhere. Therefore, the level of the activity should be increased. Once benefit and cost are equal on the margin, the scarce resources are used just as well in that activity as elsewhere, but no better. If the cost of the next unit of activity exceeds the benefit, however, the scarce resources are better employed elsewhere. Therefore, the activity should not continue beyond the point at which benefit and cost are equal on the margin.

Our competitive, price-taking tee shirt manufacturer is attempting to maximize its total profit, the difference between total revenue and total cost. The marginal benefit in this context is the **marginal revenue**, the increase in total revenue from selling one more shirt. The marginal revenue is the established market price for a competitive firm. For example, if the firm increases its sale of tee shirts from 10 to 11, total revenue increases from \$50 (\$50 = \$5·10) to \$55 (\$55 = \$5·11). The marginal revenue is \$5, the price of the shirt. Since the demand curve is horizontal at \$5.00, the marginal revenue between any two quantities is always \$5, the price. Therefore, equating the price and the marginal cost of producing and selling shirts is the same as equating the marginal benefit and the marginal cost of that activity. The marginal benefit = marginal cost decision rule for maximizing an economic objective appears time and again throughout this text. It is one of the more important principles in all of economics.

MARGINAL REVENUE

The increase in total revenue from selling one more unit of output; equal to price for a competitive firm.

THE SUPPLY CURVE AS MARGINAL COST CURVE The issue at hand is why the firm's marginal cost curve is its supply curve. The two are equivalent because of the price = marginal cost best-profit supply rule. A supply curve indicates the quantity the firm wants to supply at every price, with the objective of maximizing its profit. We have identified one such point on the firm's supply curve in our example. At a price of \$5.00, the firm wants to supply 150 shirts because supplying 150 shirts maximizes profit when the established market price is \$5.00.

Figure 6.5(a) represents our firm's supply curve. The price of tee shirts is on the vertical axis, and the quantity of tee shirts supplied is on the horizontal axis. Figure 6.5(b) reproduces Figure 6.4, consisting of the firm's horizontal demand curve and its marginal cost curve. The quantity-price combination (150, \$5.00) is shown on the supply curve in Figure 6.5(a), corresponding to the best-profit output in Figure 6.5(b) when the price is \$5.00.

To find the other points on the graph, consider how the firm would react if faced with different market prices. For instance, suppose that the going market price is \$6.00. In Figure 6.5(b) the firm now faces a horizontal demand curve at a height of \$6.00. The new demand curve intersects the marginal cost curve

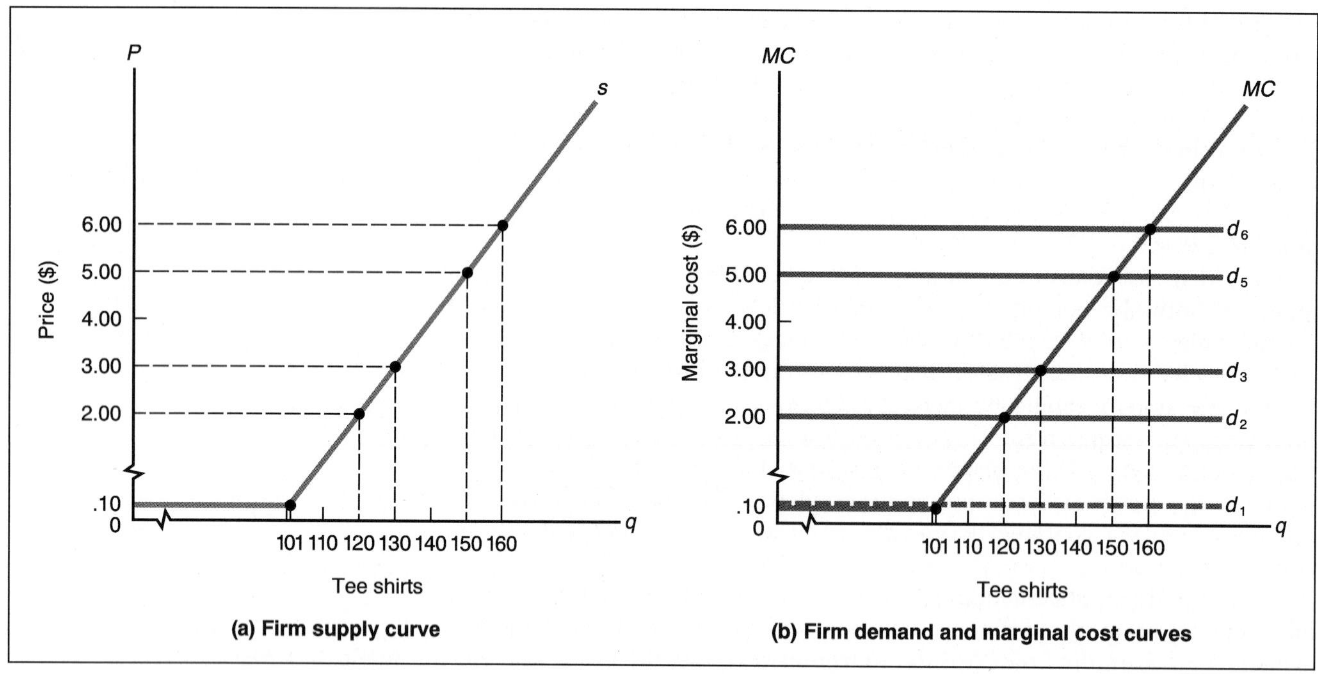

FIGURE 6.5

The Supply Curve and the Marginal Cost Curve for Tee Shirts

The supply curve, *s*, in Figure 6.5(a) indicates the quantity of tee shirts the clothing store is willing to supply at each market price. The marginal cost curve, *MC*, in Figure 6.5(b) indicates the marginal cost of producing and selling tee shirts at each quantity. The supply curve and the marginal cost curve are identical because the clothing store supplies the quantity of tee shirts at which price equals marginal cost in order to maximize its profits. A competitive firm's supply curve is its marginal cost curve.

at 160, the new best-profit output for the firm. At a price of $6.00, producing and selling shirts 151 through 159 adds to total profit, since their marginal costs range from $5.10 to $5.90. Producing and selling the 160th shirt neither increases nor decreases the firm's profit because marginal revenue (price) and marginal cost are both equal to $6.00 at 160. The price = marginal cost supply rule assumes that the firm produces and sells the 160th unit. Marginal cost exceeds marginal revenue for all shirts above 160. Therefore, at a price of $6.00 the firm wants to supply 160 units. The quantity-price combination (160, $6) is a point on the firm's supply curve in Figure 6.5(a).

Similarly, at a price of $3.00, 130 shirts is the best-profit quantity. At a price of $2.00, 120 shirts is the best-profit quantity. Hence, the quantity-price combinations (130, $3) and (120, $2) are also points on the firm's supply curve in Figure 6.5(a). The lowest price that the firm can accept and still produce shirts is just slightly greater than $.10. At a price of $.10, the firm is indifferent between producing anywhere from 1 to 101 shirts and producing no shirts at all. No profit can be made in any case. Therefore, the supply curve becomes horizontal at $.10, representing the firm's indifference to supply quantities 0 through 101 at that price.

Notice that the graphs of the firm's supply curve and its marginal cost curve are *identical.* The marginal cost curve graphs the relationship between quantity and marginal cost. The supply curve graphs the relationship between quantity and the price required to elicit that quantity from the firm. The two are one and the same because the firm supplies the quantity at which price *equals* marginal cost in order to maximize its profit. Therefore, whether price or marginal cost appears on the vertical axis makes no difference, *so long as the firm follows the* p = MC *best-profit supply rule.* If the firm pursued some objective other than maximizing profit, its supply and marginal cost curves would not be identical.

We have established proposition 1: A competitive, price-taking firm's supply curve is its marginal cost curve.

Proposition 2: Supply Curves are Upward Sloping

Earlier we presented an intuitive explanation of why supply curves are expected to be upward sloping. Proposition 2 qualifies that intuition by suggesting that the expectation applies only to the short run, not the long run. To understand why this is so, we need first to distinguish between the short run and the long run in a production context.

SHORT RUN VERSUS THE LONG RUN One obvious distinction between the short run and the long run is the passage of time—the long run refers to a longer period of time. But time is not the defining distinction between the two. Rather, economists distinguish the short run and the long run on the basis of how completely firms are able to react to changing market conditions.

In the **short run** at least one factor of production remains fixed, unable to be increased or decreased. The firm must live with past decisions made with respect to any fixed factor. The short run becomes the **long run** when the firm is able to vary all factors of production. The long run also includes the possibility of new firms entering a profitable industry or of existing firms leaving an unprofitable industry. The time at which the short run becomes the long run varies considerably from industry to industry, and even within an industry depending on how the market conditions change and on the availability of various resources.

SHORT RUN

A period of time short enough that at least one factor of production remains fixed and long enough that at least one factor is variable.

LONG RUN

A period of time long enough that the firm is able to vary all factors of production and firms can enter or leave the industry.

To clarify the distinction using our example, suppose that the market price of tee shirts rises from $5.00 to $6.00. The firm wants to increase production to exploit its improved profit opportunities. It may be able to increase production fairly quickly by hiring more labor, buying additional materials and equipment, and running a second shift in the factory from 4:00 p.m. to midnight. Or it may use its existing factors more intensively, for example, by having the employees work overtime on weekends. The firm may also want to purchase new land and build another factory if it believes the new price will hold indefinitely. This cannot be done so quickly, however. The process of finding a suitable piece of land, arranging for its purchase, engaging a contractor to build the factory, and having the factory built and made operational may take many months, perhaps even a few years. The firm could save time by renting an existing building if a suitable one is available, but even then it may need a month or two to set up a factory in the building. In this example, the *short run* lasts until the new factory is in place and ready to operate. The *long run* begins once the new factory begins producing shirts.

The process of firms entering and leaving an industry is also inherently a long-run phenomenon. New investors who want to begin producing tee shirts with the price at $6.00 have to start from scratch. They should require approximately the same amount of time to enter the industry as existing firms require to expand all aspects of their operations.

Leaving an industry in response to unfavorable market conditions may also require a considerable amount of time. A decline in the price of shirts from $5.00 to $3.00 may induce some firms to sell their plant and equipment and leave the industry. Finding a buyer and arranging for the sale take time, however, and the firm remains in the short run until the sale is final.

Capital and land are usually assumed to be the fixed factors in the short run, but this is not necessarily the case. A computer software company interested in expanding its production needs highly skilled computer programmers who may not be immediately available to the firm. The firm remains in the short run until it can hire the programmers and put them to work.

In any event, proposition 2 applies only to the short run, when at least one factor of production is fixed.

LAW OF DIMINISHING RETURNS

As increasing amounts of a variable factor of production are added to one or more fixed factors of production, the marginal product of the variable factor eventually declines.

THE LAW OF DIMINISHING RETURNS The expectation of upward-sloping short-run supply curves is based on a property of production that applies to virtually every firm—the Law of Diminishing Returns. The **Law of Diminishing Returns** says that as increasing amounts of a variable factor of production are added to one or more fixed factors of production, the marginal product of the variable factor eventually declines.

Notice two points about the Law of Diminishing Returns before turning to an explanation of its meaning. First, the law applies only to the short run—there must be at least one fixed factor of production. Second, the law introduces a new margin for us to consider, the marginal product of a factor of production.

MARGINAL PRODUCT OF LABOR

The additional output produced by hiring one more unit of labor, holding all other factors of production constant.

THE MARGINAL PRODUCT OF LABOR Marginal products are defined analogously to marginal benefits, marginal costs, and marginal grades. Think of labor (L) as the variable factor of production, producing some output (q). The **marginal product of labor** (MP_L) is the additional output produced by hiring one more unit of labor, holding all other factors of production constant. Units of labor are usually defined in terms of numbers of workers or hours of work. The marginal product of labor is sometimes labeled MPP_L, the marginal *physical* product of labor, to indicate that a marginal product measures the additional output in physical units of output, not dollar values.

In general,

$$MP_L = \Delta q/\Delta L$$

As with marginal cost, the marginal product of labor is defined on a per unit basis if labor cannot be added in single units.

The marginal products of the other factors of production are defined similarly.

AN AGRICULTURAL EXAMPLE OF MARGINAL PRODUCT The following simple agricultural example illustrates the Law of Diminishing Returns. Imagine that you own a plot of farmland and are hiring workers to farm the land. Each worker receives the same set of tools, so the tools need not be considered separately from the workers. The unit of labor is a single worker, and output is measured in bushels of produce over some period of time. The land is uniformly fertile, and all workers have identical skills.

Table 6.3 indicates how output might increase in this example as workers are added to your land. The numbers are hypothetical, constructed to illustrate the Law of Diminishing Returns. According to the table, the first worker pro-

TABLE 6.3 **The Law of Diminishing Returns**

NUMBER OF WORKERS	TOTAL PRODUCT (BUSHELS)	MARGINAL PRODUCT (BUSHELS)
1	100	100
2	200	100
3	300	100
4	400	100
5	475	75
6	525	50
7	550	25
8	550	0
9	525	−25

duces 100 bushels of output. Therefore, the marginal product of the first worker is 100. Also, marginal product and total product are the same with only one worker.

Assume that the first worker is able to farm only ¼ of the land. If so, the second worker hired will also be able to farm only ¼ of the land, and the production should increase by another 100 bushels. The marginal product of the second worker is 100 bushels, and the total product received from both workers is 200 bushels. Similarly, the third and fourth workers are able to farm only ¼ of the land, so their marginal products are also 100 bushels. The total product of all four workers is 400 bushels.

The marginal product of labor begins to decline when the fifth worker is hired because the land now truly becomes a fixed factor of production. The fifth worker cannot simply be given more open land to farm as the first four were. Instead, you must rearrange the land allocated to *every* worker so that each farms, on average, ⅕ of the parcel rather than ¼ of the parcel. According to the hypothetical numbers in Table 6.3, the total product with five workers increases, but to 475 bushels, not 500 bushels. The marginal product of the fifth worker declines to 75 bushels. The Law of Diminishing Returns takes effect at this point precisely because each worker now has less of the fixed land to work with. The marginal product of labor continues to decline without any natural limit once diminishing returns set in, as the fixed land is spread ever thinner among the workers. Table 6.3 illustrates the force of the law.

Adding a sixth worker increases total product to 525 bushels. The marginal product of the sixth worker declines to 50 bushels, since each worker is now assigned only ⅙ of the parcel. With seven workers, total product increases again to 550 bushels, but the marginal product of the seventh worker declines to only 25 bushels. With eight workers, the land becomes so crowded that total product does not increase at all. The marginal product of the eight worker is zero. Finally, crowding becomes so severe with nine workers that they manage to get in each other's way. The marginal product of the ninth worker is −25 bushels, as total product declines from 550 to 525. The example is not outlandish. The total productivity on farms in less-developed countries often increases when excess workers leave the farms to seek employment in urban areas.

Diminishing returns are as common in manufacturing as they are on the farm. Hiring labor to work overtime does not necessarily increase output in proportion to the increase in hours worked. Human capacities for work are limited—people tire when working long hours. Employing a second shift overcomes the human fatigue factor, but, as with overtime work, it puts increasing strain on fixed plant and equipment. Fatigue transfers to the machinery, which breaks down more frequently, causing more down time. As a result, running two shifts in a factory does not usually double the output obtained from running one shift. Diminishing returns is a very general phenomenon, hence a "law" of production.

DIMINISHING RETURNS AND SUPPLY CURVES The Law of Diminishing Returns causes supply curves to be upward sloping in the short run because of its effect on marginal cost. Returning to the agricultural example, suppose that you hire workers to farm your land. Because your farm is small, you can hire as many workers as you want at a fixed wage, equal to P_L. Think in terms of hiring one worker at a time, and consider what happens to the marginal cost of your output.

Recall that, in general, marginal cost is the ratio of the change in total cost to the change in output.

$$MC = \Delta TC/\Delta q$$

As you hire one more worker, your costs increase by the amount of the fixed wage, P_L. Therefore, $\Delta TC = P_L$. Your output increases by the marginal product of labor, by definition of a marginal product. Therefore, $\Delta q = MP_L$. Hence, the marginal cost of output can be rewritten as

$$MC = P_L/MP_L$$

in terms of each new worker hired.

The Law of Diminishing Returns ensures that the marginal product of labor will eventually decline as more and more workers are hired. Once diminishing returns set in, therefore, the denominator of the marginal cost ratio declines, and the marginal cost of output rises. In our example, marginal cost begins to rise with the fifth worker hired. It continues to increase as more workers are hired until, finally, marginal cost becomes large without limit at the eighth worker, whose marginal product is zero. Intuitively, the marginal cost of output increases because you receive less and less for your money. Each new worker costs the same to employ, the wage P_L, but each is increasingly less productive. Increasing marginal cost in the short run is not limited to our example. It occurs whenever diminishing returns arise, which is to say in most production settings.

The final link to the individual firm's supply curve relies on proposition 1. The Law of Diminishing Returns causes the firm's marginal cost curve to be upward sloping in the short run. But, from proposition 1, the firm's marginal cost curve *is* its supply curve. Therefore, the Law of Diminishing Returns also ensures that the individual firm's supply curve is upward sloping in the short run. We have established proposition 2: A competitive firm's supply curve is expected to be upward sloping in the short run.

No such expectation exists with respect to supply in the long run, when all factors of production are variable and firms can enter or leave the industry. Long-run supply curves may be upward sloping horizontal, or downward sloping depending on the nature of the firm's production technology and on what happens to factor prices when all firms expand their output and bid for factors of production.

We will explore the long run in depth in Chapter 13. At this point we are primarily interested in understanding how price and quantity are determined in competitive markets, and the short-run supply curve is sufficient for this purpose.

MARKET SUPPLY

Analyzing market events requires knowledge of market supply. The relationship between the market supply curve and the individual firms' supply curves is exactly analogous to the relationship between the market demand curve and the individual consumers' demand curves. The overall **market supply schedule** indicates the total quantity all firms in the market want to supply at each price, other things equal. It is the sum, at each price, of the individual's firms' supply schedules. The **market supply curve** is the graph of the market supply schedule. Because an industry consists of all firms supplying a particular product, the market supply curve is also referred to as the *industry supply curve.* The market, or industry, supply curve is the horizontal summation of all the individual firms' supply curves, just as the market demand curve is the horizontal summation of all the individual consumers' demand curves. We will use S to represent the market, or industry, supply curve and s to represent an individual firm's supply curve. Similarly, we will use Q to represent the total quantity supplied by all firms in the market and q to represent the quantity supplied by an individual firm.

MARKET SUPPLY SCHEDULE

The total quantity that all firms in the market are willing and able to supply at each price, other things equal; the sum of the individual firms' supply schedules.

MARKET SUPPLY CURVE

A graphical representation of the market supply schedule, showing the total quantity that all firms in the market are willing and able to supply at each price, other things equal; equal to the horizontal summation of the individual firms' supply curves; also called the *industry supply curve.*

Finally, note that the market supply curve is upward sloping: The Law of Supply applies to the market supply curve. This must be so because each individual firm's supply curve is upward sloping.

Change in Quantity Supplied versus Change in Supply

Using supply curves to analyze markets requires the same subtle distinction in terminology that we met with demand curves. You must keep straight the difference between a change in quantity supplied and a change in supply. A **change in quantity supplied** refers to movements along the supply curve as price changes, other things equal. A **change in supply** refers to a shift in the entire supply curve, as illustrated in Figure 6.6. A shift in the supply curve up and to the left from S to S' represents a *decrease* in supply. The quantity supplied has decreased at every price. A shift in the supply curve down and to the right from S to S'' represents an *increase* in supply. The quantity supplied has increased at every price.

CHANGE IN QUANTITY SUPPLIED

A movement along the supply curve as price changes, other things equal.

CHANGE IN SUPPLY

A shift in the entire supply curve.

A change in supply occurs when one of the "other things" influencing quantity supplied, such as the factor prices, the production technologies, the prices of other products, taxes, and the number of firms in the industry, changes or when special events, such as severe weather or a strike by a union, occur. These variables are not shown on the graph of a supply curve. They lie behind the supply curve, determining the position and slope of the curve. If one or more of these variable change, the entire supply curve shifts to a new position.

Events that cause the supply curve to shift can be grouped into two categories: events that change the costs of production and events that change the

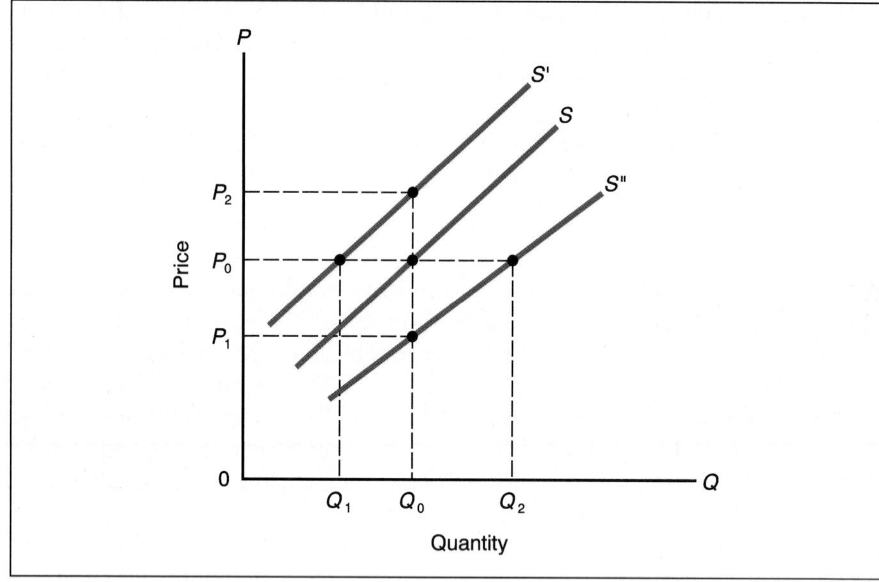

FIGURE 6.6

Shifts in the Market Supply Curve

The entire market supply curve shifts when one of the factors that influences supply, other than the price of the product, changes. For example, an increase in wages increases firms' marginal costs and causes a decrease in supply. The supply curve shifts up and to the left, from S to S'. Conversely, a decrease in wages decreases firms' marginal costs and causes an increase in supply. The supply curve shifts down and to the right, from S to S''.

total quantity supplied to the markets. The principal cost shifters are changes in factor prices or taxes and in the underlying production technology. The principal quantity shifters are changes in the prices of other products, changes in the number of firms in the industry, and special events such as severe weather or union strikes.

Changes in Supply

COST-INDUCED CHANGES IN SUPPLY Anything that increases marginal cost shifts the supply curve up and to the left. Higher wage rates, rising fuel costs, and morale problems among the employees that reduce their productivity all increase marginal cost at every output and thereby decrease supply. They cause a shift in the supply curve from S to S' in Figure 6.6. Whether the shift from S to S' is viewed as an upward shift or a shift to the left is a matter of interpretation. The supply curve shifts up in the sense that firms require higher prices to supply any given quantity. For example, a price P_0 was sufficient to elicit an overall quantity supplied of Q_0 on the original supply curve S. Now P_2 is required to cover the higher marginal cost at Q_0 on the new supply curve S'. Alternatively, the supply curve shifts to the left in the sense that the willingness to supply decreases from Q_0 on S to Q_1 on S' at price P_0, and similarly at every price. The shift-up interpretation is perhaps the more natural one for cost-induced decreases in supply.

Conversely, anything that decreases marginal cost shifts the supply curve down and to the right. Reduced wage rates, declining fuel costs, and technological change that increases factors' (marginal) productivity all lower marginal cost at every output and lead to an increase in supply. They cause a shift in the supply curve from S to S'' in Figure 6.6. The price required to elicit an overall supply of Q_0 drops from P_0 to P_1 because of the decrease in marginal cost (a shift down). Alternatively, at price P_0 the willingness to supply increases from Q_0 to Q_2 (a shift to the right).

Take care to note that upward and downward shifts in supply and demand curves have opposite interpretations. An *upward* shift in a demand curve represents an *increase* in demand, whereas an *upward* shift in a supply cuve represents a *decrease* in supply. Conversely, a *downward* shift in a demand curve represents a *decrease* in demand, whereas a *downward* shift in a supply curve represents an *increase* in supply. The left-right shifts have the same interpretation for each curve, however.

QUANTITY-INDUCED CHANGES IN SUPPLY Quantity-induced shifts in the supply curve may be either direct or indirect. Direct shifts in quantity supplied are caused by such events as widespread crop failures in agriculture or large numbers of firms leaving the industry because the market price is too low for them to earn a profit. Both events cause a decrease in supply to the market. The market supply curve shifts to the left, as from S to S' in Figure 6.6. Conversely, favorable weather conditions in agriculture or widespread entry into the industry by new firms responding to a high and profitable price causes an increase in supply to the market. The market supply curve shifts to the right, as from S to S'' in Figure 6.6.

Indirect quantity effects result from changes in the prices of other products that firms in the industry also supply or are capable of supplying. An increase in some other price *decreases* supply in this market as firms shift resources to the other product. The market supply curve shifts to the left. Conversely, a decrease in the price of another product *increases* supply in this market. The market supply curve shifts to the right.

THE ELASTICITY OF SUPPLY

The **price elasticity** of supply measures the responsiveness of quantity supplied to changes in price along a supply curve. The mechanical aspects associated with measuring and graphically representing supply elasticity are similar to those associated with demand elasticity. Supply and demand elasticity share the following properties:

1. The elasticity of supply is defined as the ratio of the percentage change in quantity supplied to the percentage change in price:

   $$E_S = \text{(percentage change in quantity)/(percentage change in price)}$$

   Unlike demand, however, supply elasticity *cannot* be defined by the direction of change in total revenue as price changes, since price and quantity move in the same direction along an upward-sloping supply curve. An increase in price always increases the total revenue; a decrease in price always decreases total revenue. Notice, too, that the definition of supply elasticity does not use absolute values. Elasticity is always positive along an upward-sloping supply curve.

(PRICE) ELASTICITY OF SUPPLY
A measure of the responsiveness of quantity supplied to a change in price along a supply curve; specifically, the percentage change in quantity supplied divided by the percentage change in price.

2. If $E_S > 1$, supply is *elastic* between the prices. The percentage change in quantity exceeds the percentage change in price. Quantity supplied is relatively responsive to a change in price in percentage terms.

   If $E_S = 1$, supply is *unit-elastic* between the prices. The percentage change in quantity equals the percentage change in price.

If E_S <1, supply in *inelastic* between the prices. The percentage change in quantity is less than the percentage change in price. Quantity supplied is relatively unresponsive to a change in price in percentage terms.

3. The reasonable limits to supply elasticity are the same as for demand elasticity. A *vertical* supply curve is *perfectly inelastic.* Quantity supplied is completely unresponsive to changes in price, and $E_S = 0$. A *horizontal* supply curve is *perfectly elastic.* Quantity supplied is infinitely responsive to even the smallest change in price, and E_S is infinitely large.

Both limiting cases have realistic applications. Suppose U.S. wheat farmers have made their spring plantings. Shortly thereafter they learn that a terrible drought has destroyed much of the Russian wheat crop and that Russia will turn to the U.S. market to replace its wheat when the U.S. crop arrives. The Russian misfortune is obviously favorable to the U.S. farmers. They know that the price of wheat will rise as the unexpected Russian demand increases the overall demand for their wheat. But the U.S. farmers cannot respond by increasing quantity because the crop is already in the ground. Supply is perfectly inelastic until the next planting. Another example of perfectly inelastic supply is the auctioning of a famous painting, such as Rembrandt's *Night Watch.* The painting is unique: Its supply is perfectly inelastic at a quantity of one.

Perfectly elastic supply is also possible in the long run. Suppose that all the firms in an industry can expand production by duplicating what they have already done. They produce twice as much output by hiring exactly twice as many factors of production and employing them in precisely the same way. If duplication is possible and if bidding for new factors of production does not increase the prices of these factors, then the long-run supply curve will be horizontal, perfectly elastic at the going market price. The market price is said to be cost determined. The price is just sufficient to cover all costs of production, and these costs do not change as industry output expands and contracts. Whether an industry supply curve ever remains perfectly flat as output expands is open to question, but perfectly elastic supply might be a reasonable approximation of reality for certain markets over a limited range of output. Perfectly elastic supply is unlikely in the short run, however, because of the Law of Diminishing Returns.

The Determinants of Supply Elasticity

Four principal factors determine the price elasticity of supply: the characteristics of the production technology, the ability of firms to switch production from one product to another, the amount of excess capacity in the industry, and the passage of time.

1. *The characteristics of the production technology:* The production technology used to produce a product is central to the question of supply elasticity because the technology determines the relationship between the factor inputs and the output. When firms hire more factors of production to increase production, the production technology determines whether the resulting increase in output is large or small. The more labor, materials, fuel, and machines needed to produce a given increase in output, the higher the costs of producing the additional output, and the more inelastic (steeper) the firms' supply curves. Firms require higher prices to cover the higher costs. Con-

versely, the smaller the increase in factor inputs required to produce a given increase in output, the lower the costs of producing that output, and the more elastic (flatter) the firms' supply curves.

2. *Substitutability in production:* In a production context, substitutability refers to the ability of firms to switch production among alternative products. As such, it relates to the production technologies of all the products a firm might produce. The more easily firms can shift production to other products, the more *elastic* the supply is; the more difficult it is for firms to shift production to other products, the more *inelastic* the supply is. Increases in the price of one product make it relatively more profitable than other products, whose prices remain constant. Firms want to shift resources from their other products to this product. The opposite is true when the price of one of their products decreases. The incentive to shift resources as price changes always exists. The substitutability among production processes determines how easily firms can respond to this incentive.
3. *The amount of excess capacity in the industry:* The elasticity of supply depends on how close the industry is operating to its full capacity, the limit of its production capability. The closer the industry is to full capacity, the more *inelastic* supply is; the farther the industry is from full capacity, the more *elastic* supply is. When firms have considerable excess capacity, some of their plant and equipment lies idle. If market conditions turn more favorable and if the firms hire additional workers in order to increase output, these workers can more fully utilize the idled plant and equipment. Output can be increased fairly easily and without large additional costs, since the firms have already purchased the idle resources. Near capacity, however, production is straining against the firms' plant and equipment, and output is more difficult and more costly to increase. The firms may be forced to pay workers overtime or to run more costly second and third shifts. Productivity also suffers if workers tire and the equipment breaks down more often, which reduces the additional output produced. The supply response becomes increasingly inelastic. Once firms reach their absolute maximum capacities the market supply curve becomes perfectly inelastic. Further increases in output are impossible regardless of the price.
4. *The passage of time:* The supply elasticities of most products increase with the passage of time following a change in price, just as the demand elasticities do. Firms, like consumers, are better able to respond to changing market conditions as time passes. As with demand, economists distinguish three "runs," or time periods: the momentary run, the short run, and the long run. Figure 6.7 represents the three runs.

The Russian wheat example that we used earlier to represent the case of a perfectly inelastic supply curve is an appropriate illustration. The situation immediately following the spring planting is the **momentary run**, the period of time for which output is set and a supply response is impossible. The momentary supply elasticity is zero, and the momentary supply curve, S_{MR}, is perfectly inelastic. Farmers know that the price will rise, say, from P_0 to P_1, but they are unable to respond.

MOMENTARY RUN

The period of time during which output is set and a supply response is impossible.

Suppose that the price remains at P_1 for a number of years as Russia and other foreign countries continue to experience weather problems. The next planting season begins the short run, when the farmers can first expand their production. After enough time passes, the short run turns into the long run.

Recall from our discussion of the firm's supply decision that the distinction between the short run and the long run in supply is more precise than the

FIGURE 6.7

The Supply Elasticity of Wheat Over Time

Supply becomes more elastic with the passage of time following a change in price. An increase in the price of wheat from P_0 to P_1 that catches farmers by surprise leads to no increase in output above Q_0 in the momentary run immediately following the price increase, because farmers cannot increase their output. The perfectly inelastic momentary-run supply curve S_{MR} applies. The momentary run is followed by the short run when farmers can plant more wheat by increasing some but not all of their factors of production. The short-run supply curve S_{SR} applies; the quantity supplied increases to Q_{SR}. The short run is followed by the long run when farmers can vary all of their factors of production and new farms can start up. The long-run supply curve S_{LR} applies; the quantity supplied eventually increases to Q_{LR}.

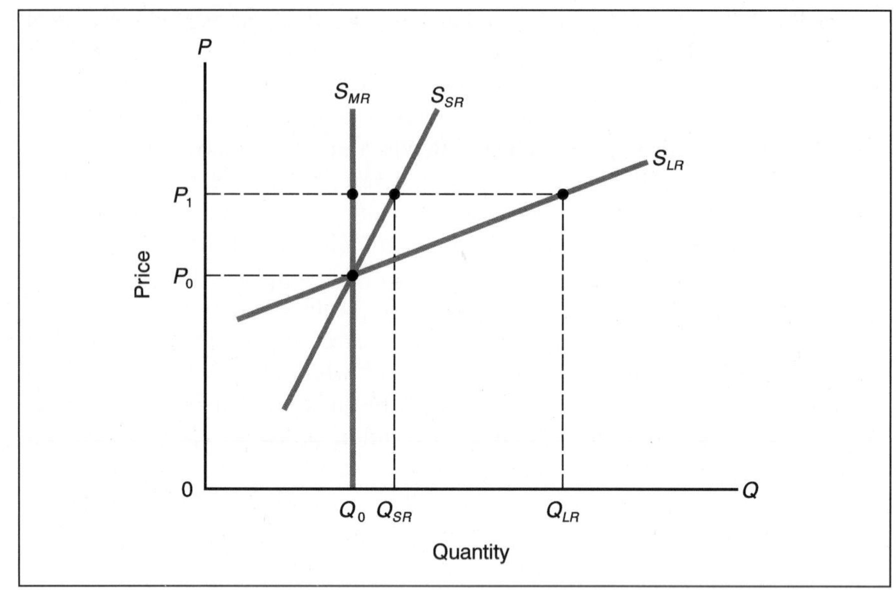

distinction between the short run and the long run in demand. In the *short run*, at least one factor of production is fixed, unable to be increased or decreased. The short run becomes the *long run* when the firm (farm) is able to vary all factors of production and new firms (farms) can enter the market.

Land is likely to be the fixed factor in the short run in our agricultural example. Farmers can respond to the higher price by farming their land more intensively. They can employ more workers, buy more seed and fertilizer, and purchase more equipment. They can also plant wheat on land that they had previously used for other crops. Output increases from Q_0 to Q_{SR} along the short-run supply curve, S_{SR}. In the long run farmers bring more farmland under cultivation, and new wheat farms come into existence. Output increases once again, now to Q_{LR} along the long-run supply curve, S_{LR}.

Table 6.4 reports estimates of both short-run and long-run supply elasticities for a number of agricultural commodities. Notice that the long-run elasticity is considerably larger for every crop.

TABLE 6.4 **Short-Run and Long-Run Price Elasticities of Supply for Selected Agricultural Products**

PRODUCT	ELASTICITY	
	Short-Run	**Long-Run**
BEETS	0.13	1.00
CARROTS	0.14	1.00
CUCUMBERS	0.29	2.20
GREEN PEAS	0.31	4.40
MILK	0.11	6.69
ONIONS	0.34	1.00
SPINACH	0.20	4.70
TOMATOES	0.16	0.90

SOURCE: M. Nerlove and W. Addison, "Statistical Estimation of Long-Run Elasticities of Supply and Demand," *Journal of Farm Economics* (November 1958).

The Concept Summary table summarizes the various determinants of supply elasticity.

CONCEPT SUMMARY

DETERMINANTS OF SUPPLY ELASTICITY

FACTOR	MORE ELASTIC	LESS ELASTIC
Production technology	Fewer inputs required for a given increase in output	More inputs required for a given increase in output
Substitutability	Easy to switch to other products	Difficult to switch to other products
Capacity	Far below capacity	Close to capacity
Passage of time	In long run with all factors variable and with entry and exit of resources	In short run because of Law of Diminishing Returns

Looking Ahead

Chapter 5 on product demand and Chapter 6 on product supply have set the stage for an analysis of competitive markets that are guided by the Laws of Supply and Demand. The key concepts in these chapters are the market demand and the market supply curves. Chapter 7 will show how these two curves interact to determine price and quantity and will indicate why the Laws of Supply and Demand promote an efficient allocation of society's scarce resources.

SUMMARY

The first section of Chapter 6 discussed the nature of competitive markets, for which the Laws of Supply and Demand apply, and the characteristics of firms that supply to competitive markets.

1. A competitive market is one in which a large number of firms supply very similar or identical products and consumers are well informed about the prices charged by each firm. Competitive markets are also characterized by the free flow of resources into and out of the market in response to profits and losses.
2. Firms in competitive markets are price takers, and it is reasonable to assume that their sole objective is to maximize profit.
3. The Laws of Supply and Demand do a good job of explaining market exchanges in a large percentage of the product markets in the United States.

The second section of Chapter 6 showed how an individual firm's supply of a product arises from the firm's economic problem and discussed the properties of the individual firm's supply curve.

4. The supply of a product is the amount that firms are willing and able to sell over a certain period of time. The structure of the firm's economic problem indicates that supply is determined by the price of the product, the prices of other products that the firm can supply, production technologies, factor prices, and taxes.
5. A supply schedule shows the quantity supplied at different prices, other things equal. A supply curve is a graph of a supply schedule. Supply schedules and supply curves obey the Law of Supply: The higher the price, the greater the quantity supplied, and vice versa.
6. The Law of Supply is based on the fact that the cost of producing additional output increases the more output firms are already producing. Therefore, firms require higher prices in order to increase supply.

The third section of the chapter showed how a firm solves its economic problem and developed the two fundamental propositions about the individual firm's supply curve that support the Law of Supply.

7. A price-taking, profit-maximizing firm supplies the output at which price equals marginal cost. Marginal cost is the additional cost of producing one more unit of output.
8. The profit-maximizing decision rule is the basis of the first fundamental proposition of supply: The competitive, price-taking firm's supply curve is its marginal cost curve. Because competitive, price-taking firms equate price to marginal cost, points on a market supply curve indicate the marginal cost at any given quantity, as well as the total quantity supplied by all firms in the industry at any given price.
9. The second fundamental proposition of supply is that short-run supply curves are expected to be upward sloping. This Law of Supply results from the Law of Diminishing Returns, which says that as a firm adds more and more of a variable factor of production, such as labor, to a fixed factor of production, such as capital, the marginal product of the variable factor eventually declines.
10. The marginal product of labor is the additional output produced by adding one more unit of labor.
11. The short run in a production context refers to the period of time over which at least one factor of production is fixed. In the long run, the firm can vary all factors of production, and firms can enter or leave the industry.

The fourth section of the chapter discussed the market or industry supply curve.

12. The market supply schedule is the sum of the individual firms' supply schedules, and the market supply curve is the horizontal summation of the individual firms' supply curves.
13. Market supply curves shift when one of the other variables influencing supply changes. The principal supply shifters are changes in the prices of other products the firm supplies, the factor prices, taxes, the production technologies, the number of firms in the industry, and special events such as bad weather in agriculture.

The fifth section of Chapter 6 discussed supply elasticity.

14. Supply elasticity is defined analogously to demand elasticity. It is the ratio of the percentage change in quantity supplied to the percentage change

in price. Supply is elastic, unit-elastic, or inelastic as the ratio is greater than, equal to, or less than 1, respectively.

15. The principal determinants of supply elasticity are the characteristics of the production technology, substitutability in production, the amount of excess capacity in an industry, and the passage of time.

KEY TERMS

change in quantity supplied
change in supply
competitive market
(price) elasticity of supply
individual firm's supply curve
Law of Diminishing Returns
Law of Supply
long run
marginal benefit
marginal cost
marginal product of labor
marginal revenue
market supply curve
momentary run
price taker
short run
supply

QUESTIONS

1. What is the Law of Supply? What are the "other things equal" with respect to the supply curve?
2. a. What are the characteristics of a competitive market?
   b. Why do competitive markets cause firms to be price takers?
   c. Give several examples of product markets that are highly competitive.
3. Three firms have the following individual supply schedules for product X.

PRICE	FIRM 1	FIRM 2	FIRM 3
$1	5	0	8
2	10	7	15
3	15	14	21
4	20	21	28
5	25	28	30

   The number in columns two through four are the quantities supplied at each price in the first column.
   a. What is the market supply schedule for product X? (Assume that the three firms are the only sellers.) Also draw the market supply curve.
   b. Why might the three firms have different supply schedules?
   c. Is firm 1's supply curve elastic or inelastic between the prices of $1 and $2? Between $4 and $5?
4. a. What is the competitive firm's supply rule for maximizing profit?
   b. Why is it an application of the general principle that any activity should be continued to the point at which marginal benefit equals marginal cost?
5. Does the Law of Diminishing Returns apply to the following production relationship? (Assume that labor is the only factor of production that can vary in the short run.)

NUMBER OF WORKERS	TOTAL OUTPUT
0	0
1	2
2	8
3	12
4	14
5	15

6. Would the following tend to increase or decrease the supply of American automobiles?
   a. The wages of American auto workers fall by 10 percent.
   b. Consumers' incomes rise by 20 percent.
   c. The use of robots on the American assembly line reduces the costs of production.
   d. One of the major American auto manufacturers goes out of business.
   e. The cost of automobile insurance decreases.
7. a. What are the distinctions among the momentary-run, short-run, and long-run supply curves?
   b. Along which of the curves is the elasticity of supply the highest? The lowest? Why?
8. a. Define *marginal cost* and the *marginal product of labor.* What is the relationship between these two concepts?
   b. Define *marginal revenue.* Why is price the same as marginal revenue for a price-taking, competitive firm?
9. Why do we expect a competitive firm's supply curve to be upward sloping in the short run?
10. *Extra credit:* Consider the following production data for a firm in industry X. Labor is the only factor of production, and the hourly cost of labor is $5.

NUMBER OF WORKERS	TOTAL PRODUCT
0	0
10	100
20	200
30	295
40	370
50	420
60	445

a. Calculate the marginal product of labor at each level of output in the table.
b. Calculate the marginal cost for each level of output in the table.

CHAPTER

7

Market Equilibrium: The Laws of Supply and Demand

LEARNING OBJECTIVES

CONCEPTS TO LEARN

The competitive market equilibrium

The results of shifting demand and supply curves

The net value from producing and consuming a product

Consumer and producer surplus from market exchange

Prices as a reflection of benefits and costs on the margin

CONCEPTS TO RECALL

Opportunity cost [1]

Efficiency [2]

Positive and normative analysis [2]

The margin in economic analysis [2]

The production possibilities frontier [3]

Elasticity of demand and supply [5, 6]

The market demand and the market supply curves [5, 6]

The marginal benefit equals marginal cost decision rule [6]

We saw in Chapter 4 that prices are asked to do all the work in a market system. They must incorporate all relevant economic information and bring buyers and sellers together in exchange.

Sometimes prices appear to carry out their tasks in strange ways. Adam Smith, the father of modern economics, puzzled over the relative prices of diamonds and water. He could not understand why diamonds, an inessential bauble, were so expensive, whereas water, a basic necessity of life, was so cheap. The market's valuation of diamonds and water seemed backward to Smith. Along the same lines, consumers in the northern climates clearly prefer the plump, tasty, homegrown tomatoes of summer to the small, tasteless, gas-injected tomatoes shipped north in the winter. Yet the winter tomatoes are much more expensive.

In addition, market prices driven by the Laws of Supply and Demand can behave most dramatically. A crop freeze in northern Florida may easily double or triple the price of orange juice. The Dow Jones Industrial Index of stock prices on the New York Stock Exchange dropped 500 points on October 19, 1987, losing 20 percent of its value in a matter of hours. Football teams purchased for $10 million 15 years ago now sell for over $100 million. The prices of personal computers are plummeting today at a time when the price of almost everything else is rising.

In fact, the prices in these examples are exactly as they should be. They are conveying just the right information: what is in demand and what is not, and what is costly to supply and what can be supplied cheaply. In doing so, they are helping to promote orderly and efficient exchanges between buyers and sellers, even when those prices are moving rapidly up or down.

Chapter 7 discusses the principles of exchange in competitive markets that operate according to the Laws of Supply and Demand. The focus throughout the chapter is on market prices: how prices bring buyers and sellers together in the marketplace and why they promote an efficient allocation of society's scarce resources.

THE LAWS OF SUPPLY AND DEMAND

Having developed the market demand curve in Chapter 5 and the market supply curve in Chapter 6, we are now in a position to bring the two curves together and see how competitive markets operate.

Suppose that 1 million consumers of compact discs meet up with 100 firms supplying compact discs in the competitive marketplace. The consumers' market demand schedule for a few selected prices is given in the second column of Table 7.1, and the firms' market supply schedule is given in the third column of that table. The quantities represent the total number of discs demanded and supplied during the course of a year. All the numbers are hypothetical.

The market demand and the market supply curves, D and S, in Figure 7.1 correspond to the market demand and the market supply schedules in Table 7.1. The two curves are drawn as solid lines to show the total quantities de-

TABLE 7.1 **One-Year Market Demand and Market Supply Schedules for Compact Discs (Hypothetical Data)**

PRICE OF COMPACT DISCS	QUANTITY DEMANDED OF COMPACT DISCS (MILLIONS)	QUANTITY SUPPLIED OF COMPACT DISCS (MILLIONS)	EXCESS SUPPLY OR EXCESS DEMAND (MILLIONS)	
$28	3	15	12	·
24	4	14	10	Excess supply
20	6	11	5	·
16	9	9	0	*Equilibrium*
12	12	6	6	·
8	14	3	11	Excess demand
4	18	1	17	·

manded and supplied at prices other than those in the table. What will price and output be in the market for compact discs?

Our eye is naturally led to the point of intersection of *D* and *S* in Figure 7.1, at which the price of a disc is $16 and 9 million discs are exchanged between producers and consumers. This turns out to be the correct answer. Consumers in the aggregate purchase 9 million discs at a price of $16 per disc. Their total expenditures on discs, price times quantity, equal $144 million ($144 million = $16 · 9 million). The total expenditures are represented by the area of the rectangle 0*abc* in Figure 7.1. The height of the rectangle, 0*a*, is the price, $16. The base of the rectangle, 0*c*, is the quantity exchanged, 9 million. The area of the rectangle, base times height, is total expenditures. Conversely, the firms in the aggregate supply 9 million discs at a price of $16 per disc, receiving total revenues of $144 million.

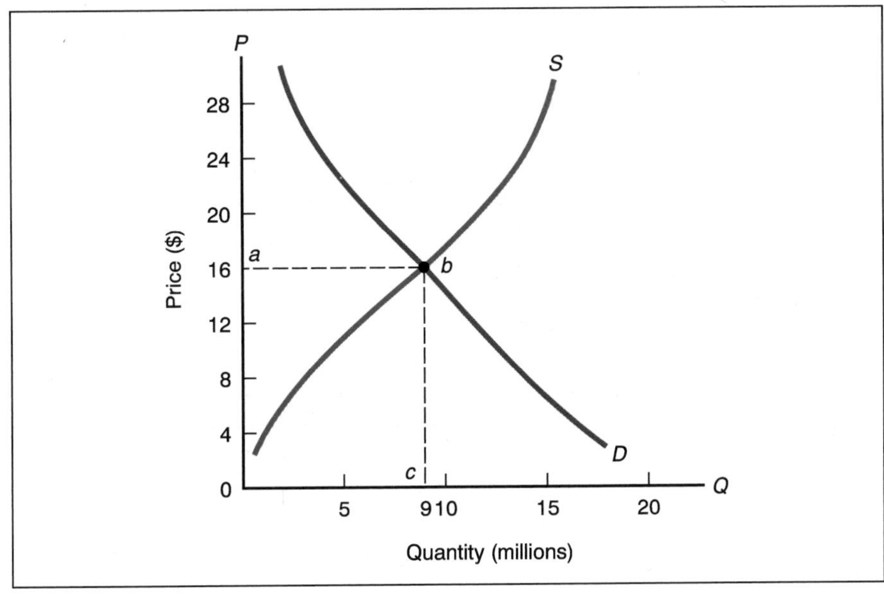

FIGURE 7.1

The Market for Compact Discs

The market demand (*D*) and supply (*S*) curves are graphs of the hypothetical market demand and supply schedules in Table 7.1. The equilibrium occurs at the intersection of the demand and supply curves. The equilibrium price is $16, and the equilibrium quantity is 9 million compact discs.

MARKET EQUILIBRIUM

The intersection of the market demand and the market supply curves at which the quantity demanded equals the quantity supplied.

The intersection of the market supply and the market demand curves is referred to as the **market equilibrium**. In this market $16 is the equilibrium price, and 9 million discs is the equilibrium quantity.

Market Equilibrium

You should view the quantity-price combination of 9 million discs and $16 as something far more than a single point on a supply and demand diagram. To understand how markets operate, you must appreciate that the equilibrium price of $16 brings the demanders and suppliers of compact discs together in a manner shared by no other price.

EQUILIBRIUM

A state of rest, or balance, due to the equal action of opposing forces or influences; in economics, a situation from which no one has any incentive to change.

An **equilibrium** is a state of rest or balance due to the equal action of opposing forces or influences. In the context of the marketplace the opposing forces are the Laws of Supply and Demand. They oppose one another in their response to prices. The Law of Demand says that demand curves slope down and to the right. A higher price reduces the quantity demanded, and a lower price increases the quantity demanded. The corresponding Law of Supply says that supply curves slope up and to the right. A higher price increases the quantity supplied, and a lower price decreases the quantity supplied. At the equilibrium price of $16, and *only* at that price, do these opposing forces strike a balance: The quantity demanded by all the consumers exactly matches the quantity supplied by all the firms. Consumers *want* to buy 9 million discs, and firms *want* to supply 9 million discs at the equilibrium price of $16. Since both sides of the market are exchanging exactly the amount they want to exchange, the market is at rest, or in balance. No one has an incentive to change the market outcome.

An equilibrium does *not* imply that either the consumers or the business firms are necessarily happy with the result. Consumers no doubt wish that the price were lower than $16; firms would just as surely prefer a price higher than $16. Equilibrium is not about happiness, however. Rather, it is simply a matter of the equilibrium price matching desires on both sides of the market.

Excess Supply and Excess Demand

To appreciate this unique property of the equilibrium price, consider the state of the market at any price other than $16. For example, suppose that the price is greater than the equilibrium price—say, $24. Refer to Table 7.1 and Figure 7.2(a). The two graphs in the figure reproduce the market demand and the market supply curves from Figure 7.1. At a price of $24 firms in the aggregate want to supply 14 million discs. Consumers, however, want to buy only 4 million discs. The quantity supplied exceeds the quantity demanded. At a price of $24 the market is in **excess supply** in the amount of 10 million discs, the difference between the quantity supplied and the quantity demanded (10 million = 14 million − 4 million). Desires do not match, nor do they at any price above $16. The market is in excess supply at *any* price above the equilibrium. The fourth column of Table 7.1 records the amount of excess supply at all prices above $16. Excess supply reveals itself as a surplus of goods that firms are unable to sell.

EXCESS SUPPLY

The amount by which quantity supplied exceeds quantity demanded when price is above the equilibrium price.

EXCESS DEMAND

The amount by which quantity demanded exceeds quantity supplied when price is below the equilibrium price.

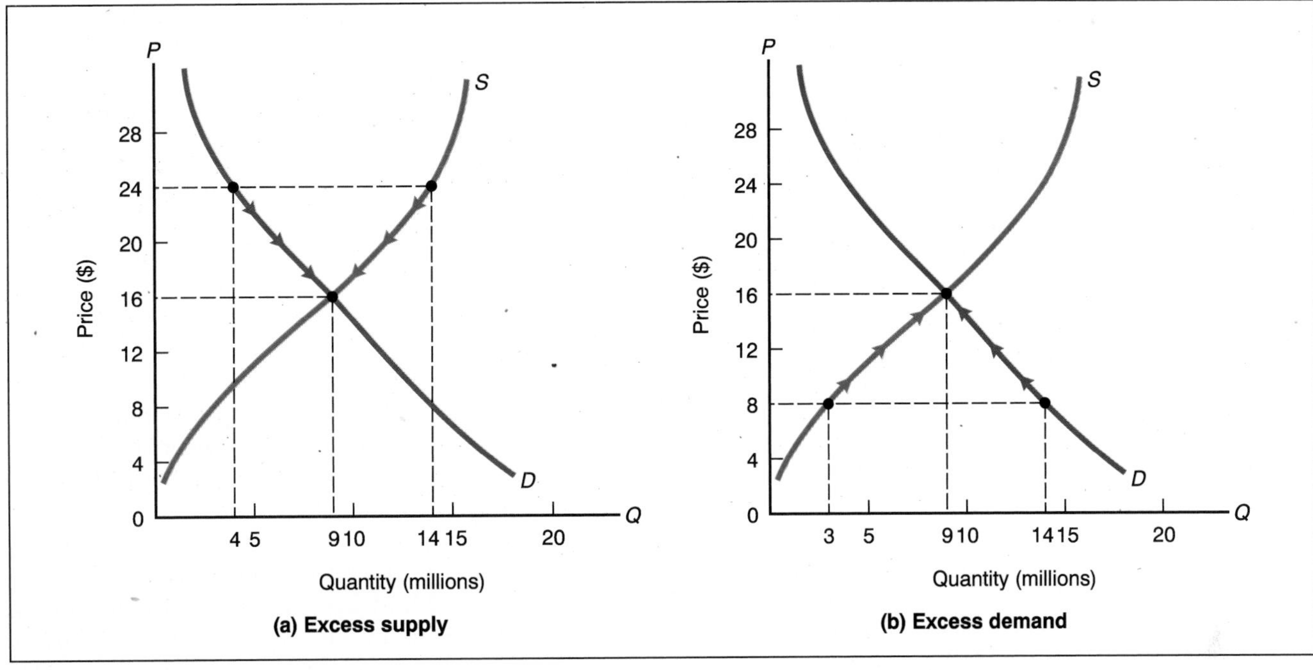

FIGURE 7.2

Excess Supply and Excess Demand in the Compact Disc Market

The market demand and supply curves correspond to the market demand and supply schedules in Table 7.1. In Figure 7.2(a), the market is in excess supply at a price of $24. The quantity supplied is 14 million compact discs and the quantity demanded is 4 million compact discs, for an excess supply of 10 million discs. A market is in excess supply at any price above the equilibrium price. The combined actions of the suppliers and demanders will automatically drive the price back down to the equilibrium price of $16. In Figure 7.2(b), the market is in excess demand at a price of $8. The quantity demanded is 14 million compact discs and the quantity supplied is 3 million compact discs, for an excess demand of 11 million discs. A market is in excess demand at any price below the equilibrium price. The combined actions of the suppliers and demanders will automatically drive the price back up to the equilibrium price of $16.

Alternatively, suppose that the price is less than the equilibrium price—say, $8. Refer to Table 7.1 and Figure 7.2(b). At a price of $8 firms in the aggregate want to supply 3 million discs. Consumers, however, want to buy 14 million discs. The quantity demanded exceeds the quantity supplied. At a price of $8 the market is in **excess demand** in the amount of 11 million discs, the difference between the quantity demanded and the quantity supplied (11 million = 14 million − 3 million). Once again desires do not match, nor do they at any price less than $16. The market is in excess demand at *any* price below the equilibrium. The fourth column of Table 7.1 records the amount of excess demand at all prices below $16. Excess demand reveals itself as a shortage of goods available for consumers to buy.

Two points from these examples deserve emphasis. First, the market conditions of equilibrium, excess supply, and excess demand must be associated with particular prices. In Figures 7.1 and 7.2 the same market is in equilibrium at a price of $16, in excess supply at a price of $24, and in excess demand at a price of $8. All three situations are possible in any market. The level of the market price determines which situation applies at any given time.

Second, the quantity purchased in the market *always* equals the quantity sold no matter what the price. The equality of purchases and sales is true by definition because a purchase and a sale are the opposite sides of any one market transaction. The amount bought and sold at any price is the lesser of the quantity supplied and the quantity demanded at that price. For example, in Figure 7.2(a), 4 million discs are bought and sold at a price of $24. Firms cannot force consumers to buy what they do not want to buy. In Figure 7.2(b), 3 million discs are bought and sold at a price of $8. Consumers cannot force firms to sell what they do not want to sell. The identity between purchases and sales is different from the concept of equilibrium, however, which is a matching of desires. Only at the equilibrium price of $16 is the amount bought and sold, 9 million discs, equal to the amount consumers and firms *want* to buy and sell.

Stability

The quantity-price combination of 9 million discs and $16 is more than an equilibrium. It is a *stable* equilibrium, meaning that the market will automatically return to the equilibrium from any other quantity-price combination. In other words, 9 million discs exchanged at a price of $16 is the only sustainable quantity-price combination in the market.

Think of the stability of an equilibrium in terms of a pendulum. The point at the bottom of the pendulum's swing is the only possible equilibrium, the only point of rest. Bring the pendulum to any other point and let go. As the pendulum swings back and forth, it is out of equilibrium, but the pendulum eventually returns to its equilibrium. The equilibrium point at the bottom is stable. The market's equilibrium is analogous to the pendulum's equilibrium in this respect. Whenever the desires of consumers and firms do not match, the economic self-interests of business firms and consumers cause price and output to change until desires do match, and the market returns to equilibrium.

To see why the equilibrium is stable, return to the case of the market in excess supply at a price of $24. Refer again to Figure 7.2(a). Let's begin with the firms' adjustments, since they make the production and pricing decisions. Firms produce 14 million discs with the expectation that they can sell this amount at price of $24. The firms have misread the market, however. They are unable to sell all they would like to sell at $24. Consumers only want to buy 4 million discs. Unsold discs begin to accumulate at an annual rate of 10 million discs, the amount of the excess supply. Producing goods that cannot be sold is clearly unprofitable, the signal to the firms that the current market situation is not sustainable.

The firms will not continue to set their prices at $24 and supply 14 million discs year after year, knowing that consumers will only purchase 4 million discs. Rather, the firms can be expected to respond to the situation of excess supply in two ways. First, they sell off the unsold discs at special, one-time-only bargain prices. We have all seen these "inventory reduction sales." Once the discs have been produced, selling them at any price is more profitable than leaving them unsold. According to the demand curve in Figure 7.2(a), the price must fall all the way to $8 to induce consumers to purchase 14 million discs, the total amount of discs produced this year. Second, the firms assume that $24 is not a sustainable price, that the market price will soon decline. Because firms expect the price to fall, they lower their annual rate of production. Each firm moves back down its supply curve, with the result that both price and quantity supplied decline next year.

Firms make the production and pricing decisions, but consumers are equally important to the process of reaching the equilibrium. The fact that consumers only want to buy 4 million discs at a price of $24 contributes to the original excess supply. Then, as the price falls, consumers' economic self-interest of trying to maximize utility leads them to move down their demand curves. Their quantity demanded increases, further reducing the excess supply in the marketplace.

If some excess supply remains at the new lower price, firms adjust once again. Price continues to fall, quantity supplied decreases, and quantity demanded increases. The process of firms adjusting their sights downward continues until the price reaches the equilibrium price of $16, at which point all excess supply has been removed from the market. Firms are able to sell 9 million discs at a price of $16, exactly the amount they want to sell. The market has returned to equilibrium.

Choosing $24 as the starting price in this example is entirely arbitrary. The same argument applies for *any* price above the equilibrium price of $16. The profit motive of business firms, combined with consumers' desires to maximize utility, eventually drives all prices greater than $16 back down to $16. As a result, the quantity exchanged in the market returns to 9 million discs.

Prices below $16 are also not sustainable. They, too, will be driven back to equilibrium. Return to the case of the market in excess demand at a price of $8, shown in Figure 7.2(b). The firms believe the market price is $8 and plan to sell 3 million discs. The firms will soon realize that they have misread the market, however, this time being overly pessimistic. Eager consumers quickly remove all the product from the shelves. The quantity demanded, 14 million discs, exceeds the available supply of 3 million discs. Faced with a shortage of discs some customers offer to pay far more than the current market price of $8 "under the table." According to the demand curve in Figure 7.2(b), all 3 million discs can be sold at a price as high as $28.

The signals of empty shelves and "under the table" payments when the price is $8 are unmistakable. Firms know that they should increase both price and quantity supplied in order to increase their profits. Each firm moves up its supply curve. As the price increases, the self-interest of consumers leads them to reduce their quantity demanded, further decreasing the amount of excess demand. The price continues to increase each period until it reaches the equilibrium price of $16, at which point all the excess demand is removed from the market. The same adjustment applies starting at any price below $16. The profit motive of business firms, combined with consumers' desires to maximize utility, eventually drives all prices less than $16 back up to $16. As a result, the quantity exchanged in the market returns to 9 million discs.

Of all the possible quantity-price combinations, therefore, only one need concern us—9 million discs and a price of $16, the point of intersection of the market supply and the market demand curves. If the market is there, it will stay there; if it is not there, it should quickly and automatically go there. By a happy coincidence, this is exactly the point our eye is led to on a supply and demand diagram.

The importance of a **stable market equilibrium** can hardly be overstated. If price and quantity could settle anywhere, no theory could possibly explain market events, past, present, or future. Economic analysis of a market economy would simply be impossible. Markets events become understandable, and predictable, only with the assurance that quantity and price will settle at their equilibrium values.

STABLE MARKET EQUILIBRIUM

A property of the market equilibrium such that the market automatically returns to the equilibrium from any other quantity-price combination.

Analyzing Markets Using Supply and Demand Curves

Prices and quantities in individual markets are forever changing. How can this be if the market quickly settles on one equilibrium price and quantity? The answer is that these changes in prices and quantities represent movements from one equilibrium to another.

The market equilibrium changes in response to *shifts* in the market demand curve, in the market supply curve, or in both. These shifts in turn are caused by changes in one or more of the variables determining quantity demanded or supplied, *other than the price of the product itself.* As we have seen, events causing the market demand curve to shift include changes in consumers' incomes (including changes in taxes and transfer payments), tastes, the prices of substitutes and complements, and the size and composition of the population. Events causing the market supply curve to shift include changes in production technologies, factor prices, the prices of other products, and direct changes in the quantity supplied resulting from crop failures or the presence of new firms in the industry. The following examples illustrate how shifts in the market demand and the market supply curves affect the equilibrium price and the equilibrium quantity.

SHIFTS IN THE DEMAND CURVE Suppose that consumers' incomes increase. The increase in incomes increases the demand for all normal goods and services. Figure 7.3 shows the independent effect of the increase in incomes on the market equilibrium for a typical product.

S is the market supply curve, and D is the market demand curve before the increase in incomes occurs. The original equilibrium is (Q_0, P_0), at the intersection of D and S. The increase in incomes shifts the market demand curve up and to the right from D to D'. The market establishes a new equilibrium, (Q_1, P_1), at the intersection of D' and S. *The increase in demand increases both the equilibrium quantity and the equilibrium price.*

SHIFTS IN THE SUPPLY CURVE Prices and quantities do not necessarily both increase over time, however; the computer industry is an obvious example of

FIGURE 7.3

A Shift in Demand

The market is originally in equilibrium at Q_0,P_0, at the intersection of D and S. An increase in consumers' incomes increases demand, and the demand curve shifts up and to the right from D to D'. The new equilibrium is Q_1,P_1, at the intersection of D' and S. An increase in demand tends to increase both the equilibrium price and the equilibrium quantity.

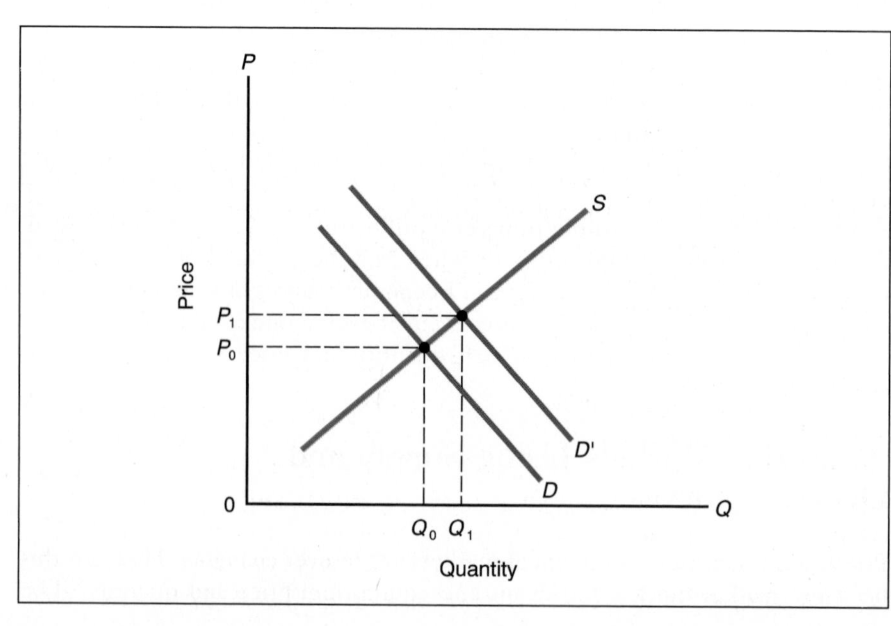

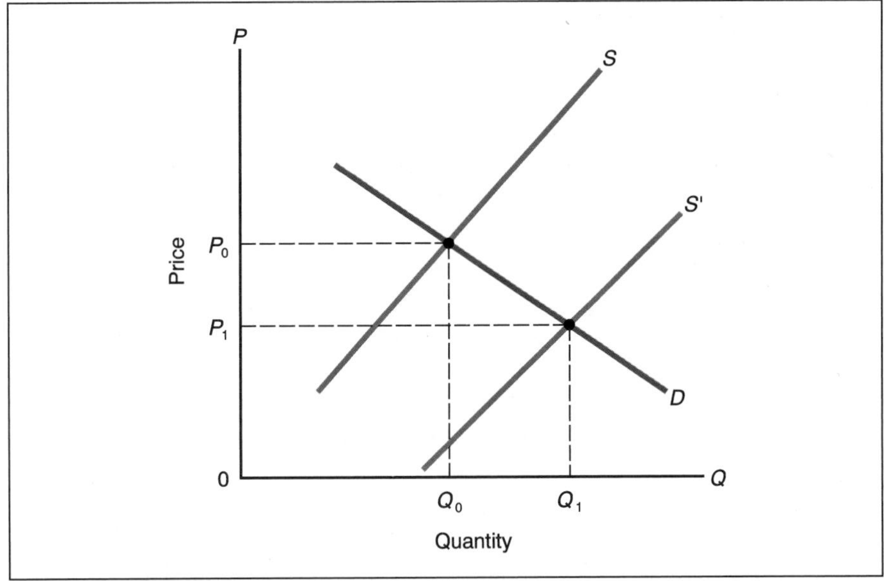

FIGURE 7.4

A Shift in Supply: Technological Change in Computers

Rapid technological change increases supply in the market for computers and drives down computer prices. The equilibrium in the computer market is Q_0,P_0 before the latest technological change, at the intersection of D and S. The technological change increases supply, and the supply curve shifts down and to the right from S to S'. The new equilibrium is Q_1,P_1, at the intersection of D and S'. An increase in supply tends to increase the equilibrium quantity and decrease the equilibrium price.

this fact. The use of computers has grown enormously over the past 20 years, while the price of a given amount of computing power has plummeted. Quantities have increased, and prices have decreased because the market for computers has been dominated by rapid technological change. The progression from vacuum tubes, to transistors, to silicon microchips, to microprocessors has substantially lowered the (marginal) cost of producing a given amount of computing power. The technological change has greatly increased supply. Figure 7.4 shows the independent effect of technological change on the market equilibrium in the computer market.

D is the market demand curve, and S is the market supply curve prior to the invention of the latest technology, the microprocessor. The original equilibrium is (Q_0, P_0), at the intersection of S and D. The technological change brought on by the invention of the microprocessor decreases costs and causes an increase in supply, shifting the market supply curve down from S to S'. The new equilibrium is (Q_1, P_1), at the intersection of S' and D. *The increase in supply increases the equilibrium quantity and lowers the equilibrium price.* (The demand curve has also shifted out rapidly over time, but not by enough to overcome the even more rapid shift in the supply curve.) Thanks to technological progress, consumers can now buy personal computers for a few thousand dollars with computing power that, 10 years ago, was only available to businesses at prices of $100,000 and more.

The first four rows of the Concept Summary table on page 165 indicate the expected effects on equilibrium quantity and equilibrium price of all possible shifts in either the demand curve or the supply curve. The two examples above correspond to rows 1 and 3. Developing a facility for analyzing market events using supply and demand curves is absolutely essential to successful economic analysis. You should think carefully about each row and then ask yourself why equilibrium price and equilibrium quantity move as indicated and what changes could cause increases and decreases in demand or supply.

CURRENT ISSUE: The development of new substitute products can sharply reduce market demand. Television has long had that effect on city newspapers, and the competition from television has become much worse for the newspapers with the advent of cable TV. The cable news stations are cutting deeply into newspaper circulation, and many advertisers are switching from newspapers to cable. *The Economist* reports that the 1990s have witnessed the worst slump in the newspaper industry in 50 years in the United States, Western Europe, and Japan. (*The Economist*, October 31, 1992, p. 67).

FIGURE 7.5

Shifts in Both Supply and Demand: Legalizing Marijuana

The market for marijuana is originally in equilibrium at Q_0,P_0 before legalization, at the intersection of D and S. Legalizing marijuana would increase supply as more people grow marijuana for market. The supply curve shifts down and to the right from S to S'. Legalizing marijuana would also increase demand as more people are willing to use it. The demand curve shifts up and to the right from D to D'. The new equilibrium is Q_1,P_1 after legalization, at the intersection of D' and S'. Increases in both supply and demand tend to increase the equilibrium quantity. The equilibrium price may increase, stay the same, or decrease depending on the relative size of the shifts in supply and demand.

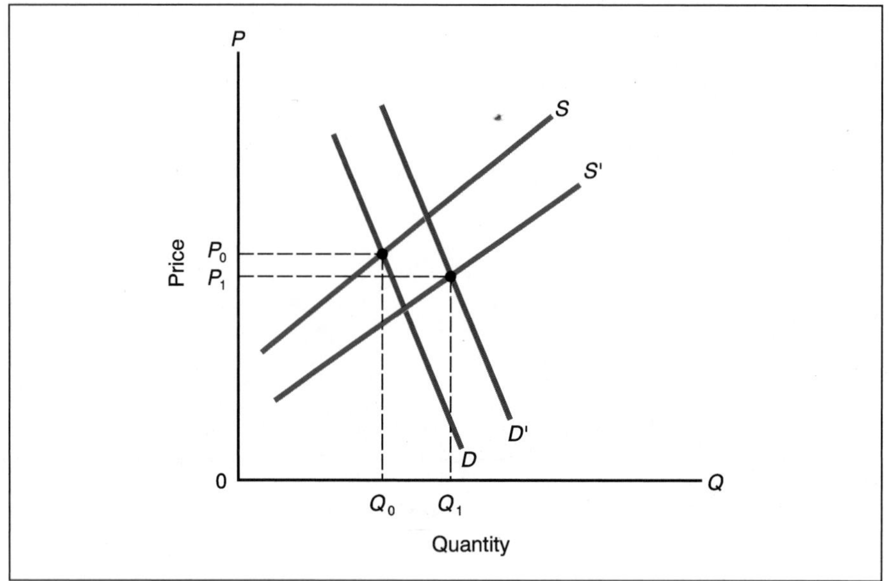

SHIFTS IN BOTH THE DEMAND AND THE SUPPLY CURVES A single event that affects a market usually causes a shift in *either* the demand curve *or* the supply curve, but not both, as in the two examples above. There are exceptions, however. Suppose that the government were to legalize the production and sale of marijuana. This policy would undoubtedly increase both supply and demand. Regarding the supply side of the market, producing and selling marijuana is highly profitable. It must be to offset the risk of being caught and punished. If selling marijuana suddenly were to become legal, many new firms would enter the market in search of the profits, and supply would increase. Regarding the demand side of the market, many consumers might now be willing to try marijuana absent the legal sanctions against its use. Demand is also likely to increase.

Figure 7.5 shows the effect of legalization on the market for marijuana. The market demand and the market supply curves before legalization are D and S. The market equilibrium before legalization is (Q_0, P_0), at the intersection of S and D. As a result of legalization, supply increases from S to S′, and demand increases from D to D'. The new equilibrium is (Q_1, P_1), at the intersection of S' and D'. According to Figure 7.5, the equilibrium quantity of marijuana increases substantially, but the equilibrium price of marijuana hardly changes at all.

The different amounts that quantity and price change illustrate an important general principle. *When both the supply and the demand curves shift, the direction of change in the equilibrium can confidently be predicted for quantity or for price, but not for both.* For example, legalizing marijuana would almost certainly increase the equilibrium quantity of marijuana exchanged in the market. Both increases in supply and increases in demand tend to increase the equilibrium quantity. The effect on price is uncertain, however. The increase in demand tends to increase the equilibrium price; the increase in supply tends to decrease the equilibrium price. Therefore, whether the equilibrium price increases, decreases, or remains the same depends on the amount that each curve shifts. Figure 7.5 shows the supply shift slightly dominating the demand shift, so that the equilibrium price declines somewhat. But this does not necessarily have to be true. Were marijuana legalized, its price could rise if the increase in demand were strong enough to overcome the increase in supply.

The second four rows in the Concept Summary table indicate the predicted effects on equilibrium quantity and equilibrium price when both curves shift. Usually both curves shift as a result of two separate events, one event shifting each curve. A question mark (?) indicates that the predicted effect is uncertain. Once again, you should practice shifting demand and supply curves to make sure you understand the entries in each row.

CONCEPT SUMMARY

Effects on Equilibrium Quantity and Price of Shifts in Demand and Supply Curves

SHIFT	EFFECT ON EQUILIBRIUM QUANTITY	EFFECT ON EQUILIBRIUM PRICE
Demand increases Supply constant	Increases	Increases
Demand decreases Supply constant	Decreases	Decreases
Supply increases Demand constant	Increases	Decreases
Supply decreases Demand constant	Decreases	Increases
Demand increases Supply increases	Increases	?
Demand decreases Supply increases	?	Decreases
Demand increases Supply decreases	?	Increases
Demand decreases Supply decreases	Decreases	?

Elasticities and Market Outcomes

The preceding section showed the *direction* that equilibrium price and equilibrium quantity change in response to changes in demand and supply. Knowledge of demand and supply elasticities adds to our understanding of market outcomes because these elasticities determine, in part, the *amount* by which the equilibrium price and the equilibrium quantity change in response to changes in supply and demand. In the limit, elasticity can override some of the expected effects on price and quantity listed in the Concept Summary table.

The four graphs in Figure 7.6 show the effects of an increase in demand against four supply curves, ranging from perfectly elastic to perfectly inelastic.

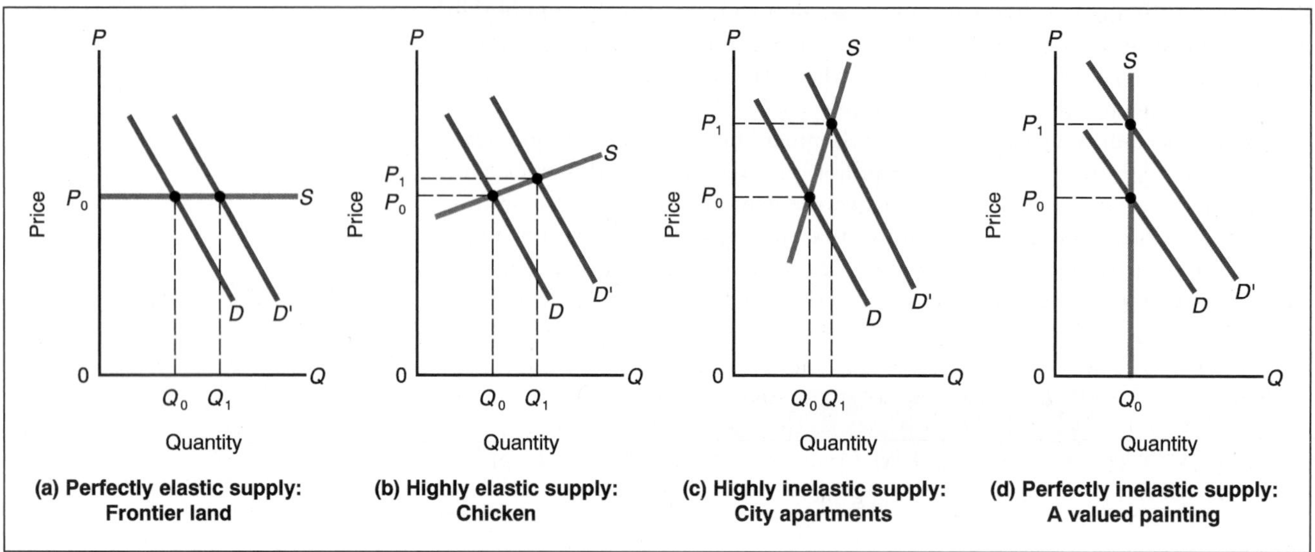

(a) Perfectly elastic supply: Frontier land

(b) Highly elastic supply: Chicken

(c) Highly inelastic supply: City apartments

(d) Perfectly inelastic supply: A valued painting

FIGURE 7.6

Elasticities and Market Outcomes

An increase in demand has different effects on the equilibrium quantity and equilibrium price depending on the elasticity of supply. In Figure 7.6(a), the supply of frontier land is perfectly elastic. The increase in demand for frontier land increases the equilibrium quantity from Q_0 to Q_1, but has no effect on the equilibrium price. In Figure 7.6(b), the supply of chicken is highly elastic. The increase in demand for chicken leads to a relatively large increase in the equilibrium quantity from Q_0 to Q_1, and a relatively small increase in the equilibrium price from P_0 to P_1. In Figure 7.6(c), the supply of city apartments is highly inelastic. The increase in demand for apartments leads to a relatively small increase in the equilibrium quantity from Q_0 to Q_1, and a relatively large increase in the equilibrium price (rent) from P_0 to P_1. In Figure 7.6(d), the supply of a famous painting is perfectly inelastic. The increase in demand for the painting increases the equilibrium price from P_0 to P_1, but has no effect on the equilibrium quantity.

In each instance (Q_0, P_0), the intersection of the market supply curve, S, and the original market demand curve, D, is the original equilibrium. The new market demand curve after the increase in demand is D'.

When supply is perfectly elastic [Figure 7.6(a)], the increase in demand affects only the equilibrium quantity. Quantity increases, as expected, from Q_0 to Q_1. However, the equilibrium price remains at P_0 because suppliers are willing to supply any amount of the product at P_0. An example is the market for land on the frontier in colonial America. As the settlers pushed westward seeking new homesteads, the demand for frontier land increased. But uninhabited land was so plentiful that its supply was essentially perfectly elastic. Landowners could not raise the prices of their land because if they tried to do so, the settlers could find other plots of land that were selling for the going market price, P_0 in the diagram.

The next two graphs illustrate the intermediate cases. In Figure 7.6(b) the supply curve is highly elastic (gently sloped). In Figure 7.6(c) it is highly inelastic (steeply sloped). When demand increases, both the equilibrium quantity and the equilibrium price increase, as expected, from (Q_0, P_0) to (Q_1, P_1) in both cases. But the amounts of the price and the quantity increases differ considerably. When supply is highly elastic [Figure 7.6(b)], the equilibrium quantity increases substantially, and the equilibrium price increases very little. When supply is highly inelastic [Figure 7.6(c)], the equilibrium quantity increases very little, and the equilibrium price increases substantially.

The market for chicken is an example of the second case. Over the past 20 years health-conscious Americans turned from beef to chicken to reduce their intake of fat and cholesterol. Fortunately for consumers, chickens can be raised cheaply in large quantities. The supply of chickens is highly elastic. Therefore, suppliers were able to meet the increased demand for chicken with very little increase in the price of chicken.

Apartments in urban areas illustrate the third case. As the population of the United States grew and became concentrated in the urban areas, the demand for apartments increased substantially. But urban land is scarce and highly valued for commercial and industrial uses. Increasing the supply of apartments is extremely costly because landlords have to bid the land away from potential industrial and commercial users. The supply of apartments is highly inelastic. Therefore, the increased demand for apartments has caused apartment rents to soar in many of the nation's cities.

Figure 7.6(d) shows the effect of an increase in demand when supply is perfectly inelastic. The equilibrium price increases, as expected, from P_0 to P_1, but the quantity remains at Q_0. Since the quantity supplied is Q_0 regardless of the price, it cannot respond to the price pressures resulting from an increase (or decrease) in demand. A good example of this case is the market for the famous paintings of the old masters. The demand for art has skyrocketed, but the supply of the old masters' paintings cannot be increased. Consequently, the increase in demand has served only to bid up the prices to dizzying heights. Private art collectors now pay tens of millions of dollars for masterpieces such as Van Gogh's *Water Lilies,* much to the consternation of museum directors. The leading art museums are now being bid out of the market for the best works of art.

The four graphs in Figure 7.6, and the examples, establish the following general principles:

An increase or decrease in demand has a *larger* effect on the equilibrium *quantity* and a *smaller* effect on the equilibrium *price,* the *higher* the elasticity of supply. Conversely, an increase or decrease in demand has a *smaller* effect on the equilibrium *quantity* and a *larger* effect on the equilibrium *price,* the *lower* the elasticity of supply. In the limit of *perfectly elastic* supply, only *quantity* changes. Conversely, in the limit of *perfectly inelastic* supply, only *price* changes.

Using the same four graph technique, see if you can verify the corresponding general principles with respect to a shift in the supply curve:

An increase or decrease in supply has a *larger* effect on the equilibrium *quantity* and a *smaller* effect on the equilibrium *price,* the *higher* the elasticity of demand. Conversely, an increase or decrease in supply has a *smaller* effect on the equilibrium *quantity* and a *larger* effect on the equilibrium *price,* the *lower* the elasticity of demand. In the limit of *perfectly elastic* demand (unlikely), only *quantity* changes. Conversely, in the limit of *perfectly inelastic* demand, only *price* changes.

Supply, Demand, and Inflation

A word of caution is in order about interpreting supply and demand diagrams during the inflationary times in which we live. A general price inflation poses a frame of reference problem for supply and demand analysis.

Supply and demand curves are drawn under the assumption that all the variables affecting quantity supplied and quantity demanded, other than the price of the product itself, are being held constant. The list of "other things equal" includes the prices of all other products. In other words, a supply and demand diagram implicitly assumes that there is no general price inflation. In fact, the prices of most goods and services are rising year by year. Therefore, a price change shown on a supply and demand diagram must be reinterpreted *relative* to the general rate of inflation. The price change is interpreted as a **real price change,** equal to the actual change in the price less the general rate of inflation.

REAL PRICE CHANGE
The actual change in a price less the general rate of inflation.

HISTORICAL NOTE: A case of Budweiser sold for about $6.00 in the late 1960s when many of the parents of today's college students were in college. Today a case of Budweiser sells for about $15.00, two and a half times as much. But prices generally are over four times higher today than they were in the late 1960s, which means that the real price of Budweiser is much lower now than it was 25 years ago.

For example, in 1992 the prices of goods and services purchased by consumers rose at an average rate of 2.9 percent. If a supply and demand analysis of some market shows that the price of the product increased during 1992, then the analysis is indicating that the price increased *relative* to the average of all other prices. Not only did the actual price of the product increase; it also increased by *more than* 2.9 percent. If the supply and demand analysis shows no change in the product's price during 1992, then the price did not change relative to the average of all other prices. The actual price increased by 2.9 percent, the overall rate of inflation. If the supply and demand analysis shows a decrease in price, then the price fell relative to the average of all other prices. The actual price may or may not have decreased. All the analysis indicates is that the price increased by *less than* 2.9 percent. Relative, or real, price decreases are common, even if actual price decreases are not. The prices of many products rise each year by less than the overall rate of inflation.

SUPPLY, DEMAND, AND THE ALLOCATION OF RESOURCES

A nation's economy cannot produce unlimited quantities of all goods and services. Resources are scarce and have to be allocated to the various goods and services that are produced each year. Now that you understand how competitive markets work you can begin to answer one of the more important questions in economic analysis: How do competitive markets allocate scarce resources?

A perfectly good answer to this question is that competitive markets allocate resources according to the Laws of Supply and Demand. Supply and demand interact in a particular market to establish the equilibrium price, labeled P_e, which in turn selects the equilibrium quantity, labeled Q_e. Q_e, the quantity exchanged between buyers and sellers, represents the allocation in that market.

Here is an alternative answer to the allocation question: Prices allocate resources in competitive markets by equating the value and the cost of the last good exchanged between buyers and sellers. We want to understand this alternative answer because it explains why competitive markets promote an efficient allocation of society's scarce resources and why markets form so easily.

Equilibrium Price, Marginal Cost, and Marginal Value

Consumers and business firms exhange goods and services in the marketplace in order to help solve their economic problems. They are very different economic agents, however. They enter into market exchanges with different motives, indeed, with entirely different economic problems. During their exchanges they have a common interest in only one piece of information, the prices of the products. Therefore, prices have to coordinate the market exchange between consumers and business firms. Nothing else can perform this function. Moreover, in the process of coordinating the market exchanges, prices have to incorporate all the economic information that is relevant to the exchanges. Consumers do not necessarily know anything about the firms they are dealing with other than the prices at which the firms are willing to sell their products. Similarly, firms do not necessarily know anything about their customers other than the prices at which they are willing to buy the firm's products. So prices have to incorporate all the economic information that leads to firms' willingness to sell and consumers' willingness to buy. What exactly is the economic information that market prices incorporate in a competitive market environment?

Business firms enter a market in search of profit. The price of a product indicates how much revenue a firm receives for each additional unit sold. We saw in Chapter 6 that a competitive firm arrives at its supply schedule by comparing the market price with the cost of producing additional units, the marginal cost of producing the product. The firm supplies output to the market as long as the price exceeds the marginal cost, stopping when price just equals marginal cost. Therefore, market prices incorporate information about a firm's costs of production in a competitive market. *Price equals marginal cost,* the cost of the last unit of output produced by the firm.

Since every firm determines its supply schedule in the same way, the market price must equal the cost of producing the last good supplied to the market no matter which firm actually supplies the good. In other words, *the market supply curve is the marginal cost curve for the entire industry.* At each quantity the vertical distance to the supply curve measures marginal cost, the cost of producing the last unit of output supplied to the market.

Consumers enter a product market to receive the value, or utility, from consuming the good or service. They balance the value received against the price of the good, which indicates how much scarce income they must sacrifice for each unit of the good consumed. In the process of determining the best possible balance between price and value, the price of the good must represent some value associated with consuming the good. In fact, the price represents the **marginal value,** the value of the last good consumed by each consumer.

MARGINAL VALUE
The value of the last good consumed by each consumer.

The relationship between price and marginal value on the demand side of the market is less direct than the relationship between price and marginal cost on the supply side. Price cannot literally *equal* the value of the last good consumed because value, or utility, cannot be measured. But price can be said to *represent* the value of the last good consumed by the following line of reasoning.

Suppose that over a certain period of time you consume 10 cassette tapes at a price of $8.00 each. You would not be able to say how much value, or utility, you receive from any of these tapes, including the tenth one. Nonetheless, because you chose not to buy an eleventh tape, you do perceive that the value you place on tapes falls below $8.00 between the tenth and eleventh tape. The tenth tape is worth at least $8.00 to you and the eleventh less than $8.00, although you cannot express either value directly in terms of utility. Instead, the link between price and marginal value comes indirectly from the perspective of opportunity cost, by the following argument.

The price of $8.00 establishes the opportunity cost of consuming another tape in terms of the utility that you could receive by purchasing $8.00 worth of other products. The $8.00 buys 1/2 of a $16.00 compact disc, or 8 $1.00 ball point pens, and so on. If you buy 10 tapes, you have decided that the utility received from the tenth tape, however measured, just equals or exceeds the utility you could have received from $8.00 worth of other products. Having purchased 10 tapes, however, $8.00 worth of other products offers more utility than does an eleventh tape. You are not willing to give up those products for an eleventh tape. So the $8.00 price *represents* marginal value by indicating the number of *units* of other goods that give the same utility as the tenth tape, rather than by measuring the utility received directly. Therefore, market prices incorporate information about the value that a consumer places on goods and services. *Price represents marginal value,* the value to the consumer of the last unit purchased.

Since all consumers are going through the same thought processes with respect to cassette tapes or any other product, the market price represents the value of the last good consumed no matter who consumes it. *The market demand curve represents marginal value in terms of the opportunity cost of consuming the last unit.* At each quantity the vertical distance to the demand curve measures marginal value, the value of the last good consumed.

At a supply and demand equilibrium, therefore, the equilibrium price, P_e, is simultaneously

1. marginal cost, the cost to some firm of supplying the last unit of the equilibrium quantity, Q_e; and
2. marginal value, the value to some person of consuming the last unit of the equilibrium quantity, Q_e.

In Chapter 2 we noted that the question "What is true on the margin?" is crucial for solving the economic problem and applied it to the problem of studying for tests. We have now shown that the margin is also fundamental to the process of exchange in competitive markets. *Prices link buyers and suppliers together on the margin.* They encourage exchange until the value and the cost of the last unit exchanged are equal.

The Diamonds-Water Paradox of Value

Economists did not understand that prices reflect marginal values and costs until the end of the nineteenth century. Before then they were often confused by the market's evaluation of goods and services. Adam Smith, the father of modern economics, posed what was for him the classic puzzle of market valuation, the market's relative valuation of diamonds and water.

Diamonds sold to consumers are nothing more than baubles, lovely, but inessential, pieces of jewelry. Yet diamonds command a very high price. Water is essential to life; its value is immeasurable. Yet the price of water is usually extremely low. Smith wondered why the prices of diamonds and water do not reflect the true values of these goods to consumers. He termed the market's valuation of diamonds and water the paradox of value.

The diamonds-water paradox of value is not a true paradox. It was resolved once economists understood that prices reflect marginal values and marginal costs. The flaw in the paradox is that the values it refers to are the *total* values of diamonds and water. But the market prices of diamonds and water (and any other good or service) bear no necessary relationship to total values. Instead, they correctly represent the values (and the costs) of the *last* diamond and *last* drops of water consumed.

Figure 7.7 compares the market for diamonds and water. Figure 7.7(a) pictures the market for diamonds; Figure 7.7(b) pictures the market for water. Diamonds are costly to mine, cut, and polish. The marginal cost of diamonds is quite high, even at relatively small quantities, as indicated by the position of the supply curve for diamonds, S_D. Consequently, the demand curve for

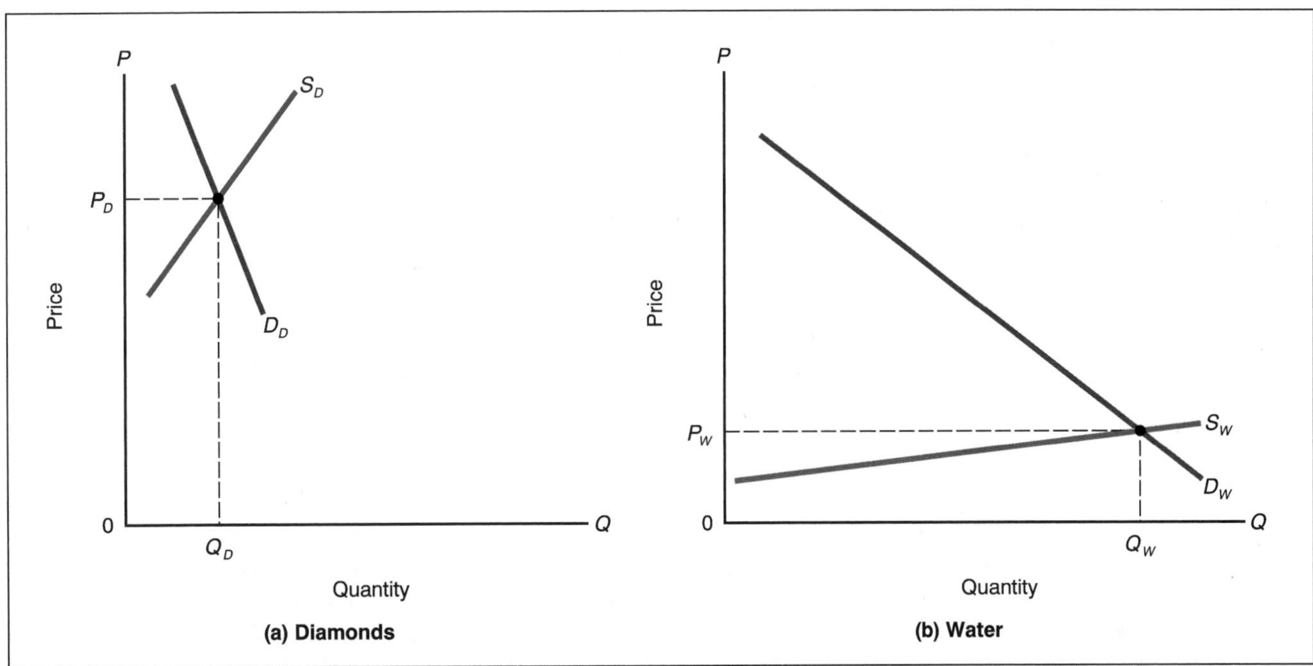

FIGURE 7.7

The Diamonds-Water Paradox of Value

Supply and demand analysis resolves the diamonds-water paradox: why diamonds are more expensive than water. Prices reflect marginal cost and marginal value. The marginal cost of producing diamonds is high. Therefore, the supply and demand for diamonds intersect at a high price, P_D, in Figure 7.7(a), and the value to consumers of the last diamond purchased is high. Conversely, the marginal cost of supplying water is low. Therefore, the supply and demand for water intersect at a low price, P_W, in Figure 7.7(b), and the value to consumers of their last glass of water is low.

diamonds, D_D, intersects the supply curve at a relatively high price, P_D. Because the marginal cost of diamonds is always high, the value to some consumer of the *last* diamond purchased at the equilibrium quantity, Q_D, must also be high. The equilibrium price, P_D, correctly reflects the high marginal value of diamonds.

In contrast, drinking water is relatively cheap to provide. The marginal cost of supplying water usually remains quite low, even at enormously high quantities, as indicated by the position of the supply curve for water, S_W. Consequently, even though the demand for water, D_W, is very great, the demand and the supply curves for water intersect at a relatively low price, P_W. With the marginal cost of water remaining so low, consumers enjoy the luxury of consuming water until the value they place on the *last* unit of water consumed is also quite low. P_W correctly reflects the low marginal value of water.

Water may be essential to life, but the marginal value of water really is remarkably low under normal circumstances. To convince yourself of this, imagine walking to the nearby water fountain for a drink before class begins. Just as you reach the fountain, someone jumps in front of you, claims ownership of the fountain, and insists on payment for a drink of water. The chances are you would forego the drink at any price higher than a few pennies (assuming you accept the claim of ownership!). Another glass of water just is not worth very much.

Should prices reflect marginal values rather than total values? The answer is decidedly yes, for two reasons. The equating of marginal values and marginal costs through the interaction of supply and demand is exactly what is required for achieving economic efficiency in market exchanges. In addition, the fact that prices reflect marginal values and marginal costs is the reason why markets form so easily in a free market system.

The Efficiency of Competitive Markets

NET VALUE

At any quantity exchanged in the market, the difference between the total value as perceived by the consumers and the total cost as experienced by the firms.

As discussed in Chapter 2, economic efficiency for society as a whole requires that the Law of Substitution hold with respect to people—no one can be made better off without making at least one other person worse off. In each individual product market the efficiency norm translates into maximizing the net value from producing and consuming the product. **Net value** is the difference between total value as perceived by the consumers and total cost as experienced by the business firms.

Promoting the economic well-being of individuals is the ultimate goal of an economic system in a humanistic society. Therefore, the total value consumers receive from their purchases of goods and services is obviously an important part of the efficiency objective. But total value cannot stand as the objective by itself. Maximizing total value in each market would be equivalent to allowing consumers to purchase every product free of charge. With prices set equal to zero, people would consume each product until the last unit had no further utility whatsoever. Although this may sound attractive from a consumer's perspective, it is a futile objective. The Law of Scarcity guarantees that no society has enough resources to provide that many goods and services.

Producing more of any one product uses scarce resources that could be used to produce other products of value to consumers. The value that consumers receive from these other products defines the opportunity cost of providing more of any one product. Firms experience this opportunity cost directly when they pay for scarce factors of production to produce their products, bidding the factors away from competing uses. The firms' total costs of production must be balanced against the total value that consumers receive in the exchange of any one good or service.

The best society can strive for, then, is to maximize net value, the amount by which total value exceeds total cost, in each market. Maximizing net value is the appropriate economic objective from a social perspective because it recognizes both the individuals' well-being that every humanistic society tries to promote and the opportunity cost of using society's scarce resources. The question, then, is how a society can maximize net value in each product market.

Selecting the Efficient Output

Society's economic problem of trying the maximize net value market by market is no different in principle from any other economic problem, such as the consumer's or the firm's economic problem. In every instance the goal is to maximize the difference between the benefits incorporated in the objective and the costs incorporated in the constraints. We described the general decision rule for solving the economic problem in Chapter 6: *An activity should be continued to the point at which the marginal benefit of the activity equals the marginal cost of the activity. Marginal benefit* is the additional benefit, measured in terms of the objectives, of the next unit of activity. *Marginal cost* is the opportunity cost of the activity.

In the context of a market for a good or service, marginal benefit is marginal value, the value to some consumer of the last unit exchanged in the market. Marginal cost is the cost to some firm of producing the last unit exchanged in the market. The decision rule implies that a product should be exchanged

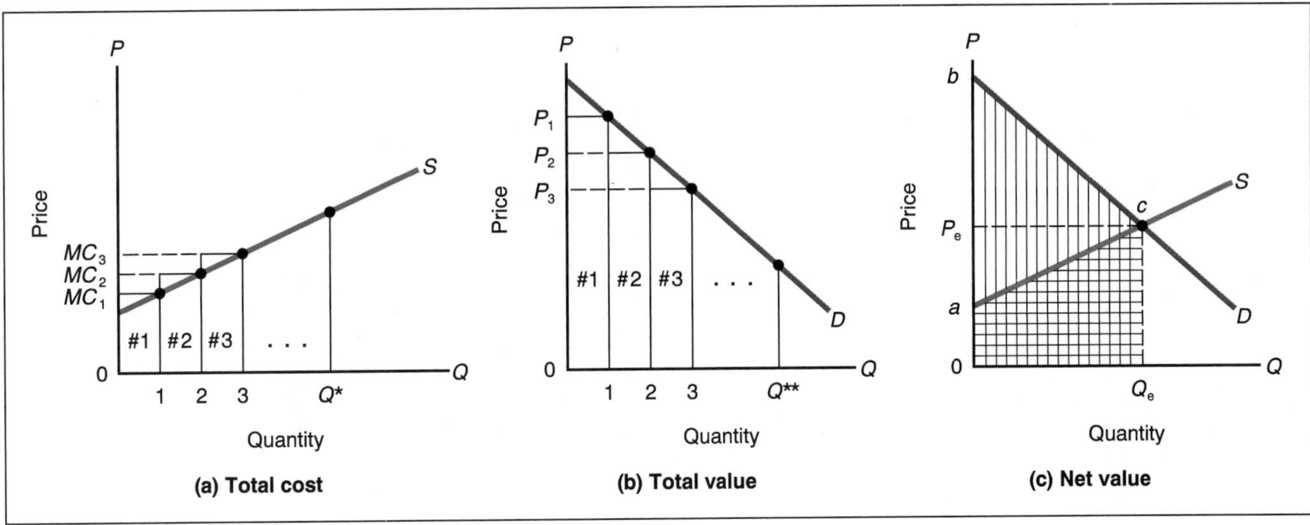

FIGURE 7.8

Total Cost, Total Value, and Net Value

The vertical distance to the market supply curve at each quantity is the marginal cost of supplying the last unit. Therefore, in Figure 7.8(a), the total cost of supplying output Q^* is approximately equal to the area under S up to Q^*. The vertical distance to the market demand curve at each quantity is the amount consumers are willing to pay for the last unit. As such, it represents the marginal value of the last unit purchased. Therefore, in Figure 7.8(b), the total value of Q^{**} is represented by the area under D up to Q^{**}. In Figure 7.8(c), the net value of producing and consuming the product is the shaded area *abc*, the area below D and above S up to equilibrium quantity Q_e. Net value in this market is as large as it can possibly be at Q_e.

between buyers and sellers until the marginal value of consuming the product equals the marginal cost of producing the product. As we have seen, this is exactly what happens in a competitive market. At the supply and demand equilibrium the marginal value and the marginal cost of the last unit exchanged are both equal to the equilibrium price. Therefore, the net value from producing and consuming the good is as large as it can possibly be.

Figure 7.8 shows how to represent the net value from producing and consuming a product on a supply and demand diagram. Refer to Figure 7.8(a), which pictures the market supply curve, S. Select any quantity, such as Q^*. The total cost of producing Q^* is (approximately) equal to the area under the supply curve up to Q^*. To see why, recall that the market supply curve indicates the marginal cost of production at each quantity. Think of producing each unit of output up to Q^* one at a time. The marginal cost of the first unit is the height of the supply curve, labeled MC_1 in the diagram. Therefore, the total cost of producing 1 unit is equal to the area of the rectangle labeled #1, whose height is MC_1 and whose base is 1 unit. The cost of producing the second unit is MC_2, equal to the area of the rectangle labeled #2, whose height is MC_2 and whose base is 1 unit. The total cost of producing 2 units is the sum of the areas of rectangles #1 and #2. Continuing unit by unit up to Q^*, the total cost of producing Q^* equals the sum of the areas of rectangles #1, #2, #3, and so on. The area under the supply curve up to Q^* closely approximates the combined areas of the rectangles.

Refer, next, to Figure 7.8(b), which pictures the market demand curve, D. Select any quantity, such as Q^{**}. The total value of consuming Q^{**} can be represented as the area under the demand curve up to Q^{**}. This time think about consuming each unit of output up to Q^{**} one at a time. Suppose that consumers were offered only the first unit of the product. According to the market demand curve, some consumer would be willing to pay a price equal to P_1 for the unit. Therefore, P_1 represents the marginal value to that consumer in terms of opportunity cost interpretation of marginal value. The total value of consuming 1 unit equals the area of the rectangle labeled #1, whose height is P_1 and whose base is 1 unit. Since someone is willing to pay P_2 for the

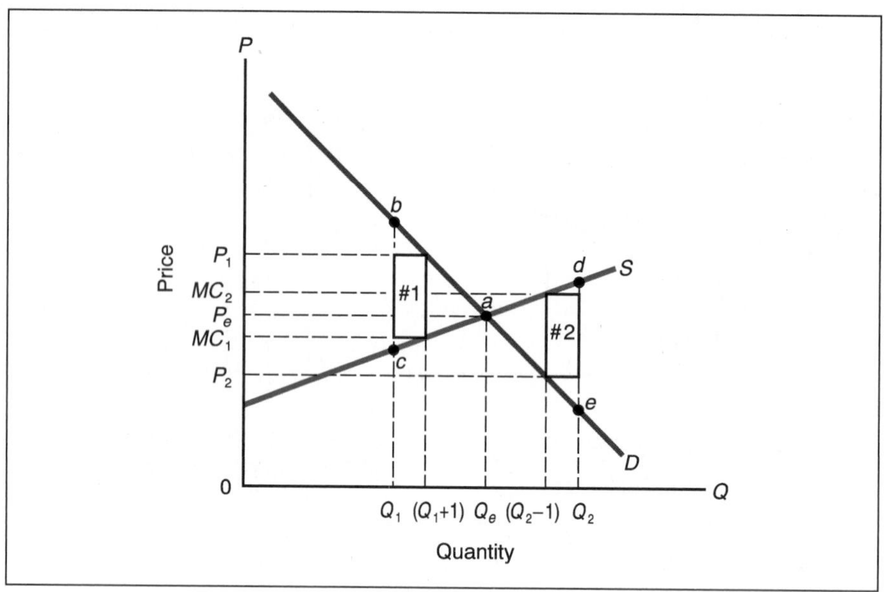

FIGURE 7.9

Inefficient Exchange

Society loses net value whenever the quantity exchanged differs from the supply and demand equilibrium quantity Q_e. Suppose the quantity exchanged is Q_1, less than Q_e. Consumers would be willing to pay P_1 to consume one more unit, whereas the cost of producing one more unit is only MC_1. Net value is increased by $(P_1 - MC_1)$ by producing and consuming one more unit area #1. Conversely, suppose the quantity exchanged is Q_2, more than Q_e. The last unit costs MC_2 to produce, but consumers are willing to pay only P_2 for the last unit. Net value is increased by $(MC_2 - P_2)$ by producing and consuming one less unit area #2. The maximum net value occurs when Q_e is exchanged, the equilibrium quantity.

second unit, the marginal value of the second unit is represented by the area of the rectangle labeled #2, whose height is P_2 and whose base is 1 unit. The total value of consuming the first 2 units is the sum of the areas of rectangles #1 and #2. Continuing unit by unit up to Q^{**}, the total value of consuming Q^{**} can be represented by the sum of the areas of rectangles #1, #2, #3, and so on. The area under the market demand curve up to Q^{**} closely approximates the combined areas of the rectangles.

Figure 7.8(c) puts the supply and the demand curves together and shows the equilibrium quantity, Q_e. The total value of consuming Q_e is represented by the area under the demand curve up to Q_e, highlighted by the vertical lines. The total cost of producing Q_e is equal to the area under the supply curve up to Q_e, highlighted by the horizontal lines. The vertical-lined area between the demand and the supply curves, area *abc*, is the net value from producing and consuming Q_e, the difference between total value and total cost at Q_e. In general, the net value of producing and consuming any output is the difference between the areas under the market demand and the market supply curves up to that output.

The difference between the areas under the two curves is greatest at the equilibrium, Q_e. Net value is as large as it can possibly be at the supply and demand equilibrium. Q_e is the efficient allocation in this market. To see why, refer to Figure 7.9, which illustrates the loss in net value from producing and consuming any quantity other than Q_e.

Suppose that for some reason quantity is less than Q_e—say, Q_1 (we will see examples of this in Chapter 8). Net value would increase if the market could somehow exchange 1 more unit because some consumer would be willing to pay P_1 for a good that only cost some producer MC_1 to produce. Marginal value exceeds marginal cost at $(Q_1 + 1)$ by $(P_1 - MC_1)$. The loss in net value from not exchanging the unit is equal to the area of the rectangle labeled #1, whose height is $(P_1 - MC_1)$ and whose base is 1 unit. Since marginal value exceeds marginal cost for all units between Q_1 and Q_e, the total amount of net value sacrificed by producing and consuming at Q_1 rather than Q_e is approximately equal to the triangular area *abc*.

Suppose, instead, that the quantity exchanged is greater than Q_c—say, Q_2. Now net value would increase if the market exchanged 1 less unit because marginal cost exceeds marginal value. Producers would save resources that cost MC_2, but that are currently producing a unit of output valued only at P_2 by consumers. The resources are better used elsewhere. The loss from exchanging that unit is equal to the area of the rectangle labeled #2, whose height is $(MC_2 - P_2)$ and whose base is 1 unit. Since the cost of producing all units from Q_e to Q_2 exceeds their value to consumers, producing and consuming Q_2 reduces the net value available at Q_e by an amount approximately equal to the triangular area *ade*.

Of course, competitive markets do not normally select outputs such as Q_1 and Q_2. Supply and demand interact to select Q_e, the efficient allocation. Furthermore, what is true for one market is true for all markets. If every product were allocated by the Laws of Supply and Demand, a free market economy would automatically maximize the total net value of producing and consuming all goods and services. No other system of economic exchange could possibly do any better in terms of promoting economic efficiency.

Adam Smith foresaw the efficiency property of competitive markets without benefit of a precise notion of economic efficiency. He marveled at how the economic self-interests of consumers and producers lead them, as if by an invisible hand, to engage in free market transactions that promote the social good. Smith equated the social good with the total wealth of a nation.

Prices and the Incentives for Exchange

People sometimes have the impression that market transactions are entirely one-sided. Business firms are taking advantage of consumers, or consumers are taking advantage of firms, usually the former. This cannot possibly be true, however, except in the most unusual circumstances. The overwhelming evidence to the contrary is simply that markets form so easily in a free market system. Market exchange is voluntary; no one forces anyone to buy or sell anything. Therefore, market exchanges must be *mutually* beneficial to buyers and suppliers for markets to form.

Reflect for a moment on the thousands of products that trade in the marketplace. The list of products runs well beyond the commonplace, to the bizarre and even the illegal. Whenever a demand for a good or service develops, someone appears ready and willing to supply it. Lonely teen-agers in the United States can speak for hours on the telephone to other lonely teen-agers whom they have never met. Each year brings scores of new "perfect gifts" for people who have everything—pet rocks, electric forks, folding bicycles, whatever. Poor families in Calcutta rent their babies to beggars because tourists are more likely to give to beggars with babies in tow. Many controlled substances appear to be readily available despite severe legal sanctions against their sale and use. The list could go on and on.

The incentives to form markets are so strong that many people earn their living as "middlemen," doing nothing more than helping to bring buyers and suppliers together. Real estate brokers, investment bankers, talent and sports

FIGURE 7.10

Consumer Surplus and Producer Surplus

The total market value of a product is $P_e \cdot Q_e$, the amount of dollars exchanged between consumers and producers, equal to the rectangular area $0P_ecQ_e$. The total value to consumers is represented by the area under D up to Q_e, the area $0bcQ_e$. Consumers receive a consumer surplus equal to the area P_ebc, the difference between their total value and the total market value. The total cost to producers is the area under S up to Q_e, the area $0acQ_e$. Producers receive a producer surplus equal to the area aP_ec, the difference between the total market value and their total cost. Market exchange is mutually beneficial; consumers and producers both receive a surplus in the market.

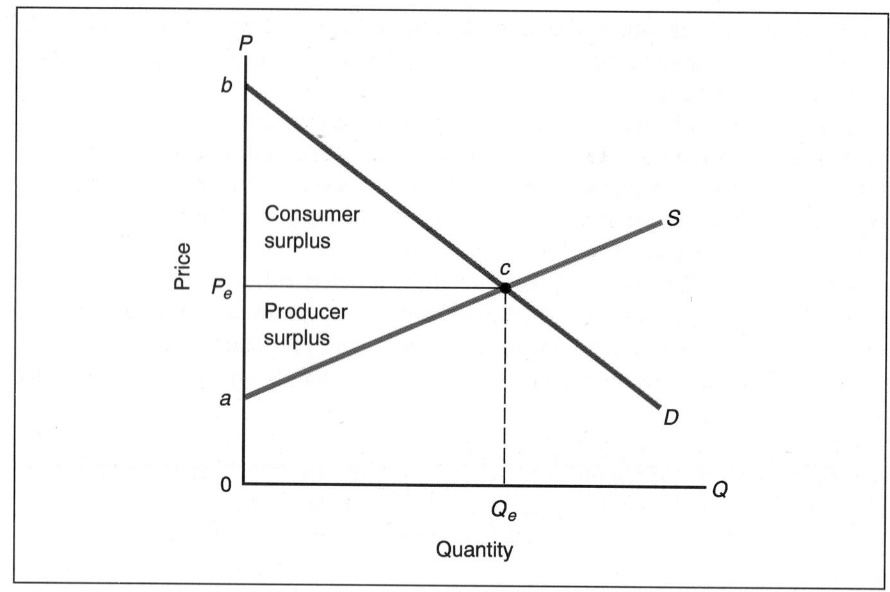

CURRENT ISSUE: Enterprising Russian soldiers are earning thousands of dollars a week by stripping metals from closed Russian military bases and selling the metals illegally to the West. (*The Economist*, November 7, 1992, p. 59).

agents, and employment agents are all examples of middlemen whose services buyers and suppliers are gladly willing to pay for.

The easy formation of markets is all the more remarkable because no one is directing the markets. The process of exchange is simply driven by the knowledge that market exchange is mutually beneficial to consumers and producers as they attempt to solve their economic problems.

THE MUTUAL GAINS FROM EXCHANGE: CONSUMER AND PRODUCER SURPLUS

Figure 7.10 illustrates the mutual gains from exchange in a competitive market. The **total market value** of the quantity Q_e exchanged in equilibrium is $P_e \cdot Q_e$, the dollars exchanged between consumers and producers. The total market value is simultaneously the total expenditures paid by the consumers and the total revenues received by the firms. In Figure 7.10 the total market value is equal to the area of rectangle $0P_ecQ_e$.

TOTAL MARKET VALUE

The dollars exchanged between the consumers and the producers in the market, equal to the total expenditures paid by the consumers and the total revenues received by the firms.

The gains to consumers arise because the total market value of Q_e is *less than* the total value they receive from consuming Q_e. The difference between the total value to consumers and the total market value is the **consumer surplus** from the market exchange. The total value that consumers receive is the entire area under the demand curve up to Q_e, area $0bcQ_e$. As noted above, the total market value is the area of the rectangle $0P_ecQ_e$. Therefore, the consumer surplus is equal to the area P_ebc, the difference between area $0bcQ_e$ (total value) and area $0P_ecQ_e$ (total market value). Alternatively, consumer surplus is the area below the market demand curve, D, and above the price line, P_ec, up to Q_e. Consumers receive a surplus because the product is worth more to them than they have to pay for it.

CONSUMER SURPLUS

At any quantity exchanged in the market, the difference between the total value to consumers and the total market value.

The gains to producers arise because the total market value of Q_e is *greater than* the total cost of producing Q_e. The difference between the total market value and the total cost of production is the **producer surplus** from the market

PRODUCER SURPLUS

At any quantity exchanged in the market, the difference between the total market value and the total cost of production.

exchange. The total market value is the area of the rectangle $0P_ecQ_e$. The total cost of producing Q_e is the area under the supply curve up to Q_e, area $0acQ_e$. Therefore, the producer surplus is equal to the area aP_ec, the difference between area $0P_ecQ_e$ (total market value) and area $0acQ_e$ (total cost). Alternatively, producer surplus is the area below the price line, P_ec, and above the supply curve, S, up to Q_e. Producers receive a surplus because the revenue that they receive from selling the product exceeds the cost of producing the product.

In summary, Figure 7.10 shows that the net value from the market exchange, area abc, is split between the consumers and the producers. The consumers' share of the net value is area P_ebc, the consumer surplus. The producers' share of the net value is area aP_ec, the producer surplus. In general, both consumers and producers benefit from market exchange.

CONSUMER SURPLUS AND THE MARGIN Market exchanges are *mutually* beneficial because competitive prices reflect marginal values and marginal costs. Consumers gain from market exchanges because they are able to buy *all* units of a good at a price that represents the value to them of the *last* unit consumed. The values of all units up to the last unit exceed the value of the last unit. Returning to our earlier example, if you buy 10 cassette tapes at a price of $8.00, the individual values of tapes 1 through 9 exceed $8.00, and the value of tape 10 may as well. You gladly forego $80 worth of other goods and services to purchase 10 tapes.

That market exchanges yield us a surplus is evident from our everyday experiences. We have all been in the position of deciding to buy a product without knowing beforehand exactly how much it will cost. When we purchase the product, we are pleasantly surprised—the price is considerably less than we thought it would be. Since we are willing to pay more, there is clearly a surplus of value over expenditure in this instance. More generally, we often pay less for a product than the maximum we would have been willing to pay, but we never willingly pay more for a product than we think it is worth to us. This is not to say that we do not regret some of our purchases. You may have the misfortune someday of owning a real lemon of an automobile and may regret having bought it. If so, your regret comes only with the advantage of hindsight. You obviously thought the car was worth the price when you purchased the car. Market exchanges clearly benefit consumers. They have to, or consumers would not be so willing to engage in exchange.

PRODUCER SURPLUS AND THE MARGIN Firms gain from market transactions because they are able to sell *all* units of a product at the cost of producing the *last* unit. Marginal cost rises as output is increased. Therefore, the marginal costs of all units up to the last unit are less than the marginal cost of the last unit. But since firms sell *all* units at the going market price, the revenue obtained on every unit up to the last unit exceeds the cost of producing each of those units. The difference between total revenue and total cost on all units is the firms' producer surplus. Market exchanges clearly benefit producers. They have to, or firms would not be so willing to engage in exchange.

In summary, consumers and business firms eagerly and voluntarily engage in market exchanges because the market price offers something for each of them, a consumer surplus and a producer surplus.

SUMMARY

The first section of Chapter 7 showed how markets operate when they are guided by the Laws of Supply and Demand.

1. The equilibrium price and the equilibrium quantity occur at the intersection of the market demand and the market supply curves.
2. Any price greater than the equilibrium price causes excess supply. Any price lower than the equilibrium price causes excess demand. The market equilibrium is also stable. Price automatically returns to the equilibrium price, so it is the only sustainable price.
3. Equilibrium prices and equilibrium quantities change when either the market demand curve or the market supply curve shifts. When the market demand curve shifts, price and quantity move in the same direction; for example, an increase in demand increases both equilibrium price and equilibrium quantity. When the market supply curve shifts, price and quantity move in opposite directions; for example, an increase in supply decreases the equilibrium price and increases the equilibrium quantity.
4. An increase or decrease in demand has a larger (smaller) effect on the equilibrium quantity and a smaller (larger) effect on the equilibrium price, the higher (lower) the elasticity of supply. In the limit of perfectly elastic (inelastic) supply, only quantity (price) changes. A similar principle applies to an increase or decrease in supply.
5. The price changes shown on supply and demand diagrams are real price changes. A real price change is the actual price change less the overall rate of inflation.

The second section of Chapter 7 showed how prices encourage consumers and producers to engage in efficient market exchanges.

6. Competitive prices bring consumers and producers together on the margin. The equilibrium price established by the interaction of supply and demand is equal to both marginal value and marginal cost. The marginal value is the value to some consumer of the last unit of output exchanged. The marginal cost is the cost to some firm of producing the last unit of output exchanged.
7. A market exchange is efficient if it maximizes the net value from consuming and producing a product. Net value is the difference between the total value of the product as perceived by consumers and the total cost of producing the product as experienced by business firms. Net value is maximized at a competitive equilibrium because marginal value and marginal cost are equal at the equilibrium output.
8. The net value of exchanging a certain quantity of a product is represented on a supply and demand diagram as the area between the market demand and the market supply curves up to that output. The total value of any quantity is represented by the area under the market demand curve up to that quantity. The total cost of producing any quantity is approximately equal to the area under the market supply curve up to that quantity. Net value is as large as possible at the equilibrium quantity, the intersection of the market demand and the market supply curves.
9. The fact that prices reflect marginal values and marginal costs explains why markets form so easily. Market exchange is mutually beneficial. Consumers gain a consumer surplus because they are able to buy all units of a product

at a price equal to the value to them of the last unit. Producers gain a producer surplus because they are able to sell all units at a price equal to the cost of producing the last unit.

KEY TERMS

consumer surplus
equilibrium
excess demand
excess supply
marginal value
market equilibrium
net value
producer surplus
real price change
stable market equilibrium
total market value

QUESTIONS

1. Suppose that the new digital compact cassettes (DCCs) are sold for $10 (assume that DCC players are affordable and that all kinds of music are available on DCCs).
   a. What effect is this new invention likely to have on the demand for conventional compact discs (CDs)? On the supply of CDs?
   b. What is the likely effect on the equilibrium price and the equilibrium quantity of CDs? Illustrate using supply and demand curves.
2. Suppose that the market demand and the market supply for compact discs (CDs) for various prices are as follows:

PRICE	QUANTITY DEMANDED	QUANTITY SUPPLIED
32	0	56
28	5	48
24	9	38
20	14	28
16	18	18
12	23	9
8	28	0

   a. What is the equilibrium price? The equilibrium quantity?
   b. Are the market demand and the market supply schedules consistent with the Laws of Demand and Supply?
   c. Would you expect the equilibrium identified in part a to be a stable equilibrium?
3. Refer again to the data in question 2.
   a. Is the market in excess demand or excess supply when the price is $24? When the price is $12? For each case calculate the amount of excess demand or excess supply.
   b. What is the amount bought and sold when the price is $12? Why?
4. How will each of the following affect the equilibrium price and the equilibrium quantity of gasoline? Illustrate using demand and supply curves.
   a. A million consumers this year purchase smaller, more fuel efficient cars.
   b. A new outbreak of hostilities in the Persian Gulf leads to a sharp increase in the price of a barrel of crude oil.
   c. Events a and b happen at the same time.
5. Discuss how the elasticity of demand determines the effects on the market equilibrium of a change (increase or decrease) in supply.
6. Suppose that the demand for some product is highly (price) elastic, but not perfectly elastic, and that the supply is (price) inelastic, but not perfectly inelastic. If supply decreases, what will happen to total expenditures (revenues) on the product? Illustrate using demand and supply curves.
7. a. Define *marginal cost* and *marginal value*, and describe their relationships to the market demand and the market supply curves and to the market price.
   b. In question 2, what are marginal cost and marginal value at a quantity of 28?
8. Using a supply and demand diagram, illustrate the following concepts at the market equilibrium: total cost, total value, net value, consumer surplus, producer surplus.
9. Using supply and demand analysis, depict a situation in which
   (i) producers capture all the net value from producing and consuming the good.
   (ii) consumers capture all the net value from producing and consuming the good.
   Can you describe conditions that might generate the first situation? The second situation? Are the conditions realistic?
10. We know that over the last 10 years both the demand for and the supply of personal computers have increased dramatically. What factors might explain the huge increase in demand? What factors might explain the huge increase in supply? Which do you think has been greater, the increase in demand or the increase in supply? Why?
11. Robberies soar in central cities after a federal drug bust as addicts desperately try to get more money to buy the drugs remaining on the street. How does the soaring crime rate relate to the addicts' elasticity of demand for drugs? (*Hint:* Is their demand highly elastic or inelastic, and what difference does this make?)

CHAPTER

8

Applications of Supply and Demand

LEARNING OBJECTIVES

CONCEPTS TO LEARN

Supply and demand in agriculture

Markets in chronic excess demand or supply

Legislated price ceilings and price floors

The economic effects of taxes

CONCEPTS TO RECALL

The Laws of Supply and Demand [5, 6, 7]

The net value from producing and consuming a good [7]

People in the United States believe in the free market system and are generally quite willing to let markets allocate resources. On occasion, though, they have reason to complain about market outcomes, and in those instances they often petition the government to "do something" about the problems that they see.

Farmers, for one, are not so thrilled about the Laws of Supply and Demand. The prices of their crops have fallen steadily throughout the twentieth century relative to prices generally. The crop prices are the source of farmers' incomes, which means that farmers' incomes have not kept pace with the growth in incomes generally. Crop prices are also highly unstable, so that farmers never know from year to year what their incomes will be. To add insult to injury, farmers pray for good weather, yet good weather actually lowers total farm income.

Farmers are not the only ones with complaints about the market system. Some people argue that the prices of basic social necessities such as housing and medical care are too high. They know that many poor families cannot afford decent housing or adequate medical care, and they think this is unfair. Others complain that the things they want are sometimes unavailable, such as a ticket to watch their favorite team in the playoffs or a parking space downtown. Then there are taxes. The federal, state, and local governments have managed to tax almost everything, and people resist the taxing of their purchases or their incomes.

Can governments do anything about these problems? Well, taxes will always be with us. As for the other complaints, we will see that government intervention into the competitive marketplace can only change the nature of these problems. It cannot fully solve the problems.

Chapter 8 applies the principles of supply and demand to a number of important U.S. policy issues relating to the kinds of complaints mentioned above. The applications emphasize how demand and supply elasticities influence both market outcomes and the results of government interventions in the marketplace. The chapter begins with the difficulties of the farmers.

AGRICULTURE

No sector of any economy is more important than the agricultural sector. A nation's first economic thoughts always turn to the problem of feeding itself. People in the United States lose sight of this fact because U.S. agriculture is so large and productive. The United States easily feeds itself, with plenty to spare, so that Americans hardly ever experience a food crisis. They enjoy the luxury of taking their food supply for granted. You can be sure that people in other nations pay close attention to U.S. agriculture, however. Exports of food from the United States account for 20 percent of the world's agricultural trade.

The U.S. agricultural sector also happens to be an excellent vehicle for illustrating the Laws of Supply and Demand in action. Agriculture at the level of the farm is the most highly competitive sector in the U.S. economy. The markets for most agricultural commodities exhibit the four requirements for a competitive market discussed in Chapter 6: identical products, good information about prices, a large number of farms, and the free flow of resources into and out of the industry. The crops supplied by different farms are literally indistinguishable. Number 2 hard wheat is Number 2 hard wheat no matter where it is grown. The national market for agricultural products is well organized and fully integrated. Information on prices, and on market conditions generally, is readily available to all buyers and sellers. There are approximately 2.2 million farms in the United States. Finally, entry into and exit from farming in the long run are relatively easy. For all these reasons, the Laws of Supply and Demand capture virtually all relevant economic information about market exchange in agriculture.

Well-functioning competitive markets are not normally targets of government policy initiatives in a free market economy. Agriculture is the outstanding exception in the United States. In 1990 the federal government paid over $10 billion to farmers under various price support programs that had their beginnings in the Great Depression of the 1930s. These programs are designed both to stabilize crop prices and to protect the incomes of small farmers when crop prices are especially low. Part of the government's willingness to support farmers can be explained by their unquestioned political power, but only in part. The Laws of Supply and Demand are not always kind to farmers. We want to explore the various market pressures on farmers that have aroused the sympathies of the American public.

Proper market analysis is a two-step process. First, learn as much as you can about the characteristics of both market demand and market supply, paying particular attention to demand and supply elasticities. Then put demand and supply together to see what their interaction implies about the behavior of price and quantity. Our discussion of agriculture follows this two-step procedure. We begin with a look at each side of the market.

The Demand for Agricultural Products

The demand for agricultural products has two distinct components, domestic demand and export demand. Domestic demand is approximately three-fourths of the total demand and export demand one-fourth, although these proportions vary substantially for individual products.

DOMESTIC DEMAND As indicated in Chapter 5, the demand for agricultural products is highly price and income inelastic. In other words, the market demand curve is extremely steep (price inelastic). It also shifts out slowly over time (income inelastic). Farmers in the United States have not particularly benefited from the substantial growth in U.S. income throughout the twentieth century. People's eating habits do change as they become wealthier; they eat out more often in restaurants and purchase more processed food. But little of this filters down to the farm. Farmers care more about how much people eat than how they eat, and total food consumption per person in the United States has remained virtually constant since 1910. Nearly all increases in demand are the result of population growth. This bodes ill for farmers, since U.S. population growth has slowed considerably in recent years.

EXPORT DEMAND The export component of total demand is considerably different. It is price elastic rather than price inelastic for the same reason that a firm's demand curve is far more elastic than is the industry demand curve. The U.S. food exports face substantial competition in world markets. When U.S. prices increase, other things equal, foreign demanders are quick to substitute the now-cheaper food supplied by other countries. When U.S. prices fall, they substitute in favor of U.S. suppliers. Domestic demand is much more inelastic because government policies have tended to isolate domestic buyers from the rapidly growing world agricultural markets.

Export demand is also far less predictable year to year than is the domestic component. It depends on such variable factors as the state of foreign economies, the extent to which other countries restrict imports of food and subsidize their own food exports, and the value of the dollar relative to other currencies.

OVERALL MARKET DEMAND The characteristics of domestic demand for food dominate overall market demand simply because domestic demand is so much more important than is export demand. The market demand curve is price inelastic and shifts out slowly over time, subject to occasional bursts and declines from its trend rate of growth caused by the volatility of the export component. This could change in the near future, however. The market demand curve could become price elastic if export demand continues to grow and the government permits more domestic exposure to world markets. That has not been the case up to now, however.

The Supply of Agricultural Products

The supply of most agricultural commodities has three characteristics of note: increasing price elasticity over time, substantial advances in productivity over time, and considerable instability in the short run.

SUPPLY ELASTICITIES We saw in Chapter 6 that the price elasticity of supply increases substantially with the passage of time. Agriculture experiences a long momentary run during which supply responses to changing market conditions are minimal. Crops are planted and harvested once a year and then stored. Sales come out of storage until the next harvest. Farmers are effectively locked into their previous planting decisions for a year, or even two, depending on how soon after planting market conditions change.

Supply elasticity increases as the momentary run gives way to the short run, but not by very much. Recall that the estimated short-run supply elasticities are very low, on the order of .2 for food as a whole. Attempts to increase supply run into the Law of Diminishing Returns as farmers attempt to squeeze more output from a fixed amount of land. Farmers could reduce supply significantly whenever demand decreases by planting only a part of their land, but they tend not to do this. The setup costs of preparing land for planting are a significant percentage of the total costs. Consequently, farmers usually plant an entire plot of land rather than part of it. They project that the extra revenues from the additional crops will exceed the minimal extra costs of planting the entire plot of land.

The supply responses are considerable once land can be varied and the short run gives way to the long run. The long-run elasticities of most crops are much larger than their short-run elasticities and are actually elastic for many crops.

INCREASES IN PRODUCTIVITY OVER TIME The market supply curve for nearly all agricultural commodities has shifted out steadily and substantially year after year throughout most of the twentieth century. That supply has continued to increase rapidly since the 1950s may seem surprising in light of the exodus from rural to urban areas noted in Chapter 4. Farm employment declined steadily from 7.2 million workers in 1950 to 3.2 million workers in 1985 and has remained fairly constant since then. But the decline in employment has been more than offset by enormous increases in labor productivity.

Table 8.1 records agriculture's impressive productivity gains during the 30-year period from 1960 to 1990. Labor productivity increased more than fourfold from 1960 to 1990 (second column). As a result, farm output increased by 58 percent (third column) despite the exodus from the farms.

The gains in labor productivity have come from two sources, the substitution of other inputs for labor and continued technological change. Farmers have effectively substituted land and capital for labor. From 1930 to 1980 the amount of land per worker increased fivefold and the amount of capital per worker fifteenfold. Agriculture is now one of the most capital intensive industries in the entire U.S. economy. Data for 1979 showed that farms used an average of $43,000 of capital per worker, compared with $21,500 of capital per worker for the economy as a whole, and even these averages are misleading. Agriculture contains a mixture of large and small farms, with large farms dominating overall production. Seventy percent of all farms are small operations with annual gross income of less than $40,000. They account for only 10 percent of all gross farm income, and their owners receive the vast majority of their incomes from off-farm activities. Most of the nation's agricultural output comes from approximately 300,000 large, highly mechanized "commercial farms," those with annual gross incomes of $100,000 and more. These large farms account for 70 percent of all gross farm income, and farming is their principal source of income. The commercial farms are very large, highly capitalized businesses.

TABLE 8.1 **Productivity Growth in Agricuture, 1960–90 (1960 = 100)**

YEAR	LABOR PRODUCTIVITY (OUTPUT PER HOUR)	FARM OUTPUT	TOTAL FACTOR PRODUCTIVITY (OUTPUT PER UNIT OF TOTAL INPUT)
1960	100	100	100
1970	178	111	113
1975	241	125	129
1980	305	137	131
1985	420	157	157
1990	429	158	164

SOURCES: U.S. Department of Commerce, Bureau of the Census, *Statistical Abstract of the United States, 1987* (Washington, DC: U.S. Government Printing Office, 1987); *Economic Report of the President 1993* (Washington DC: Government Printing Office, 1993).

Agricultural production has also achieved an impressive record of continual technological advance. More productive equipment, the development of hybrid seeds, improved livestock feeding methods, better fertilizers and pesticides, and effective programs for teaching farmers about these advances have all contributed to a record of productivity growth unmatched by any other major sector of the economy. Moreover, the end is nowhere in sight. Agriculture appears to be on the verge of new productivity breakthroughs in the areas of biotechnology and genetic engineering.

SHORT-RUN INSTABILITY Agriculture is the one sector of the economy that remains at the mercy of Mother Nature. Warm sunshine and gentle rains, blistering heat waves and droughts, disease, and infestations of insects all cause dramatic shifts in the market supply curve over the short run. Wide swings in output from year to year for individual crops are common, against a long-run trend that is decidedly upward. For example, the Corn Belt experienced a severe drought in 1983. Corn production declined from 8.2 million bushels in 1982 to 4.2 million bushels in 1983. When good weather returned in 1984 and 1985, corn production recovered along with it, rising to 7.8 million bushels in 1984 and 8.9 million bushels in 1985.

Market Equilibrium

What kinds of market outcomes result from these characteristics of agricultural demand and supply? And why has the national government been unwilling to let the natural market forces prevail in agriculture? The most important issues center on the behavior of agricultural prices.

There are two stories to tell of agricultural prices, one about the long run and one about the short run. Both are commonly perceived as tales of woe for the farmer.

PARITY

The ratio of prices received by farmers for their output to the prices farmers pay for their inputs.

LONG-RUN PRICE BEHAVIOR Over the long run, prices of agricultural products have fallen relative to prices generally. The U.S. Department of Agriculture (USDA) follows long-run price trends by means of a concept called **parity.** Parity is the ratio of prices received by farmers for their output to the prices farmers pay for their inputs.

$$\text{Parity} = \frac{\text{output prices received by farmers}}{\text{input prices paid by farmers}}$$

The input prices include family cost of living expenses as well as the usual factors of production. Parity in 1914 is arbitrarily defined as 100, with all subsequent price ratios defined relative to the 1914 value.

The steady decline in parity throughout this century is shown in Table 8.2. Only in the immediate post–World War II years did parity achieve its 1914 level. Since 1950, however, the relative decline in farm prices has been sharp and fairly persistent.

The different rates of increase in the market demand and the market supply curves explain the persistent decline in parity. Both curves shift out over time. But, as indicated above, the large shifts in the supply curve caused by pro-

TABLE 8.2 **Parity Ratio: Prices Received/Prices Paid (1914 = 100)**

YEAR	PARITY RATIO
1914	100
1920	99
1930	83
1940	81
1950	101
1960	80
1970	72
1975	76
1980	65
1985	52
1990	54

SOURCES: U.S. Department of Commerce, Bureau of the Census, *Statistical Abstact of the United States, 1987*, and *1992* (Washington, DC: U.S. Government Printing Office, 1987, 1992); U.S. Department of Commerce, Bureau of the Census, *Historical Statistics of the United States: Colonial Times to 1970* (Washington, DC: U.S. Government Printing Office, 1975).

ductivity growth far outpace the fairly moderate shifts in the demand curve that arise mostly from population growth. The net result is persistent downward pressure on agricultural prices, as indicated in Figure 8.1.

The market demand and the market supply curves, D and S, refer to the state of the market in some initial base year in the past. The demand curve is highly inelastic (steep). The (long-run) supply curve is much more elastic (less steep). The equilibrium price is P_0. After a number of years, demand increases modestly to D'. During that same period, supply increases far more than demand, to S'. The increase in demand puts upward pressure on price, and the increase in supply puts downward pressure on price. The supply effect dom-

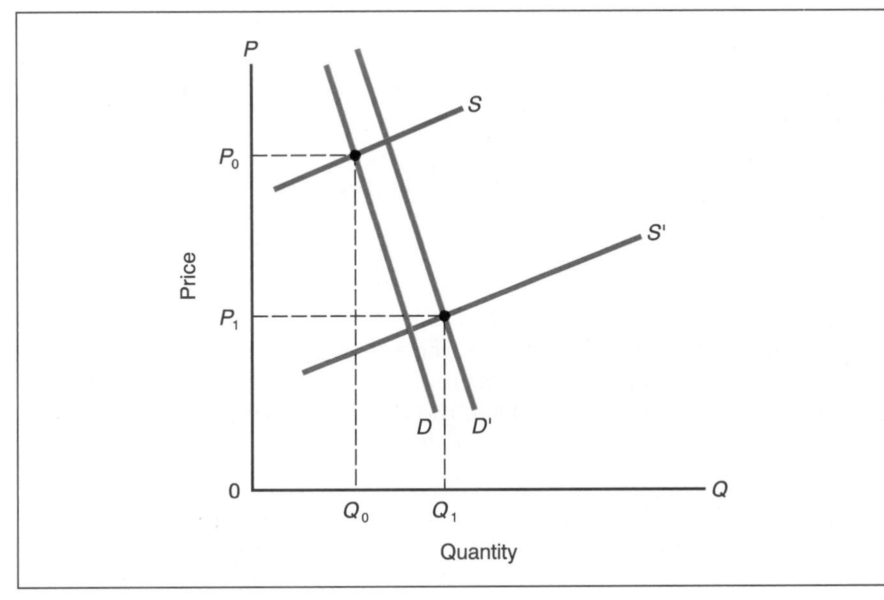

FIGURE 8.1

The Long-run Decline in Parity in Agriculture

The figure illustrates the long-run decline in parity, the ratio of output prices received by farmers to the input prices paid by farmers. Parity is initially P_0 in some base year, at the intersection of D and S. Over time, the demand curve shifts out modestly from D to D', mostly because of increases in population. The supply curve shifts out much more than the demand curve, from S to S', because of rapid technological change in agriculture. The relatively larger shift in the supply curve lowers parity over time to P_1, at the intersection of D' and S'.

inates in agriculture, and prices fall over time, from P_0 to P_1. Moreover, the decline in price is large because demand is so inelastic.

Declining parity has always been the major justification for having the government support agricultural prices above their natural equilibrium levels. The argument is that falling relative prices translate into below-average incomes for farm families. The Laws of Supply and Demand, if allowed to operate, are therefore viewed as unfair to farmers.

In fact, farm incomes *are* generally far less than nonfarm incomes. In 1980, for example, the median income of farm families was only 74 percent of the nonfarm median family income. Nonetheless, the leap from prices to income is a bit misleading. Falling prices do not necessarily imply lagging incomes when the decline in prices is due to productivity growth. The loss in revenue from the lower prices can be more than offset by the savings from cost-reducing productivity growth. This appears to have been the case on the larger commercial farms. Median family income on the commercial farms equals or exceeds the nonfarm median. The large commercial farmers in trouble are those who got themselves heavily into debt in the early 1980s on the expectation that the buoyant 1970s would continue. But these farms represent only a small minority of all commercial farms. Since the commercial farms provide 70 percent of the total agricultural output, the agricultural sector overall is in reasonably good shape despite the persistent decline in parity.

Falling prices do hurt the small farmers, whose farms are not highly capitalized and have not experienced large increases in labor productivity. As noted above, however, these families receive the vast majority of their incomes from nonfarm sources. Therefore, they have below-average incomes in large part because their nonfarm sources of income are not particularly good ones.[1]

SHORT-RUN PRICE BEHAVIOR The short-run story about agricultural prices is one of volatility. Agricultural prices fluctuate much more than do prices generally. Table 8.3 compares the annual rates of change in the prices received by farmers (second column) and in the prices of all products purchased by consumers, excluding food (third column) for the 16-year period from 1970 to 1985. The point to notice is that the *actual* prices received by farmers both rise and fall, whereas the prices of all other products only move in one direction, upward.

The volatility of farm prices results primarily from a combination of two factors, the short-run instability of the market supply curve, caused by periods of good and bad weather, and the price inelasticity of both the market demand and the market supply curves. Figure 8.2 illustrates the effect of weather on agricultural markets.

The market demand and the market supply curves in Figure 8.2 are both relatively steep, reflecting their low price elasticities. The supply curve S represents the market supply in a year of normal weather conditions. The price in a year of "normal" weather is P_0, at the intersection of S and D. When the weather is bad, the supply curve shifts to the left, to S'. The equilibrium price rises significantly, from P_0 to P_1. When the weather is especially favorable, the

[1]The analysis and data on agriculture in this chapter rely heavily on an excellent overview of U.S. agriculture in Chapter 4, *The Economic Report of the President 1986* (Washington, D.C.: U.S. Government Printing Office, 1986), 129–158.

TABLE 8.3 **Farm Prices and Farm Incomes, 1970–85**

YEAR	PRICES RECEIVED BY FARMERS (ANNUAL PERCENTAGE CHANGE)	PRICES PAID BY CONSUMERS FOR ALL ITEMS EXCEPT FOOD (ANNUAL PERCENTAGE CHANGE)	GROSS FARM INCOME ($ BILLION)
1970	1.7	6.0	$ 58.8
1971	3.3	4.6	62.1
1972	11.3	3.0	71.1
1973	42.0	3.9	98.9
1974	7.1	9.9	98.2
1975	−3.8	9.3	100.6
1976	1.0	6.6	102.9
1977	−2.0	6.5	108.8
1978	15.0	7.2	128.4
1979	14.8	11.4	150.7
1980	1.5	14.6	149.3
1981	3.7	10.9	166.3
1982	−4.3	6.6	163.4
1983	1.5	3.4	152.4
1984	5.2	4.4	174.4
1985	−9.9	3.9	166.6

SOURCE: *Economic Report of the President 1986* (Washington, DC: U.S. Government Printing Office, 1986).

supply curve shifts to the right, to S''. The equilibrium price falls significantly, from P_0 to P_2. The instability of supply translates into fairly large price changes *because demand is so inelastic.* Price would change by only a small amount if demand were highly elastic. Supply instability, by itself, is not sufficient to generate volatile prices.

The dramatic effect of weather on farm prices can be seen in the price changes reported in Table 8.3. The severe drought of 1983 pushed prices up by 5.2 percent during 1984 despite continued declines in export demand. When good weather returned in 1984 and 1985, prices plummeted by 10 percent in 1985.

Farmers are burdened by short-run price instability because volatile prices translate directly into volatile incomes. Farmers cannot expect a steady flow of income year after year. Return again to the case of good and bad weather illustrated by Figure 8.2. When a supply curve shifts along an inelastic demand curve, price and total revenues move together. For instance, when good weather shifts the supply curve out to S'' and the equilibrium price declines from P_0 to P_2, total revenue (gross farm income) also declines. $P_2 \cdot Q_2$ is less than $P_0 \cdot Q_0$ because demand is inelastic. Conversely, when bad weather shifts the supply curve in to S', the inelasticity of demand causes total revenue to increase. $P_1 \cdot Q_1$ exceeds $P_0 \cdot Q_0$.

The fourth column of Table 8.3 highlights the ebbs and flows of gross farm income during the 16-year period from 1970 to 1985. That incomes fell in five of those years (1974, 1980, 1982, 1983, and 1985) is really quite striking. Total incomes in other major sectors of the economy seldom decline during inflationary times. Agriculture is truly distinctive in this regard.

FIGURE 8.2

Weather, Agricultural Prices, and Farmers' Incomes

S is the supply curve for a crop in a normal weather year. The equilibrium quantity and price are Q_0, P_0, at the intersection of D and S. Exceptionally bad weather decreases supply. The supply curve shifts to the left from S to S' and the equilibrium quantity and price are Q_1, P_1, at the intersection of D and S'. Because demand is inelastic, farmers' total income increases; $P_1 \cdot Q_1 > P_0 \cdot Q_0$. Exceptionally good weather increases supply. The supply curve shifts to the right from S to S'' and the equilibrium quantity and price are Q_2, P_2, at the intersection of D and S''. Because demand is inelastic, farmers' total income decreases; $P_2 \cdot Q_2 < P_0 \cdot Q_0$.

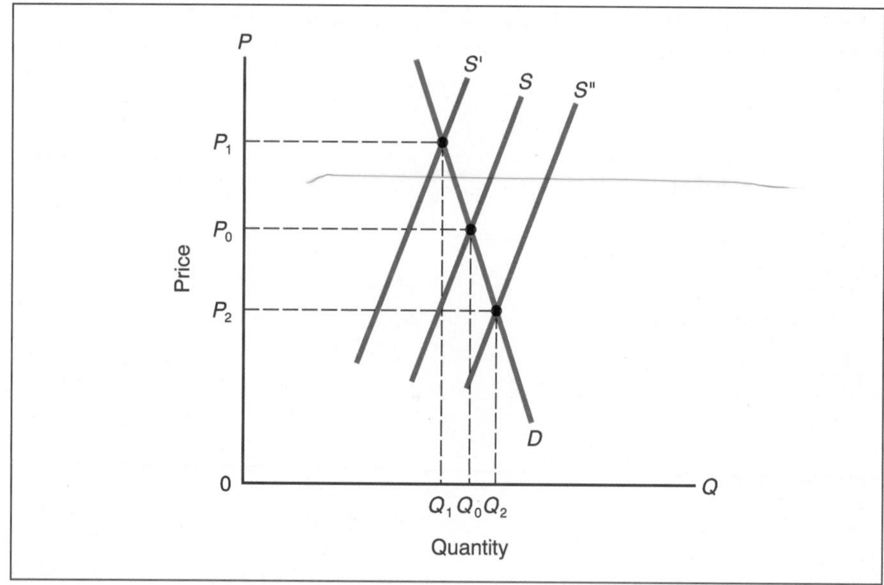

The situation in agricultural markets is especially ironic. Farmers pray for good weather, but, as Figure 8.2 indicates, good weather is not necessarily good for all farmers. Good weather lowers total farm income. The best of all worlds for an individual farmer is to be spared the ravages of poor weather when most others' crops are failing. Not only is total revenue higher when the weather is bad and the supply curve shifts in, but also the revenue is distributed over fewer farms. A large number of farmers do suffer when the weather turns bad. But the farmers who are spared can make huge incomes. Notice in Table 8.3 that gross farm income rose substantially in 1984 following the drought of 1983 and then dropped sharply in 1985 following the return of good weather in 1984.

NONCLEARING MARKETS

Societies that choose capitalism as their economic system rely on markets to allocate resources, with every expectation that markets will perform satisfactorily. The United States is no different in this respect. Fortunately, markets usually do perform satisfactorily, but occasionally they do not.

People often become distressed when markets malfunction because their instincts are to trust the market system. Market problems also breed confusion. People may not fully understand the nature of the problem because in the normal course of events they do not have to think about how markets operate. Also, capitalistic societies always experience a tension between a desire to have the government do something about a market problem and an inherent distaste for any government intervention into economic affairs. Government policies always generate controversy, whatever the context. Moreover, the distaste for government action is well founded. Government intervention in the marketplace often creates a whole new set of problems.

This section, as well as the next two, illustrates the problems that can plague even reasonably competitive markets and the various confusions that surround the problems themselves and the government's attempts to solve them. We begin with the problems that arise when markets are prevented from reaching their natural equilibrium.

Parking on City Streets

Life in these United States has its share of petty annoyances. High on many people's lists is the pain of trying to find a metered parking space in any downtown urban area. People complain that there are not enough parking spaces and badger local officials to provide more parking.

The call for more parking is a common reaction whenever people perceive a quantity problem—if there is not enough of something, ask someone to provide more of it. Having now studied the Laws of Supply and Demand, however, your thoughts should turn immediately to price, not quantity, whenever you hear a quantity complaint. A quantity complaint is the symptom of a pricing problem. For some reason the price is not settling at its equilibrium value as it normally does. If price were at its equilibrium value, consumers and producers would be buying and selling exactly what they want to buy and sell, the equilibrium quantity. People might not like the equilibrium, but, if not, they will complain about the price, not the quantity.

A quantity complaint that there is not enough of something indicates that the price is below its equilibrium value and that the market is in a state of chronic excess demand. The first step toward solving the problem is to understand what is holding the price below equilibrium. What countervailing forces are undermining the Laws of Supply and Demand? The quantity problem will disappear if the normal market forces can be resurrected and the price returned to its equilibrium value. At the same time, simply providing more supply to meet all the quantity demanded at an artificially low price is hardly a compelling solution. It would probably be a terrible waste of resources.

The urban parking problem illustrates these principles. The demand and supply curves in Figure 8.3 represent the market for metered on-the-street parking. The demand curve has a moderate slope. Economists have no direct knowledge of the price elasticity for on-the-street parking, nor any reason to believe that it is unusually elastic or inelastic. In contrast, the supply curve is very steep. Remember that the supply curve represents the marginal costs of providing additional parking spaces, and that marginal cost is an opportunity cost. The opportunity cost of providing more on-the-street parking is clearly very high because urban land is extremely valuable. Widening streets to provide more parking or metering vacant lots uses land that has enormous commercial or residential value. Also, clogging existing streets with more parked cars impedes the city's entire transportation and distribution network, another substantial opportunity cost.

The actual price of on-the-street parking P_A, is surely well below the equilibrium price, P_e, as shown in Figure 8.3. Metered rates seldom exceed 25 cents for every 15 minutes and are usually well below that. Compare those prices with the much higher prices at competing parking garages. The market remains in a state of chronic excess demand at the below-equilibrium price, P_A, with Q_D automobiles vying for Q_S spaces. No wonder people have trouble finding a place to park.

Why is the price not at its equilibrium value? Two possibilities come to mind. First, city officials may be pressured by the voters and the merchants to

FIGURE 8.3

The Market for Metered On-the-Street Parking

The market for metered on-the-street parking is in a state of chronic excess demand. The equlibrium parking meter price is P_e, at the intersection of D and $S(MC)$. The actual parking meter price is P_A, well below P_e, because of political pressures to keep the meter prices low and scofflaw behavior. At P_A, the quantity of metered parking spaces demanded is Q_D and the quantity supplied is Q_S. The market is in chronic excess demand in the amount $(Q_D - Q_S)$, and people complain that they cannot find a parking space.

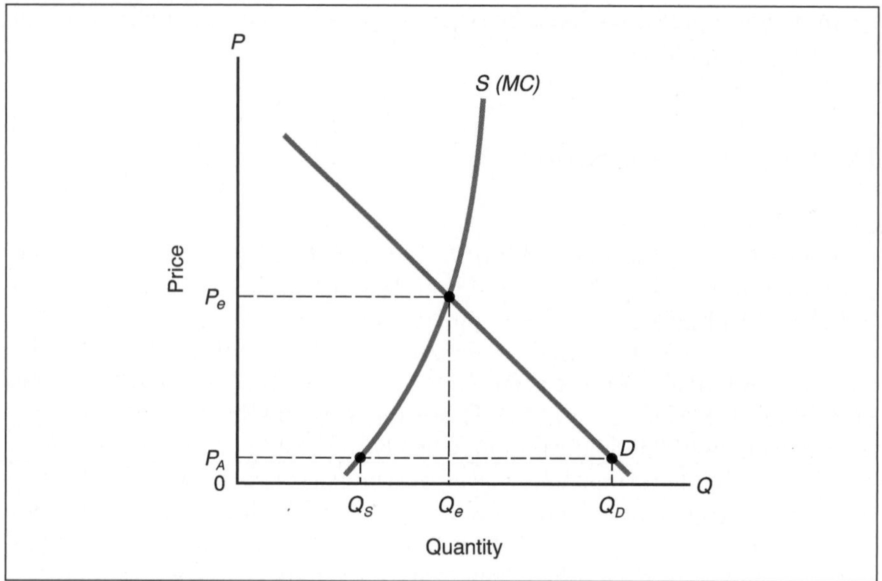

keep the metered rates low. On-the-street parking is designed primarily to serve shoppers on a short-term, high-turnover basis. In many cities feeding meters hour after hour is illegal. Apparently merchants and consumers alike have decided that below-equilibrium meter rates are in their mutual best interests. Second, parking hardly brings out the best civic behavior in people. Many otherwise law-abiding citizens become scofflaws and refuse to feed meters at all. They gamble, betting that the police will fail to notice the expired meter. Consequently, the actual price is below even the metered price. It may well be close to zero in cities where scofflaw behavior is especially prevalent. Set the price in any market near zero, and excess demand inevitably results.

What should cities do about the parking problem? The answer is not at all clear. City officials often mount aggressive campaigns against scofflaws, towing cars and booting the worst offenders. Such efforts do reduce illegal parking by raising the penalty for getting caught, but only at considerable cost to all concerned. And people still park illegally. These campaigns also fail to address the fundamental cause of the problem—the meter price is still far below the equilibrium price. People will continue to complain that there are not enough parking spaces unless officials are willing to raise the prices. Unfortunately, higher meter prices also increase the incentive to gamble. Setting the meter price at P_e does not guarantee that the actual price will rise to P_e, given people's scofflaw tendencies.

Should local officials simply provide the parking spaces that people want? Certainly not. The parking example highlights the folly of trying to supply the quantity demanded at an artificially low price. With reference to Figure 8.3, providing $(Q_D - Q_S)$ additional parking spaces is enormously wasteful. Urban land is so highly valued in alternative uses that providing many more parking spaces beyond Q_e entails far larger costs than almost anyone would be willing to pay. The supply curve lies well above the demand curve in that region.

Sid Caesar put it best: "Parking is such sweet sorrow." Perhaps this is as it must be.

REFLECTION: Sports fans, which would you prefer at play-off time: (1) A market-clearing price for the tickets or (2) the current system in which the ticket price is below the market-clearing price and the tickets are sold either by lottery (NCAA basketball tournament) or on a first come–first served basis (baseball play-offs and World Series)?

The Urban Transportation Mess

On-the-street parking is hardly one of life's pressing problems. But it is indicative of a far greater problem, the entire urban transportation mess that has afflicted cities ever since the ascendancy of the automobile. Everyone has known for a long time that we rely far too much on the automobile, and far too little on bus and rail transit, to move people through our cities.

The typical response has always been a quantity response—build more transportation capacity. At first, in the 1950s, we built highways to accommodate the cars, but demand always outpaced the supply. So in the 1960s and 1970s we turned to mass transit. A number of cities built new rail systems, or refurbished existing systems, all heavily subsidized by the national government. Bus transit also grew, especially as commerce and industry became more dispersed geographically. Rail transit works best when there are only a few central hubs. Despite the increased supply of bus and rail transit, vast numbers of people choose to stay in their cars. Traffic remains choked during the rush hours, both in and around our cities.

Underlying all efforts to improve the urban transportation network is a fundamental pricing problem—the price of automobile travel during the peak rush hours is far below its marginal cost. A major component of that cost is the value of time people lose when they are forced to crawl along congested highways. Unless people are required to pay these congestion costs, they will overuse the automobile and underuse transit no matter how good the transit services. Never underestimate people's love for their cars. Quantity solutions, by themselves, are doomed to fail.

UNFAIR PRICES

Ask consumers which prices are too high, and many would reply: "The price of everything is too high." People are concerned about general price inflation, and they expect that the federal government will act to keep inflation under control. But the concern about rising prices seldom translates into a call for government control of prices in individual markets, at least not in the United States.

Occasionally, though, high prices for the necessities of life—food, clothing, shelter, proper medical care—do arouse a heightened sense of injustice. When the poor have to pay more than 25 percent of their incomes for rent or are forced to go without proper medical care because they cannot affort it, people's faith in the operation of competitive market forces becomes strained. Many petition their governments to lower the price below its natural equilibrium price in order to bring these necessities within reach of the poor. On the other side of the market, suppliers would always like to receive higher prices. If too-low prices are perceived to create special hardships, producers will petition governments to increase the price above the market's equilibrium price. The farmers are an example here.

Price Ceilings and Price Floors

When governments in the United States respond to pressure to change the market price, they usually do not simply dictate a different price. Rather, they

FIGURE 8.4

Price Ceilings and Price Floors

The equilibrium price is P_e, at the intersection of D and S. People who consider the equilibrium price to be too high or too low petition the government to change the price. A price floor, P_F, is a legislated price below which the market price cannot fall. A price floor is set above the equilibrium price. A price ceiling, P_C, is a legislated price above which the market price cannot rise. A price ceiling is set below the equilibrium price.

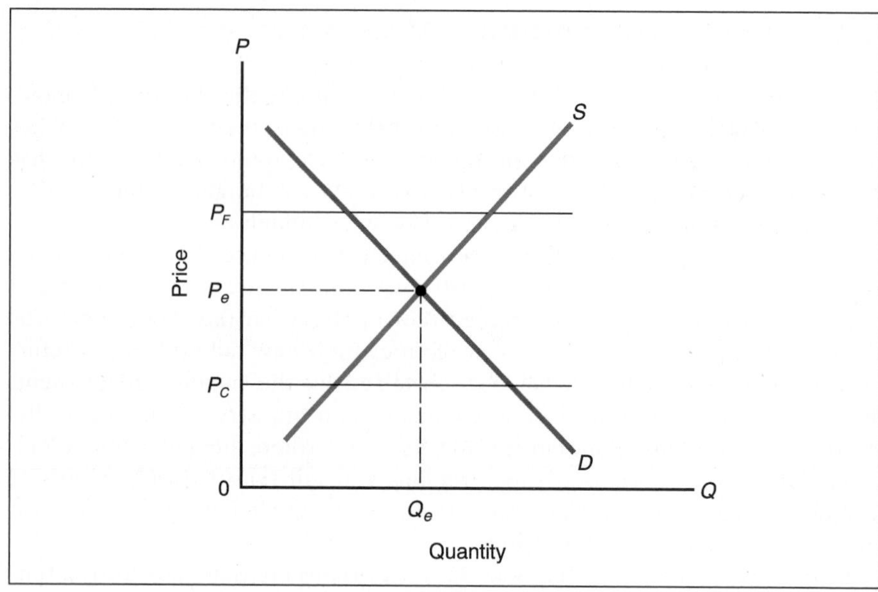

are more likely to impose a legal limit on the allowable range of prices in the form of price ceilings or price floors.

PRICE CEILING

A legislated amount above which the market price is not allowed to rise.

A **price ceiling** is an amount above which the price is not allowed to rise. Refer to Figure 8.4. The natural equilibrium price is at P_e. If P_e is perceived to be too high because it causes hardship for the poor, the government may legislate a price ceiling at P_C. P_C is the legal upper limit on the price. Notice that a price ceiling must be set *below* the equilibrium price to have an effect on a market. If P_C were set above P_e, the market would simply remain at P_e.

Helping the poor by establishing price ceilings on particular goods and services is not common practice in the United States. A few U.S. cities, most notably New York City, have instituted rent controls on apartments on the grounds that the poor are more likely to rent than to own their own homes. But rent control is really the only important ongoing example of a price ceiling in the United States. The United States prefers, instead, to provide direct aid for necessities by means of in-kind transfer payments. Transfers have an advantage over price ceilings in that they can be more easily targeted to poor families. Food stamps, rent subsidies, and subsidized medical care are available only to families and individuals whose incomes fall below certain levels. The nonpoor pay the full price. Other developed market economies have been far more willing to legislate prices for the social necessities. Canada and Great Britain, for example, offer medical care free to all citizens, paid for out of general tax revenues, and many countries make subsidized public housing widely available.

PRICE FLOOR

A legislated amount below which the market price is not allowed to fall.

A **price floor** is an amount below which the price is not allowed to fall. If the equilibrium price, P_e, in Figure 8.4 is perceived by suppliers to be too low, the government may legislate a price floor at P_F. P_F is the legal lower limit on the price. Notice that a price floor must be set *above* the equilibrium price to have an effect on the market. If P_F were set below P_e, the market would simply remain at P_e.

The United States has been more willing to use price floors to protect producers than to use price ceilings to protect consumers. The outstanding example of direct support by means of price floors occurs in agriculture. Grains and dairy products have been subject to price floors since the 1930s, when agricultural prices first fell sharply from parity. The agricultural price support program has been the one constant in a rapidly changing agricultural environment. The United States has also been willing to protect industries subjected to foreign competition by placing tariffs and quotas on imported goods. Tariffs and quotas protect U.S. producers by allowing them to charge U.S. consumers higher prices and are justified primarily as a means of protecting jobs for U.S. workers.

Another important price floor is the federal minimum wage, which has been in effect since 1935. As of 1993 it was set at $4.25 an hour. The minimum wage is designed to protect low-wage workers and their families from falling into poverty.

Let's consider one example of a price ceiling, rent control, and one example of a price floor, the agricultural price supports. Chapter 9 discusses the federal minimum wage and Chapter 39 the effects of tariffs and quotas.

Rent Control

The United States' reluctance to adopt price ceilings is understandable. Any price ceiling substitutes a state of legislated excess demand for the natural market equilibrium, and whether chronic excess demand is to be preferred to the natural equilibrium is always an open question. **Rent control** is a perfect case in point. No one can deny the hardships imposed on poor families when they must pay a large portion of their monthly incomes for rent. But rent control does not eliminate the problem of providing decent rental housing for the poor. By legislating excess demand, rent control merely changes the symptoms of the problem.

RENT CONTROL
A price ceiling on the rents that landlords can charge low-income tenants.

Figure 8.5 illustrates the new set of problems with rent control. The demand and supply curves, *D* and *S*, represent the market for rental apartments sought by low-income families. The equilibrium rent without rent control is R_e, a price that the public feels is more than poor families should have to pay. The city government responds by imposing a price ceiling below R_e at R_C, which now becomes the maximum legal rent for these apartments. The apartments are rent controlled. With rent controls the quantity of apartments demanded increases from Q_e to Q_D, and the quantity of apartments supplied decreases from Q_e to Q_S. The market for the rent-controlled apartments is in chronic excess demand in the amount $(Q_D - Q_S)$.

Who gains and who loses from rent control, and what are its other economic effects? The landlords are clear losers under rent control. The total rents they receive (and tenants pay) drop from $R_e \cdot Q_e$ to $R_C \cdot Q_S$. Someone must lose whenever a market price increases or decreases, but proponents of rent control gladly support a policy that redistributes income from the landlords to low-income tenants through lower rents. Also, rent control boards try to set the rent at a level that brings landlords a fair rate of return. They see themselves as merely preventing excessive rents made possible by the competing commercial, industrial, and residential demand for urban land.

Landlords are not swayed by the argument of the rent control board that R_C provides a "fair" rate of return. They seek the highest return on their investment in the land and buildings, just as all investors do. Once rent control is

FIGURE 8.5

Rent Control for Low-income Apartments

The equilibrium rent for low-income apartments, R_e, at the intersection of D and S, takes a huge chunk of poor families' monthly incomes. Local governments sometimes respond with rent control, creating a different set of problems. The controlled rent R_C increases the quantity of low-income apartments demanded to Q_D and reduces the quantity of low-income apartments supplied to Q_S, generating an excess demand in the amount $(Q_D - Q_S)$. Some of the poor families that the government is trying to help are shut out of these apartments. Rent control causes an efficiency loss of net value equal to the triangular area *abc*.

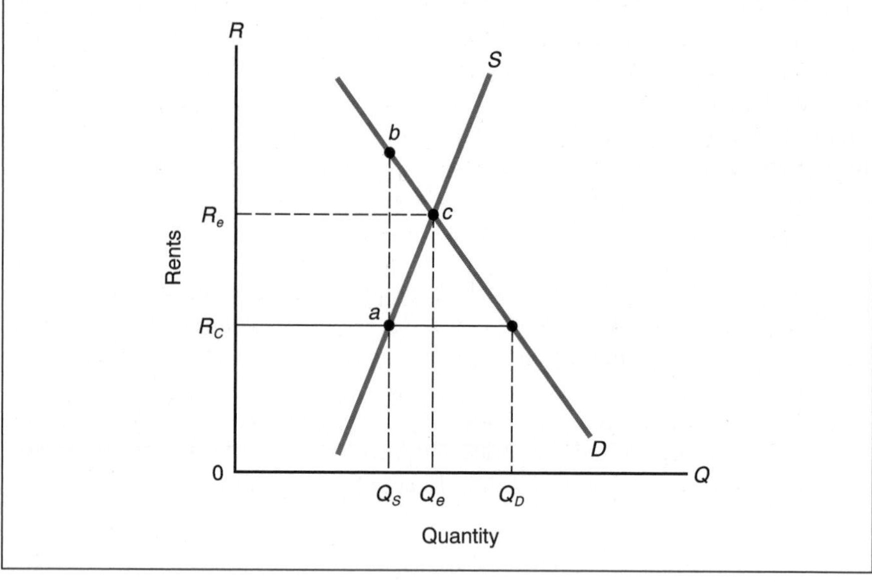

instituted, landlords know that alternative uses of the land bring a higher rate of return, and they want out. The decrease in quantity supplied comes about in one of two forms, either conversions to other types of property or a decline in the quality of existing units. Some landlords convert the apartments to non-controlled cooperative or condominium arrangements or sell out to commercial and industrial developers. If the rent control law restricts the ability to convert, landlords attempt to lower their costs by decreasing maintenance services. By lowering their costs, they can restore the original rate of return on their investment despite receiving lower rents. The maintenance adjustment takes time, as long as 10 years, and throughout this period the quality of the apartment units steadily declines. Hence, even if the number of apartment units were to stay at Q_e, the supply of apartments *of a given quality* would drop below Q_e. Eventually many of these apartments fall below minimal building code standards and are abandoned.

HISTORICAL NOTE: The supply response to rent controls in Cairo, Egypt has had tragic consequences. The rent controlled apartment buildings are so poorly maintained that many simply collapse, killing hundreds of people each year. Some landlords take measures to hasten the collapse of their buildings, because new apartment buildings are not rent controlled. (*The Economist*, October 17, 1992, p. 48).

The decline in the supply of apartments creates a number of problems. One unfortunate problem is that not all low-income renters gain from the rent control, even if we ignore the new market entrants from Q_e to Q_D. Only those families lucky enough to obtain the Q_S remaining units gain. Families numbering $(Q_e - Q_S)$, who used to live in apartments of this quality, are also now shut off from this market. Presumably they are forced into even lower quality housing. Some families may have to double and triple up with relatives and friends. Are the people who are forced out better off than before rent control, when their rents were too high? It is difficult to say. The nature of their housing problem has changed; it certainly has not been resolved.

In addition, the supply response entails an efficiency loss as rent control drives the market below its natural equilibrium quantity, Q_e. Families are willing to pay more for the displaced units $(Q_e - Q_S)$ than it would cost landlords to provide them. But the resources that would normally go to these apartments are diverted to less valued uses under rent control. The loss in net value is represented by the area between the demand and the supply curves from Q_S to Q_e, the triangular area *abc*.

Finally, rent controls create powerful incentives for graft and corruption, as do all price ceilings. In the normal market situation supply is rationed by price: All buyers willing to pay the equilibrium price are able to buy the good. Price ceilings such as rent control replace rationing by price with rationing by some other means. Who determines which of the Q_D demanders get the Q_S apartments? Under standard rent control procedures the available Q_S rent-controlled apartments are supposed to be rationed to low-income families on a first come–first served basis. But all families along the demand curve except the last family at Q_D are willing to pay more than R_C for the apartment. A family will pay any price up to the point on its demand curve. Moreover, the families who are first in line are not necessarily those who are willing to pay the most. Both landlords and potential renters know these facts.

In this situation landlords can easily extract side payments from anxious families willing to pay more than R_C for an apartment in exchange for moving them to the front of the line. The merits of rent control become highly questionable once a system of side payments develops. On the one hand, the poorest families are most likely to be shut out. On the other hand, those families situated on the demand curve above the original market rent, R_e, may actually end up paying more for the apartment under rent control. So even some "lucky" families who get the rent-controlled apartments may be worse off under rent control. They would prefer the natural market equilibrium, with the apartments rationed by price.

Note, finally, that the problems with rent control increase the more elastic demand and supply are, since higher elasticities increase the amount of excess demand. The same general principle applies to all price ceilings. They work best if both demand and supply are highly inelastic.

CURRENT ISSUE: President Clinton wants to extend health care benefits to everyone and at the same time hold down the costs of health care. This will almost certainly require some system of rationing medical care other than by means of price.

THE NEW YORK CITY EXPERIENCE[2] New York City has the oldest and most extensive rent control program in the United States. It is the only city that has imposed controls on rental apartment units continuously since World War II. New York chose to continue the national rent controls imposed by Washington in 1943 as part of an emergency wartime program that controlled the prices of a broad range of goods and services. All other major cities with rent controls waited until the 1960s and 1970s to impose them.

Virtually all rental apartment units in New York have been under some form of rent control since 1973. The city's long experience with rent control has been much as theory would predict:

1. From 1965 through 1980 housing officials estimate that 300,000 apartment units were lost to abandonment, and tens of thousands more to co-op or condominium conversion.
2. Virtually no new rental units were built during that period, except at the luxury end of the market.
3. Vacancy rates on rental units are extremely low. A percentage of the total apartment units in any housing market are always vacant at any given time. People move, or die, and their apartments remain vacant until new tenants move in. An average vacancy rate of 5 percent is generally considered the

[2]The data in this section were taken from testimony before the Subcommittee on Housing and Community Development of the House Committee on Banking, Finance, and Urban Affairs, Ninety-Sixth Congress, February 1980.

rate at which the rental market is excessively tight; renters have great difficulty finding apartments. New York City's vacancy rates on rental units are usually in the 2 to 3 percent range, a sure indication of extreme excess demand.
4. Finally, evidence of extralegal side payments abounds, as when new tenants pay key money for the "privilege" of obtaining keys to their apartments.

The problems with rent control do not necessarily argue against it relative to the free market solution. A situation in which poor people pay a large percentage of their meager incomes for rent is also distressing. One can certainly sympathize with New York's attempts to control rents in the face of large-scale immigration and extremely high land values.

Agricultural Price Supports

The *agricultural price support* programs are the outstanding example of price floors in U.S. product markets. Unfortunately, price floors are every bit the mixed blessing price ceilings are, and for the same reason. They change the symptoms without solving the underlying problem, in this case substituting a state of chronic, legislated excess supply for the market's natural equilibrium.

THE ORIGINAL PRICE SUPPORTS Government price supports began with the establishment of the Commodity Credit Corporation (CCC) in 1933. Using funds supplied to it by Congress, the CCC was authorized to set prices at which it would purchase, and store, all quantities that farmers were unable to sell in the private market. In short order the CCC was supporting the prices of wheat, corn, upland cotton, rice, soybeans, peanuts, sugar, and three storable dairy products, nonfat dry milk, butter, and cheese. The support programs for these products have continued uninterrupted to this day, albeit with modifications.

The support prices are determined as a percentage of parity, typically 75 to 90 percent. So long as the support price is above the natural equilibrium price, the price supports serves as a price floor. Figure 8.6 indicates the effects on a supported market when the price floor is effective.

The demand curve is inelastic, as in our previous agricultural examples. However, this time the supply curve is represented as being fairly elastic, reflecting the more elastic supply responses of agricultural products in the longer run. The longer-run elasticities are relevant here because the price supports have been in existence for such a long time and farmers are confident they will remain in existence.

If left alone, the market would establish an equilibrium at (Q_e, P_e). Judging that the price P_e would spell disaster for too many farmers, the CCC agrees to buy all unsold product at the higher price, P_F. As a result:

1. Farmers refuse to sell any output to private demanders at a price below P_F. Private quantity demanded is thereby limited to Q_D.
2. With a price no lower than P_F guaranteed by the government, farmers produce an amount Q_S. The market is placed in chronic excess supply in the amount of ($Q_S - Q_D$).

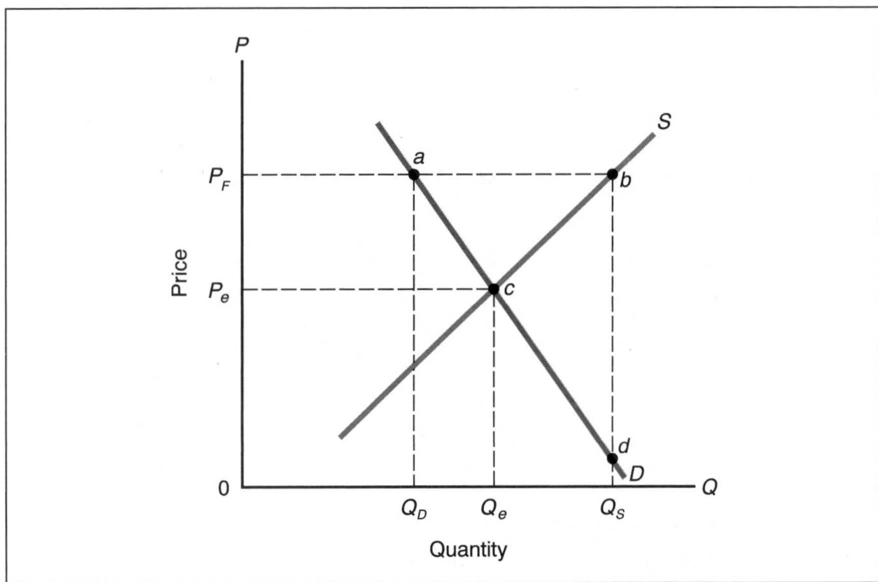

FIGURE 8.6

Agricultural Price Supports

The federal government established a set of price floors, or price supports, for major crops during the Great Depression in response to declining crop prices. The equilibrium quantity and price without the price supports would be Q_e,P_e, at the intersection of D and S. The government support price, P_F, places the market in chronic excess supply. Consumers buy Q_D at a price of P_F and farmers supply Q_S. The government buys, and stores, the excess supply, $(Q_S - Q_D)$, at a cost of $P_F \cdot (Q_S - Q_D)$, equal to the rectangular area abQ_SQ_D. The loss in net value caused by the price supports is the triangular area *cbd*, the area between S and D beyond the natural market equlibrium quantity Q_e.

3. The government ends up buying and storing the excess supply. The cost to the CCC is $P_F \cdot (Q_S - Q_D)$, the rectangular area abQ_SQ_D in Figure 8.6 (and any additional storage costs, not pictured in the figure).

Farmers gain considerably under this program. They are able to sell more output (Q_S versus Q_e) at a higher price (P_F versus P_e). Consumers and taxpayers lose. Do the gains to the farmers more than offset the losses to consumers and taxpayers? The answer is no. The price supports are incredibly wasteful for three reasons.

The first cost is the pure efficiency loss that results from encouraging production beyond the natural equilibrium quantity, Q_e. All units from Q_e to Q_S cost more to produce than anyone is willing to pay for. The resources employed in producing these units are better used elsewhere. The loss in net value is represented by the area between the supply and the demand curves from Q_e to Q_S, the triangular area *cbd*.

Second, what can the government do with the surplus? It cannot sell the surplus on the market without undermining its own price floor unless shifts in either demand or supply temporarily send the equilibrium price well above the support price. Dumping the product on foreign markets is also unattractive. It would surely bring protests from abroad. Some of the surplus can be used to provide lunches for schoolchildren and to carry out other such acts of public charity. But none of these uses is subject to the direct approval of taxpayers. As a result, many citizens might well consider the entire taxpayer costs of the program a complete waste of resources—tax dollars literally thrown away.

Third, the government must place trade restrictions on foreign imports that raise their effective prices to the price floor. Otherwise, foreign suppliers could undercut the support price with sales to U.S. consumers. These trade restrictions waste additional resources by substituting high-cost U.S. supplies for low-cost foreign supplies. Sugar is the classic example. Price supports and trade

FIGURE 8.7

Target Prices and Deficiency Payments

The federal government added a second price floor for major crops in 1973 in the form of a target price. Farmers are guaranteed a target price, P_T, and they supply Q_S at the target price. All the quantity supplied is sold on the private market. The market price must fall to P_1 to induce consumers to buy the quantity Q_S. The government then pays the farmers the difference between the target price P_T and the market price P_1 for the output sold. The "deficiency payment" is $(P_T - P_1) \cdot Q_S$, equal to the rectangular area $P_T bc P_1$. The government does not buy and store crops under this program, but the target price still causes a loss in net value equal to the triangular area *abc*.

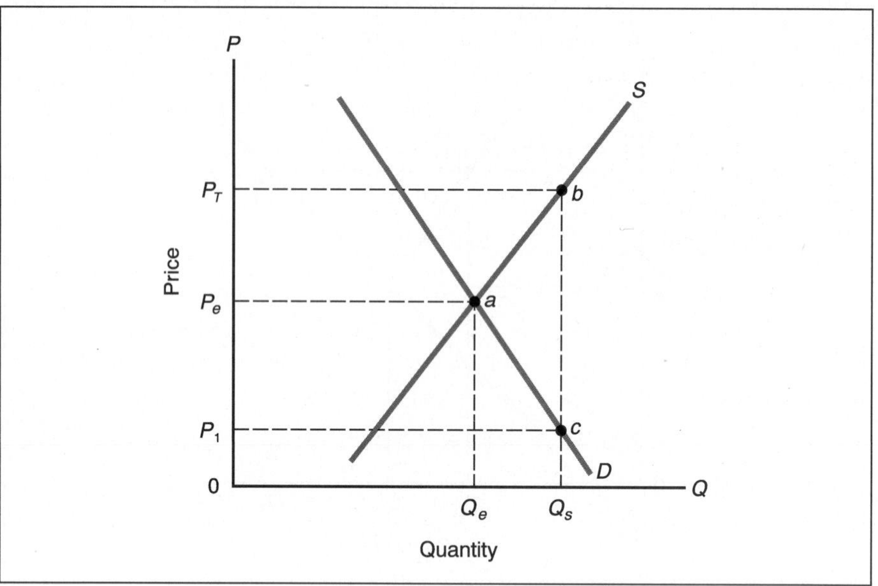

restrictions keep the price of sugar in the United States three to four times higher than its price on world markets.

TARGET PRICES AND DEFICIENCY PAYMENTS The price support system became more complex in 1973 with the introduction of a new target price–deficiency payment scheme. Under this program the USDA sets target prices for each product. The farmers sell all their output on the private market. If the equilibrium price is less than the target price, the government pays farmers the difference between the target price and the market price.

The operation of this system is depicted in Figure 8.7. The target price is P_T. Assured of the target price, farmers produce Q_S. Consumers are only willing to purchase Q_S at a price of P_1, so the market price falls to P_1. The government pays farmers the difference between P_T and P_1 on all output sold, the deficiency payment. In Figure 8.7 the total deficiency payments equal the rectangular area $P_T bc P_1$.

The target price–deficiency payment scheme has four advantages over the traditional price support program, even if farm output is the same under either program. First, the government does not end up storing any output. Second, consumers as well as producers gain because the price to them drops from P_e to P_1. Third, with the price on the free market lowered to P_1, U.S. farmers are better able to compete in the important price-elastic export market. Finally, waste is reduced. This program avoids the wastes associated with storing produce and raising import prices. The losses are confined to the loss in net value from producing and consuming beyond the natural market equilibrium of Q_e, area *abc*. What individuals appear to gain as producers and consumers they more than lose as taxpayers. The taxpayer cost of the deficiency payments (area $P_T bc P_1$) exceeds the combined gains in consumer surplus (area $P_e ac P_1$) and producer surplus (area $P_e ab P_T$).

THE CURRENT HYBRID PROGRAM When the government instituted the target price–deficiency payment scheme, it did not replace the original price support system. Both programs remain in effect. The target price is set above the old support price, and deficiency payments are limited to the difference between the target price and the support price.

As a result of the limitation on the deficiency payment, the support price serves as an absolute price floor on the free market price. If the natural forces of supply and demand drive the market price significantly below the support price, farmers sell to the government at the support price rather than to private demanders at the free market price. The government stores its purchases, just as under the original program. In fact, agricultural markets were so weak throughout the 1980s that government stocks of grains and dairy products have increased substantially under this hybrid support program.

DISTRIBUTIONAL IMPLICATIONS The overriding goal of these complex price support mechanisms is distributional, to support sagging farm incomes whenever prices fall far below parity. Whether price supports available to all farmers serve this purpose well is debatable for two reasons. First, not all farmers need income support. As noted earlier, the average income of families on the large commercial farms, those that supply the majority of the nation's agricultural output, are above the average of all nonfarm families. The two classes of farms in trouble are some commercial farms that went heavily into debt in the late 1970s and early 1980s and the small farms whose families receive the majority of their income from nonfarm sources. Second, price supports available to all farmers cannot possibly target support only to the low-income farm families. Just the opposite occurs. Since price supports tie the subsidies to the amount of output produced, the larger, more efficient farmers must inevitably receive the lion's share of the support payments. Once again, economists favor general tax-transfer schemes that target transfers specifically to the poor and are independent of production.

The price support programs could be viewed as a stabilization device in which the government acts to keep the price near its long-run equilibrium price in the face of short-run instabilities. While this is a possible justification, it is clearly only a secondary consideration in the agricultural programs. Stabilization schemes require that the support price be set at the long-run equilibrium price. However, the target prices are set well above the long-run equilibrium, as were the support prices before them. Parity as experienced in 1914, not the steadily declining long-run equilibrium prices, is the implied target. The primary motive is clearly distributional.

RECENT EXPERIENCE UNDER PRICE SUPPORTS Recent experience with the USDA's price support programs is closely in line with theoretical expectations. This is hardly surprising—competitive markets are quite predictable. The principal effects of these programs are the following:

1. The combination of high target prices, elastic supply in the long run, and the natural downward long-run trend of agricultural prices has created an enormous farm support program. The CCC expenditures peaked at $25.9 billion in 1986, when crop prices were extremely low. CCC expenditures have been on the order of $10 billion during the 1990s.

2. Agriculture is awash in excess supply. The USDA estimates that excess capacity in corn, wheat, and rice is one-third of annual production and that dairy farmers typically produce 12 billion pounds of dairy products beyond what private demand will absorb. In order to curb the excess supply, crop farmers receiving deficiency payments are required to keep a percentage of their acreage out of production. Dairy farmers are paid to slaughter livestock. The idea in each instance is to shift the supply curve back so that the target price becomes the market's natural equilibrium.

   The USDA concedes that acreage restriction as not been successful in reducing grain output, despite huge acreage reductions. By 1983 U.S. farmers had idled more land than the total amount of land devoted to crops in all of Western Europe. The restrictions fail because farmers retire their least productive land and shift the resources formerly used there to the land still under production. Their behavior is hardly surprising, given the strong incentive to produce at the inflated target price. Also, many of the largest and most efficient farmers forego the deficiency payments entirely, choosing instead to plant all their land and sell at the free market price. The efficient farms clearly do not need the target price supports.

   High support prices also put U.S. farmers at a competitive disadvantage in foreign markets, which only increases the excess supply.
3. The price support programs, combined with the trade restrictions necessary to make them stick, generate serious inefficiencies. Government estimates place the combined net loses on all support programs at $4.4 to $6.5 billion.
4. Farm aid is not effectively targeted to the farms with low incomes. Fully one-third of the aid goes to commercial farms with sales in excess of $250,000, only about 4 percent of all farms. The smallest farmers, those with annual sales of $40,000 or less, receive less than 10 percent of the farm aid.

The Clinton administration will have to decide whether price supports are really the best way to help struggling farmers.

THE ECONOMIC EFFECTS OF TAXATION

Quick, name a product or factor of production that is not taxed. That is a difficult challenge. Faced with tax revenue requirements of approximately $2 trillion each year, the federal, state, and local governments of the United States have managed to tax just about everything.

Taxes distort competitive markets by forcing markets away from their natural equilibrium. Unlike the case of price controls, however, changing a market's equilibrium is not usually the primary goal of tax policy. All the major taxes are levied primarily to raise revenue. As a secondary goal, taxes may also be designed to discourage or encourage certain types of activity such as cigarette smoking or to change the distribution of purchasing power among certain groups of people. Only occasionally, though, do governments levy a tax for the sole purpose of influencing behavior in individual markets. Nonetheless, all taxes, whatever their purpose, do distort individual markets, and the market effects of taxation have important economic consequences.

Economists have a natural interest in the efficiency and distributional consequences of tax-induced market distortions. Understanding how taxes affect markets is crucial in this regard, because *the precise way that markets react to taxation determines both the efficiency and the equity implications of any tax.* An economic analysis of a tax without reference to the market setting in which it appears is quite literally useless.

Income taxes levied on factors of production are far more important in the United States than are sales and individual excise taxes levied on products. This is true in most developed market economies. But since the examples in this chapter are all taken from individual product markets, we will use the individual excise tax to illustrate the economic effects of taxation. Fortunately, the choice of which tax to analyze is of no consequence because the general principles to be developed in this section apply to all taxes.

An *excise tax* is a tax levied on the sale of a product, paid by the producers. That is, the producers are required to send a check covering the tax liability to the government. Excise taxes are designed as either per unit or ad valorem levies. A *per unit tax* collects a given amount of revenue on each unit sold, for instance, \$.20 per gallon of gasoline or \$.50 per pack of cigarettes. An *ad valorem tax* collects a percentage of the sales price, such as a 5 percent tax on restaurant meals or hotel rooms. A *sales tax* is an ad valorem tax covering a broad set of products, usually taxing the sale of each product at the same rate. Excise and sales taxes are the primary revenue sources of the state governments.

We will use a per unit excise tax for our example. A per unit tax is easier to analyze using supply and demand diagrams than is an ad valorem tax, and the underlying principles are identical for both kinds of taxes.

The Market's Reaction to Taxation

Figure 8.8 illustrates how a competitive market reacts to an excise tax on some product. Suppose that the product is not taxed initially. The market demand and the market supply curves without any tax are D and S, and the no-tax equilibrium is (Q_e, P_e). The government then levies a \$1 per unit excise tax on the sale of the product, to be paid by the producers.

Since the producers pay the tax, they are the ones that react first to the tax. They now require \$1 more to supply a given unit of output because the marginal cost of supplying each unit has risen by the amount of the tax. For example, they were previously willing to supply Q_e at a price of P_e. They now require a price of $(P_e + \$1)$ to supply Q_e. The same is true for all quantities: The market supply curve shifts up everywhere by exactly \$1, from S to S'. The market establishes a new equilibrium at (Q_T, P_{gt}), the intersection of D and S'. Firms receive revenues of $P_{gt} \cdot Q_T$ from their sales to consumers, but they must send \$1 on each unit sold to the government. The total tax revenue collected by the government is $\$1 \cdot Q_T$. The tax revenue is equal to the area of rectangle $P_{gt}abP_{nt}$, whose height, ab, is \$1 and whose base is Q_T.

Notice that the tax drives a wedge between the prices faced by consumers and firms. The relevant price from the consumers' point of view is the actual market price, P_{gt}, commonly called the **gross-of-tax price** because it includes the tax. The effective price from the firms' point of view is P_{nt}, the so-called **net-of-tax price.** The net-of-tax price, P_{nt}, reflects the fact that firms must send \$1 received on each unit to the government, so that only P_{nt} is available

GROSS-OF-TAX PRICE
The price including the tax, which is the price that the consumers pay under an excise or sales tax.

NET-OF-TAX PRICE
The price excluding the tax, which is the price that producers receive to cover their costs under an excise or sales tax.

FIGURE 8.8

The Market Response to a \$1 Per Unit Excise Tax

The equilibrium quantity and price before the tax is $Q_e P_e$, at the intersection of D and S. A \$1 per unit excise tax shifts the market supply curve up by \$1 from S to S' because the firms' marginal costs have increased by \$1 at every output. The equilibrium quantity and price with the tax is Q_T, P_{gt}, at the intersection of D and S'. P_{gt} is the gross-of-tax price, the market price paid by the consumers. P_{nt} is the net-of-tax price, the price received by the firms after paying the \$1 tax. $P_{gt} - P_{nt} =$ \$1. The government tax revenue is $\$1 \cdot Q_T$, equal to the rectangular area $P_{gt}abP_{nt}$. The tax burden is shared by consumers and producers. Consumers lose because the price to them rises from P_e to P_{gt}. Producers lose because the price to them falls from P_e to P_{nt}. The tax causes a dead weight loss in net value equal to the triangular area *abc*, the area between D and S from Q_T to Q_e.

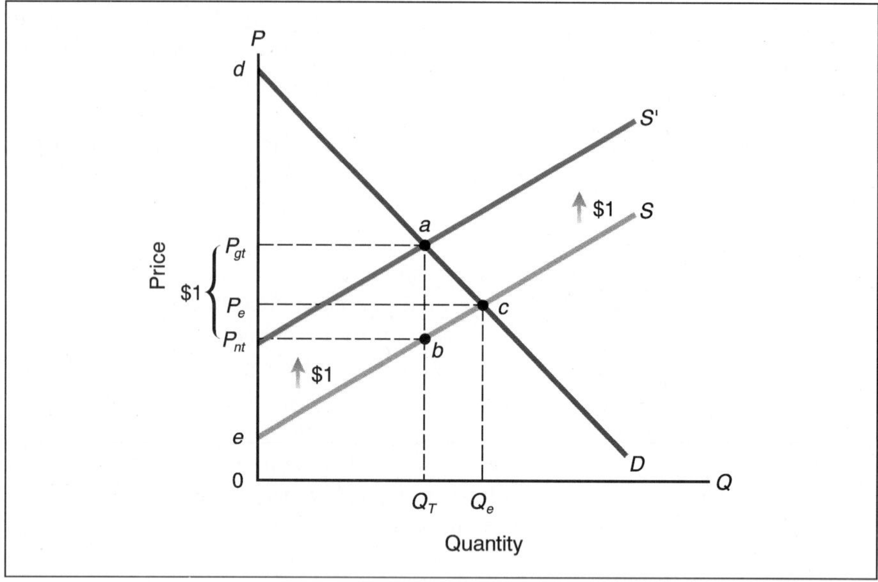

to them to cover their costs of production. The difference between the gross- and net-of-tax prices is always the amount of the tax per unit, \$1 in our example.

$$P_{gt} = P_{nt} + \text{tax} = P_{nt} + \$1$$

The Distributional Implications of Taxation

IMPACT OF A TAX

Refers to the levying of the tax; that is, who actually writes the tax check to the government.

INCIDENCE OF A TAX

Refers to the true burden of the tax; that is, how the burden of the tax is split between demanders and suppliers.

Who bears the burden of the tax? In answering this question, economists distinguish between the impact and the incidence of the tax. The **impact** of the tax refers to the levying of the tax, who actually writes the tax check to the government. In our example the excise tax is levied on the firms, as is true for all excise and sales taxes. The firms bear the impact of the tax. The **incidence** of the tax refers to the true burden of the tax, which depends on how the market splits the burden between suppliers and demanders. The sharing of the tax burden is the question of ultimate interest, and it has *nothing* to do with the impact of the tax, that is, whom the legislature chooses to tax. Instead, the incidence depends *entirely* on how the market reacts to the tax. Few principles of economics are less well understood by the general public.

As drawn in Figure 8.8, consumers and producers share the burden of the \$1 tax. Consumers lose because the effective price to them rises from P_e to P_{gt}. Producers lose, too, because the market price does not rise by the full amount of the tax. The new market price, P_{gt}, is \$1 above P_{nt} and therefore less than \$1 above P_e. The effective price from the firms' perspective falls from P_e to P_{nt}.

The incidence of the tax can be represented as losses in consumer surplus and producer surplus. In the original no-tax equilibrium consumers used to receive a consumer surplus equal to the triangular area dP_ec below the demand curve and above P_e. After the tax their consumer surplus is only $dP_{gt}a$. Firms originally enjoyed a producer surplus equal to the triangular area eP_ec above the original supply curve, *S*, and below P_e. After the tax their producer surplus is only $eP_{nt}b$.

The split in tax burden between consumers and firms appears to be roughly equal, but this is only because of the particular shapes of the demand and supply curves in Figure 8.8. In general, the incidence of a tax depends on the relative elasticities of demand and supply. The principle is this: *The more inelastic demand is relative to supply, the more the burden of a tax falls on the demanders.* Conversely, *the more elastic demand is relative to supply, the more the burden of a tax falls on the suppliers.* In other words, the side of the market that responds relatively less to changes in price tends to get stung by a tax.

The principle is most easily seen by considering the extreme cases. Suppose, first, that demand is perfectly inelastic, as in Figure 8.9(a). Consumers do not respond at all to price changes. As before, the tax shifts the supply curve up by $1, from *S* to *S′*. This time, however, the market price rises by the full amount of the tax. The effective price to consumers, P_{gt}, is $1 above P_e. The effective price to the firms, P_{nt}, remains at P_e. Consumers bear the full burden of the tax. An excise or sales tax on table salt would be a reasonably good example of this case.

Producers bear the full tax burden if the supply curve is perfectly inelastic, as in Figure 8.9(b). Shifting up a vertical supply curve by $1 leaves it unchanged because *S* and *S′* coincide. The market price, P_{gt}, remains at P_e, and the price net-of-tax received by the suppliers falls by $1. Think of the auction of a single painting as an example. Suppose that the government suddenly announces a 20 percent tax on the proceeds of the sale as the auction is proceeding. The announcement has no effect on the auction because the amount that the highest bidder is willing to pay remains the same. The tax just reduces the seller's income by 20 percent.

FIGURE 8.9

Tax Incidence and Inefficiency: The Extreme Cases

Consumers bear the entire burden of an excise tax when demand is perfectly inelastic. In Figure 8.9(a), the market price rises by $1 from P_e to P_{gt} as the supply curve shifts from *S* to *S′* in response to the $1 tax. The net-of-tax price to the firms, P_{nt}, remains at P_e. Conversely, producers bear the entire burden of an excise tax when supply is perfectly inelastic. In Figure 8.9(b), the tax cannot shift the vertical supply curve; *S* and *S′* are identical. The market price to consumers, P_{gt}, remains at P_e, and the net-of-tax price to the firms, P_{nt}, falls by $1. Firms cannot pass any of the tax burden on to the consumers by charging a higher price. There is no dead weight loss in net value in either case, because the equilibrium output does not change in response to the tax.

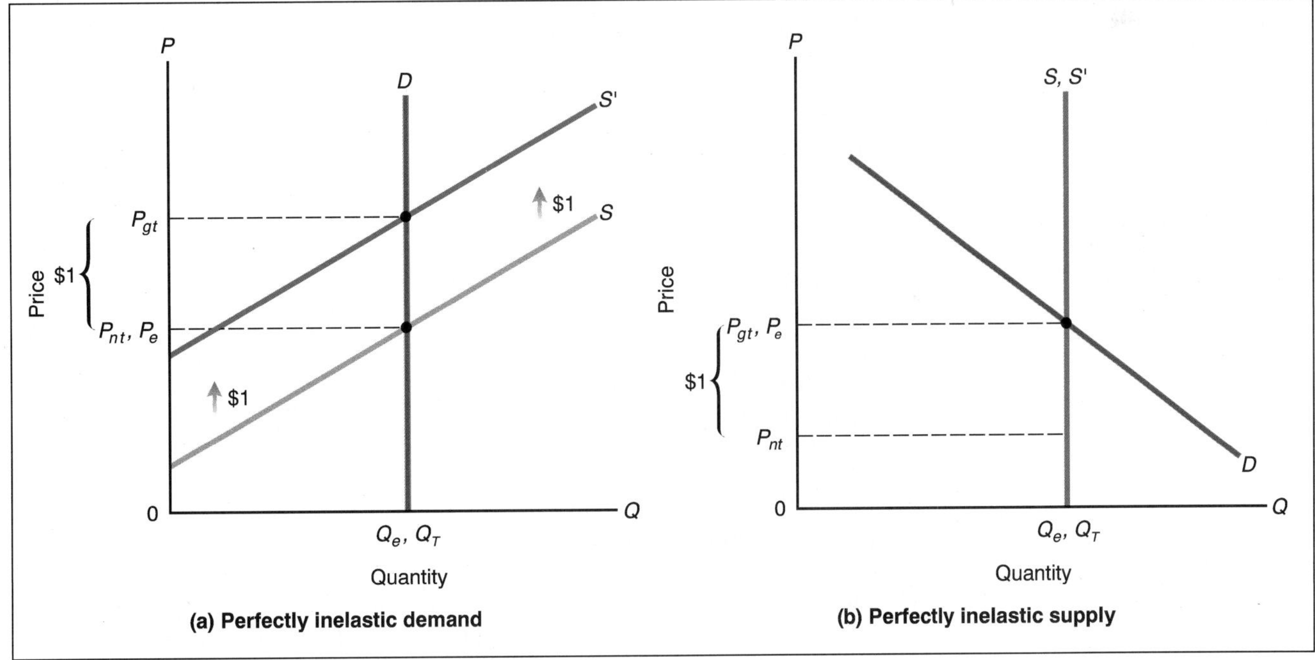

(a) Perfectly inelastic demand

(b) Perfectly inelastic supply

Confusions About Tax Incidence

People are often confused by the true incidence of a tax. One of the most common mistakes is equating impact with incidence: Because I write the check to the government, I must bear the full burden of the tax. This is not true, of course. We have just seen that firms bear no burden at all from an excise tax if demand is perfectly inelastic, even though firms write the check to the government.

The opposite error typically occurs with sales and excise taxes. Consumers often believe that they bear the full burden of these taxes because of the way in which bills of sale are written. Here is a familiar example. Suppose that you enjoy a $10 meal at your favorite restaurant on December 31, one day before a new 5 percent state meals tax goes into effect. You return to the restaurant on June 1 next year and have the same meal. Suppose that the meal still costs $10. Now, however, your check includes one more line for the 5 percent meals tax. The tax is $.50, and the final cost of the meal is $10.50. You certainly appear to bear the burden of the tax. Consumers always appear to bear sales and excise tax burdens, since these taxes are simply added on at the bottom of any bill of sale.

The bills of sales are misleading, however, because they fail to report a crucial, and hypothetical, piece of information: What would the price of the meal have been on June 1 had there been no tax? Suppose that the restaurant's costs have risen over the six-month period, so that the owners need $10.25 in June to make the same profit on your meal that they made at a price of $10 on December 31. By charging you only $10, they are bearing part of the tax burden.

If their costs have risen, why would the owners not raise the price to $10.25, plus the 5 percent tax? The answer is that the demand may not be sufficient to support that strategy. For instance, if the firms depicted in Figure 8.8 tried to keep their prices $1 above P_e, the market would be in excess supply. The Laws of Supply and Demand would quickly drive the price down to P_{gt}, as drawn. P_e is that hypothetical price that we need to know, but cannot know once a product is taxed.

Firms will always *try* to pass on the full amount of the tax. Their attempt is represented in Figure 8.8 by the $1 shift in the supply curve from S to S'. Whether they succeed or not depends on the relative supply and demand elasticities. The same is true of the restaurant owners. Given the state of demand, $10 plus the tax may be the profit-maximizing price, not $10.25 plus the tax.

In summary, all a bill of sale ever shows is the difference between the gross- and net-of-tax prices, which is always equal to the amount of the tax. The line on the bill before the tax is P_{nt}, and the final line on the bill after the tax is P_{gt}. But a bill of sale does not indicate how the market has reacted to the tax and, therefore, who bears the incidence of the tax. It does not tell us what the price would have been without the tax.

Impact Irrelevance

The limiting cases of perfectly inelastic demand or supply highlight a final point about tax incidence that is widely misunderstood: The impact of a tax is irrelevant to the burden of the tax. The tax incidence, or burden, is the same whether the legislature chooses to tax the suppliers or the demanders in a market. To see why, return to the example of auctioning a painting in which the seller bears the entire burden of a 20 percent tax on the proceeds of the auction. Suppose, instead, that the buyers had to pay the tax. In that case all bidders would simply lower their bids by 20 percent, so that the winning bid would be 20 percent lower. After paying the tax, the winning bidder is no worse off than without the tax. The supplier, however, receives 20 percent less revenue, which is exactly what happens when the supplier pays the tax. Demand and supply elasticities, not legislatures, determine who bears the burden of a tax.

The principle of impact irrelevance requires one qualification. Some goals of tax policy are easier to achieve by taxing suppliers or demanders. For instance, a sales tax on firms is much easier to administer than is a similar tax levied on the consumers. Also, protecting low-income people from undue tax burdens is much more easily accomplished with taxes levied on individuals than with taxes levied on firms. In principle, though, taxes on either side of the market can be designed to achieve identical results.

The Efficiency Implications of Taxation

The same efficiency principle that applies to government price controls applies to taxes. *Any government intervention into a market that forces a market away from its natural equilibrium quantity,* Q_e, *entails an efficiency loss.* In the case of taxes, the net value received by demanders and suppliers declines by more than the tax revenue collected by the government.

The efficiency loss is represented by the triangular area *abc* in Figure 8.8. Consumers' and producers' combined losses of consumer surplus and profit as a result of the tax are equal to the area $P_{gt}acbP_{nt}$. Some of their losses represent a transfer of purchasing power to the government as tax revenues, the rectangular area $P_{gt}abP_{nt}$. But no one recovers the area *abc*, the area between the demand and the supply curves between Q_T and Q_e. It represents a pure dead weight loss, the result of removing units of output whose value to consumers exceeds the cost of producing them. The resources freed up by the tax move into less valued uses.

Demand and supply elasticities are as important to determining the amount of efficiency loss of a tax as they are to pinning down tax incidence. Higher elasticities tend to produce larger changes in the equilibrium quantity. Therefore, as a general principle: *The more elastic the market demand and the market supply curves, the larger the efficiency loss for any given amount of tax revenue collected.*

Once again the extreme cases are instructive. When demand or supply is perfectly inelastic, as in Figure 8.9, the equilibrium quantity does not change. Consequently, the entire loss of consumer surplus [Figure 8.9(a)] or producer surplus [Figure 8.9(b)] is captured by the government as tax revenue. There is no pure dead weight loss, only a transfer from the household or business sector to the government sector.

The Efficiency/Equity Trade-Off

Efficiency and equity can work at cross-purposes in designing tax policy. For instance, states wrestle with efficiency/equity trade-offs when deciding whether food purchased in grocery stores for home consumption should be included in the sales tax base. The demand for such food is highly inelastic. Taxing it would raise large amounts of revenue with relatively low efficiency losses. At the same time, however, the low demand elasticity guarantees that consumers would bear most of the burden of the tax. Since poor families spend a higher percentage of their incomes on food than do nonpoor families, the burden of the tax would fall disproportionately on the poor. Most people find this unattractive from an equity standpoint.

The unattractive equity implications often carry the day among state legislatures. Many states have chosen to pass up an easy and efficient source of revenue by exempting food for home consumption from their sales taxes.

SUMMARY

The first section of Chapter 8 analyzed the agricultural sector of the economy, the most highly competitive sector in the U.S. economy. The analysis reached two principal conclusions about the prices of agricultural commodities, one relating to prices in the long run and one relating to prices in the short run.

1. Prices of agricultural commodities have been falling steadily throughout the twentieth century (relative to prices generally) because productivity increases have increased supply faster than demand has been increasing. The price declines have been large because the market demand curve is highly inelastic.
2. The prices of agricultural commodities are highly volatile in the short run because good and bad weather shifts the market supply curve along a highly inelastic demand curve. Farm incomes follow the pattern of prices because demand is inelastic. Prices and total farm income both decrease when the weather is good and supply increases, and they both increase when the weather is bad and supply decreases.

The last three sections of Chapter 8 considered three problems that can afflict even highly competitive markets: markets do not clear; the equilibrium prices are considered to be unfair; and taxes.

3. On-the-street parking in cities is an example of a market that does not clear. The price of metered parking is well below the equilibrium, so the market remains in a state of chronic excess demand and people have difficulty finding a place to park. The solution of building more parking spaces to meet the quantity demanded at the metered prices would be a terrible waste of resources. The best solution would be to raise the price to its equilibrium level, but this is difficult to do.
4. People complain that particular prices are unfair, either too high or too low, in the sense that they place an undue burden on the poor. Governments in the United States sometimes respond to these complaints with price ceilings and price floors. A price ceiling is an amount above which the market price cannot rise. A price floor is an amount below which the market price cannot fall. Price ceilings and price floors substitute legislated excess demand and excess supply, respectively, for the natural market equilibrium. Whether they are preferred to the natural equilibrium is an open question.
5. Rent control is an example of a price ceiling. The intent is to help low-income families find affordable rental housing. But rent control has a num-

ber of undesirable effects. It lowers the supply of available housing, shuts out some of the deserving poor from the rent-controlled housing market, encourages graft and corruption at the expense of the tenants, and causes an efficiency loss by decreasing the amount of net value in the housing market.

6. The agricultural price supports started during the Great Depression of the 1930s are an example of a price floor. Their intent is to support the incomes of poor farmers and stabilize crop prices, but they also have a number of undesirable effects. The price supports generate chronic excess supply, reduce the competitiveness of U.S. farmers in foreign markets, and funnel much of the farm aid to the wealthiest farmers.
7. A tax forces a market away from its natural equilibrium. Excise taxes raise the price to consumers, lower the effective price received by firms, and decrease the equilibrium quantity. The side of the market that is relatively more price inelastic bears more of the burden of the tax. Taxes cause an efficiency loss by decreasing the amount of net value in a market, and the amount of loss rises the more the equilibrium quantity responds to the tax. Taxes on products that have highly inelastic demands are good on efficiency grounds, but can be bad on equity grounds. The loss in net value is small with inelastic demand, but the burden of the tax is easily passed on to consumers, especially consumers with low incomes.

KEY TERMS

impact of a tax
incidence of a tax
parity
price ceiling
price floor

QUESTIONS

1. What attributes of the demand and the supply for agricultural produce have contributed to the steady decline in parity?
2. How do you explain the huge increase in the supply of agricultural products in the United States since World War II despite the large migration of people off the farms and into urban areas?
3. Why is good weather not necessarily "good" for all farmers? How does your answer depend on the price elasticity of demand?
4. The direct costs of creating an on-the-street parking space are not very high. All you have to do is to paint some lines and install a parking meter. Yet the supply curve for metered parking spaces is very steep in the central city. How do you explain this?
5. What are the arguments in favor of rent control for low-income housing? What kind of problems does it cause? Do you favor rent control for low-income housing?
6. "The attractiveness of price ceilings or price floors depends in part on the elasticities of supply and demand." Demonstrate the truth of this statement.
7. Compare and contrast
   a. the original agricultural price support scheme, in which the government buys crops at the price floor; and
   b. the target price scheme, in which the government lets the market price prevail and gives the farmers cash grants.

   Who gains, who loses, and what are the efficiency implications of each type of price floor?
8. Many people have long supported very high taxes on cigarettes to discourage people from smoking. Do you think that the burden of a high cigarette tax is likely to fall more on the smokers or on the cigarette manufacturers, or to be shared somewhat equally between them? Why?
9. a. For a given amount of tax revenue collected, how is efficiency loss related to the elasticities of demand and supply?
   b. Give an example of a product that, if taxed, would lead to a low efficiency loss and another example of a product that, if taxed, would lead to a high efficiency loss. Explain your choices.
10. "The market, and not the legislature, ultimately determines who bears the burden of tax." Discuss the truth of this statement.
11. (Extra Credit) The market for a certain product is such that there is no demand when price is equal to $20 and no supply when price is equal to $1. The initial equilib-

rium in the market is reached when price is $5 and quantity exchanged is 20 (in other words, the demand curve cuts the vertical axis at price equals 20, the supply curve cuts it a price equals 1, and the two curves intersect at price equals 5 and quantity equals 20). Illustrate this market using demand and supply curves. (Assume both curves are straight lines.)

a. Suppose that the government imposes a $2 per unit excise tax on the sale of the product and the new equilibrium quantity is 15 at a price of $6. Illustrate this new equilibrium.
b. What are the gross-of-tax and the net-of-tax prices at the new equilibrium?
c. Who appears to bear more of the burden of the tax, consumers or producers?
d. Does the tax cause any loss of economic efficiency?

CHAPTER

9

Supply and Demand in Competitive Labor Markets

LEARNING OBJECTIVES

CONCEPTS TO LEARN

- The supply of labor
- The demand for labor
- The profit-maximizing decision rule for hiring labor
- How competitive markets help determine the distribution of wage and salary income
- Competition as the great equalizer in economic affairs
- The economic effects of the federal minimum wage

CONCEPTS TO RECALL

- Opportunity cost [1]
- Equality of opportunity [2]
- Horizontal equity [2]
- The margin in economic analysis [2]
- Substitution and income effects [5]
- The Laws of Supply and Demand [5, 6, 7]
- The marginal product of labor [6]

Chapters 5 through 8 considered the Laws of Supply and Demand as they apply to product markets, the top half of the circular flow of economic activity. Chapter 9 shifts the focus of attention to factor markets, the bottom half of the circular flow.

The markets for the primary factors of production—labor, capital, and land—are vitally important to resolving the four fundamental economic questions. The prices determined in factor markets guide business firms to an efficient resolution of the How *question. Firms conserve on their use of relatively expensive (scarce) inputs in favor of relatively cheap (abundant) inputs, exactly as required for the efficient use of society's scarce resources. Factor prices are also directly involved in resolving the* For Whom *question. The amounts of income that people earn in a market economy depend on the quantity and quality of the resources they possess* and *on the prices that these resources command in the factor markets. The incomes people earn then feed directly into the* What *question. Consumers with relatively high incomes have more dollar "votes" in determining what goods and services business firms will produce; consumers with relatively low incomes have fewer dollar "votes." Finally, factor prices help determine the rate of economic growth, the* Now versus the Future *question. The level of interest rates throughout the economy influences both the amount individuals want to save and the amount firms want to invest. As we saw in Chapter 3, the volume of saving and investment has a marked impact on long-run economic growth. Also, individuals have a natural incentive to provide more of the high-priced, highly valued resources and fewer of the low-priced, less valued resources. This, too, increases the economy's production possibilities over time.*

In everyday language we do not refer to wages and salaries, interest rates on savings deposits and loans, and rents paid to landlords as "prices," but they are prices just the same. Wages are the prices at which firms purchase labor from individuals. Interest rates are the prices at which money is exchanged between lenders and borrowers. Similarly, land and building rents are the prices that households and firms pay owners for the use of these resources. Furthermore, if factor markets are competitive, these factor prices are determined by the Laws of Supply and Demand, just as the prices of goods and services are determined by the Laws of Supply and Demand in competitive product markets. The only difference is that the roles of supplier and demander are reversed. In factor markets the individuals are the suppliers, and the business firms are the demanders.

Chapter 9 concludes the five-chapter section on Supply and Demand with an analysis of competitive labor markets. The markets for capital and land are covered in Chapters 20 and 21, as part of the consideration of factor markets and the distribution of income in the United States.

We will assume throughout Chapter 9 that the conditions required for the Laws of Supply and Demand to operate all hold. They are the same conditions that are required for competitive product markets: (1) large numbers of buyers and sellers in a given labor market; (2) homogeneous labor from the perspective of the buyer, that is, any number of workers would be equally productive to a firm; (3) accurate information about wages and market conditions that is available to everyone; and (4) easy entry into and exit from a market by both suppliers and demanders. Under these conditions no one individual or firm has any control over the market wage; everyone is a price taker. In addition, no one on either side of the market can gain a lasting, unfair advantage over anyone else.

We begin by analyzing how the Laws of Supply and Demand determine wages and employment in a single labor market, or occupation.

THE SUPPLY AND DEMAND FOR LABOR

The Supply of Labor

How much labor will be supplied to a given labor market at different wages, other things equal? In answering this question, let's begin with a representative individual's decision to work at any job.

THE CONSUMER'S MODIFIED ECONOMIC PROBLEM The decision about how much to work is part of the solution to the individual's economic problem. We need to modify the consumer's economic problem of Chapter 5, however, because it assumed that the consumer had a fixed amount of income to spend on goods and services. The labor supply decision had already been made. The amount of income to be earned is the heart of the matter in the labor supply decision.

To keep the modified economic problem as simple as possible, assume that each individual has a single option—to work at one job at a fixed hourly wage. People are free to choose how many hours they work each day. What are the objectives, alternatives, and constraints in this situation?

Objectives: Individuals want to maximize utility, or satisfaction, as before, but the way they go about this depends on their motivation for working. In particular, do people work to live or live to work?

The standard economic model of the work decision assumes people work to live. They value their leisure time. Time spent working is a "bad," a necessary sacrifice undertaken as a means of earning income. The income in turn allows people to enjoy goods and services, to "live." The two "goods" that give utility, then, are income and leisure time.

The workaholics of the world live to work. They consider working a good in and of itself. Although a number of people do live to work, economists do not view them as representative of the general population.

Alternatives: The labor supply decision adds a new alternative, how much time to spend working. People must also decide what goods and services to purchase with the income they earn, but we will suppress that part of the economic problem to focus on the decision to work. The only remaining decision is the split of available time between working and leisure.

Constraints: Time, not income, is now the scarce resource. If people sleep 8 hours, they have only 16 hours each day to divide between work and leisure.

We noted in Chapter 5 that prices are an important part of a consumer's constraint. The same remains true here. The wage that the individual receives determines the amount of income earned for each hour of leisure time sacri-

TABLE 9.1 **Possible Income-Leisure Combinations at Wages of $8/Hour and $10/Hour**

INCOME (WAGE = $8/HR.)	LEISURE (16 HOURS MAX.)	INCOME (WAGE = $10/HR.)	LEISURE (16 HOURS MAX.)
$ 0	16	$ 0	16
8	15	10	15
16	14	20	14
24	13	30	13
32	12	40	12
40	11	50	11
48	10	60	10
.	.	.	.
.	.	.	.
.	.	.	.
128	0	160	0

ficed. For example, if the wage is $8.00 per hour, the possible income-leisure combinations available to the individual are those given in the first two columns of Table 9.1. The individual's problem is to select the combination that yields the maximum amount of satisfaction.

THE INDIVIDUAL SUPPLY CURVE In this simple model of labor supply the number of hours a person decides to work depends on the wage rate and preferences for leisure time versus income. Holding preferences constant, how many hours does a representative individual want to work at different wage rates? This is the question underlying an individual's supply curve for labor. It is exactly analogous to the question underlying the individual demand curve for a product: Other things equal or constant, how much of the product does a consumer want to buy at different prices?

Furthermore, the shape of the labor supply curve depends on the combined interaction of the substitution and the income effects of a wage change, just as these effects determine the shape of the demand curve for a product. But there is one important difference. The Law of (Downward Sloping) Demand has no counterpart for the supply of labor (or of any other factor of production). *The supply curve for labor need not be upward sloping.* The reason is that, unlike the case for product demand, the substitution and the income effects tug in opposite directions on the desire to work.

THE SUBSTITUTION EFFECT Recall that the substitution effect is a relative price effect. The price ratio between two goods defines the rate at which consumers can trade one good for another. As the price ratios change, the substitution effect says that consumers substitute toward the relatively cheaper item. In the case of labor supply the wage rate defines the rate of trade between income and leisure. As shown in the first two columns of Table 9.1, the individual can trade 1 hour of leisure for $8.00 of income. If the wage rises to $10.00, the rate of trade is now more favorable to earning income. Earning $10.00 used to "cost" 1 hour and 15 minutes of leisure time. Now the cost is only 1 hour. Earning income is relatively cheaper. Alternatively, leisure time is now relatively more expensive. Each hour of leisure taken sacrifices $10.00 of income rather than $8.00. The substitution effect of a wage increase favors additional hours of work. Conversely, if the wage rate decreases, leisure is less costly in terms of income foregone, so the individual substitutes toward leisure and works fewer hours.

In other words, the substitution effect causes the labor supply curve to be *upward* sloping. Hours of work increase as the wage increases and decrease as the wage decreases.

THE INCOME EFFECT Recall that the income effect is an absolute price, or purchasing power effect. Consumers tend to buy more of all goods if purchasing power increases and less of all goods if purchasing power decreases. In the case of labor supply an increase in the wage increases purchasing power by increasing the income-leisure combinations available to the individual. Compare the income-leisure combinations in the third and fourth columns of Table 9.1, when the wage is $10.00, to the income-leisure combinations in the first two columns of the table, when the wage is $8.00. At the higher wage the individual can have more income for the same amount of leisure (for example, $40 versus $32 with 12 hours of leisure), or more leisure for the same amount of income (for example, 12 hours versus 11 hours of leisure for an income of $40), or more income and more leisure (for example, $50 and 11 hours of leisure versus $48 and 10 hours). Since income and leisure are both goods, the individual tends to consume more of both. But more leisure time means fewer hours of work. The income effect of a wage increase *decreases* the supply of labor. Conversely, a wage decrease reduces purchasing power, which tends to reduce both income and leisure time. Hours of work increase. Therefore, the income effect of a wage decrease *increases* the supply of labor.

In other words, the income effect causes the labor supply curve to be *downward sloping.* Hours of work decrease as the wage increases and increase as the wage decreases.

Whether the individual supply curve for labor is upward or downward sloping, then, depends on the relative strength of the substitution and the income effects.

LABOR SUPPLY IN THE UNITED STATES A casual look at labor supply behavior in the United States suggests that the overall supply of labor has been downward sloping throughout the twentieth century. Workers have decided to enjoy much more leisure time as wage rates have risen. Non-agricultural production workers averaged 54.3 hours of work per week in 1901. Their average work week had fallen to 34.5 hours by 1990. The income effect appears to have dominated the substitution effect.

Simple comparisons between wages and hours worked over time are misleading, however, because other things affecting hours worked have not been constant over time. Statistical studies that attempt to determine the *independent* effect of wages on hours worked have uncovered a rather striking result. There are two distinct "representative individuals" in the labor force. Men and women respond quite differently to changes in wages.

The labor supply curve for men appears to be slightly downward sloping. The income and the substitution effects more or less offset one another, with the income effect being just a bit stronger. The consensus among labor economists is that a 10 percent increase in wages reduces the labor supply of males by 1 to 2 percent. By contrast, the labor supply curve for women is definitely upward sloping and quite elastic. The substitution effect strongly dominates the income effect for women. Estimated female labor supply elasticities exceeding 1 are not uncommon.

Why are men's and women's labor supply responses so different? No one knows for sure. There is certainly no reason to believe that men and women have fundamentally different preferences with regard to working. Rather, economists believe that their labor supply responses differ because men and women face different conditions when deciding how much to work. This is certainly true in two respects.

First, women earn far less than do men in the United States. In 1990 the average wage for women was only two-thirds of the average wage for men. This could account for part of the difference if, as is commonly believed, the labor supply curves for men and women alike are backward bending.

Refer to Figure 9.1. At low wages, below W_0, the substitution effect dominates, and the labor supply curve is upward sloping. People prefer increased income to increased leisure time as wages rise. At high wages the situation reverses. People already have relatively high incomes, so they take part of the gains from increased wages as more leisure time. The income effect dominates, and the supply curve bends backward.

Suppose that men and women have the same backward-bending supply curves. The difference in their labor supply responses can be explained by their positions on the supply curve. The majority of relatively "low-wage" women are on the upward sloping portion of their supply curves, while the majority of relatively "high-wage" men are on the downward sloping portion of their supply curves.

A second important difference between men and women lies in their different roles within the household. The stereotype of women as full-time homemakers died years ago. As of 1992, 57.8 percent of all women worked in the marketplace, and most of those who worked were married. Nonetheless,

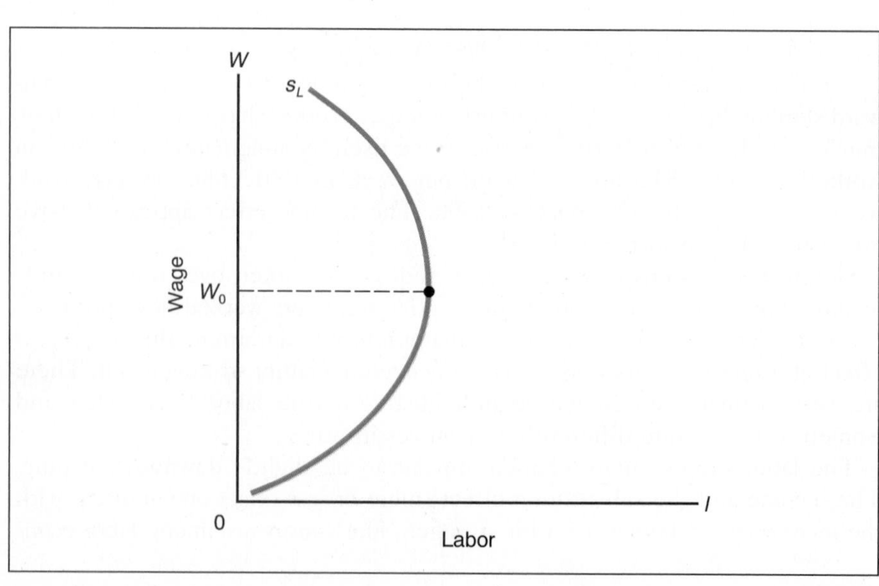

FIGURE 9.1

A Backward Bending Labor Supply Curve?

Some economists believe that the individual supply curve for labor, s_L, is backward bending. At low wages below W_0, the substitution effect of a wage increase dominates the income effect of a wage increase, so people substitute income for leisure and work more. The labor supply curve is upward sloping. At high wages above W_0, the income effect of a wage increase dominates the substitution effect of a wage increase, so people take more leisure and work less. The labor supply curve is downward sloping.

women still spend much more time than men do maintaining the household. Among women and men who work full time, women average 24 hours per week in "household production," men only 16 hours per week. As a result, the simple labor-leisure model described above may be more accurate for men than for women.

The argument is that men are more likely to see the work decision as a straight income-leisure choice and that income and leisure are not close substitutes. As a result, men simply do not respond very much to a change in their wages. Women, however, are more likely to see their choices as threefold: work in the marketplace, work at home, and leisure. If they also view work in the marketplace and work at home as close substitutes, this could explain why the substitution effect appears to be so strong for women. Women reduce hours worked at home for hours worked in the marketplace as their market wages rise and substitute in the opposite direction as their market wages fall.

The labor supply literature offers still other explanations for why men and women respond so differently to wage changes, but these two are the most popular.[1]

THE VALUE OF TIME The simple income-leisure model highlights a very important economic principle, the value of time in economic decision making. The applications of this principle go far beyond the decision to work.

The fact that people prefer to fly rather than taking the train when traveling long distances is a clear example of the value of time. Folklore has it that Americans love trains. Perhaps they do—federal subsidies to maintain Amtrak's passenger service are fast approaching $1 billion a year. By the same token, a number of people dread flying. Taking the train has another advantage over flying: It is often much cheaper. In March 1993, for example, regular coach fare on Amtrak, Boston to Washington, was $128 round-trip. Regular coach airfare was $662 round-trip. Why, then, do so many travelers between Boston to Washington choose to fly? The obvious answer is that by flying they save time, the value of which more than offsets both the public's alleged preference for trains over planes and the price advantage of the train.

The airplane-train example underscores an important distinction that economists make between the price of a product and the **full price** of the product. The full price includes the value of the time spent shopping for the product and actually consuming it. A train ticket may often be far cheaper than an airline ticket is. But the full price of the train exceeds the full price of the airplane for most people, and people base their purchases on the full price of consuming a product.

FULL PRICE

The price of a product plus the value of the time spent shopping for and actually consuming the product.

The value of time also plays a crucial role in one of the more important ongoing trends in the U.S. economy, the flight of women out of full-time homemaking and into the market labor force over the past 30 years. The shift of women out of full-time homemaking has exceeded the shift of workers out of agriculture in the post–World War II period.

REFLECTION: Elderly retired couples are more likely than young adult couples to go on long ocean cruises, in part because they place a lower value on their time. Can you think of other ways in which the behavior of the elderly differs from young adults that can be explained, in part, by differences in the value of time to each?

As noted above, 57.8 percent of all women worked in the marketplace in 1992. In 1960 only 36.5 percent of all women worked in the marketplace. What

[1]For an excellent discussion of the differences between male and female labor supplies see R. Ehrenberg and R. Smith, *Modern Labor Economics: Theory and Public Policy*, second edition (Glenview, IL: Scott, Foresman and Company, 1985), Chap. 6.

caused such a revolutionary change in women's behavior? Part of the explanation is that women's real wages have grown rapidly since 1950. As we have seen, women are apparently quite willing to substitute market production for home production, given the opportunity to earn higher wages. In fact, the President's Council of Economic Advisers attributes approximately half of women's increased labor force participation to the wage effect alone. The council's estimate is on the high side relative to those of other researchers, but the increase in wages has certainly had an important effect on women's labor force participation.

Another large part of the explanation lies in the changes that have occurred in the value of time spent in home production. The time required to produce a given level of home services has declined significantly over the past 30 years. Time-saving devices have affected all aspects of home production, most especially the preparation of meals. Preparing meals was once a highly time consuming operation. This is no longer true, thanks to innovations such as prepared and instant foods and the microwave oven. Also, the "baby bust" of the 1970s significantly reduced the value of time spent in home production. Smaller households are less time consuming to maintain than are larger households, even more so without young children to care for. One study estimated that the annual value of home services increases from $26,700 to $35,600 (1992 dollars) when children under the age of six are present in the household.

A closely related development is the migration of families from rural to urban areas, which has made it easier for women to adjust the time they spend working at home or in the marketplace. Families can more easily purchase inputs for home production in an urban setting. Urbanization also increases the job opportunities available close to the home, including opportunities for part-time and other flexible working arrangements.

Changes in wages and the value of time spent in home production do not explain all of the increase in women's labor force participation, by any means. Other factors such as changes in the type of education women have received, reduced discrimination in the workplace, and changes in attitudes about women working have also played a role. We will consider these additional factors in later chapters of this text. Women now comprise 46 percent of all workers. Their experience in the labor force is one of the more important issues affecting the U.S. economy, and we want to understand it as fully as possible.[2]

THE OVERALL MARKET SUPPLY CURVE We have been considering an individual's decision of how many hours to work at any job. The market supply curve obtained from adding up these individual supply curves indicates the overall labor force participation for the nation as a whole. It shows, at various average wage rates, how much labor individuals want to supply across all occupations.

This overall labor supply curve is nearly vertical in the United States, a blend of males' downward-sloping supply curves and females' upward-sloping supply curves. If female labor force participation continues to increase and male labor force participation continues to decrease, overall labor force participation may become more sensitive to wages. But this depends on how men and women

---

[2]Two excellent sources on women in the labor market are *The Economic Report of the President, 1987* (Washington D.C.: U.S. Government Printing Office, 1987), chap. 7, and R. Gronau, "Home Production—A Forgotten Industry," *Review of Economics and Statistics* 62 (August 1980): 408–415.

share home production. The men's share has been steadily increasing since 1970. The overall labor supply curve may not change very much if this trend continues because women's supply curves would become more inelastic.

SUPPLY TO AN OCCUPATION The relevant market supply curve in many microeconomic applications is the overall supply to a particular occupation—steelworker, high school mathematics teacher, entertainer, and the like. These occupation-specific market supply curves are analagous to the market demand curves for individual products. They are almost certainly upward sloping because different occupations are natural substitutes for one another so long as individuals are willing and able to work in more than one occupation.

People compare the wages and working conditions of a number of jobs before deciding where to work. So, for example, whenever local school boards raise the salaries of high school mathematics teachers, the supply response comes form two sources. Some people who are currently out of the labor force may now decide to teach high school mathematics. As noted above, this supply response may not be very strong, if indeed it exists at all. In addition, the higher wages attract people who are currently working in other jobs because the wages of mathematics teachers have risen relative to wages in competing occupations. Conversely, decreases in wages drive people toward competing occupations.

Occupational choice enhances the substitution effect, which tends to make the occupation-specific supply curve upward sloping. This occurs for essentially the same reason that female labor supply curves are upward sloping and elastic. Home production is a close substitute for work in the marketplace, just as different occupations are often close substitutes for one another.

The Demand for Labor

Analyzing an individual firm's demand for labor does not require any modification of the firm's economic problem as presented in Chapter 6, only a change in emphasis. In Chapter 6 we concentrated on the supply of output and suppressed the part of the firm's economic problem relating to the hiring of factors of production. Here we suppress the output question and focus directly on the decision to hire labor.

A competitive firm's decision about how much labor to hire is analagous enough to its decision about how much output to supply that it pays to recall the main elements of the output supply decision from Chapter 6:

1. Because the firm is a price taker, it can sell as much of the product as it wants at the going market price, P_e. As a result, the demand curve facing the firm is perfectly elastic, horizontal, at P_e.
2. Since the firm's goal is to maximize profit, it supplies the output at which price, or marginal revenue, equals marginal cost. This decision rule is the basis of the first proposition of supply in Chapter 6: A competitive firm's supply curve is its marginal cost curve.
3. Most supply curves are upward sloping in the short run because of the Law of Diminishing Returns. This is the second proposition of supply in Chapter 6.

AN INDIVIDUAL FIRM'S DEMAND FOR LABOR The development of the firm's demand curve for labor proceeds along the same lines, with the roles of supply and demand reversed.

THE SUPPLY OF LABOR TO A FIRM The firm has no control over the wage it pays for a particular kind of labor in a competitive labor market because it is one of many firms hiring the labor. Instead, it faces the established market wage, and it can hire as much labor as it wants at that wage. In other words, the *supply* of labor to the firm is perfectly elastic, horizontal, at the market wage, W_e, as illustrated in Figure 9.2

The market wage, W_e, defines the *marginal cost* of hiring additional labor. For example, if the market wage is $250 per week, each new worker hired increases total cost by $250 no matter how many workers have already been hired.

THE FIRM'S DEMAND FOR LABOR A firm's demand curve for labor indicates how much labor it wants to hire at each market wage. Since the firm's goal is to maximize profit, it will hire labor until the wage, or marginal cost, equals the marginal revenue from hiring labor, the additional revenue obtained from the last worker hired. The hiring decision rule is just another specific application of this general principle: Continue an economic activity until marginal benefit equals marginal cost.

The value of labor's marginal product: The key to the demand for labor, then, is the marginal revenue from hiring labor, just as the key to the supply of output is the marginal cost of output. To see how the wage and the marginal revenue of labor interact, recall the example in Chapter 6 of a farmer hiring labor to farm a plot of land. The first three columns of Table 9.2 reproduce Table 6.3, showing the total and marginal products at each quantity of labor hired.

MARGINAL (PHYSICAL) PRODUCT OF LABOR

The additional output produced by each additional unit of labor.

The **marginal product** (MP_L), or marginal physical product, refers to the additional *physical* units of output produced by each additional worker. To obtain the marginal revenue from hiring each additional worker, the physical units must be multiplied by the price that the farmer receives for each unit of

FIGURE 9.2

The Supply of Labor to a Firm in a Competitive Labor Market

The supply of labor to a firm hiring in a competitive labor market, s_L, is horizontal, or perfectly elastic, at the going market wage, assumed to be $250 in the figure. The firm is a wage taker. It can hire as much or as little as it wants at the going market wage.

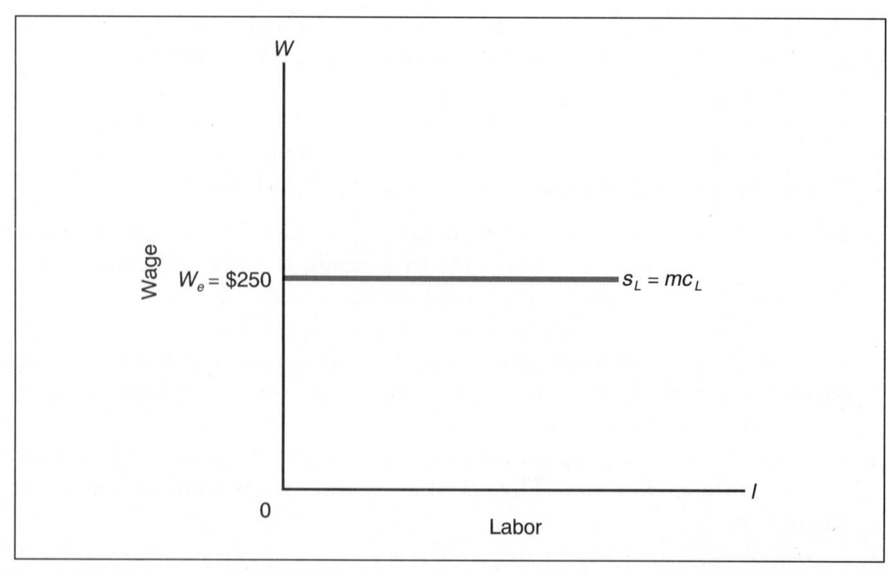

TABLE 9.2 The Value of Labor's Marginal Product

NUMBER OF WORKERS	TOTAL PRODUCT (BUSHELS)	MARGINALPRODUCT (MP_L)	PRICE OF OUTPUT (P_g)	VALUE OF MARGINAL PRODUCT ($VMP_L = MP_L \cdot P_g$)
1	100	100	$5	$500
2	200	100	5	500
3	300	100	5	500
4	400	100	5	500
5	475	75	5	375
6	525	50	5	250
7	550	25	5	125
8	550	0	5	0
9	525	−25	5	−125

additional output produced. If the product market is competitive, the price received for each unit of output is the same no matter how much output the farmer sells. Assume that the price of output is $5 (column 4). Therefore, the marginal revenue from hiring additional labor, called the **value of labor's marginal product** (VMP$_L$), is $MP_L \cdot \$5$, column 5 of Table 9.2. In general,

$$VMP_L = MP_L \cdot P_g$$

where P_g is the price of the good or service produced by the labor.

Refer to Table 9.2. The first four workers each produce 100 units of output. With the output selling for $5, the value of each worker's marginal product is $500 ($500 = 100 · $5). Hiring the fifth worker increases output by 75 units. Therefore, the value of the fifth worker's marginal product is $375 ($375 = 75 · $5), and so on for each additional worker hired.

Figure 9.3 depicts the VMP_L for the farm workers. By connecting each point from Table 9.2 (column 5), the graph assumes that the farmer can hire fractional amounts of each worker's time.

VALUE OF LABOR'S MARGINAL PRODUCT

The marginal revenue from hiring an additional unit of labor in a competitive labor market, equal to the marginal (physical) product of labor times the price of the good or service that the labor is producing.

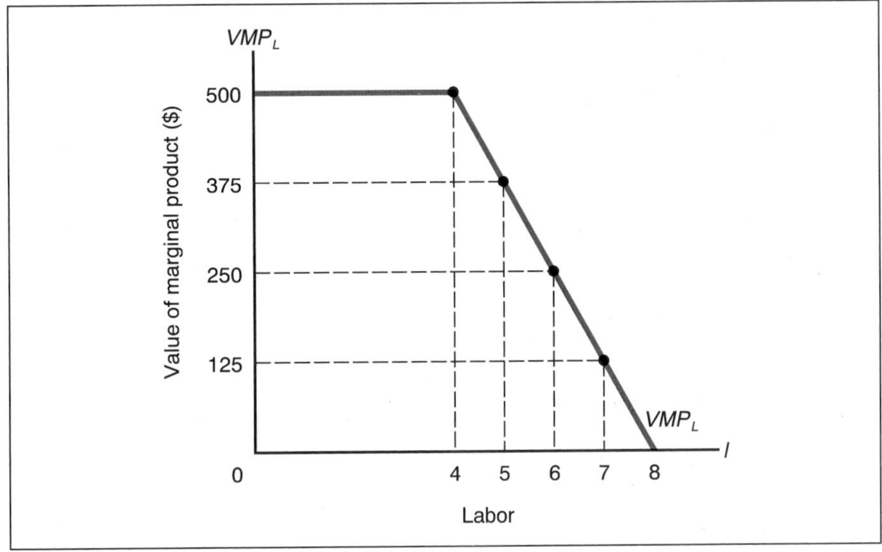

FIGURE 9.3

The Value of Labor's Marginal Product on the Farm

The curve VMP_L is a graph of the value of labor's marginal product in our farm example from Table 9.2. The value of labor's marginal product is the additional revenue received from hiring one more farm worker—$VMP_L = MP_L \cdot P_g$. VMP_L is $500 for workers 1 through 4, and then declines because of the Law of Diminishing Returns.

FIGURE 9.4

Hiring Labor to Maximize Profit

The figure combines the supply curve of labor to the farm in our example, s_L, from Figure 9.2, with the value of labor's marginal product, VMP_L, from Figure 9.3. The marginal revenue from hiring additional labor is given by VMP_L. The marginal cost of hiring additional labor is $250, the market wage. Profits are maximized by hiring the number of workers at which the marginal revenue equals the marginal cost, or the wage = VMP_L. The profit-maximizing number of workers is 6 in our example, at the intersection of s_L and VMP_L.

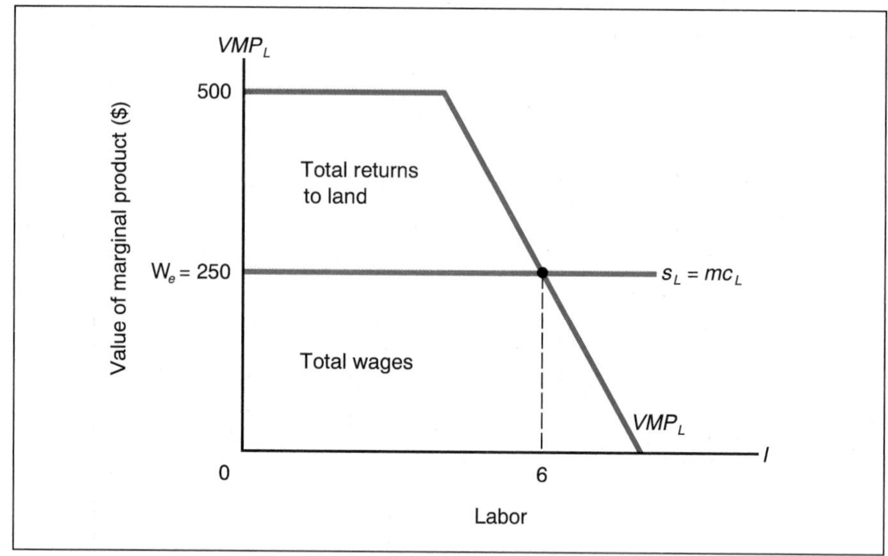

The best-profit point: Suppose that the going wage for these farm workers is $250. How many workers should the farmer hire? Figure 9.4 combines the VMP_L curve from Figure 9.3 and the horizontal supply curve at the wage of $250 from Figure 9.2.

The farmer should hire 6 workers, the point of intersection of the two curves. The marginal revenue of all workers up to 6, given by the VMP_L curve, exceeds the wage. Workers 1 through 4 each bring in $500 in revenue, yet they cost the farmer only $250 each. The profit from hiring each of these workers is $250. Hiring the fifth worker increases revenue by $375 at a cost of $250, for an increase in profit of $125. Hiring the sixth worker brings in $250 of extra revenue at a cost of $250, for no net gain or loss. However, if the farmer can hire a fraction of the worker's time, the extra revenue from hiring all but the last fraction of the sixth worker's time exceeds the wage the farmer must pay.

Hiring the seventh worker decreases profit. The marginal revenue is only $125, yet that worker also costs the farmer $250. Hiring workers beyond the seventh reduces profits even more. So hiring 6 workers maximizes profit from farming the land.

The demand curve for labor: The labor-wage combination (6, $250) is a point on the farmer's demand curve, depicted in Figure 9.5. At a wage of $250, the farmer wants to hire 6 workers. Total wages are 6 · $250 = $1500, the rectangular area below the wage up to 6 workers in Figure 9.5. Total profits to the farmer, in the form of returns to the fixed land, equal the area above the wage and below the VMP_L curve, up to 6 workers.

By the same argument, the farmer would hire 7 workers if the wage were $125, would hire 5 workers if the wage were $375, and would be indifferent to hiring anywhere from 0 to 4 workers at a wage of $500. Therefore, the labor-wage combinations (0–4, $500), (5, $375), and (7, $125) are also points on the farmer's demand curve for labor.

The demand for labor is the value of labor's marginal product because the farmer hires the quantity of labor at which $W_e = VMP_L$. This is the first fundamental proposition of the demand for labor, analogous to the first proposition of supply in product markets.

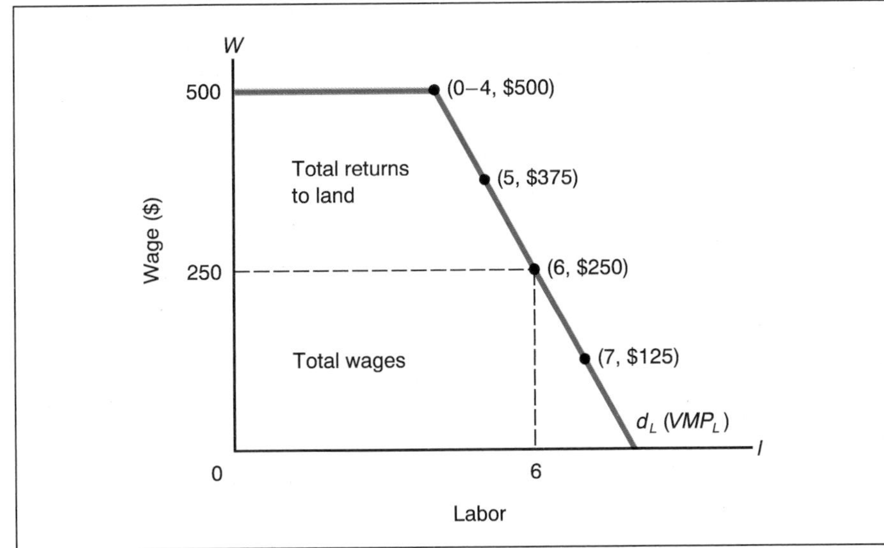

FIGURE 9.5

The Farmer's Demand Curve for Labor

The farmer's demand curve for labor in our example, d_L, indicates the number of workers that the farmer wants to hire at each market wage. Because the farmer hires the number of workers at which $W = VMP_L$ in order to maximize profit, the farmer's demand curve for labor is identical to the value of labor's marginal product curve, VMP_L.

THE LAW OF DIMINISHING RETURNS The second fundamental proposition of the demand for labor is that *a competitive firm's demand curve for labor is expected to be downward sloping in the short run.* This is so because of the Law of Diminishing Returns, the same reason why product supply curves are expected to be upward sloping.

The Law of Diminishing Returns says that the marginal (physical) product of labor eventually declines as more workers are hired. But this means that the value of labor's marginal product must also eventually decline, since VMP_L is just MP_L times a constant, the price of output. If VMP_L declines, so, too, must the demand curve for labor, since the two are one and the same.

THE MARKET DEMAND CURVE FOR LABOR The market demand curve for a particular kind of labor is the horizontal summation of all the individual firms' demand curves for that labor. Since each firm's demand curve is downward sloping, the market demand curve is also downward sloping.

Labor Market Equilibrium

If the market supply and the market demand curves for a particular occupation are as drawn in Figure 9.6, the Laws of Supply and Demand will drive the market to (L_e, W_e), the intersection of the two curves. The reasoning is exactly analogous to that of product markets. W_e is the equilibrium wage because it is the only wage at which desires match on both sides of the market. At W_e, firms want to buy L_e units of labor, exactly the amount that individuals want to supply.

No wage other than W_e can be maintained in the market. If the wage is temporarily above W_e—say, at W_1—the market is in excess supply. More workers want to work than firms are willing to hire. Workers scrambling for jobs offer their services for lower wages. At the lower wages the quantity of labor demanded by the firms increases, and the quantity of labor supplied decreases.

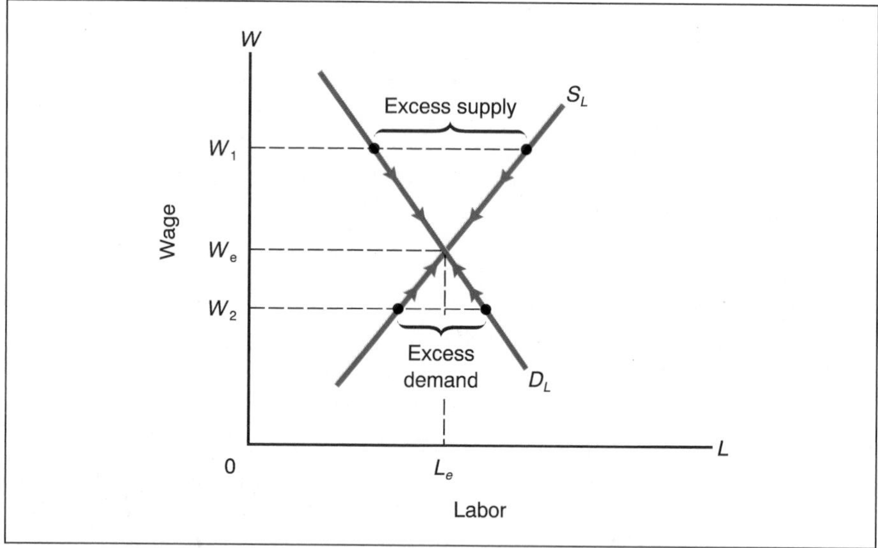

FIGURE 9.6

Equilibrium in the Market for Labor

The Laws of Supply and Demand operate in labor markets just as they do in product markets, with the roles of the suppliers and demanders reversed. In a labor market for a particular occupation, the individuals are the suppliers and the firms are the demanders. The equilibrium quantity of labor hired and the wage are L_e, W_e, at the intersection of the market demand and supply curves D_L and S_L. The labor market is in excess supply at any wage above the equilibrium wage, such as W_1. Excess supply puts downward pressure on the wage and drives it back to the equilibrium wage, W_e. Conversely, the labor market is in excess demand at any wage below the equilibrium wage, such as W_2. Excess demand puts upward pressure on the wage and drives it back to the equilibrium wage, W_e.

The wage continues to fall until it reaches W_e, at which point all excess supply disappears from the market.

If the wage is temporarily below W_e—say, at W_2—the market is in excess demand. Firms want to hire more workers than are available at that wage. They offer higher wages to attract workers. The higher wages simultaneously increase the quantity of labor supplied and reduce the quantity of labor demanded by the firms. The wage continues to rise until it reaches W_e, at which point all excess demand disappears from the market.

THE DISTRIBUTION OF WAGE AND SALARY INCOME

We are now in a position to see how the Laws of Supply and Demand apply to the For Whom or Distribution question by showing how competitive market forces help determine the distribution of labor incomes. Why do some people earn high wages and others low wages in the United States, or in any other market economy? Any judgment about whether the U.S. economy treats people fairly requires an answer to this question because wages and salaries account for nearly 80 percent of total factor income in the United States. Unfortunately, economists do not fully know the answer. It is an extremely broad and complex question that Chapter 9 only begins to address by considering how normal competitive market forces can generate differences in the wages that people earn. We will discuss other forces that determine wages and salaries in the U.S. economy later in Section V of this text.

Identical People, Identical Jobs

Competitive market forces do not promote wide disparities in wages and salaries in and of themselves. Quite the contrary. Competition is the great equalizer in a market economy. Competitive markets promote both equality of opportunity and horizontal equity, the equal treatment of equals. Equality of opportunity follows directly from the conditions required to have a competitive market environment. With accurate information about prices and market conditions available to everyone and with easy entry into and exit from markets, individuals and business firms have equal access to whatever advantages arise in the marketplace that they are capable of pursuing. Equal access, in turn, tends to promote equality of end results. No one who enjoys a temporary advantage can maintain that advantage by preventing others who want the same advantage from entering the market. Once others enter the market, the advantage is "competed away." Ultimately, the competitive marketplace achieves horizontal equity. It treats identical individuals and identical business firms identically, whether in factor or in product markets.

EQUALITY WITHIN OCCUPATIONS To see the equalizing tendencies of competitive labor markets and their implications for wages, return to our example of the farmer hiring workers to farm the land. Suppose that there are 2,000 such farms, 1,000 in each of two regions of a country, and that 12,000 workers are seeking employment on these farms. The farms, and workers, are identical in every respect. Also, workers know the wages on every farm and are free to move from farm to farm both within a region and between regions of the country, in line with the conditions required for competitive markets.

Suppose initially that 5,000 workers seek employment on the 1,000 farms in the first region, 5 to each farm, and that 7,000 workers seek employment on the 1,000 farms in the second region, 7 to each farm. The situation on each type of farm is as pictured in Figure 9.7, with Figure 9.7(a) representing the farms in the first region and Figure 9.7(b) the farms in the second region.

Finally, assume that the 5 workers on the farms in the first region receive a competitive wage of $375, equal to the VMP_L at 5 workers. The 7 workers on the farms in the second region also receive a competitive wage of $125, equal to the VMP_L at 7 workers.

FIGURE 9.7

Equality of Wages Within Occupations

Figure (a) shows each of 1000 identical farms in the first region of a country and Figure (b) shows each of 1000 identical farms in the second region of a country. The farms are the same as in our example. Originally, 5000 farm workers seek employment in the first region and are hired at a wage of $375, equal to the VMP_L with 5 workers on each farm. 7000 farm workers seek employment in the second region and are hired at a wage of $125, equal to the VMP_L with 7 workers on each farm. Workers in the lower-wage second region will soon move to the higher-wage first region. The final equilibrium in Figure (c) occurs when there are 6000 workers in both regions each earning $250, equal to the VMP_L with 6 workers on each farm. The movement of workers equalizes the wages of identical workers within occupations in competitive labor markets.

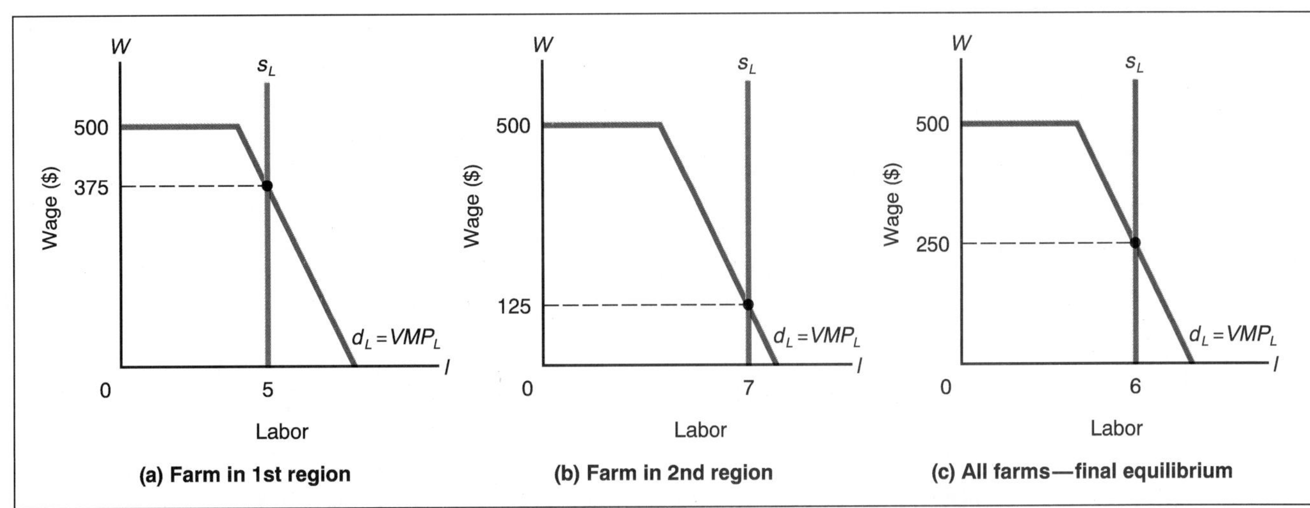

This initial situation cannot persist. The workers on the farms in the second region soon learn of the higher wages paid on the farms in the first region and migrate to those farms. As the result of the migration, the farms in the first region experience an excess supply of workers at a wage of $375, and the farms in the second region experience an excess demand for labor at the wage of $125. The wage falls on the farms in the first region and rises on the farms in the second region until the wages equalize, at which point the incentive to migrate ends. The final equilibrium is depicted in Figure 9.7(c). All 2,000 farms hire 6 workers, with each worker receiving a wage of $250.

The general principle illustrated by this example is that *competitive labor markets tend to equalize the wages of identical individuals within each occupation.*

EQUALITY ACROSS OCCUPATIONS The equalizing tendency of competitive markets applies across occupations as well as within occupations, so long as large numbers of workers are equally willing and able to work at different jobs. The argument is the same that for the equalizing tendency within each occupation.

Figure 9.8 shows the markets for two occupations, occupation 1 in Figure 9.8(a) and occupation 2 in Figure 9.8(b). The supply and the demand curves originally intersect at a wage of W_1 in occupation 1 and W_2 in occupation 2.

These wage differentials cannot persist so long as workers in the two markets are willing and able to work at either job. Workers will migrate from low-wage occupation 2 to high-wage occupation 1. Supply increases in the first market from S_L to S_L' to S_L'' and decreases in the second market from S_L to S_L' to S_L'' until the single equilibrium wage W_{Final} exists in both markets. Only at that wage does the migration of workers cease.

In general: *If all workers are equally willing and able to work in all jobs, then the Laws of Supply and Demand guarantee that everyone earns the same wage.*

FIGURE 9.8

Equality of Wages Across Occupations

The wage in occupation 1 is originally W_1 and the number of workers employed is L_1, at the intersection of D_L and S_L in Figure 9.8(a). The wage in occupation 2 is originally W_2 and the number of workers employed is L_2, at the intersection of D_L and S_L in Figure 9.8(b). So long as the workers are willing and able to work in either occupation, workers will move from low-wage occupation 2 to high-wage occupation 1. Supply increases in occupation 1 from S_L to S_L' to S_L'', and decreases in occupation 2 from S_L to S_L' to S_L''. The movement of workers continues until the wages are equal at W_{Final} in each occupation, at the intersection of D_L and S_L'' in both graphs. L_{e_1} workers are employed in occupation 1 and L_{e_2} workers are employed in occupation 2.

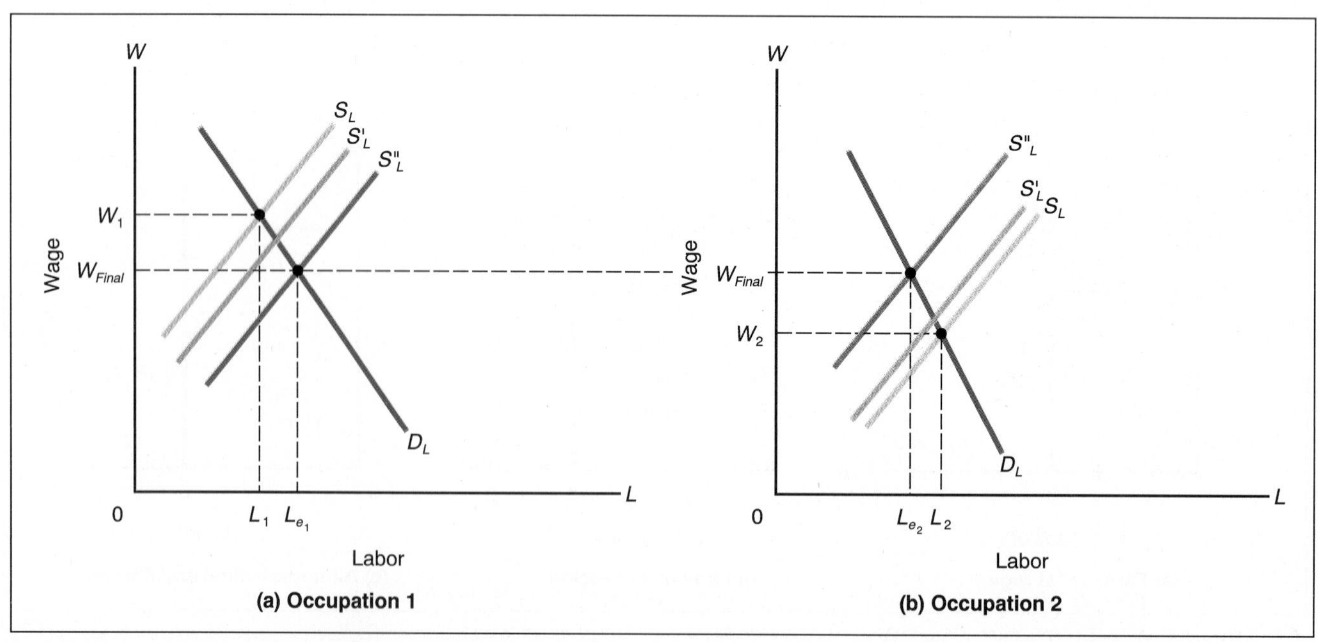

Disparities in Wage Income

Wages and salaries in the United States are not equal across all occupations, of course. Nor would they be even if all labor markets were highly competitive. The reason is that people differ in both their ability and their willingness to perform different jobs.

IDENTICAL PEOPLE, JOBS DIFFER: EQUALIZING WAGE DIFFERENTIALS Jobs differ significantly from one another, enough so that people are not equally able or willing to work at different jobs. For starters, jobs clearly differ in their educational requirements in terms of both the formal schooling they require and the amount of on-the-job training provided by firms after employment begins. People are excluded from many jobs simply because they are unable to perform them.

Jobs also differ in their attractiveness. Adam Smith identified four characteristics of jobs that affect workers' willingness to accept them:

1. *Constancy of employment:* Most people dislike jobs in which they are likely to be laid off periodically. Construction work is a case in point. Many workers shy away from construction jobs because of the seasonal nature of the work.
2. *The probability of success:* People like to succeed in whatever they do. This helps explain why relatively few young adults seriously consider careers as professional athletes. Despite the enormous rewards to the lucky few, the minute odds of succeeding prevent most people from even trying.
3. *The amount of responsibility:* This characteristic can work either way. Many people dislike responsibility. Others thrive on it, much preferring to "be their own boss." Whatever the case, few people are indifferent to the amount of responsibility a job entails. It is always an important factor in assessing the attractiveness of a particular job.
4. *Working conditions:* This is a catch-all for many different characteristics. Is the job easy or strenuous? Challenging or boring? Prestigious? Is the working environment safe or hazardous? Quiet or noisy? Clean or dirty? Attributes such as these clearly affect people's willingness to accept a particular job.

Movement of workers between occupations does not equalize wages across occupations when jobs differ. Return again to Figure 9.8, in which the wages of occupations 1 and 2 are initially W_1 and W_2, respectively. Workers in occupation 2 know that the wage is higher in occupation 1. But suppose that they do not possess the education or skills required for occupation 1 or that they find it relatively unattractive for any of the four reasons listed above. In either case, they do not move from occupation 1, and the wage differential persists in the final equilibrium.

Economists call these lasting wage differences in competitive labor markets **equalizing wage differentials.** The term *equalizing* highlights an important point: *Competitive markets still treat equal people equally, but in terms of overall satisfaction, not wages.* People with identical preferences and innate abilities who work in different occupations for different wages are equally well off, so long as they have the same opportunities. The wage differences exactly compensate for the differences in the jobs that make them relatively desirable or undesirable.

EQUALIZING WAGE DIFFERENTIAL
A difference in the wages for different jobs that just compensates workers for the relative attractiveness of the jobs.

In terms of Figure 9.8, people willingly accept the lower wage, W_2, to work in occupation 2 as compensation for the fact that this occupation is more desirable. It may be safer, more pleasant, or more challenging, or it may require less investment in formal schooling. Conversely, the higher wage, W_1, in occupation 1 is required to attract workers away from occupation 2. In the final equilibrium, the wage differential ($W_1 - W_2$) is such as to make the workers indifferent between the two jobs. Workers receive the same level of satisfaction in either occupation.

Equalizing wage differentials are an important feature of labor markets. The two characteristics that have been studied the most by economists are differences in formal educational requirements and hazardous working environments.

Occupations that require a college education definitely pay more, on average. Investing in a college education significantly increases lifetime earnings. One study estimated that the average increase in lifetime earnings for men is equivalent to receiving a one-time payment of $130,000 upon beginning college. The equivalent increase for women is $80,000.[3] (These are the other-things-equal increases, independent of all other factors that influence lifetime earnings.)

The returns for men, at least, appear to more than compensate for the cost of a college education. They are more than just an equalizing differential. This suggests either that the markets for occupations requiring a college education are not yet at their final equilibrium or that the market for college education is not fully competitive. People of equal abilities do not have equal access to a college education. The returns to a college education would just compensate for the investment of time and money to receive the education if the market for a college education were competitive and in equilibrium.

Studies of hazardous work environments find that workers are compensated for enduring the hazards. One widely cited study concludes that wages increase by $20–$35 per year for every 1 in 10,000 increase in the probability of dying from a job-related accident.[4]

PEOPLE DIFFER, JOBS DIFFER: NONCOMPETING LABOR MARKETS The discussion to this point has assumed that all people are identical. This is not true, of course. People have very different preferences about the kinds of jobs they enjoy and very different innate abilities. Some of us prefer the comfort of working indoors at a desk; others of us are restless and much prefer to work outdoors. Most people dislike working at night; others do not mind at all. Some people are particularly bright. Still others are blessed with special athletic or musical talents.

When both people and jobs differ, the overall market for labor divides into a number of separate noncompeting labor markets because people are no longer so willing to move from one occupation to another. The Laws of Supply and Demand determine the wage in each submarket, so that wages tend to differ across occupations. The wage differences are not necessarily compensating wage differences, however. *Unequals* can be treated very unequally in competitive labor markets.

The following example, involving day work and night work, illustrates these points for the case of different preferences for work. Suppose that there are

---

[3]These estimates are for the 1960s and 1970s. The earnings advantage of a college education appears to be increasing for both men and women in the 1990s. B. Kaufman, *The Economics of Labor Markets*, second edition (Chicago: The Dryden Press, 1989), 87.

[4]Ehrenberg and Smith, *Modern Labor Economics*, 235.

two types of workers: the vast majority who prefer to work during the day rather than at night and a small minority who do not care when they work. A firm hiring these workers runs a day shift and a night shift in its factory. It has to pay its workers on the night shift 25 percent more than its workers on the day shift to attract enough workers to the night shift. The night shift ends up with both types of workers, those who prefer daytime work and those who do not care when they work.

For those workers who prefer daytime work, but are working the night shift, the 25 percent premium represents a compensating difference in pay for working at night. They are no better off than if they worked for lower pay during the day, and no better off than those who actually do work the day shift. For those workers who do not care when they work, however, the night-shift premium is pure economic gain. They would have accepted the day rate because they are equally happy working the day shift or the night shift. They are better off than the other night-shift workers, even though they earn the same pay, because they do not suffer any inconvenience from working at night. They are also better off than the day-shift workers because they earn the 25 percent premium.

The night-shift workers who do not care when they work are said to receive an economic rent for working at night. **Economic rent** is the difference between the wage a worker receives and the wage required to attract the worker to the job. As such, economic rent measures the pure economic gain from accepting a particular job. In our example the entire 25 percent night-shift premium is an economic rent for the workers who do not care when they work. If some workers actually prefer to work at night, they would receive an even larger economic rent because they would have been willing to work the night shift for less than the day-shift pay.

ECONOMIC RENT

The difference between the wage a worker receives and the wage required to attract the worker to the job.

REFLECTION: Professors' salaries at private colleges and universities differ substantially across disciplines for people with the same seniority and rank. Professors in the natural sciences, finance, and economics tend to be on the high end of the pay scale, and professors in the humanities and foreign languages tend to be on the low end of the pay scale. Do you think that most of the differences in pay are equalizing pay differentials?

SUMMARY The following Concept Summary table summarizes the effects of competitive labor markets on the distribution of wage and salary income.

CONCEPT SUMMARY

The Distribution of Wage and Salary Income in Competitive Labor Markets

PERSONAL AND JOB CHARACTERISTICS	MARKET RESULT
People are identical, jobs are identical	Everyone earns the same wage
People are identical, jobs differ in desirability or skills required	Equalizing wage differentials occur across occupations All people are equally well off—have the same level of utility
People differ, jobs differ	Noncompeting labor markets form Wages are determined by supply and demand in each market Identical people receive the same level of utility Nonidentical people earn different amounts of economic rent

VMP_L and the Distribution of Wages

Labor markets in the United States produce enormous disparities in wages and salaries. The 10 percent of the wage earners at the top of the wage distribution earn, on average, over ten times as much as the 10 percent of the wage earners at the bottom of the wage distribution. Some individuals earn millions of dollars a year. Others work hard and still live in poverty. Why?

One can always appeal to the Laws of Supply and Demand to the extent competitive market forces can explain these differences. The reason for these disparities must be that the supply and the demand curves intersect at very high wages in some cases and at very low wages in other cases. In addition, many labor markets are noncompeting because both people and jobs differ. As a result, relatively few people are able or willing to move between the high-wage and low-wage markets, so that the wage differences persist.

Appealing to the Laws of Supply and Demand in this way is not terribly revealing, however. We can gain additional insight into why people earn different wages from the result that competitively determined wages equal the value of labor's marginal product in each occupation. That single term, $VMP_L = MP_L \cdot P_g$, reveals three important determinants of wage differentials in a competitive market environment: workers' productivity or skills, the number of workers in any one labor market, and the markets for the goods and services that the workers are producing.

MARGINAL PRODUCT The first term, the marginal product of labor, tells us two things. It reminds us, first, of the obvious point that workers' productivity, or skills, in part determine their wages. Workers' marginal *products*, and not anything else about them, matter to their employers. There are any number of examples. Skilled blue-collar workers earn more than unskilled blue-collar workers do in part because they are more skilled. For instance, in 1992 the median weekly salary of auto mechanics in the United States was approximately 66 percent higher than the salary of the service station attendants who only pump gas. We noted in Chapter 3 that the major economic difference between the rich and the poor countries is the amount of capital they possess. The rich countries have been able to provide their workers with a large amount of capital, whereas the poor countries have not. Capital increases workers' wages by making them more productive. Finally, the skills and general knowledge learned in college pay off in the marketplace, as noted above.

Skills and productivity alone do not determine wages, however. *Marginal* product, the productivity of the last worker hired, is the key. In other words, the number of people who possess a particular skill matters as well. This is just another example of the general principle that competitive market prices reflect what is true on the margin.

Young economists with Ph.D.s entering the academic market for the first time in the mid-1980s were more knowledgeable, and possessed far better research skills, than did their counterparts 15 to 20 years earlier. Basic knowledge advances at a very rapid pace. Yet the salaries for first-year assistant professors in economics were only about 75 percent as high in real terms (correcting for inflation) as they were at the end of the 1960s. The younger academics were more skilled, but the numbers did them in. One consequence of the post–World War II baby boom was a glut of new Ph.D.s seeking university positions in most academic fields during the 1980s. The market reacted as expected in the face of an excess supply. Real wages fell in order to clear the market.

The professors' students suffered the same fate in the 1970s and early 1980s, and for the same reason. The starting salaries of graduating seniors failed to keep pace with inflation as the baby boomers poured into the market scrambling for jobs. Thanks to the baby bust of the 1970s, today's graduating seniors have it much better. The employers are doing the scrambling these days, and the real wages of college graduates are rising. The turnaround is hardly surprising, given the magnitude of the baby bust. Reduce supply in any market considerably, and prices are likely to rise.

THE PRICE OF THE PRODUCT Productivity and numbers are only part of the explanation as to why wages differ. The second term in the value of labor's marginal product, P_g, indicates that the demand for labor is a **derived demand.** It depends in part on the market for the product or service that the workers are providing. The higher the price of the product, the higher the wage of the workers producing the product. When the worker is producing a service, the connection between the market for the service and the worker's wage is especially direct.

DERIVED DEMAND
The principle that the demand for labor depends in part on the market for the product that the workers are producing; the higher the price of the product, the higher the wages, other things equal.

PHYSICIANS VERSUS ACADEMICS In 1991, the median salary of physicians was 26 percent higher than the median salary of college and university teachers.[5] The difference in their salaries was not primarily due to differences in numbers or skills. The baby boom increased the supply of physicians just as it did the supply of new Ph.D. economists. Nor are physicians necessarily more skilled than are academics. Comparing their skills is admittedly an apples and oranges exercise, but the fact remains that the training of physicians and academics is remarkably similar. Physicians take courses during the first two years of medical school. They then spend the next two years learning their way around a hospital and then, often, four more years as residents learning a narrow specialty. Academics also take two years of course work, followed by a two- to four-year period in which they learn their way around a classroom and become an expert in the area of their doctoral dissertation. They then spend up to six more years as nontenured faculty members. Despite these similarities, however, physicians have fared much better in the marketplace. Why?

The answer lies in the respective markets for their services. The demand for medical care has been shifting out rapidly over the past 20 years for two reasons. First, the demand for medical care is income elastic. As peoples' incomes have increased, they have devoted a larger share of their budgets to medical care. Second, the federal government gave physicians a considerable boost with the passage of Medicare and Medicaid in the mid-1960s. Medicare provides hospital insurance for the aged. Medicaid provides a broad range of medical services for families and individuals receiving public assistance and for other low-income, "medically needy" people as well. Both programs are financed by tax dollars and have grown enormously. Neither the aged nor the

[5]The data on salaries here and above comes from U.S. Department of Labor, Bureau of Labor Statistics, *Employment and Earnings* 40, No. 1 (January 1993), Table 56.

poor would have spent anywhere near as much on medical care as the federal, state, and local governments have on their behalf. Overall, the growth in demand for physicians outpaced the growth in their supply over the past 20 years. As a result, physicians' salaries rose faster than prices generally.

Academics have not been so fortunate. Demand for a college education grew briskly through the 1970s on the heels of the baby boom, but then slowed considerably in the 1980s following the baby bust. Even in the boom years, though, the growth in demand for academics paled in comparison to the growth in demand for medical care. As indicated above, it did not keep pace with the increase in the supply of new Ph.D.s. Consequently, academics' salaries fell far behind physicians' salaries.

ATHLETES AND ENTERTAINERS The role of the demand for the service in determining salaries is especially evident in the sports and entertainment fields. Young, aspiring professional athletes, actors and actresses, musicians, and dancers single-mindedly devote themselves to developing a particular talent, gambling that the market will support them. In effect, their supply curves are perfectly inelastic above a very low wage, as in Figure 9.9. How well they do depends ultimately on the demand for their services. If the general public likes what they do, they win; if not, they lose. Talent certainly matters to some extent within a given sport or line of entertainment. But the demand factor is so important that the relationship between talent and salary in these fields is often quite tenuous.

In sports, television is often the decisive factor in determining salaries. The most popular boxers earn far more than do all other athletes for a single sporting event. They do so not because they are any more skilled, but rather because boxing promoters have long understood the principle that television has much more value to viewers than to advertisers. Producers of television programs are usually forbidden to charge viewers each time they turn on their sets, but if they could, they would earn far more than they currently receive from selling advertising time. Boxing promoters are not so restricted. They offer the top boxing matches on a pay-to-view basis in theaters and arenas throughout the world. As a result, boxers have tapped into millions of dollars of revenue that

FIGURE 9.9

The Labor Supply Curve of Athletes and Entertainers

The labor supply curve of athletes and entertainers, s_L is perfectly inelastic above a very low reservation wage, $W_{Reservation}$. The reservation wage is the wage required for them to remain in their professions. The wages of these people depend largely on the demand for their talents.

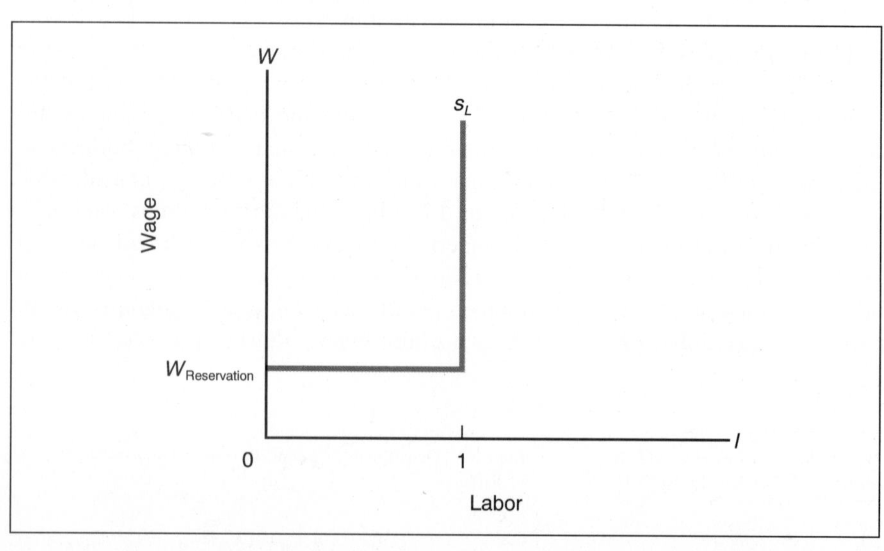

other athletes have been unable to exploit. Along the same lines, the average professional basketball player makes more than the average professional hockey player primarily because the National Basketball Association has a much richer television contract than does the National Hockey League.[6]

Horse racing exploits a different angle. The top jockeys earn fabulous salaries because society has decided that betting at the racetrack is an acceptable form of gambling, and people love to gamble. How many people would watch horses run around a track without the opportunity to bet on the outcome?

In the entertainment field, salaries are determined to a great extent by how the public prefers to be entertained. Movie stars, television personalities, and rock musicians enjoy an adoring public. Serious actors, dancers, and classical musicians perform in relative obscurity simply because the vast majority of people are uninterested in what they do.

The market reacts strongly to the public's preferences. Sylvester Stallone has parlayed a macho image into fame and a vast fortune. Recent estimates place his *annual* earnings at tens of millions of dollars. By contrast, Ian McKellen, acknowledged by many to be the greatest living classical actor, is a virtual unknown. Although McKellen undoubtedly derives enormous satisfaction from his accomplishments in the theater, his earnings are only a small fraction of Stallone's. McKellen's consummate talent on the stage is no match in the marketplace for Stallone's macho movie image, given the public's tastes.

Competitive versus Noncompetitive Market Forces

Competitive market forces cannot explain all the differences in the wages that people earn. Not all labor markets are highly competitive. Nonetheless, competitive market forces are an important determinant of relative wages, and VMP_L provides a convenient summary of the three factors that determine competitive wages: productivity or skills, the numbers of workers who are willing and able to enter a given occupation, and the market for the good or service being produced. Analyzing the combined interaction of these three factors is a good place to start when thinking about why different people earn different wages.

Chapters 18, 19, and 22 will discuss a number of other factors that determine the distribution of wage income. They fall into one of four categories:

1. special institutional arrangements such as the long-term employment relationships that exist between large corporations and many of their employees
2. noncompetitive market forces, including the market power of big business firms and labor unions
3. discrimination by race and sex
4. noneconomic factors such as inherited ability, marriage patterns, social status, and luck

Labor economists do not know the extent to which these other factors override the standard competitive market forces, but most are convinced that the Laws of Supply and Demand remain an important determinant of the distribution of wage income in the U.S. economy.

---

[6]Pay-per-view television may soon be commonplace in the other sports simply because it is so much more profitable than advertiser-supported television. The fans will resist it, though. They do not want to pay to watch their favorite teams.

THE FEDERAL MINIMUM WAGE[7]

MINIMUM WAGE (FEDERAL)

A wage floor legislated by the federal government, set at $4.25/hour in 1993, which is the lowest wage that firms can pay their workers.

We noted in Chapter 8 that the United States has generally been unwilling to institute price ceilings or price floors in response to complaints that free market prices represent an undue burden on the poor. There are two notable exceptions: price supports in agriculture and **minimum wage legislation,** which places a floor under the wages that firms can pay their production workers. Both policies came into being during the Great Depression of the 1930s and have remained in effect continuously since then. Chapter 9 concludes with an analysis of the minimum wage.

History and Current Status

The federal government passed a minimum wage for nonsupervisory employees in 1938 as part of the Fair Labor Standards Act, the first piece of labor legislation ever enacted at the federal level. The minimum was set at $.25 an hour, approximately 45 percent of the average hourly wage in manufacturing at the time. It applied to 43 percent of all hourly employees.

Congress has legislated increases in the minimum wage 16 times since 1938, the last time in 1989, effective April 1, 1990. Each adjustment targeted the minimum at between 40 and 50 percent of the average hourly wage in manufacturing. Congress has also periodically extended the percentage of workers covered by the legislation. As a result of these adjustments and extensions, the minimum wage in 1993 was $4.25 per hour and applied to 85 percent of all hourly production workers. The workers not covered are concentrated in agriculture and in small firms within the retail and the service sectors that employ a large proportion of part-time workers.

A U.S. Bureau of the Census survey undertaken in 1986 indicated that 5.1 million workers paid by the hour received a wage equal to the prevailing minimum wage of $3.35 (3.5 million) or less (1.6 million), representing 8.8 percent of all hourly workers. The workers most affected by the minimum wage tended to be young, female, working part-time, and concentrated in the service and the retail sectors. Of these 5.1 million workers, 37 percent were teen-agers, and 60 percent were less than 24 years of age. Sixty-five percent were women. Sixty-seven percent worked only part time. Slightly more than half worked in the service and the retail sectors. An additional 4.5 million workers received wages between $3.35 and $4.45 in 1986. They had nearly the same characteristics as those working at or below the minimum.

Economic Effects of a Minimum Wage

The goal of minimum wage legislation is clear enough, to ensure that all people who work escape the ravages of poverty. This was an especially compelling goal during the Great Depression of the 1930s. As we discovered in Chapter

[7]The analysis in this section relies on two sources: "Research Summaries," *Monthly Labor Review* 110, No. 7 (July 1987): 34–38 (for much of the data); and C. Brown et al., "The Effect of the Minimum Wage on Employment and Unemployment," *Journal of Economic Literature* XX, No. 2 (1982): 487–528 (for the analysis and the responses to the minimum wage).

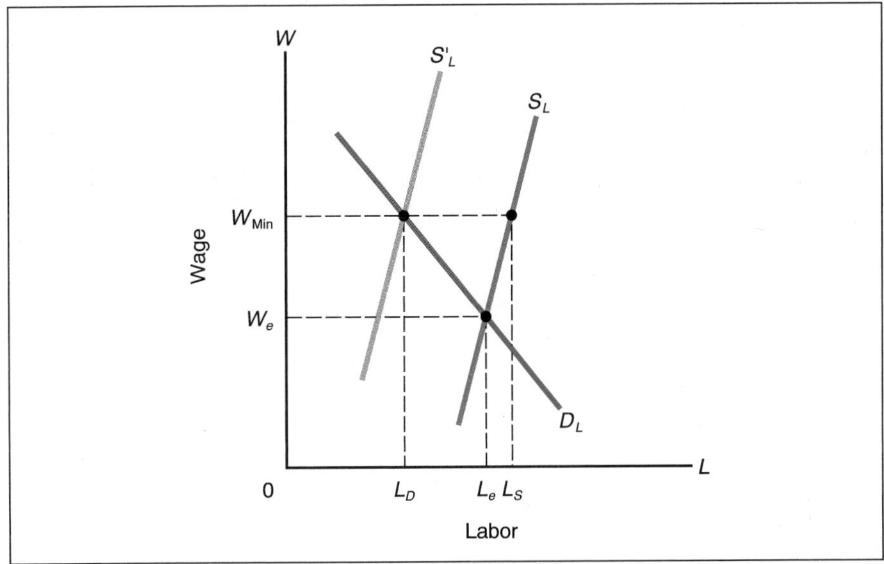

FIGURE 9.10

The Minimum Wage

The equilibrium quantity of labor and the wage is L_e, W_e without a minimum wage, at the intersection of D_L and S_L. The minimum wage, W_{Min}, is a price floor on wages set above W_e. At W_{Min}, L_S workers seek employment but firms hire only L_D workers. ($L_S - L_D$) workers are unemployed, equal to the amount of the excess supply in the unskilled labor markets at W_{Min}. There will be no unemployment if workers become discouraged trying to find employment and drop out of the labor force. In this case supply decreases to S'_L, and the number of workers supplied at W_{Min} equals L_D, the number of workers that the firms hire.

8, however, price ceilings and price floors are never totally effective; they end up trading one problem for another. A minimum wage floor is no different. It substitutes the problem of unemployment for an equilibrium wage that society has determined is too low, with the result that some low-income workers gain, while others lose. Whether low-income workers as a whole are better off is open to debate.

Figure 9.10 illustrates the effects of a minimum wage. The figure represents the market for a low-paying occupation, assumed to be highly competitive.

The market clears at L_e,W_e without a minimum wage, at the intersection of the market supply and the market demand curves, S_L and D_L. Society judges W_e to be unacceptably low, however, so it legislates a minimum wage of W_{Min}. As a result, firms reduce their quantity demanded to L_D workers, and the quantity supplied increases slightly to L_S. Hence, the policy generates unemployment equal to $L_S - L_D$. L_S people are willing to work at W_{Min}, but only L_D are hired. As with all price floors, the minimum wage substitutes a situation of chronic excess supply for the market's natural equilibrium.

The L_D workers who remain employed under the minimum wage are clearly better off. But $L_e - L_D$ of the unemployed workers are just as clearly worse off because they would have been willing to work at the market wage, W_e. The unemployed workers numbering $L_S - L_e$ might also be considered losers from this policy, since they do want to work at the higher minimum wage. (Firms are worse off, too, because they are forced to pay a higher wage, although minimum wage supporters are presumably more concerned about the low-income workers than they are about the firms.)

Do the gains of the gainers more than offset the losses of the losers? The answer is a matter of personal taste, but opinions one way or the other are likely to be influenced by the elasticities of the supply and the demand curves. Unemployment is higher with a minimum wage the more elastic supply and demand are. Also, the total wages receive by low-income workers decline if demand is elastic. $W_{\text{Min}} \cdot L_D < W_e \cdot L_e$. The reverse is true if demand is inelastic.

The Minimum Wage and Teen-age Unemployment

Some policy makers and economists have been especially concerned about the connection between the minimum wage legislation and the high teen-age unemployment rates. Knowing that teen-agers constitute a disproportionate share of the low-wage hourly workers and suspecting that the demand for unskilled teen-agers is highly elastic, they fear that the minimum wage is an important cause of teen-age unemployment. This fear has led to proposals for a two-tiered minimum wage, with a lower minimum for teen-agers than for all other workers.

Economic research has not been able to find a strong relationship between the minimum wage and teen-age unemployment, however. The consensus opinion is that a 10 percent increase in the minimum wage reduces teen-age *employment* only slightly, by 1 to 3 percent. In other words, the demand for teen-age labor appears to be highly inelastic. Moreover, increases in the minimum wage have essentially no effect whatsoever on teen-age *unemployment*.

The difference between the employment and the unemployment responses indicates that teen-agers faced with the prospect of unemployment quickly become "discouraged workers" and simply drop out of the labor force. In terms of Figure 9.10, the supply curve shifts to the left as discouraged workers leave the market, all the way to line S'_L. With the S'_L intersecting the demand curve at L_D, *employment* has dropped from L_e to L_D as a result of the minimum wage, but *unemployment* is zero. The market is in equilibrium at $L_D, W_{\min}$, not in a state of chronic excess supply. The employment effect is more important than the unemployment effect with discouraged workers, however, because the discouraged workers are losers under a minimum wage.

The question remains why the demand for teen-age labor should be so inelastic. Some labor economists believe this is a false estimate, caused by the fact that employers maintain employment either by paying an illegal wage below the minimum or by cutting nonwage fringe benefits to offset the higher wage payments. Whatever the explanation, the estimated employment effect does seem to be too low.

The Minimum Wage and Poverty

The minimum wage is justified as a means of protecting workers from poverty, but it is not a very effective policy tool to that end. The problem is that it does not target effectively on the poorest members of society. The majority of workers who benefit from the legislation are members of families that are not poor.

Theoretical studies show that general tax and transfer programs are potentially far more effective anti-poverty policies than is the minimum wage. But if the appropriate tax-transfer programs are not forthcoming, then the minimum wage may be the only way to protect immigrants, poorly trained U.S. citizens, people who can only work part time, and other workers who also happen to be poor.

Erosion of Effectiveness

Finally, whatever the various effects of the minimum wage legislation have been, they were seriously eroded during the 1980s by Congress's refusal to increase the minimum between 1981 and 1989. In 1981, the minimum wage of $3.35 was 42 percent of the average hourly wage in manufacturing, but by 1986 it was only 34 percent of the average. Not surprisingly, the percentage of hourly workers earning the minimum wage or less fell sharply during that time, from 15 percent in 1981 to 8.8 percent in 1986.

In some parts of the country the minimum wage became irrelevant by the mid-1980s. It was essentially a price floor set *below* the natural market equilibrium. For example, fast food restaurants in eastern Massachusetts were offering teen-agers $6.00 to $7.00 per hour in 1987. A 10 percent increase in the minimum wage that year to $3.69 could not possibly have raised the wages of these teen-agers or affected their employment opportunities. Even the recent 27 percent increase in the minimum wage to $4.25 left the minimum wage below the market wage for teen-agers in Massachusetts in 1992 (although not in other parts of the country). Congress must ensure that the minimum wage keeps pace with the natural increase in market wages caused by productivity growth and inflation if it wants to maintain the effectiveness of the minimum wage legislation.

SUMMARY

The first section of Chapter 9 demonstrated that competitive labor markets operate exactly as do competitive product markets, with the roles of supply and demand reversed. Individuals are the suppliers, and business firms the demanders.

Regarding the supply of labor:

1. Individuals experience the cost of supplying labor in terms of the leisure they sacrifice in order to earn income. The labor-leisure trade-off, and therefore an individual's labor supply curve, depends on substitution and income effects. The supply curve is not necessarily upward sloping because the substitution and the income effects pull in opposite directions. The substitution effect of a wage increase favors working harder, whereas the income effect of a wage increase favors taking more leisure.
2. Men and women in the United States appear to have very different supply curves. For men the income effect slightly dominates—their labor supply curves are downward sloping and highly inelastic. For women the substitution effect dominates—their labor supply curves are upward sloping and highly elastic.
3. The supply curve to a given occupation is almost certainly upward sloping, since occupations bear a substitute relationship to one another in the eyes of workers.
4. The desire for leisure places a substantial value on time. The time spent buying and consuming goods and services is an important element of their full cost, and the time costs are higher the higher a person's wage.

Regarding the demand for labor:

5. For competitive firms the extra revenue obtained from hiring additional labor is the value of labor's marginal product, equal to the marginal product of the last worker times the price of the product that the worker produces. $VMP_L = MP_L \cdot P_g$. Competitive firms maximize profit by hiring the amount

of labor at which the market wage equals the VMP_L. Consequently, the VMP_L is the firm's demand curve for labor.

The second section of the chapter discussed the distributional implications of competitive labor markets.

6. Identical workers within the same occupation earn the same wage no matter where they work.
7. Workers in two different occupations earn the same wage so long as they are equally willing and able to work in either occupation.
8. If workers are identical, but occupations differ in their required skills or attractiveness, then equalizing wage differentials result, which reflect the relative desirability of different jobs. The identical workers receive the same total utility, consisting of the wage plus the occupation's characteristics, no matter what job they take.
9. If people differ and jobs differ, then the overall market for labor separates into a number of individual, noncompeting labor markets with wages determined in each market by the Laws of Supply and Demand. Identical workers are treated equally, but nonidentical workers may receive different amounts of economic rent. Economic rent is the difference between the actual wage received and the wage required to keep a worker employed in a particular occupation.
10. Given that wages differ across occupations and that the wage = VMP_L, the VMP_L suggests three important determinants of wages in competitive markets: a worker's productivity or skill, the number of other workers with the same skill, and the market for the good or service that the worker is producing.

The final section of Chapter 9 analyzed the federal minimum wage.

11. The minimum wage, established in 1938, is a price floor that currently applies mostly to teen-agers, women, and part-time employees. Despite fears that the minimum wage would decrease employment, research studies find that the employment effects are quite small. Even so, the minimum wage has not been a very effective weapon against poverty, as originally intended, because only a minority of individuals working at the minimum wage come from poor families. Also, the minimum wage has lost some of its effectiveness because Congress did not adjust the minimum wage between 1981 and 1989. As a result, market wages exceed the minimum wage in some regions of the country.

KEY TERMS

derived demand
economic rent
equalizing wage differential
full price
marginal (physical) product of labor
minimum wage (federal)
value of labor's marginal product

QUESTIONS

1. Describe the roles of the income and the substitution effects in determining the slope of an individual's labor supply curve. What would the labor supply curve look like if
   a. the substitution effect is larger than the income effect?
   b. the substitution effect is smaller than the income effect?

2. What are some factors that may explain why the supply of labor for women is so much more elastic than is the supply of labor for men in the United States? Can you think of others besides those mentioned in the chapter?
3. Why do wages equal the value of labor's marginal product in competitive labor markets?
4. Suppose that a company is considering hiring a production expert who is expected to increase production by 10,000 units per year. The product sells for $40. The person applying for the job is asking for a salary of $500,000. Should the company hire this person? How would your answer change if
   a. the person asks for $380,000?
   b. the person asks for $500,000, but the price of the product increases to $55?
5.

NUMBER OF WORKERS	TOTAL PRODUCT	MARGINAL PRODUCT OF LABOR (MP_L)	VALUE OF LABOR'S MARGINAL PRODUCT (VMP_L)
0	0		
1	10		
2	18		
3	25		
4	31		
5	35		
6	37		
7	37		

   a. Complete the table. Assume the price of the product is $10.
   b. Does the Law of Diminishing Returns apply to these data ?
6. Refer again to the table in question 5.
   a. How many workers should the firm hire if the wage is $90? If the wage is $65?
   b. Assume the wage is $90. How many workers should the firm hire if the price of the product rises to $20?
7. Under what conditions are wages likely to be equal for two occupations? What conditions cause wages to differ for different occupations? Assume the labor markets are competitive.
8. "Competitive labor markets satisfy the principle of horizontal equality: Equals are treated equally." Do you agree or disagree with this statement? Explain.
9. Define *economic rent.* Do you think professional baseball players in the United States earn an economic rent? Explain.
10. Suppose that the government of a certain country is thinking about establishing a minimum wage for unskilled labor. The government is worried that the minimum wage may cause some unemployment. The government is also worried about the effect of the minimum wage on the total wages received by the unskilled labor. Given the government's concerns, which would it prefer?
    (i) Both the demand and the supply for unskilled labor are highly elastic.
    (ii) Both the demand and the supply for unskilled labor are highly inelastic. Illustrate using demand and supply curves.

CASE

Will The North American Free Trade Agreement (NAFTA) Hurt The U.S. Textile Industry?*

Few economic issues in the U.S. today have generated as much controversy as the North American Free Trade Agreement (NAFTA). NAFTA would eliminate trade barriers such as tariffs and quotas between the U.S., Canada, and Mexico. President Clinton supports ratification of NAFTA, as did President Bush, but NAFTA has a number of prominent opponents, including Ralph Nader, Jesse Jackson, Ross Perot, and organized labor. The opponents fear that free trade with Mexico, a relatively low wage country, will result in reduced employment and lower wages in the United States, as U.S. companies relocate to Mexico to take advantage of the lower wages there. Ross Perot made NAFTA one of the focal points of the 1992 presidential election debates. He stated that NAFTA would create a "great sucking sound as jobs head south to Mexico."

Chapter 39 will analyze the effects of NAFTA in the context of a more general, international trade model. Here we are concerned with how NAFTA may affect a specific industry, the U.S. textile and apparel industry.

The effects of NAFTA on the U.S. textile and apparel industry are of particular concern because the industry faced increased competition from foreign producers throughout the 1980s, especially from Asian countries. In 1980, imports accounted for approximately 20 percent of all clothing sales in the U.S. markets. By 1991, the market share of imports had risen to 60 percent. As a result of the increased foreign competition, employment in the U.S. textile and apparel firms decreased by more than 35 percent, from 2.4 million to 1.6 million workers. Despite these losses, the textile and apparel industry has remained a very important industry for the U.S., employing 9 percent of all U.S. manufacturing workers. It is the largest employer of women and minorities.

Will NAFTA lead to a further reduction in U.S. textile and apparel production, and thereby further reduce wages and employment opportunities for women and minorities in the U.S.? The answer appears to be "no."

In 1991 the value of textile and apparel imports from Mexico into the U.S. was approximately 1.2 million dollars. The value of exports from the U.S. to Mexico was 1.1 million dollars. If NAFTA is implemented all duties on goods made from North American yarn will be eliminated within a six year period. Industry experts estimate that U.S. textile and apparel imports from Mexico will rise about 60 percent as a result of NAFTA, and U.S. exports to Mexico will rise approximately 30 percent.

The increase in U.S. exports to Mexico will occur because Mexico will have to eliminate its 17 percent tariff on U.S.-made clothing within the six-year time span. The resulting increase in Mexican demand for U.S. textile and apparel products will benefit both U.S. textile firms and U.S. textile workers. Also, because the U.S. textile and apparel industry is relatively capital intensive, the U.S. firms are unlikely to relocate to Mexico to take advantage of lower Mexican wages. The higher costs of other inputs in Mexico, especially electricity, would outweigh any reduction in costs from using cheaper Mexican labor.

The estimated 60 percent increase of Mexican imports into the U.S. sounds threatening to the U.S. industry, but these imports will be primarily at the expense of Asian imports, most notably textile and apparel goods produced in Hong Kong, Singapore, and Taiwan. NAFTA puts the Asian exporters at a substantial disadvantage relative to the Mexican exporters since the Asian products, which are not made from yarn spun and woven within North America, will still be subject to tariffs and quotas in the United States. Also, wages in these countries have risen lately, putting the Asian producers at a further disadvantage relative to the Mexican producers.

ECONOMIC ADVISOR'S REPORT

Suppose that you are hired as an economic advisor by the U.S. textile workers union to address concerns they have about the effects of NAFTA on their members.

1. The union leaders ask you to explain to them what effect the estimated 30 percent increase in textile and apparel exports to Mexico will have on wages and employment of U.S. textile workers. Use a demand and supply diagram of the market for U.S. textile workers to answer their question, in which the demand curve is the demand for labor by U.S. textile and apparel firms and the supply curve is the supply of U.S. labor to U.S. textile and apparel firms. Put the wage on the vertical axis and employment on the horizontal axis.
2. The union leaders are also very concerned about the estimated 60 percent increase in imports of textile and apparel goods from Mexico to the U.S. Why are the increased Mexican imports not likely to have much effect on the wages and employment of U.S. textile workers?

*Provided by Klaus G. Becker, Texas Tech University.

PART

III

The Economic Problems of Consumers and Business Firms

CHAPTER

10

The Theory of Consumer Choice

LEARNING OBJECTIVES

CONCEPTS TO LEARN

How consumers maximize their utility

Applying the substitution and the income effects

CONCEPTS TO RECALL

The consumer's three-part economic problem [1]

The margin in economic analysis [2]

The substitution and income effects [5]

Imagine that you are relaxing and listening to one of your favorite cassette tapes. Listening to the tape is satisfying, but suppose that your friend asks you just how satisfying: "Excuse me. How much utility are you receiving as you listen to your tape?" You cannot possibly answer this question; no one could. We have no way of directly measuring our preferences, of knowing the exact amount of utility or satisfaction that we receive from the goods and services we consume. Does this mean that we cannot say anything about decisions that involve preferences? The answer, fortunately, is that we can solve economic problems that involve preferences. Economics would be in deep trouble if this were not the case because preferences appear in all forms of decision making.

Preferences are obviously central to the consumer's economic problem. They also play an important role in the business world. Two business managers reviewing five prospective investment projects may reach different decisions about them simply because the managers have different preferences. Suppose that the company's research department estimates that each project will have a satisfactory rate of return. Even so, preferences enter into the decision of whether to finance the projects because all investment projects are risky. Estimated rates of return are never guaranteed in the uncertain future. The first manager may be a bit of a gambler and decide to finance all five projects. The second manager, a more cautious person, may decide that only two of the five should be financed; the other three are too risky. Neither manager is necessarily right or wrong at the time the decision is made. They just have different preferences with regard to exposing the company to risk.

Preferences are also central to any social issue concerned with equity, which is to say almost all social issues. Should governments give aid to the poor, and, if so, should the aid be in cash or in kind? Some people believe that families and private charities, not the government, should provide for the poor. Other people believe that the government should provide for the poor. Among those people who favor government aid, some prefer that the government give cash grants. They are willing to let poor families decide how to spend the aid. Others adopt a more paternalistic stance. They prefer in-kind aid that directly provides those goods or services that they believe are necessary for the poor.

Economists in the nineteenth century actually did try to measure utility. Needless to say, their attempts were not very successful. A crowning achievement of economic theory during the twentieth century was to show how to solve economic problems involving preferences without having to measure utility directly.

Chapter 10 takes a close look at people in their role as consumers. The chapter analyzes the theory of consumer choice, which explains how consumers choose among the goods and services that they are able to purchase in order to maximize their utility. The principles developed in the chapter apply to all economic problems involving preferences.

One of the more important implications of the theory of consumer choice is the Law of (Downward-Sloping) Demand. We want to understand how our attempt to maximize utility leads to downward-sloping demand curves for nearly all of the goods and services we buy.

THE MODERN THEORY OF CONSUMER CHOICE

Think of yourself as a representative consumer trying to solve your own economic problem. To keep the analysis as simple as possible, let's consider just one small part of your problem. Suppose that you enjoy listening to recorded music on both compact discs (D) and cassette tapes (T). You have decided to allocate \$160 of your income during the year to purchase both discs and tapes. This is much less money than you would like to spend on discs and tapes, but you believe that is all you can afford. The price of a compact disc (P_D) is \$16, and the price of a cassette tape (P_T) is \$8. How many discs and tapes should you purchase in order to maximize your utility?

This simple example is detailed enough to capture all three parts of the consumer's economic problem. The *objective* is to maximize the utility that you receive from listening to discs and tapes. The *alternatives* are the various combinations of discs and tapes that you are able to buy. The *constraints* consist of your limited budget of \$160 combined with the prices of the discs and tapes. You are constrained because you cannot buy as many discs and tapes as you would like to buy. Because our simple example captures all parts of the consumer's economic problem, it is also detailed enough to reveal all aspects of the solution to the problem.

The first requirement for maximizing utility is simple enough. You must spend the entire \$160 on discs and tapes. Letting scarce income remain unused when it could be purchasing valued discs or tapes is obviously not the way to maximize utility. Therefore, you must choose one of the combinations of discs and tapes listed in Table 10.1. These are the combinations of discs and tapes that use up your entire budget of \$160, given that the price of discs is \$16 and the price of tapes is \$8. At one extreme you can choose to spend the entire \$160 on tapes. If you do, you can buy 20 tapes at a price of \$8.00 each. At the other extreme you can choose to spend the entire \$160 on compact discs. If you do, you can buy 10 discs at a price of \$16 each. The other combinations in the table are the alternatives in which you spend some of the \$160 on discs and some on tapes. For example, the combination of 4 discs and 12 tapes cost \$160. You spend \$64 on discs (\$64 = \$16 · 4) and \$96 on tapes (\$96 = \$8 · 12); \$160 = \$64 + \$96.

TABLE 10.1 Possible Combinations of Compact Discs and Cassette Tapes (Budget = \$160; P_D = \$16; P_T = \$8)

QUANTITY OF DISCS	QUANTITY OF TAPES
0	20
1	18
2	16
3	14
4	12
5	10
6	8
7	6
8	4
9	2
10	0

Spending all of your budget on discs and tapes is only one part of the solution to your economic problem. The second, and more difficult, part is an allocation problem. Exactly how do you spend your scarce income? You must choose the one combination of discs and tapes in Table 10.1 that maximizes your utility. In general, how should consumers allocate their scarce income among the alternative goods and services available to them in order to maximize their utility?

Choosing Discs and Tapes to Maximize Utility

Economists view the allocation process as proceeding in a series of continual, small adjustments until utility is maximized. Consumers make an initial choice and then ask themselves whether small, or marginal, adjustments in their choices would increase their utility. Recall that *marginal* refers to small changes. In terms of our example, suppose that you initially choose to buy 2 discs and 16 tapes. You then think about the possibility of making a small adjustment in your purchases, adding a disc at the expense of a few tapes or adding some tapes at the expense of a disc.

ABILITY TO TRADE

The rate at which consumers can trade one good for another in their budgets, equal to the price ratio of the two goods.

You adjust your purchases and maximize utility by comparing the ability to trade tapes for discs in the marketplace with your willingness to trade tapes for discs on the margin. The ratio of the market prices of discs and tapes indicates the **ability to trade** one good for the other. In our example P_D/P_T = \$16/\$8 = 2/1. You can trade two \$8 tapes for one \$16 disc or one \$16 disc for two \$8 tapes without spending any more or less income. You must then decide whether trading 2 tapes for 1 disc or 1 disc for 2 tapes increases your utility.

(MARGINAL) WILLINGNESS TO TRADE

The rate of trade between any two goods that leaves the consumer's level of utility unchanged; also called the *marginal rate of substitution* between the two goods.

At this point some introspection is required. You must have an idea of the rate at which you are willing to trade small quantities of tapes for discs. Giving up tapes lowers utility, and adding discs raises utility. Conversely, adding tapes raises utility, and giving up discs reduces utility. At some rate of trade the two opposing effects on utility just balance each other out, and your utility remains unchanged. This rate defines your **willingness to trade** small quantities of tapes for discs on the margin. You are willing to trade because a trade that leaves your utility unchanged makes no difference to you. You are equally well off whether you make the trade or not.[1]

You should adjust your spending between tapes and discs whenever your (marginal) willingness to trade differs from the ability to trade as determined by the ratio of the two prices. The ability to trade always remains the same so long as the prices remain the same. The market allows you to trade at the rate of 2 tapes for 1 disc in our example. Your willingness to trade on the margin changes, however, depending on how many tapes and discs you have purchased.

Refer to Table 10.2. Having initially purchased 2 discs and 16 tapes, the third column of the table indicates that you are willing to trade small quantities of tapes for discs at a rate greater than 2 to 1. If so, you should take advantage

[1]Economists refer to the willingness to trade on the margin as the marginal rate of substitution, labeled *MRS*. We will continue to use the terms *willingness to trade on the margin* and *(marginal) willingness to trade* in the text because they are more intuitive. The term *MRS* appears in Appendix 10:1, which has a more formal graphical analysis of the theory of consumer choice.

TABLE 10.2 (Marginal) Willingness to Trade Cassette Tapes for Compact Discs (Ratio of Tapes to Discs)

QUANTITY OF COMPACT DISCS	QUANTITY OF CASSETTE TAPES	(MARGINAL) WILLINGNESS TO TRADE	HYPOTHETICAL (MARGINAL) WILLINGNESS TO TRADE
0	20	greater	17/1
1	18	than	12/1
2	16	2/1	9/1
3	14	·	6/1
4	12	·	4/1
5	10	·	3/1
6	8	2/1	2/1
7	6	·	1/1
8	4	·	1/2
9	2	less than	1/4
10	0	2/1	1/16

of the market's offer to trade at 2 to 1. Buy 2 fewer tapes and 1 more disc, so that you now purchase 3 discs and 14 tapes. Since you are willing to give up more than 2 tapes to consume 1 more disc, trading at the rate of 2 tapes for 1 disc must increase your utility.

The fourth column of the table makes the example more concrete by providing a set of hypothetical numbers for your (marginal) willingness to trade at each combination of tapes and discs. You do not actually need to know precisely what your (marginal) willingness to trade is. Simply knowing that you are willing to trade tapes for discs at a rate greater than the rate at which the market allows you to trade, 2 to 1, is enough. However, the numbers help our intuition. According to the table, you are willing to trade at the rate of 9 tapes for 1 disc when you have initially purchased 2 discs and 16 tapes. Since you only have to give up 2 tapes to add 1 more disc, trading tapes for discs at the rate of 2 to 1 clearly increases your utility.

Having now adjusted your purchases to 3 discs and 14 tapes, you ask if a further adjustment increases your utility. According to Table 10.2, it does. You are still willing to trade tapes for discs at a rate greater than 2 tapes for 1 disc. The precise (marginal) willingness to trade is listed as 6 tapes for 1 disc in the fourth column of the table. Therefore, you should accept the market's offer to trade 2 tapes for 1 disc and adjust your purchases to 4 discs and 12 tapes. The adjustment increases your utility.

The adjustments continue until you are purchasing 6 discs and 8 tapes. At that point your willingness to trade tapes for discs on the margin is 2 for 1. Therefore, if you trade at the market rate of 2 tapes for 1 disc, your utility remains the same. Once your (marginal) willingness to trade equals the ability to trade, you have reached an equilibrium in the adjustment process because no further trades are beneficial. You have maximized your utility by purchasing 6 discs and 8 tapes.

The same principle applies if you adjust your purchases from the other direction. Suppose that you initially purchase 7 discs and 6 tapes. According to Table 10.2, your willingness to trade tapes for discs on the margin is less than the ability to trade at 2 tapes for 1 disc. So long as the (marginal) willingness to trade tapes for discs is less than the ability to trade, you should adjust by adding more tapes at the expense of discs. The fourth column of the table indicates that you are willing to give up 1 disc to consume 1 more tape. However, the market allows you to add 2 tapes if you give up 1 disc. Therefore, adding 2 tapes at the expense of 1 disc must increase your utility. Since you are now at 6 discs and 8 tapes after the trade, no further adjustment can increase your utility.

The adjustment process has established the following principles of consumer choice:

UTILITY-MAXIMIZING DECISION RULE

The (marginal) willingness to trade one good for another is equal to the ability to trade them according to the ratio of their prices.

1. **Utility** is **maximized** when the (marginal) willingness to trade between any two goods equals the ratio of their prices.
2. If the (marginal) willingness to trade between any two goods differs from the ratio of their prices, utility can be increased *with no additional expenditure of income* by buying more of one good and less of the other.

In terms of our example, if the (marginal) willingness to trade tapes for discs is greater than P_D/P_T, buy more discs and fewer tapes. If the (marginal) willingness to trade tapes for discs is less than P_D/P_T, buy more tapes and fewer discs.

The only remaining question is whether our example is realistic. Does the willingness to trade on the margin change, so that it eventually equals the ability to trade as consumers adjust their purchases? In our example your willingness to trade tapes for discs diminishes steadily as you add discs and subtract tapes. Is this pattern of diminishing willingness to trade to be expected?

LAW OF DIMINISHING (MARGINAL) WILLINGNESS TO TRADE

For a consumer, the marginal willingness to trade one good for some other good decreases as more and more of the one good is exchanged for the other good.

The answer is definitely yes. The pattern of diminishing willingness to trade holds with such regularity that it is elevated to the status of a law. The **Law of Diminishing (Marginal) Willingness to Trade** is the backbone of the theory of consumer choice. It is based on the well-tested psychological principle that the grass is always greener on the other side of the fence. People tire of things that they have in abundance and long for things that they have little of. In terms of our example, your willingness to trade tapes for discs is relatively high when you are purchasing only 2 discs and 16 tapes. Since you have many tapes and only a few discs, you are willing to give up a large number of tapes for another disc. As you continue to add discs and subtract tapes, however, your willingness to trade tapes for additional discs steadily diminishes. By the time you reach 7 discs and 6 tapes, your willingness to trade tapes for another disc has fallen to 1 for 1. Beyond that point your willingness to trade tapes for discs changes direction. For instance, if you are purchasing 9 discs and only 2 tapes, you are now tiring of discs and longing for tapes. According to Table 10.2, you are willing to trade 4 of your discs in exchange for 1 more tape.

The best evidence supporting the Law of Diminishing (Marginal) Willingness to Trade is simply that consumers tend to purchase a wide variety of goods and services. In our example if your willingness to trade never declined as far as 2 for 1, you would keep trading tapes for discs at the market rate of 2 for 1 until you end up purchasing only discs. In practice, consumers tend not to adjust their purchases to the point of completely removing goods and services from their budgets. This suggests that their willingness to trade goods and services for one another eventually reaches equality with their price ratios, in line with the Law of Diminishing (Marginal) Willingness to Trade.

We saw in Chapter 5 that the substitution and the income effects of a change in price lie behind the Law of Demand. The two effects follow directly from the solution to the consumer's economic problem.

The Substitution Effect

Recall that the substitution effect is a relative price effect: Consumers tend to substitute in favor of products that have become relatively cheaper and away from products that have become relatively more expensive. We can see how the substitution effect of a change in price arises in our example from the principle that you equate your (marginal) willingness to trade with the ability to trade tapes for discs in order to maximize utility.

Suppose that the price of discs decreases from $16 to $8. The ratio of the prices is now 1/1 (P_D/P_T = $8/$8 = 1/1). The ability to trade tapes for discs has decreased from 2 tapes for 1 disc to 1 tape for 1 disc. However, your willingness to trade tapes for discs is 2 for 1 at the combination of 6 discs and 8 tapes. Therefore, your willingness to trade tapes for discs exceeds the ability to trade tapes for discs, and your utility is no longer maximized. You should take advantage of the new ability to trade at 1 for 1 and substitute discs for tapes in your budget. Since you are willing to trade 2 tapes for 1 disc, the gain in utility from adding 1 more compact disc exceeds the loss in utility from purchasing 1 less tape. As you continue to add discs and subtract tapes, your willingness to trade tapes for discs declines because of the Law of Diminishing (Marginal) Willingness to Trade. You keep substituting discs for tapes in your budget until the willingness to trade tapes for discs declines to 1/1, the new market price ratio. At that point the adjustment process has reached a new equilibrium, and your utility is once again maximized.

In conclusion, the decrease in the price of discs, other things equal, induces you to substitute in favor of discs and against tapes in order to maximize your utility. The quantity of discs demanded increases because of this substitution effect.

The Income Effect

Recall that the income effect of a change in price is an absolute price effect: A change in price changes consumers' purchasing power, or real income, and a change in purchasing power tends to affect the quantity demanded of all goods. Our example gives us a more precise understanding of what purchasing power is.

Purchasing power refers to the quantities of goods and services that consumers are able to purchase with their limited incomes. It is not a single number, but the whole set of choices available to consumers, assuming they spend all their income. In our example your purchasing power when the price of compact discs is $16 and the price of tapes is $8 is the entire set of choices listed in Table 10.1

A change in one or more prices changes purchasing power, even if income remains the same. Suppose that you still allocate $160 to purchase discs and tapes, but that the price of compact discs falls to $8.00. Now if you spend all $160 on discs and tapes, the new choices available to you have greatly expanded. Table 10.3 displays a partial listing of your new options.

TABLE 10.3 **Possible Combinations of Compact Discs and Cassette Tapes (Budget = \$160; P_D = \$8; P_T = \$8)**

QUANTITY OF DISCS	QUANTITY OF TAPES
0	20
2	18
4	16
6	14
8	12
10	10
12	8
14	6
16	4
18	2
20	0

The decrease in the price of discs from \$16 to \$8 has clearly increased your purchasing power because you can

1. Buy more tapes without sacrificing any discs (for example, 6 discs and 14 tapes at the new prices versus 6 discs and 8 tapes at the old prices),
2. Buy more discs without sacrificing any tapes (for example, 12 discs and 8 tapes at the new prices versus 6 discs and 8 tapes at the old prices), or
3. Buy more discs and more tapes (for example, 10 discs and 10 tapes at the new prices versus 6 discs and 8 tapes at the old prices).

Notice that the decrease in the price of discs permits increased consumption of tapes as well, with only one exception: If you always choose to purchase only tapes, the decrease in the price of discs has no effect on your purchases. However, the exception does not apply in our example. When the price of discs was \$16, you bought 6 discs and 8 tapes.

In general, a decrease in any price increases purchasing power, and an increase in price decreases purchasing power. The change in purchasing power is the source of the *income effect* of a price change. A decrease in the price of any good tends to increase the quantity demanded of all normal goods. Conversely, an increase in the price of any good tends to decrease the quantity demanded of all normal goods.

To summarize, the substitution and the income effects combine to support the Law of Demand. When the price of discs decreases, other things equal, both effects lead to an increase in the quantity of discs demanded in order to maximize utility. Your demand curve for compact discs slopes downward and to the right.

FOOD STAMPS—SUBSTITUTION AND INCOME EFFECTS APPLIED

The substitution and the income effects underlie all analysis of consumer behavior. Sometimes the effects are considered directly. At other times reference to the Law of Demand is sufficient, with the understanding that the demand curve summarizes the operation of both effects simultaneously. The analysis in this text will most often require only the Law of Demand, but occasionally we will look at each effect separately. The U.S. government's food stamp program is an excellent vehicle for illustrating how the separate effects can be useful in economic analysis.

Americans are a charitable people, but they are ambivalent about how to offer charity, in cash or in kind. An **in-kind gift** takes the form of a particular good or service. In-kind aid has the apparent advantage of accountability. The donors want the recipients to have more of a particular good, and they believe in-kind aid will guarantee this result. Aid in the form of cash has the advantage of honoring the principle of consumer sovereignty. Cash assistance allows the recipients to decide how to spend the aid. Americans are always a bit uncomfortable forcing people to spend resources in a certain way, despite the oft-expressed fears that gifts of cash will be spent irresponsibly.

IN-KIND GIFT

A charitable donation or transfer in the form of a particular good or service.

REFLECTION: Have you ever received a gift and wished that you had been given the equivalent amount of cash instead? Do you prefer to give gifts or cash to your relatives and friends? If gifts, why is that?

The government follows both impulses in its public assistance programs for the poor. For example, Aid to Families with Dependent Children is a cash grant program to the poor. It provides a monthly check to low-income families headed by a single parent. The food stamp program is an in-kind aid program. When it began in 1971, low-income families received coupons that allowed them to purchase food at a discount. The lower the family's income, the higher the discount. Does offering families discount coupons affect their expenditures differently than if they were offered an equivalent amount of cash? The substitution and the income effects helps us answer this important policy question.

For the sake of comparison, assume that a family receives 30 percent food coupons, so that each dollar spent on food costs the family only $.70. Suppose that the family spends $100 on food each month, $70 out of its own pocket and $30 paid by the government. Alternatively, suppose that the family receives a cash grant of $30 each month, to be spent as it wishes. Would the family spend the same amount on food and all other goods and services each month under the two programs?

The answer is no, in general, because the food discount has both an income effect and a substitution effect associated with it, whereas the cash grant has only an income effect. The food stamp program lowers the effective price of food by 30 percent. As a result, the family's purchasing power has been increased by $30 because it spends $100 on food. This increase is the income effect of the price discount. The price of food relative to all other goods has also decreased, which generates a substitution effect in favor of food. In contrast, the cash grant is simply a $30 increase in purchasing power. It causes no change in relative prices between food and all other goods.

The additional substitution effect of the food discount causes the family to buy more food, and less of all other goods, than the cash grant does. Another way to think of this is that in order to receive $30 with the food stamps, the family has to purchase $100 worth of food. Under the cash grant it receives $30 no matter how it spends the money. The cash grant provides no additional incentive to purchase food. Therefore, offering discounts on a particular item does induce families to spend more on that item than does a cash grant for the same dollar expenditure by the government. This inducement is the intent of in-kind aid.

There is a catch, however. The government does not offer families unlimited food stamps to buy as much food as they want for a very good reason. Families would then have an incentive to purchase enormous amounts of food and resell it at a profit. In our example the family could buy food at a 30 percent discount; then resell it at, say, a 20 percent discount; and make a huge profit. Consequently, the government has always limited the amount of coupons available to any one family.

For most families this limitation destroys the substitution effect. To see why, suppose that each month the family is limited to $30 in coupons, but spends $200 on food. The last $100 spent on food is purchased at full price. Hence, there is no change in the relative price of food for the last $100—and no substitution effect.

The family would not care if it received $30 in cash or $30 worth of discounts on its first $100 of food expenditures each month. The family members are equally well off in either case because there is only an income effect with either program. The family will spend the same amounts on food and all other goods and services under either program.

This example demonstrates that the substitution effect is a *marginal* price effect. For it to apply, the change in price must apply to the very last goods purchased. In fact, most families receiving food stamps spend more on food each month than their allotment of coupons. For this reason economists view the food stamp program as essentially just another cash grant program for low-income families. Taxpayers may not see it this way, but substitution and income effect analysis argues strongly in favor of the economists' point of view.[2]

SUMMARY

The first section of Chapter 10 presented the modern theory of consumer choice, which describes how consumers solve their economic problem.

1. The first requirement for maximizing utility is that consumers spend all of their scarce incomes.
2. According to the modern theory of consumer choice, consumers compare their willingness to trade small quantities of any two goods with the price ratios of the goods in order to maximize utility. The (marginal) willingness to trade is the rate of trade of the two goods that leaves utility unchanged. Consumers are indifferent to a trade at that rate. The ratio of the prices indicates the ability to trade the two goods.
3. With reference to the discs-tapes example, utility is maximized when the (marginal) willingness to trade tapes for discs equals the ratio of the price of discs to the price of tapes.
4. If the willingness to trade tapes for discs exceeds the price ratio, consumers substitute toward discs in order to increase utility. If the willingness to trade tapes for discs is less than the price ratio, consumers substitute toward tapes in order to increase utility.
5. The Law of Diminishing (Marginal) Willingness to Trade says that the willingness to trade tapes for discs decreases the fewer tapes and more discs the consumer has, and vice versa.

The second section of the chapter analyzed the federal food stamp program in terms of the substitution and the income effects.

---

[2]A number of years ago the government switched from discount coupons to coupons with a given cash value. The cash coupons can only have an income effect because they do not change the relative price of food. They are clearly equivalent to an equal-value cash grant unless a family chooses not to use all its coupons, which is rare.

6. The substitution and the income effects answer the question of whether low-income families will react differently to food stamps than to an equivalent amount of aid in cash. Discount food stamps increase a family's purchases of food relative to a cash grant of equal value because of a substitution effect that is missing from a cash grant. However, if a family purchases more food than is subsidized by its allotment of food stamps, then food stamps and cash grants are equivalent. The substitution effect of the food stamps disappears. Most families in the United States do purchase more food than is subsidized by their allotment of food stamps, so the food stamp program is effectively a cash grant.

KEY TERMS

ability to trade
law of diminishing (marginal) willingness to trade
utility-maximizing decision rule
(marginal) willingness to trade

QUESTIONS

1. a. What are the income and the substitution effects of a price change?
   b. How is each of them related to the Law of Demand?
2. a. Suppose that a consumer buys only two goods, *X* and *Y*. The consumer has income of \$200 to spend on these two goods, and the prices of *X* and *Y* are P_X = \$5 and P_Y = \$10. Explain why it is difficult to define the consumer's purchasing power (real income) unambiguously. How might you define the consumer's purchasing power (real income)?
   b. What happens to the consumer's purchasing power (real income) in terms of your definition if P_X rises to \$10?
3. Suppose that a consumer's marginal willingness to trade hot dogs for hamburgers is 3 to 1, that is, 3 hot dogs for 1 hamburger. Also, hamburgers are twice as expensive as hot dogs are.
   a. Is the consumer purchasing hot dogs and hamburgers so as to maximize utility?
   b. If not, how should the consumer adjust his purchases of the two goods to increase utility? Why?
4. State the Law of Diminishing (Marginal) Willingness to Trade, and demonstrate how it supports the Law of Demand.
5. a. What is an in-kind gift? Give an example.
   b. Why might people prefer to receive gifts of cash rather than in-kind gifts?

APPENDIX

10:1

Consumer Choice Using Indifference Curves

Appendix 10:1 presents a graphical analysis of the modern theory of consumer choice. The graphical analysis extends the discussion in the text by taking a closer look at the nature of preferences, or tastes.

The appendix uses the same example as in Chapter 10. You have decided to allocate \$160 of your income to purchase compact discs (D) and cassette tapes (T). The price of compact discs, P_D, is \$16, and the price of cassette tapes, P_T, is \$8. Compact discs and cassette tapes are desirable goods that provide utility, and you would always like to have more of each no matter how many you already own. Your problem is to determine the combination of discs and tapes that yields the most satisfaction, given your limited budget of \$160.

THE STRUCTURE OF PREFERENCES

Ordering Preferences

To solve their economic problems, consumers must be able to determine a *complete ordering* of their preferences with respect to the combinations of goods and services available to them.

The notion of an **ordering** has two properties. Suppose that you are presented with two combinations of compact discs and cassette tapes, A and B, and asked which combination you prefer. Combination A contains 10 discs and 5 tapes; combination B contains 7 discs and 7 tapes. An ability to *order* your preferences for these combinations means, first, that you are able to decide that

1. You prefer combination A to combination B, or
2. You prefer combination B to combination A, or
3. You are indifferent between A and B (each yields the same amount of utility or satisfaction).

There is a fourth possibility: You cannot decide how you feel about the two combinations. This is the possibility that an ordering rules out. If your preferences are such that you cannot decide among various alternatives, then you cannot solve your economic problem.

Notice that ordering pairs of alternatives according to preference or indifference is an ordinal, or rank-ordering, procedure. If you prefer one combination of goods to the other, you are *not* required to say by *how much* you prefer the one, but simply that you prefer it. A is first and B is second, or B is first and A is second, or they are tied. That is an ordinal ranking—and all any consumer (or a decision maker in any context) needs to know.

TRANSITIVITY

A condition on an ordering of consumer preferences requiring that all pairwise rankings of alternative combinations be consistent with one another.

A preference ordering must also satisfy a consistency requirement known as **transitivity.** Transitivity requires that all pairwise rankings of alternative combinations be consistent with one another. For example, suppose that you are presented with a third combination, C, containing 5 discs and 8 tapes and you are asked to order all pairwise comparisons of A, B, and C. You decide that you prefer A to B and B to C. Then transitivity requires that you also prefer A to C. Indifference works the same way. If you are indifferent between A and B, but prefer B to C, then you must prefer A to C.

ORDERING OF PREFERENCES

When faced with two combinations of goods and services, the ability to determine either that one combination is preferred to the other or that the two combinations give the same level of utility; an ordering must also satisfy the condition of transitivity.

Transitivity removes the possibility of the following type of inconsistency. Suppose that you prefer A to B and B to C, but that you also prefer C to A, in violation of transitivity. You begin with combination A. Someone forces you to exchange A for B. According to your ranking of A and B, this exchange makes you worse off. Next, you are forced to exchange B for C. According to your ranking of B and C, this exchange makes you worse off again and therefore certainly worse off than when you had A. But your direct ranking of C and A indicates that you are better off than when you had A. Transitivity rules out an exchange that makes you simultaneously better off and worse off.

COMPLETE ORDERING OF PREFERENCES

The ability to provide an ordering of all alternative combinations of goods and services potentially available to the consumer.

A **complete ordering** means that you are able to order *all* alternatives potentially available to you. You are never in a position of saying "I cannot decide how I would rank these alternatives."

Preferences and the Indifference Map

An *indifference map* is an abstraction that provides a convenient graphical representation of a complete ordering of preferences. Imagine that you are placed in a room for hours on end and asked to order, pairwise, hundreds of combinations of compact discs and cassette tapes. You do this without any regard to what you can actually afford to buy, that is, without regard to the amount of income you have or the prices of discs and tapes. The questioning is simply an exercise to determine your preferences for the two goods.

If you are able to provide a complete ordering of the various combinations, a graph of your preferences would probably appear as represented in Figure

FIGURE 10:1.1

The Indifference Map for Compact Discs and Cassette Tapes

The indifference map represents a typical ordering of preferences for compact discs and cassette tapes. It is the set of all the indifference curves, I_0, I_1, I_2, etc., for the two goods. The consumer is indifferent between all combinations of discs and tapes on any one indifference curve, such as *A*, *B*, *C*, *D*, and *E* on I_0; these combinations give the same level of utility. All combinations of discs and tapes on a higher numbered indifference curve are preferred to any combination of discs and tapes on a lower numbered indifference curve. The consumer's goal is to reach the highest possible indifference curve.

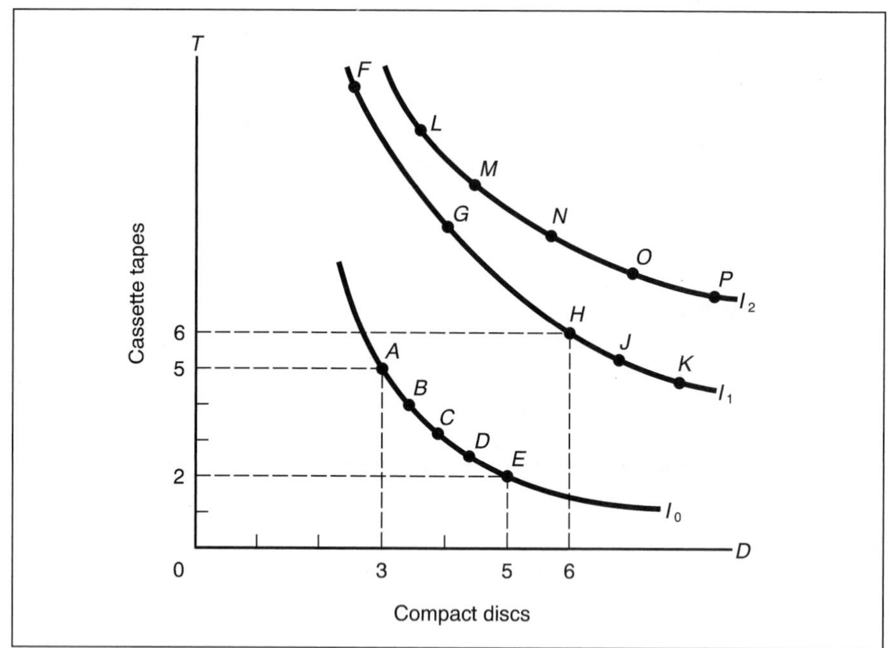

INDIFFERENCE CURVE

A graphical representation of the different combinations of goods and services that an individual is indifferent to because they yield the same level of utility.

10:1.1. Cassette tapes are on the vertical axis, and compact discs are on the horizontal axis. Each point on the graph represents a combination of discs and tapes that you were asked to consider. Your preferences would reveal the following pattern. You would register indifference between some combinations of discs and tapes, such as *A*, *B*, *C*, *D*, and *E* on curve I_0. The curve I_0 is called an **indifference curve.** An indifference curve contains a set of disc-tape combinations to which you are indifferent. For instance, *A* and *E* might refer to these combinations: *A* = (3 discs, 5 tapes) and *E* = (5 discs, 2 tapes). Relative to *A*, *E* provides 2 additional discs, which alone raises your utility. But *E* also contains 3 fewer tapes, which alone lowers your utility. If the two effects on your utility just cancel one another out in your mind, you would register indifference between these two combinations.

You would prefer other combinations, such as *H* on indifference curve I_1, to all the combinations on I_0. For example, *H* might contain 6 discs and 6 tapes. So long as discs and tapes are desirable, *H* is certainly preferred to either *A* or *E*, since *H* contains more of both goods. Therefore, by the transitivity requirement, *H* must also be preferred to all points on I_0, combinations for which you are indifferent to either *A* or *E*. However, you would be indifferent between *H* and a number of other combinations. All these combinations, such as *F*, *G*, *J*, and *K*, lie on indifference curve I_1, along with point *H*. Each one of them is preferred to any combination on I_0, again because of transitivity.

Similarly, points *L*, *M*, *N*, *O*, and *P* on indifference curve I_2 are all combinations to which you are indifferent, but you prefer each of these combinations to any combination on either I_1 or I_0. Notice that higher numbered indifference curves contain disc-tape combinations that provide increasing amounts of utility.

INDIFFERENCE MAP

The set of all the indifference curves.

The set of all the indifference curves, the **indifference map,** represents your complete ordering of all possible combinations of discs and tapes. The indif-

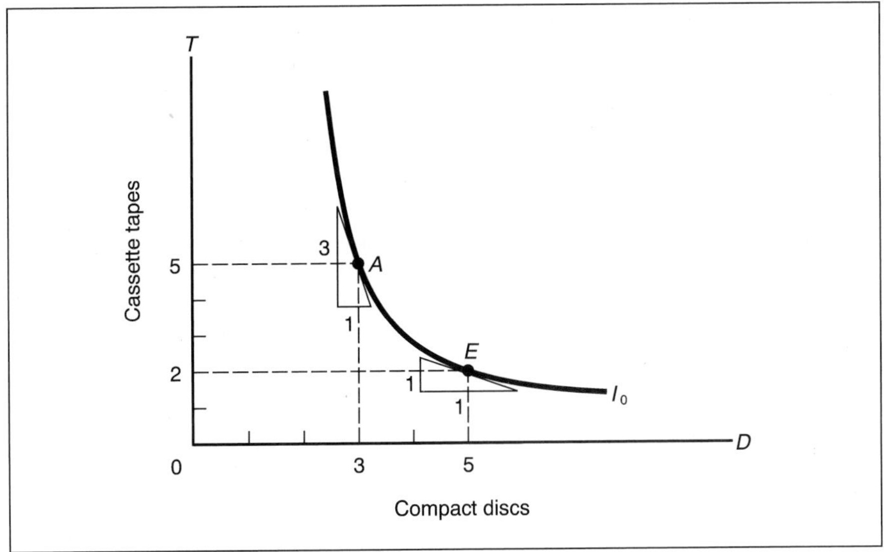

FIGURE 10:1.2

The Marginal Rate of Substitution Between Compact Discs and Cassette Tapes

The marginal rate of substitution (MRS) between compact discs and cassette tapes is the slope of an indifference curve. It is the same concept as the marginal willingness to trade, the rate at which the consumer is willing to trade small quantities of tapes for discs in the sense that the consumer's utility remains unchanged by the trade. The MRS declines as the consumer moves down and to the right along an indifferene curve consuming more discs and fewer tapes, for example, from 3/1 at point *A* to 1/1 at point *E* on I_0. The decline in the MRS reflects the Law of Diminishing Marginal Rate of Substitution.

ference map does not mean to suggest that you ever actually sit in a room for hours on end thinking about alternatives. Rather, it indicates how you would order any combinations that might actually become available to you, combinations that you certainly would think about.

Willingness to Trade: The Marginal Rate of Substitution

The indifference map allows us to represent the concept of the (marginal) willingness to trade developed in Chapter 10. Consider any one combination of discs and tapes, represented by a point on some indifference curve. The willingness to trade away from that combination is the *slope* of the indifference curve at that point.

Figure 10:1.2 reproduces indifference curve I_0 from the indifference map of Figure 10:1.1. Suppose that you are at point *A*, consisting of 3 discs and 5 tapes. According to the diagram, the slope of I_0 at point *A* is 3. Giving up 3 tapes for 1 new disc or giving up 1 disc for 3 new tapes leaves you on indifference curve I_0.[1] Since the trade of 3 for 1 leaves you on the same indifference curve, your utility has remained the same. But that is the definition of the (marginal) willingness to trade: the rate of trade to which you are indifferent in the sense that your utility neither increases or decreases.

MARGINAL RATE OF SUBSTITUTION

The rate at which an individual is willing to trade one good for another so as to leave utility unchanged; the slope of an indifference curve.

The slope of an indifference curve is called the **marginal rate of substitution (MRS)** between the two goods pictured on the axes. The MRS is *marginal* because it refers to small exchanges between the goods. It is a rate of *substitution* in the sense that the consumer is indifferent to the exchange. Values of the MRS are negative numbers because one of the goods is decreas-

[1]This is only approximately true. Along a smooth curve the slope refers to infinitesimal exchanges of discs and tapes, exchanges in small fractions of a unit. Since fractional units are impossible, the slope only approximates unit exchanges of discs and tapes.

ing while the other is increasing along an indifference curve. Finally, the MRS is synonymous with the (marginal) willingness to trade.

LAW OF DIMINISHING MARGINAL RATE OF SUBSTITUTION

The more of a good that consumers have, the fewer units of another good they are willing to trade to consume an additional unit of the good.

Notice that the indifference curves in Figures 10:1.1 bow inward to the origin. They are said to exhibit **diminishing marginal rate of substitution:** The slope of each indifference curve declines as the consumer moves downward and to the right along the curve. Refer to Figure 10:1.2. Because of the shape of I_0, the MRS at A exceeds the MRS at E. At A you are willing to trade 3 tapes for 1 disc; at E you are willing to trade only 1 tape for 1 disc. This makes sense. You desire both discs and tapes. At A you have many tapes and few discs relative to E. Therefore, to remain at the same level of utility you should be willing to trade more tapes for discs at A than at E. Adding a new disc is worth a sacrifice of 3 tapes at A, but only 1 tape at E. As discussed in Chapter 10, the diminishing marginal rate of substitution (willingness to trade) holds with such regularity that it is elevated to the status of a law of consumer behavior, the Law of Diminishing Marginal Rate of Substitution (Marginal Willingness to Trade).

SOLVING THE CONSUMER'S ECONOMIC PROBLEM

The indifference map defines the preference relationship between the alternatives and the objective. Your *objective* in terms of the indifference map is to reach the highest possible indifference curve. Which indifference curve this is depends on your budget constraint.

The Budget Constraint

BUDGET CONSTRAINT

The maximum combination of goods and services that a consumer is able to purchase, given the consumer's income and the prices of the goods and services.

The **budget constraint** determines the combinations of goods and services that a consumer is actually able to purchase based on the consumer's income and the prices of the goods and services. The budget constraint says that total expenditures on the goods and services must equal income. In our example total expenditures on tapes and discs equal \$160, the portion of your income that you have allocated to these goods. The algebraic expression of your budget constraint is

$$16 \cdot D + 8 \cdot T = 160$$

where D is the number of discs that you purchase, T is the number of tapes that you purchase, the price of discs is \$16, and the price of tapes is \$8. At \$16 per disc, $16 \cdot D$ is your total expenditure on discs. At \$8 per tape, $8 \cdot T$ is your total expenditure on tapes. The sum of the expenditures on discs and tapes is \$160.

We want to graph the budget constraint with tapes on the vertical axis and discs on the horizontal axis so that we can combine it with the indifference map. To graph the budget constraint, solve the algebraic expression for T.

$$8 \cdot T = -16 \cdot D + 160$$

$$T = -(16/8) \cdot D + 160/8$$

$$T = -2 \cdot D + 20$$

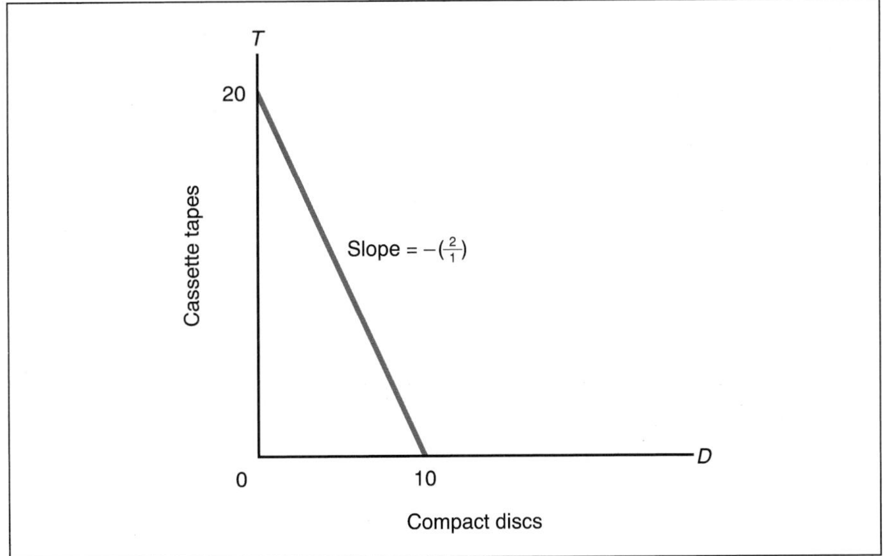

FIGURE 10:1.3

The Budget Line for Compact Discs and Cassette Tapes

The budget line is a graph of the consumer's budget constraint for compact discs and cassette tapes. The consumer can buy all combinations of discs and tapes that are on or under the budget line, but cannot afford the combinations above the budget line. The slope of the budget line is the (negative of the) ratio of prices, $(-)\ P_D/P_T = (-)\ \$16/\$8 = (-)\ 2/1$, the ability to trade tapes for discs. The distance of the budget line from the origin depends on how much income the consumer allocates to purchasing discs and tapes, $160 in our example. The intercept on the vertical axis indicates that the consumer can buy 20 tapes by spending all $160 on tapes at $8 per tape.

The graph of the budget constraint is the straight line pictured in Figure 10:1.3, called the budget constraint line or simply the **budget line.** The slope of the budget line equals -2, the (negative of the) ratio of the price of discs to the price of tapes. The slope indicates the *ability to trade* 2 tapes at $8 for 1 disc at $16 without any change in total expenditures. The ability to trade is a negative number because tapes and discs move in opposite directions in the exchange. The intercept on the vertical axis is 20, the quantity of tapes you can purchase if you spend your entire budget on tapes. At the vertical intercept, $D = 0$. The combinations of discs and tapes that you can actually purchase lie on or below the budget constraint. Combinations above the line are unattainable.

BUDGET LINE

A graphical representation of the consumer's budget constraint.

Changes in the Budget Constraint

The position of the budget line changes if income or one of the prices changes. Suppose that the income you allocate to tapes and discs increases from $160 to $320. The new budget constraint is

$$16 \cdot D + 8 \cdot T = 320$$

$$T = -(16/8) \cdot D + 320/8$$

$$= -2 \cdot D + 40$$

The slope of the budget line stays the same, but the vertical intercept has doubled from 20 to 40 tapes. Hence, the increase in income shifts the budget line out parallel to the original budget line, as depicted in Figure 10:1.4(a). In general, an increase in income shifts the budget line out parallel to the original line, and a decrease in income shifts the budget line in parallel to the original line.

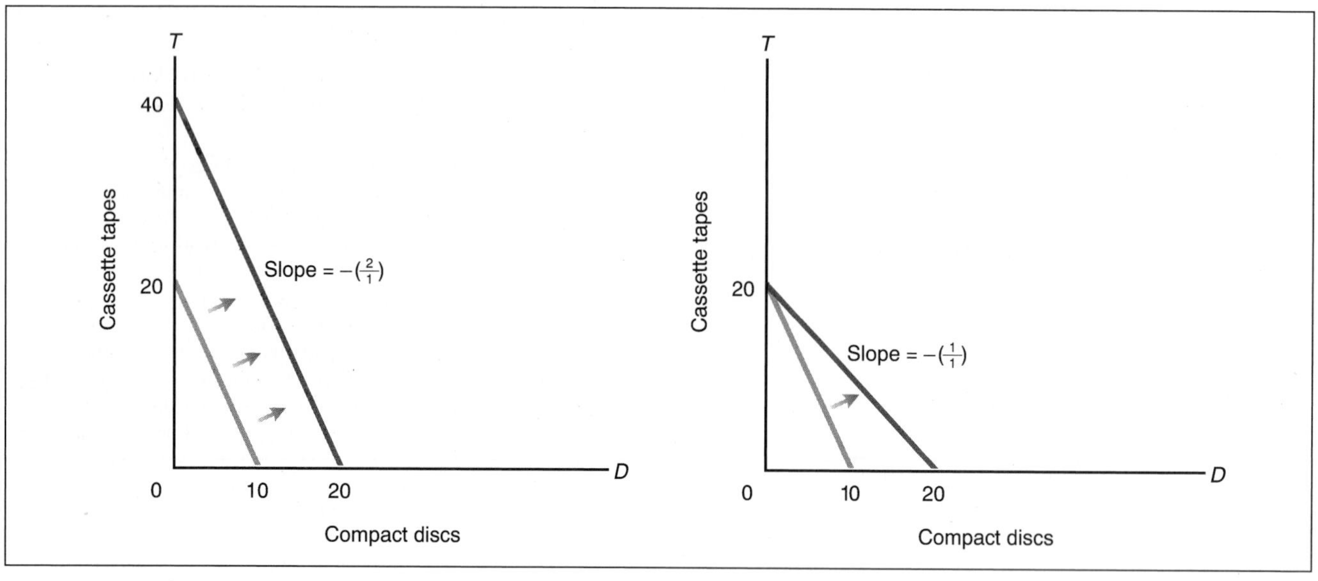

FIGURE 10:1.4

Changes in the Budget Line

Increases or decreases in income cause a parallel shift in the budget line outward or inward. In Figure 10:1.4(a), a doubling in the income allocated to discs and tapes from $160 to $320 shifts the budget line parallel outward. The intercept on the vertical axis doubles from 20 tapes to 40 tapes, because the consumer can now buy 40 tapes by spending all $320 of income on tapes at $8 per tape. Increases and decreases in the price of one of the goods rotate the budget line. In Figure 10:1.4(b), a decrease in the price of discs, P_D, from $16 to $8 rotates the budget line out along the horizontal axis. The slope of the budget line decreases from (−) 2/1 to (−) 1/1. (−) *PD*/*PT* = (−) $8/$8 = (−) 1/1. The intercept on the vertical axis remains the same because the price of tapes, P_T, has not changed. The consumer can still buy only 20 tapes by allocating all $160 to tapes at $8 per tape.

In contrast, a change in one of the prices causes the budget line to rotate. For instance, suppose that P_D falls from $16 to $8. The budget constraint is now

$$8 \cdot D + 8 \cdot T = 160$$

$$T = -(8/8) \cdot D + 160/8$$

$$= -1 \cdot D + 20$$

Figure 10:1.4 (b) depicts the new budget line. The slope is now −1, but the vertical intercept remains at 20. The budget line has rotated outward, with the vertical intercept serving as the fixed point. If you spend all your income on tapes, you can still buy only 20 tapes. Except for that one point, however, the decrease in P_D increases your purchasing power, as discussed in Chapter 10. All the original combinations are available to you, as well as many combinations that were beyond the original budget constraint. In general, a decrease in one of the prices rotates the budget line outward, whereas an increase in one of the prices rotates the budget line inward. You should practice rotating the budget line by representing the effect on the budget line of (1) an increase in P_D and (2) both an increase and a decrease in P_T (Hint: The original horizontal intercept becomes the fixed point of rotation when P_T changes).

Maximizing Utility: The Consumer's Equilibrium

Let's return to the original budget constraint. You allocate $160 to purchase tapes and discs, the price of discs is $16, and the price of tapes is $8. Which of the available combinations of discs and tapes should you purchase?

To determine the combination of discs and tapes that maximizes utility, combine the budget line of Figure 10:1.3 with the indifference map of your preferences, Figure 10:1.1, as in Figure 10:1.5.

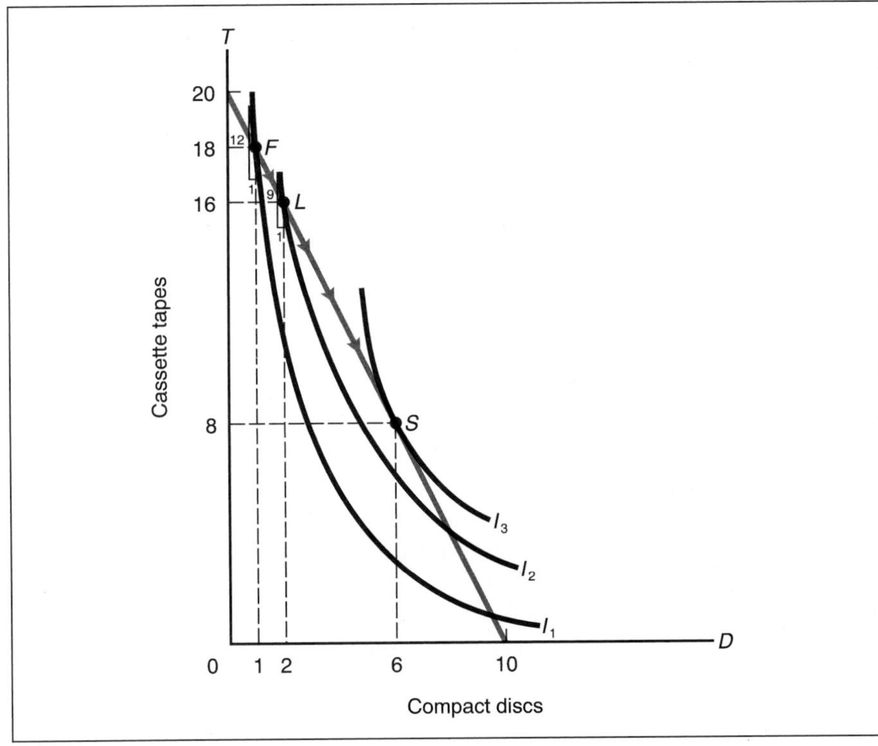

FIGURE 10:1.5

Maximizing Utility: the Consumer's Equilibrium

This figure combines the indifference map for compact discs and cassette tapes from Figure 10:1.1 with the budget line for discs and tapes from Figure 10:1.3. The consumer is in equilibrium, receiving the maximum possible amount of utility, at point *S*, the point of tangency between indifference curve I_3 and the budget line. At the point of tangency, the slope of the indifference curve, the MRS, equals the slope of the budget line, the ratio of the prices P_D/P_T. At any other points on the budget line, such as *F* and *L*, MRS $\neq$ P_D/P_T. The consumer is on a lower indifference curve than I_3 and can increase utility by reallocating purchases of discs and tapes without spending any more on discs and tapes.

Your objective is to reach the highest possible indifference curve, given the combinations actually available to you. That combination is at point *S* in the diagram, consisting of 6 discs and 8 tapes. Point *S* is the point at which the budget line is *tangent* to one of the indifference curves. You are able to reach indifference curve I_3, but only at point *S*. You are in equilibrium at point *S* because you have no incentive to change your allocation of 6 discs and 8 tapes. Any other combination of discs and tapes along the budget line moves you to a lower indifference curve and makes you worse off.

Two properties of note apply to point *S*. First, you are spending all your scarce budget. Point *S* is *on*, not under, the budget line. Letting income go idle when both of the goods are desirable is clearly inefficient—a waste of scarce resources.

Second, because *S* is a point of tangency, the slopes of the budget line and the indifference curve I_3 are equal at point *S*. The slope of the budget line is the negative of the ratio of the prices, $-(P_D/P_T) = -(\$16/\$8) = -2$, the ability to trade tapes for discs. The slope of I_3 at *S* is the MRS at *S*, the (marginal) willingness to trade tapes for discs at *S*. Hence, at point *S*

$$\text{MRS} = \text{(the negative of) the ratio of the prices}$$

In other words, at point *S*

$$\text{the (Marginal) willingness to trade} = \text{the ability to trade}$$

This is the allocational rule for maximizing utility developed in Chapter 10.

CONSUMER EQUILIBRIUM

A situation in which the marginal rate of substitution between any two goods equals the ratio of their prices; the consumer is maximizing utility.

EQUILIBRIUM

A situation in which there is no incentive to change a decision.

To see why this rule must hold for maximum utility, consider another point on the budget line, point *F* on indifference curve I_1. You spend all your income at *F*, purchasing 18 tapes and 1 disc. But the allocational rule does not hold. According to Figure 10:1.5, at *F* the MRS is 12/1 on I_1. You are willing to trade 12 tapes for 1 disc. However, the ability to trade remains at 2/1 everywhere along the budget line, equal to the ratio of the prices. Therefore, you should trade 2 tapes for 1 disc and move along the budget line in the direction of the arrows toward *S*. Total expenditures remain the same at \$160, but you move to a higher indifference curve—say, to point *L* on I_2.

Since you have added discs and decreased the quantity of tapes, the willingness to trade tapes for discs declines. The MRS at point *L* is 9/1, according to Figure 10:1.5. However, the MRS still exceeds 2/1, the ability to trade. Hence, you should once again exchange 2 tapes for 1 disc, moving further along the budget line toward point *S*. Continue exchanging 2 tapes for 1 disc until you reach point *S* on indifference curve I_3. At point *S* the MRS and the ratio of prices are both (−)2/1. With total expenditures fixed at \$160 no further exchanges can move you to a higher indifference curve (improve utility).

At point *S* you have reached an **equilibrium.** In economic analysis an equilibrium exists when no one has an incentive to change. Since you have attained the highest possible utility at point *S*, given your limited budget, you have no incentive to change from *S*. Conversely, no other point on or under the budget line is a point of equilibrium. At all these other points there is an incentive to reallocate your purchases, since you can move to higher indifference curves without any increase in total expenditures on discs and tapes.

Deriving the Individual Demand Curve

The indifference map and the budget constraint line embody all aspects of the consumer's problem: the objective, the alternatives, and the constraint, along with a complete ordering of the alternatives according to the consumer's preferences. As such, the indifference map–budget line diagram can be used to derive the individual demand curve.

Recall that an individual demand curve is an other things equal relationship between price and quantity demanded. Figure 10:1.6 (a) depicts the equilibrium point *S* for our sample problem, at which you purchase 6 discs and 8 tapes. Figure 10:1.6 (b) shows the corresponding point, *S*′, on the demand curve for discs. The demand curve is drawn under the assumptions that P_T = \$8, your income = \$160, and your tastes are as represented by the indifference map in Figure 10:1.6 (a). These assumptions are the "other things" determining quantity demanded that are being held constant along the demand curve. Given those values, the demand curve indicates that if P_D is \$16, then you want to buy 6 compact discs.

To determine the other points on the demand curve, hold income, P_T, and tastes constant and vary P_D in the indifference map–budget constraint diagram. The budget line rotates as P_D varies, with the fixed point on the vertical axis. Figure 10:1.6 (a) shows the new position of the budget line for various values of P_D. A new equilibrium exists along each new budget line at the point where the budget line is tangent to an indifference curve. These points are labeled *B*, *J*, and *W* in Figure 10:1.6 (a), with the values of discs indicated in each instance. In other words, the change in P_D establishes a new combination of discs and tapes for which MRS = (−) P_D/P_T.

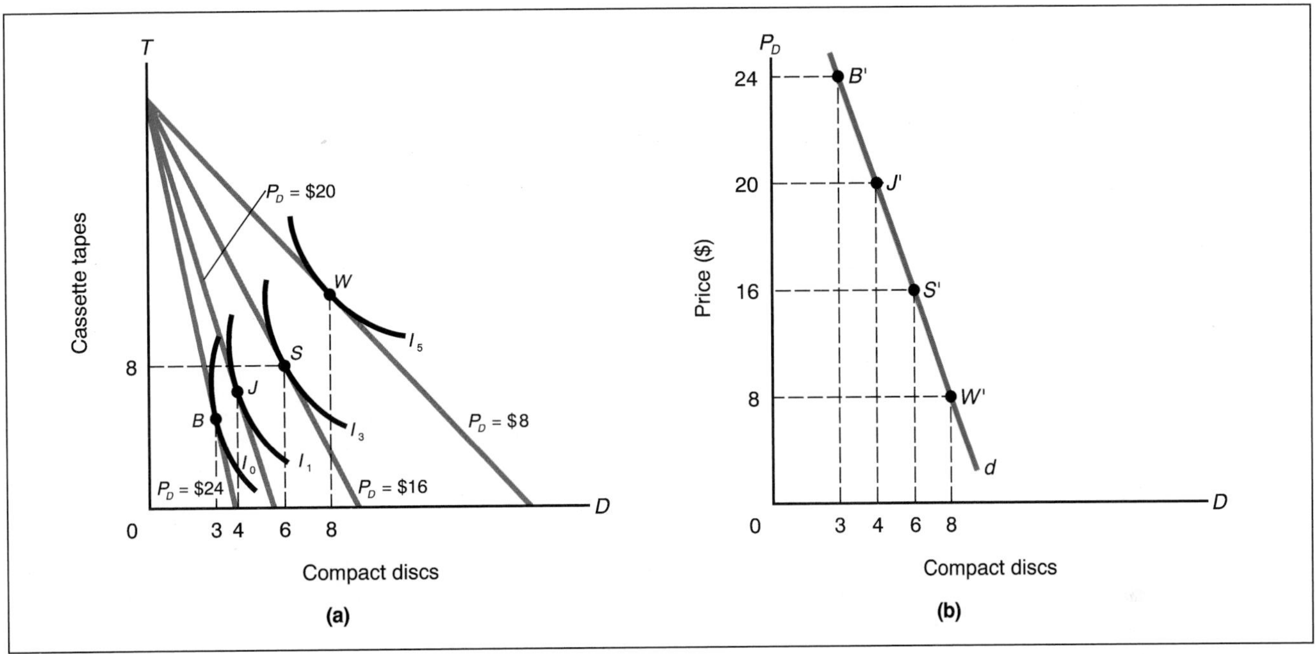

FIGURE 10:1.6

The Demand Curve for Compact Discs and the Consumer's Equilibrium

All points on the individual demand curve for compact discs in Figure 10:1.6(b) are points of consumer equilibrium in Figure 10:1.6(a) in which the consumer is maximizing utility. The demand curve shows the quantity of discs demanded as the price of discs, P_D, varies, while holding constant tastes, income at $160, and the price of tapes, P_T, at $8. For example, when P_D = $16, Figure 10:1.6(a) shows that the consumer maximizes utility at point S, and purchases 6 discs. Therefore the corresponding point on the demand curve in Figure 10:1.6(b) is S', showing that the quantity of discs demanded is 6 when P_D = $16, other things equal or constant such as tastes, income, and P_T.

The points B, J, and W in Figure 10:1.6 (a) correspond to points B', J', and W' along the demand curve in Figure 10:1.6 (b). For instance, B' indicates that the quantity of discs demanded is 3 when P_D = $24 (and income = $160, P_T = $8, and tastes are as represented by the indifference map). So the demand curve indicates how much you want to buy at each price, P_D, in the sense that points on an demand curve are points of consumer equilibrium, or maximum utility.

The Substitution and the Income Effects

The substitution and the income effects that underlie the individual demand curve can also be represented on the indifference map–budget line diagram. Consider points S and W in Figure 10:1.6 (a). At S, P_D = $16, and you purchase 6 discs (and 8 tapes). At W, P_D = $8, and you purchase 8 discs. Therefore, when the price of discs falls from $16 to $8, the substitution and the income effects combined cause quantity demanded to increase by 2 discs. Figure 10:1.7 conceptually decomposes the substitution and the income effects of the decrease in P_D into their separate components.

Recall that the substitution effect is a relative price effect. It involves a direct comparison of willingness to trade with the price ratios. In order to isolate the substitution effect in the move from S to W, the income or purchasing power effect of the price decrease must be removed. The increase in purchasing power as a result of the price decrease is what allows you to achieve a higher level of utility. Therefore, by removing the purchasing power effect you are constrained to enjoy the same level of utility as when the price was $16. In terms of the diagram, you are constrained to move along the original indifference curve.

FIGURE 10:1.7

The Substitution and the Income Effects

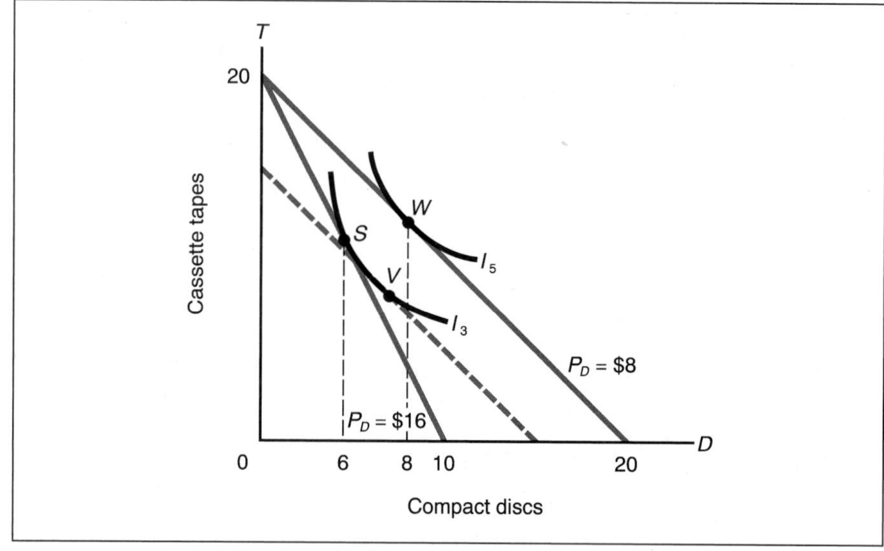

In our example, a decrease in the price of compact discs, P_D, from \$16 to \$8 leads to an increase in the quantity of discs demanded from 6 discs to 8 discs as the consumer moves to a new equilibrium from *S* to *W*. The figure shows how to decompose the increase in quantity demanded into two components, one resulting from the substitution effect and one resulting from the income effect. The substitution effect is the move from *S* to *V*. It shows how the consumer would react to facing the new price ratio, P_D/P_T = \$8/\$8 = 1/1, but having income taken away so as to remain on the initial indifference curve I_3 (that is, being forced to remain at the same level of utility). The income effect is the move from *V* to *W*. It is the result of returning the income that was taken away to keep the consumer on I_3 in order to measure the substitution effect.

To isolate the substitution effect, then, engage in the following conceptual procedure. You are allowed to purchase discs and tapes at the new price ratio, P_D/P_T = \$8/\$8 = 1/1. However, you must also relinquish income so that your utility remains the same. As income is taken away, the new budget line shifts in parallel until it is just tangent to the original indifference curve, I_3, at point *V* (the dotted line). The difference between the quantity of discs demanded at *V* and the quantity of discs demanded at *S* is the measure of the *substitution effect* of the price decrease. The amount of income taken from you in order to remain on I_3 is a measure of the value to you of the decrease in the price of discs from \$16 to \$8. It indicates how much of your income you would be willing to pay to have the price decrease from \$16 to \$8, in the sense that the payment would make you indifferent to the original situation.

Because of the assumption of diminishing marginal rate of substitution, the direction of the substitution effect is unambiguous. A decrease in price increases quantity demanded *if utility is held constant.* Since the new budget constraint is flatter because of the decrease in P_D, *V* must be on a flatter portion of I_3 than is point *S*. You buy more discs and fewer tapes. Likewise, an increase in price decreases quantity demanded *if utility is held constant,* and you move along indifference curve I_3.

To measure the income effect, return the income that was taken away to hold you on I_3. Returning the income shifts the dotted budget line through *V* out parallel until it reaches the actual new budget line. You now consume at point *W*, the actual equilibrium. The difference between the quantity of discs demanded at V and the quantity of discs demanded at W is the measure of the *income effect,* or purchasing power effect, of the price decrease. It is the difference between the combined substitution and income effects (S to W), and the substitution effect (S to V). The income effect further increases the quantity of discs demanded because discs are a normal good. If discs were an inferior good, point W would be to the left of point V. For inferior goods an increase in income reduces quantity demanded.

FOOD STAMPS OR CASH GRANTS

The indifference map–budget line diagram is useful for demonstrating the differences between in-kind aid such as the U.S. food stamp program and an equal dollar amount of aid in the form of cash. To conclude the appendix, we will reproduce Chapter 10's analysis of the original food stamp program using the indifference map–budget line framework.

Figure 10:1.8 depicts the recipient family's position both prior to and after receiving aid. Food is on the horizontal axis, and all other goods are on the vertical axis. The indifference map shows the family's preferences for food and all other goods. The budget line, JK, is the family's budget constraint if it receives no aid. The prices of food (P_F) and all other goods (P_O) are both assumed to equal \$1, so that the slope of the budget line, JK, is -1. Using only its own income, the family reaches point A on indifference curve I_0. At A the slope of I_0 is equal to -1, the slope of budget line JK. Purchases of food and all other goods are F_A and O_A, respectively.

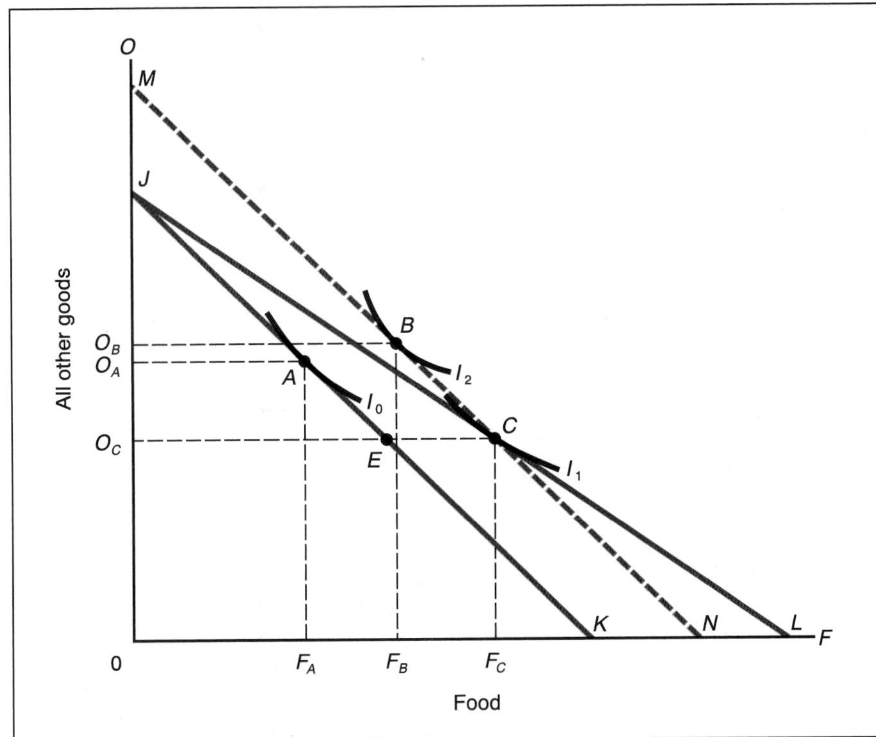

FIGURE 10:1.8

Food Stamps versus Cash Grants

The 30 percent food stamp coupons rotate the family's budget line from JK to JL, and the family moves from point A on indifference curve I_0 to point C on indifference curve I_1. The family spends O_CE of its own funds on food and receives food stamps worth EC from the government. A cash grant of EC would shift the family's budget line out parallel to the dotted line MN, and the family would move to point B on indifference curve I_2. Because of the substitution effect, the food stamps induce the family to consume more food than it would with the equal value cash grant, F_C versus F_B. The family is also worse off with the food stamps than with the cash grant, reaching point C on I_1 versus point B on I_2.

Following the example in Chapter 10, suppose that the family receives food stamp coupons that reduce the price of food by 30 percent. Since the effective price of food has decreased to \$.70, the budget line rotates outward to the new solid budget line, *JL*. The family moves to point *C* on indifference curve I_1. At *C* the slope of I_1 is equal to 0.7, the slope of new budget line *JL*. The family now purchases F_C of food and O_C of all other goods. It spends O_CE of its own funds on food, the amount of food on the no-aid budget line, *JK*, and receives *EC* worth of coupons from the U.S. government. O_CE is 70 percent of O_CC.

Suppose, instead, that the family receives a cash grant in the amount of *EC*, the same amount that the government spends on food coupons. The cash grant causes the original budget line to shift out parallel to *JK*, to the dotted line, *MN*. The family now maximizes its utility at point *B* on indifference curve I_2. At *B* the slope if I_2 is equal to -1, the slope of budget line *MN*. The family purchases F_B of food and O_B of all other goods.

Three facts stand out in comparing points *C* and *B*. First, the two aid programs create different sets of alternatives for the family, even though the dollar amounts of aid are the same. The food stamp program increases the family's purchasing power indirectly by reducing the price of food. In contrast, the cash program increases the family's purchasing power directly by increasing its income. Second, because the food stamp program changes the price ratio between food and all other goods, it introduces a substitution effect in favor of purchasing food that is absent from the cash grant program. F_C is larger than F_B because of the substitution effect. Third, the family is better off with the cash grant than with the equal dollar amount of food stamps. It is able to reach indifference curve I_2 with the cash grant, but it can only reach indifference curve I_1 with the food stamps. The cash grant is better because the family is free to spend the grant however it wants to. In contrast, the food stamp program induces the family to purchase food by artificially lowering its price. In effect, the family has to bias its purchases towards food to generate *EC* dollars worth of aid. This bias reduces the family's utility relative to a no-strings-attached cash grant. In-kind aid substitutes in part the paternalistic desires of the donor for the desires of the recipient.

Food Stamps as a Cash Grant

Chapter 10 indicated that most economists have always considered the food stamp program to be equivalent to a cash grant program because the amount of food stamps any one family can receive is limited. So long as the family spends more on food each month than is covered by its allotment of food stamps, the program is equivalent to a cash grant. Figure 10:1.9 pictures the situation with limited coupons.

The family receives 30 percent food coupons, with a total dollar limit of *DG* in government aid. The budget line rotates as before, but only until the amount of government aid reaches *DG*. Beyond point *G* the new budget line is parallel to the original line, at a horizontal distance of *DG*. The new budget line is *JGP*.

Suppose that the family moves from *A* on the original budget line to *H* on the new budget line when it receives the food stamps. The family purchases F_H of food, but the 30 percent subsidy applies only to the amount F_G. The family pays full price of \$1 on all food purchases between F_G and F_H. The

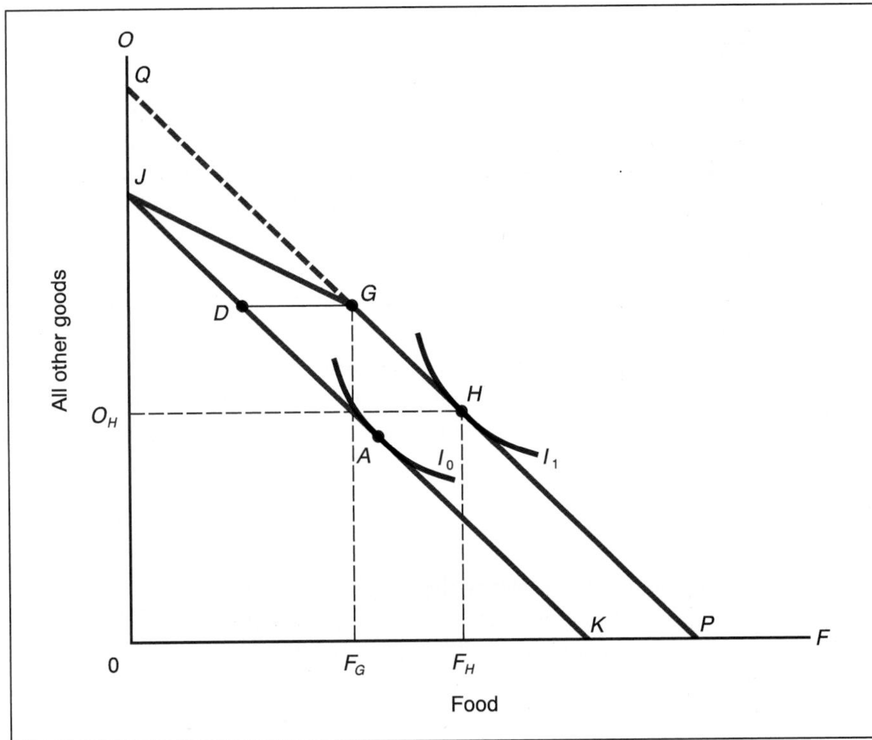

FIGURE 10:1.9

Limited Food Stamps Are Equivalent to a Cash Grant

The government limits the amount of food stamp coupons that a family can receive, equal to the amount *DG* in the figure. As a result, the 30 percent food stamp coupons rotate the budget line out from *JK* to *JG*, beyond which the new budget line *GP* is parallel to the original budget line *JK*. The family moves to point *H* on indifference curve I_1. A cash grant of *DG* shifts the budget line to *QGP*, and the family moves to point *H* on indifference curve I_1, the same as with the food stamps. The cash grant and the food stamps are equivalent from the family's point of view as long as the family spends more on food each month than its allotment of food stamps. Limiting the food stamps to an amount *DG* removes the substitution effect of the food stamps.

total subsidy is *DG*. In contrast, a cash grant of *DG* shifts the original budget line parallel to the right by amount *DG*. The family moves to point *H*, *exactly as it does under the food stamp program.* The only difference in the budget lines under the two aid programs lies in the region above and to the left of point *G*. Under the food stamp program the combinations of food and all other goods available to the family lie on the segment *JG*. Under the cash grant the combinations of food and all other goods available to the family lie on the segment *QG*. But the family is not in the region above and to the left of *G* under the food stamp program because it purchases more food each month than F_G, the amount subject to the 30 percent discount.

Most families on food stamps do purchase more food than is covered by their allotment of coupons. For them, the limit on the coupons effectively removes the substitution, or relative price, effect. Only the income effect of the subsidy remains. As a result, cash and food stamps become identical forms of aid in every respect.

SUMMARY

Appendix 10:1 began with a discussion of the structure of preferences that is required to solve any economic problem involving preferences.

1. Decision makers must be able to provide a complete ordering of their preferences. In terms of our consumer problem, a complete ordering means that, when presented with any two combinations of discs and tapes, you can always determine whether you prefer one combination to the other or are indifferent between the two. A complete ordering also requires tran-

sitivity of preferences: If you prefer combination A to combination B, and combination B to combination C, then you must prefer combination A to combination C.

2. A complete ordering of discs and tapes gives rise to an indifference map, a graphical representation of preferences. The indifference map is the set of all indifference curves. Each indifference curve contains the combinations of discs and tapes to which you are indifferent because the combinations give you the same level of utility.
3. The slope of an indifference curve is the marginal rate of substitution (MRS) between tapes and discs. The MRS indicates the rate at which you are willing to trade tapes for discs. Indifference curves bow inward to the origin, reflecting the Law of Diminishing Marginal Rate of Substitution.
4. The further an indifference curve is from the origin, the higher the utility level it represents. A consumer's objective is to reach the highest possible indifference curve.

Appendix 10:1 then presented a graphical solution to the consumer's economic problem.

5. The budget constraint indicates the combinations of goods and services actually available to the consumer, assuming that total expenditures equal total income. In our example the budget constraint depends on the income allocated to purchase discs and tapes and the prices of discs and tapes.
6. The graph of the budget constraint is the budget line. The budget line is a straight line whose slope is the (negative of the) ratio of the price of discs to the price of tapes. The price ratio indicates the ability to trade discs for tapes. Changes in income shift the budget line in or out in a parallel manner. A change in one of the prices causes the budget line to rotate.
7. The consumer is in equilibrium, and maximizes utility, at the point of tangency between the budget line and one of the indifference curves. At the point of tangency the marginal rate of substitution between discs and tapes equals the ratio of the price of discs to the price of tapes. Alternatively, the (marginal) willingness to trade discs for tapes equals the ability to trade discs for tapes.
8. To obtain points on the individual demand curve for discs, hold income, the price of tapes, and preferences constant, and vary the price of discs. The new points of tangency between the budget lines and the indifference curves determine the quantity of discs demanded at each price of discs, other things equal.
9. The substitution effect of a price change shows the increase in quantity demanded if the consumer is forced to move along the original indifference curve so that utility remains unchanged. The substitution effect is always negative: A decrease in price leads to an increase in quantity demanded along an indifference curve, and vice versa. Having moved along an indifference curve, the income, or purchasing power, effect is the additional change in quantity demanded when the budget line is shifted out parallel until it reaches the actual new budget line. The income effect of a price decrease (increase) increases (decreases) the quantity demanded for normal goods.

Appendix 10:1 concluded with a comparison of food stamps and cash grants using the indifference map–budget line framework. The analysis reached the same conclusions as the discussion in Chapter 10.

10. Discount food stamps increase a family's purchases of food relative to a cash grant of equal value because of a substitution effect that is missing from a cash grant. However, if a family purchases more food than is subsidized by its allotment of food stamps, then food stamps and cash grants are equivalent. The substitution effect of the food stamps disappears. Most families in the United States do purchase more food than is subsidized by their allotment of food stamps, so the food stamp program is effectively a cash grant.

KEY TERMS

budget constraint
complete ordering of preferences
consumer equilibrium
indifference curve
indifference map
law of diminishing marginal rate of substitution
marginal rate of substitution
ordering of preferences
transitivity

QUESTIONS

1. What are the assumptions about preferences that underlie the theory of consumer choice? Indicate why each assumption is important for solving the consumer's economic problem.
2. a. What is the marginal rate of substitution (MRS) between two goods?
   b. What is the relationship between the MRS and an indifference curve between the two goods?
   c. What is the relationship between the MRS and the marginal willingness to trade one of the goods for the other?
3. a. What is an indifference curve?
   b. Draw three reasonable-looking indifference curves from the indifference map for compact discs and cassette tapes, and explain why you drew them as you did (that is, explain their shapes).
   c. Which of the three indifference curves in part b represents the highest level of utility? The lowest level of utility?
   d. Can indifference curves between two goods ever cross? Why or why not?
4. Suppose that Mr. Smith likes to consume hot dogs and hamburgers. He has $100 to spend on these two goods. A hamburger costs $2.00, and a hot dog costs $1.00.
   a. Draw Mr. Smith's budget line for hamburgers and hot dogs.
   b. Show how each of the following affects Mr. Smith's budget line:
      (i). an increase in the price of hamburgers to $4.00
      (ii). an increase in the income that Mr. Smith spends on hamburgers and hot dogs to $200.
      (iii). a decrease in the price of hot dogs to $0.50
5. Return to the original conditions in question 4: income is $100; the price of hamburgers is $2.00 and the price of hot dogs is $1.00. Redraw Mr. Smith's budget line.
   a. Add reasonable-looking indifference curves for hamburgers and hot dogs to your diagram of the budget line, and show the utility-maximizing quantities of hamburgers and hot dogs.
   b. What must the marginal rate of substitution (MRS) between hamburgers and hot dogs be at the utility-maximizing point?
   c. Suppose that the price of hamburgers falls to $1.00. Show on your diagram the new utility-maximizing quantities of hamburgers and hot dogs. Does your diagram honor the Law of Demand for hamburgers?
6. Demonstrate the Law of Demand using an indifference map and a series of budget lines.
7. *Extra credit:* Draw reasonable-looking indifference curves for the following pairs of goods:
   a. two kinds of soft drinks that are perfect substitutes in a 1-to-1 ratio
   b. hot dogs and hot dog buns that are perfect complements in a 1-to-1 ratio
   c. unspoiled wetlands and toxic dump sites

APPENDIX

10:2

The Utility Theory of Consumer Choice

The theory of consumer choice can be described very directly, and simply, if we are willing to assume that consumers can measure the amount of utility, or satisfaction, that they receive from consuming goods and services. Utility cannot be measured, of course, but assuming that it can adds considerably to our intuition about the consumer's economic problem. Measuring utility also allows us to present the consumer's economic problem in the same way that we presented the student's economic problem in Chapter 2, and in the same way that we will present the firm's economic problem in the chapters to come. We can take a direct approach to the student's and the firm's economic problems because we can measure the grade point average and the profit that each is trying to maximize. Thus, the utility approach to the consumer's economic problem highlights the similarities among all economic problems.

We will illustrate the utility theory of consumer choice with our example in Chapter 10. You are trying to decide how many compact discs and cassette tapes to purchase with $160 of income in order to maximize your utility. The price of discs is $16, and the price of tapes is $8.

MARGINAL UTILITY

If the utility you receive from consuming compact discs could be measured, it would have a pattern similar to the hypothetical numbers presented in Table 10:2.1. The second column shows the total utility, or satisfaction, that you receive by consuming each possible quantity of discs, from 0 to 10. Total utility

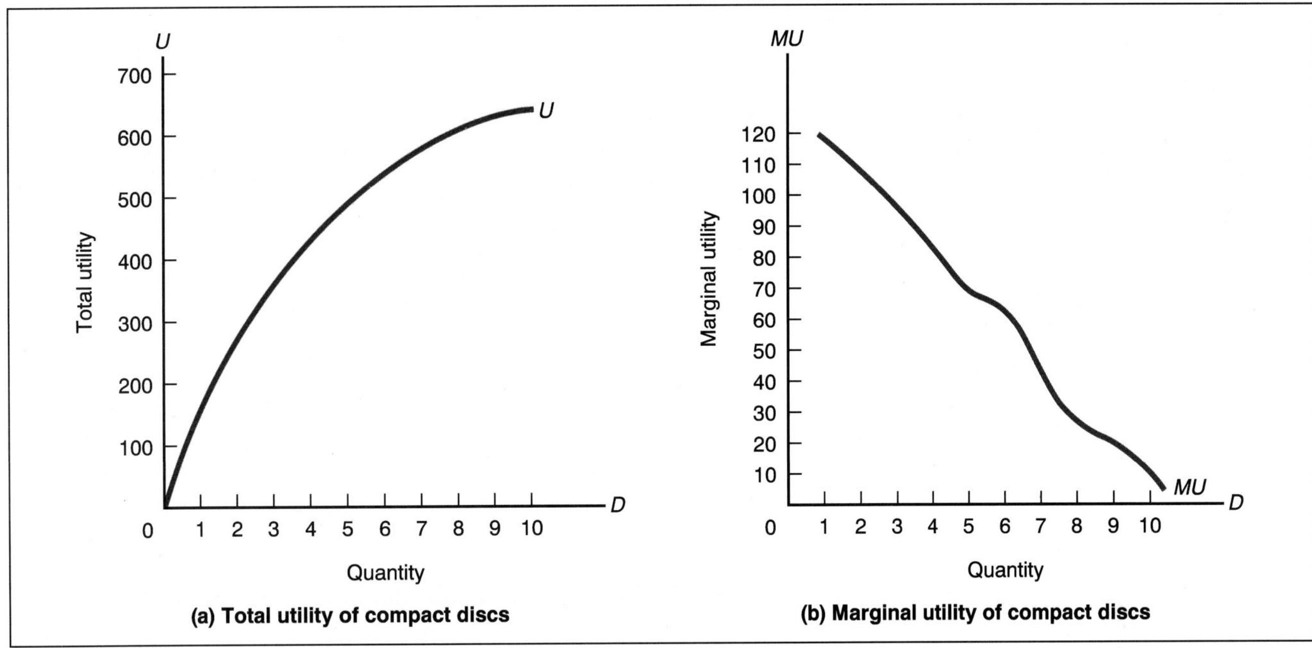

FIGURE 10:2.1

Total Utility and Marginal Utility of Compact Discs

This figure is a graph of the hypothetical numbers on the total utility and the marginal utility obtained from consuming compact discs that are listed in Table 10:2.1. In Figure 10:2.1(a), the total utility obtained from consuming compact discs rises with the number of discs consumed, but not in direct proportion. Total utility increases at a decreasing rate because of the Law of Diminishing Marginal Utility, which is illustrated in Figure 10:2.1(b). The marginal utility of consuming discs, the increase in utility from consuming one more disc, decreases as the quantity of discs consumed increases.

is zero if you consume no discs, and then it increases as the quantity of discs consumed increases. Figure 10:2.1(a) provides a graph of total utility for each quantity of discs based on the numbers from Table 10:2.1.

Total utility does not increase by the same amount for each additional disc consumed, however. The third column of Table 10:2.1 records the marginal utility obtained from consuming discs. **Marginal utility** here is the increase in utility obtained from consuming an additional disc. At any quantity it is the addition to utility of the last disc consumed. For example, the total utility you receive from consuming 4 discs is 408, and the total utility from consuming 5 discs is 478. Therefore, the marginal utility you receive from consuming the fifth disc is 70, the difference between the total utilities at 4 and 5 discs (70 = 478 − 408). Notice that the definition of marginal utility is analogous to the definition of the marginal grade from studying in the student's problem from Chapter 2. Recall that the marginal grade in a subject was the increase in your test score obtained from studying the subject for an additional hour.

MARGINAL UTILITY

The increase in utility obtained from consuming one more unit of a good.

According to the hypothetical numbers in the table, the marginal utility you receive from consuming discs diminishes with each new disc consumed. The graph of marginal utility in Figure 10:2.1(b) clearly demonstrates the pattern of diminishing marginal utility. There is nothing special about compact discs. The pattern of diminishing marginal utility holds with such regularity that it is elevated to the status of a law, the Law of Diminishing Marginal Utility.

LAW OF DIMINISHING MARGINAL UTILITY

The marginal utility of consuming a product decreases as the amount of the product consumed increases.

The **Law of Diminishing Marginal Utility** is based on the well-tested psychological principle that we can have too much of a good thing. Think of the food you most enjoy eating. Suppose that it happens to be deep-dish pizza. Now imagine eating deep-dish pizza over and over again, for breakfast, lunch, and dinner, every day. Eventually you will tire of deep-dish pizza. The marginal utility you receive from eating yet another pizza becomes smaller and smaller. That is what the Law of Diminishing Marginal Utility says.

MAXIMIZING UTILITY

Marginal utilities and prices are the keys to maximizing utility. If you can measure the marginal utility at different quantities consumed of each good, all you will need to do is compute the ratio of marginal utility to price for each good. Then you adjust your purchases until the ratios of marginal utility to price are equal for all goods. At that point your utility is maximized. The reason is as follows.

The ratio of marginal utility to price indicates the additional utility per dollar from consuming one more unit of a good. Returning to our example, suppose that you consume 6 discs. According to Table 10:2.1, the marginal utility of consuming the sixth disc is 64. The price of a disc is \$16. Therefore, the ratio of marginal utility to price is 4 for discs.

$$MU_D/P_D = 64/\$16 = 4/\$1$$

In purchasing the sixth disc you spent \$16 to receive an increase in utility of 64. Therefore, at 6 discs the additional utility per dollar from consuming 1 more disc is 4.

You have spent \$96 to purchase 6 discs (\$96 = \$16 · 6). Therefore, you have \$64 left to spend on tapes (\$64 = \$160 − \$96), which allows you to purchase 8 tapes (\$64 = \$8 · 8). Suppose that the marginal utility of the eighth

TABLE 10:2.1 Total and Marginal Utilities from Consuming Compact Discs (hypothetical data)

QUANTITY OF COMPACT DISCS	TOTAL UTILITY	MARGINAL UTILITY
0	0	0
1	120	120
2	228	108
3	324	96
4	408	84
5	478	70
6	542	64
7	582	40
8	606	24
9	626	20
10	634	8

tape happens to be 32. The price of a tape is \$8. Therefore, the ratio of marginal utility to price for tapes is also 4.

$$MU_T/P_T = 32/\$8 = 4/\$1$$

In purchasing the eighth tape you spent \$8 to receive an increase in utility of 32. Therefore, at 8 tapes the additional utility per dollar from consuming 1 more tape is 4.

The ratios of marginal utility to price are equal for 6 discs and 8 tapes, at a value of 4.

$$MU_D/P_D = MU_T/P_T = 4/\$1$$

Consequently, no small adjustment in your purchases of discs and tapes can increase your level of satisfaction. Suppose that you purchase fewer discs and more tapes. Each dollar you save on the discs decreases your utility by 4 units of satisfaction per dollar. Spending those dollars on tapes increases your utility by 4 units of satisfaction per dollar. The decreases and increases in utility cancel one another, and total utility remains the same. Your total utility is maximized by purchasing 6 discs and 8 tapes because no exchange of discs for tapes or tapes for discs can increase your utility.

You can only increase total utility by adjusting your purchases of discs and tapes if the ratios of marginal utility to price are unequal for discs and tapes. For example, suppose that you purchase 3 discs and 14 tapes. According to Table 10:2.1, the marginal utility of the third disc is 96. Therefore, at 3 discs the ratio of marginal utility to price is 6.

$$MU_D/P_D = 96/\$16 = 6/\$1$$

In purchasing the third disc you spent \$16 to receive an increase in utility of 96. Therefore, at 3 discs the additional utility per dollar from consuming 1 more disc is 6.

Although we do not have a table of marginal utilities for tapes, we know from the Law of Diminishing Marginal Utility that the marginal utility at 14 tapes is less than the marginal utility at 8 tapes. Suppose that the marginal utility of the fourteenth tape is 8. Therefore, at 14 tapes the ratio of marginal utility to price is 1.

$$MU_T/P_T = 8/\$8 = 1/\$1$$

In purchasing the fourteenth tape you spent \$8 to receive an increase in utility of 8. Therefore, at 14 tapes the additional utility per dollar from consuming 1 more tape is 1.

Now you can increase your total utility by purchasing 1 more disc and 2 fewer tapes. The \$16 you save by purchasing 2 fewer tapes decreases your utility at the rate of 1 unit of satisfaction per dollar. Spending the \$16 on an additional disc increases your utility at the rate of 6 units of satisfaction per dollar. Your total utility is increasing at the rate of 5 units of satisfaction per dollar.

You should continue to add discs and subtract tapes until the ratios of marginal utility to price are equal for both goods, at 6 discs and 8 tapes in our example. The ratios do eventually become equal because of the Law of Diminishing Marginal Utility. As you add discs, the marginal utility of discs decreases. Therefore, the ratio of marginal utility to price also decreases because the price of a disc never changes. It remains at \$16. Conversely, as you purchase fewer tapes, the marginal utility of tapes increases, and so does the ratio of marginal utility to price. In our example the two ratios eventually become equal at a value of 4.

Our analysis has established the following two principles of consumer choice:

UTILITY-MAXIMIZING DECISION RULE

Utility is maximized when the ratios of marginal utility to price are equal for all goods.

1. **Utility** is **maximized** when the ratios of marginal utility to price, MU/P, are equal for all goods.
2. If the ratios of marginal utility to price are unequal, utility can be increased *with no additional expenditure of income* by buying more of the good with the higher ratio and less of the good with the lower ratio. In terms of our example:

- If $MU_D/P_D > MU_T/P_T$, buy more discs and fewer tapes.
- If $MU_D/P_D < MU_T/P_T$, buy more tapes and fewer discs.

THE SUBSTITUTION EFFECT

Recall that the substitution effect is a relative price effect: Consumers tend to substitute in favor of products that have become relatively cheaper and away from products that have become relatively more expensive. We can see how the substitution effect of a change in price arises in our example from the principle that you equate the ratios of marginal utility to price for both discs and tapes in order to maximize utility.

Suppose that you are maximizing your utility, purchasing 6 discs and 8 tapes. Then the price of discs decreases to \$8. With the price of discs now at \$8 the ratio of the marginal utility of discs to the price of discs rises to 8.

$$MU_D/P_D = 64/\$8 = 8/\$1$$

The ratio of the marginal utility of tapes to the price of tapes remains at 4, however. The ratios are now unequal, and your utility is no longer maximized. The additional utility per dollar from purchasing an additional disc exceeds the additional utility per dollar from purchasing an additional tape. Therefore, you can increase your utility by substituting discs for tapes in your budget. The gain in utility per dollar from adding 1 more disc exceeds the loss in utility per dollar from purchasing 1 less tape. As you continue to add discs, the marginal utility of discs declines because of the Law of Diminishing Marginal Utility, and the ratio MU_D/P_D falls below 8. Similarly, subtracting tapes increases the marginal utility of tapes, and the ratio MU_T/P_T rises above 4. Substituting the now cheaper discs for tapes tends to drive the ratios of marginal utility to price back to equality, so that you can once again maximize your utility.

THE INCOME EFFECT

The substitution effect is not the entire story, however. The income effect also comes into play in maximizing utility. Recall that the income effect of a change in price is an absolute price effect: A change in price changes a consumer's purchasing power, or real income, and a change in purchasing power tends to affect the quantity demanded of all goods.

The decrease in the price of discs from \$16 to \$8 increases your purchasing power and allows you to buy more discs and more tapes. The income effect, along with the substitution effect, serves to increase the quantity of discs demanded. But tapes are also desirable, so you may use some of your increased purchasing power to buy more tapes as well. In any event, your utility is maximized when the ratios of marginal utility to price are once again equal for discs and tapes.

To summarize, the decrease in the price of discs, other things equal, generates both a substitution effect and an income effect that increase the quantity of discs demanded in order to maximize utility. The decrease in the price of discs is also likely to increase your demand for tapes in order to maximize utility because of the income effect.

SUMMARY

The utility theory of consumer choice assumes that consumers can measure the utility they receive from consuming goods and services. Appendix 10:2 illustrated the theory with the example in Chapter 10 of purchasing compact discs and cassette tapes with a fixed budget of \$160.

1. Consumers compare the ratios of marginal utility to price for each product in order to maximize utility. Marginal utility is the increase in utility from consuming one more unit of a good. The ratio of marginal utility to price measures the increase (decrease) in utility per dollar from buying one more (less) unit of the product.
2. With reference to the discs-tapes example, utility is maximized when the ratio of marginal utility to price is equal for both discs and tapes.
3. If the ratios of marginal utility to price are unequal, the consumer substitutes toward the product with the higher ratio to increase utility because it gives higher utility per dollar.
4. The Law of Diminishing Marginal Utility says that the marginal utility of consuming a product declines as the amount of the product consumed increases.

KEY TERMS

Law of Diminishing Marginal Utility

marginal utility

utility-maximizing decision rule

QUESTIONS

1. What is the Law of Diminishing Marginal Utility? Demonstrate how this concept supports the Law of Demand.
2. Suppose for some consumer that the marginal utility of a tofu hot dog is 3, and its price is \$1; the marginal utility of a decaf cappuccino is 4, and its price is \$2. Is the consumer maximizing utility? If not, how should the consumer adjust her purchases of these goods to increase utility? (Assume the consumer has enough income to buy plenty of hot dogs and cappuccino.)
3. If one good is 100 times as expensive as another good, can we assume that someone consuming both goods receives 100 times more total utility from the more expensive good than from the cheaper good? Why or why not?

CHAPTER

11

The Firm's How Problem and the Total Cost of Production

LEARNING OBJECTIVES

CONCEPTS TO LEARN

The long-run and the short-run total cost curves
The economic costs of production
The firm's How or input problem
The production function
The least-cost production rule
Economies and diseconomies of scale
How to control and combat industrial pollution
The United States' anti-pollution policies

CONCEPTS TO RECALL

Opportunity cost [1]
The firm's three-part economic problem [1]
The margin in economic analysis [2]
The How or input question [3]
The production possibilities frontier [3]
Marginal cost [6]
The marginal product of labor [6,9]

How often we hear this complaint: "Darn, they just don't make things the way they used to." And that's right, "they" don't.

Old-timers fondly remember radios and other small appliances that seemed to last forever. They came in sturdy cases, and when they broke, they were taken to be repaired "as good as new." Today's appliances often seem chintzy and shoddy by comparison. They are housed in thin plastic casings, with little attention to detail and workmanship. Moreover, when they break, they are simply replaced. Over the past thirty years or so we have witnessed a change from "maintain and repair" appliances to "discard and replace" appliances.

The same is true of automobiles. Mechanics used to tinker with carburetors and engines for hours on end until they ran smoothly again. No longer with today's computerized engines. Now when something goes wrong, the mechanic simply unbolts the malfunctioning part, tosses it away, and replaces it with a new part. Also, auto manufacturers today are increasingly using lightweight plastics and aluminum in the engines and body panels rather than the heavier, longer-lasting steel of yesteryear.

Chapter 11 will help us understand why "they don't make things the way they used to" and, more to the point, why we wouldn't want them to.

Chapter 11 presents an analysis of the firm's decisions relating to its costs of production. As such it addresses the How or input question, one of the four basic economic questions that all societies must answer. Business firms answer the How question in a market economy. Fortunately for society the goals of business firms and society are entirely compatible. Firms try to produce their output as cheaply as possible to increase their profits. If they succeed, they answer the How question efficiently; society gets the maximum possible output from its scarce resources. We want to understand how firms attempt to minimize their costs of production.

The chapter begins with an overview of production costs from an economic perspective. The overview focuses on the *total cost curve,* which indicates the total cost of producing each level of output the firm might choose to produce. All the other cost curves used in this text are derived from the total cost curve.

THE TOTAL COST OF PRODUCTION

The total cost of production for a typical business firm follows the pattern represented by the cost data in Table 11.1. The table shows the total cost and the marginal cost of production at each level of output in both the long run and the short run. Although the cost data are hypothetical, they are consistent with all the attributes that economists normally associate with a firm's costs of production. We will use these cost data again in Chapters 13 and 14.

LONG-RUN TOTAL COST CURVE
The other things equal relationship between output and total cost in the long run.

SHORT-RUN TOTAL COST CURVE
The other things equal relationship between output and total cost in the short run.

Figure 11.1 graphs the total cost data in Table 11.1, with total cost on the vertical axis and output on the horizontal axis. Figure 11.1(a) depicts the **long-run total cost (LRTC) curve,** the other things equal relationship between output and total cost in the long run (the first and second columns in the table). Figure 11.1(b) depicts the **short-run total cost (SRTC) curve,** the other things equal relationship between output and total cost in the short run (the first and fourth columns in the table).

TABLE 11.1 **Long-Run and Short-Run Costs for a Representative Firm**

	LONG RUN		SHORT RUN			
QUANTITY	Total Cost	Marginal Cost	Total Cost	Marginal Cost	Variable Cost	Fixed Cost
0	$ 0	$ —	$ 320	$ —	$ 0	$320
1	146	146	391	71	71	320
2	264	118	444	53	124	320
3	359	95	484	40	164	320
4	432	73	512	28	192	320
5	488	56	533	21	213	320
6	528	40	548	15	228	320
7	560	32	560	12	240	320
8	576	16	576	16	256	320
9	590	14	593	17	273	320
10	600	10	623	30	303	320
11	611	11	654	31	334	320
12	625	14	713	59	393	320
13	641	16	777	64	457	320
14	659	18	853	76	533	320
15	706	47	958	105	638	320
16	762	56	1,088	130	768	320
17	835	73	1,247	159	927	320
18	936	101	1,436	189	1,116	320
19	1,055	119	1,660	224	1,340	320
20	1,200	145	1,920	260	1,600	320

Recall from our discussion of marginal cost in Chapter 6 that marginal cost is the change or increase in total cost from producing one more unit of output. As such, marginal cost is the *slope* of the total cost curve at each level of output. For instance, when the firm increases its production from 11 units to 12 units, Table 11.1 indicates that long-run total cost increases by $14, from $611 to $625. Therefore, the firm's long-run marginal cost is $14 at an output of 12 units (third column).

Figure 11.1 and Table 11.1 reveal two important characteristics of the relationship between total cost and output: the pattern of total cost and the distinction between total cost in the long run and total cost in the short run.

The Shape of the Total Cost Curves

The first characteristic relates to the shape of the total cost curves. Notice that both curves are upward sloping. Total cost continually increases as output increases and continually decreases as output decreases. This makes sense because if a firm wants to increase output, it must hire more factors of production, and hiring more factors of production increases total cost.

Total cost does not increase proportionally with output, however. Refer to the long-run total cost curve in Figure 11.1(a). The *LRTC* curve would be a straight line from the origin if total cost increased in direct proportion to output. The firm's marginal cost would be constant at every level of output, equal in value to the slope of the line. Instead, the *LRTC* curve is bowed inward toward the origin over the range of output from 0 to 10. Total cost is increasing *at a*

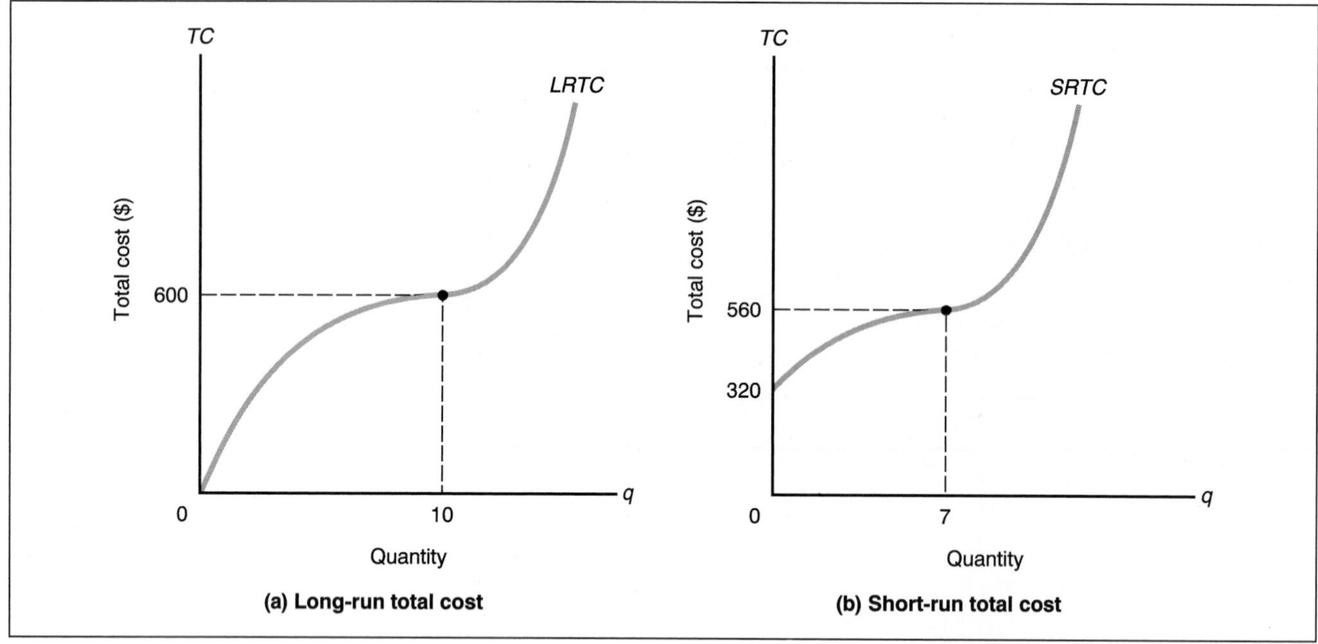

FIGURE 11.1

The Long-run and Short-run Total Cost Curves

The figure is a graph of the hypothetical data on a firm's long-run and short-run total costs of production from Table 11.1. The long-run total cost curve in Figure 11.1(a), *LRTC*, applies in the long run when the firm can vary all its factors of production. Long-run total costs at first rise proportionally more slowly than output and then rise proportionally more rapidly than output. The short-run total cost curve in Figure 11.1(b), *SRTC*, applies in the short run when at least one factor of production is fixed. Short-run total costs also rise proportionally more slowly than output at first and then rise proportionally more rapidly than output.

decreasing rate; the slope of the curve is steadily decreasing. We can see this by referring to the long-run marginal costs in Table 11.1 (third column). Marginal cost is steadily decreasing over the first 10 units of output.

The *LRTC* curve is bowed outward away from the origin at output levels greater than 10. Total cost is now increasing *at an increasing rate;* the slope of the curve is steadily increasing. We can see this from the table as well. Marginal cost is steadily increasing above 10 units of output.

The same pattern applies to the short-run total cost curve in Figure 11.1(b). According to the short-run marginal cost data in Table 11.1 (fifth column), the bow of the curve changes direction at 7 units of output. Short-run marginal cost is steadily decreasing from 0 to 7 units of output and steadily increasing beyond 7 units of output.

We will explain why the total cost curves have this shape later on in the chapter, after we understand how the firm's hiring decisions determine the relationship between total cost and output.

Total Cost in the Long Run and in the Short Run

The distinction between long-run and short-run total costs relates to the position of the curves. Notice that the *LRTC* curve begins at the origin, whereas the *SRTC* curve intersects the total cost axis well above the origin, at a total cost of $320. The different positions of the two curves reflect the difference between the long run and the short run.

Recall that in the long run all factors of production are variable. If the firm chooses to expand or contract output, it can rethink its hiring decisions with respect to all its factors of production. Therefore, all costs associated with hiring factors of production are also variable in the long run. In particular, should the firm decide not to produce at all, it will hire no factors of production and incur no costs. This is why the *LRTC* curve begins at the origin.

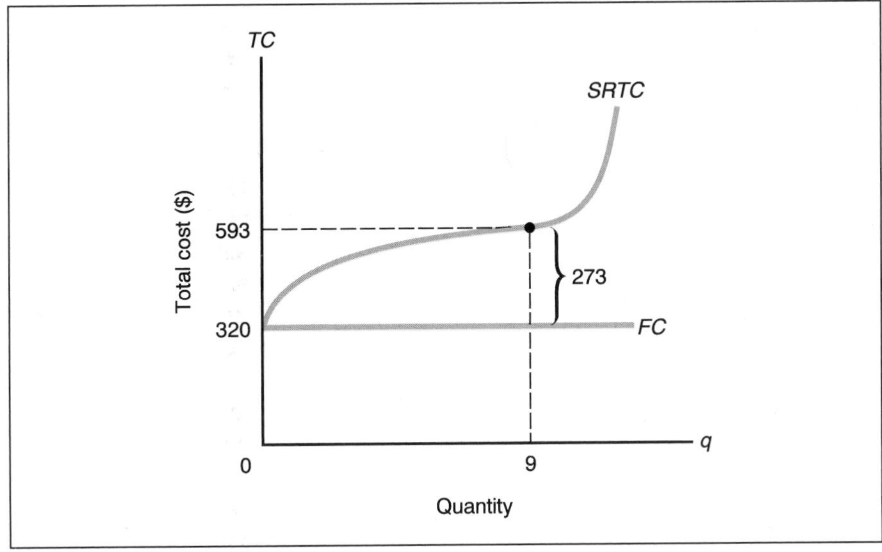

FIGURE 11.2

Short-run Total Cost, Short-run Variable Cost, and Fixed Cost

The figure is a graph of the hypothetical short-run cost data from Table 11.1. Short-run total cost is the sum of short-run variable cost plus fixed cost. The fixed cost curve, *FC*, is horizontal at $320, the amount of the firm's fixed cost; it does not vary with output. Short-run variable cost at each output is the vertical distance between the short-run total cost curve, *SRTC*, and the fixed cost curve *FC* (= $320). *SRTC* intersects the vertical axis at $320, the fixed cost, because the firm would incur the $320 of fixed cost associated with its fixed factor(s) of production even if it shut down and ceased production.

In the short run at least one of the factors of production is fixed. Fixed factors can be neither increased nor decreased for the duration of the short run no matter what level of output the firm chooses to produce. As a result, the costs associated with purchasing the fixed factors are also fixed regardless of the level of output. These costs are the result of past commitments the firm has made, and they cannot be changed until the short run becomes the long run. In other words, total cost in the short run naturally divides into two components, fixed cost (*FC*) and short-run variable cost (*SRVC*).

$$SRTC = FC + SRVC$$

Fixed cost is the cost associated with the fixed factors of production. **Variable cost** is the cost associated with the variable factors of production. Only the variable cost component of short-run total cost varies with output in the short run.

FIXED COST

The cost associated with the fixed factors of production in the short run.

VARIABLE COST

The cost associated with the variable factors of production.

Refer to Figure 11.2, which reproduces the short-run total cost curve from Figure 11.1(b). The horizontal line *FC* is the amount of the firm's fixed cost. The fixed cost is $320 no matter what the level of output (seventh column in the table). The vertical distance between *SRTC* and *FC* at any level of output is the amount of the firm's variable cost at that output. For example, if the firm produces 9 units of output, it incurs short-run total cost of $593, consisting of fixed cost of $320 and variable cost of $273. Should the firm decide to shut down and cease producing, its variable cost would be zero, since it would not hire any of the variable factors of production. But it still must pay the $320 of fixed cost associated with the fixed factors. Therefore, *SRTC* intersects the total cost axis at $320.

Here is an example to illustrate the distinction between fixed and variable costs in the short run. Suppose that an airline decides to offer daily flights between two cities that it has not previously serviced. To operate the new flights the airline rents terminal and hangar space at each of the cities' airports and rents two additional airplanes from another airline. Assume that the combined rent on the airport space and airplanes is $1 million per year and that the rental contracts are one-year contracts. That is, the airline is committed to these rents for a minimum of one year.

As the airline operates the flights during the first year, it incurs a number of additional costs: fuel for the planes; salaries for the pilots, flight attendants, baggage handlers, and ticket takers; food for the passengers; cleaning services for the planes; and so forth. The more daily flights the airline provides, the higher these costs are; the fewer daily flights, the lower these costs.

The short run lasts for one year in this example. The airline's fixed costs are the $1 million paid on the rental contracts for airport space and the airplanes. The variable costs are the costs associated with operating the flights. The total cost of the new service is the sum of the variable operating cost and the $1 million in fixed cost. Notice that only the variable cost changes with the number of flights offered. The airline must pay $1 million in rent whether it offers five flights daily, one flight daily, or no flights at all.

At the end of a year's time the airline can decide whether to renew the rental contracts on the existing airport space and airplanes. It may even decide to rent more or less airport space and more or fewer airplanes, depending on the profitability of the service. At that point the short run has become the long run. All factors of production are variable, as are all costs associated with providing the service. In the long run, then, there is no distinction between long-run total cost (*LRTC*) and long-run variable cost (*LRVC*).

$$LRTC = LRVC$$

Fixed cost in the long run is zero because there are no fixed factors of production.

Additional Characteristics of the Total Cost Curves

Total cost curves have a number of important characteristics that are not directly revealed by the diagrams themselves. Four should be kept firmly in mind whenever you see a total cost curve: the time dimension of output and cost, the other things equal qualification of the total cost curve, total cost as opportunity cost, and the total cost curve as a representation of production efficiency.

THE TIME DIMENSION Points on a total cost curve are implicitly defined over a given period of time. Output on the horizontal axis is a flow variable, the *rate* of production over a specific length of time. In our airline example the output, q, might refer to the number of flights per day, or per week, or per year. Therefore, total cost is also a flow variable measured over the same length of time as the output. For instance, if a graph of the airline's short-run cost represents the fixed cost as the $1 million of *annual* rental fees, then output must refer to the number of flights each *year*. If output refers to the number of *daily* flights, then the $1 million of fixed cost must be scaled down appropriately from an annual to a *daily* figure, as by dividing the $1 million by 365.

OTHER THINGS EQUAL A total cost curve is an *other things equal* relationship between the total cost and the level of output. The total cost of production for a firm depends on a number of variables, such as output (because of the

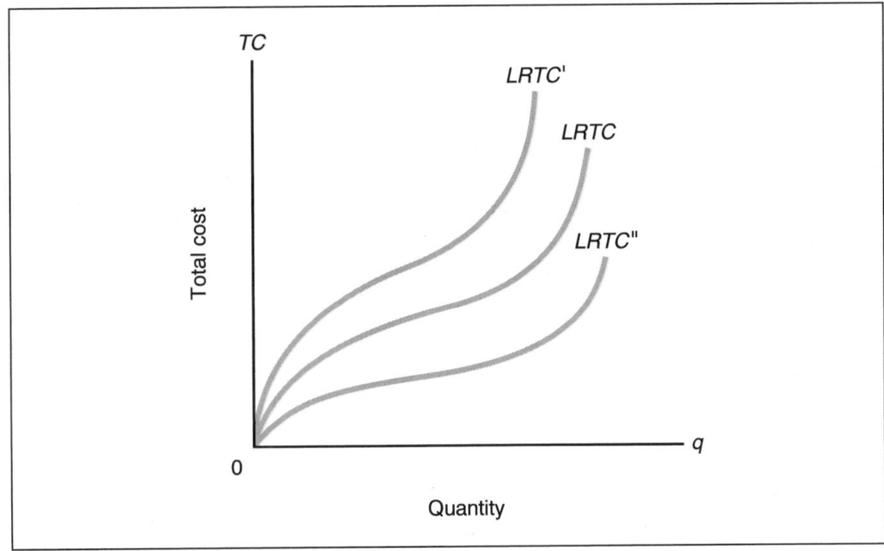

FIGURE 11.3

Shifts in the Long-run Total Cost Curve

The long-run total cost curve *LRTC* shifts up or down whenever one of the variables that affect the cost of production, other than output, changes. These variables include factor prices, taxes, and production technologies. For example, an increase in wages shifts the long-run total cost curve up from *LRTC* to *LRTC'*. Long-run total cost increases at every level of output. Conversely, a cost-saving technological change shifts the long-run total cost curve down from *LRTC* to *LRTC.''* Long-run total cost decreases at every level of output.

inputs needed to produce the output), factor prices, taxes, and the production technologies available to the firm. A total cost curve pictures the relationship between total cost and output on the assumption that all the other variables besides output that affect total cost are being held constant. In this respect a total cost curve is analogous to demand and supply curves, which highlight the relationship between quantity and price, holding constant all the other variables that affect demand or supply.

Having selected output for the horizontal axis, the effect on total cost of changes in any one of the other variables must be represented as a shift up or down in the entire total cost curve. For example, if our airline signs a new contract with its pilots at a higher wage, the total cost curve shifts up at every output, as pictured in Figure 11.3

LRTC represents the original long-run total cost curve and *LRTC'* the long-run total cost curve under the new pilot contract. Long-run total cost has increased at *every* level of output (except at $q = 0$).

Similarly, cost-saving innovations in production technology shift the total cost curve down at every level of output. For example, new automated baggage conveyors that lower the airline's loading and unloading costs might shift the long-run total cost curve from *LRTC* to *LRTC''*.

ECONOMIC (OPPORTUNITY) COST VERSUS ACCOUNTING COST A total cost curve depicts the total *economic* cost of production at every output. Recall from Chapter 1 that cost in economic analysis refers to opportunity cost. Thus, the **total economic cost** at any given output is the total opportunity cost of supplying that output. In a production context, opportunity cost is the value that a firm's inputs would have in their next best use.

TOTAL ECONOMIC COST

For any given output, the total opportunity cost of the factors of production used in producing and selling that output.

Many standard accounting definitions of cost are not the same as economic or opportunity cost because they are used for different purposes. For example, tax accountants must define cost in line with the requirements of the tax laws. The federal and state corporation and personal income taxes define taxable income, or taxable "profit," in the usual manner, as the difference between total revenue and total cost. But the total cost in the tax laws refers just to the annual operating expenses of the firm. The total economic or opportunity cost includes the annual operating expenses *plus* the opportunity cost of capital and in some cases the opportunity cost of labor supplied by the owners of the firm. Let's look briefly at each component of total economic cost.

OPERATING EXPENSES
The total accounting costs incurred by the firm by producing and selling its output, including the explicit monetary costs and certain nonmonetary costs.

EXPLICIT MONETARY (OPERATING) COSTS
The firm's out-of-pocket payments for its factors of production plus the general sales and excise taxes paid by the firm on the sale of its products.

NONMONETARY OPERATING COSTS
Costs of production that do not involve out-of-pocket payments for factors of production, the most important being an estimate of the depreciation of the firm's stock of capital.

DEPRECIATION
The decline in the market value of the firm's stock of capital during the year.

OPPORTUNITY COST OF CAPITAL
The return that the owners of the firm could earn if the value of the capital they own were invested in their next best investment alternatives.

OPERATING EXPENSES A firm's annual **operating expenses** that the tax laws count as total cost include explicit monetary costs and certain nonmonetary costs. The **explicit monetary costs** are principally the out-of-pocket payments for the firm's factors of production, including the wages and salaries of the firm's employees, land rents, rental payments on rented capital, interest payments on borrowed funds, and payments for intermediate inputs such as materials and fuels. Also included in the explicit monetary costs are the general sales and excise taxes paid by the firm on the sale of its products. The most important **nonmonetary operating cost** is an estimate of the depreciation of the firm's stock of capital. In economic analysis, **depreciation** refers to the decline in the market value of the firm's stock of capital during the year. In practice, firms estimate the depreciation on their capital stock following guidelines established by the U.S. Internal Revenue Service.

THE OPPORTUNITY COST OF CAPITAL All firms incur an **opportunity cost of capital** in addition to their operating expenses. Suppose that the market value of a firm's plant and equipment is $10 million, of which 30 percent has been paid for with borrowed funds and 70 percent with funds supplied by the owners. The cost of the borrowed capital is represented by the interest payments on the firm's debt, which are part of the firm's operating expenses. But the cost of the funds supplied by the owners is not part of the firm's operating expenses as defined by the U.S. tax laws. The reason is that the cost of owner-supplied funds is an opportunity cost, not an operating expense. It is the amount the owners could earn if the value of the capital they own were invested in their next best investment alternatives.

Suppose that the owners can earn a 10 percent rate of return on any investments they make outside the firm. They always have the option of ceasing production, selling off the assets of the firm, and investing the proceeds of the sale at 10 percent. In our example, selling the assets brings in $10 million. Three million dollars of the proceeds (30 percent) would go to the bondholders to pay the principal on the firm's debt. The remaining $7 million (70 percent) would be distributed to the owners. This is the amount of the capital they own, their *equity* in the firm. At a 10 percent rate of return, the owners can earn $700,000 on the $7 million. Therefore, $700,000 represents the annual opportunity cost of owner-supplied capital. It is the return that must be made available to the stockholders to justify keeping their capital tied up in the firm.

The *actual* returns to the stockholders come in one of two forms, dividends and retained earnings. Together they represent the taxable income or profit of the firm under the U.S. tax laws.

DIVIDENDS
The portion of after-tax profits that managers of the firm pay to the stockholders.

Dividends are direct payments by the firm to the stockholders, just as interest payments are direct payments to the bondholders. The income tax laws do not allow a firm to deduct dividends as an operating expense, however. They are considered part of taxable profit. Only the interest payments to the bondholders are counted as part of the operating expenses.

Retained earnings are the funds remaining from total revenues after paying all operating expenses, income taxes, and dividends. They are retained by the firm to provide funds for future investment. The sum of dividends plus retained earnings reflects the actual performance of the firm, the actual return on the capital owned by the stockholders. The actual return to capital is not necessarily equal to the opportunity cost of owner-supplied capital, however. The opportunity cost is the return available to the owners if the value of the capital they own were used *outside* the firm in alternative investments.

RETAINED EARNINGS

The funds of the firm remaining from total revenues after paying all operating expenses, income taxes, and dividends; used to finance future investment.

THE OPPORTUNITY COST OF LABOR Sometimes the owners of a firm do not pay themselves a salary for the time they spend working at the firm. Family-owned businesses are common examples. Those running the firm may pay other family members explicit salaries, but they often draw no salary for themselves. The value of their time is hidden as part of the after-tax income of the business.

Whether or not an owner draws a salary is irrelevant to a proper economic accounting of the cost of running the business, however. An owner could presumably choose to work at another firm for a salary, and the salary available in the next best alternative defines the **opportunity cost of the owner's labor** to the family business. As such, it is a legitimate component of the total economic or opportunity cost of the business.

OPPORTUNITY COST OF LABOR

The wage or salary available to the employees of a firm in their next best employment alternatives.

TOTAL ECONOMIC COST To summarize, total economic cost measures the total opportunity cost of the factors of production. The operating expenses of the firm presumably equal the opportunity costs of using these factors of production. For instance, we saw in Chapter 9 that wages in competitive markets equal the value of labor's marginal product and that wages tend to equalize for comparable jobs. Thus, the wage any one firm pays a worker is an opportunity cost; it equals the value of that worker in the worker's next best alternative line of employment. The same principle applies to the other factors of production, since firms must bid these resources away from other firms. Therefore, adding the opportunity costs of owner-supplied capital and owner-supplied labor to the firm's operating expenses captures the total opportunity cost, or total economic cost, of supplying the firm's output. This is the total cost represented by a total cost curve.

AN EXAMPLE The following example illustrates the distinction between the economic and the tax accounting definitions of total cost.

Suppose that two friends start a business by supplying a total of $1 million of their own funds to the business to purchase plant and equipment. They could each earn 10 percent on the $1 million, equal to $100,000, if they invested it elsewhere. In addition, both owners work in the business without drawing a salary. They could each earn $50,000 in some other line of work.

During the first year of operation the business generates $900,000 in total revenues from the sale of a product. The firm has out-of-pocket expenses for sales taxes, labor, and material inputs (intermediate products) totaling $450,000. The capital stock depreciates in value at the rate of 20 percent per year, so that depreciation on the $1 million of capital is $200,000. Refer to Table 11.2.

The owner's tax accountant would report a taxable profit during the first year of $250,000, equal to $900,000 of total revenues less $650,000 of operating

TABLE 11.2 **Revenues, Costs, and Profit of a Hypothetical Firm**

REVENUES:	$900,000
OPERATING EXPENSES:	
Out-of-pocket expenses (sales taxes, labor, material inputs)	$450,000
Depreciation of capital	200,000
Total operating expenses	650,000
TAXABLE ACCOUNTING PROFIT:	250,000
NONMONETARY OPPORTUNITY COSTS:	
Owner-supplied labor	100,000
Owner-supplied capital	100,000
Total nonmonetary opportunity costs	200,000
TOTAL ECONOMIC (OPPORTUNITY) COSTS:	850,000
ECONOMIC PROFIT:	50,000

expenses. The operating expenses consist of the $450,000 out-of-pocket costs, plus the $200,000 allowance for depreciation of the firm's capital stock.

The total economic cost of the business during the first year is $850,000. In addition to the $650,000 of expenses, the owners incur opportunity costs of

1. $100,000 interest on the $1 million they supplied to the firm to purchase plant and equipment and
2. $100,000 on their own labor they supplied to the firm.

ECONOMIC PROFIT
The difference between total revenue and total (economic) cost.

The **economic profit** is therefore only $50,000, the difference between total revenues and total *economic* cost ($900,000 − $850,000). The taxable profit overstates the economic profit because it ignores the opportunities the owners have to use their funds and their labor elsewhere.

The concept of economic profit answers the question that an economist always asks: What is the best use of scarce resources? Suppose that instead of starting this business the two friends had each worked elsewhere and invested their funds in other ventures earning a 10 percent rate of return. Combined they would have received income of $200,000 during the year: $100,000 interest on their $1 million, plus $100,000 in salary. So supplying their labor and financial resources to this business is profitable from an economic perspective only if total revenues exceed operating expenses by more than $200,000. The $50,000 of economic profit, then, represents the friends' gain, or "profit," from supplying their labor and capital to their own business rather than to their next best alternatives.

THE TOTAL COST CURVE AND ECONOMIC EFFICIENCY The final point to understand about the total cost curve is that it does not describe just any relationship between total cost and output. The points on a total cost curve depict *the best possible relationship* between output and total cost at every level of output. For instance, the point (q_1, TC_1) on the total cost curve in Figure 11.4 is interpreted in one of two ways:

1. TC_1 is the *minimum cost* of producing output q_1; or
2. q_1 is the *maximum output* attainable for a cost of TC_1.

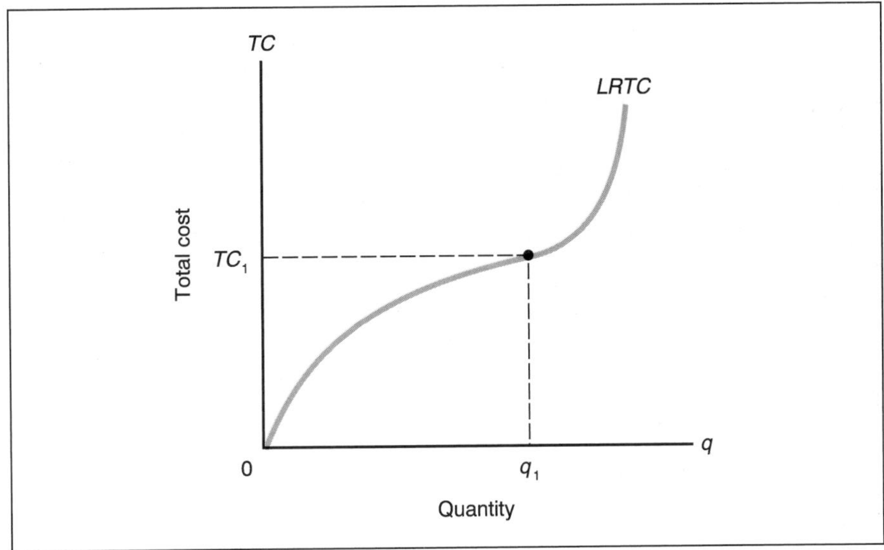

FIGURE 11.4

The Long-run Total Cost Curve and the Firm's How Problem

The long-run total cost curve *LRTC* represents the best possible relationship between output and total cost for a firm. The point (q_1, TC_1) has one of two interpretations: (1) q_1 is the maximum output that the firm can produce for a total cost of TC_1 or (2) TC_1 is the minimum total cost that the firm must incur to produce output q_1. *LRTC* depicts an efficient solution to the firm's How problem.

A firm can achieve these quantity-cost combinations only if it makes efficient choices in hiring factors of production. In other words, a total cost curve depicts an efficient solution to the firm's How question.

We can easily think of ridiculous ways to produce any good or service that would lead to very different quantity-cost combinations. For example, suppose that a computer software company wants to produce user manuals for its latest piece of software. It could do this by purchasing 10 million monkeys, equipping each one with a personal computer, and having the monkeys bang away on the keyboards. A monkey may occasionally produce an acceptable manual by pure luck.

Refer to Figure 11.5. Suppose that the monkey strategy costs TC_{10} and produces q_0 user manuals in a year's time. The firm can obviously do much better than this. More reasonable production techniques can produce many more manuals for the same total cost of TC_{10}. The introduction of better and better techniques increases output from q_0 to q_1, q_2, q_3, and so on. Finally, the firm's managers discover the best possible combination of factors of production for producing user manuals. When they do, output increases to q_{10} for a total cost of TC_{10}. (q_{10}, TC_{10}) is a point on the firm's long-run total cost curve, *LRTC*.

TOTAL COST CURVE

The best possible relationship between a firm's total cost and its output; it indicates either the minimum total cost of producing each level of output the firm might choose to produce or the maximum output obtainable for each given amount of total cost.

The output–total cost combination (q_{10}, TC_{10}) defines the limit of the firm's production possibilities. For a total cost of TC_{10}, q_{10} is the *maximum* number of user manuals the firm can produce. This is the second interpretation of points on the total cost curve given above.

Alternatively, think of the monkeys producing q_{10} user manuals every year. The manuals would cost far more than TC_{10}—say, TC_{100}. As the firm employs better production techniques, the total cost of producing q_{10} user manuals decreases. The best technique reduces the cost to TC_{10}, but no further. According to the *LRTC* curve, TC_{10} is the *minimum* total cost of producing q_{10} user manuals. This is the first interpretation of points on the total cost curve given above.

In other words, the total cost curve is an efficiency frontier for the firm. All output–total cost combinations in the region above and to the left of *LRTC* in Figure 11.6 are possible, but inefficient, combinations. The software company

FIGURE 11.5

Inefficient and Efficient Production of Software Manuals

If a firm hired monkeys at a cost of TC_{10} to produce manuals for its software, the monkeys may be able to produce q_0 acceptable manuals in a year. More reasonable production techniques would increase output from q_0 to q_1, q_2, q_3, etc., for the same cost TC_{10}, until output reached q_{10}. q_{10} is the maximum number of manuals that the firm can produce for a total cost of TC_{10}, because the point (q_{10}, TC_{10}) is on the long-run total cost curve *LRTC*. Alternatively, monkeys may be able to produce q_{10} manuals in a year, but only at a total cost of TC_{100}. More reasonable production techniques would reduce the cost of producing q_{10} manuals, but only to TC_{10}. TC_{10} is the minimum total cost the firm must incur to produce q_{10} manuals.

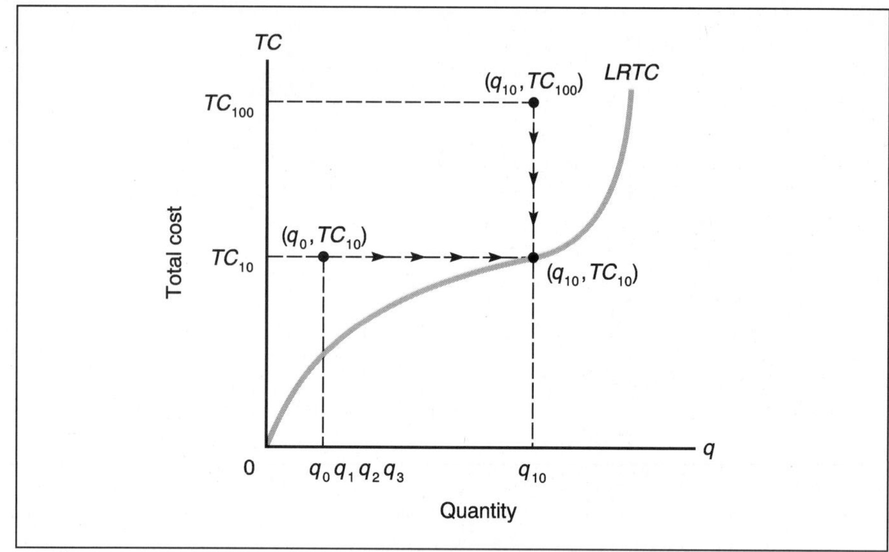

can produce quantity q_4 user manuals for a total cost of TC_6. But in doing so, it is making incorrect choices in hiring factors of production. The output–total cost combinations in the region below and to the right of *LRTC* are impossible for the firm to achieve. The firm simply cannot produce q_4 user manuals for a total cost of only TC_2. To produce q_4 user manuals the firm must spend at least TC_4 on factors of production. Points on *LRTC* define the efficiency frontier, the limits of the firm's output–total cost possibilities. The total cost curve of the firm is analogous to the production possibilities frontier for the economy as a whole in this sense. *LRTC* pictures the efficient solution of the How question for an individual firm; the production possibilities frontier pictures the efficient solution of the How question for the entire economy.

LEAST-COST PRODUCTION

Achieving the efficient quantity-cost combinations on the total cost curve is a very difficult economic problem for most business firms. One difficulty is that there are often many ways to produce the same good or service. Think of the choices involved in the generation of electricity as just one example. The sources of power for generating electricity include hydro (water), coal, oil, and nuclear power. The power source chosen in turn dictates choices with respect to all the other factors of production: the electric utility's plant and equipment, the amount of labor to be hired and the skill requirements of the labor force, and the material inputs (intermediate products) consistent with the power source. Moreover, the firm may use either newer or older plant and equipment, and the age of the capital stock has a direct bearing on the best choices for most of the other factors of production. What is the best way to produce electricity? An electric utility clearly faces a wide range of choices in trying to answer this question.

Another difficulty is that the precise information a firm needs about each of the methods of production is not easily obtained. To understand the informational problem, we must first describe the structure of the economic problem

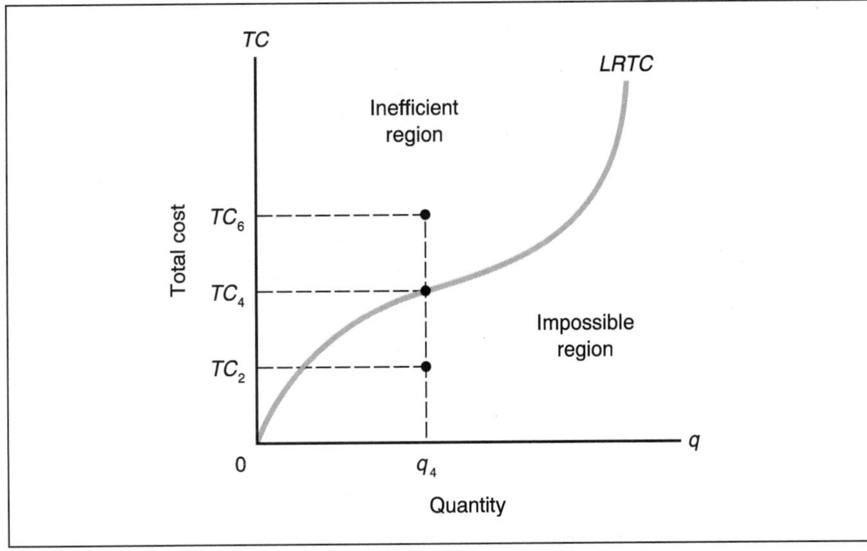

FIGURE 11.6

The Total Cost Curve as an Efficiency Frontier

The total cost curve *LRTC* is an efficiency frontier for the firm just as the production possibilities frontier is an efficiency frontier for the entire economy. All points above and to the left of *LRTC*, such as (q_4, TC_6), are possible but inefficient. The firm is spending more than it has to in order to produce q_4. All points below and to the right of *LRTC*, such as (q_4, TC_2), are impossible. The firm cannot produce ouput q_4 for a total cost of only TC_2. All points on *LRTC*, such as (q_4, TC_4) represent an efficient solution to the firm's How problem. If the firm is on *LRTC*, it can increase output only by hiring more factors of production and increasing its total cost.

in the usual manner. What are the objectives, alternatives, and constraints for the firm's How problem?

The Structure of the How Problem

The firm's economic problem can be described in one of two ways, depending on how one views the points on the firm's total cost curve. Let's adopt the second interpretation given above: Points on the curve describe the maximum output obtainable for a given amount of total cost. Under this interpretation, the firm's *objective* is to produce the most output it can, subject to the *constraint* that it spends a given amount of money on factors of production. The *alternatives* are the different combinations of factors of production that the given amount of money can buy. Each combination of factors produces a different level of output. The efficient solution to the **firm's How problem** involves finding the factor combination that produces the largest amount of output.

FIRM'S HOW PROBLEM

The goal of producing the maximum output for a given total cost spent on factors of production; alternatively, the goal of producing a given output for the minimum total cost spent on factors of production.

A firm needs two pieces of information to solve its How problem: (1) the total cost of purchasing any combination of factors of production and (2) the maximum output attainable from any combination of the factors.

TOTAL COST The total cost is the easy part. The cost of any one factor is the product of its price times the quantity of the factor hired. Total cost is the sum of the costs for each factor. Think of a firm hiring three generic kinds of factors, labor (L), material inputs (M), and capital (K), whose prices are P_L, P_M, and P_K, respectively. The total cost of hiring a combination of these three factors is

$$TC = P_L \cdot L + P_M \cdot M + P_K \cdot K$$

where L, M, and K refer to the quantities of each factor hired. Firms presumably know the prices and quantities of the factors they hire, so total cost is easily determined. The only possible exception concerns owner-supplied resources. Firms may not be sure what rate of return (that is, P_K) measures the opportunity cost of the owner-supplied funds used to purchase plant and equipment. Could the owners obtain a 5 percent return elsewhere? Or 10 percent? Or 15 percent? They may not know the answer.

For the record, a recent study of 46 industries in the United States found that material inputs (including fuel) are by far the most important factor of production in terms of their share of total factor cost. They are the largest share of total cost in 37 of the 46 industries. Moreover, the material input share of total cost exceeds 50 percent in 30 of the industries and 60 percent in 16 industries. By contrast, labor is the largest share of total cost in only seven industries and capital in only two. Capital is a distant third in overall importance. Its share of total cost is 15 percent or less in 30 of the industries.[1]

THE PRODUCTION FUNCTION The second piece of information needed to solve the How problem is the sticking point, knowing the maximum output attainable from any combination of factors. This is clearly a difficult requirement. A firm may not even be sure of the maximum output it can produce from the factors of production it is currently using, much less what would be the case if it changed its production decisions. In any event, understanding this relationship between its factor inputs and its outputs requires all the engineering and the managerial talent the firm can muster. The engineers must be familiar with the capabilities of the firm's plant and equipment. The firm's managers have to know how best to coordinate the various factors of production and how to keep their workers motivated to perform at their full potential.

PRODUCTION FUNCTION
The relationship between a firm's outputs and its inputs that indicates the maximum output attainable from all possible combinations of inputs that the firm might use.

Economists define the relationship between the factors of production employed by a firm and the maximum output attainable as the firm's **production function.** We first met the idea of a production function in our agricultural example in Chapter 6. The example described a very simple production function in which a crop was produced using only labor and land, and labor was the only variable factor of production in the short run. Looking at such a simple production function was useful for understanding the Law of Diminishing Returns and for establishing the relationship between marginal product and marginal cost. We also used the example in Chapter 9 to show that wages equal the value of labor's marginal product in competitive labor markets. Now we want to consider a more realistic setting in which firms can adjust many factors of production simultaneously, even in the short run. When a firm expands its production in the short run, it typically adds many different kinds of labor, material inputs, and equipment, all the factors that are not fixed. It does not just add one factor of production.

To capture the more realistic case, assume that the firm produces its output (q) using the three generic factors of production as above, labor (L), materials (M), and capital (K). Write the firm's production function as

$$q = q(L, M, K)$$

The expression means that q is the maximum output the firm can produce using the amounts of labor, materials, and capital represented by L, M, and K.

[1]D. Jorgenson and B. Fraumeni, "Productivity and U.S. Economic Growth, 1979–1985," unpublished manuscript, 1987.

Understand that the production function does *not* necessarily describe the relationship between the output the firm is currently producing and the inputs the firm is currently using. The firm might not be squeezing every last bit of output from its inputs. Also, the production function does much more than describe the firm's current production process. It indicates the maximum output attainable from *all possible* combinations of inputs, not just the factors of production the firm is currently using. As such, the production function summarizes all the output-input *alternatives* available to the firm when solving the How problem, the entire set of production possibilities for the firm.

In terms of electricity generation, the production function allows for all possible power sources and all ages of the capital stock. For example, if the electric utility chooses to use nuclear power with the latest plant and equipment and its associated labor and materials requirements, q is the maximum output attainable from these resources. The factors associated with different power sources, and/or different ages of capital, are implicitly set equal to zero, since they are not being used. And so on for different choices.

REFLECTION: Think for a moment about the production function for your college or university. What are some of the inputs? How would you measure the output?

Maximum Output/Least-Cost Production

Assume for the moment that the firm does know its production function and the total cost of hiring any combination of inputs. How does the firm determine the factor combination that maximizes its output for a given amount of cost? The key, as always, is to ask what happens on the margin. How do cost and output change when the firm adds or releases small quantities of each factor of production? This is what the firm has to know to solve its How problem.

Changes in cost and output on the margin are given by the price of the factor and the factor's marginal product, respectively. The price indicates the change in total cost for each unit change in the factor. For example, if a particular kind of skilled labor earns $20 per hour, total cost increases by $20 per hour when one more worker is hired. (We are assuming that the firm hires factors in competitive markets, so that it has no effect on factor prices.)

Recall from Chapters 6 and 9 that the marginal product of a factor is the additional output produced by hiring one more unit of the factor. For example, if the skilled laborer works 1 more hour and produces 100 additional units of output, the worker's marginal product is 100 units of output per hour. Information on each factor's marginal product comes from the firm's production function.

The Least-Cost Production Rule

Solving the How problem is a straightforward two-step process, at least in principle. First, the firm computes the ratio of the marginal product to the price for each of its factors of production:

$$MP_F/P_F$$

Then it adjusts the amount of each factor of production until the ratio MP_F/P_F is equal for all factors. Equalizing the factor ratios places the firm on its total cost curve.

To see why the ratio MP_F/P_F is the key to solving the How problem, we must first understand what the ratio means. Think of the firm adding 1 more unit of a particular kind of labor. MP_L is the additional output from adding 1 unit of labor. P_L, the wage, is the addition to total cost from adding 1 unit of labor. Therefore, the ratio is the additional output divided by the additional cost, or

$$MP_L/P_L = \Delta q/\Delta TC$$

Equivalently, the ratio measures the additional output per dollar obtained from additional units of the labor.

For example, suppose that $MP_L = 10$ units of output per hour and $P_L =$ \$5 per hour. Then

$$MP_L/P_L = 10/5 = 2$$

The firm obtains 2 units of output per dollar of expenditure when it hires 1 more unit of labor.

To see why the firm must equalize output per dollar on the margin for all factors to be on its total cost curve, suppose that a firm hires two kinds of labor, L_1 and L_2. The firm computes MP_L/P_L for each type of worker and discovers that the ratios are unequal.

$$MP_{L_1}/P_{L_1} = 2 \quad \text{and} \quad MP_{L_2}/P_{L_2} = 1$$

With the ratios unequal, the firm can produce more output *at no additional cost* by releasing L_2 and hiring more L_1. If the firm spends \$1 less on L_2 and \$1 more on L_1, its total cost remains unchanged, but its output increases. According to the ratios, by releasing \$1 worth of L_2, the firm sacrifices 1 unit of output. By hiring \$1 worth of L_1, the firm gains 2 units of output. Net, the firm obtains 1 more unit of output *at no additional cost.*

With the ratios unequal, therefore, the firm must be operating somewhere in the inefficient region above and to the left of its total cost curve—say, at point A in Figure 11.7. By releasing \$1 worth of L_2 and adding \$1 worth of L_1, the firm moves horizontally to the right from point A, in the direction of the arrows. It is increasing its output, but not its total cost.

So long as $MP_{L_1}/P_{L_1} > MP_{L_2}/P_{L_2}$, the firm can always obtain additional output at no additional cost by substituting equal dollar amounts of L_1 for L_2. Once the ratios have equalized, however, the ability to obtain additional output costlessly ends. For example, suppose that the ratios equalize at 1.7 to 1. At that point, spending \$1 less on L_2 reduces output by 1.7 units, and spending \$1 more on L_1 increases output by 1.7 units. Neither total cost nor output changes; the firm has reached a point on its total cost curve. It can only increase output by increasing its total expenditures on factors of production. The firm must move upward along its total cost curve.

Will the ratios tend to equalize as the firm substitutes in favor of L_1? The answer is yes because of the Law of Diminishing Returns. Recall that the Law of Diminishing Returns is a law about the behavior of marginal products. It says that the marginal product of a variable factor tends to decline as the firm uses more of the factor. According to the law, therefore, the marginal product of L_1 tends to decline as the firm adds more L_1. Conversely, the marginal

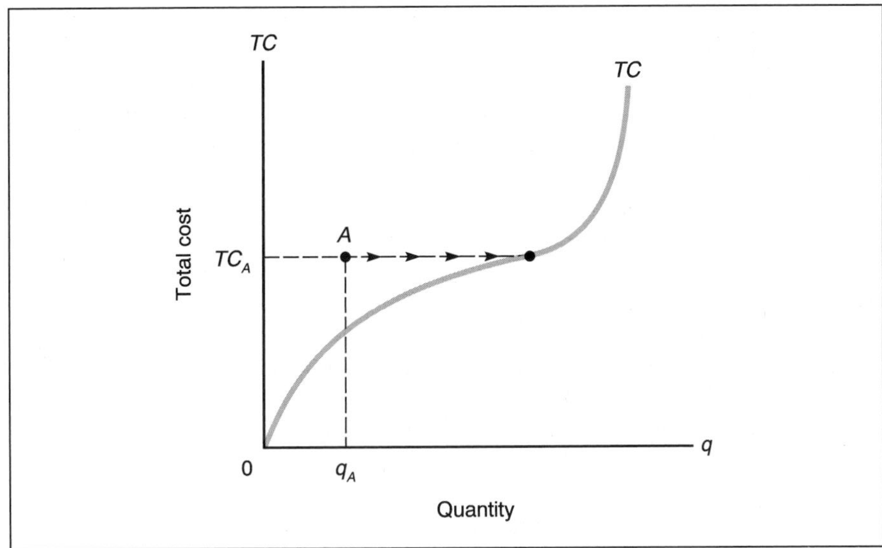

FIGURE 11.7

The Total Cost Curve and the Least-cost Production Rule

Suppose that a firm hires two types of labor, L_1 and L_2, and that their ratios of marginal products to prices (wages) are unequal: $MP_{L_1}/P_{L_1} > MP_{L_2}/P_{L_2}$. The firm would be at an inefficient point such as A in the figure, producing output q_A for a total cost of TC_A. By substituting L_1 for L_2, the firm can produce more output at no additional cost, and move horizontally from point A toward its long-run total cost curve *LRTC*. The firm reaches *LRTC* when the least-cost production rule $MP_{L_1}/P_{L_1} = MP_{L_2}/P_{L_2}$ holds, and it produces the most output possible for a total cost of TC_A.

product of L_2 tends to increase as the firm releases L_2. Therefore, substituting L_1 for L_2 causes M_{L_1}/P_{L_1} to decline below 2 and MP_{L2}/P_{L2} to increase above 1. The two ratios will tend to equalize at a value somewhere between 2 and 1.

Whether the ratios actually do equalize at some point depends on how much the first ratio declines and the second ratio increases. If they do equalize, then the firm continues to employ both types of labor. If MP_{L_1}/P_{L_1} remains above MP_{L_2}/P_{L_2} as the last unit of L_2 is released, the firm should not use L_2. The output per dollar that L_2 brings to the firm is too low to justify its employment.

What holds for these two kinds of labor holds for all the firm's factors of production. The firm should engage in the same pairwise comparison between all its factors of production and *substitute toward the factor with the higher output per dollar on the margin.* By doing so, the firm obtains additional output at no additional cost. When all pairwise MP_F/P_F ratios have been equalized, the firm is on its total cost curve.

To summarize the **least-cost production rule:**

LEAST-COST PRODUCTION RULE

The solution to the firm's How problem, in which the firm equalizes the ratio of marginal product to price across all factors of production.

1. Equalize MP_F/P_F across all factors of production.
2. If the MP_F/P_F ratios are unequal between two factors, substitute toward the factor with the higher ratio.

The least-cost production rule applies to both the short run and the long run, which is why we did not indicate whether the total cost curve in Figure 11.7 is the short-run or the long-run curve. The only difference is that the rule applies just to the variable factors of production in the short run, since these are the only factors the firm can adjust. The fixed factors are just that—fixed. Once the short run gives way to the long run, the rule applies to all factors of production.

The Problem of Measuring Marginal Products

The least-cost production rule is easy to describe in principle, but very difficult for firms to achieve in practice. The problem comes in measuring the marginal products of the various factors of production. A marginal product is an other things equal concept. It measures the change in output when only one factor of production is changing. Firms almost never change one factor of production at a time, however. As noted earlier, they usually change many factors of production simultaneously when they increase or decrease their output, even in the short run.

Measuring the separate marginal product of each factor requires sophisticated statistical techniques that most firms do not even try to use. Instead, they simply intuit the marginal products the best they can through experimentation and observation as they try to achieve the least-cost production rule. They make small changes in their production processes and see what happens to output (and total cost). Firms have a strong incentive to experiment in this way because they must lower their costs of production as much as possible to maximize profit. After all, profit is the difference between total revenue and total cost. Firms cannot maximize profit unless the cost of producing their output is as low as possible.

ECONOMIES OF SCALE

- *In terms of long-run total cost:* the region of the long-run total cost curve along which the percentage change in total cost is less than the percentage change in output.
- *In terms of the production function:* an equal proportionate increase in all the firm's inputs by an amount *k* leads to a proportionate increase in the firm's output by more than *k* (for example, a doubling of all the firm's inputs leads to more than a doubling of the firm's output); also called increasing returns to scale.

DISECONOMIES OF SCALE

- *In terms of long-run total cost:* the region of the long-run total cost curve along which the percentage change in total cost is greater than the percentage change in output.
- *In terms of the production function:* an equal proportionate increase in all the firm's inputs by an amount *k* leads to a proportionate increase in the firm's output by less than *k* (for example, a doubling of all the firm's inputs leads to less than a doubling of the firm's output); also called decreasing returns to scale.

CONSTANT RETURNS TO SCALE

- *In terms of long-run total cost:* the region of the long-run total cost curve along which the percentage change in total cost is equal to the percentage change in output.
- *In terms of the production function:* an equal proportionate increase in all the firm's inputs by an amount *k* leads to a proportionate increase in the firm's output equal to *k* (for example, a doubling of all the firm's inputs leads to a doubling of the firm's output).

The Shape of the Total Cost Curve Once Again

Now that we understand what the total cost curve represents and how it is derived, let's return to the discussion of its shape, beginning with the long run.

THE LONG RUN Economists characterize the long-run total cost curve as exhibiting economies of scale at low levels of output and diseconomies of scale at high levels of output. The notion of scale economies is an elasticity concept—in this case, the elasticity of total cost with respect to output. It compares the percentage changes in total cost and output as follows:

1. The total cost curve exhibits **economies of scale** if the $\%\Delta TC/\%\Delta q < 1$. Our hypothetical total cost curve in Figure 11.1 exhibits economies of scale at low levels of output, when the curve is bowed inward toward the origin. Refer back to the data on long-run total cost in Table 11.1. If the firm increases output from 4 to 6, a 40 percent increase, long-run total cost increases from \$432 to \$528, only a 20 percent increase. The $\%\Delta TC/\%\Delta q = 20/40 = .50$.[2]
2. The total cost curve exhibits **diseconomies of scale** if the $\%\Delta TC/\%\Delta q > 1$. The long-run total cost curve in Figure 11.1 exhibits diseconomies of scale at high levels of output, in the region somewhat beyond the point at which the curve begins to bow outward away from the origin. Referring again to Table 11.1, if the firm increases output from 18 to 20, an 11 percent increase, long-run total cost increases from \$936 to \$1,200, a 25 percent increase. Thus, $\%\Delta TC/\%\Delta q = 25/11 = 2.3$.
3. The total cost curve exhibits **constant returns to scale** if $\%\Delta TC/\%\Delta q = 1$. The long-run total cost curve in Figure 11.1 happens to exhibit constant

[2]A refresher on computing elasticities may be helpful. The percentage change in output is the ratio of the change in output to the mean of the two outputs, multiplied by 100 to turn the ratio into a percentage. $\Delta q = 6 - 4 = 2$. $q_{mean} = (6 + 4)/2 = 5$. Thus, $\%\Delta q = (2/5) \cdot 100 = 40\%$. Similarly, the percentage change in total cost is the ratio of the change in total cost to the mean of the two total costs, multiplied by 100. $\Delta TC = 528 - 432 = 96$. $TC_{mean} = (528 + 432)/2 = 480$. Thus, $\%\Delta TC = (96/480) \cdot 100 = 20\%$.

returns to scale at a single point somewhat beyond the output at which the bow changes directions. A straight-line long-run total cost curve has constant returns to scale throughout, but economists do not believe most firms have straight-line long-run total cost curves.

The nature of a firm's scale economies in the long run depends on its production function. Suppose that a firm doubles its expenditures on factors of production. The production function determines how much additional output the firm can produce if it continues to satisfy the least-cost production rule as it adds new factors of production. Notice that the firm does not necessarily double the amount of every variable factor of production when it doubles its factor costs. It may well change the relative proportions of each factor. In any event, whether output more than doubles, just doubles, or less than doubles determines whether the firm experiences economies of scale, constant returns to scale, or diseconomies of scale, respectively.[3]

ECONOMIES OF SCALE AT LOWER OUTPUTS Firms are likely to experience economies of scale at low levels of output for a number of reasons. **Factor indivisibilities** come into play at very low levels of output. Think back to the two friends starting their own business. In order to produce any output at all, they have to supply their own labor and purchase some material inputs and capital—paper and pens, fuel, electricity, desks, phones, personal computers, and so on. They may even hire one or two workers to help them. As they begin to produce, they may only need to buy some more material inputs until output reaches a certain critical point. Within that initial range of output the firm experiences substantial economies of scale; output increases, yet costs hardly increase at all.

FACTOR INDIVISIBILITY

The inability to use a fraction of a particular factor of production, as when a self-employed catering service owner has to use at least one truck.

The firm should still be able to experience some economies of scale as output continues to expand because of **specialization,** or **division of labor** (and other factors). For example, the two owners may at first have to serve as jacks-of-all-trades, overseeing and participating in production, marketing, sales, and accounting. As output increases and they hire more labor, they and each of their employees can specialize more narrowly in specific tasks. Some of the new employees are accountants, some sales representatives, and so forth. Freed from these tasks, the two owners can concentrate their efforts on long-range planning. This division of labor can be expected to increase output faster than it increases total cost (in percentage terms).

DIVISION OF LABOR

The process by which each task within a firm is defined narrowly and assigned to different people who perform only these specific tasks.

The firm can take advantage of complex highly efficient plant and equipment as output expands still further. For example, larger computer systems generally offer greater computing capacity and more flexibility per dollar than do smaller systems. But output has to grow sufficiently to justify the cost of the larger systems. The automobile assembly line is another prime example of

[3]An older, and narrower, definition of scale economies that is still widely used defines scale economies only in terms of the production function, as follows:

- *Economies of scale*—an equal proportionate increase in all the firm's inputs by an amount k leads to a proportionate increase in the firm's output by more than k (for example, a doubling of all the firm's inputs leads to more than a doubling of the firm's output); also called *increasing returns to scale*
- *Constant returns to scale*—an equal proportionate increase in all the firm's inputs by an amount k leads to a proportionate increase in the firm's output equal to k
- *Diseconomies of scale*—an equal proportionate increase in all the firm's inputs by an amount k leads to a proportionate increase in the firm's output by less than k; also called *decreasing returns to scale*

economies of scale through plant and equipment. Producing 300,000 to 500,000 cars per year on the largest, most automated assembly lines is less than three to five times as expensive as producing 100,000 cars per year on smaller, less automated assembly lines.

DISECONOMIES OF SCALE AT HIGHER OUTPUTS Economists usually attribute the long-run diseconomies of scale at higher outputs to two phenomena: lowered employee morale and managerial inefficiencies. As firms become larger and more specialized, employee morale suffers because employees tend to lose interest in their jobs. Individual tasks become ever more routinized and less challenging, and highly specialized employees are also less able to identify with the final product. An uninterested work force is a less productive work force; firms receive less output per dollar spent on wages and salaries. The managerial inefficiencies arise in trying to cope with an ever-expanding managerial structure. A managerial hierarchy consisting of layer upon layer of vice-presidents and other middle managers eventually becomes unwieldy and ineffective. Information flows with increasing difficulty throughout the hierarchy. Accountability suffers as well, and along with it some of the incentive middle managers have to be efficient. The net result is that managerial costs eventually grow faster than output.

Whether these potential sources of scale diseconomies are very important is debatable. The effect of firm size on employee morale is not well understood. Counteracting any possible loss of interest is the fact that large firms tend to pay higher salaries, on average, than do small firms. Larger paychecks can do wonders for employees' morale. The managerial inefficiency argument is also problematic. Large firms tend to split up their companies into separate, largely autonomous divisions in an effort to avoid an unwieldy managerial structure. Also, computers have greatly reduced the problems of passing information through the managerial hierarchy.

Probably the best argument for diseconomies of scale is the simple observation that most industries consist of a fairly large number of firms. Markets would tend to be dominated by one large firm if economies of scale persisted all the way to total market demand. In contrast, markets will contain a large number of firms if diseconomies of scale kick in at output levels that are only a small fraction of the total market demand. If one firm tried to take over the market, its costs would rise rapidly as its production increased into the region of scale diseconomies. New small and medium-sized firms would enter the market and undercut the existing firm's costs. In fact, most markets do have a large number of small and medium-sized firms.

EVIDENCE ON SCALE ECONOMIES The arguments for economies and diseconomies of scale are persuasive, but they remain somewhat speculative. In truth, economists have very little reliable information on individual firms' total cost curves. Discovering a firm's total cost curve is not simply a matter of plotting its total cost against output year by year. Remember that the total cost curve is an other things equal relationship between output and total cost. It holds constant all other variables affecting total cost. These other variables are not constant over time, however, and as they change, they affect the firm's total cost each year, just as changes in output do. We saw in our airline example how a new labor contract would increase total cost even if output were to remain constant from one year to the next. The new contract shifts the total cost curve upward.

Uncovering the total cost curve requires a sophisticated statistical analysis of firm-specific data that allows the researcher to estimate the *separate,* or *independent,* effect of output on total cost. Only a careful statistical analysis can distinguish between movements along the curve as output changes and shifts in the curve as one of the other variables affecting total cost changes.

This kind of statistical analysis is just now beginning to take place for private-sector firms. Statisticians had not developed reliable statistical techniques for estimating total cost curves until the 1970s. Moreover, researchers did not have access to the data needed to estimate individual firm cost curves even after the statistical techniques became available. Information on a firm's production techniques, output levels, and factor costs is privileged. Firms are reluctant to reveal their production and cost data to anyone, lest the data wind up in the hands of their competitors.

The U.S. Department of Commerce does collect firm-specific data for its annual Census of Manufactures, but it keeps the data strictly confidential. Only industrywide totals appear in published summaries of each census. A breakthrough finally occurred in the mid-1980s, when the Census Bureau gave researchers access to the firm-level data, providing the research maintained the confidentiality of individual firms. Over the next 5 to 10 years we should begin to have a better understanding of the actual nature of firms' total costs.

Our knowledge of firms' total cost curves prior to these ongoing studies came from two sources, neither very reliable. One approach consisted of economists and their graduate students interviewing a firm's engineers and managers to try to learn as much as they could about the firm's production techniques and costs. Unfortunately, even engineers and managers very close to the production process are unlikely to have a very precise understanding of the other things equal relationship between total cost and output. They, too, would have to apply the same sophisticated statistical techniques that economists now use to isolate the effect of output on cost.

The only other alternative was to apply the new statistical techniques to the industry-level data published in the Census of Manufactures. But most industries contain a fairly large number of firms that vary considerably in size and in the exact mix of products that they produce. As a result, a total cost curve estimated on industry data may not accurately represent any one firm's total cost curve.

The only notable exceptions to this state of affairs are the regulated industries, including the recently deregulated transportation sector. Production and cost data for regulated firms have always been a matter of public record, so economists first applied the new statistical techniques to these firms. The best data, and the most consistent set of results, come from the electric utilities. The cost studies typically find that the electric utilities exhibit economies of scale over the entire range of output up to market demand. This is hardly surprising because, as we will see in Chapter 14, the electric utilities are natural monopolies within the regions they serve. Economies of scale are likely to be much more important for the electric utilities than for private-sector firms.

For what it is worth, the engineering and industrywide cost studies suggest that the typical long-run total cost curve exhibits substantial economies of scale at low levels of output. Thereafter, the total cost–output relationship is essentially constant returns to scale. Virtually no one has found evidence of substantial diseconomies of scale at higher output levels in the long run. The "conventional wisdom" of diseconomies of scale, as represented by the hypothetical data in Table 11.1, is somewhat a matter of faith among economists.

THE SHORT RUN The relationship between short-run total cost and output depends on the pattern of short-run variable cost, since the fixed-cost component of short-run total cost never changes. The short-run variable cost curve has the same general shape as the long-run total cost curve, even though the firm cannot vary all its factors of production in the short-run. Economies and diseconomies of scale are strictly long-run concepts.

Nonetheless, factor indivisibilities and specialization cause output to increase proportionately more than does variable cost at low levels of output for the same reasons that they generate long-run economies of scale. The fixed factors do not restrict output very much when output is low. Adding new, complex capital is almost certainly just a long-run phenomenon, however.

Because of the Law of Diminishing Returns, short-run variable cost must eventually rise proportionately more than output does as output increases. The fixed factors of production eventually limit the firm's ability to expand output as each of the variable factors has smaller and smaller amounts of the fixed factors to work with. The Law of Diminishing Returns does not apply to the long run, however.

Marginal Product and Marginal Cost

Our agricultural example from Chapters 6 and 9, in which a farmer adds identical farm workers to a plot of land, is useful for illustrating the typical pattern of short-run variable cost. This time, though, we allow the marginal product of labor to increase at first in order to represent the gains from the division of labor. The first worker has to do everything himself. With two workers one can till the ground, and the other can plant the crop, presumably with some gain in their overall productivity. With three workers one can till, another can plant, and the third can water and fertilize the crop. And so on. Recall that four workers are needed to farm all the land, so that the gains from the division of labor apply to the first four workers. Once the fifth worker is added, though, the Law of Diminishing Returns kicks in as the land truly becomes a fixed factor and each worker has less land to farm.

Refer to Table 11.3. The marginal product of labor (MP_L) in the second column reflects the pattern of specialization followed by the Law of Diminishing Returns. MP_L rises over the first four workers and then falls.

The fourth column shows what happens to the marginal cost (MC) of producing the crop, assuming that the farmer can hire workers at a wage of \$250, as in Chapter 9. We saw in Chapter 6 that marginal cost is the wage divided by the marginal product of labor. The wage, P_L, is the change in total cost from hiring 1 more worker, and MP_L is the change in output.

$$MC = \Delta TC/\Delta q = P_L/MP_L$$

The pattern of marginal costs depends entirely on the marginal product of labor because the wage is constant at \$250. Notice that MC falls over the first four workers when MP_L is rising. Then MC rises from the fifth worker on, once the Law of Diminishing Returns sets in and MP_L is falling. This is the same general pattern of short-run marginal cost illustrated in Table 11.1. It implies that short-run variable cost is rising proportionately less than output over the first four workers and proportionately more than output from the fifth worker on.

TABLE 11.3 **The Relationship Between Marginal Product and Marginal Cost for a Hypothetical Farm**

NUMBER OF WORKERS	MARGINAL PRODUCT (MP_L) (BUSHELS)	TOTAL PRODUCT	MARGINAL COST ($MC = P_L/MP_L$) (P_L = \$250)
1	100	100	\$ 2.50
2	110	210	2.27
3	140	350	1.79
4	150	500	1.67
5	75	575	3.33
6	50	625	5.00
7	25	650	10.00
8	0	650	∞

Table 11.3 also illustrates the very powerful effect that the Law of Diminishing Returns can have on short-run costs at high levels of output. Marginal cost rises without limit at the eighth worker in our example because adding that worker increases total cost by \$250, but does not increase output at all.

APPLICATIONS OF THE LEAST-COST PRODUCTION RULE

Economists understand that the least-cost production rule is an ideal guideline resulting from a simple model of the firm's How problem. They realize that few business firms are producing as efficiently as they possibly can. Whether firms follow the least-cost production rule to the letter is unimportant, though. What matters is whether the model yields useful predictions about how firms actually behave.

The model of the firm's How problem has turned out to be a highly useful tool of economic analysis. Not only does the least-cost production rule help explain firms' input decisions. It also sheds light on a number of important government policy issues that turn on the question of production efficiency. The following examples offer a sampler of applications illustrating how the least-cost production rule helps us better understand firms' economic behavior.

Hire the Most Productive Worker?

Do firms always hire the most productive worker? The answer is no because the most productive worker might not be the most cost-effective. Suppose that a firm can hire a "more skilled" worker or a "less skilled" worker and that the more skilled worker is 2 times as productive as the less skilled worker on the margin. That is,

$$MP_{\text{more skilled}} = 2 \cdot MP_{\text{less skilled}}$$

For example, with respect to units of output per hour:

$$MP_{\text{more skilled}} = 36 \quad MP_{\text{less skilled}} = 18$$

Productivity is not the only consideration, however; price, or cost, matters, too. Suppose, also, that the wage of the more skilled worker is 3 times the wage of the less skilled worker:

$$P_{\text{more skilled}} = 3 \cdot P_{\text{less skilled}}$$

For example,

$$P_{\text{more skilled}} = \$12/\text{hour} \quad P_{\text{less skilled}} = \$4/\text{hour}$$

The MP/P ratio for each worker indicates that

$$MP_{\text{more skilled}}/P_{\text{more skilled}} < MP_{\text{less skilled}}/P_{\text{less skilled}}$$

$$36/12 = 3 < 4.5 = 18/4$$

The firm should hire the less skilled worker because that worker brings the firm a higher output per dollar on the margin. Additional output per dollar is the proper hiring criterion, not output (productivity) alone.

Sports fans and team owners do battle over just this point. The fans always want their team to sign the most skilled player available. All they care about is winning the championship. The team owner, however, is forced to pay attention to the "bottom line." If the most skilled player available is a superstar with an enormous salary, the owner may well decide to sign a lesser player who is still helpful to the team, and far more cost-effective.

"They Just Don't Make Things the Way They Used To"

The least-cost production rule also explains why firms do not make things the way they used to and why we would not want them to.

Some people may long for the good old days of sturdy, long-lasting, "maintain and repair" appliances, but the changeover to flimsier, "discard and replace" appliances makes perfect economic sense. In the United States, with its huge and growing stock of capital, labor has become ever more expensive, whereas capital has remained relatively cheap. Producing "discard and replace" appliances is the proper way to take advantage of these relative factor prices.

Why pay a repair company $50 and more to repair a clock radio when a new one costs only $20? Why pay a jeweler $30 to repair a $20 jogger's watch? Even more expensive appliances, such as television sets, are often replaced when they first break down. Should someone spend $150 to repair a five-year-old television set or spend $250 for a new one? People faced with this decision often choose to buy a new television set. Furthermore, if appliances are likely to be replaced every few years, why house them in casings designed to last for thirty years? Thin plastic casings are much cheaper—and perfectly functional for "discard and replace" appliances.

The same point applies to automobiles. We do not want to pay mechanics $60 an hour to tinker very long with a part that costs $50 to replace. And building cars with heavyweight steel today would make them prohibitively expensive.

Are we worse off for these changes? Not at all. We do not really want appliances and automobiles that last "forever." Rather, we want to enjoy the *services* these products offer us "forever" at the lowest possible cost. "Discard and replace" is far cheaper over the long haul than is "maintain and repair" in a high-wage economy. Not surprisingly, competition has steered appliance manufacturers to the least-cost alternative. And we are better off for it.[4]

DIFFERENCES IN PRODUCTION TECHNIQUES THROUGHOUT THE WORLD

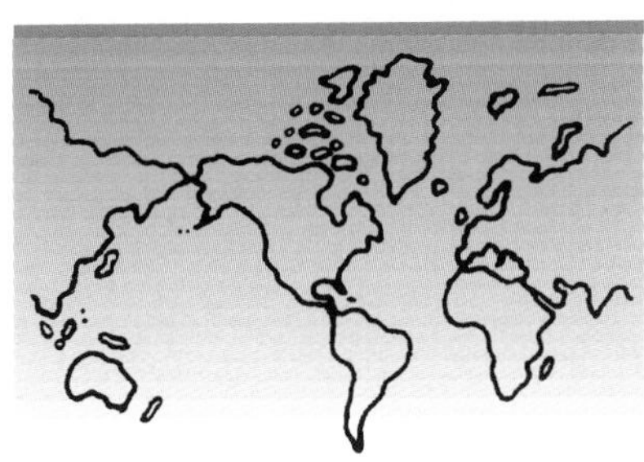

The same products are produced very differently in different parts of the world. For instance, textiles are produced in both the United States and India, but by very different methods. Textile production in India is highly labor-intensive; in the United States it is highly capital-intensive. These choices are dictated by different prices for labor and capital in the two countries. The least-cost production rule indicates why.

Suppose that a textile manufacturer in India duplicated the techniques of U.S. manufacturers, using the same amount and kinds of labor and capital to produce the same amount of cloth. Suppose, further, that production in the United States is efficient, so that

$$MP_K^{US}/P_K^{US} = MP_L^{US}/P_L^{US}$$

If the Indian manufacturer duplicates the production techniques of the U.S. manufacturers, the marginal products in the two countries would be equal:

$$MP_K^{US} = MP_K^I \quad \text{and} \quad MP_L^{US} = MP_L^I$$

But the prices of capital and labor are very different in the two countries. In India, unlike the United States, capital is very scarce, and labor is far more plentiful. Consequently, in India the price of capital is much higher, and the price of labor is much lower.

$$P_K^{US} << P_K^I \quad \text{and} \quad P_L^{US} >> P_L^I$$

Therefore, by duplicating the U.S. production techniques the Indian manufacturer would not be producing in a least-cost manner.

$$MP_K^I/P_K^I << MP_L^I/P_L^I$$

The output per dollar from hiring additional labor would far exceed the output per dollar from using additional capital. The Indian manufacturer should substitute labor for capital until the two ratios are equal.

[4]The only caveat is that the "discard and replace" technologies increase the social costs of properly disposing of the appliances, in the form of increased litter and pollution. Neither the consumers who use the appliances nor the firms that make them bear the direct costs of the litter and pollution, so they tend to ignore these costs. The full social costs of the newer "discard and replace" technologies are probably still less than the full social costs of the older "maintain and repair" technologies. But the cost advantage is not nearly so large as it appears to consumers.

Indian manufacturers know this, of course, which is why they do *not* imitate U.S. production techniques. They use much more labor per unit of output and equip their workers with older, less sophisticated, and less expensive capital.

People often use labels such as "modern" or "backward" to describe different production technologies. For instance, Indian textile manufacture might be described as "backward" and U.S. textile manufacture as "modern." "Backward" and "modern" are emotionally loaded words, suggesting that some managers know something that other managers do not know. This is seldom the case, however. Once new production technologies and new kinds of capital are invented, their existence is generally widely known. Moreover, people everywhere presumably make equally intelligent choices about how best to solve their economic problems. The differences one sees are not reflections of "knowledge" versus "ignorance," of being "backward" or "modern." Rather, they reflect intelligent production choices by managers operating in very different factor markets. Indian textile manufacturing is not "backward" at all. It is "least-cost" and "efficient," given the available resources in India.

CURRENT ISSUE: Agriculture provides obvious examples of producing the same product with different techniques, even among the developed countries. European farmers use much more labor and much less land and capital than do farmers in the land- and capital-rich United States. Farmers in the United States remove more land from cultivation under the federal government's acreage restriction program than the total amount of land farmed in Western Europe.

The Federal Government's War Against Industrial Pollution

Our final application of the least-cost production rule concerns the federal government's policies aimed at reducing industrial air and water pollution. In the early 1970s the federal government decided to wage an all-out war against industrial polluters. The 1970 Amendments to the Clean Air Act established 247 air quality control regions throughout the United States and defined a target level of ambient air quality to be met in each region. The amendments called for uniform reductions of emissions at all sources of pollution within each region. If a region did not meet these standards by 1975, no new sources of pollution would be allowed in that region.

The 1972 Amendments to the Federal Water Pollution Control Act were even more ambitious. They established maximum levels of waste discharge at each point source of pollution, with the ultimate objective of making all inland bodies of water suitable for fishing and swimming by 1983.

Economists have been highly critical of the federal government's anti-pollution policies from the onset. If economists agree on anything, it is the nature of industrial pollution in a market economy—why it exists and what to do about it. They understand the existence of industrial pollution as a straightforward application of the firm's How problem and see the least-cost production rule as the proper guideline for designing an anti-pollution strategy. The federal government's anti-pollution strategy has failed because it favors a regulatory command-and-control approach to fighting pollution that ignores the principles of least-cost production. As a result, the battle against pollution is far more costly than it needs to be. The 1990 Amendments to the Clean Air Act finally offered a ray of hope when they introduced a least-cost pricing strategy to control the electric utilities' emissions of sulfur dioxide, the source of acid rain. We will illustrate the government's problems in fighting pollution with an analysis of industrial water pollution, although the same principles apply to air pollution.

THE INCENTIVE TO POLLUTE The economic analysis of industrial water pollution begins with the fact that water is a valuable factor of production to many firms. Water is an essential component of many liquid products, such as soft drinks. Beyond this, however, many manufacturing firms use water as a cleansing agent, a cooling agent, a means of transportation, or a convenient means of disposal for industrial waste products. All these other uses, and especially the last one, pollute the water.

Since water is a factor of production, it becomes part of the least-cost production rule. Think of a firm situated along a river and producing some output (q) using labor (L), capital (K), and water (W), according to the production function

$$q = q(L, K, W)$$

Assume that the firm uses the water in one or more of the four ways listed above.

The firm tries to satisfy the least-cost production rule for all three factors to produce efficiently, so that

$$MP_L/P_L = MP_K/P_K = MP_W/P_W$$

Water is different from labor and capital, however—it is a common-use resource. No one owns the water, so no one charges the firm (or anyone else) for its use; $P_W = 0$. But since P_W is in the denominator of the third ratio, that ratio is large without limit. Therefore,

$$MP_L/P_L = MP_K/P_K < MP_W/(P_W = 0)$$

The firm should substitute water for both capital and labor to minimize its production costs.

The ratios will never equalize with $P_W = 0$. The best the firm can do is drive the MP_W to zero so that the value of the third ratio is 0/0. In other words, the firm should think of every possible way to use water until water literally has no additional uses. Since water is free, its output per dollar on the margin always exceeds the output per dollar from using any other factor of production, until $MP_W = 0$. Firms have a powerful economic incentive to use and pollute water (and air).

Our analysis shows that industrial pollution is a pricing problem. Because no one owns the property rights to water (air), firms treat clean water as a free good, even though it is a scarce and highly valued resource. The way to solve the problem is clear: Force firms to pay a price for using clean water that reflects its value to society. A tax on water does the trick.

An ideal tax policy would levy a separate tax rate on each pollutant, with higher tax rates applied to more harmful pollutants and lower tax rates applied to less harmful pollutants. Monitoring each pollutant is a difficult task, however, so that the government is more likely to levy a single tax on water usage. We will assume that this is what the government does in the discussion that follows.

The tax rate should also follow the general principle that prices reflect what is true on the margin. In this case, the principle means setting the tax rate equal to the aggregate damage to all third parties from the last unit of pollution at each firm. The third parties may include commercial fishing firms and people who use the river for recreational purposes. Here, too, practical considerations dictate an alternative strategy. Existing scientific knowledge of the damage caused by water (and air) pollution is fairly sketchy, enough so that no one can accurately estimate the value of the damages caused by various pollutants. Consequently, governments have little choice other than to set a target level of pollution. The policy objective then becomes meeting the target level of pollution at the least possible cost.

A pollution tax does fight pollution at the least cost because it is directed to the firm's profit motive, the same motive that generates pollution in the first place. A tax changes the value of the MP_W/P_W ratio and thereby gets to the heart of the problem. With a tax, t_W, on water usage, the ratio is now MP_W/t_W. Assuming that firms have driven MP_W down to zero, the ratio is no longer undefined as 0/0. The ratio now equals zero because the denominator is positive ($0/t_W = 0$). Therefore,

$$MP_L/P_L = MP_K/P_K > MP_W/t_W = 0$$

Given the tax on water, labor and capital now both offer the firm a higher output per dollar on the margin than does water. Firms must substitute away from water in favor of both labor and capital to minimize their production costs. The substitution continues until the three ratios are again equal. As firms use less water, the amount of pollution decreases. All the government has to do is increase the tax rate until pollution decreases to the aggregate target level.

The tax guarantees that the pollution target will be met at the least possible cost because it gives each firm complete freedom to respond as it sees fit. Some firms will decide to pay the tax and continue polluting. Other firms will find that alternative methods of cleaning, or cooling, or disposing of industrial wastes are now cheaper than continuing to use water. They will substitute these other methods and reduce their water tax liability. With each firm responding to the tax to minimize its own cost, the aggregate cost of reducing pollution is also minimized.

The tax reduces pollution in another way, by feeding through to the markets for goods and services. The process is illustrated in Figure 11.8, which shows the market supply and the market demand curves of a product whose production causes water pollution. Recall that the market supply curve is the sum of the firms' marginal cost curves. The market supply curve is S_0 prior to the tax; it reflects the firms' marginal cost of producing the product, but it ignores the cost of the pollution. The market equilibrium without the pollution tax is (Q_0, P_0), at the intersection of D and S_0.

The firms' marginal costs increase as a result of the pollution tax because they now have to pay for a resource that used to be free of charge. Therefore, the tax shifts the market supply curve up to S_1. S_1 incorporates the full social marginal costs of producing the product, equal to the firms' private marginal costs of production plus the marginal costs of the pollution. The new equilibrium is (Q_1, P_1), at the intersection of D and S_1. The price of the polluting good has risen, and resources have shifted toward untaxed, nonpolluting goods whose prices are now relatively cheaper. These price and output changes help in the battle against pollution by steering consumers and producers away from polluting goods.

The only remaining question is whether firms really are able to use alternative methods of cleaning, cooling, transporting, and disposing of wastes in

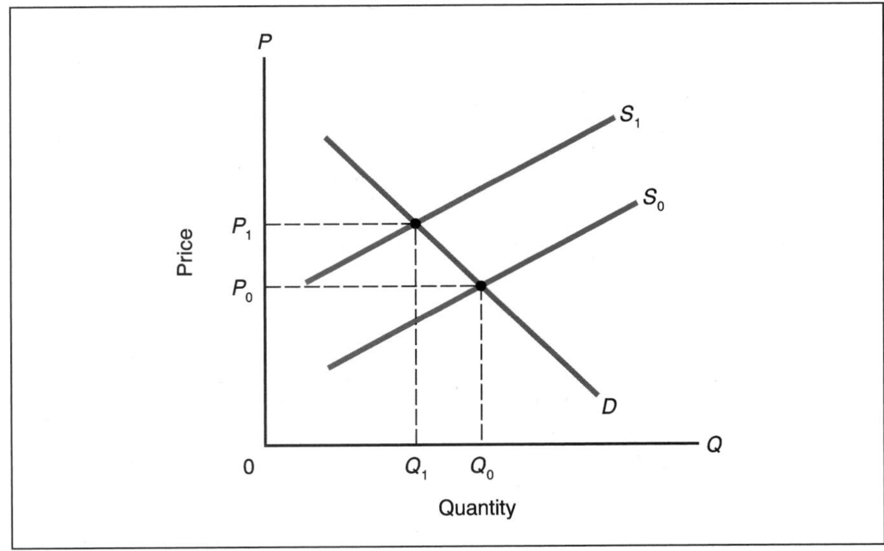

FIGURE 11.8

A Pollution Tax and the Output of Polluting Firms

A tax on the use of water by firms that pollute the water raises the firms' marginal cost of production. The market supply curve shifts up from S_0 to S_1 by the amount that marginal cost increases. The equilibrium changes from (Q_0,P_0) at the intersection of D and S_0 to (Q_1,P_1) at the intersection of D and S_1. The pollution tax on water helps fight pollution by raising the prices of polluting goods, which induces people to consume less of these goods.

response to taxation. The cost of reducing pollution is lower the more easily firms are able to substitute away from water. If firms must use water for these purposes, then society must rely entirely on the output effects pictured in Figure 11.8 to reduce pollution. Fortunately, water is a highly substitutable factor of production. The German experience with pollution taxes has shown that the tax strategy is highly effective.

In the 1960s West Germany decided to clean up four of the five rivers in the Ruhr River Basin. At the time the Ruhr supported much of the West German manufacturing base, and the rivers in the basin were predictably choked with pollutants. The West Germans attacked the problem with a combination of taxes on firms to reduce the flow of pollutants into the four rivers and waste treatment plants to remove any remaining pollutants in excess of the target levels.

The combination tax-and-waste-treatment strategy worked very well. In particular, the pollution taxes were highly effective in reducing pollution at its source. Firms were easily able to find substitutes for water, with the result that West German firms use *far* less water than do their counterparts in other countries. West German steel mills, for example, reduced water usage to 2.6 cubic meters per ton of steel produced in response to the tax. The worldwide average for steel production at the time was 130 cubic meters of water per ton of steel. The West German experience left no doubt that charging firms for using water is an effective anti-pollution strategy.[5]

U.S. POLICY Until 1990 the United States chose to ignore both economic theory and the West German experience. Instead of establishing a price for the use of clean water (clean air), the United States adopted a regulatory command-and-control approach to combating pollution. Each firm receives a set of permits that indicate how much pollution can be discharged from each

[5]M. Goldman, "Pollution: the Mess Around Us," in M. Goldman, ed., *Controlling Pollution: the Economics of a Cleaner America* (Englewood Cliffs, NJ: Prentice-Hall, 1967), 36.

source. In addition, the government often specifies in great detail the technologies that firms must employ to control or treat waste discharges. A central thrust of the U.S. strategy is an "even-handed" approach to meeting pollution targets, in the sense that every firm is required to reduce its pollution in more or less equal amounts.

The command-and-control approach is much less cost-effective than is the tax approach. Its most basic failing is that the price of clean water (air) remains at zero, which gives firms an enormous incentive to cheat and pollute the water anyway. The government is then forced to take the initiative to prosecute cheaters, and the burden to prosecute usually falls on the state governments. Prosecution does not work very well. Firms pressure the state governments not to prosecute by threatening to leave, and firms will cheat anyway if the fines are not set high enough to deter cheating. In fact, very few firms have been successfully prosecuted since the new laws have been in effect, and the fines have not been especially burdensome even when prosecution has succeeded. In contrast, with a pollution tax the firms must take the initiative to reduce their tax liabilities. True, firms can cheat under the tax approach, but the incentive to cheat is far less than under the regulate-and-prosecute approach. Once firms have changed their production techniques to reduce their tax liabilities, they are unlikely to switch back.

The command-and-control approach is also far less flexible than is the tax approach. Firms are not free to pursue their least-cost strategies for avoiding pollution as they are with a pollution tax. An even-handed strategy may sound fair, but it is highly inefficient. Under the least-cost tax strategy, the aggregate pollution target is met with highly varied pollution reductions firm by firm, depending on the nature of each firm's production technology. Firms that can easily substitute away from water will do so to reduce their tax liabilities. Firms that cannot easily substitute may find that paying the tax is the cheaper alternative. Society should not care what each firm does. All it should care about is meeting the aggregate pollution target as cheaply as possible.

The U.S. policies have succeeded in reducing pollution. For example, in 1990 the Environmental Protection Agency estimated that airborne concentrations of lead and particulate matter had declined by 95 percent and 38 percent, respectively, since 1970. These are two of the more harmful air pollutants. Reductions in water pollution are more difficult to verify, but few question that the government's policies have made some progress in cleaning up the nation's waters.[6]

REFLECTION: In the 1970s the federal government set a goal of zero air and water pollution. Do you think this makes economic sense? (*Hint:* Think in terms of opportunity cost.)

The problem, though, is that these reductions in pollution have been far more costly than they needed to be. One economic study of 11 cases of industrial air pollution and 6 cases of industrial water pollution estimated that a pricing strategy would have dramatically reduced costs for the same reduction in pollution. The estimated cost reductions ranged from 42 percent to 93 percent in 10 of the 11 air pollution cases and from 11 percent to 68 percent in the 6 water pollution cases. With the United States spending over $90 billion on pollution abatement and control, cost savings of these magnitudes represent a considerable saving of scarce resources.[7]

[6]P. Portney, "Economics and the Clean Air Act," *Journal of Economic Perspectives* 4, No. 4 (Fall 1990): 176.

[7]A. Blinder, *Hard Heads, Soft Hearts* (Reading, MA: Addison-Wesley, 1987), 152–153.

MARKETABLE DISCHARGE PERMITS The 1990 Amendments to the Clean Air Act represented a dramatic shift in the federal government's anti-pollution strategy toward the pricing solution. The oil- and coal-burning electric utilities emit sulfur dioxide into the atmosphere, which is the source of acid rain. Prior to 1990 each utility received pollution permits that limited the amount of sulfur dioxide it could emit. The 1990 amendments made the permits transferable and marketable for the first time; the utilities now can buy and sell the permits among themselves as they wish. (This new provision is subject to the approval of each state legislature, so it may not yet apply to utilities in all the states.)

Marketable pollution permits offer the same incentives to reduce pollution as a pollution tax does. Utilities that wish to keep polluting buy additional permits from other utilities. They pay for the right to pollute, just as with the tax. Conversely, utilities that can easily substitute away from emitting sulfur dioxide sell their permits to other utilities. The revenues from selling the permits are equivalent to the reduction in tax liabilities under the pollution tax. In other words, the market price of the permits defines the cost to firms of additional pollution or the benefits of additional reductions in pollution, just as a pollution tax does.

MARKETABLE PERMIT (POLLUTION)

A government-issued allowance to emit a certain amount of a pollutant that firms can buy and sell; used in the United States to control the emission of sulfur dioxide by the electric utilities under the Clean Air Act.

Marketable pollution permits have a number of practical advantages over pollution taxes. They make it easier to meet the target level of pollution. All the government has to do is issue a total number of permits equal to the overall target level. With a tax the target must be approached in trial-and-error fashion by adjusting the tax rates. In addition, the price of the permits naturally rises with economic growth and inflation. A pollution tax must be adjusted periodically to ensure that it retains the proper "bite." Finally, marketable permits were easy to implement because the utilities were already receiving nontransferable permits. Instituting a pollution tax would have required an entirely new administrative regime.

CURRENT ISSUE: The market for trading the discharge permits began operation in March 1993.

Economists have some evidence that marketable permits are highly effective. In the 1980s Wisconsin decided to allow firms along the Fox River to exchange water pollution permits. The Fox contains the highest concentration of paper mills of any river in the world. The Wisconsin experiment has been a huge success. Preliminary estimates indicate that the marketable permits have reduced the costs of pollution control by 80 percent relative to the old command-and-control approach. The permits have also proved to be readily adaptable to variations in temperature and water flow along the river.[8]

Economists are hoping that the federal government will extend the pricing approach to the control of water pollution and to the other sections of the Clean Air Act that attempt to control urban air pollution and 190 chemicals classified as hazardous air pollutants. The marketable permits for controlling sulfur dioxide emissions are the only exception so far to the government's regulatory command-and-control approach to reducing water and air pollution.

---

[8] W. Oates, "Markets for Pollution Control," *Challenge* 27, No. 2 (May–June 1984): 15–16.

SUMMARY

Chapter 11 began with an overview of the individual firm's total cost curve, one of the more important analytical constructs in all of economic analysis. The total cost curve is the basis of all the cost relationships used in this text. The overview stressed five attributes of a firm's total cost of production.

1. *Other things equal:* A total cost curve depicts the other things equal relationship between the firm's output and its total cost of production. All other variables that affect total cost, such as factor prices and the firm's production technology, are held constant. Changes in these other variables shift the curve up or down.
2. *The short run versus the long run:* Total cost in the short run naturally divides into fixed cost and variable cost. Fixed cost is associated with the firm's fixed factors of production and does not vary with output. Variable cost is associated with the firm's variable factors of production and does vary with output. In the long run, total cost and total variable cost are one and the same, since all factors of production can be varied. Fixed cost is zero.
3. *Shape of the total cost curve:*
   a. The long run: Economists believe that the long-run total cost curve is bowed inward toward the origin at low levels of output and bowed outward away from the origin at high levels of output. This shape reflects the belief that firms experience economies of scale ($\%\Delta TC/\%\Delta q < 1$) at low levels of output and diseconomies of scale ($\%\Delta TC/\%\Delta q > 1$) at high levels of output. The initial economies of scale are attributed to factor indivisibilities, specialization, and the use of large, highly efficient capital. The changeover to diseconomies of scale is attributed to lowered worker productivity and managerial inefficiencies. The strongest evidence for diseconomies of scale is the fact that most markets support a large number of firms.
   b. The short run: The short-run variable cost curve and the total cost curve have the same general shape as the long-run total cost curve. Factor indivisibilities and specialization cause short-run variable cost to rise proportionately less than output at low levels of output. But because of the Law of Diminishing Returns, variable cost must eventually rise proportionately more than output as output increases. The fixed factors eventually limit the firm's ability to increase output in the short run without sharply increasing cost.
4. *Economic cost versus tax accounting cost:* The total cost represented on a total cost curve is total economic cost, the total opportunity cost of producing the firm's output. Accounting cost for income tax purposes includes only the operating expenses of the firm. Economic cost includes operating expenses plus the opportunity cost of capital and labor supplied to the firm by the owner(s). Economic profit is the difference between total revenue and total economic cost.
5. *Economic efficiency:* The total cost curve is an efficiency frontier, the output–total cost combinations that represent an efficient solution to the firm's How problem. All points (q, TC) on a total cost curve have one of two interpretations:

a. q is the maximum output attainable for total cost of TC, or
b. TC is the minimum total cost required to produce the output q.

The second section of the chapter described the least-cost production rule that firms must follow to be on their total cost curves.

6. According to the least-cost production rule, firms should hire factors of production so as to equalize the MP_F/P_F ratio across all factors of production.
7. If the ratios between two factors are unequal firms should substitute toward the factor with the higher ratio. Doing so increases output at no additional cost.

The third section of Chapter 11 considered a number of applications of the least-cost production rule. Economists recognize that marginal products are very difficult to measure. But the assumption that firms attempt to equalize the MP_F/P_F ratios to reduce their costs has helped economists understand the nature of firms' production decisions.

8. The least-cost production rule explains why firms do not necessarily hire the most skilled workers, why the same products are produced very differently in different countries, and why "they just don't make things the way they used to." The reason is the same in each instance: Firms economize on relatively expensive inputs and make liberal use of relatively cheap inputs.
9. The federal government's war against industrial pollution is far more costly than it needs to be because the government favors a regulatory command-and-control approach to fighting pollution that ignores the principles of least-cost production. Firms pollute the water and air because these resources are free to them. An anti-pollution policy must place a price on the use of water and air, as by means of a pollution tax, to give firms an incentive to substitute away from using and polluting water and air.
10. The 1990 Amendments to the Clean Air Act introduced a pricing strategy for the sulfur dioxide emissions of electric utilities, which are the source of acid rain. The utilities can now buy and sell their permits to emit sulfur dioxide. Marketable permits are equivalent to a pollution tax and encourage the utilities to find the least-cost means of reducing their sulfur dioxide emissions.

KEY TERMS

Constant returns to scale
Depreciation
Diseconomies of scale
Dividends
Division of labor
Economic profit
Economies of scale
Factor indivisibility
Firm's How problem
Fixed cost
Least-cost production rule
Marketable permit (pollution)
Operating expenses
Opportunity cost of capital
Opportunity cost of labor
Production function
Retained earnings
Total cost curve (short-run and long-run)
Total economic cost
Variable cost

QUESTIONS

1. A competitive firm's production function is as follows in the short run, with labor the only variable input.

QUANTITY OF LABOR	TOTAL OUTPUT PER YEAR
0	0
1	4.0
2	7.0
3	9.0
4	10.0
5	10.5

The owners of the firm have $10,000 invested in the capital used by the firm. They can earn a return of 10 percent on these funds in their next best investment alternatives. The wage rate is $25 per unit of labor.

a. Determine the fixed cost, the variable cost, and the short-run total cost of the firm at every level of output listed in the table.

b. Sketch the firm's fixed cost curve, its variable cost curve, and its short-run total cost curve. Are the shapes of these curves realistic? Explain.

2. Refer again to the data in question 1. Suppose that the firm signs a new contract with the labor union and that the new wage rate is $30 per unit of labor. Show the effects of this change on each of the three curves you drew in question 1.
3. Refer again to the data in question 1. Do you have enough information to determine the long-run total cost of the firm? Why or why not?
4. Explain some of the main differences between a firm's accounting costs for tax purposes and its economic costs. Also, which would you expect to be larger at any given output, the accounting costs or the economic costs?
5. A college graduate gets the following job offers:

	JOB 1	JOB 2
Salary per year	$25,000	$20,000
Medical insurance	None	$5,000

The college graduate accepts job 1. What is his/her opportunity cost of accepting job 1?

6. Why is a firm's total cost curve (short-run or long-run) an efficiency frontier for the firm, much like the production possibilities curve is an efficiency frontier for the entire economy?
7. a. Why does the typical firm's long-run total cost curve tend to bow outward from the origin at high output levels?

   b. Why does the typical firm's short-run total cost curve tend to bow outward from the origin at high output levels?
8. Suppose that a competitive firm rents two different kinds of machines that it uses in its factory to produce its output. The marginal product of machine 1 is 6 units per hour, and the rental price of this machine is $12 an hour. The marginal product of machine 2 is 4 units per hour, and the rental price of this machine is $6 an hour. Is the firm using these two machines in the most efficient manner? If yes, explain why. If no, explain why not, and indicate how the firm should adjust its use of the two machines.
9. A firm has the following cost structure in the long run:

TOTAL COST	OUTPUT
$0	0
25,000	1
40,000	2
60,000	3
100,000	4

Over what range of output does the long-run total cost curve exhibit economies of scale? Constant returns to scale? Diseconomies of scale? (Assume that the firm increases output 1 unit at a time.)

10. The United States has preferred a command-and-control approach to reducing industrial pollution. Economists recommend instead a policy of taxing polluters based on the amount that they pollute the air and water. What are the economic advantages of a pollution tax over the command-and-control approach for reducing industrial pollution?
11. *Extra credit:* The 1990 Amendments to the Clean Air Act instituted a system of marketable permits to control the emission of sulfur dioxide by the electric utilities. Compare and contrast marketable permits with a tax on the utilities' emission of sulfur dioxide.

CHAPTER

12

Private Investment Analysis

LEARNING OBJECTIVES

CONCEPTS TO LEARN

Compounding to future value
Discounting to present value
The discount rate
The present value of an investment
The yield (rate of return) on an investment
Levered investments
Government cost-benefit analysis

CONCEPTS TO RECALL

Opportunity cost [1]
The profit maximizing decision rule for hiring labor [9]

Imagine that you are the executive vice-president in charge of a large corporation's long-range planning. You are trying to decide whether to purchase a newly invented machine for each of the company's factories. The machine costs \$10,000, which the company will pay for now, in cash. You expect the machine to yield net revenues of \$1,200 each year for 10 years. The net revenues are the difference between the revenues from selling the product that the machine produces and the costs of operating and maintaining the machine. You believe that the machine will have no further value to the company, or to anyone else, after 10 years. Is this machine a good investment?

Business women and men wrestle with investment decisions like this all the time. The art of doing business at the top management levels involves peering into the uncertain future and deciding which investment projects are worthwhile and which are not. Successful business people will tell you that you do not have to be right all the time, but you do have to be right the majority of the time.

Public officials also have to confront the investment decision. President Clinton has said that more public investments in education facilities, highways, and the like should be among the nation's top priorities. Many of these public investments will bring in no revenues at all, and the returns on them may not be realized until far in the future. How can we be sure that our tax dollars are well spent on these kinds of projects?

Chapter 12 develops the principles needed to analyze private investment projects, such as the hypothetical machine above. The principles developed in the chapter apply as well to your own saving decisions, when you are trying to decide how much money to place in bank accounts, stocks, and bonds and whether to buy a house.

The appendix to Chapter 12 discusses the special problems associated with the analysis of government investment projects, which is called **cost-benefit analysis.** Although the underlying principles of government cost-benefit analysis are the same as those for private investment analysis, governments encounter a whole host of evaluation problems that tend to be absent in private investment analysis. The appendix discusses some of the more important problems.

Let's begin with the firm's investment decision.

DURABILITY: THE SPECIAL FEATURE OF CAPITAL

Investing in plant and equipment is no different from hiring labor, in principle. We saw in Chapter 9 that in order to maximize profit a competitive firm should hire labor until the wage equals the value of labor's marginal product. Similarly, in order to maximize profit a competitive firm should add capital until the price of capital equals the value of capital's marginal product. The price of capital, P_K, is the marginal cost of adding capital; the value of the marginal product of capital, $VMP_K = MP_K \cdot P_{\text{good}}$, is the marginal revenue of adding capital. Profits are maximized when the marginal cost and the marginal revenue of adding capital are equal.

Purchasing capital differs from hiring labor in one crucial respect, however, the time dimension. The price of labor and the value of labor's marginal product can be evaluated over the same period of time. For example, a firm can compare the hourly wage it pays to its blue-collar workers with the value of the output that the workers produce each hour. In contrast, capital is durable. Firms expect the plant and equipment purchased today to be productive and yield additional revenues for a number of years. A piece of machinery may last 10 years or more, a new factory 25 or 50 years. Therefore, firms must peer into the future when analyzing an investment project. The price paid for capital today must be compared with a value of marginal product consisting of a stream of returns that the firm expects to receive for a number of years.

The machine mentioned in the introduction will serve as our example. The price of the machine, P_K, is $10,000. The value of capital's marginal product, VMP_K, consists of the stream of $1,200 of net returns for each of the next 10 years. If $VMP_K > P_K$, invest in the machine. The marginal revenue obtained from the machine exceeds its marginal cost. Conversely, if $VMP_K < P_K$, do not invest.

The profit-maximizing rule is simple enough, but evaluating the *VMP* of the machine is not a simple task. Two special problems arise: comparing dollars received or spent in different time periods and coping with the uncertainties about what might actually happen in the future.

Dollars over time are not equivalent. The $1,200 you expect to receive six years from now is not worth the same as the $1,200 you expect to receive two years from now, and neither amount is equivalent to $1,200 worth of the total cost incurred today in buying the machine. You cannot simply add the annual $1,200 net returns for 10 years and compare the total, $12,000, with the $10,000 cost of the machine. The $12,000 is a meaningless figure; it is *not* the *VMP* of the machine.

In addition, no one can be certain what the future will bring. You *expect* the machine to earn $1,200 each year for 10 years and nothing thereafter, but this is only a guess on your part. The actual results could be quite different, either far better or far worse.

Evaluating dollars over time and peering into the uncertain future are central features of any investment analysis.

EVALUATING DOLLARS OVER TIME

You should have no trouble convincing yourself that dollars over time are not equivalent. Suppose that someone offers you the choice of a dollar today or a dollar one year from now. You would surely take the dollar today. Anyone would, for a number of reasons.

For starters, the future is uncertain. One or both of you might not be here one year from now. Even if you are able to meet one year from now, the person offering the dollar might not make good on the promise to pay. Inflation is a second reason to take the dollar now. With prices steadily rising, the dollar today buys more than a dollar will buy one year from now. Finally, everyone has access to some very safe financial investment opportunities, such as federally insured bank deposits and U.S. government bonds. Suppose that you do not really want to spend the dollar until next year. Even so, you can take the dollar now, deposit it in a bank account or buy a one-year government bond, and earn interest on the dollar for the year. At the end of the year you will have more than a dollar to spend.

The financial investment opportunities that all people have are the key to valuing dollars over time. To focus on this key point we will assume for the moment that the future is certain and that there is no inflation.

Suppose that you always have the option of earning an annual rate of return of 10 percent by placing your money in a perfectly safe bank account (10 percent may be too high, but it makes for easy calculations). Consider the option of receiving a dollar now or a dollar one year from now. We know a dollar received one year from now is not worth as much to you as a dollar received today. The question is this: How much money received one year from now is equivalent to receiving $1 today? The answer is $(1 + .10)$ dollars, or $1.10, if you can always save at an interest rate of 10 percent.

The reason is this. Suppose that you take $1 today and place it in your bank account where it earns interest at a rate of 10 percent (.10, when expressed as a decimal fraction). In one year you will have $(1 + .10)$ dollars, $1.10, equal to the original dollar, the principal, plus interest of $.10 on the dollar. Therefore, you are indifferent between receiving $1 today or receiving $\$(1 + .10)$, $1.10, one year from now. Equivalence of dollars over time is defined in terms of indifference: For example, $1 today and $\$(1 + .10) = \$1.10$ one year from now are equivalent in value because you are indifferent between receiving one or the other.

In general, any amount of money, X dollars, received today is equivalent to $X \cdot (1 + .10)$ dollars received one year from now at an interest rate of 10 percent. An amount X invested at 10 percent for one year returns the principal, X, plus interest of $.10 \cdot X$, for a total of $X + .10 \cdot X = X \cdot (1 + .10)$. For example, $75 invested for one year at 10 percent returns $\$75 + .10 \cdot \$75 = \$75 \cdot (1 + .10) = \$82.50$ one year from now. So receiving $75 today is equivalent to receiving $82.50 one year from now if you can save at a 10 percent rate of interest.

The same method of evaluating dollars over time applies to all future years. To find the sum of money received two years from now that is equivalent to $1 received today, think of taking the dollar today and placing it in your bank account for two years. During the first year the value of your dollar grows to $\$(1 + .10)$. Then, at the end of the first year the *entire* $\$(1 + .10)$ earns interest at a rate of 10 percent for a second year. At the end of the second year you receive $\$(1 + .10)$, the principal entering the second year, plus interest on that principal equal to $.10 \cdot (1 + .10)$, for a total of

$$\begin{aligned}(1 + .10) + .10 \cdot (1 + .10) &= (1 + .10) \cdot (1 + .10) \\ &= \$(1 + .10)^2 = \$1.21\end{aligned}$$

Therefore, at an interest rate of 10 percent, $1 today is equivalent to $(1.10)^2 = \$1.21$ two years from now.

In general, any amount of money X received today is equivalent to $X \cdot (1 + .10)^2$ received two years from now if you can always save at a rate of 10 percent. For example, $75 invested for two years at 10 percent grows to $90.75 in two years [$\$90.75 = \$75 \cdot (1 + .10)^2$]. So $75 received today is equivalent to $90.75 received in two years if you can save at a 10 percent rate of interest.

The pattern continues for three years, four years, five years, and so on. The money grows by the factor $(1 + .10)$ for each additional year it is invested.

Therefore, \$1 received today is equivalent to $\$(1 + .10)^3$ received three years from now, to $\$(1 + .10)^4$ received four years from now, and to $\$1(1 + .10)^n$ received n years from now. Similarly, any amount of money, X dollars, received today is equivalent to $X \cdot (1 + .10)^3$ dollars received three years from now, to $X \cdot (1 + .10)^4$ dollars received four years from now, and to $X \cdot (1 + .10)^n$ dollars received n years from now.

Discounting to Present Value

Computing the future value of current dollars is called **compounding.** The more natural calculation when analyzing investment projects is in the opposite direction. Managers want to known how a future stream of net revenues compares with project costs incurred today. To make this comparison they need to know the *current* value of *future* revenues and costs. Computing the current value of future dollars is called **discounting to present value.**

Discounting future dollars to present value is the inverse of compounding current dollars to future value. If \$1 received today is equivalent to \$(1 + .10) received one year from now, then \$1 received one year from now is equivalent to \$1/(1 + .10) received today. Multiply by (1 + .10) to convert current dollars into equivalent dollars received one year from now; divide by (1 + .10) to convert dollars received one year from now into current dollars.

To see why discounting to present value is the inverse of compounding, suppose that you had \$1/(1 + .10) = \$.91 today. If you invest that sum of money for one year at an interest rate of 10 percent, it will grow to $[\$1/(1 + .10)] \cdot (1 + .10) = \$1$. So you would be indifferent about receiving \$1/(1 + .10) = \$.91 today and \$1 one year from now. In general, any amount of money, X dollars, received one year from now is worth $X/(1 + .10)$ dollars received today if you can save at 10 percent. Thus, $X/(1 + .10)$ dollars is said to be the **present value** of X dollars received one year from now; the term $1/(1 + .10)$ is the **discount factor;** and .10 (10 percent) is the **discount rate** or **rate of discount.**

The same pattern applies to all future years. The value two years from now of X dollars today saved at an interest rate of 10 percent is $X \cdot (1 + .10)^2$. Therefore, the present value of X dollars received two years from now is $X/(1 + .10)^2$. The present value of X dollars received three years from now is $X/(1 + .10)^3$; the present value of X dollars received n years from now is $X/(1 + .10)^n$. When the discount rate is .10 (10 percent), $1/(1 + .10)^n$ is the discount factor applied to dollars received in year n.

Returning to an earlier example, the present value of \$90.75 received two years from now, applying a discount rate of 10 percent, is \$75 [$\$75 = \$90.75/(1 + .10)^2$]. This is just the inverse of the statement that \$75 received today will be worth \$90.75 two years from now, compounded at a 10 percent rate of interest.

COMPOUNDING

The process of computing the equivalent future value of current dollars.

DISCOUNTING TO PRESENT VALUE

The process of computing the current value of future dollars.

PRESENT VALUE

The equivalent current value of future dollars, equal to the future dollars multiplied by the relevant future discount factor.

DISCOUNT FACTOR

The factor by which future dollars are multiplied to determine their present value; it is equal to $1/(1 + r)^n$, where r is the discount rate and n is the time in the future when the dollars are received or spent.

DISCOUNT RATE

The interest rate used to calculate the present value of future dollars; alternatively, the interest rate used to compound current dollars to their future value.

The Investment Decision Rule

The whole point of discounting to present value is to place dollars received or spent in different time periods on an equal footing so that they can be directly compared with one another. In effect, discounting to present value standardizes all dollars to a single time period, the present.

Let's now return to the \$10,000 machine that returns \$1,200 a year for each of the next 10 years. You must compare the 10-year stream of returns to the price, or cost, of the machine. Since the \$10,000 of cost is incurred now, the natural way to compare the two is to discount the stream of net returns to present value. The value of the discounted stream of net returns, at a 10 percent discount rate, is

$$\$1{,}200/(1 + .10) + \$1{,}200/(1 + .10)^2 + \cdots + \$1{,}200/(1 + .10)^{10}$$

VALUE OF MARGINAL PRODUCT OF CAPITAL (VMP_K)

The present value of the additional revenue received over time from adding one more unit of capital to the existing capital stock.

The first term is the present value of the \$1,200 to be received one year from now; the second term is the present value of the \$1,200 received two years from now; and so on up to the last term, which is the present value of the last \$1,200 received 10 years from now.

The discounted stream of net returns converts all future dollars to their present values, their values in today's dollars, and is directly comparable to the \$10,000 cost of the machine. In other words, the *discounted* stream of net returns is the appropriate VMP_K of the machine in the P_K versus VMP_K comparison.

The investment decision rule is as follows:

1. If the discounted stream of net returns exceeds \$10,000, invest in the machine. The returns, appropriately discounted to present value, exceed the cost.
2. If the discounted stream of net returns is less than \$10,000, do not invest. Instead, distribute the \$10,000 to the stockholders, and let them place the funds in their safe bank accounts at a 10 percent rate of return. The safe alternative is a better investment than is the machine.
3. If the discounted stream of returns just equals \$10,000, investing in the machine is no better or worse for the stockholders than placing their funds in the safe alternative at an interest rate of 10 percent.

Whether or not the machine is a good investment, then, depends directly on the general savings opportunities of the company's stockholders. The discount rate defines the opportunity cost of funds when evaluating investment projects. This point is central to investment analysis—and deserves careful thought.

In deciding whether to purchase the machine, you are really considering two choices: (1) Give up the \$10,000 in exchange for a machine that, you project, will bring net returns of \$1,200 per year for 10 years, or (2) distribute the \$10,000 to the stockholders, and let them save at a 10 percent rate of return. If you distribute the \$10,000, the stockholders have \$10,000 in today's dollars. If you buy the machine, your firm receives a stream of returns whose present value (value in today's dollars) is the discounted stream of returns. Hence, comparing the discounted stream of returns with the initial cost of the machine explicitly considers the opportunity cost of funds.

Another way to see that the discount rate serves as the opportunity cost of funds is to compare the value of the alternatives 10 years from now. If you distribute the funds to the stockholders, the \$10,000 will grow in value to $\$10{,}000 \cdot (1 + .10)^{10}$ in 10 years. If you buy the machine, your firm receives \$1,200 in the first year, which you will distribute to the stockholders at that time for them to invest at 10 percent for nine years; another \$1,200 in the second year, which you will distribute to the stockholders at that time for them to invest at 10 percent for eight years; and so on, up to the final \$1,200 received in the tenth year. The value of the stream of net returns to your stockholders 10 years from now is therefore

$$\$1{,}200(1 + .10)^9 + \$1{,}200(1 + .10)^8 + \cdots + \$1{,}200.$$

This stream can be compared with the $10,000 invested for 10 years at 10 percent, or $\$10{,}000 \cdot (1 + .10)^{10}$. Notice that the comparison 10 years from now is nothing more than the previous present value comparison in which both the costs of the machine and the discounted stream of returns are multiplied by $(1 + .10)^{10}$.

Compounding to the future in this way highlights the implicit assumption behind all present-value calculations, that stockholders always place funds into saving at the discount rate as soon as they are received. As such, it underscores the role of the discount rate as reflecting the opportunity cost of funds—the rate of return available to stockholders generally.

The straight (undiscounted) sum of net returns ignores the opportunity cost of funds and gives a completely misleading reading of the value of the machine. True, the machine returns more than its cost, $12,000 in total, over the 10-year period. But the $12,000 total is irrelevant if your stockholders have alternative investment opportunities at a reasonable rate of return. In fact, the machine is probably a poor investment. The discounted stream of returns falls below $10,000 at a discount rate between 3 and 4 percent. Your stockholders probably can find safe investment alternatives yielding more than 4 percent.

A final point is a matter of terminology. Investment analysts define the **present value of an investment** as the difference between the discounted stream of net returns and the initial investment cost. In other words, the present value of an investment is $(VMP_K - P_K)$. Alternative statements of the investment decision rule using this concept are

PRESENT VALUE OF AN INVESTMENT

The difference between the discounted stream of net returns on the investment and the initial investment cost.

1. Accept all investment projects whose present value is positive.
2. Reject all investment projects whose present value is negative.
3. If the present value of a project equals zero, investing in the project is no better or worse for the stockholders than placing their funds in the safe alternative at the rate of discount (10 percent in our example).[1]

The Power of Discounting

Present value calculations may seem tedious, but they are absolutely essential to the analysis of business investments and your own personal savings opportunities. Failure to discount future dollars to the present (or, alternatively, failure to compound current dollars to the future) can be grossly misleading. Never underestimate the power of discounting (compounding). The following two examples illustrate the point.

---

[1] *Correcting for inflation:* We noted in the beginning of the chapter that dollars today are worth more than dollars in the future because of inflation. But once dollars over time are standardized by the discount factors $[1/(1 + .10), 1/(1 + .10)^2$, and so on, in our example], inflation makes no difference at all to the calculation of present values. The reason is that in a present-value calculation inflation increases both the numerator and the denominator of each term by the same proportion, so that the value of each term is unchanged. Therefore, use expected future nominal, or observed, revenues, costs, and interest rates when computing the present value of an investment. Expected future inflation requires no correction in the present value formula. Advanced texts in investment analysis prove this result.

THE MILLION DOLLAR LOTTERY Many states now have lotteries that offer prizes of $1 million and more. The prize money is quite misleading, however, because "million-dollar winners" do not receive the million dollars all at once. Instead, the prize money is spread out over many years. A typical million dollar prize is $50,000 a year for 20 years.

The present value of $50,000 per year for 20 years is nowhere near $1 million for most people. At a discount rate of 10 percent, the present value of the $50,000 received in the 4th year is only $34,151; the present value of the $50,000 received in the 10th year is only $19,277; and the present value of the last $50,000 received in the 20th year is only $7,432. The present value of the entire stream discounted at 10 percent is $425,700. For someone with a rate of discount of 5 percent, the present value of the stream of winnings is $623,200. These are hefty prizes to be sure, but nowhere near $1 million. States clearly get away with a bit of false advertising when claiming lottery prizes of $1 million.

If you are still not convinced that the timing of the winnings matters, imagine winning $1 a year for 1 million years. This does not seem like such a fabulous prize, and it is not. The present value of this prize is only $10 at a rate of a discount of 10 percent (see the discussion of long-lived investments below).

MANHATTAN ISLAND A favorite example of the power of compounding is the sale of Manhattan Island for $24. We learn in our high school history courses how badly the Dutch took the Indians on that deal. Well, not really. Remember, the sale took place in 1620. If $24 had been placed in a bank account earning 5 percent in 1620 and left to accumulate for 370 plus years, it would have grown to an enormous sum, approximately $1.7 billion. This sum happens to be about equal to the current estimated value of Manhattan Island (the land only, not the structures).

The lesson to take from the sale of Manhattan Island is not that the Dutch duped the Indians. The proper lesson is the one stressed in Chapter 7: Market exchanges are usually mutually beneficial. The Indians appear to have received a reasonable price for their island.

The Value of Your College Education

We are now in a position to evaluate perhaps the most important investment you have made to this point in your life, the investment in your college education. Is it a good investment? To decide if it is, you have to compute the present value of your education.

The main difference between your college education and our hypothetical machine is the timing of the initial investment costs and of the stream of net returns. The initial investment costs of a college education are spread over the four undergraduate years. These costs include all the out-of-pocket expenses directly related to your education, principally tuition, other school fees, and textbooks (but not room and board, at least not all of it; if you were not in school, you would still have to live somewhere and eat). In addition to these direct costs, there are the opportunity costs of not working, the wages you could have earned had you not attended college. These opportunity costs are substantial. Even at the minimum wage of $4.25 an hour (in 1993), a 40-hour-a-week job for 50 weeks pays $8,500 a year ($4.25 · 40 · 50 = $8,500). The initial investment cost of your education is the discounted stream of the direct and opportunity costs over the four years of college.

The net returns begin in the fifth year, the year after you graduate. They are the *increase* in the salaries you expect to earn each year throughout your working lifetime as a result of your education. The present value of the net returns is the discounted stream of salary increases from the fifth year to the year that you plan to retire.

The present value of your education, then, is the difference between the discounted stream of the annual expected salary increases and the discounted stream of the costs. In Chapter 9 we reported that the present value of an undergraduate education in the United States averaged $130,000 for men and $80,000 for women in the 1960s. These estimates assume a discount rate of 5 percent, which means that the rate of return on a college education in the 1960s exceeded 5 percent, on average. The present value of your education could well be much more or much less than these estimates, depending on your career choice and on what you consider to be your relevant rate of discount. Education is a less attractive investment for you if your investment opportunities generally earn more than 5 percent.

Economists believe that the average returns to a college education are rising substantially in the 1990s, although it is far too early to know whether the overall returns to a college education have risen. After all, the stream of returns to someone in the class of 1993 will continue until sometime around 2040.

REFLECTION: Do you view your education primarily as an investment? If so, are you thinking primarily in terms of the potential monetary benefits, of other types of benefits, or of both? What might be some of the nonmonetary benefits?

ADDITIONAL CONSIDERATIONS IN INVESTMENT ANALYSIS

The Yield on an Investment

In everyday conversation, people are more likely to describe the return on investments as an annual rate of return rather than as a present value. "This office building yields an annual return of 16 percent," or "My stocks earned 13 percent last year." This is perfectly acceptable, so long as the meaning of each rate of return is clearly understood. The annual rate of return on an investment is a tricky concept.

The proper way to define the annual rate of return on an investment relies on the present-value calculation. The annual rate of return, called the **internal yield on an investment,** is the rate of discount that just sets the present value of an investment equal to zero. In other words, the internal yield is the discount rate that would make one indifferent between accepting and rejecting the project.

INTERNAL YIELD ON AN INVESTMENT
The rate of discount that just sets the present value of an investment equal to zero.

Investment analysts use computer programs to solve for the annual rate of return on an investment. One common method selects different rates of discount to compute the present value of an investment. The computer program begins with a discount rate equal to zero and then increases the discount rate in small increments [for example, .1 percent (.001)] until the program finds the discount rate for which the present value of the investment is just equal to zero. That discount rate is the internal yield, or annual rate of return, on the investment. (Advanced texts show that this method may not find a solution, or it may find multiple solutions. We will ignore this technicality throughout this text when referring to the internal yield, or annual rate of return, on an investment.)

A word of warning is in order on calculating rates of return. The machine in our example earns $1,200 per year on an initial investment of $10,000. A simple "back of the envelope" calculation suggests that the annual return on the machine is 12 percent, equal to the annual $1,200 return divided by the $10,000 investment (.12 = 1,200/10,000). *Avoid these simple calculations.* The internal yield on the machine is only 3.45 percent, not even close to 12 percent.

The problem with these "back of the envelope" calculations is that they ignore the timing of the net returns. The machine does not have a 12 percent annual rate of return because a large portion of the stream of net returns occurs in the distant future. A rate-of-return calculation must consider the timing of the returns.

To see why, suppose that three $10,000 machines (1, 2, and 3) each yield a total (undiscounted) stream of net returns of $12,000 over a 10-year period, but that the timing of the net returns is quite different. The pattern of net returns for each machine is as follows:

- Machine 1: $1,200 every year for years 1–10 (the machine in our example)
- Machine 2: $11,999 in year 1; 0 in years 2–9; $1 in year 10
- Machine 3; $1 in year 1; 0 in years 2–9; $11,999 in year 10

Machine 2 is a much better investment than machine 1 is, and machine 1 is a much better investment than machine 3 is. Early returns are better than later returns, other things equal. Calculating the internal yield of an investment by means of the present-value formula takes the timing of the returns into consideration. A simple "back of the envelope" calculation does not. It would represent the annual rate of return for each of the three machines as 12 percent, reflecting the fact that each yields an average net return of $1,200 per year over the 10-year period. In fact, the proper internal rates of return are approximately 3.45 percent (machine 1), 20 percent (machine 2), and 1.8 percent (machine 3).

Long-lived Investments

The present-value calculation has a simple approximation when the stream of net returns is very long-lived. If a stream of net returns, R, literally occurs every year forever, the present value of that stream at a discount rate r is given by the formula

$$PV = R/r$$

For example, if the machine in our example yielded annual returns of $1,200 forever, the present value of the stream of returns, using a discount rate of 10 percent, would be

$$PV = \$1{,}200/0.10 = \$12{,}000$$

A machine lasting forever is far-fetched, but some governments do issue bonds, called *consols*, that yield a fixed interest payment forever. Moreover, the approximation formula is quite accurate for very long-lived investments, those lasting 50 to 100 years. Some structures, such as factories, office buildings, and railroad tracks, actually are productive for that length of time.

The approximation formula highlights very clearly the inverse relationship between the rate of discount and the present value of a stream of returns. At a rate of discount of 10 percent, for example, $1,200 per year received forever is worth $12,000 in today's dollars. At a rate of discount of 5 percent, the present value of $1,200 received forever doubles to $24,000 ($1,200/0.05 = $24,000). The reason for the inverse relationship is just that the rate of discount serves as the opportunity cost of funds. The prospect of receiving $1,200 a year forever is worth less to a person who can invest generally at 10 percent than it is to another person who can invest generally at only 5 percent.

THE PROBLEM OF FUTURE UNCERTAINTY

Discounting future dollars to present value is absolutely essential for analyzing investments. When all is said and done, however, discounting is nothing more than a mechanical device for comparing dollars over time. The real attraction in analyzing potential investments lies in the uncertainty of peering into the future. No one can know for sure what the future will bring. People who enjoy making investment decisions have a bit of the gambler in them. They are willing to take risks, undaunted by the possibility that they might guess wrong on occasion.

Discounting to present value encounters two main areas of uncertainty: (1) how the rate of discount will change over time and (2) what the future stream of net returns will be. The analysis of how to adjust for changes in the discount rate over time is somewhat technical and best left to an advanced text on investments. We will focus instead on the uncertainty associated with the future stream of net returns, which is usually the greater uncertainty in investment analysis.

Future Net Returns

Evaluating the future net returns in a present value calculation is very much a guessing game, especially if the investments are fairly long-lived. The value of future net returns will depend on a number of unknown variables, such as the state of the economy, government policy, and the rate of technical progress within the industry, many of which are beyond the control of the firm. The following simple example is representative of the nature of the uncertainty and the decision that managers have to confront.

Suppose that your company sells a product that faces stiff competition from foreign producers. Congress is currently debating whether to place a high tariff on imports of the product. If the tariff passes, you will be able to charge a much higher price in the future and earn large profits. If Congress decides against the tariff, you will continue to lose customers to the foreign firms.

In addition, the success of your product depends on the overall state of the economy. It is no different from most other products in this respect. When the economy is booming, business is good for you, too. When the economy is mired in a recession, your sales slow down considerably. Assume that the tariff and the state of the economy are the only two unknown variables that affect the future sales of your product.

TABLE 12.1 **Payoff Matrix of Internal Yields**

STATE OF ECONOMY	TARIFF POLICY	
	Tariff	**No Tariff**
Boom	30%	3%
Recession	10%	−12%

PAYOFF MATRIX

A listing of the present values or the internal yields of an investment under every possible future environment.

Return to the example of our $10,000 machine. Faced with future uncertainties concerning both the tariff and the state of the economy, you will not be able to plug a single number for the net returns, such as the $1,200 per year we had been using in our previous examples, into the present-value formula. Instead, you will have to choose different numbers, depending on the different possibilities that the future holds in store. The result of the analysis is a payoff matrix such as in Table 12.1. A **payoff matrix** indicates either the present value or the internal yield of the machine under each possible future environment. Table 12.1 reports the possible internal yields of the machine.

Along the left-handed side of the matrix are the two possibilities for the economy: boom and recession. Along the top of the matrix are the two possibilities for the tariff: tariff and no tariff. The four cells, or entries, of the matrix indicate the internal yield of the machine under each of the four possibilities.

The top left-hand corner is the best of all worlds for your company: a booming economy and a tariff. Sales will be brisk if both those events occur. You estimate that the internal yield of the machine will be 30 percent, a very good investment indeed. The bottom right-hand corner of the matrix represents the worst of all worlds for your company: a recession and no tariff. In this case the present value of the machine is negative, with an internal yield of − 12 percent. The machine is a terrible investment under those circumstances.

The remaining two cells of the payoff matrix give the intermediate cases, when one aspect of the future environment is favorable and one unfavorable. According to the hypothetical numbers in the table, the tariff is more important to your company than is the state of the economy. With a tariff and a recession (bottom left-hand corner), the yield on the machine falls to 10 percent. With no tariff and a booming economy (top right-hand corner), the yield drops to 3 percent.

Is this machine a good investment or not? Different investment analysts could easily reach different conclusions, even if they agree on the numbers in the payoff matrix. The decision is ultimately a subjective one that depends on two factors. The first is a guess about the future. How likely is each of the four possible outcomes? Is the passage of the tariff virtually assured or still a 50–50 proposition at this point? Some economists are predicting a booming economy over the next few years. Others fear a prolonged recession. Who is right? You would probably support the project if you believe that the tariff is a cinch to pass and the economy will boom. Thirty percent is a hefty rate of return. You would surely say no to the investment if you are "certain" that the tariff will fail to pass and the economy is headed for a recession. The perception of the future is crucial to the decision—and highly subjective. No investment analyst knows for sure what will happen.

The second factor is people's attitudes toward taking risks. Suppose that everyone believes there is a 25 percent chance of the best of all worlds occurring and a 25 percent chance of the worst of all worlds occurring. Those with gamblers' instincts may be enticed by the chance of a big success and decide to go for it. More cautious types may look at the 25 percent chance of taking a big loss and back off. Any investment decision is ultimately a matter of personal taste in an uncertain world. Is this project a good investment? This question often has no right or wrong answer.

"HOME" ECONOMICS

The decision to purchase a home is the largest single investment decision that many people make during their lifetimes. Our analysis of private investment decisions concludes with some principles relating to investing in a house.

Those of you now in college will undoubtedly suffer through the following conversation sometime during the next 10 years. A friend of yours will have bought a house, while you are still renting an apartment. Your friend will corner you at a party and scold you for continuing to live in an apartment. "Why throw your hard-earned money away each month by giving it to your landlord? Do what I did. Build up equity in a house. I have something to show for my money."

Do not fall for this line. The notion that the relevant choice is building up equity in a home versus throwing money away on rent is nonsense. The actual alternative is building up equity in a home versus building up equity in some other kind of asset.

Your friend's equity in the home is the down payment made to purchase the house. If you continue to rent, you can invest the same amount of money elsewhere. Investing in housing has been a good investment, on average, in the United States over the entire period since World War II. But other forms of investment have done well, too. People who chose to tie up their money over that same time period in the stocks of successful companies such as Wal-Mart or Polaroid may well be far wealthier today than they would have been had they chosen instead to buy real estate. Housing is by no means the best investment for all people in all situations.

Leverage

Housing *is* different from most financial investments in one important respect. It is the one major investment that the average person can make on a highly levered basis. A **levered investment** is one purchased in part with borrowed funds. In the case of housing, buyers need only pay 20 percent (or less) of the purchase price out of their own funds. They can borrow the remainder by taking out a mortgage on the property. Stocks, bonds, certificates of deposit, pensions, and other typical forms of saving for the average person must be purchased entirely (or largely) out of their own funds.

LEVERED INVESTMENT
An investment that is financed in part with borrowed funds.

Buying assets on a levered basis has two special characteristics. On the one hand, borrowing can substantially increase the return on the investment. Do not be afraid of going into debt if you want to make a killing by investing. The term *leverage* suggests that borrowing acts as a lever and fulcrum, serving to increase the return on your investments. On the other hand, borrowing has a serious downside: It is extremely risky. Borrowing can "lever" a modest loss into an outright disaster.

The following simple example illustrates these two features of levered investments. Suppose that you buy a $10,000 asset that you intend to sell one year from now. You pay for the asset by investing $2,000 of your own funds and borrowing $8,000 from Uncle Fred. Uncle Fred does not charge you any interest, but you do agree to pay him back the $8,000 after you sell the asset. Your equity in this asset is the $2,000 of your own funds.

Suppose that the asset increases in value from $10,000 to $11,000 during the year. Had you purchased it entirely with your own funds, your return would have been 10 percent, a gain of $1,000 on the $10,000 invested. Borrowing, however, increases your return to 50 percent. After selling the asset for $11,000 and repaying Uncle Fred his $8,000, you are left with $3,000. But you only had $2,000 to start with. So you have gained $1,000 on the original $2,000, a return of 50 percent.

Borrowing, therefore, has "levered" your return fivefold, from 10 percent to 50 percent. The fivefold gain results from having paid only ⅕ of the purchase price with your own funds. The leverage factor is just the inverse on the proportion represented by the equity (5 versus ⅕). Had you put up ½ of the purchase price, the leverage factor would be 2 (a $1,000 gain on $5,000, for a 20 percent return).

So much for the good news. The bad news occurs if the asset declines in value. Suppose that the value of the asset drops 10 percent during the year from $10,000 to $9,000. Had you put up the full $10,000, you would have lost 10 percent. By borrowing, however, your loss increases to 50 percent. After selling the asset for $9,000 and repaying Uncle Fred his $8,000, you are left with $1,000. Since you started with $2,000, you lost half your money, a loss of 50 percent. Leverage is clearly a very risky strategy.

The risks increase if you have to pay interest on the loan, which, of course, most of us do. Borrowing with interest pays off only if the investment increases in value by *more* than the rate of interest. Otherwise, you lose by levering, and the losses can be substantial. The leverage factor is no longer symmetric. The downside risk greatly increases.

To see this, consider the same example, but this time suppose that you agree to pay Uncle Fred interest of 10 percent. That is, you will pay him back $8,800 at the end of the year, the $8,000 that you borrowed plus $800 interest. Now if the asset increases in value from $10,000 to $11,000, all you gain is 10 percent. Selling the asset for $11,000 and repaying Uncle Fred $8,800 leaves you with $2,200, which represents a 10 percent gain on your original $2,000. Leverage gains you nothing.

Should the asset decline in value from $10,000 to $9,000, however, the 10 percent loss is magnified considerably. After selling the asset for $9,000 and repaying Uncle Fred $8,800, you only have $200 left. Your original $2,000 has shrunk by 90 percent, a ninefold leverage factor on the downside.

The lesson of this example is that you must recognize a mortgaged housing investment for what it is, a highly risky levered investment. The recent collapse of the housing market in New England underscores the risks of owning a home. Many New Englanders who bought houses in the mid-1980s lost all the equity in their homes, and more, by 1991. When you face the decision of whether to buy a house or rent an apartment, be sure to give some thought to the risks involved in purchasing a home.

Tax Considerations

Our brief tour of the investment decision has ignored one very important element, the tax implications of purchasing particular kinds of assets. Federal and state personal and corporation income taxes, and local property taxes, combine to tax the returns from different kinds of assets very differently. These tax differences enter importantly into virtually all investment decisions, and every good investment analysis includes a careful study of the tax laws. Unfortunately, the tax implications of particular forms of investment happen to be extremely subtle and complex, enough so that we can do no more than offer one brief example by way of illustration.

The returns to stockholders of a corporation are taxed at least twice if they are received in the form of dividends: first by federal and state corporation income taxes and again by federal and state personal income taxes. Corporations might also pay local property taxes on some assets, particularly structures. Housing, by contrast, receives a number of tax breaks. For instance, both local property taxes and mortgage interest payments can be taken as deductions against income on the federal personal income tax. Also, capital gains on the sale of a home are not subject to federal income tax if the seller subsequently purchases another home of equal or greater value. In contrast, capital gains on the sale of stocks are subject to federal income taxation. In short, the tax laws generate an enormous bias in favor of investing in real estate relative to investing in corporate assets. Stocks must have a significantly higher before-tax rate of return than do houses to yield the same after-tax return.

SUMMARY

The first section of the chapter discussed the distinctive feature of capital, its durability.

1. Firms expect capital inputs purchased today to be productive for a long period of time. The durability of capital gives rise to two special problems when analyzing investments: Dollars over time are not equivalent in value, and the future is uncertain.

The second section of the chapter discussed the principles involved in evaluating dollars over time.

2. Dollars of revenues and costs in different time periods must be standardized to one time period. The natural choice is the present; future dollars are discounted to their present value. The present value of an amount of money, X dollars, received n years from today is $X/(1 + r)^n$ dollars, where r is the discount rate reflecting the opportunity costs of funds (the rate of return available on a safe investment alternative), and $1/(1 + r)^n$ is the discount factor for year n.
3. The present value of an investment is the difference between the discounted stream of net returns and the initial investment cost.

4. The investment decision rule is as follows:
   a. Accept an investment project if it has a positive present value;
   b. Reject an investment project if it has a negative present value; and
   c. If the present value of an investment project is zero, the return on the project is no better or worse than the return that the stockholders can earn generally on their financial investments.

The third section included two additional considerations in analyzing investment projects.

5. The annual rate of return on an investment, called the *internal yield*, is the rate of discount that sets the present value of the investment equal to zero.
6. For long-lived investments, the present value of an annual stream of returns, R, occurring over a very long period of time is (approximately) $PV = R/r$, where r is the rate of discount.

The fourth section of the chapter discussed the problem of uncertainty about the future.

7. Uncertainties regarding future net returns center around such factors as the future state of the economy, government policy, and the rate of technological progress within an industry, many of which are beyond the control of the firm. The best one can hope for is to develop a payoff matrix that indicates the present value or internal yield of a project under each possible state of the future.
8. An investment decision is ultimately subjective. It depends on the analyst's subjective view of what the future will be and the analyst's attitude toward taking risks.

Chapter 12 concluded with a discussion of the decision to purchase a house, the largest investment decision many people make during their lifetimes.

9. Housing is usually a highly levered investment: People pay only a small percentage of the purchase price with their own funds; the rest is borrowed through a mortgage.
10. Borrowing gives an investment leverage by greatly increasing the rate of return if the investment is successful. Leverage is a very risky strategy, however, because borrowing also greatly increases the losses if the investment is unsuccessful.
11. Tax considerations are always a very important part of any investment analysis. Housing receives highly favorable tax treatment under the federal personal income tax, especially relative to corporate investment.

KEY TERMS

compounding
cost-benefit analysis
discount factor
discount rate
internal yield on an investment
levered investment
payoff matrix
present value
present value of an investment
value of marginal product of capital (VMP_K)

QUESTIONS

1. What are the similarities in the decisions to hire labor and to purchase capital? What are the differences?
2. What is the relationship, if any, between compounding current dollars to their future value and discounting future dollars to their present value?
3. A business firm with $100 to invest is considering the following projects:

PROJECT	INITIAL COST	NET RETURN IN YEAR		
		1	2	3 (and forever after)
A	100	150	150	0
B	100	0	300	0
C	100	290	0	0

   a. If the stockholders can earn 10 percent (r = 0.10) generally on their investment, which project should the firm pick, if any? Why?
   b. Would your answer change if the stockholders had no profitable invetment alternatives other than these projects? Explain.
   c. If, instead, the stockholders can earn 100 percent (r = 1.0) generally on their money, are all the projects still a good investment? Demonstrate. Which is best?
4. Choose a rate of interest that you think is the correct discount rate for you, and answer the following questions:
   a. Why did you choose the rate that you did?
   b. Given the rate that you chose, would you rather have $2.00 one year from now or $2.20 three years from now?
5. a. What is the internal yield on an investment?
   b. In question 3, what is the internal yield of project C?
6. Describe how you would determine whether your college education is a good investment. In particular, address the following questions:
   a. What are the main costs of your education? The main benefits?
   b. When do these costs and benefits occur?
   c. How would you compare the stream of benefits and costs?
7. Suppose that you have the opportunity to buy a piece of land that you believe you could rent for $5,000 per year, forever. Assume that there are no costs associated with maintaining the land.
   a. How much would you be willing to pay for the land if you could earn 5 percent on your investments generally?
   b. How would your answer to part a change if you could earn 20 percent on your investments generally?
8. Comment on the following statement: Because the future is uncertain, decisions about choosing investment projects ultimately depend on the personal tastes of the person making the decision.
9. Suppose that you borrow $1,000 from a friend to purchase a rare coin. The annual interest rate on the loan is 10 percent, and you are expected to pay your debt in full after one year. The cost of the coin is $2,000. You pay $1,000 of the cost from your own funds. You sell the coin after one year for $2,500.
   a. Calculate your return on this investment.
   b. Calculate your return on this investment if you purchased the coin entirely with your own funds.
   c. How would your answers to parts a and b change if you sold the coin for $2,100?

CASE

Bringing Home The Gold And Then Some*

Businesses try to influence consumers' tastes for their products through advertising and other marketing strategies. The 1992 Summer Olympic Games in Barcelona, Spain was the scene of one of the more successful marketing promotions in recent years.

The United States sent the so-called "Dream Team" to the Summer Games in Barcelona. Many basketball experts believe that the Dream Team was the best team in the history of basketball. It consisted of eleven of the National Basketball Association's brightest stars: Charles Barkley, Larry Bird, Clyde Drexler, Patrick Ewing, Michael Jordan, Ervin "Magic" Johnson, Karl Malone, Chris Mullin, Scottie Pippen, David Robinson, and John Stockton. It also included one college player, Christian Laettner from Duke University.

Basketball fans would say that the Dream Team's mission was to bring home the gold medal and, by doing so, to show the rest of the world that the country that invented and so dearly loves the game was also the best at playing it. This mission took on special import because the U.S. fans' pride had been badly wounded in recent years. The United States, fielding its usual team of college all stars, had lost to the Soviet Union in the 1988 Olympics, coming home with a disappointing bronze medal. Further losses to foreign teams during the World Championship Games were the last straw. The time had come to send the professional players from the National Basketball Association (NBA) to the Olympics.

The Dream Team had another mission besides restoring the nation's basketball pride, however. It was also on an international marketing mission for the NBA. The NBA, under the leadership of Commissioner David Stern, had been pursuing an aggressive marketing strategy of selling the NBA game and its licensed products both at home and abroad. The NBA's outreach to international markets began well before the Dream Team went to Spain. NBA teams had played pre-season games in the Soviet Union, Spain, and France. Two NBA teams, the Houston Rockets and the Seattle Supersonics, played their first two games of the regular 1992-93 season in Japan. The NBA had also set up stores to sell NBA-licensed merchandise in several European cities, including Paris and Munich.

So, besides bringing home the gold medal, the Dream Team was sent to Barcelona to showcase the NBA game and NBA merchandise. The NBA wanted to make sure that consumers in other countries, particularly Europeans, would continue to develop their taste for the NBA. Twenty-seven companies were designated as official licensees of U.S. Men's Olympic Basketball team merchandise. Their products included replica game jerseys, sweatpants, banners, coffee mugs and glasses, sportbags, basketballs, team hats and caps, pennants, keychains, bumper stickers, and T-shirts, sweatshirts, and shorts featuring graphics of the USA team and its individual players.

The Dream Team brought home the gold in more ways than one. It was every bit as successful in the marketplace as on the basketball court. Consumers all over the world embraced the Dream Team and were eager to buy NBA and Dream Team memorabilia. Michael Jordan and his Dream Teammates now sell shoes, soft drinks and other merchandise throughout Europe, Asia, and South America. Thanks to the Dream Team, the taste for the NBA game and its products is worldwide and here to stay.

ECONOMIC ADVISOR'S REPORT

1. Suppose that National Hockey League (NHL) officials, having observed how successful the NBA was in marketing its game and merchandise worldwide, ask you what they should do to develop a taste for the NHL game and its merchandise in other countries. What advice would you give them? Do you believe that the NHL can be as successful as the NBA was?
2. In 1994 the World Cup of Soccer will be played in the U.S. The best soccer players from all over the world will come to the U.S. and play before American audiences. ABC will televise 11 of the 51 games and ESPN will televise the remaining 40. Do you think that Americans will finally develop a taste for soccer as a result of the World Cup matches and rush to buy World Cup and soccer related merchandise?

*Provided by Klaus G. Becker, Texas Tech University.

APPENDIX

12

Cost-Benefit Analysis

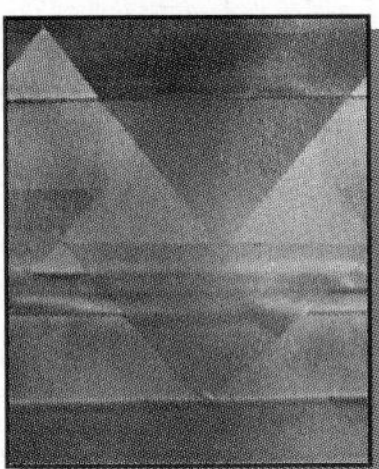

Expenditures on intercontinental ballistic missiles, bridges and public highways, elementary school buildings, post offices, and manpower training programs are all examples of government, or public-sector, investments. The analysis of these government investments is called *cost-benefit analysis.* In principle, cost-benefit analysis is no different from private investment analysis. Both public- and private-sector managers should try to determine the present value of each proposed project, which involves evaluating the future stream of net returns and choosing an appropriate rate of discount. Having calculated present values, they then follow the same decision rule: Accept projects having a positive present value, and reject projects having a negative present value.

In practice, however, government cost-benefit analysis encounters a number of difficulties that are absent in private investment analysis. We will consider three of the more serious problems in evaluating government investments: (1) evaluating the future stream of net returns; (2) accounting for the distributional implications of public projects; and (3) overcoming political realities, which often interfere with the proper evaluation of government investment alternatives.

EVALUATING THE STREAM OF NET RETURNS

The objective of private investment analysis is to help a firm maximize its profits over the long run. Therefore, the stream of net returns in a present-value calculation is the difference between projected revenues and costs measured at going market prices.

In contrast, the stream of net returns in a cost-benefit analysis is seldom, if ever, just the difference between projected revenues and costs measured at going market prices. Government investment analysis is called cost-benefit analysis to highlight the fact that net benefits might not take the form of net revenues. Investing in missiles, school buildings, and public highways certainly has nothing to do with the profit motive. Nonetheless, a cost-benefit analysis is useful only if the government's investment analysts can place dollar values on the net stream of returns from public projects.

Two difficulties that often arise in trying to quantify the benefits and costs of government projects are caused by the presence of intangibles and non-marketed benefits. Neither is a serious problem in private investment analysis.

Intangibles

INTANGIBLE

A benefit or a cost that cannot be evaluated in dollar terms.

An **intangible** is a benefit or a cost that cannot be evaluated in dollar terms. An obvious example of an intangible benefit is the increase in national security provided by a particular weapon such as the Patriot missile. No one can hope to place a dollar value on a nation's security, and the Pentagon does not even try. Military objectives are not subjected to a cost-benefit analysis. Instead, the Department of Defense simply defines a set of military objectives that it believes will contribute to national security. Then its only economic concern is how to meet each military objective at the lowest possible cost.

Intangibles are much less important in other areas of government activity, but they are seldom entirely absent. Examples of intangible benefits include the prestige of being the first country to put a man on the moon and the nation's supposed love affair with rail travel. A particularly troubling intangible cost is the possibility that some workers will die during the construction of a project.

The presence of intangibles can seriously undermine a cost-benefit analysis, even in nonmilitary applications. Proponents and opponents of government projects can always find some intangible benefits and costs to support their arguments for and against the projects. The key question with intangibles is whether they should be allowed to override the quantifiable information contained in a cost-benefit analysis. Suppose that a government project has a positive present value on the basis of all quantifiable benefits and costs. Should the presence of an intangible cost rule the project out? The possibility that some workers may lose their lives while building the project is a difficult case in point.

Suppose that a state highway department is considering building a suspension bridge. Past experience in building suspension bridges suggests that two workers will die during the construction of the bridge. The projected deaths of two workers are clearly a cost of the project, but how should they be evaluated?

One argument is that the costs of the bridge need not be adjusted for the expected loss of life. Construction workers presumably consider the possibility of dying when they agree to work on the bridge. Therefore, the risk of dying is already built into the wages required to attract workers to the job. According to this view, costs need to be adjusted only if workers underestimate the risks of dying.

The counterargument is that the government should have a different perspective on the expected loss of life. Workers adopt a before-the-fact perspective. Each workers assesses the *probability* that he or she will die prior to accepting the job. Those who take the job do so because the probability of dying is extremely low. Some economists believe that the government should adopt an after-the-fact perspective, however. The government knows that two people will almost certainly die, and it should not care who those two individuals might be. According to this view, the virtual certainty that two workers will die is an undeniable additional cost of the project and ought to be included in the analysis. After all, suppose that an all-knowing being tapped two construction workers in advance and told them they would be the two who would die. Presumably no wage would be high enough to induce these two people to work on the bridge.

The question remains how to value the loss of life if the government adopts the all-knowing, after-the-fact perspective. If the value of a life is infinitely large, suspension bridges (and many other government projects) would never be built. The costs would always exceed the benefits. This is hardly an reasonable solution. Alternatively, the government could set some value on the certain loss of life—say, the loss in lifetime earnings of the individual—to be used in all cost-benefit studies. This is not an altogether reasonable solution either. People may well feel that their lives are far more valuable than just their lifetime earnings. Perhaps loss of life according to this view is truly an intangible cost that has no "reasonable" value. Decision makers may simply have to decide whether the projected loss of life is "too high" for projects that otherwise have positive present value.

Nonmarketed Benefits

Government agencies often do what private firms never do: They give away some or all of the benefits of government investments free of charge. For example, people can drive toll-free on the interstate highway system in most parts of the country.

Giving away the benefits of public projects raises two questions: (1) Should the benefits be given away? (2) If so, how should the government evaluate the benefits?

The surprising answer to the first question is quite often yes, the benefits should be given away. The marginal cost of an additional vehicle entering the highway is virtually zero on the more rural, noncongested sections of the interstate. If the marginal cost is zero, efficiency dictates that the price should also be zero. People should not be discouraged from driving on the interstate if they impose no costs on anyone.

Regarding the question of evaluating benefits that are given away, often the only choice is to evaluate the benefits indirectly by trying to place a value on each source of benefit. The four-lane interstate superhighways generate a number of benefits. They are much safer than are the narrower roadways they replaced. They also benefit consumers and businesses in the form of better gasoline economy, less wear and tear on tires and other parts, and reduced travel time.

Placing dollar values on these separate sources of benefit is not at all straightforward. For instance, what is the value to each driver of the increase in safety? Presumably a researcher would compare the incidence of accidents on the interstate and other roadways and then use medical expenses to place a dollar value on each type of accident. But a reduction in fatal accidents begs the loss-of-life question again. Should the government always build a four-lane highway if it will save one life? Determining the value of reduced travel time is also problematic. Some people use the road for business, others for pleasure. What is the value of leisure time saved? Of business time saved?

We see once again the beauty of market prices. They summarize the value of all benefits (and costs) in a single number. Absent prices, the only choice is to proceed indirectly and introduce some subjectivity into the analysis. Still, one should not be too pessimistic. Researchers have been able to provide reasonable estimates of indirect value for many different kinds of government projects.

ACCOUNTING FOR THE DISTRIBUTIONAL IMPLICATIONS OF PUBLIC PROJECTS

Public officials are frequently concerned with who gains and who loses from government projects. Such distributional concerns are absent in private investment analysis. All firms (or individuals) care about is whether the aggregate present value of an investment is positive or negative.

Suppose that a state government is considering building a new highway through its capital city to ease congestion problems there. No one doubts that the highway has positive present value. Commuters applaud it, businesses are ecstatic, and the city's residents support it as well—with one nagging exception. The proposed highway cuts through a very poor neighborhood, and many families in the neighborhood will have to be relocated. The state agrees to pay the costs of relocating, but the people in the neighborhood resist. They do not want to lose their homes and neighbors.

Suppose that society cares about helping the poor. Should the losses suffered by these families be given an extra weight in the cost-benefit analysis of the highway *because they are poor?* Or is counting the costs of relocating the families as part of the highway's total costs sufficient?

Distributional concerns almost always arise in government investment analysis. Some people stand to gain from public projects, and others stand to lose. As a result, government officials must confront the basic ethical question of end-results equity that we described in Chapter 2: How should the gains of the gainers be balanced against the losses of the losers? Should project benefits and costs be given special distributional weights that depend on who receives the benefits or bears the costs? Or should the government just add unweighted benefits and costs to determine the present value of proposed investments? Good arguments exist on either side of this issue.

The case for giving extra weight to the benefits and costs experienced by the poor is persuasive on strictly theoretical grounds. If society truly believes that an extra dollar is worth more to a poor person than to a rich person or that the poor are somehow ethically more deserving, then the poor should receive extra weight in a cost-benefit analysis. A straight sum of project costs and benefits is incorrect because it treats additional dollars of cost and benefit as equal for all.

At the same time, practical considerations argue strongly against the distributional weighting of costs and benefits. Distributional weights are entirely subjective. What is the proper difference in weights for the rich and the poor? This is an important question because the weighting scheme can easily overwhelm the analysis. If one gives the poor a high enough weight, distributional concerns alone will determine if the present value of any investment is positive or negative. Yet the government certainly does not want to adopt the position of accepting any project that helps the poor and rejecting any project that hurts the poor. Public officials ought to pay some attention to the underlying productivity of government investments, which is really what the present-value formula is designed to measure.

Another practical consideration is that the distributional implications of any one project pale in comparison with the distributional implications of the government's tax and transfer policies. Restructuring the Social Security System, or the public assistance programs, or the federal personal income tax would have a distributional impact far greater than the distributional impact of any one government investment. Still, one project can have an enormous impact on a small group of people, as when a new highway destroys a neighborhood. The case against including distributional considerations is weaker whenever the gains and the losses are narrowly focused.

Perhaps the best solution is to treat the distribution of project benefits and costs as another intangible, to be considered when all other aspects of the project's benefits and costs have been quantified.

OVERCOMING POLITICAL REALITIES

In the best of all worlds a single government agency would oversee and coordinate the analysis of all investment projects. That agency would standardize the measurement of all quantifiable benefits and costs, adopt a common public rate of discount for all projects, and isolate cost-benefit analysis from undue political pressures.

The reality is quite different. Each government agency jealously guards its political turf. Bureau chiefs are reluctant to surrender any decision-making authority to another agency if they do not have to. At all levels of government, cost-benefit analysis is primarily an agency-specific undertaking, with little or no effective coordination across agencies. The results—widely varying methods of analysis and a process that is highly susceptible to outside political pressures—are entirely predictable.

The influence of political pressures is best seen in the obsession with the employment and wage effects of government projects. Private consulting firms have made a small fortune contracting with government agencies to study how proposed projects will affect regional employment and wages. These studies are then included as part of an agency's overall cost-benefit analysis.

Politicians' concerns with employment are understandable. The political attraction of supporting a new superhighway that will employ 10,000 construction workers for two years at an average wage of $15 an hour is undeniable. Jobs and high wages translate directly into votes. But focusing on the employment question is a terrible way to conduct a cost-benefit analysis.

Cost-benefit analysis is supposed to help government officials decide how best to use society's scarce resources. Employment studies introduce two biases into a cost-benefit analysis that completely defeat the purpose of the analysis. The first bias is counting the wages earned in constructing a project as a benefit of the project. In fact, the wages paid construction workers are part of a project's *costs*. Taking a significant part of a project's costs and moving it to the benefit side of the ledger can make almost any project look worthwhile.

The wages of construction workers are a benefit only if the workers were previously unemployed, *and unemployable in any other economic activity*. In that case their opportunity costs are zero, and any wages they receive are a true benefit. But most of the workers employed on government projects are already gainfully employed or, if unemployed, only temporarily so. They do have viable employment alternatives, in which case the wages they receive are a true opportunity cost. They represent the payment required to get workers to work on the project rather than elsewhere.

Employment studies introduce a second bias into cost-benefit analysis by including as a benefit a number of secondary income gains attributable to the project. For instance, constructing a dam in a wilderness area gives rise to a whole host of additional economic activity. Construction workers have to be housed, fed, and clothed while building the dam, as do the maintenance workers and managers after the dam is completed. A town, complete with restaurants, banks, shopping malls, movie theaters, and the like, could spring up where none previously existed. The earnings associated with these businesses are counted as a secondary benefit of the project. These secondary benefits are usually enormous, often far larger than the direct benefits of the project.

Adding secondary employment benefits to the project is inappropriate. All public projects give rise to such benefits. The secondary benefits of constructing an office building in downtown St. Louis may be less obvious than are those associated with building a dam in the wilderness, but they exist nonetheless. Who can say for sure that two different projects of the same size give rise to different amounts of secondary benefit? Counting secondary benefits does not help in comparing the relative merits of different projects. All it does is generate an unwarranted bias toward selecting larger projects over smaller projects, since larger projects naturally give rise to larger secondary benefits.

The bias toward larger projects is unwarranted because secondary benefits are largely offset by secondary losses. In a fully employed economy the resources used in constructing and maintaining a government project have to come from somewhere. The regions that lose resources to these projects presumably suffer a whole series of secondary losses as the economies of these regions contract. For example, a hydroelectric project that lowers the price of electricity to a region hurts the oil and the natural gas industries. Some consumers will switch from oil and gas ranges and furnaces to electric ranges and electric heating. As the oil and the gas industries decline, the regions that rely on these industries for their incomes will suffer secondary losses. An oil-burning electric utility that had been supplying the region may shut down. Also, public investments come at the expense of private production, which also gives rise to secondary benefits. Presumably these lost secondary benefits are part of the project's opportunity cost. Politicians who support the job-creating aspects of a superhighway forget about the jobs that are lost in the private sector when taxes are raised to pay for the highway.

The most reasonable assumption is that the secondary benefits and the secondary losses of a project should just about cancel one another out no matter how large the project. The best strategy is to ignore secondary benefits and losses in a cost-benefit analysis.

To summarize, a project is worthwhile only if a proper accounting of its *direct* benefits and costs yields a positive present value. Politically motivated employment studies undermine cost-benefit analyses by counting some direct project labor costs as benefits and by otherwise "discovering" secondary benefits that are not truly net benefits for the economy as a whole. Unfortunately, public debate on the relative merits of government projects tends to focus in on these employment effects, often to the exclusion of true project benefits and costs.

CONCLUSION

The difficulties of calculating the present values of government investment projects should by no means rule out attempts at careful cost-benefit analysis. Cost-benefit analysis is the proper framework for evaluating government investments. It directs attention toward the correct issues and away from the bogus issues. Government officials should be thinking about how to measure the true benefits and costs of a project and how to factor in distributional concerns. They should be less concerned with how many workers the project will employ or with the many secondary benefits that the project will generate.

Issues such as intangibles and distributional concerns raise difficult questions, to be sure, questions that are absent in private investment analysis. Nonetheless, a good cost-benefit study can place these tough issues in their proper perspective by weighing their importance relative to the benefits and costs that can reasonably be quantified. In short, good cost-benefit analysis promotes better government decision making.

SUMMARY

Appendix 12 discussed some of the special problems that arise in cost-benefit analysis, the evaluation of government investment projects.

1. Evaluating the net stream of returns on government investments often encounters two difficulties that are not serious problems for private investment analysis:
   a. Intangibles—benefits and costs that cannot be evaluated in dollar terms, such as the national security provided by a missile or the deaths of some construction workers in building a bridge.
   b. Nonmarketed benefits—benefits that are given away and that have to be evaluated indirectly in terms of the sources of the benefit. An example is the benefit of a toll-free interstate highway, which derives from the combined benefits of having a roadway that is safer, reduces the operating costs of cars and trucks, and reduces travel time.
2. Government projects invariably benefit some people and harm others, so that a cost-benefit study must decide how to weigh the gains of the gainers against the losses of the losers. If society cares about helping the poor, then the benefits and the costs to the poor should be given extra weight. Practical considerations argue against including distributional judgments in cost-benefit analysis, however, because they are highly subjective and can easily overwhelm the analysis.
3. Political realities often undermine good cost-benefit analysis. Government agencies guard their own turf, so that cost-benefit analysis is not applied evenhandedly to all government projects. Also, employment considerations

tend to dominate the debates on public projects, even though they undermine the purpose of cost-benefit analysis, which is to determine the best use of society's scarce resources. Employment studies count wages as part of the benefits of a public project when they are actually part of the project's costs, and they add in a number of secondary benefits that are not net benefits for the economy as a whole.

4. Cost-benefit analysis is an important aid to government decision making because it provides the proper framework for analyzing government investments. It helps focus attention on the true benefits and costs of public projects.

KEY TERMS

intangible

QUESTIONS

1. To what extent is government cost-benefit analysis similar to private investment analysis? To what extent is it different?
2. In your opinion, should the government include distributional considerations in its cost-benefit analyses of government projects?
3. a. Name a government project that is likely to have an intangible benefit associated with it, and describe the benefit.
   b. Name a government project that is likely to have an intangible cost associated with it, and describe the cost.
4. A government project has the following properties:
   a. It will create new housing for the poor, but it will destroy an historical site.
   b. It will create new business opportunities in the community.
   c. From past experience with housing projects of this kind, it is known that at least one worker will die during the construction of the project.

   Discuss the problems involved in quantifying each of these cost and benefits.
5. The federal government is in the process of closing military bases throughout the country. Evaluate the following statement: The government should close the smallest bases first, since they employ fewer people and have less of an impact on their surrounding communities.

PART

IV

The Structure of Product Markets in the United States

Chapters 13 through 17 analyze different types of markets for goods and services, with primary emphasis on two questions: (1) How does the structure of a market itself affect business decisions? (2) To what extent are business decisions in different market settings consistent with society's twin goals of efficiency and equity?

Attempts to answer these questions run smack into the staggering complexity and diversity of any modern economy. Thousands of goods and services are bought and sold in a wide variety of market settings. Moreover, business people are quick to emphasize the distinctive features of their own products and markets that, they believe, make their products quite different from any other product. The first problem in addressing these questions, then, is a modeling problem. Is there a simple classification of market structures that yields some useful general principles about the relationships among market structure, market behavior, and market outcomes?

THE CLASSIFICATION OF PRODUCT MARKETS

PERFECT COMPETITION

A product market characterized by a large number of firms, identical products, perfect information, no strategic behavior, a free flow of resources into and out of the industry, and prices and quantities determined by the Laws of Supply and Demand.

PURE MONOPOLY

A product market in which a single firm comprises the entire industry and has complete control over all supply decisions.

Economists have found it most useful to classify markets on the basis of how competitive they are. The end-points on a spectrum of competitiveness are easy enough to set. The most competitive market structure is **perfect competition,** in which prices and quantities are determined by the Laws of Supply and Demand. The least competitive market structure is **pure monopoly,** in which a single firm comprises the entire industry and has complete control over all supply decisions. *Monopoly* is the Greek word for "one seller."

Unfortunately, perfect competition and pure monopoly characterize only a very small percentage of total economic activity in modern economies. Perfectly competitive markets are found mostly in the agricultural sector of the U.S. economy. Overall, perfect competition accounts for no more than 4 to 5 percent of total U.S. economic activity.

Pure monopoly is even less common, accounting for less than 3 percent of national output in the United States. Also, the most important instances of pure monopoly owe their existence to government policies. An act of Congress passed in 1790 gave the U.S. Postal Service a pure monopoly in the delivery of first class mail. State governments grant public utilities exclusive franchises to operate in certain parts of the state. Federal patents sometimes protect firms from any competition whatsoever. For instance, prior to World War II the Hartford Empire Company had a monopoly patent on glass bottling machinery. The patent effectively gave Hartford complete control over every aspect of the glass bottling industry, including whom the bottlers could supply and the size and shape of bottle to be used for each purpose. Hartford established different sizes and shapes for different uses so that bottlers could not easily supply markets that they were not supposed to supply. This in part explains why we see such a variety of glass containers. A more recent example is the series of patents that has protected Polaroid from competition in the instant camera segment of the photography market, a market otherwise dominated by Kodak.

Absent government sanctions such as these, pure monopoly is virtually nonexistent at the national level. Most of the remaining examples are small local businesses, such as newspapers in one-newspaper towns and lone country stores in the middle of the wilderness.

Perfect competition and pure monopoly may constitute only a small percentage of real-world markets, but they are extremely important to the analysis of market structure. They provide the analytical foundations for all market analysis because economists view all other real-world markets as containing features of these two extremes. Also, the efficiency and equity properties of perfect competition are the ideal standards against which economists judge all other market structures.

No consensus exists on how to classify the 90-plus percent of all markets that lie between perfect competition and pure monopoly. Yet nearly all classification schemes share one broad goal. They attempt to place real-world market structures into one of two broad categories: (1) those markets that are effectively competitive and (2) those markets that are noncompetitive. Markets are **effectively competitive** if individual firms have very little control over price and other market outcomes. In this sense they approximate perfectly competitive firms, which have absolutely no control over the market. Markets are **noncompetitive** if individual firms have considerable control over price and other market outcomes. In this sense they approximate the conditions associated with pure monopoly. Dividing markets into one of these two classes makes sense at the introductory level.

EFFECTIVELY COMPETITIVE PRODUCT MARKET

A product market in which individual firms have very little control over price and other market outcomes.

NONCOMPETITIVE PRODUCT MARKET

A product market in which individual firms have considerable control over price and other market outcomes.

The model most commonly used to represent effectively competitive markets is monopolistic competition. As the name suggests, **monopolistic competition** is a blend of the elements found in perfect competition and pure monopoly. The combination of competitive and monopolistic features is heavily weighted toward the competitive end of the spectrum, however, because under monopolistic competition individual firms have relatively little control over their markets. Many local retail and service markets—grocery stores, restaurants, clothing stores, hair salons, electricians, and so forth—are accurately described by the model of monopolistic competition. We will follow the convention of using monopolistic competition as the primary example of an effectively competitive market, with the understanding that other types of market structures can also be effectively competitive.

MONOPOLISTIC COMPETITION

A product market characterized by a large number of firms producing slightly differentiated products, with easy entry and exit, and in which strategic behavior is unimportant.

The model most commonly used to represent the noncompetitive sector of the economy is oligopoly. *Oligopoly* is the Greek word for "a few sellers." Hence, an **oligopoly** is a market dominated by a few large firms. We will be interested primarily in the national oligopolies, in which a few very large firms dominate the entire U.S. market for a particular product.

OLIGOPOLY

A product market dominated by a few large firms.

The standard measure of market dominance is the four-firm concentration ratio, abbreviated CR4. **CR4** is the percentage of total *domestic* sales accounted for by the four largest firms in the industry. A common rule of thumb among industrial organization economists is that an industry is "highly concentrated" if it has a CR4 of 50 percent or more. The automobile industry is an example of a highly concentrated national oligopoly. The "Big Three" (General Motors, Ford, and Chrysler) supply the majority of the domestically produced cars in the United States.

CR4

The four-firm concentration ratio, equal to the percentage of total domestic sales accounted for by the four largest firms in the industry.

The Department of Commerce recognizes 452 distinct manufacturing industries or markets in its Standard Industrial Classification (SIC) of industries

TABLE IV.1 **The Structure of Product Markets in the U.S. Economy**

MARKET STRUCTURE	SECTOR OF THE ECONOMY	NUMBER OF FIRMS IN THE INDUSTRY	DEGREE OF PRODUCT DIFFERENTIATION
PERFECT COMPETITION	Primarily agriculture 4–5% of national output	Very large number	None
PURE MONOPOLY	Primarily sanctioned by government Postal Service, public utilities, certain patented products 3% of national output	One	Total
MONOPOLISTIC COMPETITION (EFFECTIVELY COMPETITIVE)	Majority of markets in all sectors of the economy except transportation and public utilities 72–73% of national output	Very large number	Some
OLIGOPOLY (NONCOMPETITIVE)	Transportation and public utilities; heavy manufacturing (for example, photographic equipment, chemicals); some consumer products (for example, beer, cereal, soup) 20% of national output	A few large firms dominate each industry CR4 > 50%	Some or none Real or imagined

in the United States. Of these, 127 are highly concentrated using the 50 percent benchmark. Oligopolies exist in every sector of the economy, but these markets tend to be concentrated in transportation, public utilities, and heavy manufacturing. In addition to automobiles, aluminum, chemicals, diesel engines, mainframe computers, photographic equipment and supplies, airframe manufacturers and airlines, and railroads are all examples of oligopolies. Some markets that are strictly consumer-oriented—for example, beer, cereal, and soup—are oligopolies as well. As a general rule, though, firms in the national oligopolies tend to sell intermediate products to other businesses as well as final products to consumers.[1]

We will follow the convention of using oligopoly as our primary model of a noncompetitive market, with oligopoly understood to mean a national oligopoly. The presumption is that when a few very large firms dominate the entire national market, the industry is probably more like pure monopoly than perfect competition. In point of fact, though, many of the national oligopolies are quite competitive.

[1]A widely-cited overview of market structure in the United States is W. Shepherd, "Causes of Increased Competition in the U.S. Economy," *Review of Economics and Statistics* 64, No. 4 (November, 1982): 613–626. The SIC data are from W. Baldwin, *Market Power, Competition, and Antitrust Policy* (Homewood, IL: Richard D. Irwin, 1987), 156.

INDEPENDENT OR INTERDEPENDENT DECISIONS (STRATEGIC BEHAVIOR)	BARRIERS TO ENTRY OR EXIT	ABILITY TO CONTROL PRICE AND OTHER MARKET OUTCOMES
Independent No strategic behavior	None	None
Independent No strategic behavior	Blocked entry and exit	Total control of price and other market outcomes
Interdependent to some extent Strategic behavior unlikely to be important	Very low to nonexistent	Some
Tightly interdependent Strategic behavior evidenced in many decisions	Substantial	Considerable

THE FOUR MODELS OF MARKET STRUCTURE

Table IV.1 summarizes the four principal economic models of market structure—perfect competition, pure monopoly, monopolistic competition (representing effectively competitive markets), and oligopoly (representing noncompetitive markets). The table includes the sectors of the economy to which the market structure applies, the percentage of total national output each represents, and the characteristics that economists believe are most important in determining how competitive a market is. These characteristics include the number of firms in the industry, the degree of product differentiation by firm, the extent to which individual firms' decisions are mutually interdependent and lead to strategic behavior, and barriers to entering or leaving the industry.

The number of firms in the industry refers to the number of firms nationwide unless otherwise qualified. Qualifications are sometimes in order, however, because we saw in Chapter 4 that the geographic extent of a market or industry can vary considerably for different products. For example, the public utilities are considered to be natural monopolies, yet the markets for which they have an exclusive franchise are regional, not national.

Product differentiation refers to differentiation by individual firms: Do buyers distinguish specific products by the firm that produced it? We do, for most products. We care what we buy (for example, Coke versus Pepsi, GAP

PRODUCT DIFFERENTIATION

A situation in which buyers distinguish or identify products by the firms that produce them; also refers to firms' attempts to distinguish their products from similar products produced by other firms in the industry, by either real or illusory means.

jeans versus Levis) and where we shop (for example, at the local supermarket or at the supermarket in the next town). In contrast, buyers of wheat do not know, or care, which farm the wheat came from. "Wheat is wheat." The buyers consider wheat to be a homogeneous product. The same is true for most agricultural products. Perfect competition is the only market structure with no product differentiation by firm (farm).

STRATEGIC BEHAVIOR
Any decision by a firm that considers how other firms will react to the decision.

Strategic behavior refers to a decision by one firm that takes into consideration how other firms will react to the decision. Strategic behavior, by definition, can occur only in an interdependent market environment. For this reason strategic behavior is not a factor in perfectly competitive markets or in pure monopolies. The decisions of perfectly competitive farmers are independent, not interdependent. Farmer Smith may think about the overall market conditions for wheat when deciding how much wheat to plant, but he does not think about how much wheat Farmer Jones might plant. The same holds true for Farmer Jones. They both know that they are much too small to have any effect on the market for wheat. As a result, there is no scope for strategic behavior. At the other end of the competitive spectrum, a pure monopolist does not behave strategically because there is no other close competitor for its product. You buy your electricity from the local electric utility or go without it.

Business decisions are almost always interdependent and strategic to some extent in all other market structures. Very few firms change their prices without giving some thought to how their competitors might react. Nonetheless, strategic behavior is unlikely to be an important feature of markets that are structured as monopolistic competition because markets with large numbers of firms are just not conducive to strategic behavior. Firms have too many competitors—not only their current competitors, but potential competitors as well—to keep track of to act strategically. They can do little more than assess the overall market conditions and act accordingly, much as the perfectly competitive wheat farmers do.

This is why Table IV.1 indicates that strategic behavior is important only in an oligopoly. A market dominated by a few large firms is made to order for strategic behavior. The firms cannot help but recognize their mutual interdependence because the actions of any one large firm have a significant impact on the overall market and, therefore, on the prospects of any other firm in the industry. In such an environment each firm must try to predict how other firms will react to its decisions and factor those expected reactions back into its own decisions. For example, Ford cannot set the prices on its line of cars without thinking about how General Motors, Chrysler, and the major foreign auto makers will react to its prices.

BARRIER TO ENTRY OR EXIT
Anything that restricts or prevents the free flow of resources into or out of an industry.

A **barrier to entry or exit** is anything that restricts or prevents resources from entering or leaving an industry. An example is the exclusive franchise given to electric utilities or cable TV operators that prevents other investors from entering the market and offering these services. Barriers to entry (and exit) are anti-competitive because they undermine the role of profits and losses in guiding resources to their most valued uses. Absent barriers to entry, existing firms will expand, and new firms will enter an industry if the industry is profitable. Conversely, existing firms will contract and some investors will exit the industry to seek profits in other markets if the industry is unprofitable. Barriers to entry (exit) reduce or prevent these responses. As such, they make the market system less responsive to the desires of consumers and give some investors an undue advantage in the pursuit of profits. Barriers to entry (exit) are a distinguishing feature of all noncompetitive markets.

The combination of all these market characteristics determines firms' ability to control price and other market outcomes, the final column of Table IV.1. This is the single most important test of market competitiveness.

The boundary between effectively competitive markets and noncompetitive markets is necessarily fuzzy. Many industries do not fit easily into one group or the other. The best we can offer is a reasonable rule of thumb. If an industry contains a large number of firms, if the barriers to entry are low, and if strategic behavior is unimportant, then consider it to be effectively competitive. If an industry contains a few dominant firms, if the barriers to entry are substantial, and if strategic behavior is important, then consider it to be noncompetitive. Beyond that, think about the characteristics listed in Table IV.1, and use your best judgment. Refer back to Table IV.1 as you study each of the market structures in Chapters 13 through 17. It will give you a quick summary of the principal features of each model.

CHAPTER

13

Perfect Competition

LEARNING OBJECTIVES

CONCEPTS TO LEARN

Perfectly competitive markets

The all-or-none profit test

Shut-down and break-even production points

Average total, fixed, and variable costs

The zero-profit long-run competitive equilibrium

The long-run market supply curve

The three criteria for judging market outcomes:

1. Allocational efficiency
2. Production or technical efficiency
3. Equity

The relationship between short-run and long-run costs

CONCEPTS TO RECALL

Opportunity cost [1]

Equality of opportunity [2]

Horizontal equity [2]

The conditions for a competitive market [6]

Marginal cost [6]

The profit-maximizing supply rule [6]

The Laws of Supply and Demand [5,6,7]

The maximum net value efficiency property of competitive markets [7]

Economists joke that most students take a micro principles course to learn how to make a killing in the stock market. The course cannot teach you how to do this, however. The problem is simply that the stock market is a highly competitive market, essentially perfectly competitive. Investors trade millions of shares of stock each day in a free and open exchange. No one can be assured of continued success over a long period of time in such a highly competitive environment.

Playing the stock market is a guessing game about what the future might bring. Buyers are willing to buy because they believe the prices of certain stocks are about to rise. Conversely, sellers are willing to sell because they believe the prices of these same stocks are about to fall. In any exchange, therefore, someone is guessing correctly, and someone incorrectly. Guess right most of the time and you will make your killing. Unfortunately, competitive market forces are hard at work against you. The analysis of perfectly competitive markets in Chapter 13 will indicate why you cannot reasonably expect to make a fortune over the long haul by playing the stock market.

Perfect competition is the natural starting point for analyzing different types of market structures because it is the standard of perfection against which all other market structures are judged. Perfect competition is the only market structure that operates strictly in accordance with the Laws of Supply and Demand. As such, it is the only market structure that can achieve an efficient allocation of society's scarce resources without government intervention in the marketplace. Perfectly competitive product markets also appeal to people's sense of equity and fair play because they offer everyone equal access to market opportunities and treat identical individuals equally. No other market structure can match perfect competition in promoting both efficiency and equity. Capitalist societies would be very well served if all product markets were perfectly competitive.

Chapter 13 has two primary objectives: (1) to explain how perfect competition achieves society's twin goals of efficiency and equity and (2) to develop specific market tests of efficiency and equity from the outcomes of a perfectly competitive market structure. These market tests will then serve as the criteria for evaluating market outcomes under pure monopoly, monopolistic competition, and oligopoly.

We progressed a long way toward these two objectives in Chapters 5 through 8 when we analyzed the Laws of Supply and Demand in markets for goods and services. Our earlier discussion was incomplete in two respects, however. It did not fully explain the role of profit in the operation of competitive markets. Also, the analysis focused exclusively on the short run, and we need to understand how competitive markets behave in the long run as well. Chapter 13 fills in these remaining gaps.

The chapter begins with a quick review of the material in Chapters 5 through 8 related to the operation of perfectly competitive product markets.

REVIEW OF PERFECT COMPETITION

Chapter 6 described the characteristics of a perfectly competitive market, which are reproduced in Table IV.1:

1. The industry consists of a very large number of firms.
2. The firms produce identical products: "Wheat is wheat." There is no product differentiation by firm.
3. Consumers and firms have correct information about all relevant aspects of the market, such as the prices charged by each firm.
4. There are no barriers to the entry or exit of firms in the long run. Resources are free to move into or out of the market in response to profits and losses.

Also, firms cannot behave strategically because there are so many firms in the industry. A farmer will consider overall market conditions when deciding how much to plant, but he will not care what any particular farmer does.

We saw that agriculture is the one sector of the economy that most closely approximates these conditions.

Chapters 5 through 8 established the following principles concerning the operation of perfectly competitive markets in the short run.

1. *Determination of price and quantity:* Equilibrium quantity and equilibrium price are determined by the combined interaction of market supply and market demand. Refer to Figure 13.l(b). The market demand curve, *D*, is the sum of all the individual consumers' demand curves. The market supply curve, *S*, is the sum of all the individual firms' supply curves, that is, their marginal cost curves. The equilibrium quantity and the equilibrium price (Q_e, P_e), occur at the intersection of *D* and *S*. The market and the industry are one and the same.
2. *The demand curve for an individual firm:* Figure 13.1(a) represents one of the thousands of individual firms, all assumed to have identical costs and to produce an identical product. The demand curve facing an individual firm, d_f, is horizontal, or perfectly elastic, at the level of the equilibrium price, P_e, regardless of the shape of the market demand curve. This is so because

FIGURE 13.1

A Perfectly Competitive Market: the Short Run

The equilibrium quantity and price (Q_e,P_e) in the market is determined by the intersection of the market supply and demand curves, *S* and *D*, in Figure 13.1(b). Each of the representative firms in Figure 13.1(a) takes the market price as a given. Its demand curve, d_f, is horizontal, perfectly elastic at the equilibrium price P_e. The firm maximizes profit by selecting the output q_e, at the intersection of the firm's demand curve, d_f, and its marginal cost curve, *MC*. Price equals marginal cost at q_e, which is the profit-maximizing supply rule for a competitive firm.

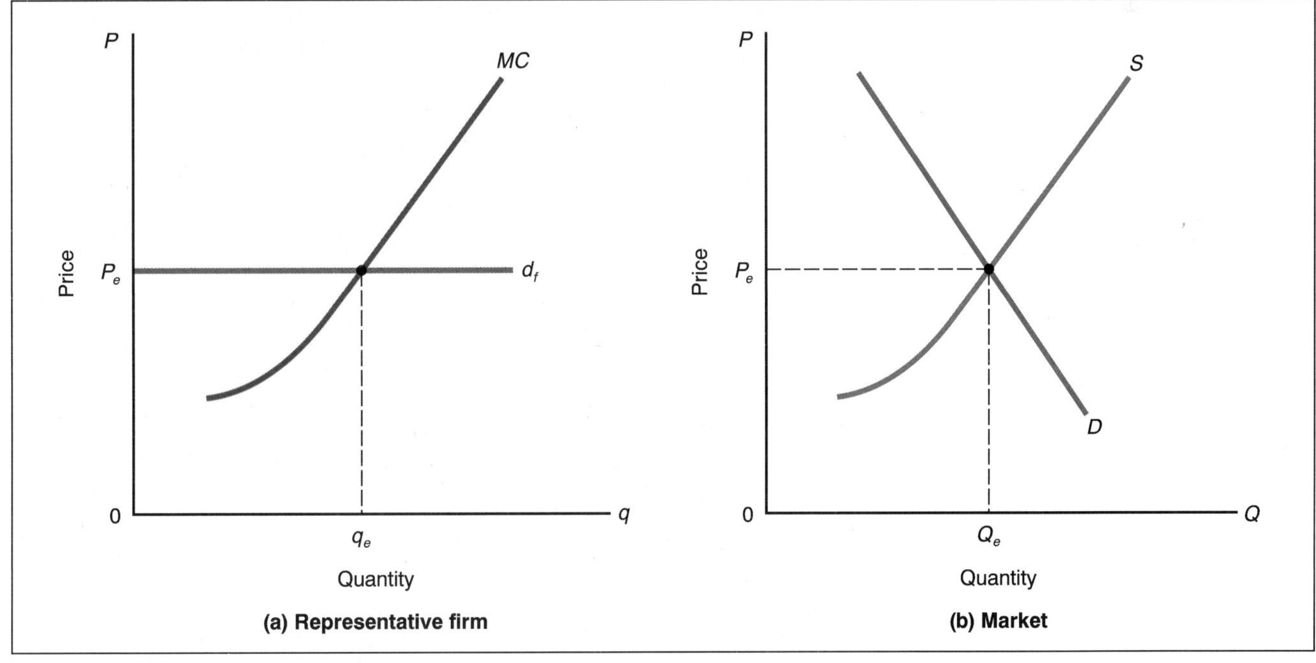

PERFECT COMPETITION

A product market characterized by a large number of firms, identical products, perfect information, no strategic behavior, a free flow of resources into and out of the industry, and prices and quantities determined by the Laws of Supply and Demand.

the firms are small and they produce identical products. Each firm is such an insignificant player in the overall market that its actions, by themselves, have no effect on market price. A firm can double or halve its output, and the market will hardly notice. Also, consumers do not care which firm produces the products they buy because they view the firms' products as identical. Therefore, if one firm raises its price above the equilibrium price, its customers will simply buy the same product from another firm. These two properties force perfectly competitive firms to be price takers. They can sell as much or as little as they want at the equilibrium price, but they cannot affect that price.

3. *The profit-maximizing supply rule,* P = MC: To maximize profit, each firm produces and sells the output, q_e, at which price equals marginal cost. The $P = MC$ supply rule is a specific example of the general principle that any economic activity should continue to the point at which marginal benefit equals marginal cost. For a firm, marginal benefit is the marginal revenue from selling additional units of the product. Under perfect competition, marginal revenue is always the equilibrium price, since the firm receives P_e on every additional unit sold. The marginal cost of producing additional units of output is given by the marginal cost curve. The $P = MC$ supply rule establishes the firm's marginal cost curve as its supply curve, since the marginal cost curve indicates how much output the firm is willing to supply at any given market price.

INDIVIDUAL FIRM'S SUPPLY CURVE

The output that a competitive firm is willing and able to supply at every price; alternatively, a competitive firm's marginal cost curve above the minimum of its average variable cost curve.

MARKET SUPPLY CURVE

—**Short run**—the horizontal summation of the individual firms' supply or marginal cost curves, above the minimum of average variable cost.

A useful way to summarize the operation of a perfectly competitive market for analytical purposes is to think of it as occurring in three distinct steps:

1. Consumers and firms bring their individual demand and supply curves to the marketplace. In other words, consumers and firms make known how much they are willing to buy and sell at all possible market prices. In the process they form the market demand and the market supply curves.
2. The combined interaction of all the demanders and the suppliers as they bargain over price establishes the equilibrium price that just clears the market. Total quantity demanded equals total quantity supplied at the intersection of the market demand and the market supply curves.
3. Once the equilibrium price is established, every consumer and firm decides exactly how much to buy and supply at that price. Consumers demand the quantity that maximizes their satisfaction. Firms supply the quantity that maximizes their profit, by following the $P = MC$ supply rule. In this way consumers and firms determine their individual share of the overall quantity exchanged in equilibrium.

The points recalled in this brief review should all be familiar. If you are unclear on any of them, reread the relevant material in Chapters 5 through 8.

A final comment concerns the device of graphing a representative firm and the market (industry) side by side, as in Figure 13.1. We will use this technique throughout Chapter 13. It is extremely useful for analyzing competitive markets because it allows us to see how the individual firms fare under different market conditions. The technique is made possible by the fact that the two graphs have the same scale on the vertical axis, dollars per unit of output. Price is a per unit measure, the number of dollars spent or received on each unit of output. Marginal cost is also a per unit measure, the cost of the last unit of output produced. Furthermore, the two graphs have a direct link to one another. The position of the firm's demand curve is set by the level of the equilibrium price, P_e, on the market graph. Remember, though, that the scale on the horizontal axis is quite different in the two graphs. The market output, Q, is many thousands of times larger than each individual firm's output, q.

PROFIT AND LOSS

Profit figured prominently in our earlier development of competitive supply. We assumed that competitive firms would select the output at which price equals marginal cost *because this is the output that maximizes profit.* But our analysis in Chapters 5 through 8 stopped short of asking just how good the maximum amount of profit really is. The maximum profit could be spectacular, with the owners earning a fabulous rate of return on their capital. Or the maximum profit could be just average, with the owners doing about as well as investors anywhere. In a declining market the maximum profit could be unacceptable, with the firm actually incurring a loss. We simply assumed in the earlier chapters that the firm's maximum profit was "good enough," that it would actually supply the best-profit output in the short run. To complete the analysis of perfect competition we need to consider whether firms are making profits or losses and how the market responds to either situation.

The All-or-None Profit Test

Let's begin by asking a fundamental, all-or-none question about the downside: How bad can market conditions be? What is the *minimum* level of profit that the owners can accept in order to continue supplying to the market? The answer turns out to very simple: *A firm will continue to produce only if total revenue is at least as large as the variable cost of production.* This simple all-or-none rule requires some careful thought, however. It has very different implications for the short run and the long run, and it takes some getting used to in either case.

THE SHORT-RUN SHUT-DOWN POINT Recall from our discussion of cost in Chapter 11 that a firm's total cost in the short run divides naturally into two components, fixed cost and variable cost.

$$SRTC = FC + SRVC$$

Fixed cost is the cost associated with the fixed factors of production. Variable cost is the cost associated with the variable factors of production. The fixed cost is a **sunk cost** from the point of view of the firm for the duration of the short run. It is the result of previous decisions related to the fixed factors of production and cannot be avoided or changed in any way until the short run gives way to the long run. The firm can vary its output in the short run only by hiring or releasing the variable factors of production. Therefore, it has control only over its variable cost.

SUNK COST
A firm's fixed cost in the short run, arising from decisions about factors of production that were made in the past.

Notice that the all-or-none rule implies that the firm might continue producing in the short run even if it incurs losses. According to the rule, total revenue need only be sufficient to cover the firm's variable cost, not its total cost. The reasoning is as follows. A firm has two choices in the short run: (1)

produce the profit-maximizing level of output at which $P = MC$ or (2) shut down its operations entirely and cease production. Suppose that the firm chooses to shut down. By doing so it avoids all its variable cost, but not its fixed cost. The obligation to pay its fixed commitments continues for the duration of the short run no matter what the firm does. So the decision to shut down is a decision to incur a loss equal to the value of the firm's fixed cost. In other words, the firm's fixed cost sets a floor on the amount of loss the firm is willing to sustain.

The firm should continue to produce if it can do better than this. The firm does better if total revenue exceeds variable cost because, after paying all the variable factors of production, some revenue is left over to pay off part of the fixed cost. The firm loses less than its fixed cost, which is all that is required. If total revenue is less than variable cost, the firm should shut down. By continuing to produce, it loses its fixed cost *plus* some of its variable cost. The situation in which total revenue just equals variable cost is called the **shut-down point.** The firm is indifferent between shutting down and continuing to produce. Either way, it loses an amount equal to the value of its fixed cost.

SHUT-DOWN POINT

A market situation in which a firm's total revenue equals its variable cost (price equals average variable cost), so that the firm is indifferent between producing and not producing.

The general principle operating here is that economic decisions are always forward looking. In deciding whether to produce, a firm should compare projected future revenue with projected future variable cost because these are the only things it can control. The firm should forget its fixed cost because the fixed cost is a bygone, the result of past decisions that cannot be undone.

Letting bygones be bygones is a perfectly sound economic principle that people have great difficulty accepting. How often we hear: "I can't stop now. Look at all the time and effort I have put into this." But if plowing onward only adds to the losses, the person should stop and do something else. Perhaps the psychologists can tell us why people often have such difficulty letting go of losing propositions.

THE LONG-RUN BREAK-EVEN POINT The implications of the all-or-none rule are very different in the long run. All factors of production are variable in the long run, so there is no distinction between total cost and variable cost.

$$LRTC = LRVC$$

Thus, the all-or-none rule implies that total revenue must cover the full cost of production. The firm cannot accept losses in the long run. The situation in which total revenue just equals total cost is called the **break-even point.** At that point the owners of the firm are just indifferent between keeping their capital invested in the firm and investing it elsewhere. The owners will leave the industry for other investment alternatives if total revenue falls short of total cost in the long run.

BREAK-EVEN POINT

A market situation in which a firm's total revenue equals its long-run total cost (price equals long-run average cost), so that economic profit is zero.

You may wonder why the owners would accept break-even production. Where is the return on their capital? The answer turns on the distinction between total cost based on standard tax accounting principles and total cost measured from an economic perspective, which we discussed in Chapter 11. Profit is always defined as the difference between total revenue and total cost, and loss is a negative profit. But the interpretations given profit and loss depend on how cost is defined.

In standard tax accounting usage, total cost equals total operating expenses. Therefore, making a profit means earning a positive return on the owners' capital invested in the firm, and making a loss means earning a negative return on the owners' capital. The firm breaks even if it earns a zero return on its capital; total revenue is just sufficient to cover total operating expenses. Breaking even in a tax accounting sense would not be acceptable to the firm's owners.

In economic usage, a firm's total cost is the sum of all the operating expenses of the firm *plus* the opportunity cost of owner-supplied capital.[1] The opportunity cost of capital is the return the owners could earn on their capital if it were not tied up in the firm. Breaking even in economic terms is defined relative to the opportunity cost of capital. A firm is breaking even if the total revenue is sufficient to pay all the firm's operating expenses *with enough left over to provide the owners a return on their capital equal to the return available from the next best investment alternatives.* For instance, if the owners can earn 10 percent on capital elsewhere, the firm is breaking even if the owners are earning 10 percent on their capital invested with the firm. This is why the owners are indifferent between remaining with the firm and taking their capital elsewhere at the break-even point.

A market situation in which a firm makes a profit in economic terms is a highly favorable situation. Not only are the owners earning a positive return on their capital, but also they are earning a higher return than investors are earning generally. For example, the owners may be earning a 15 percent return on their capital while everyone else is earning 10 percent. Other investors will be eager to enter the industry and earn the 15 percent return themselves. Indeed, any return greater than 10 percent is a profitable market situation that will attract other investors. Conversely, loss from an economic perspective does not necessarily imply a negative return to capital, only that the owners are earning a lower return on their capital than they could earn elsewhere. For example, they may be earning only a 7 percent return when they could get a 10 percent return outside the firm. Any return below 10 percent is low enough to cause them to withdraw their capital from the firm and place it elsewhere to earn the 10 percent.

THE ALL-OR-NONE TEST—AN EXAMPLE A simple example taken from Chapter 11 will serve to illustrate the firm's all-or-none production decision in the short and the long runs. In that chapter we described an airline that decides to run daily flights between two cities it had not previously serviced. To provide the service the airline must commit itself to $1 million of *fixed cost* for one year, in the form of rental contracts for airport space and two airplanes. Once the planes begin to fly, the airline receives revenue from ticket sales and incurs additional costs associated with operating the service. The airline's *variable cost* includes expenses for fuel; salaries for pilots, flight attendants, and baggage handlers; food and other supplies; and so forth.

Suppose that one or two weeks after beginning the service the airline realizes it has made a serious mistake. Demand for the service is nowhere near as strong as it was expected to be. Refer to Table 13.1. The projected total revenue for the year, $800,000, falls far short of the projected total costs of $1,500,000, consisting of $500,000 of variable operating cost and $1 million of fixed rental cost. The airline projects a loss of $700,000 on the service for the year.

[1]Recall that total cost also includes the oppportunity cost of owner-supplied labor when the owner-operators do not pay themselves a salary. The discussion here ignores this opportunity cost.

TABLE 13.1 **Annual Projected Revenue and Cost of Flights**

Total revenue:	$800,000	Total cost:	$1,500,000
		Variable cost:	500,000
		Fixed cost:	1,000,000

The service has just begun. Should the airline discontinue the flights or continue to operate them for the remainder of the year? According to the all-or-none rule, the airline should continue to operate the flights. The projected total revenue of $800,000 exceeds the projected *variable cost* of $500,000. Were the airline to shut down the service, it would lose $1 million, the fixed rental cost (ignoring the revenues and variable costs during the first week or two of operation). By continuing, the airline receives $300,000 in revenue over and above the variable cost of operation that it can use to offset part of its fixed cost. Its loss is reduced to $700,000.

The long run arrives at the end of the year when the airline has the option of renewing the rental contracts. Now all factors of production are variable, and the airline will renew the rental contracts only if it decides to continue the service. Total cost and variable cost are one and the same. If the airline projects the same experience for a second year, it will obviously choose to discontinue the service at the end of the year. Total revenue is not sufficient to cover *total cost* in the long run.

The Various Average Cost Curves

One final step remains in preparation for the analysis of perfect competition in the long run. We need to be able to measure profit and loss on the standard graph of the representative firm in a way that allows us to see the shut-down and break-even points. So far that graph contains only the firm's marginal cost curve and its horizontal demand curve. We have to incorporate the firm's total and variable costs to represent the break-even and shut-down points. To do so, total and variable costs must be expressed on a per unit basis because, as noted above, marginal cost and price are both per unit measures.

Consider the relevant per unit short-run cost curves. Per unit costs at any level of output are just the total costs divided by that output. Short-run total cost equals fixed cost plus short-run variable cost.

$$SRTC = FC + SRVC$$

Therefore, on a per unit basis,

$$SRTC/q = FC/q + SRVC/q$$

or

$$AC_{sr} = AFC + AVC$$

Short-run total cost divided by output, AC_{sr}, is *short-run average total cost,* or simply *short-run average cost.* It is also referred to as *short-run unit cost.*

TABLE 13.2 **Short-Run Costs for a Representative Firm**

QUANTITY	TOTAL COST (SRTC)	MARGINAL COST (MC_{sr})	VARIABLE COST (VC)	FIXED COST (FC)	AVERAGE COST (AC_{sr})	AVERAGE VARIABLE COST (AVC)	AVERAGE FIXED COST (AFC)
0	$ 320	$ —	$ 0	$320	$ —	$—	$ —
1	391	71	71	320	391	71	320
2	444	53	124	320	222	62	160
3	484	40	164	320	161	55	107
4	512	28	192	320	128	48	80
5	533	21	213	320	107	43	64
6	548	15	228	320	91	38	53
7	560	12	240	320	80	34	46
8	576	16	256	320	72	32	40
9	593	17	273	320	66	30(30.33)	36
10	623	30	303	320	62	30(30.30)	32
11	654	31	334	320	59(59.45)	30(30.36)	29
12	713	59	393	320	59(59.42)	33	27
13	777	64	457	320	60	35	25
14	853	76	533	320	61	38	23
15	958	105	638	320	64	43	21
16	1,088	130	768	320	68	48	20
17	1,247	159	927	320	73	55	19
18	1,436	189	1,116	320	80	62	18
19	1,660	224	1,340	320	87	71	17
20	1,920	260	1,600	320	96	80	16

NOTE: All average variables are rounded to the nearest whole number. AVC plus AFC may not add exactly to AC_{sr} because of rounding error.

These three terms are used interchangeably. Similarly, fixed cost divided by output is *average fixed cost (AFC)*, and short-run variable cost divided by output is *average variable cost (AVC)*. (The qualifier "short-run" is unnecessary for average fixed and variable costs, since these terms only need to be defined in the short run.)

Table 13.2 reproduces the short-run cost data from Table 11.1, with the addition of the three new average cost concepts. Recall that these are hypothetical cost data for a representative firm. They capture all the important properties that the costs of actual firms are most likely to exhibit. These properties apply to nearly all firms, not just to perfectly competitive firms. Let's explore how the three new average cost concepts behave as output increases from 0 to 20.

AVERAGE FIXED COST Figure 13.2 displays average fixed cost (AFC), the final column of Table 13.2. The numerator of AFC, the fixed cost, is constant at \$320, so that AFC declines continuously as output increases. AFC is large without limit at an output of zero because the fixed cost of \$320 remains, even if the firm shuts down (\$320/0 $\rightarrow \infty$). At $q = 1$, $AFC = FC =$ \$320 (\$320/1 = \$320). By the time output reaches 20, AFC has declined to \$16 (\$320/20 = \$16). AFC eventually approaches zero as output grows larger and larger.

AVERAGE FIXED COST
At every output, the firm's fixed cost divided by its output.

FIGURE 13.2

Average Fixed Cost

The average fixed cost curve, *AFC*, is a graph of the average fixed cost data in Table 13.2. *AFC* declines continuously as output increases because fixed cost is the unchanging sunk cost associated with the firm's fixed factors of production in the short run.

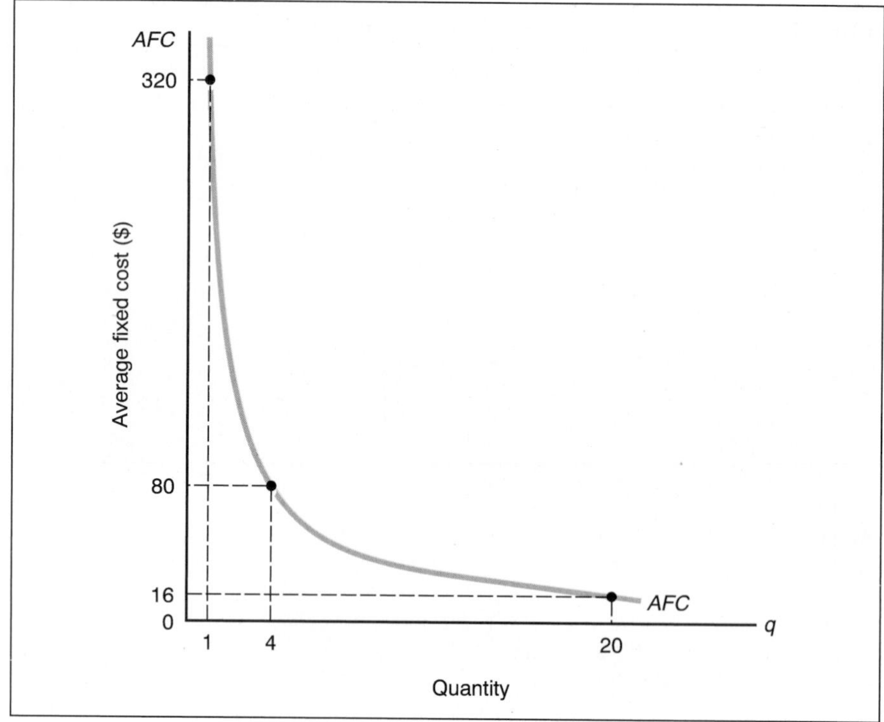

Business people often refer to the pattern of declining average fixed cost as the "spreading of overhead expenses." The expenses of maintaining the corporate headquarters, the salaries of the chief executive officers, the costs of running the annual sales meeting, and similar overhead expenses are essentially fixed costs of doing business that do not vary as output increases or decreases. Nonetheless, they are part of the firm's total cost that has to be covered by sales revenue. As output increases, these overhead expenses are spread ever thinner in the sense that they constitute an ever-smaller proportion of the unit cost of the product. In terms of our numbers, *AFC* is 5/8 of AC_{sr} at an output of 4 ($80/128 = 5/8), but only 1/6 of AC_{sr} at an output of 20 ($16/96 = 1/6).

Having described average fixed cost, we can ignore it for the most part. As noted earlier, fixed cost is sunk cost, a bygone that does not figure into the firm's decision-making process.

AVERAGE (TOTAL) COST

At every output, the firm's total cost divided by its output.

AVERAGE COST Short-run average cost (AC_{sr}, sixth column of Table 13.2) is U-shaped, reflecting the fact that short-run total cost rises proportionately less than output at low levels of output and then rises proportionately more than output at higher levels of output. Refer to Figure 13.3. AC_{sr} is large without limit at $q = 0$ because of the influence of *AFC*, and then it declines steadily over the first 12 units of output. It reaches its minimum value of $59 (approximately) at $q = 12$ and then rises steadily as output increases beyond 12.

Two further points about the shape of AC_{sr} are worth noting for future reference. First, AC_{sr} is not sharply curved near its minimum point. The changes in short-run average cost over the range of output from 9 to 15 are relatively small. The largest value in that range is $66 ($q = 9$), and the smallest is $59

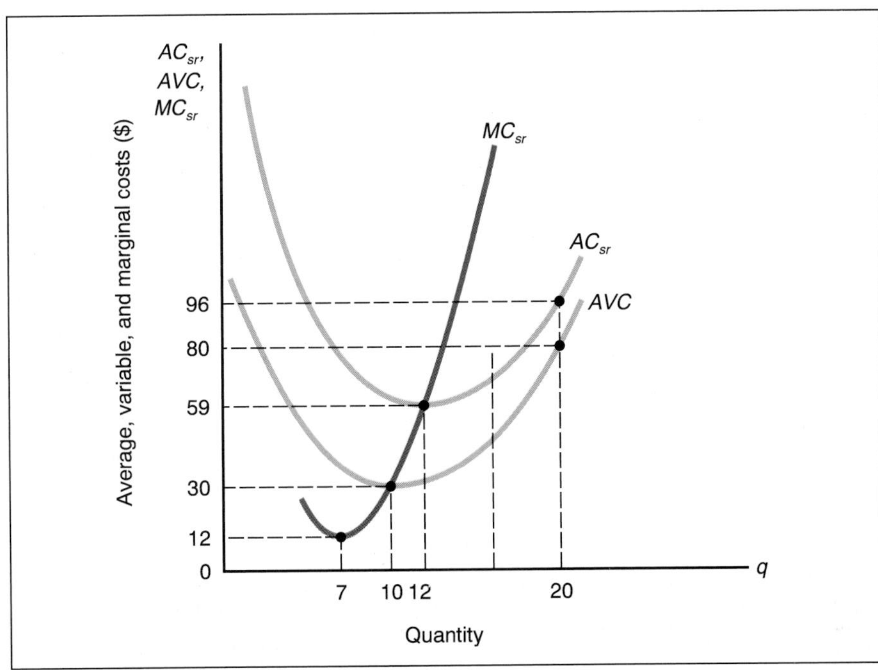

FIGURE 13.3

Short-Run Average Total Cost, Average Variable Cost, and Marginal Cost

The short-run average total cost curve, AC_{sr}, the short-run average variable cost curve, AVC, and the short-run marginal cost curve MC_{sr}, are graphs of the short-run average and marginal cost data in Table 13.2 AC_{sr} and AVC are both U-shaped. Per-unit total and variable costs first decline because of factor indivisibilities and the division of labor, and then rise because of the Law of Diminishing Returns. The short-run marginal cost curve, MC_{sr}, goes through the bottom of AC_{sr} and AVC. MC_{sr} is below AC_{sr} and AVC when these average cost curves are falling and above AC_{sr} and AVC when they are rising.

($q = 12$). Many economists believe that real-world average cost curves are relatively flat near their minimum values. Second, AC_{sr} increases sharply over the highest range of output, from 17 to 20. This, too, is realistic. The Law of Diminishing Returns takes over with a vengeance as production nears the physical limits of its capacity in the short run, causing sharp increases in unit cost.

AVERAGE VARIABLE COST Average variable cost (AVC, seventh column in Table 13.2) is also U-shaped, for the same reason that AC_{sr} is U-shaped. Variable cost is the portion of total cost that changes as output increases or decreases, so AVC reflects the way that total cost increases as output increases, just as average cost does.

AVERAGE VARIABLE COST

At every output, the firm's variable cost divided by its output.

AVC is included in Figure 13.3 for easy comparison with AC_{sr}. Since $AC_{sr} = AFC + AVC$, AVC is well below AC_{sr} at low levels of output when AFC is still a substantial percentage of total unit cost. As output increases, AFC approaches zero, and AVC approaches AC_{sr}. At $q = 20$, AVC is already 83 percent of AC_{sr} ($\$80/96 \cdot 100 = 83\%$). Notice, too, that AVC reaches its minimum value of \$30 (approximately) at $q = 10$, which is 2 units before AC_{sr} reaches its minimum value. AC_{sr} takes longer to bottom out because of the effect of AFC pulling average total cost down.

MARGINAL COST We discussed the U-shaped short-run marginal cost curve in Chapter 11 (MC_{sr}, third column of Table 13.2). Recall that MC_{sr} declines over the range of output where the total cost curve is bowed inward and increases over the range of output where the total cost curve is bowed outward.

MC_{sr} attains its minimum value at the output where the bow of the total cost curve changes direction (the minimum value is \$12 at $q = 7$ for our data). Note also the rapid increase in marginal cost at the higher output levels, reflecting the Law of Diminishing Returns.

The important point to add here is that *the* MC_{sr} *curve passes through the minimum points of both the* AVC *and the* AC_{sr} *curves.* Refer to Figure 13.3. MC_{sr} equals \$30 at $q = 10$, the minimum point of the AVC curve. Also, MC_{sr} equals \$59 at $q = 12$, the minimum point of the AC_{sr} curve. This is not a coincidence peculiar to our hypothetical data. It results from the special relationship between a margin and its corresponding average, as follows. For an average to increase, the margin must be above the average, pulling the average up. For an average to decrease, the margin must be below the average, pulling the average down. Therefore, the only point at which the margin and the average can be equal is where the average is neither increasing nor decreasing. AC_{sr} and AVC are neither increasing nor decreasing at only one point, their minimum points. So the marginal cost curve must intersect the two average cost curves at their minimum points.

This relationship between the margin and the average applies to the margin and average of anything, not just marginal and average cost. Course grades are a more familiar example. Suppose that the end of the semester has arrived, with only the final examination remaining in the economics course. Your average to date on all papers and examinations is 90. Think of the final examination as the *marginal* grade, the grade on the next assignment. The final examination grade will be factored in with your current grade *average* to determine your overall semester *average* in economics.

Suppose that your overall semester average turns out to be a 91. What must have been true of the grade on your final examination, the marginal grade? The answer is that it must have been higher than 91 or it could not have pulled your overall average up from 90 to 91. *The margin must exceed the average to pull the average up.* (Note that the margin, the final examination grade, has to be greater than both the initial average (90) and the final average (91).) Similarly, if your overall semester average turns out to be 89, then the grade on your final examination must have been below 89. *The margin must be below the average to pull the average down.* Finally, your overall semester average remains at 90 only if the grade on your final examination is also 90. *The average remains the same only if the margin and the average are equal.*

The Short-Run Equilibrium

With the average cost curves in hand we can now undertake a complete analysis of a short-run competitive equilibrium. Figure 13.4 depicts a competitive market consisting of 1,000 identical firms. Figure 13.4(b) shows the state of the overall market or industry. Figure 13.4(a) shows the situation of one of the 1,000 firms, whose costs are those listed in Table 13.2. The analysis proceeds in four distinct steps, as follows:

1. *The equilibrium quantity and price:* The equilibrium quantity and the equilibrium price, (Q_e, P_e), are determined by the intersection of the market demand and the market supply curves, D and S, in Figure 13.4(b). According to the graph, the intersection occurs at $Q_e = 16{,}000$ and $P_e = \$130$.

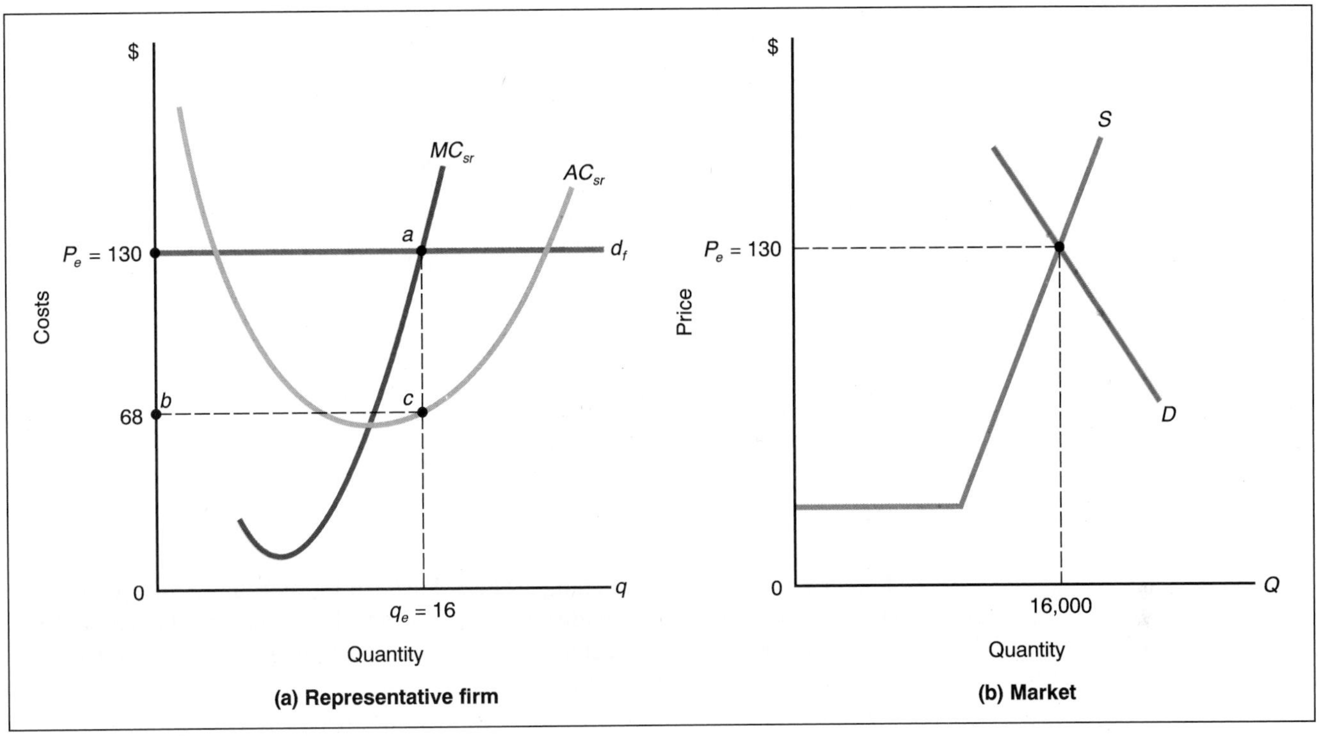

2. *The demand curve of a representative firm:* The demand curve for each of the 1,000 firms is perfectly elastic at the equilibrium price of \$130. It is the horizontal line, d_f, in Figure 13.4(a). The firms are price takers, able to sell as much or as little as they want at the going market price of \$130.
3. *The* P = MC_{sr} *profit-maximizing supply rule:* The firm's goal is to maximize profit. The profit-maximizing output occurs at the intersection of d_f and MC_{sr}. Price and marginal cost both equal \$130 at an output of 16. As a result, each firm supplies 16 units of output to the market if it supplies any output at all.
4. *Computing profit or loss in the short run:* The first three steps are review. The new and final step is to represent each firm's short-run profit or short-run loss in Figure 13.4(a).

$$\text{Profit} = \text{total revenue} - \text{total cost}$$

Total revenue at any quantity is price times that quantity, or $TR = P_e \cdot q$. At the profit-maximizing level of output, q_e, total revenue is represented by the area of rectangle $0P_eaq_e$. The base of the total revenue rectangle is the profit-maximizing level of output, q_e, and the height is the equilibrium price, P_e, (the height of d_f). In our example, the profit-maximizing quantity is 16, and the equilibrium price is \$130.

$$\text{Total revenue} = \$130 \cdot 16 = \$2{,}080$$

Total cost at any quantity is average total cost times that quantity, or the cost per unit times the number of units produced.

FIGURE 13.4

Measuring Profit (or Loss) for a Representative Firm

The equilibrium quantity and price, (Q_e,P_e) are determined by the intersection of the market supply and demand curves, *S* and *D*, in Figure 13.4(b). Q_e = 16,000 and P_e = \$130. The demand curve, d_f, for each of the 1000 representative firms pictured in Figure 13.4(a) is horizontal at the equilibrium price of \$130. Each firm maximizes profit by producing 16 units, at the intersection of d_f and MC_{sr}. The market situation is profitable for the firms because the market price of \$130 is greater than the average cost of \$68 at the best-profit output, qe = 16. Each firm's profit is $(P_e - AC_{sr}) \cdot q_e$, equal to the rectangular area P_eacb. The profit is (\$130 − \$68) · 16 = (\$62) · 16 = \$992. Each firm would make a loss if P_e were less than AC_{sr} at the best-profit output.

$$SRTC = AC_{sr} \cdot q$$

$$AC_{sr} \cdot q = (SRTC/q) \cdot q = SRTC$$

At the profit-maximizing level of output, q_e, short-run total cost is represented by the area of rectangle $0bcq_e$. The base of the total cost rectangle is the profit-maximizing level of output, q_e, and the height is c, the value of AC_{sr} at q_e. In our example, the profit-maximizing quantity is 16, and AC_{sr} at that quantity is \$68.

$$\text{Short-run total cost} = \$68 \cdot 16 = \$1{,}088$$

Therefore,

$$\begin{aligned} \text{Profit} &= \text{total revenue} - \text{total cost} \\ &= \$2{,}080 - \$1{,}088 = \$992 \end{aligned}$$

The profit is the area of rectangle bP_eac. This can be seen in one of two ways: (1) Rectangle bP_eac is the difference between the total revenue rectangle, $0p_eaq_e$, and the total cost rectangle, $0bcq_e$; or (2) profit is the difference between price and average cost, multiplied by the profit-maximizing level of output. P_e is the revenue the firm receives *per unit of output,* and AC_{sr} is the cost to the firm *per unit of output.* Thus, profit is the difference between revenue and cost *per unit,* or the profit *per unit,* times the number of units.

$$\begin{aligned} \text{Profit} &= \text{total revenue} - \text{total cost} \\ &= P_e \cdot q_e - AC_{sr} \cdot q_e \\ &= (P_e - AC_{sr}) \cdot q_e \\ &= \$(130 - 68) \cdot 16 \\ &= \$62 \cdot 16 = \$992 \end{aligned}$$

Return to the profit rectangle, bP_eac. The base of the rectangle, bc, is q_e. The height of the rectangle, bP_e $(= ac)$, is the difference between price, P_e, and average cost, AC_{sr}, at q_e, the profit per unit. So the area of the rectangle is $(P_e - AC_{sr}) \cdot q_e$, profit per unit times the number of units, or profit.

The second interpretation of the profit rectangle points to a simple visual test of whether a market situation is profitable or not at the profit-maximizing level of output. Compare the equilibrium market price, P_e, with the firm's average cost, AC_{sr}:

1. If price exceeds average cost ($P_e > AC_{sr}$), the firm makes a profit.
2. If price is less than average cost ($P_e < AC_{sr}$), the firm incurs a loss.
3. If price equals average cost ($P_e = AC_{sr}$), the firm just breaks even.

Figure 13.5 explores the various possibilities. Interpret the four parts of the figure as describing a steadily deteriorating market situation in which demand for the product declines from D^1 to D^2 to D^3 to D^4 in parts 1 through 4. As before, the industry consists of 1,000 identical firms, each with the cost structure given in Table 13.2. The cost curves are the same in each part of the figure.

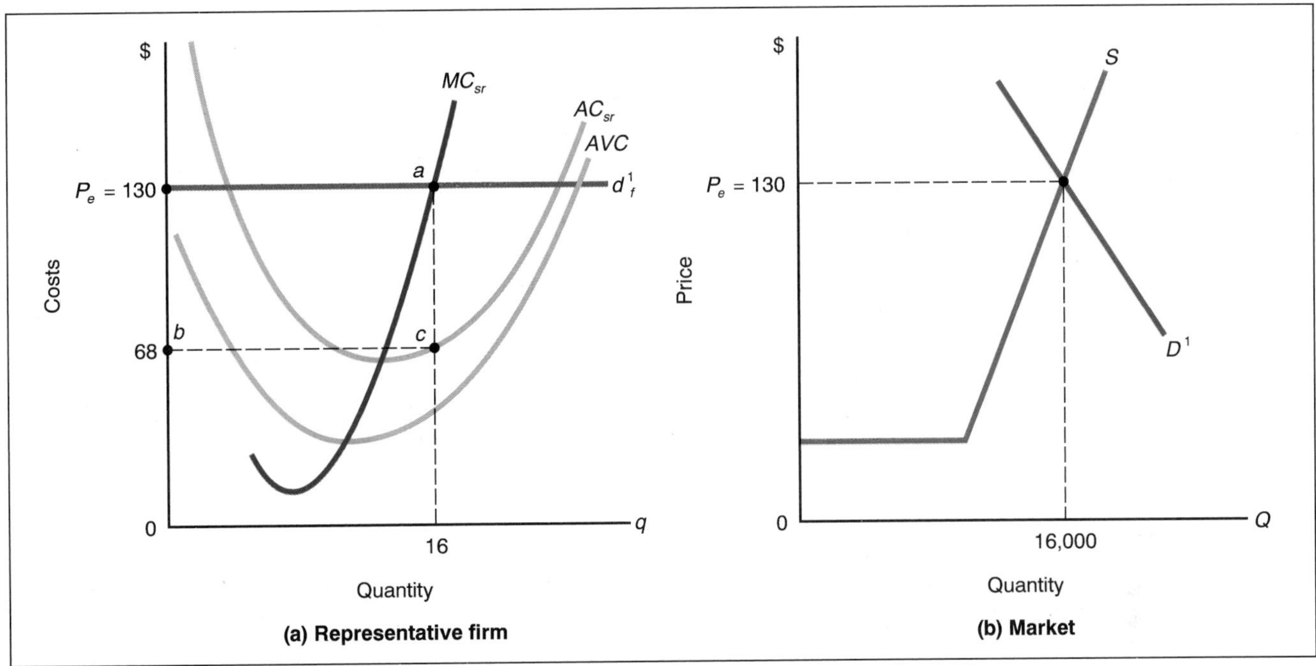

Part 1: This graph reproduces the profitable situation from Figure 13.4. The market supply and demand curve, S and D^1, in Part 1 (b) intersect at a price of \$130. At that price each of the 1000 firms in Part 1(a) supplies 16 units to the market, at the intersection of d_f^1 and MC_{sr}. The price of \$130 is greater than the average cost of \$68 at the best profit output of 16 units, and each firm earns a profit of \$992, equal to the rectangular area bP_eac.

FIGURE 13.5

From Profits to Shut-Down in a Declining Market

Figure 13.5 pictures the representative firm going from a situation of profits to the shut-down point as the market demand curve steadily declines from D^1 in Part 1 to D^4 in Part 4.

PART 1: THE FIRMS MAKE A PROFIT D^1 in part 1 reproduces the market situation depicted in Figure 13.4. Q_e = 16,000, and P_e = \$130. P_e is represented by d_f^1 in Figure 13.5(a). Each firm contributes 16 units to the total market equilibrium and makes a profit of \$992. Firm profit is represented by the area of rectangle bP_eac.

PART 2: THE FIRMS BREAK EVEN Once demand decreases to D^2 in part 2, the best each firm can do is break even. The intersection of D^2 and S occurs at Q_e = 12,000 and P_e = \$59. P_e is represented by d_f^2 in Figure 13.5(c). As price falls to \$59, the profit-maximizing level of output at each firm decreases from 16 to 12. d_f^2 intersects MC_{sr} at q = 12; 12 is also the output at which MC_{sr} intersects AC_{sr}. Therefore, $P_e = AC_{sr}$ = \$59, and the firm just breaks even.

$$\text{Total revenue} = P_e \cdot q_e$$
$$= \$59 \cdot 12 = \$708.$$

$$\text{Total cost} = AC_{sr} \cdot q_e$$
$$= \$59 \cdot 12 = \$708$$

Therefore, total revenue = total cost, and economic profit = 0. (Note that the total cost calculations in this example, and in the examples following, are

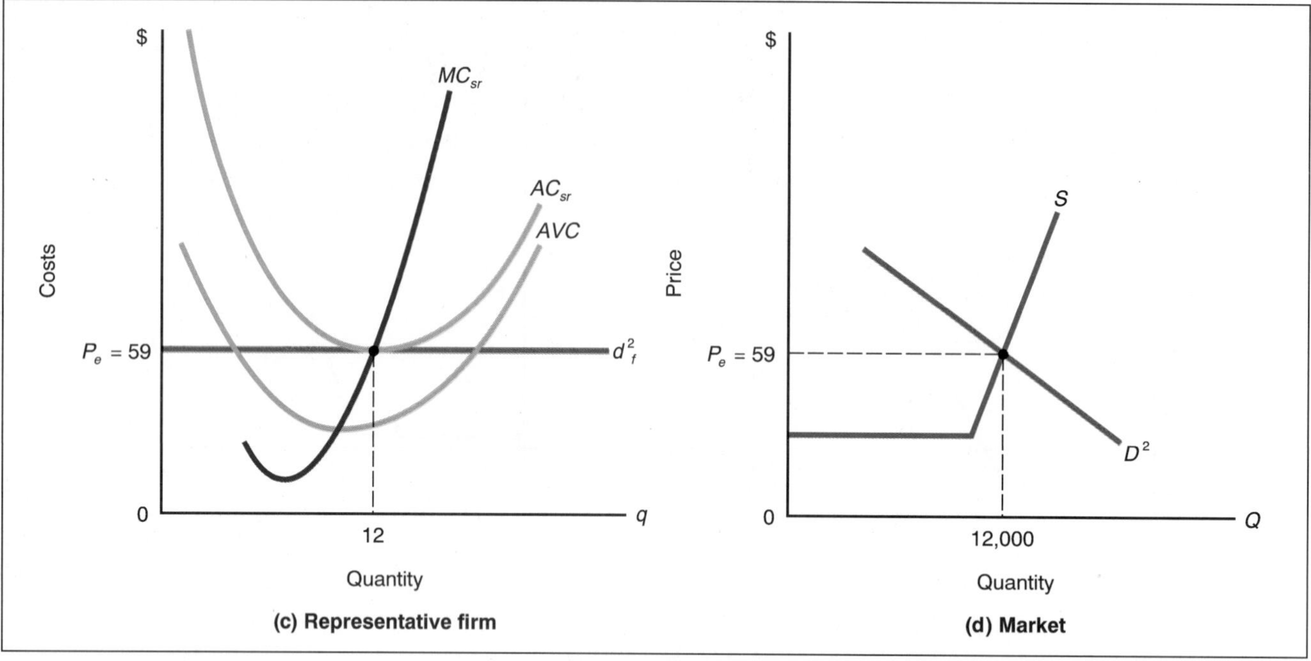

FIGURE 13.5 (continued)

From Profits to Shut-Down in a Declining Market

Part 2: When the market demand curve declines to D^2, the market price falls to \$59, at the intersection of S and D^2 in Part 2(b). Each of the 1000 firms in Part 2(a) supplies 12 units to the market, at the intersection of d_f^2 and MC_{sr}. The price of \$59 equals average cost at the best profit output of 12 units, so the best the firms can do is break even. Each firm earns zero profit, the break-even point.

based on the rounded average cost entries in Table 13.2. Therefore, they will not exactly match the total cost entires in the second column of the table.)

PART 3: THE FIRMS MAKE A LOSS, BUT KEEP PRODUCING When market demand declines further to D^3 in part 3 each firm experiences a loss. The intersection of D^3 and S occurs at $Q_e = 11{,}000$ and $P_e = \$31$. P_e is represented by d_f^3 in Figure 13.5(e). At a price of \$31 each firm reduces output further to 11, the intersection of d_f^3 and MC_{sr}. Price is now well below AC_{sr}, which equals \$59 at $q = 11$. Total revenue $= P_e \cdot q_e = \$31 \cdot 11 = \$341$. Total cost $= AC_{sr} \cdot q_e = \$59 \cdot 11 = \$649$. Each firm loses \$308 (profit = total revenue − total cost = \$341 − \$649 = −\$308). The loss is represented by the area of rectangle *defg*, whose base, *dg*, is q_e and whose height, *de* (= *fg*), is the difference between AC_{sr} and P_e at $q = 11$. The area is $\$28 \cdot 11 = \$308$. In other words, the firm loses \$28 per unit (\$59 − \$31) on each of 11 units.

Will firms continue to produce in the short run with losses of \$308? The answer is yes because total revenue exceeds variable cost. Variable cost $= AVC \cdot q_e = (VC/q_e) \cdot q_e$. At $q_e = 11$, $AVC = \$30$, and variable cost equals \$330 ($\$30 \cdot 11 = \$330$), which is less than the total revenue of \$341. Alternatively, the loss of \$308 is less than the fixed cost of \$320, which each firm would lose in the short run if it shut down.

On a per unit basis, then, the test for shutting down is whether the equilibrium market price P_e exceeds AVC, at the profit-maximizing level of output.

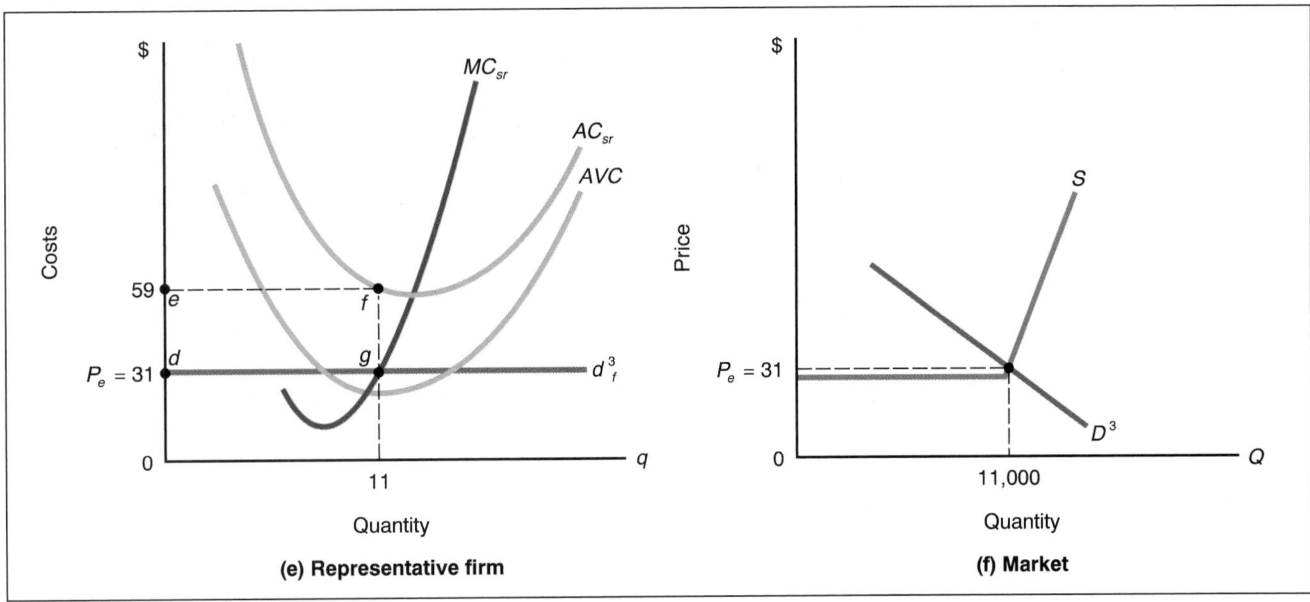

Part 3: When the market demand curve declines further to D^3, the market price falls to $31, at the intersection of S and D^3 in Part 3(b). Each of the 1000 firms in Part 3(a) supplies 11 units to the market, at the intersection of d^3_f and MC_{sr}. The price of $31 is less than the average cost $59 at the best profit output of 11 units, so the best each firm can do is make a loss. The loss is $(AC_{sr} - P_e) \cdot 11 = (\$59 - \$31) \cdot 11 = (\$28) \cdot 11 = \$308$, equal to the rectangular area *defg*. The firms keep producing in the short-run because the price of $31 exceeds the average variable cost of $30 at 11 units of output. Each firm more than covers its variable cost and loses less than its fixed cost.

FIGURE 13.5 (continued)

From Profits to Shut-Down in a Declining Market

With the market demand at D^3, the equilibrium price of $31 is greater than *AVC* of $30, so each firm keeps producing despite the losses.

PART 4: THE FIRMS ARE AT THE SHUT-DOWN POINT: When market demand decreases to D^4 in part 4, each firm is at its shut-down point. The equilibrium price, P_e, is now at $30, represented by d^4_f in Figure 13.5(g). At that price the best-profit output for each firm is $q = 10$, the output at which d^4_f and MC_{sr} intersect; 10 is also the output at which MC_{sr} and *AVC* intersect, so that $P_e = AVC = \$30$. Total revenue equals variable cost equals $300, the shut-down point ($\$30 \cdot 10 = \$300$). Alternatively, total cost $= AC_{sr} \cdot q_e = \$62 \cdot 10 = \$620$. Each firm loses $320 by producing, exactly the amount they would lose by shutting down and paying the fixed cost of $320. So each firm is indifferent between supplying 0 and 10 units to the market. Should market demand decrease further, the output supplied goes to zero. At an equilibrium price below $30 each firm cannot even cover its variable cost.

PROFIT-MAXIMIZING SUPPLY RULE

A perfectly competitive firm supplies the output at which price equals marginal cost as long as price is greater than (short-run) average variable cost.

The analysis of the firm's shut-down point leads to a most important conclusion. Proposition 1 of Chapter 6 said that, in the short run, a competitive firm's supply curve is its marginal cost curve. That proposition is now modified as follows: *In the short run a competitive firm's supply curve is the portion of its marginal cost curve that lies above the minimum value of its average variable cost*

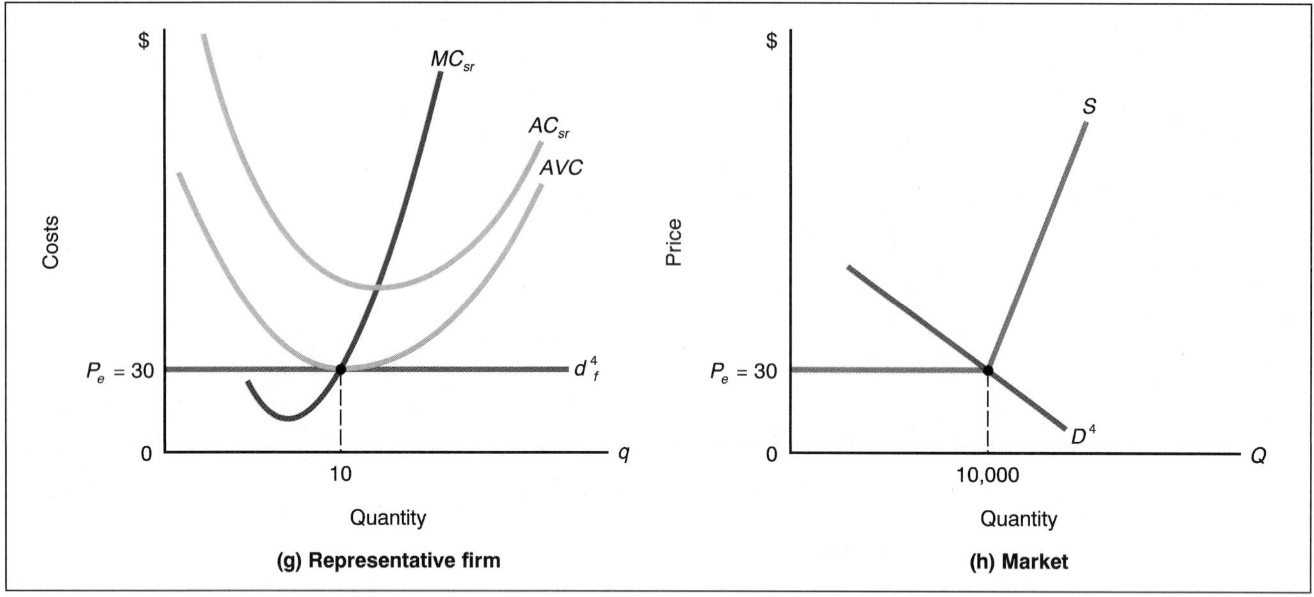

FIGURE 13.5 (continued)

From Profits to Shut-Down in a Declining Market

Part 4: When the market demand curve declines still further to D^4, the market price falls to \$30, at the intersection of S and D^4 in Part 4(b). Now each of the 1000 firms in Part 4(a) is at its shut-down point. The firms are indifferent between supplying 10 units to the market, at the intersection of d_f^4 and MC_{sr}, or shutting down. The price of \$30 equals each firm's average variable cost at the best profit output of 10 units, so the best the firms can do is just cover their variable cost. They lose an amount equal to their fixed cost, which is what they lose if they shut down. The market supply curve S in Part 4(b) becomes horizontal at the shut-down price of \$30.

curve. The minimum value of *AVC* defines the shut-down point at which a firm's willingness to supply, even in the short run, ceases.

In our example, firms only supply output at equilibrium prices greater than \$30, the minimum value of *AVC*. This is why the market supply curve, *S*, becomes horizontal at a price of \$30. With each firm indifferent between supplying 0 and 10 units at that price, total market supply could be anywhere between 0 and 10,000 units. At any price below \$30, market supply is zero.

THE LONG RUN IN PERFECT COMPETITION

Two new possibilities arise as enough time passes and the short run turns into the long run:

1. Existing firms can adjust all the factors of production that were fixed in the short run. They review their input decisions in the long run, with the goal of minimizing their costs of production.
2. New firms can enter the industry, and existing firms can leave the industry. The decision to enter or leave an industry depends on investors' expectations of future profits.

The decision on adjusting previously fixed factors naturally precedes any decision to enter or exit the industry. Investors cannot estimate how profitable selling a product might be without undertaking a complete analysis of what the costs of production are in the long run.

Adjusting Previously Fixed Factors of Production

Suppose that each of the 1,000 firms from our previous examples has the long-run total costs of production (*LRTC*) given in Table 11.1 The long-run total and the long-run marginal cost data are reproduced in Table 13.3, with the addition of long-run average total cost (AC_{lr}) in the fourth column. Recall that average total cost and average variable cost are one and the same in the long run:

$$AC_{lr} = LRTC/q$$

Figure 13.6 depicts the long-run average and the long-run marginal cost curves. They are similar to their short-run counterparts in two respects:

1. Both AC_{lr} and MC_{lr} are U-shaped because of the presence of economies of scale at low levels of output and diseconomies of scale at high levels of output. AC_{lr} is also relatively flat over a wide range of output on either side of its minimum point. From $q = 10$ to $q = 20$, AC_{lr} is gently sloped, varying only between \$60 and \$47.

TABLE 13.3 Long-Run Costs for a Representative Firm

QUANTITY	TOTAL COST (*LRTC*)	MARGINAL COST (MC_{lr})	AVERAGE COST (AC_{lr})
0	\$ 0	\$ —	\$ —
1	146	146	146
2	264	118	132
3	359	95	120
4	432	73	108
5	488	56	98
6	528	40	88
7	560	32	80
8	576	16	72
9	590	14	66
10	600	10	60
11	611	11	56
12	625	14	52
13	641	16	49
14	659	18	47(47.071)
15	706	47	47(47.067)
16	762	56	48
17	835	73	49
18	936	101	52
19	1,055	119	56
20	1,200	145	60

NOTE: Average cost is rounded to the nearest whole number.

FIGURE 13.6

Long-Run Average and Marginal Costs

The long-run average total cost curve, AC_{lr} and the long-run marginal cost curve MC_{lr}, are graphs of the long-run average and marginal cost data in Table 13.3. AC_{lr} is U-shaped. Per-unit long-run total costs first decline because of economies of scale, and then rise because of diseconomies of scale. MC_{lr}, goes through the bottom of AC_{lr}. MC_{lr} is below AC_{lr} when AC_{lr} is falling and above AC_{lr} when AC_{lr} is rising. The long-run curves assume that the firm has adjusted all factors of production, including previously fixed factors, so that it produces each output at the lowest possible cost.

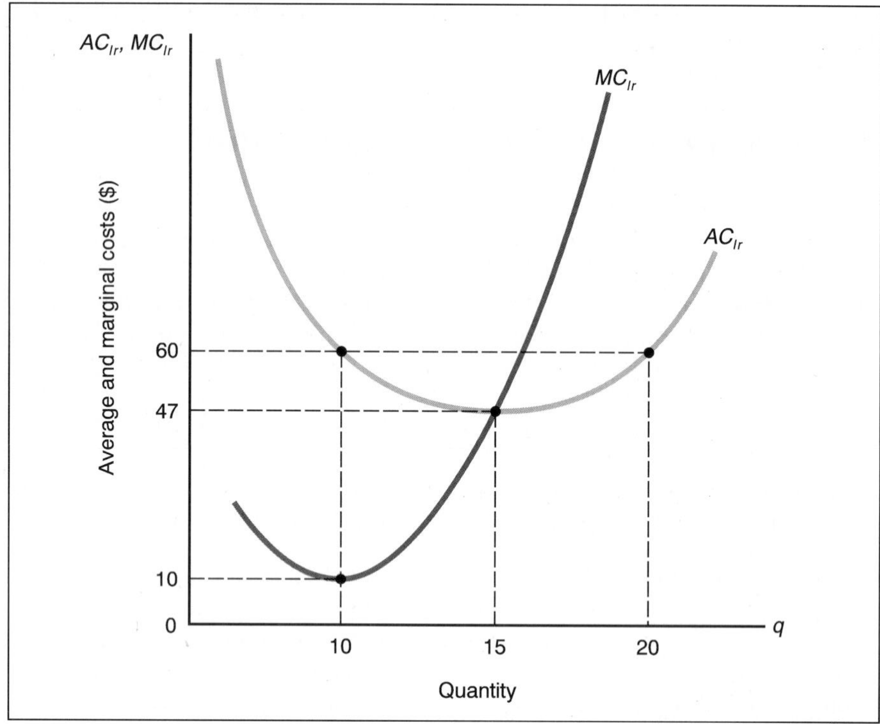

2. MC_{lr} intersects AC_{lr} at its minimum value of $47 (approximately) at $q = 15$. MC_{lr} is less than AC_{lr} at outputs less than 15 and greater than AC_{lr} at outputs greater than 15. The output at which the long-run marginal and long-run average cost curves intersect is of particular interest because it is the **minimum efficient scale of operation (MES)** of the firm. The MES is the output at which long-run economies of scale are fully exhausted and long-run diseconomies of scale are about to begin. Alternatively, the MES is the level of output that minimizes the average cost of production (cost per unit) in the long run.[2] When firms produce at the MES, they supply their output to the market at the lowest possible total cost, since cost per unit is at a minimum. Their scale of operation is efficient because they use the least possible amount of society's scarce resources for the amount of output supplied.

MINIMUM EFFICIENT SCALE OF OPERATION (MES)

The minimum of the long-run average cost curve; alternatively, the output at which economies of scale end and diseconomies of scale begin.

SHORT-RUN AND LONG-RUN AVERAGE COST CURVES Short-run total and short-run average costs tend to be greater than long-run total and long-run

[2]Relating the MES to the point of intersection on our graph requires some manipulation. At the MES the long-run total cost curve exhibits constant returns to scale. The elasticity of total cost with respect to output equals 1, or $\%\Delta TC/\%\Delta q = 1$. To express the elasticity in terms of marginal and average cost, rewrite the percentage changes as

$$(\Delta TC/TC)/(\Delta q/q) = 1$$

Rearranging terms,

$$(\Delta TC/\Delta q)/(TC/q) = MC_{lr}/AC_{lr} = 1$$

Therefore, $MC_{lr} = AC_{lr}$ at the MES.

average costs are because firms cannot vary their fixed factors of production in the short run to reduce their costs of production. Our hypothetical cost data reflect this cost disadvantage in the short run. Compare *SRTC* in Table 13.2 (second column) with *LRTC* in Table 13.3 (second column). Short-run total cost is higher at all outputs except $q = 7$ and $q = 8$.

The short-run cost disadvantage arises because firms may be caught using the wrong level of the fixed factors of production. Suppose that the firm has minimized the cost of producing its output by combining its factors of production according to the least-cost production rule of Chapter 11. Suddenly market conditions change, and the firm wants to increase or decrease its output. It can add or release variable factors of production, such as labor and materials, in order to change its output, but it cannot vary its fixed factors of production, such as capital. As a result, the firm is stuck with the wrong amount of capital at the new level of output for the duration of the short run. Once the short run becomes the long run, the firm can add or release capital and produce the new output at the lowest possible cost. Until then, short-run total and short-run average costs are higher than long-run total and long-run average costs are at the new level of output.

Firms are always in the short run in the sense that the short-run cost curves represent their *actual* costs of production. The long-run cost curves define the *limit* of how low the costs of production can possibly be at any given output. The limit is reached if the firm is producing its output in the short run with the same combination of all its factors of production that it would use in the long run. Only in this case are the short-run costs of production equal to the long-run costs of production, including total, average, and marginal costs.

Refer back to our short-run analysis of firms in a declining market. The firms broke even in the short run at a price of $59, producing 12 units of output. However, $59 is not the long-run break-even price for the firm. It is just the break-even price in the short run for the given amount of capital in place.

If the price were to remain at $59, firms would change the amount of capital in the long run to reduce their costs. Ultimately they would produce the output at which $P = MC_{lr}$ ($= MC_{sr}$ with the new capital stock) after adjusting for the right amount of capital and would be able to make a profit. According to Table 13.3, MC_{lr} increases to $59 somewhere between 16 and 17 units. Suppose that the firms choose $q = 16$. AC_{lr} at $q = 16$ is only $48 with the new capital stock, less than the price of $59, so the firms can make a profit in the long run. Total revenue is $944 ($59 · 16 = $944). Long-run total cost is $762 (from Table 13.3). Therefore, a price of $59 yields a profit of $182 ($944 − $762 = $182) in the long run. In this case, $59 is not a long-run break-even price.

The appendix to Chapter 13 explores the relationship between short-run and long-run costs of production in more detail. At this point we want to move on to the process of entry and exit, which is a hallmark of competitive markets in the long run.

Entry and Exit

Unfortunately for our firms the price will not remain at $59, or at any other profitable level, in the long run. The entry (or exit) of firms always tends to drive competitive prices to the long-run break-even point.

In analyzing the effects of entry and exit we will assume that long-run factor adjustments occur prior to entry or exit, so that short- and long-run average and marginal costs are equal at the output currently being supplied to the market. This assumption allows us to represent any one firm's costs using only AC_{lr} and MC_{lr}. We will also assume that *all* firms, both existing firms and new entrants, have the same costs of production—the costs given in Table 13.3.

Since the entry of new firms into a competitive industry occurs whenever the industry is profitable, let's begin with a market situation in which each of our 1,000 firms is making a profit. Suppose that the equilibrium price has settled at $73 long enough so that each of our 1,000 firms has adjusted its fixed factors and is producing on its long-run cost curves. The best-profit output is $q = 17$, the output at which $P = MC_{lr}$ ($= MC_{sr}$, assuming firms have adjusted their capital for an output of 17 units). Therefore, the total quantity supplied to the market is 17,000 units. The industry is profitable at that price. Total revenue for each firm is $1,241 ($73 · 17 = $1,241). Total cost is $835 (from Table 13.3). So each firm makes a profit of $406 ($1,241 − $835 = $406).

A market situation in which perfectly competitive firms make a profit cannot persist for very long. Remember that the cost of capital, the return available on investments generally outside the industry, is built into long-run total cost. The existence of profit means that the owners of these firms are making a return on their capital greater than the returns available to them, and to other investors, outside the industry. Other investors see this and want to enter this industry. They are able to enter because there are no barriers to entry in perfect competition. The entry of new firms increases overall market supply and puts downward pressure on price.

Figure 13.7 illustrates the process of entry triggered by industry profit. The initial market situation prior to entry is given by the intersection of D and S^0 in Figure 13.7(b). $Q_e = 17{,}000$, and $P_e = \$73$. Note that S^0 is the *short-run* market supply curve, the sum of the firms' *short-run* marginal cost curves. The sum of the firms' long-run marginal cost curves is not a relevant market concept, as the example will illustrate. However, MC_{sr} does equal MC_{lr} at the level of output actually supplied, assuming that firms have correctly adjusted capital to that output.

Turning to Figure 13.7(a), each firm produces $q = 17$, at the intersection of d_f^0 (= $73) and MC_{lr} ($= MC_{sr}$ at $q = 17$), and each earns a profit of $406, equal to the area *abcd*.

As new firms enter, the industry supply curve shifts to the right, to S^1, S^2, and S^3 in the graph, putting continual downward pressure on price. As price falls, each firm reduces its output and earns less profit. For example, when industry supply reaches S^2, the equilibrium price has fallen to $56. The best profit output for each firm declines to $q = 16$, the intersection of d_f^2 (= $56) and MC_{lr} ($= MC_{sr}$ at $q = 16$, with the proper adjustment of capital). Total revenue for each firm is now only $896 ($56 · 16 = $896). Total cost is $762 (from Table 13.3). Profit has fallen to $134 ($896 − $762 = $134).

Entry continues until market supply increases to S^3, driving price down to the break-even point, $47 for our cost data. With the equilibrium price at $47, the intersection of d_f^3 and MC_{lr} ($= MC_{sr}$ at that output) occurs at the minimum of AC_{lr}. Each firm produces $q = 15$ and earns zero profit. Investors can no longer earn a larger return on their capital in this industry than they can elsewhere. The incentive to enter the industry ends, and the industry has achieved its final long-run equilibrium.

Notice that industry output is much greater than when price was $73, even though each firm has reduced its output from 17 to 15, simply because there

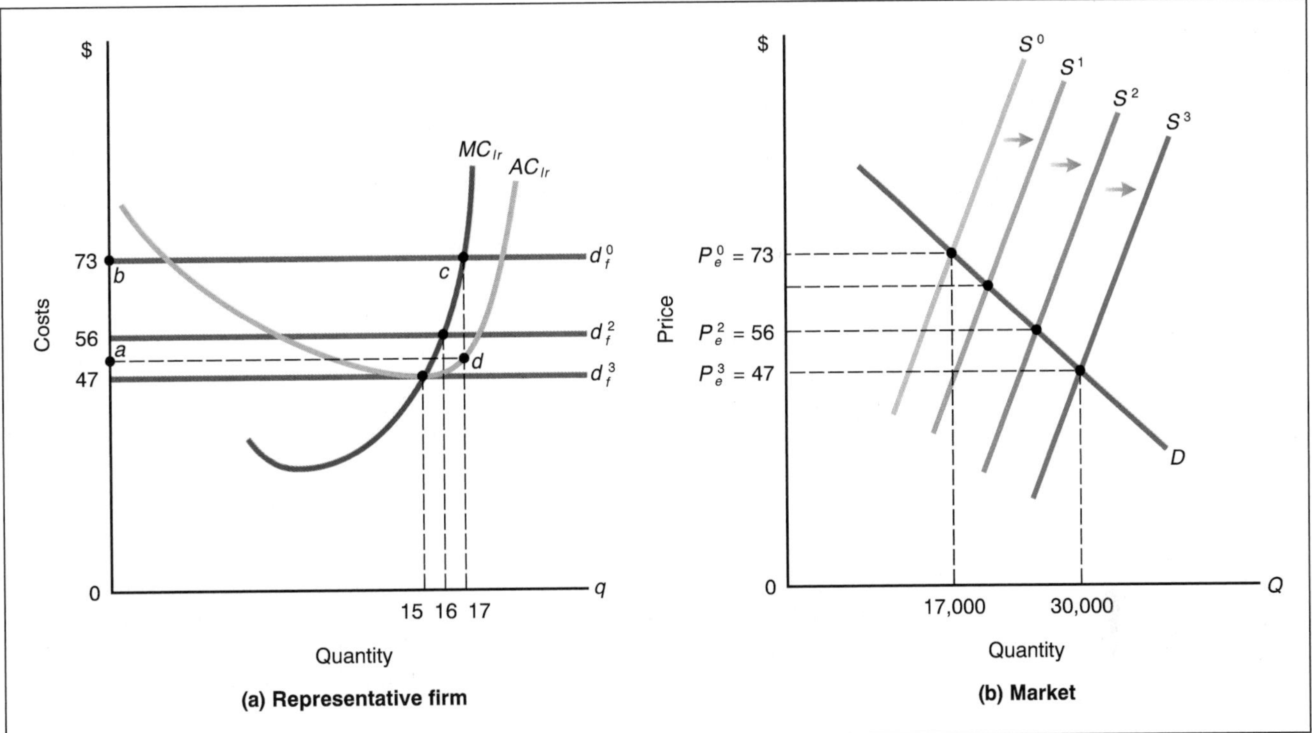

FIGURE 13.7

Adjustment to the Long-Run Equilibrium

The market is initially in short-run equilibrium at the intersection of S^0 and D in Figure 13.7(b). The equilibrium price is $73 and the equilibrium quantity is 17,000. Each of the 1000 representative firms pictured in Figure 13.7(a) produces 17 units, at the intersection of d_f^0 and MC_{lr}, and makes a profit equal to the rectangular area *abcd*. The existence of profits induces entry into the industry, and the market supply curve in Figure 13.7(b) shifts out from S^0 to S^1, etc., until it reachs S^3. The equilibrium price is $47 at the intersection of S^3 and D. The best any firm can do is break even, making zero profits, by producing 15 units at the intersection of d_f^3 and MC_{lr}. The total market quantity has risen to 30,000 since there are now 2,000 firms in the market. Entry stops, and the market is in long-run equilibrium, once the price falls to the firms' long-run break-even point of $47.

are now many more firms in the industry. The final long-run equilibrium quantity, Q_e, depends on how many new firms are needed to drive the price down to $47. Figure 13.7 assumes that the long-run equilibrium contains 2,000 firms, so that $Q_e = 30{,}000$ units ($15 \cdot 2{,}000 = 30{,}000$).

Price is driven to the break-even point from either direction. Loss induces exit just as surely as profit induces entry, and for the same reason—investors want to earn the highest return possible on their capital. The scenario of exit restoring the break-even price is entirely symmetric to the entry scenario. At any price less than $47, firms are experiencing losses. A loss means that the owners are earning a lower return on their capital in this industry than they could earn elsewhere. They want out. Some firms begin to exit the industry as their owners find the better investment opportunities elsewhere. With fewer firms, market supply decreases (shifts to the left), putting upward pressure on price. The market price rises to the break-even price, at which point the incentive to exit the industry ends. The market is once again in long-run equilibrium.

To summarize, the long-run equilibrium in perfect competition has two distinct characteristics:

1. zero (economic) profit for firms
2. price equal to the minimum of long-run average cost (In effect, price is determined only by cost in the long run. The long-run equilibrium price has to be $47 in our example *because* the minimum unit cost of production is $47 in the long run.)

Both results depend on the process of entry and exit. As such, they underscore how important the profit motive is to the operation of the free market system.

REFLECTION: What is an example of an industry in which rapid entry is occurring? In which exit is occurring?

The zero-profit result is the more general of the two characteristics. Profit tends toward zero over time in almost any industry without significant barriers to entry (and exit). The market structure need not be perfectly competitive. Price equal to *minimum* AC_{lr} is unique to perfect competition, however. It depends on the price-taking behavior of perfectly competitive firms, that each firm's demand curve is perfectly elastic at the equilibrium market price. Nonetheless, it is suggestive of what happens in other market structures. As a general rule, prices are closer to minimum long-run average costs the freer entry and exit are.

THE EQUALIZING TENDENCY OF COMPETITION The natural long-run tendency toward break-even production highlights another property of competitive markets that we first met in Chapter 9, the equalizing tendency of the competitive process. In Chapter 9 the issue was what wage workers can expect to earn in the marketplace. We saw that if labor markets are perfectly competitive, identical workers receive the same level of satisfaction no matter what their occupation. Any differences in wages they might earn are equalizing differences. They exactly compensate for the relative attractiveness of each occupation—whether the job is especially pleasant, tedious, or hazardous; requires extensive formal training; and the like. The same equalizing principle applies to the returns to capital. If all markets were perfectly competitive, investors could expect to earn the same rate of return on their funds over the long run no matter where they placed them. Any lasting differences in returns would be equalizing differences, compensating for differences in risk. Most investors are willing to invest in highly risky ventures only if they receive higher rates of return on average than investors receive on safer investments.

This is not to say that competitive firms never make a profit. The owners of small firms in highly competitive market environments can make enormous returns on their capital if they develop a new product that consumers like or a new technology that reduces their costs of production. These returns can only be temporary, however—a short-run phenomenon. The entry into the industry of new investors who imitate the idea is sure to follow, lowering prices and competing away the profits over the long run.

HAND CALCULATORS The introduction of hand calculators in the early 1970s is a good case in point. In 1971 the simplest calculator that performed essentially only the four arithmetic functions—addition, subtraction, multiplication, and division—cost around $80.00 (well over $300 in today's prices). By the end of the decade, the price had fallen to around $10. Part of the price decrease was due to cost-saving advances in technology, such as more highly integrated circuitry, which dramatically reduced assembly costs. But a good part of the price reduction resulted from the competitive effect of entry. Only a handful of firms were producing calculators in 1971, whereas the industry contained dozens of firms by the end of the decade. The market became so saturated that some of those firms eventually dropped out; the market price had fallen below their break-even points.

There is an important lesson here. If you want to make a killing in the competitive marketplace, having an idea for a product that will appeal to consumers is not enough. You must be the *first* one to enter the marketplace with the idea. If you let others test the market before you enter, you may well be too late. Never underestimate how quickly investors flock to profitable opportunities. Such is the nature of the competitive struggle for profit—people with good ideas gain a toehold only to see imitators compete their advantages away. Staying ahead of the game requires one good idea after another—and the courage to be among the first to take the plunge into new markets.

THE STOCK MARKET The stock market provides another good example of the equalizing tendency of competitive markets. Here is why you cannot reasonably expect to make a killing in the stock market over the long run.

Suppose that you devise a sure-fire method of buying when stock prices are low and selling when they are high. You will begin to make your fortune, but only for awhile. Word of your success will spread quickly through the market, and other investors will study the pattern of your purchases and sales. Once they learn your method and follow it, your run is over. Now everyone will want to buy when you want to buy and sell when you want to sell. Your sure-fire method becomes a formula for buying high and selling low, hardly a formula for success. In effect, the other investors have competed away whatever advantages your method enjoyed, just as surely as investors compete away profitable opportunities in any competitive market.

CURRENT ISSUE: The Securities and Exchange Commission watches closely over the financial markets to ensure that investors do not buy and sell stocks and other financial securities based on "insider information" about companies' prospects. Insider information is information that is available to only a few people. It gives the people who have it an unfair advantage over other investors that they can turn into a guaranteed profit.

Studies of the stock market uphold what the theory of competitive markets predicts. No one method of selecting stocks emerges as the best method. In fact, selecting stocks at random appears to be just about as effective as using any systematic method of selection over the long haul. So when you are ready to take the plunge into the stock market, tape the stock market listings from your newspaper to the wall, step back 10 paces, blindfold yourself, toss darts at the listings, and buy whatever stocks the darts land on. This "method" is probably as good as any other.

The Long-Run Market Supply Curve

The short-run and long-run market supply curves are very different concepts. The short-run market supply curve is the sum of the firms' short-run marginal cost curves (above the minimum of average variable cost). The long-run market supply curve is *not* the sum of the firms' long-run marginal cost curves, however. A **long-run market supply curve** indicates the aggregate quantity supplied to the market at each price, given that the market has reached its full long-run equilibrium. As such, the long-run market supply curve incorporates both long-run phenomena, the adjustment of previously fixed factors and the entry or exit of firms.

MARKET SUPPLY CURVE

—**Long run**—the total quantity supplied by the firms in the market at each price, when each firm is producing at the MES, the minimum of its long-run average cost.

The long-run marginal cost curve is an individual firm's long-run supply curve (above the minimum of AC_{lr}) in that it shows how much output the firm is willing to supply in the long run at each market price. Why, then, can these individual supply curves not be summed to produce the long-run market supply curve? The answer is that each firm's long-run marginal cost curve incorporates the adjustment of previously fixed factors, but not the entry or exit of firms. Only one price, the break-even price, can maintain itself as a long-run equilibrium price after entry or exit occurs. Firms know this and would be reluctant to lock themselves into an amount of fixed capital other than the amount that would be appropriate for the output they intend to produce at the

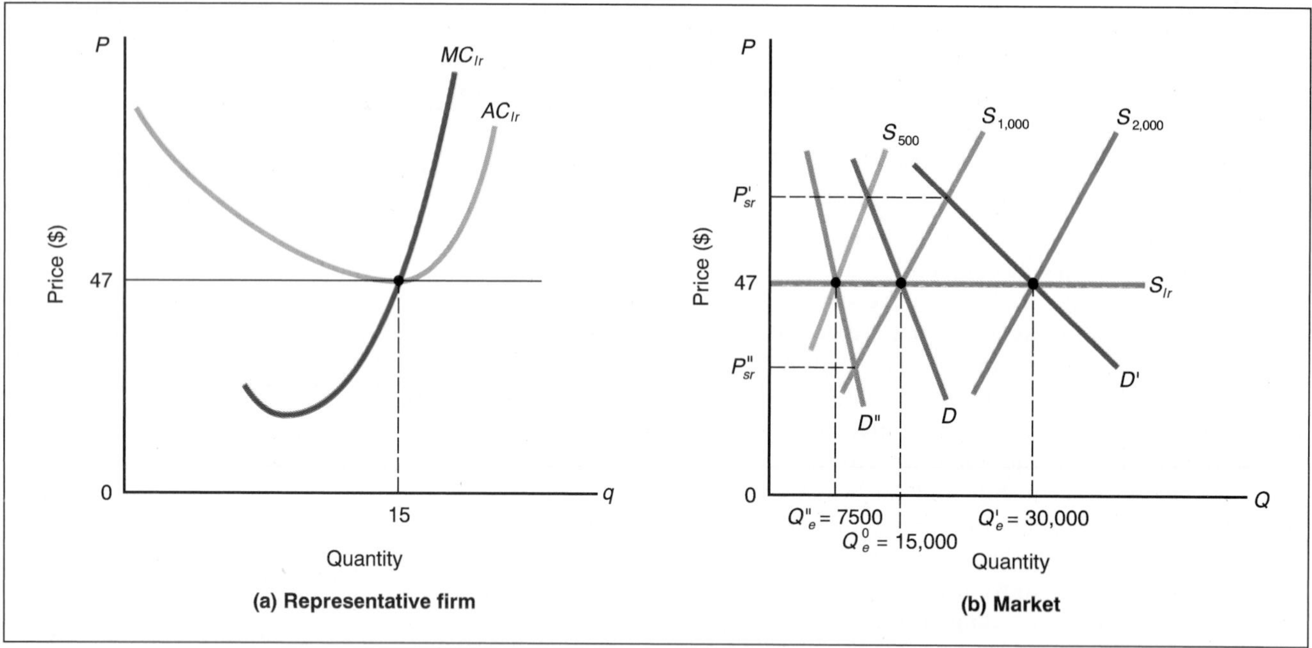

FIGURE 13.8

The Long-Run Supply Curve

The market is initially in a long-run equilibrium in Figure 13.8(b) at a price of \$47 and a quantity of 15,000 units, with each of 1000 firms pictured in Figure 13.8(a) supplying 15 units to the market. An increase in demand from D to D' increases price to P'_{sr} in the short run, at the intersection of D' and S_{1000}. The profits at the higher price induce entry of new firms until the equilibrium price returns to \$47, the break-even point. The new long-run equilibrium quantity is 30,000, with 2000 firms in the industry each producing 15 units. A decrease in demand from D to D'' decreases price to P''_{sr} in the short run, at the intersection of D'' and S_{1000}. The losses at the lower price cause exit of firms until the equilibrium price returns to \$47, the break-even point. The new long-run equilibrium quantity is 7,500, with 500 firms in the industry each producing 15 units. Points on the long-run supply curve S_{lr} in Figure 13.8(b) assume that entry and exit of firms has driven the price to the zero-profit, break-even point of \$47.

break-even price. Hence, only that one break-even point on each firm's long-run marginal cost curve, not the entire marginal cost curve, is relevant to the overall market supply in the final long-run equilibrium.

In terms of our example, firms would not really adjust capital to an output level of 17 when price is \$73 or to an output of 16 when price is \$56. They know that entry is bound to occur and that price will soon be driven to the break-even price of \$47. Therefore, adjusting capital to production at 15 units of output in the long run is the only sensible strategy. In other words, the adjustment of previously fixed factors and entry or exit occur simultaneously as the market adjusts to its long-run equilibrium. The example separated the two events only to distinguish them analytically.

Figure 13.8 illustrates the derivation of the long-run market supply curve. The derivation relies on the adjustment process described in Figure 13.7. Suppose that our industry of 1,000 firms is initially in long-run equilibrium at the break-even price of \$47 when the market demand curve is at D. The total market supply, output Q_e, is 15,000 units, with each firm supplying 15 units. So the point (Q_e = 15,000, P_e = \$47) is one point on the long-run supply curve, S_{lr}. The supply curve $S_{1,000}$ is a *short-run* market supply curve, the sum of the 1,000 firms' *short-run* marginal cost curves.

Suppose that demand increases from D to D'. Price rises temporarily to P'_{sr} in the short run. With price above the break-even price, each firm is now earning a profit. Other investors see that the industry is profitable, and new firms enter. Assuming that new and existing firms have the same costs, as above, entry continues until the price is driven back down to the break-even price of \$47. If, as in our previous example, 2,000 firms are needed to restore the break-even price, the new long-run equilibrium output is 30,000 units, with each firm producing 15 units. The new short-run market supply curve is the

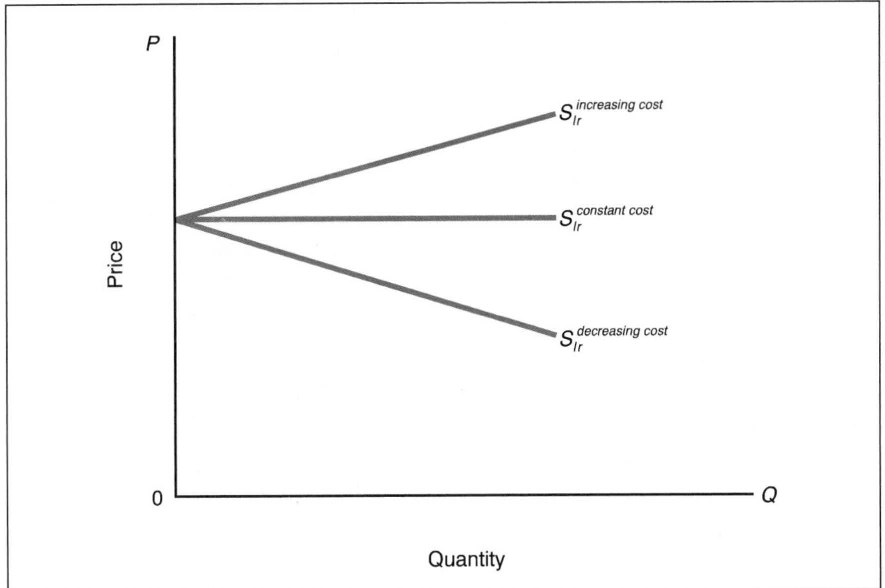

FIGURE 13.9

Constant, Increasing, and Decreasing Cost Industries

The figure represents the three cases of constant, increasing, and decreasing cost industries. In a constant cost industry, expansion and contraction of output has no effect on the minimum of firms' long-run average costs. The long-run supply curve, $S^{\text{constant cost}}$, is horizontal, perfectly elastic. In an increasing cost industry, expansion of output increases firms' average costs, usually bcause the bidding for more resources drives up factor prices. The long-run supply curve, $S^{\text{increasing cost}}$, is upward sloping. This is the most common case. In a decreasing cost industry, expansion of output decreases firms' average costs, possibly because the cost of a key input declines. The long-run supply curve, $S^{\text{decreasing cost}}$, is downward sloping. This case is unusual.

line $S_{2,000}$. The point (Q_e = 30,000, P_e = \$47) is a second point on the long-run market supply curve, S_{lr}.

Similarly, a decrease in demand from D to D'' temporarily decreases price to P''_{sr}. With price below the long-run break-even price, each of the 1,000 firms incurs a loss. The owners can earn a higher return to their capital elsewhere. Firms exit, and the quantity supplied decreases, putting upward pressure on price. Exit continues until price rises to the break-even price of \$47. Figure 13.8 assumes that price can be \$47 along D'' only if the number of firms declines to 500. The new long-run equilibrium output Q_e is 7,500 units, with each firm producing 15 units ($15 \cdot 500 = 7{,}500$). The new short-run market supply curve is S_{500}. The point (Q_e = 7,500, P_e = \$47) is a third point on S_{lr}.

CONSTANT, INCREASING, AND DECREASING COSTS The long-run market supply curve is horizontal, that is, perfectly elastic, at the break-even price of \$47. The industry is said to be a **constant cost industry** because the minimum of AC_{lr} remains constant at \$47 no matter how much output is supplied to the market. This results from the simplifying assumption that new firms can always enter by replicating how existing firms produce without any effect whatsoever on long-run cost.

CONSTANT COST INDUSTRY

An industry in which the minimum long-run average cost of the firms remains constant no matter how much output is supplied to the market, so that the long-run market supply curve is horizontal.

In fact, constant cost industries are the exception, not the rule. Empirical studies of competitive markets verify that long-run supply curves are often far more elastic than are short-run supply curves, but they are seldom perfectly elastic. Instead, most industries are **increasing cost industries.** Their supply curves are upward sloping, such as $S_{lr}^{\text{increasing cost}}$ in Figure 13.9.

INCREASING COST INDUSTRY

An industry in which the minimum long-run average cost of the firms increases as output supplied to the market increases, so that the long-run market supply curve is upward sloping.

A case in point is a well-known study comparing the short- and long-run supply elasticities of 19 vegetables. The study found that only one vegetable, green snap beans, has a long-run supply elasticity that is virtually infinite (perfectly elastic). One other vegetable, kale, has essentially identical long- and short-run price elasticities (0.23 versus 0.20). The long-run supply curves of the remaining 17 vegetables are upward sloping, with long-run supply elasticities anywhere from 2 to 23 times larger than the short-run elasticities. The long-run supply elasticities range in value from 0.16 (lettuce) to 4.70 (spinach).[3]

The long-run equilibrium price is still driven to the break-even point in increasing-cost industries. The difference from the constant cost case is that the minimum of AC_{lr} increases as new firms enter the industry, so that price cannot return to its original value as quantity supplied increases. Instead, it settles on a higher, break-even equilibrium level.

Cost increases with expansion are certainly to be expected. In agriculture, for example, farmers plant their best land first. As price rises, they bring increasingly poorer land into cultivation. Similarly, existing farms presumably own the best land. If price increases induce the entry of new farms, these farms will probably have poorer land on average than do the existing farms. The cost of producing a given amount of output is higher on the poorer land. As a result, the long-run price must be permanently higher to support larger supplies in the long run.

Increasing cost is not unique to agriculture. Whenever any industry expands, it must bid resources away from other uses. Increasing demand for factors tends to increase their prices, and higher factor prices mean higher production costs. For instance, when the Organization of Petroleum Exporting Countries (OPEC) engineered dramatic oil price increases during the 1970s, oil companies throughout the world scrambled to find new reserves of oil that they could bring to the market. The newer reserves were less accessible than were existing reserves, requiring much higher drilling costs per barrel of crude oil. Also, the demand for people trained in geology skyrocketed. By the end of the decade college graduates with majors in geology were being hired right out of college for salaries approaching $30,000, more than double that of most of their classmates. When oil prices collapsed in the 1980s, some of the newer pools of reserves became unprofitable. Firms supplied crude oil only from their cheaper, more accessible reserves. The market for geology majors also collapsed along with oil prices. Unit costs and prices fell as firms moved back down their long-run supply curves.

The computer industry provides still another example. In the late 1980s the rapid expansion of computer sales to home and business outpaced the supply of silicon chips. The price of the chips rose sharply and increased the average cost of producing the computers.

These are not isolated examples. Prices of labor and materials often increase as an industry expands and decrease as an industry contracts, especially if the factors are highly specialized, as with mineral reserves, geologists, and silicon chips. Only industries producing simple products with readily available, unspecialized resources are likely to approach the constant cost case. Even in those industries, though, long-run supply curves are usually somewhat upward sloping, not perfectly elastic.

Expanding industries might also suffer from a phenomenon called external diseconomies that drive up costs. External diseconomies refer to actions by some firms that adversely affect the production functions of other firms. A

[3]M. Nerlove and W. Addison, "Statistical Estimation of Long-run Elasticities of Supply and Demand," *Journal of Farm Economics* (November 1958).

classic example is fishing. As more and more boats fish the same waters and deplete the fish population, they make it more difficult for all boats to catch fish. The entry of new boats changes the underlying production function for catching fish; the same amounts of resources and effort are less and less productive.

Fishing is somewhat distinctive, however, because examples of external diseconomies are not so common. By and large, long-run supply curves are upward sloping because firms bid up factor prices as an industry expands.

A **decreasing cost industry** with a declining long-run supply curve, such as $S_{lr}^{\text{decreasing cost}}$ in Figure 13.9, is a theoretical possibility, but highly unlikely. This is so even though average costs do decline over time for many products. The hand calculator is an example, as are computers generally. However, these cost decreases are the result of technological advances that lower production costs at every level of output and that occur independently of whether an industry is expanding or contracting. As such, they represent a continual downward shifting of S_{lr} over time, not a movement along a single declining supply curve as required for the decreasing cost case. Decreases in minimum long-run average costs caused by the expansion of an industry, *other things equal*, are difficult to imagine.

DECREASING COST INDUSTRY

An industry in which the minimum long-run average cost of the firms decreases as output supplied to the market increases, so that the long-run market supply curve is downward sloping.

DO COSTS DIFFER AMONG FIRMS? Before leaving the long-run supply curve a comment is in order regarding our assumption that all firms have the same costs. This is not an assumption made for convenience; it is the correct assumption. All firms in a competitive industry do have the same economic costs, even though some firms may appear to have a cost advantage because they happen to own some highly productive resources. Understanding why these costs are identical is a good test of your understanding of economic cost as opportunity cost.

Figure 13.10 depicts an agricultural market consisting of two types of farms, one with good land, the other with poor land. The long-run equilibrium price,

FIGURE 13.10

All Farms Have the Same Opportunity Costs of Production

The market equilibrium is (Q_e, P_e), at the intersection of the market supply and demand curves S and D in Figure 13.11(c). The price P_e is just high enough to allow the farms with poor land in Figure 13.11(b) to break even and earn a normal return on the land. The land on the good farms in Figure 13.11(a) earns an economic rent, or profit, equal to the rectangular area aP_ebc. The profit is an opportunity cost of farming the good land because a farmer could rent the land for this amount to some other farmer. Therefore, the true opportunity cost of producing on the good land is given by the dotted average cost curve AC_{lr}, and both farms have the same opportunity costs of production.

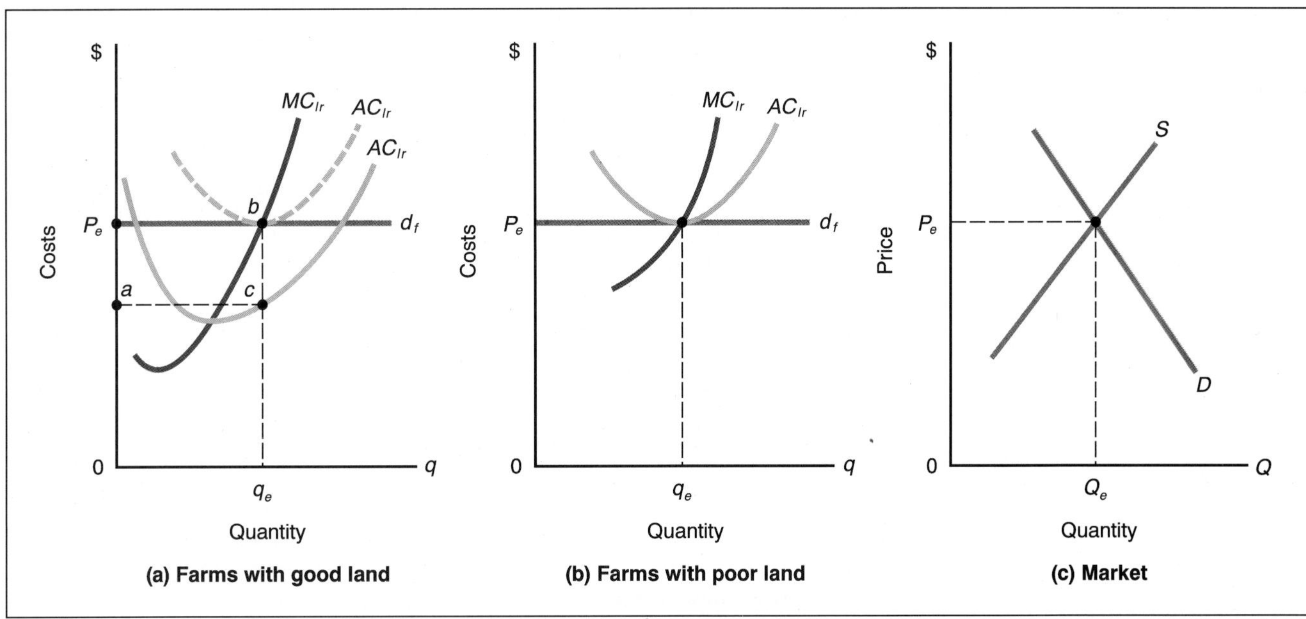

P_e, determined by the intersection of the market supply and the market demand curves [Figure 13.10(c)] is just high enough to allow the farms with poor land to break even [Figure 13.10(b)]. The farms with good land [Figure 13.10(a)] have a lower break-even point and appear to make an economic profit equal to the area of rectangle aP_ebc. However, the rectangular area is not a true economic profit; it is part of the opportunity cost of operating these farms. The reason is that the farmers who own the good land have the option of farming it themselves or renting it out to others. If they were to rent the land, they would receive a rental payment exactly equal to the area of rectangle aP_ebc because everyone knows that the good land is that much more valuable. Therefore, the opportunity cost of farming the land themselves has increased by that amount, and their average *economic* cost is properly represented by the dotted line AC_{lr}, not by the solid line AC_{lr}. All farms have the same economic cost, even though owning the good land is an advantage. The rectangular area aP_ebc is simultaneously a rent to the land over and above the rent required to keep it in farming and an opportunity cost to whomever chooses to farm the land.

The same point applies to firms whose advantage lies in employing particularly talented managers. The managers' skills would soon be known to all other firms in a competitive market environment. Unless firms pay these managers the full value of the advantages they bring to the firms, other firms will bid them away for that amount. Only the managers can gain from possessing special managerial talents in a competitive market; the owners of firms cannot.

For example, Lee Iacocca was generally credited with rescuing Chrysler Corporation from the brink of bankruptcy, and he earned a multimillion dollar annual salary from Chrysler as a result. Chrysler stockholders did not have the option of retaining his services for a few hundred thousand dollars and pocketing for themselves the additional millions of dollars his skills brought to the company.

THE NORMATIVE PROPERTIES OF COMPETITIVE MARKETS

The development of the long-run supply curve completes the analysis of perfectly competitive product markets that began in Chapters 5 through 8. Throughout we have stressed two issues above all others: (1) how prices and profit serve as the signals that guide the allocation of scarce resources and (2) how competitive markets promote society's twin goals of efficiency and equity. Chapter 13 concludes by summarizing the key points related to each of these issues.

Prices, Profit, and Resource Allocation

A primary test of any economic system is how well it responds to the desires of individuals. Scarce resources must flow toward products in greater demand and away from products in lesser demand. A market economy relies on prices and profit to allocate resources in response to individuals' desires, and we have seen that prices and profit perform that task extremely well when markets are perfectly competitive. The complete scenario is represented in Figure 13.11, which shows how a perfectly competitive market, operating according to the Laws of Supply and Demand, responds to a change in consumer tastes.

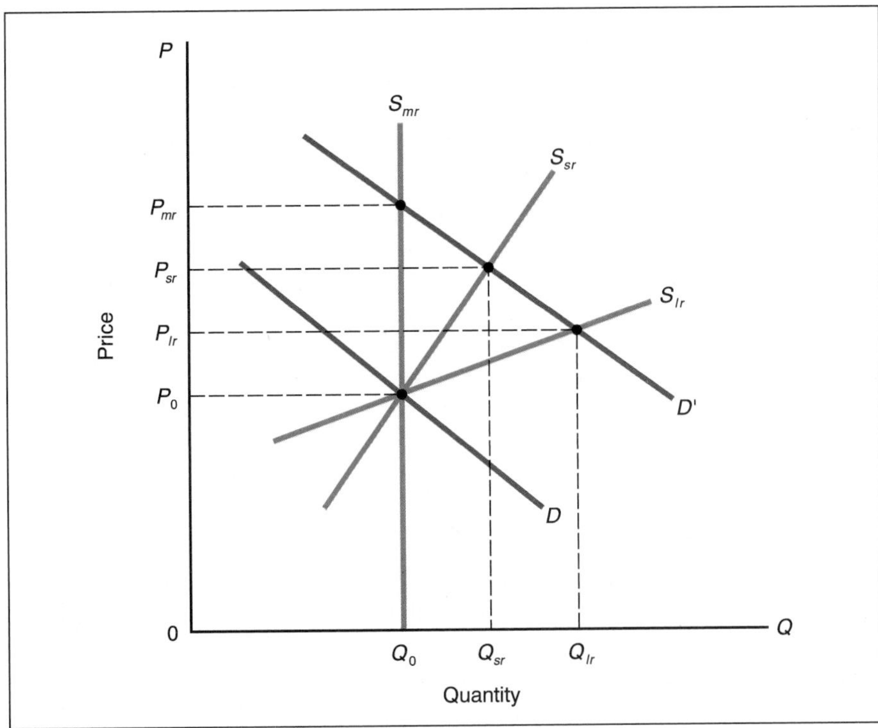

FIGURE 13.11

How Competitive Markets Respond to an Increase in Demand

The figure shows how prices and profits guide firms to respond to an increase in demand. The market is initially in long-run equilibrium at (Q_0, P_0), at the intersection of D and the three supply curves. Then demand increases from D to D'. Immediately after the increase in demand, in the momentary run, firms cannot increase output and the momentary supply curve, S_{mr}, is perfectly inelastic. The price rises to P_{mr}, at the intersection of D' and S_{mr}. The higher price is profitable, so that in the short-run firms move along their short-run supply curves. Output increases to Q_{sr} and price falls to P_{sr} in the short-run, at the intersection of D' and S_{sr}. The industry is still profitable, so new firms enter the industry and output increases along the long-run supply curve, S_{lr}. The final long-run equilibrium is (Q_{lr},P_{lr}), at the intersection of D' and S_{lr}. Production ultimately increases from Q_0 to Q_{lr} in response to the increase in demand.

The equilibrium quantity and the equilibrium price are originally at (Q_0, P_0), at the intersection of the market demand curve, D, and the various supply curves. The market is in long-run equilibrium along the long-run supply curve, S_{lr}, so that the firms in the industry are just breaking even. The industry exhibits increasing costs—S_{lr} is upward sloping.

Suppose that consumers' tastes then change in favor of the product. The market demand shifts upward and to the right to D'. The market responds in three distinct stages—the momentary run, the short run, and the long run:

MOMENTARY RUN

The time period during which changing market conditions catch the firms by surprise and they are unable to change their supply of output to the market.

1. *The momentary run:* The change in tastes at first catches the firms by surprise, and they are unable to increase supply immediately. The supply curve for the moment, S_{mr}, is perfectly inelastic at the existing quantity, Q_0. The price rises to P_{mr} along S_{mr} as consumers bid for Q_0. The market equilibrium settles at (Q_0, P_{mr}) for the duration of the momentary run.
2. *The short run:* At the higher price, P_{mr}, firms that were previously breaking even now make a profit. P_{mr} is also greater than their short-run marginal cost at Q_0, since MC_{sr} is given by the short-run supply curve, S_{sr}. Therefore, the firms can make an even larger profit if they expand production to the output at which price equals MC_{sr}. They bid labor, materials, and other *variable* factors of production away from other uses and increase the quantity supplied to the marketplace. The increased output puts downward pressure on the market price. The market equilibrium settles at (Q_{sr}, P_{sr}) for the duration of the short run.
3. *The long run:* Once the short run gives way to the long run, the firms are able to bid previously fixed factors away from other uses in order to lower their cost of production. With lowered production costs, P_{sr} is above long-run marginal cost, so firms can make even greater profits by expanding

output further. In addition, new firms enter the industry as other investors want to share in the profits being made at P_{sr}. The new firms bring even more scarce resources into the industry, increasing supplies and putting further downward pressure on the market price. Eventually the market returns to long-run equilibrium at (Q_{lr}, P_{lr}) along S_{lr}. All firms are once again just breaking even, ending the incentive to enter the industry.

Overall, the consumers' new-found desire for the product elicits an increase in quantity supplied from Q_0 to Q_{lr}. No one has to direct firms to allocate more resources to the product and increase supply. They are entirely driven by the profit motive as changes in prices generate profitable opportunities for increasing production. The interaction of prices and profit, therefore, guides the allocation of scarce resources over time in the appropriate manner.

Efficiency and Equity

Responding to consumers' desires is not enough. An economic system must also promote society's twin goals of efficiency and equity. Perfect competition does exceedingly well on this score as well. Competitive prices, in equilibrium, settle on values that are both efficient and equitable.

Under perfect competition, the equilibrium price always equals the short-run marginal cost. In the long run, the equilibrium price also equals the minimum of the long-run average cost (and the long-run marginal cost).

(always)	(in long-run equilibrium)
$P_e = MC_{sr}$	$P_e = \text{minimum } AC_{lr}$

These are the values required for allocational efficiency, production or technical efficiency, and equity.

ALLOCATIONAL EFFICIENCY

Achieved in a product market when the quantity exchanged in the market maximizes the net value of producing and consuming a good; the market test is price equal to short-run marginal cost.

ALLOCATIONAL EFFICIENCY **Allocational efficiency** in market exchange requires that the exchange maximize the net value from producing and consuming each good. The market test for allocational efficiency is $P = MC_{sr}$. Chapter 7 gave the reason why.

To review briefly, net value is maximized when the value to some consumer of the last exchanged equals the cost to some firm of producing the last unit, or

$$MV_{\text{consumption}} = MC_{\text{production}}$$

The competitive price links consumers and producers exactly as required.

Every consumer equates price and marginal value in consumption, where marginal value is defined as an opportunity cost. The last unit purchased at price P_e yields the same level of satisfaction that consumers could obtain from any combination of other goods available to them for the same cost, P_e. Thus, $P_e = MV_{\text{consumption}}$.

On the other side of the exchange, every perfectly competitive firm supplies the output at which $P_e = MC_{sr}$. Short-run marginal cost always measures the actual cost of producing the last unit, whether or not the industry is in long-run equilibrium. Thus, $P_e = MC_{\text{production}}$.

Bringing the two sides of the market exchange together, competitive pricing satisfies $MV_{consumption} = MC_{production}$ ($= P_e$), as required for allocational efficiency.

PRODUCTION EFFICIENCY **Production efficiency,** also known as **technical efficiency,** requires that the total quantity supplied to the marketplace use up the least amount of society's scarce resources. The market test for production efficiency is that production at each firm occurs at the minimum efficient scale of operation (MES), the output that minimizes AC_{lr}. With each firm producing at minimum per unit cost, every unit of the total market supply is also produced at minimum per unit cost. Therefore, the total resource cost of supplying the market is also as low as possible. (Production efficiency also requires that firms hire factors of production so as to minimize the costs of producing whatever output they choose to supply. We have been assuming throughout Chapter 13 that firms do minimize production costs by efficiently solving their How problems, as described in Chapter 11.)

Perfectly competitive markets satisfy production efficiency in the long-run equilibrium when the price is driven to the break-even point and P_e = minimum AC_{lr}. Notice, too, that consumers capture all of the cost savings. With P_e = minimum AC_{lr}, they are able to buy the product at the lowest possible price that covers the firms' production costs.

PRODUCTION (TECHNICAL) EFFICIENCY

Achieved when the output supplied to the market uses the least amount of society's scarce resources; the market test is that each firm produces in the long run at the minimum of its long-run average cost curve, the minimum efficient scale of operation (MES).

EQUITY We noted in Chapter 2 that citizens of the United States have long embraced two principles of equity: equality of opportunity and horizontal equity (the equal treatment of equals). Equality of opportunity is a process notion of equity. Horizontal equity is an end-results notion of equity. Yet the two principles are very closely related, since equal opportunity makes equal treatment of equals possible. Perfect competition in product markets promotes both types of equity.

EQUITY

In the context of product markets, the presence of equality of opportunity and horizontal equity; the inability of firms to maintain economic profits in the long run.

EQUALITY OF OPPORTUNITY The market test of **equality of opportunity** is twofold: (1) the absence of barriers to entry or exit and (2) equal access to all relevant market information. Perfect competition necessarily meets these tests because they are defining characteristics of a perfectly competitive market. Under perfect competition everyone does have equal access to all relevant market information, and individuals are always free to pursue whatever opportunities yield them the greatest advantage.

EQUALITY OF OPPORTUNITY

In the context of product markets, all investors have equal access to profitable market opportunities because of the absence of barriers to entry and equal access to all relevant market information.

HORIZONTAL EQUITY The market test of **horizontal equity** in product markets is break-even production in the long run, such that price equals long-run average cost. Perfect competition satisfies horizontal equity in the long-run equilibrium, when P_e = minimum AC_{lr}. Once price reaches the break-even point, all profit is competed away, and investors earn the same rate of return to capital that they can earn anywhere else, standardizing for risk. This strikes people as fair. A dollar of saving channeled into investment is the same no matter who supplies it. Why should one person's dollar of saving earn more than another person's dollar?

Understand that dollars of investment are not treated equally at all times under perfect competition. The market often rewards good ideas with hefty returns and bad ideas with equally hefty losses in the short run. This is per-

HORIZONTAL EQUITY

In the context of product markets, all owners of firms earn the same return to their capital in the long run (standardizing for risk).

fectly okay. After all, profits and losses guide the allocation of scarce resources. The question underlying horizontal equity is whether investors can *maintain* an advantage indefinitely. Horizontal equity applied to markets is inherently a long-run test of equity. All that matters is that equals are eventually treated equally, and that profits are eventually competed away. Perfectly competitive markets pass this test.

The inability of competitive firms to maintain their profits may be a mixed blessing. It leads to the criticism that perfectly competitive product markets might not be conducive to long-run economic growth. The argument, first put forward by Harvard's Joseph Schumpeter in the 1930s, is that firms need a steady stream of profits to finance research and development efforts into new products and production technologies. As we saw in Chapter 2, technological change is the key to long-run economic growth. Schumpeter believed that profitable firms in less competitive market environments are likely to be more technically progressive over time.

Schumpeter's argument is controversial. We will explore the evidence for and against it in Chapter 17. Whatever the truth of the matter, however, one point is beyond contention. Perfect competition does as well as any market structure possibly can in promoting equity and efficiency in product markets at any one point in time. Economists use the four market outcomes of perfect competition summarized in the following Concept Summary table as standards for evaluating all product market outcomes.

CONCEPT SUMMARY

DESIRABLE MARKET OUTCOMES ACHIEVED BY PERFECT COMPETITION

MARKET OUTCOMES	DEFINITION	MARKET TEST
Efficiency		
Allocational efficiency	Maximum net value in exchange	$P = MC_{sr}$
Production (technical) efficiency	Goods supplied at lowest possible resource cost	Production at MES or minimum AC_{lr}
Equity		
Equality of opportunity	Equal access to all market opportunities	Absence of barriers to entry, exit; equal access to all market information
Horizontal equity	Equal treatment of equals in long run	$P = AC_{lr}$; Zero maintained profits

SUMMARY

Chapter 13 completed the analysis of perfect competition begun in Chapters 5 through 8. As such, it provides the groundwork for the analysis of all other market structures in Chapters 14 through 17 because perfect competition sets the standards for efficiency and equity against which all other product markets are judged.

The first section of the chapter reviewed the main points about the operation of perfectly competitive product markets in the short run from Chapters 5 through 8.

1. The market demand curve is the sum of the individual consumers' demand curves. The short-run market supply curve is the sum of the firms' marginal cost curves. The short-run market equilibrium occurs at the intersection of the market demand and the market supply curves.
2. The demand curve for each firm is horizontal, perfectly elastic, at the equilibrium price. The firms are price takers. Each firm supplies the output at which $P_e = MC_{sr}$ in order to maximize profit.

The second section of the chapter described the all-or-none profit test that applies to all profit-maximizing firms.

3. Firms have the option of producing the output that maximizes profit or of not producing at all. They will choose the profit-maximizing output so long as total revenue exceeds variable cost. In per unit terms, price must exceed average variable cost ($P > AVC$).
4. The all-or-none profit test in the short run implies producing as long as losses are less than fixed cost, since the firm loses its fixed cost if it shuts down. The point at which total revenue just equals variable cost (in per unit terms, $P = AVC$) is the shut-down point. The firm is indifferent between producing or shutting down at that point.
5. The all-or-none profit test in the long run implies that the total revenue must cover the total cost of production (in per unit terms, $P > AC_{lr}$). The point at which total revenue just equals total cost ($P = AC_{lr}$) is the break-even point. Since total economic cost includes the opportunity cost of capital, break-even production (zero economic profit) implies that the owners of the firm are earning a rate of return on their capital equal to the highest return they can earn elsewhere. They are indifferent between producing in this market or elsewhere.

The second section also developed a number of short-run and long-run average cost concepts that we will use in our analysis of the other market structures in Chapters 14 through 17. The section stressed the following properties of these cost curves.

6. Since $SRTC = FC + SRVC$, $AC_{sr} = AFC + AVC$.
7. The margin of any variable intersects its corresponding average when the average is neither increasing nor decreasing. Thus, MC_{sr} intersects AC_{sr} and AVC at their minimum values, and MC_{lr} intersects AC_{lr} at its minimum value. The output at which AC_{lr} achieves its minimum value is the minimum efficient scale of operation (MES) for the firm.
8. Economists believe that both long-run and short-run average cost curves are relatively flat in the region of minimum average cost.

The third section of the chapter described the operation of perfectly competitive markets in the long run, when (1) firms can adjust previously fixed factors of production and (2) new firms can enter or existing firms can exit the industry. Regarding the adjustment of previously fixed factors:

9. Short-run total and short-run average costs tend to be greater than long-run total and long-run average costs are because firms are restricted from adjusting their fixed factors of production in the short run.
10. Short-run and long-run total, average, and marginal costs are the same for a given level of output if firms choose the same combination of factors of production in the short run that they would choose in the long run.
11. Short-run total cost is the actual cost of production that the firm experiences. Long-run total cost is the limit of how low short-run total cost can be at each level of output.

Regarding the entry and exit of firms:

12. A market situation in which perfectly competitive firms make profits or losses cannot persist in the long run. Profits lead to entry of new firms, which increases industry supply and puts downward pressure on the market price. Losses cause some firms to leave the industry, which decreases industry supply and puts upward pressure on the market price. Entry or exit continues until all firms just break even and P_e = minimum AC_{lr}.
13. The long-run market supply curve shows how much output the industry is willing to supply at each possible price, once the industry reaches its full long-run equilibrium. The full equilibrium occurs when all firms have adjusted previously fixed factors of production and when entry or exit has driven profits or losses to zero, the break-even point. The long-run market supply curve is *not* the sum of the firms' long-run marginal cost curves because the long-run marginal cost curves incorporate the adjustment of previously fixed factors, but not the entry or exit of firms.
14. Long-run market supply curves may exhibit constant costs (horizontal), increasing costs (upward sloping), or decreasing costs (downward sloping). Increasing costs are most likely. The long-run market supply curve is far more elastic than is the short-run market supply curve for most products.

The final section of Chapter 13 discussed the desirable normative properties of perfect competition.

15. Perfectly competitive product markets are responsive to consumers' desires. The full adjustment of a perfectly competitive market to an increase in consumer demand is driven by changes in prices and profits in three stages: (1) prices rise in the momentary run when output is fixed, and firms earn profits; (2) firms increase production in the short run in reaction to the higher prices and profits; and (3) production increases even more in the long run as firms lower their production costs by adjusting previously fixed factors and new firms enter the industry. Supply continues to increase until price is driven down to minimum AC_{lr}, and all firms are breaking even once again. The reverse applies to a decrease in demand, which leads to price decreases, losses in the short run, and exit from the industry in the long run.
16. Perfect competition leads to four desirable efficiency and equity properties that are the standards against which all other market structures are judged: allocational efficiency, production (technical) efficiency, equality of opportunity, and horizontal equity.
    a. *Allocational efficiency:* maximizing the net value of consuming and producing each good. The market test is $P_e = MC_{sr}$, which is the profit-maximizing supply rule for perfectly competitive firms.

b. *Production (technical) efficiency:* producing the total output supplied to the market at the least total cost, thereby conserving society's scarce resources. The market test is production at each firm's MES, the minimum AC_{lr} (in addition to least-cost production by each firm). Perfectly competitive markets achieve production efficiency in the long run as entry or exit drives price to the minimum AC_{lr}.

c. *Equality of opportunity:* the absence of barriers to entry or exit and equal access for everyone to all relevant market information. These two properties are defining characteristics of perfectly competitive markets.

d. *Horizontal equity:* the equal treatment of equals which, in product markets, means equal rates of return on investment, adjusted for risk. The market test is break-even production, or $P_e = AC_{lr}$, which is satisfied in the long-run equilibrium when P_e = minimum AC_{lr}.

KEY TERMS

allocational efficiency
average (total) cost
average fixed cost
average variable cost
break-even point
constant cost industry
decreasing cost industry
equity
increasing cost industry
individual firm's supply curve
market supply curve (short-run and long-run)
minimum efficient scale of operation (MES)
momentary run
perfect competition
production (technical) efficiency
profit-maximizing supply rule (competitive firm)
shut-down point
sunk cost

QUESTIONS

1. a. When economists say that a market is (perfectly) competitive, what do they mean?
   b. What is the relationship between a competitive firm's demand curve and its marginal revenue curve?
2. The following table gives the short-run costs and the market price for a competitive firm for the range of output supplied (q) from 0 to 6. Fill in the blanks.

q	TOTAL COST	FIXED COST	VARIABLE COST	MARGINAL COST	PRICE	PROFIT
0	$500	____	$ 0	$0	$200	____
1	____	____	100	____	200	____
2	____	____	150	____	200	____
3	____	____	225	____	200	____
4	____	____	325	____	200	____
5	____	____	450	____	200	____
6	____	____	700	____	200	____

3. Refer again to the data in question 2.
   a. Calculate average cost (AC), average variable cost (AVC), and average fixed cost (AFC) at each output.
   b. What must be true about the relationship among these three average cost concepts? Do your calculations illustrate this relationship?
   c. What output maximizes the firm's profit?
   d. Explain how the profit-maximizing output illustrates the output supply rule for a competitive firm.
4. Suppose that a competitive firm has fixed cost of $2,000 and variable cost of $3,000 when its produces 100 units of output. The market price for the firm's product is $25. Assume also that producing 100 units of output gives the firm the highest possible profit it can earn if it chooses to produce anything at all.
   a. Does the firm make a profit or incur a loss by producing 100 units of output?
   b. Would you advise the firm to shut down or to keep producing in the short run?
5. Suppose that a firm incurs a total cost of $1,200 to produce 100 units of a product and that the marginal cost of producing the 101st unit is $10. Is average cost rising, falling, or constant between 100 units and 101 units?
6. What is the minimum efficient scale of operation (MES) for a firm, and why would society want firms producing at the MES?
7. Farmer Jones has much better land for growing corn than does Farmer Smith. Jones can grow twice as many bushels of corn as Smith can for the same expenditures on factors of production other than land (for example, seed, labor, tractors). Why, then, do Farmers Jones and Smith have the same costs of growing corn from an economic perspective?
8. a. Can perfectly competitive firms ever make a profit?
   b. Why do perfectly competitive firms continue to operate even when they earn zero economic profits in the long run?

9. Demonstrate the truth of the following statement as it applies to the product market: Competition is a great equalizer in economic affairs.
10. The short-run market supply curve is the horizontal summation of each firm's short-run marginal cost curve (above the minimum of average variable cost). Why is the long-run market supply curve not the horizontal summation of each firm's long-run marginal cost curve? What is the long-run market supply curve?
11. a. What factors might cause the long-run market supply curve of a competitive industry to be upward sloping?
    b. What factors might cause the long-run market supply curve of a competitive industry to be downward sloping?
12. a. What are the goals of allocational efficiency and production (technical) efficiency?
    b. What are the market tests for each of these goals?
    c. Why does a perfectly competitive market structure meet both of these goals?

APPENDIX

13

The Relationship Between Long-Run and Short-Run Costs

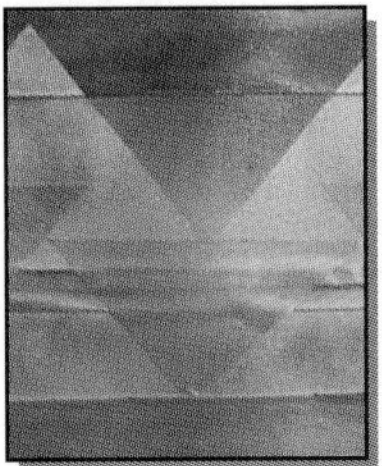

All total, average, and marginal cost curves, both short-run, and long-run, are drawn under the assumption that firms have achieved an efficient solution to their How problems. They have found the combination of factor inputs that minimizes the total cost of producing any given output (and therefore the average and the marginal costs as well). As described in Chapter 11, the solution to the How problem involves equalizing ratios of marginal products to factor prices, MP_{factor}/P_{factor}, across all *variable* factors of production. The important distinction between the long run and the short run lies in the number of variable factors. In the long run the firm can equalize the MP_{factor}/P_{factor} ratios across *all* factors of production. In the short run the firm can equalize the ratios only across all *variable* factors of production. The MP_{factor}/P_{factor} ratios of the fixed factors are the result of past decisions. They are not necessarily equal to the ratios for the variable factors in the short run.

For instance, suppose that each of our 1,000 firms uses capital (K), labor (L), and material inputs (M) to produce its output. Capital is fixed in the short run, but the firms can always vary labor and materials. Cost minimization in the long run implies

$$MP_K/P_K = MP_L/P_L = MP_M/P_M$$

The *LRTC*, AC_{lr}, and MC_{lr} curves are drawn under the assumption that the three ratios are equal. Cost minimization in the short run implies only that

$$MP_L/P_L = MP_M/P_M$$

MP_K/P_K may or may not be equal to the other two ratios. This is the assumption underlying the *SRTC*, AC_{sr}, *AVC*, and MC_{sr} curves.

At best, short-run total cost (and short-run average cost) can equal long-run total cost (and long-run average cost) at any given output. This occurs if the $MP_{\text{factor}}/P_{\text{factor}}$ ratios of the fixed factors happen to be equal to the ratios of the variable factors. In general, though, the ratios of the fixed and variable factors differ. In this case, the short-run total cost exceeds the long-run total cost of producing the output that the firm is supplying to the market. The firm's actual costs are higher than they need to be. The reason the firm adjusts the previously fixed factors once the long run arrives is to equalize all ratios and thereby lower its actual (that is, short-run) cost of production to the limit represented by the long-run curves.

The cost data illustrate the relationship between short-run and long-run costs. Figure 13:1.1 reproduces the short-run average and the short-run marginal cost curves from Figure 13.4 and the long-run average and the long-run marginal cost curves from Figure 13.6.

Suppose that each firm produces an output of 16, as in Figure 13.4. At q = 16, AC_{lr} = \$48, and MC_{lr} = \$56. The corresponding short-run values are much higher: AC_{sr} = \$68, and MC_{sr} = \$130.

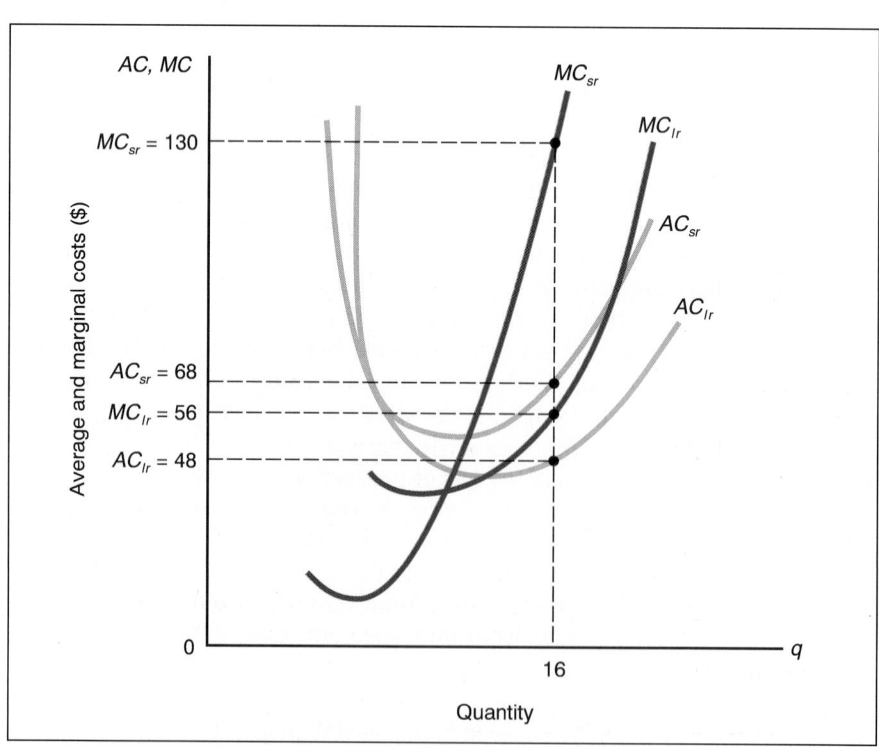

FIGURE 13:1.1

Short-Run Versus Long-Run Average and Marginal Costs

The short-run average and marginal cost curves MC_{sr} and AC_{sr}, are based on the data in Table 13.2. They indicate the firm's *actual* costs of production at each output, given the amount of fixed capital in place, assuming that the firm combines all its *variable* factors of production in the least-cost manner. The long-run average and marginal cost curves, MC_{lr} and AC_{lr}, are based on the data in Table 13.3. They indicate the firm's *minimum possible* costs of production at each output, because they assume that the firm combines *all* its factors of production in the least-cost manner. MC_{sr} and AC_{sr} are greater than MC_{lr} and AC_{lr} in our example because the firm is struck with too little capital in the short-run to produce the output of 16 with the lowest possible costs.

The implication of these data is that our firms are stuck in the short run with the wrong amount of capital. For example, the capital stock may be too low for an output of 16, so that

$$MP_K/P_K > MP_L/P_L = MP_M/P_M$$

On the margin, the output per dollar spent on capital exceeds the output per dollar spent on the other two factors (review Chapter 11 if you are unclear about this).

If the firms had put more capital in place, their short-run cost would have been lower. Figure 13:1.2 illustrates. AC^0_{sr} and AC_{lr} are the initial curves we have been using all along. At higher levels of fixed capital AC_{sr} shifts downward as indicated by the dotted lines AC^1_{sr} and AC^2_{sr} (the corresponding marginal costs for these curves are not shown). At just the right amount of capital, when $MP_K/P_K = MP_L/P_L = MP_M/P_M$, the short-run average cost curve just touches the long-run average cost curve. It cannot shift down any lower. The lowest AC_{sr} for an output of 16 is AC^2_{sr} in Figure A13.2.

With the right amount of capital, therefore, short-run and long-run average (and total) costs are equal. They have to be because the firm is using the same quantities of all factors in the short run to produce 16 units of output that it would use if it were in the long run. Notice, however, that AC^2_{sr} and AC_{lr} are not equal at any output other than 16. The amount of capital that is just right when $q = 16$ is the wrong amount of capital for any other output. As a result, AC^2_{sr} must be greater than AC_{lr} at any output other than 16.

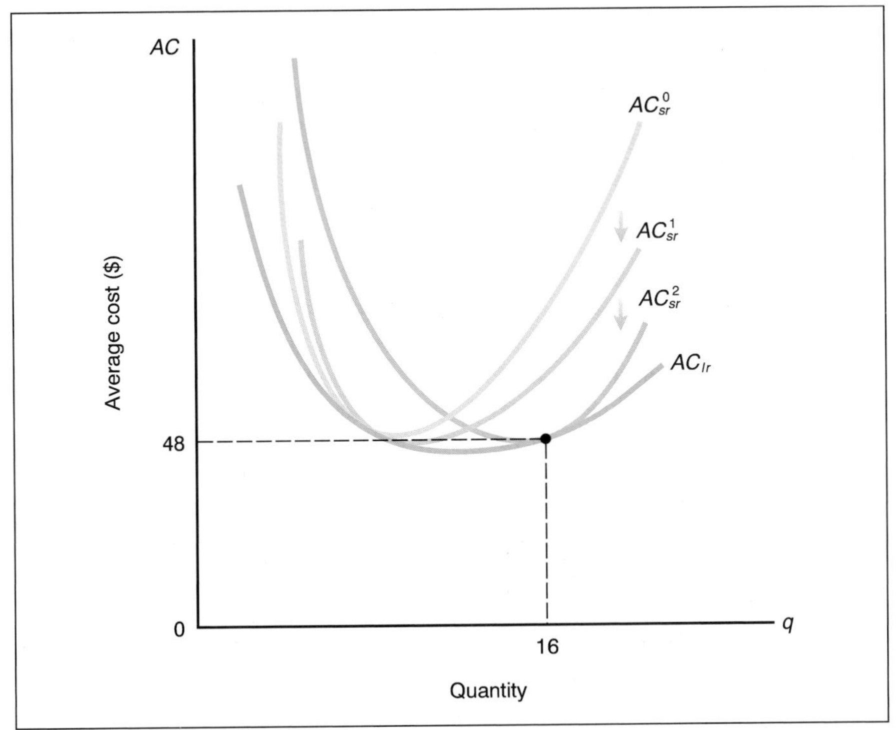

FIGURE 13:1.2

Increasing the Stock of Capital to Reduce Costs

The firm is initially producing 16 units of output with too little capital, so its actual average cost is on the average cost curve AC^0_{sr}. Successively increasing the stock of capital lowers the firm's actual average costs of producing the 16 units to the points on the average cost curves AC^1_{sr} and AC^2_{sr}. The actual average cost can be no lower than the point on AC^2_{sr}, because AC_{lr} indicates the minimum possible average cost when the firm produces 16 units of output, $48 in our example.

FIGURE 13:1.3

Producing with the Optimal Amount of Capital

Short-run and long-run average and marginal costs are equal at 16 units of output if the firm is using the amount of capital that minimizes the cost of producing the 16 units. But AC_{sr} is above AC_{lr}, and MC_{sr} does not equal MC_{lr}, at any output other than 16 units, because the amount of capital that minimizes the cost of producing 16 units is not the amount of capital that minimizes the cost of producing any other quantity. Therefore, production at any output other than 16 raises the actual average cost, AC_{sr}, above the minimum, possible average cost, AC_{lr}.

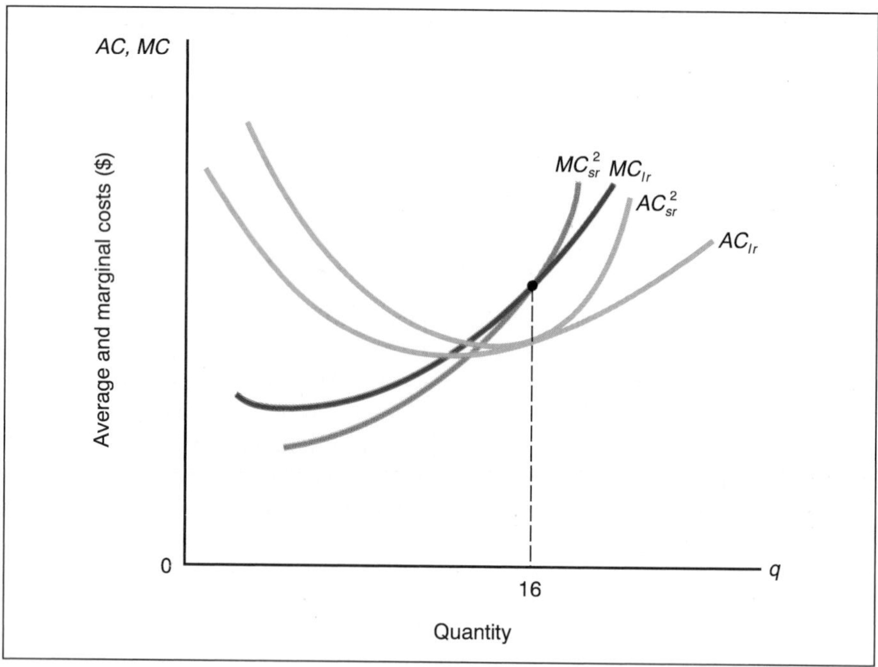

Short- and long-run marginal costs must also be equal when all factor ratios are equal. This can be seen by inverting the factor ratios as P_{factor}/MP_{factor}. The inverted ratio is interpreted as the marginal cost of increasing any one factor. The numerator, P_{factor}, is the additional cost of adding one more unit of a factor. The denominator, MP_{factor}, is the additional output obtained from adding one more unit of a factor. Therefore, the ratio is the additional cost per unit of output, that is, the marginal cost of adding one more unit of a factor. With the ratios equal, marginal costs are equal no matter what factors are added—"long-run" capital or "short-run" labor or materials. So marginal costs are equal in both the short- and the long runs.

Figure 13:1.3 illustrates. MC^2_{sr} is the marginal cost curve associated with AC^2_{sr}. At $q = 16$, $MC^2_{sr} = MC_{lr}$. Notice, also,that MC^2_{sr} and MC_{lr} differ at any other output. $MC^2_{sr} > MC_{lr}$ at higher outputs, and $MC^2_{sr} < MC_{lr}$ at lower outputs.

The relationship between short-run and long-run costs at $q = 16$ applies to any other output as well. There is one correct amount of capital that equalizes AC_{sr} and AC_{lr} (and short-run and long-run marginal costs) for any output that the firm chooses to produce. Otherwise, AC_{sr} is greater than AC_{lr} at that output. For the hypothetical cost data in Chapter 13, the amount of capital lying behind the short-run costs is just the right amount for an output of 8 units. At $q = 8$, $AC_{sr} = AC_{lr} = \$72$, and $MC_{sr} = MC_{lr} = \$16$ (compare the entries in Tables 13.2 and 13.3).[1]

Figure 13:1.4 shows that AC_{lr} is a lower boundary of the best possible AC_{sr} curves at every output. The minimum value of AC_{lr}, \$47 at $q = 15$ in our hypothetical data, defines the *break-even point* for the firm. If price in the long

[1]Short- and long-run average costs are also equal at outputs of 7 and 9 in the tables because of rounding error and the discrete, single-unit nature of the cost data. Notice, though, that MC_{sr} and MC_{lr} are equal only at $q = 8$.

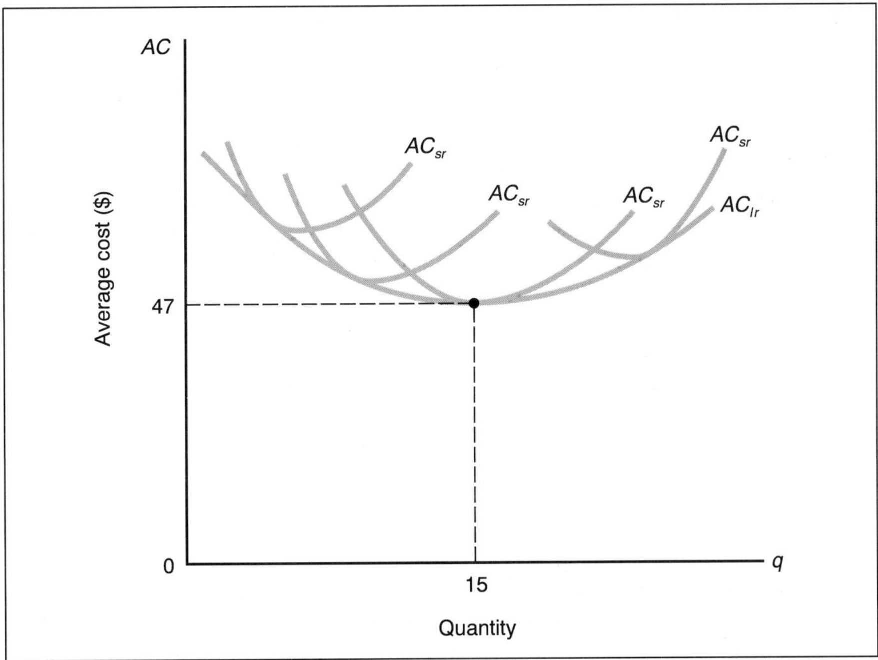

FIGURE 13:1.4

Long-Run Average Cost—the Boundary of the Short-Run Averge Cost Curves

The long-run average cost curve, AC_{lr}, defines the lower limit, or boundary, of each possible short-run average cost curve, AC_{sr}. There is one AC_{sr} curve for each amount of capital chosen, and the amount of capital will be the cost-minimizing amount for just one output. That is the output at which an AC_{sr} curve just touches AC_{lr}. The minimum efficient scale of operation, the *MES*, is the lowest possible unit cost of production, the minimum of AC_{lr}. It is $47 at an output of 15 in our example, so $47 is the firm' break-even point in the long run.

run were expected to be $47, the owners of these firms would just be indifferent between staying in the industry and producing 15 units and leaving the industry and investing in their next best alternatives.

SUMMARY

The appendix developed the relationship between the short-run and the long-run costs of production.

1. Short-run and long-run costs are related by a firm's desire to produce its output at the lowest possible cost. As discussed in Chapter 11, firms produce at least cost by equalizing the ratios of marginal products to prices, $MP_{\text{factor}}/P_{\text{factor}}$, for all variable factors of production.
2. In the short run the firm equalizes the $MP_{\text{factor}}/P_{\text{factor}}$ ratios for all but the fixed factors of production. In the long run the firm equalizes the $MP_{\text{factor}}/P_{\text{factor}}$ ratios for all factors of production. The ability to equalize all the factor ratios in the long run is what drives long-run total cost (and long-run average cost) below short-run total cost (and short-run average cost) in general.
3. The short-run total and the short-run average costs are the actual costs of production experienced by the firm. The long-run total and the long-run average costs are the lower limit of the short-run total and the short-run average costs at any given output.
4. The long-run average cost curve is the lower boundary of the best possible short-run average cost curves at every level of output.
5. Short-run and long-run marginal costs are equal at any given output level only if the short-run and the long-run average costs are equal at that output level.

QUESTIONS

1. State the conditions for cost minimization in the short run and the long run.
2. Draw a typical long-run average cost curve and one short-run average cost curve for a competitive firm.
   a. Why do the short-run and the long-run average cost curves have the same general shape?
   b. Do the two curves ever meet? If not, why not? If yes, why?
   c. Why is short-run average cost greater than long-run average cost at most output levels?
   d. Can the short-run average cost curve ever be below the long-run average cost curve?

CHAPTER

14

Pure Monopoly

LEARNING OBJECTIVES

CONCEPTS TO LEARN

Pure monopoly

Market (monopoly) power

Effective market (monopoly) power

The profit-maximizing output rule for firms with market power

The social costs of pure monopoly

Rent-seeking behavior

Price discrimination

Windfall profits taxes

Public utility regulation

CONCEPTS TO RECALL

The marginal benefit equals marginal cost decision rule [6]

Marginal cost [6,13]

Average total cost [13]

The three criteria for judging market outcomes [13]

Market power! The term conjures up images of corporate fat cats in plush boardrooms high above the metropolis plotting evil against consumers and workers alike. Alas, economists are not such dramatic folk. In economic analysis the concept of market power relates to the individual firm's demand curve. A firm possesses **market power** *if it faces a downward-sloping demand curve for its product, as in Figure 14.1.* d_f *is the demand curve for an individual firm,* not *the overall market demand curve. Economists also commonly refer to market power as* monopoly power. *The two terms are synonymous.*

Virtually every business firm in the United States has market or monopoly power according to the economic definition. A firm usually loses some of its business when it raises its price, but not all of its business as a perfectly competitive firm would. According to Figure 14.1, an increase in price from P_0 *to* P_1 *reduces the firm's quantity demanded, but only from* q_0 *to* q_1*. Similarly, quantity demanded increases when a firm lowers its price, but not infinitely so. A reduction in price from* P_0 *to* P_2 *in Figure 14.1 increases the quantity demanded, but only from* q_0 *to* q_2*.*

Market power is the one sure way of distinguishing perfect competition from all other market structures. Perfectly competitive firms have no market power. They are price takers, having no choice but to accept the going market price determined by the Laws of Supply and Demand. Their demand curves are horizontal at the market price. In contrast, firms with market power are price setters. They alone decide which price to set along their downward-sloping demand curves. Market structures may have some attributes in common with perfect competition, such as ease of entry and exit or homogeneous products. But if firms in a particular market have market power, that market differs fundamentally from perfect competition. As we shall see, it does not operate according to the Laws of Supply and Demand.

Chapter 14 begins the analysis of market power with the extreme case of **pure monopoly,** in which the industry consists of a single firm. The one firm produces a product for which consumers have no close substitutes, and entry into the market by other firms is virtually impossible. Pure monopoly is hardly the most important market structure in the United States. Recall from our preview of market structures that pure monopoly accounts for only 2 or 3 percent of total output. Also, the most important examples result from government legislation—for instance, the public utilities, local cable television service, the postal service (first class mail), and certain products with patent protection, such as Polaroid's instant camera. Nonetheless, beginning with pure monopoly has a number of virtues from an analytical standpoint.

The model of pure monopoly allows us to explore the effects of market power in and of itself without having to consider the endless possibilities associated with strategic interaction among firms. With no close substitutes available to consumers and with entry virtually impossible, a pure monopolist need not worry about how other firms react to its decisions.

In addition, understanding pure monopoly is an important prerequisite to an analysis of oligopoly. Economists assume that oligopolists aspire to the life of a pure monopolist. They would love to isolate themselves from competition

MARKET POWER (MONOPOLY POWER)

A market situation in which an individual firm faces a downward-sloping demand curve for its product.

PURE MONOPOLY

A product market in which a single firm comprises the entire industry and has complete control over all supply decisions.

HISTORICAL NOTE: Although Congress gave the U.S. Postal Service a pure monopoly in delivering first class mail, the development of new communication technologies, such as the fax machine and E-mail, is fast eroding the value of that monopoly power. These developments point out how substitute products can undermine the exercise of monopoly power.

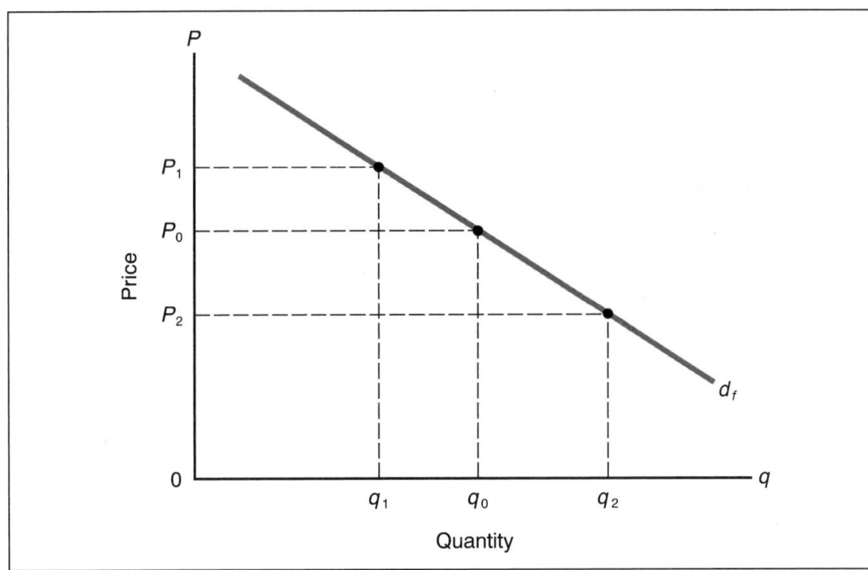

FIGURE 14.1

Market Power and the Firm's Demand Curve

A firm has market, or monopoly, power if it faces a downward sloping demand curve for its product. The only firms without market power are perfectly competitive firms, whose demand curves are horizontal, perfectly elastic, at the equilibrium market price.

with other firms in their industry. The reason is that profits for the *industry as a whole* are never higher than when the market is structured as a pure monopoly. In this sense pure monopoly defines the limit that the giant firms can hope to achieve, assuming that their objective is to maximize profit.

Only rarely does a firm manage to take over the industry and become a pure monopolist itself. Nonetheless, large firms always have an incentive to cooperate with one another and "speak with one voice," so that the industry behaves as if it were a pure monopoly. By cooperating, the firms maximize the total profits collectively available to them.

Finally, pure monopoly is the natural analytical counterpoint to perfect competition. If perfect competition is the best of all market structures for a society committed to the pursuit of efficiency and equity, then pure monopoly is in many respects the worst of all market structures. Firms may aspire to pure monopoly, but society most certainly does not. Pure monopoly is unlikely to be either efficient or equitable.

The first task is to see how a pure monopolist sets its output and price to maximize profit.

PROFIT MAXIMIZATION UNDER PURE MONOPOLY

All firms, whether they have market power or not, maximize profit by following the same general principle: Produce the output at which marginal revenue equals marginal cost. We saw in Chapter 6 how this principle led to the supply rule for a perfectly competitive firm: Produce the output at which price equals marginal cost. Firms with market power produce a different level of output and set a different price because they face downward-sloping demand curves rather than horizontal demand curves. To understand why they behave differently, we need to appreciate three implications of facing a downward-sloping demand curve for a firm attempting to maximize profit.

Implications of a Downward-Sloping Demand Curve

PRICE-SETTING BEHAVIOR VERSUS PRICE-TAKING BEHAVIOR A firm with market power does not have a supply curve. Unlike a perfectly competitive firm, it does not consider how much it would be willing to supply at each possible market price. Instead, a firm with market power sets the price of the product itself. The firm's goal is to determine the *single* price-quantity combination along its downward-sloping demand curve that maximizes profit.

THE DEMAND CURVE AND THE TOTAL REVENUE FRONTIER People sometimes have the impression that the giant corporations have the power to do whatever they want—for instance, sell any quantity they choose to at any price that suits their fancy. Do not fall for that myth. Even a pure monopolist cannot sell any quantity at any price. A firm's downward-sloping demand curve is a fundamental constraint that limits its price and quantity options. The firm can either set its price and sell the corresponding quantity on the demand curve or choose its quantity and charge the corresponding price on the demand curve. It cannot set price and quantity independently.

Having chosen price or quantity, the demand curve defines the total revenue frontier for the firm, just as the total cost curve defines the total cost frontier for the firm and the production possibilities frontier defines the output frontier for society as a whole. The point (q_1, P_1) on the demand curve in Figure 14.2 has one of two interpretations:

1. q_1 is the *maximum* quantity the firm can sell if it sets its price at P_1, or
2. P_1 is the *maximum* price the firm can charge if it chooses to sell output q_1.

Suppose that the firm sets its price at P_1, in line with the first interpretation. It then wants to sell as much output as it can at that price. q_1 is the most output the firm can sell at P_1, generating a maximum total revenue of $TR_{max} = P_1 \cdot q_1$. It would like to sell more output—say, q_2—but the firm's customers

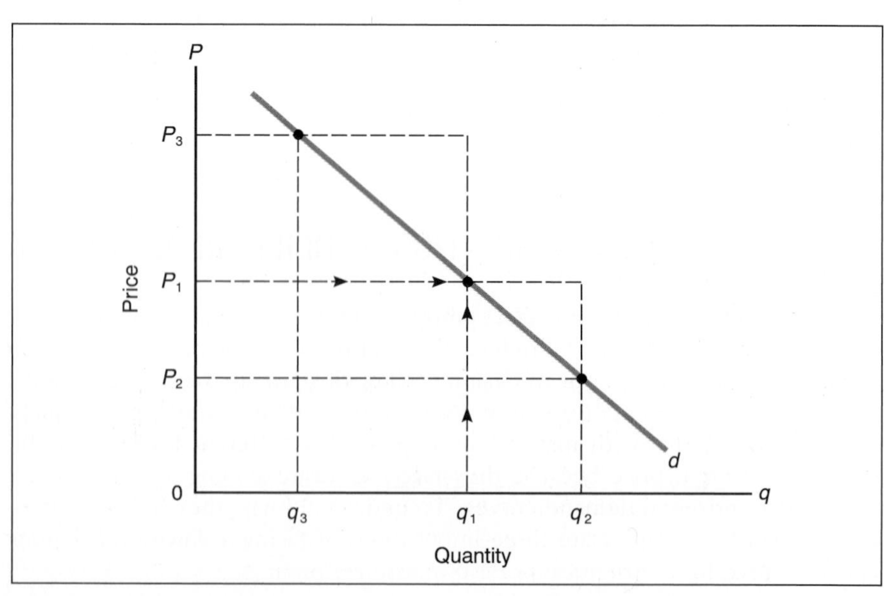

FIGURE 14.2

The Firm's Demand Curve and Its Total Revenue Frontier

A firm with market power must decide what quantity to produce and what price to charge. The firm's demand curve defines the best quantity-price combinations available to the firm. If the firm sets its price at P_1, the most output it can sell is q_1. It cannot sell q_2 units of output at the price P_1. If the firm decides to produce quantity q_1, the highest price it can charge is P_1. It cannot charge P_3 and sell q_1 units of output. The demand curve defines the total revenue frontier for the firm.

will not buy q_2 when the price is P_1. They will buy q_2 only at a price of P_2. The quantity-price combination (q_2, P_1) is beyond the total revenue frontier established by the demand curve. The firm can sell any quantity less than q_1 at the price of P_1, but doing so needlessly sacrifices total revenue.

Alternatively, suppose that the firm decides to produce quantity q_1, in line with the second interpretation. It would then like to sell the output at the highest possible price. P_1 is the highest possible price, commonly referred to as the "price the traffic will bear." Once again, the maximum total revenue is $TR_{max} = P_1 \cdot q_1$. The firm would like to charge a higher price—say, P_3—but the firm's customers will not purchase q_1 at that price. They will only purchase an amount q_3. The quantity-price combination (q_1, P_3) is beyond the demand curve, which defines the total revenue frontier. The firm could charge a lower price than P_1 and sell q_1, but doing so would needlessly sacrifice total revenue.

DEMAND AND MARGINAL REVENUE The final important implication of a downward-sloping demand curve is that the marginal revenue from selling additional output is less than the price of the product. To see why, consider the straight-line, downward-sloping demand curve, *d*, in Figure 14.3. The first two columns of Table 14.1 give the quantity-price demand schedule corresponding to *d* for the range of output between 0 and 20. At prices of \$152 and above, quantity demanded is zero. Below \$152, every decrease in price of \$6 increases quantity demanded by 1 unit. Quantity demanded is 1 at a price of \$146, 2 at a price of \$140, 3 at a price of \$134, and so forth. In other words, the slope of the demand curve is −6.

The third column of Table 14.1 indicates the total revenue ($P \cdot q$) received by the firm at each price-quantity combination along the demand curve. For

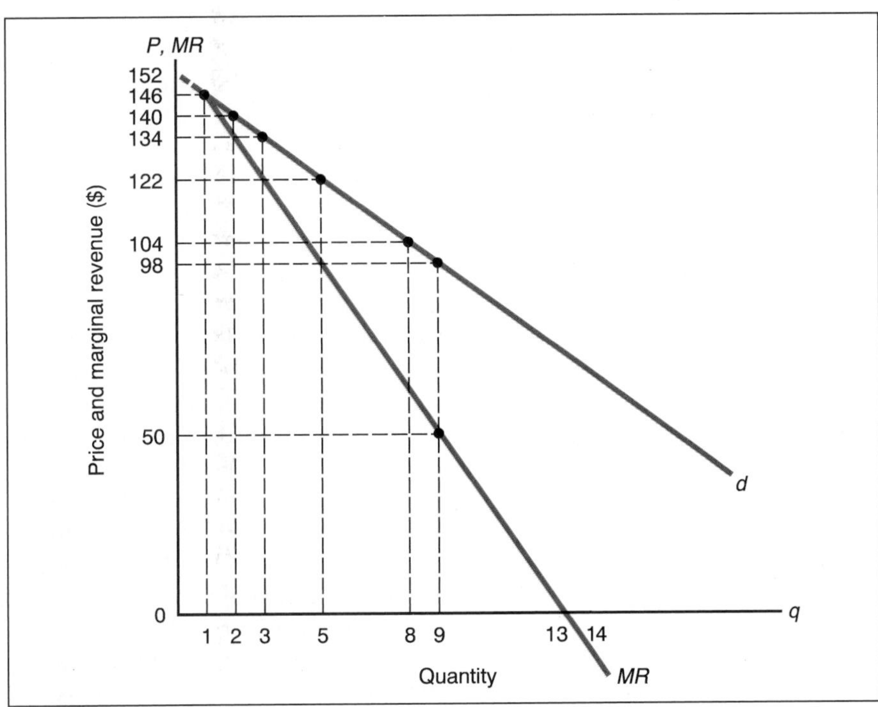

FIGURE 14.3

Demand and Marginal Revenue

The demand curve, *d*, and the marginal revenue curve, *MR*, are graphs of the price and the marginal revenue at each output from Table 14.1. The figure shows that the marginal revenue curve lies below the demand curve when a firm has market power. The firm must lower its price on all units of output to sell more output each time period, so its marginal revenue is below its price at every output beyond one unit. For example, the firm charges a price of \$98 when output is 9 units but the marginal revenue of increasing sales from 8 units to 9 units is only \$50.

TABLE 14.1 **Demand and Marginal Revenue for a Downward-Sloping Demand Curve**

QUANTITY (q)	PRICE (P)	TOTAL REVENUE ($TR = P \cdot q$)	MARGINAL REVENUE ($MR = \Delta TR$)
0	$152	$ 0	$ —
1	146	146	146
2	140	280	134
3	134	402	122
4	128	512	110
5	122	610	98
6	116	696	86
7	110	770	74
8	104	832	62
9	98	882	50
10	92	920	38
11	86	946	26
12	80	960	14
13	74	962	2
14	68	952	−10
15	62	930	−22
16	56	896	−34
17	50	850	−46
18	44	792	−58
19	38	722	−70
20	32	640	−82

instance, the total revenue at $P = \$146$, $q = 1$ is \$146 (\$146 = \$146 · 1); the total revenue at $P = \$140$, $q = 2$ is \$280 (\$280 = \$140 · 2); and so forth. The fourth column of Table 14.1 shows the marginal revenue at each output. Recall that marginal revenue is the increase in total revenue from selling one more unit of output. For example, the total revenue from selling 2 units is \$280, and the total revenue from selling 3 units is \$402. As a result, the marginal revenue when the quantity sold increases from 2 to 3 units is \$122 (\$402 − \$280 = \$122).

The firm's marginal revenue curve, MR, in Figure 14.3 depicts the marginal revenue combinations from the first and fourth columns in Table 14.1. Beyond $q = 1$, MR lies below d—marginal revenue is less than price. For example, at $q = 3$, $MR = \$122$, and $P = \$134$.

Marginal revenue is less than price because the firm has to lower its price in order to increase the quantity sold. Suppose that the firm is considering whether to increase sales from 8 to 9 units of output over a given period of time. The firm has two choices. It can sell *all* 8 units at a price of \$104 each, or it can sell *all* 9 units at a price of \$98 each. (Refer to the first and second columns in Table 14.1.) Therefore, an increase in sales from 8 to 9 units has two separate effects on total revenue. First, by selling 9 units rather than 8, the firm *increases* its total revenue by \$98 on the additional 9th unit. Second, to sell all 9 units the firm must now sell units 1 through 8 at \$98 rather than \$104. (It cannot sell the first 8 units for \$104 and the 9th unit at \$98. All 9 units must sell at a price of \$98.) Therefore, relative to selling only 8 units, the firm loses \$6 each on units 1 through 8 (\$6 = \$104 − \$98). The total revenue received from all 8 units *decreases* by \$48 (\$48 = \$6 · 8). Net total revenue increases by

\$50 (\$50 = \$98 − \$48), the marginal revenue at $q = 9$ (from the fourth column of Table 14.1), and \$50 is less than the price of \$98.

To summarize, the two effects on marginal revenue of increasing sales from 8 to 9 units are

1. An addition to total revenue from selling the 9th unit at \$98:	+ \$98
2. A decrease in total revenue from selling units 1–8 at \$98 rather than \$104:	− \$48
Marginal revenue at $q = 9$:	+ \$50

Notice that marginal revenue becomes negative at $q = 14$ and beyond. When output is this large, the negative effect on total revenue from lowering the price to increase the quantity sold dominates the positive effect on total revenue from selling an additional unit of output.

Contrast this relationship between price and marginal revenue with the perfectly competitive firm facing a horizontal demand curve. Our tee shirt manufacturer in Chapter 6 can sell as many shirts as it wants at a price of \$5. Since the firm does not have to lower the price to sell more shirts, the second effect on total revenue described above is absent. Selling each additional shirt simply increases total revenue by \$5. Marginal revenue always equals price—the competitive firm's marginal revenue curve *is* its demand curve.

The relationship between price and marginal revenue is another example of the relationship between averages and margins discussed in Chapter 13. Price is average revenue, the amount of revenue received per unit of output. Therefore, the firm's demand curve is its **average revenue curve.** Average revenue is constant at the going market price along the horizontal demand curve of a perfectly competitive firm. Since average revenue is neither increasing nor decreasing, marginal revenue and average revenue (price) must be equal. By contrast, average revenue (price) decreases along the downward-sloping demand curve of a firm with market power. Therefore, marginal revenue must be below average revenue, pulling average revenue down. The marginal revenue curve lies below the demand curve.

AVERAGE REVENUE CURVE
An individual firm's demand curve.

Average and Marginal Cost

A primary goal of this chapter is to compare the market outcome under pure monopoly with the market outcome under perfect competition. In order to sharpen the comparison, let's assume that the pure monopolist has the same cost structure as the perfectly competitive firms of Chapter 13. This is not such an unrealistic assumption. The presence or absence of market power relates to a firm's demand curve, not to its costs. The fundamental properties of the costs of production that we developed in Chapters 11 and 13 apply to all firms. For instance, the average and the marginal cost curves of a pure monopolist are likely to be U-shaped in both the short and the long runs, with the marginal cost curve passing through the minimum of the average cost curve; short-run total cost is the sum of fixed and variable costs, whereas long-run total cost is the same as long-run variable cost; and so forth. The main difference between a pure monopolist and a perfectly competitive firm is a matter of scale: A pure

TABLE 14.2 Long-Run Costs of the Pure Monopoly

QUANTITY (Q)	TOTAL COST ($LRTC$)	MARGINAL COST (MC_{lr})	AVERAGE COST (AC_{lr})	
0	$ 0	$ —	$ —	
1	146	146	146	
2	264	118	132	
3	359	95	120	
4	432	73	108	
5	488	56	98	
6	528	40	88	
7	560	32	80	
8	576	16	72	
9	590	14	66	
10	600	10	60	
11	611	11	56	
12	625	14	52	
13	641	16	49	
14	659	18	47	(47.071)
15	706	47	47	(47.067)
16	762	56	48	
17	835	73	49	
18	936	101	52	
19	1,055	119	56	
20	1,200	145	60	

NOTE: Average cost is rounded to the nearest whole number.

monopolist is likely to be a much larger firm than is a perfectly competitive firm. But the difference in size is not important in understanding how a firm with market power sets price and quantity to maximize profit, so we can ignore it for now.

Table 14.2 reproduces the data on long-run total cost, average cost, and marginal cost from Table 13.3. We chose the long-run data because the distinction between the short run and the long run is not as interesting under pure monopoly as it is under perfect competition. Given that entry and exit are impossible, the only important difference between the short and the long runs is that the monopolist can adjust previously fixed factors of production in the long run. The process of adjustment is the same as in a perfectly competitive firm and has the same objective: to reduce the actual costs of production to the limits defined by the long-run cost curves. There is no need to repeat that analysis. We will assume that the monopolist has made the appropriate adjustments and is operating on its long-run cost curves.

Maximizing Profit

Figure 14.4 combines the demand curve (D) and marginal revenue curve (MR) from Figure 14.3 with the average cost curve (AC) and marginal cost curve (MC) corresponding to the data in Table 14.2. These are the four curves needed to analyze the profit-maximizing decision of the firm. (Notice that the

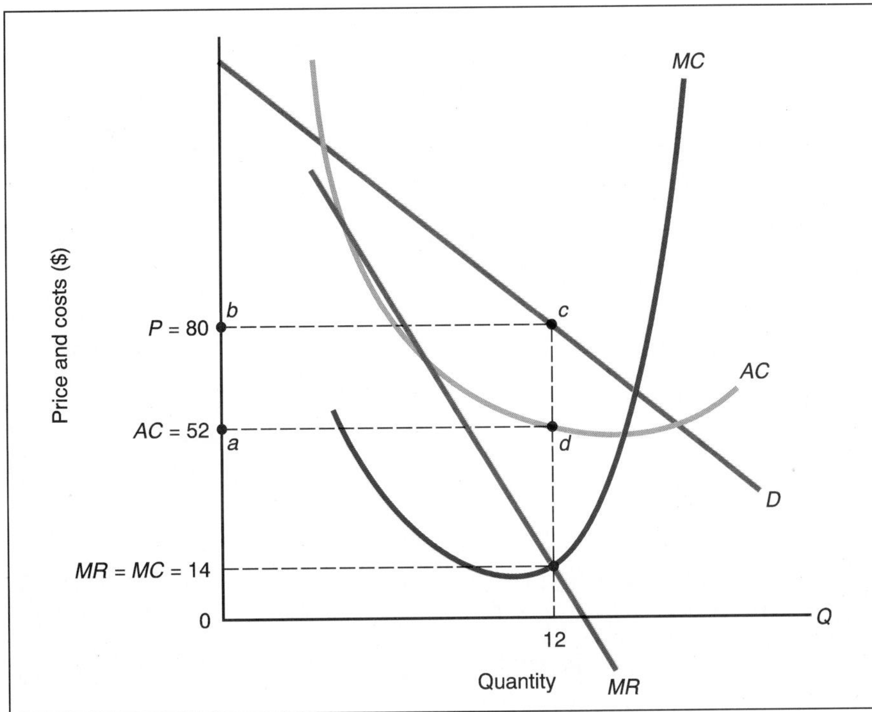

FIGURE 14.4

Maximizing Profit: Pure Monopoly

The figure combines the demand curve, *D*, and marginal revenue curve, *MR*, from Figure 14.3 with the monopolist's average cost curve, *AC*, and marginal cost curve, *MC*, from the long-run cost data in Table 14.2. The monopolist maximizes its profit by producing and selling 12 units of output, at the intersection of the *MR* and *MC* curves, and charging a price of $80 on *D*. This is how any firm with market power maximizes profit. The monopolist earns a profit equal to the rectangular area *abcd* and is able to maintain this profit in the long-run because entry is impossible. The monopolist has effective market, or monopoly, power.

demand curve is labeled *D* rather than *d*, and output *Q* rather than *q*, to indicate that the firm and the industry are one and the same under pure monopoly.) Table 14.3 records the monopolist's price, marginal revenue, marginal cost, total revenue, total cost, and profit at each level of output.

The analysis of profit-maximization proceeds in three steps: from output, to price, to the measurement of profit. It applies to *any* firm with market power, not just to a pure monopoly.

PROFIT-MAXIMIZING OUTPUT RULE

A firm produces the output at which marginal revenue equals marginal cost (and charges the price on its demand curve corresponding to this output).

1. *Which output should the firm produce?* The profit-maximizing supply rule says that a firm should select the output at which marginal revenue equals marginal cost. Marginal revenue equals marginal cost at the intersection of the *MR* and *MC* curves. In Figure 14.4, *MR* and *MC* intersect at $Q = 12$, when marginal revenue and marginal cost both equal $14 (refer to Table 14.3).
2. *Which price should the firm charge?* Having chosen $Q = 12$, the firm wants to sell the output at the highest possible price. To find that price, go up to the demand curve, *D*, at $Q = 12$. The profit-maximizing price is $80, the highest price the firm can charge and still sell all 12 units of output.
3. *Does the firm make a profit or incur a loss?* Profit (loss) is represented exactly as it is for the perfectly competitive firm.

$$\text{Profit} = \text{total revenue} - \text{total cost}$$
$$= P \cdot Q - AC \cdot Q = (P - AC) \cdot Q$$

The market situation depicted in Figure 14.4 is favorable to the monopolist. At $Q = 12$, the price of $80 far exceeds the average cost of (approximately) $52. The firm's profit equals the area of rectangle *abcd*, a profit of $335 (refer to Table 14.3).

TABLE 14.3 **Revenue, Cost, and Profit for a Pure Monopoly**

QUANTITY (Q)	PRICE (P)	MARGINAL REVENUE (MR)	MARGINAL COST (MC)	TOTAL REVENUE (TR)	TOTAL COST (TC)	PROFIT ($TR - TC$)
0	$152	$ —	$ —	$ 0	$ 0	$ 0
1	146	146	146	146	146	0
2	140	134	118	280	264	16
3	134	122	95	402	359	43
4	128	110	73	512	432	80
5	122	98	56	610	488	122
6	116	86	40	696	528	168
7	110	74	32	770	560	210
8	104	62	16	832	576	256
9	98	50	14	882	590	292
10	92	38	10	920	600	320
11	86	26	11	946	611	335
12	80	14	14	960	625	335
13	74	2	16	962	641	321
14	68	−10	18	952	659	293
15	62	−22	47	930	706	224
16	56	−34	56	896	762	134
17	50	−46	73	850	835	15
18	44	−58	101	792	936	−144
19	38	−70	119	722	1,055	−333
20	32	−82	145	640	1,200	−560

Table 14.3 confirms that $335 is the maximum profit the monopolist can earn. At levels of output less than 12, marginal revenue exceeds marginal cost. The firm should increase production and sales to increase profit. For example, the marginal revenue of increasing sales from 9 to 10 units is $38, whereas the marginal cost is only $10. Increasing production from 9 to 10 units increases profit by $28, from $292 to $320. Beyond 12 units of output, marginal cost exceeds marginal revenue. Producing and selling in that range reduces total profit. For example, the marginal revenue of increasing sales from 12 to 13 units is $2, whereas the marginal cost is $16. Increasing production from 12 to 13 units reduces profit by $14, from $335 to $321.

Notice that the firm is indifferent between producing 11 units and producing 12 units because the marginal revenue and the marginal cost of increasing production from 11 to 12 units are both $14. The "tie" happens because the table assumes that the firm can only produce single, whole units of output. The smooth curves in Figure 14.4 assume that the firm can produce partial units of output, in which case the firm would produce right up to the limit of 12 units, where MR and MC intersect.

Figure 14.5 displays the monopolist's total revenue, total cost, and profit corresponding to the data in Table 14.3. Figure 14.5(a) shows the total revenue and the total cost curves. The shape of the total cost curve is familiar from Chapter 11. Total revenue has an inverted U-shape. Total revenue increases whenever marginal revenue is positive, and marginal revenue is positive in the range of output from 0 to 13 for our firm. Conversely, total revenue decreases whenever marginal revenue is negative, and marginal revenue is negative in

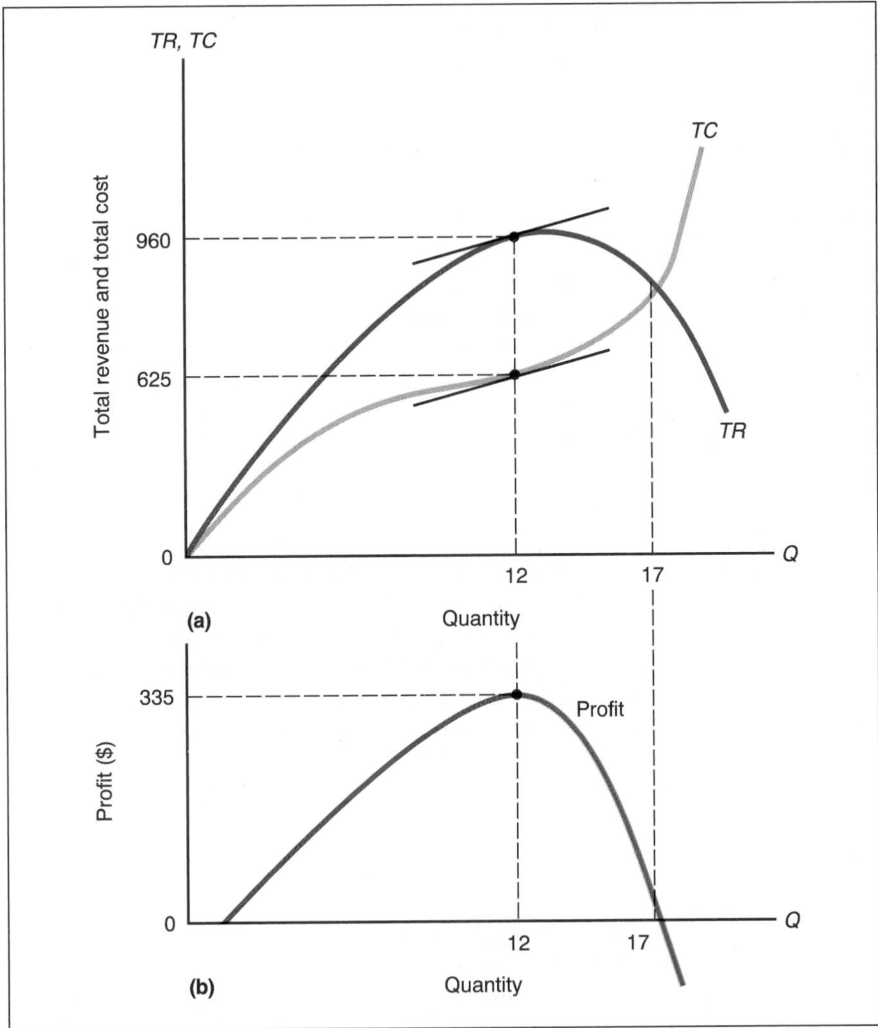

FIGURE 14.5

Total Revenue, Total Cost, and Profit for the Pure Monopolist

Figure 14.5(a) graphs the total revenue and total cost data, and Figure 14.5(b) graphs the profit data, from Table 14.3 for the pure monopolist. The total revenue curve, *TR*, rises when marginal revenue is positive, reaches its peak when marginal revenue is zero, and falls when marginal revenue becomes negative. The total cost curve, *TC*, has the shape of the long-run total cost curve described in Chapter 11. Profit, the difference between *TR* and *TC*, first rises and then falls. It reaches its peak of \$335 at the profit-maximizing output of 12 units, when the slope of *TR*, marginal revenue, equals the slope of *TC*, marginal cost.

the range of output beyond 14. Total revenue reaches its peak when marginal revenue is zero, between 13 and 14 units of output.

Figure 14.5(b) displays the firm's profit. Profit is the vertical distance between the total revenue and the total cost curves at each output. Profit first increases and then decreases, reaching its maximum value of \$335 at $Q = 12$. Refer again to Figure 14.5(a). We learned in Chapter 11 that marginal cost is the slope of the total cost curve. Similarly, marginal revenue is the slope of the total revenue curve. The difference between total revenue and total cost, profit, attains its maximum value at $Q = 12$ when the slopes of the two curves (the dotted lines) are equal. In other words, profit is maximized when marginal revenue equals marginal cost.

EVALUATION OF PURE MONOPOLY

Pure monopoly is not an attractive market structure from society's point of view. The market outcome depicted in Figure 14.4 fails all three efficiency and equity norms established in Chapter 13. It is characterized by allocational inefficiency, production (technical) inefficiency, and inequities.

Allocational Efficiency

Allocational efficiency requires that market exchanges extract the maximum net value from producing and consuming a good. The market test is price equal to marginal cost. In our example, price is far greater than marginal cost. The price is \$80 at the profit-maximizing output of 12 units, whereas marginal cost is only \$14. This result is not unique to pure monopoly; price is necessarily greater than marginal cost whenever a firm has market power. The reason is that firms with market power set *marginal revenue* equal to marginal cost in order to maximize profit. Since the firm's demand curve is downward sloping, the marginal revenue curve lies below the demand curve. Price is greater than marginal revenue and therefore greater than marginal cost. Market power is incompatible with the goal of allocational efficiency.

Firms with market power set too high a price and produce too little output. $P = MC$ at the intersection of the *demand curve* and the marginal cost curve, not the intersection of the marginal revenue and the marginal cost curves. Refer to Figure 14.6, which reproduces the demand, the marginal revenue, and the cost curves of Figure 14.4. D and MC intersect at $Q = 16$ when $P = MC = \$56$. $Q = 16$ is the output that maximizes the net value of producing and consuming the good.

CONTRIVED SCARCITY

The market situation generated by a pure monopolist (or any firm with market power), in which the monopolist (firm) consciously reduces its output below the efficient level of output to maximize its profit.

The monopolist is said to create a **contrived scarcity** by selling only 12 units of output at a price of \$80. The output is "scarce" relative the efficient level of output and "contrived" because the monopolist consciously reduces

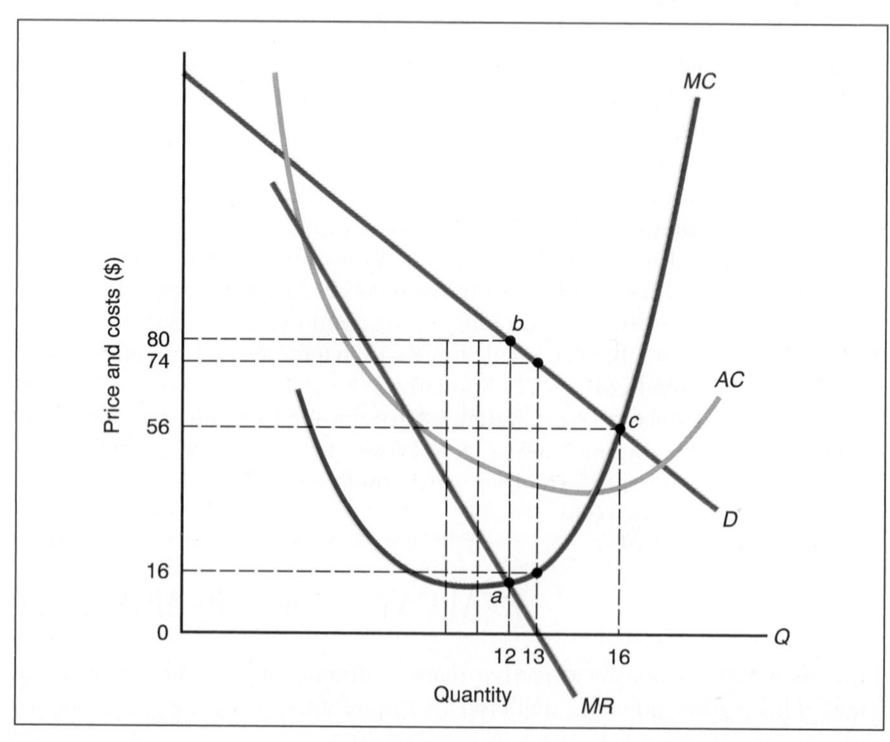

FIGURE 14.6

Market Power and Allocational Inefficiency

The figure reproduces the demand (D), marginal revenue (MR), average cost (AC), and marginal cost (MC) curves from Figure 14.4. The net value from producing and consuming the good is maximized when price equals marginal cost. This occurs at the intersection of D and MC, with an output of 16 units and a price of \$56. The monopolist maximizes its profit by producing 12 units of output at the intersection of MR and MC, and charging a price of \$80, which is much higher than marginal cost. As such, the monopolist creates a contrived scarcity, keeping output too low and price too high relative to the efficient quantity-price combination. The loss in net value equals the triangular area *abc*, the area below D and above MC between 12 and 16 units of output. All firms with market power give rise to allocational inefficiencies in this way.

output and raises price in order to maximize profit. The monopolist's contrived scarcity undermines Adam Smith's comforting notion of the "Invisible Hand," which Smith saw as automatically guiding market exchanges undertaken for private gain to an efficient allocation of society's scarce resources. Unfortunately, the profit motive automatically guides the market system *away* from efficient exchanges when firms possess market power.

ELABORATION: Understand that market power, not profit maximization, is the villain here. Competitive firms also maximize profit. But by maximizing profit they also maximize net value from a social perspective because their prices equal marginal cost.

The social cost of market power is that firms refuse to supply goods whose value to consumers exceeds their cost of production. Recall that the prices along the demand curve are a reflection of marginal value to consumers. In our example, consumers are willing to pay $74 for the 13th unit. The marginal cost of producing the 13th unit is only $16 (see Table 14.3), however. By not producing the 13th unit, society loses $58 of net value ($58 = $74 − $16). The lost net value is a deadweight efficiency loss because no one captures it. Similarly, society suffers a deadweight loss in net value on all units above 12 for which demand exceeds marginal cost, all units up to 16 in our example. The total deadweight loss in Figure 14.6 is the area *abc* under *D* and above *MC* between the profit-maximizing level of output, 12, and the efficient level of output, 16.

Market power would appear to be a very serious problem for a capitalist economy because nearly all firms possess market power. In other words, allocational inefficiency is pervasive in product markets; it is the rule, not the exception. Only perfectly competitive markets are allocationally efficient, and perfect competition accounts for no more than 4 to 5 percent of total output in the United States.

In fact, though, the total amount of allocational inefficiency may not be very high. Markets for goods and services in the United States are impressively competitive according to economist William Shepherd, one of the nation's foremost experts in the analysis of market structures. In his widely cited study of the U.S. economy, Shepherd concluded that in 1980 over three-fourths (76.7 percent) of total output in the United States was supplied in effectively competitive product markets. Moreover, effective competition prevails in all sectors of the economy, with the exception of transportation and public utilities. Of the remaining seven sectors (agriculture; mining; construction; manufacturing; retail trade; finance, insurance, and real estate; and services), only in manufacturing (69 percent) is the effectively competitive share of total output less than 80 percent. Shepherd's "effectively competitive" category includes perfectly competitive markets (unimportant except in agriculture), markets structured as monopolistic competition, and markets structured as oligopolies that he judges to be effectively competitive.[1]

The upshot of Shepherd's analysis is that few firms possess very much market power. Individual firms' demand curves tend to be quite flat, so that prices in most markets are close to marginal costs. Chicago economist Arnold Harberger estimated that the total amount of deadweight loss resulting from market power in the United States is less than .1 percent of total output, roughly $6 billion in a $6 trillion economy. Moreover, Harberger formed his estimate using data from the 1920s, and the U.S. economy is far more competitive today than it was in 1920.[2]

[1]W. Shepherd, "Causes of Increased Competition in the U.S. Economy," *Review of Economics and Statistics* 64, No. 4 (November, 1982): 613–626.

[2]A. Harberger, "Monopoly and Resource Allocation," *American Economic Review* 44, No. 2 (May 1954): 77–87.

Production (Technical) Efficiency

Production, or technical, efficiency requires that the firm produce its output using the least possible amount of society's scarce resources. The market test is production at the minimum efficient scale of operation (MES), the minimum of the long-run average cost curve, so that per unit cost is as low as possible. In our example, the firm's MES occurs at $Q = 15$, when per unit or average cost is \$47. (Refer to Table 14.2.) By producing only 12 units, the firm experiences a per unit cost slightly in excess of \$52. The monopolist is technically inefficient.

Technical inefficiency is also not unique to pure monopolists. Any firm with market power and a U-shaped average cost curve is unlikely to produce at its MES. Firms select the output at which their marginal revenue and marginal cost curves intersect to maximize profit. The profit-maximizing output will also be the MES only if the marginal revenue and the marginal cost curves happen to intersect at the MES, where the average cost curve and the marginal cost curve intersect. This is very unlikely.

Even so, the problem of technical inefficiency may not be as bad as it might appear for a market economy. Most economists believe that firms' average cost curves are fairly flat around the region of their MES. If so, the actual average cost of production may not be much higher than the minimum possible average cost. This point is reflected in our hypothetical cost data. The per unit cost of producing at $Q = 12$ is \$52, only about 10 percent higher than the minimum per unit cost of \$47 at $Q = 15$. Average costs of production in many businesses may be even closer than this to their minimum possible values.

In addition, economies of large-scale production are a fact of life in many industries. Some firms have to be quite large in order to approach their minimum efficient scale of operation, and because they are large, they often acquire a high degree of market power. In these instances, the issue is not so much whether the firm is producing exactly at its MES. Rather, the question is whether these firms should be allowed to become large in order to exploit the economies of scale, or whether society is better off having many smaller firms, each producing with much higher unit costs.

In terms of our example, which is better:

1. one firm supplying the market at $Q = 12$, with an average cost of \$52; or
2. 12 or more small firms each supplying 1 unit of output at a per unit cost of \$146? (Total cost = \$146 at $Q = 1$. Refer to Table 14.2.)

Production efficiency is far better served by having one firm and capturing the cost savings of large-scale production. But with size comes market power, and therein lies the dilemma for a market economy. The problem is that consumers do not necessarily capture the cost savings if the large firms exercise their market power. Consumers pay \$80 for a product that costs \$52 to produce in our example. The firm captures much of the cost savings of large-scale production as profit.

A final qualification is the Schumpeter argument noted in Chapter 13, that large firms with market power may be more technically efficient than are small competitive firms over time. Schumpeter felt that profits were necessary to support the research and development of better technologies and new products. We will consider the relationship between market power and research and development in Chapter 17.

Equity

Recall that the criterion of equity or fairness as applied to product markets has two components, a process component and an end-results component. The process component is equality of opportunity: All investors should have equal access to profitable market opportunities. The end-results component is horizontal equity: All owners of firms should earn the same return to their capital in the long run, standardizing for risk.

When governments create pure monopolies through exclusive territorial franchises or patents, they necessarily undermine the process equity principle of equality of opportunity. The franchise or patent acts as an absolute legal barrier to entry into the industry. Other firms cannot enter the industry because they are not allowed to. If these pure monopolies are then left to their own devices, they will almost certainly violate the end-results principle of horizontal equity. The owners will probably receive higher returns on their capital than do investors generally.

HISTORICAL NOTE: George Steinbrenner is certainly thankful for major league baseball's exemption from the antitrust laws, which effectively prevents new teams from entering the lucrative New York market. He purchased the New York Yankees for under $10 million in the 1970s and in the 1980s signed a television contract for $500 million over 25 years.

Our example illustrates the point very clearly. The owners of the monopoly make a profit of $335 by selling 12 units of output at $80. This profit represents a return to their capital over and above the return that investors can earn generally. Other investors see the profit, but they are not allowed to enter the industry and compete for it. As a result, the owners of the monopoly are able to enjoy the profit year after year. The firm possesses **effective market power,** or **effective monopoly power,** defined as the ability to maintain profit over the long run.

EFFECTIVE MARKET (MONOPOLY) POWER

The ability of a firm to maintain an economic profit in the long run

Be very careful to distinguish market (monopoly) power from effective market (monopoly) power. Market power simply means that the firm faces a downward-sloping demand curve. Effective market (monopoly) power refers to one particular market outcome, the ability to maintain profit in the long run. As such, effective market (monopoly) power requires the existence of barriers to entry.

Although virtually all firms possess market power, relatively few are able to turn that market power into effective market power. In other words, relatively few firms can prevent other investors from entering their markets and competing away their profits. The long-run equalizing tendency of competitive market forces is the rule, not the exception, in any modern economy. The case of pure monopoly is one obvious exception, however.

The idea that some firms enjoy effective market power and are able to earn profits year after year requires two qualifications. The first is that these profits are difficult to see and, in any event, may not be shared by all the owners of these firms. The second is that profits of individual firms may be an illusion from a broader social perspective. The maintained "profit" area *abcd* in Figure 14.4 enjoyed by our pure monopolist may be largely offset by losses encountered in the pursuit of that profit. Worse yet, the "profit" area might actually represent an additional efficiency loss for society as a whole.

WHO CAPTURES THE PROFIT? A series of patents has given Polaroid Corporation a monopoly in the production of instant cameras for over 40 years. Without question, Polaroid earned enormous profits in many of those years. Edwin Land, the camera's inventor and the founding father of Polaroid, became one of the wealthiest individuals in the United States. But not all past and current investors in Polaroid stock became millionaires or even enjoyed an unusually high return on their investment. Buying stock in a profitable company with effective market power does not guarantee investors a hefty rate of return. As we saw in Chapter 13, timing is of the essence in playing the stock market.

The problem for investors is that the stock market reacts very quickly to profitable opportunities. Suppose that a company is just breaking even and that purchasing the company's stock yields a return of 10 percent, the same return that investors can earn generally. Suddenly a new patented invention generates an unending stream of profits for the company equal to $1 per year per share of stock outstanding. If investors can earn 10 percent on their money generally, they would be willing to pay $10 for the opportunity to receive $1 per year forever.[3] Upon hearing of the invention, therefore, investors rush to buy the stock, and the price of the stock begins to rise. Once the price of the stock rises by $10, purchasing the stock again brings a return of 10 percent. The stock market is said to *capitalize* the annual stream of profits into the value of the firm's stock. After capitalization occurs, the stream of profits from the invention becomes invisible, and unavailable to any future investors in the company.

Three groups of investors enjoy a return greater than 10 percent from the $1 stream of profits: (1) those who owned the stock originally and still do, (2) those who owned the stock originally and sold after the price began to rise, and (3) those new investors who were able to buy the stock before it rose by the full amount of $10. Investors who wait until the value of the stock rises by the full $10 are too late.

Returning to the example of Polaroid, Edwin Land became wealthy because he owned Polaroid stock from the beginning. Other investors who bought and sold Polaroid stock in later years may or may not have done well, depending on the timing of their purchases and sales. Identifying exactly who gains from monopoly profits is never an easy task.

RENT SEEKING The second qualification about profits is that effective monopoly power usually does not just fall into the laps of those firms that have it. Profits most often have to be pursued. Indeed, the pursuit of profit lies at the heart of all entrepreneurial activity. It is an economic activity unto itself, involving expenditures of resources and competition among entrepreneurs.

For instance, firms in a number of industries engage in patent races with one another. They each finance large research and development operations with the hope that their scientists and engineers will be the first to discover new products or production technologies that can be patented and turned into a stream of profits. The biotech firms are a leading example today. Most of them are little more than research and development outfits scrambling to be the first to produce marketable products through gene-splitting techniques, products such as an effective vaccine against AIDS or a dramatic new hybrid crop.

The firms that win these patent races often do enjoy monopoly profits under the protection of government patents. But the profits of the successful firms overstate the profits to research and development activity generally. They do not take into account the costs expended by the unsuccessful firms that came

---

[3] Recall from Chapter 12 the simplified present value formula for long-lived investments, $PV = R/r$, where R is the stream of annual returns and r is the discount rate. $R = \$1$, and $r = 0.10$ in our example. Therefore, $PV = \$1/0.10 = \$10$.

up empty. Competition among research and development outfits reduces the overall profits from the activity, just as competition reduces profits generally in the marketplace. In fact, if research and development activity were perfectly competitive, firms could expect to earn no profit from it on average. The costs of the firms' unsuccessful projects would just offset the profits from their successful projects.

Profits areas such as the rectangle *abcd* in Figure 14.4 miss these costs of competing for the profits. Furthermore, the fact that firms can compete for an effective monopoly position reduces somewhat the inequity of one firm eventually gaining such an advantage. Nonetheless, society has an interest in reducing artificial barriers to entry so that opportunities to compete for a maintained profit position are kept to a minimum.

The competitive pursuit of profit by entrepreneurs raises an important question: Are the resources spent competing for profits simply wasted from society's point of view? In the case of research and development the answer is almost surely no. Some duplication of research effort is unavoidable, but new products and cost-reducing improvements in technology do have substantial value to consumers.

Other examples are less clear-cut, however. Advertising campaigns that appeal more to image and lifestyle than to a product's attributes are certainly suspect. Successful advertising can be enormously profitable. But if consumers are persuaded to buy products for reasons that are more imagined than real, has anyone except the owners of the advertising companies and their client firms really gained anything of value? Economists are especially skeptical of entrepreneurial profit-seeking activity when it is directed toward government agencies. Private companies spend huge sums of money lobbying government officials for legislation favorable to their industry. Government contractors sometimes engage in frivolous lawsuits against the government, attempting to block the awarding of a contract to a competitor. Restaurant owners may make payments to local officials "under the table" to secure a liquor license. Activities of these sorts appear to undermine the public interest in efficiency and equity in favor of the narrow interests of the entrepreneurs.

Economists define entrepreneurial profit-seeking activity as **rent seeking** when it is directed toward unproductive, socially wasteful ends. The term is meant to distinguish the activities described in the preceding paragraph from the socially useful quest for profits through developing new products and employing more efficient production technologies. When profits are maintained through rent-seeking behavior, profit areas such as *abcd* in Figure 14.4 are doubly misleading from a social perspective. Not only do they fail to take account of the costs incurred in competing for the profits, but also they fail to recognize that these costs are a total waste of society's scarce resources. If the profits just equal the costs of competing, then the profit area *abcd* represents a gross efficiency loss from rent-seeking activity that should be added to the deadweight efficiency loss from monopoly power described in Figure 14.6. Some economists believe that these costs are substantial, perhaps as large as 10 percent of total corporate output, which is many times greater than Harberger's estimate of the deadweight loss from monopoly power.

RENT SEEKING
The pursuit of profitable market opportunities by entrepreneurs that is directed toward unproductive, socially wasteful ends.

Not all economists believe that the costs of rent seeking are that high. Nor is the distinction between productive and unproductive profit-seeking activity always clear-cut. But economists are in widespread agreement on one point: Entrepreneurs operating in a market economy should not be counted on to have much of a social conscience. Their natural incentive is to pursue profitable

HISTORICAL NOTE: Political rent seeking has been one of the leading growth industries in the United States over the past 30 years. In 1960, there were 365 paid lobbyists registered with the Senate. By 1992, the number had swelled to 40,111, with 7,556 of the paid lobbyists considered active. (*The Economist*, October 10, 1992, p. 21.)

opportunities through whatever avenues are available to them, productive or not.

The profit motive itself is not the issue; it is central to the smooth and efficient operation of a market economy. Rather, the important policy issue is to avoid creating opportunities for rent-seeking behavior in order to ensure that the private interest of entrepreneurs coincides with society's interest in efficiency and equity. In other words, governments in capitalist societies must design rules of exchange that direct the profit motive toward productive ends. A large part of this goal involves eliminating artificial barriers to entry as much as possible so that entrepreneurs do not think in terms of competing for maintained profit positions in the first place.

The following Concept Summary table summarizes the social costs of monopoly.

CONCEPT SUMMARY

THE SOCIAL COSTS OF PURE MONOPOLY

OBJECTIVES	MARKET TEST	ACHIEVED? MARKET OUTCOMES
EFFICIENCY		
Allocational efficiency	$P = MC$	No $MR = MC$; $P > MC$ Contrived scarcity; price too high; output too low
Production (technical) efficiency	Production at MES or minimum AC_{lr}	Generally no; only by chance *Caveat:* large firm may be necessary to capture economies of scale (for example, natural monopolies such as the public utilities)
EQUITY		
Equality of opportunity	Absence of barriers to entry, exit; equal access to all market information	No Absolute barrier to entry; no close substitutes for the product
Horizontal equity	$P = AC_{lr}$; zero maintained economic profit	No, generally Firm maintains economic profit in long run; effective market power; rent seeking generates additional inefficiencies

PRICE DISCRIMINATION

The analysis so far has assumed that the monopolist charges all customers the same price for its product. In fact, firms with monopoly power often engage in

price discrimination, charging different customers different prices that are unrelated to differences in the cost of serving the customers. The airline industry is a prime example. The next time you fly ask seven passengers sitting near you what they paid for their tickets. You may well receive seven different answers—same destination, same food, same movie, yet many different prices.

PRICE DISCRIMINATION
Charging different customers different prices that are unrelated to differences in the cost of serving the customers.

The airlines and other firms price discriminate because it can increase their profits far beyond what they can earn by charging a single price. The profit rectangle *abcd* in Figure 14.4 understates the effective market power of the pure monopolist if it can engage in price discrimination.

Two points about the definition of price discrimination should be noted before proceeding with the analysis. First, cost-based price differences do not constitute price discrimination. Suppose that a firm supplies two customers, A and B, with goods sent directly from its factory. Customer A lives 50 miles from the factory, and customer B lives 100 miles from the factory. If the firm charges customer B a higher price to cover the additional cost of transporting the goods an extra 50 miles, the higher price to customer B is not discriminatory. Prices have to be unrelated to the costs of supplying customers to constitute price discrimination. Second, the costs referred to in the definition are ambiguous. Are they differences in marginal cost or in some form of average cost? Presumably economists would favor defining price discrimination in terms of marginal cost. The courts, however, have not settled on one particular definition of cost in cases involving price discrimination.

Airlines are certainly not the only firms that price discriminate. A moment's reflection will indicate that price discrimination is fairly widespread. Movie theaters charge less for their afternoon matinee showings than for their evening showings and frequently offer discounts to students and senior citizens. Some doctors and lawyers charge their poorer patients and clients less than they do their wealthier patients and clients. Magazines and record clubs give first-time subscribers discounts relative to renewal subscribers. In each instance, the costs of serving the different customers are unlikely to be much different.

Firms that engage in price discrimination try to put the best light on it by suggesting that they are giving their lower-price customers a special break. Airlines offer families special vacation "discounts," just as magazines offer one-time special "introductory" prices to new subscribers. Doctors and lawyers are showing compassion for their low-income patients and clients. The implication is that the higher price is the "normal" price. Economists are skeptical of this implication, however, because price discrimination is such an easy and effective strategy for increasing profit. Not all firms with market power are able to price discriminate, but if they can, they have every incentive to do so. Both the higher and lower prices are "normal" when seen in light of the profit motive. They are each profit-maximizing prices.

Profit Maximizing Through Price Discrimination

Let's use the airlines as an example to see how price discrimination increases profit. To keep the example simple, assume that an airline has only two distinct classes of customers, business travelers and family vacation travelers. Further, assume that the average costs of serving each class of customer are equal and constant at all levels of service. With average cost constant, marginal cost is also constant and equal to average cost, so there is no ambiguity about the

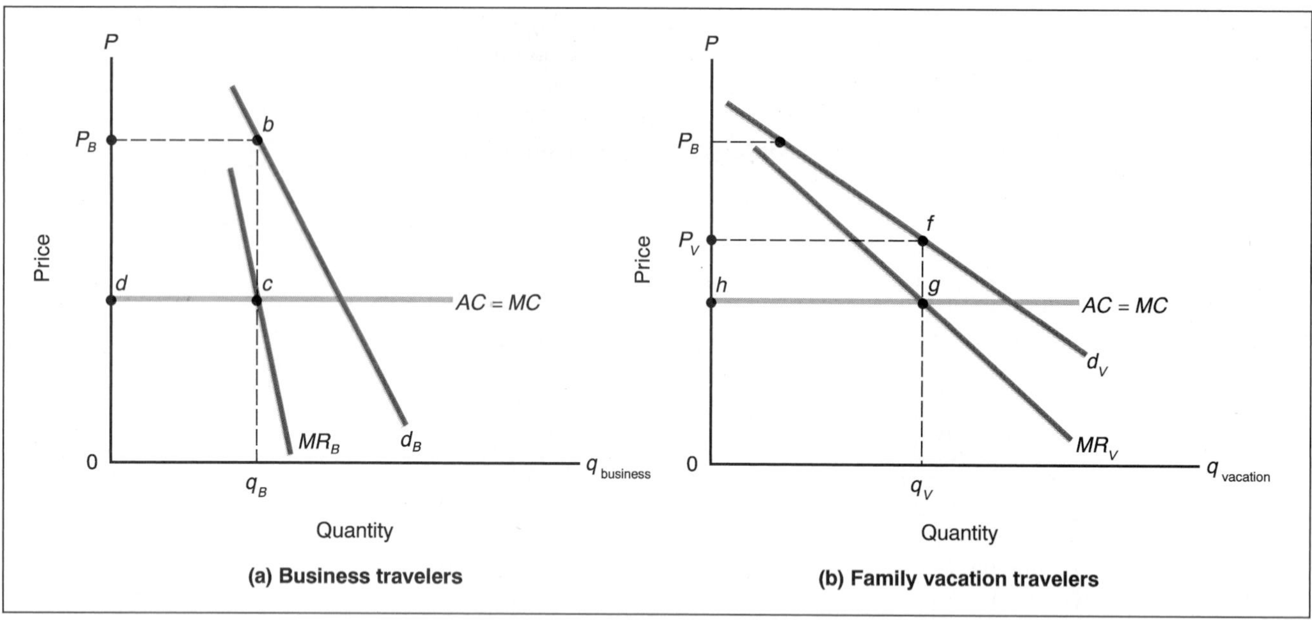

FIGURE 14.7

Price Discrimination by the Airlines

The airlines know that they have two distinct classes of customers, the business travelers in Figure 14.7(a) whose demand curves are relatively inelastic, and the family vacation travelers Figure 14.7(b), whose demand curves are relatively elastic. The average and marginal costs of serving the two classes of customers are the same. The airlines maximize profit by price discriminating. They set the output at $MR = MC$ for each class, and charge the relatively high price P_B to the business travelers and the relatively low price P_V to the vacation travelers. They do this by charging the higher price on short-term tickets that business travelers buy and the lower price on tickets purchased well in advance that vacation travelers buy. Price discrimination increases profits considerably relative to charging the same price to all customers.

costs of serving different customers. (Recall that average and marginal costs are equal when average cost is neither increasing nor decreasing.)

From the airlines' point of view their business and vacation customers constitute two separate markets, even though they are offering the same service to each. The markets are distinguished on the basis of demand elasticity. Figure 14.7 illustrates the two markets.

Figure 14.7(a) shows the market for business travel, and Figure 14.7(b) shows the market for vacation travel. With average cost (AC) and marginal cost (MC) the same for each customer, the only differences in the two markets are the demand curves (d) and their associated marginal revenue curves (MR). The demand for business travel (d_B) is very steep, that is, highly inelastic. When businesses send their employees to faraway places, they consider the trip a *necessity*, and they want the employees to arrive in a hurry. Time is money in business dealings. There is *no substitute* for air travel. Also, the airfare is a *negligible cost* to the business. In short, the demand for business air travel has all the characteristics of highly inelastic demand. By contrast, the demand for vacation travel (d_V) is much flatter, that is, much more elastic. Vacation travel is a *luxury* for most consumers for which there may be *substitute* means of transportation in some cases, for example, auto, bus, or train. Also, airfare represents a *significant cost* to most families. Vacation travel has all the characteristics of elastic demand.

The profit-maximizing strategy for the airlines is to exploit the differences in the demand elasticities. The airline should set $MR = MC$ in each market, offering q_B seats to business customers at a price of P_B and q_V seats to vacationers at a price of P_V. The separate prices are discriminatory because they are clearly unrelated to differences in cost. In charging separate prices the airline is just setting prices inversely to the elasticities of demand.

The total profit obtained by price discrimination is the sum of areas P_Bbcd in Figure 14.7(a) and P_Vfgh in Figure 14.7(b). No single price offered to both classes of customers can provide as large a profit because the separate prices

P_B and P_V maximize profits in each market individually. Any other pricing strategy must sacrifice profits in at least one of the markets. For example, charging the higher price, P_B, in both markets maximizes profit from the business customers, but it sacrifices potential profit from the vacationers because P_B is too high up on the vacationers' demand curve; marginal revenue exceeds marginal cost at that price. Better to fill more seats with vacationers by lowering the price to P_V, the point at which $MR = MC$ in that segment of the market.

The Conditions Necessary for Price Discrimination

Why don't all businesses price discriminate if price discrimination is so profitable? The answer is that two conditions must hold for price discrimination to work: (1) A firm must have some way of identifying its customers on the basis of their demand elasticities; and (2) the different classes of customers must be kept separate, so that the firm really can divide its sales into distinct markets.

Firms are sometimes able to identify customers by means of a direct signal, such as age or income, that clearly divides them into different classes. Movie theaters can fairly easily distinguish students and elderly (elastic demand) from the rest of the population (inelastic demand). Magazines can just as easily distinguish first-time subscribers (elastic demand) from renewal subscribers (inelastic demand). Doctors and lawyers often know who among their patients and clients are poor (elastic demand) and who are rich (inelastic demand).

Even when such direct signals are not available, businesses may be able to get their customers to identify themselves by offering different pricing options that appeal to different classes of customers. This is exactly what the airlines do. They know that they have distinct classes of business and vacation travelers, but they cannot tell which is which when they sell the tickets. Most ticket sales are completely impersonal, carried out over the phone and often through a travel agency. Yet the airlines also know that business travelers are likely to buy tickets on short notice and travel on weekdays. Vacationers, by contrast, often plan far ahead and travel on weekends. Therefore, the airlines vary their airfares by time of purchase, charging high prices for short-notice weekday flights and offering large "discounts" for tickets purchased far in advance and for weekend travel packages. Sure enough, business travelers buy most of the short-notice, high-priced tickets, and vacationers buy most of the in-advance, "discounted" tickets. The two classes self-select, identifying themselves and their demand elasticities by the options they choose.

Many businesses, however, are not so lucky. They know little about their customers and have no good way of getting them to identify themselves through different pricing options. These businesses cannot price discriminate.

Once the different classes of customers have been identified, they must be kept separate to prevent resales of the service or product among customers. This second condition is also met in our examples. Most business travelers would hardly be interested in purchasing the airline tickets that vacationers tend to buy. Poor patients and clients cannot resell the medical and the legal services they receive. Moviegoers attending the matinee performance receive tickets that are not honored at the evening performance.

In other markets, however, the possibility of reselling the product completely undermines any attempt to price discriminate. To see why, suppose that Figure 14.7 referred to the market for raincoats in the wet Northwest and the dry Southwest. Now Figure 14.7(a) represents the (demand inelastic) Northwest, and Figure 14.7(b) represents the (demand elastic) Southwest. If the raincoat manufacturers try to establish a substantially higher price in the Northwest on the basis of differing demand elasticities, consumers in the Southwest will soon do them in. Southwest consumers can earn an easy profit by acting as middlemen, buying raincoats cheaply in the Southwest, shipping them to the Northwest, and selling them just slightly below the Northwest price. The increase in demand for raincoats in the Southwest drives up the price in the Southwest; the increased supply of raincoats in the Northwest drives down the price in the Northwest. The prices in the two regions tend to equalize, with the only remaining difference equal to the cost of shipping the raincoats from the Southwest to the Northwest. The possibility of buying and reselling prevents the suppliers from establishing two separate markets for their products.

REFLECTION: Find a common example of price discrimination other than those mentioned in the text.

The two conditions necessary for successful price discrimination explain why price discrimination is more widespread for services than for manufactured products. Sellers of services are more likely to know something about their customers' demand elasticities than are sellers of manufactured products. Also, services tend to be more difficult to resell than are manufactured products.

PURE MONOPOLY AND PUBLIC POLICY

Our analysis of pure monopoly revealed two clear social costs from the exercise of market power, allocational inefficiency and inequity. Firms with market power set prices above marginal costs and produce too little output. In doing so they may also earn a profit, which they can maintain if barriers to entry prevent other investors from entering the industry. Any pure monopoly would almost certainly be able to earn a profit and maintain it. Large firms with market power may also be technically inefficient and waste resources, but the issue there is less clear-cut.

Governments in the United States have been willing to tolerate the existence of large firms that have considerable market power. They have even granted certain firms the right to operate as pure monopolies. At the same time, though, governments have recognized the potential inefficiencies and inequities associated with market power, all the more so when firms approach the status of pure monopoly. When the exercise of market power threatens to become excessive, governments combat it by one of four means: (1) windfall profits taxes, taxes on the portion of profits considered to be excessive by some arbitrary legislative standard; (2) industry regulation; (3) government ownership; and (4) antitrust legislation.

Chapter 14 concludes with a discussion of windfall profits taxes and the regulation and ownership of public utilities. These policies are directed to markets that correspond most closely to the pure monopoly case. Each policy attempts to safeguard the public interest by restraining the exercise of market power and otherwise promoting the social goals of efficiency and equity. (The fourth option, antitrust legislation, is targeted specifically at the oligopolies with the goal of preventing them from becoming pure monopolies, or of acting too much as pure monopolies would. We will discuss antitrust legislation in Chapter 17.)

Windfall Profits Taxes

In 1973 the Organization of Petroleum Exporting Countries (OPEC) seized control of the world oil market and engineered a series of price increases that led to an eightfold increase in the price of a barrel of crude oil by the end of the decade. Profits in the oil industry skyrocketed worldwide. For all intents and purposes the industry was operating as if it were a pure monopoly, with OPEC directing industrywide price and output decisions.

The federal government was unable to break OPEC's stranglehold on the world market. But the government did not want U.S. companies to earn excessive and unfair profits as a direct result of OPEC's blatant exercise of market power. At first Congress responded by setting price ceilings on domestically produced oil, which lasted until April 1979. Once the ceilings were removed, U.S. companies were in a position to increase their prices to the world price established by OPEC and enjoy enormous "windfall" increases in their own profits. Knowing this, Congress responded by passing the Windfall Profits Tax of 1980, an excise tax ranging from 30 to 70 percent of the price of each barrel of domestic crude oil. The 1980 tax on oil was not the first special tax on industries that Congress passed when it felt that industry profits were excessive, but it remains the most recent example.

Windfall or **excessive profit** is the same as economic profit, the return to capital over and above the opportunity cost of capital, which is the return investors can earn generally in the marketplace. If the tax base of a windfall profits tax were truly windfall profit, then the tax would work as intended. The firm would simply transfer some of its profit to the U.S. Treasury. The tax would have no other effect on the firm.

WINDFALL (EXCESSIVE) PROFIT
A return to capital over and above the opportunity cost of capital that society considers to be excessive.

To see why, return to the example of our pure monopolist. Without a tax the monopolist produces 12 units of output, sets its price at $80, and earns a windfall profit of $335. Suppose that Congress announces a new windfall profits tax equal to 80 percent of all windfall profits. How will the monopolist react? If the tax is truly a tax on profit, the monopolist will not react at all. The tax allows the monopolist to keep 20 percent of whatever profits it earns, and 20 percent of a larger number is larger than 20 percent of a smaller number. So the best the monopolist can do is earn the maximum amount of profit possible, send 80 percent of it to the government, and keep the remaining 20 percent of the maximum profit for itself. Twenty percent of the maximum profit is more than 20 percent of any other profit level. But the monopolist is already maximizing its profit by selling 12 units at $80. So the best strategy is to stay put, earn a profit of $335, and pay a tax of $268 ($268 = .8 · $335). The after-tax profit of $67 ($67 = .2 · $335) is the maximum possible after-tax profit.

Unfortunately, the tax base of a windfall profits tax is never just the profit portion of the return to capital. Prevailing corporate and personal income tax law does not count the opportunity cost of capital as a legitimate business expense of the firm. Neither do windfall profits taxes, so these taxes end up taxing the total return to capital, or something else entirely. Notice, for example, that the 1980 Windfall Profits Tax was not a tax on the return to capital at all, despite its name. It was an excise tax on output, a tax levied on each barrel of oil sold.

Excise taxes and taxes on factor costs do have output effects because they increase a firm's marginal cost. We learned in Chapter 8 that an excise tax levied on competitive firms increases their marginal costs by the full amount of the tax per unit. The firms' willingness to supply decreases, leading to a reduction in the equilibrium level of output, an increase in the equilibrium price, and a deadweight loss. The same effects occur in a pure monopoly and for the same reason: An excise tax also increases a monopolist's marginal cost by the full amount of the tax per unit. As a result, *MR* and *MC* intersect at a lower level of output than before, the monopolist charges a higher price, and deadweight loss increases. The tax increases the allocational inefficiency of monopoly by making the contrived scarcity worse. The Windfall Profits Tax of 1980 was certainly not intended to reduce U.S. production of oil. If anything, Congress wanted U.S. production to increase in order to reduce the nation's reliance on imported oil from the OPEC members. Nonetheless, the tax did reduce U.S. production.

As a practical matter, then, windfall profits taxes are a mixed blessing. They do promote equity by diverting some "ill-gotten" excessive profits to the public treasury, but the intended gains in equity come at the expense of unintended efficiency losses. Windfall profits taxes are hardly unique in this respect. We will see in Chapter 22 that weighing equity gains against efficiency losses is always a central issue whenever governments attempt to redistribute income.

Public Utility Regulation

Regulation and government ownership apply to the public utilities, such as electricity, telephones, water, and sewerage. The utilities are considered natural monopolies at the regional level because a single firm can supply the region at lowest cost. State governments allow the utilities to operate as monopolies, but they do not let them behave as profit-maximizing monopolists. They either regulate them or take them over completely.

Private ownership with regulation is the more common choice for the electric utilities and the local telephone service. State governments give private investors an exclusive territorial franchise to provide electricity or phone service. They then regulate the utilities to ensure that they do not exploit their advantage and behave as pure monopolists. Public ownership is the more common choice for water and sewerage. Whatever approach the states choose, their goal is to promote the public interest, that is, to promote efficiency and equity. Our discussion describes how the state electric utility commissions regulate the private electric utilities with the public interest in mind.

THE UTILITIES' COST STRUCTURE A regulatory commission's task would be fairly straightforward, in principle, if public utilities had demand and cost characteristics similar to those of our pure monopolist in the first part of the chapter. (Refer back to Figure 14.4 and Table 14.3.) The commission would force the utility to operate at the intersection of the demand and the marginal cost curves, producing 16 units of output and charging a price of \$56. As we have seen in Figure 14.6, this quantity-price combination, (16, \$56), maximizes the net value of producing and consuming the good—it satisfies the goal of allocational efficiency. Moreover, the utility would be willing to accept that solution because it is profitable. The price of \$56 exceeds the average cost of (approximately) \$48 at $Q = 16$. The utility makes a profit of \$134 (seventh column of Table 14.3). Even if the commission forced the utility to turn the \$134 of profit over to the public treasury in the interests of equity, the utility would still break even and cover its cost of capital. The investors could live with this solution as well.

Unfortunately, achieving efficiency and equity is not that simple for the regulatory commissions. The problem is that the demand and the cost characteristics of our pure monopolist are not representative of the public utilities.

Governments allow the utilities to operate as pure monopolies for reasons of technical efficiency. Utilities are characterized by extremely high setup costs and relatively low operating costs. For example, providing electricity to a region requires a huge initial investment in generating capacity and in constructing a distribution network of poles and lines to homes and businesses. Once the generating capacity and the distribution network are in place, the variable costs of supplying the electricity are quite low. The combination of high setup costs and low operating costs creates substantial economies of scale. The scale economies are so large that a utility's average cost continues to decline all the way to the region of *market* demand (*D*), as represented in Figure 14.8. Note, also, that with average cost (*AC*) declining, marginal cost (*MC*) is everywhere below average cost up to market demand.

The utilities are said to be **natural monopolies** because a single utility can produce at or near its minimum efficient scale of operation (MES) only if it is allowed to supply the entire market. Allowing a number of utilities to supply each region in the interest of promoting competition would simply waste resources. Each utility would be producing at much higher average costs than a single monopoly utility could achieve. Just imagine the duplication and waste of having three or four utilities supplying electricity to your hometown, with each investing in its own generating facilities and constructing its own distribution network of poles and lines.

NATURAL MONOPOLY

A market situation in which the MES (the minimum of the long-run average cost curve) of a single firm is at or beyond the entire market demand for the product.

EFFICIENCY AND EQUITY The government's goal of pursuing efficiency and equity is not so easy to carry out in the face of declining average cost. The government essentially has three options, each illustrated in Figure 14.8: (1) Do not regulate at all, (2) regulate by setting price equal to marginal cost in the interest of allocational efficiency, or (3) regulate by setting price equal to average cost.

NO REGULATION The first option is to allow the utility to operate as it wishes, without any regulatory oversight at all. If the utility then maximizes profit, it would produce output Q_M, at the intersection of *MR* and *MC*; charge a price of P_M; and earn a profit equal to the area aP_Mbc. Some economists favor this option. They believe that the utilities are more likely to operate efficiently if they are unregulated. In a normal market setting, the profit motive provides the incentives to produce efficiently. A regulatory environment that denies a utility a chance to earn a profit destroys any incentives to introduce new cost-reducing technologies or improve the quality of service, or even try to produce at the lowest possible cost. Also, leaving the utilities on their own saves the considerable costs associated with the regulatory process itself. Finally, these economists believe that an unregulated utility would not maximize profits for fear of incurring the public's wrath. They would set prices well below P_M to keep the public's trust and maintain their monopoly position.

FIGURE 14.8

Regulating the Electric Utilities

The electric utilities are natural monopolies because their average costs (AC) decline all the way to total market demand (D). The government has three choices: (a) let a private monopolist run the service unregulated which, if the monopolist maximizes profit, leads to output Q_M at the intersection of marginal revenue (MR) and marginal cost (MC), and a price P_M, (b) force the monopolist to set the efficient quantity-price combination (Q_{eff},P_{eff}) at the intersection of D and MC, and subsidize the utility out of general tax revenues in the amount equal to the rectangular area $P_{eff}def$; or (c) set the average cost price P_{AC} at the intersection of D and AC, and provide output Q_{AC}. The regulations choose the average cost pricing option despite its inefficiency because they want the users of electricity to pay the full cost of supplying electricity to the region, in line with the benefits-received principle.

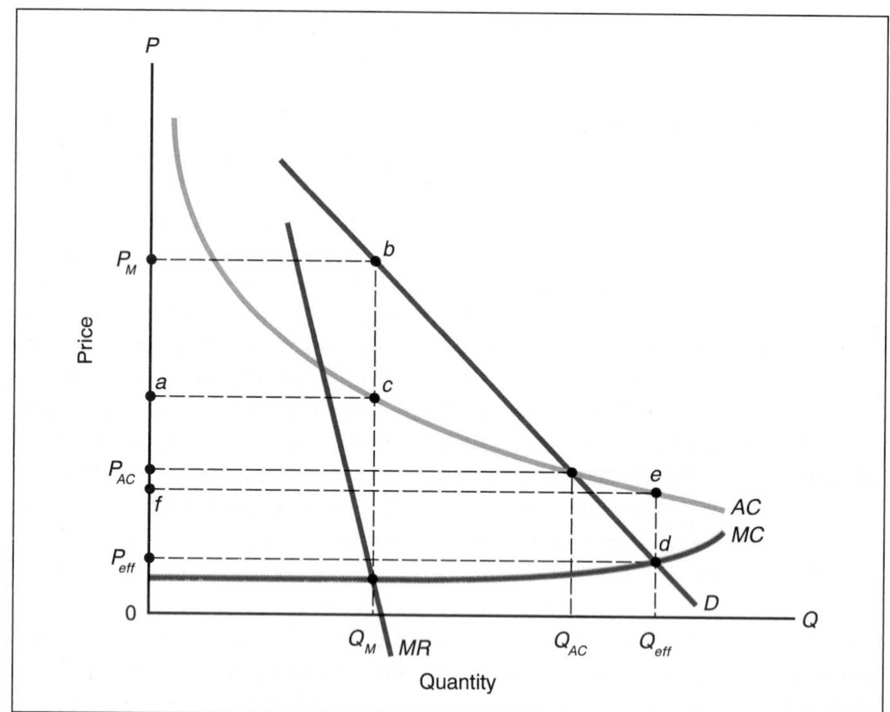

These advantages are counterbalanced by two serious disadvantages. An unregulated utility would certainly set price above marginal cost. It would not be allocationally efficient. In addition, the government has no guarantee that the utility will not exercise some of its market power and take a profit. Granting a utility a pure monopoly in the interests of technical efficiency is one thing. But no government wants to be open to the charge that a utility is abusing its privilege and profiting at the public's expense.

These disadvantages apparently have been persuasive, since governments have chosen either to regulate utilities or to operate them as public enterprises. The question remains how best to regulate the private utilities.

MARGINAL COST PRICING: ALLOCATIONAL EFFICIENCY One option is to pursue the goal of allocational efficiency so that the public receives the maximum net value from operating the utility. Allocational efficiency is achieved at the intersection of the demand and the marginal cost curves, with $P = MC$. Under this option, the regulatory commission forces the utility to set its price at P_{eff} and to offer Q_{eff} units of service. The public gains the dual advantages of both allocational and technical efficiency.

The equity implications of this option are not entirely acceptable, however. The problem arises because marginal cost is below average cost. With P_{eff} set equal to marginal cost, price is also below average cost at Q_{eff}. The owners of the utility experience a loss equal to the area $P_{eff}def$. Therefore, if the commission chooses this option, the government must be prepared to cover the loss with a subsidy to the owners out of general tax revenues. The owners of the utility cannot be expected to accept a return on their investment that is below the returns they can earn generally.

Governments have not been willing to do this. Subsidizing utilities out of general tax revenues violates a time-honored equity principle called the benefits-received principle of public pricing and taxation. The **benefits-received principle** says that citizens ought to pay for public services in accordance with the benefits they receive from them. The public utilities are a natural candidate for applying the benefits-received principle. Users are easily distinguished from nonusers, and more intensive users from less intensive users. According to the benefits-received principle, therefore, users should pay the full costs of the service, and more intensive users should pay a larger share of the costs than should less intensive users. Setting price equal to marginal cost is at odds with the benefits-received principle. The price P_{eff} itself is fine. Only users pay it, and more intensive users do pay more in total for the service than do less intensive users. But the part of the costs that would be covered by general tax revenues breaks the link between payments and benefits received. All citizens throughout the state end up subsidizing, through their tax payments, those citizens who are receiving the services of a local utility. The subsidies might not cancel one another throughout the state, and this is considered unfair.

BENEFITS-RECEIVED PRINCIPLE

A pricing principle for public services, which says that citizens should pay for public services in accordance with the benefits they receive from them.

AVERAGE COST PRICING The unwillingness to subsidize the utilities has led the regulatory commissions to a third option, average cost pricing. The commission forces the utility to set its price at P_{AC} and to offer Q_{AC} units of service. Under this option the owners just cover their cost of capital. Average cost pricing is viewed as an acceptable compromise between the other two options. It is preferred to no regulation at all because it achieves a price closer to the efficient marginal cost price and it avoids any possible charge that the owners are profiting at the public's expense. Average cost pricing is also preferred to marginal cost pricing because it satisfies the benefits-received principle. With $P_{AC} = AC$, users pay the full costs of the service, and they pay in proportion to the amount they use the service. This gain in equity apparently more than offsets the loss in allocational efficiency from setting price above marginal cost.

The average cost pricing strategy is not unique to the public utilities. When governments charge for a service, they almost always do so on the basis of average costs. Parking fees at public beaches are set to cover the costs of operating the beach. Tolls on bridges, tunnels, and highways are set to cover the costs of constructing and maintaining the various facilities under the jurisdiction of the metropolitan transportation authority. In each instance the benefits-received principle is the operating principle in setting the price.

Each electric utility regulatory commission sets electricity prices, or rates, only periodically, usually every three to five years. The commission determines the appropriate average cost price through a discovery process in which the utility presents data on its revenues and costs of providing the services, both past data and estimates of future revenues and costs. The process of setting the price then proceeds in two steps.

The first step involves constructing an average cost curve for the utility. The commission begins with the utility's estimates of its operating expenses at each level of service for such items as labor and materials. The commission then adds an allowable cost of capital to the operating expenses to determine the utility's total cost.

$$\text{Total cost} = \text{operating expenses} + \text{the allowable cost of capital}$$

The allowable cost of capital is the product of (1) a "fair" rate of return, r_{fair}, which the commission permits the owners to earn on their capital and (2) the value of the utility's capital stock in place, K. The allowable cost of capital = $r_{fair} \cdot K$. Note that the fair rate of return must equal or exceed the owner's opportunity cost of capital.

The second step makes use of the revenue data to estimate the quantity-price combination that will set total revenue equal to total cost, or $P_{AC} = AC$. A utility can apply for a rate (price) change at any time between the hearings if it believes either demand or cost has changed significantly.

The regulation of public utilities has proved to be reasonably successful. The American public certainly accepts the average cost pricing philosophy of the regulatory commissions. In addition, economists' fears that the utilities would not be technically progressive under regulation have not been realized. Quite the contrary. The utilities generally have an admirable record of introducing new cost-cutting technologies. To cite just one example, long-distance telephone calls are much cheaper today than they were 25 years ago.

The technical record of the utilities really is a puzzle to economists because everything about the regulatory process argues against having any incentive to produce efficiently. The utilities face no competition, and they are not allowed to earn a profit. Moreover, the demand for their services is price inelastic. If they are careless and inefficient, they can always cover any resulting cost increases by raising prices. Raising price increases total revenues when demand is inelastic. The standard explanation of the puzzle is that the utilities really are allowed to earn a profit after all. The argument is that with rates set only every three to five years the utilities can capture some profit for awhile by introducing new cost-reducing technologies. Also, regulators may be prone to set the fair rate of return comfortably above the owners' opportunity cost of capital.

One study of the actual rates of return earned by the electric utilities has cast some doubt on this explanation, however. The study found that, on average, the actual rates of return were less than the allowable rates of return from 1977 to 1982 and that the allowable "fair" rates of return were *less* than the owners' cost of capital in 1980–81.[4] The admirable performance of the utilities remains somewhat of a puzzle.

SUMMARY

Chapter 14 explored the implications of market power in the context of pure monopoly, when the industry supplying the market consists of a single firm. The first section of the chapter established the following principles.

1. A firm possesses market, or monopoly, power if its demand curve is downward sloping. Almost every firm in a market economy possesses market power by that definition.
2. Any firm having market power is a price setter. It does not have a supply curve, unlike a perfectly competitive firm. Rather, the firm must determine the single price-quantity combination on its demand curve that maximizes profit. The demand curve defines the total revenue frontier for the firm.

[4]G. Rothwell and K. Eastman, "A Note on Allowed and Realized Rates of Return of the U.S. Electric Utility Industry," *Journal of Industrial Economics* XXXVI, No. 1 (September, 1987): 105–110.

3. When a firm's demand curve is downward sloping, its marginal revenue curve lies below the demand curve. Only for a perfectly competitive firm is the firm's demand curve the same as its marginal revenue curve.
4. To maximize profit, the firm selects the output at which marginal revenue equals marginal cost and charges the price on the demand curve corresponding to the chosen output.

The second section of the chapter discussed the normative properties of pure monopoly.

5. The market outcome under pure monopoly is not very satisfactory from society's point of view. It is characterized by allocational inefficiency, production (technical) inefficiency, and inequity.
    a. *Allocational inefficiency* exists because the monopolist produces at the intersection of the marginal revenue and the marginal cost curves. As a result, price is greater than marginal cost, and the net value from producing and consuming the good is not maximized. All firms having market power generate allocational inefficiency. They engage in a contrived scarcity, keeping output below the efficient level in order to maximize profit.
    b. *Production (technical) inefficiency* exists if the monopolist does not produce at the MES, the minimum of its long-run average cost curve. A firm with market power produces at the MES only by chance, if the marginal revenue and the marginal cost curves happen to intersect at that point. The potential loss in production efficiency is tempered somewhat by the cost savings of very large scale production, which may require a few very large firms, each having considerable market power.
    c. The *inequity* of pure monopoly takes two forms. Pure monopoly violates the process equity principle of equality of opportunity because the barriers to entry that create the monopoly keep other investors out of the market. As a result, pure monopoly also violates the end-results equity principle of horizontal equity. The monopolist can earn and *maintain* excess profit. Effective market or monopoly power is the ability to maintain profit in the long run. Investors in markets with barriers to entry can earn a higher rate of return on their capital than other investors earn generally.
6. Monopoly profits are often invisible because the stock market capitalizes the stream of profits into the value of the stock. Once capitalization occurs, purchasing the stock of a profitable company yields only the same return available to all investors generally.
7. The monopoly profits earned by one firm overstate the gains to society because they ignore the costs borne by unsuccessful entrepreneurs in the competition for maintained profits. If the competition involves unproductive rent-seeking activity, then the profits earned by the successful firms represent a gross efficiency loss from the point of view of society. Rent-seeking behavior simply wastes resources.

The third section of the chapter showed how firms can enhance their effective market power through price discrimination, charging different customers different prices that are not justified by cost differences in supplying the customers.

8. Firms price discriminate on the basis of their customers' demand elasticities, charging higher prices to customers with lower demand elasticities.

9. Successful price discrimination requires two conditions: (a) Firms must be able to identify distinct classes of customers who have different demand elasticities, and (b) customers must not be able to resell the output to one another. These conditions are most often met with services as opposed to manufactured products.

The final section of Chapter 14 discusses two policy issues that are closely related to pure monopoly, windfall profits taxes and public utility regulation.

10. Congress levies windfall profits taxes on an industry when it believes that firms are earning excessive profits as the result of a blatant exercise of market power. If Congress could really levy a tax on windfall profits, these taxes would transfer some profits to the public treasury without changing firms' production decisions. Windfall profits are difficult to define, however, so that these taxes end up taxing something else, either costs of production or output. As a result, windfall profits taxes capture profits at a cost of restricting output even further and increasing allocational inefficiency.
11. States grant electric utilities the status of pure monopolies for reasons of technical efficiency: The utilities' average costs decrease all the way to market demand. The states then regulate the utilities, forcing them to operate at the intersection of their demand and average cost curves, with price equal to average cost. Average cost pricing is viewed as an acceptable compromise between letting the utilities operate as they wish and profit from their monopoly status and regulating them at the allocationally efficient marginal cost price. Setting price equal to marginal cost is unacceptable because it would require a subsidy to the utilities out of general tax revenue. The subsidy violates the benefits-received principle of pricing for public services.

KEY TERMS

average revenue curve
benefits-received principle
contrived scarcity
effective market (monopoly) power
market power (monopoly power)
natural monopoly
price discrimination
profit-maximizing output rule
pure monopoly
rent seeking
windfall (excessive) profit

QUESTIONS

1. Market power differentiates perfect competition from all other market structures. What is market power?
2. Both perfectly competitive firms and pure monopolies want to maximize profits. Also, both types of firms maximize profits by producing the output at which marginal revenue equals marginal cost. Yet perfect competition is consistent with the social goal of allocational efficiency, and pure monopoly is not. Why is this?
3. A pure monopolist has the following cost and demand data. The price in column 4 refers to the price along the monopolist's demand curve as each output level in column 1.

q	TOTAL COST	MARGINAL COST	PRICE	TOTAL REVENUE	MARGINAL REVENUE
0	$ 500	—	$1,000	____	$
1	600	$100	900	____	____
2	650	50	800	____	____
3	725	75	700	____	____
4	825	100	600	____	____
5	950	125	500	____	____
6	1,200	250	400	____	____

a. Fill in the blanks in the last two columns.

b. Calculate the monopolist's profit at each output from 0 to 6.
c. What output maximizes the monopolist's profit?
d. Explain how the profit-maximizing output illustrates the profit-maximizing rule for a pure monopolist.
e. How do the data show that this firm has market power?

4. Write an essay on the potential evils of pure monopoly from society's point of view.
5. Suppose that you buy stock in a firm that has effective market (monopoly) power. Why might you not be able to earn a higher return on this stock than if it were the stock of a perfectly competitive firm?
6. What is rent-seeking behavior, and why does it add to the inefficiencies of monopoly power? Give several examples of rent seeking as part of your answer.
7. Discuss the truth of this statement: Most firms in the United States have monopoly power, but relatively few have effective monopoly power. Among other things, be sure to indicate the difference between monopoly power and effective monopoly power and to discuss the factors that turn the former into the latter.
8. Do the following represent price discrimination? Explain your answers.
   a. Colleges give more financial aid to students the lower their families' incomes.
   b. Students receive special discount rates for subscriptions to the *Wall Street Journal.*
   c. The monthly cost of purchasing a particular magazine at a newstand is $10, but it costs a consumer $11 to have it delivered at home.
9. The airlines do not know their customers any better than hardware store owners know their customers. Yet airlines are easily able to price discriminate, whereas hardware stores cannot price discriminate. What differences between the two kinds of businesses explain their different abilities to price discriminate?
10. The state regulatory commissions require the electric utilities to charge a price equal to the average cost of supplying electricity. Discuss the advantages and disadvantages of average cost pricing as opposed to marginal cost pricing of electricity.
11. Comment on the following statements: In theory, a windfall profits tax just captures some of the excessive economic profits of firms without causing them to change their output. In practice, however, windfall profits taxes usually do cause the taxed firms to reduce their output.

CHAPTER

15

Softening Competition: From Collusion to Effectively Competitive Markets

LEARNING OBJECTIVES

CONCEPTS TO LEARN

- Cooperative versus noncooperative behavior among firms
- The industry cartel
- The Prisoners' Dilemma
- Monopolistic competition
- Product differentiation
- The pros and cons of licensing

CONCEPTS TO RECALL

- The three criteria for judging market outcomes [13]
- The zero-profit long-run competitive equilibrium [13]
- Market (monopoly) power [14]
- Effective market (monopoly) power [14]
- The profit-maximizing output rule for firms with market power [14]

Chapters 15 through 17 tackle the real-world complexities of effective competition and oligopoly, the two market structures that characterize more than 90 percent of all product markets in the U.S. economy.

Business women and men will tell you that it is tough out there in the real world. Firms compete vigorously with one another, in both the short run and the long run. They compete in the short run by means of price, advertising, and other sales promotions. They compete in the long run by varying the characteristics of their products and by developing new products and new production technologies. Moreover, the business environment is often highly strategic. Businesses play games with one another, each trying to guess how other firms will react to their decisions. No one is guaranteed success under these conditions. Everyone works hard, but hard work alone may not be enough. Success is often a combination of hard work, timing, and, yes, pure dumb luck.

At the same time, the world out there is not perfectly competitive by any stretch of the imagination. Most firms have market power and set their prices above marginal cost. Many firms enjoy effective market power and are able to maintain a profitable market position for a long, long time. In truth, the thousands of product markets in a modern economy are incredibly diverse, and firms display an enormous variety of behavior.

Economists have come to understand much of firms' behavior in product markets as an attempt to soften competition. The central idea is that firms try to capture customers and distance themselves from other firms so that they can earn, and maintain, profits. Chapter 15 begins with two examples of firm behavior that lie at opposite ends of the competitive spectrum.

COOPERATIVE BEHAVIOR

Collusion by two or more firms in which they explicitly agree not to compete with one another.

The first example is **cooperative,** or collusive, **behavior,** in which firms soften the competition among themselves by simply refusing to compete with one another. Instead of setting their prices independently and competing, the firms get together and agree to sell at a common price greater than average cost. Our analysis of cooperative behavior focuses on the industry cartel, one of the most blatant forms of collusion.

The second example is an effectively competitive market made so because the industry contains a very large number of firms and minimal barriers to entry. The model that economists use to describe this market is monopolistic competition. Cartels and monopolistic competition define the limits of noncompetitive and competitive behavior when markets are neither pure monopolies nor perfectly competitive.

COOPERATIVE BEHAVIOR: THE CASE OF AN INDUSTRY CARTEL

History tells us that the surest way for firms to soften competition among themselves is simply to refuse to compete. Cooperation among firms extracts the maximum possible profit from the market by turning the industry into a pure monopoly.

In the 1920s General Electric and the German firm Freidrich Krupp were the only producers of tungsten carbide, a material used in the manufacture of cutting tools, dies, and other industrial products. Near the end of the decade GE and Krupp decided to quit competing with one another; they joined forces to form a monopoly. Immediately after they joined together, the firms were able to raise the price of tungsten carbide from \$50 a pound to \$453 a pound. The price remained between \$255 and \$453 a pound until 1942, when the monopoly was successfully challenged by the U.S. Department of Justice under the antitrust statutes and dissolved. Thereafter, when the two firms were once again forced to compete, the price of tungsten carbide ranged from \$27 to \$45 a pound.[1]

CARTEL

An organization of some or all of the firms in an industry established for the purpose of maximizing the total profits of the cooperating firms.

The tungsten carbide monopoly is an example of an industry cartel. A **cartel** is an organization of some or all the firms in an industry established for the purpose of maximizing the total profits of the cooperating firms. The cartel performs two functions for its members. First, it determines the price and the total cartel output that maximizes profits for the firms as a whole. Second, it divides up the total cartel profits by setting production quotas for each firm. All firms agree to honor the cartel price and their individual production quotas.

Cartels and other forms of cooperative behavior do not always ensure smooth sailing, however. Cartels and other cooperative arrangements are difficult to maintain because each member has a strong incentive to cheat.

Let's take a look at how cartels gain and exercise market power and why they are vulnerable to cheating.

Maximizing Cartel Profits

Understanding how cartels maximize group profits is best achieved with an example in which an industrywide cartel is formed in a perfectly competitive market. Cartels arise out of oligopolies, not highly competitive markets, but beginning with perfect competition serves to sharpen the analysis. Therefore, suppose that a perfectly competitive market is originally in a long-run competitive equilibrium, with each of the firms just breaking even. Refer to Figure 15.1. Figure 15.1(b) pictures the market or industry demand (D) and supply (S) curves. Figure 15.1(a) pictures the marginal cost curve (MC) and the average cost curve (AC) of a representative firm, along with the firm's demand curves (d) at various market prices. The market is originally in equilibrium at (Q_e, P_e), the intersection of D and S. Each firm supplies q_e to the market, the output at which the price P_e equals MC, and just breaks even. $P_e = MC = AC$.

Then some genius comes along and figures out how to organize all the firms into a cartel. Because the firms have agreed to cooperate, each is able to view the market as a pure monopolist would, rather than as one small firm among many would. In other words, the cartel sees the market demand and the market supply curves in Figure 15.1(b).

We learned in Chapter 14 that a pure monopolist maximizes profit by producing at the intersection of its marginal revenue and marginal cost curves and by charging the corresponding price along its demand curve. The cartel max-

[1]W. Adams, "Public Policy in a Free Enterprise Economy," in W. Adams, ed., *The Structure of American Industry*, Seventh Edition (New York: Macmillan, 1986), 397–398.

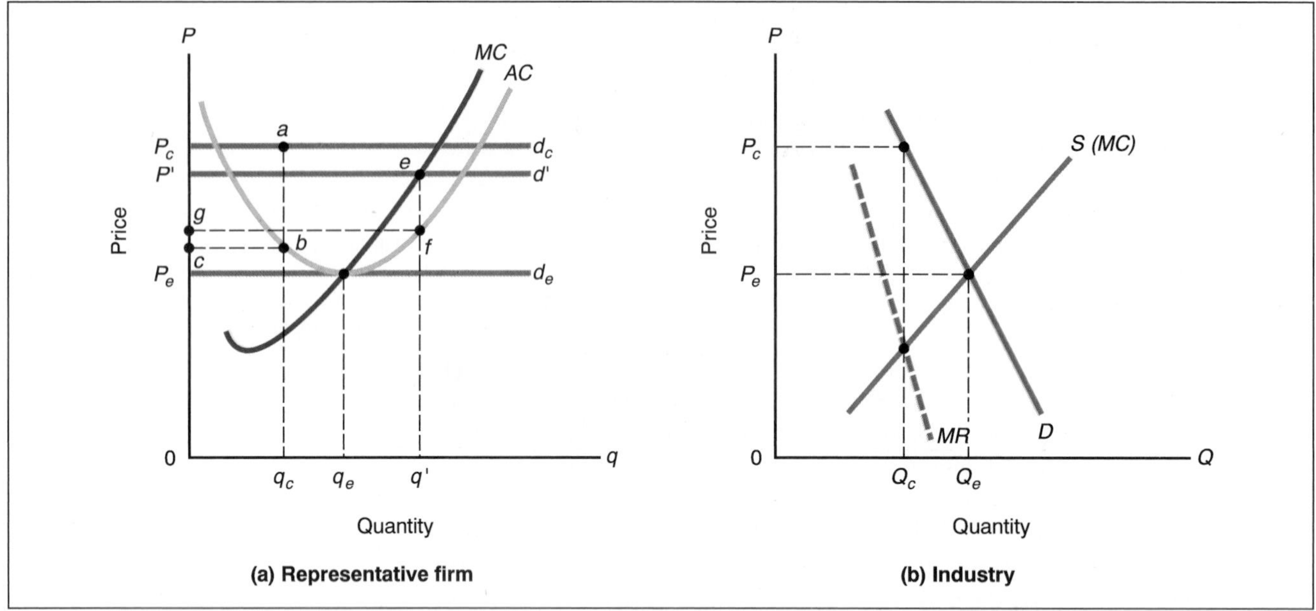

FIGURE 15.1

An Industry Cartel

A perfectly competitive industry is initially in long-run equilibrium with the quantity and price (Q_e,P_e) at the intersection of the industry supply and demand curves *S* and *D* in Figure 15.1(b). Each of the representative firms in Figure 15.1(a) supplies output q_e at the intersection of d_e and *MC* and is just breaking even. Then someone organizes the firms into a cartel and sets price and output to maximize total industry profits. Industry profits are maximized with an output of Q_c, at the intersection of industry *MR* and *S*(*MC*) in Figure 15.1(b). The profit-maximizing cartel price is P_c. Each firm is given a quota of q_c and earns a profit equal to the rectangular area $abcP_c$. Firms have an incentive to cheat by charging a price of P' and selling q' at the intersection of d' and *MC*. Once the cheating is detected, however, all firms lower their prices, the cartel falls apart, and the firms return to the original zero-profit competitive equilibrium.

imizes industrywide profit in the same way. Recall that the market supply curve is the sum of the individual firms' marginal cost curves. Therefore, *S* represents the marginal cost of supplying industry output. The dotted line *MR* is the marginal revenue curve associated with the market demand curve, *D*. The profit-maximizing cartel output is Q_c, at the intersection of *MR* and *S*. The profit-maximizing cartel price is P_c on the market demand curve, *D*.

Having determined the price and the total output, the cartel must then set production quotas for each of the firms. Refer to Figure 15.1(a). d_c is the representative firm's demand curve at the cartel price, P_c. Each firm would like to increase production beyond q_e to the intersection of *MC* and d_c in order to maximize its profit. But the cartel cannot allow the firms to do this. Total industry output was Q_e before the cartel, with each firm supplying q_e of the total. The cartel has to enforce a *reduction* of total output from Q_e to Q_c in order to maximize industry profits. Therefore, the cartel imposes production quotas on each firm *below* q_e—say, at q_c—such that the sum of every firm's q_c equals Q_c. By agreeing to sell output q_c at the cartel price, P_c, each firm makes a profit equal to the area of rectangle $abcP_c$.

Cheating: The Prisoners' Dilemma

Cooperating through a cartel obviously works to the advantage of each of the firms. Even so, the cartel contains the seeds of its own destruction. The problem is that each firm would like to increase production beyond its quota and has an easy way of doing so. All a firm needs to do is cheat on its fellow members by secretly lowering its price slightly below the cartel price—say, to P'. If all other firms honor the cartel price, the cheater can sell as much as it wants at P'. Its demand curve is the horizontal curve d', and the profit-maximizing output is q', at the intersection of d' and *MC*. The profits from cheating, equal to the area of rectangle $efgP'$, are far greater than the profits are from sticking to the cartel agreement. Once someone cheats and the word gets out, however, all firms lower their prices to protect their share of the market, and the cartel agreement falls apart. The market returns to the zero-profit competitive equilibrium.

Will the firms really cheat, knowing that cheating threatens the cartel? The answer is most likely yes. The problem for the cartel is that the obvious incentive to cheat breeds distrust, and the firms become caught in a game known as the Prisoners' Dilemma. The **Prisoners' Dilemma** is so named because it was first described in terms of two prisoners choosing whether or not to confess to a crime. The game applies equally to firms in a cartel, however, with "cheat" and "do not cheat" replacing "confess" and "do not confess."

PRISONERS' DILEMMA
In the context of an industry cartel, a game played among the member firms in which the equilibrium outcome is for the firms to cheat and destroy the profits made possible by the cartel.

The firms' dilemma is that they are led through strategic considerations to an outcome that they know is not in their best interests. To see why, suppose that the cartel consists of only two firms, 1 and 2, each deciding whether to cheat or not. Refer to Table 15.1.

The options for firm 1 are listed down the left-hand side of the table, and the options for firm 2 are listed along the top of the table. The four cells of the table list the possible outcomes. The bottom left-hand corner of each cell shows the outcome for firm 1; the top right-hand corner shows the outcome for firm 2. If neither cheats (top left-hand cell), each firm earns the cartel profit, corresponding to area $abcP_c$ in Figure 15.1. If both cheat (the bottom right-hand cell), the cartel unravels, and they each break even, corresponding to the competitive equilibrium in Figure 15.1. If firm 1 does not cheat, but firm 2 does (top right-hand cell), firm 2 gains the maximum possible profit, corresponding to the area $efgP'$ in Figure 15.1. These profits come at the expense of firm 1, which ends up with a loss. The reverse is true if firm 1 cheats and firm 2 does not (bottom left-hand cell).

The dilemma is that cheat-cheat is the only equilibrium for this game, even though both firms know that they are better off if neither cheats. Consider the situation from the point of view of firm 1. Firm 1 cannot be sure what firm 2 will do, so its goal is to maximize its profit no matter what firm 2 does. Suppose that firm 1 assumes that firm 2 will not cheat. Then its best-profit strategy is to cheat. Not cheating earns firm 1 the cartel profit, but cheating earns the maximum possible profit. Suppose, instead, that firm 1 assumes that firm 2 will cheat. Once again its best strategy is to cheat. If firm 1 does not cheat, it earns a loss as firm 2 captures the maximum possible profit. By cheating, firm 1 at

TABLE 15.1 The Prisoners' Dilemma

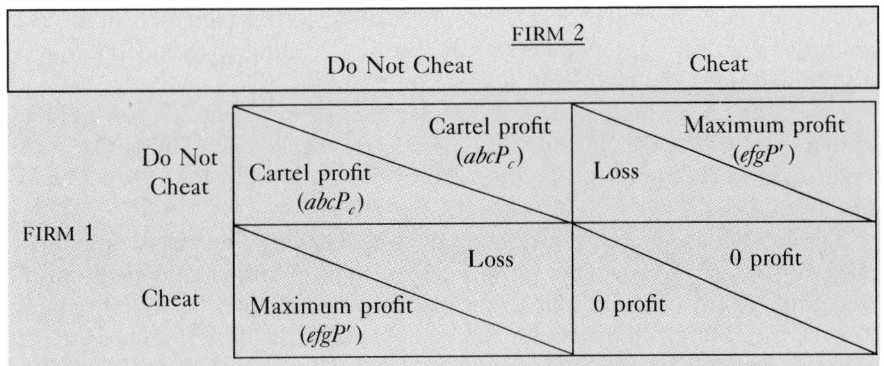

		FIRM 2: Do Not Cheat	FIRM 2: Cheat
FIRM 1	Do Not Cheat	Cartel profit ($abcP_c$) (firm 2) Cartel profit ($abcP_c$) (firm 1)	Maximum profit ($efgP'$) (firm 2) Loss (firm 1)
	Cheat	Loss (firm 2) Maximum profit ($efgP'$) (firm 1)	0 profit (firm 2) 0 profit (firm 1)

least breaks even. So cheating is the dominant strategy. It brings firm 1 the highest profit no matter what firm 2 does. Firm 2 reasons exactly the same way. Therefore, both firms cheat, the cartel unravels, and the firms break even.

The incentive to cheat is so strong that cartels are unlikely to survive unless they build in some method for dealing with cheating right from the beginning. The best safeguards are early detection and an agreed-on rule for dishing out swift and harsh punishment to cheaters. Building in safeguards against cheating is often easier said than done, however. Preventing cheating is particularly difficult if demand is highly unstable, or if the firms have very different costs, or if the cartel makes infrequent sales to large buyers such as government agencies. Unstable demand makes detection of cheating more difficult because a firm is never quite sure whether a decline in its sales is the result of falling demand or cheating by another firm in the cartel. If firms' costs differ, the cartel may have difficulty agreeing on a single price. Also, high-cost firms may not be able to enforce the punishment of low-cost firms if the low-cost firms choose to undercut the cartel price. With large, infrequent sales, a firm may decide that the short-run gains of cheating and making a large sale more than offset the long-run losses of undermining the cartel agreement.

In point of fact, cartels and other forms of cooperation have been difficult to maintain. Successful, long-standing cooperation among firms is the exception rather than the rule.

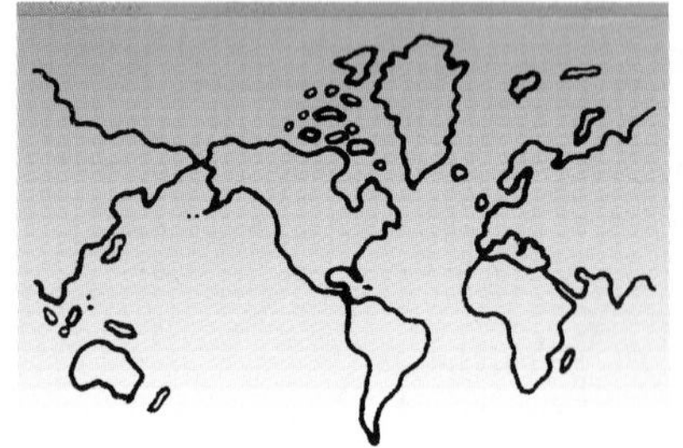

OPEC: THE RISE AND FALL OF A CARTEL

OPEC, the Organization of Petroleum Exporting Countries, offered the world a prime example of both the power and the instability of cartels in the 1970s and early 1980s. In 1973 OPEC members agreed to set oil prices and maintain production quotas, and they took control of the world oil market. The cartel was spectacularly successful for awhile. OPEC was able to engineer a series of price increases that raised the price of a barrel of crude oil from $2.00 in 1973 to $34 by October 1981. The arrangement brought in hundreds of billions of dollars in additional oil revenues to OPEC members.

October 1981 marked the height of OPEC's monopoly power. Shortly thereafter OPEC began to lose its grip on the oil market, and the price of crude oil plummeted, falling as low as $10 a barrel by mid-decade. The OPEC cartel was done in by two factors, the artificially high price of oil and cheating within the cartel. The high cartel price led to a glut of oil on the world market as the quantity of oil demanded decreased and supplies of oil increased from other countries that were not members of the cartel. Cheating on production quotas also undermined the cartel and finally tore it apart.

Few economists predicted in 1973 that OPEC would be able to hold together because they were sure that the countries would cheat. OPEC's continued success throughout the 1970s and into the early 1980s took almost everyone by surprise.

The prediction of cheating turned out to be correct. The smaller producers such as Nigeria, Algeria, and Libya violated their production quotas from the beginning. They behaved as if all they cared about was short-run profit taking. Yet the cartel survived despite the cheating because Saudi Arabia chose to play the role of benefactor and was in a position to do so. Saudi Arabia is many times over the largest oil producer among the OPEC members. Whenever the other members cheated, the Saudis reduced their own production to maintain the overall output target and the cartel price. Had the Saudis not reduced their output, the cartel would have quickly dissolved.

By the early 1980s, however, the Saudis had had enough. Their production had dropped to about one-third of its 1973 level, and they were unwilling to make further cuts to support the cartel. Saudi Arabia's change of heart, combined with increasing supplies of oil from non-OPEC countries, finally destroyed the market power of the cartel.

U.S. Policy Toward Cooperative Behavior

The United States decided long ago that it would not rely on the incentive to cheat to undermine cooperative arrangements among firms. Cartels and other forms of explicit collusion among firms were outlawed by the Sherman Antitrust Act of 1890. Firms are forced to make decisions on their own, that is, to behave noncooperatively. Violators of the Sherman Act are subject to both criminal and civil penalties.

CURRENT ISSUE: The National Collegiate Athletic Association is an example of an industry cartel that the federal government has decided to allow. The leading Division I schools are able to recruit star athletes in football and basketball who are literally worth millions of dollars to their schools; yet they do not have to pay them more than room, board, and tuition. Small wonder that many of these athletes leave college prematurely so that they can offer their talents on a more open market.

Most of the major U.S. antitrust cases involving outright collusion have been brought against industries characterized by highly variable demands and large fixed costs, such as cement, steel, and coal. The firms in each instance sought to establish a single price in order to avoid bouts of excessive price cutting and huge losses during periods of low demand. They were seeking price stability, not necessarily maximum cartel profits.

We will assume from now through Chapter 17 that firms **behave noncooperatively** since cooperation among firms is illegal. A key question throughout is how firms attempt to soften competition among themselves when they cannot explicitly cooperate. The remainder of this chapter analyzes this question in the effectively competitive sector of the economy, using monopolistic competition as an example of an effectively competitive market.

NONCOOPERATIVE BEHAVIOR
Independent decision making by firms in which they openly compete with one another.

MONOPOLISTIC COMPETITION

Recall from our preview of market structures that the model of **monopolistic competition** is much closer to perfect competition than it is to pure monopoly. The reason why is that it shares three structural characteristics with perfect competition. The model assumes that the industry consists of a very large number of firms, that barriers to entry and exit are minimal, and that firms do not behave strategically. (Refer to Table IV.1 for a list of the characteristics.)

MONOPOLISTIC COMPETITION
A market structure characterized by a large number of firms producing slightly differentiated products, by easy entry and exit, and by the unimportance of strategic behavior.

The assumption of a large number of firms is certainly accurate for most retail and service markets nationwide. Think of the thousands of restaurants, bars, hair salons, electricians, banks, real estate brokers, automotive body shops, and so forth throughout the United States. The overwhelming majority of business firms in the United States are fairly small businesses operating under conditions of monopolistic competition. Virtually all the proprietorships and partnerships and most of the small corporations can be viewed as monopolistically competitive firms.

The assumption of minimal barriers to entry and exit is also true of the vast majority of product markets in the United States. Resources respond to profits and losses in most markets, much as they do in the perfectly competitive agricultural markets. We noted in Chapter 4 that hundreds of thousands of new firms start up each year in the United States, and tens of thousands fail. Nearly all these firms are operating in the effectively competitive sector of the economy, in markets that are monopolistically competitive.

The assumption that firms do not behave strategically is not entirely accurate; even small retailers interact strategically to some extent. Nonetheless, ruling out strategic behavior is a reasonable assumption because markets with a large number of firms and minimal barriers to entry are just not conducive to strategic behavior. Firms have too many competitors—not only their current competitors, but potential competitors as well—to keep track of to act strategically. They can do little more than assess the overall market conditions and act accordingly, much as the perfectly competitive farmers.

Product Differentiation—The Monopolistic Element

PRODUCT DIFFERENTIATION

A situation in which buyers distinguish or identify products by the firms that produce them; also refers to firms' attempts to distinguish their products from similar products produced by other firms in the industry by either real or illusory means.

The one noncompetitive element of monopolistic competition is the assumption that products are differentiated by firm. A shirt is not just any shirt, nor a bar just any bar, nor a hair salon just any hair salon. Consumers do care where they shop and what brand of product they buy. The degree of **product differentiation** in monopolistic competition is nowhere near as strong as it is in pure monopoly, though. The product of any one firm always has reasonably close substitutes, namely, the similar products available from other firms in the industry. The firms' products are definitely not identical in the eyes of consumers, however, as they are in a perfectly competitive market.

Product differentiation is no accident. Firms in effectively competitive markets consciously attempt to differentiate their products to soften competition. They search for a niche in the marketplace that will distance them from their competitors in the eyes of consumers and allow them to capture a share of the market. To the extent firms succeed, they achieve a degree of market power—their demand curves are downward sloping. If a firm raises its price above its competitors' prices, it does not lose all its business, in contrast to the demand conditions of perfect competition.

Economists have identified four principal strategies for differentiating products: (1) horizontal differentiation, (2) vertical differentiation, (3) varying product characteristics, and (4) advertising and sales promotion. Let's spend a moment discussing these strategies. They are a large part of what "doing business" is all about in market economies.

HORIZONTAL DIFFERENTIATION

A form of product differentiation in which a firm distinguishes its product from the products of other firms in the industry by choosing where to locate its place of business.

HORIZONTAL DIFFERENTIATION **Horizontal differentiation** refers to the choice of where, physically, to locate a business. Geography is a natural, and very important, product differentiator in the retail trade and service sectors of the economy simply because most retail and service businesses have to locate near their customers. For instance, the thousands of supermarkets in the United States all sell essentially the same products, but they are not in the same markets. The three supermarkets in town A may compete fiercely with each other for customers, but they do not compete so much with the three supermarkets in town B 40 miles away. Even if prices in the town B supermarkets were substantially higher than were those in the town A supermarkets, consumers in town B would not necessarily rush to town A to do their shopping.

The full price to them of buying anything in town A includes the time and expense of traveling the 80 miles round trip. Distance, therefore, serves to differentiate products in the eyes of consumers and soften competition among firms. This is why retail trade and service businesses always think long and hard about where to locate. They know that the costs of shopping naturally divide the retail trade and the service sectors into fairly small regional submarkets, and they want to choose the submarket that is best for them.

VERTICAL DIFFERENTIATION **Vertical differentiation** refers to differentiation on the basis of quality. Some firms choose to offer high-quality versions of a product, others low-quality versions. Stereo equipment is a good example. Think of the wide range of quality available in every component of a stereo system—receivers, tape decks, turntables, compact disc players, speakers, even the headphones.

VERTICAL DIFFERENTIATION
A form of product differentiation in which a firm distinguishes its product from the products of other firms in the industry on the basis of quality.

Vertical differentiation is primarily a strategy of targeting consumers on the basis of their incomes. Other things equal, everyone prefers higher-quality products to lesser-quality products, including stereo systems. Yet other things, such as income, are not equal. For the most part high-income people buy the higher-quality stereo systems, and low-income people buy the lower-quality systems. The same holds true for other products differentiated by quality. Therefore, when firms choose to supply a particular quality of product, they are essentially targeting their sales to a particular income class.

VARYING PRODUCT CHARACTERISTICS Some products are quite complex in the sense that they have a large number of individual characteristics. Manufacturers of these products can attempt to differentiate their products by *varying the characteristics* they make available. In doing so, they are differentiating their products primarily on the basis of tastes. They know people have different preferences for different characteristics.

An automobile is a good example. People do not just buy "a car." Rather, they are purchasing an entire bundle of characteristics best suited to their particular tastes. The number of bundles to choose from is really quite staggering, even from one manufacturer and in one general price range. Begin with the basic choices: body type (sedan, hatchback, wagon, van, convertible); color; size of engine; standard or automatic transmission. Then add a page or two of options, and one can choose from tens of thousands of different automobiles in that one make and price range. By offering such a wide range of choices, the auto manufacturers are obviously trying to cater to every conceivable preference.

ADVERTISING AND SALES PROMOTION Advertising and other forms of sales promotion serve to differentiate products by providing information to consumers in conjunction with the other three means of product differentiation. Firms use advertising campaigns and sales promotions to make consumers aware of the location of their store and of the quality and characteristics of their products or services. Firms also use advertising campaigns and sales promotions in and of themselves to generate brand or store loyalties. This strategy relies on consumers having incomplete information about competitors' products. Firms know that consumers might not be willing or able to obtain full information on all the options available to them, so they try to entice consumers to buy their product. If consumers do try the product and like it and if they do not devote much time or effort to learning about other products, they may become loyal and captive customers. They will switch to another firm's product only if they are convinced that the competing product is *substantially* better or if its price is *significantly* lower. In effect, firms hope consumers substitute the advertising message for their own efforts to obtain information.

REFLECTION: What kind(s) of product differentiation do colleges practice in trying to attract students?

A simple example of horizontal differentiation—the location decision—will illustrate how firms soften competition by differentiating their products.

GEOGRAPHIC DIFFERENTIATION: THE LOCATION DECISION Suppose that the population of a relatively new town is now large enough to support two supermarkets. The town is long and narrow, represented by line segment *AB* in Figure 15.2, and the population is evenly distributed along the line segment. Two supermarkets, S1 and S2, decide to enter the town and have to choose a location somewhere along *AB*. Assume that each supermarket has the same constant average and marginal costs in order to focus solely on how the location decision affects the demand for their products. Finally, assume that shopping is costly and that the costs of time and effort to shop rise sharply with distance from the store. Other things equal, consumers strongly prefer to shop at the nearest store.

If one of the supermarkets could have the town to itself, it would locate in the middle of the town (*M*) to maximize the number of customers. It would not want to lose some customers to smaller neighborhood grocery stores by locating away from the middle. When two supermarkets enter simultaneously, the location decision is not so clear-cut. On the one hand, each has an incentive to locate near the center of town to maximize its share of the market. On the other hand, locating near the center of town runs the risk of causing very sharp price competition between the stores. Supermarkets are very similar to one another. If the townspeople view the two stores as identical, then the store with the lower prices captures the entire market. The fear of being shut out of the market may well lead to disastrous price wars in which each store throws away its profits by trying to undersell the other store.

The stores are most likely to back off somewhat from competing so vigorously and locate at the outskirts of the town with, say, S1 at *A* and S2 at *B*, as shown in Figure 15.2. Now if their prices happen to differ, the higher-priced store is no longer necessarily shut out of the market. Suppose that the prices at S1 are slightly higher than are the prices at S2. Some customers to the left

FIGURE 15.2

The Location Decision of Supermarkets

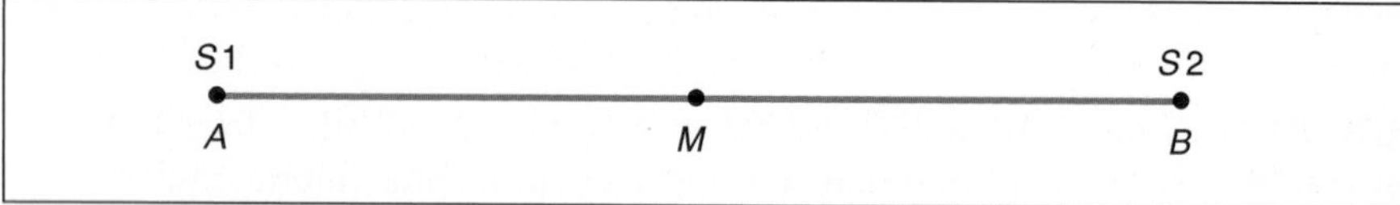

Two supermarkets have to decide where to locate in the long, narrow town represented by the line segment *AB*. If they both locate in the center of town at *M* the competition between them will be very sharp. They will have to charge the same prices and they risk getting into disastrous price wars. They can soften the competition between themselves if they locate at the opposite ends of the town and capture the customers near to them. This strategy, an example of horizontal differentiation, is best if the cost of shopping rises sharply with distance to the store.

of M will switch to S2, but not everyone will switch as long as the costs of shopping increase rapidly with distance. The people near S1 will continue to shop there.

Therefore, by differentiating themselves on the basis of their location and softening the price competition between them, the supermarkets capture part of the market in the town and gain market power. They each face a downward-sloping demand curve, given the prices of the competitor. Furthermore, the supermarkets may well have effective market power. Being the higher-priced store is not disastrous, so the supermarkets are not necessarily led into price wars that sacrifice their profits. Instead, they can coexist, with each earning and maintaining a profit.

Our simple example is actually quite realistic. Retail stores selling similar products usually do try to distance themselves from one another. The exceptions occur under fairly special circumstances. Ice cream parlors and bookstores in university towns tend to cluster near the campus because they literally have no other choice. Similarly, fast-food restaurants locate around major interchanges of the interstate highways because they cannot make a profit if they are out in the boondocks. In these cases the stores usually try to differentiate themselves by other means. University bookstores may specialize in selling certain kinds of books, and the fast-food restaurants may feature different foods. The incentive to differentiate products to capture customers and soften competition applies to all forms of product differentiation, not just to the location decision.

Equilibrium Under Monopolistic Competition

Although our supermarket example is useful for seeing the potential advantages of product differentiation, it misses an essential feature of many retail markets—ease of entry and exit. We want to see what happens under monopolistic competition as investors respond to profits and losses and the industry moves from a temporary short-run equilibrium to its final long-run equilibrium.

THE SHORT-RUN EQUILIBRIUM Describing a market structure as monopolistic competition implies that the firms have successfully differentiated their products from one another. Otherwise, the market structure would be perfect competition. Moreover, since each firm faces a downward-sloping demand curve, the monopoly model of Chapter 14 is the proper model for analyzing monopolistic competition. The firms are price setters, not price takers.

Figure 15.3(a) describes the short-run equilibrium for one of the representative firms in a monopolistically competitive market. The diagram essentially reproduces Figure 14.4 on profit maximizing under pure monopoly, without reference to the specific demand and cost data we used there. As in the case of pure monopoly, the four relevant curves are the demand curve (d_{sr}), the associated marginal revenue curve (MR_{sr}), the marginal cost curve (MC_{sr}), and the average cost curve (AC_{sr}). They all have the standard shapes. The use of lower case letters for the demand curve (d) and for output (q) indicates that the firm is one among many in the industry.

The firm maximizes profit by producing q_{sr}, at the intersection of MR_{sr} and MC_{sr}, and by charging the corresponding price, P_{sr}, along the demand curve. According to the graph, the market situation is profitable for the firm because

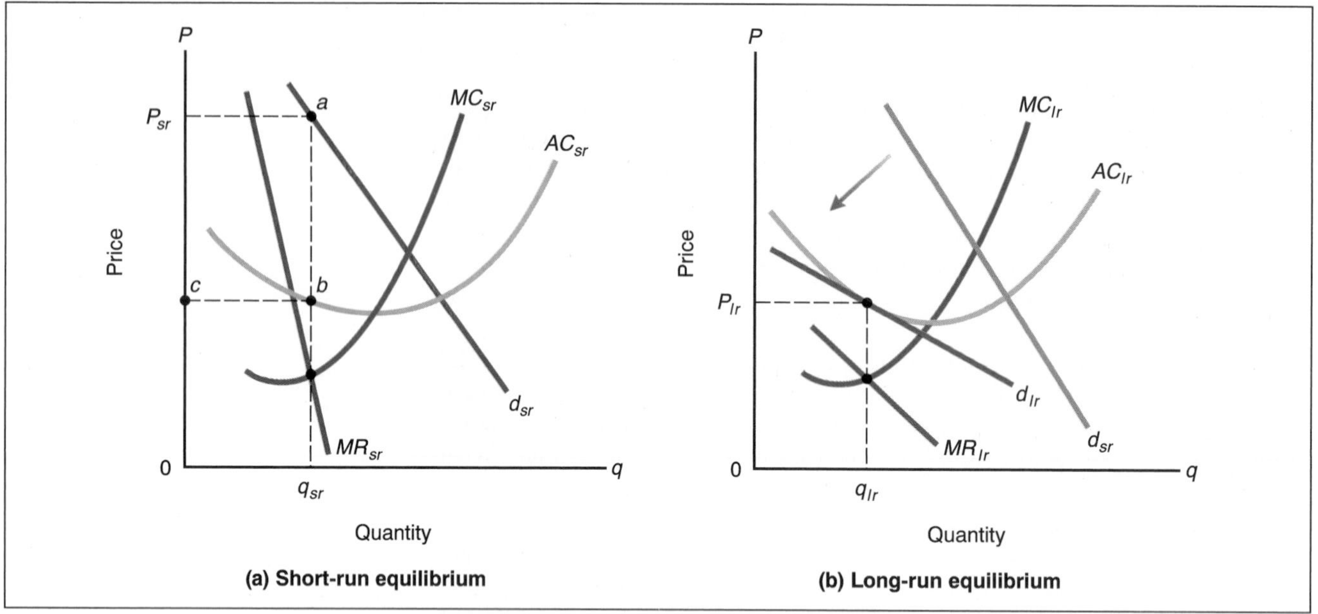

FIGURE 15.3

Monopolistic Competition in the Short Run and the Long Run

The figure shows a representative firm operating in a monopolistically competitive market. The firm faces a downward sloping demand curve because its product is differentiated from the products of other firms, so it maximizes profit just as a pure monopolist does. In the short-run equilibrium, Figure 15.3(a), the firm produces output q_{sr} at the intersection of marginal revenue (MR_{sr}) and marginal cost (MC_{sr}), and charges the price P_{sr}. The firm makes a profit equal to the rectangular area $P_{sr}abc$. The firm cannot expect to maintain its profit in the long-run, however. Profits cause new firms to enter the industry, which shifts each firm's demand curve in and flattens it. The industry reaches its long-run equilibrium in Figure 15.3(b) when the demand curve of the average firm, d_{lr}, just touches its average cost curve AC_{lr} and the profits are competed away. The best that a firm can expect to do is break even in the long run, producing q_{lr}, and charging a price P_{lr}.

P_{sr} is above AC_{sr} at q_{sr}. The firm's profit equals the area of rectangle $P_{sr}abc$ $[=(P_{sr} - AC_{sr}) \cdot q_{sr}]$.

THE LONG-RUN EQUILIBRIUM The similarity between monopolistic competition and pure monopoly ends with the short run. In the long run, monopolistic competition is much more like perfect competition than it is like pure monopoly. The reason is that the short-run equilibrium cannot maintain itself. Investors outside the industry see the short-run profits being made and want to enter the industry. Unlike pure monopoly, new firms can enter because barriers to entry are low or nonexistent. Each firm earns less and less profit as the new firms enter and the market is split up among the larger number of firms. The incentive to enter the industry continues until the best a new firm can do is break even. At that point the market has reached its long-run equilibrium.

The tendency toward a zero-profit long-run equilibrium is pictured in Figure 15.3(b). The graph assumes that each firm has adjusted all its previously fixed factors of production appropriately, so that production occurs along the long-run cost curves, MC_{lr} and AC_{lr}. The demand curve labeled d_{sr} is the original demand curve from Figure 15.3(a). As new firms enter, each firm's demand curve shifts downward and flattens, as indicated by the dotted arrow. The demand curve shifts down because each firm captures less of the overall market. It flattens because new firms generate more similar products and therefore more choices, more substitutes for consumers. The demand for any one firm's product becomes more elastic. (We represented the entry of new firms under perfect competition in Chapter 13 by shifting out the short-run market supply curve. Here the firms have market power, so there is no supply curve. This is why we now represent the process of entry by shifting the demand curve inward as new firms divide up the market.)

The industry reaches its long-run equilibrium when the demand curve has shifted down to d_{lr} and just touches AC_{lr} at a single point (that is, it becomes tangent to AC_{lr}). The best the representative firm can do is break even by producing q_{lr} and charging P_{lr}. Any other quantity-price combination along d_{lr} brings a loss to the firm because price is below average cost. Notice, also, that MR_{lr} and MC_{lr} must intersect at q_{lr}, as shown, since q_{lr} is the firm's best-profit point. Zero profit is the best profit available to the firm.

Figure 15.3 depicts a profitable short-run market situation that causes entry of new firms. If the firms were originally experiencing losses in the short run, the market would still tend toward a zero-profit equilibrium in the long run. Losses cause *exit* from the industry as investors seek to place their funds elsewhere. When some firms exit, the remaining firms each have a larger share of the market, and their demand curves shift *up*. Exit from the industry continues until the remaining firms' demand curves just touch their average cost curves. The process of entry and exit leading to break-even production is entirely symmetric.

The Competitive Struggle

Doing business under conditions of monopolistic competition is a constant struggle, just as it is in perfectly competitive markets. Firms try any way they can to differentiate their products. To the extent they succeed they attract more consumers. Their demand curves shift outward and steepen; that is, they become more inelastic. For example, a successful advertising campaign or a higher-quality product might shift a firm's demand curve from d_{lr} to d_{sr} in Figure 15.4.

The firm might be able to make a profit with demand at d_{sr}, just as the firm does in Figure 15.3. The profits will be short-lived, however, because profits act as a signal attracting more resources to the industry. Other investors will soon imitate what the successful firm has done, enter the industry, and take away some customers. As the imitators arrive, the firm's demand curve shifts back down to d_{lr}, and the profits disappear. In other words, the long-run equalizing tendency of competitive market forces operates here just as it does in perfect competition. To be successful you must be the first to act upon a good idea. If you wait, the opportunity to make a profit will already have been competed away. *Investors can never expect to maintain a profitable position in the long run when there are no significant barriers to entering their industry.*

We have been careful to describe the long run as "tending" toward zero-profit, break-even production. Entry into profitable situations and exit from

FIGURE 15.4

The Competitive Struggle

The figure represents the nature of the competitive struggle under monopolistic competition, which most firms engage in. Firms try to differentiate their products from other firms. If they are successful, their demand curves shift out and become more inelastic, and they may be able to earn a profit in the short run. New firms will inevitably imitate what the successful firms have done, however, because there are no significant barriers to entry. The entry of new firms in the long run shifts the firm's demand curve back down, makes it more elastic, and tends to compete away any short-run profits.

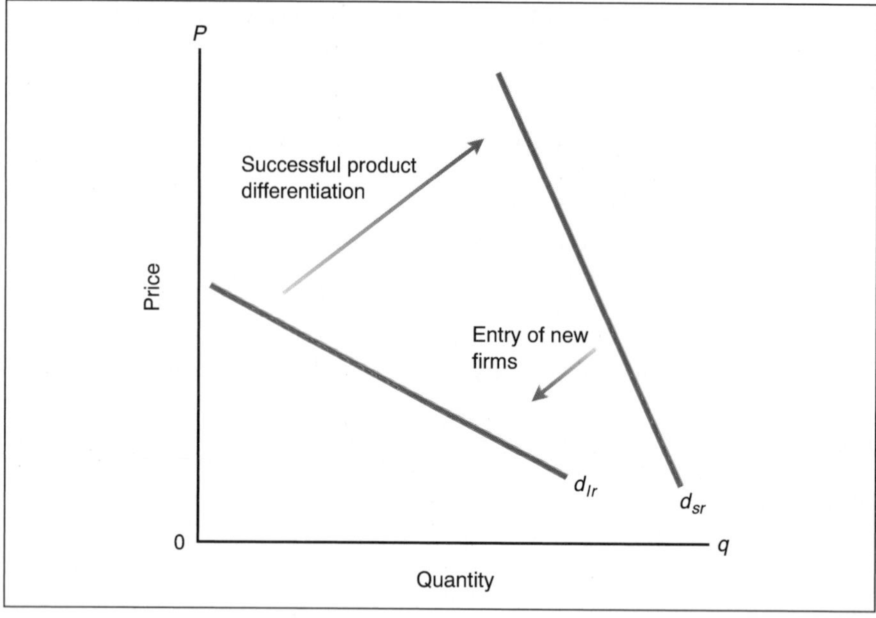

losing situations certainly are the norm. Remember that hundreds of thousands of new businesses start up each year in the United States, and tens of thousands of firms fail. Nonetheless, the long-run equilibrium pictured in Figure 15.3(b) should be thought of as an average, or expected, outcome. It does not necessarily apply to all firms.

Some firms operating in monopolistically competitive markets are able to maintain profits in the long run; they do have effective market power. The McDonald's Corporation is a case in point. McDonald's is hardly lacking for fast-food competitors. It has scores of imitators. Nonetheless, the individual McDonald's franchises remain highly profitable, on average. Other firms have copied the McDonald's line of products, but they have not been able to duplicate the magic of the McDonald's name. The name itself acts as an effective barrier to entry, protecting the corporation's profits in the long run.

By the same token, some firms appear to be perpetual losers. Many of those small, family-run, corner grocery stores that stay open from six in the morning until late at night are undoubtedly experiencing losses by any proper economic accounting. The family members would be far better off financially if they sold the store and hired themselves out to some other line of work. Yet they continue on because running a small, family grocery store is what they are most comfortable doing.

A final possibility is illustrated by our example of the supermarkets in the new town. Suppose that the two supermarkets can each earn a profit if they locate at the outskirts of the town, but that the town is not large enough to support three supermarkets. They all make losses if a third supermarket enters the town. Knowing this, the third store does not enter. Therefore, the two stores are able to maintain profits in the long run, even though there are no barriers to entry.

These examples notwithstanding, the general principle holds: Firms cannot *expect* to enjoy effective monopoly power if there are no barriers to entering the industry. Entry always tends to compete away profits in the long run by driving price to average cost, the break-even point.

Evaluation of Monopolistic Competition

Market outcomes under monopolistic competition have both good and bad qualities, as the name suggests they might. The market structure is equitable because of its competitive feature that resources are free to move into and out of the market. But monopolistic competition fails to achieve either allocational efficiency or production (technical) efficiency because of its monopoly feature that each firm has some market power. Refer to Figure 15.5, which reproduces Figure 15.3(b), the long-run equilibrium.

ALLOCATIONAL EFFICIENCY Monopolistic competition does not satisfy allocational efficiency because product differentiation gives each firm some market power. Since the firms' demand curves are downward sloping, the results from pure monopoly apply. Price exceeds marginal cost, and too little output is produced. The net value from producing and consuming the firm's output is maximized at q_{eff}, the output at which demand and marginal cost intersect. By producing only q_{lr}, each firm engages in a contrived scarcity for the purposes of maximizing its own profit, and society loses some potential net value. A firm cannot possibly produce q_{eff}, however, because it would experience a loss. The demand curve is below the average cost curve at q_{eff}.

PRODUCTION (TECHNICAL) EFFICIENCY Since the demand curve remains downward sloping even in the long run, the demand and the average cost curves meet to the left of q_{MES}, the minimum efficient scale of operation. Each firm has excess capacity in the sense that it has not fully exhausted all economies of scale, and cost per unit are not as low as they could be. Therefore, monopolistic competition wastes some of society's scarce resources because total industry output is not produced at the lowest possible cost. For example, when four gasoline stations appear at one intersection, they may each be serving too few customers. The stations do not produce at their MES for the same reason that they do not produce at q_{eff}. Lowering price in order to increase output to q_{MES} would bring a loss.

EQUITY Monopolistic competition satisfies both equality of opportunity and horizontal equity as well as could be expected. Barriers to entry are low or nonexistent for the most part, so that investors generally have equal access to profitable opportunities. As in perfect competition, equal access generates horizontal equity. Entry (and exit) of firms drives price to average cost in the long run, the test for horizontal equity. Owners of firms in these markets cannot earn higher returns to their capital, on average, than investors can earn generally.

Equity is not unique to monopolistic competition. All markets characterized as effectively competitive have low barriers to entry and prices close to average costs in the long run. In other words, roughly three-quarters of all output in the U.S. economy is produced in markets that are reasonably fair according to the criteria of equality of opportunity and horizontal equity.

How Inefficient is Monopolistic Competition?

The inefficiencies associated with monopolistic competition and other effectively competitive market structures are probably not very troublesome for two reasons: The inefficiencies are likely to be small, and they "buy" consumers some choice.

Regarding the size of the inefficiencies, most firms in highly competitive markets have very little market power in the long run. As new firms enter and generate more substitute products for consumers, any one firm has less of a hold on its customers, less market power. The individual firms' demand curves become highly elastic, nearly horizontal. The flatter the demand curve is, the closer the marginal revenue curve is to the demand curve, and the closer q_{lr}, q_{eff}, and q_{MES} are in Figure 15.5. Recall that in perfect competition, where the demand curve *is* horizontal, q_{lr}, q_{eff}, and q_{MES} coincide. The perfectly competitive long-run equilibrium occurs at the intersection of AC_{lr} and MC_{lr}. Indeed, if a new entrant's product is viewed as identical to an existing firm's product in the eyes of consumers, then both firms' demand curves become horizontal. The long-run equilibrium is the perfectly competitive equilibrium because the products are not differentiated.

In short, most firms cannot soften competition very effectively. They try to capture customers and maintain profits by differentiating their products, but they end up looking very much like perfectly competitive firms anyway, with price nearly equal to marginal cost and without much effective market power. The "culprit" is entry. Product differentiation does not help firms very much if they cannot keep imitators out of the industry by erecting barriers to entry. That is precisely why supply and demand analysis is such a powerful tool. It approximates the market outcomes of most effectively competitive markets, even though firms are not, strictly speaking, perfectly competitive.

FIGURE 15.5

Efficiency and Equity Under Monopolistic Competition

Monopolistic competition generates some allocational and technical inefficiency. The allocational efficiency arises because price exceeds marginal cost. The firm sets marginal revenue equal to marginal cost, and price is greater than marginal revenue; q_{lr} is below q_{eff}, at the intersection of d_{lr} and MC. The technical inefficiency occurs because q_{lr} is less than q_{mes} at the minimum of AC_{lr}, the minimum efficient scale of output. The industry has excess capacity. Monopolistic competition is equitable, however, in the sense that profits are competed away in the long run. P_{lr} equals average cost for the averge firm.

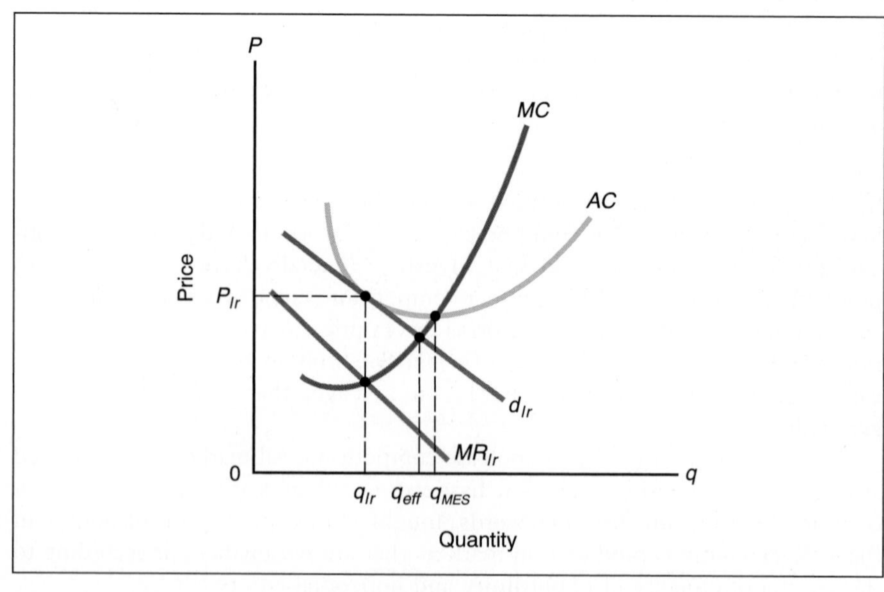

The second point, the issue of product choice, relates to the source of the inefficiencies. Firms have market power because of product differentiation. Consumers care where they shop and which products they buy, so that markets give rise to some allocational and production inefficiencies. Consumers value choice, though, and the ability to choose may well be worth more than the resulting efficiency costs. Perfect competition achieves allocational and production efficiency only through complete standardization. All firms' products must be identical—"wheat is wheat." Faced with the alternatives of standardization and choice, most consumers would prefer choice, providing the inefficiencies are not too large. If so, then society is better off with product differentiation and monopolistic competition than with standardization and perfect competition.

The following Concept Summary table summarizes the market outcomes under monopolistic competition.

CONCEPT SUMMARY

EVALUATION OF MONOPOLISTIC COMPETITION

OBJECTIVES	MARKET TEST	ACHIEVED? MARKET OUTCOMES
EFFICIENCY		
Allocational efficiency	$P = MC$	No $MR = MC$; $P > MC$ *Caveat:* P often close to MC; most firms face highly elastic demand curves *Caveat:* consumers gain choice, but not the optimal amount of product differentiation
Production (technical) efficiency	Production at MES or minimum AC_{lr}	Generally no; only by chance *Caveat:* production often close to MES
EQUITY		
Equality of opportunity	Absence of barriers to entry, exit; equal access to all market information	Generally yes Barriers to entry usually absent; information easily obtained
Horizontal equity	$P = AC_{lr}$; Zero maintained economic profit	Generally yes Firms cannot maintain economic profits in long run, on average; little to no effective market power
Overall: a satisfactory market structure		

The Optimal Amount of Product Differentiation[2]

Because consumers prefer choice, another interesting efficiency question arises that we have not considered before: Do effectively competitive markets naturally generate the optimal amount of product differentiation? The answer is no, in general. A free market system has no built-in mechanism for generating the correct amount of product differentiation. This is true even under the two simplifying assumptions we have been making throughout this section: that firms are interested only in maximizing profit and that they do not engage in strategic behavior.

A market system relies on the profit motive to guide the allocation of resources. Unfortunately, the profit motive does not necessarily provide firms with the correct signals when they are deciding where to locate or what kinds of products to provide. To see why, consider the example of a group of investors trying to decide whether to open a new singles bar downtown. They plan to offer the usual features that appeal to young singles along with one special gimmick unique to their bar—a round of free drinks at 9:00 p.m. Their market analysis indicates that their bar will be profitable, so they open the bar.

Suppose that the bar is profitable. The investors clearly made the correct decision from their point of view, but their decision may not be correct from a broader social perspective. The problem is that some of their business comes at the expense of other singles bars already operating in the city as some people change their allegiance to the new bar. The other bars experience a decline in demand, which in turn lowers their profits. Economists call this the *business-stealing effect* of product differentiation. Some of the original bars could actually be experiencing losses if the business-stealing effect is strong enough. If so, the possibility arises that the combined losses of the original bars exceed the profit of the new bar. In this case society would prefer that the new bar not exist; too many resources, overall, are allocated to single bars. The business-stealing effect is an external effect that private investors never include in their profit and loss calculations. It results in a tendency to provide too much product differentiation.

Countering the business-stealing effect is a second effect that tends to produce too little product differentiation, firms' inability to capture consumer surplus. Suppose that the investors' market analysis indicates (correctly) that the bar will not be profitable, so they decide against opening it. Even though the bar is unprofitable, society might still prefer that it exist. Figure 15.6 illustrates this possibility.

The market analysis shows that the bar's demand curve (d) is everywhere below average cost (AC), so that the investors experience a loss at any price-quantity combination along d. However, imagine the following scenario. The owners agree to open the bar and operate it efficiently. They charge the marginal cost price, P_{MC}, at the intersection of d and MC. In exchange for opening the bar, the customers agree to cover any loss the owners experience by paying a separate one-time charge. The loss at (q_{eff}, P_{MC}) equals the area of rectangle $P_{MC}ace$ [$=(AC - P_{MC}) \cdot q_{eff}$]. Would the consumers be willing to cover the loss? The answer is yes, in principle, so long as the loss is less than the consumer surplus they receive from patronizing the bar. The consumer surplus is

[2]This is a more advanced topic that can be skipped in shorter courses.

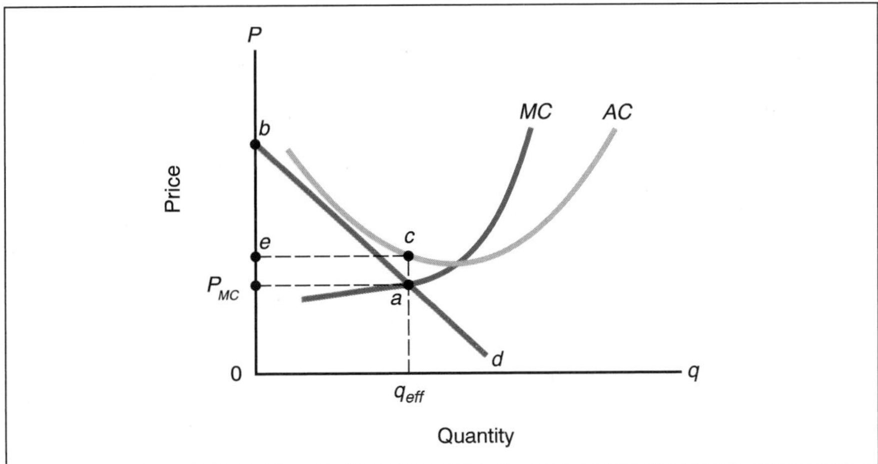

FIGURE 15.6

Too Little Product Differentiation

The figure indicates why there may be too little product differentiation under monopolistic competition. The firm will not offer this product because the demand curve, *d*, is everywhere below the average cost curve, *AC*. The best it can do is make a loss. Suppose, however, that the firm did produce the efficient level of output, q_{eff}, at the intersection of *d* and *MC*, and charged the price P_{MC}. The firm makes a loss equal to the area $P_{MC}ace$. The consumer surplus is the triangular area $P_{MC}ab$. Producing the product is worthwhile if the consumer surplus exceeds the firm's loss. But firms have no way of capturing the consumer surplus so they do not offer the product.

the triangular area $P_{MC}ab$, the area below *d* and above P_{MC} up to q_{eff}. The consumer surplus exceeds the loss in Figure 15.6, so opening the bar is worthwhile from the broader social perspective. It increases net value.

The problem in this case is that the owners cannot easily extract any of the consumer surplus from their customers. Individual customers will not volunteer to cover the loss unless they can be assured that all customers are paying the one-time charge. Realistically, all the owners can do is charge a price and collect revenue in the usual fashion, and the revenue is not sufficient from their point of view. Therefore, *the inability to capture consumer surplus* creates a bias toward providing too little product differentiation.

Whether or not a market generates just the right amount of product differentiation depends on the relative strengths of the business-stealing effect and the inability to extract consumer surplus. No market mechanism exists to guarantee that they exactly cancel one another. Therefore, any one market may have too much or too little product differentiation.

Many economists now suspect that the potential allocational inefficiencies of having too much or too little product differentiation are far more important than are the fairly small allocational and technical inefficiencies caused by the existence of market power. However, no one has yet been able to develop a reliable test to measure the correct amount of product differentiation in an actual market.

GOVERNMENT POLICY AND EFFECTIVE COMPETITION: LICENSING

A capitalistic society would be very pleased if all product markets were effectively competitive. As we have seen, effectively competitive markets are reasonably fair and not terribly inefficient. These markets may not generate the correct amount of product differentiation, but not much can be done about that. Government intervention in such an economy would be limited to setting the ground rules for market exchange, such as defining property rights and enforcing contracts.

Leaving well enough alone has generally been the policy stance of U.S. governments in effectively competitive markets. Government market policy has typically been directed toward the oligopolies and the natural monopolies. The one notable exception is **licensing.** The federal, state, and local governments have seen fit to license a number of occupations and industries that fall within the effectively competitive sector of the economy.

LICENSING

A type of government regulation that restricts entry into an industry as a means of assuing service quality and standards or as a means of controlling the spread of socially undesirable activities.

Governments justify licenses as a means of assuring standards or controlling vice. The argument has merit in each case. People do want some assurance that the electricians wiring their houses and the surgeons operating on their loved ones are competent to perform these tasks. Occupational licensing provides a governmental certification of quality for services that most consumers have very little knowledge of. Liquor licenses for package stores and restaurants serve a different function. They give governments some control over the availability of alcohol in their communities. A society might want to limit the sale of alcohol beverages to prevent the spread of alcohol abuse.

The merits of these arguments notwithstanding, most economists are highly skeptical of licenses because licenses have a number of disturbing economic effects. At very least, society must bear the expense of operating a licensing bureau. Beyond that, licenses act as a legal barrier to entry in industries that would otherwise be effectively competitive if governments had not chosen to limit their supply. As such, licenses have the potential to harm consumers and promote graft and corruption. Finally, licenses often have very little effect on quality or vice. For all these reasons economists are doubtful that the benefits of licensing outweigh the costs in most cases.

To see the potential economic costs of licenses, consider the case of restaurants licensed to serve alcoholic beverages. Restaurants cannot serve alcohol unless they obtain a liquor license issued by either a state or a local government licensing bureau, and the bureau controls the total number of licenses available.

Figure 15.7 pictures the market situation for one licensed restaurant, given the current supply of liquor licenses. d_{LC} is the demand curve for the restaurant's meals; the corresponding marginal revenue curve is MR_{LC}. The price refers to the average price of a meal, including drinks. MC and AC are the marginal and the average costs of serving meals to customers. The graph assumes that owning a licensed restaurant is profitable, given the limited supply of licenses. The restaurant maximizes profit by serving q_{LC} customers, at the intersection of the MR_{LC} and the MC curves, and by charging an average price of P_{LC}. The profit equals the area of rectangle $P_{LC}abc$ [$=(P_{LC} - AC) \cdot q_{LC}$].

This favorable market situation could not persist without the licenses because the market for restaurants is highly competitive. Investors would see the profits to be made and begin opening new restaurants that sell alcoholic beverages. Each restaurant's demand curve would shift down and flatten to d_{lr}, and all profits would be competed away. Consumers would have a wider choice of restaurants in the long run, and the average price of a meal with drinks would fall to P_{lr}. By limiting the supply of licenses, however, the licensing bureau prevents the market from reaching its natural long-run equilibrium. The licensing system establishes a legal barrier to entry that perpetuates effective monopoly power and higher prices to consumers.

Restricting entry through licensing has another drawback. It creates an environment ready-made for graft and corruption. The administrators of the government licensing bureaus have a strong economic incentive to limit the number of licenses, whatever the avowed social purpose of the license may be.

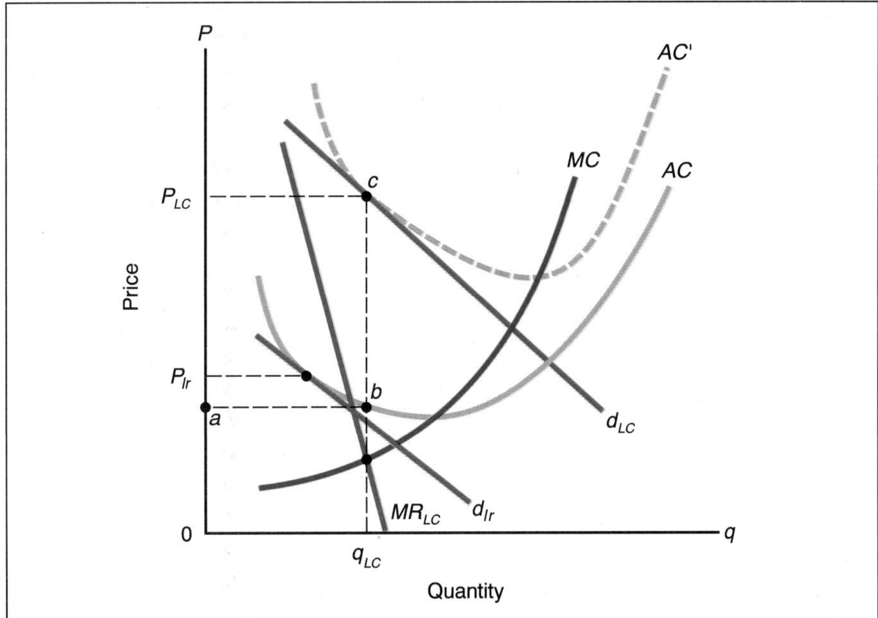

FIGURE 15.7

The Economic Costs of Liquor Licenses in Restaurants

The figure shows the market situation of an average restaurant with and without liquor licenses. With the liquor licenses, the restaurant's demand curve is d_{LC}. The restaurants serves q_{LC} meals, at the intersection of MR_{LC} and MC, charges an average price per meal of P_{LC}, and makes a profit equal to the rectangular area $P_{LC}abc$. The restaurant can maintain the profits in the long-run because licensing restricts entry into the industry. Without liquor licenses, new restaurants would start up, the demand curve of the average restaurant would fall to d_{lr} in the long run, the average meal would cost only P_{lr}, and the restaurant would just break even. Licensing also encourages corruption, because the government officials who issue the licenses can extract an annual under-the-table payment for the licenses up to the amount of the restaurant's profit. The fee shifts the restaurant's average cost curve up, to a maximum of AC'.

They know that restricting supply gives a license an economic value. Prospective restaurant owners also realize that a liquor license is valuable. In our example they would be willing to pay any amount up to profit area $P_{LC}abc$ to obtain a license. Therefore, even though the charge for a license might be a small annual fee set by the legislature, a government administrator can easily extract an additional "under-the-table" payment for a license. The illegal payment is a yearly fee that increases a restaurant owner's fixed cost of doing business. It shifts the average cost curve upward (but does not shift the marginal cost curve because the payment is unrelated to the number of customers served). The restaurant's average cost curve could shift up to the dotted line, AC'. In this case the government administrator captures all the profit made possible by limiting the supply of licenses, and the restaurant owner just breaks even. If the administrator and the restaurant owner split the profit, the average cost curve would shift up, but not all the way to AC′. In this case both government administrators and already licensed restaurant owners have an interest in limiting the number of licenses.

Never underestimate the economic value of restricting entry into a market. Illegal payments are difficult to estimate, but the overall value of licenses can be determined if the licenses are transferable from one licensee to another. A good example is taxicab medallions in New York City, which are fixed in number and transferable. The price of a medallion exceeds $100,000.

Liquor licenses (and other licenses designed to control vice) must necessarily be limited, given their social purpose, so that the economic costs and potential for corruption are unavoidable. A key question, then, is whether licensing the distribution and sale of liquor really does limit access and reduce the incidence of alcohol abuse. Even if the answer is yes, society must still decide if the benefits of licensing exceed the costs.

Occupational licenses are potentially less costly because they are usually available to anyone who completes the necessary training course and passes a qualifying examination. In practice, though, licensing bureaus often do control entry by varying the training requirements and/or the pass rates on the qualifying examinations. To the extent entry is restricted the previous analysis applies. The licensing system reduces consumers' choice, increases prices and industry profits, and promotes graft and corruption.

A final issue with occupational licenses is whether they have much effect on the overall quality of service within the industry. For instance, does licensing electricians assure competency and raise standards? We know that there are better and worse electricians despite the fact that they all have the same license. Moreover, reputation tends to spread by word of mouth. You like (or do not like) the work of a particular electrician and tell your friends, who then tell their friends, and so on. Suppose that electricians could practice without a license. Would things really be that much different? Someone who chooses to make a living as an electrician would have every incentive to learn the trade well and develop a good reputation. Those who develop the best reputations would earn the highest incomes, which is essentially what happens anyway. The most important effect of licensing on overall quality may be a negative one, to protect the incomes of the bad electricians by preventing the entry of potentially better electricians.

In summary, the argument for licensing occupations may be compelling in some cases, for example, the licensing of medical doctors. But the burden of proof is on licensing. In most cases the benefits would appear to be fairly small and the potential costs fairly large. Licensing bureaus can usually restrict entry if they want to, and they certainly have a strong incentive to do so.

SUMMARY

Chapter 15 began with a discussion of cooperative behavior as the ultimate means of softening competition among firms, using the industry cartel as an example.

1. A cartel has the effect of turning a market into a pure monopoly. The cartel establishes the monopoly price and restricts output in order to maintain that price by setting production quotas for each firm.
2. Firms have a strong incentive to cheat, which they can easily do by lowering price just below the cartel price. The firms are trapped in a game known as the Prisoners' Dilemma. The dilemma is that each firm cheats, even though they all know that the best solution is for everyone not to cheat and to maintain the cartel. The incentive to cheat results from mistrust. Cheating is the best strategy for each firm if the other firms cheat or if they do not cheat. Since each firm is unsure what the others will do, they all cheat.

3. Cheating is easier to prevent the more similar the firms are, the quicker the cartel can detect cheating, and the more severe the punishment for cheating is.

Cartels and other forms of cooperative behavior are illegal in the United States. Therefore, the remainder of Chapters 15 through 17 assumes that firms behave noncooperatively. The second section of Chapter 15 considered the effectively competitive sector of the economy, using monopolistic competition as the model exemplifying an effectively competitive market.

4. Monopolistic competition differs from perfect competition in only one important respect. The firms are able to differentiate their products from one another by means of (1) horizontal (geographic) differentiation, (2) vertical (quality) differentiation, (3) varying product characteristics, and (4) advertising and sales promotions. The section began by showing how geographic differentiation—the location decision—can soften price competition by giving firms market power, a downward-sloping demand curve. Product differentiation is often the only way that firms in the effectively competitive sector of the economy can hope to capture customers and maintain profits.
5. Firms operating under conditions of monopolistic competition are not entirely successful in softening competition. Profits tend toward zero in the long run because of the absence of barriers to entry or exit. Therefore, monopolistic competition satisfies the equity principles of equality of opportunity and horizontal equity. Equity results from the competitive aspect of the market structure. However, monopolistic competition fails to achieve either allocational efficiency or production (technical) efficiency. Price exceeds marginal cost, and the output of each firm is less than the minimum efficient scale of operation (MES). The inefficiencies result from the monopolistic aspect of the market structure.
6. The inefficiencies may be unimportant, however, for two reasons. First, the inefficiencies are likely to be small in most markets. The firms' demand curves are often fairly elastic in the long run, which means that price is close to marginal cost and output is near the MES. Second, consumers like the choice among products that product differentiation brings. They may prefer monopolistic competition to perfect competition, with its standardized products, providing the inefficiencies associated with monopolistic competition are not too large.
7. The market system might not produce the correct amount of product differentiation. Firms have an incentive to produce too much product differentiation because of a business-stealing effect. Some of a firm's profits come at the expense of other firms' profits, so that a firm overestimates the value to society of introducing a new product. Firms also have an incentive to produce too little product differentiation because they cannot capture the consumer surplus arising from a new product. The profit from introducing a new product could be negative, whereas the consumer surplus is positive. No market mechanism exists to balance these two incentives and produce the correct amount of product differentiation. A market can have too many or too few products.

The chapter concluded with a discussion of U.S. government policy relating to effectively competitive product markets.

8. Governments in the United States leave effectively competitive markets alone for the most part. The only government policy directed primarily toward the effectively competitive sector of the economy is licensing.

9. Occupational licenses are justified as a means of assuring service quality and standards; liquor licenses are justified as a means of controlling vice. Economists are skeptical of licenses because they can act as a legal barrier to entry if their supply is limited and prevent a market from reaching its natural long-run equilibrium. The results are higher prices to consumers, profits where none would otherwise exist, and an environment that is ready-made for political graft and corruption. Licenses have economic value if their supply is limited, and administrators of licensing bureaus can easily extract some or all of the value through illegal side payments. Also, licenses may have little effect in ensuring service quality or in limiting the spread of undesirable activities.

KEY TERMS

cartel
cooperative behavior
horizontal differentiation
licensing
monopolistic competition
noncooperative behavior
prisoners' dilemma
product differentiation
vertical differentiation

QUESTIONS

1. a. Why can a cartel earn profits for its member firms when the firms cannot earn profits by themselves?
   b. Why do cartel members have a strong incentive to cheat on the cartel agreement?
   c. What factors are likely to increase (decrease) cheating by cartel members?
2. a. Why is cheating the expected outcome when firms are caught in the Prisoners' Dilemma?
   b. Why is the Prisoners' Dilemma a dilemma?
3. Suppose that an industry consists of two large firms. The owners of the firms consider two forms of cooperative behavior: (1) merge together into one large firm to form a pure monopoly; or (2) maintain separate firms, but form a cartel. How and why might the market outcomes differ under these two forms of cooperative behavior?
4. Give examples of industries in which the firms attempt to differentiate their products
   a. by varying product characteristics.
   b. by horizontal differentiation.
   c. by vertical differentiation

   Do some of the industries you selected practice more than one type of product differentiation?
5. a. What are the main similarities and differences between a perfectly competitive firm and a monopolistically competitive firm?
   b. Answer the same question after replacing "perfectly competitive firm" with "pure monopoly."
6. Suppose that a monopolistically competitive firm is making an economic profit in the short run. What will happen to this firm's demand if one of its rivals introduces a new and improved product? Would this affect the original firm's market power? What will happen to the firms' short-run profits?
7. a. Why does monopolistic competition not satisfy the goal of allocational efficiency?
   b. Why is the amount of allocational inefficiency not likely to be very large in most industries?
8. a. What factors might cause two firms selling very similar products to locate right next to each other? Give some examples.
   b. What factors might cause two firms selling very similar products to locate some distance from one another? Again, give some examples.
9. Many cities license taxicabs.
   a. What might be the reasons for licensing taxicabs?
   b. What effect does licensing have on cab fares and on the profits of the cab companies?
   c. On balance, do you favor the licensing of taxicabs?
10. Discuss this statement: All monopolistically competitive firms have market power, but very few of these firms have much, if any, effective market power.
11. *Extra credit:* Explain what is meant by too little and too much product differentiation. Why does a monopolistically competitive industry not necessarily generate the optimal amount of product differentiation?

CHAPTER

16

Oligopoly

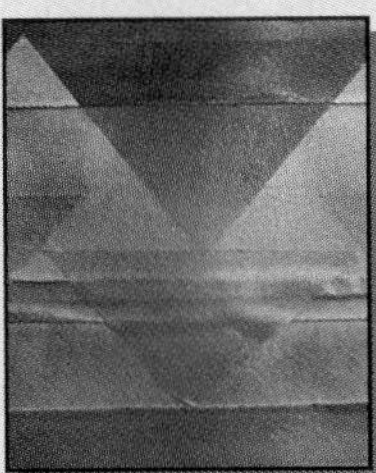

LEARNING OBJECTIVES

CONCEPTS TO LEARN

Oligopoly

The Law of Large Numbers

Strategic behavior

Tacit collusion and nonprice competition

The trigger strategy and mark-up pricing models

Sales maximization versus profit maximization

Tender takeovers

CONCEPTS TO RECALL

The firm's three-part economic problem [1]

The marginal benefit equals marginal cost decision rule [6]

The profit-maximizing output rule for firms with market power [14]

Chapters 16 and 17 analyze market behavior under oligopoly, the market structure in which a few large firms dominate the industry. The common rule of thumb is that an industry is an oligopoly if the combined sales of the four largest firms are at least 50 percent of the total sales by all domestic firms. Approximately 20 percent of the national product of the United States is sold in industries that are oligopolies by this measure.

The markets structured as national oligopolies contain the headline-grabbing giant corporations, the Fortune 500 firms, the IBMs, Exxons, General Motors, Boeings, Coca-Colas, and Kodaks of the business world. Their presence is felt throughout the United States and often worldwide.

The giant U.S. corporations are truly enormous. The 200 largest corporations in the United States produce over 44 percent of total national output and hold about two-thirds of all business assets. Many individual companies have annual sales exceeding $10 billion. The large corporations are also multiplant and multiproduct businesses, almost without exception. Many are multinational corporations as well. To give some examples, the 15 largest manufacturing corporations in the United States operate an average of 87 plants each. General Electric alone operates over 200 domestic plants and 100 foreign plants. ITT is a well-known multiproduct and multinational corporation. Since 1962 ITT has purchased approximately 250 domestic and foreign companies. ITT was even accused of helping the CIA in its attempt to overthrow the government of Chile in the 1970s. The major U.S. oil companies now have extensive interests in other energy sources, primarily coal, uranium, and solar energy. And so it goes. The largest firms often have a commanding presence in a number of different markets.

Congress directs most of its legislative attention to the oligopolies, and this is as it should be. The large corporations are likely to exhibit the noncompetitive behavior and performance associated with pure monopoly. They bear close watching because they represent a potential threat to society's pursuit of efficiency and equity.[1]

OLIGOPOLY
A product market dominanted by a few large firms.

Understanding how firms behave when they operate under conditions of **oligopoly** is clearly a top priority of economists and policy makers alike. Unfortunately, achieving that understanding is among the more difficult challenges in all of economics. Economists have uncovered very few principles of market behavior that apply with much generality across these industries, or even within one industry over time. No general model exists for analyzing the noncompetitive oligopoly sector. Certainly economists have developed nothing comparable to the Laws of Supply and Demand, which have proved to be such a useful general model or framework for analyzing the effectively competitive sector of the economy. Many economists are convinced that a good general model of oligopoly can never be found. They believe that industry-specific case studies are the only sure means of achieving an understanding of the beer industry, the automobile industry, the chemical industry, or any of the oligopolies.

[1]The data in the introduction are from two sources: W. Adams, "Public Policy in a Free Enterprise Economy," in W. Adams, ed., *The Structure of American Industry*, Seventh Edition (New York: Macmillan 1986), 395–427; and W. Baldwin, *Market Power, Competition, and Antitrust Policy* (Homewood, IL: Richard D. Irwin, 1987), 29, 149–179.

Chapter 16 discusses why general principles of market behavior under oligopoly are so hard to come by.

WHY NO GENERAL PRINCIPLES OF OLIGOPOLY?

Economists have been unable to develop broad general principles of market behavior under oligopoly because of the very nature of an oligopoly: The industry is dominated by a few large firms that are somewhat protected from the pressures of competition by barriers to entry. Attempts to model market behavior encounter two severe difficulties when the actions of a few large firms determine market outcomes. The first is that the distinctive features of the industries, including the idiosyncrasies of the individual firms, matter fundamentally in shaping market outcomes. How much competition exists within the industry? Does the government have a major influence on the firms' behavior? What are the objectives of the firms? These are important questions in determining market behavior under oligopoly, and their answers differ from industry to industry. In addition, the market environment is highly interdependent, which means that all behavior is strategic. When a firm is deciding what price to charge for its product, it must consider how the other firms in the industry might react to its decision. Let's take a closer look at each of these features.

Domination by a Few Firms

All industries are distinctive in certain respects, and all firms have certain idiosyncrasies that set them apart from the other firms in the industry. But when an industry consists of a large number of firms, all roughly the same size, economists can rely on the Law of Large Numbers to develop general principles of industry behavior. **The Law of Large Numbers** is a law of statistics. It says that the average behavior of a large group of firms (or people) becomes highly predictable even if the behavior of individual members of the group is highly unpredictable. In effect, the differences that set individual members of the group apart from one another tend to average out for the group as a whole.

LAW OF LARGE NUMBERS

A property of statistics, which says that the average behavior of a large group of firms (or people) becomes highly predictable, even if the behavior of individual members of the group is highly unpredictable.

For example, the admissions officers at your state university know that if they accept 15,000 students from the pool of applicants for the freshman class, approximately 6,000 of those students will in turn accept the offer of admission. (The numbers are hypothetical.) Only rarely are they surprised. Actual enrollments are usually within a percentage point or two of projected enrollments. But suppose that the admissions officers selected a handful of the applications and tried to guess how many of those students would accept the offer of admission. They would often be quite wrong. The state university may happen to be the first choice of all these students; the fifth choice of all these students; or the first choice of one student, the third choice of another, and the fifth choice of yet another. The officers have no sure way of knowing what the mix of preferences is within the small group. Fortunately, they do not have to worry about individual preferences when predicting the number of acceptances from the entire group of applicants. They know from experience that the entire group of applicants contains about the same mixture of first-, third-, and fifth-choice students year after year. Therefore, the admissions officers can be highly confident that approximately 6,000 students will accept the university's offer of admissions.

The same principle applies to market structures. Thanks to the Law of Large Numbers we can confidently predict average market outcomes under monopolistic competition without concerning ourselves very much about the attributes of each individual firm, or even the distinctive features of each industry. By contrast, the Law of Large Numbers is no help at all in predicting market behavior under oligopoly. The differences among individual firms do not average out for the industry as a whole when only a handful of firms dominates the industry. Each firm's distinctive characteristics, such as the goals and managing style of its top executives or the particular way in which the firm chooses to differentiate its product, matter very much in determining market outcomes over time. So does the market environment in which the firms operate. Trying to predict market behavior under oligopoly is analogous to the admissions officers trying to predict how many students among a handful of selected applicants will accept their offer of admissions. We cannot be sure how the firms within any one industry will respond to changing events over time. And if we cannot be sure how any one industry might behave, we obviously have little hope of developing general principles of market behavior that apply across industries producing different products and operating in very different market environments.

AUTOMOBILES, AIRPLANES, AND OIL To see the difficulties of formulating general principles of market behavior compare briefly three industries: automobiles (General Motors, Ford, and Chrysler), airframe manufacturers (Boeing, Lockheed, and McDonnell-Douglas), and oil (Exxon, Texaco, Sunoco, and others).

The automobile industry is almost entirely a market-directed industry. The Big Three sell their cars to millions of consumers and thousands of business firms and buy their material inputs from over 40,000 suppliers. They face intense competition from foreign producers. Most large corporations interact directly with a number of agencies of the federal government, and the automobile industry is no exception. The auto manufacturers have to meet various federal regulations pertaining to safety, pollution control, and the miles per gallon achieved by their overall fleet of cars. The federal government succeeded in persuading the Japanese to limit the number of Japanese cars exported to the United States throughout the 1980s, a policy that helped support higher prices for U.S. cars. General Motors is also a major contractor with the Department of Defense. But none of these governmental interactions affects the industry in any fundamental way. For the most part, the Big Three automobile manufacturers respond to standard economic market forces. The principles of competition and monopoly power developed in Chapters 13 and 14 go a long way toward explaining their behavior.

The airframe industry differs from the automobile industry in two important respects, the nature of the product and the interrelationships with the government. Regarding the product, building an airplane is far more complicated than building a car. New airplanes typically incorporate a number of state-of-the-art technological advances that require testing and redesigning along the way. The time from the initial design to the production of a new airplane is measured in years. By contrast, automobiles have undergone only minor changes over the past 30 years. A new line of cars appears every year, even more quickly in some years. Airplanes and cars are also sold differently. Airframe manufacturing is strictly a production-to-order business. The manufacturers do not design and produce a new airplane unless a customer has agreed to purchase a number of the planes in advance. Some cars are also built on a production-to-order basis. Customers select the options they want, and then the car is ordered and produced. But the majority of cars are sold "off the lot." The automobile manufacturers produce cars, ship them to their dealers, and hope people will buy them.

Another big difference between the two industries is their relationship with the federal government. The three airframe manufacturers and the Department of Defense have forged a very tight relationship that neither side can live without. The Department of Defense is the firms' single most important customer, and the firms, of course, are the primary suppliers of military aircraft. Thousands of employees at Boeing, Lockheed, and McDonnell-Douglas began their careers in the Department of Defense. The interrelationships between the buyer and the sellers are very tight indeed. The process by which the Department of Defense contracts for new aircraft is also an important feature of this industry. The structure of the contract can affect delivery times, reliability, and the costs of developing and producing an airplane. An economic analysis of the airframe industry must consider how the Department of Defense and the airframe manufacturers interact. Nothing comparable exists in the automobile industry.

The oil industry introduces yet another wrinkle that differs from the other two industries. Governments always play a major role on the *supply* side of oil markets. In the United States, the federal government owns the rights to all offshore sites that are believed to contain oil and to some inland sites as well. The private companies bid for the rights to explore and develop these sites in government-run auctions. State governments also influence the supply of oil taken from their lands by means of prorationing laws that dictate how quickly a company can remove oil from a common resource pool. The laws exist because the total amount of oil that can be extracted from a pool depends on the rate at which it is extracted. Therefore, if three companies have tapped into a common pool, the rate at which each firm extracts oil has an external effect on the other two firms. The prorationing laws are a response to this external effect. In addition, the oil industry has always enjoyed special federal and state tax treatment designed to encourage exploration and production by domestic producers. When all is said and done, however, intervention into oil markets by U.S. governments pales in comparison to the influence of the Organization of Petroleum Exporting Countries (OPEC) on the oil industry worldwide. OPEC's control of the world oil market in the 1970s has no parallel in any other major industry over the past 30 years. The price of oil during the 1970s was influenced as much by Middle Eastern politics as by standard market forces. OPEC's monopoly power slipped badly in the 1980s, but do not be too quick to write OPEC off. It may well make a comeback. Many Western countries, including the United States, are still heavily dependent on oil imports from the Middle East.

Developing a set of general principles for industries as diverse as the automobile, airframe, and oil industries is clearly a difficult task. If these industries contained a large number of small firms, the differences among them would not matter so much. We could confidently predict that competition among the firms would drive prices close to marginal and average costs and keep profits low. But with only a few firms in each industry the particular features of the industry matter in predicting behavior and market outcomes.

Strategic Behavior Over the Long Run

REFLECTION: Think of some situations in which you behaved strategically and what motivated you to do so.

The difficulties of predicting behavior are compounded by strategic interactions among the few dominant firms. Gamesmanship is a fact of life for the large corporations because their fortunes are so intertwined. Should Ford raise the prices of its luxury cars? The answer very much depends on whether Ford thinks General Motors, Chrysler, and the foreign producers are about to raise the prices of their luxury cars. What bids will Boeing and Lockheed and McDonnell-Douglas enter for the new jet fighter contract? They are each thinking along the same lines. They know that a lower bid increases the chances of winning the contract. But a lower bid also increases the probability of an embarrassing cost overrun if they do win, which would threaten the credibility of their bids on future projects. What is the best bidding strategy under these circumstances? Should Exxon increase its exploration for new oil reserves? The answer surely depends on whether Exxon thinks OPEC will be able to regain its dominance of the world oil market and raise the price of oil.

Strategic behavior need not lead to unpredictable outcomes, even when only a few firms are involved. For instance, we saw that firms in a cartel have a powerful incentive to cheat despite the obvious advantages of maintaining the cartel. But the firms in an oligopoly are not attempting to cooperate and collude. Instead, they are openly competing among themselves and trying to gain the upper hand. In addition, large corporations are long-lived institutions. The ability to compete effectively in any of the oligopolistic industries requires large-scale investments and the accumulation of a considerable amount of technical expertise. Finally, the oligopolies are often protected from the entry of new firms by substantial barriers to entry. These factors combine to create an environment in which a fairly stable number of firms engage in repeated strategic interactions over a long period of time. The firms do not make once-and-for-all strategic decisions about price or anything else. They continually reassess their decisions as they learn how other firms have reacted to them.

What happens when competing, noncooperating firms interact strategically over a long period of time? The answer, unfortunately, is that almost anything is possible. Market outcomes can vary all the way from marginal cost pricing and zero economic profits to the pure monopoly price and maintained profits for every firm. About all one can say for sure is that the market outcomes in these games depend on the timing and frequency of decisions and on the information available to each firm. Referring to the examples above, Ford can roll back its price increase if General Motors and Chrysler refuse to increase their prices. In contrast, Boeing, Lockheed, and McDonnell-Douglas can make only one bid for a jet fighter contract. The more information Exxon has about the political maneuverings within the OPEC cartel, the more confident it can be about its exploration decisions. These kinds of considerations certainly matter in an ongoing strategic environment. But understanding what factors affect strategic decision making has not brought economists closer to a set of general principles about actual market outcomes.

The truth is that the oligopolies exhibit an enormous variety of behavior, and economists have developed theory upon theory attempting to explain the behaviors they observe. No one theory has stood up very well, however, when applied across industries or even within one industry over time. We will see some of the theoretical difficulties in the next section when we consider pricing behavior under oligopoly.

SETTING PRICES IN OLIGOPOLY: STICKY PRICES AND NONPRICE COMPETITION

We learned when studying the Laws of Supply and Demand that prices in competitive markets react quickly to changes in supply and demand. In fact, prices can increase or decrease dramatically if the market supply curve and/or the market demand curve is highly inelastic (steep). Prices simply do not behave that way in oligopolistic markets.

Prices in the highly concentrated industries vary much less than do prices in the effectively competitive industries, especially in the downward direction. Annual price decreases of 20 percent and more are not uncommon in agriculture and other highly competitive industries. Not so in the oligopolies. For example, one study computed annual price changes for 39 highly concentrated producer goods industries in each of four years when demand was exceedingly sluggish: 1961, 1970, 1975, and 1980. The study found only two instances where prices fell by more than 20 percent among the 156 observations (39 industries · 4 years = 156 price changes).[2]

The prices just referred to are actual market prices, not list prices. Be sure to keep in mind the distinction between list prices and actual market prices when thinking about price behavior in an oligopoly. Many large corporations sell a variety of products whose prices are published in booklets for the benefit of their dealers and customers. The published prices are the *list prices.* (The list price of a consumer product is often referred to as the "manufacturer's suggested retail price".) Firms change their list prices only infrequently, simply because revising and publishing new price booklets is costly.

The behavior of list prices is misleading, however. The relevant prices are the actual prices of market transactions, not the list prices. We know from our experience buying automobiles that actual new car prices can differ considerably from their list prices. New cars, especially new American cars, almost never sell at their list prices. Moreover, actual prices do respond to market conditions. Car dealers offer smaller discounts from the list price when demand is brisk and larger discounts from the list price when demand is soft. The behavior of new car prices is typical of most industries; actual market prices vary far more than do list prices. Even so, actual market prices are much stickier in the highly concentrated industries than in the effectively competitive sector of the economy. We want to understand why this is so.

Tacit Collusion

Price stickiness under oligopoly is hardly a new phenomenon. In the 1920s Harvard economist Edward Chamberlin commented that the giant corporations appeared to be engaging in a **tacit collusion** with one another, silently (tacitly) agreeing to maintain their prices above competitive levels. The firms could not openly agree to fix prices in cartel-like fashion, but their pricing behavior was hardly much different than if they had openly colluded. Their tacit agreements did not extend to nonprice methods of competition, however. The large corporations did and still do compete vigorously with one another through means

TACIT COLLUSION
An implicit agreement among the large corporations in an oligopoly, most often in the form of an agreement not to compete in terms of prices.

[2] I. Domowitz, R. Hubbard, and B. Petersen, "Oligopoly Supergames: Some Empirical Evidence on Prices and Margins," *Journal of Industrial Economics* XXXV, No. 4 (June, 1987): 377–398.

other than price—for example, geographic and quality product differentiation, advertising and sales promotions, and research and development into new products and production processes. They seem as comfortable with nonprice competition as they are uncomfortable with price competition.

The fact that different firms charge essentially the same price for similar products is not an issue. Firms selling similar products have no choice but to charge the same price, or the higher-priced firms will be shut out of the market. Corporate executives do not have to call each other and share price information to reach this result. After all, every farmer's wheat sells at the same price in a perfectly competitive market. The real issue is why the large firms are able to maintain their prices above average (and marginal) costs and earn a profit. In other words, how do they manage to soften competition among themselves?

Economists now believe that a large part of the answer lies in the nature of their strategic interactions. As noted in the preceding section, firms do not make once-and-for-all pricing decisions. They engage in repeated strategic interactions with their competitors over a very long period of time. Firms have the opportunity to adjust their own prices as they receive new information about the pricing decisions of other firms. The opportunity to engage in repeated interactions can lead to prices above average costs and to maintained profits for all firms.

Repeated Interaction: The Trigger Strategy Model

TRIGGER STRATEGY

A punishment strategy within the context of a tacit collusion to maintain prices above average cost, in which the rival firms threaten to cut their prices to average cost forever if one of the firms cheats on the pricing agreement.

A popular story of tacit collusion in an ongoing strategic environment is the **trigger strategy** model. The model assumes that all firms in an industry produce an identical product and have identical and constant average costs. The story begins with all firms tacitly agreeing to set their prices above average cost so they each can earn a profit. The agreement also includes the following (tacit) understanding: Should any firm undercut the agreed-on price, all other firms will slash their prices to average cost as soon as they learn of the transgression. Moreover, their prices will remain at average cost forever since all trust will have been destroyed. The price cut is said to trigger the other firms' reactions because they react automatically and with perfect certainty—hence the name *trigger strategy* for the model.

The price may stay above average cost forever under these strategic ground rules, depending on the benefits and the costs of cheating. Each firm thinks along the following lines. If the firm cheats and cuts price, it steals customers from other firms and earns much larger profits than if it does not cheat. The extra profits continue only for a short time, however, until the other firms discover what has happened. At that point the agreement falls apart, prices are slashed to average cost, and all firms earn zero profits forever. If each firm decides that the short-run gains from cheating are less than the long-run costs of earning zero profits forever after being discovered, then no firm cheats, and the collusive price is maintained. The agreement falls apart only if the reverse is true—if the short-run gains from cheating exceed the long-run losses of the other firms' trigger strategy. In short, the model has many of the same features as the cartel model of explicit collusion. The collusive price has a better chance of being maintained the quicker firms can detect cheating and the harsher the punishment for cheating is. The firms must also sell similar products and have similar costs of production, so that they can agree on an initial price.

The trigger strategy model is not an entirely satisfactory explanation of price stickiness. It suffers two troubling flaws. First, it cannot explain what price the firms initially agree on or even how they reach an agreement. The initial price can be anywhere between the average cost price and the price that would exist if the market were organized as a pure monopoly. This is too wide a range for the model to be an accurate predictor of oligopoly prices. Second, the automatic trigger reaction is not entirely believable. Suppose that the agreement breaks down because someone cheats, so that the firms begin earning zero profits. The firms obviously have a strong incentive to renegotiate a new price that will allow them to make a profit. If they could agree on a price once, why not again? Why accept zero profits forever if the market is potentially profitable for everyone? But if firms believe they can renegotiate their way out of the trigger response, they have all the more incentive to cheat in the first place. The costs of cheating are not nearly so high. Therefore, the possibility of renegotiating an agreement works against the model from both sides.

Economists have tried to improve on the trigger strategy model in two ways. One approach has firms make their decisions in different time periods. A second approach introduces various kinds of uncertainties, particularly with regard to the information each firm has about the other firms in its industry. These more complex models of repeated gamesmanship are well beyond the scope of this book. Suffice it to say that these models have achieved only a limited success in describing actual market behavior, and then only for particular industries over short periods of time.

Incentives for Nonprice Competition

Although the trigger strategy model may not be very successful in explaining price behavior, it has left us with one important insight. The model suggests why firms favor nonprice competition over price competition. The key is the difference in the predictability of the two forms of competition. If one firm cuts its price, the results are highly predictable. Either that firm steals other firms' customers, or a destructive price war ensues. The results of nonprice competition are much less predictable, however. If one firm engages in a more extensive advertising campaign or increases its research and development efforts, it may or may not gain a larger share of the market. Sometimes advertising campaigns and research and development projects succeed, and sometimes they fail. Firms feel much less compelled to reach an agreement banning nonprice competition when the results are so uncertain.

Firms might not be able to ban nonprice competition, even if they wanted to. Suppose that firms did agree to ban nonprice competition. The unpredictability of nonprice competition would then undermine the effectiveness of the trigger strategy in maintaining the agreement. For example, I might break a tacit agreement with you not to advertise, even though I know that you will advertise as soon as you find out that I have. My hope is that my advertising firm will come up with a successful advertising campaign and yours will not. Retaliation through advertising is not nearly so threatening as retaliation through a price war, so every firm has that much more incentive to cheat and to compete. Yet another problem with avoiding nonprice competition is that it can take so many different forms. Firms would have to reach a large number of tacit agreements to ban nonprice competition entirely, and this is unlikely.

We will not pursue the analysis of nonprice competition any further at this point. The motivation for product differentiation that we discussed in Chapter 15 is the same for the large corporations as for the smaller monopolistically competitive firms. In each instance the firm is trying to find just the right niche in the market that will distance it from its competitors and maximize its market power. We will consider two of the more important kinds of nonprice competition for the large corporations, advertising and research and development, when we analyze barriers to entry in Chapter 17. They each have the potential for blocking the free movement of resources that is so vital to the equity and efficiency of a market economy.

The theory of repeated strategic interaction is one of the newest fields of economic analysis. Until 10 to 15 years ago models of strategic interaction were all essentially static, single-play models. The newer models are much more realistic, if only because of their ongoing time dimension. The older models are still useful, though. They show very clearly how strategic considerations modify the standard analysis of market power contained in Chapters 14 and 15. Let's compare one of the earliest strategic models, called the mark-up pricing model, with the standard profit-maximizing model of market power.

Mark-up Pricing

MARK-UP PRICING

A rule-of-thumb method of pricing in which a firm sets its price at a constant percentage above its unit or average cost.

The **mark-up pricing** model attempts to explain why the large corporations appear to respond so differently to changes in demand and changes in cost. Macro economists tell us that prices respond quickly to changes in the costs of production in the noncompetitive sector of the economy. The large firms tend to raise their prices almost immediately whenever the price of oil increases or unions bargain for higher wages, and they lower their prices just as quickly whenever the price of oil falls or unions accept a wage cut. In contrast, their prices respond only slowly to changes in demand. When demand increases, the large firms respond by increasing production right away, but they hold the line on price. Demand has to remain strong for a number of months before prices begin to rise significantly. The same is true in reverse. When demand slackens, the firms respond by cutting production immediately, but not price. Prices begin to fall significantly only when demand has remained weak for a number of months. Prices appear to be sticky because changes in demand occur more often than do changes in costs.

The model of pricing behavior known as mark-up pricing can explain this pattern of price changes. The mark-up pricing story has two main components, one relating to the strategic environment in which these firms operate and one relating to the nature of their production costs.

A fundamental property of the strategic environment is its staggering complexity. Many of the large corporations are multiproduct firms, producing literally hundreds of different products. They also buy material and capital inputs from thousands of different suppliers. This means that the firms are buying and selling simultaneously in a huge number of different markets, each with its own set of customers, competitors, and strategic considerations. Designing strategies that maximize profit, or any other objective, market by market in such an environment is a hopelessly complex task. According to the mark-up model the multiproduct firms do not even try to meet specific objectives. Instead, they base all their decisions on simple rules of thumb that can be applied

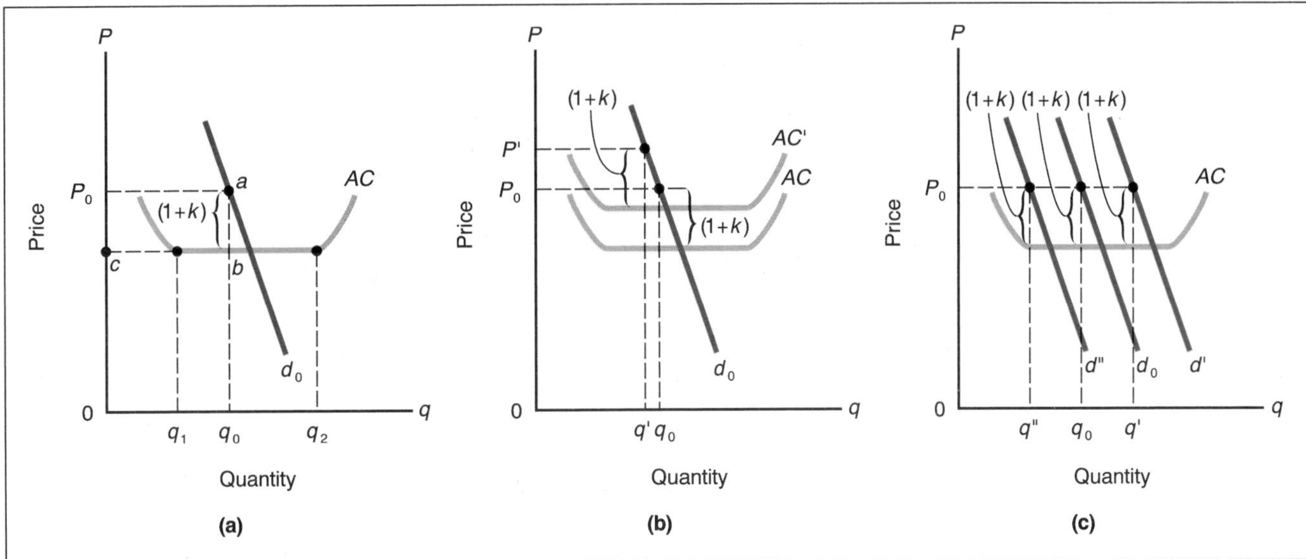

FIGURE 16.1

Mark-up Pricing

The mark-up pricing model assumes that firms set their prices equal to a constant mark-up above average costs, and that the average cost curve is essentially flat over a wide range of output. The mark-up by the firm in Figure 16.1(a) is k percent, for a mark-up factor of $(1 + k)$, and AC is flat over the range of output from q_1 to q_2. An increase in average costs from AC to AC' in Figure 16.1(b) causes the firm to increase its price from P_0 to P', as it maintains the $(1 + k)$ mark-up between average cost and price. In contrast, an increase or decrease in demand to d' or d'' in Figure 16.1(c) has no effect on the firm's price. The demand curve continues to intersect the AC curve in its flat region so neither average cost nor price changes.

across all markets and are known to produce satisfactory results. Mark-up pricing is one such rule of thumb. The idea is that a firm tries to calculate the unit or average cost of producing each product as best it can and then simply sets price equal to a constant percentage above unit cost. In other words, $P = (1 + k) \cdot AC$, where k is the constant mark-up applied to all products. For example, if the mark-up is 20 percent, $k = .2$.

The second component of the mark-up pricing story is that average costs are approximately constant over a wide range of output. We noted in Chapter 11 that this cost assumption is widely held among economists, even though it has not been verified by careful statistical analysis.

The three graphs in Figure 16.1 combine the two components of the model. Refer to Figure 16.1(a). The average cost curve (AC) reflects the standard assumption about production costs. AC declines up to q_1, remains constant from q_1 to q_2, and then rises beyond q_2. The firm's demand curve is initially at d_0. The firm sets its price at P_0, a mark-up of k percent above the constant average cost, and produces q_0. **Mark-up pricing** generates a profit equal to the area of rectangle $abcP_0$.

We have not bothered to include the marginal revenue and the marginal cost curves because the firm is not maximizing profit. The firm's objective here is to deal with complexity in a reasonable and effective manner by following a simple rule of thumb. As a result, the profit rectangle $abcP_0$ is not necessarily the largest possible profit the firm could obtain, but it is presumably a satisfactory amount of profit. This is the first time in the text that we have assumed that the objective of the firm is something other than maximizing profit.

The mark-up model represented in Figure 16.1 can reproduce both characteristics of pricing behavior actually observed in the U.S. economy at the macro level: the quick responsiveness to changes in cost and the slow responsiveness to changes in demand. Changes in the firm's costs are completely and immediately passed through to prices. Refer to Figure 16.1(b). If the average cost curve shifts up to AC' and the mark-up percentage, k, remains constant, the price increases to P'. Since P is k percent above AC and P' is k percent above AC', the price increases by the full amount of the shift in costs, assuming the new quantity remains in the flat region of AC. Similarly, any decrease in AC causes an equal, proportional decrease in P.

In contrast, price can be unresponsive to changes in demand. Refer to Figure 16.1(c). If the firm's demand increases to d' and the firm maintains the mark-up percentage at k, output increases to q', but price remains at P_0. Similarly, a decrease in demand to d'' reduces output to q'', but leaves price unaffected. The firm changes its price only if demand shifts outside the region of constant AC.

The mark-up pricing model fits the facts of the U.S. macro economy reasonably well, but does it really explain pricing behavior under oligopoly? The best evidence in its favor is anecdotal: Many business executives claim that their companies follow mark-up pricing in setting prices. The most prominent example is General Motors, which has long maintained that it sets the price of its cars as a simple mark-up above costs. Statistical analysis does not generally support these claims, however. Most studies find that the *price-cost margin*, the ratio of price to average cost, varies with market conditions. For instance, a recent study computed the average price-cost margins within 312 U.S. manufacturing industries each year from 1958 to 1981. These 312 industries represent approximately 70 percent of all U.S. manufacturing industries. The study found that the price-cost margins generally behave as one might expect. When business is booming, the price-cost margin increases; when demand slackens, the price-cost margin decreases. Moreover, the tendency for price-cost margin to follow market conditions is *more* pronounced the more concentrated the industry.[3]

Firms that claim to follow mark-up pricing obviously know how they set their prices, but they are undoubtedly referring to their list prices, not their actual prices. When it comes to determining the actual market prices, more is going on than a simple mark-up rule of thumb. For starters, demand factors appear to be just as important as cost factors are in determining actual market prices.

We have now considered two models that attempt to explain the stickiness of prices under oligopoly in very different ways and have seen that neither of them is completely convincing. In truth, economists do not have a simple, unified theory of how the giant corporations set their prices. The theory of pricing under oligopoly remains one of the outstanding puzzles in modern economics.

THE OBJECTIVES OF THE LARGE FIRMS

Throughout the text we have been assuming that firms have a single objective, to maximize profits. They try to squeeze every last bit of profit out of the marketplace. (The mark-up pricing model has been the only exception.) The assumption is reasonably accurate for relatively small firms operating in highly competitive market environments, but it may not be accurate for the large firms in an oligopoly. Many economists believe that the large corporations are not

[3]In addition to the Domowitz, *et. al.* study cited in the previous footnote, see: I. Domowitz, R. Hubbard, and B. Petersen, "The Intertemporal Stability of the Concentration-Margins Relationship," *Journal of Industrial Economics* XXXV, No. 1 (September 1986): 13–34.

profit maximizers. Nobel Laureate Herbert Simon dubbed them **profit satisficers,** meaning that they are interested in profit only to the point of achieving a satisfactory level of profit. Having achieved that level, the big firms then pursue other objectives.

PROFIT SATISFICERS
Large corporations that are interested in profit only to the point of achieving a satisfactory level of profit and then pursue other objectives.

Why should the large corporations behave differently from the smaller firms in more competitive market environments? One part of the answer is that profits come easier to the large firms. Economic profits are difficult to measure, but empirical studies of accounting profits, the difference between sales and expenses, strongly suggest that size pays. They all find that the average ratio of accounting profits to sales within an industry tends to rise the more concentrated the industry. One study of the Fortune 500 firms found that the largest firm in an industry was the most profitable firm more than 25 percent of the time.[4] The idea, then, is that the large firms do not have to work as hard as the smaller, more competitive firms to earn a profit. They have the leeway to pursue other objectives.

Why, though, do the firms bother pursuing other objectives? The stockholders of a corporation are presumably interested only in profit maximization. Like all investors, they want to earn the highest possible return on the funds they have invested in the company. Why should they allow their firms to forego profitable opportunities? Economists have given two different kinds of answers to that question.

The first answer is suggested by our analysis of pricing behavior: Strategic considerations force firms away from maximizing profits at every point in time. The trigger strategy model argues for adopting a long-run perspective; the aggressive pursuit of profit in the short run will destroy the opportunity to earn a profit in the future. Investors are still interested in maximizing profit according to that model, but their objective is maximizing long-run profit, not short-run profit. The mark-up model suggests another possibility: The strategic environment is too complex to even consider a profit-maximizing strategy. According to that model, firms have no choice but to resort to simple rules of thumb that produce a satisfactory level of profit.

The second answer relates to the separation of management and ownership in large corporations. The argument here is that stockholders and managers have different objectives and that managers have enough control over the corporation to pursue their objectives. Stockholders may be interested in profits, but managers are concerned primarily with longevity, with maintaining their jobs over the long haul. Consequently, managers may forego some profit opportunities in favor of other objectives that help ensure the continuation of the firm.

Sales Maximization

For instance, managers seem particularly interested in **market share,** defined as the ratio of the firm's sales to total industry sales. They may assume, rightly or wrongly, that a larger firm is more likely to survive than is a smaller firm. Maximizing sales is not the same as maximizing profit. Let's compare these two objectives as one example of how the interests of managers and stockholders might conflict.

MARKET SHARE
The ratio of a firm's sales (total revenue) to the total industry sales.

[4] W. Baldwin, *Market Power, Competition, and Antitrust Policy* (Homewood, IL: Richard D. Irwin, 1987), 311–312.

FIGURE 16.2

Profit Maximization Versus Sales Maximization

The firm maximizes profit by producing output q_{PM}, at the intersection of marginal revenue (MR) and marginal cost (MC), and charging the price P_{PM}. The maximum profit is the rectangular area $P_{PM}abc$. The firm maximizes sales (total revenue) by producing output q_{SM}, where MR equals zero, and charging the price P_{SM}. The firm makes a profit equal to the rectangular area $P_{SM}efg$. Sales maximization increases the firm's market share relative to profit maximization, at the cost of sacrificing some profit.

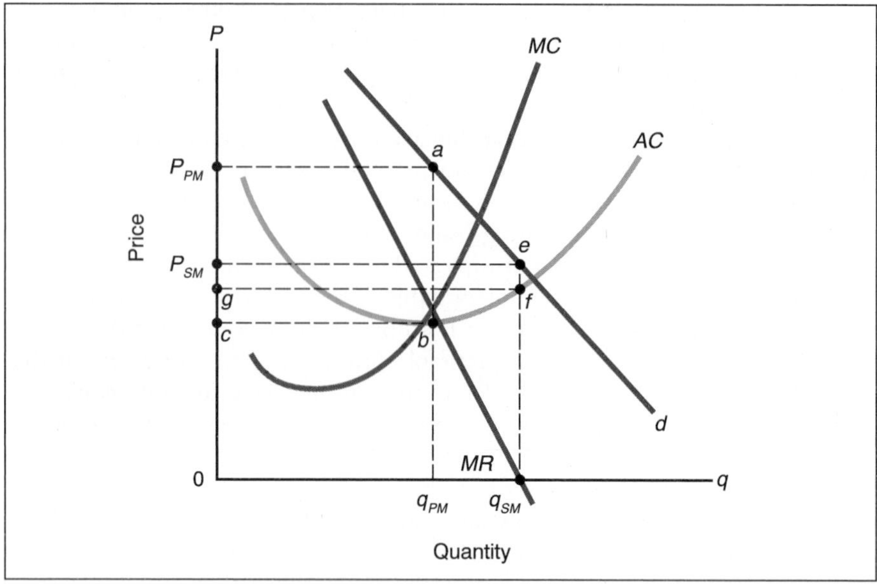

SALES MAXIMIZATION

The goal of maximizing total revenue or sales by producing the output at which marginal revenue is zero.

Figure 16.2 is the familiar graph that we have been using to analyze profit maximization when firms have market power. It contains the firm's demand curve (d), marginal revenue curve (MR), average cost curve (AC), and marginal cost curve (MC). Assume that the market is in the long run, and ignore all strategic considerations.

We know what the firm does if its objective is to maximize profit. The firm selects the output q_{PM}, at the intersection of MR and MC, and charges a price of P_{PM} (the subscript $_{PM}$ stands for profit maximizing). The maximum amount of profit is equal to the area of rectangle $P_{PM}abc$.

What should the firm do if, instead, its objective is maximizing the dollar value of sales, or total revenue? To find the quantity-price combination that maximizes total revenue, all we need consider are the demand and the marginal revenue curves. Total revenue is maximized at q_{SM}, the output at which MR is zero (the subscript $_{SM}$ stands for sales maximizing). The reason is as follows. At any output below q_{SM} marginal revenue is positive; increasing output in that range adds to total revenue. Conversely, at any output above q_{SM} marginal revenue is negative; selling output in that range reduces total revenue. So the maximum total revenue occurs at q_{SM}, when $MR = 0$. Finally, if the firm produces q_{SM}, it charges a price of P_{SM} and earns a profit equal to the area of rectangle $P_{SM}efg$. By maximizing sales, the managers charge a lower price and sell more output than the stockholders would like them to.

Figure 16.2 also captures Simon's notion that firms are profit satisficers. Maximizing sales sacrifices some profit. The profit rectangle $P_{SM}efg$ under sales maximization is necessarily smaller than the profit rectangle $P_{PM}abc$ under profit maximization. However, a profit of $P_{SM}efg$ is presumably satisfactory to the owners, which may be why they give the managers some leeway to pursue other goals. The owners would not be so understanding if sales maximizing led to negative profits.

The clash between maximizing profit and maximizing sales can also arise between employees and owners. The National Basketball Association (NBA) offers a nice example. The NBA players and management have negotiated an agreement that places a total salary cap on each team. The salary cap is defined as a percentage of the teams' revenues, not profits. Therefore, the players would like lower ticket prices than the owners would because they want their teams to maximize sales revenue, not profit.

Some major league baseball stars have attendance clauses in their contracts. This is a different matter entirely. These players would presumably like the owners to give tickets away so as to maximize q, the number of people attending.

Who Really Controls the Giant Corporations

Do corporate managers really act independently of the wishes of the stockholders, enough so that it makes a difference to market outcomes? Some economists believe that they do not, although the reason why they do not is a matter of some dispute. Those who believe that the interests of managers and stockholders are fairly closely aligned tend to fall into one of two groups. One group argues that managers have to give primary consideration to profit because the corporation cannot survive unless it at least breaks even. So the first order of business for any manager is assuring that the firm is comfortably above the long-run break-even level. Having achieved a satisfactory level of profit, to use Simon's term, anything else the managers do is relatively unimportant. Referring to our example comparing profit and sales maximization, these economists would argue that the difference between P_{PM} and P_{SM} (alternatively, q_{PM} and q_{SM}) is unlikely to be very large.

A second group argues that managers can indeed behave quite differently than the stockholders would like them to. Since the early 1980s, however, the balance of power between managers and stockholders has been shifting in favor of stockholders. One reason for the shift in power is that financial markets have become increasingly dominated by large institutional investors, such as pension fund managers, investment banks, and brokerage houses, which are interested only in profits. These institutional investors have leverage over corporate managers because they can shift huge amounts of money in and out of corporate stocks and bonds. In particular, they can threaten to sell a large block of the company's stocks and bonds should the managers become lax in the pursuit of profit. Selling the stocks and bonds would depress the company's stock and bond prices and make it more difficult to raise funds for new investment. Carrying out the threat would undoubtedly anger the stockholders, who may respond by replacing the top management. The managers therefore have to pursue profit opportunities aggressively to protect their jobs.

TENDER TAKEOVERS Corporate managers also became vulnerable to tender takeovers in the 1980s. A tender takeover works essentially as follows. A group of investors issues large amounts of new debt and uses the proceeds to buy the existing stock of the target corporation. The debt often carries very high interest rates, the so-called junk bonds. The takeover investors offer ("tender") the existing stockholders a deal that they cannot refuse, a price well above the current market price of the stock. Tender takeovers are called *hostile* takeovers because they are opposed by the current managers. The current managers know that the new owners typically sell off parts of the business to pay back some of the debt and replace many of the current managers with their own people.

The increase in tender takeovers that started in the mid-1980s is viewed as strong evidence that managers had been pursuing their own objectives to the detriment of the stockholders. After all, how can the takeover investors afford to pay such a high price for the stock of the target company? The standard answer is bad management. The managers were concerned with themselves, not the stockholders. In the process they allowed the company to become top heavy with managers and administrators, excessively costly, and not nearly as profitable as it could be. The takeover investors believe that by streamlining the company and installing new managers who will restore the rightful emphasis on profit maximization, they can increase the company's profit enough to justify the high stock prices.

The managers also refused to take full advantage of the U.S. corporate tax laws, which strongly favor debt financing of new investment over equity financing through retained earnings or new stock issues. Corporations can deduct interest payments on their debt from before-tax profits as an expense of doing business, but they cannot deduct dividends or any other allowance for the cost of equity funding. Given the corporate tax rate of 35 percent, a dollar of interest payment on corporate debt costs the stockholders only 65 cents; 35 cents of the interest is returned as a reduction in their corporate tax liability. By contrast, a dollar of dividends costs one dollar. That is a fairly strong bias in favor of debt financing.

A tender takeover necessarily takes advantage of the tax laws because the takeover group issues debt to buy the company's stock. Trading debt for equity increases after-tax earnings per share on the remaining stock and helps justify the high buy-in price. Of course, it also increases the riskiness of the firm. If business turns sour, the company may not be able to meet the principal and interest payments on the debt. The increasing risk of bankruptcy is what kept the current managers from taking full advantage of the tax laws. They did not want to put their own jobs at risk.

THE EVIDENCE ON CORPORATE CONTROL Have institutional investors and tender takeovers really tilted the objectives of management toward profit maximization? As in most matters pertaining to oligopoly, the evidence is unclear. The tender takeovers themselves provide a direct test of the hypothesis. The target firms should be significantly more profitable after the takeover if the former managers of the target firms were pursuing their own objectives at the expense of profit. In fact, just the opposite has occurred. A recent study of 96 tender takeovers found that the before-tax profitability of the target firms *decreased substantially*, on average, after the takeover. Moreover, the decrease in before-tax profits was so steep that the tax advantages of the takeover could not possibly have offset them. The study revealed another interesting point. The 96 tender takeovers represented only 1.6 percent of the 6,000 corporate mergers that occurred during the same time period. Tender takeovers make great stories for the news media. But the vast majority of mergers between corporations result from friendly negotiations between the managers of the merging firms, just as they always have. In short, the tender takeovers themselves offer no direct evidence of a shift in the objectives of management toward profit maximization.[5]

---

[5]D. Ravenscraft and F. Scherer, "Life After Takeover," *Journal of Industrial Economics* XXXVI, No. 2 (December, 1987): 147–156.

At the same time, corporations are now routinely issuing more debt and engaging in other sophisticated kinds of financial maneuvering to increase short-term profits and reduce the threat of a tender takeover. This behavior is commonly attributed to the disciplining effect of institutional investors and the threat of tender takeovers. Some close observers of the business community do believe that there has been a clear shift in management objectives toward profit maximization. They also believe that the shift has been damaging. The new knock against corporate managers is that they spend too much time and energy on short-run financial matters. They should redirect their energies to the fundamentals of business that matter over the long-haul—production, marketing, and research and development. Critics also worry that the increase in corporate debt is risky. They believe that U.S. businesses have become more vulnerable to bankruptcy should the economy suffer another deep recession like the recession of 1981–82.

HISTORICAL NOTE: Debt-financed tender takeovers fell off considerably in the late 1980s through the first two years of the 1990s, perhaps because they were not particularly successful, or because stock prices were fairly high on average, or because managers learned how to defend against them. They did make a slight comeback in 1992, however.

These criticisms may well be overstated, however. We saw in the section on pricing behavior how strategic considerations may drive firms away from profit maximization no matter who controls the firm. Suffice it to say that the question of who controls the large corporations, and to what ends, remains unanswered.

Conclusion: What is the Economic Problem?

In Chapter 1 we emphasized that the first step in understanding economic events begins with this question: What are the objectives, alternatives, and constraints of the individual agents involved? In other words, what economic problems are they trying to solve? If we cannot describe the agents' economic problems, we cannot hope to predict how they will behave in different market situations. This first principle of economic analysis is especially applicable to the large corporations. The structure of the firm's economic problem is not at all clear under oligopoly. We have just seen that economists are uncertain about the objectives of the large corporations. Earlier sections of the chapter described the uncertainties surrounding their alternatives and constraints. What exactly are the rules of the games that oligopolies play with one another? Can the firms sort through the enormous complexities of their market environments to define their alternatives and constraints, or are they forced to rely on simple rules of thumb such as mark-up pricing? How do the idiosyncrasies of each firm and each market come into play, given that only a small number of firms are involved? Economists cannot develop a general theory of oligopoly without being able to define a common economic problem for the oligopolies. Many economists believe that there is no common economic problem to be found.

ELABORATION: Even the demand curve facing an individual firm is difficult to determine when firms behave strategically. A demand curve is an other things equal concept; it assumes that the prices of the other firms are being held constant. But this is not often a reasonable assumption in an oligopoly. Can a firm assume that its rivals will not adjust their prices if it should raise or lower its price?

SUMMARY

Chapter 16 examines why generalizations about market behavior are so difficult to achieve when the market is structured as an oligopoly. Economists have no satisfactory, unified model of oligopoly, and they are unlikely to develop one. Many economists believe that industry-specific case studies are the only effective means of analyzing markets in the highly concentrated sector of the economy.

The chapter began with a discussion of the two attributes of oligopoly that work against generalizing about any aspect of market behavior: (1) The actions of a few large firms dominate the industry, and (2) the firms engage in repeated strategic interactions over a long period of time.

1. Market behavior is predictable when industries contain a large number of firms because of a law of statistics known as the Law of Large Numbers. The law says that the average behavior of a large group of firms (or people) is highly predictable, even if the behavior of each individual is not. This law does not apply to oligopoly, in which a few firms dominate the industry. In that case, individual differences among firms and the overall market environment in which the industry operates matter in determining market outcomes. The automobile, airframe, and oil industries serve as illustrations of this.
2. Large firms competing in a oligopoly engage in repeated strategic interactions over a long period of time, continually adjusting their decisions once they see how the other firms have reacted to them. Almost any market outcome is possible in such a strategic environment, from the competitive marginal cost price and zero economic profits to the pure monopoly price and maintained profits. The theory of strategic interactions has not yielded many useful general principles of market behavior. All one can say of a general nature is that market outcomes in a repeated strategic environment depend on the frequency and timing of decisions and on the information available to each firm.

The chapter then turned to the uncertainties surrounding the question of how the giant corporations set their prices.

3. Prices in the highly concentrated industries are stickier than those in the effectively competitive sector of the economy. The large corporations behave as if they have engaged in a tacit collusion to avoid price competition in favor of nonprice competition. Also, the large corporations have succeeded in softening competition among themselves. Their prices generally exceed both marginal and average costs.

The chapter considered two models of pricing behavior—the trigger strategy and mark-up pricing—which capture some likely reasons for price stickiness in an ongoing strategic environment.

4. The trigger strategy model directly addresses the idea of tacit collusion in an ongoing strategic environment. The model says that firms reach an initial, tacit agreement to set price above average cost. Part of their agreement includes a trigger strategy, in which it is understood that all firms will lower their prices to average cost immediately and forever if any one firm is caught cheating. Prices stay above average cost so long as the short-term gains from cheating are less than are the long-term losses of earning zero profits forever after the cheating is discovered. The model has two weaknesses. It cannot explain what initial price the firms agree to. It is also undermined by the possibility of renegotiation after cheating occurs. Having once negotiated an agreement, the firms might well renegotiate an agreement after cheating has occurred, rather than accepting zero profits forever. However, the possibility of renegotiating increases the incentive to cheat in the first place.

5. The trigger strategy model does suggest why firms favor nonprice competition over price competition. The key is that the effects of nonprice competition are far less certain that are the effects of a price war. Therefore, firms have less incentive to maintain any agreement on nonprice competition. Also, nonprice competition can take many forms. Negotiating an initial agreement on every possible variation of nonprice competition is unlikely.
6. The mark-up pricing model attempts to explain the actual pattern of price changes in the big business sector. Its central idea is that the strategic environment is so complex for multiproduct corporations that they resort to simple rules of thumb in setting prices. They do not try to maximize profits, or anything else. Under mark-up pricing, a firm marks up the prices of all its products by a constant percentage above unit or average costs. If average costs are also reasonably flat, as many economists believe, then the firm's prices do not respond to changes in demand, but do respond to changes in unit costs. The model fits the facts noted above, but it cannot explain another fact: why the mark-ups vary in response to changes in demand and other market conditions. The model appears to apply better to list prices than to actual market prices.

The final section of Chapter 16 discussed another possibility about firms in the highly concentrated industries: Their managers may not be profit maximizers. They may pursue other goals such as market share. The explanation for this possibility runs along the following lines.

7. Profits come easily to the giant corporations, so that their managers have the luxury of being profit satisficers rather than profit maximizers. They seek a satisfactory level of profits to please the stockholders and then turn to other goals that help to ensure the continued existence of the corporation.
8. Corporate managers and stockholders have different objectives, and managers have the power to carry out their own wishes. The stockholders' objective is profit maximization, whereas the managers are interested more in long-run stability. The tension between the two was demonstrated by comparing the objectives of sales maximization and profit maximization. Maximizing sales increases the size of the firm, which may help ensure its continuation. Sales are maximized by selecting the output at which marginal revenue is zero. Output is larger, and price lower, than under profit maximization, which selects the output at which marginal revenue equals marginal cost.
9. The combination of large institutional investors gaining control of the stock and bond markets and the recent increase in tender takeovers has supposedly disciplined managers to seek profit maximization. The evidence with respect to tender takeovers does not support this view, however. Firms that have been subjected to a tender takeover have seen their profits decline, not increase, after the takeover. The question of who controls the large corporations, and to what ends, remains unanswered.
10. Economists have not been able to describe a common economic problem for the oligopolies. This in turn has prevented economists from developing a general theory of oligopoly.

KEY TERMS

law of large numbers
market share
mark-up pricing
oligopoly
profit satisficers
sales maximization
tacit collusion
trigger strategy

QUESTIONS

1. Strategic behavior is a central feature of an oligopolistic market structure, whereas it is unimportant in any of the other market structures that we have studied. Why are the oligopolies different in this respect?
2. a. What are the conditions that lead to an oligopolistic market structure?
   b. What is the common rule of thumb for characterizing a market structure as an oligopoly?
   c. Is oligopoly the dominant market structure in the United States?
   d. Give some examples of industries that are oligopolies in the United States.
3. Use one of the three industries mentioned early in the chapter (the automobile, airframe, and oil industries) to illustrate why the Law of Large Numbers does not apply to oligopolistic markets. What are some of the implications of this?
4. Oligopolies appear to be reluctant to compete against one another in terms of price, but quite willing to compete against one another by nonprice means.
   a. How does the trigger strategy model try to explain this behavior?
   b. What forms does the nonprice competition take? Give some examples.
5. a. What is the difference between the list price and the actual price of a product?
   b. Are list prices or actual prices likely to vary more over time?
   c. Think back to competitive markets that operate according to the Laws of Supply and Demand. Describe a government policy in this context that is likely to cause a list price to differ from an actual price.
6. In the noncompetitive sector of the economy, prices appear to be sticky in response to changes in the demand for firms' products, but quite responsive to changes in firms' costs.
   a. How does the mark-up pricing model attempt to explain this behavior?
   b. What are some of the weaknesses of the model in this regard?
7. Many economists believe that short-run profit maximization is not the objective of the oligopolistic firms. What factors support this view?
8. Compare and contrast sales maximization and profit maximization in terms of their effects on price, output, and profit.
9. To what extent did the tender takeovers that occurred during 1980s provide evidence that profit maximization is not the objective of an oligopolistic firm?
10. What are some of the difficulties in describing the economic problem that an oligopolistic firm is trying to solve when deciding how much output to produce and what price to charge?

CHAPTER

17

Public Policy and the Big Business Sector

LEARNING OBJECTIVES

CONCEPTS TO LEARN

Barriers to entry:

1. Legal
2. Natural
3. Behavioral

The economic effects of advertising

Innovation, creative destruction, and dynamic efficiency

The patent dilemma

Rivalry among the few

Evaluating oligopoly from a social perspective

The U.S. antitrust laws and their recent enforcement

CONCEPTS TO RECALL

The three criteria for judging market outcomes [13]

Market (monopoly) power [14]

Effective market (monopoly) power [14]

Oligopoly [16]

Virtually all economists agree that the giant corporations in the oligopolistic sector of the economy have effective monopoly power. Their returns to capital as measured by accounting profits exceed the opportunity cost of capital, on average, and the returns to capital tend to increase the more concentrated the industry. These facts are well documented and widely accepted. Economists and legal experts disagree, however, on why the more concentrated industries are more profitable.

The majority opinion is associated with Joseph Bain, a leading industrial organization economist of the 1940s and 1950s. Bain attributed the positive relationship between profits and industry concentration to a combination of collusion and barriers to entry. He believed that collusion among firms, either tacit or explicit, to set price above average cost is easier to maintain the more concentrated the industry. Then, having agreed to a profitable price, firms in the more concentrated industries are better able to erect barriers to entry against outside investors intent on capturing some of the industry's profits. Bain's definition of a barrier to entry*—anything that allows existing firms to earn economic profits without the threat of entry—is also widely accepted.*

The minority opinion, led by Judge Robert Bork and UCLA economist Harold Demsetz, argues that the highly concentrated industries are more profitable because they are more efficient. Judge Bork, one of the nation's leading legal experts on antitrust policy, believes that "a market position that creates output restriction and higher prices will always be eroded if it is not based on superior efficiency." Demsetz agrees. He believes that the positive relationship between profits and industry concentration arises because "where efficiency differences are important, efficient firms obtain large market shares and earn rents [profits], and both concentration and industry-level profitability are thus high."

MIT's Richard Schmalensee tried to settle the issue by testing each hypothesis on a sample of 70 manufacturing industries. His results were inconclusive, as are most results in the study of oligopoly: "It would appear likely that the relative importance of collusion and differential efficiency vary considerably among industries and over time."[1]

CURRENT ISSUE: An outstanding example of the better-efficiency view is Microsoft. Microsoft has achieved a commanding position in the computer industry in large part because Bill Gates and his companions keep developing superior computer software products year after year.

Chapter 17 assesses the economic consequences of the giant corporations. The central policy question is this: What gives large firms effective monopoly power—barriers to entry or better efficiency? If barriers to entry are the source of maintained profits, then the government is more likely to adopt a watchdog role to protect the public's interest in efficiency and equity. If the large firms are more profitable because they are more efficient, then the need for government policy is less compelling. We present evidence supporting both sides in the chapter and then conclude with an analysis of the federal government's antitrust laws, which are designed to promote competition and limit the exercise of market power.

[1]H. Demsetz, *The Market Concentration Doctrine* (Washington, D.C.: American Enterprise Institute for Public Policy Research, 1973); R. Bork, *The Antitrust Paradox: A Policy at War with Itself* (New York: Basic Books, 1978), 133. R. Schmalensee, "Collusion versus Differential Efficiency: Testing Alternative Hypotheses," *Journal of Industrial Economics* XXXV, No. 4 (June 1987): 420. See, also, W. Baldwin, *Market Power, Competition, and Antitrust Policy* (Homewood, IL: Irwin, 1987), Chapter 13. The Demsetz quote is on pp. 310–311.

The chapter begins with an analysis of barriers to entry as a source of effective market power.

EFFECTIVE MONOPOLY POWER AND BARRIERS TO ENTRY

A **barrier to entry** is anything that impedes or prevents the free flow of resources into an industry to compete away existing economic profits. Barriers to entry (and exit) are a distinguishing feature of all noncompetitive markets. A market is never classified as noncompetitive if resources are free to move in and out of the industry. At the same time, however, the presence of barriers to entry does not guarantee that a market is noncompetitive.

BARRIER TO ENTRY (OR EXIT)
Anything that restricts or prevents the free flow of resources into or out of an industry

The Three Categories of Barriers to Entry

The most important barriers to entry fall into three broad categories: legal barriers, natural barriers, and behavioral barriers. Many of the national oligopolies in the United States are protected by one or more of these barriers.

LEGAL BARRIERS **Legal barriers to entry** are those erected by governments. They are created by exclusive franchises (public utilities, cable television), public ownership (U.S. Postal Service in the United States, nationalized industries in other countries), patents (Polaroid camera), copyrights (books and songs), licenses (electricians, taxicabs, medical doctors, television stations), specific exemptions from the antitrust laws granted by Congress (Major League Baseball), and tariffs or quotas on foreign imports (chemicals, steel). Needless to say, government sanctions can impose a total barrier to entry. As we noted in Chapter 14, virtually all instances of pure monopoly in the United States are the result of legal barriers to entry.

LEGAL BARRIER TO ENTRY
Any government policy, such as an exclusive franchise or a patent, that restricts or prevents the free flow of resources into or out of an industry.

The United States is strongly committed to free enterprise, enough so that the federal, state, and local governments never impose legal barriers to entry for their own sake. They can always point to other motives—tariffs to protect certain jobs, licenses to ensure standards, exclusive franchises to avoid duplication of facilities, antitrust exemptions to preserve quality and competition in baseball, and so on. The fact remains, though, that these legal sanctions are anti-competitive, and the costs of reducing competition must always be weighed against the perceived benefits of the sanctions.

NATURAL BARRIERS **Natural barriers to entry** come in two forms: limited access to a vital factor of production, most often a nonreproducible natural resource, and economies of scale in production. They are natural barriers to entry in that they are inherent features of production or supply.

NATURAL BARRIER TO ENTRY
Features inherent in production or supply, such as economies of scale and limited access to a vital factor of production, that restrict or prevent the free flow of resources into or out of an industry.

NATURAL RESOURCES Industries that rely on nonreproducible natural resources, such as steel (iron ore), aluminum (bauxite), and petroleum (crude oil), often become structured as oligopolies with high barriers to entry. The reason is that large pools of easily accessible reserves of these minerals are available in only a few geographic areas. Also, exploration for new reserves is costly and very risky; explorations often come up empty. The firms that find the most accessible reserves early on often obtain a dominant position in the industry, one that can be difficult for other investors to overcome. The outstanding example in the United States was the aluminum industry. Alcoa owned virtually all known reserves of bauxite prior to World War II and enjoyed a pure monopoly in the production of new aluminum. Its only source of competition was in the secondary market, from small firms that produced aluminum products from scrap aluminum. Only the government was able to bring a semblance of competition to the primary market. The Department of Justice brought an antitrust case against Alcoa in 1945 and won. Alcoa was forced to share its reserves with Reynolds Metals and Kaiser Aluminum and to give each firm a part of its production facilities as well.[2]

ECONOMIES OF SCALE The production of some products exhibits substantial economies of scale such that the minimum efficient scale of operation (MES) can only be achieved by a very large firm. We saw in Chapter 14 that this poses a dilemma for a market economy. On the one hand, each firm must be large relative to the overall market to save on resource costs. Society would not want a large number of small firms, each producing at very high costs. On the other hand, a market with only a few firms is likely to be noncompetitive. In the case of the public utilities, where markets naturally regionalize, the MES encompasses the entire regional market. This is why the public utilities are referred to as natural monopolies.

No natural monopolies exist at the national level. But when the MES is even as high as 3 to 5 percent of total national output, as it appears to be for many products, an industry cannot support the very large number of firms required for monopolistic competition. The individual firms will be very large, and the market may well become an oligopoly, with size itself imposing a substantial barrier to entry.

Beer is an example. The MES of a single brewery is on the order of 45 million gallons a year, a truly enormous brewery costing in excess of $250 million. Only a company intent on competing for a significant position in the national market would even consider building a brewery that large. The MES for automobiles is even larger. A fully integrated, efficient automobile plant produces between 200,000 and 400,000 automobiles a year and costs over $3 billion to build. Clearly, investors thinking of entering either industry are not going to do so casually.

BEHAVIORAL BARRIER TO ENTRY

A strategic decision on the part of a firm that is specifically designed either to deter entry entirely or to accommodate entry by forcing new firms to enter on a smaller scale

BEHAVIORAL BARRIERS TO ENTRY **Behavioral barriers to entry** are various strategies specifically designed to discourage the entry of new firms. The principal strategies that firms are alleged to use are product differentiation, predatory pricing, and investment in excess capacity. We say "alleged" because strategies that are too successful in discouraging entry could lead to antitrust suits for attempting to monopolize a market. The Justice Department has never successfully prosecuted a firm for engaging in a behavioral barrier to entry.

Successful *product differentiation* is inherently a barrier to entry because it allows firms to capture certain customers and shields them somewhat from potential competitors. Product differentiation can be a very effective barrier to

[2]For a discussion of the Alcoa case, see Baldwin, *Market Power*, 347–349.

entry in certain instances. The development of brand loyalties through intense advertising campaigns is an example. Consumer loyalties to Pepsi and Coke make entry into the cola soft drink market very difficult. Another example is the research and development of new product characteristics that consumers will find attractive. Research and development can be viewed as a race among firms for patents. If an existing firm wins the race, the patent can be substantial legal barrier to further entry into the industry. If a new entrant wins, the patent serves as its ticket to enter. It may then also protect the new firm from competition from the firms already in the industry.

Predatory or **limit pricing** is a price-cutting strategy intended to discourage entry. The incumbent (existing) firm lowers its price and willingly accepts a lower level of profits, perhaps even losses, for a short period of time in order to discourage new firms from entering the market. The hope is that potential entrants will be unable or unwilling to compete at that price. Once potential competitors are driven off, the firm then raises its price above the original level and enjoys even larger profits in the long run. Thus, predatory pricing is a strategy of incurring short-run losses in return for long-run gains.

PREDATORY PRICING

A strategy used by an incumbent firm to deter entry in which the firm sets its price so low that a new entrant could not possibly make a profit.

Investment in excess capacity is strategy similar to predatory pricing. The incumbent firm purchases more plant and equipment than it needs. It then threatens to use the excess capacity to flood the market with output should a new firm try to enter the industry.

Predatory pricing and investment in excess capacity sound pretty threatening, but their effectiveness is problematic. We will see below why most economists doubt that either strategy is, or ever has been, an effective barrier to entry. Successful product differentiation is probably the only important behavioral barrier to entry, and then only in a few industries.

Economists are particularly interested in the question of what makes something an effective barrier to entry. Let's begin with a closer look at economies of scale.

Size and the Nature of Capital

Economists are becoming increasingly convinced that size alone is not enough to deter entry or restrict mobility. Never underestimate how large the U.S. economy is or how well developed its capital markets are. The $3 billion needed to build an efficient automobile plant is a lot of money, but consider that a group of investors raised $25 billion to buy out Nabisco in 1988. The finances required to enter at the MES are not likely to be a problem if investors really want to enter an industry.

Another way to put size in perspective is to consider that the MESs for most industries are usually 10 percent or less of total industry output, and often far less. For example, the MES for beer is roughly 10 percent of total industry output; the MES for automobiles is only 3 to 6 percent of total industry output. In other words, if economies of scale were the only barrier to entry most oligopolies would support 10 or more equal-sized firms. An industry with that many firms is likely to be effectively competitive. Indeed, one of the leading puzzles about oligopolies in the United States is why they are often far more concentrated than their production technologies would suggest. Anheuser-Busch and Miller account for over 50 percent of all domestic beer sales, and the Big Three automobile manufacturers account for the large marjority of domestic car sales. Factors in addition to size must be protecting these firms from domestic competitors.

COMMITMENT, SUNK COSTS, AND IRREVERSIBILITY Economists point to the nature of the capital stock as one of the more important factors contributing to entry barriers. Two key concepts in the modern analysis of barriers to entry are *commitment* and *irreversibility*. When investors decide to enter an industry, to what extent are they committed to that move? The answer depends on how long a period of time the short run is for that industry, and the length of the short run depends in turn on the nature of the capital stock. The more specific the capital is to that particular industry, or the more slowly it depreciates in value, or the less developed the secondhand market is for the capital, the longer the short run is. Recall that once an investment is made, the costs associated with the investment are sunk costs. They cannot be recovered for the duration of the short run. So the decision to enter an industry with a long short run is an irreversible decision that commits the investors to that industry for a number of years.

Existing firms have a tremendous first-mover advantage over new entrants in an industry with large sunk costs. For the firm already in, the incumbent, price need only exceed average *variable* cost, the shut-down point, to enable it to continue to produce throughout the duration of the short run. The sunk capital costs are irrelevant. For a new entrant, however, price must exceed average *total* cost including the cost of capital, the break-even point, to justify entering the industry. As a result, an entrant is vulnerable to the pricing policies of the incumbents. The fear is that the incumbents will respond to entry by setting price above average variable cost, but below average cost, so that a new firm cannot make a profit, a fear that could deter entry in the first place.

Both the beer and the automobile industries are good examples of the principle of commitment. Much of the capital that goes into the brewing of beer is so highly specific to brewing that it essentially has no other use. The costs of the brewery are sunk until the brewery fully depreciates. Therefore, the decision to enter the beer industry with a modern $250 million MES brewery commits the investors to the industry for a long period of time. Investors cannot easily back out once they take the plunge. The same is true for automobiles. The capital might not be quite so specific there, but the entry fee is substantially higher, and the short run is still a considerable number of years. In each industry, therefore, size combines with commitment and irreversibility to deter new domestic entrants.

The airline industry provides a nice contrast to the beer and the automobile industries. The size is there, but not the commitment. Jet airliners cost tens of millions of dollars, but most airlines rent their planes, rather than buying them. They are able to take advantage of a well-developed rental market that exists for both new and used planes. As a result, the short run is fairly short for the airlines. They can test a new market and, if it fails, pull out fairly quickly to cut their losses. As a result, barriers to entry are fairly low. This was borne out during the 1980s following the deregulation of the industry in 1978. Prior to deregulation the industry was tightly controlled by the Civil Aeronautics Board (CAB). The CAB dictated the markets the airlines could service, the fares they could charge, entry into the industry, and mergers between airlines. Under CAB regulations, entry was essentially blocked in most markets. Only one trunk carrier, Northeast, was allowed to enter the industry after 1938, and the airlines were granted monopolies on 70 percent of the available city-to-city routes. After deregulation the industry took on the fluid characteristics of an effectively competitive industry. Inefficient airlines failed; price competition developed in many markets; many city-to-city routes became competitive; and a large number of new firms appeared, offering either commuter service or low-fare, no-frills service on short and medium flights between 200 and 1,000 miles.

CONTESTABLE MARKETS The airlines are representative of a market structure known as a **contestable market,** so named by the two economists who first described this type of market, William Baumol of New York University and John Panzar of Bell Laboratories. The principal feature of a contestable market is the absence of any significant barriers to entry. In particular, there are no important sunk costs associated with capital. The short run is extremely short—so short, in fact, that hit-and-run entry becomes a possibility. If investors see that an industry is profitable, they can enter, take a share of the profits, and exit before the existing firms have a chance to react. Under these conditions price is driven to average cost *even if the industry consists of a single firm.* Baumol and Panzar named these markets contestable rather than competitive because the zero-profit result does not depend on having a large number of firms.

CONTESTABLE MARKET

A market structure in which the existing firm or firms have market power and are subject to the possibility of hit-and-run entry by new firms.

Figure 17.1 illustrates the idea of a contestable market. In this example the industry consists of a single firm whose demand and average cost curves are D and AC. Suppose that the firm tries to set its price above average cost in order to earn a profit, say, at P_2. That price is not sustainable if hit-and-run entry is possible. A new entrant with the same costs could enter at any price below P_2 and above P_0—say, P_1—capture the entire market by selling Q_1, earn a profit equal to the area of rectangle P_1abc, and then exit the industry before the incumbent has a chance to react. Knowing that this type of entry is possible, the incumbent has no choice but to price at P_0 and do no better than break even. The break-even price-quantity combination, (P_0, Q_0), is the only sustainable equilibrium for the industry.

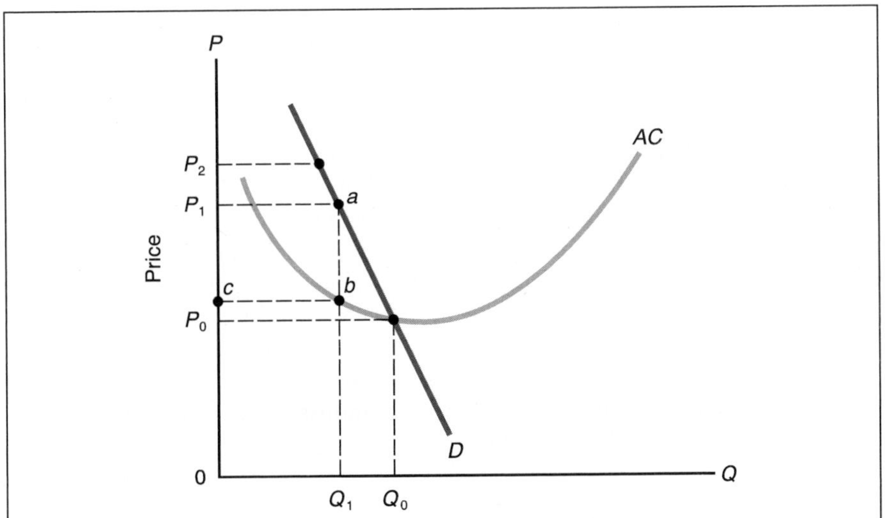

FIGURE 17.1

A Contestable Market

Suppose that a pure monopolist with the demand curve D and average cost curve AC were to set its price at P_2 above average cost in order to make an economic profit. If the market is contestable, a new entrant could enter, capture the entire market by charging a lower price P_1, earn a profit equal to the rectangular area P_1abc, and exit the industry before the monopolist has a chance to respond. The mere threat of such profitable "hit-and-run entry" forces the monopolist to set its price at P_0, at the intersection of D and AC, and do no better than break even.

The model of a contestable market is flawed in certain respects. For one, output reacts more quickly than does price; the incumbent is not able to lower price immediately when the new firm enters, yet the new entrant can produce output immediately. The model also assumes that both entrant and incumbent have the same costs, which might not be true. Nonetheless, the model of contestable markets underscores two important principles. The first is that any industry should tend toward break-even production if resources are free to flow into and out of the industry. Effective monopoly power depends far more on barriers to entry than on the number of firms in the industry. The second principle is that entry does not actually have to occur to drive price to average cost. The mere threat of entry can be enough to prevent any blatant exercise of market power and keep industry profits low.

Size and Imperfect Capital Markets: The Long-Purse Theory

LONG-PURSE THEORY

The theory that, in the absence of perfect capital markets, large firms have an advantage over new entrants in undertaking investment, since they can finance their investment out of past profits retained by the firms, whereas new entrants have to borrow to invest; this advantage acts as a barrier to entry.

Size can be a very effective barrier to entry when combined with highly imperfect capital markets. This combination has been called the **long-purse theory** of a barrier to entry. The theory begins with the fact that most business investment in the United States is financed out of retained earnings rather than new issues of stocks and bonds. This suggests that capital markets might be imperfect, that consumers and financial institutions are somewhat reluctant to lend to firms because they cannot judge how good the firms' investment opportunities really are. If this is true, then large incumbent firms have a decided advantage over new entrants. They can finance new investments out of past profits retained by the firm, whereas new entrants have to borrow to invest. Size matters in this instance because larger firms have higher levels of retained earnings, that is, "longer purses." Therefore, the incumbents get to invest the most, even if they do not have the best investment opportunities.

Miller's rise to the number two position in the beer industry in the 1970s and 1980s, right behind Anheuser-Busch, is supposedly a classic case of the long-purse theory in operation. Miller was stuck in the middle of the pack until the early 1970s. It was not a very profitable company and trailed far behind Anheuser-Busch, the clear industry leader at the time. All that changed when retail giant Philip Morris bought Miller in 1972. Philip Morris decided to push Miller's two newest beers, Lowenbrau and Miller Lite, by undertaking an all-out advertising blitz and investing in new brewing facilities. Advertising expenditures on Miller Lite alone increased 100-fold, from $525,000 in 1973 to $53 million by 1983. The total amount of capital investment in brewing facilities increased from $228 million in 1972 to over $1 billion by 1979. Throughout this period Philip Morris showed no particular concern for earning a return on these expenditures. Its Miller division lost money through 1975 and barely did better than break even until the mid-1980s, a substandard performance compared with other divisions of the corporation. Philip Morris even built one brewery that it never opened. Of course, the strategy eventually paid off in terms of market share, if not profits. The beer industry has never been a profit leader among the nation's oligopolies.[3]

---

[3]The rise of Miller under Philip Morris is discussed in W. Mueller, "Conglomerates: A Nonindustry," in W. Adams (ed.), *The Structure of American Industry*, third edition (New York: Macmillan, 1986), 367–371.

The long-purse theory is potentially very troubling for a market economy. Philip Morris's long purse undoubtedly gave Miller an advantage in chasing Anheuser-Busch that none of the other beer manufacturers had. At the same time, the long-purse theory is unlikely to apply to many industries for two reasons. First, capital markets in the United States, including markets for venture capital, really are well developed. Even though most investment is financed by retained earnings, plenty of outside funding is readily available for potentially profitable investment opportunities. Beer may be an exception in that the industry was never very profitable and therefore was unable to attract funds for expansion. This leads to the second point: Few companies are likely to be as tolerant as Philip Morris was of Miller's subpar return to capital year after year. Perhaps Philip Morris kept going because so much of its investment in brewing facilities turned into a sunk cost. If so, then investments in other industries are unlikely to be so irreversible.

Behavioral Barriers to Entry and Credibility

Four behavioral strategies have received the lion's share of attention in the economics literature on barriers to entry: predatory or limit pricing, investment in excess capacity, creation of brand loyalties through product differentiation and advertising, and races to win patents for new products and production processes. We will use predatory pricing and advertising to develop principles relating to behavioral barriers to entry. Investment in excess capacity is a strategy so similar to predatory pricing that we only need consider one of them. We will discuss patent races in the next section on the relationship between market structure and long-run economic growth because patents and patent races play a central role in that relationship.

PREDATORY PRICING John D. Rockefeller was accused of using predatory pricing in the late 1800s to drive out competitors and establish market dominance for his company, Standard Oil of New Jersey. The accusation against Standard Oil was never proved, but Congress obviously thought that predatory pricing was widespread enough at the turn of the century to represent a serious threat to competition. The Clayton Antitrust Act of 1914 specifically outlaws predatory pricing. The Clayton Act did not define what constitutes a predatory price, however, leaving that up to the courts to determine. In the last 15 years some (but not all) courts have ruled that a price is predatory if it is below a firm's average variable cost. The presumption is that a price set below the shut-down point could have only one purpose, to drive away competitors.

Economists are not convinced that predatory pricing, by itself, can be an important barrier to entry. It lacks *credibility*, the one quality that all strategic behavior must have to be an effective barrier to entry. To see why, consider the following example. Suppose that an industry consists of a single firm earning a monopoly profit. A second firm is thinking about entering the industry. If the second firm does enter, total industry profits will fall as output expands beyond the monopoly output, but assume that each firm will still be able to earn a profit. In order to focus on the pricing strategy, assume also that the second firm has the same cost structure as the monopolist and that there are no important sunk costs associated with investment. Average total cost and average variable cost are virtually identical.

Suppose that the monopolist tries to keep the second firm out by cutting price below average cost and threatening to keep price there if the second firm enters. The second firm will not fall for the threat. The monopolist would be foolish to keep its price low if the second firm enters. Why should the monopolist accept losses when it can raise price along with the new firm and earn a profit? Maintaining a low price after entry is especially foolhardy if the monopolist is the much larger firm because then it has more to lose. Furthermore, even if the monopolist did succeed in driving that firm away, another firm would soon want to enter the industry, since there are no other barriers to entry. The monopolist would have to accept losses forever to maintain its monopoly position. The second firm knows all this, so it calls the monopolist's bluff, enters the industry, and shares the profits.

Predatory pricing can be rescued as a effective barrier to entry by introducing uncertainty. Suppose that the second firm does not know much about the costs or objectives of the monopolist. Under those conditions the second firm might interpret an unexpectedly low price by the monopolist as a signal that the monopolist actually has lower costs or that the monopolist is willing to play "hardball," pricing and competing aggressively in the future. These signals might scare off a new entrant, but, then again, they might not. Pricing strategies suffer a severe handicap as a barrier to entry—they are easily reversible. As a result, they tend to lack the quality of commitment that is so necessary to erecting entry barriers.

The uncertainty version of predatory pricing raises a troubling point: The price set by the monopolist does not necessarily have to be below average variable cost, or any other cost measure, to be predatory. It just has to be "unexpectedly low" in the eyes of potential entrants to scare them off. As a result, the courts have no easy test of whether or not a price is predatory.

BRAND LOYALTIES THROUGH ADVERTISING Businesses try to develop customer loyalties through product differentiation, sales promotions, and advertising. To the extent they succeed, these techniques give firms market power in the form of downward-sloping demand curves. The question remains whether they are also capable of giving firms *effective* market power by erecting barriers to entry. Advertising is particularly intriguing in this regard. Over the past 30 to 40 years in the United States the industries experiencing the biggest increase in four-firm concentration ratios have generally been consumer goods industries with high advertising-to-sales ratios.

Advertising can be either pro-competitive or anti-competitive, depending on the nature of the product, the content of the advertising message, and the medium of the message. The distinction that matters in terms of the nature of the product is whether the product is a search good or an experience good. A *search good* is a product whose qualities are obvious upon inspection. Examples include articles of clothing, prescription drugs, and eyeglasses. We can determine while shopping whether a particular style, material, and weight of shirt or jacket is right for us. Prescription drugs have to have a certain chemical make-up. We judge the style and fit of eyeglasses as we buy them. The key issue with search goods is product selection: What varieties of products are available to consumers, and how do consumers learn about them? An *experience good*, by contrast, is a product whose qualities can be determined only by actually consuming the good. Examples include most foods and drinks and automobiles. Do you like the taste of bran flakes? Of Dr. Pepper? What car gives you all the qualities you seek in an automobile? The only sure way to answer these questions is to buy the products and try them. A key issue with experience goods is the type of information consumers have available to them when they purchase the product.

The advertising message can provide either hard or soft information. *Hard information* describes the qualities of the product, including price, product attributes, and where and when consumers can buy the product. *Soft information* focuses on image rather than content. Soft messages try to convince you that a product is really tasty, or is the product of choice among the "in crowd," or will somehow make you more appealing to members of the opposite sex.

Finally, advertising messages are conveyed through print (signs in storefront windows, circulars, newspapers, and magazines) or the broadcast media, radio and television. Most hard information is conveyed through print and radio. Television is the preferred medium for the soft image messages.

PRO-COMPETITIVE ADVERTISING Advertising that conveys *hard information* about *search goods* is clearly pro-competitive. Such advertising provides consumers with better information about product selection. Better information in turn promotes product quality, reduces the market power to be gained by imagined as opposed to real differences among products, and facilitates entry of new firms by making consumers aware of new products. Hard information about search goods is also cost-efficient because it substitutes for consumers having to bear the cost of searching for products themselves. To give one example, your local drugstore sells brand-name aspirin at prices well above the price of the generic store-brand aspirin. Local newspaper ads that remind people that aspirin is aspirin and make them aware of the generic store brands can only serve to lower the prices and profits of the brand names.

The pro-competitive effects of hard information in search goods advertising are well documented. One widely cited study compared the price of prescription eyeglasses in states that prohibit the advertising of glasses with the price in states that allow optometrists and opticians to advertise their glasses. The study found that the price of prescription glasses was more than twice as high in those states than ban advertising. A similar study of attorneys' fees found that advertising definitely lowers fees and profits for standard services, such as wills and real estate title searches. Hard-information advertising of search goods clearly promotes efficiency and equity in a market economy.[4]

ANTI-COMPETITIVE ADVERTISING The troubling, potentially anti-competitive effects of advertising arise in connection with the *soft advertising* of *experience goods* on network television. Soft advertising of experience goods does not help consumers make more informed choices. Quite the contrary. It is designed to capture customers and increase a firm's market power by creating brand loyalties. Firms know that consumers are reluctant to change brands of experience goods once they find a good that is satisfactory. Changing brands means actually buying a competing product and trying it. Shopping alone is not enough,

[4]L. Benham, "The Effect of Advertising on the Price of Eyeglasses," *Journal of Law and Economics* 15, No. 2 (October 1972): 337–352; J. Schroeter, S. Smith, and S. Cox, "Advertising and Competition in Routine Legal Service Markets: An Empirical Investigation," *Journal of Industrial Economics* XXXVI, No. 1 (September 1987): 49–60. An excellent source on the economics of advertising is W. Comanor and T. Wilson, "Advertising and Competition: A Survey," *Journal of Economic Literature* XVII, No. 2 (June 1979): 453–476.

unlike with search goods. Also, providing hard information in the ads is pointless, since consumers have to experience the products themselves to know whether they like them. So the game is one of trying to capture customers with image-oriented messages that appeal to the emotions rather than the intellect.

Using network television as the medium for these ads introduces another potentially anti-competitive factor, economies of scale. Television advertising is very expensive, but ads that reach millions of consumers are actually cheaper per message received than less expensive ads conveyed through other media. Also, the ability to repeat the same message a number of times throughout a television program appears to enhance the impact of soft, image advertising. These economies of scale in delivering the message mean that size itself matters. The large corporations that can afford to advertise on network television buy more cost-effective advertising, not just more advertising, than do smaller firms.

The combination of brand loyalties and economies of scale in network television advertising certainly has the potential for creating an effective barrier to entry in experience-goods consumer industries. But there are also good reasons for believing that advertising might not be able to prevent entry. New entrants to an oligopoly are likely to be able to afford national television advertising campaigns. If they can, why should the advertising campaigns of the incumbent firms necessarily be more effective than those of the new entrants? Incumbents do have a first-mover advantage, but initial advantages built on emotion and image are shaky at best. Also, much soft advertising of experience goods is self-canceling. Once one firm in an industry engages in an extensive advertising campaign, the other firms are sure to follow for fear of losing their markets. Consumers end up being bombarded by ads from all the firms and may well become immune to their messages. Although many people do develop brand loyalties when buying experience goods, their loyalties may have little to do with any one firm's advertising campaign. A consumer's experience with the product surely counts for something.

These caveats notwithstanding, the fact remains that the corporate giants in the experience-goods consumer industries spend staggering sums on advertising. The advertising budgets of each of the Big Three auto makers exceed $500 million annually. The ready-to-eat cereal manufacturers—Kellogg's, General Foods (Post), General Mills, and Quaker—allocate 10 percent of their sales revenues to advertising. In beer the ratio of advertising to sales revenue is around 4 percent.[5] Although much of these advertising expenditures may be self-canceling, the advertising industry can point to some spectacular successes. Comet cleanser captured one-third of the market shortly after it was introduced. The ads promoting Comet stressed its remarkable innovation: Comet was green, whereas all other cleansers at the time were white. Coca-Cola and Kimberly-Clark achieved the pinnacle of advertising success. Consumers came to use their brand names to identify the product. "I'll have a Coke," and "Please pass me a Kleenex"; not "I'll have a cola drink," and "Please pass me a facial tissue." Such strong brand-name identification is a very difficult obstacle for competitors to overcome. The huge advertising budgets and the isolated successes cannot easily be brushed aside. Advertising undoubtedly is and has

CURRENT ISSUE: Years ago the advertisers promoted color for cleansers. Today we see the reverse in the Pepsi-Coke battle. Pepsi is betting on clear for cola.

[5] K. Elzinga, "The Beer Industry," F. Scherer, "The Breakfast Cereal Industry," and W. Adams and J. Brock, "The Automobile Industry," all in Adams (ed.), *Structure of American Industry*, 218–220; 189; 137, 143–144.

been an important barrier to entry in some of the experience-goods consumer industries.

How Important are Barriers to Entry?

Our discussion of potential barriers to entry has emphasized a common theme throughout: The case supporting each potential barrier is not entirely convincing. One can tell isolated stories of how a particular characteristic or strategy appears to have been effective in deterring entry. But an isolated story does not prove that something is generally effective in deterring entry. In fact, no single characteristic or strategy that we have considered would seem to be an important barrier to entry in and of itself.

At the same time, however, some industries have proved to be very difficult to enter. The various characteristics and strategies can pose insurmountable barriers to entry when present in combination. For instance, a new entrant into the automobile industry must plan on capturing 3 to 6 percent of the market to produce at the MES. The obstacles to achieving entry at this level include large sunk capital costs upon entry, the need to establish a national network of reliable dealers (General Motors has over 10,000 dealerships), and brand loyalties to existing firms nurtured by huge advertising campaigns. These are indeed imposing obstacles. The only successful entrants into the U.S. market in the last 50 years have been large established foreign firms such as Toyota, Honda, and Mercedes-Benz. No entirely new firm has been able to enter the market.

The beer industry has also had no important new entrants on a national scale since World War II and for many of the same reasons as in the automobile industry. The MES is approximately 10 percent of industry output, brewing beer entails very high sunk capital costs, and a national brewer would have to break down existing brand loyalties.

The ready-to-eat cereal market has also been nearly impenetrable. The special wrinkle there is brand proliferation. The existing cereal manufacturers introduced 84 new brands from 1950 to 1983 in an effort to fill every possible niche in the market. As a result, no new entrant could reasonably expect to capture more than 1 percent of the market; yet the MES is roughly 3 to 6 percent of the market. In addition, a new entrant would have difficulty fighting for grocery shelf space. The only successful new entrants since 1940 were a few small firms producing natural granola cereals in the 1970s. Granola turned out to be a profitable niche in the market that the incumbents had overlooked. But most of the new firms quickly departed when the incumbents began producing their own granola cereals.[6]

A fair summary statement about barriers to entry and oligopoly would read much like a summary statement about any aspect of oligopoly. Many large corporations enjoy effective market power primarily because their industries are protected by extremely high barriers to entry. But determining what, if anything, is creating barriers to entry in a particular industry requires a case study of that industry. The usual candidates—size, sunk costs, and various kinds of strategic decisions, including price, investment, product differentia-

[6]Ibid.

tion, and advertising—may combine to form highly effective barriers in one market setting and be completely ineffective in another market setting.

LONG-RUN ECONOMIC GROWTH AND MONOPOLY POWER

In his great treatise on economic systems, *Capitalism, Socialism, and Democracy*, published in 1942, Harvard economist Joseph Schumpeter startled the economics profession by offering a vigorous defense of the large corporation and effective monopoly power. His defense consisted of three parts.

DYNAMIC EFFICIENCY
The reduction in firms' costs of production over time due to technical change and increased productivity.

INNOVATION
The process of recognizing the practical uses of an invention and understanding the steps required to make it commercially viable.

DIFFUSION
The final post-research stage of the process of invention and innovation in which firms are actually using a new production technology or producing and selling a new product.

First, Schumpeter argued that the **dynamic efficiency** of an economy, its record of technical change and long-run economic growth, is far more important than are the static, one-point-in-time efficiencies of having prices equal marginal costs (allocational efficiency) and least-cost production (production efficiency). Dynamic efficiency evolves from the three-step process of invention, innovation, and diffusion. *Invention* in an economic context is the discovery of a new production technology or a new product or material input. Innovation and diffusion are the stages that bring an invention into the economic sphere of activity. **Innovation** refers to the process of recognizing the practical uses of an invention and understanding the steps required to make it commercially viable. *Innovators* are the business entrepreneurs who see how to put a new cost-reducing production technology into place or how to produce and market a new product, including any changes in the organization of the business that might be required. **Diffusion** refers to the final post-research stage in which firms are actually using a new production technology or producing and selling a new product. Diffusion brings the fruits of inventions to consumers in the form of lower prices or new products. Schumpeter was not arguing that static allocational efficiency and production efficiency are unimportant, only that society should be willing to sacrifice some static efficiency if doing so promotes dynamic efficiency.

This led directly to the second part of Schumpeter's defense, that there is indeed a trade-off between static and dynamic efficiency. Schumpeter believed that invention and innovation flourish best in a market environment characterized by large firms and monopoly profits for two reasons. First, inventions and innovations are more likely to occur if firms commit resources to the research and commercial development of new ideas. Unfortunately, investment in research and development (R&D) is highly risky. Much time, money, and effort are devoted to ideas that never pan out commercially. Also, firms engage in R&D races with one another to patent new, commercially viable production technologies and products. The first-place finishers in these patent races may win big; the others often come up empty. Schumpeter thought that only large corporations with effective monopoly power would be willing to bear these risks of investing in R&D. Second, invention and innovation are both little more than ideas that anyone can easily steal. To avoid profiting from others' ideas, governments issue patents to inventors and innovators that grant them a monopoly in the commercial use of their ideas. The U.S. patent laws offer monopoly protection for a period of 17 years. Governments would rather not erect legal barriers to entry through patents that give someone the right to earn monopoly profits, but no one would have any incentive to engage in inventive and innovative activity without monopoly protection for some length of time.

Private citizens cannot protect themselves from others who would steal their ideas.

The third part of Schumpeter's defense of big business is that society need not be overly concerned about the monopoly power necessary to support invention and innovation, particularly monopoly power gained after the fact. The reason is that the process of invention, innovation, and diffusion is not a marginal process. Schumpeter characterized it as a process of **creative destruction** that causes drastic changes in the economic environment, simultaneously destroying markets and bankrupting some firms while creating new markets and profitable opportunities for other firms. He believed that any monopoly position is likely to be fairly short-lived in such an environment. A firm that enjoyed monopoly profits as the result of some innovation would soon be undone by other innovations at other firms.

CREATIVE DESTRUCTION
The process by which invention, innovation, and diffusion cause drastic changes in the economic environment, simultaneously destroying markets and bankrupting some firms while creating new markets and profitable opportunities for other firms.

The computer industry during the past 30 years is a good example of what Schumpeter had in mind. IBM came up with the best inventions and innovations early on and established a dominant position in nearly every segment of the computer market by the early 1960s. But the technological environment in computers was so fertile that IBM could not hold its position. Subsequent inventions and innovations by other firms chipped away at IBM for the next 20 years. By the early 1980s most of the computer market was effectively competitive, and IBM is now a troubled corporation.

Schumpeter believed that the process of creative destruction through invention and innovation was the driving force behind the evolution and growth of capitalist economies. The process was to be encouraged, not discouraged, even if it required some market power and monopoly profits to keep it going.

Evaluating the Schumpeter Hypothesis

Schumpeter's thesis about the nature of creative destruction under capitalism and its relationship to monopoly power is a landmark in economic analysis. Only one part of his analysis—the idea that inventions and innovations are more likely to occur in large firms with a high degree of market power—has clearly failed either theoretically or empirically to stand up over time. Let's turn first to the theory of innovative activity. (Schumpeter was primarily concerned with innovation, so we will lump invention and innovation together for the remainder of the section.)

THE INCENTIVE TO INNOVATE Economists now realize that size is not critical to the process of innovation. Large and small investors alike are willing to take risks, and venture capital markets provide ample funding for innovative activity. The real issue is a matter of incentives, whether large or small firms have a greater incentive to try to innovate. The issue cannot be settled on theoretical grounds. To see why, think of the simplest market environment consisting of a monopolist earning a monopoly profit and a small potential entrant.

The potential entrant clearly has some incentive to be the first to patent an innovation. A patent on a new cost-reducing production technology or a new product can serve as its entry ticket into a profitable industry. If the innovation is really drastic, the entrant could conceivably drive the existing firm from the market and establish itself as a new monopolist. The monopolist also has a strong incentive to be the first to patent an innovation in order to protect its market. It is not clear which firm has the stronger incentive to innovate.

WHICH FIRMS INNOVATE? Recent empirical studies of patented innovations have been unable to establish any clear relationship between firm size and innovation. Schumpeter was right in arguing that risky R&D activity would be dominated by large firms. In 1981 in the United States 141 large firms, each with more than 25,000 employees, accounted for 76 percent of all private R&D activity. But he was wrong in assuming that the R&D divisions of large established corporations are the natural breeding grounds for innovative activity.

A research team recently completed a massive study of innovative activity in England, covering 4,378 innovations from 1945 to 1983. The three principal conclusions of the study are roughly consistent with what most research on patented innovations tends to find in both Europe and the United States:[7]

1. The number of innovations per employee is highest in small firms with less than 1,000 employees and in very large firms with more than 10,000 employees. The small firms more than hold their own in generating innovations. They accounted for only 3 to 4 percent of total R&D expenditures during the period covered by the study; yet they produced roughly 35 percent of the total innovations.
2. The small firms are best at generating cost-reducing process innovations, whereas the large firms are best at generating new product innovations. The process innovations of the small firms most often take the form of new, highly specialized inputs that they sell to larger firms. The large innovators are most often multiproduct, multinational companies that use new product innovations to help them diversify into related product markets.
3. Innovation occurs primarily in the manufacturing sector, not the service sector, of the economy. Ninety percent of the innovations were commercialized by firms whose principal activity is manufacturing.

Overall, the study supports the current conventional wisdom among economists on the relationship between size and innovative activity. It is that some degree of industry concentration is necessary to support innovative activity, but the necessary degree of concentration is not so large in most industries as to prevent the industry from being effectively competitive. Schumpeter overstated the connection between market power and innovation.

DYNAMIC VERSUS STATIC EFFICIENCY The other parts of Schumpeter's thesis have stood the test of time, by and large. In particular, most economists today would agree that dynamic efficiency is more important than is static efficiency and that preserving incentives for innovation requires some form of monopoly protection after the fact.

This text has already made the case for the relative importance of dynamic efficiency. In Chapter 3 we noted that long-run economic growth made possible by continued increases in factor productivity is one of the primary deter-

---

[7]K. Pavitt, M. Robson, and J. Townsend, "The Size Distribution of Innovating Firms in the UK: 1945–1983," *Journal of Industrial Economics* XXXV, No. 3 (March 1987): 297–316. For an excellent discussion of Schumpeter's views, and research and development generally, see Baldwin, *Market Power*, Chapter 12, 266–302.

minants of a nation's economic well-being. Whether productivity grows at the rate of 3 percent per year or 1 percent per year, or not at all, makes a tremendous difference to the nation's standard of living over time. Small differences in the rate of growth will eventually dwarf any conceivable static allocational and production efficiency losses associated with prices that exceed marginal costs, or wasteful rent seeking, or production that occurs at other than the minimum efficient scale of operation.

THE PATENT DILEMMA The notion that innovations require monopoly patent protection in order to avoid free-riding is also uncontroversial. Schumpeter saw that the process of invention, innovation, and diffusion poses a true dilemma for society. On the one hand, patents preserve the incentive to invent and innovate. One can argue whether patent protection ought to extend for 17 years as it does in the United States, but establishing legal barriers to entry that offer some degree of effective monopoly power is absolutely essential. On the other hand, the monopoly power that patents create partially undermines the diffusion of innovations to society. We have seen that monopolists set higher prices and produce less output than do competitive firms, thereby reducing the net value available from producing and consuming goods and services. Patent protection has the same effects. It allows the innovator (inventor) to capture some of the potential gains to consumers as higher profits and reduces the overall net value of the innovation to society as a whole.

The patent dilemma is a true dilemma; there is no escaping it. The interesting question is how much monopoly power patents actually create. Fortunately, the answer appears to be not very much in most industries. Many patents can be imitated within the guidelines of the patent laws. For instance, IBM personal computer clones appear within months after IBM patents and markets a new personal computer. The longstanding protection that Polaroid enjoyed for its instant camera is the decided exception, not the rule. Also, patents are unlikely to create long-lasting monopoly power in fertile technological environments where innovations are continually forthcoming. This was precisely Schumpeter's third point in his defense of monopoly power. Patents may protect firms better in stagnant technological environments, but the issue is less pressing in stagnant environments. Also, stagnant industries tend to be protected by other kinds of barriers to entry, as we saw above in the case of the automobile industry.

CURRENT ISSUE: On Bill Gates again—Microsoft products are so good that Gates has amassed a fortune despite widespread cheating by his own customers. Word, Excel, and other Microsoft programs are protected by the patent and copyright laws, but people often let friends copy their programs anyway in violation of the laws. The copyright protection of computer software is almost impossible to enforce.

THE LIMITS OF MARKET POWER

Our discussion in Chapters 16 and 17 has focused so far on the attributes of oligopoly that are similar to the attributes of pure monopoly, particularly prices set above marginal costs and barriers to entry that create effective monopoly power. Oligopoly is certainly closer to pure monopoly than it is to perfect competition, but competition is by no means absent in oligopoly. Even the largest corporations are subject to the competitive pressures of the marketplace. The giant corporations face vigorous competition from firms within their own industry and, to a lesser extent, from firms in related industries. Moreover, the competition stretches across national borders. Foreign firms now have a substantial share of the U.S. market in a number of industries.

Rivalry Among the Few

We have seen that the competition among large firms within an industry is quite different from the competition among perfectly competitive firms. Perfectly competitive firms compete only by means of price. The large corporations shy away from price competition in favor of product differentiation, advertising, patent races, and various other forms of nonprice competition. Economists call the competition within an oligopoly **rivalry** among the few to distinguish it from the price competition that occurs in highly competitive markets. Call it what you will, large firms often compete intensely for market share, profits, and entry into markets. In most industries their rivalry serves to discipline managers to produce more efficiently and to limit firms' market power.

RIVALRY
The name commonly used to describe nonprice competition among oligopolistic firms.

The market often severely penalizes even the largest corporations when their managers make poor business decisions. Whenever it does, the disciplining function of rivalry is painfully evident. Every decade since World War II has witnessed its share of corporate giants in trouble. In the 1950s and early 1960s the major U.S. steel manufacturers lagged well behind foreign manufacturers in adopting a new and cheaper technology for converting iron ore to steel. That mistake opened the U.S. market to foreign firms, and they were quick to take advantage. By 1970 the foreign firms had captured over one-sixth of the U.S. market, and the U.S. manufacturers were never able to recover their former dominance. The share of imports in the U.S. market continued to rise steadily throughout the 1970s and 1980s, reaching 23 percent by 1986.[8]

In the early 1960s Lockheed made some unfortunate design and engine decisions that pushed it to the brink of bankruptcy. The Defense Department decided it could not afford to lose one of its primary suppliers of aircraft, so the federal government loaned Lockheed $200 million to ensure its survival. The loans represented the first federal bailout of a major U.S. corporation.

Chrysler Corporation was the most famous troubled giant of the 1970s. Chrysler was too slow to change over to smaller cars following the oil price increases in 1973–74. The federal government decided to step in once again, with a $1 billion bailout this time, because it did not want 120,000 auto workers to lose their jobs.

The 1980s was a decade of turmoil in the airline industry. A number of the major airlines had great difficulty adjusting to a competitive environment following deregulation of the industry in 1978. Braniff filed for bankruptcy in 1982 and returned to operation only after a complete reorganization. Eastern performed poorly throughout the decade and ultimately failed.

CURRENT ISSUE: Auto giant General Motors is also a troubled firm. Its share of the U.S. market has declined steadily from 50 percent in the late 1970s to just over 30 percent today, and it remains saddled with inefficient factories and a bloated staff of salaried employees. Industry experts estimated that, in 1992, its average production costs per car were nearly $800 more than those of Chrysler or Ford. (*The Economist*, October 24, 1992, p. 83.)

In the 1990s some of the biggest names in the computer industry have run into deep trouble. The companies on the East Coast, such as Digital and Wang, failed to see the popularity of the personal computer and lost out to their West Coast competitors. Kenneth Olsen, Digital Equipment Corporation's founding father, was pushed aside, and Digital laid off tens of thousands of workers. Wang Corporation stopped producing computer hardware altogether.

Business failures are usually fairly quiet events, not nearly so dramatic as some of the preceding examples. Large corporations typically do not completely fail in the sense that the company literally closes its doors and goes out

[8]See W. Adams and H. Mueller, "The Steel Industry," in Adams (ed.), *Structure of American Industry*, 74–125.

of business. Instead, a healthy company buys out a failing company at bargain basement prices and reorganizes the business. Or a troubled multiproduct company sells off its unprofitable lines of business and continues operation with its remaining products lines. Nonetheless, oligopolies are definitely not immune to failure.

Foreign Competition

Increasing competition from foreign producers has been one of the leading economic stories of the past 25 years. All of us are aware of the foreign invasion in electronics and automobiles, but it has been much broader than that. We presented data in Chapter 14 from a study by William Shepherd, indicating that 76.7 percent of U.S. industries were effectively competitive in 1980. This percentage was up dramatically from 1958, when Shepherd estimated that only 56.4 percent of U.S. industries were effectively competitive. Shepherd believes that competition from imports was the dominant reason for increased competitiveness in 13 U.S. industries, and he attributes one-sixth of the increase in competitiveness overall to competition from foreign producers.[9]

Competition from Related Industries

Competition from related industries is more like standard price competition. Customers always pay close attention to price when products are fairly close substitutes. They care much less about the size of the firm selling the product.

Competition from substitute products is not as important a factor as rivalry within an industry is for most of the giant corporations. It can be very important, though, in isolated cases. Think of containers for drinks, which are made of glass, plastic, cardboard, aluminum, steel, and other metals. When the bottlers of soft drinks and beer switched their bottles from glass to plastic, and their cans from steel to aluminum, the switch obviously had a substantial impact on both the favored and the displaced industries. Middle-aged men remember a rite of passage during their teen-age years: finally becoming strong enough to grab a soft-drink can with both hands and crush it with their thumbs. Only the strongest teen-agers could crush the cans one-handed. The switch from steel to aluminum cans not only added to the woes of the sagging U.S. steel industry. It also removed forever that rite of passage from the American scene. Now any eight-year-old can crush a soft-drink can.

All there factors limit the market power of the large corporations more than one might think. In Chapter 16 we referred to a recent study of 312 U.S. manufacturing industries representing approximately 70 percent of all U.S. manufacturing industries. The study computed the difference between price and average operating expenses (roughly, average variable cost) within each industry from 1958 to 1981. The study found that price exceeded average operating expenses by a greater percentage in the highly concentrated oligopolies than in the unconcentrated, effectively competitive industries, as one would expect. The differences were not very large, however. Over the 24-year

[9]W. Shepherd, "Causes of Increased Competition in the U.S. Economy," *Review of Economics and Statistics* 64, No. 4 (November, 1982): 613–626.

period, prices were 24 percent above average operating expenses for all the unconcentrated industries in the sample and just 29 percent above average operating expenses for a selected group of 57 highly concentrated producer goods industries. Moreover, the price-expense differences between the highly concentrated group and the unconcentrated industries declined throughout the sample period. These findings are consistent with other recent studies of industry profitability in manufacturing, which show that the highly concentrated industries are only slightly more profitable than are the unconcentrated industries. Firms in the highly concentrated oligopolies do not appear to have *substantially* more effective market power than do firms in less concentrated market structures.[10]

HISTORICAL NOTE: The mighty do fall from their perches. Each year *Fortune* magazine lists the 500 largest corporations in the United States, the "Fortune 500" companies. Only three corporations that were among *Fortune's* top twenty in 1970 remain in the top twenty today.

In conclusion, life under oligopoly is hardly a quiet life. The managers of large corporations have to work hard to maintain the health of their corporations, and sometimes they fail. Contrary to what some would have us believe, buying stock in a giant "blue-chip" company is no guarantee of a nice, steady return to our savings.

EVALUATION OF OLIGOPOLY

Our analysis in Chapters 16 and 17 has indicated that the oligopolies generally fail to achieve the social goals of allocational efficiency and equity. Large corporations may be a net benefit to society, but, if so, the case for them rests on superior technical efficiency.

Allocational Inefficiency

The large corporations have a considerable amount of market power and are able to maintain their prices well above marginal costs. Society does not receive the maximum possible net value from producing and consuming goods and services when the market is structured as an oligopoly.

Inequities

Many highly concentrated industries in the United States are protected by substantial barriers to entry. Barriers to entry inherently violate equality of opportunity as new investors are prevented from entering these industries or can enter only on a relatively small scale. As such, barriers to entry create the *potential* for effective market power by preventing new firms from competing away industry profits. The firms then find a way to *realize* the potential for earning excessive monopoly profits by finding ways of softening competition among themselves. The analysis in Chapters 15 through 17 identified the two main avenues of escape:

1. differentiating their products (for example, the supermarkets in Chapter 15, the advertising and patent races in Chapter 17) and

[10] I. Domowitz, R. Hubbard, and B. Petersen, "Oligopoly Supergames: Some Empirical Evidence on Prices and Margins," *Journal of Industrial Economics* XXXV, No. 4 (June 1987): 377–398.

2. engaging in some form of tacit collusion to maintain price above average cost (for example, trigger strategies or mark-up pricing rules of thumb in Chapter 16).

Monopoly profits also violate the end-results principle of horizontal equity because investors' dollars are not treated equally.

There is some good news, however. The U.S. economy is more competitive today than it was 30 years ago. Many industries have moved from being highly concentrated oligopolies to being effectively competitive industries. Those that have remained highly concentrated have lost some of their market power. Finally, the margins between prices and costs in the highly concentrated industries are moving closer to the price-cost margins in effectively competitive industries.

Technical (Production) Efficiency

The evaluation of oligopoly in terms of technical efficiency is a mixed bag, but it probably tends to favor the large corporations overall. The issue of technical efficiency has both static elements (performance at one point in time) and dynamic elements (performance over time).

The key static efficiency issue concerns economies of scale. Very large corporations are necessary in the production of some products in order to take advantage of economies of scale. Having highly competitive markets with large numbers of small firms would waste scarce resources in the minimum efficient scale of operation (MES) can be achieved only by a very large firm. A market economy cannot, and should not, avoid having some markets structured as oligopolies. Whether the oligopolies have exploited economies of scale as effectively as possible remains an open question, however.

The University of Chicago's Sam Pelzman argues that the large corporations are generally a good deal for consumers. He concedes that their prices are much higher than their marginal costs. Yet he believes the large firms are so much more efficient because of economies of scale, that their prices are still well below what they would be if the large firms were broken up into smaller firms.[11] Countering his position somewhat is the fact that most U.S. oligopolies are much more highly concentrated than could possibly be justified by economies of scale. The MES for nearly all products is under 10 percent, whereas the market shares of the leading firms in many industries are much higher than that. A firm that is too large may experience serious diseconomies of scale and therefore have much higher average costs than necessary. The issue remains controversial.

The dynamic efficiency issue concerns the relationship between firm size and innovation. Once again the evidence is mixed. Some degree of market power is probably necessary to provide funds for research and development. Also, innovators (and inventors) must receive some monopoly protection for their ideas in order to maintain incentives to innovate (invent). But market structures do not have to become highly concentrated to support innovative activity. Small firms in both effectively competitive and oligopolistic markets

[11] S. Peltzman, "The Gains and Losses from Industrial Concentration," *Journal of Law and Economics* 20, No. 2 (October 1977): 229–263.

account for a disproportionate share of patented innovations, especially cost-reducing process innovations. The large firms are somewhat better at product innovation.

In conclusion, oligopoly ends up looking much more like pure monopoly than like perfect competition. The large corporations have effective monopoly power, on average. We have seen, however, that an evaluation of oligopoly must always include the following disclaimer: Market outcomes may differ substantially from industry to industry. Each industry must ultimately be judged on a case-by-case basis.

The following Concept Summary table summarizes our evaluation of oligopoly.

CONCEPT SUMMARY

EVALUATION OF OLIGOPOLY

OBJECTIVES	MARKET TEST	ACHIEVED? MARKET OUTCOME
EFFICIENCY		
Allocational efficiency	$P = MC$	No Prices of large firms above MC, on average; tacit collusion to support prices, compete by nonprice means
Production (technical) efficiency	Production at MES or minimum AC_{lr}	Generally no Largest firms are often much larger than required for MES
		Caveat: dynamic efficiency Profits of large firms support R&D, promote invention and innovation, make economy more productive (but evidence suggests large firms are better at new product development than cost-reducing innovation)
EQUITY		
Equality of opportunity	Absence of barriers to entry, exit; equal access to all market information	Generally no Large firms are often protected by substantial barriers to entry; tacit collusion may impede spread of information
Horizontal equity	$P = AC_{lr}$; zero maintained economic profit	Generally no Large firms more profitable, on average; have effective market power
		Caveat: the largest firms may face stiff competition and lose much of their effective market power
Overall: mixed; some advantages, disadvantages		

THE FEDERAL GOVERNMENT'S RESPONSE TO OLIGOPOLY: ANTITRUST LEGISLATION

The business climate around the end of the nineteenth century was marked by a wave of mergers between companies that created a number of giant corporations with dominant market positions. The mergers during those years gave birth to such well-known U.S. companies as Standard Oil, U.S. Steel, American Tobacco, International Harvester, Du Pont, U.S. Rubber, General Motors, and IBM. The newly merged companies were referred to as trusts at the time. The public grew increasingly fearful of the trusts, and the federal government responded with a two-pronged approach to control their exercise of market power, industry regulation and antitrust legislation. Both policies date from the late 1800s.

Federal regulation of oligopoly began in 1887 with the regulation of the nation's railroads under the auspices of the Interstate Commerce Commission. Regulation subsequently spread to the other transportation industries (water, air, and trucking) and to a number of other industries as well, most notably communications (telephone, radio, and television) and the financial sector (banking and securities and commodities brokers). The industries targeted for regulation were those for which some degree of monopoly power was unavoidable because of high costs of entry and for which unregulated competition would produce wasteful duplication of facilities.

Washington soured on the regulation of oligopolies in the mid-1970s. By 1980 Congress had passed legislation deregulating the transportation industries and most of the financial sector. Only a few industries remain under close regulation today. For that reason our discussion of government policy is limited to the antitrust statutes. Suffice it to say that economists generally applaud the move toward deregulation of oligopoly. The regulatory commissions had appeared to place the interests of the industry above the public's interest in efficiency and equity.

Congress passed three landmark pieces of antitrust legislation to curb the market power of the new trusts. The first was the Sherman Antitrust Act of 1890, followed in 1914 by the Clayton Antitrust Act and the Federal Trade Commission Act. These three acts have remained the pillars of the federal government's antitrust policy to this day. In the words of Judge Bork, all antitrust legislation since 1914 has merely been an elaboration.[12]

The Three Principal Antitrust Statutes

THE SHERMAN ANTITRUST ACT OF 1890 The Sherman Antitrust Act contains three sections that have important economic impacts, Sections 1, 2, and 7.

Section 1 outlaws every contract, combination, or conspiracy in restraint of interstate trade or commerce. Restraints of trade include the price-fixing and market-sharing agreements typically associated with cartels. The courts quickly ruled that colluding to restrain trade or commerce is illegal per se, without regard to intent or consequences.

[12]Bork, *Antitrust Paradox*, 47.

Section 2 forbids anyone from monopolizing, or attempting to monopolize, interstate trade or commerce. The courts have usually (although not always) subjected the Section 2 stricture against monopolizing to the *rule of reason*, meaning that the government must prove an intent to monopolize. Simply having monopoly or market power is not illegal.

Section 7 allows individuals or firms that suffer financial injury resulting from violations of Sections 1 and 2 to sue for triple damages.

Enforcement of the Sherman Act is the responsibility of the Antitrust Division of the U.S. Department of Justice. Violations of Sections 1 and 2 are criminal offenses subject to fines and/or imprisonment.

THE CLAYTON ANTITRUST ACT OF 1914 Congress passed the Clayton Antitrust Act to remedy a serious defect of the Sherman Act. Section 2 of the Sherman Act came to be viewed as flawed because it attacked only existing monopoly power. Its entire thrust was remedial and trust-busting. The Clayton Act was designed to be preventive, to nip monopoly in the bud. It outlawed certain types of conduct that are likely to lessen competition and lead to a monopoly position. Sections 2, 3, and 7 contain the key provisions from an economic perspective.

Section 2 outlaws price discrimination if the effect is to substantially lessen competition or create a monopoly in any line of commerce. Although Section 2 applies to all forms of price discrimination, it has been used primarily to prevent predatory pricing.

Section 3 outlaws tying or exclusive dealing contracts between manufacturers and retailers in which the retailer cannot sell products supplied by any of the manufacturer's competitors. As in Section 2, such contracts are illegal only if they substantially lessen competition or create a monopoly in any line of commerce.

Section 7 prevents one company from buying the stock of another company if the effect is to lessen competition between the two companies. Section 7 also forbids the merger of two or more companies to form a holding company if it lessens competition among the companies. The Cellar-Kefauver Act of 1950 amended Section 7 to turn it into a full-fledged anti-merger law. It prevents one company from acquiring the assets of another company, not just its shares of stock, and extends the lessening-of-competition test beyond the immediate companies to a lessening of competition in any line of commerce anywhere within the country.

HORIZONTAL MERGER

A merger between firms selling the same product.

VERTICAL MERGER

A merger between firms that operate in different stages in the production and marketing of a single product.

CONGLOMERATE MERGER

A merger between firms operating in different product markets.

The government has used Section 7 to block both horizontal and vertical mergers between firms. A **horizontal merger** is a merger between two or more firms selling the same product, for example, the 1986 merger of Chrysler and American Motors. A **vertical merger** is a merger between two or more firms in different stages in the production and marketing of a single product. The large oil corporations are examples of vertically integrated firms formed by merging all stages of the process of bringing oil products to the market—from drilling, to refining, to shipping oil and natural gas to retail markets, to franchising retail outlets for heating oil and gasoline.

The government has never succeeded in blocking conglomerate mergers under Section 7, however. **Conglomerate mergers** are mergers between firms operating in different product markets. ITT is the prime example of a corporate giant formed through conglomerate mergers. It sells in hundreds of different product markets. The courts have never found that a conglomerate merger would substantially lessen competition in any one product market.

The penalties for violating Sections 2, 3, and 7 of the Clayton Act are civil rather than criminal. Offenders must simply cease any violations or otherwise correct them. They do not face fines and imprisonment. However, Section 4 of the Clayton Act extends the right to sue for triple damages to violations of any of the antitrust laws.

The Clayton Act represents a completely different approach to the control of market power than does the Sherman Act. In addition to being preventive rather than remedial, it shifts the focus of attention from the intent of market behavior to the effects of market behavior—namely, the extent to which market behavior actually lessens competition. The Clayton Act is also prospective in the sense that the test of lessening competition applies to the future, not to the present.

THE FEDERAL TRADE COMMISSION ACT OF 1914 The Federal Trade Commission Act strengthened the government's antitrust posture in two ways. First, it created an independent commission, the Federal Trade Commission (FTC), and gave it authority to enforce the substantive provisions of both the Federal Trade Commission Act and the Clayton Act (but not the Sherman Act). The FTC can investigate alleged violations of either act and issue cease and desist orders. Its decisions are binding, subject only to appeal in the courts. Second, Section 5 of the act outlaws certain unfair methods of competition, such as bribery, false disparagement of a competitor's product, and industrial espionage. The Wheeler-Lea Act of 1938 amended Section 5 to prohibit unfair or deceptive practices in commerce. The 1938 amendments have been used to prosecute instances of deceptive and misleading advertising.

The Goals of Antitrust Legislation

Economists naturally think of antitrust legislation as an instrument for promoting efficiency and equity. The legislation should help ensure that the giant corporations set their prices close to marginal costs (allocational efficiency), that they are innovative and produce near their MES (technical efficiency, both dynamic and static), and that they do not enjoy very much effective monopoly power (equity). In short, economists would define the ultimate goals of antitrust legislation in terms of market outcomes, how businesses actually perform.

Congress never spelled out exactly what its antitrust legislation was supposed to achieve, but it clearly never intended to hold firms directly accountable for their performance. The antitrust laws are defined in terms of market structure and business conduct, not business performance. The underlying philosophy behind the legislation appears to be more process-oriented than results-oriented. The central idea is to preserve and promote competition, with the implicit understanding that a more competitive economy is inherently more efficient and more equitable. The legislation implies that the principal enemies of competition are concentration (Sherman, Section 2; Clayton, Section 7), collusion (Sherman, Section 1), predatory pricing (Clayton, Section 2), exclusionary behavior (Clayton, Section 3), and deceptive practices and other unfair methods of competition (FTC Act, Section 5).

Congress may have little choice but to pursue efficiency and equity indirectly through structure and conduct provisions. Performance criteria are very difficult to interpret and enforce. For instance, suppose that the antitrust laws specified that prices had to equal marginal costs. Marginal cost happens to be very difficult to measure because it is an other things equal concept. Marginal cost defines how total cost changes as output changes, holding constant all other variables that can cause total cost to change, such as factor prices or production technology. Measuring the other things equal effect of output on cost requires sophisticated statistical techniques that are still as much art as science in their application. Suppose that the government and a firm it is prosecuting both hire expert economists to undertake a statistical analysis of a firm's marginal cost. The two experts could easily come up with very different values for the firm's marginal cost. If they did, a court of law would be hard pressed to determine which value, if either, accurately measures the firm's true marginal cost.

Going after profits through antitrust legislation in the name of promoting equity is also problematic. A firm could have excessive profits because (1) the demand for its product suddenly increased, (2) it developed a successful new product or a much cheaper production technology, (3) it undertook a highly risky investment that happened to pay off, or (4) it has effective market power because of high barriers to entry and is able to maintain price well above average costs. Only the fourth reason for high profits is a matter of concern. The first three events would generate temporary profits for a firm even if it were perfectly competitive. The government would certainly not want to prevent firms from earning profits in these instances. Quite the contrary. We have seen that profits are absolutely essential to the effective operation of a market economy. Profits are the signals, and the rewards, that encourage innovation and risk-taking and that guide firms to produce the products that consumers want to buy at the lowest possible cost. Profits gained by exercising market power serve none of these purposes, but a court of law may well have trouble distinguishing ill-gotten monopoly profits from the other three sources of profits. Governments in a capitalistic society cannot afford to be overly aggressive in denying firms opportunities to earn profits.

Standards of conduct are also difficult to interpret and enforce. The Clayton Act requires the FTC or the courts to determine whether certain types of behavior would lessen competition in the future. This is not an easy task by any means. But developing reasonable guidelines for judging the competitiveness of a market is not nearly so difficult as estimating a firm's marginal cost or determining the source of a firm's profits.

Recent Trends in Antitrust Enforcement

Prosecution under the antitrust laws has undergone a complete turnaround in the past 40 years. The 1950s and 1960s were marked by vigorous prosecution of the antitrust laws. The government attempted to block both horizontal and vertical mergers, even if they involved fairly small firms, and it challenged most vertical arrangements between firms. Price cuts by large firms were often interpreted as instances of predatory pricing and therefore were challenged. Then in the early 1970s the government suddenly decided to back way off from its watchdog stance on big business. For example, during the period from

1960 to 1964 the FTC brought 530 price discrimination (that is, predatory pricing) cases against businesses under Section 2 of the Clayton Act. By the early 1970s the number of such cases had dropped to around 10 per year. In 1969 the government charged IBM with attempting to monopolize the computer industry in violation of Section 2 of the Sherman Act. That was the last monopoly case involving horizontal structure brought by the government. The new attitude favoring deregulation went hand in hand with the relaxed stance toward antitrust prosecution.

The new direction in antitrust policy was set firmly in place under the Reagan administration. FTC activity against predatory pricing under Section 2 of the Clayton Act ceased entirely in 1982. In that same year the government dropped its suit against IBM and settled a vertical integration suit against AT&T by consent decree, under which no verdict was rendered. The government subsequently dropped suits involving a vertical merger within the petroleum industry and a new concept of shared monopoly allegedly used by the cereal manufacturers. Most antitrust cases today are private triple-damage suits brought by one firm against another.

The Merger Guidelines

In addition to dropping a number of major cases, the Justice Department established new guidelines for prosecuting mergers (1982, modified in 1984) and vertical restraints, such as tying and exclusive dealer arrangements (1985). The Justice Department still follows the Reagan guidelines.

The vertical restraint guidelines are extremely permissive. The Justice Department has admitted that virtually all nonprice vertical restraints would be allowed under its guidelines. The merger guidelines are a bit tougher, although they still reflect a fairly relaxed attitude toward antitrust prosecution.

The principal test in deciding whether to allow a merger under the 1984 guidelines is the degree of concentration in the industry. The Justice Department discarded the traditional four-firm concentration ratio (CR4) for measuring industry concentration in favor of a new index called the **Herfindahl-Hirschman Index (HHI),** which takes into account the market shares of all the firms in the industry. The HHI is the sum of the squares of each firm's market share.

HERFINDAHL-HIRSCHMAN INDEX (HHI)

An index of industry concentration, equal to the sum of the squares of each firm's market share within the industry.

$$HHI = (s_1)^2 + (s_2)^2 + \cdots + (s_i)^2 + \cdots + (s_n)^2$$

Where s_i is the market share of the ith firm, expressed as a decimal fraction, and n is the number of firms in the industry. For example, if an industry consists of three firms with market shares of .50, .30, and .20, the HHI $= (.5)^2 + (.3)^2 + (.2)^2 = .25 + .09 + .04 = .38$. The highest possible value of the HHI is 1, when the industry is a pure monopoly.

The guidelines consider an industry to be highly concentrated if the HHI exceeds 0.18 and competitive if the HHI is less than 0.10. To lend some perspective to these numbers, suppose that an industry consists of equal-sized firms, all with identical market shares. In this case the value of the HHI would be $1/n$, where n is the number of firms in the industry. In other words, an industry of 10 equal-sized firms has an HHI of .10 (= 1/10); an industry of five equal-sized firms has an HHI of .20 (= 1/5). According to the guidelines, therefore, an industry consisting of 10 or more equal-sized firms is competitive, and an industry consisting of five or fewer equal-sized firms is highly concentrated.

The 1984 merger guidelines distinguish between horizontal mergers and nonhorizontal mergers (that is, vertical and conglomerate mergers). The guidelines for horizontal mergers are fairly complex. Roughly speaking, the Justice Department will not challenge a merger if the industry is competitive (HHI < 0.10). Otherwise, it will challenge if the proposed merger increases the HHI by more than 0.10.

The Justice Department's determination of whether a merger substantially lessens competition turns on such factors as the ease of entry into the industry, the likelihood of fixing prices through tacit collusion, the financial health of the firms, the significance of foreign competition, and the probable impact of the merger on innovation. The Justice Department is also willing to consider arguments that a merger increases production efficiency by exploiting economies of scale. The courts had never before accepted economies of scale arguments as a basis for justifying a merger.

The standards for judging nonhorizontal (vertical and conglomerate) mergers are much simpler. The Justice Department is unlikely to challenge any vertical merger unless the industry HHI exceeds .18. The Justice Department does not judge conglomerate mergers on the basis of market concentration at all. The only basis for challenging a conglomerate merger is a lessening of potential competition.

The 1984 merger guidelines would disallow some mergers, but they are certainly in keeping with the new relaxed attitude toward big business. The 1980s witnessed a new wave of horizontal mergers, including the headline-grabbing hostile takeovers. Often the mergers involved very large firms—Texas Air and Eastern Airlines, Standard Oil of California and Gulf Corporation, Heileman and Pabst Brewing Companies, Chrysler and American Motors. The government typically allowed the mergers, insisting only that the companies eliminate any possible anti-competitive aspects prior to merger. For example, Gulf had to sell off about one-third of its wholesale and retail business before Standard Oil of California could acquire it. Mergers between such large firms never would have been permitted in the 1950s and 1960s.

Reactions to the New Policy Direction

Economists are sharply divided over the new policy direction in antitrust enforcement. The critics are dissatisfied with both the performance and the behavior of big business. With regard to performance, they believe that the large corporations fail to achieve any of the standard criteria for judging market outcomes—allocational efficiency, technical efficiency, and equity. When they look at oligopoly in the United States, they see prices set well above marginal costs, industry concentrations already well beyond what is required either to exploit economies of scale or to support innovative activity, and high barriers to entry in many industries that give firms effective monopoly power. The critics also distrust the behavior of the large corporations. They point to the enormous amount of rent-seeking behavior by corporate lobbyists in Washington. They also believe that collusive behavior is widespread. A common complaint about the large multiproduct corporations is that they develop an "I'll pat your back if you pat my back" attitude because they meet each other at so many points of contact. Finally, the critics argue that vigorous enforcement of the antitrust laws has played a major role in increasing the competitiveness of the U.S. economy. William Shepherd attributes 40 percent of the rise in effective competition in the U.S. economy from 1958 to 1980 to the antitrust activity of the 1950s and 1960s. His estimate rises to 57 percent when he includes the newly deregulated industries that were also affected by antitrust activity.

In short, critics of the new relaxed attitude toward antitrust argue that vigorous prosecution of the antitrust laws is essential to preserving competition in the big business sector and thereby promoting the efficiency and the equity of the economy. They would agree with Shepherd's conclusion: "If antitrust were suddenly to cease, then a large wave of new mergers and collusion would soon raise the degree of market power in a wide range of sectors."[13]

Supporters of the new policy direction in antitrust believe that the big business sector is reasonably competitive, enough so that an aggressive antitrust policy is simply unnecessary. They see a number of indications of sufficient competitiveness. First, price-cost margins are not appreciably higher in the highly concentrated industries than in the unconcentrated industries. Second, only a few industries are so dominated by a single firm that industry performance could conceivably warrant a structural monopolizing case under Section 2 of the Sherman Act. According to the supporters, just a handful of rivals is sufficient to ensure that an industry remains effectively competitive. They believe that tacit collusion is very difficult to maintain, even among a small number of firms. Third, the giant U.S. corporations generally earn high marks for technical efficiency, with only a few exceptions. They have successfully exploited cost-reducing economies of scale, and they have an admirable record with regard to both product and process innovation. Fourth, the competition from foreign producers has forever changed the big business sector in the United States. People today are not so worried about the market power of the large corporations. The new worry is whether U.S. companies can withstand the invasion of foreign competitors. We need not fear a decline in competitiveness under the new antitrust guidelines.

Another argument in favor of the new policy direction is that the structural monopoly and merger cases simply have become too unwieldy and costly. The IBM case dragged on for 13 years and 700 trial days before it was finally dropped. The pretrial discovery process took six years, and the presentation of the government's case another three years. The court received 104,000 pages of transcript and 17,000 exhibits, and the total cost of the case exceeded $100 million. Many issues that were relevant in 1969 when the case began were irrelevant by 1982 when the case ended. Surely the time, effort, and money expended on the IBM case could have been put to better use.[14]

Economists will probably never fully agree on the proper role of antitrust policy, given the uncertainties that abound in the analysis of oligopoly. However, the arguments favoring a reduced role for antitrust activity do appear to be winning the day among the majority of economists. The emerging view is that prosecution under antitrust should be limited to instances of outright collusion and predatory behavior aimed at eliminating competitors, erecting bar-

[13]Shepherd, "Causes of Increased Competition," 623.

[14]Baldwin, *Market Power*, 363–364.

riers to entry, or disciplining other firms. Lester Thurow, former dean of MIT's Sloan School of Management, aptly summarizes the emerging view when he says that the only stricture under antitrust should be that firms cannot agree not to compete with one another.[15] We saw in Chapter 15 that cooperative behavior is the surest way of softening competition and protecting effective market power. The government must prevent firms from choosing this option.

SUMMARY

Chapter 17 began with a discussion of barriers to entry, which the majority of economists believe are an important factor in maintaining profits in the highly concentrated industries.

1. A market economy will inevitably contain some very large firms because of economies of scale, but size itself is probably not an effective barrier to entry. Size combined with large sunk costs or imperfect capital markets can be a very effective barrier, however.
2. Capital that is highly specific to an industry, that is slow to depreciate, and that cannot easily be sold in a secondhand market gives rise to large sunk costs and implies that the industry has a long short run. A decision to enter an industry with a long short run has the elements of commitment and irreversibility that are essential to creating an effective barrier to entry. Once a firm enters, it has to cover only its average variable costs to remain in business, whereas a new entrant has to cover its average total costs. Therefore, sunk costs give incumbents an important first-mover advantage.
3. A market without any significant sunk costs of capital and with no other barriers to entry is a contestable market. In its purest form, a contestable market permits hit-and-run entry. A new entrant can enter, make some profits, and exit before the incumbent can respond. Hit-and-run entry is unrealistic in certain respects, but it points out that entry does not have to occur to drive price to average cost. The threat of entry is enough and applies even to a pure monopolist.
4. Size combined with imperfect capital markets can also create an imposing barrier to entry. Corporations finance the majority of their investments from their own retained earnings. If investors are reluctant to lend to corporations, then large firms with huge amounts of internal funds, long purses, have a natural advantage in financing new investments. Miller supposedly rose to number two in the beer industry on the long purse of Philip Morris. The long-purse theory may not have much general relevance, though, since venture capital markets are well developed in the United States. Also, few companies are willing to stick with a losing investment strategy for long on the hope that it will eventually turn a profit.
5. The section also considered two behavioral barriers to entry, predatory pricing and advertising. Predatory pricing is a strategy in which the incumbent sets its price below the level at which a new entrant could make a profit. Most economists doubt that firms could use predatory pricing to

[15]Thurow's position on antitrust appears in W. Adams, "Public Policy in a Free Enterprise Economy", in Adams (ed.), *Structure of American Industry*, 417. For an excellent history and analysis of U.S. antitrust policy, see Baldwin, *Market Power*, Chs. 5, and Part III, Chs. 15–20. Baldwin discusses the 1984 Merger guidelines on pp. 381–383.

deter entry. Prices are easy to change; therefore, a pricing strategy lacks the key ingredients of commitment and irreversibility. Also, if a new firm enters, the incumbent would often be foolish to continue fighting by keeping its price low. It can usually do better by raising its price, accommodating the new firm, and sharing the industry profits. In short, the strategy of predatory pricing lacks credibility.

6. Advertising can be a pro-competitive activity or an anti-competitive barrier to entry, depending on the nature of the good, the kind of information conveyed by the advertising message, and the medium of the message. Advertising for search goods that conveys hard information through print media such as newspapers is a pro-competitive activity. It improves consumers' information about products, and it substitutes for the searching consumers would have to do for themselves. Advertising for experience goods that conveys soft information over network television can be an anti-competitive barrier to entry by building up brand loyalties that are difficult to overcome. Network television advertising also has some economies of scale associated with it that give an advantage to large firms with huge advertising budgets.
7. Research shows that large firms generally use behavioral barriers to discipline smaller firms and to limit their share of the market. Behavioral barriers seldom keep new firms from entering an industry in the first place.
8. No one potential barrier to entry seems very important when considered by itself. However, a number of barriers in combination can present a formidable barrier to entry. In truth, some of the highly concentrated industries have been very difficult to enter. Automobiles, beer, and ready-to-eat cereals are examples.

The chapter then turned to Schumpeter's defense of monopoly power. Shumpeter believed that large firms with monopoly power were necessary to support the process of invention, innovation, and diffusion of new products and production processes that is essential to long-run economic growth.

9. According to Schumpeter, monopoly power before the fact is necessary to finance research and development. Monopoly power after the fact through patent protection is necessary to prevent the stealing of new ideas and thereby preserve incentives for inventive and innovative activity. Schumpeter argued that the dynamic efficiency of the economy, embodied in its record of long-run economic growth, is more important than static efficiencies such as allocational efficiency and production efficiency. Also, monopoly power is not a problem because it cannot perpetuate itself. Economic growth is a process of creative destruction, in which invention and innovation destroy old markets as they create new ones. Firms with monopoly power will soon be replaced by other firms.
10. The one part of Schumpeter's defense that has not stood the test of time is his view that large corporations are necessary to support invention and innovation. Research has shown that small firms take out a disproportionate share of all patents. The small firms are better at developing new production processes; the large firms are better at developing new products.
11. The other aspects of Schumpeter's defense of monopoly power have stood the test of time. Dynamic efficiency is more important than is static efficiency. Inventions and innovations do require patent protection. Patents give rise to a true dilemma. Monopoly protection is necessary after the fact

to preserve incentives for invention and innovation, but at the same time monopoly protection inhibits the diffusion of new ideas throughout the economy. Fortunately, monopoly power after the fact has not been a problem in most industries, primarily because most patents are fairly easily to imitate around. Personal computer clones are a good example.

The third section of the chapter discussed the sources of competition within the highly concentrated industries.

12. Even the largest corporations face competition from other firms within the industry and from industries producing substitute products. Competition within the industry is called rivalry among the few and usually takes the form of nonprice competition. Increasing rivalry from foreign producers has been a leading story in the U.S. economy for the past 35 years. William Shepherd attributes one-sixth of the increase in competition in the economy since 1958 to foreign competition, concentrated in 13 industries. Competition across industries is generally less important, but it can be very important in certain cases. The competition for containers is an example. Competition within the highly concentrated industries is vigorous enough so that price-cost margins, and profits, are not substantially greater in the highly concentrated industries than in the effectively competitive sector of the economy.

The fourth section of the chapter presented an evaluation of the oligopolies along the standard lines of efficiency and equity.

13. The highly concentrated industries fail to achieve the goals of allocational efficiency and equity. Barriers to entry give firms the potential of setting their prices above marginal and average costs. The firms realize this potential by means of product differentiation and tacit collusion over price in an ongoing strategic environment. The large corporations score better in terms of technical efficiency, both static (exploiting economies of scale) and dynamic (compiling a good record of invention and innovation). However, the highly concentrated industries are generally much more concentrated than they need to be to realize either the static or the dynamic efficiencies that large firms make possible.

Chapter 17 concluded with a discussion of the federal government's antitrust policy.

14. The three pillars of the nation's antitrust policy are the Sherman Antitrust Act of 1890, the Clayton Antitrust Act of 1914, and the Federal Trade Commission Act of 1914.
15. The three acts, and their subsequent amendments, are designed to foster competition by addressing market structure and business conduct. The Sherman Act outlaws cooperative restraints of trade and any attempts to monopolize an industry. The Clayton Act forbids predatory pricing, certain vertical arrangements, and mergers if any of these practices serves to lessen competition. The Federal Trade Commission Act outlaws unfair and deceptive business practices.
16. The Reagan administration established a set of merger guidelines that are still in force today. The guidelines first judge the effect of mergers on industry concentration. Concentration is measured by the Herfindahl-Hirschman Index (HHI), equal to the sum of the squares of each firm's

market share within the industry. An industry with a post-merger HHI of .10 or less is considered to be competitive; an industry with an HHI of .18 or more is considered to be highly concentrated. Horizontal mergers in a competitive industry will not be challenged; horizontal mergers in a highly concentrated industry are likely to be challenged. [The Justice Department also considers the potential effect of a merger on competition within an industry.] Vertical mergers are subject to less stringent tests, and conglomerate mergers are judged only by their effect on competition.

17. Antitrust cases were vigorously prosecuted by the Justice Department in the 1950s and 1960s. Then prosecutions declined substantially in the 1970s and 1980s. Some economists favor a return to vigorous enforcement of the antitrust laws. They believe that the antitrust activity of the 1950s and 1960s was instrumental in making the economy more competitive and that the economy will become less competitive under lax enforcement. Supporters of the new relaxed antitrust policy believe that the economy is competitive enough today that vigorous enforcement of the laws is unnecessary. They also point to the enormous costs of the big antitrust cases.

KEY TERMS

barrier to entry (or exit)
behavioral barrier to entry
conglomerate merger
contestable market
creative destruction
diffusion
dynamic efficiency
Herfindahl-Hirschman Index (HHI)
horizontal merger
innovation
legal barrier to entry
long-purse theory
natural barrier to entry
predatory pricing
rivalry
vertical merger

QUESTIONS

1. The large corporations tend to earn higher profits than firms do generally.
   a. What are the two main explanations that economists give for why the large corporations are more profitable on average?
   b. To what extent are these two explanations compatible with one another?
2. What factors tend to limit the effective market power of even the largest corporations? Give some examples of large corporations that have lost some of their effective market power in recent years.
3. What are the three main kinds of barriers to entry? Give several examples of each.
4. a. What factors lead to high sunk costs for firms in the short run?
   b. Why do economists believe that the presence of high sunk costs can act as an effective barrier to entry?
   c. Give some examples of industries with high sunk costs; with low sunk costs.
5. a. What is the key factor that makes a market a contestable market?
   b. What is the predicted outcome of a contestable market?
   c. How does a contestable market differ from a perfectly competitive market?
6. Economists are not convinced that predatory pricing is a credible strategy for deterring entry. Why not?
7. Discuss the notion that advertising can be either pro-competitive or anti-competitive. Give examples of pro-competitive and anti-competitive advertising as part of your discussion.
8. Joseph Schumpeter argued that large firms with effective market power are necessary to support invention and innovation.
   a. What is the basis of Schumpeter's argument?
   b. Why does his argument place market power in a more favorable light from a social perspective?
   c. What does economic research say about the relationship between firm size and innovation?
9. a. What types of behavior are illegal under the U.S. antitrust laws?
   b. What are the arguments in favor of and against more vigorous prosecution of firms under the antitrust laws?
10. How well do the oligopolies satisfy the three goals of allocational efficiency, technical efficiency, and equity?

CASE

Some Skies are Contestable, Others Are Not*

The airline industry was heavily regulated during the forty-year period from the 1930s to the 1970s. The Civil Aeronautics Board (CAB) not only limited entry into and exit from the industry, but also designed a formula that airlines had to apply to their airfare calculations. Then, in 1978, the Carter administration and Congress decided to deregulate the airlines. The 1978 Airline Deregulation Act phased out all entry and exit restrictions by 1982, and gave the airlines complete freedom to determine their fares as they saw fit by 1983. The decision to deregulate the airline industry was based on two premises: that the industry lacked the characteristics that would support economic regulation, and that regulation had led to higher fares than would have prevailed under unrestricted competition. The theoretical foundation for these views was the theory of contestable markets. Airplanes—"capital on wings"—are easily moved from market to market. Therefore, even if a route between two cities or countries is served by just a few airlines, or only one airline, the threat of potential entry would force these airlines to set competitive fares. Otherwise a new entrant could fly the route, undercut the incumbent airlines' fare, and earn a profit.

Deregulation has successfully promoted competition and lowered airfares. Forty-three U.S. air carriers served the U.S. market in 1978. In 1991, there were 63 U.S. carriers, a 45 percent increase since deregulation. Average airfares decreased by about 25 percent over the same time period. U.S. airfares are approximately 5 percent below the world average for short distance travel (150 miles), and 40 percent below the world average for long distance travel (2400 miles). Furthermore, deregulation has not prevented the airlines from earning a reasonable return on their capital. Industry profits were negative in the early 1980s, primarily because of the deep 1981–82 recession, and a few carriers suffered huge losses in the more competitive deregulated market environment (Eastern in 1990, for example). On the whole, though, the industry has been profitable since 1984.

The U.S. has recently attempted to open up the skies on an international level. As more international airlines seek to enter the United States, the world's biggest passenger market, the U.S. is asking other countries such as Great Britain, Germany, and Japan to make their skies more contestable for U.S. carriers in return. The U.S. airlines face sizeable government-imposed entry barriers in many international markets, particularly in Europe. The barriers take the form of restrictions on the number of cities that U.S. airlines are allowed to serve, and on the number of flights per week that the U.S. airlines can offer on the routes that they are allowed to fly. The Netherlands signed an open-sky agreement with the United States in 1992, the first European country to do so. Great Britain, Germany, and Japan, however, are still not willing to relax their route limitations and landing restrictions (as of 1993).

The major U.S. airlines depend on expansion of their overseas markets to remain profitable, and the European market for passenger travel is expected to grow rapidly throughout the 1990s. But the barriers imposed on the U.S. airlines in Europe may prevent them from increasing the number of flights on their current routes and offering flights to new destinations, steps that will be necessary to maintain their share of the expanding European market.

In conclusion, the U.S. airlines operate in two completely different market environments. The U.S. markets became contestable following deregulation, with more airlines and lower airfares. The international markets are still far from being contestable for the U.S. airlines, however, because of government-imposed barriers to entry.

ECONOMIC ADVISOR'S REPORT

1. In the busy U.S. Northeast corridor takeoff and landing slots are restricted because of airport capacity constraints and air traffic control limitations. These restrictions limit the number of flights in and out of the certain major airports, such as National in Washington and Logan in Boston, thereby reducing potential entry and competition. The federal government asks you to advise them on what they should do to ration the limited flight capacity among the competing airlines eager to serve the Northeast markets. In particular, should the federal government once again regulate flights in the Northeast corridor, or can the market be counted on to ration the flights efficiently?
2. Suppose that you are sent to Europe as a representative of the U.S. Government and the U.S. airline industry. Your task is to convince the European governments that both the United States and Europe would benefit by increasing the number of European cities that U.S. airlines are allowed to serve, and by lifting the restrictions on the number of flights per week that the U.S. airlines can offer. What would be your line of argument?

*Prepared by Klaus G. Becker, Texas Tech University.

PART

V

Factor Markets and the Distribution of Income

CHAPTER

18

Wages and Salaries in the United States

LEARNING OBJECTIVES

CONCEPTS TO LEARN

- The four main facts about wages and salaries in the United States
- The age-earnings profile
- Monopsony power of business firms
- The history of labor unions in the United States
- The economic effects of labor unions
- Segmented labor markets
- Collective bargaining and bilateral monopoly

CONCEPTS TO RECALL

- The marginal benefit equals marginal cost decision rule [6]
- How competitive markets help determine the distribution of wage and salary income [9]
- The profit maximizing decision rule for hiring labor [9]
- Market (monopoly) power [14]

When economists look at labor markets in the United States, they see four main facts about wage and salary income that need to be explained. First, and foremost, is the extreme variation in wages and salaries within any one year. Earnings vary considerably from occupation to occupation, and even within occupations. Just knowing what jobs people have does not necessarily tell us whether they earn high or low incomes. Second is the pattern of earnings over the lifetime of an average worker. Earnings tend to rise steadily from young adulthood to late middle age and then decline for a few years before retirement. Although there are exceptions, this pattern applies to most workers and most occupations. Third is the relationship of earnings to years of formal education. You will be pleased to know that labor markets tend to reward additional years spent in school with higher wages and salaries at all ages. Also, the earnings of the more educated workers tend to increase much more rapidly during the years when earnings are rising. The fourth main fact is that earnings vary systematically by race and gender, which raises the specter of discrimination. On average, nonwhite workers earn much less than do white workers, and women of all races earn much less than do men of all races. Women's earnings also increase much less rapidly than do men's earnings up to middle age. This raises an obvious and troubling question: To what extent are these differences in earnings caused by outright discrimination against minorities and women?

When you finish college and enter the labor force in your chosen occupation, will your starting salary be high or low? Can you expect your salary to grow rapidly over time? Chapters 18 and 19 will help you answer these questions by analyzing the main factors that determine the pattern of wages and salaries in the United States.

Chapter 18 begins with an extended discussion of the four main facts about wage and salary income in the United States. It then attempts to explain the first of these four facts, the variability of earnings within any one year. Chapter 19 addresses the other three facts.

THE FOUR MAIN FACTS ABOUT LABOR MARKET EARNINGS

Economists who specialize in labor economics devote much of their research effort to explaining the four main facts about wage and salary income noted in the introduction. Let's take a closer look at each of them.

Fact 1: The Variation in Earnings

The most striking fact about the distribution of earnings in the United States is how differently the marketplace values different people's labor. For example, the 20 percent of the labor force at the top of the earnings distribution earn approximately 10 times more, on average, than do the 20 percent of the labor force at the bottom of the earnings distribution. Moreover, the 10-fold difference in the average earnings of the highest-paid and lowest-paid workers conceals an even greater variation among individuals' wages and salaries. Some people at the top of the distribution—athletes, movie stars, top corporate executives—earn millions of dollars annually. Some people at the bottom of the distribution—unskilled blue-collar workers with little education—work full time, yet cannot escape the clutches of poverty.

People earn such widely different incomes because earnings vary considerably across occupations, and even within occupations. The Bureau of Labor Statistics reported that the average weekly earnings of physicians was $1007 in 1992. That same year engineers earned an average of $862 per week, accountants $600, teachers (primary and secondary) $561, masons $480, secretaries $373, sales clerks $252, and cleaners and servants only $191 per week.[1] We have come to accept the fact that rates of pay differ for different kinds of jobs. Somewhat more surprising, though, is the considerable variation in earnings within occupations. For instance, executives at the very top of the corporate hierarchy often earn three to four times as much as other "top" executives just one step down in the hierarchy. The variation in earnings is also substantial even within lesser-paying occupations. A 1986 study of secretarial positions in the Chicago area found that Level I secretaries (the lowest level) received an average pay of $300 per week. However, 38 percent of these secretaries earned either less than $260 per week or more than $340 per week.

Large variations in pay within occupations are not unique to the United States. A detailed 1981 survey of earnings in England uncovered the fact that on average, within all occupations, the 10 percent of the workers with the highest earnings were paid 2.5 times as much as the 10 percent of the workers with the lowest earnings. With earnings variations of this magnitude, just knowing peoples' occupations does not tell you all that much about how well off they are.[2]

Why do different people receive such different rates of pay for their labor? This is the overriding question that needs to be answered. The remaining three facts offer some clues to that answer.

Fact 2: The Age-Earnings Profile

A second fact about labor market earnings is that earnings vary systematically with the age of the worker. For most workers, earnings rise steadily into middle age and then decline. A graph relating annual earnings to age throughout a worker's lifetime is called the worker's **age-earnings profile.** Figure 18.1(a) displays the average age-earnings profile for all people of working age in the United States during 1991. The horizontal axis records the age of the people; the vertical axis measures the average annual earnings, in thousands of dollars, of all people within each age category. Therefore, a point on the age-earnings profile indicates the *average* earnings in 1991 of all people in a given age group.

AGE-EARNINGS PROFILE

A graph displaying the average annual earnings by age within the labor force.

An average age-earnings profile for a country indicates the pattern of earnings that young people can expect to receive over their lifetimes, but not the actual level of their earnings. Since the points on the average age-earnings profile in the figure apply to a single year, they capture the other things equal effect of

---

[1]U.S. Department of Labor, Bureau of Labor Statistics, *Employment and Earnings* 40, No. 1 (January 1993): 233–237. The average earnings are the median earnings.

[2]For a discussion of the Chicago secretaries data see B. Kaufman, *The Economics of Labor Markets*, third edition (Hinsdale, IL: The Dryden Press, 1991), 224–235. The English data are reported in A. Atkinson, *The Economics of Inequality*, second edition (Oxford: Clarendon Press, 1983), 98.

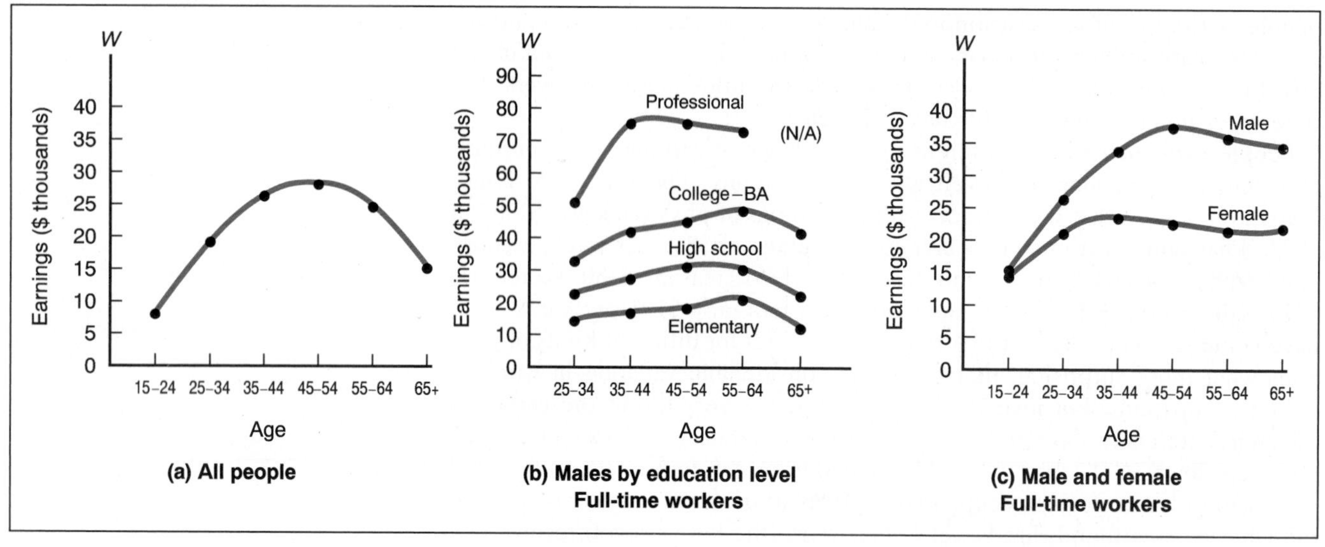

FIGURE 18.1

Age-Earnings Profiles in the United States, 1991

The age-earnings profile shows the average earnings of people within each age on the horizontal axis. Figure 18.1(a) displays the age-earnings profile of all persons. It is hump-shaped; average earnings rise into middle age and then decline in the later working years and through retirement. Figure 18.1(b) compares the age-earnings profiles of males who work full time and who have attained different levels of education. The age-earnings profiles show the average earnings increase with the level of education and also rise more steeply in the early adult years the higher the level of education. Figure 18.1(c) compares the age-earnings profiles of males and females who work full time and shows that they have very different patterns of average lifetime earnings. The average earnings of females are much less than those of males, rise and fall much less over time, and reach their peak at a much earlier age.

age on earnings. They do not allow for future increases in earnings resulting from inflation in wages and prices generally or from increases in the average productivity of workers over time.

Notice the distinct humped pattern to the age-earnings profile. Average earnings rise steadily until ages 45–54 and then decline steadily thereafter. An interesting question is why earnings should behave this way instead of, say, rising steadily or remaining constant throughout a person's lifetime.

Fact 3: Education and Earnings

The third main fact about labor market earnings is that additional years of formal education increase lifetime earnings and change the shape of the age-earnings profiles. These two effects can be seen very clearly in Figure 18.1(b). This graph displays the average age-earnings profiles of male full-time workers in the United States who have received different amounts of formal education, ranging from elementary school to a professional education. The data are from 1991. For instance, each point on the elementary school age-earnings profile indicates the average earnings of all heads of households who are the age measured on the horizontal axis *and* who have only an elementary school education. Points on the other age-earnings profiles have the same interpretation for the years of education indicated.

Notice that annual earnings increase at every age level as the amount of education increases. Also, the age-earnings profiles become steeper as the amount of education increases; annual earnings increase more rapidly the more education a worker has. As a result, workers with more education not only earn more as young adults than do workers with less education; the difference in annual earnings between them also grows consistently larger year by year well into middle age.

The fact that lifetime earnings increase with years of education is not very surprising. People would not invest so much time and money in education if it did not pay off, on average, in the form of higher wages and salaries. But why should formal schooling received prior to joining the work force have such lasting effects on the rate of increase in earnings? The effect of education on the shape of the age-earnings profile is much more difficult to explain.

Fact 4: Possible Discrimination in Labor Markets

The fourth stylized fact about labor market earnings that cries out for explanation is the apparent disadvantage of nonwhite minorities and women in U.S. labor markets. The average earnings of full-time black male workers in the United States were only 71 percent of the average earnings of full-time white male workers in 1991. Full-time female workers did even less well, on average, earning only 65 percent as much as full-time male workers in 1991. Moreover, the ratio of female to male earnings has remained essentially unchanged for 50 years. The ratio of female to male earnings stood at 63 percent in 1939. Blacks have at least made some progress toward equality with whites over the past 50 years, although they started much further behind. Black male earnings were only 45 percent of white male earnings in 1939. The ratio narrowed fairly rapidly until 1970, when it stood at 68 percent. Progress toward equality for black males since then has obviously been much slower. Curiously, the earnings of black women have reached near equality with the earnings of white women. This accomplishment loses some of its luster, however, considering that women generally lag far behind men in labor market earnings.

Women's earnings differ from men's earnings in one other respect. Women have a much flatter age-earnings profile than do men, as indicated by Figure 18.1(c). The age-earnings profiles in that graph depict the average earnings of females and males in the United States who worked full time in 1991. The profiles show that, on average, young women start out behind young men in the world of work and fall further behind as they grow older. Women's earnings also peak at an earlier age.

The differences in earnings between nonwhites and whites and between women and men are large and persistent. Economic research has tried to determine the extent to which these differences are the result of free choice and standard competitive market forces as opposed to outright discrimination that denies minorities and women equal opportunity and isolates them from the equalizing forces of competition. Sad to say, the evidence suggests that discrimination has been an important factor in holding down the wages and salaries of minorities and women in the United States. We will review the evidence on discrimination in Chapter 19.[3]

PERFECT COMPETITION AND THE DISTRIBUTION OF EARNINGS

We made a start toward understanding the pattern of wages and salaries in Chapter 9 when we discussed the distributional implications of perfectly competitive labor markets. The Laws of Supply and Demand provide an accurate explanation of market behavior whenever resources are free to move to better market opportunities and prices are flexible and responsive to underlying mar-

[3]The 1991 data in this section and for Figure 18.1 are taken from U.S. Department of Commerce, Economics and Statistics Administration, Bureau of the Census, "Money Income of Households, Families, and Persons in the United States: 1991," *Consumer Income*, Current Population Reports, Series P-60, No. 180 (August 1992). For excellent discussions of the history of wages in the United States for women and nonwhite minorities see B. Kaufman, *The Economics of Labor Markets*, third edition (Hinsdale, IL: The Dryden Press, 1991), Chapter 9; and R. Ehrenberg and R. Smith, *Modern Labor Economics: Theory and Public Policy*, fourth edition (New York: Harper Collins, 1991), Chapter 14.

ket conditions. These conditions apply to a substantial portion of U.S. labor markets.

The U.S. labor force is remarkably mobile. One-fifth of the adult population moves out of county or state every five years, most often as the result of a job change. Of all workers in the United States, more than 28 million individuals (25 percent) change the *industry* in which they work during every three-year period, and only one-half of all full-time workers have held the same job for more than 3½ years.[4] Workers in the United States are clearly willing and able to respond to market opportunities.

Wages and salaries are also quite flexible and responsive to market conditions in a large number of labor markets. For example, the market for college graduates was in excess demand throughout the period from 1961 to 1969; then it turned to excess supply from 1969 to 1974 as the first of the post–World War II baby boomers graduated. During the first period the starting salaries of college graduates grew more rapidly than did wages and prices generally. During the second period their starting salaries grew less rapidly than did wages and prices generally. Now, with the baby bust generation graduating from college, the starting salaries of college graduates are once again growing more rapidly than are wages and prices generally. In other words, the starting salaries of college graduates behaved exactly as predicted by the Laws of Supply and Demand.

CURRENT ISSUE: Today's graduating seniors have an additional advantage. The computerization of the workplace has increased the demand for young adults with a college education. The earnings gap between those with only a high school education and those with a college education has widened considerably in the 1990s.

Not all labor markets are competitive, to be sure. Nonetheless, we saw in Chapter 9 that the theory of competitive labor markets can give us considerable insight into why different people earn different wages. Let's briefly review the theory as it applies to the distribution of income.

The Competitive Outcomes

A principal result from Chapter 9 is that competitive wages equal the value of labor's marginal product in an occupation. The value of marginal product is labor's marginal physical product times the price of the good or service that the labor produces.

$$W = VMP_L = MP_L \cdot P_g$$

The marginal product term, MP_L, tells us that wages depend on workers' skills or productivity and on the number of other workers who have the same skills. Other things equal, wages are higher the more skilled or productive the workers and the smaller the number of workers with the same skills. Conversely, wages are lower the lower the workers' skills and the larger the number of workers with the same skills. The price of the good or service, P_g, reminds us that the demand for labor is derived demand. The more highly valued the good or the service, the higher the wages and the salaries of the workers who produce it.

In addition, the distribution of wages in competitive labor markets depends on individual preferences for different kinds of work and the attributes of various jobs, as follows:

[4]Ehrenberg and Smith, *Modern Labor Economics*, 264 and 360.

1. *All workers and all jobs are identical.* If all workers and all jobs are identical, so that anyone is willing and able to do anyone else's job, then all workers earn the same wage in equilibrium. If wages temporarily differ among the jobs, workers will move from the low-paying jobs to the high-paying jobs until wages are equal for all.
2. *All workers are identical, but jobs differ.* If workers have identical preferences for different kinds of work, but jobs differ in terms of how desirable they are or the skills that they require, then wages differ among jobs in equilibrium. Less-desirable jobs and jobs requiring a greater amount of training pay higher wages, and more-desirable and low-training jobs pay lower wages. Nonetheless, all workers are equally well off despite earning different wages because the differences in their wages are equalizing, or compensating, wage differences. The wage premiums paid to workers for risking their lives to build skyscrapers, or for handling hazardous chemicals, or for enduring the disruptions of constant travel, or for working the night shift just offset the loss in satisfaction from these less-desirable working conditions.

   The theory of equalizing wage differences underscores a very important point. We tend to judge how well off people are by the amount of income that they earn. In fact, income is a very imperfect measure of an individual's well-being. Other factors, such as working conditions, job satisfaction, and the amount of leisure time people have, are also important determinants of economic well-being.
3. *Both workers and jobs differ.* People are definitely not all alike. We often have very different preferences for the types of jobs we enjoy. When people's preferences for jobs differ and the jobs themselves differ, the overall market for labor divides into a number of noncompeting markets. Individual labor markets are noncompeting because people are no longer so willing or able to move from one occupation to another. Wages are determined by the Laws of Supply and Demand in each submarket and differ across occupations, just as in the second case. Moreover, the wage differences are not necessarily equalizing wage differences. Instead, some workers earn a economic rent. They receive a wage greater than the wage required to keep them working in their particular jobs. Different workers are not necessarily equally well off when markets give rise to economic rents, even if they earn the same wage.

In summary, the competitive model of Chapter 9 can begin to explain part of the first main fact about wage and salary income, the wide variation in earnings across occupations. The competitive model has more trouble explaining the extreme variation in wages within occupations, however. Some equalizing wage differences can be expected to exist within occupations because each broadly defined occupation includes specific jobs having different working conditions, such as day shifts versus night shifts in factories or secretarial positions with more- or less-flexible hours. As a general rule, though, differences in pay within occupations should diminish the more competitive the market. The differences in pay actually observed within occupations, on the order of 2 or 3 to 1 between the highest- and lowest-paid workers, are unlikely to be just equalizing differences. Something beyond the Laws of Supply and Demand appears to be determining wages and salaries in many labor markets.

The competitive model of Chapter 9 simply did not address the other three stylized facts about wages and salary income. That chapter presented a short-run model of labor markets that is not designed to explain either the age-earnings profiles of workers over their lifetimes or the effect of education on future earnings. Chapter 9 also did not consider the possibility of labor market discrimination because discrimination is inherently noncompetitive. It undermines the Laws of Supply and Demand.

The remaining sections of this chapter consider two noncompetitive elements in labor markets that can have important effects on labor market earnings, the market power of firms and labor unions. We continue to assume a short-run model and focus on the variability of earnings within a given year.

THE MARKET POWER OF BUSINESS FIRMS

Labor receives a wage equal to the value of its marginal product, $W = VMP_L$, when both labor markets and output markets are perfectly competitive. This fundamental result derives from the hiring decisions of profit-maximizing competitive firms. All firms maximize profit by hiring labor until the cost of the last worker hired just equals the extra revenue from selling the product produced by the last worker. If labor markets are competitive, a firm can hire all the labor it wants at the going market wage, W. Therefore, the wage, W, is always the marginal cost of hiring additional labor. If product markets are also competitive, the firm can sell all the output it produces at the going market price, P_g. The last worker hired produces an amount of output equal to the marginal (physical) product of labor, MP_L. Since all units of output are sold at the price P_g, the marginal revenue from hiring the last worker is $MP_L \cdot P_g = VMP_L$, the value of labor's marginal product.

Labor receives a wage less than the value of its marginal product when firms possess market power in *either* product markets *or* factor markets. Profit-maximizing firms with market power are able to gain some of their profits at the expense of labor by forcing wages below the competitive wage. We will begin with the case of market power in product markets only and then consider the case of a firm having market power in both markets.

Monopoly Power in Product Markets

Firms with monopoly power in product markets do not necessarily have market power in hiring labor. They may be only one of a large number of firms hiring a particular kind of labor, in which case they are likely to have little or no influence over the wage. If their labor markets are truly perfectly competitive, then they have no control over the wage. They are wage takers and can hire as much labor as they wish at the going market wage, W. Therefore, the marginal cost of hiring additional labor always equals the wage, W, no matter how much labor they hire. In this respect they are no different from firms that are also selling their products in a perfectly competitive market.

The difference between competitive and monopolistic firms lies in the marginal revenue from hiring additional labor. For firms with monopoly power the marginal revenue from hiring additional labor is no longer the value of labor's marginal product. The last worker hired by a monopolistic firm increases output by the marginal (physical) product of labor, MP_L, just as it does for a competitive firm. However, the extra revenue a monopolistic firm receives for this output is measured by the marginal revenue from selling output, MR_g, not the price of the product, P_g. Therefore, the marginal revenue from hiring an ad-

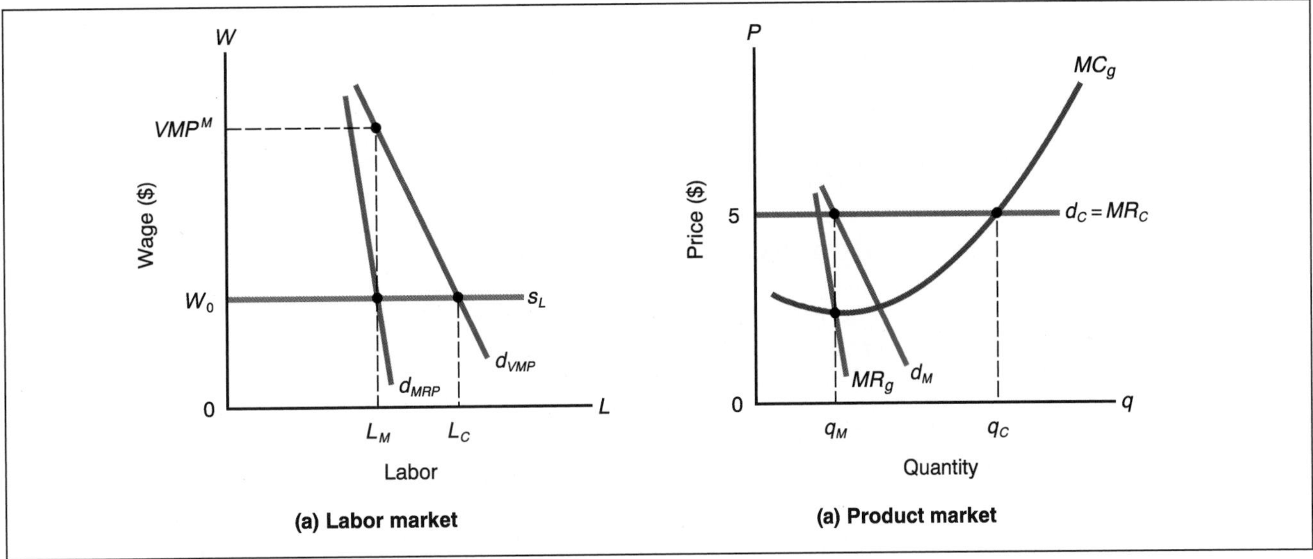

FIGURE 18.2

The Demand for Labor by Monopolistic and Competitive Firms

Figure 18.2 compares the demand for labor between a competitive firm and a monopoly firm. Both firms buy labor in competitive labor markets, at the wage W_0. In Figure 18.2(b), d_C is the horizontal demand curve of the competitive firm, d_M and MR_g are the demand and marginal revenue curves for the monopoly firm, and MC_g is their common marginal cost curve. They both charge the same price of $5. In Figure 18.2(a), the demand curve for labor is d_{VMP} for the competitive firm and d_{MRP} for the monopoly firm, reflecting the value of labor's marginal product and the marginal revenue product respectively. d_{MRP} lies to the left of d_{VMP} and is more steeply sloped because MR is below price for the monopoly firm, and MR falls as the firm increases its output. The monopoly firm hires less labor than the competitive firm, L_M versus L_E, because it produces less output. Also, the value of labor's marginal product in the monopoly firm, VMP^M, exceeds the wage.

ditional worker is the product of the marginal (physical) product of labor and the marginal revenue from selling output, $MP_L \cdot MR_g$. This product is called the **marginal revenue product of labor** and is labeled MRP_L. A firm with monopoly power hires labor until $W = MRP_L$. Since the marginal revenue from selling output is always less than the price for a firm with monopoly power, $MP_L \cdot MR_g < MP_L \cdot P_g$. A firm with monopoly power pays its workers less than the value of their marginal product.

Figure 18.2 illustrates the difference in the demand for labor between a competitive firm and a monopolistic firm that charge the same price for their output. Figure 18.2(b) depicts the product market. It assumes that both firms have the same marginal cost curve, MC_g, and that the price of the product is $5. The competitive firm faces the perfectly elastic demand curve, d_C, and produces output, q_C, at the intersection of d_C and MC_g. The monopolistic firm faces the downward-sloping demand curve, d_M, and the corresponding marginal revenue curve, MR_g. The firm produces output q_M, at the intersection of MR_g and MC_g, and charges a price of $5.

Figure 18.2(a) shows the demand for labor for each firm at the competitive market wage, W_0. The horizontal line, W_0, is the perfectly elastic supply curve of labor facing each firm, s_L. Workers will supply as much labor as each firm wants at a wage of W_0. The demand curve for labor of the competitive firm is d_{VMP}, reflecting the value of marginal product, $MP_L \cdot P_g$, at each quantity of labor hired. The demand curve for labor of the monopolistic firm is d_{MRP}, reflecting the marginal revenue product of labor, $MP_L \cdot MR_g$, at each quantity of labor hired.

Notice that d_{MRP} lies to the left and below d_{VMP} and is steeper than d_{VMP}. d_{MRP} lies to the left and below d_{VMP} because $MR_g < P_g$. If the two firms charge the same price, the monopolistic firm always demands less labor because it produces less output. d_{MRP} is steeper than d_{VMP} because MR_g declines as output increases for the monopolistic firm, whereas P_g is constant for the competitive firm no matter how much output it produces.

MARGINAL REVENUE PRODUCT OF LABOR

The marginal revenue from hiring an additional worker, equal to the product of the marginal (physical) product of labor and the marginal revenue from selling the output produced by that labor.

The competitive firm hires L_C workers to produce its output, q_C, at the intersection of W_0 and d_{VMP}. The firm with monopoly power hires L_M workers to produce its output, q_M, at the intersection of W_0 and d_{MRP}. The wage for workers in the competitive firm equals the value of their marginal product at L_C. Workers in the firm with monopoly power receive the same wage, but the wage is only equal to the workers' marginal revenue product at L_M. The value of their marginal product, VMP^M, exceeds their marginal revenue product, MRP_L. Therefore, any profits earned by the monopolistic firm come partly at the expense of their workers.

Monopsony Power

The harm caused labor by the exercise of monopoly power may not be very great. We saw in Chapters 14 and 17 that prices are close to marginal costs in most product markets, which means that MRP_L is close to VMP_L in most competitive labor markets. We will also see in Chapter 19 that large firms actually pay higher wages than do small firms, presumably as a means of keeping their employees motivated to work hard over the long run.

Firms do have the potential to cause substantial harm to labor, however, if their market power extends to labor markets. In this case they may be able to set a wage far below the value of labor's marginal product.

MONOPSONY POWER
Market power in labor markets (or in any factor markets) such that firms are able to set the wage of the workers (or cost of the factors) they hire.

Firms with market power in labor markets (or in any factor market) are said to possess monopsony power. *Monopsony* is the Greek word for "one buyer." **Monopsony power** means that the individual firm faces an upward-sloping supply curve for labor. In order to hire more workers the firm must pay higher wages to the new workers *and* to all its existing workers. Conversely, if the firm lays off workers, then the wage it must pay to the remaining workers declines. In other words, firms with monopsony power are wage setters, not wage takers. Notice that monopsony power is defined analogously to monopoly power in product markets, in which the firm faces a downward-sloping demand for its output. Firms with monopoly power lower or raise their prices to sell more or less output. They are price setters, not price takers. Firms tend to have monopsony power when they are important buyers of a specialized kind of labor. For instance, IBM and Digital undoubtedly exercise some monopsony power in the market for computer scientists.

PURE MONOPSONY
The limiting case of monopsony power in which one firm is the only buyer of a particular kind of labor (or of any factor).

The limiting case of monopsony power is **pure monopsony,** in which one firm is the only buyer of a particular kind of labor. Pure monopsony is analogous to pure monopoly in product markets. Like pure monopoly, instances of pure monopsony are uncommon, but not unheard of. Hospitals located in rural areas are often the only source of employment for trained nurses living in the area. Coal mines have market power over coal miners that approaches pure monopsony. And major league sports teams were virtually pure monopsonists prior to the institution of free agency in the 1970s. Before free agency, players' contracts contained reserve clauses that bound the players to the team that first signed them. They played for that one team or not at all, unless they were traded, in which case they had no choice but to play for their new team. In those days rival leagues provided the only source of competition for players, but leagues were difficult to establish at the top levels. Major League Baseball and the National Hockey League have never been seriously challenged by a rival league. In the 1960s the American Football League successfully competed for players against the National Football League, and the American Basketball Association somewhat less successfully competed against the National Basketball Association. In each case, though, the old and new leagues merged after a few years, re-establishing the monopsony power of the teams' owners.

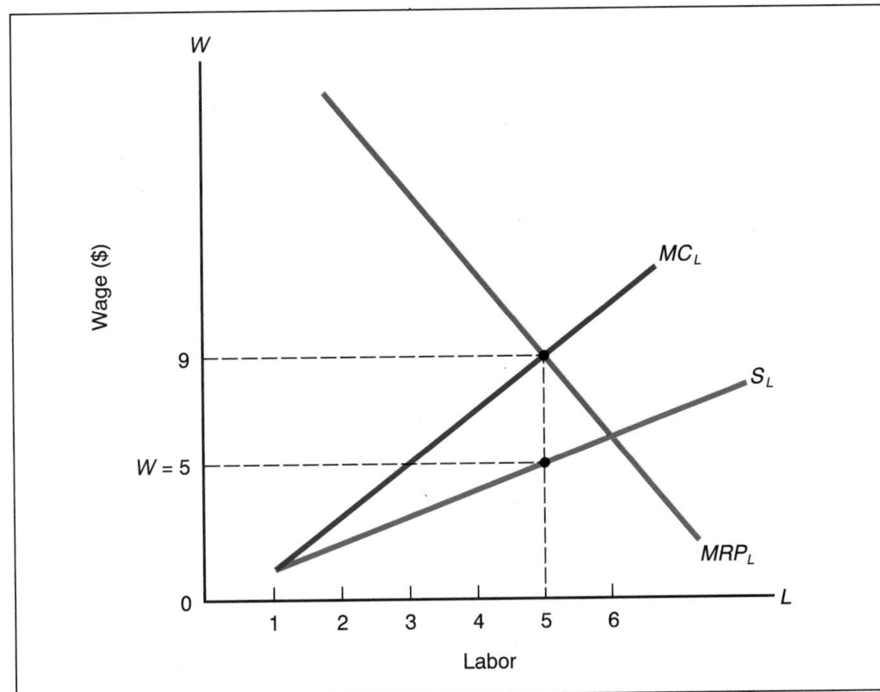

FIGURE 18.3

Monopsony Power

A firm with monopsony power faces an upward-sloping supply curve for labor, S_L, because it must pay more to all its workers to hire an additional worker. As a result, the marginal cost of hiring labor, MC_L, exceeds the wage at each quantity of labor hired. MC_L is above S_L. The firm's demand for labor is the marginal revenue product of labor, MRP_L. The firm maximizes profit by hiring labor such that the marginal revenue from hiring labor equals the marginal cost of labor, at the intersection of MRP_L and MC_L. The firm hires 5 workers, and pays a wage of $5, the corresponding wage on S_L.

Let's consider the case of pure monopsony to illustrate how firms set wages when they have monopsony power. We will assume that the firm also has monopoly power in its product market, so that its demand curve for labor is labor's marginal revenue product curve, not labor's value of marginal product curve.

Figure 18.3 and Table 18.1 offer a simple representation of a labor market under pure monopsony. The firm's demand curve for labor, its MRP_L, is a straight line. Refer to the second column of Table 18.1. The MRP_L is $21 for the first worker hired and declines by $3 for each additional worker hired. The firm faces an upward-sloping supply curve for labor, S_L, that is also a straight line. Refer to the third column of the table. The firm can hire one worker at a wage of $1. Then the wage rises by $1 for each additional worker hired. If the firm wants to hire 2 workers, it must pay a wage of $2 to *each* worker; if it wants to hire 3 workers, it must pay a wage of $3 to *each* worker; and so on for additional workers.

TABLE 18.1 **Pure Monopsony**

QUANTITY OF LABOR (L)	MARGINAL REVENUE PRODUCT (MRP_L)	WAGE (W)	TOTAL WAGES ($W \cdot L$)	MARGINAL COST OF LABOR (MC_L)
1	$21	$1	$ 1	$ 1
2	18	2	4	3
3	15	3	9	5
4	12	4	16	7
5	9	5	25	9
6	6	6	36	11

The firm follows the standard hiring rule to maximize its profit: Hire workers until the marginal revenue obtained from the last worker equals the marginal cost of hiring the last worker. As before, the marginal revenue obtained from the last worker is the MRP_L. However, the wage is no longer the marginal cost of hiring labor. The marginal cost exceeds the wage because to hire one more worker the firm must pay higher wages to *all* its workers. Refer to the fourth and fifth columns of the table. If the firm hires 1 worker, the total wage bill, $W \cdot L$ (fourth column), is \$1 (\$1 = \$1 · 1 worker). If the firm hires 2 workers, the total wage bill increases to \$4 (\$4 = \$2 · 2 workers). The marginal cost of hiring a second worker is \$3 (fifth column), equal to the difference in the total wages paid for 2 workers and for 1 worker (\$3 = \$4 − \$1). Similarly, the firm must increase the wage to \$3 for all workers to hire a third worker. The total wage bill for 3 workers is \$9 (\$9 = \$3 · 3 workers), so that the marginal cost of hiring the third worker is \$5 (\$5 = \$9 − \$4). The marginal cost of hiring labor (fifth column) exceeds the wage (second column) for all workers beyond the first.

Refer again to Figure 18.3. The supply curve of labor, S_L, indicates the wage the firm must pay for each number of workers hired. As such, S_L is the average cost curve for hiring labor from the firm's perspective because the wage is the cost per worker, the unit cost of labor. The marginal cost of hiring labor is the curve labeled MC_L, which comes from the fifth column of Table 18.1. MC_L lies above S_L for all workers beyond the first. Note once again the analogy to monopoly power in product markets. In product markets a monopolist's demand curve is its average revenue curve. The marginal revenue curve lies *below* the demand curve because the firm must *lower* its price on *all* units of output to sell more output. Here MC_L lies *above* S_L because the monopsonist must *raise* its wage to *all* workers to hire more workers.

The profit-maximizing number of workers is given by the intersection of the MRP_L and the MC_L curves, at which point the marginal revenue and the marginal cost of hiring labor are equal. The intersection occurs at 5 workers, and the marginal revenue and the marginal cost of hiring labor are both equal to \$9. The firm does not pay a wage of \$9, however. The firm need only pay a wage of \$5 to attract 5 workers, according to supply curve S_L. So the firm hires 5 workers at a wage of \$5.

To see why hiring 5 workers at a wage of \$5 maximizes profits, suppose that the firm hired a different number of workers. If it hires fewer than 5 workers, the marginal revenue from hiring an additional worker exceeds the marginal cost. MRP_L lies above MC_L. The firm can add to its profit by hiring additional workers. For example, if the firm were to hire 3 workers at a wage of \$3, it is sacrificing profit. A fourth worker has a marginal revenue product of \$12 and a marginal cost of \$7. Therefore, by hiring a fourth worker the firm increases its profit by \$5 (\$5 = \$12 − \$7). The straight-line curves in Figure 18.3 implicitly assume that the firm can hire parts of a worker's time. If so, the monopsonist should continue to hire labor until it has 5 workers, at which point MRP_L and MC_L are equal. Similarly, MC_L lies above MRP_L beyond 5 workers. Each additional worker (or part-time worker) hired in that range costs the firm more in additional wages than the revenue that the worker brings to the firm from selling the output it produces. The firm's profits decline beyond 5 workers. Therefore, hiring 5 workers at a wage of \$5 maximizes the firm's profit.

Labor suffers a double disadvantage when firms have market power in both product and labor markets. The wage is not only less than the value of labor's marginal product. Also, it is less than labor's marginal revenue product to the firm. In our example, the fifth worker brought in $9 of additional revenue to the firm, but received a wage of only $5.

Our simple example illustrates a very important principle: Firms can set wages far below the marginal value of their workers to them when they have considerable monopsony power. This principle has been amply demonstrated time and again in the world of sports. The courts in 1976 directed Major League Baseball to grant free agency to all players signed prior to 1971, the first time free agency in any form appeared in professional sports. The average salaries of those players jumped from $54,330 to $77,292 from 1976 to 1977, a 42 percent increase in one year.[5] The same thing is happening today in professional football. Unrestricted free agency is making millionaires out of the best offensive and defensive linemen. Only the players at the "skill" positions—quarterbacks, running backs, and wide receivers—earned such large salaries when the players were less free to join new teams.

The baseball and football examples are dramatic, but not very representative of most labor markets in the United States. While monopsony power has not been as widely studied as monopoly power has been, we can guess that the average amount of monopsony power in the United States is fairly small. Most workers have a number of employment alternatives. They are not as captive as baseball and football players were in the days before free agency. Even the largest corporations face stiff competition for much of their work force, especially at the entry-level positions. For example, IBM and Digital face vigorous competition for talented computer scientists. They undoubtedly have some monopsony power in this market, but probably not very much. Finally, whatever monopsony power large corporations do have may be largely offset by the presence of powerful labor unions, which we turn to in the next section. Nonetheless, society may well want to protect workers from the occasional blatant exercise of monopsony power, just as the U.S. courts decided to protect professional athletes from the reserve clause. The exchange of labor services is hardly ever an even-handed exchange when monopsony power approaches pure monopsony. The firm usually has a decided advantage.

REFLECTION: Do you think your college or university is likely to have more monopsony power in hiring classics professors or accounting professors?

LABOR UNIONS

Workers have long relied on the labor union to counter the market power of the corporations and otherwise to promote their general economic interests. The essence of union activity is **collective bargaining,** in which elected union representatives bargain with management on behalf of the members of the union over pay and other terms of employment. The union's representatives negotiate with management secure in the knowledge that the members are willing to strike the employer if the union's demands are not met. The threat of a strike, or a strike itself, is the primary method that unions use to achieve their objectives.

COLLECTIVE BARGAINING
A process in which elected union representatives bargain with management on behalf of the members of the union over pay and other terms of employment.

The collective bargaining process increases workers' market power by allowing them to speak with one voice, and to act as one, should a strike become necessary. In this respect the union is analogous to an industrial cartel, which allows a collection of individual firms to set price as a pure monopolist would.

[5] Kaufman, *Economics of Labor Markets,* 261–262.

The union, through collective bargaining, gives the workers monopoly power in selling their labor.

History of the Union Movement

CRAFT UNION

A labor union in which every member of the union is engaged in one particular craft or trade.

THE EARLY YEARS Unions have existed in the United States since the 1790s. The first unions were **craft unions,** in which every member of the union engaged in one particular craft or trade. The craft union remained the only form of union organization until the 1930s.

The early unions were strictly local in scope and had little economic power. The legal environment throughout the 1800s was hostile to unions, and employers were not required to bargain with the unions. The union movement received a much-needed shot in the arm at the end of the nineteenth century in the person of Samuel Gompers, who became known as the father of the modern labor movement in the United States. Gompers founded the American Federation of Labor (AF of L), a national organization whose purpose was to oversee and advise the local craft unions. The individual unions continued to bargain locally with their employers, however. Gompers established the principles that the unions should pursue only the economic interests of their members and that the strike should be used only to achieve particular economic objectives. By convincing the local unions to follow these principles, Gompers prevented the unions from becoming highly politicized, a fate that befell and weakened the labor union movement in Europe.

The AF of L was not able to increase the economic power of the local craft unions, however. They remained relatively weak until the 1930s for two reasons. One was that the courts continued to be hostile to the union movement. Employers could easily obtain court injunctions against a strike. They were also able to force new hires to sign "yellow dog" contracts in which workers agreed that they would not join a union as a condition of employment. The courts upheld these contracts. In addition, the craft unions were increasingly ineffective in the emerging mass-production, factory environment of the early 1900s. The automobile manufacturers and other mass producers hired vast numbers of unskilled workers who did not belong to any one craft or trade.

THE 1930s TO THE PRESENT The 1930s was a watershed in the U.S. labor union movement, ushering in a 40-year period of union growth and prosperity during which the unions achieved a considerable amount of economic power. Two sets of events were primarily responsible for turning around the fortunes of the unions, the birth of the industrial union and two landmark pieces of federal legislation.

INDUSTRIAL UNION

A labor union organized according to industry rather than the tasks that the workers perform within the industry.

John L. Lewis succeeded in organizing the coal miners into the nation's first industrial union. An **industrial union** is a union organized according to industry rather than the tasks the workers perform within the industry. The industrial union was tailor-made for the new industrial environment and spawned such powerful unions as the United Auto Workers and the International Brotherhood of Teamsters (the Teamsters has evolved into a *general union*, containing elements of both craft and industrial unions). In 1935 Lewis founded the Congress of Industrial Organizations (CIO), a national organization of the individual industrial unions. The CIO and AF of L merged in 1955.

The new industrial unions would not have prospered to the extent they did without the help of the federal government. The Norris-LaGuardia Act of 1932 and the National Labor Relations Act of 1935 (also called the Wagner Act) completely reversed the government's previous hostility toward union activity. The Norris-LaGuardia Act prevented employers from obtaining court-ordered injunctions against union activities and contained additional provisions that rendered unenforceable the yellow dog contracts. Having thus turned the tide in favor of unions, Congress followed with the National Labor Relations Act (NLRA), which greatly encouraged union formation and activity. The NLRA has been called the Magna Carta of the labor movement. It prohibits firms from engaging in unfair labor practices, including firing, demoting, or otherwise harassing employees for engaging in union activities. It also established a set of procedures for forming a union. Briefly, union organizers can force an election to have a union if they receive authorizing signatures from 30 percent of the potential members of the union. Then, if a majority of the potential members vote in favor of the union, the union is established, and the employer must engage in collective bargaining with the union's representatives. Finally, the act established the National Labor Relations Board (NLRB) to oversee and administer the NLRA. Among its other duties, the NLRB determines the appropriate electoral unit for voting on the establishment of a union. The NLRB has tended to favor industrial unions over craft unions.

There have been only two important pieces of legislation directed at union activities since 1935, the Taft-Hartley Act of 1947 and the Landrum-Griffin Act of 1959. Both acts were amendments to the NLRA. They each modified the decidedly pro-union stance of the 1930s legislation.

The Taft-Hartley Act of 1947 was passed to protect the rights of workers and, in particular, their right not to join a union. The Taft-Hartley Act outlawed the **closed shop,** which required a worker to join an established union upon being hired. It continued to allow the **union shop,** which requires a worker to join a union within 30 days of being hired. But the Taft-Hartley Act gave states the option of outlawing the union shop as well by legislating right-to-work laws. So far 21 states have passed right-to-work laws. Finally, the Taft-Hartley Act gave the president the power to obtain an 80-day back-to-work court injunction to halt a strike if he believes that the strike threatens the nation's health or safety. Organized labor quite naturally viewed the Taft-Hartley Act as a significant step backward to the days of government hostility toward unions.

CLOSED SHOP

A labor union rule that requires a worker to join an established union upon being hired.

UNION SHOP

A labor union rule that requires a worker to join a union within 30 days after being hired.

The Landrum-Griffin Act of 1959 was a reaction to spreading corruption within the unions. It stipulated that all union procedures and elections must be democratic and required that the union representatives provide the members with a full financial disclosure of the union's operations.

Union Membership

Unions flourished in the 50 years from 1930 to 1980. As Table 18.2 indicates, union membership grew in two spurts, from 1930 to 1954 and again from 1964 to 1970. During the first growth period the increase in union membership exceeded the increase in the labor force, so that the percentage of the labor force in unions increased. The reverse was true after that period. The percentage of the labor force in unions has declined steadily since its peak in

TABLE 18.2 Union Membership in the United States, 1930–91

YEAR	PERCENTAGE OF NON-AGRICULTURAL EMPLOYMENT	MILLIONS OF WORKERS
1930	11.6	3.4
1940	26.9	8.7
1950	31.5	14.3
1954	33.7 (peak)	17.0
1960	31.5	17.0
1964	28.9	16.8
1970	27.3	19.4
1974	25.8	20.1
1980*	24.7	22.4
1986	18.0	17.0
1991	16.1	16.6

*Data from 1980 on include members in associations, such as the National Education Association, as well as members in unions. Association membership in 1980 was approximately 2.5 million employees.

SOURCES: U.S. Department of Commerce, Economics and Statistics Administration, Bureau of the Census, *Statistical Abstract of the United States, 1992* (Washington, D.C.: U.S. Government Printing Office, 1992); R. Ehrenberg and R. Smith, *Modern Labor Economics: Theory and Public Policy* (New York: HarperCollins, 1991), 446.

1954. Nonetheless, organized labor obtained a commanding presence in the U.S. economy that it retained until the 1980s. During the 1950s and 1960s roughly one-third of all non-agricultural wage and salary workers in the private sector and one-half of all blue-collar workers were members of unions. The troubled 1970s were testimony to the economic power that the unions had achieved. Union wages and salaries increased much more rapidly than did wages and salaries generally from 1970 to 1980.

Students today may well be surprised to learn that unions had achieved such success. The leading story about the unions in recent years has been the sharp decline of union membership and power, at least in the private sector. Refer again to Table 18.2. Union membership in the private sector plummeted from 1980 through 1986. Since the labor force continued to grow during that same period, the percentage of the labor force in unions fell even more rapidly. By 1986 only 14 percent of all non-agricultural wage and salary workers were members of unions (not counting associations). Union membership has continued to fall into the 1990s, although not so rapidly since 1986.

A less-publicized story during the 1980s was an equally dramatic rise in unionism within the public sector. Membership in public-sector unions increased rapidly from 1980 to 1986, so that by 1986, 40 percent of all union members belonged to public-sector unions. During the 1950s and 1960s public-sector unions accounted for only 14 percent of total union membership.[6]

The recent trends in public- and private-sector union membership have turned organized labor into a highly concentrated activity. In 1986, 40 percent of all union members belonged to one of six large unions, four in the private sector and two in the public sector: International Brotherhood of Teamsters

[6]For a complete discussion of the different experiences of private and public sector unions, see R. Freeman, "Contraction and Expansion: the Divergence of Private Sector and Public Sector Unionism in the United States," *Journal of Economic Perspectives* 2, No. 2 (Spring 1988): 63–88.

(IBT); United Auto Workers (UAW); International Ladies Garment Workers Union (ILGWU); Transportation Communications Union (TCU); National Education Association (NEA); and American Federation of State, County, and Municipal Employees (AFSCME).[7]

What caused the dramatic decline in private-sector union membership in the 1980s? Labor economists point to a whole host of causes, ranging from unfavorable structural and demographic changes within the economy, to increasing government hostility, to increasing and very effective employer hostility. Roughly speaking, everything that could go wrong for the unions did go wrong.

Regarding the structural and demographic changes within the economy, the unions' traditional base of support has been among male blue-collar workers in the oligopolistic manufacturing industries located in the North and Northeast. Every part of the unions' traditional base has been eroding over the past 20 to 30 years. The labor force has become increasingly female and white-collar, and the economy has been producing relatively more services and fewer manufactured goods. Also, economic activity has been leaving the North and Northeast, the "Rustbelt," for the South and Southwest, the "Sunbelt." Plant closings increased significantly in the North and Northeast during the 1980s, and with them large numbers of union members lost their jobs. Also, states in the South and Southwest tend to favor right-to-work laws. The citizens in those states are not particularly sympathetic to the unions.

As if these structural and demographic changes were not enough, the unions were subjected to increasing hostility from both the government and the employers. The Reagan administration was hardly a friend of the unions. President Reagan began his first term by firing all the striking air traffic controllers and replacing them with non-union labor. He also appointed a pro-management administrator to head the NLRB.

Employer hostility also greatly intensified during the 1980s. Employers had good reason to fear the unions. As noted above, the unions had succeeded in raising union wages faster than non-union wages during the 1970s, and an increasing number of studies were finding that the existence of a union reduces profits in and of itself. In addition, deregulation of the heavily unionized transportation industries and increased foreign competition had made the business environment more competitive. Managers did not want to be saddled with tough union demands in the new competitive environment.

Equally important, employers also had the means to resist the unions. The union organization and election procedures established by the NLRB forbid employers from engaging in unfair labor practices intended to discourage the formation of unions. But employers are allowed to try to persuade their employees to vote against the union during the organizing and election process. The persuasion of employees grew into a thriving business. Firms spent millions of dollars on consulting firms that specialize in dissuading employees from forming a union. Employers also harassed employees who tried to organize unions, by all accounts. The number of unfair labor practices filed with the NLRB skyrocketed. Employers had every incentive to engage in unfair practices, since the penalties for first-time offenders under the NLRA are virtually non-existent.

The employers' persuasion and harassment tactics worked beautifully, according to Harvard's Richard Freeman: "the preponderance of evidence is that

---

[7]Kaufman, *Economics of Labor Markets*, 461–463.

the extent of management opposition substantially determines the outcomes of organizing campaigns."[8] Today only a trickle of workers are being organized through NLRB procedures, and fewer still eventually win collectively bargained contracts. Freeman also believes that employer opposition to unions is by far the leading cause of the decline in private-sector union membership. The same structural and demographic changes that occurred in the U.S. economy also occurred in many other industrialized market economies; yet only the United States experienced a sharp decline in union membership. The feature that differentiates the United States is the NLRB union organizing and election process. No other country affords its employers such a golden opportunity to resist the unionization of its work force.

The incentives to resist unions do not exist in the public sector. Quite the contrary; public-sector employees are voters. Politicians who resist their efforts to organize risk being removed from office during the next election. Also, unions can help administrators win larger budget increases. The interests of administrators and the unions are not necessarily adversarial, as they are in the private sector. These political incentives, combined with a number of recent changes in state and federal laws that were more favorable to public-sector unions, fostered the rapid growth in union membership in the public sector.

Collective Bargaining

Collective bargaining, the essence of union activity, can have a profound effect on labor market outcomes. Let's return to the example of the pure monopsonist in the preceding section to see how collective bargaining changes the relationship between a firm and its workers. Imagine that the workers form a union and enter into collective bargaining with the monopsonist. At the very least the union wants to improve on the pure monopsony outcome, in which the firm hires 5 workers at a wage of $5. To keep the example as simple as possible assume that the union and the firm bargain only over the wage. Once the wage has been determined, the firm can then hire as many workers as it wants at the bargained wage.

Collective bargaining fundamentally alters how both the firm and the workers view the market. The crucial change from the firm's perspective is the marginal cost of hiring labor. Once the bargaining process sets the wage, that wage becomes the marginal cost of hiring labor. For example, if the firm and the union agree on a wage of $6, then the firm can hire as many workers as it wants at $6. Therefore, the marginal cost of hiring an additional worker is always $6. In effect, the supply curve from the firm's point of view becomes horizontal at $6, just as it would be if the firm were hiring in a competitive market at the same wage. The supply and the marginal cost curves, S_L and MC_L, in Figure 18.3 are no longer relevant to the firm.

The firm continues to hire the number of workers at which marginal cost and marginal revenue are equal in order to maximize profit. Since the bargained wage is the marginal cost and the MRP_L is the marginal revenue, the firm always hires along its MRP_L curve. Refer back to Figure 18.3 and Table 18.1. If the bargained wage is $6, the firm hires 6 workers, since the MRP_L is $6 at 6 workers; if the bargained wage is $12, the firm hires 4 workers, since the

[8] Freeman, "Contraction and Expansion," 83.

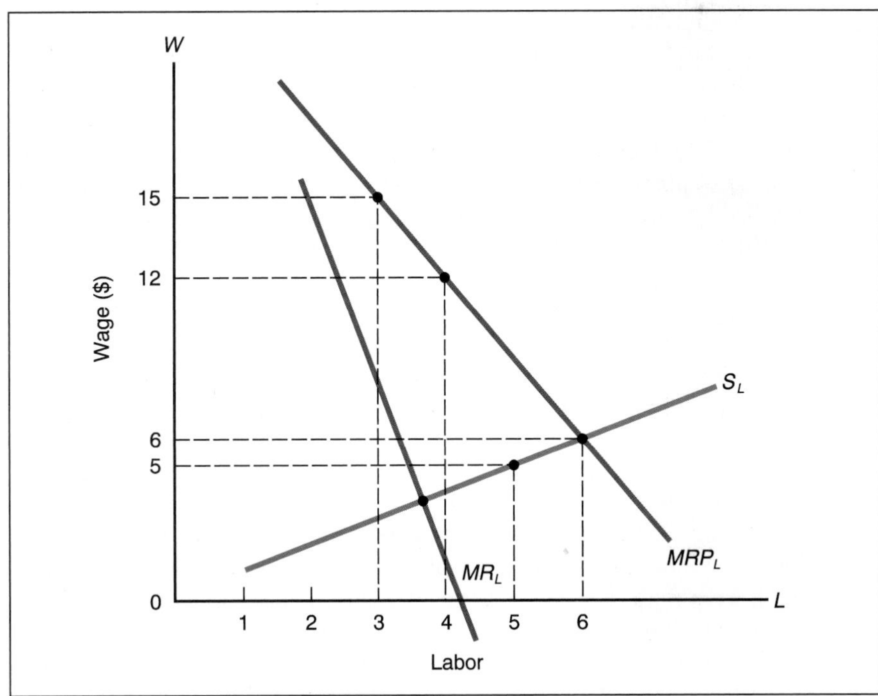

FIGURE 18.4

The Bargaining Options for a Labor Union

The figure shows the various bargaining options for a labor union when it confronts a firm with monopsony power. The firm will hire along its marginal revenue product of labor curve, MRP_L, at whatever the bargained wage is. As a result, the marginal revenue from the union's point of view, MR_L, lies below MRP_L. The marginal cost of supplying labor from the union's point of view, is the labor supply curve, S_L. Three possible wage options are: 1) maximize employment at a wage of \$6, with 6 workers hired; 2) maximize the total wages received by the workers, which occurs when MR_L equals zero. Assuming no part-time labor, the wage is \$12, with 4 workers hired; 3) maximize the workers' surplus, which occurs at the intersection of MR_L and S_L Assuming no part-time labor, the wage is \$15, with 3 workers hired.

MRP_L is \$12 at 4 workers; and so forth. The MRP_L curve is the firm's demand curve for labor at each bargained wage.

The presence of the union completely changes the workers' perspective of the marketplace. No longer are the workers powerless individuals offering labor along the supply curve, S_L, in Figure 18.3. Instead, they are able to view the market through their elected representatives exactly as a pure monopolist views a product market. The union representatives see the firm's MRP_L curve as its demand curve for labor. They have to decide which wage-labor combination on the MRP_L curve is in the best interests of the union's members.

Table 18.3 reproduces the data from Table 18.1 in a manner that emphasizes the perspective of the union. Figure 18.4 corresponds to Table 18.3. The first and second columns of Table 18.3 reproduce points on the supply curve of labor, S_L, from Figure 18.3. The wages that the individual workers require in

TABLE 18.3 Collective Bargaining from the Union's Perspective

QUANTITY OF LABOR (L)	WAGE ALONG SUPPLY CURVE (W)	MARGINAL REVENUE PRODUCT (MRP_L)	TOTAL WAGES ($MRP_L \cdot L$)	MARGINAL REVENUE (MR_L)
1	\$1	\$21	\$21	\$21
2	2	18	36	15
3	3	15	45	9
4	4	12	48	3
5	5	9	45	−3
6	6	6	36	−9

order to offer their labor to the firm have not changed. Therefore, *from the union's perspective,* S_L is the marginal cost of supplying labor; it indicates the wage that is necessary to bring forth each additional worker. The third column of Table 18.3 reproduces the MRP_L from Table 18.1. It is the demand for labor from the union's perspective. The fourth column of Table 18.3 indicates the total wages paid at each quantity of labor hired. It differs from the total wage column in Table 18.1 because the bargaining process causes the firm to hire along its MRP_L curve, not the supply curve of labor, S_L, as before. So, for example, if the firm hires 5 workers, the bargained wage must have been \$9, for a total wage bill of \$45 (\$9 · 5 workers = \$45). The firm no longer hires 5 workers for a wage of \$5 as it did prior to establishment of the union.

Notice also that the MRP_L is not the marginal revenue received from supplying labor from the union's perspective. Instead, the marginal revenue is the change in the total wages received by the union members for each additional worker hired. The marginal revenue from the union's perspective at each quantity of labor is given in the fifth column of Table 18.3. For example, when the number of workers hired increases from 1 to 2, total wages increase from \$21 to \$36 (fourth column). The change in the total wages received is \$15 (\$15 = \$36 − \$21). Therefore, \$15 is the marginal revenue from supplying the second worker from the union's perspective. The marginal revenue from supplying labor is represented as MR_L in Figure 18.4. Notice that it lies everywhere below the MRP_L curve, just as MR lies below the demand curve for a pure monopolist in a product market.

The Goals of the Union

The union is trying to improve on the pure monopsony outcome of 5 workers hired at a wage of \$5. Which labor-wage combination on the firm's MRP_L should it choose? The answer is unclear. The union will surely try to raise the wage to \$6 if it can. At a bargained wage of \$6 the firm hires 6 workers. The union's members clearly gain because both the wage and the total number of workers hired increase relative to the pure monopsony outcome. In fact, the \$6 wage, at the intersection of the MRP_L and the S_L curves, maximizes the employment of union workers. At a bargained wage greater than \$6, the firm hires fewer than 6 workers. At a bargained wage less than \$6, fewer than 6 workers will want to work for the firm. In general, the intersection of the firm's demand curve, MRP_L, and the workers' supply curve, S_L, is the employment-maximizing solution under collective bargaining.

Bargaining for a wage above \$6 poses a dilemma for the union relative to the maximum employment solution because the firm hires fewer than 6 workers at any wage above \$6. Those workers who continue to work at the higher wage gain. The workers who are laid off because of the higher wage lose. So the union's representatives have no clear-cut best wage to bargain for. The wage they finally decide to shoot for most likely results from a political calculation: Who stands to gain from a higher wage, who stands to lose, and how much voting power do the gainers and losers have within the union? The elected representatives cannot please everyone, but they have to satisfy the majority of the members to remain in office.

Economic considerations alone suggest that the representatives bargain for one of two wages above \$6: (1) the wage that maximizes the total wage bill or

(2) the wage that maximizes the total surplus of the union members. The total wage bill is at a maximum when the marginal revenue that the workers receive from supplying labor is zero. In Figure 18.4, MR_L hits the horizontal axis between 4 and 5 workers. If we assume that only 4 or 5 workers can be hired, the union will choose 4 workers, the last full unit at which MR_L is positive. The bargained wage that causes firms to hire 4 workers is the firm's MRP_L at 4 workers, a wage of \$12. Total wages are \$48 (\$48 = \$12 · 4 workers). We can see from column 4 in Table 18.3 that \$48 is the largest value of total wages. The maximize total wages strategy is equivalent to the maximize sales revenue strategy of a firm with monopoly power in a product market. Recall that the firm chooses the output at which *MR* is zero in order to maximize sales.

The total surplus of the union members is the difference between the total wages they receive and the total cost to them of supplying their labor. The members' total surplus is at a maximum when the marginal revenue and the marginal cost from supplying labor are equal from the workers' point of view. $MR_L = MC_L$ at the intersection of the MR_L and the S_L curves, between 3 and 4 workers in Figure 18.4. Again, if work must be supplied in whole units, the union will choose 3 workers, the last whole unit at which MR_L exceeds MC_L (S_L). The bargained wage that will cause the firm to hire 3 workers is the firm's MRP_L at 3 workers, a wage of \$15. The maximize workers' surplus strategy is equivalent to the maximize profit strategy of a firm with monopoly power in a product market. Recall that the firm chooses the output at which $MR = MC$ in order to maximize profits.

Whether the union's representatives will choose either of these economic solutions is problematic, however, because the interests of the union members are not analogous to the interests of the stockholders of a firm. For instance, if a firm maximizes profit, all stockholders share in the profit in proportion to the amount of stock that they hold. By contrast, if the union's representatives follow the maximize workers' surplus strategy, the 3 workers who remain employed capture all the surplus. Workers 4, 5, and 6 lose relative to the maximize employment strategy. Economic theory alone cannot predict what the union's representatives will choose to do.

Uncertainty about the goals of the union is not the only reason why the outcome of a collective bargaining process is uncertain. A second reason is that both the firm and the union have considerable market power. In our example, the firm enters the bargaining process as the only buyer, a pure monopsonist. The union enters the bargaining process as the only seller, a pure monopolist. Economists refer to a market situation consisting of one buyer confronting one seller as a **bilateral monopoly.** The final outcome of a bilateral monopoly depends on the relative strengths of each party: For instance, who has the resources and patience to wait out a strike? Presumably the wage will be somewhere between \$5, the pure monopsony outcome, and \$12, the maximize workers' surplus outcome. Beyond that, all economic analysis can offer is the obvious generalization: The stronger the firm, the lower the wage; the stronger the union, the higher the wage.

BILATERAL MONOPOLY
A market situation consisting of one buyer confronting one seller.

Other Union Methods to Raise Wages

Unions employ other means besides the threat of a strike to promote higher wages, better working conditions, and more jobs for their members. Generally speaking, the other strategies fall into one of two categories: (1) attempts to restrict the supply of workers to unionized jobs and (2) attempts to increase the demand for union workers. These strategies follow standard market principles: Other things equal, the lower the supply of a service or the higher its demand, the higher the price. In this case, price refers to union wages and other fringe benefits.

Supply restrictions involve targeting particular categories of workers and preventing them from applying for full union membership. Targeting by age is one such strategy. The crafts and trades have apprenticeship programs that prevent younger workers from becoming full-fledged union members until the period of apprenticeship ends. Unions have also supported compulsory retirement laws that remove older workers from the market. Minorities were also an easy target in the past. Some unions blatantly discriminated against minorities before discrimination in hiring was outlawed by the federal government. The construction trades were particularly guilty of discrimination against blacks.

Attempts to increase the demand for union members take many different forms. Some unions finance advertising campaigns for the products that their members produce. The television ads that urge us to buy clothing with the union label are an example. Product advertising recognizes the economic principle that the demand for labor is a derived demand; it depends in part on the demand for the product that the labor produces. A second strategy involves limiting the number of substitutes for union labor. The unions have used their political muscle to support minimum wage legislation, which raises the cost to firms of hiring unskilled non-union labor. Unions have championed tough anti-immigration laws for the same reason. They fear that new waves of immigrants will offer employers a large supply of low-wage labor that firms could use to undermine the bargaining power of the unions. Bargaining for tight job classifications and rigid work rules is another strategy that limits firms' ability to substitute away from union labor. On construction jobs, for instance, union contracts may stipulate that electricians have to install the electrical fixtures, but that carpenters have to cut the holes for the fixtures. At their worst the work rules lead to **featherbedding,** in which firms are forced to hire workers who are of no value to them whatsoever. When the railroads introduced diesel engines to replace coal-burning engines, the unions won the right to have a coal fireman on the diesels to save the firemen's jobs.

FEATHERBEDDING

A work rule in which firms are forced to hire workers who are of no value to them.

The various union strategies for restricting supply and increasing demand have no doubt been helpful to organized labor. But the fact remains that the strike is far and away the most effective weapon in the unions' arsenal.

The Economic Effects of Unions

Have unions been good or bad for the U.S. economy? Few economic questions stir the emotions as much as this one. Some people see the unions as the savior of working men and women. Others blame the unions for just about everything they see wrong with the economy. Economists have focused on two issues in trying to provide an objective answer to the question: (1) the effect of unions on efficiency and productivity and (2) the effect of unions on wages.

A general point needs to be understood before turning to the specific evidence on each issue. Whether unions are beneficial or harmful depends to a large extent on whether they serve primarily to reduce monopsony power or

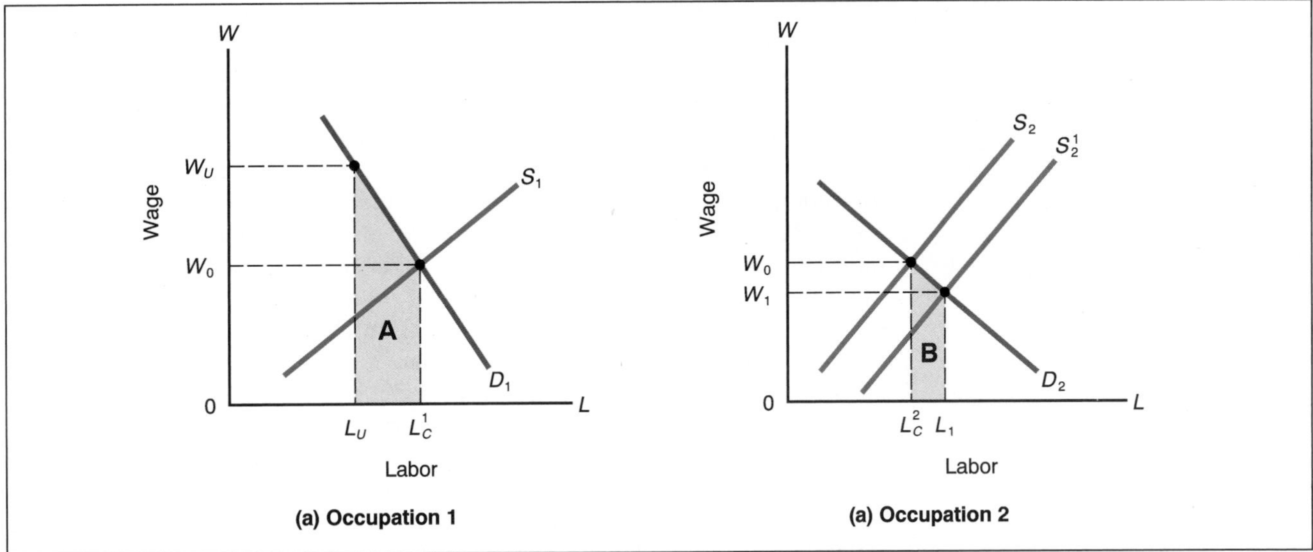

FIGURE 18.5

Labor Unions Segment Labor Markets

The labor markets for occupation 1 in Figure 18.5(a) and occupation 2 in Figure 18.5(b) would be competitive without a labor union, and workers are willing and able to work in either occupation. The equilibrium wage would be W_0 in both occupations, at the intersection of D_1 and S_1 in Figure 18.5(a), and D_2 and S_2 in Figure 18.5(b). Suppose a labor union organizes the workers in occupation 1 and sets a wage of W_U. At the higher wage, firms employ only L_U workers in occupation 1 instead of L_C^1 workers. The displaced worker move to occupation 2, shifting the supply curve out to S_2^1, and establishing a new equilibrium at (L_1, W_1). The union has segmented the labor markets, causing the wage in occupation 2 to decrease from W_0 to W_1. Also, the loss in productivity from the displaced workers in occupation 1, the shaded area A in Figure 18.5(a), exceeds their productivity in occupation 2, the shaded area B in Figure 18.5(b). The labor union is inefficient.

to reduce competition in labor markets. Unions are clearly beneficial when they counteract and reduce firms' monopsony power through collective bargaining. Their actions in this case tend to increase employment and output, lower prices to consumers, and reduce profits ill-gotten through the exercise of market power. Unfortunately, unions do not come into being solely to counteract the monopsony power of large corporations. Unions often form in markets that would otherwise be highly competitive. When this happens, unions tend to segment labor markets and reduce competition.

A labor market is **segmented** whenever workers who are qualified for a particular job are denied access to that job. Two equally qualified and productive workers can earn different wages in a segmented labor market. This cannot happen in a perfectly competitive labor market. When labor unions segment competitive markets, organized labor gains at the expense of equally qualified and productive non-union labor, and the efficiency of the economy suffers.

SEGMENTED LABOR MARKET

A labor market in which workers who are qualified for a particular job are denied access to that job.

Figure 18.5 illustrates the effects of unions when they reduce competition by segmenting labor markets. The two graphs depict competitive labor markets for two occupations, 1 and 2, with market demand and supply curves D_1, S_1, D_2, and S_2, respectively. We assume that the occupations require the same skills and are equally attractive to workers. Therefore, if the Laws of Supply and Demand are free to operate in both markets, the equilibrium wage, W_0, must be the same in each market. L_C^1 workers are employed in occupation 1, and L_C^2 workers are employed in occupation 2 in the competitive equilibrium.

Suppose that union organizers are able to form a union in occupation 1 and win a wage of W_U through collective bargaining. The quantity of labor demanded by all the firms hiring in occupation 1 declines to L_U as a result of the higher wage. The $(L_C^1 - L_U)$ workers who lose their jobs in occupation 1 turn to occupation 2 for employment. The supply curve shifts outward in that market from S_2 to S_2^1, establishing a new equilibrium for occupation 2 at (L_1, W_1).

The supply and demand analysis shows that labor unions have the effect of segmenting markets that would otherwise be competing. Market segmentation is pernicious because it violates the principle of horizontal equity: Equals are treated unequally. Differences in pay among identical individuals are not equalizing differences. Instead, people earn different incomes just because they happen to work in different industries or because of irrelevant personal characteristics such as race, gender, or family background. Furthermore, the differences in earnings persist; they are not broken down by the usual competitive market forces.

In our example, the $(L_C^1 - L_U)$ displaced workers are fully willing and able to work in occupation 1, but are prevented from doing so by the actions of the union. Market segmentation benefits the union workers who remain employed in occupation 1. Their wages rise from W_0 to W_U. But *all* other workers lose; their wages decline from W_0 to W_1.

In addition, the overall efficiency of the economy declines. Recall that the market demand curve for labor under competition is the value of labor's marginal product. The height of the demand curve at each quantity of labor measures the value to a firm of the last worker hired. The $(L_C^1 - L_U)$ workers who transfer from occupation 1 to occupation 2 had values of marginal product between W_0 and W_U in occupation 1. The total value of production lost in occupation 1 is the shaded area A under D_1 and between L_C^1 and L_U in Figure 18.5(a). The values of these workers' marginal products are only between W_0 and W_1 in occupation 2. The total value of production gained by employing them in occupation 2 is the shaded area B under D_2 and between L_C^2 and L_1 in Figure 18.5(b). The difference in the shaded areas, $(A - B)$ is the deadweight efficiency loss arising from the misallocation of labor. The union prevents some workers from being employed where they have the most value to society.

In summary, unions can be quite harmful when they serve to segment markets and undermine competitive market forces. Unions often claim to represent the interests of all workers. In fact, when they reduce competition, their gains come partially at the expense of non-union workers.

EFFICIENCY AND PRODUCTIVITY Economists cannot agree whether unions are harmful or beneficial to the overall efficiency and productivity of the economy. The traditional view is that unions are harmful for the most part. Proponents of this view argue that unions serve primarily to reduce competition rather than to counter monopsony power. Consequently, they cause labor to be misallocated and reduce economic efficiency, as we have just seen. Unions also prevent firms from achieving least-cost methods of production by blocking the introduction of new technologies that would replace union workers and by insisting on tight job classifications and rigid work rules that reduce firms' ability to substitute among factors of production. Finally, union contracts call for promotions on the basis of seniority rather than merit. All these practices impede the efficient operation of the economy.

Two Harvard economists, Richard Freeman and James Medoff, have recently mounted a serious challenge to the traditional view. They argue that unions actually improve efficiency and productivity in a variety of ways. First, the mere existence of a union has a shock effect, inspiring management to run a tighter ship. Second, the union creates a more productive work force. The advantages begin at the hiring stage. Because the unions restrict entry, they generate an excess supply of workers. This enables firms to choose the best workers from the pool of candidates. Then, once the workers join the firm, the union improves their morale and productivity. To cite one example, promotion by seniority removes the potential for destructive competition between older and younger workers. Finally, the presence of a union reduces turnover because workers can express their dissatisfactions through the union rather than by quitting. Lower turnover reduces firms' hiring and training costs and provides them with a more experienced work force.[9]

The Freeman-Medoff challenge is well taken. About all one can say is that the effect of unions on efficiency and productivity remains an open question.

UNION VERSUS NON-UNION WAGES The question of the unions' effect on wage income has two parts: (1) Do unions raise the wages of their members? (2) What effect have unions had on the overall distribution of income?

Unions appear to have a considerable effect on the wages of their members. In 1988, for example, the average weekly earnings of union workers were $476, whereas the average weekly earnings of non-union workers were $356. The union wage was 34 percent higher. Fringe benefits also average 30 to 35 percent more in union firms.[10] These data overstate the effect of the unions on wages (and fringe benefits), however. The proper question is the effect of unions on wages *other things equal.* What percentage of the wage difference is attributable to unions independently from all other factors that might cause union wages to be higher?

Correcting for the effect of other factors that might influence wages is important because all is not equal between union and non-union workers. Union and non-union workers are employed in different occupations and industries and have different personal characteristics, on average. Relative to non-union workers, union workers tend to be concentrated in the capital-intensive manufacturing oligopolies in the North and Northeast, working in blue-collar occupations that are either unpleasant or dangerous. Also, union workers are disproportionately male and black, and they have more experience than do non-union workers. Each of these differences could explain some of the difference in the union wage. To give just a few examples, men earn much more than women, on average. Their wage advantage may be due to discrimination against women or to a more stable employment record, not to the fact that men are more likely to belong to a union. Providing workers with more capital makes them more productive and raises their wages. Workers employed in dangerous or unpleasant jobs typically receive equalizing pay increases that compensate them for working under these conditions. Union wages could be higher than non-union wages for any or all of these reasons, none of which has anything to do with union membership itself.

Another point to remember is that market forces nearly always have an important effect on wages. Sellers of any good or service tend to do well when the demand for their product is highly inelastic and growing rapidly. Conversely, sellers do poorly when the demand for their product is highly elastic and stagnant. The same holds true for labor. Long-distance truckers are a good example of the importance of market forces. Truckers' wages grew rapidly in the post–World War II period up to 1980. They no doubt benefited from the strength of the Teamsters union, one of the nation's largest and most powerful unions. But market forces played a large role in their success, too. The construction of the interstate highway system and innovations such as placing

---

[9]R. Freeman and J. Medoff, *What Do Unions Do?* (New York: Basic Books, 1984).

[10]Kaufman, *Economics of Labor Markets*, 583–584.

trucks on trains made trucking the lowest-cost method of shipping products for many manufacturers. The demand for trucking grew rapidly, and along with it the demand for truck drivers. The demand for drivers is also highly inelastic. The elasticity of demand for any factor of production depends on three qualities: (1) the elasticity of demand for the product that the factor produces, (2) the ability of firms to substitute away from the factor as factor prices change, and (3) the importance of the factor in the overall costs of the firm. The elasticity of demand is *lower* the *lower* the elasticity of demand for the product, the *less easily* firms can substitute the factor in production, and *less important* the factor is in overall costs.

The demand for truck drivers is inelastic on all counts. Long-distance trucking was heavily regulated prior to 1980, with the result that unionized long-distance trucking firms faced little or no competition. The demand for their services was highly inelastic. Also, trucking firms cannot substitute other factors of production for a driver. Finally, the drivers' salaries are a relatively small part of the overall costs of producing goods and shipping them to market. In summary, the long-distance truckers had all the market forces aligned in their favor prior to 1980. We can safely conclude that their wages would have grown rapidly even without the Teamsters union.

The deregulation of the industry just prior to 1980 illustrates very dramatically the potent effect of market forces on wages. Deregulation opened the industry up to non-union carriers. As a result, the demand for unionized carriers fell and became much more elastic. The effect on the unionized drivers was devastating. Over 100,000 union truck drivers lost their jobs between 1980 to 1986, and their wage advantage over non-union drivers fell by 40 percent. Even the powerful Teamsters union could not hold fast against the forces of competition.

What, then, is the independent, other things equal effect of the unions on wages? Economists have devoted a large amount of research to this question without reaching any definite conclusions. The consensus opinion is that unions raise the wages of their members anywhere from 10 to 30 percent. Since the actual union–non-union wage difference is 34 percent, unions may account for anywhere from 29 percent ($29 = 10/34 \cdot 100$) to 86 percent ($88 = 30/34 \cdot 100$) of the actual difference in union wages.[11]

UNIONS AND THE DISTRIBUTION OF INCOME Unions affect the distribution of income in five ways, one of which tends to make the distribution less equal and four of which tend to make the distribution more equal. The unequalizing tendency is the market segmentation effect analyzed above. Unions artificially increase union wages at the expense of non-union wages when they segment otherwise competitive labor markets. In doing so, they make wage incomes less equal. This effect is weakened somewhat by two factors. Some workers who are laid off by union firms do not move to other markets and drive wages down elsewhere. Instead, they go on unemployment and wait out the unionized market in the hope that a union job will eventually become available. Also, some non-union firms grant wage increases in line with the wage increases at union firms in order to appease their workers so that they will not form a union.

---

[11]Kaufman, *Economics of Labor Markets*, 588–594. The data on truck drivers is on p. 602.

Unions equalize the distribution of income in four ways. First, unions redistribute income from profits to wages to the extent that they reduce monopsony power. Since profit income is highly concentrated in the hands of the rich, the effect of this redistribution is equalizing. Second, union contracts stipulate that all workers in a given job classification receive the same pay regardless of age or experience. Hence, unions tend to flatten the age-earnings profile. The gap between the highest and the lowest wages is 42 percent smaller, on average, in union plants than in non-union plants. Third, national unions such as the United Auto Workers negotiate the same contract for all workers within a company no matter where the plants are located. They also tend to equalize wages throughout the industry. By doing so, unions tend to reduce wage differences within occupations. Finally, unions tend to reduce the gap between higher-income white-collar workers and lower-income blue-collar workers. The incomes of white-collar workers are 50 percent higher, on average, than the incomes of blue-collar workers in non-union firms in the United States. In union firms, the incomes of white-collar workers are only 33 percent higher.

Harvard's Richard Freeman believes that the four equalizing effects more than offset the one unequalizing effect. He estimates that unions make the distribution of income about 3 percent more equal.[12]

In thinking about the economic effects of unions, one point made earlier should be kept firmly in mind. Union membership has declined sharply in the 1980s, to the point where now only 14 percent of the labor force in the private sector is unionized. Much of our knowledge of the economic effects of unions comes from studies using data prior to 1980, when the unions' membership was larger and the unions more powerful. Therefore, the results of these studies must represent an upper limit to the effect of unions. The overall impact of the unions on the U.S. economy has clearly diminished since 1980.

SUMMARY

Chapter 18 began by presenting the four main facts about labor market earnings that economists have tried to explain.

1. Earnings are highly variable both across and within occupations.
2. The average age-earnings profile, the pattern of average earnings by age, is hump-shaped, rising from young adulthood into middle age and then declining during the last years of work.
3. Age-earnings profiles are higher and increase more steeply as years of education increase.
4. Women and nonwhite minorities earn considerably less than do white males, on average, and women have flatter age-earnings profiles than do men.

Labor markets are fairly competitive overall, which means that competitive market forces explain much of the variation in earnings. The second section of the chapter reviewed the principal results from Chapter 9 on perfectly competitive labor markets.

5. The equilibrium wage in perfectly competitive labor markets is the value of labor's marginal product, equal to the marginal (physical) product of labor times the price of the good or the service that the worker is producing.

[12]For a complete discussion of the distributional effects of labor unions, see Kaufman, *Economics of Labor Markets*, 602–605.

6. If all workers are identical and all jobs are equal, then everyone earns the same wage. If workers are identical, but jobs differ in terms of attractiveness or skill requirements, then wages differ across occupations. Everyone is equally well off, however, because all wage differences are equalizing wage differences that just compensate workers for the relative desirability of their jobs. If both people and jobs differ, then labor markets are noncompeting, and wages are determined by supply and demand in each market. Some workers earn an economic rent, the difference between their wage and the wage required to keep them on the job.

The third section of the chapter explored how the market power of large firms affects the pattern of wages.

7. If firms have monopoly power in product markets, but hire in competitive labor markets, then the wage is the marginal revenue product of labor, equal to the marginal (physical) product of labor times the marginal revenue that the firm receives from selling its output. The marginal revenue product is less than the value of marginal product because marginal revenue is less than price. Therefore, firms extract some of their monopoly profit at the expense of labor.
8. Firms with market power in labor markets are said to possess monopsony power. Firms with monopsony power face an upward-sloping supply curve for their labor and are wage setters. They hire labor such that the marginal revenue product of labor equals the marginal cost of labor, which is above the wage. Consequently, monopsony power can drive wages far below the value of labor's marginal product.
9. Although extreme examples of monopsony power can arise in certain markets, as in the professional sports leagues, significant monopsony power is unlikely to be widespread in the United States.

Labor unions arose to counteract the market power of business firms and to promote the interests of labor generally. The final section of the chapter explored the economic practices and consequences of labor unions.

10. The essence of union activity is collective bargaining, in which elected representatives bargain with management on behalf of the union members over wages and other working conditions. The primary bargaining chip of the representatives is the threat of a strike by the members.
11. The first unions in the United States were craft unions, which had little economic power. The union movement gained considerable momentum during the 1930s with the advent of the industrial union and the passage of two landmark pro-labor laws, the Norris-LaGuardia Act and the National Labor Relations or Wagner Act. The Wagner Act is considered the Magna Carta of the union movement. Among other provisions, the act established procedures for organizing unions under the supervision of the National Labor Relations Board.
12. Union membership in the United States grew rapidly from the 1930s to the 1960s, reaching a high point of 33.7 percent of the non-agricultural labor force in 1954. The unions wielded considerable economic power throughout the 1960s and 1970s. Union membership in the private sector then declined precipitously from the late 1970s through the mid-1980s, so that unions now account for only about 14 percent of the labor force. The decline in membership resulted from a variety of factors, including unfa-

vorable structural and demographic changes, increasing government hostility toward unions, and increasing and highly effective employer hostility toward the unions. Membership in public-sector unions continued to grow throughout this same period.

13. Collective bargaining gives workers monopoly power in selling their labor. The goals of the union are unclear, though, because an increase in the bargained wage can reduce the total employment of union members. Two likely economic goals of unions are to maximize worker surplus and to maximize the total wage bill.
14. A bargaining situation in which a pure monopsonist confronts a single labor union is called a bilateral monopoly. The final outcome of a bilateral monopoly depends on the relative bargaining strengths of the two parties.
15. Unions use other methods besides the strike to promote their interests. They attempt to restrict the supply of union labor by such means as establishing apprenticeship programs and lobbying for early retirement legislation. Some unions engaged in outright discrimination prior to the passage of the civil rights laws. They attempt to increase the demand for union labor by such means as mounting buy-union advertising campaigns, bargaining for restrictive work rules, and lobbying for tough anti-immigration laws.
16. The economic effects of unions depend largely on whether they serve to counteract monopsony power or to restrict competition in labor markets. To the extent they counteract monopsony power, they can be highly beneficial, increasing employment and wages, lowering prices, and reducing monopoly profits. To the extent they reduce competition, they can be quite harmful, segmenting labor markets so that union members gain at the expense of all other workers, and the overall efficiency of the economy is reduced.
17. Unions appear to raise wages from 10 to 30 percent, other things equal. Unions also tend to have a slightly equalizing effect on the overall distribution of income.
18. Economists have not reached a consensus on whether unions make the work force more or less productive. The traditional view is that unions retard productivity through such practices as restrictive work rules. This view is now being challenged by economists who believe that unions enhance productivity by allowing firms to choose from a larger pool of job applicants, by reducing turnover, and by improving worker morale.

KEY TERMS

age-earnings profile
bilateral monopoly
closed shop
collective bargaining
craft union
featherbedding
industrial union
marginal revenue product of labor
monopsony power
pure monopsony
segmented labor market
union shop

QUESTIONS

1. List and briefly describe the four main facts about labor market earnings in the United States.
2. What factors determine the distribution of wages and salaries in competitive labor markets? In your answer, be sure to include the concepts of equalizing wage differences and economic rent as they apply.
3. What is the marginal revenue product of labor (MRP_L)? How does it differ from the value of labor's marginal product (VMP_L), as defined in Chapter 9?
4. a. What is monopsony power?
   b. What factors determine the degree of monopsony power that a firm possesses?
   c. Give some examples of factor markets in which monopsony power is likely to be present.
5. Consider the following firm with a demand curve for labor given by MRP_L and a labor supply curve given by the column denoted W, the wage:

QUANTITY OF LABOR	MRP_L	W
1	30	2
2	25	3
3	20	4
4	15	5
5	10	6
6	5	7

   a. What type of firm and labor market do the data in the table above represent?
   b. What is the average cost of labor to the firm?
   c. Calculate the marginal cost to the firm of hiring labor.
   d. What is the profit-maximizing number of workers?
6. Refer again to the data in question 5. This time suppose that the firm's employees become union members.
   a. How does the process of collective bargaining change the employment outcome you found in question 5?
   b. Find the marginal revenue from hiring each additional worker from the union's perspective.
   c. If the bargained wage is $15, how many workers will the firm hire?
7. Two goals that union representatives might bargain for are (1) maximizing the total wage bill and (2) maximizing the total surplus of the union members. Can economic theory predict what the union's representatives will choose to do? Which of the two goals would you choose if you were the union representative?
8. Comment on the following statement: Unions have a different effect on the overall distribution of income if they serve primarily to counteract monopsony power than if they segment labor markets that would otherwise be competitive.
9. a. How do unions attempt to promote higher wages and better working conditions for their members?
   b. How do these methods differ in their relative success in achieving the unions' goals?
   c. Which (if any) of these methods would be preferable from the firms' point of view?
10. a. What are some of the factors that led to the increase in union membership from the 1930s to the 1970s?
    b. What are some of the explanations offered for the sharp decline in private-sector union membership during the 1980s?
    c. Why did the public-sector unions not experience the same decline in membership during the 1980s?
11. *Extra credit:* "Recession, unification and de-industrialization have put Germany's mighty unions under pressure. Employers are gaining the upper hand" (*The Economist*, January 23, 1993, p. 63). Explain how the factors mentioned in this quote could weaken the position of unions in Germany.

CHAPTER

19

Human Capital Theory and Discrimination

LEARNING OBJECTIVES

CONCEPTS TO LEARN

- Human capital theory
- Formal education, on-the-job training, and earnings
- Internal labor markets
- Efficiency wages and corporate tournaments
- The segmentation theory of labor markets
- Discrimination in labor markets
- The federal laws against labor market discrimination

CONCEPTS TO RECALL

- The marginal benefit equals marginal cost decision rule [6]
- How competitive markets help determine the distribution of wage and salary income [9]
- The profit maximizing decision rule for hiring labor [9]
- The four main facts about wages and salaries in the United States [18]
- The age-earnings profile [18]
- Segmented labor markets [18]

Chapter 19 discusses the effects of education and labor market discrimination on wages and salaries. Combining these two topics in one chapter may seem odd at first sight, but they have a natural connection. They are the leading hypotheses for explaining the fourth main fact about U.S. labor markets from Chapter 18: why women and nonwhite minorities do not fare as well as white males do in the U.S. labor markets. One hypothesis is that women and nonwhite minorities suffer lower earnings and poorer job opportunities because they receive less education than do white males. The competing hypothesis is that outright discrimination against women and nonwhite minorities holds down their earnings and job opportunities. The two hypotheses are not mutually exclusive; most economists believe that lack of education and discrimination both contribute to the labor market disadvantages of women and nonwhite minorities. The only disagreement is over the relative importance of the two explanations.

Education and discrimination are not only relevant to the labor market experiences of women and nonwhite minorities. They also go a long way toward explaining the other three facts about labor market outcomes that we discussed in Chapter 18: the variability of earnings, the average age-earnings profile, and the effect of education on the age-earnings profile. In particular, they help explain what lies ahead for those of you who see yourselves entering the corporate "fast track" after college.

The first section of Chapter 19 analyzes the relationship between education and earnings. The second section then adds the problem of discrimination in labor markets, the most pernicious form of market segmentation. Space limitations prevent a complete analysis of discrimination by race as well as gender. Therefore, we have chosen to focus on discrimination against women. Many of the issues discussed apply to racial discrimination as well. We will note the similarities and differences between gender and racial discrimination as the discussion proceeds.

EDUCATION AND EARNINGS: HUMAN CAPITAL THEORY

Economists refer to expenditure on education as an investment in human capital because education makes people more productive and increases their earnings, just as investment in physical capital makes business firms more productive and increases firms' profits. The analysis of the relationship between education and earnings is called the **theory of human capital.** Workers receive two distinct kinds of education: formal schooling prior to joining the work force, ranging from elementary and secondary school to graduate school; and on-the-job training supplied by their employers once they enter the work force.

HUMAN CAPITAL THEORY

A theory that analyzes the relationship between education and earnings, on the assumption that education increases people's earnings by making them more productive.

Citizens in the United States have long chosen to invest heavily in their human capital. A 1973 study of wealth in the United States commissioned by the U.S. Congress estimated that U.S. citizens had accumulated over $8 trillion of human capital through education, approximately $39,000 per person. The value of human capital was somewhat larger than the value of physical capital in place in 1973, which the study estimated to be $7.6 trillion.[1] Small wonder, then, that economists believe that education is an important determinant of wage and salary income in the United States.

Formal education and on-the-job training each has a significant impact on the pattern of wages and salaries. Taken together, they go a long way toward explaining the four main facts about wage and salary income.

Formal Education

Formal education refers to all schooling received in institutions outside the labor force, from elementary school through graduate school. It also includes general vocational training by institutions established for that purpose and not associated with any one business firm. Formal education gives people **general training** from a labor market perspective. It teaches basic skills—reading, writing, arithmetic, analytical thinking, familiarity with computers, and so forth—that are useful in a number of occupations and that workers can take with them whenever they change jobs.

FORMAL EDUCATION

Refers to all schooling received in institutions outside the labor force, from elementary school through graduate school, and includes general vocational training by institutions established for that purpose and not associated with any one business firm.

GENERAL TRAINING

In a labor market context, the training people receive that teaches basic skills—reading, writing, arithmetic, analytical thinking, familiarity with computers, and so forth—that are useful in a number of occupations and that workers can take with them whenever they change jobs.

Why do earnings increase with years of formal education, on average? The standard answer accepted by most economists is fully compatible with perfectly competitive markets for both labor and education. On the demand side, firms are willing to pay higher wages for more highly educated workers because additional education increases workers' productivity. On the supply side, more highly educated workers require higher wages to offset the costs of obtaining additional education. From the workers' point of view the higher wage is an equalizing wage difference.

To see why the Laws of Supply and Demand imply a positive relationship between years of formal education and earnings let's consider a model of formal education that makes the simplest possible assumptions regarding the nature of jobs, of workers, and of the costs of education. Regarding jobs, assume that the economy offers workers a fixed number of jobs regardless of the wage for each type of job. Picture the jobs as though they are arranged along the rungs of a ladder, bottom to top, according to the skills required for the job. The jobs on the ground floor are unskilled jobs requiring no formal education. The jobs on the first rung of the ladder require some skills that workers can obtain with one year of formal education. The jobs two rungs up the ladder require still greater skills that workers can obtain with two years of formal education. The pattern continues up the job ladder, with jobs on each succeeding rung requiring additional skills that workers can obtain with an additional year of formal education. The jobs on the top rung are the most highly skilled jobs, requiring the most years of formal education.

Regarding the workers, assume that the number of workers equals the number of jobs and that all workers are identical. They have the same natural abilities and the same preferences for the various jobs on the job ladder. In any one year people are either in school or working, but not both. Also, all workers retire at the same age. Therefore, the more years people spend in school, the fewer years they spend working throughout their lifetimes.

[1]R. Ehrenberg and R. Smith, *Modern Labor Economics: Theory and Public Policy*, fourth edition (New York: Harper Collins, 1991), 299–300.

Finally, assume that the costs of obtaining each additional year of formal education are equal for all workers. Costs can vary by year of schooling. For instance, a year of high school might be cheaper than a year of college. But no individual has a cost advantage in obtaining formal education.

A model with all these assumptions is obviously highly simplified. Nonetheless, it is representative of the way in which the majority of economists approach the theory of human capital.

The labor markets must allocate workers to jobs, so that each worker fills one of the available jobs. In our simple model this can happen only if wages increase steadily rung by rung up the job ladder. To see why, think about people trying to decide whether to accept a job on the ground floor or a job on the first rung of the ladder. The advantage of choosing the lowest-skilled job is that people can begin working and earning income immediately, since the job requires no formal education. For the sake of discussion, suppose that the ground-floor wage is the minimum wage, $4.25 an hour (1993). In order to choose a job one rung up on the job ladder workers must have a year of formal education. Therefore, workers choosing those jobs bear two costs relative to choosing the lowest-skilled job: (1) the out-of-pocket costs of the education and (2) the opportunity costs of delaying work for one year, equal to $4.25 an hour times the number of hours the lowest-skilled worker works each year. Because of these costs, no one will accept jobs on the next rung unless the wage they receive is higher than the minimum wage. Firms would presumably be willing to pay higher wages in these jobs because the workers are more productive, having received a year of education. The only possible equilibrium is when the workers believe that the increase in pay *throughout their lifetimes* for jobs on the first rung just offsets the full costs of the education, both the direct costs and the opportunity costs, for that one year.[2] Everyone would want the higher-skilled job if the increase in pay is larger than the full costs of the education. Conversely, everyone would want the lower-skilled job if the increase in pay is less than the full costs of the education. In other words, wages in the two sets of labor markets are in equilibrium when workers do not care which job they take.

The relationship between the wages of jobs one and two rungs up the job ladder is arrived at by the same line of reasoning. People choosing a job two rungs up the ladder rather than one rung up must acquire an additional year of education. They bear the direct costs of education and the opportunity costs of the lost wages by not working for a year at a one-rung job. Therefore, equilibrium in the two job markets requires that the two-rung jobs pay higher wages, so that the increase in pay throughout the workers' lifetimes just equals the full costs of the additional year of education. With any other difference in the wages everyone would prefer either one-rung or two-rung jobs. Furthermore, the wages for these two sets of jobs are naturally tied to the minimum wages paid for the lowest-skilled jobs. For instance, suppose that the wages for one-rung and two-rung jobs are out of equilibrium, so that everyone prefers the two-rung jobs. In other words, the two-rung wages are too high. If the wages for one-rung and ground-floor jobs are in equilibrium, so that people are indifferent between these two sets of jobs, then everyone would want two-rung jobs. Since two-rung jobs are better than one-rung jobs, they are also necessarily better than ground-floor jobs. Everyone would choose two years of

[2]In other words, the present value of the increased lifetime income must equal the full costs of the education.

education, and the jobs on the bottom two rungs of the job ladder would remain vacant. However, with two-rung jobs in excess supply and the other two sets of jobs in excess demand, wages would naturally adjust until the proper wage differences exist among all sets of jobs if the markets are competitive.

The same analysis applies throughout the job ladder. The increase in lifetime wages from one rung to the next must always exactly compensate people for the direct plus opportunity costs of the additional year of formal education required to move one rung up the job ladder. Therefore, the model predicts that wages increase with years of formal schooling. The prediction that wages are positively related to the amount of investment in education, other things equal, is common to all standard models used in the theory of human capital.

Our model, simple as it is, yields an important insight about the relationship between education and earnings. Although people with more education earn higher wages, they are not necessarily better off than are less-educated people earning lower wages. Some or all of the higher earnings are an equalizing wage difference, compensating for the direct and opportunity costs of obtaining the education. For example, medical doctors receive the highest average salaries of all the professions. But they also spend the most time in school, and the direct costs of their education are enormous. Some of their apparent salary advantage is just offsetting the extra cost of their education.

In our simple model *all* wage differences among jobs are equalizing differences. No one is any better off than anyone else is because in the final equilibrium people do not care which jobs they perform or how much education they receive. This result arises from the assumptions that everyone is identical and that markets are competitive. We see once again that competitive markets honor the principle of horizontal equity: They treat equals equally. Although the assumptions of our model are oversimplified, the model underscores the warning that income may not be an accurate measure of economic well-being.

THE RETURNS TO FORMAL EDUCATION Our model also helps to explain the third fact about earnings in the United States that we noted in Chapter 18, the relationship between formal education and labor market earnings. Wages and salaries do rise with the number of years of formal education. People with more education tend to have higher age-earnings profiles. On average, wages and salaries increase with years of formal schooling at every age level in the population. The annual returns to a college education appear to be in the 5 to 15 percent range.[3] The returns to a college education were in the lower end of that range during the 1970s when the baby boom generation graduated and the market for college graduates was in excess supply. The returns appear to be moving toward the high end of the range during the 1990s as the market for college graduates has changed over to one of excess demand.

Our model cautioned that income may be a poor measure of economic well-being. The same warning applies to interpreting the returns to education. Studies of the returns to education compute the returns as the increase in lifetime earnings from an education, other things equal, just as in our simple model. These income measures of the return of education could easily overstate or understate the true returns, however, because it is difficult to keep other things

[3]Ehrenberg and Smith, *Modern Labor Economics*, 320.

equal. For instance, suppose that high-ability people tend to receive the most education and that high-ability people earn more than do low-ability people, independently of education. In that case, studies on the returns to education are comparing the earnings of more-educated, high-ability individuals with the earnings of less-educated, low-ability individuals. The proper comparison is between more-educated, high-ability and less-educated, *high*-ability individuals (or between more-educated, low-ability and less-educated, low-ability individuals). The standard comparison may overstate the return to education because it includes the effect of ability on earnings.

Attempts to separate the effects of ability from the effects of education on earnings are highly controversial. Researchers who use IQ test scores to measure ability find that IQ has very little independent effect on earnings. Education appears to have a far more important effect. IQ test scores have always been suspect as a measure of innate ability, however.

A study of identical twins undertaken by economist Paul Taubman at the University of Pennsylvania reaches the opposite conclusion about the effect of ability on earnings. Taubman discovered that the earnings of identical twins are much more highly correlated than are the earnings of two individuals generally. That is, if one twin has high (low) income, the other twin is likely to have high (low) income, much more so than for pairs of individuals generally. Identical twins are identical genetically, so they have the same innate abilities. They are also likely to be raised in highly similar family and social environments. Taubman found that the twins' similarities in ability and background were far more important than were their educations in explaining why their incomes tend to be so similar. Extrapolating his study of identical twins to the entire population, he concluded that fully two-thirds of the measured returns to education are actually due to innate ability and background. His conclusion is disturbing because it suggests that success or failure in the labor market is largely predetermined by birth and upbringing. Many researchers are highly critical of that conclusion, however, claiming that the results from Taubman's study of identical twins do not apply to the entire population. Suffice it to say that the effect of ability (and childhood background) on labor market earnings remains highly controversial and unsettled.[4]

The connection between ability and education suggests that the returns to education may be less than they appear. Other considerations suggest that the returns to education may be greater than they appear. The standard human capital model rests on the two assumptions that people view education strictly as an investment and that the only returns to education are in the form of increased earnings. Neither assumption may be warranted. Some students may view part of their education as a consumption good that they undertake for pure enjoyment. If so, not all the costs of the education should be counted as investment costs. The consumption portion does not have to be covered by future increases in earnings. Also, some of the returns to education are not monetary in nature. A college education is far more than a ticket to a higher-paying job. It is also a ticket to a different lifestyle, enabling one to seek white-collar work as opposed to blue-collar work and to enjoy a more cultured and

---

[4]P. Taubman, "The Relative Influence of Inheritable and Environmental Factors and the Importance of Intelligence in Earnings Functions," in W. Krelle and A. Shorrocks (eds.), *Personal Income Distribution* (Amsterdam: North Holland, 1978). Harvard's Zvi Grilliches was an early, and widely cited, critic of Taubman's study. See Z. Grilliches, "Sibling Models and Data in Economics: Beginnings of a Survey," *Journal of Political Economy* 87, No. 5, Part 2 (1979): S37–S64.

examined life. If we add the nonmonetary returns to the increase in wages and subtract the consumption portion from the investment costs, the actual returns to education could be far greater than 5 or 10 or even 15 percent. No one knows for sure the true value of formal education.

Perhaps the most surprising conclusion arising from the extensive research on the returns to formal education is that education alone accounts for only about 10 percent of the difference in earnings among individuals. That is, while almost everyone agrees that earnings rise with years of formal education, other things equal, the *separate* effect of education on the distribution of earnings is small. Simply knowing how much formal education people have does not tell you very much about how much they earn. Many other elements come into play in determining the distribution of earnings. One very important element is the education that people receive in the form of on-the-job training from their employers, which we turn to next.

On-the-job Training

The employment relationship typically begins with a training period during which employees learn a set of skills that make them more productive to the firm. The theory of **on-the-job training (OJT)** is closely analogous to the theory of formal education, with the training period corresponding to the time spent in formal schooling and the post-training period corresponding to the period when the individual is employed in the higher-skilled job. Let's begin by considering on-the-job training from the employer's perspective. We will assume that newly hired, untrained workers have a value of marginal product of VMP_0 to a large number of firms and that labor markets are competitive. Untrained workers can always find employment at a wage $W_0 = VMP_0$. All workers immediately enter a training program upon joining a firm.

ON-THE-JOB TRAINING

Training offered by firms to their employees that teaches them skills that make them more productive to the firm.

During the training period the cost of labor to the firm exceeds the value of labor's marginal product. Employees are not very useful to firms while they are being retrained. The value of their marginal product during training, VMP_{TR}, is less than VMP_0 ($VMP_{TR} < VMP_0$). Also, firms incur training costs in addition to the wages paid each employee. The full cost of a new employee during training is $W_0 + T$, where W_0 is the wage paid during training and T is the cost of training each employee. $(W_0 + T) > VMP_{TR}$ for the trainees. The difference, $(W_0 + T) - VMP_{TR}$, represents the net cost of each trainee to the firm during the training period.

Suppose that training raises the value of labor's marginal product to VMP_1. Employees have to accept a wage lower than VMP_1 after the training period so that firms can recover the net costs of training them. If W_1 is the post-training wage, then $VMP_1 - W_1$ represents the post-training net return on each employee, for each period that the employee remains with the firm. A firm cannot know for sure how long any one trained worker will stay with the firm, but it does know the average tenure of its trained workers. Suppose that trained workers remain with the firm for an average of five years. Then the firm will hire and train new workers up to the point at which the annual net returns $(VMP_1 - W_1)$ over five years are just sufficient to offset the initial net cost of training $[(W_0 + T) - VMP_0]$.[5]

[5]That is, the present value of the net returns over five years just equals the net cost of training.

SPECIFIC TRAINING

In a labor market context, the skills that employees learn during on-the-job training that are useful only to the firm offering the training, such as learning how to operate highly specialized equipment used only by that firm.

An immediate implication of the human capital theory of hiring labor is that firms' willingness to train workers depends on the nature of the training. Firms make a clear distinction between general training and specific training. As noted earlier, general training refers to the teaching of basic skills such as reading, problem solving, and word processing. **Specific training** refers to skills that are useful only to the firm offering the training. An example would be learning how to operate highly specialized equipment used only by that firm.

Firms are reluctant to offer general training because it is easily transferable to other firms. Suppose that general training raises the value of marginal product of employees to VMP_1 in all firms. If a firm offers general training, it may not be able to recover the net costs of training. Another firm can easily bid the worker away after training by offering a wage between W_1 and VMP_1, up to the limit of VMP_1. The competing firm can afford to pay more because it does not have to recover any of the initial training costs. The U.S. Army well understands the costs of offering general training. The Army spends a considerable amount of time and money teaching newly enlisted men and women valuable general skills, such as regular work habits, teamwork, and problem solving. When the enlistment period is up, many soldiers choose to leave military service and transfer their skills to jobs in the private sector. The Army has to start over again training new recruits. Private firms do not want to be caught in the Army's bind.

Specific training, by contrast, ties the employee to the firm after the training period ends because it does not increase the employee's productivity to other firms. If all training is specific, then trained workers have a value of marginal product of VMP_1 to the firm that trains them and a value of marginal product of VMP_0 to all other firms. The competing firms cannot offer a wage higher than W_0 to a trained worker.

All training programs undoubtedly offer some general training that is transferable to competing firms. This is certainly true of managerial training programs. Firms know this and try to minimize paying for the more general components of training in these cases. For example, they may offer managerial trainees lower pay (lower than W_0) during the training period.

So far we have considered OJT from the employer's perspective. Employees clearly have an incentive to receive specific OJT because it raises their productivity and wages over time. In fact, employees may also be willing to share some of the costs of specific training, either directly or indirectly by accepting a wage less than W_0 during the training period. The higher the employees' share of the training costs, the higher the post-training wages that firms can afford to pay them, up to the limit of VMP_1.

The desire, or need, to provide workers with specific training helps explain many of the hiring and wage-setting practices of U.S. firms. We will consider a selection of these practices that have an important and direct bearing on the four main facts about wage and salary income. Assume from now on that all training is specific training, since the specific component of training drives all the results.

OJT AND THE VARIATION IN EARNINGS Specific OJT helps to explain the large differences in earnings both across and within occupations. In the one-period competitive model of Chapter 9, wages always equal the value of labor's marginal product. Specific OJT breaks the link between wages and the value of marginal product, even in competitive labor markets. In our simple model above, the post-training wage can take on a whole range of values between W_0, the wage for untrained workers, and VMP_1, the marginal product of trained workers. Generally speaking, occupations requiring a larger amount of specific training pay higher post-training wages. Also, specific training causes wages to differ within occupations for a number of reasons. Workers in training receive lower wages than do already trained workers. Beyond that, different firms may experience different costs of training the same general category of worker and therefore pay different post-training wages. However, post-training wages can differ even if training costs are the same for all firms. Because training is firm-specific, firms cannot lose their trained workers to a better wage offer so long as they maintain the wage somewhere within the range of W_0 to VMP_1. Since firms are under no competitive pressure to offer any one wage within that range, other considerations peculiar to each firm may dictate the post-training wages that firms choose to pay. This is one of the most important implications of specific OJT. We will consider some of these other considerations below.

OJT AND THE AGE-EARNINGS PROFILE The theory of specific on-the-job training helps explain three features of the age-earnings profile: (1) why the age-earnings profile is humped, rising through middle age and then falling near retirement, (2) why the age-earnings profile rises more steeply for more educated workers, and (3) why women have lower and flatter age-earnings profiles than do men.

According to human capital theory, the hump in the age-earnings profile arises because younger workers are more likely to receive OJT than are older workers. This is so because the gains from training occur in the post-training period for both employees and employers. When workers undertake training, they sacrifice some wage income in return for higher post-training wages. Employers bear the costs of specific training in return for paying workers less than the value of their marginal products during the post-training period. Therefore, both employees and employers have more to gain the longer the post-training period. As workers age, the incentive to provide *and* to receive training falls. So productivity and earnings increase early on in the working relationship as the result of continual doses of training, and then they stop growing as training ceases.

Why, though, should earnings fall in the last years of employment? The answer lies in the eventual erosion of skills learned early on. Older workers are not as dexterous, as mentally alert, as healthy, or perhaps even as knowledgeable as newly trained workers. In other words, human capital depreciates over time just as physical capital depreciates with its continued use in production. The combination of no further training and depreciation of skills and knowledge is a double handicap for older workers that eventually causes their productivity and earnings to fall.

FORMAL EDUCATION, OJT, AND THE AGE-EARNINGS PROFILE The standard explanation for why age-earnings profiles rise more steeply for more educated workers is that people who choose more formal education are also more receptive to on-the-job training. They are more likely to seek out jobs with a higher training component, and they benefit more from any given amount of training. As a result, workers with more formal education become increasingly more productive than do workers with less formal education in the early working years. Thus, the two main branches of human capital theory—formal education and on-the-job-training—combine to explain why the earnings gap between more- and less-educated workers increases with age.

OJT AND WOMEN'S AGE-EARNINGS PROFILES The human capital explanation for why women experience lower and flatter age-earnings profiles than do men centers on the fact that women are far more likely to interrupt their working careers because of their greater responsibilities at home. Men spend an average of 3 percent of their potential work years away from work, women an average of 31 percent. Interruptions in work are not conducive to on-the-job training. If women expect to interrupt their post-training careers, the number of years in which they can enjoy the returns to training in the form of higher wages are correspondingly reduced. Their skills are also likely to depreciate faster with frequent career interruptions. Relative to men, therefore, women desire jobs with a lower training component because their expected returns from receiving training are less. Sacrificing wage income during training is not as good an investment for women as it is for men, on average. Training women is also less advantageous from the employers' perspective, since employers expect to have less time to recover the initial training costs.

Thus, human capital theory predicts that women will tend to be employed in low-training, less-productive occupations that pay lower wages. The facts are roughly consistent with the theory. In 1989, 64 percent of all full-time female employees worked in one of six broad occupational categories: nurses and health technicians, elementary and secondary school teachers, retail sales clerks, clerical workers, apparel and textile workers, and service workers. The last four of these are low-training occupations. The first two require a substantial amount of training, but most of it is general training that women can retain and transfer to new jobs if they interrupt their working careers. Largely because they are concentrated in these occupations, women receive less than half as much on-the-job training as do men in the United States. Consequently, their productivity and wages rise less steeply in the early years of work. Their age-earnings profiles are flatter than are men's profiles.

Normal competitive market forces also come into play in explaining why women earn low wages. Because women seek out employment in a relatively small number of low-training occupations, they create excess supply pressures in these markets that hold their wages down. The combined effects of low training and high supply pressures keep women's wages at 65 percent of men's wages.

Human capital theory offers an explanation for the differences in age-earnings profiles between women and men that fits the facts, but it might not be the only explanation. Many people believe that outright labor market discrimination against women is another important reason, perhaps the more important reason, why women's wages lag behind those of men. We will explore the discrimination hypothesis in the second section of this chapter.[6]

OJT AND THE DISTRIBUTION OF EARNINGS The amount of specific on-the-job training workers receive appears to be about twice as important as their

---

[6]B. Kaufman, *The Economics of Labor Markets*, third edition (Hinsdale, IL: The Dryden Press, 1991), 336–337 and 364–365.

formal education in determining the level of their earnings. On-the-job training is difficult to measure directly, so researchers use years of work experience as a proxy variable for the amount of on-the-job training a worker has received. The consensus opinion from a large number of studies is that experience accounts for about 20 percent of the difference in earnings among workers, whereas formal education accounts for only 10 percent of the difference. Taken together, these percentages suggest that investment in human capital is a very important determinant of wage income. It is by no means the only determinant, however. Over two-thirds of the difference in earnings among workers is due to factors other than the amount of human capital that workers have acquired.[7]

Internal Labor Markets

We noted in Chapter 18 that a substantial portion of the labor force in the United States is highly mobile and changes jobs frequently. By the same token, another substantial portion of the labor force chooses to stay put and work at the same job for a very long time. One-half of all men in the labor force and one-quarter of all women work for the same employers for more than 20 years, and 8 percent of all men aged 45 to 49 have worked for only one employer.[8]

Specific on-the-job training fosters these long-term working relationships because once training occurs, both employee and employer have strong incentives to maintain their relationship. Trained employees want to remain with the firms that trained them because they can earn higher wages there than elsewhere. Employers want to retain trained workers because they can recover the initial training costs by paying workers less than the value of their marginal products during the post-training period. The longer a worker remains with the firm, the higher the return to the investment in training is from the employer's point of view. Also, replacing trained workers with new workers entails new training costs, with no guarantee that the firm can recover the costs. The costs of hiring and training a new worker are not at all trivial. One study estimates that replacing a blue-collar worker costs between two days' and two weeks' pay; replacing a white-collar workers costs between two weeks' and two months' pay (these figures include hiring and firing costs as well as training costs). Moreover, the costs of replacing workers are rising, on average, simply because the U.S. labor force is becoming increasingly a white-collar labor force. In 1950, 37.5 percent of all workers held white-collar jobs. By 1989, 56.3 percent of all workers held white-collar jobs.[9]

Many of the larger corporations in the United States have further encouraged long-term employment relationships by adopting internal labor markets. An **internal labor market** is a method of hiring and promotion in which firms hire new employees from outside the firm only into the lowest-level jobs within the corporate hierarchy and then promote from within to all higher-level jobs. Not surprisingly, internal labor markets are most prevalent in industries that require large amounts of specific training, such as the steel, petroleum, and chemical industries. Hiring experienced workers from outside the firm is dif-

INTERNAL LABOR MARKET
A method of hiring and promotion in which firms hire new employees from outside the firm only into the lowest-level jobs within the corporate hierarchy and then promote from within to all higher-level jobs.

[7]B. Kaufman, *Economics of Labor Markets*, 318.
[8]R. Ehrenberg and R. Smith, *Modern Labor Economics: Theory and Public Policy*, third edition (Glenview, IL: Scott, Foresman, 1987), 417; and Kaufman, *Economics of Labor Markets*, 5.
[9]Kaufman, *Economics of Labor Markets*, 10 and 185–186.

ficult when much of the training is specific to a particular firm. Internal labor markets are much less common in industries for which specific training is unimportant, such as the garment and shoe industries.

Both employees and employers have come to accept internal labor markets. Employees apparently believe that promotion from within gives them more control over their own destinies. Firms like internal labor markets because they can learn about those personal qualities of their employees that are difficult to judge when hiring from the outside: honesty, motivation, acceptance of criticism, ability to work with other employees, and so forth. The cost to employer and employee alike is that internal labor markets isolate experienced employees from competition in the broader marketplace. Each side may let better opportunities pass them by if they are looking only within the firm.

Internal labor markets arise in large part from the need to train and retain workers. Once internal labor markets come into existence, however, they introduce new possibilities for explaining differences in wages and salaries that go well beyond the confines of human capital theory. The competing theories all derive from the fact that firms with internal labor markets have chosen to isolate themselves from the marketplace for experienced workers. Each firm has to develop its own set of rules for deciding who gets promoted and for determining the rate of pay of every job beyond the lowest entry-level positions. These rules respond to a complex set of motives within the firm. They are not just passive reactions to the Laws of Supply and Demand.

To conclude this section we will briefly explore two theories of how firms set wages that are based on the presence of specific training, stable long-term employment relationships, and internal labor markets. The first describes wage and salary policies designed to maintain workers' morale over the long haul. The second views the internal labor market as an instrument for segmenting markets, so that equally productive workers do not receive the same wages. Both theories are alternatives to human capital theory for explaining the four main facts about wage and salary income. The three theories are not mutually exclusive, however. Each one uncovers some of the reasons why wages and salaries differ among individuals.

Motivational Theories of the Age-Earnings Profiles

We have seen that both employers and employees desire long-term working relationships whenever specific training is an important component of the job. Employers, however, face two serious obstacles in keeping their employees motivated and productive throughout their tenure with the company: the method of paying wages and salaries and the pyramidal structure of corporations.

INCENTIVE-BASED PAY

A method of payment used by employers that relates pay directly to the results of an employee's work, such as the commissions received by salespeople.

TIME-BASED PAY

A method of payment used by employers that consists of a straight payment per unit of time independent of the results of the employee's work, such as a manager's annual salary.

Regarding the method of payment, employers can pay their employees on either an incentive basis or a time basis. **Incentive-based pay** relates pay directly to the results of an employee's work. Examples include the commissions received by salespeople and the rates that auto mechanics receive for each type of repair they undertake. **Time-based pay** is a straight payment per unit of time independent of the results of the employee's work, such as a laborer's hourly wage and a manager's annual salary. Eighty-six percent of all workers are paid on a time basis.

Employers have good reasons for shying away from incentive-based pay. The most general problem is that output is often difficult to measure precisely, especially for white-collar workers. How much does each of a corporation's financial managers, or lawyers, or even the president contribute to the overall revenues of the firm? Rather than trying to answer such questions as a basis for pay, firms choose to pay their employees a straight annual salary based of their positions within the corporate hierarchy. Even when incentive-based pay is possible, it has often proved to be unsatisfactory. Employees have an incentive to strive for quantity—to produce as much as possible—and the quality of their work suffers. Employees also prefer the more certain incomes associated with time-based pay. They require a wage premium to accept incentive-based pay, and firms are often not willing to pay it. For all these reasons, then, employers have chosen overwhelmingly to pay on a straight time basis.

Time-based pay is not entirely satisfactory, however, since employees receive the same pay regardless of the quality of their work. Employers have to find other means of assuring that their employees remain motivated to do good work. They essentially have two options, the stick approach and the carrot approach.

The stick approach involves careful supervision and monitoring of employees, along with well-understood penalties for those employees who shirk their duties. The most drastic penalty is firing the shirkers. Less drastic measures are demotions or reductions in pay. The stick approach has obvious drawbacks. Close monitoring of employees is costly and tends to undermine their morale. Firing employees increases turnover, as do other types of penalties if workers become disgruntled and quit. We have seen that firms like to avoid turnover whenever specific training is an important component of the job.

THE EFFICIENCY WAGE The carrot approach is called the efficiency wage. The idea is that firms pay their employees more than they have to in order to keep them. Remember, firms offering specific training can choose a wage within a fairly wide range of wages in the post-training period. Increasing the wage (salary) within that range brings three benefits: (1) It increases employees' morale and productivity, (2) it reduces turnover and thereby saves on training costs, and (3) it reduces the need for costly monitoring. The sum of these three benefits is the marginal benefit from an increase in the wage. The marginal cost is the increase in the wage itself necessary to create these benefits. Firms compare the three sources of marginal benefits from additional increases in the wage with the marginal cost of the wage increase itself in determining what wage to pay. The **efficiency wage** is the wage at which the marginal benefits and the marginal costs of further increases in the wage are equal. As such, the efficiency wage is the wage that maximizes profit within the range of wages that firms could pay.

EFFICIENCY WAGE

The wage at which the marginal benefits and the marginal costs to the firm of further increases in the wage are equal; alternatively, the wage that maximizes the firm's profit within the range of wages it could pay.

The theory that firms pay an efficiency wage to reduce shirking has been offered as the explanation for why larger firms pay higher wages than do smaller firms. The wage premium in larger firms is really quite substantial. Other things equal, firms with 100 to 500 employees pay an average of 6 percent more than do firms with fewer than 100 employees. Firms with more than 500 employees pay 12 percent more.[10] According to the efficiency wage theory, both large and small firms are maximizing profit by paying an efficiency wage. The difference in pay arises because monitoring employees is more costly the larger the firm. Therefore, starting from the same wage, an increase in pay has greater marginal

[10]Ehrenberg and Smith, *Modern Labor Economics*, fourth edition, 424–425.

benefit to larger firms because it allows them to save more on monitoring costs. As a result, the efficiency wage at which the marginal benefits and the marginal costs of further wage increases are equal is higher for larger firms.

THE CORPORATE TOURNAMENT The need to keep employees motivated over the long haul can also explain why top executives often earn enormous salaries that are many times higher than are the salaries of the executives immediately below them in the corporate hierarchy. This salary pattern is seen as a response to the pyramid structure of corporations. Many eager young college or MBA graduates join management training programs knowing full well that only a handful of the trainees can make it all the way to the top. How can firms keep their managers productive and continually striving for the top positions when the odds of succeeding are so stacked against them? Many large corporations have solved this problem by designing the struggle for the top along the lines of professional sporting tournaments, such as golf and tennis tournaments. The winners receive enormous prizes (salaries). Equally important, the losers must also be treated well, or people might not be willing to compete against such long odds despite the ample rewards for winning. Corporations reward the losing managers by agreeing to keep them employed at a good salary until retirement, even though they know that the losers have no further incentive to perform well. They are likely to become "dead wood." The tournament salary structure also explains why corporations desire a mandatory retirement age. They want to be able to remove the deadwood losers in a reasonable period of time.

The corporate tournament is the most dramatic example of a general policy of delaying rewards in order to maintain incentives throughout a long-term employment relationship. Generous pension plans are also consistent with a motivational strategy, as are certain fringe benefits such as vacation time that increases with years of experience. A delayed payment strategy has one final advantage: It automatically self-selects a good pool of job applicants for the firm. Firms can be assured that only people who are seeking a long-term employment relationship will apply for the managerial positions. These people are less likely to suffer morale problems or to quit, thereby reducing the efficiency wage that the firms must pay. The self-selection aspect of delayed payment strategies may also explain why employees accept these strategies, even though they are highly risky. After all, employees run the risk of being fired before they receive the big payoffs. People seeking long-term working relationships are probably more willing to accept the risk.

CURRENT ISSUE: The federal government has phased out mandatory retirement. This may have played a role in the widespread layoff of older middle-management employees in the early 1990s. Mandatory retirement is an essential component of the corporate tournament because it sets a limit on the number of years that the corporations have to carry those who do not make it to the top. One wonders how these layoffs will affect the morale of the younger workers.

Delayed payment strategies modify the post-training relationship between wages and values of marginal product in our simple model of on-the-job training as follows. Firms pay wages way below the value of employees' marginal products in the early years. Then they raise wages (and other fringe benefits) close to or even above the value of marginal product in the later years. The firm makes a large enough return on employees while they are younger to cover both the net costs of specific training and the net costs during the later working years in the form of huge salaries to the top executives, generous salaries and fringe benefits to older "deadwood" managers, and pensions to retirees.

COMPARING MOTIVATIONAL AND HUMAN CAPITAL THEORIES Motivational theories of corporate wage and salary policies compete with human capital theory as an explanation of the age-earnings profile. Proponents of the motivational theories argue that the rising portion of the age-earnings profile does not result from continual doses of training, as suggested by human capital theory. They point out that most training occurs at the beginning of the working relationship. Experience in and of itself might make workers somewhat more productive, but productivity increases cannot explain why the age-earnings profile increases so sharply. Instead, firms increase pay steadily over time primarily to keep their employees motivated over the long haul and attached to the firm. Notice, though, that motivational theories have difficulty explaining why the age-earnings profile declines in the later years. Human capital theory does better on this score.

REFLECTION: Japanese firms supposedly have an advantage over U.S. firms because they give their workers lifetime contracts. What are some advantages of a lifetime employment arrangement? Do you see some disadvantages as well?

Market Segmentation

Internal labor markets clearly segment markets for all positions above the entry-level positions. Two identical employees working in higher-level positions at different firms can earn different salaries simply because their firms have chosen different salary structures. The employees in the lower-salary firm cannot move to the higher-salary firm except in an entry-level position. Therefore, they tend to stay with their firm, and the salary structures in the two firms never equalize as they would if the markets for the upper-level positions were openly competitive.

The **segmentation theory** of internal labor markets argues that segmentation extends to the entry-level positions as well. The theory turns on the premise that productivity is tied primarily to the job, not to the worker. In its purest form the segmentation theory says that businesses teach their employees *all* they need to know to perform the various tasks within the company. In other words, on-the-job training is the only form of investment in human capital that matters. Any formal education that employees have received is irrelevant to their productivity. Firms use formal education strictly as a screening device to choose desirable employees for the entry-level positions. They select high school graduates for certain jobs and college graduates for other jobs simply because the degrees indicate that workers have the appropriate basic skills, work habits, expectations, and attitudes necessary to function on these jobs within a corporate structure.

SEGMENTATION THEORY
In the context of labor markets, the theory that businesses teach their employees all they need to know in order to perform the various tasks within a company, so that on-the-job training is the only form of investment in human capital that determines a worker's productivity.

Many nongraduates can also be trained to be perfectly capable employees, but why should employers take the risk? The high school and the college graduates have already been certified by their schools, in effect, so employers are fairly confident that they know what they are getting. The result is that the markets for the lowest entry-level jobs are segmented. High school and college graduates enter internal labor markets in larger firms that offer stable careers, high pay, and opportunities for advancement. Nongraduates are denied access to these "primary" jobs. They are forced into "secondary" jobs in smaller firms that are unstable, low paying, and essentially dead-end (as, for example, custodians, delivery persons, night security guards, and so forth). Because the jobs are so unattractive, many workers in these secondary markets maintain only a loose attachment to the labor force. They move in and out of employment and never develop the work habits, attitudes, and skills necessary for the primary jobs in the larger corporations. They remain trapped in the secondary market, forever segmented from the primary internal labor markets.

The segmentation theory of internal labor markets has another disturbing implication: The private returns to formal education far exceed the social returns. Formal education has value to individuals because it is their ticket of entry to a good job. But formal education has little social value because it does not increase workers' productivity. In fact, the social returns to formal education may well be negative. Society can surely find cheaper methods of screening potential workers if formal education is little more than a screening device.

The segmentation theory of internal labor markets has not been accepted by the majority of economists. The best evidence in its favor is that the returns to completing the last year of high school and the last year of college are much higher than are the returns for completing all other years of school. This suggests that the degrees themselves have special significance as a credential or screening device. The theory is deficient in a number of respects, however. It cannot so easily explain why *every* extra year of education yields returns in the form of higher earnings. Nor can it explain why societies have not developed cheaper screening devices, if this is all formal education is. Most economists accept the human capital view that formal education increases productivity in and of itself. In other words, productivity is at least somewhat embodied in the employees independently of the jobs that they perform. A final problem with the segmentation theory is that labor markets are not as firmly segmented into primary and secondary jobs as the theory suggests.

Despite these shortcomings, segmentation theory is instructive in showing how institutional factors within the economy, such as internal labor markets, can segment markets and undermine the equalizing tendencies of competitive market forces. For instance, internal labor markets provide a mechanism through which employees' personal characteristics can have a separate influence on their earnings. At their best, internal labor markets allow innate ability to come to the fore because employers have the luxury of viewing their employees over a long period of time. They learn who the most able people are and promote them to the top positions. Innate ability is much more difficult to judge when hiring from outside. In this way internal labor markets serve to make the economy more productive. At their worst, internal labor markets foster "good old boy" networks in which employers reward and promote employees on the basis of arbitrary and irrelevant characteristics, such as race or gender, family background, and social connections. Although such practices should eventually place companies at a competitive disadvantage, the widespread use of internal labor markets can long delay the day of reckoning. Also, if discrimination occurs in hiring at the ports of entry, the people discriminated against never have a chance to prove their worth. We will see below that lasting discrimination in labor markets is difficult to explain without the support of segmenting institutions, such as internal labor markets.

LABOR MARKET DISCRIMINATION AGAINST WOMEN

Discrimination against women and nonwhites appears to be an important source of labor market segmentation in the United States. We will consider the possibility of discrimination against women in this section of the chapter. Many of the same principles apply to discrimination against nonwhites.

Women and men have such different labor market experiences in the United States than an outside observer who did not know better might wonder if they are working in the same country. Women earn 65 percent as much as do men, on average, a percentage that has not changed much since 1939. The return to formal education is much lower for women. In 1990 the average earnings of female *college* graduates were less than the average earnings of male *high school* graduates. Women's age-earnings profiles are flatter than are men's. The female profile essentially stops rising after age 30. The male profile continues to rise into late middle age.[11] Women are not promoted as rapidly as are men. A recent study of Harvard MBAs found that men and women graduating in 1972 received the same starting salaries that year. By 1984 the women's salaries were $4,000 below the men's salaries, correcting for all factors other than gender that might reasonably account for the difference in their salaries. Finally, men and women work in different jobs for the most part. We noted earlier that 64 percent of all women work in one of six occupations. But even that statistic does not indicate just how segregated men and women are in the labor market. A survey of 400 California establishments, covering 61,000 employees from 1959 through 1979, discovered that if men and women worked in the same occupation, they usually worked for different companies. If they worked for the same company, they usually had different job titles. In the entire sample, only 10 percent of the workers with the same job titles worked in a mixed-gender environment.

Even federal employees are highly segregated by gender. In 1983, 78 percent of all federal workers in civil service grades 1–6 were female; 85 percent of all workers in civil service grades 10–15 were male.[12]

Why do women have such different labor market experiences from men? One possible explanation is that the differences result from a combination of conscious choices that women make and competitive market forces reacting to their choices. Another possible explanation is that the differences result from discrimination against women in the labor market. Most economists believe that both explanations have some validity. They disagree, however, on their relative importance.

The choice and competition explanation is based on the human capital view of women in the labor market that we discussed above. To review briefly, women's disadvantages in the labor market stem from the fact that they continue to bear most of the responsibilities for rearing children and managing the household. Thus, when women enter the labor market to work for pay, the majority choose jobs with characteristics that allow them to maintain their household responsibilities. They seek jobs that have flexible hours (often part time), are close to home, involve little or no travel, and require only minimal amounts of specific on-the-job training. Women have to be prepared to interrupt their careers, and low-training jobs permit them to do so. We have seen that women receive only about half as much on-the-job training as men do and interrupt their careers much more frequently, on average. The result is that women choose among a few occupations that have the desired characteristics.

Competitive market forces take over at this point. As more and more women joined the labor force and sought employment in a handful of occupations,

---

[11]Refer to Figure 18.1 and the discussion in Chapter 18 of the facts about earnings in the United States.

[12]J. Olsen and I. Frieze, "Woman Accountants: Do They Earn as Much as Men?", *Management Accounting* LXVII, No. 12 (June 1986): 27–31. W. Bielby and J. Baron, "Sex Segregation Within Occupations," *AEA Papers and Proceedings* 76, No. 2 (May 1986): 43–47. A letter from Mickey Leland, Chairman, Congressional Black Caucus, to the Honorable Mary Rose Oakar, Chairman, Subcommittee on Compensation and Employee Benefits, House of Representatives, Washington, D.C., July 22, 1985.

they drove down the wages in these occupations. Employers would only hire the influx of women into the market if they were willing to accept lower wages. This is just standard supply and demand analysis: Excess supply drives down prices in competitive markets.

Stanford's Victor Fuchs, a leading proponent of the human capital explanation, believes that women's responsibility for child rearing in the United States is the greatest single barrier preventing them from achieving earnings equality with men. He points out that a woman's earnings decline significantly with each additional child, so that women without children have very different labor market experiences than do women with children. For example, by age 40 married women earn only 85 percent as much as unmarried women. Also, 50 percent of all women earning $25,000 or more in 1986 were childless, whereas only 24 percent of women earning less than $25,000 were childless. According to Fuchs, the government should concentrate on child-focused policies, such as providing or subsidizing day care centers, if it wants to improve the labor market earnings of women. These policies would have a much greater impact on women's earnings than would anything the government might do to combat discrimination against women.[13]

Proponents of the discrimination explanation argue that the human capital explanation ignores the role of discrimination in the choices that women make. True, women "choose" to raise the children and take low-training jobs when they do enter the labor market, but these choices result in large part from discrimination. According to this view, women know that they confront two kinds of discrimination in the labor market. They receive lower pay than men do for the same jobs. This is why they "choose" less on-the-job training. The payoff to training is not as large for them. They also face discrimination in hiring, which tends to steer them into a relatively few occupations, those with low pay, low training, and little chance for advancement.

These two forms of discrimination create a vicious circle for women that forces them back into the home. Married couples understand that the husband receives better pay and has better chances for advancement in the labor market. Therefore, the rational choice for them is to have the husband spend relatively more time working for pay and the wife spend relatively more time working at home and raising the children. The circle is complete because once the women accept the brunt of the responsibilities in the home, their labor market options really are more limited. What look like conscious choices, then, are actually decisions forced upon women because of discrimination in the labor market.

The discrimination explanation of women's labor market experiences is certainly plausible. Economists have undertaken a large number of studies that attempt to explain the difference in men's and women's pay on the basis of all the factors we have been discussing in this chapter and Chapter 18, such as years of formal education, years of working experience, age, membership in a union, and various job characteristics. These studies come up far short of achieving a complete explanation. They find that anywhere from one-third to two-thirds of the wage difference between men and women cannot be explained by these factors. What is the missing piece of the puzzle? An obvious candidate is discrimination against women.

---

[13] V. Fuchs, "Women's Quest for Economic Equality," *Journal of Economic Perspectives* 3, No. 1 (Winter 1989): 25–42.

Two questions remain to be answered if discrimination is an important factor in explaining the labor market experiences of women: (1) Why are women discriminated against? (2) Why does discrimination persist? In answering these questions economists distinguish between two different types of discrimination, pre-market discrimination and current market discrimination. **Pre-market discrimination** exists when people are denied equal opportunities to develop their natural abilities to the fullest extent possible in their formative years before they enter the labor market. For example, children might be denied access to the best schools because of their race or gender. Pre-market discrimination lowers the average productivity of the people being discriminated against and therefore lowers their wages and job options when they do enter the labor market. **Current market discrimination** refers to unequal treatment of people in the labor market on the basis of personal characteristics such as race or gender that are unrelated to differences in their productivity. Unequal treatment can take the form of unequal pay for the same work, or unequal access to training programs and promotions, or discrimination in hiring that segregates people into particular occupations or jobs.

PRE-MARKET DISCRIMINATION

Denying people equal opportunities to develop their natural abilities to the fullest extent possible in their formative years before they enter the labor market, as when children are denied access to the best schools because of their race or gender.

CURRENT MARKET DISCRIMINATION

In the context of labor markets, unequal treatment of people on the basis of personal characteristics, such as race or gender, that are unrelated to differences in their productivity, taking the form of unequal pay for the same work, unequal access to jobs, and unequal access to training programs and promotions.

The majority view among economists is that, since World War II, pre-market discrimination has been relatively more important in holding down the earnings of blacks and current market discrimination has been relatively more important in holding down the earnings of women, although both types of discrimination have been present for both groups. Blacks began the post–World War II period far behind whites in educational achievement. The educational gap between blacks and whites has been closing rapidly since then, especially after 1960. This has been the principal factor behind the decline in the black-white earnings gap. By 1970 the average returns to a high school education had equalized for blacks and whites, other things equal, and the average returns to a college education had become somewhat larger for blacks.

Current market experiences have been more important in maintaining the large earnings gap between men and women. The crowding of women into a relatively few occupations and the tendency of women to interrupt their careers have been particularly influential. For this reason we will focus on the possibility of current market discrimination against women in the remainder of this section.

The Causes of Discrimination

Economists have identified three plausible employer motives for discrimination against women: prejudice, statistical discrimination, and social custom.

Prejudice against women, if it exists, is an obvious cause of discrimination against women. The only point to add is that the employers themselves need not be prejudiced to practice discrimination. The prejudice can come from male employees or even customers. Employers are likely to discriminate against women if their male employees refuse to work with women or if their customers refuse to buy from women. Customer prejudice appears to have been a factor in denying women access to positions in law firms and brokerage houses. Until very recently legal and financial clients strongly preferred to work with male lawyers and brokers. Males employed in these professions may also have been uncomfortable working with women.

Statistical discrimination occurs when employers attribute to each member of a group the average characteristics of the entire group of people. The group-

STATISTICAL DISCRIMINATION

Attributing to each member of a group the average characteristics of the entire group of people, which become the basis for hiring, training, or promoting any one individual within the group.

wide average characteristics become the basis for hiring, training, or promoting any one individual within the group.

The source of statistical discrimination is imperfect information, not prejudice. An employer does not know enough about any one individual woman to predict how she will behave, so he uses the average behavior of all women as a simple screening device to predict her behavior. For example, suppose that a male and a female, both college graduates, apply for a single opening in the managerial training program of a large corporation. Having interviewed the two candidates, the employer considers them identical in every respect but one, their gender. Looking ahead, he also knows that if the woman never marries, her career should be identical to the man's career. Never-married women are no more likely to interrupt their careers than are men. If the woman does marry, however, she is more likely to interrupt her career. The employer has no idea if the woman will eventually marry, but he knows that many women do marry and that married women are more likely to interrupt their careers than are married men. So he hires the male based on the average behavior of men and women generally. Notice that statistical discrimination is not discriminatory against women *on average.* But it does discriminate against individual women whose characteristics differ from the average characteristics of all women.

Discrimination resulting from social custom is often difficult to distinguish from discrimination resulting from prejudice, since prejudice itself arises from the socialization of attitudes. Prejudice, though, implies unthinking bigotry. Social custom usually refers to a more innocent process of gender stereotyping, although it leads to the same result—discrimination. We are socialized into thinking that men and women have distinctive attributes. Men are typically viewed as being strong, aggressive, decisive, and even good at mathematics. Women are typically viewed as being patient, caring, and sympathetic. Such stereotyping of attributes can easily lead to occupational stereotyping. Certain jobs are considered "male" jobs because they require the male attributes; examples include carpenters, engineers, mechanics, truck drivers, and police. Other jobs are "female" jobs because they require the female attributes; examples include nurses, secretaries, cashiers, dental hygienists, and librarians. Employers accept these stereotypes. They would not think of hiring a woman to do "man's" work, and vice versa. In the five "male" occupations listed above, more than 80 percent of the employees are male. In the five "female" occupations listed above, more than 80 percent of the employees are female. Gender stereotyping may explain why certain occupations are so predominantly male or female.[14]

The Persistence of Discrimination

Identifying possible underlying causes of discrimination against women is fairly easy. Explaining why the discrimination persists is much more difficult because discrimination is extremely vulnerable to competitive market forces. Employers who discriminate place themselves at a substantial competitive disadvantage relative to nondiscriminating employers. In other words, the profit motive ought to drive discrimination out of the marketplace. And if the market cannot

[14]Kaufman, *Economics of Labor Markets*, 365, Table 8.2.

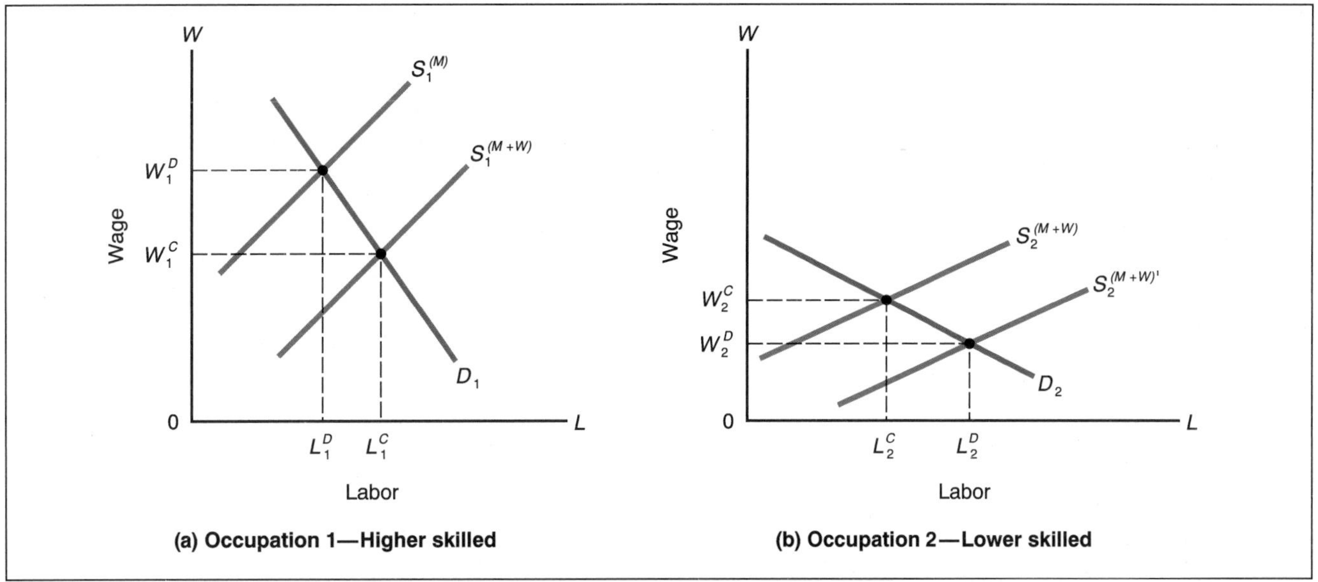

FIGURE 19.1

The Economic Effects of Discrimination Against Women

The labor markets for higher-skilled occupation 1 in Figure 19.1(a) and lower-skilled occupation 2 in Figure 19.1(b) would be competitive without discrimination against women. The competitive equilibrium in occupation 1 would be (L_1^C, W_1^C) at the intersection of D_1 and $S_1^{(M+W)}$; the competitive equilibrium in occupation 2 would be (L_2^C, W_2^C) at the intersection of D_2 and $S_2^{(M+W)}$. Discrimination against hiring women in occupation 1 shifts the supply curve to the left to $S_1^{(M)}$. The new equilibrium is (L_1^D, W_1^D), at the intersection of D_1 and $S_1^{(M)}$. The displaced women from occupation 1 move into occupation 2, shifting the supply curve out to $S_2^{(M+W)'}$. The new equilibrium is (L_2^D, W_2^D), at the intersection of D_2 and $S_2^{(M+W)'}$. The discrimination against women raises the wages of men working in occupation 1, and lowers the wages of all women and also of the men working in occupation 2.

eliminate discrimination, then the courts stand ready to assist. Discrimination is illegal. Federal law prohibits all forms of current market discrimination.

DISCRIMINATION AND COMPETITION To see why discrimination is vulnerable to competitive market pressures consider the simple example illustrated by Figure 19.1. The example relates to men and women, but it can also represent whites and nonwhite minorities, with whites substituting for men and nonwhite minorities for women. The figure depicts the markets for two occupations, 1 and 2, both of which are potentially perfectly competitive. Occupation 1 is more highly skilled and requires more formal education. If both men and women are free to work in occupation 1, the relevant market supply curve is $S_1^{(M + W)}$. The market equilibrium occurs at the intersection of D_1 and $S_1^{(M + W)}$. Employers hire L_1^C men and women at a wage of W_1^C. Similarly, the equilibrium for occupation 2, absent discrimination, occurs at the intersection of D_2 and $S_2^{(M + W)}$. Employers hire L_2^C, men and women at a wage of W_2^C.

Suppose that employers in occupation 1 refuse to hire women because they are prejudiced against women. With the supply to occupation 1 now restricted to qualified men, the supply curve shifts back to $S_1^{(M)}$. Employers hire L_1^D men at a wage of W_1^D. Any women displaced from occupation 1 who still want to work are forced to work in occupation 2, assumed to be their next best alternative. The market supply curve for occupation 2 shifts out to $S_2^{(M + W)'}$ with the influx of women into that market. Employers now hire L_2^D men and women at a wage of W_2^D.

Prejudice against women has the effect of segmenting the two markets. Women who are willing and qualified to work in occupation 1 are prevented from doing so. As a consequence, they receive lower pay than do men, although they are identical to men in every relevant respect.

The analysis should look familiar because the economic consequences of segmentation through discrimination are identical to the economic consequences of segmentation by labor unions that we analyzed in Chapter 18. Notice that the economic consequences spread far beyond the women discriminated against. Men who are qualified to work in occupation 1 gain from the discrimination against women. Their wages rise from W_1^C to W_1^D. But *all* other workers lose, including all men and women qualified to work in occupation 2. Their wages fall from W_2^C to W_2^D. Also, society as a whole loses because labor is misallocated. Some women are not allowed to work where their labor is most valuable. Therefore, discrimination moves society inside its production possibilities frontier.

The question, though, is how this discrimination can persist. There surely must be some entrepreneurial individuals who are not prejudiced against women. If so, then the unprejudiced entrepreneurs have an easy opportunity for earning a profit. They can start their own firms that employ workers in occupation 1 and hire the women who have been discriminated against by the prejudiced employers. Presumably these women will work at the new firms for any wage greater than W_2^D The unprejudiced entrepreneurs do not have to pay them a wage as high as W_1^D, which the prejudiced employers are paying to the men in occupation 1. Therefore, the unprejudiced entrepreneurs have a decisive cost advantage over the prejudiced employers. They can charge lower prices for their products than can the prejudiced employers and still make a profit.

The prejudiced employers will be driven out of business unless they lower their wages or start hiring the lower-cost women themselves. The only possible final equilibrium in occupation 1 is the nondiscriminatory equilibrium, with L_1^C men and women employed at a wage of W_1^C. Similarly, with the women qualified to work in occupation 1 now back in this market, the supply curve in occupation 2 shifts back to $S_2^{(M + W)}$. The wage there returns to W_2^C, with L_2^C men and women employed.

Some employers hiring into occupation 1 may still be prejudiced and continue to hire only men. Other employers may hire only women into occupation 1. Still others may have a mixed labor force in occupation 1. Regardless, all men and women working in occupation 1 must receive a wage of W_1^C no matter where they work. The market is free of *discrimination*, even if *prejudice* remains. The lesson of our simple example is clear: Prejudice can have no lasting economic consequences in a competitive market environment.

Discrimination is more likely to persist if it results from statistical discrimination or social custom. Employers will undoubtedly practice statistical discrimination so long as women with children interrupt their careers to care for the children. Occupational stereotyping can also be very persistent if people are socialized to accept the stereotypes from childhood, especially if many women themselves accept the stereotypes. Even so, both forms of discrimination are vulnerable to competitive market forces.

Markets segmented by gender (or race) have the same effects as analyzed above no matter what the underlying cause of the discrimination. Some women are receiving wages far below their true value to some group of employers, and the profit motive should drive employers to hire these women. For example, the employers may offer women day care services in exchange for some decrease in their wage. Women who have been discriminated against may be willing to accept this option. With women's wages well below their true value, both they and the firms have a lot of room to bargain in reaching employment arrangements that make both the firms and the women better off. Similarly, once employers realize that gender stereotypes are inaccurate, they have every economic incentive to ignore the stereotypes and hire women into traditionally "male" jobs. Governments do not have to order enterprising employers to cease discriminating in a competitive market environment. The profit motive is sufficient to end discrimination.

Perhaps discrimination persists because it is supported by other noncompetitive institutions in the labor market, such as the internal labor markets of large corporations. For instance, statistical discrimination could exist against women at the ports of entry to the internal markets and severely restrict their access to the most desirable, primary-sector jobs. Even if women are hired at the entry levels, continued statistical discrimination or social custom may determine which positions women are permitted to hold within the corporate hierarchy. Women who continue to suffer discrimination after hiring may decide to stay with their present job rather than accept an entry-level position with another firm, even if the other firm is known to be less discriminatory. These forms of discrimination can persist because internal labor markets shield discriminatory practices from the discipline of competition. Another possible explanation for the persistence of discrimination is that labor unions have contributed to occupational stereotyping when defining job characteristics and work rules. These possibilities are admittedly speculative, but the persistence of discrimination is difficult to explain in a competitive market environment. Segmenting institutions, such as internal labor markets and labor unions, must play some role in maintaining current market discrimination against women to the extent it exists.

REFLECTION: Assuming that current labor market discrimination against women exists, which of the three explanations offered in the text for this phenomenon seems most plausible to you: prejudice, statistical discrimination, or socialization of male and female jobs? Do other explanations come to mind?

DISCRIMINATION AND THE LAW The federal government launched an all-out attack against labor market discrimination in the 1960s and 1970s with the passage of the Equal Pay Act of 1963, the Civil Rights Act of 1964, and Executive Orders 11246 and 11375, the first signed by President Lyndon Johnson in 1965 and the second signed by President Jimmy Carter in 1977.

The Equal Pay Act, an amendment to the Fair Labor Standards Act, was the first piece of federal legislation to address current labor market discrimination. The act stipulates that men and women must receive equal pay for equal work. Equal work is defined as work requiring the same degree of skill, effort, and responsibility and taking place under similar working conditions. The Equal Pay Act also overturned a number of protective labor laws which, among other things, "protected" women from being asked to work evenings or to engage in heavy lifting.

The Equal Pay Act was seriously deficient because it did not cover discrimination in hiring or promotion. The Civil Rights Act of 1964 corrected this oversight. Title VII of the act prohibits discrimination by race, gender, color, or religion in hiring, in compensation, and in the terms, conditions, and privileges of employment, including promotion and job training. The act also established the Equal Employment Opportunity Commission (EEOC) to enforce the provisions of the act.

Executive Order 11246 of 1965 stipulates that no company doing business with the federal government can discriminate on the basis of race in any aspect of employment. In addition, every contractor having more than $50,000 worth of business with the federal government must establish an affirmative action program. Executive Order 11375 of 1977 added discrimination against women to affirmative action.

Affirmative action requires employers to undertake a statistical analysis of their work force to determine whether it is unbalanced in terms of race or gender. Companies with low percentages of nonwhite minorities or women must make an extra effort to seek out and hire applicants from these groups. The Office of Federal Contract Compliance (OFCC) administers affirmative action to ensure that employers comply with the hiring guidelines.

These four laws remain the cornerstones of the federal government's efforts to eradicate discrimination from the labor market. The consensus opinion among economists is that they have been highly successful. Harvard's Richard Freeman believes that the civil rights legislation is the single most important factor behind the relative economic gains of blacks since 1964. Georgia State's Bruce Kaufman believes that affirmative action caused a virtual revolution in company personnel policies in the hiring of women. He notes that affirmative action might have been even more successful had the OFCC focused its efforts on the firms with the lowest percentages of nonwhite minorities and women. Instead, the OFCC targeted large corporations with a high percentage of white-collar workers. These companies were not the worst offenders, but targeting the large corporations led to the hiring of more nonwhite minorities and women.[15]

Optimism or Pessimism?

What lies ahead for women in the U.S. economy? One can find reasons for optimism and reasons for pessimism. The optimists point to recent improvements in the female-male earnings gap. The ratio of female wages to male wages rose from 60 percent to 65 percent from 1980 to 1986, the sharpest gain in this century. The relative position of young females has also shown marked improvement recently. In 1978 the ratio of female wages to male wages in the 20 to 24 age category stood at 78 percent. By 1986 the ratio had increased to 86 percent. The optimists also point to a number of favorable trends in the human capital characteristics of women. Years of formal education are increasing faster for women than for men. Also, women in college now study the same subjects as men. This was not always so. As recently as 1960, 46 percent of all women college students majored in education. By 1986 women were distributed among college majors in roughly the same proportions as men. Business had become the most popular major for both, the first choice among 28 percent of both men and women students. Women are also pursuing advanced degrees to a much greater extent today. As a result, their labor market positions have improved dramatically in the managerial and professional occupations. The proportion of females in managerial and professional occupations increased from 34 percent to 43 percent from 1970 to 1986. Finally, women are less prone to interrupt their careers today than they were even 10 years ago. The optimists believe that all these positive trends will continue.

The pessimists counter that much of the recent improvement in the female-male earnings gap was recovering ground lost in the 1970s. The earnings gap

---

[15] R. Freeman, "The Changing Labor Market for Black Americans," *Brookings Papers on Economic Activity* 1 (1973): 67–120; and Kaufman, *Economics of Labor Markets*, 450–451. For additional analysis of discrimination against women and nonwhite minorities in the United States, see Kaufman, *Economics of Labor Markets*, Chapter 9, 411–459, and Ehrenberg and Smith, *Modern Labor Economics*, fourth edition, Chapter 14, 529–574. Much of our data and analysis in this section comes from there two sources.

stood at 63 percent in 1939. Furthermore, even if women's wages are increasing relative to men's wages, women are suffering in other ways. The number of female-headed households continues to grow, which means that women have less leisure time. They also bear even more of the responsibilities for raising children, including the financial responsibility. The feminization of poverty is the most disturbing aspect of the breakup of the traditional family structure. Of all female-headed households, 35 percent fell below the poverty line in 1991. A final note of pessimism is sounded by those who believe that labor market discrimination against women is both pervasive and persistent in the U.S. economy and that the discrimination is rooted in social custom. According to this view, women cannot improve their economic positions very much unless they are able to change people's attitudes about the "proper" role of men and women in the household and in business, a formidable task indeed.[16]

Should one be optimistic or pessimistic about the economic prospects of women? The jury is still out on this all-important social question.

SUMMARY

The first section of Chapter 19 discussed the relationship between investment in education and labor market earnings, which economists call the theory of human capital. A main goal of human capital theory is to explain the fact that earnings increase systematically with additional investment in education.

1. Investment in education takes two forms: (a) formal education received in schools and vocational institutions and (b) on-the-job training received in the workplace.
2. According to human capital theory, people view formal education as an investment whose costs are the direct costs of the education plus the opportunity costs of the income lost by attending school and whose returns are the increase in wages they receive because more education leads to higher-paying jobs. Firms are willing to pay higher wages to more educated workers because each additional year of formal education increases a worker's productivity.
3. The text developed a simple model of formal education in which the value of the increase in wages that workers receive over their lifetimes from spending an additional year in school just equals the full costs of the year spent in school.
4. The returns to a college education in the United States are estimated to be between 5 and 15 percent per year, on average.
5. The theory of on-the-job training (OJT) is similar to the theory of formal education. Firms are willing to offer training because it makes their workers more productive. Workers are willing to undertake training because it leads to higher wages in the post-training period.
6. Firms try to offer specific training that is useful only within the firm itself. They try to avoid general training, such as problem solving, because workers can take general training with them to other firms.
7. Specific OJT breaks the equality between wages and the value of labor's marginal product in competitive labor markets. During the training period,

[16]"Symposium: Women in the Labor Market," *Journal of Economic Perspectives* 3, No. 1 (Winter 1989): 3–75. See, especially, the summary article by E. Lazear, "Symposium on Women in the Labor Market," 3–7.

wages plus the direct costs of training exceed the value of the workers' marginal product. Therefore, wages must be sufficiently below the value of marginal product throughout the post-training period to allow firms to recover the net costs they incur during training.

8. Specific OJT can explain a number of the features of the age-earnings profile:
   a. The rising portion of the hump-shaped age-earnings profile is the result of continual doses of OJT given to young workers, which increases their productivity and earnings into middle age. The training eventually stops, and wages stop rising, because the post-training period is not long enough to justify the costs of training for workers or employers. Wages begin to decrease in the later years as workers' human capital depreciates.
   b. Workers with more years of formal education are more receptive to OJT, which explains why the age-earnings profile rises more steeply the more educated the worker.
   c. Women have lower and flatter age-earnings profiles than do men because women choose careers offering less OJT than those chosen by men. Women bear most of the responsibilities for child raising and home keeping, so they interrupt their careers much more often than do men. Therefore, OJT is not as valuable to women or to their employers. The crowding of women into a few low-training occupations keeps their wages relatively low.
9. Differing amounts of formal education and OJT explain about 30 percent of the difference in earnings among people, with formal education accounting for about 10 percent of the difference and OJT accounting for about 20 percent of the difference.
10. The need for specific OJT has led to long-term employer-employee relationships in some large firms in the form of internal labor markets, in which firms hire from the outside for the entry-level positions and then promote from within to upper-level positions.
11. The presence of internal labor markets has spawned two hypotheses competing with human capital theory to explain the pattern of earnings, a motivation-based theory of wages and the segmentation hypothesis.
12. The motivational theory says that large firms design their wage and salary policies to keep their employees motivated over the long haul. Common practices include efficiency wages designed to keep morale high, reduce costly monitoring of employee effort, and reduce costly turnover; corporate tournaments in which the firms pay the winning top executives huge salaries and benefits and agree to keep the "deadwood" losers employed at good salaries until retirement; and delayed fringe benefits, such as pension plans. The motivational theory can explain the rising portion of the age-earnings profile, but not the falling portion in the later years.
13. The segmentation hypothesis says that productivity is tied to the job, not the worker. Firms use formal schooling only as a screening device to choose people for the entry-level positions in their internal labor markets and then teach employees all they need to know to perform their jobs through OJT. As a result, labor markets become segmented into a primary sector, offering good jobs with chances for promotion within internal labor markets, and a secondary sector, offering low-paying dead-end jobs. Also, the social re-

turns to formal education may be negative since formal education does not increase productivity.

14. While most economists believe that the segmentation theory is overstated, internal labor markets do segment labor markets beyond the entry-level positions and allow for the possibility of discrimination and "good old boy" networks to come into play in hiring, promotion, and salary decisions.

The second section of Chapter 19 discussed labor market discrimination, with emphasis on possible labor market discrimination against women.

15. Women's labor market experiences are quite different from those of men. Women earn substantially lower pay, the majority of women work in one of six occupations, and men and women most often hold different jobs within any one company.
16. These facts raise the possibility of labor market discrimination against women, meaning that women are denied equal treatment with respect to hiring or promotion or salaries simply because they are women. Discrimination can explain why so many women "choose" low-training occupations. Women know that training is not as valuable to them as it is to men because they face discrimination during the post-training period. As a result, they "choose" to spend the majority of time raising children and working at home, and their earnings remain permanently lower than men's earnings.
17. Labor market discrimination against women has three likely sources: outright prejudice; statistical discrimination, in which employers ascribe to any one woman the average attributes and behavior of women as a whole; and social customs, which designate certain occupations as "male" or "female."
18. Competitive market forces tend to eliminate discrimination so long as some employers do not discriminate. The nondiscriminating employers can hire those who are discriminated against at relatively low wages, which gives them a decisive cost advantage in selling their products. The discriminating employers must cease their discriminatory practices to remain in business.
19. The federal government mounted a strong attack against labor market discrimination in the 1960s with the passage of civil rights legislation that prohibits discrimination in all aspects of employment. These civil rights acts were buttressed by the affirmative action program, which requires all employers with federal contracts to make a special effort to hire women and nonwhite minorities if their work forces contain low proportions of either group. Economists believe that the federal anti-discrimination policies have been very successful in promoting the labor market opportunities of blacks and women.
20. If discrimination against women persists, as many economists believe, it is probably due to statistical discrimination or social customs operating in combination with noncompetitive institutions, such as internal labor markets and labor unions.
21. Some economists are optimistic and others pessimistic about the labor market prospects of women in the United States. The optimists point to recent improvements in women's pay generally and marked progress toward equality with men in the high-education, high-paying managerial and professional occupations. The pessimists point to the continued child-raising and home-keeping responsibilities of women, the rise of female-headed households, and the disturbing feminization of poverty.

KEY TERMS

current market discrimination
efficiency wage
formal education
general training
human capital theory
incentive-based pay
internal labor market
on-the-job training
pre-market discrimination
segmentation theory
specific training
statistical discrimination
time-based pay

QUESTIONS

1. a. Why does the theory of human capital predict a positive relationship between years of formal education and earnings?
   b. Would this prediction remain the same if some individuals had a cost advantage in obtaining formal education? If not, how would the prediction change in your opinion? (That is, to what extent will the resulting wage differences remain "equalizing" wage differences?)
2. a. How is the return to formal education usually measured?
   b. Why might this method overstate the returns to education? Understate the returns to education?
3. Discuss the differences between general and specific training
   a. from the firm's point of view.
   b. from the employees' point of view.
4. Discuss the role of specific on-the-job training in explaining the following features of the age-earnings profile:
   a. The age-earnings profile is humped, rising through middle age and then falling near retirement.
   b. The age-earnings profile rises more steeply for more educated workers.
   c. Women have lower and flatter age-earnings profiles than do men.
5. a. What are internal labor markets, and why do they exist?
   b. Briefly describe why the presence of internal labor markets plays a role in explaining wage and earnings differences.
   c. Briefly summarize the advantages and disadvantages of internal labor markets.
6. What are efficiency wages? Explain how the theory of efficiency wages can account for the fact that larger firms pay considerably higher wages than do smaller firms.
7. a. What is the basic premise of the segmentation theory of labor markets?
   b. What are its main implications with respect to the structure of labor markets?
   c. Is the theory capable of explaining any of the main facts about earnings in the United States?
8. Compare and contrast the human capital explanation and the discrimination explanation for why women have different labor market experiences from men. What is the available evidence supporting each explanation?
9. Years ago, before the civil rights movement, it was charged that many skilled blue-collar nonwhite workers were prohibited by outright racial discrimination from entering the normal labor markets for skilled workers. Instead, they were forced to seek unskilled blue-collar jobs, working at low-paying tasks well below their capabilities. Assume that this was true. Answer the following three questions, with appropriate explanations:
   a. What effects does this form of discrimination have on employment and wages in both the skilled and the unskilled labor markets? Show these effects graphically using supply and demand analysis.
   b. Do all whites benefit from the discrimination against nonwhite minorities?
   c. What effect does discrimination have on the nation's production possibilities? (Give an intuitive explanation.)
10. a. Why is the persistence of current labor market discrimination in the United States difficult to explain?
    b. What are some explanations for its persistence?
    c. Which of the explanations do you find the most persuasive?

CHAPTER

20

The Market for Capital

LEARNING OBJECTIVES

CONCEPTS TO LEARN

The flow of funds from savers to investors in the U.S. financial markets

Financial intermediaries

National net worth

The household's lifetime economic problem

Saving, investment, and interest rates

Capital market equilibrium

Why different financial securities have different rates of return

CONCEPTS TO RECALL

The household's three-part economic problem [1]

Substitution and income effects [5]

The Laws of Supply and Demand [5,6,7]

Private investment analysis [12]

The market for capital is one of the more important markets in the economy. For starters, it is the market where savers and investors meet to determine the level of saving and investment in the economy. As we saw in Chapter 3, saving and investment is vital to the process of long-run economic growth, and long-run economic growth is the single most important determinant of a nation's economic well-being.

The market for capital also contributes to the inequality of incomes in the United States, as it does in all capitalist economies. Income from capital accounts for slightly less than 20 percent of the total income generated in the U.S. factor markets, about one-fourth as much as income from labor. Nonetheless, it has a substantial impact on the personal distribution of income because capital is owned disproportionately by people with high incomes. Twenty percent of the U.S. population owns over 95 percent of all the accumulated wealth from saving, the source of funds for capital. Also, the larger a person's income is, the greater the percentage of income received from capital tends to be. With few exceptions, the very richest individuals receive the majority of their income from capital.

Chapter 20 analyzes the market for capital. We want to see how funds flow from savers to investors in the United States through the nation's financial markets and how the rates of return in financial markets bring the market for capital into equilibrium. The chapter also explains why rates of return are so different on the various kinds of financial instruments available to savers, such as bank deposits, corporate stocks, and bonds of all varieties.

THE FLOW OF FUNDS FROM SAVERS TO INVESTORS

Investment, Saving, and the Income from Capital

We first met the market for capital in Chapter 3 when we considered the relationships among capital, investment, and long-run economic growth. You must be sure that you understand two points from the discussion in Chapter 3 before analyzing the market for capital.

The first is the distinction between capital and investment. *Capital* is the factor of production, the total amount of equipment and structures (for example, mainframe computers, factories, office buildings) *in place* that firms use to produce their goods and services. Capital is a stock variable—it can be measured at a given point in time. *Investment* is the *addition* to the nation's stock of capital during the year, the purchase of *new* plant and equipment. Investment is a flow variable—it can be measured only with reference to a period of time because the amount that the capital stock has changed depends on the amount of time that has passed. A year is the natural unit of time for measuring investment.

The second point to recall from Chapter 3 is the distinction between physical and human capital. *Physical capital* refers to the stock of plant and equipment.

Human capital refers to the total amount, or stock, of education that people have acquired. We discussed investment in human capital in Chapter 19. Chapter 20 is concerned only with investment in physical capital. Review the discussion of these points in Chapter 3 if you are unclear about either of them.

Our primary focus in this chapter is on the income generated by capital. Households receive all the income from capital, but they do so in a roundabout manner that requires careful study. In particular, the income generated by a unit of capital may come to households from sources that are far removed from the capital itself.

The ultimate source of income from capital is the productivity of capital, just as it is for labor (or any other factor of production). Capital added to other factors of production increases the firm's output and therefore its total revenues. The increased revenues allow the firm to pay income to the suppliers of the capital. Capital differs from labor in two important respects, however. First, capital is a *produced input.* Firms do not buy capital directly from individuals. They buy capital from other firms, the manufacturing and construction firms that produce equipment and build structures. Second, the capital is *durable,* meaning that it remains productive for more than a year's time, usually far more than a year. Most equipment purchased today will remain in production for at least three years, and structures often last 35 years and more. Because of these two characteristics, the income generated by capital is not received directly by individuals in the same way that income generated by labor is.

When a firm hires labor, the hourly wage or annual salary of the worker is simultaneously the cost of the worker to the firm as the buyer of labor and the income received by the worker as the supplier of labor. The dollars of cost and income flow directly through a labor market at the point of the market exchange for the labor. In contrast, when a firm buys a machine, the cost of the machine does not translate directly into the income generated by the machine and received by anyone. It is, instead, revenue received by the firm that built the machine. In other words, the market exchange for capital goods is more like a product market transaction than a labor market transaction. The exchange generates income directly for the factors that are used to build the capital, but not from the capital itself.

A capital good does not begin to generate income until the firm that buys it begins using it in production. Then, once capital is in place, it can remain productive and continue to generate a stream of income for a number of years. How, then, is the stream of income ultimately received by individuals?

The answer is that individuals receive the income from capital in a roundabout way as a return to their saving because their saving is the ultimate source of funds for investment by business firms. The reason lies in the circular flow of economic activity. Individuals receive all the income generated by the producers in the economy from employing the primary factors of production: labor, capital, and land. They can dispose of their income in one of two ways: They can either spend it on consumer goods or save it. Firms meanwhile produce two kinds of products: semi-finished products and final products. The semi-finished products are those that are sold to other firms as material inputs to be further altered and refined in production. The final products are those that leave the production hierarchy. They consist of consumer goods and capital goods. Goods (and services) sold to consumers (and governments) for consumption are obviously final products. So, too, are the equipment and structures sold to other firms, the capital goods. Firms buy equipment and structures to help them produce their own products. They do not further refine capital goods and sell them, as they do semi-finished products/material inputs.

Now put the individuals and the firms together. The portion of the revenues from sales that firms spend on material inputs stays within the business sector. The remainder of the revenues is spent on purchasing the primary factors of production and enters the circular flow of economic activity as income received by individuals for the purchase of final products. The portion of their incomes that individuals consume is spent on consumer goods. Therefore, the portion of their incomes that individuals save must ultimately be used by business firms to purchase new capital goods, the other final products besides consumer goods. Saving must equal investment for the entire economy. No other source of funds is available for purchasing capital goods.

The flow of funds from savers to investors through a nation's financial markets is very complex. Funds do not travel in a simple, direct line from households to businesses. Rather, the flow of funds involves all four sectors of the economy—household, business, government, and foreign—and individuals and institutions within each sector can be either suppliers or demanders of funds. Also, dollars of saving often pass through many layers of institutions called financial intermediaries along their journey to the investors. To understand how the financial markets work we have to understand what kinds of transactions take place in the financial markets and the special role of the financial intermediaries in channeling funds from savers to investors.

Internal Financing

The majority of the total saving in the economy is channeled directly to investment by the business firms themselves. For example, in 1992, firms in the United States raised $770.4 billion to finance current and future investment projects. Of this total, $735.9 billion (95.5 percent) consisted of their own funds generated by the production and sale of their products. Although internal funding of investment may not seem like saving by individuals, remember that all businesses are owned by individuals, the stockholders of the firm. If the managers had not used these internal funds for investment, they would have distributed the funds to the stockholders as dividends, a source of income. Therefore, when managers set aside funds for investment, the stockholders are essentially allowing the managers to save in their behalf a portion of the income earned from the business.

Internal funding of investment comes from two sources of saving, capital consumption allowances and retained earnings. **Capital consumption allowances** are funds that firms set aside to replace equipment and structures as they age and lose their productive capacity. Capital consumption allowances for each unit of capital are supposed to match the **depreciation** of the capital, defined as the decline in the capital's economic value during the course of a year. In practice, firms estimate the depreciation of their capital stock based on guidelines established by the U.S. Internal Revenue Service (IRS). The IRS recognizes depreciation of capital as a legitimate operating expense and permits firms to deduct the capital consumption allowances set aside when computing the taxable profits of the firm. In principle, capital consumption allowances enable the firm to maintain its existing stock of capital without

CAPITAL CONSUMPTION ALLOWANCES

Funds that firms set aside to replace equipment and structures as they age and lose their productive capacity, equal in principle to the economic depreciation of capital.

DEPRECIATION

The decline in capital's economic value during the course of a year.

having to resort to outside funding. The firm replaces each unit of capital using funds accumulated from the capital consumption allowances on that unit while it was part of the production process.

HISTORICAL NOTE: Capital consumption allowances increased dramatically in the 1980s and 1990s as firms invested more and more in computers and computer-driven technologies. Computers tend to depreciate rapidly, not so much because they wear out, but because they become obsolete so quickly.

Retained earnings are part of the accounting profits of the firm, the difference between total revenues and total operating expenses. Accounting profits end up as one of three things: as taxes, as dividends, or as retained earnings. Corporations pay taxes on their profits under the federal and state corporate income taxes. Partnerships and proprietors pay taxes on their profits under the federal and state personal income taxes. The profits remaining after taxes are either distributed to the firm's stockholders as dividends or retained in the company as retained earnings. The retained earnings are earmarked for future investment projects. Since capital consumption allowances are designed to replace existing capital, the retained earnings finance additions to the firm's stock of capital. In other words, retained earnings are funds set aside to help finance the continued expansion of the firm.

RETAINED EARNINGS

The portion of the accounting profits of the firm that is not paid out as taxes or as dividends to stockholders, but is set aside to help finance the continued expansion of the firm.

Capital consumption allowances are by far the more important source of internal funding for the firm and the single most important source of funds for investment. In 1992, for example, capital consumption allowances in the United States were $653.4 billion and retained earnings only $82.5 billion. Thus, capital consumption allowances accounted for 88.8 percent of all internal funds and 84.8 percent of all funds raised to finance U.S. investment in 1991.[1]

Capital consumption allowances and retained earnings are called **business saving.** As noted above, though, business saving is really saving by stockholders that they then channel directly to investment through the firms that they own. The stockholders assure the continued operation of their firm and help provide for its future expansion by allowing the managers to save in their behalf.

BUSINESS SAVING

The sum of capital consumption allowances and retained earnings held by firms.

External Financing and the Financial Markets

Not all the funds for investment come from the firms themselves. As the figures for 1992 illustrate, U.S. firms raised $34.5 billion of the financing for their investments from external sources of saving. This is where the nation's financial markets enter the picture. The role of the **financial markets** is to transfer money throughout the economy from surplus agents to deficit agents. The **surplus agents** are the savers, or lenders, the suppliers of funds in financial markets. Surplus agents have more income than they desire to spend in any one year. The **deficit agents** are the borrowers, the users of funds in financial markets. Deficit agents have less income than they desire to spend in any one year. Investment is one of the uses of funds, but not the only one.

FINANCIAL MARKETS

Markets that play the role of transferring money from surplus agents to deficit agents throughout the economy.

SURPLUS AGENTS

Economic agents who are the savers, or lenders, or the suppliers of funds in financial markets because they have more income than they desire to spend in any one year.

DEFICIT AGENTS

Economic agents who are the borrowers or the users of funds in financial markets because they have less income than they desire to spend in any one year.

EQUITY AND DEBT The transfer of money from surplus agents to deficit agents occurs in one of two ways: either through the creation of equity or debt, or through trades of money for existing equity or debt.

In an equity-creating transaction, a surplus agent transfers funds to a business firm in exchange for new shares of common stock. The agent becomes one of

[1]U.S. Department of Commerce, Economics and Statistics Administration, Bureau of Economic Analysis, *Survey of Current Business*, 73, No. 3 (March 1993): Table 5.1, p. 14.

the owners of the firm, and the stock, or *equity*, entitles the agent to share in the profits of the firm. Transferring funds through equity is a gamble for surplus agents. They earn a return on their saving only if the firm is successful.

Transferring funds through debt is somewhat less of a gamble. In a debt-creating transaction, a deficit agent and a surplus agent form a borrower-lender relationship. The debt instrument can take one of two forms, a promise to repay or an order to repay. A *promise to repay* may take many different forms, but it always stipulates that the borrower will repay the lender certain amounts of money at specific dates in the future. One example is a corporate bond, which firms can use instead of issuing stock to raise funds for investment. The saver (lender) transfers funds to the corporation (borrower) in return for the corporate bond. The typical corporate bond includes a face value, an interest payment, and a date of maturity. The face value, often $1,000 or multiples of $1,000, is the principal on the bond, the amount the firm repays at the date of maturity. If the date of maturity is 10 years in the future, the bond is said to be a 10-year bond. The interest payment is an amount the firm pays the holder of the bond each year until the bond matures, for example, $80 per year for 10 years. The annual interest payments are in addition to the repayment of the principal when the bond matures. Holders of corporate bonds are not owners of the firm. They have no claim on the profits of the firm other than the principal and interest stipulated on the bond.

A variation of the standard bond is the *Treasury bill,* which the U.S. government uses to borrow money for less than a year's time. Treasury bills specify only a face value and a date of maturity. They do not pay interest. For example, you might lend the government $950 today in return for a Treasury bill that pays you $1,000 (the face value) in 180 days (the date of maturity). Still another variation of a promise to repay that consumers are familiar with is *installment debt,* the form used for automobile loans and home mortgages. In an installment contract the borrower repays the lender both principal and interest in equal monthly installments until the principal is entirely repaid. The monthly installments are computed by a complicated formula that takes into account the interest owed on the principal remaining after each installment.

An example of an *order to repay* is a checking account at a bank. You might not think of a checking account as a loan, but it is. When you place money in a checking account, you are lending the bank your money in return for an order to repay. When you write a check on your account, the bank must transfer the funds to whomever you have made the check payable. Checking accounts may or may not pay interest. Even if they do not, the account yields a return in the form of a service, the convenience of being able to pay for goods and services by check. Also, checking accounts have no specific date of maturity. You may close your account at any time, thereby terminating your loan to the bank.

Financial markets give rise to another type of transaction in which two agents trade existing equity and debt. Once common stock, corporate bonds, Treasury bills, and mortgages have been created, or issued, they can be traded. For example, you might have some money that you want to exchange for shares of common stock in IBM. Someone else, unknown to you, owns shares of IBM common stock and wants to exchange the stock for money. So the two of you exchange money for the IBM stock through a broker who has a license to trade stock on the New York Stock Exchange. In fact, most exchanges of stock are trades of existing stock, not issues of new stock that transfer funds directly from savers to firms. Stocks are not unique in this respect. There are also active markets for trading most existing debt instruments, such as the corporate and the government bond markets. Exchanges of existing equity and debt affect the rates of return available to savers on these financial instruments, but they do not transfer funds from savers to investors.

Equity and debt instruments are assets from a surplus agent's (lender's) point of view. An **asset** (credit) is something an agent owns or a claim the agent has against someone. Equity and debt instruments are debits or liabilities from a deficit agent's (borrower's) point of view. A **liability** is a something an agent owes, a financial claim against the agent due someone else. The difference between an agent's asset and its liabilities is its **net worth,** also referred to as **wealth.** An agent's wealth at any one time is the result of all its past lending and borrowing decisions up to that point. Notice that net worth or wealth need not be positive. An agent has negative net worth if its liabilities exceed its assets.

ASSET

Something an agent owns or a financial claim an agent has against someone.

LIABILITY

Something an agent owes, or a financial claim against the agent due to someone else.

NET WORTH/WEALTH

The difference between an agent's assets and its liabilities.

FINANCIAL INTERMEDIARIES Financial markets give rise to many different kinds of financial intermediaries. A **financial intermediary** is any institution involved in the process of transferring funds from suppliers to users that positions itself between the ultimate suppliers and the ultimate users of funds. An example is a commercial bank, which borrows funds from households in exchange for checking or savings deposits and then lends the funds to businesses to help them finance their investment projects. In this set of transactions the holders of the checking and savings deposits are the ultimate suppliers of funds (lenders), the businesses are the ultimate users of funds (borrowers), and the commercial bank is the financial intermediary, serving to channel the funds from households to businesses.

FINANCIAL INTERMEDIARY

Any institution involved in the process of transferring funds from suppliers to users that positions itself between the ultimate suppliers and the ultimate users of funds in financial markets, such as a commercial bank.

Besides commercial banks, the most important financial intermediaries in the U.S. economy are savings banks, insurance companies, pension funds, and automobile finance companies. In the broadest sense these other financial intermediaries all operate in the same way as commercial banks when they transact with ultimate suppliers and ultimate users of funds. They accept funds from ultimate suppliers in exchange for which they offer a range of financial services that may or may not include a rate of return for the use of the funds. They then lend the funds to ultimate users. The rate of return they receive on their loans allows them to cover the costs of providing the financial services that they specialize in and to earn an acceptable return on their capital. (Financial intermediaries also transact with other financial intermediaries, but we will ignore that possibility for now as an unnecessary complication. Suffice it to note that many layers of financial intermediation can separate the ultimate suppliers and ultimate users of funds.)

Financial intermediaries provide three important services to savers and investors. They increase the options available to savers, they serve as brokers between savers and investors, and they sharply reduce the cost of transferring funds. These services increase the total amount of saving and investment by facilitating the transfer of funds from savers to investors. Let's look briefly at each of them.

INCREASING THE OPTIONS FOR SAVERS Most households do not offer all their saving directly to business firms by purchasing corporate bonds or stocks. Instead, they seek a variety of financial services from their saving. Households

TABLE 20.1 Financial Assets Held by Households, End of Year 1992

ASSET	VALUE (BILLIONS)
DEPOSITS	$ 3,351
PENSION FUND RESERVES	4,586
EQUITY IN NONCORPORATE BUSINESS	2,264
EQUITY IN CORPORATIONS	2,535
LIFE INSURANCE RESERVES	434
CORPORATE AND FOREIGN BONDS	131
OTHER NONGOVERNMENT SECURITIES	1,630
SUBTOTAL: FINANCIAL ASSETS OTHER THAN GOVERNMENT SECURITIES	$14,931
GOVERNMENT SECURITIES	1,250
TOTAL FINANCIAL ASSETS	$16,181

SOURCE: Board of Governors of the Federal Reserve System, *Balance Sheets for the U.S. Economy, 1945–92* (Washington, D.C.: U.S. Government Printing Office, 1993), Report C.9, Table B.100.

want checking accounts that offer the convenience of paying by check, pension plans that will provide a steady income throughout the retirement years, and life insurance policies that offer the combination of a savings account and a large payment to loved ones in the event of death. Commercial and savings banks, pension funds, and insurance companies come into being because they can profitably offer these kinds of services. Not surprisingly, the profit motive works just as well in financial markets as it does in nonfinancial markets to encourage the supply of financial services that households want to buy.

Table 20.1 illustrates the importance of the various services offered by financial intermediaries. The table shows the distribution of financial assets held by U.S. households at the end of 1992. Notice that corporate and noncorporate equities and bonds amounted to only 33 percent of the total financial assets, excluding government securities. Households have chosen to place the majority of their saving over time with the financial intermediaries, particularly in deposits at commercial and savings banks and in pension funds. Households presumably would save a lot less each year if their only savings options were to purchase corporate and noncorporate stocks and bonds.

SERVING AS BROKERS Financial intermediaries also promote saving and investment by serving as brokers between savers and investors. As we saw in Chapter 4, a broker is an agent who brings buyers and sellers together in a market. Stock brokers bring buyers and sellers of stock together in well-organized stock exchanges such as the New York Stock Exchange. Investment banks serve the same function in the market for corporate bonds. When a corporation issues bonds to raise money for investment, it does not bother to seek out people and institutions who are willing to hold the bonds. Instead, it relies on an investment bank to act as the broker. Investment banks bid for the bond issue, and the firm sells the bonds to the highest bidder. The investment bank that purchases the bonds then resells them to the economic agents who ultimately want to hold the bonds as part of their assets. The bank earns its profit by selling the bonds at a higher price than it paid for them. Stock exchanges and investment banking are just two examples of the many brokerage services provided by financial intermediaries.

REDUCING THE COST OF TRANSFERRING FUNDS Financial intermediaries promote saving and investment in yet a third way, by greatly reducing the costs of transferring funds from savers to investors. Suppose that a firm wants to borrow $10 million to finance an investment project and that each of 10,000 households wants to save $1,000, for a total saving of $10 million. Without the existence of financial intermediaries, the firm would have to seek out each household and write 10,000 separate loan contracts of $1,000 each in order to raise the $10 million. Financial intermediaries such as commercial banks can effect the transfer of funds from the households to the firms at a much lower cost. For example, each of the households might choose to open a $1,000 checking account at a commercial bank, so that the bank receives the $10 million in saving. Then the firm and the loan officers of the bank can negotiate a single $10 million loan contract to finance the investment. True, opening 10,000 checking accounts and negotiating the bank loan entail some costs. But transferring the $10 million from the households to the firm through the commercial bank is obviously much less costly and time-consuming than directly negotiating 10,000 loan contracts between the firm and the households.

A final point to note about financial intermediaries relates to the way in which individuals earn income from capital. A large portion of their capital income derives from the assets they hold with the financial intermediaries, such as interest earned on checking and savings accounts and pension annuities received during the retirement years. The income does not all come directly from the business firms whose capital is the ultimate source of the income. Financial intermediaries channel some of the income from capital from businesses to individuals in the process of channeling some of the saving of individuals to businesses for investment.

THE SUPPLIERS AND DEMANDERS OF FUNDS We are now in a position to trace the flow of funds from savers to investors through the financial markets. As we do, we will see that a substantial amount of the funds potentially available to finance investment is diverted to other uses and never reaches the business firms. The diversion of funds begins in the household sector.

HOUSEHOLD SECTOR When consumers save, they do not just buy financial assets. They also buy real assets in the form of houses or consumer durables, such as automobiles and major appliances. Houses and consumer durables are considered real assets because they are similar to plant and equipment, the real assets of business firms. The house or automobile or stove purchased today generates a stream of housing or automotive or cooking services well into the future, just as plant and equipment purchased today generates a stream of goods or services for many years to come. Therefore, purchases of houses and consumer durables are more like a simultaneous act of saving and investment than an act of consumption, analogous to the financing of investment by business firms out of retained earnings. In fact, the purchase of a new home is so similar to the purchase of business capital that residential structures are included as part of the nation's stock of physical capital. All other real assets purchased by the household sector are considered to be consumer goods in the form of consumer durables, and not part of the capital stock.

Purchases of real assets are an important component of household saving. In 1992, for example, households increased their holdings of financial assets by $471.3 billion. In that same year households increased their holdings of real assets by $258 billion, consisting of a $189 billion increase in owner-occupied homes and a $69 billion increase in the stock of consumer durables (these figures are net of depreciation on these assets).[2] Furthermore, the purchase of real assets feeds back directly into the nation's financial markets because households often borrow to finance these purchases. They take out mortgages on new homes, borrow from banks or finance companies to purchase automobiles, and borrow on their credit cards to finance purchases of major appliances. In other words, the household sector is not only a supplier of funds to a nation's financial markets; it is also an important demander of funds.

For example, in the latter half of the 1980s households took advantage of newly created home equity loans, which allow them to borrow against the equity they have built up in existing homes. They have used the home equity loans to finance such things as home improvements, major appliances, cars, and their children's college educations. As a result, the increase in their mortage debt in recent years has far exceeded the increase in the stock of housing.

GOVERNMENT SECTOR The federal, state, and local governments are also important players in the financial markets, and they can be either net demanders or net suppliers of funds. Governments levy taxes and fees to pay for their expenditures. If these revenues are used to purchase public investment goods, such as schools, highways, and office buildings, then they are in effect forced saving that increases the nation's stock of capital. Otherwise, government expenditures are either acts of public consumption or transfer payments that simply return the tax dollars to the private sector.

If the taxes and fees of a government exceed its expenditures during the year, the government budget is in surplus, and the government becomes a supplier of funds to the financial markets. Government officials want to earn a rate of return on the excess revenues, so they place their funds in bank deposits and buy other interest-bearing financial assets, just as households do when they save. If expenditures exceed taxes and fees during the year, the government budget is in deficit, and the government has to borrow to cover the revenue shortfall. It becomes a net demander of funds in the financial markets. Each year since 1981 the federal government has run substantial deficits and has been a large net demander of funds. By contrast, the state and the local governments ran surpluses and were net suppliers of funds until the end of the decade, when obligations to their retirement accounts drained the operating surpluses and made them slight net demanders of funds. The federal government's annual deficits were always far greater than were the state and the local governments' annual surpluses, so that the government sector has been a large net demander of funds since 1981. In 1992, for example, the overall government sector was a net demander of funds in the amount of $407.7 billion.

---

[2]Board of Governors of the Federal Reserve System, *Balance Sheets for the U.S. Economy, 1945–92* (Washington, D.C.: U.S. Government Printing Office, 1993), Report C.9, Table B.100.

REST-OF-WORLD (FOREIGN) SECTOR U.S. households, businesses, and governments place some of their funds in foreign businesses and financial intermediaries. Similarly, foreign households, businesses, and governments place some of their funds in U.S. businesses and financial intermediaries. If the flow of funds out of the United States exceeds the flow of funds into the United States, the foreign sector is a net demander of funds in the U.S. financial markets. Conversely, if the flow of funds into the United States exceeds the flow of funds out of the United States, the foreign sector is a net supplier of funds to the U.S. financial markets. The latter has been the case throughout the 1980s and into the 1990s. The foreign sector was a very important supplier of funds and played a major role in financing the nation's investment. In 1992, for example, the net supply of funds into the United States totaled $68.9 billion.

ALL SECTORS COMBINED Table 20.2 summarizes the net flow of funds into the U.S. financial markets from the four nonfinancial sectors of the economy in 1992. The net flow of funds to financial markets (column 4) is the difference between the net acquisition of financial assets, or lending (column 2), and the net increase in financial liabilities, or borrowing (column 3). The aggregate net flow of funds is the total amount of saving that is available to finance investment by business firms. The table shows that the household, business, and foreign sectors were net suppliers of funds and that the government sector was a net demander of funds. It also shows very clearly the important role of households as both suppliers and demanders of funds in the U.S. financial markets. Households were both the largest lenders *and* the second-largest borrowers of funds among all the sectors. Finally, the table indicates that the federal government's inability to balance its budget is a serious potential drain on investment. Funds borrowed to finance government deficits are not available to business firms for investment in plant and equipment. Fortunately, the foreign sector replaced some of the funds drained off by the government sector in 1992. This same pattern held true throughout most of the 1980s as well. Investment in the United States might well have been much lower over the previous decade had foreigners not placed large amounts of their saving in U.S. financial markets.

REFLECTION: Is internal financing of investments necessarily cheaper for firms than external financing is?

TABLE 20.2 Net Flow of Funds by Sector of the Economy 1992

SECTOR	NET ACQUISITION OF FINANCIAL ASSETS (BILLIONS)	NET ACQUISITION OF FINANCIAL LIABILITIES (BILLIONS)	NET INCREASE IN FINANCIAL WEALTH (BILLIONS)
HOUSEHOLD[a]	$471.3	$221.6	$249.7
NONFINANCIAL BUSINESS	165.5	88.5	77.0
STATE AND LOCAL GOVERNMENT	1.9	48.4	−46.5
U.S. GOVERNMENT	−31.0	330.2	−361.2
FOREIGN (REST-OF-WORLD)	179.1	110.2	68.9

[a]The household sector includes personal trusts and nonprofit institutions.

SOURCE: Board of Governors of the Federal Reserve System, *Flow of Funds Accounts: Flows and Outstandings, Fourth Quarter 1992* (Washington, D.C.: U.S. Government Printing Office, 1993), Report Z.1, Tables F.100, F.101, F.105, F.106, F.109.

National Net Worth and the Income from Capital

NATIONAL NET WORTH

The net worth or wealth of an entire nation, equal to the market value of the nation's real, or tangible, assets plus the market value of its land, less any claims against these assets held by foreigners.

Two final points will conclude our overview of the flow of funds in the United States. First, **national net worth,** the net worth of an entire nation, is the market value of the nation's real, or tangible, assets plus the market value of its land, less any claims against these assets held by foreigners. The real assets include all consumer durables and all capital goods owned by the household, business, and government sectors. The capital goods consist of residential structures (homes), nonresidential plant (factories, office buildings) and equipment (computers, desks), and inventories (goods that have been produced, but not yet sold). The real assets and the land are net worth for the nation as a whole because they are the nonlabor resources that produce goods and services for the benefit of the nation's citizens.

In contrast, the financial assets owned by individuals and institutions do not produce anything. They are merely claims against the income generated by the real assets. Equity in the form of corporate stock is net worth to the individuals who hold the stock, but the market value of financial equity matches the market value of the capital that the equity has purchased. Therefore, to include financial equity as well as capital in national net worth would represent double counting. Financial debt instruments do not give rise to net worth at all because one lender's credit or asset is another borrower's debit or liability. For instance, when a firm issues corporate bonds to finance purchases of capital, the bonds are simultaneously an asset to the bondholders and a liability to the firm. This point is worth remembering when you read alarmist statements that U.S. consumers and businesses are awash in a sea of debt. A sea of debt is also a sea of credit. Being awash in a sea of credit does not sound quite so threatening.

Table 20.3 shows the national net worth of the United States at the end of 1992. Saving in the U.S. economy over time has resulted in the accumulation of over $18 trillion of productive real assets, nearly $72,000 per person. Moreover, most of the saving has come from U.S. citizens. Foreign citizens held claims to less than 4 percent of the real assets in 1992. A succinct statement of the productive activity in the U.S. economy in 1992 would read as follows: Producers in the United States combined $14 trillion of capital, $4.3 trillion of land, and a labor force of 127 million workers to produce $6 trillion worth of final goods and services.

Our final point merely summarizes how individuals receive income from capital and consumer durables. We have seen that income from capital has both an implicit component and an explicit component. The implicit component is the annual stream of services received by consumers from the houses and the consumer durables that they have purchased. The income is implicit because the housing services that members of a household receive from an owner-occupied home, or the automotive services received from their cars, do not involve a flow of dollars from one person to another. Nonetheless, the annual services provided by these assets are real, valued services and should be viewed simultaneously as consumption by, and income to, the people who have purchased the assets. The explicit component is the annual dollar return on net worth, the difference between the annual returns received on real plus financial assets and the annual payments made on financial liabilities. The returns on assets include such items as interest received on a savings account at a bank, dividends received on shares of corporate stock, and apartment rent-

TABLE 20.3 **Net Worth of the United States, End of Year 1992**

TANGIBLE ASSETS	VALUE (BILLIONS)
RESIDENTIAL STRUCTURES	$ 5,188
NONRESIDENTIAL PLANT AND EQUIPMENT	5,538
INVENTORIES	1,101
CONSUMER DURABLES	2,191
SUBTOTAL OF REPRODUCIBLE ASSETS	$14,018
LAND AT MARKET VALUES	4,289
TOTAL TANGIBLE ASSETS	$18,307
U.S. GOLD AND SDRs[a]	20
NET CLAIMS ON FOREIGN ASSETS	−618
TOTAL CONSOLIDATED DOMESTIC NET ASSETS	$17,709

[a]SDRs refer to Special Drawing Rights that are used in international transactions. Gold and SDRs are considered assets because they can be used in international trade to purchase real goods and services from foreign countries.

SOURCE: Board of Governors of the Federal Reserve System, *Balance Sheets for the U.S. Economy, 1945–92* (Washington, D.C.: U.S. Government Printing Office, 1993), Report C.9, Table B.11.

als received by landlords. The most common payment on liabilities is interest paid on a loan, such as a mortgage or an auto loan or an outstanding credit card balance.

The following example illustrates how you would compute the explicit component of your income from capital. Suppose that you have one asset and one liability. The asset is a financial asset, a $1,000 savings account that earns 6 percent interest per year. The liability is an average balance of $200 on your credit card, on which the credit card company charges you 18 percent interest per year. Your net worth is $800, the difference between the dollar amount of the savings account (the asset) and the credit card balance (the liability). Your income from capital during the year is the difference between the interest you receive on the savings account and the interest you pay on the credit card balance. The interest received on the savings account is $60 ($60 = $1,000 · 0.06). The interest paid on the credit card balance is $36.00 ($36.00 = $200 · 0.18). Therefore, your explicit income from capital during the year is $24 ($24 = $60 − $36).

Unlike labor income, an individual's income from capital can be negative if payments on liabilities exceed returns from assets. Income from capital is decidedly positive for the United States as a whole, however, accounting for just under 20 percent of all income earned in the nation's factor markets. This income derives from the productivity of the $14 trillion stock of capital in place.

REFLECTION: Do you have positive or negative net worth?

Interest received on a savings account, the annual income from a pension annuity, and many other forms of income from capital may seem far removed from the productivity of factories or machines, but this is only because financial intermediaries have positioned themselves between savers and investors. The productivity of real assets is what ultimately allows someone to pay someone else a positive rate of return for the use of funds. Commercial banks would not pay us interest on deposits if they could not re-lend to businesses and consumers at still higher rates of interest. And businesses and consumers would not borrow from commercial banks if they could not buy real assets whose productivity exceeds the interest on their loans.

We will look at the relationships among saving, investment, and rates of interest more closely in the next section.

THE MARKET FOR CAPITAL

The market for capital can be described either directly in terms of saving and investment or indirectly in terms of the demand and the supply of funds in financial markets. Let's begin with the direct approach and analyze the supply of saving and the demand for investment.

Savers and investors are, for the most part, different economic agents facing different economic problems. When they meet in the nation's financial markets, they share one piece of information in common, the prices of lending and borrowing money in various forms. We will refer to these prices as interest rates, although they can take other forms such as dividends on shares of common stock. Interest rates are, simultaneously, the returns received by savers for lending to investors and the costs to investors of borrowing from savers.

Financial markets are highly competitive for the most part and operate according to the Laws of Supply and Demand. Therefore, our analysis of saving and investment proceeds in the usual manner. The first task is to show how saving and investment are each related to interest rates, other things equal. We then show how interest rates adjust to equate the desired levels of investment and saving, at which point the market for capital is in equilibrium. The analysis of equilibrium is where we bring in the financial markets to explain how they determine the movement of interest rates.

To keep the analysis as simple as possible, assume that consumers (households) are the only savers, that businesses are the only investors, and that there is a single rate of interest on all loans between consumers and businesses. The final section of the chapter considers a number of reasons why interest rates differ for different kinds of financial assets and liabilities.

The Supply of Saving

The ability to lend and borrow significantly changes the consumer's economic problem that we discussed in Chapter 5. There we assumed that consumers spend all their income on goods and services each year. Through lending and borrowing, however, consumers can choose a pattern of consuming goods and services over time that differs from the pattern of their earnings over time. When consumers save, they are consciously deciding to consume less than their income now in order to be able to consume more than their income in some future year(s). Conversely, consumers borrow in order to consume more than their incomes now, knowing that they will have to consume less than their income in some future year(s) to pay back the loan.

Most adults do lend and borrow to break the link between their consumption and their labor market earnings over time. Figure 20.1 illustrates the typical pattern in the United States. We learned in Chapter 18 that the average age-

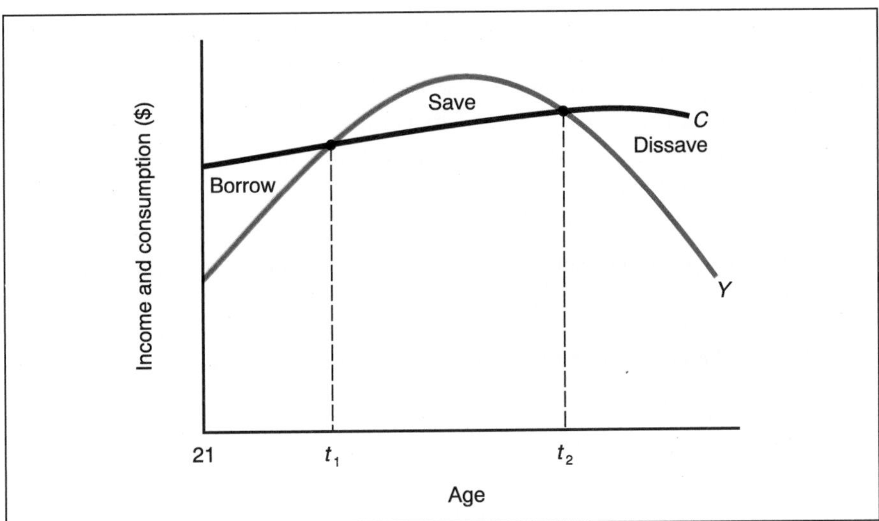

FIGURE 20.1

Lifetime Income and Consumption

The figure shows the average lifetime pattern of income and consumption of adults. Lifetime income, Y, is the average age-earnings profile. It is hump-shaped, rising to middle age and then declining. Lifetime consumption, C, is smoother than lifetime income because people borrow and lend to try to maintain a fairly constant standard of living. They are net borrowers when young, from age 21 to t_1, so consumption exceeds income. Then they become net savers in middle age, from t_1 to t_2, as they build up a nest egg for retirement. Income exceeds consumption. They dissave after t_2, the retirement years, living off their savings from middle age. Consumption once again exceeds income.

earnings profile has a humped shape. Earnings rise into middle ages and then decline in the later work years and during retirement. The curve labeled Y represents a typical age-earnings profile. Consumption throughout adulthood tends to be much smoother than are earnings. The curve labeled C represents the typical pattern of consumption over time. People prefer a much more constant standard of living than they would have if they simply spent all their earnings each year on goods and services.

Adults "smooth" their consumption over time by borrowing and lending. When adults are young, the period from age 21 to t_1 in Figure 20.1, they consume more than they earn. This is the time when people save very little of their incomes and are likely to take out a mortgage on a home and borrow to finance cars and major appliances. Borrowing is negative saving. When adults reach middle age, the period from t_1 to t_2 in the figure, they consume less than their incomes and save. Middle-aged adults save to provide for their retirement years, by contributing to company pension plans and purchasing a variety of stocks, bonds, and other financial assets. Some may pay back their debts incurred as young adults. Since borrowing is negative saving, paying off a loan is positive saving. Finally, when adults reach the age of retirement from the labor market, the period beyond t_2 in the figure, they again consume more than their incomes. They do so by drawing down the assets that they accumulated during middle age, another form of negative saving. The saving during middle age allows adults to maintain during the retirement years the standard of living they have become accustomed to, despite a sharp decline in their labor market earnings. At death, only a very small percentage of adults leave behind a substantial estate, which implies that only a very small percentage of younger adults inherit substantial amounts of wealth. For the vast majority of people in the United States the lifetime pattern of consumption and income described by Figure 20.1 is essentially self-contained.

SAVING AND THE CONSUMER'S ECONOMIC PROBLEM The pattern of consumption and saving illustrated in Figure 20.1 results from consumers solving their economic problem defined over their entire lifetimes. While the lifetime economic problem has the standard form—objectives, alternatives, and constraints—it is much more complex than the one-period economic problem defined in Chapter 5. Just writing down the elements of the lifetime economic problem is enough to give a flavor of its complexity.

Objective: The goal is to achieve the highest amount of utility or satisfaction over an entire lifetime.

Alternatives: Consumers face two sets of alternatives:

1. The various goods and services available to consumers throughout their lifetimes and
2. The pattern of lending (saving) and borrowing (dissaving) over time that will allow the consumers to purchase the goods and services they want each year.[3]

Constraints: Three constraints limit the amount of lifetime satisfaction that consumers can hope to achieve:

1. The current and future prices of the various goods and services.
2. The resources available to consumers over their lifetimes. The principal resources are inherited wealth, any transfers received from family members or the government, and labor market earnings. Consumers also have to take into consideration taxes paid to governments.
3. The current and future interest rates at which consumers can borrow and lend. From a consumer's point of view, interest rates are prices that determine the ability to trade off current consumption for future consumption. For example, at an interest rate of 10 percent, each $1.00 saved and not consumed today will allow consumers to buy $1.10 worth of goods and services one year from now (ignoring taxes).

Notice that all future values of prices, interest rates, and resources are the values consumers expect them to be, not necessarily their actual values. No one can know for sure what these values will be at anytime in the future.

The decision on how much to save and how much to consume each year is one small part of the overall solution to the lifetime economic problem. The structure of the problem suggests that the desired level of saving in any one year depends on a very large number of factors, including preferences for current and future consumption, current and expected future prices of goods and services, expected lifetime earnings, inherited wealth, current and expected future interest rates, current and expected future tax payments, and so forth.

SAVING AND INTEREST RATES Our concern here is the other things equal relationship between the desired level of saving and interest rates. How does the desired level of saving vary with the current level of interest rates, holding constant all the other factors that influence the saving decision? The standard presumption is that the desired level of saving and interest rates are directly related. Higher interest rates supposedly induce consumers to save more, and lower interest rates induce consumers to save less, other things equal. In other words, the supply of saving curve is upward sloping, as represented by the curve S in Figure 20.2(a).

---

[3]We are assuming that all job decisions have been made in order to highlight the role of saving in the lifetime economic problem.

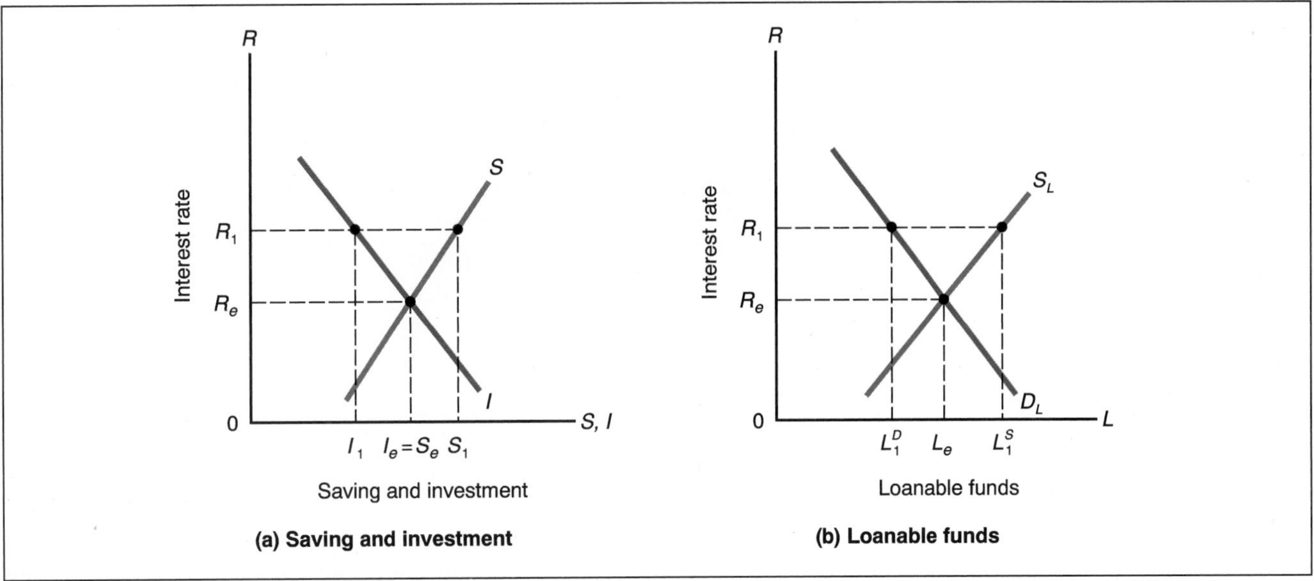

FIGURE 20.2

Saving, Investment, and the Market for Loanable Funds

Figure 20.2(a) shows the market for saving and investment. Saving demand, S, is positively related to the interest rate, R, and investment demand, I, is negatively related to R. The market for capital is in equilibrium at the intersection of S and I, with an interest rate of R_e, and saving and investment of S_e and I_e. The interest rate is determined in the market for loanable funds in Figure 20.2(b). The supply of loanable funds, S_L, corresponds to the saving demand S in Figure 20.2(a) and the demand for loanable funds, D_L, corresponds to investment demand I. The equilibrium in the loanable funds market is at (L_e,R_e), at the intersection of D_L and S_L. If the interest rate is above R_e, at R_1, the market for loanable funds is in excess supply in the amount $(L_1^S - L_1^D)$, and the excess supply will drive the interest rate back to R_e. The market for saving and investment is in equilibrium when the market for loanable funds is in equilibrium.

The supply of saving need not be upward sloping, however. In Chapter 9 we learned that the substitution and the income effects of a change in wages pull in opposite directions on an individual's supply of labor. As a result, the supply curve of labor may not be upward sloping. The same is true of the supply curve of saving. The substitution and the income effects of changes in interest rates pull in opposite directions on the desired level of saving. Depending on their relative strengths, the supply curve of saving could be upward sloping, downward sloping, or vertical.

The following simple example illustrates the substitution and the income effects of a change in interest rates. Suppose that you have earned $1,000 from working and are trying to decide how much of this income to consume today and how much of it to save in a bank account for consumption one year from now. Just as you are about to decide, the bank announces an increase in the interest rate on the savings account from 10 percent to 20 percent. (These rates are admittedly quite high, but they make for easy calculations.) How will the interest rate increase affect the amount you plan to save? The answer depends on the relative strength of the substitution and the income effects.

Recall that the substitution effect of a price change is a relative price effect. It says that consumers substitute toward goods and services that have become relatively cheaper. At a 10 percent rate of interest, each dollar of consumption sacrificed today allows you to buy $1.10 worth of goods and services one year from now. At a 20 percent rate of interest, each dollar of consumption sacrificed today allows you to buy $1.20 worth of goods and services. The increase in interest rates has made future consumption relatively cheaper because each extra dollar of saving buys more future goods and services. Therefore, you have an incentive to substitute away from current consumption in favor of future consumption. The *substitution effect* of an increase in interest rates tends to *encourage* saving.

Recall that the income effect of a price change is an absolute price or purchasing power effect. Purchasing power refers to the ability to buy goods and services. It increases if prices decrease and decreases if prices increase. The

TABLE 20.4 Current and Future Consumption from $1,000 of Income (at 10% and 20% Rates of Interest)

CURRENT CONSUMPTION (C_0)	CONSUMPTION ONE YEAR FROM TODAY (C_1) (10% RATE OF INTEREST)	CONSUMPTION ONE YEAR FROM TODAY (C_1) (20% RATE OF INTEREST)
$1,000	$ 0	$ 0
800	220	240
600	440	480
450	605	660
420	638	696
400	660	720
200	880	960
0	1,100	1,200

income effect says that consumers tend to buy more of most goods and services if they have more purchasing power and less of most goods and services if they have less purchasing power. The increase in interest rates increases your purchasing power so long as you save anything at all. Refer to Table 20.4, which shows various combinations of current consumption (C_0) and future consumption (C_1) available to you at interest rates of 10 percent and 20 percent.

At the higher interest rate, you can

1. consume more one year from now for the same amount of consumption today; for example, compare (C_0 = 600, C_1 = 480) with (C_0 = 600, C_1 = 440); or
2. consume more today for the same amount of consumption one year from now; for example, compare (C_0 = 450, C_1 = 660) with (C_0 = 400, C_1 = 660); or
3. consume more today and more one year from now; for example, compare (C_0 = 420, C_1 = 696) with (C_0 = 400, C_1 = 660).

With greater purchasing power you tend to buy more of both goods; that is, you consume more today and consume more one year from now. But more consumption today implies less saving. Therefore, the *income effect* of the increase in interest rates tends to *discourage* saving. Whether or not you save more or less depends on the relative strength of the substitution and the income effects.

Research into the relationship between interest rates and the aggregate level of saving by all consumers suggests that the substitution effect dominates the income effect, but only slightly so. The market supply curve of saving is upward sloping, but very steep, nearly vertical. The elasticity of saving with respect to interest rates in the United States is probably no higher than 0.2.

Aggregate saving may be insensitive to interest rates because many people are *target savers,* who are saving to finance a particular future expenditure. A good example is parents saving to help finance a young child's future college education. Suppose that the parents want to save $30,000 by the time the child enters college. If interest rates rise, the parents can meet their target of $30,000 with less saving each year. If interest rates fall, they have to save more each year to meet their target. The income effect dominates for target savers, so that their supply curve of saving is downward sloping. Not all people are target savers, of course. But adding individual downward-sloping supply curves of target savers to other individual upward-sloping supply curves is likely to produce a fairly steep aggregate, or market, supply curve of saving.

The upward-sloping saving curve pictured in Figure 20.2(a) embodies one further assumption about human behavior: People are impatient. Given the option of consuming an *equal* amount of goods and services today or sometime in the future, they would always choose to consume today. People forego consuming goods and services today only if they can consume a *greater* amount of goods and services in the future. Therefore, interest rates must be positive to induce people to save at all.

If people were not impatient, we might observe negative rates of interest. Consumers would willingly pay others to convert current consumption into future consumption. This possibility may seem strange, but only because the assumption of impatience is accurate. Other things equal, most people do prefer to consume now rather than later.

Investment Demand

In Chapter 12 we described how firms evaluate investment projects to determine their desired stock of capital. The key to the evaluation is discounting to present value the expected stream of net returns from a project. Discounting to present value establishes an inverse relationship between the demand for *capital* and the rate of interest available to stockholders in financial markets, which serves as the opportunity cost of funds. Because the discount rate of interest appears in the denominator of the present value calculation, the higher the interest rate, the lower the discounted stream of returns on investment projects; conversely, the lower the interest rate, the higher the discounted stream of returns on investment projects. Therefore, firms desire a larger stock of capital (accept more projects) the lower the interest rate, and a smaller stock of capital (reject more projects) the higher the interest rate. Review the material in Chapter 12 if you are unclear about the role of the interest rate in analyzing investment projects.

INVESTMENT AND INTEREST RATES The inverse relationship between demand for capital and interest rates does not necessarily imply that *investment* demand and interest rates are inversely related, however. The demand for capital refers to the *total* amount of plant and equipment a firm wants to have in place to produce its output. Investment demand refers to the number of *new* projects a firm is willing and able to put in place during the course of the year. The distinction between capital and investment is important because capital projects often take a considerable amount of time to build and place into operation. The actual investment in new plant and equipment becomes separated in time from the point at which the firm decides it wants a larger stock of capital. As a result, the rate of investment might not be sensitive to the current level of interest rates even though the demand for capital is.

For example, suppose that a decrease in interest rates increases the number of capital projects a firm wants to undertake this year from five to six, but that the firm can only construct and place into operation a maximum of three new projects each year. In that case the decrease in interest rates increases the demand for capital, but has no effect on the firm's investment during the year. The firm can add only three new projects regardless of its desire for more capital.

In fact, firms in the United States complete, on average, about one-third of their desired capital projects in any one year. This suggests that an increase in the demand for capital does translate into a higher rate of investment. If the demand for capital is inversely related to interest rates, then investment demand is also inversely related to interest rates, as indicated by the investment demand curve, *I*, in Figure 20.2(a).

The remaining question is the slope of the investment demand curve: Is it flat or steep? How sensitive is the demand for capital, and investment demand, to changes in interest rates? Economic research has not been able to arrive at a consensus opinion. One group of economists, led by Stanford's Robert Hall and Harvard's Dale Jorgenson, believes that investment demand is quite sensitive to interest rates and other factors that affect the cost of capital, such as tax policy. Their research indicates that investment demand is almost unit elastic with respect to changes in the cost of capital. A 10 percent decline in interest rates increases investment demand by nearly 10 percent, other things equal.

Another group of economists, led by Northwestern's Robert Eisner, believes that the state of the economy is far more important than interest rates are in determining the aggregate level of investment demand in the United States. His research suggests that firms invest if they predict a strong and growing demand for their products in the years ahead, and they do not invest if they predict a weak demand for their products. In the aggregate, therefore, investment demand depends primarily on the predicted growth of the economy. Interest rates have little or no additional, separate impact on the investment decision. In other words, firms appear to give far more weight to the projected stream of returns than to the discount factor in deciding whether to accept or reject capital projects.[4]

The Hall/Jorgenson–Eisner debate has not been resolved. Most economists believe that investment demand is inversely related to interest rates. But the sensitivity of investment demand to change in interest rates remains a wide open question.

Capital Market Equilibrium

Figure 20.2(a) combines the supply of saving and the demand for investment curves, *S* and *I*. The interest rate is on the vertical axis, and saving and investment are on the horizontal axis. The market for capital is in equilibrium at an interest rate of R_e, at the intersection of *S* and *I*. R_e equates the desired levels of saving and investment at values S_e and I_e.

[4]The controversy over what determines investment demand began in earnest in the late 1960s. See R. Hall and D. Jorgenson, "Tax Policy and Investment Behavior," *American Economic Review* 57 (June 1967): 291–314, and R. Eisner, "Tax Policy and Investment Behavior: Comment," *American Economic Review* (June 1969): 379–388. For a recent summary of the controversy, see R. Chirinko, "Business Investment and Tax Policy: A Perspective on Existing Models and Empirical Results," *National Tax Journal* XXXIX, No. 2 (June 1986): 137–155.

The desired levels of saving and investment are unequal, and the market for capital is out of equilibrium at any interest rate other than R_e. The interest rate has to return R_e in order to restore the equilibrium. The required adjustment in interest rates occurs in the nation's financial markets, which are represented in Figure 20.2(b). That graph pictures the supply and the demand of loanable funds for investment. The supply of funds for investment ultimately comes from the savers (lenders) and is equal to the aggregate net flow of funds in Table 20.2. The supply curve, S_L, corresponds to the supply of saving curve, S, in Figure 20.2(a). The demand for funds for investment comes from the producers (borrowers), so that the demand curve, D_L, corresponds to the investment demand curve, I, in Figure 20.2(a). The equilibrium in the financial markets also occurs at R_e, the interest rate at which both the supply and the demand of loanable funds for investment are equal. The equilibrium quantity of funds, L_e, that flows from savers to investors is equal to the equilibrium levels of saving and investment, S_e and I_e, in Figure 20.2(a).

Suppose that interest rates are above the equilibrium—say, at R_1. The market for loanable funds is in excess supply in the amount $(L_1^S - L_1^D)$. At R_1, savers want to supply L_1^S, but investors only want to borrow L_1^D. Financial markets are highly competitive and operate according to the Laws of Supply and Demand. Therefore, the excess supply of loanable funds puts downward pressure on the interest rate, just as excess supply drives down price in any competitive market. The interest rate continues to fall until it reaches R_e, at which point the market for loanable funds is in equilibrium.

The interest rate adjustment in the financial markets simultaneously restores equilibrium in the market for saving and investment. At R_1 the desired level of saving exceeds the desired level of investment by $(S_1 - I_1)$, the same amount by which the market for loanable funds is in excess supply. As interest rates fall in the financial markets, the amount of saving supplied falls, and the amount of investment demanded rises. When the interest rate returns to R_e, the desired levels of saving and investment are once again equal.

CAPITAL MARKETS AND MACROECONOMICS A final point about the adjustment to capital market equilibrium relates to macroeconomics. If both saving and investment are relatively insensitive to interest rates, as many economists suspect, then adjustments in interest rates may not be very effective in restoring and maintaining equilibrium. Imagine the limiting case in which both the saving and the investment curves are vertical, completely insensitive to interest rates. If the desired levels of saving and investment happen to be unequal, then changes in interest rates cannot restore equilibrium. Some other mechanism has to perform that task.

As noted, some economists believe that other variables besides interest rates are more important in maintaining the equilibrium between saving and investment. Indeed, one of the leading theories of macroeconomics, called Keynesian economists after its founder John Maynard Keynes, rests on the premise that the supply of saving is much more sensitive to consumers' incomes than to interest rates. Keynes believed that the supply of saving adjusts to investment demand primarily through changes in income. We will study the Keynesian view of saving and investment equilibrium very carefully in the macroeconomics section of this text.

WHY SO MANY RATES OF INTEREST?

We have been assuming throughout our analysis of the market for capital that all financial instruments have the same rate of interest. This is not true, of course. Refer to Table 20.5, which lists the average interest rates during 1992 for a broad selection of bonds, as well as the average yield on corporate equity for that same year. There was hardly one rate of interest in 1992.

Different financial instruments have different rates of return for a variety of reasons. We will briefly consider four of the most important: (1) differences in term to maturity, (2) differences in risk, (3) differences in tax treatment, and (4) the existence of pure profits or losses.

Term to Maturity

The *term to maturity* on a loan refers to the date in the future when the borrower repays the principal. Lenders can choose among an enormous range of terms to maturity, from bank deposits that they can terminate on order any time they want, to three- and six-month U.S. Treasury bills, to medium-term corporate and government bonds maturing in anywhere from 1 to 10 years, to longer-term corporate and government bonds and mortgages having terms to maturity up to 30 years (and even longer in some cases). The interest rates on shorter- and longer-term securities are directly tied to one another by savers' expectations about future rates of interest. Short- and long-term securities have the same rate of interest only if savers believe that the interest rates on short-term securities will not change in the future.

TABLE 20.5 **Average Annual Rates of Return on Selected Financial Assets, 1992**

ASSET	AVERAGE RATE OF RETURN %
U.S. TREASURY SECURITIES:	
3-MONTH BILLS	3.45
6-MONTH BILLS	3.57
3-YEAR NOTES	5.30
10-YEAR BONDS	7.01
CORPORATE BONDS (MOODY'S):	
Aaa	8.14
Baa	8.98
HIGH-GRADE MUNICIPAL BONDS (STANDARD & POOR'S)	6.41
RETURN TO STOCKHOLDER'S EQUITY (ALL MANUFACTURING CORPORATIONS)	10.1[a]

[a]The average rate of return on stockholders' equity is the ratio of profits after corporation income taxes to the value of stockholders' equity, averaged over the first three quarters of 1992.

SOURCE: *Economic Report of the President, 1993* (Washington, D.C.: U.S. Government Printing Office, 1993), Tables B.69, B.89.

The following simple example illustrates the connection between interest rates on securities having different terms to maturity. Suppose that you want to save \$1,000 for a period of two years. You consider two options: (1) purchase a two-year \$1,000 U.S. government bond, or (2) purchase a one-year \$1,000 U.S. government bond now and another one-year U.S. government bond one year from now. Suppose that the one-year and two-year bonds both have an interest rate of 10 percent.

If you purchase the two-year bond, you know that you will have \$1,000 · (1 + .10) · (1 + .10) two years from now. If you purchase the two one-year bonds, you know that you will have \$1,000 · (1 + .10) at the end of the first year. However, you cannot know for sure how much you will have at the end of two years. You can only guess, and your guess depends on what you believe the interest rate will be on a one-year government bond one year from now. Let's represent that rate as R_{11} (expressed as a decimal fraction), standing for the expected rate on the one-year bond one year from now. Having guessed that the rate will be R_{11}, you believe that you will have \$1,000 · (1 + .10) · (1 + R_{11}) two years from now.

You are indifferent between the two options only if you expect that the rate on the one-year bond one year from now will be 10 percent. If you expect R_{11} to be above 10 percent, you will purchase the two one-year bonds. If you expect R_{11} to be less than 10 percent, you will purchase the two-year bond.

All savers judge these options just as you do. If the interest rates on the two bonds are both 10 percent and savers expect R_{11} also to be 10 percent, they are indifferent between the two options. The markets for the two bonds are in equilibrium because no one wants to switch from one bond to the other. If savers expect R_{11} to be above 10 percent, however, they will all prefer the option of purchasing two one-year government bonds. The supply of funds will flow out of two-year bonds and into one-year bonds, driving up interest rates on the two-year bonds and driving down interest rates on the one-year bonds. Equilibrium in the two markets will be restored when the interest rate on the two-year bonds has risen high enough and the interest rate on the one-year bonds has fallen far enough, so that savers are once again indifferent between the two options. Conversely, suppose that the interest rates on both bonds are 10 percent and that savers expect R_{11} to be less than 10 percent. Now everyone prefers the two-year bonds. The supply of funds will flow from one-year to two-year bonds, driving up the one-year rate and driving down the two-year rate until savers are indifferent between the two bonds.

The example leads to the following conclusions:

1. Interest rates on short- and long-term bonds will be equal if savers expect no change in short-term interest rates in the future.
2. Interest rates on long-term bonds will be above interest rates on short-term bonds if savers expect short-term interest rates to rise in the future.
3. Interest rates on long-term bonds will be below interest rates on short-term bonds if savers expect short-term rates to fall in the future.

Table 20.5 shows that the interest rates on long-term U.S. Treasury securities were higher than the interest rates on short-term U.S. Treasury securities were in 1992. Since the only important difference in these securities is their term to maturity, this suggests that savers in 1992 expected short-term interest rates to rise in the future.

Risk

Most people do not like to gamble with their savings; they prefer safe securities to risky securities, other things equal. Therefore, riskier securities have to offer savers a higher return than do safer securities to compensate for their higher risk.

Investment rating services such as Moody's analyze the debt of governments and corporations and rank securities according to the probability that the borrower will be unable to repay the loan. Moody's uses a lettering system to indicate the degree of risk, with Aaa ("triple A") bonds being the safest. Bond ratings of Aa, A, and Baa indicate increasing amounts of risk.

The corporate bond yields listed in Table 20.5 show the effect of risk on rate of return. Corporate bonds rated Baa by Moody's had to offer savers an interest rate nearly one percentage point higher than the corporate bonds rated Aaa, 8.98 percent versus 8.14 percent.

Tax Considerations

Not all financial securities receive equal tax treatment under federal and state income taxes. The differences in tax treatment cause interest rates to differ because savers care about the returns available to them after the payment of taxes.

For instance, the interest income on bonds issued by state and local governments, called municipal bonds, is not taxed under the federal personal income tax. The interest income on federal bonds is taxable under the federal personal income tax. Suppose that you are in the 15 percent federal income tax bracket, meaning that any additional income you receive is taxed at the rate of 15 percent. If you purchase a $1,000 municipal bond with an interest rate of 10 percent, you receive $100 of interest income on the bond each year, and the income is not taxed. If you purchase a $1,000 U.S. government bond with an interest rate of 10 percent, you also receive $100 of interest income on that bond. However, you have to pay a tax of $15 on the income if you are in the 15 percent tax bracket, leaving you with only $85 after paying the tax. You, and all other federal taxpayers, would clearly prefer the municipal bond if both bonds had the same rate of interest. Therefore, the markets for municipal and U.S. bonds can be in in equilibrium only if the municipal bonds have a lower interest rate, reflecting their more favorable tax treatment. The general principle is that funds will flow away from more heavily taxed securities toward less heavily taxed securities until the differences in their interest rates just compensate savers for the differences in their tax treatment.

Table 20.5 shows very clearly the effect of taxes on the yields of municipal and U.S. government bonds. Compare the interest rates on 10-year U.S. Treasury securities (7.01 percent) and high-grade municipal bonds (6.41 percent). These two securities are both quite safe and have roughly the same terms to maturity. The main difference between them is their tax treatment. Not surprisingly, the interest rate on the municipal bond is significantly lower.

Pure Profits or Losses

The existence of pure economic profits or losses in the markets for goods and services can have a very dramatic impact on the return to equities. Pure profits arise primarily through changes in demand for products, innovation, the exercise of monopoly power, and the willingness to accept risky ventures.

We saw in Chapter 13 how changing market conditions can generate substantial short-run economic profits and losses, even in highly competitive markets. Firms lucky enough to experience a sudden increase in demand for their products earn pure economic profits from their good fortune. Innovators who introduce successful new products or cost-reducing production technologies also earn pure profits in the short run. In each instance the stockholders share the profits and receive a sharp increase in the yield on their equity. Conversely, firms whose products have fallen out of favor and firms that are slow to adopt new production technologies experience losses. The yield on their equity falls.

Since market conditions are always changing within an economy, we would expect to find a wide range of returns on the equity for different companies within any one year. Average annual returns on equity, such as those reported in Table 20.5, are misleading in this respect. At the same time, though, these profits and losses are temporary. Profits will be competed away in the long run as imitators enter the industry, and losses will be eliminated as some of the losing firms exit the industry. Therefore, competition does tend to push yields on equity toward the average over time.

Profits created by the exercise of monopoly power might not be competed away, however, if they are protected by barriers to entry such as economies of scale, sunk costs, licenses, and advertising. But as we discussed in Chapter 14, competition in the stock market substitutes for competition in product markets as far as new savers are concerned. If the profits are maintained, savers eager to purchase the stock will drive up the price of the stock. The price will rise until new savers earn the same return by purchasing the stock of monopolistic companies that they can earn by purchasing the stock of highly competitive companies. Therefore, savers can expect to earn approximately the same return on equity over a long period of time no matter what stocks they hold.

The one exception to this rule concerns the higher-than-average returns on stocks of especially risky industries. The profits of successful companies have to exceed the losses on failed companies in risky industries by enough to compensate savers for taking risks. Otherwise, only people who like to gamble would supply funds for risky ventures, and, as noted earlier, most of us are not gamblers.

SUMMARY

The first section of Chapter 20 traced the flow of funds from savers to investors in the United States.

1. The majority of funds for investment are provided by the businesses themselves in the form of capital consumption allowances and retained earnings. Capital consumption allowances are funds set aside to replace existing capital as it depreciates in value. Retained earnings are the profits left over after the payment of taxes and dividends. These forms of internal business saving are saving by the stockholders that they allow the firm's managers to undertake in their behalf.
2. The need to finance some investment from external funds involves the nation's financial markets. Funds are transferred from lenders to borrowers

through equity or debt instruments. An equity instrument, such as a share of corporate stock, gives the lender a share of the profits of the business. A debt instrument, such as a corporate bond or a bank account, is a promise or an order that the borrower will repay the lender certain amounts of money at some future date(s).

3. Financial intermediaries are institutions such as banks, insurance companies, and pension funds that position themselves between the ultimate savers and investors. Financial intermediaries promote saving and investment in three ways: by offering savers a wide variety of choices for their saving, by serving as brokers between lenders and borrowers, and by greatly reducing the costs of transferring funds from savers to investors.
4. All four sectors of the economy transact in the nation's financial markets. The household sector is the largest lender and one of the largest borrowers of funds. Households borrow primarily to finance their purchases of homes and consumer durables. Governments are net borrowers of funds if they run budget deficits (if receipts are less than expenditures) and net lenders of funds if they run budget surpluses (if receipts exceed expenditures). The foreign sector is a net lender of funds if foreign citizens place more savings in the United States than U.S. citizens place abroad and a net borrower of funds if the reverse is true. The household sector is a net lender of funds, and the business sector is usually a net borrower of funds (1992 was an exception). Since 1981 the foreign sector has been a net lender of funds, and the government sector has been a net borrower of funds. Total investment equals the aggregate net flow of funds to financial markets (aggregate net lending) plus the internal financing provided by business firms.
5. Individuals receive income from capital as a return to their wealth or net worth, the difference between their assets (claims against others) and their liabilities (claims others have against them). The ultimate source of income from capital, however, is the productivity of the capital itself.
6. The national net worth of a country equals the market value of its real assets plus its land, less any claims against these assets held by foreigners. The national net worth of the United States in 1992 was nearly $18 trillion, and income from capital accounted for approximately 20 percent of all income generated in the United States.

The second section of the chapter described the market for capital, first in terms of saving and investment and then in terms of the demand and the supply of loanable funds.

7. The supply of saving results from consumers solving their economic problem over their entire lifetimes. Consumers typically smooth their consumption relative to their lifetime income, borrowing to increase consumption when young, then paying back debt and accumulating net worth when they are middle-aged, and finally dissaving to support their standard of living during the retirement years.
8. Saving can be positively related, negatively related, or unrelated to the level of interest rates, other things equal. An increase in interest rates leads to a substitution effect that encourages additional saving and an income effect that discourages saving. Saving appears to be slightly positively related to interest rates in the United States, with an elasticity probably no higher than 0.2.

9. A firm's demand for investment derives from its demand for capital. We saw in Chapter 12 that the demand for capital is inversely related to the level of interest rates because interest rates define the opportunity cost of capital to the firm in present value calculations. Whether investment demand is also inversely related to the level of current interest rates depends, in part, on how quickly firms can adjust their stocks of capital. Firms in the United States appear to complete about one-third of all new projects in a year's time.
10. Some economists believe that investment demand is highly sensitive to the level of interest rates and other factors affecting the cost of capital, such as taxes. Other economists believe that investment demand is primarily related to the performance of the economy, not to the level of interest rates.
11. The market for capital is in equilibrium when the interest rate is such that the desired level of saving equals the desired level of investment. Alternatively, the market for capital is in equilibrium when interest rates equate the demand for and the supply of loanable funds in the nation's financial markets.

The final section of Chapter 20 considered why different financial instruments have different interest rates (rates of return).

12. The principal factors that affect the level of interest rates (rates of return) on financial securities are term to maturity, risk, taxes, and (for equity) the existence of pure profits and losses.
13. Term to maturity affects the level of interest rates (rates of return) because savers/lenders must expect to earn the same return over time no matter whether they purchase one long-term asset or a sequence of shorter-term assets. Other things equal, interest rates on long-term assets exceed interest rates on short-term assets when people expect future interest rates on short-term assets to rise, and vice versa. Interest rates on short-term and long-term assets are equal when people expect that interest rates on short-term assets will not change in the future.
14. Regarding the other factors, interest rates (rates of return) are higher the riskier the asset, the more it is taxed, and (for equity) the larger the profits of business firms, and vice versa.

KEY TERMS

asset
business saving
capital consumption allowances
deficit agents
depreciation
financial intermediary
financial markets
liability
national net worth
net worth (wealth)
retained earnings
surplus agents
wealth (net worth)

QUESTIONS

1. Describe the various forms of internal and external financing used by firms to finance their investments.
2. How do financial intermediaries such as commercial banks and savings institutions improve the workings of financial markets?
3. Which sectors of the U.S. economy have been net suppliers of funds to the nation's financial markets in recent years? Which sectors have been net demanders of funds?

4. Suppose that you have $10,000 that you have decided to invest in a certificate of deposit account that pays an annual interest rate of 10 percent. Your outstanding credit card balance is $400, on which the annual percentage rate (APR) is 18 percent. The remaining balance on your installment car loan is $4,000, with an APR of 6 percent.
   a. Calculate your financial net worth and your (explicit) income from capital during the year.
   b. Suppose that the interest rate on the certificate of deposit is variable. How much can this rate decrease before your income from capital becomes negative?
5. A household's saving decision evolves as the solution to a very complex lifetime economic problem. What are the principal elements of the household's lifetime economic problem?
6. One often hears the argument that a reduction in the federal personal income tax rates would increase after-tax rates of return to savers and thereby induce households to save more. Do you think this argument is necessarily correct? Explain why or why not.
7. Assume that the demand for funds (investment demand) is negatively related to interest rates and that the supply of funds (saving) is positively related to interest rates. Also assume that there is only one interest rate prevailing in the economy. Using supply and demand analysis, determine the impact, if any, of each of the following on the equilibrium interest rate:
   a. Businesses expect a higher demand for their products in the future.
   b. Young and middle-aged people worry that the Social Security System may collapse, so they decide to save more for their retirement years.
8. Suppose that you are interested in investing $1,000 for a period of two years. The one- and the two-year risk-free interest rates are 6 percent and 12 percent respectively. According to these figures, do savers expect the one-year interest rate to be higher or lower one year from now? More specifically, what should the one-year interest rate be one year from now in order for the market to be in equilibrium? Explain.
9. a. What is the difference between capital and investment?
   b. Does the inverse relationship between the demand for capital and interest rates imply that investment demand and interest rates are inversely related.
10. What factors explain why there are different rates of return on different financial securities? Briefly indicate how each factor you name affects the rate of return on a security, supported by actual examples.

CHAPTER

21

The Markets for Land and Natural Resources

LEARNING OBJECTIVES

CONCEPTS TO LEARN

The fixed supply of land

The factors that determine the demand for land

Efficient land taxes versus inefficient local property taxes

The natural resource pricing rule

Why we will not run out of natural resources

CONCEPTS TO RECALL

Opportunity cost [1]

The Laws of Supply and Demand [5,6,7]

The net value from producing and consuming a product [7]

Compounding to future value [12]

Allocational efficiency [13]

and and the natural resources contained in the land are nature's economic gifts to a nation. People sometimes wonder whether the market system makes the best use of nature's gifts.

For example, golfers decry the sale of their beloved golf courses to the real estate developers. They cannot imagine that the land is better used for yet another apartment building or shopping mall. In no country is the plight of the golfer worse than in Japan. The Japanese are absolutely crazy about golf, yet hardly anyone there actually plays the game. Land is so scarce that only a few golf courses have been built in the entire country. Some of the private clubs are able to command entrance fees in excess of $1 million, so great is the demand for golf. With fees this high, the vast majority of Japan's would-be golfers have to be content with hitting golf balls into the night at jam-packed, triple-decker driving ranges. The best golfer in Japan may never have played a round of golf!

In a more serious vein, some people worry that the market system causes us to use up our scarce natural resources too quickly. They wonder what will happen when the supply of oil runs out.

Chapter 21 will indicate why the Laws of Supply and Demand allocate land and natural resources just as well as they do any other good or service. The market system does not misuse land or natural resources. To the contrary, it helps to maximize the value of these precious gifts from nature. For example, the market system will see to it that we do not run out of oil or any other natural resource.

The markets for land and natural resources are the remaining factor markets that we have to consider. The two markets are not entirely distinct because the market value of natural resources, such as oil and minerals, determines the value of the land that contains them. Nonetheless, the prices of land and natural resources are set quite differently in the marketplace, so Chapter 21 devotes one section to each.

We would also note by way of introduction that land and natural resources do not have much effect on the overall personal distribution of income in the United States because they account for less than 1 percent of the total income generated in the nation's factor markets. Their only noticeable impact is at the very top of the income distribution. We saw in Chapter 17 that the natural resource industries tend to have substantial barriers to entry. As a result, these industries have given rise to a small number of very large fortunes. Also, some very wealthy individuals receive most of their income from land holdings. For the most part, though, the key issues in these markets are allocational in nature, not distributional. We want to focus on how the market system guides the efficient use of land and natural resources.

The chapter begins with the market for land.

THE MARKET FOR LAND

We saw in Table 20.3 that land is an important part of the national net worth of the United States. The land component of national net worth can be considered nature's gift to the nation because the supply of land is essentially fixed. True, the quality of a nation's land can be altered. Irrigation transforms the desert into rich farmland, the application of fertilizers and organic material enhances poor soils, and landfill extends the boundaries of coastal cities. But the economic value created by transforming the land in these ways results from the labor, materials, and capital used to alter the land, not from changes in the quantity of land itself. The fixity of land is its distinctive feature among the three primary factors of production.

Land Values and Economic Rent

Figure 21.1 illustrates how the market determines the value of land. The supply curve, S, is vertical, reflecting the fixed supply of land. It shows that landlords are willing to supply the total quantity of land, $\overline{T}$, regardless of the price of the land. The three demand curves, D^0, D', and D'', have the usual shape. They reflect the value of the land to the users of the land—for example, to farmers, or homeowners and renters, or commercial and industrial businesses. The demand for land is a derived demand, as is the demand for all factors of production. The value of land depends on the value of the services that it helps to produce.

If the market demand is D^0, the price of each parcel of land is P^0, at the intersection of D^0 and S. The total value of the land is $P^0 \cdot \overline{T}$. If the demand for the land rises to D'', the price of each parcel of land rises to P'', and the total value of the land is $P'' \cdot \overline{T}$. If the demand for the land falls to D', the price of each parcel of land falls to P', and the total value of the land is $P' \cdot \overline{T}$. The price, and total value, of land rises or falls with the demand for the land because only the demand curve can shift.

A comment about interpreting the price of land is in order before continuing. You can think of the price, P, as either (1) the price the user would have to

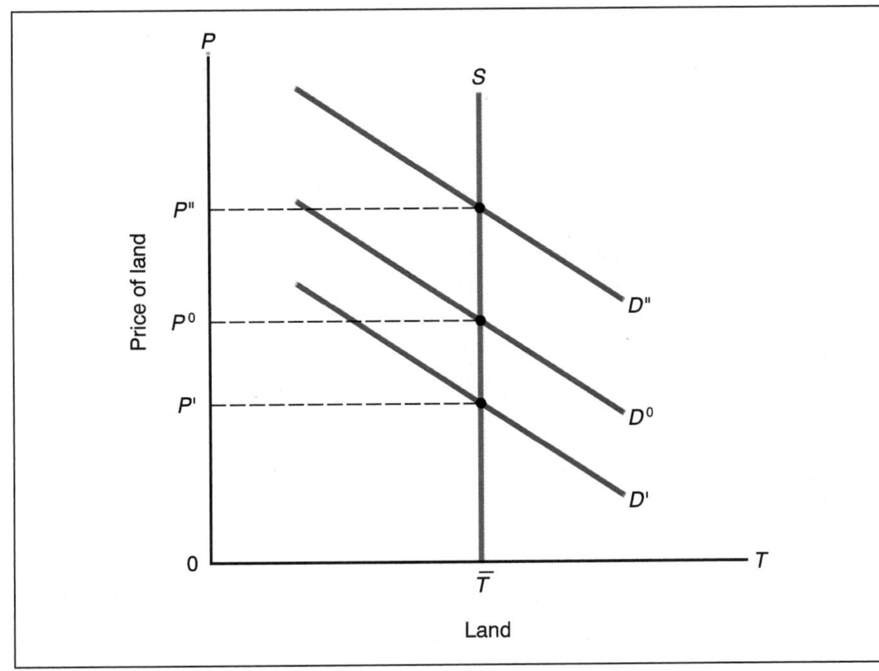

FIGURE 21.1
The Market for Land

The distinctive feature of land is that the supply of land is essentially fixed, at $\overline{T}$ in the figure. The supply curve, S, is perfectly inelastic. As a result, the price or annual rental value of land is determined by the demand for land. The price is P^0 if the demand is D^0; the price decreases to P' if the demand for land decreases to D'; and the price increases to P'' if the demand for land increases to D''. The entire price of land is an economic rent, because the opportunity cost of supplying the fixed amount of land is zero.

pay to purchase the land from the landlord or (2) the annual net rental, or income, that the landlord receives from a tenant for renting the land. The annual net rental is the rental received from the user less any costs the landlord incurs to maintain the land for its current use. In equilibrium, the present value of the stream of annual net rental payments just equals the purchase price of the land.

The entire return, or income, that landlords receive for the use of their land is an economic rent. We first met the concept of economic rent applied to wage and salary income in Chapter 9. Recall that most of the salaries of entertainment and sports superstars is economic rent. Their economic rent is the difference between their salaries and the very much lower salaries they would require to remain as entertainers or professional athletes. The lower salaries they require define the opportunity cost to them of remaining in their professions.

Economic rent applied to capital is pure economic profit, the return to capital over and above the opportunity cost of capital. The opportunity cost of capital is the return to capital required to keep investors interested in supplying capital to the business.

Economic rent has the same interpretation when applied to land. The only twist is that the opportunity cost of supplying the land is zero because the supply of land is fixed. Landlords have no choice other than to sell their land to the highest bidder, so they will continue to supply the land at any price greater than zero. Therefore, the *entire* income that landlords receive for their land is an economic rent.

The Demand for Land

If the demand for land determines its value, what attributes of the land itself determine whether the demand for it is high or low? The two most important attributes of land from an economic standpoint are its inherent qualities and its location.

THE INHERENT QUALITIES OF LAND The inherent qualities of land refer, in the broadest sense, to the fertility of the soil and whether the land is forested or sits above a pool of oil or a lode of minerals. These qualities obviously determine whether the land has value to farmers or to the lumber and extractive resources industries. Finer distinctions beyond these broad qualities also matter in determining the demand for land. For instance, soil can be better suited for certain crops, depending on such factors as climate, rainfall, slope of the land, and the exact organic and mineral content of the soil. The demand for the land will be greater if it is better suited to the crops that are themselves in greater demand. Similarly, the value of land rich in natural resources depends in part on the particular minerals that it contains. It also depends on how accessible the minerals are; that is, whether they are close to the surface and easily mined or buried deep within the earth and costly to extract.

LOCATION Location is the primary determinant of the demand for land when it is used for residential, commercial, or industrial purposes. Regarding residential land use, real estate agents joke that housing prices depend on three factors, location, location, and location. They know that the physical characteristics of a house—for example, its size, condition, number of bathrooms, architectural style, and so forth—matter in determining its value. But they also know that virtually identical houses on equal-sized plots of land can sell for very different prices, depending on where they are located.

The location factor in housing values has three separate dimensions: aesthetic, neighborhood, and cost.

THE AESTHETIC DIMENSION The aesthetic dimension is straightforward. Lakefront property typically commands a hefty premium; so does land high on a hill with a breathtaking view. By contrast, residential property bordering on railroad tracks or situated in an industrial area sells for less than the market average.

THE NEIGHBORHOOD DIMENSION The neighborhood dimension is more subtle. Houses in uniformly high-income communities tend to have much higher values than do otherwise identical houses in mixed- or low-income communities. People with high incomes prefer to live in high-income communities and can afford to pay the premium to buy into these communities. Why do high-income people have these preferences? One explanation is that people are more comfortable living "with their own kind." High-income families are likely to find more people with backgrounds, work experiences, and consumption habits similar to theirs in high-income communities than in mixed- or low-income communities. Another explanation is safety. Crime rates tend to be lower in high-income communities than in mixed- or low-income communities. A third explanation has to do with the education of their children. A number of studies have shown that family income itself is one of the more important factors in determining the effectiveness of local public schools. Students learn better if they are surrounded by students with high-income parents who are able to expose their children to numerous cultural opportunities and who stress the importance of education. Moreover, living with other high-income families reduces the cost of the public school system to any one high-income family. Given equal-sized school systems and equal expenditures per pupil, a high-income family pays a lower share of the total education costs if it lives among high-income families than if it lives among low-income families.

THE COST DIMENSION The cost dimension of location applies both to business and to residential users. Businesses have discovered that there are cost savings to be gained if commercial and manufacturing firms cluster together in downtown urban areas along with all the industries that service the firms and their employees. The service industries include banking, insurance, real estate, law, consulting, retailing, restaurants, and transportation. The clustering phenomenon explains why land rents on properties zoned for commercial and industrial purposes tend to decline systematically with distance from the center of the city. The demand for property is highest in the downtown area because the cost savings from locating there are the greatest. The demand for property away from the center declines with distance because the cost advantage from clustering declines as firms move farther from the center. The same cost-saving principle explains why, at any given distance from the center, commercial and industrial property located near major highways commands the highest rent.

Businesses cannot expect to capture any of the cost savings from a superior location, however. Because the supply of land is fixed, the bidding for the more desirable properties simply drives up their rents. Once the market for land reaches its equilibrium, the differences in rents on commercial and industrial properties throughout an urban area exactly equal the differences in cost to the firms arising from the location of the properties. All the advantages of location accrue to the landlords in the form of higher rents.

The cost-saving principle also applies to properties zoned as residential properties. Most people who live in urban areas prefer to live closer to downtown, other things equal. Living closer to the city reduces the cost of traveling downtown to shop or to enjoy the numerous cultural amenities of the city. Those who work downtown also save on commuting costs. These transportation cost savings help explain why the value of residential property also declines systematically with distance from the center of a city, other things equal. Another important factor is the one mentioned above, that land in or near the center of a city is highly valued by businesses. Businesses outbid homeowners for most of the land in the center of a city because the locational value to businesses generally exceeds the locational value to homeowners. Consequently, most homeowners live on the outskirts of the city or in the surrounding suburbs where the competition from business for the available land is less intense and the land values are lower.

When thinking about the relative values of residential land in the cities and the suburbs, do not be misled by comparing the expensive homes on one-acre lots in the high-income suburbs with the cheaper homes in the run-down sections of most U.S. cities. This comparison does not hold other things equal. The cheaper urban homes are often older, smaller, tightly crowded together with other similar homes on tiny plots of land, and situated in higher-crime areas. Instead, think what the value of the expensive suburban home would be if it were located on a one-acre lot in the center of the city, surrounded by other nice homes on one-acre lots. The price of land is so high in the downtown areas that we simply do not see suburban-style, high-income housing located there. High-income families who choose to live downtown reside in luxury high-rise apartments or condominiums, the only luxury housing valuable enough to compete with businesses for land in the central city.

Land Prices and Economic Efficiency

You may wonder what economic purpose is served by the price of land, since the supply of land is fixed. The same amount of land will be supplied no matter what its price. Therefore, why not give ownership of all land to the government and have the government offer it free of charge to all users on a first-come, first-served basis? This scheme would not reduce the amount of land supplied, and users would have the advantage of using the land for free. Isn't this the most efficient way to use our gift from nature?

The answer is decidedly no. Land is a scarce resource that provides valuable services to both consumers and producers. As we saw in Chapter 7, economic efficiency requires that society maximize the net value from supplying and using any good or factor of production. Net value is the difference between the total value to users and the total cost to suppliers. Net value is the same as total value in the case of land because the supply of land is fixed; the total (opportunity) cost of supplying land is zero.

The total value of using land can be maximized only if each parcel of land is supplied to the user that values it the most. The government giveaway proposal cannot guarantee this result. The first-come, first-served user of a parcel of land may not be the user who values the land most highly. However, parcels of land sold in competitive markets necessarily do go to the highest-valued users.

Landlords view the market for their land as pictured in Figure 21.1. Their land is in fixed supply, and the price (or annual net rental) they receive for it is an economic rent. Users of land do not view the market at all like this, however. The price of the land is the cost to them of using the land, and they buy land only if the value of the land to them exceeds the market price. Furthermore, potential users bid up the price until the total amount of a particular type of land demanded equals the fixed amount of that land supplied. As the price rises, some potential users drop out of the market; the value of the land to them no longer exceeds its cost. Therefore, when the market reaches its equilibrium price, only those users who place the highest value on the land remain in the market, exactly as required for economic efficiency. The same is true of any good or service allocated by the Laws of Supply and Demand.

For example, we have seen that businesses value land in the center of cities the most. In the process of bidding for the land they drive the price up so high that most potential residential users seek more affordable land elsewhere. The result is that very scarce urban land goes to the highest-valued users, the businesses.

In summary, selling land in a free market cannot appreciably change the overall supply of land. But market prices serve the important function of allocating the scarce land among users so that society maximizes the value to society of its precious gift from nature.

We mentioned the golfers' lament in the introduction to the chapter. Golfers in the United States may believe that their beloved golf courses should not be sold for apartment buildings or shopping malls. Unfortunately, though, society on the whole disagrees with them. The golf courses are sold because the land has much higher value in residential or commercial use. The revenue from greens fees cannot hope to match what the land developers are willing to pay for the land.

The market system is clearly allocating land properly in land-scarce Japan, even if it is frustrating the Japanese love for golf. The demand for golf courses there, great as it is, cannot match the demand for land for residential, commercial, and industrial purposes. Building golf courses would hardly be the best use of land in Japan.

CURRENT ISSUE: Do not just throw out those old golf clubs that have been lying around the basement for years. They may be worth quite a lot of money as collectors' items. Check with a nearby golf professional to be sure. And if they are worth something, try to sell them in Japan. You will get three to four times as much for them there as in the United States.

Land Taxes and Economic Efficiency

Having the government confiscate and give away land would be highly inefficient. But levying taxes on land is very appealing from an efficiency standpoint. To see why, refer again to Figure 21.1. Assume that the market demand and supply curves would be D^0 and S, without any tax, so that the price of the land is P^0.

Suppose that the government levies a tax on the landlords equal to 25 percent of the value of their land. The tax has no effect on the market for land because the landlords are willing to supply the same amount of land no matter what price they receive. Therefore, the supply curve remains unchanged, and supply and demand intersect at P^0, just as they did without the tax. With the price to users unchanged, the allocation of land among competing users is also unaffected by the tax, and land continues to be allocated efficiently. The burden of the land tax falls entirely on the landlords, who pay 25 percent of the value of their land to the government.

Support for land taxes in the United States reached its peak in the late 1800s under the leadership of Henry George, a printer who dabbled in political economy. George proposed replacing all existing taxes with a single tax on land, citing among other advantages the superior efficiency properties of land taxes. His "Single Tax Movement" gathered momentum for awhile and nearly carried George to victory in the 1886 election for mayor of New York City. Enthusiasm for the land tax faded quickly after the election, however.

The local property tax comes closest in spirit to what George had proposed, but not at all close in execution. Cities and towns levy taxes on the *combined* value of the land and the structures on the land. Since the value of the structures typically exceeds the value of the land, the local property tax is primarily a tax on capital, not land. Moreover, the supply of structures is not perfectly inelastic within a community. Therefore, as we saw in our analysis of taxes in Chapter 8, the local property tax can give rise to inefficiencies, and the property owners may be able to shift some of the tax burden to consumers or workers.

THE MARKET FOR NATURAL RESOURCES

The oil, natural gas, and minerals stored within the earth's crust are obviously an extremely valuable economic gift of nature. Natural resources share with land the characteristic that their total *quantity* is ultimately fixed. The earth's crust contains only a finite amount of these resources. However, they differ from land in that the *supply* of oil, natural gas, and minerals to the market in any one year is most definitely not fixed. As a result, the market prices of natural resources are determined quite differently from the market price of land.

INEXHAUSTIBLE RESOURCE

A resource whose quantity does not diminish as it is used in production, such as land.

EXHAUSTIBLE RESOURCE

A resource available in a finite amount whose quantity diminishes as it is used in production, such as the natural resources.

The difference in the market supply of land and of natural resources arises because land is an **inexhaustible,** or *nondepletable,* resource, whereas natural resources are **exhaustible,** or *depletable,* resources. The same quantity of land remains available for production or consumption year after year, for all intents and purposes. Therefore, landowners have no choice but to supply their fixed quantities of land each year and take whatever demanders will pay for it. By contrast, the quantity of a natural resource extracted each year and used in production or consumption can never be replaced. The total quantity remaining in the earth's crust diminishes by the amount extracted each year. Therefore, firms that own the rights to natural resources have an important supply decision to make: How much of the resource should they supply to the market each year until the quantity is completely exhausted?

The following example illustrates the nature of the supply decision. Suppose that you own the rights to a pool of oil and are trying to decide how many barrels of oil to extract and supply now versus one year from now. Many other people own rights to their own pools of oil, so that the market for oil is competitive. You can sell as much of your oil as you want each year at the going market price. The price of a barrel of oil currently is P_0. You (and all the other suppliers) expect that the price of a barrel one year from now will be P_1.

Finally, assume that everyone can extract the oil at no cost in order to keep the example as simple as possible.

Under these conditions, you earn an income of P_0 per barrel on oil supplied today, and you expect to earn an income of P_1 per barrel on oil supplied one year from now. Since dollars earned today are not equivalent to dollars earned one year from now, the two incomes have to be compared for the same period of time. Let's compare the income that you would have in one year if you extract the oil now or one year from now. Suppose that the rate of interest on a perfectly safe financial asset is 10 percent, as in our capital market examples, so that you can save any income earned from selling oil today at a rate of 10 percent. The P_0 of income per barrel received from oil supplied today grows to $P_0 \cdot (1 + .10)$ dollars of income per barrel one year from now if the income is saved at the 10 percent rate. Oil supplied one year from today is expected to earn P_1 per barrel. Therefore, you are indifferent between supplying oil today or one year from now if $P_1 = P_0 \cdot (1 + .10)$.

The example illustrates that *the price of oil one year from now must rise by the rate of interest each year.* This is the only possible equilibrium relationship between the current price and the price one year from now. To see why, suppose that the price of oil is expected to rise by less than the rate of interest, so that $P_0 \cdot (1 + .10) > P_1$. You (and all the other suppliers) would prefer to supply oil today and earn interest on the income, rather than supplying oil one year from now. But the increase in supply today decreases the price today, and the removal of supplies one year from now increases the expected future price. P_0 falls, and P_1 rises until $P_0 \cdot (1 + .10) = P_1$ and suppliers are once again indifferent between supplying oil now or one year from now. The reverse adjustment occurs if the price of oil is expected to rise by more than the rate of interest. With $P_0 \cdot (1 + .10) < P_1$, everyone prefers to supply oil one year from now. The removal of supplies today increases P_0, and the expected increase in supply one year from now decreases P_1 until the equilibrium relationship between the prices is restored.

Project our example to all future years and the same analysis applies. *The price of oil, or any other natural resource, must rise each year by the rate of interest in order to maintain equilibrium in the market.* Notice that this pricing rule has nothing whatsoever to do with price inflation. The pricing rule refers to the real price of oil. It says that oil and other natural resources will become increasingly expensive over time *relative* to all other goods, services, and factors of production. For instance, imagine a world without inflation in which the price of everything happened to be $1 in some year. The prices of natural resources would grow by the rate of interest each year, even if the prices of everything else remained at $1. At an interest rate of 10 percent, the prices of natural resources would reach $2 in approximately seven years and double again every seven years thereafter. Natural resources would quickly become very expensive relative to all other goods, services, and factors of production. The real price increase occurs because natural resources are not replaceable, a feature distinctive to them.

The History of Oil Prices

Our simple model of oil pricing would not have done a good job of predicting oil prices throughout the twentieth century. The real price of a barrel of crude oil remained essentially constant from 1900 to the early 1970s, with only occasional periods of small increases and decreases. Since 1973, the (real) price of oil has been extremely erratic. The price of crude oil rose nearly eight fold from 1973 to 1981, after which it fell more or less continuously until the end of the decade. The price of crude oil rose sharply again in 1990 following Iraq's invasion of Kuwait and then fell back as tensions eased in the Middle East. Our model fails to explain the price of oil because it is too simple to capture some important realities of the oil market.

Prices remained constant instead of rising prior to 1970 because of new oil discoveries and new drilling technologies. The oil companies kept discovering new, easily accessible supplies of oil throughout the century. The total quantity of oil available to the market was not truly constant, as required by the model. Also, new drilling technologies dramatically lowered the marginal cost of drilling for oil. Our model excludes cost considerations entirely. If the model were modified to account for drilling costs, it would yield the intuitive result that the price of oil rises more slowly than the rate of interest does if marginal costs are falling over time. The price can actually decline if marginal costs fall sharply enough. Until 1970, therefore, the combination of new oil discoveries and declining drilling costs put enough downward pressure on prices to counterbalance the natural tendency for oil prices to rise over time.

The behavior of oil prices since 1973 has largely been the result of a shifting balance of market power. Our model assumes that the market is competitive. As noted in Chapter 17, however, the natural resource markets often contain a substantial amount of market power that is protected by a natural barrier to entry. Potential entrants often have difficulty gaining access to low-cost supplies of resources.

The *existence* of market power does not alter the results of the model. If our model contained a single profit-maximizing monopolist, the monopolist would still set the price to rise at the rate of interest over time. However, *changes* in the exercise of market power can have dramatic short-term effects on prices, which is exactly what happened in the market for oil from 1973 through 1989. As described in Chapter 15, the Organization of Petroleum Exporting Countries (OPEC) formed a tight cartel in 1973 that took control of the world oil market. OPEC used its new-found market power to engineer sharp increases in the price of oil, first in 1974 and again in 1979. Then in the early 1980s OPEC lost control of the market, and the price of oil came tumbling down. The rise and fall of OPEC clearly dominated the market for oil in the 1970s and 1980s. The sharp rise in oil prices following the Iraqi invasion of Kuwait resulted from the fear that war between Iraq and the United States might temporarily shut off the flow of oil from oil-rich Saudi Arabia. Once the threat of war diminished, the prices came back down.

What does the future hold in store, assuming OPEC cannot regain control of the market? The best guess would be for continued increases in the price of oil roughly in line with our simple model. The natural tendency for the price to increase will probably not be counterbalanced as we move into the twenty-first century because the days of discovering new easily accessible supplies of oil appear to be over. Oil from the newest sources in the North Sea and Alaska is much more costly to extract than is the oil in the Middle East. Moreover, continued population growth and economic growth, especially in Third World countries, ought to ensure a growing demand for oil, unless scientists discover a new and cheap substitute for oil. Our simple model assumed a constant demand for oil over time. The price of oil rises even faster than the rate of interest if demand is growing, other things equal.

Will We Run Out of Oil?

Our simple model has an important implication for the future: The common fear that we will eventually run out of oil and minerals is groundless. We certainly will not run out of natural resources. The fear that we will ignores the fundamental principle that prices act as signals, guiding the decisions of producers and consumers.

If the world keeps using its natural resources at current rates, the real prices of these resources must eventually begin to rise. Both demanders and suppliers will respond to the price increases in ways that will prevent the ultimate depletion of any resource. Let oil continue to serve as an example.

Demanders will respond to ever-higher oil prices by substituting away from oil and oil products. Consumers may continue to drive gas-guzzling automobiles so long as the price of gasoline remains around $1 per gallon. As gasoline prices rise to $2, or $5, or $10 a gallon, however, consumers will invariably find other alternatives. They might switch fairly quickly to small, solar-charged, battery-driven cars for commuting, shopping, and other short trips. The technology is already available for producing an affordable battery-driven car that is acceptable for short trips. Similarly, producers who now use oil for their source of energy will switch to coal and switch again to nuclear fuels if the price of coal becomes too high.

CURRENT ISSUE: California has already passed a law requiring that, by the year 2000, a small percentage of each auto manufacturer's new cars sold in the state must be emission-free. *Emission free* means an "electric car," given current technology.

The supply responses to higher prices will be of two kinds. The oil producers will increase their exploration efforts to find new supplies of oil. If the newfound supplies are more inaccessible and costly to extract—deeper in the ground or under the ocean floor—the producers will work on developing new technologies to extract them as cheaply as possible. In addition, entrepreneurs will realize that users are seeking substitute products for oil and try to meet the demand. The higher oil prices rise, the more profitable the market for oil substitutes is. Consumers can rest assured that oil substitutes will be forthcoming because the profit motive will drive research and development efforts toward finding new substitutes. In 1989 scientists vigorously debated the possibility that controlled cold fusion might become a practical and virtually endless source of energy for some purposes. The initial claims about cold fusion proved to be false. However, as the prices of natural resources rise, fusion research will surely intensify, increasing the chances of a real breakthrough in this area.

Fears that the world will run out of natural resources are often supported by comparisons between annual rates of consumption and estimates of **known reserves** published by the U.S. Geological Survey and industry organizations. Known reserves will support current rates of consumption of oil and most minerals for only 20 to 50 years. But known reserves are the reserves that are profitable to extract, given *today's* prices and *existing* technologies. The U.S. Geological Survey also publishes estimates of **ultimate recovery resources,** its best guess about the amount of resources that could conceivably be profitable to recover at any time in the future. Depending on the resource, the amounts of ultimate recovery resources are anywhere from a few hundred times

KNOWN RESERVES
The amount of a natural resource that the U.S. Geological Survey estimates is profitable to extract at current prices and with current production technologies.

ULTIMATE RECOVERY RESERVES
The amount of a natural resource that the U.S. Geological Survey estimates could conceivably be profitable to extract at any time in the future.

larger to tens of thousands of times larger than the amount of known resources. As resource prices rise, some of the ultimate recovery reserves will surely turn into profitable known resources.[1]

In the case of oil the steep rise in prices engineered by OPEC led to a furious search on the part of non-OPEC producers for new reserves, in the North Sea, Alaska, Mexico, and elsewhere. By 1980 the amount of known reserves of oil was over nine times larger than the amount of known reserves in 1950. If the price of crude oil were to rise sharply above $40 a barrel, the amount of known reserves would undoubtedly jump once again. Indeed, a ready supply lies in waiting in the United States. The western states are sitting on vast quantities of ultimate recovery reserves of oil locked in shale rock. Producers cannot profitably extract shale oil at a price of $30 a barrel. But shale oil would certainly be extracted and become part of the world's known reserves if the price of oil were to rise to $100 a barrel.

HISTORICAL NOTE: Mineral experts tell us that the known reserves of all minerals almost always increase each year.

The U.S. Geological Survey publishes yet a third quantity estimate, the amount of natural resources in the earth's crust. These amounts are truly vast, typically equal to millions of years of consumption at current rates. If prices rise high enough, perhaps some of these resources will move into the Geological Survey's estimate of ultimate recovery resources and from there into its estimate of known reserves. Although no one can gaze too far into the future, there are clearly plenty of natural resources available for even the very distant future. The market system will see to that.

Two conclusions follow from our discussion of natural-resource pricing. First, consumers and producers may eventually stop using one of the natural resources, but not because the resource has been completely exhausted. Rather, its price will have risen to the point of driving the resource out of the market in favor of alternatives. Second, the inevitable rise in natural-resource prices indicates that the value of nature's gift to us naturally tends to diminish over time as these exhaustible resources are used up. Even if we succeed in substituting away from a particular resource, we are still not as well off as we were before its price began to rise.

Solar- or fusion-based technologies are our best hope for cheaper energy in the future because they both use essentially inexhaustible resources, sunlight and water. The real prices of energy derived from these sources would not have a natural tendency to rise each year at the market rate of interest, and we could conceivably enjoy cheap supplies of energy indefinitely. Absent breakthroughs in either area, though, the prospect of ever more expensive energy is a virtual certainty.

SUMMARY

The first section of Chapter 21 analyzed the market for land.

1. The distinctive economic feature of land is that its supply is essentially fixed. Consequently, the price (or annual rental value) of land is determined by the demand for land, and the entire price of land is an economic rent.

---

[1]For futher discussion of mineral reserves estimates see W. Nordhaus, "Resources as a Constraint on Growth," *American Economic Review* 64, No. 2 (May, 1974): 23.

2. The demand for land depends primarily on its location and its inherent qualities, such as whether it is suitable for farming or contains valued oil or minerals.
3. The location element in the demand for residential land has three dimensions: the aesthetic, neighborhood, and cost dimensions. The aesthetic dimension refers to such things as view and whether the land borders on a lake. The neighborhood dimension includes such elements as whether people of similar income or tastes live nearby, crime rates, and the quality of the local school system. The cost dimension refers to the money and time costs of commuting, shopping, and engaging in leisure activities.
4. The cost dimension also applies to the demand for land by businesses. Businesses can save costs by locating near other businesses, particularly those that service the businesses and their employees. These costs savings explain why businesses cluster in downtown areas and bid up land rents so high that most homeowners are forced to seek cheaper land in the suburbs. The price of land in a metropolitan area tends to decline the farther it is from the center of the city.
5. Even though each parcel of land is fixed, market prices perform the important function of allocating land efficiently among the demanders. Allocating land according to the Laws of Supply and Demand assures that each parcel of land goes to the user who values it the most, thereby maximizing the total value of land, our nation's gift from nature.
6. Henry George proposed replacing all taxes with a single tax on land because a tax on fixed land does not affect the allocation of land and is therefore efficient. Local property taxes come closest to what George had in mind. While George's proposition is correct, local property taxes are not efficient because they tax both the value of the land and the value of the structures on the land. As such, they tax both land and capital, and the supply of capital to a community is not fixed.

The second section of Chapter 21 analyzed the market for natural resources.

7. Although the total quantity of exhaustible natural resources, such as oil and minerals, is fixed, the supply of these resources is not fixed. Owners must decide how much of the resource to supply to the market each year.
8. Natural-resource prices are related to interest rates because suppliers have the choice of supplying now and saving the proceeds for a year or holding back the supply until next year. The section presented a simple model of the supply decision for oil in which the price of oil rises each year by a percentage equal to the rate of interest. Actual prices may rise faster or slower than the rate of interest does, depending on more complex demand and cost considerations than are captured by the model. Nonetheless, the prices of exhaustible natural resources do have a tendency to rise steadily year by year relative to the prices of reproducible goods and services.
9. Although the rise and fall of OPEC's monopoly power has dictated the pattern of oil prices in recent years, the long-run trend of oil prices will almost certainly be upward, as our simple model predicts.
10. Rising prices of oil and other exhaustible minerals cause demanders to seek out substitute products and suppliers to develop substitute products. These market forces are so strong that an exhaustible natural resource will price itself out of the market long before the quantity of the resource is completely exhausted.

11. Fears of running out of natural resources are based on the amount of known reserves published by the U.S. Geological Survey, which will support current rates of consumption for only 20 to 50 years. But known reserves are based on today's prices and technologies. The earth's crust contains vast quantities of oil and minerals. Some of these reserves will be tapped and added to known reserves as prices rise and new recovery technologies are developed. Some of these reserves will never be used as substitutes become available and the resources price themselves out of the market.

KEY TERMS

exhaustible resource
inexhaustible resource
known reserves
ultimate recovery reserves

QUESTIONS

1. What is the distinctive economic feature of land? How would you characterize this feature in a supply-demand diagram?
2. Suppose that a farmer irrigates a plot of desert land and turns it into rich farmland. Has he brought about an increase in the supply of land?
3. What factors determine the demand for land? Give examples of each, and indicate how your examples would affect the price of land.
4. A fancy clothing boutique has its store situated in a perfect location—it is surrounded by a large number of households with very high incomes. The boutique owners rent the store from a landlord. Who is likely to gain more from the perfect location, the landlord or the owners of the boutique?
5. Why does the value of land in and around major cities tend to decrease steadily in value the farther away from the city it is?
6. a. Why is a tax on land efficient?
   b. Based on your answer to part a, would you conclude that the local property tax is an efficient tax?
7. a. Why is the price of an exhaustible natural resource expected to rise each year at a rate equal to the interest rate?
   b. Why does this same expectation not apply to the price of land?
8. Do you believe that the United States will be dependent on oil in the distant future—say, 200 years from now? Why or why not?
9. Our model of natural-resource pricing predicts a steady increase in the (relative) price of oil, yet the price of oil has both increased and decreased very sharply over the past 20 years. What factors missing from our simple model help to explain the recent behavior of oil prices?
10. Why is the total economic value of land maximized when it is allocated by the Laws of Supply and Demand?

CHAPTER

22

The Distribution of Income and Poverty in the United States

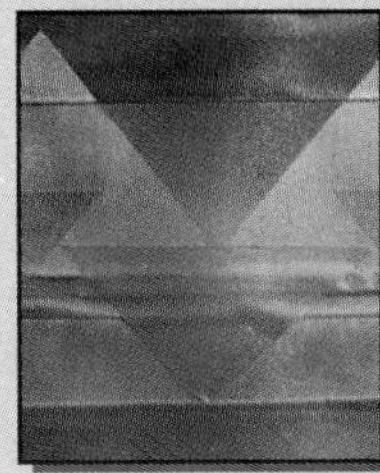

LEARNING OBJECTIVES

CONCEPTS TO LEARN

The personal distribution of income and wealth in the United States

The Lorenz curve and associated Gini coefficient

Social mobility

The incidence of poverty in the United States

The United States' War on Poverty: Successes and failures

Public insurance and public assistance in the United States

The negative income tax

CONCEPTS TO RECALL

Process equity: equality of opportunity [2]

End-results equity: horizontal equity [2]

The For Whom or Distribution Question [3]

The dominant economic image of the United States at the beginning of the 1960s was its immense wealth relative to other nations. The image was entirely accurate; the U.S. economy at the time was producing 40 percent of all the world's output and income. Harvard economist John Kenneth Galbraith solidified the image in 1958 with the publication of The Affluent Society, *which described how the great riches of the nation resulted in lifestyles that were singularly American.*

Shortly after Galbraith's book appeared, a number of economists and sociologists began reporting that all was not well in the land of plenty. Sociologist Michael Harrington's best-selling book, The Other America, *published in 1962, vividly portrayed an American landscape scarred by clusters of impoverished families living in the cities, in the countryside, and on the farms. Their lifestyles bore little resemblance to Galbraith's affluent Americans. The people Harrington described were in desperate straits.*

The Kennedy administration became alarmed about the problem of poverty and decided to count the poor, the first time a poverty count had ever been undertaken in the United States. The nation was shocked to discover that 39.5 million Americans, 22.4 percent of the entire population, were living under conditions of poverty in 1959. Poverty in the United States was every bit the problem that Harrington and others had said it was.

The Kennedy administration responded in 1963 by declaring an all-out War on Poverty whose goal was to eradicate poverty from the United States. The war has made some headway, but it is far from over. The percentage of people living in poverty has declined since 1959; it stood at 14.2 percent in 1991. But this is a smaller percentage of a much larger population than in 1959. More than 35 million people remain in the clutches of poverty, not so many fewer than in 1959.

Chapter 22 concludes the section on factor markets with a discussion of the For Whom, or distribution, question in the United States. The For Whom question is one of the four fundamental economic questions that all societies must answer. We saw in Chapter 3 that this question has two dimensions, a process dimension and an end-results dimension.

The process dimension relates to the problem of assuring equality of opportunity. Do people have equal access to whatever opportunities they are willing and able to pursue? Are the rules of the economic game fair? Our analysis throughout this text has shown that competition is the key to assuring equal opportunity in a capitalist economy. People do have equal access to opportunities when product and factor markets are highly competitive. Competition is also the great equalizer in economic affairs. Equal opportunity translates into horizontal equity—equals are treated equally in the competitive marketplace. By contrast, equality of opportunity suffers when product and factor markets are riddled with monopoly and monopsony power supported by barriers to entry and when factor markets are segmented by the presence of labor unions, internal labor markets, and discrimination in hiring and pay. In these instances some people are able to gain an economic advantage over other people who are their equals in every relevant respect. Many people consider these advantages unfair.

The end-results dimension of the distribution question typically expresses itself in two ways in a capitalist economy. The first is a general concern about inequality in the overall personal distribution of income and wealth, the fundamental problem of the haves and the have nots. How much inequality is too much? Should the government try to make the distribution more equal, and if so, how? What are the economic effects of the government's distributional policies? The second is a more focused concern about the poor, those people at the very bottom of the distribution who have fallen out of the mainstream of economic life and cannot afford what society has come to accept as a minimally adequate standard of living. Should the government attack the causes of poverty through publicly supported education and job-training programs and anti-discrimination policies? Or should the government simply treat the symptoms of poverty by transferring enough income or food or housing or medical care to the poor to bring them out of poverty? What are the economic effects of each of these options?

Chapter 22 focuses on the two end-results aspects of the distribution question. The chapter begins with an overview of the distribution of income and wealth in the United States and then turns to the problem of poverty.

THE DISTRIBUTION OF INCOME AND WEALTH IN THE UNITED STATES

Income

The U.S. Bureau of the Census collects data on income as part of a detailed annual survey of nearly 60,000 families and unrelated individuals called the **Current Population Survey.** The number of people surveyed is large enough to be an accurate representation of the entire U.S. population. The survey asks respondents to list their *total money income,* equal to their factor market income plus cash transfers from governments and private sources. Factor market income includes the principal sources of income from supplying labor, land, and capital: wages and salaries, rents, interest receipts, and dividends. Cash transfers include such items as private pensions, Social Security benefits, public assistance (welfare) checks, and unemployment insurance benefits. Total money income excludes *in-kind income* in the form of particular services received from private and public sources. The most important private sources of in-kind income are the contributions that employers make to their employees' retirement pensions and medical insurance plans. The most important public sources of in-kind income are food stamps given to the needy and payments to physicians and hospitals for medical services received by welfare recipients and the elderly.

CURRENT POPULATION SURVEY
An annual survey of approximately 60,000 families and unrelated individuals compiled by the U.S. Bureau of the Census, which is used to obtain information on income and other personal characteritics.

The Current Population Survey is the principal source of annual data on personal income for the United States. It is the basis of the federal government's "official" statistics on the distribution of income and the number of people in poverty. In addition, the survey is detailed enough to provide a breakdown of income by the personal characteristics of the respondents, in-

TABLE 22.1 **Personal Distribution of Income in the United States: Families and Households, 1991**

FAMILIES					
PERCENTAGE OF FAMILIES	BOTTOM 20%	2ND 20%	3RD 20%	4TH 20%	TOP 20%
PERCENTAGE OF TOTAL INCOME	4.4	10.7	16.6	24.1	44.2
HOUSEHOLDS					
PERCENTAGE OF HOUSEHOLDS	BOTTOM 20%	2ND 20%	3RD 20%	4TH 20%	TOP 20%
PERCENTAGE OF TOTAL INCOME	3.8	9.6	15.9	24.2	46.5

SOURCE: U.S. Department of Commerce, Economics and Statistics Administration, Bureau of the Census, "Money Income of Households, Families, and Persons in the United States: 1991," *Consumer Income,* Current Population Reports, Series P-60, No. 180 (1991): Tables B-3, B-7. The data on median and mean family incomes reported in the text are on p. 44.

cluding age, gender, race, education, record of employment during the year and size and composition of the respondents' families. We made use of some of these other data in Chapters 18 and 19.

The Census Bureau reports the distribution of total money income separately for families and households. The households include unrelated individuals. The most popular method of presenting the distribution of income is by the percentage of total income received by each quintile (20 percent) or decile (10 percent) of the population, with the families (or unrelated individuals) ordered from lowest income to highest income. Table 22.1 presents the distribution of income in 1991 for all families and households, by quintile.

Presenting the data in this way is useful because it gives us an immediate feel for the degree of income inequality in the United States. Refer to the family data. If income were equally distributed among families, all five numbers in Table 22.1 would be 20. Each quintile of families would receive 20 percent of the total income. In fact, the numbers in the table suggest that the distribution of income in the United States is quite unequal. The poorest 20 percent of the families receive only 4.4 percent of total income, whereas the richest 20 percent of the families receive 44.2 percent of total income. The richest families receive 10 times as much income as do the poorest families, on average (44.2/4.4 = 10). (The household data are slightly more unequal because the distribution of income among unrelated individuals is more unequal than is the distribution among families.)

THE LORENZ CURVE AND GINI COEFFICIENT The data in Table 22.1 form the basis for two other popular representations of income inequality: (1) a picture of inequality known as the Lorenz curve and (2) a single measure of inequality known as the Gini coefficient. The Lorenz curve and the Gini coefficient are named after the statisticians who invented them.

LORENZ CURVE

A graph of the distribution of income that relates the cumulative percentage of all families, ordered by income from lowest to highest, to the cumulative percentage of the total income (wealth) that they receive.

THE LORENZ CURVE The **Lorenz curve** is the graph that results from plotting the cumulative percentage of all families against the cumulative percentage of the total income they receive. Figure 22.1 depicts the Lorenz curve for the data on families from Table 22.1

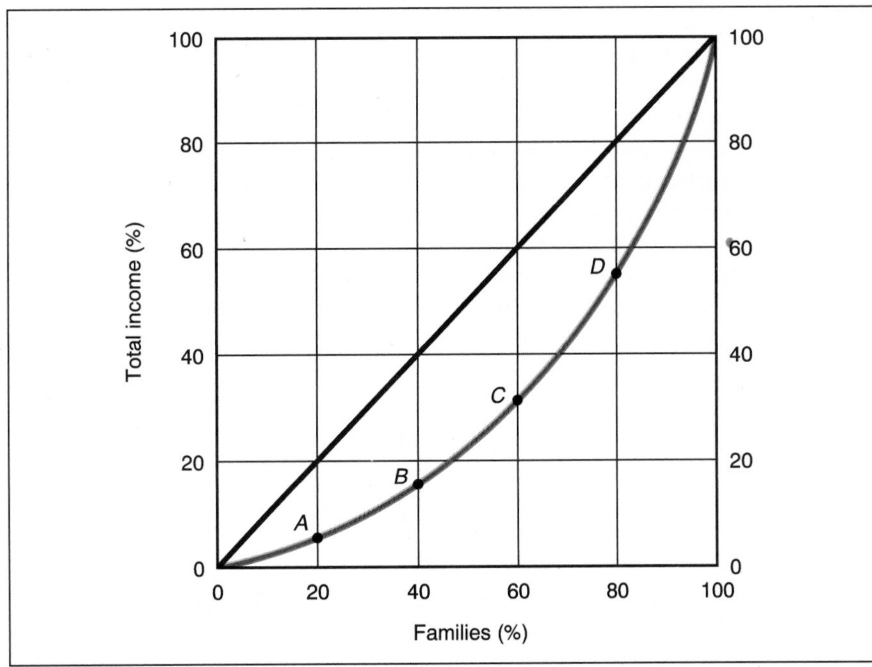

FIGURE 22.1

The Lorenz Curve for Income in the United States 1991

The Lorenz curve is a picture of the distribution of income. It graphs the cumulative percentage of total income on the vertical axes of the square against the cumulative percentage of families arranged from lowest income to highest income along the bottom of the square. The diagonal of the square is the line of perfect equality. The Lorenz curve would lie on the diagonal if all families had the same income. The further the Lorenz curve is bowed downward from the diagonal, the more unequal the distribution of income. The figure shows that the distribution of income was far from equal in the United States in 1991. For example, point *A* indicates that the poorest 20 percent of the families had only 4.4 percent of the total income.

As in Figure 22.1, a Lorenz curve is usually drawn inside a square that includes the diagonal running from the lower left-hand corner to the upper right-hand corner of the square. The bottom and sides of the square are the horizontal and vertical axes. The bottom of the square (the horizontal axis) records the percentage of all families, cumulatively from 0 to 100 percent, ordered by lowest income to highest income as in Table 22.1. The sides of the square (duplicate vertical axes) record the percentage of total income received, cumulatively from 0 to 100 percent, by the percentage of families recorded along the bottom of the square.

Notice that all Lorenz curves must begin and end at the end points of the diagonal of the square. The lower left-hand corner is the origin. It indicates that 0 percent of the families receive 0 percent of the total income. Conversely, the point in the upper right-hand corner indicates that 100 percent of the families receive 100 percent of the total income. The shape of the Lorenz curve between these two points depends on the degree of inequality in the distribution of income.

The diagonal of the square serves as a frame of reference for picturing the degree of income inequality because it is the line representing perfect equality. If all families had the same income, 20 percent of the families would receive 20 percent of the income, 40 percent of the families 40 percent of the income, 60 percent of the families 60 percent of the income, and so on up the diagonal. The Lorenz curve would lie along the diagonal.

The Lorenz curve bows downward away from the diagonal if income is not equally distributed. To see this, look again at the data in Table 22.1, which generate the Lorenz curve pictured in Figure 22.1. The four points shown on the curve come from the data, with the curve then smoothed through those four points and the end points of the diagonal. Since the first (poorest) 20 percent of the families receive only 4.4 percent of the total income, point *A* on the Lorenz curve corresponding to the first 20 percent of the population is less than one-fourth of the distance to the diagonal. Point B indicates that the first 40 percent of the families receive 15.1 percent of the total income, the sum of the first two entries in the table (15.1 = 4.4 + 10.7). Point B is also well below the diagonal. Similarly, point C indicates that the first 60 percent of the families receive 31.7 percent of the total income (31.7 = 4.4 + 10.7 + 16.6), and point D indicates that the first 80 percent of the families receive 55.8 percent of the total income (55.8 = 4.4 + 10.7 + 16.6 + 24.1). Points C and D on the Lorenz curve also lie below the diagonal.

In general, the Lorenz curve lies closer to the diagonal the more equal the distribution of income and is bowed farther away from the diagonal the more unequal the distribution of income. The substantial bow in the Lorenz curve in Figure 22.1 offers a convenient visual indication that the distribution of income in the United States is far from equal.

GINI COEFFICIENT

A common measure of the degree of inequality of income or wealth, equal to the area between the Lorenz curve and the diagonal of the square containing the Lorenz curve, divided by the entire area beneath the diagonal.

THE GINI COEFFICIENT The **Gini coefficient** makes use of the Lorenz curve to provide a single numerical measure of the degree of income inequality. It is computed as the ratio of two areas in Figure 22.1: (1) the area between the Lorenz curve and the diagonal of the square and (2) the entire area beneath the diagonal of the square.

$$\text{Gini coefficient} = \frac{\text{the area between the Lorenz curve and the diagonal}}{\text{the entire area beneath the diagonal}}$$

Notice that the Gini coefficient must have a value between zero and one. A value of zero represents perfect equality, and a value of one represents the greatest possible inequality. In the case of perfect equality the Lorenz curve and the diagonal coincide, so that the area between them is 0, and the value of the Gini coefficient is also zero. The greatest possible inequality consists of one family receiving all the income. In this case the Lorenz curve coincides with the bottom of the square through all families except the last family, since no other family has any income. Then the curve shoots up the right-hand side of the box to the top when the last family is accounted for. The area between the Lorenz curve and the diagonal equals the entire area beneath the diagonal, and the value of the Gini coefficient is one.

Between the limiting values of zero and one, the higher the value of the Gini coefficient, the more unequal the distribution of income. The reason is that the Lorenz curve bows farther away from the diagonal the more unequal the distribution. Therefore, the area between the diagonal and the Lorenz curve increases the more unequal the distribution, which increases the value of the Gini coefficient.

The Gini coefficient is most useful for comparative purposes, such as tracking the pattern of inequality over time or comparing inequality within subgroups of the population. For instance, the Gini coefficient for family income in the United States was .397 in 1991 and .365 in 1980.[1] This tells us that the distribution of income among families became more unequal between 1980 and 1991.

---

[1]U.S. Department of Commerce, Economics and Statistics Administration, Bureau of the Census, "Money Income of Households, Families, and Persons in the United States: 1991," *Consumer Income,* Current Population Reports, Series P-60, No. 180 (August 1992): Table B-3.

BUNCHING AND HIGH INCOMES The Lorenz curve and Gini coefficient hide two other characteristics of the income distribution that are worth noting. The first is that the vast majority of families are bunched near the middle of the distribution, lying in a range from one-half the average level of income to twice the average level of income. The second is that the distribution includes a small number of families or individuals with extremely high incomes, people such as computer wizard Bill Gates of Microsoft and rock star Michael Jackson who earn tens of millions of dollars annually. Because of these high-income families and individuals you should beware of statements about the "average" level of income.

We have been using "average" to stand for the *mean* level of income. Another common meaning of "average" is the *median* level of income, the income of the family in the middle of the income distribution. Half the families have less income than this family, half have more income. The median family income in the United States was only $35,939 in 1991, much less than the mean family income of $43,237. The difference between the two averages is due to those relatively few families with huge incomes, which pull the mean level of income well above the median level of income.

The two characteristics of bunching around the middle and a small group of people with very high incomes are not unique to the distribution of income in the United States. They are common features of all distributions of income, including distributions in the other developed market economies and distributions within communities throughout each country. The majority of families have similar incomes, and the mean level of income is almost always considerably larger than the median level of income is.

Wealth

Data on wealth, or net worth, are much sketchier than are data on income. Government surveys of wealth occur only infrequently and cover far fewer families than do the annual surveys of income. Also, surveys of wealth are notoriously unreliable because most people are very reluctant to divulge information about their net worth.

The last comprehensive survey of wealth undertaken by the federal government was in 1983. Called the Survey of Consumer Finances, it covered only 3,665 families, less than 8 percent of the number of families surveyed each year in the Current Population Survey. Even so, the Survey of Consumer Finances was the most comprehensive survey of wealth ever undertaken in the United States. The government's last comprehensive survey of wealth before 1983 occurred 21 years earlier, in 1962. The 1983 survey was updated in 1989.

Surveys of wealth may be few and far between, but they always show that the distribution of wealth is far more unequal than is the distribution of income. The Survey of Consumer Finances collected data on families' financial assets and liabilities and on their housing wealth. According to the survey, 28 percent of all the wealth in these forms is held by just 2 percent of the families, and 57 percent of the wealth is held by 10 percent of the families. Furthermore, 20 percent of all families have negative net worth—their liabilities exceed their assets. The Gini coefficient for the distribution of wealth is a whopping .80, twice as large as the Gini coefficient for the distribution of income.

The distribution of wealth is even more unequal if housing wealth is excluded. Financial net worth, the difference between financial assets and financial liabilities, is the accumulated savings over time that the household sector has supplied to the nation's financial markets. These savings are a principal source of the funds for business investment. Fifty-four percent of the financial net worth is held by 2 percent of the families and 86 percent by 10 percent of the families. Moreover, 55 percent of all families have negative financial net worth, meaning that they are net borrowers in the nation's financial markets. In short, most of the saving by households that provides funds for business investment comes from a tiny percentage of U.S. households.

The survey uncovered another interesting fact about household net worth. Only 20 percent of all net worth is due to inheritance. For the most part, families accumulate their wealth year by year through savings out of their incomes.

The distribution of wealth would have been more equal had the survey included consumer durables and wealth accumulated in pension plans. But including these items would not change the basic conclusion that the distribution of wealth is far more unequal than is the distribution of income in the United States.

THE VERY WEALTHY The government issued a separate report on the very wealthy, defined as the families in the survey who fall within the four highest *income* classes: annual incomes of $50,000–$100,000; $100,000–$150,000; $150,000–280,000; and $280,000 and above. These are the families who hold the majority of all household wealth. They had an average net worth of $797,000, ranging from an average of $270,800 for the $50,000–$100,000 income class to $5.4 million for the $280,000 and above income class.

The very wealthy have a number of distinctive characteristics relative to the population as a whole. They are overwhelmingly white: Ninety-two percent of the very wealthy are white, non-Hispanic Caucasians. They earn a substantial portion of their incomes from capital and land: Only 70 percent of the very wealthy receive more than half of their incomes from labor market earnings. (Recall that income from labor accounts for nearly 80 percent of income overall in the United States.) The very wealthy have not simply inherited most of their wealth: Only 17 percent of the very wealthy inherited more than half of their net worth. While they do enjoy inherited wealth to a greater extent than does the overall population, they, too, have accumulated most of their wealth through saving. Finally, if you want to be counted among the very wealthy in the next government survey of wealth, consider careers in investment banking, insurance, real estate, and the professions, especially doctors, lawyers, and accountants. These are the predominant occupations of the very wealthy. You might also start your own business and hope it succeeds. Successful entrepreneurs are also quite prominent among the wealthy elite. Microsoft's Bill Gates is an outstanding example. Gates went from Harvard drop-out to one of the wealthiest people in the United States in just a few years.[2]

---

[2]The wealth data in this section are reported in "Survey of Consumer Finances, 1983," *Federal Reserve Bulletin* 70, No. 9 (September 1984): 680–692; and "Financial Characteristics of High Income Families," *Federal Reserve Bulletin* 72, No. 3 (March 1986): 163–177. We found no comparable analysis of the updated 1989 survey. One source suggested that, if anything, the distribution of wealth became slightly more unequal from 1983 to 1989. A. Kennickelland J. Shack-Marquez, "Changes in Family Finances from 1983 to 1989: Evidence from the Survey of Consumer Finances," *Federal Reserve Bulletin* 78, No. 1 (January 1992): 1–18.

The Puzzling Distribution of Income

Let's turn back to the distribution of income for the remainder of this section. Economists have long puzzled over this question: Why do the numbers in Table 22.1 come out the way they do? Why, for instance, do 20 percent of the families command over 44 percent of the total income? In Chapters 9 and 18 through 21 we have identified a long list of factors that influence how much income people receive—their innate ability, the amount of formal education and on-the-job training they have received, whether they belong in a union, the demand for special skills they might have, their access to primary jobs in large corporations, whether they suffer discrimination, the amount of savings they supply to the nation's financial markets, the quality and quantity of land that they own, and so on. Noneconomic factors such as marriage patterns also affect the distribution of income. The question remains, though, as to just how important each of these separate factors is in determining the overall distribution of income. Economists simply do not know the answer to this question.

Our fundamental ignorance about the distribution of income was highlighted by Princeton's Alan Blinder in his well-known study of U.S. income distribution.[3] Blinder followed the distribution reported in the Current Population Surveys each year from 1947, the first year of the survey, until 1977. He concluded that the single most striking feature of the distribution of income in the United States was its constancy. The numbers hardly changed at all over the entire 31-year period.

Blinder was struck by his finding because it was so unexpected. The United States was hardly a static, unchanging entity during the years of his study. As we noted in our discussion of the U.S. economy in Chapter 4, the United States has undergone a whole host of economic and demographic changes since World War II, many of a magnitude unprecedented in the nation's history. The role of the government sector also greatly expanded during this time. The United States of 1977 bore little resemblance to the United States of 1947, yet the distribution of income remained essentially unchanged. No one knows why.

The timing of Blinder's study turned out to be ironic because sometime around 1976 or 1977 the distribution of income in the United States did begin to change. It has become steadily more unequal since that time. The Gini coefficient for families stood at .36 in 1977. By 1982 it had increased to .39 and by 1991 to .397. Roughly speaking, the top quintile of families appears to be gaining relative to the bottom two quintiles. Moreover, the same pattern appears to be true no matter how the population is subdivided—that is, by males, by females, by white-collar workers, by blue-collar workers. The distribution has become more unequal within each of these subgroups, and in the same way. The highest-income group is gaining relative to the lowest-income groups.[4]

The recent increase in inequality is every bit as puzzling as was the constancy in the distribution in the 30-year period following World War II. The

---

[3]A. Blinder, "The Level and Distribution of Economic Well-Being," in M. Feldstein (ed.), *The American Economy in Transition* (Chicago: University of Chicago Press, 1980), 415–479.

[4]U.S. Department of Commerce, Economics and Statistics Administration, Bureau of the Census, "Money Income of Households, Families, and Persons in the United States: 1991," *Consumer Income*, Current Population Reports, Series P-60, No. 180, (August 1992): Table B-3. See, also, S. Danziger and P. Gottschalk (eds.), *Uneven Tides: Rising Inequality in America* (New York: Russell Sage Foundation, 1992), 1–17.

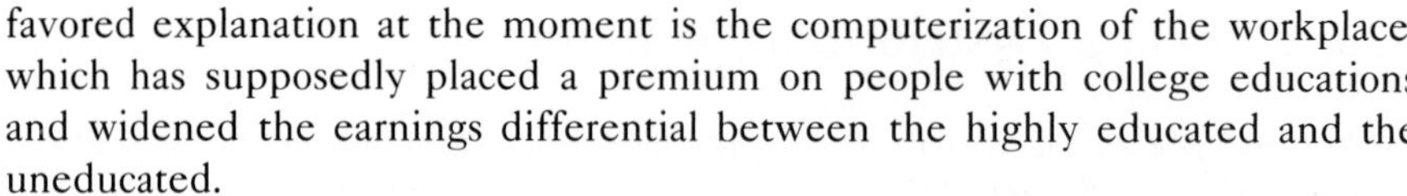

favored explanation at the moment is the computerization of the workplace, which has supposedly placed a premium on people with college educations and widened the earnings differential between the highly educated and the uneducated.

There are a number of other explanations as well for the increase in inequality. Some point to the increase in high-income two-earner families, the Yuppie phenomenon, to explain the rise in incomes at the top of the distribution. Others think that the federal tax and welfare reforms enacted during the Reagan administration helped the rich at the expense of the poor. Still another explanation points to the increasing internationalization of the economy, which has pushed the economy even more in the direction of services and away from manufacturing. According to this view, the jobs created in the service sector are low-paying, secondary-type jobs that hold down the incomes of those at the bottom of the distribution.

REFLECTION: Do you think that the increase in two-earner families has tended to increase or decrease income inequality among families as reported by the Current Population Survey?

None of these other explanations is entirely convincing, however. The increase in two-earner families, the shift of the economy toward services, and the internationalization of the economy were under way well before 1977. If these events are affecting the distribution of income now, why didn't they do so earlier? Also, the Reagan bashers have to explain why inequality began to increase well before President Reagan took office. In truth, no one really understands why the distribution of income has recently become more unequal after years of remaining essentially constant.

The computerization of the workplace is a more promising explanation because most of it has occurred since 1980. Research on the distributional implications of computerization is just now underway. We will know more about it in a few years.

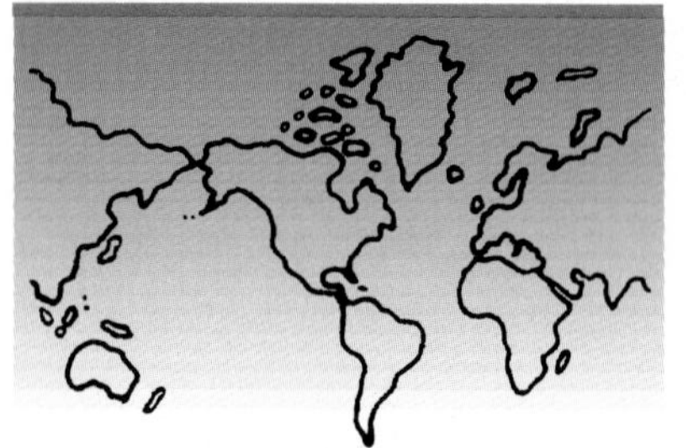

INCREASING INCOME INEQUALITY WORLDWIDE

The recent increase in income inequality has not been limited to the United States. Peter Gottschalk of Boston College computed changes in family income inequality from 1979 to 1987 in seven other industrialized countries: Australia, Canada, France, Germany, the Netherlands, Sweden, and the United Kingdom. This is the same period when income inequality began to increase in the United States. Gottschalk found that family income inequality increased in six of the seven countries. Only in Germany did the inequality of family income remain constant.

The United States experienced the largest increase in family income inequality by a wide margin, an average increase of 12.9 percent per year. The Netherlands was in second place at 6.9 percent per year. Sweden experienced the smallest increase in inequality (besides Germany), just 0.5 percent per year.[5]

Gottschalk also discovered that market forces were an important contributor to increasing equality in all these countries. He calculated changes in the inequality of the earnings of prime-aged male heads of families, ages 25–55, who worked full time. These are the workers who are most attached to the labor force, so that any changes in the inequality of their earnings are due to changes

[5]Gottschalk used a simple measure of inequality called the 90/10 ratio as the basis of comparison. The 90/10 ratio is the ratio of the average income of the families in the 90th percentile of the income distribution to the average income of the families in the 10th percentile of the distribution. The higher the 90/10 ratio, the more unequal the distribution of income.

in their relative wage rates, not their hours worked. Gottschalk found that the inequality of prime-aged male earnings increased in all the countries for which family income inequality increased. The wages of the high income workers rose relative to the wages of the low income workers. The increase in earnings inequality was largest in the United States, The United Kingdom, and Canada, approximately 10 percent per year. The increase was smallest in Sweden, only 1.4 percent per year, where market forces are not nearly as important in determining wages as in the other countries.

One other result of Gottschalk's study is worth noting. Only in the United States and the Netherlands was the increase in family income inequality greater than the increase in male earnings inequality. He attributed this to a retrenchment of transfer programs in both countries during the 1980's, especially transfers to the poor. All the other countries increased their public transfers as a percentage of national income, which lessened the impact of the increased inequality of earnings.[6]

Can the Government Change the Distribution?

Suppose that the citizens of the United States decide that they want a more equal distribution of income. The question remains whether the federal government will be able to carry out their wishes. Governments in capitalist economies suffer three severe handicaps in trying to change the distribution of income.

First, the government will certainly want to attack the underlying causes of inequality. In order to do so, however, government officials must first understand what economic factors have the most influence on the distribution. Otherwise, they cannot possibly design effective policies to make the distribution more equal. As we just indicated, economists have not been able to provide government officials with this understanding.

Second, any major redistributional policy is going to include a set of taxes and transfers that tax the haves and transfer income to the have nots. Taxes and transfers are a "quick fix" that addresses the symptoms of inequality and not the underlying causes. Nonetheless, the government may have to treat the symptoms if the citizens are anxious for change and the underlying causes of inequality cannot be changed very quickly, if at all. Unfortunately, both taxes and transfers create incentives that lead to inefficient behavior. Eventually the government will be faced with a difficult economic and political choice between efficiency and equity: Are the distributional gains of additional taxes and transfers worth the inefficiencies that they generate?

The third problem is that noneconomic social practices and customs may have a dominant influence on the distribution of income, in which case the government is essentially helpless. For example, we referred in Chapter 19 to a controversial study of identical twins, which concluded that innate ability may account for nearly 60 percent of the differences in earnings among people in the United States. If the study is correct, then the pattern of marriages is crucial in determining the distribution of income because marriage is the channel through which a society transfers ability from one generation to the next.

[6]Peter Gottschalk, "Changes in Inequality of Family Income in Seven Industrialized Countries," *American Economic Association Papers and Proceedings* 83, No. 2 (May 1993): 136–142.

Marriage patterns would be as equalizing as possible if marriages were random; that is, if a young man of high ability is equally likely to marry a woman of high ability, middle ability, or low ability, and the same for a woman. Conversely, marriage patterns promote inequality if people tend to marry within their ability levels; that is, if high-ability men marry high-ability women and low-ability men marry low-ability women. Marriages are presumably not random in terms of ability, so that marriage patterns themselves contribute to the observed inequality of income. Also, the wealthy are more likely to marry the wealthy, so that marriage patterns also contribute to the unequal distribution of wealth.

The government's distributional policies are unlikely to change the underlying social fabric of the nation, or even try to do so. If not, then the government may not be able to redistribute income or wealth very effectively.

The problems with trying to change the distribution may not matter very much in the United States because the nation has never articulated a policy regarding the overall distribution of income or wealth. We noted in Chapter 2 that U.S. citizens appear to care more about process equity than end-results equity. The prevailing attitude appears to be this: Assure equality of opportunity, promote competition, and let the chips fall where they may. Fortunately, the chips do not always fall in the same place. People can and do change their positions within the distribution, a phenomenon known as social mobility.

Social Mobility

Is a family situated in the lowest quintile of the income distribution destined to remain in that quintile forever? The answer is yes in a caste system. The members of the lowest caste will always remain at the bottom of the distribution. People do move throughout the distribution over time in more open societies, some to higher quintiles, some to lower quintiles. The overall amount of movement of families throughout the distribution is a commonly used indicator of the **social mobility** of the population.

SOCIAL MOBILITY

The extent to which families change their position over time within the personal distribution of income.

The amount of social mobility within a society is closely related to equality of opportunity because equal access to economic opportunities promotes social mobility. As such, social mobility is an excellent measure of process equity. The higher the degree of social mobility, the fairer the economic system, in the sense of giving everyone an equal chance to succeed.

Table 22.2 indicates the degree of social mobility in the United States. The table shows the extent to which families changed their positions within the distribution of income between 1971 and 1978. Each row represents a quintile of families within the distribution in 1971, starting with the lowest (poorest) quintile in the first row. Each column within a row indicates the percentages of these families that were in each of the five quintiles by 1978. For example, the third row shows what happened to families that were in the third quintile of the distribution in 1971. By 1978, 14.0 percent of these families had reached the highest quintile, 18.5 percent rose to the second-highest quintile, 30.5 percent remained in the third quintile, 23.5 percent fell to the fourth quintile, and 13.5 percent fell to the lowest quintile.

According to Table 22.2, families were always more likely to remain in the same quintile than to move to any other one quintile. Nonetheless, the United States has a considerable amount of social mobility. The majority of families

TABLE 22.2 **Social Mobility within the United States, 1971–1978**

POSITION IN INCOME QUINTILE IN 1971	PERCENTAGE IN INCOME QUINTILE IN 1978				
	Bottom 20%	**2d 20%**	**3d 20%**	**4th 20%**	**Top 20%**
Bottom 20%	55.5	22.0	9.5	7.0	6.0
2d 20%	21.5	34.5	21.5	13.5	9.0
3d 20%	13.5	23.5	30.5	18.5	14.0
4th 20%	6.0	15.0	25.5	31.5	22.0
Top 20%	3.5	4.5	14.0	29.5	48.5

SOURCE: The social mobility data are reported in R. Ehrenberg and R. Smith, *Modern Labor Economics: Theory and Public Policy*, fourth edition, (New York: Harper Collins 1991), Example 9.6, p. 342. The original source is M. Lilla, "Why the 'Income Distribution' is so Misleading," *Public Interest* 77 (Fall 1984): 62–76.

within each quintile changed quintiles from 1971 to 1978, with the single exception of the lowest quintile. Fifty-five percent of the families in the lowest quintile in 1971 remained there in 1978. Even so, families in the lowest quintile are hardly destined to remain there forever. Indeed, 13 percent of the families who were in the lowest quintile in 1971 attained the top two quintiles by 1978 (13.0 = 6.0 + 7.0).

Perhaps the high degree of social mobility in the United States explains why the United States has been willing to tolerate fairly unequal distributions of income and wealth. True, the Clinton adminstration expressed displeasure over the recent increase in equality and proposed a small increase in the income tax rates on the highest-income taxpayers, which Congress passed. Still, the federal government is unlikely to launch a frontal assault on the distribution of income (or wealth) to try to make it more equal.

The one exception to the relative lack of interest in the overall distribution of income concerns the poor. As noted in the introduction, President John F. Kennedy declared an all-out War on Poverty, and the federal government has been committed to the goal of eliminating poverty ever since. The remainder of the chapter addresses the problem of poverty in the United States.

POVERTY IN THE UNITED STATES

The Kennedy administration faced an immediate problem when it wanted to count the poor. It first had to develop a workable definition of poverty.

The Poverty Line

The administration chose to define an absolute standard of poverty. The idea was to determine a level of income, called the **poverty line,** that would allow a family to purchase the bare necessities for what Americans in the 1960s considered to be a minimally adequate standard of living, nothing more. The poverty line was adjusted for family size and for differences in the cost of living in different regions of the country. Families with incomes below the poverty line were poor, by definition; families with incomes at or above the poverty line were nonpoor.

POVERTY LINE

The amount of income that allows a family or unrelated individual to purchase the bare necessities for a minimally adequate standard of living; anyone with income below the poverty line is considered to be living in poverty.

The Kennedy administration used two methods to compute the poverty line, only one of which has survived. The more comprehensive method consisted of formulating an entire bare-bones budget that provided for food, clothing, shelter, and a few other essentials, such as transportation to and from work and minimal amounts of dental and medical care. The budget was intended to be extremely spare so that everyone would agree: A family that could not afford even those items in the poverty budget was in dire need of help. For example, the food budget allowed for adequate nutrition and little more. It paid some attention to the foods that Americans actually eat, but the family had to shop with care—no late night snacks and absolutely no dining out. The clothing allowance provided adequate protection from the elements, but no designer jeans or other frills. The budget for shelter was especially indicative of what it meant to live in poverty. It provided for hot and cold running water, heat and electricity, indoor plumbing, a stove and a refrigerator, a bed and a dresser for each person, and enough furnishings so that a family could have a common meal. For a family of four, this meant one table and four chairs. Families living on a poverty-line budget had no radio or television and no money for any other form of entertainment.

The alternative method of computing the poverty line set the line at three times the budget allowance for food, on the grounds that low-income families spend about one-third of their incomes on food. Since the two methods of computing the poverty line gave virtually identical results, the simpler food-budget-times-three calculation has survived as the method of computing the poverty line each year.

The Kennedy administration published the first "official" poverty line in 1964: $1,800 for a single person and $3,000 for a family of four, living in the urban Northeast. Notice that the official definition of poverty recognizes the substantial economies of scale that exist within a family. A family of four does not need four times as much income as a single person to escape poverty, only 1⅔ as much ($3,000/$1,800 = 1⅔).

The administration adjusts the poverty line each year for inflation. By 1991, the poverty line was $13,924 for a family of four.

History of the War on Poverty

Table 22.3 chronicles the success of the War on Poverty. Four distinct periods are evident in the data: the 1960s, 1970–78, 1979–82, and 1983–91.

The War on Poverty got off to a smashing start. The poverty rate plummeted throughout the 1960s, starting even before the official declaration of war. The 1960s were generally good times and especially good for the poor. The poverty rate fell by almost 10 percentage points from 1960 to 1970, as nearly 14 million people escaped the clutches of poverty during the decade.

The war continued to show results from 1970 to 1978, although at a much slower pace. The high point in the war effort came in 1973, with the poverty rate down to 11.1 percent and 23 million people in poverty. Those numbers were never again duplicated. The poverty rate increased slightly during the deep recession of 1974–75 and then quickly fell back again into the 11 percent range.

Many economists were feeling quite good about the War on Poverty by the mid-1970s. The economists at the Congressional Budget Office authored a

TABLE 22.3 Poverty in the United States, 1959–91

YEAR	NUMBER OF PEOPLE IN POVERTY (MILLIONS)	POVERTY RATE %
1959	39.5	22.4
1960	39.9	22.2
1965	33.2	17.3
1970	25.4	12.6
1973[a]	23.0	11.1
1975	25.9	12.3
1978	24.5	11.4
1980	29.3	13.0
1983	35.4	15.2[b]
1987	32.2	13.4
1990	33.6	13.5
1991	35.7	14.2

[a]1973 recorded both the fewest number of people in poverty and the lowest poverty rate of any year since 1959.

[b]The 15.2 percent poverty rate in 1983 was the highest recorded poverty rate since 1965.

SOURCE: U.S. Department of Commerce, Economics and Statistics Administration, Bureau of the Census, "Poverty in the United States: 1991," *Consumer Income*, Current Population Reports, Series P-60, No. 183 (1992).

report in 1977 claiming that the actual poverty rate was only about half the official rate. They noted that the official data were based on surveys of total money income, the same income concept used for the overall income distribution data. As noted above, total money income misses in-kind government transfers, such as medical payments, housing subsidies, and food stamps, all of which are very important sources of income to low-income families. When the CBO economists included the in-kind transfers in total income they found that the true poverty rate in 1976 was an impressive 5.8 percent, well below the official figure of 11.5 percent. They and many other economists were quite pleased with the government's progress against poverty.[7]

The remaining critics of the war effort by the mid-1970s were generally those economists who believe that the poverty line should be defined in relative terms, not absolute terms. A commonly proposed relative standard would set the poverty line at half the median level of income, which would have raised the poverty line to approximately $18,000 in 1991 for a family of four. By this relative standard the War on Poverty had made little progress in its first 15 years. About the same number of families had less than half the median level of income in 1978 as in 1963.

A relative income standard has the advantage of adjusting for rising expectations about what constitutes a minimally acceptable standard of living as the median level of income rises over time. Adjusting for rising expectations has merit because a poverty line is inherently a relative concept. It has meaning only against accepted community standards about what constitutes a decent standard of living. After all, most of the poor in the United States today would

[7]Congressional Budget Office, U.S. Congress, *Poverty Status of Families under Alternative Definitions of Income* (Washington, D.C.: U.S. Government Printing Office, 1977).

have been considered very well off in Elizabethan England or in Bangladesh today.

The government recognized the importance of community standards when it first defined the poverty line in 1963, but then ignored the problem of changing expectations over time. The government's absolute poverty line adjusts only for inflation. It fixes expectations about an adequate standard of living at 1963 levels, even though the median standard of living had risen substantially in the United States between 1963 and 1978 and is even higher today. For instance, shouldn't the poverty-line budget have made allowance for a television set by 1978 (or today)?

Whatever satisfaction existed about the progress against poverty in 1978 was negated by the events of the next five years. The economy soured during that period. By 1982 the United States was in the throes of its worst recession since the Great Depression of the 1930s. Low-income families and individuals were hit hard financially, and the War on Poverty beat a hasty retreat. Between 1979 and 1983 the number of people in poverty swelled by more than 10 million, and the problem of poverty was once again in the forefront of the American conscience. The low point occurred in 1983 when 15.2 percent of the population, over 35 million people, was in poverty. Numbers that high had not been seen since the early 1960s, just about the time the War on Poverty began.

The poverty rate decreased steadily from 1983 to 1990 as the economy recovered from the recession, but it never returned to the low levels experienced during the 1970s. By 1990, 13.5 percent of the population, a total of 33.6 million people, remained in poverty. The mild recession of the early 1990s drove the poverty rate up again, to 14.2 percent and 35.7 million people in 1991.

The Incidence of Poverty

Who are most likely to be poor? To avoid poverty? Table 22.4 records poverty rates in 1991 for various subgroups of the population along a number of personal characteristics: level of education, family status, race, gender, and so forth. When interpreting the data, keep in mind that in 1991 the poverty rate for all persons was 14.2 percent, and the poverty rate for all families was 12.8 percent. A number of very clear patterns emerge from the table.

EDUCATION, EMPLOYMENT, AND FAMILY A good education, full-time employment, and a stable family environment all provide excellent insurance against poverty. The relationship between level of education and poverty is very strong, and consistent with the human capital theory of wages. Adults with a high school education have lower-than-average poverty rates, and families headed by adults with a college education have much-lower-than-average poverty rates. Conversely, people are much more vulnerable to poverty if they have less than a high school education.

The relationship between work experience and poverty is also as expected. Working full time provides excellent protection against poverty. Vulnerability to poverty increases significantly for part-time workers and for workers who are unemployed.

The advantages of a stable family environment are also readily apparent from the table. The poverty rate for families headed by a married couple is only 6.0

TABLE 22.4 Incidence of Poverty in the United States: Poverty Rates for Selected Groups, 1991

OVERALL POVERTY RATES			
All persons	All families	Unrelated individuals	
14.2	12.8	21.1	
HIGHEST LEVEL OF EDUCATION COMPLETED BY PERSONS 25 YEARS AND OVER			
No high school diploma	High school diploma	Some college	Bachelor's degree or more
25.2	9.2	6.5	3.1
WORK EXPERIENCE (POVERTY RATES OF PERSONS)			
Year-round full time	Not year-round full time	Did not work during year	
2.6	13.4	22.8	
FAMILY STATUS: HEAD OF FAMILY (POVERTY RATES OF FAMILIES)			
Married couple	Male, no wife present	Female, no husband present	
6.0	13.0	35.6	
GENDER (POVERTY RATES OF PERSONS)			
Male	Female		
12.3	16.0		
RACE (POVERTY RATE OF PERSONS)			
White	Black	Hispanic	
11.3	32.7	28.7	
AGE (POVERTY RATE OF PERSONS)			
Aged (> 65)	Children (<18)		
12.4	21.8		
GEOGRAPHIC LOCATION (POVERTY RATE OF PERSONS)			
Northeast	Midwest	South	West
12.2	13.2	16.0	14.3
In metropolitan area: Total	In metropolitan area: Central cities	In metropolitan area: Outside central cities	Outside metropolitan area
13.7	20.2	9.6	16.1

Note: The poverty rate of families is the poverty rate of the head of the family.

SOURCE: U.S. Department of Commerce, Economics and Statistics Administration, Bureau of the Census, "Poverty in the United States: 1991," *Consumer Income*, Current Population Reports, Series P-60, No. 181 (1992): Tables 1, 2, 5, 7, 11, 14.

percent. The poverty rate doubles for families headed by a male with no wife present and increases more than fivefold for families headed by a female with no husband present. Living outside a family also significantly increases the risk of being in poverty. The poverty rate for unrelated individuals is 21.1 percent, well above the 14.2 percent average for all persons.

DISCRIMINATION The data raise the possibility of labor market discrimination against minorities and women. The poverty rate for blacks is nearly 3 times higher than that for whites, and the poverty rate for Hispanics is approximately 2½ times higher than that for whites. The 1991 results are not at all unusual in this regard. The poverty rate for blacks has been 3 and even 4 times higher than the poverty rate for whites every year since 1959. Similarly, the poverty rate for Hispanics has been 2 to 3 times higher than the poverty rate for whites every year since 1973, when the government first reported poverty rates for Hispanics. Women are also more vulnerable to poverty than are men, as the data on single-parent families indicate. The discrepancy between males and females is much lower among unrelated individuals. The poverty rate for males is 12.3 percent, whereas the poverty rate for females is 16.0 percent.

URBAN VERSUS RURAL POVERTY Many people living in metropolitan areas see the urban ghettos and think of poverty as primarily an urban problem. Poverty in the central cities is extremely high, as the table indicates. But poverty is, and always has been, a rural affliction as well. Notice that people living outside metropolitan areas have higher-than-average poverty rates. The incidence of poverty is also relatively high in the South, the only major region of the country with a poverty rate significantly above the national average.

CHILDREN Children in the United States are especially vulnerable to poverty. Over 20 percent of all children under the age of 18 are living under conditions of poverty. Children have always had above-average poverty rates, but their relative position has grown alarmingly worse over time. The ratio of the poverty rate for children to the poverty rate for all persons increased from 1.19 in 1960 to 1.54 in 1991.

COMBINING CHARACTERISTICS Combining the separate characteristics that make people vulnerable to poverty dramatically increases the likelihood of poverty. We have already noted that single-parent families headed by females are much more vulnerable to poverty than are single-parent families headed by males. Single-parent black and Hispanic families headed by females are even more likely to live in poverty; the poverty rates for both these types of families exceed 50 percent. The poverty rates of the children living in these families are larger still because larger families are much more likely to be poor than are smaller families. Slightly more than two-thirds of all children under 18 years of age living in black, female-headed families are in poverty. The corresponding percentage for Hispanic children is just over 70 percent.

CURRENT ISSUE: There is a lot of short-term movement in and out of poverty in the United States. Most families who have ever received a public assistance check remain on the welfare rolls for only a few months. At the same time there is a substantial amount of long-term poverty. A significant percentage of the families on public assistance in any one month have been on welfare for eight years or more.

SOURCE: (M. Bane and D. Ellwood, "Slipping Into and Out of Poverty: The Dynamics of Spells," *Journal of Human Resources* XXI, No. 1, Winter, 1986, 1–23.)

THE ELDERLY The elderly are the one group whose vulnerability to poverty has lessened significantly since 1959. The elderly were much more likely to be poor than were the non-aged in 1959. Their poverty rate was 35.2 percent, compared with a rate of 22.4 percent for all persons. Now the elderly are slightly less likely to be counted among the poor. Their poverty rate had fallen to 12.4 percent by 1991, compared with 14.2 percent for all persons. The turnaround in the fortunes of the elderly resulted from a combination of substantial increases in government transfer payments to the elderly and an increasing tendency for the elderly to work part time rather than retire completely from the labor force.

THE GOVERNMENT AND THE POOR IN THE UNITED STATES

Governmental concern for the poor in the United States did not suddenly spring forth in the 1960s. Public charity existed in early colonial times, long before private charitable organizations came into being. Private charity was not important until the last quarter of the nineteenth century.

Early government support for the poor in the United States adopted the model of public charity set forth in the English Poor Law enacted in 1601 under the reign of Queen Elizabeth I. The English believed that aid to the poor should come from local governments, not the national government, because the local governments know best the needs of their own citizens. The English also believed that aid should be **categorical.** The government should determine why someone is poor and act accordingly. The Poor Law divided the poor into three categories: (1) those who are able to work, but are lazy and unwilling to work; (2) those who are able to work, but are temporarily and involuntarily unemployed or disabled; and (3) those who are helpless. Only the latter two groups were deserving of sympathy and continued public support. Members of the first group should be forced to work as a condition for receiving aid.

CATEGORICAL ASSISTANCE
Public assistance that is based on some personal characteristic of a family or unrelated individual in addition to low income, such as whether the person is living in a family headed by a single parent.

The adult poor were housed together in publicly-supported almshouses run by overseers who had complete discretion to treat their charges as they wished. The overseers also arranged work for the able-bodied. Children either lived in the almshouses with a parent or were sent to orphanages or foster homes. Living conditions in the almshouses and orphanages were generally horrid. A few of the poor were allowed to remain with their families or relatives, but then they received almost no government support of any kind.

The United States copied the English approach to public charity until the Great Depression of the 1930s. The U.S. almshouses and orphanages were supported entirely by state and local governments, and none too well. Living conditions for the poor were every bit as brutal as in England. The only significant piece of social legislation at the federal level prior to the Great Depression was the establishment of the Children's Bureau in 1912 to protect young children from having to work. Otherwise, the federal government took no part in helping the poor.

The Great Depression: The Social Security Act of 1935

The Great Depression forced the federal government into helping the poor. Unemployment rates over 25 percent impoverished vast numbers of people, far more than the state and the local governments could possibly support. Also, the newly poor could hardly be blamed for their poverty; they were clearly the victims of a failed economy. The federal government responded with the passage of the Social Security Act of 1935, the single most important piece of social legislation in the nation's history. The Social Security Act fundamentally changed the government's approach to the problem of poverty. It established a number of income-support programs that remain to this day the government's principal weapons in its continuing battle against poverty. The inhumane almshouses and orphanages quickly faded away.

The new income-support programs represented a two-pronged approach to the problem of poverty, public insurance and public assistance. The public insurance programs were designed to protect workers and their families from becoming impoverished at any time during their lives. The public assistance programs were public charity, pure and simple. They provided both cash payments and medical support to the poor.

The original programs have been modified since 1935, and some new income-support programs have been added. But the basic strategy of public insurance and public assistance has remained the principal approach for preventing and relieving poverty. The only other anti-poverty strategies of note have been the civil rights legislation of the 1960s and a series of education, job-training, and employment subsidy programs that started in the 1960s.

We will conclude the chapter with an analysis of the income-support strategy. Chapter 19 discussed the anti-discrimination strategy. The education/employment strategy is much less important than are the other two strategies in terms of the numbers of people affected and their success in reducing poverty in the United States. The education and training programs are not unimportant; they enrolled over 3 million people in 1981. But this is still a small number compared with the number of poor helped by other strategies. Also, the education and training programs have never been entirely successful. The consensus opinion is that the programs have been able to teach people new skills, but that the new skills have not necessarily led to stable, high-paying jobs. Too many of the graduates remain in the unstable, low-paying secondary sector of the labor market and continue to move in and out of poverty.[8]

The Income-Support Programs

Table 22.5 lists the major income-support programs in the United States, those programs exceeding $10 billion in transfers. The data are for fiscal year 1992. Let's take a brief look at each of the programs.

PUBLIC INSURANCE AND PUBLIC PENSIONS

SOCIAL SECURITY The largest government income-transfer program by far is the public pension component of the Social Security System, which was the centerpiece of the Social Security Act of 1935. Social Security was designed as a public pension that would protect workers and their families during the retirement years and provide insurance benefits to dependents if the breadwinner of the family died. The public pension was supposed to imitate private pension plans. The government levied a payroll tax on a worker's salary, half to be paid by the employer and half by the employee. The taxes would accumulate in a Social Security Trust Fund and be invested by the government, just as contributions to private pensions plans are placed in trust funds and

[8]For an assessment of the successes and failures of the government training programs for low-skilled workers, see L. Bassi and O. Ashenfelter, "The Effect of Direct Job Creation and Training Programs on Low-Skilled Workers," in S. Danziger and D. Weinberg (eds.), *Fighting Poverty: What Works and What Doesn't* (Cambridge, MA: Harvard University Press, 1986).

TABLE 22.5 Income-Support Programs in the United States: Federal, State, and Local Governments, Fiscal Year 1992

	EXPENDITURES (BILLIONS)[a]
PUBLIC INSURANCE AND PENSIONS	
SOCIAL SECURITY[b]	$281
MEDICARE	129
MILITARY AND CIVIL SERVICE RETIREMENT	58
UNEMPLOYMENT COMPENSATION	35
VETERANS BENEFITS	34
AGRICULTURAL SUPPORT PROGRAMS	15
SUBTOTAL: INSURANCE AND PENSIONS	$552
PUBLIC ASSISTANCE (MEANS-TESTED)	
CASH ASSISTANCE	
AID TO FAMILIES WITH DEPENDENT CHILDREN	$ 27
SUPPLEMENTAL SECURITY INCOME (SSI)	20
IN-KIND ASSISTANCE	
MEDICAID	133
FOOD STAMPS	23
HOUSING ASSISTANCE	19
OTHER PUBLIC ASSISTANCE[c]	82
SUBTOTAL: PUBLIC ASSISTANCE	$304
TOTAL INCOME SUPPORT	$856

[a]All data are estimated outlays.
[b]Social Security includes old age, survivors, and disability benefits.
[c]Other public assistance includes 50 to 60 small programs in the areas of food, education, job training, veterans services, and other social services. Most of the aid in these programs is in-kind aid.

SOURCES: Office of Management and Budget, *Budget of the United States Government, Fiscal Year, 1993, Supplement, February 1992,* Part Five: Historical Tables, (Washington, D.C.: U.S. Government Printing Office, 1992), Table 11.3. Also author's estimates of state and local portions of public assistance for fiscal year 1992 based on data from previous years.

invested. The invested tax revenues would be sufficient to provide annual pensions to the workers and their families during retirement. Also, the larger the worker's contribution during the working years, the larger the benefit during retirement, just as under a private pension plan.[9]

The Great Depression undermined the intentions of Congress. The need to support the elderly was so great that the payroll tax collections were immediately paid out to retirees. Money never accumulated in the Social Security Trust Fund to pay for the retirement of the workers who contributed the taxes, not during the Depression or for 40 years thereafter. Instead, Social Security evolved into an enormous pay-as-you-go annual tax-transfer program from the young to the old. The payroll taxes on the current working young provided transfer payments to the *current* retired elderly.

Social Security remained on a pay-as-you-go basis until 1983. At that time Congress passed a set of reforms that made the program operate more like a true pension program. Payroll taxes were raised and benefit schedules adjusted

[9]Congress expanded Social Security benefits in 1956 to include disability insurance payments for all disabled workers covered by the Social Security System. This is a relatively small program.

so that the Social Security Trust Fund began to accumulate a surplus for the first time in its history. The surplus is designed to peak right when the baby boomers retire and will then be drawn down to pay their retirement benefits. The surplus will be entirely depleted after the baby boomers pass on, and the system will revert to a pay-as-you-go basis once again.

MEDICARE Medicare is the medical component of the Social Security System. It came into existence in 1965 as an amendment to the Social Security Act. Medicare provides hospital and other medical insurance to the elderly as part of the Social Security System. It grew rapidly right from the start and quickly became the second-largest income-support program next to the Social Security retirement benefits. The Social Security System is often referred to by its initials, OASDHI, which stand for Old Age, Survivors, Disability, and Hospital Insurance.

MILITARY AND CIVIL SERVICE RETIREMENT As the name suggests, this is a pension program for the military and the civil service employees of the federal government, neither of whom are covered by the Social Security System. The state governments have similar pension programs for their employees.

UNEMPLOYMENT INSURANCE Unemployment insurance, which also stems from the Social Security Act of 1935, is designed to protect workers from a downturn in the economy. The program provides unemployment benefits to workers who have been laid off, but not to those who voluntarily quit their jobs. Unemployment insurance is administered by the state governments, subject to broad federal guidelines, and benefits are financed by payroll taxes paid entirely by employers. Unemployment benefits are typically available for a maximum of 26 weeks, with the provision that unemployed workers make a serious effort to find work. The federal government has occasionally extended the benefit period (to as long as 65 weeks) when the rate of unemployment has been especially high. Unemployment benefits replace about 50 percent of lost income after taxes on average, although the replacement ratio varies somewhat by state.

VETERANS BENEFITS Veterans benefits are primarily disability payments to the men and women who were wounded or injured while serving in the Armed Forces. All disabled veterans are eligible.

AGRICULTURAL SUPPORT PROGRAMS The agricultural transfers are the price-support programs that we discussed in Chapter 8. They provide insurance for all farmers against low, and unstable, crop prices.

PUBLIC ASSISTANCE

MEANS-TESTED

Refers to public assistance that is given to families or individuals only if their incomes are below some predetermined amount.

AID TO FAMILIES WITH DEPENDENT CHILDREN The Social Security Act of 1935 established three categorical public assistance programs: Old Age Assistance, Aid to the Blind, and Aid to Families with Dependent Children. Aid under the public assistance programs was **means-tested,** unlike aid under the public insurance programs. Recipients had to demonstrate that they were poor to be eligible for aid. The assistance came in two forms, a monthly check paid directly to recipients and payments to physicians, hospitals, and other medical vendors for medical care provided to recipients and their families. The three programs were administered by the state governments, which determined who is eligible for aid and how much aid each person and each family receives. Eligibility requirements were subject to some broad federal guidelines, but the states had considerable latitude in interpreting the guidelines. The states were also entirely free to establish the amount of aid to be given to recipients. Some states required local government administration and/or financial participation as well. The federal government's role in these programs was primarily financial; it agreed to reimburse the states for a percentage of the total benefits paid out. The federal government recognized that richer states could more easily supply public assistance than could the poorer states. Therefore, it covered a larger share of the payments the poorer the state and the lower the average benefits paid to recipients.

Notice the influence of the English Poor Law in the design of the public assistance programs. They were essentially state (and local) programs, and they were categorical in the way that the Poor Law intended. The programs did not help all the poor, only those deemed least able to help themselves. The aged and blind are certainly not helpless, but they obviously have fewer economic opportunities than does the general adult population. Aid to Families with Dependent Children was targeted to families with only a single parent present. The two-parent nuclear family was intact in those days. Single parents were most often widows or widowers, not people who were divorced from or deserted by their spouses. Since few people had much life insurance in the 1930s, the death of a spouse was often economically devastating, especially if the husband died. Also, the surviving parent was not expected to work full time, if at all; caring for the children was the first priority. Therefore, single-parent families gained the public's sympathy and were obvious candidates for aid.

The framers of the Social Security Act had no intention of creating huge public assistance programs. They were much more interested in preventing poverty through public insurance than in offering large amounts of public charity to the poor. They assumed that Old Age Assistance would wither away as Social Security matured and ever more workers were covered by the program. Instead, Old Age Assistance grew rapidly into a very large transfer program and remained the largest public assistance program until the 1960s. The legislators also could not foresee the decay of the nuclear family that began in the 1960s. They assumed that Aid to Families with Dependent Children would remain a small program for widows and widowers, not very much larger than Aid to the Blind. Instead, Aid to Families with Dependent Children exploded in the 1960s and 1970s and became the program most people associate with "welfare" in the United States.

Public assistance remained essentially unchanged until the 1960s. The only exception was a new public assistance program for disabled workers who had become poor, Aid for the Temporarily and Permanently Disabled, established in 1950. This program was administered and financed exactly as the other three assistance programs.

MEDICAID Medicaid came into being along with Medicare as part of the 1965 amendments to the Social Security Act. It consolidated all medical payments under the four public assistance programs and greatly expanded the available medical coverage. Otherwise, it retained the basic elements of the former medical assistance programs. The states still determine the level of payments to medical vendors, and the federal government reimburses the states for a share of the costs. Medicaid quickly became the largest public assistance program as medical costs exploded after 1965. Some states provide Medicaid for "medically needy" families, those with large medical expenses who are not poor enough to qualify for the public assistance programs.

SUPPLEMENTAL SECURITY INCOME (SSI) Congress consolidated Old Age Assistance, Aid to the Blind, and Aid for the Disabled under one program, Supplemental Security Income (SSI) in January 1974. SSI is federally administered and financed, leaving Aid to Families with Dependent Children and Medicaid as the only combined federal-state plans. States are free to supplement the federal payments under SSI, and many do so. As a result, SSI retains some of the federal-state favor of the three programs it replaced.

FOOD STAMPS The federal government broke new ground in 1971 when it added a new food stamp program to the arsenal of public assistance programs. It marked the first time that Congress was willing to assist the nation's poor on a noncategorical basis. All poor families (and some nonpoor families who are close to the poverty line) are eligible for the stamps. The food stamp program is also entirely administered and financed by the federal government, unlike any of the other public assistance programs.

OTHER PUBLIC ASSISTANCE The expenditures listed in Table 22.5 for the four major public assistance programs represent about two-thirds of the total expenditures on public assistance in the United States. The federal government also funds an additional 50 to 60 smaller public assistance programs in the areas of food, education, job retraining, housing assistance, medical care, veterans benefits, and other social services. These comprise the "other public assistance" expenditures listed in the table.

REFORM THE INCOME-SUPPORT PROGRAMS?

The income-support programs are governments' primary weapon in its War on Poverty. How effective are they? Many people would argue that they are not nearly effective enough.

The primary criticism of the income-support programs is that they have failed to eliminate poverty. Federal, state, and local governments transferred over $800 billion directly to people in fiscal year 1992, yet over 35 million people remained in poverty. The failure to eliminate poverty is especially disconcerting because the total amount of transfers the poor would need to escape poverty is far less than $800 billion. Suppose that the federal government were to write checks to all poor families and unrelated individuals for the exact amount that they need to reach the poverty line. For example, if the poverty line for a family of four is $14,000, a family of four with income of $4,000 would receive a check for $10,000. Another poor family of four with income of $9,000 would receive a check for $5,000 and so forth. The total value of all such government checks is called the **poverty gap,** equal to the amount that the total income of all poor families falls short of the total income they would

POVERTY GAP

The minimum total amount of income that all poor families and unrelated individuals would have to be given to reach the poverty line and escape poverty.

need to escape poverty. The poverty gap in the United States was approximately $65 billion in 1991, not even one-tenth as large as the governments' total transfer payments to persons.[10]

The United States is clearly willing to transfer the sum of money required to eliminate poverty. The problem in terms of fighting poverty is that the government transfers are not **target efficient.** They are not necessarily targeted to the poor families who are most in need of transfers. Indeed, about half of all poor families receive no government aid of any kind.

TARGET EFFICIENCY
In the context of public assistance, transfer payments that are given only to the poor and remove them from poverty at the lowest possible expense.

Why are the $800 billion income-support transfers so ineffective in reaching the poor? The primary reason is that nearly two-thirds of the transfers are federal pension and insurance programs that are not intended to be target efficient in eliminating poverty. They are not even meant to be redistributional. The public pension and insurance programs are designed to protect *all* citizens against the possibility of experiencing periods of low income (because of, for example, retirement, unemployment, unusually low crop prices) or ruinous medical expenses. As such, they certainly prevent some families and individuals from falling into poverty. We noted earlier that the rapid growth of the Social Security System over the past 25 years has been largely responsible for reducing the risk of poverty among the elderly. The vast majority of the transfers under the public pension and insurance programs go to the nonpoor, however. This is true even of unemployment compensation: Eighty percent of all unemployment checks go to nonpoor families and individuals. The federal pension and insurance programs tax the middle and upper classes to recycle transfers back to the middle and upper classes for the most part. The poor are often out of the loop. Such is the nature of pension and insurance protection.

This leaves the $304 billion of public assistance transfers, which are means-tested and thus specifically targeted to the poor. The public assistance programs are not entirely satisfactory, either. They have a patchquilt appearance that many people find unacceptable. For starters, the government cannot decide whether it wants to give aid in cash or in kind. Cash aid is best from the perspective of the recipients because it gives them maximum flexibility to spend the aid as they wish. In-kind aid is somewhat paternalistic. The government gives aid in kind because it wants to be sure that the aid is being spent on useful items, such as food, housing, or medical care, rather than being squandered. As noted in Chapter 10, however, the goal of accounting for the funds may be partly an illusion. In the case of food stamps, the poor probably buy the same goods and services that they would if the aid were in cash instead of food stamps. In contrast, Medicaid probably does increase the medical care received by the poor. They would not buy as much medical care as the government buys for them if they received the equivalent amount of aid in cash.

The public assistance programs are also not target efficient in the sense that they do not reach all the poor. The United States has insisted on adhering to the two principles of public charity embodied in the English Poor Law: categorical aid and state and local participation. As a result, the amount of aid received by the poor depends very much on who they are and where they live.

---

[10]The size of the poverty gap was estimated by the author based on information reported in U.S. Department of Commerce, Economics and Statistics Administration, Bureau of the Census, "Poverty in the United States: 1991," *Consumer Income*, Current Population Reports, Series P-60, No. 183 (1992): xvi.

Single-parent families are often reasonably well supported by the network of public assistance programs. They are eligible for cash assistance under Aid to Families with Dependent Children (AFDC), which in turn automatically qualifies them for Medicaid. They may also be eligible for subsidies under the smaller public assistance programs in the form of housing assistance, food supplements, educational and training benefits, or other social services. Large numbers of single-parent families with children participate in as many as six public assistance programs that manage to keep them out of poverty.

Poor families with both parents present are not so fortunate. They are often ineligible for AFDC (see the discussion of workfare, below), and Supplemental Security Income (SSI) is no help to them either unless one of the parents is aged, blind, or disabled. Those ineligible for cash assistance are often ineligible as well for Medicaid and for most, if not all, of the other small public assistance programs. In truth, the safety net for married couples is very flimsy. They may receive food stamps if they are quite poor. If one or both parents work, they receive a small tax credit on their federal income tax, and they are eligible for unemployment compensation for 26 weeks or so. All too often poor married couples turn to woefully underfunded state relief programs as a last resort, or they receive no aid at all. The economic vulnerability of married couples became painfully clear during the deep recession of 1981–82, when many of them slipped into poverty. At the depth of the recession in 1982, 40 percent of all poor families were "traditional" families headed by a married couple, at least one of whom worked.

Where the poor live matters as well. As noted, AFDC and Medicaid are state-administered programs in which the states assume anywhere from one-sixth to one-half of the total expenses. The richer states can afford to pay their share of the expenses much more easily than can the poorer states. Not surprisingly, therefore, support levels vary tremendously across the country. New York paid its AFDC recipients an average cash benefit of $181 in 1988; the average AFDC benefit per recipient in Mississippi that year was only $39.48. The cost of living is higher in New York City than in Jackson, Mississippi, to be sure, but not 4½ times higher. The poor have responded to the differences in states' support payments by migrating to the high-benefit states. In 1987 six of the richest industrial states—New York, New Jersey, Pennsylvania, California, Illinois, and Michigan—accounted for 40 percent of all AFDC payments nationwide.

A Negative Income Tax

The wide variation in support for the poor in the United States has led to a call for sweeping reforms of the public assistance programs. Many critics argue that the long-standing principles of categorical aid and state-local support of public assistance are the crux of the problem. They favor replacing all the current programs with a single noncategorical public assistance program, which the federal government alone would administer and finance. The most common reform proposal along these lines is the negative income tax.

NEGATIVE INCOME TAX

A subsidy given to families or individuals whose income is below some predetermined amount and administered as part of the federal personal income tax.

A **negative income tax** incorporates public assistance into the federal personal income tax, to be administered by the U.S. Internal Revenue Service (IRS). The idea is very simple. All families and unrelated individuals are required to file an income tax form. The government designates a "cutoff" level of income, adjusted for family size. Families (taxpayers) with incomes above the cutoff level pay taxes according to the schedule of tax rates under the personal income tax. Families (taxpayers) with incomes below the cutoff level receive subsidies, or transfer payments, from the government. The schedule of subsidies can be entirely different from the schedule of tax rates for the tax-paying families. A subsidy can be thought of as a negative tax; hence, the name *negative income tax.*

A negative income tax has a number of features to recommend it relative to the categorical public assistance programs. It is much more target efficient in fighting poverty. The amount of subsidy a low-income family receives depends only on its size and level of income, not on the composition of the family, where the family lives, or other essentially irrelevant considerations. The poor receive help because they are poor, pure and simple. A negative income tax would provide much-needed aid to families who currently receive no public assistance, particularly poor married couples. Also, all public assistance under a negative income tax is cash assistance. The poor themselves decide how best to spend the funds. The nonpoor do not attempt to impose their preferences on the poor, as they do with in-kind transfers. Another plus is that a negative income tax is impersonal. Under the current system the poor have to apply in person to a welfare office to register and receive aid—in effect, they have to publicly announce their poverty. The stigma and personal shame of admitting poverty comprise one reason why many people who are eligible for assistance refuse to apply for it. Under a negative income tax a poor family can quietly mail a form to the IRS. Finally, the negative income tax saves on administrative expenses. Categorical programs, especially those offering in-kind aid, are very costly to administer. Medicaid, for example, involves two separate groups of administrators, one to attend to the needs of the welfare recipients and another to make payments to the physicians and hospitals. By contrast, the additional costs of adding a subsidy component to the federal personal income tax are relatively minor.

A negative income tax has never come to pass, nor has any other significant reform of the federal-state (and local) public assistance programs. Why is public assistance so hard to reform despite its many shortcomings? Perhaps the most fundamental reason is that no one knows how to design a fully acceptable system of public charity. The American public might well support an alternative method of public assistance if it could satisfy three goals. Ideally, it should (1) bring everyone out of poverty, (2) be relatively inexpensive, and (3) preserve the incentive to work among those who are able to work. Unfortunately, the three goals are inherently incompatible. Public assistance can at best satisfy two of the three objectives. Therefore, the American public has never been convinced that there really is a better alternative to the current system.

HISTORICAL NOTE: The closest the United States ever came to adopting a negative income tax was in 1972 during the Nixon administration. President Richard Nixon proposed a new federal Family Assistance Plan that was a modified version of the negative income tax and would have replaced the existing federal-state cash assistance programs. His Family Assistance Plan never came to a vote in Congress.

The negative income tax is a case in point. While it has much to recommend it, it cannot satisfy all three objectives. To see why not, let's consider a very simple negative income tax applied to a family of four. We will assume that the poverty line for a family of four is exactly $14,000 to simplify calculations.

In establishing a negative income tax the government must first determine the cutoff level of income at which subsidies end and taxes begin. A natural choice for the cutoff is the poverty line, so that all poor families receive subsidies and all nonpoor families pay taxes. Next, the government sets the rate (or rates) at which to subsidize the poor. Suppose that the subsidy (negative tax) rate is set at 50 percent for all poor families regardless of their income.

The subsidy, or negative tax, equals 50 percent of the difference between the poverty line and a family's income:

$$\text{Subsidy} = 0.50 \cdot (Y_{\text{poverty line}} - Y_{\text{actual}})$$

where

$Y_{\text{poverty line}}$ = the poverty line

Y_{actual} = the family's income before it receives a subsidy

With a poverty line of $14,000, the subsidy formula is

$$\text{Subsidy} = 0.50 \cdot (\$14{,}000 - Y_{\text{actual}})$$

Only families with incomes below the poverty line qualify for a subsidy.

A negative income tax of this form offers a minimum guaranteed income to all families. In our example, the minimum guaranteed income is $7,000 because a family that earns no income receives a subsidy of $7,000 [$7,000 = 0.50 · ($14,000 − $0)]. All families that earn some income end up with more than $7,000. Their total income, Y_{total}, is the sum of their actual income and the subsidy:

$$Y_{\text{total}} = Y_{\text{actual}} + \text{subsidy}$$

For example, a family that earns $5,000 receives a subsidy of $4,500 [subsidy = 0.50 · ($14,000 − $5,000) = 0.50 · ($9,000) = $4,500]. The family's total income, including the subsidy, is $9,500 ($9,500 = $5,000 + $4,500).

How well does this negative income tax meet the three objectives for public assistance programs? The answer is not well at all. It does satisfy the objective of being a relatively inexpensive program. The total amount of assistance would probably be well under $100 billion. However, the negative income tax fails totally in terms of the first objective. *All* poor families remain in poverty after receiving their subsidy. This is a consequence of setting the cutoff level of income at the poverty line. We saw that the poorest families with no income receive $7,000; they move only half way to the poverty line. At the other end of the spectrum a family with income of $13,999, just $1 short of the poverty line, also remains in poverty. The family's subsidy is $.50 [subsidy = 0.50 · ($14,000 − $13,999) = 0.50 · $1 = $.50]. Its total income including the subsidy is $13,999.50, still $0.50 short of escaping from poverty.

One way to ensure that families escape poverty is to raise the cutoff level of income. All poor families would escape poverty in our example if the cutoff level of income were raised to $28,000, twice the poverty line. The minimum guaranteed income rises to the poverty line, $14,000 [subsidy = 0.50 · ($28,000 − $0) = $14,000], and all poor families earning some income would have more than $14,000 in total income after receiving their subsidies. However, this program does not meet the second objective. It is very expensive because so many nonpoor families in the United States have incomes between $14,000 and $28,000. At a cutoff level of $28,000, 40 percent of all families would receive subsidies. The remaining 60 percent of the families with incomes above $28,000 would have to be taxed at very high rates to pay for the subsidies.

The government clearly wants to avoid offering subsidies to large numbers of nonpoor families.

Another option to help more families escape poverty is to raise the subsidy rate. Suppose that the government keeps the cutoff level of income at the poverty line of $14,000. Then the subsidy rate must be 100 percent in order for people to escape poverty, in which case everyone just escapes. The total income of every poor family is exactly $14,000 because the government pays the entire difference between the poverty line and the family income, whatever the family income may be. Conversely, no poor family escapes poverty at any subsidy rate less than 100 percent.

A 100 percent subsidy, combined with the cutoff level of income at the poverty line, also meets the second goal. The total amount of the government subsidies just equals the size of the poverty gap. Since the negative income tax would be replacing existing programs, the poverty gap would be larger than the $65 billion reported above. But the program's cost would probably be less than $200 billion, an easily manageable sum for the United States.

A 100 percent subsidy rate is terrible in terms of the third objective, however. It destroys any incentive that the poor might have to work as long as they believe they will remain poor if they work. A family ends up with total income of $14,000 whether the family members earn nothing, or $5,000, or $10,000. Why bother to work at all for low wages? In fact, all public assistance programs of this general form create strong disincentives to work if the subsidy rate is fairly high. The problem is that the subsidy rate acts as a marginal tax rate on the poor. A *marginal tax rate* is the rate of tax paid on *additional* income earned.

To see why the subsidy rate is a marginal tax rate, return to our original negative income tax example with the cutoff level of income at the poverty line and a subsidy rate of 50 percent. We saw that a family of four with earnings of $5,000 receives a total income of $9,500. Suppose that some family members work harder and increase the family's earnings to $6,000. Their subsidy is now $4,000 [subsidy = 0.50 · ($14,000 − $6,000) = 0.50 · $8,000 = $4,000], for a total income of $10,000 ($10,000 = $6,000 + $4,000). All the family cares about is its total income after receiving the subsidy. By earning an additional $1,000 the family is only $500 better off, $10,000 versus $9,500. In effect, family members are taxed at a rate of 50 percent on the additional income earned.

The marginal tax arises because the family loses $.50 of subsidy for every additional $1 earned. In our example, the subsidy drops $500, from $4,500 to $4,000, as a result of the additional $1,000 of earnings, which is why the family is only $500 better off. The government could lower the marginal tax by lowering the subsidy rate, but then it would not be providing as much help to the poor.

The best way to encourage the poor to work harder is to subsidize additional work effort, not tax it. But this requires a subsidy of this form: Subsidy = $0.50 \cdot Y_{\text{actual}}$. (The subsidy rate need not be 50 percent.) Under this subsidy formula the poor keep all additional dollars of income earned, plus they receive a subsidy of 50 percent on the additional income. This is a ridiculous public assistance program, however. The poorest families receive the lowest subsidies; a family with no income receives nothing at all. Also, poor families near the poverty line become better off than nonpoor families just above the poverty line are. They have no incentive to lift themselves out of poverty by working a little harder. For example, a poor family with earnings of $10,000 would receive a subsidy of $5,000 under this plan, for a total income of $15,000. A nonpoor family earning $14,500 receives nothing; $14,500 is the family's total income. Therefore, members of the poor family have no incentive to earn an additional $3,000 and to escape poverty on their own. We can see why public assistance programs subsidize the difference between some cutoff level of income and actual income, even though this form of subsidy can create very high marginal tax rates.

The cash public assistance programs all use subsidy formulas similar to the one in our negative income tax example. Consequently, they have all the same problems in trying to meet the three objectives. The subsidy rates and cutoff income levels vary considerably from program to program. AFDC has a 100 percent subsidy rate on all wage income above the income earned during the first four months of work. Income earned during the first four months is disregarded in computing this subsidy; it has a subsidy rate of zero. Each state is free to set the cutoff level of income, and most states have chosen a cutoff well below the poverty line. A negative income tax therefore simply standardizes the subsidy formula and applies it to all poor families.

A great irony of public assistance in the United States is that the poor who qualify for assistance face extremely high marginal tax rates, much higher than any nonpoor taxpayer faces. The highest marginal tax rate under the federal personal income tax is 39.6 percent. Taxpayers would object strenuously if the rates were 50 percent or more. Indeed, concern about the effect of high marginal tax rates on work incentives was a major factor in lowering income tax rates under the 1986 Tax Reform Act.

By contrast, the marginal tax rates on most of the poor who receive aid are many times higher than 39.6 percent. As noted, the subsidy rate on AFDC is 100 percent after the first four months of earnings, implying a marginal tax rate of 100 percent. Moreover, single-parent families who receive AFDC payments often receive assistance under a number of in-kind programs, all of which use the same general formula for determining aid. Therefore, if family members earn more income, the family may suffer cutbacks in food stamps, medical payments, housing allowances, and other services, along with the dollar-for-dollar loss of their cash subsidy. The cumulative effect of these cutbacks amounts to far more than 100 percent of the additional income earned, so that the attempt to improve their lot by working harder leaves them worse off. Few people would be anxious to work harder under those penalties.

Workfare

One of the reigning American myths is that most poor people are poor because they are lazy and willing to live off the public dole. This myth ignores three facts. First, large numbers of people who are eligible for public assistance simply refuse to accept public charity because they feel it is too demeaning. Second, the poor receiving public assistance in the United States have very strong financial incentives not to work harder, much more so than any other Americans have. And, third, many of the poor are unable to work to the extent required to escape poverty. Dr. Blanche Bernstein, former director of the New York City Department of Welfare, estimates that two-thirds of the teen-age mothers receiving AFDC are not realistically employable because they lack the skills required in today's workplace.[11]

The Reagan administration and Congress abandoned the goal of preserving work incentives in the AFDC aid formula when they increased the subsidy rate to 100 percent in 1982. The rate had previously been 67 percent. They opted instead to increase the total amount of aid to the poor without greatly increasing the costs of public assistance. As we have seen, a 100 percent subsidy rate does well by these other two goals.

The administration and Congress certainly want the able-bodied poor to work to the extent they can. The problem, though, is how to offset the overwhelming disincentive to work in the aid formula. The government chose the stick approach—workfare. **Workfare** is a state-administered program in which the state welfare office identifies the poor who are able to work, helps them find a job, and then forces them to work as a condition for receiving aid. Some states had established workfare programs in the 1960s to help control spiraling welfare costs. Now the federal government is insisting that all states establish and enforce workfare programs. Also, benefits under Aid to Families with Dependent Children must be available to two-parent families, but only if the adults accept workfare.

WORKFARE
A state-administered program in which the state welfare office identifies the poor who are able to work, helps them find a job, and then makes work a prerequisite for receiving public assistance.

Unfortunately, workfare has never been very successful. Social workers today are not at all like the almshouse overseers of old. They are generally sympathetic to their clients and unwilling to force them to work. Also, the federal government does not reimburse states in full for the costs of finding jobs for the poor and monitoring their work effort. Consequently, many states have made only halfhearted attempts at workfare. In truth, the treatment of the able-bodied poor remains very haphazard throughout the United States.

Remaining Poverty Problems

Design a public assistance program that eliminates poverty, is not too expensive, and maintains work incentives and you will be famous. Until you or someone else figures out how to do this, the United States will probably not undertake a sweeping reform of its public assistance programs. The bulk of public assistance will retain the basic features it has had since the Great Depression. It will provide aid on a *categorical basis* through *state-administered programs* that are heavily subsidized by the federal government. The fundamental principles of the English Poor Law continue to dominate the approach to public charity in the United States.

The current public assistance programs have not been failures by any means. They are reasonably effective at reaching the desperately poor and helpless. Also, the poor who face the highest marginal tax rates are, for the most part, those who are least able to work: single mothers with children, the elderly, the blind, and the disabled. Nonetheless, the current programs have been ineffective in addressing three of the more pressing social problems in the government's War on Poverty: poverty among married couples, long-term poverty among teenage mothers, and the financial devastation caused by long-term illness.

[11]B. Bernstein, "Welfare Dependency," in W. Bawden (ed.), *The Social Contract Revisited: Aims and Outcomes of President Reagan's Social Welfare Policy* (Washington, D.C.: Urban Institute Press, 1984), 125–156.

MARRIED COUPLES Married couples have fallen through the government's safety net of income support. As noted earlier, these families represent a considerable percentage of all poor families, yet they often receive little or no public assistance.

TEEN-AGE MOTHERS The rapidly increasing number of families headed by teen-age mothers has been a major factor in the feminization of poverty in the United States. These young women often have poor educations and few marketable skills. They face the prospect of remaining on public assistance for a long period of time, and their children run a very high risk of starting their own adult lives in poverty.

LONG-TERM HEALTH CARE FOR THE ELDERLY Almost everyone is vulnerable to the financial devastation caused by long-term illness, but none more so than the elderly. Medicare, the medical component of the Social Security System, is seriously deficient in providing health insurance for the elderly. It covers short-term hospitalization for acute illness, but not long-term care in a nursing home for chronic illness or disability, which so many of the elderly require. By failing to pay for long-term care, Medicare covers only about 60 percent of the total medical expenses of the elderly.

Under the current system a family has to pay for nursing home care out of its own resources until those resources are almost completely exhausted. At that point the family is considered medically needy and can qualify for nursing home coverage under Medicaid in most states. Recall that Medicaid is the medical component of public assistance for the poor. Nursing home care is so expensive that a long-term illness can easily impoverish all but very wealthy families.

As this is being written, the Clinton adminstration is hard at work drafting a plan for health care reform under the leadership of Hillary Rodham Clinton.

SUMMARY

The first section of Chapter 22 provided an overview of the personal distribution of income and wealth in the United States.

1. The government has collected data on income annually since 1947 as part of its Current Population Survey, which covers nearly 60,000 families and unrelated individuals. The income reported is money income, equal to factor market income plus cash transfers from governments and private sources. The income data exclude in-kind sources of income such as employer contributions to employee pension and insurance plans and food stamps and medical services under the governments' public assistance programs.
2. Government surveys of wealth are few and far between. The most recent survey was the 1983 Survey of Consumer Finances, which covered 3,655 families. The last comprehensive government survey of wealth before 1983 was in 1962. The 1983 survey was updated in 1989.
3. Two popular measures of the degree of inequality in income and wealth are the Lorenz curve and the Gini coefficient. The Lorenz curve is a graph

of the percentage of income (wealth) received against the percentage of population. The Gini coefficient is based on the Lorenz curve. It is bounded between zero (perfect equality) and one (one family has all the income/wealth), and its value increases the more unequal the distribution.

4. Neither income nor wealth is very equally distributed in the United States. The Gini coefficient for income from the Current Population Survey is approximately 0.4. The Gini coefficient for wealth from the Survey of Consumer Finances was a whopping 0.8, and the survey revealed that the vast majority of saving for investment comes from a relatively few families. Fifty-four percent of all financial wealth is held by 2 percent of the families. The very wealthy tend to have careers in investment banking, insurance, real estate, and the professions, or they are successful entrepreneurs.
5. Economists have very little understanding of why income and wealth are distributed as they are. For instance, the distribution of income remained essentially constant from 1947 to 1976, a period of enormous economic and demographic changes in the United States. Since 1977, income inequality has been steadily increasing, with the families in the top 20 percent of the distribution gaining at the expense of the families in the bottom 40 percent. Economists have been unable to explain the pattern of the income distribution in either period. A promising explanation of the more recent period is the computerization of the workplace, which has put a premium on a college education, but this explanation has not yet been adequately tested.
6. Noneconomic factors can have a significant influence on the distribution of income and wealth. One example is marriage patterns. Marriage patterns influence the distribution of income if innate ability is an important determinant of people's earnings. The most equalizing pattern is random marriages by ability, but marriages are almost certainly not random by ability. If not, they contribute to inequality of income. Marriage patterns also contribute to the inequality of wealth if the wealthy tend to marry the wealthy.
7. Governments may not be able, or willing, to redistribute income or wealth if noneconomic factors are important determinants of income and wealth.
8. One popular measure of equality of opportunity is social mobility, the extent to which families change their positions within the distribution of income over time. Social mobility appears to be fairly high in the United States, which may help explain why the United States is willing to tolerate substantial inequalities of income and wealth.

The second section of Chapter 22 discussed the extent and incidence of poverty in the United States since 1963, when the federal government declared its War on Poverty.

9. The War on Poverty was a response to the first systematic survey of the poor as part of the 1960 census, which showed that 39.5 million Americans, 22 percent of the population, were living under conditions of poverty.
10. The Kennedy administration chose an absolute definition of poverty. The poverty line is the level of income that allows a family to purchase the bare necessities for a minimally adequate standard of living. The poverty line is adjusted for family size, region of the country, and inflation. The actual poverty rate is always much lower than the official, published pov-

erty rate is because the available income data exclude in-kind public assistance transfers such as food stamps and medical care.

11. The official poverty rate fell fairly steadily from 1963 through 1977, reaching its low point of 11.1 percent in 1973. The poverty rate then rose sharply in the early 1980s to a high of 15.2 percent by 1983, primarily because of the deep recession of 1981–82, and then declined slowly until 1990 as the economy grew. The mild recession of the early 1990s caused a small increase in the poverty rate, which stood at 14.2 percent in 1991. The War on Poverty is far from over.
12. People are more likely to be poor the less education they have, the less steadily they work, and the less stable their family situation is. Women suffer a higher incidence of poverty than do men, and blacks and Hispanics have much higher poverty rates than do whites. Twenty percent of all children live in poverty. Poverty rates are slightly higher in rural areas than in metropolitan areas and highest in the South. Combining attributes that cause a high incidence of poverty leads to very high poverty rates. For example, slightly more than two-thirds of all children living in black, female-headed families are poor. The incidence of poverty has remained much the same since 1963 with one notable exception, the elderly. The elderly now have a lower-than-average rate of poverty, whereas they used to have a much-higher-than-average rate of poverty. The elderly poverty rate has improved because government transfers to the elderly have expanded and the elderly are increasingly choosing part-time employment over full retirement.

The third section of the chapter offered an overview of the income-support strategies and programs of the federal, state, and local governments.

13. U.S. governmental support for the poor has generally embraced three principles of public charity set forth in the English Poor Law of 1601: Local governments should support the poor, aid should be categorical, and governments should not help the able-bodied who refuse to work. Until the Great Depression, the United States adopted the English approach of placing the poor in almshouses run by overseers and supported by state and local governments.
14. The Great Depression forced the federal government into providing income support, and the government responded with the Social Security Act of 1935, the most sweeping piece of social legislation in the nation's history. The Social Security Act pursued a combined strategy of public insurance and public assistance, with overwhelming reliance on public insurance. The two insurance programs, Old Age and Survivors Insurance (Social Security) and Unemployment Insurance, provided insurance against periods of low income. They were available to all citizens. The three public assistance programs, Old Age Insurance, Aid to the Blind, and Aid to Families with Dependent Children, were directed toward the poor. The federal government set broad eligibility guidelines for the public assistance programs and shared in their financing. Otherwise, they were administered by the states (and by local governments in some states).
15. The strategy of income support embodied in the Social Security Act has remained the fundamental strategy to the present. Notable changes since 1935 include (a) the addition of a new public assistance program for the disabled (in 1950); (b) the consolidation of all medical payments under

public assistance into a single program, Medicaid, and a new medical insurance program for the elderly as part of Social Security, Medicare (both in 1965); (c) the addition of food stamps for the needy, the first major all-federal, noncategorical public assistance program (in 1971); (d) the consolidation of the first three public assistance programs into a single federal program, Supplemental Security Income (SSI) (in 1974); many states supplement federal SSI benefits; and (e) the addition of a number of relatively small job-training and education programs (1960s as part of the War on Poverty) and the periodic addition of small social service programs as part of public assistance. At present, the public insurance programs account for approximately 70 percent and the public assistance programs approximately 30 percent of all government transfers to persons.

The final section of Chapter 22 addressed the issue of reforming income support in the United States.

16. Critics of the government's income-support programs point out that the programs have not eliminated poverty despite a level of transfers that far exceeds the poverty gap, the minimum total income required to lift everyone out of poverty. Also, the amount of support that the poor receive depends on who they are and where they live. Nearly half of all poor families receive no aid.
17. Many economists favor replacing all current public assistance programs with a single federal negative income tax.
18. Public assistance is difficult to reform because people would like a new approach to meet three goals: lift everyone out of poverty, not be too expensive, and preserve work incentives among the able-bodied. These three goals are incompatible; one of them has to give.
19. The current public assistance programs have been reasonably effective in supporting the poor who are least able to work. However, the public assistance and social insurance programs have not been effective in addressing three pressing social problems: poverty among married couples, long-term poverty among women who become pregnant during their teens, and the financial devastation caused by long-term illness.

KEY TERMS

categorical assistance
Current Population Survey
Gini coefficient
Lorenz curve
means-tested
negative income tax
poverty gap
poverty line
social mobility
target efficiency
workfare

QUESTIONS

1. a. What is a Lorenz curve?
   b. Sketch a Lorenz curve for wealth based on the following statistics:

POPULATION:	BOTTOM ¼	SECOND ¼	THIRD ¼	TOP ¼
% of Wealth Held:	25%	10%	15%	50%

   c. Are these numbers representative of the distribution of wealth in the United States?
2. Describe how the Gini coefficient is calculated, and indicate why it must have a value between zero and one.
3. a. What has been happening to the distribution of income in the United States since the late 1970s?
   b. What are some of the explanations offered for the re-

cent changes in the distribution?

c. Which of these explanations do you find convincing, if any?

4. Evaluate the success of the United States' War on Poverty. What gains have been made against the problem of poverty, and what problems still remain?

5. a. Which groups of people are especially vulnerable to poverty in the United States?

b. Which groups among the poor are not very well protected by the U.S. public assistance programs? Which groups are fairly well protected?

6. What have been the principal U.S. strategies for preventing and reducing poverty since the Great Depression? Give several examples of programs associated with each strategy.

7. a. Why do some economists believe that a negative income tax would be an improvement over the current public assistance programs?

b. Discuss some of the drawbacks of a negative income tax.

8. The amount of government transfers to persons each year in the United States is very much larger than the poverty gap, yet over 35 million Americans remain in poverty. Why are the government transfers not more effective in reducing poverty?

9. The poor face the highest marginal tax rates on additional income earned of any U.S. citizens—in some cases greater than 100 percent. What features of the U.S. public assistance programs cause the poor to face such high marginal tax rates?

10. a. Discuss the strengths and weaknesses of a public assistance subsidy to the poor in which the subsidy is based on the following formula (adjusted for family size):

$$\text{Subsidy} = x\% \cdot (Y_{\text{poverty line}} - Y_{\text{actual}})$$

where Y is a family's income and x is between 0 and 100 percent.

b. Briefly compare that subsidy formula to the following formula in terms of its effects on the poor:

$$\text{Subsidy} = x\% \cdot Y_{\text{actual}}$$

where Y_{actual} is less than $Y_{\text{poverty line}}$.

CASE

The Falling Wages of High School Graduates*

High school graduates entering the labor market are faring ever more poorly compared with college graduates. For example, the wage premium for a college degree relative to a high school degree was 40 percent in 1978 among young white males with one to five years of work experience. The college premium is over 75 percent today. High school graduates are suffering in an absolute sense as well. The average hourly wage paid to young white males with only a high school diploma has fallen 24 percent between 1979 and 1991, when adjusted for inflation.[a]

The wages of less educated, unskilled workers have been falling because the supply of these workers has been increasing while the demand for them has been decreasing. The main problem for unskilled U.S. workers has been the decrease in demand. The demand for less educated workers has been dampened by rising supplies of substitutes in production, particularly computers and foreign workers. Recall that an increase in the supply of a substitute lowers the demand for a good or service.

Consider the computer revolution first. With word processing, a secretary types more letters in a day. With computerized routing, a truck driver delivers more tonnage. With automated typesetting, a press worker creates many more newspaper column inches. Firms do not need to hire as many secretaries, truck drivers, and press workers.

New technology displacing workers is hardly a new phenomenon. Decades ago automated switchboards displaced telephone operators, the interstate highway system speeded up freight delivery, and supermarkets put corner grocers out of business. Technological change always destroys certain kinds of jobs while creating other new kinds of jobs. Why has the computer revolution been particularly tough on less educated workers? The answer is that computers are especially good substitutes for these workers. Keep in mind, though, that technological change has been displacing unskilled workers in the manufacturing sector of the U.S. economy for at least forty years.

The second substitute for unskilled U.S. workers, foreign workers, is a more recent phenomenon, and it may be the more important of the two in depressing their wages. Suppose that the United States were to open its borders to anyone, from anywhere in the world, who wanted a job here. Millions of workers earning $150 a month overseas would emigrate to the United States in search of higher paying jobs, and drive down the wages of unskilled U.S. workers.

Our borders are not going to open completely of course, at least not to unskilled workers. But they are nearly open to goods. With dramatic gains in communications, and a more friendly attitude towards capitalism among governments worldwide, it has become easier to build modern factories in the low-income, developing countries. If Nike can make shoes in Taiwan for $100 a pair that would cost $280 to produce here, the jobs will move to Taiwan. As a result, our workers must now compete in a global labor market. If we import shoes from Taiwan, brooms from Mexico, textiles from Brazil, and consumer electronics from Indonesia, we are supporting foreign unskilled workers at the expense of U.S. unskilled workers. Whether workers come here or factories go there, the result is the same: the wages of unskilled U.S. workers decrease.

Does this mean that we should keep out foreign-made goods? Not at all. Countries that shield domestic industries behind tariffs and quotas cost their consumers dearly. They also tend to become stagnant and inefficient backwaters, as their producers comfortably avoid the discipline of foreign competition.

If the demand for unskilled U.S. workers is falling because of the computer revolution and increased foreign competition, then the demand for unskilled workers should also be falling in Europe, Japan, and the other industrialized market economies. And it is. Relative to college graduates, high school graduates in nearly every advanced industrial economy see their wages falling.

There is one difference in the United States, however; the wages of young high school graduates are falling faster here. No one knows why for sure, but one reason may be that European and Japanese high school graduates are better prepared for work. They are more skilled on average than American high school graduates. Most European students go to school 210 days a year, instead of 180 as here. At the end of twelve years, they have the equivalent of an extra two years of school. Japan's school year is 240 days. European and Japanese students also have more homework each day. Consequently, a diploma from a high school there may be equivalent to a degree from a community college here.

European and Japanese companies also provide more training for young workers who are not college graduates than U.S. companies do. Should Congress ask taxpayers to

(continued on next page)

Provided by David Denslow, University of Florida.

[a]K. Murphy and F. Welch, "Inequality and Relative Wages," *American Economic Review* 83, No. 2 (May 1993): 104–109.

The Falling Wages of High School Graduates (continued)

fund training that companies provide in the other countries? Opponents contend that our companies would pay for the training if it were useful. Why should taxpayers support job training? Let workers and firms come up with the money.

Jobs in Europe and Japan are more likely to be permanent, however. Fewer workers move from one company to another, so firms are confident that investing in their workers will pay off. Moreover, the training tends to be specific training that is more finely tuned to particular jobs, since workers already have attained good general skills from the public educational system. In the U.S. a firm may be forced to invest more in teaching basic skills in reading, writing, and math, only to watch its trainees move to another firm that takes advantage of the training without paying for it. A large portion of government-funded job training in the United States would do what public education does in Europe for those not planning to attend college.

Therefore, perhaps Congress should fund training programs to keep our unskilled workers ahead of the unskilled workers in the developing countries, both for their own sake and to keep spending on welfare from mushrooming. At the same time, though, voters want Congress to reduce the federal deficit, without raising taxes or cutting spending on Social Security and other entitlement programs. Because of these constraints, Congress may instead require firms to furnish training at their own cost or mandate that the states support more technical education.

ECONOMIC ADVISOR'S REPORT

Suppose that President Clinton asks you to advise him on how to improve the wages and job prospects of unskilled U.S. workers who have only a high school diploma. He asks you to compare and contrast four specific proposals: 1) Provide government-funded training programs for unskilled workers; 2) Impose additional tariffs or quotas to reduce imports of foreign goods; 3) Increase the school year to 240 days; and 4) Do nothing—let the free market adjust to the changing demand for unskilled labor.

1. What are the advantages and disadvantages of each proposal?
2. Which proposal(s) would you recommend, if any?
3. Do you think some other policy is better than any of these four proposals?

PART

VI

Government in the U.S. Economy

CHAPTER

23

The Role of Government in the U.S. Economy and Government Expenditures

LEARNING OBJECTIVES

CONCEPTS TO LEARN

Vertical equity
The economics of information
The principal-agent problem
Adverse selection
Moral hazard
Externalities
Non-exclusive public goods

CONCEPTS TO RECALL

Equality of opportunity [2]
Horizontal equity [2]
The for whom or distribution question [3]
Natural monopoly [14]
Oligopoly [16, 17]

Government spending in the United States exceeds $2 trillion, approximately 35 percent of the total national output produced each year. Why does a society that is fundamentally committed to free market capitalism, and distrustful of government intervention, tolerate such massive government expenditures? The answer is that U.S. citizens are of two minds regarding the proper role of the government in the economy. They distrust the government, yet they willingly turn to the government to solve pressing economic problems. These two mind sets have been very much in evidence in recent presidential politics.

The distrust of government intervention in the economy runs deep in the United States. Ronald Reagan correctly sensed the growing disenchantment with ever-expanding government programs and rode a promise to "get the government off our backs" to a landslide victory in the 1980 presidential election. His administration failed to keep this promise, however. President Reagan inherited a federal budget of $600 billion, equal to 22.5 percent of the national output. In the final year of his administration, expenditures by the federal government had grown to $1.1 trillion, equal to 22.8 percent of the national output. President George Bush also campaigned on a promise to streamline the federal budget. He believed that the United States should rely more on the private sector to solve social problems and likened private initiatives to "a thousand points of light." President Bush was even less successful than President Reagan was in keeping his campaign promise. The growth in federal spending accelerated under his administration. By 1992 federal expenditures were nearly $1.5 trillion, equal to 24.4 percent of the national output.

Presidents Reagan and Bush were unable to reduce federal spending for many political and economic reasons. One of the more important economic reasons is that a market economy needs a strong government sector. Markets often fail to perform satisfactorily. When this happens, the American public has been quite willing to set aside its distrust of the government and accept government intervention into economic affairs.

President Bill Clinton rode this other mind set to victory in 1992. He campaigned on the need for change in the United States. Far from "getting the government off our backs," he saw the federal government leading the way in a frontal assault on a broad range of economic problems: reducing unemployment, reforming health care, cleaning up the environment, restoring quality in education, rebuilding the nation's infrastructure, and addressing a host of other issues. In 12 short years presidential policies had come full circle, tugging at the ambivalence that the people of the United States feel toward their government.

Chapters 23 and 24 discuss the economic role of the government sector in a market economy, with particular emphasis on the United States. Chapter 23 begins with the legitimate economic functions of the government in a market economy.

Governments have a very important economic role to play in a market economy. We noted in Chapter 4 that a market economy can hardly function at all without a government-imposed legal structure that, at a minimum, defines the property (ownership) rights to capital and land and enforces contracts between buyers and sellers. The government must also ensure that there is enough money available to "grease the wheels of commerce." Economic development would come to a halt without the use of money that people have confidence in.

The federal, state, and local governments in the United States have expanded their economic responsibilities far beyond these basic functions, however. We also saw in Chapter 4 that the government sector has been one of the leading growth sectors of the U.S. economy since World War II.

Even so, the distrust of government places an absolute condition on when the government can legitimately become involved in economic affairs. Government intervention is justified *only* on the basis of market failure in the United States. The American public clearly believes that the free market economy is the natural mechanism for answering the four basic economic questions outlined in Chapter 3: What? How? For Whom? Now versus the Future? Government intervention is justified only when the market system performs badly, or not at all. People may disagree in a particular instance about whether the market is performing sufficiently badly to warrant government intervention. But few people in the United States would support government intervention without evidence of significant market failure.

The belief in the market system also places limits on the appropriate forms of government intervention. Government policies must try to facilitate the operation of the market economy, not undermine it. The idea is that government economic policy should steer the free market back on the path toward efficiency and equity, not replace the market entirely with a set of government institutions. In some cases replacing the market is the only possible option, but this is definitely not the option of first choice.

The first section of Chapter 23 considers the economic problems that plague a market economy and lead to a call for government intervention. We want to understand how and why markets fail, how the government should respond to each instance of market failure, and how the government's policies can help promote efficiency and equity. The second section of the chapter then looks at actual government expenditures in the United States and shows that they are consistent with the legitimate functions of government. All the major U.S. government programs can be viewed as a response to market failure.

MARKET FAILURES JUSTIFYING GOVERNMENT INTERVENTION

Chapters 5 through 9 and 13 described the market system working as well as it possibly can, when markets are (perfectly) competitive and operate according to the Laws of Supply and Demand. We saw that competitive markets have an impressive set of strengths:

1. They give individuals and business firms the *freedom* to pursue their own self-interests and to solve their economic problems as they see fit.
2. Market exchanges are *orderly* rather than chaotic, even though no one is directing the exchanges.
3. Competitive markets are *responsive* to the desires of consumers. Prices and profits guide firms to produce the goods and the services that consumers want.
4. Finally, competitive markets promote society's twin goals of *efficiency* and *equity*.

Regarding efficiency, competitive markets help society achieve an efficient allocation of its scarce resources. Society receives the maximum net value from producing and consuming goods and services when markets operate according to the Laws of Supply and Demand. In addition, competitive factor markets ensure the *full employment* of all productive resources. For example, anyone who wants to work at the going market wage is able to do so in a competitive labor market. No workers are unemployed. In other words, the Laws of Supply and Demand automatically bring the economy to its production possibilities frontier.

Regarding equity, competitive market exchanges ensure *equality of opportunity*, an important component of process equity. Everyone has equal access to whatever market opportunities they are capable of pursuing. Equality of opportunity in turn leads to *horizontal equity:* Equals are treated equally in competitive markets. Horizontal equity is an important component of end-results equity.

Freedom, order, responsiveness, and the potential for efficiency and equity—those are certainly impressive qualities arguing in favor of letting the free market economy solve society's economic problems. Where, then, does the market system go wrong? What problems justify a substantial economic role for the government as a corrector of market failure?

The truth of the matter is that a fair number of things go wrong, and all the capitalist nations have chosen to combat the ills afflicting their market economies with heavy doses of government intervention. Some nations intervene more aggressively than others, but no nation is anywhere close to the textbook ideal of pure market capitalism.

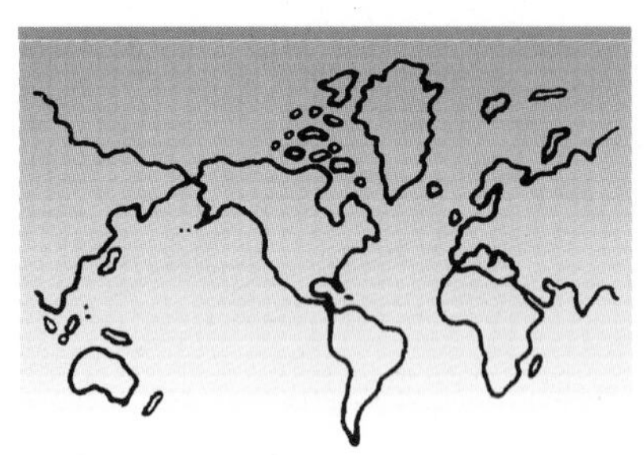

THE GOVERNMENT SECTOR IN THE INDUSTRIALIZED MARKET ECONOMIES

The World Bank publishes a selection of data on government spending and taxation for all nations. The data for the industrialized market economies reveal a number of similarities and differences among them.

The clearest indication of the relative sizes of the government sectors are the ratios of general government consumption by all levels of government to gross domestic product (GDP). General government consumption includes only the resource-using government purchases of goods and services; it does not include transfer payments. Therefore, these ratios indicate the percentage of a nation's resources that are allocated to the public sector.

The ratios reported for 19 of the industrialized market economies in 1989 were remarkably similar. Fourteen were within a range of 15 to 20 percent, including the United States at 20 percent. Denmark and Sweden were the exceptions on the high end, with ratios of 25 percent and 26 percent, respectively. Japan was the outstanding exception on the low end, with a ratio of 9 percent. The other low-end countries were Ireland, New Zealand, and Switzerland, at 14, 14, and 13 percent respectively. The message from these ratios is that the industrialized market economies have all chosen a mixed capitalist system. Their economies are predominantly private, but their commitment to capitalism has not precluded the development of substantial government sectors.

The World Bank also publishes data on total expenditures by the central governments, which include both government purchases and transfer payments. Data on transfer payments by lower-level governments are not widely available. The ratios of total central government expenditures to GDP, when set against the ratios of government consumption to GDP, give a sense of the willingness to redistribute purchasing power nation-wide through taxes and transfer payments, either cash or in-kind. Here we see much more variation among the industrialized market economies. In 1989, the ratios ranged from a high of 57.9 percent in Ireland to a low of 16.5 percent in Japan. The high-transfer countries, with ratios above 40 percent, were: Ireland (57.9); the Netherlands (54.5); Belgium (50.7); Italy (47.9); New Zealand (45.9); Norway (42.7); France (42.6); Denmark (41.8); and Sweden (40.6). The low-transfer countries, with ratios below 30 percent, were: Finland (29.3); Germany (29.0); Canada (23.1); United States (23.0); and Japan (16.5).

The World Bank data also show that only the United Kingdom and the United States devoted more than 10 percent of their central government expenditures to defense. The United States was the major outlier by far in 1989, at 24.6 percent, which explains why its government consumption ratio was relatively high. The United Kingdom was much closer to the rest of the pack, at 12.5 percent.

A word of warning is in order on using government data to judge a nation's commitment to free enterprise. Japan would appear to be the most committed to free enterprise on the basis of the government data. It is the low-end outlier on both government purchases and central government transfer payments. Yet Japan has long had a policy of targeting and subsidizing particular industries that it wants to develop. It also permits huge business combines among firms in the manufacturing and financial sectors that would be considered anticompetitive and illegal under U.S. antitrust laws. In fact, many observers have concluded that Japan is much less committed to unfettered free enterprise than the United States is, despite its much smaller government sector.[1]

Distributional, Allocational, and Stabilization Functions

Economists classify market failures, and the government policies designed to correct them, in three broad categories: distributional, allocational, and stabilization. The **distributional** problems and policies relate to the goal of achieving fair and evenhanded market exchanges and an acceptable distribution of income. The **allocational** problems and policies relate to the goal of achieving an efficient use of society's scarce resources. The **stabilization** problems and policies relate to achieving the macroeconomic goals of long-run economic growth, full employment, price stability, and satisfactory economic relations with foreign countries.

Keep in mind that the three categories are highly interdependent. For instance, any major government policy designed to correct perceived distributional inequities is likely to have important allocational and macroeconomic effects as well. Nonetheless, the three-way classification is a useful way of describing the various functions of government in a market economy.

DISTRIBUTIONAL POLICIES
Government economic policies that respond to market failures relating to the goals of achieving fair and evenhanded market exchanges and an acceptable distribution of income.

ALLOCATIONAL POLICIES
Government economic policies that respond to market failures relating to the goal of achieving an efficient use of society's scarce resources.

STABILIZATION POLICIES
Government economic policies that respond to market failures relating to the macroeconomic policy goals of achieving long-run economic growth, full employment, price stability, and satisfactory economic relations with foreign countries.

[1]The World Bank, *World Development Report 1991: The Challenge of Development* (Oxford, England: Oxford University Press, 1991), Table 9, p. 221 and Table 11, p. 225.

Distributional Problems

Chapter 22 discussed why the government has a fundamental role to play in resolving the distribution question. The problem for a market economy concerns the distribution of income.

Left to its own devices, a market economy completely determines the distribution of income. The factor markets set values for all factor prices—the wage rates and salaries for every occupation, the rates of return on all forms of saving, and the rental values for every parcel of land. These factor prices combine with the quantities of factors that individuals supply to the marketplace to determine the income each person receives.

The market does well in achieving equality of opportunity and horizontal equity if markets are competitive. But another important component of end-results equity is **vertical equity,** which asks how unequals should be treated. The market system cannot guarantee that the distribution of income will satisfy society's notion of vertical equity, even if all markets were perfectly competitive.

VERTICAL EQUITY

A principle of end-results equity that asks how unequals should be treated; specifically, how much redistribution should society undertake among people with different amounts of income or wealth.

The sticking point surrounds the ownership of resources. By and large, a market economy takes the initial ownership of resources as a given. Those who are able to bring large amounts of highly valued resources to the factor markets earn high incomes. Conversely, those with meager amounts of property, little savings, and few marketable skills earn low incomes. The market economy helps promote equal treatment of equals, but unequals can be treated very unequally. Is this fair?

Unfortunately, the ownership of resources happens to be far from equal in any of the world's market economies. People begin the race for economic success each year at very different starting lines. Some people inherit large amounts of wealth; others are born into poverty. Some people are blessed with great intelligence or coordination; others are rather dull or uncoordinated. Some people are fortunate enough to have received college and even graduate educations; others are high school drop-outs. Not surprisingly, the results in the marketplace also tend to be very unequal. We saw that the distribution of income is highly unequal in the United States and that the distribution of wealth is even more unequal. Also, large numbers of people are simply left behind in the economic race. Over 35 million people in the United States live under conditions of poverty.

Suppose that society wants to change the distribution of income. A market system has no way of responding to this desire because significant changes in the personal distribution of income require significant changes in the current distribution of resources. Only the government can be counted on to change the distribution of resources in line with society's preferences. In a free market economy, changes in the distribution of resources are best accomplished by a policy of broad-based taxes and transfer payments that take income from some and give it to others. We saw in Chapter 8 the difficulties of trying to achieve distributional goals by tinkering with individual markets through price ceilings and price floors.

PROBLEMS WITH GOVERNMENT INTERVENTION Saying that the government *can* achieve a desirable distribution of income through general tax and transfer policies is a far cry from saying that government policies will actually achieve a desirable distribution of income. Chapter 22 enumerated the difficulties that government redistributional policies are sure to encounter.

To review briefly, the first problem is that political debate may fail to reach a consensus on the distribution question, especially if public opinion is sharply divided. Resolving differences of opinion is especially problematic under democratic voting procedures, a point we will discuss in Chapter 24. In addition, those who are taxed may resent being taxed, especially if they disagree with the majority's views on the distribution. Finally, both taxes and transfers introduce inefficiencies into the market economy. Society, therefore, is faced with yet another tough question: What is the best trade-off between equity and inefficiency in redistributing income? The need to preserve efficiency may prevent society from redistributing income as much as it would like.

For all these reasons, governments are unlikely to achieve an entirely satisfactory solution to the distribution question. Nonetheless, only the government has any hope of succeeding. Left to its own devices, the market system simply cannot resolve the distribution question, *even if all markets are perfectly competitive.*

NONCOMPETITIVE MARKETS The distributional problems in a market economy increase when markets are not competitive. They violate people's sense of process equity. We have seen in previous chapters how market power and barriers to entry in product markets and segmentation in labor markets undermine the competitive properties of equality of opportunity and horizontal equity.

Barriers to entry in product markets, whether they are legal, natural, or behavioral, deny outside investors access to profitable markets. When large firms with market power are protected by barriers to entry, their owners can earn and *maintain* economic profits. Investors in these markets receive a higher rate of return on average than do investors generally. Similarly, when labor markets become segmented by the use of internal labor markets, or by labor unions, or by sexual and racial discrimination, some people are denied access to jobs that they are able to perform. The result is horizontal inequity. People who are equally productive and capable receive different pay based on economically irrelevant distinctions such as the color of their skin or whether they happen to belong to a union.

The market system looks especially unfair when people are denied equal access and equals are treated unequally. Small wonder that the United States has responded to these inequities with a battery of weapons, including antitrust legislation, regulation, windfall profits taxes, civil rights legislation, affirmative action, and legislation to monitor both the formation of labor unions and labor union practices. Chapters 14, 17, 18, and 19 have discussed these policy responses to the inequities of noncompetitive markets.

Allocational Problems

Free market economies are particularly effective at allocating society's scarce resources, but all is not smooth sailing. Market economies encounter two kinds of obstacles along the way, market problems and technical problems. The two can occur independently, but they are often closely related. The technical problems are usually the source of the market problems.

The market problems relate to the fact that markets are almost never *perfectly* competitive. The conditions required for a perfectly competitive market are too strong—they usually do not hold in the real world. When the conditions fail to hold, markets become noncompetitive, which gives rise to inefficiencies (and inequities, as we have just seen). The two conditions for perfectly competitive markets most frequently violated are the requirements (1) that there be a very large number of firms in the market and (2) that buyers and sellers all have access to the same information.

In addition to noncompetitive markets, capitalism suffers from a number of technical problems that lead to a call for government intervention. We will consider three of the more important technical problems in this section: incomplete markets, with reference to insurance; externalities; and public goods.

NONCOMPETITIVE MARKETS AND ECONOMIES OF SCALE The problems that arise when markets become dominated by a few large firms were analyzed in Chapters 14 through 17 and will only be reviewed briefly here.

Approximately 25 percent of all goods and services in the United States are produced in noncompetitive markets. These markets are often structured as national oligopolies, in which a few giant corporations exercise considerable control over the entire market.

Markets dominated by large, price-setting firms upset Adam Smith's comforting vision of the Invisible Hand. Firms with market power still pursue their own self-interests, but, unlike competitive firms, their self-interests are no longer consistent with society's interests. They set their prices above marginal cost, which means that the net value from producing and consuming their products is no longer maximized. These markets fail to achieve allocational efficiency.

Markets become dominated by large firms not because the managers of these firms are smarter than the managers of smaller firms are. Rather, their market power most often has a technological basis, the presence of significant economies of scale. Production on a very large scale is often much cheaper, per unit of output, than is production on a small scale.

We saw that economies of large-scale production pose a dilemma for supporters of a free market economy. On the one hand, allowing firms to become large promotes production (technical) efficiency by reducing the overall resource costs of production. On the other hand, big firms with market power do not necessarily behave in a manner that transfers the cost savings through to consumers. Consumers gain only if the lower costs translate into lower prices. But if large firms set prices well above marginal costs, society loses some of the potential net value of the cost savings. Also, the owners of the firms capture an undue proportion of the cost savings as increased profits.

Noncompetitive markets pose a very difficult question for society: Are the inefficiencies and inequities sufficiently harmful to warrant government action? The existence of market power creates a potential role for the government, but reasonable people can and do disagree on the question of whether government intervention can improve matters. The uncertainty of how to react to the market power of large firms has been reflected in the United States' antitrust posture. Tough antitrust laws have been on the books since the early 1900s, but enforcement of the laws has varied considerably over time. For instance, we saw in Chapter 17 that the Reagan administration ushered in a much more relaxed stance against market power than had been true in the previous two decades. The U.S. Justice Department approved a number of mergers between large firms in the 1980s and 1990s that it would not have allowed in the 1960s and 1970s.

NATURAL MONOPOLIES The call for government intervention in the United States has been more persuasive when economies of scale lead to a natural monopoly, in which a single firm can supply the entire market demand most cheaply. Natural monopolies tend to arise when the start-up costs of production are very large relative to the operating costs of providing a good or a service once the production facilities are in place. In Chapter 14 we analyzed one class of natural monopolies, the public utilities—electricity, water, sewage, and telephone. A number of other natural monopolies, including highway transportation, recreational facilities such as parks and beaches, and radio and television broadcasting, have also been subject to government intervention in the United States. Let's take a brief look at highway transportation since it is a major component of government spending in the United States.

HIGHWAY TRANSPORTATION Highways, bridges, and tunnels have the cost characteristics of a natural monopoly because the construction costs are such a high percentage of the total costs. Think of the output on a highway as the number of vehicles using the highway over a given period of time. Once the highway has been built, the cost of another car or truck using the roadway is minimal, at least up to the point of congestion. (Congestion is an example of an externality, another technical problem to be discussed below.) In northern climates even a substantial portion of the ongoing maintenance costs is due to weathering, not roadway usage. Therefore, the average cost of highway transportation steadily declines as the fixed construction and maintenance costs are spread over an ever-larger number of vehicles.

The case for government provision of highways is especially compelling because large parts of a nation's highway network would never be provided by the private sector. Travel is so light in many rural areas that no private investor could charge a toll that would cover the full cost of the roadway. Charging tolls is not even feasible on most local streets. Therefore, if a nation desires a complete highway network, the government must provide it.

U.S. POLICY RESPONSES TO SCALE ECONOMIES Previous chapters have described the four principal strategies used by governments in the United States to maintain efficiency and equity in the presence of giant firms and natural monopolies: antitrust legislation (Chapter 17), windfall profits taxes (Chapter 14), direct regulation (Chapter 14), and government provision of services (Chapter 14). We will not repeat those discussions here.

NONCOMPETITIVE MARKETS AND IMPERFECT INFORMATION The free flow of information, equally available to all, is very important to the proper functioning of a market economy. This may seem like a fairly innocuous requirement, but the truth is that parties to market transactions often have very poor information. Since people who lack information are extremely vulnerable in a market setting, informational problems are a common justification for government intervention.

THE ECONOMICS OF OBTAINING INFORMATION Business firms often have an informational advantage over their customers regarding the products and the services they sell. Will the product do what it is supposed to do? Will it last? Firms usually know the answers to such questions, but consumers may not, short of buying the product and learning after the fact. More important, consumers may not be willing to obtain full information about a product prior to purchase. They are not just being lazy. To the contrary, their ignorance is most often a rational solution to an economic problem, in this case the problem of obtaining information.

The benefit of obtaining information is clear enough. The more information consumers have, the greater their knowledge is about the qualities of the product prior to purchase. But consumers may not acquire complete information because the process of obtaining information on products or services is costly. At the very least, consumers must spend time asking other consumers about a product's qualities. At worst, properly testing a product may require special equipment, perhaps even a laboratory setting, that individual consumers are unlikely to own or have easy access to.

As with any other economic activity, consumers want to maximize the *net* benefit of obtaining information, the difference between total benefit and total cost. Following our general principle for maximizing net benefit, consumers should seek information on a product only to the point at which the marginal benefit just equals the marginal cost. For many products and services, this point may occur well before consumers have full information. As a result, firms retain their informational advantage, and consumers are vulnerable to being disappointed.

Governments have a distinct advantage over individuals in obtaining information on products. One reason is that the process of obtaining information is subject to considerable economies of scale. Once any one person obtains the relevant information, no one else need duplicate that person's efforts. The information can be published and made available fairly cheaply to all. Having a single government agency test products and monitor services, and then publish the findings, is much less costly than having all consumers do their own testing and monitoring.

Another advantage to government testing is that the marginal benefits of additional testing are millions of times greater from the government's perspective than from the individual's perspective. The government takes the broad social perspective and sees that testing can benefit everyone. Individuals, in contrast, are interested only in the benefits to themselves. Consequently, the government will bear the additional costs of obtaining full information about products and services, whereas an individual may not.

These are the reasons why governments establish various agencies to test products and monitor services, such as the Food and Drug Administration and the Bureau of Standards.

INCOMPLETE INSURANCE MARKETS Uncertainty is an unavoidable fact of life. No one can know for sure what the future might bring. This is unfortunate, since most of us dislike uncertain situations, especially those that can have a significant impact on our lives. In the jargon of economics, we are *risk adverse.* We would gladly give up some income to turn an uncertain, risky environment into a certain, riskless environment.

The desire to avoid risks leads to a demand for insurance against the random misfortunes of life: accidents, sickness, untimely death, loss of job, and the like. Firms are willing to provide insurance against risky events if three conditions hold: (1) They can insure large numbers of people, (2) the probability that any one individual will suffer misfortune is unrelated to the probability that any other individual will suffer misfortune, and (3) the firm has good information about the people being insured. These conditions are not always satisfied, however, and when they are not, insurers cannot profitably insure against the risks. The private insurance markets are incomplete—a demand exists for a product that no one is willing to supply. When this happens, people naturally turn to the government to fill in the gaps with public insurance programs financed by tax dollars.

The two most common problems in insurance markets are that the events being insured against are not independent of one another and that the insurers cannot obtain all the information about those being insured that they need to write profitable policies.

DEPENDENT EVENTS Unemployment insurance and flood insurance are good examples of the first problem. Workers want to insure themselves against spells of unemployment, but unemployment tends not to be an independent event. When the economy experiences a recession, large numbers of workers lose their jobs more or less at the same time. When the economy improves, large numbers of the unemployed return to work. In other words, the probability that one worker will lose his or her job is not independent of the probability that other workers will lose their jobs.

The same is true of flooding. People living along a river want insurance against the possibility of a flood. But when the river overflows its banks, they all suffer together.

If everyone suffers misfortune at once, the insurance company is exposed to the same risk as any one individual, but the losses are magnified if the misfortune occurs. No company could profitably supply insurance under these conditions.

THE PRINCIPAL-AGENT PROBLEM The informational difficulties are more subtle. Insurance markets suffer from a condition of unequal access to information known as the **principal-agent problem.** The *principal,* the insurance company, would like to know everything about the risks of the *agents,* those being insured, so that they can write profitable insurance policies. But the insurers usually have only limited information about those being insured. The more incomplete the information about those being insured, the more vulnerable the insurer is to the problems of moral hazard and adverse selection.

PRINCIPAL-AGENT PROBLEM

An informational problem in which one individual (the principal) tries to monitor and control the behavior of another individual (the agent), but does not have enough information to do so, and the two individuals have different goals.

Moral hazard. **Moral hazard** arises when the individuals being insured can influence the probability of the event being insured against, unbeknownst to the insurer. In the case of unemployment insurance, for example, insurance companies would be willing to offer policies only against the event that workers are laid off by the employer. Companies could not possibly write policies that paid off if a worker quit because any worker could then decide to quit and collect on the policy.

MORAL HAZARD

In the context of insurance, arises when individuals who are being insured can influence the probability of the event being insured against, unbeknownst to the insurer.

If companies attempted to write unemployment insurance policies against layoffs, however, they would be extremely vulnerable to moral hazard. Quitters could falsely claim that they were temporarily laid off and therefore were eligible for insurance. An insurance company might have no way of learning the truth, especially if employers agreed to go along with the workers' story in return for a kickback on the payout. If enough workers lied about their status, the actual payout on the policies could far exceed the expected payout, and the insurance companies would lose money.

Medical insurance is also vulnerable to moral hazard because people's behavior can influence the probability of their becoming ill. Insurance companies may not be able to monitor the behavior of their policyholders sufficiently to protect themselves from smokers, heavy drinkers, and the like. Contrast this with the case of suicide under life insurance policies. Insurance companies are not willing to pay if death is self-inflicted, but they are protected because suicides are fairly easy to detect. Moral hazard is not much of a problem for life insurance. The extent to which ill health is self-induced is obviously much more difficult to determine.

Adverse selection. The group of people covered by a particular kind of insurance policy varies in the risk each member of the group represents to the insurance company. For instance, any group of insured drivers includes good and bad drivers, and the bad drivers are more likely to make claims against their insurance policies. The differences in risk are not a problem by themselves. If the insurance company can distinguish among those being insured on the basis of risk, it can vary the premiums by risk. The automobile insurers are an example. They use the accident records of individual drivers to divide the drivers into normal and high-risk pools and then charge the accident-prone high-risk drivers a higher premium.

ADVERSE SELECTION

In the context of insurance, arises when the insurance company is forced to set one premium because it cannot distinguish between high-risk and low-risk individuals, with the result that low-risk individuals cancel their policies.

The problem of **adverse selection** occurs when insurance companies are unable to distinguish high-risk individuals from low-risk individuals. In this case the companies are forced to charge one premium to everyone despite the differences in risk. Insurance markets become shaky whenever this happens because the single premium discriminates against the low-risk individuals in favor of the high-risk individuals. If the premium is more than the low-risk individuals are willing to pay, they drop out and try to form an insurance pool with other low-risk individuals. The company is left with a more adverse (high-risk) pool and may experience losses because of excessive payouts.

Adverse selection may prevent an insurance market from ever developing. Forming a pool of only low-risk individuals may be impossible if the information problems are severe. Moreover, if low-risk individuals do drop out, companies stuck with ever-increasing percentages of high-risk individuals may be forced to charge higher premiums than the high-risk individuals are willing to pay. So high-risk individuals, too, may be forced out of the private insurance market. The normal market incentives that bring suppliers and demanders together are clearly absent in this instance.

Medical insurance is particularly vulnerable to the problem of adverse selection. The medical profession's understanding of the factors that predispose individuals to many kinds of illness is rudimentary at best. And even if the factors were better known, insurance companies might well have great difficulty in detecting some of them, such as genetic predispositions to disease.

ADDITIONAL MOTIVES FOR PUBLIC INSURANCE Public insurance programs for the elderly in the United States have been motivated, in part, by two additional concerns that are not strictly allocational in nature. One is distributional and the other is paternalistic.

The distributional concern is suggested by the adverse selection problem. Certain individuals that the private insurers can identify as high risk may not be able to afford the premiums required to insure against their risks. The leading example is comprehensive medical care for the elderly. The risk of ill health obviously increases with age, so insurance companies require a higher premium to cover the elderly. Yet many of the elderly simply do not have enough income to pay the higher premium.

If the government steps in and provides the insurance, its motive is partly distributional. Medical insurance is being viewed as a **merit good,** a good that society considers a virtual necessity, but that is beyond the means of those with low incomes. The public insurance program acts as an in-kind transfer to the elderly.

MERIT GOOD

A good that society considers a virtual necessity, but that is priced beyond the means of those with low incomes.

The paternalistic motive applies to public pensions. People can save throughout their working lives to provide income for their retirement years. Large numbers of people may choose to live for the present, however, and not save enough for their retirement. These people risk becoming wards of the state after they retire. To remove this possibility, society asks the government to establish a public pension plan and force all workers to participate. The government has to force everyone to participate if its motive is paternalistic because it cannot tell in advance who will save enough for retirement and who will not.

PUBLIC INSURANCE IN THE UNITED STATES The various problems that undermine private insurance markets are among the more serious problems afflicting a market economy if the United States is any indication. Governments in the United States have become major providers of insurance. For example, unemployment insurance, medical insurance for the aged, and public pensions that protect the aged against the loss of income at retirement are each among the largest programs in the federal budget. Taken together, public insurance represents the biggest single category of government expenditures, bigger even than defense. Citizens of the United States have been quite willing to call on the government when private insurance markets fail.

EXTERNALITIES When a buyer and a seller engage in a market transaction, they normally experience all the value and the cost associated with the transaction. Occasionally, though, some of the value or cost spills over onto third parties who have no direct role in the transaction. When this occurs, the transaction is said to involve an externality.

An **externality** is a third-party effect of a transaction that directly affects either consumers' satisfaction or firms' production possibilities. For example, you, your fellow students, and millions of other consumers and firms have an ongoing demand for paper products, a demand that paper manufacturers are quite willing to supply. In the process of producing paper, however, the paper companies pollute both water and air.

EXTERNALITY

A third-party effect of a transaction that directly affects either consumers' satisfaction or firms' production possibilities.

Air pollution ruins the paint on people's houses and cars and may cause health problems. Water pollution alters the recreational qualities of streams and lakes. They may no longer be fit for swimming, or game fishing, or pleasure boating. Polluted water may also pose a hazard to health. People suffer third-party losses that have no direct connection to the purchase and sale of paper.

POLLUTION Externalities such as air and water pollution create serious allocational problems for all economic systems. A market economy is particularly vulnerable to externalities because markets have no way of accounting for them. Consequently, no incentives exist to correct for them. Industrial pollution is a perfect case in point.

COMMON-USE RESOURCE

A resource such as water or air that no one owns.

As we discussed in Chapter 11, air and water are **common-use resources,** meaning that no one owns the rights to them. Since no one owns them, no private market can exist for air and water. They are available to everyone free of charge, including the paper companies.

We saw that paper companies minimize their costs of production by using water and air for every conceivable purpose they can think of, since these resources are costless to them. If they happen to pollute the water or air in the process, no matter. They will not receive a bill for the third-party damages they have caused because no one owns these resources.

Can we expect paper companies to be public spirited and voluntarily choose not to pollute? Not at all. The normal market incentives argue against any public-spirited impulses that firms might have. Suppose that one public-spirited paper company decides to produce in a nonpolluting manner. Unless it can be assured that other paper companies will do the same, it will soon think better of the idea. The firm raises its costs of production by not polluting, which puts it at a competitive disadvantage relative to other firms that continue to pollute. Also, one paper company acting alone may have very little effect on the overall level of pollution if a number of companies are polluting. In this case the company's public-spirited impulse is not only costly; it is also futile.

POLLUTION AND ECONOMIC EFFICIENCY Externalities do serious damage to the goal of economic efficiency. The best a market economy has to offer for promoting efficiency is the perfectly competitive market. But even competitive markets are inefficient when market transactions give rise to externalities.

A market for a good or a service is efficient if it maximizes the net value of producing and consuming the product. We saw in Chapter 7 how the Laws of Supply and Demand interact to maximize net value. But competitive markets are efficient only if buyers and sellers experience all the value and the cost associated with consuming and producing goods and services. When value or cost spills over onto third parties, competitive markets end up maximizing the wrong net value.

To see this, suppose that the market for paper products is perfectly competitive, represented by Figure 23.1. The market demand curve, D, reflects, at each quantity, the marginal value of paper to consumers of paper. The market supply curve S^{priv} indicates, at each quantity, the marginal cost experienced by the paper companies in producing the paper. Left to its own devices, the market clears at Q_0, at the intersection of D and S^{priv}.

MARGINAL COST OF POLLUTION

The additional cost of pollution experienced by all third parties combined when a polluting activity is increased by one unit.

Q_0 is not the efficient output, however, because it ignores the external damage caused by the pollution. The full social marginal cost of producing paper is given by the supply curve S^{soc}. S^{soc} adds to S^{priv}, at every output, the **marginal cost of pollution,** which is the additional cost of pollution experienced by all third parties combined when an additional unit of paper is produced.

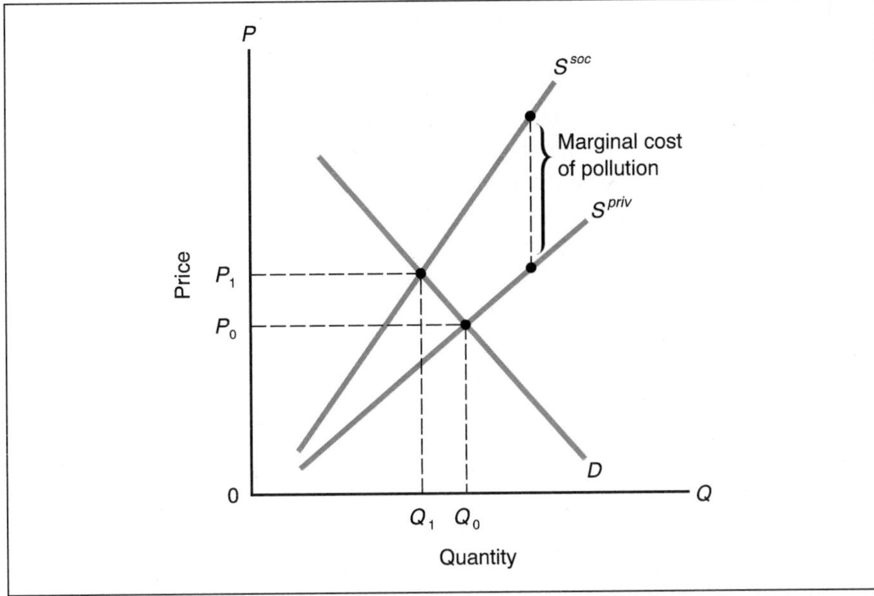

FIGURE 23.1

Pollution and the Market for Paper

At every output, the demand curve D indicates the marginal value of paper to consumers, and the supply curve S^{priv} indicates the marginal cost to the paper companies of producing paper. The equilibrium in the market for paper would be (Q_0, P_0), at the intersection of D and S^{priv}, without government intervention. The supply curve S^{soc} indicates the full social marginal cost of producing paper at every output. It adds to S^{priv} the marginal cost to all third parties combined of the pollution generated when the paper companies produce additional paper. The optimal output of paper is Q_1, at which the marginal value of paper equals the full social marginal cost of producing paper. The government can achieve Q_1 by means of a pollution tax on the paper companies which raises their effective market supply curve to S^{soc}. The higher price P_1 at the intersection of D and S^{soc} encourages consumers to conserve on their use of paper.

The efficient allocation is Q_1, the intersection of D and S^{soc}. At Q_1 the marginal value of consuming paper equals the full social marginal cost of producing paper. The market goes beyond that point because it only takes into account the direct marginal cost that paper firms experience in producing the paper. As a result, the market maximizes the difference between value and cost associated with the direct exchange of paper, rather than the difference between value and cost experienced by all of society. The market chooses to maximize the wrong net value.

As we saw in Chapter 11, correcting for industrial pollution requires government intervention in the form of pollution taxes or other policies that are equivalent to taxes, such as marketable discharge permits. These policies have the effect of setting a price on the use of the scarce, and valued, clean air and water. A properly designed pollution tax shifts S^{priv} up to S^{soc} from the firms' perspective, so that they supply their paper along the correct social supply curve.

EDUCATION: AN EXTERNAL ECONOMY Pollution is an example of a harmful externality. Economists refer to such harmful third-party effects as *external diseconomies.* Third-party effects can also be beneficial, in which case they are referred to as *external economies.*

Education is a good example of an external economy. A democratic society can function effectively only if all voters have a minimum level of education. They must be literate and able to understand issues of social policy. Therefore, the education of each person makes everyone else better off, at least up to a point.

Left to its own devices, however, a free market economy is likely to produce too little education. People would decide how much education to buy on the basis of their personal gains from the education. They would have no incentive

REFLECTION: Do you favor public primary and secondary education, or would you prefer that the government get out of the education business? A longstanding proposal in the United States that has broad support calls for a private education system in which the government's only role would be to provide tuition vouchers (subsidies) to children of low-income families so that they would be as free to choose among the private schools as anyone else. Is this a good idea?

to consider the external benefits that their education gives to others because the market has no way of rewarding them for these benefits.

In the mid-1800s the United States chose to attack educational externalities directly by establishing the local public school system and mandating a minimum level of primary and secondary education for all its citizens. Government provision of education is not the only way to correct for the externality; subsidizing private education is another possible approach. Nonetheless, the United States obviously felt that an educated citizenry is so important that it was willing to replace the market with the government in this instance.

NONEXCLUSIVE (PUBLIC) GOOD

A good such as national defense that is consumed by everyone once any one person or the government buys it; no one can be excluded or exclude themselves from consuming the good.

EXCLUSIVE GOOD

A good whose benefits are received only by the person who consumes it.

NONEXCLUSIVE GOODS The final important allocational problem for a market economy involves **nonexclusive goods,** of which defense is the classic example.

Most goods and services are **exclusive goods.** When you purchase a hamburger, it is yours alone to eat and enjoy. The hamburger is *exclusive* to you. Defense expenditures are quite different, however. When the government buys a new missile, the services provided by that missile, whatever they may be, are entirely nonexclusive. The government cannot exclude anyone from consuming the services. Moreover, individuals cannot exclude themselves from consuming the services even if they would want to. In effect, nonexclusive goods such as missiles are the ultimate externality. Purchase of the good by anyone directly affects everyone.

Markets are helpless in the presence of nonexclusive goods. If society wants them, they must be purchased collectively through a government agency. This is why nonexclusive goods are usually referred to as *public goods.*

THE FREE-RIDER PROBLEM To see why the market system has difficulty with nonexclusive goods, imagine that you are a member of a small island nation that is continually being harassed by other nations. One day a salesman visits the island offering a missile so destructive that, he claims, the mere threat of using it will deter others from ever bothering your country again. The salesman is very persuasive, and everyone wishes that the country owned the missile. Furthermore, the missile happens to be inexpensive; each person can afford it. Will anyone step forward and buy the missile? The chances are they will not.

FREE-RIDER

A person who consumes a nonexclusive (public) good without paying for any of the costs of the good.

Suppose that you buy the missile. This is exactly what the others want you to do. Once you buy it, they can enjoy the same services you do, and it does not cost them a dime. They become **free-riders** on your purchase, and you end up being the sucker. Better to let someone else be the sucker and free-ride on his/her purchase. But if everyone thinks alike, no one ends up buying the missile, *even though everyone wants it.* The incentive to free-ride destroys the normal incentive to engage in market transactions.

The free-rider problem exists for all nonexclusive goods. Lighthouses are another example. No one shipping company wants to pay for a lighthouse, given that all shipping companies will have equal access to its warning signal free of charge. This is why lighthouses are usually publicly provided.

Notice that the free-rider problem is absent with exclusive goods. If consumers want the services of exclusive goods, they must purchase the goods for themselves. This is the basis of the normal incentive to engage in market transactions.

EFFICIENT ALLOCATION OF NONEXCLUSIVE GOODS Having the government purchase nonexclusive goods such as defense by no means solves the problem of properly allocating these goods. Deciding how much defense to purchase is one of the most difficult economic questions a government must wrestle with, even ignoring the thorny question of what services defense expenditures actually provide for a nation in the nuclear age. The basic problem is an information problem. The government must know the value that each consumer places on additional units of defense expenditure in order to allocate defense efficiently. Unfortunately, the government has no good way of obtaining this information.

Suppose that people sense that there is a direct connection between their stated preferences and their tax payments in support of a good such as defense. If so, the free-rider problem reappears. Defense enthusiasts have an incentive to understate their preferences. If there is no direct connection between preferences and tax payments, the more likely case, defense enthusiasts may well have an incentive to overstate their enthusiasm. Those who dislike defense should overstate their displeasure no matter how they are asked to pay. The government cannot easily force people to reveal their true preferences.

A nonexclusive good such as defense is certain to breed disagreements, as indeed it does. The crux of the matter from an economic perspective is that everyone is forced to consume the same amount. Whatever quantity the government chooses, some people are sure to want more spent on defense and others less spent on defense.

Macroeconomic Stabilization Problems

Free market economies are not always capable of achieving the four macroeconomic policy goals of long-run economic growth, full employment, price stability, and satisfactory economic relations with other nations. We noted in Chapter 2 that the U.S economy has not performed particularly well with respect to any of these goals since the early 1970s.

Most economists believe that government intervention through monetary and fiscal policies can help guide free market economies toward each of these goals. The entire second half of this text, from Chapter 25 on, describes how the macroeconomy operates and how fiscal and monetary policies can achieve the policy goals. At this point we would only note that many of the nation's macroeconomic problems result from various kinds of market failure. For instance, unemployment would not be a serious problem if all markets were perfectly competitive.

GOVERNMENT EXPENDITURES IN THE UNITED STATES

What do governments in the United States actually do? By and large, exactly what you would expect them to do. Table 23.1 shows the composition of expenditures for the federal government in fiscal year 1992 and for state and local governments in fiscal year 1991. The major expenditure items correspond very closely to the legitimate functions of government discussed in the preceding section. Governments in the United States are clearly responding to instances of market failure. Moreover, the primary economic functions of the federal, state, and local governments have changed very little since World War II. The growth in the government sector has been more an increase of support within existing functions than an expansion of the government into new areas.

The Federal Government

Federal expenditures are concentrated in three areas that pose very difficult problems for market economies: national defense, insurance, and the distribution of income.

REFLECTION: The recent cutbacks in defense spending are providing the United States with a long-awaited "peace dividend." How would you prefer that the dividend be used: Give it back to the private sector in the form of tax cuts? Use it to fund other domestic public services? If the latter, which public services?

DEFENSE We noted in Chapter 4 that the federal government is primarily a tax and transfer operation, with the single exception of national defense. Defense and defense-related activities account for approximately 70 percent of the federal government's expenditures on goods and services, the resource-using component of the federal budget. The remaining nondefense expenditures on goods and services largely pay the operating expenses of the various federal transfer agencies.

Most of the federal transfers to persons fall into one of three categories: (1) public insurance and pensions, (2) subsidies to farmers and veterans, and (3) public assistance. We discussed each of these transfer programs in Chapter 22 when describing the federal government's income-support strategy. Let's briefly review the highlights.

SOCIAL INSURANCE AND PENSIONS Table 23.1 shows that public insurance and retirement pensions dominate the transfer component of the federal budget. In fact, they account for approximately 70 percent of all transfer payments to persons by all governments in the United States. The transfers under these programs are mostly cash payments made directly to individuals. Also, eligibility under these programs is independent of a person's income. Consequently, most of the insurance and pension transfers go to the nonpoor.

The three major insurance and pension programs are Social Security, other federal pensions, and unemployment insurance.

SOCIAL SECURITY Social Security is the largest domestic expenditure program in the entire U.S. fiscal system. Employees, and their employers, contribute to the Social Security System throughout their working lives by means of a payroll tax on wages and salaries. These tax payments entitle employees (and their dependents) to two kinds of support:

1. retirement pensions, life insurance, and disability insurance under OASDI (Old Age, Survivors, and Disability Insurance); and
2. medical insurance covering hospitalization, physicians' services, medicines, and supplies under Medicare. Coverage begins at age 65. Nearly all people working in the private sector participate in the Social Security System.

CIVILIAN AND MILITARY PENSIONS Federal civil service and military employees have a separate retirement pension plan, as do many state and local government employees. The federal pensions are one of the largest items in the entire federal budget.

UNEMPLOYMENT INSURANCE Unemployment insurance provides cash payments to workers who have been laid off by their employers, but not to those workers who have quit their jobs. The maximum length of time workers may receive unemployment payments varies by state, but most states have adopted a 26-week maximum. Unemployment insurance is financed by a payroll tax. Unlike the Social Security payroll tax, however, the tax is levied only on employers.

SUBSIDIES TO FARMERS AND VETERANS The federal government has singled out two groups for special subsidies, farmers and veterans.

AGRICULTURAL PRICE SUPPORTS Chapter 8 noted that the market economy has not been particularly kind to U.S. farmers, either in the long run or in the short run. The long-run problem is that farm prices and farm incomes have not kept pace with prices and incomes generally throughout the twentieth century. Rapid technological change in the form of better fertilizers, pesticides, hybrid crops, and farming techniques has led to huge increases in supply over time that have outpaced the more modest increases in demand. The result is steadily downward pressure on prices, which has been particularly damaging to small farmers. The short-run problem is price instability caused by yearly changes in the weather. Good weather increases supply, which, because demand is highly inelastic for most crops, sharply reduces crop prices. Conversely, bad weather decreases supply, which sharply increases crop prices.

The federal government first responded to these problems during the Great Depression of the 1930s. The government chose to implement a price-support strategy that set a price floor for the major crop prices. The price-support programs have been modified on occasion since the Great Depression, but price supports remain the primary means of subsidizing farmers' incomes.

The agricultural price-support programs combine insurance and income-support motives. By stabilizing prices, they provide insurance to all farmers against the short-run variability of prices caused by good and bad weather. By supporting prices above the market price, they provide income support for the small-scale, lower-income farmers (although the majority of the support payments are received by the large-scale, higher-income farmers).

VETERANS BENEFITS All veterans are eligible for a number of in-kind transfers, such as subsidized education and housing. Disabled veterans receive additional cash allowances and subsidized health care.

PUBLIC ASSISTANCE The other set of transfer programs listed in part A of Table 23.1 is comprised of the public assistance or "public welfare" programs. They constitute the remaining 30 percent of all government transfers to persons. The public assistance programs differ from the public insurance and pension programs in three respects: They are means-tested, that is, targeted to the poor; much of the assistance is distributed in kind rather than in cash (as with Medicaid and food stamps); and many of the programs are jointly financed by the federal and state governments (and the local governments in some states).

TABLE 23.1 Expenditures by Federal, State, and Local Governments in the United States

	Expenditures (Billions)	*Percentage of Subcategory*	EXPENDITURES (BILLIONS)	PERCENTAGE OF TOTAL EXPENDITURES
A. FEDERAL GOVERNMENT (FISCAL YEAR, 1992)[a]				
Government expenditures on goods and services			$478.1	32.4
Defense and defense related	$341.5[b]	71.4		
Non-defense expenditures	136.6	28.6		
Domestic transfers to persons (direct expenditures)			616.3	41.8
Social insurance and pensions				
Social Security benefits (OASDI)	288.3	46.8		
Medicare	129.2	21.0		
Civilian and military retirement	59.5	9.7		
Unemployment insurance	34.7	5.6		
Agricultural support payments	14.7	2.4		
Veterans benefits[c]	32.4	5.3		
Public Assistance				
Food and nutrition (Food stamps: 21.1)	21.3	3.5		
Supplemental Security Income (SSI)	18.3	3.0		
Net interest payments			198.8	13.5
Grants-in-aid			182.2	12.3
Payments to individuals	114.6	62.9		
AFDC	15.1	8.3		
Medicaid	72.5	39.8		
Other	67.6	37.1		
Total Expenditures			1475.4	100.0

[a]The data for the federal government are estimated outlays.
[b]Includes national defense; general science, space, and technology; and international affairs.
[c]Includes education benefits; medical benefits; insurance benefits; and compensation, pension and burial payments.

State and Local Governments

For the most part state and local expenditures are responding to two kinds of allocational market failure: externalities and natural-monopoly, decreasing-cost production. The major expenditure categories provide examples of each.

EDUCATION Recall that education found its way into the public sector in the nineteenth century because of the externality component of education: All

TABLE 23.1 **Expenditures by Federal, State, and Local Governments in the United States** (continued)

			EXPENDITURES (BILLIONS)	PERCENTAGE OF TOTAL EXPENDITURES
B. STATE GOVERNMENTS (FISCAL YEAR, 1991)[d]				
Direct Expenditures			442.3	70.3
Public welfare	100.1	22.6		
Education	80.5	18.2		
Highways	38.9	8.8		
Health and hospitals	38.5	8.7		
Other	184.3	41.7		
Grants-in-aid			186.5	29.7
Total General Expenditures			628.8	100.0
C. LOCAL GOVERNMENTS (FISCAL YEAR, 1991)[d]				
Education			229.2	36.8
Utilities			70.8	11.4
Health and hospitals			43.5	7.0
Police and fire protection			41.7	6.7
Public Welfare			26.9	4.3
Highways			26.0	4.2
Other			185.3	29.6
Total General Expenditures			623.4	100.0

[d]Data for state and local governments were available through fiscal year 1991 only.

SOURCES: Part Five: Historical Tables, Executive Office of the President of the United States *Budget of the United States Government, Fiscal Year 1993, Supplement, February 1992.* (Washington D.C.: U.S. Government Printing Office, 1992), Table 3.1, p. 5–42; Table 3.2, pp. 5–46, 47; Table 11.1, p. 5–136; Table 11.2, pp. 5–143, 161, 162; Table 12.1, p. 5–165; Table 12.3, pp. 5–199, 200. U.S. Department of Commerce, Economics and Statistics Administration, Bureau of Census, *Government Finances: 1990–91 (Preliminary Report),* (Washington, D.C.: U.S. Government Printing Office, 1993), Series GF/91-5P, p. 1.

citizens in a democracy benefit from any one person's education. State governments mostly provide higher education through state colleges and universities. The localities concentrate on primary and secondary education.

POLICE AND FIRE PROTECTION Local police protection and fire protection also have significant externality components. The police externality is much like the defense externality, only on a smaller scale. Fire protection also generates external economies: Protecting your house from fire protects your neighbors' houses to some extent as well.

HIGHWAYS We noted in the previous section that highways are a prime example of a decreasing-cost service. So is mass rail transit.

OTHER The "Other" category in state and local budgets is comprised of a wide range of services, including parks and recreation, natural resources, water and sewage, nonhighway transportation, correctional facilities, and general government. Either externalities or decreasing costs of production have driven all these services into the public sector.

State and local governments also participate in the nation's efforts to protect people from poverty, mostly through the provision of public assistance and public hospitals.

PUBLIC ASSISTANCE We have already discussed the state and local commitment to the nation's public assistance effort in Chapter 22. The states' commitment is substantial enough to make public welfare the largest category of states' own general expenditures.

Public welfare is also the fifth-largest category in local budgets, although this figure is a bit misleading. Most states do not require local contributions to the state's share of public assistance, although a few of the largest states do, most notably California and New York. Since these two states also have the largest welfare programs, their welfare expenditures end up being a noticeable percentage of total local government expenditures. For most local governments, though, public welfare is not a major item of expenditure.

HEALTH AND HOSPITALS The health and hospitals component of state and local budgets can be viewed as a form of in-kind public assistance. A majority of these expenditures finance state mental and psychiatric hospitals or municipal general hospitals, which primarily serve patients who cannot afford private hospital care.

The Federal Regulatory Agencies

Our tour of the government sector in the United States concludes with some brief comments on federal regulation.

The budget data in Table 23.1 hide the many regulatory functions of the federal government because expenditures by each regulatory agency are fairly small. Make no mistake about it, though. Regulation has been a principal response to market failure in the United States ever since the Great Depression of the 1930s. Forty-one new federal regulatory agencies came into being in the 40-year period from 1930 through 1979. The Carter and Reagan administrations finally called a halt to the growth in regulation.

Federal regulation is concentrated in five broad areas: banking and finance, competition and trade, employment and discrimination, energy and the environment, and safety and health. The regulatory agencies in each of these areas are responding to particular kinds of market failure, most of which we discussed in the preceding section. Familiar examples from each area include the Federal Reserve Banking System (control of the money supply), the Federal Trade Commission (antitrust and consumer protection from deception and fraud), the National Labor Relations Board (union and business labor practices), the Environmental Protection Agency (pollution control), and the Occupational Safety and Health Administration (worker health and safety).

SUMMARY

The first section of Chapter 23 described the market failures that lead to a call for government intervention. The section began by reviewing the strengths of a market economy when markets are perfectly competitive and work as well as they possibly can. These are strengths that government policies should try to emulate and preserve.

1. Perfectly competitive markets give individuals freedom to do as they wish, bring order to economic exchanges, are responsive to the desires of consumers, and promote society's twin goals of efficiency and equity.
2. Regarding efficiency, perfectly competitive markets promote allocational efficiency because the Laws of Supply and Demand choose the output that maximizes the net value of consuming and producing goods and services. They also promote production or technical efficiency by assuring that goods and services are produced as cheaply as possible with the minimum use of society's scarce resources. Competitive factor markets also bring the economy to its production possibilities frontier.
3. Regarding equity, competitive markets promote process equity by assuring equality of opportunity for all. Equal opportunity in turn leads to horizontal equity, the equal treatment of equals, which is a major component of end-results equity.

Despite these strengths, the government has an important economic role to play in a free market economy. The market system fails in a number of ways that require government intervention to correct. All capitalist countries have chosen a system of mixed capitalism, with the market system and the government working hand in hand in the quest for efficiency and equity. Market failures fall into three broad categories—distributional, allocational, and macroeconomic stabilization.

4. *Distributional:* Markets generate a distribution of income in the process of setting prices in the factor markets for labor, land, and capital. But no market economy can guarantee that the resulting distribution of income is satisfactory, even if all markets are perfectly competitive. By and large, the factor markets take the ownership of resources as a given. Those who begin with a lot of valuable resources end up with a lot of goods and services, and vice versa. Government intervention is necessary to correct perceived distributional imbalances, and general tax and transfer policies are the best way to redistribute purchasing power.

   The distributional problems increase when markets are not competitive. Market power and barriers to entry in product markets and segmentation in labor markets deny investors and workers equal opportunity and lead to horizontal inequities—equals are treated unequally.
5. *Allocational:* Market economies are vulnerable to a number of market and technical problems that give rise to inefficiencies that the government has to correct. The market problems arise because of economies of scale and imperfect information, which tend to make markets noncompetitive.
6. *Economies of scale:* Earlier chapters in this text discussed how economies of scale can lead to markets dominated by large firms with considerable market power. The large firms set their prices above marginal costs, resulting in allocational inefficiency. Economies of scale sometimes give rise to a natural monopoly, in which one firm can supply the entire market most

cheaply. Examples include the public utilities, highway transportation, parks and recreation facilities, and radio and television broadcasting. Governments have tried to curb the exercise of market power through windfall profits taxes, regulation, government provision of services, and antitrust legislation.

7. *Imperfect information:* Market imperfections arise when certain economic agents enjoy informational advantages over other agents. People lacking information are extremely vulnerable in a market economy and are hesitant to engage in market exchanges. Government agencies that test and monitor products are examples of government intervention motivated by informational problems.

Market economies are plagued by other technical allocational problems that only the government can resolve. The section considered three of the most important: incomplete insurance markets, externalities, and nonexclusive public goods.

8. *Incomplete insurance markets:* Consumers want insurance against the misfortunes of life, and private insurers are only partially willing to fulfill this need. Private insurers are reluctant to write policies when the events being insured against do not occur independently from one another. Unemployment insurance is a leading example. Insurance markets are also afflicted with the principal-agent problem—insurers (the principals) cannot know all they need to know about those being insured (the agents) in order to write profitable policies. The principal-agent information problem leaves insurers vulnerable to the twin problems of moral hazard and adverse selection. Medical insurance is a prime example. The government also provides public insurance for distributional and paternalistic reasons. Medical insurance for the elderly is an example of the former motive; it is viewed as a merit good. Public pensions are an example of the latter motive; society fears that people will not adequately provide for their retirement unless they are forced to.
9. *Externalities:* Even perfectly competitive markets lose their efficiency properties in the presence of external third-party effects. Markets end up maximizing the wrong net value because they have no way of taking the external effects into account. Industrial pollution is a prime example of a harmful external effect. Education generates beneficial external effects. Only government policies can force consumers and producers to account for the external effects of their transactions when large numbers of people are affected.
10. *Nonexclusive goods:* Non-exclusive goods such as defense are the ultimate externalities: Purchase of a nonexclusive good by anyone directly affects everyone. Nonexclusive goods are vulnerable to the free-rider problem and are therefore virtually impossible to market. Government provision is the only viable option.
11. *Macroeconomic stabilization:* A free market economy does not always achieve the macroeconomic policy goals of long-run economic growth, full employment, price stability, and stability in a country's economic relations with foreign countries. Government fiscal and monetary policies can help achieve these goals. We will see in the macroeconomic section of the text that the need for monetary and fiscal policies is largely the result of various kinds of market failures.

The final section of Chapter 23 offered an overview of federal, state, and local expenditures. Government expenditures in the United States are primarily a response to the market failures identified in the first section of the chapter.

12. The federal government concentrates its spending in three areas: defense, redistribution, and public pensions and insurance. It also performs a number of necessary regulatory functions. The state and the local governments concentrate their spending on a wide range of allocational problems caused by externalities and economies of scale—the most important being education (externality) and highways and transportation (economies of scale). They also provide aid to the poor by participating with the federal government in the public assistance programs and by operating both psychiatric and general hospitals for those who cannot afford private hospital care.

KEY TERMS

adverse selection
allocational policies
common-use resource
distributional policies
exclusive good
externality
free-rider
merit good
moral hazard
nonexclusive (public) good
principal-agent problem
stabilization policies
vertical equity

QUESTIONS

1. What are the desirable attributes of competitive markets that operate according to the Laws of Supply and Demand? Answer from society's point of view.
2. If all markets operated according to the Laws of Supply and Demand, there would be no need for a government to solve economic problems in a capitalist economy. Do you agree or disagree with this statement? If you disagree, give some examples of remaining economic problems that the government would have to solve and why the problems would exist.
3. Economists classify market failures into three broad categories. What are they? Give an example of a market failure within each category that is important in the U.S. economy.
4. Match the following list of publicly provided goods and services with one (or more) of these categories of allocational problems: nonexclusive (public) good, natural monopoly, externality, economies of scale, information problem.
   a. public water and sewage
   b. education
   c. national defense
   d. the interstate highway system
   e. public health insurance
5. Why can a market system not be expected to solve the for whom or distribution question?
6. a. Give two examples of market problems that are caused by poor information, and explain briefly the nature of the problem.
   b. What can the government do to help overcome the problems that you described? Will government intervention necessarily be effective in either case?
7. Name five major areas of expenditure in the federal budget, and indicate how each can be viewed as a response to market failure. Then do the same for any three major areas of expenditure in state and local budgets.
8. An ardent environmentalist might argue that the optimal amount of industrial air and water pollution is zero pollution. Do you agree or disagree? Might your answer differ for different kinds of pollutants?
9. Many environmentalists believe that the Brazilian rain forests provide a significant portion of the earth's oxygen supply, and they express concern about the ongoing destruction of these forests.
   a. What kind of good is a rain forest?
   b. Why are the rain forests being destroyed if they are such an important source of the oxygen that we need to live?
10. In 1980 Ronald Reagan promised to "get the government off our backs." In terms of government expenditures, did he accomplish that goal? What significant changes have taken place in government spending in the United States over the past 10 to 15 years? What do you foresee as likely changes over the next 10 years?

CHAPTER

24

Government Revenues, the Principles of Taxation, and the Economics of Democracy

LEARNING OBJECTIVES

CONCEPTS TO LEARN

The five major U.S. taxes
Debt financing
The normative criteria for tax design
Progressive, proportional, and regressive taxes
The theory of public choice
Arrow's Impossibility Theorem
Special-interest lobbying

CONCEPTS TO RECALL

Horizontal equity [2]
The economic effects of taxes [8]
Vertical equity [23]

In the late 1970s a Californian named Howard Jarvis became the new hero of the fiscal conservatives when he led a successful property tax revolt in protest against ever-increasing government spending and taxes. Jarvis and his followers collected enough signatures to place a referendum on the ballot; called Proposition 13, this proposal placed a cap on local property taxes equal to 1 percent of property values. California voted yes on Proposition 13, and conservatives everywhere hailed the vote as a landmark victory. Jarvis proved that the people had the power to hold the government in check.

Enthusiasm for tax limitation swept through the country on the heels of Proposition 13. Similar property tax limitations quickly followed in Texas, Massachusetts, and a number of other states. On the national scene Ronald Reagan rode the sentiment for tax limitation to a landslide victory over Jimmy Carter in the 1980 presidential election. Shortly after taking office Reagan joined with conservative Congressman Jack Kemp of New York in persuading Congress to cut the personal income tax by 23 percent across the board. This was the largest tax cut of any kind in the history of the United States.

Liberals complained that Jarvis and his conservative followers had switched the debate over the role of the government from the expenditure side to the tax side in order to play on people's emotions. Rather than debating the proper role of government and what expenditures this role required, the conservatives simply painted taxes as an evil that took away people's spendable incomes. People naturally prefer to pay lower taxes, but that is not the issue according to the liberals. They should think first about what kinds of public services they want and then ask themselves whether they are willing to pay the taxes needed to finance the services.

Conservatives countered that public officials do not behave responsibly. They do not think in terms of the public's interest in efficiency and equity and what the government can do to achieve these goals. Instead, they use the government to pursue their own self-interest, and their self-interest is to keep raising taxes and spending. Only by limiting and even cutting taxes can citizens curb public officials' insatiable appetite for more spending.

The liberal-conservative debate over the government sector continues to rage in the United States.

Our discussion of the government's role in a market economy in Chapter 23 focused almost exclusively on government expenditures. Chapter 24 begins with a look at the revenue side of federal, state, and local budgets. The chapter then concludes our discussion of the government sector on a political note. The United States and most of the industrialized capitalist nations have chosen a representative democracy as their form of government. The final section of the chapter asks the practical question raised by the conservatives: To what extent is government economic policy really able to improve the efficiency and equity of the economy under a representative democracy? The answer is by no means clear.

THE PRINCIPAL SOURCES OF GOVERNMENT REVENUES

Governments in the United States use four main sources of revenue to finance their expenditures: (1) taxes; (2) direct charges to users of public services; (3) debt; and (4) grants-in-aid received from higher-level governments in the hierarchy of the federal, state, and local governments.

Tax collections are by far the most important source of revenues in the United States. They have financed between 70 percent and 75 percent of total government expenditures since 1981. Also, five taxes account for nearly all the tax revenue collected. They are, in order of importance, (1) the federal and the state personal income taxes, (2) the federal payroll tax earmarked for the Social Security Trust Fund, (3) general sales and excise taxes (primarily state), (4) property taxes (primarily local), and (5) the federal and the state corporation income taxes.

Grants-in-aid differ from the other three revenue sources because they are transfers of funds among governments rather than transfers of funds from the private sector to the public sector. Therefore, the ultimate sources of funds for financing public-sector programs are taxes, direct user charges, and debt. Grants-in-aid net out to zero for the fiscal system as a whole.

Table 24.1 lists the principal revenue sources of the federal government for 1992, and the state and local governments for 1991. The table shows that the governments have chosen very different means of financing their expenditures.

The Federal Government

The federal government relies almost entirely on two of the four revenue sources, taxes and debt. Tax collections account for 96 percent of all nondebt receipts. The federal government makes use of all of the taxes listed above, with the exception of property taxes, but the federal personal income tax and the Social Security payroll tax predominate. These two taxes account for approximately five-sixths of total federal tax revenues, and they are the two most important taxes in the entire U.S. fiscal system.

The use of debt financing requires some explanation. Governments issue debt to finance their budget deficits. A government's budget is in **deficit** when the government's expenditures exceed its revenues from taxes, direct user charges, and grants-in-aid. Conversely, a government's budget is in **surplus** when the government's revenues from these three sources exceed its expenditures. Governments finance their deficits by borrowing money from private and foreign citizens, business firms, and other governments. They issue new debt to the lenders in the form of government bonds in exchange for the money. A **government bond** is a promissory note that pays the bondholder (the lender) an amount equal to the principal or face value of the bond at a specified future date. The bond may also pay the lender interest on the principal each year until the government repays the principal.[1] The total amount of debt (borrowing) outstanding is the sum of all past budget deficits, less all

BUDGET DEFICIT

Exists when a government's expenditures exceed its revenues from taxes, direct user charges, and grants-in-aid.

BUDGET SURPLUS

Exists when a government's revenues from taxes, direct user charges, and grants-in-aid exceed its expenditures.

GOVERNMENT BOND

A promissory note issued by a government that pays the bondholder (the lender) an amount equal to the principal, or face value, of a bond at a specified future date.

[1]The federal government distinguishes among Treasury bills, notes, and bonds, depending on when it repays the principal. A Treasury bill repays the principal within 1 year, a Treasury note repays the principal within 1 to 10 years, and a Treasury bond repays the principal more than 10 years in the future.

TABLE 24.1 **Revenue Sources of Federal, State, and Local Governments**

	REVENUES (BILLIONS)	PERCENTAGE OF TOTAL EXPENDITURES
A. FEDERAL GOVERNMENT (FISCAL YEAR 1992)[a]		
Total receipts: Tax revenues and charges	$1075.7	72.9%

	REVENUES (BILLIONS)	PERCENTAGE OF TOTAL RECEIPTS
Personal income tax	478.7	44.5
Contributions for social insurance	410.9	38.2
Corporation income tax	89.0	8.3
Other taxes and charges	97.1	9.0

	REVENUES (BILLIONS)	PERCENTAGE OF TOTAL EXPENDITURES
Debt financing	399.7	27.1
Total expenditures	1475.4	100.0

B. STATE GOVERNMENTS (FISCAL YEAR 1991)[b]

	REVENUES (BILLIONS)	PERCENTAGE OF GENERAL REVENUE
Federal grants-in-aid	$ 134.9	24.5
Total taxes	310.5	56.3

	REVENUES (BILLIONS)	PERCENTAGE OF TOTAL TAXES
General sales and excise taxes	$153.5	49.4
Personal income tax	99.3	32.0
All other taxes	57.7	18.6

	REVENUES (BILLIONS)	PERCENTAGE OF GENERAL REVENUE
Direct user charges and miscellaneous revenues	106.3	19.2
Total general revenue	551.7	100.0

[a]The data for the federal government are estimated receipts and expenditures.
[b]Data for state and local governments were available through fiscal year 1991 only.

(continued)

TABLE 24.1 **Revenue Sources of Federal, State, and Local Governments** (continued)

			REVENUES (BILLIONS)	PERCENTAGE OF GENERAL REVENUE
C. LOCAL GOVERNMENTS (FISCAL YEAR 1991)[2]				
Grants-in-aid			$201.9	37.3
	REVENUES (BILLIONS)	PERCENTAGE OF TOTAL GRANTS		
From federal government	19.1	9.5		
From state governments	182.7	90.5		
Total taxes			214.7	39.6
	REVENUES (BILLIONS)	PERCENTAGE OF TOTAL TAXES		
Property tax	161.7	75.3		
Other taxes	53.0	24.7		
Direct user chargers and miscellaneous revenues			125.2	23.1
Total general revenue			541.8	100.0

SOURCES: Executive Office of the President of the United States, *Budget of the United States Government, Fiscal Year 1993, Supplement, February 1992* (Washington D.C.: U.S. Government Printing Office, 1992), Part Five: Historical Tables, Table 1.1, p. 5–14; Table 2.1, p. 5–22. U.S. Department of Commerce, Economics and Statistics Administration, Bureau of Census, *Government Finances: 1990–91 (Preliminary Report)* (Washington, D.C.: U.S. Government Printing Office, 1993), Series GF/91-5P, p. 1.

past surpluses that were used to retire some of the debt. In other words, debt is a stock variable defined at a point in time, and a deficit is a flow variable defined over the course of a year, as are expenditures and revenues.

Heavy reliance on debt financing to fund annual expenditures was new to the Reagan administration and has continued ever since. The amount of federal debt held by the public was $709 billion at the end of 1980, right before President Reagan took office. The debt had grown to $2,050 billion by the end of 1988, Reagan's last year in office. By 1992, at the end of the Bush presidency, the federal debt held by the public was $2,687 billion, and it climbed above $3 trillion in 1992.

Even though President Clinton has made deficit reduction one of his top economic priorities, the debt will continue to grow rapidly. The projected federal deficit for 1993 is over $300 billion, and the President's deficit reduction plan, which congress just barely approved, will only reduce the deficit by $100 billion per year from 1993 to 1998.[2]

[2]The data on the public debt in this section are in Table 7.1, p. 5–89 of the February, 1992 *Supplement* to the *Budget of the United States Government, Fiscal Year 1993*, referenced in Table 24.1.

Previous administrations had also routinely issued new debt to help finance expenditures; the federal budget has been in deficit in all but two years since World War II. But the annual federal deficits were in magnitudes of billions and tens of billions of dollars, not hundreds of billions of dollars. Prior to the Reagan administration, the federal government relied almost exclusively on taxes to finance its expenditures.[3]

The State and Local Governments

State and local governments raise their revenues quite differently than does the federal government. They do not routinely use debt to finance their annual expenditures, and they rely much less on taxes than does the federal government.

Unlike the federal government, state and local governments ran surpluses every year throughout the 1980s. The recession of 1990–91 threw some of the large state governments into a deficit position as tax collections fell off. But these states are now raising taxes and user charges, and cutting expenditures, in order to bring their budgets into balance. Most state constitutions prohibit the use of debt to finance state or local operating expenditures (as opposed to capital expenditures).

Tax collections accounted for only 56.3 percent of state revenues and 39.6 percent of local revenues in 1991. As Table 24.1 indicates, these governments make up the revenue shortfall from two main sources, grants-in-aid from higher-level governments and direct user charges for public services. The most notable difference between the local and the state governments is their choice of taxes. Local governments collect three-fourths of all tax revenues from property taxes, and the property tax is the only significant source of tax revenue for most communities. By contrast, states make use of a number of taxes. They rely most heavily on the general sales tax and the personal income tax, but neither tax dominates, as the property tax does at the local level. The category "All other taxes" listed in Table 24.1 consists primarily of excise taxes earmarked to special state funds, such as the state gasoline taxes and motor vehicle excise taxes that are earmarked to state highway funds.

Let's now take a brief look at each of the major revenue sources.

The Five Major Taxes

FEDERAL AND STATE PERSONAL INCOME TAXES

THE FEDERAL PERSONAL INCOME TAX The federal personal income tax is the largest single source of revenue in the entire U.S. fiscal system. It accounts for over 80 percent of total federal and state personal income tax revenues and serves as the model for most of the state personal income taxes.

---

[3]The one exception was during World War II, which was primarily debt financed. The war years from 1941 to 1945 brought about the largest increase in the federal debt as a percentage of national product in U.S. history. In 1946, the federal debt held by the public stood at 114 percent of the national product, compared with 53 percent of the national product in 1992.

A personal income tax is a tax on income received, levied either on individuals or on married couples. Married couples may file either one joint tax return or two individual tax returns. The federal personal income tax embodies the following general principles:

1. All factor income is subject to taxation, whether it derives from labor, capital, or land. As such, it represents a tax on the supply of these factors. (There are some important exceptions to this principle, to be noted below.)
2. The tax protects individuals and families with very low incomes by exempting a certain level of income from taxation. All taxpayers receive a personal exemption for themselves and for each family member and an additional standard deduction that is independent of family size.[4] Only income in excess of the exempt income is subject to tax. Income subject to tax is referred to as *taxable income.*

   In 1992 taxpayers received a personal exemption of $2,300 for each family member and an additional standard deduction of $6,000 (for married couples filing jointly). Therefore, a family of four paid tax only on income in excess of $15,200 ($15,200 = (4 · 2,300) + 6,000 = 9,200 + 6,000). The exemptions and standard deduction increase automatically each year with the rate of inflation.
3. In 1992, income was taxed at three different rates, 15, 28, and 31 percent, depending on the level of income. The rate schedule for married couples filing jointly in 1992 was as follows:

HISTORICAL NOTE: The Tax Reform Act of 1986 significantly increased the amount of low income protection from taxation. The exemption for each family member increased immediately from $1080 to $2000, and the standard deduction for married couples filing joint returns increased from $3600 to $5000. As a result, the level of income exempt from taxation for a family of four jumped nearly $5100, from $7920 to $13,000.

TAXABLE INCOME	MARGINAL TAX RATE
$0–35,800	15%
$35,801–86,500	28
Above $86,500	31

MARGINAL TAX RATE

The rate of tax applied to additional income received under a personal income tax.

The tax rates are said to be *graduated,* meaning that they increase as income increases. Each income range is referred to as the *tax bracket* for the applicable marginal rate. For example, the 28 percent tax bracket includes the portion of taxable income ranging from $35,801 to $86,500.

Beginning in 1993, taxable incomes from 140,001 to 250,000 are subject to a marginal tax rate of 36 percent, and taxable income above 250,000 is taxed at a rate of 39.6 percent. The limits for the 15, 28, and 31 percent brackets increase from their 1992 amounts by the rate of inflation in 1993.

HISTORICAL NOTE: The Tax Reform Act of 1986 replaced an eleven-bracket structure of graduated rates ranging from 11 percent to 50 percent with a four-bracket rate structure of 15–28–33–28 percent. The new rate structure was the culmination of a series of reforms over a 25 year period designed to reduce the number of tax brackets and lower the rates. In 1963 there were 24 tax brackets, with rates ranging from 20 percent to 91 percent. The rate structure was changed again in 1990 to 15–28–31 percent, and again in 1993.

STATE PERSONAL INCOME TAXES Forty-three states levy personal income taxes. Most of these taxes embody the three principles just described, including the graduated rate schedule. The most important difference between the federal and the state taxes is that the state tax rates are much lower, ranging in 1991 from 0.4 percent on the lowest level of taxable income in Iowa to 12 percent on the highest level of taxable income in North Dakota. (Massachusetts also taxes income from capital at a 12 percent rate.) This is why the federal tax looms larger in the economic decisions of most people than does their own state's income tax.

[4]Taxpayers may itemize deductions for certain expenditures instead of taking the standard deduction if itemizing increases the amount of the deduction. Most low-income taxpayers do not choose to itemize, however.

THE SOCIAL SECURITY PAYROLL TAX When Congress established the Social Security System in 1935, it decided to fund the system with a separate payroll tax on the wage incomes of all covered workers. Half of the tax is levied on the worker and half on the employer. In 1992 workers and employers each paid a tax of 6.2 percent on wage income up to a limit of $55,500 to provide for retirement and other cash benefits. Income in excess of the limit is untaxed. Hence, the maximum payroll tax liability for workers (and their employers) in 1992 was $3,441 (= 0.062 · $55,500). There is also now a separate payroll tax earmarked for the Medicare program. In 1992 the Medicare tax rate was 1.45 percent on all wage income up to a limit of $130,000. The upper limit will be removed in 1994.

The growth in payroll tax revenues has kept pace with the growth in Social Security benefits since 1935, to the point where the payroll tax is now the second most important tax in the U.S. fiscal system. For the majority of taxpayers the payroll tax is the most important tax; their payroll tax liability exceeds their federal personal income tax liability.

Congress adjusts the payroll tax revenues by periodically changing both the rate of tax and the income limit. The most recent set of adjustments resulted from the 1983 amendments to the Social Security Act. The 1983 amendments were designed to forestall an impending crisis that threatened to undermine the entire Social Security System. By the late 1970s annual benefit payments began to exceed annual payroll tax collections. Beyond that, the system was heading for disaster down the road when the huge baby boom generation, those people born between 1947 and 1964, retired.

The 1983 amendments made substantial changes in both the benefit schedules and the payroll tax that were designed to build up a huge surplus of funds until the baby boomers begin to retire. The surplus would then be drawn down to cover the baby boomers' retirement benefits. Included in the reforms was a series of increases in the payroll tax rates and income limits during the five-year period from 1983 to 1988.

The income limit on the retirement benefits portion of the tax increases each year with the rate of inflation. But with no new tax rate increases scheduled beyond 1988, the future growth in payroll tax revenues should be less rapid than it has been in the recent past.

GENERAL SALES AND EXCISE TAXES An excise tax is a tax on the sale of a single commodity. A general sales tax is levied on a broad range of commodities, usually at a common rate.

General sales taxes have long been the leading source of tax revenue at the state level, although personal income taxes may soon overtake them. Forty-five states make use of the general sales tax. In 1991 the tax rates varied from a low of 3 percent in Wyoming to a high of 7 percent in New Jersey and Rhode Island.

The primary appeal of sales (and excise) taxes is that they are easy to administer. Most businesses keep careful records of sales receipts for their internal accounting purposes, and state departments of revenue can use these records as a basis for determining a business's sales tax liability.

Ease of collection is another reason why the low-income, developing countries rely heavily on sales taxes rather than personal income taxes. A broad-based personal income tax is just not possible for a developing country because such a large percentage of the population is illiterate. The burden of operating a personal income tax falls largely on the people; individuals must keep accurate records of their income and file a tax return. People cannot be expected to keep records and file tax returns if they cannot read or write. Consequently, the developing countries have to tax their businesses, and the sales tax has been a popular choice.

The principal complaint against the sales tax is the perception that it unduly burdens those with low incomes. Low-income people spend a higher percentage of their incomes on consumer goods and services than do high-income people. Thus, they suffer a disproportionately higher tax burden under a general sales tax. Twenty-eight states have attempted to reduce the burden of the sales tax on their poorer citizens by exempting food purchased for home consumption from taxation.

THE LOCAL PROPERTY TAX Local property taxes account for 96 percent of all property tax revenues in the United States. Only a handful of states use the property tax as a major source of revenue, and the federal government does not tax property at all except after death as part of an estate tax.

The property tax is the only major tax that is not levied on a component of the circular flow of economic activity. It is a tax on a component of wealth, not on the expenditures or incomes that flow through goods and factor markets. The majority of property tax revenue is raised from local taxes on residential housing, although taxes on commercial and industrial property also raise substantial amounts of revenue. Taxes on other forms of personal property, such as cars, home furnishings, and pleasure boats, are far less common and are unimportant in terms of the total revenue they collect.

Survey after survey reveals that the property tax is the least popular of the major taxes. If the tax on residential property is so universally disliked, why do all local governments use it? They use it because the property tax is the only tax that is fairly easy to levy and administer at the local level. The value of residential property within a community offers every local government a natural, broad tax base. In contrast, sales taxes may not raise sufficient amounts of revenue in towns with little commercial or industrial activity.

REFLECTION: Does your state have a property (or other) tax cap? If so, have you noticed a decline in public services—for example, cutbacks in the curriculum or extracurricular programs at the high school or less frequent garbage collection? Even if your state does not have a tax cap, have public services declined over the past five years because of budgetary pressures?

The property tax is also easy to administer because property stays put, certainly relative to income. If localities levied income taxes, problems would arise over the issue of where the income was earned. If localities tried to tax the incomes of their residents, they would have difficulty collecting taxes on income earned outside their jurisdiction. If the localities tried to tax income earned within the community, they would have difficulty tracking down and collecting taxes from individuals who earn their incomes within the community, but live elsewhere. Residential property is so much easier to keep track of than income is.

Finally, sales and income taxes might well drive businesses and workers to neighboring communities without such taxes. Because existing residential property stays put, there is less risk of losing the tax base with a property tax. True, raising or lowering the property tax rate may affect the amount of new construction in the community and therefore the value of the tax base. But, more than any other tax, the property tax gives local governments the independence they need to finance the public services desired by the community.

FEDERAL AND STATE CORPORATION INCOME TAXES

THE FEDERAL CORPORATION INCOME TAX As the name implies, the federal and the state corporation income taxes are levied only on the income earned by corporations. The earnings of proprietors and partnerships are considered to be regular factor income received by the owners of these firms and are taxed under the federal and the state personal income taxes.

Corporate "income" or "profit" subject to the federal tax is roughly equivalent to the returns to capital invested in the corporation by the stockholders (owners), but only roughly. The actual tax base is extremely complex and varies by type of business. Broadly speaking, though, taxable profit is the difference between revenues from sales and two categories of costs, operating expenses and depreciation. The operating expenses of the corporation include out-of-pocket expenses for factors of production such as the wages and salaries of the firm's employees and the costs of material inputs and fuels, the sales and excise taxes paid on the sale of the products, and the interest paid to holders of corporate bonds who have loaned the corporation money for investment. Depreciation is an estimate of how much the value of the firm's stock of plant and equipment declines during the year, based on guidelines established by the U.S. Internal Revenue Service.

The federal corporation income tax employs a three-step graduated rate schedule, much like that for personal income tax. The corporate rates are 15, 25, and 34 percent. However, the 34 percent rate takes effect at only $75,000 of taxable income, so that virtually all corporate income is taxed at the 34 percent rate.[5]

STATE CORPORATION INCOME TAXES Forty-three states levy corporation income taxes, most of which are modeled after the federal tax. The main difference between the state and the federal taxes is the tax rate. The state tax rates are much lower, just as they are with the personal income taxes. In 1991, the tax rates ranged from a low of 1 percent in Alaska to a high of 12.25 percent in Pennsylvania. States are naturally reluctant to raise their corporate tax rates for fear that business firms will leave for states with lower tax rates. This reluctance has prevented the corporation income tax from becoming a major source of state revenues.[6]

Tax collectors like the corporation income tax because it is an easy source of revenue. Economists, on the other hand, generally dislike the tax. They were not pleased when the Tax Reform Act of 1986 increased federal corporation income tax revenues at the expense of personal income tax revenues.

Economists complain that the corporation income tax introduces a whole host of distortions into capital markets that would otherwise function fairly closely to the perfectly competitive ideal. The tax distorts capital markets by causing different kinds of assets to be taxed at very different rates. Demanders and suppliers of capital have a natural incentive to gravitate toward relatively

---

[5]In 1993 Congress increased the marginal tax rate to 35 percent on corporate income in excess of $10 million.

[6]All data on state taxes are from U.S. Advisory Commission on Intergovernmental Relations, *Significant Features of Fiscal Federalism 1992* (Washington, D.C.: U.S. Government Printing Office, February 1992), Table 22, pp. 68–72 (State personal income tax rates); Table 25, pp. 76–78 (State corporation income tax rates); and Table 29, pp. 89–90 (State sales tax rates and exemptions).

lightly taxed assets and shy away from highly taxed assets. As a result, the allocation of capital is quite different, and far less efficient, than it would be if all assets were taxed at the same rate.

For example, the tax encourages investment in the noncorporate sector at the expense of the corporate sector because only corporate income is taxed. The tax also encourages firms to engage in debt financing because they can deduct interest from the tax base, but not dividends. With more debt outstanding, firms become riskier than they otherwise would be. Firms can lay off workers to save on costs if business turns sour, but the obligation to repay their debts, with interest, remains no matter what happens. Finally, the complexities of the tax base happen to generate a very strong bias in favor of short-term investments, such as equipment, and against longer-term investments, such as physical plant.

Direct User Charges for Public Services

Direct user charges for public services go by many names: *rates* charged by the electric and water utilities, *tolls* on bridges and highways, *fares* on bus and rail transit, and admission *fees* to parks and beaches. The state gasoline *tax* is also considered by many to be a charge for the use of the state's roadways, especially since these taxes are earmarked to the state highway funds.

Call them what you will, direct user charges are extremely popular. They appeal to a deeply held principle of equity in the collection of government revenues that we first met in Chapter 14, the **benefits received principle of taxation.** The benefits received principle says, simply, that taxes and other means of payment are fair if they bear a direct relationship to the benefits people receive from the public services being financed. The principle dates from seventeenth-century England, when landowners paid taxes to the king in return for the state's promise to maintain public order.

BENEFITS RECEIVED PRINCIPLE OF TAXATION

The principle that the taxes and other means of payment for public services are fair if they bear a direct relationship to the benefits people receive from the public services.

Direct user charges honor the benefits received principle as closely as possible. Users pay for the services, and nonusers do not; more-intensive users pay more for the service than do less-intensive users. This is exactly what the benefits received principle is all about.

The benefits received principle is bound to appeal to a capitalistic society because the market system operates on the same principle. Buyers pay only for those goods and services that give them benefit. They are not forced to buy anything that they do not want. Since user charges are nothing more than prices set by a public agency, they bear the same relationship to benefits received as do market prices.

REFLECTION: Is your town substituting direct user charges for the property tax in order to pay for town services, such as contracting out garbage collection to private firms and charging fees to participate in town recreation programs or high school sports; is it relying on hidden user charges, as when parents volunteer to coach town soccer teams that used to be coached by town recreation personnel?

Direct user charges would undoubtedly be used even more if they could be, but they are often not a practical option. The majority of public expenditure programs are just not amenable to payment according to benefits received. Paying for the nation's defense is one example. Any attempt to levy taxes for defense on the basis of benefits received would be undermined by the free-rider problem. People would refuse to reveal their true preferences if they thought that their tax payments would bear any close relationship to their stated preferences.

Pinning down the benefits of many public goods and services is problematic even without the free-rider problem. Public education is justified because o the external benefits it confers. But does anyone seriously believe that citizens could be taxed accurately on the basis of the external benefits that they receive from public education? Trying to use the benefits received principle to pay for highways also raises difficult questions. How much benefit does each member of a community receive from the local roadways? What fraction of the benefits accrue to people outside the jurisdiction? Can outsiders be made to pay for these benefits, given that tolls are impractical for most local roadways? Even if tolls could be charged, should they be? If the marginal costs of traveling on the road are (near) zero, economic efficiency dictates that the price should be (near) zero. In this case the dictates of equity and efficiency are inconsistent with one another.

Redistributional transfer payments are still another category of expenditures that cannot be financed according to the benefits received principle. The primary beneficiary of a transfer payment is the person who receives it. Therefore, taxing to pay for transfers according to the benefits received principle would result in no net transfer at all.

We can now see why the federal government makes so little use of user charges. With defense, transfers to the poor, interest payments on the debt, and grants-in-aid dominating federal expenditures, the federal government must rely on general taxes such as the personal and the corporation income taxes that offer taxpayers no direct connection between the taxes they pay and the benefits they receive.

The only possible exception at the federal level is the Social Security payroll tax. The Social Security System was not a true pension plan prior to the 1983 amendments. It was essentially a pay-as-you-go, tax-transfer scheme that transferred income each year from the young to the elderly. The payroll tax revenues collected from employers and workers did not accumulate in an investment pension fund to pay for future retirement benefits. Instead, the tax revenues were immediately paid out to current retirees. Still, some economists argued that the payroll taxes came with an implied promise of future pension benefits and medical insurance and were therefore consistent with the benefits received principle. The 1983 amendments tightened the benefits received justification for the payroll tax by allowing for a surplus to accumulate to pay for the baby boomers' retirement years. By accumulating a surplus, the Social Security System now operates more like a standard private pension plan. The system is scheduled to return to a pay-as-you-go, tax-transfer scheme, however, after the baby boomers retire.

State and local governments also have to rely on general taxes to finance the majority of their expenditures, including each of the five major categories identified in Chapter 23: education, highways, public welfare, health and hospitals, and local police and fire protection.

Once the link between taxation and benefits received is broken, judging the merits of taxes requires a completely different set of principles. We will consider the principles governing the design of general taxes in the next section of this chapter.

Debt Financing

Issuing government bonds to raise funds is appropriate for only one purpose in the normal course of events: to finance public capital expenditures, such as school buildings, highways, and other public works construction projects. Governments are not supposed to issue bonds to finance the annual operating expenses associated with government programs. In this respect the accepted rules of public finance are similar to the rules of private business finance. Corporations routinely issue bonds to finance their investments in plant and equipment, but not to finance their annual production expenses.

The main difference between public and private debt is that most government projects are not expected to generate revenues to pay back the principal and interest on the bonds, although some projects are financed on that basis. High schools and rural highways do not generate revenues, whereas a debt-financed college dormitory at a state university might be able to pay back bondholders from student room fees.

When no revenues are expected from a capital project, governments issue **full faith and credit bonds** that are backed by the power to tax. The full faith and credit guarantee is that the government will raise sufficient tax revenues in future years to pay back the principal and interest on the debt. Bonds used to pay for self-financing projects such as college dormitories are called **revenue bonds.**

FULL FAITH AND CREDIT BOND

Government bonds issued to finance capital projects that are not expected to bring in revenues; the bonds are backed by the government's power to tax.

REVENUE BOND

Government bonds that are used to pay for self-financing capital projects.

Raising taxes to repay full faith and credit bonds is perfectly legitimate. Highways and schools may not generate any revenues directly. But they do expand the nation's production possibilities frontier and allow national income to grow if they are productive. Taxing some of the additional income to repay the debt is appropriate, just as firms set aside some of their revenues to repay debt that was used to finance productive private investments.

Most economists recognize two other extraordinary circumstances in which the federal government can appropriately issue debt, wars and recessions. The first large infusion of public debt in the United States occurred during World War II. The government felt it had little choice but to borrow from the public at the time, with military expenditures running as high as 25 percent of total national output. The federal government may also issue debt whenever the circular flow of economic activity slows down and the economy experiences a recession. We will see in the macroeconomic chapters of this text that requiring a balanced budget during a recession can make the recession worse. Moreover, debt-financed government expenditures, or tax cuts with tax revenues replaced by issuing debt, can help pull the economy out of a recession. But debt financing of operating expenses or transfer payments during a recession comes with the understanding that revenues from nondebt sources will meet or exceed these expenditures once the economy recovers.

State and local governments do follow the accepted rules of debt financing for the most part. Nearly all state governors and local administrators are required by state law to submit balanced operating budgets. Projected revenues from taxes, direct user charges, and grants-in-aid must be sufficient to cover all projected operating expenses during the upcoming year. State and local debt is used primarily for capital expenditures.

THE REAGAN-BUSH-CLINTON DEFICITS The same cannot be said of the federal government. The huge federal budget deficits that began in 1981 have forced the government to issue debt to finance operating expenses as well as capital expenditures, and the debt cannot be justified by either of the extraordinary circumstances noted above. The deficits came about when President

Reagan persuaded Congress to pass two large programs that sharply increased expenditures and reduced tax revenues. The expenditure program was a huge military buildup to counter a perceived threat to the nation's security from the Soviet Union. The tax program was the 23 percent reduction in the personal income tax that we mentioned in the introduction. The purpose of the tax cut was to help stimulate the economy. The Reagan deficits began when the economy was in the throes of a deep recession, but the administration itself projected that the huge deficits would continue once the economy had recovered to full employment. And, of course, the Reagan-Bush-Clinton deficits have been peacetime deficits.

We will return to the deficits in Chapter 31 when we consider the various macroeconomic issues associated with large ongoing deficits and a large public debt.

NORMATIVE CRITERIA FOR TAX DESIGN

What principles should apply to the design of general taxes, those for which there is no necessary connection between tax payments and benefits received? Economists judge general taxes on the basis of five criteria: (1) ease of administration, (2) simplicity, (3) flexibility, (4) efficiency, and (5) equity.

The Properties of "Good" Taxes

EASE OF ADMINISTRATION Ease of administration is really the foremost requirement of any general tax. Above all else, revenue departments have to be able to collect large amounts of revenue fairly easily. If a general tax is difficult to administer, a government simply will not use it.

We noted above that ease of administration was a principal appeal of three of the major U.S. taxes: general sales and excise taxes, local property taxes, and corporation income taxes. Personal income taxes and the Social Security payroll tax are also easy to administer. They have to be, or they would not have become the two leading U.S. taxes.

SIMPLICITY Simplicity and ease of administration are closely related. The difference is that the simplicity criterion adopts the taxpayer's point of view. Taxpayers must understand the nature of their tax liability and be able to compute and pay their taxes with a minimum of time and effort. In particular, complying with the tax should not require taxpayers to maintain a detailed set of records that they would not otherwise keep.

The more complex a tax is, the more taxpayers will evade paying their proper tax liability, out of either ignorance or spite. Once tax evasion becomes widespread, the tax is no longer a useful source of revenue. Revenue departments cannot chase down everyone. This is why simplicity and ease of administration are so closely linked.

FLEXIBILITY The flexibility criterion refers to the ability of a tax to respond appropriately to market failure. For general taxes this boils down to (1) flexibility in the pursuit of equity and (2) flexibility in the conduct of macroeconomic policy. As such, the flexibility criterion applies mostly to the design of federal taxes.

The federal personal income tax is potentially very flexible in both respects. Regarding equity, personal income taxes have a natural advantage over all the other major taxes in that they can be tailored most easily to the personal circumstances of the taxpayer. For instance, protecting poor families from the burden of taxation under a personal income tax is easily achieved by personal exemptions that remove the first dollars of income from taxation and vary by family size. Protecting the poor from tax burden is much more difficult under a payroll or property tax and virtually impossible under sales and excise taxes.

Flexibility in the conduct of macroeconomic policy refers to how quickly the government can change tax collections in response to changes in the state of the economy. The government must be able to change the structure of a tax quickly, for example, by adjusting tax rates up or down. Then the change in the tax structure must translate quickly into changes in actual tax collections.

The federal personal income tax is potentially a very flexible macroeconomic policy tool. Congress can enact temporary across-the-board surcharges or cuts in the tax rates in response to economic conditions. Then, given that the tax is withheld from workers' paychecks, the change in actual tax liabilities occurs with only about a month's delay. Workers see an almost immediate increase or decrease in their take-home pay.

In fact, the macroeconomic flexibility of the tax has not been exploited very often. Congress has usually been reluctant to change the tax structure without undertaking a full set of time-consuming congressional hearings. We will pursue this point, along with other macroeconomic issues of federal tax policy, in Chapter 30.

EFFICIENCY Tax policy can contribute to the efficient operation of the economy in certain situations. For instance, we saw in Chapter 11 that taxing polluters is an efficient, least-cost solution to the problem of pollution externalities. In the macroeconomic chapters of this text we will consider how tax policy can help achieve the various macroeconomic policy goals.

For the most part, however, general broad-based taxes impede the efficient operation of a market economy. Chapter 8 showed how sales and excise taxes generate deadweight efficiency losses of potential net value by forcing competitive markets for goods and services away from their natural equilibriums. Income and property taxes also cause deadweight efficiency losses, the only difference being that they do their damage in the factor markets for labor, capital, and land. All major taxes inevitably cause some efficiency loss. We learned in Chapter 8 that the amount of efficiency loss depends on two factors, the level of the tax rate and the elasticities of supply and demand.

Therefore, the efficiency criterion takes on a negative slant when applied to tax policy. The goal is to select and design taxes that minimize the efficiency losses per dollar of revenue raised. The way to minimize efficiency loss is to keep tax rates low or to tax markets whose supplies or demands are highly inelastic.

EQUITY What is the fairest way to raise general tax revenue? Since the benefits received principle is inoperable for general taxes, society must develop a whole new set of equity norms to guide the design of tax policy. No one can give a definitive answer to the question of what the fairest general tax is. As in all matters of equity, people are free to believe whatever they want to believe. Nonetheless, we can say that economists would vote overwhelmingly for one of two taxes as being the most fair: the personal income tax or a tax on personal consumption expenditures. The equity principles favoring these taxes trace their ancestry to the writings of Adam Smith and John Stuart Mill in the late 1700s and early 1800s.

THE ABILITY-TO-PAY PRINCIPLE OF TAXATION Smith and Mill argued that citizens should view the payment of general taxes as a necessary sacrifice for promoting the common good. The key equity question as they saw it was this: What is the fairest way to ask people to sacrifice? They both concluded that the government should ask citizens to sacrifice in accordance with their *ability to pay*. In addition, they believed that taxes levied according to taxpayers' ability to pay should honor the principles of horizontal equity and vertical equity. **Horizontal equity** requires equal treatment of equals. **Vertical equity** says that unequals may be treated unequally.

HORIZONTAL EQUITY (TAXATION)

The principle that two people with equal levels of utility before a tax should have equal levels of utility after a tax.

VERTICAL EQUITY (TAXATION)

The principle that unequals may be treated unequally, that is, two people with different values of a tax base may legitimately pay different amounts of tax.

As principles guiding tax design, horizontal and vertical equity raise two very important questions. First, in what sense are people to be considered equals, or unequals? In other words, what is the best measure of a person's ability to pay taxes? Both principles require an answer to these questions. Second, just how unequally may unequals be treated? The answer to this question defines society's notion of vertical equity.

The answer to the first question is directly tied to the choice of the tax base. The reason is that any tax is levied by applying a tax rate to a tax base. Two people whose tax bases have the same value are necessarily subjected to the same rate of tax and therefore pay the same tax. They are treated equally. So the tax base implicitly defines the sense in which two people are considered equal, in line with horizontal equity. By the same token, two people whose tax bases have different values are necessarily unequal. So differences in the tax base implicitly define the extent to which people are unequal for the purposes of applying the principle of vertical equity.

Having determined the proper tax base, satisfying the principle of vertical equity relates to the structure of the tax. The two elements of the tax structure that primarily determine just how unequally society intends to treat unequals are (1) the tax rates to be applied to different levels of the tax base and (2) the manner in which portions of the tax base are exempt from taxation.

HORIZONTAL EQUITY: CHOOSING THE TAX BASE Let's turn first to the problem of choosing the tax base. Which tax base best measures a taxpayer's ability to pay? Most economists would answer either income or consumption. Proponents of an income tax argue that income earned during the course of a year is the best measure of a person's utility or economic well-being. Therefore, two people with equal income are equally well off and should pay the same tax. The income subject to tax should include all sources of income because people's well-being depends on how much income they have, not how it was received. Income received from all factors of production, income received from transfer payments, and **capital gains** or losses received from assets should all be part of the tax base. A capital gain on a stock or bond or other asset is the difference

CAPITAL GAIN (ANNUAL)

The difference between the value of an asset at the end of the year and its value at the beginning of the year.

between the value of the asset at the end of the year and its value at the beginning of the year. Income defined broadly in this way is commonly referred to as the **comprehensive tax base** (CTB). Finally, the Internal Revenue Service should not care how people use their incomes, whether they save or consume, or how they save or consume.

COMPREHENSIVE TAX BASE

A broad-based measure of the personal income subject to tax under a personal income tax that includes all income received from factors of production, all transfer payments received, and net capital gains on assets received during the year.

Proponents of a consumption tax argue that consumption is the best measure of utility or well-being because it is the act of consumption that actually yields utility. Furthermore, people's well-being should be judged over their entire lifetimes, not from year to year. The vast majority of people lead self-contained economic lives. They inherit very little wealth at the beginning of their lives and bequeath very little wealth to their heirs when they die. Once people become adults, they make decisions about how to earn income throughout their lives, and they eventually consume virtually all their income before they die. For those few individuals who do bequeath a significant amount of wealth, the bequest can be viewed as a final act of consumption for the purposes of taxation.

When interpreted in the context of individuals' lifetimes, horizontal equity requires that two people with equal utility *over their lifetimes* before tax should have equal utility *over their lifetimes* after tax. Since the act of consumption is the best measure of utility, the pattern of lifetime consumption is the best surrogate measure for lifetime utility. Therefore, lifetime horizontal equity translates into the following proposition for taxation: Two people with the same amount of consumption each year of their lives should pay the same tax each year. This requirement can be met only with a personal consumption tax when taxes are collected annually.

For example, two people with equal consumption each year would pay equal taxes under a personal consumption tax, but not necessarily under a personal income tax. The problem with the income tax is that two people with the same pattern of lifetime consumption might not receive the same amount of income every year. Through saving and borrowing, many different patterns of income can result in the same pattern of consumption. If the two people's incomes do differ and if income is the tax base, then their tax payments would also differ year by year. Lifetime horizontal equity would not be achieved.

A personal consumption tax would be administered much as the personal income tax is now, with taxpayers filing once a year and tax payments withheld from each paycheck. The main difference is that taxpayers would deduct all saving from their income in determining the tax base. Since income can only be consumed or saved, the difference between income and saving is consumption.

The idea of changing the federal personal income tax into a personal consumption tax received a serious hearing in the debates leading up to the Tax Reform Act of 1986. The debate considered more than just the equity implications of switching the tax base. Efficiency and administrative issues were also involved. In the end, both the administration and the Congress decided in favor of retaining the personal income tax.

VERTICAL EQUITY: CHOOSING THE TAX STRUCTURE Exactly how unequally should unequals be treated? This is a fundamental question of end-results equity, and no attempt to answer it has ever come close to gaining widespread acceptance. The best that the United States has been able to do is to recast the question in fairly general terms: Should taxes be progressive, proportional, or regressive? A consensus appears to exist that taxes should be at least mildly progressive.

The terms *progressive, proportional,* and *regressive* refer to the general pattern of tax burdens as income rises. The idea for an income tax is to compute the ratio of income taxes paid to income for each family (or unrelated individuals). The ratio defines the average tax burden (ATB) for each family:

$$ATB = T / Y$$

where T is the tax payment by the family and Y is the family's (comprehensive) income. Now observe what happens to the ATB as family income increases:

PROGRESSIVE TAX

A tax for which the average tax burden increases as the taxpayer's income increases.

PROPORTIONAL TAX

A tax for which the average tax burden remains constant as the taxpayer's income increases.

REGRESSIVE TAX

A tax for which the average tax burden declines as the taxpayer's income increases.

1. The tax is **progressive** if the ATB increases as income increases. Taxpayers not only sacrifice more income as their ability to pay increases; they also sacrifice an ever-increasing proportion of their income.
2. The tax is **proportional** if the ATB remains constant as income increases. Taxpayers sacrifice more in absolute amount as their ability to pay increases, but the proportion of income sacrificed remains constant.
3. The tax is **regressive** is the ATB declines as income increases. Taxpayers may or may not sacrifice more in absolute amount as their ability to pay increases, but the proportion of income they are asked to sacrifice declines.

The terms *progressive* and *regressive* are laden with emotion. A progressive tax is presumably good in that it contributes to society's attempt to redistribute income from rich to poor. It takes a *relatively* larger bite out of the rich. By the same token a regressive tax is presumably bad because it is counter to society's redistributional efforts. The poor sacrifice *relatively* more than do the rich. Similarly, a proportional tax is considered to be distributionally neutral, since rich and poor suffer tax burdens in the same proportion to their income.

VERTICAL EQUITY: THE U.S. TAX SYSTEM The consensus among public-sector economists is that the U.S. tax system is approximately proportional throughout all but the lowest, poverty-level income range, where it is mildly progressive. The proportionality results from the offsetting effects of the five major taxes, some of which are progressive, others regressive, and still others proportional.

The two major federal taxes somewhat offset one another. The federal personal income tax is among the more progressive of the major taxes. It is sharply progressive at the low end because of the personal exemptions and the standard deduction, and then it becomes mildly progressive to nearly proportional as income increases. The progressive effect of the graduated rate schedule is largely offset by the many deductions available to the middle- and high-income taxpayers. State personal income taxes follow the same pattern because they are modeled after the federal tax for the most part. Overall, they are slightly less progressive than is the federal tax. The federal and the state personal income taxes are so large that their low-end progressivity makes the entire U.S. tax system mildly progressive at the lowest income levels.

The Social Security payroll tax, in contrast, is the most regressive of the major taxes. The income cutoff in the tax base earmarked for cash benefits means that taxpayers with very high income pay the same tax as do taxpayers in the $50,000 to $60,000 income range, a very regressive feature. The payroll tax also hits low-income families very hard because it does not exempt any wage income from the tax.

Sales and excise taxes are proportional to mildly regressive. As noted earlier, they are perceived to be highly regressive because, in any one year, low-income families consume a much higher percentage of their incomes than do high-income families. From a lifetime perspective, though, the tax becomes roughly proportional as the vast majority of people consume virtually all the income that they earn over their entire lives.

Economists are divided on the local property tax. The tax used to be viewed as highly regressive because economists thought that landlords could pass the tax on to renters, who have lower incomes than do homeowners. A newer, and emerging, view is that property owners bear most of the burden of the tax. If so, the tax is quite progressive because property is owned disproportionately by the rich. Still a third, and decidedly minority, view holds that the property tax is essentially a payment for local services in line with the benefits received principle. This is so because people seek out the communities that best match their preferences for local services and taxes. Issues of progressivity, proportionality, and regressivity are irrelevant for benefits received taxes because taxpayers get what they pay for. Benefits received taxes are distributionally neutral.

The federal and the state corporation income taxes are generally considered to be progressive. The majority of economists believe that corporate stockholders bear most of the burden of the tax, and income from capital is highly concentrated among the rich.

To summarize, the consensus is that the personal and the corporation income taxes are progressive, the state sales and excise taxes are proportional to mildly regressive, and the Social Security payroll tax is highly regressive. No one knows what to conclude about the local property tax, but this does not matter so much because the property tax is among the smaller of the major taxes. Overall, the mix of progressive, proportional, and regressive taxes makes the U.S. tax system roughly proportional throughout all but the lowest income ranges, where it is slightly progressive.

DEMOCRACY AND THE THEORY OF PUBLIC CHOICE

The political choices that nations make have important economic consequences. The final section of Chapter 24 analyzes the economic consequences of representative democracy, the form of government chosen by the United States and by most of the industrialized capitalist countries.

Chapter 23 discussed the appropriate economic role of the government as a corrector of market failures. The practical question, though, is whether government economic policy can actually hope to realize its potential for correcting market failures. Most economists were fairly confident 20 to 30 years ago. They taught that government policy could help an economy become more efficient and more equitable. Since that time, however, economists have become increasingly skeptical of government intervention.

The skeptics are rallying around an emerging economic view of political behavior known as the **theory of public choice,** whose central idea is that people behave the same way in the political arena as they do in the economic arena. The traditional view holds that people are self-motivated in their economic activities, but public spirited in their political activities. Not so, according to the new view. People do not suddenly change their stripes when they

THEORY OF PUBLIC CHOICE

A theory of government based on the premise that people behave in the same self-interested manner in the political arena as they do in the economic arena.

enter the political arena; they continue to pursue their own self-interests. In politics as in the market, people act to maximize their own utility.

Self-interest is fine in the economic sphere. We have seen how self-interested economic behavior can lead to market transactions that are both efficient and equitable. Public choice theorists are much less sanguine about self-interested political behavior, however, especially in democratic forms of government. They believe that democratic political institutions and procedures can be a major stumbling block to the conduct of effective economic policy when behavior is self-motivated. The theory of public choice helps us understand why democratic forms of government so often encounter difficulties with the conduct of economic policy.

In Chapter 1 we noted that the traditional lines between the social sciences have become increasingly blurred of late. The theory of public choice is a leading example of this trend. A number of economists, led by Nobel laureates Kenneth Arrow and James Buchanan, have applied standard economic principles to political behavior, with fairly striking results. Foremost among them is the conclusion that democratic political institutions and procedures may hinder the quest for economic efficiency and equity.

Economic Efficiency and Democratic Voting Rules

The economic problems with democracy begin with the fact that democratic voting rules are not necessarily consistent with the pursuit of economic efficiency. Democratic voting rules come in many forms, from unanimous consent down to a simple (50 percent) majority. Of all the possible voting rules, only unanimity is fully consistent with economic efficiency.

Government policies clearly promote economic efficiency if they make some people better off without making anyone else worse off. Only unanimity can assure that all such policies, and only those policies, will be adopted. Under unanimous voting, any policy that makes some people better off without making anyone else worse off would pass. Those who stand to gain would vote in favor of the policy. Those who would not be any worse off would presumably abstain from voting. Conversely, any policy that generated losses for some would be blocked by the potential losers. In principle, then, government policy can achieve efficiency under a unanimous voting rule. The electorate would adopt all efficiency-improving policies until such opportunities were exhausted.

Democratic societies never choose unanimity, however, because the costs of obtaining unanimous agreement on a course of action are just too high. Voting by unanimous consent works well only with very small groups. Once the number of voters becomes fairly large, designing policies in which no one loses is virtually impossible. Since potential losers can always defeat a policy under unanimous voting, the unanimity requirement leads to political paralysis. This is why democracies choose less-stringent majority voting rules, such as a simple or a two-thirds majority.

Notice, though, that any voting rule short of unanimity introduces a cost into the political process, the cost of being on the losing side. These costs have not prevented societies from choosing majority voting rules, but majority voting can wreak havoc on economic policy formation under self-motivated behavior.

The economic problems with majority voting rules arise because majority voting is not fully consistent with economic efficiency. Policies that generate both gainers and losers cannot be judged by the efficiency criterion alone, yet such policies can pass under majority voting. This is not necessarily a bad outcome. Virtually all economic policies generate gains and losses, and voters in a democracy have to accept the possibility that they may be on the losing side of a vote. What is troubling, though, is that under majority voting rules voters can accept policies that reduce the overall level of economic well-being and reject policies that just as clearly increase the overall level of economic well-being.

To see these possibilities, suppose that everyone has the same income and is viewed by society as equally deserving, so that distributional considerations are not an issue. Imagine that a vote is taken on a policy in which voters totaling 51 percent of the electorate each receive small benefits and voters totaling 49 percent of the electorate each suffer substantial losses. The policy would pass under a simple majority vote, even though the aggregate losses greatly exceed the aggregate gains. Overall economic well-being has diminished.

Now reverse the situation. Imagine a policy in which voters totaling 51 percent of the electorate each suffer small losses and voters totaling 49 percent of the electorate each receive enormous benefits. The policy would fail a majority vote, even though the aggregate gains greatly exceed the aggregate losses. In this instance, majority voting rules cause voters to miss an opportunity to improve overall economic well-being.

Arrow's Impossibility Theorem

The potential efficiency problems with majority voting rules pale in comparison to a second problem uncovered by Nobel laureate Kenneth Arrow. He showed that majority voting rules might not generate a consistent set of social priorities when people disagree about what those priorities should be. His result, known as **Arrow's Impossibility Theorem,** stands as one of the foremost intellectual achievements of the twentieth century. It was especially disheartening to those who believe that personal freedom is best safeguarded by a democratic form of government. Arrow showed that majority voting procedures can come apart at the seams when social priorities are inconsistent.

ARROW'S IMPOSSIBILITY THEOREM
The proposition that individuals' preferences for particular government policies might not aggregate into a consistent set of social preferences for those policies under democratic voting rules.

We will illustrate Arrow's theorem with a simple example of choosing a policy that affects the distribution of income. Despite its simplicity, our example cuts right to the heart of the For Whom or distribution question, one of the four fundamental questions that any society must answer. The example shows why democracies might not be able to resolve the distribution question. The economic problems with democracy are certainly not limited to the pursuit of efficiency.

SOCIAL INCONSISTENCY Suppose that three individuals, 1, 2, and 3, are considering three different policies for transferring $100 among the three of them. The policies A, B, and C are listed in Table 24.2.

The rows in the table indicate how much each individual receives under each policy. For instance, policy A transfers $50 to individual 1, $20 to individual 2, and $30 to individual 3; policies B and C are similar.

Suppose that the three people vote their own self-interest in line with the theory of public choice, so that their preferences for the three policies depend

TABLE 24.2 **Distribution of $100 Under Three Different Policies**

POLICY	INDIVIDUAL 1	INDIVIDUAL 2	INDIVIDUAL 3
A	$50	$20	$30
B	30	50	20
C	20	30	50

only on the size of the transfer they receive under each policy. Their self-interested preferences are as follows:

- Person 1 prefers A to B, B to C, and A to C.
- Person 2 prefers B to C, C to A, and B to A.
- Person 3 prefers C to A, A to B, and C to B.

Although all three people know exactly what they prefer, the social preferences determined by a majority vote on the three policies are muddled. Two of the three individuals (1 and 3) prefer policy A to policy B. Two of the three (1 and 2) also prefer B to C. Since society prefers A to B and B to C under majority voting, consistency requires that society prefer A to C. Instead, two of the three (2 and 3) prefer C to A. Majority voting cannot determine which is the best policy, given the inconsistency.

The important conclusion to draw from this example is that majority voting cannot be expected to resolve the distribution question when voting behavior is self-interested. Democracies *may* be able to resolve the question if there is a broad consensus on what to do. No social inconsistency arises if everyone has the same preferences. But, as we discussed in Chapter 22, notions about what constitutes a fair distribution of income are likely to breed sharp disagreements. So attempts to reach a political consensus on the distribution question are especially prone to Arrow's social inconsistency problem.

Representative Governments

Our discussion so far relates to direct democracies such as the local town meeting, in which people vote directly on government policies. In fact, all democratic nations have chosen representative forms of government over direct democracies for the simple reason that direct democracies become unwieldy with large numbers of people. Unfortunately, representative forms of government are as vulnerable to inefficiencies and to Arrow's inconsistency problem as direct democracies are. With respect to Arrow's inconsistency problem, the three individuals in our example could have been legislators representing three equal-sized constituencies, with the dollar amounts referring to the amount received by each member of the constituency. None of the results change, so long as the legislators vote in the best interests of their constituencies.

Elected representatives can also vote for inefficient policies and defeat efficient policies. These possibilities are enhanced by two features that come into play with representative governments, special-interest lobbying and logrolling.

SPECIAL-INTEREST LOBBYING AND LOGROLLING Representative government encourages special-interest lobbying because it drastically reduces the number of people voting. Lobbyists can much more easily target their efforts to sway the vote than they can under direct democracy. Special-interest lobbying is made even easier if the legislators engage in logrolling, in which one legislator votes for another member's pet project providing the second member agrees to return the favor. Special-interest groups only have to persuade a handful of legislators to get what they want when a system of logrolling is in place.

Special-interest lobbying generates a political bias in favor of small, well-organized groups with much to gain or lose and against large, poorly organized groups, the members of which stand to gain or lose only a small amount. Since this bias exists regardless of the merits of the positions taken, it can do severe damage to the quest for efficiency. Under the representative form of government, the gainers from a policy do not even have to be in the majority.

A favorite example among economists of the harmful economic effects of lobbying is tariff policy, which we will discuss in detail in Chapter 39. Briefly, a tariff is a tax levied on goods imported into the country. Tariffs protect the investors and the workers in import-competing industries, such as automobiles, that produce products similar to those being imported. By raising the price of imports, tariffs allow these industries to charge higher prices and employ more workers. At the same time, tariffs hurt all consumers by forcing them to pay higher prices for the protected goods.

Study after study reaches the same conclusion regarding tariffs (and other forms of trade restriction): The costs to consumers, in the aggregate, far exceed the benefits to the protected industries. Tariffs reduce the overall efficiency of the economy. Nonetheless, tariffs pass because the protected industries and their workers have much to gain and are easily organized. They have well-heeled special-interest groups in Washington who lobby intensely for the tariffs. In contrast, each consumer loses only a relatively small amount from a tariff, and the millions of individual consumers are much less well represented in Washington. The political cards are stacked against both the consumer and economic efficiency.

To be fair, special-interest lobbyists do perform a useful informational function in a representative system of government. Lobbying helps overcome a nasty political problem that arises in all large democratic societies: Self-interested citizens have little or no incentive to become actively involved in the political process, or even to vote. Learning about issues, conveying preferences to elected officials, and voting are all costly endeavors, in time and effort if nothing else. Unfortunately, the expected benefits of a citizen's time and effort are negligible because one voice or one vote just does not count for very much. Therefore, the standard economic marginal benefit–marginal cost calculation tells self-interested voters not to bother becoming involved with political issues or voting.

Special-interest groups offer citizens a means of conveying their desires to public officials that has some political clout, much as the labor union gives individual workers market power that they would otherwise not have. Whether this informational advantage more than offsets the harm that these groups can do is an open question.

Bureaucrats

The theory of public choice also questions the motives of the bureaucrats who control the various governmental agencies. Bureaucrats are supposed to operate their agencies in the public interest, promoting efficiency and equity. But public choice theorists argue that they might not do so because bureaucrats have plenty of leeway to pursue their own self-interests.

For starters, government agencies often have a virtual monopoly on the services they provide. Only government agencies provide for the nation's defense, or supply water to communities, or build the nation's roadways. The bureaucrats who run these agencies do not have to worry about competing in the marketplace. All they need do is convince the legislature to provide them with funding.

Moreover, the legislators may be easy prey for the bureaucrats because the bureaucrats usually have a decided informational advantage. The provision of public services suffers from the same general principal-agent problem that plagues the insurance industry. In this case the legislature is the principal, and the bureaucrat is the agent. The legislature (the principal) presumably tries to monitor the bureaucrats (the agents) to ensure that they are behaving in the public interest. But legislatures may not be able to monitor the bureaucrats very effectively because only the bureaucrats know for sure what it costs to provide the services of the bureau.

If bureaucrats have personal objectives other than serving the public interest, they may well be able to use their informational advantage for their own personal gain. For example, they may overstate the costs of providing the service. If the legislature gives them sufficient revenues to cover the inflated cost estimates, they and their subordinates can pocket the difference between the revenues and the true costs. Simply overstating the salaries required to retain the top managers would do the trick if legislators do not have much knowledge of the market for managers. The excessive revenues may be used for expensive perquisites such as meals in fancy restaurants, plush offices, vacation jaunts during supposed business trips, and the like.

To give one other example of possible bureaucratic inefficiency, bureau chiefs may obtain some satisfaction from the sheer size of the agencies they run. If so, they can satisfy their desire for a larger agency by overstating the amount of labor required to provide the services. Since the legislature is unlikely to know the actual labor requirements, it may well agree to finance excessive amounts of labor. These are just some of the ways that bureaucrats can waste scarce resources for their own personal gain if they are self-interested rather than public spirited.

The Political Process: A Concluding Assessment

How damaging is the political process to the conduct of economic policy? This is a difficult question to answer. The theory of public choice has uncovered a number of potential problems, and many of its predictions ring true. Democracies do have trouble resolving sharp differences of opinion. Special-interest lobbying is a major industry in Washington, logrolling is commonplace, and we do suffer foolish policies by catering to narrow interests. Stories of outrageous bureaucratic excesses surface from time to time. Yet the evidence is not entirely one-sided. Much political behavior runs counter to the theory of public choice, as the following examples illustrate.

U.S. distributional policy— We know that people disagree sharply about redistributional policy, yet their disagreements have not appeared to generate much social inconsistency about the appropriate policy stance. To the contrary, U.S. redistributional policy has been remarkably stable since the 1930s, when the federal government entered the picture for the first time. We saw in Chapter 22 that the strategy for income support set down in the Social Security Act of 1935, a combination of public insurance and categorical assistance to the poor, remains the foundation of the government's income-support policy to this day.

Special-interest lobbying— Special interest groups do not always have their way with elected officials. The special interest bias in policy making was notably absent in the deregulation of the trucking industry during the late 1970s. Trucking deregulation occurred despite vehement lobbying by the trucking industry and the Teamsters union, and the fact that the benefits of the deregulation to each consumer were minimal. Also, the United States has generally been a champion of free trade despite intense lobbying pressure for trade restrictions.

Civic-minded behavior— There is much evidence of civic-minded behavior. Many citizens do take the trouble to study the issues and cast their votes. Top-level federal bureaucrats often agree to serve the president at great sacrifice to their personal incomes. In truth, many people do appear to change their stripes and become public spirited when they enter the political arena.

Bureaucratic inefficiency— The alleged inefficiencies of bureaucracies are difficult to pin down. If bureaucrats can hide inefficiencies from their legislative overseers, they can also hide them from economic researchers. In any event, the empirical evidence on bureaucratic inefficiency is mixed.

Overall, there can be little doubt that the U.S. economy is more efficient and more equitable because of government intervention. To cite some of the most obvious examples, the market system would hardly be able to provide an adequate level of national defense or the network of roadways that we enjoy. And government income-support programs protect millions of families from slipping into poverty.

At the same time, however, the theory of public choice has introduced a proper note of caution about expecting too much from government policy. Remember, too, that the political difficulties that we have discussed ignore the considerable resource costs of government policy. These costs take two forms, the direct costs of operating the various government programs and the indirect costs of raising tax revenues in the form of administrative costs, taxpayer compliance costs, and efficiency losses.

President Reagan's conservative administration succeeded in driving home to the American public the caution about expecting too much from the government. Reagan laid to rest the old liberal notion, born during Franklin Roosevelt's administration, that the government is a sure-fire panacea for the ills of the marketplace. This is all to the good. Yet Reagan's announced intention to "get the government off our backs" just as surely overstated the case. A market economy cannot operate efficiently and equitably without a large dose of government intervention. The Clinton administration seems determined to sell the public on the potential value of government intervention when appropriately applied.

SUMMARY

The first section of Chapter 24 offered an overview of the principal sources of revenue used by the federal, state, and local governments.

1. The federal government relies primarily on two revenue sources, taxes and debt financing. The personal income tax and the payroll tax earmarked for Social Security are the two most important federal taxes, and by far the largest revenue raisers in the entire U.S. fiscal system.
2. State governments raise revenue from a variety of taxes, with general sales taxes and personal income taxes the most important. Grants-in-aid from the federal government and direct user charges for public services are also important sources of state revenues.
3. Local governments rely on three main revenue sources: local property taxes, federal and state grants-in-aid, and direct user charges for public services.
4. Direct user charges are popular among state and local governments because they are consistent with the benefits received principle of paying for public services. Users pay for the services, and nonusers do not pay, exactly as in free market exchanges. Most people consider this the fairest method of paying for public goods and services.
5. Issuing debt to finance public capital expenditures is appropriate. Issuing debt to finance government operating expenditures is not. The federal government may issue debt to fight wars or overcome a recession.

Unfortunately, the benefits received principle cannot be applied to many important government expenditures—for example, defense, education, many roadways, and redistributional transfer programs. These goods and services must be paid for with general taxes, such as the personal income tax. The second section of the chapter discussed the economic principles relating to the design of general taxes, with emphasis on the personal income tax.

6. The five economic norms applied to general taxes are ease of administration, simplicity, flexibility, efficiency, and equity.
7. Equity in general taxation requires that taxes be levied in accordance with a taxpayer's ability to pay. The two guiding subprinciples within the ability-to-pay principle are (a) horizontal equity—equal treatment of equals; and (b) vertical equity—unequals may be treated unequally.
8. Most economists divide into two camps with respect to what best measures a person's ability to pay taxes, income or consumption. Whichever measure is chosen as the best measure of ability to pay is necessarily the ideal tax base under horizontal and vertical equity. In the deliberations preceding the Tax Reform Act of 1986, the federal government chose income over consumption as the best tax base.
9. Ideally, the income subject to tax should be broad-based and include (a) all income from supplying factors of production; (b) all transfers received, whether public or private; and (c) capital gains. The sum of these three sources of income is called the comprehensive tax base (CTB) and is considered to be the best measure of utility, or ability to pay, by proponents of the income tax.

10. No consensus exists on the question of vertical equity. All one can say is that the United States appears to prefer a mildly progressive tax system, meaning that average tax burdens rise slightly as incomes rise.
11. The U.S. tax system is roughly proportional throughout the entire range of incomes except at the lowest income levels, where it is mildly progressive. The consensus opinion among economists is that the federal and the state personal and corporation income taxes are progressive, the general sales and excise taxes are proportional to mildly regressive, and the Social Security payroll tax is highly regressive. Economists are not sure whether to view the property tax as a benefits received tax or a general tax. If the latter, the emerging view is that it is a progressive tax borne by property owners.

The final section of Chapter 24 discussed the economic pitfalls of democratic political institutions.

12. The theory of public choice argues that people tend to pursue their own self-interests in their political affairs, just as they do in their economic affairs.
13. Majority voting rules are not necessarily consistent with economic efficiency. A majority vote can pass economic policies that reduce economic efficiency and reject policies that would improve economic efficiency.
14. Majority voting rules are also susceptible to Arrow's Impossibility Theorem, which says that a consistent set of social preferences on policy issues may not emerge when citizens disagree on the issues. Redistributional policies are especially prone to social inconsistencies.
15. Representative government is as vulnerable to promoting economic inefficiency as direct democracy is. Special-interest lobbying of elected representatives enhances the possibility of accepting inefficient policies by giving undue political influence to a small minority of voters. At the same time, special-interest lobbying improves economic decision making by giving a collective voice to individual voters. If self-interested voters are forced to act independently, the standard marginal benefit–marginal cost calculation argues against voting at all.
16. The theory of public choice also cautions that any political system is vulnerable to the whims of bureaucrats who run the public agencies. They may care far more for their own personal objectives than for the public's interest in efficiency and equity, and they also have considerable leeway to pursue their own interests. Bureaucrats do not face the usual competitive market pressures that automatically direct private-sector managers toward the public interest. Moreover, they have a decided informational advantage over the legislators who are trying to monitor their behavior. Only the bureaucrats know the true costs of running their agencies.
17. Although the theory of public choice has raised some troubling points, not all the evidence supports the theory. Redistributional policy in the United States has been remarkably consistent since the 1930s. Special-interest lobbyists do not always get their way. Public officials often display public-spirited behavior that appears to run counter to their narrow economic self-interests. Research shows that public agencies are not always inefficient.

KEY TERMS

Arrow's Impossibility Theorem
benefits received principle of taxation
budget deficit
budget surplus
capital gain (annual)
comprehensive tax base
full faith and credit bond
government bond
graduated tax rates
horizontal equity (taxation)
marginal tax rate
progressive tax
proportional tax
regressive tax
revenue bond
theory of public choice
vertical equity (taxation)

QUESTIONS

1. A government had the following expenditures and revenues in 1993 (billions of dollars):

YEAR	EXPENDITURES	TAX RECEIPTS	GRANTS-IN-AID	USER CHARGES
1993	1224.4	886.0	103.2	200.8

   a. Was the government's budget in surplus or deficit in 1993, and by how much?
   b. Was the government adding to its outstanding debt in 1993?
   c. Are these data more likely to apply to a national government or to a state government?
2. What are the five major taxes in the United States, and which governments use them to raise a significant percentage of their tax revenues?
3. a. What does it mean to say that a tax is progressive? Proportional? Regressive?
   b. Of the five major taxes in the United States, select the tax that you think is the most progressive and the tax that you think is the most regressive, and explain your choices.
4. a. Under what conditions might it be appropriate for a government to run a deficit? Why?
   b. Are the recent federal budget deficits justified by any of the conditions you mentioned in part a?
5. Some politicians are proposing that Congress exclude capital gains from taxation under the federal personal income tax.
   a. Is this proposal consistent with the principle of horizontal equity under an income tax?
   b. Would excluding capital gains make the federal income tax more or less progressive?
   c. What arguments can be made for excluding capital gains from taxation?
6. In 1993, Congress raised the highest marginal tax rate under the federal personal income tax from 31 percent to 39.6 percent for taxable incomes above $250,000. What are the equity and efficiency implications of increasing the highest marginal tax rate?
7. a. What is the main assumption about people's behavior that underlies the theory of public choice?
   b. Why does the theory of public choice suggest that the government might not realize its potential to correct market failures? Give a few examples by way of illustration.
8. a. What democratic voting rule is entirely consistent with the goal of economic efficiency? Why is this voting rule not often used?
   b. Why might a simple majority voting rule lead to inefficient government policies?
   c. Why does Arrow's Impossibility Theorem cast doubt on the ability of democratic societies to answer the For Whom or distribution question?
9. a. How might special-interest lobbying undermine the goal of economic efficiency? Give an example.
   b. What useful role does special-interest lobbying play in a representative democracy? Give an example.
10. *Extra credit:* Suppose that Rhonda, Steven, and Theresa use a majority voting rule to decide how to divide $12. They must choose among the options listed below.

	R	S	T
Option 1:	5	4	3
Option 2:	3	5	4
Option 3:	4	3	5

For example, option 1 would give $5 to Rhonda, $4 to Steven, and $3 to Theresa. The voting rules are that two of the options are pitted against each other and then the winner goes up against the remaining option.
Suppose that Steven ends up with the most money. Which of the two options were pitted against each other first?

CASE

A Free Ride to Cross-border Shopping*

The Peace Bridge over the Niagara River connecting Fort Erie, Ontario, Canada with Buffalo, New York, is packed with so many returning Canadian shoppers on weekends that a two-hour wait to clear customs is not unusual. Similar congestion occurs at most of the major border crossings between Canada and the United States. In 1991 Canadians made over 50 million U.S. border crossings, an average of two per person, double the 1986 level.

The border crossings are motivated by Canadians seeking bargains in the United States. Canadian prices for most goods and services are much higher than are the prices for the same items in the United States, sometimes two to three times higher. Even Canadian-made goods are often cheaper in the U.S. stores.

There are many reasons why prices are higher in Canada. One of the more important is that wages are a bigger expense in Canada because the minimum wage is higher in Canada and labor unions are stronger there. The higher wages are a major reason why the cost of doing business in Canada is 20 percent to 30 percent higher than in the U.S., on average. Indeed, the wholesale cost in Canada exceeds the retail cost in the United States for many goods. In addition, a number of government policies serve to raise production costs or prices. Canadian retailers are forced by law to re-label U.S.-made goods in both French and English. Canada has higher import duties on consumer goods than the United States. The tariffs on shoes, for example, make the price of imported shoes twice as high in Canada. Stiff production quotas on dairy and poultry products raise their prices by 60 percent. Extremely high "sin taxes" on gasoline, alcohol, and cigarettes make them two to three times more expensive in Canada. Many Canadians cross the border just to fill up their gas tanks. The 7 percent federal goods and services tax (GST) that went in effect on January 1, 1991 further increased the Canadian-U.S. price differences.

The U.S. price advantage might be less enticing to Canadians if transportation costs to the United States were higher. But 90 percent of Canada's 26.6 million people live within a 90-minute drive of the 3,000–4,000 mile long border.

The price differences are considerably narrowed after Canadians pay taxes and duties on their purchases at Canadian customs. But this is true only if Canadians declare all their purchases at customs, and many items are easily smuggled across the border. The Canadian government has imposed penalties to increase the voluntary declaration of purchases. Customs officials confiscate smuggled cigarettes or alcohol and impose heavy fines on offenders. Fines are also imposed on other undeclared goods, if they are discovered. But Canadian customs agents are too overwhelmed by the volume of traffic at the major border crossings to undertake a careful search of every car crossing back into Canada.

Some price differences would remain even if all the taxes and duties were collected. The much lower distribution costs of stateside factory outlets, discount warehouses, and megastores, coupled with less restrictive U.S. government regulations and lower sales taxes, remain formidable competitive advantages for the U.S. retailers. Moreover, the inconvenience of not being able to shop on Sundays in Canada (it is illegal for stores to be open on Sundays in many communities) would still attract cross-border shoppers, as would the greater variety of goods available in the U.S. stores.

Total spending by cross-border Canadian shoppers reached an estimated $5 billion (U.S. $4.3 billion) in 1991, an average of $100 per trip. Many new stateside shopping facilities have been set up to cater to Canadian shoppers. Bonwit Teller, one of the anchor stores in Buffalo's Galleria Mall, attributed 45 percent of its 1991 sales to Canadian shoppers. Some Canadian merchants are quietly expanding their operations in the United States to serve Canadian shoppers while others are closing down their operations in Canada. Forty percent of the retail space in Windsor, Ontario, Detroit's neighboring city, was vacant by the summer of 1993. One study estimated that Ontario residents spent $2.2 billion in the United States in 1991 and cost the province 14,000 jobs. The businesses and jobs that are lost in Canada are gained on the U.S. side.

Other related businesses have also prospered in the United States, such as hotels and restaurants. Canadians receive a $100 duty-free exemption on U.S. goods brought back to Canada if they stay in the United States for at least 48 hours. U.S. hotels offer special discounts to Canadians to encourage them to stay and claim the exemption, and Canadians have responded to the discounts. The hotel occupancy rate in Buffalo was 18 percent higher than the U.S. national average in 1991, matching occupancy rates in the popular U.S. vacation cities.

Cutting Canada's taxes to stem the flow of cross-border shoppers would not be easy because Canada needs the tax

(continued on next page)

*Provided by K. K. Fung, Memphis State University.

A Free Ride to Cross-border Shopping (continued)

revenues to fund its universal health care system and the many other government services that Canadians enjoy. One of the reasons that the government is so concerned about cross-border shopping is that the shoppers are free riding on the government services by avoiding the federal and provincial sales taxes. Changing government regulations to reduce production costs or prices would arouse fierce opposition from vested interests. Removing the high tariffs, or the diary and poultry production quotas, or the French/English labeling requirement would all be very risky politically.

ECONOMIC ADVISOR'S REPORT

Suppose that the Canadian government hires you to advise them on cross-border shopping. The government officials ask your advice on the following policies that they are considering to reduce cross-border shopping:

a. Impose higher tariffs, or levy special sales taxes, on imported goods;
b. Reduce the number of customs agents at the major crossings to increase the wait time for returning shoppers;
c. Increase the penalties for undeclared goods;
d. Remove the federal GST and replace the lost tax revenues with higher federal personal income taxes.

1. Give your assessment of each policy. In particular, will the policy reduce cross-border shopping? Will it have any other desirable or undesirable effects? Which policy, if any, do you favor?
2. The government officials have noted that many states in the U.S. are relying less on their sales taxes and more on their personal income taxes to raise tax revenues. They ask you how this shift in states' tax revenues will affect cross-border shopping. How would you answer?
3. In general, the government officials wonder how much freedom the Canadian government has to set its own economic and social policies when shoppers can vote with their feet (or cars) and travel to a neighboring country with different policies to avoid paying taxes. What would you say to them? How can the Canadian government increase its freedom to pursue its own economic and social policies?

Sources: "Border Shopping Becomes a Habit," *The Globe and Mail*, Toronto, August 9, 1993, A1 and A4.
"Fear and Clothing in Canada. Surge in Cross-border Shopping Alarms Government," *Chicago Tribune*, May 27, 1991, 1.
"Invasion of the Booty Snatchers," *Business Week*, June 24, 1991, 66–69.
"No End in Sight for Canadians' U.S. Shopping Spree," *The Reuter Business Report*, January 27, 1992.
"Shopping Smugglers May Face Stiff Fines," *The Toronto Star*, June 8, 1991, Al.
"Smugglers Face Stiffer Penalties," *The Toronto Star*, June 11, 1991, Al.
"Think-Tank Blames Sin Taxes, Unions for Cross-border Sales," *The Vancouver Sun*, August 19, 1992, D2.

PART

VII

Introduction to Macroeconomic Theory and Policy

CHAPTER

25

The Macroeconomic Policy Goals I: Long-Run Economic Growth and Full Employment

LEARNING OBJECTIVES

CONCEPTS TO LEARN

- The macroeconomic policy goals
- Full employment
- Cyclical unemployment
- Frictional/search unemployment
- Structural unemployment
- The natural rate of unemployment
- The Rule of 72

CONCEPTS TO RECALL

- Long-run economic growth [3]
- The circular flow of economic activity [4]
- The Laws of Supply and Demand [5, 6, 7]

The United States has been the world's dominant economy in the last half of the twentieth century. In 1960, 40 percent of all the output produced for market worldwide was produced in the United States. As late as 1990, the figure was still impressive—27 percent.

There are some very dark clouds on the horizon, however. The United States has experienced a significant decline in long-run economic growth since 1973. The United States pushed its production possibilities frontier out at an average rate of 3 percent per year throughout the entire twentieth century up to 1974. Since then the growth in potential output has never been as high as 3 percent in any one year, and the average rate of growth over the past 20 years has been closer to 1 percent than to 3 percent.

A two-percentage-point decline in long-run economic growth may not seem like very much, but if the low rate of growth continues, it will eventually have disastrous consequences. Suppose that the U.S. economy grows at slightly more than 1 percent per year throughout the twenty-first century, as it has since 1974. By the end of the century the U.S. economy will be only about one-third as large as it would have been had it returned to its previous growth rate of 3 percent per year. The United States will also surely be a second-rate economic power.

A ROAD MAP FOR MACROECONOMICS

Chapter 25 begins our study of macroeconomics, which looks at the performance of the entire economy. The macroeconomics chapters of the text address the three fundamental questions of macroeconomic analysis:

1. What factors determine the circular flow of economic activity through a nation's product and factor markets, which we described in Chapter 4?

The circular flow behaves very erratically in all the developed market economies, expanding in some years and contracting in others. A far more sobering thought is that the ebbs and flows of the market economies occasionally become extreme and cause tremendous suffering. Unemployment reached 25 percent of the labor force in the United States in 1933, the worst year in the Great Depression of the 1930s. Prices rose 8 trillion percent in Germany in the early 1920s. What causes the circular flow to increase or decrease? How can the extremes of depression and rampant inflation happen, and how can they be avoided? Explaining the behavior of the circular flow of economic activity is the focal point of macroeconomic analysis.

The two remaining questions are policy questions, and they both involve the circular flow of economic activity.

2. How does the circular flow of economic activity relate to the four macroeconomic policy goals that we identified in Chapter 2: long-run economic growth, full employment (low unemployment), price stability (a low rate of inflation), and stability in economic relations with foreign countries (a balance between imports and exports and a stable value of the currency)?

The macroeconomic policy goals are vitally important because they determine the economic well-being of a nation. We want to understand how the performance of the economy affects each one of them.

3. How can the government influence the level and the composition of the circular flow and thereby help society achieve the macroeconomic policy goals?

We noted in Chapter 2 that the United States does not usually attack the policy goals directly by hiring the unemployed in make-work government programs, by using price controls to halt inflation, and so forth. Instead, the federal government tries to achieve the policy goals indirectly by influencing the overall performance of the economy. The two policies that the federal government relies on most are fiscal policy and monetary policy. Fiscal policy is budgetary policy. It refers to changes in the federal government's expenditures and taxes made for the specific purpose of changing the level or the composition of the circular flow. Monetary policy refers to changes in the nation's money supply made for the specific purpose of changing the level or the composition of the circular flow. How can the federal government use its fiscal and monetary policies to achieve the macroeconomic policy goals? This is the central macroeconomic policy question in the United States.

Chapters 25 and 26 begin our study of macroeconomics with a close look at the four macroeconomic policy goals in the context of the U.S. economy. The main purpose of studying macroeconomics is to gain an understanding of how a nation can best achieve these goals. Therefore, we must have a clear idea of what the goals are, what the government is trying to achieve, before analyzing the performance of the U.S. economy.

Chapter 25 discusses the goals of long-run economic growth and full employment. As noted in Chapter 3, these two goals have the greatest impact on the economic health of any nation. Chapter 26 then discusses the remaining goals of price stability and stability in U.S. economic relations with other countries. Achieving these goals is also important to the economic health of a nation, but not nearly as important as long-run economic growth and full employment are.

LONG-RUN ECONOMIC GROWTH

We discussed the fundamental principles associated with long-run economic growth in Chapter 3. You should have a firm understanding of the following four points from Chapter 3 as you begin your study of macroeconomics.

1. Long-run economic growth refers to *persistent increases in the potential of the economy to produce goods and services.* The words to emphasize in the definition are *persistent* and *potential.* Long-run economic growth is an ongoing process. Success or failure in achieving long-run growth is measured not over a period of years, but over decades, or generations, or even centuries. An economy that grows for a few years and then stops has not experienced long-run economic growth. Also, long-run economic growth refers to year-by-year increases in the *potential,* or *maximum, amount* of goods and services that could possibly move through the circular flow of economic activity, as opposed to increases in the *actual amount* of goods and services that move

through the circular flow. We pictured the process of long-run economic growth in Chapter 3 as an ever-expanding production possibilities frontier. The economy may or may not be operating on its frontier in any given year, but the actual performance of the economy is irrelevant in measuring long-run economic growth.

2. The economic constraints on a nation that determine its production possibilities are the quantity and the quality of its resources and the production technologies that are available for turning the resources into goods and services. In order to grow, therefore, a nation must continuously increase the quantity and the quality of its resources and place new, more productive technologies into production. Also, nations are ultimately interested in the growth in output per person rather than the growth in output itself. The amount of goods and services that an economy can deliver to each person, on average, determines a nation's standard of living.
3. Investment is the key to increasing the standard of living. Investment includes both investment in physical capital, such as plant and equipment, and investment in human capital, or education. Investment promotes long-run economic growth in every possible way. Investment in physical capital increases the stock of plant and equipment, which is one of the three primary factors of production. Also, new plant and equipment is usually better, higher-quality plant and equipment. New machines and factories embody the new production technologies that scientists and engineers have developed. Investment in human capital, which includes formal education in school and on-the-job training in businesses, is also essential to the process of long-run economic growth. For growth to continue, an economy needs scientists and engineers who can develop new production technologies, managers who are trained to operate large and complex businesses, and an educated labor force that can adapt to new technologies. In short, investment is the key to improving the productivity of all resources. A nation cannot enjoy an ever-higher standard of living unless its resources are becoming ever more productive over time.
4. The question of how fast an economy will grow lies at the heart of the Now versus the Future question, one of the four basic economic questions that all societies must answer. Business firms can produce only two kinds of final goods and services, investment goods and consumer goods. Therefore, more investment this year to promote economic growth implies less consumption this year. Future generations benefit from the more rapid economic growth made possible by a higher level of investment. Current generations bear the opportunity costs of growth because they are sacrificing consumer goods. They must save a higher percentage of their incomes to provide the funds for investment. Higher saving and higher investment go hand in hand.

Review the discussion of long-run economic growth in Chapter 3 if any of these points are unclear. We will only add to them a sense of the magnitudes involved with long-run economic growth in the United States.

How Fast Can the Economy Grow?

The process of economic growth requires an enormous amount of patience because countries can only push their production possibilities out very slowly over time. Most economists would place the upper limit of the long-run growth in output for the United States at 4 percent per year, and even 4 percent may be a little high. The average annual rate of growth in output in the United States throughout the entire twentieth century has been just a shade below 3 percent. A reasonable long-run growth report card for the United States might be as follows: 3.0–4.0 percent, excellent; 2.5–3.0 percent, good; 2.0–2.5 percent, fair; 2.0 percent or less, poor.

The potential growth in the U.S. standard of living, as measured by the growth in output per person, is even more modest. The growth in output per person is approximately equal to the growth in output minus the growth in population. Therefore, if population is growing at 1 percent per year, the figures on the growth scorecard must each be reduced by 1 percentage point to put them on an output-per-person basis.

The difference between rates of growth in output of 4 percent and 2 percent may not seem like much, but do not be fooled by the small numbers. Countries whose output grows at 4 percent per year will eventually be much better off than will countries whose output grows at 2 percent per year.

THE RULE OF 72 When thinking about rates of growth you should be aware of a handy rule of thumb known as the Rule of 72. The rule indicates how quickly something that grows at a certain annual percentage rate doubles in value. It works as follows. Divide 72 by the annual rate of growth, *g*, expressed as a percentage:

$$R_{72} = 72/g\%$$

The ratio R_{72} gives the number of years it takes for something growing at g percent per year to double in value.

For example, if the output of economy A is growing at 4 percent per year, then

$$R_{72} = 72/4 = 18$$

The output of economy A doubles in value every 18 years. If the output of economy B is growing at 2 percent per year, then

$$R_{72} = 72/2 = 36$$

The output of economy B doubles in value every 36 years.

Suppose that our two hypothetical economies, A and B, were the same size in 1900. Economy A grows at 4 percent per year throughout the twentieth century and beyond, while economy B grows at 2 percent per year throughout the twentieth century and beyond. By 2008, 108 years later, economy A will have doubled its capacity to produce output six times ($6 = 108/18$). In other words, it will be 64 times larger in 2008 than in 1900 ($64 = 2 \cdot 2 \cdot 2 \cdot 2 \cdot 2 \cdot 2$). Economy B will have doubled its capacity to produce output only three times ($3 = 108/36$). It will be eight times larger in 2008 than in 1900 ($8 = 2 \cdot 2 \cdot 2$). Starting from the same point as economy B in 1900, economy A's two-percentage-point growth advantage allows it to be *eight times* larger than economy B by the beginning of the next century ($8 = 64/8$). Small percentage point differences in economic growth eventually make an enormous difference to the economic health of a nation.

The Recent U.S. Growth Report Card

How fast has the United States grown over the past few decades? This question is difficult to answer because long-run economic growth is difficult to measure. Remember that we are interested in the rate of growth of the *potential* or *maximum* output that the economy can produce, not in the actual rate of growth in output. Economists use two methods to estimate the rate of growth in potential output.

One method simply uses the actual rate of growth in output over a long period of time as the measure of long-run economic growth. The assumption is that the rate of growth in actual output approximates the rate of growth in potential output over the very long run. Our statement above that the U.S. economy has grown at a rate just shy of 3 percent per year throughout the twentieth century to 1974 made use of this method. The 3 percent growth rate refers to growth in actual output, not potential output, although the two were assumed to be one and the same over a 74-year period.

A second method attempts to measure long-run economic growth directly by building a simple model of the entire economy and then using the model to estimate what the level of national product (income) would be if the economy were operating on its production possibilities frontier. In other words, how much output could the economy produce if it were efficiently answering the How question, employing all its scarce resources and doing so as efficiently as possible? Changes in the estimated potential output year to year define the annual rate of economic growth.

Robert Gordon of Northwestern University used the second method to estimate the potential output of the U.S. economy every year since 1875. Part A of Table 25.1 records his estimates of long-run economic growth in the United States for each decade since 1950. The second column gives his estimate of the average annual rates of growth in total potential output for each decade; the third column records the average annual rates of growth in the U.S. population for each decade; the fourth column records the average annual rates of growth in potential output per person for each decade. Recall that the rate of growth in potential output per person is the best measure of the increase in a nation's standard of living. Notice that the rate of growth in potential output per person is approximately equal to the difference between the rate of growth in output and the rate of growth in population (within a few hundredths of a percentage point).

Gordon's estimates of potential output could well be inaccurate. No one can say for sure what the potential output of any economy is in any given year. Nonetheless, the estimates of the growth in potential output for the United States in Table 25.1 are the considered opinion of a recognized expert in macroeconomics, and we can safely assume that they are reasonably accurate. Gordon's estimates are also consistent with the pattern of long-run economic growth that most researchers find for the U.S. economy during the past 40 years.

We can see from the table that the rate of long-run economic growth in the United States has been steadily decreasing throughout the post–World War II

TABLE 25.1 Long-Run Economic Growth in the United States

A. AVERAGE ANNUAL RATES OF GROWTH BY DECADE, 1950–89

DECADE	GROWTH IN POTENTIAL OUTPUT %	GROWTH IN POPULATION %	GROWTH IN POTENTIAL OUTPUT PER PERSON %
1950–59	3.73	1.72	1.98
1960–69	3.51	1.27	2.21
1970–79	3.08	1.06	2.00
1980–89	2.36	0.98	1.37

B. AVERAGE ANNUAL RATES OF GROWTH BEFORE AND AFTER 1975

YEARS	GROWTH IN POTENTIAL OUTPUT %	GROWTH IN POPULATION %	GROWTH IN POTENTIAL OUTPUT PER PERSON %
1950–74	3.59	1.43	2.13
1975–90	2.54	1.02	1.50

SOURCE: R. Gordon, *Macroeconomics*, Fifth edition (Glenview IL: Scott, Foresman/Little, Brown, 1989), Appendix A, pp. A1–A7. Council of Economic Advisors, *Economic Report of the President, 1993* (Washington, D.C.: U.S. Government Printing Office, 1993), Table B-2, p. 351, Table B-3, p. 352, Table B-29, p. 381. The data on potential output for 1990 and 1991, in the table and in the text, are from R. Gordon, *Macroeconomics*, sixth edition (New York: Harper Collins, 1993), Appendix A, p. A6.

era. The decline in the rate of growth in the standard of living, as measured by the growth in output per person, was tempered somewhat by a corresponding decline in population growth.

Part B of the table shows that a distinct break in the rate of growth in output occurred in 1974, shortly after the Organization of Petroleum Exporting Counties (OPEC) engineered a fourfold increase in the price of oil. The annual rate of growth in potential output averaged 3.59 percent from 1950 through 1974, but only 2.54 percent since 1974. In fact, Gordon estimates that the rate of growth in potential output was 3 percent or better in *every* year between 1950 and 1974 and never again reached 3 percent in *any* year after 1974. For almost 20 years now the rate of long-run economic growth has been below the overall average rate of growth for the entire twentieth century.

The declining rate of growth is very troubling for the U.S. economy. Even a small decline in the rate of long-run economic growth, if it persists, has enormous implications for a nation's standard of living. For example, if the rate of long-run economic growth were to recover to its 1950–74 level and remain there, the U.S. economy would be 34 times larger 100 years from now than it is today. If, instead, the rate of long-run economic growth were to remain at its post-1974 level, the U.S. economy would be only twelve times larger 100 years from now than it is today. A permanent one-percentage-point decline in the rate of growth in output eventually has a very dramatic impact on the economy.

The first years of the 1990s were not at all encouraging, according to Gordon. He estimates that the growth in potential output fell to 1.02 percent in 1990 and 1991. With population growing at an annual rate of 1.01 percent, the growth in potential output per person was essentially zero.

These figures, and the comparison above of the hypothetical economies growing at 4 percent and 2 percent per year, point out a fundamental principle of macroeconomics: *Small changes in the rate of long-run economic growth have an impact on a nation's standard of living over the long run that dwarfs any other factor affecting the standard of living.* How a society answers the Now versus Future question is vitally important to the economic health of the nation over the long haul. We will look closely throughout the macroeconomics chapters at the factors that determine the levels of saving and investment in the economy. Since saving and investment are the most important determinants of long-run economic growth, they in turn are the single most important determinants of a nation's standard of living in the long run.

Every U.S. president since the mid-1970s has emphasized the need to save and invest more to increase the rate of growth. President Clinton is no exception. He stressed repeatedly during his campaign and while in office the need to "grow the economy," as he put it. The United States can certainly afford to bear the opportunity costs of growth, but one wonders if President Clinton will be any more successful in his quest for higher growth than his predecessors were. Citizens of the United States have apparently not been willing to give up any of their good life today to increase investment in physical capital or education for the benefit of future generations. As we saw in Chapter 3, saving and investment are low in the United States, both absolutely and relative to our major economic competitors such as Japan and Germany.

Actual Versus Potential Growth

One final point to note about economic growth is that an economy can grow faster than its rate of long-run economic growth if it starts from a position well below its production possibilities frontier. Output can grow very rapidly for a short while if producers are hiring workers who were unemployed and using machines that were lying idle. Once the economy reaches the frontier, however, the rate of growth in output year by year is limited by the rate of growth in potential output. For example, OPEC engineered a fourfold increase in the price of crude oil in 1973 that pushed the United States way below its production possibilities frontier in 1974 and 1975. The economy recovered starting in 1976 and moved rapidly back to the frontier. Output grew by 4.9 percent in 1976, 4.7 percent in 1977, and 5.3 percent in 1978. These rates of growth could not continue, however, once the economy reached the production possibilities frontier. In 1979, when the economy was essentially operating on its frontier, the rate of growth in output fell to 2.5 percent. This was approximately equal to Gordon's estimate of the rate of growth in potential output from 1976 to 1979.[1]

FULL EMPLOYMENT

Long-run economic growth is only half the prescription for a healthy economy. A nation must also realize its potential. It must make sure that its resources are fully employed so that the economy remains on or near its production

[1]Council of Economic Advisors, *Economic Report of the President, 1993* (Washington, D.C: U.S. Government Printing Office, 1993), Table B-2, p. 351.

possibilities frontier as the frontier shifts out over time. We turn next to the goal of full employment, concentrating on the full employment of labor.

The Employment Act of 1946 commits the federal government to pursue the goal of full employment. As part of its responsibility, the government goes to great lengths to determine how many people are unemployed, who the unemployed are, and why they have become unemployed.

Measuring the Unemployed

The Bureau of Labor Statistics (BLS), a division of the U.S. Department of Labor, surveys over 60,000 people each month to determine their labor market status. A survey of 60,000 people is large enough to be representative of the entire nation.

The people in the survey can be employed, unemployed, or not in the labor force. The **employed** are those who have worked at least one hour during the survey week. The **unemployed** are those who are actively seeking employment, but who are unable to find a job. In particular, a person is counted as unemployed if he or she (1) has not worked at all during the survey week and (2) is available for work and (3) either has searched for work within the previous four weeks or has been temporarily laid off and is waiting for recall by the employer. An economist would add, for those searching for work, that the search has to be appropriate. People must be seeking jobs consistent with their skills and must be willing to accept the going market wages for those jobs. An out-of-work blue-collar laborer cannot apply for a vacancy on the surgical staff of Columbia Presbyterian Hospital and claim to be unemployed. Similarly, a teen-ager who insists on a wage of $100 an hour to work at McDonald's is not unemployed. The BLS surveyors do not ask whether the unemployed are searching in an appropriate manner, they presume that their search is appropriate.[2]

EMPLOYED

People who have worked for at least one hour during the week of the Bureau of Labor Statistics employment survey.

UNEMPLOYED

Those people who are actively seeking employment, but are unable to find a job.

The **labor force** is the sum of the people, aged 16 and older, who are either employed or unemployed.

LABOR FORCE

All people, aged 16 and older, who are either employed or unemployed.

$$\text{Labor force} = \text{employed} + \text{unemployed}$$

The remaining category of teen-agers and adults in the survey are those who are *not in the labor force.* They are not in the labor force because they are not interested in working at the time of the survey.

The **unemployment rate,** labeled U, is the ratio of the unemployed to the labor force, expressed as a percentage. It is the most widely reported statistic on overall labor market conditions.

UNEMPLOYMENT RATE

The ratio of the unemployed to the labor force, expressed as a percentage.

Based on its surveys, the BLS estimated in 1992 that the U.S. labor force numbered approximately 127 million people, of whom 117.6 million were employed and 9.4 million were unemployed. (These data are for civilian workers; they exclude resident members of the Armed Services, approximately 1.6 million people.) The unemployment rate in 1992 averaged 7.4 percent throughout the year. Notice that, with a labor force of 127 million people, even very small changes in the unemployment rate affect a large number of people. Every one percentage point increase in the unemployment rate—say from 6 percent to 7

[2]For a more detailed description of how the BLS surveys and measures unemployment see J. Norwood, "The Measurement of Unemployment," *American Economic Review* 78, No. 2 (May 1988): 284–288.

TABLE 25.2 Unemployment in the United States

A. THE RATE OF UNEMPLOYMENT SINCE 1980

YEAR	RATE OF UNEMPLOYMENT %
1980	7.1
1981	7.6
1982	9.7
1983	9.6
1984	7.5
1985	7.2
1986	7.0
1987	6.2
1988	5.5
1989	5.3
1990	5.5
1991	6.7
1992	7.4

B. AVERAGE ANNUAL RATE OF UNEMPLOYMENT BY DECADE, 1950–92

DECADE	RATE OF UNEMPLOYMENT %
1950–59	4.5
1960–69	4.7
1970–79	6.2
1980–89	7.3
1990–1992	6.5

C. INCIDENCE OF UNEMPLOYMENT DURING THE 1980s

CATEGORY	AVERAGE ANNUAL RATE OF UNEMPLOYMENT %
All workers	7.3
Males	7.3
Females	7.0
Whites	6.3
Blacks	15.0
Teen-agers (16–19)	18.6
Black teen-agers (16–19)	39.8
Adult white males	6.4

SOURCE: Council of Economic Advisors, *Economic Report of the President, 1993* (Washington, D.C.: U.S. Government Printing Office, 1993), Table B-37, p. 390, Table B-38, p. 391.

percent—represents an additional 1.27 million people who want to work, but do not have a job.[3]

The BLS surveys have been ongoing since 1947. They have revealed a number of facts about unemployment in the United States that you should keep in mind as you think about the problem of unemployment. Table 25.2 presents some data illustrating these facts.

---

[3]*Economic Report of the President, 1993,* Table B-30, p. 382.

THE CYCLICAL NATURE OF UNEMPLOYMENT The unemployment rate cycles inversely with the performance of the economy, rising when the circular flow of economic activity declines and falling when the circular flow increases. Part A of Table 25.2 records the annual unemployment rate during the 1980s. The unemployment rate tracks the performance of the economy very closely. When the economy went into a steep recession in 1982, the unemployment rate rose by two percentage points. As the economy recovered steadily throughout the remainder of the decade, the unemployment rate declined just as steadily, reaching a decade low of 5.3 percent by 1989. The recession starting off the 1990s increased the unemployment rate once again; it stood at 7.3 percent at the end of 1992.[4] The close inverse relationship between the unemployment rate and the performance of the economy has existed throughout the post–World War II era. It is one of the more important macroeconomic features of the U.S. economy.

THE WORSENING UNEMPLOYMENT RATE Unemployment appears to be an ever-worsening problem in the United States, despite the government's commitment to reduce unemployment. Part B of Table 25.2 shows that the average unemployment rate has increased in every full decade since 1950. Moreover, the increases have been quite large. To put the numbers in perspective, suppose that the United States can reduce the unemployment rate from the 1980s average of 7.3 percent to the 1950s average of 4.5 percent. If so, an additional 3.5 million people who are currently unemployed would be able to find jobs.

Many economists have argued that the average unemployment rate will fall substantially during the 1990s for a number of reasons that we will discuss below. The first three years of the 1990s have not been particularly encouraging to that view, however. The unemployment rate increased steadily from 5.2 percent in January of 1990 to 7.3 percent by December of 1992, and averaged 6.5 percent from 1990 to 1992.[5]

THE UNEVEN INCIDENCE OF UNEMPLOYMENT Unemployment does not strike all groups of people evenhandedly. Part C of Table 25.2 compares the average unemployment rates throughout the 1980s by gender, race, and age, relative to the unemployment rate for all workers. The data show that the chances of being unemployed vary tremendously by race and age. The unemployment rate for blacks was nearly 2½ times greater than the unemployment rate for whites was throughout the decade, 15 percent for blacks versus 6.3 percent for whites. Teen-agers also suffer very high unemployment rates. The teen-age unemployment rate for males was almost three times as high throughout the decade as the unemployment rate for adult white males was. The combined disadvantages of race and age are particularly damaging for black teen-agers. Nearly 40 percent of all black teen-agers in the labor force were unemployed during the 1980s.

---

[4]Council of Economic Advisors, *Economic Indicators, March 1993* (Washington, D.C.: U.S. Government Printing Office, 1993), 12.

[5]The unemployment rate for January 1990 is reported in Council of Economic Advisors, *Economic Report of the President, 1991* (Washington, D.C.: U.S. Government Printing Office, 1991), Table B-39, p. 330. The unemployment rate for December 1992 is reported in *Economic Indicators, March 1993*.

The relative disadvantages of blacks and teen-agers have been fairly constant over the past 40 years. The only major change in the incidence of unemployment has been among males and females. The female unemployment rate during the 1980s was slightly below the male unemployment rate. This is a reversal from past decades; the female unemployment rate typically exceeded the male unemployment rate prior to 1980.

UNDEREMPLOYED AND DISCOURAGED WORKERS The unemployment rate may not be an accurate measure of how far society is from the goal of full employment. The Department of Labor attempts on occasion to estimate two other categories of people who are very dissatisfied with their labor market experiences, the underemployed and discouraged workers.

UNDEREMPLOYED

Workers who are counted as employed, but who are working below their full capacities, either part time when they want to work full time or at jobs below their skill levels.

The **underemployed** are workers who are counted as employed, but who are working below their full capacities. They may be working only part time when they want to work full time. Recall that a person need only work one hour during the survey week to be counted as employed. Or they may be working full time at a job below their skill levels, earning wages that are below their full earnings capacity. An example would be a high school teacher who has been let go after 20 years of teaching and is now driving a taxicab to try to make ends meet. A very large number of workers are underemployed in the United States. A 1986 Department of Labor study estimated that 6 million people were underemployed, about the same number of people who were unemployed at the time.

DISCOURAGED WORKERS

Those people who have become so discouraged trying to find an acceptable job that they have dropped out of the labor force.

Discouraged workers are people who have become so discouraged trying to find an acceptable job that they have dropped out of the labor force. A 1987 Department of Labor study estimated that approximately 1 million people were discouraged workers. This estimate is highly problematic, however, because many discouraged workers have only a loose attachment to the labor market. Over half of them had not searched for work within the past year. In any event the problem of underemployment appears to be far more serious than is the problem of discouraged workers in the United States.[6]

Some economists argue that the unemployment rate overstates the nation's employment problems. They point out that many unemployed workers refuse to take available jobs because they consider the jobs "beneath them," with wages that are unacceptably low. Should these people be counted as unemployed? The question is especially important because these same people may be eligible for unemployment insurance financed by working taxpayers. Should taxpayers support these people? These economists would answer no to both questions. They believe that people should be willing to accept underemployment over unemployment. In their view the economy is performing well enough if it generates a job for each person who wants to work. The economy cannot be expected to generate the "perfect" job for each person.

In summary, the unemployment rate as measured by the monthly BLS surveys may not give an entirely accurate picture of overall labor market conditions in the United States. Nonetheless, it is the primary statistic that government officials use when judging how well the economy is performing with respect to the goal of full employment.

---

[6]For a more complete discussion of underemployed and discouraged workers, and references for the Department of Labor Studies, see B. Kaufman, *The Economics of Labor Markets*, second edition (Chicago: The Dryden Press, 1989), 601–603.

Unemployment as a Macroeconomic Policy Problem

Despite the wealth of information on the unemployed, the nature of unemployment as a policy problem remains a slippery concept. We noted earlier that the United States does not attack the problem of unemployment directly by employing anyone who cannot find a job. Instead, the federal government directs its policies at the performance of the economy. The government attempts to reduce unemployment by using its fiscal and monetary policies to increase the circular flow of economic activity and create jobs in the private sector. Therefore, a key policy question is this: How much does the unemployment rate respond to fiscal and monetary policies?

In 1992, 7.4 percent of the labor force were unemployed, nearly 9 million people. Could the government have used fiscal and monetary policies to create decent private-sector jobs for some or all of these people? In trying to answer this question economists have found it useful to divide total unemployment into three distinct analytical categories: cyclical unemployment, frictional and search unemployment, and structural unemployment. Let's take a close look at each category.

Cyclical Unemployment

Cyclical unemployment is the only category of unemployment that is highly responsive to the performance of the economy and therefore to fiscal and monetary policies. The problem of cyclical unemployment arises because labor markets do not always operate according to the Laws of Supply and Demand. Wages tend to be sticky in many labor markets. When supply or demand shifts, wages do not adjust quickly to the new equilibrium level. The wage stickiness results in a pattern of unemployment that rises and falls with the overall performance of the economy.

Figure 25.1 compares what happens to measured unemployment in a competitive labor market [Figure 25.1(a)] versus a labor market with sticky wages [Figure 25.1(b)]. The demand curve for labor, D_L, indicates the amount of labor that firms want to hire at each wage. The supply curve for labor, S_L, indicates the number of people who want to work at each wage. In other words, S_L indicates the size of the labor force at each wage. The initial equilibrium in each graph is given by the labor-wage combination (L_0, W_0), at the intersection of D_L and S_L. Labor in this market is fully employed initially. L_0 people want to work at the equilibrium wage, W_0, and this is exactly the number who are working. The measured unemployment rate is zero.

Suppose that the economy goes into a recession and business falls off. Firms find that they cannot sell as many goods and services as they could before the economy softened. Consequently, they do not need as many workers, and their demand for labor falls from D_L to D_L' in both panels.

Figure 25.1(a) shows what would happen if the labor market were competitive and operated according to the Laws of Supply and Demand. The market quickly seeks a new equilibrium at the intersection of D_L' and S_L. The wage falls from W_0 to W_1, and the level of employment from L_0 to L_1. The labor force now consists of L_1 workers, those who want to work at the new equilibrium wage, W_1. Since L_1 is exactly the number of people who are working, unemployment remains at zero despite the recession.

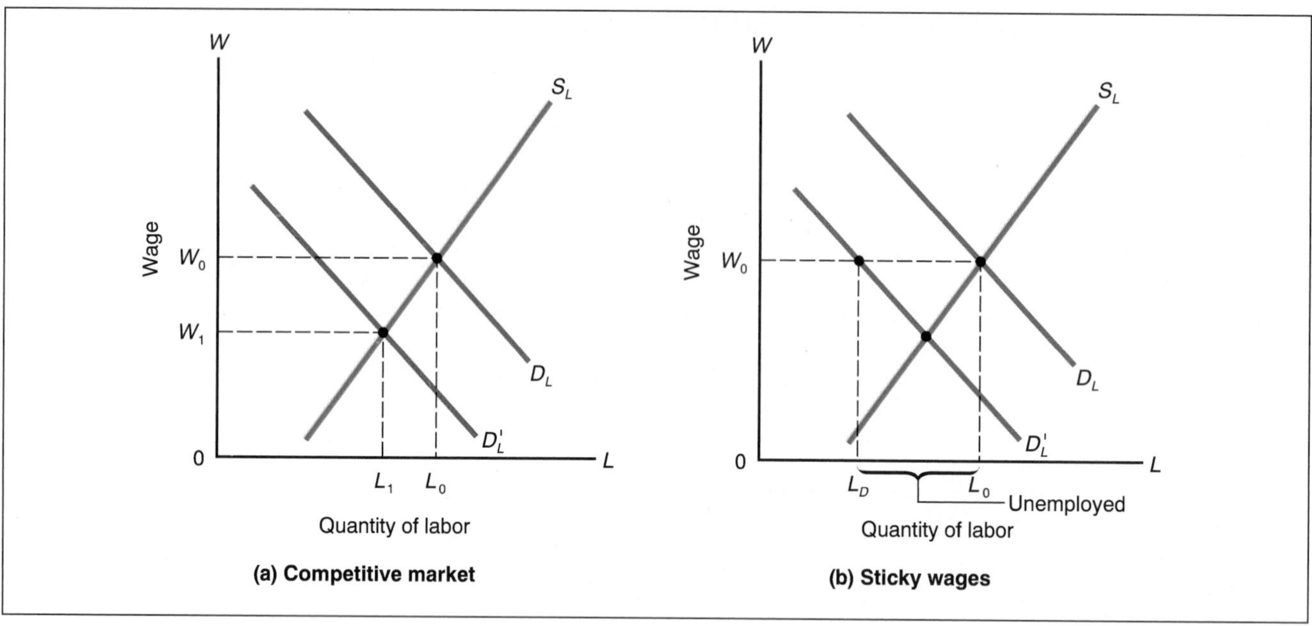

FIGURE 25.1

Recessions, Competitive Labor Markets, and Sticky Wages

The figure compares how a labor market responds to a recession if it is competitive [Figure 25.1(a)] and if wages are sticky [Figure 25.1(b)]. The initial equilibrium is (L_0, W_0) in both graphs, at the intersection of D_L and S_L, and there is no unemployment. Then the economy experiences a recession and the demand for labor decreases to D'_L in each graph. If the labor market is competitive as in Figure 25.1(a), the new equilibrium is (L_1, W_1), at the intersection of D'_L and S_L. The L_1 workers who continue to work receive a lower wage, and $(L_0 - L_1)$ workers drop out of the labor force. No workers are unemployed. If wages are sticky at W_0 as in Figure 25.1(b), the decrease in demand causes an excess supply in the labor market. L_0 workers want to work, but firms are willing to hire only L_D workers. $(L_0 - L_D)$ workers are unemployed, equal to the amount of the excess supply at the sticky wage W_0. Sticky wages give rise to involuntary cyclical unemployment that rises and falls with the performance of the economy.

Workers do suffer because of the recession, but they take their losses in forms other than becoming unemployed. Some workers, $(L_0 - L_1)$ in number, drop out of the labor force; they are willing to work at the old wage, W_0, but not at the new, lower wage, W_1. Other workers, the L_1 people who continue to work, receive a lower wage.

Figure 25.1(b) shows what happens when wages are sticky. Suppose that workers resist a cut in their wages and employers agree to keep the wage at W_0. Now when the recession hits, the quantity of labor demanded by the firms falls to L_D at the **sticky wage,** W_0. The quantity of labor supplied remains the same as before the decline set in; L_0 workers still want to work at the wage W_0. The labor market is in excess supply at W_0 in the amount of $(L_0 - L_D)$. L_0 workers are looking for work, but the firms are willing to hire only L_D of them. The remaining $(L_0 - L_D)$ workers are unemployed. In other words, measured unemployment shows up as excess supply on a supply and demand diagram of a labor market.

When the economy recovers and the demand curve returns to D_L, the firms are once again willing to hire L_0 workers. Unemployment returns to zero. With sticky wages, therefore, the economy experiences **cyclical unemployment** that fluctuates with the state of the economy. Unemployment rises when the economy goes into recession and falls when the economy recovers and expands.

Cyclical unemployment does respond to fiscal and monetary policies. When an economy goes into decline and cyclical unemployment rises, the government can use fiscal and monetary policies to help the economy recover and reduce the level of employment. In terms of our example, proper fiscal and monetary policies can restore the demand for labor to D_L and return the economy to full employment at L_0. Moreover, the government has every incentive to reduce the level of unemployment because cyclical unemployment is involuntary. The $(L_0 - L_D)$ workers who are unemployed in our example want to work at a wage of W_0.

Wage stickiness is an important feature of the U.S. economy. Many wages and salaries do not respond quickly to changing labor market conditions. Twenty percent of all U.S. labor works under a three-year wage contract, which is the standard contract for labor unions in the United States. Not all of these workers are unionized, however; only 14 percent of the U.S. labor force belongs to a labor union. An additional 5 percent of the labor force works under two-year contracts. Some of these multiyear labor contracts contain provisions that adjust wages automatically for changes in inflation year by year, but they do not adjust wages automatically for changing labor market conditions. The vast majority of the remaining 75 percent of the labor force works under one-year contracts.[7] With most wages set for periods of one to three years, the ebbs and flows of the economy produce increases and decreases in the measured unemployment rate as represented by Figure 25.1(b).

WAGE STICKINESS

The existence of impediments that prevent wages from moving to their equilibrium level at the intersection of the supply and demand curves for labor.

CYCLICAL UNEMPLOYMENT

Unemployment that fluctuates with the state of the economy because wages are sticky.

WHY ARE WAGES STICKY? The fact of wage stickiness in U.S. labor markets cannot be denied. What has long puzzled economists is why workers and firms have agreed to fixed-wage contracts over more flexible wage contracts. Why, for instance, do workers prefer to increase the risk of losing their jobs when the economy softens instead of accepting wage cuts so that more of them can keep their jobs? Referring to Figure 25.1, are workers on the whole necessarily better off at the sticky-wage equilibrium, (L_D, W_0), than at the flexible-wage equilibrium, (L_1, W_1)? The answers to these questions are not at all clear.

Sticky wages are hardly a new phenomenon, or peculiar to the United States. The great British economist John Maynard Keynes noticed that wages were sticky in the 1920s and 1930s in England. His observation led him to reject the existing theories of how the macro economy operates, which were all based on competitive labor markets with flexible wages. Keynes developed a new theory of the macro economy based on noncompetitive labor markets and sticky wages that remains one of the most widely embraced macroeconomic theories to this day—and one that we will develop in this text.

CONCERN FOR RELATIVE WAGES Keynes believed that workers resist wage cuts because they want to maintain their relative position in the hierarchy of all wage earners. Their concern for relative wages leads them to prefer a 10 percent increase in the prices of goods and services to a 10 percent cut in their wages, even though each decreases their purchasing power by 10 percent. When prices rise, they know that all workers are affected similarly; when their wages are cut, they have no guarantee that everyone else's wages have also been cut.

THE INSIDER/OUTSIDER THEORY More recent research on wage stickiness has explored a number of other possibilities. One of the more popular theories today is based on the control of decision-making power within unions and corporations. Consider the case of labor unions. The wage policies bargained for by union representatives must be approved by a majority vote of the union members. The older, more experienced members have more votes, and more political clout with the union representatives, than do the younger, less ex-

[7]J. Abraham, "Income Redistribution During a Disinflation," *Journal of Macroeconomics* 9, No. 2 (Spring 1987): 205.

perienced members. Small wonder, then, that the unions bargain for fixed-wage contracts, with layoffs determined by seniority. This is clearly the type of contract that the older, more experienced workers prefer. When a recession comes, they get to keep both their jobs and their incomes; the least experienced members get laid off and bear the entire brunt of the decline.

The same type of political maneuvering may take place among the managers of large corporations. The more experienced managers can secure their jobs and their incomes with a fixed-salary, layoff-by-experience strategy, which places all the risks of the ebbs and flows of the economy on the younger managers.

INSIDER/OUTSIDER THEORY

A theory of wage stickiness that says that the older, more experienced employees, the "insiders," have the decision-making power and use it to place all the risks of a business downturn on the younger, less experienced employees, the "outsiders."

Economists refer to this politically determined wage policy as the **insider/outsider theory of wage setting.** The older, more experienced "insiders" have the decision-making power and use it to place all the risks of a business downturn on the younger, less experienced "outsiders."

EFFICIENCY WAGES Another popular explanation of wage stickiness relates to the long-term relationships that corporations have with many of their employees. Large corporations often make use of internal labor markets, in which they hire people into entry-level positions and then promote employees from within to higher-level positions in the corporation. Internal labor markets arose, in part, because corporations have to train new hires to turn them into productive employees. To the extent the training is specific to the firm, both the employees and the employers have an incentive to maintain their relationship after the training period ends. On the one hand, employees who receive firm-specific training are more productive to the firm that trains them than to any other firm, so they cannot earn as high a wage elsewhere. On the other hand, employers earn a return on their training programs only if the trained employees stay with the firm. If a trained employee leaves, the corporation loses the productivity of the employee and has to bear the costs of hiring and retraining a new employee. The practice of training new hires and promoting from within can lead to long-term employment relationships. Of all males over 40 in the United States 8 percent have worked for only one company.

The large corporations have adopted a number of salary and employment policies that are designed specifically to reduce turnover. For one, they have been willing to err on the high side and pay their experienced employees somewhat larger salaries than necessary in order to keep them. A higher-than-necessary salary policy has the added benefit of improving employee morale over the long haul, so that employees will remain happy and productive and not shirk their duties. These high salaries have been called **efficiency wages** because they are profitable (efficient) from the firms' point of view. The benefits of improved morale and reduced turnover more than offset the costs of paying higher-than-necessary salaries.

EFFICIENCY WAGE

A wage that is higher than necessary to retain the employees, but that firms are willing to pay to improve the morale of the employees so that they will remain happy and productive and not shirk their duties; the wage that maximizes the profits of the firm.

Corporations are also reluctant to cut salaries for fear that morale will suffer and their employees will begin to look elsewhere. Layoffs are much better than an across-the-board cut in salaries for maintaining morale if the corporation has to reduce its labor costs in the face of declining sales. Employees know that business is suffering when layoffs occur because the firm is obviously reducing its production and sales. In contrast, a cut in salaries is more difficult for employees to interpret. The firm may be cutting salaries to reduce costs in response to declining sales. But the firm may also be cutting wages simply to increase profits. A salary cut, then, is likely to breed suspicion and reduce morale. Also, the employees who avoid a layoff when times are bad are happy to have kept their jobs and their high salaries. Their emotional attachment to the corporation becomes stronger, if anything. When faced with a general economic decline, then, corporations would rather lay off some of their employees than cut salaries to reduce costs.

Long-term employment relationships through internal labor markets also foster the insider/outsider strategy of placing the employment and income risks on the least experienced employees. The entry-level employees can most easily be replaced from outside the firm when the economic recovery occurs.

EVIDENCE ON STICKY WAGES Two Princeton economists, Alan Blinder and Don Choi, recently surveyed the personnel directors and employees of 19 manufacturing firms in New Jersey and Pennsylvania to see if the more popular theories of wage stickiness were at all valid. Their survey results confirmed some of the theories. Nearly every employer gave the desire to avoid turnover as a reason for resisting wage cuts. They did not want to bear the costs of hiring and training new workers. Also, fairness in setting wages was very important to both employers and employees, and they agreed on what constituted a fair wage policy. The firms could cut wages only if it were necessary to stay in business or to place wages in line with the wages at comparable firms; cutting wages simply to increase profits was definitely seen as unfair. The personnel directors stressed that management was very reluctant to cut wages because this might be viewed as unfair by the employees. Gaining a reputation for treating employees unfairly is disastrous and must be avoided above all else. The best employees would leave, and the firm would not be able to attract good job applicants. Finally, when offered a choice between price increases and wage cuts that would have the same effect on their purchasing power, the employees overwhelming preferred the price increases, just as Keynes had surmised.[8]

If the attitudes expressed in this small survey are widespread, and one suspects that they are, then U.S. workers will have to live with cyclical unemployment. Firms have to lay off workers to reduce costs when their business falls off if they are not allowed to reduce wages. Sticky wages appear to have become socialized into employer-employee relationships.

THE REASONS FOR UNEMPLOYMENT The cyclical pattern of unemployment is very evident in the official survey data. The BLS surveyors ask the unemployed how they became unemployed. They record the responses in one of four categories: job losers, job leavers, re-entrants, and new entrants. **Job losers** are those who have been laid off or fired by their employers. **Job leavers** are those who have voluntarily quit their jobs and are actively looking for another job. The **re-entrants** are those who were once employed, then dropped out of the labor force, and have now re-entered the labor force. The **new entrants** are those who are seeking employment for the first time; they have never worked before.

Table 25.3 records the percentages of unemployment accounted for by the four categories of unemployment, along with the total unemployment rate, for 1982, 1987, and 1992. The U.S. economy was mired in a deep recession in

JOB LOSERS

Those people who have been laid off or fired by their employers.

JOB LEAVERS

Those people who have voluntarily quit their jobs and are actively looking for other jobs.

RE-ENTRANTS

Those people who were once employed, then dropped out of the labor force, and have now re-entered the labor force.

NEW ENTRANTS

Those people who are seeking employment for the first time, having never worked before.

[8] A. Blinder and D. Choi, "A Shred of Evidence on Theories of Wage Stickiness," *Quarterly Journal of Economics* CV, Issue 4 (November 1990): 1003–1015.

TABLE 25.3 **Reasons for Becoming Unemployed, 1982 and 1987, and 1992**

CATEGORY	PERCENTAGE POINTS OF TOTAL UNEMPLOYMENT RATE		
	1982	**1987**	**1992**
JOB LOSERS	5.7	3.0	4.2
JOB LEAVERS	0.8	0.8	0.8
RE-ENTRANTS	2.2	1.6	1.8
NEW ENTRANTS	1.1	0.8	0.7
TOTAL UNEMPLOYMENT RATE[1]	9.7	6.2	7.4

[1]The numbers in the four categories do not always add to the total unemployment rate because of rounding error.

Source: Council of Economic Advisors, *Ecnomic Report of the President, 1993* (Washington, D.C.: U.S. Government Printing Office, 1993), Table B-39, p. 392.

1982, operating well below its production possibilities frontier. By 1987 the economy had undergone four years of rapid growth and was operating at or near the limits of its production possibilities frontier. The recession of 1990–91 sent the economy well below its frontier once again, where it remained in 1992.

The prospects of finding employment are obviously quite sensitive to the state of the economy. For example, the 3.5-percentage-point difference between the unemployment rates in 1982 and 1987 represents approximately 4 million additional people who were actively seeking employment and were unable to find a job in 1982. Moreover, the data show that the cyclical component of unemployment is highly concentrated among the job losers. They become unemployed against their wishes when the economy suffers, victims of the preference for sticky wages over flexible market clearing wages.

Fortunately, the government can reduce cyclical unemployment with its fiscal and monetary policies. The question that remains, though, is how much of the unemployment rate is accounted for by cyclical unemployment. In particular, how much of the 6.2 percent unemployment rate in 1987 was cyclical unemployment? The majority of economists would answer "Not too much, if any."

The data in Table 25.3 show that the other three categories of unemployment besides job losers are not as sensitive to the state of the economy. Also, job losers still accounted for about half of the unemployed in 1987, when the economy was near its production possibilities frontier. These data suggest that many factors other than the state of the economy determine the measured unemployment rate in the United States. These other factors explain the remaining two categories of unemployment, frictional and search unemployment and structural unemployment. They have very different causes than does cyclical unemployment and are not so responsive to fiscal and monetary policies.

Frictional and Search Unemployment

The concepts of frictional and search unemployment are so closely related that we have chosen to place them in a single category. They both result from imperfect information in labor markets.

A quick glance at the Help Wanted pages of your local newspaper will convince you that most people seeking employment have an enormous variety of options to choose from. There are many different occupations, and the various occupations differ considerably in their working conditions, their skill or educational requirements, and the wages that they offer. Wages may also differ from firm to firm within the same occupation. Matching people with available jobs is not a simple process, given all this variety. At the very least, people need to invest some time and effort to learn about their options. Even so, they may not have very good information about the job opportunities available to them.

Frictional and search unemployment both result from the need to obtain information. Roughly speaking, we can associate frictional unemployment with the job losers and search unemployment with the other three categories of the unemployed.

FRICTIONAL UNEMPLOYMENT Frictional unemployment refers to the unemployment that inevitably exists in an economy as large, diverse, and dynamic as the U.S. economy. New job opportunities are forever being created, and other jobs eliminated, as consumers' tastes change from one set of products to another or as technological advances change the way that the goods and the services are produced. Labor markets remain in a constant state of flux, with workers losing their jobs in some sectors of the economy and being forced to find new jobs in other sectors. These sectoral shifts in the demand for labor occur independently of the overall state of the economy. For example, labor has been steadily shifting out of the manufacturing sector and into the service sector in the United States for the past 20 years, to the point where almost all new employment growth is in the service sector. The relative decline in manufacturing jobs is due primarily to labor-saving technological changes that have drastically reduced the amount of labor required to produce manufactured products. Increased competition from foreign manufacturers has also contributed to the job loss, although it is not nearly so important as labor-saving technological change. The percentage of U.S. national product accounted for by the manufacturing sector has held fairly steady at about 20 percent as the employment opportunities have fallen.

The movement of workers from sector to sector that goes on beneath the surface of the economy is sure to generate some measured unemployment, even if all labor markets are highly competitive and operate according to the Laws of Supply and Demand. The needs to gather information and to relocate act as frictions in the economy that produce the unemployment, which explains why this kind of unemployment is called **frictional unemployment.** Notice that frictional unemployment has nothing to do with sticky wages or with the overall state of the economy. Instead, the amount of frictional unemployment depends on two factors: the amount that the demand for labor shifts from product to product (sector to sector); and how quickly workers can move to new employment opportunities.

FRICTIONAL UNEMPLOYMENT
Unemployment caused by the continuously shifting employment opportunities from sector to sector that go on beneath the surface of the economy; gathering information about job opportunities and relocating take time and act as frictions in the economy that generate unemployment.

The unemployed are concentrated in two categories. One is the job losers who have been let go against their wishes. The other is the job leavers who voluntarily quit their jobs in the contracting sectors to seek out better jobs in the expanding sectors. Many economists would categorize the unemployment that the job leavers experience as search unemployment rather than frictional unemployment. The difference between frictional and search unemployment is somewhat arbitrary, but the distinction between voluntary and involuntary unemployment is important in thinking about unemployment as a policy problem.

SEARCH UNEMPLOYMENT
Unemployment caused by employees who leave their jobs voluntarily and are looking for other jobs, or by re-entrants or new entrants to the labor force who are looking for a job.

SEARCH UNEMPLOYMENT The concept of **search unemployment** rests on the simple idea that we are always trying to improve ourselves in all aspects of our lives. Part of our self-improvement is a continual search for better job opportunities once we decide to enter the labor force.

People who already have jobs are constantly on the lookout for better jobs. Changing jobs is commonplace in the United States; 25 percent of all U.S. workers move to a different industry every 3 years.[9] If job changers quit their jobs before searching for a new job, they are unemployed until they land the new job.

In fact, though, the vast majority of job changers never experience any unemployment. For example, when university professors search for better academic positions, they make contacts with colleagues throughout the profession. They may even apply to several faculties and arrange to give a number of seminars on their current research. But they do not have to give up their current positions to engage in the job search. If they do decide to join another university, they arrange to have their new contract begin the day after their old contract ends, so they are never unemployed. Similarly, managers can pick up the phone and discretely inquire about other job opportunities. They may even hire "headhunter" firms to search for them. Still, the data in Table 25.3 show that nearly 1 million people do quit their jobs before they have found a new position. Job leavers are an important component of the unemployed.

First-time entrants into the labor force and people who re-enter the labor force are also likely to experience some search unemployment. College graduates often engage in extensive searches before accepting their first permanent jobs. If their searches extend beyond graduation, they join the ranks of the unemployed until the searches end. Many teen-agers looking for summer or part-time employment experience short periods of unemployment. Teen-agers are also prone to become job leavers, searching yet again for another job. They stay with one job for less than three months, on average, in part because they are still in school and living at home, and in part because most of the jobs available to them are not very attractive.

Leaving and re-entering the labor force is much more common among women than men, at least among adults. Women spend an average of 31 percent of their potential work years away from work, compared with 3 percent for men. Nearly 70 percent of adult men who drop out of the labor force do so because they have become sick or disabled. Many of the sick and disabled men never return to work. Women, in contrast, tend to move between work at home and work in the marketplace. They most often drop out of the labor force to care for children or assume other household responsibilities. When the children have grown or the home responsibilities have lessened, women quite often return to work either part time or full time. When women do decide to re-enter the labor force, they are very likely to search for a while before accepting employment. In addition to seeking high-paying jobs, they may search

[9]R. Ehrenberg and R. Smith, *Modern Labor Economics: Theory and Public Policy*, fourth edition (New York: Harper Collins, 1991), 360.

for flexible working conditions that allow them to balance the various demands of the household and workplace.[10]

SEARCHING AS PRODUCTIVE ACTIVITY Unemployment that results from voluntary search activity has very different policy implications from those of unemployment that results from being fired or laid off. Searching for better job opportunities is a type of investment in a person's future that is beneficial to both the individual and society alike.

Search unemployment arises because job leavers, labor force re-entrants, and new entrants do not necessarily take the first job available to them. No one wants to be unemployed, but both the individual and society gain from the search activity. The individual gains because searching uncovers valuable information about employment opportunities that leads to a higher-paying job. The higher pay more than compensates for the time spent unemployed. Society gains because searching produces a better match between workers and available jobs. The labor force overall is more productive despite the periods of unemployment while people are searching.

Search unemployment, like frictional unemployment, is not very sensitive to the overall state of the economy. An improving or declining economy pulls both ways on the amount of search activity. For instance, wages tend to increase more rapidly when the economy moves closer to its production possibilities frontier. The increase in wages increases the potential benefit of additional time spent searching. At the same time, however, the opportunity cost of additional time spent searching increases because the wages foregone while searching increase as well. With both the benefit and the cost of additional time spent searching increasing, the time spent searching may increase, decrease, or stay the same. The same argument applies in reverse when the economy is declining.

The data in Table 25.3 suggest that search unemployment does move somewhat with the economy. Unemployment among labor force re-entrants and new entrants was somewhat lower in 1987 than in 1982, while unemployment among re-entrants was somewhat higher in 1992 than in 1987. Even so, there are good reasons to believe that the government cannot affect the amount of search unemployment very much through fiscal and monetary policies. The primary cause of search unemployment is poor information about job opportunities, not the state of the economy. Therefore, efforts to reduce search unemployment have to focus on improving labor market information. A nationwide computerized job bank that helps match workers with jobs would be far more effective in reducing search (and frictional) unemployment than would fiscal and monetary policies.

In addition, many institutional factors within the economy have an important effect on search activity. The two-worker family sharply reduces the cost of searching for the second wage earner. Unemployment insurance, which replaces about half of the average worker's earnings for a period of 26 weeks, also reduces the cost of searching. Congress established the unemployment insurance program during the Great Depression to provide desperately needed

---

[10]The data in this paragraph are from B. Kaufman, *The Economics of Labor Markets*, third edition (Chicago: The Dryden Press, 1991), 336; and B. Shiller, *The Economics of Poverty and Discrimination*, fifth edition (Englewood Cliffs, N.J.: Prentice-Hall, 1989), Chapter 3.

income for people who had lost their jobs. Unemployment insurance is no doubt beneficial; it has prevented many families from falling into poverty while the breadwinner was unemployed. But it does have the unfortunate side effect of increasing the unemployment rate somewhat by reducing the cost of searching. One study estimates that every 10-percentage-point increase in the ratio of unemployment insurance to wages increases the average duration of a spell of unemployment by half a week. This is enough to have a noticeable effect on the measured rate of unemployment because the longer people search, the more likely a BLS surveyor will happen upon them when they are unemployed.[11]

A final point to remember is that search (and frictional) unemployment is not the policy problem that cyclical unemployment is. Search activity is voluntary and productive. It is also very short term. Sixty percent of all spells of unemployment last for a month or less, and much of the short-term unemployment is search (or frictional) unemployment.

Structural Unemployment

STRUCTURAL UNEMPLOYMENT
Unemployment caused by severe and lasting mismatches between people who are looking for work and the jobs that are available to them; the mismatches are typically geographic or skills-related.

Structural unemployment refers to severe and lasting mismatches between the people looking for work and the jobs that are available to them. The mismatches are most often geographic or skills-related.

Geographic mismatches can occur whenever a region is heavily dependent on one industry. Thirty years ago the classic example of structural unemployment was the Appalachian coal miner. Coal mines throughout the Appalachian Mountains had closed down as oil and natural gas had replaced coal as the preferred fuel for generating electricity and heating homes. Appalachia was so heavily dependent on coal that the unemployed miners were unable to find work in other occupations near their homes. The entire region remained chronically depressed for years on end, with unemployment rates much higher than the national average. Job opportunities were plentiful in other parts of the country, but the unemployed miners were understandably reluctant to pack up their families and head elsewhere. Appalachia was their home, after all. It had a culture and a lifestyle all its own. Many families chose to stay, even though the costs of staying were extremely high; they suffered chronic unemployment.

A more recent example of chronic regional unemployment is the state of Michigan with its unemployed automobile workers. For the past 10 to 15 years Michigan's unemployment rate has been at or near the top of the list among all industrial states, a distinction Michigan could do without. The auto workers who lost their jobs to foreign competitors know that job opportunities exist in other states, yet they do not want to leave their homes any more than the Appalachian coal miners did before them. They also know that they cannot duplicate the high wages they received as auto workers no matter where they move, which only increases their reluctance to move.

COMMENT: If the European consortium Airbus, which is heavily subsidized by a number of European governments, outcompetes McDonnell-Douglas and Boeing in international markets, this will cause an increase in structural unemployment in Seattle and St. Louis, where these companies have a major presence. California is also experiencing a sharp increase in structural unemployment with the cutbacks in defense spending.

Chronic skills mismatches most often result from educational failures or technological change or a combination of both. The increasing numbers of dropouts from the central-city high schools throughout the United States are an example of the former. The students who drop out often lack even the most

[11]R. Ehrenberg and R. Smith, *Modern Labor Economics: Theory and Public Policy*, second edition (Glenview, IL: Scott, Foresman, 1985), 617.

basic skills needed for steady employment—the ability to read and follow a set of instructions, write a short memo, do basic arithmetic, or show enough sense of responsibility just to report for work each day. Dr. Blanche Bernstein, the former head of public welfare in New York City, estimated that two-thirds of all teen-age welfare mothers in New York were simply unemployable for these reasons. No business would want to hire them, even if they were willing to work.[12]

Technological change can also lead to structural unemployment by changing the skill requirements of the labor force. A recent study of adult males tried to determine why men's labor force experiences have deteriorated markedly over the past 20 years. In 1970, 3.5 percent of adult men were either unemployed or had dropped out of the labor force. By 1990, before the recent recession hit, the percentage had risen to 5 percent. The study determined that almost all of the increase had occurred among the lowest-wage, lowest-skilled men. Technological change, such as the computer revolution, has reduced the overall demand for unskilled workers. Also, foreign competition in the manufacturing sector reduced the demand for unskilled blue-collar workers. The composition of unemployed men has definitely shifted over the past 20 years toward the unskilled workers.[13]

A new phenomenon that bears watching is a potential employment mismatch based on age. Faced with increasing international competition, many large corporations in the United States realized that they had too many middle managers. The first years of the 1990s witnessed a downsizing of managerial positions that occurred independently of the recession during that period. The downsizing targeted middle-aged managers, who were especially vulnerable on two counts: They had larger salaries than did the younger employees, and getting rid of them opened up the corporate structure to new blood. Many corporations did not simply fire the excess managers. They chose instead to buy them out with early retirement offers that were much more attractive financially than waiting and taking the normal retirement plan. The employees who accept the buyouts may decide after a few years that retiring at age 50 or 55 is too young and try to return to the labor force. If so, they are likely to have difficulty finding employment for the same reasons that they were offered the buyouts in the first place: Firms prefer to hire younger workers. The result would be an increase in structural unemployment on the basis of an age mismatch between job seekers and employers. Time will tell if this turns out to be an important phenomenon in the United States.

Structural unemployment, like search or frictional unemployment, is not very sensitive to the state of the economy. True, firms are more willing to hire and train unskilled (and older) workers when the economy is booming than when the economy is in a recession. Some of the decline in unemployment from 1982 to 1987 reported in Table 25.3 was no doubt due to a slight decline in mismatch, structural unemployment. Nonetheless, the government cannot hope to make a substantial dent in structural unemployment with its fiscal and monetary policies. Reducing structural unemployment requires entirely different strategies, such as relocation subsidies to the regionally unemployed, or

---

[12]B. Bernstein, "Welfare Dependency," in W. Bawden (ed.), *The Social Contract Revisited: Aims and Outcomes of President Reagan's Social Welfare Policy* (Washington, D.C.: Urban Institute Press, 1984), 125–156.

[13]W. Howe, "Labor Market Dynamics and Trends in Male and Female Unemployment," *Monthly Labor Review* 113, No. 11 (November 1990): 3–11.

subsidized job-training programs for the unskilled, or public-service jobs for the long-term unemployed.

The federal government did offer relocation subsidies under the Trade Adjustment Assistance Program, which was instituted in 1974. The subsidies were targeted at employees such as the auto workers whose jobs had been lost to foreign competition. The consensus opinion is that the program was generally ineffective. The unemployed were reluctant to move to other parts of the country, even with the benefit of a government subsidy. The federal government has also supported a variety of job-training programs since the 1960s, either directly or in partnership with private business, as part of its War on Poverty. These programs have been modestly successful. Job training is expensive, though, and the programs reached only a small minority of the structurally unemployed. Finally, as noted in Chapter 2, governments at all levels in the United States have been reluctant to offer public-service jobs to the long-term unemployed simply for the sake of employing them. In short, structural unemployment will remain an important feature of the U.S. economy for the foreseeable future.

Full Employment: The Natural Rate of Unemployment

The federal government has chosen to fight unemployment primarily through fiscal and monetary policies. Because of this, economists do not define the goal of full employment as achieving a zero rate of unemployment. Instead, they define full employment in terms of reaching the natural rate of unemployment, written U_{NR}, or, equivalently, the non-accelerating inflationary rate of unemployment, written U_{NAIR}.

The concept of the natural rate of unemployment relates to the fact that any large market economy will naturally experience some unemployment, whatever the state of the economy. The total rate of unemployment is the sum of cyclical unemployment, frictional and search unemployment, and structural unemployment.

$$U_{\text{total}} = U_{\text{cyclical}} + U_{\text{frictional/search}} + U_{\text{structural}}$$

Of the three components, we saw that only cyclical unemployment is highly responsive to the overall state of the economy and therefore to the government's fiscal and monetary policies. The remaining two components depend more on other inherent features within the economy, such as the amount of misinformation within labor markets, the natural frictions involved with changing jobs, the amount of voluntary job search people undertake, and mismatches between the unemployed and the available jobs. Therefore, the sum of frictional and search unemployment and structural unemployment comprises a **natural rate of unemployment** that cannot be reduced very much with fiscal and monetary policies.

NATURAL RATE OF UNEMPLOYMENT

The sum of frictional and search unemployment and structural unemployment; the rate of unemployment that corresponds to production on the production possibilities frontier and that cannot be reduced very much by fiscal and monetary policies. Also called the *non-accelerating inflationary rate of unemployment.*

$$U_{NR} = U_{\text{frictional/search}} + U_{\text{structural}}$$

The best the federal government can do is drive U_{cyclical} down to zero with its fiscal and monetary policies. Its goal, in other words, is to reduce unemployment to U_{NR}. Setting U_{cyclical} equal to zero, or U_{total} equal to U_{NR}, is a realistic meaning of full employment, given the policy choices of the federal government.

The equivalent concept of U_{NAIR}, the **non-accelerating inflationary rate of unemployment,** brings together the twin goals of full employment and price stability, with reference to the production possibilities frontier. The idea is this. All resources, including labor, are fully employed when the economy is on its production possibilities frontier. Also, we learned in Chapter 3 that a market economy must experience inflation if it tries to live beyond the boundaries of its production possibilities frontier. We will see in Chapter 38 that the inflation actually accelerates if the economy persists in trying to live beyond its means. A 10 percent inflation this year may become a 50 percent inflation next year, a 150 percent inflation the year after that, and then . . . who knows? Inflation can blow sky-high once it begins to accelerate.

NON-ACCELERATING INFLATIONARY RATE OF UNEMPLOYMENT

The minimum that the rate of unemployment can be without starting an ever-accelerating inflationary process; also called the *natural rate of unemployment.*

The federal government clearly wants to avoid starting an accelerating inflation. It wants its fiscal and monetary policies to bring the economy to the production possibilities frontier, but no further. The question, then, is what level of unemployment constitutes being at full employment on the frontier, and the answer is the one just given. The economy has reached the frontier when

$$U_{\text{cyclical}} = 0 \quad \text{and} \quad U_{\text{total}} = U_{\text{frictional/search}} + U_{\text{structural}}$$

Any attempt to reduce the unemployment rate further runs the risk of starting an ever-accelerating inflationary process. Therefore,

$$U_{\text{NAIR}} = U_{\text{frictional/search}} + U_{\text{structural}} = U_{NR}$$

The natural rate of unemployment and the non-accelerating inflationary rate of unemployment are just alternative ways of defining the goal of full employment when it is to be pursued with fiscal and monetary policies.

Economists tend to prefer U_{NAIR} over U_{NR} because there is nothing truly natural about the natural rate of unemployment. It can be reduced by other policies such as cuts in unemployment insurance benefits to reduce the incentive to search or relocation subsidies to reduce geographic mismatches. Nonetheless, we will refer to full employment as U_{NR} in this text simply because U_{NAIR} is such a mouthful to say.

HOW LARGE IS U_{NR}? How large is the natural rate of unemployment in the United States? This is a very important macroeconomic policy question, yet economists are not all in agreement on the answer. Estimates of U_{NR} vary widely, with most falling within the 4 percent to 7 percent range. Within these estimates, two to three percentage points are commonly attributed to structural unemployment, with the remainder attributed to frictional and search unemployment.

A range of three percentage points may not seem like much of a disagreement, but, remember, every percentage point of unemployment represents approximately 1.27 million workers. If the federal government targets its monetary and fiscal policies on a U_{NR} of 7 percent when the true U_{NR} is 4 percent, it may be unnecessarily forcing 3.8 million workers into involuntary cyclical unemployment. Conversely, if the federal government targets on a U_{NR} of 4 percent when the true U_{NR} is 7 percent, it risks starting a rampant inflationary process that may be very costly to stop. Clearly, a lot is riding on the estimate of U_{NR}.

Those economists who estimate a high U_{NR} point to the high-turnover nature of unemployment. Sixty percent of all spells of unemployment last for less than one month. This suggests that a great deal of unemployment is frictional or search unemployment, with a lot of short-term movement between jobs in different sectors of the economy and a lot of movement into and out of the labor force. High turnover also suggests that U_{NR} is quite high, since the rapid turnover occurs independently of the state of the economy.

Those economists who estimate a low U_{NR} look at the same unemployment data and notice a hard core of unemployment lying behind the turnover. Only 2.4 percent of the labor force suffers spells of unemployment that last six months or more, yet these workers account for 45 percent of the total weeks of unemployment experienced by all workers during the course of a year.[14] Also, 45 percent of all spells of unemployment end with the worker becoming discouraged and dropping out of the labor force. If discouraged workers re-enter the labor force, they appear to have suffered two relatively short spells of unemployment when they have actually been out of work for a fairly long period of time. The hard core of longer-term unemployment suggests that a significant percentage of unemployment is either cyclical or structural, not search or frictional. This in turn implies a lower estimate of U_{NR}, since $U_{\text{structural}}$ is unlikely to be more than two or three percentage points.[15]

IS U_{NR} RISING OR FALLING? Another important question is whether U_{NR} is rising or falling, whatever its current level may be. We saw in Table 25.2 (part B) that total unemployment has been rising steadily in the United States over the past 40 years. Whether all the increase is due to an increase in the natural rate of unemployment is unclear. The 1970s and the 1980s each experienced a severe recession that drove cyclical unemployment way up for a few years. Unemployment reached a high of 8.3 percent during the recession of 1974–75 and 9.5 percent during the recession of 1981–82. The 1950s and the 1960s escaped recessions of these magnitudes.[16] Nonetheless, most economists believe that the U_{NR} was also increasing fairly steadily from the 1950s into the 1980s.

Four percent unemployment seemed like a reasonable "full employment" target for fiscal and monetary policies in the 1950s. In 1971 President Nixon's Council of Economic Advisers raised the full employment target to 5 percent. In 1981 President Reagan's Council of Economic Advisers raised the target once again to 6.5 percent. Economists may have disagreed with the numbers chosen for the U_{NR} by the president's advisers, but nearly everyone agreed that the U_{NR} was increasing during this period. There is less agreement on whether the U_{NR} is now rising, falling, or leveling off.

---

[14]The two sets of data are not inconsistent with one another, as the following simple example indicates. Suppose that nine workers experience 1 week of unemployment and one worker experiences 11 weeks of unemployment. Most spells of unemployment are short term, yet one worker experiences more than half of the 20 total weeks of unemployment. This is roughly the pattern of unemployment that we see in the United States.

[15]For a more complete discussion of the debate on the nature of unemployment see Kaufman, *Economics of Labor Markets*, 622–629.

[16]*Economic Report of the President, 1993*, Table B-37, p. 390.

Those economists who believe that U_{NR} is now falling point to a decline in the high-unemployment teen-age population and the more stable employment pattern of adult women, which has lowered their unemployment rate below that of adult men. Another factor arguing for a declining U_{NR} is the recent decrease in government transfer payments that support labor market searching, such as unemployment insurance and public assistance. Unemployment insurance benefits are now subject to federal income tax, and cash payments under public assistance programs have fallen sharply in real terms over the past ten years. They have not kept pace with the rate of inflation. These changes raise the costs of searching and reduce search unemployment.

The principal factors arguing for a steady or even a rising U_{NR} are the rapid pace of technological change and the increasing internationalization of the economy, both of which have contributed to the decline in low-skilled manufacturing jobs and raised the unemployment rate of adult males. Another possible factor increasing U_{NR} is the downsizing of managerial staffing in large corporations which, as noted above, may lead to an age-based increase in structural unemployment.

The net effect of these various factors on the U_{NR} is unclear. Economists are as divided on the trend in U_{NR} as they are on the size of U_{NR}.[17]

The Psychological Effects of Unemployment

The economic effects of unemployment on families and individuals are clear enough. Unemployment is one of the two main events that cause families to fall into poverty in the United States (along with separations of husbands and wives). What about the psychological effects of unemployment: Do spells of unemployment exact a large emotional toll as well?

Psychologists became extremely interested in the effects of unemployment on mental health during the Great Depression of the 1930s. The first systematic psychological study of unemployment followed a group of people who worked in a flax factory in Marienthal, Austria. The workers became unemployed when the factory closed in 1933. Since the factory was the main source of employment in Marienthal, most of the workers remained unemployed for a long time.

The Marienthal study spawned nearly 100 other psychological studies of unemployment during the Great Depression, mostly in the United States and Europe. The Great Depression studies generally uncovered a pattern of deteriorating mental health following unemployment that proceeded in a series of three stages. Workers initially reacted with shock to their unemployment. Once the shock wore off, they moved into a period of alternating optimism and pessimism. This second stage finally gave way to a sense of fatalism and resignation as the unemployment persisted. The psychologists attributed the deterioration of the workers' mental health to the loss of time structure and regular, habitual activity in their lives, which undermined their sense of purpose. Another important contributing factor was the reduction in social contacts following unemployment, which led to a loss of stature and identity. The Great

[17]For further discussion of the factors affecting U_{NR} see R. Krashevski, "What Is So Natural About High Unemployment?," *American Economic Review* 78, No. 2 (May 1988): 289–293; and Howe, "Labor Market Dynamics," 3–11.

Depression studies generally corroborated Freud's view that steady employment is a person's strongest tie to reality among people in the labor force.

Studies of the psychology of unemployment have continued to proliferate to this day. Psychologist Norman Feather undertook an exhaustive review of all the psychological research on unemployment in the 50-year period from the Great Depression to the mid-1980s.[18] Feather believes that two general conclusions have emerged from all the research, whatever else the individual studies may show: (1) Unemployment has a larger effect on mental health the greater the financial strain on the individual or family, and (2) unemployment acts primarily as a catalyst in the process of deteriorating mental health.

The relationship between financial strain and mental health explains why unemployment typically causes more psychological and emotional distress among middle-aged men than among teen-agers. The unemployed men are usually the breadwinners of the family, whereas unemployed teen-agers are often still attached financially to their families. Psychologists also see the relationship between financial strain and mental health as a powerful argument for unemployment insurance programs. Unemployment insurance provides both good financial insurance *and* good emotional insurance for the nation's labor force.

Unemployment is a psychological catalyst in the sense that it intensifies whatever psychological and emotional problems already exist when the unemployment occurs. There is very little evidence that emotionally healthy individuals suffer any lasting psychological effects from unemployment. When psychological stress is present, however, unemployment increases the stress by removing the structure in people's lives and threatening their sense of purpose. This finding is generally consistent with the earlier psychological studies during the Great Depression, with one important exception. The more recent research has not found the deterioration-by-stages pattern that was so prominent in the Great Depression studies.

No other general conclusions have emerged from the research as strongly as these two, according to Feather. The main reason why not is that psychologists have not been able to agree on the appropriate model for studying the effects of unemployment on mental health. The relationship between unemployment and mental health is obviously a varied and complex problem. Feather conjectures that psychological theory may not yet be developed enough to reach a general understanding of the emotional consequences of unemployment.

SUMMARY

The first section of Chapter 25 posed the three fundamental questions of macroeconomics.

1. What factors determine the circular flow of economic activity?
2. How does the circular flow of economic activity relate to the four macroeconomic policy goals that we identified in Chapter 2: long-run economic growth, full employment (low unemployment), price stability (a low rate of inflation), and stability in economic relations with foreign countries (a balance between imports and exports and a stable value of the currency)?

[18]N. Feather, *The Psychological Impact of Unemployment* (New York: Springer-Verlag, 1989). See, especially, his summary comments in Chapter 10, pp. 244–253. Feather discusses the Great Depression studies in Chapter 2, pp. 10–19.

3. How can the government influence the level and the composition of the circular flow with its fiscal and monetary policies and thereby help society achieve the macroeconomic policy goals?

The second section of the chapter discussed the macroeconomic goal of long-run economic growth.

4. Long-run economic growth refers to lasting increases in the potential of the economy to produce goods and services. It involves pushing the production possibilities frontier out continuously over time.
5. Investment is the key to long-run economic growth, both investment in physical capital and investment in human capital (education). Investment changes the quantity and the quality of the nation's resources and embodies new production technologies, all of which help promote long-run economic growth.
6. Countries must be patient when pursuing long-run growth. The outer limits of growth in the United States are on the order of 4 percent per year.
7. Long-run economic growth is the most important factor in determining the overall economic health of a nation over the long haul. Even one-percentage-point differences in the rate of growth can have an enormous effect on a nation's standard of living in the long run.

The final section of Chapter 25 discussed the goal of full employment/low unemployment.

8. People are unemployed if they are actively seeking employment, but are unable to find a job, or if they have been temporarily laid off and are waiting to be recalled.
9. The average rate of unemployment has increased every decade in the United States since 1950. Also, the incidence of unemployment varies considerably by race and age. Blacks have much higher unemployment rates than do whites, and teen-agers have much higher unemployment rates than do adults.
10. Economists distinguish three types of unemployment for the purposes of analysis: cyclical unemployment, frictional and search unemployment, and structural unemployment.
11. Cyclical unemployment is highly sensitive to the ebbs and flows of the economy and is therefore affected by fiscal and monetary policies. It exists because wages are sticky; workers and employers have settled on a sticky-wage policy with layoffs and recalls rather than a flexible-wage policy that would preserve workers' jobs when the economy goes into a recession. We considered three popular explanations why wages may be sticky: (a) Workers resist wage cuts because they want to preserve their position in the hierarchy of wages, (b) according to the insider/outsider theory, experienced workers prefer layoffs and rehires because the newer workers bear the burden of this system, and (c) employers with internal labor markets pay high wages and resist wage cuts to preserve worker morale and reduce costly turnover. Cyclical unemployment is concentrated among job losers.
12. Frictional unemployment and search unemployment are based on misinformation. Frictional unemployment refers to the unemployment resulting from the natural frictions of the economy as new jobs are forever being created and other jobs destroyed. Workers need time to discover the new job opportunities. Search unemployment is concentrated among the job leavers, re-entrants, and new entrants who search for the best job oppor-

tunity before accepting a job. Searching is voluntary and rational behavior for the individual. Some search unemployment is also desirable for society since it creates better matches between employer and employee.

13. Structural unemployment refers to severe mismatches between the unemployed and the jobs that are available. The most common mismatches are skills mismatches or geographic mismatches. Neither frictional/search unemployment nor structural unemployment is as sensitive to the performance of the economy as cyclical unemployment is.
14. The natural, or non-accelerating inflationary, rate of unemployment is the sum of frictional/search unemployment plus structural unemployment. It is the level of unemployment that exists when the economy is on its production possibilities frontier. Cyclical unemployment is zero on the frontier. The best that fiscal and monetary policies can hope to do is to reduce total unemployment to the natural rate of unemployment.
15. Unemployment has psychological costs as well as economic costs. Psychological studies of unemployment have shown that unemployment causes more emotional distress the more financial strain it puts on the family or the individual. Unemployment also intensifies whatever emotional problems are present at the time the unemployment occurs.

KEY TERMS

cyclical unemployment
discouraged workers
efficiency wage
employed
frictional unemployment
insider/outsider theory
labor force
natural rate of unemployment
non-accelerating inflationary rate of unemployment
search unemployment
structural unemployment
underemployed
unemployed
unemployment rate
wage stickiness

QUESTIONS

1. a. What are the four main macroeconomic policy goals in the United States?
   b. Does the federal government try to achieve the goals directly for the most part?
   c. Briefly describe the two main policies that the federal government uses to try to achieve the four macroeconomic policy goals.
2. What is long-run economic growth? Would you expect the following to promote long-run economic growth?
   a. Firms invest heavily in research and development.
   b. Firms invest heavily in advertising to increase sales.
   c. The government establishes five new public universities.
3. Do you agree or disagree with the following statement? The decrease in long-run economic growth in the United States from an average of about 3 percent per year before 1973 to an average of about 1 percent per year since 1973 is too small a decrease to worry about.
4. a. How does the Bureau of Labor Statistics define and attempt to measure unemployment?
   b. What are the limitations of the rate of unemployment as an indication of the nation's employment problems?
5. a. What are the three categories of unemployment that economists have defined to help them analyze and understand the problem of unemployment?
   b. What government policies are needed to reduce each category of unemployment?
   c. Which of the categories of unemployment does each of the following headlines describe?
      (i) "College graduates are having difficulty finding that first job"
      (ii) "Auto sales depressed, 2000 autoworkers laid off"
      (iii) "High school drop-outs seen as unfit for today's computerized workplace"
      (iv) "The Home Shopping Network may replace the sales clerk by the year 2010"
6. a. What is wage stickiness, and why is it important to the problem of unemployment?
   b. What are some of the popular theories economists have developed to explain sticky wages? Which of these theories do you find most persuasive? Which least persuasive?
7. What are the advantages and the disadvantages of unem-

ployment insurance?

8. Do you agree or disagree with the following statement? Macroeconomic policy cannot be viewed as successful until we have achieved zero percent unemployment.
9. a. What is the natural rate of unemployment?
   b. Will the following policies undertaken by the government serve to reduce the natural rate of unemployment?
      (i) Tax relief for firms that relocate to economically depressed, high-unemployment areas of the country
      (ii) Government training programs for unskilled workers
      (iii) Fiscal and monetary policies designed to restore the economy to full employment.
10. a. What factors may be causing the natural rate of unemployment to increase during the 1990s?
    b. What factors may be causing the natural rate of unemployment to decrease during the 1990s?

CHAPTER

26

The Macroeconomic Policy Goals II: Price Stability and Stable International Economic Relations

LEARNING OBJECTIVES

CONCEPTS TO LEARN

Inflation
Consumer price index
Hyperinflation
Fisher equation
Imports and exports
The balance of trade
Dollar depreciation/appreciation

CONCEPTS TO RECALL

The circular flow of economic activity [4]
The Laws of Supply and Demand [5, 6, 7]

Inflation is Public Enemy #1 in the United States according to the pollsters. The Gallup organization has asked the American public every year since 1935 to name the most pressing problem—military, social, economic, or otherwise—facing the country. The answer most often given during peacetime is inflation.

The federal government has certainly responded to the public's concern about inflation. The Employment Act of 1946 commits the administration and Congress to the goal of price stability, and the government goes to great lengths to measure and track the rate of inflation in the United States. The goal of price stability remains an elusive target, however. Prices have risen every year but two since the end of World War II (1949 and 1954).

The internationalization of the U.S. economy has been another major economic story of the past 25 years, and it will continue to be for the foreseeable future. From the end of World War II until the early 1960s the United States enjoyed a truly dominant position in the world economy, one without any important challengers. Since then, of course, Japan, Western Europe, and many other countries have risen up to become serious competitors to U.S. producers, both here and abroad. The overriding concern now among the American people is whether the United States can compete effectively in world markets. People worry about the loss of manufacturing jobs to foreign imports and about foreign ownership of U.S. businesses.

The Employment Act of 1946 does not commit the federal government to any particular international economic goals, nor has any subsequent legislation. Nonetheless, the unwritten "rules of the game" in international trade commit all nations to maintaining a reasonable balance between their imports and their exports and a stable exchange value of their currencies relative to other currencies. The United States has not always played by the rules, even though every administration and every Congress pays lip service to them. The United States' imports have greatly exceeded its exports every year since 1984. Also, the dollar has moved up and down considerably year by year against the Japanese yen, the German mark, the British pound, and the other major currencies ever since 1973, when the major currencies were set free from government support to seek their own levels in the foreign exchange markets.

Chapter 26 discusses the two remaining macroeconomic policy goals, price stability and stability in our economic relations with foreign countries.

PRICE STABILITY/LOW INFLATION

INFLATION

Continuing increases in the level of prices generally, usually expressed as a percentage rate of increase.

Inflation refers to a process of *continuing increases in the level of prices generally*, with particular emphasis on the words *generally* and *continuing*.

To say that prices *generally* are increasing means that the prices of a large number of goods and services must be increasing simultaneously to constitute an inflation from a macroeconomic perspective. For example, the price of medical care has been increasing rapidly every year for the past 20 years and more. If this were the only price that was rising, we could speak of an inflation in the price of medical care. But the United States would not be experiencing an

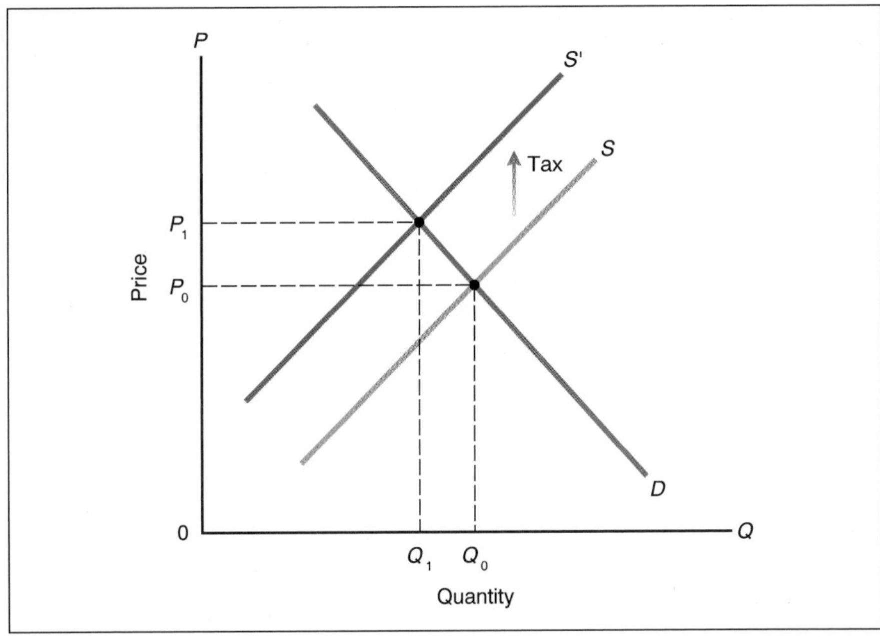

FIGURE 26.1

Taxes and Inflation

The price of some product is initially P_0 at the intersection of D and S, and there is no inflation. A tax on the product shifts the supply curve up by the amount of the tax from S to S'. The price of the product increases until it reaches its new equilibrium level P_1, at the intersection of D and S', at which point the price stops increasing. A tax causes a one time shift in the supply curve that leads to a permanently higher price level, but not to an inflation.

inflation as the term is properly understood. Medical care would just become ever more expensive relative to other goods and services year after year. In fact, though, most other prices have been rising as well, so that the rising price of medical care is contributing to the general price inflation in the United States.

To say that the price increases must be *continuing* indicates that inflation is an ongoing process, not just a temporary, one-time increase in prices. You must take care to distinguish between higher price *levels* and *continuous increases* in price levels when thinking about the problem of inflation. Figure 26.1 illustrates the distinction. Think of the figure as picturing the market for any representative good or service. The market is originally in equilibrium at the intersection of the market demand and supply curves, D and S. The equilibrium quantity and price are Q_0 and P_0, respectively.

We saw when studying the Laws of Supply and Demand that the price of a product tends to increase whenever demand increases or supply decreases. Suppose that the supply decreases because the government levies a tax on the product. The tax shifts the supply curve up by the amount of the tax, from S to S' in the figure. The new equilibrium is (Q_1, P_1), at the intersection of D and S'.

Tax increases are often considered inflationary because they drive up prices. The figure shows, however, that a tax increase does not cause an inflationary process in and of itself. The price increases for awhile after the government levies the tax as the market moves to its new equilibrium. But the increase in price would not be considered an inflation because the period when the price is increasing is only temporary. The price stops rising once it reaches P_1, the new equilibrium price level. There was no inflation in the original equilibrium, and there is no inflation at the new equilibrium.

True, the price is higher in the new equilibrium, and it will not come back down. A tax increase does drive up the price. But a higher price *level* does not constitute an inflation. Prices must be *continuously increasing* to term the process an inflation. In other words, something has to shift up the supply curve and/or the demand curve continuously over time to cause an inflation, so that prices are continuously rising. A tax increase does not do this. It causes only a one-time shift in the supply curve and therefore only a one-time increase in the price level.

One final point about the definition of inflation is worth noting. Inflation is expressed as the percentage rate of change in a price over a period of time, most often a year. The annual rate of inflation is the ratio of the change in price during the year to the price at the beginning of the year, multiplied by 100 to convert the ratio into a percentage.

$$\text{Annual rate of inflation} = [(P_{\text{end of year}} - P_{\text{end of previous year}})/P_{\text{end of previous year}}] \cdot 100$$

For example, suppose that the price of a gallon of milk was \$2.00 at the end of 1992 and \$2.20 at the end of 1993. Then the annual rate of inflation in the price of milk during 1993 was 10 percent:

$$\text{Annual rate of inflation}_{\text{milk}} = [(\$2.20 - \$2.00)/\$2.00] \cdot 100 = (\$.20/\$2.00) \cdot 100 = 10\%$$

The standard shorthand expression for the rate of inflation is $\Delta P/P$. Δ is the Greek symbol for "change," so that $\Delta P/P$ is the change in price divided by the price, or the rate of change in the price. The P in the denominator refers to the price level at the end of the previous period (1992 in our milk example). The term $\Delta P/P$ is understood to be the percentage rate of change in the price, even though the final multiplication by 100 is usually left out of the expression.

Computing a Price Index and an Overall Rate of Inflation

The federal government reported that the rate of inflation in the United States during 1992 was 2.9 percent. Calculating a single number to represent "the" overall rate of inflation requires some explanation because the prices of individual goods and services do not all rise at the same rate. In 1992 many prices rose by more than 2.9 percent, many prices rose by less than 2.9 percent, and the prices of some products even fell (personal computers and floppy discs, for example). The reported 2.9 percent rate of inflation is an average of many different price changes. The question, then, is this: What is a sensible way to compute an average overall rate of inflation from the individual rates of inflation of many different products?

THE REFERENCE MARKET BASKET The standard method of computing an overall rate of inflation, and the one used by the federal government, is a two-step process. The government begins by defining a market basket of goods and services that is purchased by a typical member of some reference group. The reference group may consist of households (consumers), or business firms, or governments, or even all the purchasers of final goods and services in the entire economy. Next, the government determines how much the market basket of goods and services costs each month and converts the monthly costs into a price index. The annual rate of inflation is then calculated as the percentage increase in the cost of the market basket from year to year or, equivalently, the percentage increase in the price index from year to year. Each reference group has its own price index and rate of inflation, based on the relevant market basket for the group.

The most closely watched price index is the **consumer price index,** the CPI, which is based on a market basket of consumer goods and services purchased by the typical household. The rate of inflation refers to the annual percentage change in the CPI unless otherwise qualified, an example being the 2.9 percent rate of inflation for 1992 reported above. The CPI has very important economic consequences. It is used as the basis for adjusting wages in labor union contracts that contain annual *cost-of-living-adjustment clauses* (COLA clauses) and for adjusting government transfer payments, such as Social Security retirement benefits and public assistance. The adjustments are designed to protect workers and transfer recipients from increases in the cost of living caused by inflation. Some private pensions are also adjusted annually on the basis of the CPI.

CONSUMER PRICE INDEX
A price index based on a market basket of consumer goods and services purchased by the typical household.

CONSTRUCTING A PRICE INDEX We can illustrate how to construct the CPI and the corresponding rate of inflation with a simple market basket consisting of two goods. The procedures for constructing the CPI, or any other price index, are the same no matter how many goods the market basket contains. Therefore, assume for the purposes of our example that every household purchases just two goods, a single kind of food and a single type of clothing.

Suppose that the typical household buys 10 units of the food and 20 units of the clothing during the year. Therefore, the market basket for consumers that we will use to compute our hypothetical CPI and the rate of inflation consists of 10 units of food and 20 units of clothing.

Let's assume that the price of the food was \$12 per unit and the price of the clothing was \$4 per unit on December 31, 1987. Therefore, the total cost of the market basket at the end of 1987 was \$200:

$$\text{Cost of market basket}_{1987} = (\$12 \cdot 10) + (\$4 \cdot 20) = \$120 + \$80 = \$200$$

Suppose that the price of the food had risen to \$18 and the price of the clothing had risen to \$5 by December 31, 1988. Therefore, the total cost of the market basket at the end of 1988 is \$280:

$$\text{Cost of market basket}_{1988} = (\$18 \cdot 10) + (\$5 \cdot 20) = \$180 + \$100 = \$280$$

The rate of inflation during 1988 is the percentage increase in the cost of the market basket from December 31, 1987, to December 31, 1988:

$$\begin{aligned}\text{Rate of inflation}_{1988} &= [(\$280 - \$200)/\$200] \cdot 100 \\ &= (\$80/\$200) \cdot 100 \\ &= 0.4 \cdot 100 = 40\%^{1}\end{aligned}$$

[1]An equivalent way to compute the percentage change is to divide the cost of the market basket on December 31, 1988, by its cost on December 31, 1987, and subtract 1:

$$\begin{aligned}\text{Rate of inflation}_{1988} &= [(\$280/\$200) - 1] \cdot 100 \\ &= (1.4 - 1) \cdot 100 = .4 \cdot 100 = 40\%\end{aligned}$$

Working with the cost of an actual market basket is unwieldy because the market basket contains a large number of goods and services. For example, the actual expenditures on goods and services by a typical household may have been something like \$20,590.15 at the end of 1987. Rather than publish numbers such as these, the government turns the annual costs of the market basket into a simpler price index. The only purpose of determining the costs of the market basket each year is to compute rates of inflation, and the simple price index is sufficient for this.

A price index is constructed by dividing the cost of the market basket every year by the cost of the market basket in the base year. The price index is multiplied by 100 to turn it into a percentage relative to the base year. Therefore, the CPI in our example is constructed by dividing the cost of the market basket in each year by the cost in 1987, the base year. The CPI for 1987 is arbitrarily set equal to 100:

$$\begin{aligned} CPI_{1987} &= (\text{cost of market basket}_{1987}/\text{cost of market basket}_{1987}) \cdot 100 \\ &= (\$200/\$200) \cdot 100 = 1.0 \cdot 100 = 100 \end{aligned}$$

The consumer price index for 1988 is 140:

$$\begin{aligned} CPI_{1988} &= (\text{cost of market basket}_{1988}/\text{cost of market basket}_{1987}) \cdot 100 \\ &= (\$280/\$200) \cdot 100 = 1.4 \cdot 100 = 140 \end{aligned}$$

The rate of inflation during 1988 is the percentage change in the CPI from 1987 to 1988:

$$\text{Rate of inflation}_{1988} = [(140-100)/100] \cdot 100 = 40\%$$

The percentage change in the CPI gives the same rate of inflation as the percentage change in the cost of the market basket. This must be so because the CPI simply divides the cost of the market basket each year by the same number, the cost of the market basket in the base year 1987. Therefore, the cost of the market basket in the base year cancels out when computing the percentage changes from one year to the next.

Continuing with our example, suppose that the cost of the market basket rises to \$300 by December of 1989. The CPI for 1989 is

$$\begin{aligned} CPI_{1989} &= (\text{cost of market basket}_{1989}/\text{cost of the market basket}_{1987}) \cdot 100 \\ &= (\$300/\$200) \cdot 100 = 1.5 \cdot 100 = 150 \end{aligned}$$

CPI_{1989} tells us that the cost of the market basket was 50 percent higher in 1989 than in the base year of 1987. The annual rate of inflation during 1989 is the percentage change in the CPI from 1988 to 1989:

$$\begin{aligned} \text{Rate of inflation}_{1989} &= [(150-140)/140] \cdot 100 \\ &= (10/140) \cdot 100 = .071 \cdot 100 = 7.1\% \end{aligned}$$

In general, the rate of inflation between any two years is the percentage change in the consumer price index between the two years. In our example, the rate of inflation between 1987 and 1989 is 50 percent.

INFLATION: A WEIGHTED AVERAGE OF PRICE INCREASES Defining the rate of inflation as the percentage increase in the cost of a market basket of goods and services leads to an equivalent and very intuitive definition of the overall rate of inflation. The *overall rate of inflation* turns out to be a weighted average of the rates of inflation of each item in the market basket, where the individual weights reflect the importance of each item to the consumer in the base year. Specifically, the weights are the proportion of total expenditures devoted to each item in the base year. Deriving the weighted average interpretation of the rate of inflation is tedious, so we will just demonstrate it with the numbers in our simple example.

In 1987, our base year, the typical household spent 60 percent of its income on food [(\$120/\$200) · 100 = 60%] and 40 percent of its income on clothing [(\$80/\$200) · 100 = 40%]. Therefore, the rate of inflation in any one year is .6 times the rate of inflation in food during the year plus .4 times the rate of inflation in clothing during the year.

$$\text{Rate of inflation} = .6 \cdot (\Delta P/P)_{\text{food}} + .4 \cdot (\Delta P/P)_{\text{clothing}}$$

In 1988 the price of food rose from \$12 to \$18, a 50 percent in crease [(\$18 − \$12)/\$12 = \$6/\$12 = .5 = 50%]; the price of clothing rose from \$4 to \$5, a 25 percent increase [(\$5 − \$4)/\$4 = \$1/\$4 = .25 = 25%]. Therefore, the rate of inflation during 1988 was

$$\text{Rate of inflation}_{1988} = .6 \cdot (50\%) + .4 \cdot (25\%) = 30\% + 10\% = 40\%$$

the same answer obtained by using the percentage change in the CPI.

Notice that the overall rate of inflation is closer to the rate of inflation of food than that of clothing, since food is more important in the typical household's budget. This makes sense. An increase in the price of automobiles has a much greater impact on our cost of living than does an increase in the price of toothpicks. Therefore, a 10 percent inflation in the price of automobiles ought to get much more weight than a 10 percent inflation in the price of toothpicks when constructing an overall rate of inflation. Our simple example shows that the market basket/price index method of computing the rate of inflation does give more weight to products that are more important in consumers' budgets.

The Consumer Price Index

The CPI is constructed and published by the Bureau of Labor Statistics (BLS), the same agency that measures the rate of unemployment. The actual CPI contains many more than two items. Indeed, the BLS goes to great lengths to track the rate of inflation for consumer goods and services. The bureau sends representatives to over 19,000 retail establishments in 85 urban areas throughout the United States to sample the prices of a few thousand consumer products. The prices of food, fuel, and a few other items are sampled every month. All other prices are sampled at least every other month, and every month in the five largest urban areas. In all, the BLS representatives collect data on more than 100,000 individual prices every other month. These are actual prices, not the list or "manufacturer's suggested retail prices." For example, the representatives try to determine the actual prices of new cars sold during the month at the dealerships that they visit; they do not record the sticker prices posted on the car windows.

The market basket of goods and services to be sampled each month is based on detailed Consumer Expenditure Surveys undertaken by the Census Bureau every 10 years or so. The most recent Consumer Expenditure Survey was conducted from 1982 through 1984; approximately 57,000 households participated in the survey. The last Consumer Expenditure Survey before that was in 1972–73. The BLS used the results of the 1982–84 survey to construct a new base-year market basket of goods and services for 1987. The market basket applies to a "typical" household living in an urban area; urban households represent about 80 percent of all households. The previous base year had been 1981, based on the 1972–73 survey results.

Part A of Table 26.1 records the proportion of total expenditures accounted for by the seven major categories of consumer products in the 1987 market basket: food, housing, apparel and upkeep, transportation, medical care, entertainment, and other goods and services. These percentages are the combined weights given to the rates of inflation of the products within each category in constructing the overall rate of inflation. Part A of the table also records the average annual rates of inflation during the 1980s for each of the seven categories and for all products. We can see from the table that the rates of inflation varied considerably across the categories during the decade. The prices of medical care and other goods and services rose more than did the overall average, and the prices of food, apparel and upkeep, and transportation rose less than the average. Inflation in housing and entertainment was just about at the overall average.

Part B of Table 26.1 records the change in price over the entire decade for a selection of items. Hospital rooms had the highest rate of inflation of all the items recorded by the BLS, and televisions had the lowest rate of inflation. The negative 27 percent for televisions indicates that the price of televisions fell by 27 percent during the decade. Televisions experienced *price deflation*, the opposite of price inflation. The list of items contains good and bad news for college students. The bad news you no doubt already suspected: The price changes for college tuition and school books and supplies were among the 10 highest rates of inflation across all products. The good news is that sound equipment, interstate telephone calls, and televisions, each popular items among students, were the only broad categories of products whose prices fell during the 1980s.

CORE RATE OF INFLATION

The rate of inflation that is based on a restricted market basket of goods and services, which excludes items that have highly volatile prices and that have significant weight in computing the overall rate of inflation.

THE CORE RATE OF INFLATION The BLS also publishes an underlying or **core rate of inflation,** which is based on a restricted market basket that excludes all items of food, shelter (within housing), and energy (within housing and transportation). The prices of these items are highly volatile, and each has a fairly high weight in the overall rate of inflation. Consequently, they have an undue influence on the monthly changes in the rate of inflation.

Food prices are highly volatile because they are determined by the Laws of Supply and Demand for the most part. They rise and fall with every shift in the market supply or the market demand curve. Food also has nearly an 18 percent weight in computing the overall rate of inflation (refer to part A of Table 26.1). The shelter category includes mortgage interest rates, which oc-

TABLE 26.1 The Consumer Price Index

A. THE SEVEN MAJOR CATEGORIES OF CONSUMER PRODUCTS IN THE 1987 CPI MARKET BASKET

CATEGORY	PROPORTION OF TOTAL EXPENDITURES IN MARKET BASKET %	AVERAGE ANNUAL RATE OF INFLATION DURING THE 1980s %
Food	17.8	4.4
Housing	42.9	5.2
Apparael and upkeep	6.3	3.1
Transportation	17.2	4.3
Medical care	5.4	8.1
Entertainment	4.4	5.1
Other goods and services	6.0	7.9
All items	100.0	5.1
Core rate of inflation (excludes food, shelter, energy)		5.4

B. PERCENTAGE CHANGE IN PRICE DURING THE 1980s—SELECTED ITEMS

ITEM	PERCENTAGE CHANGE IN PRICE DECEMBER 1979–DECEMBER 1989 %
Hospital rooms	161.9
College tuition	149.0
School books and supplies	140.5
Automobile insurance	119.9
Cereal	117.4
Rent	75.5
Electricity	68.8
Snacks	65.4
Postage	64.2
Maintenance and repair services	63.2
Cosmetics	60.3
New Cars	44.0
Motor fuel	3.5
Women's suits	2.5
Coffee	2.1
Sound equipment	− 2.5
Telephone calls—interstate	− 14.7
Television	− 27.0
All items	64.0

SOURCES: M. Schmidt, "Comparison of the Revised and the Old CPI," *Monthly Labor Review* 110, No. 11 (November 1987): Table 1, p. 4; and P. Jackman, "Consumer Prices in the 1980's: the Cooling of Inflation," *Monthly Labor Review* 113, No. 8 (August 1990): Table 1, p. 20, Table 2, p. 22, and Table 3, pp. 23–25.

casionally increase or decrease by 5 to 10 percent within a month. Energy prices have been extremely volatile ever since 1973, when the Organization of Petroleum Exporting Countries (OPEC) first took control of the world oil market. OPEC used its market power to increase the price of crude oil eightfold from 1973 to 1980. Then, in 1981, OPEC fell into disarray and lost its grip on the world oil market countries. The price of crude oil plummeted, declining by almost one-third between 1981 and 1984. OPEC has never regained control of the market, and the price of oil has tended to fluctuate quite a bit.

By removing these three important and highly volatile items, the core rate of inflation gives a better indication of the month-by-month changes in the rates of inflation for all consumer products. For example, suppose that the price of food rises generally by 10 percent in one month, which has happened on occasion. This alone would increase the overall rate of inflation by 1.8 percentage points ($.18 \cdot 10\% = 1.8\%$) during the month.

REFLECTION: The next time your morning newspaper reports a big increase or decrease in the rate of inflation from the preceding month, notice how much of the change is due to changes in the prices of food, or shelter, or energy.

The distinction between the core and the overall rates of inflation becomes less important over longer periods of time, however, because the ups and downs of food, shelter, and energy prices tend to cancel out over time. According to Table 26.1, the annual average core rate of inflation during the 1980s was 5.4 percent, just about the same as the annual average overall rate of inflation of 5.1 percent.

Other Important Price Indexes

The federal government publishes a number of other price indexes and inflation rates for other reference groups besides households. Two of the more important are the producer price index (PPI) and the GDP deflator.

PRODUCER PRICE INDEX

A price index that is designed to track changes in the cost of production over time; it has three components derived from three separate market baskets: crude materials; intermediate materials, supplies, and components purchased from other firms; and finished manufactured goods.

THE PRODUCER PRICE INDEX The **Producer Price Index** (PPI) is designed to track changes in the costs of production over time. It is derived from three separate market baskets: crude materials; intermediate materials, supplies, and components purchased from other firms; and finished manufactured goods. The finished goods prices in the PPI are wholesale prices, not retail prices. The BLS obtains information on producer prices from a monthly mail survey sent to thousands of firms, and publishes each component of the PPI as a separate index.

The components of the PPI are closely watched because they are considered to be good leading indicators, or predictors, of future changes in the CPI. Firms in the United States are quick to pass increases or decreases in their costs of production on to their customers by raising or lowering their prices. Therefore, changes in the PPI are typically followed by changes in the CPI within the next few months.

THE GDP DEFLATOR The GDP deflator is derived from a very broad market basket of final goods and services purchased in all four sectors of the economy: the household sector, the business sector, the government sector, and the rest-of-world sector. GDP stands for gross domestic product; it refers to the value of all the final products that flow through the markets for goods and services.

The GDP deflator plays a very important role in tracking the growth of the economy over time. Suppose that the dollar value of the circular flow of economic activity in the United States increases by 10 percent during the year. The GDP deflator is used to determine how much of the 10 percent increase is due to increases in the flow of real goods and services through the product and the factor markets and how much is simply due to price increases. We will return to the GDP deflator in Chapter 27, which discusses how the government's accountants measure the circular flow of economic activity.

The Costs of Inflation

Inflation is undoubtedly Public Enemy #1 because of the common perception that inflation robs everyone of purchasing power. This perception is certainly understandable. We noted in Chapter 25 that most labor contracts set wages for anywhere from one to three years. Once people's wages have been set, they naturally hope for stable prices because every percentage point of inflation lowers the purchasing power of their paychecks.[2] Also, everyone feels the effects of inflation, whereas unemployment affects only a small percentage of the labor force. Most people are fairly secure in their jobs; they do not see unemployment as a serious threat to their well-being. Small wonder, then, that people most often select inflation as the leading problem facing the nation.

The notion that inflation robs everyone of purchasing power is not correct, however. It flies in the face of a fundamental principle of macroeconomics, the circular flow of economic activity. The dollar value of goods and services that flow through a nation's product markets must equal the dollar value of incomes earned in a nation's factor markets. Therefore, if inflation is driving up the prices of goods and services that people buy, it must also be increasing the wages, interest rates, and rents that are the sources of their incomes.

The only way that inflation can affect the overall purchasing power of a nation is through imports and exports, the one leak in the circular flow. Higher import prices caused by inflation translate into higher incomes for foreign citizens, not U.S. citizens. Therefore, inflation in import prices does transfer purchasing power to foreign countries. The United States lost hundreds of billions of dollars of purchasing power to the OPEC countries from 1973 to 1980.

The loss in purchasing power in imports is counterbalanced, however, by inflation in export prices, which transfers purchasing power from foreign citizens to U.S. citizens. The *net* transfer of purchasing power, therefore, depends on the relative sizes of imports and exports and the rates of inflation in each. This net transfer is not very important in the United States because the difference between imports and exports each year is always only a small percentage of the total national income and product. Throughout the 1980s, for example, the value of imports exceeded the value of exports by an average of $38 billion, less than 1 percent of the national product.

The people who see inflation robbing them of purchasing power forget that their wage increases each year depend in part on the underlying rate of inflation in the economy. Wage increases will be higher if the economy has been experiencing a 10 percent rate of inflation than if prices have been stable—in fact, about 10 percent higher, on average. The circular flow of economic activity

---

[2]Some of the three-year labor union contracts contain cost-of-living adjustment clauses, known as COLA clauses, that automatically increase wages each year to match the increases in the CPI. Most employee contracts do not have this built-in inflation protection, however.

naturally tends to protect the purchasing power of people's incomes during periods of inflation.

HYPERINFLATION

An inflation in which prices are increasing very rapidly, causing people to lose confidence in the currency.

THE THREAT OF HYPERINFLATION Inflation may not rob everyone of purchasing power, but economists consider inflation to be a very serious problem nonetheless. For starters, governments must take care to keep inflation under control because the process of inflation is driven by an internal dynamic that feeds upon itself. The following scenario can easily occur if governments are not careful. Prices begin rising at the rate of 10 percent per year, then 20 percent, then 100 percent, then 1,000 percent; finally, the process blows sky high into a **hyperinflation,** in which new higher prices are quoted every hour. The point at which hyperinflation sets in is the point at which people lose confidence in their currency. No one wants to hold the nation's money because they have no idea what they will be able to buy with it; the entire financial structure of the economy is threatened. During hyperinflations the political cartoonists draw consumers entering stores with shopping carts full of money and leaving with a single loaf of bread.

With hyperinflation comes real economic hardship. Businesses go bankrupt, people lose their jobs, and many economic exchanges revert to barter, with goods and services traded directly for other goods and services. Economic growth grinds to a halt until the government takes steps to reissue a new money and restore people's confidence in it.

The United States has always managed to keep inflation under control and avoid the hardships of a hyperinflation. Not so other countries' economies, however. Prices exploded in the Central Powers of Europe during the early 1920s. Prices in Austria were 242 times higher in June 1924 than in January 1921; in Hungary, 504 times higher in March 1925 than in July 1921; and in Poland, 9,620 times higher in April 1924 than in January 1921. These inflations paled in comparison with the German hyperinflation, however. Prices in Germany were 80 *billion* times higher in June 1924 than in January 1921! A more recent hyperinflation occurred in Bolivia during 1985, when prices rose by 11,750 percent in that year alone.[3]

Many countries today have uncomfortably high rates of inflation. Poland and Yugoslavia are struggling with inflation as they try to convert their economies to capitalism. Prices rose over 580 percent in each country during 1990. Argentina and Brazil experienced four-digit inflation during 1990, 2,314% and 2,937%, respectively. These countries may not yet be in hyperinflations, but they are clearly flirting with financial disaster.

Experience has taught that even a moderate amount of inflation is very difficult to stop once it takes hold and that an inflationary process can blow up into a hyperinflation if the government does not keep inflation under control. The good news is that governments can easily control inflation if they want to. The bad news is that stopping an inflationary process can be very costly for a short period of time. Governments are sometimes unwilling to bear the costs, so they let the inflation feed upon itself and run out of control.

We will return to the internal dynamic that drives inflation in Chapter 38, after we understand how the macro economy operates. At this point we want

---

[3]T. Sargent, "The Ends of Four Big Inflations," in R. Hall, ed., *Inflation* (Chicago: University of Chicago Press, 1982), 51, 62–63, 70–71, 74–75. *International Financial Statistics Yearbook, 1992,* (Washington, D.C.: International Monetary Fund, 1992), pp. 189, 235, 243, 579, 749.

to focus on the costs associated with moderate and controlled amounts of inflation, such as the United States has been experiencing. The costs take the form of inefficiencies and redistributions of purchasing power.

THE COSTS OF MODERATE INFLATION The costs of inflation depend on three factors: (1) whether the inflation is balanced or unbalanced, (2) whether economic contracts and institutions have adjusted to the inflation, and (3) whether the level of inflation each year is anticipated or unanticipated.

An inflation is **balanced** if the prices of all goods and services, including all factors of production, are rising at exactly the same rate. An inflation is **unbalanced** if prices are rising at different rates, some faster than and others slower than the overall average rate of inflation.

BALANCED INFLATION

An inflation in which the prices of all goods and services, including all factors of production, are rising at exactly the same rate.

UNBALANCED INFLATION

An inflation in which the prices of individual goods and services are rising at different rates, some faster than and others slower than the overall rate of inflation.

Economic contracts are adjusted to inflation if all the dollar values stipulated in the contracts, including all prices, increase and decrease automatically in proportion to the overall rate of inflation. Contracts with this feature are said to be *indexed,* or tied, to the CPI; if the CPI rises by 10 percent, then all dollar values in the contract automatically rise by 10 percent. One institutional feature of the economy that has an important effect on the costs of inflation is a nation's tax system. A tax is adjusted for inflation if the purchasing power of the taxes paid to the government, the so-called real tax payment, is independent of the rate of inflation. For example, suppose that you would owe $1,000 under an income tax if there were no inflation and $1,100 if prices were to rise by 10 percent. Your real tax payment is the same in either case; you owe 10 percent more in taxes when prices rise by 10 percent. The income tax is adjusted for inflation.

Inflation is **fully anticipated** if everyone always knows what the inflation rate will be, this year, next year, and forever after. Inflation is **unanticipated** if it catches people by surprise: Everyone expects a 5 percent inflation in the year 2000, and the actual rate of inflation turns out to be 10 percent. Inflations are always unanticipated to some extent; no one can peer into the future with an unerring crystal ball.

FULLY ANTICIPATED INFLATION

This exists if everyone knows what the inflation rate will be in all future years.

UNANTICIPATED INFLATION

This exists when people are unable to guess correctly what the rate of inflation will be in all future years.

Notice that the three factors are interrelated. Inflation will be more balanced the more contracts are indexed to the CPI. Also, a balanced inflation with indexing is somewhat easier to anticipate than is an unbalanced inflation without indexing. Conversely, the better people can anticipate inflation, the more likely contracts and institutions are to be indexed to inflation, and the more balanced the inflation will be.

PURE INFLATION: BALANCED, ADJUSTED, AND ANTICIPATED Let's begin the analysis of the costs of inflation with the purest type of inflation. Imagine an inflation that is balanced and fully anticipated, with all contracts and institutions adjusted to the inflation. Inflation has been 10 percent forever and will continue to be 10 percent forever. Everyone correctly anticipates that inflation will be 10 percent, so all contracts are indexed to the 10 percent inflation and the inflation is balanced. All goods and factor prices rise by 10 percent. This pure case is unrealistic, to be sure, but it gives us a baseline for comparing the costs of inflation under different assumptions about the three factors.

The costs of a balanced, fully adjusted to, and fully anticipated inflation would be extremely small so long as the inflation remained moderate—say, 10 percent of less. A pure inflation of this kind gives rise to only two kinds of inefficiencies: (1) the costs to consumers and businesses of reducing the amount of cash they hold and (2) the printing costs to businesses of continually updating the prices of products listed in catalogs, in brochures, and on restaurant menus.

The shoe-leather costs of inflation. The dollar bills and coins that we all carry as a matter of convenience for small day-to-day transactions become ever less attractive when prices are rising. They do not offer a rate of return, so they cannot be protected from inflation. Every percentage point of inflation erodes the purchasing power of our cash by a percentage point each year; a dollar bill buys 10 percent less each year when the rate of inflation is 10 percent. Consequently, we all have an incentive to reduce our cash holdings in favor of other assets that are protected from a pure inflation, such as savings accounts, certificates of deposit, stocks, and bonds. But this means that we have to make more trips to our bank to take money out of our savings accounts or make more calls to our broker to sell some stocks or bonds whenever we want to buy the small items that require payments in cash. Economists refer to the extra costs of managing our cash in this way as the *shoe-leather costs of inflation.*

The shoe-leather costs are not very large in the United States, in part because we already do economize on cash through the use of credit cards and checks. The most common estimate of the shoe-leather costs is approximately $0.5 billion for every one-percentage-point increase in the rate of inflation.[4] This is a minuscule cost in a $6 trillion economy.

The menu costs of inflation. The menu costs of having to continually update price lists because of inflation are also extremely small. Firms would update price lists fairly regularly even without an inflation as their demand and cost conditions changed. A moderate inflation would probably not change the pattern of updating price lists very much. Economists do not have good estimates on the *menu costs of inflation,* but they are undoubtedly smaller even than the shoe-leather costs of inflation.

A pure inflation would not have any important redistributional effects either. Everyone is treated symmetrically by the balanced inflation, and no one is caught by surprise with a sudden unexpected change in inflation, so there are no channels for realigning purchasing power throughout the population. The only loss in purchasing power is through the shoe-leather and the menu costs. The former is likely to be felt by everyone, and the latter is too small to be of any consequence.

In summary, then, a moderate pure inflation that is balanced, fully adjusted to, and fully anticipated is hardly a burden at all to an economy. The circular flow of economic activity largely protects the purchasing power of people's incomes, and nothing else happens of much consequence.

The costs of inflation rise sharply when the inflation is unbalanced, unadjusted to, and unanticipated, however. Let's look at some of the ways in which actual inflations give rise to inefficiencies and redistribute purchasing power.

UNBALANCED INFLATION Inflation in the United States is typically highly unbalanced. We saw above that, throughout the 1980s, the price of hospital rooms rose over two and one-half times faster than the average rate of inflation, and the price of television sets actually fell.

---

[4]See, for example, S. Fischer, *Indexing, Inflation, and Economic Policy* (Cambridge, MA: MIT Press, 1986), 12. Fischer's book is widely cited on the costs of inflation. See, especially, the introduction and Chapters 1 and 2.

Most of the unbalance in measured inflation is due to differences in the demand and supply conditions across individual markets. For example, demand could be growing in some markets and declining in other markets. Nonetheless, inflation will tend to be unbalanced even when the impetus for inflation is an across-the-board increase in the demand for goods and services caused by an increase in the money supply. The reason why is that some firms respond quickly and others more slowly to changes in the average rate of inflation. David Stockton undertook a study of 91 industries in the United States to determine how quickly they respond to changes in inflation. His data covered 32 years, from 1949 to 1980. He found tremendous variation in the response to inflation. Eight of the industries reacted almost instantaneously to changes in inflation. These were highly competitive industries to which the Laws of Supply and Demand apply, including food products, textiles, home electric equipment, office machinery, and toys and sporting goods. At the other end of the spectrum were the regulated and highly concentrated final goods industries, including the electric utilities, capital equipment, and transportation equipment. These industries take two to three years to fully adjust to changes in inflation.[5]

Stockton's findings have important implications for the costs of inflation. An increase in inflation leads to more variation in *relative* prices when industries adjust at different rates to the inflation. Prices in the quick-to-adjust industries rise relative to prices in the slow-to-adjust industries, the more so the bigger the increase in inflation. In other words, the higher the inflation becomes, the more unbalanced it becomes. The increased variation in relative prices in turn generates inefficiencies and haphazard redistributions of purchasing power throughout the economy.

Inefficiency. An unbalanced inflation misallocates resources by knocking individual markets out of equilibrium and substituting a pattern of excess supplies and demands. The relatively higher prices in the quick-to-adjust industries induce producers to bring more resources into these markets and increase the quantities supplied. At the same time, the higher prices drive consumers to seek out substitute products and decrease the quantities demanded. The reactions of producers and consumers result in excess supply in the quick-to-adjust markets. Conversely, the relatively lower prices in the slow-to-adjust markets decrease the quantities supplied and increase the quantities demanded. The result is excess demand in the slow-to-adjust markets. The inflation-induced pattern of excess supplies and demands wastes society's scarce resources because the resources do not go to the markets where they are most highly valued.

Redistribution. An unbalanced inflation also redistributes purchasing power from consumers who favor the products of the relatively higher priced, quick-to-adjust industries to the consumers who favor the products of the relatively lower priced, slow-to-adjust industries. Whether this redistribution is likely to be pro-poor or pro-rich is difficult to say, however. The poor spend a higher percentage of their incomes than do the rich on the basic necessities—food, clothing, and shelter. If we knew that the basic necessities were mostly produced by the quick-to-adjust industries, then we could conclude that an unbalanced inflation redistributes purchasing power from the poor to the rich.

[5] D. Stockton, "Relative Price Dispersion, Aggregate Price Movement, and the Natural Rate of Unemployment," *Economic Inquiry* XXVI, No. 1 (January 1988): 1–22.

The reverse would be true if the basic necessities were mostly produced by the slow-to-adjust industries. Stockton's data do not show any consistent pattern along these lines, however. His quick-to-adjust industries are a mixture of basic necessities (food products, textiles) and luxury items (home electronics, toys and sporting goods). Also, his slow-to-adjust industries include electricity, a basic necessity.

Not surprisingly, studies of past U.S. inflations have not uncovered any definite pro-poor or pro-rich pattern to the purchasing power effects of the inflations. The redistributions of purchasing power are more or less haphazard. They tend to vary from one episode of inflation to the next, depending on which items are leading the overall rate of inflation and which are lagging behind.

UNADJUSTED INFLATION As indicated above, economists are primarily interested in the extent to which two institutional features of the economy—contracts for products and factors of production and the nation's tax laws—are adjusted to inflation.

Unadjusted contracts. The analysis of unbalanced inflation has already indicated that most contracts are not indexed to the CPI. This is unfortunate because the economy would be much more efficient if all contracts were indexed. All prices would adjust immediately to changes in the rate of inflation, inflation would be balanced, and the economy would avoid the pattern of excess supplies and demands brought about by an unbalanced inflation.

Business firms and workers are reluctant to index contracts to the CPI, however, despite the economywide advantages to indexing. They would be comfortable indexing only if they were assured that everyone is indexing simultaneously. Otherwise, they know that inflation is sure to be unbalanced and the individual firms and workers that do index become vulnerable to changes in the overall rate of inflation in this situation.

Business firms are primarily concerned about two sets of prices: the prices they receive for their products and the prices of the inputs needed to produce their products. They are much less concerned about prices generally. Any firm that thinks about indexing the price of its products to the CPI would be wary of the following scenario. Suppose that the CPI rises by 10 percent, but that the prices of a firm's inputs rise by much less than 10 percent. This is entirely possible with an unbalanced inflation. Assume for the sake of discussion that the firm's input prices do not rise at all. The firm would be forced to raise the prices of its products by 10 percent if it is indexed to the CPI, even though its costs of production have not increased. The 10 percent price increases would put the firm at a severe disadvantage if its competitors were not indexed to the CPI because the competitors would not have raised their prices. A 10 percent *decrease* in the CPI might be even worse for the indexed firm; it could force the firm to lower its prices below its costs of production. Small wonder that firms are reluctant to index their prices to the CPI unless every firm indexes simultaneously.

Workers are equally wary of having their wages indexed to the CPI. Their big fear is a decrease in the CPI, which would lower their wages relative to other workers whose wages are not indexed. The unions that fought for COLA clauses in their contracts assumed that the CPI would only increase, not decrease. They would not have been so interested in COLA clauses if the CPI were equally likely to move up or down.

The costs to an economy of not having indexed contracts in times of inflation are the same as those noted in the previous section on unbalanced inflation. Unindexed prices generate a pattern of excess supplies and demands that misallocates scarce resources and causes haphazard redistributions of purchasing power.

Unadjusted taxes. Taxes in the United States are only partially indexed for inflation. The taxpayers who receive income from capital are the most vulnerable to inflation because income from capital is not indexed to inflation under either the federal personal or the federal corporation income taxes. The tax laws relating to income from capital are extremely complicated. We will illustrate the problem that inflation causes for income from capital with one example, the capital gain received on the sale of stock.

Suppose that you bought a share of stock in some company for $100 in 1980 and sold the stock in 1990 for $200. Your *capital gain* on the stock is $100, the difference between the price you sold it for in 1990 and the price you bought it for in 1980 ($100 = $200 − $100). The capital gain is counted as part of your taxable income in 1990 under the federal personal income tax. You would pay a tax of $28 on the capital gain if you were in the 28 percent tax bracket.

If prices remained the same between 1980 and 1990, your $100 capital gain represents an increase in purchasing power. After paying the $28 tax, you still have an increase in purchasing power of $72, which represents your real return on the stock. Suppose that prices doubled between 1980 and 1990, however. In this case your $100 capital gain has not increased your purchasing power at all because it takes $200 to buy in 1990 what $100 bought in 1980. The $172 remaining after paying the $28 tax does not buy as much in 1990 as the $100 bought in 1980. The return on your stock is actually negative; you have transferred purchasing power to the government.

The government can protect capital gains from inflation by indexing the purchase price of stocks to the CPI. Taxpayers would be allowed to increase the purchase price of a stock by the increase in the CPI since the time of purchase when computing their capital gains. In our example, you would increase the purchase price to $200 and show no taxable capital gain on the stock if the CPI doubled between 1980 and 1990. This calculation correctly indicates that the $100 capital gain merely protected your purchasing power. It did not represent an increase in purchasing power, and you should not pay a tax on it.

The government's failure to index capital gains and other sources of capital income is anti-rich because the rich own the vast majority of the nation's capital. It also artificially raises the cost of capital during times of inflation, which discourages investment and slows down economic growth. Reforming the tax laws to protect capital income from inflation would undoubtedly make the economy more productive and efficient.

UNANTICIPATED INFLATION The inability to anticipate inflation correctly adds to the efficiency losses of an unbalanced and unadjusted inflation by increasing the overall uncertainty in the economy. People may react to the uncertainty by purchasing unproductive assets such as gold as a hedge against inflation. They may also be reluctant to enter into long-term contracts that lock them into a highly uncertain future. The federal government may have more difficulty issuing 30-year bonds, and banks may be unwilling to write 25- and 30-year mortgages to homeowners. The unexpected pattern of inflation has not had these effects in the United States, perhaps because inflation has moved within fairly narrow bounds. It has never been lower than −2.1 percent (1949) or higher than 18.1 percent (1946) since World War II. No one knows for sure how people would react if the swings in inflation year to year were quite a bit larger or what the additional costs would be.

The main cost of unanticipated inflation is distributional. It increases the likelihood of haphazard redistributions of purchasing power throughout the economy. We will illustrate with three of the more important redistributional effects: (1) redistributions among wage earners, (2) redistributions from people with unearned incomes to people with earned incomes, and (3) redistributions from lenders to borrowers.

Redistributions among wage earners. We noted in Chapter 25 that 5 percent of all employees in the United States work under two-year contracts, 20 percent work under three-year contracts, and most of the rest work under one-year contracts. The three-year contract is the standard union contract. The wage increases negotiated in these contracts would presumably take into account the average rate of inflation so long as the inflation is correctly anticipated. Suppose, though, that a spurt of inflation catches employees by surprise. Imagine that inflation has been zero for some time and that the employees negotiate their contracts expecting that inflation will continue to be zero. Suddenly inflation jumps to 10 percent per year and remains there. The employees are now saddled with negotiated annual wage increases that are too low each year by 10 percentage points. They lose some of the purchasing power that they expected to enjoy.

The sudden increase in inflation affects the employees differently depending on the length of their contracts. The employees with one-year contracts can adjust to the higher inflation next year. The other employees are locked into the wrong contracts for two and three years (we are ignoring COLA clauses to focus on the effects of unanticipated inflation). The result of the unexpected surge in inflation is a redistribution of purchasing power from the employees with longer contracts to the employees with shorter contracts. The amount of the redistribution among workers through this channel appears to be substantial. A recent study by Jesse Abraham suggests that every one-percentage-point increase in unexpected inflation may redistribute purchasing power equal to 1 percent of *total wages* among employees with contracts of different lengths.[6]

Unearned incomes versus earned incomes. People who rely on unearned sources of income are especially vulnerable to unexpected inflation. These include the elderly who are living off private pensions and Social Security retirement benefits and the poor who receive public assistance from the government. Pensions and public transfers are not naturally protected from inflation by the circular flow of economic activity as are sources of earned income, such as wages, interest income, and rents. Every one-percentage-point increase in inflation reduces purchasing power by one percentage point if these unearned sources of income are truly fixed.

The ability to anticipate inflation correctly is an important factor in determining how well unearned incomes are protected from inflation. Companies want to know how much their future pension commitments will be each year as they engage in long-range planning. They will be more willing to index the pensions to the CPI if they can anticipate future inflation than if inflation rises

---

[6]J. Abraham, "Income Redistribution During a Disinflation," *Journal of Macroeconomics* 9, No. 2 (Spring 1987): 218.

and falls unexpectedly. Similarly, administrators and legislators want to know what their future commitments will be under the various public transfer programs as they struggle to keep their budgets in balance. They, too, are more likely to index the transfers to the CPI if they believe that they can anticipate future inflation.

The record of protecting unearned incomes from inflation is mixed in the United States. Most private pensions are not indexed to the CPI; they are truly fixed sources of income to the retirees who receive them. The few private pensions that are indexed usually stipulate a maximum amount of inflation adjustment, such as 3 percent per year. Congress indexed Social Security retirement benefits to the CPI in the early 1970s. Social Security is the largest government transfer program and the main source of income for a large number of the elderly. The largest cash public assistance program for the poor, Aid to Families with Dependent Children (AFDC), is not indexed to the CPI, however. AFDC provides monthly cash benefits to single-parent families with children who are living in poverty. The monthly benefit levels are determined by the state governments, and the states have not been willing to protect the poor from inflation, in large part because they have been pressed to keep expenditures down to balance their budgets. The average monthly benefit level nationwide fell by 14 percent from 1975 to 1988 after adjusting for inflation.

Inflation in the United States almost certainly transfers purchasing power from unearned income to earned income, although the size of the transfer is unknown. Moreover, the transfer is just as certainly pro-rich and anti-poor because the poor rely much more on sources of unearned income than do the rich.

Redistributions from lenders to borrowers. Unexpected inflation transfers substantial amounts of purchasing power from lenders to borrowers. The following simple example illustrates why.

Suppose that your friend wants to borrow $100 from you for one year. Assume for the moment that the rate of inflation is zero, always has been zero, and is expected to remain at zero for the foreseeable future. You and your friend have to decide on the interest rate to charge for the loan. As a lender you think along the following lines. Your friend is asking you to give up $100 of purchasing power today. You are willing to do that, but only if you receive more than $100 of purchasing power when he pays you back one year from now. In other words, you want some return for your sacrifice. You decide that 5 percent is an appropriate return, so you ask him to pay you back $105 one year from now: the $100 that he borrowed plus 5 percent interest on the $100. Your friend agrees to the 5 percent interest charge. As the borrower, he understands that in order to receive $100 of purchasing power today he must be prepared to sacrifice even more purchasing power in the future. This is the opportunity cost of borrowing. So he is willing to sacrifice $105 of purchasing power one year from now. If all lenders and borrowers think along these lines, the interest rate on loans will be 5 percent in a world without inflation.

Now assume that everyone expects the rate of inflation to be 10 percent during the next year. You would no longer be willing to accept a 5 percent rate of interest on the loan. You need $110 one year from now to buy the same goods and services that $100 buys today, so you have to charge your friend a 10 percent rate of interest just to protect your purchasing power. Then, if you require an additional 5 percent in purchasing power to make the loan, you have to add five percentage points of interest on top of the 10 percent, for a total interest rate of 15 percent. You now ask your friend to pay you back $115 one year from now: $110 to protect your purchasing power and an additional $5 of purchasing power. Your friend will agree to the 15 percent rate of interest because he was willing to give up 5 percent more purchasing power one year from now than he borrowed today. He expects to have 10 percent more income with all prices, including factor prices, expected to rise by 10 percent. So paying back $115 in a world of 10 percent inflation is the same burden as paying back $105 in a world without inflation. If all borrowers and lenders think along these lines, the interest rate on loans will be 15 percent when the expected rate of inflation is 10 percent.

The situation we are interested in here is one in which the 10 percent inflation occurs, but catches people by surprise—everyone expected inflation to remain at zero. In this case you and your friend will agree to a 5 percent rate of interest because neither of you expects that the interest rate needs to be adjusted for inflation. At the end of the year, however, your friend turns out to have made a great deal and you a terrible deal. Your friend repays you $105, which is less than the purchasing power that you lent him one year ago now that prices are 10 percent higher. You have, in effect, paid your friend to lend him money. The effective interest rate on your loan is *minus* 5 percent once you adjust for inflation, equal to the loss in your purchasing power.

HISTORICAL NOTE: Many farmers in the United States went bankrupt in the early 1980s as inflation fell from 13 percent to less than 3 percent in three years. They were locked into high-interest loans taken out in 1979 and 1980 and could not make the principal and interest payments once the inflation subsided.

Our simple example illustrates the principle that an *unexpected* inflation redistributes purchasing power from lenders to borrowers. The reverse is also true: An unexpected deflation (reduction in inflation) redistributes purchasing power from borrowers to lenders (rework the above example with an unexpected 10 percent decrease in prices and see how you gain at the expense of your friend).

The redistribution of wealth through unanticipated inflation is the most important redistributional effect of inflation in the United States. Every 1 percent increase in unanticipated inflation redistributes approximately $60 billion of purchasing power from creditors (net lenders) to debtors (net borrowers), an amount equal to 1 percent of the national product.[7] The creditors are concentrated among the highest- and lowest-income families, and the debtors are in the middle of the distribution. Therefore, the redistribution of wealth favors the middle classes at the expense of both the rich and the poor in the United States. In addition, the federal government is a large net debtor. The federal debt exceeds $4 trillion. Therefore, unanticipated inflation transfers a substantial amount of purchasing power from the private sector to the federal government.

THE FISHER EQUATION

The relationship between observed, or nominal, interest rates and the underlying real interest rates that says that the observed interest rate on a financial security equals the real interest rate plus the expected rate of inflation.

THE FISHER EQUATION Our simple example when the rate of inflation is expected illustrates a very important formula in macroeconomic analysis known as the Fisher equation, after economist Irving Fisher who first discovered it. The Fisher equation says that the observed, or nominal, interest rate on a loan equals the underlying real rate of interest plus the expected rate of inflation.

$$i_{\text{observed, nominal}} = r_{\text{real}} + \Delta P/P_E$$

The underlying real rate of interest, r_{real}, is the additional purchasing power that the lender requires and the borrower is willing to pay. r_{real} is 5 percent in our example. $\Delta P/P_E$ is the expected rate of inflation. $i_{\text{observed, nominal}}$ is the

[7]Fischer, *Indexing* Ch. 1, pp. 25–26.

interest rate that appears on the loan contract, that is, the actual amount of interest that the borrower pays the lender. $i_{\text{observed, nominal}}$ is 15 percent in our example when the expected rate of inflation is 10 percent; it is 5 percent when the expected rate of inflation is zero.

The Fisher equation says that observed or nominal interest rates consist of two components: the expected rate of inflation, which protects the purchasing power of the loan, and an underlying real rate of interest, which reflects the additional purchasing power that the lender requires and the borrower is willing to pay.

Notice another very important implication of the Fisher equation. *Interest rates increase and decrease point for point with increases and decreases in the expected rate of inflation.* Countries that are free of inflation have interest rates on the order of 5 percent. Countries that have been experiencing 20 percent inflation have interest rates on the order of 25 percent. And countries that have been experiencing triple-digit inflation of 300 percent have interest rates on the order of 305 percent. Interest rates have to adjust to the expected inflation in order to protect the purchasing power in loan contracts. The Fisher equation will play a central role in our analysis of inflation later on in the text.[8]

SUMMING UP: THE COSTS OF INFLATION Judging the costs of inflation ultimately depends on one's point of view. The University of Chicago's Robert Lucas argues that the only costs of inflation, per se, are the shoe-leather and the menu costs of a balanced, fully adjusted, and anticipated inflation. These costs are trivial, as we have seen. He attributes all the other inefficiencies and redistributional effects described above to other factors. Lucas blames the costs of an unbalanced inflation on the various institutional and political forces that prevent contracts and the tax system from being indexed to the CPI. Inflation itself is not the culprit. He also believes that the ebbs and flows of inflation, which make inflation so hard to anticipate, are the result of misguided fiscal and monetary policies that only serve to destabilize the economy. Lucas notes that these policies also cause changes in output and employment that are likely to be far more important than are any changes in the rate of inflation.

MIT's Stan Fischer disagrees with Lucas. Fischer argues that the costs of inflation have to be viewed within the existing institutional context of the economy. He would count all the costs described above as costs of inflation, which leads him to conclude that the costs of even a moderate amount of inflation are quite large in the United States. Fischer believes that a 10 percent rate of inflation would redistribute substantial amounts of purchasing power and generate efficiency losses on the order of 2 percent of the national product. Two percent of the national product is around $120 billion, or about $500 per person per year. Fischer does concede that the costs of inflation are mostly avoidable. He agrees with Lucas that most of the costs would disappear if prices and the tax system were indexed to the CPI and if the government maintained a steadier policy course.[9]

CURRENT ISSUE: Many of the industrialized market economies have had low rates of inflation in the 1990s and they want to keep inflation low. By the end of 1992, the central banks of Canada, Germany, Great Britain, Japan, and New Zealand had announced target rates of inflation of 2 percent or less. In mid-1993, Fed Chairman Alan Greenspan expressed concern about inflation even though the rate of inflation in the United States was less than 3 percent at the time. (*The Economist*, November 7, 1992, p. 23.)

[8]The point-for-point relationship between interest rates and expected inflation would not be expected to hold precisely because of real-world complications such as taxation, which our simple example ignores. Nonetheless, the point-for-point relationship is approximately true in the United States.

[9]Fischer, *Indexing*, p. 4; and R. Lucas, "Discussion," of S. Fischer, "Towards an Understanding of the Costs of Inflation," in K. Brunner and A. Meltzer, eds., *The Costs and Consequences of Inflation*, vol. 15 of *Carnegie-Rochester Conference Series on Public Policy* (Amsterdam: North Holland, 1981), 43–50.

Whatever their views on the costs of inflation, most economists agree that inflation is nowhere near as serious a problem as high levels of unemployment and slow economic growth are. The only caveat, and a crucial one, is the need to keep inflation tightly under control. A nation should never allow itself to start down the path of ever-increasing inflation and face the threat of a runaway hyperinflation. A modern economy cannot function without the use of money, and people will have confidence in the nation's currency only if they are assured that the government will act to keep inflation under control. We will see that governments can control inflation if they want to, and they really have no choice but to do so.

IMPORTS, EXPORTS, AND THE VALUE OF THE DOLLAR

Nations engage in trade with one another to increase their standards of living. We saw in Chapter 3 how international trade allows a nation to push its consumption possibilities beyond the limits of its own production possibilities frontier.

Imports are the key to the increase in living standards made possible by trade. Nations import to gain access to goods and services that they cannot produce at all, or at least not as well as other nations can. For example, the United States could grow bananas under tightly controlled hothouse conditions that artificially produce a tropical climate. But this would use a lot of scarce resources, and the bananas would be very expensive. Far better to let the tropical countries grow the bananas in their natural habitat and import the bananas. Consumers in the United States wind up with cheaper bananas, and the resources that would be needed to grow bananas in the United States can be put to much more productive uses.

Automobiles are a less clear-cut example than bananas, but the same principle applies. If Honda, Mitsubishi, and Toyota can build cars that the American public likes more cheaply than can General Motors, Ford, and Chrysler, then the United States should increase its imports of the Japanese cars and reduce its own production of cars. The American public resists the principle in the case of automobiles because more Japanese imports mean fewer jobs for American auto workers. In fact, imports generally have a bad name in the United States because people equate imports with loss of jobs. You can be sure that some politician will call for trade restrictions on imports whenever they threaten American producers. Bananas may not be a threat, but foreign automobiles certainly are.

The concern for jobs is understandable. The jobs lost by the American auto workers to foreign competition represent a big loss to each of the displaced auto workers and their families, and the loss of a job is highly visible. Moreover, the job losses tend to be concentrated geographically; witness the high unemployment among auto workers in Michigan.

Balanced against these losses, however, are the gains to the American consumers who are able to buy better and cheaper automobiles. These gains draw much less attention than do the losses because the benefits to each consumer are fairly small and not very visible. Moreover, the benefits are also not at all concentrated; they are shared broadly by millions of consumers throughout the United States. Make no mistake about it, though. Study after study shows that the small gains received by the millions of consumers are many times larger in the aggregate than are the large losses suffered by the tens of thousands of auto workers who lose their jobs. The losses to the auto workers are real. But the nation as a whole is far better off by importing automobiles and having the displaced auto workers seek employment elsewhere.

Always remember that imports are the ends of international trade. Gaining access to imported products is the sole purpose for engaging in trade with foreign nations. Imports are good, not bad, for a nation.

The Balance of Trade

If imports are the ends of international trade, then exports are the means to those ends. Countries are not willing to produce goods and send them to other countries unless they receive goods in exchange. In other words, a nation must export in order to be able to import. A nation's **balance of trade** is the difference between the value of its exports and the value of its imports. Most nations are forced by the unwritten rules of international trade to have a balance of trade approximately equal to zero: The value of their exports must equal the value of their imports. The following simple example will illustrate why this is so.

BALANCE OF TRADE
The difference between the value of a nation's exports and the value of its imports (merchandise exports and imports only; excludes trade in services).

Suppose that all of U.S. trade consists of a single British importer selling wool sweaters in the United States and a single U.S. exporter selling food in London. The British importer sells $180 worth of sweaters. The U.S. exporter sells food valued at £100.

The importer is a British citizen. She does not want dollars; she wants pounds sterling that she can take back to England and spend there. Similarly, the exporter is a U.S. citizen. He does not want pounds sterling; he wants dollars that he can take back to the United States and spend there. So the importer and the exporter bring their currencies to the foreign exchange market, where the currencies of different nations are exchanged. The foreign exchange markets establish exchange rates at which the different currencies can be exchanged.

Assume that the exchange rate of dollars for pounds sterling is $1.80 per pounds sterling.

$$\text{Exchange rate} = \$1.80/£$$

The importer and the exporter meet and exchange their currencies at this rate. The exchange is even. The importer gives her $180 to the exporter in exchange for his £100, and they both now have their own currencies.

Notice that before they exchange the currencies, we know the *dollar* value of the imported sweaters ($180) and the *pound sterling* value of the exported food (£100). The two values cannot be compared because they are denominated in different currencies. The exchange of currencies sets the *dollar* value of the food exports ($180), and we can now compare the dollar value of the exports with the dollar value of the imports. The two values are equal (at $180), indicating that England and the United States have made an even exchange of goods for goods, sweaters for food. The balance of trade in each country is zero.

Suppose, instead, that the foreign exchange market has established an exchange rate of $1.60 per pound sterling.

$$\text{Exchange rate} = \$1.60/\pounds$$

At this rate, the exchange of currencies between the importer and the exporter is no longer even. The U.S. exporter gives the British importer his £100 and receives $160 from her in exchange. The importer has $20 left over. The dollar value of the imports remains at $180 as before, but the dollar value of the exports is only $160. From the U.S. point of view, the value of imports exceeds the value of exports by $20, exactly the amount that the British importer has left over after the exchange of currencies. The United States is said to have a **deficit** in its balance of trade because its balance of trade is negative $20. Conversely, England has a **surplus** in its balance of trade; the value of its exports exceeds the value of its imports.

BALANCE-OF-TRADE DEFICIT
The value of a nation's imports exceeds the value of its exports.

BALANCE-OF-TRADE SURPLUS
The value of a nation's exports exceeds the value of its imports.

A balance-of-trade deficit is a good deal for the United States and a bad deal for England. Citizens of the United States are receiving sweaters in part for pieces of paper, dollar bills. They are not required to exchange goods for goods, food for sweaters, even up. Conversely, British citizens are producing and sending sweaters to the United States and are not receiving an equal value of goods, food, in exchange. Part of their scarce resources used to produce the sweaters are being exchanged for pieces of paper, dollar bills. The British importer may be willing to place the dollars in U.S. financial securities as a form of saving (see below), but suppose that she does not want to. Then the trade imbalance cannot continue. The British will insist on an even exchange of goods for goods. Although our example is highly simplified, it shows why nations must export in order to import.

Stable Value of the Currency

Nations want their currencies to be stable in value relative to the currencies of other nations in addition to striving for a zero balance of trade. These two goals are closely related, as we will see in a moment.

Stable currency values create a more certain business environment for firms engaged in international trade. For example, firms exporting food to England know that sometime in the future they will be exchanging pounds sterling for dollars. They have to guess what the exchange rate of dollars for pounds will be six months, one year, two years from now as they plan their production and marketing strategies for the English market. The more stable the dollar is, the better they are able to predict the future exchange rates, and the more confidence they have in their business plans. A stable value of the dollar helps to promote international trade by reducing uncertainty.

In addition, movements in the value of a nation's currency generate a pattern of gainers and losers within the country that are best avoided. Let's begin with a few definitions before demonstrating this point.

DEPRECIATION (CURRENCY)
The value of a nation's currency falls relative to the value of other currencies.

A nation's currency is said to **depreciate** if its value falls relative to other currencies. For example, suppose that the dollar–pound sterling exchange rate changes from $1.80/£ to $2.00/£. The value of the dollar has fallen relative to the pound. It used to take $1.80 to buy one £; now it takes $2.00 to buy one £. The dollar has depreciated in value relative to the pound. A depreciating dollar is commonly referred to as a weaker dollar.

APPRECIATION (CURRENCY)
The value of a nation's currency rises relative to the value of other currencies.

Conversely, a nation's currency is said to **appreciate** if its value rises relative to other currencies. For example, suppose that the dollar–pound sterling exchange rate changes from $1.80/£ to $1.60/£. The value of the dollar has risen relative to the pound. It used to take $1.80 to buy one £; now it only takes $1.60 to buy one £. The dollar has appreciated in value relative to the pound. An appreciating dollar is commonly referred to as a stronger dollar.

The common terms *weaker dollar* and *stronger dollar* suggest that a depreciation of the dollar is bad for everyone in the United States and an appreciation of the dollar is good for everyone. This is not so. Some people gain and others lose when the dollar exchange rate moves in either direction. The three groups most directly affected by a change in the exchange rates are consumers, import-competing industries, and export industries. Import-competing industries are those that face direct competition from foreign imports. The U.S. automobile and textile industries are examples. The three groups are affected differently when the dollar depreciates or appreciates.

Suppose that the dollar depreciates in value from $1.80/£ to $2.00/£. This is bad for consumers, but good for exporters and import-competing industries. Consumers lose because British goods have become more expensive for them. A fine wool sweater priced at £100 in London used to cost U.S. consumers $180. Now they must pay $200 for it. Notice that the price rises to U.S. consumers even if the sweater is no more costly to produce and continues to sell for £100 in London. The depreciation of the dollar has made the sweater more expensive in the United States.

Import-competing industries, unlike consumers, gain from the depreciation. Consumers are more likely to buy domestically produced products because the imported products have become more expensive. Staying with our example, some consumers will refuse to pay $200 for the British sweater. They will buy a sweater from a U.S. producer instead. Similarly, the Big Three U.S. auto manufacturers have a much easier time selling their cars when the dollar depreciates against the Japanese yen.

Finally, U.S. exporters gain when the dollar depreciates. A depreciating dollar simultaneously makes imports more expensive to U.S. consumers and U.S. exports cheaper for foreign consumers. Suppose that an IBM personal computer sells for $1,800 in the United States. The computer cost a British citizen £1,000 before the dollar depreciated. After the dollar depreciates to $2.00/£, the same computer costs the British citizen less than £1,000 because £1,000 now exchanges for $2,000. IBM's sales of personal computers in England increase when the dollar depreciates relative to the pound, even though the dollar price of the computer, $1,800, has not changed.

The reverse is true when the dollar appreciates in value—say, from $1.80/£ to $1.60/£. Consumers gain because imported British goods are now cheaper for them. Import-competing industries lose because U.S. consumers are more likely to buy the relatively cheaper foreign imports. Exporters also lose because U.S. products are now more expensive to foreign customers. These points were driven home in the mid-1980s when the dollar appreciated sharply against most of the world's currencies. As a result, U.S. imports increased substantially, and import-competing manufacturers suffered badly; U.S. exports also fell sharply as exporters had great difficulty selling products that were suddenly much more expensive to foreign consumers and businesses. Complaints grew that U.S. manufacturing was unable to compete anymore with the foreign manufacturers. But productivity in U.S. manufacturing was not declining during that period, either absolutely or relative to foreign manufacturers. The import-competing and the export manufacturers simply had difficulty selling their products in the face of the appreciating dollar. Not surprisingly, the fortunes of the U.S. manufacturers improved when the dollar began depreciating against the major currencies in 1986. The dollar has continued to depreciate against most of the major currencies into the 1990s, and the fears of being outcompeted have subsided a bit.

The effects on consumers when the exchange rate depreciates or appreciates are much larger in the aggregate than are the effects on the import-competing and the export industries. This is why the labels "weaker dollar" for a depreciating dollar and "stronger dollar" for an appreciating dollar make sense. As we have just seen, a weaker (depreciating) dollar is bad for consumers, and a stronger (appreciating) dollar is good for consumers, and consumers' losses and gains are the most important.

The Value of the Dollar and the Balance of Trade

We noted above that the goals of a zero balance of trade and a stable value of the currency are closely related to one another. Let's return to our simple example of a single British importer and a single U.S. exporter to see why.

When the exchange rate is $1.80/£, both countries achieve a zero balance of trade, and the British importer's $180 trades even up for the U.S. exporter's £100. There is no pressure on the exchange rate to change, and the value of the dollar is stable relative to the pound. A zero balance of trade and a stable dollar go hand in hand. This is no accident. The dollar can be stable relative to the pound only if the two countries in our example have achieved a zero balance of trade.

Consider the situation when the exchange rate is $1.60/£. The dollar value of U.S. imports exceeds the dollar value of U.S. exports, and the British importer is holding $20 that she does not want. This situation cannot be an equilibrium period after period. The British importer will try to get rid of all her dollars and exchange them for pounds. Her desire to sell her excess dollars puts downward pressure on the value of the dollar, and the dollar begins to depreciate. The dollar continues to depreciate until the exchange rate reaches $1.80. At this point the importer's $180 trades even up for the exporter's £100. Moreover, the dollar value of U.S. imports equals the dollar value of U.S. exports, at $180; the depreciation of the dollar restores the equality of exports and imports.

This example gives us another perspective on the principle that countries have to export to be able to import. Suppose that a country's exports begin to lose out to foreign competition so that the value of the country's imports exceeds the value of its exports. The trade imbalance causes the currency to depreciate, which raises the costs of imports. Therefore, the loss of the export markets eventually makes the country's imports more expensive and reduces the gains from international trade.

The United States: An Exception to the Rule

The principle that a nation must achieve a zero balance of trade in order to stabilize the value of its currency holds for most nations of the world. The United States is one exception, however. The value of the dollar can be stable even if the values of U.S. imports and U.S. exports are very unequal. The reason why is that foreign citizens may be quite willing to hold dollars.

Return one last time to our simple example of the British importer and the U.S. exporter in the case when the exchange rate is $1.60/£ and the importer ends up with an additional $20. We assumed above that the importer does not want the $20; she only wants pounds sterling. Suppose that the importer were willing to hold the $20, however, by purchasing a certificate of deposit or a U.S. government bond. If so, there would be no pressure for the exchange rate to change. She would be willing to exchange $160 for the U.S. exporter's £100 and hold onto her remaining $20 as a form of saving. The exchange rate would remain stable at $1.60/£.

Why might the importer be willing to hold the $20? One reason is the special role of the dollar in international trade. The United States has been such an important player in international markets for so long that the dollar has gained the status of a worldwide money. People can use dollars to buy goods and services in almost any country. As a result, they are as willing to hold dollars as they are their own currencies. Our importer knows that she can always trade the dollars for goods and services anywhere. The same is not true of the Mexican peso or the Russian ruble. She would probably not be willing to hold these currencies.

A second reason why people might want to have dollars is that they look to U.S. financial markets as a good place to put their savings. Money managers of large corporations, banks, insurance companies, and pension trust funds are on the lookout worldwide for financial securities such as stocks, bonds, and certificates of deposit that will earn them a good rate of return. Consequently, U.S. financial securities are always an attraction. One reason is that the U.S. financial markets are the most highly developed in the world. Money managers can choose from a huge variety of financial securities, and exchanges of securities are easily accomplished. The United States is also very stable politically; the managers know their funds are relatively safe in the United States. Foreign money managers need dollars to invest in the U.S. financial markets, so there is always a demand for dollars that is independent of the trade in imports and exports. Our British importer may be willing to hold the $20 because she wants to save $20 and she believes that buying, say, a U.S. certificate of deposit is the best way for her to save.

In summary, the rules of international trade are somewhat different for the United States (and for the other industrialized nations with highly developed capital markets). The value of U.S. imports can exceed the value of U.S. exports, and the dollar can still be stable. The requirement for dollar stability is as follows: *The dollar is stable if the amount of dollars that foreign citizens are willing to hold is equal to the difference between U.S. imports and exports.*

This turns out to be a difficult condition to satisfy because the willingness to hold dollars in the United States is itself not very stable. Flows of funds into and out of the United States are very sensitive to conditions in financial markets worldwide. Funds flow in when interest rates rise in the United States. Funds flow out when interest rates rise in Europe. An inflow of funds causes the dollar to appreciate as money managers seek to buy dollars with Japanese yen and French francs and German marks; an outflow of funds causes the dollar to depreciate as the money managers sell their dollars for foreign currencies. Achieving a stable dollar is extremely difficult in the face of the worldwide flow of funds.

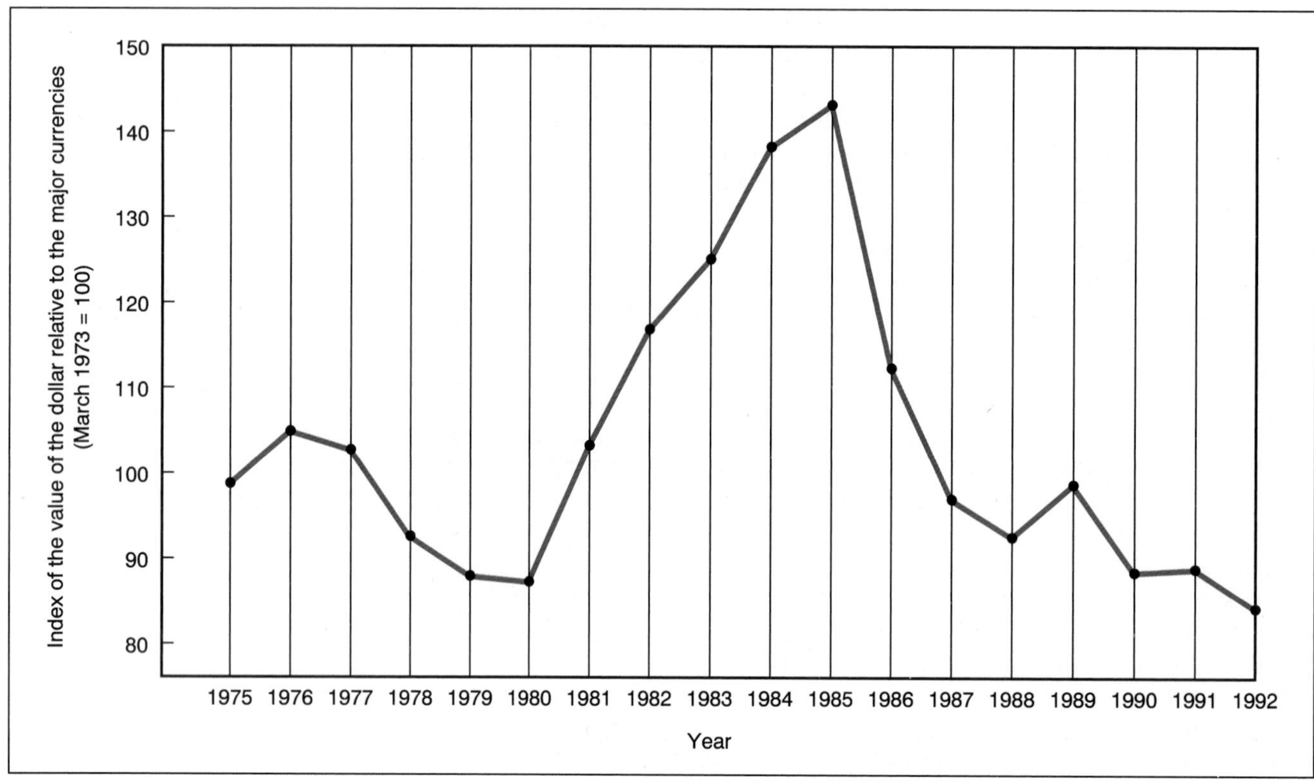

FIGURE 26.2

The Dollar versus Foreign Currencies, 1975–92

The figure shows an index of the value of the dollar relative to a weighted average of the currencies of a number of the industrialized market economies, from 1975–1992. The index sets the relative value of the dollar equal to 100 in March, 1973. The value of the dollar has not been stable since 1975. In particular, the dollar appreciated steadily and substantially against the major currencies from 1980 to 1985, and then depreciated steadily and substantially against the major currencies from 1985 to 1992.

SOURCE: Council of Economic Advisors, *Economic Report of the President, 1993* (Washington, D.C.: U.S. Government Printing Office, 1993), Table B-107, p. 470.

Figure 26.2 shows the value of the dollar relative to an index of the major currencies from 1975 to 1992. The figure indicates just how elusive the goal of a stable dollar has been for the United States.

The United States has also failed to achieve a zero balance of trade throughout most of the post–World War II period, although this goal is somewhat less important for the United States than for other countries. Table 26.2 records the average difference between the value of exports and the value of imports for each decade since 1950. We can see that the United States has switched from being a large net exporter of goods and services to being a very large net importer of goods and services. The switch occurred for many reasons that we will discuss in the remaining chapters of the text.

One final point is that even the United States cannot import more than it exports indefinitely. Foreign citizens will not save forever; they will eventually want to cash in their savings and consume. When they do, either the dollar will depreciate as they trade the dollars for their own currencies, or they will buy U.S. goods. Either way, U.S. exports will rise, and U.S. imports will fall,

TABLE 26.2 **Average Annual Value of the Difference Between Exports and Imports by Decade Since 1950**

DECADE	EXPORTS MINUS IMPORTS ($ BILLION)
1950s	$ 3.4
1960s	7.5
1970s	12.6
1980s	−38.3
1990–92	−40.4

SOURCES: Council of Economic Advisors, *Economic Report of the President, 1991* (Washington, D.C.: U.S. Government Printing Office, 1991), Table B-1, p. 287. Council of Economic Advisors, *Economic Report of the President, 1993*, (Washington, D.C.: U.S. Government Printing Office, 1993), Table B-1, p. 349. Council of Economic Advisors, *Economic Indicators, March 1993*, (Washington, D.C.: 1993), p. 1.

turning the balance-of-trade deficit into a surplus. Over time, therefore, even the United States must maintain an equality between its exports and its imports. It, too, has to export to be able to import.

SUMMARY

The first section of Chapter 26 discussed the problem of inflation.

1. Inflation refers to a process of continuous increases in the level of prices generally.
2. The federal government tracks inflation by defining a market basket of goods and services for some reference group. The annual rate of inflation is the increase in the cost of the market basket during the year. The government computes a price index by dividing the value of the market basket each year by its value in the base year, assigning the base year a value of 100. The rate of inflation is then the percentage change in the price index over time. This method of computing inflation makes the overall rate of inflation a weighted average of the rates of inflation of each item in the market basket. The weights are assigned to each item in proportion to expenditures on the item within the market basket. Three closely watched price indexes are the consumer price index (CPI), the producer price index (PPI), and the GDP deflator.
3. The consumer price index is based on a market basket of consumer goods and services. It is used to adjust for inflation in wage and pension contracts and to protect government transfer payments from inflation.
4. The producer price index is based on three market baskets of producer inputs: crude materials; intermediate materials, supplies and components; and finished manufactured goods sold at wholesale. Changes in the PPI lead to future changes in the CPI as producers pass their cost increases through to consumers.
5. The GDP deflator is based on a market basket of final goods purchased by all sectors of the economy. It is used to divide changes in the value of the circular flow of economic activity into real changes and price changes.

6. Governments should strive to keep inflation low for two reasons:
   a. An inflationary process has an internal dynamic that can feed upon itself if the government allows it to. A 10 percent inflation this year becomes a 100 percent inflation next year, and so on, leading to a hyperinflation in which prices are changing every hour. Hyperinflation goes hand in hand with loss of confidence in the currency and the financial system generally. Economic exchange reverts to a straight barter of goods for goods, and economic growth grinds to a halt.
   b. Even moderate amounts of inflation lead to efficiency losses and haphazard redistributions of purchasing power.
7. The inefficiencies and redistributions caused by a moderate amount of inflation depend on the extent to which the inflation is (a) unbalanced, (b) unadjusted to, and (c) unanticipated. An inflation is unbalanced if prices of individual goods and services are rising at different rates. An inflation is unadjusted to when economic contracts and/or the tax system are not indexed to the rate of inflation. An inflation is unanticipated when year-to-year changes in the rate of inflation catch people by surprise. The three conditions are interrelated. For example, a balanced, anticipated inflation is much easier to adjust to than is an unbalanced, unanticipated inflation. All three conditions are present in every inflation.
8. There would be only two very small costs to a balanced, fully adjusted to, fully anticipated inflation: the shoe-leather costs of managing cash more closely and the menu costs of firms having to change their prices more frequently. Neither cost is of much consequence.
9. An unbalanced inflation leads to inefficiencies by increasing the variation in relative prices. The high-inflation markets tend to be in excess supply, and the low-inflation markets tend to be in excess demand. An unbalanced inflation also leads to haphazard redistributions of purchasing power. People who favor the high-inflation products lose relative to people who favor the low-inflation products.
10. Inflations are unadjusted to because neither firms nor workers are interested in indexing their prices and wages to the CPI unless they can be assured that everyone is indexing to the CPI simultaneously. The failure to index economic contracts to inflation leads to potentially large efficiency losses. The U.S. tax system is also not fully indexed to inflation, which means that the amount of taxes people pay in relation to their incomes varies with the rate of inflation. Income from capital is particularly vulnerable to inflation.
11. The main effect of an unanticipated inflation is that it greatly increases the amount of haphazard redistributions of purchasing power through the economy. Workers on long-term labor contracts lose relative to workers on short-term labor contracts. People with fixed incomes lose relative to people with earned incomes. Debtors/borrowers gain at the expense of creditors/lenders. An unanticipated inflation also increases the efficiency costs of inflation by increasing the amount of uncertainty in the economy.
12. Economists disagree on the costs of a moderate inflation. One view holds that the costs of inflation, per se, are minuscule. They consist only of the shoe-leather and the menu costs. All the other costs are due not to the inflation, but to the factors that make the inflation unbalanced, unadjusted to, or unanticipated. Another view holds that the costs of inflation must be

counted within the institutional context of the economy. According to this view, the costs of a moderate inflation in the United States are substantial, but avoidable.

The second section of the chapter discussed the goals of an equality between imports and exports and a stable value of the currency.

13. Imports are the ends of trade: Countries import to gain access to goods that are produced better or more cheaply in foreign countries.
14. Exports are the means to the end. Countries have to export in order to import. Foreign countries will not send goods to a country unless they receive goods in exchange.
15. Most countries are forced to have a zero balance of trade, in which the value of their imports equals the value of their exports. If the value of their imports exceeds the value of their exports (a balance-of-trade deficit), the importers end up holding the other nation's currency, which they may not want to do.
16. A currency depreciates when its value falls relative to other currencies. A currency appreciates when its value rises relative to other currencies. Nations seek a stable value of their currency because a stable currency makes for a more certain environment for international trade and investment. Also, changes in the value of a nation's currency lead to a pattern of gains and losses that are best avoided. A depreciating currency is bad for consumers who buy imports and good for exporters and import-competing firms. The reverse is true of an appreciating currency.
17. The two goals of a zero balance of trade and a stable currency are related. For example, if the value of imports exceeds the value of exports for a small country, the value of its currency depreciates.
18. The United States does not have to have a zero balance of trade each year to maintain a stable dollar because people are willing to hold dollars. In any event, the United States has not achieved a zero balance of trade or a stable value of the dollar over the past 15 to 20 years.

KEY TERMS

appreciation (currency)
balanced inflation
balance of trade
consumer price index
core rate of inflation
depreciation (currency)
Fisher equation
fully anticipated inflation
hyperinflation
inflation
producer price index
unanticipated inflation
unbalanced inflation

QUESTIONS

1. Describe how the federal government constructs the consumer price index (CPI).
2. Name two other price indexes published by the federal government other than the CPI. Indicate how they differ from the CPI and why they are useful.
3. The values of the CPI for the United States from December 1989 through December 1992 were

   1989: 109.2
   1990: 115.1
   1991: 119.9
   1992: 123.5

   a. What were the rates of inflation in the United States as measured by the CPI in 1990, 1991, and 1992?

b. What was the cumulative rate of inflation from December 1989 through December 1992?

4. Suppose that you learn that inflation in a certain country is *balanced* and *fully anticipated*.
   a. What do the italicized terms mean?
   b. What are the economic costs of a balanced and fully anticipated inflation?
   c. Is inflation likely to be balanced? To be fully anticipated? Why or why not?
5. a. Why is it not true that inflation robs everyone of purchasing power?
   b. What is a hyperinflation, and why is it a policy problem?
6. To what extent is the U.S. economy indexed against inflation? Support your answer with some specific examples.
7. Discuss the following statement, making use of the Fisher equation where appropriate: Unanticipated inflation causes a redistribution from lenders to borrowers, whereas a fully anticipated inflation does not.
8. a. Has the dollar been stable relative to other currencies in the recent past?
   b. What are the advantages to the United States and to other countries of having a stable value of the dollar relative to other currencies?
9. a. What does it mean to say that the dollar has appreciated in value?
   b. Who gains and who loses in the United States from an appreciation of the dollar?
   c. Who gains and who loses in Germany from an appreciation of the dollar against the German mark?
10. a. Why must the value of imports equal the value of exports for most countries?
    b. Why do large industrialized countries like the United States not have to maintain an equal value of imports and exports every year? Why, though, must the value of their imports and their exports be approximately equal over time?

CHAPTER

27

The National Income and Product Accounts

LEARNING OBJECTIVES

CONCEPTS TO LEARN

National income
Gross domestic product (GDP)
Value added
Consumption
Investment
Government purchases of goods and services
Net exports
The national income = national product accounting identity
The total saving = investment accounting identity
Disposable income
GDP deflator

CONCEPTS TO RECALL

The circular flow of economic activity [4]

Harvard's Simon Kuznets is generally credited with giving birth to modern macroeconomics in the 1930s. His innovation? Kuznets invented the national income and product accounting system for the macro economy.

This may sound like a fairly mundane accomplishment, but Kuznets's national accounts were a tremendous breakthrough in economic analysis for policy makers and economists alike. For the first time, governments had a framework for collecting and organizing macroeconomic data that allowed them to monitor the performance of their economies. Likewise, Kuznets's national accounting system enabled economists to put various macroeconomic theories to the test against actual data. Before Kuznets's national accounts, individual statistics on various parts of the economy were just that—individual statistics. They had no coherent story to tell.

The national income and product accounts perform two tasks that are absolutely essential to the study of macroeconomics. They measure the overall level of economic activity during the course of a year in a consistent manner, and they identify various components within the economy, such as the consumption and saving of households, that have an important bearing on the overall performance of the economy.

Chapter 27 describes the national income and product accounts of the United States. We need to have a clear and coherent picture of the entire economy before we try to understand how the macro economy operates.

The national income and product accounts measure the overall level of economic activity in terms of the circular flow of economic activity. As such, the fundamental accounting problem is to ensure that the value of the circular flow is the same everywhere on the circle. The two natural places to measure the flow of economic activity are the factor markets and the product markets. The value of the labor, capital, and land exchanged in the nation's factor markets during the year is called the **national income.** The value of the final goods and services exchanged in the nation's product markets during the year is called the **national product.** The national income and product accounts must define the two so that they are always equal to one another. The fundamental accounting identity for the economy as a whole is that national income equals national product.

NATIONAL INCOME

The value of the labor, capital, and land exchanged in the nation's factor markets during the year.

NATIONAL PRODUCT

The value of the final goods and services exchanged in the nation's product markets during the year.

A secondary goal in describing the overall level of economic activity is to divide changes in national income or product into real changes and price changes. If national product increases by 10 percent during the year, what portion of the 10 percent represents increases in the amount of real goods and services exchanged, and what portion is the result of price increases? The national income and product accounts can give us the answer. This is important because we want to be able to monitor the real growth of the economy.

The national income and product accounts do much more than describe the overall level of economic activity. Economists and policy makers want to understand how consumption and saving by households, investment by business firms, government expenditures and taxes, and other components of the circular flow influence the macro economy and the four macroeconomic policy goals. The national income and product accounts help them think about these issues by showing how all the components fit together.

TABLE 27.1 **Income Statement of a Hypothetical Corporation**

Value of Sales	= Cost of Goods Sold
Sales	Intermediate goods Compensation of employees Rental payments to persons Net interest paid Corporate profits

The national income and product accounts for the United States are compiled by the Bureau of Economic Analysis (BEA), a division of the U.S. Department of Commerce. Thanks to the BEA you can follow the U.S. economy very closely if you want to. The BEA publishes detailed statistics on national income and national product four times a year, and a selection of statistics every month, in the *Survey of Current Business*. The bureau has put together a consistent set of national accounts going all the way back to 1929. The BEA accountants have provided us with the framework and the language that we need to analyze the economy.[1]

Chapter 27 has four objectives:

1. to describe how the BEA accountants define national income and national product so that national income equals national product;
2. to define a number of the components of the circular flow that are important in understanding how the economy operates and to indicate how the components are related to one another;
3. to show how to divide changes in national product into real changes and price changes; and
4. to reflect upon what the national income and product accounts can tell us about a nation's standard of living.

NATIONAL INCOME AND NATIONAL PRODUCT

The Income Statement of the Firm

The fundamental accounting identity between national income and national product is best understood if we begin at the microeconomic level, with the income statement of a business firm. An **income statement** records the value of the output and the income generated by the firm during the course of the year. As such, the income statement is a miniature version of the national accounts.

INCOME STATEMENT

A record of the value of the output and income generated by the firm during the course of the year; a record of a firm's sales and the cost of goods sold.

Table 27.1 presents a highly simplified income statement of a hypothetical corporation. The left-hand side of the statement records the value of the firm's sales, the output of the firm. The right-hand side of the statement lists the

[1]An excellent reference on the national income and product accounts and other statistics published by the U.S. government is Albert Sommers, *The U.S. Economy Demystified*, revised edition (Lexington, MA: D. C. Heath, 1988).

costs of goods sold, the costs of purchasing the inputs needed to produce the goods (or services). The inputs are intermediate goods and the three primary factors of production, labor, land and capital. *Intermediate goods* include fuels, such as oil and gas; other raw materials, such as iron ore; and semi-finished products used in the production of the firm's product, such as tires and glass for automobiles. Firms purchase intermediate goods from other firms.

The costs to the firm of purchasing labor, land, and capital are simultaneously the incomes received by the households supplying these primary factors of production to the firm. **Compensation of employees** is the payment to, and income received by, labor. It includes wages, salaries, and fringe benefits, such as employer contributions to health insurance and pension plans. **Rental payments to persons** are combined payments to land and to capital. The rent paid for space in an office building is in part a payment for the use of the land that the building sits on and in part a payment for the use of the building itself. The portion of the rent allocated to the land is a source of income for the owner of the land. The portion of the rent allocated to the building is a source of income to those who supplied the funds to build the building. **Net interest paid** is the difference between any interest paid and any interest received by the firm. Firms receive interest when they place funds temporarily in certificates of deposit, government bonds, and other financial securities. Most of the interest paid by firms is interest on bonds that they have issued to raise funds for investment. Therefore, net interest paid is a source of income from borrowed capital. It represents a return to the firm's bondholders who have loaned funds to the firm for the purchase of capital. The final cost of goods sold is **corporate profits,** a payment to the firm's stockholders who own the firm. The owners supply funds for investment in return for stock certificates that entitle them to share in the profits of the firm. Therefore, corporate profits are a source of income from owner-supplied capital.

COMPENSATION OF EMPLOYEES

The payment to, and the income received by, labor, including wages, salaries, and in-kind fringe benefits.

RENTAL PAYMENTS TO PERSONS

The combined payments to land and to capital in the form of rents.

NET INTEREST

The difference between interest paid and interest received by firms.

CORPORATE PROFIT

The difference between the value of sales and the cost of goods sold; the income received by the stockholders who own the firm.

The income statement represents an accounting identity: *The value of sales always equals the cost of goods sold.* Corporate profits are the residual item that guarantees the two sides of the income statement balance. The profits are the funds remaining after the firm pays all its other costs of production out of the revenues from its sales. Profits can be positive, zero, or negative. For example, if profits are zero, then the firm pays nothing that year for owner-supplied capital, and the stockholders receive no income on the funds they have supplied to the firm. The principle that profits are the residual item in the cost of goods sold is very important to the structure of the national income and product accounts. We will see that all the adjustments made by the national income accountants to ensure that national income equals national product turn on the role of profits as the residual item in the firm's income statement.

National Income

National income is the sum of all payments to, or income received by, the primary factors of production—labor, land, and capital. It includes the four sources of income listed on the income statement—compensation of employees, rental income of persons, net interest paid, and corporate profits—summed over all the firms in the economy. Data on compensation of employees are gathered primarily from the states' unemployment insurance systems, which have detailed wage and salary data on almost all private-sector employees. The other three items are compiled primarily from corporate tax returns, which list the sources of income separately as part of the costs of goods sold.

A fifth, and final, component of national income is **proprietors' income,** which is the income earned by noncorporate forms of business, principally partnerships and sole proprietorships. The data on proprietors' income are collected primarily from personal income tax returns, which often do not list the sources of income separately. For example, college professors who write textbooks often establish sole proprietorships so that they can deduct their home offices as an expense to reduce their income taxes. The income that they report to the U.S. Internal Revenue Service (IRS) as the "profit" from their textbooks is a mixture of the different sources of income. A portion of the income is really a salary for the time spent writing the text. Another portion is an implicit rental payment for the land on which the house was built. Still another portion is a return to capital, which includes the office and any equipment in the office, such as a personal computer. The BEA does not attempt to break down the income into its separate sources. Instead, it records proprietors' income as a separate component of national income.

PROPRIETORS' INCOME

Income or profit earned by unincorporated forms of business, principally partnerships and sole proprietorships.

To summarize:

National income = compensation of employees + rental income of persons + net interest paid + corporate profits + proprietors' income

These are the five payments to and sources of income received by the primary factors of production—labor, land, and capital.

Value Added

The next task is to see how the national income accountants define national product so that it equals national income. The best way to do this is not to proceed directly to the product markets. Instead, we will take an intermediate step and define a concept called the value added of a business firm (or other producer). Value added measures the circular flow of economic activity at the sites where the goods and the services are produced.

The concept of value added views the firm as beginning its production process with the intermediate goods purchased from other firms. The firm then adds the primary factors of production—labor, land, and capital—to the intermediate goods and produces its own products, which have a greater value than did the intermediate goods it started with. The value of its own products is equal to the sales of the firm. The difference between the value of its sales that it ends with and the cost of the intermediate goods that it starts with is the **value added** of the firm.

VALUE ADDED

For a single producer, the difference between the value of sales and the cost of the intermediate goods that it buys from other producers; for the economy, the sum of the value added by each producer.

Value added = sales − cost of intermediate goods

The overall value added for the economy is the sum of the value added by each producer.

The value added by a firm derives from the addition of the primary factors of production. Notice that value added equals the sum of the four payments to the primary factors listed on our hypothetical income statement in Table 27.1. Sales equals the total cost of goods sold, which is the sum of all five items of cost on the right-hand side of the income statement. Value added, in effect, brings the cost of intermediate goods over to the left-hand side of the income statement, where it is subtracted from sales. Therefore, the value added by the firm must equal the sum of the remaining four items on the right-hand side, the payments to the primary factors of production. Also, the overall value added for the economy must equal national income (proprietors' income is also the difference between sales and the cost of intermediate goods for partnerships and proprietorships).

The concept of value added illustrates that national product is not equal to total sales of all goods and services. It includes only the sales of final or finished products, that is, products that are sold to final users and not to other firms as intermediate goods.

The following example will clarify the relationships among national income, value added, and national product. Imagine a very simple economy consisting of three producers: farmers who grow wheat, millers who grind the wheat into flour, and bakers who use the flour to bake bread. All the wheat grown is sold to the millers for flour. All the flour milled is sold to the bakers for bread. The bread is the final product. It is sold to the households, who consume it. Also, the only scarce primary factor of production in this economy is labor, so that wages are the only source of income. The land for growing wheat is so plentiful that it is free, and the producers somehow manage to produce their products without any capital.

Table 27.2 records the production activity of this economy, which begins with the growing of wheat. The wheat seeds are manna from heaven. They are simply lying on the ground for the farmers to pick up and plant, so that the cost of intermediate goods is zero for the wheat farmers. The farmers' labor is worth \$5, according to the table. The value of the wheat sold is \$5, equal to the cost of producing the wheat, and the farmers sell their wheat to the millers. The value added by the wheat farmers is also \$5, the difference between the farmers' sales (\$5) and the cost of intermediate goods, the wheat seeds (\$0). Notice that the value added in wheat farming equals the income earned by the farmers.

The millers take the \$5 worth of wheat, add \$10 worth of labor, and produce \$15 worth of flour, which they sell to the bakers. The \$15 equals the cost of producing the flour. The value added by the millers is \$10, the difference between their sales (\$15) and the cost of intermediate goods, the wheat (\$5). The value added in milling equals the income earned by the millers.

TABLE 27.2 Value Added, National Income, and National Product for a Hypothetical Economy

PRODUCTION ACTIVITY	COST OF INTERMEDIATE GOODS	LABOR	SALES	VALUE ADDED
FARMING WHEAT	\$ 0	\$ 5	\$ 5	\$ 5
MILLING FLOUR	5	10	15	10
BAKING BREAD	15	20	35	20
TOTALS	20	35	55	35
CONSUMPTION: \$35 (BREAD)				

The treatment of investment in the national accounts is very complicated. The BEA defines three separate categories of investment expenditures: (1) nonresidential fixed investment, (2) residential fixed investment, and (3) the increase in the final goods inventories of manufacturers. Each category is important to the study of macroeconomics and requires some comment.

NONRESIDENTIAL FIXED INVESTMENT **Nonresidential fixed investment** is what we normally think of as investment by business firms: purchases of new plant and equipment. The BEA accountants refer to the building of new plant as construction of nonresidential structures, which consist of factories, warehouses, office buildings, and retail outlets. They refer to machinery and other equipment as nonresidential producers' durable equipment.

NONRESIDENTIAL FIXED INVESTMENT
Purchases of new plant and equipment during the year.

Investment versus existing capital. The BEA counts only *new* construction activity and purchases of *new* equipment as part of investment. The purchase and sale of an *existing* structure or an *existing* machine is not counted as part of investment. The distinction between new and existing structures and equipment is essential in recording the flow of production activity during the year and in maintaining the equality between national income and national product.

Recall from Chapter 3 that investment is a flow variable and capital is a stock variable. Investment represents new production activity during the year, which is part of the overall circular flow of economic activity and generates income. In fact, the BEA records construction activity as part of investment while the construction activity is ongoing because an ongoing construction project is generating income at the same time. The BEA does not wait until the structures are completed to count them as part of investment.

In contrast, an existing building or machine was produced in some past year and generated income in the past. It is part of the existing stock of capital, but not part of investment. The purchase and sale of the building this year is just a transfer of part of the existing stock of capital from one owner to another. Therefore, to count the purchase and sale of existing buildings or machines as part of investment would overstate the current year's production activity. It would also break the equality between national income and national product; national product would increase without any corresponding increase in national income.

Investment versus intermediate goods. Businesses buy two kinds of goods from other businesses: intermediate goods and investment goods. Both kinds of goods are used as inputs in the production of goods and services. Yet intermediate goods are netted out of national product, whereas investment goods are counted as final goods and become part of the national product. What is the distinction between them? The answer is durability—how long they are expected to last—with a year's time being the dividing line. Intermediate goods are expected to be used up within the year; investment goods are expected to last for more than a year. An example of the distinction between them is the purchase of a new blast furnace to be used in the production of steel and the coal used to fire the furnace. The coal is used up immediately as it is purchased and counted as an intermediate good. The blast furnace is expected to last for more than a year, so it is counted as part of the investment of the firm.

Depreciation/capital consumption allowance. Business firms distinguish between intermediate goods and investment goods just as the national income accountants do. A steel producer would record the purchase of the coal as an intermediate good on the income statement of the firm. In contrast, the firm would count the value of the blast furnace as an addition to the firm's stock of capital and record it on the balance sheet of the firm, which lists the firm's assets and liabilities. The blast furnace would not appear as a cost of goods sold on the income statement, nor would any investment in plant and equipment.

Capital goods are used up in the process of producing goods and services, however. Blast furnaces, personal computers, and factories depreciate in value as they continue to produce goods and services no matter how well they are maintained. The process of depreciation can be very slow. Machines and equipment may remain productive up to 10 years, or even longer. Some structures may last 35 years and more. Eventually, though, every firm expects to replace its existing capital stock.

Firms set aside funds to replace their existing capital stock in an account called depreciation, which is recorded on the income statement as a cost of goods sold. The amount entered as depreciation is not an out-of-pocket expense. Rather, it is an estimate of how much the firm's capital stock has depreciated in value during the year. Table 27.3 reproduces the income statement of our hypothetical corporation from Table 27.1, with depreciation added on the right-hand side. Firms want to record an estimate of depreciation as part of their costs because every dollar of depreciation lowers their profits by one dollar. The smaller their profits, the smaller their tax liability.

ECONOMIC DEPRECIATION

The decline in the market value of a firm's capital stock over a given period of time.

Economists define **economic depreciation** as the decline in the market value of the firm's capital stock during the year. The depreciation could be due to wear and tear, or accidental damage, or obsolescence as a better technology is discovered, or simply aging. Notice that depreciation applies to the *entire* capital stock of the firm, not just to the investments of the current year.

The U.S. Internal Revenue Service (IRS) recognizes depreciation as a legitimate cost of production for tax purposes, but it does not ask each firm to estimate the economic depreciation of its capital stock. Instead, the IRS provides guidelines to firms for computing depreciation on different kinds of capital for ease of administration. The guidelines indicate how long each type of capital is expected to last.

The BEA accountants also recognize the depreciation of the capital stock as a legitimate cost of production. They do try to estimate the economic depreciation of the nation's capital stock, rather than relying on the IRS guidelines, however, because they want to generate the best possible estimate of the capital stock. They call their estimate of economic depreciation the **capital consumption allowance** (*CCA*).

CAPITAL CONSUMPTION ALLOWANCE

An estimate by the Bureau of Economic Analysis of the economic depreciation of the nation's stock of capital during the year.

Gross investment and net investment. The capital consumption allowance drives a wedge between national income and national product that has to be accounted for. To see why, refer to the income statement in Table 27.3. Re-

TABLE 27.3 Income Statement of a Hypothetical Corporation

Value of Sales =	Cost of Goods Sold
Sales	Depreciation Intermediate goods Compensation of employees Rental payments to persons Net interest paid Corporate profits

member that whatever amount the firm enters for the depreciation of its capital stock reduces corporate profits by the same amount. Depreciation has no effect on the total cost of goods sold or on the value of sales. The same holds true at the national level. The BEA reduces corporate profits and proprietors' income by the amount of its estimate of capital consumption allowance. As a result, national income falls below gross domestic product by the amount of the capital consumption allowance.

The BEA corrects this discrepancy by distinguishing between gross investment (I_G) and net investment (I_N). **Gross investment** is value of new capital put in place during the year, the three categories of investment defined above. **Net investment** equals gross investment minus the BEA's estimate of the capital consumption allowance on the entire stock of capital.

GROSS INVESTMENT
The value of new capital put in place during the year, equal to the sum of purchases of new plant and equipment, increases in firms' inventories, and purchases of new homes.

NET INVESTMENT
The difference between gross investment and the BEA's estimate of the capital consumption allowance (depreciation).

$$I_N = I_G - CCA$$

In Chapter 3 we defined investment as the change in the stock of capital without distinguishing between gross and net investment. Now we can say that net investment is the better measure of the change in the value of the stock of capital. The value of a nation's capital stock changes in two ways: (1) it increases by the addition of new capital during the year, the amount of gross investment, I_G; and (2) it decreases by the depreciation of the existing stock of capital, the capital consumption allowance, CCA. Net investment captures both changes.

The difference between gross and net investment in the United States is substantial because the annual decline in the value of the capital stock is very large. In 1992, for example, I_G was \$770.4 billion, and I_N was only \$117.0 billion. The capital consumption allowance is so large primarily because the U.S. stock of capital is so large, in excess of \$12 trillion. In other words, producers in the United States had to invest over \$650 billion in 1992 just to maintain the value of the existing stock of capital.

Gross domestic product and net domestic product. The distinction between gross and net investment in turn leads to a distinction between gross domestic product and **net domestic product** (NDP). GDP includes gross investment, and NDP includes net investment. The difference in the treatment of investment is the only difference in these two measures of national product, so that GDP and NDP differ by the amount of the capital consumption allowance. NDP is the measure of national product that is conceptually equal to national income.

NET DOMESTIC PRODUCT (NDP)
The difference between gross domestic product and the BEA's estimate of the capital consumption allowance (depreciation).

To summarize:

$$\begin{aligned} I_G &= I_N + CCA \\ \text{GDP} &= C + I_G + G + (Ex - Im) \\ \text{NDP} &= C + I_N + G + (Ex - Im) \end{aligned}$$

Therefore,

$$\text{GDP} = NDP + CCA$$

RESIDENTIAL FIXED INVESTMENT The BEA treats all purchases by households as consumption with one exception, purchases of new houses. A new house is a real asset so similar to an office building or any other business structure that the BEA counts the construction of new houses as part of total investment under the category of residential fixed investment. Residential fixed investment also includes apartments and condominiums, anything built for use as a residence.

The same accounting rules apply to residential construction as apply to nonresidential construction. The value of the construction is counted as it is put in place to correspond to the income that is simultaneously being generated in building the house. Also, residential fixed investment includes only the purchase of newly constructed houses and other residences. The purchase and sale of existing houses is simply a transfer of ownership; it is not a current production activity that generates income.

Residential fixed investment accounts for about 30 percent of total investment and only 4 percent of total GDP. Nonetheless, the housing market is very important to the study of macroeconomics because the demand for new homes is very sensitive to the level of interest rates. Most new homes are purchased with the help of a mortgage, which is a loan to a home buyer that uses the house as collateral. If you default on your mortgage payments, you forfeit ownership of your home to the bank. The standard mortgage is paid back with level monthly payments over 15 to 30 years. Each percentage point increase in mortgage rates increases the monthly payment by $50 to $100 on a $100,000 mortgage, so that the demand for mortgages is very sensitive to the level of interest rates.

CHANGE IN INVENTORIES GDP and national income are designed to measure the overall level of economic activity. As such, they need to account for the change in manufacturers' inventories during the year.

Manufacturers and retailers often hold inventories of manufactured goods. For example, a toy manufacturer may ship the toys it produces to a warehouse and then sell the toys out of the warehouse to the retailers. General Motors, Ford, and Chrysler ship cars to their dealers that the dealers sell off their lots. The amount of toys in the warehouse and the amount of cars on the dealers' lots are the inventories of toys and cars. The value of a firm's inventory is one of the assets of the firm; it is considered part of the firm's stock of capital.

Suppose that the amount of inventories held by manufacturers increases during the year. For example, a toy manufacturer produces more toys than it sells during the year, so the amount of toys in the warehouse increases. Production activity has occurred; the firm has manufactured toys and generated income in the process. Yet none of the increase in inventory appears on the income statement of the firm. The toys are not reflected in the firm's sales on its income statements because they were not sold. Producing the toys did generate payments to factors of production that appear on the income statement; the firm bought some intermediate goods and paid wages, rents, and interest attributable to the production of the additional toys in its warehouse. But since the toys were not sold, all these costs of production simply decrease the firm's profits by the same amount. Therefore, the production of the additional toys does not change the firm's total cost of goods sold. Since the production of the additional toys is not reflected in either the firm's sales or its cost of goods sold, this production activity does not appear in either national product or national income. The BEA accountants adjust for this by (1) counting the increase in inventory as part of investment, which increases national product, and (2) adding the increase in inventory to corporate profits (or proprietors' income), which increases national income. The increase in inventory is considered to be a sale by the firm to itself on its investment account. The purchase of inventory represents an increase in the assets of the firm in the form of inventory capital.

Similarly, the BEA accountants subtract any decrease in inventories from investment and profits to more accurately reflect the amount of production activity during the year. Suppose that the toy manufacturer has sold more toys than it has produced during the year, so that its inventory has decreased from the beginning to the end of the year. The amount that the inventory decreased represents sales of toys that were produced in past years, not this year. Nonetheless, selling these toys increases the firm's sales and profits, so the toys appear in both national product and national income for the current year. The BEA accountants correct for this by adjusting investment and profits downward by the decrease in inventory, thereby preserving the national income and product accounts as a measure of production activity during the year.

The change in inventories is a very small component of total investment, less than 5 percent in most years. Even so, inventories play a central role in the study of macroeconomics. We will see that firms adjust their inventories in a manner that drives the economy to an equilibrium level of national income. Also, *changes* in inventories often account for the majority of *changes* in gross domestic product from year to year.

GOVERNMENT PURCHASES OF GOODS AND SERVICES The government sector is central to the study of macroeconomics. After all, the federal government is responsible for pursuing the four macroeconomic policy goals through its fiscal and monetary policies.

The national income and product accounts record the various items in the budgets of the federal, state, and local governments. For the purposes of macroeconomic analysis it is useful to distinguish three broad categories within the governments' budgets: government purchases of goods and services, transfer payments, and taxes. Government purchases of goods and services and transfer payments are the two types of government expenditures. Taxes are the main source of government revenues.

Recall that fiscal policy is budgetary policy; it involves changes in government purchases of goods and services, or transfer payments, or taxes. We will see that changes in these three broad categories have very different effects on the economy. You will better understand why this is so once you understand how each category fits into the national income and product accounts.

GOVERNMENT PURCHASES **Government purchases of goods and services** (G) are part of gross domestic product. We noted in Chapter 1 that governments play roles of both consumer and producer in the economy. When the government purchases goods or services in its role as a consumer, it is much like a household purchasing goods and services. For example, the purchase of a land-based missile can be thought of as an act of public consumption that contributes to the national security. As such, it belongs in both the national income and the national product. On the income side, the missile was produced by a private firm and generated income in the form of wages and salaries, rents, interest payments, and profits. On the product side, the missile is a final prod-

GOVERNMENT PURCHASES OF GOODS AND SERVICES

Aggregate purchases of final goods and services by the federal, state, and local governments; the services are primarily the labor services of government employees.

uct, and the government is the final demander. The missile will sit in its silo, one hopes never to be used.

The government's role as a producer is accounted differently from that of a private business firm. The only major source of income from government production is the compensation of government employees. Governments take land by eminent domain for schools, military bases, and the like. They rarely pay rent to anyone. The BEA counts the interest on the government debt as a transfer payment because most of the interest is not a payment for borrowed capital. The majority of government debt outstanding is federal debt, and most of the federal debt was issued to pay for past wars or for current transfer payments and operating expenses. Very little of the federal debt has been issued to finance public investments. Finally, government production is not-for-profit. Indeed, much of the output from government production is not even sold; for example, the operating expenses of local schools and military bases are covered out of tax revenues. Whenever the output is sold, the price is set to cover the operating expenses, so there is no return to capital. Therefore, all that is left to include in the circular flow of economic activity from government production is the compensation of government employees, which is part of national income. The BEA maintains the equality between national income and national product by counting the compensation of government employees as part of the governments' purchases of goods and services. In fact, nearly all of the services purchased by governments are the labor services of government employees.

TRANSFER PAYMENTS Transfer payments are not counted as part of the national product because they do not correspond to any production activity during the year. People receive transfer payments because of who they are, not because they have provided a service to anyone during the year. Families on welfare receive monthly checks from the government because they are poor. Retirees receive Social Security monthly benefits because they contributed payroll taxes to the Social Security System during their working lifetimes. Their payroll contributions were made in the past, not the present. In contrast, a check paid to a public school teacher is a payment for services rendered during the current year.

Raising taxes to finance transfer payments redistributes resources within the private sector. It does not change the level of the circular flow or economic activity. Income leaves the private sector when the government collects the taxes and returns to the private sector when the government makes the transfer payments. In contrast, raising taxes to finance government purchases of goods and services does increase the circular flow of economic activity. People hired to teach in the public schools are engaged in productive activity, just as they would be if they were hired by a private firm.

TAXES All taxes levied on the suppliers of labor, capital, and land are automatically included in national income and national product. This includes the federal and the state personal and corporation income taxes, the Social Security payroll tax, and the local property tax. These taxes are part of the circular flow because the BEA values labor, land, and capital at the cost to the firms of hiring these factors of production. The cost to the firm includes any taxes paid by these factors on the income earned.

For example, suppose that you begin to work for a corporation after college at a salary of $20,000. Your take-home pay is less than $20,000 because the firm deducts federal and state personal income taxes and the Social Security payroll tax from your paycheck. The BEA accountants record your entire

TABLE 27.4 **Income Statement of a Hypothetical Corporation**

Value of Sales	= Cost of Goods Sold
Sales	Indirect business taxes Depreciation Intermediate goods Compensation of employees Rental payments to persons Net interest paid Corporate profits

$20,000 salary as part of the compensation for employees because that is what the firm pays to hire you. Although the firm may deduct in your behalf the income taxes that you owe, these deductions do not change the fact that the firm is paying you a salary of $20,000. Similarly, the rental payments to persons, net interest paid, corporate profits, and proprietors' income recorded in national income all include any taxes paid on these sources of income. Moreover, since the cost of goods sold on the income statement includes all income taxes, the value of sales also includes all income taxes. Income taxes are part of national product as well as national income. Finally, local property taxes are also included in national income because households pay these taxes out of their take-home pay.

Indirect business taxes (*IBT*) are the one exception to the rule that all taxes are included in national income and national product. **Indirect business taxes** are primarily the sales and excise taxes that firms pay on the sale of their products. Firms list indirect business taxes as a separate cost on their income statements, as illustrated in Table 27.4. As a result, these taxes drive a wedge between sales and the sources of income regardless of who bears the burden of the tax.

INDIRECT BUSINESS TAXES
Sales and excise taxes that firms pay on the sale of their products.

Suppose that the firm succeeds in passing the tax on to its customers by raising its prices. In this case the value of sales increases by the amount of the tax, and corporate profits remain the same. Suppose, instead, that the firm cannot raise its prices, and it bears the full burden of the tax. In this case the value of sales remains constant, and the firm's profits fall by the full amount of the tax. In either case the tax has driven a wedge between sales, which appear as part of the national product, and profits, which appear as part of the national income. Indirect business taxes are the main break in the equality between national income (*NI*) and net domestic product (NDP). The BEA adjusts by adding indirect business taxes to national income to maintain the equality.

To summarize:

$$\text{NDP} = NI + IBT$$
$$\text{GDP} = \text{NDP} + CCA = NI + IBT + CCA$$

NET EXPORTS The increasing internationalization of the U.S. economy has been one of the major ongoing macroeconomic stories of the past 30 years. Exports and imports are now each approximately 11 percent of GDP; in 1965 they were only 5 percent of GDP. Exports and imports are now large enough to have a substantial impact on overall economic activity.

We saw in Chapter 4 that net exports are the one leakage in the circular flow of economic activity. The BEA accountants have to include net exports in GDP both to record the amount of production activity in the United States and to maintain the equality between national income and national product.

EXPORTS
Goods and services produced domestically and sold in foreign countries.

Exports (*Ex*) are goods and services that are produced domestically and sold in foreign countries. As such, they are part of the annual production activity in the United States and contribute to U.S. national income. But they are not included as part of the expenditures by U.S. final demanders because they are purchased by households, business firms, and governments in foreign countries. The BEA accountants adjust by adding exports to GDP.

IMPORTS
Goods and services produced in foreign countries and sold in the domestic country.

The reverse holds true for imports. **Imports** (*Im*) are goods and services that are produced in foreign countries and sold in the United States. As such, they are not part of the annual production activity in the United States, and they do not contribute to U.S. national income. But they are included as part of the expenditures by U.S. final demanders because they are purchased by U.S. households, business firms, and governments. The BEA accountants adjust by subtracting imports from GDP.

NET EXPORTS
The difference between exports and imports.

The adjustment for exports and imports is typically combined into one term, **net exports,** which is the difference between exports and imports.[2]

$$\text{Net exports} = Ex - Im$$

Summary: National Income and Product

This concludes our tour of the circular flow of economic activity as recorded in the national income and product accounts of the United States. The key concepts are national income, the value of the income earned by the labor, land, and capital exchanged in the nation's factor markets; gross (net) domestic product, the value of the final goods and services exchanged in the nation's product markets; and the fundamental accounting identity between national income and gross domestic product. The only differences between national income and gross domestic product are the capital consumption allowance and the indirect business taxes. Gross domestic product is more widely reported than is national income as the measure of the total economic activity.

DISPOSABLE INCOME, SAVING, AND INVESTMENT

We next want to look at two components of the circular flow of economic activity that are crucial to the study of macroeconomics: disposable income and saving. We also want to develop a second important accounting identity: total saving in the economy must equal the level of investment.

[2]Earlier we distinguished between gross domestic product (GDP) and gross national product (GNP) in terms of where the final goods and services are produced. The difference between GDP and GNP in terms of expenditures occurs in net exports. Net exports in GDP consist of all merchandise trade in goods and services. Net exports in GNP include merchandise trade plus the net flow of factor incomes to the United States from the rest of the world. The net income flow equals receipts of income by U.S. citizens earned in foreign countries minus receipts of income by foreign citizens earned in the United States. In terms of our previous example, the income earned by the U.S. tax accountant in London is an example of the former, and the income earned by the British tax accountant in New York is an example of the latter. Technically, only GNP corresponds to national income because the U.S. national income only includes income earned by U.S. citizens.

Disposable Income

Households earn all the income generated in the economy because they own all the labor, land, and capital supplied to the nation's factor markets. Households do not receive all the income that they earn, however. Some of their income is siphoned off by the government and business sectors before they have a chance to use it.

The income actually available to households for their own use is called **disposable income.** Macroeconomists are particularly interested in disposable income because households base their consumption and saving decisions on disposable income, not on national income.

DISPOSABLE INCOME

The income available to households for their own use, to be consumed or saved.

The main difference between national income and disposable income results from the taxes and the transfers of the federal, state, and local governments. The taxes that households pay out of national income are not part of their disposable income. Federal and state personal income taxes and the Social Security payroll tax are often withheld from our wages and salaries even before we receive our paychecks. If we then pay a property tax to a local government or if the corporation in which we own stock pays federal or state corporation income taxes before paying us our dividends, these taxes further reduce the income available to us for our own spending and saving. Governments give as well as take, however. Transfer payments such as Social Security benefits and public assistance checks increase the disposable incomes of the households that receive them. Therefore, to go from national income to disposable income we must subtract all taxes paid to governments and add back in all transfer payments received from governments. The only exception to this rule is the amount of indirect business taxes paid by business firms. Indirect business taxes are not part of national income to begin with.

The second important difference between national income and disposable income is the retained earnings of business firms. *Retained earnings* are a portion of the profits that managers set aside to finance future investment projects. These funds are not available to households as disposable income.

The combined effect of taxes and retained earnings means that only a fraction of corporate profits and proprietors' income ends up as disposable income of households, even though they are both part of national income. Consider corporate profits. National income includes the corporate profits before any tax has been paid out of them. As we have just seen, the portion of the profits that corporations pay in corporation income taxes to federal and state governments is not available to households. The corporate profits that remain after the taxes have been paid have one of two destinations. The managers can pay out the after-tax profits as dividends to the stockholders, or they can retain these profits as retained earnings. Only the portion of corporate profits that is paid out in dividends becomes part of the disposable income of households. The retained earnings remain with the corporation.

$$\text{Corporate profits} - \text{corporate income taxes} = \text{corporate after-tax profits}$$
$$\text{Corporate after-tax profits} = \text{dividends} + \text{retained earnings}$$

Retained earnings are called **business saving** (S_{business}) because they are part of the national income that is saved to finance investment. Retained earnings can be thought of as saving that managers do on behalf of the stockholders. The stockholders/households own all the after-tax profits, but they let the man-

BUSINESS SAVING

The portion of the profits that managers set aside to finance future investment projects; also called *retained earnings.*

agers keep part of the profits as retained earnings for further investment in the corporation.

To summarize, disposable income differs from national income because of taxes, government transfer payments, and retained earnings.

Disposable income (DI) = national income (NI)
− all taxes (Tx) [except indirect business taxes]
+ government transfer payments (Tr)
− retained earnings of business firms (S_{business}) [business saving]

$$DI = NI - Tx \text{ (except } IBT) + Tr - S_{\text{business}}$$

National income is quite a bit larger than disposable income is in the United States. In 1992 national income was $4,744.1 billion, and disposable income was $4,430.8, a $300 billion difference.

Finally, households can do two things with their disposable income: They can consume their income, or they can save it. Saving by households is called **personal saving** (S_{personal}).

PERSONAL SAVING
The portion of disposable income that households do not consume.

$$DI = C + S_{\text{personal}}$$

PERSONAL INCOME The BEA publishes another measure of household income, personal income, that is closely related to disposable income. The only difference between them is that personal income includes personal taxes, which consist primarily of the federal and the state personal income taxes. Disposable income excludes these taxes.

$$\text{Personal income} = \text{disposable income} + \text{personal taxes}$$

Personal income in the United States was $5,058.1 in 1992, about $627 billion more than disposable income.

Personal income receives more attention in the news media than does disposable income because the BEA publishes estimates of personal income each month. The BEA can estimate disposable income only on a quarterly basis since some of the tax data needed to compute disposable income are not available on a monthly basis. Although personal income is more widely reported, disposable income is more relevant to macroeconomic analysis. Households base their spending and saving decisions on their disposable income, not on their personal income.

The Saving = Investment Accounting Identity

We have seen that the circular flow of economic activity causes an identity between national income and national product. The national income flowing through the nation's factor markets must equal the national product flowing through the nation's product markets. Lying beneath the surface of the circular flow is another accounting identity of fundamental importance to the study of macroeconomics, the identity between saving and investment. If the national income accountants define national income and national product so that the two are equal, then the total saving in the economy must equal the level of investment.

Deriving the equality between saving and investment from the equality between national income and national product is tedious, but well worth the effort. We saw in Chapter 3 that investment is the key to long-run economic growth. The identity between saving and investment indicates that saving and investment go hand in hand. Policies designed to stimulate investment are of little use if the level of saving cannot be increased. Conversely, policies designed to stimulate saving are of little use if firms do not increase their level of investment. We always have to think about saving and investment together. In addition, the equality between saving and investment highlights the interrelationships among three of the leading macroeconomic issues of the day in the United States: the low level of investment, the large federal budget deficit, and the trade imbalance between imports and exports. A little work now to understand the identity between saving and investment will pay great dividends in your study of macroeconomics.

Our goal is to begin with the equality between national income and national product and show that it implies the equality between saving and investment. We will begin with the equality between national income (*NI*) and net domestic product (*NDP*), which leads to an equality between total saving and net investment.

We know that national income (*NI*) and net domestic product (NDP) are not quite equal; they differ by the amount of indirect business taxes (*IBT*).

$$\textit{National income} = \textit{national product}$$

$$NI + IBT = \text{NDP}$$

Write NDP in terms of its components, the expenditures by final demanders.

$$NI + IBT = C + I_N + G + (Ex - Im)$$

Next, we want to replace national income with disposable income. To do this, we have to built up from disposable income to national income. We did the reverse above in going from national income to disposable income. To go from disposable income to national income, add taxes (except indirect business taxes) and retained earnings (business saving) to disposable income, and subtract government transfer payments from disposable income.

$$NI = DI + Tx \text{ [except } IBT\text{]} - Tr + S_{\text{business}}$$

Therefore,

$$\textit{National income} = \textit{national product}$$

$$DI + Tx \text{ [except } IBT\text{]} - Tr + S_{\text{business}} + IBT = C + I_N + G + (Ex - Im)$$

Combine the two tax terms of the left-hand side so that *Tx* refers to *all* taxes from now on.

$$DI + Tx - Tr + S_{\text{business}} = C + I_N + G + (Ex - Im)$$

Next, replace disposable income with the sum of its components, consumption plus personal saving.

$$C + S_{\text{personal}} + Tx - Tr + S_{\text{business}} = C + I_N + G + (Ex - Im)$$

Notice that consumption (C) appears on both sides of the equation, so that we can cancel it. Also, combine personal and business saving into one term.

$$(S_{\text{personal}} + S_{\text{business}}) + Tx - Tr = I_N + G + (Ex - Im)$$

We want net investment (I_N) by itself on the right-hand side. Therefore, bring government purchases of goods and services (G) and net exports ($Ex - Im$) over to the left-hand side, and combine all the government terms.

$$(S_{\text{personal}} + S_{\text{business}}) + (Tx - Tr - G) + (Im - Ex) = I_N$$

The three terms on the left-hand side show the three sources of saving in the economy from every sector of the economy. The first term is saving by the private sector, consisting of personal saving by the household sector and business saving by the business sector. The second term is saving by the government sector. The third term is saving by the foreign or rest-of-world sector.

$$S_{\text{private sector}} + S_{\text{government sector}} + S_{\text{foreign sector}} = I_N$$

The sum of the saving by each sector is the total saving in the economy. Therefore, we have shown that total saving equals net investment.

$$S_{\text{total}} = I_N$$

Some comments on each source of saving are in order.

PRIVATE-SECTOR SAVING
The sum of personal saving and business saving.

SAVING BY THE PRIVATE SECTOR Personal saving and business saving are typically combined as saving by the private sector because the households own all the private business firms in the economy. Any after-tax profits earned by corporations and other businesses are really income earned by the stockholders of the firm. As indicated above, a decision to retain some of the profits for future investment is a saving decision by the managers of the firm on behalf of the stockholders. The stockholders presumably take into account any retained earnings saved on their behalf when deciding how much to save out of their own disposable income. Therefore, business saving and personal saving are closely linked.

GOVERNMENT SAVING
The difference between government revenues and government expenditures.

SAVING BY THE GOVERNMENT SECTOR Saving by a government is the same as running a budget surplus. A government's budget is in surplus if its tax revenues (and other fees) exceed its total expenditures on transfer payments and purchases of goods and services (budget surplus: $Tx - Tr - G > 0$). Conversely, a government's budget is in deficit if its tax revenues (and other fees) are less than its total expenditures on transfer payments and purchases of goods and services (budget deficit: $Tx - Tr - G < 0$). A budget deficit represents negative saving, or dissaving, by a government. In other words, a budget deficit is a negative budget surplus. Saving by the government sector is the combined saving, or budget surpluses, of the federal, state, and local governments.

A budget surplus is a form of saving because a government disposes of excess tax revenues that it has not spent much as a household disposes of funds that it decides to save and not spend. The government's treasurer places the funds in checking and savings accounts, certificates of deposit, and other financial instruments that the government is allowed to buy. The funds then move through the financial markets to their ultimate destination, investment by business firms. (Chapter 20 discusses how funds flow through the nation's financial markets from savers to investors. The pathways are often very complex; funds can travel through many layers of financial institutions on their journey to the investors.)

SAVING BY THE FOREIGN SECTOR To see why the difference in the value between imports and exports represents saving by the foreign sector, return to our simple example in Chapter 26 of the U.S. food exporter and the British clothing importer. Recall that the exporter sells 100£ worth of food in London, and the importer sells $180 worth of sweaters in the United States. Once the importer and the exporter exchange pounds sterling for dollars on the foreign exchange market, we know the dollar value of the food exports. We considered one example in which the exchange rate was $1.60/£. At this exchange rate the importer gives up $160 for the exporter's 100£, and the dollar value of the exports is $160. The dollar value of the imports ($180) exceeds the dollar value of the exports ($160) by $20, exactly the amount that the importer has left over after the exchange of currencies. The importer in our example has no choice but to hold the $20 in the United States. She may place the funds in a bank account or buy another kind of financial asset such as a certificate of deposit, a stock, or a bond. This is exactly what households do when they save and what governments do when they run a surplus.

FOREIGN SAVING
The difference between imports and exports.

Our simple example illustrates the following general principle: Whenever the dollar value of imports exceeds the dollar value of exports, importers are holding dollars that become part of the total saving in the economy. Dollars saved by foreign citizens finance U.S. investments just as do the dollars saved by U.S. households, businesses, and governments.[3]

TOTAL SAVING
The sum of personal saving, business saving, government saving, and foreign saving.

Accounting Identities and Economic Behavior

The saving = investment identity places before us the interrelationships among three of the leading macroeconomic stories in the United States: a disappointingly low level of net investment, large government budget deficits fueled by record federal deficits, and a huge trade imbalance of imports over exports. These stories have been ongoing in tandem since 1982, shortly after President Reagan first took office, and we will return to them time and again in the macroeconomic chapters that follow. Some of the key issues are evident from just looking at the accounting identity, however. For example, we can see that large budget deficits reduce total saving in the economy dollar for dollar. This may have a depressing effect on net investment if funds saved in the private sector end up buying government bonds rather than financing private investment. At the same time, the huge trade imbalance counteracts the budget deficits to some extent by providing a huge source of saving from foreign citizens. Foreign citizens have been buying some of the federal debt.

[3] $S_{\text{foreign sector}}$ also includes the net interest flows to and from the United States on assets held by U.S. citizens in foreign countries and assets held by foreign citizens in the United States.

They have also been directly financing investment by business firms in the United States. Investment in the United States might have been even lower without the influx of funds from abroad.

A word of caution is in order, however—*extreme* caution. Be sure you understand the equality between saving and investment for what it is, a national income accounting identity. Saving must equal investment by definition, given the circular flow of economic activity. The equality between saving and investment has no behavioral content in and of itself; it cannot explain cause and effect. For example, huge budget deficits may not cause a decrease in total saving or investment. Instead, the deficits may induce households and firms to save more if they believe that their taxes will be increased sometime in the future to pay off the debt. Households and firms may then increase their saving to have more funds available to pay the higher future taxes. Or the budget deficits may induce a trade imbalance as foreigners rush in to buy the safe, high-yielding federal bonds. The value of the dollar appreciates when foreign money managers with pounds and francs and yen are seeking dollars. An appreciating dollar causes imports to rise and exports to fall. These are just two of any number of possibilities. One cannot infer cause and effect from a national income accounting identity.

Nonetheless, the accounting identity must hold. Any explanation of macroeconomic events must be consistent with the fact that total saving from all sectors of the economy must equal the level of investment. We will return often to the equality of saving and investment in our study of macroeconomics.

Summary of the U.S. National Income and Product Accounts

Table 27.5 on pages 786–87 summarizes the relationships we have developed in the chapter and includes 1992 values of all items for the United States.

CONSTANT DOLLAR GDP AND THE GDP DEFLATOR

CURRENT DOLLAR (NOMINAL) GROSS DOMESTIC PRODUCT

The actual dollar value of the gross domestic product generated during the year.

CONSTANT DOLLAR (REAL) GROSS DOMESTIC PRODUCT

The value of the gross domestic product generated each year, evaluated at the prices that existed in a given base year.

The BEA publishes two values of gross domestic product: current dollar, or nominal, GDP; and constant dollar, or real, GDP. **Current dollar or nominal GDP** is the actual dollar value of the GDP during the year. **Constant dollar or real GDP** measures the value of the GDP generated each year at the prices that existed in a given base year. The current base year is 1987. Therefore, the constant dollar or real GDP for each year is the value that the GDP would be had it been purchased at 1987 prices. Changes in the constant dollar GDP from year to year represent changes in the real quantities of goods and services flowing through the nation's product markets because the prices of the goods and services are held constant at their base year values. Constant dollar GDP removes the effect of inflation on the circular flow of economic activity.

The GDP Deflator

GDP DEFLATOR

A price index based on a market basket of consumption goods, investment goods, government purchases, and net exports; used to convert current dollar GDP into constant dollar GDP.

The BEA converts current dollar GDP to constant dollar GDP by means of a price index called the **GDP deflator.** The GDP deflator is constructed along the lines of the consumer price index (CPI) that we described in Chapter 26.

The BEA accountants define a market basket of goods and services that are representative of the items in the GDP. The GDP market basket contains a selection of consumer goods and services, investment goods, goods and services purchased by governments, and net exports. The GDP deflator then tracks changes in the cost of purchasing the market basket over time.

The only difference between the GDP deflator and the CPI is that the GDP market basket changes each year to reflect the current components of the GDP. The CPI market basket is representative of a household's purchases in a chosen year and remains constant from year to year.

Changes in the CPI are most often used to represent the overall rate of inflation. The main purpose of constructing a GDP deflator is to convert the actual current dollar GDP to the constant dollar GDP. The conversion is simple: Divide the actual current dollar GDP by the GDP deflator (expressed as a decimal fraction) to compute the constant dollar GDP. Division by the GDP deflator is said to "deflate" the actual value of the GDP to its constant dollar value. For example, the actual current dollar GDP for 1992 was $5,951 billion, and the GDP deflator for 1992 was 120.9. Therefore, the constant value GDP was $4,922 billion.

$$\begin{aligned}\text{Constant value GDP}_{1992} &= \text{current value GDP}_{1992}/\text{GDP deflator}_{1992} \\ &= \$5{,}951 \text{ billion}/1.209 = \$4{,}922 \text{ billion}\end{aligned}$$

Because the GDP deflator uses the current year's market basket, dividing actual GDP by the GDP deflator has the effect of computing the dollar value of GDP each year using the base year (1987) prices.[4]

Using constant dollar GDP rather than current dollar GDP to monitor the growth of an economy over time is important during times of inflation, such as the United States has been experiencing since World War II. The rate of growth in actual current dollar GDP is a combination of the rate of growth in real goods and services and the rate of growth in prices. Inflation can easily dominate the rate of growth in nominal current dollar GDP. For example, suppose that the U.S. economy is operating on its production possibilities frontier and that output is growing at its limit of 3 to 4 percent per year. Inflation happens to be 10 percent per year. Current dollar GDP would be growing at 13 to 14 percent per year (approximately), far more than the real growth of the economy. The majority of the growth in current dollar GDP is due to inflation.

The effect of inflation on the rate of growth in current dollar GDP increases over time. Compare the current and the constant dollar GDP figures for 1950 and 1992 (in $ billion):

	1950	1992
Current dollar GDP	$ 286	$5,951
Constant dollar GDP	1,400	4,922

---

[4]To see this, express the GDP deflator for 1992 as GDP $\text{deflator}_{1992} = (P_{92} \cdot Q_{92})/(P_{87} \cdot Q_{92})$. Notice that the quantities are the current year (1992) quantities. The actual current dollar $\text{GDP}_{1992} = P_{92} \cdot Q_{92}$. Therefore, dividing the current dollar GDP_{1992} by the GDP deflator_{1992} to compute the constant dollar GDP_{1992} yields

$$\text{Constant dollar GDP}_{1992} = (P_{92} \cdot Q_{92})/[(P_{92} \cdot Q_{92})/(P_{87} \cdot Q_{92})] = P_{87} \cdot Q_{92}$$

$P_{87} \cdot Q_{92}$ is the dollar value of the 1992 components of the GDP using the 1987 prices.

TABLE 27.5 The National Income and Product Accounts of the United States, 1992 ($ billions)

A. NATIONAL INCOME AND NATIONAL PRODUCT			
National Income			
National income			$4,744.1
Compensation of employees		3,525.2	
+			
Rental income of persons		4.7	
+			
Net interest paid		415.2	
+			
Corporate profits		394.5	
+			
Proprietors' income		404.5	
Gross Domestic Product			
Gross domestic product			5,950.7
Consumption		4,095.8	
+			
Gross investment		770.4	
+			
Government purchases of goods and services		1,114.9	
+			
Net exports		−30.4	
Exports	636.3		
−			
Imports	666.7		
Gross and Net Investment			
Gross investment			770.4
Net investment	117.0		
+			
Capital consumption allowance	653.4		
Net Domestic Product			
Net domestic product			5,297.3
Gross domestic product	5,950.7		
−			
Capital consumption allowance	653.4		
Gross Domestic Product and National Income			
Gross domestic product[a]			5,950.7
National income		4,744.1	
+			
Indirect business taxes		504.2	
+			
Capital consumption allowance		653.4	

[a]The three components listed do not add to gross domestic product because of the exclusion of minor items that we ignored in the chapter, and because of statistical discrepancies that arise in collecting the data.

(table continued on next page)

TABLE 27.5 The National Income and Product Accounts of the United States, 1992 ($ billions) (continued)

B. DISPOSABLE INCOME, PERSONAL INCOME, CONSUMPTION, AND PERSONAL SAVING			
Disposable Income			
Disposable income			4,430.8
National income		4,744.1	
−			
Taxes (except indirect business taxes)		918.4	
+			
Transfers (government + private)		866.1	
−			
Retained earnings		103.2	
+			
Other[b]		(−)157.8	
Personal Income			
Personal income			5,058.1
Disposable income		4,430.8	
+			
Personal taxes		627.3	
Consumption and Personal Saving			
Disposable income			4,430.8
Consumption (and other personal outlays)[c]		4,218.2	
+			
Personal saving		212.6	
C. INVESTMENT AND SAVING			
Net Investment = Total Saving			117.0
Total saving			117.0
Saving: private sector		315.8	
Personal saving	212.6		
+			
Business saving (retained earnings)	103.2		
+			
Saving: government sector		(−)282.2	
+			
Saving: foreign sector[d]		83.4	

[b]The path from national income to disposable income is somewhat more complicated than represented in the chapter. The Other category includes portions of compensation of employees and net interest that households do not have at their disposal, and other minor items. It also includes some statistical discrepancies.

[c]Consumption here includes personal transfers of interest and other items that are in addition to the consumption of goods and services listed under gross domestic product.

[d]Saving by the foreign sector includes interest earned on assets held by foreign citizens in the United States and by U.S. citizens in foreign countries, as well as other minor transfers. These items are excluded from net exports listed under gross domestic product. Foreign saving also includes a large statistical discrepancy, which is inevitable when trying to account for transactions across international borders.

SOURCES: U.S. Department of Commerce, Economics and Statistics Administration, Bureau of Economic Analysis, *Survey of Current Business* 73, No. 3 (March 1993): Table 1.1, p. 6; Table 1.9, p. 8; Table 1.14, p. 9; Table 2.1, p. 10; and Table 5.1, p. 14. The historical data in the chapter are from Council of Economic Advisors, *Economic Report of the President, 1993*, (Washington, D.C.: U.S. Government Printing Office, 1993), unless otherwise noted (and earlier editions of the *Economic Report of the President* in some cases).

Current dollar GDP increased nearly 21-fold during the 42-year period (5,951/286 = 20.8), whereas constant dollar GDP increased only 3.5-fold (4,922/1400 = 3.5). The increase in the constant dollar GDP best measures the growth in real goods and services because both the 1950 GDP and the 1992 GDP are evaluated using 1987 dollars. We can see that much of the 21-fold increase in current dollar GDP was due to inflation. The lesson is clear: Use data on constant dollar GDP to track the real increases in the circular flow of economic activity over time.

REAL GDP AND THE STANDARD OF LIVING

Growth in real GDP per person is the best single measure available to economists for judging how much the standard of living has improved over time within a country. But how good a measure is it? For instance, real GDP per person in the United States was $9,194 in 1950 (1987 prices). By 1992 real GDP per person had grown to $19,274, slightly more than twice its value in 1950. These data tell us that the United States was producing and delivering two times as many goods and services to its citizens, on average, in 1992 than in 1950. Can we conclude from this that the average citizen in the United States was twice as well off in 1992 as in 1950? The answer is almost certainly no.

The main problem with attempting to link real GDP per person to economic well-being is that GDP is really not designed to measure economic well-being. GDP is primarily a measure of the amount of marketed activity that takes place within an economy during the course of a year: the value of final goods and services exchanged in a nation's product markets. As a result, real GDP per person misses a number of factors that affect the standard of living.

Imputing Values to Nonmarketed Activity

The first problem in trying to link real GDP per person with the standard of living is that GDP ignores a lot of nonmarketed activity that contributes to people's economic well-being. The BEA accountants do attempt to adjust GDP figures for some kinds of nonmarketed activity. The two most important adjustments are the value of food consumed on the farm that produced it and the value of housing services consumed by homeowners.

The BEA accountants try to estimate the market value of the food that farmers set aside for their own families. The estimated value of the food is counted simultaneously as a source of income for the farmer and as consumption by the family. Imputing a value of housing service to homeowners is an attempt to treat home ownership and renting symmetrically. If a family rents an apartment, the rent they pay is a source of rental income to the landlord and a form of consumption by the family. No such payment exists when a family owns its own home, yet the family is consuming housing services just as the renting family is. To maintain consistency between renting an apartment and owning a home, the BEA accountants impute a value of rent on the owned home equal to what an equivalent house would rent for. Homeowners are seen as paying the imputed value of the rent to themselves as income and using it to consume an equal amount of housing services. Notice that the imputed values of food or rent simultaneously increase one component of national income (farmers' income or rental income to persons) and one component of national product (consumption). Any adjustment to the national income and product accounts must maintain the equality between national income and national product.

The Underground Economy

The BEA adjustments for nonmarketed activity still miss a large amount of nonmarketed activity, both legal and illegal, that has come to be known as underground economy. The legal segment of the underground economy includes such activities as barter—the straight exchange of goods and services—and home production. The illegal segment of the underground economy includes criminal activities such as the drug trade and the more general problem of tax evasion.

Regarding the legal activities, suppose that I have a green thumb and my neighbor is an auto mechanic, so we agree to exchange our services without pay. I tend his gardens, and he fixes my car. If I were to hire a mechanic and he were to purchase a landscaping service, national income and product would rise by the value of each service. Given that we exchange the services in a barter arrangement, however, our services remain "underground" and are not recorded in the accounts, even though they are just as valuable to us as if we had purchased them. The same point applies to the child rearing, cooking, cleaning, and repair work that people do for themselves in their own homes and apartments. National income and product increase when people take the children to a daycare center, or go to a restaurant, or hire a domestic to clean the house, or hire a carpenter to repair the bathroom ceiling. These valued activities go unreported when people do them themselves.

REFLECTION: What routine, day-to-day services does your household provide for itself that your family could purchase in the market if it chose to do so?

Regarding the illegal activities, criminal behavior such as illicit drug dealing raises an interesting ethical question. Crime pays on average, sad to say. Criminal behavior contributes to the economic well-being of many who engage in it. But should the ill-gotten gains from crime be counted as part of society's well-being? If the answer is no, then income and consumption from the sale of illegal drugs does not belong in national income or national product.

Tax evasion, although illegal, is a somewhat different issue since it is often associated with legal activities. For example, operating a bar is largely a cash-run business, and hiding cash transactions from the tax authorities is much easier than hiding credit card transactions. Suppose that the otherwise law-abiding owners of a bar decide that the combined bite of the state sales tax, the federal and the state income taxes, and the federal payroll tax is just too much to bear, so they hide some of their sales from the tax authorities. The sale of drinks is legal and ought to be recorded as part of national income and national product, but the BEA accountants will not pick up the hidden sales and income. Domestics are another example. People who clean houses or do light repair work and yard chores often insist on being paid in cash so they can avoid paying taxes on the income. They, too, are part of the underground economy.

The size of the underground economy is an important issue for macroeconomic analysis. Consider the example of an increase in income taxes. Macroeconomic theory predicts that an income tax increase will lower the level of economic activity, as we will see. The presence of a large underground economy could well make the effect of the tax increase seem larger than it really is, however. The problem is that tax increases drive more activity underground. Some people may quit their jobs and do more of the household chores themselves rather than hiring others to do them. In addition, tax evasion on marketed activities is likely to rise. Therefore, although the recorded level of national income and product decreases following an income tax increase, much of the decrease could be offset by increases in underground activities. Since economists cannot see the underground activities, they tend to overestimate the reaction of the economy to the tax increase.

CURRENT ISSUE: We have had tax accountants tell us that they estimate the underground economy to be about one-third of the GDP. Of course, many of their clients operate on the fringes of the underground economy.

Estimating the size of the underground economy is obviously a very difficult task. A recent study of the underground economy in Great Britain found it to be 3 to 5 percent of the recorded British GDP.[5] Whether this estimate is accurate, or whether it reflects the size of the underground economy in the United States, is anyone's guess.

Quality Changes and the GDP Deflator

Still another problem in linking changes in constant dollar GDP to changes in economic well-being is that the market basket used to compute the GDP deflator keeps changing over time. Earlier we compared the constant dollar GDPs for 1950 and 1992. The 1950 constant dollar GDP is based on a representative market basket of goods from 1950, and the 1992 constant dollar GDP is based on a representative market basket of goods from 1992. Those are very different market baskets. Just think about the consumer portion of the basket. Very few households had a television in 1950, and now our homes are filled with many other electronic gadgets that did not exist at all in 1950: CD players, microwave ovens, videocassette recorders, and so on.

The BEA accountants do try to account for quality changes in some of the more important products such as automobiles. If the price of a new car increases by 10 percent, the BEA tries to estimate how much of the 10 percent increase is the result of real quality improvements, such as air bags and antilock brakes, and how much is a pure price increase. Adjustments of this kind are limited though, and the accountants can hardly adjust adequately for quality changes when entirely new products appear and other products disappear. Just what is the appropriate 1987 price of a 1950 vacuum tube, 9-inch, black-and-white television? Constant dollar GDP comparisons are clearly less accurate the longer the time period being compared. This is unfortunate because we would like to be able to track real economic growth, and changes in the standard of living, over a very long period of time.

Pollution, Depleted Resources, and Other Economic Bads

Economic growth is somewhat of a mixed blessing. With growth and industrial development come a number of economic "bads": pollution of the environment, destruction of forests and wetlands, depletion of oil and mineral reserves, an increase in work-related accidents and fatalities, crowding and crime in major cities, and so forth. The national income and product accounts do not subtract out most of these bads.

---

[5]S. Smith, "European Perspectives on the Shadow Economy," *European Economic Review* 33 (1989): 592.

The treatment of pollution in the national accounts is especially one-sided. The costs of pollution are ignored, yet fighting pollution raises GDP, as when manufacturers buy scrubbers for their smokestacks to reduce pollution. The BEA accountants estimate the depreciation of the capital stock each year, but they do not bother to estimate the annual destruction or depletion of our natural resources. The costs of industrial accidents are also misrepresented in the national accounts. The working time lost because of accidents does reduce GDP, but the medical care required to treat the accidents increases GDP. Given the high cost of medical care, an industrial accident probably increases GDP!

The BEA's decision on these matters is undoubtedly pragmatic. How does one value the decline in health or, worse, the loss of life from pollution? What is the cost of destroying or depleting our irreplaceable natural resources? By how much does living in fear of crime reduce the quality of life? Any method of evaluating these costs would be fairly arbitrary. Nonetheless, ignoring the economic bads that are the inevitable consequences of growth clearly overstates the increase in economic well-being as measured by the growth in real GDP per person.

HISTORICAL NOTE: The reverse is also true. Industrial air and water pollution has declined substantially in the United States since 1970. The gains in reduced pollution are missed in the GDP so the growth in GDP per person understates the increase in the U.S. standard of living since 1970 on this score.

Leisure Time

Valuing changes in leisure time is yet another difficult problem in trying to link the growth in real GDP to economic well-being. Manufacturing workers in the United States have enjoyed ever more leisure time throughout the twentieth century. The average workweek in manufacturing was 54.3 hours in 1900.[6] It had decreased to 38.6 hours by 1953 and has remained fairly constant since then. Increases in constant dollar GDP since 1900 clearly understate the growth in economic well-being by failing to include the value of the increased leisure time.

The value of leisure time can cut the other way, too. The past 35 years have witnessed a steady increase in the percentage of women in the labor force. Married women with families who work in the labor market no doubt have much less leisure time than did their counterparts of 35 years ago who worked only in the home. Two-earner families make real GDP grow more rapidly, but the growth in GDP overstates the growth in economic well-being because it misses the loss in leisure time that many women have suffered.

The Distribution of Income

One final point needs to be made about using real GDP as a measure of economic well-being. Suppose that we could somehow ignore all the measurement problems noted above. Even so, growth in real GDP per person is not all that societies care about. They also care how the additional output (income) is distributed.

The 1980s were hailed as a decade of steady economic growth in the United States. Indeed, the economy did enjoy over 100 months of uninterrupted growth in real GDP per person from the third quarter of 1982 onward, as the economy returned to the production possibilities frontier from the depths of the 1981–82 recession. On closer inspection, however, economists discovered

[6]R. Ehrenberg and R. Smith, *Modern Labor Economics: Theory and Public Policy*, Second edition, (Glenview, IL: Scott, Foresman, 1985) Table 6.3, p. 152.

that the economic growth was extremely unbalanced. The rising tide of growth did not lift all of the boats during the 1980s; the distribution of income became much more unequal. The people at the very top of the income distribution received a hugely disproportionate share of the income gains, while the people at the bottom of the distribution hardly gained at all. Economic growth in the 1980s had little effect on the number of people living in poverty.

Did the decade of the 1980s improve the overall economic well-being of the United States? Your answer to this question depends on how you weigh the size of the economic pie against the distribution of the pie, that is, the gains in real GDP per person against the increasing inequality of income. People have come out strongly on both sides of this question.[7]

A Concluding Comment

Let's end on a positive note. Real GDP per person may be a very imperfect measure of the standard of living, but it is the best measure available to us. And it tells the right story, by and large.

Economic historians have attempted to trace U.S. real GDP back to the early years of the nation. One study estimates that real GDP per person was $1,285.50 in 1820 (1987 prices). As noted earlier, it was $19,274 in 1992, 15 times larger than in 1820. The population of the United States was 28 times larger in 1992 than in 1820, but the real GDP was over 400 times larger![8]

Is the U.S. standard of living 15 times higher now than in 1820? Perhaps not. The GDP figures may overstate the improvement in the standard of living because of the increase in marketed activity since 1820 and the numerous economic bads associated with growth. Then again, the GDP figures may understate the improvement in the standard of living because we enjoy so much more leisure time than did our ancestors. Scratching out a living on the farms and the frontier in the early 1800s took backbreaking labor every waking hour of the day.

Whatever the truth of the matter, there can be no doubt that the U.S. standard of living has improved many times over since 1820. The GDP figures testify loud and clear to the stunning economic success of American capitalism.

SUMMARY

Chapter 27 described the national income and product accounts of the United States, which are compiled by the Bureau of Economic Analysis within the U.S. Department of Commerce. Table 27.5 summarized the most important accounting relationships. Some of the key principles underlying the accounts are the following.

---

[7]Economists also rely on GDP per person to compare the relative standards of living in different countries. Unfortunately, comparisons of GDP across countries may be a worse gauge of relative economic well-being than are comparisons of GDP within countries over time. We will consider these problems in Chapter 41, which discusses the low-income developing countries.

[8]The estimate of GDP per person in 1820 is from A. Maddison, *Phases of Capitalist Development* (Oxford: Oxford University Press, 1982), 8. (Conversion to 1987 prices for purposes of comparison was done by author.)

1. The national income and product accounts measure the circular flow of economic activity. As such, the fundamental accounting identity is that national income must equal national product.
2. If national income is defined to equal national product, then saving must equal investment. The three components of saving are
   a. saving by the private sector, consisting of the personal saving of households and business saving (or retained earnings out of profits);
   b. saving by the government sector, equal to the combined budget surpluses of the federal, state, and local governments. Government deficits represent negative government saving; and
   c. saving by the foreign sector, equal to the difference between imports and exports.
3. The value added by business firms measures the circular flow at the point of production. It is equal to total sales less the cost of intermediate goods.
4. A very important component of the circular flow is disposable income, which is the income available to households. Households base their consumption and saving decisions on their disposable income. Consumption is by far the most important component of gross domestic product, and personal saving helps finance the investment of business firms.
5. Current dollar or nominal GDP is the actual value of GDP in a given year. Constant dollar or real GDP evaluates the GDP in a given year using base-year prices. The current base year is 1987. The GDP deflator is a price index of final goods and services that is used to convert current dollar GDP to constant dollar GDP. Dividing the current dollar GDP by the GDP deflator has the effect of evaluating the GDP in the base-year prices.
6. The best available measure of the overall economic well-being of a nation is real GDP per capita. It is used to track improvements in a nation's standard of living over time and to compare relative standards of living across countries.
7. Even so, real GDP per capita is a flawed measure of economic well-being because it is not designed for that purpose. Its intent is to measure the amount of marketed activity during the year. As such, it misses or miscalculates the effects on economic well-being of all of the following:
   a. the underground economy, consisting of legal bartering of goods and services, household production, and illegal activities such as criminal behavior and tax evasion;
   b. many of the economic bads that inevitably accompany economic growth, such as air and water pollution, destruction and depletion of natural resources, the increase in industrial accidents, and crowding and crime in major cities;
   c. quality changes in goods and services, including the introduction of new products and the disappearance of other products over time;
   d. changes in leisure time; and
   e. changes in the distribution of income.
8. Real GDP per person in the United States has grown 15-fold since 1820. The standard of living in the United States may or may not be 15 times higher than in 1820, but the growth in real GDP per person clearly shows that American capitalism has been a stunning economic success.

KEY TERMS

capital consumption allowance
compensation of employees
constant dollar (real) gross domestic product
consumption
corporate profit
current dollar (nominal) gross domestic product
disposable income
economic depreciation
exports
foreign saving
government purchases of goods and services
government saving
gross domestic product
gross investment
gross national product
imports
income statement
indirect business taxes
national income
national product
net domestic product
net exports
net interest
net investment
personal saving
private-sector saving
proprietors' income
rental payments to persons
retained earnings
total saving
value added

QUESTIONS

1. a. Why must national income equal national product?
   b. What is value added, and why must it equal national income?
2. Which of the following are included in the measurement of GDP?
   a. An increase or decrease in firms' inventories during the year.
   b. Purchases of the products of one firm by another firm to be used as material inputs.
   c. Purchases of foreign cars by domestic citizens.
   d. Purchases of houses built 10 years ago.
   e. The decline in pollution from paper mills during the year.
3. What is the capital consumption allowance, and how might it differ from economic depreciation?
4. a. Can net investment ever be negative?
   b. Can gross investment ever be negative?
5. a. What is the difference between disposable income and national income?
   b. Why is each of these income concepts important to the study of macroeconomics?
6. a. What are the three components of total saving?
   b. Why must total saving equal investment for the entire economy?
7. Suppose that the national income accountants find the following data for an economy during 1992 (data in $ billion).

   Consumption = $8,000
   All taxes = $3,000
   Disposable income = $12,000
   Retained earnings = $2,000
   Capital consumption allowance = $1,000
   Government purchases = $1,000
   Government transfers = $1,500
   Exports = $3,000
   Imports = $1,000

   Compute the values of personal saving, gross domestic product, net domestic product, net and gross investment, and total saving.
8. You are given the following data on the current dollar GDP and the GDP deflator for some country:

YEAR	CURRENT DOLLAR GDP ($ BILLION)	GDP DEFLATOR (1987 = 100)
1991	$5,000	125
1992	6,000	200

   Did constant dollar (real) GDP increase or decrease in 1992?
9. Suppose that a country had a real GDP per person of $10,000 in 1950 and now has a real GDP per person of $15,000. Can we conclude that the citizens of the country are better off now than they were in 1950?
10. The data in the table below refer to the same simple economy described in the chapter. Wheat is used to make flour, flour is used to make bread, and bread is sold to consumers as a final product. Labor is the only primary factor of production. Fill in the missing entries in the table.

	INTERMEDIATE MATERIALS	LABOR	SALES	VALUE ADDED
Wheat	0	10		
Flour		20		
Bread		50		

   Also calculate the national income, total value added, total sales in the economy, and consumption of bread

CHAPTER

28

Modeling the Macro Economy: New Classical and New Keynesian Perspectives

LEARNING OBJECTIVES

CONCEPTS TO LEARN

The business cycle
Fiscal policy
Monetary policy
New classical economics
New Keynesian economics
Aggregate demand and aggregate supply
Aggregate demand and aggregate supply shocks

CONCEPTS TO RECALL

The three-part economic problem [1]
The circular flow of economic activity [4]
The Laws of Supply and Demand [5, 6, 7]
The macroeconomic policy goals [25, 26]
  a. Long-run economic growth [25]
  b. Full employment [25]
  c. Price stability [26]
  d. Stable international economic relations [26]
The national income = national product accounting identity [27]

Bill Clinton's victory over George Bush in the 1992 presidential election was more than a changing of the political guard in Washington. It was a profound changing of the economic guard as well.

There are two main schools of macroeconomics today, new classical economics and new Keynesian economics. The new classical economists believe that the macro economy performs about as well as can be expected on its own in the short run. "Hands off" is their general advice to the government. In their view, doses of fiscal and monetary policies cannot expect to do much good and may actually be harmful. They tend to limit their policy prescriptions to long-run problems, such as policies to increase long-run economic growth. The new Keynesians, in contrast, believe that the economy can perform very badly in the short run if left on its own. They favor active intervention with fiscal and monetary policies to help the economy pursue the macroeconomic policy goals.

Presidents Reagan and Bush kept counsel with economists whose leanings were more toward the new classical view. They both agreed that the economy can best solve its own problems for the most part. President Clinton swept the new classical economists out of Washington and surrounded himself with some of the very best new Keynesian economists. The president made it quite clear in his first State of the Union address to Congress that he wants the federal government leading the way on any number of economic problems. The administration's economic policy stance is interventionist again, more so than at any time since the Nixon administration in the early 1970s.

Having discussed the four macroeconomic policy goals and described the national income and product accounts, we are now in a position to study the overall operation and performance of the U.S. economy.

Chapter 25 identified the three fundamental questions of macroeconomic analysis: (1) What factors determine the circular flow of economic activity? (2) How does the circular flow of economic activity relate to the four macroeconomic policy goals? (3) How can the government influence the level and the composition of the circular flow with its fiscal and monetary policies and thereby help society achieve the macroeconomic policy goals. Chapter 28 begins with some observations on these three questions that will serve as a guide to where we are heading in the chapters that follow.

Macro economists have not come close to reaching an agreement on how to answer the fundamental questions. One reason why they have not has to do with the size and the complexity of any modern economy. No one can hope to understand the U.S. economy in all its details. Instead, economists are forced to study the economy with highly simplified models, and they cannot agree on the best model for analyzing the economy.

Chapter 28 considers the all-important first step in macroeconomic analysis: how to build a model of the macro economy. The discussion includes an overview of the two leading macro models in use today, the new classical model and the new Keynesian model. We will make use of both models in our analysis of the U.S. economy.

THE CIRCULAR FLOW OF ECONOMIC ACTIVITY AND MACROECONOMIC POLICY

The Business Cycle

The central question that macro economists wrestle with is the determination of the circular flow: What factors determine the level and the composition of the circular flow of economic activity?

The study of the circular flow is interesting in its own right because the circular flow does not simply increase in a smooth and orderly fashion from year to year. Far from it. As we noted in Chapter 25, the circular flow of economic activity is highly erratic in all the world's developed market economies. In some years market economies perform well below their production possibilities frontiers. Resources lie idle, and the production of goods and services is much smaller than it could be. In other years market economies strain against their production possibilities frontiers. Resources are fully utilized, and the production of goods and services is as large as possible.

Furthermore, erratic behavior is the rule, not the exception. The circular flow of economic activity moves continually over time in a pattern of expansions and contractions, booms and busts, called the **business cycle.** The circular flow may grow for awhile, but each period of growth eventually comes to an end and is followed by a period of decline, a recession. Fortunately, each recession also eventually comes to an end and is followed by a period of growth.

BUSINESS CYCLE
The continuing pattern over time of expansions and contractions, booms and busts, in the circular flow of economic activity in capitalist economies.

The periods of growth and recession vary in duration and intensity. An economy may experience uninterrupted growth for a number of years or for just a few months; similarly, the recessions may last for years or months. When economies are growing, the rate of growth may be rapid or slow; when economies are in decline, the rate of decline may also be rapid or slow. Long or short, intense or mild, the business cycle is a fundamental macroeconomic fact of life in a market economy.

We can see these patterns in Figure 28.1, which illustrates the behavior of the circular flow of economic activity for the U.S. economy from 1977 through 1992. The horizontal axis lists each quarter (three-month period) from the beginning of 1977 to the end of 1992. For example, 1978:4 refers to the fourth quarter of 1978, the three-month period from October through December. The vertical axis records the real gross domestic product of the United States, in billions of dollars, using 1987 prices as the base year. The values of real gross domestic product listed for each quarter are annual rates, that is, the value that would result if the flow of domestic product during the quarter were maintained for an entire year. The solid line represents the production possibilities frontier for the economy during each quarter. It is an estimate of maximum value of real gross domestic product that the economy could sustain without causing any severe inflationary pressures.

The uneven performance of the U.S. economy, including the cyclical pattern of growth and recession, is evident from the figure. At the beginning of 1977 we see that the economy was operating below its production possibilities frontier. Large oil price increases in 1973–74 had pushed the economy into a deep recession. By 1977 the economy had entered a period of growth and was proceeding to march back to its frontier. The progress was temporarily halted by

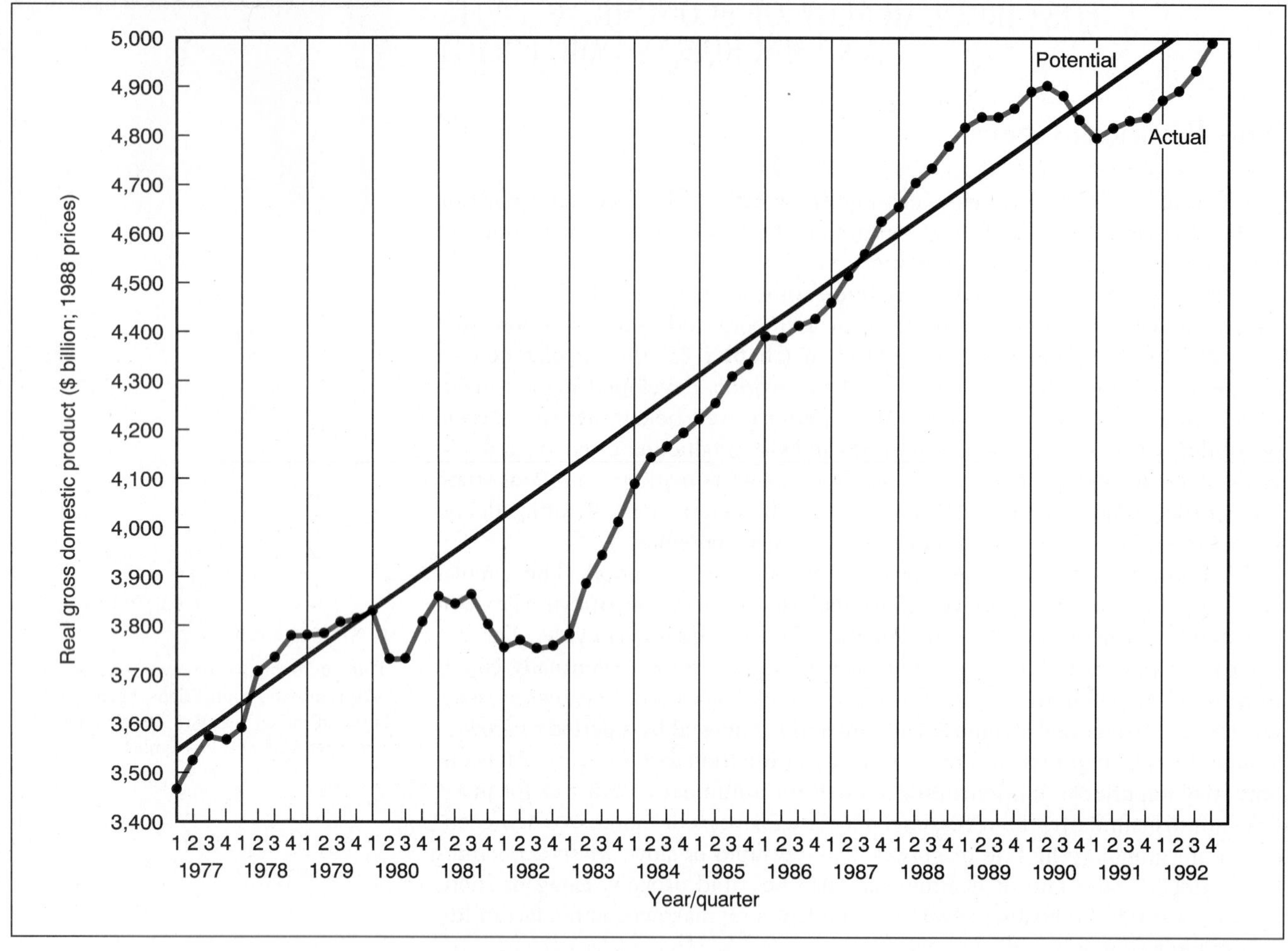

FIGURE 28.1

The United States Economy—1977–92

The figure tracks the real gross domestic product (GDP) of the United States in each quarter from 1977 to 1992. The straight line is an estimate of the sustainable productive capacity of the economy, corresponding to the production possibilities frontier. The performance of the U.S. economy during this period reflects the erratic, cyclical ebbs and flows that are typical of all the industrialized market economies. At times real GDP was increasing and at other times it was decreasing. Sometimes the economy strained against its productive capacity, and at other times it operated well below the production possibilities frontier.

SOURCE: R. Gordon, *Macroeconomics*, sixth edition (New York: Harper Collins, 1993), Appendix A, p. A6; and Council of Economic Advisors, *Economic Indicators, March 1993* (Washington, D.C.: U.S. Government Printing Office, 1993), 2. The potential GDP line was drawn as a straight line through Gordon's estimate of potential real GDP for 1977:1 and 1992:2 to serve as a simple visual approximation of Gordon's time series of estimated potential real GDP for each quarter.

a slight decline in fourth quarter of 1977, but the economy quickly recovered, reached the frontier in early 1978, and essentially remained at the frontier through the first quarter of 1980. At that point the period of prosperity came to an end, as the economy declined sharply during the second quarter of 1980. The economy began to recover over the next year, but before it could return to the frontier, it suffered a very sharp recession that lasted for over a year. By the middle of 1982 the U.S. economy was farther below its production possibilities frontier than at any time since the Great Depression of the 1930s. The economy finally reversed direction near the end of 1982 and entered a long period of virtually uninterrupted growth back to the frontier. The period of growth continued until 1990, when the economy experienced another brief recession that lasted through the first quarter of 1991. In summary, the period from 1977 to 1992 exhibited all the typical macroeconomic features of developed market economies: some years when the economy is straining at the limits of its capacity, other years when the economy is operating well below its capacity, and a cyclical pattern of growth and recession that varies considerably in duration and intensity. The study of macroeconomics tries above all else to understand why market economies behave in this erratic fashion.

HISTORICAL NOTE: In 1993 the U.S. economy was growing, but very slowly—not even fast enough to reduce the unemployment rate significantly.

The Circular Flow and the Macroeconomic Policy Goals

Economists are not interested in the question of what determines the circular flow of economic activity just for its own sake. The question is important because the ebbs and flows of the economy have a direct impact on each of the four macroeconomic policy goals. We talked about one obvious example in Chapter 25, the problem of cyclical unemployment. People have a much easier time finding good, high-paying jobs and avoiding unemployment if the economy is growing rapidly and pushing against its production possibilities frontier than they do if the economy is declining and operating far below its production possibilities frontier. Similarly, inflation is likely to increase when the economy moves close to the frontier and begins to strain against its productive capacity. Investment is also influenced by the performance of the economy. Business firms are more likely to invest if the economy is booming than if the economy is languishing in the depths of a recession. These are just a few of the ways that the level of the circular flow affects the macroeconomic policy goals.

The composition of the circular flow also has a direct impact on the macroeconomic policy goals. We noted in Chapter 3 that the only final goods an economy can produce are investment goods and consumer goods. The rate of long-run economic growth depends crucially on the investment/consumption mix within the economy. Another important compositional issue relates to the distinction between current dollar gross domestic product (GDP) and constant dollar GDP. What factors determine how much of the growth in current dollar GDP is growth in real GDP and how much of the growth is just price increases?

Part and parcel to understanding what determines the level and the composition of the circular flow is understanding the linkages between the circular flow and the macroeconomic policy goals. We will emphasize these linkages throughout the macroeconomics chapters of the text because the macroeconomic policy goals ultimately determine the overall economic health of a nation.

Fiscal and Monetary Policies

The national governments of all countries engage in macroeconomic policy. Broadly speaking, **macroeconomic policy** is an attempt to achieve the macroeconomic policy goals by intervening in some form in the operation of the economy. Macroeconomic policy is typically associated with the national gov-

MACROECONOMIC POLICY

An attempt to achieve the macroeconomic policy goals by intervening in some form in the operation of the economy.

ernment because only the national government can hope to influence the overall level of economic activity.

As noted in Chapter 2, the United States has generally been unwilling to pursue the macroeconomic goals directly. The federal government does not typically offer "make-work" government jobs to anyone who is unemployed, or control prices to prevent inflation, or commandeer people's savings to increase the level of investment, or block the flow of imports and exports to any great extent. The government would have to control economic activity with a very heavy hand to pursue the macroeconomic policy goals so directly, and this is inconsistent with the U.S. commitment to market capitalism. Instead, the United States has chosen an indirect approach to achieving the macroeconomic policy goals. The macroeconomic policies of the federal government target the economy itself, not the policy goals. The government attempts to influence the level and the composition of the circular flow of economic activity and thereby achieve the macroeconomic policy goals. This is why understanding what determines the circular flow of economic activity and how the circular flow links to the policy goals is so important. The federal government cannot possibly hope to conduct effective macroeconomic policy without this understanding, given the way it has chosen to proceed.

We noted in Chapter 25 that the two principal macroeconomic policies of the federal governments are fiscal policy and monetary policy. We will focus on these two policies throughout the text.

FISCAL POLICY

Changes in the federal budget made for the specific purpose of influencing the level and the composition of the circular flow of economic activity; includes changes in government spending on goods and services, changes in transfer payments, or changes in taxes.

FISCAL POLICY Recall that **fiscal policy** refers to changes in the federal budget made for the specific purpose of influencing the level and the composition of the circular flow of economic activity. These budgetary changes could be changes in government spending on goods and services, or changes in transfer payments, or changes in taxes; in other words, they could be changes in any component of the federal budget. The conduct of fiscal policy is the joint responsibility of the administration and the Congress, since they have joint control over the federal budget.

A word on the motivation for budgetary changes is in order. The administration and the Congress undertake changes in the federal budget for all kinds of reasons, most of which have nothing to do with trying to affect the performance of the economy. In the early 1990s, for example, the administration proposed and the Congress approved large reductions in military expenditures following the disintegration of the Eastern European Communist bloc and the Soviet Union. These reductions were clearly motivated by strategic military considerations, the belief that the military threat to Western Europe and the United States had been substantially reduced. We would not tend to think of the military cutbacks as an act of fiscal policy. In contrast, when the Congress passes a temporary reduction in personal income taxes to stimulate the economy or extends the period that unemployed workers can collect unemployment insurance, these are clearly instances of fiscal policy.

Ascribing motives to individual budgetary changes is problematic, however. We will learn that changes in government expenditures and taxes affect the level and the composition of the circular flow regardless of why they were undertaken. Therefore, when the administration and the Congress are deciding on the appropriate fiscal policy stance, they have to take into consideration all the legislated budgetary changes that are expected to occur throughout the year for whatever reason. They may or may not decide to make additional changes in government expenditures or taxes for the sake of the economy. Whatever they decide, though, the total of all the changes in government expenditures and taxes during the year defines the fiscal policy stance of the government.

To give a recent example, the Clinton administration decided in 1993 that the projected cuts in military spending were not enough. President Clinton wanted to reduce the federal budget deficit considerably for reasons that we will explore in later chapters. So the administration proposed spending cuts in other areas to bring the total cut in spending to about $250 billion over a five-year period. The administration also proposed $250 billion in tax increases over the same five years. Congress approved these changes in the summer of 1993.

MONETARY POLICY **Monetary policy** refers to changes in the money supply made for the specific purpose of influencing the level and the composition of the circular flow of economic activity. The two most important components of the money supply in the United States are the dollar bills of various denominations and the checking accounts in commercial banks and other depository institutions. The money supply has a direct effect on the circular flow because most economic transactions are paid for with dollars or checks.

MONETARY POLICY
Changes in the money supply made for the specific purpose of influencing the level and the composition of the circular flow of economic activity.

The conduct of monetary policy in the United States is the responsibility of the Board of Governors of the **Federal Reserve Banking System,** which is the nation's central bank. The Federal Reserve is commonly referred to as the "Fed." Congress established the Fed in 1913 as a public agency separate from the administration and the Congress. The chairman of the Board of Governors is required to appear before the Congress each year to report on the board's intended monetary policy. But the Board of Governors is free to increase or decrease the money supply as it chooses.

FEDERAL RESERVE BANKING SYSTEM
The central bank of the United States, commonly referred to as the "Fed."

Motivation is not an issue with monetary policy. The Fed is a non-profit institution whose primary responsibility is to manipulate the money supply in a manner consistent with achieving the macroeconomic policy goals. Virtually all changes in the money supply engineered by the Fed are motivated by a desire to affect the performance of the economy.

The Three-Part Economic Problem for the Entire Economy

The conduct of fiscal and monetary policies can be thought of as the government's attempt to solve the standard three-part economic problem for the entire macro economy, consisting of objectives, alternatives, and constraints.

Objectives: The objectives are the four macroeconomic policy goals. One might think that the government should try to reach each of the four goals simultaneously. Unfortunately, this is not always possible, given the choice to pursue the goals indirectly by manipulating the economy. Fiscal and monetary policies that move the economy closer to one of the goals often move the economy farther away from one or more of the other goals. For example, policies that stimulate the economy and move it closer to the production possibilities frontier create jobs for unemployed workers. They may also induce more investment by business firms, which increases long-run economic growth.

But policies that stimulate the economy are also likely to increase the rate of inflation, reduce the value of the dollar relative to other currencies, and increase the balance-of-trade deficit. The government is thus often forced to choose. The policy question is this: What set of policies provides the best compromise among the macroeconomic policy goals?

Alternatives: The alternatives are the policy options available to the government for achieving the macroeconomic policy goals, principally fiscal and monetary policies.

Constraints: The primary constraint in the macroeconomic policy problem is the economy itself, which determines how the application of fiscal and monetary policies affects each of the macroeconomic policy goals. The economy also determines the extent to which the four goals are compatible with one another. Suppose that the Fed increases the money supply. What effect does this have on unemployment? On long-run economic growth? On inflation? On the value of the dollar? The economy holds the answers to these questions. Understanding what determines the circular flow of economic activity simultaneously helps us define the menu of policy choices that are available to the government.

The study of macroeconomics can be thought of as an attempt to understand the structure of the three-part macroeconomic policy problem and to determine how best to solve it. This has not proved to be an easy task.

Economists are not at all in agreement about how to solve the macroeconomic policy problem. Divisions run deep. One source of disagreement is largely a matter of taste and centers on the objectives. Economists may disagree on the importance that policy makers should attach to each of the policy goals. Some economists may favor an all-out attack on unemployment; others may be concerned about holding down the rate of inflation. If so, their policy recommendations are likely to be quite different. A more important and fundamental disagreement centers on the constraint, that is, on the operation and the performance of the economy. Macro economists cannot agree on what factors are most important in determining the circular flow of economic activity. They have not settled on the best model for analyzing the economy. To understand why not, we have to think a bit about the problem of how to build a model of the entire economy.

THE NEED FOR A MACRO MODEL

Trying to understand the operation of a modern market economy is a truly daunting task. Nowhere is the need for the modeling approach to economic analysis more obvious than in the study of macroeconomics. Think back for a moment to the description of the U.S. economy in Chapter 4: more than 250 million consumers, 18 million business firms producing tens of thousands of products, $2 trillion of government expenditures, hundreds of billions of dollars of international trade with over 100 nations, $6 trillion worth of goods and services produced every year. No one can hope to understand such a huge and complex economy in all its details, and economists do not even try. They approach the study of macroeconomics by building highly simplified models of the macro economy that, they believe, capture the essential features of how the economy operates.

Macro economists understand that their models are much, much simpler than are the complex economies that they are trying to describe. They know that they are ignoring many aspects of the economy and that their models may sometimes be wide of the mark in predicting the unemployment rate, the level of inflation, or the pace of economic growth. Nonetheless, one has no choice but to think about the modern macro economy in an extremely simplified way. Building a model of the economy is the necessary first step in macroeconomic analysis.

Even highly simplified models of the economy can be extremely complicated. Private economic consulting firms, such as DRI–McGraw-Hill and Chase Econometrics, build huge mathematical models that are designed to forecast, or predict, various aspects of the economy. They sell their forecasts to businesses who want to know where the economy is heading in order to help them with their production and marketing plans. Many government agencies have also built large mathematical forecasting models to help them design fiscal and monetary policies that will best meet the macroeconomic policy goals. Agencies with their own forecasting models include the Federal Reserve, which is in charge of controlling the nation's money supply; the Congressional Budget Office, which offers economic analysis and advice to the Congress; the Council of Economic Advisers, which advises the president and writes the annual *Economic Report of the President;* and the U.S. Treasury and the states' departments of revenue, which are interested in forecasting future tax collections.

The private and the government forecasting models are exceedingly complex. The largest forecasting models contain hundreds of economic variables embedded in thousands of interrelated equations that only very large mainframe computers are capable of solving. Even so, these large forecasting models look very simple when set against the staggering complexity of the U.S. economy. They, too, miss much of the detail of the economy, with the result that they all have their good and bad years. At times one of the forecasting models may be right on the mark. At other times it may miss by a wide margin, as when it predicts a decrease in unemployment over the next six months and the unemployment rate actually rises.

Our goals in this text are much more modest than those of the giant forecasting models. We want to describe a few simple relationships that will give us a good first-pass understanding of how the U.S. economy operates. We are after a qualitative analysis of the key macroeconomic variables, such as national income, investment, interest rates, and the unemployment rate, not accurate quantitative predictions of their values. For instance, the models we will be using are far too simple to be able to predict the rates of unemployment and inflation to the nearest percentage point. They are detailed enough, however, to indicate what forces cause unemployment and inflation to rise or fall, and this is enough for our purposes.

Whether simple or complex, all models of the macro economy have the same basic goal in mind. They are all trying to explain what forces determine the level and the composition of the circular flow of economic activity. Why does the circular flow increase by 6 percent one year and not at all the next? Why is the level of saving and investment so low in the United States? Macro models are useful to business and the government only to the extent they can answer questions such as these. To give one example, the better we understand the circular flow of economic activity, the better we can answer the two fundamental macroeconomic policy questions: (1) How do the level and the composition of the circular flow affect the four macroeconomic policy goals? (2) How can the government help to achieve the macroeconomic policy goals through its monetary and fiscal policies?

Modeling the Circular Flow

Since all macro models are trying to explain the circular flow of economic activity, they all begin with the same relationship, one that describes the circular flow. The first relationship, or equation, of every macro model represents the circular flow through the market for goods and services. It is written

$$Y = C^d + I^d + G^d + (Ex^d - Im^d)$$

The Y on the left-hand side of the equation stands for national income. The terms on the right-hand side are the demands, or desired expenditures, of the four sectors of the economy. C^d is consumption demand by the household sector, I^d is investment demand by the business sector, G^d is the demand for goods and services by the government sector, and $(Ex^d - Im^d)$ is the demand for net exports [the demand for exports (Ex^d) minus the demand for imports (Im^d)] by the foreign sector.

The equation represents the supply and the demand sides of the product markets. The left-hand side of the equation indicates the total, or aggregate, value of final goods and services that producers are willing to supply to the product markets. Producers generate the national income in the process of producing their goods and services. Since national income equals national product, the value of the national income generated in production equals the value of all the final goods and services produced during the year. As noted above, the right-hand side of the equation indicates the total, or aggregate, demand for the final goods and services in the product markets by all four sectors of the economy.

The equation serves as a statement of equilibrium for the economy as a whole. It says that the circular flow of economic activity has achieved its equilibrium value when the total amount of final goods and services that producers are willing to supply is equal to the total amount of final goods and services that demanders are willing to buy. The equation is analogous to the equilibrium condition for a single market: A market is in equilibrium when the supply of the product equals the demand for the product.

The remaining task in building a macro model is to specify what economic variables determine each side of the equation. What variables determine how much total product the producers in the economy are willing to supply? What variables determine how much total product the final demanders are willing to buy? These turn out to be among the more controversial questions in all of economics. Economists have debated long and hard over the key variables that determine the circular flow of economic activity in a modern capitalist economy such as the United States, and the debate continues to rage. The professional economics literature contains at least five different basic models of the U.S. economy. The models differ in the emphasis they place on the supply and the demand sides of the product markets and on the variables that are most important in determining aggregate supply and demand. Macro economists cling tenaciously to their preferred models.

The debate among macro economists is difficult to resolve precisely because macroeconomic models are so simple relative to the economy they are trying to describe. Simplicity requires sweeping assumptions about how the economy operates. Every model of the economy contains some assumptions that are realistic and others that are unrealistic, with the result that each has its strong and weak points. At best, a macro model will be useful for explaining and predicting some events and not so useful for explaining and predicting other events. No one macro model can hope to explain and predict everything with unerring accuracy.

Everyone is striving toward the same end—a consensus best model of the macro economy. But finding that "best model" has proved to be an elusive goal. The truth is that macroeconomics is a much less settled discipline than is microeconomics. The vast majority of economists are in agreement about the basic principles of microeconomics. Macroeconomics, in contrast, has been perpetually in turmoil, no more so than today.

THE NEW CLASSICAL AND THE NEW KEYNESIAN PERSPECTIVES

Two models, the new classical model and the new Keynesian model, have emerged from the pack to become the leading macroeconomic models of the day. New classical economists and new Keynesian economists have very different views about the variables that determine the circular flow of economic activity. The differences between them are important because their models also have very different implications for government policy. New classical economists do not believe that the government can do much to improve the performance of the private economy in the short run. In their view, occasional doses of fiscal and monetary policies are bad medicine. These measures are unnecessary because they cannot bring the economy closer to the macroeconomic policy goals, on average. They are also undesirable because they cause the economy to behave erratically. The best course for the government is steady-as-she-goes. The government should announce its intended fiscal and monetary policies and stick to its plans so that the private economy knows exactly what the government is doing. This helps individuals and business firms perform more confidently and effectively.

The new Keynesians, in contrast, believe that fiscal and monetary policies have an important role to play in managing the economy. In their view market economies can perform very badly if left to their own devices, straying far from any one or all of the macroeconomic policy goals. Occasional doses of fiscal and monetary policies, correctly administered, are just the right medicine for an ailing economy. They can significantly improve the overall performance of the economy and help a nation achieve its macroeconomic policy goals.

We want to highlight the main differences between the new classical and the new Keynesian models because they will be featured throughout the macroeconomics chapters of this text. Unfortunately, a consensus between the two leading branches of macroeconomic analysis appears to be a long way off.

The New Classical Model

The so-called classical economists of the 1800s and early 1900s had one prevailing model of how individual product and factor markets operated—supply and demand. To the extent they thought about macroeconomics, they simply assumed that the overall level of economic activity was also governed by the Laws of Supply and Demand. They analyzed the exchanges in a nation's product markets as if these markets comprised a single competitive market blown up to encompass the entire economy. The new classical economists of today embrace the old classical view that the macro economy is best modeled as if it were competitive and governed by the Laws of Supply and Demand.

A reasonable case can be made for the assumption that the Laws of Supply and Demand determine the overall level of economic activity in the United States. Industrial organization economists who study individual product markets tell us that the majority of output in the U.S. economy is marketed under highly competitive conditions. A common estimate is that the Laws of Supply and Demand are a useful tool for analyzing how prices and quantities change in approximately 70 percent of all the product markets in the United States.

There also appears to be a substantial amount of competition in the markets for labor and capital, the two most important primary factors of production. Of all the workers in the United States, 25 percent (more than 31 million individuals) change the *industry* in which they work within every three-year period, and only one-half of all full-time workers have held the same job for more than 3½ years.[1] Workers in the United States are clearly willing and able to respond to market opportunities. Wages and salaries are also quite flexible and responsive to market conditions in a large number of labor markets. For example, the starting salaries of college graduates fell relative to salaries generally in the 1970s when the baby boom generation was graduating and flooding the job market. The starting salaries of college graduates are rising today relative to salaries generally as the first members of the small baby bust generation are now graduating and entering the job market.

Similarly, U.S. financial markets are responsive to the rates of return available on various financial securities. If the interest rate on government bonds rises slightly relative to the return available on common stocks, money tends to pour out of the stock market and into the government bond market. Also, the average level of interest rates in the financial markets rises and falls with the amount of money that the Federal Reserve makes available in the economy. The free flow of resources among markets and flexible prices that respond to market conditions are the hallmarks of competitive markets.

The point is that modeling the overall economy as if it were competitive and governed by the Laws of Supply and Demand ought to be a good approximation of reality if the majority of the nation's individual product and factor markets are highly competitive.

PREDICTIONS OF THE NEW CLASSICAL MODEL Modeling the macro economy as competitive leads to a number of predictions about the behavior of prices and quantities, some of which are highly controversial.

---

[1] R. Ehrenberg and R. Smith, *Modern Labor Economics: Theory and Public Policy*, fourth edition (New York: Harper Collins: 1991), 360.

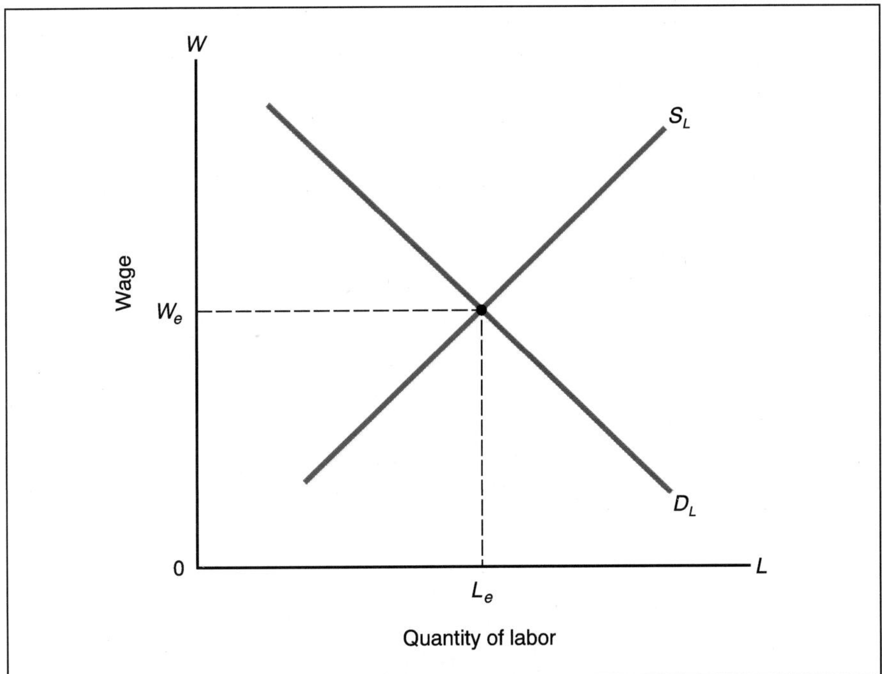

FIGURE 28.2

Full Employment in a Competitive Labor Market

A competitive labor market operates in accordance with the Laws of Supply and Demand. The supply curve S_L indicates how many people are willing to work at each wage and the demand curve D_L indicates how much labor the firms are willing to hire at each wage. The equilibrium is (L_e, W_e), at the intersection D_L and S_L. Everyone who wants to work at the wgae W_e is working, so there is full employment. Also, firms use the labor that they hire where it is most valued, so the output produced with the labor L_e is as large as possible. Therefore, if all labor (and other factor) markets were competitive, the economy would operate on its production possibilities frontier.

Perhaps the most striking prediction of the competitive new classical model is that the U.S. economy will almost always be on, or at least very near, its production possibilities frontier. This prediction follows from the assumption that factor markets are competitive. To see why, let's consider the simplest possible case in which there is only one kind of labor, and labor is the only primary factor of production. Figure 28.2 illustrates the market for labor.

D_L is the market demand curve for labor. It is the sum of the individual demand curves from all the producers in the economy. S_L is the market supply curve for labor. It is the sum of the individual supply curves from all the workers in the economy. The interaction of the market demand and the market supply curves establishes an equilibrium wage of W_e and an equilibrium quantity of labor exchanged of L_e. Each firm takes the share of L_e that it has purchased and produces the maximum amount of output that it can. Since no workers are unemployed and each firm is producing as much output as possible, the total output produced in the economy is as large as it can possibly be, given the amount of labor that the workers are willing to supply. The economy is operating on its production possibilities frontier.[2]

Figure 28.3 illustrates this result in terms of the overall markets for final goods and services. The graph is the analogue to the single-market supply and demand graph for the entire economy. The output, Q, on the horizontal axis represents the total flow of final goods and services through the nation's product markets. It is the real, or constant dollar, gross domestic product (or net domestic product), the value of the final goods and services expressed in 1987

[2]The conclusion remains the same if we add capital, land, and many different kinds of labor. Each firm takes the resources that it purchases in the factor markets and combines them to produce as much output as it possibly can. No resources are unemployed if the factor markets are competitive, so the economy is operating on its production possibilities frontier.

FIGURE 28.3

Aggregate Demand and Aggregate Supply in the New Classical Model

The aggregate demand curve, *AD*, indicates the total amount of output, *Q*, demanded by all final demanders in the economy at each overall price level, *P*. The aggregate supply curve, *AS*, indicates the total amount of output supplied by all producers at each overall price level. The new classical assumption that factor markets are competitive implies that *AS* is vertical at Q^*, the value of real gross domestic product (GDP) corresponding to the production possibilities frontier. Real GDP is entirely determined by the quantity and quality of a nation's resources and by the available production technologies, the same factors that determine the production possibilities frontier. The overall price level adjusts the aggregate quantity demanded to the frontier level of output. The equilibrium overall price level is P_0 at the intersection of *AD* and *AS*.

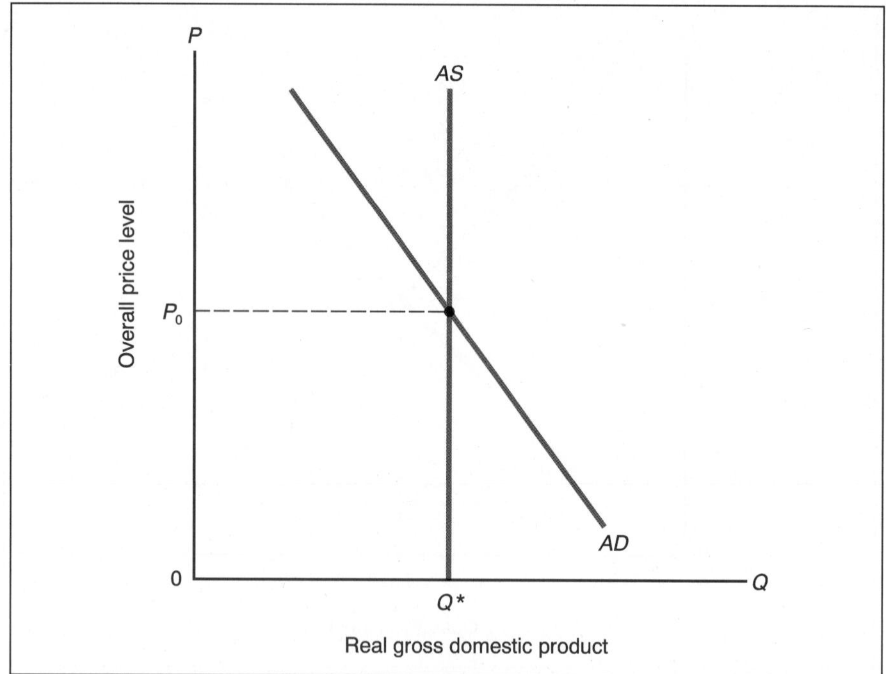

AGGREGATE DEMAND

The total quantity of final goods and services demanded at each overall price level by all the final demanders in the economy; the aggregate demand curve, labeled *AD*, is a graph of aggregate demand.

AGGREGATE SUPPLY

The total quantity of final goods and services supplied at each overall price level by all the producers in the economy; the aggregate supply curve, labeled *AS*, is a graph of aggregate supply.

prices. The price, *P*, on the vertical axis is the overall level of the prices of final goods and services as measured by a broad-based price index such as the GDP deflator. The demand and supply curves are labeled *AD* and *AS*, respectively, to indicate that they are the aggregate, or total, demand and supply curves for the economy as a whole. *AD*, **aggregate demand,** indicates the total quantity of final goods and services demanded at each overall price level by all the final demanders in the economy. *AS*, **aggregate supply,** indicates the total quantity of final goods and services supplied at each overall price level by all the producers in the economy.

We have drawn *AD* to be downward sloping in the usual manner for reasons that will be explained in Chapter 37. *AS* must be vertical as drawn, however, at the value of real gross domestic product that the firms produce with the resources they have purchased in the competitive factor markets. We are assuming that Q^* is the total amount of final goods and services that the producers supply, given the total amount of labor, L_e, made available to them (from Figure 28.2).

The vertical *AS* curve at Q^* is the one-dimensional representation of the nation's production possibilities frontier. It is the maximum amount of real or constant dollar gross domestic product that the economy can produce, given the quantity and quality of the resources supplied in the factor markets and the production technologies available to the producers. We have seen that the economy will actually produce Q^* and be on its production possibilities frontier if the factor markets are competitive.

Notice that the firms will supply Q^* once they have hired the amount of labor, L_e, no matter what the price level, *P*, is. The role of the price level is to adjust the aggregate quantity demanded to the aggregate supply of Q^*. The aggregate quantity demanded is Q^* when the price level is P_0. Therefore, the

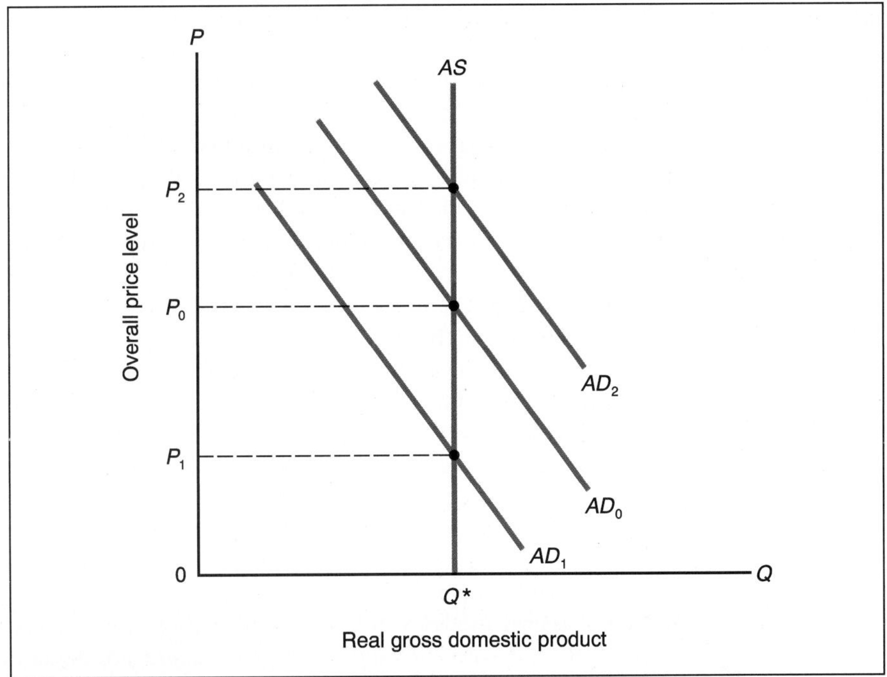

FIGURE 28.4

Changes in Aggregate Demand in the New Classical Model

In the new classical model, real gross domestic product (GDP) is the frontier level of output for all intents and purposes, Q^* in the figure, because of the assumption that factor markets are competitive. Therefore, changes in aggregate demand only affect the overall price level. A decrease in aggregate demand from AD_0 to AD_1 may briefly bring the economy below its production possibilities frontier. But the excess supplies in the product markets cause the overall price level to decrease from P_0 to P_1, which quickly brings the economy back to equilibrium on the frontier, at the intersection of AD_1 and AS. Similarly, an increase in aggregate demand from AD_0 to AD_2 causes excess demands in the product markets which increase the overall price level from P_0 to P_2. The economy quickly returns to equilibrium on the frontier, at the intersection of AD_2 and AS.

equilibrium for the competitive macro economy pictured in Figure 28.3 is an overall price level of P_0 and a real gross domestic product of Q^*.

Shifts in aggregate demand may move the economy above or below the frontier, but these situations can only be short-lived. We saw when studying the Laws of Supply and Demand that prices adjust quickly in competitive markets to restore equilibrium. Similarly, a competitive macro economy quickly returns to equilibrium on the production possibilities frontier. Figure 28.4 illustrates.

Aggregate demand is originally at AD_0, and the economy is in equilibrium at P_0 and Q^*, as in Figure 28.3. If aggregate demand should decrease to AD_1, producers can no longer sell Q^* at the price level P_0. The product markets are in excess supply at P_0, and the quantities purchased by the final demanders drop. The economy has moved below its production possibilities frontier. The situation will soon correct itself, however, because the excess supplies put downward pressure on the product prices and increase the aggregate quantity demanded. The overall price level continues to decrease until it reaches P_1, at which point equilibrium is restored on the production possibilities frontier. The quantity demanded along AD_1 equals Q^* when the overall price level is P_1.

Similarly, an increase in aggregate demand to AD_2 creates a situation of excess demands throughout the nation's product markets. This situation is also short-lived. The excess demands put upward pressure on the product prices. The overall price level continues to rise until it reaches P_2, at which point equilibrium is restored on the frontier.

The implications of the competitive new-classical model are clear: The United States should almost always be operating on, or very near, its production possibilities frontier. Therefore, real gross domestic product is determined entirely by the supply side of the economy, that is, by the quantity and quality of a nation's resources and the production technologies available to producers. These are the same factors that determine the production possibilities frontier. The new classical economists argue that periods of rising unemployment are primarily the result of increases in frictional and search or structural unemployment, that is, increases in the natural rate of unemployment.

New Keynesian economists do not agree. They believe that the United States has experienced many periods of very high cyclical unemployment when the economy is operating well below its production possibilities frontier. Moreover, the periods of high unemployment are not always short-lived. They can persist for years at a time. The U.S. economy remained in the grip of the Great Depression for the entire decade of the 1930s. Nothing so disastrous as the Great Depression has happened since. Even so, the economy remained below the production possibilities frontier for a few years during and following the recessions of the mid-1970s, the early 1980s, and the early 1990s. The problem of recurring periods of high and lasting cyclical unemployment plagues all the developed market economies. Indeed, a major weakness of capitalism as an economic system is that capitalist economies all too often waste scarce resources by allowing them to lie idle. The new Keynesian view is certainly the majority view among macro economists.

The competitive new classical model yields a second, closely related prediction that appears to be at odds with the facts: Changes in aggregate demand primarily cause changes in prices. Any changes in output caused by a change in aggregate demand are temporary and inconsequential. We saw this in Figure 28.4. The principal effect of the decrease in aggregate demand from AD_0 to AD_1 is a decrease in the overall level of prices from P_0 to P_1. Any resulting decline in output is fleeting; the economy quickly recovers to Q^* on the production possibilities frontier. Similarly, the principal effect of the increase in aggregate demand from AD_0 to AD_2 is an increase in the overall level of prices from P_0 to P_2.

Numerous studies have shown that the facts in the United States are quite different, unless the economy is operating right up against its production possibilities frontier. Changes in aggregate demand cause both prices and output to change at even modest levels of unemployment, and the changes in output persist for a very long time. The change in output is more pronounced, and longer lasting, the higher the level of unemployment.[3]

In addition, the pattern of the price and the quantity changes in response to a shift in aggregate demand is directly opposite to the pattern of the price and the quantity changes that we observe when demand shifts in a single competitive market. In individual competitive markets, prices and profits are the signals that show firms how they should change their output. Therefore, when demand shifts in a competitive market, prices and profits change first, and then firms respond by changing their output.

Figure 28.5 illustrates how prices and output respond to a shift in demand in a single competitive market. The market is initially in equilibrium at (Q_0, P_0), at the intersection of the initial demand curve, D_0, and the three supply curves shown in the graph. Suppose that demand increases suddenly to D_1.

[3]Of course, the new classical economists would argue that the economy is never much below its frontier. We will see in Chapter 37 that changes in aggregate demand can change aggregate output in the new classical model, but only if the change in demand leads to events that cause the frontier to move in or out as well. The links between demand and the frontier are problematic, however. In any case, the point remains that only changes in aggregate supply have any important impact on aggregate output in the new classical model.

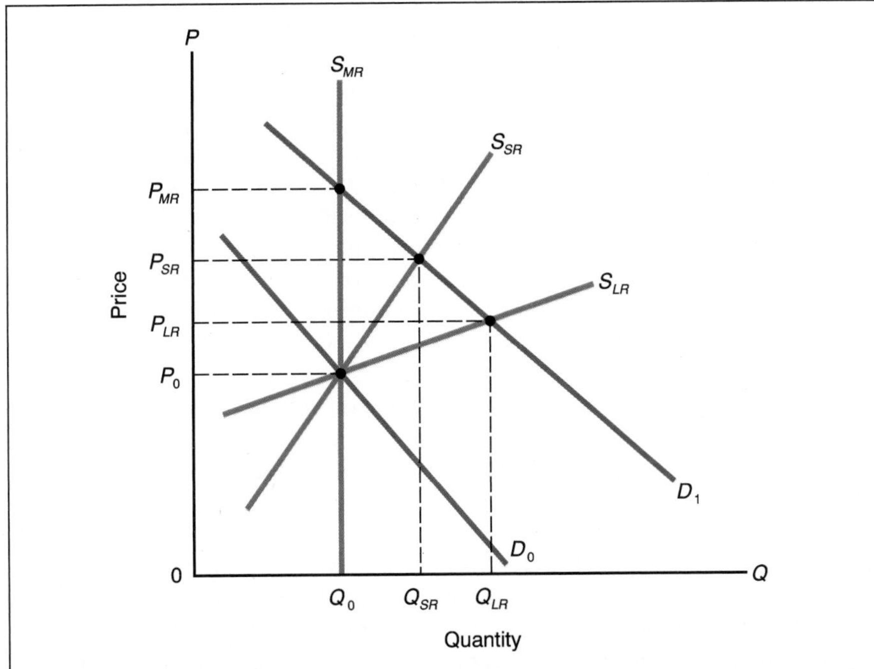

FIGURE 28.5

An Increase in Demand in a Single Competitive Market

The figure shows how a single competitive market responds over time to an increase in demand. The original equilibrium is (Q_0,P_0) at the intersection of D_0 and the three supply curves. Demand then increases from D_0 to D_1. In the momentary run, producers cannot adjust output and the vertical momentary supply curve S_{MR} applies. Price rises to P_{MR}, at the intersection of S_{MR} and D_1. As time passes, producers increase output along the short-run supply curve S_{SR}. The short-run equilibrium is (Q_{SR},P_{SR}), at the intersection of D_1 and S_{SR}. As more time passes and the short-run becomes the long-run, the long-run supply curve S_{LR} applies. The final equilibrium is (Q_{LR},P_{LR}), at the intersection of D_1 and S_{LR}. Over time, therefore, the increase in price moderates and the increase in output builds. This is exactly the opposite of how the macro economy responds to an increase in aggregate demand when there are unemployed resources. In such an economy the increase in the overall price level builds and the increase in real gross domestic product moderates over time.

The response to the increase in demand occurs in three stages, called the momentary run, the short run, and the long run.

The **momentary run** is the period immediately following the increase in demand. The firms are caught by surprise and have already decided to supply the quantity Q_0 to the market. They cannot change their production decisions for the moment. Therefore, the market supply curve during the momentary run, the curve labeled S_{MR} in the figure, is vertical at Q_0. The price rises sharply from P_0 to P_{MR} to restore equilibrium along the new demand curve, D_1. The firms' profits increase, since they are selling the same output as before at much higher prices.

MOMENTARY RUN

The period immediately following a change in supply or demand when producers cannot change their output supplied to the market.

The higher prices and profits are the signals to the firms to increase their output as soon as they can, when the momentary run becomes the short run. During the **short run** the firms can increase their output by varying some of their factors of production, but not all of their factors of production. For instance, the firms may be able to hire more labor, but they cannot build or buy new factories until more time has passed. So they respond by running second or third shifts in their existing factories. Now output increases along the short-run supply curve, labeled S_{SR}, and the market establishes a new equilibrium at (Q_{SR}, P_{SR}) for the duration of the short run. Notice that the increase in output has put downward pressure on the price, which falls from P_{MR} to P_{SR}. Nonetheless, the firms are still earning handsome profits at the price P_{SR}.

SHORT RUN

The period following a change in supply or demand over which firms can vary some of their factors of production, but not all of them.

The short run gives way to the **long run** when firms can vary all their factors of production. They can now put new factories into operation, which should lower their costs of production and increase their profits even more. Also, new firms can enter the market, which they will do because the market is profitable. Now output increases along the flatter long-run supply curve, S_{LR}. In the final long-run equilibrium, output increases to Q_{LR}, and the price decreases further from P_{SR} to P_{LR}.

LONG RUN

A period of time over which firms can vary all of their factors of production, and can enter or exit an industry.

In summary, an increase in demand in a competitive market causes price to increase first, followed by increases in output. Moreover, the increases in output build over time, from Q_0 to Q_{SR} to Q_{LR} in Figure 28.5. In contrast, the increases in price moderate over time, from P_{MR} to P_{SR} to P_{LR} in the figure. P_{LR} is not far above the original P_0. The same pattern of responses follows a decrease in demand, but in reverse. First prices and then profits fall, leading eventually to decreases in output. The decreases in output build over time, and the decreases in price moderate over time as the price moves back toward P_0.

The responses of price and output at the macro level to an increase in aggregate demand are exactly the opposite of the responses in Figure 28.5 when the economy is operating below its production possibilities frontier. It is as if the labels of the three supply curves were reversed. An increase in aggregate demand leads almost immediately to an increase in aggregate output, in real gross domestic product, whereas the overall price level increases very little at first. The increase in aggregate demand may not lead to a significant increase in prices for six months or more. As a general rule, prices are slower to rise the higher the initial rate of unemployment. In any event the output response precedes the price response at the macro level. Moreover, as time passes, the price increases build, and the output increases moderate. The aggregate supply curve, *AS*, becomes steeper, not flatter, over time.

The same pattern applies to a decrease in aggregate demand, but in reverse. Real gross domestic product decreases first, followed by decreases in the overall price level. As time passes, the price decreases build, and the decreases in real gross domestic product moderate.[4]

To summarize, the new classical competitive model does not do well in predicting how the U.S. economy responds to changes in aggregate demand. Aggregate output does change in response to changes in aggregate demand, and the changes in output can persist for a long time, perhaps five years or more. Also, the changes in aggregate output tend to precede the changes in the overall price level. These responses of output and price are directly opposite to the predictions of the competitive model.

The actual behavior of prices and output in the United States suggests that certain kinds of market imperfections have an important role to play in explaining the operation of the macro economy. The economy does not operate strictly in accordance with the Laws of Supply and Demand.

The New Keynesian Model

The new Keynesians come at the problem of explaining the ebbs and flows of the economy from the opposite direction. They believe that output responds to changes in aggregate demand because the economy is riddled with market imperfections. Market imperfections are the centerpiece of the new Keynesian model of the economy.

The great British economist John Maynard Keynes offered the first systematic challenge to the competitive model of the macro economy in the 1930s. The economies of Western Europe, Great Britain, and United States were caught in the throes of the Great Depression at the time. Unemployment in-

[4]For an excellent discussion of the behavior of aggregate prices and quantities in the United States, see R. Gordon, *Journal of Economic Literature* XXVIII, No. 3 (September 1990): 1115–1171.

creased to 25 percent of the labor force in the United States by 1933 and rose even higher in England. The story is that Keynes looked out his office window at the unemployed workers in the bread lines and concluded that the Laws of Supply and Demand were not operating in the British labor markets. He disagreed with the classical view that the unemployment was temporary and would disappear once wages and prices had adjusted to return the capitalist economies to their production possibilities frontier. Wages and prices fell substantially from 1929 to 1933, yet the unemployment persisted.

The events of the day led Keynes to reject the classical competitive model of the macro economy, which was essentially the only macro model of his day. He formulated an entirely new macroeconomic theory of a developed market economy which he set forth in *The General Theory of Employment, Interest, and Money*, published in 1936. Many consider Keynes's *General Theory* to be the greatest intellectual achievement in economics of the twentieth century. It introduced a completely new set of ideas about how the macro economy operates, ideas that his new Keynesian disciples believe have stood the test of time for the most part.

Keynes's theory of the macro economy came to be called Keynesian economics. The new Keynesian economists of the present day have mostly refined the basic ideas of Keynes's original theory to give them sounder theoretical underpinnings. We will consider four of Keynes's main ideas, which remain as central features of the modern-day new Keynesian model.

MAIN IDEAS OF THE NEW KEYNESIAN MODEL *Idea 1: Wages and prices are sticky.* The most basic tenet of the new Keynesian model is that modern capitalist economies are riddled with market imperfections that cause many wages and prices to be sticky. Keynes focused on sticky wages and labor market imperfections. The new Keynesians are turning more of their attention to price stickiness and product market imperfections—why, for example, the overall price level does not respond quickly to changes in aggregate demand. They are also emphasizing imperfections in capital markets.

We discussed in Chapter 25 why wages appear to be sticky in many labor markets and why sticky wages generate a pattern of cyclical unemployment with layoffs and rehires. We will present the new Keynesian views on sticky prices and capital market imperfections in later chapters. It is enough at this point to note one of the fundamental assumptions of the new Keynesian model: Wages and prices are too sticky to serve the function of bringing the macro economy quickly to equilibrium when the economy is operating below its production possibilities frontier. In contrast to the new classical economists, the new Keynesians do not believe that wages and prices are the key variables determining the circular flow of economic activity in the short run. And the short run in macroeconomics can last for a considerable period of time, perhaps as long as five years.

What, then, is the key economic variable that drives the economy in the short run? The answer given by Keynes and his new Keynesian disciples is national income itself. In effect, the circular flow of economic activity feeds on itself. The amount of income generated today has a significant effect on the amount of income that will be generated tomorrow. Moreover, income changes with the ebbs and flows of the economy not because factor prices are changing, but because the amount of productive activity itself is changing. When aggregate demand declines, firms do not immediately lower their wages and prices as the new classical competitive model suggests. Instead, firms lay off workers, vacate their factories and office buildings, and suffer a decline in profits. The income received by households declines because fewer people are working and because rental payments and profits decrease. Conversely, when aggregate demand increases, firms hire more workers, rent or build more factories and office buildings, and enjoy an increase in profits. Households have more income because the circular flow of real economic activity has increased, not because factor prices have risen.

CURRENT ISSUE: Unemployment in Western Europe and Canada is higher, on average, than in the United States, and it responds less to an economic recovery. Economists are not sure why this is.

Income affects the circular flow of economic activity through the demand side of the product markets. To see why, we need to turn to Keynes's second fundamental idea, that aggregate demand is a very important determinant of the circular flow of economic activity.

Idea 2: Aggregate demand is an important determinant of real gross domestic product. In the competitive new classical model the total output produced is completely determined by the supply side of the economy. The economy is always driven to the production possibilities frontier, so that the real gross domestic product depends on the quantity and the quality of the nation's resources and the production technologies available to the firms. The level of aggregate demand simply determines the overall price level; it has no important effect on total output.

In Keynes's view of the macro economy, the roles of aggregate supply and aggregate demand are essentially reversed. He argued that the total output in the economy was primarily determined by the level of aggregate demand, at least in the short run. The reason why turns on the fact that wages and prices are sticky.

Once firms choose to set their prices and wages, they essentially become passive actors in the economy and simply react to the demand for their products. The idea is that firms guess what the demand for their products will be and produce the output required to meet that demand. Should they happen to guess wrong the first time, they guess again and adjust their production accordingly. They keep adjusting production until their output just matches the actual demand for their products.

According to this view, the circular flow of economic activity is primarily determined by the level of aggregate demand. Aggregate supply passively adjusts to whatever the level of aggregate demand happens to be. If aggregate demand increases, firms hire more resources and increase production to meet the increase in demand. If aggregate demand decreases, firms lay off resources and reduce production to match the lower level of demand. Therefore, the level of real gross domestic output is primarily determined by the level of aggregate demand in the short run when wages and prices are sticky.

Notice that the Keynesian story is consistent with the fact that when aggregate demand changes, output changes first before price does. The firms' first reaction to a change in the demand for their products is to change their level of production. The firms may eventually change their prices, but the price changes come later.

We said earlier in the chapter that the first relationship in any macro model is the statement of equilibrium in the market for final goods and services:

$$Y = C^d + I^d + G^d + (Ex^d - Im^d)$$

The next step in building the new Keynesian model of the economy is to specify what factors determine the individual components of aggregate demand. According to the new Keynesian perspective, the better we understand what determines the components of aggregate demand, the better we will understand the performance of the macro economy in the short run. Therefore, all Keynesian macro models feature six key relationships: the statement of equilibrium plus five additional relationships that explain the determinants of aggregate demand, one each for consumption demand (C^d), investment demand (I^d), government demand for goods and services (G^d), export demand (Ex^d), and import demand (Im^d). The basic idea behind the new Keynesian model is that national income (or national product), Y, adjusts to meet the level of aggregate demand, $C^d + I^d + G^d + (Ex^d - Im^d)$.

A model of this form could be very simple. For instance, one factor that determines the government's demand for goods and services, G^d, is whether or not the country is fighting a war. Suppose that a war does break out and the government's demand for military weapons increases by $10 billion. According to the Keynesian view of the economy, the weapons manufacturers will increase their production by $10 billion to meet the increase in demand. The result is that national product and national income increase by $10 billion. A $10 billion increase in aggregate demand leads to a $10 billion increase in national income—very simple.

Unfortunately, the reaction of the economy to an increase in aggregate demand is not quite that simple because the level of national income is itself one of the more important determinants of aggregate demand. As a result, the circular flow of economic activity feeds on itself. A change in aggregate demand leads to a change in national income, which leads to a further change in aggregate demand, which leads to yet another change in national income, and so on, indefinitely.

Income is an important determinant of aggregate demand primarily because consumption demand is closely related to the level of national income, and consumption is the most important component of aggregate demand. An increase in national income leads to an increase in households' disposable income. The more disposable income households have, the more consumer goods they will want to buy. Conversely, a decrease in national income leads to a decrease in households' disposable income and a decrease in their consumption demand.

Let's return to our example of the $10 billion increase in the government's demand for weapons, keeping in mind the relationship between consumption demand and national income. As before, the weapons manufacturers increase their production by $10 billion, and national income increases by $10 billion. The $10 billion increase in national income is received by a large number of people: employees of the weapons manufacturers, employees of the firms that supply materials to the weapons manufacturers, stockholders of these firms, and so forth. The people who receive the additional income will spend some of it, not on weapons, of course, but on consumer goods and services—food, clothing, cars, medical care, movies, and the like. The producers of these consumer goods and services will increase their production to meet this new demand, so that national product and national income increase once again. But the increase in national income causes a further increase in consumption demand, which leads to yet another increase in national product and income, and so on, indefinitely. The $10 billion increase in the government's demand for weapons ultimately generates much more than a $10 billion increase in national income and national product.

Keynes argued that the process of national income feeding back on itself through aggregate demand is a dominant feature of the economy in the short run. In his view, income is much more important than are prices in explaining the short-term performance of the economy. And, remember, the short run can last for a considerable period of time. Understanding how national income affects each component of aggregate demand is obviously very important from a Keynesian perspective, since the relationship between national income and aggregate demand determines the nature of the feedback mechanism.

The final two ideas of Keynes that we want to consider relate directly to the question of economic policy. Keynes's macroeconomic theories gave birth to the notion that the government had an important role to play in improving the overall performance of the economy.

Idea 3: Left to its own devices, the macroeconomic performance of the economy may not be very desirable. An economy with highly competitive markets governed by the Laws of Supply and Demand, in which wages and prices are the key economic variables determining the circular flow of economic activity, is a highly desirable economy. Prices automatically drive the economy to its production possibilities frontier, so that society derives the maximum possible output from its scarce resources.

In contrast, an economy with sticky wages and prices—in which the circular flow of economic activity is driven by the level of aggregate demand, and national income itself is one of the more important variables determining the level of aggregate demand—can perform very poorly. Aggregate demand may lead the economy to a position well below its production possibilities frontier, with high levels of involuntary cyclical unemployment. Or aggregate demand may try to bring the economy beyond its production possibilities and fuel a serious inflationary process. Moreover, the economy can remain off its production possibilities frontier for a long time. Wages and prices are the variables that adjust to drive the economy to its frontier. If wages and prices are sticky, they cannot perform this task very well, and no other economic variables can take their place. Aggregate demand does not tend to return to the production possibilities frontier when it is driven by the overall level of economic activity instead of by prices.

The classical economists of the 1930s viewed the Great Depression as a temporary aberration that would quickly correct itself once wages and prices did their work. Keynes argued otherwise. He believed that the Great Depression would continue on for years unless governments acted to increase the level of aggregate demand. His fourth novel idea was that government policies could substantially improve the performance of the economy in the short run.

Idea 4: The government's fiscal and monetary policies can help achieve the macroeconomic policy goals. Keynes saw that fiscal and monetary policies can affect the performance of the economy because they change the level (and the composition) of aggregate demand. Fiscal policies involve changes in government spending on goods and services, or transfer payments, or taxes. Changes in government spending on goods and services have a direct effect on aggregate demand because they are part of aggregate demand. Changes in transfer payments and taxes affect aggregate demand indirectly by influencing the levels of consumption demand and investment demand. Monetary policy involves changes in the nation's money supply. It also affects aggregate demand indirectly by influencing the levels of consumption demand and investment demand.

The government's ability to manage the level of aggregate demand through its fiscal and monetary policies is very important in an economy with sticky wages and prices because aggregate demand affects the level of output. Keynes was among the first economists to appreciate the usefulness of fiscal and monetary policies. He argued that governments could lead their economies out of the Great Depression by using fiscal policies to increase the level of aggregate demand. Producers would respond to the increase in aggregate demand by hiring more resources and increasing production. Unemployment would fall, and the economies would move closer to their production possibilities frontier. The classical economists of his day missed this possibility because their competitive view of the macro economy led them to believe that aggregate demand had essentially no effect on the level of output. As we have seen, the competitive macro model suggests that an increase in aggregate demand increases only prices, not output.

Keynes was primarily interested in the question of how fiscal and monetary policies could be used to reduce unemployment because unemployment was the pressing issue of his day. In fact, the level (and the composition) of aggregate demand has a direct effect on all four macroeconomic policy goals. A primary objective in our study of macroeconomics is to understand how the government's fiscal and monetary policies relate to all four of the macroeconomic policy goals.

LIMITATIONS OF THE NEW KEYNESIAN MODEL Keynes's views on the ability of fiscal and monetary policies to improve the performance of the economy were widely embraced by economists and policy makers. All of the highly developed capitalist nations try to manage their economies with fiscal and monetary policies. This does not mean that Keynes and his new Keynesian followers have completely won the day in macroeconomics, however. Far from it. The modern new Keynesian model remains a highly simplified model of the macro model, and, as such, it has its strengths and weaknesses. The competitive new classical macro model is better suited for many purposes.

We have argued that the Keynesian model outperforms the new classical model in explaining how the economy reacts in the short run to changes in aggregate demand. This is a considerable advantage because fiscal and monetary policies affect the economy by changing aggregate demand. The economy is often hit with other kinds of "shocks" to aggregate demand as well, such as a sudden burst of investment demand or a large decrease in defense spending. The Keynesian model has been very useful in explaining how the economy reacts to these demand-side events.

AGGREGATE DEMAND SHOCK
Any event that directly affects the total demand for goods and services at each overall price level.

But the economy is also hit with shocks to aggregate supply, and in these cases the competitive new classical model may well have the advantage. An **aggregate supply shock** is any event that directly affects either firms' costs of production or their ability to supply output to the market. Common examples of cost-changing supply shocks are cost-reducing technological change, such as the introduction of robotics into the automobile assembly line, and changes in the prices of key inputs. The eightfold increase in oil prices engineered by the Organization of Petroleum Exporting Countries (OPEC) during

AGGREGATE SUPPLY SHOCK
Any event that directly affects producers' costs of production or the quantity that they can supply to the market.

FIGURE 28.6

Aggregate Supply Shocks

The figure shows how the macro economy responds to aggregate supply shocks. The initial equilibrium is (Q^*, P_0), at the intersection of the aggregate demand and aggregate supply curves AD and AS_0. An adverse aggregate supply shock, such as an increase in oil prices or a severe drought, shifts the aggregate supply curve to the left, from AS_0 to AS_1. The new equilibrium is (Q_1, P_1), at the intersection of AD and AS_1. An adverse aggregate supply shock reduces real gross domestic product (GDP) and increases the overall price level. Conversely, a favorable aggregate supply shock, such as cost reducing technological change or exceptionally good weather for farming, shifts the aggregate supply curve to the right, from AS_0 to AS_2. The new equilibrium is (Q_2, P_2), at the intersection of AD and AS_2. A favorable aggregate supply shock increases real gross domestic product (GDP) and decreases the overall price level.

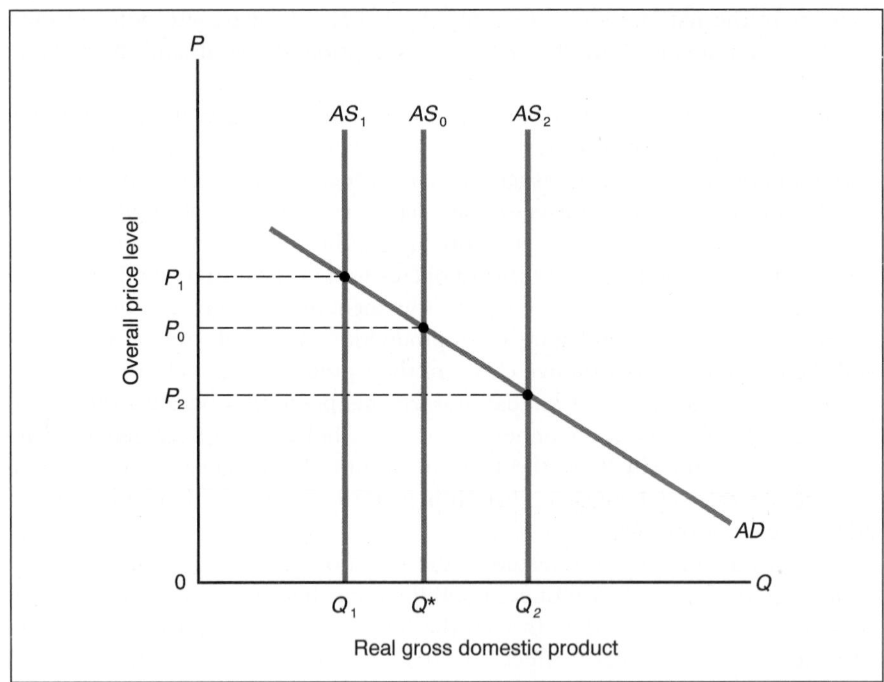

the 1970s was an enormously adverse supply shock to the U.S. economy. Conversely, the steep decline in oil prices in the early 1980s following the demise of OPEC's market power was a very favorable supply shock to the U.S. economy. Examples of output-changing supply shocks are a serious drought that affects crops and widespread strikes by labor unions that bring industries to a halt.

Cost-changing aggregate supply shocks are more important in the United States. Moreover, U.S. producers tend to pass cost changes through to the prices of their products very quickly, which is exactly what happens in competitive markets. Shifts up or down in the market supply curve quickly raise or lower the equilibrium price, respectively. This suggests that the competitive new classical macro model, with its flexible prices, is a good model for analyzing the effects of aggregate supply shocks. It is certainly better than the new Keynesian model, which is based on the assumption of sticky, sluggish price responses to market events.

Figure 28.6 illustrates the effects of aggregate supply shocks, using the competitive new classical model. Assume that the economy is originally in equilibrium at (Q^*, P_0), on its production possibilities frontier at the intersection of AD and AS_0, as in Figure 28.3.

An adverse supply shock, such as an oil price increase, shifts the aggregate supply to the left, from AS_0 to AS_1. The equilibrium quantity falls to Q_1, and the equilibrium price rises to P_1. An adverse supply shock is terrible for the economy. It simultaneously increases prices and lowers output, and it reduces the economy's production possibilities.

A favorable supply shock, such as productivity-enhancing technological change, shifts the aggregate supply to the right, from AS_0 to AS_2. The equilibrium quantity rises to Q_2, and the equilibrium price falls to P_2. A favorable supply shock is a blessing for the economy. It simultaneously lowers prices and increases output, and it increases the economy's production possibilities.

The effects pictured in Figure 28.6 are an accurate representation of how the U.S. economy actually responds to adverse and favorable supply shocks, even when the economy is operating below its production possibilities frontier. Prices and output respond quickly to supply shocks, as if the economy were highly competitive. The new classical model performs well in this instance.

New classical economists claim that aggregate supply shocks such as technological change affect the U.S. more often, and more substantially, than do aggregate demand shocks. This claim is controversial, but if it is correct, it is a strong argument in favor of using the new classical model to analyze the U.S. economy.

Another limitation of the new Keynesian model is a practical one. The potential to manage the economy in the short run with fiscal and monetary policies is quite different from the reality. Both fiscal and monetary policies take time to formulate and to work their way through the economy. As a result, knowing when to apply the policies can be a nasty problem. Also, fiscal and monetary policies are difficult, if not impossible, to coordinate because the Fed is independent of the Congress and the administration. We will see that the government is unlikely to be able to manage the economy very tightly in the short run.

The Long Run: Areas of Agreement

The competitive new classical model is an excellent model for analyzing long-run macroeconomic issues such as predicting the economic effects resulting from the aging of the U.S. population over the next 50 years, or describing the cumulative effects of the slowdown in productivity growth in the United States that began in 1973, or understanding how to control inflation. Most new Keynesian economists concede that wages and prices are reasonably flexible in the long run, so that the macro economy appears to be ever more competitive with the passage of time. Furthermore, long-run economic growth, the ability of the economy to push out its production possibilities frontier, dominates the economic landscape over the long haul. We saw in Chapter 3 that long-run economic growth requires increases in the quantity and the quality of a nation's resources and the development of new production technologies. These are all supply-side phenomena. Aggregate demand may pull the economy below its production possibilities frontier on occasion, but this is not very important when analyzing long-run issues. The actual growth in output over 25 or 50 years should be very close to the growth in potential output. Therefore, nothing much is lost by adopting the new classical assumptions that the economy is competitive and that it operates on its production possibilities frontier. In fact, economists almost always assume that the macro economy is competitive when analyzing long-run macroeconomic issues.

Consequently, the policy prescriptions of new classical and new Keynesian economists are often identical when they are addressing ways to promote long-run economic growth, or to keep a moderate inflation from gaining momentum and building to a runaway hyperinflation, or when analyzing the economic consequences of running large federal budget deficits year after year. The primary differences between them center on the short run.

WHERE TO BEGIN

We will begin our analysis of the macro economy from the new Keynesian perspective. Our first goals are to understand how the economy responds to changes in aggregate demand in the short run and how fiscal and monetary policies affect the level of aggregate demand. The new Keynesian model is the better model for these purposes.

To keep the analysis as simple as possible, we will assume that wages and prices are fixed rather than just sticky, so that any changes in national income or national product are changes in real income or output. We will also assume that the economy is operating well below its production possibilities frontier so that real income or output can both increase and decrease.

Our simple new Keynesian model will give us some important insights about how the performance of the economy affects three of the four macroeconomic policy goals: full employment, long-run economic growth, and the balance of trade and the dollar exchange rate. It is not useful for analyzing the problem of inflation.

Beginning with the new Keynesian model has an additional advantage. As noted in the introduction, new Keynesian thinking has swept into Washington following the Clinton election victory. All three members of Clinton's Council of Economic Advisers—Chairwoman Laura Tyson, Alan Blinder, and Joseph Stiglitz—received their graduate training at MIT, one of the centers of new Keynesian economics in the United States. Each one has made important contributions to the development of the new Keynesian perspective. The concepts that you will learn in the next few chapters are guiding the formulation of macroeconomic policy in Washington these days.

SUMMARY

Chapter 28 began with an overview of the three fundamental questions in macroeconomics.

1. The three fundamental questions are as follows:
   a. What determines the circular flow of economic activity?
   b. How do the level and the composition of the circular flow relate to the four macroeconomic policy goals of long-run economic growth, full employment, price stability, and stability in economic relations with foreign nations?
   c. How can the government help achieve the macroeconomic policy goals through its fiscal and monetary policies, which influence the level and the composition of the circular flow?
2. In all the developed market economies, the circular flow of economic activity moves through a pattern of booms and recessions over time called the business cycle. The periods of boom and recession vary both in intensity and in duration.
3. Fiscal policy is budgetary policy. It involves changes in government expenditures on goods and services, or transfer payments, or taxes to influence the level and the composition of the circular flow. Fiscal policy is the responsibility of the administration and the Congress.
4. Monetary policy involves changes in the money supply intended to influence the level and the composition of the circular flow. Monetary policy

is the responsibility of the Board of Governors of the Federal Reserve, the nation's central bank.

5. The conduct of macroeconomic policy can be thought of as an attempt to solve the three-part economic problem for the entire economy. The objectives are the four macroeconomic policy goals. The alternatives are fiscal and monetary policies. The constraint is the economy itself, which determines how the macroeconomic policies relate to the policy goals and the extent to which the four policy goals are compatible with one another.

Chapter 28 then turned to the problem of how to build a macroeconomic model of a highly developed market economy such as the U.S. economy. The second section of the chapter discussed the need for a macroeconomic model and the limitations of any such model.

6. A macroeconomic model of a highly developed market economy must be extremely simple relative to the economy it is trying to explain. It cannot hope to describe and predict every aspect of the economy. At best, a macro model will have both strengths and weaknesses. It will be useful for explaining and predicting some events and not so useful for explaining and predicting other events.
7. Even the largest mathematical forecasting models used by private firms and government agencies fail to capture many important details of the U.S. economy.
8. The primary goal of any macroeconomic model is to explain the forces that determine the circular flow of economic activity. As such, the first relationship or equation in all macro models is a representation of the circular flow through the product markets:

$$Y = C^d + I^d + G^d + (Ex^d - Im^d)$$

   Y is national income and the terms on the right-hand side are the demands by each sector of the economy: household (C^d), business (I^d), government (G^d), and foreign ($Ex^d - Im^d$). The relationship describes the supply and the demand sides of the product markets. Firms generate the national income as they supply the final goods and services, the national product, which is equal in value to the national income. The right-hand side is the aggregate demand for the final goods and services.

9. Macro economists sharply disagree about how to complete the model. At least five different macro models appear in the professional literature. The models differ in the emphasis they give to the two sides of the product markets and in the variables they consider important in determining the supply and the demand of final goods and services.

The third section of the chapter contrasted and compared the two leading macroeconomic models of the day, the new classical model and the new Keynesian model.

10. The new classical economists have returned to the view of the classical economists of the late 1800s and early 1900s, that the macro economy is best modeled as if it is highly competitive and operates in accordance with the Laws of Supply and Demand. The model has a number of very strong implications:
    a. Factor markets are highly competitive and automatically bring the economy to equilibrium on, or very near, its production possibilities frontier.

They do this without any significant amount of unemployed resources. Wages and prices are highly flexible.

b. Real gross domestic product is determined entirely by the supply side of the economy. The factors determining output are the quantity and the quality of the resources supplied in the factor markets and the production technologies available to producers. These are the same factors that determine the production possibilities frontier.
c. Changes in aggregate demand affect prices, but not output. Any change in output in response to a change in aggregate demand is temporary and of no consequence. Wages and prices soon adjust to return the economy to the production possibilities frontier.
d. Frequent doses of fiscal and monetary policies are uncalled for since the economy performs well enough on its own. Governments policies should be steady and predictable so that households and business firms can better plan their economic affairs.

11. Some of the predictions of the new classical model appear to be wide of the mark. Most economists would say that capitalist economies often operate below their production possibilities frontiers, with high levels of cyclical unemployment. Also, when economies are below their frontiers, changes in aggregate demand cause changes in output that can last for a number of years. Moreover, output responds first and then price to a change in aggregate demand. This is exactly the opposite of what happens in a single competitive market when demand changes.
12. The new Keynesian economists are disciples of John Maynard Keynes, who developed a completely different theory of how the macro economy operates. Keynes's thinking was motivated by the Great Depression, when unemployment in England exceeded 25 percent.
13. The chapter highlighted four of Keynes's main ideas.
    a. The economy is riddled with imperfections that cause wages and prices to be sticky and prevent them from performing the function of returning the economy quickly to equilibrium on the production possibilities frontier. In the short run, which can last for many years, national income itself is a more important determinant of the circular flow than are wages and prices.
    b. With wages and prices sticky, the supply side of the product markets becomes passive and simply reacts to changes in demand. If aggregate demand increases, producers hire more resources and increase their production. If aggregate demand decreases, producers lay off resources and decrease their production. Aggregate demand drives the economy in the short run, and income itself is one of the key determinants of aggregate demand. The economy feeds back on itself. An increase in aggregate demand increases production and national income, which leads to further increases in aggregate demand, and so on.
    c. Aggregate demand may not lead the economy to a very desirable level of income. It may drive the economy well below its production possibilities at times and cause high levels of cyclical unemployment; at other times aggregate demand may try to bring the economy beyond its frontier and fuel an inflationary process. With wages and prices sticky, there is no mechanism to return the economy quickly to the frontier.
    d. Fiscal and monetary policies change the level of aggregate demand. Since changes in aggregate demand affect output, frequent doses of

fiscal and monetary policies can improve the performance of the economy. Keynes argued that governments should use fiscal policies to increase aggregate demand and lead the market economies out of the Great Depression.

14. The new Keynesian model appears to outperform the new classical model in explaining how the economy reacts to changes in aggregate demand in the short run. The new classical model has its own advantages, however. It does a better job of explaining how the economy reacts to aggregate supply shocks. An aggregate supply shock is anything that directly affects the costs of production or the ability to supply output to the market, such as technological change, or an increase in the price of an important input such as oil, or a drought. Supply shocks quickly affect both price and output at the macro level, exactly as one would expect if markets were highly competitive.
15. The disagreements between the two schools center on the short run. New Keynesians agree that the new classical model is appropriate for analyzing long-run macroeconomic issues, such as long-run economic growth, the need to keep inflation under control, and the dangers of running large federal budget deficits.

KEY TERMS

aggregate demand
aggregate demand shock
aggregate supply
aggregate supply shock
business cycle
Federal Reserve Banking System
fiscal policy
long run
macroeconomic policy
momentary run
monetary policy
short run

QUESTIONS

1. What is fiscal policy, and who is responsible for the conduct of fiscal policy in the United States?
2. What is monetary policy, and who is responsible for the conduct of monetary policy in the United States?
3. Why do economists need to build a model of the macro economy to think about how the economy operates?
4. What assumptions of the new classical model of the economy led to the conclusion that the economy always operates on or near the production possibilities frontier?
5. a. How do price and output respond to an increase in demand in a single market that operates according to the Laws of Supply and Demand? Consider the responses of price and output in the momentary run, the short run, and the long run.
   b. Is this the way that the overall price level and the national product respond to an increase in aggregate demand in the U.S. economy? If not, what are the differences between the macro responses and the single-market responses?
6. New Keynesian economists believe that wages and prices are sticky. How does this belief lead them to conclude that aggregate demand determines national product (income) in the short run? What are some other important assumptions of the new Keynesian model?
7. a. Under what conditions, or for what events, does the new Keynesian model appear to be the better model for explaining the performance of the macro economy?
   b. Under what conditions, or for what events, does the new classical model appear to be the better model for explaining the performance of the macro economy?
8. Describe the different roles that aggregate demand and aggregate supply play in the new classical and the new Keynesian models of the economy.
9. Compare and contrast the new classical and the new Keynesian models in terms of their policy recommendations for achieving (a) the macroeconomic policy goal of full employment and (b) the macroeconomic policy goal of robust long-run economic growth.
10. Describe the macroeconomic policy problem in terms of the three-part economic problem consisting of objectives, alternatives, and constraints.

CASE

An International Comparison of Unemployment Rates*

How have unemployment rates in the United States compared with unemployment rates in the other industrialized market economies over the past twenty-five to thirty years? Table CS 7.1 lists the unemployment rates in the United States, Canada, Japan, Germany (formerly West Germany), France, Italy, and the United Kingdom for the years 1965–92. These countries are the seven industrial countries of the world with the highest per capita incomes. They are often referred to as the G7 (Group of Seven) countries. The table presents data on average annual unemployment rates over four subperiods: 1965–73; 1974–82; 1983–1989; and 1990–92. The period from 1974 to 1982 contained two large OPEC-induced oil price increases, one in late 1973 and the other in 1979, that threw most of the G7 countries into recessions in 1974 and again in 1981. The period from 1983–89 was generally a period of steady recovery and economic growth from the deep recession of 1981–82. The recovery lasted until 1990, when most of the G7 countries again experienced recessions followed, at best, by slow recoveries.

Comparing unemployment rates over a long period of time gives us a sense of the differences in the natural rates of unemployment among the G7 countries. Since the booms and recessions in these economies tend to move together, any large differences in average unemployment rates, or in the long-run trends in the unemployment rates, are likely to reflect differences in the underlying natural rates.

A number of facts stand out from the table.

- Japan is in a class by itself. It alone has experienced only a slight upward trend in unemployment since 1965, and its average unemployment rate over the entire period is much lower than that of any other G7 country. The United States and Canada have never had such low rates of unemployment since 1965.
- European unemployment rates were somewhat comparable to Japan's until the first OPEC-induced oil price increase in 1973–74. Since then unemployment in Europe has exhibited a definite upward trend that economists refer to as Eurosclerosis. Notice that the period of recovery and growth from 1983 to 1989 did not push the European unemployment rates down, as it did in the United States. West Germany's upward trend was interrupted by the fall of the Berlin Wall and the subsequent unification of Germany, but the German unemployment rate has jumped sharply again above 8 percent in 1993.
- The average rates of unemployment in the United States and Canada were approximately equal during the first two periods, after which a substantial gap has opened between the two countries.

What can account for these differences in the long-run behavior of unemployment rates among the G7 countries? One possible explanation is differences in the countries' unemployment insurance benefits. This is one likely reason why the Canadian unemployment rate has become so much higher than the U.S. rate. Canada's labor market looks remarkably similar to that of the U.S. as far as the composition of the labor force is concerned. There is more unionization in Canada, but the unions are concentrated in the public sector. The two countries also had similar unemployment

*Provided by Manfred W. Keil, Northeastern University.

TABLE CS 7.1 Average Annual Unemployment Rates in the G7 Countries, 1965–1992 (percent)

United States	4.5	7.2	6.9	6.5
Canada	4.8	7.7	9.6	9.9
Japan	1.3	2.0	2.7	2.1
Germany	0.7	3.4	6.7	4.7
France	2.4	5.6	10.0	9.6
Italy	3.5	4.2	7.0	6.9
United Kingdom	3.2	6.7	10.3	8.5

SOURCE: Council of Economic Advisors, *Economic Report of the President 1993* (Washington, D.C.: U.S. Government Printing Office, 1993), Table B-106, p. 469. The 1992 unemployment data are through the third quarter of the year.

An International Comparison of Unemployment Rates (cont.)

insurance systems until 1971, when Canada considerably liberalized its program. The Canadian government raised the monthly unemployment benefits well above U.S. levels, and sharply reduced the time that people had to be previously employed to collect the benefits. The only puzzle is why the Canadian unemployment rate did not rise above the U.S. rate until 1976 (Canada's unemployment rate has been higher than the U.S. rate in every year since 1976, with the single exception of 1981, when it was .1 percent lower). The answer appears to lie in the fact that Canada is a raw material exporting country. Unlike the United States, Canada benefited from the two OPEC-induced oil price shocks of the 1970s. This same factor is now working against Canada, however, following the collapse of oil prices in the 1980s. Canada's more liberal unemployment insurance system and its heavier reliance on raw material exports may well be the principal reasons why Canada's unemployment rate has been two and three percentage points above the U.S. rate since 1983.

Unemployment benefits are also generally far more liberal in Europe than in the United States. The standard duration of unemployment benefits in the United States is 26 weeks, with occasional extensions to 39 and even 52 weeks in times of recession. In contrast, France pays unemployment benefits for almost 4 years, and Germany and the U.K. have no effective time limit on the duration of unemployment benefits. This may also explain another feature of European unemployment lying behind the data in the table. The European countries have been plagued by a very high percentage of long-term unemployment, people who have been unemployed for over a year. In 1988, the long-term unemployed accounted for only 7 percent of the total unemployed in Canada and the United States. The corresponding percentages in the European countries that year were: Germany, 47 percent; France, 45 percent; Italy, 69 percent; and the U.K., 45 percent. People who are unemployed for a long time tend to lose some of their skills, which makes them less likely to find employment. As a result, the Europeans experience an unemployment phenomenon called hysteresis, in which the unemployment rate does not return to the previous natural rate of unemployment once it rises above the natural rate. Instead, a period of high unemployment increases the underlying natural rate. We can see this phenomenon clearly in the period from 1983 to 1989, when the economic recovery in Europe did not reverse the upward trend in unemployment there.

How can we explain Japan's exceedingly low unemployment rates since 1965? The answer here may be that attitudes and institutions can have a substantial effect on unemployment. Japan is considered a corporatist economy (Germany was, too, until 1979). This term means that the unions, the employers, and the government work together to set national wage levels for each sector of the economy. National wage bargaining takes aggregate unemployment levels into account, which makes wages more responsive to cyclical situations. As a result, a corporatist economy such as Japan avoids large increases in unemployment following adverse aggregate demand or supply shocks to the economy.

ECONOMIC ADVISOR'S REPORT

Suppose that President Clinton hires you to advise him on unemployment insurance.

1. Explain to the president why most economists believe that increases in unemployment insurance benefits increase the natural rate of unemployment.
2. Suppose the economists are correct. Would you advise President Clinton to scrap the unemployment insurance program, or at least sharply curtail the monthly benefits (either their amount, or the duration for which unemployment benefits are paid, or both)?

PART

VIII

National Income Determination, Fiscal Policy, and Unemployment

CHAPTER

29

National Income Determination

LEARNING OBJECTIVES

CONCEPTS TO LEARN

Consumption function
Saving function
Marginal propensity to consume
Marginal propensity to save
Life-Cycle Hypothesis
Investment demand
Cost of capital
Equilibrium level of national income
The saving = investment equilibrium

CONCEPTS TO RECALL

The circular flow of economic activity [4]
New Keynesian economics [28]
Aggregate demand and aggregate supply [28]

The final decade of the twentieth century has gotten off to a disappointing start in the United States, economically speaking. The United States experienced a mild recession in 1990, which was then followed by a barely perceptible recovery. The recovery was so weak that the growth in output was not enough to lower unemployment throughout 1992 and the first half of 1993.

Economists all the while were bemoaning the lack of consumer confidence. Household surveys showed that people were not very confident about the future, and their lack of confidence made them hesitant to increase their spending. Economists knew that the economy could not pick up until consumers started spending because, as we saw in Chapter 27, consumption is almost two-thirds of GDP.

Investment was just as sluggish as consumption in the early 1990s. With consumers not spending, firms had little need to expand their production capacities. The low level of investment also bodes ill for the future because we know that investment is the key to long-run economic growth.

Consumption and investment hold center stage as we take our first look at the operation of the macro economy. They are the linchpins of macroeconomic analysis.

Chapter 29 analyzes the effects of aggregate demand on the circular flow of economic activity from the new Keynesian perspective. The analysis assumes that the economy is operating well below its production possibilities frontier, with lots of unemployed resources, so that changes in aggregate demand affect the real level of economic activity and not just the overall price level. Also, our focus is on the short run, when changes in real output and income are more important than are changes in prices. Therefore, we begin the analysis of the macro economy with a simplified version of the new Keynesian model in which wages and prices are not just sticky, but fixed.

Chapter 29 has one main goal: to explain how the economy operates when aggregate demand is the driving force behind the circular flow of economic activity. Government policy will come later. You must understand the operation of the economy before you can think about how the federal government might influence the economy through its fiscal and monetary policies. Therefore, the chapter develops the simplest possible macro model that can illustrate the operation of the macro economy.

THE SIMPLEST MACRO MODEL

A macro model must contain the household sector and the business sector at a bare minimum to illustrate how a market economy functions. The government and the foreign sectors can be added later; they do not change the fundamental principles relating to how the economy operates.

In the simplest possible economy the business sector hires all the primary factors of production supplied by the households and produces all the final goods and services supplied to the product markets. The two sources of demand for the final goods and services in the product markets are consumption by the household sector and investment by the business sector. Therefore, the statement of product market equilibrium for this economy is

$$Y = C^d + I^d$$

Recall that the left-hand side of the equation represents the supply side of the product markets. Y is the level of national income generated by the business firms in the process of producing the goods and the services that they supply to the product markets. The value of all the goods and the services supplied to the product markets, the national product, is equal to the value of the national income generated in production by virtue of the circular flow of economic activity. The right-hand side of the equation represents the demand side of the product markets, the sum of consumption demand by the households (C^d) and investment demand by the business firms (I^d). The product markets are in equilibrium when the aggregate supply of the final goods and services, Y, equals the aggregate demand for the final goods and services, $C^d + I^d$.[1]

Here are some points of review from earlier chapters to keep in mind as we build the simplest new Keynesian model.

Active Demand and Passive Supply

A major tenet of the new Keynesian perspective is that aggregate demand is the driving force that determines the circular flow of economic activity. Supply reacts passively to demand. Business firms set their wages and prices and then base their production decisions on their best guesses about what the demands for their products will be. The firms then adjust their production until the amount of goods and services supplied just equals the amount demanded. Therefore, the key to understanding the operation of the economy lies in understanding the factors that determine the level of aggregate demand, both consumption demand by the households and investment demand by the business firms. The aggregate supply of goods and services follows wherever aggregate demand happens to lead it. The second and third sections of the chapter describe the various factors that determine consumption demand and investment demand.

National Income and Aggregate Demand

A particularly important issue is how consumption demand and investment demand are themselves related to the level of national income or product.

[1]Gross domestic product (GDP), or national product, and national income are not quite equal. They differ by the sum of indirect business taxes and the capital consumption allowance on the stock of capital in the actual U.S. economy. Nonetheless, we can safely ignore these differences. In the first place, the simplest economy has no indirect business taxes because it has no government sector. In addition, the capital consumption allowance is an estimate of the depreciation of the *entire* stock of capital, most of which was put into place in previous years. As a result, the estimate of the capital consumption allowance by the Bureau of Economic Analysis (BEA) is essentially a constant that does not vary with the level of economic activity. Therefore, we can disregard it in distinguishing between GDP and national income. In fact, the text will ignore indirect business taxes even after we add the government sector, so that GDP (or national product) and national income will always be used interchangeably to refer to the circular flow of economic activity.

Also, Y is usually referred to as national income rather than as national product in macroeconomic analysis, a convention we will adopt in this text.

Chapter 28 described the dual relationship between aggregate demand and national income in which aggregate demand determines the level of national income and the level of national income in part determines aggregate demand. This dual relationship creates a feedback mechanism that magnifies the effects of changes in aggregate demand on the economy. The fourth section of the chapter puts consumption demand and investment demand together and shows how aggregate demand determines the equilibrium level of national income.

Saving, Investment, and Equilibrium

The final section of Chapter 29 develops an alternative and very useful way of describing the macro equilibrium, through saving and investment. We learned in Chapter 27 that if national income equals national product, then the total saving in the economy must equal the level of investment by business firms. Therefore, the circular flow of economic activity is in equilibrium when the amount that savers want to save is equal to the amount that producers want to invest.

Real Versus Nominal Values

Chapter 27 distinguished between the real, constant dollar, and nominal, current dollar values of macroeconomic variables. Macroeconomic theory attempts to explain the real, constant dollar value of the circular flow of economic activity and its various components. Since we are assuming that prices and wages are fixed, the nominal, current dollar value and the real, constant dollar value of the circular flow of economic activity are one and the same. Therefore, the values of all the economic variables—consumption, investment, national income, and so forth—are understood to be their real, constant dollar values, as required by the theory.

CONSUMPTION DEMAND

Think for a moment of the many factors that determine how much the members of your household choose to spend on consumer goods and services during the course of a year. Your list could be quite lengthy. It might include, at a minimum, your household's disposable income; its wealth in the form of stocks, bonds, savings accounts, and the value of your house if you own your home; the prices of the goods and services that you buy; interest rates; expectations about what prices, interest rates, and your household's disposable income and wealth will be in the future; the tastes and ages of every household member; and whether each member is employed or in college. Many factors shape each household's demand for goods and services, but one of the factors—disposable income—is far and away the most important for most households. The amount of goods and services that the typical household is willing and able to buy during the course of a year depends primarily on the amount of (real) disposable income that it receives during the year.

The Keynesian Consumption Function

John Maynard Keynes was the first economist to see that the link between consumption demand and disposable income had a substantial impact on the overall performance of the macro economy. He believed that a household's consumption demand has two components, a small component that is unrelated to the household's disposable income and a larger component that varies directly with the household's disposable income, although less than dollar for dollar. What is true for a representative household's consumption demand is true for the economy as a whole.

A HYPOTHETICAL CONSUMPTION FUNCTION The hypothetical data in Table 29.1 are consistent with Keynes's views on the relationship between aggregate consumption and aggregate disposable income. The first column records the consumption demand at every level of disposable income in the second column. All data are real, constant dollar values in billions of dollars, to approximate the values of consumption and disposable income for the United States in the early 1990s.

Notice, first, that consumption demand equals disposable income when disposable income is $2,000. Thus, $2,000 is called the **break-even level of disposable income.**

BREAK-EVEN LEVEL OF DISPOSABLE INCOME

The level of disposable income at which households' consumption demand equals their disposable income.

Consumption demand is less than disposable income when disposable income is above $2,000. Since all that households can do is either consume or save their disposable incomes, households in the aggregate are saving over that range of disposable income. For example, consumption demand is only $4,400 when disposable income is $5,000. The amount of saving is $600, the difference between disposable income and consumption demand ($600 = $5,000

TABLE 29.1 **Consumption Demand: Consumption Function/Propensity to Consume ($ billion)**

CONSUMPTION DEMAND (C^d)	DISPOSABLE INCOME (Y_d)	MARGINAL PROPENSITY TO CONSUME (MPC = $\Delta C^d/\Delta Y_d$)	AVERAGE PROPENSITY TO CONSUME (APC = C^d/Y_d)
$ 400	$ 0	—	—
1,200	1,000	.80 (= 800/1,000)	1.20
2,000	2,000	.80	1.00
2,800	3,000	.80	.93
3,600	4,000	.80	.90
4,400	5,000	.80	.88
5,200	6,000	.80	.87
6,000	7,000	.80	.86
6,800	8,000	.80	.85
7,600	9,000	.80	.84
8,400	10,000	.80	.84
9,200	11,000	.80	.84
10,000	12,000	.80	.83
10,800	13,000	.80	.83

− \$4,400). Households can save in many ways, such as holding on to cash; depositing some of their disposable income in a savings account; buying financial assets such as stocks, bonds, and certificates of deposit; buying real assets such as a piece of land or a house; and paying back loans.

Consumption demand is greater than disposable income when disposable income is below \$2,000. Households in the aggregate are dissaving over that range of disposable incomes; the amount of saving is negative. For example, consumption is \$1,200 when disposable income is \$1,000. Households in the aggregate are dissaving \$200 (− \$200 = \$1,000 − \$1,200). At these low levels of disposable income many households are trying to maintain their standards of living by dissaving. They may sell some stocks or real estate, draw down savings accounts, or borrow. These are all forms of dissaving that bring in money to households so that they can buy consumer goods and services that they could otherwise not afford out of their disposable incomes. Households cannot go on dissaving forever, but when their incomes fall sharply, they will dissave for awhile in an attempt to maintain their standards of living.

Note, finally, that consumption demand is \$400 even when disposable income falls to zero. This is the amount of consumption demand that Keynes said was independent of disposable income and determined by all the other factors that influence consumption demand. You can think of this amount of consumption as being present at every level of disposable income. Households then increase their consumption demand above this base amount as they receive disposable income.

Figure 29.1 pictures the relationship between consumption demand and disposable income for the hypothetical data in Table 29.1. Aggregate (real) consumption demand, C^d, is on the vertical axis, and aggregate (real) disposable income, Y^d, is on the horizontal axis.

The 45° line is a frame-of-reference line that allows us to see each level of disposable income in the vertical direction. The distance from the origin to a given level of disposable income on the horizontal axis is equal to the height of the 45° line at that level of disposable income. For example, the point on the 45° line at a disposable income of \$2,000 has a value of \$2,000 measured in the vertical direction, the point on the 45° line at a disposable income of \$5,000 has a value of \$5,000 measured in the vertical direction, and so forth. Having a vertical measure of disposable income makes it easy to compare the levels of consumption demand and disposable income, since consumption demand is also measured in the vertical direction.

CONSUMPTION FUNCTION

The relationship that indicates how much households in the aggregate are willing and able to consume during the year at every level of total disposable income, other things equal; also called *consumption demand.*

The line C^d is called the **consumption function,** or the *propensity to consume.* It shows the aggregate consumption demand during the year at each level of total disposable income, other things equal. The other things being held equal or constant are all the other factors that influence the households' demands for goods and services, such as wealth, tastes, and expectations about the future.

The consumption function, C^d, crosses the 45° line at the break-even level of disposable income, which is \$2,000 in our example. The vertical distance to the 45° line at Y_d^1 = \$2,000 is the aggregate disposable income, \$2,000. The vertical distance to C^d at Y_d^1 = \$2,000 is the aggregate consumption demand at that level of disposable income, also \$2,000. Since the two lines intersect at Y_d^1 = \$2,000, aggregate consumption demand equals aggregate disposable income.

C^d is below the 45° line at all levels of disposable income above \$2,000, indicating that households in the aggregate choose to save some of their dis-

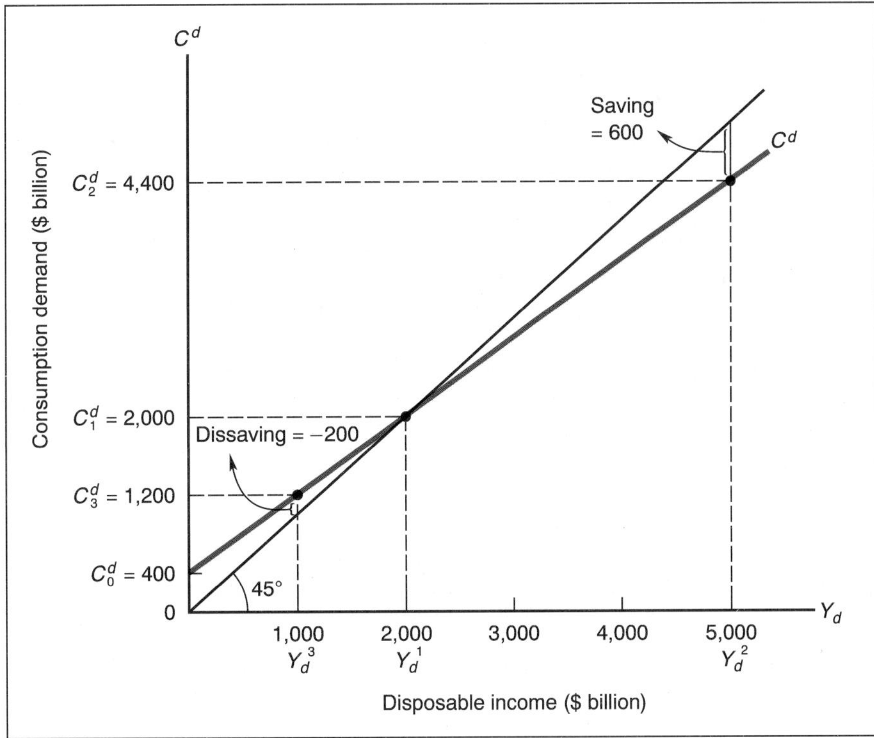

FIGURE 29.1

The Consumption Function

The consumption function, C^d, is a graph of the aggregate consumption demand by households at each level of disposable income, Y_d, from Table 29.1. Disposable income is on the horizontal axis and aggregate consumption demand is on the vertical axis. The consumption and income data are in real terms, billions of constant dollars. Points on the 45-degree line show the level of disposable income in the vertical direction. The break-even level of disposable income when households consume all their income is $2,000, at the intersection of C^d and the 45-degree line. Households save some of their disposable income at all income levels above $2,000. For example, when disposable income is $5,000, households consume $4,400 and save $600. The $600 of saving is the vertical distance between the 45-degree line and C^d. Households dissave at all income levels below $2,000. For example, when disposable income is $1000, households consume $1,200; their saving is (−)$200, the vertical distance between the 45-degree line and C^d.

posable income over this range. The amount of saving is the vertical distance between the 45° line and the consumption function at each level of disposable income. For example, at Y_d^2 = $5,000, the vertical distance to C_2^d is $4,400, the aggregate consumption demand, and the vertical distance to the 45° line is $5,000, the aggregate disposable income. Aggregate saving is $600, the vertical distance between C_2^d and the 45° line. Both consumption demand and saving demand increase the farther disposable income rises above $2,000.

C^d is above the 45° line at all levels of disposable income below $2,000, indicating that households in the aggregate are dissaving over this range. The amount of dissaving is the vertical distance between C^d and the 45° line at each level of disposable income. For example, at Y_d^3 = $1,000, the vertical distance to C_3^d is $1,200, the aggregate consumption demand, and the vertical distance to the 45° line is $1,000, the aggregate disposable income. Aggregate dissaving is −$200, the vertical distance between C_3^d and the 45° line. The amount of dissaving increases the farther disposable income falls below $2,000.

C^d intersects the vertical axis at C_0^d = $400. This is the amount of aggregate consumption demand that is independent of the level of disposable income.

THE MARGINAL PROPENSITY TO CONSUME Our discussion of the consumption function so far has described how the level of consumption demand relates to the level of disposable income. Economists are also very interested in how consumption demand changes as disposable income changes with the ebbs and flows of the business cycle. Changes in consumption demand have a very important effect on changes in the circular flow of economic activity simply because consumption is around 60 to 65 percent of GDP.

FIGURE 29.2

The Marginal Propensity to Consume

The marginal propensity to consume, labeled MPC, is the slope of the consumption function, C^d. MPC = $\Delta C^d / \Delta Y_d$. The MPC = 0.80 at all levels of disposable income for the consumption function in Table 29.1. Households increase their consumption by \$800 for every \$1,000 increase in disposable income.

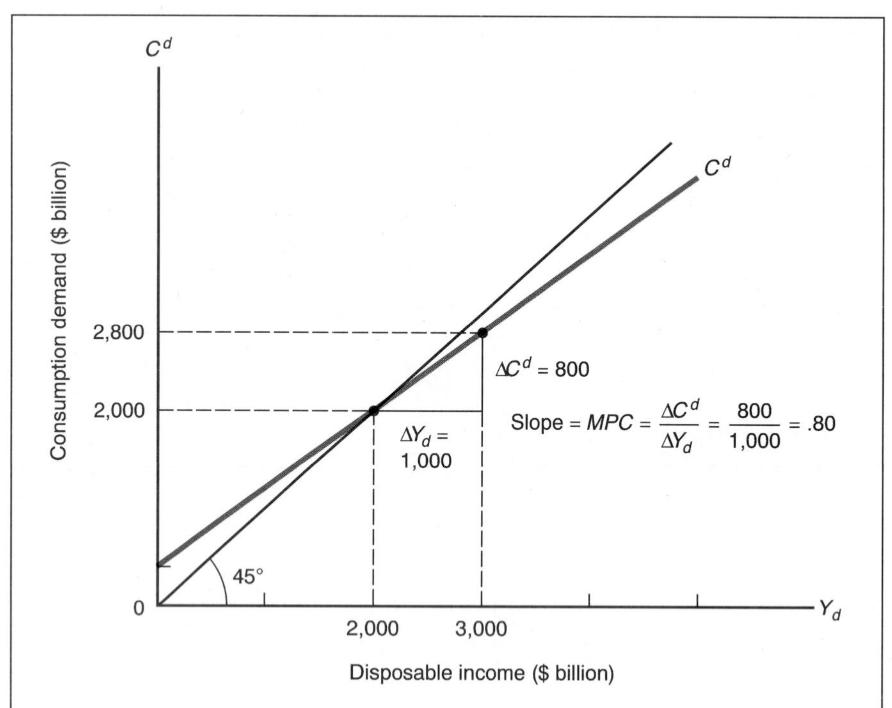

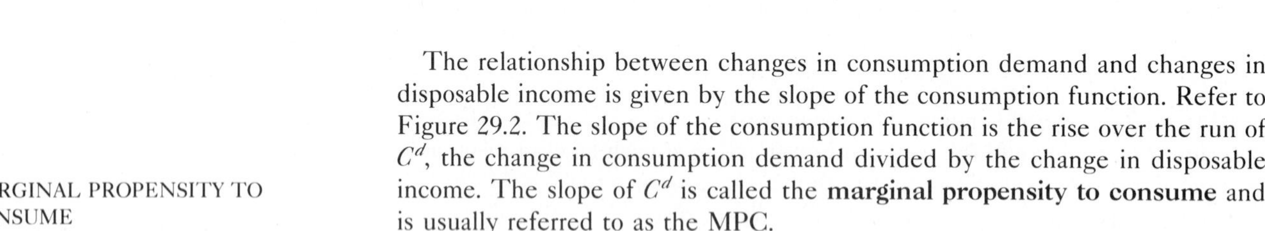

The relationship between changes in consumption demand and changes in disposable income is given by the slope of the consumption function. Refer to Figure 29.2. The slope of the consumption function is the rise over the run of C^d, the change in consumption demand divided by the change in disposable income. The slope of C^d is called the **marginal propensity to consume** and is usually referred to as the MPC.

MARGINAL PROPENSITY TO CONSUME

The portion of each additional dollar of disposable income that households consume; the ratio of the change in consumption demand to the change in disposable income.

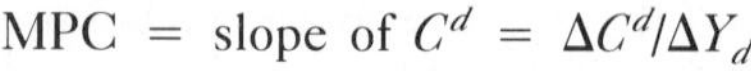

$$\text{MPC} = \text{slope of } C^d = \Delta C^d / \Delta Y_d$$

The MPC indicates the portion of each *additional* dollar of disposable income that the household consumes. As such, the MPC must have a value between zero and one, inclusive, since a household can only consume or save each additional dollar of disposable income.

$$0 \leq \text{MPC} \leq 1$$

An MPC equal to one says that households consume all, and save none, of each additional dollar of disposable income. An MPC equal to zero says that households consume none, and save all, of each additional dollar of disposable income. An MPC between zero and one means that households both consume and save a portion of each additional dollar of disposable income, which is the realistic case.

The MPC for our hypothetical consumption function is .80, as indicated in the third column of Table 29.1. Households in the aggregate consume 80 cents and save 20 cents of each additional dollar of disposable income. For example, consumption demand increases from \$2,000 to \$2,800, an increase of \$800, when disposable income increases from \$2,000 to \$3,000, an increase of \$1,000.

MPC = \$800/\$1,000 = .80. Our hypothetical consumption function is consistent with Keynes's belief that consumption demand varies directly with disposable income, but less than dollar for dollar.

REFLECTION: Is your marginal propensity to consume very high or very low? Is it higher or lower than your parents' MPC?

Note, finally, that the consumption function is flatter than the 45° line. The slope of the 45° line is 1, whereas the slope of C^d is the MPC, which is .80.

THE AGGREGATE U.S. CONSUMPTION FUNCTION Does our hypothetical consumption function accurately reflect the relationship between aggregate consumption and aggregate disposable income over time in the United States? The answer is yes and no.

There have been innumerable studies of the aggregate U.S. consumption function because consumption is so important to the overall performance of the economy. The weight of the evidence from all the research is that our hypothetical consumption function is a reasonably accurate representation of the aggregate consumption function in the United States over the short run. The only wrinkle is that the aggregate consumption function becomes much steeper as time passes. The MPC in the short run, within a year or so, is on the order of .60 to .80. That is, every dollar increase or decrease in disposable income raises or lowers consumption spending by 60 to 80 cents within one year after the increase. Keynes was right: Consumption demand in any given year is very sensitive to the current level of disposable income being generated in the economy.

The research also consistently finds that the MPC builds over time. Permanent changes in disposable income that last for a number of years ultimately raise consumption spending over 90 cents on the dollar. The ratio of consumption spending to disposable income has averaged .91 each year since 1929, the first year that the Bureau of Economic Analysis collected data for the national income and product accounts. The .91 ratio is consistent with the estimates of the long-run MPC from the consumption function studies, which are on the order of .90 to .93. Our hypothetical MPC of .80 should therefore be viewed as a compromise between the short-run and the long-run MPCs in the United States. An MPC of .80 also happens to be a particularly easy number to work with in numerical examples. We will use it throughout the macroeconomics chapters of the text.[2]

Finally, the break-even level of aggregate disposable income is very low in the United States. Aggregate consumption equaled or exceeded aggregate disposable income only in the depths of the Great Depression, when unemployment was 20 to 25 percent of the labor force. Personal saving has been positive every year since 1940.

THE AVERAGE PROPENSITY TO CONSUME The final column of Table 29.1 reports the **average propensity to consume (APC)** at each level of disposable income, which is the ratio of consumption to disposable income:

AVERAGE PROPENSITY TO CONSUME

The ratio of consumption demand to disposable income.

[2]For a summary of the research on the consumption function in the United States, and further discussion of the MPC in the short run and the long run, see R. Hall and J. Taylor, *Macroeconomics: Theory, Performance, and Policy*, 2nd edition (New York: W. W. Norton, 1988): 195–205. Hall and Taylor are among the more prominent macro economists in the United States. They place the short-run MPC at .76 and the long-run MPC at .91 (Table 8-1, p. 195).

$$\text{APC} = C^d/Y_d$$

Notice that the APC declines steadily as disposable income increases.

The declining APC for our hypothetical consumption function is consistent with the short-run aggregate consumption function in the United States. It is also consistent with the behavior of individual households throughout the United States in any given year. High-income households consume a lower portion of their disposable incomes than do low-income households. A declining APC is not consistent with the long-run aggregate consumption function in the United States, however. The APC has been essentially constant over the long run. As noted above, consumption has averaged about 91 percent of disposable income since 1929, even though real disposable income increased nearly sixfold from 1929 to 1990.

Take care to note the difference between the MPC and the APC. The MPC refers to the ratio of *changes* in consumption demand to *changes* in disposable income. The APC refers to the ratio of *levels* of consumption demand to *levels* of disposable income. The MPC is much more important to the study of the macro economy.

We will use the hypothetical consumption function in Table 29.1 and Figure 29.1 throughout the macroeconomics chapters of this text. Make sure that you understand its properties before proceeding.

Saving Demand

SAVING FUNCTION

The relationship that indicates how much households in the aggregate are willing and able to save during the year at every level of total disposable income, other things equal; also called *saving demand.*

The relationship between saving demand and disposable income follows immediately from the relationship between consumption demand and disposable income. The **saving function,** or the *propensity to save,* indicates how much households in the aggregate are willing and able to save at every level of total disposable income, other things equal. As we have already seen, the amount households save must always equal the amount they choose not to consume, since all that they can do with their disposable income is either consume it or save it. In other words, the aggregate saving function is the mirror image of the aggregate consumption function.[3]

Table 29.2 and Figure 29.3 present the hypothetical saving function that corresponds to our hypothetical consumption function. The first and third columns of Table 29.2 reproduce the hypothetical consumption and disposable income data from Table 29.1. Figure 29.3 also reproduces the hypothetical consumption function, C^d, from Figure 29.1 so that we can easily compare C^d with the saving function, S^d.

Notice, first, that consumption and saving in the first and second columns of Table 29.2 always add up to the disposable income in the third column. For example, when disposable income is \$6,000, consumption is \$5,200, and saving is \$800 (\$5,200 + \$800 = \$6,000).

Saving demand is zero at \$2,000, the break-even level of disposable income when households in the aggregate are consuming all their disposable income. Therefore, the aggregate saving function, S^d, in Figure 29.3 cuts the horizontal axis at the disposable income of \$2,000.

[3]The two potential sources of saving in our simplest economy are business saving, or retained earnings, and the personal saving of households. We will assume that the firms pay out all their profits as dividends, so that the only source of saving in our simplest economy is the personal saving of households.

TABLE 29.2 **Saving Demand: Saving Funciton/Propensity to Save ($ billion)**

CONSUMPTION DEMAND (C^d)	SAVING DEMAND (S^d)	DISPOSABLE INCOME (Y_d)	MARGINAL PROPENSITY TO SAVE (MPS = $\Delta S^d/\Delta Y_d$)	AVERAGE PROPENSITY TO SAVE (APS = S^d/Y_d)
$ 400	$(−) 400	$ 0	—	—
1,200	(−) 200	1,000	.20 (= 200/1,000)	(−) .20
2,000	0	2,000	.20	0
2,800	200	3,000	.20	.07
3,600	400	4,000	.20	.10
4,400	600	5,000	.20	.12
5,200	800	6,000	.20	.13
6,000	1,000	7,000	.20	.14
6,800	1,200	8,000	.20	.15
7,600	1,400	9,000	.20	.16
8,400	1,600	10,000	.20	.16
9,200	1,800	11,000	.20	.16
10,000	2,000	12,000	.20	.17
10,800	2,200	13,000	.20	.17

S^d is positive when disposable income is greater than $2,000. For example, when disposable income is $5,000, households in the aggregate are consuming $4,400 and saving $600.

S^d is negative when disposable income is below $2,000. This is the range of incomes when households are consuming more than their disposable incomes and dissaving. For example, when disposable income is $1,000, C^d is $1,200, and S^d is −$200.

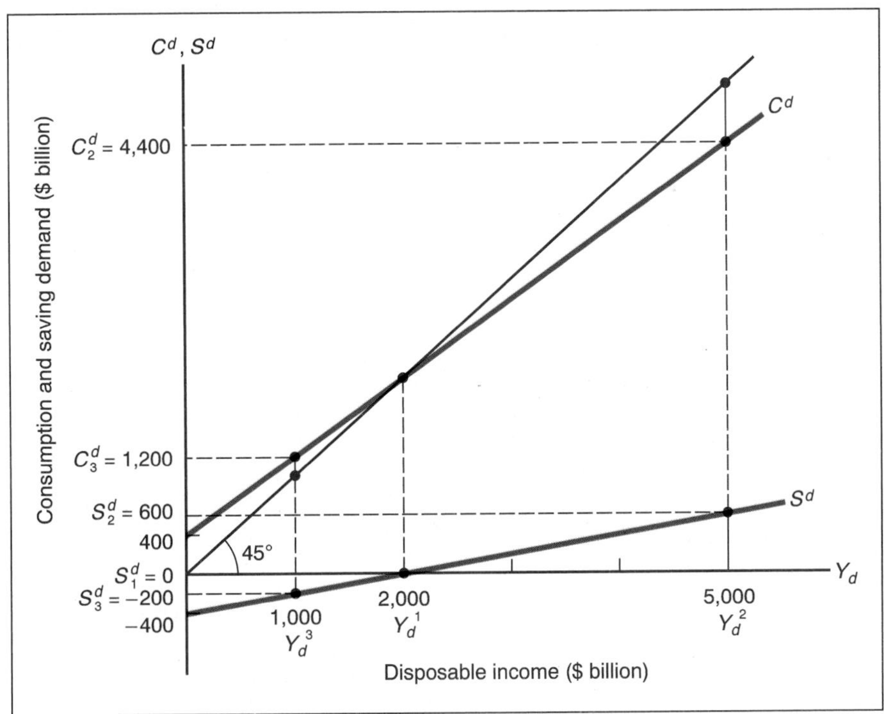

FIGURE 29.3

The Saving Function

The saving function, S^d, is a graph of the aggregate saving demand by households at each level of disposable income, Y_d, from Table 29.2. S^d is the mirror image of the consumption function, C^d, because households can either consume or save their disposable income. Saving is zero at the break-even level of disposable income, $2,000, when households consume all their disposable income. Saving is positive at all levels of disposable income above $2,000. For example, when disposable income is $5,000, households save $600. Saving is negative at all levels of disposable income below $2,000; households are dissaving. For example, when disposable income is $1,000, saving is (−)$200. The marginal propensity to save, labelled MPS, is the slope of the saving function. MPS = $\Delta S^d/\Delta Y_d$. The MPS = 0.20 for the saving function in Table 29.2

S^d hits the vertical axis at $-\$400$. This is the component of saving demand that is determined by the factors other than disposable income that influence the level of consumption demand and saving demand. The $-\$400$ of saving is the mirror image of the \$400 of consumption demand that is independent of disposable income.

MARGINAL PROPENSITY TO SAVE

The portion of each additional dollar of disposable income that households save; the ratio of the change in saving demand to the change in disposable income.

THE MARGINAL PROPENSITY TO SAVE The slope of the saving function is the rise over the run of S^d, the change in saving divided by the change in disposable income. The slope of S^d is called the **marginal propensity to save** and is commonly referred to as the MPS.

$$\text{MPS} = \text{slope of } S^d = \Delta S^d/\Delta Y_d$$

The MPS indicates the portion of each *additional* dollar of disposable income that the household saves. The MPS for our hypothetical saving function is .20. Every additional \$1,000 of disposable income increases saving by \$200 (refer to the fourth column of the table).

Notice that the MPC and the MPS add up to one for our hypothetical consumption and saving functions (.80 + .20 = 1). In the aggregate the households in our simplest economy spend 80 cents and save 20 cents of each additional dollar of disposable income. The MPC and the MPS must always add up to one because each additional dollar of disposable income must be either consumed or saved.[4]

$$\text{MPC} + \text{MPS} = 1$$

We noted above that studies of the aggregate U.S. consumption function have found a short-run MPC in the range of .60 to .80 and a long-run MPC in the range of .90 to .93. Equivalently, these studies have found a short-run MPS in the range of .40 to .20 and a long-run MPS in the range of .10 to .07.

Also, the MPS must be between zero and one, inclusive, just as the MPC is.

$$0 \leq \text{MPS} \leq 1$$

AVERAGE PROPENSITY TO SAVE

The ratio of saving demand to disposable income.

The final column of Table 29.2 records the **average propensity to save (APS)** at each level of disposable income, which is the ratio of saving demand to disposable income:

$$\text{APS} = S^d/Y_d$$

The average propensity to save is also the mirror image of the average propensity to consume (APC) because the average propensities to consume and save must add up to one.

$$\text{APC} + \text{APS} = 1$$

[4]The derivation of the MPC, MPS relationship is as follows. $Y_d = C^d + S^d$. Therefore, in terms of changes, $\Delta Y_d = \Delta C^d + \Delta S^d$. Divide both sides by ΔY_d:

$$(\Delta C^d/\Delta Y_d) + (\Delta S^d/\Delta Y_d) = \Delta Y_d/\Delta Y_d = 1$$
$$\text{MPC} + \text{MPS} = 1$$

The APS rises steadily as disposable income increases for our hypothetical data, just the opposite of the APC. The MPS is much more important than the APS is to the study of the macro economy.

Other Factors Influencing Consumption Demand

The consumption function shows the independent, *other things equal* effect of disposable income on consumption demand. Changes in disposable income cause movements along the consumption function. The other factors that influence households' consumption demand—expectations about the future, prices, tastes, and so forth—are not pictured on the consumption function graph. They are lying behind the scene, determining the position of the consumption function. Changes in any of these other factors shift the entire consumption function up or down to a new position. Moreover, any change that shifts the consumption function must shift the saving function in exactly the opposite direction. Otherwise, consumption and saving would no longer add up to disposable income, which is unchanged.

For example, suppose that the households in our simplest economy have a change in tastes in favor of consumption. They want to consume $300 more at every level of disposable income. We would represent this by shifting C^d up by $300 in Figure 29.1 and adding $300 to the consumption data in Tables 29.1 and 29.2. C^d would now intersect the vertical axis at $700.

By deciding to consume $300 more at every level of disposable income, households have simultaneously decided to save $300 less at every level of disposable income. Therefore, we would also have to shift S^d down by $300 in Figure 29.3 and subtract $300 from the saving data in Table 29.2. S^d would now intersect the vertical axis at −$700.

With these points in mind, let's take a look at some of the other factors that influence consumption demand and saving demand.

FUTURE EXPECTATIONS: THE LIFE-CYCLE HYPOTHESIS Consumers do not base their consumption and saving decisions just on their current situations. Their future prospects also come into play. College students are a good example. Many students (or their parents) are spending far more than their current disposable incomes to attend college because they view a college education as a good investment in their future. They are borrowing and otherwise dissaving now with the expectation that their college degrees will gain them access to high-paying jobs after college.

The chief competitor to the Keynesian consumption function for explaining aggregate consumption assumes that consumers look far into the future, indeed over their entire lifetimes, in making their consumption and saving decisions. The competing model, called the **Life-Cycle Hypothesis,** was developed jointly in the late 1950s by Albert Ando of the University of Pennsylvania and Franco Modigliani of MIT.[5] We want to take some time with the Life-Cycle Hypothesis because it is one of the building blocks of the new classical model of the economy.

LIFE-CYCLE HYPOTHESIS

A theory of household consumption demand that attempts to explain the average pattern of lifetime income and consumption given by the age-earnings profile.

[5]A. Ando and F. Modigliani, "The Life-Cycle Hypothesis of Saving: Aggregate Indications and Tests," *American Economic Review* 53, No. 1, Part I (March 1963): 54–84. A precursor to the Ando, Modigliani paper was F. Modigliani and R. Brumberg, "Utility Analysis and the Consumption Function," in K. K. Kurihara, ed., *Post-Keynesian Economics* (New Brunswick, NJ: Rutgers University Press, 1954).

FIGURE 29.4

The Age-Earnings Profile and Lifetime Consumption

The figure shows the typical pattern of earnings and consumption over people's lifetimes. Age is on the horizontal axis, and consumption and income are on the vertical axis. The age-earnings profile, *Y*, indicates the average earnings of people at each age during their lives. Average earnings rise until middle age and then decline, falling sharply during retirement. The line *C* indicates the average consumption of people at each age during their lives. People smooth their consumption over their lifetimes to enjoy a fairly constant standard of living. They borrow when young, save during middle age to pay off their debts and build a nest egg for retirement, and dissave during their retirement. The Life-Cycle Hypothesis is based on this average pattern of lifetime earnings and consumption.

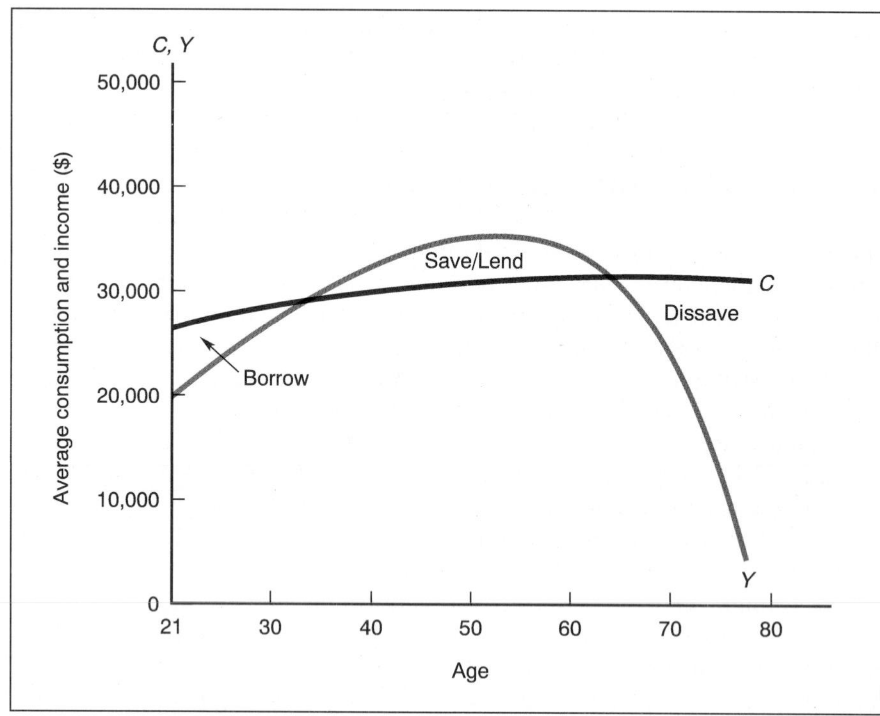

The Life-Cycle Hypothesis was an attempt to explain the average pattern of lifetime income and consumption observed in the United States, which is illustrated in Figure 29.4. The horizontal axis lists each age within the population, starting with age 21. The vertical axis records the average values of earned income and consumption per person by all people of the corresponding age on the horizontal axis. The hump-shaped curve labeled *Y* is the **age-earnings profile** of the population, the average earnings per person at each age. Income rises steadily until late middle age and then begins to decline, falling sharply during the retirement years. The curve labeled *C* shows the average consumption per person at each age.

AGE-EARNINGS PROFILE

The average earnings per person at each age within the population.

The figure shows that lifetime consumption is much smoother than is lifetime income. On average, people borrow when they are young to support a level of consumption above their annual incomes. Young adults may borrow heavily to buy big-ticket items, such as houses and cars, or to further their educations, or they may use credit card debt simply to increase their current standard of living. As people reach middle age, they consume less than their incomes and save. They pay back their earlier debts and begin to build up a nest egg for their retirement years. In their retirement years they once again consume more than their incomes, living off the accumulated savings during their high-income, middle-age years.

Modigliani and Ando hypothesized that this pattern of lifetime income and consumption is the result of people making consumption plans over their entire lifetimes and adjusting each year as new information becomes available. First, they project what their lifetime resources will be. The two main types of lifetime resources are their projected labor market earnings over their working lifetimes and inherited wealth. (Inherited wealth is inconsequential for most people, however.) They also take into account both current and projected future taxes and government transfers such as Social Security to calculate their projected disposable incomes. People then borrow and lend as necessary to smooth consumption so that they enjoy a fairly constant standard of living out of their lifetime resources.

The Keynesian and Life-Cycle views of the consumption and saving decision could hardly be more different. Keynes linked consumption demand to current disposable income each year. The Life-Cycle Hypothesis links consumption demand to lifetime resources. Not surprisingly, the two theories have very different implications.

For starters, the Life-Cycle Hypothesis suggests that the short-run MPC out of current disposable income ought to be very low. To see why, suppose that a household receives an increase in disposable income during the year. The change in income could have been anticipated or unanticipated, and it could be viewed as either permanent or temporary. Consider the expected reaction to each type of change under the Life-Cycle Hypothesis.

An anticipated change in disposable income—An example of a fully anticipated change in disposable income might be a 3 percent salary increase (after taxes) received by a tenured faculty member at a major university. The professor has taught at the university for 15 years, has always planned to stay there until retirement, and expects to receive after-tax salary increases on the order of 3 percent each year. Because the 3 percent salary increase was fully anticipated, it has already been factored into the professor's lifetime consumption plan. Therefore, it has absolutely no effect on his consumption; the short-run MPC out of the salary increase is zero. In general, only *unanticipated* changes in disposable income can change consumption under the Life-Cycle Hypothesis. The only remaining question is whether households view unanticipated changes as permanent or temporary.

An unanticipated change in disposable income, viewed as permanent—An example of this case might be a young executive who wins a promotion to vice-president in charge of marketing and receives a huge increase in salary along with the promotion. The executive was in competition with many other managers for the position; she could not assume that she would get the promotion so it could not have been fully anticipated. Having received the promotion, however, she views the salary increase as permanent. She now expects to receive much higher salaries in future years than she would have received without the promotion. The unanticipated, permanent increase in her annual salary shifts her age-earnings profile up by the full amount of the salary, so she increases her consumption by the full amount of the salary as well. The short-run MPC out of a *permanent,* but *unanticipated,* increase in annual income is one. (The short-run MPC would be even greater than one if the change in income this year suggests even bigger changes in future years, as it might in this example.)

An unanticipated change in disposable income, viewed as temporary—Unanticipated, temporary changes in disposable income would include one-time windfall gains such as gambling winnings, an unexpected tax rebate, or, in the other direction, a short spell of unemployment. The short-run MPC out of temporary changes in income such as these would be very low. They represent an increase or decrease in lifetime resources, but because they are one-time changes, people spread the consumption from these changes over their remaining lifetimes.

For young people the immediate effect on consumption is very low, probably little more than 5 percent of the change in disposable income. For example, suppose that a young adult wins a $1,000 prize in the state lottery for guessing most of the numbers correctly. If he is a Life-Cycle consumer, he will not consume the $1,000 immediately because he wants to smooth his consumption over his lifetime. Instead, he might place the $1,000 in a savings account earning 5 percent so that he can increase his consumption each year by $50. He may also consume a small portion of the $1,000 each year, but his short-run increase in consumption is likely to be very small.

In summary, only *unanticipated* changes in disposable income that are expected to be *permanent* generate a short-run MPC that is very much different from zero. Not all changes in disposable income are likely to be of this kind, however. Many unanticipated changes in disposable income are undoubtedly viewed as temporary, given the endless ebbs and flows of the business cycle. For instance, most spells of unemployment are temporary, and probably unanticipated. Also, many changes in disposable income are probably anticipated to a large extent, especially among those employees with long-term employment relationships. Therefore, the short-run MPC should be quite low if people behave according to the Life-Cycle Hypothesis.

HISTORICAL NOTE: A recent study found that blue collar workers reduce their consumption by one-fourth as much as white collar workers per dollar of income lost during a spell of unemployment. This is consistent with the Life-Cycle Hypothesis. Blue collar workers are likely to view a spell of unemployment as a temporary reduction in their incomes, whereas white collar workers are likely to view a spell of unemployment as leading to a permanent reduction in their incomes. M. Dywarski and S. Sheffrin, "Consumption and Unemployment," (*Quarterly Journal of Economics* CII, Issue 2 (May 1987): 411–428.)

How does the Keynesian consumption function stack up against the Life-Cycle Hypothesis? As with most models, they both have their strengths and weaknesses.

The biggest problem for the Life-Cycle Hypothesis is explaining the high short-run MPC of .60 to .80 in the United States. Consumption demand is highly sensitive to changes in current disposable income, in line with the Keynesian consumption function. Economists have long puzzled over why the short-run MPC is so high, and the issue is far from resolved.

The main advantage of the Life-Cycle Hypothesis is that it provides a theory for explaining why many factors other than disposable income might influence consumption demand. We will briefly mention a few of them to conclude the discussion of consumption demand.

WEALTH Wealth should certainly have some effect on consumption. Suppose that two people each earn $25,000 per year, but one has recently inherited $10 million. The person with the inheritance would be expected to consume more each year because he has much greater lifetime resources to draw on.

A famous instance of wealth affecting aggregate consumption in the United States occurred after World War II. Many economists were expecting a return to the Great Depression once the war wound down and aggregate demand was no longer supported by enormous amounts of government military expenditures. Instead, the nation transformed itself fairly quickly back to a peacetime economy, and the economy performed very well. The savior was consumption demand, which turned out to be much stronger than anyone had expected. The federal government had financed the war by issuing large amounts of debt to the American public. After the war, when people were once again free to buy consumer goods and services, they viewed their holdings of the government's bonds as a huge increase in their wealth and went on a consumption binge. Their consumption had been low for many years because of the Great Depression and the War.

Changes in private wealth do not always have such a large effect on consumption demand, however. The stock market crashed on October 19, 1987; the Dow Jones Industrial Index lost 500 points on that day, fully 20 percent of its value. Some people feared that the crash would depress consumption demand and lead the economy into a recession, but consumption demand hardly changed at all. Economists are not sure why. One explanation is that most households own stocks indirectly through their pension funds. Only about 20 percent of households hold stocks directly. Another explanation is that the stock market had been rising rapidly during the previous year, so that the 500-point loss merely returned the Dow Jones to its level of the year before. In any event the crash of 1987 confirmed the widespread belief that changes in stock prices have little effect on consumption demand in the United States.

PRICES The effect of prices on consumption demand has been incorporated into our analysis for the most part because we have been referring to real consumption and real disposable income. An increase in the consumer price index lowers real disposable income, other things equal. Prices also have wealth effects that can affect consumption demand, however. An increase in prices reduces the value of our money holdings and thereby reduces our real wealth. We also saw how unanticipated changes in the rate of inflation can transfer purchasing power between debtors and creditors. These wealth-induced price effects are likely to be quite small, however.

INTEREST RATES Interest rates can affect the timing of consumption in the Life-Cycle model. Higher interest rates make saving more attractive, so people save more now and consume more later on in their lives. Conversely, lower interest rates discourage saving, so people consume more now and consume less later on in their lives. Many economists question whether these Life-Cycle effects are very important, however. Most studies do not find that consumption and saving are very sensitive to changes in interest rates.

THE AGE DISTRIBUTION OF THE POPULATION The Life-Cycle Hypothesis suggests that aggregate consumption and saving ought to vary with the age distribution of the population. The reason is simply that the young and the old tend to dissave, and the middle-aged tend to save. This prediction, if true, could be a ray of sunshine for the United States.

Most economists believe that the United States needs to increase its saving and investment in order to increase productivity and long-run economic growth, yet personal saving has been abnormally low over the past 15 years. The huge baby boom generation that was born between 1947 and 1964 may have been largely responsible for the decline in personal saving. The baby boomers were in their young adult years for the most part over the past 15 years, a period of dissaving according to the Life-Cycle Hypothesis. They are now approximately 30 to 50 years of age, in or just entering their middle-age years. The Life-Cycle Hypothesis predicts that their saving should increase sharply as they pay off the debts of their youth and begin to build a retirement nest egg. If the Life-Cycle Hypothesis is correct, the baby boomers will usher in a new period of high saving and high investment in the United States and put an end to the low-saving, low-investment, low-growth scenario that the United States has been stuck in since 1974.

INVESTMENT DEMAND

Investment demand is the other component of aggregate demand in our simplest economy.

The most striking feature of investment is its volatility. Investment moves with the business cycle just as consumption does, increasing when national income is increasing and decreasing when national income is decreasing. But the swings in investment are much more pronounced than are the swings in consumption. Northwestern's Robert Gordon calculated the change in gross investment during eight business cycles in the United States from 1948 to 1982. Gross investment fell by an average of 20 percent during the downturns and rose by an average of 33 percent during the upturns. These percentage changes were about six times larger than the percentage changes in consumption, or any other component of GDP. And net investment is even more volatile than is gross investment.[6]

The volatility of investment makes it highly unpredictable. Economists have tried long and hard, and without much success, to pin down the factors that determine investment demand. How much does investment demand respond to changes in national income? Tax policy? Interest rates? Stock market prices? Corporate profits? To what extent is investment demand driven by technological change? Economists cannot agree on the answers to these questions, and their disagreements extend to all three components of investment—plant and equipment, inventories, and housing. Every component of investment is highly volatile and difficult to predict.

Our main concern in this chapter is whether investment demand is closely related to the current level of economic activity. We will focus on investment in plant and equipment in answering this question because it is the most important component of investment.

Investment in Plant and Equipment

Investment in plant and equipment increases and decreases with the business cycle, but it is *not* closely related to the level of economic activity. To understand why not, you must keep firmly in mind the distinction between capital and investment.

The stock of capital is the factor of production that firms combine with labor, land, and material inputs to produce their output. Investment is the *change* in the stock of capital during the year. Given this distinction, the investment decision can be viewed as a two-step process that takes place at the beginning of each year. First, firms determine their desired stock of capital, the amount of capital that they would like to have in place by the end of the year. Then they decide on a level of investment during the year that will increase their

[6]R. Gordon, *Macroeconomics*, fifth edition (Glenview, IL: Scott, Foresman/Little, Brown 1989), 579–581; Table 1, p. 580. Also, E. Prescott, "Theory Ahead of Business Cycle Measurement," Federal Reserve Bank of Minneapolis, *Quarterly Review* (Fall 1986), p. 9.

existing stock of capital either part way or all the way to the new desired stock of capital. Let's look at both parts of the decision, with an eye toward how each part is related to the current production or sales of the firm.

THE DESIRED STOCK OF CAPITAL The desired stock of capital is certainly related to the level of output that the firm expects to be producing and selling in the future. A higher level of output requires more capital and all other factors of production; a lower level of output requires less capital and all other factors of production. Moreover, the output that the firm expects to be producing and selling in the future ought to bear some relationship to its current level of production and sales, which means that the desired stock of capital is related to the current level of production and sales.

The relationship between the desired stock of capital and the current level of production and sales may not be all that close, however, because capital is durable. Most equipment can be expected to last for anywhere from 3 to 10 years, and some structures may last for 30 years or even longer. Therefore, in deciding on their desired stock of capital, firms are not just going to consider their current level of sales. They will also try to guess what their sales will be for a number of years into the future. Guesses about the future are uncertain at best, but firms have to guess, and they are likely to consider much more than their current level of sales in making their guesses. For example, suppose that a firm's sales are 10 percent higher this year than last year. Does this mean that the firm's sales will remain at the new level next year, or increase by another 10 percent, or change by some other amount? The managers of the firm will bring more information to bear in answering the question than just the 10 percent increase in sales this year. They will consider the trend of sales over the past five years or so; they will also factor in their best guess about where the overall economy is heading in the near future.

Keynes believed that uncertainty about the future was the key element in the investment decision. He described investment demand as being driven by unpredictable "animal spirits," by which he meant waves of optimism and pessimism about future sales as managers peered into a highly uncertain future.

In any event, a firm's desired stock of capital may not be very closely related to its current level of sales.

THE INVESTMENT DECISION Even if the desired stock of capital were closely related to the current level of sales, investment would not be. Investment is the *change* in the stock of capital. Therefore, if the desired stock of capital is related to the current *level* of sales, the rate of investment would be related to the *change* in the firm's sales. In other words, investment depends on the expected *growth* of sales *regardless* of what the current *level* of sales happens to be.

Any possible relationship between investment and the current level of production or sales is further clouded by the fact that many investment projects take a long time to complete. Firms cannot necessarily increase their existing stock of capital to the desired stock of capital within one year.

The time to completion has a substantial effect on the rate of investment in the United States. Firms in the aggregate complete only about one-third of their planned investment in plant and equipment in any one year.[7] The ma-

[7]Hall and Taylor, *Macroeconomics*, p 238.

jority of plant and equipment investment undertaken each year is the result of decisions made in previous years.

In summary, the rate of investment in plant and equipment does not bear a close relationship to the current level of production. Therefore, we will assume for simplicity that the plant and equipment component of investment demand is entirely unrelated to the level of national income.

A HYPOTHETICAL INVESTMENT DEMAND CURVE Figure 29.5 illustrates the investment demand curve for plant and equipment for our simplest economy. Investment demand is on the vertical axis, and national income, labeled Y, is on the horizontal axis. The investment demand curve, I^d_{P+E} is horizontal at a level of \$400 (as with consumption and saving, all data are in billions of constant dollars). In other words, we are assuming that firms in the aggregate want to invest \$400 in plant and equipment during the year regardless of the level of national income.

You should not take this too literally. Investment demand would surely fall if national income were to fall to zero, and just as surely rise if national income were to triple in value. Interpret the investment demand curve as referring to a "reasonable" range of national income. If national income is currently at \$6,000, it is unlikely to rise above \$7,000 or fall below \$5,000. Therefore, we are assuming that investment demand remains at \$400 for all values of national income that are likely to occur.

The \$400 of investment demand is determined by factors other than the current level of economic activity. Changes in these other factors shift I^d_{P+E} up and down. As we have already seen, one such factor is the expected change

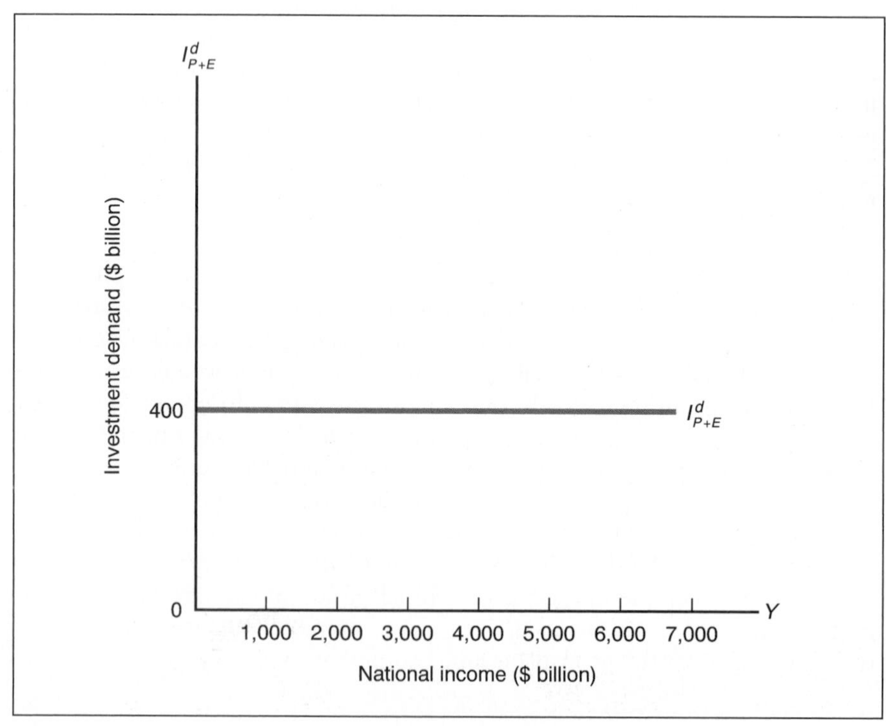

FIGURE 29.5

Investment in Plant and Equipment and National Income

Firms' investment in plant and equipment is not closely related to the level of national income. It is determined, instead, by such factors as the projected growth in national income and the cost of capital. Therefore, our simplest model assumes that the demand for investment in plant and equipment is unrelated to the level of national income, Y. In particular, we are assuming that investment in plant and equipment is \$400 over the range of values that national income is likely to have (in billions of constant dollars). Therefore, the graph of investment in plant and equipment, I^d_{P+E}, is horizontal at a value of \$400. Changes in the other factors that influence plant and equipment investment shift I^d_{P+E} up or down.

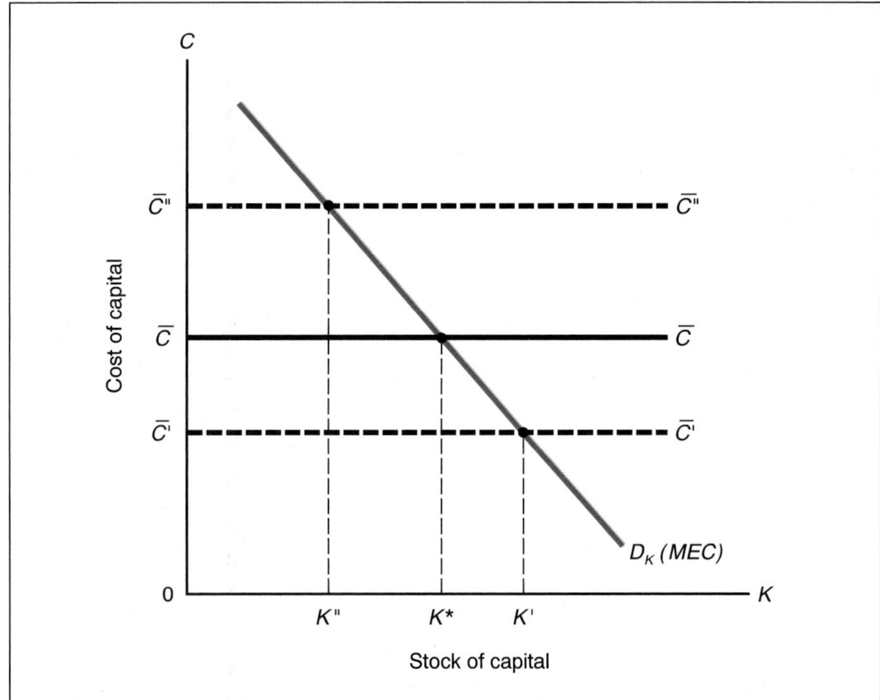

FIGURE 29.6

The Desired Stock of Capital and the Cost of Capital

The figure shows that a firm's desired stock of capital is inversely related to the cost of capital. The demand curve for capital, D_K, is called the marginal efficiency of capital (MEC). It indicates the returns to adding another unit of capital at each level of the firm's capital stock. The returns are the amount that the new unit of capital reduces the firm's costs of production. C is the cost of capital, which depends on four factors: the price of new capital, interest rates, the rate of depreciation of the capital stock, and the tax system. C is a constant, $\overline{C}$, because no one firm is large enough to affect the cost of capital. The firm's desired stock of capital is the amount of capital at which the marginal efficiency of capital equals the cost of capital, the intersection of D_K and $\overline{C}$. The desired stock of capital is K^* when the cost of capital is $\overline{C}$. A decrease in the cost of capital from $\overline{C}$ to $\overline{C}'$ increases the desired stock of capital to K'. An increase in the cost of capital from $\overline{C}$ to $\overline{C}''$ decreases the desired stock of capital to K''.

in the level of economic activity. Let's consider briefly some of the other factors that economists believe have an important effect on investment demand.

OTHER FACTORS AFFECTING INVESTMENT DEMAND Most of the factors that affect investment demand do so by influencing the desired stock of capital. Earlier we said that firms base their desired stock of capital on their expected output or sales. The other factors affect the desired stock of capital by influencing the amount of capital that firms want to use to produce each unit of output, called the **capital/output ratio.** The two most important factors determining a firm's capital/output ratio are the production technologies available to the firm and the cost of capital.

CAPITAL/OUTPUT RATIO

The amount of capital required to produce each unit of output.

THE DEMAND FOR CAPITAL, PRODUCTION TECHNOLOGY, AND THE COST OF CAPITAL When choosing their desired stock of capital, firms compare the returns from each additional unit of capital with the cost of the capital. Adding capital has value to the firm if it reduces the operating costs of producing the output. The returns to each additional unit of capital are the amount that the capital reduces the operating costs. The firm adds capital to the point at which the returns from the last unit of capital just equal the cost of the capital. The total amount of capital at that point is the desired stock of capital.

Figure 29.6 illustrates the capital decision. Dollars of return and cost are on the vertical axis, and the total amount of capital is on the horizontal axis. The demand curve for capital, D_K, is often referred to as the **marginal efficiency of capital,** labeled MEC. The marginal efficiency of capital refers to the re-

MARGINAL EFFICIENCY OF CAPITAL

The returns to capital from the last unit of capital put in place; also, the demand curve for capital.

turns from the last unit of capital put in place. The MEC depends primarily on the firm's available production technologies, which determine how readily the firm can substitute capital for other factors of production and reduce its operating costs.

D_K (MEC) is downward sloping, as expected, because the returns to capital decline the more capital the firm already has in place. For instance, many firms have found that microcomputers drastically reduce the costs of various secretarial, accounting, and record-keeping activities by replacing more costly office personnel, secretaries, bookkeepers, and the like. Even so, a firm can only use so many microcomputers. The returns to buying additional microcomputers must eventually decline.

COST OF CAPITAL

The annual cost to a firm of purchasing an additional unit of capital.

$\overline{C}$ is the annual **cost of capital** to the firm. It is constant at $\overline{C}$ because each firm is usually an insignificant buyer in the overall national market for capital. A firm cannot influence its cost of capital no matter how much capital it buys.

The desired stock of capital, K^*, is at the intersection of the D_K (MEC) and $\overline{C}$. The returns to the last unit of capital at K^* as measured by the demand for capital, the MEC, just equal the cost of capital, $\overline{C}$.

THE COST OF CAPITAL AND THE DESIRED STOCK OF CAPITAL The figure shows that the cost of capital has a direct effect on the desired stock of capital. A decrease in the cost of capital from $\overline{C}$ to $\overline{C}'$ induces the firm to increase its capital/output ratio, so that its desired stock of capital increases from K^* to K'. Conversely, an increase in the cost of capital from $\overline{C}$ to $\overline{C}''$ induces the firm to decrease its capital/output ratio, so that its desired stock of capital decreases from K^* to K''.

The cost of capital to a firm depends primarily on four elements: the prices of the capital goods, interest rates, the rate at which the capital depreciates, and the tax system.

The price of the capital. The price that the firm has to pay for a machine, a factory, or an office building is the obvious component of the cost of capital. The cost of microcomputers clearly depends on whether the firm pays \$10,000 or \$12,000 for each computer.

Interest rates. Suppose that a microcomputer costs a firm \$10,000 and that the firm borrows the \$10,000 to pay for it at an interest rate of 8 percent. The annual interest charge of \$800 (\$800 = 8% of \$10,000) is part of the annual cost of the computer.

The firm is more likely to pay for the computer out of its retained earnings simply because the firms in the United States finance almost two-thirds of their investment from retained earnings. In this case the interest charge is no longer an out-of-pocket cost to the firm, but it remains an opportunity cost associated with the computer. The firm always has the option of giving the stockholders the \$10,000, rather than buying a computer. If the stockholders can earn 8 percent on their savings, then \$800 is the annual opportunity cost of investing \$10,000 in a microcomputer.

Depreciation. All capital begins to depreciate as soon as it is placed into production, and the firm has to set aside funds in its depreciation account to replace capital as it wears out. The annual depreciation charges are part of the annual cost of capital. Suppose that the \$10,000 microcomputer is expected to last for 10 years and depreciates in value at the constant rate of 10 percent per year over the 10 years. The annual depreciation charge is \$1,000 (\$1,000 = 10% of \$10,000). The sum of the \$800 interest charge and the \$1,000 depreciation charge, \$1,800, defines the basic annual cost of capital associated with the computer.

Tax policy. The tax system has a significant effect on the cost of capital. All returns to capital are subject to tax, either by the corporation income tax or by the personal income tax (for proprietorships and partnerships). These taxes raise the cost of capital by increasing the returns that firms require on their capital to cover the other components of the cost of capital.

Congress has used three main tax instruments to affect the cost of capital: corporation income tax rates, depreciation allowances, and investment tax credits. Congress can raise the cost of capital by increasing the corporation income tax rate or lower the cost of capital by reducing the corporation income tax rate. In addition, the U.S. Internal Revenue Service (IRS) determines how quickly firms can depreciate various kinds of capital for tax purposes. The faster the allowable rate of depreciation is, the less tax the firms have to pay and the lower the cost of capital is. An **investment tax credit** allows firms to deduct a portion of the total value of their investment during the year against their taxable profits. The most recent example was a 10 percent tax credit on certain equipment investment that was in effect from 1964 to 1986. An investment tax credit also lowers the cost of capital.

INVESTMENT TAX CREDIT

A tax credit under the federal corporation income tax that allows firms to deduct a portion of the total value of their investment during the year from their taxable profits.

INVESTMENT DEMAND AND THE COST OF CAPITAL Economists are sharply divided on the question of whether the government can influence investment demand very much by changing the cost of capital through tax policies, at least in the short run. All economists would agree that the demand for *capital* is inversely related to the cost of capital as drawn in Figure 29.6, both for the individual firm and for the entire economy. The point of contention is the extent to which *investment* in plant and equipment is also inversely related to the cost of capital.

Refer to Figure 29.7, which relates the investment demand curve for plant and equipment, I_{P+E}, to the cost of capital. Is the investment demand curve quite steep, such as I^1_{P+E}, so that investment in plant and equipment is not very sensitive to changes in the cost of capital? Or is the investment demand curve relatively flat, such as I^2_{P+E}, so that investment in plant and equipment is quite sensitive to changes in the cost of capital?

Some economists think that the investment demand curve looks like I^1_{P+E}, very steep. They believe that investment in plant and equipment depends primarily on the expected growth in sales. Firms invest when they think their sales will grow, and they do not invest when they think their sales will be flat. The cost of capital makes very little difference beyond that. The link between investment and the cost of capital is weak because firms cannot easily substitute capital for other factors of production. In other words, the desired stock of capital itself is not very responsive to the cost of capital. Also, the delays associated with investing weaken the link between investment demand and changes in the cost of capital still further. Investment responds slowly to changes in the cost of capital, too slowly for tax policy to be an effective tool for spurring investment demand in the short run. So, for example, if the economy is languishing in a recession, tax policies that reduce the cost of capital do not induce firms to invest very much at all. Instead, the government should pursue policies to stimulate aggregate demand so that firms' sales will grow. A growing economy is the key to promoting a high level of investment.

Other economists think that the investment demand curve looks like I^2_{P+E}, relatively flat. They argue that firms can easily substitute capital for other fac-

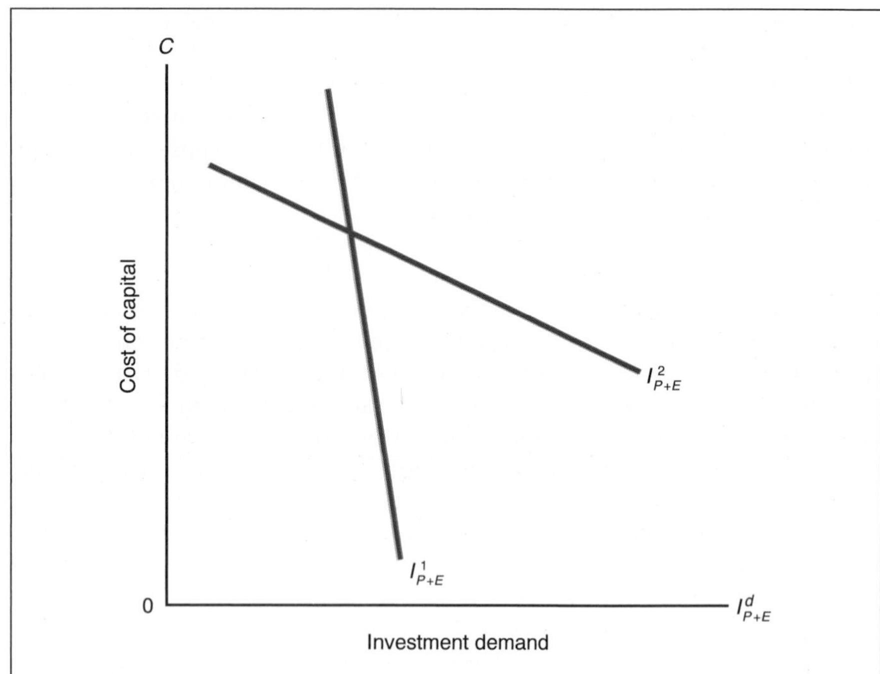

FIGURE 29.7

Investment Demand and the Cost of Capital

Economists agree that the desired stock of capital is closely related to the cost of capital, *C*. They disagree on the extent to which investment in plant and equipment in a given year is determined by the cost of capital in the same year. Some economists believe that investment demand is not very sensitive to changes in the cost of capital, that the investment demand curve is very steep, like I^1_{P+E}. In their view, investment demand depends mostly on the growth in aggregate demand. Other economists believe that investment demand is quite sensitive to changes in the cost of capital, that the investment demand curve is relatively flat, like I^2_{P+E}. In their view, Congress can increase investment demand with tax policies, such as an investment tax credit, that lower the cost of capital.

tors of production, so that the demand for capital is quite responsive to changes in the cost of capital. They also believe that the investment response is quick enough to make tax policy an effective spur to investment demand.

The differences between these two views have been difficult to resolve, in part because of the volatility in investment demand, and in part because of the lags in investment. So much of this year's investment in plant and equipment is the result of decisions made in past years that economists have difficulty untangling exactly what determines the level of investment each year.[8]

OTHER FACTOR PRICES Our discussion of the cost of capital assumed that the prices of other factors of production are held constant. Changes in wages, the price of oil, and other factor prices also affect the firm's desired capital/output ratio because the other factors of production are either substitutes or complements to capital in the production. For instance, labor and capital tend to be substitutes in production. An increase in wages induces firms to substitute capital for labor, raising the desired stock of capital, and presumably the level of investment. High wages in the United States no doubt spurred the development of the fast-food restaurants such as McDonald's and KFC. The fast-food restaurants are much more capital intensive than are the diners and the family-style restaurants they replaced.

[8]Robert Eisner of Northwestern is a leading proponent of the view that the investment demand curve is more responsive to growth in demand than to the cost of capital. Robert Hall of Stanford and Dale Jorgenson of Harvard are leading proponents of the view that the investment demand curve is quite responsive to the cost of capital. Their seminal studies are: R. Eisner, *Factors in Business Investment* (Cambridge, MA: Ballenger, 1978) and R. Hall and D. Jorgenson, "Tax Policy and Investment Behavior," *American Economic Review* 57, No. 3 (June 1967): 391–414.

Investment in Inventory

Goods held in inventory are either goods in process that are being used as material inputs in production, such as the engines to be placed in the cars on the assembly line, or finished goods that are sitting in warehouses or on the shelves of the retailers. American manufacturers, wholesalers, and retailers hold an enormous amount of inventory, about 40 cents for every dollar of GDP.

The amount of goods in inventory at any given time is the stock of inventory capital. *Investment* in inventory is the amount that inventories *change* from the beginning to the end of the year. Unlike the stock of inventory, investment in inventory is quite small, usually less than 5 percent of total investment expenditures. Nonetheless, inventory investment is very important to the operation of the economy. Decreases in inventory investment accounted for 87 percent of the decreases in GDP, on average, during the eight recessions from the end of World War II to 1990. Inventory investment is also the most volatile component of investment demand.[9]

The analysis of inventory investment proceeds along the same lines as the analysis of plant and equipment investment. Firms first decide on their desired stock of inventory capital based on their expected sales during the year. Then they invest in inventory to adjust their current stock of inventory to the desired stock.

The only difference, and an important one, is that firms can adjust their inventories very quickly. The average investment in inventory is just a few days' worth of production in most industries. As a result, the desired stock of inventory is very closely related to the current level of production and sales, and the investment quickly adjusts the inventories to the desired stock. This does not mean, however, that investment in inventory is closely related to the level of production or sales. As with plant and equipment, it is the stock of inventories that is related to the current level of production or sales. Investment in inventory, the change in the stock, is related to the *change* in production or sales, whatever the *level* of production or sales may be.

There is no close relationship between inventory investment and the level of production or sales, either for the individual firm or for the economy as a whole.

Therefore, we will assume that investment demand for inventories, I^d_{INV}, is unrelated to the level of national income in our simplest economy. In other words, a graph relating I^d_{INV} to national income, Y, would be horizontal, just as the graph of I^d_{P+E} is in Figure 29.5. For the purposes of our model, we will assume that firms in the aggregate want their inventories to increase by \$25 during the course of the year regardless of the overall level of economic activity. The \$25 is determined by factors other than national product or income, such as the expected change in sales or the cost of capital.

The only wrinkle in inventory investment is that the desired investment in inventories could just as easily be zero or negative as positive. $I^d_{INV} = 0$ means that firms in the aggregate want their stock of inventories to remain the same. $I^d_{INV} < 0$ means that firms in the aggregate want to lower their stock of inventories during the year.

[9] A. Blinder and L. Maccini, "Taking Stock: A Critical Assessment of Recent Research on Inventories," *Journal of Economic Perspectives* 5, No. 1 (Winter 1991): 73–96. The data on inventory are on pages 73 through 75.

INVENTORY INVESTMENT AND NATIONAL INCOME The ability of firms to adjust their inventories quickly plays a very important role in the operation of the macro economy. We will make the following assumption in our model: Once firms decide how much they want their inventories to change, they stick to that decision. They do not tolerate *unwanted* increases or decreases in their inventories.

This is a very realistic assumption. Firms monitor their inventories very closely because unwanted changes in inventory in either direction can be very costly. Think of a car dealer who happens to sell Buicks as an example. Detroit manufactures the cars and ships them to the dealer on a regular schedule. Suppose that the dealer's sales fall off, yet Detroit keeps shipping the cars. The inventory of cars on the lot begins to build up, and the dealer may eventually have to rent lot space from other firms to store the unsold cars. This situation obviously cannot continue. The dealer will eventually call the manufacturer and tell it to stop shipping the cars. If Detroit gets similar calls from a number of Buick dealers, it will lay off auto workers, cut production, and ship fewer Buicks to the dealers. The Buick dealers will sell the cars on their lots, that is, sell out of inventory, until their desired level of inventory is restored.

Suppose, instead, that the dealer's sales are greater than expected. The dealer begins to sell cars at a faster clip than Detroit is shipping them, and the dealer's inventory of cars on the lot begins to decline. This situation cannot continue either because no dealer wants to stock out of cars. The great fear of car dealers, and other merchants, is losing customers to competitors. Customers come in to buy mid-sized Buicks, but cannot find the cars they want on the lot. So they go to the Honda, Ford, and Dodge dealers to buy their mid-sized cars and never again purchase a mid-sized Buick. Therefore, the dealer, fearing lost sales, calls the manufacturer and asks it to ship more cars. If Detroit gets similar calls from a number of Buick dealers, it will hire more auto workers, increase production, and ship more Buicks to the dealers.

REFLECTION: Your own experiences should convince you that firms do not want to stock out of inventory. How many times during the past year have you tried to buy something and not been able to because the item was temporarily out of stock? It happens, but not often.

Car dealers are no different from most other sellers of manufactured goods. Unwanted changes in inventories lead to predictable changes in employment and production, as follows:

SITUATION	REACTION
Unwanted inventory accumulation	Lay off workers and cut production National income decreases
Unwanted inventory depletion	Hire more workers and increase production National income increases

We will see in the next section how the adjustment in inventories brings the economy to its equilibrium.

Investment in Housing

Most investment in housing is undertaken by households, not firms. As such, the decision to build a new home is part of the consumption decision. It is clearly a long-run decision, one that is determined by more than the current level of the household's disposable income. Therefore, we will assume that the investment demand for housing, I^d_H, is also unrelated to the current level of economic activity. In other words, a graph relating I^d_H to national income, Y, would be horizontal, just as the graph of I^d_{P+E} is in Figure 29.5. For the purposes of our model, we will assume that investment demand for housing is \$175 (billion) regardless of the level of national income.

Investment in housing is noteworthy because it is the one component of investment demand that everyone agrees is highly sensitive to the cost of capital, in particular, to mortgage interest rates. A one-percentage-point change in the interest rate on a 30-year, \$100,000 mortgage changes the monthly payment by about \$50 to \$75. Changes of this magnitude are enough to trip the balance for many households on the decision of whether or not to take out a mortgage and buy a new home.

Total Investment Demand

The **total investment demand** is the sum of the three components of investment demand: investment demand for plant and equipment, investment demand for inventory, and investment demand for housing. Since we are assuming that each component of investment demand is unrelated to the current level of economic activity, total investment demand is also unrelated to the current level of economic activity.

TOTAL INVESTMENT DEMAND
The sum of the three components of investment demand: investment demand for plant and equipment, investment demand for inventory, and investment demand for housing.

$$I^d = I^d_{P+E} + I^d_{INV} + I^d_H$$
$$I^d = \$400 + \$25 + \$175$$
$$I^d = \$600$$

I^d is horizontal at \$600 (billion) at every level of national income, as pictured in Figure 29.8. The \$600 of investment demand is determined by factors other

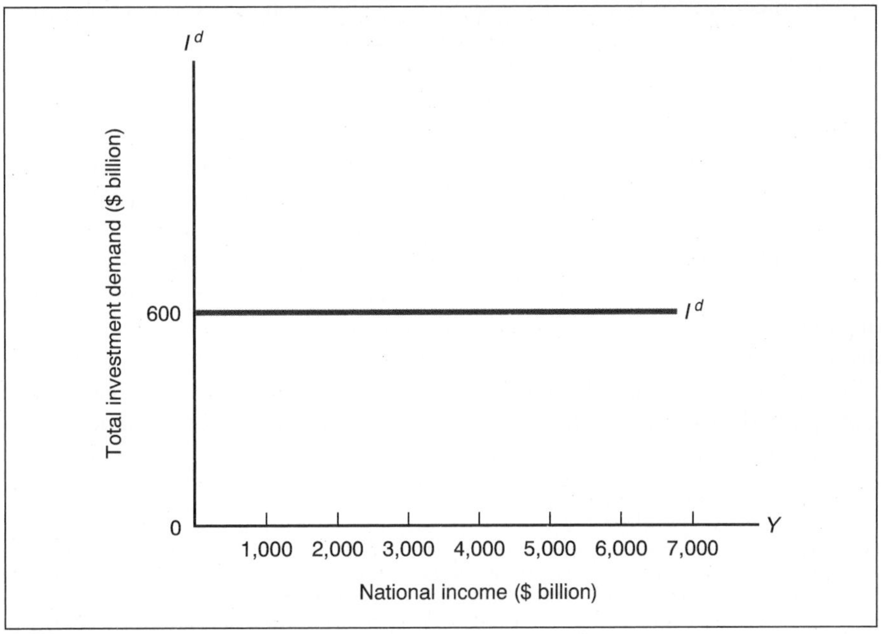

Total investment demand ($ billion)
I^d
600
0
I^d
Y
1,000 2,000 3,000 4,000 5,000 6,000 7,000
National income ($ billion)

FIGURE 29.8
Total Investment Demand

Total investment demand, I^d, is the sum of the demands for investment in plant and equipment, in inventory, and in housing. Our simplest model assumes that each component of investment demand is independent of the level of national income, Y. We are assuming that total investment demand is \$600 over the range of values that national income is likely to have. Therefore the graph of total investment demand, I^d, is horizontal at a value of \$600. Changes in factors other than national income that influence any one of the components of total investment demand shift I^d up or down.

than the level of economic activity, such as expected future sales or the cost of capital. Changes in these factors shift I^d up or down.

THE EQUILIBRIUM LEVEL OF NATIONAL INCOME

Having described how consumption demand and investment demand are related to national income, we are now in a position to describe the equilibrium for the economy.

The equilibrium condition in our simplest economy is

$$Y = C^d + I^d$$

Firms guess what the demand for their products will be and produce to meet that demand. The total amount of final goods and services they produce is the national product, which is also equal to the national income received by the households for their factors of production. Our simplest economy is in equilibrium when the aggregate demand for the final goods and services equals the value of the national income that the firms have produced. The aggregate demand for the final goods and services is the sum of consumption demand and investment demand.

Table 29.3 and Figure 29.9 demonstrate the equilibrium for our simplest economy based on the hypothetical consumption demand and investment demand relationships from the previous two sections. The first column of Table 29.3 reproduces the hypothetical consumption function from Table 29.1. It records the consumption demand, C^d, at each national income listed in the fourth column of the table.[10] The second column of the table records the total investment demand, I^d, which is \$600 regardless of the level of national income. The third column is aggregate demand, the sum of consumption demand and investment demand at every level of national income. For example, when national income is \$4,000 (fourth column), consumption demand is \$3,600, and investment demand is \$600. Aggregate demand is \$4,200, the sum of \$3,600 (C^d) and \$600 (I^d). As above, the data on consumption, investment, and national income are in real terms, in billions of constant dollars.

Figure 29.9 pictures aggregate demand at every level of national income, *Y*. The vertical axis measures aggregate demand, and the horizontal axis measures national income. The 45° line is again a frame-of-reference line that shows the value of national income in the vertical direction. Aggregate demand at each level of national income is measured by the line *ADE*, the sum of C^d (from Figure 29.1) and I^d (from Figure 29.8). Economists often use the letters *ADE* to represent the graph of aggregate demand in terms of national income to distinguish it from the aggregate demand curve labeled *AD* in Chapter 28, in which price is the variable determining aggregate demand. *ADE* stands for **aggregate desired expenditures** or **aggregate demand for expenditures.** Both terms are just different ways of describing aggregate demand. We will

AGGREGATE DESIRED EXPENDITURES (AGGREGATE DEMAND FOR EXPENDITURES)

The relationship between the aggregate demand for final goods and services and national income, other things equal.

[10] Consumption demand is related to disposable income, not national income, but disposable income and national income are equal in our simplest economy. Disposable income differs from national income by the amount of government taxes and transfers and the retained earnings of the business firms. Government taxes and transfers are zero in the simplest model, and we are assuming that firms pay out all profits as dividends, so that retained earnings are also zero.

TABLE 29.3 **The Equilibrium Level of National Income for the Simplest Economy: Household and Business Sectors ($ billion)**

CONSUMPTION DEMAND (C^d)	INVESTMENT DEMAND (I^d)	AGGREGATE DEMAND ($C^d + I^d$)	NATIONAL INCOME (Y)	INVENTORIES AND PRODUCTION RESPONSE
$ 400	$600	$ 1,000	$ 0	Unwanted inventory
1,200	600	1,800	1,000	depletion
2,000	600	2,600	2,000	Increase production
2,800	600	3,400	3,000	.
3,600	600	4,200	4,000	.
4,400	**600**	**5,000**	**5,000**	**Equilibrium**
5,200	600	5,800	6,000	.
6,000	600	6,600	7,000	.
6,800	600	7,400	8,000	Unwanted inventory
7,600	600	8,200	9,000	accumulation
8,400	600	9,000	10,000	.
9,200	600	9,800	11,000	.
10,000	600	10,600	12,000	.
10,800	600	11,400	13,000	Decrease production

continue to refer to *ADE* as aggregate demand, however, because aggregate demand is the standard terminology.

Geometrically, *ADE* is obtained by adding I^d vertically to C^d. Since I^d is constant at $600, *ADE* is just $600 larger than C^d at every level of *Y*. In other words, *ADE* has the same shape as C^d. Most important, the slope of *ADE* is

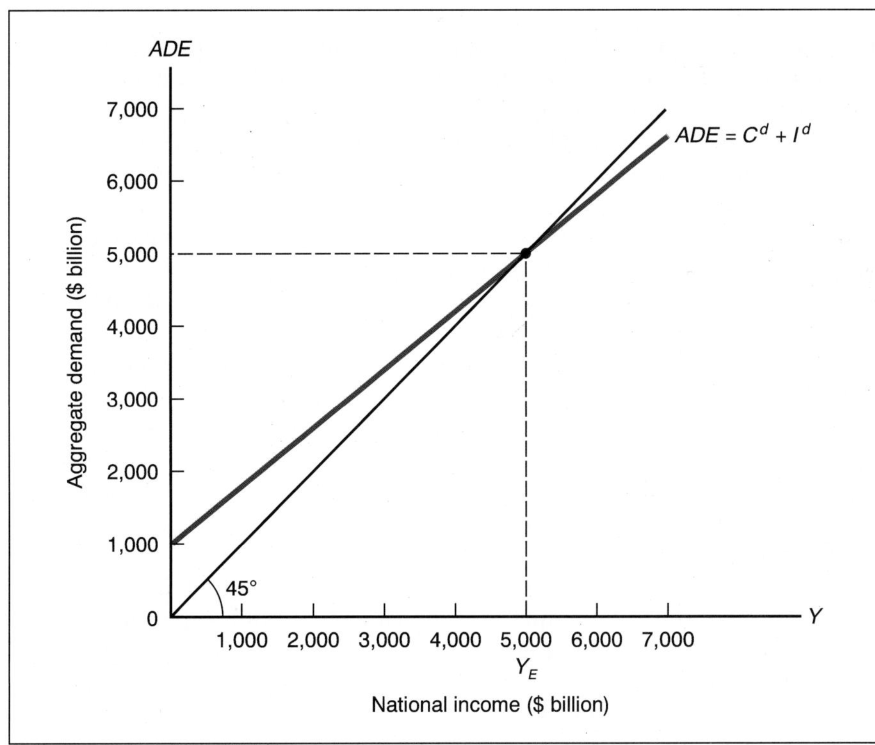

FIGURE 29.9

The Equilibrium Level of National Income

The figure is a graph of the equilibrium level of national income for our simplest economy from the data in Table 29.3. The line ADE indicates the aggregate desired expenditures, or aggregate demand, at each level of national income, *Y*. ADE in our simplest model is the sum of consumption demand by households, C^d, and total investment demand by business firms, I^d. National income is on the horizontal axis and aggregate demand is on the vertical axis. The aggregate demand and income data are in real terms, in billions of constant dollars. The equilibrium level of national income is at the intersection of the ADE line and the 45-degree line, $5,000 in our simplest model. At the equilibrium, national income equals aggregate demand. $Y_E = C^d + I^d$. The value of income, or output, generated by the producers equals the value of goods and services that the final demanders want to buy.

the same as the slope of C^d, the MPC, which is equal to .80 in our simplest economy. Refer again to Table 29.3, and notice that every $1,000 change in *Y* increases *ADE* by $800. For example, when *Y* increases from $2,000 to $3,000, *ADE* increases from $2,600 to $3,400, an increase of $800.

EQUILIBRIUM LEVEL OF NATIONAL INCOME

The level of national income at which aggregate demand equals national income; alternatively, the level of national income at which saving demand equals investment demand.

The **equilibrium level of national income,** labeled Y_E, occurs at the intersection of *ADE* and the 45° line in Figure 29.9, when national income is $5,000. The equilibrium level of national income is $5,000 because $5,000 is also the value of aggregate demand when *Y* is $5,000. The firms have guessed that the aggregate demand for their output will be $5,000, so they produce that level of GDP and generate that level of national income. The firms have guessed correctly. Refer to Table 29.3. When national income is $5,000, households want to buy $4,400 worth of consumer goods and services (first column of the table), and firms want to buy $600 worth of investment goods (second column of the table). In the aggregate, therefore, households and firms want to buy $5,000 worth of final products ($5,000 = $4,400 + $600), exactly the value of final products that the firms have produced.

The equilibrium condition for our simplest economy is satisfied:

$$Y = C^d + I^d \quad \text{at } Y = \$5{,}000$$

Aggregate supply in the product markets, the left-hand side, equals aggregate demand in the product markets, the right-hand side, so that nobody has any incentive to change their decisions. The economy stays at $5,000, the equilibrium level or Y_E, unless something causes the *ADE* line to shift.

Adjusting to Equilibrium

The economy automatically moves to the equilibrium if it does not happen to be there. Figure 29.10 and the fifth column of Table 29.3 illustrate why the economy always adjusts quickly to its equilibrium.

Consider, first, any level of national income above the equilibrium, $Y_E =$ $5,000. For example, suppose that firms guess the aggregate demand for their output will be $8,000, so they produce that level of output and generate that level of national income, labeled Y_1 in Figure 29.10(a). The firms have guessed wrong this time. Aggregate demand is only $7,400, equal to $6,800 of consumption demand and $600 of investment demand. Therefore, $8,000 cannot be an equilibrium level of income.

We have to return to the national income and product accounts to understand why firms do not continue to produce $8,000 worth of output. The national accounts tell us that the sum of *actual* consumption expenditures (C^A) and *actual* investment expenditures (I^A) must be $8,000 when national income is $8,000. National income equals the sum of expenditures by final demanders—this is a national income and product accounting identity that is true at *every* level of national income. $Y_1 = C_1^A + I_1^A = \$8{,}000$.

Therefore, aggregate *actual* expenditures are given by the height of the 45° line at $8,000 in the figure, equal to national income. But aggregate demand, or aggregate *desired* expenditures, is only $7,400, the height of the *ADE* line at $8,000. $ADE = C_1^d + I_1^d = \$7{,}400$. Someone is buying $600 worth of goods that they do not want to buy. That someone turns out to be the business firms. They are "buying" unwanted goods for their inventories.

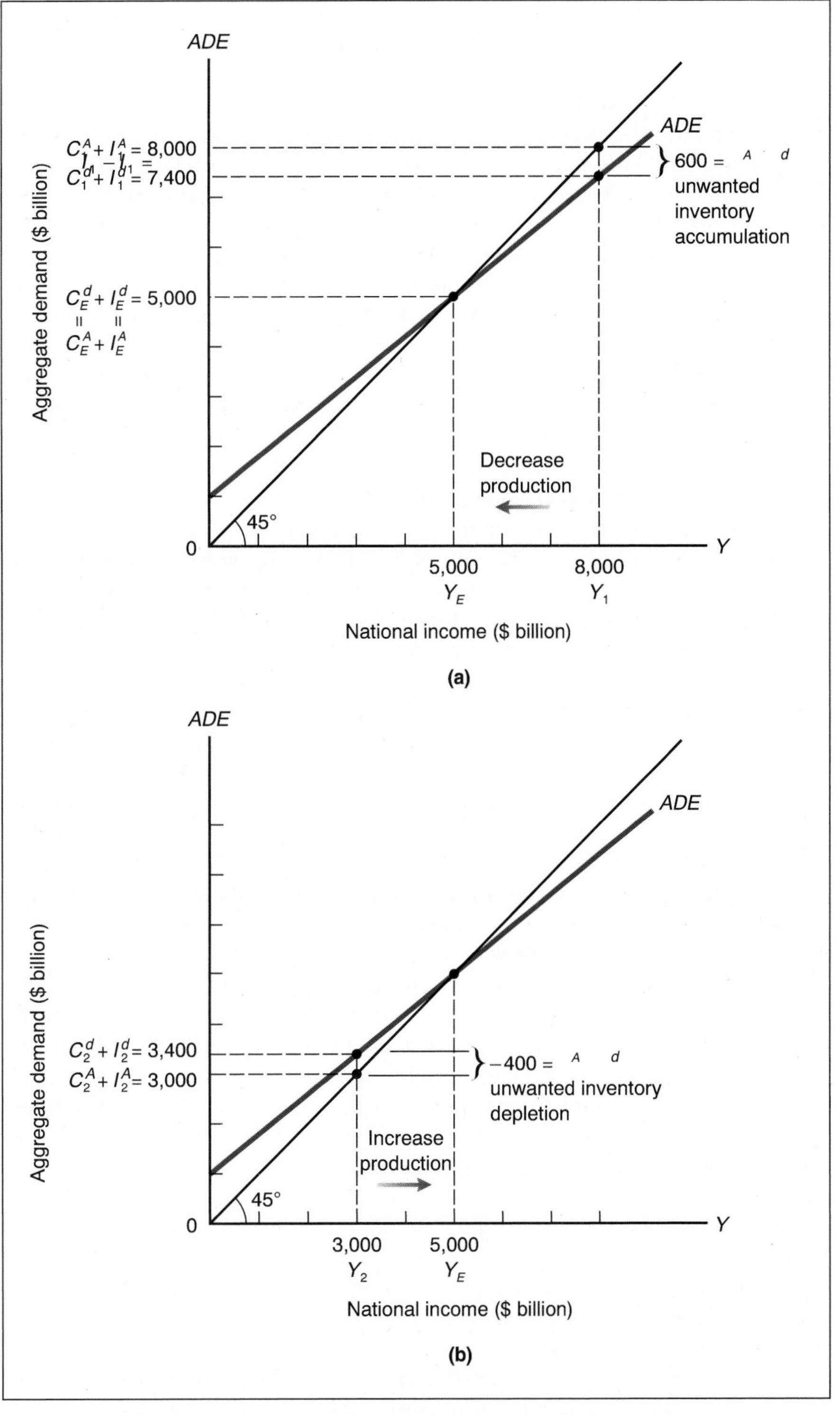

FIGURE 29.10

Adjusting to the Equilibrium Level of National Income

The figure shows how the economy automatically adjusts to the equilibrium level of income, $5,000 in our simplest model, at the intersection of the ADE and 45-degree lines. In Figure 29.10(a), the economy is initially above the equilibrium at $Y_1 = \$8{,}000$. Aggregate demand, $C_1^d + I_1^d$, is only $7,400. The difference between national income and aggregate demand, $600, is the vertical distance between the ADE and 45-degree lines at $8,000. The $600 is unwanted inventory accumulation; firms are not selling as much as they thought they would. The firms respond by cutting production to reduce their inventories until national income returns to $5,000, the equilibrium level. At the equilibrium, firms' actual and desired investment in inventory are equal. $I_E^d = I_A^d$. In Figure 29.10(b), the economy is initially below the equilibrium at $Y_2 = \$3{,}000$. Aggregate demand, $C_2^d + I_2^d$, is $3,400. The difference between national income and aggregate demand, (−)$400, is the vertical distance between the ADE and 45-degree lines at $3,000. The (−)$400 is unwanted inventory depletion; firms are selling more than they thought they would. The firms respond by increasing production to increase their inventories until national income returns to $5,000, the equlibrium level.

Households can presumably consume and save whatever amounts they want to consume and save out of their incomes. Therefore, we assume that actual consumption expenditures always equal consumption demand. $C_1^A = C_1^d =$ \$6,800 at $Y_1 =$ \$8,000. Similarly, we assume that investment in plant and equipment and investment in housing are whatever firms and households want them to be. But firms cannot always control the amount of investment in their inventories. Should they guess wrong about the demand for their products, they end up investing more or less in inventory than they want to. In this example they guessed that consumers and firms would buy \$8,000 worth of final products. In fact, consumers and firms only want to buy \$7,400 worth of final products. The remaining \$600 worth of unsold goods piles up in the firms' inventories, representing unwanted inventory investment.

Refer to the ninth line in Table 29.3. $I^d =$ \$600, as always. When $Y =$ \$8,000, $C_1^A = C_1^d =$ \$6,800. Therefore, $I_1^A =$ \$1,200, the difference between Y_1 and C_1^A (\$1,200 = \$8,000 − \$6,800). This is the national income and product accounting identity. Finally, $I_1^A - I_1^d =$ \$600, the amount of the unwanted inventory investment (\$600 = \$1,200 − \$600).

This situation cannot continue because firms do not let unwanted goods pile up in their inventories. As we saw in the preceding section, they react by cutting production until the amount that they are investing in inventory is exactly what they want it to be. Lower production means a lower level of national income, so that Y falls below \$8,000.

Firms experience unwanted inventory accumulation whenever aggregate demand is less than national income. But *ADE* is less than Y for any value of Y greater than \$5,000. For example, at $Y =$ \$7,000, aggregate desired expenditures are only \$6,600, and firms experience \$400 of unintended and unwanted inventory accumulation. Therefore, firms continue to cut production until $Y_E =$ \$5,000, at which point $I^d = I^A =$ \$600, and investment in inventory is exactly what firms want it to be.

To summarize: *At any* Y *greater than* Y_E, ADE *is below the 45° line, which means that aggregate demand is less than national income. Firms cut production to* Y_E *to avoid unwanted inventory accumulation.*

The reverse situation applies for any level of national income below the equilibrium level. Refer to Figure 29.10(b). Suppose that firms guess that the demand for their products will be \$3,000, so they produce $Y_2 =$ \$3,000. Once again the firms have guessed wrong; only this time aggregate demand exceeds \$3,000. Households want to consume \$2,800, and firms want to invest \$600, for an aggregate demand of \$3,400. *ADE* = \$3,400 at $Y_2 =$ \$3,000. The households and the firms are buying \$400 more worth of goods than the firms thought they would buy.

The national income and product accounting identity says that actual expenditures must equal \$3,000. $Y_2 = C_2^A + I_2^A =$ \$3,000. But $C_2^A = C_2^d =$ \$2,800. Therefore, $I_2^A =$ \$200, the difference between Y_2 and C_2^A (\$200 = \$3,000 − \$2,800). The \$400 difference between the actual expenditures and the desired expenditures represents unwanted inventory depletion. $I_2^A - I_2^d$ = −\$400 (−\$400 = \$200 − \$600). This situation cannot continue because firms do not want to stock out of inventory. They react by increasing production and Y increases above \$3,000.

Firms experience unwanted inventory depletion whenever aggregate demand is greater than national income. But *ADE* is greater than Y for any value of Y less than \$5,000. So firms increase production to \$5,000, the equilibrium level of income.

To summarize: *At any* Y *less than* Y_E, ADE *is above the 45° line, which means that aggregate demand exceeds national income. Firms increase production to* Y_E *to avoid unwanted inventory depletion.*

In conclusion, the *equilibrium* level of national income, *the point at which* ADE *cuts the 45° line*, is the only sustainable level of national income for the economy. The desire of firms to keep their inventories under control automatically drives the economy to its equilibrium.

EQUILIBRIUM IN TERMS OF SAVING AND INVESTMENT

The national income and product accounts teach us that if national income equals national product, then saving must equal investment. This implies that the equilibrium for the economy can be described in terms of saving and investment, which is called the leakages-and-injections approach to equilibrium.

Households receive all the national income, but they do not spend all their income. They save part of it. The amount they save represents a *leakage* from the product markets because the dollars of saving do not return directly to the firms as sales of consumer goods and services. The saving has to be made up by the investment of the firms, which the saving ultimately finances. The investment is the *injection* into the product markets that offsets the saving leakage. The circular flow of economic activity can only be in equilibrium if saving demand equals investment demand: The amount that the households want to save has to match the amount that the firms want to invest. In other words, the desired leakages from the circular flow equal the desired injections into the circular flow at the equilibrium.

The households do all the saving in our simplest economy, and the firms do all the investment (except for investment in housing), and households and firms have different motives for saving and investing. Households save to be able to consume more in the future. Firms invest to maximize their profits. Therefore, although *actual* saving must equal *actual* investment, saving demand, the amount that households *want* to save, does not necessarily equal investment demand, the amount that firms *want* to invest. We can see this in our simplest economy. Investment demand is \$600 (billion) at all levels of economic activity. Saving demand varies with the level of economic activity, however. It equals \$600 only at one level of national income—the equilibrium level.

Table 29.4 and Figure 29.11 represent the savings = investment equilibrium for our simplest economy. The first column of Table 29.4 records the level of saving at each level of national income listed in the third column. The saving data reproduce the data from Table 29.2 (remember that disposable income equals national income in our economy). The second column of the table records the constant investment demand of \$600.

Saving and investment are on the vertical axis of Figure 29.11, and national income, Y, is on the horizontal axis. The saving function, S^d, reproduces the saving function from Figure 29.3. The investment demand curve, I^d, is horizontal at \$600 as before. S^d reaches \$600 and intersects I^d when Y equals \$5,000, the equilibrium level of national income from the preceding section. (Refer to the sixth line of Table 29.4 to confirm that saving is \$600 when national income is \$5,000.) The equilibrium level of national income has to be the same as before because S^d corresponds to the consumption function, C^d, from the previous section.

TABLE 29.4 **The Equilibrium Level of National Income for the Simplest Economy: Household and Business Sectors—Saving = Investment Approach—($ billion)**

SAVING DEMAND (S^d)	INVESTMENT DEMAND (I^d)	NATIONAL INCOME (Y)	ACTUAL SAVING AND INVESTMENT ($S^A = I^A$)	UNWANTED INVENTORY DEPLETION (−) OR ACCUMULATION ($I^A - I^d$)
$(−) 400	$600	$ 0	$(−) 400	$(−) 1,000
(−) 200	600	1,000	(−) 200	(−) 800
0	600	2,000	0	(−) 600
200	600	3,000	200	(−) 400
400	600	4,000	400	(−) 200
600	**600**	**5,000**	**600**	**0 (Equilibrium)**
800	600	6,000	800	200
1,000	600	7,000	1,000	400
1,200	600	8,000	1,200	600
1,400	600	9,000	1,400	800
1,600	600	10,000	1,600	1,000
1,800	600	11,000	1,800	1,200
2,000	600	12,000	2,000	1,400
2,200	600	13,000	2,200	1,600

To summarize: *The equilibrium level of national income occurs at the intersection of* S^d *and* I^d.

No other level of national income can be an equilibrium. If the economy happens to be operating at some other level, the firms quickly adjust their production and return the economy to the equilibrium. The story is the same as before.

Suppose, for example, that Y is temporarily above the equilibrium, at $7,000. The level of saving demand is $1,000 when Y_1 = $7,000, which is $400 more than the investment demand of $600. Households are saving more, and consuming less, than firms thought they would. The result is unwanted inventory accumulation that the firms do not allow to continue. They cut production and quickly return the economy to the equilibrium Y of $5,000.

We can see the unwanted inventory accumulation if we remember that *actual* saving (S^A) must equal *actual* investment (I^A). This is a national income and product accounting identity that is true at *every* level of national income. We are also assuming that the households save what they want to save. $S_1^A = S_1^d$ = $1,000. Therefore, actual investment must also equal $1,000, which is $400 more than the firms' intended investment of $600. I_1^A = $1,000; I^d = $600. $I_1^A - I^d$ = $400. Therefore, $400 is the unwanted investment in inventory (refer also to the fourth and fifth columns of the table).

At the equilibrium, when Y = $5,000:

$$S_E^d = S_E^A = \$600 = I_E^A = I_E^d$$

The amount that households want to save equals the amount that firms want to invest. In particular, the firms are investing exactly what they want to in their inventories. The economy remains at $5,000 unless some event causes S^d or I^d to shift. (Refer to the fourth and fifth columns of the table.)

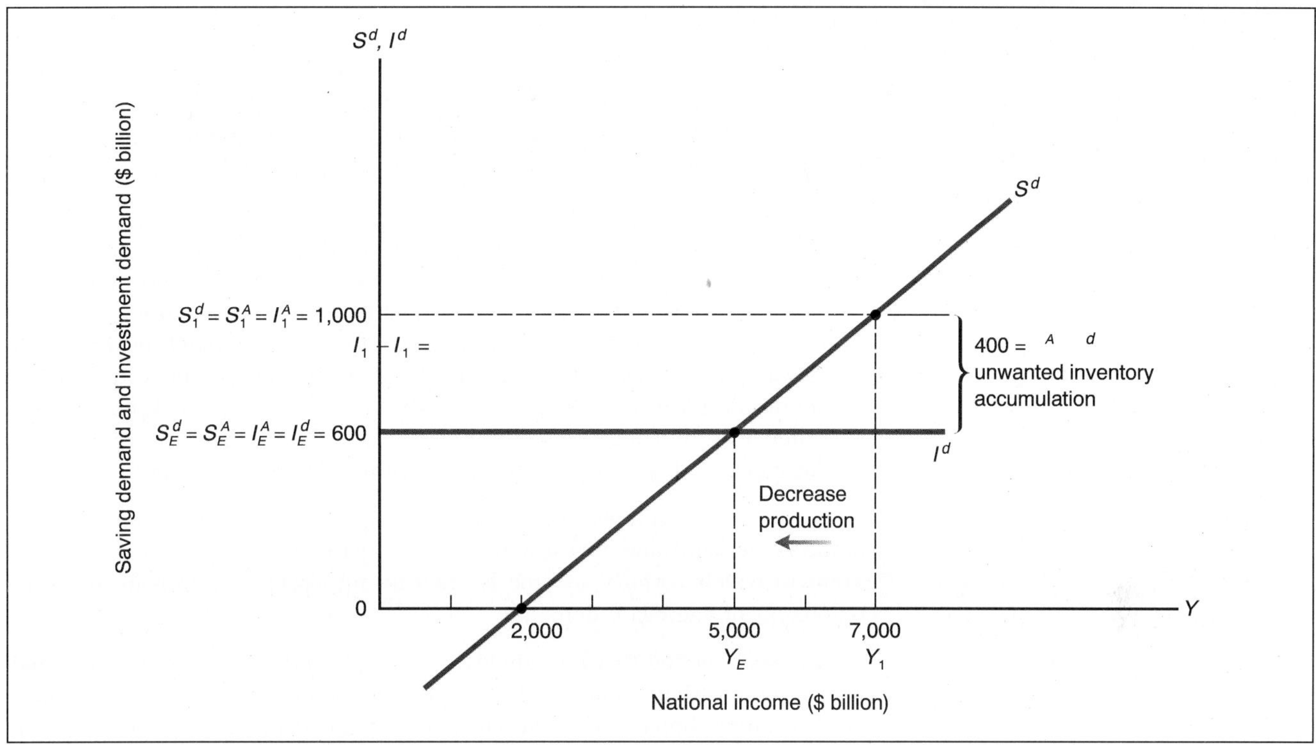

The figure is a graph of the equilibrium level of national income for our simplest economy from the data on saving and investment demand in Table 29.4. The economy is at its equilibrium level of national income when saving demand, S^d, the amount that households want to save, equals investment demand, I^d, the amount that business firms want to invest. The equilibrium level of national income is at the intersection of S^d and I^d in the figure, $5,000 in our simplest model. At Y_1 = $7,000, above the equilibrium, the actual level of saving and the actual level of investment both equal $1,000. Actual saving always equals actual investment; that is a national income accounting identity. But the actual investment of $1,000 is greater than the firms' desired investment of $600. The difference, $400, represents unwanted investment in inventory. The firms respond by cutting production until national income falls to the equilibrium level of $5,000. The equilibrium is the same as in Figure 29.9, because $S^d = I^d$ at the same level of national income for which $Y = C^d + I^d$.

FIGURE 29.11

Saving, Investment, and Equilibrium

Test your understanding of the equilibrium level of national income one last time by describing what happens in terms of saving and investment when the economy is operating below the equilibrium of $5,000—say, at Y = $4,000. Can you see that the firms are experiencing unwanted inventory depletion at Y = $4,000 and that they respond by increasing production until the economy returns to the equilibrium?

Looking Ahead

We are now ready to see how the economy moves from one equilibrium to another in response to changes in aggregate demand. This is one of the main topics of Chapter 30.

SUMMARY

Chapter 29 began by developing the simplest possible new Keynesian model of the macro economy, in which wages and prices are fixed in the short run, some resources are unemployed, and demand is the driving force in the economy. The model describes how the nation's product markets reach an equilibrium.

1. The simplest possible economy consists of the household and the business sectors, in which aggregate demand consists of consumption demand by the households and investment demand by the business firms.
2. With wages and prices fixed, firms guess about the demand for their products and adjust their production to the demand. The product markets are in equilibrium when the level of national income or national product generated in producing goods and services equals the aggregate demand for the goods and services, consumption demand plus investment demand.

The next two sections of the chapter discussed the determinants of consumption demand and investment demand, with particular emphasis on the extent to which national income is itself an important determinant of either component of aggregate demand.

3. Keynes believed that households' consumption demand consists of a small component that is unrelated to disposable income and a larger component that varies directly with the current level of disposable income, but less than dollar for dollar. The other things equal relationship between consumption demand and disposable income is the consumption function, or the propensity to consume. The other things being held constant are all the factors that influence consumption demand besides disposable income—wealth, expectations about the future, the age distribution of the population, and so forth. Changes in these variables increase or decrease consumption demand at every level of disposable income—they shift the consumption function up or down.
4. The marginal propensity to consume, labeled the MPC, is the slope of the consumption function, the ratio of the change in consumption demand to the change in disposable income. The MPC is a fraction between zero and one, inclusive.
5. The saving function, or the propensity to save, is the mirror image of the consumption function because all that households can do with their disposable income is either consume it or save it. The marginal propensity to save, labeled the MPS, is the slope of the saving function, the ratio of the change in saving demand to the change in disposable income. The MPS is also a fraction between zero and one, inclusive. Also, MPC + MPS = 1.
6. The Keynesian consumption function appears to be consistent with aggregate consumption over time in the United States. Research on consumption demand typically finds that the short-run MPC is between .60 and .80 and the long-run MPC is slightly above .90.
7. The chief competitor to the Keynesian consumption function is the Life-Cycle Hypothesis, which assumes that households plan their consumption over their lifetimes, borrowing and lending to smooth consumption relative to income. They adjust their lifetime consumption plans to changes in their

lifetime resources, which consist of current and expected labor market earnings and inherited wealth. They also take into account current and expected future government transfers and taxes, which affect their lifetime disposable incomes. The Life-Cycle Hypothesis is an important component of the new classical model of the economy.

8. A principal implication of the Life-Cycle Hypothesis is that the MPC out of changes in current disposable income is very low, close to zero, if the change is either anticipated or, if unanticipated, viewed as temporary. The MPC out of unanticipated changes in current disposable income that are viewed as permanent is close to one. In fact, the MPC out of temporary changes in disposable income does appear to be much smaller than the MPC out of permanent changes in disposable income in the United States, as predicted by the model. The Life-Cycle Hypothesis also provides a theory to explain how other factors, such as wealth and the age distribution of the population, affect consumption demand. Its main weakness is that it underpredicts the aggregate MPC in the United States.

None of the three components of investment demand—plant and equipment, inventory, and housing—is closely related to the level of national income. Therefore, we are assuming that each is a constant, independent of the level of national income in the simplest model. The third section of the chapter made the following additional points about each component of investment demand.

Plant and Equipment

9. The desired stock of *capital* is related to a firm's expected output or sales, which implies that *investment* in plant and equipment is related to the *change* in output or sales, not to the level. The desired stock of capital also depends on the firm's capital/output ratio, which is determined primarily by the firm's production technology, the cost of capital, and other factor prices.
10. The cost of capital depends primarily on four factors: the price of each unit of capital, interest rates, the rate of depreciation of the capital, and the tax system. Changes in corporate tax rates, depreciation allowances, and investment tax credits are the primary fiscal policy tools that Congress uses to influence the cost of capital.
11. Economists agree that changes in the cost of capital affect the desired stock of capital, but they do not agree on whether changes in the cost of capital have an immediate and important effect on investment demand. One problem in trying to estimate the effect of the cost of capital on investment demand is that many investment projects take such a long time to order, build, and put into place. The result is that much of the investment in any one year is the result of investment decisions made in past years, so that the relationship between the cost of capital and current investment is difficult to determine.

Inventory Investment

12. Unlike plant and equipment, firms can adjust their inventories quickly to their desired stock of inventory. An important assumption of the new Keynesian aggregate demand model is that firms do not tolerate unwanted inventory accumulation or depletion. If demand is higher than anticipated

and inventories are depleting, firms hire more workers and increase production. If demand is lower than anticipated and inventories are accumulating, firms lay off workers and decrease production.

Housing Demand

13. Investment in housing is the one component of investment demand that is highly sensitive to changes in the cost of capital, in particular, to changes in mortgage interest rates.

The fourth section described how the macro economy automatically seeks an equilibrium level of national income and national product.

14. The equilibrium occurs when aggregate demand equals the level of national income generated in production. In terms of the aggregate demand–45° line graph, the equilibrium occurs at the intersection of the aggregate demand line *ADE* and the 45° line.
15. When national income is above the equilibrium, aggregate demand is less than national income, and firms experience unwanted inventory accumulation. They cut production to the equilibrium. When national income is below the equilibrium, aggregate demand is greater than national income, and firms experience unwanted inventory depletion. They increase production to the equilibrium.

The final section of Chapter 29 described the equilibrium in terms of saving demand and investment demand.

16. The equilibrium level of national income occurs when saving demand equals investment demand. Actual saving always equals actual investment—this is a national income and product accounting identity. But the amount households *want* to save, saving demand, equals the amount firms *want* to invest, investment demand, only at the equilibrium.

KEY TERMS

age-earnings profile
aggregate desired expenditures (aggregate demand for expenditures)
capital/output ratio
consumption function
cost of capital
equilibrium level of national income
Life-Cycle Hypothesis
marginal efficiency of capital
marginal propensity to consume
marginal propensity to save
saving function
total investment demand

QUESTIONS

1. What is the marginal propensity to consume? What is the marginal propensity to save? How are the two concepts related? Explain.
2. The text assumed that the demand for investment in plant and equipment is unrelated to the current level of national income, even though the demand for capital (the desired stock of capital) may be closely related to the current level of national income. Explain why there is a difference between the demand for capital and the demand for investment in this regard.
3. Answer the following questions about the cost of capital.
   a. What is the cost of capital, and what are the principal components that make up the cost of capital?
   b. How does the U.S. Congress attempt to influence the cost of capital?
   c. Virtually all economists assume that the demand for capital (the desired stock of capital) is closely related to the cost of capital. Why? At the same time, economists disagree about whether investment demand is closely related to the cost of capital. Explain why there is a difference between the demand for capital and the demand for investment in this regard.

4. Name two events that might cause the consumption function to shift up (or down). Explain how, and why, they cause the consumption function to shift.
5. Answer the following questions about inventory investment.
   a. Can the demand for inventory investment be negative? Why or why not?
   b. What is happening to firms' investment in inventory when the level of national income is above the equilibrium level of income? In answering this question, distinguish between firms' actual investments in inventory and their desired investments in inventory (their investment demand).
6. Explain why the economy adjusts to one equilibrium level of national income for a given level of aggregate demand (that is, for a given *ADE* line in the *ADE*–45° line graph).
7. Compare and contrast the Keynesian consumption function and the Life-Cycle Hypothesis. Your answer should cover the following points, with appropriate explanations.
   a. What assumptions does each one make about how households form their consumption plans?
   b. What does each one imply about the relationship between aggregate consumption demand and current disposable income?
   c. How well does each one fit the facts about consumption demand in the United States?
8. Suppose that a star baseball player is scheduled to receive a $750,000 increase in salary next year according to the terms of his contract. Next year is the third year of his five-year contract with the club. The contract stipulates how much his salary is to be during each year of the contract. Would you expect his consumption to increase next year? Indicate how your answer to this question depends on whether he is a Life-Cycle consumer or a Keynesian consumer.
9. The baby boom generation, born between 1947 and 1964, is the largest group within the U.S. population. The baby boomers are now in their middle-age years.
   a. Why, and how, might the passage of the baby boomers through middle age affect the level of saving in the United States? Indicate how your answer depends on whether the baby boomers are likely to be Life-Cycle or Keynesian consumers. Which do you think they are likely to be? Why?
   b. Why is the level of saving an important issue in the United States (or in any nation)?
10. An economy has the following consumption data.

DISPOSABLE INCOME ($ BILLION)	CONSUMPTION DEMAND ($ BILLION)
0	200
1,000	1,100
2,000	2,000
3,000	2,900
4,000	3,800
5,000	4,700

Answer the following questions based on these data, giving appropriate explanations.
   a. What is the break-even level of disposable income? Over what range of disposable incomes are households saving? Over what range of disposable incomes are households dissaving?
   b. What is the marginal propensity to consume for this economy? What is the marginal propensity to save?
   c. Define the average propensity to consume. What happens to the average propensity to consume as disposable income increases in this economy? Is this pattern realistic?
   d. Name some events that might cause consumption demand to increase (or decrease) at every level of disposable income, and indicate why. For each event, explain also what is happening to saving demand.
   e. These data are reasonably consistent with the Keynesian consumption function. Are they likely to be consistent with consumption according to the Life-Cycle Hypothesis?
11. Suppose that our simplest economy has the consumption demand and the investment demand relationships pictured below. Show how you would combine the two relationships to determine the equilibrium level of national income for the economy.

Also, select a level of national income different from the equilibrium level on your diagram. Discuss how and why the economy would automatically return to the equilibrium level of national income from the level of national income that you selected.

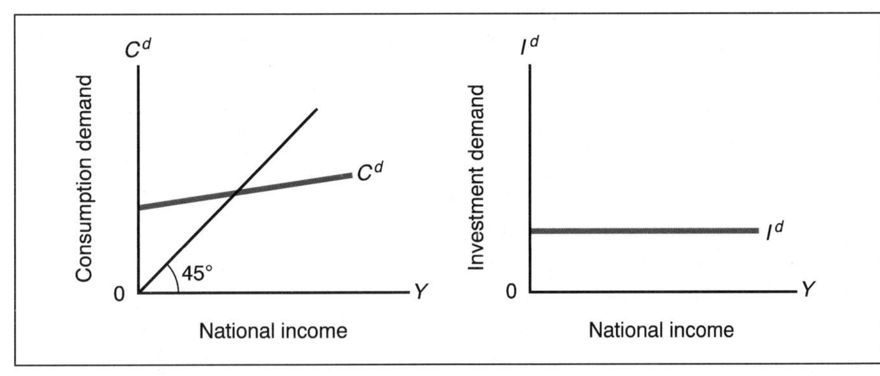

APPENDIX

29 Algebraic Analysis of Equilibrium

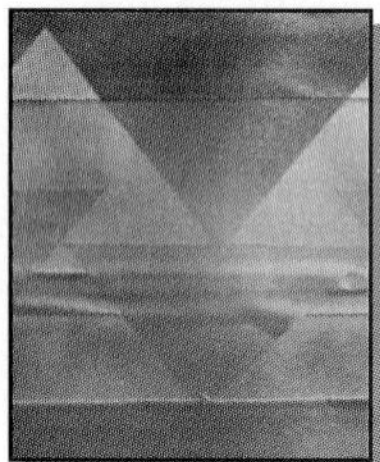

This appendix shows how to derive the equilibrium in Chapter 29 algebraically, using both the aggregate demand and the saving = investment methods. It also shows what happens when the economy is out of equilibrium.

THE AGGREGATE DEMAND METHOD

The general form of the straight-line Keynesian consumption function used throughout Chapter 29 is

$$C^d = C_0 + \text{MPC} \cdot Y$$

C^d is consumption demand, and Y stands for either disposable income or national income in our simplest economy. C_0 is the intercept on the vertical axis, the value of consumption demand when $Y = 0$. MPC, the marginal propensity to consume, is the slope of the consumption function, the ratio $\Delta C^d/\Delta Y$. $C_0 = 400$, and MPC $= 0.8$ in the chapter, so that our hypothetical consumption function is

$$C^d = 400 + 0.8 \cdot Y$$

(All dollar values in the appendix are in billions of constant dollars.)

The general form of the total investment demand used throughout Chapter 29 is

$$I^d = \bar{I}$$

I^d is total investment demand, and $\bar{I}$ is a constant independent of the level of Y. $\bar{I} = 600$ in the chapter, so that our hypothetical investment demand is

$$I^d = 600$$

The equilibrium level of national income is the level that equals aggregate demand, the sum of $C^d + I^d$.

$$\text{Equilibrium condition:} \quad Y = C^d + I^d$$

Substitute the equations for C^d and I^d on the right-hand side of the equilibrium condition:

$$Y = [400 + 0.8 \cdot Y] + 600$$
$$Y = 1{,}000 + 0.8 \cdot Y$$

Bring all Y terms to the left-hand side and solve for Y:

$$Y - 0.8 \cdot Y = 1{,}000$$
$$0.2 \cdot Y = 1{,}000$$
$$Y = 1{,}000/0.2 = 5{,}000$$

The equilibrium level of Y, or Y_E, is 5,000.

To check that 5,000 is the equilibrium, add C^d and I^d at $Y = 5{,}000$:

$$C^d = 400 + 0.8 \cdot 5{,}000 = 400 + 4{,}000 = 4{,}400$$
$$I^d = 600$$
$$C^d + I^d = 5{,}000$$

THE SAVING DEMAND EQUALS INVESTMENT DEMAND METHOD

The general form of the straight-line saving function used throughout Chapter 29 is

$$S^d = S_0 + \text{MPS} \cdot Y$$

S^d is saving demand. S_0 is the intercept of the saving function on the vertical axis, the value of saving demand when $Y = 0$. MPS, the marginal propensity to save, is the slope of the saving function, the ratio $\Delta S^d/\Delta Y$. The saving function is the mirror image of the consumption function because households can only consume or save their incomes.

$$C^d + S^d = Y$$

at every level of Y, including $Y = 0$. Therefore, the intercepts of the two functions must add to zero. $C_0 + S_0 = 0$. Since $C_0 = 400$, $S_0 = -400$.

Also, the proportions of any change in income that are consumed and saved must add to one. $\Delta C^d/\Delta Y + \Delta S^d/\Delta Y = 1$. Therefore, the slopes of the two functions must add to one.

$$MPC + MPS = 1$$

The MPS = 0.2 when the MPC = 0.8.

Therefore, our hypothetical saving function that corresponds to our hypothetical consumption function is

$$S^d = -400 + 0.2 \cdot Y$$

Investment demand is as above:

$$I^d = 600$$

The equilibrium level of national income is the level at which saving demand equals investment demand.

$$\text{Equilibrium condition:} \quad S^d = I^d$$

Substitute the equations for S^d and I^d in the equilibrium condition:

$$-400 + 0.2 \cdot Y = 600$$

Isolate Y on the left-hand side, and solve for Y:

$$\begin{aligned} 0.2 \cdot Y &= 1{,}000 \\ Y &= 5{,}000 \end{aligned}$$

To check that 5,000 is the equilibrium, compared S^d and I^d at $Y = 5{,}000$:

$$S^d = -400 + 0.2 \cdot 5{,}000 = -400 + 1{,}000 = 600 = I^d$$

THE ECONOMY OUT OF EQUILIBRIUM

Let's consider one example of the economy out of equilibrium—say, at $Y = 7{,}000$.

Aggregate Demand Versus National Income

At $Y = 7{,}000$:

$$\begin{aligned} C^d &= 400 + 0.8 \cdot 7{,}000 = 400 + 5{,}600 &&= 6{,}000 \\ I^d &= &&\underline{600} \\ C^d + I^d &= &&6{,}600 < 7{,}000 \end{aligned}$$

Aggregate demand is less than Y by 400, so the firms experience 400 of unwanted inventory accumulation. They cut production back to the equilibrium of 5,000.

Saving Demand Versus Investment Demand

At $Y = 7{,}000$:

$$S^d = -400 + 0.2 \cdot 7{,}000 = -400 + 1{,}400 = 1{,}000 > 600 = I^d$$

Saving demand exceeds investment demand by 400. The saving leakage from the product markets exceeds the investment injection into the product markets by 400, so the firms experience 400 of unwanted inventory accumulation. They cut production back to the equilibrium of 5,000.

QUESTIONS

Given the following information for an economy, find the equilibrium level of national income, Y_E.

$C^d = 300 + 3/4 \cdot Y$	$C^d =$ consumption demand
$I^d = 40$	$I^d =$ investment demand
	$Y =$ income (national and disposable)

Also:

a. What is the value of the marginal propensity to consume?
b. Find the relationship between saving demand (S^d) and national income (Y). What is the value of the marginal propensity to save?
c. Show that $S^d = I^d$ at the equilibrium level of income computed above.
d. How large is aggregate demand when national income equals 1,000?
e. Describe how the economy will adjust to the equilibrium level of national income when national income is temporarily at 1,000.

CHAPTER

30

The Spending Multiplier, Fiscal Policy, and Unemployment

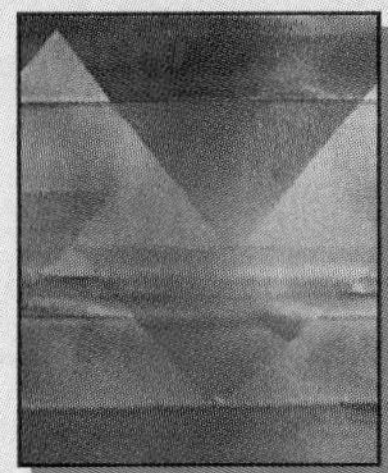

LEARNING OBJECTIVES

CONCEPTS TO LEARN

- The macroeconomic policy problem
- Spending multiplier
- Tax multiplier
- Transfer multiplier
- Balanced budget multipliers
- Recessionary and inflationary gaps
- Practical limitations of U.S. fiscal policy

CONCEPTS TO RECALL

- The production possibilities frontier [3]
- The circular flow of economic activity [4]
- Full employment [25]
- Fiscal policy [28]
- Consumption function [29]
- Saving function [29]
- Marginal propensity to consume [29]
- Marginal propensity to save [29]
- Equilibrium level of national income [29]

The United States faced a mixed blessing in the early 1990s. The collapse of the Soviet Union reduced the threat of war in Europe and allowed the United States the luxury of making substantial cuts in defense spending. The defense cutbacks were doubly welcome because of the huge federal budget deficit, which was approaching $400 billion by 1992.

At the same time, however, the economy was mired in a recession. The timing of the defense cutbacks could not have been worse for the economy. Defense spending is almost entirely purchases of goods and services, and, as we will see in Chapter 30, reducing government purchases has the most powerful negative effect on the equilibrium level of national income of all possible budgetary changes. The large cuts in defense spending served to deepen the recession and slow down the recovery, especially in states such as California, Connecticut, Massachusetts, Texas, and Washington whose industries rely heavily on defense contracts.

Normally the federal government could have countered the effects on the economy of the military cutback by reducing taxes or increasing spending in other nondefense areas. Indeed, many people had long awaited the day when the government could divert some of its spending from defense to domestic purposes. But Ross Perot's presidential campaign had successfully hammered away on the evils of the large federal budget deficit, and Congress was not about to make any move that would increase the deficit.

President Clinton was extremely worried about the negative impact of the defense cutbacks. In his first months in office he pushed hard for a modest $16 billion package of spending increases to help boost the economic recovery. Most economists thought that Clinton's stimulus package was too small to make much of a difference to the economy, but it did not matter anyway. Congress refused to pass even $16 billion in spending increases and handed Clinton his first political defeat on economic policy.

Chapter 30 focuses on John Maynard Keynes's two great insights into macroeconomic policy that paved the way for government intervention into the macro economy. His first insight was that aggregate demand may not lead the economy to a very desirable equilibrium. The market economies of the United States, Great Britain, and Western Europe were operating way below their production possibilities frontiers during the Great Depression of the 1930s, when Keynes was formulating his ideas about how the macro economy operates. His second insight was that wages and prices could not be counted on to bring an economy to its frontier, at least not in any reasonable period of time. Nonetheless, Keynes argued that the capitalist countries did not have to wait for the Depression to run its course. The government could lead the economy back to the frontier with proper doses of fiscal and/or monetary policies.

Chapter 30 begins by describing the macroeconomic policy problem as Keynes and his new Keynesian disciples define it.

THE MACROECONOMIC POLICY PROBLEM

We saw in Chapter 29 how aggregate demand leads the economy to one equilibrium level of national income when wages and prices are sticky and firms react passively to the demand for their products. The policy problem is that the equilibrium determined by the level of aggregate demand may not be a very desirable equilibrium. Figure 30.1 illustrates two possibilities that have plagued all the developed market economies from time to time.

Figure 30.1 pictures both the production possibilities frontier for the economy and the aggregate demand–45° line graph from Chapter 29. The axes of the production possibilities frontier are consumer goods and services and investment goods, the two kinds of final products in our simplest economy.

Figure 30.1(a) represents the situation that Keynes saw during the Great Depression. Refer, first, to the aggregate demand–45° line graph. Aggregate demand at every level of national income is given by the solid aggregate demand line, ADE_0. ADE_0 intersects the 45° line at Y_0^A, the equilibrium level of national income for the economy. Unfortunately, Y_0^A is not a very desirable equilibrium, as illustrated by the production possibilities frontier graph. Y_0^A lies well inside the production possibilities frontier. Aggregate demand is not sufficient to fully employ all the resources in the economy; willing and able workers are unemployed, and machines lie idle. The economy is in a recession or worse, as in the 1930s.

Return once more to the aggregate demand–45° line graph. The line Y_{FE} is called the full-employment level of national income. It indicates the level of national income that would be necessary to fully employ all resources, so that the economy is operating on its frontier. In other words, Y_{FE} is the representation of the two-dimensional production possibilities frontier in one dimension, national income. Since Y_{FE} is drawn to the right of the equilibrium Y_0^A, the graph shows that the economy is operating inside its frontier.

Notice one important difference between the equilibrium and the full-employment levels of national income. The position of Y_0^A is determined by the level of aggregate demand. It must occur at the intersection of ADE_0 and the 45° line. In contrast, the position of Y_{FE} is somewhat arbitrary because we cannot be sure where to draw Y_{FE}. We do not know what the full-employment level of national income really is, just as we do not know how far out from the origin to draw the production possibilities frontier. Nonetheless, drawing Y_{FE} somewhere to the right of Y_0^A indicates that the economy is operating below its frontier. The farther Y_{FE} is to the right of Y_0^A, the farther the economy is below the frontier. Representing the state of the economy in this way is sufficient for our purposes.

Recessions and depressions are not the only undesirable possibilities. Market economies occasionally try to push beyond their means, which can only build up inflationary pressures that, at worst, lead the economy down the path to hyperinflation. Figure 30.1(b) illustrates the inflationary scenario. The equilibrium level of national income, Y_0^B, on the aggregate demand–45° line graph, at the intersection of the solid aggregate demand line ADE_0 and the 45° line, is beyond the production possibilities frontier. Y_{FE}, the one-dimensional representation of the frontier, is to the left of the equilibrium Y_0^B. Drawing Y_{FE} anywhere to the left of the equilibrium level of national income on the aggregate demand–45° line graph represents an economy trying to live beyond its means.

No economy can really live beyond its means, of course. Y_{FE} is the highest possible level of *real* or constant dollar national income. An equilibrium such as Y_0^B beyond Y_{FE} has to be interpreted as nominal or current dollar national income. The difference in dollar value between Y_0^B and Y_{FE} is all due to inflation which, as we will see later on in the text, accelerates if the economy continues to try to live beyond its means.

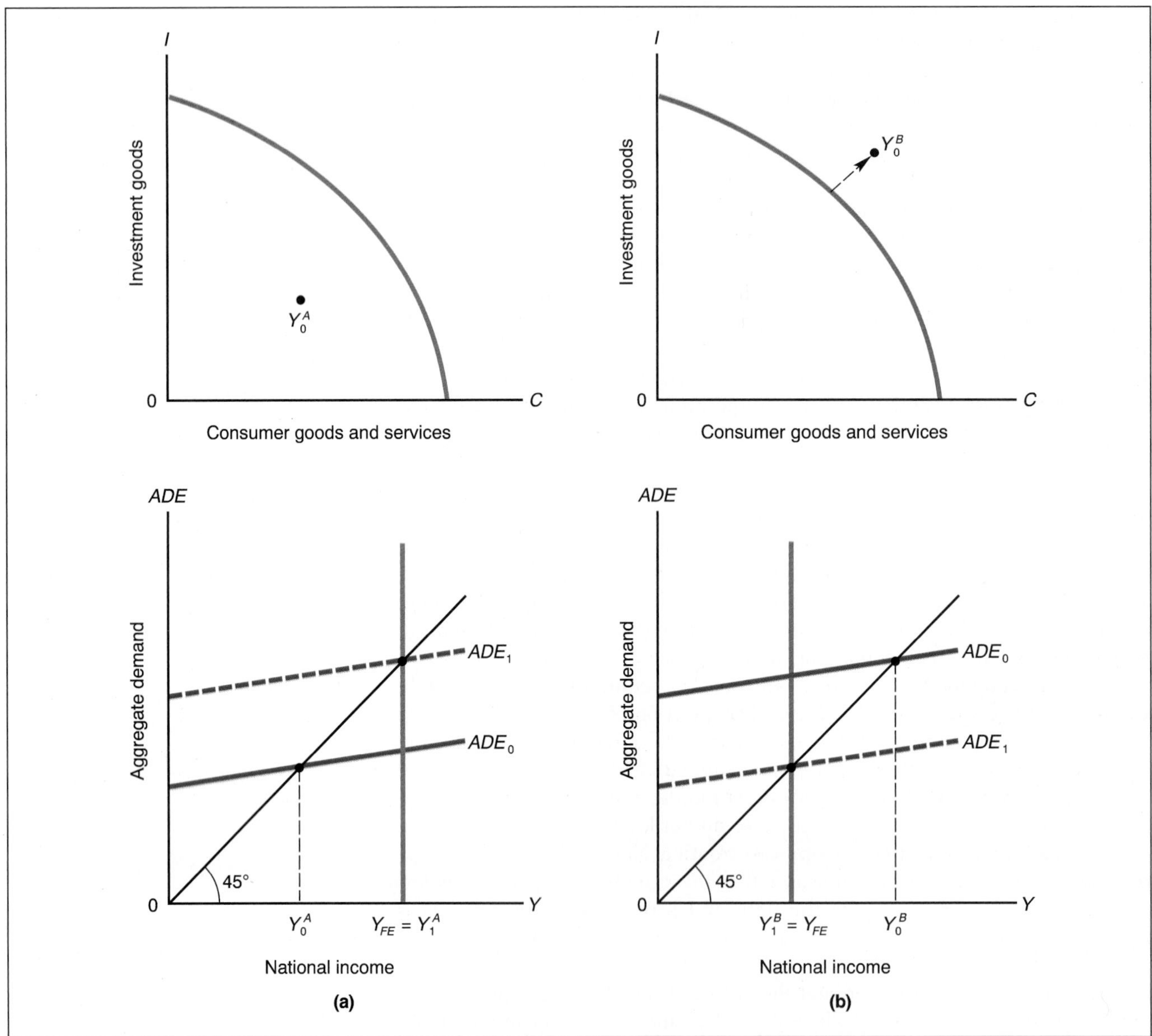

FIGURE 30.1

Unemployed Resources and Inflation

The figure shows two problems that afflict market economies, unemployed resources and inflation, analyzed from a new Keynesian perspective. In Figure 30.1(a), the equilibrium level of income is Y_0^A, at the intersection of ADE_0 and the 45-degree line in the bottom graph. The top graph shows that Y_0^A, is below the production possibilities frontier; the economy has unemployed resources. The vertical line Y_{FE} in the bottom graph represents the production possibilities frontier. It is the level of national income that would fully employ all resources and place the economy on the frontier. The government's policy problem is to increase aggregate demand from ADE_0 to ADE_1 through expansionary fiscal and/or monetary policies to bring the economy to equilibrium on the frontier. In Figure 30.1(b), the equilibrium level of income is Y_0^B, at the intersection of ADE_0 and the 45-degree line in the bottom graph. The top graph shows that Y_0^B is beyond the production possibilities frontier; the economy is trying to live beyond its means, which can only result in an inflation. The vertical line Y_{FE} in the bottom graph is the maximum real output that the economy can produce. Y_0^B is nominal, current dollar national income. The government's policy problem is to decrease aggregate demand from ADE_0 to ADE_1 through contractionary fiscal or monetary policies to bring the economy to equilibrium on the frontier.

Keynes's first policy insight was that, left to its own devices, an economy driven by aggregate demand could continue to operate above or below the frontier for a long time. In particular, Keynes disagreed with the prevailing classical theory of his day that wages and prices would quickly adjust to bring the economy back to the frontier. Keynes did not think wages and prices could be counted on to re-establish an equilibrium on the frontier in any reasonable period of time.

This led to Keynes's second policy insight, that the government could bring the economy to its frontier fairly quickly by means of fiscal and/or monetary policies. The production possibilities frontier is more or less fixed in the short run. Y_{FE} on the aggregate demand–45° line graphs in Figure 30.1 depends on the quantity and the quality of the nation's resources and on the available production technologies, which are difficult to change in the short run. But the government does not have to change the frontier. Instead, fiscal and monetary policies work by changing the level of aggregate demand, which changes the equilibrium level of national income. Aggregate demand can be changed fairly quickly. The short-run policy goal, then, is to change the equilibrium level of national income so that the equilibrium is on the frontier.

An economy in a recession, or depression, operating well below its production possibilities frontier, requires a dose of expansionary fiscal and/or monetary policy. **Expansionary** fiscal and monetary policies are policies that increase the level of aggregate demand. Refer to Figure 30.1(a). The short-run policy goal is to use expansionary fiscal and/or monetary policy to shift the level of aggregate demand up from the solid line, ADE_0, to the dotted line, ADE_1. ADE_1 intersects the 45° line at Y_{FE}, so that the new equilibrium level of national income, Y_1^A, coincides with Y_{FE} and the economy is now operating on its production possibilities frontier.

EXPANSIONARY POLICY

A fiscal or monetary policy that increases the level of aggregate demand.

An economy trying to live beyond its production possibilities frontier requires a dose of contractionary fiscal and/or monetary policy. **Contractionary** fiscal and monetary policies are policies that decrease the level of aggregate demand. Refer to Figure 30.1(b). The short-run policy goal is to use contractionary fiscal and/or monetary policy to shift the level of aggregate demand down from the solid line, ADE_0, to the dotted line, ADE_1. ADE_1 intersects the 45° line at Y_{FE}, so that the new equilibrium level of national income, Y_1^B, coincides with Y_{FE} and the economy is now operating on its production possibilities frontier.

CONTRACTIONARY POLICY

A fiscal or monetary policy that decreases the level of aggregate demand.

Economists refer to fiscal and monetary policies as *aggregate demand management* because they keep the economy operating on or near its production possibilities frontier by manipulating the level of aggregate demand. The economy always operates at its equilibrium. The short-run policy goal as Keynes described it is to match the equilibrium with the frontier.

The Steps in Doing Policy

Aggregate demand management is essentially a three-step process.

Step 1. Policy makers first have to decide on an appropriate target level of national income, Y_{Target}, that they want to establish as the equilibrium. Keynes naturally thought in terms of achieving the full-employment level of income, Y_{FE}, because unemployment was the overriding problem during the Great Depression. Policy makers always give full employment very high priority, but there are three other macroeconomic policy goals besides full employment: long-run economic growth, price stability, and a zero balance of trade and a stable dollar. We saw in Chapter 28 that the four macroeconomic policy goals are often conflicting, so that policy makers have to compromise. For example, increasing aggregate demand to reduce unemployment can make inflation worse and lower the value of the dollar. If unemployment is near the natural rate of unemployment, U_{NR}, but inflation is worsening, the government may decide that a lower equilibrium level of national income is desirable to fight inflation, even if it increases unemployment somewhat. The target level of national income that the policy makers choose is the one that they believe represents the best compromise or balance among the four policy goals.

Step 2. The second step for the policy makers is to build a reliable model of the economy. The model performs three essential functions. It tells the policy makers what the equilibrium level of national income would be without any government policies. It also indicates how the equilibrium changes in response to particular doses of fiscal and monetary policies. Finally, the model shows how different levels of national income affect each of the macroeconomic policy goals. Policy makers cannot set the target level of national income unless they understand the links between the macroeconomic policy goals and the economy. We have begun to build our own model of the economy, the model from Chapter 29, to help us understand the government's policy options.

Step 3. The third and final step for the policy makers is to design specific fiscal and/or monetary policies that will match the equilibrium level of national income, Y_E, with the target level, Y_{Target}.

One of the goals of this chapter is to see how fiscal policy affects the equilibrium level of national income. To do this, we need to understand how changes in aggregate demand affect the equilibrium through a process called the spending multiplier. This is best accomplished with our simplest model, before we add the government sector.

THE SPENDING MULTIPLIER

As noted in Chapter 28, an economy led by aggregate demand has a feedback nature to it. Firms respond to an increase in aggregate demand by increasing production and generating more income in the economy. The workers, landlords, and capitalists who receive the income consume some of it, which generates still more demand. Producers of consumer goods and services respond to the increase in consumption demand by increasing production, which generates more income, which leads to still more consumption, and so on. The result is that an initial change in aggregate demand leads to a much greater change in the equilibrium level of income. The feedback nature of the economy through consumption demand multiplies the effects of the increase in aggregate demand on the economy. A concept called the spending multiplier indicates the ultimate effect of the feedback process on the equilibrium.

SPENDING MULTIPLIER

The ratio that relates the change in the equilibrium level of national income to an initial change, or shift, in aggregate demand.

Suppose that aggregate demand increases or decreases at every level of national income. In other words, *ADE* in the aggregate demand–45° line graph shifts up or down. The **spending multiplier,** labeled M_{Spending}, relates the change in the equilibrium level of national income to the initial change, or shift, in aggregate demand.

Saving, Investment, and the Spending Multiplier

The saving = investment view of equilibrium is the easiest way to see the spending multiplier graphically. Figure 30.2 illustrates the spending multiplier.

The economy is originally in equilibrium at Y_0 = \$5,000, at the intersection of the saving function, S^d, and the original investment demand curve, I_0^d. S^d, I_0^d, and the original equilibrium are taken from our simplest economy in Chapter 29. The slope of S^d, the marginal propensity to save (MPS), is .20. I_0^d is \$600 at every level of Y. (All data are in billions of constant dollars.)

Suppose that firms become more optimistic about the future and investment demand increases by \$100, from I_0^d = \$600 to I_1^d = \$700. Y_0 can no longer be the equilibrium level of national income because I_1^d exceeds S^d at Y_0 = \$5,000. Now that demand has increased, firms would experience unwanted depletion of their inventories if they continued to produce \$5,000 worth of goods and services. Instead, firms increase production in response to the increase in demand to rebuild their inventories. The new equilibrium occurs at Y_1 = \$5,500, at the intersection of S^d and the new investment demand curve, I_1^d.

Notice that the change in the equilibrium level of national income is \$500, which is five times more than the \$100 increase in investment demand (Y_1 − Y_0 = \$5,500 − \$5,000 = \$500). The feedback nature of the economy has multiplied the change in investment demand by a factor of five. How do we know that the new equilibrium is \$500 greater than the original equilibrium? The answer lies in the marginal propensity to save, the MPS.

The ratio of the change in I^d to the change in Y_E is the rise over the run of the saving function S_d, the slope of S^d, or the MPS.

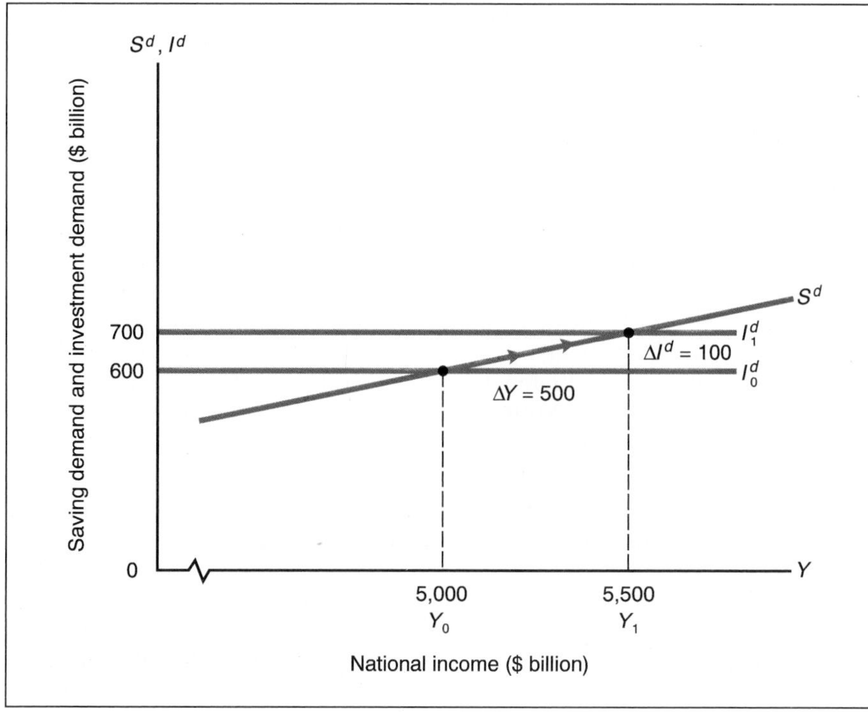

FIGURE 30.2

The Spending Multiplier

The economy is initially in equilibrium at Y_0 = \$5,000 in our simplest economy, at the intersection of the saving function, S^d, and investment demand curve I_0^d. The data are in billions of constant dollars. Then investment demand increases by \$100, from I_0^d = \$600 to I_1^d = \$700. The new equilibrium is Y_1 = \$5,500, at the intersection of S^d and I_1^d. The \$100 increase in investment demand leads to a multiplied \$500 increase in the equilibrium level of national income. The value of the spending multiplier is [1/MPS]. MPS, the slope of S^d, equals 0.20. Therefore the value of the spending multiplier is 5 (= 1/0.20).

$$\text{Slope of } S^d = \text{MPS} = \Delta I^d/\Delta Y$$

The MPS is .20, and $\Delta I^d = \$100$. To solve for the change in national income, bring ΔY to the left-hand side of the equation and MPS to the right-hand side.

$$\begin{aligned} \Delta Y &= (1/\text{MPS}) \cdot \Delta I^d \\ &= (1/.20) \cdot \$100 \\ &= 5 \cdot \$100 \\ &= \$500 \end{aligned}$$

The term 1/MPS is the spending multiplier, M_{Spending}.

$$M_{\text{Spending}} = 1/\text{MPS}$$

M_{Spending} multiplies the change in investment demand to compute the change in the equilibrium level of national income. $M_{\text{Spending}} = 5$ when MPS = .20. Every \$1 increase in investment demand increases the equilibrium level of national income by \$5.

M_{Spending} can also be expressed in terms of the slope of the consumption function, the marginal propensity to consume (MPC). We know that MPC + MPS = 1, or MPS = 1 − MPC. Therefore,

$$M_{\text{Spending}} = 1/(1 - \text{MPC})$$

For example, when the MPS is .20, MPC = .80, the slope of the consumption function in our simplest economy.

$$M_{\text{Spending}} = 1/(1-.80) = 1/.20 = 5$$

the same value of M_{Spending} as above. The spending multiplier is more commonly expressed in terms of the MPC than the MPS.

Properties of the Spending Multiplier

Two properties of the spending multiplier are worth noting before developing the intuition behind the multiplier process.

THE MPS, THE MPC, AND M_{SPENDING} *The higher the value of the MPC, the higher the value of* $M_{Spending}$. Alternatively, *the lower the value of the MPS, the higher the value of* $M_{Spending}$. Table 30.1 illustrates the different values of M_{Spending} for different values of the MPC and the MPS. When the MPC and the MPS are both .50, $M_{\text{Spending}} = 2$. As the MPC rises from .50 to .90 in the table (alternatively, as the MPS falls from .50 to .10), M_{Spending} increases from 2 to 10. The numbers in the table indicate that changes in aggregate demand can have a very powerful effect on the equilibrium level of national income.

THE SPENDING MULTIPLIER IS SYMMETRIC *The feedback multiplier process is symmetric. Changes in aggregate demand have the same powerful effect on the economy whether aggregate demand is increasing or decreasing.* In our example a \$100 de-

TABLE 30.1 **The Marginal Propensities to Save and Consume and the Spending Multiplier**

MARGINAL PROPENSITY TO SAVE (MPS)	MARGINAL PROPENSITY TO CONSUME (MPC)	SPENDING MULTIPLIER [M_{Spending} = 1/MPS = 1/(1 − MPC)]
.50	.50	2
.33(1/3)	.67(2/3)	3
.25	.75	4
.20	.80	5
.10	.90	10

crease in investment demand would lead to a \$500 decrease in the equilibrium level of national income. To see why, return to Figure 30.2, and reverse the initial and the final equilibria in your mind's eye. Think of I_1^d = \$700 and Y_1 = \$5,500 as the initial equilibrium, and imagine that investment demand decreases by \$100, from I_1^d = \$700 to I_0^d = \$600. The new equilibrium occurs at the intersection of S^d and I_0^d, at Y = \$5,000. The decrease in Y is \$500, five times as large as the change in I^d.

Saving Demand and the Spending Multiplier

Why does a change in aggregate demand lead to a multiplied change in the equilibrium of national income? The intuition in terms of saving and investment is the following. Return to our first example of the \$100 increase in investment demand.

The economy can be in equilibrium only if saving demand equals investment demand. Therefore, when investment demand increases by \$100, saving must also increase by \$100 to return the economy to equilibrium. What causes saving to increase? The answer is the increases in national income as firms respond to the increase in demand by increasing production. Households move upward along the aggregate saving function, S^d, in the direction of the arrows as they receive the additional income. The equilibrium is restored when national income increases enough to generate \$100 more saving demand.

One dollar of additional national income does not generate one dollar of additional saving demand, however. It generates only \$.20 of additional saving in our example, since the MPS is .20. Five dollars of additional national income are needed to generate one dollar of additional saving. Therefore, national income must increase by \$500 to generate the additional \$100 of saving.

In general, each additional dollar of national income generates only MPS times one dollar worth of additional saving. This means that 1/MPS dollars of additional national income are required to raise saving by one dollar. Therefore, each dollar increase in investment demand requires 1/MPS dollars of additional income to restore the saving demand = investment demand equilibrium. Thus, 1/MPS is the spending multiplier.

The same argument applies in reverse to a decrease in investment demand. Saving demand must decrease by the same amount as investment demand in order to restore the equilibrium. Therefore, national income must fall by

1/MPS times the decrease in investment demand to reduce saving demand by the required amount.

Consumption, National Income, and the Multiplier

The intuition behind the feedback multiplier process is most evident from the interrelationship between consumption demand and national income. Table 30.2 illustrates the round-by-round feedback between consumption and national income that generates the multiplied increase in national income. The MPC is .80, as above.

The first row of the table shows the immediate effect of the $100 increase in investment demand. The $100 change in investment demand appears in the second column. Producers of investment goods see the increase in demand, so they produce $100 more investment goods and generate $100 more national income. National income increases immediately by $100, as indicated by the fourth column.

The economy continues to expand, however. The workers, landlords, and capitalists associated with the investment goods industries now have $100 more income. They spend MPC times the $100, or $80 ($80 = 0.80 · $100), on consumer goods and services: food, clothing, entertainment, cars, and the like. Consumption demand in the second round has increased by $80 (third column, second row). Producers of these consumer goods and services see the increased consumption demand and increase their production by $80, generating $80 more national income in the process. The $80 increase in national income appears in the fourth column, second row of the table. National income has now increased by $180: $100 in the first round in the investment goods industries and $80 in the second round in the consumer goods industries.

The economy expands still further in the third round. The $80 of additional national income generated in the second round is received by workers, landlords, and capitalists associated with the consumer goods industries. They

TABLE 30.2 The Multiplier Process Round by Round ($ billion)

ROUND	CHANGE IN INVESTMENT DEMAND (ΔI^d)	CHANGE IN CONSUMPTION DEMAND (ΔC^d)	CHANGE IN NATIONAL INCOME (ΔY)
1	$100	$ —	$100
			+
2	—	.80 · $100 = $80	80
			+
3	—	.80 · $ 80 = $64	64
		·	+
4		·	·
·		·	·
·		·	·
·		·	+
·		·	·
		·	
			Final ΔY = $500

spend MPC times the \$80, or \$64 (\$64 = 0.80 · \$80) on consumer goods and services, the same kinds of goods and services that households bought in the second round. Consumption demand in the third round has increased by \$64 (third column, third row). Producers of these consumer goods and services see the increased consumption demand and increase their production by \$64, generating \$64 more national income in the process. The \$64 increase in national income appears in the fourth column, third row of the table. National income has now increased by \$244: \$100 in the first round in the investment goods industries; \$80 in the second round in the consumer goods industries; and \$64 in the third round, also in the consumer goods industries.

The process continues indefinitely as the households that receive more income each round spend MPC of it on consumer goods and services in the next round. The interaction between consumption demand and national income drives the round-by-round increases in national income. Notice, though, that each new round is only MPC, or .80, as large as the preceding round. The additions to national income become ever smaller, and the economy homes in on a new higher equilibrium level of national income.

The final change in national income in response to the initial \$100 increase in investment demand is the sum of the changes listed in the fourth column of the table. The change in the equilibrium is

$$\Delta Y = \$100 + \$80 + \$64 + \ldots$$

which can be written as

$$\Delta Y = \$100 + (0.80 \cdot \$100) + (0.80 \cdot 0.80 \cdot \$100) + \ldots$$
$$\Delta Y = \$100 + (0.80 \cdot \$100) + [(0.80)^2 \cdot \$100] + \ldots$$

Each successive round is smaller than the previous round by .80, the MPC. The sum of the round-by-round changes in the limit turns out to be

$$\Delta Y = \$100 \cdot [1/(1 - 0.80)] = \$100 \cdot [1/(1 - \text{MPC})]$$
$$= \$100 \cdot M_{\text{Spending}} = \$100 \cdot 5 = \$500$$

\$100 is the initial change in aggregate demand, the increase in investment demand; 1/(1 − MPC) is the spending multiplier. The change in income is M_{Spending} times the initial change in aggregate demand, or \$500, as expected.

REFLECTION: The spending multiplier gives us another perspective on why the marginal propensity to consume is less than one. What would the value of the spending multiplier be if the MPC were one or greater than one?

The Spending Multiplier, Recessions, and Expansions

The multiplier process explains why, when aggregate demand declines, the newspapers are filled for awhile with stories about the economy going from bad to worse. Recessions tend to build in strength before they bottom out, whether at the national level or the state level. Suppose, for example, that the U.S. automobile industry suffers a very bad year—car sales fall way off. As a result, General Motors, Ford, and Chrysler cut production and lay off auto workers, and unemployment begins to rise in Michigan. The decline of the Michigan economy spreads far beyond the auto industry, however. The unemployed auto workers have less income, so they spend less on consumer goods and services. Retailers see that the demand for their products has fallen, so they cut production and reduce their work forces. Income in the state falls still further, round by round, until the majority of the multiplier process has been completed. Within a year or so storefronts are boarded up, downtown office space lies vacant, new housing starts have declined, and the Michigan unemployment rate reaches 10 percent or more. The majority of the newly unemployed during the year are not even auto workers. The multiplier process magnifies the steep decline in new car sales into a statewide recession in Michigan.

That's the bad news. The good news is that the multiplier process helps the entire state economy recover when auto sales pick up again. The recovery begins with the auto workers being recalled and then spreads round by round as the increased income and consumption demand interact to produce a booming economy once again.

The Michigan story illustrates another very important point about the spending multiplier. The initial \$100 increase in aggregate demand in our example does not have to be an increase in investment demand. The spending multiplier applies equally to all components of aggregate demand. The initial increase could have been a \$100 increase in consumption demand, such as an increase in the demand for new cars. Or the \$100 could have been a combined increase in investment demand and consumption demand totaling \$100, such as a \$75 increase in consumption demand and a \$25 increase in investment demand. A \$100 increase in aggregate demand generates a \$500 increase in the equilibrium level of national income no matter what component or components of aggregate demand increase in the first round to start the process going. The interrelationship between consumption demand and disposable income takes over from the second round onward to add \$400 of new national income and complete the multiplier process following the initial increase in aggregate demand in the first round.

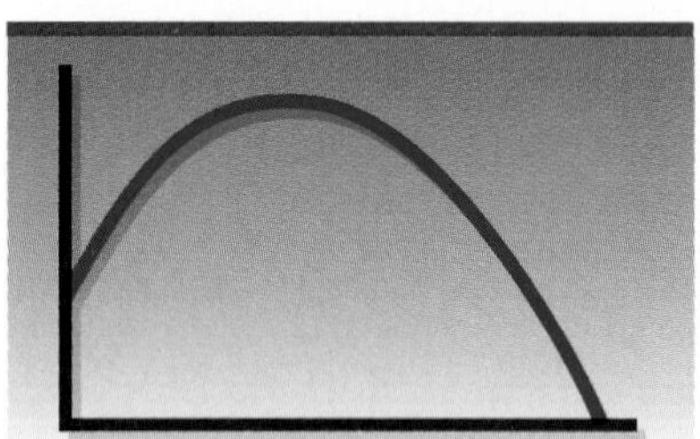

THE SPENDING MULTIPLIER IN THE UNITED STATES

Our simplest economy is adequate for illustrating the round-by-round nature of the multiplier process. But the model is far too simple to capture some of the more important features of the actual spending multiplier in the United States.

We noted in Chapter 29 that the actual MPC in the United States increases over time, from around .75 in the short run to a value slightly above .9 in the long run. An MPC of .9 implies a spending multiplier of 10 in our simplest economy:

$$M_{\text{Spending}} = 1/(1 - \text{MPC}) = 1/(1 - .9) = 1/0.1 = 10$$

In fact, the actual spending multiplier in the United States is far below 10. Economists Gary Fromm and Lawrence Klein surveyed 11 of the leading forecasting models in the United States. Six of the models that have a distinct Keynesian orientation place the actual U.S. spending multiplier within a range of 1.0 to 3.0, far below 10. In addition, five of these six models show a hump-shaped pattern for the multiplier process, illustrated in Figure 30.3.

The horizontal axis records the passage of time, by quarters. The vertical axis indicates the change in national income in response to a \$1 increase in

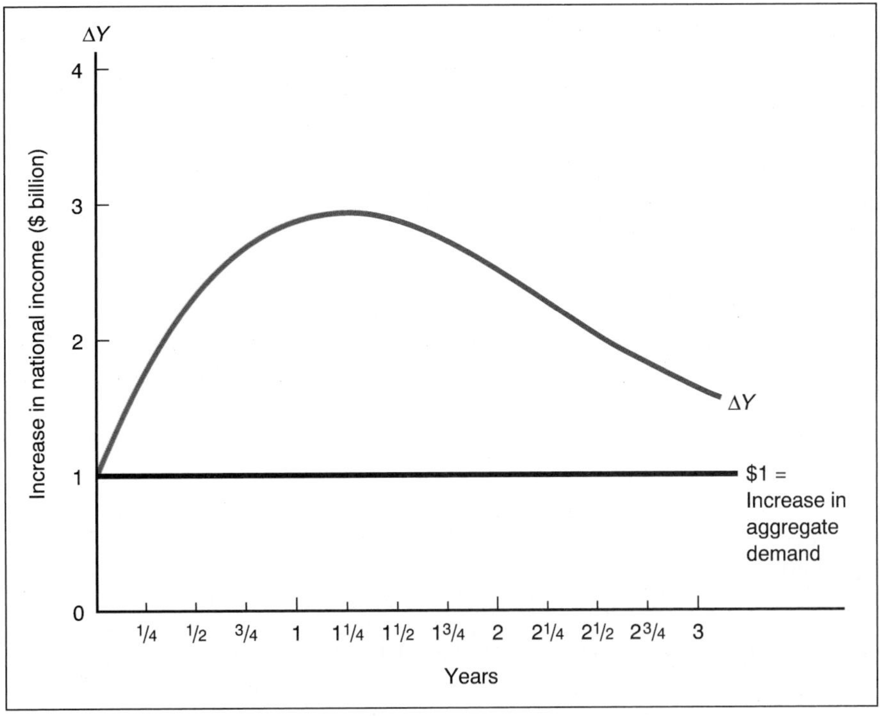

FIGURE 30.3

The Spending Multiplier in the United States

The figure illustrates the properties of the actual spending multiplier in the United States, as estimated by the large forecasting models that have a new Keynesian perspective. The horizontal axis records the passage of time, by quarters, after an increase in aggregate demand. The vertical axis records the increase in national income resulting from a $1 increase in aggregate demand. The spending multiplier is hump-shaped. The increase in national income builds to its peak value within 6 months to a year and three quarters after the increase in aggregate demand, and then declines to its final value between 1.0 and 2.5 after about three years.

aggregate demand. According to the forecasting models, the spending multiplier builds to its peak between 1.5 and 3.0 anywhere from six months to a year and three-quarters after the increase in aggregate demand. It then declines to a final value between 1.0 and 2.5 within three years. Our simplest model does not have this hump-shaped feature. The multiplier process described above builds continuously over time to its final value.[1]

Our simplest model is consistent with one feature of the U.S. spending multiplier, however: the speed of the multiplier process. The forecasting models suggest that the spending multiplier reaches its peak value fairly quickly. The same is true in our simplest model in the sense that the majority of the change in national income occurs in the early rounds. The change in national income in our example is $244 after only three rounds ($244 = $100 + $80 + $64), approximately half of the final change of $500. The change in national income is $336 after five rounds, two-thirds of its final value, and nearly $450 after 10 rounds, 90 percent of its final value. Three to five rounds of the multiplier would probably occur within six months of calendar time, and 10 rounds within a year, a time frame roughly consistent with the large forecasting models.

Nonetheless, we clearly have a way to go in building a model that adequately describes the operation of the U.S. economy, even qualitatively. Subsequent chapters will complicate the simplest model in a number of ways that both reduce the value of the spending multiplier and generate the hump-shaped pattern of Figure 30.3. A section on the U.S. spending multiplier will appear

[1]L. Klein and G. Fromm, "A Comparison of Eleven Econometric Models of the United States," *American Economic Review* 63, No. 2 (May 1973): 385–393. Table 5, p. 391 has a summary of the multipliers.

each time we add a new feature to the model that brings the spending multiplier more in line with its actual value.

FISCAL POLICY

We are now in a position to add the government sector to our model and explore the possibilities of fiscal policy. Recall that fiscal policy is budgetary policy. Fiscal policy refers to changes in the federal government's purchases of goods and services (G), and/or transfer payments (Tr), and/or taxes (Tx) undertaken for the specific purpose of changing the level or the composition of the circular flow of economic activity.

Can fiscal policy affect the level of aggregate demand and the equilibrium level of national income? Yes indeed. Changes in government purchases, transfer payments, and taxes each have a powerful, multiplied effect on the circular flow of economic activity. Let's consider each component of the federal budget separately.

Government Purchases of Goods and Services

Changes in government purchases of goods and services have a direct, dollar-for-dollar effect on aggregate demand because government purchases of goods and services are part of aggregate demand. With the government sector added to our model, aggregate demand is now the sum of the household sector's consumption demand (C^d), the business sector's investment demand (I^d), and the government sector's demand for goods and services (G^d). The new equilibrium condition in the product markets is

$$Y = C^d + I^d + G^d$$

The right-hand side of the equation is the aggregate demand for final goods and services by households, business firms, and the federal, state, and local governments. The left-hand side of the equation is the supply of final goods and services to the product markets by the producers, the value of the national product or national income. The product markets are in equilibrium when aggregate demand equals national income.

G^d AND NATIONAL INCOME The first question to ask is whether government purchases are closely related to the current level of national income. The answer is no. Federal and state and local purchases of goods and services are primarily determined by factors other than the current level of economic activity.

Most federal purchases are for defense or are defense-related, about 80 percent of the total federal G. Defense purchases are clearly determined by national security and other military considerations, not the current level of national income.

State and local government purchases are larger than federal purchases in the United States, approximately 60 percent of total G, and cover a whole range of functions. Public education is the largest component of state and local G,

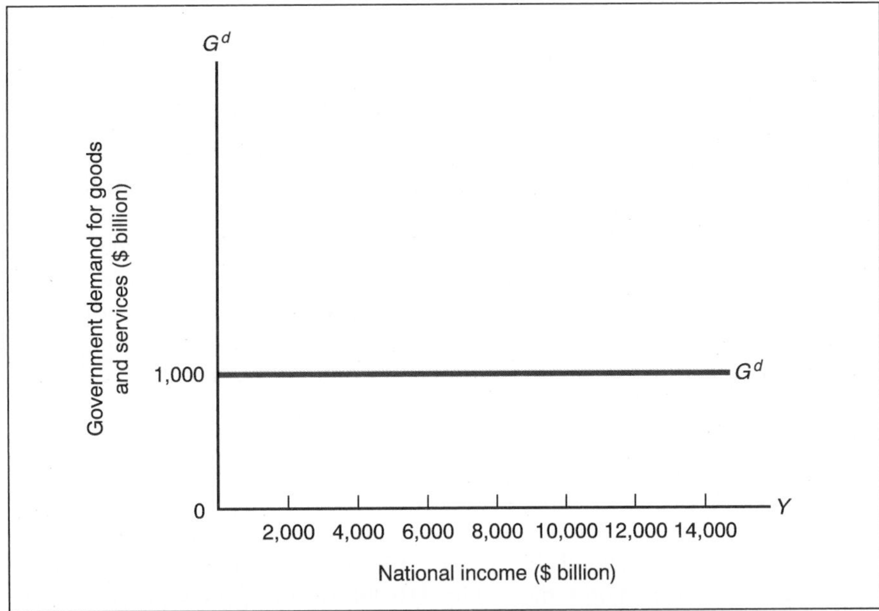

FIGURE 30.4

Government Spending on Goods and Services and National Income

Purchases of goods and services by the federal, state, and local governments are not closely related to the level of national income. They are determined, instead, by such factors as national security considerations and the number of children to be educated by the local public schools. Therefore, our simplest model assumes that government purchases are unrelated to the level of national income, *Y*. In particular, we are assuming that government spending on goods and services is $1,000 over the range of values that national income is likely to have (in billions of constant dollars). Therefore, the graph of government spending on goods and services, G^d, is horizontal at a value of $1,000. Changes in the other factors that influence government purchases shift G^d up or down.

about 35 percent of the total. Other important areas of state and local spending are the construction and maintenance of highways; public safety, including police, fire, and correctional institutions; the public hospitals; and general government, which covers the operating expenses of the administrative, legislative, and judicial branches of the governments.

Many factors besides income have an important influence on each of these components of state and local *G*. For example, local education expenditures are driven as much or more by the number of children to be educated than by a community's income. Expenditures on highway maintenance and construction depend heavily on weather conditions and the traffic density on the roadways. Police and correctional expenditures vary with crime rates. And so on. State and local income is just one of many factors determining the size of the state and local public sector, and probably not the most important factor.

Therefore, we will assume that the total government demand for goods and services is unrelated to the current level of national income, just as we did for investment demand. Figure 30.4 illustrates.

Government demand for goods and services is on the vertical axis, and the current level of national income, *Y*, is on the horizontal axis. G^d is horizontal, equal to $1,000 (billion) regardless of the level of *Y*. *G* was approximately $1,000 billion ($1 trillion) in the United States during 1992. The $1,000 of G^d is determined by factors other than the current level of national income. Changes in these other factors, such as more or fewer children to be educated, shift G^d up or down. We are also assuming that governments can buy what they want to buy, just as with consumption demand. The government demand for goods and services is the same as the actual government purchases of goods and services.

The assumption that G^d is unrelated to *Y* in the short run is very realistic for the United States. Even the huge private and government mathematical forecasting models assume that there is little or no feedback from the current level of national income to federal, state, and local government purchases.

EQUILIBRIUM WITH THE GOVERNMENT SECTOR Since G^d is a constant, adding the government sector to our model does not change the properties of the simplest model. Only the equilibrium level of national income is different because government demand is added to aggregate demand. Table 30.3 and Figure 30.5 show the new equilibrium with the government sector.

The first two columns of Table 30.3 reproduce the hypothetical consumption function and the investment demand relationship from Chapter 29. (As before, all data are in billions of dollars.) The MPC = .80, and investment demand is constant at $600. The third column of the table records the constant $1,000 of government demand for goods and services. The fourth column shows the level of aggregate demand at each level of national income listed in the fifth column. Aggregate demand in the fourth column is the sum of the first three columns, C^d (first column) + I^d (second column) + G^d (third column).

The equilibrium level of national income is $10,000, when aggregate demand (fourth column) equals national income (fifth column). The reason why $10,000 must be the equilibrium is the same as in the simplest economy without a government sector. Firms guess about the demand for their products and produce to meet the demand. In this case $10,000 is the only level of national income at which firms guess right. The $10,000 worth of final goods and services that they produce is exactly equal to the value of final goods and services that households, firms, and governments in the aggregate want to buy. Therefore, no one has any incentive to change from the equilibrium.

The firms have guessed wrong about the demand for their products at any level of national income other than the equilibrium and experience unwanted inventory depletion or accumulation as a result. Firms quickly adjust their guesses about demand and their production to the equilibrium level, so that their inventories behave as they want them to. Refer to the sixth column of the table to see the adjustment to the equilibrium.

Figure 30.5 pictures the new equilibrium on the aggregate demand–45° line graph. The aggregate demand line, *ADE*, in Figure 29.9 for the simplest econ-

TABLE 30.3 The Equilibrium Level of National Income: Household, Business, and Government Sectors ($ billion)

CONSUMPTION DEMAND (C^d)	INVESTMENT DEMAND (I^d)	GOVERNMENT DEMAND (G^d)	AGGREGATE DEMAND ($C^d+I^d+G^d$)	NATIONAL INCOME (Y)	INVENTORIES AND PRODUCTION RESPONSE
$ 400	$600	$1,000	$ 2,000	$ 0	Unwanted inventory
1,200	600	1,000	2,800	1,000	depletion
2,000	600	1,000	3,600	2,000	Increase production
2,800	600	1,000	4,400	3,000	.
3,600	600	1,000	5,200	4,000	.
4,400	600	1,000	6,000	5,000	.
5,200	600	1,000	6,800	6,000	.
6,000	600	1,000	7,600	7,000	.
6,800	600	1,000	8,400	8,000	.
7,600	600	1,000	9,200	9,000	.
8,400	**600**	**1,000**	**10,000**	**10,000**	**Equilibrium**
9,200	600	1,000	10,800	11,000	
10,000	600	1,000	11,600	12,000	Unwanted inventory
10,800	600	1,000	12,400	13,000	accumulation
					Decrease production

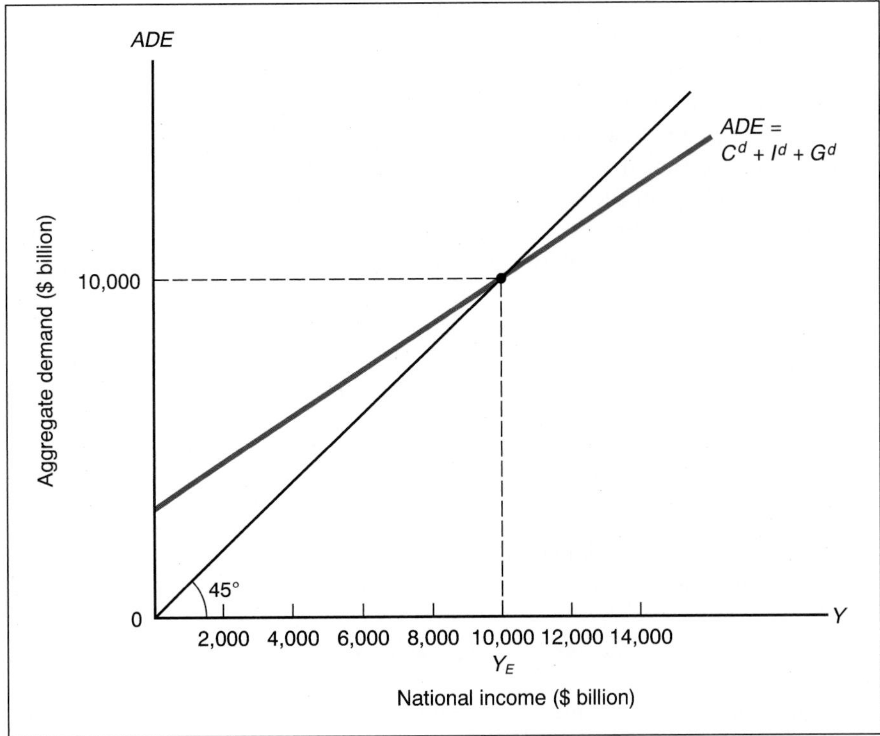

FIGURE 30.5

The Equilibrium Level of National Income with the Government Sector

The figure is a graph of the equilibrium level of national income for our economy from the data in Table 30.3. Adding the government sector to our model means that aggregate desired expenditures, *ADE*, or aggregate demand, is the sum of consumption demand by households (C^d), investment demand by business firms, (I^d), and government spending on goods and services by the federal, state, and local governments (G^d). $ADE = C^d + I^d + G^d$. Adding the government sector does not change the basic properties of our simplest model without a government sector from Chapter 29. The equilibrium level of national income is at the intersection of the *ADE* and the 45-degree lines, equal to $10,000 (in billions of constant dollars). Also, since G^d is a constant, the slope of the *ADE* line remains the marginal propensity to consume (MPC), and the value of the spending multiplier is still $M_{\text{Spending}} = 1/(1 - \text{MPC})$.

omy without the government was the vertical sum of the consumption function, C^d, from Figure 29.1 and the investment demand curve, I^d, from Figure 29.8. Because I^d is a constant, *ADE* had the same shape as C^d. The new *ADE* line in Figure 30.5 simply adds another constant in the vertical direction, the horizontal government demand curve, G^d, from Figure 30.4. Since I^d and G^d are both constant at every level of *Y*, *ADE* continues to have the same shape as C^d. *ADE* is now $1,600 above C^d, the sum of I^d ($600) and G^d ($1,000), but *ADE* still has the same slope as C^d, the MPC, equal to .80. Refer to the fourth and fifth columns of Table 30.3. Aggregate demand increases by $800 for every $1,000 increase in national income. For example, aggregate demand increases by $800 from $10,000 to $10,800 when national income increases by $1,000 from $10,000 to $11,000.

The equilibrium occurs at the intersection of *ADE* and the 45° line, just as in the simplest economy. The new equilibrium is $Y_E = \$10,000$; Y_E used to be $5,000 without the $1,000 of government demand. Otherwise, the graphical analysis of the equilibrium is the same as in the simplest economy.

G^d AND THE SPENDING MULTIPLIER The value of the spending multiplier remains the same with the addition of the government sector: $M_{\text{Spending}} = 1/(1 - \text{MPC})$ as before. Therefore, M_{Spending} is still equal to 5 because the MPC out of changes in national income is still equal to .80. Every $1 change, or shift, in aggregate demand leads to a $5 change in the equilibrium level of income. Furthermore, the spending multiplier applies to changes in G^d because G^d is part of aggregate demand. Every $1 increase or decrease in *G* increases or decreases aggregate demand by $1 and leads to a $5 increase or decrease in the equilibrium level of national income. Changes in government purchases give the federal government a very powerful tool indeed for influencing the level of economic activity.

The effect of a change in G^d on the equilibrium level of national income is most easily seen by referring to Table 30.2, which illustrated the multiplier process. Suppose that the initial \$100 increase in aggregate demand had been an increase in G^d from \$1,000 to \$1,100 rather than a \$100 increase in I^d. The analysis would carry through exactly as before. Rounds two and beyond are driven by the interrelationship between consumption demand and national income, which is unchanged by the addition of a constant level of government demand for goods and services. All that matters in the first round to start the multiplier process going is that producers of some type of goods and services see an increase in demand, increase production to meet the new demand, and generate \$100 more national income. The demand for consumer goods and services takes over from there on to complete the multiplier process.

The same principle regarding the spending multiplier holds as before: The spending multiplier applies equally to initial changes, or shifts, in any and all components of aggregate demand, whether ΔC^d, or ΔI^d, or ΔG^d.

In conclusion,

$$\Delta Y_E = M_{\text{Spending}} \cdot \Delta G^d$$

Note, for example, that adding \$1,000 worth of government purchases of goods and services to the simplest model increased the equilibrium level of national income by \$5,000, from $Y_E = \$5{,}000$ to $Y_E = \$10{,}000$.

FINANCING GOVERNMENT EXPENDITURES Any change in a government's budget always involves at least two separate steps because the government's total expenditures must be matched by the receipt of funds to finance them. For instance, an increase in government purchases has to be financed somehow. The first step is the increase in G^d. The second step is the financing, and the government has a number of options. One option is to "finance" the increase in G^d by decreasing other expenditures in the same amount, which keeps all the changes on the expenditure side of the budget. The other option is to increase government revenues, and here governments have three main choices: (1) print new money, (2) issue new debt, or (3) increase taxes.

Printing new money, dollar bills, to finance new expenditures is an option available only to the federal government because state and local governments do not issue their own money. The federal government has occasionally financed some of its expenditures by printing money, although the usual sources of revenue are new debt and taxes. In any event we will hold off analyzing the print-money option until the chapters on money and monetary policy. An increase in government expenditures financed by printing money is a combined fiscal and monetary policy. In contrast, an increase in government expenditures financed by issuing new debt or raising taxes is a pure fiscal policy.

DEBT FINANCING Governments run a deficit when their expenditures exceed their revenues from tax collections and fees. They borrow to finance their deficits by issuing new debt in the form of promissory notes that they sell to the public. A *promissory note* is a promise to repay the face value of the note, usually $1,000, at some date in the future, called the maturity date. The note may or may not pay interest to the holder each year until the maturity date. The amount that the buyers/lenders are willing to pay for the notes is the amount of money borrowed to cover the deficit.

The U.S. Treasury issues three kinds of promissory notes: bills, notes, and bonds. Treasury bills mature within 1 year; Treasury notes mature within 1 to 10 years; and Treasury bonds mature anytime beyond 10 years, usually from 10 to 30 years. Treasury bills do not pay interest to the holders, whereas Treasury notes and bonds do.

The federal government has the luxury of borrowing to finance its expenditures because it can always find willing buyers for its debt. Treasury bills, notes, and bonds are highly desirable financial securities. They offer competitive rates of return and a variety of maturity dates. Savers can purchase anything from 180-day Treasury bills to 30-year Treasury bonds. The existing securities are also easily bought and sold, so that savers/lenders can switch the maturity of their debt holdings or exchange their Treasury debt for some other form of saving at any time and in virtually any amount. The final attraction is safety. U.S. Treasury securities are considered to be the safest of all financial securities worldwide: The federal government will be the very last institution to default on its debt payments. Safety is one reason why foreign citizens and institutions have been eager buyers of the federal debt. We noted in Chapter 4 that the federal government has exploited the attractiveness of its debt and has increased its reliance on debt financing ever since 1981, the first year of the Reagan administration. The record annual deficits have continued throughout the Bush administration and into the Clinton administration, with no end in sight.

Chapter 31 will take a close look at the economic implications of an expanding federal debt. Our concern in this chapter is the effect of debt financing on aggregate demand in the short run.

New debt can affect the level of aggregate demand only if it changes the level of saving by households and businesses. We will assume at this point that issuing new federal debt affects the *composition* of saving, but not the *level* of saving. Given the opportunity to buy new issues of Treasury bills, notes, and bonds, some households and businesses choose to buy the Treasury securities rather than placing their saving in bank accounts or purchasing other financial securities, such as stocks, corporate bonds, and certificates of deposit. But they do not increase their saving to buy the new debt. Therefore, issuing new debt has no affect on aggregate demand. Consumption demand and investment demand remained unchanged.

The effect of this assumption is that the spending multiplier applies to a debt-financed increase in government purchases of goods and services. In terms of our model, a $1 increase in G^d financed with new debt increases the equilibrium level of national income by $5, just as above. The spending multiplier also applies to a decrease in government purchases of goods and services if the government reduces its borrowing by the same amount. With less new debt being issued, households and businesses buy other financial securities with the portion of their saving that they would have used to buy the new debt. They do not decrease the level of their saving.

The assumption that increases or decreases in government borrowing have no effect on aggregate demand is an assumption of convenience at this point. It is useful for comparing the relative effects of government purchases, taxes, and transfers on aggregate demand. It is not an accurate assumption, however. Most economists believe that government borrowing does affect aggregate demand even in the short run because it changes the level of interest rates throughout the economy, and some components of aggregate demand are sensitive to interest rates. An analysis of interest rates goes hand in hand with the role of money in the economy, so we will wait until the money chapters of the text to analyze the effects of debt financing on aggregate demand.

The remaining option to finance government purchases, raising taxes, does have a powerful, multiplied effect on the economy. We turn next to the analysis of taxes.

Taxes

Taxes, unlike government purchases, are not part of aggregate demand because they are not a direct payment for a good or a service. Tax checks written to governments do not pass through the product or factor markets within the circular flow of economic activity. Therefore, increases or decreases in taxes have no *immediate* impact on the level of gross domestic product (GDP) or national income. Nonetheless, changes in taxes have a powerful, multiplied effect on the equilibrium level of national income through their indirect effects on consumption demand and investment demand.

An *increase* in taxes *decreases* aggregate demand by decreasing either consumption demand or investment demand, or both. The decrease in aggregate demand leads to a multiplied decrease in the equilibrium level of national income. Conversely, a *decrease* in taxes *increases* aggregate demand by increasing either consumption demand or investment demand, or both. The increase in aggregate demand leads to a multiplied increase in the equilibrium level of national income.

Let's look more closely at the relationships among taxes, consumption demand, and the equilibrium level of national income, using our model as an example. We will consider a $100 increase in taxes to compare the effects with the $100 increase in government purchases analyzed above.

TAX MULTIPLIER

The ratio that relates the change in the equilibrium level of national income to a change in taxes on households.

THE TAX MULTIPLIER Our goal is to develop a tax multiplier along the lines of the spending multiplier. The **tax multiplier,** labeled M_{Tax}, relates the change in the equilibrium level of national income to a change in taxes on households. The derivation of the tax multiplier proceeds in four steps.

Step 1: Taxes, national income, and disposable income. The first step is to recall that taxes drive a wedge between national income and disposable income. We can no longer assume that the two are equal. In particular, although an increase in taxes has no immediate impact on national income, it does reduce households' disposable income dollar for dollar. Therefore, a $100 increase in taxes paid by households reduces their disposable income by $100.

$$\Delta Y_d = (-)\Delta Tx = (-)\$100$$

The minus sign indicates that disposable income and taxes change in the opposite direction. An increase in taxes decreases disposable income; a decrease in taxes increases disposable income.

Step 2: Consumption demand and disposable income. The second step relates the change in disposable income to the change in consumption demand. The two are related through the marginal propensity to consume (MPC). Every \$1 change in disposable income changes consumption demand by MPC times \$1. The MPC = .80 in our model.

$$\Delta C^d = 0.80 \cdot \Delta Y_d$$

The change in disposable income is equal to the change in taxes, but in the opposite direction. Therefore, every \$1 *increase* in taxes *reduces* consumption demand by MPC times \$1.

$$\Delta C^d = \text{MPC} \cdot (-)\Delta Tx = 0.8 \cdot (-)\Delta Tx = 0.8 \cdot (-)\$100 = (-)\$80$$

Consumption demand decreases by \$80 when taxes increase by \$100, equal to MPC times the change in taxes.

Step 3: Consumption demand and the equilibrium. The third step relates the change in consumption demand to the change in the equilibrium level of national income. The two are related through the spending multiplier.

$$\Delta Y_E = M_{\text{Spending}} \cdot \Delta C^d = [1/(1 - \text{MPC})] \cdot \Delta C^d$$

ΔY_E refers to the change in the equilibrium level of national income. $M_{\text{Spending}} = 5$ in our model.

$$\Delta Y_E = 5 \cdot (-)\$80 = (-)\$400$$

Step 4: The tax multiplier. The last relationship shows that a \$100 increase in taxes decreases the equilibrium level of national income by \$400. Therefore, the tax multiplier in our model is (−)4.

$$\begin{aligned} \Delta Y_E &= M_{\text{Tax}} \cdot \Delta Tx \\ (-)\$400 &= M_{\text{Tax}} \cdot \$100 \\ M_{\text{Tax}} &= (-)4 \end{aligned}$$

The minus sign indicates that taxes and the equilibrium move in opposite directions. Taxes are a *drain* on aggregate demand. An increase in taxes reduces consumption demand and decreases the equilibrium level of national income. Conversely, a decrease in taxes increases consumption demand and increases the equilibrium level of national income. A \$100 decrease in taxes increases the equilibrium level of national income by \$400.

Notice that the tax multiplier is not as large as the spending multiplier. In particular, the tax multiplier is MPC times the spending multiplier, as well as having the opposite sign.

$$M_{\text{Tax}} = (-)4; \quad M_{\text{Spending}} = 5; \quad (-)4 = (-)0.80 \cdot 5$$

Changes in taxes have a less potent effect on the equilibrium than do changes in aggregate demand because they work indirectly in changing aggregate demand. Every \$1 change in taxes changes conumption demand by only MPC times \$1. The remaining portion of the tax change changes saving demand by MPS times \$1. In our example consumption demand decreases by \$80, and saving demand decreases by \$20 in response to the \$100 increase in taxes. Therefore, aggregate demand changes, or shifts, by only \$80, not by the full \$100. The \$20 of the tax increase that comes out of saving would not have been spent in any case, so it has no effect on aggregate demand. In contrast, the \$100 change in government purchases in our earlier example changes aggregate demand by the full \$100.

In terms of the aggregate demand–45° line graph in Figure 30.5, a \$100 increase in government purchases of goods and services shifts *ADE* up by \$100. A \$100 increase in taxes decreases consumption demand by \$80, so *ADE* shifts down by \$80.

The relationship between the tax multiplier and the spending multiplier in our model is true for any value of the MPC. M_{Tax} is always MPC times M_{Spending} and has the opposite sign. The general expression for the spending multiplier is

$$M_{\text{Spending}} = 1/(1 - \text{MPC})$$

Therefore, the general expression for the tax multiplier is

$$\begin{aligned} M_{\text{Tax}} &= (-)\text{MPC} \cdot M_{\text{Spending}} \\ &= (-)[\text{MPC}/(1 - \text{MPC})] \end{aligned}$$

For an MPC of .80,

$$M_{\text{Tax}} = (-)[0.80/(1 - 0.80)] = (-)[0.80/0.20] = (-)4$$

In conclusion, changes in taxes on households, such as a change in the federal personal income tax, have a powerful, multiplied effect on the equilibrium level of national income. Note, also, that the federal government can change taxes to affect the economy without having to change its expenditures. It can finance a tax cut by increasing its borrowing and issuing new debt, and it can raise taxes and simultaneously reduce its borrowing. The tax multiplier applies to all tax changes affecting households that are offset by changes in borrowing, just as the spending multiplier applies to changes in government purchases that are offset by changes in borrowing.

REFLECTION: Test your understanding of the tax multiplier by seeing if you can rework each step of our example for a \$100 decrease in taxes.

Transfer Payments

Changes in transfer payments are the third tool of fiscal policy, along with changes in government purchases and taxes. Transfer payments are analytically equivalent to negative taxes because the only difference between transfer payments and taxes is the direction in which the money flows. Households and businesses write checks to governments when they pay taxes; governments write checks to households and businesses when they make transfers to them. Otherwise, transfer payments and taxes are identical. Transfer payments, like taxes, are not direct payments for a good or a service, so transfer payments do not enter the circular flow of economic activity and are not part of aggregate demand. Therefore, changes in transfer payments, like changes in taxes, have no immediate impact on GDP or national income. They do, however, have the same powerful, multiplied effect on the equilibrium level of national income as do taxes through their indirect effects on consumption demand and investment demand. The only difference is the direction of the effect. Transfer payments are a contributor to aggregate demand. An *increase* in transfer payments *increases* aggregate demand and the equilibrium level of national income; a *decrease* in transfer payments *decreases* aggregate demand and the equilibrium level of national income.

THE TRANSFER MULTIPLIER The **transfer multiplier,** labeled M_{Transfer}, relates the change in the equilibrium level of national income to a change in government transfer payments. The derivation of the transfer multiplier proceeds exactly as the derivation of the tax multiplier did. Only the direction of the effects changes. We will again consider a \$100 increase in transfer payments and an MPC equal to 0.8. The four steps, briefly, are as follows.

TRANSFER MULTIPLIER
The ratio that relates the change in the equilibrium level of national income to a change in government transfer payments.

Step 1: Transfers, national income, and disposable income. Although the \$100 increase in transfer payments has no immediate impact on national income, it does increase households' disposable income by \$100.

Step 2: Consumption demand and disposable income. Consumption demand increases by MPC times the \$100 increase in disposable income, or \$80. Equivalently, consumption demand increases by MPC times the \$100 increase in the transfer payments.

Step 3: Consumption demand and the equilibrium. The equilibrium level of national income changes by M_{Spending} times the change in consumption demand. $M_{\text{Spending}} = 5$, and $\Delta C^d = \$80$. Therefore,

$$\Delta Y_E = 5 \cdot \$80 = \$400$$

Step 4: The transfer multiplier. A \$100 increase in transfer payments leads to a \$400 increase in the equilibrium level of national income. Therefore, the value of the transfer multiplier is (+)4.

$$M_{\text{Transfer}} = 4$$

M_{Transfer} is MPC times M_{Spending} and has the same sign. The transfer multiplier is smaller than the spending multiplier is because transfer payments work indirectly on aggregate demand. The \$100 increase in transfer payments increases consumption demand by MPC times \$100, or \$80, not by the full \$100. The remaining \$20 of the transfer payments is saved and does not affect aggregate demand.

The general expression for the transfer multiplier is

$$M_{\text{Transfer}} = \text{MPC}/(1 - \text{MPC})$$

M_{Transfer} applies to all debt-financed changes in transfer payments.

Notice that M_{Transfer} is the same as M_{Tax} except for the sign. An increase in transfer payments increases the equilibrium, whereas an increase in taxes decreases the equilibrium. Otherwise, the tax and the transfer multipliers are both MPC times the spending multiplier.

The Balanced Budget Multipliers

BALANCED BUDGET CHANGE

An equal change in government expenditures and revenues.

So far we have been considering changes in expenditures and tax revenues that are "financed" by changes in borrowing. A government can also increase or decrease its expenditures and tax revenues by the same amount. An equal change in expenditures and tax revenues is called a **balanced budget change** because it does not change the size of the government's deficit.

Balanced budget changes are particularly appealing to so-called fiscal conservatives who want to hold the line on government spending. They argue that debt financing makes it too easy to vote for new government programs, whereas balanced budget increases promote fiscal responsibility. Administrators and legislators are more likely to scrutinize proposals for new spending programs if they know that they have to raise taxes to pay for them.

Two kinds of balanced budget changes must be distinguished for macro economic purposes: (1) a change in the government's purchases matched by an equal change in taxes and (2) a change in transfer payments matched by an equal change in taxes. These two budgetary changes leave the government's budget deficit unchanged, but they have quite different effects on the economy.

$\Delta G^d = \Delta Tx$ A balanced budget change in government purchases and taxes changes the equilibrium level of national income. Our previous examples indicate why.

Earlier we considered a \$100 increase in government purchases and a \$100 increase in taxes. The net effect on the equilibrium of a \$100 balanced budget change in G^d and Tx is the sum of the two changes taken individually.

The spending multiplier gives the change in the equilibrium level of national income resulting from a change in government purchases. Since $M_{\text{Spending}} = 5$ in our model, a \$100 increase in G^d increases the equilibrium level of national income by \$500.

$$\Delta Y_E = M_{\text{Spending}} \cdot \Delta G^d = 5 \cdot \$100 = \$500$$

The tax multiplier gives the change in the equilibrium level of national income resulting from a change in taxes. Since $M_{\text{Tax}} = (-)4$ in our model, a \$100 increase in taxes decreases the equilibrium level of national income by \$400.

$$\Delta Y_E = M_{\text{Tax}} \cdot \Delta Tx = (-)4 \cdot \$100 = (-)\$400$$

Therefore, the net change in the equilibrium from a \$100 increase in G^d and Tx is \$100.

$$\Delta Y_E = \$500 - \$400 = \$100$$

The increase in government purchases increases aggregate demand and increases the equilibrium level of national income. The increase in taxes decreases aggregate demand and decreases the equilibrium level of national income. The two effects do not cancel out, however, because the spending multiplier is greater than the tax multiplier is. Changes in government purchases have a greater effect on aggregate demand than do equal-dollar changes in taxes, so the equilibrium level of national income increases.

Notice that the change in the equilibrium is exactly equal to the balanced budget change in government purchases and taxes, \$100. This result is not peculiar to our model, with its MPC of .80. It holds for any MPC and the corresponding values of $M_{Spending}$ and M_{Tax}. *Equal changes in* G^d *and* Tx *change the equilibrium level of national income by the same amount and in the same direction.* A \$25 increase in G^d and Tx increases the equilibrium level of national income by \$25, a \$33 decrease in G^d and Tx decreases the equilibrium level of national income by \$33, and so forth.

The **balanced budget multiplier** *for government purchases and taxes,* labeled $M_{\Delta G^d = \Delta Tx}$, relates the change in the equilibrium level of national income to a balanced budget change in G^d and Tx. Since the equilibrium changes in the same direction and amount as the balanced budget change, the value of the balanced budget multiplier is one.

BALANCED BUDGET MULTIPLIER
The ratio that relates the change in the equilibrium level of national income to a balanced budget change in government purchases and taxes.

$$M_{\Delta G^d = \Delta Tx} = 1$$

The algebra needed to derive this result for any MPC is messy and will be left to the appendix to Chapter 30.

$\Delta Tr = \Delta Tx$ Balanced budget changes in transfer payments and taxes leave the equilibrium level of national income unchanged. The *balanced budget multiplier for transfers and taxes,* labeled $M_{\Delta Tr = \Delta Tx}$, relates the change in the equilibrium level of national income to a balanced budget change in transfer payments and taxes. Since $M_{Tax} = (-)M_{Transfer}$, the value of the multiplier is zero. Our previous examples are once again instructive.

$M_{Transfer} = 4$ in our model. A \$100 increase in transfer payments increases the equilibrium level of national income by \$400. $M_{Tax} = (-)4$. A \$100 increase in taxes decreases the equilibrium level of national income by \$400. Therefore, a \$100 balanced budget increase in transfer payments and taxes has no effect on the equilibrium.

$$\Delta Y_E = \$400 - \$400 = 0$$
$$M_{\Delta Tr = \Delta Tx} = 0$$

Summary: The Fiscal Policy Multipliers

The following Concept Summary table lists the five fiscal policy multipliers developed in this section. The multipliers are a convenient way of thinking about the effects of virtually any budgetary changes on the equilibrium level of national income.

CONCEPT SUMMARY

THE FISCAL POLICY MULTIPLIERS

FISCAL POLICY	FISCAL POLICY MULTIPLIER
Change in government purchases (ΔG^d)	$M_{\text{Spending}} = 1/(1 - \text{MPC})$
Change in transfer payments (ΔTr)	$M_{\text{Transfer}} = \text{MPC}/(1 - \text{MPC})$
Change in taxes (ΔTx)	$M_{\text{Tax}} = (-)\text{MPC}/(1 - \text{MPC})$
Balanced Budget Multipliers:	
a. Equal change in government purchases and taxes ($\Delta G^d = \Delta Tx$)	$M_{\Delta G^d = \Delta Tx} = 1$
b. Equal change in transfer payments and taxes ($\Delta Tr = \Delta Tx$)	$M_{\Delta Tr = \Delta Tx} = 0$

Following are some examples that show how the multipliers can help us understand some important fiscal policy issues. Our first example relates to the limitations of macroeconomic policy at the state level.

STATES' ECONOMIC POLICIES State governors are always talking a good economic game. They claim that their administrations are pursuing economic policies to promote a healthy state economy, and they are quick to take credit when their economies perform well. Voters are just as quick to blame the governors when their states' economies turn sour. In fact, the idea that states can pursue effective macroeconomic policies is largely a myth. State governments have very little control over their economies.

The first problem governors face in trying to manage their economies is that the fate of their economies is largely determined by events happening beyond the states' borders. Suppose that we were to build a set of national income and product accounts for a state. The "national" income = "national" product accounting identity is

$$Y = C + I + G + (Ex - Im)$$

The main difference between a state's and the nation's accounts is that net exports are much more important at the state level. Much of what a state's own firms produce, especially the output of the large manufacturing corporations, is exported to citizens and firms in other states. Automobile manufacturers, computer companies, and the larger manufacturing firms sell most of their products out of state. Also, many firms depend greatly on federal defense contracts. Similarly, many of the goods and services that a state's own citizens buy are imported from firms located in other states. In effect, each state is like a small nation surrounded by large nations. Its economic destiny is largely tied to the economies of the other states and to the federal government.

In addition, states have a very limited set of policy options for managing their economies. They cannot isolate themselves from outside events. The Constitution of the United States prohibits states from using tariffs, quotas, export taxes, or any other commercial devices that would limit the free flow of goods and services across their borders. Monetary policy is also out because states do not issue their own money. So states are essentially left with fiscal policies as the only means of managing their economies, and they are limited to balanced budget moves, by and large.

All but a few states have laws that require their governors to submit balanced operating budgets each year, and the U.S. financial markets would force the states into balancing their operating budgets even if these laws did not exist. State debt is not as readily accepted as federal debt is. States can issue debt to finance specific capital projects, but, unlike the federal government, they cannot routinely issue debt to cover operating deficits. A state that persisted in running operating deficits would soon find its bond rating lowered to junk bond status, and the financial markets may eventually cut it off entirely from borrowing. States do run operating deficits on occasion, but they have to promise to raise taxes and/or cut expenditures to restore balance as a condition for continued access to borrowing.

The problem for state fiscal policies is that the balanced budget multipliers are too low. Suppose that a state government increases its expenditures to try to stimulate the economy. Since the majority of state expenditures are purchases of goods and service, G^d, the potential stimulus from increased spending is quite large. But the state also has to raise taxes to finance the new expenditures, so the best that it can hope for is a balanced budget multiplier of one. $M_{\Delta G^d = \Delta Tx} = 1$. Unfortunately, a multiplier of one is too low, given the current resistance to larger governments and higher taxes. State governments simply cannot raise spending and taxes by enough to have a significant effect on their economies.

Governors trumpet the job-creating benefits of policies to lure new business into the state. States commonly offer businesses space in government-subsidized industrial parks, complete with water, sewage, electricity, and ample parking. They may also throw in state and local tax abatements as an added inducement. The industrial parks no doubt do attract new business into the state, creating new jobs and stimulating the economy. But the governors conveniently ignore the depressing effect of the additional taxes needed to pay for these kinds of business subsidies. The net effect on the economy of the subsidies and new taxes combined is unlikely to be very large.

States are in a worse bind if the increased expenditures are transfer payments because the balanced budget multiplier for transfers and taxes is zero. $M_{\Delta Tr = \Delta Tx} = 0$. A state's public assistance expenditures naturally increase when the state economy goes into a recession, as some of the unemployed are eventually forced onto the welfare rolls. The increased transfer payments do give a boost to the economy. But the increase in taxes needed to finance the transfers exactly offsets the stimulating effect of the transfers.

CURRENT ISSUE: California is in the midst of taking a big hit with the decrease in defense spending, and Californians will no doubt turn to the state for help to create new jobs. The government may not be able to help very much, though. The immediate impact of the defense cutbacks is to throw the state's budget into deficit because California has a huge public assistance program. The state may have to raise taxes, which will cause more job loss.

In conclusion, state macroeconomic policy is vastly overrated. Only the federal government can hope to articulate and carry out policies to achieve the macroeconomic policy goals.

THE FISCAL POLICY OPTIONS Our second example is a simple numerical exercise that illustrates the nature of the macroeconomic policy problem and the various fiscal policy options that the federal government might use to solve the problem. The exercise uses our model of the economy from Table 30.3 and Figure 30.5, in which the MPC = .80.

SETTING THE TARGET LEVEL OF NATIONAL INCOME As indicated in the first section of the chapter, the first step in solving the policy problem is determining a target level of national income that offers the best compromise among the four macroeconomic policy goals. To keep things simple, let's assume that the government's policy makers are concerned only about unemployment and they determine that the full-employment level of national income is $12,000 (billion).

BUILDING A MODEL OF THE ECONOMY The next step in solving the policy problem is building a model of the economy that shows what the equilibrium level of national income is and how the economy would react to different kinds of policies. We already have a model. Figure 30.6 reproduces the aggregate demand–45° line graph from Figure 30.5. The equilibrium level of national income, Y_0, is $10,000, at the intersection of the solid aggregate demand line, ADE_0, and the 45° line. The full-employment level of national income, Y_{FE}, is $12,000, as indicated by the solid vertical line.

RECESSIONARY GAP

Exists when the equilibrium level of national income is less than the full-employment level of national income; the size of the gap is the amount that aggregate demand has to increase to bring the equilibrium level of national income to the full-employment level of national income.

RECESSIONARY AND INFLATIONARY GAPS The economy is experiencing a **recessionary gap:** The equilibrium level of national income, Y_E, is below the full-employment level of national income, Y_{FE}. The economy is operating below its production possibilities frontier, and resources are unemployed. For

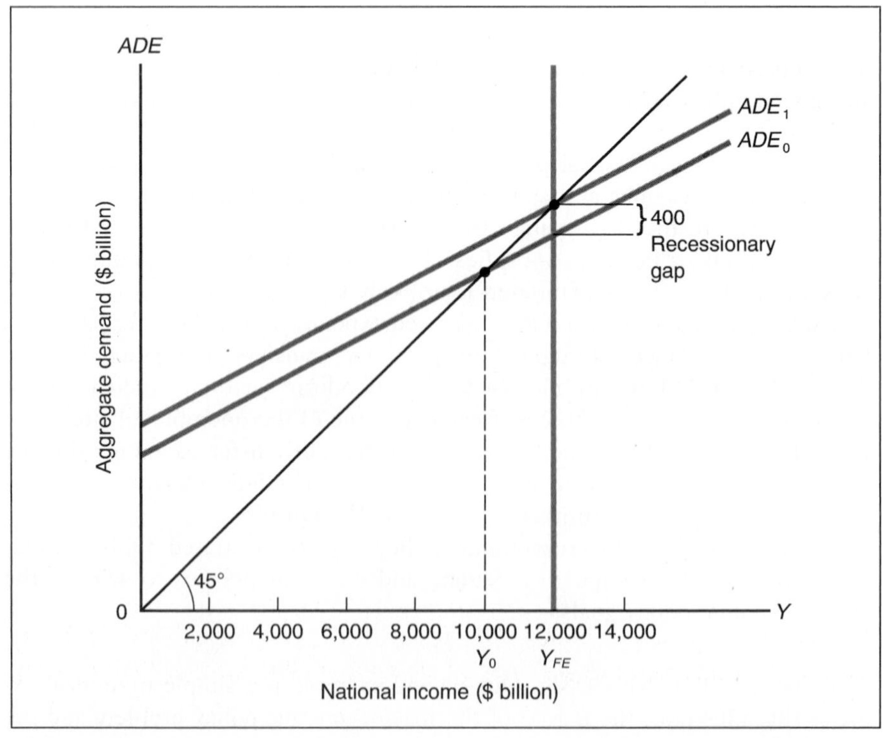

FIGURE 30.6

A Recessionary Gap

The economy is in equilibrium at Y_0 = $10,000, at the intersection of the aggregate demand line ADE_0 and the 45-degree line. Y_0 is less than the full-employment level of national income, Y_{FE} = $12,000, so the economy is experiencing a recessionary gap. The size of the gap is $400, the amount that aggregate demand has to increase to bring the economy to equilibrium at the full-employment level of income Y_{FE}. The size of the gap is the required change in national income, $2,000, divided by the spending multiplier, which is 5 is our model. [$400 = $2,000/5].

future reference, the reverse situation when the equilibrium level of national income, Y_E, is above the full-employment level of national income, Y_{FE}, is an **inflationary gap.** The economy is trying to push beyond its production possibilities frontier, leading to an inflation.

INFLATIONARY GAP

Exists when the equilibrium level of national income is greater than the full-employment level of national income; the size of the gap is the amount that aggregate demand has to decrease to bring the equilibrium level of national income to the full-employment level of national income.

The *size* of the recessionary gap is *not* the difference between Y_E and Y_{FE}, however. Instead, it is the amount that aggregate demand has to increase to bring the equilibrium level of national income to the full-employment level of national income. In other words, the size of the recessionary gap is the vertical distance between ADE_0 and ADE_1 in Figure 30.6. As such, the size of the recessionary gap is the required change in income ($Y_{FE} - Y_E$) divided by the spending multiplier.

$$\text{Size of the recessionary gap} = (Y_{FE} - Y_E)/M_{\text{Spending}}$$

The required change in income ($Y_{FE} - Y_E$) is \$2,000 (\$2,000 = \$12,000 − \$10,000); $M_{\text{Spending}} = 5$ in our model. Therefore,

$$\text{Size of the recessionary gap} = \$2{,}000/5 = \$400$$

Government policies have to increase (shift) aggregate demand by \$400 to remove the recessionary gap. Once aggregate demand has shifted, the multiplier process increases national income by the additional \$1,600 necessary for Y_E to reach Y_{FE} at 12,000.

FISCAL POLICY OPTIONS The final step is to design an expansionary fiscal policy that will increase aggregate demand by \$400 and thereby increase Y_E by \$2,000. A number of different expansionary fiscal policies can remove the recessionary gap. Here are three of them, each of which makes use of the fiscal policy multipliers summarized in the previous Concept Summary table.

1. *A debt-financed increase in government purchases of goods and services.* The spending multiplier applies to debt-financed increases in G^d. Therefore, the required increase in G^d is \$400.

$$\Delta Y_E = M_{\text{Spending}} \cdot \Delta G^d$$
$$\$2{,}000 = 5 \cdot \$400$$

Since G^d is part of aggregate demand, a \$400 increase in G^d does increase aggregate demand by \$400, as required to remove the recessionary gap.

2. *A decrease in taxes "financed" by an increase in debt.* The tax multiplier applies to the decrease in taxes. $M_{\text{Tax}} = (-)4$ in our model. Therefore, the required decrease in taxes is \$500.

$$\Delta Y_E = M_{\text{Tax}} \cdot \Delta Tx$$
$$\$2{,}000 = (-)4 \cdot (-)\$500$$

The \$500 cut in taxes increases consumption demand by MPC times \$500, or \$400 (\$400 = 0.8 · \$500). Since C^d is part of aggregate demand, a \$500 tax cut does increase aggregate demand by \$400, as required to remove the recessionary gap.

REFLECTION: See if you can design still other expansionary fiscal policies to remove the recessionary gap. Try one or two fiscal policies involving changes in transfer payments.

3. *A balanced budget increase in government purchases of goods and services and in taxes.* $M_{\Delta G^d = \Delta Tx} = 1$. Therefore, G^d and Tx must increase by \$2,000 to increase Y_E by \$2,000. The increase in G^d increases aggregate demand by \$2,000. The \$2,000 tax increase reduces C^d by MPC times \$2,000, or \$1,600 (\$1,600 = 0.80 · \$2,000). The net increase in aggregate demand is \$400 (\$400 = \$2,000 − \$1,600), as required to remove the recessionary gap.

FISCAL POLICY IN PRACTICE

These simple numerical exercises demonstrate the theoretical possibilities for fiscal policy, what fiscal policy can achieve in principle. The actual conduct of fiscal policy is not quite so routine as these exercises make it seem, however. The government cannot just pick out a target level of national income and expect to reach it with a set of fiscal policies any time it wants to.

FINE TUNING

Using fiscal or monetary policies to keep the economy at or very near the target level of national income.

COUNTERCYCLICAL POLICY

A fiscal or monetary policy that counteracts the movements in aggregate demand whenever aggregate demand tends to move the economy away from the target level of national income.

Economists ask: Can the government hope to fine tune the economy through countercyclical fiscal and monetary policies? **Fine tuning** means keeping the economy at or very near the target level of income. An obvious example is keeping the economy operating on or very near the production possibilities frontier at all times. **Countercyclical policies** are policies that counteract movements in aggregate demand that threaten to move the economy away from the target level of national income. An example is an expansionary fiscal policy that increases aggregate demand to counteract a fall in consumption demand that would otherwise plunge the economy into a recession. An opposite example is a contractionary fiscal policy that decreases aggregate demand to counteract a rise in consumption demand that would otherwise attempt to move the economy beyond its production possibilities frontier and build up unwanted inflationary pressures.

Can the government fine tune the economy? The answer is almost certainly no. Most economists agree that the best the government can hope to do is "lean against the wind," that is, prevent the economy from heading toward disaster. The government cannot prevent recessions, but it can prevent a recession from turning into another Great Depression. Similarly, the government cannot prevent occasional bouts of inflation, but it can prevent an inflation from developing into an explosive hyperinflation.

We can only consider the problems associated with fiscal policy at this point.

The Fiscal Policy Lags

The conduct of fiscal policy is fraught with practical difficulties. Foremost among them are the time lags involved with fiscal policy, the time required to enact a fiscal policy and have it take effect. The time lags occur in three stages, one right after another: (1) the recognition lag, (2) the administrative lag, and (3) the operational lag.

RECOGNITION LAG (FISCAL OR MONETARY POLICY)

The time required for policy makers to realize that the economy is in trouble and needs a dose of countercyclical policy.

THE RECOGNITION LAG The **recognition lag** is the time required for policy makers to realize that the economy is in trouble and needs a dose of countercyclical policy. The length of the recognition lag depends on the time required to collect reliable data on macroeconomic variables and on the ability to forecast the future performance of the economy. Data on GDP, inflation, and unemployment are available with only about a one-month lag. As noted in Chapter 28, however, forecasting remains more an uncertain art than an exact science. The large macroeconomic forecasting models, private and government, have not been very successful at predicting recessions or inflations. Especially disconcerting was their utter failure to predict three of the more dramatic economic episodes of the past 20 years: the recession of 1974–75, the recession of 1981–82, and the abrupt recovery in 1983–84.

The 1974–75 recession was the deepest recession in the United States since the Great Depression of the 1930s, yet the forecasting models failed to see it coming in 1973. The average prediction of the large models at the time was that real gross national product (GNP) would *grow* by 2.2 percent from the first quarter in 1974 to the first quarter of 1975. Instead, real GNP *fell* by 3.8 percent.

The recession of 1981–82 supplanted the 1974–75 recession as the deepest since the Great Depression. Once again the forecasting models were wide of the mark. The average forecast was that nominal GNP would fall by 2.1 percent from the third quarter of 1981 to the third quarter of 1982. In fact, nominal GNP fell by 10.8 percent.

The forecasting models also missed the ensuing recovery. Unemployment had risen sharply during the recession and was still at 9.6 percent at the end of 1983. The average forecast in 1983 was that unemployment would remain above 9 percent in 1984. Instead, the recovery was much stronger than predicted, and unemployment fell to 7.5 percent by the end of 1984.[2]

The inability to forecast accurately is a serious handicap for fiscal (and monetary) policy. The government can hardly hope to fine tune the economy if it cannot predict where the economy will be over the next six months to a year. In truth, the economy is often far from its target before the policy makers recognize the nature of the problem.

THE ADMINISTRATIVE LAG The **administrative lag** is the time required to enact legislation to change government purchases, or transfer payments, or taxes. The standing joke around Washington is that as soon as the policy makers recognize that the economy is in trouble, the government springs into inaction. The budgetary process is extremely cumbersome and time-consuming in the United States.

ADMINISTRATIVE LAG (FISCAL POLICY)

The time required to enact legislation to change government purchases, transfer payments, or taxes.

The budgetary cycle normally begins in the fall when the administration starts to put together its entire proposed budget for the next fiscal year, which begins the following October. The budget proposal incorporates the administration's forecasts for the economy over the next fiscal year. The budget is submitted to Congress in January. The House and the Senate then work from January to September to pass the legislation needed to authorize all the individual expenditure and revenue components of the budget and to appropriate the actual expenditures for each program. Committees in both houses hold hearings on the various parts of the budget, taking testimony from experts and

[2]The data in this section are taken from the discussion of macroeconomic forecasting difficulties in R. Gordon, *Macroeconomics*, fifth edition (Glenview, IL: Scott, Foresman/Little, Brown, 1989), 466–469. See, also, S. McNees, "Which Forecast Should You Use?", *New England Economic Review* (July/August 1985): 36–42. McNees is a recognized authority on the performance of the various forecasting models.

other interested parties. The committees then draft bills and send them to the full House and Senate for a vote.

The final House and Senate bills usually differ. If so, the bills relating to economic policy are sent to the Joint Economic Committee, which holds its own hearings and drafts a compromise bill. The compromise bill is then sent back to the House and Senate for another vote. The legislative process is never entirely completed by October, so parts of the budget each year are supported by temporary continuing resolutions until the final legislation is passed.

Needless to say, all this takes a considerable amount of time. One study of 10 major tax bills enacted from 1948 to 1965 found that the average time from administrative proposal to final passage was 8 months, with a range of 1 to 18 months.[3] The situation has hardly improved since then. The 1986 Tax Reform Act was signed in October of 1986. The Reagan administration published its first proposal for tax reform in November of 1984.

Any hope of fine tuning the economy with fiscal policy is clearly out of the question with such long administrative lags. The administrative lag has been a serious obstacle to the conduct of effective fiscal policies.

OPERATIONAL LAG (FISCAL POLICY)

The time period from the passage of new legislation to the final change in the equilibrium level of national income.

THE OPERATIONAL LAG The final lag is the **operational lag,** the time period from the passage of new legislation to the final change in the equilibrium level of national income. The operational lag has two distinct stages: (1) the time required to change expenditures or taxes once the legislation to do so has been enacted and (2) the length of the multiplier process. Fiscal policies cannot affect the economy until the expenditures or taxes are actually changed. Once the changes occur, the multiplier process determines how quickly changes in government expenditures and taxes affect the circular flow of economic activity.

CHANGING EXPENDITURES AND TAXES Government purchases, especially military and public works projects, are often very difficult to change quickly. Sophisticated military weapons systems and major construction projects such as highways or public office buildings take years to complete. Congress passes legislation that authorizes and appropriates the expenditures in one year, and then the actual expenditures take place over a period of years. Perhaps the outstanding example is the federal interstate highway system. Funds for the interstate system were appropriated in 1956, yet parts of the interstate are still not completed! The long operational lags involved with most government purchases virtually rule them out as a tool for fine tuning the economy.

The time required to change transfer payments depends on exactly what is being changed. Consider public assistance as an example. The lags could be quite long if the legislation changes the eligibility rules, which determine who qualifies for welfare. Each state or local welfare office would have to review both its existing caseload and potential new cases before new welfare checks could be written. In contrast, a simple increase in the monthly benefit levels could be enacted within a month.

A common anti-recession policy is the extension of the time period that the unemployed can receive unemployment insurance, typically from the standard period of 26 weeks to 39 weeks or even a year. Extending unemployment

[3]J. Pechman, *Federal Tax Policy* (Washington, D.C.: The Brookings Institution, 1966), Ch. 3 and Table 3.1, p. 32.

insurance can lead to increases in unemployment benefits within a month or two.

Changes in the personal income tax can also occur very quickly because the majority of taxpayers have taxes withheld from their paychecks. Payroll offices can easily change the amount of taxes withheld within a month or two after the legislation is enacted.

THE MULTIPLIER PROCESS The final lag in the conduct of fiscal policy is the multiplier process. We saw earlier in the chapter that the multiplier process is reasonably quick. The majority of the multiplier works its way through the economy well within a year's time.

Add up the recognition, administrative, and operational lags and the conclusion is clear: Fiscal policy is unlikely to be able to fine tune the economy. The best it can hope to do is "lean against the wind" to help prevent an economic disaster, and most economists are convinced that fiscal policy is flexible enough to do this.

A Long-Standing Tax Proposal

The most serious lag in the conduct of fiscal policy is the lengthy and cumbersome administrative lag. For this reason many economists have long proposed that Congress give the president the power to raise or lower the personal income tax rates temporarily according to some well-defined rule that is based on the performance of the economy. For example, the administration could cut the tax rates by any amount up to 10 percent for one year if real GDP falls for two consecutive quarters. Alternatively, the administration could raise the tax rates by any amount up to 10 percent for one year if inflation exceeds 10 percent. The idea is that an automatic tax rule would circumvent the administrative lag and be an effective countercyclical policy tool. The administration could act quickly in response to a problem, actual tax collections could be changed within a month or two, and these changes in taxes would have a powerful, multiplied effect on the economy.

Many economists now believe that an automatic tax rule would not be very effective. The issue turns on the last point, that changes in taxes have a powerful, multiplied effect on the economy. Tax changes do have a powerful, multiplied effect if they are viewed as permanent. But these tax changes are specifically designed to be temporary, and temporary tax changes may not change aggregate demand very much.

As we saw in Chapter 29, the Life-Cycle Hypothesis suggests that households distinguish between permanent and temporary changes in their disposable income. They increase their consumption by almost the full amount of a permanent change, whereas they hardly increase their consumption at all in response to a temporary change. Temporary increases or decreases in disposable income mostly lead to temporary increases or decreases in saving. In other words, the MPC from a temporary change in disposable income is very low, close to zero. If this is true, then the tax multiplier is also quite small. Temporary tax changes cannot change aggregate demand or the equilibrium level of national income very much at all.

The federal government has given economists two good opportunities to put the Life-Cycle Hypothesis to the test with regard to taxation. In 1968 the government enacted a 10 percent across-the-board increase in the personal income tax rates to counteract inflationary pressures that had been building in the economy. The increase took effect in July of 1968 and was to be removed at the end of 1970. In 1975, Congress enacted a one-time 10 percent rebate of 1974 tax payments with a ceiling of $200 to help pull the economy out of the recession. Taxpayers knew at the outset that both the 1968 tax surcharge and the 1975 tax rebate were temporary. Studies of these events strongly suggest that the MPC out of temporary tax changes is much less than the MPC out of permanent tax changes, as predicted from the Life-Cycle Hypothesis. The estimates range from MPC = 0 (temporary tax changes only affect saving) to MPC = 0.5 (half of a temporary tax decrease is consumed, half is saved), with the majority of the estimates near the low end.[4]

These studies suggest that giving the administration the discretion to change tax rates temporarily according to a set rule may not be an effective countercyclical policy tool. Suppose that the "temporary" MPC is only .20. Then the "temporary" tax multiplier is only (−).25 [$M_{\text{Tax}} = (-)\text{MPC}/(1 - \text{MPC}) = (-)0.20/(1 - 0.20) = (-)0.20/0.80 = (-).25$]. With a tax multiplier this low, temporary tax rate changes on the order of 5 to 10 percent would change the equilibrium level of national income by about $10 billion, a change hardly noticeable in a $6 trillion economy.

The issue is moot in any event, since Congress has never been willing to give up any of its tax powers to the administration. The United States will have to live with the long administrative lag associated with changes in tax policy.

SUMMARY

Chapter 30 began with a description of the macroeconomic policy problem that the federal government tries to solve with its fiscal and monetary policies.

1. The essence of the policy problem is that aggregate demand may not lead the economy to a very desirable equilibrium level of national income. For example, the equilibrium may be well below the production possibilities frontier, with high levels of unemployment. Alternatively, aggregate demand may try to bring the economy beyond its production possibilities frontier, leading to inflation.
2. The conduct of fiscal or monetary policy is a three-step process.
   a. First, policy makers must set a target level of national income that represents the best compromise among the four macroeconomic policy goals of long-run economic growth, full employment, low inflation, and a zero balance of trade and stable value of the dollar.
   b. Then policy makers need a model of the economy that indicates (i) what the equilibrium would be without any dose of policy, (ii) how the economy would respond to specific fiscal or monetary policies, and (iii) how changes in the equilibrium would affect the four macroeconomic policy goals.

[4]For a review of the literature on the different reactions to permanent and temporary changes in taxes and transfers, see R. Hall and J. Taylor, *Macroeconomics: Theory, Performance, and Policy*, second edition (New York: Norton, 1988), 211–212. Also: A. Blinder and A. Deaton, "The Time Series Consumption Function Revisited," *Brookings Papers on Economic Activity* 2 (1985): 465–511; J. Poterba, "Are Consumers Forward Looking? Evidence from Fiscal Experiments," *American Economic Review* 78, No. 2 (May 1988): 413–417.

c. The final step is designing fiscal and/or monetary policies to meet the target level of national income. Fiscal and monetary policies are called aggregate demand management because they change aggregate demand to move the equilibrium to the target level of national income. Expansionary fiscal and monetary policies increase aggregate demand. Contractionary fiscal and monetary policies decrease aggregate demand.

The second section of Chapter 30 described the spending multiplier.

3. The spending multiplier, labeled M_{Spending}, relates changes in the equilibrium level of national income to changes or shifts in aggregate demand. A change in aggregate demand leads to a multiplied change in the equilibrium level of national income because of the feedback between national income and consumption demand. An increase in national income increases disposable income, which increases consumption demand, which further increases national income, and so on, round by round. A change or shift in any component of aggregate demand can start the round-by-round multiplier process.
4. $M_{\text{Spending}} = 1/(1 - \text{MPC})$ for the simplest economy. The higher the MPC is, the higher M_{Spending} is, and vice versa. Also, the multiplier process is symmetric. Equal increases and decreases in aggregate demand lead to equal multiplied increases and decreases in the equilibrium level of national income.

The third section of the chapter added the government sector to the simplest model and explored the various options for fiscal policy.

5. Fiscal policy consists of changes in government demand for goods and services (government purchases), transfer payments, or taxes made with the intention of changing the equilibrium level of national income.
6. Government purchases are part of aggregate demand. The equilibrium condition for an economy consisting of the household, business, and government sectors is that the level of national income equals the sum of consumption demand, investment demand, and government demand for goods and services. $Y = C^d + I^d + G^d$.
7. The spending multiplier applies to changes in government purchases because government purchases are part of aggregate demand.
8. Taxes and transfers are not part of aggregate demand. Nonetheless, changes in taxes and transfers have a powerful, multiplied effect on the equilibrium level of national income because they affect consumption demand (and investment demand). The tax multiplier relates changes in the equilibrium level of income to changes in taxes. The transfer multiplier relates changes in the equilibrium level of income to changes in transfer payments. $M_{\text{Tax}} = (-)\text{MPC}/(1 - \text{MPC})$; $M_{\text{Transfer}} = \text{MPC}/(1 - \text{MPC})$. The tax and the transfer multipliers are smaller than the spending multiplier is because changes in taxes and transfers affect aggregate demand indirectly rather than directly, as in the case of changes in government purchases. The Concept Summary table on page 898 lists the various fiscal policy multipliers.

The final section of Chapter 30 discussed the three time lags involved with the actual conduct of fiscal policy: the recognition, administrative, and operational lags.

9. The recognition lag is the time required for policy makers to recognize that the economy is in trouble and needs a dose of fiscal (or monetary) policy. The length of this lag depends in part on the ability to forecast the future performance of the economy, which is an uncertain art at best.
10. The administrative lag is the time between the recognition of a problem and the passage of legislation that changes government purchases, transfer payments, or taxes. The administrative lag is very long for fiscal policy, often a year or more.
11. The operational lag is the time from the change in the legislation to the change in the equilibrium level of national income. It has two parts: (a) the time required to actually change government expenditures or revenues and (b) the length of the multiplier process. Government purchases often take years to change. The time required to change transfer payments and tax revenues depends on the nature of the legislated changes. Changes in tax rates, or extensions of unemployment insurance benefits, can occur within a month or two. Fundamental structural changes in transfer programs or taxes may take much longer. Once the fiscal changes are made, the multiplier process works fairly quickly.
12. The combined time lags are considerable, long enough to rule out fiscal policy as a means of fine tuning the economy, that is, keeping the equilibrium level of national income close to the target level at all times. The best fiscal policy can hope to do is "lean against the wind" and help prevent an economic disaster such as the Great Depression or a hyperinflation.
13. Tempoary changes in taxes and transfer payments intended to increase or decrease aggregate demand have been used on occasion in the United States. Research suggests that these policies have not been very successful because the MPC out of temporary tax changes appears to be very low, probably much less than one-half, in line with the prediction of the Life-Cycle Hypothesis. A low MPC implies a low tax multiplier and not much effect on aggregate demand.

KEY TERMS

administrative lag (fiscal policy)
balanced budget change
balanced budget multiplier
contractionary policy
countercyclical policy
expansionary policy
fine tuning
inflationary gap
operational lag (fiscal policy)
recessionary gap
recognition lag (fiscal or monetary policy)
spending multiplier
tax multiplier
transfer multiplier

QUESTIONS

1. What is expansionary fiscal policy? Contractionary fiscal policy? Give some examples of each. During his first year in office President Clinton proposed, and Congress approved, cutting government expenditures by about $250 billion and increasing taxes by about $250 billion over the five-year period from 1993 to 1998. Is this policy expansionary or contractionary?
2. a. Describe the steps involved in making macroeconomic policy.
   b. Why is making policy as much an art as a science? For example, why might two different policy makers with access to the same data on the economy reach different conclusions about what fiscal policy to pursue?
3. Use the spending multiplier to calculate the change in na-

tional income that would result from a $200 decrease in government spending. Assume that the MPC = 0.90.

4. Explain why an increase in aggregate demand of $1 leads to more than a $1 increase in the equilibrium level of national income.
5. a. Calculate the change in national income if the government increases its transfer payments by $500 and finances the transfers by issuing debt. Assume that the MPC = 0.75.
   b. How would your answer change if the transfers were financed by a $500 increase in taxes?
6. Suppose that the economy is at the full-employment level of national income and the federal government cuts defense spending by $100 billion. By how much must the government change taxes, and in what direction, to keep the economy at the full-employment level of national income? Assume that the MPC = 2/3.
7. Suppose that the equilibrium level of national income is $1,000 and the full-employment level of income is $1,500.
   a. Is the economy experiencing an inflationary gap or a recessionary gap?
   b. Represent this situation on the *ADE*–45° line graph, and show the size of the gap on your diagram.
   c. Calculate the size of the gap, assuming that the MPC = 0.80.
   d. Describe two fiscal policies that would close the gap, and indicate why they would work.
8. a. Describe the three lags in the conduct of fiscal policy.
   b. Why do these lags suggest that the federal government is unable to fine tune the economy with fiscal policies? Be sure to indicate what it means to fine tune the economy.
9. The text assumed that government spending on goods and services (*G*) is unrelated to the level of national income.
   a. Why is this a reasonable assumption for a macro model?
   b. What components of *G*, either federal or state/local, do you think might possibly be related to national income and why?
10. Why is it so much more difficult for state governments to control their economies than it is for the federal government to control the national economy?
11. You are given the following diagrams representing consumption demand (C^d), investment demand (I^d), and government spending on goods and services (G^d). How would you put these diagrams together to find the equilibrium level of national income?

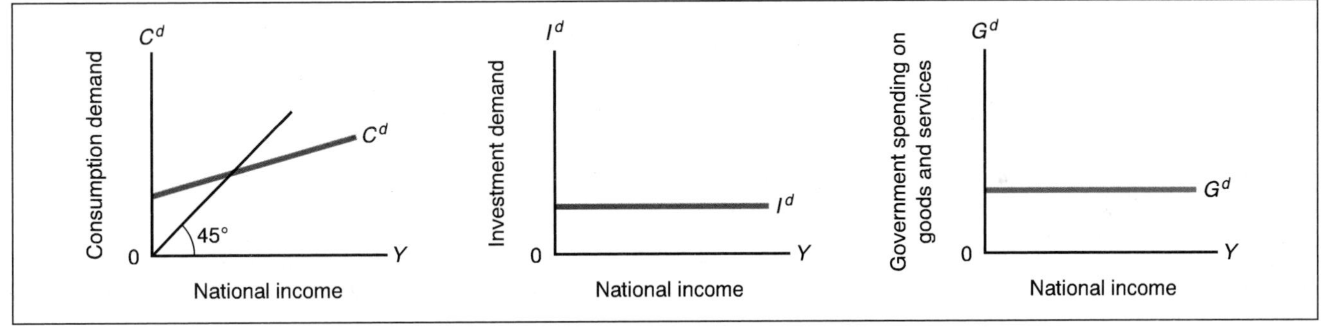

APPENDIX

30

Algebra of the Spending Multiplier and the Fiscal Policy Multipliers

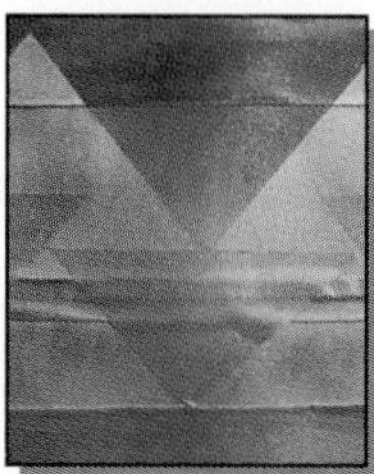

The appendix derives algebraically the various multipliers presented in Chapter 30.

THE SPENDING MULTIPLIER IN THE SIMPLEST ECONOMY

The equilibrium condition in the simplest economy with only the household and the business sectors is

$$Y = C^d + I^d$$

The Keynesian consumption function, C^d, is

$$C^d = C_0 + \text{MPC} \cdot Y$$

Investment demand is a constant independent of gross domestic product (GDP)/national income:

$$I^d = \bar{I}$$

Substitute the equations for C^d and I^d into the equilibrium condition, and solve for the equilibrium, Y_E.

$$
\begin{aligned}
Y &= C_0 + (\text{MPC} \cdot Y) + \bar{I} \\
Y - (\text{MPC} \cdot Y) &= C_0 + \bar{I} \\
Y \cdot (1 - \text{MPC}) &= C_0 + \bar{I} \\
Y_E &= [1/(1 - \text{MPC})] \cdot (C_0 + \bar{I})
\end{aligned}
$$

The spending multiplier relates changes in the equilibrium level of national income to changes, or shifts, in aggregate demand. Therefore, write the equilibrium equation in terms of changes.

$$\Delta Y_E = [1/(1 - \text{MPC})] \cdot (\Delta C_0 + \Delta \bar{I})$$

ΔC_0 is the change or shift in the consumption function, $\Delta \bar{I}$ is the change or shift in investment demand, and the sum of $\Delta C_0 + \Delta \bar{I}$ equals the shift in aggregate demand. $M_{\text{Spending}} = 1/(1 - \text{MPC})$. The MPC in our simplest economy is .80, so that $M_{\text{Spending}} = 5$ $[5 = 1/(1 - 0.8) = 1/0.2]$. The multiplier equation indicates that the spending multiplier applies equally to changes in consumption demand and investment demand.

THE FISCAL POLICY MULTIPLIERS

Adding the government sector to our model involves two changes. First, government purchases of goods and services, G^d, are part of aggregate demand. Therefore, the equilibrium condition with the government sector is

$$Y = C^d + I^d + G^d$$

We are assuming that G^d is a constant independent of national income.

$$G^d = \overline{G}$$

$\overline{G} = 1{,}000$ in our simple economy.

Second, taxes and transfers drive a wedge between national income, Y, and disposable income, Y_d.

$$Y_d = Y - Tx + Tr$$

Consumption demand is related to disposable income, not national income.

$$C^d = C_0 + (\text{MPC} \cdot Y_d)$$

Substituting the equation for disposable income into the consumption demand equation gives consumption demand in terms of *national income.*

$$C^d = C_0 + [\text{MPC} \cdot (Y - Tx + Tr)]$$

Also, I^d is a constant in our simple economy.

$$I^d = \bar{I} \ (= 600)$$

Substitute C^d, I^d, and G^d into the equilibrium condition, and solve for the equilibrium, Y_E. Note that C^d must be expressed in terms of national income, not disposable income.

$$\begin{aligned}
Y &= C_0 + [\text{MPC} \cdot (Y - Tx + Tr)] + \bar{I} + \bar{G} \\
Y &= C_0 + (\text{MPC} \cdot Y) - (\text{MPC} \cdot Tx) + (\text{MPC} \cdot Tr) + \bar{I} + \bar{G} \\
Y - (\text{MPC} \cdot Y) &= C_0 - (\text{MPC} \cdot Tx) + (\text{MPC} \cdot Tr) + \bar{I} + \bar{G} \\
Y \cdot (1 - \text{MPC}) &= (C_0 + \bar{I} + \bar{G}) - (\text{MPC} \cdot Tx) + (MPC \cdot Tr) \\
Y_E &= \{[1/(1 - \text{MPC})] \cdot (C_0 + \bar{I} + \bar{G})\} \\
&\quad + \{[-\text{MPC}/(1 - \text{MPC})] \cdot Tx\} + \{[\text{MPC}/(1 - \text{MPC})] \cdot Tr\}
\end{aligned}$$

Write the equilibrium equation in terms of changes to determine the various fiscal policy multipliers.

$$\begin{aligned}
\Delta Y_E &= \{[1/(1 - \text{MPC})] \cdot (\Delta C_0 + \Delta\bar{I} + \Delta\bar{G})\} \\
&\quad + \{[-\text{MPC}/(1 - \text{MPC})] \cdot \Delta Tx\} + \{[\text{MPC}/(1 - \text{MPC})] \cdot \Delta Tr\}
\end{aligned}$$

$M_{\text{Spending}} = 1/(1 - \text{MPC})$ and applies to changes in G^d, as well as to changes in consumption demand and investment demand.

$M_{\text{Tax}} = -\text{MPC}/(1 - \text{MPC})$ and applies to changes in taxes.

$M_{\text{Transfer}} = \text{MPC}/(1 - \text{MPC})$ and applies to changes in transfer payments. Note that M_{Tax} and M_{Transfer} are both MPC as large as M_{Spending} and that $M_{\text{Tax}} = (-)\, M_{\text{Transfer}}$.

For an MPC = .80,

$$\begin{aligned}
M_{\text{Spending}} &= 1/(1 - \text{MPC}) = 1/(1 - 0.8) = 1/0.2 = 5 \\
M_{\text{Tax}} &= -\text{MPC}/(1 - \text{MPC}) = -0.8/(1 - 0.8) = -0.8/0.2 = -4 \\
M_{\text{Transfer}} &= \text{MPC}/(1 - \text{MPC}) = 0.8/(1 - 0.8) = 0.8/0.2 = 4
\end{aligned}$$

The balanced budget multiplier, $M_{\Delta Gd = \Delta Tx} = 1$, combines the separate effects on Y_E of changes in G^d and Tx. The effect of ΔG^d on the equilibrium is

$$\Delta Y_E = M_{\text{Spending}} \cdot \Delta G^d = [1/(1 - \text{MPC})] \cdot \Delta G^d$$

The effect of ΔTx on the equilibrium is

$$\Delta Y_E = M_{\text{Tax}} \cdot \Delta Tx = [-\text{MPC}/(1 - \text{MPC})] \cdot \Delta Tx$$

The combined effect on the equilibrium is

$$\Delta Y_E = \{[1/(1 - \text{MPC})] \cdot \Delta G^d\} + \{[-\text{MPC}/(1 - \text{MPC})] \cdot \Delta Tx\}$$

But $\Delta G^d = \Delta Tx$ for a balanced budget change. Therefore, substitute ΔG^d for ΔTx in the equation for ΔY_E, and factor out ΔG^d.

$$\Delta Y_E = \{[1/(1 - \text{MPC})] - [\text{MPC}/(1 - \text{MPC})]\} \cdot \Delta G^d$$

Combine the two terms in the brackets, which have a common denominator.

$$\Delta Y_E = [(1 - \text{MPC})/(1 - \text{MPC})] \cdot \Delta G^d = 1 \cdot \Delta G^d$$

The balanced budget multiplier is one. The equilibrium level of national income changes by the same amount as the change in G^d (= ΔTx), and in the same direction.

QUESTIONS

a. Given the following information for an economy, find the equilibrium level of income, Y_E.

$C^d = 200 + 2/3 \cdot Y_d$	Y_d = disposable income
$I^d = 20$	Y = national income
$G^d = 70$	C^d = consumption demand
$T = 24$	I^d = investment demand
	G^d = government demand for goods and services
	T = taxes—transfer payments

b. What is the value of the spending multiplier for this economy? Of the tax multiplier? Of the$\Delta G^d = \Delta Tx$ balanced budget multiplier? (*Hint:* What is the MPC?)

c. If government spending on goods and services, G^d, decreases by 10, what will the change in Y_E be?

d. If the government matches the decrease in G^d by a cut in taxes of 10, how will your answer to part c change?

e. If the economy is at the full-employment level of income and the government increases G^d by 10, how can it change taxes to keep the economy at full employment? If government transfer payments increase by 12, by how much will the equilibrium level of income change? If the government increases taxes by 12 to finance the transfer payments, what will the net effect on Y_E be?
Suppose that the government decides that the target level of income is 900. Relative to the equilibrium computed in part a, is the economy experiencing a recessionary or an inflationary gap? What is the size of the gap? Design two government policies that will eliminate the gap.

CHAPTER

31

Automatic Stabilizers, Net Exports, and Budget Deficits

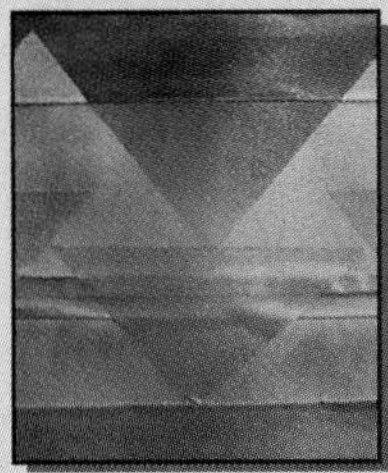

LEARNING OBJECTIVES

CONCEPTS TO LEARN

Automatic stabilizers
Marginal propensity to import
Cyclical budget deficit
Structural budget deficit
The burden of the federal debt

CONCEPTS TO RECALL

Dollar depreciation/appreciation [26]
Net exports [26, 27]
The total saving = investment accounting identity [27]
Fiscal policy [28, 30]
Marginal propensity to consume [29]
Equilibrium level of national income [29]

The great policy dilemma of the 1990s centers on the combination of a sluggish economy and large federal budget deficits.

Most economists believe that the large federal deficits are very bad for the economy. They reduce saving, investment, productivity, and long-run economic growth, and in doing so they place a tremendous burden on future generations who are helpless to defend themselves politically. Yet reductions in the deficit require either cuts in government spending or increases in taxes, or both. We just saw in Chapter 30 that both spending cuts and tax increases have powerful, multiplied depressing effects on the economy.

President Clinton opted for going after the deficit. His first major macroeconomic policy initiative was a five-year, $500 billion deficit reduction plan containing approximately equal amounts of spending reductions and tax increases. His deficit reduction plan just barely squeaked by the Senate and the House in the summer of 1993. Clinton's plan has merit; the deficit will have to be reduced sooner or later, and the benefits of reducing the deficit appear to be substantial over the long haul. But the members of Congress were a tough sell, in large part because they knew that deficit reduction of this magnitude would almost certainly increase unemployment and cause a fair amount of economic misery over the next five years. Is the nation willing to bear the short-run costs of unemployment for the long-run benefits of deficit reduction? This may well be the leading macroeconomic question in the United States today.

The dilemma will be turned around the other way on President Clinton's other large policy initiative, health care reform. Estimates of the annual cost of a comprehensive federal health care program are on the order of $100 to $150 billion. Will Congress enact such a program, given the large budget deficit? Time will tell whether the federal government stays the course on reducing the budget deficit.

Chapter 29 demonstrated the feedback nature of the new Keynesian model, which occurs through the relationship of consumption demand to disposable income. Consumption demand is not the only channel through which national income feeds back to aggregate demand, however. Changes in national income directly affect business saving in the business sector, tax collections and transfer payments in the government sector, and imports in the foreign sector.

These other three channels of feedback differ from the consumption feedback channel in one very important respect. The consumption demand channel makes national income highly sensitive to changes in aggregate demand. It is the basis of the spending multiplier by which an increase in aggregate demand leads to a multiplied increase in national income. The other three feedback channels have the opposite effect. They are called automatic stabilizers because they make national income less sensitive to changes in aggregate demand. They lower the value of the spending multiplier.

Chapter 31 develops the three remaining feedback channels from national income to aggregate demand. The most important of the three in the U.S. economy is the feedback through taxes and transfers in the government sector. Not only is this feedback the most important automatic stabilizer, but also it has a sizable impact on the federal government's budget deficit, one of the leading macroeconomic issues of the day.

The federal government began running huge budget deficits in the first years of President Reagan's administration and has continued to do so ever since. President Reagan inherited a public debt of approximately $1 trillion. By 1993 the public debt had surpassed $4 trillion and was increasing even more rapidly than during the Reagan years. Much has been written about the evils of the huge federal budget deficits and the ever-expanding public debt, some fact and some fiction. You cannot begin to separate fact from fiction until you understand how the economy feeds back into the federal budget deficit through its effect on taxes and transfers.

Chapter 31 begins with an analysis of the automatic stabilizers. In the process we will complete our new Keynesian model of the economy by adding net exports to aggregate demand.

AUTOMATIC STABILIZERS

An **automatic stabilizer** is any component of the economy that is related to the level of national income and lowers the value of the spending multiplier. As such, an automatic stabilizer stabilizes the economy by making it less responsive to aggregate demand shocks. The lower the value of the spending multiplier is, the less the equilibrium level of national income changes in response to an increase or a decrease in aggregate demand. Also, an automatic stabilizer is automatic in the sense that its stabilizing effect is built into the economy. It is not the result of any conscious decision by government policy makers or anyone else.

AUTOMATIC STABILIZER
Any component of the economy that is related to the level of national income and lowers the value of the spending multiplier; automatic stabilizers make the economy less responsive to aggregate demand shocks.

The four principal automatic stabilizers in the U.S. economy are taxes, transfer payments, business saving, and imports.

Taxes

The federal, state, and local governments collected nearly $1.8 trillion of taxes in 1992, approximately 38 percent of the national income. Whatever other economic effects these taxes may have, they are far and away the most important automatic stabilizer in the U.S. economy.

Our analysis of the tax multiplier in Chapter 30 assumed that governments can raise any given amount of tax revenue that they want to during the course of a year. The specific example in the chapter was a $100 billion federal tax increase. The hidden assumption we made there to illustrate the tax multiplier is that the federal government is continually adjusting the structure of its taxes behind the scenes to hit its revenue target. The **tax structure** consists of the tax rates and the tax base, that is, which items of income or output are subject to tax, and which are exempt from tax.

TAX STRUCTURE
The tax rates and the tax base of any particular tax.

In fact, governments do not continually adjust the tax structure during the course of the year. They set the tax structure and let the tax revenues fall where they may. The result is that tax collections are directly related to the state of the economy. Tax revenues rise when national income increases and fall when national income decreases, as illustrated in Figure 31.1.

The horizontal axis records the level of national income, and the vertical axis records the total tax revenues collected by the federal, state, and local governments. The line, *Tx*, shows the total tax revenues collected at each level

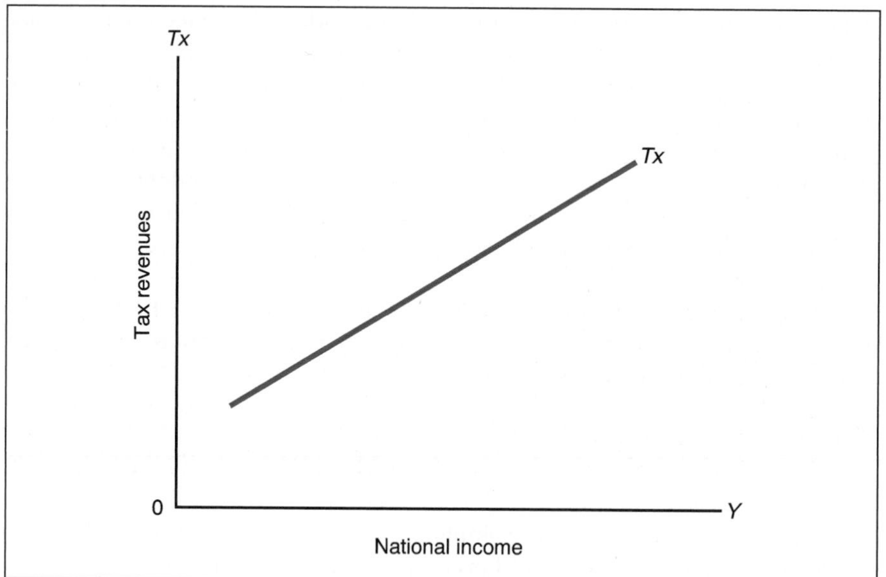

FIGURE 31.1

Tax Revenues and National Income

Four of the five major taxes in the United States—the federal and state personal income taxes, the payroll tax for Social Security, the federal and state corporation income taxes, and the state sales taxes—all tax components of the circular flow of economic activity. Therefore, tax revenues vary directly with the level of national income. The upward-sloping line, *Tx*, shows the direct relationship between tax revenues and national income. National income, *Y*, is on the horizontal axis and tax revenues, *Tx*, are on the vertical axis. An increase in national income increases tax revenues and a decrease in national income decreases tax revenues.

of national income. *Tx* is upward sloping to indicate that tax revenues rise and fall along with the state of the economy. The straight line, *Tx*, actually understates somewhat the sensitivity of tax revenues to the economy. A 1 percent increase in national income raises tax revenues by slightly more than 1 percent.

The reason why tax revenues vary directly with the sate of the economy is obvious just from listing the five major taxes in the United States (in order of importance): the federal and the state personal income taxes, the federal Social Security payroll tax, general sales and excise taxes (primarily state), the property tax (primarily local), and the federal and the state corporation income taxes. The personal income, payroll, and corporation income taxes are levied on all or part of the national income received in the factor markets, and the general sales and excise taxes are levied on sales in the product markets. The revenues collected by these taxes clearly depend on the circular flow of economic activity. The property tax is the one exception among the five taxes. It is not directly related to the circular flow because it is a levy on wealth, not income. Even so, property values do tend to rise and fall with the state of the economy.

Taxes act as an automatic stabilizer because they are a drain on aggregate demand. Suppose that aggregate demand increases and national income begins to increase round by round in the multiplier process. The additional tax dollars siphoned off by the government each round as national income increases reduce households' disposable income, which reduces their consumption demand. As a result, the increases in national income during each round of the multiplier process are less than they would be if tax collections were unrelated to national income. The value of the spending multiplier declines.

True, governments might spend the additional tax revenues on government purchases or transfer payments, but what governments do with the tax revenues is a separate issue. They might also choose to retire some of their debt. The point is that the tax revenues in and of themselves act as a drain on aggregate demand that reduces consumption demand and partially offsets the multiplier process.

TABLE 31.1 **The Multiplier Process Round by Round ($ billion)**

ROUND	CHANGE IN INVESTMENT DEMAND (ΔI^d)	CHANGE IN CONSUMPTION DEMAND (ΔC^d)	CHANGE IN NATIONAL INCOME (ΔY)	CHANGE IN TAX REVENUES ($\Delta Tx = .25 \cdot \Delta Y$)	CHANGE IN DISPOSABLE INCOME ($\Delta Y_d = \Delta Y - \Delta Tx$)
1	$100	$—	$100	$.25 \cdot \$100 = \$25$	$75
			+		
2	—	$.80 \cdot \$75 = \$60$	60	$.25 \cdot \$\ 60 = \$15$	45
			+		
3	—	$.80 \cdot \$45 = \$36$	36	$.25 \cdot \$\ 36 = \$\ 9$	27
			+		
4					
⋮		⋮	⋮		
		FinalΔY	= $250		

We can see how income and sales taxes act as an automatic stabilizer by expanding our round-by-round example of the multiplier process from Chapter 29, which was represented in Table 29.2. Recall that the example begins with a $100 (billion) increase in investment demand and that the marginal propensity to consume (MPC) is .80. We assumed in Chapter 29 that the government changed the tax structure behind the scenes to keep tax revenues constant. Table 31.1 represents the multiplier process under the more realistic assumption of a fixed tax structure and automatically changing tax revenues.

Columns two through four in the table are the same as in Table 29.2: the change in investment demand (second column), the change in consumption demand (third column), and the change in national income (fourth column). Table 31.1 adds the change in taxes (fifth column) and the change in disposable income (sixth column) each round. Our new example assumes that the change in taxes each round is 0.25 (25 percent) times the change in national income, which is roughly the case for all taxes combined in the United States. Twenty-five percent is called the *marginal tax rate,* the tax rate on additional income. The change in disposable income each round (sixth column) is the difference between the change in national income (fourth column) and the change in taxes (fifth column). The MPC out of *disposable income* is .80.

The multiplier process begins, as in our previous example, with a $100 increase in investment demand. Producers of investment goods increase production to meet the new demand, and national income increases by $100 in the first round, just as before (fourth column, first row). Rounds two and beyond are different, however. The government now takes 25 percent of the $100 increase in national income for taxes. Tax revenues increase by $25 (fifth column, first row) ($\$25 = .25 \cdot \$100$). Households are left with a $75 increase in disposable income (sixth column, first row) ($\$75 = \$100 - \$25$).

Households base their consumption demand in the second round on the increase in their *disposable income,* not on the increase in national income. Therefore, the increase in consumption demand in the second round is $MPC \cdot \Delta Y_d$, or $60 (third column, second row) ($\$60 = 0.80 \cdot \$75$). Producers of consumer goods increase production to meet the new consumption demand, and national income increases by $60 in the second round (fourth column, second row). The government takes 25 percent of the $60 increase in national income for taxes. Tax revenues increase by $15 (fifth column, second row)

(.25 · \$60 = \$15). Households are left with a \$45 increase in disposable income (sixth column, second row) (\$45 = \$60 − \$15).

Households' consumption demand in the third round increases by MPC · ΔY_d, or \$36 (third column, third row) (0.80 · \$45 = \$36). Producers of consumer goods increase production to meet the new consumption demand, and national income increases by \$36 in the third round (fourth column, third row). The multiplier process continues in this way indefinitely.

The change in national income after three rounds is the sum of the entries in the fourth column: ΔY = \$100 + \$60 + \$36 = \$196. Compare this with the \$244 change in national income after three rounds in our previous example without income and sales taxes: ΔY = \$100 + \$80 + \$64 = \$244. The 25 percent tax rate on additional national income substantially lowers the increase in consumption demand and national income from the second round on.

The final change in the equilibrium level of national income with a 25 percent marginal tax rate turns out to be \$250, compared with \$500 in our previous example. The income and the sales taxes are a very potent automatic stabilizer, indeed. They lower the value of the spending multiplier by 50 percent, from 5 to 2.5. National income is only half as responsive to the change in aggregate demand in our model with a built-in 25 percent marginal tax rate.

Transfer Payments

Government transfer payments, unlike taxes, are contributors to aggregate demand. Transfer payments increase households' disposable incomes and their consumption demand. Nonetheless, some government transfer payments act as an automatic stabilizer because they are inversely, or negatively, related to the level of national income, as shown in Figure 31.2.

The horizontal axis records the level of national income, and the vertical axis records the total amount of government transfer payments, most of which are federal. The line, *Tr*, shows the total level of government transfer payments at every level of national income. *Tr* is downward sloping to indicate that government transfer payments move inversely to the state of the economy. Transfer payments increase when national income decreases and decrease when national income increases.

The two most important transfer programs that vary with the economy are unemployment insurance and public assistance ("welfare"), particularly Food Stamps, Aid to Families with Dependent Children (AFDC), and Medicaid. Unemployment rises when the economy goes into a recession, and more people apply for unemployment insurance benefits. Conversely, unemployment falls when the economy is booming, and fewer people apply for unemployment insurance benefits. Unemployment insurance benefits rose to approximately \$25 billion during the depths of the 1981–82 recession. By 1987, when the economy had returned to its production possibilities frontier, unemployment insurance benefits had fallen to \$15 billion.[1]

Similarly, unemployment is one of the two events that is most likely to cause a spell of poverty in a family (separation of husband and wife is the other).

---

[1]Executive Office of the President of the United States, *Budget of the United States Government, Fiscal Year 1993, Supplement, February 1992* (Washington, D.C.: U.S. Government Printing Office, 1992), Part Five: Historical Tables, Table 11.1, p. 5–136.

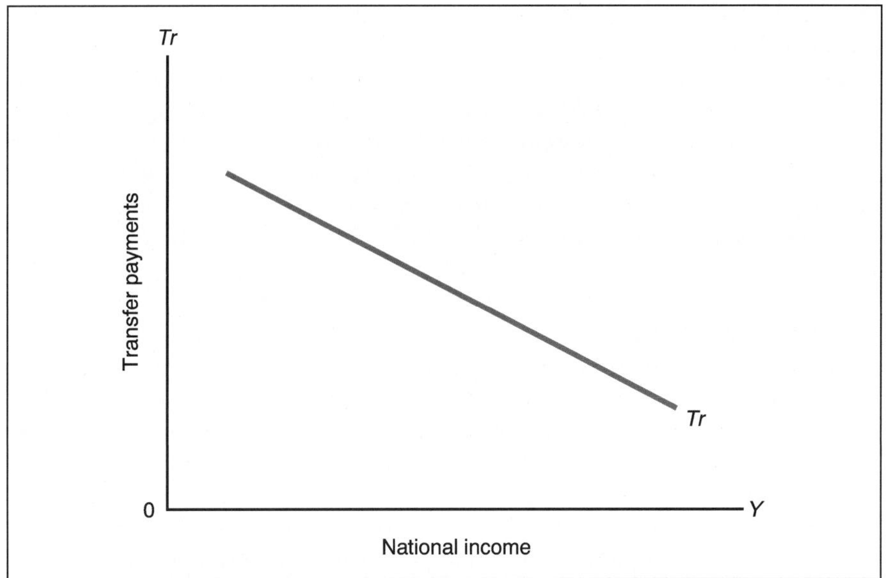

FIGURE 31.2

Transfer Payments and National Income

Some transfer programs, such as Unemployment Insurance and Public Assistance, are sensitive to the level of national income. When national income decreases and people lose their jobs, unemployment insurance benefits and public assistance payments increase. The reverse is true when national income increases and more people are employed. The downward-sloping line, *Tr*, shows the inverse relationship between transfer payments and national income. National income, *Y*, is on the horizontal axis and transfer payments, *Tr*, are on the vertical axis. An increase in national income decreases transfer payments and a decrease in national income increases transfer payments.

The poverty rate rises when the economy is in a recession, and more people apply for Food Stamps and AFDC. People who qualify for AFDC automatically qualify for Medicaid benefits, so Medicaid costs increase as well. The reverse is true when the economy recovers and the poverty rate falls. Public assistance does not respond to the state of the economy as strongly as unemployment insurance does, but public assistance is definitely inversely related to the level of national income.

To see why government transfer programs such as unemployment insurance and public assistance act as an automatic stabilizer, return to our multiplier example above with transfer payments substituted for taxes. Suppose that government transfer payments *decrease* by 25 percent of the *increase* in national income. In other words, when national income increases by $100 in the first round, unemployment insurance benefits, public assistance, and other income-sensitive government transfer payments decrease by a total of $25. The analysis carries through exactly as above. With transfer payments down by $25, households' disposable income has increased by only $75, equal to the $100 increase in earned national income minus the $25 decrease in transfer payments. Therefore, consumption in the second round increases by .80 · $75 = $60, and so on, as before. The final change in the equilibrium level of national income is once again $250.

The actual marginal transfer rate is much less than 25 percent in the United States. Government transfer payments are not nearly as important an automatic stabilizer in the United States as taxes are. The combined spending on unemployment insurance, public assistance, and other income-sensitive transfer payments was approximately $250 billion in 1992, far less than the $1.8 trillion of tax revenues.[2] Nonetheless, our example indicates why income-sensitive

[2]*Budget of the United States Government,* Part Five: Historical Tables, Tables 3.2, 11.1, and 11.2.

government transfer payments automatically lower the value of the spending multiplier.

The tax and transfer examples point out an important principle relating to automatic stabilizers: *Any drain on aggregate demand that is directly (positively) related to national income acts as an automatic stabilizer.* Taxes are an example.

Conversely, *any contributor to aggregate demand that is inversely (negatively) related to national income acts as an automatic stabilizer.* Government transfer programs such as unemployment insurance and public assistance are examples.

Business Saving

Business saving, the retained earnings of corporations, is another important automatic stabilizer in the U.S. economy. As with taxes, business saving is a drain on aggregate demand that is directly (positively) related to national income.

Corporate profits before taxes are the most volatile component of national income. Also, corporate profits are usually the first component to change when the growth in national income increases or decreases. For example, the current dollar value of national income increased each year throughout the 1980s, within a range of 3.1 percent (1981) to 11.4 percent (1984). In contrast, corporate profits before taxes increased in the five years when the rate of growth in national income was increasing and decreased in the five years when the rate of growth in national income was decreasing.

The corporation income taxes paid on corporate profits are an automatic stabilizer and have already been accounted for in the discussion of taxes. The after-tax corporate profits have one of two destinations: They are either paid out as dividends or held as retained earnings, business saving. The dividends become part of households' disposable income, but the retained earnings do not. Therefore, retained earnings are, like taxes, a drain on aggregate demand that reduces disposable income and consumption demand.

Retained earnings are also directly, and very dramatically, related to national income. Corporations do not often change their dividend payout policies, with the result that dividends do not fluctuate very much. Dividends increased steadily each year throughout the 1980s at an average annual rate of 8.5 percent. With dividends growing fairly steadily, retained earnings bear the brunt of the swings in corporate profits. Retained earnings exhibited the same pattern as did before-tax corporate profits during the 1980s, increasing when the rate of growth in national income was increasing and decreasing when the rate of growth in national income was decreasing. But the volatility of retained earnings was much greater than that of before-tax corporate profits. The average annual rate of change in before-tax corporate profits was 11.8 percent, plus or minus, during the 1980s. The average annual rate of change in business saving was a whopping 41.4 percent, plus or minus.[3] Therefore, although business saving is a minor component of national income, its extreme sensitivity to changes in national income makes it an important automatic stabilizer in the U.S. economy.

---

[3]Council of Economic Advisors, *Economic Report of the President, 1993* (Washington, D.C.: U.S. Government Printing Office, 1993), Table B-22, p. 373.

Net Exports

The United States is the least dependent on international trade of all the developed market economies and has been throughout the entire post–World War II era. Twenty years ago U.S. exports and imports were small enough, each less than 5 percent of gross domestic product (GDP), that their macroeconomic effects could be ignored for the most part. This is no longer true. The increasing internationalization of the U.S. economy has been one of the leading economic stories over the past 30 years. Exports and imports are now about 11 percent of GDP and have a number of important effects on the U.S. economy.[4]

One of the more important is that the foreign sector has become the second largest automatic stabilizer in the United States behind taxes. The feedback from national income to aggregate demand through the foreign sector is now a significant feature of the U.S. economy. This feedback has always been important in the other developed market economies.

In order to understand why the foreign sector acts as an automatic stabilizer we need to take some time to add the foreign sector to our simple model of the economy. The demand for net exports, the difference between export demand (Ex^d) and import demand (Im^d), is the final component of aggregate demand. The foreign sector will play a key role in our analysis of the economy from here on.

NET EXPORTS AND AGGREGATE DEMAND Aggregate demand is the sum of the demands for the national product by all four sectors of the economy: the household sector (C^d), the business sector (I^d), the government sector (G^d), and the foreign sector ($Ex^d - Im^d$). Therefore, the equilibrium condition in the product markets for the entire economy is

$$Y = C^d + I^d + G^d + (Ex^d - Im^d)$$

The product market for final goods and services is in equilibrium when the value of national income (national product) generated by the producers, Y, equals the aggregate demand for the national product by all four sectors of the economy.

The two principal determinants of the demand for both exports and imports are the level of national income and the exchange rates. Let's begin with the key question that we asked of the other components of aggregate demand: How are export demand and import demand related to the level of national income?

IMPORT DEMAND AND NATIONAL INCOME The household and the business sectors both purchase a large amount of imported goods from foreign producers. Their demand for imports is such that the overall demand for U.S. imports is closely and directly (positively) related to the level of U.S. national income.

The demand for imported goods and services by U.S. households is part and parcel of their demand for consumer goods and services generally. When

[4]Council of Economic Advisors, *Economic Indicators, March 1993* (Washington, D.C.: U.S. Government Printing Office, 1993), 1.

TABLE 31.2 **Import Demand ($ billion)**

IMPORT DEMAND (Im^d)	NATIONAL INCOME (Y)
$ 50	$ 0
150	1,000
250	2,000
350	3,000
450	4,000
550	5,000
650	6,000
750	7,000
850	8,000
950	9,000
1,050	10,000
1,150	11,000
1,250	12,000
1,350	13,000

households have more disposable income, their demand for Sony televisions, German Audis, Irish sweaters, and other foreign products increases along with their demand for domestic products. Conversely, when households have less disposable income, their demand for foreign products decreases along with their demand for domestic products. Since national income and disposable income move together, the demand for U.S. imports of consumer goods and services is directly related to U.S. national income.

The link between U.S. import demand and U.S. national income is just as direct in the business sector. Approximately two-thirds of U.S. imports are raw materials, intermediate products, and capital goods purchased by U.S. producers. When U.S. firms increase production and generate more national income, they import more of these inputs from foreign firms. Conversely, when U.S. firms decrease production and generate less national income, they import fewer of these inputs from foreign firms.

In conclusion, the overall demand for U.S. imports by both U.S. households and U.S. business firms is closely and directly (positively) related to the level of national income. Table 31.2 and Figure 31.3 present a hypothetical import demand function for our simple economy.

The import demand function has the same general shape as our hypothetical consumption function from Chapter 29. It has one component that is unrelated to the level of national income and another component that is positively related to the level of national income. Refer to Table 31.2, which shows the level of imports demanded (first column) at every level of national income (second column). As before, all data are in billions of constant dollars.

Import demand is $50 when the level of national income is zero. This is the component that is unrelated to the level of national income. It is determined by other factors that affect import demand, such as exchange rates. Import demand then increases by $100 for every $1,000 increase in national income. For example, import demand is $150 when national income is $1,000; it increases by $100 to $250 when national income increases to $2,000.

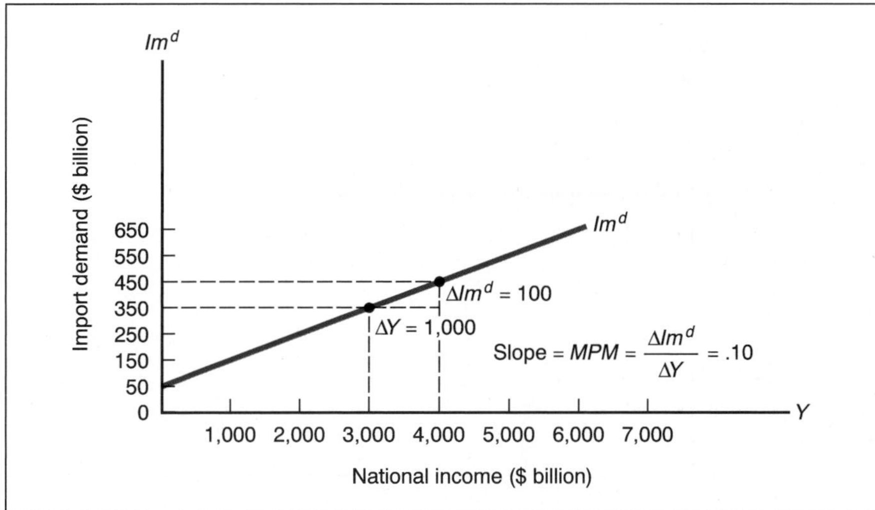

FIGURE 31.3

Import Demand and National Income

The figure is a graph of the hypothetical demand for imports in Table 31.2. National income, Y, is on the horizontal axis and the demand for imports, Im^d, is on the vertical axis. The data are in billions of constant dollars. The import demand function, Im^d, is upward sloping; imports vary directly with the level of national income. As national income rises, consumers buy more imported products and firms import more capital goods and intermediate products. The reverse is true as income falls. The slope of the import demand function is the marginal propensity to import (MPM). MPM = $\Delta Im^d/\Delta Y$. The MPM for our import demand function equals 0.10.

The **marginal propensity to import,** labeled the MPM, is analogous to the marginal propensity to consume. The MPM is the ratio of the change in import demand to the change in national income.

MARGINAL PROPENSITY TO IMPORT

The additional amount of import demand resulting from a $1 increase in national income; the ratio of the change in import demand to the change in national income.

$$\text{MPM} = \Delta Im^d/\Delta Y$$

The MPM = .10 in our example, approximately its value for the U.S. economy.

Figure 31.3 pictures our hypothetical import demand function. The vertical axis records the level of import demand, and the horizontal axis records the level of national income. The straight line, Im^d, the import demand function, shows the level of import demand at every level of national income. Im^d intersects the vertical axis at \$50, indicating that import demand is \$50 when national income is zero. The slope of Im^d, the rise over the run, is .10, the MPM. Changes in factors other than national income that affect the demand for imports, such as exchange rates, shift Im^d up or down.

EXPORT DEMAND AND NATIONAL INCOME The demand for U.S. exports is also closely related to the level of national income, but not to *U.S.* national income. U.S. exports are sales to consumers, producers, and governments in foreign countries. As such, the demand for U.S. exports is the same as the demand for U.S. imports within foreign countries. Consequently, the demand for U.S. exports is directly (positively) related to the national incomes of *foreign countries*. When the economies of Japan and Western Europe are booming, U.S. exporters find the demand for their food, computers, and airplanes increasing. Conversely, when the economies of Japan and Western Europe fall into a recession, the demand for these U.S. exports decreases.

Any connection between the demand for U.S. exports and *U.S.* national income occurs only indirectly through the effect of the U.S. economy on other economies. For instance, Canada is the leading trading partner of the United States. A booming U.S. economy tends to pull the Canadian economy along

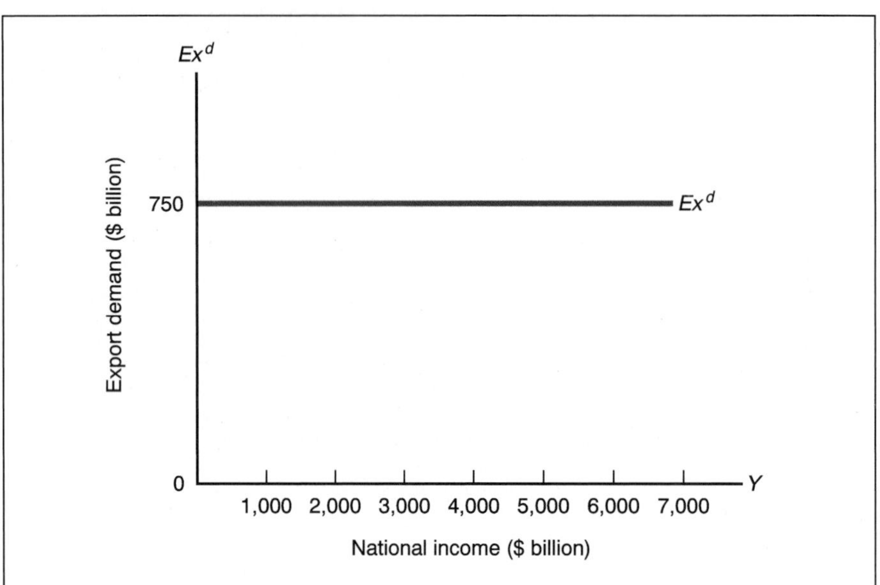

FIGURE 31.4

Export Demand and National Income

The demand for U.S. exports depends on the level of national income in foreign countries, but does not depend closely on the level of U.S. national income. Therefore, our model assumes that export demand is independent of the level of U.S. national income. In particular, we are assuming that export demand is $750 over the range of values that U.S. national income is likely to have (in billions of constant dollars). Therefore, the graph of export demand, Ex^d, is horizontal at a value of $750. Changes in factors that influence the demand for U.S. exports, such as a depreciation or appreciation of the dollar, shift Ex^d up or down.

with it because Canadian exports to the United States increase, and an increase in Canadian exports increases Canadian aggregate demand and national income. The larger Canadian national income in turn feeds back to an increased demand for U.S. exports to Canada.

The indirect relationship between U.S. exports and U.S. national income is not nearly as strong as the direct relationship between U.S. imports and U.S. national income, however. Therefore, we will assume for simplicity that the demand for U.S. exports is unrelated to the level of U.S. national income, as illustrated in Figure 31.4.

The demand for U.S. exports is assumed to be $750 (billion) at every level of U.S. national income. The export demand line, Ex^d, is horizontal at $750. The $750 is determined by factors other than U.S. national income, such as exchange rates or foreign national incomes. Changes in these other factors shift Ex^d up or down.

EQUILIBRIUM WITH THE FOREIGN SECTOR Figure 31.5 completes our model of the economy by adding net exports to the model of Chapter 30. All data are in billions of dollars, as before. The aggregate demand line, *ADE*, in Figure 30.5 for the simpler economy excludes the foreign sector. To build the new aggregate demand line from the old aggregate demand line we need to (1) add, vertically, the export demand line, Ex^d, from Figure 31.4; and (2) subtract, vertically, the import demand function, Im^d, from Figure 31.3.

Adding export demand geometrically to aggregate demand is straightforward. Since export demand is constant, $750, at every level of national income, adding Ex^d just shifts up the old *ADE* line by $750. In other words, Ex^d changes the position, but not the slope, of the *ADE* line.

Subtracting import demand vertically from aggregate demand is a bit trickier. Since import demand increases as national income increases, ever-larger amounts of import demand are subtracted from the old *ADE* line at higher

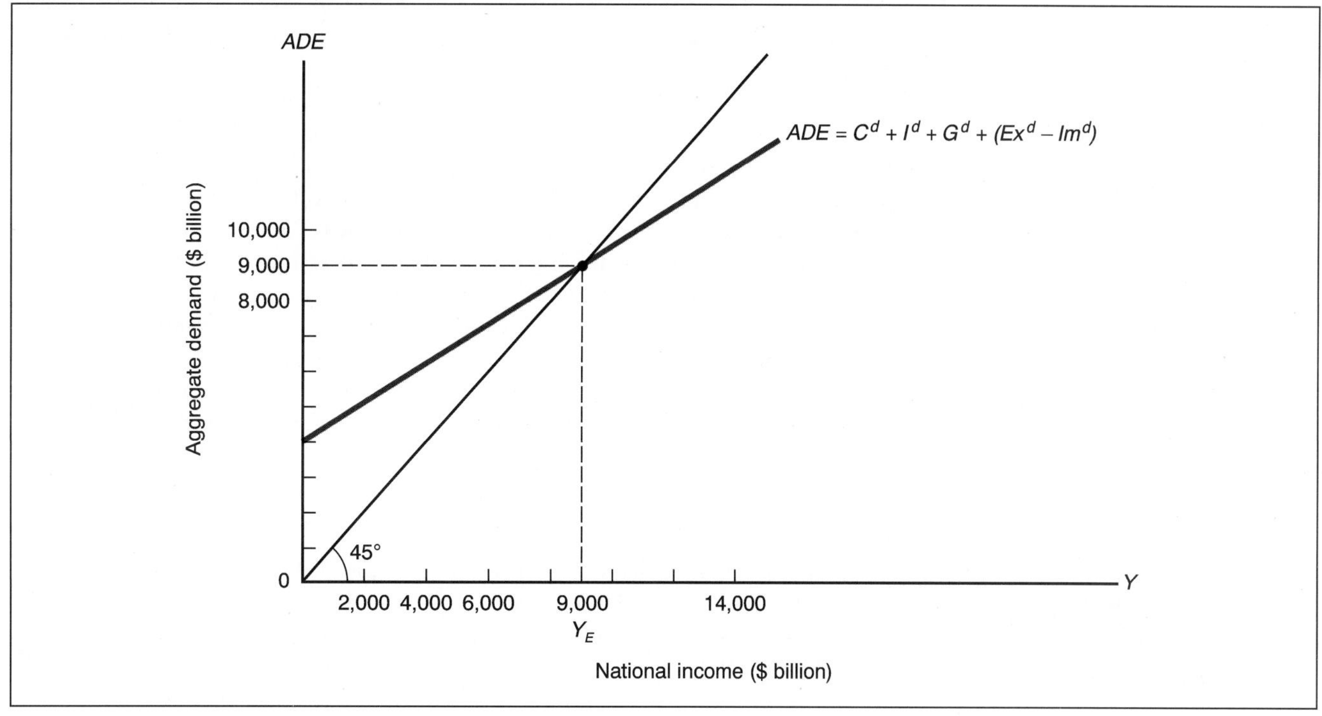

FIGURE 31.5

The Equilibrium Level of National Income in the Complete Model of the Economy

Adding the foreign sector completes the list of final demanders in the economy. *ADE*, or aggregate demand, is the sum of consumption demand by households (C^d), investment demand by business firms (I^d), government spending on goods and services by the federal, state, and local governments (G^d), and net exports in the foreign sector ($Ex^d - Im^d$). $ADE = C^d + I^d + G^d + (Ex^d - Im^d)$. As always, the equilibrium level of national income is at the intersection of the ADE and the 45-degree lines, $9,000 in our model (in billions of constant dollars). Adding the foreign sector flattens the ADE line somewhat because import demand is positively related to national income. As the level of national income increases, ever more important demand is subtracted from aggregate demand.

levels of national income. Refer to Table 31.2. At $Y = 0$, $Im^d = \$50$, so that the new *ADE* line is \$50 below the old *ADE* line. At $Y = \$5,000$, $Im^d = \$550$, so that the new *ADE* line is \$550 below the old *ADE* line. At $Y = \$12,000$, $Im^d = \$1,250$, so that the new *ADE* line is \$1,250 below the old *ADE* line. Therefore, subtracting import demand both *lowers* and *flattens* the *ADE* line. The *ADE* line for the full economy has a smaller slope than did the *ADE* line for the simpler economy without a foreign sector. We will return to the slope of the *ADE* line below.

As always, the equilibrium level of national income is at the intersection of the aggregate demand line, *ADE*, and the 45° line. $Y_E = \$9,000$ according to Figure 31.5.

NET EXPORTS AND EXCHANGE RATES We saw in Chapter 26 that changes in the dollar exchange rate for foreign currencies affect both export demand and import demand simultaneously. A brief review will be helpful.

Recall that an appreciation of the dollar is an increase in its value relative to foreign currencies. Suppose that the dollar appreciates in value from \$1.80/£ to \$1.60/£. British imports have become cheaper to U.S. households and businesses because they can now buy a pound sterling for only \$1.60 instead of \$1.80. The demand for British imports increases. Conversely, U.S. exports have become more expensive to British households and businesses because a pound now buys only \$1.60 instead of \$1.80. The demand for U.S. exports decreases.

In general, an appreciation of the dollar increases the demand for imports and decreases the demand for exports. It shifts Im^d upward in Figure 31.3, and it shifts Ex^d downward in Figure 31.4. Net exports are the difference between export demand and import demand. Therefore, *an appreciation of the dollar decreases the demand for net exports, which decreases aggregate demand and the equilibrium level of national income.*

A depreciation of the dollar is a decrease in its value relative to foreign currencies. Suppose that the dollar depreciates in value from $1.80/£ to $2.00/£. British imports have become more expensive to U.S. households and businesses because they now must pay $2.00 to buy a pound sterling instead of $1.80. The demand for British imports decreases. Conversely, U.S. exports have become cheaper to British households and businesses because a pound now buys $2.00 instead of $1.80. The demand for U.S. exports increases.

In general, a depreciation of the dollar decreases the demand for imports and increases the demand for exports. It shifts Im^d downward in Figure 31.3, and it shifts Ex^d upward in Figure 31.4. Therefore, *a depreciation of the dollar increases the demand for net exports, which increases aggregate demand and the equilibrium level of national income.*

Let's now return to the analysis of automatic stabilizers.

IMPORTS AS AN AUTOMATIC STABILIZER The demand for imports satisfies the conditions for an automatic stabilizer. It is a drain on aggregate demand—import demand is subtracted from aggregate demand—and it is positively related to the level of national income. With imports now 11 percent of GDP and a marginal propensity to import of about .10, imports have become a very important automatic stabilizer for the U.S. economy.

Think back to the round-by-round multiplier process to see why imports act as an automatic stabilizer. Suppose that an initial increase in aggregate demand starts a round-by-round increase in national income, as in our previous examples. To the extent that households spend some of their increased income on imported goods, the increase in production to meet their demand increases national income in *foreign* countries, not in the United States. That additional income earned by foreign workers, landlords, and capitalists leaks out of the multiplier process. It is not available to U.S. households for consumption in the next round. The result is that the final change in U.S. national income is less than it would have been without the leakage of income to imports. The spending multiplier is smaller.[5]

HISTORICAL NOTE: In August of 1993 the Fed sold Japanese yen for dollars to depreciate the Yen relative to the dollar. It did this to help support the sagging Japanese economy, which was mired in a deep recession at the time. A depreciation of the Yen against the dollar encourages Japanese exports to the United States and discourages Japanese imports from the United States, thereby increasing aggregate demand in Japan.

THE INCREASINGLY IMPORTANT FOREIGN SECTOR The increasing importance of the foreign sector in the United States was driven home in the 1980s, when the economy struggled to recover from the recession of 1981–82. The recovery took five years—the economy did not return to the production possibilities frontier until 1987—and the foreign sector played a key role in slowing down the pace of the recovery.

Part of the problem was the natural increase in import demand as national income increased, which acted as an automatic stabilizer. The increase in imports reduced the value of the spending multiplier and reduced the growth in national income.

---

[5]The only difference between imports and the other automatic stabilizers is that the leakage occurs in the first round of the multiplier process. Refer back to Table 31.1, and suppose that 25 percent of all U.S. purchases are imports. If so, then national income would only increase by $75 in the *first* round, since $25 of the initial increase in investment is purchased from foreign producers. The value of the spending multiplier would be slightly smaller than in our tax example.

The stabilizing effect of import demand is always present and, by itself, would not have slowed the recovery all that much. Taxes and transfers are much more important automatic stabilizers than is import demand. But a second factor kicked in that greatly increased the foreign sector's drag on the economy, a dramatic appreciation of the dollar. The dollar appreciated by 38 percent against the major currencies between 1981 and 1985, as the United States became the favored nation for savers and investors worldwide.[6] Foreigners were anxious to invest in U.S. real estate and private companies and to otherwise place their savings in all kinds of U.S. financial securities, including U.S. government bonds, certificates of deposit, and corporate stocks and bonds. They needed dollars to transact in the U.S. markets, so they offered their currencies for dollars in the foreign exchange markets and drove up the value of the dollar. As expected, the appreciation of the dollar simultaneously reduced export demand and increased import demand, further reducing net exports and holding down the growth of the economy.

The experience of the 1980s is likely to be repeated. We will see in later chapters that an increase in aggregate demand can cause an appreciation of the dollar, which reduces net exports and removes some of the increase in aggregate demand. The 1980s have taught us that the foreign sector is now large enough to exert a significant drag on aggregate demand when the dollar is appreciating.

The Overall Impact of Automatic Stabilizers

Automatic stabilizers offer the U.S. economy a fair amount of protection against aggregate demand shocks. Income and sales taxes, income-sensitive government transfer payments, business saving, and import demand combine to reduce the value of the spending multiplier by about 40 percent. In other words, a change in aggregate demand changes the equilibrium level of national income by only 60 percent as much as it would without the automatic stabilizers.

Geometrically, automatic stabilizers flatten *ADE* in the aggregate demand–45° line graph. We have already seen how import demand directly flattens *ADE*. Income and sales taxes, income-sensitive transfer payments, and business saving indirectly flatten *ADE* by making consumption demand less sensitive to changes in national income. They do so by causing disposable income to change by less than national income changes. Take the federal personal income tax as an example. Because income taxes increase when national income increases, households do not receive the full benefit of the increase in national income. The increase in their disposable income equals the increase in national income minus the increase in their federal income taxes. Since consumption demand depends on disposable income and not on national income, the change in consumption demand is smaller than it would be without an income tax.

Figure 31.6 shows that a change in aggregate demand produces a smaller change in the equilibrium level of national income the flatter *ADE* is. The steeper line, $ADE_0^{w/oAS}$, is the aggregate demand line without automatic stabilizers. The flatter line, $ADE_0^{w/AS}$, is the aggregate line with automatic stabilizers. The initial equilibrium level of national income is Y_0, at the intersection of each ADE_0 line and the 45° line.

[6]*Economic Report of the President, 1993,* Table B-107, p. 470.

FIGURE 31.6

Aggregate Demand with and without Automatic Stabilizers

The figure shows how automatic stabilizers flatten the aggregate demand line, *ADE*, and make the economy less sensitive to changes in aggregate demand. $ADE^{w/oAS}$ is the relatively steep aggregate demand line that would exist without automatic stabilizers. $ADE^{w/AS}$ is the actual, relatively flat aggregate demand line with automatic stabilizers such as income taxes and import demand. The equilibrium level of national income is initially Y_0; at the intersection of $ADE_0^{w/oAS}$, $ADE_0^{w/AS}$, and the 45-degree line. A decrease in aggregate demand in the amount *ab* shifts the two aggregate demand lines down to $ADE_1^{w/oAS}$ and $ADE_1^{w/AS}$. Without automatic stabilizers, the equilibrium level of national income would fall to $Y_1^{w/oAS}$, at the intersection of $ADE_1^{w/oAS}$ and the 45-degree line. With automatic stabilizers, the equilibrium level of national income falls to $Y_1^{w/AS}$, at the intersection of $ADE_1^{w/AS}$ and the 45-degree line. The automatic stabilizers reduce the decline in national income by about 40 percent.

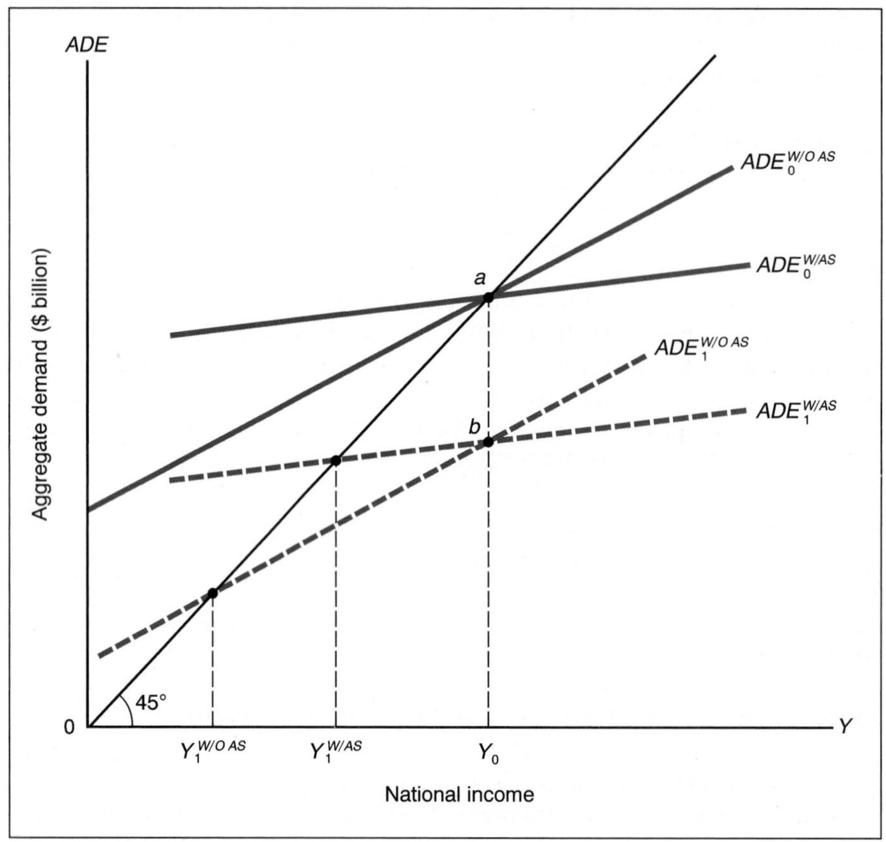

Suppose that aggregate demand decreases by the amount *ab*. The equilibrium level of national income falls to $Y_1^{w/AS}$ with automatic stabilizers, at the intersection of the dotted line $ADE_1^{w/AS}$ and the 45° line. In contrast, the equilibrium level of national income falls all the way to $Y_1^{w/oAS}$ without automatic stabilizers, at the intersection of the dotted line $ADE_1^{w/oAS}$ and the 45° line. The distance between Y_0 and $Y_1^{w/AS}$ is approximately 60 percent of the distance between Y_0 and $Y_1^{w/oAS}$ for the U.S. economy.

Automatic Stabilizers: Good or Bad?

Are automatic stabilizers good or bad for the U.S. economy? The answer depends on where the economy happens to be.

Automatic stabilizers are good when the economy is operating close to the target level of national income because the economy stays closer to the target when aggregate demand shifts up or down. Suppose that Y_0 is the target level of national income in Figure 31.6. When aggregate demand falls by *ab*, the economy stays closer to the target with automatic stabilizers than without automatic stabilizers.

Automatic stabilizers are definitely a blessing when the economy begins to go into a recession because they break the fall in national income. The annual unemployment rate reached 8.5 percent during the recession of 1974–75 and 9.7 percent during the recession of 1981–82. As bad as these figures were, the unemployment rate would have been several percentage points higher each time without the automatic stabilizers. More recently, import demand fell by \$6 billion in 1991, which helped support aggregate demand during the recession of 1990–91. It had risen by \$38 billion in 1990, and rose again by \$47 billion in 1992 as the economy began to recover.[7]

Whenever the economy moves into a recession, you can bet that the news media will ask economists this question: Are we headed for another Great Depression? Almost all economists answer no for at least two good reasons.

The first is that the economy has much more automatic stability now to break the fall than it had during the Great Depression. When the Depression hit in 1930, income and sales taxes were minuscule compared with today, the federal government had no public assistance or unemployment insurance programs (they began with the passage of the Social Security Act of 1935), and imports were unimportant. Today, because of the automatic stabilizers, a recession is much less likely to snowball into another Great Depression.

According to Victor Zarnowitz of the National Bureau of Economic Research, a dollar increase in GNP led to a \$.95 increase in disposable income in the period from 1912 to 1945, but only a \$.39 increase in disposable income in the period from 1945 to 1982. As a result, he estimates that the spending multiplier has decreased from a range of 3.2 to 5.1 in the earlier period to a range of 1.8 to 2.5 in the latter period.[8]

A second reason is that most economists have faith that the federal government will use its fiscal and monetary policies to prevent a disaster like the Great Depression. In contrast, macroeconomics was not well developed in the 1930s, and policy makers at the time did not understand how to use fiscal and monetary policies to get the economy growing again. The fiscal policies that were tried were hardly expansionary at all, and monetary policy was disastrous. The Fed sat back and watched the money supply decrease by one-third in the first years of the Great Depression. Economists are confident that the government will not repeat those mistakes.

Automatic stabilizers are not so desirable if the economy is operating far from its target, however, because then a larger change in aggregate demand is necessary to bring the economy back to the target. Returning again to Figure 31.6, suppose that the target level of national income is $Y_1^{w/oAS}$, so that the economy is initially suffering an inflationary gap at Y_0. Without automatic stabilizers, contractionary policies have to shift aggregate demand down by *ab* to close the gap. With automatic stabilizers, contractionary policies have to shift aggregate demand down by much more than *ab* to close the gap. A decrease in aggregate demand of *ab* only brings the economy to $Y_1^{w/AS}$, about 40 percent above the target. The required change in aggregate demand with automatic stabilizers may be larger than is politically feasible if the economy strays from its target. Therefore, automatic stabilizers that are a blessing when the economy begins to move into a recession become something of a curse when the economy is trying to recover from the depths of a recession. As already noted, automatic stabilizers slowed the recovery from the deep 1981–82 recession. They also exerted a drag on the economy in the early 1990s as the economy struggled to recover from the recession of 1990–91.

---

[7]The unemployment data are from the *Economic Report of the President, 1993*, Table B-37, p. 390. The import data are from *Economic Indicators*, March 1993, 1.

[8]Victor Zarnowitz, "Facts and Factors in the Recent Evolution of Business Cycles in the United States," in *NBER Working Paper #2865* (Cambridge, MA: National Bureau of Economic Research, 1989), 26 and 28.

THE SPENDING MULTIPLIER IN THE UNITED STATES

The previous section on the spending multiplier in Chapter 30 noted that the simple models of Chapters 29 and 30 vastly overstated the value of the spending multiplier. $M_{\text{Spending}} = 1/(1 - \text{MPC})$ in those simple models. Since the long-run MPC for the United States is on the order of .90, those models predict an M_{Spending} of about 10, whereas the actual M_{Spending} in the United States is in the neighborhood of 1 to 3.

The automatic stabilizers bring us part of the way to the actual spending multiplier. By knocking out 40 percent of the value of the spending multiplier, the automatic stabilizers reduce M_{Spending} in our model from 10 to 6.

MARGINAL PROPENSITY TO SPEND
The portion of the change in national income that feeds back into further changes in aggregate demand during each round of the multiplier process; the slope of the aggregate desired expenditures (*ADE*) line.

The appendix to this chapter presents the detailed algebra of the spending multiplier with automatic stabilizers. The basic idea is that M_{Spending} depends on the slope of the *ADE* line in the aggregate demand–45 ° line graph. The slope of *ADE* is called the **marginal propensity to spend** out of national income. It indicates what portion of the change in national income feeds back into a further change in aggregate demand during each round of the multiplier process.

$$M_{\text{Spending}} = 1/(1 - \text{marginal propensity to spend})$$

The slope of *ADE* is the MPC in the simple models of Chapters 29 and 30 without automatic stabilizers. As we have seen, automatic stabilizers decrease the slope of *ADE*, the marginal propensity to spend; in the process they lower the value of M_{Spending}.

Automatic Stabilizers Versus Discretionary Policies

A final point about automatic stabilizers needs to be stressed: The government cannot rely on automatic stabilizers to keep the economy at a target level of national income. If a change (shift) in aggregate demand moves the economy off its target, the automatic stabilizers help by reducing the resulting change in the equilibrium. But this is all they can do. Automatic stabilizers cannot reverse the change (shift) in aggregate demand to return the economy to the target.

Return again to Figure 31.6, and assume that the initial equilibrium, Y_0, is the target level of national income. When aggregate demand decreases by *ab*, the automatic stabilizers help by breaking the fall of national income. The economy moves to $Y_1^{w/AS}$ instead of $Y_1^{w/oAS}$. But the economy will stay at $Y_1^{w/AS}$ unless the government responds with expansionary fiscal or monetary policies to shift the dotted line $ADE_1^{w/AS}$ back up to its initial position.

The fact that income-tax collections automatically decrease and unemployment insurance benefits automatically increase as national income decreases cannot reverse the direction of aggregate demand. Any changes in the federal budget that respond automatically to the level of national income, as well as the other automatic stabilizers, just flatten the *ADE* line; they do not shift *ADE*. Only discretionary fiscal and monetary policies can shift *ADE* up or down to match the equilibrium with the target level of national income.

BUDGET DEFICITS AND FISCAL POLICY

The president and the Congress have every political incentive to talk a good fiscal policy game. They often claim that they are pursuing expansionary fiscal policies to get the economy moving or contractionary policies to hold down the growth of aggregate demand—whatever is necessary to help achieve the macroeconomic policy goals. How can you put them to the test and judge for yourself the direction and the magnitude of fiscal policy?

The federal government publishes a wealth of information on fiscal policy. You might begin by reading through the federal budget line by line to see what has been appropriated for each agency. The Office of Management and Budget publishes the federal *Budget of the United States Government* each year, along with supporting *Special Analyses of the Federal Budget*, over a thousand pages of detailed information on the federal budget. You might also read the comments on fiscal policy in the annual *Economic Report of the President*, put together by the president's Council of Economic Advisers, as well as the numerous budget studies undertaken by the Congressional Budget Office, the research arm of the Congress.

Of course, neither you nor most anyone else has the time or the inclination to pore over all the published information on the government's fiscal policies. What you want instead is a simple, "quick and dirty" measure of the direction and the magnitude of the government's discretionary fiscal policy stance for any one year. At the very least, the measure should indicate whether fiscal policy is expansionary or contractionary and give a sense of how expansionary or contractionary. The simple measure of fiscal policy most often reported in the news media is the change in the federal budget deficit from one year to the next.

The change in the federal budget deficit would appear to be a reasonably good measure of the government's fiscal policy stance. The **budget deficit** is the difference between expenditures and revenues, that is, government purchases plus transfer payments minus taxes (and other fees):

ACTUAL BUDGET DEFICIT
The difference between government expenditures and government revenues.

$$\text{Deficit} = G + Tr - Tx$$

The change in the deficit is the change in these three items:

$$\Delta\text{Deficit} = \Delta G + \Delta Tr - \Delta Tx$$

Changes in government purchases, transfer payments, and taxes are the three main tools of fiscal policy. Therefore, the change in the deficit from one year to the next summarizes the net change in all three fiscal policy tools.

An increase in the deficit is commonly interpreted as an indication of expansionary fiscal policy. The deficit can increase only if the increase in government purchases and increase in transfer payments exceed the increase in taxes, which would tend to increase aggregate demand. The more the deficit increases, the more expansionary the fiscal policy is. Conversely, a decrease in the deficit is commonly interpreted as an indication of contractionary fiscal policy. The deficit can decrease only if the increase in government purchases plus the increase in transfer payments is less than the change in taxes, which would tend to decrease aggregate demand. The more the deficit decreases, the more contractionary the fiscal policy is.

Unfortunately, the change in the federal budget deficit is not a very reliable measure of the government's fiscal policy stance. The problem is that changes in the deficit depend on two factors: (1) discretionary changes in expenditure programs or taxes, which is what we want to measure; and (2) changes in the state of the economy, whether the equilibrium level of national income is increasing or decreasing. The deficit is very sensitive to the state of the economy because both taxes and transfer payments vary with the level of national income. When the economy moves into a recession and unemployment increases, tax collections automatically decrease and income-sensitive transfer payments automatically increase. The budget deficit increases. Conversely, when the economy is booming and unemployment decreases, tax collections automatically increase and income-sensitive transfer payments automatically decrease. The budget deficit decreases. Changes in the state of the economy have an enormous effect on the size of the federal deficit. Every one percentage point increase in the unemployment rate increases the deficit by approximately $50 billion.

The Structural Deficit

A single measure, the change in the deficit, cannot untangle the separate effects of these two factors on the budget deficit. The effect of the economy on the deficit has to be removed to assess the government's fiscal policy stance. In 1955 economists at the Bureau of Economic Analysis devised a deficit concept that does this; they called it the high-employment deficit. President Reagan's economic advisers changed the name of the high employment deficit to the structural deficit, which is the name more commonly used today.

The structural deficit standardizes the measure of the deficit at one level of national income. The natural choice is the full employment level of national income or, alternatively, the natural rate of unemployment, U_{NR}, which we will assume is 6 percent. Therefore, the **structural deficit** is an estimate of what the federal deficit would be *if* the economy were at the natural rate of unemployment, regardless of where the economy actually is. Having standardized the structural deficit measure at U_{NR}, changes in the structural deficit from year to year indicate the government's fiscal policy stance.

STRUCTURAL BUDGET DEFICIT

An estimate of what the government's budget deficit would be if the economy were at full employment (the natural rate of unemployment), regardless of where the economy actually is; it increases and decreases with discretionary changes in government spending on goods and services, transfer payments, or taxes; formerly referred to as the *high-employment budget deficit*.

The structural deficit removes the effect of the economy on the deficit because the structural deficit is always measured at $U_{NR} = 6$ percent each year. The only way that the structural deficit can change is if the federal government makes discretionary changes in its expenditure or tax programs that increase or decrease the budget deficit at every level of national income, including the full employment level of national income. This is what fiscal policy is all about. Therefore, changes in the structural deficit are a reliable measure of the government's fiscal policy stance:

- *An increase in the structural deficit indicates that fiscal policy has been expansionary.* The federal government has undertaken programmatic changes in its expenditure and tax programs that increase the budget deficit at every level of national income.
- *A decrease in the structural deficit indicates that fiscal policy has been contractionary.* The federal government has undertaken programmatic changes in its expenditure and tax programs that decrease the budget deficit at every level of national income.

Some Pitfalls With the Structural Deficit

The change in the structural deficit is not a perfect measure of the government's fiscal policy stance, however. An immediate problem is that the structural deficit is only an estimate, not an actual number. Different economists may arrive at different estimates of what the deficit would be *if* unemployment were at the natural rate.

Another problem is that the natural rate of unemployment is a moving target. The level of national income required to keep the unemployment rate at 6 percent increases as the production possibilities frontier expands over time and labor becomes more productive. The higher the full-employment level of national income is, the larger tax collections are and the smaller some of the transfer payments are. In other words, the structural deficit measured at $U_{NR} = 6$ percent has a natural tendency to decrease over time. A decrease in the structural deficit may be due to economic growth rather than a contractionary fiscal policy.

Still another problem is that changes in government purchases have a greater multiplied effect on the equilibrium level of national income than do changes in taxes or transfer payments. Suppose that the government's fiscal policy is a balanced budget change, consisting of equal increases in government purchases and taxes. The balanced budget multiplier is one; this fiscal policy is expansionary. Yet balanced budget changes leave the structural deficit unchanged, suggesting that fiscal policy has been neither expansionary nor contractionary.

Finally, many economists recommend computing the ratio of the structural deficit to the full employment level of national income or GDP and using changes in the ratio as the measure of fiscal policy. Changes in the ratio give a better indication of the *magnitude* of the government's fiscal policy initiatives than does the structural deficit itself.

These problems notwithstanding, the change in the structural deficit (or in the ratio of the structural deficit to national income) is a fairly reliable "quick and dirty" measure of the government's fiscal policy stance. It is far better than the change in the actual deficit. Unfortunately, the news media almost always report changes in the actual deficit rather than the structural deficit. You may have to search through government publications such as the *Economic Report of the President* to find data on the structural deficit.

The Cyclical Deficit

The **cyclical deficit** is the difference between the actual deficit and the structural deficit.

CYCLICAL BUDGET DEFICIT

The component of the government's budget deficit that fluctuates with the state of the economy; the difference between the actual budget deficit and the structural budget deficit.

$$\text{cyclical deficit} = \text{actual deficit} - \text{structural deficit}$$

Since the structural deficit is measured at the natural rate of unemployment, the size of the cyclical deficit depends entirely on the state of the economy. It increases and decreases with the business cycle, hence the name cyclical deficit.

The cyclical deficit mirrors the performance of the economy:

- *The cyclical deficit is positive when* $U > U_{NR}$ *and becomes larger the farther* U *is above* U_{NR}. For example, at $U = 8\%$ the actual deficit is larger than the structural deficit, which assumes that U = 6%. The cyclical deficit is positive.

- *The cyclical deficit is zero when* U = U_{NR}. If the actual unemployment rate were 6 percent, then both the actual deficit and the structural deficit would be equal. The cyclical deficit would be zero.
- *The cyclical deficit is negative (a surplus) when* U < U_{NR} *and becomes more negative the farther* U *is below* U_{NR}. Suppose that the unemployment rate is 3 percent and the actual deficit is in balance. Since the structural deficit is the deficit at U = 6%, it is positive. With the actual deficit = 0, the cyclical deficit is negative (a surplus).

Summary: The Structural and the Cyclical Deficits

To summarize, economists conceptually divide the actual federal budget deficit into two components, the structural deficit and the cyclical deficit.

$$\text{Actual deficit} = \text{structural deficit} + \text{cyclical deficit}$$

Therefore, changes in the deficit from year to year consist of changes in the structural and the cyclical deficits.

$$\Delta\text{Actual deficit} = \Delta\text{structural deficit} + \Delta\text{cyclical deficit}$$

HISTORICAL NOTE: Unemployment increased by two percentage points from 1990 to 1993. This alone has added over $100 billion each year to the federal deficit.

The change in the structural deficit results from the government's discretionary fiscal policy. An increase in the structural deficit indicates an expansionary fiscal policy, and a decrease in the structural deficit indicates a contractionary fiscal policy. The change in the cyclical deficit results from automatic changes in tax collections and income-sensitive transfer payments as the level of national income increases and decreases. An expanding economy reduces the cyclical deficit, and a contracting economy increases the cyclical deficit.

Budget Deficits During the 1980s

Table 31.3 presents the actual, structural, and cyclical federal budget deficits during the 1980s, when the federal deficit leaped to the forefront as a leading macroeconomic issue. The estimates of the structural deficit were made by Northwestern's Robert Gordon and assume that U_{NR} = 6 percent. The cyclical deficit is the difference between the actual deficit and Gordon's estimated structural deficit. The data illustrate a number of the principles about budget deficits discussed above.

THE CYCLICAL DEFICITS Notice first how the cyclical deficits mirror the performance of the economy. The economy moved into the deepest recession since the Great Depression during 1981–82, and the unemployment rate rose briefly above 10 percent. The deep recession caused a dramatic increase in the cyclical deficit, as personal and corporation income tax collections fell off and income-sensitive transfer payments such as unemployment insurance benefits increased. Following the recession the economy began a long, slow recovery

TABLE 31.3 **The Federal Budget Deficits, 1980–89 ($ billion)**

YEAR	ACTUAL DEFICIT[a]	STRUCTURAL DEFICIT[b]	CYCLICAL DEFICIT	RATIO OF STRUCTURAL DEFICIT TO NATIONAL INCOME (%)
1980	$ 68.0	$ 35.4	$ 32.6	1.6
1981	96.0	42.5	53.5	1.7
1982	202.6	98.8	103.8	3.9
1983	169.2	105.4	63.8	3.9
1984	187.0	154.7	32.3	5.1
1985	212.2	192.3	19.9	5.9
1986	189.0	160.4	28.6	4.7
1987	164.3	176.0	(−) 11.7	4.8
1988	167.4	203.6	(−) 36.2	5.1
1989	137.0	180.2	(−) 43.2	4.3

[a]Actual deficit = structural deficit + cyclical deficit.
[b]Structural deficits assume U_{NR} = 6 percent.

SOURCE: R. Gordon, *Macroeconomics*, 5th edition (Glenview, IL: Scott, Foresman/Little, Brown, 1989), Appendix A, pp. A5–A7. Council of Economic Advisors, *Economic Report of the President, 1993* (Washington, D.C.: U.S. Government Printing Office, 1993), Table B-21, p. 371.

that continued through the remainder of the decade. The steady recovery led to a steady decrease in the cyclical deficit, as tax collections rose and income-sensitive transfer payments declined. The cyclical deficit turned negative (became a surplus) beginning in 1987, when the unemployment rate dipped below Gordon's assumed natural rate of 6 percent. The unemployment rate had fallen to 5.3 percent by 1989.

THE STRUCTURAL DEFICITS The structural deficits increased substantially each year from 1981 through 1985, indicating that fiscal policy was highly expansionary during that time. The increases were largely the result of a massive military buildup combined with a 23 percent cut in the personal income tax (more on these below). The expansionary fiscal policy was just the right medicine for an ailing economy trying to recover from a recession, according to the new Keynesian perspective. Indeed, many new Keynesian economists believe that the government's fiscal policy stance was the main reason for the recovery.

The structural deficit decreased somewhat in 1989, indicating that fiscal policy was mildly contractionary. This may have contributed to precipitating the mild recession of 1990.

ACTUAL DEFICITS AND FISCAL POLICY The data also reveal how changes in the actual deficit can be a misleading indicator of the government's fiscal policy stance, both its magnitude and its direction. Compare the changes in the actual and the structural deficits from 1987 to 1988. The actual deficit hardly changed at all, whereas the structural deficit increased by more than $27 billion. Using the change in the actual deficit as the measure of fiscal policy would suggest that fiscal policy was essentially neutral, whereas the increase in the structural deficit correctly shows that fiscal policy was somewhat expansionary.

Worse yet, changes in the actual deficit can misrepresent the direction of fiscal policy. Compare the changes in the actual and the structural deficits from

1986 to 1987. The actual deficit *decreased* by about $25 billion, suggesting that fiscal policy was contractionary. In contrast, the structural deficit *increased* by nearly $16 billion, correctly indicating that fiscal policy was mildly expansionary. The cyclical deficit column shows that the decrease in the actual deficit was due to the continued rapid growth of the economy. The lesson is clear: Use changes in the structural deficit, not in the actual deficit, to assess the government's fiscal policy stance.

LARGE STRUCTURAL DEFICITS AND THE BURDEN OF THE DEBT

The increased reliance on deficit financing that began during the Reagan/Bush administrations represented a major and an unprecedented shift in federal budgetary policy. The federal government had run very large budget deficits only once before, during World War II to finance the war effort. The World War II deficits were actually a much larger percentage of national income than were the Reagan/Bush deficits. The difference, though, is that the Reagan/Bush deficits were peacetime deficits, and the federal government had never before even considered running such large peacetime deficits for years on end.

Particularly noteworthy was the increase in the structural deficits, to $200 billion and more. When the deficits first began to appear, President Reagan assured the American public that the economy would grow its way out of the deficits as it returned to full employment. His economic advisers admitted, however, that economic growth would not reduce the projected structural deficits because the structural deficits are calculated *at* full employment.

To put the numbers in Table 31.3 in perspective, the average actual and structural deficits from 1970 to 1979 were $31.4 billion and $26.1 billion. The average actual and structural deficits from 1980 to 1989 were $159 billion and $135 billion, each five times as large as its 1970s counterpart.[9]

Each year that the government runs a deficit it increases the amount of public debt outstanding. The Reagan/Bush deficits were so large that the debt is growing faster than the growth in the national product. President Reagan inherited a public debt of $909 billion, equal to 34 percent of the gross national product (GNP). By 1992 the public debt had increased to $4002 billion, equal to 67 percent of the GDP.[10] The public debt continued to grow faster than did the national product into the Clinton administration.

The dramatic increase in deficit financing came about immediately after President Reagan took office in 1981. Reagan proposed three major budgetary changes:

1. A massive increase in defense expenditures to counter what he perceived to be a growing military threat from the Soviet Union.
2. A 23 percent cut in personal income tax rates, by far the largest federal tax cut ever, to stimulate the economy. The proposed tax cut was especially intriguing because it was based on a new supply-side theory of how the

---

[9]R. Gordon, *Macroeconomics*, fifth edition (Glenview, IL: Scott, Foresman/Little, Brown, 1989), Appendix A, pp. A5–A7.

[10]*Economic Indicators, March 1993*, 1, 32. *Economic Report of the President, 1993*, Table B-1, p. 348. Executive Office of the President of the United States, *Budget of the United States Government, Fiscal Year 1993, Supplement, February 1992* (Washington, D.C.: U.S. Government Printing Office, 1992), Part Five: Historical Table, Tables 7.1, p. 5–89.

economy responds to tax policy that had nothing in common with the Keynesian tax multiplier theory of Chapter 30. We will explore the supply-side theory of tax policy in Chapter 38.

3. Huge cuts in nondefense purchases and transfer payments to keep the budget in balance. President Reagan was a staunch fiscal conservative who did not believe in running budget deficits. He also wanted to reduce federal social welfare expenditures, which had been growing rapidly since the early 1960s.

Congress agreed with President Reagan's assessment of the Soviet military threat and authorized the increase in defense spending. It also approved the income tax cuts. The economy was suffering from the double whammy of high unemployment and high inflation, and no one seemed to know what to do. In its frustration Congress considered the new supply-side theory and said in effect: "What the heck, let's give it a try." Congress balked at most of the cuts in social welfare expenditures and other nondefense purchases, however. It refused to slash the major social welfare programs such as Social Security, Medicare, Medicaid, and Aid to Families with Dependent Children. The net results were a huge increase in defense spending and a record tax cut, which meant a huge increase in the structural deficit. The structural deficits took awhile to reach their full value because the tax cuts were phased in over three years: a 5 percent cut in the first year, followed by 10 percent cuts in each of the next two years. The military spending increases were also phased in over time.

The tax cuts have never been restored. Defense spending was cut back significantly after the breakup of the Soviet Union, but not enough to counter the growth of federal expenditures in other areas, particularly social welfare programs, interest on the debt, and the savings and loan bailout. Consequently, the structural deficits continued to be in the $200 billion range in the 1990s, and the public debt is still growing faster than is the national product.

Are large structural deficits a problem? Is a large and growing public debt a burden on the economy? Before answering these questions, take note of the emphasis on structural deficits in the discussion so far. Economists always focus on the structural deficit when thinking about the economic implications of deficits and the public debt. The cyclical deficit responds automatically to the ebbs and flows of the economy and is essentially beyond the control of the government. It does serve as an important automatic stabilizer as we have seen, but it is otherwise irrelevant to an economic analysis of budget deficits and the public debt.

The question of whether structural deficits are a problem has a different answer in the short run and the long run.

Temporary Structural Deficits

Keynes taught economists and policy makers not to fear temporary, short-run structural deficits. On the contrary, running a deficit can be extremely beneficial if the economy is moving into a recession. Increasing government expenditures or cutting taxes increases aggregate demand, which can nip the recession in the bud and save millions of people their jobs.

Furthermore, the government will not always be running temporary deficits. Sometimes aggregate demand grows too rapidly and tries to bring the economy beyond its production possibilities frontier. When this happens, the government might respond by decreasing government expenditures or increasing taxes to decrease aggregate demand, which is likely to cause a temporary structural budget surplus.

The temporary structural deficits and surpluses may not cancel out over time, but the public debt would remain small and inconsequential. The ratio of public debt to national income would undoubtedly decline over time.

A BALANCED BUDGET? President Bush pushed hard throughout his administration for an amendment to the Constitution that would require the administration to submit a balanced operating budget each year, just as most of the state governors are required to do. He had the support of many legislators as well. Proponents of the balanced budget amendment argue that it would bring much needed fiscal discipline to the budgetary process. The amendment would stop the rapid growth of the public debt immediately and force the administration and the Congress to be more careful in assessing new government expenditure programs.

The fiscal discipline argument has merit. Even so, the vast majority of economists oppose the balanced budget amendment on macroeconomic grounds. As a practical matter, any balanced budget legislation would have to be defined in terms of the actual budget, not the structural budget. Unfortunately, requiring the federal government to balance the actual budget each year has perverse macroeconomic consequences. It forces fiscal policy to become pro-cyclical rather than countercyclical.

Economists worry about the following scenario. Suppose that the administration and the Congress design a balanced budget for the year, as required. During the course of the year national income decreases unexpectedly, and the economy begins to move into a recession. The decrease in national income reduces tax collections and increases income-sensitive transfer payments, moving the budget from balance to a deficit. Since the administration and the Congress are forced to balance the budget, they have to respond to the deficit by decreasing government spending and/or raising taxes for the next year. But decreases in government spending and tax increases both lead to multiplied *decreases* in national income, which makes the recession worse.

The government needs to *increase* the deficit still further to fight the recession, not balance the budget. Instead, a balanced budget requirement forces the government into pro-cyclical fiscal policies that follow the economy and increase the ebbs and flows of the business cycle. Most economists believe that this is too high a price to pay for whatever fiscal discipline a balanced budget amendment may bring.

The balanced budget amendment has never gotten off the ground. Nonetheless, Congress became so exasperated with the large budget deficits that it enacted two separate pieces of legislation to force the government to balance the budget. The Gramm-Rudman-Hollings Act of 1985 (GRH) mandated a gradual reduction in the deficit each year, with a target of balancing the budget by 1991. GRH was essentially ignored, so Congress tried again in 1990 with the Omnibus Budget Reconciliation Act of 1990 (OBRA). The new law raised taxes somewhat and scheduled a series of reductions in expenditures each year, with a target of balancing the budget by 1996. OBRA is headed for the same fate as GRH. The budget deficit kept increasing in 1991 and 1992, and no one takes the 1996 target date seriously anymore.

President Clinton does not support a balanced budget amendment, but he did call for a $500 billion reduction in the deficit over five years. We will return to this policy below.

Perhaps these balanced budget laws are ineffective in part because the administration and the Congress instinctively respond to the macroeconomic implications of changes in the deficit. They are not willing to bear the short-run costs of deficit reduction.

Long-Run Structural Deficits

Large structural deficits that continue for years on end and build up a large public debt are a different matter entirely from temporary structural deficits that are responding to a recession. They can be a substantial burden to the economy. The analysis of continuing structural deficits differs as well. Economists assume that resources are fully employed when analyzing the long-run burden of a growing public debt. The short-run ebbs and flows of the business cycles are not so relevant in a long-run context.

PUBLIC INVESTMENT OR PUBLIC CONSUMPTION? The first question to ask about a policy of continuing structural deficits is this: What are the deficits financing? Is the government issuing debt to finance investment in public capital, such as schools, highways, and hydroelectric projects? Or is the government issuing debt to finance the current operating expenses of the government agencies and transfer payments?

Issuing debt to finance public investment is perfectly sound. After all, the business sector is a net debtor. Businesses routinely issue debt to finance their investments, and governments can, too. The only issue in this case concerns the investments themselves: Are the investments productive?

A debt-financed private investment is productive if it brings in enough additional revenues to cover all the operating expenses of the project, pay off the principal and the interest on the debt, and have enough profit left over to give the stockholders an acceptable return on their investment. The same productivity test applies to debt-financed public investments, with one twist: Governments do not always sell the output of the public projects. Families with schoolchildren do not pay tuition to the local public schools, and most highways are toll-free. Instead, the government raises taxes to cover the expenses of building and maintaining public schools and highways. Nonetheless, public investments expand the nation's production possibilities frontier and increase the national income whether or not they bring in any revenues. If a public investment is productive, the government can raise taxes to cover the operating expenses of the project, pay off the principal and the interest on the debt, and still leave citizens with plenty of additional disposable income to enjoy. Indeed, public education may well have contributed more to long-run economic growth in the United States than has any comparable amount of private investment.

Issuing debt to finance annual operating expenses and transfer payments can be a burden, however. A business cannot issue debt year after year to finance its operating expenses and hope to survive. Governments can do this because of their power to tax, but they should avoid the temptation.

Unfortunately, this is essentially what the federal government has been doing since 1981. The government does not keep a separate capital budget, so it is difficult to know how much of federal purchases are public investments. The best estimates, though, are that gross federal investment is much less than $100 billion each year, and most of this is military investment. Net federal investment is probably on the order of $20 billion annually. The majority of the recent structural deficits have been supporting operating expenses and transfer payments.

The nature of the burden in this case depends on whether the public debt is external or internal. **External debt** is debt held by foreign citizens, businesses, and governments. **Internal debt** is debt held by U.S. citizens, businesses, and government agencies. Most of the federal debt is internal debt; foreign citizens and businesses own only about 20 percent of the privately held federal debt.

EXTERNAL DEBT (PUBLIC)

Public debt that is held by foreign citizens, businesses, and governments.

INTERNAL DEBT (PUBLIC)

Public debt that is held by U.S. citizens, businesses, and government agencies.

EXTERNAL DEBT External public debt is analogous to private debt. Suppose that you go into debt to buy a stereo system. You purchase the stereo with a credit card and pay back the card company over the next two years. Borrowing to consume goods and services today involves a trade-off of future consumption for present consumption. In borrowing the money to buy the stereo system today, you have agreed to sacrifice even more purchasing power in the future because you have to pay interest on the debt. This is the burden of the debt to you.

External debt issued to pay for current operating expenses or transfer payments places a nation in the same position. The burden of the external debt is the transfer of purchasing power to foreign citizens in the future as the nation pays back the debt, with interest. One reason why debt financing is so tempting is that the present generations can enjoy the current consumption and place the payback burden on future generations.

INTERNAL DEBT The burden of financing current operating expenses and transfers with internal debt is extremely subtle, far more so than is commonly understood. People are led astray in thinking about the burden of the public debt because they draw an analogy between public and private debt. The analogy holds true only for external public debt, however. Internal public debt is not at all analogous to private debt because the citizens owe the debt to themselves. It is as if one of your hands could borrow from and pay back the other hand.

The false analogy between private and internal public debt leads people to worry that the public debt will bankrupt the nation, but bankruptcy is not the problem. The government can always raise taxes to pay off its internal debt. The money leaves the private sector when the taxes are paid and returns to the private sector as the government buys back its debt with interest. No resources leave the country as they do when the government pays off its external debt.

The federal government is not about to retire its internal debt, however, because taxes reduce the efficiency of the market system. Raising taxes by about $3 billion to pay off the internal debt would entail enormous efficiency costs. In addition, retiring the internal debt would redistribute resources toward the wealthy who hold a disproportionate share of the debt. Still, bankruptcy is not the problem.

Instead, the potential problem with internal debt is that it can reduce private investment, leaving future generations with a smaller capital stock, a less productive economy, and slower long-run economic growth. The deficit is said to crowd out private investment. This is a very serious problem because, as we have seen, long-run economic growth is the most important determinant of a nation's overall economic well-being.

To see the effect of debt financing on private investment, recall the investment = saving accounting identity from Chapter 27.

$$\text{Investment} = S_{\text{Private}} + S_{\text{Government}} + S_{\text{Foreign}}$$

The two sources of **national saving** are S_{Private}, saving by the household and the business sectors, and $S_{\text{Government}}$, saving by the government sector. We will ignore foreign saving, S_{Foreign}, for the moment, to concentrate on internal debt.

NATIONAL SAVING
The amount of saving generated by the domestic economy during the year, equal to the sum of saving by the private sector and saving by the government sector; the difference between total saving and foreign saving.

$S_{\text{Government}}$ is the government budget surplus, so that deficit financing reduces $S_{\text{Government}}$ dollar for dollar. Whether deficit financing also reduces national saving depends on how S_{Private} responds to the budget deficit. Most economists believe that S_{Private} does not increase dollar for dollar with the decrease in $S_{\text{Government}}$. Consequently, deficit financing reduces national saving, which must then reduce the level of investment. The reasoning is as follows.

The first point to understand is that the burden of the debt is a long-run problem. Therefore, when thinking about the debt burden economists typically assume a fully employed economy. Since the only final goods the economy can produce are consumer goods or investment goods, any increase in consumption must come at the expense of saving and investment at full employment. Economists also assume that households are making long-run consumption decisions in line with the Life-Cycle Hypothesis, and smoothing consumption over their lifetimes.

A growing public debt is likely to reduce national saving, and investment, under these two assumptions. The government cannot keep expanding public debt faster than the economy is growing, as has been the case since 1981, and still be able to sell its bonds. Eventually the government has to raise taxes again and reduce the resources of future generations. The effect of deficit financing in a Life-Cycle model is a redistribution of resources from older generations to younger generations under this scenario.

CURRENT ISSUE: President Clinton's $500 billion deficit reduction plan will not eliminate the federal budget deficits. But it may cause the debt to grow more slowly than GDP, in which case the burden of the debt will steadily diminish over time.

The net result of the transfer across generations is an increase in consumption and a decrease in saving and investment. The reason why is that older generations have a higher MPC than do younger generations. Suppose that the government cuts taxes by $100 today, issues $100 of new debt, and announces that it will increase taxes by enough 20 years from now to pay back the ensuing debt, with interest. Compare the reactions of two groups of people: the elderly, who expert to live only two more years, and the young, who expect to live 40 more years.

The elderly have a net increase in resources because they do not have to pay the future taxes. They also spend most of their tax cuts because they only have two years left to live.

The young buy the majority of the debt and adjust their consumption over the remainder of their lives, taking into account the new debt and the anticipated future tax increase. By buying the debt and receiving interest on it they obtain the funds that they will eventually need to pay the future tax increase. But they still lose on net because they have to pay back enough taxes to cover both their own tax cuts and the tax cuts of the elderly. Overall, their lifetime resources are reduced by the amount that the elderly gain, and they reduce their consumption as a result.

The increase in consumption by the elderly exceeds the decrease in consumption by the young because the elderly are spreading their gains over two years, whereas the young are spreading their losses over 40 years. Consequently, total consumption increases, and total saving and investment decrease.

Models designed to study these intergenerational consumption effects show that their impact on saving and investment can be very large when the government runs large structural deficits for 10 or 20 years, as is the case today. The current generation's consumption and transfer binge places an enormous burden on future generations through reduced productivity and long-run economic growth.[11]

FOREIGN SAVING AND INVESTMENT So far we have been ignoring saving by the foreign sector, $S_{Foreign}$, to concentrate on the effects of internal debt. Purchase of the debt by foreigners, external debt, is a source of foreign saving. Therefore, deficit financing with external debt substitutes for the decrease in $S_{Government}$ dollar for dollar and does not decrease total saving or crowd out investment. Foreigners did purchase an increasing proportion of the government debt during the 1980s, which helped prevent U.S. investment from declining. Remember, though, that external debt is still a burden because it requires transfers of future resources out of the United States. Substituting external debt for internal debt just changes the nature of the burden on future generations.

The Great Policy Dilemma Once Again

President Clinton buys the argument that large structural deficits reduce long-run economic growth. He continually stresses the need to "grow the economy" and believes that deficit reduction is the place to start. At the same time, the sluggish economy argues strongly against large spending cuts and tax increases.

Many economists who dislike the structural deficits nonetheless argue that putting people back to work should be the first priority. They believe that the Congress and the administration should forget the deficit for the moment and engage in expansionary fiscal policies to stimulate employment. In their view deficit reduction can wait until the private sector is back on its feet and better able to take the spending cuts and tax increases.

The dilemma posed by the large structural deficits and a sluggish economy is a real one. The right course for fiscal policy is not at all clear. Although Congress did enact Clinton's deficit reduction plan, it remains to be seen whether Congress will actually reduce the structural budget deficit over the next five years.

---

[11]A minority of economists argue that structural deficits have virtually no effect on national saving and investment. Harvard's Robert Barro is the leading proponent of this view. Barro believes that the majority of households behave according to the Life-Cycle Hypothesis *and* that they are altruistic toward future generations. They will not let the government transfer resources from the future generations to the present generations through deficit financing. In particular, the elderly, because they are altruistic, do not increase their consumption. Instead, they buy government bonds with their tax cuts and bequeath the bonds so that their heirs are not burdened by the inevitable future tax increase. The result is that $S_{Private}$ increases by the same amount that $S_{Government}$ decreases. Deficit financing has no effect at all on national saving and investment.

Most economists doubt that Life-Cycle consumers are so altruistic toward future generations. They believe that deficit financing does transfer resources across generations, reduce national saving, and crowd out private investment as described above.

SUMMARY

Chapter 31 began with a discussion of automatic stabilizers in the U.S. economy.

1. National income feeds back to aggregate demand through four channels in addition to consumption demand: income and sales taxes, income-sensitive government transfer payments, business saving (retained earnings), and import demand. The feedback in each instance serves as an automatic stabilizer, which is defined as any component of the economy that is related to national income and lowers the value of the spending multiplier. As such, these automatic stabilizers make the economy less sensitive to changes in aggregate demand.
2. Income and sales taxes, income-sensitive transfer payments, and business saving act as automatic stabilizers because they cause disposable income to change by less than national income changes. Since consumption demand is related to disposable income, consumption demand changes by a smaller amount during each round of the multiplier process, which reduces the value of the spending multiplier.
3. Import demand acts as an automatic stabilizer because imports remove some of the round-by-round change in national income from the circular flow of economic activity during the multiplier process. Expenditures on imports become sources of income to foreign producers, not domestic producers.
4. Any drain on aggregate demand that is positively related to the level of national income acts as an automatic stabilizer. Income taxes, business saving, and import demand are examples. Any contributor to aggregate demand that is negatively related to the level of national income also acts as an automatic stabilizer. Income-sensitive government transfer payments are an example.
5. The four automatic stabilizers reduce the value of the spending multiplier in the United States by about 40 percent.
6. Automatic stabilizers are helpful if the economy is operating close to its target level of national income because changes or shocks to aggregate demand do not move the economy as far away from the target. They are a hindrance if the economy is far from the target because larger increases in aggregate demand are needed to return to the target. For example, automatic stabilizers break the fall of an economy heading into a recession, but they make it more difficult for the economy to recover from a recession.

The first section of the chapter also added the foreign sector to our model to complete the new Keynesian aggregate demand model of the macro economy.

7. Aggregate demand for the complete economy, which consists of the household, business, government, and foreign sectors, is the sum of consumption demand, investment demand, government demand for goods and services, and net export demand. Net export demand is the difference between export demand and import demand. The product markets are in equilibrium when aggregate demand equals the level of national income generated in production.
8. Export demand depends on the levels of national income in foreign countries, not on the level of domestic national income. Import demand is directly related to the level of domestic national income, in part because

some of consumption demand is for imports and in part because businesses import some of the raw materials, intermediate products, and capital goods used as inputs in production. This is why import demand is an automatic stabilizer.

The second section of the chapter discussed how changes in the federal budget deficit can be used to measure the direction and the magnitude of discretionary fiscal policy.

9. Changes in the deficit from year to year result from two factors: (a) any discretionary or programmatic changes in government purchases, transfer payments, or taxes, which is what discretionary fiscal policy means; and (b) changes in the state of the economy.
10. Economists conceptually divide the actual budget deficit into two components, the structural budget deficit and the cyclical budget deficit, in order to measure the independent effects of these two factors. The structural budget deficit is an estimate of what the deficit would be if the economy were operating at the natural rate of unemployment. The cyclical deficit is the difference between the actual deficit and the estimated structural deficit.
11. Changes in the structural deficit year to year measure the direction and the magnitude of discretionary fiscal policy during the course of the year. An increase in the structural deficit indicates that the government undertook an expansionary fiscal policy. A decrease in the structural deficit indicates that the government undertook a contractionary fiscal policy. Changes in the cyclical deficit mirror the state of the economy, which affects the deficit through taxes and income-sensitive transfer payments. For example, the cyclical deficit increases when the economy enters a recession because tax collections fall and income-sensitive transfer payments rise.

One of the more striking features of the Reagan/Bush presidencies was the increased reliance on debt financing, which led to very large structural deficits and caused the public debt to grow more rapidly than did national income. The large structural deficits continued into the Clinton administration. The final section of Chapter 31 analyzed the effects of large structural deficits and a growing public debt.

12. Incurring a temporary structural deficit to head off a recession can be very useful. It supports aggregate demand and can save millions of workers their jobs. For this reason most economists oppose a balanced budget amendment to the Constitution, which would force the federal administration to submit balanced (actual) budgets each year as most state governors are required to do. A balanced budget amendment would no doubt promote fiscal discipline, but at the cost of causing fiscal policy to be pro-cyclical, amplifying the ebbs and flows of the business cycle.
13. A policy of long-run structural deficits can be a serious burden to the economy, however. The first question to ask is this: What are the deficits financing? Issuing debt to finance public investments in school buildings, highways, and the like is a sound budgetary practice, equivalent to businesses issuing debt to finance their private investments. The only issue in this case is whether or not the public investments are productive.
14. The burden arises if the structural deficits are primarily financing current operating expenses and transfer payments, as the recent deficits have been.

The nature of the burden depends on whether the debt is external (owed to foreigners) or internal (owed to the country's own citizens). Most of the privately held U.S. debt is internal debt.

15. External debt is analogous to private debt. The burden lies in the fact that the nation eventually has to transfer purchasing power to foreign citizens in order to pay back the debt, with interest. Public debt cannot grow faster than national income forever.
16. Internal debt is not analogous to private debt because citizens owe the debt to themselves. The burden with internal debt lies in the fact that it can crowd out private investment, thereby lowering productivity and long-run economic growth. National saving consists of the saving by the private sector and the government sector. Deficit financing reduces saving by the government sector dollar for dollar. Most economists believe that saving by the private sector increases by less than the deficit, so that national saving decreases, and investment along with it. Issuing external debt is a source of foreign saving, which supports investment. But external debt still results in a burden because of the future transfer of purchasing power that is required.

KEY TERMS

actual budget deficit
automatic stabilizer
cyclical budget deficit
external debt (public)
internal debt (public)
marginal propensity to import
marginal propensity to spend
national saving
structural budget deficit

QUESTIONS

1. Taxes are a drain on aggregate demand, and government transfer payments are a contributor to aggregate demand. Yet they both act as automatic stabilizers. How can this be?
2. Suppose that the consumption expenditures of U.S. citizens shift from domestic goods to imported goods, while leaving the total demand for goods and services unchanged. What effect does this change in tastes have on the equilibrium level of national income? On the balance of trade (= exports minus imports)?
3. Show the effect of a depreciation of the dollar on the import demand and export demand functions. Explain how the depreciation of the dollar affects net export demand and the equilibrium level of national income.
4. The following table gives the value of import demand at each level of national income.

IMPORT DEMAND	NATIONAL INCOME
100	1,000
150	2,000
250	3,000
400	4,000
600	5,000

Calculate the marginal propensity to import (MPM) for each $1,000 change in national income. Is the slope of the import demand function constant? Would you expect households' MPM to rise as their incomes rise?

5. Suppose that the government announces that the federal budget deficit increased by $10 billion last year. Based on this information can you decide whether the government pursued an expansionary fiscal policy last year? Why is the change in the federal budget deficit not a reliable measure of fiscal policy?
6. a. Why is the change in the structural federal budget deficit a better measure of the government's fiscal policy stance than is the change in the actual federal budget deficit?
   b. Why is the change in the structural budget deficit not a perfect measure of the government's fiscal policy stance?
7. Assume that a country has a balanced budget initially. The country's economic structure has automatic, built-in stabilizers in the form of taxes and government transfers. Suppose that national income decreases as a result of a decrease in consumption demand.
   a. What is the effect of the decrease in consumption demand on the actual budget deficit? On the structural budget deficit?
   b. If the government is required by law to maintain a balanced (actual) budget, what further impact would this

law have on aggregate demand and national income as the government tries to re-balance the budget?

8. a. How does the burden of an external public debt differ from the burden of an internal public debt?
   b. Are there any conditions under which neither external debt nor internal debt is a burden to a nation?
9. In a certain economy, transfer payments by the government increase by $0.30 for every $1 decrease in the national income. Also, total tax revenue increases by $0.40 for every $1 increase in national income. The MPC = 0.8. Suppose that something causes aggregate demand to increase by $10,000, so that national income increases by $10,000 in the first round of the multiplier process.
   a. Given the above tax and transfer structure of the economy, what is the increase in national income in the second round of the multiplier process?
   b. How would your answer to part a change if national income had decreased by $10,000?
10. *Extra credit:* Suppose that the government cuts taxes, issues new debt, and announces that it will raise taxes in the future to pay back this debt. There are only two generations in the economy: the young and the old. There are more old people than young people. What will happen to total saving and investment as a result of this tax cut? How would your answer change if all the old people had bequest motives and wanted to leave as much inheritance as possible to their children and grandchildren?

APPENDIX

31

Algebraic Analysis of Income Taxes and Net Exports

The appendix contains two sections. The first section presents an algebraic treatment of income taxes as an automatic stabilizer. The second section completes the new Keynesian aggregate demand model of the economy by adding net exports to aggregate demand.

INCOME TAXES AS AN AUTOMATIC STABILIZER

The algebraic model of the economy in the appendix to Chapter 30 assumed that tax revenues were a constant that was independent of the level of national income. As we saw in Chapter 31, tax revenues vary directly with the level of national income. A more realistic tax equation is

$$T = T_0 + t \cdot Y$$

T_0 is a constant representing the portion of tax revenues that is independent of national income; t is the marginal tax rate, the slope of the Tx line in Figure 31.1; and Y is national income. The text assumed a value of $t = .25$.

Taxes affect consumption demand by reducing disposable income below national income. Consumption demand is

$$C^d = C_0 + \text{MPC} \cdot Y_d$$

where Y_d is disposable income.

$$Y_d = Y - T$$

Substituting the income tax equation for T

$$Y_d = Y - (T_0 + t \cdot Y)$$

Substituting the equation for disposable income into the consumption demand equation gives consumption demand in terms of *national income.*

$$\begin{aligned} C^d &= C_0 + \text{MPC} \cdot [Y - (T_0 + t \cdot Y)] \\ &= C_0 + \text{MPC} \cdot Y - \text{MPC} \cdot T_0 - \text{MPC} \cdot t \cdot Y \end{aligned}$$

Combining the Y terms,

$$C^d = C_0 + \text{MPC} \cdot (1 - t) \cdot Y - \text{MPC} \cdot T_0$$

The two remaining components of aggregate demand are investment demand and government purchases, which are both unrelated to the level of national income.

$$I^d = \bar{I}$$

$$G^d = \bar{G}$$

The equilibrium condition is

$$Y = C^d + I^d + G^d$$

Substitute the equations for the three components of aggregate demand in the right-hand side of the equilibrium condition, and solve for Y.

$$\begin{aligned} Y &= C_0 + \text{MPC} \cdot (1 - t) \cdot Y - \text{MPC} \cdot T_0 + \bar{I} + \bar{G} \\ Y - \text{MPC} \cdot (1 - t) \cdot Y &= (C_0 + \bar{I} + \bar{G}) - \text{MPC} \cdot T_0 \\ Y \cdot [1 - \text{MPC} \cdot (1 - t)] &= (C_0 + \bar{I} + \bar{G}) - \text{MPC} \cdot T_0 \\ Y &= [1/[1 - (1 - t) \cdot \text{MPC}]] \cdot (\text{C}_0 + \bar{I} + \bar{G}) \\ &\quad - [\text{MPC}/[1 - (1 - t) \cdot \text{MPC}]] \cdot T_0 \end{aligned}$$

The change in the equilibrium in response to changes in the components of aggregate demand or T is

$$\begin{aligned} \Delta Y = {} & [1/[1 - (1 - t) \cdot \text{MPC}]] \cdot (\Delta C_0 + \Delta \bar{I} + \Delta \bar{G}) \\ & - [\text{MPC}/[1 - (1 - t) \cdot \text{MPC}]] \cdot \Delta T_0 \end{aligned}$$

The spending and the tax multipliers with an income tax are

$$\begin{aligned} M_{\text{Spending}} &= 1/[1 - (1 - t) \cdot \text{MPC}] \\ M_{\text{Tax}} &= -\text{MPC}/[1 - (1 - t) \cdot \text{MPC}] \end{aligned}$$

An income tax reduces the values of both multipliers. To see this, compare M_{Spending} without and with an income tax.

WITHOUT AN INCOME TAX	WITH AN INCOME TAX
$M_{\text{Spending}} = 1/(1 - \text{MPC})$	$M_{\text{Spending}} = 1/[1 - (1 - t) \cdot \text{MPC}]$

The income tax increases the value of the denominator and lowers the value of the spending multiplier. For example, the text assumed an MPC of .80 and a marginal tax rate, t, of .25. M_{Spending} without the income tax is 5. With the income tax

$$\begin{aligned} M_{\text{Spending}} &= 1/[1 - (1 - .25) \cdot .80] \\ &= 1/[1 - (.75 \cdot .80)] \\ &= 1/(1 - .60) \\ &= 1/.40 = 2.5 \end{aligned}$$

The 25 percent marginal tax rate reduces the value of the spending multiplier by half. The income tax is a powerful automatic stabilizer.

THE COMPLETE MODEL WITH THE FOREIGN SECTOR

The demand for net exports, exports minus imports, is the final component of aggregate demand.

Export demand in the United States is independent of U.S. national income.

$$Ex^d = \overline{X}$$

Import demand in the United States is directly related to U.S. national income, according to the relationship

$$Im^d = M_0 + \text{MPM} \cdot Y$$

M_0 is the portion of import demand that is unrelated to the level of national income, and MPM is the marginal propensity to import.

The equilibrium condition for the full model is

$$Y = C^d + I^d + G^d + (Ex^d - Im^d)$$

Substitute the equations for all the components of aggregate demand into the right-hand side of the equilibrium condition, and solve for Y.

$$Y = C_0 + \text{MPC} \cdot (1 - t) \cdot Y - \text{MPC} \cdot T_0 + \bar{I} + \overline{G} + [\overline{X} - [M_0 + \text{MPM} \cdot Y]]$$

$$Y - \text{MPC} \cdot (1 - t) \cdot Y + \text{MPM} \cdot Y = (C_0 + \bar{I} + \overline{G} + \overline{X} - M_0) - \text{MPC} \cdot T_0$$

$$Y \cdot [1 - \text{MPC} \cdot (1 - t) + \text{MPM}] = (C_0 + \bar{I} + \overline{G} + \overline{X} - M_0) - \text{MPC} \cdot T_0$$

$$Y = [1/[1 - (1 - t) \cdot \text{MPC} + \text{MPM}]] \cdot (C_0 + \bar{I} + \overline{G} + \overline{X} - M_0) - [\text{MPC}/[1 - (1 - t) \cdot \text{MPC} + \text{MPM}]] \cdot T_0$$

The change in the equilibrium in response to changes in the components of aggregate demand or T_0 is

$$\Delta Y = [1/[1 - (1 - t) \cdot \text{MPC} + \text{MPM}]] \cdot (\Delta C_0 + \Delta \bar{I} + \Delta \bar{G} + \Delta \bar{X} - \Delta M_0) - [\text{MPC}/[1-(1 - t) \cdot \text{MPC} + \text{MPM}]] \cdot \Delta T_o$$

The value of the spending multiplier is now

$$M_{\text{Spending}} = 1/[1 - (1 - t) \cdot \text{MPC} + \text{MPM}]$$

Imports lower M_{Spending} still further because MPM increases the value of the denominator. For example, the text assumed MPM = .10. The value of M_{Spending} with MPC = .80, t = .25, and MPM = .10 is

$$\begin{aligned} M_{\text{Spending}} &= 1/[1 - (1 - .25) \cdot .80 + .10] \\ &= 1/[1 - (.75 \cdot .80) + .10] \\ &= 1/(1 - .60 + .10) \\ &= 1/.5 = 2 \end{aligned}$$

Compare this with M_{Spending} = 2.5 above, with an income tax, but no import demand.

Taxes and import demand act as automatic stabilizers because they reduce the *marginal propensity to spend out of national income* from .80 (the MPC) in the simplest model of the economy to .50 in the complete model. The income tax takes \$.25 of every \$1 of national income generated out of the circular flow of economic activity during each round in the multiplier process, leaving consumers with a \$.75 increase in disposable income. They spend .80 (the MPC) of their disposable income, or \$.60 of the \$1 increase in *national income,* in the next round of the multiplier process (\$.60 = .80 · \$.75). But \$.10 of their spending is on imports, which leaks out of the circular flow of economic activity into the pockets of foreign producers. Therefore, the increase in *domestic* aggregate demand and national income is \$.50 in the next round of the multiplier process for every \$1 of *national income* generated in the preceding round. The marginal propensity to spend out of national income is .50, which is the denominator of the spending multiplier.

QUESTIONS

1. a. Given the following information for an economy, find the equilibrium level of national income, Y_E.

$C^d = 200 + .8 \cdot Y_d$ — Y_d = disposable income
$I^d = 10$ — Y = national income
$G^d = 70$ — C^d = consumption demand
$T = 100 + .3 \cdot Y$ — I^d = investment demand
G^d = government demand for goods and services
T = income taxes (transfer payments are zero)

b. What is the value of the spending multiplier for this economy?

2. Now add net exports to the economy in question 1.

$Ex^d = 50$ — Ex^d = export demand
$Im^d = 10 + .2 \cdot Y$ — Im^d = import demand

a. Find the new equilibrium level of national income, Y_E.
b. What is the value of the marginal propensity to import?
c. What is the value of the spending multiplier for this economy?

CHAPTER

32

Business Cycles: The Multiplier-Accelerator Model and the Real Business Cycle

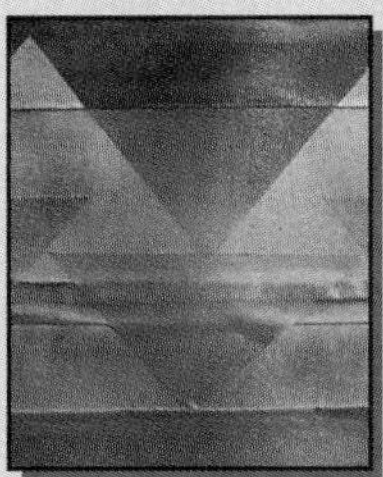

LEARNING OBJECTIVES

CONCEPTS TO LEARN

The business cycle	Multiplier-accelerator model
Indexes of cyclical indicators	Real business cycle model

CONCEPTS TO RECALL

Laws of Supply and Demand [5, 6, 7]	Equilibrium level of national income [29]
Gross domestic product (GDP) [27]	Investment demand [29]
Aggregate demand and aggregate supply [28]	Life-Cycle Hypothesis [29]

We saw in Chapter 4 that there is no such thing as a perfect economic system. The centrally planned socialist economies of Eastern Europe and the Soviet Union collapsed under the weight of oppressive central bureaucracies and grossly misallocated resources that made their economies highly unproductive. Their citizens believed that capitalism was the better alternative.

Capitalism is not a perfect economic system either, however. The Achilles' heel of capitalism is the business cycle, the continual ebbs and flows of economic activity that at times throw people out of work and at other times send prices spiraling upward. Capitalist countries live perpetually in the shadows of the Great Depression of the 1930s and the hyperinflations in Western Europe following each of the world wars.

Understanding the causes of business cycles has always been the number one research goal of modern macroeconomics, yet economists are still a long way from reaching that goal. The business cycle is perhaps the least understood and most controversial topic in all of economics.

You certainly will not find a definitive answer to the question of what causes business cycles in this text. Chapter 32 turns to an analysis of the business cycle with two more modest goals in mind. The chapter begins with a discussion of how economists and policy makers monitor the performance of the economy and what they have learned about business cycles in the United States. We then consider two popular models of the business cycle. One, called the multiplier-accelerator model, is widely embraced by new Keynesian economists. The other, called the real business cycle, has become the principal model used by new classical economists to explain how the macro economy operates.

MONITORING THE BUSINESS CYCLE IN THE UNITED STATES

Most economic historians credit Wesley C. Mitchell with being the founding father of modern research on the business cycle. Mitchell's treatise *Business Cycles,* published in 1913, was the first detailed, systematic study of the macroeconomic performance of the developed market economies. Then, in 1920, Mitchell was instrumental in forming the National Bureau of Economic Research (NBER), whose primary research agenda in the beginning was to monitor the economic performance of the United States and 16 other developed market economies. The NBER quickly became recognized as the center of business cycle research in the United States, a position it holds to this day.

The Traditional View of the Business Cycle

Mitchell and his colleagues at the NBER established the traditional view of macroeconomic fluctuations. They pictured the developed market economies as moving through a recurring series of temporary expansions and contractions that cycle around a more permanent trend rate of growth in real national prod-

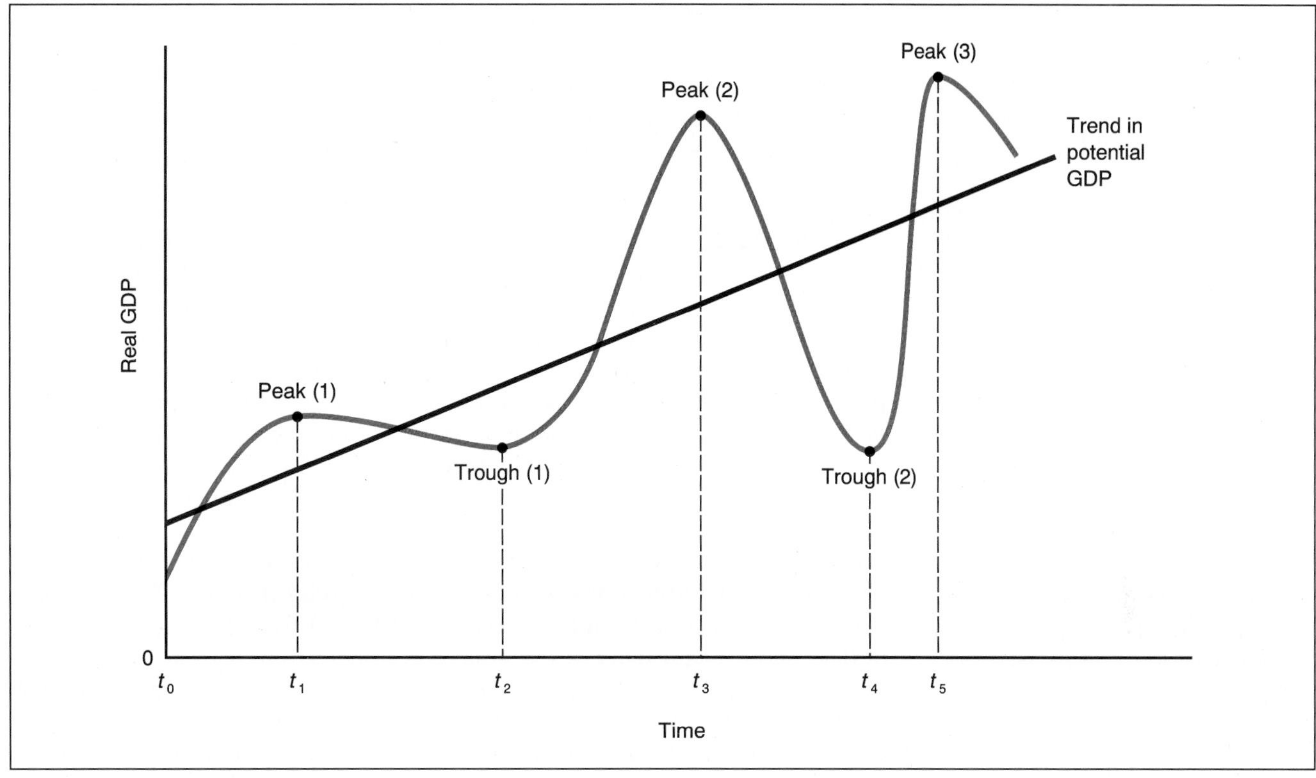

FIGURE 32.1

The Phases of the Business Cycle

The figure illustrates the different phases of the business cycle. Time is on the horizontal axis and real GDP is on the vertical axis. The straight line represents the production possibilities frontier, the maximum sustainable level of real GDP, which is assumed to grow at a constant rate over time. At time t_0 the economy is an expansion phase of the cycle, which ends at time t_1 when the cycle reaches its peak. Then the economy moves into the contraction phase of the cycle which lasts until t_2, when the cycle reaches its trough. A new expansion phase begins after t_2 and continues until the cycle reaches another peak at t_3. The economy continues to cycle indefinitely. The figure shows two complete peak-to-peak business cycles. The length of the first business cycle is $(t_3 - t_1)$, and the length of the second cycle is $(t_5 - t_3)$. The first of the two business cycles is both longer and shallower than the second business cycle.

uct; hence the term *business cycles.* This is the view we used when describing the performance of the U.S. economy since 1977 in Chapter 25. The NBER's view of the macro economy was essentially unchallenged until the new classical real business cycle theory came along in the 1980s.

Figure 32.1 illustrates the traditional view. Real gross domestic product (GDP) is on the vertical axis, and time is on the horizontal axis. The straight line through the cycles is the permanent, trend rate of growth in potential GDP. It represents the rate at which the production possibilities frontier is moving out over time, or the rate of long-run economic growth. We saw in Chapter 3 that increases in potential GDP require changes in the quantity or the quality of a nation's resources and changes in production technologies. Mitchell and his colleagues at the NBER presumed that these changes occur fairly slowly, and fairly steadily, over time. They recognized that the rate of long-run economic growth could change over time, as it did in the United States after 1973. But they believed that these changes would happen only infrequently, so that it was reasonable to think in terms of a fairly permanent, underlying trend rate of economic growth.

The cycles track the actual performance of the economy over time, the temporary expansions and contractions of real GDP year by year. Following the graph, the economy is in the midst of an **expansion phase** at time t_0. The expansion phase continues until time t_1, when the economy reaches a **peak.** The peak represents a turning point, after which the economy enters a **contraction phase,** commonly referred to as a *recession*. The contraction phase continues until time t_2, when the economy reaches a **trough.** The trough represents another turning point, after which the economy rebounds and enters a second expansion phase. The second expansion phase reaches its peak at time t_3, after which the economy enters a second contraction phase. The contraction phase continues until the trough at time t_4, after which a new expansion phase begins again. The pattern continues on indefinitely, with alternating periods of expansion and contraction cycling around the permanent trend line.

EXPANSION PHASE (BUSINESS CYCLE)

The period of time during which economic activity is increasing; commonly referred to as a *boom*.

PEAK (BUSINESS CYCLE)

A turning point in the business cycle when the expansion phase ends and the contraction phase begins.

CONTRACTION PHASE (BUSINESS CYCLE)

The period of time during which economic activity is declining; commonly referred to as a *recession*.

TROUGH (BUSINESS CYCLE)

A turning point in the business cycle when the contraction phase ends and the expansion phase begins.

Economists describe business cycles in terms of their length and severity, both of which can vary considerably from cycle to cycle. The *length* of one complete business cycle is the time from one peak to the next.[1] The peak-to-peak measure identifies two complete business cycles in Figure 32.1, the first one lasting from t_1 to t_3 and the second one lasting from t_3 to t_5. The *severity* of the cycle is the distance of the peaks and troughs from the underlying trend line, which can vary within each cycle. For example, economists speak of a shallow or a deep recession, depending how far the trough of the cycle is below the production possibilities frontier. The first business cycle in the figure is both longer and shallower than is the second business cycle.

CYCLICAL INDICATORS Mitchell and the other NBER economists pioneered a method of monitoring the performance of the overall economy by following over time a large number of data series, which they called cyclical indicators. A **cyclical indicator** is a data series that meets three criteria: economic significance, current availability and reliability, and timing.

CYCLICAL INDICATOR

A monthly or quarterly data series that contains reliable and significant information concerning the performance of the economy over time and that moves in a pattern consistent with the movement of the overall business cycle.

A data series can satisfy the criterion of economic significance in one of two ways. It can be an important component of one of the four elements of the economy that the NBER monitors over time: output, income, employment, or trade (both domestic and international). Or it can be something that macro economists believe has a significant influence on one or more of these elements, such as the nation's money supply. The NBER has never just monitored the growth of GDP alone.

The criterion of current availability and reliability means that the data are available periodically over a very short period of time, preferably monthly, but no longer than quarterly. The data also must be of good quality, collected from reputable and reliable sources and comparable over a long period of time. A data series is not useful for monitoring the performance of the economy if the information contained in the series keeps changing over time.

The third criterion, timing, is the heart of the matter. The data series must move over time in a pattern consistent with the movement of the overall business cycle. Most important, the peaks and the troughs of the data series must bear a reasonably consistent relationship to the peaks and the troughs of the business cycle.

[1]A complete cycle could also be measured from trough to trough, which would identify a different business cycle, with a different length, from the peak-to-peak measure. The peak-to-peak measure is the one commonly used.

The NBER began publishing its list of cyclical indicators in 1938, and the list has since grown to include over 100 series. The U.S. Department of Commerce elevated the NBER to semi-official status as the monitor of the economy when the department agreed, in 1961, to publish the NBER's cyclical indicators each month in its *Business Conditions Digest.* That publication remained in existence until 1990; the department now incorporates the cyclical indicators within its monthly *Survey of Current Business.*[2]

THE INDEXES OF CYCLICAL INDICATORS The Department of Commerce pushed the method of cyclical indicators one step further in 1968 when it developed and began publishing three indexes based on the cyclical indicators: the index of leading indicators, the index of coincident indicators, and the index of lagging indicators. Each index is a composite of cyclical indicators that have similar timing, but that cover different sectors of the economy or different types of economic activities. The department chooses the "best" cyclical indicators for each of the indexes according to the three criteria mentioned above.

The **index of leading indicators** is designed to forecast aggregate economic activity and to predict the turning points of the business cycle, both the peaks and the troughs. Therefore, the peaks and the troughs of the cyclical indicators chosen for this index must precede the peaks and the troughs of the business cycle. The index consists of the 11 cyclical indicators listed in Table 32.1.

INDEX OF LEADING INDICATORS
An index of 11 cyclical indicators that is designed to forecast aggregate economic activity and predict the turning points of the business cycle.

The **index of coincident indicators** is designed to track the expansion and the contraction phases of the business cycle, and its turning points, as they occur. The index consists of the four cyclical indicators listed in Table 32.1. Notice that each cyclical indicator corresponds to one of the four elements of the economy that the NBER attempts to monitor: employment, income, output (production), and trade.

INDEX OF COINCIDENT INDICATORS
An index of four cyclical indicators that is designed to track the expansion and the contraction phases of the business cycle, and its turning points, as they are occurring.

The **index of lagging indicators** is designed to confirm the existence of the various phases of the business cycle and its turning points. As such, it is expected to move over time in the same pattern as the index of coincident indicators, with a few months' delay. The peaks and the troughs of the cyclical indicators chosen for this index must come after the peaks and the troughs of the business cycle. The index consists of the seven cyclical indicators listed in Table 32.1.

INDEX OF LAGGING INDICATORS
An index of seven cyclical indicators that is designed to confirm the existence of the various phases of the business cycle and its turning points with a few months' delay.

The leading, coincident, and lagging indexes are the most closely watched indicators of overall economic activity in the United States. They are widely reported each month in the news media because they are generally perceived to be a reasonably accurate gauge of the current state of the economy and where it is heading. The Department of Commerce has revised the composition and the construction of the indexes frequently since 1968 in a continuing effort to improve their ability to track the business cycle. The last revision was in January of 1989.

DATING THE PEAKS AND THE TROUGHS The Department of Commerce has left to the NBER the task of dating the peaks and the troughs of each business cycle. The NBER's reputation in U.S. business cycle research is such that its estimates of the peaks and the troughs are virtually the only estimates ever published or cited.

[2]The early history of the National Bureau of Economic Research and its approach to describing business cycles can be found in D. Zerwitz, "Business Cycles," *NBER Reporter: Program Report* (Spring 1989).

TABLE 32.1 **The U.S. Department of Commerce Indexes of Leading, Coincident, and Lagging Indicators, as of January 1989**

INDEX OF LEADING INDICATORS

1. Average weekly hours of production for nonsupervisory workers, manufacturing
2. Average weekly initial claims for unemployment insurance, state programs
3. Manufacturers' new orders in 1982 $, consumer goods and material industries
4. Contracts and orders for plant and equipment in 1982 $
5. Index of new private housing units authorized by local building permits
6. Index of stock prices, 500 common stocks
7. Money supply (M2) in 1982 $[1]
8. Vendor performance, percentage of companies receiving slower deliveries
9. Change in sensitive materials prices, weighted moving average, smoothed
10. Change in manufacturers' unfilled orders in 1982 $, durable goods industries, smoothed
11. Index of consumers' expectations, compiled by the University of Michigan Survey Research Center

INDEX OF COINCIDENT INDICATORS

1. Employees on nonagricultural payrolls
2. Personal income less transfer payments in 1982 $
3. Index of industrial production
4. Manufacturing and trade sales in 1982 $

INDEX OF LAGGING INDICATORS

1. Average duration of unemployment in weeks (inverted)
2. Ratio, manufacturing and trade inventories to sales in 1982 $
3. Average prime rate charged by banks
4. Commercial and industrial loans outstanding in 1982 $
5. Ratio, consumer installment credit outstanding to personal income
6. Change in index of labor cost per unit of output, manufacturing, smoothed
7. Change in CPI for services, smoothed

[1]M2 is a broad measure of the money supply that will be discussed in Chapter 33.

SOURCE: M. Hertzberg and B. Beckman, "Business Cycle Indicators: Revised Complete Indexes," *Business Conditions Digest* 29, No. 1 (1989): 97–102.

The NBER formalized the process of dating peaks and troughs in 1980 when it established an ongoing Business Cycle Dating Committee. The sole function of the committee is to meet on occasion to decide if a peak or a trough in the business cycle has occurred.

The committee does not use any simple objective rule to select a peak or a trough. Instead, it relies heavily on the NBER's cyclical indicators, and its decisions are ultimately quite subjective. For example, the committee reported that it identified a trough in November of 1982 by looking at data series on real GNP, real retail sales, real personal income, industrial production, and unemployment, "among others." The problem with this approach is that the cyclical indicators reach their own peaks or troughs at different times, so that the committee has to make a best-judgment call on whether the overall business cycle has reached its peak or trough.

A widely used simple rule of thumb is that the economy is in a recession if real GDP declines for two consecutive quarters. Presumably a recession is over by this rule as soon as real GDP grows for one quarter, since it has then no longer declined two quarters in a row. The Business Cycle Dating Committee could easily reach a different conclusion by looking at an entire set of cyclical indicators, however, as it did during the recession of the early 1990s.

The committee had identified July 1990 as the peak of the long expansion phase that began following the trough of November 1982. Real GDP subsequently fell during the last two quarters of 1990, a recession by the common rule of thumb. Real GDP then grew briefly during the first half of 1991, signaling the end of the recession by the common rule of thumb. The committee disagreed that the recession had ended, though, arguing that it would not want to identify a trough until the cyclical indicators it was following had returned to their previous peaks. Only then could the committee be sure, in retrospect, that the economy had entered an expansion phase. In fact, the recovery stalled in mid-1991, and the cyclical indicators stayed well below their previous peaks. Consequently, the committee declined to identify a business cycle trough at that time; in its judgment it was too early to tell if the economy had reached a trough. Finally, the committee met in December of 1992 and announced, with the advantage of hindsight, that the trough had occurred in March of 1991. As of mid-1993 the economy was still in a mild expansion phase heading toward the next peak.[3]

Evidence on Business Cycles in the United States

The NBER has identified nine peaks and nine troughs from the first post–World War II peak of December 1948 to the last trough in March 1991, eight full peak-to-peak U.S. business cycles over that 42 year period. Table 32.2 lists all the post-war peaks and troughs.

Victor Zarnowitz, a professor at the University of Chicago Business School and a senior research associate of the NBER, has recently completed a study that compared the six complete peacetime business cycles in the United States from 1912 to 1945 with the six complete peacetime business cycles from 1945 through 1982.[4] His study uncovered some very good news.[5]

For starters, the U.S. economy has become far more stable since World War II. Business cycles are much less severe in the more recent period, both the expansions and the contractions. As one example, Zarnowitz compared the changes in industrial activity and employment during the expansion and the contraction phases of the cycles during both periods. Industrial activity increased by 50 percent and employment by 22 percent, on average, during the expansion phases of the earlier period. The comparable figures for the later period are 26 percent for industrial activity and 11 percent for employment, roughly half as large. The decrease in the severity of the contraction phases has been even more pronounced. Industrial activity decreased by 27 percent and employment by 18 percent, on average, during the contraction phases of the earlier period. The comparable figures for the later period are 11 percent for industrial activity and only 3 percent for employment.

[3]For further discussion of the methods of the business cycle dating committee see R. Hall, "The Business Cycle Dating Process," *NBER Reporter: Program Report* (1991/92).

[4]The peacetime cycles exclude the two cycles that occurred during the world wars in the earlier period and the two cycles that occurred during the Korean and Vietnam wars in the later period.

[5]V. Zarnowitz, "Facts and Factors in the Recent Evolution of Business Cycles in the United States," *NBER Working Paper # 2865* (February 1989). See, especially, Tables 2 and 3. For an exhaustive study of the business cycle, see V. Zarnowitz, *Business Cycles: Theory, History, Indicators and Forecasting,* NBER Studies in Business Cycles, 27 (1990).

TABLE 32.2 Peaks and Troughs of U.S. Business Cycles Since World War II (year: quarter)

PEAK	TROUGH
1948:4	1949:4
1953:2	1954:2
1957:3	1958:2
1960:2	1961:1
1969:4	1970:4
1973:4	1975:1
1980:1	1980:3
1981:3	1982:4
1990:3	1991:1

SOURCE: V. Zarnowitz, "Facts and Factors in the Recent Evolution of Business Cycles in the United States," *NBER Working Paper #2865* (February 1989): Table 8. R. Hall, "The Business Cycle Dating Process," *NBER Reporter: Program Report* (Winter 1991/92): 1–3. Also, a telephone conversation with the NBER to determine the 1991:1 trough.

Zarnowitz offers a number of plausible explanations of why the economy has become so much more stable. Foremost among them is one that we noted in Chapter 31, a dramatic rise in the impact of automatic stabilizers, particularly within the government sector. He also believes that the shift to services in the later period has been stabilizing because the demand for services is much less sensitive to the business cycle than is the demand for manufactured products.

Another piece of good news is that the average proportion of time spent in the expansion phase during a complete business cycle has increased dramatically. In the earlier period 53 percent of the average cycle was spent in the expansion phase and 47 percent in the contraction phase. In the later period 75 percent of the average cycle was spent in the expansion phase and only 25 percent in the contraction phase.

The only characteristic that has not changed is the average length of a complete business cycle, which was 45 months in both periods. One wonders if this conclusion would stand had Zarnowitz extended the later period to the 1990s. The most recent peak-to-peak cycle ran from July 1981 to July 1990, 108 months, one of the longest complete cycles ever. The more recent data do appear to be consistent, however, with Zarnowitz's finding that the expansion phases are becoming longer and the contraction phases shorter. The expansion phase from November 1982 to July 1990 was among the longest expansion phases of the entire twentieth century.

A final comment concerns the ability of the index of leading indicators to forecast the business cycle. We noted in Chapter 28 that the large macroeconomic forecasting models have not done particularly well in forecasting the business cycle. In truth, the index of leading indicators has not fared any better. The index is an accurate predictor in the limited sense that since the index was first published in 1968, each peak and trough of the business cycles has been preceded by corresponding peaks and troughs in the index. This is hardly surprising, since the cyclical indicators in the index are chosen in large part because their turning points precede the turning points in the business cycle. But the forecasting value of the index of leading indicators is diminished because the lead time of the index has been highly variable. At times the index turning point is a month or two ahead of the business cycle turning point, at other times six months or more ahead. The index also has the distressing habit of issuing false signals in the form of extra turning points. The index has reached a peak or a trough four more times than the business cycle has since 1968, each time predicting a turning point that did not come. The Department of Commerce's frequent revisions notwithstanding, the index of leading indicators is not a dependable forecasting tool. This is hardly surprising, given that both the length and the severity of the business cycles are so variable in the United States.

Internal Versus External Business Cycles

Having now taken a look at the pattern of business cycles in the United States, let's return to the fundamental question of macroeconomics that we posed in the beginning of the chapter. Why do market economies have such a strong inherent tendency to move in cycles over time, through an endless succession of expansions and contractions? The aggregate demand models of Chapters 29 through 31 are not well equipped to answer this question because they are inherently static rather than dynamic. They show how the economy tends to move automatically to a single equilibrium level of national income for a given level of aggregate demand. They are not designed to show how the level of national income tends to move in cycles over time.

The equilibrium level of national income can change in these models, but only in one way—through shocks to aggregate demand. An aggregate demand shock is any event that causes aggregate demand to increase or decrease at every level of aggregate demand. In terms of the aggregate demand–45° line graph, an aggregate demand shock shifts the aggregate demand line *ADE* up or down. Increases or decreases in aggregate demand kick in the multiplier process, which causes the level of national income to increase or decrease for awhile until national income reaches its new equilibrium.

Economies are continually bombarded by aggregate demand shocks of all kinds, and these shocks certainly play a role in pushing national income up and down. Changes in consumer confidence often trigger large increases or decreases in consumption demand. Government purchases increase whenever nations enter into wars with other nations and then decrease when the wars end. Depreciations and appreciations of the dollar cause net export demand to rise and fall. Expansionary and contractionary fiscal and monetary policies can cause many or all of the components of aggregate demand to shift up and down simultaneously. Indeed, we noted in Chapter 26 that the University of Chicago's Robert Lucas, a leading new classical economist, believes that misguided fiscal and monetary policies have been a major cause of instability in the U.S. economy.

Our earlier models can analyze only aggregate demand shocks, but economies are also continually buffeted by aggregate supply shocks that directly affect production. Especially good or bad weather often has a dramatic impact on agricultural production. Strikes in a key industry such as steel can cripple production in a number of industries for awhile. Inventions and innovations often lead to long waves of investment demand as firms replace their outmoded capital. An obvious example has been the computerization of production after World War II following the invention of the analog computer. An earlier example was the electrification of both households and business firms in the late

1800s. Aggregate supply shocks must also play an important role in explaining economic fluctuations.

POLITICAL BUSINESS CYCLE

A theory that attributes the business cycle to attempts by the incumbent administration to manipulate the economy to increase its chances of re-election, consisting of expansionary pre-election policies and contractionary post-election policies.

Some economists even believe that they have found evidence of a **political business cycle,** in which the incumbent administration manipulates the economy to increase its chances of re-election. According to this theory, the administration engages in expansionary fiscal and monetary policies right before the election to reduce unemployment because it knows that jobs mean votes. Then, after the election, the administration engages in contractionary fiscal and monetary policies to offset the inflationary pressures that have built as a result of its pre-election expansionary policies. Most economists find this theory unpersuasive, however, if only because an administration is unlikely to be able to fine tune the economy in this manner, even if it were inclined to do so. The fiscal and monetary policy lags are simply too long and too uncertain for this strategy to work.

Aggregate demand and supply shocks may well play the leading role in explaining the economic fluctuations of the market economies. Even if this were so, however, a theory of the business cycle based entirely on these shocks is not entirely satisfactory. Aggregate demand and supply shocks are, by their nature, events that hit the economy in a largely random, unpredictable fashion. Yet the inherent tendency for market economies to move in cycles is so pronounced that any theory of the business cycle based solely on these shocks would have a gravity/anti-gravity feel to it: What goes up must come down, and what goes down must come up.

For this reason economists have long searched for internal mechanisms built into the economy that inherently cause the economy to move in cycles over time. The problem with built-in mechanisms is that they tend to predict business cycles that are far more regular and smooth than are actual business cycles. The idea, though, is that the internal mechanisms generate a tendency for regular cycles, and then outside aggregate demand and supply shocks upset the regular pattern somewhat. The combination of the internal mechanisms and the outside shocks generates the highly irregular business cycles that we observe.

Most of the early theories of the business cycle in the era of modern macroeconomics stressed internal mechanisms over outside shocks. The theories of the past 10 years or so have switched their primary emphasis to the role of outside shocks in explaining business cycles. We will look at one model of each type for the remainder of the chapter.

THE MULTIPLIER-ACCELERATOR MODEL

MULTIPLIER-ACCELERATOR MODEL

An internal model of the business cycle that is based on the instability of investment demand and its relationship to national income through both the demand side and the supply side of the economy.

One of the most successful and influential of the internal-mechanism business cycle models was also one of the first, the **multiplier-accelerator model** of investment demand developed by MIT's Paul Samuelson in 1939. Samuelson set out to modify Keynes's new theory of the macro economy so that it would generate business cycles.[6]

Samuelson reasoned that investment demand is likely to be an important cause of business cycles because it is by far the most volatile component of

[6]P. Samuelson, "Interactions between the Multiplier Analysis and the Principle of Acceleration," *Review of Economic Statistics* 21, No. 2 (May 1939): 75–78.

aggregate demand. The volatility of investment demand is to be expected. It is inherent in the stock-flow relationship between capital and investment. A small change in the demand for capital leads to a much larger change in investment demand.

To see why, suppose that a small firm has been using a stock of 100 personal computers and that the computers last an average of five years before they have to be replaced. Twenty computers wear out each year. Therefore, the firm has to invest in 20 new computers each year just to maintain the stock of computers at 100.

This year the firm decides to expand and determines that it will now need 110 computers. As a result, it has to invest in 30 computers this year, 20 to replace the worn-out computers and 10 to increase the stock to 110. Notice what has happened. A 10 percent increase in the firm's demand for capital, from 100 to 110 computers, has resulted in a 50 percent increase in the firm's investment demand, from 20 to 30 new computers.

In addition to the inherent instability of investment demand, Samuelson saw that investment demand for plant and equipment is related to national income in two ways, one through the demand side of the economy and one through the supply side. Investment is related to national income through the demand side of the economy because investment demand is one of the components of aggregate demand. Investment is related to national income through the supply side of the economy because firms need capital to produce goods and services, and they increase their stock of capital by investing in plant and equipment. The two-way relationship between investment and national income generates an inherent tendency for the economy to move in cycles. The theory is as follows.

The expansion phase—Suppose that the economy is initially in equilibrium. Consumers then become more confident about the future and increase their consumption demand. The increase in consumption demand begins to generate a multiplied increase in national income. The firms that produce consumer goods have to increase their production capacity to meet the increase in consumption demand, so they increase investment to increase their stock of capital. This is the supply side relationship between investment and national income that we have ignored in our previous analysis of the multiplier process.

The increase in investment demand leads to a further increase in aggregate demand and propels the economy to an even higher multiplied level of national income. The economy is going through its expansion phase. Samuelson saw the increase in investment demand as accelerating the multiplier process that was started by an increase in the consumption demand. This is why he called his theory the multiplier-accelerator model of the business cycle.

The peak—The expansion cannot continue indefinitely, however. Once firms increase their investment they are increasing the rate at which they are adding to their stock of capital. Remember, investment is the change in the stock of capital.

$$I = \Delta K$$

At some point they will decide that the *level* of investment, that is, the *rate of increase* in their stock of capital, is sufficient. Once they do, investment demand stops increasing and so does aggregate demand. The economy homes in on an equilibrium level of income, the peak of the business cycle.

The contraction phase—The economy cannot stay at the peak because the capital stock eventually catches up to the amount required to produce the peak level of goods and services. When it does, the firms do not need to invest at all. Investment demand declines to zero, which decreases aggregate demand and leads to a multiplied decrease in national income. The decrease in investment demand brings the economy into its contraction phase.

The trough—The economy homes in on a new equilibrium level of national income, the trough of the business cycle. Fortunately, the recession must end as well for the simple reason that capital depreciates as it is used in production. At some point enough capital will wear out that firms do not have enough capital left to produce even the recession-level of goods and services. Firms need to invest to replenish their capital stocks. The increase in investment demand increases aggregate demand and leads to a multiplied increase in national income. The economy is back in an expansion phase once again.

The pattern of expansions and contractions continues indefinitely. Notice that the cycles are internally generated by the dual demand—and supply-side relationships between investment and national income. The only outside shock to the economy was the initial increase in consumption demand at the beginning of the story.

Other Applications of the Theory

INVENTORY INVESTMENT In 1941, shortly after Samuelson published his theory, the University of Chicago's Alan Metzler discovered that the two key relationships underlying the multiplier-accelerator model applied to inventory investment as well.[7] Metzler's extension of Samuelson's theory was important. It showed that economies have at least one built-in mechanism that tends to keep recessions short because stocks of inventory are depleted very quickly once firms stop investing in inventory. In addition, changes in inventories tend to be a very large component of the changes in national income in the United States, especially during the contraction phase. Decreases in inventories accounted for 87 percent of the decreases in GDP, on average, during the eight contractions from World War II to 1990.[8]

CONSUMER DURABLES The multiplier-accelerator model also applies to consumer durables such as automobiles and major appliances because they have essentially the same attributes as capital goods. The stock of consumer durables and the purchase of new consumer durables bear the same stock-flow relationship to each other as do capital and investment. Not surprisingly, consumer durables are the most unstable component of consumption demand. Also, the stock-flow relationship leads to the same dynamic over time described above for investment demand.

For example, car sales are likely to move in cycles. A run of a few good years of car sales is almost certain to be followed by a bad year. As the stock

---

[7]L. A. Metzler, "The Nature and Stability of Inventory Cycles," *Review of Economic Statistics* 23 (August 1941): 113–129.

[8]A. Blinder and L. Maccini, "Taking Stock: A Critical Assessment of Recent Research on Inventories," *Journal of Economic Perspectives* 5, No. 1 (Winter 1991): 73–74. This is an excellent overview of the economic research on inventory investment.

of cars becomes ever newer, large numbers of consumers will eventually decide that they do not need to buy a new car. Conversely, a run of a few bad years of car sales is almost certain to be followed by a good year. Consumers can hold off their purchases of new cars only so long. As the stock of cars ages and their cars spend more time in the repair shop, large numbers of consumers will eventually decide that the time has come to buy a new car. This appears to have been the case in 1993, a particularly good year for the auto manufacturers. The average age of the cars on the road at the beginning of 1993 was about as high as it ever gets. Consumers could not delay buying those new cars any longer.

INVESTMENT, AGGREGATE DEMAND, AND THE COST OF CAPITAL The multiplier-accelerator theory rests on the notion that firms invest only if they see the demand for their products growing. As such, the theory is favored by those economists who believe that the growth in aggregate demand, and not the cost of capital, is the key to investment demand. These economists also tend to be new Keynesians because the multiplier-accelerator theory offers an important reason to worry about the level of aggregate demand. Remember, investment is the key to long-run economic growth. The multiplier-accelerator theory suggests that a high level of investment demand can occur only in an environment of rapidly growing aggregate demand.

EMPIRICAL RELEVANCE Samuelson's multiplier-accelerator theory has stood up pretty well to the test of time. As noted in Chapter 29, economists have had great difficulty isolating the factors that determine investment demand. Nonetheless, many economists have had some success predicting investment demand in both plant and equipment and in inventories using models based on the multiplier-accelerator theory. Moreover, whatever success the theory has in explaining inventory investment translates directly into an ability to track the U.S. business cycles, since changes in inventory investment account for such a large portion of the changes in national income. The overall weight of the investment research has convinced a large number of economists that the multiplier-accelerator mechanism is an important feature of the U.S. economy and an important force driving U.S. business cycles.

At the same time, many economists, especially those of the new classical persuasion, disagree with this position. The new classical economists have developed a completely different theory to explain the business cycle called the real business cycle, which we turn to next. The real business cycle model challenges virtually every aspect of the new Keynesian view of the macro economy, from how to interpret the business cycle, to how the economy operates, to whether fiscal and monetary policies can hope to improve the overall performance of the economy.

THE REAL BUSINESS CYCLE THEORY

New classical and new Keynesian economists have completely different explanations of the business cycle. Their differences begin with two fundamentally different assumptions about how the macro economy operates that we discussed in Chapter 28. The new classical economists assume that the economy is essentially competitive, with flexible wages and prices; the new Keynesian economists assume that the economy is riddled with market imperfections that give rise to sticky wages and prices. In addition, the new classical economists assume that consumers are Life-Cycle consumers for the most part; the new Keynesian economists assume that the typical consumer is a Keynesian consumer.

Recall that the new classical assumption of competitive factor markets implies that all resources are fully and efficiently employed so that the economy operates on its production possibilities frontier. Therefore, only one level of real GDP is possible in equilibrium, the full employment level of real GDP on the production possibilities frontier. The *AS* curve in the product markets is vertical at that output. Furthermore, only changes in aggregate supply can change the equilibrium level of output in the economy. These are changes in the quantity and quality of the nation's resources, or changes in production technologies, the same changes that cause the production possibilities frontier to shift out over time. Changes in aggregate demand, in and of themselves, only affect the equilibrium price level.

The study of the business cycle is inherently a long-run exercise because it follows the performance of the economy over a long period of time. Consistent with the long-run perspective, the new classical economists assume that households are forward-looking consumers who behave according to the Life-Cycle Hypothesis. They smooth their consumption over their entire lives in order to maximize their lifetime utility or satisfaction out of what they perceive to be their lifetime resources. Households adjust their consumption year by year as they receive new information about their lifetime resources, but always in a way that smooths lifetime consumption. An important implication of the Life-Cycle Hypothesis is that the marginal propensity to consume out of temporary changes in current disposable income is very low. In contrast, the Keynesian consumption function assumes that the marginal propensity to consume out of all changes in disposable income, temporary or permanent, is quite high.

Shocks Versus Internal Mechanisms

In addition to their different assumptions about the macro economy, the new classical economists have shifted the emphasis on what drives the economic fluctuations in market economies. They de-emphasize internal mechanisms, such as the multiplier-accelerator theory, and emphasize the role of outside shocks to the economy. According to the new classical view, market economies are driven by continual shocks to the fundamental structure of the economy, which consists of household preferences, resources, and production technologies. These are shocks to the real side of the economy as opposed to the monetary or the financial side; hence the term **real business cycle** to describe their theory.

REAL BUSINESS CYCLE THEORY

A theory to explain the business cycle developed by new classical economists that is based on outside shocks to the fundamental structure of the economy, which consists of household preferences, resources, and production technologies.

An example of a shock to preferences is a shift against saving and in favor of current consumption, such as appears to have occurred in the United States over the past 20 years. Examples of resource shocks are natural disasters, such as floods and hurricanes that destroy crops and property, and changes in the prices of imported raw materials, such as the dramatic increases and decreases in crude oil prices that buffeted the U.S. economy in the 1970s and 1980s. The most common type of technology shock is a technological change that increases the productivity of the nation's resources, particularly the productivity of labor because labor is the most important resource. Technological change can lead to the development of new products or to new, less costly ways of producing existing products. Also, the technological changes can arise in either the domestic economy or the foreign economies. If foreign firms are leading the way in technological change, the domestic firms may lose their markets to the foreign competitors, forcing resources to shift to new industries. An obvious example is the technological and competitive edge that Japanese firms have recently enjoyed over U.S. firms in many consumer electronic products, such as television and stereo equipment. Production in some of these areas has virtually ceased in the United States.

These real shocks may be temporary or permanent. Even if they are temporary, however, their effects on the economy persist for awhile and cause a period of expansion or contraction that has the appearance of a business cycle. New classical economists do not like the term *business cycle,* however, because it implies an underlying regular pattern to the expansions and contractions that they do not believe exists. Instead, the shocks are random and unpredictable and lead to the highly irregular pattern of expansions and contractions that we observe in all market economies. For this reason they prefer to call the irregular ups and downs of the economy *economic fluctuations* to remove any connotation of a regular cycle. The name *real business cycle theory* is something of a misnomer in this regard.

Technological Change and Economic Fluctuations

The real business cycle theory is still relatively new, having first appeared in the early 1980s. The theory to date has emphasized continuing, random productivity shocks in all sectors of the economy as the primary engine that drives economic fluctuations. In addition, the productivity shocks are assumed to result primarily from technological change, both domestic and foreign. The productivity shocks are positive, on average, so that the economy grows over time, but there is considerable variation around the average. This explains why the pattern of expansions and contractions is so irregular.

The emphasis on productivity shocks is understandable, given that only changes in aggregate supply can change real output in the competitive new classical macro model. A productivity shock is an aggregate supply shock that shifts the vertical AS curve to the right for a favorable shock and to the left for an unfavorable shock. A favorable shock makes the nation's resources more productive, thereby expanding the nation's production possibilities frontier. National product and national income also increase as the competitive economy remains on the frontier. Conversely, an unfavorable shock makes the nation's resources less productive, thereby decreasing the nation's production possibilities frontier. National product and national income also decrease as the competitive economy remains on the frontier.

Productivity shocks generate economic fluctuations in the new classical competitive model that are consistent with two well-documented facts about economic fluctuations in the United States:

1. *All the aggregate real variables in the private sector tend to move together.* Output, consumption, investment, and employment all tend to increase during an expansion. Conversely, output, consumption, investment, and employment all tend to decrease during a contraction.

2. *Real wages are pro-cyclical.* Real wages refer to purchasing power, the ratio of wages to the prices of the goods and the services that workers buy with their wages.

$$W_{real} = W/P$$

Where W is the wage and P is a broad price index of goods and services such as the consumer price index (CPI) or the GDP deflator. Real wages tend to increase during expansions and decrease during contractions, although only slightly.

A theory of economic fluctuations ought to be consistent with these two facts, and the new classical real business cycle theory is. Let's consider the standard real business cycle story of an expansion driven by a positive productivity shock as an example.

Suppose that some new technological change leads to a temporary increase in labor productivity throughout the economy. The increase in labor productivity increases the production possibilities frontier and allows output and income to expand. Also, because labor is more productive, it commands a higher real wage, and households' real disposable incomes rise. The households do not consume all of their additional income, however, because they are Life-Cycle consumers. They realize that the increase in disposable income is only temporary, so they consume only a small part of it and save the rest. The saving allows them to spread the consumption gains over their lifetimes.

The increase in saving finances an increase in investment. Remember, the only two final products that firms can produce are consumption goods and investment goods, and the competitive factor markets keep the economy on its production possibilities frontier. Therefore, the saving by households translates directly into more investment by firms.

The increase in investment increases the capital stock and allows firms to increase production. The investment alone cannot increase output very much, however, because it is only a small percentage of the capital stock. For example, net investment in the United States in 1992 was approximately $120 billion, which represented less than a 1 percent increase in the $14 trillion stock of capital.[9] Employment has to increase to get a significant increase in output because labor is by far the more important factor of production. The workings of the labor market are crucial in any analysis of economic fluctuations.

Real business cycle theory assumes that labor markets are competitive, operating according to the Laws of Supply and Demand. The temporary, productivity-enhancing technological change does increase employment, as illustrated in Figure 32.2.

The vertical axis records the real wage, not the nominal wage, and the horizontal axis the quantity of labor. People base their labor supply decisions on the real wage because they know that the real wage defines how much purchasing power they have to buy goods and services. They do not jump at a 10 percent wage increase if they know that prices are also rising by 10 percent.

---

[9]Board of Governors of the Federal Reserve System, *Balance Sheets for the U.S. Economy, 1945–92* (Washington, D.C: U.S. Government Printing Office, 1993), Table 11.1. U.S. Department of Commerce, Economics and Statistics Administration, Bureau of Economic Analysis, *Survey of Current Business* 73, No. 3 (March 1993): Table 1.1, p. 6 and Table 1.9, p. 8.

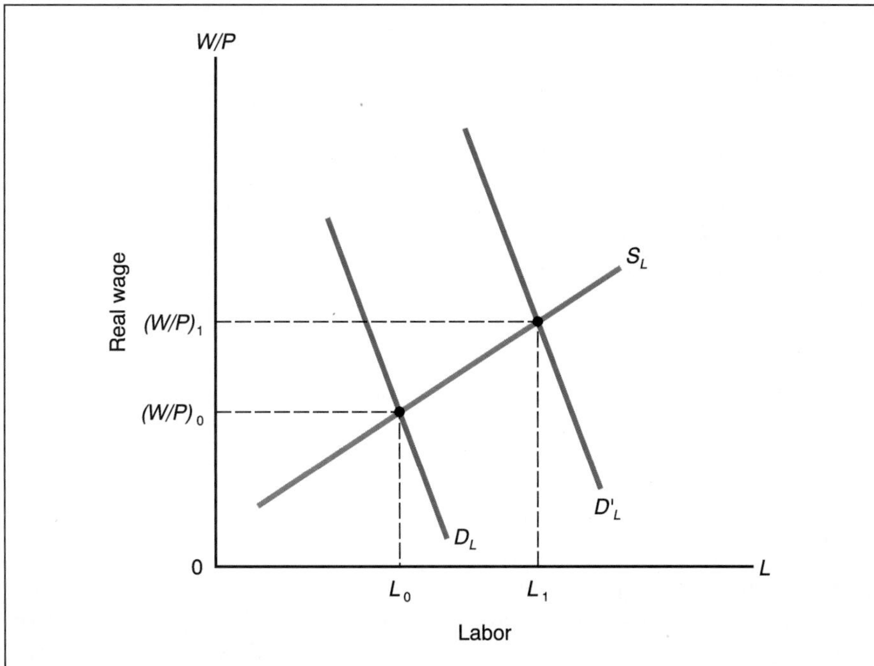

FIGURE 32.2

Competitive Labor Markets and the Real Business Cycle

Real business cycle theory assumes that labor markets are competitive for the most part, as in the figure. The quantity of labor is on the horizontal axis. The real wage, W/P, is on the vertical axis because firms base their hiring decisions on the real wage and workers base their labor supply decisions on the real wage. The initial equilibrium is $(L_0,(W/P)_0)$, at the intersection of the labor demand and supply curves D_L and S_L. An increase in labor productivity increases the firms' demand for labor from D_L to D_L^1. The new equilibrium is $(L_1, (W/P)_1)$, at the intersection of D_L^1 and S_L. Workers increase the amount of labor they supply from L_0 to L_1 in response the higher real wage, and the larger labor supply allows firms to increase production. Measured unemployment is always at the natural rate of unemployment when labor markets are competitive. The new classical economists argue that any reduction in measured unemployment as the economy expands is primarily due to a decrease in voluntary search unemployment or in frictional unemployment.

Similarly, employers base their hiring decisions on the real wage, which they compare to the productivity of the workers. They, too, think in real terms, comparing wages to the prices of their products. The original equilibrium before the technological change occurs at $[L_0, (W/P)_0]$, at the intersection of D_L and S_L.

The technological change makes workers more productive to firms, so their demand for labor shifts from D_L to D_L'. The new equilibrium is $[L_1, (W/P)_1]$, at the intersection of D_L' and S_L. Both the real wage and employment rise, and the increase in employment is the primary reason why firms are able to increase their output.

In summary, the standard real business cycle story of an economic expansion driven by technological change is entirely consistent with the two basic facts about economic expansions in the United States. Output, consumption, investment, and employment all increase, and the real wage rises. Also, the desire of households to smooth consumption and increase saving, which increases investment, provides a mechanism for the expansion to continue after the immediate impact of the technological change ends. Firms will be increasing the capital stock and expanding output and income for quite some time after the technological change occurs.

REFLECTION: You should think through the opposite case of a decrease in productivity by reversing all the steps of the story above. See how it generates a contraction in which output, consumption, investment, and employment all decrease and the real wage falls.

Does Real Business Cycle Theory Fit the Facts?

How well does real business cycle theory fit the facts of economic fluctuations in the United States? It has the direction right; how about the magnitudes?

Two leading new classical economists, Finn Kydland and Edward Prescott, gave real business cycle theory a tremendous boost in 1982 when they published a paper showing that the theory fits the facts remarkably well.[10] They built a very simple macro model and used estimates from various empirical studies to specify the various components of the model, such as the aggregate demand for consumer goods, the total supply of labor, and aggregate production as a function of labor, capital, and technological change. The idea was to make the various components of their model consistent with the U.S. economy. They then hit their model with a series of productivity shocks and traced the reaction to the shocks over time. The productivity shocks were the actual shocks to aggregate production in the United States, defined as the changes in aggregate output that could not be explained by changes in the quantities of labor and capital. The aggregate productivity shocks defined in this way move up and down over time in the United States, essentially at random.

Their simple model explained the facts of U.S. economic fluctuations extremely well, capturing about 70 percent of the annual changes in output, consumption, investment, employment, and the real wage overall. The percentages were somewhat higher than 70 percent for output, consumption, and investment and somewhat lower than 70 percent for employment and the real wage. The success rate was especially noteworthy because the Kydland and Prescott model was so incredibly simple. Among other simplifications it had a single representative consumer, one consumer good, nothing but competitive markets operating according to the Laws of Supply and Demand, no government or international sectors, and no money or other financial variables. New classical economists were convinced that the competitive real business cycle model was an appropriate benchmark model for thinking about the U.S. economy.

Real business cycle theory quickly became the leading theory within the new classical perspective, without any serious competitors. The research agenda was set. New classical economists went about refining the basic Kydland/Prescott model, adding financial variables and accommodating different kinds of shocks, such as changes in preferences. Real business cycle theory is so new that this research is still in its preliminary stages. We will consider some of the refinements that have been published in later chapters.

Implications of Real Business Cycle Theory

Real business cycle theory has cast a completely new light on the nature of economic fluctuations.

EXTERNAL SHOCKS VERSUS INTERNAL MECHANISMS As already noted, the theory changes the emphasis from internal mechanisms to external shocks as the driving force behind economic fluctuations. The previous emphasis on internal mechanisms assumed that economies had an inherent tendency to move in regular cycles because of built-in features, such as the multiplier-accelerator process of investment. The outside shocks to the economy made the patterns of expansion and contraction irregular, but the internal mechanisms were still

[10] F. Kydland and E. Prescott, "Time to Build and Aggregate Fluctuations," *Econometrica* 50, No. 6 (1982): 1345–1370.

the principal driving forces in the economy. Real business cycle theory argues that the internal mechanisms are relatively unimportant. Almost all the changes in the economy are due to the external shocks.

THE NATURE OF ECONOMIC FLUCTUATIONS The most remarkable implication of real business cycle theory is its interpretation of the economic fluctuations themselves. The traditional NBER view that the fluctuations are temporary cycles moving around a more or less permanent, trend rate of growth in potential GDP had dominated macroeconomic thinking for nearly 60 years. According to the traditional view, the business cycle was an economic bad, something to be avoided and overcome through the application of fiscal and monetary policies. The goal of fiscal and monetary policies, stated in terms of the business cycle, was to dampen both the expansion and the contraction phases of the cycles so that the economy operates closer to the trend rate of growth. Dampening the cycles avoids periods of overheating, which build up inflationary pressures, and periods of slack with lots of unemployed resources.

Real business cycle theory offers a completely different and quite remarkable interpretation of the expansions and the contractions. The economy is so highly competitive that it is always operating either on or very near its production possibilities frontier. As a result, the economy does not cycle around a more or less permanent, trend rate of growth in potential GDP, as represented in Figure 32.1. The trend line simply does not exist. The fluctuating line in the figure is not just the actual performance of the economy; it is also the *potential* of the economy as well. *The economy and the production possibilities frontier move together over time, for all intents and purposes.* Actual GDP and national income move up and down over time because aggregate supply shocks, such as technological change, move the production possibilities frontier in and out over time, thereby allowing actual output to change.

In essence, households and firms are always reacting as best they can to a series of continuing random shocks to the economy. Since they interact in competitive markets for the most part, their reactions are as efficient as can be expected.

NO ROLE FOR FISCAL AND MONETARY POLICIES The interpretation that economic fluctuations are efficient reactions to outside shocks leads immediately to the main policy conclusion of real business cycle theory. *Fiscal and monetary policies cannot improve the performance of the economy in the short run.*

Budgetary policy, properly conceived, is just a matter of microeconomic resource allocation. A nation must decide what functions it wants the government to perform and how to raise the revenues needed to pay for these functions. Budgetary policy has no short-run macroeconomic stabilizing purpose in the sense of reacting to the business cycle. The only potentially useful macroeconomic function for the government is to influence the rate of long-run economic growth by running structural budget surpluses or deficits to increase or decrease national saving.

Likewise, the government should make sure that the money supply is large enough to accommodate the overall level of production and spending. Beyond that, the government should not try to manipulate the economy in the short run through monetary policy. Needless to say, these implications for fiscal and monetary policies are quite different from the new Keynesian implications.

The New Keynesian Attack

The new Keynesians have mounted a fierce attack against the real business cycle on a number of different fronts.

DOES REAL BUSINESS CYCLE THEORY FIT THE FACTS? The first issue is whether a real business cycle model really does fit the facts all that well. Martin Eichenbaum of Northwestern University reworked the original Kydland/Prescott model to see if its results stood up to small changes in the underlying parameters and in the sample period over which it was simulated.[11] Eichenbaum found that even slight changes in either the parameters or the sample period do significantly change the results. His analysis suggests that the Kydland/Prescott model could explain anywhere from 5 to 200 percent of U.S. economic fluctuations. Eichenbaum concluded that the Kydland/Prescott real business cycle model is not a reliable benchmark model of the U.S. economy.

WHAT TECHNOLOGICAL CHANGES? New Keynesian economists also wonder what these large technological changes are that are supposedly driving the economy. Fairly large productivity changes are needed to change output significantly in the standard real business cycle model, yet the only obvious large supply shocks to the U.S. economy in recent years have been the oil price changes in the 1970s and 1980s. Also, technological changes that increase productivity are understandable. What, though, is an example of technological regress that lowers productivity and brings on an economic contraction?

LABOR HOARDING IS THE SOURCE OF PRODUCTIVITY CHANGES New Keynesians concede that the productivity measure Kydland and Prescott used to shock their model rises and falls over time. But the standard explanation of the movement in labor productivity is labor hoarding in a new Keynesian unemployment environment, not technological change. According to new Keynesians, firms lay off workers during contractions, but they retain many experienced employees who have established long-run employment relationships with their firms. They keep the experienced employees because they do not want to bear the costs of hiring and retraining new employees when the economy recovers. The retained, or "hoarded," workers are underemployed during the downturn; they are not working to full capacity. The result is that output falls more rapidly than does employment during a contraction, and measured labor productivity declines rather sharply. Then, as the economy recovers into the expansion phase, the firms hire new workers, but not as many as they would if they had not hoarded some of their experienced employees during the downturn. The result is that output increases more rapidly than does employment during expansions, and measured labor productivity increases rather sharply.

COMMENT: In the early 1990s the media reported an upsurge in labor productivity in the United States. Much of the surge is bogus, however, the result of the downsizing phenomenon. Companies are subcontracting more of their work to outside firms, rather than performing the work in-house. As a result, the ratio of their sales to their own labor costs rises dramatically. Also, many salaried employees are working longer hours, but this does not show up in the firms' labor costs.

An interesting study by NBER research associates Robert Barsky and Jeffrey Miron strongly supports the labor-hoarding explanation of productivity changes.[12]

---

[11]M. Eichenbaum, "Real Business Cycle Theory," *Journal of Economic Dynamics and Control* 15 (1991): 607–626. The 5 to 200 percent estimate is on p. 608.

[12]R. Barsky and J. Miron, "The Seasonal Cycle and the Business Cycle," *NBER Working Paper # 2688* (August 1988).

Barsky and Miron studied the well-known, highly regular cycle-within-a-cycle that happens every year in the United States, the seasonal pattern of expansion and contraction during the course of the year. Output regularly surges in the second and fourth quarters and declines in the first and third quarters. The second-quarter surge is due to an increase in construction activity in the northern part of the country as the weather warms up and allows construction workers to return to outside work. The fourth quarter surge is the result of the Christmas season and is by far the larger surge. These seasonal patterns are so regular that the national income accountants typically "seasonally adjust" their data to remove the seasonal effects and get a better picture of the underlying movement in the data. Barsky and Miron realized that the seasonal patterns may help resolve some of the issues that the new Keynesians and the new classical economists have been debating.

The seasonal data strongly support the labor-hoarding story. Labor productivity tends to increase sharply in the fourth quarter each year during the Christmas surge. The Christmas season is clearly a demand-led phenomenon in line with the new Keynesian view of the economy; it has nothing to do with technological change.

LABOR MARKETS ARE NOT SO COMPETITIVE The new Keynesians also question the competitive labor market story that underlies the real business cycle model. Both employment and unemployment vary considerably during expansions and contractions in the United States. New classical real business cycle theory assumes that the employment fluctuations are voluntary responses to changes in the real wage—workers move along their labor supply curves as the real wage increases and decreases. New classical economists also believe that most of the change in measured unemployment lies in voluntary search unemployment or frictional unemployment. In their view, unemployment declines during the upswing because the unemployed reduce the average time searching for new jobs in order to take advantage of higher real wages. Conversely, unemployment rises during the downswing as real wages fall and search time increases.

New Keynesians point out that the real wage is pro-cyclical, but only slightly so. The magnitude of employment changes actually observed in the United States could only occur if the supply of labor is highly responsive to changes in the real wage. Yet virtually all labor market research concludes that exactly the opposite is true—the labor supply does not respond much at all to changes in the real wage. The truth, according to the new Keynesians, is that most of the changes in employment and unemployment are the result of increases and decreases in involuntary unemployment in an environment of imperfect labor markets and sticky wages. Most of the changes in measured unemployment are in the involuntary job loser category, as firms fire workers during contractions and hire workers during expansions. This is why output, consumption, investment, and employment all move together over the business cycle. It has little to do with voluntary changes in labor supply. Many new Keynesians find preposterous the notion that economic downturns are efficient responses to outside shocks and require no policy intervention.

WAGES AND PRICES ARE STICKY Along those same lines, new Keynesians also deny the competitive assumption of the real business cycle model. They believe that sticky wages and prices, and nonclearing markets, are the most important features of developed market economies. New Keynesian research is focused on the question of how very different kinds of households and firms react in different kinds of market settings. New classical research is focused on the question of how representative households and competitive firms respond to changing economic conditions. The new Keynesians believe that the new classical research agenda is the wrong agenda for understanding the U.S. economy.

MONEY MATTERS Finally, the new Keynesians ask the new classical real business cycle proponents to explain why real GDP appears to be so responsive to changes in the money supply, which is a financial shock to the economy rather than a real shock.

The New Classical Counterattack

The new classical economists are not without their defenses against the charges and can mount an impressive counterattack on a number of points as well.

PRODUCTIVITY SHOCKS They argue that aggregate productivity changes are not the result of large, visible events, but rather the cumulation of thousands of small changes in industries throughout the economy. On average, the economy experiences technological progress and grows, but there is much variation around the average.

MICRO VERSUS MACRO LABOR SUPPLY RESPONSES Regarding the working of the labor markets, they would argue that the empirical estimates of labor supply responsiveness are misleading. The labor market research has been focused at the micro level, on the labor supply response of individuals. Most of the change in hours of work during expansions and contractions, however, is the result of a relatively small number of people making large, all-or-none, 40-hour-per-week movements in and out of the labor force. This explains why the macro employment response to small changes in real wages is large, whereas the micro individual response appears to be quite small. Real wages change enough over the cycle to drive a fair number of people over the all-or-none line, so that total hours of work change substantially.

MONEY FOLLOWS OUTPUT New classical economists concede that changes in the money supply and changes in real GDP are highly correlated. Both increase and decrease together. But they argue that the new Keynesians have cause and effect reversed. The money supply follows and accommodates changes in output; it does not cause changes in output. We will have to wait a few chapters to pursue this issue. Suffice it to say that the Barsky/Miron study of the seasonal cycle comes down strongly on the new classical side here. The money supply typically surges in the fourth quarter, along with the surge in Christmas sales. The government is clearly increasing the money supply to accommodate the Christmas demand. The increase in the money supply is certainly not causing the Christmas demand.

WHERE ARE THE NEW KEYNESIAN MICRO FOUNDATIONS? When they go on the attack, the new classical economists argue that the new Keynesians are simply assuming wage and price stickiness. The new Keynesians, they say, have not yet been able to explain convincingly how wage and price stickiness is compatible with the idea that households and firms are trying to solve their economic problems as best they can by engaging in exchange. How do sticky prices and wages, and involuntary unemployment, maximize the economic interests of either households or firms? The new classical economists charge that the new Keynesians have not been able to answer this fundamental question. In contrast, competitive markets with flexible prices do maximize their economic interests, which is why it is a good assumption.

REAL BUSINESS CYCLE THEORY IS MUCH LESS DEVELOPED Finally, the new classical economists point out that Keynesian theory is over 60 years old, whereas real business cycle theory is little more than 10 years old. They believe that the real business cycle is a good and proper benchmark model for understanding the U.S. economy and that the best research agenda is to continue to develop and refine the model.

A Reconciliation?

Are you confused about how the economy operates and what policies the government should undertake to manage the economy, if any? If you are, be assured that you are not alone. The new Keynesian and the new classical economists have put forth completely different views about the nature of economic fluctuations, how the macro economy operates, and whether fiscal and monetary policies are useful. Moreover, the two views are a long way from a reconciliation. Listen to what some of the leading economists from each school have to say.

Charles Plosser of the University of Rochester is a strong proponent of the real business cycle model. He chides the new Keynesians for their lack of convincing and consistent micro foundations based on the choices people make to solve their economic problems, which leads the new Keynesians into ad hoc theorizing, such as the multiplier-accelerator model. He sees this as an "essential flaw," a "fundamental problem" with the new Keynesian theory, so essential and fundamental that "the underpinnings of our understanding of economic fluctuations are likely to be found somewhere other than a suitably modified version of the Keynesian model."

New Keynesians Gregory Mankiw and Lawrence Summers, both of Harvard University, are just as strident on the other side.

Mankiw: "[Real business cycle theory] will, I predict, ultimately be discarded as an explanation of observed fluctuations."

Summers: "[Real business cycle theory] has no ability to explain economic fluctuations in the United States or other capitalist economies."

Plosser, Mankiw, and Summers do not sound like economists who are about to reconcile their differences, do they?[13]

---

[13]C. Plosser, "Understanding Real Business Cycles," *Journal of Economic Perspectives* 3, No. 3 (Summer 1989): 51–77. The quotes are on pp. 51 and 52. N. G. Mankiw, "Real Business Cycles: A New Keynesian Perspective," *Journal of Economic Perspectives* 3, No. 3 (Summer 1989): 79–90. The quote is on p. 89. L. Summers, "Some Skeptical Observations on Real Business Cycle Theory," *Quarterly Review*, Federal Reserve Bank of Minneapolis (Fall 1986): 23–27. The quote is on p. 24.

Unfortunately, empirical research using aggregate macroeconomic data is unlikely to be able to resolve the differences between the new Keynesian and the new classical economists in a convincing fashion. Bits and pieces of evidence supporting one side or the other of the kinds mentioned above will undoubtedly continue to emerge; but decisive evidence one way or the other, probably not. The conclusion is inescapable: Macroeconomics these days is truly in a state of turmoil when it comes to explaining the short-run ebbs and flows of the economy and what to do about them.

SUMMARY

Chapter 32 began with a discussion of how economists and policy makers monitor the performance of the economy and what they have learned about business cycles in the United States.

1. The National Bureau of Economic Research (NBER) has been recognized as the center of research on the U.S. business cycle since its founding in 1920. The NBER established the traditional view of the business cycle as a temporary, recurring series of expansions and contractions moving around a more or less permanent, trend rate of growth in potential real GDP. The trend rate of growth is the rate at which the production possibilities frontier moves out over time.
2. The NBER also pioneered the technique of monitoring the performance of the economy by means of a broad set of cyclical indicators. Cyclical indicators are data series that are reliable, are currently available, are economically significant, and reflect the timing of the overall business cycle to some degree. The NBER has traditionally monitored the behavior of output, income, employment, and trade.
3. The Department of Commerce publishes three indexes that are composites of the NBER's cyclical indicators.
   a. *The index of leading indicators* is designed to forecast aggregate economic activity and predict the peaks and the troughs of the business cycle.
   b. *The index of coincident indicators* is designed to track the expansion and contraction phases of the business cycle, and the peaks and the troughs, as they are occurring.
   c. *The index of lagging indicators* is designed to confirm the existence of the phases of the business cycle and its turning points.

These three indexes are the most closely watched indicators of overall economic activity in the United States.

4. The Business Cycle Dating Committee of the NBER is charged with identifying the peaks and the troughs of the business cycle in the United States, and everyone uses its estimates. The committee relies on a broad set of cyclical indicators, and a fair amount of judgment, in determining the peaks and the troughs. The NBER has identified nine peaks and nine troughs since the first post–World War II peak in December of 1948, eight complete peak-to-peak business cycles in all.
5. A recent study by the NBER's Victor Zarnowitz compared the U.S. business cycles from 1945 to 1982 with the cycles from 1912 to 1945. He found that the business cycle has become much less severe in the recent period,

on average, due in large part to the increased automatic stability in the economy. Zarnowitz also found that the expansion phase has increased substantially relative to the contraction phase. The average length of the complete cycle has not changed; it was 45 months in each period. Business cycles are highly irregular, however. There is considerable variation around the average length and severity of the cycles.

The second section of the chapter presented Samuelson's multiplier-accelerator model of investment demand.

6. The multiplier-accelerator model is an example of an internal mechanism built into the economy that tends to generate business cycles.
7. Investment demand is inherently unstable because of the stock-flow relationship between capital and investment. A small percentage change in the demand for capital leads to a much larger percentage change in the demand for investment.
8. Investment demand bears a dual relationship to national income, one operating through the demand side of the economy and one operating through the supply side of the economy. The demand-side relationship is that investment demand is part of aggregate demand. The supply-side relationship is that firms need capital to produce goods and services, and they increase their stock of capital by investing.
9. Investment "accelerates" the expansion phase of the cycle because firms need to invest in order to increase their production capacity to meet the growing demand. Investment also brings about and accelerates the contraction phase of the cycle because firms do not need to add to their production capacity when the economy is at its peak, or when the economy is declining. Investment demand falls at these times. The economy eventually recovers from the recession as capital depreciates and firms have to increase investment again to replenish their capital stocks.
10. Many new Keynesian economists believe that the multiplier-accelerator mechanism is an important driving force behind the business cycle in the United States.

The final section of Chapter 32 presented the new classical real business cycle theory of economic fluctuations, which is now the main branch of the new classical school.

11. Real business cycle theory stresses outside shocks to the real structure of the economy as the driving force behind economic fluctuations. The real structure consists of preferences, resources, and production technologies. The models of the past 10 years have assumed that the principal shocks are productivity shocks caused by technological change.
12. The basic real business cycle story of an expansion is that a temporary technological change expands the production possibilities frontier and increases households' incomes by increasing the real wage. Households are Life-Cycle consumers. They save most of the temporarily higher real wage, which leads to an increase in investment. They also increase their labor supply because of the higher real wage, which increases employment and allows output to expand. The story is consistent with the two main facts of economic fluctuations in the United States: Output, consumption, investment, and employment all tend to increase (and decrease) simultaneously, and real wages are pro-cyclical.

13. Since the new classical economists assume that the economy is competitive, they do not view economic fluctuations in the traditional way (that is, as temporary cycles around a permanent trend). There is no permanent trend in potential real GDP distinct from the actual performance of the economy. The shocks expand and contract the production possibilities frontier, and the competitive economy remains on its frontier for all intents and purposes.
14. The economic fluctuations result when households and business firms react as well as they can to the continuing random shocks to the economy. Furthermore, their reactions are as efficient as can be expected because markets are essentially competitive. Therefore, fiscal and monetary policies cannot improve the performance of the economy in the short run.
15. The new Keynesians challenge the real business cycle theory on a number of grounds. They believe that wages and prices are sticky, that much unemployment is involuntary, and that changes in involuntary unemployment explain why all the real economic variables move together over the cycle. They also believe that the swings in labor productivity are the result of labor hoarding, not technological change. They refuse to believe that economic downturns are efficient responses to economic shocks and see the need for corrective fiscal and monetary policies.
16. The principal new classical counterargument is that the new Keynesians have been unable to explain how their assumptions of wage and price stickiness are compatible with the economic interests of households and firms who are trying to solve their economic problems through exchange.

KEY TERMS

contraction phase (business cycle)
cyclical indicator
expansion phase (business cycle)
index of coincident indicators
index of lagging indicators
index of leading indicators
multiplier-accelerator model
peak (business cycle)
political business cycle
real business cycle theory
trough (business cycle)

QUESTIONS

1. What are some reasons why the U.S. economy has become more stable in the second half of the twentieth century than it was in the first half of the twentieth century?
2. What are some of the difficulties that economists at the NBER face in trying to determine the peaks and the troughs of a business cycle?
3. Is each of the following events an aggregate demand shock or an aggregate supply shock to the economy, or both?
   a. OPEC countries increase the price of oil.
   b. The U.S. government sends military troops to Somalia for a relief operation.
   c. Scientists discover a new form of energy that decreases production and transportation costs.
   d. The Clinton administration increases public investment in infrastructure throughout the country.
4. Why must both the contraction phase and the expansion phase of a business cycle eventually come to an end, according to the multiplier-accelerator model of the business cycle?
5. a. Suppose that producers believe that an increase in demand for their goods will be followed by an even larger increase in demand in the future. What would be the effect of such a demand increase on net investment, according to the multiplier-accelerator theory of the business cycle?
   b. Suppose, instead, that producers believe that the increase in demand will last only for one year and then return to its current level. How would this affect net investment?

6. Discuss the major differences between the multiplier-accelerator theory and the real business cycle theory in their attempts to explain the persistence of business cycles.
7. Suppose that an economy enters a recession; national output decreases, and unemployment increases. The government asks two economists for policy advice. One of the economists is a proponent of new Keynesian theory, and the other one is a devoted new classical economist. Based on your knowledge of these two theories, explain what policy advice you think that each economist would give.
8. a. What are the main points of the new Keynesian critique of real business cycle theory?
   b. What are the main points of the new classical critique of the new Keynesian theories?
9. What is the major difference between the traditional view (represented by the NBER) and the new classical view of the business cycle? In particular, how do they differ in interpreting the cyclical changes in output?
10. How do the new classical economists explain large fluctuations in employment accompanied by small changes in real wages?

CASE

Hard Times in California*

The U.S. standard of living sagged over the three years from 1989 to 1992, reflecting four years of recession and slow economic growth. The national unemployment rate rose from 5.3 percent in 1989 to 7.4 percent in 1992, and income per person dropped by $170 in constant 1992 dollars.

Californians bore more than their share of the downturn. Their income per person fell by $960 in constant 1992 dollars, the largest decrease suffered by any state, and their unemployment rate soared from 5 percent to 9 percent. From 1990 to 1991 alone, California employers shed over half a million workers from their payrolls.

One major blow to the California economy was the cutback in national defense spending. In 1988, federal spending on military contrasts in California was double the national average on a per person basis. But as the United States spent less on aircraft and munitions after the fall of the Soviet Union, defense workers found pink slips in their pay envelopes. For example, over 150,000 California aerospace workers lost their jobs.

A second large shock hit the construction sector. Developers across the nation built thousands of office towers and shopping malls in the early 1980s in response to special incentives in the Economic Recovery and Tax Act of 1981. Just as it was becoming clear that they had overbuilt, the Tax Reform Act of 1986 knocked out the tax incentives that were propping up the commercial construction sector, and the worsening savings and loan crisis removed much of its funding. The construction sector collapsed nationwide. The collapse was particularly severe in California because it was accompanied by slowing population growth. Knowing that jobs were unavailable in California, fewer people moved into the state and ever more people moved out. The slower population growth meant reduced demand for new houses, as well as for offices and shopping malls.

Battered by the defense cutbacks and the collapse of its construction sector, California would have plunged into depression, not merely a recession, were it not for the presence of a considerable amount of automatic stability in the California economy. One major source of automatic stability is "import" demand, where imports refer to purchases from other states. When Californians buy fewer automobiles, part of the impact is felt in Michigan. When they buy fewer carpets and less furniture, the profits of factories in the Carolinas decline. Consequently, some of the multiplier effect from reduced defense and construction activity is felt by other states, not California.

The second important automatic stabilizer for the California economy is federal taxes and transfer payments. As Californians were becoming poorer relative to the rest of the country, they sent smaller amounts from their paychecks to the U.S. Treasury. They also received more federal transfers in the form of public assistance and unemployment compensation. As a result, while the average income of Californians fell by $960 over three years, their average *disposable* income fell by only about $460, nearly $500 less. Much of

(continued on next page)

*Provided by David Denslow, University of Florida.

Hard Times in California (cont.)

the difference came from lower federal taxes and higher federal transfers.[1]

Every state, not just California, has the advantage of being partially insured against severe regional recessions by federal taxes and transfers. For example, the Midwest economy suffered during the early 1980s as the soaring value of the dollar overseas slashed the demand for American food and industrial products. Other regions of the country shared their losses as the proportion of national taxes paid by the Midwest fell and the proportion of federal transfers received increased. When the turn came for the East and West coastal regions to tumble in the late 1980s and early 1990s, the Midwest helped out by paying a larger fraction of national taxes and receiving a smaller share of federal transfers.

The nationwide scope of our insurance against regional downturns intrigues Europeans, as they attempt to move toward a single currency. If Europe adopts a single currency, then no nation will have an independent monetary policy. Just as California cannot fight its recession by expanding its money supply to cut interest rates, so France would be unable to push its interest rates below those in the rest of Europe. With a single currency, all the Western European nations would have the same interest rates.

The Europeans know that if California were a separate country, it might enjoy some advantages from having its own monetary policy. Also, the California dollar could float against the U.S. dollar, just as the Canadian dollar does now, and help cushion shocks to the economy. But any such gains would be more than offset by the loss of the insurance against local recessions through federal taxes and transfers. Knowing this, some economists are questioning whether Europe would be wise to adopt a single currency if the European nations are unwilling to forge a community-wide system of taxes and government transfer payments.

[1]The California income data are from U.S. Bureau of Economic Analysis (BEA) diskettes, May 1993 release. The employment data are from recent BEA county diskettes, which also contain state data.

ECONOMIC ADVISOR'S REPORT

Suppose that the governor of California hires you to advise him on how the state government can help fight the recession in California.

1. What policies that you might recommend to President Clinton to fight a national recession would be unavailable to the governor to fight the California recession?
2. Do you think that the governor has any highly effective policy tools for getting the state's economy back on its feet? If yes, what are they and why are they effective? If no, why not?

   Now suppose that you are advising the European Community (EC) in the year 2000, and assume that they have adopted a single currency.
3. Would you advise the EC to adopt a community-wide unemployment insurance program financed by an EC income tax? What are the advantages and disadvantages of such a plan?

PART

IX

Money and Monetary Policy

CHAPTER

33

The Nature of Money and Banking: First Principles

LEARNING OBJECTIVES

CONCEPTS TO LEARN

U.S. money supply
Balance sheets, assets, and liabilities
Demand for money
Velocity of circulation
The equation of exchange
The properties of money
The Fed
Commercial banks (depository institutions)
Open Market Operation

CONCEPTS TO RECALL

The circular flow of economic activity [4]
Hyperinflation [26]

Chapters 33, 34, and 35 turn to a topic that is near and dear to all of us—money. Money is the magical, mystical side of economics. It is not a resource or factor of production like labor, capital, or land. The dollar bills that you carry with you are just pieces of paper with no inherent value of their own. They are not backed by anything—you cannot turn them in at the nearest bank for gold or silver or anything else. Your checking account balance that you write checks against to buy things is nothing more than a configuration of electrons on some computer storage disk. Yet most economists believe that the amount of dollar bills and checking account balances has a profound effect on the circular flow of **real** *goods and services. We want to understand why and how this can be so in the next three chapters.*

Chapter 33 begins our study of money with two specific goals in mind. We want to understand the nature of money and to see why money is so important to the functioning of the macro economy.

The study of money and monetary policy is chock full of details about financial institutions and financial markets that are unfamiliar to most beginning students of economics. Rather than dive right in, Chapter 33 begins with some general principles relating to money that apply to all market economies regardless of their particular financial arrangements. Institutional details of the U.S. monetary system are kept to a bare minimum. These general principles will prepare us for the various institutional details relating to the supply of money in the United States that appear in Chapters 34 and 35.

WHAT IS MONEY?

The natural starting point in our analysis of money is to pin down what it is that we are talking about. What exactly is money? This turns out to be a difficult question to answer. Many things have served as money throughout history, and the nature of money tends to change and evolve within a country over time.

MONEY

Anything that is routinely used to pay for goods and services or to pay off debts.

We have to begin somewhere, though, so let's accept for now the most common definition of money. **Money** is anything that is routinely used to pay for goods and services and to pay off debts. According to this definition, the money supply in the United States and in all the other developed market economies consists of three items: currency, checking accounts with unlimited checking privileges (providing the account has sufficient funds), and traveler's checks.

CURRENCY

The dollar bills and coins of various denominations circulating in the economy.

FEDERAL RESERVE BANKING SYSTEM

The central bank of the United States.

FEDERAL RESERVE NOTE

A dollar bill of any denomination that is the paper currency of the United States.

Table 33.1 lists the average daily amount of each item in the United States during 1992. The table indicates that currency and checking accounts are the only two components of the money supply of any consequence. We can safely ignore traveler's checks in our analysis of money.

Currency refers to the dollar bills and coins of various denominations circulating throughout the economy. Dollar bills are called Federal Reserve Notes because they are issued by the **Federal Reserve Banking System,** the "Fed" for short, which is the central bank of the United States. (Take out a bill, and notice that "Federal Reserve Note" appears along the top of the face side.) Economists usually refer to dollar bills as **Federal Reserve Notes,** labeled

TABLE 33.1 The Money Supply in the United States, 1992 (Average Daily Amount)

COMPONENT		AMOUNT (BILLIONS)
Currency		$279.4
Transactions deposits		679.1
Demand deposits	319.2	
Other checkable deposits	359.9	
Travelers checks		8.1
Total money supply		$966.6

SOURCE: Council of Economic Advisors, *Economic Indicators, March 1993* (Washington, D.C.: U.S. Government Printing Office, 1993), 26–27.

FRN, a practice we will follow in this text. The issuing of paper currency today is controlled by the central banks in all the developed market economies.

Coins used to be an important component of all currencies, but they are relatively unimportant today. Pennies, nickels, dimes, and so on amount to only a few billion dollars in the United States.

Checking accounts with unlimited checking privileges are called **transactions deposits.** They include *regular checking accounts* that do not pay interest and the various kinds of *NOW and Super NOW* accounts that do pay interest. NOW stands for negotiable order of withdrawal.

TRANSACTIONS DEPOSIT
A checking account with unlimited checking privileges.

The U.S. government's publications list the regular checking accounts as "demand deposits" because the balances in these accounts are payable to the owners on demand. In contrast, banks have the right to hold up payment on NOW accounts for a few days, although they almost never exercise the right. The government lists them as "other checkable deposits."

Businesses own most of the regular checking accounts in the United States because they are not allowed to hold NOW accounts. Households own most of the NOW accounts. The vast majority of transactions deposits are held with commercial banks.

You or someone in your family may have a deposit account at a bank with limited checking privileges, such as a money market deposit account with a three- or a six-check limit per month. These accounts are not considered to be part of the money supply because they are not *routinely* used to pay for goods and services or to pay off debts.

Notice, also, that credit card transactions are not part of the money supply. You may buy something with a credit card, but you do not literally *pay* for it with the card. A credit card transaction is really a short-term loan from a merchant to you, with the credit card company standing in the middle. Your credit card allows you to take possession of goods and services before you pay for them. The credit card company pays the merchant with a check at the end of the month, and you then pay the credit card company, usually by check. Most credit card companies allow you to spread the payment over a number of months with an interest charge, at which point they become the lenders, not the merchant. The point is that the actual payment for goods and services in credit card transactions in made by check, not by credit card.

Two final words of caution are in order when thinking about money because of the way that the term *money* is used in everyday speech. First, people tend to think of money only in terms of currency, as in "I have to get some 'money' out of my NOW account." Don't fall into that trap. Balances in NOW accounts and regular checking accounts are money, too. Indeed, as Table 33.1 shows, they are the most important component of the money supply. You do not increase the amount of money that you have when you go to the bank and write a $50 check for "Cash" against your NOW account to get $50 worth of Federal Reserve Notes (FRN). Instead, you are merely changing the form of your money, substituting $50 of FRN for $50 in your NOW account. Get used to thinking of checking account balances as money.

In addition, take special care to distinguish between money and income. They are very different concepts, yet they tend to be used interchangeably in everyday speech. The confusion arises because we are paid in money for our work. For instance, suppose that you have a work-study job and your friend asks you: "How much money did you make last semester?" Everyone understands the meaning of this question. Still, "making money" refers to printing new money in economic analysis, and private citizens cannot do this, at least not legally. Better to ask: "How much income did you earn last semester?"

Income is a flow variable, such as the amount earned over a given period of time—an *hourly* wage, an *annual* salary, or work-study earnings over a *semester*. Money is a stock variable; it does not have a time dimension. The data in Table 33.1 were computed by measuring the amount of money in the economy at the end of each business day during 1992 and then calculating the average of the daily amounts for the year. The average amount of currency, checking accounts, and traveler's checks held by the public in 1992 is a very different concept from the flow of national income received by the public in the nation's factor markets during 1992. The distinction between money and income is crucial in macroeconomic analysis.

THE CIRCULAR FLOW AND THE EQUATION OF EXCHANGE

The importance of money to the operation of the economy can best be understood with reference to the circular flow of economic activity. Chapter 27 presented three different measures of the circular flow: national income, national product, and value added. They calculate the circular flow at three different points on the circle. National income measures the flow of activity through the nation's factor markets. National product measures the flow of activity through the nation's product markets. And value added measures the contribution to overall economic activity by the producers in the economy.

National income, national product, and value added essentially measure the total amount of *marketed* activity within the economy during the year. This suggests that the circular flow can also be measured in terms of money because money is the second part of all market exchanges. Goods and services (including factors of production) pass from the sellers to the buyers in exchange for money, which passes from the buyers to the sellers. Therefore, the circular flow of (marketed) economic activity must be equal to the product of two terms: the average amount of money in the economy multiplied by the number of times that money changes hands from buyers to sellers during the course of a year.

The measure of the circular flow in terms of money is called the **equation of exchange,** written

$$M \cdot V = Y$$

Y is the current dollar value of the national income; M is the average amount of money in the economy; and V is the **velocity of circulation,** or velocity for short, the number of times that money changes hands to pay for final goods and services (or, alternatively, for primary factors of production) during the year.

The equation of exchange is another national income accounting identity because the velocity of circulation is defined as the ratio of the national income to the money supply:

$$V = Y/M$$

In other words, the velocity of circulation converts the average *stock* of money, the money supply, into a *flow* of national income during the course of a year.

For example, in 1992 the average money supply (M) in the United States was $966.6 billion, and the national income (Y) was $4,744.1 billion.[1] Therefore, the velocity of circulation in1992 was 4.91.

$$V = Y/M = \$4{,}744.1/\$966.6 = 4.91$$

Alternatively,

$$Y = M \cdot V = \$966.6 \cdot 4.91 = \$4744.1$$

Viewed from the perspective of the equation of exchange, the U.S. economy generated a national income of $4,744.1 in 1992 because the money supply of $966.6 changed hands between buyers and sellers 4.91 times during the year.

The equation of exchange is also commonly represented in terms of the national product and written

$$M \cdot V = P \cdot Q$$

The right-hand side of the equation represents the current dollar value of the national product as prices times the quantities: the prices of the goods and services times the quantities of the goods and services flowing through the nation's product markets. The national product version of the equation of exchange has the advantage of separating out price changes (inflation) from quantity changes within the circular flow from year to year.

EQUATION OF EXCHANGE
The measure of the circular flow of economic activity in terms of money; a national income accounting identity, which says that the dollar value of national income or national product equals the product of the money supply times the velocity of circulation.

VELOCITY OF CIRCULATION
The ratio of the dollar value of national income or national product to the money supply; the number of times the money supply changes hands during the year to buy final goods and services (or primary factors of production).

Velocity and the Demand for Money

The velocity of circulation depends on the demand for money by households, businesses, and government agencies. To understand the connection between

[1]Council of Economic Advisers, *Economic Indicators, March 1993* (Washington, D.C.: U.S. Government Printing Office, 1993), 4, 26, and 27.

velocity and the demand for money you must understand what the demand for money means.

DEMAND FOR MONEY

The average amount of money that a person or an institution wants to hold and not spend.

Our demand for money is *not* the answer to this question: Would we like more money? (Sure we would, in unlimited amounts!) Instead, the **demand for money** is the amount of money that we want to hold at any one time and not spend. This is a tricky concept, however, because we do not want money for its own sake, unlike any other good or service. Money is useful to us only because we can get rid of it in exchange for goods and services. Also we do not tend to hold a given amount of money. Quite the contrary; our money holdings vary considerably over time. The amount of money that we have increases when we cash or deposit our paychecks and then decreases as we spend our money. Consequently, the demand for money has to be interpreted as an average amount of money held over a period of time.

The following simple example illustrates the concept of demand for money. Suppose that you earn $200 each month from a work-study job and get paid once a month. You place your entire work-study check in your NOW account at the beginning of the month and write checks on your account during the month to buy goods and services, drawing your account down to zero on the last day of the month. You then replenish your account with another $200 work-study check on the first day of the next month and proceed to write checks as before, drawing the account down to zero at the end of the month. The same pattern continues each month. To keep the example simple, assume also that you do not use Federal Reserve Notes. The balance in your NOW account is the only money that you have.

The amount of money that you hold in this example varies from $200 to zero and is hardly ever constant for more than a day at a time. Therefore, your demand for money has to be interpreted as the average of your money holdings each day during the month. You hold relatively large amounts of money during the first days of the month, near $200, and relatively small amounts of money during the last days of the month, nearer to zero. Suppose that you spend your money evenly over the month, the same amount each day. In this case, the average of your daily money holdings would be $100, the midpoint between the beginning-of-month $200 balance and the end-of-month zero balance. The $100 average balance is your demand for money.

Interpreting the demand for money as an average amount held establishes the link between velocity and the demand for money. Your personal velocity of circulation in our example is equal to 2 (measured on a monthly basis). You support $200 of income or spending each month with an average of $100 of money.

$$\begin{aligned} V_{\text{Personal}} &= \text{monthly income/average amount of money held} \\ &= \$200/\$100 = 2 \end{aligned}$$

Turning the ratio upside down, your demand for money, an average daily balance of $100, is equal to one-half of your monthly income of $200. In other words, velocity is just the inverse of the demand for money expressed as a proportion of income. The velocity is 2; the demand for money as a proportion of income is one-half. The inverse relationship between velocity and the demand for money is an important link in understanding how money affects the economy.

The Importance of Money in the Economy

The equation of exchange is a simple, yet powerful, tool for seeing the potential economic effects of money on the economy. For example, suppose that the velocity of circulation happened to be a constant equal to $\overline{V}$. All households, businesses, and government agencies want to hold an amount of money that is a constant proportion of their incomes for some reason. The equation of exchange in this case is

$$M \cdot \overline{V} = P \cdot Q$$

We can see that monetary policy has a very potent effect on the economy with V constant. A change in the money supply must lead to a change in prices, P, or to a change in real output, Q, or to both. And therein lies the magic of money. Money, after all, is nothing more than pieces of paper, in the case of Federal Reserve Notes and configurations of electrons stored on computer disks, in the case of checking accounts. Yet changes in the money supply can directly affect the circular flow of economic activity. That the amount of money in the economy can affect the prices of goods and services is not so surprising. What is surprising, though, is that money can affect the real side of the economy. This substance called money can determine whether or not someone has a job! Other pieces of paper and other configurations of electrons stored on computer disks do not have this power. Call them money, however, and they are able to affect the rate of inflation and unemployment, two of society's macroeconomic policy goals. We want to understand why money has such power.

Let's stay with the example of constant velocity to explore further the potential consequences of money for the real side of the economy. Chapters 29 through 31 analyzed the effects of changes in aggregate demand on the economy without any mention of the money supply. When economists do not mention an economic variable, they are implicitly assuming that the variable is constant, the other things equal assumption. Therefore, the analysis in those chapters implicitly assumed that the money supply was constant. We also assumed that prices were constant in order to focus on changes in real income or output when there are lots of unemployed resources. If velocity is constant as well, then the equation of exchange implies that real income or output must also be constant. Constant M, V, and P imply a constant Q. Remember, the equation of exchange is a national income accounting identity; it has to be true at all times.

But a constant Q means that the value of the spending multiplier (and all the other fiscal policy multipliers) must be zero because real income or output cannot change. A change in one component in aggregate demand must necessarily be completely offset by equal changes in aggregate demand in the opposite direction to maintain the economy at a constant equilibrium level of real income. Fiscal policy is useless; only monetary policy can affect the economy.

Don't worry, though. All that you learned in Chapters 29 through 31 has not been for naught. The point of the constant velocity example is simply to show that the presence of money in the economy has an impact on all aspects of the economy. In fact, the velocity of circulation is not constant; it varies somewhat from year to year.

For example, velocity defined in terms of national income ranged from a high of 5.60 to a low of 4.71 between 1980 and 1990. The average annual change in velocity, plus or minus, during the 1980s was only 0.22, or 4.2 percent of its average value. Velocity fell steadily from 1981 to 1986, with the exception of one upward tick in 1984, and then rose steadily from 1986 to 1990.[2]

Velocity tends not to be highly variable in normal times because it is largely determined by institutional factors that change only slowly, such as how often people are paid and how they pay for goods and services. We will see in Chapter 35 that the demand for money, and thus velocity, also responds to changes in economic variables such as the level of national income and interest rates.

Changes in aggregate demand can affect real national income or output if velocity can change, even if money and prices are constant. Indeed, the equation of exchange gives us a whole new perspective on aggregate demand. It indicates that changes in aggregate demand affect the equilibrium level of real national income *because* they change the velocity of circulation. No other possibility exists if money and prices are constant.

For instance, an increase in aggregate demand increases the equilibrium level of real national income by activating idle money that was being held and not spent and by getting that money to change hands. The demand for money has to decrease so that velocity can increase. An example is a debt-financed increase in government purchases. The federal government induces people to reduce their money holdings in exchange for Treasury bonds and then activates the money with its purchases. The result is that the money supply turns over more rapidly. Velocity increases, which increases the equilibrium level of real national income.

In conclusion, looking at the economy through the equation of exchange teaches us two valuable lessons. The first is that the federal government can affect the macro economy with both monetary and fiscal policies. Monetary policies work by changing the money supply. Fiscal policies work by changing the velocity of circulation against a constant money supply (as do all changes in aggregate demand). The second is that the impact of money reaches far beyond the narrow confines of monetary policy. Money affects all aspects of the macro economy, including how the economy responds to changes in aggregate demand.

THE NATURE OF MONEY

Now that we have seen the power of money, let's look more closely at the nature of money to understand the source of its power and how its power is maintained.

The Various Forms of Money

The first point to understand is that the power of money has no necessary connection with the form that it takes. All kinds of substances have served as money throughout history.

[2]Council of Economic Advisers, *Economic Report of the President, 1993* (Washington, D.C.: U.S. Government Printing Office, 1993), Table B-22, p. 372 and Table B-65, p. 423.

The line distinguishing money from nonmonies in terms of the medium-of-exchange property is difficult to draw with any precision. Checks written on money market demand deposits with limited checking privileges are accepted as a medium of exchange as commonly as checks written on regular checking or NOW accounts. Is the limit on the number of checks allowed per month really an important distinction? Furthermore, most savings accounts without checking privileges are highly **liquid,** meaning that they are easily converted to money. If households and businesses consider them as good as money, should they not be considered part of the money supply?

LIQUID ASSET

A financial asset that is easily converted into money.

These questions have no hard and fast answers. For this reason the federal government publishes three different versions of "the money supply" in the United States, labeled M1, M2, and M3. **M1** is the narrowest transactions definition of money, the most common definition, and the one we have been using. It consists of the items in Table 33.1, those financial securities that are routinely used for transactions. **M2** consists of M1 plus limited-checking money market deposit accounts and various kinds of very highly liquid small savings accounts with balances under $100,000, such as money market mutual funds, passbook savings accounts, and certificates of deposit. It also includes some very short-term deposit accounts in European financial institutions held by U.S. citizens. M2 is much larger than M1, $3,473.6 billion on average in 1992, compared with $966.6 billion for M1. **M3,** the broadest definition of money, consists of M2 plus various kinds of large deposit accounts with balances exceeding $100,000, including institutional money market mutual funds and European accounts held by U.S. citizens. M3 in 1992 was $4,177.4 billion. Table 33.2 summarizes the three different versions of the U.S. money supply.

M1

The narrowest definition of money, consisting of those financial securities that are routinely accepted for transactions; the sum of currency and balances in checking accounts with unlimited checking privileges.

M2

A definition of money, consisting of M1 plus limited-checking money market deposit accounts and various kinds of very highly liquid small savings accounts with balances under $100,000.

M3

A broad definition of money, consisting of M2 plus various kinds of large deposit accounts with balances exceeding $100,000, including institutional money market mutual funds and European accounts held by U.S. citizens.

Many economists favor M2 over M1 as the better definition of money because money market deposit accounts are used for transactions and small savings accounts are routinely converted into Federal Reserve Notes or checking accounts for spending purposes. Also, the velocity of circulation defined in terms of M2 is slightly more stable than is the velocity defined in terms of M1. The average annual change in M2 velocity during the 1980s, plus or minus, was 3.6 percent, compared with 4.2 percent for M1.[4] This implies that controlling the amount of M2 has more predictable effects on national income than does controlling the amount of M1. In contrast, only a few economists favor M3 as the definition of money because large savings accounts are seldom converted directly into Federal Reserve Notes or checking accounts. We will continue to use the narrow M1 definition in this text because it is most closely tied to the defining characteristic of money as the medium of exchange.

THE UNIT OF ACCOUNT The **unit of account** is the standard that defines the value of goods and services in exchange. The dollar is the unit of account in the United States; the value in exchange of each good or service is its price expressed in terms of dollars. All the developed market economies use their currencies as the unit of account. The yen is the unit of account in Japan, the franc in France, and so forth.

UNIT OF ACCOUNT

The standard that defines the value of goods and services in exchange.

Having a unit of account is absolutely essential to the operation of a modern developed economy. Economic agents have to know the relative values of goods and services when deciding how much of any one good to buy or sell.

[4]The data for M2 velocity are from the same sources as M1 velocity on page 987.

TABLE 33.2 **Three Measures of the Money Supply in the United States: M1, M2, and M3, 1992 (Average Daily Amount)**

M1			amount (billions)
Currency			$ 279.4
Transactions deposits			679.1
Demand deposits		319.2	
Other checkable deposits		359.9	
Travelers checks			8.1
	Total M1		$ 966.6
M2			
M1			966.6
Savings deposits and Money market deposit accounts			1130.4
Money market mutual funds[a]			351.6
Small time deposits (<$100,000)			950.8
Overnight Eurodollars + other			74.2
	Total M2		3473.6
M3			
M2			3473.6
Money market mutual funds[b]			204.3
Large time deposits (>$100,000)			387.3
Term Eurodollars + other			112.2
	Total M3		$4177.4

[a]General purpose and broker/dealer
[b]Institution only

SOURCE: Council of Economic Advisors, *Economic Indicators, March 1993* (Washington, D.C.: U.S. Government Printing Office, 1993), 26–27.

HISTORICAL NOTE: The only exceptions to using the currency as the unit of account occur when the domestic currency is no longer accepted as a medium of exchange, such as during a period of extreme instability in the government or during a hyperinflation. For example, many contracts in Israel for awhile after its establishment in 1947 were stipulated in terms of U.S. dollars rather than the Israeli shekel.

How many apples trade for a set of bath towels, and how many apples and sets of towels trade for a new car or an hour of labor, and so forth? People would have to keep track of all the possible pairwise combinations of goods and services without a unit of account, quite literally making apples versus oranges comparisons. With a unit of account, they only have to know the price of each good or service. Once they know their prices, the relative value of any two goods or services is easily computed as the ratio of the prices.

The savings in informational requirements with the currency serving as the unit of account are phenomenal. Ten goods and services can be paired in 45 different ways; far easier to remember just 10 prices. The possible pairwise combinations of tens of thousands of goods and services are astronomically large, numbering in the hundreds of millions. We would clearly be lost without prices to compute the relative values.

STORE OF VALUE
A means of holding wealth from one period to the next.

A STORE OF VALUE Holding money is one way of saving for future consumption. As such, money serves as a **store of value,** a means of holding wealth from one period to the next.

Money has many strong competitors as a store of value, of course; households and businesses can save in many ways. Real estate, consumer durables, passbook savings accounts, stocks, bonds, and insurance are some of the other savings possibilities. Each form of saving, or store of value, has distinctive characteristics that make it attractive. Money has a unique attraction, its function as the medium of exchange. At the same time, other forms of saving offer a higher rate of return than does money, or they offer other services such as health insurance that money cannot provide as well. Households and businesses tend to save in a variety of ways so that their savings provides them with a wide range of services.

The introduction of NOW accounts throughout the United States in the early 1980s provided competition within money itself. The only checking accounts prior to NOW accounts in most states were regular checking accounts that did not (and still do not) offer a rate of return. NOW accounts dominate both regular checking accounts and Federal Reserve Notes for transactions in which checks were accepted. They effectively combine many of the transactions services of a regular checking account with the rate of return and safety of a passbook savings account. Not surprisingly, the ratio of FRN to checking accounts held by households fell sharply throughout the 1980s, and very few households have regular checking accounts anymore.

Establishing a Medium of Exchange

If the medium of exchange is the defining property of money and the source of its power, how does something become a medium of exchange? The answer is that it does so in one of two ways: by government fiat or by custom.

All societies have an enormous incentive to establish something as a medium of exchange because, as we saw in Chapter 3, economic development is virtually impossible without money. The alternative to a money economy is a barter economy in which all exchanges are straight trades of goods and services. The problem with a barter economy is that bartered exchange requires a double coincidence of wants. An economist who wants a new suit has to find a tailor who wants some economic advice. Money removes this requirement. We can earn our livings as we choose and use the money we receive to buy what we want. Money, in other words, permits specialization in production and the expansion of markets, both of which are essential for economic development.

The incentive to have a money is so strong that governments usually do not wait for it to arise. They simply declare a currency as money by government fiat or law. Federal Reserve Notes are government fiat money. Take out a Federal Reserve Note, and notice what it says on the front: "This note is legal tender for all debts, public and private." This is the federal government's declaration that Federal Reserve Notes are a medium of exchange, or money. It says that if you owe a merchant or a lender $25 and tender (offer) him or her $25 worth of Federal Reserve Notes, you have legally fulfilled your obligation. Sellers of goods and services and lenders must accept Federal Reserve Notes as payment.

Checking accounts are not government money; they are issued and maintained by private banks. They are also not legal tender; some merchants will not accept your personal check, and they do not have to. Nonetheless, most merchants do accept checks, at least checks written on local banks, and most large transactions are made by check.

Checks became a medium of exchange simply by custom. They proved to be such a convenient and reliable means of payment that everyone just became accustomed to using them. As noted above, checks were first used on a widespread scale during the Renaissance in Europe, and they have been an important medium of exchange in Europe and North America ever since.

Governments do not have to issue a fiat currency. Society's need for a money that can serve as a convenient medium of exchange is so compelling that some form of money is sure to arise in the private sector even without the government. Remember that the first paper currencies in the United States were notes issued by private banks, not governments. The United States did not issue a paper currency from the time of its founding until 1863.

Most governments today do issue fiat currencies, yet the government currencies hardly drive out the private bank money. We have seen that private checking account balances are the most important component of the money supply in the United States, as they are in all the developed market economies. The common use of checks is perhaps the best testimony to society's overwhelming need to have a convenient medium of exchange.

What Gives Money Value?

Many people believe that money has value because it is backed by something tangible. This used to be true for the most part. Full-bodied coins were backed by the value of the metal in the coins, and many government and private bank currencies used to be fully convertible into gold or silver. This is no longer true today, however. Government fiat currencies and checking deposits have become the main forms of money throughout the world, and these monies are not backed by anything tangible. You cannot convert a Federal Reserve Note into gold, silver, or anything else. The truth is that a Federal Reserve Note has no inherent value other than its value as money, as a medium of exchange. The same holds true for the Swiss franc and the Japanese yen. Yet the U.S. dollar, Swiss franc, and Japanese yen are all accepted and valued currencies worldwide.

Similarly, you cannot convert your checking account balances into anything more tangible than Federal Reserve Notes. Yet checks written against these balances are accepted and valued in the United States and elsewhere.

What, then, does give money value today? The answer is nothing more than confidence, the confidence of knowing what real goods and services the money can buy. The money in use today has value only because it is the medium of exchange. Moreover, people will continue to value the money and accept it for real goods and services only if they are confident that they can exchange the money some time in the future for other goods and services.

Confidence is a pretty flimsy basis for value. The moment that confidence disappears—pffft!—the money becomes worthless. People will not accept money for real goods and services if they do not know what they can get for the money. The money ceases being a medium of exchange, which is to say it ceases being money.

Money must be kept scarce and under control to maintain its value in exchange. This is why all the developed nations have asked their national governments to take over control of the money supply. Nations desperately need money to keep their economies operating smoothly, and their citizens want assurance from the government that confidence in the money will be maintained. This is also why price stability is such an important macroeconomic policy goal. Inflation erodes confidence in the money because it erodes the exchange value of the money percentage point by percentage point with the rate of inflation. For example, an ongoing 5 percent inflation lowers the exchange value of a one dollar bill or one dollar in a checking account by 5 percent each year.

Nations can live with moderate amounts of inflation. Your Federal Reserve Notes may buy 5 percent fewer goods and services next year if prices are rising by 5 percent, but you still have a good idea of what you can buy with your money. An accelerating inflation leading to a hyperinflation is disastrous, however, because then confidence in the money cannot be maintained. Hyperinflations render checking accounts worthless and force people to exchange shopping carts full of paper currency for a loaf of bread, if they can exchange the currency at all for any good or service. We will see that controlling the money supply and controlling inflation go hand in hand; they are essentially opposite sides of the same goal.

Not surprisingly, people tend to lose confidence in the government's ability to control the money supply whenever they lose confidence in the ability of the government to govern at all. Most hyperinflations occur when the government is highly unstable, as during wartime or shortly after a war in the nations that have lost.

HISTORICAL NOTE: The Continental became worthless in the midst of the Revolutionary War when citizens began to doubt that the new government would win the war.

Congress has entrusted the Fed with the control of the money supply in the United States, both the Federal Reserve Notes and the checking account balances. The Fed has direct control over the Federal Reserve Notes because it issues them. Increasing or decreasing the amount of Federal Reserve Notes outstanding is a routine exercise and easily understood. We will see how the Fed does this in the final section of this chapter. The more subtle money supply issue is how the Fed gains leverage and control over the checking account balances. Private banks issue checking accounts and largely determine the amount of checking accounts balances at any one time. Moreover, private banks have no direct interest in the size of the money supply. They are private, profit-maximizing business firms, no different in this regard from IBM or the corner grocery store. The amount of checking account balances that they are willing to hold is determined by considerations of profit, not the size of the money supply.

We will see in Chapter 34 how the Fed brings the banks under its wing to ensure that the banks' profit motive does not drive the money supply in a direction that is counter to the Fed's goals for monetary policy. The Fed must have some control over the banks in order to conduct an effective monetary policy because checking accounts are the major portion of the money supply.

BALANCE SHEETS, ASSETS, AND LIABILITIES

Accountants keep track of transactions involving money by means of balance sheets. A **balance sheet** is a listing of a person's or an institution's assets, liabilities, and net worth.

BALANCE SHEET

A listing of a person's or an institution's assets, liabilities, and net worth.

Assets, Liabilities, and Net Worth

ASSET

Something that is owned, real or financial; a claim against someone or some institution.

An **asset** is something that is owned, real or financial. Examples of real assets owned by households are a plot of land, a house, and any consumer durable. Financial assets most often take the form of a claim against some person or institution. Examples are corporate and government bonds, corporate stocks, savings accounts, and money. For instance, a corporate bond is a claim against a corporation that entitles the owner to the principal or face value of the bond on the date when the bond matures, plus interest each year until the maturity date. Corporate stock is a claim against the corporation that entitles the owner to a share of the corporation's profits.

LIABILITY

Something that is owed; a claim against someone by some other person or institution.

A **liability** is something that is owed. Liabilities are usually financial rather than real and most often take the form of a claim that some person or institution has against the holder of the liability. Examples are Stafford loans that students take out to finance their educations, car loans, and home mortgages. In each case the lending institution has a claim against the borrower. Also, someone's financial asset is almost always someone else's financial liability. For example, any corporate bonds and stocks that you may own are simultaneously your assets and the liabilities of the corporations that issued them. A Stafford loan is simultaneously an asset of the bank that lent the money and a liability to the student who borrowed the money.

NET WORTH

The difference between a person's assets and liabilities; also called *wealth.*

Net worth, or **wealth,** is the difference between someone's assets and liabilities, that is, the difference between what is owned and what is owed. Net worth is negative if liabilities exceed assets, in which case the person or the institution is said to be *insolvent.* The amount owed, the liabilities, exceeds the amount that is owned, the assets, to cover the debts.

Balance sheets are arranged in the form of a capital T, which is why they are commonly called T accounts. Table 33.3 illustrates. Assets appear on the left side of the T and liabilities and net worth on the right side of the T. The two sides of a balance sheet must always balance because net worth is the residual item that makes them balance. It takes on whatever value is necessary to satisfy the fundamental balance sheet identity that

$$\text{Assets} = \text{liabilities} + \text{net worth}$$

Those of you who applied for financial aid to help pay for your college educations were required to prepare a mini balance sheet. The federal Financial Aid Form (FAF) asks for a partial listing of your, and your parents', assets, liabilities, and net worth in terms of these assets and liabilities. The assets include a mix of real and financial assets such as the value of your family's home, any savings and checking account balances, certificates of deposit, and cash. The liabilities include such items as the home mortgage, car loans, credit card debt, and all previous student loans. The net worth you reported was factored in with your income and your parents' income in determining your financial need for college expenses.

REFLECTION: Write down your own personal balance sheet with your most important assets and liabilities listed. Is your personal net worth (independent of that of your family) positive or negative?

TABLE 33.3 A Balance Sheet

Assets	Liabilities + Net worth

Balance Sheet Transactions

Two kinds of balance sheet transactions play the central role in the study of money: an exchange of assets between two parties; and a loan, in which two parties establish a borrower-lender relationship. The exchange of assets and the loan are the transactions most commonly used to get money to change hands, from people or institutions who have money and are not interested in spending it to others who do not have enough money to finance all that they want to buy. In addition, the exchange of assets and the loan are the principal transactions used by banks to increase or decrease the amount of money that they issue. The Fed primarily uses the exchange-of-assets transaction to increase or decrease the amount of Federal Reserve Notes outstanding. Commercial banks and other depository institutions primarily use the loan transaction to increase or decrease the amount of transactions deposits, the checking accounts balances. All central banks other than the Fed also rely primarily on the loan transaction to increase or decrease their nation's currencies because, unlike the Fed, they do not have anything convenient to exchange. Let's take a close look at these transactions.

AN EXCHANGE OF EXISTING ASSETS Table 33.4 illustrates how we will record an exchange of existing assets on the balance sheet of the traders. The two "persons" exchanging the assets could be households, businesses, or government agencies. Person 1 starts off with money, M, and wants to buy some corporate bonds. Person 2 starts off with corporate bonds and wants to exchange some of the bonds for money to buy goods and services. The two get together and agree on the price for each bond and the number of bonds they will exchange (the exchange is likely to be carried out by a broker on a bond market who acts as middleman, in which case the two persons never actually meet). The plus and minus signs indicate the direction of the exchange. A plus sign means that the person takes on that asset, and a minus sign means that the person gives up that asset in the exchange. The two persons' balance sheets must remain in balance because they have just substituted one asset for another in equal dollar amounts.

A LOAN: THE BORROWER-LENDER RELATIONSHIP Table 33.5 illustrates how we will record the loan transaction on the balance sheets of the lender and the borrower. Person 1 is the lender, and person 2 is the borrower in this example. Person 1 starts off with money that she is willing to lend. Person 2 wants some money to buy goods and services, but is either unable or unwilling to exchange any assets to acquire the money. Instead, he is looking to borrow the money.

TABLE 33.4 **An Exchange of Existing Assets: Money for Corporate Bonds**

PERSON 1			PERSON 2		
Assets		Liabilities	Assets		Liabilities
M	(−)		Corporate bonds	(−)	
Corporate bonds	(+)		M	(+)	

TABLE 33.5 The Borrower-Lender Relationship: Lending Money

PERSON 1			PERSON 2	
Assets		Liabilities	Assets	Liabilities
M	(−)		M (+)	Loan (+)
Loan	(+)			

So the two persons agree to a loan contract that stipulates the amount of the loan and the terms of repayment. The loan is simultaneously a new asset to person 1, the lender, and a new liability to person 2, as indicated by the plus signs on their balance sheets. The money that changes hands from lender to borrower is the second half of the transaction, as indicated by the minus sign after the M on person 1's balance sheet and the plus sign after the M on person 2's balance sheet.

The two balance sheets remain in balance. The loan is essentially an exchange of assets from the lender's point of view. Person 1 has substituted the loan for money in equal dollar amounts on her balance sheet. The borrower, person 2, has a new asset, money, and a new liability, the loan, of equal dollar amounts on his balance sheet. (The subsequent paying back of the loan has further balance sheet repercussions that need not concern us.)

Notice that the loan contract simultaneously creates a new asset for the lender and a new liability for the borrower on the balance sheets. This is how nearly all financial securities—stocks, bonds, bank deposits, and so forth—came into existence. They were originally contracts between two persons engaged in a borrower-lender relationship. This also explains why nearly all financial securities are simultaneously some person's financial asset and some other person's financial liability. They have to be for all balance sheets to remain in balance.

Furthermore, many financial securities are routinely traded as part of an exchange-of-assets transaction after they have been created as loan contracts. The original creation, or issue, of a financial security is said to occur in the *primary market* for that security. Exchanges of the existing financial security then take place in the *secondary market* for that security.

For example, the corporate bonds that are exchanged in Table 33.4 originally came into being as part of a borrower-lender relationship. The corporation, the borrower, issued the bonds to raise money to finance its planned investment. The purchasers of the corporate bonds, the lenders, gave the firm money in return for the bonds. New corporate bonds are typically issued through investment banks who buy the bonds and then resell them to the ultimate purchasers/lenders. The issuing of new bonds through investment banks occurs on the primary market for bonds.

Once corporate bonds have been issued, they are then routinely traded in secondary bond markets. You can find the prices of hundreds of corporate bonds listed every day in the financial pages of any big city newspaper. Many of the exchanges in the secondary bond markets are exchanges of bonds for money, as in the example in Table 33.4. The company that originally issued the bond is not directly involved in these exchanges on the secondary market. The exchange of an existing bond just changes the ownership of the bond, the name of the person who receives the principal and the interest that the corporation must pay to the bondholder.

Creating and Destroying Money

Banks for the most part use either the exchange-of-assets transaction or the loan transaction to create and destroy the money that they issue. The recording of the bank's transactions on the balance sheets looks somewhat different from the previous examples because of two accounting rules that apply to money.

1. *Money is a liability of the bank that issues the money and appears on the liability side of the issuing bank's balance sheet.* Federal Reserve Notes are a liability of the Fed, and transactions deposits, the checking accounts, are a liability of the commercial banks and other depository institutions that issue them.

Listing money as a liability of the bank that issues it is consistent with the principle that most financial securities must simultaneously be someone's asset and someone else's liability for all balance sheets to balance. Federal Reserve Notes and checking account balances are assets to whoever holds them. Households, nonbank businesses, and government agencies own the money that they hold, so that the money appears on the asset side of their balance sheets. Notice in the examples above that money always appears on the asset side of all the balance sheets. Therefore, money must be a liability of the bank that issues it.

2. *Banks do not have to have money to exchange it or lend it.* They, and they alone, have the ability to create the money that they issue. This rule is also consistent with the principle that all institutions that issue financial securities as liabilities create the securities that they issue. For example, corporations create the new stocks and bonds that they issue to raise money for investment, and the U.S. Treasury creates the bonds that it issues to raise money for government spending.

With these two rules in mind, let's now look at how the Fed and the depository institutions create and destroy Federal Reserve Notes and balances in checking accounts.

CREATING AND DESTROYING FEDERAL RESERVE NOTES A central bank like the Fed can routinely use the exchange-of-assets transaction to increase or decrease the amount of currency outstanding if there happens to be something convenient for it to exchange. *Convenient* really does mean "convenient." The Fed has to be able to exchange some asset for its Federal Reserve Notes at any time in huge quantities, tens and hundreds of millions of dollars per exchange, as either buyer or seller, with a simple telephone call or two, and all without unduly disrupting the asset market it is trading in. The Fed happens to have just such an asset available to it—the $4 trillion of existing U.S. Treasury debt. The world's other central banks do not have anything so convenient to trade, so they have to rely primarily on the loan transaction to increase or decrease their currencies.

Treasury bills, notes, and bonds are loan contracts just like corporate bonds. The only difference is that they are created when the U.S. Treasury engages in a borrower-lender relationship with the public in order to finance the annual federal budget deficits. The Treasury is the borrower, and the public is the lender. The amount of Treasury debt outstanding increases each year that the federal government runs a deficit.

The majority of the Treasury securities outstanding, about $4 trillion worth as of 1993, are actively exchanged in a secondary market called the Open

Market. All exchanges in the Open Market are exchanges of assets because a Treasury security is a financial asset to anyone who holds it. It appears as a financial liability only on the U.S. Treasury's balance sheet.

The Fed holds just under 10 percent of the Treasury securities that are exchanged on the Open Market, and it actively exchanges Treasury securities in the secondary Open Market for the sole purpose of controlling the money supply. One of its main objectives in this regard is to ensure that the public has enough Federal Reserve Notes to conduct its day-to-day business.

The Fed trades its Treasury securities with securities dealers at 12 large commercial banks such as Citicorp and at 20 to 25 other large financial institutions, principally large investment banks such as Goldman, Sachs and large brokerage houses such as Merrill Lynch. The securities dealers in these financial institutions are the main dealers in government securities on both the primary market and the secondary Open Market. They are responsible for "making" the Open Market in Treasury securities, and in the other financial securities that they trade, meaning that they agree to buy and sell securities at reasonable prices in order to ensure that the securities markets remain orderly.

The secondary Open Market in Treasury securities is perfect for the Fed's needs. The Fed can exchange the securities with the securities dealers over the phone in any amount required, in either direction, and at any time. Treasury securities can always be bought or sold at some price. Moreover, the volume of exchanges on the Open Market is so huge that even the Fed's large trades are not at all disruptive.

OPEN MARKET OPERATION

A purchase or sale of Treasury securities by the Fed for the purpose of controlling the money supply.

The Fed executes all exchanges at the Trading Desk of the New York Fed. An exchange of its Treasury securities is called an **Open Market Operation.** The Fed *buys* Treasury securities to *increase* the amount of Federal Reserve Notes outstanding. The Fed *sells* Treasury securities to *decrease* the amount of Federal Reserve Notes outstanding. Increasing and decreasing the amount of Federal Reserve Notes outstanding is routine, thanks to the existence of the huge Treasury debt outstanding and the well-developed secondary Open Market for the Treasury securities.

INCREASING THE AMOUNT OF FEDERAL RESERVE NOTES OUTSTANDING Suppose that the Fed wants to increase the amount of Federal Reserve Notes outstanding by $10 million. The Fed's Trading Desk calls some of the securities dealers and indicates that it wants to buy $10 million worth of Treasury securities. The dealers indicate the prices at which they are willing to sell the securities, and the Fed buys from the dealers offering the lowest prices until it has purchased $10 million worth of securities. The Fed pays for the securities with newly created Federal Reserve Notes that are printed and sent to the Fed by the Bureau of Engraving and Printing, a division of the U.S. Treasury.

Table 33.6 shows how the Fed's Open Market Operation to increase the amount of Federal Reserve Notes affects the balance sheets of the Fed and the securities dealer that it trades with. (The table assumes a single securities dealer for convenience.) It is the exchange-of-assets transaction described above with a twist.

The securities dealer has made a straight trade of assets, taking on $10 million in Federal Reserve Notes (FRN) in exchange for $10 million of Treasury securities that it sells to the Fed. The Fed's balance sheet looks somewhat different from the exchange-of-assets example above, however. Its holdings of

TABLE 33.6 **Increasing Federal Reserve Notes with an Open Market Operation: The Fed Buys Treasury Securities**

THE FED		SECURITIES DEALER	
Assets	Liabilities	Assets	Liabilities
Treasury Securities $10 million (+)	FRN $10 million (+)	Treasury securities $10 million (−) FRN $10 million (+)	

Treasury securities, an asset to the Fed, increase by $10 million. But the corresponding $10 million increase in FRN appears on the liability side of the Fed's balance sheet because it is the bank issuing the FRN. Moreover, the Fed did not have the FRN to begin with; it paid for the securities with $10 million of newly printed Federal Reserve Notes. The effect of the Open Market Operation is that the amount of FRN in the hands of the nonbank public has increased by $10 million. The FRN are literally new money and are simultaneously an asset to the securities dealer that sold the Treasury securities to the Fed and a liability to the Fed.

DECREASING THE AMOUNT OF FEDERAL RESERVE NOTES OUTSTANDING Decreasing the amount of Federal Reserve Notes is just as routine. Suppose that the Fed wants to decrease the amount of Federal Reserve Notes outstanding by $10 million. The Fed's Trading Desk calls some of the securities dealers that it trades with and indicates that it wants to sell $10 million worth of its Treasury securities. The dealers indicate the prices at which they are willing to buy the securities, and the Fed sells to the dealers offering the highest prices until it has sold $10 million worth of its securities. The Fed has taken $10 million of FRN out of circulation. (Any old FRN that it receives are put through a shredder and destroyed. You can get packages of some of the shredded dollar bills if you go on a tour of one of the Federal Reserve Banks.)

The Fed's Open Market Operation to decrease the amount of Federal Reserve Notes affects the balance sheets of the Fed and the securities dealer that it trades with exactly as in Table 33.6, with all the signs reversed. The dealer's holdings of Treasury securities *increase* by $10 million, and its holdings of FRN *decrease* by $10 million. The Fed has $10 million *less* of Treasury securities on the asset side of its balance sheet, matched by $10 million *less* of FRN outstanding on the liability side of its balance sheet. The amount of FRN in the hands of the nonbank public has decreased by $10 million.

CREATING AND DESTROYING CHECKING ACCOUNT BALANCES Commercial banks and other financial institutions that accept deposits with unlimited checking privileges are financial intermediaries who position themselves between the ultimate lenders and borrowers in the economy. Households and businesses lend to banks when they deposit a portion of their savings in a checking account. The banks then turn around and lend some of the funds deposited with them to households and businesses who are borrowing to finance consumer durables such as automobiles and to invest in houses, plant, equipment, and inventories. Banks earn a profit by charging higher interest on their loans than the interest they pay on their deposits. For example, they may charge 9 percent interest on car loans, yet pay only 4 percent interest on their NOW accounts.

The practice of banks lending the funds deposited with them is reputed to have started with the goldsmiths in England during the eighteenth century. Before the reign of Charles I, merchants in England stored the full-bodied gold coins that they received from selling their wares in the Tower of London for safekeeping. Charles I broke the trust by expropriating some of the gold, at which point the merchants began storing their gold with private goldsmiths. The goldsmiths originally earned their profit by charging a fee for storing the coins. They soon realized, however, that they did not have to keep all the gold coins in storage because not all the depositors would seek to withdraw their coins at the same time. They could greatly increase their profits by lending some of the gold coins, with interest, to other merchants. All they had to do was keep some coins on hand to meet day-to-day requests for withdrawal. The result was that more gold coins circulated throughout the economy; the money supply increased.

Modern banks follow the same principle as the goldsmiths. They keep only a small fraction of the funds deposited with them on hand for day-to-day transactions and lend the rest. The result is that the amount of checking account balances increases.

LENDING TO INCREASE THE AMOUNT OF CHECKING ACCOUNT BALANCES The easiest way to see that bank loans create new checking account balances is to consider the line-of-credit arrangement that banks commonly have with businesses. A line of credit means that the bank stands willing to lend to the business any amount up to some maximum amount, the line of credit. In return, the business may agree to keep a certain checking account balance with the bank, on average.

Suppose that a business negotiates a $10 million loan with the loan officer of a bank as part of its $50 million line of credit. The loan transaction begins just as in the borrower-lender transaction described above. The bank draws up a loan contract that stipulates the terms of the loan, which is simultaneously a new asset for the bank/lender and a new liability for the business/borrower. The second half of the transaction differs from the earlier example, however. Instead of transferring funds that it has on hand, the loan officer goes to her computer terminal and simply creates a new $10 million checking account balance for the business. The business can then write checks on the $10 million account. The $10 million account is quite literally a new configuration of electrons created and stored on a computer disk.

Table 33.7 illustrates how the line-of-credit loan affects the balance sheets of the bank and the business. The $10 million loan, as indicated, is simultaneously an asset for the bank and a liability for the business. The newly created $10 million checking account balance is simultaneously an asset of the business and a liability of the bank. Remember the rule: Money is an asset to anyone who holds it and a liability to the bank that issues it. The money in this case is the checking account. The money supply has increased by $10 million as a result of the bank loan.

Central banks in other countries increase the amount of their nations' currencies in essentially the same way. They make loans and give the borrowers newly printed currency—francs, yen, deutsche marks—which is simultaneously an asset of the borrower and a liability of the central bank.

TABLE 33.7 Commercial Bank Loans and Checking Accounts: Creating a New Checking Account Balance by Making a Loan

COMMERCIAL BANK		BUSINESS BORROWER	
Assets	Liabilities	Assets	Liabilities
Loan $10 million (+)	Checking account $10 million (+)	Checking account $10 million (+)	Loan $10 million (+)

Most loans to individuals are not line-of-credit loans. A bank does not create a new checking account for us when we take out a home mortgage or a car loan.[5] Instead, the bank gives us a cashier's check. Even so, the loan creates new checking account balances. We immediately give the check to the seller of the house or to the car dealer, and he or she deposits the check in his or her bank. New checking account balances are created as soon as the seller deposits the cashier's check.

Remember this whenever you have doubts that bank loans create new money in the form of checking account balances: Checking account balances are the most important component of the U.S. money supply, more than twice as large as the amount of Federal Reserve Notes in the United States. Banks do not simply lend FRN. We will take a closer look at the money creation process in Chapter 34. Our purpose here is just to establish the principle that bank loans create new money.

CALLING IN LOANS TO DECREASE THE AMOUNT OF CHECKING ACCOUNT BALANCES The mortgage or the car loan that we take out is *secured* by the house or the car that is being financed; that is, the bank assumes ownership of our house or car if we default on the loan. In contrast, many business loans are *unsecured* loans. The bank cannot take ownership of any particular asset of the business if the business defaults on the loan. In return for getting unsecured loans, businesses often have to accept a *call feature* in the loan contract, which means that the bank has the right to call for immediate and full repayment of the loan at any time. Calling in unsecured loans decreases the amount of checking account balances as the loan is paid back.

The balance sheet implications of calling in a $10 million loan are exactly the reverse of the entries in Table 33.7. Just reverse all the signs. Calling in the loan *subtracts* both the loan and the checking account balances from the balance sheets of both the bank and the borrower. The checking account balances *decrease* by $10 million.

Calling in loans is a drastic measure that banks do not take under normal business conditions. When loans and checking account balances decrease in the banking system, they usually do so by a process of attrition. Old loans are being repaid and new loans issued all the time. Banks reduce the amount of their loans and checking account balances when they decide not to issue new loans as the old loans are repaid. The point is that the total amount of bank loans outstanding largely determines the total amount of checking account balances in the banking system. Similarly, central banks in other countries can

[5]An exception is the home equity loan, in which we receive a line of credit to write checks up to a maximum amount.

decrease the amount of loans and currency outstanding by deciding not to issue new loans as old loans are repaid. They do not have to call in loans.

Illiquid Banks and Bank Runs

One final point about the banking industry deserves mention. Banks are inherently *illiquid*, meaning that they cannot meet all the potential claims of their depositors. Depositors expect to be able to close their checking accounts and receive Federal Reserve Notes for the full amount of their checking account balances any time they want. Once banks make loans, however, the amount of checking account liabilities on their balance sheets exceeds the amount of Federal Reserve Notes they have on hand. They are stuck if all depositors come to them at once seeking Federal Reserve Notes. The early English goldsmiths were in the same position once they began to make loans. The amount of gold coins remaining in storage was far less than their deposit liabilities.

BANK RUN

An attempt by large numbers of depositors to close their checking (and savings) accounts in exchange for currency.

An attempt by large numbers of depositors to close their checking (and savings) accounts in exchange for currency is called a run on a bank. A **bank run** occurs whenever the depositors begin to lose confidence in their bank. Bank runs have a tendency to spread from bank to bank, which, if unchecked, can lead to a full-blown financial panic. The panic thrusts the economy into a recession as bank lending virtually ceases and large numbers of people lose their deposits. Nations turned to central banking largely to prevent bank runs and financial panics. We will see in Chapter 34 that Congress established the Federal Reserve Bank System in 1913 primarily for this reason.

Having considered the nature of money and how banks create and destroy it, we are now prepared to study the details of the U.S. monetary system in Chapter 34.

SUMMARY

The first section of Chapter 33 described the money supply in the United States.

1. The most commonly accepted definition of the money supply is the sum of currency, checking account balances with unlimited checking privileges, and traveler's checks. Currency is the coins and dollar bills, or Federal Reserve Notes. These are the items that are routinely used to pay for goods and services.
2. Paper currency and checking accounts are the major components of the U.S. money supply, as they are in all the developed market economies.

The second section of the chapter explored the importance of money by means of the equation of exchange.

3. The equation of exchange, $M \cdot V = P \cdot Q$, measures the circular flow of economic activity in terms of money. $P \cdot Q$ is the dollar value of national product, M is the money supply, and V is the velocity of circulation, the number of times that money turns over during the course of a year to purchase final goods and services. Velocity turns the stock of money into the dollar flow of goods and services.
4. Velocity moves slowly up and down over time. It is largely determined by

institutional factors, such as how often we are paid and how we pay for goods and services.

5. The demand for money is the amount of money that we want to hold at any given time. The ratio of the overall demand for money to the national product or income is the inverse of velocity.
6. The equation of exchange indicates that changes in the money supply can affect the rate of inflation, the rate of growth in output, and unemployment.

The third section of the chapter looked more closely at the nature of money.

7. The power of money does not depend on what form it takes. Money has been many substances throughout history, including coins made of various metals, beads, paper currencies, and checking account balances.
8. The power of money derives from what it does rather than from what it is. Money serves three functions: the medium of exchange, the unit of account, and a store of value.
   a. The medium of exchange is the defining characteristic of money. Something is money if it is routinely accepted in exchange for goods and services.
   b. The unit of account is the standard that defines the value in exchange of every good and service. The currency is the unit of account in nearly all countries. In the United States, goods and services are valued in dollars.
   c. Money is a store of value because holding money is one of the ways in which we can save for future consumption.
9. The line distinguishing money from nonmonies is difficult to determine precisely. The United States publishes three different measures of money, M1, M2, and M3. M1 is the narrow transactions definition defined above. M2 consists of M1 plus a number of highly liquid short-term financial securities, such as money market deposit accounts and mutual funds, and small savings and time deposits (< \$100,000). M3 consists of M2 plus large savings and time deposits (> \$100,000) and some other securities. (Refer to Table 33.2.)

The final section of Chapter 33 described balance sheets and some common balance sheet transactions.

10. A balance sheet is a listing of someone's assets, liabilities, and net worth.
11. An asset is something that is owned. A liability is something that is owed. Net worth, or wealth, is the difference between assets and liabilities.
12. Two balance sheet transactions are especially important to the study of money: (a) an exchange of existing assets; and (b) a loan, in which two persons engage in a borrower-lender relationship. These two transactions are the most common means of transferring money from those who have it to those who do not have enough money to buy what they want to buy. They are also the most common methods used by banks to increase or decrease the money that they issue.
13. The Fed, which is the central bank of the United States, uses the exchange-of-assets transaction to increase and decrease Federal Reserve Notes (FRN). It exchanges Treasury securities with a few large securities dealers in the secondary Open Market for Treasury securities. The Fed buys Treasury securities from the dealers to increase the amount of FRN outstanding. The Fed sells Treasury securities to the dealers to decrease the amount of FRN outstanding.

14. Commercial banks and the other depository institutions primarily use the borrower-lender transaction to increase and decrease the amount of their checking account balances. Banks create new checking account balances when they make loans. Banks reduce the amount of checking account balances when they call in loans or decide not to write new loans as old loans are repaid. Central banks in other countries primarily use the borrower-lender transaction to increase and decrease their currencies because, unlike the Fed, they do not have anything as convenient as the outstanding Treasury debt to trade.
15. Money is an asset to anyone who holds it; it is a liability of the bank that issues it.

KEY TERMS

asset	Federal Reserve Note	money
balance sheet	liability	net worth
bank run	liquid asset	open market operation
currency	M1	store of value
demand for money	M2	transactions deposit
equation of exchange	M3	unit of account
Federal Reserve Banking System	medium of exchange	velocity of circulation

QUESTIONS

1. a. Who owns most of the regular checking accounts, and why do they use them? Who owns most of the NOW accounts, and why do they prefer them over regular checking accounts?
   b. Why are credit card transactions not classified as part of the money supply?
2. What is the difference between money and income?
3. a. What is the velocity of circulation, and how is it related to the national product?
   b. Suppose that the velocity of circulation is 5 and the dollar value of the economy's national product (national income) is \$6 trillion. How large is the money supply in the economy?
4. a. How would you measure your demand for money?
   b. What are some of the reasons why you and others hold money? Do your motives differ somewhat for Federal Reserve Notes and for checking account balances?
5. What are the main functions of money? Does money have competitors (actual or potential) for any or all of these functions? If yes, give an example of a competitor.
6. a. What is the difference between the M1 and M2 definitions of money?
   b. Why do some economists favor M2 over M1 as the better definition of money?
   c. What arguments can be made for using M1 as the definition of money?
7. a. Are Federal Reserve Notes backed by anything tangible?
   b. Why are Federal Reserve Notes considered to be part of the money supply?
   c. Are they the most important component of the money supply?
   d. Why has paper currency replaced full-bodied coins made of precious metals as the primary form of currency throughout the world?
8. Show how the following transactions affect the balance sheets (assets and liabilities) of Joe and Sue.
   a. Joe initially has \$5,000 of Federal Reserve Notes, and Sue initially has 1,000 shares of stock valued at \$25 per share. Joe then buys 100 shares of stock from Sue.
   b. Joe initially has \$5,000 of Federal Reserve Notes. Instead of selling her stock, Sue borrows \$3,000 from Joe.
9. a. How does the Fed increase or decrease the amount of Federal Reserve Notes outstanding through Open Market Operations? Show how the balance sheets of the Fed and the securities dealers are affected by these Open Market Operations.
   b. How do central banks in other countries that do not have large amounts of government debt increase and decrease their money supplies?
10. Why does the money supply increase when a commercial bank makes a loan to a business customer as part of a line-of-credit agreement? Show how the balance sheets of the commercial banks and the business customers are affected by these loans.

CHAPTER

34

The Monetary System of the United States

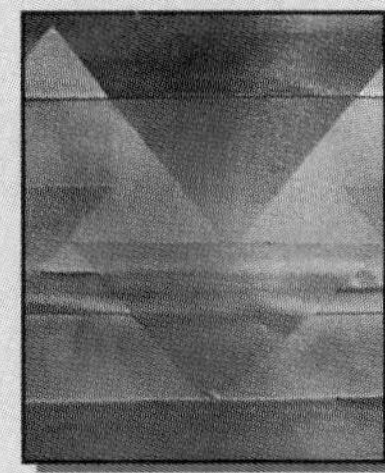

LEARNING OBJECTIVES

CONCEPTS TO LEARN

Federal Reserve Banking System
Reserves
The reserve requirement
Money multiplier
Savings and loan associations

CONCEPTS TO RECALL

U.S. money supply [33]
The Fed [33]
Commercial banks (depository institutions) [33]
Open Market Operation [33]
Balance sheet, assets, and liabilities [33]

Chapter 34 considers the institutional details of the U.S. monetary system that play a role in determining the growth of the money supply. Most beginning economics students have very little knowledge of the U.S. monetary system. They have heard of the Fed and the depository institutions, but the world of money and finance is one big puzzle to them. If this is true of you, keep in mind as you begin that there are three main pieces to the puzzle: the Federal Reserve Banking System (the Fed), the depository institutions, and the nonbank public.

The Fed is the nation's central bank. It is in charge of issuing the nation's currency, the Federal Reserve Notes, and of conducting monetary policy. The depository institutions are the hub of the monetary system, standing in the middle between the Fed and the nonbank public. They are private-sector firms that issue the largest component of the U.S. money supply that the Fed is charged with controlling, the transaction deposits or checking accounts. The households, businesses, and government agencies within the nonbank public are the direct link between the money supply and the overall performance of the economy. They hold the money and use it to finance purchases of goods and services and of various kinds of financial securities, such as stocks and bonds.

After reading Chapter 34 you will understand the basic functions of the Fed and the depository institutions. You will also see how the three pieces of the monetary puzzle fit together in such a way that the Fed is able to gain control over the amount of checking account balances in the depository institutions. The Fed cannot hope to control the growth of the money supply and conduct an effective monetary policy if it cannot limit the depository institutions' ability to make loans and create new checking accounts.

Our tour of the U.S. monetary system begins with the Federal Reserve Banking System, the nation's central bank, which sits at the top of the system.

THE FEDERAL RESERVE BANKING SYSTEM

Federal Banking Legislation

The Federal Reserve Banking System evolved to its current structure and functions in a series of distinct steps since its founding in 1913. The three main pieces of legislation relating to the Fed are the Federal Reserve Act of 1913, the National Banking Acts of 1933 and 1935, and the Depository Institutions Deregulation and Monetary Control Act of 1980.

FEDERAL RESERVE ACT OF 1913
An act of Congress that established the Federal Reserve Banking System, the first true central bank in the United States.

THE FEDERAL RESERVE ACT OF 1913 The Congress established the nation's first true central bank with the passage of the **Federal Reserve Act of 1913.** Its motives for having a central banking system were essentially twofold. The Treasury wanted a central bank to serve as its financial agent in international transactions and currency exchanges with England and the rest of Western Europe. Trade between the United States and these countries was increasing, and most of them had central banks. Closer to home, and far more important,

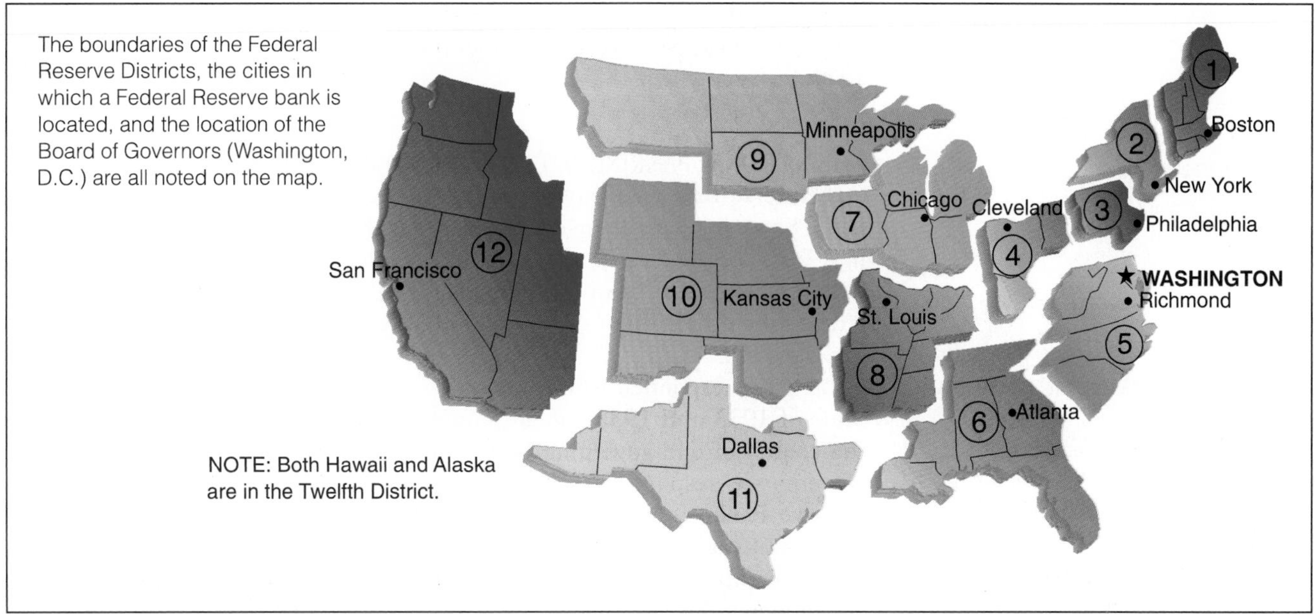

FIGURE 34.1

The Federal Reserve System

The Federal Reserve Banking System is divided into twelve geographic districts throughout the United States. Each district is served by a Federal Reserve Bank located in one of the major cities within each district. The map indicates the geographical boundaries of each Federal Reserve district and the location of the twelve Federal Reserve Banks.

SOURCE: Reprinted by permission from *Economics*, second edition, by Roger A. Arnold.

the Congress wanted a central bank that would act as a lender of last resort to the nation's private banks to prevent runs on the banks.

The United States had just been through a serious run on its banks that resulted in the Panic of 1907, the latest in a series of financial panics that had plagued the country throughout its history. Bank runs can easily feed on themselves and cause widespread bank failures without a central bank. If one major bank gets into financial trouble, its depositors begin a run on the bank as they rush to close their deposit accounts in exchange for currency. The bank is then sure to fail because it cannot meet all the depositors' claims for currency. Depositors in other healthy banks see what is happening, become nervous, and begin runs of their banks, which also cannot met the depositors' claims. So other banks begin to fail. Finally, sheer panic sets in when enough large banks have failed, and the entire banking system is threatened with a domino-like collapse.

A central bank can prevent the bank runs by standing ready to lend currency to any private bank threatened by a run. Once nervous depositors realized that they can exchange their deposits for currency, the bank runs are nipped in the bud, calm is restored, and the nation avoids a financial panic. Congress envisioned in 1913 that preventing bank runs would be the primary function of the Fed.

The Congress set up the Federal Reserve Banking System as a separate and independent nonprofit governmental body that was not subject to the direct control and oversight of either the Congress or the administration. The United States was divided into 12 geographic regions, each with its own Federal Reserve Bank located in a major city within the region. Figure 34.1 shows the current regional structure of the Federal Reserve Banking System and indicates where the 12 Federal Reserve Banks are located.

The 12 Federal Reserve Banks operated more or less as separate entities in the beginning, responsible only to their own regions. The banks even carried on their own Open Market Operations. The result was that the New York Fed

ELABORATION: Most diehard conservatives who are extremely skeptical of government intervention in the economy concede the need for a central bank to take control of the money supply. The supply of money could be determined privately by the Laws of Supply and Demand, but this arrangement tends to make financial markets highly unstable. The frequent financial panics in the United States before 1913 are testimony to the need for a guiding hand over the money supply.

immediately came to dominate the entire Federal Reserve Banking System, simply because New York City was the nation's financial center in the early 1900s.

THE NATIONAL BANKING ACTS OF 1933 AND 1935 Having 12 autonomous Federal Reserve Banks was not conducive to operating an effective monetary policy. The arrangement proved disastrous at the onset of the Great Depression in 1929. The Federal Reserve Banks stood by and let bank after bank fail within their regions from 1929 to 1933. The money supply fell by one-third at a time when the money supply should have been increasing to support aggregate demand.

NATIONAL BANKING ACTS OF 1933 AND 1935

Acts of Congress that brought the 12 Federal Reserve Banks under the control of one governing body, the Board of Governors.

BOARD OF GOVERNORS (FEDERAL RESERVE)

The seven-member governing body that oversees and controls the Federal Reserve Banking System.

FEDERAL OPEN MARKET COMMITTEE (FOMC)

A 12-member committee of the Fed that formulates and executes the Fed's purchases and sales of Treasury securities on the Open Market in the conduct of monetary policy.

Congress responded to the monetary debacle with the **National Banking Acts of 1933 and 1935,** which brought the 12 Federal Reserve Banks under the control of one governing body, the **Board of Governors.** The Board of Governors is responsible for overseeing the operations of the entire Federal Reserve Bank System. It consists of seven members appointed by the president to 14-year terms, with one member replaced every two years. The long-term appointments are designed to keep the Board of Governors free of political influence.

The National Banking Acts also established the **Federal Open Market Committee (FOMC)** to formulate and execute a single, nationwide Open Market policy. The FOMC is made up of the seven members of the Board of Governors plus five presidents of Federal Reserve Banks, one of whom is the president of the New York Fed. Today the FOMC meets about eight times each year to set the course of monetary policy consistent with the four macroeconomic policy goals. As noted in Chapter 33, the Trading Desk at the New York Fed conducts the purchases and sales of Treasury securities on behalf of the FOMC.

Finally, the National Banking Acts gave the Board of Governors a number of financial regulatory powers, including the ability to set interest rate ceilings on various savings and time deposits and margin (borrowing) limits on purchases of common stock on the stock exchanges.

THE DEPOSITORY INSTITUTIONS DEREGULATION AND MONETARY CONTROL ACT OF 1980 The final landmark piece of legislation in the evolution of the Federal Reserve Banking System was the **Depository Institutions Deregulation and Monetary Control Act of 1980 (DIDMCA).** DIDMCA brought all financial institutions that accept deposit accounts of any kind, the **depository institutions,** under the control of the Fed. The depository institutions include the commercial banks and the so-called thrifts, which consist of the savings and loan associations, savings banks, and credit unions. In return, the depository institutions receive all the banking services offered by the Fed, including lender-of-last-resort protection. Before 1980 the Fed's control extended only to the commercial banks, and then only to those commercial banks that chose to be members of the Federal Reserve Banking System.

DEPOSITORY INSTITUTIONS DEREGULATION AND MONETARY CONTROL ACT OF 1980 (DIDMCA)

An act of Congress that brought all depository institutions under the control of the Fed.

DEPOSITORY INSTITUTION

A financial institution that accepts deposit accounts of any kind.

DIDMCA also phased out all interest rate ceilings on savings accounts and other time deposits, such as certificates of deposit, between 1980 and 1986. The only important restrictions on deposit accounts today are the two noted in Chapter 33: Depository institutions cannot offer an interest rate on regular checking accounts, and most businesses cannot own interest-bearing NOW accounts.

The Functions of the Federal Reserve Bank System

The Federal Reserve Banking System performs a number of important functions and services as the nation's central bank. The Fed

1. issues the national paper currency, the Federal Reserve Notes.
2. acts as a lender of last resort to prevent runs on banks.
3. supervises the depository institutions to ensure that they engage in sound banking practices.
4. operates 48 clearinghouses nationwide that keep track of the entire stream of payments among the depository institutions. For instance, the clearinghouses inform every institution at the end of each day of the volume of checks written against its deposit accounts and the volume of checks deposited to its accounts. Having large clearinghouses keep track of the flow of checks is much cheaper than having each institution keep track of its own deposit accounts.
5. acts as the fiscal agent of the U.S. Treasury. The Treasury maintains its own checking accounts at the Federal Reserve Banks. It deposits checks from taxes and fees into these accounts as they come in and writes checks against these accounts to finance government purchases and transfer payments. The Federal Reserve Banks also engage in exchanges of international currencies with other central banks and hold gold certificates that are backed by the gold owned by the federal government. The gold certificates are a holdover from the days prior to 1971 when the federal government stood willing to convert dollars held by foreign citizens into gold certificates. Until 1993 the Fed also served as the broker for selling all new issues of Treasury securities. Now securities dealers perform this function.
6. holds reserves against deposits for the depository institutions (these reserve accounts are described below).
7. is fully responsible for formulating and conducting the nation's monetary policy. The Fed's Open Market Operations are the primary means that it uses to control the growth of the money supply.

CURRENT ISSUE: The volume of transactions recorded by the Fed's clearinghouse system, called CHIPS, equals the value of the GDP, approximately $6 trillion, every 2½ days. (*The Economist*, October 17, 1992, p. 95.)

The rest of the chapter will focus on the first, sixth, and seventh functions, which are closely related and lie at the heart of increases and decreases in the nation's money supply.[1]

The Depository Institutions

The commercial banks hold the lion's share of all the transactions deposits, both the regular checking accounts and the NOW accounts, so we will concentrate on them in describing the U.S. monetary system. The appendix to Chapter 34 discusses the widespread failures of the savings and loan associations during the 1980s and the subsequent taxpayer bailout of their depositors. The savings and loan failures were a serious matter because they ended up wasting a lot of resources on bad investments. They had little effect on the U.S. money supply, however.

[1]For a booklet that describes the history, structure, and functions of the Federal Reserve System, see Board of Governors of the Federal Reserve System, *The Federal Reserve System: Purposes and Functions* (Washington, D.C.: U.S. Government Printing Office, 1984). Another excellent source on the history of the Federal Reserve System is T. Simpson, *Money, Banking, and Economic Analysis*, third edition (Englewood Cliffs, NJ: Prentice-Hall, 1987), chapter 10, pp. 195–215.

The term *commercial bank* is a remnant of the 1800s when these banks lent money almost exclusively to businesses. The loans were very short term, usually much less than a year, to cover either temporary imbalances of receipts and payments or investments in inventory. These short-term business loans were called commercial loans; hence the name *commercial bank*. Nowadays commercial banks offer a broad range of services, including long-term mortgages, medium-term car loans to consumers, credit cards, and pension fund management. The name *commercial bank* has stuck, however, even though it is no longer accurate.

The Nonbank Public

The nonbank public plays two key roles in determining the money supply, both of which were introduced in Chapter 33. One is the role of the securities dealers who exchange Treasury securities with the Fed in the Fed's Open Market Operations. The other is the role of the households and the businesses who seek loans from commercial banks in order to finance consumer durables, houses, and investments in plant and equipment and in inventories. As we saw in Chapter 33, these loans increase the amount of checking account balances in the commercial banking system.

The Balance Sheets of the Three Key Players

Table 34.1 provides a bird's-eye view of the U.S. monetary system. It lists those assets and liabilities of the Fed, the commercial banks, and the nonbank public that have a major role to play in determining the size of the money supply.

We can place all the items in the balance sheets based on the discussion so far in Chapters 33 and 34, except for the two items in boldface type. Let's briefly review what we know about each of the items at this point.

THE MONEY SUPPLY The two main forms of money in the United States are paper currency, the Federal Reserve Notes (FRN), and checking account bal-

TABLE 34.1 The U.S. Monetary System

THE FED		COMMERCIAL BANKS		NONBANK PUBLIC (HOUSEHOLDS AND BUSINESSES)	
Assets	Liabilities	Assets	Liabilities	Assets	Liabilities
Gold certificates and other international reserves	FRN	**Reserves**	Checking accounts	Money: FRN, Checking accounts	Bank loans
Treasury securities	**Reserves**	Treasury securities	Other deposit accounts	Other deposit accounts	
Discount loans to banks		Loans	**Discount loans from Fed**	Treasury securities	

ances. Money is an asset to anyone in the nonbank public who holds it. The Federal Reserve Notes are issued by the Fed and are a liability of the Fed. The checking accounts are issued by the commercial banks (and other depository institutions, which we are ignoring) and are a liability of the commercial banks.

TREASURY SECURITIES All three players in the monetary system hold substantial amounts of Treasury securities as one of their assets. The Treasury securities are a liability of the Treasury, which is not included in the table. The Fed exchanges Treasury securities with securities dealers in the nonbank public in order to increase or decrease the amount of Federal Reserve Notes outstanding and to otherwise control the growth of the money supply.

COMMERCIAL BANK LOANS Commercial bank loans are simultaneously an asset of the commercial banks, the lenders, and a liability of the nonbank public, the borrowers. Increases and decreases in bank loans increase and decrease the amount of checking account balances in the commercial banks. The borrowers are primarily consumers and businesses who use the loans to finance purchases of consumer durables and investment in houses, plant, equipment, and inventory.

GOLD CERTIFICATES AND OTHER INTERNATIONAL RESERVES The gold certificates are an asset of the Fed equal in value to the gold that the federal government owns. The gold certificates used to be part of the payments mechanism for international transactions, but no longer serve that purpose. We will ignore them from now on. The other international reserves are the currencies (and other very short term financial securities) of other nations that are held by the Fed. The currencies are received as part of international transactions with other countries, for example, when U.S. exporters exchange pounds sterling for dollars at a Federal Reserve Bank. The foreign currencies are an asset of the Fed. We will return to them later in this text when we discuss the United States's international economic relations. Gold certificates and the other international reserves have no corresponding liabilities on U.S. balance sheets. They are part of the net worth of the United States.

The last two items in boldface, reserves and discount loans, have not appeared before.

Reserves

The Fed requires the commercial banks (and all other depository institutions) to keep accounts at the Fed against their checking account balances called reserve accounts, or **reserves** for short. The Fed can also require reserves against savings and time deposit accounts, but it has chosen not to since early in 1991. Each reserve account is a non-interest-bearing deposit account that is an asset of the commercial banks and a liability of the Fed.

RESERVES
A non-interest-bearing account against deposits that commercial banks (and other depository institutions) must keep with the Fed; used by the Fed to control the amount of loans and deposits that banks can create.

A commercial bank's reserves at the Fed increase whenever Federal Reserve Notes enter the bank as part of *any* transaction. Common, everyday examples are a deposit of FRN in a checking or a savings account, FRN received from selling some of its Treasury securities, and FRN received from someone paying

TABLE 34.2 **Exchanging Federal Reserve Notes for a Checking Account**

THE FED		COMMERCIAL BANKS		NON-BANK PUBLIC (HOUSEHOLDS AND BUSINESSES)	
Assets	Liabilities	Assets	Liabilities	Assets	Liabilities
	FRN (−) Reserves (+)	Reserves (+)	Checking accounts (+)	FRN (−) Checking accounts (+)	

off a loan. All banks hold some FRN in their vaults as vault cash to carry out day-to-day transactions, but no bank wants to keep too many FRN on hand. Banks ship most of the FRN they receive to the regional Federal Reserve Bank in armored trucks. Whether shipped or held in their vaults, all Federal Reserve Notes received are credited to the commercial banks' reserve accounts.

Table 34.2 illustrates how the deposit of FRN in a checking account affects the balance sheets of the three players in the monetary system.

- *Nonbank public:* The nonbank public is trading one form of money for another. Its holdings of FRN decrease, and its checking account balances increase in equal amounts on the asset side of its balance sheet.
- *Commercial banks:* The assets and the liabilities of the commercial bank both rise by the amount of the deposit. The bank records the increase in the checking account balances on the liability side of its balance sheet. The bank also receives credit for the FRN in its reserve account with the Fed, so its reserves rise by the amount of the deposits on the asset side of its balance sheet.
- *The Fed:* The Fed views the deposit of FRN as an exchange of its two most important liabilities. FRN outstanding in the nonbank public decrease, and reserves held by the commercial banking system increase by the amount of the deposit.

The withdrawal of FRN from a checking account drains reserves from the commercial bank, as does any transaction in which FRN leave the bank. Just reverse the signs in Table 34.2. The nonbank public, by withdrawing FRN, changes the form of its money holdings from checking account balances to FRN. The commercial bank's reserves and checking account balances go down by the amount of the withdrawal. The Fed records an increase in FRN outstanding and an equal decrease in reserves held for the commercial banks.

THE RESERVE REQUIREMENT The Fed established the reserve accounts as a means of limiting the amount of checking account balances that the commercial banks (and the other depository institutions) can create by making loans. The Fed cannot hope to control the overall money supply without some control over checking account balances.

RESERVE REQUIREMENT

The minimum average ratio of reserves to deposit account balances that commercial banks (and other depository institutions) must maintain over every two week period.

The control mechanism works as follows. The Fed sets a **reserve requirement** (RR), defined as a ratio of reserves to checking account balances. The commercial banks (and other depository institutions) must then maintain a ratio of reserves to checking account balances at least as large as the reserve requirement.

$$RR \leq \text{reserves / checking account balances}$$

Specifically, the banks must show that they meet the reserve requirement, on average, over every two-week period.

Congress allows the Fed to set the reserve requirement for checking accounts anywhere between 8 and 14 percent. The reserve requirement is currently 10 percent (as of 1993).[2] Therefore,

$$.10 \leq \text{reserves / checking account balances}$$

Suppose that a commercial bank has $100 million of checking account balances. Then it must have at least $10 million of reserves in its account with the Fed (.10 = 10/100). The $10 million of reserves are the bank's **required reserves.** Any reserves above $10 million are **excess reserves.** For example, if the bank happened to have $17 million in its reserve account, then $10 million of its total reserves are required reserves, and $7 million are excess reserves.

RESERVE REQUIREMENT

The minimum average ratio of reserves to deposit account balances that commercial banks (and other depository institutions) must maintain over every two week period.

EXCESS RESERVES

The difference between a commercial bank's total reserves and its required reserves; the amount of reserves that a commercial bank can lend and still be able to satisfy the reserve requirement.

Notice that the reserve requirements does not force the commercial banks to have a particular amount of checking account balances. All it does is place a ceiling on the amount of their balances.

To see that the reserve requirement limits a commercial bank's ability to make loans and create new checking account balances, turn the previous example around. Suppose that the bank has $10 million of reserves. We have seen in Chapter 33 that making new loans under a line-of-credit arrangement creates new checking accounts. With $10 million of reserves, the bank can only make new loans until the total of its checking account balances reaches $100 million. The bank is said to be *fully loaned up* at that point because all its reserves are required reserves. Any additional loans would increase the checking account balances above $100 million and put the bank below the reserve equipment. Put differently, banks have to have excess reserves in order to make new loans and create new checking account balances.

RESERVES AND OPEN MARKET OPERATIONS The reserve requirement ceiling on bank loans is fairly effective because the Fed has a great deal of control over the total reserves in the banking system through its Open Market Operations. We have seen that Federal Reserve Notes are one source of reserves for commercial banks and that the Fed can increase or decrease the amount of Federal Reserve Notes through Open Market purchases and sales of Treasury securities.

The Fed can also adjust the total amount of reserves directly through its Open Market Operations. In fact, this is the usual Open Market transaction. Suppose that the Fed buys $15 million worth of Treasury securities from one of the securities dealers. Instead of sending the dealer $15 million of FRN, the Fed simply notifies one of its clearinghouses of the transaction. The clearinghouse adds $15 million to the dealer's checking account balance at

---

[2]Congress also allows the Fed to set reserve requirements anywhere from 0 to 9 percent on all other deposit accounts, including savings accounts, certificates of deposit, money market deposit accounts, and the European dollar accounts. The current reserve requirements are 3 percent on the European dollar accounts and 0 on all the other deposit accounts (as of 1993).

TABLE 34.3 **The Fed's Open Market Purchase of Treasury Securities, Creating Checking Account Balances and Reserves**

THE FED		COMMERCIAL BANK USED BY SECURITIES DEALER		SECURITIES DEALER	
Assets	Liabilities	Assets	Liabilities	Assets	Liabilities
Treasury securities $15 million (+)	Reserves $15 million (+)	Reserves $15 million (+)	Checking accounts $15 million (+)	Checking accounts $15 million (+)	
				Treasury securities $15 million (−)	

whatever commercial bank the dealer uses and credits the bank with $15 million of new reserves. These large Open Market transactions are executed by computer over an electronic network called FedWire. No checks are written, and no currency changes hands. Table 34.3 shows how this electronic Open Market purchase affects each balance sheet.

- *Securities dealer:* The securities dealer exchanges $15 million of its Treasury securities for a $15 million increase in its checking account balances on the asset side of its balance sheet.
- *Securities dealer's commercial bank:* The commercial bank's reserves increase by $15 million on the asset side of its balance sheet, and its checking account balances increase by $15 million on the liability side of its balance sheet.
- *The Fed:* The Fed's holdings of Treasury securities increase by $15 million on the asset side of its balance sheet, and its reserves increase by $15 million on the liability side of its balance sheet.

The Open Market purchase increases the total reserves in the commercial bank by $15 million, which permits the bank to make new loans and create new checking account balances. With its Open Market Operations the Fed has created new reserves, not new FRN as in the example in Chapter 33.

Test your understanding of this reserve transaction by tracing through the effects of a $15 million Open Market sale of Treasury securities by the Fed. Do you see that the Open Market sale reduces reserves in the commercial banks by $15 million, which reduces the total amount of loans the bank can write and checking account balances it can create?

In summary, the receipt of FRN from any source and the Fed's Open market purchase of Treasury securities are the two main sources of reserves for the commercial banks (and other depository institutions).

CHECK WRITING AND RESERVES Another transaction that has a direct effect on a commercial bank's reserves is the writing and depositing of checks in its checking accounts. A check written against an account reduces the bank's checking account balances on the liability side of its balance sheet and reduces reserves by an equal amount on the asset side of its balance sheet. Conversely, the deposit of a check into an account increases the bank's checking account balances on the liability side of its balance sheet and increases reserves by an equal amount on the asset side of its balance sheet.

TABLE 34.4 **The Writing and Depositing of Checks: Clearing Checks from One Bank to Another**

COMMERCIAL BANK 1		COMMERCIAL BANK 2	
Assets	Liabilities	Assets	Liabilities
Reserves $100 (−)	Checking accounts $100 (−)	Reserves $100 (+)	Checking accounts $100 (+)

Table 34.4 shows the balance sheet effects of a $100 check written against an account in Commercial Bank 1 and deposited in Commercial Bank 2. Reserves and checking account balances fall by $100 in Commercial Bank 1 and rise by $100 in Commercial Bank 2. Notice that the writing and depositing of checks does not change the total amount of reserves in the commercial banks. It merely shuffles existing reserves from bank to bank. The Fed's clearinghouses keep track of the end-of-day reserve balances in each bank, along with the checking account deposits and withdrawals, as part of their services to the banks.

RESERVES: CONTROL VERSUS SAFETY A final point about the reserve accounts is that they are a control mechanism pure and simple. Reserves have nothing to do with ensuring the safety of the depositors' accounts. After all, the Fed requires the commercial banks to hold reserves equal to only 10 percent of their deposits. The banks are allowed to be illiquid as a result: they cannot convert all their deposits into FRN with the reserves available in their reserve accounts with the Fed.

In 1935 Congress established a separate public insurance agency, called the **Federal Deposit Insurance Corporation (FDIC),** to insure deposits at commercial banks. The FDIC operates much like a private insurance company. The commercial banks pay premiums to the FDIC in return for insurance protection of their depositors. The FDIC builds up a fund by investing the premiums, which it uses to insure deposits up to the current limit of $100,000 per deposit. The depositors are paid from the FDIC fund in the event that the bank fails. You have no doubt seen the $100,000 FDIC insurance guarantee posted at your bank.

FEDERAL DEPOSIT INSURANCE CORPORATION (FDIC)

A public agency established by Congress that insures deposit accounts at commercial banks (and other depository institutions).

In the 1930s Congress also established a separate insurance agency, the Federal Savings and Loan Insurance Corporation (FSLIC), to insure deposits at the savings and loan associations (S&Ls). The widespread failure of the S&Ls in the 1980s swamped the capacity of the FSLIC to meet its insurance obligations and led to the Federal tax bailout of the depositors. The appendix to this chapter describes the S&L debacle.

The Discount Window

The Fed gives the commercial banks an out if they cannot meet their reserve requirements; they can borrow reserves temporarily from the Fed. The loans are called discount loans and are said to pass through the Fed's discount window. The **discount rate** is the rate of interest that the Fed charges the banks for these loans.

DISCOUNT RATE

The rate of interest that the Fed charges commercial banks for loans of reserves to help the banks meet their reserve requirements.

The discount window loans are the final items that appear on the balance sheets in Table 34.1. They are simultaneously an asset to the Fed and a liability to the commercial banks. The Fed credits the reserve account of the borrowing bank by the amount of the loan.

Congress believed that discount window loans would be the most important function of the Fed when it established the Federal Reserve Bank System. The discount window was the channel that the Feds could use to lend FRN to banks that were threatened with a run, in the Fed's capacity as the lender of last resort. The discount window still serves that function to some extent. The Fed occasionally makes extended loans to small banks who are under pressure and cannot get reserves from other sources. But most discount window loans today are very short term loans, often for only a day, to help banks meet temporary shortfalls in their required reserves.

Banks are not supposed to exploit the discount window. The Fed expects them to exhaust other sources of reserves or restrain their borrowing before turning to the discount window. In this sense the discount loans remain loans of last resort. In truth, though, commercial banks routinely use the discount window to cover temporary reserve shortfalls. A bank would have to abuse its borrowing privileges and return to the discount window repeatedly to get reserves before the Fed would refuse to lend the bank any more reserves.

The Fed may try to discourage borrowing through the discount window by raising the discount rate. For the most part, though, the Fed uses the discount rate as a signal for the future direction of monetary policy. An increase in the discount rate is a signal that the Fed intends to restrain the growth of the money supply with its Open Market Operations. Conversely, a decrease in the discount rate is a signal that the Fed intends to increase the growth of the money supply with its Open Market Operations. Open Market Operations, not changes in the discount rate, are the primary instrument that the Fed uses for conducting monetary policy.

THE MONEY MULTIPLIER

The fractional reserve requirement does more than give the Fed some control over the commercial banks. It causes the money supply to be highly sensitive to the Fed's Open Market Operations.

The Fed's Open Market Operations increase or decrease the amount of reserves in the commercial banks, which in turn increases or decreases the banks' abilities to make new loans and create new checking accounts. The result is that every dollar's worth of Treasury securities that the Fed buys or sells on the Open Market leads to more than a dollar change in the money supply. The relationship between the Fed's purchase or sale of Treasury securities and the resulting change in the money supply is called the **money multiplier.**

MONEY MULTIPLIER

The ratio that relates the total change in the money supply to the value of Treasury securities that the Fed purchases or sells on the Open Market.

Two Simplifying Assumptions

The easiest way to see the money multiplier is to make the following two simplifying assumptions:

1. *No one ever wants to hold Federal Reserve Notes.* This assumption is that the nonbank public pays for all its transactions by check. Consequently, any

FRN received are immediately deposited in checking accounts. The assumption is clearly false, but it greatly simplifies the presentation of the money multiplier. We will consider the implications of holding FRN after presenting the money multiplier.

2. *Commercial banks never want to hold excess reserves; banks always want to be fully loaned up.* This assumption is approximately true for the commercial banking system as a whole. Excess reserves average less than 0.25 percent of the money supply.

   A commercial bank with excess reserves may not want to make loans because it does not see any attractive lending possibilities at the moment. It surely does not want to hold excess reserves either, though, because reserves do not earn a rate of interest. Fortunately, the bank has the option of lending the excess reserves to other commercial banks who do have good lending opportunities and are looking for additional reserves to be able to make the loans. Loans of excess reserves among banks occur on the Federal Funds Market, and the rate of interest on these loans is the **federal funds rate.** As a general rule, the banks with excess reserves to lend are the smaller rural banks, and the banks borrowing their excess reserves are the larger banks in the financial centers. The loans tend to be very short term, often no more than a day. Let's now look at the round-by-round money multiplier under these two assumptions.

FEDERAL FUNDS RATE

The rate of interest that banks charge other banks on loans of excess reserves.

The Open Market Operation

The change in the money supply begins with the Fed's Open Market Operation executed by the Trading Desk at the New York Fed. Suppose that the Fed wants to increase the money supply, so the Fed's Open Market Committee instructs the Trading Desk to buy $1,000 worth of Treasury securities from one of the securities dealers. Assume that the Fed pays with Federal Reserve Notes so that we can show later on how the desire to hold some Federal Reserve Notes affects the value of the money multiplier.

We know how the Open Market purchase affects the balance sheets of the Fed and the securities dealer. The securities dealer replaces $1,000 of Treasury securities with the $1,000 of FRN on the asset side of its balance sheet. The Fed's holdings of Treasury securities increase by $1,000 on the asset side of its balance sheet, and FRN outstanding increase by $1,000 on the liability side of its balance sheet. The Open Market purchase immediately increases the money supply by $1,000, the newly printed FRN that the Fed used to buy the Treasury securities from the securities dealer.

The money supply continues to increase well beyond $1,000 because of the assumption that the securities dealer does not want to hold the FRN. The dealer immediately deposits the FRN in a checking account at its bank, Commercial Bank 1. This gives Commercial Bank 1 a source of excess reserves that it can use to make new loans and increase its checking account balances.

DEPOSIT CREATION BY THE COMMERCIAL BANKS

COMMERCIAL BANK 1 The role of Commercial Bank 1 in further increasing the money supply occurs in three distinct steps: the deposit by the securities

TABLE 34.5 The Securities Dealer Deposits the FRN in Its Bank

THE FED		COMMERCIAL BANK 1 USED BY SECURITIES DEALER		SECURITIES DEALER	
Assets	Liabilities	Assets	Liabilities	Assets	Liabilities
	FRN $1,000 (−) Reserves $1,000 (+)	Reserves $1,000 (+)	Checking accounts $1,000 (+)	FRN $1,000 (−) Checking account $1,000 (+)	

dealer, the loan of excess reserves by the bank, and the use of the loan by the borrower.

1. *The securities dealer makes the deposit.* The securities dealer's deposit of FRN into its checking account does not increase the money supply; it simply changes the form of the money supply. The dealer is just exchanging FRN for a checking account balance. The deposit does give Commercial Bank 1 a new source of reserves, however. Table 34.5 shows how the deposit affects the balance sheets of the securities dealer, Commercial Bank 1, and the Fed.

The securities dealer has $1,000 less in FRN and $1,000 more in checking account balances on the asset side of its balance sheet. Commercial Bank 1 receives credit in its reserve account for the FRN whether it holds the FRN in its vault or sends the FRN to the regional Federal Reserve Bank. Reserves increase by $1,000 on the asset side of its balance sheet, and checking account balances increase by $1,000 on the liability side of its balance sheet. The Fed records both the $1,000 increase in reserves and the $1,000 decrease in FRN outstanding on the liability side of its balance sheet.

2. *The bank makes the loan.* We are assuming that Commercial Bank 1 was fully loaned up prior to the Fed's Open Market purchase; that is, all its reserves were required reserves. The bank now has excess reserves after the deposit. The reserve requirement is 10 percent. Therefore, the bank needs only $100 of reserves to meet the reserve requirement for the new $1,000 deposit ($100 = 0.10 · $1,000). Thus, $900 of the bank's $1,000 of new reserves are excess reserves ($900 = $1,000 − $100). The excess reserves allow the bank to make new loans and create new checking account balances.

We will see in a moment that the bank cannot lend more than the amount of its excess reserves and expect to meet the reserve requirement in the future. So the bank lends $900 to some borrower and creates a new $900 checking account balance in a line-of-credit arrangement. Table 34.6 shows the bank's balance sheet immediately after making the loan.

The original $1,000 deposit by the securities dealer remains on the balance sheet, as does the $1,000 of reserves associated with this deposit. The loan of $900 appears on the asset side of the balance sheet, matched by the borrower's new $900 checking account balance that was created by the loan. Notice that the money supply has increased by an additional $900, the amount of the loan. The increase in the money supply is now $1,900, consisting of the additional $1,000 in the checking account of the securities dealer plus the new $900 checking account that the bank created for the borrower.

3. *The borrower uses the loan.* Consumers and businesses do not borrow to hold money in a checking account; they borrow to purchase goods and services.

TABLE 34.6 **Commercial Bank 1 Makes a Loan, Creating More Checking Account Balances**

COMMERCIAL 1		HOUSEHOLD OR BUSINESS BORROWER	
Assets	Liabilities	Assets	Liabilities
Reserves $1,000 (+) Loan to household or business $900 (+)	Checking account of securities dealer $1,000 (+) New checking account of borrower $900 (+)	New checking account from loan $900 (+)	Bank loan $900 (+)

This is why Commercial Bank 1 cannot lend more than the amount of its excess reserves. The bank may assume that the securities dealer will hold on to its $1,000 deposit. But it must assume that the borrower will eventually write $900 worth of checks against the new account, and the writing of checks reduces the bank's reserves. Assume for simplicity that the borrower is a consumer who writes one $900 check for a new stereo system. Table 34.7 shows Commercial Bank 1's balance sheet after the borrower writes the check against the new account.

The liability side of the bank's balance sheet now contains only the $1,000 deposit by the securities dealer. The writing of the check reduces the bank's reserves by $900, leaving $100 of reserves on the asset side of the balance sheet. The $900 loan remains on the asset side as well. Additional assets and liabilities total $1,000.

The bank is once again fully loaned up. It has $100 of reserves against the securities dealer's deposit of $1,000. New reserves equal 10 percent of new deposits, as required. If the bank had lent more than its $900 of excess reserves, it would have had less than $100 of new reserves remaining after the borrower wrote the check, and it would be short of the reserve requirement. This is why the bank can only lend an amount equal to its excess reserves.

COMMERCIAL BANK 2 The store that sold the stereo system receives a $900 check from the borrower and deposits the check in its bank, Commercial Bank 2. The same three-step process of lending and expanding the money supply that occurred in Commercial Bank 1 repeats itself.

1. *The stereo merchant makes the deposit.* The $900 check deposited by the stereo merchant increases reserves in Commercial Bank 2, as shown in Table 34.8. Reserves increase by $900 on the asset side of Commercial Bank 2's balance sheet, and checking account balances increase by $900 on the liability

TABLE 34.7 **Commercial Bank 1, Final Position**

Assets	Liabilities
Reserves $100 (+) Loan to household or business $900 (+)	Checking account of securities dealer $1,000 (+)

TABLE 34.8 Commercial Bank 2 Receives a Deposit

Assets		Liabilities	
Reserves $900	(+)	Checking account of stereo merchant $900	(+)

side of its balance sheet. Notice that Commercial Bank 2 now has the $900 of reserves that Commercial Bank 1 lost.

2. *The bank makes the loan.* Commercial Bank 2 was fully loaded up prior to the Fed's Open Market purchase. The bank now has excess reserves after the stereo merchant's deposit. The reserve requirement is 10 percent. The bank's required reserves against the new deposit are $90, 10 percent of the $900 ($90 = .10 · $900). The bank has $810 of excess reserves that it can lend ($810 = $900 − $90).

The bank finds a customer who wants to borrow $810 and makes a loan by creating a new checking account balance of $810 in a line-of-credit loan. Table 34.9 shows the bank's balance sheet immediately after making the loan.

The original $900 deposit by the stereo merchant remains on the balance sheet, as does the $900 or reserves associated with the merchant's deposit. The loan of $810 appears on the asset side of the balance sheet, matched by the new $810 checking account of the borrower that was created by the loan. Notice that the money supply has increased by an additional $810, the amount of the loan. The increase in the money supply is now $2,710, consisting of the additional $1,000 in the checking account of the securities dealer in Commercial Bank 1, plus the additional $900 in the checking account of the stereo merchant in Commercial Bank 2, plus the new $810 checking account created for the borrower in Commercial Bank 2 ($2,710 = $1,000 + $900 + $810).

3. *The borrower uses the loan.* The borrower will soon spend the $810 loan on goods and services. Assume as before that the borrower buys one item costing $810—say, a very old used car—and gives the used car dealer a check for $810. Table 34.10 shows the final position of Commercial Bank 2's balance sheet.

The writing of the check reduces the bank's reserves and its checking account balances by $810. The asset side of the balance sheet has an additional $90 of reserves and the new $810 loan. The $900 of new assets matches the $900 increase in new liabilities, the stereo merchant's checking account deposit of $900. Commercial Bank 2 is again fully loaned up. The $90 of reserves are 10 percent of the stereo merchant's $900 deposit.

TABLE 34.9 Commercial Bank 2 Makes a Loan, Creating More Checking Account Balances

COMMERCIAL BANK 2				HOUSEHOLD OR BUSINESS BORROWER			
Assets		Liabilities		Assets		Liabilities	
Reserves $900	(+)	Checking account of stereo merchant $900	(+)	New checking account from loan $810	(+)	Bank loan $810	(+)
Loan to household or business $810	(+)	New checking account or borrower $810	(+)				

TABLE 34.10 **Commercial Bank 2, Final Position**

Assets		Liabilities	
Reserves $90	(+)	Checking account of stereo merchant $900	(+)
Loan to household or business $810	(+)		

COMMERCIAL BANK 3 The money supply creation process continues on as the used car dealer deposits the $810 check in his bank, Commercial Bank 3. That bank receives credit for $810 of new reserves, $81 of which are required reserves against the new deposit and $729 of which are excess reserves (required reserves = .10 · $810 = $81; excess reserves = $810 − $81 = $729). The bank makes a loan of $729, the amount of the excess reserves, and creates a new deposit of $729 for the borrower. The loan increases the money supply by an additional $729 to $3,439 ($3,439 = $1,000 + $900 + $810 + $729). Another merchant receives the borrower's $729 check and deposits it in a fourth commercial bank.

THE MONEY MULTIPLIER AND THE RESERVE REQUIREMENT The money supply continues to increase, round by round, indefinitely, as the original $1,000 of new reserves created by the Fed's Open Market purchase of Treasury securities gets reshuffled through the commercial banks. The loans each round, and the writing and depositing of checks, create more money in the form of new checking account balances, but not more reserves. For instance, the new reserves at the beginning of round four are as follows: $100 in Commercial Bank 1; $90 in Commercial Bank 2; $81 in Commercial Bank 3; and $729 in Commercial Bank 4, which are about to be reduced by Commercial Bank 4's loan. The total new reserves in the four banks have remained at $1,000 ($1,000 = $100 + $90 + $81 + $729).

Notice that the increase in the money supply is getting smaller in each successive round. The increase in any one round is .9 of the increase in the preceding round.

$$\begin{aligned}\Delta \text{ Money supply} &= \$1{,}000 + \$900 + \$810 + \$729 + \ldots \\ &= \$1{,}000 + (0.9 \cdot \$1{,}000) + (0.9 \cdot \$900) \\ &\quad + (0.9 \cdot \$810) + \ldots\end{aligned}$$

The money supply eventually increases by $10,000.[3]

The money multiplier relates the total change in the money supply to the Fed's initial purchase of Treasury securities in the Open Market. The $1,000 Open Market purchase led to a $10,000 increase in the money supply. Therefore, the value of the money multiplier is 10.

---

[3]
$$\begin{aligned}\Delta\text{Money supply} &= \$1{,}000 + \$900 + \$810 + \$729 + \ldots \\ &= \$1{,}000 + (.9 \cdot \$1{,}000) + (.9^2 \cdot \$1{,}000) + (.9^3 \cdot \$1{,}000) + \ldots \\ &= \$1{,}000 \cdot (1 + .9 + .9^2 + .9^3 + \ldots) \\ &= \$1{,}000 \cdot [1/(1 - .9)] = \$1{,}000 \cdot (1/.1) \\ &= \$1{,}000 \cdot 10 = \$10{,}000\end{aligned}$$

$$\text{Money multiplier} = \text{total } \Delta \text{ money supply / initial Open Market purchase}$$
$$= \$10{,}000/\$1{,}000 = 10$$

The money multiplier has a value of 10 because the reserve requirement is 10 percent. The money multiplier equals one divided by the reserve requirement under the assumptions that no one holds FRN and banks are always fully loaned up.

$$\text{Money multiplier} = 1/\text{reserve requirement}$$

A reserve requirement of .10 leads to a money multiplier of 10 (10 = 1/.10).

Properties of the Money Multiplier

The money multiplier process has a number of properties worth noting.

1. *The value of the money multiplier is inversely related to the reserve requirement.* The higher the reserve requirement, the lower the value of the money multiplier, and the lower the reserve requirement, the higher the value of the money multiplier. For example, a reserve requirement of 20 percent (.20) leads to a money multiplier of 5 (5 = 1/.20). A reserve requirement of 5 percent (.05) leads to a money multiplier of 20 (20 = 1/.05).

Changing the reserve requirement is a powerful mechanism for increasing or decreasing the money supply. A decrease in the reserve requirement creates instant excess reserves in all banks and allows them to make loans. An increase in the reserve requirement instantly places most banks below the reserve requirement and forces many of them to call in loans.

Changing the reserve requirement has such a potent effect on the money supply that it is seldom used. For example, a doubling of the reserve requirement from 10 percent to 20 percent would cut the money supply in half. Banks would be forced to call in half their loans! Therefore, whenever the Fed does change reserve requirements, it tends to offset the effects of the change with Open Market Operations that work in the opposite direction. Changes in reserve requirements would otherwise be unnecessarily disruptive to the loan markets.

The Fed changed the reserve requirements once between 1980 and 1993. In 1991 it lowered the reserve requirement on checking accounts from 12 percent to 10 percent, and it removed a 3 percent reserve requirement on certain savings and time deposits.

2. *The money multiplier is symmetric.* Open Market sales of Treasury securities by the Fed lead to a multiplied decrease in the money supply. The Fed drains reserves from the commercial banks when it sells some of its Treasury securities, forcing the banks to reduce their loans and deposits. In our example, a \$1,000 sale of Treasury securities by the Fed would reduce the money supply by \$10,000, with the same changes occurring each step of the way in the opposite direction. Banks would be short of reserves each round by an amount equal to (1 − reserve requirement) times the loss in their deposits, forcing them to call in loans by the amount of the reserve shortfall.

3. *The form of an Open Market Operation is irrelevant to the money multiplier process.* Our example considered a \$1,000 purchase of Treasury securities financed with new FRN. Suppose, instead, that the Fed paid for the Treasury

securities with an electronic FedWire transaction that directly credited the securities dealer's checking account at its bank. As noted earlier, this is the usual Open Market transaction.

The example would carry through as above. To see why, return to the first step within Commercial Bank 1 and Table 34.5. All the balance sheets would be the same as they were after the securities dealer deposits the FRN in the bank. The dealer's holdings of Treasury securities would be $1,000 less, and its checking account balance would be $1,000 larger, which is the initial increase in the money supply. Commercial Bank 1 would have $1,000 more reserves, and the Fed would have $1,000 more Treasury securities and a $1,000 increase in its reserve liabilities. The rest of the example is unaffected from then on; the money supply eventually increases by $10,000.

4. *The form of the bank loans is irrelevant to the money multiplier process.* Our example considered a line-of-credit loan to emphasize that bank loans create new money in the form of new checking account balances. The same increase in the money supply occurs if the banks gave the borrowers FRN or, as is more common, cashier's checks each round.

To see this, return to step 3 within Commercial Bank 1. Giving a borrower FRN from its vault cash or a cashier's check reduces the bank's reserves. Therefore, a $900 loan in either of these forms would reduce the bank's reserves by $900. The asset side of the balance sheet would show $100 of new reserves and the $900 loan, exactly as in Table 34.7. Moreover, the increase in the money supply would still be $1,900 at this stage, consisting of the $1,000 increase in the checking account of the securities dealer, plus either $900 of FRN or the $900 cashier's check that the borrower now has. The bank loan creates new money even if the bank does not create a new deposit. FRN in the vault of a bank are part of reserves. FRN in the hands of a borrower within the nonbank public are part of the money supply. Moreover, the $900 becomes an increase in a checking account balance as soon as it is deposited in Commercial Bank 2.

5. *The value of the money multiplier is very sensitive to the amount of Federal Reserve Notes that the nonbank public chooses to hold.* Our example produced a very high value of the multiplier because of the assumption that the nonbank public does not want to hold FRN. This is far from true, of course. We saw in Table 33.1 that FRN are about 40 percent of the money supply. As a result, the actual value of the money multiplier is on the order of 2.5 in the United States, much less than 10.

Our example suggests how sensitive the value of the money multiplier is to the holding of FRN. Suppose in the very first round that the securities dealer had chosen to hold on to 40 percent of its FRN, or $400. The dealer would then deposit only $600 its checking account in Commercial Bank 1. The bank would have had only $540 in excess reserves to lend rather than $900, or 90 percent of $600 rather than 90 percent of $1,000 ($540 = 0.9 · $600). The final change in the money supply would be quite a bit smaller than 10. In subsequent rounds, if the stereo merchant or the used car dealer had also deposited only 60 percent of the checks he received and had held on to 40 percent as FRN, the increase in the money supply would be smaller still.

6. *The money multiplier and the spending multiplier are very different concepts.* The money multiplier appears similar to the aggregate demand spending multiplier from Chapter 30 because they are both the outcome of a round-by-round process. The two multipliers are very different concepts, however. The money

multiplier relates the total change in the money supply to an initial Open Market Operation by the Fed. The spending multiplier relates the change in the equilibrium level of national income to an initial change or shift in aggregate demand. Take care not to confuse these two multipliers.

Commercial Banks and the Money Multiplier

The money multiplier exercise is very misleading in one respect. It views the commercial banks as entirely passive entities that simply react to the amount of reserves that the Fed creates. In fact, the commercial banks are aggressive, profit-maximizing firms that have some ability to affect the amount of reserves in the banking system. The Fed has to watch the banks closely to be sure that their actions in search of profits do not undermine the monetary policy stance of the Fed.

Suppose that a commercial bank is fully loaned up, yet has some attractive lending opportunities that it would like to pursue. The bank does not have to wait for the Fed to increase the reserves in the banking system with an Open Market Operation and hope that some of the new reserves come its way. It can increase its reserves on its own. Here are some of the more common methods that banks use to obtain excess reserves.

1. Induce the nonbank public to reduce its holdings of FRN by offering higher interest rates on its NOW accounts and on its other savings and time deposit accounts or by offering cash incentives or gifts to customers who open new accounts.
2. Sell some of its Treasury securities. Most banks, including all the large city banks, hold Treasury securities as one of their assets. They can sell their Treasury securities to a securities dealer to get more reserves in an exchange-of-assets transaction.
3. Borrow reserves on the Federal Funds market, which reduces even further the small amount of excess reserves in the banking system.
4. Borrow reserves through the Fed's discount window.
5. Borrow FRN from foreign branch banks. Many large city banks have offices in foreign countries.
6. Induce consumers and businesses to switch some funds out of checking accounts and into savings and other time deposits that do not have a reserve requirement. This switch converts some of the bank's required reserves into excess reserves. To the extent banks succeed in getting excess reserves by any of these methods, they can make new loans and cause the money supply to grow more rapidly.

The Fed has to be especially watchful of the leeway that banks have to scramble for reserves because the business fortunes of the commercial banks tend to follow business fortunes generally. As a result, the profit motive of the banks tends to make the money supply pro-cyclical and intensifies the business cycle.

More households and businesses seek to borrow during the expansion phase of the business cycle, which increases the spread between interest rates on bank loans and interest rates on bank deposits. The banks' loan opportunities are most attractive at this time, and they become especially aggressive in scrambling for reserves and making loans. In other words, the profit motive of the banks causes bank loans and the money supply to increase most rapidly when aggregate demand is growing most rapidly. Yet this is precisely the time when the Fed may want to slow down the growth of the money supply to prevent the economy from overheating.

Conversely, fewer consumers and businesses seek to borrow during the contraction phase of the business cycle, which decreases the spread between interest rates on bank loans and interest rates on bank deposits. The banks' loan opportunities are least attractive at this time, and they become less aggressive in scrambling to obtain reserves and to make loans. In other words, the profit motive of the banks causes bank loans and the money supply to increase most slowly when aggregate demand is stagnant or contracting. Yet this is precisely the time when the Fed may want to increase the growth of the money supply to pull the economy out of a recession.

The Fed has not been entirely successful in counteracting the profit motive of the commercial banks. The Fed can control the **monetary base,** which is the sum of FRN plus reserves, fairly tightly through its Open Market Operations. But it does less well in predicting the value of the money multiplier, which determines the size of the money supply that results from a given monetary base. The Fed's forecasts of the money multiplier just three months into the future have an average error of about 2 to 3 percent. The forecast errors are mostly due to variations in the ratio of FRN to deposit accounts held by the nonbank public. The ratio varies unpredictably, in large part because the commercial banks become more or less aggressive in attracting FRN to get reserves over the course of the business cycle. As we saw above, the value of the money multiplier is quite sensitive to changes in the ratio of FRN to deposits.

MONETARY BASE
The sum of Federal Reserve Notes plus bank reserves.

The truth is that the Fed has had a difficult time controlling the growth of the money supply throughout its history. Nonetheless, we will assume that the Fed can control the money supply to the dollar in Chapter 35 in order to focus on the question of how changes in the money supply affect the economy.

SUMMARY

The first section of Chapter 34 presented an overview of the monetary system of the United States, featuring the three key players: the Federal Reserve Bank System, the commercial banks and the other depository institutions, and the nonbank public.

1. Congress established the Federal Reserve Bank System in 1913 as an independent, nonprofit government agency to be a lender of last resort to the banks to prevent bank runs and to facilitate international transactions.
2. The Fed's main responsibilities today are to conduct the monetary policy of the United States; act as the fiscal agent of the federal government; and oversee the operation of the commercial banks and other depository institutions, which are now all members of the Federal Reserve Bank System.
3. The commercial banks hold the vast majority of all checking account deposits.
4. The nonbank public is the link between the financial and the real sectors of the economy. Households, business firms, and government agencies hold the money supply and use it to buy real goods and services.

5. The Fed requires the commercial banks (and other depository institutions) to hold reserve accounts with the Fed, which the Fed uses as a means of limiting their ability to make loans and increase checking account balances.
6. Banks must have a ratio of reserves to deposits at least as large as the reserve requirement, which in 1993 was 10 percent on checking account balances.
7. Reserves equal in amount to the reserve requirement multiplied by the checking account balances are called required reserves. Any reserves greater than required reserves are excess reserves.
8. The banking system as a whole gets new reserves primarily in two ways (a) whenever FRN enter a bank and (b) whenever the Fed conducts an Open Market Operation in which it buys Treasury securities from a securities dealer and credits the dealer's bank with new reserves. Banks can also borrow reserves through the Fed's discount window.
9. The writing and depositing of checks redistributes existing reserves throughout the banking system. A check written against an account reduces the bank's reserves by the amount of the check. A check deposited to an account increases the bank's reserves by the amount of the check.

The second section of Chapter 34 described the money multiplier.

10. The money multiplier relates the total change in the money supply to the Fed's initial purchase or sale of Treasury securities on the Open Market.
11. The money supply changes by a multiple of the Fed's Open Market Operation because the Fed's purchase (sale) of Treasury securities increases (decreases) reserves in commercial banks. Excess reserves allow banks to make loans and create new checking account balances. A reduction in reserves forces banks to reduce their lending, which decreases the amount of checking account balances.
12. The money multiplier equals 1/reserve requirement under two assumptions: (a) No one wants to hold FRN, and (b) banks never want to hold excess reserves. The public's desire to hold FRN lowers the value of the money multiplier.
13. Commercial banks have some leeway to obtain reserves on their own. Moreover, they are profit-maximizing firms whose profit motive tends to make the money supply pro-cyclical. Banks scramble to obtain reserves and to create more checking accounts when the economy is booming, the demand for loans is strong, and loans are most profitable. They are less aggressive in seeking reserves and creating checking accounts when the economy is sluggish, the demand for loans is weak, and loans are less profitable. The actions of the banks cause the money multiplier to be somewhat unpredictable, which makes it more difficult for the Fed to control the money supply.

KEY TERMS

Board of Governors (Federal Reserve)
depository institution
Depository Institutions Deregulation and Monetary Control Act of 1980 (DIDMCA)
discount rate
excess reserves
Federal Deposit Insurance Corporation (FDIC)
federal funds rate
Federal Open Market Committee
Federal Reserve Act of 1913
monetary base
money multiplier
National Banking Acts of 1933 and 1935
required reserves
reserve requirement
reserves

QUESTIONS

1. Why did Congress establish a central banking system in 1913?
2. a. Why does the Fed require commercial banks to hold reserves?
   b. How do commercial banks acquire reserves? Name as many ways as you can.
   c. What causes commercial banks to lose reserves? Again, name as many events as you can.
3. What role does the nonbank public play in determining the size of the money supply?
4. a. What are required reserves and excess reserves?
   b. Why do banks not want to hold excess reserves?
   c. Why can banks safely make loans only in the amount of their excess reserves?
5. Suppose that the Fed wants to decrease the money supply by $15 million. Would the Fed buy or sell Treasury debt on the Open Market to do this? Would the Fed trade less than, more than, or exactly $15 million of its Treasury debt to decrease the money supply by $15 million?
6. What is the purpose of the Fed's loans to banks through the discount window? How does the Fed try to influence the amount that commercial banks borrow through the discount window?
7. Suppose that the reserve requirement is 0.2. How much would the money supply decrease if the Fed sells $5 million of Treasury debt on the Open Market? What assumptions are you making in your answer?
8. Why does the Fed have to monitor the actions of the commercial banks closely as it attempts to control the growth of the money supply?
9. What are some of the problems that the Fed faces in trying to control the growth of the money supply? As part of your answer, indicate why the value of the money multiplier does not remain constant over time.
10. For the following items, indicate on whose balance sheet each would appear as an asset and on whose balance sheet each would appear as a liability.
    a. Federal Reserve Notes
    b. Treasury debt
    c. commercial bank loans
    d. checking account balances

APPENDIX

34

The Troubled Savings and Loan Industry

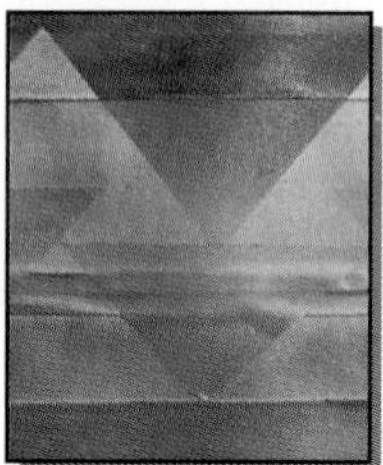

The savings and loan associations (S&Ls) ran into deep trouble during the 1980s. Hundreds of S&Ls become insolvent, meaning that the value of their assets was less than the value of their deposit liabilities; they had negative net worth. Many of the insolvent S&Ls, including some of the largest ones, failed completely and ceased to operate. The United States had not witnessed a banking failure of this magnitude since the Great Depression, when a third of all the commercial banks went out of business.

THE FEDERAL BAILOUT

Congress stepped in to try to resolve the mess in August of 1989 with the passage of the Federal Institutions Reform, Recovery, and Enforcement Act (FIRREA). FIRREA brought a number of the insolvent S&Ls under the ownership and control of a new federal agency, the Resolution Trust Corporation (RTC), in an effort to salvage and revitalize them. The RTC would sell off the assets of the S&Ls that it could not save. FIRREA also established the Savings Association Insurance Fund (SAIF) to continue to protect S&L depositors by insuring their deposits. SAIF replaced the insurance protection offered by the Federal Savings and Loan Insurance Corporation (FSLIC), which could not meet its insurance obligations once so many large S&Ls began to fail.

FIRREA in effect guaranteed that federal taxpayers would bail out the troubled S&L industry and protect its depositors by providing whatever funds were necessary to do so. The S&L bailout was initially estimated to cost the taxpayers $500 billion over five years, but it could be much larger. Boston College's Edward Kane, one of the nation's leading experts on the S&L industry, has offered these sobering estimates of the state of the industry. As of the first quarter of 1990, approximately 2,900 S&Ls were in operation and insured by SAIF. Of these, 333 were insolvent and already under the ownership of the government, and 311 were insolvent, but still under private ownership. Another 311 S&Ls had dangerously low net worth and were good bets to fail. Still another 620 were struggling with moderately low net worth; they probably could raise enough capital to survive, but the jury was still out on them. Only 1,264 S&Ls, well less than half of the total, were deemed to have sufficient net worth by the usual accounting standards for the industry. The S&L mess is far from being resolved, the RTC and SAIF notwithstanding.

THE CAUSES OF THE PROBLEM

The S&L troubles stemmed from three factors mixing together and reinforcing one another: the inherent weakness of the S&Ls' balance sheets; bank regulators who refused to close down insolvent S&Ls, and federal deposit insurance.

Balance Sheet Weakness

S&Ls suffer from an extreme imbalance between their assets and their liabilities. Their assets are primarily long-term mortgages on commercial and residential properties. Mortgages typically have terms to maturity ranging from 15 to 30 years. Their liabilities, in contrast, are extremely short term. Savings deposits can be withdrawn virtually on demand, and many of their certificates of deposit have maturities of one year or less. The problem with this mismatch is that the S&Ls are extremely vulnerable in periods of rising interest rates. They can easily become insolvent because they are locked into long-term mortgages at low rates of interest, while they are forced to pay the current higher interest rates on their deposits to keep them.

For example, suppose that an S&L has $100 worth of assets in the form of a 30-year mortgage with a 4 percent yield. The $100 mortgage earns the bank interest income of $4 per year (approximately). The bank's liabilities consist of $90 of savings deposits on which the bank also pays 4 percent interest. The bank's net worth is $10, the difference between its mortgage asset and its deposit liabilities. A net worth of 10 percent of assets is an acceptable level of capitalization.

Now suppose that interest rates double to 8 percent. The bank has to pay the 8 percent interest on its deposits in order to retain the $90 of deposits. Were it to lose its deposits, it would have to sell the mortgage to pay off the depositors. At the same time, the value of its mortgage has fallen by half to $50. To see why, think about how much someone would be willing to pay for the mortgage if the bank tried to sell it. The mortgage still earns only $4 per year in interest income, yet interest rates are now 8 percent. Therefore, a buyer would pay only $50 for the mortgage, since $4 of interest income earned on a $50 asset is an 8 percent yield. The S&L is insolvent. It has an asset worth $50, deposit liabilities of $90, and a negative net worth of $40 (−$40 = $50 − $90).

Short-term interest rates skyrocketed in the early 1980s, reaching levels of 15 to 20 percent, and drove large numbers of S&Ls into insolvency. Kane estimates that between 600 and 800 S&Ls were insolvent by 1984. At this point the role of the bank regulators comes into play.

Regulatory Failure

Private firms that become insolvent normally declare bankruptcy and go out of business, or they reorganize their operations on a sounder footing and continue to operate. They may also be sold and reorganized by the new owners. The S&Ls have always been regulated by the federal government in order to ensure sound banking practices. The bank regulators are supposed to either close or force a reorganization of insolvent S&Ls. In practice, however, they did neither in the 1980s. Regulators had always shown a bias toward allowing insolvent S&Ls to remain in operation without interfering when interest rates had risen in the past, and they behaved no differently in the 1980s. They could get away with pretending that the S&Ls under their supervision were not insolvent by reporting their mortgage assets at par or book value rather than at market value. In our example above they would continue to show the mortgage as an asset with a value of $100, its book value, after the interest rates had risen to 8 percent. This produces a book value net worth of $10, the same as when interest rates were at 4 percent. Reporting book values of assets and liabilities on balance sheets is standard accounting practice, but the regulators know full well what the true values of the assets are.

Why did the regulators do this? The answer is that their narrow self-interests are not the same as the taxpayers' interests. The taxpayers want a healthy S&L industry over the long term. The regulators are interested in looking good over the short term so that they can keep their jobs. As such, they did not want to admit that the S&Ls under their supervision were in trouble—it would not look good for their careers. In addition, a number of large S&L stockholders contributed heavily to congressional political campaigns during the 1980s in order to keep the elected representatives from looking too closely at the regulatory process. The S&L mess is a classic example of regulatory failure.

We now come to the third and final part of the story, federal deposit insurance.

Federal Deposit Insurance

The federal government began to insure the deposits at commercial banks and the thrifts in the aftermath of massive bank failures during the Great Depression. Thousands of low-income families lost their entire life's savings when their banks failed, and Congress wanted to make certain that this would never happen again. So it established the Federal Deposit Insurance Corporation (FDIC) to insure deposits at the commercial banks and the FSLIC to insure deposits at the S&Ls and the savings banks.

Although one can certainly understand the rationale for federal deposit insurance, it has a nasty side effect—it allows failed S&Ls to remain in business. Insolvent private businesses are forced to go out of business or reorganize, even though they, too, record their assets and liabilities at book value, because private investors see right through the accounting practices. They understand the true market value of a firm and simply refuse to buy stock in or make loans to insolvent firms. In contrast, insolvent S&Ls usually do not have any problem attracting funds, thanks to the federal deposit insurance. People do not care very much whether they place their funds in healthy or troubled S&Ls because they are insured in any case. So they have no incentive to learn about the true market value of the S&Ls.

Now consider the point of view of the investors in an S&L. Once their institution becomes insolvent, they have lost all their equity in the firm, and they have nothing more to lose. Instead, they have every incentive to pay whatever interest is required to attract more deposits and to take gambles on highly risky investments in the hope of that a big payoff will put them back into the black. Their gambles are fully backed by the federal deposit insurance, so they are playing with the taxpayers' money at this point, not their own. And taxpayers have very deep pockets; the investors can play forever if the regulators will let them.

Keeping the insolvent S&Ls in business weakens the market position of the otherwise healthy S&Ls and can easily lead to a snowballing of insolvencies. The healthy S&Ls are forced to raise the interest on their deposits in order to compete for deposits with the insolvent firms and to lower the interest received on their investments in order to compete successfully against the insolvent S&Ls. Kane likens the insolvent S&Ls to zombies, who eat up previously healthy S&Ls and turn them into insolvent zombies who then join in the hunt to eat up still other healthy S&Ls.

THE 1980s

The three factors described above had long been in place, but they finally brought the industry to its knees in the 1980s. The special feature of the 1980s was that the real estate industry also became a highly troubled industry. As a result, the real estate gambles that had sometimes paid off in the past produced a series of spectacular failures in the 1980s. The countryside is now full of half-finished shopping malls, empty office buildings, and vacant houses built for speculation and, along with them, hundreds of insolvent and shaky S&Ls. The S&L troubles are sure to continue unless the bank regulators force insolvent S&Ls to close or to reorganize into going concerns.

One final note of optimism is that the current S&L mess is fairly small potatoes compared with the bank failures of the Great Depression, and even many of the episodes of bank panics before then. A cost of $500 billion over five years is not such a disaster in an economy that generates $6 trillion of gross domestic product every year. The main costs are the resources wasted in building commercial and residential structures that no one wanted to buy at prices that would yield a profit to the investors. Someone will buy them at fire-sale prices, however, and the nation can go on from there. The structures will eventually have some use.[1]

[1]The sources for this appendix are: E. Kane, *The S and L Insurance Mess: How Did it Happen?* (Washington, D.C.: The Urban Institute Press, 1987); E. Kane, "Long-Run Benefits in Financial Regulation From Increased Accountability and Privatization," unpublished manuscript, August 3, 1992; and discussions with Professor Kane.

CHAPTER

35

Monetary Policy

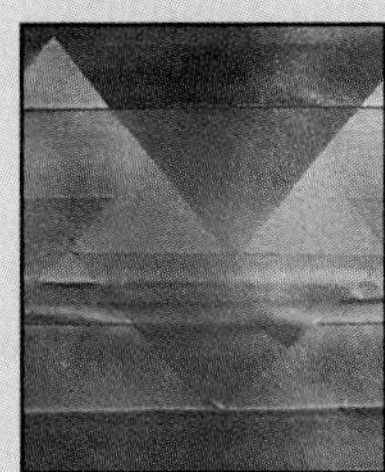

LEARNING OBJECTIVES

CONCEPTS TO LEARN

Transactions demand for money
Precautionary demand for money
Speculative demand for money
Loan markets
Practical limitations of U.S. monetary policy
Interest rates

CONCEPTS TO RECALL

Long-run economic growth [3, 25]
Laws of Supply and Demand [5, 6, 7]
New Keynesian economics [28]
Monetary policy [28, 34]
Equilibrium level of national income [29]
Balance sheet, assets, and liabilities [33]
Demand for money [33]
Open Market Operation [33, 34]
Money multiplier [34]

The chairmanship of the Fed may well be the most powerful economic position in the world. The current chairman, Alan Greenspan, controls the money supply of the world's largest economy and does so without having to answer directly to the Congress, the administration, or anyone else.

Most economists believe that changes in the money supply affect both the circular flow of goods and services and the interest rates in U.S. financial markets. This means that Greenspan has considerable influence over each of the four macroeconomic policy goals in the United States. It also means that the whole world hangs on Greenspan's every word about U.S. monetary policy. Imports by the United States are nearly 20 percent of all the world's imports. The economic fate of most nations is closely tied to that of the United States; it has been said that the world sneezes when the United States catches a cold. Also, money flows into and out of U.S. financial markets from all corners of the earth as U.S. interest rates rise and fall.

The power of the chairmanship has its limitations, however. Paul Volcker, chairman of the Fed under Presidents Carter and Reagan, is often credited with helping to bring down inflation from 13 percent in 1979 to 3.8 percent by 1982 when he clamped down on the growth of the money supply. He is also credited with plunging the economy into the recession of 1981–82, the worst recession in the United States since the Great Depression. The chairman of the Fed cannot overcome the inherent conflicts among the macroeconomic policy goals, the power of the chairmanship notwithstanding. We will also see that monetary policy cannot hope to fine tune the economy any more than fiscal policy can.

Chapter 35 analyzes the effects of monetary policy on the economy. The Fed has full responsibility for the conduct of monetary policy in the United States.

Any discussion of monetary policy must begin by acknowledging that monetary policy lies at the center of the controversy between the new Keynesian and the new classical economists. The new Keynesian economists believe that monetary policy has a significant impact on the circular flow of goods and services. In their view, changes in the money supply affect the level and the composition of aggregate demand, which in turn affects real national income and influences each of the four macroeconomic policy goals. The new classical economists believe that the causal link between the money supply and the real side of the economy is just the reverse. In their view, changes in the money supply follow, rather than cause, the circular flow of real goods and services for the most part. They argue that monetary policy has a direct and a significant causal effect only on the rate of inflation in both the short run and the long run.

Our analysis of monetary policy in Chapter 35 continues with the new Keynesian assumptions employed in Chapters 29 through 32. The policy horizon is the short run. Wages and prices are fixed, and the economy is operating far below its production possibilities frontier with lots of unemployed resources, so that changes in aggregate demand affect real national income. Macro economists agree that monetary policy does have short-run effects described in this chapter under these assumptions. The issue that divides the new Keynesian and the new classical economists is whether these are the proper assumptions for modeling the economy in the short run.

Chapter 38 will consider the effects of monetary policy over the long run when wages and prices are flexible, as the new classical economists believe. Macro economists agree that the primary effect of monetary policy is on inflation under these conditions.

Our main goal in Chapter 35 is to understand the short-run effects of monetary policy on two key economic variables, the equilibrium level of (real) national income and interest rates (and other rates of return on assets). Chapter 35 brings interest rates into our analysis of macroeconomics for the first time. They are not one of the four macroeconomic policy goals, but they have a direct impact on many of the goals.

THE ECONOMIC EFFECTS OF MONETARY POLICY

The economic effects of monetary policy depend to some extent on the nature of the financial sector within a country: the kinds of financial institutions and markets it has, how they are structured, and how they operate. The financial sectors of the developed market economies differ considerably from one another. For instance, we noted in Chapter 33 that the Fed alone among the world's central banks relies primarily on the exchange-of-assets method to increase or decrease the money supply. In addition, the United States has far and away the largest and most highly developed financial sector. It has the largest number of banks and other financial institutions positioned between the ultimate savers and the ultimate investors in the economy, and by far the largest volume and the widest variety of financial securities are traded on its financial markets. Another difference among the developed market economies is the degree of independence between their financial and their nonfinancial business sectors. For example, many of the leading financial institutions in Japan are closely aligned with leading manufacturing firms, whereas in the United States the financial sector operates far more independently from the manufacturing sector.

These differences notwithstanding, the principal economic effects of monetary policy are essentially the same in all the developed market economies. For this reason we want to begin our analysis of monetary policy in a simple way that abstracts from the particular institutional details of the U.S. financial sector. This will allow us to see the fundamental principles of monetary policy that apply to any developed market economy. With the fundamental principles in hand, we can then add some of the important institutional details that influence the conduct and the effectiveness of monetary policy in the United States.

A Money Rain: Expansionary Monetary Policy

The abstract device that economists use to understand the main economic effects of expansionary monetary policy is called a **money rain.** The idea is this. Imagine that the economy is initially in complete equilibrium. Supply equals demand in *all* markets, real or financial, every product market, every factor market, and the markets for every financial security, including money. Suddenly the central bank decides to engage in an expansionary monetary policy and inject new money into the economy. It prints the money and loads

MONEY RAIN

An abstract device used by economists to represent an increase in the money supply that imagines the new money falling from the sky.

it into helicopters, which fly over the countryside dropping the money. The skies are filled with a rain of money, and people from households and business firms rush out to grab the money as it falls to the ground.

Another less dramatic way of imaging a money rain is to think of the central bank mailing the newly printed money to some households and businesses that it has selected at random. This then gives us a simple way of describing a contractionary monetary policy that decreases the money supply. The central bank could write to randomly selected households and businesses and require them to send back some of their money.

The rain of new money upsets the initial equilibrium in the economy as the households and businesses react to the infusion of new money. Their immediate reaction centers on the asset side of their balance sheets because money is an asset to households and businesses. Every household and business firm had the exact composition of assets that it wanted as part of the overall equilibrium in the economy before the money rain. The new money upsets the composition of their assets; they now have too much money and too few of all other assets. The economic effects of the expansionary monetary policy result when households and businesses try to restore the proper proportions of assets on their balance sheets. Let's take a look at the assets held by households and businesses to see exactly what happens.

THE ASSETS HELD BY HOUSEHOLDS AND BUSINESS FIRMS Table 35.1 lists the more important assets that appear on the balance sheets of households and business firms. The assets are both real and financial assets. Each household or business firm might not have every asset listed, but these are the assets that we would find on the aggregate balance sheets of the household and the business sectors.

We will begin with the households. Their real assets are houses, other real estate, and consumer durables, such as automobiles and the major household appliances—refrigerators, washing machines, and the like. These real assets are

TABLE 35.1 Assets of Households and Business Firms

HOUSEHOLDS			BUSINESS FIRMS		
	Assets			Assets	
Financial assets	FRN Checking accounts Savings deposits Certificates of deposit Money market accounts Stocks Corporate bonds Treasury bonds State and local bonds Insurance		Financial assets	FRN Checking accounts Savings deposits Certificates of deposit Money market accounts Stocks Corporate bonds Treasury bonds State and local bonds Insurance Accounts receivable	
Real assets	Consumer durables Houses Other real estate		Real assets	Plant and equipment Inventories	

all goods that are expected to last more than a year. As noted in Chapter 27, the purchase of a consumer durable is really a form of saving, even though it is counted as a component of consumption expenditures in the national accounts and is a part of aggregate demand. Households buy real assets today to receive and consume a future stream of services associated with using the asset—transporation from their cars, the storage of food in their refrigerators, and so forth. The purchase of a house is also a form of saving. Once again, households are trading consumption today when they buy houses in exchange for future consumption in the form of housing services. The purchase of a new home is simultaneously considered to be part of investment in the national accounts and part of aggregate demand.

The purchase or holding of financial assets is the other way in which households save. They have a lot of choices—money, various kinds of savings and time deposits such as passbook savings accounts and certificates of deposit, stocks, corporate and government bonds, and insurance. The items listed in the table are just a partial menu of the kinds of financial securities available to households as a means of saving some of their current income for future consumption.

Turn next to the business firms. The real assets are the productive capital of the firms, that is, the plant, equipment, and inventories that they use in producing and selling their products. Purchases of new plant and equipment and increases in inventories represent investment in physical capital, which is part of aggregate demand.

The financial assets are the various ways in which businesses can save to finance their future investments. Their choices are generally the same as for households, with a few exceptions. The most notable difference is *accounts receivable*, which refers to the value of goods that a firm has sold, but has not yet received payment for. Accounts receivable are an important financial asset for many firms, whereas they would seldom appear on households' balance sheets. In addition, corporations are restricted in the types of stocks that they can hold in other corporations, and corporations hold most of the non-interest-bearing regular checking accounts.

Households and business firms tend to hold a variety of assets for two reasons. The first is that different assets offer different kinds of services. Each real asset provides a future stream of specific consumption services to households or a future stream of specific productive services to business firms. In contrast, financial assets usually provide a future stream of income that can be used to purchase a variety of goods and services. Many financial assets offer their own distinctive services as well. Money provides transactions services in its role as the medium of exchange. Savings deposits are very safe and highly liquid short-term assets. Corporate stocks provide equity in the form of a share in the profits of the firm. The future income stream with stocks is fairly uncertain, but has the potential for very large gains in some instances. Corporate and government bonds, in contrast, yield a known stream of future income if they are held until they mature. Insurance provides financial protection against ill health, an accident, or an untimely death much more cheaply than do other kinds of assets. In short, households and firms can buy a variety of valued services by spreading their saving over a broad range of assets. They are said to diversify their portfolios of assets in this way.

Diversifying assets has the additional advantage of reducing risk. Buying assets is inherently risky because the future returns on most assets cannot be known with certainty. We do not know for sure what interest rates or stock prices will be a year from now, or whether the roof on our house will leak and cost $6,000 to replace. Savers can reduce the risk they expose themselves to by purchasing a variety of assets whose returns are uncorrelated with one another. Roughly speaking, two assets are uncorrelated if the economic conditions that tend to make the returns on one of the assets exceptionally high (exceptionally low) are different from the economic conditions that tend to make the returns on the other asset exceptionally high (exceptionally low). A portfolio containing a mixture of money, deposits of various kinds, stocks, bonds, and real estate is less risky than is a portfolio with the same average rate of return that contains only one kind of stock. In short, people know that they should not put all their eggs in one basket.

Households have to determine the proper size and composition of their asset holdings as part of solving their economic problems. How much do they want to save for the future? What kinds of services do they want from their assets, both real and financial? What trade-offs are they willing to accept between risk and return? The answers to these questions determine the level and the composition of the assets on their balance sheets.

The same point applies to business firms. Firms have to decide how much and what kinds of capital to use in producing and selling their goods and services. This is the how-to-produce part of their economic problem, and the decisions they make determine the level and the composition of the real assets on their balance sheets. They also have to decide how much they should save for future investment and in what form—how much money they should hold, what kinds of insurance they need and how much of each, and how many accounts receivable they are willing to carry. These decisions determine the level and the composition of the financial assets on their balance sheets.

ADJUSTING TO NEW MONEY The central bank's money rain upsets the equilibrium that households and firms have achieved on the asset side of their balance sheets. They now have more money than they had planned on holding, and their reaction is entirely predictable. They will get rid of some of the money and buy other assets to restore the proper composition of assets on their balance sheets. Each person might not buy more of every asset. Some people may use the new money to buy a car; others may buy more insurance or a certificate of deposit; still others may exchange the money for a mix of assets. The same holds true for each business firm. In the aggregate, though, the demand for all other assets increases. The excess supply of money creates an excess demand for all other assets, real and financial, throughout the economy. The effects of monetary policy result when people and firms exchange the new money for other real and financial assets.

Notice, though, that the new money gives rise to an apparent paradox. People and firms are trying to get rid of the money, but in the aggregate they cannot succeed. The new money does not disappear. The only way that the economy can return to equilibrium is if the demand for money increases to meet the new higher supply of money. For example, suppose that the money supply was initially $100 and the money rain increases the money supply to $150. The demand for money must have been $100 before the money rain for the economy to be in equilibrium. Immediately after the money rain the supply of money is $150, but the demand still only $100. Money is in excess supply, which is what leads households and firms to seek out other assets.

The equilibrium in the economy can be restored only when the demand for money rises to \$150 to meet the new supply of \$150. But the demand for money is the amount of money that households and firms are willing to *hold*, and not spend on other assets. In other words, the process of trying to get rid of money has to generate economic effects that simultaneously increase the demand for money so that households and firms are eventually willing to hold the new money.

The study of monetary policy, then, raises two questions:

1. What are the effects of an expansionary monetary policy? What happens in the economy as households and firms try to get rid of the new money and buy other assets?
2. How do the effects of an expansionary monetary policy feed back into the demand for money so that households and firms are eventually willing to hold the new money and stop trying to buy other assets? In other words, how does the economy return to equilibrium with a new, higher money supply?

THE DEMAND FOR REAL ASSETS The first important effect of an expansionary monetary policy is that it increases the demand for real assets. Some households use their new money to buy houses and other consumer durables. They may also buy nondurable goods and services—food, entertainment, and so forth—that would not appear on a balance sheet, in which case their net worth decreases. In either event, the increase in money leads to an increase in consumption demand.

Similarly, some firms use their new money to buy new capital goods. They invest in plant and equipment or increase the level of their inventories. The increase in money also leads to an increase in investment demand.

The increase in consumption demand and investment demand represents an increase in aggregate demand, which increases the equilibrium level of income. Figure 35.1 illustrates.

Aggregate demand before the money rain is ADE_0, and the equilibrium level of national income is Y_0, at the intersection of ADE_0 and the 45° line. (We are ignoring the foreign sector at this point to keep the analysis as simple as possible.) The injection of new money into the economy through the money rain increases aggregate demand to ADE_1, as consumption demand increases from C_0^d to C_1^d and investment demand increases from I_0^d to I_1^d. The increase in aggregate demand leads to a multiplied increase in national income through the spending multiplier. The new equilibrium level of national income is Y_1, at the intersection of ADE_1 and the 45° line.

The analysis indicates that the amount of money in the economy is one of the "other things equal" that determines the level of aggregate demand on the ADE–45° line graph. The more money in the economy, the higher the level of aggregate demand, which is certainly what our intuition would suggest. The analysis also reveals the first important effect of an expansionary monetary policy on the economy: *An increase in the money supply increases aggregate demand and the equilibrium level of national income.*

NATIONAL INCOME AND THE DEMAND FOR MONEY The increase in national income also increases the demand for money, which is necessary to restore

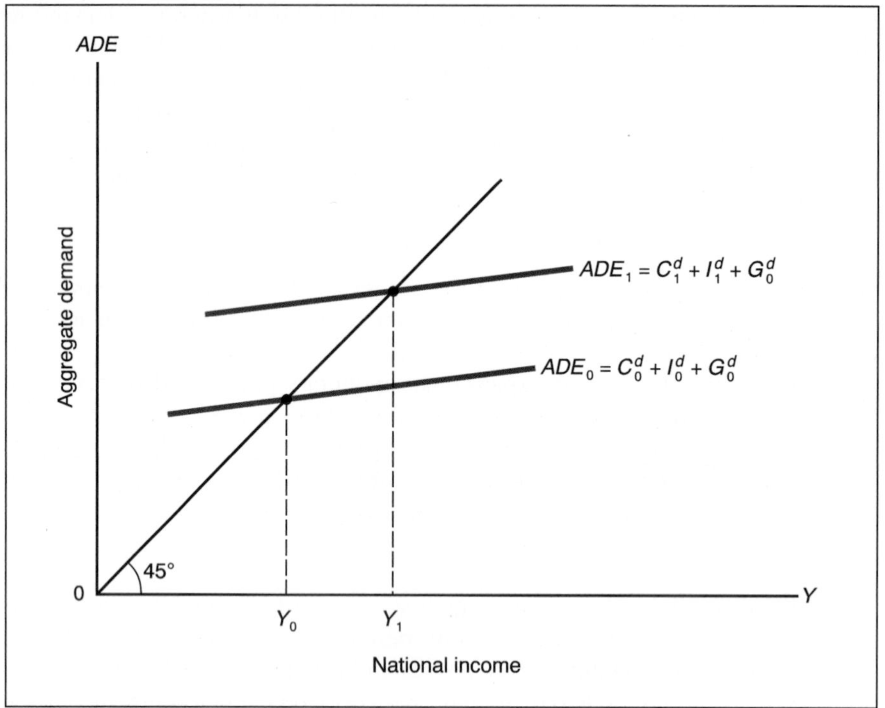

FIGURE 35.1

The Money Rain, Aggregate Demand, and National Income

A "money rain" that increases the supply of money increases aggregate demand as households and businesses exchange their excess money for real assets. The initial equilibrium level of national income is Y_0 before the money rain, at the intersection of ADE_0 and the 45° line. Households buy more consumer durables, which increases consumption demand from C_0^d to C_1^d. Households also buy new houses, and firms increase their purchases of plant and equipment and inventory, which increases invest demand from I_0^d to I_1^d. Therefore, aggregate demand increases to ADE_1 as a result of the money rain, and the new equilibrium level of national income is Y_1, at the intersection of ADE_1 and the 45° line. An increase in the money supply increases the equilibrium level of national income.

equilibrium to the households' and firms' balance sheets. The reason why is that money is the medium of exchange.

The primary motive supporting the demand for money is a transactions motive, to facilitate the purchases of goods and services. Households and businesses would have to take money out of other deposit accounts or call their brokers to sell stocks and bonds every time they wanted to buy something if they did not hold money. These transactions take time and energy and may even require the payment of fees such as bank service charges or brokerage fees. The value of holding money is that it avoids these transactions costs.

Money would not be an attractive asset if it were not the medium of exchange. Federal Reserve Notes and regular checking accounts do not offer a rate of return. NOW accounts do pay interest, but other equally safe and highly liquid assets such as passbook savings accounts, short-term certificates of deposit, and Treasury bills typically offer slightly higher rates of return than do NOW accounts.

Furthermore, the value of holding money increases the more that households and businesses spend. This is why high-income, high-spending individuals carry more FRN and keep larger checking account balances, on average, than do low-income, low-spending individuals. People can economize on money to some extent. Credit cards allow people to hold less money because they can pay off their credit card balances as soon as they deposit their paychecks. To the extent they do this, they do not have to hold money at all to pay for credit card transactions. Not all transactions use credit cards, however, so that the demand for money varies directly with households' spending and income. Similarly, larger businesses hold more money on average than do smaller businesses.

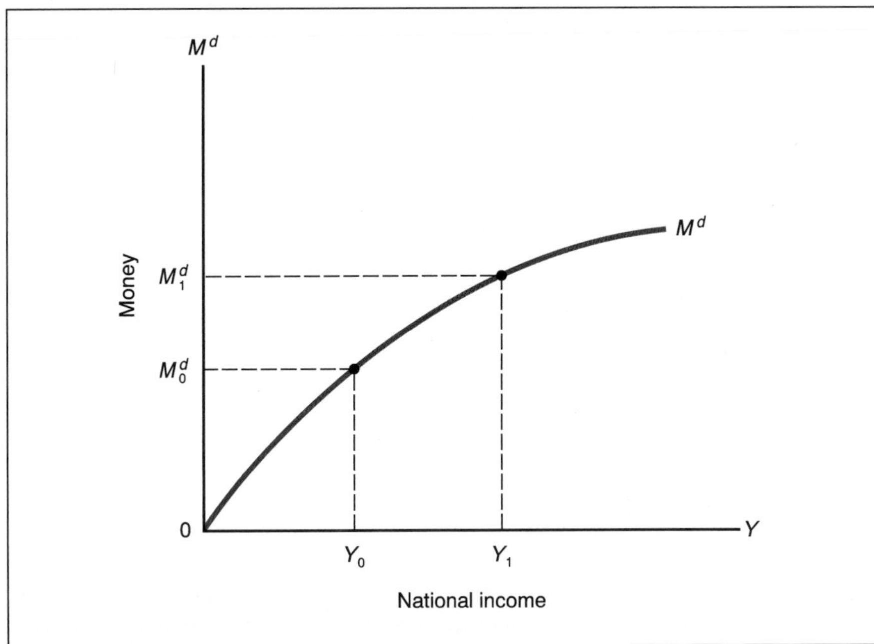

FIGURE 35.2

The Transactions Demand for Money

Households and businesses have a transactions demand for money because money is the medium of exchange for purchasing goods and services and factors of production. The quantity of money demanded for transactions purposes is directly related to the level of real national income as indicated by the transactions demand for money curve M^d. Real national income is on the horizontal axis and the transactions demand for money is on the vertical axis. The curve M^d is bowed downward because households and businesses can economize on their holdings of money as income increases. The money rain in our example increases the equilibrium level of national income from Y_0 to Y_1, which increases the quantity of money demanded for transactions purposes from M_0^d to M_1^d. The increase in the quantity of money demanded helps to restore the equilibrium between the supply of money and the demand for money following the money rain.

What is true for individual households and business firms applies to the entire economy. Refer to Figure 35.2. The demand for money is on the vertical axis, and (real) national income is on the horizontal axis. The figure shows that the demand for money varies directly with the level of national income. The quantity of money demanded is larger the higher national income is, and the quantity of money demanded is smaller the lower national income is. The direct relationship between the demand for money and national income is called the **transactions demand for money** because it derives from money's role as the medium of exchange. More national income means more spending in the nation's factor and product markets, and more spending causes households and firms to hold more money to facilitate the spending.

TRANSACTIONS DEMAND FOR MONEY

The fundamental motive for holding money that derives from money's role as the medium of exchange; it says that the aggregate demand for money is directly related to real national income, directly related to the overall price level, and inversely related to interest rates and rates of return on other assets.

Notice that the demand for money is not a straight line. It bows downward to reflect the ability to economize on money as income and spending rise. Empirical studies suggest that the demand for money is nowhere near proportional to national income. A 1 percent increase in national income increases the quantity of money demanded by only about 0.6 percent in the United States.[1]

The two income levels pictured in Figure 35.2 are the same as those in Figure 35.1. Y_0 is the equilibrium level of national income before the money rain, and Y_1 is the equilibrium level of national income after the money rain. The increase in national income in turn increases the quantity of money demanded for transactions purposes from M_0^d before the money rain to M_1^d after the money rain. The transactions demand for money increases because households and firms are spending more at the new equilibrium.

[1]This is the income elasticity reported in D. Jaffe, *Money, Banking, and Credit* (New York: Worth Publishers, 1989), 395.

FIGURE 35.3

The Overall Price Level and the Transactions Demand for Money

The quantity of money demanded for transactions purposes is directly proportional to the overall price level as indicated by the straight line M^d because money is denominated in nominal terms. A doubling of the overall price level from P_0 to P_1 on the horizontal axis doubles the quantity of money demanded from M_0^d to M_1^d on the vertical axis.

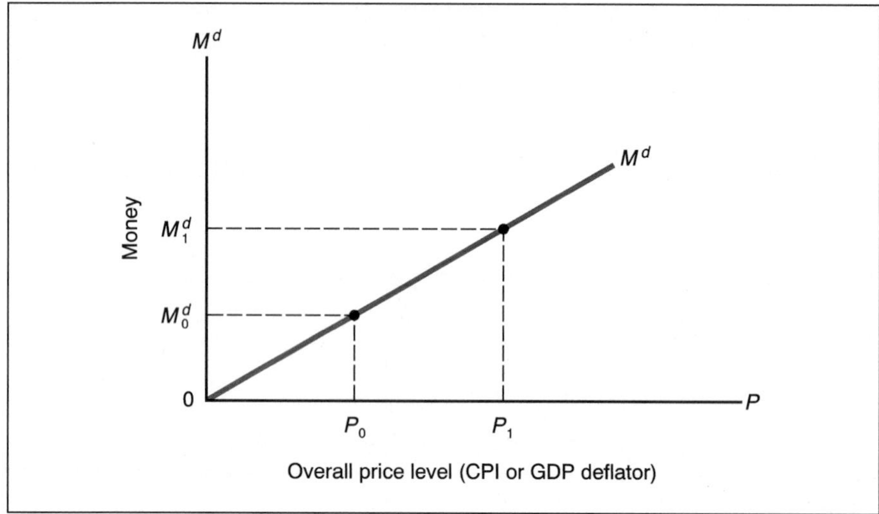

In conclusion, one of the important effects of the expansionary monetary policy, the increase in national income, simultaneously serves to increase the demand for money. The higher demand for money helps bring households' and firms' balance sheets back into an equilibrium in which the demand for money matches the new higher supply, so that the desire to get rid of the new money eventually ends.

One final point about the transactions demand for money needs to be stressed. The levels of national income pictured in Figures 35.1 and 35.2 refer, as always, to *real* or *constant dollar* national income. The transactions demand for money, however, is determined by the *nominal* or *current dollar* level of national income because Federal Reserve Notes and checking accounts are denominated in nominal dollar amounts. Figure 35.2 relates the demand for money to real income and spending, to the *number* of transaction that are made in the economy. But the demand for money also depends on the *dollar value* of those transactions, on the *prices* of the goods and services. Suppose, for example, that you are forced to spend twice as much to buy the same goods and services because the prices of all goods and services double. The doubling of prices doubles your transaction demand for money because you need twice as much money to pay for the same goods and services.

Figure 35.3 pictures the relationship between the transactions demand for money and a broad-based index of prices for goods and services, such as the consumer price index (CPI) or the gross domestic product (GDP) deflator. The level of real income or spending, the number of transactions, is being held constant in the figure. The relationship is a straight line because the demand for money increases in direct proportion to the increase in the price index, for a given number of transactions. For example, the quantity of money demanded for transactions purposes doubles from M_0^d to M_1^d when the price level doubles from P_0 to P_1.

THE DEMAND FOR FINANCIAL ASSETS The new money in the economy also increases the demand for financial assets of all kinds, as households and business firms seek to exchange their money for other financial assets. The increase in the demand for financial assets decreases the interest rates and other rates of return on these assets. The decrease in interest rates and other rates of return on financial assets is the second important economic effect of an expansionary monetary policy.

We will illustrate the relationship between the demand for assets and their rates of return for two assets that households and businesses hold—savings deposits and corporate and government bonds—since this is the first time we have talked about rates of return on assets.

SAVINGS DEPOSITS The following simple example shows why an increase in the demand for savings deposits decreases the interest rate on these deposits. Suppose that a commercial bank decided just before the money rain to attract $10 million in new saving deposits in order to increase its reserves so that it can make new loans. The bank managers figure that they have to offer an interest rate of 7 percent on the accounts to reach their $10 million target. The money rain occurs just as they are about to announce the 7 percent rate.

The money rain causes the bank managers to change their thinking about the interest rate needed to attract the $10 million of new savings deposits. They realize that households and businesses now have an excess supply of money that they are eager to exchange for other assets, including savings deposits. Consequently, they should be willing to accept a lower return on the deposits. So the bank managers decrease their interest rate offer to 6 percent, confident that 6 percent is now sufficient to attract $10 million of new deposits.

The example of savings deposits applies to any financial security that offers a rate of interest, such as money market deposit accounts and certificates of deposit. The attempt to get rid of the new money puts downward pressure on the interest rates of all interest-bearing financial securities.

CORPORATE OR GOVERNMENT BONDS The increased demand for corporate and government bonds also lowers the rate of return available on them. We have to understand how to compute the rate of return on a bond to see why.

The standard bond contract between a borrower and a lender stipulates three conditions: the face value or principal on the bond, the annual interest *payment* on the bond (*not* the interest *rate)*, and the date that the bond matures. The *face value*, usually $1,000, is the amount the borrower agrees to pay back to the lender on the date when the bond matures. The annual interest payment is an additional payment that the borrower agrees to make each year to the lender until the maturity date. These three conditions never change throughout the life of the bond.

The *price* of the bond is the amount that someone pays for the bond contract with the three stated conditions. The price is a variable, even at issue when the contract is written. The price at issue is the amount of money the lender loans to the borrower, either a corporation or the government. It can be equal to, more than, or less than the face value of the bond, the amount of money that the borrower agrees to repay the lender when the bond matures. Once most corporate and government bonds are issued, they are traded on a secondary market through bond brokers and securities dealers, where the price is again a variable. The purchase and sale of an existing bond just changes the person to whom the borrower owes the annual interest payment and the $1,000 principal at the maturity date.

The rate of return available to a bondholder is inversely related to the price of the bond. To see why, suppose that today you purchase a $1,000 bond (the face value), which offers an annual interest payment of $80 and matures one year from now. You plan to hold the bond until it matures.

Your return on the bond during the year has two components. The first is the $80 interest payment. The second is the difference between the $1,000 that you will receive one year from today and the amount that you pay for the bond today. Call the purchase price today P_{Today}. The return on the bond is

$$\begin{aligned}\text{Return} &= \text{interest payment} + (\text{face value} - P_{\text{Today}}) \\ &= \$80 + (\$1{,}000 - P_{\text{Today}})\end{aligned}$$

Dividing the return by the purchase price today converts the return into a rate of return, labeled R_{Bond}.

$$\begin{aligned}R_{\text{Bond}} &= [\text{interest payment} + (\text{face value} - P_{\text{Today}})]/P_{\text{Today}} \\ &= [\$80 + (\$1{,}000 - P_{\text{Today}})]/P_{\text{Today}}\end{aligned}$$

For example, suppose that you pay $995 for the bond. Then your rate of return during the year is 8.5 percent (to the nearest tenth of a percent).

$$\begin{aligned}R_{\text{Bond}} &= [\$80 + (\$1{,}000 - \$995)]/\$995 \\ &= (\$80 + \$5)/\$995 \\ &= \$85/\$995 = .085 = 8.5\%\end{aligned}$$

The rate of return on the bond decreases the higher the price of the bond. P_{Today} appears in both the numerator and the denominator in the rate-of-return calculation. The larger P_{Today}, the smaller the numerator and the larger the denominator, both of which decrease R_{Bond}. Conversely, the lower the price of the bond, the higher its rate of return.

For example, we saw that the rate of return is 8.5 percent if you pay $995 for the bond. The rate of return on this bond drops to 8 percent if you pay $1,000 for the bond.

$$\begin{aligned}R_{\text{Bond}} &= [\$80 + (\$1{,}000 - \$1{,}000)]/\$1{,}000 \\ &= \$80/\$1{,}000 = .08 = 8\%\end{aligned}$$

The rate of return on the bond falls below 8 percent if you pay more than $1,000 for the bond. For example, at a price of $1,025, the rate of return is 5.4 percent.

$$\begin{aligned}R_{\text{Bond}} &= [\$80 + (\$1{,}000 - \$1{,}025)]/\$1{,}025 \\ &= (\$80 - \$25)/\$1{,}025 \\ &= \$55/\$1{,}025 = .054 = 5.4\%\end{aligned}$$

You may wonder why anyone would pay more than $1,000 for a $1,000 bond. As the last example indicates, however, bonds priced at more than their face value still can yield a positive rate of return. You might be quite willing to pay $1,025 for this bond if the rates of return on other assets were in the 4 percent range.[2]

[2] If you plan to sell the bond before it matures, then the expected sales price replaces the $1,000 face value in the calculation, and the rate of return is an expected rate of return.

Many short-term bond contracts, such as Treasury bills that mature within one year, do not even have an interest payment. They just stipulate the $1,000 face value and a maturity date—say, six months from the date of issue. The price on Treasury bills must always be below $1,000 to yield a positive rate of return.

To summarize: *The price of a bond and the rate of return on a bond are inversely related.* The higher the price of a bond, the lower its rate of return; the lower the price of a bond, the higher its rate of return. This makes sense intuitively: The more you have to pay for a bond (or any asset), the less it is worth to you, other things equal.

Now return to our example of the money rain. Some households and firms with the new money are looking to exchange the money for corporate and government bonds. The increased demand for these bonds drives up their prices and decreases their rates of return to the new buyers.

You may have noticed that the sellers of the bonds after the money rain, those who had purchased the bonds sometime in the past, experience an increase in their rate of return as the bond prices rise. But the return to the sellers is irrelevant because it is a return on decisions made in the past. The relevant rate of return is the prospective return to the purchasers, the rate of return available to the households and firms that are trying to exchange their new money for bonds. The rate of return from their point of view decreases. Indeed, the sellers of the bonds are now in the same position. Having sold the bonds, they now have money to spend. If they try to buy other bonds with the money or put it is savings deposits, they will find that the rates of return on these assets have decreased.[3]

EXPANSIONARY MONETARY POLICY AND RATES OF RETURN The examples of the savings deposits and bonds illustrate the general principle that an increase in demand for any financial asset lowers the rate of return on the asset to the purchasers. The money rain, by creating an excess supply of money and an excess demand for all other financial assets, lowers the rates of return on the financial assets. In conclusion: *An expansionary monetary policy lowers interest rates and other rates of return on financial assets.*

We will usually refer to the rates of return on financial securities as interest rates from here on, even though many rates of return are not in the form of interest rates, as we have just seen for bonds.

INTEREST RATES AND THE DEMAND FOR MONEY The decline in interest rates following the money rain feeds back into the demand for money. It increases the quantity of money demanded and helps the economy return to equilibrium with the new, higher money supply.

The transactions demand for money is sensitive to the interest rates available on other financial assets because those interest rates define the opportunity cost of holding money. The higher the interest rates, the higher the opportunity cost of holding money, and the lower the interest rates, the lower the opportunity costs of holding money. For example, if one-year certificates of deposit offer a 10 percent rate of return, every $100 held as Federal Reserve Notes or deposited in a regular checking account sacrifices $10 of interest in-

[3]The same analysis applies to common stocks. The money rain increases the demand for stocks, which drives up stock prices and lowers the rate of return available on stocks to the new purchasers.

come that could have been earned on the certificate of deposit. In contrast, if one-year certificates of deposit offer only a 3 percent rate of return, holding $100 as Federal Reserve Notes or in a regular checking account sacrifices only $3 of interest income.

When deciding how much money to hold for transactions purposes, households and businesses have to compare the interest available on other assets with the time and the expense of converting these other assets to money whenever they want to buy something. The $10 of interest income offers more compensation for the time and the expense of converting to money than does the $3 of interest income. Therefore, the transactions demand for money is inversely related to interest rates on other financial assets. The higher the interest rates, the less money held for transactions purposes, and the lower the interest rates, the more money held for transactions purposes.

The opportunity cost of holding money in a NOW account is less than these examples indicate because NOW accounts pay interest. Interest rates on NOW accounts are typically less than interest rates on other liquid assets, however, because of their advantage as a medium of exchange. Therefore, the opportunity cost of holding a NOW account is still positive, so that the demand for NOW accounts is also inversely related to interest rates on other financial assets.

Economists have described two other motives for holding money besides the transactions motive; the precautionary motive and the speculative motive. These other motives also suggest an inverse relationship between the demand for money and interest rates.

PRECAUTIONARY DEMAND FOR MONEY

The motive for holding money to cover temporary and unexpected expenses or losses of income.

The **precautionary motive** says that households and businesses may keep some money on hand to cover temporary and unexpected expenses or losses of income, such as a medical emergency, a temporary spell of unemployment, or an unexpected increase in the price of heating oil. Money held for these purposes is undoubtedly quite small. These situations happen only infrequently, and households and firms can find many safe, highly liquid short-term assets to hold as a precautionary reserve that yield higher rates of return than does money. Money market mutual funds, U.S. Treasury bills, and passbook savings accounts are three such assets. To the extent a precautionary demand for money exists, however, the demand is likely to be highly sensitive and inversely related to interest rates on other highly liquid assets.

SPECULATIVE DEMAND FOR MONEY

The motive for holding money based on expectations of future interest rates.

Keynes proposed a **speculative motive** for holding money based on expectations of future interest rates. His idea was that people have a notion about what the "normal" or average rate of interest is on various financial assets. Interest rates move in cycles over time, just as national income and employment do. When interest rates rise above the "normal" range, people see this as a temporary situation because they expect interest rates to return to the "normal" levels. Therefore, they reduce their money holdings in exchange for the other assets in order to take advantage of the opportunity. Conversely, when interest rates fall below the "normal" range, people also see this as a temporary situation. They hold more money because they do not want to lock themselves into other financial assets when interest rates are unusually low. Instead, they are content to sacrifice some interest now and wait until the interest rates return to "normal." The speculative motive therefore also generates an inverse relationship between the demand for money and interest rates.

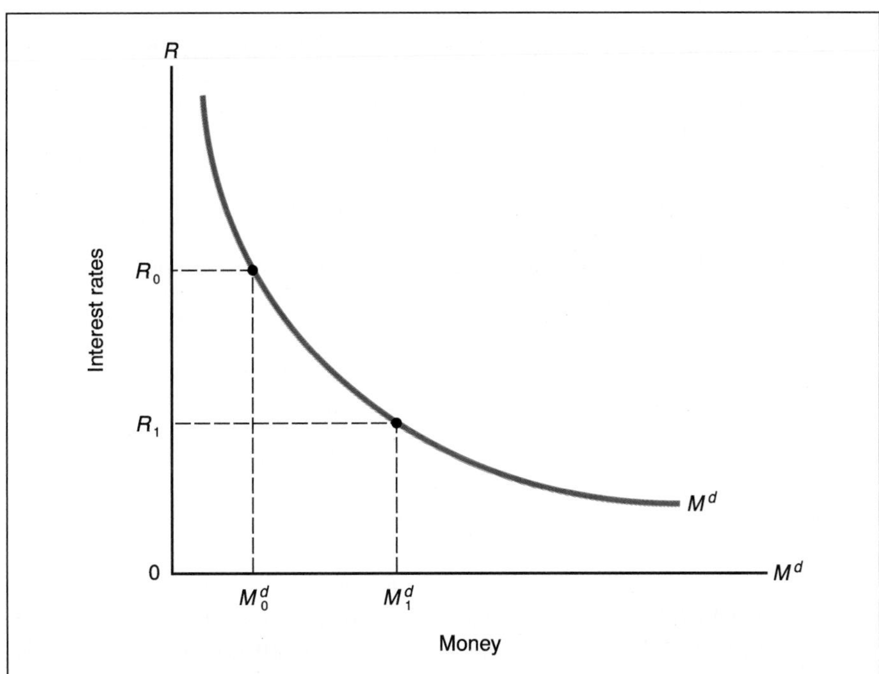

FIGURE 35.4

Interest Rates and the Demand for Money

The interest rate available on other financial assets defines the opportunity cost of holding money. Therefore, the demand for money is inversely related to the level of interest rates on other financial assets, as indicated by the demand for money curve M^d. The quantity of money demanded is on the horizontal axis and the average interest rate on other financial assets is on the vertical axis. The money rain in our example lowers the average interest rate on other financial assets from R_0 to R_1, which increases the quantity of money demanded from M_0^d to M_1^d. The increase in the quantity of money demanded helps to restore the equilibrium between the supply of money and the demand for money following the money rain.

The speculative motive may have been important in the recession of the early 1990s. Interest rates on money market funds, certificates of deposit, and other highly liquid assets fell to very low levels in 1991 and 1992, in the 2 to 4 percent range. Such low interest rates had not been observed for 20 years or more. At the same time, the demand for money skyrocketed, especially the demand for NOW accounts, which grew at annual rates in excess of 10 percent.[4] Households may have been waiting for interest rates to rise and were willing to sacrifice the small interest advantage of staying in other liquid assets. Interest rates on these assets were only about one percentage point above the interest rates on NOW accounts, so the sacrifice of holding NOW accounts in the meantime was not very large.

Figure 35.4 illustrates the inverse relationship between the demand for money and interest rates. Interest rates are on the vertical axis, and the demand for money is on the horizontal axis. For Federal Reserve Notes and regular checking accounts, interpret the interest rate on the vertical axis as the average interest rate on other liquid assets. For NOW accounts, interpret the interest rate as the difference between the average interest rate on other liquid assets and the interest rate on the NOW accounts. Notice that the quantity of money demanded remains fairly low for medium and high values of interest rates. Households and business firms prefer other liquid assets to money when interest rates are in this range because the opportunity cost of holding money is high. The quantity of money demanded increases substantially at very low interest rates, however, consistent with Keynes's speculative motive for holding money and the experience of 1991 and 1992.

[4]Council of Economic Advisers, *Economic Indicators, March 1993* (Washington, D.C.: U.S. Government Printing Office, 1993), 26.

Figure 35.4 also shows how the money rain feeds back into the demand for money. Suppose that the average interest rate on other assets falls from R_0 to R_1 as households and firms are trying to exchange their new money for other financial assets. The decrease in the return on these assets in turn increases the quantity of money demanded from M_0^d to M_1^d. The decline in interest rates induces people to want to hold more of the new money as other financial assets become less attractive. This helps to return the economy to equilibrium by increasing the demand for money to match the new, higher supply of money.

SUMMARY: AN EXPANSIONARY MONETARY POLICY Our analysis of the money rain as an example of an expansionary monetary policy is now complete. To summarize, the steps of the analysis are as follows:

1. The injection of money into the economy leads to an excess supply of money and an excess demand for all other assets. Households and businesses want to exchange the new money for both real and financial assets.
2. The demand for real assets, for both consumer durables and capital goods, increases. The result is an increase in consumption demand and investment demand, which increases aggregate demand and the equilibrium level of national income. The demand for financial assets also increases, which decreases interest rates (and other rates of return) on these assets. Therefore, *an expansionary monetary policy has two important effects on the economy: It increases the equilibrium level of national income and reduces the average level of interest rates.*
3. The two effects of the expansionary monetary policy feed back into the demand for money and return the economy to equilibrium. The increase in national income increases the quantity of money demanded for transactions purposes because there is more spending on goods and services in the aggregate. The decrease in interest rates decreases the opportunity cost of holding money and further increases the quantity of money demanded.
4. The economy returns to equilibrium when national income increases by enough, and interest rates fall by enough, to increase the demand for money to the new, higher supply of money. Households and businesses are content to hold the new money at this point and they stop trying to exchange money for other real and financial assets. Their portfolio of assets is once again in equilibrium.

A Contractionary Monetary Policy

The analysis of a contractionary monetary policy, in which the central bank reduces the money supply, follows the analysis of an expansionary monetary policy step for step, with all the results reversed. Suppose that the Fed asked all households and businesses to mail some of their money back to the Fed. The reaction of the households and the businesses, and the return to equilibrium, would be as follows:

1. The reduction of money upsets the equilibrium that households and businesses had achieved in their portfolio of assets. They now have too little money and too much of all other assets. Money is in excess demand, and all other assets are in excess supply. Therefore, households and businesses

want to exchange real and financial assets for money to build up their money holdings.

2. The demand for real assets, both consumer durables and capital goods, decreases. This results in a decrease in consumption demand and investment demand, which decreases aggregate demand and the equilibrium level of national income. The demand for financial assets also decreases, which raises interest rates (and other rates of return) on these assets. Households and businesses are now taking money out of other deposit accounts and trying to sell assets such as corporate and government bonds. Interest rates on the deposit accounts rise as bank managers are forced to offer higher interest to hold on to these accounts. Bond prices fall in the sell-off, which raises the rates of return available on these assets to new purchasers.

Therefore, *a contractionary monetary policy has two important effects on the economy: It decreases the equilibrium level of national income and increases the average level of interest rates.*

3. The two effects of the contractionary monetary policy feed back into the demand for money and return the economy to equilibrium. The decrease in national income decreases the quantity of money demanded for transactions purposes because there is less spending on goods and services in the aggregate. The increase in interest rates increases the opportunity cost of holding money and further decreases the quantity of money demanded.
4. The economy returns to equilibrium when national income decreases by enough, and interest rates rise by enough, to decrease the demand for money to the new, lower supply for money. Households and businesses are content to hold the reduced amount of money at this point and they stop trying to exchange other real and financial assets for money. Their portfolio of assets is once again in equilibrium.

The following Concept Summary table summarizes the effects of expansionary and contractionary monetary policies on the equilibrium level of national income and interest rates.

CONCEPT SUMMARY

THE EFFECTS OF MONETARY POLICY ON REAL NATIONAL INCOME AND INTEREST RATES

MONETARY POLICY	REAL NATIONAL INCOME	INTEREST RATES
Expansionary (Fed buys Treasury securities on the Open Market)	Increase Y	Decrease R
Contractionary (Fed sells Treasury securities on the Open Market)	Decrease Y	Increase R

We are now in a position to consider the institutional details of how monetary policy works its way through the economy in the United States.

MONETARY POLICY IN THE UNITED STATES

The Fed does not drop money from helicopters or ask households and firms to mail money back to the Fed. We saw in Chapter 33 that the primary method of conducting monetary policy is the Open Market Operation in which the Fed buys and sells existing Treasury securities. The Fed *buys* Treasury securities from securities dealers to *increase* the money supply and *sells* Treasury securities to securities dealers to *decrease* the money supply.

The ultimate effects on the economy of the Fed's Open Market Operations are the same as those summarized above. The Fed's method of conducting monetary policy simply changes somewhat the pathway that the economy takes to reach those effects. The same holds true for any of the developed market economies. The effects of monetary policy are the same; the pathway to the effects depends on the particular monetary and financial institutions within the country.

The Open Market Operation changes the story about the money rain in two ways. The first is that the commercial banks (and other depository institutions) become key players in bringing about the two effects. The Fed's Open Market Operations are designed, first and foremost, to throw the commercial banks' portfolios of assets out of line. It is the commercial banks' reactions that are counted on to change the level of national income and the interest rates. The second is that the effects on national income and interest rates do not occur simultaneously. Instead, the Fed sets off a causal chain of events in which its Open Market Operation first changes interest rates, which then change the levels of aggregate demand and national income. Moreover, the key interest rate is the interest rate on commercial bank loans to households and businesses.

The causal chain of events is as follows:

- *Expansionary monetary policy*

  Fed's purchase of Treasury securities $\rightarrow R \downarrow \rightarrow C^d \uparrow$ and $I^d \uparrow \rightarrow Y_E \uparrow$

- *Contractionary monetary policy*

  Fed's sale of Treasury securities $\rightarrow R \uparrow \rightarrow C^d \downarrow$ and $I^d \downarrow \rightarrow Y_E \downarrow$

Expansionary Monetary Policy

EXPANSIONARY MONETARY POLICY
An increase in the money supply undertaken by the Fed for the purpose of increasing aggregate demand; the Fed buys Treasury securities on the Open Market.

Let's consider an **expansionary monetary policy** in the United States.

THE OPEN MARKET OPERATION As we saw in Chapters 33 and 34, the policy begins when the Trading Desk at the New York Fed calls the securities dealers at a few large commercial banks, brokerage houses, and investment banks and announces its intention to buy some of its Treasury securities. The securities dealers offer prices at which they are willing to sell, and the Fed buys from the dealers offering the lowest prices.

Suppose that the Fed buys entirely from the securities dealers at Merrill Lynch in order to keep the story simple. No money or checks change hands in most of these transactions. Instead, the Fed takes ownership of the Treasury securities and, in return, has one of its clearinghouses adjust the balance sheet

TABLE 35.2 The Fed's Open Market Purchase of Treasury Securities

THE FED		COMMERCIAL BANK OF MERRILL LYNCH		MERRILL LYNCH	
Assets	Liabilites	Assets	Liabilities	Assets	Liabiliites
Treasury securities (+)	Reserves (+)	Reserves (+)	Checking account (+) of Merrill Lynch	Checking account (+) Treasury securities (−)	

of the commercial bank that Merrill Lynch uses. The clearinghouse increases the bank's reserves by the amount of the Open Market purchase on the asset side of the bank's balance sheet and also increases Merrill Lynch's checking account with the bank by the same amount on the liability side of the bank's balance sheet. Table 35.2 records the effects of the Open Market purchase on the balance sheets of Merrill Lynch, the commercial bank, and the Fed.

Merrill Lynch exchanges Treasury securities for an equal increase in its checking account balance on the asset side of its balance sheet. The commercial bank's reserves and checking accounts increase on the asset and the liability sides of its balance sheet, respectively. The Fed's holdings of Treasury securities increase on the asset side of its balance sheet, matched by an equal increase in reserves due commercial banks on the liability side of its balance sheet. The money supply increases immediately by the amount of the Open Market purchase, in the form of the increase in Merrill Lynch's checking account balance.

The increase in the money supply has almost no immediate impact on aggregate demand and the equilibrium level of national income. Merrill Lynch receives the new money, yet the composition of its assets is not necessarily thrown out of equilibrium. The Merrill Lynch securities dealers have willingly exchanged some of their Treasury securities for the checking account. Also, Merrill Lynch and the other financial institutions that the Fed trades with on the Open Market use very little real capital. So even if their portfolios were out of line, they would not purchase much more real capital with the new checking account balance and cause a noticeable increase in investment demand.

THE COMMERCIAL BANKS AND THEIR LOANS The commercial banks (and other depository institutions) are the key to the real effects of monetary policy in the United States because it is their portfolios of assets that are thrown out of equilibrium most dramatically by the Fed's Open Market Operations. In our example the Open Market purchase by the Fed gives the commercial bank excess reserves. The bank now has too many reserves and too few loans. This position is costly to the bank because reserves do not offer a rate of return, whereas the return on bank loans is the principal source of revenue for the bank.

The Fed counts on the fact that commercial banks have a strong incentive to seek out new borrowers and to exchange their excess reserves for new loans. The market for bank loans occupies center stage in the conduct of monetary policy in the United States.

Figure 35.5 illustrates the market for bank loans. The interest rate on bank loans is on the vertical axis, and the quantity of loans to households and busi-

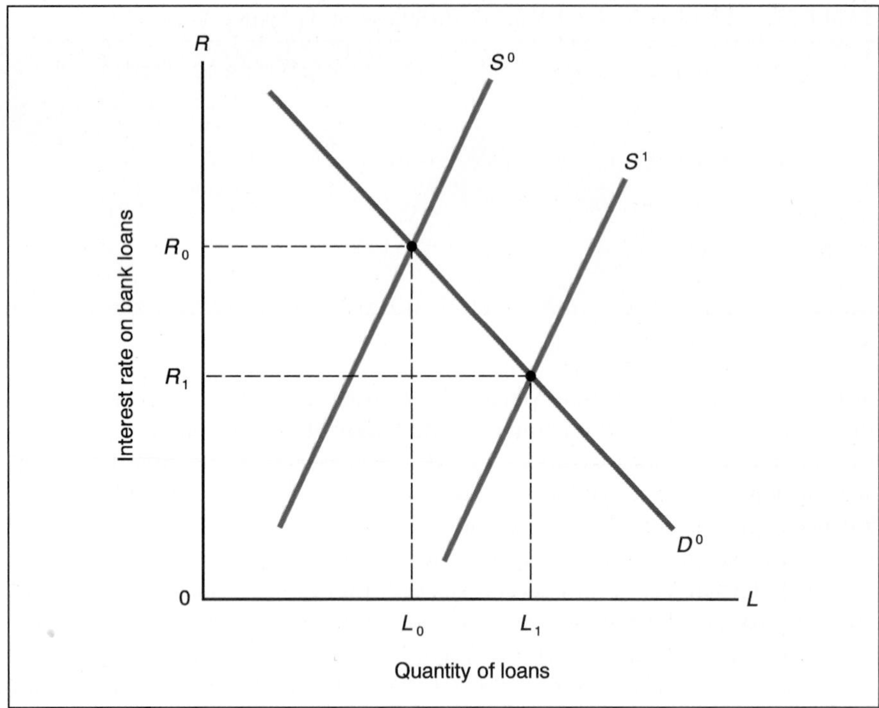

FIGURE 35.5

Expansionary Monetary Policy and the Market for Bank Loans

In the market for bank loans the commercial banks are the suppliers/lenders and the households and businesses are the demanders/borrowers. The quantity of bank loans is on the horizontal axis and the interest rate on bank loans is on the vertical axis. The supply curve, S, is upward sloping because banks are willing to lend more money the higher the interest rate. The demand curve, D, is downward sloping because households and businesses are willing to borrow more money the lower the interest rate. The initial equilibrium in the loan market is (L_0,R_0), at the intersection of D^0 and S^0. An expansionary monetary policy increases banks' excess reserves, which the banks want to lend. The supply of bank loans increases from S^0 to S^1, and the new equilibrium is (L_1,R_1), at the intersection of D^0 and S^1. The expansionary monetary policy lowers the interest rate on bank loans, which induces households and businesses to increase their borrowing and spending.

nesses is on the horizontal axis. The market supply and the market demand curves, S^0 and D^0, represent the initial situation before the Fed's Open Market purchase. The supply curve represents the banks' willingness to lend at various interest rates. S^0 is upward sloping, as usual. The interest rate on loans represents the rate of return on the loan to the bank. The higher the loan interest rate is, the more the banks are willing to lend; the lower the loan interest rate is, the less the banks are willing to lend. The demand curve, D^0, represents the households' and business firms' willingness to borrow at various interest rates. D^0 is downward sloping, as usual. The interest rate on loans represents the cost of borrowing to the borrowers. Therefore, the higher the loan interest rate is, the less the households and the firms are willing to borrow; the lower the loan interest rate is, the more the households and the firms are willing to borrow. The initial equilibrium is at the intersection of S^0 and D^0. L_0 bank loans are written at an interest rate of R_0.

A general point about loan markets is worth noting before continuing. In any supply and demand diagram of a loan market, the *supplier* is always the *lender*, for whom the loan is an asset, and the *demander* is always the *borrower*, for whom the loan is a liability. Only the identity of the lenders and the borrowers changes from market to market. For instance, when you open a passbook savings account, you are lending money to a bank. The savings account is your asset and the bank's liability. Therefore, in a supply and demand graph of passbook savings accounts, the households are the lenders, and the banks are the borrowers.

Return to the market for bank loans in Figure 35.5, in which the banks are the lenders and the households and the firms are the borrowers. The increase in reserves because of the Fed's Open market purchase increases the banks' willingness to lend at every interest rate. The supply curve shifts down and to the right, from S^0 to S^1. The banks' increased willingness to supply puts downward pressure on the interest rate. Banks are anxious to find new borrowers to get rid of their non-interest-bearing excess reserves, and they are willing to offer lower rates to borrowers. The loan interest rate falls from R_0 to R_1, which induces households and firms to move downward along their demand curves and increase their borrowing. The quantity of loans increases from L_0 to L_1.

THE INCREASE IN AGGREGATE DEMAND The decrease in the interest rate on bank loans is the key interest rate effect that the Fed hopes for. A primary goal of an expansionary monetary policy is to increase aggregate demand and the equilibrium level of national income. The mechanism for increasing aggregate demand is the increase in bank loans. Households and firms borrow from commercial banks and other depository institutions primarily to finance purchases of real assets. Households borrow to buy big-ticket items, such as houses, cars, and major appliances. Firms borrow to pay for investment in plant and equipment and in inventory. Therefore, the downward-sloping demand curve for bank loans implies that the demand for consumer durables and for investment is also sensitive to the interest rate on bank loans.

Figure 35.6 illustrates. Figure 35.6(a) shows the demand for consumer durables, and Figure 35.6(b) shows investment demand. Both demands are related to the interest rate on bank loans, which is on the vertical axis. According to the graphs, the decrease in the interest rate on bank loans from R_0 to R_1 increases the quantity of consumer durables demanded from C_0^{Dur} to C_1^{Dur} and increases the quantity of investment demanded from I_0^d to I_1^d. The combined increase in consumption spending and investment spending demanded by households and firms corresponds to the increase in their borrowings from L_0 to L_1 in Figure 35.5.

Chapter 29 discussed the extent to which the demand for consumer durables and investment demand are sensitive to interest rates on bank loans. The

FIGURE 35.6

The Interest Rate on Loans, Consumer Durables, and Investment

Households borrow to finance consumer durables and new houses, and businesses borrow to finance their investments in plant and equipment and inventory. Therefore, the demands for consumer durables and investment are inversely related to the interest rates on bank loans, as shown by the curves C^{Dur} and I^d in Figure 35.6(a) and Figure 35.6(b), respectively. An expansionary monetary policy that reduces the interest rate on bank loans from R_0 to R_1 increases the quantity of consumer durables demanded from C_0^{Dur} to C_1^{Dur} in Figure 35.6(a). It also increases the quantity of investment demanded from I_0^d to I_1^d in Figure 35.6(b). The increase in spending on consumer durables and investment as a result of an expansionary monetary policy increases aggregate demand and the equilibrium level of national income.

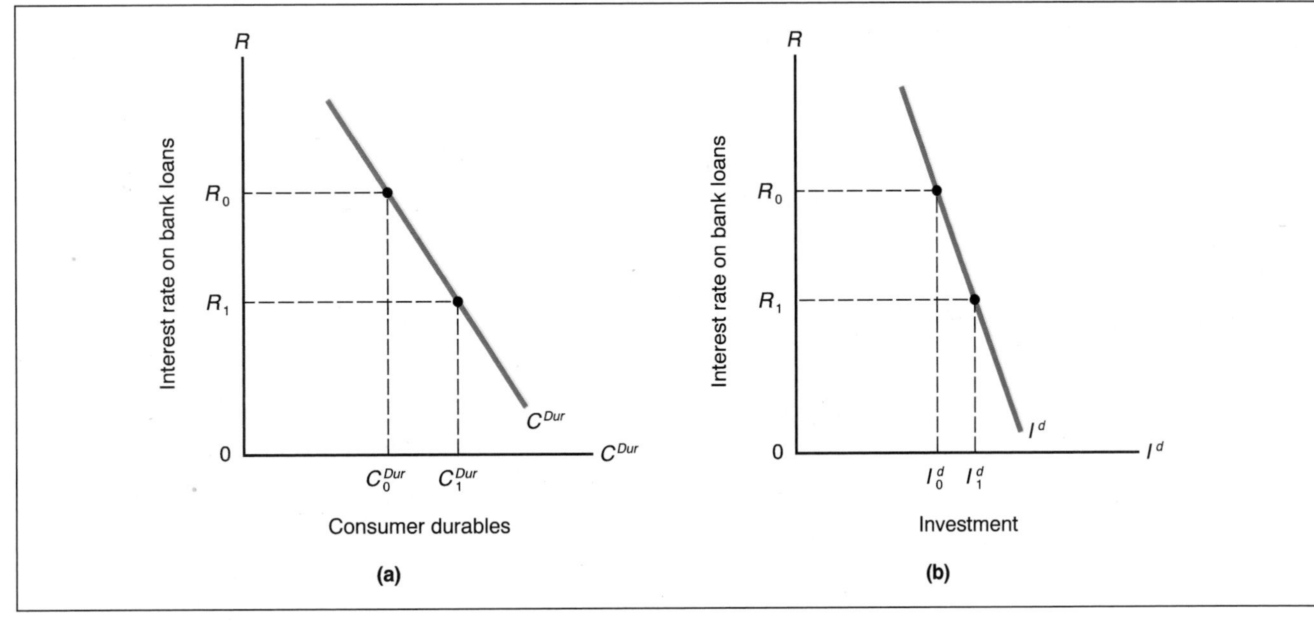

conclusion was as follows. The demand for mortgage loans to finance new homes appears to be quite sensitive to mortgage interest rates. The purchase of new homes is part of investment demand. The demand for consumer durables, particularly the demand for automobiles, also appears to be fairly sensitive to loan rates. The relationship between interest rates and investment in plant and equipment and in inventories is a source of controversy among economists. Everyone agrees that the demand for *capital* is related to interest rates, but economists disagree sharply on whether investment in plant and equipment and in inventories is sensitive to interest rates.

In any event, the Fed hopes to stimulate consumption demand and investment demand by pumping reserves into the banking system and inducing banks to reduce the interest rates on loans so that they can turn the reserves into loans. We saw in Chapter 34 that the money supply increases ultimately by a multiple of the Fed's Open Market purchase of Treasury securities as the banks make the new loans. The new money being created by the bank loans supports the increase in consumer demand and investment demand. Aggregate demand increases and leads to a multiplied increase in the equilibrium level of national income, as illustrated in Figure 35.1.

Our analysis of an expansionary monetary policy is now complete. To summarize, the pathway from the Fed's Open Market purchase of Treasury securities, to the lowering of interest rates, to the increase in national income proceeds in the following steps:

1. The Open Market purchase creates excess reserves in the commercial banks and throws their holding of assets out of equilibrium. The banks want to exchange the non-interest-bearing excess reserves for loans.
2. The banks' desire to make loans drives down the interest rate on bank loans, which induces households and firms to increase their borrowing in order to finance increases in consumer durables and investment. The increase in consumption demand and investment demand increases aggregate demand, which increases the equilibrium level of national income.
3. In conclusion: *An expansionary monetary policy increases national income and decreases interest rates on assets.* This is the same conclusion that we reached for the money rain.

Contractionary Monetary Policy

CONTRACTIONARY MONETARY POLICY

A decrease in the money supply undertaken by the Fed for the purpose of decreasing aggregate demand; the Fed sells Treasury securities on the Open Market.

The Fed begins a **contractionary monetary policy** by having the Trading Desk at the New York Fed sell some of its Treasury securities, mostly Treasury bills, to the securities dealers that it trades with. The Open Market sale works its way through the economy exactly as the Open Market purchase, except in reverse. Make sure that you understand the following step-by-step summary of the effects of a contractionary monetary policy.

1. The Open Market sale drains reserves from the commercial banks and throws their holdings of assets out of equilibrium. The banks are now below their reserve requirements and have to reduce the amount of their loans in order to build up their reserve accounts.
2. The banks' decreased willingness to make loans drives up the interest rate on bank loans. Refer again to Figure 35.5. This time, think of S^1 as the initial supply curve for loans made prior to the Fed's Open Market sale and

the initial equilibrium as (L_1, R_1), at the intersection of D^0 and S^1. The banks' decreased desire to lend shifts the supply curve up and to the left to S^0 and establishes a new equilibrium at (L_0, R_0), at the intersection of D^0 and S^0. The increase in the interest rate from R_1 to R_0 induces households and firms to decrease their borrowing to finance increases in consumer durables and investment. Borrowing decreases from L_1 to L_0. In Figure 35.6, the quantity of consumer durables demanded decreases from C_1^{Dur} to C_0^{Dur}, and the quantity of investment demanded decreases from I_1^d to I_0^d in response to the higher interest rate on loans. The decreases in consumption demand and investment demand decrease aggregate demand, which decreases the equilibrium level of national income.

3. In conclusion: *A contractionary monetary policy decreases national income and increases interest rates on assets.* This is the same conclusion that we reached if the Fed asked people at random to mail in some of their money.

The previous Concept Summary table summarizes how expansionary and contractionary monetary policies in the United States affect the equilibrium level of national income and interest rates.

Practical Problems with U.S. Monetary Policy

In Chapter 30 we noted that the administration and the Congress cannot fine tune the economy with their fiscal policies because of the many practical difficulties that arise in the conduct of fiscal policy. The best that fiscal policy can hope to do is "lean against the wind" and help prevent the economy from straying too far from whatever target level of national income the administration may set. The same is true of monetary policy. The conduct of monetary policy is plagued with its own set of practical difficulties that prevent the Fed from being able to fine tune the economy.

THE POLICY LAGS For starters, the Fed's Board of Governors faces the same three policy lags as the administration does in the conduct of fiscal policy: the recognition lag, the administrative lag, and the operational lag.

RECOGNITION LAG The **recognition lag** is the time required for the Board of Governors to recognize that the economy is in trouble and needs a dose of expansionary or contractionary monetary policy. Recall that the length of the recognition lag depends on the ability to collect reliable data and forecast the future performance of the economy. As noted in the discussion of fiscal policy, forecasting is the problem. The Board of Governors is no better at economic forecasting than anyone else is. Monetary and fiscal policies suffer an equal handicap here.

RECOGNITION LAG (MONETARY POLICY)

The time required for the Board of Governors to recognize that the economy is in trouble and needs a dose of expansionary or contractionary monetary policy.

ADMINISTRATIVE LAG The **administrative lag** is the time required to change the course of monetary policy once the Board of Governors decides to do so. Here the Board of Governors has a decided advantage over the administration and the Congress. We saw that the administrative lag was an enormous problem in the conduct of fiscal policy; the budgetary process is lengthy and cumbersome. Not so in the conduct of monetary policy. The administrative lag is extremely short, virtually non-existent. The Board of Governors instructs the

ADMINISTRATIVE LAG (MONETARY POLICY)

The time required to change the course of monetary policy once the Board of Governors decides to do so.

Fed's Open Market Committee (FOMC) on its goals for monetary policy, and the FOMC meets almost monthly to discuss the state of the economy in relation to the Board of Governors' goals. Should the FOMC decide that a dose of monetary policy is required, all it need do is call the Trading Desk at the New York Fed with instructions to begin an Open Market Operation. The Trading Desk then places calls to the securities dealers it trades with and begins to execute either a purchase or a sale of Treasury securities on the Open Market. The whole process takes only a day or two.

OPERATIONAL LAG Recall that the operational lag in fiscal policy has two parts. The first is the time from the passage of legislation to the actual change in government purchases, transfer payments, or tax collections. The second is the multiplier process, the time required for the changes in spending or taxes to affect the equilibrium level of national income.

OPERATIONAL LAG (MONETARY POLICY)

The time required for a change in the money supply to affect the equilibrium level of national income.

The first half of the corresponding **operational lag** under monetary policy does not exist because the money supply increases or decreases simultaneously with the Open Market Operation. The Fed's purchase of Treasury securities increases the money supply by the amount of the purchase. The Fed's sale of Treasury securities decreases the money supply by the amount of the sale.

The operational lag that matters for monetary policy is the time required for the change in the money supply to affect the equilibrium level of national income. Here is where the conduct of monetary policy suffers its main practical problems. The consensus among economists is that the lag between the change in the money supply and the change in the equilibrium level of national income is very long, at least a year to a year and a half on average. What is worse, the lag is highly variable, both in timing and in effect. In truth, the Fed never has a very clear idea of when its Open Market Operations will affect the economy, and with what force. The operational lag is every bit the practical difficulty for the conduct of monetary policy that the administrative lag is for the conduct of fiscal policy.[5]

The Fed's difficulties with the operational lag stem from two main sources: uncertainties about the size of the money multiplier and uncertainties about the demand for money.

THE SIZE OF THE MONEY MULTIPLIER Chapter 34 noted the uncertainties with respect to the size of the money multiplier, which relates the final change in the money supply to the Fed's initial Open Market Operation. Recall that the problem here is the commercial banks (and other depository institutions). They are not the passive economic agents that they are represented to be in the simple money multiplier exercise. Instead, they are profit-maximizing business firms whose actions tend to make the growth of the money supply pro-cyclical rather than countercyclical. The Fed has not always been able, or even willing, to counteract the pro-cyclical tendencies of the banks. (Review the discussion of the commercial banks at the end of Chapter 34 if you are unclear about these points.)

UNCERTAINTIES ABOUT THE DEMAND FOR MONEY The Fed must be able to predict the demand for money accurately in order to conduct an effective mon-

[5]For further discussion of the operational lag associated with monetary policy, see R. Hall and J. Taylor, *Macroeconomics: Theory, Performance, and Policy*, second edition (New York: Norton, 1988), 350–351.

etary policy because the demand for money determines how the economy reacts to a change in the money supply. As we have seen, a change in the money supply causes national income and interest rates to change, which in turn feeds back into the demand for money. The economy returns to equilibrium when national income and interest rates change by enough so that the change in the demand for money matches the change in the money supply. Therefore, the Fed has to know how the demand for money is related to national income and interest rates in order to be able to predict how its monetary policies will affect national income and interest rates.

Unfortunately, the demand for money has been hard to pin down. The money demand curves in Figures 35.2 and 35.4 shift around quite a bit over time, and the Fed has not always foreseen the shifts. Two celebrated cases of the Fed misreading the demand for money occurred 10 years apart, in 1981 and 1991.

Paul Volcker was chairman of the Board of governors during the Carter administration and the first term of the Reagan administration. Volcker decided, in October of 1979, to clamp down on the growth of the money supply over the next few years to fight inflation. The CPI had increased by 13.3 percent in 1979. Then in 1980 Congress passed the Depository Institutions Deregulation and Monetary Control Act of 1980 (DIDMCA), which authorized the interest-paying NOW checking accounts nationwide, beginning in 1981. NOW accounts had been available in only a few states before DIDMCA. The NOW accounts became part of the money supply and were an instant hit among households.

The result was a huge, and unanticipated, increase in the demand for money, which is also contractionary. Households reduced their demand for houses and consumer durables, and sold other financial assets, to build up their NOW accounts. The increase in the demand for money following DIDMCA made Volcker's contractionary monetary policy far more contractionary than it would otherwise have been. Many economists believe that the combination of the contractionary monetary policy and the large increase in the demand for money was largely responsible for bringing on the recession of 1981–82, the deepest recession in the United States since the Great Depression. The combination also helped to produce record-high short-term interest rates, in the 17 to 20 percent range. Volcker certainly did not want either of these results.

In 1991 Alan Greenspan, the chairman of the Board of Governors under President Bush, decided to increase the money supply to pull the economy out of the recession. The money supply as measured by M1 increased at an annual rate of 10 percent throughout 1991 and 1992. Many economists thought this was the appropriate policy at the time and predicted that the economy would begin to grow sometime in 1992 before the presidential election. Instead, the economy remained stagnant until the last quarter of 1992 and contributed to President Clinton's victory over President Bush that November. The problem again was an unexpected increase in the demand for money.

The increase in the money supply drove down interest rates on short-term assets to levels that had not been seen in the United States for 20 years or more. As noted earlier, NOW accounts, savings deposits, money market funds, and short-term certificates of deposit were paying interest rates in the 2 to 4 percent range in October of 1992. Households and businesses responded by increasing their holdings of regular and NOW checking accounts and by pulling out of the other short-term financial assets. M1 grew rapidly, whereas M2 hardly grew at all. The quantity of money demanded had grown much more rapidly than the Fed had foreseen, and the monetary policy was not nearly as expansionary as anticipated.

These two episodes are obviously instances when the demand for money changed very dramatically. The demand for money is normally more stable than it was at these times, but it is never entirely predictable. As a consequence, the Fed can never be certain just how expansionary or contractionary its monetary policies will be.

CONTRACTIONARY VERSUS EXPANSIONARY MONETARY POLICY[6] Many economists believe that a contractionary monetary policy is more immediately effective than is an expansionary monetary policy. They argue that the Fed can stop a booming economy from overheating with contractionary monetary policy, but that the Fed might not be able to bring an economy out of a recession with expansionary monetary policy. They liken the economy to a train moving along a track dragging a long rope. The Fed's contractionary policy can pull on the rope and halt the economy in its tracks, but the Fed's expansionary policy can only push on the rope and cannot thereby move the economy forward.

The commercial banks may actually help the Fed with its contractionary monetary policy, assuming the Fed does remove reserves from the banking system. The banks make the policy even more contractionary if they engage in credit rationing at high interest rates, and many economists believe that they do. Figure 35.7 illustrates the effects of credit rationing.

Figure 35.7(a) shows the traditional explanation of how a contractionary monetary policy affects the market for bank loans, the explanation given above. The loan interest rate is on the vertical axis, and the quantity of loans is on the horizontal axis. The initial equilibrium prior to the contractionary policy is (L_0, R_0), at the intersection of the initial supply and demand curves, S^0 and D^0. The Fed sells some of its Treasury securities on the Open Market and drains reserves from the banking system. The banks have to reduce their loans to meet the reserve requirements, so the supply curve shifts up and to the left from S^0 to S^1. The new equilibrium is (L_1, R_1), at the intersection of S^1 and D^0. The decrease in the supply of loans increases the loan interest rate and decreases the quantity of loans. Less borrowing means less spending on consumer durables and investment and a lower level of aggregate demand.

Banks, however, may not let the interest rate on loans rise by enough to clear the market, to R_1 in our example. They worry that very high interest rates are likely to attract more and more loan applications for highly risky projects. The high interest rates force households and firms into riskier projects that have higher average rates of return, but also a higher likelihood of failure and default on the loan. Therefore, rather than granting a loan to any borrower who is willing to pay the high rate, R_1, banks hold the line on the increase in the interest rate and engage in credit rationing.

Figure 35.7(b) illustrates the loan market with credit rationing. Supply decreases from S^0 to S^1, as in Figure 35.7(a), when the Fed drains reserves from the banking system. Instead of letting the interest rate rise to R_1 and clear the market, banks refuse to let the interest rate rise above R_2. Households and firms want to borrow an amount L_2^D at the interest rate R_2, whereas the banks are only willing to lend an amount L_2^S. The market for loans is in excess demand in the amount $L_2^D - L_2^S$.

CREDIT CRUNCH

A condition of excess demand in the loan markets in which potential borrowers complain that they cannot get loans even when they are willing to pay the quoted interest rate for the loans.

[6]The material in this section is more advanced and may be skipped in shorter courses with no loss in continuity.

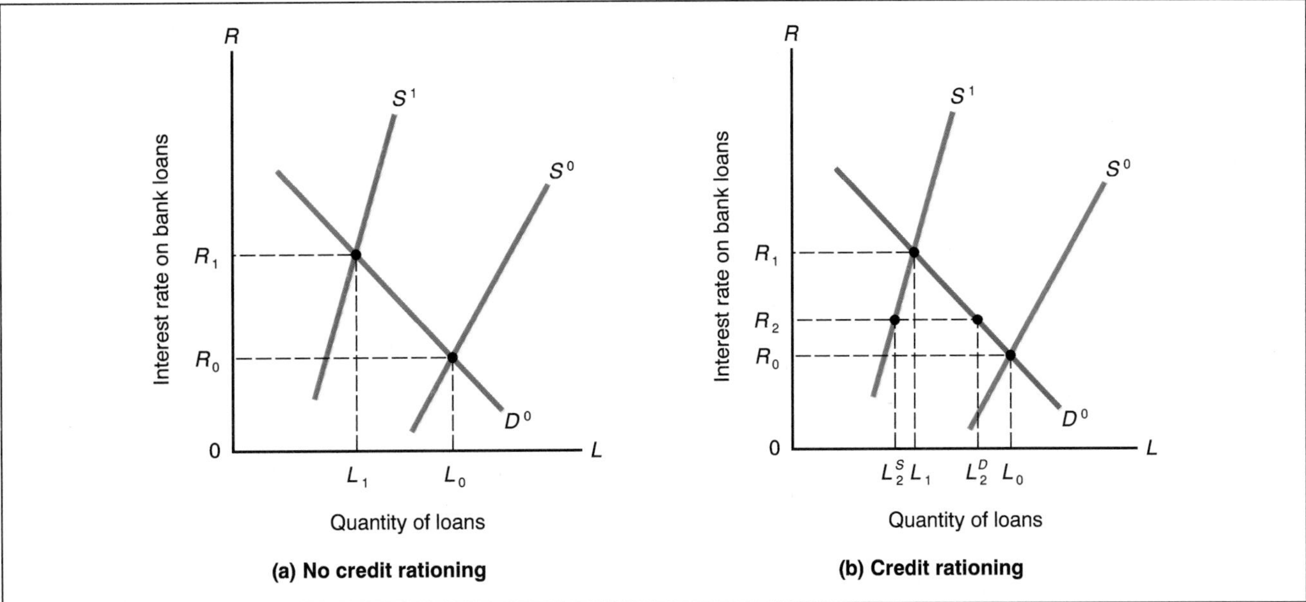

FIGURE 35.7

Credit Rationing and Contractionary Monetary Policy

Figure 35.7(a) shows how the market for bank loans would respond to a contractionary monetary policy without credit rationing. The initial equilibrium is (L_0,R_0), at the intersection of the demand curve for loans D^0 and the supply curve for loans S^0. The contractionary monetary policy drains reserves from the commercial banks, which decreases the supply of loans from S^0 to S^1. The new equilibrium is (L_1,R_1) at the intersection of D^0 and S^1. Banks do not let the interest rate rise to R_1, however, because that high an interest rate induces borrowers to finance very risky projects and increases the default rate on the loans. Instead, the banks engage in credit rationing as shown in Figure 35.7(b). They set the interest rate at R_2, which creates an excess demand for loans equal to $(L_2^D - L_2^S)$. The excess demand allows the banks to screen out the riskiest borrowers and reduces the default rate of the loans. The quantity of loans drops from L_1 without credit rationing to L_2^S with credit rationing, which makes the monetary policy even more contractionary.

The advantage to the banks of holding down the interest rate is that they can review and compare the relative risks of the L_2^D loan requests and ration the L_2^S loans they are willing to make to the best customers. What they lose with the lower interest rate they more than make up by screening out the worst customers and lowering the default rate on their loans. Notice that credit rationing reduces the amount of loans relative to the market-clearing solution from L_1 to L_2^S, which means that spending on consumer durables and investment is lower as well. Credit rationing makes the contractionary monetary policy even more contractionary.

The evidence that commercial banks and other depository institutions do engage in credit rationing is fairly substantial. The economy is said to experience a **credit crunch** when potential borrowers complain that they cannot get loans even when they are willing to pay the quoted interest rate for the loans. Credit crunches have been fairly common in the United States. They occurred in 1966, 1969–70, 1974–75, and 1980, and the Fed was undertaking a contractionary monetary policy in each instance. The commercial banks (and other depository institutions) do appear to ration credit when reserves are scarce.

The commercial banks cannot be so helpful to the Fed during an expansionary monetary policy. The problem during a recession is on the demand side of the loan market, as illustrated in Figure 35.8.

The supply and demand curves, S^0 and D^0, represent the state of the market for bank loans prior to both the recession and the expansionary monetary policy. The pre-recession, pre-policy equilibrium is (L_0, R_0). The recession occurs first and decreases the demand for loans from D^0 to D^1. Workers are laid off, and businesses see little or no growth in the demand for their products. Consequently, the demands for consumer durables and investment decrease, along with the demand for loans to finance these goods. Notice, too, that the demand curve has become steeper as well as shifting down and in. Laid-off workers and managers who see little growth in demand become less responsive to the interest rates on loans. Lower interest rates do not increase the quantity of loans demanded as much during a recession as they do in a healthier economy.

FIGURE 35.8

Expansionary Monetary Policy in a Recession

The figure shows why the Fed might not be able to bring the economy out of a recession with expansionary monetary policy. The initial equilibrium in the market for bank loans before the recession is (L_0,R_0), at the intersection of D^0 and S^0. A recession reduces the demand for loans by households and businesses and makes their demand for loans more inelastic. The demand curve shifts down from D^0 to D^1. The equilibrium in the market for bank loans during the recession, but before the expansionary monetary policy, is (L_1,R_1), at the intersection of D^1 and S^0. The expansionary monetary policy creates excess reserves in the commercial banks and increases the supply of bank loans from S^0 to S^1. The final equilibrium after the expansionary monetary policy is (L_2,R_2), at the intersection of D^1 and S^1. The expansionary monetary policy causes a relatively large decrease in the interest rate on bank loans from R_1 to R_2, but only a modest increase in loans from L_1 to L_2. The modest increase in borrowing by households and businesses means that aggregate demand does not increase very much, and the economy remains in a recession.

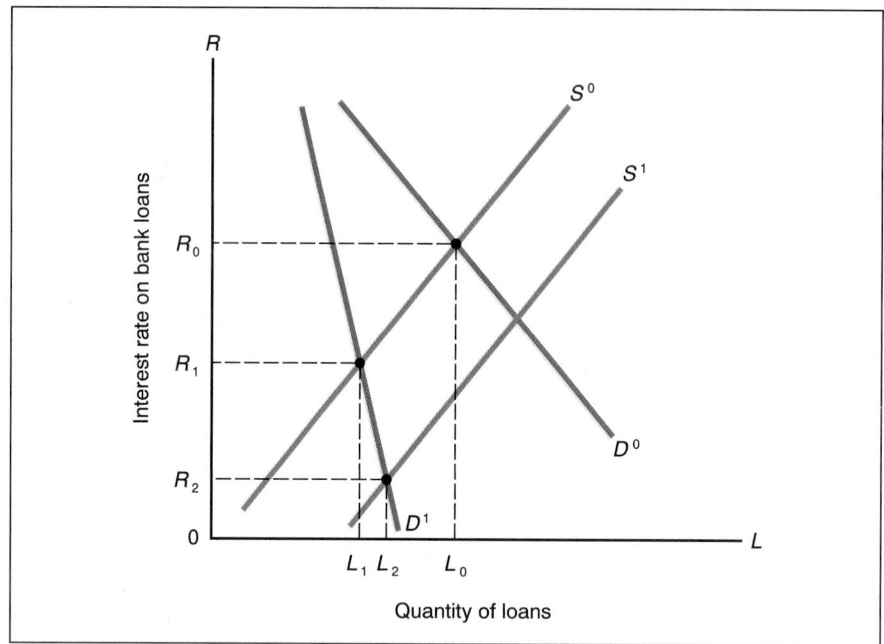

The equilibrium in the loan market during the recession, but before the expansionary monetary policy, is (L_1, R_1), at the intersection of S^0 and D^1.

Suppose that the Fed tries to counteract the recession with an expansionary monetary policy. It buys some Treasury securities on the Open Market and injects more reserves into the banking system. The new reserves increase the bank's willingness to lend, and the supply curve shifts out and down from S^0 to S^1. The new equilibrium is (L_2, R_2), at the intersection of S^1 and D^1.

The expansionary monetary policy mostly affects the interest rates on loans and not the quantity of loans. The interest rate decreases substantially, from R_1 to R_2; the equilibrium quantity of loans increases only slightly, from L_1 to L_2. Spending on consumer durables and investment also increases only slightly, which means that aggregate demand increases only slightly, and the economy remains in a recession.

The problem is that the decline in interest rates does not induce much additional borrowing from households and firms. This is exactly what happened in 1991 when the Fed undertook an expansionary monetary policy to pull the economy out of the recession. Banks took the new reserves created by the Fed and bought financial securities, mostly Treasury securities, from other financial institutions and from the government. They did not write many new loans because there just was not much demand for loans. The financial institutions that sold the securities to the banks simply held on to their newly created checking account balances.

The pull on a rope, push on a rope analogy goes back at least as far as John Maynard Keynes. Keynes believed that monetary policy could not pull the market economies out of the Great Depression because new bank reserves would not lead to much more borrowing. He argued that expansionary fiscal policies were needed because they increase aggregate demand directly. In fact, U.S. commercial banks had large amounts of excess reserves during the Great Depression. The banks could not find borrowers for these funds, as Keynes had predicted. And, since interest rates on short-term financial securities were near zero, they simply chose to hold excess reserves.

WHAT TO TARGET? The practical problems discussed above raise an interesting question for the Fed: What economic variable or variables should the Fed try to control with its Open Market Operations? An ideal target variable would have two properties. It would be a variable that the Fed could control very tightly and one that has a well-defined relationship to national income and interest rates, particularly national income. Unfortunately, there does not appear to be such an ideal target variable.

The Fed can most closely control the monetary base, the sum of Federal Reserve Notes plus reserves, with its Open Market purchases and sales. The monetary base is, in turn, closely related to the narrow M1 transactions definition of the money supply. As we have just seen, however, increasing or decreasing M1 does not always have highly predictable effects on the level of national income. Some economists argue that the Fed should target M2 instead because the velocity of circulation is somewhat more stable with respect to M2 than to M1. In other words, changes in M2 have the more predictable effect on national income through the equation of exchange, $M \cdot V = P \cdot Y$. The drawback to this suggestion is that the Fed probably cannot control the level of M2 very tightly just with Open Market Operations.

The Fed has never resolved the target variable problem and has shifted targets often throughout its history. The Fed currently looks at a broad range of financial indicators in setting its monetary policy, including broad money aggregates such as M2 and M3, the amount of reserves borrowed from the discount window, and a wide spectrum of interest rates. One implication of this broad-based approach is an admission that monetary policy cannot fine tune the economy. The Fed knows that the best it can hope to do is "lean against the wind."

REFLECTION: According to the newspapers, what are the Fed's policy intentions, and why? Do you agree with the chairman's statements about the nature of the economy's problems? Do you have the same priorities as the chairman does regarding the macroeconomic policy goals?

INTEREST RATES AS A MACROECONOMIC POLICY VARIABLE

Chapter 35 has added a second layer of complexity to our study of the macro economy by bringing interest rates into the analysis. We had been concerned with a single policy variable, the level of (real) national income, before this chapter. From now on, though, we will keep track of two policy variables simultaneously, the level of (real) national income and interest rates.

Interest rates certainly capture the attention of the public throughout the world. Big-city newspapers publish daily the interest rates and rates of return on a large number of financial securities. Small changes in key interest rates, such as the Fed's discount rate or the commercial banks' prime lending rate, often cause a flurry of excitement worthy of front-page headlines.

The attention given interest rates is hardly surprising. Households and business firms have an obvious interest in the behavior of interest rates. Changes in interest rates affect the return on their assets and the cost of their debt and other liabilities. Interest rates are important from a broader social perspective as well. They have a direct impact on some of the macroeconomic policy goals and on other goals that societies care about.

Should interest rates be low or high from a social perspective? The question has no clear-cut answer. Some of society's goals argue for low interest rates, whereas others argue for high interest rates. The usual arguments for keeping interest rates low are that low interest rates promote long-run economic growth, encourage home ownership, and help the poor. The counterargument for keeping interest rates high is that high interest rates protect and strengthen the value of the dollar relative to foreign currencies. One suspects that the arguments for low interest rates have won the day in the United States, judging from the uproar that always accompanies a sharp increase in interest rates. Let's take a brief look at the arguments on each side.

The Benefits of Low Interest Rates

LONG-RUN ECONOMIC GROWTH The connection between interest rates and long-run economic growth runs through investment in plant and equipment and in human capital (education). We have seen that investment in both physical and human capital is the most important determinant of long-run economic growth. In addition, many economists believe that investment demand is inversely related to the cost of capital, and interest rates are an important component of the cost of capital. The higher interest rates are, the higher the cost of capital is, and the lower investment demand is; the lower interest rates are, the lower the cost of capital is, and the higher investment demand is.

The argument, then, is that low interest rates stimulate investment demand and promote long-run economic growth. Low interest rates encourage firms to borrow or use their retained earnings to finance investment in plant and equipment. Similarly, low interest rates encourage people to borrow to further their educations.

The connection between interest rates and long-run economic growth is a powerful argument for favoring low interest rates, simply because long-run economic growth is so crucial to the overall economic well-being of any nation. The call for lowering interest rates to promote economic growth is especially compelling for the United States. We saw in Chapter 25 that the United States has been stuck in a low-investment, low-growth profile ever since 1973. Nothing would improve U.S. living standards more than an increase in investment and growth. In addition, long-term interest rates have been exceedingly high by historical standards throughout the 1980s and into the 1990s. As a result, the cost of capital in the United States is very high, among the highest of the industrial market economies. This may explain in part why the United States devotes a lower percentage of its resources to investment than do nearly all the other industrial market economies.

Politicians and economists have been advocating higher investment and growth as a top economic priority for the past 20 years. Many economists believe that the government cannot hope to achieve that goal unless long-term interest rates are substantially reduced.

The only caveat in the lower-interest-rate argument concerns the presumed relationship between interest rates and investment in plant and equipment. As noted in Chapter 29, economists disagree on the sensitivity of plant and equipment investment to interest rates, and to the cost of capital generally. Some economists believe that demand for plant and equipment investment is highly sensitive to interest rates. Other economists disagree. The latter believe that plant and equipment investment is determined primarily by the rate of growth in aggregate demand and that interest rates play only a minor role in the investment decision. Still, virtually all economists would agree that low interest rates are more conducive to investment and long-run economic growth than are high interest rates. The only disagreement is over how low interest rates would need to be to stimulate investment.

HOME OWNERSHIP Owning a home is part of the American dream, and the federal government has tried a number of different approaches to help people achieve that dream.

During the Great Depression, Congress established and initially funded the savings and loan associations (S&Ls) and the savings banks, the so-called thrifts, whose sole function at the time was to accept deposits and issue home mortgages. The thrifts operated under the auspices of the Federal Home Loan Bank Board, which bore roughly the same relationship to the thrifts as the Fed did to the commercial banks.

Congress also offers numerous incentives for home ownership through the federal personal income tax. For example, homeowners can deduct both the interest paid on their mortgages and their local property taxes from their incomes in computing their taxable incomes. In addition, homeowners are not taxed on the capital gains from selling a house if they buy another house of equal or greater value. Renters are not given any comparable tax advantages.

Finally, the government has tried to keep interest rates low to encourage home ownership. Most homes are bought with the aid of a mortgage loan, and the demand for mortgages is highly sensitive to mortgage interest rates. For this reason, investment in new homes is the most interest-sensitive component of investment demand.

Congress tried at first to ensure low mortgage interest rates through direct regulation. It authorized interest-rate ceilings on the savings deposits of thrifts shortly after the thrifts began operation. The theory behind the ceilings was that low interest rates on deposits would permit the thrifts to offer low interest rates on their mortgages. One problem with this theory is that it required a whole host of additional interest-rate ceilings on other financial securities to ensure that households would keep their deposits at the thrifts. The Depository Institutions Deregulation and Monetary Control Act of 1980 finally removed all the interest-rate ceilings and allowed other financial institutions to write mortgages. The point still holds, though, that lower interest rates encourage households to take out mortgages and invest in new homes.

HELPING THE POOR The distributional argument for low interest rates is based on a perception that, on average, high-income people are net lenders, or creditors, and low-income people are net borrowers, or debtors. Therefore, low interest rates are pro-poor because they help debtors by reducing the cost of borrowing and hurt creditors by reducing the return to lending.

The perception is not quite accurate for the United States. The people in both the top 20 percent of the income distribution and the bottom 20 percent of the income distribution are net lenders or creditors, on average. The 60 percent of the people in between are net borrowers or debtors, on average. Therefore, low interest rates redistribute income from the top and the bottom of the income distribution to the middle.

The reason that the people at the bottom of the distribution are net lenders, on average, is that this group contains a large percentage of the nation's elderly, who are living off the savings accumulated during their working years. Low interest rates really hurt the elderly because interest income is a major component, often the main component, of their total income. The elderly took a very big hit during the early 1990s when interest rates on their certificates of deposit and other savings accounts plummeted in response to the Fed's expansionary monetary policy.

Concern for the poor has often been used as a justification for low interest rates, the misperception about the distribution of net lenders and net borrowers notwithstanding.

The Benefits of High Interest Rates

The primary argument for keeping interest rates high is that high interest rates support the value of the dollar. The connection between interest rates and the value of the dollar arises because financial markets no longer honor national boundaries. They are truly international in scope. Money managers in large manufacturing corporations, insurance companies, commercial banks, and other financial institutions search worldwide for financial securities that offer the best rate of return and other financial services. Moreover, financial markets are always open for business in some part of the world, so that financial transactions can be made around the clock.

The worldwide linking of financial markets has meant that small changes in U.S. interest rates generate a huge flow of funds across U.S. borders that affects the dollar exchange rate. Suppose, for example, that the Fed undertakes a contractionary monetary policy that raises U.S. interest rates. Money managers in London, Bonn, Paris, and Tokyo react immediately by selling financial securities in their own markets and buying financial securities in the United States to take advantage of the higher U.S. interest rates. They need dollars to buy securities in the U.S. financial markets, however, so they first have to exchange their currencies for dollars. Their offerings of pounds sterling, deutsche marks, francs, and yen for dollars in the foreign exchange markets drive up the value of the dollar against all these currencies. Therefore, an increase in U.S. interest rates very quickly causes the dollar to appreciate. The "stronger" dollar in turn helps U.S. consumers because imported goods are now cheaper to them. (The stronger dollar hurts U.S. exporters and import-competing firms, however. Review the analysis in Chapter 26 of the gains and losses from changes in the dollar exchange rate if you are unclear on these points.)

Conversely, a decrease in U.S. interest rates leads to an immediate outflow of funds from the United States. The dollar depreciates as money managers trade dollars for foreign currencies in the foreign exchange markets so that they can buy financial securities in London, Tokyo, and other foreign markets. If the dollar is already "weak," the government may be reluctant to pursue monetary or fiscal policies that lower interest rates and weaken the dollar still further, despite the many arguments for lowering interest rates.

The Concept Summary table summarizes the relationship between interest rates and the various policy goals.

CONCEPT SUMMARY

INTEREST RATES AND POLICY GOALS

ADVANTAGES OF LOWER INTEREST RATES
- —Promote long-run economic growth (through investment in plant and equipment and in education)
- —Promote home ownership (through lower mortgage rates)
- —Improve the distribution of income (helps net debtors, hurts net creditors)

ADVANTAGES OF HIGHER INTEREST RATES
- —Increase the value of the dollar (dollar appreciates relative to foreign currencies)

SUMMARY

The first section of Chapter 35 explored the economic effects of monetary policy in terms of a money rain that abstracts from the institutional details of a nation's financial sector. The analysis is short run and assumes a new Keynesian policy environment of sticky wages and prices and unemployed resources.

1. Households and businesses hold a variety of real and financial assets. The real assets of households include consumer durables, houses, and other real estate. The real assets of businesses are their productive capital—plant, equipment, and inventories. The financial assets held by both households and businesses include money, other deposit accounts, stocks, bonds, and insurance; businesses also hold accounts receivable.
2. The injection of new money into the economy upsets the composition of assets on the balance sheets of households and businesses. They now have too much money and too few of all other assets.
3. The economic effects of an expansionary monetary policy result when households and businesses exchange the new money for both real and other financial assets. The economy returns to equilibrium because the economic effects that result from trying to get rid of the money eventually cause the demand for money to rise to match the new, higher supply of money.
4. The desire to buy real assets with the new money increases consumption demand and investment demand, which increases aggregate demand and leads to a multiplied increase in real national income.
5. The increase in national income increases the transactions demand for money. The primary motive for holding money is related to its function as the medium of exchange. The larger national income is, the more households and businesses spend, and the larger their transactions demand for money is. A 1 percent increase in national income increases the quantity of money demanded by 0.6 percent.

6. The quantity of money demanded for transactions purposes also increases in direct proportion to the overall level of prices because FRN and checking account balances are denominated in nominal dollar values.
7. The desire to buy financial assets with the new money decreases interest rates (and rates of return) on these assets. For example, the increase in demand for corporate or government bonds drives up their prices. The prices of bonds are inversely related to their (expected) returns.
8. The demand for money is inversely related to interest rates because the interest rates on financial assets define the opportunity cost of holding money. Therefore, the decrease of interest rates as a result of the new money in the economy further increases the quantity of money demanded.
9. An expansionary monetary policy increases (real) national income and decreases interest rates on financial assets. The economy returns to equilibrium when national income increases by enough, and interest rates decrease by enough, that the demand for money increases to equal the new, higher supply of money.
10. Conversely, a contractionary monetary policy decreases (real) national income and increases interest rates on financial assets. The economy returns to equilibrium when national income decreases by enough, and interest rates increase by enough, that the demand for money decreases to equal the new, lower supply of money.

The second section of the chapter explained the institutional details associated with the conduct of monetary policy in the United States, in which the commercial banks and the market for bank loans play the major role.

11. *Expansionary monetary policy:* The Fed buys Treasury securities, which increases excess reserves in the banking system and allows banks to make more loans. The increased supply of loans lowers the interest rate on bank loans and induces households and businesses to borrow more. They borrow to finance purchases of consumer durables and investment goods, so that the increased borrowing increases aggregate demand and national income. Interest rates, especially interest rates on bank loans, decrease first, and then aggregate demand and real national income increase.
12. *Contractionary monetary policy:* The Fed sells Treasury securities, which decreases reserves in the banking system and forces banks to reduce their lending. The decreased supply of loans raises the interest rate on bank loans and induces households and businesses to borrow less. They purchase fewer consumer durables and investment goods, so that the decreased borrowing decreases aggregate demand and national income. Interest rates, especially interest rates on bank loans, increase first, and then aggregate demand and real national income decrease.
13. The Fed cannot fine tune the economy with its monetary policies. The operational lag is a major stumbling block in the conduct of monetary policy. The time from the Fed's Open Market Operation to the change in national income is very long, more than a year on average, and highly variable. Two practical problems for the Fed are uncertainty about the value of the money multiplier and uncertainty about the demand for money. Also, the Fed is better able to slow down the growth in aggregate demand with a contractionary policy than to increase the growth in aggregate demand with an expansionary policy.

14. The Fed currently looks at a broad range of financial indicators in setting its monetary policies, including broad money aggregates such as M2 and M3 and a large number of interest rates.

The final section of Chapter 35 considered the advantages of higher or lower interest rates from a social perspective.

15. The main advantages of low interest rates are that they promote investment and long-run economic growth, promote home ownership, and help net debtors who are perceived to be among the poorer citizens.
16. The main advantage of high interest rates is that they increase the value of the dollar against foreign currencies.

KEY TERMS

administrative lag (monetary policy)
contractionary monetary policy
credit crunch
expansionary monetary policy
money rain
operational lag (monetary policy)
precautionary demand for money
recognition lag (monetary policy)
speculative demand for money
transactions demand for money

QUESTIONS

1. a. What are some of the financial and the real assets held by households? By businesses?
   b. Why do households and businesses hold such diversified portfolios of assets?
2. a. What effect does an increase in the supply of money have on the equilibrium level of national income, and why?
   b. What effect does an increase in the supply of money have on interest rates and other rates of return on assets, and why?
3. Why does a money rain eventually cause an increase in the demand for money that matches the new, higher supply of money?
4. Suppose that you buy a corporate bond in the secondary market that has exactly one year left until it matures. The bond has a face value of $1,000 and pays an annual interest of $100. You pay $1,050 for the bond and plan to hold it until it matures. Calculate your rate of return on the bond.
5. a. Suppose that you buy a share of stock whose price is currently $50. You plan to sell the stock one year from now, and you expect the price of the stock to be $60 when you sell it. The stock pays an annual dividend of $3. Calculate your expected rate of return on the stock.
   b. Given the other savings options available to you today, would you actually be interested in buying this stock?
   c. How would your answers to parts (a) and (b) change if the current price of the stock is $60?
6. The demand for money in the economy is closely related to three economic variables: real national income, the overall level of prices, and interest rates on financial assets. Why is the demand for money related to each of these variables? Name one other factor besides these three that might affect the demand for money, and indicate why it would do so.
7. Most economists believe that expansionary and contractionary monetary policies in the United States first affect interest rates and then affect the equilibrium level of national income. Why is this?
8. Discuss the various motives behind the demand for money. What are some of the disadvantages of holding money as an asset?
9. Identify the three main lags in the conduct of monetary policy. Compare and contrast these lags with the three main lags in the conduct of fiscal policy. To what extent are the lags similar? To what extent are they different? Can the Fed expect to be able to fine tune the economy with its monetary policies?
10. Discuss this statement: The Fed conducts the monetary policy in the United States, but the commercial banks are largely responsible for the success or failure of monetary policy.

CHAPTER

36

Fiscal Policy, Monetary Policy, and the Macroeconomic Policy Goals

LEARNING OBJECTIVES

CONCEPTS TO LEARN

Crowding out:

1. through consumer durables and investment
2. through net exports

Short-run Phillips Curve

Okun's Law

CONCEPTS TO RECALL

The macroeconomic policy goals [25, 26]

New Keynesian economics [28]

Fiscal policy [28, 30, 31]

Monetary policy [28, 34, 35]

Equilibrium level of national income [29]

The macroeconomic policy problem [30]

Spending multiplier [30]

Multiplier-accelerator model [32]

The equation of exchange [33]

Balance sheet, assets, and liabilities [33]

Interest rates [35]

In 1992, the United States had not succeeded in reaching any of the four macroeconomic policy goals. Personal saving was 5 percent of disposable income, and net investment was less than 2 percent of gross domestic product (GDP). The United States remained stuck in its low-saving, low-investment, low-growth scenario of the past 20 years. Unemployment was 7.3 percent, at least one percentage point above the natural rate of unemployment, and maybe more. Inflation was 2.9 percent. The balance-of-trade deficit was $84 billion, and the dollar depreciated 3.5 percent against the yen and a number of the other major currencies, continuing a pattern that began in 1986.[1]

Everyone is striving toward the same macroeconomic goals, Democrat, Republican, and independent, liberal and conservative alike. We all want higher long-run economic growth in the 3 to 4 percent range, unemployment no higher than 5 or 6 percent, stable prices, a near-zero balance of trade, and a stable dollar in the foreign exchange markets. The outstanding macroeconomic policy question, though, is this: How do we get there?

Chapter 36 pulls together the new Keynesian analysis of the macro economy that began in Chapter 29. The chapter describes how the government can use its fiscal and monetary policies to pursue the four macroeconomic policy goals over the short run, in an economy with sticky wages and prices and unemployed resources. We will see that there is not necessarily any one best policy.

The chapter begins by tying up one loose end before turning to the macroeconomic policy goals. Our analysis of monetary policy in Chapter 35 showed how expansionary and contractionary monetary policies affect both national income and interest rates. To complete the analysis of the macro economy, we need to see how increases and decreases in aggregate demand, which include expansionary and contractionary fiscal policies, affect the level of interest rates. Previous chapters considered the effect of changes in aggregate demand on the equilibrium level of national income, but not on interest rates.

AGGREGATE DEMAND, FISCAL POLICY, AND INTEREST RATES

Our previous analysis of aggregate demand and fiscal policy described how changes in aggregate demand affect the equilibrium level of national income. To review briefly, the multiplier analysis in Chapter 30 showed that changes or shifts in aggregate demand lead to a multiplied change in the equilibrium level of national income. An increase in any component of aggregate demand leads to a multiplied increase in the equilibrium level of national income, and a decrease in any component of aggregate demand leads to a multiplied decrease in the equilibrium level of national income. Moreover, the increases and the decreases in aggregate demand could result from expansionary or contrac-

[1]U.S. Department of Commerce, Economics and Statistics Administration, Bureau of Economic Analysis, *Survey of Current Business* 73, No. 3 (March 1993): Table 2.1, p. 10 (personal saving); Table 1.1, p. 6 and Table 1.9, p. 10 (net investment). Council of Economic Advisers, *Economic Indicators, March 1993* (Washington, D.C.: U.S. Government Printing Office, 1993), 12 (unemployment), 24 (inflation), and 35 (balance of trade).

tionary fiscal policies, which involve changes in the government's purchases of goods and services, or transfer payments, or taxes.

We need to ask how changes in aggregate demand affect interest rates to complete the analysis of aggregate demand. The answer is that an *increase* in aggregate demand, including an expansionary fiscal policy, *increases* interest rates, and a *decrease* in aggregate demand, including a contractionary fiscal policy, *decreases* interest rates. Note the difference in fiscal and monetary policies with regard to interest rates. Expansionary fiscal and monetary policies both increase aggregate demand and the equilibrium level of national income. This, after all, is the definition of an expansionary policy. But an expansionary fiscal policy increases interest rates, whereas an expansionary monetary policy decreases interest rates. Similarly, contractionary fiscal and monetary policies decrease both aggregate demand and the equilibrium level of national income. But a contractionary fiscal policy decreases interest rates, whereas a contractionary monetary policy increases interest rates. The different effects on interest rates turn out to be crucial to the government's ability to hit whatever targets it sets for national income and interest rates.

Consumption Demand and Interest Rates

AN INCREASE IN CONSUMPTION DEMAND Let's use changes in consumption demand to illustrate how changes in aggregate demand affect interest rates. Any component of aggregate demand will do, so we may as well begin with the one that we are most familiar with. Begin with an increase or shift up in consumption demand. We want to see why an increase in consumption demand increases interest rates.

The key to the analysis lies in the adjustments to the households' balance sheets that are necessary to accommodate the increase in consumption demand. Table 36.1 reproduces the typical household's balance sheet from Table 35.1, with loans added on the liability side. The loans represent borrowing from

TABLE 36.1 Balance Sheet of Households

ASSETS		LIABILITIES
Financial assets	FRN Checking accounts Savings deposits Certificates of deposit Money market accounts Stocks Corporate bonds Treasury bonds State and local bonds Insurance	Loans
Real assets	Consumer durables Houses Other real estate	

banks, or from other financial institutions such as credit unions, or borrowing against credit cards.

When households decide to buy more consumer durables and other consumer goods and services, they have to obtain money somehow to finance their increased expenditures. The balance sheet in Table 36.1 shows that they have three ways of getting the money:

1. They can use their own money that they have on hand;
2. They can reduce their holdings of other financial assets, exchanging them for money; or
3. They can borrow the money.

What they cannot do is finance the new spending with new income that they may have earned because an increase in consumption demand means an increase in demand at *every* level of income. They have to match the increase in consumption demand with a decrease in their saving demand, which means either reducing their holdings of money and other financial assets or increasing their borrowing.

USING MONEY Suppose that all households just used their money on hand to finance their increased consumption demand. This would have no effect on interest rates because no one would ever enter the financial markets.

REDUCING OTHER FINANCIAL ASSETS Not all households will be able, or willing, to finance the entire increase in their consumption demand with their own money, however. They have to seek money from other sources, and this is what drives up interest rates.

One way households can raise the money is to reduce their holdings of other financial assets. For example, a household seeking money may call up its broker and place an order to sell some of its bonds. The broker finds someone else who is willing to buy the bonds and arranges the sale and purchase. The household and the other party engage in a trade of assets through the broker, as illustrated in Table 36.2.

Household 1 wants the money to finance new spending and exchanges some of its bonds for money. Household 2 is willing to exchange money for the bonds. Household 1 then takes the money and spends it on consumer goods.

Selling bonds is not the only possibility, of course. Households may get the money they need by drawing down their savings accounts and money market deposit accounts, cashing their certificates of deposit, and calling their brokers to sell some stocks as well as bonds. The transactions increase the interest rates and rates of return on all these assets.

The situation is the reverse of the analysis of the money rain in Chapter 35, when households were trying to get rid of the new money and increase their holdings of other financial assets. Now, with households drawing down their savings accounts, money market deposit accounts, and certificates of deposit,

TABLE 36.2 An Exchange of Existing Assets: Money for Corporate Bonds

HOUSEHOLD 1			HOUSEHOLD 2		
Assets		Liabilities	Assets		Liabilities
M	(+)		Corporate bonds	(+)	
Corporate bonds	(−)		M	(−)	

TABLE 36.3 Borrowing from a Credit Union

CREDIT UNION		EMPLOYEE	
Assets	Liabilities	Assets	Liabilities
Checking account (−) Loan (+)		Checking account (+)	Loan (+)

bank managers have to offer higher interest rates to maintain the dollar balances that they want in these accounts. Likewise, households are now entering the stock and the bond markets looking to sell. The desire to sell stocks and bonds decreases stock and bond prices and increases the rates of return on these assets to prospective buyers. After all, the household that buys the bonds in our example above, Household 2, will buy only at a "good" price, that is, a lower price. The lower price raises the expected return on the bond, which is what induces Household 2 to give up some of its money for the bonds. Remember that the demand for money is inversely related to the interest rates on competing assets. The higher return on the bonds reduces the amount of money that households want to hold. Those with money will exchange their money for other financial assets only if those other financial assets become more attractive.

In conclusion: *The desire to reduce holdings of financial assets in order to finance an increase in consumption demand raises the interest rates and rates of return on these assets.*

BORROWING THE MONEY Still other households will choose to borrow the money needed to finance their increase in consumption demand. Most loans to households are made by banks, automobile finance corporations, credit unions associated with their places of employment, and credit card companies. Table 36.3 illustrates a loan from a credit union. It is a common example of the borrower-lender relationship described in Chapter 33.

An employee applies to his credit union for a loan. Once the credit union approves the loan, it writes a loan contract that is simultaneously an asset of the credit union/lender and a liability of the employee/borrower. The credit union issues a check drawn on its checking account at a bank in the amount of the loan and gives it to the employee who deposits it in his bank. The transfer of money from lender to borrower is the transfer of checking account balances between the two. The employee then writes checks against the deposit to finance the new spending.

The increased demand for borrowing by households drives up interest rates in the loan markets, as illustrated in Figure 36.1.

The figure represents the market for loans from all sources. The interest rate on loans is on the vertical axis, and the quantity of loans is on the horizontal axis. The market supply and the market demand curves are S^0 and D^0 prior to the increase in consumption demand. The banks, credit unions, credit card companies, and the like are the suppliers/lenders, and the households are the demanders/borrowers (along with the business firms).[2] The loan market is initially in equilibrium at (L_0, R_0), at the intersection of S^0 and D^0.

[2]The figure lumps all the lenders together, even though they charge different interest rates. The main reason the rates differ is that the terms of the loans—for example, the payback period and the level of security—differ. Think of the interest rate as an average of the various loan rates charged by the different lenders.

FIGURE 36.1

Consumption Demand and the Market for Loans

The figure pictures the market for loans to households from the main institutions that lend to households—banks, automobile finance companies, credit unions, and credit card companies. S is the supply curve of loans from these lenders and D is the demand curve for loans by households. The initial equilibrium is (L_0,R_0), at the intersection of D^0 and S^0. An increase in consumption demand increases the demand for loans from D^0 to D^1 as some households borrow to finance their increased consumption expenditures. The new equilibrium is (L_1,R_1), at the intersection of D^1 and S^0. An increase in consumption demand increases the interest rate on loans, as does an increase in any component of aggregate demand, including an expansionary fiscal policy.

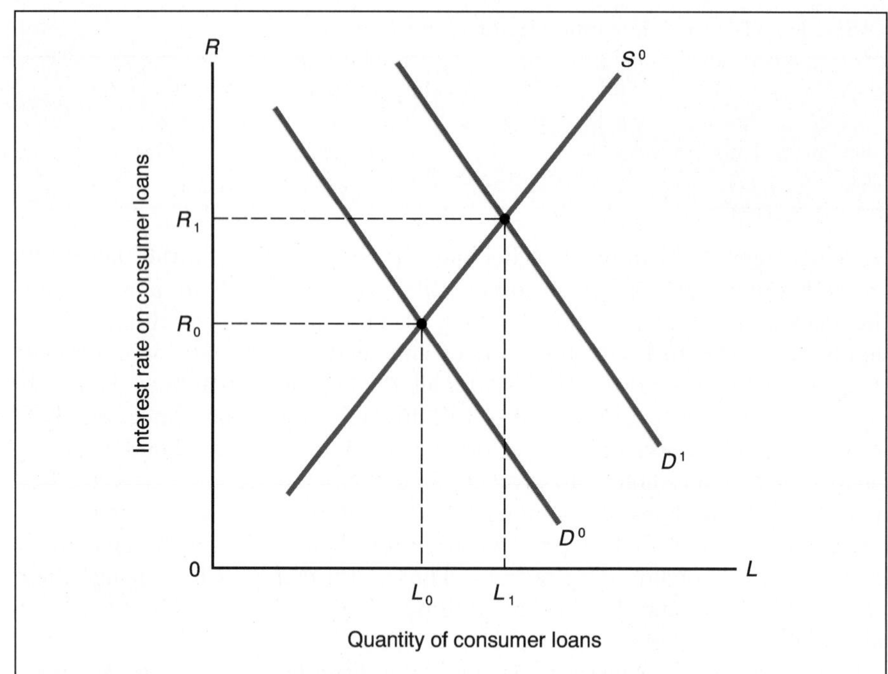

The increase in consumption demand increases the demand for borrowing by some of the households and shifts the demand curve up and to the right from D^0 to D^1. The new equilibrium is (L_1, R_1), at the intersection of S^0 and D^1. The increased demand for loans puts upward pressure on interest rates as the lenders realize that they can make more loans at higher rates. The loan rate increases from R_0 to R_1. Also, the quantity of loans written increases from L_0 to L_1 to support the increase in consumption demand.

In conclusion: *An increase in the demand for loans increases the interest rate on loans.*

To summarize, an increase in consumption demand leads some households to reduce their holdings of financial assets or borrow to raise money in order to finance the new consumption spending. Either method of obtaining money increases interest rates.

A DECREASE IN CONSUMPTION DEMAND A decrease in consumption demand lowers interest rates. The analysis is exactly the opposite of an increase in consumption demand. A decrease in consumption demand is equivalent to an increase in saving demand. Households want to buy fewer consumer goods and increase their saving. They can increase saving by holding more money, increasing their holdings of other financial assets, or paying back their loans and reducing their borrowing.

Interest rates would not change if all the households decided just to hold more money. But this is unlikely. Households will undoubtedly use some of the funds saved from the reduced spending to increase their holdings of other financial assets. They will place some of the funds in savings and money market deposit accounts, buy certificates of deposit, and tell their brokers to buy more stocks and bonds. The increased demand for financial assets reduces the interest rates and rates of return on these assets, as we saw in the case of the money rain. Other households will pay back loans and reduce their borrowing. The demand for loans decreases and lowers the interest rate on loans.

Refer again to Figure 36.1 to see how the decrease in the demand for loans affects the interest rate on loans. This time, think of (L_1, R_1) as the initial equilibrium, at the intersection of D^1 and S^0. The decrease in consumption demand decreases the demand for loans and shifts the demand curve down and to the left, from D^1 to D^0. The decreased demand for loans puts downward pressure on interest rates as the lenders have difficulty finding borrowers. The loan rate decreases from R_1 to R_0, and the quantity of loans written decreases from L_1 to L_0 along with the decrease in consumption demand.

To summarize, a decrease in consumption demand leads some households to increase their holdings of financial assets or reduce their borrowing. Either form of increased saving decreases interest rates.

The analysis of consumption demand illustrates this principle: *An increase in any component of aggregate demand increases interest rates, and a decrease in any component of aggregate demand decreases interest rates.* There is nothing special about consumption demand. Any increase in aggregate demand from any source has to be financed, which means that some people or institutions are reducing their holdings of financial assets or borrowing to obtain money and are putting upward pressure on interest rates. Conversely, any decrease in aggregate demand from any source increases saving in the economy, which means that some people or institutions are increasing their holdings of financial assets or reducing their borrowing and are putting downward pressure on interest rates.

Fiscal Policy and Interest Rates

Fiscal policy affects the economy by directly changing or shifting aggregate demand. Therefore, the effects of fiscal policy on interest rates must be the same as for changes in aggregate demand: *An expansionary fiscal policy increases aggregate demand and raises interest rates. A contractionary fiscal policy decreases aggregate demand and lowers interest rates.*

EXPANSIONARY FISCAL POLICY We saw in Chapter 30 that a debt-financed increase in government purchases is highly expansionary. It increases the equilibrium level of national income by the spending multiplier times the increase in government purchases. A debt-financed increase in government purchases also increases interest rates because the Treasury is borrowing more from the public to raise the money it needs to pay for the new purchases.

Borrowing by the Treasury is a standard borrower-lender transaction of the kind described in Chapter 33. The loan contracts in this case are the Treasury bills, notes, and bonds, which the Treasury creates and issues for sale to the public in return for money. The newly issued Treasury bills, notes, and bonds are simultaneously a new liability of the Treasury, the borrower, and an asset to whoever purchases them, the lender. The Treasury receives a check from the lender, which it then uses to finance the new government purchases. As we have seen, once the Treasury securities are issued, they are actively traded in the secondary Open Market by the Fed and others.

The increased borrowing by the Treasury adds to the overall demand for loans in the economy and increases the interest rates on loans. The effects on the nation's loan markets are identical to those described in Figure 36.1. The demand curve for loans shifts up and to the right, and both the interest rate and the quantity of loans increase. The intuition for the increase in interest rates is that the Treasury has to offer the lenders a higher return so that the lenders will accept the new debt. It does this by offering to sell the new Treasury bills, notes, and bonds at lower prices, which raises the rate of return on these securities to the buyers/ lenders. The higher returns on the Treasury securities raise interest rates in all markets as borrowers compete for the increasingly scarce funds.

What is true for this example holds for all expansionary fiscal policies. An expansionary fiscal policy increases interest rates.[3]

CONTRACTIONARY FISCAL POLICY All contractionary fiscal policies have the opposite effect—they reduce interest rates. For example, suppose that the federal government reduces its purchases and matches the reduction in expenditures with a reduction in borrowing. We saw in Chapter 30 that this fiscal policy is highly contractionary. The equilibrium level of national income decreases by the spending multiplier times the decrease in government purchases.

The reduction in government spending also lowers interest rates because the Treasury is decreasing its borrowing from the public and reducing the demand for loans in the economy. The demand curve for loans in Figure 36.1 shifts down and to the left, and both the interest rates on loans and the quantity of loans decline. The direct intuition for the decrease in interest rates is that the Treasury can sell its bills, notes, and bonds at higher prices because it is not offering as many of them. The higher prices lower the rate of return on the Treasury securities. The lower returns on the Treasury securities reduce interest rates in all loan markets because more funds are available to borrowers.

The same analysis applies to all contractionary fiscal policies. A contractionary fiscal policy decreases interest rates.

Aggregate Demand and the Velocity of Circulation

The equation of exchange

$$M \cdot V = P \cdot Q = Y$$

gives us another perspective on why an increase in aggregate demand increases interest rates and a decrease in aggregate demand decreases interest rates.

Changes in aggregate demand occur against a background of a constant money supply. Only a given amount of money is available to finance whatever amount of spending is desired in the aggregate by the household, business,

[3]A balanced budget increase in government purchases and taxes also increases interest rates even though the Treasury is not increasing its borrowing. The reason is that households are paying a portion of their taxes out of their savings, an amount equal to MPS times the increase in their taxes. Some households have to sell assets or borrow to meet their tax liabilities, which increases interest rates in the financial markets.

government, and foreign sectors. We have also been assuming that prices are constant. With money (*M*) and prices (*P*) constant, the equation of exchange indicates that any increase in aggregate demand, including an expansionary fiscal policy, increases real national product or income (*Q* or *Y*) by increasing the velocity of circulation (*V*). The constant supply of money turns over at a faster rate, and national product or income increases. Conversely, any decrease in aggregate demand, including a contractionary fiscal policy, decreases real national product or income by decreasing the velocity of circulation (*V*). The constant supply of money turns over at a slower rate, and national product or income decreases. The rquired increases and decreases in the velocity of circulation are brought about by the increases and the decreases in interest rates.

Consider an increase in aggregate demand. Since not everyone who wants to spend more has the money on hand, money has to change hands from those who have money that they are not going to spend on goods and services to those who do not have enough money to buy all the goods and the services they want to buy. Those without money attempt either to sell financial assets to those with the money or to borrow from them. The increase in interest rates induces those with the money to reduce their holdings of money and either buy the assets being offered or lend. The money is now in the hands of those who want to spend it, and aggregate demand increases as the money is spent. Transferring the money in this way gets the constant money supply to turn over faster, and the higher velocity of circulation allows for the multiplied increase in national income.

The same analysis applies in reverse to a decrease in aggregate demand. Interest rates falls as the demand for financial assets increases and the demand for loans decreases. The decrease in interest rates increases the quantity of money demanded, the constant money supply turns over more slowly, and the lower velocity of circulation allows for a multiplied decrease in national income.

Crowding Out, Interest Rates, and the Spending Multiplier

Our analysis of the spending multiplier and the various fiscal policy multipliers in Chapter 30 ignored the change in interest rates that results from a change in aggregate demand. We need to correct this oversight because the change in interest rates feeds back into aggregate demand in a way that substantially reduces the value of the multipliers. The interest rate feedback occurs through two distinct channels. One channel is through the demands for consumer durables and investment in the domestic economy. The other channel is through net exports in the foreign sector. The change in interest rates is said to **crowd out** these components of aggregate demand and lower the value of the multipliers. In effect, the constant supply of money constrains the amount that aggregate demand can change.

CROWDING OUT: CONSUMER DURABLES AND INVESTMENT Consider first the crowding out of consumer durables and investment. Suppose that the federal government increases its purchases of goods and services and finances the increase by issuing debt. Chapter 30 analyzed a debt-financed increase in government purchases with the aggregate demand–45° line graph, as follows.

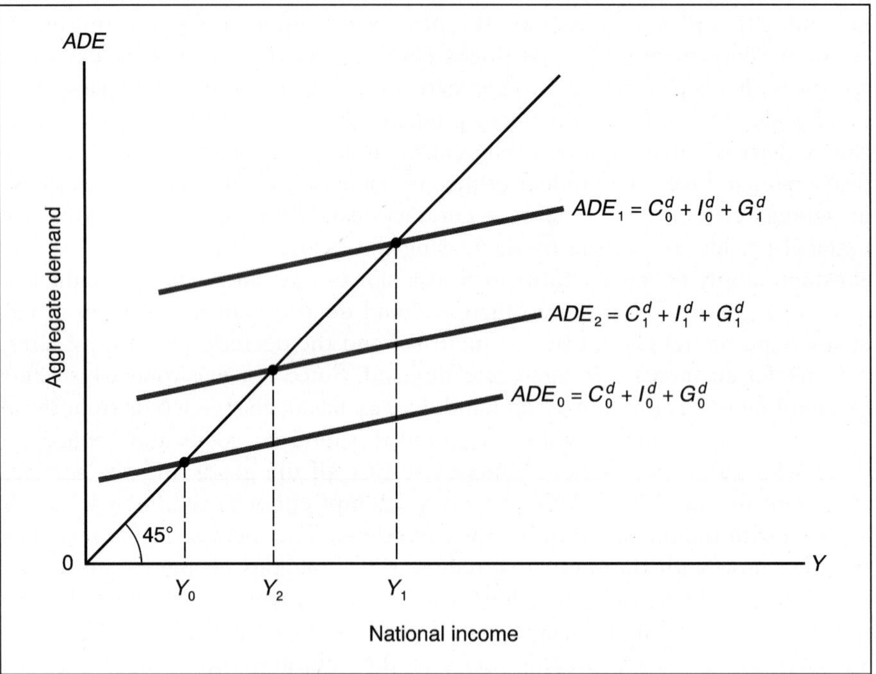

FIGURE 36.2

Crowding Out: Consumer Durables and Investment

The initial equilibrium level of national income is Y_0, at the intersection of ADE_0 and the 45° line. A debt financed increase in government purchases increases G^d from G_0^d to G_1^d, and aggregate demand shifts up from ADE_0 to ADE_1. The new equilibrium level of national income would be Y_1, at the intersection of ADE_1 and the 45° line, if interest rates did not rise. The increase in aggregate demand does increase interest rates, which increases the cost of borrowing to households and firms. As a result, households reduce their purchases of consumer durables and new houses, and firms reduce their purchases of plant and equipment and inventory. Consumption demand increases from G_0^d to C_1^d, investment demand decreases from I_0^d to I_1^d, and aggregate demand shifts down from ADE_1 to ADE_2. The final equilibrium level of national income is Y_2, at the intersection of ADE_2 and the 45° line. The rise in interest rates crowds out consumer durables and investment, which reduces the value of the spending multiplier.

Refer to Figure 36.2. The equilibrium level of national income is initially Y_0, at the intersection of aggregate demand line ADE_0 and the 45° line. The increase in government purchases increases G^d from G_0^d to G_1^d, which shifts up the aggregate demand line from ADE_0 to ADE_1. The new equilibrium level of national income is Y_1, at the intersection of ADE_1 and the 45° line.

Our previous analysis assumed that the change in G^d was the only change (shift) in aggregate demand because it ignored the increase in interest rates that accompanies the increase in aggregate demand. In fact, the increase in interest rates feeds back into the demands for consumer durables and investment and shifts these two components of aggregate demand down.

Figure 36.3 illustrates the interest rate feedback. The figure reproduces Figure 35.6, which indicated how the demands for consumer durables and investment are related to interest rates. Figure 36.3(a) shows the relationship between interest rates and the demand for consumer durables, C^{Dur}. Figure 36.3(b) shows the relationship between interest rates and investment demand, I^d. Both demands are downward sloping, inversely related to interest rates, because interest rates are an important component of the cost of buying consumer durables, new houses, plant and equipment, and inventory.

Suppose that interest rates were initially R_0 before the increase in government spending. At R_0 the demand for consumer durables is C_0^{Dur}, and the investment demand is I_0^d. C_0^{Dur} is the consumer durables component of the initial consumption demand, C_0^d, in Figure 36.2, and I_0^d is the same as I_0^d in Figure 36.2. The increase in government spending raises interest rates to R_1 as the Treasury increases its borrowing. The increase in interest rates raises the cost of borrowing to households and firms. Households respond by reducing their spending on consumer durables to C_1^{Dur} in Figure 36.3(a). Firms respond by reducing their investment spending to I_1^d in Figure 36.3(b).

Return again to Figure 36.2. The increase in interest rates reduces consumption demand from C_0^d to C_1^d and investment demand from I_0^d to I_1^d. There-

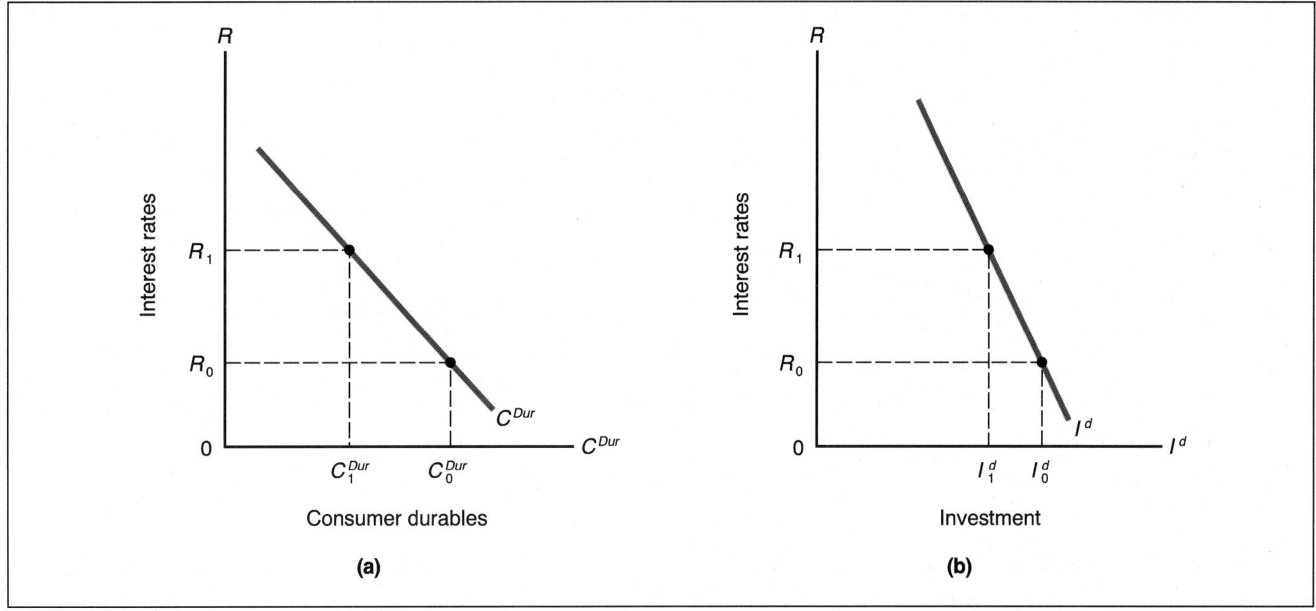

FIGURE 36.3

Interest Rates, Consumer Durables, and Investment

The increase in aggregate demand in Figure 36.2 increases interest rates from R_0 to R_1. As a result, households reduce their purchases of consumer durables and houses and firms reduce their purchases of plant and equipment and inventory. Figure 36.3(a) pictures the demand curve for consumer durables, C^{Dur}, in terms of the interest rate on loans, which is on the vertical axis. The increase in interest rates from R_0 to R_1 reduces households' purchases of consumer durables from C_0^{Dur} to C_1^{Dur}. Figure 36.3(b) pictures the investment demand curve, I^d, in terms of the interest rate on loans. The increase in interest rates from R_0 to R_1 reduces purchases of investment goods from I_0^d to I_1^d. The reduction in consumer durables and investment is one source of the crowding out effect as interest rates change in response to a change in aggregate demand.

fore, aggregate demand shifts down from ADE_1 to ADE_2. The final equilibrium level of national income is Y_2, at the intersection of ADE_2 and the 45° line. The increase in interest rates feeding back into consumption demand and investment demand has reduced the value of the spending multiplier. The increase in government purchases increases the equilibrium level of national income from Y_0 to Y_2, instead of from Y_0 to Y_1 without the interest rate feedback.

The increase in government purchases crowds out consumption demand and investment demand because the money supply is constant and there is only so much money to go around. The government, by borrowing money to finance its expenditures, leaves less money available for households and businesses to borrow. Interest rates rise to reflect the increasing scarcity of funds and choke off some consumption demand and investment demand.

The interest rate feedback through consumption demand and investment demand is symmetric. It also reduces the impact of a decrease in aggregate demand. To see why, suppose that the federal government decreases its purchases and borrows less as a result. The Treasury's reduced demand for loans decreases interest rates, which induces households to spend more on consumer durables and housing and induces firms to buy more plant and equipment and more inventory. Refer again to Figure 36.3, and think of R_1 as the initial interest rate and R_0 as the new lower interest rate. C^{Dur} and I^d both increase in response to the lower rates. The higher demand for consumer durables and investment increases aggregate demand relative to what it would be without the interest rate effect and reduces the multiplied decrease in national income brought on by the decrease in government purchases.

CROWDING OUT: NET EXPORTS The crowding out of net exports occurs because interest rates have a substantial impact on the value of the dollar. We saw in Chapter 35 that an increase in U.S. interest rates causes funds to flow into the United States from abroad in search of U.S. securities and increases the value of the dollar. The dollar appreciates relative to the other major currencies. Conversely, a decrease in U.S. interest rates causes funds to flow out

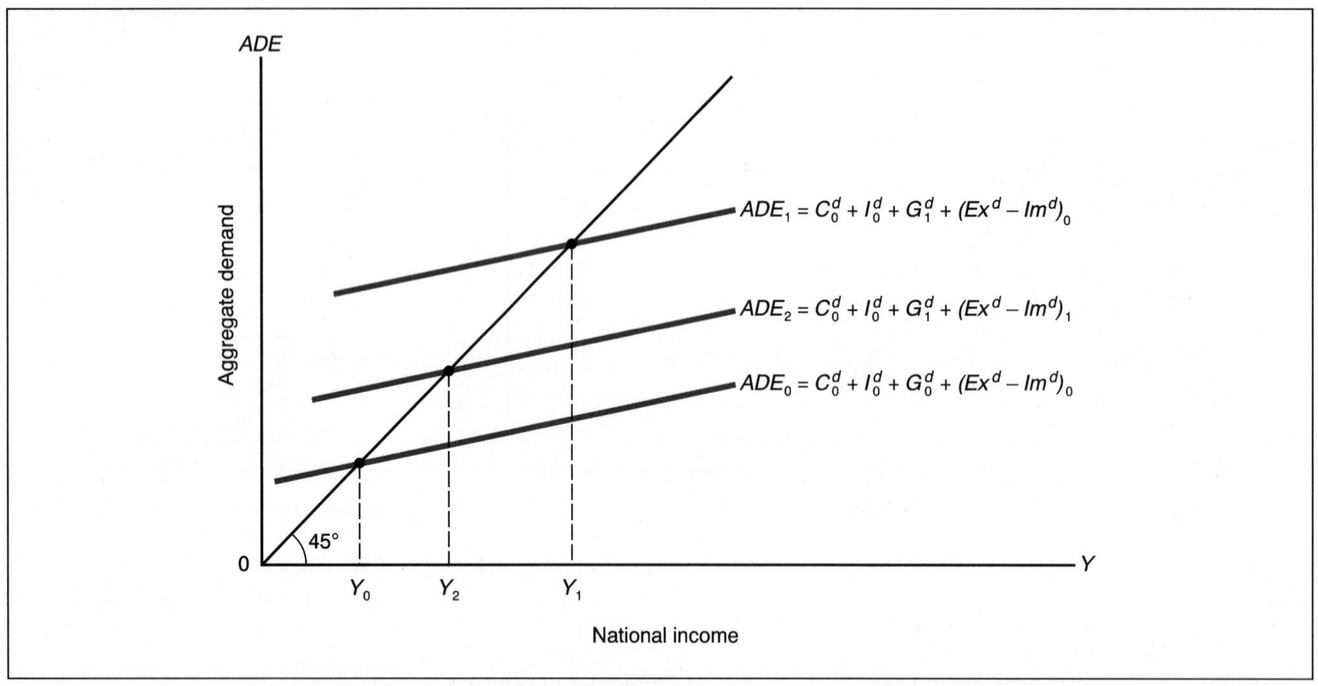

FIGURE 36.4

Crowding Out: Net Exports

The initial equilibrium level of national income is Y_0, at the intersection of ADE_0 and the 45° line. As in Figure 36.2, an increase in government purchases increases G^d from G_0^d to G_1^d, and the equilibrium level of national income would rise to Y_1, at the intersection of ADE_1 and the 45° line, if interest rates did not rise. The increase in interest rates attracts funds from foreign countries into the United States, which appreciates the value of the dollar. An appreciation of the dollar increases import demand, from Im_0^d to Im_1^d, and reduces export demand, from Ex_0^d to Ex_1^d. The demand for net exports decreases from $(Ex^d - Im^d)_0$ to $(Ex^d - Im^d)_1$, and aggregate demand shifts down from ADE_1 to ADE_2. The final equilibrium level of national income is Y_2, at the intersection of ADE_2 and the 45° line. The rise in interest rates crowds out net exports, which lowers the value of the spending multiplier.

of the United States in search of foreign securities and decreases the value of the dollar. The dollar depreciates relative to the other major currencies. An appreciation or depreciation of the dollar in turn feeds back into net exports.

Figure 36.4 illustrates the crowding out of net exports. The figure reproduces the initial shift in aggregate demand from ADE_0 to ADE_1 in Figure 36.2, resulting from the increase in government demand. As before, the equilibrium level of national income would increase from Y_0 to Y_1 without the interest rate feedback to aggregate demand. The increase in aggregate demand increases U.S. interest rates, however, so that funds flow into the United States and the dollar appreciates relative to the other major currencies. The appreciation of the dollar makes imports cheaper to U.S. consumers and U.S. exports more expensive to foreign consumers.

For example, suppose that the dollar appreciates in value from \$1.80/£ to \$1.60/£. British goods priced at 1£ used to cost U.S. consumers \$1.80. Now they cost only \$1.60. The lower price of imports to U.S. consumers increases the quantity of imports demanded. Conversely, U.S. goods priced at \$1.80 used to cost British consumers 1£. Now they cost more than 1£ because 1£ buys only \$1.60 in the foreign exchange markets. The higher price of U.S. exports to British consumers decreases the quantity of U.S. exports demanded.

The increased demand for imports and the reduced demand for U.S. exports both reduce the demand for net exports. Net exports shift down from $(Ex^d - Im^d)_0$ to $(Ex^d - Im^d)_1$ in Figure 36.4, which shifts aggregate demand down from ADE_1 to ADE_2. The reduction in net exports induced by the appreciation of the dollar reduces the value of the spending multiplier. The increase in government purchases increases the equilibrium level of national income from Y_0 to Y_2, instead of from Y_0 to Y_1.

The interest rate feedback through net exports is also symmetric; it reduces the impact of a decrease in aggregate demand. To see why, suppose that the government reduces its purchases of goods and services and borrows less. The chain of events that follows is exactly the reverse of the above. Because the Treasury is borrowing less, U.S. interest rates fall, and funds flow out of the United States in search of higher returns in foreign markets. The outflow of funds depreciates the dollar—say, from $1.60£ to $1.80/£—which makes imports more expensive to U.S. consumers and U.S. exports cheaper to British consumers. The decreased demand for imports and the increased demand for U.S. exports both increase the demand for net exports. The higher demand for net exports increases aggregate demand relative to what it would be without the interest rate/exchange rate feedback and reduces the multiplied decrease in national income brought on by the decrease in government purchases.

The two crowding-out channels are either/or propositions to some extent; the more one occurs, the less the other occurs. For example, suppose that aggregate demand increases and funds really pour into the United States as U.S. interest rates begin to rise. The increased supply of foreign funds represents an increase in saving by the foreign sector and increases the total saving in the economy. As such, it makes more funds available to those who are selling assets or borrowing to raise money, and it mitigates the increase in interest rates. The less interest rates rise, the less consumer durables and investment are crowded out. At the same time, however, the more foreign funds that enter the United States, the greater the appreciation of the dollar. The more the dollar appreciates, the more net exports are crowded out. Conversely, suppose that the United States were totally isolated from the rest of the world, so that net-export crowding out is impossible. Then U.S. rates would rise by the maximum amount and enhance the crowding out of consumer durables and investment.

CROWDING-OUT EFFECT
Changes in the demands for consumer durables, investment, and net exports that are induced by the change in interest rates following a change (shift) in aggregate demand, and that lower the value of the spending multiplier.

Twenty-five years ago net-export crowding out was essentially ignored in the macroeconomic analysis of the U.S. economy. Not so any more. The increasing internationalization of the U.S. economy has made net-export crowding out an important phenomenon for policy makers to consider. Net-export crowding out may be even more important today than consumer durable–investment crowding out is.

Net-export crowding out was certainly a significant factor in slowing down the recovery of the economy from the deep recession of 1981–82. As noted in Chapter 31, the government undertook an extremely expansionary fiscal policy to pull the economy out of the recession. The economy responded, but did not return to the production possibilities frontier until 1987. A major reason for the long recovery period was that the dollar appreciated 23 percent against the major currencies from 1982 through 1985, in part because U.S. interest rates were very high.[4] The large appreciation of the dollar decreased net exports and held down the growth of aggregate demand as the economy was trying to recover. At the same time, the influx of foreign funds supported investment and consumer durables. These two components of aggregate demand grew at their usual pace during the recovery.

CURRENT ISSUE: The United States is lobbying hard to make its economy even more internationalized. President Clinton is pressing other nations to open up government contracts for telecommunications equipment to worldwide competitive bidding. At present, most European governments require that this equipment be purchased from domestic producers.

CROWDING OUT AND THE POLICY OPTIONS The crowding-out phenomenon has some interesting implications for the timing of fiscal and monetary policies.

[4]Council of Economic Advisers, *Economic Report of the President, 1993* (Washington, D.C.: U.S. Government Printing Office, 1993), Table 107, p. 470.

Fiscal policy tends to stimulate the economy more rapidly than does monetary policy because it directly affects aggregate demand. But the crowding-out phenomenon ultimately reduces the ability of fiscal policy to stimulate or slow down the economy regardless of whether crowding out occurs through the consumer durables–investment channel or the net export channel. Crowding out does not apply to monetary policy, however. For example, an expansionary monetary policy reduces interest rates, and the reduction in interest rates stimulates consumer durables demand and investment demand. It does not crowd them out. Also, the reduction in interest rates leads to an outflow of funds from the United States, which depreciates the dollar and stimulates net export demand. Therefore, sustaining a recovery from a recession may well require a dose of expansionary monetary policy at some point to counteract the crowding-out problem with fiscal policy.

The same point holds in reverse. If the federal government really wants to hold down the growth of aggregate demand, it might start with a contractionary fiscal policy. But it should also consider slowing down the growth of the money supply at some point in order to shore up interest rates. Higher interest rates help to reduce spending on consumer durables and investment. They also support the value of the dollar, which reduces net export demand as well.

The need for monetary policy to help maintain the growth in aggregate demand is even more compelling now that the U.S. economy has become more international in scope. Net-export crowding out can significantly reduce the effectiveness of fiscal policy without some help from monetary policy.

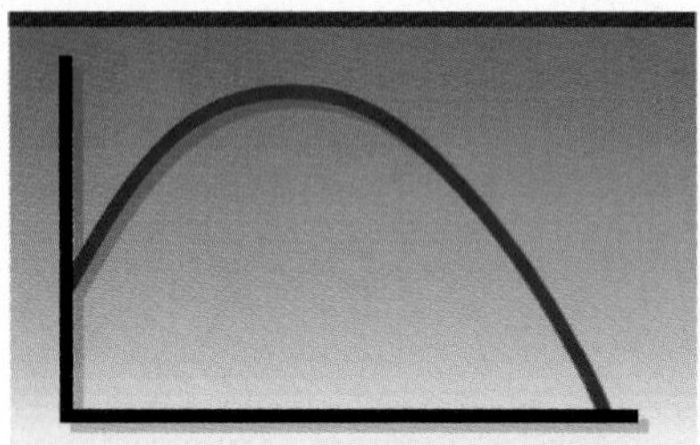

THE SPENDING MULTIPLIER IN THE UNITED STATES

Chapter 30 introduced the spending multiplier in the context of the simplest possible economy as

$$M_{\text{Spending}} = 1/(1 - \text{MPC})$$

We noted at the time that although the simple spending multiplier captures the idea of the multiplier process, it is unrealistic in two respects. First, it greatly overstates the actual value of the spending multiplier in the United States. The MPC is approximately .9 in the long run, which implies a spending multiplier of 10. In fact, the actual spending multiplier is on the order of 1 to 3. In addition, the multiplier process is hump-shaped, as illustrated in Figure 30.3. A change in aggregate demand produces a multiplied change in national income that builds continuously for about a year and a half, after which the change in national income begins to decline and settle in on its final value.

We saw in Chapter 31 that automatic stabilizers reduce the value of the simple spending multiplier by approximately 40 percent, from a value of 10 to a value of 6. The automatic stabilizers result when national income feeds back into aggregate demand through taxes, transfer payments, business saving, and import demand. Now we have seen that interest rates also feed back into aggregate demand, crowding out consumer durables, investment, and net exports and reducing the spending multiplier still further. Adding the crowding-out phenomenon to automatic stabilizers brings the actual spending multiplier most of the way down into the 1 to 3 range.

The crowding-out phenomenon also explains the hump-shaped pattern of the multiplier process. Refer again to Figures 36.2 and 36.4. The movement of the economy from Y_0 to Y_2 can be thought of as occurring in two steps over time, first from Y_0 to Y_1 and then from Y_1 to Y_2. The increase in government spending starts a multiplier process going that builds continuously to a peak of Y_1. Then, after about a year and a half, the increase in interest rates begins to take effect. The rise in interest rates eventually decreases consumption demand and investment demand, as represented in Figure 36.2, and net export demand, as represented in Figure 36.4. National income declines from its peak of Y_1 and settles on its final value of Y_2. The multiplier process is hump-shaped, as required.

AGGREGATE DEMAND MANAGEMENT: THE POLICY OPTIONS

The federal government attempts to control aggregate demand over the short run through its fiscal and monetary policies. The Concept Summary table lists the short-run effects of fiscal and monetary policies on two key economic policy variables, (real) national income and interest rates.

CONCEPT SUMMARY

THE EFFECTS OF FISCAL AND MONETARY POLICIES ON REAL NATIONAL INCOME AND INTEREST RATES

FISCAL POLICY	REAL NATIONAL INCOME	INTEREST RATES
Expansionary (increase G, Tr; decrease Tx)	Increase Y	Increase R
Contractionary (decrease G, Tr; increase Tx)	Decrease Y	Decrease R

MONETARY POLICY	REAL NATIONAL INCOME	INTEREST RATES
Expansionary (Fed buys Treasury securities on the Open Market)	Increase Y	Decrease R
Contractionary (Fed sells treasury securities on the Open Market)	Decrease Y	Increase R

To review:

- *An expansionary fiscal policy increases both national income and interest rates.* Expansionary fiscal policies include increases in government purchases of goods and services, increases in transfer payments, and decreases in taxes. Fiscal policy is the responsibility of the administration and the Congress.
- *A contractionary fiscal policy decreases both national income and interest rates.* Contractionary fiscal policies include decreases in government purchases of goods and services, decreases in transfer payments, and increases in taxes.
- *An expansionary monetary policy increases national income and decreases interest rates.* The Fed conducts an expansionary monetary policy by buying Treasury securities on the Open Market from securities dealers at a few large commercial banks, brokerage houses, and investment banks. The Fed's purchase of Treasury securities increases the reserves in the commercial banks, which allows them to make more loans and create new checking account balances.
- *A contractionary monetary policy decreases national income and increases interest rates.* The Fed conducts a contractionary monetary policy by selling some of its Treasury securities on the Open Market to the securities dealers. The Fed's sale of Treasury securities decreases the reserves in the commercial banks, which forces them to reduce their loans and checking account balances.

Notice that expansionary and contractionary fiscal and monetary policies have the same effect on national income, but the opposite effect on interest rates. An easy way to remember the different interest rate effects is to recall how the policies affect the market for loans. Fiscal policy changes the *demand* for loans, whereas monetary policy changes the *supply* of loans.

For example, an expansionary fiscal policy increases the demand for loans, as in Figure 36.1, primarily because of increased borrowing by the Treasury. The increased demand for loans increases the average interest rates on loans. In contrast, an expansionary monetary policy increases the supply of loans, as in Figure 35.5, because it gives banks excess reserves to lend. The increased supply of loans decreases the average interest rates on loans. The quantity of loans increases with both policies and the economy expands, but with opposite effects on interest rates. Test your understanding of these points by thinking about how contractionary fiscal and monetary policies affect the market for loanable funds.

Hitting National Income and Interest Rate Targets

Chapter 31 concluded with a simplified example of the government's economic policy problem in which the government used different kinds of fiscal policies to reach the full-employment level of national income. Now we are in a position to consider a more complex policy problem in which the government uses two economic policies, fiscal policy and monetary policy, to manipulate two economic policy variables, national income and interest rates. Let's briefly review the nature of the economic policy problem before proceeding.

Recall that solving the economic policy problem is a three-step process. The government's policy makers first have to decide what goals they are trying to achieve. The four macroeconomic policy goals are long-run economic growth, full employment, price stability, and a balance of trade approximately equal to zero along with a stable value of the dollar. These goals are often conflicting, and the federal government does not pursue them directly in any case. Instead, it pursues them indirectly, primarily by managing aggregate demand through its fiscal and monetary policies. Changes in aggregate demand directly affect the equilibrium level of national income and interest rates, which in turn influence the four macroeconomic policy goals. Therefore, the second step is to set target values for national income and interest rates that the policy makers believe represent the best possible compromise in terms of achieving the four macroeconomic policy goals. The third and final step is to design a combination of fiscal and monetary policies to hit the national income and interest rate targets.

The different interest rate effects of fiscal and monetary policies are crucial to hitting both targets because they give the federal government two independent policy instruments for managing aggregate demand. With two independent policy instruments, the federal government has the flexibility it needs to manipulate both national income and interest rates as it desires. In principle, the federal government can simultaneously hit whatever target values of national income and interest rates it has set with a suitable combination of fiscal and monetary policies.

In practice, the possibilities for fiscal and monetary policies are far more limited. We have seen that the federal government cannot fine tune the economy with either fiscal or monetary policy. The best either policy can hope to do is "lean against the wind" and nudge the economy in the right direction. Nonetheless, the independence of fiscal and monetary policies is still useful because it allows the government to "lean" independently on national income and interest rates. The government can decide whether it would like national income to increase, stay about the same, or decrease and whether it would like interest rates to increase, stay about the same, or decrease. Then, it can use its fiscal and monetary policies, either alone or in combination, to achieve simultaneously any one of the three choices for national income and any one of the three choices for interest rates. Manipulating the direction of national income and interest rates is not the same as hitting exact target values for national income and interest rates, to be sure. But it is enough to give the federal government a considerable amount of influence over the four macroeconomic policy goals.

The following eight examples indicate how the federal government can manipulate the direction of national income and interest rates with its fiscal and monetary policies. The first four examples are the simplest; they require only one policy, either fiscal policy or monetary policy. The last four examples are more complex; they require a combination of fiscal and monetary policies.

When thinking about these examples, you may want to refer back to the Concept Summary table on page 1087, which summarizes the effects of fiscal and monetary policies on national income and interest rates.

SINGLE POLICIES Four desired directional targets for national income and interest rates are possible with single policies.

1. *Increase national income and decrease interest rates.* Suppose that the government's policy makers decide that they want to increase aggregate demand and national income in order to reduce unemployment. They also want to decrease interest rates to spur investment demand and long-run economic growth. An

expansionary monetary policy produces the desired result. The Fed should buy Treasury securities on the Open Market to increase reserves in the commercial banks. An expansionary monetary policy simultaneously increases aggregate demand and national income and decreases interest rates.

The remaining examples will indicate the directional targets for national income and interest rates without indicating why the government might want these targets. The next section of the chapter looks closely at how changes in national income and interest rates influence the four macroeconomic policy goals.

2. *Increase national income and increase interest rates.* Expansionary fiscal policy moves the two variables in the desired direction. The administration and the Congress should increase government purchases, increase transfer payments, or cut taxes, either singly or in combination. An expansionary fiscal policy simultaneously increases aggregate demand and national income and increases interest rates.

3. *Decrease national income and decrease interest rates.* Contractionary fiscal policy is the answer if the government wants to decrease aggregate demand and national income while simultaneously decreasing interest rates. The administration and the Congress should decrease government purchases, decrease transfer payments, or raise taxes, either singly or in combination. A contractionary fiscal policy simultaneously decreases aggregate demand and national income and decreases interest rates.

4. *Decrease national income and increase interest rates.* The correct policy in this case is a contractionary monetary policy. The Fed should sell Treasury securities on the Open Market to drain reserves from the commercial banks. A contractionary monetary policy simultaneously decreases aggregate demand and national income and increases interest rates.

COMBINATION POLICIES The following four examples require a combination of fiscal and monetary policies. They illustrate the principle that the government has the flexibility to hit national income and interest rate targets simultaneously with a suitable combination of fiscal and monetary policies.

5. *Increase national income and keep interest rates about the same.* Suppose that the government's policy makers decide that they want to increase aggregate demand and national income, but that they are satisfied with the level of interest rates. Conducting only one of the policies changes both national income and interest rates. Therefore, these two targets require a combination of fiscal and monetary policies.

A combination of expansionary fiscal policy and expansionary monetary policy produces the desired result. Expansionary fiscal policy increases both national income and interest rates. Expansionary monetary policy increases national income and decreases interest rates. The two policies both serve to increase aggregate demand and national income. At the same time, they pull in opposite directions on interest rates and tend to cancel each other out. Therefore, a suitable combination of expansionary fiscal policy and expansionary monetary policy can increase aggregate demand and national income while leaving interest rates just about the same.

6. *Decrease national income and keep interest rates about the same.* The proper policy this time is a combination of contractionary fiscal policy and contractionary monetary policy. The contractionary fiscal policy decreases both na-

tional income and interest rates. The contractionary monetary policy decreases national income and increases interest rates. The two policies serve to decrease national income while pulling in opposite directions on interest rates. Therefore, a suitable combination of the two can decrease aggregate demand and national income while leaving interest rates just about the same.

7. *Leave national income about the same and increase interest rates.* These two targets require a combination of expansionary fiscal policy and contractionary monetary policy. The expansionary fiscal policy increases both national income and interest rates. The contractionary monetary policy decreases national income and increases interest rates. The two policies pull in opposite directions on national income. At the same time, they both serve to increase interest rates. Therefore, a suitable combination of the two can leave aggregate demand and national income just about the same while increasing interest rates.

8. *Leave national income about the same and decrease interest rates.* These two targets require a combination of contractionary fiscal policy and expansionary monetary policy. The contractionary fiscal policy decreases both national income and interest rates. The expansionary monetary policy increases national income and decreases interest rates. Once again, the two policies pull in opposite directions on national income. This time, though, they both serve to decrease interest rates. Therefore, a suitable combination of the two can leave aggregate demand and national income just about the same while decreasing interest rates.

These combination policy strategies suggest other possibilities. For example, suppose that the government's policy makers want aggregate demand and national income to increase substantially. They also want interest rates to increase, but only a little. The proper policy response might be a very expansionary fiscal policy coupled with a mildly expansionary monetary policy. The mildly expansionary monetary policy keeps aggregate demand and national income growing while counteracting somewhat the increase in interest rates brought on by the expansionary fiscal policy.

REFLECTION: What combination of fiscal and monetary policies would help drive interest rates down substantially while increasing national income only slightly?

Coordinating Fiscal and Monetary Policies

The attempt to manipulate national income and interest rates with a combination of fiscal and monetary policies encounters one serious practical problem that we have not stressed previously, the problem of coordinating the two policies. Fiscal and monetary policies are not conducted under one umbrella. Fiscal policy is the responsibility of the administration and the Congress, and monetary policy is the responsibility of the Fed. Moreover, Congress established the Federal Reserve Banking System as a separate and independent government agency. The Fed is not under the direct oversight of either the Congress or the administration. The chairman of the Fed's Board of Governors does have to appear before Congress twice a year to indicate the Fed's views on the state of the economy and its intentions regarding monetary policy. Other than this, the federal government makes no specific attempt to coordinate its fiscal and monetary policies.

The result of the Fed's independence is that fiscal and monetary policies can, and often do, work at cross-purposes. An outstanding example occurred in response to the deep recession of 1981–82. The administration and the Congress embarked on the most expansionary fiscal policy in the nation's history. The Fed, meanwhile, was still pursuing a very tight monetary policy that it had begun in 1979 to squeeze inflation out of the economy. The combination of a very expansionary fiscal policy and a very tight monetary policy served to slow down the recovery from the recession. It also produced very high interest rates, much higher than the nation wanted, given its concern about low levels of investment and sluggish long-run economic growth.

Congress has been willing to bear the occasional costs to macroeconomic policy of an independent Fed. It had good reasons for wanting the central bank to operate without undue political influence from the administration or the Congress, and few in Washington are seriously proposing that the Fed give up its independence.

AGGREGATE DEMAND MANAGEMENT: THE POLICY GOALS

Now that we have seen how the government can use its fiscal and monetary policies to manipulate the direction of national income and interest rates, one final policy question remains: How do changes in national income and interest rates relate to the four macroeconomic policy goals of long-run economic growth, full employment, price stability, and a zero balance of trade along with a stable value of the dollar?

The following Concept Summary table defines the menu of choices that are available to policy makers over the short run. It pulls together all that we have said in the previous chapters about the relationship of national income and

CONCEPT SUMMARY

NATIONAL INCOME (*Y*), INTEREST RATES (*R*), AND THE MACROECONOMIC POLICY GOALS (SHORT-RUN)

	LONG-RUN ECONOMIC GROWTH (INVESTMENT)	FULL EMPLOYMENT	PRICE STABILITY	BALANCE OF TRADE, STABLE DOLLAR
Increase *Y*	Increase investment multiplier accelerator model	Decrease unemployment	Increase inflation	Increase imports Worsen balance of trade
Decrease *Y*	Decrease investment (multiplier accelerator model)	Increase unemployment	Decrease inflation	Decrease imports Improve balance of trade
Increase *R*	Decrease investment (increase cost of capital)			Inflow of foreign currencies Dollar appreciates in value
Decrease *R*	Increase investment (decrease cost of capital)			Outflow of dollars Dollar depreciates in value

interest rates to the macroeconomic policy goals. Understand that the table is a menu of policy choices under a very particular set of assumptions. It assumes that the changes in national income and interest rates are the result of the government's fiscal and monetary policies. As such, the changes are driven by changes in aggregate demand. It also assumes a new Keynesian policy environment in which wages and prices are sticky in the short run and the economy may be operating far beneath its production possibilities frontier with lots of unemployed resources.

Let's run through each entry in the table to recall what we have learned so far.

National Income and the Policy Goals

Changes in national income have a significant impact on all four of the macroeconomic policy goals.

LONG-RUN ECONOMIC GROWTH Investment in plant and equipment is a key determinant of long-run economic growth, and the link between national income and investment is the multiplier-accelerator model of Chapter 32. The main insight of that model is that firms invest only when they project an increasing demand for their products. Otherwise, they do not need to expand their production capacity. Therefore, rapid growth in aggregate demand is absolutely essential in order to have a high-investment economy. Firms simply will not invest very much if aggregate demand is stagnating and the economy is suffering from high unemployment and excess capacity. This is true no matter how low the cost of capital may be, either because interest rates are low or because the federal government is offering firms special tax incentives to invest.

Some economists believe that investment in plant and equipment is determined more by the growth of aggregate demand than by the cost of capital. Although this point is controversial, most economists would agree that a stagnating economy is not especially conducive to investment in plant and equipment.

Many new Keynesian economists would also argue that the crowding-out phenomenon does not apply when the economy is far from full employment. They believe that an increase in aggregate demand in this situation stimulates investment demand through the multiplier-accelerator mechanism, rather than crowding it out. They talk about investment being "crowded in" when unemployment is very high.

FULL EMPLOYMENT/LOW UNEMPLOYMENT The connection between national income and unemployment is very direct in a world of sticky wages and prices. The unemployment rate rises and falls with the ebbs and flows of the business cycle. A decrease in aggregate demand and national income leads firms to reduce production and lay off workers, which increases the unemployment rate. An increase in aggregate demand and national income leads firms to increase production and hire more workers, which decreases the unemployment rate. We saw in Chapter 25 how the involuntary job losers category of the unemployed swings with the business cycle. In response to the business cycle, workers and firms in the United States appear to have adopted a policy of layoffs and rehires instead of a flexible wage policy that would maintain full employment at all times.

PRICE STABILITY/LOW INFLATION The previous chapters have said little about inflation because they were assuming fixed wages and prices in order to capture the essence of the new Keynesian view of the economy in the short run. A full analysis of price inflation appears in Chapter 38. Controlling inflation is by its very nature a long-run policy problem, and new Keynesian and new classical economists agree on how to keep inflation under control in the long run.

Changes in aggregate demand do change the rate of inflation even in the short run, however, and in the way that one would expect. An increase in aggregate demand increases the rate of inflation, and a decrease in aggregate demand decreases the rate of inflation. The basic insight into why comes from the Laws of Supply and Demand. An increase in aggregate demand places more product markets and factor markets in a state of excess demand and fewer in a state of excess supply. The results are upward pressure on prices generally throughout the economy and a higher rate of inflation. Conversely, a decrease in aggregate demand places more product markets and factor markets in a state of excess supply and fewer in a state of excess demand. The results are downward pressure on prices generally throughout the economy and a lower rate of inflation.

THE SHORT-RUN PHILLIPS CURVE Notice that the goals of full employment and price stability are in direct conflict with one another in the short run. An increase in aggregate demand reduces the unemployment rate, but increases the rate of inflation. A decrease in aggregate demand reduces the rate of inflation, but increases the unemployment rate.

The inverse relationship between unemployment and inflation in response to changes in aggregate demand was first documented by British economist A. W. Phillips for the British economy. Subsequent research by U.S. economists verified the same inverse relationship for the U.S. economy. The relationship, pictured in Figure 36.5, became known as the short-run Phillips Curve.

The rate of inflation is on the vertical axis, and the unemployment rate is on the horizontal axis. The vertical line highlights the natural rate of unemployment, U_{NR}, the unemployment rate when the economy is operating on its production possibilities frontier. U_{NR} is assumed to be 6 percent in the graph. The **short-run Phillips Curve** shows how the rate of inflation and the unemployment rate respond to a change in aggregate demand in the short run. Note that the curve is quite flat at high unemployment rates, becomes steeper as the unemployment rate approaches the natural rate, and then becomes very steep as the unemployment rate reaches and falls below the natural rate. The shape of the curve indicates that the inflation and the unemployment rates respond quite differently to changes in aggregate demand depending on the state of the economy when aggregate demand changes.

SHORT-RUN PHILLIPS CURVE

A curve that shows how the rate of inflation and the unemployment rate respond to a change in aggregate demand in the short run.

For example, suppose that the government undertakes expansionary fiscal and monetary policies that increase aggregate demand in order to reduce the unemployment rate. According to the figure, the increase in aggregate demand can reduce the unemployment rate substantially with only a slight increase in

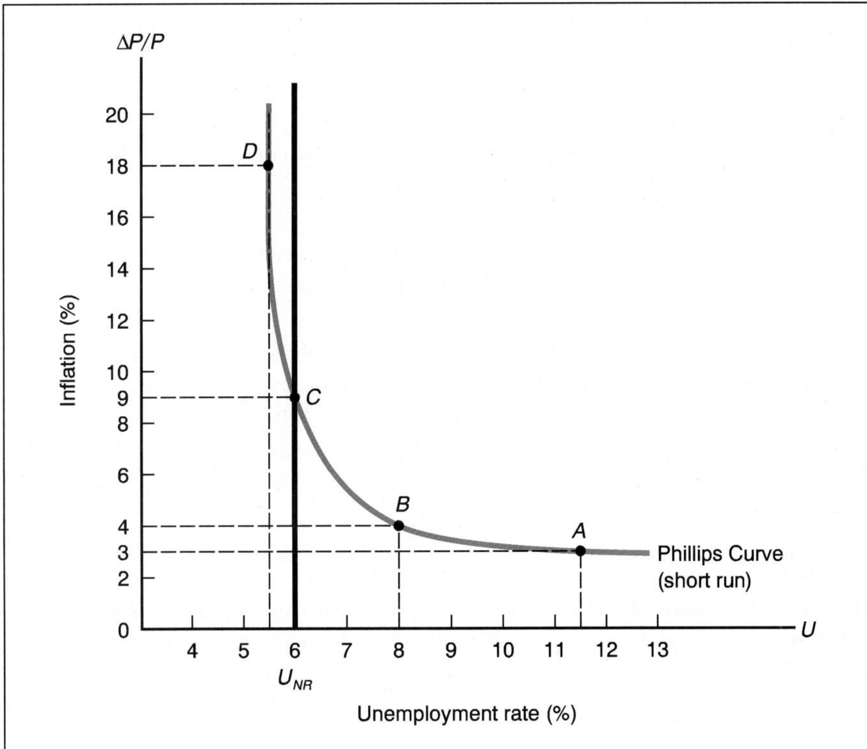

FIGURE 36.5

The Short-Run Phillips Curve

The short-run Phillips Curve shows how unemployment and inflation respond to a change in aggregate demand in the short run. The unemployment rate, U, is on the horizontal axis, and the inflation rate, $\Delta P/P$, is on the vertical axis. An increase in aggregate demand has different effects on unemployment and inflation depending on the state of the economy. The movements from *A* to *B*, *B* to *C*, and *C* to *D* are the result of equal increases in aggregate demand. The increase in aggregate demand at point *A*, when the unemployment is 11.5 percent, reduces unemployment by 3.5 percentage points to 8 percent, and increases the rate of inflation by only 1 percentage point, from 3 percent to 4 percent. As the economy moves closer to and even beyond its production possibilities frontier represented by the natural rate of unemployment, U_{NR} (= 6 percent), the same increase in aggregate demand generates a smaller reduction in unemployment and a larger increase in inflation. For example, starting at point *C*, when unemployment is 6 percent, the same increase in aggregate demand as at point *A* reduces the unemployment rate by only half a percentage point, from 6 percent to 5.5 percent, and increases the rate of inflation by 9 percentage points, from 9 percent to 18 percent.

inflation in the short run if the unemployment rate is very high to begin with. Fiscal and monetary policies reduce the unemployment rate from 11.5 percent at point A to 8 percent at point B with only a one-percentage-point increase in inflation, from 3 percent to 4 percent. The same expansionary fiscal and monetary policies reduce the unemployment rate less and the inflation rate more in the short run if the unemployment rate is nearer the natural rate to begin with. The movement from B to C assumes the same increase in aggregate demand as for the movement from A to B. This time, however, the unemployment rate declines by only two percentage points, from 8.0 percent to 6.0 percent, while the rate of inflation increases by five percentage points, from 4 percent to 9 percent. Finally, suppose that the same expansionary fiscal and monetary policies are applied when the economy is on its sustainable production possibilities frontier and the unemployment rate is at 6 percent, the natural rate. Now most of the increase in aggregate demand simply causes higher inflation. The unemployment rate drops by only a half of a percentage point, from 6 percent at point C to 5.5 percent at point D, while the rate of inflation increases by nine percentage points, from 9 percent to 18 percent. The numbers are hypothetical, but they illustrate how a given dose of expansionary policy has a very different impact on unemployment and inflation in the short run, depending on the state of the economy.

The same analysis applies in reverse to contractionary fiscal and monetary policies. The same dose of contractionary policy reduces inflation more, and increases unemployment less, the lower the unemployment rate is to begin with.

The short-run Phillips Curve underscores a very important point that we have not emphasized earlier. In a world of changing prices, fiscal and monetary policies directly control the growth of *nominal* aggregate demand and *nominal* national income and output, the growth of $P \cdot Q$ and not just the growth of Q. Moreover, the growth of nominal aggregate demand is the *sum* of the growth in prices (inflation) and the growth in output.

$$\begin{aligned} \text{Rate of growth in } P \cdot Q &= \text{rate of growth in } P + \text{rate of growth in } Q \\ &= \text{rate of inflation} + \text{rate of growth in } Q \end{aligned}$$

OKUN'S LAW

An observed relationship between output growth and unemployment, which states that every 2.5-percentage-point increase in the rate of growth of output reduces the unemployment rate in the United States by 1 percentage point.

The rate of growth in Q determines how much the unemployment rate declines. A common rule of thumb for the U.S. economy is called **Okun's Law:** Every 2.5-percentage-point increase in Q reduces the unemployment rate by 1 percentage point. Okun's Law is named after economist Arthur Okun, who first described the relationship between output growth and unemployment in the 1970s.

The short-run Phillips Curve indicates that the growth in nominal aggregate demand is split differently between inflation and growth in real output, depending on the state of the economy. Suppose that the increase in the growth of nominal aggregate demand in our example is 10 percent. The implied breakdown into inflation and growth in output in Figure 36.5 is roughly as follows:

	RATE OF INFLATION	RATE OF GROWTH IN Q
A to B	1%	9%
B to C	5	5
C to D	9	1

The numbers on each line must add up to 10 percent, the growth in nominal aggregate demand. The unemployment numbers and the rate of growth in output numbers in the example are roughly in accord with Okun's Law. For instance, the 5 percent increase in Q from B to C reduces unemployment by two percentage points (from 8 percent to 6 percent), exactly as Okun predicted (5%/2.5 = 2%). The other rate-of-growth numbers are not exactly right, but close.

We cannot stress strongly enough that the short-run Phillips Curve applies only in the short run, as its name suggests, and only in response to changes in aggregate demand. The long-run analysis of inflation in Chapter 38 will show that the inverse relationship between inflation and unemployment breaks down over time and disappears entirely in the long run. There is no long-run relationship at all between inflation and unemployment. In addition, inflation and unemployment respond very differently in the short run to a change in aggregate supply. An adverse aggregate supply shock, such as an increase in the price of crude oil, increases both inflation and unemployment. A favorable aggregate supply shock, such as an improvement in productivity, decreases both inflation and unemployment. Inflation and unemployment bear a direct relationship to one another in the short run when changes in national income are being driven by the supply side of the economy.

THE BALANCE OF TRADE AND THE VALUE OF THE DOLLAR The balance of trade is the difference between the values of imports and exports. National income and the balance of trade are connected through the marginal propensity to import, which as we saw in Chapter 31, is approximately equal to .1 in the United States. An increase in national income increases imports of consumer goods, raw materials, intermediate inputs, and capital goods and worsens the balance of trade. A decrease in national income decreases imports of these goods and improves the balance of trade.

The change in imports also feeds back somewhat into the value of the dollar. Consider the case of an increase in national income leading to an increase in imports. The importers who sell their goods in the United States are foreign citizens who eventually want to exchange the dollars that they receive into their own currencies. The desire to exchange dollars for foreign currencies lowers the value of the dollar; the dollar depreciates. Conversely, a decrease in imports reduces the exchange of dollars for foreign currencies and raises the value of the dollar; the dollar appreciates.

Interest Rates and the Policy Goals

Changes in interest rates have a significant impact on two of the macroeconomic policy goals, long-run economic growth and the value of the dollar.

LONG-RUN ECONOMIC GROWTH Interest rates influence long-run economic growth through their impact on investment demand. Interest rates are a major component of the annual cost of capital to business firms. The lower interest rates are, the lower the cost of capital is, and the higher the firms' desired stock of capital is. The presumption is that the increase in the desired stock of capital induces firms to increase their annual rate of investment. Conversely, the lower interest rates are, the higher the cost of capital is, and the lower the firms' desired stock of capital is. Presumably investment demand also decreases.

Economists cannot agree on whether interest rates and investment demand are closely related in the short run. Nearly all economists would agree, however, that low interest rates are more conducive to investment than are high interest rates over the long run, which is the relevant horizon for long-run economic growth. Economists have been uniformly critical of the high long-run interest rates in the United States that have persisted throughout the 1980s and into the 1990s. They believe that the high interest rates have contributed to the nation's low rate of economic growth. The main reason why most economists favor reducing the federal government's structural budget deficit is to reduce interest rates and stimulate investment demand.

THE BALANCE OF TRADE AND THE VALUE OF THE DOLLAR The relationship between interest rates and the value of the dollar is strong and immediate. We have seen that an increase in U.S. interest rates leads to an immediate inflow of foreign funds, which increases the value of the dollar. The dollar appreciates relative to the world's major currencies. Conversely, a decrease in U.S. interest rates leads to an immediate outflow of funds to foreign financial markets, which decreases the value of the dollar. The dollar depreciates relative to the world's major currencies. The impact of interest rates on the dollar exchange rate is much stronger and more immediate than is the impact of national income, which operates indirectly through import demand.

What Should the Targets Be?

The menu of policy choices in the Concept Summary table indicates that choosing target levels of national income and interest rates over the short run is never an easy decision. The table is full of conflicts among the goals. For instance, the federal government may want to increase national income in order to reduce unemployment and to spur investment and growth, but then it has to live with a higher rate of inflation and a worsening balance of trade. Or the government may want to decrease interest rates to encourage investment, but lower interest rates weaken the value of the dollar and make imports more expensive to consumers. The choice of national income and interest rate targets is always a judgment call. Which goals are the most important to pursue at the moment? Which combination of national income and interest rates represents the best possible compromise among the goals? Reasonable people can reasonably disagree on the best answers to these questions.

Political considerations also enter into the policy decision and lead to their own set of compromises. A good recent example occurred in 1991. The Bush administration desperately wanted to pull the economy out of the recession in time for the 1992 election. Most economists would agree that the quickest way to get the economy moving is with expansionary fiscal policy, since it directly increases aggregate demand. The large budget deficit had tied the administration's hands, however. Increasing the deficit even more in 1991 was considered political suicide by both the administration and the Congress. So the Bush administration relied on expansionary monetary policy, which increases aggregate demand only indirectly and much more slowly. As we saw in Chapter 35, the lags from increases in the money supply to increases in aggregate demand during a recession can be very long, well over a year. This appeared to be the case in 1991–92. The Fed began pumping reserves into the commercial banks in the second quarter of 1991, but the economy did not show any signs of life until the third quarter of 1992, too late to save the Bush presidency.

REFLECTION: The introduction mentioned that the United States has been having problems meeting all four macroeconomic policy goals. Which ones would you give highest priority to, and what policies would you recommend to pursue them? What would be some of the costs of your policies?

Add together the conflicts among the macroeconomic policy goals, the practical difficulties in conducting fiscal and monetary policies, and the various political considerations that appear from time to time, and the recipe for concocting just the right short-run policy mix is an exceedingly tricky one indeed.

SUMMARY

Chapter 36 pulled together the analysis of the macro economy in Chapters 29 through 35, which looked at the operation of the economy in the short run from a new Keynesian perspective of sticky wages and prices and unemployed resources.

The first section of the chapter considered how changes in aggregate demand affect interest rates. It began with a change in consumption demand.

1. An increase in consumption demand increases interest rates because some households have to reduce their holdings of financial assets or borrow to obtain the money they need to buy goods and services. Both transactions increase interest rates. For example, the desire to sell stocks and bonds lowers their prices and raises their rates of return. An increased demand for loans increases interest rates on loans.

2. Conversely, a decrease in consumption demand is an increase in saving demand. Households increase their demand for financial assets and reduce their borrowing, both of which decrease interest rates.
3. An expansionary fiscal policy increases aggregate demand directly, so it increases interest rates. Increased deficit financing requires the Treasury to borrow more, which increases the demand for loans throughout the economy.
4. Conversely, a contractionary fiscal policy decreases aggregate demand directly, so it decreases interest rates. Reducing the deficit results in less borrowing by the Treasury, which decreases the demand for loans throughout the economy.
5. The change in interest rates following a change in aggregate demand crowds out consumer durables, investment, and net exports and lowers the value of the spending multiplier. For example, an increase in aggregate demand increases interest rates, which reduces the demand for consumer durables and investment. Higher interest rates also increase the value of the dollar as funds flow into the United States, seeking the higher returns. An appreciation of the dollar reduces the demand for exports and increases the demand for imports, both of which reduce the demand for net exports.
6. Crowding out through interest rates also explains the hump-shaped pattern of the multiplier process. For example, an increase in aggregate demand causes national income to increase rapidly at first, but then the increase in interest rates reduces the demand for consumer durables, investment, and net exports, and national income declines to its final value.

The second section of the chapter showed how the government can, in principle, hit target values of national income and interest rates with a suitable combination of fiscal and monetary policies.

7. Fiscal and monetary policies give the government two independent policy tools to hit national income and interest rate targets because they have opposite effects on interest rates. Expansionary fiscal and monetary policies both increase aggregate demand and national income, but expansionary fiscal policy increases interest rates, whereas expansionary monetary policy decreases interest rates. Contractionary fiscal and monetary policies both decrease aggregate demand and national income, but contractionary fiscal policy decreases interest rates, whereas contractionary monetary policy increases interest rates.
8. The best the federal government can hope to do is influence the direction of national income and interest rates, rather than hitting target values exactly. The chapter considered a number of possibilities. For example, a desire to increase both national income and interest rates requires an expansionary fiscal policy. A desire to increase national income, but leave interest rates about the same, requires a combination of expansionary fiscal policy and expansionary monetary policy.

The final section of Chapter 36 summarized how national income and interest rates relate to the four macroeconomic policy goals.

9. Changes in national income influence all four goals in the short run. For example, increases in aggregate demand and national income
   a. promote investment demand and long-run economic growth through the multiplier-accelerator process,
   b. lower unemployment,

c. increase inflation, and
d. worsen the balance of trade by increasing the demand for imports.
Decreases in aggregate demand and national income have the opposite effects.

10. The short-run Phillips Curve illustrates the inverse relationship between inflation and unemployment in response to a change in aggregate demand. The relationship varies, depending on the state of the economy. For example, an increase in aggregate demand decreases unemployment less and increases inflation more the lower the initial rate of unemployment, and vice versa.
11. Changes in interest rates primarily affect long-run economic growth and the value of the dollar. For example, a decrease in interest rates
    a. stimulates investment demand and long-run economic growth because interest rates are an important component of the cost of capital, and
    b. causes the dollar to depreciate in value as funds flow out of the United States, seeking higher returns elsewhere.

    An increase in interest rates has the opposite effects.

KEY TERMS

crowding-out effect

Okun's Law

short-run Phillips Curve

QUESTIONS

1. What effect does each of the following policies have on the rate of inflation and the unemployment rate in the short run?
    a. a 10 percent tax cut
    b. a 12 percent rise in government expenditures
    c. a 5 percent cut in government transfer payments
2. Why does an increase in aggregate demand cause interest rates to rise?
3. a. Explain what is meant by the crowding out of consumer durables and investment and by the crowding out of net exports.
    b. Discuss the role of interest rates in the crowding-out phenomenon.
    c. What effect does crowding out have on the value of the spending multiplier?
4. What is Okun's Law? Suppose that output is $1,000, and the unemployment rate is 6 percent initially. If output increases to $1,050, what does Okun's Law predict the new rate of unemployment will be?
5. Draw the short-run Phillips Curve, and explain why you drew it as you did. What appears on the axes? What do points along the short-run Phillips Curve represent?
6. Discuss the directional effects on the equilibrium level of national income and the level of interest rates in the short run when the government engages in the following policies:
    a. Congress passes a 6 percent increase in all personal income tax rates.
    b. The Fed sells $200 million of Treasury debt on the Open Market.
    c. The Fed increases the reserve requirement on checking account deposits by one percentage point.
    d. The federal government increases government spending on goods and services by $5 billion, financed by increasing the debt.
    e. Both (a) and (b) occur simultaneously.
    f. Both (c) and (d) occur simultaneously.
7. Suppose that the government is satisfied with the current level of interest rates (rates of return) throughout the economy, but is dissatisfied with the growth in national income. Design a set of monetary and fiscal policies that will increase national income, but leave interest rates unchanged. Be specific about your policy choices, and indicate why your policies would work.
8. Suppose that the federal government undertakes the following combination of fiscal and monetary policies. Congress raises all personal income tax rates by 5 percent, and the Fed buys $20 million of Treasury debt on the Open Market. Discuss what qualitative effects this combination of policies has on each of the four macroeconomic policy goals in the short run.
9. Suppose that the federal government wants to increase output growth without worsening the balance of trade. What fiscal and monetary policies should the government undertake?

10. Suppose that the federal government is interested in increasing investment demand. Answer the following questions.
    a. Why might the government want to increase investment demand?
    b. Which of the following four policy options is the best for increasing investment demand, and why: expansionary fiscal policy, expansionary monetary policy, contractionary fiscal policy, or contractionary monetary policy?
    c. Describe one possible undesirable side effect of the policy option that you chose in part (b). (*Note:* Your answers to parts (a) and (c) should relate to the macroeconomic policy goals.)
11. Suppose that
    (i) prices are rising at the rate of 6 percent per year,
    (ii) output is rising at the rate of 3 percent per year, and
    (iii) the money supply is rising at the rate of 4 percent per year.
    a. What must be happening to the income velocity of circulation (*V*)? Why?
    b. What must be happening to the demand for money? Why?

CASE

The Accord of 2006: The End of Fiscal Policy?*

This case takes you into the future and asks you to consider the ramifications of a drastic change in federal economic policy.

In 2005, Andrew Mackintosh was appointed Chairman of the Board of Governors of the Federal Reserve System, having served as a board member since 2003. Although Mackintosh's background is in academia rather than banking, he comes from a new generation of economists that is tired of the theoretical debates between new Keynesian and new classical economists. Mackintosh favors a more pragmatic approach to monetary and fiscal policy.

It comes as a surprise, then, when in 2006 the President of the United States (who had just appointed the Chairman the previous year) and Mackintosh agree that the United States Treasury will stop selling new issues of Treasury securities to the public. Instead, as old Treasury bills, notes, and bonds mature, the government will have two options. It can redeem the maturing securities with funds received from taxes or other revenues, or it can redeem them by issuing new securities. But—and here is the shocker—it must sell the new securities only to the Federal Reserve, not to the public.

Furthermore, whenever the Treasury seeks to turn over old, maturing securities, the Fed will be obligated to buy the newly issued replacement securities. But the Fed will have the discretion to buy, or not to buy, newly issued Treasury securities that represent additional indebtedness as the result of a federal budget deficit. If the Fed chooses not to buy the new offerings, then there can be no new debt and no new increase in government spending over its revenues for any given fiscal year.

These new stipulations regarding the issuing and purchase of Treasury securities are referred to as "The Accord of 2006."

Under the Accord of 2006, it is theoretically possible that after 15 years, in 2021 (when most of the pre-2006 indebtedness would have matured), either the national debt will have been lowered toward zero with payoffs from government revenues, or (more likely) the national debt will be owned entirely by the Federal Reserve System, itself a government agency. In effect, the national debt will be owed by the government to itself.

The Accord of 2006 is a pragmatic attempt to end, or at least reduce, the huge structural federal budget deficits that the government has been running ever since 1981. The Gram-Rudman-Hollings Act of 1985, the Omnibus Budget Reconciliation Act of 1990, and the 1993 passage of President Clinton's $500 billion deficit reduction plan all failed to reduce the deficits. President Clinton's plan failed because of the enormous increases in federal expenditures for health care following the passage of the National Health Care program. Providing 37 million Americans with quality health care turned out to be far more expensive than the administration and Congress had anticipated, and they were unwilling to raise taxes to pay for the program. The current President and Chairman Mackintosh feel it is time for a more drastic approach to reducing the deficit, one which gives the Fed the power to limit deficit spending by the administration and Congress.

*Provided by James J. McLain, University of New Orleans

(continued on next page)

The Accord of 2006: The End of Fiscal Policy? (cont.)

ECONOMIC ADVISOR'S REPORT

Suppose that you are the economic advisor to the Assistant Secretary of the Treasury for Central Bank Affairs, and are asked to lead a team that will consider several questions raised by the Accord of 2006.

1. The first question Treasury wants you to answer is this: What interest rate should the Fed pay for any Treasury securities that it buys? How was the interest rate determined before the Accord, and should the Fed try to duplicate the results of that system?
2. Is the Accord of 2006 better than the old system of essentially independent fiscal and monetary policies for:
   (a) Holding down aggregate demand when the economy is booming and straining against its production possibilities frontier?
   (b) Increasing aggregate demand when the economy is operating far below its production possibilities frontier, with lots of unemployed resources?

Indicate how your answers to these questions depend on the following possible choices by the Fed:

(i) The Fed will not buy newly issued Treasury securities if they are intended to finance a federal budget deficit.
(ii) The Fed will buy newly issued Treasury securities if they are intended to finance a federal budget deficit, but only up to a limit of $150 billion each year.
(iii) The Fed will buy all newly issued Treasury securities regardless of why the Treasury is selling them.

3. The Employment Act of 1946 made the President responsible for promoting non-inflationary, full-employment economic growth.
   (a) Will the federal government's attempt to reach these goals be freer from political pressures under the Accord of 2006?
   (b) Does the Accord remove fiscal policy as a means of fulfilling the goals of the Employment Act of 1946?
   (c) Does the Accord allow the Fed to conduct a monetary policy that is independent of federal budgetary policy?
4. Does it matter whether the national debt is owned by the Fed or by private U.S. citizens?

PART

X

The Role of Prices and the Problem of Inflation

CHAPTER

37

Aggregate Supply and Aggregate Demand

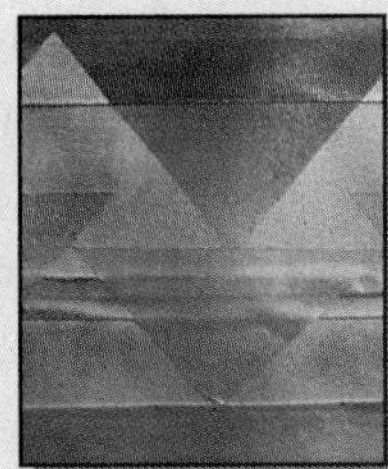

LEARNING OBJECTIVES

CONCEPTS TO LEARN

Aggregate demand curve
Short-run aggregate supply curve
Long-run aggregate supply curve
Stagflation

CONCEPTS TO RECALL

Laws of Supply and Demand [5, 6, 7]
Aggregate demand and aggregate supply [28]
New Keynesian economics [28]
New classical economics [28]
Aggregate demand and aggregate supply shocks [28]
Real business cycle model [32]

il has been one of the leading macroeconomic stories of the past 20 years. It is the prime example of the tremendous effect that supply shocks can have on an economy.

When the Organization of Petroleum Exporting Countries (OPEC) increased the price of crude oil eightfold from 1973 to 1979, it threw the industrialized market economies into turmoil. They suffered the double whammy of rising unemployment and rising inflation and were helpless to do much about it. In 1980, inflation in the United States was 12.5 percent and unemployment was 7.1 percent. Congress in its exasperation passed the largest tax cut in U.S. history on the basis of a new and untried supply-side theory of how tax cuts work, which the media dubbed Reaganomics. The Western European nations were so panicked by the specter of inflation that they tied their currencies to the German mark. They knew that the Germans feared inflation more than anyone and would do everything in their power to hold down the growth of their money supply to keep the mark strong and prevent inflationary pressures from building. The other nations of Western Europe were not sure they had the resolve to fight the inflation on their own. The oil price increases also brought enormous hardships to the low-income developing nations. Many were forced to borrow heavily at very high interest rates in order to finance their imports, and a number of them eventually defaulted on their debt.

OPEC lost its market power in 1980, and the price of oil came tumbling down almost as sharply as it had risen in the 1970s. The collapse of the oil prices ushered in a new period of prosperity. Inflation in the United States fell to 3.7 percent by 1982, and the economy grew steadily from December 1982 to July 1990, one of the longest periods of uninterrupted growth in the United States during the twentieth century. Inflation also ceased to be a serious threat in Western Europe, and many of the Western European economies enjoyed rapid growth as well. Oil was not solely responsible for the reversal of fortunes in the United States and Europe, but it certainly deserved a large part of the credit. By the end of the 1980s the debt problem had also subsided a bit for the developing nations, except for countries like Mexico that rely heavily on oil exports. For the Mexicans the earlier rise in oil prices was a blessing, and the subsequent collapse of oil prices was a curse. Most nations, though, are very thankful that oil prices are not expected to rise rapidly anytime in the near future.[1]

Chapters 37 and 38 explore the role of prices in the macro economy. Chapter 37 describes how prices help to bring the economy to an equilibrium in both the short run and the long run. Chapter 38 then concludes our study of macroeconomics with a discussion of some current policy issues. Its main focus, though, is on the problem of keeping inflation under control.

Chapter 37 begins by developing the aggregate supply–aggregate demand (AS–AD) model of the macro economy that we introduced in Chapter 28. The AS–AD model highlights the role of prices in bringing the economy to its

1. Council of Economic Advisers, *Economic Report of the President, 1993* (Washington, D.C.: U.S. Government Printing Office, 1993), Table 37, p. 390 (unemployment) and Table 58, p. 415 (inflation).

equilibrium. We will then use the AS–AD model to compare and contrast the new Keynesian and new classical perspectives on how the macro economy operates.

AGGREGATE DEMAND AND AGGREGATE SUPPLY: AN OVERVIEW

We began our study of the macro economy in Chapter 28 with the observation that the first relationship in every macro model is

$$Y = C^d + I^d + G^d + (Ex^d - Im^d)$$

The relationship describes the overall equilibrium in the nation's product markets in terms of supply and demand. The left-hand side of the relationship represents aggregate supply. Y is the (real) national income or national output generated by producers in supplying goods and services. The right-hand side of the relationship represents the aggregate demand for goods and services, broken down into its four components by sector of the economy. Aggregate demand is the sum of consumption demand (C^d) by the household sector, investment demand (I^d) by the business sector, demand for goods and services (G^d) by the government sector, and net export demand ($Ex^d - Im^d$) by the foreign sector. The relationship says that the nation's product markets are in equilibrium when the aggregate supply of goods and services equals the aggregate demand for goods and services.

Our analysis of supply and demand for a single product in the introductory chapters of the text emphasized the role of price in bringing a competitive market to equilibrium because the price is what draws suppliers and demanders together in exchange. The price of each good and each service is the one variable that households and firms share in common as they try to solve their economic problems through exchange. For the same reason, prices also play a crucial role in bringing the overall macro economy to its equilibrium.

Nonetheless, our analysis of the macro economy following Chapter 28 kept prices in the background by assuming that they are constant. We did this to highlight the new Keynesian view of how the economy operates over the short run when lots of resources are unemployed and prices (and wages) are fairly sticky. The new Keynesians argue that national income or national output is primarily determined by aggregate demand in that environment and that aggregate supply responds passively to aggregate demand. They also believe that national income is more important than are prices in determining the level of aggregate demand in the short run.

New Keynesian economists do not ignore prices, however. They acknowledge that prices vary more and become more important in the short run as the economy nears or reaches its production possibilities frontier and that prices are flexible enough in the long run to bring the macro economy to its long-run equilibrium. New Keynesian economists also acknowledge that the economy is occasionally hit by significant aggregate supply shocks that change firms' costs of production and feed through quickly to prices.

The new classical economists argue that prices are always the most important variable bringing the macro economy to its equilibrium, both in the short run and in the long run. In their view the vast majority of product markets and

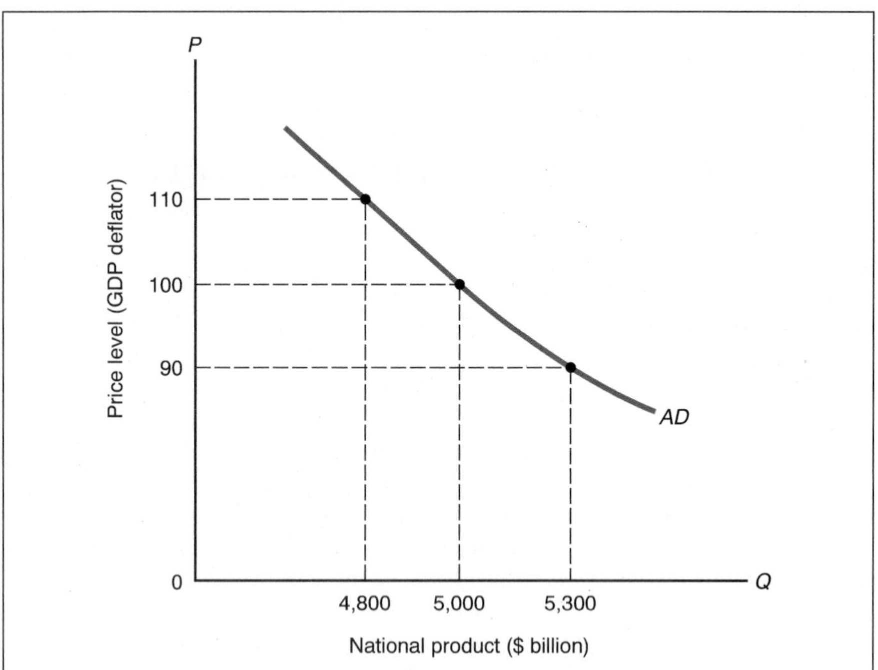

FIGURE 37.1

The Aggregate Demand Curve

The aggregate demand curve, *AD*, is a graph of the aggregate demand schedule, which indicates the aggregate quantity of final goods and services demanded by all the final demanders—households, businesses, governments, and the foreign sector—at each overall price level. Real national product, *Q*, is on the horizontal axis, measured in $billions, and the overall price level, *P*, represented by the GDP deflator, is on the vertical axis. *AD* is downward sloping. In the figure, an increase in the GDP deflator from 100 to 110 decreases the aggregate quantity of final goods and services demanded from $5,000 to $4,800. A decrease in the GDP deflator from 100 to 90 increases the aggregate quantity of final goods and services demanded from $5,000 to $5,300. The inverse relationship between the aggregate quantity demanded and the overall price level arises principally because the quantity of money demanded for transactions purposes is directly related to the overall price level.

factor markets are highly competitive and operate roughly in accordance with the Laws of Supply and Demand. Prices (and wages) are flexible for the most part, not sticky. Therefore, the best model of the macro economy is one in which prices equate aggregate supply and aggregate demand at all times as a natural by-product of equating supply and demand in each individual market.

We need to develop the AS–AD model of the economy in order to compare and contrast the new Keynesian and the new classical views of the economy. The development here extends the earlier introductory presentation of the model in Chapter 28 and pulls together some material from other chapters. Let's begin with aggregate demand because it is not a source of controversy between new Keynesian and new classical economists.

AGGREGATE DEMAND

AGGREGATE DEMAND SCHEDULE

A schedule that indicates the quantity of national output demanded by the four sectors of the economy at each overall level of prices.

AGGREGATE DEMAND CURVE

A graph of the aggregate demand schedule that shows the quantity of national output demanded by the four sectors of the economy at each overall level of prices.

An **aggregate demand schedule** describes the quantity of national output demanded by the four sectors of the economy at each overall level of prices. The **aggregate demand curve,** labeled *AD*, is a graph of the aggregate demand schedule. It is downward sloping, as illustrated in Figure 37.1.

P on the vertical axis represents the overall or average level of the prices of all products. It is a broad-based price index of goods and services, such as the gross domestic product (GDP) deflator. *Q* on the horizontal axis is a measure of real national product, such as constant dollar GDP, in billions of dollars. It represents the real quantities of goods and services demanded in the nation's product markets by the household, business, government, and foreign sectors combined. The aggregate demand curve, *AD*, shows that price and aggregate quantity demanded are inversely related, as expected. The national product demanded is $5,000 when the GDP deflator is 100. The national product demanded decreases to $4,800 when the GDP deflator rises to 110; the national product demanded increases to $5,300 when the GDP deflator falls to 90. (The numbers are hypothetical.)

The aggregate demand curve and the demand curve for a single product are both downward sloping, but the similarity between the two ends there. They are very different concepts.

The downward-sloping, single-market demand curve is a picture of the Law of Demand. It describes the relationship between the quantity demanded and the price of the product under the assumption of *other things equal*. In particular, the single-market curve assumes that all other prices and consumers' incomes are being held constant. Therefore, when the price rises, the product becomes more expensive relative to all other products, and the purchasing power of the consumers' incomes falls. When the price falls, the product becomes cheaper relative to all other products, and the purchasing power of the consumers' incomes rises. The changes in relative prices and purchasing power are the sources of the substitution and income effects that support the Law of Demand.

The aggregate demand curve, *AD*, in contrast, does not hold other things equal. The GDP deflator on the vertical axis is a broad-based price index. When it rises from 100 to 110, the assumption is that the prices of *all* goods and services are changing simultaneously. Some prices may be rising by more than 10 percent and some by less than 10 percent, but the overall level of all prices is increasing by 10 percent, on average. Moreover, the aggregate demand curve allows for the possibility that all factor prices are changing as well, even though many factor prices are not part of the GDP deflator. The standard assumption lying behind the aggregate demand curve is that factor prices always change by the same percentage as product prices do, so that the purchasing power of the national income generated in the nation's factor markets does not change. For example factor prices are assumed to increase by an average of 10 percent when the GDP deflator increases from 100 to 110. Therefore, the standard substitution and income effects of a single price change do not apply at the aggregate level. When all product and factor prices change simultaneously by the same percentage, neither relative prices nor the purchasing power of national income changes.

The downward slope of the *AD* curve results from the relationship between the overall price level and the transactions demand for money. We saw in Figure 35.3 that the transactions demand for money is directly proportional to the overall price level. A 10 percent increase in the overall level of prices causes a 10 percent increase in the transactions demand for money. The reason why is that Federal Reserve Notes and checking account balances are denominated in nominal terms. Therefore, if the prices of goods and services rise by 10 percent on average, people need 10 percent more money to buy the same amount of goods and services as before the price increase.

The 10 percent increase in the overall price level forces people to readjust their balance sheets. They need to obtain the extra money, setting off the chain of events described in Chapter 36. They draw down their deposits in savings and money market accounts and sell other financial assets, such as stocks and bonds, which drives up interest rates and rates of return on these financial assets. The higher interest rates in turn decrease the interest-sensitive components of aggregate demand, principally consumer durables and investment, especially investment in housing. In other words, the increased demand for money causes people to hold fewer real assets as well as fewer financial assets. The higher interest rates also attract foreign funds, which drives up the value of the dollar. The appreciating dollar in turn increases the demand for imports and decreases the demand for exports; the demand for net exports decreases. The decreased demand for consumer durables, investment, and net exports reduces the aggregate quantity demanded.

To summarize:

$$P \uparrow \rightarrow \text{transactions demand for money} \uparrow \rightarrow R \uparrow \rightarrow$$
$$C^{Dur}, I^d, (Ex^d - Im^d) \downarrow \rightarrow \text{aggregate quantity demanded} \downarrow$$

The same argument applies in reverse. A decrease in the overall price level causes a proportionate decrease in the transactions demand for money, which causes people to adjust their balance sheets in the opposite direction. They add to their savings and money market accounts and buy more stocks and bonds, which drives down interest rates on these financial assets. The decrease in interest rates increases interest-sensitive components of aggregate demand, such as consumer durables and investment. People buy more real assets as well as more financial assets. The decrease in interest rates also leads to an outflow of funds to foreign markets, which causes the dollar to depreciate and increases the demand for net exports.

To summarize:

$$P \downarrow \rightarrow \text{transactions demand for money} \downarrow \rightarrow R \downarrow \rightarrow$$
$$C^{Dur}, I^d, (Ex^d - Im^d) \uparrow \rightarrow \text{aggregate quantity demanded} \uparrow$$

A number of other factors support the inverse relationship between aggregate demand and the overall price level as well. For instance, corporate and government bonds are also denominated in nominal terms. Therefore, the purchasing power of bondholders' wealth decreases when prices rise, which may reduce consumption demand and investment demand. In addition, many pensions are not indexed to a broad-based price index such as the consumer price index (CPI) or the GDP deflator. The retirees with unindexed pensions do lose purchasing power when the overall price level increases, which lowers their consumption demand. The same holds true for many of the poor who receive public assistance transfers. Their welfare checks have not kept pace with the CPI over the past 20 years in the United States. None of these other factors is nearly so important as the transactions demand for money, however, in producing a downward-sloping aggregate demand curve.

AD and the *ADE*–45° Line Graph

The aggregate demand line, *ADE*, on the *ADE*–45° line graph that we have been using up to now shows the other things equal relationship between aggregate demand and (real) national income or output. It assumes that the overall price level is constant, one of the "other things" being held equal that fix the position of the curve. Increases and decreases in the overall price level shift the *ADE* line up and down. Figure 37.2 illustrates the relationship between the aggregate demand curve, *AD*, specified in terms of prices, and *ADE*, specified in terms of national income. It uses the hypothetical numbers in Figure 37.1.

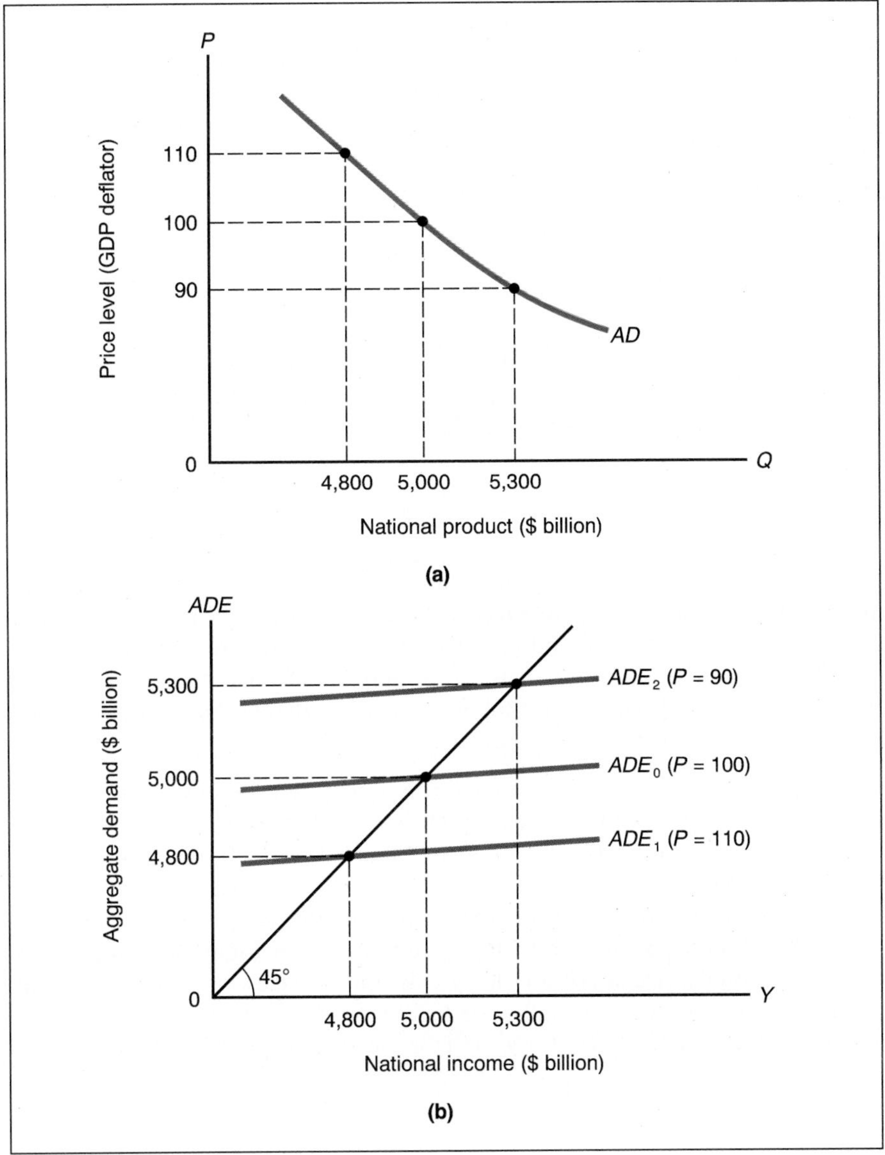

FIGURE 37.2

The *AD* Curve and *ADE*-45° Line

Figure 37.2(a) pictures the aggregate demand curve, *AD*, from Figure 37.1. Figure 37.2(b) pictures aggregate desired expenditures, *ADE*, which are determined by the level of real national income, *Y*. Real national product and real national income are assumed to be equal. Every ADE line corresponds to one value of the GDP deflator. For example, ADE_0 shows aggregate desired expenditures at every level of national income when the GDP deflator is 100. Conversely, every point on the *AD* curve corresponds to an intersection of the *ADE* and 45° lines in Figure 37.2(b), because aggregate demand equals real national product (national income) only at the equilibrium level of national income. Therefore, when the GDP deflator is 110, the *ADE* line is ADE_1, and the equilibrium level of national income is $4,800. When the GDP deflator is 90, the *ADE* line is ADE_2, and the equilibrium level of national income is $5,300.

AD is in Figure 37.2(a), and *ADE* is in Figure 37.2(b). *Q* in Figure 37.2(a), national product, has the same value as *Y* in Figure 37.2(b), national income. The values of *Q* and *Y* are in billions of dollars. Each *ADE* line in Figure 37.2(b) is associated with one value of the GDP deflator on the vertical axis in Figure 37.2(a). ADE_0 is the relationship between aggregate demand and national income (national output) when the GDP deflator is 100. Also, each level of national product on the *AD* curve corresponds to the equilibrium level of national income in Figure 37.2(b), the intersection of *ADE* and the 45° line. National income (national product) is equal to aggregate demand only at the equilibrium. Figure 37.2(a) indicates that aggregate demand is $5,000 when the GDP deflator is 100. Therefore, the equilibrium level of national income (national product) in Figure 37.2(b) associated with ADE_0 is $5,000.

An increase in the GDP deflator to 110 shifts the *ADE* line down to ADE_1. The equilibrium level of national income decreases to $4,800, the corresponding level of national product on *AD* in Figure 37.2(a). A decrease in the GDP deflator to 90 shifts the *ADE* line up to ADE_2. The equilibrium level of national income (national product) increases to $5,300, the corresponding level of national product on *AD* in Figure 37.2(a).

AGGREGATE SUPPLY

AGGREGATE SUPPLY SCHEDULE

A schedule that indicates the quantity of national output supplied by all producers at each overall level of prices.

AGGREGATE SUPPLY CURVE

A graph of the aggregate supply schedule that shows the quantity of national output supplied by all producers at each overall level of prices.

An **aggregate supply schedule** describes the quantity of national output supplied by all producers at each overall level of prices. The **aggregate supply curve,** labeled *AS*, is a graph of the aggregate supply schedule.

Aggregate Supply: The Long Run

The disagreement between the new Keynesian and the new classical economists centers on the aggregate supply curve, and then only in the short run. Both sides agree that wages and prices are flexible enough that markets essentially operate according to the Laws of Supply and Demand in the long run. In Chapter 28 we discussed the following macroeconomic implications of assuming that the economy is competitive.

1. Competitive factor markets automatically bring the economy to the production possibilities frontier. Consequently, the long-run aggregate supply curve, AS_{LR}, is vertical, as pictured in Figure 37.3. Q_0 is the frontier level of national product.
2. The national product is entirely determined by the supply side of the economy. Producers generate the frontier output, Q_0, in Figure 37.3 regardless of the overall price level for the goods and services. Aggregate demand simply determines the overall price level at the frontier, P_0, in Figure 37.3. The long-run equilibrium is (Q_0, P_0), at the intersection of *AD* and AS_{LR}.

Review the discussion in Chapter 28 if you are unclear about any of these points.

This consensus among economists underscores why long-run economic growth is ultimately the most important of the four macroeconomic policy goals. Refer again to Figure 37.3. A nation must shift AS_{LR} to the right and increase output to improve its standard of living over the long run. But shifting AS_{LR} is possible only if the nation can push out its production possibilities frontier through the process of long-run economic growth. As we saw in Chapter 3, expanding the frontier requires investment in physical and human capital, both of which make the nation's resources more productive. Without long-run economic growth, AS_{LR} stays put, and the standard of living stagnates. Nations must be patient, however, because long-run economic growth is a slow process. For example, the United States can shift out AS_{LR} only about 3 to 4 percent per year, at best.

Both new Keynesian and new classical economists advocate government policies to promote investment and long-run growth. Common proposals include increasing public investment in the nation's transportation and communications networks; reducing the structural budget deficits to keep interest rates low and

FIGURE 37.3

Aggregate Supply in the Long Run

The aggregate supply curve is a graph of the aggregate supply schedule, which indicates the aggregate quantity of final goods and services supplied by all producers in the economy at each overall price level. Real national product, Q, is on the horizontal axis, and the overall price level, P, represented by the GDP deflator, is on the vertical axis. New Keynesian economists agree with new classical economists that markets are competitive enough, and prices are flexible enough, to bring the economy to its production possibilities frontier in the long run. Both schools agree that the long-run aggregate supply curve, AS_{LR}, is vertical at Q_0, the frontier level of real national product. The role of the overall price level in the long run is to adjust the aggregate quantity demanded along the aggregate demand curve, AD, to the frontier output, Q_0. The long-run equilibrium is (Q_0,P_0), at the intersection of AD and AS_{LR}.

encourage investment demand; subsidizing education of all kinds, from training programs for unskilled high school drop-outs to student loans and grants for higher education; supporting research and development for new products and new production technologies; and easing the tax burden on saving and investment, the most radical suggestion being to replace the federal personal and corporation income taxes with a personal consumption tax that exempts saving and investment from taxation.

The Clinton administration has embraced all these proposals for promoting long-run economic growth, with the single exception of the tax reforms. President Clinton does support tax credits for investment. Yet he also supported, and Congress passed, an increase in the top federal personal income tax rate from 31 percent to 39.6 percent, to ensure that the burden of reducing the budget deficit falls disproportionately on the rich. This will tend to reduce saving and investment, because the high-income taxpayers do most of the saving in the United States.

People joke that all they hear from macro economists these days is "invest, invest, invest." Maybe so—the need to stimulate investment to promote long-run economic growth is one of the few macroeconomic policies that new Keynesian and new classical economists agree on—that, and the need to control inflation, another long-run policy issue.

Aggregate Supply: The Short Run

New Keynesian and new classical economists disagree completely about the behavior of prices and output in the short run. Their disagreement centers on the nature of the aggregate supply curve in the short run.

New Keynesian economists look at the macro economy and see a market system riddled with imperfections that produce sticky wages and prices and a short-run aggregate supply curve that is far from vertical. In their view, changes in aggregate demand produce substantial changes in output in the short run, especially when the economy is operating well below its production possibilities frontier. Moreover, the changes in output can persist for a very long time, five years and more. The long-run adjustment back to AS_{LR} is so slow that the government should not wait for the economy to return to the production possibilities frontier on its own. Instead, it should use fiscal and monetary policies to change the level of aggregate demand and bring the economy back quickly to the frontier. This is especially imperative in times of recession and high unemployment.

New classical economists look at the macro economy and see a highly competitive market system in which wages and prices are flexible in the short run as well as the long run. In their view there are no important differences between the long-run and the short-run aggregate supply curves, at least none that have any relevance for policy. Fiscal and monetary policies cannot hope to improve the performance of the economy in the short run, and they can actually do some harm. The economy functions as well as can be expected on its own over the short run.

AS_{SR}: THE NEW KEYNESIAN PERSPECTIVE Figure 37.4 pictures the new Keynesian view of the short-run aggregate supply curve, AS_{SR}. The curve is fairly flat when the economy is far below its production possibilities frontier represented by AS_{LR}, becomes steeper as the economy approaches the frontier, and becomes very steep as the economy reaches and moves beyond its sustainable, long-run frontier. The shape of AS_{SR} mirrors the shape of the short-run Phillips Curve described in Chapter 36 and for the same reason. The economy is never completely in equilibrium, according to the new Keynesians. Some individual markets are in excess supply, and others are in excess demand at any one time. The markets in excess supply put downward pressure on the overall price level, and the markets in excess demand put upward pressure on the overall price level.

When the economy is at point *A*, well below the frontier, many markets are in excess supply, and relatively few markets are in excess demand. An increase in aggregate demand at that point removes much of the excess supply without causing much upward pressure on wages or prices. Most of the increase in aggregate demand results in an increase in output, and the economy moves from *A* to *B*. A similar increase in aggregate demand starting at point *B* causes more of an increase in prices and less of an increase in output than at point *A*. More markets are already in excess demand, so that there is more upward pressure on prices throughout the economy. The upward pressure on prices becomes especially strong as the economy reaches the sustainable frontier at point *C*. Supply is difficult, if not impossible, to increase in most markets. Many firms experience supply bottlenecks for key resources; they want to buy more to expand production, but the resources are temporarily unavailable. The result is that a similar increase in aggregate demand at point *C* generates a relatively large increase in prices and very little increase in output. New Keynesians also believe that market economies often operate in the *A* to *B* range with lots of unemployed resources.

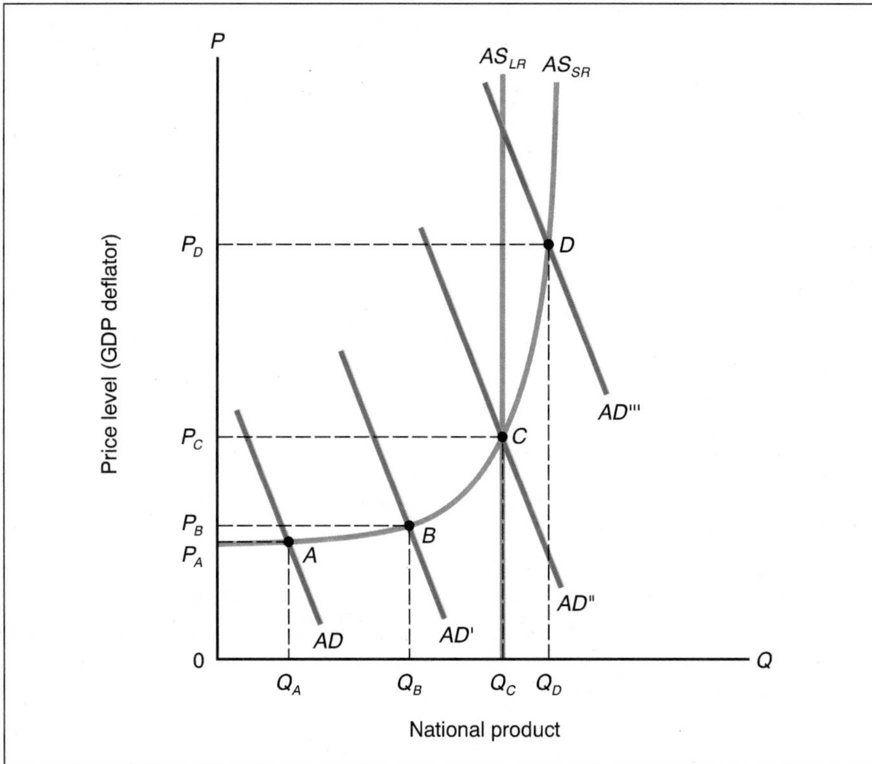

FIGURE 37.4

The Short-run Aggregate Supply Curve: New Keynesian Perspective

The figure shows how new Keynesian economists view the short-run aggregate supply curve, AS_{SR}. AS_{SR} is relatively flat at low levels of real national product when there are a lot of unemployed resources, and then becomes steeper as the economy approaches its production possibilities frontier represented by Q_C and the long-run aggregate supply curve AS_{LR}. AS_{SR} becomes very steep as the economy tries to push beyond Q_C, which is the maximum sustainable level of real national product in the long run. Consequently, increases in aggregate demand have different effects in the short run depending on the state of the economy. An increase in aggregate demand from AD to AD' increases real national product substantially from Q_A to Q_B, with only a slight increase in the overall price level from P_A to P_B. In contrast, an increase in aggregate demand from AD'' to AD''' increases real national product only slightly from Q_C to Q_D, but causes a big increase in the overall price level from P_C to P_D. The shape of AS_{SR} mirrors the shape of the short-run Phillips curve in Figure 36.5.

The wage and price stickiness that underlies new Keynesian theory has two sources. One is a set of noncompetitive labor market institutions that cause *real wages* to be sticky and generally set above the equilibrium level. The other is a set of product market imperfections that cause *nominal prices* to be sticky. The combination of real wage stickiness and nominal price stickiness produces the flat and then upward-sloping AS_{SR} in Figure 37.4. It explains why output responds to changes in aggregate demand in the short run.

REAL WAGE STICKINESS When new Keynesian economists look at the labor market, they focus their attention on labor market institutions in the so-called primary sector of the labor market, in which turnover is fairly low and employees and employers are likely to engage in long-term employment relationships. We discussed in Chapter 25 why workers and firms in the primary labor markets have generally chosen a system of rigid wages, which leads to layoffs and rehires as the economy ebbs and flows, rather than a system of highly flexible wages, which would ensure full employment at all times. The explanations turn on such concepts as internal labor markets, efficiency wages, insider/outsider theories of wage setting, and workers' concern for their relative position in the hierarchy of wages.

Review the discussion in Chapter 25 if you are unclear about these explanations. Rigid (real) wages are a crucial underpinning of the new Keynesian theory because they explain the existence of cyclical unemployment, which is involuntary and ebbs and flows with the economy. Always keep in mind that some kind of factor market imperfections, such as those just described, must lie behind any theory of the macro economy in which output responds significantly to changes in aggregate demand. Otherwise, with competitive factor markets, the economy always operates on or near its production possibilities frontier, and changes in aggregate demand cannot affect output very much.

NOMINAL PRICE STICKINESS Real wage stickiness can cause output to respond to changes in aggregate demand by increasing and decreasing involuntary unemployment. A more direct reason why output responds to changes in aggregate demand, according to the new Keynesians, is that prices themselves are sticky. This is especially true of the prices of final manufactured goods, which constitute approximately 20 percent of the gross domestic product.

Markets tend to become more concentrated and dominated by very large firms as manufactured products move up through the production hierarchy from semi-finished products to the final products that are part of gross domestic product. The final goods manufacturers at the top of the hierarchy are often huge and complex firms that produce a wide range of products and buy inputs from hundreds and even thousands of suppliers. IBM and General Motors are examples.

The giant corporations are far removed from the small firms operating in highly competitive market environments whose prices are essentially dictated to them by the Laws of Supply and Demand. The large final goods manufacturers are price setters, not price takers. In addition, the very complexity of their operations makes their prices somewhat sticky. They are likely to react to an increase in demand at first by hiring more workers and increasing production, while leaving their prices unchanged. They may eventually increase price, but only if they perceive that the increase in demand is permanent. Similarly, they first react to a decrease in demand by laying off workers and decreasing production, while leaving their prices unchanged. In contrast, an increase in demand in a highly competitive market drives up price almost immediately, and a decrease in demand drives price down almost immediately.

The price stickiness of the large firms in response to changes in demand is the result of two factors. One is that changing their prices is not costless. The other is that they may not have the information they need to determine if they should change their prices.

Regarding the costs of changing prices, the large firms typically publish catalogs that list the prices of their products. A decision to change their prices means that they have to publish new price catalogs and inform their customers of the price changes. Economists refer to these as the **menu costs** of changing prices. The menu costs are not very large, to be sure. But they do exist, so the firms need to be sure that their demand and cost conditions have changed sufficiently to warrant changing the prices of their products.

MENU COSTS

The costs to producers of publishing new price catalogs and informing customers of price changes.

Regarding the information requirements, the key issue for macroeconomics is how quickly the final goods manufacturers change their prices after a change in aggregate demand. Their price response could be fairly slow simply because of the sheer complexity of their operations. Firms care about the relationship between the demands for their own products and the costs of producing their own products. They do not care directly about aggregate demand or aggregate supply. Suppose that the Fed increases the money supply, which increases aggregate demand. The increase in aggregate demand puts upward pressure on prices throughout the economy, yet the large final goods manufacturers may be slow to see the price trend developing. On the demand side, the demands for their products may not increase immediately with the increase in aggregate demand. On the cost side, the increase in aggregate demand drives up prices on semi-finished inputs and increases firms' costs. But the input price increases percolate slowly and haphazardly up through the production hierarchy. Since the final goods manufacturers buy from hundreds of suppliers, they may not be aware for awhile that their input costs are increasing. Some firms may not even experience much of a cost increase at first, especially if some of the firms' suppliers are reluctant to increase prices to their largest and most loyal customers. In addition, many of the final goods manufacturers make use of internal labor markets and unionized labor, which means that their wages are also somewhat sticky. Labor and material inputs comprise the vast majority of most firms' total production costs. Therefore, sticky wages and slow-to-respond input costs make for sticky overall costs of production that do not increase immediately with an increase in aggregate demand.

Combine the menu costs of changing prices with sticky production costs and a pattern of product demands that may not follow aggregate demand, and it becomes clear why the final goods manufacturers are often slow to increase their prices when aggregate demand increases. Instead, they hold the line on their prices for awhile and simply increase production to meet whatever increase they see in the demands for their own products.

The same argument applies in reverse. A decrease in aggregate demand puts downward pressure on prices throughout the economy. But the downward price pressure may not immediately lower these firms' costs. Nor do the demands for their individual products necessarily decrease in step with the decrease in aggregate demand. As a result, firms are reluctant to bear the menu costs of lowering their prices. Instead, they react by laying off workers and reducing production if the demands for their own products fall off.

THE COSTS OF STICKY WAGES AND PRICES Sticky real wages and nominal prices are very costly to society precisely because they cause such large changes in output as aggregate demand changes. Figure 37.5 illustrates.

The GDP deflator on the vertical axis represents the overall price level; national product is on the horizontal axis. Suppose that the economy is initially in equilibrium on the production possibilities frontier at the intersection of AD^0 and AS_{LR}. The GDP deflator is 100, and GDP is Q_0, the output on the frontier. Aggregate demand then decreases from AD^0 to AD^1, which happens to be a 10 percent decrease. Because real wages and prices are sticky, the economy moves down along the short-run aggregate supply curve, AS_{SR}. The GDP deflator declines only slightly to 98, and GDP falls substantially from Q to Q_1 in the short run. The economy has moved below its production possibilities frontier, and unemployment increases.[2]

Suppose, instead, that all wages and prices were indexed to the growth in nominal aggregate demand. Now, as aggregate demand falls by 10 percent to AD^1, all wages and prices fall in lockstep by 10 percent. With all wages and prices (and therefore costs) falling by the same amount, neither workers nor firms have any incentive to change their employment or production decisions. The economy remains on AS_{LR} at the frontier, Q, instead of moving down along

2. We will draw AS_{SR} as a straight line from now on to make the graphs easier to read, unless the more realistic curved AS_{SR} curve is essential to the analysis.

FIGURE 37.5

The Social Costs of Sticky Wages and Prices

The figure illustrates the social costs of sticky wages and prices. The economy is initially in its long-run equilibrium on the production possibilities frontier at the intersection of AD^0, AS_{LR}, and AS_{SR}. The frontier level of real national product is Q_0 and the overall price level is 100. Then aggregate demand decreases to AD^1. With flexible wages and prices, the overall price level would fall to 90 and the economy would remain on its production possibilities frontier at Q_0, at the intersection of AD^1 and AS_{LR}. With sticky wages and prices, the overall price level falls only to 98. Real national product decreases to Q_1, at the intersection of AD^1 and AS_{SR}. The sticky wages and prices cause society to lose output ($Q_0 - Q_1$) in the short run, and the losses in output continue as the economy slowly returns to its long-run equilibrium on the frontier.

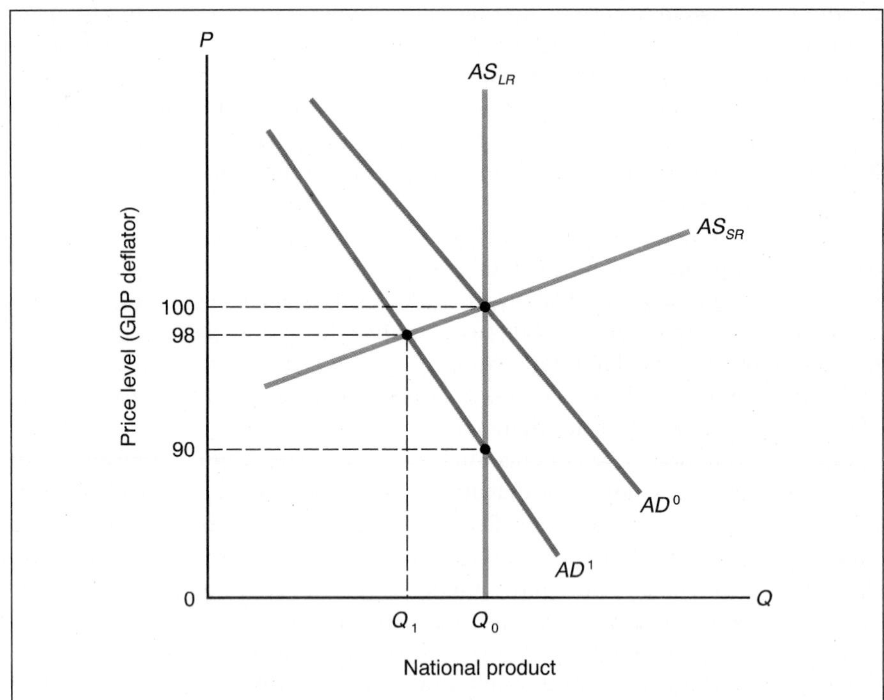

AS_{SR}. The GDP deflator eventually falls by 10 percent, equal to the decrease in nominal aggregate demand, in order to maintain the equilibrium on the frontier.

The loss of output and employment due to the sticky real wages and nominal prices when aggregate demand decreases is an enormous cost for society to bear. The economy would operate much more efficiently and generate far more output over time if all wages and prices were indexed to the GDP deflator. The problem, though, is that no one firm is willing to index its wages and prices to the growth in nominal aggregate demand unless it can be assured that all firms are indexing. Otherwise, each firm wants to control its own prices and set them in relation to its own demands and costs.

We discussed in Chapter 26 why firms and workers are unwilling to index their prices and wages to the overall price index. The reason is a coordination problem. No one firm or group of workers is willing to index its prices or wages unless it can be assured that all firms and workers are indexing their prices or wages. Review that discussion if you are unclear about this point. The unwillingness to index prices is another crucial underpinning of the new Keynesian model in the short run.

THE PROBLEMS WITH GOVERNMENT INDEXING Only the government would be able to coordinate an indexing to the overall price level by forcing all firms and workers to index together. The federal government has not been willing to do this, however, nor should it. Indexing wages and prices to nominal aggregate demand would prevent relative prices from changing and would generate its own set of inefficiencies.

To see why, suppose that a change in tastes shifts consumers' demands in favor of some products and against other products without changing the value of nominal aggregate demand. Consumers spend as much as before; they just allocate their expenditures differently. Efficiency requires that the prices of the favored products rise and the prices of the out-of-favor products fall. But with all prices indexed to nominal aggregate demand, no prices would change. The result would be excess demands in the favored markets and excess supplies in the out-of-favor markets. This is inefficient because resources are not shifting to the favored markets where they are most valued. Aggregate supply shocks would cause similar problems because they change costs differently for different products. For instance, a huge increase in oil prices does not increase the costs of production equally for all products. Relative prices have to vary to reflect the cost differences in order to maintain efficiency and to prevent excess supplies and demands from developing.

Any government-imposed indexing policy would have to grant exceptions based on individual market conditions in order to avoid creating excess demands and supplies. Experience has taught that this is not practicable, however. The Nixon administration tried to index wages and prices in the early 1970s in an attempt to control inflation directly. The commission in charge of implementing the indexing rule received thousands of petitions from firms seeking special considerations based on their individual market conditions, and many firms simply ignored the rule. The administration abandoned indexing within two years on the grounds that it was unworkable and unenforceable.

The only pricing system that is fully efficient is one of completely flexible wages and prices that are determined by the Laws of Supply and Demand. The Laws of Supply and Demand keep the economy on its production possibilities frontier and allow relative prices to change as needed whenever supplies and demands change in individual markets. They also cause wages and prices to move in lockstep together when nominal aggregate demand changes.

THE NEW CLASSICAL ATTACK The high costs of the swings in output and employment are the point of attack by the new classical economists against the new Keynesian theory of sticky wages and prices. The new classical economists ask, quite reasonably, why individuals and firms accept wage and pricing policies that are so costly to them. Why should workers accept rigid real wages when flexible real wages would keep them fully employed? Why should firms maintain sticky prices in the face of falling demand and lose sales and customers? If flexible real wages and nominal prices are so much more efficient, why haven't they become the norm? The new Keynesian theories about why real wages and nominal prices are sticky are simply not convincing to the new classical economists because they entail such enormous individual and social costs.

The new Keynesian economists counter by stressing the coordination problem. Their theories described above about sticky real wages and nominal prices make sense from the perspective of the individuals and the firms that have adopted them. True, society would be far better off with more flexible wage and price setting. But, as noted above, no individual or firm has any incentive to adopt the broader social perspective on its own, and the government has no good method of achieving the broader social perspective.

New Keynesian economists also believe that the facts are incontrovertible—markets are riddled with imperfections, workers are often involuntarily unemployed, and changes in aggregate demand generate substantial shifts in aggregate output when resources are unemployed. If their theories in support of these facts are not entirely convincing, then they believe that they simply have to work harder on the underlying theory. One cannot change the facts.

The new classical economists counter that the new Keynesian "facts" are not, in fact, true, as we saw in Chapter 32 and will discuss further below. For the moment, though, let's pursue some additional implications of the new Keynesian theory.

FROM THE SHORT RUN TO THE LONG RUN The new Keynesian assumptions of fairly sticky wages and prices in the short run and fairly flexible wages and prices in the long run have one very important implication. Output responds to a change in aggregate demand in the pattern of a business cycle. Figure 37.6 illustrates.

The economy is initially in equilibrium on the frontier at (Q_0, P_0) in each graph, at the intersection of AD^0, AS^0_{SR}, and AS_{LR}. Figure 37.6(a) shows how the economy reacts to a decrease in aggregate demand—say, as the result of a contractionary monetary policy. AD shifts down and to the left from AD^0 to AD^1. The economy moves down along AS^0_{SR} to its short-run equilibrium at the intersection of AD^1 and AS^0_{SR}. As expected, the decrease in aggregate demand decreases both price and quantity. The overall price level falls from P_0 to P_1, and the output falls from Q_0 to Q_1. The economy is now operating below its production possibilities frontier, with unemployed resources.

The economy does not stay at the short-run equilibrium, however, because the product markets (and labor markets) are in excess supply overall. The excess supply puts downward pressure on prices (and wages), which lowers firms' costs of production and shifts the short-run aggregate supply curve down and to the right. AS_{SR} keeps shifting until it reaches AS^2_{SR}, and the economy returns to equilibrium on the frontier. The final long-run equilibrium is (Q_0, P_2), at the intersection of AD^1, AS^2_{SR}, and AS_{LR}. In the long run, therefore, a decrease in aggregate demand cannot affect output. It just lowers the overall price level, from P_0 to P_2 in this example. In the meantime, though, output moves in a business-cycle pattern. It first falls from Q_0 to Q_1 after the decrease in aggregate demand and then rises back to Q_0.

The same conclusion applies to an increase in aggregate demand—say, as the result of an expansionary monetary policy. Figure 37.6(b) shows how the economy reacts to an increase in aggregate demand.

AD shifts up and to the right from AD^0 to AD^1. The economy moves up along AS^0_{SR} to its short-run equilibrium at the intersection of AD_1 and AS^0_{SR}. As expected, the increase in aggregate demand increases both price and quantity. The overall price level rises from P_0 to P_1, and the output temporarily rises above the sustainable frontier from Q_0 to Q_1.

The economy does not stay beyond its production possibilities frontier in the long run. Product markets (and labor markets) are in excess demand overall. The excess demand puts upward pressure on prices (and wages), which raises firms' costs of production and shifts the short-run aggregate supply curve up and to the left. AS_{SR} keeps shifting until it reaches AS^2_{SR}, and the economy returns to equilibrium on the frontier. The final long-run equilibrium is (Q_0, P_2), at the intersection of AD^1, AS^2_{SR}, and AS_{LR}. In the long run, therefore, an increase in aggregate demand cannot affect output. It just raises the overall price level, from P_0 to P_2 in this example. Once again, though, output moves

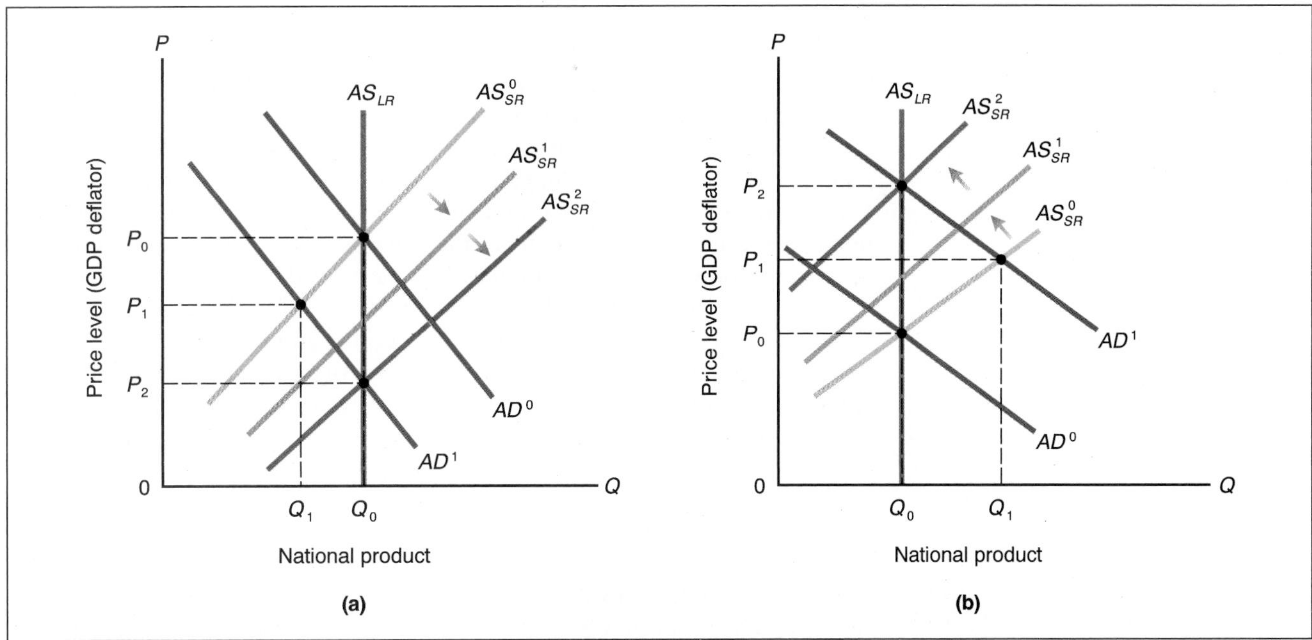

FIGURE 37.6

The Adjustment From the Short Run to the Long Run

The figure illustrates how the economy moves in a business-cycle pattern in response to a change in aggregate demand, under new Keynesian assumptions. Figure 37.6(a) shows how the economy responds to a decrease in aggregate demand and Figure 37.6(b) shows how the economy responds to an increase in aggregate demand. The economy is initially in its long run equilibrium (Q_0,P_0) on the production possibilities frontier in both graphs, at the intersection of AD^0, AS_{LR}, and AS^0_{SR}. In Figure 37.6(a), aggregate demand decreases from AD^0 to AD^1. The economy moves to the short-run equilibrium (Q_1,P_1) below the frontier, at the intersection of AD^1 and AS^0_{SR}. With more goods and factor markets in excess supply, prices and wages drop and reduce firms' costs of production. The short-run aggregate supply cruve shifts down and to the right from AS^0_{SR} to AS^1_{SR} to AS^2_{SR}. The economy returns to a long-run equilibrium (Q_0,P_2) on the frontier, at the intersection of AD^1, AS_{LR}, and AS^2_{SR}. Output first decreases from Q_0 to Q_1 and then increases from Q_1 to Q_0, in a business-cycle pattern. In Figure 37.6(b), aggregate demand increases from AD^0 to AD^1. The economy moves to the short-run equilibrium (Q_1,P_1) above the frontier, at the intersection of AD^1 and AS^0_{SR}. With more goods and factor markets in excess demand, prices and wages rise and increase firms' costs of production. The short-run aggregate supply curve shifts up and to the left from AS^0_{SR} to AS^1_{SR} to AS^2_{SR}. The economy returns to a long-run equilibrium (Q_0,P_2) on the frontier, at the intersection of AD^1, AS_{LR}, and AS^2_{SR}. Output first increases from Q_0 to Q_1 and then decreases from Q_1 to Q_0 in a business-cycle pattern.

in a business-cycle pattern. It first rises from Q_0 to Q_1 after the increase in aggregate demand and then falls back to Q_0.

In conclusion, a decrease in aggregate demand that brings on a recession is followed by a period of falling prices and rising output as the economy moves back to the frontier. Citizens can expect some good economic news for awhile following a recession.

Similarly, an increase in aggregate demand that increases output and pushes hard against the production possibilities frontier is followed by a brief period during which prices rise and output declines. Citizens can expect some bad economic news for awhile following a boom period.

POLICY IMPLICATIONS The adjustment from the short run to the long run in either case is not very relevant to new Keynesian economists, however. Regarding the decrease in aggregate demand, they believe that the adjustment back to the long-run equilibrium is very slow if the economy falls far below the production possibilities frontier into a deep recession. The recovery period may be five years, or even longer. Therefore, the sensible strategy is to intervene with expansionary fiscal and monetary policies that shift up aggregate demand and return the economy to the frontier much more quickly. Why wait for the economy to recover and allow people to suffer in the meantime?

Indeed, Keynes believed that the adjustment would never occur. He argued that falling wages and prices would hurt debtors and keep aggregate demand below the frontier level. For example, suppose that someone borrows $100 and agrees to pay it back next year. Meanwhile, wages and prices fall by half. Now paying back the $100 involves the sacrifice of twice as much purchasing power as did the original $100 given to the borrower. Many debtors may well go bankrupt at the lower prices, in which case their consumption demand would certainly decrease. Although some new Keynesian economists still follow Keynes in this respect, most believe that falling prices and wages do eventually bring the economy back to the frontier. The disagreement is not important, though, because all new Keynesians agree that the use of expansionary fiscal and monetary policies in order to increase output and reduce unemployment is the proper response to a recession.

New Keynesians believe that the adjustment to the frontier is much quicker in the case where aggregate demand increases beyond the frontier. Most markets are thrown into excess demand, firms experience supply bottlenecks for many of their inputs, and prices rise rapidly throughout the economy. Still, why allow price pressures to build? Once again, the sensible strategy is to respond to the increase in aggregate demand with contractionary fiscal and monetary policies that bring *AD* back to its original position and remove the price pressures.

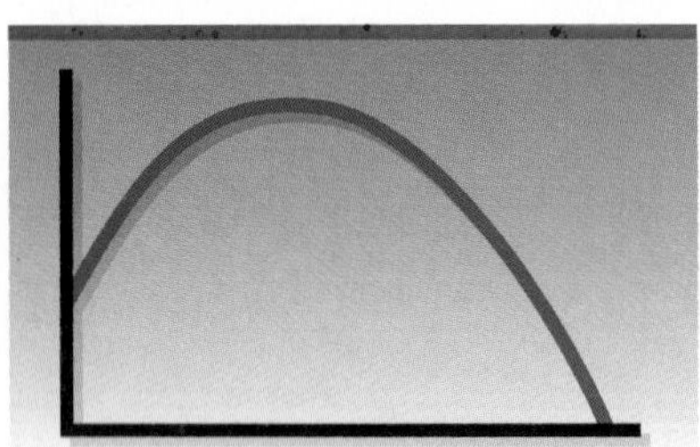

THE SPENDING MULTIPLIER IN THE UNITED STATES

The price changes that follow a change in aggregate demand are the final chapter in our story about the spending multiplier in the United States. Recall that the value of the multiplier is in the range of one to three after a period of a few years. Moreover, the multiplier process is hump-shaped. National income increases steadily for about one and a half years following an increase in aggregate demand and then decreases to its final value of one to three.

Our simple model of the economy in Chapter 29 predicted a very high value of the spending multiplier, around 10, based on a marginal propensity to consume (MPC) that builds to about 0.9 over a few years. Chapter 31 introduced the automatic stabilizers, such as income taxes and income-sensitive transfer payments, and noted that they reduce the spending multiplier by about 40 percent. Chapter 36 added the interest rate changes that follow a change in aggregate demand and argued that they reduce the spending multiplier still further by crowding out consumer durables, investment, and net exports. The interest-rate effect also generates the hump-shaped pattern of the multiplier process.

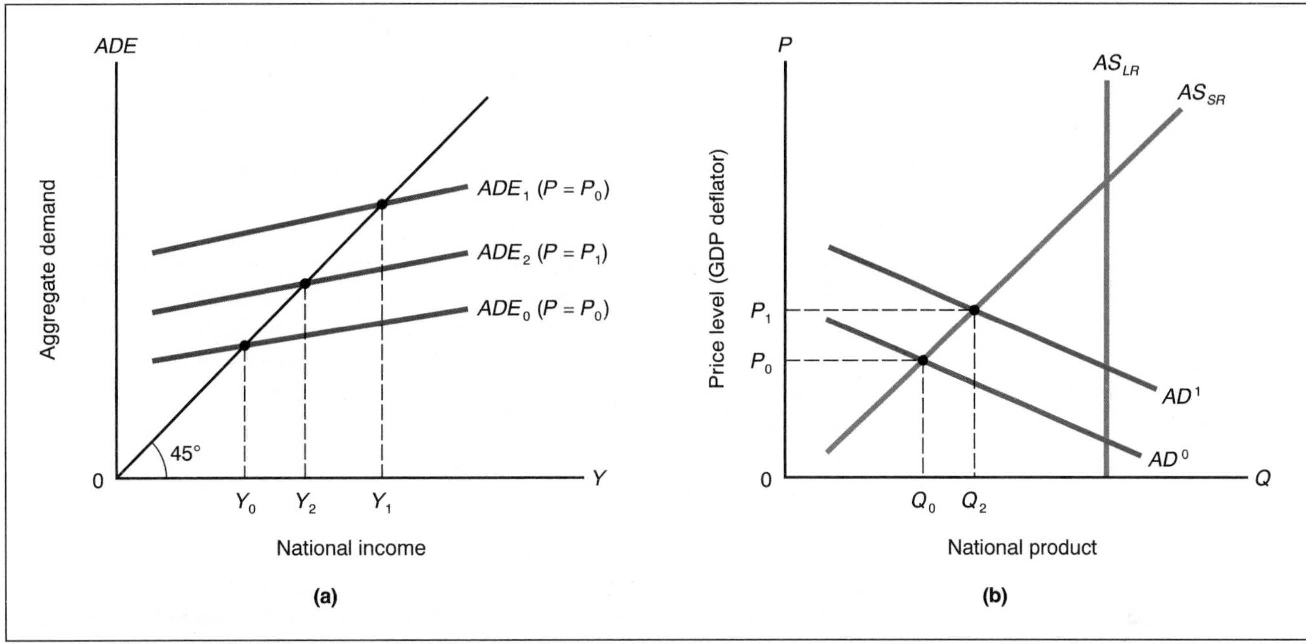

The figure shows how changes in the overall price level lower the value of the spending multiplier. Figure 37.7(a) pictures the *ADE*-45° line diagram, with aggregate desired expenditures determined by the level of real national income, *Y*. Figure 37.7(b) pictures aggregate demand and aggregate supply, *AD* and *AS*, with real national product, *Q*, on the horizontal axis and the overall price level, *P*, on the vertical axis. The economy is initially in a short-run equilibrium at Y_0 $(=Q_0)$ on both graphs, at the intersection of ADE_0 and the 45° line in Figure 37.7(a), and at the intersection of AD^0 and AS_{SR} in Figure 37.7(b). In Figure 37.7(a), an increase in aggregate demand shifts the *ADE* line from ADE_0 to ADE_1, and the economy heads to a new equilibrium level of national income, Y_1, at the intersection of ADE_1 and the 45° line. But the increase in aggregate demand increases the overall price level from P_0 to P_1, as illustrated in Figure 37.7(b). Aggregate demand shifts from AD^0 to AD^1, and the new short-run equilibrium is (Q_2,P_1), at the intersection of AD^1 and AS_{SR}. The increase in the overall price level shifts the *ADE* line down from ADE_1 to ADE_2 in Figure 37.7(a). The final short-run equilibrium level of national income is Y_2 $(=Q_2)$, at the intersection of ADE_2 and the 45° line. The rise in the overall price level has reduced the value of the multiplier; the equilibrium level of national income increases to Y_2 instead of Y_1.

FIGURE 37.7

Changes in the Overall Price Level and the Spending Multiplier

The price changes that follow a change in aggregate demand also reduce the value of the spending multiplier and contribute to its hump-shaped pattern. Figure 37.7 illustrates, for an increase in aggregate demand.

Figures 37.7(a) presents the *ADE*–45° line graph that we have been using to illustrate the spending multiplier. Figure 37.7(b) shows the *AS*–*AD* representation of the economy. The two graphs assume that the economy is initially in a short-run equilibrium well below its production possibilities frontier with lots of unemployed resources. In Figure 37.7(a), aggregate demand is ADE_0, and the equilibrium level of national income is Y_0, at the intersection of ADE_0 and the 45° line. The corresponding aggregate demand curve in Figure 37.7(b) is AD^0. The economy is in equilibrium at the intersection of AD^0 and AS_{SR}. National output is Q_0, corresponding to national income, Y_0, and the overall price level is P_0.

Refer again to Figure 37.7(a). Suppose that aggregate demand increases from ADE_0 to ADE_1. The new equilibrium level of national income is Y_1, at the intersection of ADE_1 and the 45° line. Now refer to Figure 37.7(b). The corresponding increase in aggregate demand is to AD^1, and the economy moves to a new short-run equilibrium, (Q_2, P_1), at the intersection of AD^1 and AS_{SR}. The equilibrium national output, Q_2, does not correspond to the equilibrium national income, Y_1, because ADE_1 in Figure 37.7(a) assumes that the overall price level remains at P_0. We had been assuming constant prices in our previous analysis of the spending multiplier. The increase in price to P_1 shifts down the ADE line from ADE_1 to ADE_2 and establishes a new equilibrium level of national income at Y_2. Y_2 corresponds to national output, Q_2, in Figure 37.7(b).

The price increase following the increase in aggregate demand reduces the value of the spending multiplier. National income increases from Y_0 to Y_2, rather than from Y_0 to Y_1 without the price increase. Also, the price increase contributes to the hump-shaped pattern of the multiplier process. The economy begins building to Y_1, but then backs down to Y_2 as prices increase and choke off some of the aggregate demand.

The value of the spending multiplier must be zero in the long run because the economy always operates on its production possibilities frontier in the long-run equilibrium. As we have seen, a change in aggregate demand changes only prices in the long run. The spending multiplier is inherently a short-run concept, however, that is meant to apply when the economy is operating well below its production possibilities frontier. Showing how the economy responds to a change in aggregate demand under these conditions over a period of three years or so is useful information to new Keynesian economists. It helps them determine what fiscal and monetary policies achieve the best balance among the four macroeconomic policy goals.

AGGREGATE SUPPLY SHOCK

Any event that directly affects firms' costs of production or the quantity that they can supply to the market.

AGGREGATE SUPPLY SHOCKS The new Keynesian theory allows for **aggregate supply shocks** once the assumption of constant wages and prices is dropped.

Recall that an adverse supply shock is any event that increases production costs or reduces output directly. Examples are an increase in the price of crude oil engineered by OPEC and a widespread drought that destroys crops. An adverse supply shock shifts AS_{SR} up and to the left. It may also shift AS_{LR} to the left if it is a lasting event that reduces the nation's production possibilities. A permanent increase in oil prices would affect AS_{LR}; a one-year drought would not. Figure 37.8(a) illustrates the effects of an adverse supply shock. It assumes that the supply shock is lasting and has long-run effects, to be as general as possible.[3]

The economy is initially in equilibrium on the frontier where AD^0, AS^0_{SR}, and AS^0_{LR} intersect. The overall price level is P_0, and the output is Q_0, the frontier output. A lasting adverse supply shock shifts AS_{SR} from AS^0_{SR} to AS^1_{SR}, and AS_{LR} from AS^0_{LR} to AS^1_{LR}. The price level rises to P_1, and the output falls to Q_1 in the short run.

The economy is in overall excess supply in the short run relative to the new long-run supply curve, AS^1_{LR}. Therefore, the price level falls to P_2, restoring equilibrium on the new frontier at output Q_2 in the long run. The economy

3. We are assuming that AS_{SR} shifts more than AS_{LR} because producers are better able to adjust to a supply shock as time passes.

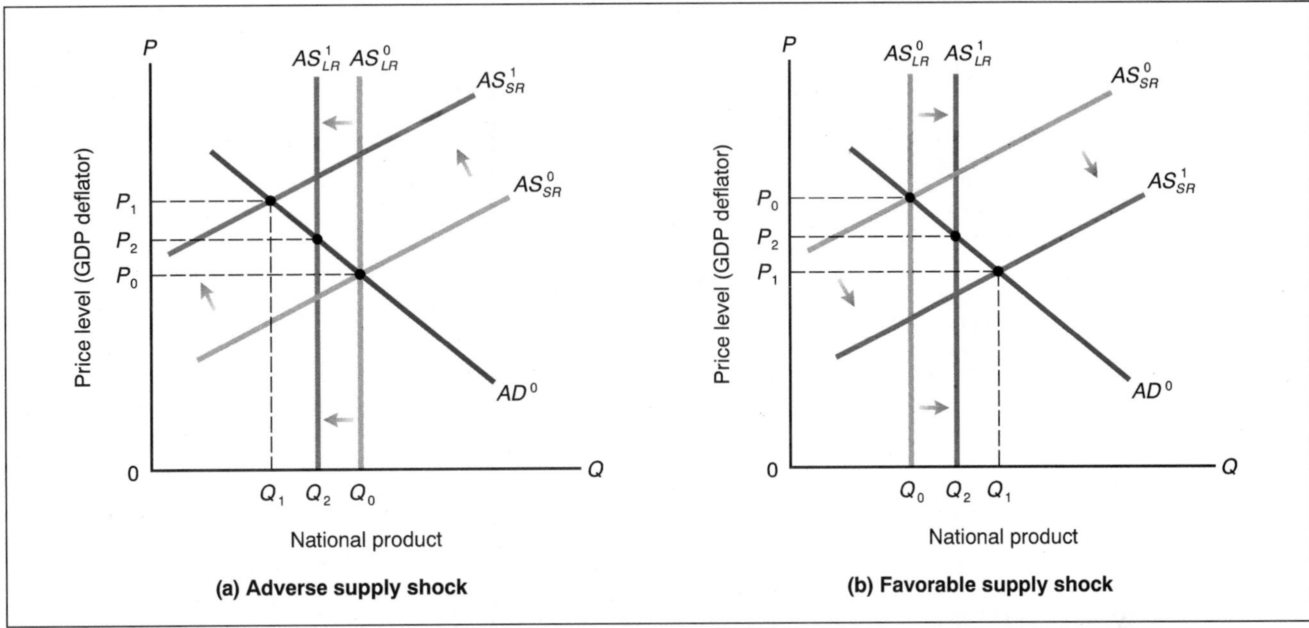

FIGURE 37.8

Aggregate Supply Shocks

The figure shows how the economy responds in a business-cycle pattern to an aggregate supply shock. Figure 37.8(a) pictures an adverse aggregate supply shock and Figure 37.8(b) pictures a favorable aggregate supply shock. The economy is initially in its long-run equilibrium (Q_0,P_0) on the production possibilities frontier in both graphs, at the intersection of AD^0, AS^0_{LR}, and AS^0_{SR}. In Figure 37.8(a), the adverse supply shock shifts both AS_{LR} and AS_{SR} to the left, from AS^0_{LR} to AS^1_{LR}, and from AS^0_{SR} to AS^1_{SR}, respectively. The new short-run equilibrium is (Q_1,P_1), at the intersection of AD^0 and AS^1_{SR}. With the economy now below its frontier and more markets in excess supply, prices and wages drop and reduce firms' costs of production. AS_{SR} shifts back down and to the right. The economy eventually returns to a long-run equilibrium (Q_2,P_2) on its new frontier, at the intersection of AD^0 and AS^1_{LR}. Output at first decreases from Q_0 to Q_1 and then increases from Q_1 to Q_2 in a business-cycle pattern. In Figure 37.8(b), the favorable supply shock shifts AS_{LR} and AS_{SR} to the right, to AS^1_{LR} and AS^1_{SR}. The new short-run equilibrium is (Q_1, P_1) at the intersection of AD^0 and AS^1_{SR}. Wages and prices rise and AS_{SR} shifts back to the left. The long-run equilibrium is (Q_2, P_2) at the intersection of AD^0 and AS^1_{LR}. Output increases from Q_0 to Q_1, and then decreases from Q_1 to Q_2, in a business-cycle pattern.

would return to a long-run equilibrium at (Q_0, P_0) if the adverse supply shock were temporary and only affected AS_{SR}.

A favorable supply shock is any event that decreases production costs or increases output directly. Examples are a cost-reducing technological change such as the ongoing improvements in computer technology and particularly favorable weather that increases crop yields. A favorable supply shock shifts AS_{SR} down and to the right. As with an adverse supply shock, it may also shift AS_{LR} to the right if it is a lasting event that increases the nation's production possibilities. Cost-reducing technological changes shift AS_{LR}; favorable weather for one year does not. Figure 37.8(b) illustrates the effects of a favorable supply shock. It also assumes that the supply shock is lasting and has long-run effects, to be as general as possible.

The overall price level is initially P_0, and the output is Q_0, the frontier output, as in Figure 37.8(a). A lasting favorable supply shock shifts AS_{SR} from AS^0_{SR} to AS^1_{SR}, and AS_{LR} from AS^0_{LR} to AS^1_{LR}. The price level falls to P_1, and output rises to Q_1 in the short run.

ELABORATION: New classical economists would argue that the business cycle pattern as the economy adjusts to its frontier is the only important internal mechanism within the economy that contributes to the ebbs and flows of economic activity over time. Even so, they see the business cycle as resulting primarily from an endless series of outside aggregate demand and aggregate supply shocks, mostly the latter.

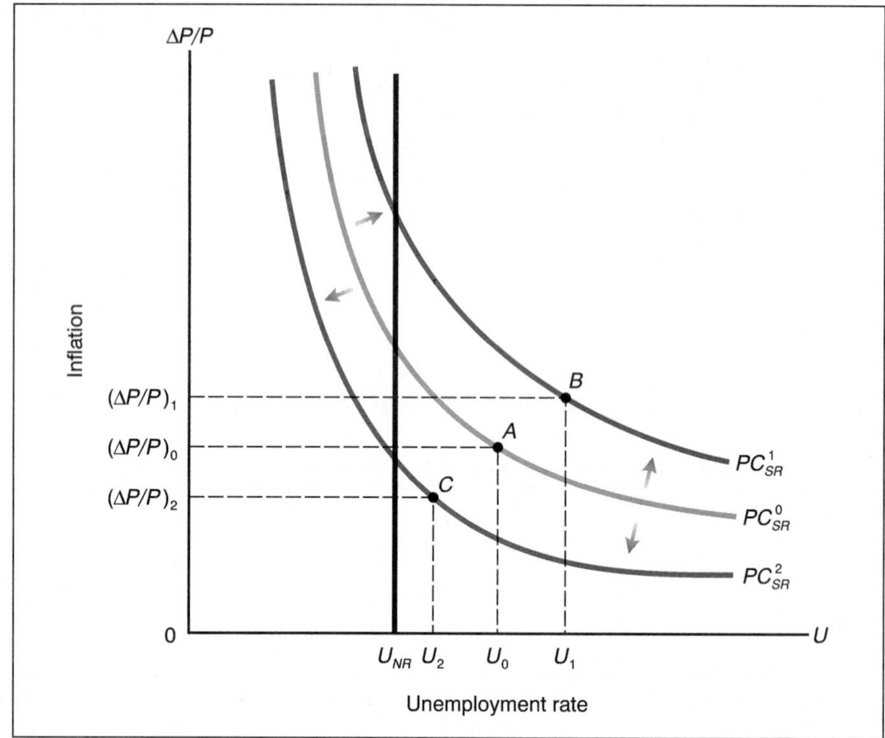

FIGURE 37.9

Aggregate Supply Shocks and the Short-Run Phillips Curve

The economy is initially in equilibrium at point A on the short-run Phillips Curve PC^0_{SR}, with an unemployment rate of U_0 and a rate of inflation of $(\Delta P/P)_0$. Point A is below the production possibilities frontier represented by the natural rate of unemployment, U_{NR}. An adverse supply shock shifts the short-run Phillips Curve up and to the right from PC^0_{SR} to PC^1_{SR}, and the economy moves to point B on PC^1_{SR}. The adverse supply shock causes stagflation, as unemployment increases from U_0 to U_1 and inflation increases from $(\Delta P/P)_0$ to $(\Delta P/P)_1$. A favorable supply shock shifts the short-run Phillips Curve down and to the left from PC^0_{SR} to PC^2_{SR}, and the economy moves to point C on PC^2_{SR}. The favorable supply shock brings the double blessing of lower unemployment and lower inflation. Unemployment decreases from U_0 to U_2 and inflation decreases from $(\Delta P/P)_0$ to $(\Delta P/P)_2$.

The economy is in overall excess demand in the short run relative to the new long-run supply curve, AS^1_{LR}. Therefore, the price level rises to P_2, restoring equilibrium on the new frontier at output Q_2 in the long run. The economy would return to a long-run equilibrium at (Q_0, P_0) if the favorable supply shock were temporary and only affected AS_{SR}.

Notice that adverse supply shocks such as an increase in oil prices are a double whammy for the economy. They both increase prices and reduce output. Conversely, favorable supply shocks such as cost-reducing technological changes are a double blessing. They both reduce prices and increase output. Also, output responds in a business-cycle pattern to aggregate supply shocks, just as it does to changes in aggregate demand.

Aggregate supply shocks also affect the short-run Phillips curve described in Chapter 36. Refer to Figure 37.9. The rate of inflation is on the vertical axis, and the unemployment rate is on the horizontal axis. The initial short-run Phillips Curve before the aggregate supply shock is PC^0_{SR}. Assume that the economy is at point A, with an inflation rate of $(\Delta P/P)_0$ and an unemployment rate of U_0.

An adverse aggregate supply shock such as an OPEC-engineered increase in oil prices shifts the short-run Phillips Curve up and to the right, from PC^0_{SR} to PC^1_{SR} in the figure. The Phillips Curve representation illustrates the double whammy of an adverse supply shock directly in terms of the macroeconomic policy goals of inflation and unemployment. An adverse supply shock tends to increase both inflation and unemployment in the short run. For example, suppose that the economy moves from point A on PC^0_{SR} to point B on PC^1_{SR}. The adverse supply shock has increased the inflation rate from $(\Delta P/P)_0$

to $(\Delta P/P)_1$, and it has also increased the unemployment rate from U_0 to U_1. MIT's Paul Samuelson dubbed the situation of increasing inflation and increasing unemployment a situation of **stagflation.**

STAGFLATION
A period of increasing inflation, falling output, and rising unemployment that follows an adverse aggregate supply shock.

A favorable aggregate supply shock such as the cost-reducing technological change in computers shifts the short-run Phillips Curve down and to the left, from PC^0_{SR} to PC^2_{SR} in the figure. A favorable supply shock has the happy effect of decreasing both inflation and unemployment in the short run. For example, suppose that the economy moves from point A to point C on PC^2_{SR}. The favorable supply shock has decreased the inflation rate from $(\Delta P/P)_0$ to $(\Delta P/P)_2$, and it has also decreased the unemployment rate from U_0 to U_2. No one has yet coined a phrase for this double blessing.

We can see why the OPEC-induced oil price increases in the 1970s were such a curse and why the collapse of oil prices in the 1980s was such a blessing for all oil-importing countries. Oil prices are a very important aggregate supply shock, undoubtedly the single most important aggregate supply shock of the past 20 years.

AS_{SR}: THE NEW CLASSICAL PERSPECTIVE The new classical economists believe that the new Keynesian analysis of the U.S. economy is dead wrong. They especially disagree with the Keynesian analysis of how the economy responds to changes in aggregate demand.

When they look at the labor markets, they see the high turnover of the American workforce, the substantial amount of wage flexibility in many markets, and the frequent spells of short-term unemployment that they interpret as increases and decreases in search or frictional unemployment.

When they look at the product markets, they point to the research of industrial organization economists, which concludes that as many as 70 percent of all products in the United States are marketed under reasonably competitive conditions. The new classical economists are convinced that the macro economy should be viewed as if it operates according to the Laws of Supply and Demand at all times. They know that this is not entirely accurate (just as the new Keynesians know that their model is not entirely accurate). But the new classical economists believe that it is the most reasonable representation of the macro economy.

REAL BUSINESS CYCLE THEORY The prevailing view of the economy among new classical economists is the real business cycle model, which we described in Chapter 32. To review briefly, the theory is securely anchored to the long-run aggregate supply curve. It sees the economy as competitive enough that it is *always* operating on or very near its production possibilities frontier, that is, on or very near AS_{LR}. The ebbs and flows of the economy represent movements in the frontier itself for the most part, as the frontier is buffeted by increases and decreases in productivity. The erratic behavior of productivity shifts AS_{LR} to the right and left and causes the business-cycle-like changes in output and employment that we observe. In other words, the economy is driven by the supply side, not the demand side as in new Keynesian theory.

In addition, real business cycle theory assumes that households adopt the most extreme long-run point of view in solving their economic problems. They behave according to the Life-Cycle Hypothesis and plan both their consumption and their labor supply decisions over their entire lifetimes.

Any notion of a short-run aggregate supply curve different from AS_{LR} is essentially unimportant in a world of competitive markets, life-cycle consumers, and production that is continually buffeted by increases and decreases in productivity. Only shifts in AS_{LR} can significantly affect the real side of the economy.

Real business cycle theorists concede that a change in aggregate demand can have real effects, even over the short run, *but only if it simultaneously causes* AS_{LR} *to shift as well, so that the nation's production possibilities change.* Otherwise, a change in aggregate demand can affect only prices. Moreover, as we saw in Chapter 32, changes in output over the short run require changes in people's decisions to supply more or less labor. Producers can significantly increase production in the short run only if people are willing to supply more labor to them. Conversely, producers must cut production if the supply of labor falls. Also, what looks like a short-run aggregate supply response is really a shift in the long-run aggregate supply curve. More labor supply expands the nation's production possibilities frontier by giving producers more resources; it shifts AS_{LR} to the right. Less labor supply contracts the nation's production possibilities frontier by giving producers fewer resources; it shifts AS_{LR} to the left. Finally, voluntary employment and output move hand in hand according to the real business cycle theory. The changes in the rate of unemployment over time measured by the Bureau of Labor Statistics surveys are virtually all changes in frictional or voluntary search unemployment. The natural rate of unemployment ebbs and flows along with the production possibilities frontier.

The requirement that a change in aggregate demand must shift AS_{LR} to affect output means that the source of the change in aggregate demand matters. An increase or a decrease in one of the components of aggregate demand can have real effects. This includes expansionary and contractionary fiscal policies. A change in the money supply cannot have real effects. Let's compare the two cases to see why they have different effects.

A direct change in aggregate demand. The link between changes in aggregate demand and the nation's production possibilities runs through interest rates, according to real business cycle theory. Consider an increase in aggregate demand. We saw in Chapter 36 that an increase in any component of aggregate demand increases interest rates as some people (or firms, or the government) have to sell financial assets or borrow to finance the increase in expenditures. Here is yet another way to think about why interest rates rise in the competitive new classical environment. An increase in any one component of aggregate demand must crowd out other components of aggregate demand, since the economy is already on its production possibilities frontier and there are only so many resources to go around. Therefore, interest rates have to rise to crowd out consumer durables, or investment, or net exports.

The crowding out is not complete, however. The increase in interest rates increases the supply of labor, which expands the frontier and allows total output to increase to meet some of the increase in demand. The link between interest rates and labor supply arises because of the assumption that people plan their labor supply decisions over their lifetimes. They are continually reassessing how much they want to work in total throughout their lives and when they want to work. The increase in interest rates gives them an incentive to change the timing of their employment toward the present. The reason is that any income earned now and saved earns a higher rate of return right away,

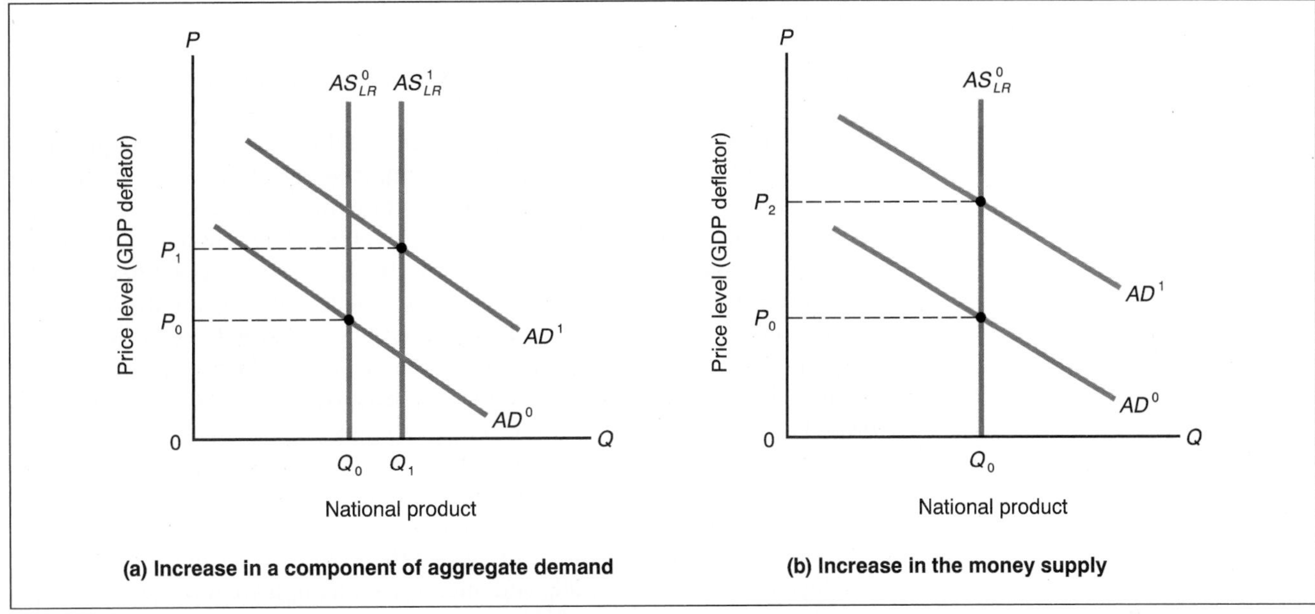

FIGURE 37.10

Changes in Aggregate Demand: New Classical Perspective

The new classical economists concede that an increase in aggregate demand can increase real national product, but only if the increase causes the production possibilities frontier to shift out as well. Figure 37.10(a) shows that an increase in a component of aggregate demand, such as that caused by an expansionary fiscal policy, can increase output. The initial equilibrium is (Q_0,P_0) on the frontier, at the intersection of AD^0 and AS^0_{LR}. An expansionary fiscal policy increases aggregate demand from AD^0 to AD^1 and causes interest rates to rise. The increase in interest rates induces people to supply more labor, which shifts out the production possibilities frontier from Q_0 to Q_1 and allows firms to increase production. The new equilibrium is (Q_1,P_1) on the new frontier, at the intersection of AD^1 and AS^1_{LR}. In contrast, Figure 37.10(b) shows that an increase in the money supply cannot increase output. Aggregate demand increases from AD^0 to AD^1 following the increase in the money supply, which places markets in excess demand and causes prices to rise. The increase in prices increases the quantity of money demanded for transactions purposes in direct proportion to the price increase, so the households and businesses just hold the new money. Output remains at Q_0, and the new equilibrium is (Q_0,P_2), at the intersection of AD^1 and AS^0_{LR}. An increase in the money supply only increases the overall price level.

so that people choose to work more now and less in the future in order to take advantage of the higher interest rates. The increase in labor supply in turn allows firms to expand production. Therefore, the increase in aggregate demand increases both employment and output as the production possibilities frontier expands.

Figure 37.10(a) shows the effects of the increase in aggregate demand in terms of the aggregate demand and the aggregate supply curves. The initial equilibrium before the increase in aggregate demand is (Q_0, P_0), at the intersection of AD^0 and AS^0_{LR}. The increase in aggregate demand shifts the aggregate demand curve up and to the right, from AD^0 to AD^1. Simultaneously, the rise in interest rates increases the supply of labor and shifts the long-run aggregate supply curve to the right, from AS^0_{LR} to AS^1_{LR}. The new equilibrium is at (Q_1, P_1), at the intersection of AD^1 and AS_{LR} along the new expanded production possibilities frontier.

To summarize:

$$\text{Aggregate demand} \uparrow \rightarrow R \uparrow \rightarrow \text{labor supply} \uparrow \rightarrow \text{employment, output} \uparrow$$

Notice that the increase in aggregate demand does not increase employment and output by reducing involuntary unemployment, as it does in the new Keynesian theory. The increase in labor supply in response to the increase in interest rates is entirely voluntary. Unemployment as measured by the Bureau of Labor Statistics may decrease, but new classical economists assume that this is almost entirely a reduction in voluntary search unemployment. People see the rise in interest rates and reduce the time spent searching for jobs, since they are more willing to accept employment. The reduction in search time reduces the measured unemployment rate because people are less likely to be picked up as unemployed by the BLS surveyors.

A decrease in aggregate demand has exactly the opposite effect on labor supply. The decrease in demand lowers interest rates as people buy financial assets and reduce their borrowings. The lower interest rates induce people to postpone employment to the future, since the returns to saving are lower. Both employment and output fall, and measured unemployment rises as people spend more time searching for jobs.

To summarize:

$$\text{Aggregate demand} \downarrow \rightarrow R \downarrow \rightarrow \text{labor supply} \downarrow \rightarrow \text{employment, output} \downarrow$$

The main problem with this theory is that the connection between interest rates and labor supply is very weak. Our intuition tells us that interest rates do not have much of an impact on how much we decide to work, and empirical research bears this out. Labor economists have not been able to find any significant relationship between interest rates and labor supply.

New classical economists are not particularly troubled by this research, however, because they do not believe that changes in aggregate demand are an important cause of changes in output and employment in any event. They believe output and employment are primarily driven by changes in productivity that directly shift the long-run aggregate supply curve. The aggregate quantity demanded follows shifts in AS_{LR}, and not the other way around for the most part.

A change in the money supply. A change in the money supply does not affect aggregate supply at all. It changes only prices. To see why, suppose that the Fed doubles the money supply. The new money shifts up the aggregate demand curve and creates excess demand in all markets. The excess demands increase prices, but this is all that happens.

The reason why has to do with the demand for money. Recall from Chapter 35 that the transactions demand for money is directly proportional to the overall price level because Federal Reserve Notes and the checking account deposits are denominated in nominal terms. Therefore, the demand for money increases in step with the prices as they rise. Eventually all prices double, which doubles the demand for money to match the doubling of the money supply. At this point the economy is once again in equilibrium.

The expansionary monetary policy is ineffective because every household and every firm simply accepts the new money into their balance sheets to cover the doubling of the prices. No one attempts to buy other financial or real assets with the new money, as they would in a new Keynesian environment of sticky prices. Consequently, the increase in the money supply has no effect whatsoever on the real side of the economy. Output, employment, interest rates, consumption, and all other real economic variables remain unchanged.

Figure 37.10(b) shows the effect of a doubling of the money supply in terms of the aggregate demand and the aggregate supply curves. The initial equilibrium before the increase in the money supply is (Q_0, P_0), at the intersection of AD^0 and AS^0_{LR}, just as in Figure 37.10(a). The new money shifts the aggregate demand curve up from AD^0 to AD^1. The new money does not shift the long-run aggregate supply curve. Therefore, the new equilibrium is (Q_0, P_2), at the intersection of AD^1 and AS_{LR}. Output remains the same, and the overall price level doubles from P_0 to P_2.

Similarly, a decrease in the money supply only lowers prices. The decrease in the money supply shifts aggregate demand down and creates excess supplies throughout the economy. The excess supplies lower prices, and the demand for money falls in step with the fall in prices. Eventually the decrease in the demand for money matches the decrease in the money supply, and equilibrium is restored without any effect on the real side of the economy.

The new Keynesian economists see this analysis and ask: How can one ignore the strong correlation between the money supply and output? Output increases when the money supply increases, and output decreases when the money supply decreases. In their view changes in the money supply clearly cause changes in output.

The new classical economists answer: True, output and the money supply move together over time. But the new Keynesians reverse cause and effect. Most of the money supply consists of checking account deposits, which are created by banks making loans. When a favorable productivity shock causes output to expand, businesses and consumers come to the banks seeking loans. More bank loans are issued, and checking account deposits expand. When an unfavorable productivity shock causes output to contract, businesses and consumers are less interested in borrowing. Fewer bank loans are issued, and checking account deposits contract. Output drives the money supply, not the other way around.

In conclusion, real business cycle theory rejects virtually all of the new Keynesian analysis of Chapters 29 through 36. Changes in aggregate demand do not have a significant effect on real national income and output precisely because economies never operate far from their production possibilities frontier. The spending multiplier is close to zero, even in the short run. More to the point, fiscal and monetary policies have *no* role to play in keeping the economy on its frontier. The competitive market economy does this job, and does it well. Fiscal and monetary policies cannot improve the performance of the economy in the short run.

Fiscal and monetary policies can affect output only to the extent that they can change the quantity and the quality of resources or induce firms to develop and adopt new technologies. These are the only things that can affect the real side of the economy because they alone determine the production possibilities frontier. They are also long-run, not short-run, phenomena.

For example, an expansionary fiscal policy that increases interest rates may increase output in the short run by increasing the supply of labor. But new classical economists are more likely to argue for a mix of fiscal and monetary policies that keep interest rates low in order to stimulate investment and long-run economic growth. Long-run growth is far more important than is any short-run increase in output that the higher interest rates may induce. The government must also keep inflation under control, another long-run policy problem that, as we will see in Chapter 38, is accomplished by keeping the growth of the money supply under control.

SUMMARY

Chapter 37 explored the role of prices in bringing the macro economy to equilibrium, using the aggregate supply–aggregate demand (AS–AD) model. The chapter also compared and contrasted the new Keynesian and the new classical theories on how the economy operates, using the AS–AD model as the basis for comparison.

The first section of the chapter developed the aggregate demand curve.

1. The aggregate demand curve, *AD*, shows the aggregate quantity demanded by all four sectors of the economy at each overall price level.
2. *AD* is downward sloping primarily because of the effect of prices on the demand for money. An increase in the overall price level increases the transactions demand for money, which in turn increases interest rates as people sell financial assets to increase their money holdings. The higher interest rates reduce the demand for consumer durables, investment, and net exports, which reduces aggregate demand. The opposite analysis applies to a decrease in the overall price level.

The second section of the chapter developed the aggregate supply curve.

3. The aggregate supply curve shows the aggregate quantity of output supplied by all producers at each overall price level.
4. New Keynesian and new classical economists agree that the economy is competitive enough, and wages and prices flexible enough, over the long run that the long-run aggregate supply curve, AS_{LR}, is vertical at the output corresponding to the production possibilities frontier. Competitive factor markets guarantee that the economy operates on its frontier. Real national product (national income) is determined entirely by the supply side of the economy in the long run. Aggregate demand serves only to set the overall level of prices; prices adjust so that the aggregate quantity demanded equals the frontier output.

The disagreement between the two schools centers on the nature of aggregate supply in the short run.

The New Keynesian View of Aggregate Supply in the Short Run:

5. The short-run aggregate supply curve, AS_{SR}, is distinctly different from AS_{LR}. AS_{SR} is relatively flat when the economy is far below the frontier, becomes steeper as the economy approaches the frontier, and becomes quite steep as the economy moves beyond its sustainable frontier. Therefore, changes in aggregate demand change real national product (national income) in the short run, and the short run can persist for quite a long time.

6. AS_{SR} is relatively flat because of a combination of sticky real wages and sticky nominal prices. Sticky real wages result from labor market institutions such as internal labor markets and labor unions, which lead to layoffs and rehires in response to the ebbs and flows of the economy, rather than leading to a flexible wage policy that maintains full employment at all times. Sticky nominal prices result from a combination of the menu costs of changing prices and the size and the complexity of the final goods manufacturers. Firms care about the relationship of their demands to their costs, and they do not always move in line with aggregate demand. The result is that the final goods manufacturers are often slow to adjust their prices.
7. The economy eventually adjusts to the production possibilities frontier in the long run. A decrease in aggregate demand that leads to a short-run equilibrium output below the frontier creates excess supplies in markets generally, which lower prices and costs of production. AS_{SR} shifts down and to the right until equilibrium is restored on the frontier. Conversely, an increase in aggregate demand that leads to a short-run equilibrium output above the frontier creates excess demands in markets generally, which raise prices and costs of production. AS_{SR} shifts up and to the left until equilibrium is restored on the frontier. In either case, output moves in a business-cycle pattern.
8. The adjustment to the long-run equilibrium is so slow when there are unemployed resources that the government should not wait for it to happen. Instead, the government should use fiscal and monetary policies to keep the economy operating on or near its production possibilities frontier.
9. The change in prices that follows a change in aggregate demand reduces the value of the spending multiplier and contributes to the hump-shaped pattern of the multiplier process.
10. An adverse aggregate supply shock such as an increase in oil prices increases firms' costs of production, which increases prices and reduces output in the short run. It produces a stagflation—both unemployment and inflation increase. A favorable aggregate supply shock such as cost-reducing technological change has the opposite effects.

The New Classical View of Aggregate Supply in the Short Run:

11. The economy is highly competitive, wages and prices are flexible, and the economy always operates on or near its production possibilities frontier. There is no essential difference between the short-run and the long-run aggregate supply curves, at least none that has any relevance to policy in the short run. The government cannot improve the performance of the economy in the short run. Real business cycle theory is now the prevailing theory of the new classical school. It says that real national product (national income) is determined by the supply side of the economy and can change only if the production possibilities frontier itself (AS_{LR}) shifts in or out.
12. Changes in aggregate demand can change output, but only if they affect the nation's production possibilities. This means that the source of the change in aggregate demand matters.
13. An increase in any component of aggregate demand does affect production possibilities because it causes interest rates to change, and the change in

interest rates changes the supply of labor. For example, an increase in aggregate demand increases interest rates, which causes people to supply more labor today. The increased supply of labor lowers real wages, firms hire more workers, and output expands. A decrease in any component of aggregate demand has the opposite effects. The problem with this theory is that economists cannot find any evidence that interest rates influence the supply of labor. This is not troublesome to new classical economists, however, because they believe that most changes in output are due to changes in productivity, and not to changes in aggregate demand.

14. A change in the money supply changes aggregate demand, but it has no effect on the real side of the economy. For example, a doubling of the money supply simply doubles prices. People's demand for money doubles along with the prices, so that they just hold on to the new money and nothing else happens.

KEY TERMS

aggregate demand curve
aggregate demand schedule
aggregate supply curve
aggregate supply schedule
aggregate supply shock
menu costs
stagflation

QUESTIONS

1. a. Draw a reasonable aggregate demand curve with the overall price level and national product on the axes, and explain why you drew it as you did.
   b. How does an aggregate demand curve for the economy as a whole differ from an aggregate demand curve for an individual market?
2. a. Draw a reasonable aggregate supply curve with the overall price level and national product on the axes.
   b. Is the curve that you drew a short-run aggregate supply curve or a long-run aggregate supply curve, or could it be both the short-run and the long-run aggregate supply curves?
   c. How does an aggregate supply curve for the economy as a whole differ from an aggregate supply curve for an individual market?
3. Consider the following aggregate demand schedule.

GDP Deflator	Aggregate Demand
105	4,900
100	5,000
95	5,200

   a. Draw the aggregate demand curve for this aggregate demand schedule.
   b. Next, represent this aggregate demand schedule using the ADE–45° graph with national income on the horizontal axis and aggregate desired expenditures on the vertical axis.
   c. Comment on the relationship between the aggregate demand curves in the two graphs.
4. Compare and contrast the principal assumptions of the new Keynesian and the new classical theories of macroeconomics, as well as their theories about how the macro economy operates. Be sure to highlight areas of agreement between the two schools as well as areas of disagreement.
5. Draw reasonable-looking aggregate supply curves for the short run and the long run, using new Keynesian assumptions. Explain why you drew them as you did. How would each curve change, if at all, under new classical assumptions?
6. Some aggregate supply shocks shift both the long-run and the short-run aggregate supply curves, and some aggregate supply shocks shift only the short-run aggregate supply curve. Give one example of each type of aggregate supply shock, and explain why they have different effects on the long-run aggregate supply curve.
7. Consider the aggregate supply–aggregate demand framework under new Keynesian assumptions. Assume the economy is in long-run equilibrium where output is 5,000 and the price level is 100.
   a. If the government undertakes a combination of contractionary fiscal and monetary policies, what effects will these policies have on output and prices?
   b. How would your answer change as the economy moves from the short run to the long run following the policy changes?
8. What is meant by nominal price stickiness? What are the causes of nominal price stickiness, according to the new Keynesian school?

9. a. Give some examples of adverse aggregate supply shocks.
   b. Demonstrate graphically the effects of these shocks, using the AS–AD framework under new Keynesian assumptions. Consider both the short-run and the long-run reactions to the shocks.
   c. Give some examples of favorable aggregate supply shocks, and repeat the analysis in part (b) for the favorable shocks.
10. a. What is stagflation?
    b. What type of shocks to the economy might cause a period of stagflation?
    c. Depict stagflation graphically, using the AS–AD framework and also using the Phillips Curve framework.
    d. What policies might new Keynesian economists recommend in response to the problem of stagflation?
    e. What policies might new classical economists recommend in response to the problem of stagflation?
11. Why does the economy respond to aggregate demand or supply shocks in the pattern of a business cycle under new Keynesian assumptions about the macro economy?

CHAPTER

38

Controlling Inflation and Other Policy Issues

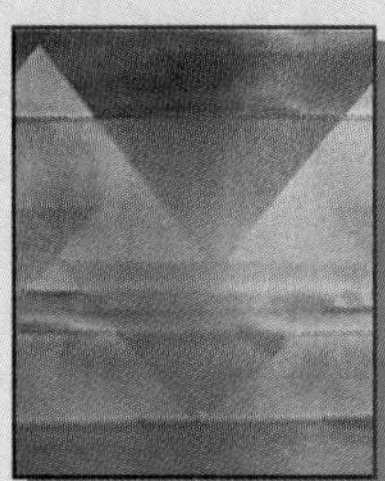

LEARNING OBJECTIVES

CONCEPTS TO LEARN

Rational expectations
Long-run Phillips Curve
Supply-side economics
Policy credibility

CONCEPTS TO RECALL

Laws of Supply and Demand [5, 6, 7]
Inflation [26]
Fisher equation [26]
New Keynesian economics [28, 37]
New classical economics [28, 37]
Aggregate demand and aggregate supply [28, 37]
Aggregate supply shock [28, 37]
The equation of exchange [33]
Short-run Phillips Curve [36]

There is a standing joke among economists about their worst professional nightmare. It is being cornered at a party and asked a macroeconomic policy question: What should the government do about ______________? Everything hangs on the blank at the end of the question.

The situation becomes especially uncomfortable if the blank is a short-run issue such as reducing unemployment. The economist stammers a bit to buy some time as he begins thinking about the rift between the new Keynesian and the new classical schools over the short run. His thoughts turn down the new Keynesian path for awhile, and he ponders the various policy options that we discussed in Chapter 36. Coming up with policies to reduce unemployment is easy enough, but he knows that before he blurts out an answer, he has to worry about how each policy affects the other macroeconomic policy goals. His thoughts then turn down the new classical path, and he is tempted to answer: "Why nothing, of course. The government's fiscal and monetary policies cannot hope to improve the performance of the economy over the next year." The poor economist becomes completely tongue-tied as the guests drift away.

The nightmare is avoided if the blank at the end of the question refers to a long-run policy issue such as increasing investment and growth, or reducing the burden of the ever-increasing public debt, or keeping inflation under control. New Keynesian and new classical economists are pretty much in agreement on these issues. The economist breathes a heavy sigh of relief and quickly offers an opinion with some degree of confidence.

Chapter 37 emphasized the sharp disagreement between the new Keynesian and the new classical economists about the operation of the macro economy in the short run. They do not disagree about everything, however. Chapter 38 concludes the macroeconomic section of the text with an analysis of three policy issues that the two schools agree on. The first is the nature of inflation and how to keep it under control. The second is whether the government has any effective leverage over the supply side of the economy in the short run. The third is the need for consistent and believable government policies.

THE NATURE OF INFLATION AND HOW TO CONTROL IT

Few economic variables are watched as closely as is inflation in the United States. Chapter 26 described how the Department of Commerce samples nearly 100,000 prices of goods and services every month and uses these price data to update broad-based price indexes such as the consumer price index (CPI) and the gross domestic product (GDP) deflator. The department's monthly announcements of the rate of inflation as measured by these indexes receive a great deal of attention in the news media.

What determines the rate of inflation in the United States? Economic research on inflation has focused mostly on the average rate of inflation during the course of a year rather than on the monthly inflation rates reported by the Department of Commerce. This research has shown that the annual rate of inflation depends primarily on four factors: the growth in nominal aggregate demand, the state of the economy relative to the production possibilities frontier, the presence of aggregate supply shocks, and people's expectations about the future rate of inflation.

A word on perspective is in order before analyzing how each of these factors affects the rate of inflation: The distinction between the short run and the long run is crucial to the analysis of inflation. Tracking the rate of inflation month by month as the Department of Commerce does is a clear case of statistical overkill. Even a year is too short a time horizon to get an accurate picture of an underlying inflationary process.

Remember, inflation refers to *sustained* increases in prices generally, with emphasis on the word *sustained.* An inflationary process is inherently a long-run phenomenon, a pattern of general price increases that is projected to continue year after year after year. An increase in prices of 5 percent on an annual basis that lasts for a few months, or even a year or two, and then stops altogether hardly constitutes an inflationary process, at least not one that has any relevance for government policy.

The important question is this: What can *sustain* an inflationary process more or less indefinitely? The four factors listed above all push the rate of inflation up and down from one year to the next or even from one month to the next. As such, they all have some influence on the underlying inflationary process because the short-run pattern of inflation can feed into inflation over the longer run. But we will see that only two of the factors—the growth in nominal aggregate demand and people's expectations of inflation—can truly sustain an inflation over the long run. These two factors are the twin engines that drive an inflationary process and are therefore the keys to the problem of keeping inflation under control.

Chapters 36 and 37 described how the first three factors affect the rate of inflation over the short run. Let's briefly review what we have said about these factors and consider whether their effects on inflation over the short run carry over the long run. The review in hand, we can then add the fourth factor—people's expectations of inflation—and move from the short run to the long run, where the analysis of inflation properly belongs.

Our analysis of the first three factors is based on the new Keynesian view of the short run. We will briefly indicate in each instance how the new classical real business cycle theory would modify the analysis. The differences between the two schools are unimportant, however, because they reach essentially the same conclusions about the nature of inflation in the short run.

The Growth of Nominal Aggregate Demand

The final section of Chapter 36 described how a 10 percent increase in nominal aggregate demand affects the rate of inflation; the growth in real national product, or output; and unemployment in the short run. The short-run Phillips curve, pictured in Figure 36.5, shows how the increase in aggregate demand is split between an increase in inflation and a decrease in unemployment.

Our analysis at the time did not consider whether the 10 percent growth in aggregate demand was a one-shot increase that would last for only a year or a steady rate of growth that would continue indefinitely. The distinction between a one-shot increase and continuous steady growth in aggregate demand is crucial to the analysis of inflation, however. A one-shot increase in aggregate

FIGURE 38.1

A One-time Increase in the Money Supply and Inflation

The figure shows that a one time increase in the money supply causes a higher price level but not a sustained inflation. The initial long-run equilibrium before the increase in the money supply is (Q_0,P_0) on the production possibilities frontier, at the intersection of AD^0, AS_{LR}, and AS^0_{SR}. There is no inflation. The increase in the money supply increases aggregate demand from AD^0 to AD^1 and prices start to rise as the economy moves to the short run equilibrium (Q_1,P_1), at the intersection of AD^1 and AS^0_{SR}. Markets are generally in excess demand at Q_1 so prices and wages rise further, which increases firms' costs of production. AS_{SR} shifts up and to the left until it reaches AS^2_{SR} and removes the excess demand. The new long-run equilibrium is (Q_0,P_2) on the frontier, at the intersection of AD^1, AS_{LR}, and AS^2_{SR}. Prices stop rising once they reach P_2. The increase in the money supply raises the overall price level from P_0 to P_2 but does not cause a sustained inflation.

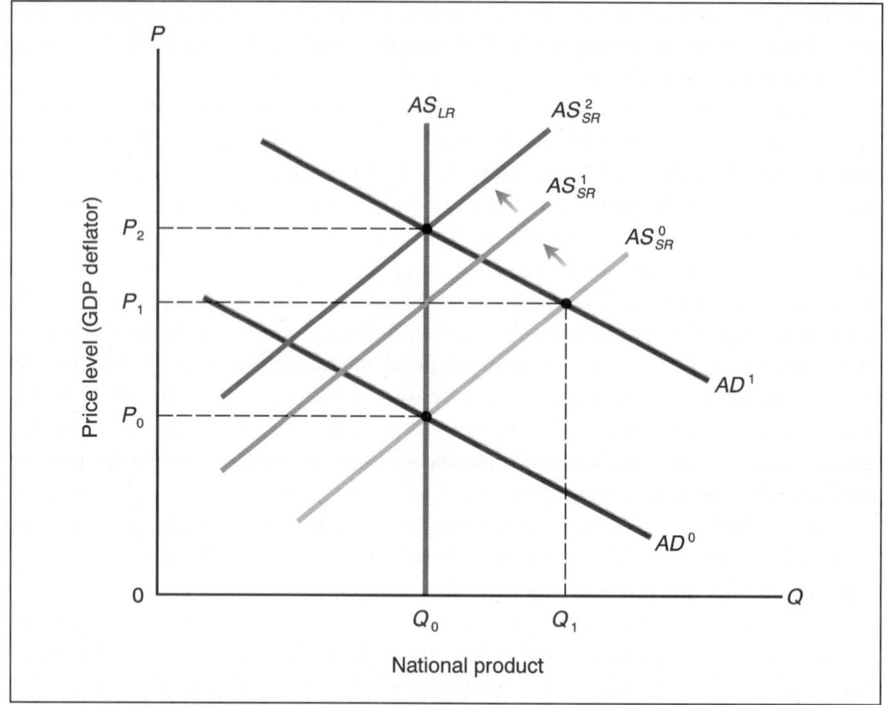

demand cannot sustain an inflation, whereas a steady growth in aggregate demand is absolutely essential for sustaining an inflation. The distinction between the two is best seen with reference to the aggregate supply–aggregate demand (AS–AD) framework pictured in Figure 38.1.

Suppose that the economy is initially in long-run equilibrium on its production possibilities frontier at the intersection of AD^0, AS_{LR}, and AS^0_{SR}. The frontier output is Q_0, and the overall price level as measured by the GDP deflator is P_0. The rate of inflation is zero. Suddenly the Fed increases the money supply and keeps it at its new higher *level* indefinitely. The result is a one-time increase in aggregate demand from AD^0 to AD^1.

The one-time increase in aggregate demand produces some fairly dramatic effects for awhile, but it cannot sustain an inflationary process in and of itself. At first, prices and output rise, and unemployment falls, as the economy heads to the temporary short-run equilibrium, (Q_1, P_1), at the intersection of AD^1 and AS^0_{SR}. The Department of Commerce's monthly price data begin to show an inflation developing, since prices are now rising from P_0 to P_1.

The short-run equilibrium cannot maintain itself, however, because the economy is now beyond its sustainable production possibilities frontier. The excess demand in the economy continues to drive up prices of both goods and factors, and the increase in factor prices increases firms' costs of production. The rising production costs act as a series of adverse aggregate supply shocks that shift the short-run aggregate supply curve up and to the left. AS_{SR} shifts from AS^0_{SR} to AS^1_{SR} to AS^2_{SR}, returning the economy to a long-run equilibrium on the frontier. The economy experiences a period of stagflation as the economy returns to the frontier. Prices continue to rise from P_1 to P_2, output falls from Q_1 to Q_0, and unemployment increases.

Notice, though, that all the action ends when the economy returns to the frontier. The inflation stops once the price level rises to P_2, and the unemployment rate returns to the natural rate at the frontier output, Q_0. The one-time increase in aggregate demand has increased the price *level* from P_0 to P_2, but it has not generated a lasting inflation.

The new classical real business cycle analysis of the one-time increase in the money supply reaches the same conclusion. The only difference is that real business cycle theory assumes that the economy moves immediately to the new long-run equilibrium, (Q_0, P_2), without all the short-run drama of the new Keynesian analysis.

Both schools agree that the inflation can continue only if the *growth* in aggregate demand is *maintained*, if there is a 10 percent increase year after year, indefinitely. With aggregate demand growing steadily year by year, the *AD* curve continues to shift up and to the right every year, and the overall price level never settles down to a new higher equilibrium *level*. Instead, the overall price level increases steadily year after year, which is the definition of an inflationary process. We will return to the role of aggregate demand growth in sustaining an inflation later on in the analysis.

The State of the Economy

The state of the economy relative to the production possibilities frontier affects the rate of inflation in the short run because it determines whether markets generally are in excess demand or excess supply throughout the economy. The state of the economy is embodied in the shape of the short-run Phillips Curve. We saw that the Phillips Curve is quite flat when the economy is operating far beneath the production possibilities frontier, with high unemployment and markets generally in excess supply. An increase in nominal aggregate demand under those conditions mostly increases output and decreases unemployment. It causes only a small increase in the rate of inflation. The Phillips Curve becomes steeper as the economy approaches the frontier, and very steep as the economy reaches and exceeds the frontier in the short run. The steepening of the Phillips Curve indicates that a given increase in nominal aggregate demand increases inflation more and more, and reduces unemployment less and less, as the economy approaches and exceeds the frontier. Output becomes ever more difficult to expand near the frontier, since most of the nation's resources are already employed. Under those conditions the increase in nominal aggregate demand translates mostly into an increase in inflation.

The independent, other things equal effect of the state of the economy on inflation should wash out over the long run as the economy moves through the ebbs and flows of the business cycles. At times the economy will be below the frontier, which tends to lower the rate of inflation; at other times the economy will be near or even above the frontier, which tends to increase the rate of inflation. These periods of upward and downward pressure on inflation should essentially cancel one another out over the long run. The one exception, as we will see below, is if the government tries to keep the economy permanently above or below the frontier. But this is really a decision about how fast the government will let nominal aggregate demand grow. The growth in nominal aggregate demand determines the state of the economy in the long run, and not the other way around.

Real business cycle theory would deny that the state of the economy has any relevance to inflation because the economy is always operating on or near its production possibilities frontier. New classical economists believe that the economic research on inflation has "discovered" this effect only because it has mismeasured the position of the frontier. In any event, both schools agree that the state of the economy is not an essential factor in explaining inflation over the long run.

Aggregate Supply Shocks

Aggregate supply shocks have a pronounced effect on inflation in the short run because they change the costs of production, and firms in the United States are quick to pass cost changes through to price changes. An adverse supply shock, such as the increase in the price of crude oil induced by the organization of Petroleum Exporting Countries (OPEC), quickly leads to higher prices. The quadrupling of the price of crude oil in late 1973 and early 1974 was largely responsible for the jump in inflation from 3.4 percent in 1972 to 8.7 percent in 1973 to 12.3 percent in 1974. Similarly, a favorable supply shock, such as the collapse of OPEC in 1980, leads just as quickly to lower prices. The price of crude oil fell from over $30 a barrel to around $10 a barrel during 1980 and 1981 and was a major contributor to the decrease in inflation from 12.5 percent in 1980 to 8.9 percent in 1981 to 3.8 percent in 1982.[1]

The changes in oil prices in the 1970s and in the early 1980s were one-time events, and the same point applies to a one-time-only aggregate supply shock as to a one-time-only increase in aggregate demand. A one-time-only aggregate supply shock can affect the rate of inflation in the short run, but not in the long run. Figure 38.2 illustrates.

The economy is initially in long-run equilibrium on its production possibilities frontier at the intersection of AD^0, AS_{LR}, and AS^0_{SR}. The frontier output is Q_0, and the overall price level is P_0. There is no inflation. Then a one-time-only adverse aggregate supply shock, such as an increase in oil prices, hits the economy. The supply shock shifts the short-run aggregate supply curves up and to the left, to AS^1_{SR}. The economy experiences stagflation for awhile as prices rise, output falls, and unemployment increases. The stagflation ends, however, when the economy reaches the new short-run equilibrium, (Q_1, P_1), at the intersection of AD^0 and AS^1_{SR}.

The period of stagflation is then followed by a period of deflation and increasing output as the economy adjusts back to its long-run equilibrium on the frontier. The reason why is that markets throughout the economy are generally in excess supply at the short-run equilibrium, (Q_1, P_1). The excess supply puts downward pressure on prices and costs, and the short-run aggregate supply curve begins to shift back down and to the right. It keeps shifting until it returns to AS^0_{SR}, and the initial long-run equilibrium, (Q_0, P_0) is restored on the frontier.

We noted in Chapter 37 that an adverse supply shock shifts the short-run Phillips Curve up and to the right, increasing both inflation and unemployment. This is the initial period of stagflation. Eventually, however, the effect of the shock wears off if it is a one-time-only event, and the short-run Phillips Curve tends to shift back down to its original position.

---

[1]Unless otherwise noted, all data on U.S. inflation rates and unemployment in this chapter are from the Council of Economic Advisers, *Economic Report of the President, 1993* (Washington, D.C.; U.S. Government Printing Office, 1993), Table B-58, p. 415 (inflation) and Table B-37, p. 390 (unemployment).

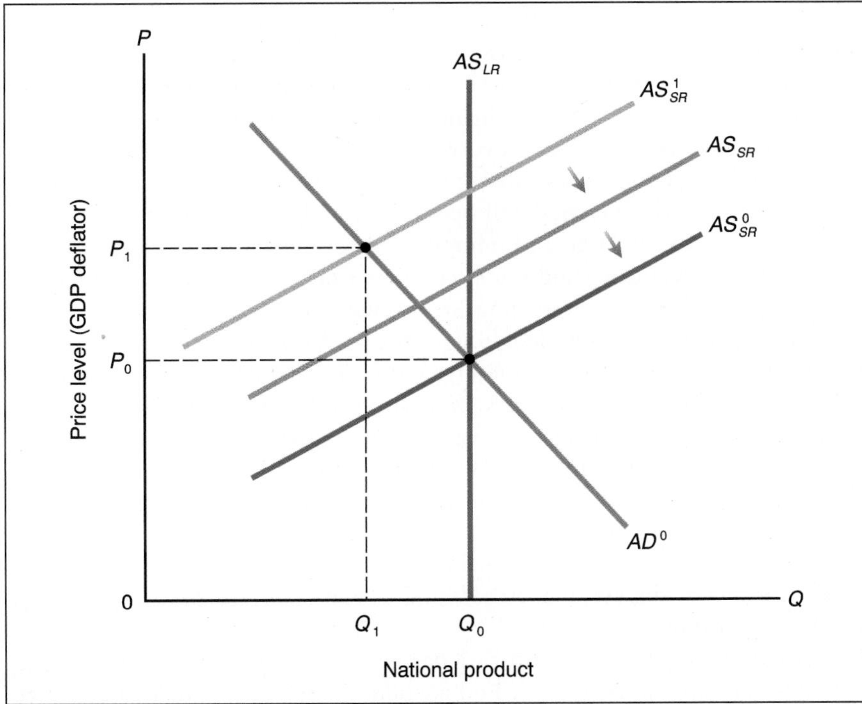

FIGURE 38.2

An Adverse Supply Shock and Inflation

The figure shows that an adverse supply shock causes prices to rise for a short time but has no lasting effect on the overall price level. The initial long-run equilibrium before the adverse supply shock is (Q_0,P_0) on the production possibilities frontier, at the intersection of AD^0, AS_{LR}, and AS^0_{SR}. There is no inflation. The adverse supply shock shifts the short-run aggregate supply curve up and to the left from AS^0_{SR} to AS^1_{SR}. Prices start to rise as the economy moves to the short run equilibrium (Q_1,P_1), at the intersection of AD^0 and AS^1_{SR}. Markets are generally in excess supply at Q_1 so prices and wages begin to fall, which decreases firms' costs of production. AS_{SR} shifts back down and to the right until it reaches AS^0_{SR} and removes the excess supply. The economy returns to its original long-run equilibrium (Q_0,P_0) on the frontier, at the intersection of AD^0, AS_{LR}, and AS^0_{SR}. The adverse supply shock does not change the long-run equilibrium price, P_0.

In conclusion, the inflationary effect of the adverse supply shock is very short-lived, as it is with a one-time increase in aggregate demand.[2] Aggregate supply shocks have to continue year after year to have a continuing effect on the rate of inflation. An example would be the continuing technological change in the production of personal computers that has driven the prices of these computers steadily downward for over a decade. Many supply shocks, especially adverse supply shocks, are of the one-time-only variety, though, in which case the above analysis applies. The one-time shocks have no lasting impact on inflation. Real business cycle theory agrees with the new Keynesian analysis of aggregate supply shocks.

Expected Inflation

The one factor we have left out so far in our analysis of inflation is the role played by people's expectations of what the rate of inflation will be in the future. The role of expected inflation turns out to be crucial because the interplay between actual and expected inflation is one of the twin engines that drive and sustain an inflationary process.

Economists might be better off if expected inflation were not such an important determinant of inflation because it makes the future course of inflation somewhat difficult to predict. One problem created by expectations is that an

[2]The example assumes that the supply shock does not affect the production possibilities, so that it shifts only AS_{SR}. A one-time-only shock that shifted both AS_{SR} and AS_{LR} would still have only a short-run effect on the rate of inflation. The only difference is that the period of deflation and increasing output when the economy returns to the long-run equilibrium would be shorter or non-existent because AS_{LR} would have shifted to the left.

inflationary process takes on the characteristics of a self-fulfilling prophecy. Inflation increases this year *because* people expected that inflation would increase, or inflation decreases this year *because* people expected that inflation would decrease. The markets for financial securities are much the same in this respect. Stock prices will rise if everyone expects them to rise because then everyone will be trying to buy stocks; stock prices will fall if everyone expects prices to fall because everyone will be trying to sell their stocks. Self-fulfilling prophecies can lead to large and unpredictable swings in the behavior of economic variables over time, and this is certainly true about the path of inflation.

A second problem is that economists are not sure how people form future expectations about anything, including future inflation. People's recent experience with inflation no doubt influences their predictions about future inflation. They are likely to expect a higher rate of inflation next year if inflation has averaged 10 percent over the past three years than if it has averaged only 2 percent. At the same time, people almost certainly do more than simply extrapolate past rates of inflation into the future. Their expectations about future inflation are undoubtedly forward-looking as well. At the very least, they will give some thought to the following question: Are future economic conditions expected to remain about the same as today, or are they expected to change significantly?

For example, suppose that inflation has been 2 percent per year for as long as people can remember, yet the Fed is about to announce a dramatic change in its monetary policy. Most people have a rough idea that an increase in the money supply increases prices and that a decrease in the money supply decreases prices. Therefore, they are likely to wait until the Fed announces its new policy before forming their expectations about next year's inflation. If the Fed announces that it plans to double the money supply next year, people are likely to expect a rate of inflation much higher than 2 percent next year. Similarly, if the Fed announces that it will cut the money supply in half next year, people might well expect a deflation, even though prices have recently been rising. Expecting the rate of inflation to remain at 2 percent following either of these announcements would not be reasonable.

RATIONAL EXPECTATIONS Almost all *theoretical* research in macroeconomics assumes that people are forward-looking in forming their expectations about the future values of all economic variables, including inflation. Macro economists assume that people have **rational expectations,** meaning that they consider all relevant information currently available to them when forming their expectations of the future. In terms of predicting future inflation, the relevant information might include the rate of inflation over the recent past, the current state of the economy, whether the economy has just been hit with significant aggregate demand or supply shocks, and the government's announced intentions for fiscal and monetary policies in the near future.

RATIONAL EXPECTATIONS

The assumption that rational individuals consider all relevant information (past, present, and future) currently available when forming expectations of the future.

The key implication of rational expectations is that people's predictions of the future are correct *on average* over time. This does *not* mean that they always guess right about future inflation (or anything else): indeed, they could guess wrong all the time. To say that people are correct *on average* just means that they are equally likely to overestimate inflation or to underestimate inflation, so that their prediction errors tend to cancel out over time. In other words, they do not predict future inflation in such a way that they systematically overestimate or underestimate the rate of inflation year after year.

Rational expectations is certainly a reasonable presumption. After all, why would people continue to predict the future in ways that they know are wrong? Suppose that you were using a method of predicting future inflation that always underestimated next year's actual rate of inflation and that your predictions were about 3 percent too low on average. You would naturally adjust your predictions up by 3 percent to correct for the underestimation. After the adjustment, you are now as likely to overestimate next year's rate of inflation as to underestimate it. Of course, some new information may come to light that suggests a different adjustment is appropriate in the future. Whatever you do, however, you will not stick with a method that has proven to underestimate inflation systematically year after year.

Empirical research on how people form expectations of inflation has not entirely supported the rational expectations assumption. People appear to extrapolate past rates of inflation rather more in forming their expectations of future inflation than rational expectations would suggest. They make too little use of current and forward-looking information, such as the current state of the economy or the Fed's announcements on the future growth of the money supply. Nonetheless, people do appear to consider the government's policy announcements to some extent in predicting the future course of inflation. This is important because we will see that it can reduce the costs of stopping an inflationary process.

FROM EXPECTED INFLATION TO ACTUAL INFLATION Economists may not know how people form their expectations of inflation, but they do know that the expectation of inflation feeds back into actual inflation and helps to sustain an inflation. The feedback from expected to actual inflation occurs through the supply side of economy by driving up the costs of production. We will illustrate the feedback with two components of costs, wages and interest rates.

EXPECTED INFLATION AND WAGE RATES Imagine union leaders and management sitting down at the bargaining table to negotiate the next union contract, which will stipulate the wage rate over the next three years, among other things. The union leaders are interested in increasing their members' real wages, or purchasing power. As such, the annual wage increases they bargain for depend on their expectation of the annual rate of inflation over the next three years. For example, suppose that they want the members' purchasing power to increase by 3 percent per year. In this case the annual wage increases in the contract would have to be three percentage points higher than the union leaders' expectation of inflation. If they expect no inflation over the next three years, they would be willing to settle for 3 percent annual wage increases. If they expect inflation to average 10 percent per year, however, they will bargain for 13 percent annual wage increases. The members need a 10 percent wage increase just to match the expected inflation and an additional three percentage points to give them the 3 percent increase in their purchasing power.

Management, meanwhile, is thinking along much the same lines. It, too, is concerned about the relationship between wages and prices—in this case the wages it pays relative to the prices of the firm's products. Suppose that it is willing to grant a wage increase three percentage points higher than the increase in its prices because it projects that the union members will be 3 percent more productive each year. As such, the annual wage increase they are willing to offer also depend on their expectation of the annual rate of inflation over the next three years, assuming that they believe their prices will change the same as prices generally. Management would be willing to offer annual 3 percent wage increases if it expects no inflation over the next three years. It would be willing to offer annual 13 percent wage increases if it expects inflation to average 10 percent per year.

Therefore, with the union leaders and management both thinking in terms of the real wage, wages adjust point for point with expected inflation. Wage increases that would be 3 percent with no expected inflation jump to 13 percent when expected inflation is 10 percent and jump to 53 percent when expected inflation is 50 percent. Moreover, there is nothing special about unionized labor. All employees expect to receive wage increases that protect their purchasing power by building in the expected rate of inflation, and employers are willing to offer such wage increases. The expectation of inflation increases all firms' actual labor costs point for point with the expected inflation.

EXPECTED INFLATION AND INTEREST RATES We have already seen in Chapter 26 that interest rates also adjust point for point with the expected rate of inflation. Recall the Fisher equation, which says that

$$i_{nominal} = r_{real} + \Delta P/P_E$$

$i_{nominal}$ is the nominal interest rate, the interest rate that we actually observe on financial securities. r_{real} is the real interest rate, the purchasing power of the annual interest payment. $\Delta P/P_E$ is the expected rate of inflation.

Interest rates adjust point for point with the expected rate of inflation for the same reason that wage rates adjust. Lenders and borrowers both think in terms of purchasing power when deciding on the interest rate on a loan. Lenders insist on adding the expected rate of inflation to the interest rate in order to protect the purchasing power of the interest they receive. They want to ensure that the interest payment truly increases their purchasing power relative to the purchasing power of the money they are lending today. Borrowers are willing to pay the additional interest if they believe that their incomes will rise by the expected rate of inflation. In that case, the higher nominal interest rate does not increase the purchasing power that they sacrifice in paying back the loan with interest. Review the example in Chapter 26 if you are unclear about this.

Interest rates are an important component of the firms' costs of capital. Therefore, the expectation of inflation drives up firms' actual costs of capital point for point with the expected inflation.

With the expectation of inflation increasing their wage costs and interest costs, firms are forced to raise their prices to cover the higher costs of production.[3] This has the added effect of driving up the costs of material inputs, the semi-finished products that firms buy from other firms. The expected inflation has fed into the actual inflation and serves to keep the inflation going.

Expected inflation acts as a *continuing* adverse aggregate supply shock that shifts the short-run aggregate supply curve up and to the left over time, as illustrated in Figure 38.3. Once people expect an inflation, the expectation

[3]We will see in Chapter 40 that an expected inflation also depreciates the nation's currency point for point, so that firms also have to pay more for the raw materials, material inputs, and capital goods that they import from foreign producers.

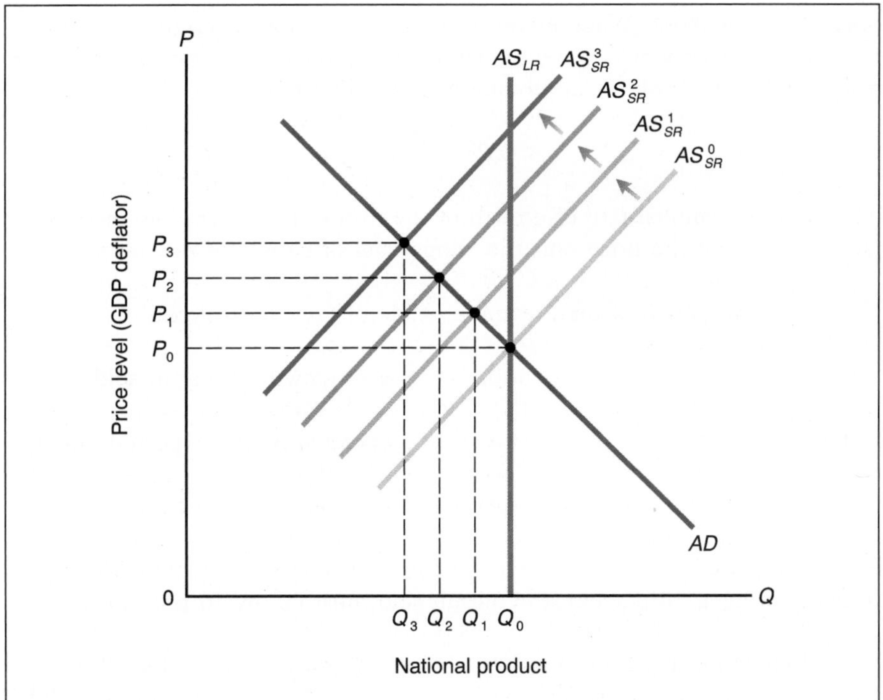

FIGURE 38.3

Expected Inflation, Actual Inflation, and Aggregate Supply

The economy is initially in a long-run equilibrium without any inflation or any expectation of inflation. The initial long-run equilibrium is (Q_0,P_0) on the production possibilities frontier, at the intersection of AD, AS_{LR}, and AS^0_{SR}. Once people begin to expect an inflation their expectations feed into an actual inflation through the supply side of the economy. An expected inflation increases wages, interest rates, and the prices of material inputs, all of which increase firms' costs of production. The short-run aggregate supply curve shifts up and to the left continuously, from AS^0_{SR} to AS^1_{SR}, AS^2_{SR}, AS^3_{SR}, indefinitely, which causes prices to rise from P_0 to P_1, P_2, P_3, indefinitely. The expectation of inflation is one of the twin engines (the other being an increase in the money supply) that drives and sustains an inflation.

drives up production costs at the same rate as the expected inflation and shifts AS_{SR} up continuously from AS^0_{SR} to AS^1_{SR} to AS^2_{SR} to AS^3_{SR}. The difference between inflation and our earlier example of a one-time-only aggregate supply shock is that AS_{SR} never stops shifting. AS_{SR} continues to shift up indefinitely as long as people continue to expect a positive rate of inflation. The economy never settles down to one short-run equilibrium, and prices never stop increasing either. Instead, the expectation of inflation drives the actual inflation indefinitely through the supply side of the economy.

Notice, too, that expected inflation shifts only AS_{SR} and not AS_{LR}. AS_{LR} represents the nation's production possibilities frontier, which is determined by the quantity and the quality of a nation's resources and its production technologies. None of these is affected by an inflation.

Nominal Aggregate Demand Growth Once Again

Expected inflation increases production costs and forces firms to raise their prices. But this cannot be the end of the inflation story because it leaves one question unanswered: Can firms sell their products at the new higher prices? The answer depends on the demand for the firm's products, which takes us back to the growth in nominal aggregate demand. The supply-side engine of the expected inflation is not enough to sustain an inflation by itself. The demand-side engine of continued growth in nominal aggregate demand must also be present to pull the prices ever upward.

Look at the problem first from the point of view of an individual firm. Assume that the expected annual rate of inflation is 10 percent, which increases the firm's costs of production by 10 percent and forces the firm to raise its prices by 10 percent. Whether the firm can sell as much output as before it raises its prices depends on the demand for its product. The total revenue the firm receives from selling its product is price times quantity:

$$TR = P \cdot q$$

Therefore, the annual rate of growth of the firm's total revenue is the annual rate of growth of the price plus the annual rate of growth of the output sold:

Rate of growth of total revenue = rate of growth of price
+
rate of growth of output sold

The rate of growth of the price is set at 10 percent by the expected inflation that is increasing the firm's production costs by 10 percent. Suppose that the firm's customers do not want to spend any more on the product, in total, than they had been spending. In that case the total revenue received by the firm is constant, and the rate of growth of total revenue is zero. With the firm's prices growing at 10 percent, the output sold must fall by 10 percent:

Rate of growth of total revenue (0%) = rate of growth of price (+10%)
+
rate of growth of output sold (−10%)

Customers have to be willing to spend 10 percent more on the firm's product for the firm to sell as much output as it did before the price increase:

Rate of growth of total revenue (10%) = rate of growth price (+ 10%)
+
rate of growth of output sold (0%)

All firms are in the same position when the expected inflation is 10 percent. Therefore, aggregate demand has to grow at the expected rate of inflation for aggregate output, the national product, to remain the same.

Figure 38.3 shows what happens when aggregate demand is not growing in the context of an expected inflation. The short-run aggregate supply curves are shifting up and to the left along the same aggregate demand curve, *AD*. Prices are continuously rising, but notice that output is continuously falling as well, from Q_0 to Q_1 to Q_2 to Q_3, indefinitely. This situation obviously cannot continue. People will not continue to expect a 10 percent inflation after output has fallen far below the production possibilities frontier, markets are generally in excess supply, and more and more workers are becoming unemployed. The only way the inflation can sustain itself is if aggregate demand grows as well in step with the expected inflation, 10 percent per year in our example. Figure 38.4 illustrates.

The short-run aggregate supply curve, AS_{SR}, shifts up by 10 percent each year, indefinitely, as in Figure 38.3, driven by the 10 percent expected inflation. This time, however, *AD* also shifts up by 10 percent each year, from AD^0 to AD^1 to AD^2 to AD^3, indefinitely, to match the shifts in the short-run aggregate supply curve. As a result of the aggregate demand shifts, the economy

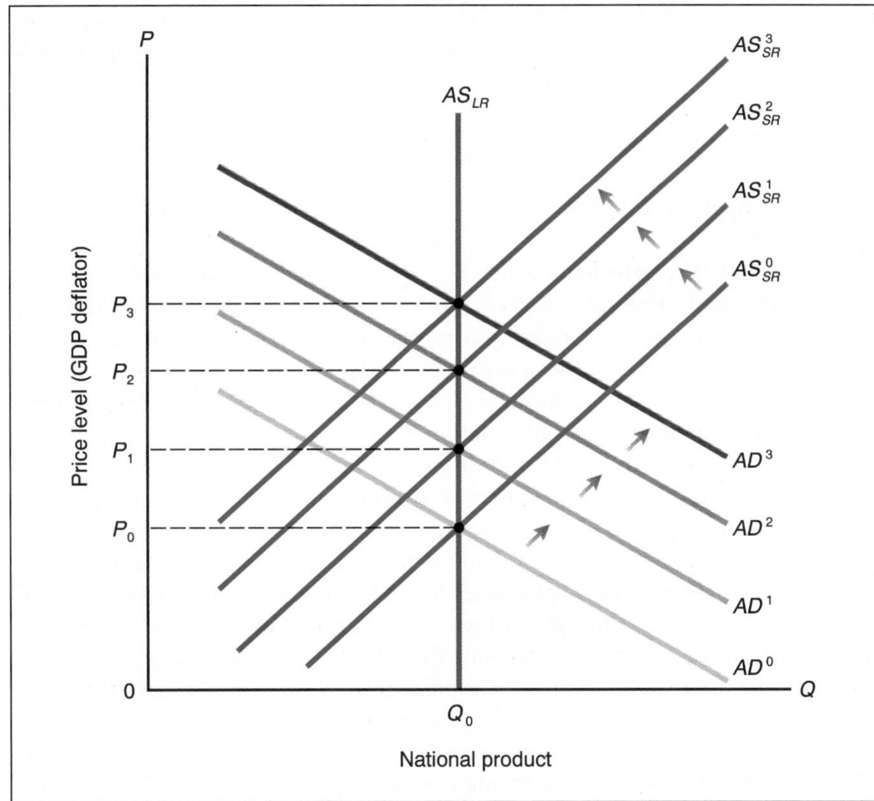

FIGURE 38.4

Increases in the Money Supply and Inflation

The figure shows how the twin engines of expected inflation and increases in the money supply drive and sustain an inflation. The initial long-run equilibrium is (Q_0,P_0) on the production possibilities frontier, at the intersection of AD^0, AS_{LR}, and AS^0_{SR}. Then people come to expect a 10 percent inflation, which begins to shift the short-run aggregate supply curve up by 10 percent indefinitely, from AS^0_{SR}, to AS^1_{SR}, AS^2_{SR}, etc. The inflation would eventually stop without an increase in aggregate demand above AD^0, however. People would not continue to expect an inflation with output falling and unemployment rising. To sustain the inflation, the government has to increase the money supply continuously so that aggregate demand increases by 10 percent indefinitely from AD^0 to AD^1, AD^2, etc. With both AS_{SR} and AD shifting up continuously by 10 percent, the economy remains on the frontier at Q_0, and the price level continues to increase by 10 percent, from P_0 at the intersection of AD^0 and AS^0_{SR}, to P_1 at the intersection of AD^1 and AS^1_{SR}, and so forth, indefinitely.

remains on the frontier at output Q_0, at each intersection of the corresponding AD and AS_{SR} curves; all resources remain fully employed; and the inflation can sustain itself indefinitely. Growth in nominal aggregate demand is clearly an essential ingredient of an inflationary process. Moreover, the growth in nominal aggregate demand must be (approximately) equal to the rate of inflation. A 10 percent inflation requires growth in nominal aggregate demand of (approximately) 10 percent; a 50 percent inflation requires growth in nominal aggregate demand of (approximately) 50 percent; and so forth.

MONEY AND INFLATION The government ultimately determines the growth in nominal aggregate demand with its fiscal and monetary policies, which means that the government has the ability to control inflation. In fact, *controlling inflation means controlling the growth of the money supply.* Nobel Laureate Milton Friedman has said that inflation is always and everywhere a monetary phenomenon, and virtually all economists would agree with him, at least for any significant amount of inflation that is sustained over the long run. The reason why money and inflation are so tightly linked can be seen from the equation of exchange:

$$M \cdot V = P \cdot Q$$

The right-hand side of the equation is nominal aggregate demand. The left-hand side is the product of the money supply and the income velocity of circulation. Write the equation of exchange in terms of annual rates of growth of each side:

Rate of growth of money		rate of growth of prices (inflation)
+	=	+
rate of growth of velocity		rate of growth of output

Look first at the right-hand side, which is the rate of growth of nominal aggregate demand. The rate of growth of output in the long run is limited by the rate of growth in the production possibilities frontier, which can be no more than about 4 percent per year in the United States. Therefore, rates of growth in nominal aggregate demand of more than 4 percent that are sustained over the long run must cause an inflation.

Regarding the left-hand side, the rate of growth of velocity is largely determined by institutional factors, such as how often people are paid and how they pay for goods and services. Consequently, velocity changes very little year by year in normal times, sometimes rising a bit and at other times falling a bit. We noted in Chapter 33 that velocity changed by an average of only 4.2 percent per year, plus or minus, throughout the 1980s. The rate of growth in the money supply, in contrast, can be any amount that the Fed wants it to be.

Putting the two sides of the equation together, we can see that the large increases in nominal aggregate demand needed to sustain a high rate of inflation require correspondingly large increases in the money supply. And this is exactly what happens in times of high inflation in all countries. If a country has been experiencing a 20 percent inflation for some time, you can be sure that its money supply has been increasing by nearly 20 percent per year. If another country has been experiencing a 300 percent inflation, you can be sure that its money supply has been increasing by nearly 300 percent per year. It cannot be otherwise.

Large increases in nominal aggregate demand without large increases in the money supply would require large increases in velocity, and this is not going to happen. For example, an ever more expansionary fiscal policy by itself would eventually crowd out consumer durables, investment, and net exports and have little impact on nominal aggregate demand. This is just another way of saying that velocity can only increase slowly in normal times. The need to have money in order to spend constrains the growth in nominal aggregate demand unless the money supply itself is growing.

THE PRESSURES TO MAINTAIN AN INFLATION Economists have long advised government officials that controlling the growth of the money supply is the key to controlling inflation. Why, then, do governments occasionally let the money supply grow rapidly and support a very high level of inflation? After all, stopping the growth of the money supply is easy to do, and high inflations are dangerous. They can easily turn into hyperinflations, which destroy faith in the currency and threaten a nation's entire financial structure.

The answer is that governments come under tremendous pressures from all sides to keep an inflation going once it gets started. Figure 38.3 illustrates the short-run costs of halting the growth in aggregate demand. Think of the government as halting the growth in aggregate demand by halting the growth in the money supply and holding aggregate demand at AD in the figure. The short-run problem is that, having just experienced inflation, people continue to expect inflation for awhile, which shifts AS_{SR} up and to the left, as in Figure 38.3. The shifting AS_{SR} curve against the now-constant AD curve reduces output below the frontier; firms go bankrupt, and workers lose their jobs. Neither business nor labor wants this result, so the business and labor leaders petition the government to keep pumping more money into the economy to maintain the growth in aggregate demand. They much prefer the result pictured in Figure 38.4, in which nominal aggregate demand grows by enough to keep the economy on its frontier, the firms in business, and the workers employed.

Worse still, additional pressure to keep the inflation going comes from within the government itself. High inflations are invariably associated with periods of high budget deficits, during which the government resorts to issuing large amounts of debt to finance its expenditures. Once an inflation is established, and people come to expect it, the interest rates that the government has to pay on its debt rise point for point with the expected rate of inflation. This is the lesson of the Fisher equation.

For example, suppose that the inflation rate has settled in at 50 percent per year and everyone expects it to continue at that rate. The government has to offer interest rates of 55 or 60 percent to issue its debt—and now has a strong incentive to keep the inflation going. If it stops printing money and ends the inflation, it would face *real* interest rates of 55 and 60 percent on its outstanding debt, which it cannot honor unless it cuts spending or raises taxes significantly. The far simpler alternative is to keep printing the money and maintain the inflation. Indeed, the government even has an incentive to *increase* the rate of inflation steadily over time so that it can pay off the interest on its debt with dollars that have less purchasing power than did the dollars it borrowed from the public. Keeping the actual inflation running ahead of the expected inflation transfers purchasing power from the private sector to the government sector when the government is debt financing.

The government's incentive to maintain and even increase inflation once it begins to debt finance its expenditures is so powerful that the University of Chicago's Robert Lucas has termed inflation a fiscal phenomenon. Lucas appreciates that growth in the money supply is what sustains an inflation. But he believes that the temptation for deficit spending is what really causes governments to give in to inflation.[4] Moreover, deficit spending gives the central bank an easy avenue for increasing the money supply. It simply buys the new Treasury debt issues with newly printed money, so that the government is effectively financing its expenditures by printing money. (The Fed is not allowed to buy new Treasury issues, but it could buy the debt in the secondary market immediately after it is issued, which would amount to the same thing. Economists call this "monetizing the debt.")

FROM INFLATION TO HYPERINFLATION Once the government decides to print whatever amount of money is necessary to sustain an inflationary process, it creates a highly unstable circular dynamic that can easily blow apart into a

[4] R. Lucas, "Discussion" of S. Fischer, "Towards an Understanding of the Costs of Inflation: II," in K. Brunner and A. Meltzer, eds., *The Costs and Consequences of Inflation*, vol. 15 of the *Carnegie Rochester Conference Series on Public Policy* (Amsterdam: North Holland Publishing Company, 1981), 43–50. The inflation-is-a-fiscal-phenomenon statement is on p. 46.

hyperinflation. Actual inflation feeds the expectation of future inflation, which feeds back into the actual inflation, which feeds into expected inflation, and so on, indefinitely. And the vicious circle is continually validated and maintained by pumping ever more money into the economy. People may eventually lose faith in the government's ability to keep the inflationary process under control. The instant this happens they lose faith in the money as a medium of exchange and refuse to hold it. The institutional factors that normally hold down the growth of velocity are overwhelmed as people become desperate to get rid of their money. Velocity skyrockets, and the inflation becomes a runaway hyperinflation. The rate of inflation increases much more rapidly than does the growth of the money supply once the hyperinflation sets in because it is fueled by the runaway growth in velocity as well as the growth in the money supply.

In conclusion, the analysis of inflation yields both good news and bad news. The good news is that governments can always stop an inflation. All they have to do is halt the growth in the money supply. The bad news is that governments may not always have the will to stop the inflation because they do not want to bear the short-run costs that go along with it. Some firms will go bankrupt, some workers will lose their jobs, and the government will be forced to cut spending or raise taxes. The tight relationship between money supply growth and inflation now cuts the other way. Governments can easily avoid these short-run costs by printing whatever money is required to sustain or even increase the inflation. But refusing to face the short-run costs of stopping an inflation runs the risk of a devastating hyperinflation down the road.

HISTORICAL NOTE: The reunification of Germany forced the government into making large social expenditures and weakened somewhat its longstanding resolve to hold down inflation as its number one priority. The weakened resolve was short-lived, however. By 1992 Germany was once again holding fast against the build-up of inflationary pressures.

Governments are well advised to keep a tight rein on the growth of the money supply over the long run and to avoid the temptation of debt-financing current expenditures. No government wants the political headache of deciding between short-run economic hardships and the long-run risk of a hyperinflation. Yet the combination of even moderate inflation and large budget deficits is a potentially explosive mixture that creates precisely these kinds of headaches.

THE SHORT-RUN AND LONG-RUN PHILLIPS CURVES Chapter 36 first described the costs of fighting an inflation in terms of the short-run Phillips Curve. Recall that the short-run Phillips Curve shows the inverse relationship between inflation and unemployment when the government manipulates aggregate demand with its fiscal and monetary policies. Expansionary fiscal and monetary policies, which increase aggregate demand, increase inflation and decrease unemployment in the short run. Contractionary fiscal and monetary policies, which decrease aggregate demand, decrease inflation and increase unemployment in the short run. We now know that contractionary monetary policy is necessary to squeeze inflation out of the economy, and the short-run Phillips Curve shows that the cost is an increase in unemployment in the short run.

At the same time, our analysis of inflation indicates that the cost of fighting inflation really is a short-run cost. The economy does not have to suffer increased unemployment forever as the cost of fighting inflation. In other words, the short-run Phillips Curve cannot be a stable relationship as time passes and the short run turns into the long run.

Economists generally agree that markets are competitive enough, and wages and prices flexible enough, that the economy eventually moves to its production possibilities frontier. The only long-run equilibrium output is the frontier

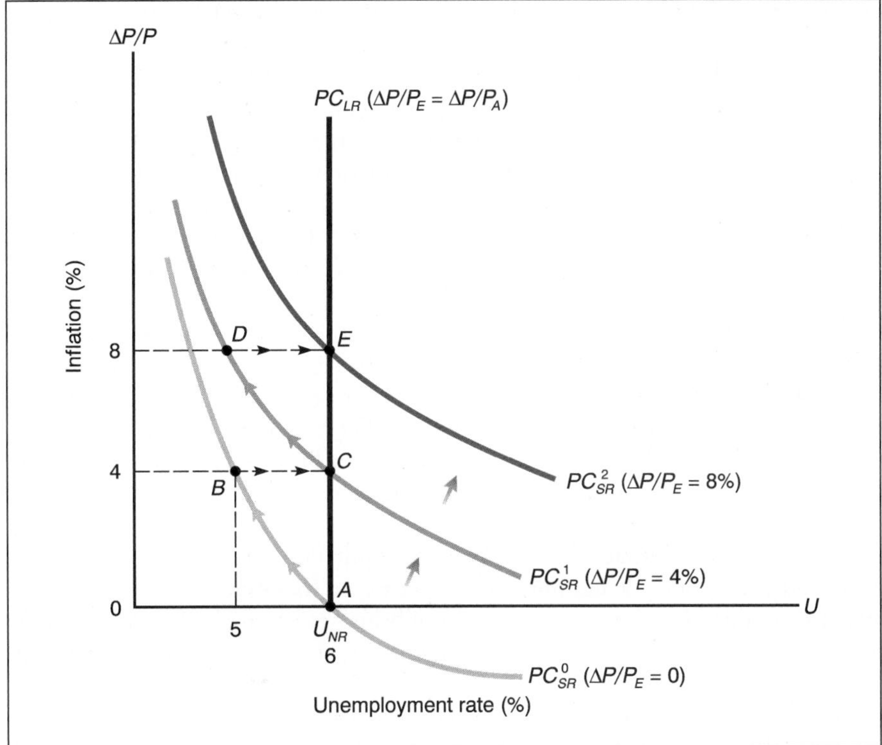

FIGURE 38.5

The Long-run Phillips Curve

The figure shows that there is no trade-off between inflation and unemployment in the long run. This is because each short-run Phillips Curve is associated with a given expected inflation and the expected inflation adjusts in the long run to the actual inflation. The economy is initially in long-run equilibrium at point A on the production possibilities frontier. Both actual and expected inflation are zero, and unemployment is at the natural rate, U_{NR}. Then an increase in the growth of aggregate demand moves the economy to point B along the short-run Phillips Curve PC^0_{SR}, which is consistent with zero expected inflation. Unemployment drops below U_{NR} to 5 percent and inflation rises to 4 percent. Eventually people come to expect a 4 percent inflation, which shifts the short-run Phillips curve up and to the right to PC^1_{SR}. PC^1_{SR} is consistent with a 4 percent expected inflation. The economy returns to point C at U_{NR}, with an actual inflation of 4 percent. A further increase in the growth of aggregate demand moves the economy to point D on PC^1_{SR}. Unemployment again falls to 5 percent, and inflation increases to 8 percent. Eventually people come to expect an 8 percent inflation, which shifts the short-run Phillips Curve up and to the right to PC^2_{SR}. PC^2_{SR} is consistent with an 8 percent expected inflation. The economy returns to point E at U_{NR}, with an actual inflation of 8 percent. The long-run Phillips curve, PC_{LR}, is vertical at U_{NR}. The economy is in long-run equilibrium on its frontier at U_{NR} when the actual inflation equals the expected inflation. This condition can hold at any rate of inflation: positive, zero or negative.

output, which is completely determined by the supply side of the economy. Aggregate demand just determines the overall price level in the long run, and any price level is consistent with the long-run equilibrium.

Now translate these results into a Phillips Curve diagram such as Figure 38.5, which has inflation on the vertical axis and unemployment on the horizontal axis. The natural rate of unemployment, U_{NR}, corresponds to the frontier level of output. Therefore, the only long-run equilibrium for the economy is at U_{NR}. Also, just as any price level is consistent with the frontier output, any rate of inflation is consistent with the natural rate of unemployment. The ver-

LONG-RUN PHILLIPS CURVE

A curve representing the idea that the economy tends to the natural rate of unemployment in the long run and that there is no long-run trade-off between inflation and unemployment; shows that any rate of inflation is compatible with the natural rate of unemployment in the long run.

tical line through U_{NR} in the figure is called the **long-run Phillips Curve.** It indicates that there is no relationship, inverse or otherwise, between inflation and unemployment in the long run.

Figure 38.5 illustrates the relationship between the long-run and the short-run Phillips Curves. The key to the relationship is that every short-run Phillips Curve assumes a given expected rate of inflation. In contrast, the long-run Phillips Curve applies after people have adjusted their expectations of inflation to the actual inflation. The story goes as follows. The economy is initially in long-run equilibrium at point *A*. Inflation is zero and has been zero for some time, so that expected inflation is also zero. Unemployment is at the natural rate, U_{NR}, assumed to be 6 percent. Suddenly the government increases the growth of the money supply, which increases the growth in nominal aggregate demand. Prices (and wages) rise at the rate of 4 percent per year. People did not expect the change in policy, however, so that they continue to expect zero inflation. The economy moves along the short-run Phillips Curve, PC^0_{SR}, which assumes zero expected inflation. The reduction in unemployment (increase in output) occurs because workers and bondholders have locked themselves into one-year or longer contracts that assumed zero inflation. As the inflation ensues, firms find their prices rising, but not their costs, so they hire more workers and increase output. The new short-run equilibrium is at point *B;* inflation rises from zero to 4 percent, and unemployment falls below the natural rate to 5 percent.

The short-run equilibrium cannot maintain itself, forever. Once people realize that the government is allowing the money supply to grow and that actual inflation is 4 percent, they come to expect a 4 percent inflation. The increase in expected inflation from zero to 4 percent causes wages and interest rates to rise and acts as an adverse aggregate supply shock that shifts the short-run Phillips Curve up and to the right to PC^1_{SR}. The economy returns to the frontier and U_{NR} at point *C*, with an inflation rate of 4 percent. The actual and expected rates are once again equal, at 4 percent, as required for long-run equilibrium.

If the government wants the unemployment rate to return to 5 percent, it has to increase the growth of the money supply even faster, so that actual inflation outstrips expected inflation once again. Suppose that the government does this and generates an 8 percent inflation. This time the economy moves along the short-run Phillips Curve, PC^1_{SR}, to point *D*. The economy cannot remain at this short-run equilibrium, however. Once people understand that the government has increased the growth of the money supply and that the actual inflation is 8 percent, they adjust their expected inflation up from 4 percent to 8 percent. The increase in expected inflation shifts the short-run Phillips Curve up and to the right once again to PC^2_{SR}, and the economy returns to the frontier and U_{NR} at point *E*. The actual and expected rates are once again equal, at 8 percent, as required for long-run equilibrium.

The relationship between the short-run and the long-run Phillips Curves leads to a number of interesting conclusions.

INFLATION IN THE LONG-RUN EQUILIBRIUM *Any* rate of inflation is consistent with the long-run equilibrium on the production possibilities frontier. The equilibrium condition is only that actual inflation equals expected inflation, which can be satisfied at any rate of inflation: zero, 200 percent, 430 percent, or anything else. This explains why economies can function with inflations of 300 percent and more. Economies can always return to their frontiers once people have adjusted to the inflation.

ACCELERATING INFLATION The only sensible unemployment target in the long run is the natural rate of unemployment. Trying to drive unemployment permanently below the natural rate does not just generate an inflation; it generates an *ever-accelerating* inflation that must ultimately become a hyperinflation. Refer again to Figure 38.5. Suppose that the government tries to keep the unemployment rate permanently at 5 percent. It can reach the target at first by generating a 4 percent inflation. But as people's expectations adjust to the new inflation, the economy begins to move back to the frontier. So the government has to increase the money supply even more rapidly and generate an 8 percent inflation. Once again expectations adjust, so the government has to increase the money supply even faster, generating, say, a 12 percent inflation. In short, the government has to keep actual inflation continually ahead of expected inflation. But expected inflation always adjusts to actual inflation, which means that still higher inflation is needed to keep unemployment at 5 percent. The cycle never ends as the short-run Phillips Curves keep shifting upward continuously. The result is an accelerating inflation that can only lead eventually to a runaway hyperinflation.

The only possible justification for trying to lower the unemployment rate is to test where the natural rate really is. Some economists believe that the natural rate of unemployment is around 4 percent. The more commonly accepted rate is in the 5 to 6 percent range. Their conjecture may well be worth testing. If they are correct, then maintaining the unemployment rate at 5 or 6 percent may be keeping 1 or 2 million people unemployed unnecessarily. If they are wrong, pushing the unemployment rate down to 4 percent for awhile would not be too costly in terms of the extra inflation it would cause.

DECELERATING INFLATION/ACCELERATING DEFLATION Perhaps the most surprising conclusion of the analysis is that keeping the unemployment rate permanently above the natural rate generates an ever-decelerating inflation or an ever-accelerating deflation. The analysis is exactly the reverse of the accelerating case.

Slowing down the growth of the money supply in order to generate a higher rate of unemployment lowers the actual rate of inflation as the economy moves along its short-run Phillips Curve. Then expected inflation adjusts to the new lower actual inflation, the short-run Phillips Curve shifts down, and the economy attempts to return to the frontier and U_{NR}. To hold the unemployment rate above U_{NR}, the government has to reduce the growth of the money supply still further, which lowers actual inflation. The lower actual inflation causes people to lower their expected inflation, the short-run Phillips Curve shifts down again, and the process continues. Inflation continues to decelerate, eventually leading to an accelerating deflation if the government persists in keeping the unemployment rate above U_{NR}.

ELIMINATING AN INFLATION The government might want to keep unemployment above U_{NR} temporarily because this is the only way economists know to squeeze inflation out of an economy. Figure 38.6 illustrates.

Suppose that the economy is initially in long-run equilibrium at point A on the long-run Phillips Curve. Unemployment is at the natural rate, U_{NR}. The rate of inflation is 12 percent and has been for some time, so that it is also the expected rate of inflation.

The government decides that 12 percent inflation is unacceptable and wants to lower inflation from 12 percent to zero. The quickest way to do this is to

FIGURE 38.6

Reducing an Inflation With a Deep Recession

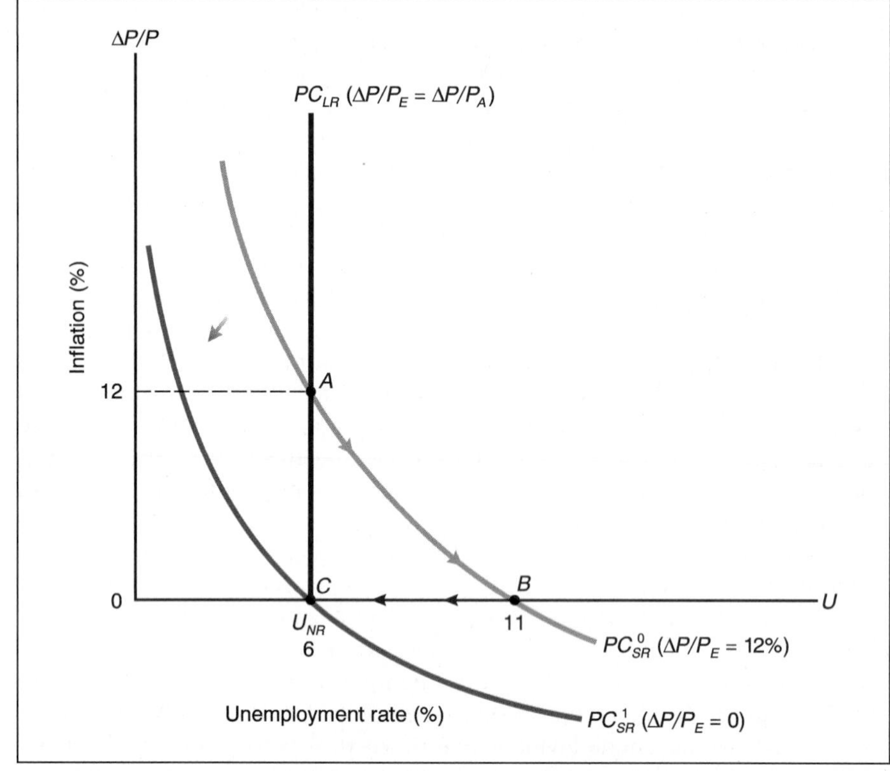

The figure illustrates how the government can reduce an ongoing inflation with monetary policy by generating a deep recession for a short period of time. The figure assumes that the economy is initially in long-run equilibrium at point *A*, at the intersection of PC_{LR} and PC^0_{SR}. Unemployment is at the natural rate, U_{NR}, and both the actual and expected inflation are 12 percent. PC^0_{SR} is consistent with an expected inflation of 12 percent. To reduce the inflation to zero the government halts the growth of the money supply and brings the economy to point *B* on PC^0_{SR}. Unemployment rises to 11 percent and inflation falls to zero. By keeping the economy at point *B*, and the actual inflation at zero, people eventually come to expect zero inflation. The reduction of expected inflation from 12 percent to zero percent shifts the short-run Phillips Curve down and to the left to PC^1_{SR}. PC^1_{SR} is consistent with zero expected inflation. The economy can then return to a long run equilibrium on the frontier at point *C* with zero inflation, at the intersection of PC_{LR} and PC^1_{SR}.

generate a short, but very deep, recession. Stop the growth of the money supply completely, or even reduce the money supply, and inflation will drop to zero right away. The economy moves to point *B* along the short-run Phillips curve, PC^0_{SR}, which is associated with the expected 12 percent inflation. Unemployment rises sharply to 11 percent as inflation falls to zero.

This move is costly in terms of higher unemployment, but the economy does not have to stay there for long. Once people realize that the government has decreased the growth of the money supply and that the actual inflation is zero, they adjust their expected inflation down to zero. The reduction in expected inflation acts as a favorable aggregate supply shock that shifts the short-run Phillips Curve down to PC^1_{SR}. The economy moves back to its long-run equilibrium at point *C*. Unemployment is once again at U_{NR}, and inflation is zero.

Another possibility is to move more slowly with a longer, shallower recession—to have the government generate, say a 7 percent unemployment rate and a 9 percent inflation in the short run. Then it would keep the unemployment rate at 7 percent as expected inflation adjusts downward until it equals zero. At this point the economy can return to its frontier with zero inflation.

Both the quick fix and the longer, slower fix are costly in the short run, but these are the only sure-fire ways of squeezing inflation out of the economy.

HISTORICAL NOTE: The Fed has kept a vigilant guard against the buildup of inflationary pressures. For example, in mid-1993 the economy was growing very slowly, yet Chairman Greenspan considered slowing down the growth of the money supply because inflation appeared to be inching up beyond the 3 percent mark.

New Keynesian and New Classical Perspectives

New Keynesian and new classical economists essentially agree with the preceding analysis of the relationship between the short-run and the long-run Phillips Curves. Their only disagreement is over the length of the short run. New Keynesians argue that an equilibrium on a short-run Phillips Curve can last for a fairly long time. Actual inflation differs from expected inflation not so much because people are fooled, but rather because wages and prices are sticky for reasons given in Chapters 25 and 37. Businesses are reluctant to change prices, and workers agree to wage and salary contracts of one year and more, so that the adjustment to changes in expected inflation is necessarily slowed down.

New classical economists argue that an equilibrium on a short-run Phillips Curve is short-lived. Wages and prices are flexible even in the short-run. Moreover, people have rational expectations; they quickly take into account what the government is doing and adjust their expectations accordingly. The result is that expected inflation adjusts quickly to match actual inflation whenever actual and expected inflation diverge, and the economy returns quickly to the frontier.

One important policy implication of their different opinions relates to how quickly the government can squeeze inflation out of the economy. The new Keynesians argue that reducing inflation requires either a deep, short recession or a prolonged, shallow recession. The new classical economists argue that inflation can be squeezed out almost immediately.

The evidence appears to favor the new Keynesians on this point. For example, inflation fell sharply from 12.5 percent in 1980 to 3.8 percent in 1982. But the new Keynesians point out that it took the deepest recession since the Great Depression to accomplish this. Unemployment rose to 9.7 percent by 1982. And there were still other favorable supply side shocks that helped reduce the inflation as well, such as the collapse of oil prices. Also, the more mild recession of the early 1990s reduced the rate of inflation more slowly. Inflation fell from 6.1 percent in 1990 to 3.1 percent by 1991 and then fell only slightly to 2.9 percent in 1992.

Stan Fischer of MIT, a leading new Keynesian economist, estimates that the cumulative costs in lost output of reducing inflation from 10 percent in 1980 to 4 percent by 1985 amounted to 25 percent of one year's national product.[5] This is an enormous cost and argues strongly for not letting inflationary pressures build if at all possible.

---

[5]S. Fischer, "Real Balances, the Exchange Rate, and Indexation: Real Variables in Disinflation," *The Quarterly Journal of Economics* CIII, Issue 1 (February 1988): 28. The 1992 inflation rate is from Council of Economic Advisers, *Economic Indicators, March 1993* (Washington, D.C.: U.S. Government Printing Office, 1993), 24.

Interest Rates One Last Time

A final point about inflation concerns the behavior of interest rates in an inflationary environment. We said in Chapter 35 that an increase in the money supply decreases interest rates. The analysis then was referring to the effects of a *one-time* increase in the money supply on the underlying *real* interest rates, the interest rates on which savers and investors base their decisions. The analysis was also short run and in a new Keynesian policy environment of sticky wages and prices.

The analysis in this chapter refers to a sustained increase in the rate of growth of the money supply, which maintains an inflation over the long run. The Fisher equation indicates that the nominal, or observed, interest rates must increase under these conditions. The continued expectation of inflation dominates any short-run decrease in interest rates brought about by an initial increase in the money supply.

Suppose, for example, that the economy has been experiencing no inflation and no growth in the money supply for some time and that both real and nominal interest rates average 5 percent. Then the Fed allows the money supply to grow by 10 percent per year, indefinitely.

Both the real and the nominal interest rates may drop below 5 percent immediately after the money supply begins to increase. Eventually, though, the nominal interest rate must rise. The continued growth in the money supply must increase both actual and expected inflation to 10 percent in the long run (approximately). Once the economy returns to the frontier and expected inflation is 10 percent, the real interest rate returns to 5 percent, and the nominal interest rate increases to 15 percent. The sustained growth in the money supply ultimately increases nominal interest rates point for point with the increase in expected inflation that it brings.

Always keep the Fisher equation in mind in an inflationary environment, especially in periods when the rate of inflation is increasing or decreasing. Interest rates tend to move in the same direction as inflation because expected inflation tends to adjust to actual inflation.

MANAGING THE ECONOMY THROUGH THE SUPPLY SIDE

Adverse aggregate supply shocks, such as an increase in oil prices, are nasty events for an economy; they increase both inflation and unemployment. Worse yet, economists are not convinced that the government has any effective remedy for them in the short run. Figure 38.7 illustrates the nature of the government's short-run policy problem.

Suppose that the economy is initially in long-run equilibrium on its production possibilities frontier at the intersection of AD^0, AS_{LR}, and AS^0_{SR}. Output is Q_0, the frontier output, and the overall price level is P_0. Suddenly the economy is hit with an adverse supply shock that shifts the short-run aggregate supply curve up and to the left from AS^0_{SR} to AS^1_{SR}. A period of stagflation sets in with rising prices, falling output, and rising unemployment as the economy moves to a new short-run equilibrium at the intersection of AD^0 and AS^1_{SR}. Output falls to Q_1 and the overall price level rises to P_1 in the shot run. (The

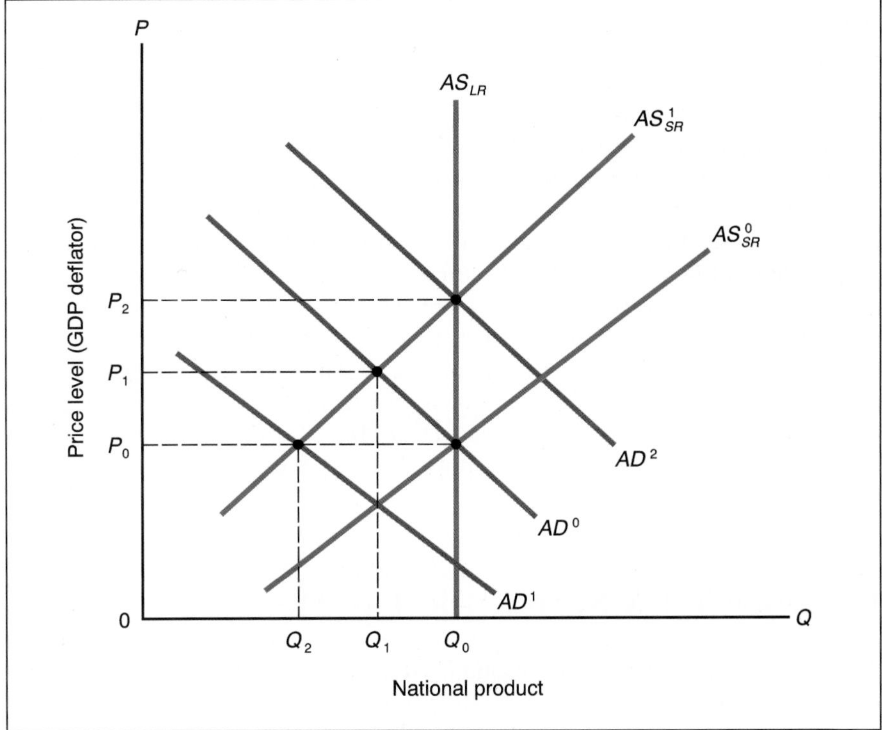

FIGURE 38.7

Responding to an Adverse Aggregate Supply Shock

The figure shows the limitations of responding to an adverse aggregate supply shock with fiscal and monetary policies, which manipulate aggregate demand. The initial long-run equilibrium before the adverse supply shock is (Q_0,P_0) on the production possibilities frontier, at the intersection of AD^0, AS_{LR}, and AS^0_{SR}. The adverse supply shock shifts the short-run aggregate supply curve up and to the left from AS^0_{SR} to AS^1_{SR}, which reduces output and increases prices. The new short-run equilibrium is (Q_1,P_1), at the intersection of AD^0 and AS^1_{SR}. The government can restore the initial price level P_0 in the short-run with contractionary fiscal and monetary policies that decrease aggregate demand from AD^0 to AD^1. The new equilibrium would be (Q_2,P_0), at the intersection of AD^1 and AS^1_{SR}. But contractionary policies reduce output even further from Q_1 to Q_2. Alternatively, the government can return the economy to the frontier output Q_0 in the short run with expansionary fiscal and monetary policies that increase aggregate demand from AD^0 to AD^2. The new equilibrium would be (Q_0,P_2), at the intersection of AD^2 and AS^1_{SR} (and AS_{LR}). But expansionary policies increase prices even further from P_1 to P_2. Neither policy response is entirely satisfactory.

supply shock may also shift AS_{LR}, but we are ignoring that possibility to focus on the short-run policy problem.)

New Keynesian and new classical economists would agree that the ideal policy response would be through the supply side of the economy. The government would like to have a set of policy tools that could quickly shift AS^1_{SR} back down and out to AS^0_{SR} and restore the original equilibrium on the frontier. The question is whether such supply-side policy tools exist. At the moment the answer appears to be no.

New classical economists have a natural interest in developing effective short-run supply-side policies. They believe that the economy is buffeted mostly by aggregate supply shocks, and they do not place much stock in managing the economy through the demand side with fiscal and monetary policies. New Keynesian economists believe that demand-side management with fiscal and monetary policies can help to improve the performance of the economy in the short run. But they, too, are interested in developing effective short-run supply-side policies because manipulating aggregate demand is not a very satisfactory policy response to an adverse aggregate supply shock.

According to new Keynesian theory, demand-side fiscal and monetary policies can restore the original price level *or* the original output, but not both. Refer again to Figure 38.7. The government can restore the original price level with contractionary fiscal or monetary policies that shift the aggregate demand curve down from AD^0 to AD^1. But this reduces output still further, from Q_1 to Q_2, and increases unemployment. Alternatively, the government can return the economy to the frontier with expansionary fiscal or monetary policies that shift the aggregate demand curve up from AD^0 to AD^2. But this increases the inflationary pressures of the aggregate supply shock by increasing the overall price level from P_1 to P_2.

Reaganomics: A Supply-Side Tax Theory

The issue of manipulating the economy from the supply side was put to the test in 1981, the first year of the Reagan administration. President Reagan inherited an economy suffering from stagflation resulting primarily from one-time adverse aggregate supply shock—OPEC had doubled the price of crude oil in 1979. Inflation rose from 9.0 percent in 1978 to 12.5 percent by 1980, and the unemployment rate rose from 6.0 percent to 7.0 percent. The administration's policy response to the stagflation ushered in one of the more interesting episodes of fiscal policy in the entire history of the United States.

The Reagan administration argued that the government could manipulate the economy through the supply side in the short run with income tax policy. In their view a cut in income taxes increases aggregate supply in the short run, shifting AS_{SR} down and to the right. Conversely, an increase in income taxes decreases aggregate supply in the short run, shifting AS_{SR} up and to the left. Therefore, they proposed a large tax cut to increase aggregate supply and effectively combat both the rising inflation and the rising unemployment simultaneously. The tax cut proposal was dubbed Reaganomics, or supply-side economics.

The tax cut proposal was particularly interesting because the theory behind it was directly counter to the prevailing view of taxes at the time, which was Keynesian. Keynes argued that tax increases and decreases affect the economy in the short run by shifting aggregate demand, not aggregate supply. Only a proverbial handful of economists believed that a tax cut could have any significant effect on aggregate supply in the short run, whether they labeled themselves new Keynesian or new classical. Nonetheless, Congress was willing to give supply-side economics a try. It passed the largest income tax cut in U.S. history, a 23 percent reduction in the personal income tax rates phased in over three years.

The Keynesian and supply-side views of tax cuts could hardly be more different, Keynes argued that a tax cut stimulates the economy by increasing people's disposable income, which increases consumption demand. The supply-side theory argued that a tax cut stimulates the economy by lowering input prices, particularly wages and interest rates, which increases aggregate supply.

TAX CUTS, LABOR SUPPLY, AND SAVING We laid out the Keynesian theory of income tax cuts in Chapter 30. The heart of the supply-side theory is that an income tax cut increases the supply of labor and saving for investment, both of which increase aggregate supply. Regarding labor, a cut in income tax rates increases the after-tax wages that workers receive—the workers' take-home pay—and encourages people to work harder, so that the supply of labor increases. The increased supply of labor puts downward pressure on the wages that firms pay their workers, which induces firms to hire more workers. Regarding saving and investment, an income tax cut increases the after-tax return that people receive on their saving, which encourages them to save more. The increase in personal saving puts downward pressure on interest rates in the financial markets, which induces firms to invest in more capital and increase production. The increase in employment and investment increases production. AS_{SR} shifts down and to the right.

SUMMARY: KEYNESIAN VERSUS SUPPLY-SIDE TAX THEORY The battle lines between the prevailing Keynesian theory and the new supply-side theory were firmly drawn in 1981 around the tax cuts.

Keynesian theory:

Income tax cut → disposable income ↑ → consumption demand ↑ → aggregate demand ↑ → real national output and income ↑

Supply-side theory:

Income tax cut→after-tax wages, interest rates↑→labor supply, savings↑→ employment, investment↑→real national output and income↑

ASSESSING THE SUPPLY-SIDE THEORY The main problem that the vast majority of economists had with the supply-side theory at the time was factual, not theoretical. The supply-side effects on labor supply and saving are possible in theory, but did not appear to be very likely. Research on labor supply had suggested that changes in wage rates have little or no short-run effect on the overall supply of labor in the United States. The same was true of interest rates and saving. Interest rates change quite a bit over time, but even large changes in interest rates appear to have very little effect on how much people save in the short run. Economists simply had no reason to believe that the tax cuts would have much effect on either labor supply or private saving in the short run, and therefore, on aggregate supply. Subsequent research since 1981 has reached essentially the same conclusions.[6]

---

[6]For a review of the economic research on the effects of income taxes on labor supply and saving, see: J. Hausman and J. Poterba, "Household Behavior and the Tax Reform Act of 1986," *Journal of Economic Perspectives* 1, No. 3 (Summer, 1987): 101–119; B. Bosworth and G. Burtless, "Effects of Tax Reform on Labor Supply, Investment, and Saving," *Journal of Economic Perspectives* 6, No. 1 (Winter 1992): 3–25.

Also, the tax cuts in and of themselves lower the government budget surplus (increase the budget deficit), which is the government component of saving. *National saving* is the sum of the private-sector saving and government saving. If the tax cuts do not increase personal saving, then they will reduce national saving.

THE EVIDENCE The economy recovered steadily from the recession of 1981–82 following the tax cut, most of which was phased in during 1982 and 1983. Unemployment fell from 9.7 percent in 1982 and 9.6 percent in 1983 to 7.5 percent in 1984 and to 7.2 percent in 1985. Was the recovery demand led or supply led? The majority of economists believe that the recovery was demand led rather than supply led. The tax cut appeared to have no effect at all on the supply of labor, exactly as most economists had predicted. Also, private saving decreased instead of increasing. How, then, did the tax cuts propel the supply side of the economy if the labor supply and private saving did not increase? These are, after all, the key components of the supply-side tax theory. Finally, federal personal income tax collections fell sharply as a result of the tax cuts, so that national saving fell sharply as well. The tax cuts appeared to stimulate the economy by increasing consumption demand, in line with the Keynesian theory.

In summary, the events following the Reagan tax cut did not convince very many economists that government tax policy is an effective tool for manipulating the economy through the supply side in the short run. What, then, can the government use to offset adverse aggregate supply shocks if tax policy cannot do it? Macro economists do not have an answer to this question. Unless they come up with something, the economy will have to suffer the occasional adverse aggregate supply shock and the stagflation that accompanies it. The only pleasant thought to offset this unhappy conclusion is that the economy will occasionally receive favorable aggregate supply shocks, as it did when the oil prices collapsed in the 1980s.

Tax Policy in the Long Run

This does *not* mean, however, that tax policy has no effect on aggregate supply in the long run. Quite the opposite is true, especially with regard to saving and investment. Changes in tax policy usually change both the after-tax rate of return to savers and the cost of capital to business firms. Saving and investment may respond only slightly in the short run to changes in the rate of return to saving and in the cost of capital. But the small short-run effects tend to build over time and can have a substantial impact on saving and investment over the long run. Since saving and investment are the key to long-run economic growth and since long-run economic growth is the most important determinant of a nation's standard of living, tax policy can make a big difference to a nation's economic well-being.

A number of economists have built simple models of the U.S. economy that are designed to track the effects of tax and other budgetary policies over very long periods of time, 50 to 100 years and more. These models always reach the same conclusions about tax policy. Tax reforms that lower tax rates on saving and investment and that raise tax rates on consumption in order to keep total tax revenues constant over time lead to much more saving and investment in the long run. The additional saving and investment increase productivity and push out the production possibilities frontier, so that the economy is eventually able to produce much more output. Completely replacing the federal personal income tax with an equal revenue expenditures tax that only taxes consumption may increase the national product by as much as 10 to 20 percent after 20 years or so, according to these models. A 20 percent increase in the national product translates into an additional $4,800 for every person every year in the United States.

These models reach the same general conclusion about budget deficits. We have seen that government borrowing to finance large structural deficits raises interest rates and the cost of capital. Large structural deficits also transfer resources from future to current generations because the government must eventually raise taxes or cut spending to reduce the deficits. All these effects significantly reduce saving, investment, productivity, and long-run economic growth over the long haul. The long-run economic models suggest that a policy of running structural deficits on the order of $200 billion for 10 to 15 years, as the federal government has been doing, may eventually reduce the national product by 10 percent or more[7].

Virtually all economists would recommended that the federal government keep taxes on saving and investment low and reduce the structural budget deficits if it is serious about promoting saving, investment, and long-run economic growth. They would also say that nothing is more important than long-run economic growth to the overall economic well-being of a nation. New Keynesian and new classical economists are in complete agreement here. So is President Clinton and a (bare) majority of Congress. In the summer of 1993, Congress passed Clinton's proposed $500 billion reduction in the deficit from 1993 to 1998.

POLICY CREDIBILITY: STEERING A STEADY COURSE

New Keynesian and new classical economists generally agree that governments need to develop a reputation for consistency and credibility. They should get in the habit of announcing their policy intentions well in advance, doing what they say they are going to do, and staying the course until their policy goals have been met. Governments that continually shift their policies may lose their credibility and end up causing quite a bit of harm.

Let's take a look at the issue of policy credibility from a new Keynesian perspective, since the new Keynesians are the ones who are prone to advise the government to intervene in the economy. The new classical economists would naturally favor a steady and credible policy stance because they see the need for policy only in a long-run context.

The new Keynesians believe that active intervention with fiscal and monetary policies can improve the performance of the economy in the short run. They strongly disagree with the current new classical view that the economy

[7]Two excellent sources on the long-run effects of tax policy and budget deficits are L. Kotlikoff, "Taxation and Savings: A Neoclassical Perspective," *Journal of Economic Literature* XXII, No. 4 (December 1984): 1576–1629; and L. Kotlikoff, "Economic Impact of Deficit Financing," *International Monetary Fund Staff Papers* 31 (September 1984): 549–582.

remains on or near its production possibilities frontier at all times. Nonetheless, the majority of New Keynesians support a steady and credible policy stance. They see a number of advantages from their own perspective.

In the first place, new Keynesians recognize the practical limitations of conducting fiscal and monetary policies. They realize that the government cannot fine tune the economy by reacting immediately to every blip in aggregate demand or aggregate supply. The best these policies can hope to do is "lean against the wind" by nudging the economy back on track when it goes astray and preventing a bad situation from turning into a disaster. "Leaning against the wind" implies a steadier course for fiscal and monetary policies than does fine tuning right from the outset.

A steady and credible policy course also has a number of advantages in terms of the allocation of resources simply because it reduces uncertainty within the economy. Three that we have talked about in previous chapters are reducing unemployment, encouraging investment, and reducing the short-run costs of fighting inflation.

A major component of unemployment is search unemployment, in which the unemployed spend time searching out various job opportunities before accepting a job. A steady and credible set of policies would generate less confusion than do sudden stop-and-go policies about what the job opportunities are, both now and in the future. People would be able to reduce their search time, which would reduce the natural rate of unemployment and expand the economy's production possibilities. (New classical economists stress this point because they believe that measured unemployment is almost entirely search or frictional unemployment at all times.)

A more certain economic environment is also conducive to investment demand. We first made this point when discussing why a stable value of the dollar is one of the four macroeconomic policy goals. The idea is that stable exchange rates promote international trade and investment by reducing uncertainty. Businesses are more willing to invest and ship goods abroad the more confidence they have in the rate at which they can convert foreign currencies earned abroad back into dollars. The same general point applies to domestic investment.

The federal government offered a good counterexample of what not to do in the first half of the 1980s. The Reagan tax cut of 1981 affected more than the personal income tax. Congress also made substantial changes in the corporation income tax that, overall, sharply reduced the cost of capital for corporations. Then, in 1982, Congress had a change of heart and passed a substantial "correction" to the 1981 law that took away many of the 1981 tax advantages and increased the cost of capital. Congress changed the corporate tax rules yet again in the Tax Reform Act of 1986 (TRA86), removing the investment tax credit and introducing a number of other features that increased the cost of capital. TRA86 was particularly tough on the real estate industry, closing a number of tax advantages that had been in existence for decades. By the end of 1986 businesses were complaining that all these changes in the tax laws had made them hesitant to invest because they no longer had any confidence about the tax implications of their investments. Their complaints had more than a ring of truth to them, and Congress called a moratorium on major tax changes for a number of years. Wrenching businesses around like that is not the kind of thing the government ought to be doing.

Finally, a credible policy stance is very useful for fighting inflation. We saw that the expectation of inflation feeds an inflation through the supply side and that the government has to convince people not to expect inflation in order to eliminate inflation. Unfortunately, the only way to do this is to generate a recession to reduce actual inflation and let expected inflation come down with actual inflation. People's expectation of inflation should adjust downward quickly if they believe that the government means business and will stick with the recession until the inflation ends. Expected inflation appears to adjust downward only slowly in the United States, however, which is why squeezing inflation out of the economy is so costly. The reason why expected inflation adjusts so slowly may well be a lack of government credibility.

People know that jobs mean votes in national elections and that the administration and the Congress are unlikely to maintain a contractionary policy stance during an election year. Therefore, they have no reason to expect inflation to fall if they believe the federal government will shortly change to an expansionary stance. We noted in Chapter 32 that the evidence for an engineered political business cycle is not very convincing. Still, fiscal and monetary policies have both changed course frequently. Thus, U.S. citizens have very little reason to believe that the federal government will ever truly stay the course.

Stanford's Robert Hall has recommended that the federal government abandon its stop-and-go policy stance of the past and commit to a policy of constant growth in nominal aggregate demand—say, 5 percent per year. Hall's recommendation is noteworthy because he is firmly associated with the new Keynesian school.[8]

To see the implications of Hall's policy recommendation, recall that nominal aggregate demand is the product of prices times quantities:

$$Y = P \cdot Q$$

Also, the rate of nominal aggregate demand is the sum of the rates of growth in prices and quantities:

$$\text{Rate of growth of } Y = \text{rate of growth of } P \text{ (inflation)} + \text{rate of growth of } Q$$

Suppose that output grows at 3 percent per year on average, equal to the rate at which the production possibilities frontier moves out over time. Then Hall's policy allows an average inflation of 2 percent per year over the long run.

The government would announce this policy and stick to it, so that it would have all the advantages of a steady and credible policy noted above. And the policy would always respond to aggregate demand and aggregate supply shocks in a set manner.

The government would simply offset any aggregate demand shocks with the appropriate fiscal and monetary policies in order to keep nominal aggregate demand growing at 5 percent year. For example, the government would

[8]Hall's proposal is presented in R. Hall and J. Taylor, *Macroeconomics: Theory, Performance, and Policy*, Second edition (New York: Norton, 1988), 498–501.

counter a decrease in the growth of consumption demand with expansionary fiscal and monetary policies that would keep the growth in aggregate demand at 5 percent.

The policy response to an adverse aggregate supply shock would be a slow and balanced offset to the price and the output effects of the shock. For example, suppose that an adverse aggregate supply shock drives up inflation to 5 percent and reduces the growth of output to zero. The government would not change the rate of growth in nominal aggregate demand, since prices and output are still growing at the rate of 5 percent combined. The result would be a shallow and prolonged recession in which the economy would return slowly to the frontier and inflation would be gradually reduced. Hall argues that a long and shallow recession is the best demand-side response to an adverse aggregate supply shock. He, like other economists, does not know how to respond quickly to the shock through the supply side.

A growing number of new Keynesian economists agree with Hall that steady growth in nominal aggregate demand is the best strategy for the government's fiscal and monetary policies. Having agreed on an overall growth target to manage output and inflation, the government can then adjust the mix of fiscal and monetary policies to increase or decrease interest rates.

Recall that interest rates primarily effect two other macroeconomic policy goals, long-run economic growth and the value of the dollar relative to foreign currencies. Lower interest rates stimulate investment and long-run economic growth and cause the dollar to depreciate in value. Higher interest rates retard investment and long-run economic growth and cause the dollar to appreciate in value. The government would presumably opt for low interest rates these days in the name of promoting growth. But a swing to high interest rates may be necessary on occasion to protect the dollar.

SUMMARY

Chapter 38 concluded the macroeconomic section of this text with a discussion of three policy issues on which new Keynesian and new classical economists are pretty much in agreement: controlling inflation, responding to adverse aggregate supply shocks, and meeting the need for consistent and credible government policies.

The first section of the chapter analyzed the process of inflation and how to keep it under control.

1. The rate of inflation year to year is determined primarily by four factors: the growth in nominal aggregate demand, the state of the economy, aggregate supply shocks, and the expectation of future inflation.
2. Inflation is inherently a long-run policy problem. Of the four factors, the growth in nominal aggregate demand and the expectation of inflation are the twin engines that drive an inflation over the long run.
3. A one-time change in aggregate demand and a one-time-only aggregate supply shock both change the rate of inflation in the short run, but they cannot sustain an inflation by themselves over the long run. Prices stop changing, and the inflation ends, when the economy returns to its long-run equilibrium on the production possibilities frontier.

4. The short-run Phillips curve indicates how the state of the economy affects the rate of inflation in the short run. Inflation tends to be lower the farther the economy is beneath its frontier, and vice versa. The effect of the state of the economy on inflation essentially washes out over the long run, however.
5. The expectation of inflation drives an inflationary process through the supply side of the economy because it increases firms' costs of production. Expected inflation feeds point for point into actual wage increases and into nominal interest rates, which affect firms' cost of capital. The increase in production costs acts as a continual adverse aggregate supply shock that shifts up the short-run aggregate supply curve, AS_{SR}, continually over time.
6. Economists assume that people have rational expectations. They are forward-looking in forming their expectations about the future course of inflation, or anything else, and take into consideration all information available to them, including the government's announced intentions for fiscal and monetary policies. The main implication of rational expectations is that people's guesses about the future course of inflation are correct, on average. They do not systematically over- or underestimate future inflation.
7. The growth in nominal aggregate demand is the other engine that drives inflation in the long run. Firms can sell their output after raising their prices because of inflation only if the demand for their products is continually growing.
8. The government ultimately controls the growth in nominal aggregate demand through its fiscal and monetary policies. The equation of exchange indicates that the key to preventing large increases in prices is to control the growth of the money supply. In that sense inflation is a monetary phenomenon.
9. Governments can easily stop the growth of the money supply in order to stop an inflation, but they may not have the will to do so. Stopping inflation entails short-run costs: Some firms go bankrupt, and workers lose their jobs. Also, governments nearly always run deficits during high inflations, so they would have to cut spending and/or raise taxes to meet the higher real interest payments on their debt. Governments sometimes choose to avoid the short-run costs and continue printing money to keep the inflation going. This runs the risk of turning a high inflation into a runaway hyperinflation.
10. There is no long-run trade-off between inflation and unemployment. The long-run Phillips Curve is vertical at the natural rate of unemployment, U_{NR}, which corresponds to the production possibilities frontier. The economy always returns to the frontier when expected inflation adjusts to the actual inflation. Each short-run Phillips Curve assumes a given expected inflation, so the short-run Phillips Curves keep shifting over time as expected inflation adjusts to actual inflation.
11. The economy can be in long-run equilibrium with any rate of inflation; all the long-run equilibrium requires is that actual inflation equal expected inflation. The only sensible long-run target for unemployment is the natural rate of unemployment. An attempt by the government to keep unemployment permanently below U_{NR} leads to an accelerating inflation. An attempt by the government to keep unemployment permanently above U_{NR} leads to an accelerating deflation.

12. The only way the government can squeeze inflation out of an economy is to engineer a recession with unemployment greater than U_{NR}, wait until expected inflation falls to zero, and then return the economy to the frontier. The costs of doing this appear to be quite high in the United States.

The second section of the chapter considered whether the government has any good short-run policy response to an adverse aggregate supply shock.

13. The Reagan administration cut the federal personal income tax rates by 23 percent across the board in 1981 in an attempt to stimulate the economy through the supply side. The goal was to combat the high inflation and the high unemployment that followed the 1979 OPEC-induced increase in oil prices. The supply-side theory was that a tax cut would increase the supply of labor and saving, which would lower costs of production and increase aggregate supply. The evidence following the tax cut suggested that it had little or no effect on either labor supply or saving. Instead, the short-run effect was to increase demand, in line with the Keynesian analysis of an income tax cut. Economists are still looking for an effective short-run response to an adverse aggregate supply shock.
14. Tax policy can have an enormous impact on saving, investment, and economic growth over the long run, however. Simple long-run models of the economy suggest that replacing the personal and the corporation income taxes with a consumption tax would promote saving, investment, and productivity and would raise the U.S. national product by as much as 20 percent. Reducing the federal budget deficit in order to reduce interest rates appears to have similar long-run benefits.

The final section of the chapter discussed the emerging consensus among all economists that the government should avoid surprises and pursue consistent and credible policies.

15. A consistent and credible government policy stance reduces uncertainty in the economy, which has a number of advantages. It reduces the search component of unemployment, promotes investment, and sharply reduces the short-run costs of squeezing inflation out of the economy.

KEY TERMS

long-run Phillips Curve

rational expectations

QUESTIONS

1. What are the principal factors that determine the rate of inflation? Which of these factors are more likely to drive the rate of inflation over the long run?
2. a. What does it mean to say that people have rational expectations? In particular, does having rational expectations mean that people always guess right about the future?
   b. Discuss some of the problems that expectations cause the government as it tries to formulate its fiscal and monetary policies.
3. a. Draw the short-run Phillips Curve and the long-run Phillips Curve. Indicate why you drew the curves as you did. Be sure to label the axes on your graph.
   b. Suppose that the government uses monetary and fiscal policies to decrease sharply the level of aggregate demand and thereby increase unemployment well above the natural rate of unemployment. Show how you would represent the short-run effect of that policy change on your graph.

c. Suppose that the government continues to keep the unemployment rate at that high level for 10 years in a row. Show what effect this long-run policy stance would have on each Phillips Curve that you drew in part (a), and explain your answer.

4. Indicate whether the following items will improve or worsen the short-run Phillips Curve (shift it down or up) or not affect the short-run Phillips Curve at all.
   a. Expected inflation rises from 5 percent to 10 percent per year.
   b. The growth in labor productivity increases from 2 percent to 4 percent per year.
   c. More people enter the labor force in search of part-time employment.
5. Describe some of the channels through which a change in the expected rate of inflation can affect the actual rate of inflation.
6. Consider an economy in long-run equilibrium at a natural rate of unemployment of 4 percent. Suppose that expected inflation is 3 percent. Using Phillips Curve analysis, show the effects of
   a. a rise in expected inflation to 5 percent.
   b. a rise in the natural rate of unemployment to 6 percent.
   c. both (a) and (b) together.
7. Suppose that Congress passes a 10 percent across-the-board increase in the personal income tax rates. Compare the effects of the tax increase on output and national saving, using Keynesian and supply-side tax theory.
8. Consider an economy with a constant velocity of circulation and sticky prices. The economy is currently in recession. If the central bank begins a policy of expanding the money supply by 4 percent per year, what can we say about the growth of output in the short run? In the long run? How does your answer change if the economy is at full employment initially?
9. What are the advantages of having the federal government follow a steady course with its fiscal and monetary policies, in which it announces its policy intentions and then maintains its policies as it said it would?

CASE

What Caused the Inflation of the 1970s?*

Aside from times of war, the worst inflation experienced by the United States was in the 1970s. From 1970 to 1980 the consumer price index more than doubled. Retirees who had invested their savings in bonds or who had fixed pensions, and who had expected to live comfortably, had to scrape by instead.

Most people blame the 1970s inflation on OPEC, the oil cartel. Following the oil embargo of 1973 that was triggered by the Yom Kippur war in October 1972, the price of oil quadrupled, roughly from $3 a barrel to $12. After the fall of the Shah of Iran in 1979, the price doubled again. Consumer prices rose at the same time. Inflation as measured by the CPI jumped from 3.4 percent in 1972 to 8.7 percent in 1973 and to 12.3 percent in 1974. Similarly, inflation jumped from 9.0 percent in 1978 to 13.3 percent in 1979 and to 12.5 percent in 1980.

Food prices also soared twice during the 1970s, and at the same times as the oil prices. Drought hit the corn crop in the United States and the wheat crop in the Soviet Union. In earlier decades silos bursting with surplus grain stored by the U.S. government dampened swings in food prices, but new agricultural policies aimed at conserving soil instead of storing grain had depleted the surpluses.

The conventional wisdom that the inflation of the 1970s arose from the oil and food markets is correct in one sense. The sharp increases in the prices of oil and food were extremely adverse aggregate supply shocks that shifted the aggregate supply curve to the left and caused brief periods of stagflation in which prices rose and real GDP fell.

There may have been a more fundamental cause of the two bursts of inflation, however. The money supply, as measured by M2 (approximately currency, checkable deposits, and time deposits under $100,000), rose rapidly in 1971–72 and again in 1975–77, periods preceding the bursts of inflation. Could it be that the rapid monetary growth was the more important cause of the inflation, but that it operated with long delays?

A useful equation for thinking about this question is the equation of exchange, which can be written $P = MV/Q$. P is the price level, M is the quantity of money, V is the velocity of circulation, and Q is output. Suppose that V and Q are constant. Then a ten percent increase in M raises prices by 10 percent.

*Provided by David Denslow, University of Florida.

But V and Q are not constant. When an expansionary monetary policy by the Fed induces the commercial banks to create money, the velocity of circulation typically drops immediately following the increase in the money supply. Then after six months or so velocity snaps back and output starts to rise. Prices may rise significantly over a year or more later. The causes of these delays, or lags, are poorly understood.

Consequently, rapid growth of the money supply, not the oil cartel or the crop failures, may have been the true cause of the inflation of the 1970s. Why, then, did oil and food prices rise so much more than most other prices? OPEC and the crop failures are certainly part of the answer. Also important, though, are the elasticities of demand and supply for oil and food, both of which are very low. Given the low elasticities, an increase in the money supply that boosted overall economic activity and raised the demands for oil and food would promote large increases in oil and food prices. The price effect is amplified if there are cutbacks in supply at the same time, as there were in oil and food.

Therefore, an alternative explanation of the inflation of the 1970s is that the Fed caused it. By increasing the money supply too rapidly, the Fed increased aggregate demand and, later, prices. Oil and food prices rose especially rapidly because of the interaction of rising demand, OPEC, crop failures, and low elasticities. Indeed without the demand boost caused by the rapid monetary growth of 1971–72, OPEC might not have become an effective cartel.

There is a potential flaw in the alternative explanation, however. It does not explain how an increase in the U.S. money supply caused *global* oil and food prices to shoot up. The 1970s was a decade of inflation in most industrial economies, not just here. How can U.S. monetary policy be blamed for that?

A plausible answer is that speculators knew that prices in the United States would go up sooner or later after the increase in the U.S. money supply. They also knew that the rise in U.S. prices would depreciate the value of the dollar in the foreign exchange markets. For example, the dollar price of a pound sterling might rise from $1.60/£ to $1.80/£. Therefore, the speculators sold dollars with the idea of buying the dollars back later on when they were cheaper. The sale of dollars by speculators drove the value of the dollar down against foreign currencies even before U.S. prices rose.

The falling dollar hurt European export industries. With U.S. prices (relative to European prices) rising less rapidly

What Caused the Inflation of the 1970s? (cont.)

than the dollar was falling in 1972 and again in 1977–78, European exporters found it hard to compete with American producers. The Europeans central banks were forced to buy dollars to try to break the free fall of the dollar. The purchases of dollars with their own currencies expanded their money supplies. In this way an inflation that began in the United States spread across the Atlantic.

Another potential flaw in the monetary explanation of the inflation of the 1970s is that the rule that inflation follows rapid growth of M2 broke down in the 1980s. But this can be explained by the passage of the Depository Institutions Deregulation and Monetary Control Act of 1980 (DIDMCA), which deregulated the banking and thrift industries and increased the demand for interest-bearing NOW accounts. Another factor breaking the previously tighter link between the growth of M2 and inflation were a number of technological changes in handling financial transactions that spread through financial markets world-wide.

SOURCE: Council of Economic Advisers, *Economic Report of the President 1993* (Washington, D.C.: U.S. Government Printing Office, 1993) Table B-59, pp. 415.

ECONOMIC ADVISOR'S REPORT

Suppose that the Fed's Board of Governors hires you to advise them on the problem of keeping inflation under control following an adverse supply shock to the economy such as the oil and food price increases of the 1970s. They ask you the following questions. How would you respond?

1. Is an adverse supply shock likely to cause a difficult policy problem for the Fed?
2. Can an adverse supply shock sustain in inflationary process by itself?
3. Should the Fed increase the growth of the money supply following an adverse supply shock, or reduce the growth of the money supply to zero, or follow a policy course somewhere between the two?
4. Do the nations of Western Europe care about how the Fed responds to an adverse supply shock?

PART

XI

International Economic Issues

CHAPTER

39

International Trade and Barriers to Trade

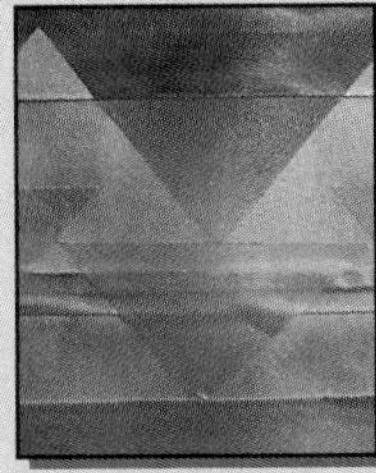

LEARNING OBJECTIVES

CONCEPTS TO LEARN

The three principal models for explaining the pattern of international trade:

1. Ricardo's comparative advantage model
2. The factor endowments model
3. The product differentiation/economies of scale model

The economic effects of tariffs, quotas, and other trade restrictions

The North American Free Trade Agreement (NAFTA)

The European Community

GATT (General Agreement on Tariffs and Trade)

CONCEPTS TO LEARN

Opportunity cost [1]

The production possibilities frontier [3]

The principle of comparative advantage [4]

The Laws of Supply and Demand [5, 6, 7]

Take a moment to look at Table 39.1. The table records the imports and the exports for the United States during 1992, by commodity and by the country of origin (for imports) and the country of destination (for exports).

The power of international trade fairly leaps from the table. It shows that U.S. citizens and businesses exchange commodities of every description with foreign citizens and businesses, and in both directions: agricultural produce, natural resources such as oil, a broad range of consumer goods and services, and both capital goods and semi-finished products that firms sell to other firms to be used as inputs in production. In addition, the United States trades with nations that are at every stage of economic and social development: the industrialized market economies, the oil-rich Organization of Petroleum Exporting Countries (OPEC), the Eastern European economies in transition, and the middle- and low-income developing nations of Central and South America, Asia, and Africa.

These international exchanges of imports and exports are voluntary exchanges between private citizens and businesses for the most part. As such, they must be mutually beneficial to buyers and sellers in the United States and elsewhere, or they would not occur. Table 39.1 reveals that the gains from international trade are very broad indeed. They are not limited to a narrow set of commodities or available to just a few countries.

Citizens and businesses in the United States have clearly recognized that international exchanges can help them solve their economic problems. Imports and exports are each about 11 percent of the gross domestic product (GDP) of the United States. Yet this is the lowest percentage of all the industrialized market economies, and a far lower percentage than for most of the world's middle- and low-income nations. Citizens of all nations understand that international trade can improve their economic well-being.

International exchanges help people solve their economic problems in the same way that domestic exchanges do. They exploit the division of labor and economies of scale that allow people to specialize in production while remaining generalists in consumption. The only difference is that the specialization occurs on a global scale.

Imports are the ends of international trade, the motivation behind specializing and trading. Nations import to gain access to goods and services that they cannot produce at all or that other nations produce better than they can, either more cheaply or with more desirable qualities. Exports are the means to these ends. Nations have to export to be able to import because foreign citizens insist on receiving real goods and services in exchange for the real goods and services they are sending abroad.

International exchanges are somewhat more limited than are domestic exchanges. The transactions costs of international exchanges tend to be higher because goods typically have to travel longer distances and pass through one or more border crossings. International transactors also have to bear the effort and the expense of exchanging their own currencies for foreign currencies in the foreign exchange markets. Political considerations may limit international exchanges as well. For example, government agencies are often required to purchase the majority of their capital and material inputs from domestic suppliers. These limitations notwithstanding, international trade has contributed greatly to improving standards of living throughout the world.

Chapters 39 through 41 conclude the text with a discussion of the global economy. Chapter 39 begins by developing the fundamental principles relating to the pattern of international trade. We want to understand why nations import or export certain goods; what the gains from international trade are; and why, despite the gains from trade, all nations choose to restrict international trade with such devices as tariffs and quotas. Chapter 40 then turns to the financial side of international trade, taking a close look at the flow of funds through the foreign exchange markets. Chapter 41 closes by analyzing the special economic problems of the low-income developing nations as they try to push out their production possibilities frontiers and improve their standards of living.

THE PATTERN OF INTERNATIONAL TRADE

The central question concerning international trade is why it is as broad as it is. People in the United States worry that U.S. industries will not be able to compete against the much lower wages of the low-income developing countries of Southeast Asia and Central and South America. At the same time people in the developing countries worry that their industries will not be able to compete against the superior technologies of the high-income industrialized nations. Yet neither low wages nor superior technologies have been a barrier to trade. To the contrary, international trade flourishes between the developing nations and the industrialized nations, to the benefit of each. Why is this? Another fact to be explained is the considerable amount of two-way trade in highly similar products. We see in Table 39.1 that two-thirds of U.S. trade is with the other industrialized nations. The majority of this trade involves the simultaneous import and export of semi-finished products and capital goods among firms—electrical equipment, machinery, computers, and the like. Another large component of this trade is in very similar consumer goods, such as beer, wine, and automobiles, which are also simultaneously imported and exported. Why do nations trade for minor variations of products that they can produce themselves?

Economists have developed three basic models to explain the variety of trade that we observe. The first is David Ricardo's theory of comparative advantage, which we met in Chapter 4. Ricardo's theory is based on differences in technologies and is useful for explaining interindustry trade between nations in different stages of economic development.

The second model stresses differences in factor endowments rather than differences in technologies as the basis for international trade. Some countries are blessed with large amounts of fertile land and natural resources and have a highly educated and skilled labor force. Other nations are resource-poor and have mostly an uneducated and low-skilled labor force. These differences in factor endowments can generate gains from trade. This model is particularly useful for seeing the distributional implications of trade. Some people gain, and other people lose from trade, even though the nation as a whole benefits. The losers from trade are the ones who fight for trade restrictions such as tariffs and quotas.

The third, and most recent, model focuses on international trade generated by the rivalry between large corporations that are competing for markets both domestically and internationally. These multinational corporations compete by

TABLE 39.1 **U.S. Merchandise Exports and Imports, 1992 ($ billion)**

	VALUE	PERCENTAGE OF TOTAL[a]	TOTAL
I. BY COMMODITY			
Exports			$448.1
Foods, feeds, beverages	$ 40.2	9.0	
Industrial supplies, materials	109.1	24.3	
Capital goods	176.7	39.4	
Autos and auto parts	46.7	10.4	
Other consumer goods	50.4	11.2	
Other	25.0	5.6	
Imports			$532.4
Foods, feeds, beverages	27.9	5.2	
Industrial supplies, materials	138.0	25.9	
Capital goods	134.4	25.2	
Autos and auto parts	91.5	17.2	
Other consumer goods	70.0	13.1	
Petroleum and petroleum related products	53.0	10.0	
Other	17.6	3.3	

[a]Percentages may not total 100 percent because of rounding error.

SOURCE: Council of Economic Advisers *Economic Report of the President 1993* (Washington, D.C.: U.S. Government Printing Office, 1993), 465, Table B-102. Council of Economic Advisers, *Economic Indicators.* (Washington D.C.: Government Printing Office, March 1993), 35.

trying to develop new products through research and development. A firm that successfully markets a new product gains a cost advantage over its rivals because of the economies of scale associated with developing and producing a narrowly defined product. This is the basic model used to explain the trade in similar products among the industrialized nations. It has also been used as a justification for trade restrictions to protect domestic industries while they are researching and developing new products.

Let's now take a closer look at each theory, beginning with Ricardo's theory of comparative advantage.

The Theory of Comparative Advantage

David Ricardo's fundamental insight about international trade was that both the pattern of trade and the gains from trade depend on differences in the opportunity costs of producing goods and services. Ricardo attributed the differences in opportunity costs to differences in the technologies used to produce the goods and the services. The newer models offer other reasons why opportunity costs of production might differ across countries, but differences in opportunity costs are still the basis for specialization and trade in these models.

The simple model that we developed in Chapter 4 to explain Ricardo's theory is useful for explaining many of the fundamental principles of international trade. Recall that we had two countries, the United States and England, each producing two goods, food (F) and clothing (C), before they trade. Labor is the only factor of production, and each country has 100 units of labor.

TABLE 39.1 U.S. Merchandise Exports and Imports, 1992 ($ billion) (cont.)

	VALUE	PERCENTAGE OF TOTAL[a]	TOTAL
II. BY COUNTRY[b]			
Exports			
Industrial countries			$263.8
Canada			
Japan	90.4	34.2	
Western Europe	47.2	17.9	
Australia	114.4	43.4	
New Zealand, South Africa	8.3	3.1	
	3.5	1.3	
Other countries			171.2
OPEC	20.7	12.1	
Eastern Europe	5.3	3.1	
Other countries[c]	145.2	84.8	
Imports			
Industrial countries			$309.1
Canada	100.2	32.4	
Japan	94.0	30.4	
Western Europe	108.1	35.0	
Australia	3.7	1.2	
New Zealand, South Africa	3.1	1.0	
Other countries			217.1
OPEC	32.5	15.0	
Eastern Europe	2.0	0.9	
Other countries	182.6	84.1	
Trade Balance (Exports − Imports)			
Industrial countries			(−)$45.2
Canada	(−) 9.8		
Japan	(−)46.8		
Western Europe	6.3		
Australia	4.6		
New Zealand, South AFrica	0.4		
Other countries			(−)45.9
OPEC	(−)11.8		
Eastern Europe	3.3		
Other countries	(−)37.4		

[b]Data by country are preliminary data for the first three quarters of 1992, annual rate.
[c]Includes Latin America, other Western Hemisphere countries, and other countries in Asia and Africa.

The United States is the more productive economy. A unit of labor in the United States produces 4 units of food and 3 units of clothing. A unit of labor in England produces 2 units of food and 2 units of clothing. Table 39.2 summarizes the production technologies in each country.

The black lines in Figure 39.1 show the production possibilities frontiers within each country, Figure 39.1(a) for the United States and Figure 39.1(b) for England.

The United States can produce 400 units of food if it puts all its labor into food production, 300 units of clothing if it puts all its labor into clothing production, and the other combinations of food and clothing along the black line frontier. The example in Chapter 4 assumed that, before trade, the United

TABLE 39.2 **Production Technologies for Food and Clothing: Output per Unit of Labor**

	FOOD	CLOTHING
United States	4F	3C
England	2F	2C

States allocates 55 units of labor to food production and 45 units of labor to clothing production, producing 220F and 135C at point *A* in Figure 39.1(a) $(220 = 4 \cdot 55;\ 135 = 3 \cdot 45)$.

England can produce 200 units of food if it puts all its labor into food production, 200 units of clothing if it puts all its labor into clothing production, and the other combinations of food and clothing along the black line frontier. The example in Chapter 4 assumed that, before trade, England allocates 72 units of labor to food production and 28 units of labor to clothing production, producing 144F and 56C at point *A′* in Figure 39.1(b) $(144 = 2 \cdot 72;\ 56 = 2 \cdot 28)$.

Both countries can gain from international trade because the opportunity cost of producing food is lower in the United States and the opportunity cost of producing clothing is lower in England. To produce 1 more unit of food, England must sacrifice 1 unit of clothing; to produce 1 more unit of food, the United States must sacrifice only ¾ of a unit of clothing. The United States has the comparative advantage in producing food; that is, it has the lower opportunity cost. Conversely, to produce 1 more unit of clothing, the United States must sacrifice ⁴⁄₃ units of food; to produce 1 more unit of clothing, England must sacrifice only 1 unit of food. England has the comparative advantage in producing clothing; that is, it has the lower opportunity cost.

Another useful way to state the comparative advantage of each country is in terms of the relative prices of food and clothing. The relative prices must reflect the opportunity costs of production along the production possibilities frontier. Therefore, the ratio of the price of food to the price of clothing in the United States is ¾, the inverse of the food-for-clothing trade-off along the frontier $(P_F/P_C = 3/4 = .75)$. The ratio of the price of food to the price of clothing in England is 1 $(P_F/P_C = 1)$. Food is relatively cheaper in the United States, and clothing is relatively cheaper in England, reflecting their comparative advantages.

COMPARATIVE ADVANTAGE

The principle that a country should specialize its production in those goods that it can produce with lower opportunity costs than other countries and trade for those goods that other countries can produce with lower opportunity costs.

As we saw in Chapter 4, Ricardo's theory of comparative advantage says that both countries can gain if they specialize in the good for which they have a **comparative advantage** and trade at any ratio of food to clothing between 4F/3C and 1F/1C, the trading ratios along each country's production possibilities frontiers. The United States exports food and imports clothing, and England exports clothing and imports food. In terms of the price ratios, producers in the United States are willing to export food at any relative price greater than .75 $(P_F/P_C > .75)$, and producers in England are willing to export clothing at any relative price less than 1 ($P_F/P_C < 1$; that is, so long as clothing is more expensive than food).

We assumed that the two countries specialize their production and trade at the rate of 5F for 4C. Equivalently, they trade at a relative price of .8, the inverse of the 5F for 4C trading ratio $(P_F/P_C = 4/5 = .8)$.

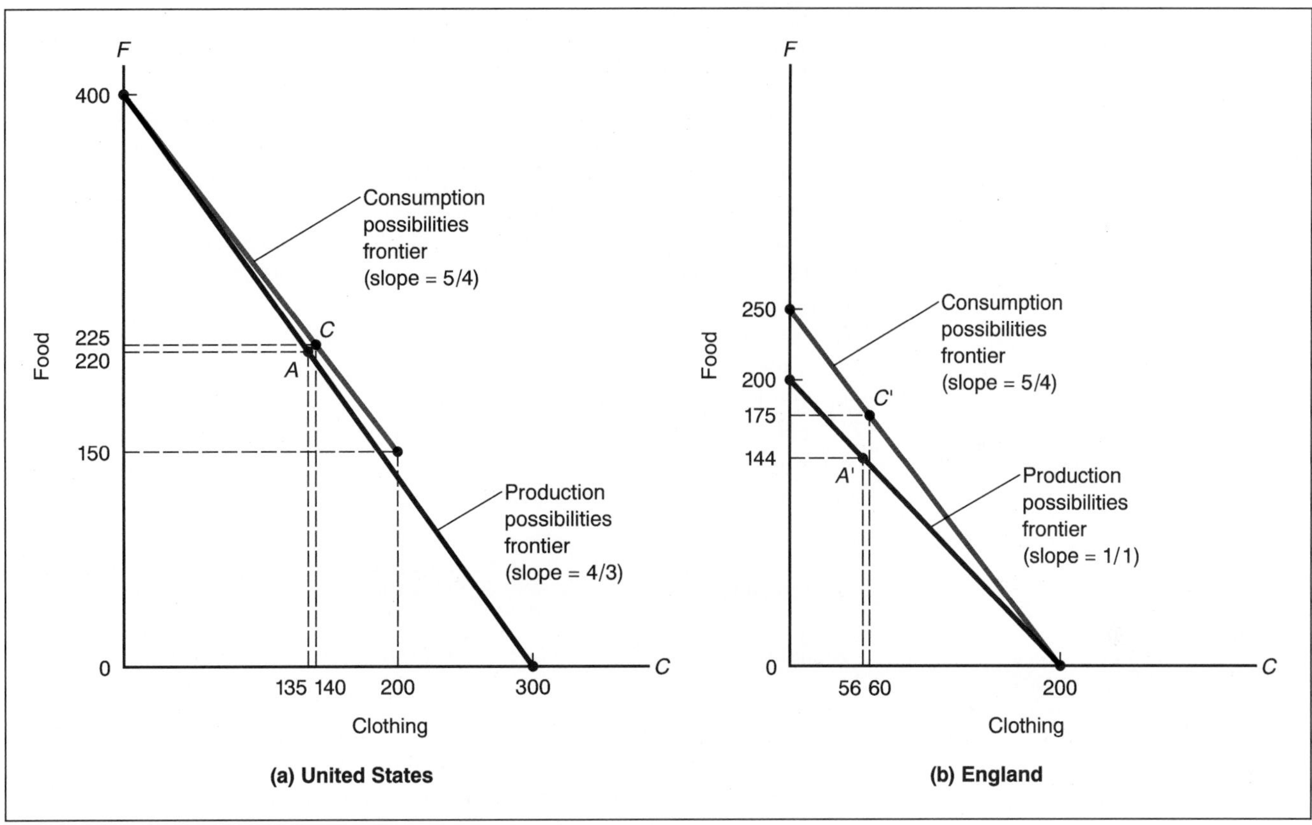

FIGURE 39.1

Comparative Advantage and the Gains From International Trade

In Figure 39.1(a), the inner black line is the production possibilities frontier of the United States, along which it can exchange food (*F*) for clothing (*C*) at the rate of 4*F* for 3*C*. The U.S. produces and consumes at point *A* (220*F*, 135*C*) without trade. By specializing its production in food, in which it has a comparative advantage, and trading with England for clothing, the U.S. can exchange food for clothing at the better rate of 5*F* for 4*C*. Specialization and trade places the U.S. on the outer purple consumption possibilities frontier. At point *C* (225*F*, 140*C*), the United States consumes both more food and more clothing than at point *A* without trade. In Figure 39.1(b), the inner black line is the production possibilities frontier of England, along which it can exchange food (*F*) for clothing (*C*) at the rate of 1*F* for 1*C*. England produces and consumes at point *A'* (144*F*, 56*C*) without trade. By specializing its production in clothing, in which it has a comparative advantage, and trading with the United States for food, England can exchange clothing for food at the better rate of 5*F* for 4*C*. Specialization and trade places England on the outer purple consumption possibilities frontier. At point *C'* (175*F*, 60*C*), England consumes both more food and more clothing than at point *A'* without trade. Both countries gain by specializing their production in the good in which they have a comparative advantage and trading for the other good.

CONSUMPTION VERSUS PRODUCTION POSSIBILITIES Specialization and trade at 5F for 4C increases the consumption possibilities of both countries beyond their production possibilities frontiers, as illustrated by the purple lines in Figure 39.1. Refer, first, to Figure 39.1(b) for England. England puts all its labor into clothing and produces 200C. Then it trades with the United States at the rate of 4C for 5F, leading to a set of consumption possibilities along the purple line. For instance, if it traded all its clothing for food, it would be able to consume 250F, the other end-point of its consumption possibilities frontier with trade [(5/4 · 200 = 250]. The slope of the purple consumption possibilities frontier is 5/4, greater than the slope of the black production possibilities frontier, which equals 1.

Turn next to Figure 39.1(a) for the United States. The United States puts all its labor into food and produces 400F. Then it trades with England at the rate of 5F for 4C, leading to a set of consumption possibilities along the purple line, whose slope is also 5/4. The consumption possibilities stop at 150F and 200C, point *C*, because England has only 200C to trade. If the United States traded for all England's clothing, it would give up 250F in return (250F/200C = 5F/4C). This trade leaves the United States with 150F and 200C (150F = 400F − 250F).

Our example in Chapter 4 assumed that the countries trade 175F for 140C (175F/140C = 5F/4C). The United States has 225F left for its own consumption, and England has 60C left for its own consumption (225F = 400F − 175F; 60C = 200C − 140C). They consume at points *C* and *C′* on their purple consumption possibilities frontiers. Both countries gain from specializing and trading; each one consumes more food *and* more clothing.

	WITH TRADE	WITHOUT TRADE
United States	225F, 140C (point *C*)	220F, 135C (point *A*)
England	175F, 60C (point *C′*)	144 F, 56C (point *A′*)

PRODUCTIVITY VERSUS OPPORTUNITY COSTS The theory of comparative advantage explains why the low-income developing nations do not have to fear the superior technologies of the high-income countries. In our example the United States is more productive in producing *both* goods, yet England can gain from trading with the United States. Differences in opportunity costs, not differences in productivity, determine the pattern and gains from trade.

To underscore this point, suppose that labor in the United States were twice as productive in producing both goods, so that 1 unit of labor produced 4 units of food and 4 units of clothing. The opportunity costs of producing food and clothing are now the same in each country. One more unit of either good entails a sacrifice of one unit of the other good in both the United States and England. Neither country can gain from trade because they would only be willing to trade at the ratio 1F for 1C, which is the same ratio that they can trade in their own countries.

Another way to see why trade is not helpful is to think in terms of the relative prices. The relative price of food to clothing would equal 1 in both countries before trade ($P_F/P_C = 1$). The United States is willing to specialize in and export food only if the relative price of food rises, or $P_F/P_C > 1$. England is willing to specialize in and export clothing only if the relative price of clothing rises, or $P_F/P_C < 1$. There is no room to maneuver. The relative price of food to clothing must remain equal to 1, and each country can do as well by producing on its own as it can by specializing and trading.

The inability to gain from trade in this case has nothing to do with superior U.S. productivity. The same would be true if the United States were equally as productive as England in producing both goods, or half as productive in both. The problem is that the opportunity costs of production are the same in both countries; no country has a *comparative advantage* in either good.

Fortunately, the equally productive case is not realistic. All nations are certain to have a comparative advantage in producing some goods no matter how unproductive they may be in an absolute sense. In other words, all nations can gain from specializing their production and trading.

THE GAINS FROM TRADE AND THE TERMS-OF-TRADE The *pattern* of trade in Ricardo's model depends only on the opportunity costs of production. Each country exports the good that it can produce relatively more cheaply. The *gains* from trade for each country depend on the **terms-of-trade,** the rate at which food and clothing are exchanged. The terms-of-trade in our example is 5F for 4C.[1]

TERMS-OF-TRADE

The rate of exchange between imported goods and exported goods; alternatively, the ratio of a nation's export prices to its import prices.

Both countries gain from trade if the terms-of-trade is between the trading ratios available in each country without trade. This is the case in our example. The terms-of-trade, 5F for 4C, is between the trading ratio of 4F for 3C along the U.S. production possibilities frontier and the trading ratio of 1F for 1C along the British production possibilities frontier. Conversely, only one country gains if the terms-of-trade is at one of the country's trading ratios. For example, only England can gain if the terms-of-trade is 4F for 3C. England can only get 3F for 3C on its own. Trading 4F for 3C makes it better off. In contrast, the United States can get 3C for 4F whether it trades for the clothing or produces the clothing itself. It does not gain from trade. International trade cannot occur outside the boundaries of the within-country trading ratios.

The actual terms-of-trade depends on the relative demands for the two products. The greater the demand for food is, the higher the relative price of food (P_F/P_C) is, the more clothing trades for each unit of food, and the more the United States gains from trade. Conversely, the greater the demand for clothing is, the lower the relative price (P_F/P_C) is, the more food trades for each unit of clothing, and the more England gains from trade.

Returning to our example, suppose that the United States wants 120C and England wants 110C. The British are willing to trade only 90C for food, so that the United States is forced to produce some of its own clothing. This means that the terms-of-trade has to be at 4F for 3C, the U.S. ratio without trade, and $P_F/P_C = .75$. The U.S. clothing producers would switch to producing food at any higher price ratio. As a result, England receives all the gains from trade.

England specializes, produces 200C, and exports 90C to the United States in exchange for 120F (120F/90C = 4F/3C). It could only have 90F without trade if it produced both food and clothing and consumed 110C.

	WITH TRADE	WITHOUT TRADE
England	120F, 110C	90F, 110C

The United States does not specialize and cannot gain from trade. The United States wants 120C, yet receives only 90C in trade from England. Therefore, it uses 10 of its labor units to produce an extra 30C [30 = 3 · 10; 120C = 90C (from England) + 30C (own production)]. This leaves 90 units of labor

[1]The terms-of-trade for a nation is usually defined as the ratio of the nation's export prices to its import prices. In our example, the terms-of-trade from the U.S. point of view is $P_F/P_C = .8$, and the terms-of-trade from the British point of view is $P_C/P_F = 1.25 = (5/4)$.

to produce 360F (360 = 4 · 90). Having exported 120F to England, the United States is left with 240F (240F = 360F − 120F). But the United States can produce 240F and 120C on its own by allocating 60 labor units to food production and 40 labor units to clothing production (240 = 4 · 60; 120 = 3 · 40). The United States does not gain from trade.

	WITH TRADE	WITHOUT TRADE
United States	240F, 120C	240F, 120C

To summarize, our example illustrates two fundamental principles about the gains from international trade. The first is that *the gains from international trade arise because trade changes a nation's terms-of-trade between goods and services.* The second is that *the gains from international trade are greater the better a nation's terms-of-trade is.*

COMPARATIVE ADVANTAGE AND EXCHANGE RATES International transactions require exchanges of one nation's currency for another nation's currency. The exchanges of currency take place in the **foreign exchange markets,** in which the exchange rates between all nations' currencies are established.

FOREIGN EXCHANGE MARKETS
The markets in which nations' currencies are exchanged and the exchange rates between all nations' currencies are established.

The real and the financial sides of international trade are closely linked. Differences in opportunity cost, comparative advantage, determine not only the pattern of international trade, but also the range of values that an exchange rate between two currencies can have. Our simple example can also illustrate this fundamental principle of international exchange. To do so, however, we have to add actual prices to the example.

Suppose that the wage rate in England is 2£ per unit of labor. Since labor is the only factor of production, the prices of food and clothing in England must equal the labor cost of producing them. (We are assuming competitive markets.) In England, 1 unit of labor can produce either 2F or 2C. Therefore, 1 unit of food or clothing requires ½ unit of labor, or a labor cost of 1£. The prices of food and clothing must each be 1£ (P_F = 1£; P_C = 1£). Notice that P_F/P_C = 1£/1£ = 1, as above.

Suppose that the wage rate in the United States is $12 per unit of labor. In the United States, 1 unit of labor can produce 4F. Therefore, 1 unit of food requires ¼ unit of labor, or a labor cost of $3. P_F = $3. Similarly, 1 unit of labor can produce 3C. Therefore, 1 unit of clothing requires ⅓ unit of labor, or a labor cost of $4. P_C = $4. Notice that P_F/P_C = $3/$4 = .75, as above.

The pound and the dollar prices of food and clothing in England and the United States determine the range of values for the dollar-pound exchange rate. In particular, the exchange rate must be equal to or between the ratios of the price of food in both countries and the price of clothing in both countries.

$$P_F^{US}/P_F^{Eng} \leq \$/£ \leq P_C^{US}/P_C^{Eng}$$
$$\$3/1£ \leq \$/£ \leq \$4/£$$

To see why this must be, consider the maximum possible value of the dollar in our example, $3/1£. England is just indifferent to trade at this exchange rate, and the United States receives all the gains from trade. English citizens can buy 1 unit of food in England for 1£, or they can exchange the pound for $3 and buy food in the United States. But $3 only buys 1 unit of food in the

United States as well. The English neither gain nor lose by importing food from the United States, rather than producing it themselves.

Citizens in the United States are eager to import clothing from England at this exchange rate, however. Clothing costs $4 per unit in the United States. Its citizens can do better by exchanging $3 for 1£ and buying 1 unit of clothing from the British for 1£. Importing clothing from England saves $1 per unit of clothing. The British are willing to exchange clothing for food when the exchange rate is $3/1£, but the United States captures all the gains from trade.

Suppose that the dollar happened to appreciate in value to $2/1£ for some reason. The dollar is said to be **overvalued** at this rate because everyone will prefer to buy food and clothing in England. British citizens can buy either 1 unit of food or 1 unit of clothing in England for 1£. If they exchange 1£ for $2, they will not have enough dollars to buy either 1 unit of food or 1 unit of clothing in the United States. Citizens of the United States will also prefer to buy in England. A unit of food costs them $3, and a unit of clothing costs them $4 in the United States. They can do better by exchanging $2 for 1£ and buying either 1 unit of food or 1 unit of clothing for 1£ in England. An overvalued dollar prices U.S. producers out of all markets in which goods are traded.

OVERVALUED CURRENCY

The value of a nation's currency relative to other currencies is greater than its equilibrium value determined by the Laws of Supply and Demand in the foreign exchange markets.

Similarly, the dollar cannot fall lower than $4/1£. Suppose that the dollar happened to depreciate in value to $5/1£. The dollar is said to be **undervalued.** Now everyone wants to buy in the United States. Citizens in the United States will not exchange $5 for 1£ to buy food or clothing in England because food costs only $3 and clothing only $4 in the United States. Conversely, British citizens are eager to exchange pounds for dollars at this rate. Why pay 1£ for food or clothing in England when they can exchange 1£ for $5 and buy more than 1 unit of food or clothing in the United States? In this case the pound is the overvalued currency, and it prices British producers out of the market.

UNDERVALUED CURRENCY

The value of a nation's currency relative to other currencies is less than its equilibrium value determined by the Laws of Supply and Demand in the foreign exchange markets.

We assumed in our original example above that the United States and England exchange at the rate of 5F for 4C and trade 175F from the United States for 140C from England. This requires an exchange rate of $3.75/1£ at the wage rate and prices given above. To see why an exchange rate of $3.75/1£ is a trading ratio of 5F for 4C, note that $3.75 for 1£ is the same as $15 for 4£ ($15 = $3.75 · 4). In the United States $15 buys 5 units of food at a price of $3 per unit; in England 4£ buys 4 units of clothing at a price of 1£ per unit. Therefore, an exchange rate of $3.75/1£ allows U.S. and English citizens to trade 5F for 4C.

Both nations gain from trade at this exchange rate. Citizens in the United States used to pay $3 for food and $4 for clothing. They still pay $3 for food, but they can now buy clothing in England for $3.75, by exchanging $3.75 for 1£ and buying the clothing for 1£. Similarly, British citizens used to pay 1£ each for a unit of food and/or clothing. They still pay 1£ for clothing, but they can now buy more than 1 unit of food in the United States for 1£, by exchanging 1£ for $3.75 and buying the food for $3 per unit.

THE VALUE OF IMPORTS EQUALS THE VALUE OF EXPORTS Note, finally, that the values of imports and exports are equal in our example. Let's compute the values in terms of dollars. We assumed that 175F exchanged for 140C. The price of food is $3 in the United States. Therefore, the dollar value of the food exports is $525 ($525 = $3 · 175). The clothing costs 140£ in England. The dollar value of the clothing imports at an exchange rate of \$3.75/£ is also \$525 (\$525 = \$3.75 · 140).

The principle that the value of a nation's imports must equal the value of a nation's exports is another fundamental principle of international trade. The values may not be equal in any one year as they are in our simple example. In fact, the dollar value of U.S. exports generally exceeded the dollar value of its imports by a wide margin in the 1950s and 1960s, and the reverse has been true since the early 1980s. Nonetheless, the value of imports and exports must eventually balance out over time. An excess of imports must eventually be followed by an excess of exports, and an excess of exports must eventually be followed by an excess of imports.

CURRENT ISSUE: Many U.S. citizens are concerned about the large U.S. trade deficit with Japan. There is no need for a nation's imports and exports to be equal with each of its trading partners, however. The equality of imports and exports applies to total imports and exports with all nations combined. The U.S.-Japanese trade deficit would not seem so troublesome if the United States had an equally large trade surplus with all other nations combined.

The reason for this is simply that nations will not export resource-using goods and services to other nations without receiving goods and services in return. For example, when the dollar value of U.S. imports exceeds the dollar value of U.S. exports, as it does now, someone is sending the United States real goods and services in exchange for dollars (or U.S. financial securities). Eventually they will want to turn these dollars into real goods and services, and when they do, the dollar value of U.S. exports must rise. We will look more closely at the financial side of international trade in Chapter 40. As we do, though, keep in mind the fundamental principle that the value of a nation's imports must eventually equal the value of its exports.

CHEAP LABOR AND INTERNATIONAL TRADE Our simple example illustrated that the low-income developing nations need not fear the superior technologies and productivity of the high-income industrial nations. Lower productivity is not a barrier to specialization and trade. The opposite side of this principle is that the industrialized nations need not fear the lower wages of the developing nations. Higher wages are not a barrier to specialization and trade either. Our simple example illustrates this important principle as well.

The 2£ wage rate in England translates into a wage rate of \$7.50 at the exchange rate of \$3.75/1£ (\$7.50 = 2£ · \$3.75/£). Although \$7.50 is well below the \$12 wage rate in the United States, the difference in wage rates between the countries has no effect on the pattern of trade or the gains from trade. The low wages in England do not drive out the U.S. food producers. All that matters is that the dollar-pound exchange rate stay somewhere between the ratios of the food prices and clothing prices in the two countries. So long as it does, the United States exports foods, England exports clothing, and both countries can gain from trade.

The chief threat to a nation's standard of living is stagnating productivity growth, not competition from other low-wage or high-productivity nations. Remember that long-run economic growth is the most important determinant of a nation's standard of living. Whether wages are high or low, growing or stagnating, depends on a nation's ability to increase productivity and push its production possibilities frontier out over time.

Economic growth always causes disruptions to the economy in the short run. In the context of international trade, unbalanced productivity growth across industries can change the pattern of comparative advantage and force nations to reallocate their resources. In our example, a doubling of labor productivity from 3C to 6C in the U.S. clothing industry would give the United States the comparative advantage in clothing. The United States would have to switch and specialize in clothing production, and England would have to switch and specialize in food production. These short-run disruptions notwithstanding, productivity growth is essential to improving a nation's standard of living over the long run.

International trade can improve the standard of living at all stages of economic development, as we have just seen. But the improvement made possible through trade is small for most nations relative to their long-term record of productivity growth.

International Trade and Factor Endowments

David Ricardo's simple model of comparative advantage reveals a number of fundamental principles of international trade and finance, but it is not a complete explanation of international exchange. A number of its predictions are at odds with what we actually observe. For instance, it predicts that nations completely specialize their production in the goods that they export. They do not produce the imported goods. In fact, specialization is nearly always incomplete. Nations typically do produce most of the products that they import. Think of clothing, food and beverages, and automobiles in the United States. The Ricardo model also assumes constant marginal costs, so that the pattern of trade is entirely determined by the supply side of the economy. In fact, marginal costs typically increase as industry output expands. As a result, the pattern of trade is determined by the interaction of supply and demand, not by supply alone.

Figure 39.2 offers a more realistic picture of the pattern of domestic production and international trade. Figure 39.2(a) shows the supply and demand for food in England, and Figure 39.2(b) shows the supply and demand for food in the United States. The supply curves in each graph refer to the domestic producers within each country and incorporate the realistic assumption of increasing marginal cost as output increases. The vertical axis records the price ratio of food to clothing, P_F/P_C, so that we can compute this figure directly with our previous model.

The intersection of the supply and demand curves in each graph shows the equilibrium in each country before trade. Supply and demand intersect at $P_F/P_C = 1$ in England and at $P_F/P_C = .75$ in the United States. The equilibrium quantity is Q_E^0 in each graph. These are the same before-trade price ratios as in our previous model. The difference here, though, is that the relative prices are determined by the interaction of supply and demand, and not just the supply side of the economy.

Opening up the countries to trade causes food to flow from the low-priced, low-cost country to the high-priced, high-cost country. As before, England imports food, and the United States exports food. The increased supply of food in England lowers the relative price of food there, and the increased demand for U.S. food increases the relative price of food there. The prices continue to change in each country until the demand for imports in England equals the supply of exports from the United States. According to Figure 39.2, the new equilibrium with trade occurs at the price ratio $P_F/P_C = .8$, also as in our previous model. This time, though, specialization is incomplete.

Refer to Figure 39.2(a). As P_F/P_C falls from 1 to .8 in England, British producers reduce their quantity supplied from Q_E^0 to Q_S^1 units of food. British

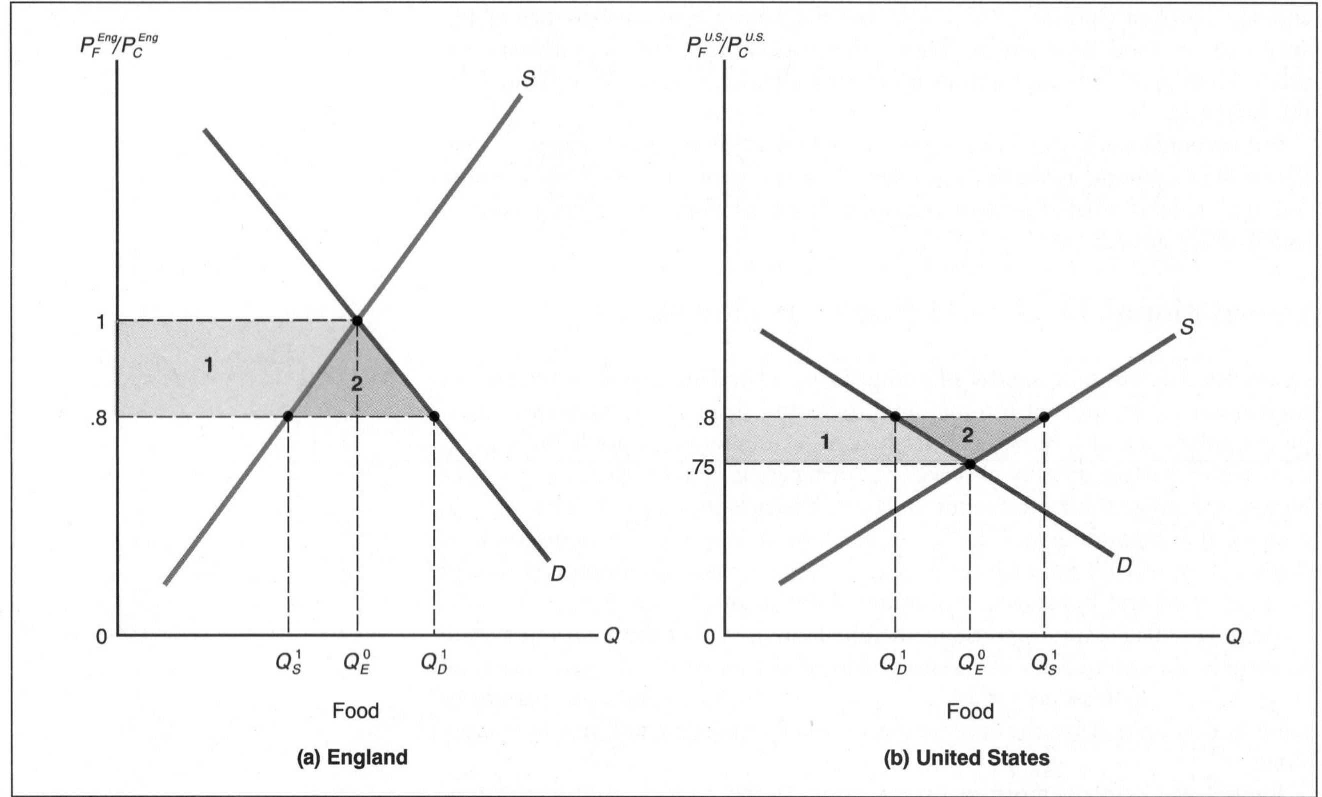

FIGURE 39.2

The Gains From Trade in the Factor Endowments Model

In the factor endowments model prices, and comparative advantage, are determined by the interaction of supply and demand. In the two figures, the demand curve, D, refers to the demand for food by the country's own consumers, and the supply curve, S, refers to the supply of food by the domestic producers. The quantity of food is on the horizontal axis and the relative price of food to clothing, P_F/P_C, is on the vertical axis. Without trade, $P_F/P_C = 1$ in England, at the intersection of D and S in Figure 39.2(a), and $P_F/P_C = .75$ in the United States, at the intersection of D and S in Figure 39.2(b). The United States is the lower price, lower cost producer, so the U.S. exports food and England imports food. The relative price of food falls in England and rises in the United States until it reaches .8 in both countries. Refer to Figure 39.2(a). At the relative price $P_F/P_C = .8$, British producers lower their quantity supplied to Q_S^1, British consumers increase their quantity demanded to Q_D^1, and England imports $(Q_D^1 - Q_S^1)$ of food. Consumer surplus increases by the sum of areas 1 + 2 because consumers now buy more food and pay a lower price. Producer surplus decreases by area 1 because producers supply less food and receive a lower price. The net gain in surplus is area 2. Refer to Figure 39.2(b). At the relative price $P_F/P_C = .8$, U.S. producers increase their quantity supplied to Q_S^1, U.S. consumers reduce their quantity demanded to Q_D^1, and the United States exports $(Q_S^1 - Q_D^1)$ of food, the same amount that England imports. Producer surplus increases by the sum of areas 1 + 2 because producers now supply more food and receive a higher price. Consumer surplus decreases by area 1 because consumers buy less food and pay a higher price. The net gain in surplus is area 2. Both countries gain from trade.

consumers increase their quantity demanded from Q_E^0 to Q_D^1 units of food. $(Q_D^1 - Q_S^1)$ is the amount of food imported from the United States. Notice that England simultaneously produces and imports food; specialization is incomplete.

Now look at Figure 39.2(b). As P_F/P_C rises from .75 to .8 in the United States, U.S. producers increase their quantity supplied from Q_E^0 to Q_S^1 units of food. Consumers in the United States decrease their quantity demanded from Q_E^0 to Q_D^1 units of food. $(Q_S^1 - Q_D^1)$ is the amount of food exported to England.

We have not shown the clothing market, but the reverse is happening there. A falling price ratio, P_F/P_C, in England is a rising price ratio, P_C/P_F. English clothing producers respond by increasing the quantity supplied, and English consumers respond by decreasing the quantity demanded. England exports clothing. Conversely, a rising P_F/P_C in the United States is a falling P_C/P_F. U.S. clothing producers respond by decreasing the quantity supplied, and U.S. consumers respond by increasing the quantity demanded. The United States imports clothing. The United States also continues to produce clothing, so that specialization is incomplete in the United States as well.

The expanded model shares a number of features with the simple Ricardo model of comparative advantage:

1. The pattern of trade is determined by differences in opportunity costs. The original high-price, high-cost producer of food, England, imports food from the original low-price, low-cost producer of food, the United States.

2. Both countries gain from trade. The gains on a supply-demand graph can be seen as follows. The demand curve shows, at every quantity, the amount that consumers are willing to pay to consume the last unit. Therefore, consumers get a surplus in the market that can be represented as the area beneath the demand curve and above the price they have to pay, up to the quantity demanded. The supply curve shows, at every quantity, the marginal cost of producing the last unit. Therefore, producers get a surplus in the market that can be represented as the area above the supply curve and below the price they receive, up to the quantity supplied.

Refer to the market for food in England in Figure 39.2(a). Consumers gain and food producers lose as the price falls from $P_F/P_C = 1$ to $P_F/P_C = .8$. The consumer surplus increases by the shaded areas labeled 1 and 2. These areas reflect the gain of consuming more food and paying a lower price for it. At the same time, the producer surplus decreases by the area labeled 1. This area reflects the loss of producing less food and receiving a lower price for it. The net gain is the area labeled 2. There will always be a net gain for the importing country because the demand curve is to the right of the supply curve over the range of prices that lead to imports.

Now refer to the market for food in the United States in Figure 39.2(b). Consumers lose and food producers gain as the price rises from $P_F/P_C = .75$ to $P_F/P_C = .8$. The consumer surplus decreases by the shaded area 1. Consumers buy less food and pay a higher price for it. At the same time, the producer surplus increases by the areas 1 plus 2. Domestic firms produce more food and receive a higher price for it. The net gain is the area 2. There will always be a net gain for the exporting country because the supply curve is to the right of the demand curve over the range of prices that lead to exports.

GAINS FROM TRADE

The amount that a nation gains through international trade relative to producing itself all the goods and the services that it consumes; alternatively, the increase in consumer surplus plus producer surplus resulting from international trade.

3. Resources are reallocated from the clothing industry to the food industry in the United States and from the food industry to the clothing industry in England. The only difference is that specialization is incomplete in both countries.

4. Although we have not shown the clothing markets, the value of imports must equal the value of exports in both countries. The intuition behind this result is that the same price ratio, $P_F/P_C = .8$, applies in both markets in each country.

The model of rising marginal costs is much richer than is the simple Ricardo model, however. In particular, it allows us to explore the important distributional implications of international trade. Although both countries gain from trade, the gains are not shared equally by all. Some factors of production gain, while others lose. To see these distributional implications we have to understand why countries might have different marginal (opportunity) costs.

FACTOR ENDOWMENTS AND COMPARATIVE ADVANTAGE Why are the costs of producing certain products lower in some countries than in others? The Ricardo model points to differences in technologies across countries. The factor endowments model points to differences in factor endowments across countries. The United States has amassed an enormous stock of sophisticated capital, is blessed with huge amounts of fertile land, and has a highly educated, highly skilled labor force for the most part. Relative to its total resources, the United States has a higher proportion of capital, land, and highly skilled labor than does almost any other country in the world. The larger the supply of a factor the lower its price, other things equal. Therefore, the United States has a cost advantage, and hence a comparative advantage, in products that use relatively large amounts of capital, land, and highly skilled labor. At the same time, most other countries have more unskilled labor relative to their other resources than does the United States. Therefore, the wages of unskilled labor tend to be lower in other countries, so that they have a cost advantage, and a comparative advantage, in products that use relatively large amounts of unskilled labor.

Furthermore, we saw in Figure 39.2 that international trade increases the producer surplus in the export industries (food in the figure). Some of this additional surplus is captured by the factors of production that are used relatively more in these industries. Therefore, international trade increases the returns to capital, land, and highly skilled labor in the United States. Conversely, international trade decreases producer surplus in the import-competing industries (clothing in the figure), and the factors that are used relatively more in these industries suffer some of the loss in the producer surplus. Therefore, international trade lowers the wages of unskilled workers in the United States. One can understand why U.S. labor unions tend to support trade restrictions.

FACTOR ENDOWMENTS MODEL OF INTERNATIONAL TRADE
A model developed to explain the pattern of international trade that is based on differences in factor endowments across countries; countries specialize their production in and export those goods that use factors of production that are relatively abundant, and they import those goods that use factors of production that are relatively scarce.

What is true for the United States is true generally throughout the world. *The relatively abundant factors, those used more intensively in the export goods, gain from trade. The relatively scarce factors, those used more intensively in the goods that compete with the imported goods, lose from trade.*[2]

THE NORTH AMERICAN FREE TRADE AGREEMENT The factor endowments model is the one that has been used to debate the merits of including Mexico in the North American Free Trade Agreement (NAFTA). NAFTA is an agreement to remove all trade barriers among Canada, the United States, and Mexico. After a long and bitter political debate, Congress voted in November 1993 to include Mexico in NAFTA.

---

[2]The factor endowments model also shows that trade tends to equalize the returns to factors worldwide. This is because the returns to factors in other countries are changing in the opposite direction to that in the United States. In the other countries, international trade decreases the returns to capital, land, and highly skilled labor, and increases the wages of unskilled labor. Advanced textbooks demonstrate that international trade would equalize the returns to all factors everywhere if factor markets were competitive worldwide. International trade substitutes for factor mobility in this sense. Barriers to factor mobility such as immigration laws, other trade restrictions, and the use of different technologies worldwide prevent returns to factors from equalizing in the real world.

Critics who wanted to exclude Mexico from NAFTA fear that expanding trade with Mexico will lower the wages of unskilled workers in the United States. The average wage of manufacturing workers in Mexico is only 1/8 the average wage of manufacturing workers in the United States. With all trade barriers removed, firms in Mexico, the United States, and elsewhere that produce goods using relatively large amounts of unskilled labor have a strong incentive to produce in Mexico and export to the United States. Unskilled U.S. workers in the import-competing industries will find their wages falling as the increased production in Mexico raises wages there. This will further increase the earnings inequality between high-wage and low-wage employees in the United States, which has been rapidly increasing since the late 1970s.

The issue takes on added emotion because of Mexico's lax environmental laws. The Mexican government has virtually no standards regarding the use of underground storage tanks, or the disposal of hazardous wastes, or the cleanup of abandoned hazardous waste sites. So U.S. firms that migrate to Mexico can also avoid the costs of complying with the U.S. environmental laws.

The movement of U.S. firms to Mexico has already begun. In the early 1980s, following the collapse of oil prices, the Mexican government established a policy called the Maquiladora program to encourage exports in order to replace the lost oil export revenues. The program allows firms, called *maquilas,* to import equipment and parts duty-free into Mexico so long as the final products are exported. By 1991 there were more than 2,000 maquilas operating in Mexico, employing 600,000 workers. More than half of the maquilas are auto parts or electronic equipment assemblers, both of which use primarily unskilled labor, and many of the maquilas are U.S. firms. The fear is that including Mexico in NAFTA will only accelerate the movement of U.S. firms into Mexico as they seek low-cost unskilled labor.

The fear that freer trade with Mexico will lower the wages of unskilled U.S. workers must be tempered by a number of considerations. First and foremost is the sheer size of the U.S. economy relative to the Mexican economy. One study critical of NAFTA estimated that investment by U.S. firms in Mexico would total $53 billion by the year 2000, an average of about $5 billion per year. This may seem like a lot until we remember that total investment in the United States exceeded $770 billion in 1992 alone. The projected investment in Mexico is less than 1 percent of total U.S. investment, a percentage much too small to have a noticeable impact on the overall U.S. market for unskilled workers, or anything else at the macro level.

In addition, suppose that the United States continues to restrict trade with Mexico in order to protect its unskilled workers. Restricting trade simply encourages unskilled Mexican workers to emigrate to the United States to seek the higher wages available here. And this has already happened, of course. No one knows for sure how many Mexican workers have entered the United States illegally to work, but one study estimates that 22 percent of the entire Mexican labor force is working in the United States.[3] The influx of Mexican workers

[3]The data on the maquilas and the projected U.S. investment in Mexico are from T. Koechlin and M. Larudee, "The High Cost of NAFTA," *Challenge* 35, No. 5 (September–October 1992): 19–26 (see, particularly, Table 1, p. 19, and p. 21). Mexico's pollution standards are described in S. Friedman, "NAFTA As Social Dumping," *Challenge* 35, No. 5 (September–October 1992): 27–32. The estimate of the percentage of the Mexican labor force in the United States is reported in W. Enders and H. Lapan, *International Economics: Theory and Policy* (Englewood Cliffs, N.J.: Prentice-Hall, 1987), 209.

has probably already lowered the wages of U.S. unskilled workers about as much as they are going to fall from the competition with Mexican labor.

A final point is that Mexico has a comparative advantage relative to the United States in products that use unskilled labor, NAFTA or no NAFTA. If U.S. firms are prevented from entering Mexico, then firms from other nations will take their place and export to the United States. Proponents of NAFTA argue that it is in the best interest of United States to allow the U.S. firms in.

On balance, including Mexico in NAFTA would not appear to have much of an effect on the wages of unskilled U.S. workers.

Product Differentiation and Economies of Scale

The third, and most recent, model of international trade attempts to explain why the high-income industrial nations both import and export very similar products. We saw in the introduction to the chapter that the two-way trade of similar products constitutes the majority of trade by the United States, and the same is true for all the industrial nations. This trade cannot be explained very well by comparative advantage or differences in factor endowments. The industrialized nations all have large stocks of sophisticated capital and highly educated and skilled labor, and their firms produce similar products using much the same technologies. A different model is clearly needed to explain this trade.

MULTINATIONAL CORPORATION

A corporation that has offices and/or factories in more than one country.

Over the past 15 years or so economists have come to understand this two-way trade as the result of competition among the large corporations of the industrialized nations. The large corporations are most often **multinational firms** with production facilities in a number of countries, and they compete on a global scale. The principal competition among them takes the form of research and development into new varieties of products, such as cars with better gas mileage, faster computer chips, beers with different tastes and alcohol content, and the like. Most of the innovation arising in large multinational corporations is product-related, not production/process-related. Each corporation is trying to carve out a niche for itself in the international marketplace.

PRODUCT DIFFERENTIATION/ ECONOMIES OF SCALE MODEL OF INTERNATIONAL TRADE

A model specifically developed to explain the two-way trade in similar products between the industrialized countries; based on the idea that multinational corporations compete with each other through the research and development of new products and successful products enjoy economies of scale, which gives them a niche in the international marketplace.

Two-way trade results from this competition in the following manner. A corporation's research and development staff works on generating new varieties and refinements of the company's products. The corporation test-markets each new product idea in the home market at first in order to save on transportation and marketing costs and to give it more flexibility to vary the products as needed. Once the corporation finds a successful product variation, economies of scale come into play. The research and development costs associated with any one product are usually an important component of the overall costs of producing the product. Furthermore, research and development costs are foregone or sunk costs that become spread over ever-larger quantities as a successful product expands its market. Consequently, the unit costs of producing the product steadily decline as sales increase, and the product gains a cost advantage through these economies of scale.

The firm expands to foreign markets once the product is a proven success at home, spreading the sunk research and development costs even further. The unit cost advantage from the economies of scale allows the corporation to compete successfully in the foreign markets against other varieties of the product. The product does find its niche in the international marketplace.

Two-way trade occurs because large corporations everywhere are playing the same game. Suppose that a U.S. corporation successfully develops one variety of a product and a German corporation successfully develops another variety of the same product. Then the U.S. firm exports its product variety to Germany, and the German firm exports its product variety to the United States. The United States and Germany engage in a two-way trade of highly similar products, which is exactly what we observe among the industrial nations.

Notice that only corporations in the industrial nations can easily play this game because only the industrial nations have economies large enough to allow them to develop their products first in their home markets and realize the economies of scale. Corporations in the smaller, middle- and low-income nations would have great difficulty developing and test-marketing new products in larger foreign markets.[4]

THE EUROPEAN COMMUNITY The product differentiation/economies of scale model is the principal model that economists have used to assess the potential economic gains from the European Community (EC), which began operation on December 31, 1992. The EC is the culmination of a 35-year effort to remove trade barriers throughout Western Europe. The effort began in 1957 when six countries—Belgium, France, Italy, Luxembourg, the Netherlands, and West Germany—signed the Treaty of Rome to form the European Economic Community (EEC). Among other goals the six nations pledged to remove all internal tariffs between them within 12 years, a goal that they achieved by 1968. Six more nations joined the EEC between 1973 and 1983—Denmark, Ireland, and the United Kingdom in 1973; Greece in 1981; and Portugal and Spain in 1983.

Then, in 1985, Jacques Delors, the president of the European Commission, authored a White Paper entitled *Completing the Internal Market,* which outlined the steps necessary to achieve complete freedom of movement for all goods and factors throughout the 12 EEC nations.[5] The EEC formally adopted Delors's recommendations in July of 1987 with the passage of the Single European Act and established December 31, 1992, as the target date for the new European Community.

Even though the internal tariffs had long since disappeared, trade within the EEC was still severely restricted in 1985. In addition to the costs and the delays of border crossings, manufacturers trying to sell in other countries encountered a host of nontariff barriers in the form of highly specific product and technical standards, local content laws, and various kinds of marketing regulations. These barriers gave local producers a significant amount of protection from foreign competitors. For example, Italy had a law requiring that all pasta sold there be made from durum wheat, which no one in Western Europe grows besides the Italians; the French required that tile meet certain specifications, which effectively excluded the German and Italian tile manufacturers; the entire EEC required that the noise from lawn mower engines be less than 90 decibels,

---

[4]A small portion of the two-way trade has more conventional origins. Tourism is one example. Ski lovers in the United States head to South America in July and August, while South American surfers pass them in the airports heading to the U.S. beaches. Also, large countries whose natural resources are concentrated geographically are likely to both export and import the resources. The United States exports its Alaskan oil to the Pacific rim countries, while the Eastern seaboard states import oil from OPEC. The high costs of transporting oil explain this two-way trade.

[5]Commission of the European Communities, *Completing the Internal Market, White Paper from the Commission to the European Council* (Luxembourg: Office for Official Publications of the European Communities, 1985).

which kept the larger U.S. tractor mowers out of Europe. Delors's White Paper set down nearly 300 directives that would eliminate all regulations and restrictions of these kinds, and most of the directives were in effect by the end of 1992. The 12 EEC nations also eliminated all border inspections among themselves.

A study undertaken by the European Commission in 1987, commonly referred to as the Cecchini Report, estimated that the gains from "completing the internal market" would be considerable, on the order of 4.3 to 6.8 percent of the EC's combined national product.[6] Most economists who have independently studied the potential gains believe that the Cecchini Report is much too optimistic. Independent estimates typically place the gains at 1 to 2 percent of the European national product. But all economists agree that the majority of the gains, 60 percent and more, will come from greater competition and reduced costs through economies of scale. The reason is that four countries, France, Germany, Italy, and the United Kingdom, account for 70 percent of the population and 80 percent of the national product within the EC. Their economies are very much alike, so that fully 80 percent of all the trade within the EC is two-way trade of similar products.

The chief inefficiencies within Western Europe prior to the EC stemmed from each country having too many small, localized firms that were protected from competition. The average European firm in 1990 was much smaller than was its counterpart in the United States, and often much too small to realize the cost-saving economies of large-scale production. Two outstanding examples were railroad locomotives and industrial boilers. Western Europe had 16 firms producing locomotives and 12 firms producing industrial boilers. The United States had two of each. The localized firms were able to charge artificially high prices to cover their higher costs, however, because of all the market and the product regulations that protected their markets. One study found enormous differences in the prices of similar products throughout Western Europe. Pharmaceuticals were 10 times more expensive in some countries than in others, new car prices varied as much as 93 percent for the same models, and telecommunications equipment prices differed by as much as 40 percent across countries. Price differences of this order of magnitude are a sure sign that markets are segmented and protected from foreign competition.

Economists predict that the EC will lead to a substantial consolidation of industries within Western Europe. They see a smaller number of multinational firms emerging and competing with one another for markets throughout Europe. The multinational firms will realize the economies of large-scale production and drive out many of the smaller, higher-cost localized firms. The increased competition for markets will also lower prices, so that consumers will capture much of the cost savings of large-scale production. The large firms will also compete with one another primarily through the research and development of new product lines as described above, so that most of the increase in trade will be two-way trade in similar products.

In summary, the majority of the gains from opening up the markets of Europe will come from cost-reducing economies of scale and increased intraindustry competition among firms producing similar products. They will not

---

[6]M. Emerson and others, *The Economics of 1992: The EC Commission's Assessment of the Economic Effects of Completing the Internal Market* (Oxford: Oxford University Press, 1988). Paul Cecchini was a principal investigator on the study.

be the traditional gains to trade achieved through comparative advantage and the specialization of production in particular industries.[7]

TARIFFS AND NONTARIFF BARRIERS TO TRADE

The three principal models used to explain international trade create an extremely strong presumption for free trade. Each model concludes that a nation can significantly improve its overall economic well-being by opening up its borders to trade.

Nonetheless, all nations restrict the flow of imports and exports to some extent through tariffs and a variety of nontariff barriers. A **tariff** is a tax on a good or a service entering a country. Nontariff barriers take many forms. The most common nontariff barrier is the **quota,** which directly limits the quantity of a good or a service that can enter a country. Quotas are the main form of trade restriction used by the United States to reduce imports. Another popular nontariff barrier is the **voluntary export restriction,** in which one country asks a second country to voluntarily restrict its exports. For example, Japan agreed to voluntarily restrict its exports of automobiles into the United States beginning in 1981. Still other nontariff barriers are the various product and marketing regulations that existed in Europe before the establishment of the European Community. Other countries also resort to these kinds of trade restrictions.

TARIFF

A tax on a good or a service entering a country.

QUOTA

A government-imposed limit on the quantity of a good or a service that can be imported into a country.

VOLUNTARY EXPORT RESTRICTION

An agreement between two nations in which one nation voluntarily limits the quantity of its exports to the other nation.

Why are countries willing to sacrifice some of the potential gains from trade by implementing these types of trade restrictions, and what harm do they cause? The remainder of Chapter 39 attempts to answer these questions. Let's begin with tariffs.

A Brief History of Tariffs

Tariffs were originally imposed by the United States and other nations as the most convenient and reliable way of raising revenues to finance government expenditures. In 1792 the federal government collected $3.43 million in tariff revenues; total federal revenues at the time were only $3.67 million. Tariff revenues remained the single most important source of federal revenues as late as 1900, when they amounted to 41 percent of total federal revenues. The advent of income taxes in the early 1900s established a far more potent source of revenues than did tariffs, and tariffs steadily diminished to insignificance as a revenue raiser. By 1980 tariff revenues were only 1.4 percent of total federal revenues.[8]

The Great Depression of the 1930s led nations to discover a new use for tariffs. They saw tariffs as a means of protecting jobs and even of stimulating

[7]An excellent economic analysis of the EC, on which much of this section is based, is H. Flam, "Product Markets and 1992: Full Integration, Large Gains?," *Journal of Economic Perspectives* 6, No. 4 (Fall 1992): 7–30. The price differences are on p. 10, and an overview of the independent estimates of the economic gains is on p. 27. Another excellent source on the economics of the EC is the "Symposium on Europe 1992," along with the invited papers, in *Brookings Papers on Economic Activity* 2 (1989): 277–381. For the micro issues, see M. Peck, "Industrial Organization and the Gains from Europe 1992," 277–299. For the macro issues, see R. Dornbusch, "Europe 1992: Macroeconomic Implications," 341–362.

[8]Enders and Lapan, *International Economics*, 132, 134.

the economy by increasing domestic demand. Modern aggregate demand theory does teach us that tariffs can stimulate the economy, at least over the short run. Remember that import demand subtracts from aggregate demand. Therefore, tariffs, by lowering import demand, raise aggregate demand and the equilibrium level of income. The increase in aggregate demand leads firms to hire more workers. The hope in the 1930s was that tariffs could help reduce the staggering levels of unemployment that existed at the time.

The U.S. Congress bought the jobs protection and unemployment arguments and passed the Smoot-Hawley tariff, which raised the average tariff on U.S. imports to 50 percent, far above what it had ever been before (or has been since). Supporters of the Smoot-Hawley tariff overlooked two points, however. The first is the principle that the value of imports must equal the value of exports. Substantially reducing U.S. imports must eventually reduce U.S. exports as well because other countries cannot export as much to the United States. The reduction in their exports lowers their aggregate demand and income and prevents them from importing as much from the United States. This point was vaguely understood. The Smoot-Hawley tariff was viewed as a **beggar-thy-neighbor policy,** a blatant attempt to export U.S. unemployment to other nations. But the supporters did not make the connection that the eventual reduction in export demand would destroy jobs in the export sector and lower U.S. aggregate demand. A beggar-thy-neighbor policy does not work in the long run.

BEGGAR-THY-NEIGHBOR POLICY

A government policy that attempts to export domestic unemployment abroad by means of tariffs and other restrictions on imports.

This fundamental principle quickly became moot, however, because of a second point that the supporters of the tariff overlooked: Other nations would not stand by and let the United States attempt to export its unemployment to them. They immediately retaliated with enormous tariffs of their own, and the predictable result was a disastrous reduction of trade worldwide that only served to deepen and prolong the Great Depression.

General Agreement on Tariffs and Trade

Chastened by the experience of the Great Depression, 23 countries met in 1947 and signed a **General Agreement on Tariffs and Trade,** commonly referred to as GATT. GATT commits the signatories to come together periodically in extended meetings called Rounds to negotiate reductions in tariffs and other trade restrictions. The negotiations must honor the **most-favored-nation principle,** meaning that any reduction in tariffs or other trade restrictions that is negotiated between any two nations automatically applies to all the nations under GATT. (That is, all nations must be treated as the most-favored nation is treated.)

GENERAL AGREEMENT ON TARIFFS AND TRADE (GATT)

A treaty originally signed by 23 capitalist nations in 1947 that commits the signatories to reduce tariffs and other trade barriers; membership in GATT has grown to nearly 100 nations.

MOST-FAVORED-NATION PRINCIPLE

A fundamental principle of GATT that states that any reduction in tariffs or other trade restrictions that is negotiated between any two nations automatically applies to all nations.

There have been eight Rounds of negotiations since 1947, with each Round typically lasting for a number of years. The most recent Round is the Uruguay Round, which began in 1986 and still had not been completed as of November 1993. Also, GATT membership has grown from the original 23 members to nearly 100.

GATT has met with mixed success in reducing trade restrictions. It has been spectacularly successful in reducing tariffs, as Table 39.3 indicates. The average level of tariffs among GATT nations has fallen steadily since World War II; the days of retaliatory tariffs are far behind. At the same time, GATT has not succeeded in reducing quotas and other nontariff barriers. Quite the contrary;

TABLE 39.3 **Average Tariff Rates on Manufactured Goods for Industrialized Countries Within GATT**

YEAR	AVERAGE TARIFF RATES
1940	40%
1950	25
1960	17
1970	12
1980	8
1990	5
GATT ROUNDS	
Geneva	1947
Annecy	1948
Torquay	1950
Geneva	1956
Dillon	1960–61
Kennedy	1964–67
Tokyo	1973–79
Uruguay	1986–

SOURCE: "World Trade Survey," *The Economist* (September 22, 1990): 7.

these other forms of trade restrictions have mushroomed since World War II and have replaced tariffs as the main form of trade restriction. The proliferation of nontariff barriers is discouraging because GATT specifically forbids quotas and export subsidies and encourages the signatories to use tariffs rather than direct quantity restrictions if they feel that they must restrict trade.

GATT has faced two major handicaps in eliminating tariffs completely and in halting the growth of the nontariff barriers. The first is that GATT is riddled with exceptions that were necessary to be able to forge the original agreement in 1947. Agricultural products have always been exempt from the provisions of GATT, as are products considered essential to national security. GATT members are permitted to arrange "voluntary" restrictions, such as the Japanese agreement to limit auto exports to the United States. Trade restrictions are also permitted to correct balance-of-payment deficits (to be described in Chapter 40). The most sweeping exception, though, is the so-called Escape Clause, which allows a nation to withdraw previous concessions and protect a domestic industry if it can show that imports have or would substantially damage domestic producers. The Escape Clause essentially gives nations free rein to restrict trade as they please because import-competing industries are almost certain to be substantially damaged by a reduction in trade restrictions. The second handicap is that GATT is unenforceable. The original 23 GATT signatories failed in their attempt to establish a supernational agency to impose sanctions on nations that violate the letter or the spirit of GATT.

CURRENT ISSUE: One major issue preventing the completion of the Uruguay Round has been the practice of subsidizing domestic agriculture. The United States, a major food exporter, has been strenuously pushing for a reduction in agricultural subsidies. Many of its competitors, France in particular, have been resisting just as strenuously.

These two handicaps have led the authors of a best-selling textbook in international economics to conclude that "Despite GATT agreements, the ability of governments to restrict trade is virtually unlimited."[9] And the means that governments have increasingly chosen are quotas and other direct quantity restrictions.

[9]Enders and Lapan, *International Economics*, 132, 134.

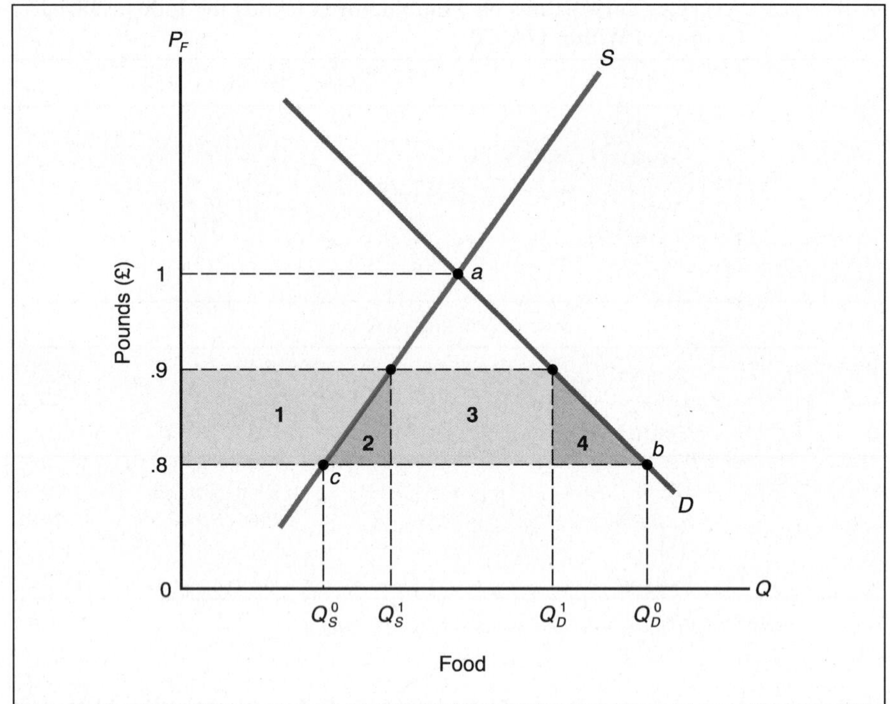

FIGURE 39.3

The Social Cost of Tariffs

The figure shows that tariffs reduce the quantity of imports and, in doing so, throw away some of the gains from trade. Without a tariff, the price of food in England is .8£ as in Figure 39.2 (assuming $P_C = 1£$), and England imports an amount of food equal to $(Q_D^0 - Q_S^0)$. A tariff of .1£ per unit of food raises the price of food to .9£. At the higher price, domestic producers increase their quantity supplied from Q_S^0 to O_S^1 and consumers reduce their quantity demanded from Q_D^0 to Q_D^1. Imports fall to $(Q_D^1 - Q_S^1)$. Consumer surplus decreases by the sum of areas 1 + 2 + 3 + 4, because consumers now buy less food and pay a higher price. Producer surplus increases by area 1, because domestic producers supply more food and receive a higher price. The government collects tariff revenue equal to area 3. Tariff revenue = $.1 \cdot (Q_D^1 - Q_S^1)$. The net loss to society from the tariff is the sum of areas 2 + 4, the amount of consumer surplus lost that no one else gains.

The Economic Costs of Tariffs and Quotas

Trade restrictions toss away some of the gains from trade that we described in Figure 39.2. Let's return to that example and consider a tariff levied by the British on imports of food in order to protect British farmers. This is a highly realistic example; agricultural products are commonly protected from free trade.

Figure 39.3 reproduces Figure 39.2(a). This time we will assume that the price of clothing is 1 ($P_C = 1£$), so that $P_F/P_C = P_F$.

The price of food is .8£ before the tariff. The quantity demanded at the free-trade price is Q_D^0. Domestic farmers Supply Q_S^0, and imports of food in the amount $(Q_D^0 - Q_S^0)$ provide the remaining quantity demanded. Suppose that the British impose a tariff of .1£ on each unit of food imported. The tariff raises the price of food in England to .9£. The higher price reduces the quantity demanded by consumers to Q_D^1 and increases the quantity supplied by domestic farmers to Q_S^1. Imports fall to $(Q_D^1 - Q_S^1)$.

We saw in Figure 39.2 that importing food without restriction gained society the triangular area *abc*. The tariff reduces some of the gain from trade as follows. Consumers lose the areas of surplus labeled 1, 2, 3, and 4 because they now pay a higher price for food and reduce their consumption. The domestic food suppliers gain the area of surplus labeled 1 that consumers lose because they now receive a higher price for food and increase their production. This is the protection effect of the tariff and represents a transfer from the consumers to the producers. The government also captures some of the area that consumers lose in the form of tariff revenue. The tariff revenue equals the height of the tariff times the amount of the imports under the tariff. This is the rectangular area labeled 3 in the figure:

$$\text{Tariff revenue} = \text{tariff} \cdot \text{imports}$$
$$= 0.1£ \cdot (Q_D^1 - Q_S^1) = \text{area 3}$$

The government presumably does something useful with the revenue, so that area 3 represents a transfer from the consumers to the government. Therefore, the net loss to society from the tariff is the sum of areas 2 and 4, the losses suffered by the consumers that no one captures. They are the portion of area *abc*, the gains from free trade, that society chooses to toss away by restricting trade with a tariff.

The economic effects of quotas and other types of direct quantity restrictions are much the same as those of tariffs. Under a quota the government issues quota licenses to individual foreign firms that place a limit on the quantity each firm can import into the country. Returning to our food example in Figure 39.3, suppose that instead of a tariff the government issues import licenses that, in total, restrict food imports to the amount $(Q_D^1 - Q_S^1)$, the same amount of imports as under the tariff. With imports limited to this amount, the domestic farmers can establish a price of .9£, the same price as with the tariff. With the price the same, the domestic supply and demand responses are the same. Domestic suppliers increase their quantity supplied to Q_S^1, and consumers reduce their quantity demanded to Q_D^1. The gains to domestic producers and the losses to consumers are also the same as with the tariff.

The only potential difference between the quota and the tariff is the tariff revenue, area 3 in Figure 39.3. The government would collect the same revenue under the quota if it auctions the quota licenses to the importers. Under the tariff, importers were willing to pay tariff revenue equal to area 3 and import $(Q_D^1 - Q_S^1)$ of food. Therefore, they would also be willing to pay the same amount for the quota licenses to import $(Q_D^1 - Q_S^1)$ food. Auctioning the quote licenses makes the quota identical to the tariff.

The common practice in the United States and in many other countries, however, is just to give the quota licenses to the importers free of charge. In this case the foreign importers capture area 3 as a pure economic profit, which economists call a **quota rent.** The quota rent arises because the quota allows the importers to sell their products at higher prices. Giving the licenses away adds area 3 to the overall economic loss, so that the total loss is the sum of areas 2, 3, and 4 in Figure 39.3.

QUOTA RENT

The economic profit earned by foreign importers under a quota when the quota licenses are given away (or sold at less than their full market value).

A final point is that the economic effects of a quota are the same whether the quota is imposed by the government of the importing country or achieved by a voluntary agreement of the exporting country. Japan's agreement to voluntarily restrict exports of their automobiles to the United States is fully equivalent to a U.S.-imposed quota of the same amount on Japanese automobile imports. The voluntary export restriction raises the price of automobiles in the United States, thereby protecting U.S. auto makers and auto workers, hurting U.S. consumers, and increasing the profits of the Japanese auto makers in the form of a quota rent.

The Politics of Trade Restrictions

Why do nations choose to sacrifice some of the gains from trade in this way? The answer lies in the distribution of the gains and the losses from trade in combination with the politics of trade. The import-competing industries lose from free trade, along with the factors of production specific to those industries. Moreover, the losses suffered by the individuals associated with these industries are large and concentrated. The farmers who are driven off their farms by food imports or the U.S. auto workers who lose their jobs to Japanese and German imports are big losers, and they tend to be concentrated in specific regions of the country. They have every incentive to lobby politicians for protection from trade to save their farms and their jobs. They may even be able to elicit sympathy from other citizens who understand the pain of losing one's livelihood.

In contrast, the gains from free trade are individually small and diverse. They accrue to millions of consumers in the form of cheaper or better products—for example, cheaper food and better cars. The gains to each individual consumer are minuscule compared with the losses suffered by the individual farmers or auto workers who lose their farms or jobs. But as Figures 39.2 and 39.3 show, the combined gains to the millions of consumers far exceed the combined losses to a few thousand farmers or auto workers. Even so, the millions of consumers have little individual incentive to lobby for free trade, and organizing them is difficult in any case. Therefore, the political outcome is predictable. The farm and automobile lobbies carry the day, the tariffs are imposed, and the nation as a whole loses.

The Costs of Trade Restrictions

A group of economists at the Federal Trade Commission (FTC) analyzed the overall costs of U.S. tariffs and quotas in 1983 and found the costs to be considerable. The U.S. tariff rates at the time averaged only 3.7 percent, yet the FTC estimated that removing all the tariffs would bring a net gain of $10.5 billion. The four largest direct quantity restrictions in 1983 were quotas on sugar, textiles, and steel and the Japanese voluntary export restraint on automobiles. The FTC economists concluded in each case that the losses to consumers far exceeded the gains to the domestic industries being protected. For example, the Japanese voluntary export restraint on automobiles cost consumers $1.1 billion in return for a $115 million gain to the U.S. auto industry. The biggest gainers were the Japanese producers, who received $824 million in quota rents. Consumers lost over $241,000 for every job saved in the U.S. auto industry. The pattern of gains and losses from the three quotas was much the same: large consumer losses, a much smaller protection gain to domestic producers, and very large quota rents to foreign producers. The overall estimated cost of the four trade restrictions was $2.2 billion, and the combined quqta rents to the foreign producers were $1.9 billion. Restricting trade and then giving away the quota rents is very costly indeed![10]

Are There Any Good Trade Restrictions?

Can tariffs and quota ever be good for the nation as a whole? Economists would seriously consider only one case in which restricting trade may be beneficial

[10]D. Tarr and M. Morkre, *Aggregate Costs to the United States of Tariffs and Quotas on Imports: General Tariff Cuts and Removal of Quotas on Automobiles, Steel, Sugar, and Textiles*, Bureau of Economics Staff Report to the Federal Trade Commission, December 1984 (Washington, D.C.: U.S. Government Printing Office, 1984), Table 1, p. 2 and Table 4, p. 8.

for a large industrial nation such as the United States, the so-called **strategic tariff** or quota. Designing strategic tariffs or quotas that are actually beneficial is very difficult, however.

STRATEGIC TARIFF
A tariff that is designed to protect domestic firms from competition while they are attempting to research and develop successful new products.

STRATEGIC TARIFFS The possibility of a strategic tariff arises in the context of the third model of international trade described above, which is based on the research and development of new product lines and economies of scale. The basic idea is that large domestic firms cannot easily protect themselves from foreign competitors while they are trying to develop new markets. They may have no believable strategy or threat to fend off the competitors. The government does have a believable threat, though: It can protect the domestic firms with tariffs and quotas (or give them direct subsidies). So the government becomes a partner in a strategy of trying to gain a first-mover advantage for its firms. Firms that are the first to develop successful products with the help of the government can then take advantage of economies of scale and gain penetration into foreign markets. The strategic tariffs (or quotas or subsidies) shift profits from foreign to domestic firms and promote exports.

A classic recent example of this strategy was the Japanese takeover of the market for computer memory chips. Texas Instruments, Intel, and National Semiconductor were among the U.S. firms that invented and developed the technology for making dynamic random access memory (DRAM) computer chips and had the semiconductor market to themselves in the early 1980s. The Japanese decided that they wanted to develop their own semiconductor memory chips, so they protected their producers from U.S. exports and went furiously to work developing and refining the chips on their own. Their research and development efforts were successful, and soon their firms were producing the most reliable memory chips. By the end of the decade NEC, Toshiba, and Hitachi had become the leading producers of the memory chips and had gained almost total control of the market.

CURRENT ISSUE: Laura Tyson, chairwoman of President Clinton's Council of Economic Advisers, is one economist who has argued in the past for trade restrictions against Japan if the Japanese refuse to open their markets further to U.S. products. In 1993 the Japanese agreed to allow more imports from the United States.

Playing the strategic tariff or subsidy game successfully is extremely problematic, however. It typically requires enormous amounts of protection or subsidy. It also requires that the government select winners in advance, and it is not at all clear that governments can do this, especially in highly fertile, rapidly changing technological environments. Careful attempts by economists to estimate the benefits and costs of these strategies always conclude that they are losers.

The Japanese takeover of the memory chip market is a perfect case in point. It is generally considered to be a spectacular success story, so successful that it has led a number of politicians to call for further trade sanctions on the Japanese in order to encourage them to open up their markets. These politicians do not want a repeat of the memory chip "fiasco" in other industries. But MIT's Paul Krugman determined that the Japanese would have been much better off to leave this industry alone and import the chips that they needed from the original U.S. manufacturers. The costs of developing their own chips were just too large.

Krugman's study does not even take into consideration the fact that the Japanese have essentially lost the memory chip market to the U.S. firms in the 1990s. A new and faster computer architecture called reduced instruction set computing, or RISC, requires a completely redesigned memory chip. U.S. firms such as Sun Microsystems, MIPS, IBM, and Digital have taken the lead in developing and producing the new chip. This time the Japanese firms have reacted by forming partnerships with the U.S. producers to market the chips; they will not try to develop and refine the new chip technology on their own.

The European Airbus Consortium is another case in point. It receives huge subsidies from a number of European governments to compete with the U.S. airframe manufacturers. One of its first planes was a mid-range commercial jet that it built to compete with Boeing's mid-range 767. Once again, a careful economic study shows that Europe would have been much better off simply buying the Boeing 767.

Picking winners in a high-tech environment is just too uncertain to be done with any confidence. Also, most of the potential gains from strategic tariffs are just shifts in profits from foreign producers to domestic producers. Consumers may not gain much from a successful strategic tariff. MIT's Krugman was a pioneer in developing the theory behind the potential gains from strategic tariffs and subsidies. Yet actual experience with these policies has led him back to the presumption for free trade. He concludes: "The economic cautions about the difficulty of formulating useful intervention and the political economy concerns that interventionism may go astray combine into a new case for free trade."[11]

SUMMARY

Chapter 39 began with a discussion of the three basic models that economists use to explain the variety of international trade that we observe: Ricardo's theory of comparative advantage, the factor endowments model, and the product differentiation/economies of scale model.

1. Ricardo's theory of comparative advantage shows that the pattern and the gains from trade depend on differences in opportunity costs in producing goods across countries. Ricardo attributed the cost differences to differences in technologies. His theory of comparative advantage says that countries can gain from trade if they specialize their production in the goods in which they have a comparative advantage (lower opportunity costs) and trade for goods in which other countries have a comparative advantage. International trade gives a country a consumption possibilities frontier beyond its production possibilities frontier.
2. Ricardo's model demonstrates many additional fundamental principles of international trade:
   a. A country gains more from specialization and trade the more that its terms-of-trade, defined as the ratio of the prices of the export goods to the prices of the import goods, improves. The terms-of-trade depends on the relative demands for the traded goods in Ricardo's model.
   b. The value of a nation's exports must equal the value of a nation's imports. Exports may not equal imports each year as in the model, but they must eventually be equal over time because nations insist on receiving real goods in exchange for their goods.

[11]Krugman quote in R. E. Baldwin, "Are Economists' Traditional Trade Policy Views Still Valid?" *Journal of Economic Literature* XXX, No. 2 (June 1992): 826. Baldwin's article is an excellent treatment of the benefits and the pitfalls of strategic trade restrictions, and cites the Airbus Study. For an analysis of the computer memory chip market, see W. Taffel, "Advantageous Liaisons," *Technology Review* 96, No. 4 (May/June 1993): 28–31, 34–36.

c. The real and the financial sides of international trade are closely linked. The exchange rate must be between the price ratios of the traded goods in each country. An exchange rate outside these ratios will price the goods of the nation with the overvalued currency out of the market.
d. Developing countries need not fear the superior technologies of the industrialized countries, and the industrialized countries need not fear the lower wages of the developing countries. Differences in opportunity costs, not in technology or wages, are the key to the gains from trade. Indeed, Ricardo's model is most useful for explaining trade between the developing and the industrialized nations.

3. The factor endowments model allows for increasing marginal costs and incomplete specialization, with a country continuing to produce the good that it imports. Countries have lower costs and a comparative advantage in producing goods that use factors that they have a relative abundance of. These are the goods that they export. For example, the United States has a comparative advantage in goods that use relatively large amounts of capital, land, and highly skilled labor. It has a comparative disadvantage in goods that use relatively large amounts of unskilled labor.
4. The factor endowments model highlights the distributional implications of trade. Trade increases the returns to the relatively abundant factors used in the export goods and lowers the returns to the relatively scarce factors used in the import-competing goods. For the United States, trade increases the returns to capital, land, and highly skilled labor and lowers the wages of unskilled workers.
5. The fear in bringing Mexico into NAFTA is that expansion of trade with Mexico will lower the wages of unskilled U.S. workers. This fear is exaggerated because the Mexican economy is so much smaller than the U.S. economy is and because so many Mexican workers are already working in the United States and have presumably already lowered the wages of unskilled U.S. workers.
6. The product differentiation/economies of scale model is used to explain the two-way trade of highly similar goods and inputs among the industrialized nations. The trade is the result of large multinational corporations competing for markets through research and development of new product varieties. Successful products enjoy economies of scale that give them a cost advantage and a niche in the international marketplace. With corporations in all countries playing this game, similar products are both imported and exported.
7. Most of the gains from the European Community will come from large multinational corporations driving out higher-cost local producers who were protected from international competitors by a host of barriers to trade in the form of product standards and marketing regulations. Most of the increase in trade will be two-way trade of similar products. The potential gains from the European Community appear to be about 1 percent of total European national product.

The second section of Chapter 39 discussed the most common barriers to trade.

8. Barriers to trade include tariffs, quotas, and other nontariff barriers. A tariff is a tax on an imported good. A quota directly restricts the quantity of an

imported good. Other nontariff barriers include the various kinds of product standards and marketing regulations that existed in Western Europe before the European Community, and voluntary export restrictions.

9. Tariffs raise the price of imported goods, resulting in losses to consumers, gains to the import-competing industries and the workers in these industries, and increased tariff revenues for the government. Quotas are identical to tariffs if the quota licenses are auctioned off to the importers. Giving the licenses away turns the government revenues into quota rents received by the foreign importers. The main political argument for trade restrictions is to protect jobs in import-competing industries.
10. Studies of trade restrictions show that the aggregate losses to consumers usually far exceed the gains to the protected industries and the tariff revenues. Yet countries restrict trade because the losses from free trade to the import-competing industries and their workers are individually large and concentrated, whereas the gains to consumers are individually small and diverse. The narrow interests of the import-competing industries and their workers carry the day politically.
11. The General Agreement on Tariffs and Trade (GATT) is an international agreement to reduce tariffs and trade restrictions that was signed in 1947 by 23 nations. It now includes nearly 100 nations. GATT has been successful in reducing tariff rates, but unsuccessful in preventing the spread of quotas and other nontariff barriers.
12. The one tariff that might possibly benefit a large industrial nation as a whole is the strategic tariff. A strategic tariff protects large multinational corporations while they try to develop new product varieties through research and development. This strategy is costly, however, and picking winners in advance is chancy. Most studies show that strategic tariffs and other direct subsidies are losers; they cost more than their benefits.

KEY TERMS

beggar-thy-neighbor policy
comparative advantage
factor endowments model of international trade
foreign exchange markets
gains from trade
General Agreement on Tariffs and Trade (GATT)
most-favored-nation principle
multinational corporation
overvalued currency
product differentiation/economies of scale model of international trade
quota
quota rent
Ricardo's model of comparative advantage
strategic tariff
tariff
terms-of-trade
undervalued currency
voluntary export restriction

QUESTIONS

1. a. To what extent do Ricardo's comparative advantage model and the factor endowments model yield similar predictions about the pattern of international trade and the gains from international trade?
   b. In what ways does the factor endowments model expand on Ricardo's comparative advantage model?
2. Why might a quota make a country worse off than does a tariff, assuming that they both restrict imports by the same amount?
3. Why does a country impose tariffs, quotas, and other trade restrictions, even if the country as a whole becomes worse off?
4. Why might similar products be both imported and exported by a country? Give some examples of two-way trade in similar products that involve the United States.
5. Suppose that in Japan 1 unit of labor is used to make 2 videocassette recorders (VCRs) and 1 unit of labor is used to make 3 television sets (TVs). In the United States 1

unit of labor is used to make 1 VCR and 1 unit of labor is used to make 1 TV. Assume that labor is the only factor of production and that each country has 200 units of labor.

a. Which country has the comparative advantage in VCRs? In TVs?

b. Show that both countries can be made better off by specializing their production in one of the products and trading.

c. Given the trading ratio of VCRs to TVs that you chose for your answer to part (b), compare the production possibilities without trade and the consumption possibilities with trade in each country.

6. What factors determine how much a country gains from international trade?

7. Switzerland exports cheese (Swiss cheese, of course) to France for \$2 a pound. Without trade, the equilibrium price in Switzerland would be \$1.50 a pound, and the equilibrium price in France would be \$2.50 a pound.

   a. Draw reasonable-looking supply and demand curves for cheese in Switzerland and France. Show on your graph the gains from international trade for both Switzerland and France.

   b. Suppose that France places a \$.20 a pound tariff on cheese. Show on your graph the gains from international trade that are lost in France and the tariff revenue that is collected by the French government.

8. Citizens in the United States are often urged to "Buy American." Do you think that "Buy American" is good advice for the United States?

9. a. What is a strategic tariff, and why might it benefit a nation?

   b. Who tends to gain more from a strategic tariff, domestic consumers or domestic producers?

   c. Why are beneficial strategic tariffs so difficult to design?

   d. Might a country like the United States be interested in strategic tariffs? If so, why? If not, why not?

10. What were the arguments in favor of and against allowing Mexico to join in NAFTA with the United States and Canada?

11. In what ways do the nations of Western Europe stand to gain from the European Community?

CHAPTER

40

International Finance

LEARNING OBJECTIVES

CONCEPTS TO LEARN

The balance of payments

Flexible exchange rates

Fixed exchange rates

The Bretton Woods fixed exchange rate system

Fiscal and monetary policies under flexible and fixed exchange rates

CONCEPTS TO RECALL

The Laws of Supply and Demand [5, 6, 7]

Fiscal policy [28, 30, 31]

Monetary policy [28, 34, 35]

The distinctive feature of international transactions is that they require an exchange of one nation's currency for another nation's currency in the foreign exchange markets. The fundamental issue of international finance is how nations will arrange for the exchange of their currencies. They have two basic choices, a system of fixed exchange rates or a system of flexible, or floating, exchange rates.

FIXED EXCHANGE RATE

An exchange rate that is set at a fixed value.

FLEXIBLE EXCHANGE RATE

An exchange rate that is determined by the Laws of Supply and Demand in the foreign exchange markets.

In a system of ***fixed exchange rates*** *the nations agree to fix the relative values of their currencies at one set of exchange rates. Then the nations' central banks agree to buy and sell foreign currencies as needed to maintain the exchange rates at the set values. In a system of* ***flexible,*** *or* ***floating, exchange rates*** *the exchange rates are determined in the free market according to the Laws of Supply and Demand. Moreover, the supplies and the demands for currencies are those of private individuals and firms. The central banks have no role to play in a pure flexible exchange rate system.*

Both exchange rate systems have their advantages and disadvantages. The ambivalence in deciding which is the best system is evident in the history of international finance since World War II. In 1944, 44 nations met at Bretton Woods, New Hampshire, and established a fixed exchange rate system based on the dollar and gold. The dollar was pegged to gold at $35 per ounce, and the United States agreed to exchange dollars for gold on demand. All other currencies were then pegged to the dollar or to gold. The Bretton Woods arrangement lasted until 1973, when most of the developed market economies decided to switch to a flexible exchange rate system and allow their currencies to float on the free market.

The 1973 arrangement lasted until the 1976 Jamaica Agreements, which allowed nations to choose one of three options: adopt a flexible exchange rate, peg the exchange rate to one currency, or peg the exchange rate to a market basket of currencies. These options have remained in effect ever since, with the result that there is now quite a mixture of exchange rate systems in effect. For example, the United States and Japan have maintained flexible exchange rates, whereas most of the Western European nations have pegged their exchange rates to the German mark since 1979.

The primary goal of Chapter 40 is to explain the economic implications of choosing fixed versus flexible exchange rates. The chapter begins with a close look at the main kinds of international transactions that give rise to the supplies and the demands for currencies in the foreign exchange markets. A knowledge of these transactions will help us understand the issues involved with choosing an exchange rate system.

THE BALANCE OF PAYMENTS

BALANCE OF PAYMENTS

The double-entry accounting system that nations use to record their international transactions during the course of a year.

The accounting structure that nations use to record their international transactions during the course of a year is called the **balance of payments.** The Bureau of Economic Analysis of the U.S. Department of Commerce compiles and publishes the balance of payments for the United States. The balance of payments records international transactions by means of a double-entry system of international credits and debits. An **international credit** is any transaction that gives rise to a demand for dollars in the foreign exchange markets (alternatively, a supply of foreign currency). An **international debit** is any transaction that gives rise to a supply of dollars in the foreign exchange markets (alternatively, a demand for foreign currency). Double-entry bookkeeping means that every credit entry has a corresponding and offsetting debit entry, and every debit entry has a corresponding and offsetting credit entry. Consequently, the sum of the international credit transactions during the year must equal the sum of the international debit transaction during the year. In other words, the balance of payments must net to zero overall.

INTERNATIONAL CREDIT

Any international transaction that gives rise to a demand for dollars in the foreign exchange markets, such as an export or a capital inflow.

INTERNATIONAL DEBIT

Any international transaction that gives rise to a supply of dollars in the foreign exchange markets, such as an import or a capital outflow.

The balance of payments contains three main subsections: the current account, the capital account, and the official settlements account. The credits and debits in each of the subaccounts do not necessarily net to zero. A subaccount is in *surplus* if credits exceed debits and in *deficit* if debits exceed credits. Let's take a closer look at each of the subaccounts.

The Current Account

The most important entries in the **current account** are the exports and the imports of manufactured goods, called merchandise exports and imports. These are the exports and the imports that were listed in Table 39.1. When U.S. exporters of food, computers, and aircraft sell their products, they receive foreign currencies—for example, Japanese yen, German marks, and English pounds—which they eventually want to exchange for dollars. Therefore, merchandise *exports* give rise to a demand for dollars; they are recorded as *credits* in the balance of payments. When foreign importers of automobiles, cameras, and wines sell their products, they receive dollars, which they eventually want to exchange for their own currencies—for example, yen, marks, and French francs. Therefore, merchandise *imports* give rise to a supply of dollars; they are recorded as *debits* in the balance of payments. The **balance of trade** is the difference between merchandise exports and merchandise imports. The word *balance* refers to the difference between the credits and the debits within each subaccount.

CURRENT ACCOUNT (BALANCE OF PAYMENTS)

The subaccount in the balance of payments that records the exports and the imports of goods and services, the receipts of factor incomes by domestic and foreign residents, and net unilateral transfers.

BALANCE OF TRADE

The difference between a nation's merchandise exports and merchandise imports.

The current account balance also includes services and flows of factor income into and out of the country. The most important services involved in international trade are tourism, travel, and financial services directly associated with exports and imports, such as insurance policies taken out on goods shipped abroad.[1] Most services that we routinely consume, such as haircuts, restaurant meals, and doctor visits, are local services that are not traded internationally. The flows of factor income are primarily interest and dividends received from saving and investment in foreign countries.

The accounting of the services and the factor income flows as debits and credits works just like the accounting of exports and incomes. For example, interest and dividend income received by U.S. residents from their saving and investment abroad gives rise to a demand for dollars as the income returns to the United States. Therefore, the *receipt of factor income by U.S. residents* is a *credit* in the balance of payments. Conversely, interest and dividend income received by foreign residents on their saving and investment in the United

[1]The purchase and sale of military goods by the federal government is also included under services in the current account.

States gives rise to a supply of dollars as the income leaves the United States. Therefore, the *payment of factor income to foreign residents* is a *debit* in the balance of payments.

BALANCE OF GOODS AND SERVICES

The sum of the balance of trade plus net exports of services plus net receipts of factor incomes.

The **balance of goods and services** is the sum of the balance of trade plus net exports of services (exports − imports) plus net receipts of factor income (receipts by U.S. citizens − payments to foreign citizens).

The final entries in the current account balance are unilateral transfers into and out of the country by persons, firms, and governments. A *transfer by a foreign "resident" to the United States* gives rise to a demand for dollars and is a *credit* in the balance of payments. A *transfer by a U.S. "resident" to a foreign country* gives rise to a supply of dollars and is a *debit* in the balance of payments. Net unilateral transfers are the difference between transfers out of (debits) and transfer into (credits) the United States. The **current account balance** equals the balance of goods and services minus net unilateral transfers.

CURRENT ACCOUNT BALANCE

The balance of goods and services minus net unilateral transfers.

Net unilateral transfers are typically a small item and are usually ignored, so that the current account balance is often used interchangeably with the balance of goods and services in discussions of the balance of payments. In 1991, however, net unilateral transfers decreased by over $40 billion as foreign countries paid their share of expenses for the Gulf War to the United States. They helped drive the U.S. current account balance to near zero ($4 billion deficit) for the first time since 1981. The current account balance returned to a substantial deficit (debits greater than credits) in 1992.[2]

To summarize:

CREDITS		DEBITS	
Merchandise exports	−	merchandise imports	= *balance of trade*
		+	
Services exports	−	services imports	
		+	
Receipts of factor income	−	payments of factor income	= *balance of goods and services*
		−	
		Net unilateral transfers (debit)	= *current account balance*

The Capital Account

CAPITAL ACCOUNT (BALANCE OF PAYMENTS)

The subaccount in the balance of payments that records capital inflows and outflows.

The **capital account** records the flow of capital into and out of a country. Capital flows across international borders whenever a resident of one country buys a financial security of a foreign country or makes a loan to a resident of a foreign country. As above, the "resident" could be an individual, a firm, or a government agency other than the central bank. The financial securities include bank deposit accounts, certificates of deposit, corporate and government bonds, corporate stocks—any financial security that represents a claim against a resident of a foreign country.

CAPITAL INFLOWS

Purchases of domestic financial securities or loans to domestic residents by foreign residents.

Purchases of U.S. financial securities and loans to U.S. residents by foreign residents are **capital inflows.** Since foreign residents need dollars to buy U.S.

[2]Council of Economic Advisers, *Economic Indicators* (Washington, D.C.: U.S. Government Printing Office, March 1993), 36.

financial securities or lend in the United States, *capital inflows* give rise to a demand for dollars. They are recorded as *credits* in the balance of payments. Purchases of foreign financial securities or loans to foreign residents by U.S. residents are **capital outflows.** Since U.S. residents need foreign currencies to buy foreign financial securities or lend in foreign countries, *capital outflows* give rise to a supply of dollars. They are recorded as *debits* in the balance of payments.

CAPITAL OUTFLOWS

Purchases of foreign financial securities or loans to foreign residents by domestic residents.

Purchases of financial securities and issues of loans with more than one year to maturity are called *long-term* capital inflows and outflows. Other purchases and loans are considered *short-term* capital inflows and outflows. Stocks are considered long-term investments and checking accounts short-term investments no matter how long someone intends to keep them. Also, purchases of stock or other assets that give the foreign buyer a controlling interest in a firm are called **direct foreign investment.** All other international capital flows are considered to be *portfolio investments.*

DIRECT FOREIGN INVESTMENT

The purchase of domestic stock or other assets by foreign residents that give them a controlling interest in a domestic firm.

The **capital account balance** equals the capital inflows minus the capital outflows.

CAPITAL ACCOUNT BALANCE

The difference between a nation's capital inflows and capital outflows.

To summarize:

CREDITS		DEBITS		
Capital inflows (purchases of U.S. financial securities or loans to U.S. residents by foreign residents)	−	Capital outflows (purchases of foreign financial securities or loans to foreign residents by U.S. residents)	=	*capital account balance*

The Official Settlements Account

Central banks hold part of their assets in the form of international reserves, consisting primarily of foreign currencies, other very short-term financial securities denominated in foreign currencies such as 180-day government bonds, and gold. They also hold, as part of their liabilities, some of the international reserves of other central banks. The entries in the **official settlements account** are purchases and sales of these international reserves. We will be concerned with their purchases and sales of foreign currencies for the most part.

OFFICIAL SETTLEMENTS ACCOUNT

The subaccount in the balance of payments that records transactions between a nation's central bank and the central banks of other nations.

A sale of foreign currency by the Fed in exchange for dollars is a *credit* in the U.S. balance of payments. A loss of foreign currency may seem like an unusual credit, but it satisfies the rule of representing an increase in either the demand for dollars or the supply of a foreign currency. Conversely, *a purchase of foreign currency* by the Fed in exchange for dollars is a *debit* in the U.S. balance of payments. It represents an increase in either the supply of dollars or the demand for foreign currency.[3]

[3]Most individuals and businesses do not deal directly with central banks. Instead, they exchange currencies at large commercial banks (and other private financial institutions). Even so, the Fed is likely to become involved in the transaction. For example, suppose that a commercial bank buys pounds from a U.S. exporter and pays with a cashier's check. The cashier's check reduces the bank's reserve account with the Fed. If the bank does not want its reserve account to decrease, it will sell the pounds to the Fed in exchange for more reserves. So the Fed ends up buying the pounds. We will speak of foreign currency purchases and sales directly with the Fed and other central banks to simplify the complexities of these transactions.

OFFICIAL SETTLEMENTS ACCOUNT BALANCE

The difference between international credit and debit transactions between a nation's central bank and the central banks of other nations.

To summarize:

CREDITS		DEBITS		
Sales of foreign currency and other international reserves by the Fed (or increases of foreign central bank deposits or securities at the Fed)	−	Purchases of foreign currency and other international reserves by the Fed (or increases of the Fed's bank deposits or securities at other central banks)	=	*official settlements balance*

Double-Entry Bookkeeping

The majority of capital flows and official settlements in the balance of payments result directly from exports and imports and from other entries in the current account. They are the second half of the current account transactions, the second entry in the double-entry method of bookkeeping, which guarantees that the overall international credits and debits must be equal.

For example, suppose that a U.S. resident buys a Nissan Maxima for $15,000 from a Japanese car dealer. The purchase of the car is an import and a debit in the current account balance. The offsetting credit entry depends on what the car dealer does with the $15,000. The dealer may deposit the customer's check in its checking account at a U.S. bank or buy other U.S. financial securities such as stocks or bonds. Each of these options is a capital inflow, an offsetting credit in the capital account. Or the car dealer may have lent the customer the $15,000. The loan is also a capital inflow, an offsetting credit in the capital account. Another possibility is that the car dealer exchanges the $15,000 for yen at the Fed to sent the funds back to Japan. The loss of $15,000 worth of yen is a loss of international reserves, an offsetting credit in the official settlements account.

The same offsetting entries in the capital and the official settlements accounts apply in reverse for U.S. exports. A sale of food in London by a U.S. exporter is an export and a credit in the current account. The exporter receives payment in pounds. If the exporter chooses to place the pounds in a London bank or purchase other financial securities in London, these transactions are capital outflows and offsetting debits in the capital account. A loan by the exporter to a British customer is also a capital outflow and an offsetting debit in the capital account. If the exporter exchanges the pounds for dollars at the Fed, the purchase of the pounds by the Fed is an offsetting debit in the official settlements account.

For small, low-income countries with poorly developed capital markets, most of the offsets to exports and imports are in the official settlements accounts. Exporters selling goods in Thailand do not want to hold many deposits in Thai banks or other financial securities denominated in the Thai currency, the bhat. They exchange most of the bhat they receive from selling their products for their own currency at the Thai central bank. This is another way of seeing why nations have to export in order to be able to import. Small nations such as Thailand have to maintain a near-equality between their exports and their imports on current account. Their exports generate the foreign currency, the international reserves, that they will need to sell to the foreign exporters selling in Thailand. They would soon run out of international reserves if they ran a large deficit on their current account, with imports exceeding exports. In other words, their official settlements account also remains in near equality as the central bank buys foreign currencies from the exporters and sells the foreign currencies to the importers in approximately equal amounts. The capital account transactions are relatively unimportant.

In contrast, a large percentage of the offsets to the current account in the industrial market economies such as the United States are in the capital account. Foreign exporters selling goods in the United States are quite willing to hold U.S. financial securities, just as U.S. exporters are willing to hold the financial securities of Japan, England, Germany, and so forth. In addition, the capital inflows and outflows can have a life of their own. They are not necessarily just offsets to the current account. The act of placing savings, or investing, in the securities of foreign countries for its own sake is called an **autonomous capital inflow** or **outflow.**

AUTONOMOUS CAPITAL INFLOW (OR OUTFLOW)

A capital inflow (or outflow) undertaken for its own sake and not as an offset to some other transaction in the balance of payments.

For example, the managers of a U.S. pension fund may decide to place some of their fund's portfolio in Japanese stocks. The managers need yen to purchase stocks on the Tokyo exchange, so they exchange dollars for yen at the Fed and then purchase the Japanese stocks in Tokyo. The purchase of the stock is an autonomous capital outflow, a debit in the capital account. The offsetting credit is the sale of yen by the Fed, which appears in the official settlements account.

Another example of an autonomous capital flow is a loan by a U.S. government agency to a developing nation, which the nation uses to buy food. Suppose that the nation buys food from the United States. The loan is an autonomous capital outflow and a debit in the capital account. The U.S. export of food to the nation is the offsetting entry in the balance of payments. It is a credit in the current account. This is an example of the **transfer mechanism,** in which first the money flows and then the goods follow. The transfer mechanism was an important feature of the Marshall Plan following World War II. The federal government poured money into Europe to help the Europeans recover from the war. Much of the money distributed through Marshall Plan grants and loans came right back to the United States through purchases of U.S. exports.

TRANSFER MECHANISM (INTERNATIONAL TRADE)

A grant or a loan to a foreign country that is then used to buy exports from the country that gave the grant or the loan; in other words, a mechanism in which first the money flows and then the goods flow.

The transfer mechanism is incomplete if the receiving government spends the money elsewhere. For example, suppose that the government buys some of the food from France and the French exporter holds the dollars in an account at a French bank denominated in dollars. Dollar-denominated accounts in foreign banks are called **Eurodollar accounts,** and they have grown very rapidly over the past 20 years. An increase in a Eurodollar account is recorded as a short-term capital inflow in the U.S. balance of payments, the offsetting credit to the original capital outflow.

EURODOLLAR ACCOUNT

Any dollar-denominated account in a foreign bank.

The fact that capital account transactions can be offsets to current account transactions means that the industrial market economies do not have to maintain a near-equality in their current account balances each year. They have the luxury of running a current account deficit for awhile, with imports exceeding exports. As noted earlier, the United States has been running large deficits in its current account every year since 1983, with the single exception of 1991. There is a limit to how long the United States or any other nation can run current account deficits, however. A deficit in the current account means that the combined capital and official settlements accounts are in surplus. Remember, overall the balance of payments must net to zero. A surplus in the official settlements balance means that the nation is losing international reserves, and it certainly cannot do this forever and maintain its trading relationships. A surplus in the capital account means that capital inflows exceed capital outflows. On net, foreign residents are willing to hold the nation's financial securities. Eventually, though, the foreign residents will want to "cash in" and consume real goods and services; they will not go on saving forever. When they do decide to cash in, the deficit in the current account will have to turn into a surplus, with exports exceeding imports, so that the nation can earn the foreign currency that will be demanded. This is why even the modern industrial nations have to export in order to import despite the attractiveness of their capital markets. A deficit in the current account must eventually become a surplus. The day when the United States has to turn its current account deficit into a surplus may not be too far in the future.

The U.S. Balance of Payments

Table 40.1 shows the U.S. balance of payments for 1992. The pattern for 1992 was typical of every year since 1986, with the single exception of 1991 noted earlier. The current account had a large deficit, offset by large surpluses in the

TABLE 40.1 U.S. Balance of Payments, 1992 ($ billion)

CURRENT ACCOUNT	
Exports	439.3
Imports	(−)535.5[a]
Balance of trade	(−) 96.3
Net services	55.1
Receipts of factor income	109.2
Payments of factor income	(−) 99.1
Balance of goods and services	(−) 31.1
Net unilateral transfers	(−) 31.3
Current account balance	(−) 62.4
CAPITAL ACCOUNT	
U.S. private capital outflows	(−) 48.7
Foreign private capital inflows	80.1
Capital account balance	31.4
OFFICIAL SETTLEMENTS ACCOUNT	
U.S. official reserve outflows	3.9
Foreign official reserve inflows	40.3
Official settlements account balance	44.2
SUMMARY	
Current account balance	(−) 62.4
Capital account balance	31.4
Official settlements account balance	44.2
Statistical discrepancy	(−) 13.2
Overall Balance of Payments	0

[a]Debits (−)

SOURCE: Council of Economic Advisers, *Economic Indicators* (Washington, D.C.: Government Printing Office, March 1993), 36–37.

capital account and the official settlements account. The current account deficits and the capital account surpluses have been large ever since 1983.

The current account deficit resulted primarily from a $96 billion balance of trade deficit, which was split fairly evenly between the industrialized market economies (−$48 billion) and all other countries (−$49 billion). Nearly all of the balance of trade deficit with the industrialized countries was accounted for by Japan (−$50 billion). Otherwise, the United States had a small trade deficit with Canada (−$11 billion) and small trade surpluses with Western Europe ($6 billion) and Australia, New Zealand, and South Africa ($11 billion, combined). The main difference in this breakdown over the preceding seven years was with Western Europe. The United States had a small trade deficit with Western Europe through 1989 and a small trade surplus since 1990.

Regarding the other countries, the United States had balance of trade deficits with both the members of the Organization of Petroleum Exporting Countries (OPEC) (−$12 billion) and all the other middle- and low-income countries (−$37 billion). This has also been true since 1986.

The large, offsetting net capital inflows since 1983 have turned the United States from a large creditor nation into the largest debtor nation. A nation is a **creditor** if the market value of assets that its citizens hold abroad exceeds the market value of assets that foreign citizens hold in the nation. Conversely, a nation is a **debtor** if the market value of assets that its citizens hold abroad is less than the market value of assets that foreign citizens hold in the nation. In 1983 the market value of assets that U.S. citizens held abroad totaled $1,069 billion, and the market value of assets that foreign citizens held in the United States totaled $801 billion. The United States was a creditor in the amount of $268 billion ($268 = $1,069 − $801). By 1991 the market value of assets that U.S. citizens held abroad had grown to $2,107 billion. But the market value of assets that foreign citizens held in the United States had grown even more because of the huge annual capital inflows, to $2,489 billion. The United States was a debtor in the amount of $382 billion ($382 = $2,489 − $2,107).[4]

CREDITOR NATION

A nation for which the market value of the assets that its citizens hold abroad exceeds the market value of the assets that foreign citizens hold in the nation.

DEBTOR NATION

A nation for which the market value of the assets that its citizens hold abroad is less than the market value of the assets that foreign citizens hold in the nation.

Foreign residents have clearly been willing to hold dollar assets in the United States. The outstanding question though, as noted above, is how much longer they will be willing to accumulate these assets before they cash them in to consume goods and services. The U.S. current account deficit and capital account surplus will reverse themselves when the foreign residents decide to cash in.

EXCHANGE RATE SYSTEMS

Having described the main kinds of international transactions, we are now in a position to compare and contrast how fixed and flexible exchange rate systems coordinate these transactions. The exchange of foreign currency is part and parcel of all international transactions, and the exchange rate systems that nations choose dictate how the foreign exchange markets operate. Let's begin with the flexible exchange rate system, since this is the system that the United States has used to exchange dollars for foreign currencies ever since 1973.

[4]The historical data on the balance of payments, and the asset holdings, are from Council of Economic Advisers, *Economic Report of the President 1993* (Washington, D.C.: U.S. Government Printing Office, 1993), Table B-99, p. 461 (asset holdings), and Table B-100, p. 462 (balance of payments).

Flexible Exchange Rates

Foreign exchange markets are highly competitive by nature. Large numbers of buyers and sellers meet in these markets, and the individual markets located in the major cities throughout the world are all interconnected electronically to form one worldwide market. Transactors have excellent, up-to-the-minute information about the exchange rates between any two currencies. As a result, exchange rates are determined by the Laws of Supply and Demand so long as central banks choose not to intervene. This is precisely what happens under a flexible, or floating, exchange rate system in its purest form. The supplies and the demands for any one currency are those of private individuals and business firms and of government agencies other than central banks. The central bankers agree to let their currencies take on whatever values are consistent with the equilibrium between supply and demand.

Figure 40.1 illustrates how the Laws of Supply and Demand determine the exchange rate between dollars and British pounds. The quantity of pounds is on the horizontal axis, and the exchange rate in terms of dollars per pound is on the vertical axis.

The demand curve for pounds, $D_£$, comes from people with dollars who want to exchange them for pounds. They might be British exporters to the United States who want to exchange the dollars that they receive from their U.S. customers for pounds so that they can return the funds to England. Or they might be U.S. pension fund managers who want pounds to buy British financial securities or real estate in London. The demand curve is downward sloping in terms of dollars per pound. The more dollars that people have to exchange

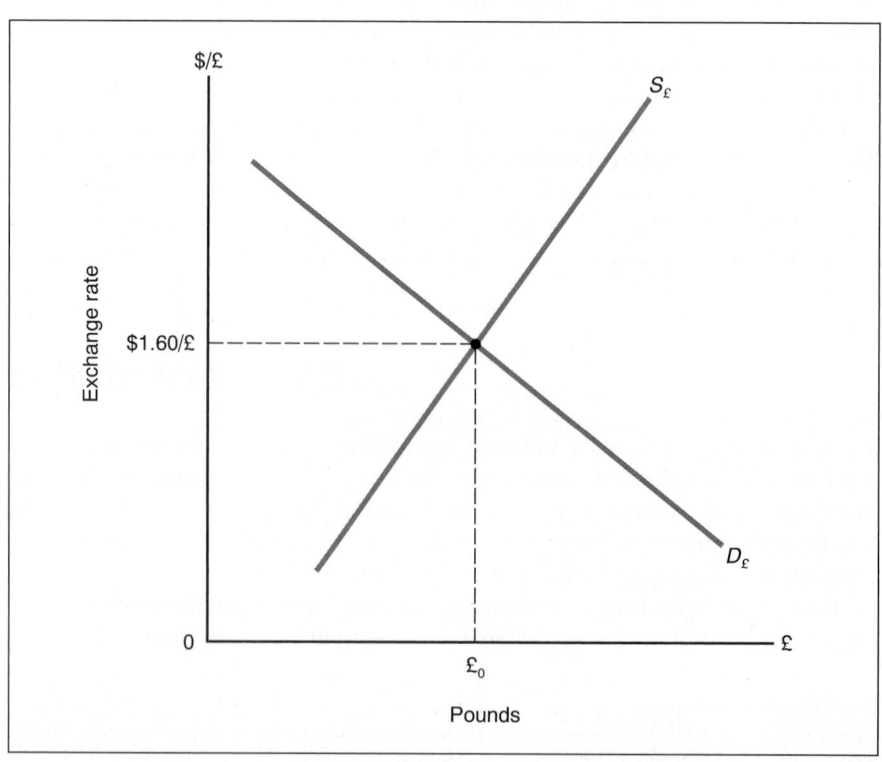

FIGURE 40.1

Flexible Exchange Rates

The value of exchange rates is determined by the Laws of Supply and Demand in a flexible exchange rate system. In the figure, the quantity of pounds sterling exchanged, £, is the horizontal axis and the exchange rate in terms of dollar per pound, $/£, is on the vertical axis. The demand curve for pounds, $D_£$, comes from sources such as British importers selling in the United States who want to convert the dollars they receive into pounds, or U.S. citizens who want pounds to buy British financial securities. The supply curve for pounds, $S_£$, comes from sources such as U.S. exporters selling in England who want to convert the pounds they receive into dollars, or from British citizens who want dollars to buy U.S. financial securities. The equilibrium exchange rate is $1.60/£, at the intersection of $D_£$ and $S_£$, and $£_0$ pounds are exchanged for dollars in the foreign exchange markets.

per pound—that is, the greater the dollar price of a pound—the smaller the quantity of pounds demanded. The fewer dollars that people have to exchange per pound—that is, the lower the dollar price of a pound—the larger the quantity of pounds demanded.

The supply curve for pounds, $S_{£}$, comes from people with pounds who want to exchange them for dollars. They might be U.S. exporters to London who want to exchange the pounds that they receive from their British customers for dollars so that they can return the funds to the United States. Or they might be British pension fund managers who want dollars to buy U.S. financial securities or real estate in New York City. The supply curve is upward sloping in terms of dollars per pound. The more dollars that people receive per pound—that is, the greater the dollar price of a pound, the larger the quantity of pounds supplied. The fewer dollars that people receive per pound—that is, the lower the dollar price of a pound, the smaller the quantity of pounds supplied.

The equilibrium value of the exchange rates occurs at the intersection of the demand and the supply curves. According to Figure 40.1, the equilibrium exchange rate is $1.60/£, with $£_0$ pounds exchanged in the foreign exchange markets.

A word on point of view is in order before continuing. The demand curve for pounds is equivalent to the supply curve of dollars because anyone with dollars who wants to buy pounds is simultaneously a supplier of dollars in the foreign exchange markets. Similarly, the supply curve of pounds is equivalent to the demand curve for dollars because anyone who wants to supply pounds for dollars is simultaneously a demander of dollars in the foreign exchange markets. Therefore, we could have represented the exchange between dollars and pounds in terms of the supply and demand for dollars. The quantity of dollars exchanged would be on the horizontal axis, and the exchange rate in terms of pounds per dollar would be on the vertical axis. The analysis of the dollar-pound exchange rate would be the same with either diagram. For example, the diagram in terms of dollars would establish an equilibrium exchange rate of .625£/$, the inverse of $1.60/£. We will continue to use Figure 40.1 to analyze exchange rates under a flexible exchange rate system.

The analysis of a single exchange rate is somewhat misleading because exchange rates are not free to take on any values whatsoever. The exchange rates between different currencies must bear a particular relationship to one another. Exchange rates must also reflect the relative prices of traded goods within each country.

RELATIVE EXCHANGE RATES: ARBITRAGE Regarding the relationship between exchange rates, suppose that the exchange rate between dollars and pounds is $2/£ and the exchange rate between the German mark (DM) and the dollar is 2DM/$. Then the exchange rate between the German mark and the pound must be 4DM/£. A mark-pound exchange rate at any other value would make arbitrage possible.

Arbitrage refers to buying and selling commodities whose prices are out of line in such a way as to guarantee a profit. It is not a gamble. To see how arbitrage works, suppose that the mark-pound exchange rate were 5DM/£, with the other exchange rates as listed above. Anyone could make a sure-fire profit. For example, a U.S. citizen could take $2.00 and buy 1£, then sell the pound

ARBITRAGE

The buying and selling of commodities whose prices are out of line in such a way as to guarantee a profit.

for 5DM, and then sell the 5DM at 2DM/1$ for $2.50. The round trip in currencies has turned $2.00 into $2.50, guaranteed. These arbitrage transactions increase the demand for pounds and the supply of marks, both of which decrease the value of the mark relative to the pound. The possibility for arbitrage ends when the mark-pound exchange rate falls to 4DM/£.[5]

Most large financial institutions such as brokerage houses and commercial banks employ arbitrageurs whose job is to keep a close watch on exchange rates throughout the day and engage in arbitrage transactions when any two exchange rates are out of line. The actions of the arbitrageurs serve to keep all exchange rates tightly related to one another at all times. Profitable opportunities from misaligned exchange rates are immediately competed away.

RELATIVE EXCHANGE RATES: PURCHASING POWER PARITY Regarding the relationship between exchange rates and the prices of traded goods, exchange rates should reflect the principle of purchasing power parity (PPP). The idea is that traded goods must cost the same in all countries where they are sold, except for transactions and transportation costs. For example, suppose that a traded good has a price of $1.50 in the United States and 1£ in England. Assuming that the good is costless to transport from one country to the other, the dollar-pound exchange rate must be $1.50/£. Any other exchange rate would lead to arbitrage in the good; anyone could make a profit by purchasing the good in one country and selling it in the other.

To see why, suppose that the exchange rate was $2/£. A U.S. citizen could buy the good in the United States for $1.50, ship it to England and sell it there for 1£, then sell the £ for $2 in the foreign exchange market. The original $1.50 has grown to $2. The demand for the good in the United States would raise its price there until it was $2. Now the relative prices of the good in the United States and England match the exchange rate, $2/£, and arbitrage is no longer possible.

PURCHASING POWER PARITY

The principle that the overall price index of one country must equal the overall price index of any other country multiplied by the exchange rate of the first country's currency to the second country's currency.

Many goods are traded between countries. Also, the relationship between traded and nontraded goods ought to be approximately the same in every country. Therefore, **purchasing power parity** relates to an overall price index of goods in two countries, such as the GDP deflator. It says, for example, that the overall U.S. price index, P_{US}, must equal the overall British price index, P_{Eng}, multiplied by the dollar-pound exchange rate, e.

$$P_{US} = e \cdot P_{Eng}$$

Purchasing power parity ties down the absolute value of exchange rates, and not just their relative values. For example, it says that a doubling of prices in the United States must depreciate the dollar by half its value (that is, double the amount of dollars needed to buy a pound).

Purchasing power parity cannot be expected to hold as tightly as does the relationship between two or more exchange rates described above. Any number of economic events cause exchange rates to move up and down, as we will see in a moment. Goods prices also change over time, but they are much stickier than exchange rates are, which can change frequently even during the course

[5]The dollar-mark and dollar-pound exchange rates may also change because of the arbitrage and establish a final equilibrium between the three currencies at different ratios than in our example. We have ignored this possibility to illustrate as simply as possible how arbitrage restores the proper equilibrium.

of a day. Also, the relationship between traded and nontraded goods might not be the same in every country. Finally, arbitrage in goods is more costly, more time consuming, and less certain than is arbitrage in exchange rates.

For all these reasons, economists expect purchasing power parity to hold approximately over the long run, but not necessarily in the short run. This appears to be the case. Recent studies have found that purchasing power parity holds reasonably well for the major currencies over a long run of about three to five years' duration, but not at all for shorter time periods.[6]

CHANGES IN EXCHANGE RATES The exchange rate in Figure 40.1 changes whenever anything causes the demand curve or the supply curve to shift. The principal shifters of currency demand and currency supply curves are changes in factors that directly affect the demand or the supply of exports or imports, changes in the state of the economy, changes in interest rates in either country, and changes in the expected future values of the exchange rate.

FACTORS AFFECTING EXPORTS AND IMPORTS Two obvious factors that have a direct impact on a nation's imports and exports are changes in tastes for traded goods and productivity changes that lower the costs and the prices of traded goods.

Suppose that British clothing becomes the new fad in the United States, so that the demand for imports from England increases. Refer to Figure 40.2(a). The curves $D^0_£$ and $S^0_£$ are the demand and the supply curves before the fad hits. The original exchange rate is \$1.60/£, just as in Figure 40.1. Once the fad hits the United States, the British clothing exporters selling in the United States have many more dollars, some of which they want to exchange for pounds to bring the funds to England. The demand for pounds increases from $D^0_£$ to $D^1_£$, and the new equilibrium exchange rate is at the intersection of $D^1_£$ and $S^0_£$. The dollar depreciates in value from \$1.60/£ to \$1.80/£.

In general, *an increase in the demand for imports increases the demand for foreign currency and depreciates the value of a nation's currency.* A clear example of this principle has been the great increase in demand for Japanese cars and consumer electronic products in the United States. The result has been a steady depreciation of the dollar against the yen over time. In 1972 a dollar traded for 303 yen in the foreign exchange markets; by the summer of 1993 a dollar traded for just over 100 yen.[7]

Productivity changes have a direct impact on the demand for traded goods. For example, rapid technological change in the production of personal computers has sharply lowered the costs of a given amount of computing power. The cost-reducing technological changes have increased the demand for U.S. personal computers in England. Figure 40.2(b) shows effects of the technological change on the dollar-pound exchange rate.

$D^0_£$ and $S^0_£$ are the demand and the supply curves for pounds before the technological change. The original exchange rate is \$1.60/£, as in Figure 40.2(a). This time U.S. exporters selling personal computers in England have

---

[6]See J. Whitt, Jr., "The Long-Run Behavior of the Real Exchange Rate: A Reconsideration," *Journal of Money, Credit and Banking* 24, No. 1 (February 1992): 72–81 (3-year estimate); and M. Manzer, "An International Comparison of Prices and Exchange Rates: A New Test of Purchasing Power Parity," *Journal of International Money and Finance* 9 (1990): 75–91 (5-year estimate).

[7]*Economic Report of the President 1993*, Table B-107, p. 470.

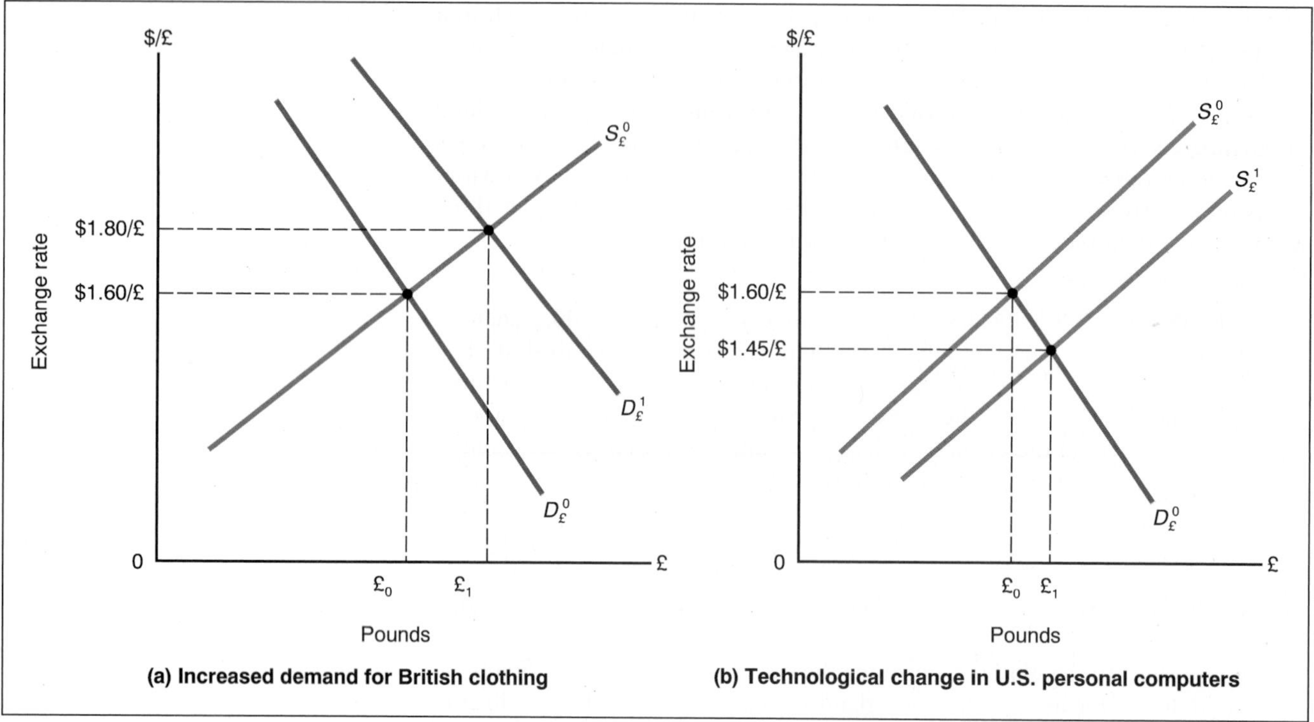

FIGURE 40.2

The Demand for Imports, Technological Change, and Exchange Rates

The figure illustrates two events that would change the exchange rate between the dollar and the pound, an increase in the demand for British clothing by U.S. consumers, and technological change in the production of U.S. personal computers. The initial equilibrium in each figure before the events occur is at the intersection of $D^0_£$ and $S^0_£$. The exchange rate is \$1.60/£ and $£_0$ pounds are exchanged for dollars in the foreign exchange markets. In Figure 40.2(a), the increased demand for British clothing in the U.S. increases the demand for pounds from $D^0_£$ to $D^1_£$, as British importers in the United States have more dollars that they want to exchange for pounds. The new equilibrium is at the intersection of $D^1_£$ and $S^0_£$. The increase in the demand for British imports causes the dollar to depreciate to \$1.80/£, and increases the quantity of pounds exchanged to $£_1$. In Figure 40.2(b), the technological change in U.S. personal computers makes them more desirable to British consumers, so exports of U.S. personal computers to England increase. The supply of pounds increases from $S^0_£$ to $S^1_£$, as U.S. exporters in England have more pounds that they want to exchange for dollars. The new equilibrium is at the intersection of $D^0_£$ and $S^1_£$. The technological change causes the dollar to appreciate to \$1.45/£, and increases the quantity of pounds exchanged to $£_1$.

more pounds that they want to exchange for dollars in order to bring the funds back to the United States. The supply of pounds increases from $S^0_£$ to $S^1_£$, and the new equilibrium exchange rate is at the intersection of $D^0_£$ and $S^1_£$. The dollar appreciates in value from \$1.60/£ to \$1.45/£.

In general, *an increase in the demand for a nation's exports increases the supply of foreign currency and appreciates the value of the nation's currency*. Increases in productivity are an important factor tending to increase the demand for exports. The purchasing power parity principle indicates that the increases in productivity do not have to be specifically in the export goods in order to appreciate the currency. Productivity changes that reduce costs and prices in any industry have the same effect. In the PPP relationship above a reduction in P_{US} reduces e, the dollar per pound exchange rate.[8]

CHANGES IN AGGREGATE DEMAND Changes in aggregate demand change the level of real national income or output and the rate of inflation. Both effects feed back into the value of the exchange rate.

For example, an increase in aggregate demand increases real national income. It also increases the rate of inflation as the economy moves along the short-run Phillips Curve. Both effects tend to depreciate the value of the currency.

The increase in national income increases the demand for imports through the marginal propensity to import. The higher income induces consumers to buy more foreign goods and induces producers to buy more foreign material inputs and capital goods in order to increase production. We have just seen that an increase in the demand for imports increases the demand for foreign currency and depreciates the value of a nation's currency.

The increase in inflation simultaneously makes imports more attractive and exports less attractive. The increased demand for imports increases the demand for foreign currency, and the decreased demand for exports decreases the supply of foreign currency. The nation's currency depreciates in value as both the demand curve and the supply curve shift up. This is another instance of the purchasing power parity principle at work. Any change in the overall price level must feed directly through to the exchange rate.

CHANGES IN INTEREST RATES Changes in interest rates have an immediate impact on the exchange rate. We described this effect in the macroeconomic chapters of the text. The idea is that money managers shop worldwide for the best returns on their funds. When U.S. interest rates rise, money managers in London, Tokyo, and Bonn want to place more funds in U.S. financial securities. To do this, however, they must first obtain dollars on the foreign exchange market, so the demand for dollars increases and the dollar appreciates in value. Figure 40.2(b) applies to the increase in U.S. interest rates. An increase in demand for dollars by British money managers is equivalent to an increase in the supply of pounds because they want to exchange pounds for dollars. The supply curve, S, shifts out, as in the figure, and the dollar appreciates in value.

Conversely, a decrease in U.S. interest rates depreciates the value of the dollar. This time Figure 40.2(a) applies. Money managers want to shift their funds out of U.S. financial securities and into British, Japanese, and German financial securities. The demand for pounds and other foreign currencies increases, and the dollar depreciates in value.

EXPECTED FUTURE CHANGES IN EXCHANGE RATES Some people enter the foreign exchange markets as speculators. They try to earn a profit by guessing what the value of exchange rates will be sometime in the future.

Speculation differs from arbitrage in two ways. First, arbitrage is guaranteed to earn a profit, whereas speculation is a gamble. Speculators win if they guess

[8]Recall, also, the U.S./British example illustrating Ricardo's model of comparative advantage in Chapter 39 where we showed what values the exchange rates could have. If U.S. labor were twice as productive, so that the goods' prices were half as large, the values of the exchange rates would also be half as large. The dollar would appreciate in value.

right and lose if they guess wrong. Second, arbitrage keeps exchange rates in the proper alignment with one another and thereby stabilizes foreign exchange markets. Speculation may also help to stabilize foreign exchange markets. But it can just as easily destabilize foreign exchange markets by causing large, volatile swings in exchange rates. For this reason, exchanges of currency motivated by speculation are commonly referred to as "hot" money.

To see the possibilities of stabilizing and destabilizing speculation, return to the example above of an increase in the demand for British imports, illustrated by Figure 40.2(a). The increased demand for imports shifts up the demand for pounds, and the dollar depreciates from \$1.60/£ to \$1.80/£. The speculators see the dollar depreciating and try to guess what it will do in the future—say, one year from now. Suppose that they believe that the surge in import demand is temporary, so they guess that the dollar will appreciate back to \$1.60/£ one year from now. The way to earn a profit based on this guess is to exchange pounds for dollars now at \$1.80/£ when the dollar is relatively cheap. Then they can sell the dollars back for pounds one year from now at \$1.60/£ when the pound is relatively cheap. The \$1.80 received for each pound now will buy more than 1£ one year from now if the speculators have guessed correctly.

This speculation is stabilizing. It creates a demand for dollars, or a supply of pounds, now when the dollar is depreciating. The supply curve for pounds, S_L, shifts out, and the exchange rate quickly moves back to \$1.60/£. The speculation has kept the dollar close to its initial value. Notice, also, that the speculation becomes a self-fulfilling prophecy. The guess that the dollar will appreciate in the future generates the demand for dollars (supply of pounds) that causes the dollar to appreciate.

Unfortunately, the self-fulfilling prophecy of speculation can also be tremendously destabilizing. Continuing with the same example, suppose that when the speculators see the dollar depreciating from \$1.60/£ to \$1.80/£, they guess that the dollar will continue to depreciate—say, to \$2.00/£ one year from now. This time the way to make a profit on the guess is to buy pounds with dollars for \$1.80/£ when the pound is relatively cheap. Then they can sell the pounds back for dollars one year from now at \$2.00/£ when the dollar is relatively cheap. The \$1.80 used to buy each pound now will grow to \$2.00 one year from now if the speculators have guessed correctly.

This speculation is destabilizing. It adds to the increased demand for pounds by the British importers, shifts D_L up further, and causes the dollar to depreciate beyond \$1.80/£. Having seen the dollar depreciate even more, what do the speculators guess now? They could revise their expectations upward beyond \$2.00/£, which increases the demand for pounds even more and further depreciates the dollar. There is no natural stopping point to the speculation. The upward revision of expectations could easily feed on itself and drive the dollar-pound exchange rate wildly upward.

MANAGED EXCHANGE RATE ("DIRTY" FLOAT)

A variation of a flexible exchange rate system in which an exchange rate is determined by the Laws of Supply and Demand within a band of values selected by the central banks; alternatively, a variation of a flexible exchange rate system in which the central banks occasionally intervene in the foreign exchange markets in order to prevent their currencies from appreciating or depreciating "too much."

MANAGED EXCHANGE RATES The possibility of destabilizing speculation is an extremely serious threat to a flexible exchange rate system. International trade cannot flourish in an environment of wildly fluctuating exchange rates driven by the psychology of speculation. It is for this reason more than any other that central banks have chosen to intervene in the foreign exchange markets from time to time, creating a hybrid exchange rate system called the **managed, or "dirty," float.**

In one version of a managed float the central banks allow the exchange rates of the major currencies to move within a fairly wide band—say, plus or minus 10 percent of their current values—in order to take advantage of the Laws of Supply and Demand. Once an exchange rate hits either the upper or the lower limit of the band, however, the central banks intervene to keep the exchange rate within the band. The intervention prevents a destabilizing speculative psychology from taking hold of the foreign exchange markets.

In terms of our example, suppose that the Fed and the Bank of London agree to allow the dollar to depreciate from \$1.60/£ to \$1.80/£, but no further. Thus, \$1.80/£ is the upper limit on the dollar-pound exchange rate band. At this point both central banks agree to supply whatever amount of pounds is needed to keep the exchange rates from rising above \$1.80/£. The message to the speculators is clear: Do not expect a further depreciation of the dollar in the future. Now that the speculators have no reason to buy pounds, D_L does not increase further, and the exchange rate stays at \$1.80/£.

The central banks do not need anything as formal as an announced band to prevent destabilizing speculation. All they need do to forestall a destabilizing speculation is to make clear their intention to intervene to prevent exchange rates from moving "too far" in either direction. An occasional intervention from time to time gives the central banks credibility. This more casual form of the managed float is the one that the Fed and the other central banks have employed since 1973 when the dollar was set free to fluctuate.

A key issue is how wide the bands should be or, alternatively, how far is "too far" under the more casual managed float. Allow the exchange rates to fluctuate within a wide range and the managed float is not much different from a pure flexible exchange rate system. The exchange rates between the major currencies may fluctuate quite a bit. Alternatively, set a narrow band explicitly or implicitly and the managed float is not much different from a fixed exchange rate system. It will require frequent interventions by the central banks.

The Fed has allowed the dollar to fluctuate substantially since 1973. Table 40.2 shows the average value of the dollar each year relative to an index of the major currencies. The data in the table are expressed as an index, with the relative value

TABLE 40.2 Index of Dollar Exchange Rate Against the Major Currencies[a] (March 1973 = 100)

Year	Index	Year	Index
1973	98.9	1983	117.3
1974	99.4	1984	128.8
1975	94.1	1985	132.4
1976	97.6	1986	103.6
1977	93.3	1987	90.9
1978	84.4	1988	88.2
1979	83.2	1989	94.4
1980	84.9	1990	86.0
1981	100.9	1991	86.5
1982	111.8	1992	83.3

[a]The value of the dollar is a trade-weighted average of exchange rates against a broad range of currencies, adjusted by changes in consumer prices.

SOURCE: Council of Economic Advisers, *Economic Report of the President 1993* (Washington, D.C.: U.S. Government Printing Office, 1993), 470, Table B-107.

of the dollar in March 1973 chosen as the benchmark and set equal to 100. The relative values are in real terms; they correct for changes in consumer prices within each country in line with the purchasing power parity idea.

The table shows that the dollar has been quite volatile since 1973. It has undergone three long swings: depreciating fairly sharply in the late 1970s, then appreciating even more sharply through 1985, and then depreciating sharply again through 1992. It has also danced around a lot from year to year; annual changes of 10 percent and more have been fairly common.

Changes of this magnitude are somewhat surprising, given that the international economy is riddled with trade restrictions. We saw in Chapter 39 how nations have tried to restrict imports through tariffs and other nontariff barriers to prevent deficits in their current accounts. The industrial nations have also resorted to various kinds of capital controls to restrict the movement of destabilizing "hot" money through the foreign exchange markets. The capital controls most commonly take the form of preventing foreign financial institutions from operating in domestic capital markets. The industrial nations have also resorted to special taxes on capital outflows to try to discourage them. Nonetheless, neither the restrictions on trade and capital flows nor the occasional intervention of the central banks has prevented the dollar from fluctuating widely against the other major currencies. The other factors that influence exchange rates—changes in tastes, worldwide productivity growth, the state of the industrial economies, interest rates, and speculation—appear to have dominated the various trade restrictions and central bank interventions in determining the value of the dollar in the foreign exchange markets.

Many economists believe that changes in the dollar of these magnitudes are not healthy for international trade. Although world trade has grown considerably since 1973, they point out that world trade grew even more rapidly under the Bretton Woods fixed exchange rate system. They prefer a return to fixed exchange rates, which we turn to next.

Fixed Exchange Rate System

Under a fixed exchange rate system the nations agree to fix the exchange rates at a given set of values. Then the central banks intervene in the foreign exchange markets as need be to maintain the fixed values. The official settlements account becomes a crucial part of a nation's balance of payments transactions.

Figure 40.3 illustrates how a fixed exchange rate system operates. It is based on the earlier examples illustrated in Figure 40.2. Refer, first, to Figure 40.3(a).

Suppose that the dollar-pound exchange rate is fixed, or pegged, at \$1.60/£ and that this exchange rate is consistent with the demand for and the supply of pounds in the foreign exchange markets. The initial demand and supply curves, $D^0_£$ and $S^0_£$, intersect at \$1.60/£, as before. The quantity of pounds exchanged is $£_0$.

An increase in the demand for British clothing increases the demand for pounds from $D^0_£$ to $D^1_£$, also as before. Under a fixed exchange rate system, however, the dollar cannot depreciate in value to clear the foreign exchange market. Instead, the Fed is committed to supply whatever pounds are necessary to meet the increased demand at the fixed, \$1.60/£ exchange rate. The

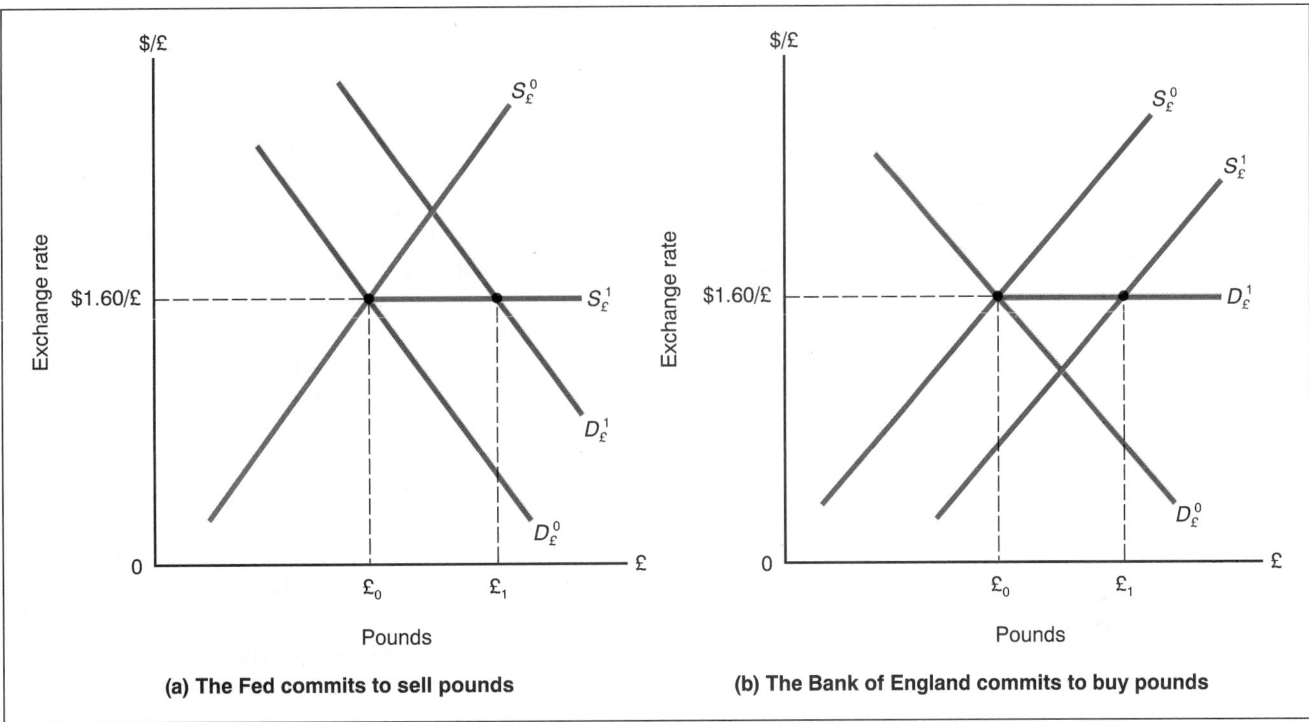

(a) The Fed commits to sell pounds **(b) The Bank of England commits to buy pounds**

FIGURE 40.3

Fixed Exchange Rates

Under a fixed exchange rate system, nations agree to fix the exchange rates between their currencies and the central banks make a commitment to buy or sell currencies as needed to maintain the values of the exchange rates. The figure assumes that the United States and England have agreed to fix the dollar-pound exchange rate at \$1.60/£, which is the current value of the exchange rate in the private foreign exchange markets. The private demand curve for pounds, $D^0_£$, and the private supply curve for pounds, $S^0_£$, intersect at \$1.60/£. In Figure 40.2(a), an increase in the demand for British imports in the United States increases the demand for pounds from $D^0_£$ to $D^1_£$, which would depreciate the value of the dollar. The Fed is commited, however, to supply whatever pounds are needed in exchange for dollars to keep the dollar at \$1.60/£. The Fed's commitment makes the supply of pounds perfectly elastic at \$1.60/£, the supply curve $S^1_£$. $£_1$ pounds are exchanged for dollars in the foreign exchange markets, at the intersection of $D^1_£$ and $S^1_£$, with the Fed supplying ($£_1 - £_0$) pounds. In Figure 40.2(b), an increase in the demand for U.S. exports in England increases the supply of pounds from $S^0_£$ to $S^1_£$, which would appreciate the value of the dollar. The Bank of England is commited, however, to buy whatever pounds are needed with dollars to keep the exchange rate at \$1.60/£. The Bank of England's commitment makes the demand for pounds perfectly elastic at \$1.60/£, the demand curve $D^1_£$. $£_1$ pounds are exchanged for dollars in the foreign exchange markets, at the intersection of $D^1_£$ and $S^1_£$, with the Bank of England buying ($£_1 - £_0$) pounds.

Fed's commitment makes the supply curve horizontal at \$1.60/£ beyond $£_0$, the line $S^1_£$. The Fed sells the importers ($£_1 - £_0$) pounds, the additional amount that they demand at the fixed, \$1.60/£ exchange rate. The same analysis would apply if the increase in the demand for pounds were due to a capital outflow from the United States to England or to speculators betting that the United States and England will soon revalue their exchange rate to \$1.80/£. The Fed is committed to exchange pounds for dollars at \$1.60/£ no matter who wants the pounds.

Figure 40.3(b) illustrates the fixed exchange rate commitment from the opposite side. The initial demand and supply curves are $D^0_£$ and $S^0_£$, as above. This time an increase in the demand for U.S. exports of food in England gives U.S. exporters pounds that they want to exchange for dollars. The supply of pounds increases to $S^1_£$. The Bank of England is committed to buy with dollars whatever amount of pounds is supplied at the fixed, \$1.60/£ exchange rate. The Bank of England's commitment makes the demand curve for pounds horizontal at \$1.60/£ beyond $£_0$, the line $D^1_£$. The Bank of England buys $(£_1 - £_0)$ pounds from the U.S. exporters, the additional amount that they supply at the fixed, \$1.60/£ exchange rate. The same analysis would apply if the increase in the supply of pounds were due to a capital inflow into the United States from England or to speculators betting that the United States and England will soon revalue their exchange rate to \$1.40/£. The Bank of England is committed to exchange dollars for pounds at \$1.60/£ no matter who wants the dollars.

These examples reveal two immediate problems with a fixed exchange rate system. First, nations must hold large amounts of foreign currencies to be able to honor their commitment to the fixed exchange rate. Second, the level at which the exchange rates are fixed or pegged is crucial to the continued operation of the system. We saw in Chapter 39 how an overvalued exchange rate can literally price a nation's goods out of international markets. Everyone in the nation wants to import foreign goods, and the nation's exporters cannot sell their goods in foreign countries. In terms of our first example above, the intersection of $D^1_£$ and $S^0_£$ is at an exchange rate of \$1.80/£. Suppose that the demand and the supply curves remain there. The fixed exchange rate of \$1.60/£ overvalues the dollar and forces the Fed to supply pounds forever. Something has to give because the Fed obviously cannot supply pounds forever.

We will uncover still another problem with fixed exchange rates below: Committing to a fixed exchange rate system sacrifices control of the domestic economy. The history of the United States under the Bretton Woods arrangement is instructive on all these points.

THE BRETTON WOODS SYSTEM As noted in the introduction, 44 nations met at Bretton Woods, New Hampshire, in 1944 and agreed to a fixed exchange rate system centered on the dollar and gold. The dollar was pegged to gold at \$35 per ounce. The United states had accumulated a huge stock of gold during the 1930s and agreed to exchange gold for dollars on demand at the pegged rate. The other nations then pegged their currencies either to the dollar or to gold. All nations wanted to avoid the chaos in international trade and finance that existed during the 1930s. Bretton Woods marked the first time that the leading capitalist nations were able to agree formally on an exchange rate system.

INTERNATIONAL MONETARY FUND (IMF)

An international agency established in 1947 by the capitalist countries that acts as a forum for resolving exchange rate and balance-of-payments problems.

Another notable accomplishment of the Bretton Woods meeting was the establishment of the **International Monetary Fund (IMF)** to act as a forum for resolving exchange rate and balance of payments problems. The IMF had to approve all changes in exchange rates greater than 10 percent. The IMF also took on the role of helping smaller nations through temporary current account deficits by lending them dollars and other currencies. The IMF never had enough lending authority to help one of the industrialized nations through a balance of payments crisis, however.

The Bretton Woods system worked beautifully at first. The United States poured military and economic assistance into Western Europe and elsewhere immediately after World War II. The aid generated huge deficits in the capital account and the military portion of the current account in the U.S. balance of payments. But the transfer mechanism worked well because the U.S. economy was virtually the only industrial economy unscathed by the war. Most of the aid dollars came right back to the United States through sales by U.S. exporters. The capital and military account deficits were offset by a huge surplus in the U.S. balance of trade. This situation persisted throughout the 1950s.

Once Western Europe (and Japan) started to recover from the war, the transfer mechanism worked less well. The U.S. aid and military dollars were increasingly spent in other countries, and the U.S. balance-of-trade surplus began to shrink. There was still no pressure on the Fed's international gold and currency reserves, however, because everyone was happy to have the dollars. The dollar had gained acceptance as an international currency that could be spent anywhere. Therefore, the injection of aid and military dollars had the effect of increasing the international supply of money, which gave the industrial nations much needed liquidity as their economies were recovering and growing. International trade flourished under the Bretton Woods system well into the 1960s.

We might also note that the IMF was reasonably successful in helping the smaller nations with their balance-of-payments problems. It even created a new reserve currency in 1967 called a **special drawing right (SDR),** which all central banks agreed to accept as an international reserve in their settlement accounts. Nations could buy SDRs with their currency and then trade the SDRs with central banks for dollars and other major currencies that they needed to settle current account deficits. The SDRs were originally valued at 1SDR = $1. Starting in 1974 their value was set at a weighted average of the dollar, pound, franc, mark, and yen. The IMF has changed the weights periodically since 1974.

SPECIAL DRAWING RIGHT (SDR)

A reserve currency created by the IMF and accepted by all central banks as an international reserve in their official settlement accounts; countries can purchase SDRs with their own currencies and then trade them to central banks for dollars and other major currencies as needed to settle current account deficits.

The first problems with the Bretton Woods system appeared in the late 1960s. The U.S. balance of trade surplus continued to shrink, and the Vietnam War brought another huge injection of dollars into the international economy. For the first time the supply of dollars exceeded the demand for dollars, and some nations began to exchange their dollars for their own currencies and for U.S. gold. The other industrialized nations also began to resent the political power that the dollar's role as an international currency gave to the United States. The United States could send dollars anywhere with impunity.

By 1970 it was clear that the dollar was highly overvalued. It also became clear that there are no really good options under a fixed exchange rate system when a key currency becomes overvalued.

"SOLUTIONS" TO MISALIGNED CURRENCIES One obvious "solution" was to devalue the dollar relative to gold—say, to $70 an ounce. The devaluation would immediately depreciate the dollar relative to all other currencies, which would make U.S. exports more competitive again and at the same time reduce U.S. imports. The improvement in the balance of trade would relieve some of the pressure on the dollar. The problem with this solution is that it creates the closest thing to a sure bet for the speculators. Upon learning that the United States was about to devalue, the speculators would try to buy up all the Fed's international reserves with dollars and then sell the reserves back to the Fed for dollars after the devaluation. The rush to buy international reserves would force the devaluation and earn enormous profits for the speculators. No one wanted to play into the hands of the speculators, so this "solution" was essentially ruled out.

Another "solution" that no one wanted was to increase trade restrictions and capital controls. The General Agreement on Tariffs and Trade (GATT) was pushing for freer trade and capital movements. The international economy already had too many trade restrictions and capital controls.

A third solution was for the United States to rein in its economy by lowering aggregate demand. This would reduce U.S. imports and improve the balance of trade, thereby lessening the pressure on the Fed's international reserves.

The reduction in aggregate demand begins automatically when the Fed exchanges gold or foreign currencies for dollars and dollar deposits. The sale of these assets for dollars or checks written against deposit accounts held by foreigners in U.S. banks removes dollars from circulation and reduces bank reserves. The effect is the same as a sale of Treasury securities by the Fed on the Open Market. The U.S. money supply decreases in either case, which leads to a decrease in aggregate demand.

The Fed may not want U.S. international transactions dictating the course of overall aggregate demand, however. If not, it can counter the decrease in the money supply caused by the loss of international reserves by purchasing an equal amount of Treasury securities on the Open Market. This is called a **sterilizing transaction** by the Fed because it is designed to leave the money supply constant. But if the Fed sterilizes the loss of international reserves, aggregate demand remains constant, the balance of trade does not improve, and the pressures on the Fed's international reserves continue apace.

STERILIZING TRANSACTION

A transaction by a central bank that is designed to offset the effect on the money supply caused by any transaction on the official settlements account; an example is the Fed's sales of Treasury securities on the Open Market to offset its purchases of foreign currencies.

Still another option is for the other industrial nations with balance of trade surpluses to stimulate their economies, which would increase U.S. exports. It would also reduce the other nations' exports if stimulating aggregate demand increases their rates of inflation. The other nations have no particular incentive to stimulate their economies, however. Under a fixed exchange rate system, only the deficit nations are under pressure to adjust their economies or risk losing all their international reserves. The surplus nations are gaining international reserves. They do not have to stimulate their economies if they do not want to. The purchase of international reserves by their central banks does automatically increase their money supplies and stimulate their economies. But they can also sterilize this effect just as easily as the Fed can sterilize in the other direction.

In any event, the United States decided by the early 1970s that the Bretton Woods system was no longer tenable. President Nixon unilaterally suspended convertibility of the dollar into gold in 1971 and then set the dollar free to float in 1973. Most economists believe that the fixed exchange rate system would not have survived the OPEC increase in oil prices that began in 1974 no matter what the United States had chosen to do.

Macroeconomic Policy and Exchange Rate Systems

The final point to make about choosing an exchange rate system is that the macroeconomic policy options are quite different under fixed and flexible exchange rates. Under flexible exchange rates, monetary policy is effective in controlling aggregate demand, whereas fiscal policy is relatively ineffective. Under fixed exchange rates, fiscal policy is effective in controlling aggregate demand, whereas monetary policy is completely ineffective. These statements assume a Keynesian world of sticky wages and prices and unemployed resources in the short run.

FLEXIBLE EXCHANGE RATES

FISCAL POLICY We saw in Chapter 36 that the effectiveness of fiscal policy in controlling demand is greatly reduced by the crowding-out effect through net exports. To review, an expansionary fiscal policy increases aggregate demand and interest rates. The increase in interest rates attracts foreign funds, which have to be converted into dollars to enter the U.S. financial markets. The increased demand for dollars causes the dollar to appreciate in value, which reduces the demand for exports and increases the demand for imports. The reduction in net exports (exports − imports) reduces aggregate demand and offsets some or all of the stimulating effect of the expansionary fiscal policy.

The analysis applies in reverse for a contractionary fiscal policy. The reduction of interest rates leads to an outflow of dollars, which depreciates the dollar and increases net exports. The increase in net exports offsets some or all of the contractionary fiscal policy.

MONETARY POLICY Monetary policy is effective in controlling aggregate demand because interest rates move in the opposite direction from fiscal policy. An increase in the money supply increases aggregate demand and decreases interest rates. The decrease in interest rates drives funds out of the United States to foreign markets looking for higher returns. The exchange of dollars for foreign currency causes the dollar to depreciate in value, which increases the demand for exports and decreases the demand for imports. The increase in net exports supports the initial increase in aggregate demand instead of offsetting it.[9]

Conversely, a decrease in the money supply decreases aggregate demand and increases interest rates. The increase in interest rates attracts funds into the United States, which causes the dollar to appreciate in value. The appreciation of the dollar in turn causes a decrease in net exports, which supports the initial decrease in aggregate demand. Therefore, both increases and decreases in the money supply are effective in controlling aggregate demand in the short run.

FIXED EXCHANGE RATES

FISCAL POLICY Fiscal policy is effective in controlling aggregate demand under fixed exchange rates. The analysis begins the same way as under flexible exchange rates. The expansionary fiscal policy increases aggregate demand and increases interest rates. The increase in interest rates attracts foreign funds as before, but this time the Fed cannot let the dollar appreciate in value. Instead, it buys all the foreign currency offered with dollars at the fixed exchange rate. The purchase of the currencies increases the U.S. money supply, which sup-

[9]We saw in Chapter 38 that continued increases in the money supply at full employment, when real aggregate demand cannot increase, simply cause price inflation. The dollar depreciates point for point with the rate of inflation.

ports the initial increase in aggregate demand and returns the interest rates to their initial levels. There is no crowding-out effect through net exports (or through consumer durables and investment). The expansionary fiscal policy, combined with the induced increase in the money supply, leads to a multiplied increase in national income.

The same analysis applies in reverse. A contractionary fiscal policy reduces aggregate demand and begins to decrease U.S. interest rates. Funds leave the United States as investors seek higher returns elsewhere, and people sell dollars to the Fed for foreign currencies. The U.S. money supply decreases and drives interest rates back up to their initial levels. The contractionary fiscal policy, combined with the induced decrease in the money supply, leads to a multiplied decrease in national income. The key to the analysis is that the supply of funds to financial markets worldwide is perfectly elastic under fixed exchange rates (assuming no capital controls). Interest rates must be the same in all financial markets.

MONETARY POLICY Monetary policy is completely ineffective under fixed exchange rates. Suppose that the Fed increases the money supply by purchasing Treasury securities on the Open Market. An increase in the money supply begins to decrease interest rates, which drives funds out of the United States. People sell dollars to the Fed for foreign currencies, which reduces the money supply and restores the initial level of interest rates. The net result is no change in the money supply, no change in interest rates, and no change in aggregate demand. All the Fed has done is exchange Treasury securities for some of its international reserves. The same analysis applies in reverse. Under fixed exchange rates the Fed cannot increase or decrease the money supply if it is the central bank that buys and sells foreign currency to maintain the fixed exchange rate.

The only wrinkle in the analysis occurs if other central banks buy and sell foreign currency in order to maintain the fixed exchange rate. Return again to an increase in the money supply. This time, however, suppose that the Bank of England supplies the pounds that U.S. money managers want for their dollars in order to buy financial securities in London. The purchase of the dollars by the Bank of England increases the British money supply as it removes the dollars from circulation. The Bank of England will not want to keep the dollars, however, since they do not earn a rate of return. So the bank ships the dollars back to the Fed and instructs the Fed to buy Treasury securities on its behalf. Once the Fed buys the securities, the dollars return to circulation in the United States. The final effect is that both the U.S. and British money supplies have increased. The U.S. monetary policy is effective in increasing aggregate demand only if the British also increase their aggregate demand.

The general principle is that *the growth of the money supply must be the same in all countries that are tied together under fixed exchange rates.* No one country can independently change its money supply. Furthermore, we saw in Chapter 38 that the growth of the money supply determines the rate of inflation in the long run. Therefore, with the growth of the money supply equal everywhere under fixed exchange rates, *every country must have the same rate of inflation in the long run.*

In conclusion, governments have much more control over their internal economies with fiscal and monetary policies under a flexible exchange rate system than under a fixed exchange rate system. Under flexible exchange rates, monetary policy remains effective in controlling aggregate demand, and fiscal policy is partially effective. Under fixed exchange rates, fiscal policy remains effective in controlling aggregate demand, but governments lose independent control of their monetary policies. Also, without independent control of the money supply, governments cannot control the rate of inflation. Macroeconomic policies have to be coordinated across countries in the long run under fixed exchange rates.

These differences in macroeconomic policy options arise because of the different ways that the two exchange rate systems react to imbalances in international transactions. Under flexible exchange rates the exchange rate itself responds to current account or capital account surpluses or deficits according to the Laws of Supply and Demand. The appreciation and depreciation of the currencies protect the internal domestic macro economy somewhat from the international economy. In contrast, the entire economy has to adjust to current account or capital account surpluses or deficits when governments commit to fixed exchange rates.[10]

These policy differences are consistent with the philosophies underlying the two exchange rate systems. The fixed exchange rate system presumes that nations should first stabilize the international economy, which then forces them to keep their internal domestic economies in order and coordinated with one another. The flexible exchange rate system presumes that nations will strive to keep their internal domestic economies in order, which then tends to stabilize the exchange rates. Neither system is foolproof, as we have seen.

The ambivalence over which exchange rate system is best is reflected in the mix of fixed and flexible exchange rates in use throughout the world today. In 1984, 91 nations had pegged their exchange rates either to another currency or to a market basket of currencies, and 55 nations had flexible exchange rates. Generally speaking, the smaller, lower-income nations favor fixed exchange rates supported by strict controls on capital inflows and outflows. The larger, higher-income nations favor flexible exchange rates.[11]

The majority of economists believe that the larger industrial nations will continue to operate under flexible exchange rates. Pegging the major currencies at an appropriate level is chancy at best, and revaluing the major currencies once they have been pegged is difficult. Also, most of the industrial nations are not willing to give up the control over their internal domestic economies as they must under a fixed exchange rate system. The one exception has been the Western European nations of the European Community.

Exchange Rates within the European Community

The ambivalence toward exchange rate systems has been especially evident in Western Europe. The Western European nations floated their exchange rates in 1973 when the United States did. The flexible exchange rates lasted until

[10]The domestic economies are not entirely protected from the international economy under flexible exchange rates, however. We saw in earlier chapters how an appreciation of the dollar helps consumers because it makes imports cheaper, but hurts exporters and import-competing industries. Conversely, a depreciation of the dollar hurts consumers because it makes imports more expensive, but helps exporters and import-competing industries. These might be called the "micro" effects of flexible exchange rates.

[11]W. Enders and H. Lapan, *International Economics: Theory and Policy* (Englewood Cliffs, N.J.: Prentice-Hall, 1987), Table 23.1, pp. 510–511.

EXCHANGE RATE MECHANISM (ERM)

The dominant feature of the European Monetary System (EMS),which pegged the currencies of the Western European nations to the German mark.

1979, when they agreed to form a new European Monetary System (EMS). The heart of the EMS was the **Exchange Rate Mechanism,** which, for all intents and purposes, pegged all the currencies of Western Europe to the German mark.

OPEC had doubled the price of oil in 1979, setting off a surge of inflation throughout Europe and the United States. The Western Europeans feared that they would not have the discipline to fight the buildup of inflationary pressures and would lose control of their money supplies. They knew, however, that the Germans feared inflation more than did any other country, having experienced a disastrous hyperinflation following World War I. West Germany would certainly retain tight control of its money supply and fight off the inflation. Also, West Germany was by far the largest economy in Europe. Therefore, by pegging their currencies to the mark, the other nations were essentially pegging the growth in their money supplies to the growth in the German money supply. The West Germans' stand against inflation would force the other nations into the same posture. Pegging their currencies to the mark had the additional advantage of reducing exchange rate volatility throughout Europe, which had been considerable following the collapse of the Bretton Woods system.

The Exchange Rate Mechanism worked quite well. West Germany did hold fast against the inflationary pressures as expected, so that inflation remained under control in Europe throughout the 1980s. There were very few currency realignments until the early 1990s (see below).

Jacques Delors went even further in his 1985 White Paper. He envisioned a complete monetary union within the European Community by the turn of the century, with all nations using a single currency controlled by a Community-wide central bank, a true United States of Europe. The members of the European Community met in Maastricht in 1991 and set down a specific plan for moving to a single currency. Broadly speaking, the central bank of each nation would bear approximately the same relationship to the Community-wide central bank as the 12 Federal Reserve districts in the United States bear to the Board of Governors in Washington. At Maastricht the members also established economic conditions within each country that, if met, would allow them to join in the monetary union by 1996. The monetary union was to be completed by January 1, 1999, under any conditions.[12]

Most economists believe that the gains to moving from the Exchange Rate Mechanism to a single currency will be fairly small because the nations' macroeconomic policies are already closely coordinated and their currencies are fairly stable. The main benefit will come from eliminating the costs of currency exchanges, which are minor.

The issues connected with forming a monetary union may be moot, however. Many observers believe that the union will never come to pass, especially since Europe appears to be moving in the opposite direction.

The worldwide recession of the 1990s has brought severe strains to the Exchange Rate Mechanism. England and Italy dropped out of the EMS entirely in September of 1992. The precipitating event for them was Germany's decision in 1991 to reduce the growth of its money supply and increase interest rates in an effort to combat the inflationary pressures that had been building in the German economy following reunification. England and Italy did not

[12]This section is based on the excellent discussion of the plan for a monetary union in C. Bean, "Economic and Monetary Union in Europe," *Journal of Economic Perspectives* 6, No. 4 (Fall 1992): 31–52.

want to be forced to reduce the growth of their money supplies at a time when their economies were in the midst of a recession.

The German resolve to fight inflation put extreme pressure on the other countries as well. In August of 1993, the nations still in the EMS agreed to allow their currencies to float against the mark within a band of 15 percent in an attempt to gain more control over their economies. The original band had been just 2.25 percent. In short, Western Europe appears to be headed more in the direction of independent, floating exchange rates than in the direction of a monetary union.

CURRENT ISSUE: Norman Lamont, English Chancellor of the Exchequer in September 1992 when England dropped out of the EMS, believes that the dream of a monetary union is finished. Immediately following the loosening of the exchange rate band he was quoted as saying: "Maastricht is now dead. The prospects of a single currency have gone out the window." (*The Globe and Mail*, Toronto, August 3, 1993, B8.)

SUMMARY

Chapter 40 began with a discussion of the balance of payments, the accounting system that nations use to record their international transactions.

1. The balance of payments is a double-entry accounting of international credits and debits that must net to zero overall. An international credit (for the United States) is anything that gives rise to a demand for dollars (a supply of foreign currency). Examples are exports, capital inflows, and sales of foreign currency by the Fed. An international debit is anything that gives rise to a supply of dollars (a demand for foreign currency). Examples are imports, capital outflows, and purchases of foreign currency by the Fed.
2. The three subaccounts in the balance of payments are the current account, the capital account, and the official settlements account.
3. The current account records the flow of exports and imports of goods and services, the receipts and payments of factor incomes, and net unilateral transfers.
   a. The balance of trade is the difference between merchandise exports and imports.
   b. The balance of goods and services is the balance of trade plus exports minus imports of services plus receipts minus payments of factor income.
   c. The current account balance is the balance of goods and services minus net unilateral transfers.
4. A current account deficit means that foreign residents and central banks are accumulating dollars and dollar assets. A current account surplus means that U.S. residents and the Fed are accumulating foreign currencies and assets. Since people will not accumulate financial assets forever, a current account deficit must eventually become a current account surplus, and vice versa.
5. The capital account balance is the difference between capital inflows and capital outflows. Capital inflows are purchases of U.S. financial securities or loans to U.S. residents by foreign residents. Capital outflows are purchases of foreign securities or loans to foreign residents by U.S. residents.
6. The official settlements balance is the difference between the sale and the purchase of international reserves by the Fed. International reserves include foreign currencies, gold, and very short-term financial securities held by central banks.
7. Many of the entries in the capital account and the official settlements account are offsets to exports and imports in the current account.

8. The United States in recent years has had large current account deficits offset by large capital account and official settlement account surpluses. As a result, the United States has become the largest debtor nation; the value of U.S. assets held by foreign residents greatly exceeds the value of foreign assets held by U.S. residents.

The second section of Chapter 40 compared and contrasted the two basic exchange rate systems, flexible exchange rates and fixed exchange rates.

9. Under a flexible exchange rate system, a nation's exchange rate is determined by the Laws of Supply and Demand. The main factors determining the demands and the supplies of foreign currencies are tastes for traded goods and worldwide productivity changes, the state of the economy, interest rates, and speculation based on expectations of the future values of exchange rates.
10. Arbitrage of exchange rates keeps currencies in proper alignment with one another. Purchasing power parity fixes the absolute value of the exchange rates. It says that the exchange rate should reflect the ratio of prices within each country.
11. The United States has had a flexible exchange rate since 1973. The dollar has been quite volatile despite numerous trade and capital restrictions and despite occasional interventions by the Fed and other central banks to prevent the dollar from fluctuating "too much." A system of flexible exchange rates with occasional central bank intervention is called a managed, or "dirty," float.
12. Under a fixed exchange rate system, nations set their exchange rates at a given value, and the central banks commit to intervene in the foreign exchange markets in order to maintain the exchange rates at the set values.
13. The market economies agreed to adopt a fixed exchange rate system in 1944 at a meeting in Bretton Woods, New Hampshire. The dollar was pegged to gold at $35 an ounce, and the other currencies were pegged to the dollar or to gold. The Bretton Woods system survived until 1973 when the United States decided to switch to a flexible exchange rate.
14. Flexible and fixed exchange rates have very different macroeconomic implications. Under flexible exchange rates, fiscal policy is relatively ineffective, and monetary policy is effective in controlling aggregate demand in the short run. Under fixed exchange rates, fiscal policy is effective in controlling aggregate demand in the short run, but nations cannot pursue independent monetary policies or have separate rates of inflation.
15. The world today consists of a variety of exchange rates. Some nations have chosen a flexible exchange rate, some have pegged their currency to a major currency, and some have pegged their currency to a market basket of major currencies. For example, the United States and Japan have flexible exchange rates, whereas most of the Western European nations have pegged their exchange rates to the German mark within a narrow band.

KEY TERMS

arbitrage
autonomous capital inflow (or outflow)
balance of goods and services
balance of payments
balance of trade
capital account (balance of payments)
capital account balance
capital inflows
capital outflows
creditor nation
current account (balance of payments)
current account balance
debtor nation
direct foreign investment
eurodollar account
exchange rate mechanism
fixed exchange rate
flexible exchange rate
international credit
international debit
International Monetary Fund (IMF)
managed exchange rate ("dirty" float)
official settlements balance
purchasing power parity
special drawing right (SDR)
sterilizing transaction
transfer mechanism (international trade)

QUESTIONS

1. Indicate what balance-of-payments entries result from each of the following transactions, what subaccount each would appear in, and whether the transaction is a credit or a debit.
   a. IBM buys $500,000 worth of superconductors from a Japanese firm.
   b. A German investor buys $1 million worth of U.S. Treasury notes.
   c. The U.S. government loans the Indian government $10 million.
   d. An American tourist exchanges $1,000 for French francs at her local Federal Reserve Bank.
   e. An American firm sends $1 million worth of VCRs to Saudi Arabia in exchange for $1 million worth of oil.
2. Suppose that an American appliance dealer buys $500,000 worth of television sets from a Japanese firm. Name three possible credit transactions that might offset these imports in the balance-of-payments accounts, two in the capital account and one in the official settlements account.
3. a. Describe how the Bretton Woods system was instituted and how it operated.
   b. Instead of abandoning its fixed exchange rate in the early 1970s, why didn't the United States choose to devalue the dollar to improve its balance of trade?
   c. Why did the United States decide to abandon the Bretton Woods fixed exchange rate system in 1973?
4. Explain how the effectiveness of a nation's fiscal and monetary policies depends on whether it has a fixed or a flexible exchange rate.
5. Suppose that the exchange rates between the dollar, German mark, and British pound are as follows:
   $1/£ 2DM/$ 4DM/£
   a. Describe how a U.S. arbitrageur can make a sure profit by buying and selling the three currencies.
   b. Next, describe how and why the arbitrage transactions restore equilibrium among the exchange rates. In particular, assuming that the first two exchange rates remain the same, what must be the equilibrium value of the German mark–British pound exchange rate?
6. How will an increase in the interest rate affect a nation's exchange rate under a flexible exchange rate system?
7. Use supply and demand analysis to show how each of the following events affects the dollar-franc exchange rate. Put the quantity of francs on the horizontal axis in your supply and demand graph.
   a. French wines become more popular in the United States.
   b. The French government purchases $1 million worth of U.S. Treasury notes.
   c. American automobile workers become more productive.
8. Suppose that wine costs 160 francs per bottle and cheese costs 2 dollars a pound. If the relative price of cheese in terms of wine is 10 pounds of cheese per bottle of wine, what is the dollar-franc exchange rate? What is the dollar price of wine? What is the franc price of cheese?
9. Describe what would happen if there is a difference in the rates of inflation between two countries that have a fixed exchange rate.
10. Why do most economists believe that the gains in moving from the Exchange Rate Mechanism to a single currency for the European Community would be small?

CHAPTER

41

Developing Nations

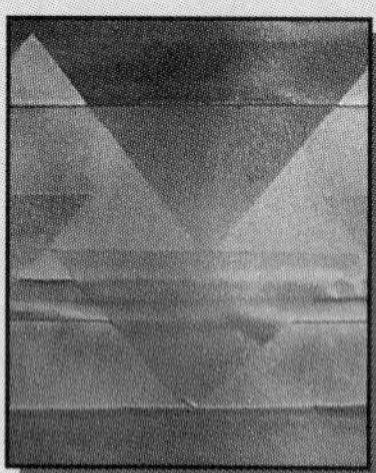

LEARNING OBJECTIVES

CONCEPTS TO LEARN

Developing countries

The determinants of long-run economic growth in developing countries

The relationship between income distribution and economic development

The supply of and the demand for children

Outward-oriented versus inward-oriented strategies for economic development

CONCEPTS TO RECALL

Opportunity cost [1]

Long-run economic growth [3]

The Laws of Supply and Demand [5, 6, 7]

The standard of living achieved in the Western industrial democracies—the United States, the countries of Western Europe, Canada, Japan, Australia, and New Zealand—is truly astounding from a global perspective. Unfortunately, most of the world's countries and people are not part of this high-income group.

In 1993 the world's population was 5.5 billion people. The vast majority of these people have far fewer creature comforts than are available to the average American, Western European, or Japanese citizen. Indeed, the standard of living throughout most of the world is appallingly low by comparison with the high-income countries. More than 3 billion people live in conditions of severe poverty, with annual incomes below $600 per person.

These people are not poor from lack of effort. They generally work long and hard throughout their lives. Work starts early in life in much of the world's rural areas. Children of six and seven weed in the fields or tend to livestock. Women play an important role in tending to crops, gathering firewood and water (often at great distance), cooking, and caring for young children. The men may work in the fields or migrate long distances seeking work in mines, plantations, or factories. In the cities young children sift through garbage dumps for bottles or cardboard that can be recycled. The sad truth is that life is very hard for most people.

Chapter 41 describes the economic circumstances that exist for most of the world's peoples who do not live in developed countries. It also examines some of the theories that seek to explain the process of economic development and analyzes a number of policy options that enhance the process of economic development.

With few exceptions, economic development is a long-term endeavor that takes place over many generations. It is also a complex process affected by cultural values, environmental constraints, political factors (both internal and external), and, not the least, economic institutions and policies.

OVERVIEW OF THE DEVELOPING NATIONS

Table 41.1 displays selected demographic and economic data by income group and region of the world for 1990.

We can see that the differences in living standards between the rich and the poor countries are enormous. The average citizen in the high-income, developed world enjoyed an income of $20,170 in 1990, which was 58 *times* that of the average citizen of the low-income, developing world ($350). Furthermore, there is every indication that this gap between the very rich and the very poor nations will continue and widen in the future. Persons from rich countries are also likely to live about 15 years longer, on average, than are their counterparts born in the lowest-income countries.

TABLE 41.1 **World Economics by Income and Region**

	POPULATION, MID-1990 (MILLIONS)	POPULATION GROWTH RATE, 1980–90 (%)	GNP PER CAPITA, 1990 ($)	LIFE EXPECTANCY AT BIRTH, 1990 (YEARS)	ADULT LITERACY, 1990 (%)
DEVELOPING ECONOMIES	4,146	2.0	840	63	74
Low income	3,058	2.0[c]	350	62[c]	60[c]
Lower middle income	629	2.0	1,530	65	75
Upper middle income	458	1.7	3,410	68	84
High income[a]	17	1.8	12,773	75	73
DEVELOPING ECONOMIES BY REGION					
South Asia	1,148	2.2	330	58	47
Sub-Saharan Africa	495	3.1	340	51	50
East Asia & Pacific	1,577	1.6	600	68	76
Latin America	433	2.1	2,180	68	84
Europe	200	0.1	2,400	70	85
DEVELOPED ECONOMIES[b]	777	0.6	20,170	77	96

[a]Israel, Singapore, Hong Kong, United Arab Emirates, and Kuwait. Kuwait's GNP was approximated from 1989 data.
[b]Western Europe, United States, Canada, Japan, Australia, and New Zealand.
[c]Excluding China and India, the population growth rate in this group rises to 2.6 percent, the life expectancy falls to 55 years, and the literacy rate falls to 55 percent.
SOURCE: The World Bank, *World Development Report 1992* (New York: Oxford University Press, 1992), Table 1, pp. 218–219.

Economic Development Defined

DEVELOPED COUNTRIES

Countries that have achieved, on average, a high standard of living, with a per capita income of at least $7,620 (as of 1990).

The Western democracies that have achieved high standards of living are called economically **developed countries.** These countries, with a combined population of less than 800 million people, comprise only 15 percent of the world's population.

Also considered developed, although struggling to adapt to free enterprise and private markets, are some of the former communist countries of Eastern Europe that were industrialized (Poland, the Czech and Slovak Republics, and Hungary) and some of the republics of the former Soviet Union (such as Russia and the Ukraine).

DEVELOPING COUNTRIES

Countries that range from the nearly developed to the very poor, with a per capita income of less than $7,620 (as of 1990); also called *less developed countries (LDCs).*

All other countries, where average incomes range from the nearly developed to the very poor, we will refer to as economically **developing countries** or, as they are often called, the **less developed countries (LDCs).**

These terms may be somewhat offensive to citizens of these countries. They are not meant to imply that people in rich countries are "advanced" in terms of human development compared to those in poor countries. Indeed, some of the poorest countries economically, such as India and China, have a much richer cultural and religious heritage than do countries with far higher incomes. Rather, this term refers to the means by which human lives can be bettered by access to economic resources—for raising life expectancy, improving literacy rates, and the like.

We might also note that some cultures would not see progress as coming from material betterment. In the Buddhist religion, which is practiced throughout much of East Asia, human advancement is spiritual in nature and comes from right living in harmony with nature. Economic growth that threatens this harmony would be a negative element in human advancement.[1]

The developing countries are also called *Third World countries.* This term arose during the Cold War to distinguish developing countries from the industrial capitalist democracies of the West (the First World) and the industrial communist countries of the Soviet bloc (the Second World).

A Geographical Comparison

There are enormous differences within the group of developing countries. For starters, recall from Table 3.2 that the World Bank groups the developing countries into three income categories: (1) low income (per capita income under $610), (2) lower middle income (per capita income between $611 and $2,465), and (3) upper middle income (per capita income between $2,466 and $7,619 (1990 figures).

The highest concentrations of world poverty are located in the rural areas of South Asia, sub-Saharan Africa, and parts of Southeast Asia. In much of Africa and South Asia, the picture of absolute poverty is bleak and pervasive.

In North Africa only Libya (with its large oil reserves) has a high per capita income; in sub-Saharan Africa only Gabon (with oil) and South Africa (with mining and manufacturing) have achieved an upper middle level of income per capita. In South Africa this accomplishment has been marred by the apartheid system of racial segregation and discrimination. In the rest of Africa average incomes are very low and have actually been falling.

There are many causes of Africa's declining per capita income over the past decade. Chief among these are war, political turmoil, self-serving authoritarian rulers, bad economic policies, drought, high population growth rates, and a colonial legacy of poor transportation systems and geographic boundaries that divide tribal groups.

South Asia has a similarly unpleasant economic situation and faces enormous challenges. Countries such as Afghanistan, Bangladesh, India, Laos, and Myanmar (Burma) are confronting internal and external political conflicts, environmental disasters, and high population growth rates. The very low incomes there provide little surplus that can be used to raise living standards. As in sub-Saharan Africa, what little surplus exists is often appropriated by a corrupt political system.

CURRENT ISSUE: The HIV (AIDS) virus is the latest scourge to hit the developing countries of Africa and Asia. The virus has gained a potentially devastating stranglehold in central Africa, particularly in Zaire, and it is spreading at an alarming rate in the major cities of Southeast Asia, particularly in Bangkok.

China is coping with the world's largest population of 1.1 billion people and a very low per capita income of $370 in 1990. Yet China's per capita income has grown by an astounding 5.8 percent a year over the period of 1965–90.[2] At this rate its per capita income will double every 12 years. In the twenty-first century China will catapult to the level of a significant world economy.

CURRENT ISSUE: Per capita income is rising by more than 10 percent annually in the southeastern coastal cities of China where the Chinese leaders have permitted free enterprise on a limited scale. The Chinese experiment with capitalism appears to be a smashing success, and it is fast spreading to the cities in the middle and northern parts of the country.

Although 60 percent of the world's peoples are living in poverty as measured by the World Bank, significant progress has been made in a number of countries over the last 50 years. Mainly this progress has come about through rapid industrialization, which has generated fast economic growth.

[1]For an interesting discussion of this point, see "Buddhist Economics" in E. F. Schumacher, *Small Is Beautiful: Economics as If People Mattered* (New York: Harper and & Row, 1974).

[2]*The World Bank Development Report* 1992, 218.

NEWLY INDUSTRIALIZING COUNTRIES (NICs)

Countries in East Asia that are rapidly industrializing and approaching or surpassing the living standards in the lower tier of developed countries.

In particular, the **newly industrializing countries (NICs)** of East Asia—the Pacific rim countries of South Korea, Taiwan, Hong Kong, and Singapore—are rapidly approaching and surpassing living standards in the lower-tier developed countries of Western Europe, such as Portugal and Greece. Fast on their heels are other Pacific rim countries, such as Malaysia and Thailand.

In Latin America a number of countries have industrialized rapidly, creating a large middle class. This is the case in Brazil, Uruguay, Venezuela, Mexico, Chile, and Argentina. However, most of these countries also face daunting social and political problems that have resulted in high inflation, huge government budget deficits, and overwhelming foreign debts. These factors lower their potential future growth by restricting the funds available for investment.

We have been making some broad comparisons of per capita gross domestic product (GDP) between countries and regions. It is appropriate at this point to examine some of the difficulties with such comparisons.

Problems in Comparing Incomes

Comparisons of income between countries can be a very tricky affair. First, there is a *measurement* problem, since each country accounts for gross domestic product (GDP) in a somewhat different way. For example, household production of subsistence crops for the family tends to be quite significant in very poor rural countries, yet this activity is probably underestimated in the GDP.

Second, calculating GDP *per capita* requires dividing the GDP estimate by the population. Population estimates can be highly inaccurate in countries with a rapidly growing population because it is expensive and difficult to carry out a nationwide census.

A third difficulty is the *conversion* problem. In order to compare GDPs between countries, these data must first be converted to a common currency such as the U.S. dollar. Using official exchange rates to convert poses a problem, since, as will be discussed later in this chapter, many governments maintain artificially high exchange rates. This distorts the true value of output produced. In addition, the value of a country's currency could rise or fall, depending on the demand for its exports. Most of what consumers buy may not be traded on the world market, however. Thus, the real purchasing power of income may be overstated or understated.

INTERNATIONAL COMPARISONS PROGRAM (ICP)

A program undertaken by the United Nations to correct for the problem of converting a country's gross domestic product (GDP) to another currency; it solves this problem by calculating a purchasing power parity exchange rate for each country.

The United Nations has an **International Comparisons Program (ICP)** to correct for the conversion problem by calculating a purchasing power parity exchange rate. The exchange rate is adjusted to reflect the costs of living in different countries and better reflects the true standards of living in different countries. Table 41.2 shows what a difference this adjustment can make.

For example, in 1990 the unadjusted gross national product (GNP) per capita of Japan ($25,430) surpassed that of the United States ($21,790) by a significant amount. But a visitor to Japan quickly notices that the typical Japanese consumer is less well off than the average American, despite Japan's supposedly higher average income level. The price of beef in Japan is $30 per pound, and the price of a very modest home in Tokyo suburbs could approach $1 million!

The higher measured GNP per capita in Japan is simply the result of the rise in the value of Japanese currency (the yen), caused by trade surpluses with the rest of the world and particularly with the United States. Thus, when Japan's entire yen economy is converted into dollars at the prevailing exchange

TABLE 41.2 **Purchasing Power Parity (PPP) Estimates of GNP Per Capita**[a]

COUNTRY	GNP PER CAPITA (NOMINAL $ 1990)	
	GNP Not Adjusted for PPP	GNP Adjusted for PPP[b]
Switzerland	32,680	$21,690
Japan	25,430	16,950
United States	21,790	21,360
Brazil	2,680	4,780
Bangladesh	210	1,050
Somalia	120	540

[a]GNP represents gross national product. The difference between GNP and GDP was explained in Chapter 27. Use of GNP rather than GDP is of little importance here.
[b]The 1990 PPP data were extrapolated from 1985 PPP estimates.

SOURCE: The World Bank, *The World Bank Development Report 1992* (New York: Oxford University Press, 1992) Table 30, 276–277.

rate (about 100 yen to the dollar in 1993), it appears as if Japan's standard of living is higher. But a nation's standard of living reflects the purchase of many products that are not traded on the world market. To reflect real living standards, the differences in purchasing power must be accounted for in making international comparisons.

The third column of Table 41.2 provides these purchasing power parity (PPP) comparisons. We see that, after accounting for differences in the costs of living, GNP per capita in Japan falls quite dramatically. It is now lower than in the United States by about 20 percent. In Bangladesh, by contrast, real per capita income rises fivefold to $1,050. This reflects the fact that Bangladesh is producing many nontradable goods. What little Bangladesh exports does not generate a strong demand for its currency. Therefore, when all the nontradable goods and services are converted to dollars at a low currency value, its GNP per capita is a low $210. Valuing what Bangladesh produces at a purchasing power parity exchange rate significantly increases the estimate of its standard of living.

Keep in mind that some heroic assumptions were made to reach these final numbers. These numbers also do not correct for the first two measurement problems of household production and population growth. In short, there is no easy or perfect method for making international comparisons, which is why they must always be done with sensitivity and caution.

Income Distribution

Even after adjusting for purchasing power parity, GDP per capita alone could give a very misleading picture of how an average family lives. This is because average income of a country can be high, yet most of that income could be going to just a small percentage of wealthy families. Some countries whose per capita incomes are very high are still considered less developed because of the unequal distribution of income. Hence, Saudi Arabia is still considered less developed despite its relatively high per capita income, since most of this income accrues to the royal family. Taking account of the *relative* income distribution is important. Later in this chapter we examine the connection between income distribution and development.

Other Measures of Development

Even if income distribution were not a large problem, GDP is by no means a perfect indicator of a nation's standard of living. GDP measures aggregate market activity, yet the quality of life depends on many factors besides marketed activity. Alternative measures of social well-being have been devised that attempt to assess directly the "quality of life." These measures include variables such as the infant mortality rate; the life expectancy rate; the literacy rate; the share of families with access to clean water; the share of families with access to electricity, gas, and the like; and the degree of political freedom, human rights, and so on.

In some cases GDP per capita is a poor indicator of the quality of life. China has a per capita income of just $370. Yet its life expectancy is 70 years, far in excess of the average of 55 years for other countries in this income group. Its adult literacy rate is 73 percent, again far superior to the average of 55 percent for countries with similar per capita incomes. Alternative measures of development are useful complements to GDP in suggesting differences in quality of life.

In many cases, though, GDP per capita is highly correlated with these alternative measures of development. Therefore, used with appropriate care, GDP can still serve as a starting point for examining social welfare and development.

THE DETERMINANTS OF LONG-RUN ECONOMIC GROWTH IN DEVELOPING COUNTRIES

Why are some countries rich and other countries poor? In some cases it is relatively easy to single out primary causes of economic success or failure. For instance, according to World Bank tables the country with the world's highest per capita income in 1990 was Kuwait (prior to the invasion by Iraq). Kuwait's high standard of living can be easily explained by its enormous oil reserves coupled with a tiny population of only 2.1 million. By contrast, the world's poorest country is Mozambique, with a per capita income of $210. Its abysmal situation can also be readily explained by decades of violent civil war.

In most cases, however, it is not possible to separate out single causes of economic success. Even for the examples given, the single explanations alone are not complete. Kuwait was a very poor nomadic sheikdom a hundred years ago with all its oil undiscovered underground. Only with the systematic application of the physical and mental capital (oil-drilling equipment, port facilities, and engineers) has Kuwait's living standard skyrocketed. Nor can Mozambique's low living standard be attributed solely to internal political strife. Mozambique was a pawn in the game of European colonization. The conditions imposed by the Portuguese colonial power led to a prolonged and bloody war for independence, which lasted until 1974. The revolutionary winners (backed by China in their independence struggle) then imposed a communist economy.

Seen from this perspective, the political and economic turmoil in Mozambique is the result of external, as well as internal, forces.

Indeed, no single variable or model can explain all the variation in income and wealth that we find around the world; rather, a complex mix of variables seems best suited to yielding useful interpretation and prediction.

Some of these variables are clearly economic and affect the long-run aggregate supply. We focus on the supply side because the factors limiting the production possibilities frontier are supply constraints. Four factors that are particularly important to expanding the frontiers of the developing countries are the labor force participation rate, the level of saving and its link to productive investment, the choice of production technologies, and the rate of population growth. Our analysis in this section will highlight these four factors.

Labor Force Participation Rate

The **labor force participation rate** is the size of a nation's labor force in relation to its total population. The rate of labor force participation depends on cultural, environmental, economic, and political forces.

LABOR FORCE PARTICIPATION RATE

The size of a nation's labor force relative to its entire population.

To see why labor force participation might vary, let's consider life in the humid tropics. In tropical climates it makes no sense to work beyond what is necessary to satisfy one's immediate needs for food, shelter, and safety. Any excess food produced or collected would spoil in the heat and humidity. Moreover, since seasonal variation is minimal, food is readily obtained in the future whenever needed. Thus, there is no incentive to save.

With the slash-and-burn agricultural system used in the tropics, the soil is thin, and plots wear out quickly, leading to migration every few years. Therefore, basic needs are obtained very simply, and no culture of accumulation for the future tends to develop. The labor supply is brief and intermittent, intended to satisfy minimal, immediate needs only. Free time is spent in highly significant ritualized activities, which provide spiritual meaning. These culturally ingrained practices do not change overnight with the introduction of industrialized goods.

By contrast, colder climates are subject to months of freezing and difficult hunting and gathering conditions. Habits of saving become culturally ingrained, such as storing grains for use in the winter months. This leads to labor force participation not just on the basis of current needs, but also on the basis of future needs.

People generally work long and hard in the developing countries, as noted in the introduction. Yet despite their efforts, their standards of living remain abysmally low for the most part. The reason why is that their labor is not very productive.

Saving, Investment, and Productivity

We saw in Chapter 3 that investment in physical and human capital (education) is the key to increases in productivity. The problem for the developing countries is the opportunity cost of investment. A higher rate of investment requires a higher rate of saving, and more saving means less consumption. With consumption at little more than subsistence levels in many of these countries, sacrificing consumption to increase investment is extremely costly.

Saving encounters additional cultural, institutional, and political impediments as well. One consequence of these additional barriers is that some of the saving that does occur does not end up financing productive investments.

So, for example, a peasant farmer in Africa might know that crop yields would rise if only irrigation water could be obtained from a river several miles away. But pipes and pumps to carry this water must be purchased at great expense. This farmer has no savings with which to purchase the pump, nor are there financial markets that would lend her the money. Even if savings were available for investment in terms of the local currency, the pumps must be imported from Europe, the United States, or Japan, and there is probably a shortage of foreign exchange needed to buy these imports. Furthermore, irrigation pumps run on electricity, which is not available in this area. Should a pump break down, obtaining spare parts, and the skills of a technician to install them, could be nearly impossible. Thus, while conceptually the problem of raising productivity is quite simple—just increase saving and investment—in practice there are innumerable roadblocks to be overcome.

For this reason, development does not happen overnight. Indeed, it took Western Europe three centuries of industrialization to achieve its current living standards. Increases in productivity must be sustained over a long period of time for a country to reach high levels of living. For example, if productivity grew by the relatively high rate of 2 percent a year, it would take more than a generation—36 years—for income to double. Thus, for a very poor country like India, with a per capita income of about $350 in 1990, it would still take slightly more than a hundred years for it to reach a per capita income of $2,800. A slower growth in productivity of 1 percent a year would mean achieving this income level only in the year 2206.[3]

Let's now take a closer look at some of the more common impediments to saving.

INSTITUTIONAL IMPEDIMENTS: SAVING AND FINANCIAL MARKETS We discussed earlier how environmental factors might lead certain cultures, but not others, to acquire a habit of saving for the future. Institutional factors can also affect the savings rate and whether the funds that are saved are used to finance productive investments that increase economic growth.

In the developed world, financial markets exist to link savers and investors. Financial institutions such as banks are readily available and are a way of life for paying bills, saving for a college education, and storing up a retirement nest egg. Banks, savings and loans, stock and bond markets, insurance companies, and pension funds are all mechanisms whereby funds from savers are made available to borrowers seeking to invest. The efficiency with which financial institutions do this can be measured by the spread between the interest rate (or return) paid to savers and the interest rate (or return) charged to borrowers. In a market setting, competitive forces will ensure that a very small spread will be earned by financial institutions for linking savers and borrowers.

The process by which savings are translated into investments is not perfect in the developed world, but by and large financial institutions are successful

---

[3]The doubling time is easily found by the Rule of 72: Take the percentage growth rate, and divide this into the number 72. This result is the number of years needed for that variable to double. For the relatively low growth rates found in economics, this formula reasonably estimates the doubling time. In this example we are also assuming that the labor force participation rate stays constant, so that as the population grows, the labor force grows at the same rate.

at achieving their functions. Occasionally there have been dramatic failures, as in the Great Depression, when bank panics caused runs on the banks. Those persons lucky enough to get their savings out before a bank failed were likely to keep their bank notes hidden in their mattress, thus breaking the link between saving and productive investment.

In many parts of the developing world, saving is carried out in traditional ways that preserve cultural values. In North Africa and the Middle East, for example, Moslems present each bride with a very valuable gift, such as a gold bracelet. This bracelet is worn by the wife her entire life and represents a significant store of wealth. Should anything happen to her husband, the Moslem wife will always have this gold bracelet to sell.

This bracelet serves the valuable economic function of a safety net for the wife. Yet savings used to buy assets such as gold bracelets and other jewelry are not available for productive investments that would increase economic growth. Although less romantic, a husband could buy a bride a savings account in her name for $5,000, to be used only in the event of separation or the death of the husband. In this case these savings would be lent out to a business seeking to invest, thereby expanding the growth rate of the economy. In addition, the woman could see her wealth grow as interest on these savings is earned.

Yet in many poor areas the old ways persist. A woman can feel her gold jewelry pressed against her flesh. She feels safe since theft is very rare. She and her husband know little of what a financial market is, nor would they feel safe entrusting her life savings to strangers to care for. Thus, the least risky thing to do is to keep saving in the old-fashioned way.

There are other institutional roadblocks to developing the link between saving and productive investment. Financial institutions like banks pay interest to depositors and charge interest to lenders. But in Moslem countries, usury ("excessive" interest) is forbidden by the holy book of Islam, the Koran. (There were similar injunctions in the Christian church in the Middle Ages.) Private financial institutions could not survive if these religious rules were strictly enforced. In some cases this is overcome by changing the rules: A depositor to a bank could "buy" a deposit, and the bank could agree to "buy it back" in the future at an agreed-on higher price. The depositor thus earns a capital gain on this deposit, not an interest payment, and has obeyed the Islamic law.

POLITICAL IMPEDIMENTS: FINANCIAL REPRESSION Sometimes governments weaken the savings–productive investment link through misguided policies that create **financial repression.**

FINANCIAL REPRESSION

A reduction in the supply of savings caused by government policies, such as a government-imposed interest rate ceiling in financial markets.

Savers will use financial markets only if the benefits outweigh the costs. Quite often government policies have unintentionally made financial instruments (like savings deposits) very unattractive to savers. What results is disintermediation in which financial institutions lose deposits, thereby restricting the investment loans that can be made.

One policy that creates financial repression is an *interest rate ceiling.* By setting a maximum legal interest rate, government officials hope to prevent banks and other financial institutions from taking advantage of borrowers. The theory is that if banks have a cheap source of funds, they can offer lower interest rate loans to borrowers, thereby encouraging investment. In practice these ceilings are self-defeating, as demonstrated in Figure 41.1.

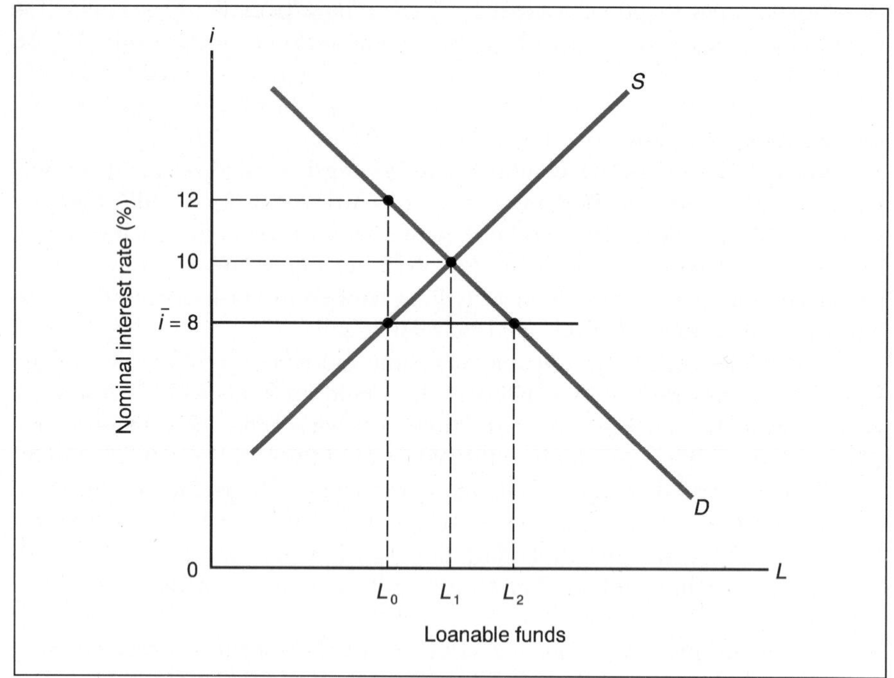

FIGURE 41.1

An Interest Rate Ceiling

The figure shows the effects of an interest rate ceiling in the market for loanable funds, which governments in developing countries often impose in an attempt to reduce their firms' costs of borrowing to invest. The quantity of loans is on the horizontal axis and the nominal interest rate is on the vertical axis. *S* is the supply curve for loans by the savers/lenders, and *D* is the demand curve for loans by the investors/borrowers. Without government intervention, the equilibrium would be at the intersection of *D* and *S*. The interest rate would be 10 percent, and the quantity of loans L_1. An interest rate ceiling of 8 percent generates an excess demand for loans equal to $(L_2 - L_0)$. Instead of encouraging investment, the policy leads to a financial repression as the amount of saving (lending) available to finance investment decreases from L_1 to L_0. The policy also encourages corruption because the amount of funds available to investors, L_0, has to be rationed to investors who want L_2 loans at the artificially low interest rate.

The interest rate on loans is on the vertical axis, and the quantity of loans is on the horizontal axis. Savers generate the supply of funds to be loaned, and investors generate the demand for funds to be borrowed. The supply curve, *S*, indicates the savers' (lenders') supply of loans at each interest rate. The demand curve, *D*, indicates the investors' (borrowers') demand for loans at each interest rate. In this example the supply and demand equilibrium occurs at a nominal interest rate of 10 percent and a volume of funds loaned equal to L_1.

Suppose that the government imposes an interest rate ceiling at 8 percent. As interest rates fall from 10 percent to 8 percent, savers will search for alternative ways to store their wealth, such as speculation in real estate, stamps, rare paintings, or foreign currencies. Savers will cut back the supply of funds to L_0, thereby reducing the funds available for investment and lowering the rate of economic growth. The fallacy of an interest rate ceiling policy is that it ignores the fact that savers have options.

Moreover, the artificially low interest of 8 percent charged to borrowers will create a *shortage* of available funds equal to $(L_2 - L_0)$. More people will want to borrow at the artificially low interest rate than there are funds available. There is a queuing up for investment loans, and months, even years, may go by before investment funds become available. Or, worse, banks (and/or the government) may distribute these scarce funds via credit rationing to favorite industries. Corruption and bribery are ways of life in countries whose governments manipulate market prices and overregulate economic activity. There is no guarantee that the industries picked by the government to receive funds will provide the largest return, since the criteria for selection are often based on political favoritism.

The firms that are shut out of the market for loans are usually small businesses and small farmers. They are forced to borrow funds on the black market at very high interest rates, if they can obtain loans at all. These are also the business firms that tend to provide the most jobs, so that the lack of investment funds has a depressing effect on output and employment.

INFLATION, SAVINGS, AND CAPITAL FLIGHT Savers care about the *real rate of interest,* which takes into account the expected inflation. The *real* rate of interest is the nominal rate of interest minus the expected inflation rate. If the nominal rate of interest is set at 8 percent and the expected inflation rate is 5 percent, then the *real* interest rate earned by the depositors is 3 percent.

Suppose that the inflation rate rises to 10 percent. The real interest earned is now *negative* 2 percent when the nominal rate is set at 8 percent (real rate of interest $= 8 - 10 = -2$). Said differently, at the end of the year the depositor will get back interest and principal that can buy 2 percent less than at the beginning of the year because of the rise in prices. If nominal interest rates are not allowed to rise with inflation (due to interest rate ceilings), then rising inflation will destroy the returns to saving, with negative consequences for the effective savings rate.

Rapid inflation in a currency will generally erode the value of all financial assets denominated in that currency. As domestic prices rise faster than foreign prices due to inflation, it becomes harder to sell exports, and imports become ever more attractive. This inevitably pushes down the value of the domestic currency and lowers the real wealth of those owning financial assets denominated in this currency.

As a hedge against losing wealth in a country with rapid inflation, people buy foreign currencies (such as the U.S. dollar). These dollars can be hoarded (thereby earning a rate of return equal to the depreciation of the local currency), or they can be invested in the United States or Europe. This is known as **capital flight.** Although the saving rate of a country may be high, the savings available to finance productive investments may be much lower because of capital flight.

CAPITAL FLIGHT

The purchase of foreign currencies or securities by domestic residents as a hedge against rapid domestic inflation.

In these last few sections we have identified various ways in which a country's savings do not find their way into productive investments. This decreases a country's growth rate, and, as we saw in Chapter 3, even a small reduction in the rate of long-run economic growth has a substantial effect on a nation's standard of living. For example, a permanent decline in the annual growth rate from 3 percent to 2 percent lengthens the time it takes income to double from 24 years to 36 years.

DIRECT FOREIGN INVESTMENT, LOANS, AND AID One way in which a country with a low savings rate can grow faster is to acquire foreign savings through direct foreign investment, loans, or gifts. Direct foreign investment occurs when a foreign firm brings in financial capital to buy or build a factory. The foreign firm also generally supplies needed foreign exchange, technological know-how, administration, product design, and marketing. It may have a local partner if required by law.

Many LDCs encourage direct foreign investment as an easy way to acquire capital and technology and to create jobs. In the last 40 years U.S. multinational corporations have set up many manufacturing plants overseas. This was done for various reasons: to "jump over" tariff walls in Europe and Latin America, to be closer to final customers and reduce transportation costs, to be closer to sources of raw materials, to utilize less expensive labor, and to gain tax advantages.

Foreign multinational corporations are involved not just in manufacturing, but also in large-scale mining and agribusiness in LDCs. For example, multinational food companies operate plantations for growing and processing pineapples in the Philippines and bananas in Honduras. Aluminum companies maintain bauxite mines in Jamaica. Oil companies engage in drilling and pumping petroleum in Kuwait.

EXPORT-ENCLAVE PRODUCTION

Refers to production by resource-using firms in the developing countries, typically multinational corporations, whose output is not consumed locally, but is exported to the First World, thereby earning foreign exchange and creating new jobs and export opportunities.

Most of these resource concerns engage in **export-enclave production.** What is produced is usually not consumed locally, but is exported to the First World. These exports of primary products constitute the bulk of foreign exchange earnings for many poor countries. By bringing in capital, along with advanced techniques for mining and agriculture, these firms create jobs and vital exports.

Direct foreign investment is a mixed blessing to many LDCs, however. Foreign ownership of factories, farms, and mines introduces a powerful political force, which can in some cases dominate the domestic political scene and may skew the distribution of income. Political domination may be matched by a cultural domination as well. With vast advertising budgets and mass-marketing techniques, foreign producers can overwhelm small local producers. Coca-Cola and television shows like "Dallas" become symbols of progress and advancement, while local cultures and traditions wither. The breakup of local cultures destroys the traditional economic system, which employs far more people than does the "modern" sector, leading to rising unemployment.

Foreign loans or gifts operate in much the same way as direct foreign investment. They raise the effective savings rate available to stimulate growth. In the 1950s and 1960s, loans to LDCs were generally made by multilateral government agencies such as the World Bank or by single government agencies such as the U.S. Agency for International Development (AID). In the 1970s private commercial banks became involved in "recycling petrodollars" to developing nations, resulting in the world debt crisis of the 1980s. The debt crisis is discussed later in this chapter.

The Choice of Production Technologies

In a free market system the amount of capital used in production is determined by the available production technologies and the prices of factors of production. In developed countries such as the United States, the price of labor has risen steadily over several centuries. This has provided an incentive for using *labor-saving* technology that substitutes capital for labor in production. A car company that builds a new factory in the United States or Japan in the 1990s will use far more capital per car—for example, robots—than Henry Ford did at the turn of this century. The reason for this is simple: The cost of labor is relatively higher now, and the cost of capital is relatively cheaper. The cost of labor to a business is not only the wage paid, but also the fringe benefits (such as health care), unemployment compensation, expenses for health and safety regulations, sick leave, and vacations and holidays. Robots require none of these!

In the developing countries where labor is plentiful and capital is scarce, one would expect to find that efficient businesses will use *more* labor and *less* capital in production. That is generally what one finds. In India it is common to see large construction projects using hundreds of day laborers, carrying sacks of cement or earth on their backs. This is cheaper than any alternative because widespread unemployment holds down wages and because capital equipment is very expensive. By contrast, in the West this same project might be done with one or two large earth diggers (costing several hundred thousand dollars each) with a skeleton crew of only a few workers.

These differences in production technique are quite appropriate if they reflect the real scarcities of labor, capital, and other factors used in production. Unfortunately, the prices of resources in a market are often distorted in LDC countries, thereby giving false signals as to scarcity. These distorted factor prices may lead to an inappropriate use of resources, thereby slowing the country's growth rate.

DISTORTED FACTOR PRICES Factor prices are distorted if the prices of resources used in production do not reflect the true scarcity of these resources. When this happens, profit-maximizing businesses may design and build factories that use a non-optimal combination of inputs in the production process. We say "may" because some techniques of production do not afford much substitution between labor and capital in production, even in the long run. For example, the manufacture of hazardous chemicals requires machinery rather than human contact. Also, many factories require a fairly fixed combination of labor and capital in the short run. Therefore, our discussion centers on the long run in which all resources in production become variable and refers specifically to the production of goods in which it is fairly easy to substitute capital for labor, as in the earth-moving example above.

Distorted factor prices mean that the economy is not producing efficiently because it is not using enough resources that are plentiful and cheap, and instead it is using resources that are scarce and expensive. This implies that the same output could be produced at a lower cost to society.

Despite the desire of most governments in the developing nations to increase jobs, they often adopt policies that distort factor prices in ways that reduce the attractiveness of hiring workers and increase the attractiveness of buying machinery as a substitute.

DISTORTIONS IN THE COST OF LABOR Effective minimum wage laws, health and safety laws, family leave laws, and other laws that artificially raise the wage or benefits package of employees send a distorted signal to the marketplace as to the scarcity of labor. The message is that labor is a scarce commodity, and hence its cost is rising compared to other inputs in production. In the short run business firms may still hire the same number of workers as before, as long as they can pass on to customers the higher costs or absorb some loss in profits to maintain output and market share.

Generally, politicians who pass such laws might believe that there are fixed factors required in production and that greedy businesses have plenty of profit to share with workers. But in the long run, as new factories are built to replace old ones, the new factories (if they are built in the same labor market as before) generally use more automated equipment, which substitutes for labor.

DISTORTIONS IN THE COST OF CAPITAL Governments unwittingly encourage businesses to substitute capital for labor in a number of ways. Usually this occurs because governments wish to industrialize quickly. To encourage the

FIGURE 41.2

An Overvalued Currency

The figure shows what would happen if the Mexican government overvalues the peso in an attempt to reduce the costs to Mexican firms of buying capital equipment from the United States. The quantity of dollars exchanged for pesos is on the horizontal axis, and the peso-dollar exchange rate in terms of pesos/\$ is on the vertical axis. The equilibrium value of the exchange rate without the Mexican government's intervention is 3 pesos/\$, at the intersection of $D_\$$ and $S_\$$, the demand curve and the supply curve for dollars. *B* dollars are exchanged for pesos in the foreign exchange markets. By setting a ceiling on the peso-dollar exchange rate of 2 pesos/\$, the government overvalues the peso and generates an excess demand for dollars equal to $(C - A)$. With fewer dollars available, Mexican firms cannot buy as much capital equipment from the United States. An overvalued peso also encourages corruption as the *A* dollars available have to be rationed among the demanders who want *C* dollars. Finally, the firms who do obtain the scarce dollars have an incentive to use production techniques that are too capital intensive because they are buying the capital at an artificially low price.

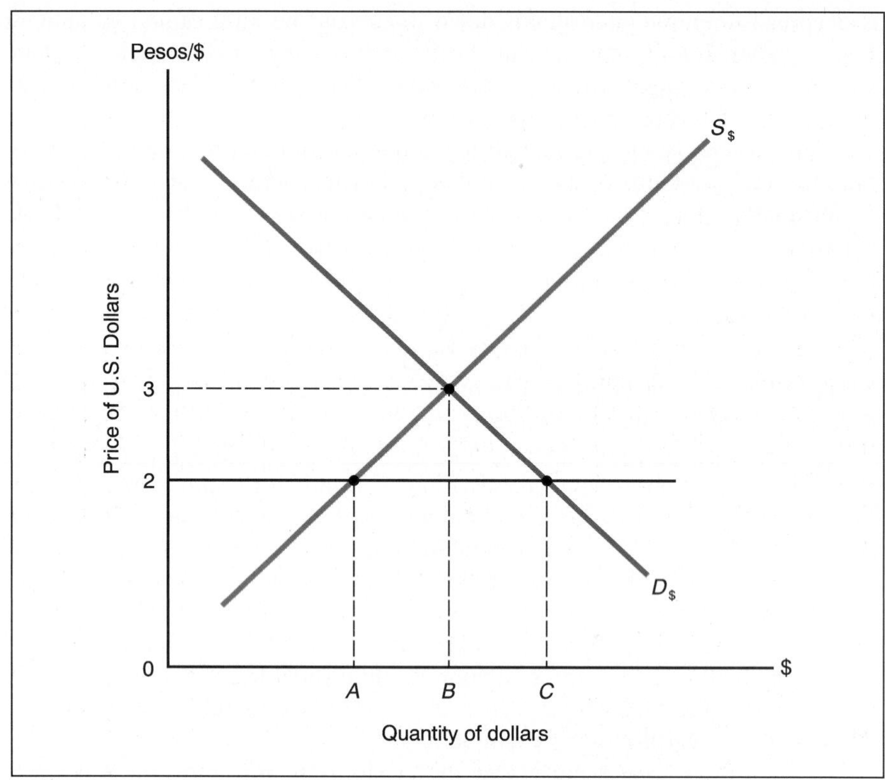

building of factories, governments often provide loans at below-market interest rates, or provide tax breaks on capital investments, or sell foreign exchange needed to buy important capital equipment at below-market rates. These programs all distort the true cost of capital, which is usually quite high in most developing countries because capital is so scarce. Yet to the business firms that receive these subsidies the most profitable way to build and operate the factory becomes more *capital-intensive*. Society loses because the capital-output ratio is higher than it otherwise would be, and many workers will not be employed.

Let's examine the last policy—manipulating the exchange rate. What would happen if a country such as Mexico decides to overvalue its own currency? It might do this in order to sell dollars more cheaply to firms wishing to industrialize.[4] Refer to Figure 41.2, which shows the supply and the demand for the U.S. dollar in foreign exchange markets. Dollars are supplied by Americans wishing to buy goods or assets in Mexico. Dollars are demanded by Mexicans wishing to buy goods or assets inside the United States. The exchange rate is on the vertical axis, and the quantity of dollars exchanged is on the horizontal axis. The exchange rate is expressed in terms of pesos per dollar.

The equilibrium exchange rate is 3 pesos to 1 dollar according to the figure. At this exchange rate the supply of dollars just equals the demand for dollars. The total number of dollars bought is the amount *B*. And, since the dollars are exchanged for pesos, the supply of pesos just equals the demand for pesos. The total number of pesos bought equals $3 \cdot B$.

[4]Mexico did this extensively in the past. Currently its exchange rate is floating and is no longer overvalued.

A company in Mexico seeking to import a $1 million machine from the United States would have to pay 3 million pesos at the equilibrium exchange rate. However, suppose that the Mexican government set a *price ceiling* of 2 pesos to the dollar. At this price the imported machine would cost the Mexican firm only 2 million pesos—a substantial savings. This is why governments set prices of foreign exchange too low or, alternatively, set their own currency price too high. The dollar is *undervalued,* and the peso is *overvalued.*

The harmful effects of an overvalued peso are twofold. By making imported capital equipment cheaper, it encourages use of more capital in production than is desirable, given the true scarcity of capital and labor. In addition, the overvalued peso creates a *shortage* (excess demand) of foreign exchange (dollars) equal to $(C - A)$. At the lower price of 2 pesos to the dollar, Mexicans want to buy more from the United States (amount C), and Americans want to buy less from Mexicans (amount A). The total amount of dollars that the Mexicans can buy drops to the amount A. Hence, less imported capital equipment can be bought than before, slowing the growth rate.

Because of the shortage of dollars, the Mexican central bank engages in rationing this scarce foreign exchange. Favoritism, bribery, and corruption are all problems that arise when the government sets a price ceiling on foreign exchange. There is no guarantee that firms with the best potential for promoting economic growth will get the funds.

The government has better means of promoting industrialization. For example, it could subsidize each unit of output produced. Business firms receive a subsidy, but only on the condition that they use technology appropriate to the actual resource conditions. Alternatively, if job creation is desired, governments could subsidize businesses for each job created. Either policy would encourage businesses to develop *capital-saving* production techniques and use more labor. Of course, these subsidies would be sensible only if unemployment were so widespread as to make the opportunity cost of labor close to zero. In this case the extra labor used would not reduce production somewhere else in the economy.

OTHER FACTORS CAUSING AN OVERUSE OF CAPITAL Even if factor prices in LDCs truly reflected scarcity conditions, factories built in these countries might be too capital-intensive for other reasons. First, most capital equipment is designed and built in the First World. Naturally the type of capital equipment built reflects the scarcity conditions existing in the developed world, not those in the developing world. Only if the LDC market for this capital equipment is large enough to encourage First World companies to redesign it will it reflect technology appropriate for the LDCs.[5]

Second, multinational companies often build similar factories in various places around the world. With design and start-up costs comprising a large part of total investment costs, it may be cheaper overall for a multinational to have one factory design, whether that factory is built in Belgium (where labor costs are high) or Brazil (where labor costs are lower).

Third, new labor-saving technology invented in the First World often comes packaged with computerized equipment that allows for a better product to be produced. Automated scanners that check for manufacturing errors can do this

---

[5]This can be overcome somewhat through the purchase of used equipment in the First World. The older vintage equipment would be more labor-intensive.

better and faster than can any combination of human workers. To produce a higher-quality product the LDC factory may have no choice but to automate.

Finally, new labor-saving equipment is a status symbol in many LDCs. A modern tractor may yield social status, even if it entails a loss of profits in the short run.

DEVELOPMENT FROM THE "BOTTOM UP" Unemployment is very high in most of the developing world. This is due partly to the overuse of capital-intensive production technologies noted above and partly to rapid population growth and rapid urbanization. In the 1970s a movement grew up to alter the technology of production in ways that would favor the creation of jobs and thereby lower unemployment rates. Instigated by the publication in 1974 of E. F. Schumacher's book *Small Is Beautiful,* the *appropriate technology movement* was born. Schumacher advocated that LDCs utilize the labor resources at hand, rather than relying on capital equipment imported from abroad. He encouraged capital-saving technological innovation. Development, he argued, should happen from the bottom up, not the top down.

For example, suppose that rural peasants in India need energy for cooking. A top-down approach would use modern imported technology (paid for with foreign loans) to dam a river so that a huge hydroelectric plant could be built. Electric lines would then be run throughout rural areas. The cost of such a project could run into the tens of billions of dollars, creating a huge foreign debt. Moreover, India would be dependent on foreigners to run the electric plant until Indians could be trained and to supply critical spare parts over the life of the equipment. Rural peasants would need to earn hard currency to pay for electricity. Collection costs would be high, given the low literacy levels.

As an alternative, Schumacher proposed a bottom-up strategy that would use local resources and lead to local self-sufficiency. This is much like Mahatma Ghandi's famous walk to the sea, which liberated India from the mindset of buying imported salt from the British colonial masters when the oceans provided all the salt Indians would need. In terms of energy, a bottom-up approach would look for energy from a local, but overlooked, source—cow dung. Given the Hindu tradition of the "sacred cow," these animals are quite plentiful and useful in production. Abundant cow manure is thus available for free on the farm. Manure can be placed in a hole in the ground and covered with a sheet of scrap metal. An inexpensive pipe from the top runs into the peasant's hut. As manure is broken down by microorganisms, methane gas is given off. This naturally produced gas can be burned cleanly as a fuel. The decomposed cow dung can later be spread on the fields as fertilizer.

The bottom-up approach uses little capital and no scarce foreign exchange. It does require more labor to collect manure every few days. But the peasant has no electric bills to pay, and the country has no foreign debt. In India today methane stoves are common. Yet it took appropriate capital-saving technology to make it available to the masses. While such an approach would not be satisfying to the average American, with a per capita income of $21,790 in 1990, it is appropriate for the average Indian peasant, with a per capita income of $350. Because India does not use scarce savings to build a hydroelectric plant, these funds become available for other investment projects that help to increase India's potential rate of growth.

The choice of technology also has important ramifications for the distribution of income in society. Aside from the important objective of making the economy more efficient, appropriate technology can reduce social tensions that might arise if capital-intensive technology leads to greater unemployment in a labor-abundant country.

The Population Growth Rate

The fourth factor that has an important impact on economic growth in the developing countries is the population growth rate. A rising population provides a larger work force, which increases the potential level of output. However, this is a two-edged sword. If population grows faster than output, *per capita* income will fall.

High population growth rates found in the poorest developing nations are troubling because they put severe strains on the limited savings available for investment in human capital. For new workers to be productive they must have food, health care, education, housing, and other types of infrastructure. Poor countries have little by way of savings to begin with. High population growth rates mean that what little savings are available must be spread over an ever-greater number of workers.

A country's population growth rate is determined by many cultural, economic, and political variables. We will consider a few of the more important variables.

POPULATION AND THE STAGE OF ECONOMIC DEVELOPMENT The richest countries contain an ever-smaller proportion of the world's population, and the poorest countries contain an ever-larger proportion. This is one of the reasons why population is a controversial topic. Efforts to curb population growth rates raise cries of racism, since the rich countries are predominantly white, while the poor countries are predominantly nonwhite.

Table 41.1 showed population growth rates by income group. The highest population growth rates are found in the poorest countries, which averaged 2.6 percent per year in the 1980s (excluding China and India). The lowest population growth rates are found in the richest developed countries, which averaged just 0.6 percent per year over the same period. Population growth rates vary widely within each category, however. In China, government laws raised the age at which young people could marry and provided severe economic penalties for those who had more than one child. China's population growth rate was only 1.4 percent per year in the 1980s. Kenya had a population growth rate almost three times that high, although it has an identical per capital GDP of $370.

A country's population growth rate is calculated as the difference between its birth rate and its death rate. (We are ignoring net immigration here.) For most of the world's history, birth rates and death rates were both high, so that population growth rates were low. Death rates fell dramatically all over the world in the twentieth century with the discovery of modern methods of inoculation against childhood diseases. In high-income countries this was accompanied by falling birth rates. In developing countries birth rates are beginning to fall, but death rates have fallen much faster. Therefore, the high population growth rates that we observe in the developing countries are the result of high birth rates and low death rates.

Does a high population growth rate *cause* a low per capita income? Or does a high per capita income *cause* a low population growth rate? Which is the horse pulling the cart? The evidence is that cause and effect runs in both directions. We have already indicated how a high population growth rate lowers the potential growth rate because investment must be spread over more workers. In the model below we examine how a higher per capita income could lead to a lower birth rate.

Families have children for a variety of reasons: love, companionship, custom, accident, religious principles, and so on. Economic factors also help determine the outcome. It may appear strange to talk about the supply of and the demand for children, yet both factors are at work in determining the population growth rate.

THE SUPPLY OF CHILDREN Supply factors look at a couple's ability to control how many offspring they will have. Genetic factors of both men and women play an important role in determining fertility and hence the potential supply. Cultural and political values also determine the age at which people marry and govern accepted practices for frequency of sexual intercourse, types of acceptable contraceptives, the legality of abortion, and so on. In some cultures males migrate seasonally in search of work, thus lowering the frequency of sexual contact.

Economics also plays a role. Poor families may lack money or information about contraceptives or sterilization procedures, and, thus, even if they wanted to limit pregnancy, they may lack the means to do so (except through abstinence). Rich families can enhance their fertility using fertility drugs, in vitro fertilization, and other methods.

Thus, the supply of children is determined by genetics, cultural habits, laws, technology, and economics.

Yet supply factors alone are not enough to explain population growth rates. For many years population control experts disseminated birth control information and free contraceptives in poor rural areas. It was assumed that high birth rates were caused by the absence of technology or income for controlling the supply of children. By making these available, birth rates were expected to decline. In reality, birth rates did not decline in many rural areas. These families desired (demanded) more children, and they threw away the contraceptives.

THE DEMAND FOR CHILDREN The demand for children refers to the desire to have children. Culture plays an important role in determining the desired family size. In some cultures children provide spiritual links to the world, so families want the most children possible. In many poor countries children have important economic functions also. They work in the fields or tend to livestock from an early age, providing food for the family. And they are the primary source of food and shelter when parents become too old to work. Having many children (especially sons) is desired to provide for security in old age.

Children are not very costly to raise in poor developing countries. Births are done at home by midwives. Babysitting is done for free by elderly relatives. Education in rural areas is limited, and out-of-pocket expenses are few. Thus, given the important benefits of children, and the limited cost, it is easy to see why in poor countries the desire to have more children is strongly ingrained.

In rich countries, by contrast, governments have outlawed child labor (except in rural areas affecting a small fraction of families). In addition, government and private pensions provide for retirement. Social Security and welfare programs provide for persons without adequate means. Hence, the economic benefits of children are greatly reduced in developed countries. The out-of-pocket costs of having children are high, including medical expenses, shelter, clothing, food, and education (including college).

Perhaps the largest expense of having children in developed countries is an "implicit" one—the time required to raise children. As economic opportunities increase for women in developing countries, so does the opportunity cost of their time. With a mobile society, nuclear families often live far away from relatives who could help with babysitting. Day care must be purchased at a high price.

In developed countries, therefore, the economic cost of having children is relatively high and the economic benefit relatively low. It is not surprising that the demand for children is lower as a consequence. Meanwhile, we have already indicated that wealthier countries can control the supply of children better as well.

Our supply and demand analysis is by no means the entire explanation for lower population growth rates in the developed countries. However, it does provide a strong theoretical model for explaining the existing evidence.

There are some important policy implications that derive from this analysis. One of these is that the best way to lower population growth rates is to raise incomes. A rising income will reduce both the demand for and the supply of children. But we should be careful to remember that per capita income is not a good measure of how the average family is living because the distribution of income is often quite unequal in the developing countries. That is why the distribution of income plays an important role in determining population growth rates, just as it does in determining the overall rate of saving. We need to consider the relationship between income distribution and economic development in order to understand the economic prospects of the developing countries.

INCOME DISTRIBUTION AND ECONOMIC DEVELOPMENT

Table 41.3 presents the 1990 distribution of income in five countries at different stages of economic development. The distribution of income in society can be measured in several ways. In Table 41.3 the population of a country is divided into five groups or quintiles. Each quintile comprises 20 percent of the total population. The percentage of income going to each quintile is shown also.

For example, the poorest 20 percent of households in Brazil earned just 2.4 percent of total household income. The second poorest 20 percent earned 5.7 percent of household income. The third and fourth quintiles earned 10.7 and 18.6 percent of household income, respectively. The richest 20 percent earned 62.6 percent of household income.

Since these data refer to shares of household income, not household income itself, these data are measures of *relative* income distribution. They do not measure absolute income differences. Thus, even though the poorest 20 percent in Bangladesh earn a greater share of household income than does the comparable group in Brazil, the *absolute* income level for the poorest 20 percent in Brazil may be higher.

TABLE 41.3 **Measures of Income Distribution**

COUNTRY	GDP PER CAPITA ($1990)[a]	YEAR	PERCENTAGE SHARE OF TOTAL HOUSEHOLD INCOME BY QUINTILE[b]					RATIO OF BOTTOM 40 TO TOP 20[c]
			Lowest 20 Percent	Second Quintile	Third Quintile	Fourth Quintile	Highest 20 Percent	
Bangladesh	1,050	1985–86	10.0	13.7	17.2	21.9	37.2	23.7/37.2
Malaysia	5,900	1987	4.6	9.3	13.9	21.2	51.2	13.9/51.2
Brazil	4,780	1983	2.4	5.7	10.7	18.6	62.6	8.1/62.6
United States	21,360	1985	4.7	11.0	17.4	25.0	41.9	15.7/41.9
Japan	16,950	1979	8.7	13.2	17.5	23.1	37.5	21.9/37.5

[a]GDP is calculated on the basis of purchasing power parity, using the United Nations International Comparisons Program.
[b]These estimates should be treated with caution. In Bangladesh the data refer to per capita expenditure. In Malaysia the data refer to per capita income.
[c]This is income going to the poorest 40 percent of households (the lowest two quintiles) compared to income going to the richest 20 percent of households.
SOURCE: The World Bank, *World Development Report 1992* (New York: Oxford University Press, 1992), Table 30, 276–277.

The Kuznets Curve

KUZNETS CURVE
A curve that shows the relationship between the income distribution and the per capita income for countries in different stages of economic development.

The data in the table suggest an interesting relationship between income distribution and per capita income known as the **Kuznets curve,** named after Simon Kuznets, who first described it. The Kuznets curve appears in Figure 41.3. Countries with very low per capita incomes tend to have relatively equal distributions of income (point *A*). Countries with high per capita incomes also tend to have relatively equal distributions of income (point *C*). Countries that are in the middle, however, tend to have income distributions that are much more unequal (point *B*). There are important exceptions to this rule, which are discussed below. And it is important to note that no country has or would desire to have a perfectly equal distribution of income.

The explanation for the hump in the Kuznets curve is not entirely clear, but there are some general tendencies that we can observe. The poorest countries of the world have a subsistence-based agricultural economy, which creates little by way of economic income. Consequently, the income distribution is relatively equal because just about everyone is very poor. As countries industrialize and income rises, however, not everyone is equally lifted out of poverty. Contrary to the axiom "A rising tide lifts all boats," in economic development some boats are anchored and flooded by the rising tide! In a growing market economy, those with the skills and the aptitudes valued by the market succeed. With access to education limited to a few, the rising demands for skilled labor cause a sharp rise in the relative wages and incomes of some and a decrease in the relative or absolute incomes of others.

This tendency toward inequality is often exacerbated by government policies that benefit industrial development at the expense of the poor in rural areas. Examples of government policies that result in a widening income distribution include overvaluing the exchange rate, which hurts the agricultural export sector in which many poor work; subsidizing credit for certain industries, which hurts the poor who are usually denied credit; and providing government education, health, and other programs only in cities, while most of the poor live in rural areas.

Inequality in land ownership (especially in Latin America) virtually precludes any chance for upward mobility in rural areas. Since colonial times in

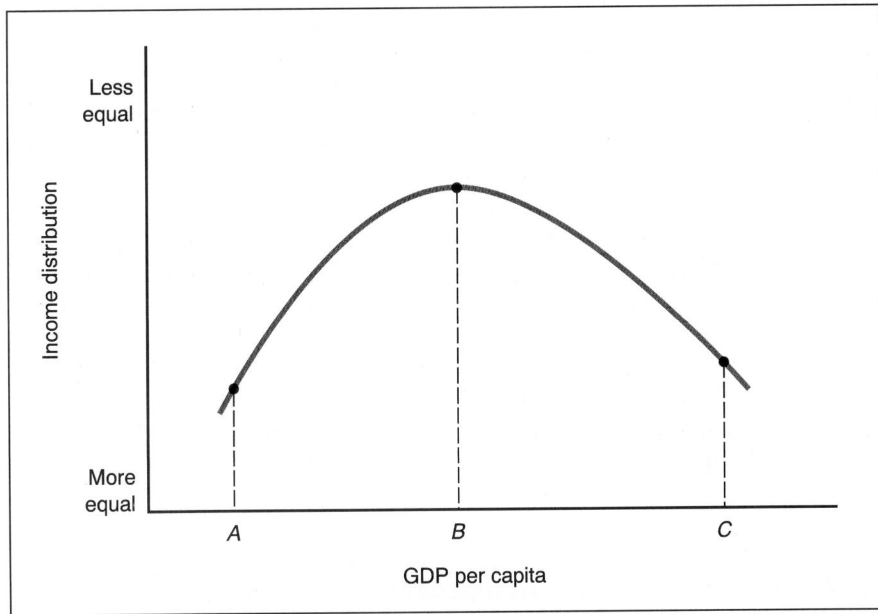

FIGURE 41.3

The Kuznets Curve

The Kuznets Curve shows the relationship between the distribution of income and per capita GDP for countries in different stages of development. GDP per capita is on the horizontal axis, and the income distribution is on the vertical axis. The income distribution tends to be most equal in the very poor and the very rich countries, and becomes much more unequal in the middle income countries that are undergoing rapid industrialization. The newly industrializing countries (NICs) of Asia are an exception to this tendency, however. They are maintaining a relatively equal distribution of income as they industrialize their economies.

Latin America, for example, most land has been held in a few large family estates called *latifundios*. Land is held often for purposes of prestige, not just income, and poor peasants cannot buy land even if someone would lend them the money to buy. There are some exceptions to this general picture. In Costa Rica land is more evenly distributed. It is no accident that Costa Rica also has one of the most stable democracies in Latin America. Since the revolution of 1917, Mexico has engaged in land reform, with mixed success.

Whatever its cause, the rise in inequality in many newly industrializing countries has proved to be a vexing problem. Those at the bottom of the socioeconomic ladder are the last to benefit from economic growth and the hardest hit during the inevitable economic downturns. Most developing countries have little by way of a social safety net for such emergencies. The terrible and grueling conditions of life at the bottom give rise to hundreds of millions of youths who are disaffected, disillusioned, and alienated from society. As England was industrializing in the nineteenth century, the masses of poor flowing into the industrial cities led to miserable and polluted living conditions—much as you find today in the megapoles of Mexico City, Rio de Janeiro, Cairo, Calcutta, and Jakarta. This gave rise to socialism and communism in England and other European countries because capitalism was not seen as a desirable system for human advancement. The anti-capitalist ideology was utilized by the communist regime in Russia following the revolution of 1917 and also was later adopted by Mao Zedong during and after his successful revolution in China in 1949.

Throughout the twentieth century, revolutionary movements sprang up around the world wherever young people had lost faith in the capitalist system. Revolutions in Cuba, Angola, Mozambique, Vietnam, and Nicaragua all led (at least initially) to the establishment of command economies that redistributed wealth and income. Communist guerrilla insurgencies to overthrow capitalism are still under way with various degrees of success in Guatemala, Peru, and the Philippines. Thus, the rise in inequality brings with it a social cost that can be quite high at times, and that can even threaten the overall stability of the nation.

As per capita income rises into the "high" range, inequality tends to lessen, as shown on the Kuznets curve. This is caused by many different factors, some market driven, others the result of political compromise. Over many generations, wages in a market may tend to equalize as higher wages in one sector attract new entrants and lower wages in another sector discourage new entrants. Assuming no barriers to entry, workers seek to better themselves by moving into higher-paying industries, and the greater supply of labor in these industries tends to depress wages in those industries and raise wages in the industries that are losing workers.

But the transition to a more equal income distribution may also require public action. Government laws help lessen income inequalities in numerous ways, for example, by creating universal public education, outlawing child labor and requiring compulsory school attendance, establishing a minimum wage, providing a legal basis for the creation of unions (as a countervailing power to monopsony), creating a progressive income tax, establishing the Social Security System, creating the G.I. bill (for educating veterans), providing for federally guaranteed student loans, and creating federal health, housing, and welfare programs, to name just a few.

The Asian NICs.

The rise in inequality is not a necessary condition for economic growth, however. In recent years the success of the Asian model has been widely noted. The Asian model is based on the success stories of the newly industrializing countries (NICs) of South Korea, Taiwan, Singapore, and Hong Kong. This basic strategy calls for redistribution of land into productive hands, redistribution and development of human capital via universal public education, and creation of labor-intensive, export-oriented industries. These economies have grown very successfully in an egalitarian way after an initial period of slow growth. Thus, the Kuznets hypothesis that a rise in inequality occurs with a rise in per capita income (up to a point) is not universally valid. However, the price to pay may be the greater authoritarian and paternalistic nature of these governments, which regulate human behavior to a greater degree than Westerners are comfortable with.

The unequal distribution of income and wealth in developing countries continues to be a source of great social tension. This social tension reduces the potential standard of living for the masses as more and more scarce resources are put into armaments to protect those who have from those who have not.

INWARD VERSUS OUTWARD GROWTH STRATEGIES

The Asian NICs represent outstanding success stories in contrast to the developing countries that pursued a diametrically opposite strategy. The NICs' strategy was outward-oriented. Its success hinged on achieving economies of scale through exports and gaining access to foreign markets (principally the United States). Other developing countries, by contrast, pursued an inward-oriented strategy. This inward strategy is called **import-substituting industrialization (ISI).**

IMPORT-SUBSTITUTING INDUSTRIALIZATION (ISI)

A strategy for economic growth and development in which a developing country produces goods that it had previously been importing.

The impetus for ISI was sound. Prior to the 1950s, developing countries exported raw materials (agricultural and mineral products) and imported finished manufactured goods. As world incomes grew, the demand for manufactured goods grew much faster than did the demand for raw materials.[6] Developing countries needed to produce more value added to their raw materials in order to prevent a fall in their terms-of-trade. The *terms-of-trade* is the ratio of export prices to import prices.

Industrialization was thus seen as the key to development. The question was which goods to produce? The Asian NICs chose to industrialize by producing goods desired in the United States. They had little choice, since their internal populations were very small and provided a limited internal market. They picked labor-intensive goods for which they had a comparative advantage in production.

The ISI countries, following a different approach, decided to produce manufactured goods that they themselves needed. In other words, they produced goods that they had previously imported—hence the term *import-substituting industrialization.* On one level this method appears logical. If a good is demanded and imported, why not produce it domestically? The economist's answer is that it may be more costly to produce it domestically and cheaper to import it. Comparative advantage should dictate which products are imported and which are exported. ISI, however, did not proceed on the basis of comparative advantage.

The Latin American Experience

ISI was the dominant strategy followed in Latin America in the 1950s and 1960s. As automobiles were a key part of the transportation system and as automobiles had been imported, the manufacture of automobiles became the leading edge of this movement. In the first phase automobiles were assembled using imported parts. In the next phase (called backward linkages) the parts themselves—steel, tires, windshields, radios, engines, transmissions, ball bearings, and so on—were manufactured.

At each stage high tariffs (sometimes over 100 percent) were placed on the imported item that was being manufactured domestically. In addition, many subsidies were provided in the form of tax breaks, low-interest-rate loans, and overvalued exchange rates. These high tariffs and subsidies were meant to be temporary to protect the "infant industry." However, domestic manufacturers, protected from competition from abroad and enjoying a near monopoly domestically, exerted significant pressure to maintain these tariffs and subsidies.

The results were quite good initially, as these economies grew substantially. The long-term effects were quite disastrous, however. Industrial products were being produced very inefficiently, with minimal economies of scale and little competition. The prices of domestic cars were far higher than were the prices of better-made imports. The overvalued exchange rates caused continual balance-of-payments problems, often requiring bailouts from the International

[6]In more technical terms, the income elasticity of demand for manufactured goods is much higher than it is for raw materials.

Monetary Fund. The traditional agricultural export sector suffered, and income distribution became more unequal. Government subsidies led to large budget deficits that were financed by printing money, thereby causing high inflation rates. The low-interest-rate loans caused financial repression, resulting in a lower effective savings rate and capital flight. To provide capital and technology, foreign multinational companies were invited in with tax breaks. These companies often exerted significant political pressures that distorted the political process.

Petrodollar Recycling and the Debt Crisis

The failure of import-substituting industrialization became evident in the 1970s. The oil price shocks of 1973–74 and 1979 led many countries (mainly in Latin America) to borrow heavily from private banks in the developed countries in order to keep their industrial economies operating. Banks were flush with deposits to loan because many members of the Organization of Petroleum Exporting Countries (OPEC) could not spend all the oil revenues they were earning. Latin American countries historically had provided high returns to investors, and bankers were eager to earn these high returns. This funneling of oil deposits to developing countries was called **petrodollar recycling.**

PETRODOLLAR RECYCLING

The practice among financial institutions of lending to the developing countries the funds that they receive from the oil-producing countries.

In the early 1980s this system collapsed under the weight of rising interest rates and economic recession in developed countries. Borrowing countries could not earn the foreign exchange needed to pay the interest on the foreign debt, which by this time totaled over $800 billion. Latin American countries experienced a debt crisis that threatened the stability of the world's financial markets. Economic progress ground to a halt throughout Latin America as new investment funds dried up.

In the 1980s most of these countries went through painful economic adjustments in order to make their economies more competitive and to get out from under the debt overload. These economic reforms are discussed in the final part of this chapter.

Economic Reform in the 1980s and 1990s

The pervasive mismanagement of economies, leading to large fiscal deficits, runaway inflation, overvalued exchange rates, and current account deficits, inevitably generates a maze of piecemeal bureaucratic regulations that give way to bribery and corruption. The incentive structure in production is distorted, and financial markets, if they exist at all, do not work well. Add to this a fair amount of political instability and it is not hard to see why many developing countries lurch from one crisis to the next.

Against this backdrop there have been some real reform measures that should pay off in the 1990s. The collapse of the Soviet empire, and its economic reform known as *perestroika* is being echoed in various other parts of the world. Governments are making serious efforts at economic reform. In broad outline this involves

1. Cutting government spending. Especially necessary are cuts in subsidies to producers and subsidies to consumers that create surpluses of unwanted goods and shortages of desired goods, respectively.

2. Privatization of industry. The selling of inefficient state-owned companies reduces the fiscal deficit.
3. Setting realistic exchange rates. Exports are encouraged by lowering exchange rates to realistic levels, which leads to an improvement in the current account balance.
4. Reducing barriers to trade. Becoming part of the world trading system ensures that domestic manufacturers cannot hide behind tariff walls. Companies that do not produce efficiently know that they will fail.
5. Reforming financial markets. Allowing savers to earn a positive real rate of return boosts the savings rate and reduces capital flight. Elimination of credit rationing ensures that these savings find their way into productive investments.

These reforms, often carried out with the advice and financial backing of the International Monetary Fund, have produced success stories in Mexico, Chile, Ghana, and other countries. All across Latin America democratic governments have replaced authoritarian military rulers and are replacing closed, inefficient economies with more open, competitive economies.

As vital as these reforms are for long-run success, they bring immediate hardship to those at the bottom of the economic ladder. The social strain of adjustment is the Achilles' heel that could be the undoing of these governments and their programs.

SUMMARY

The first section of Chapter 41 examined the standards of living in the developing countries.

1. The developing countries include the nations of Latin America, Africa, and Asia, excluding Japan. Their populations make up about four-fifths of the world's population.
2. The poorest countries of the world are located in sub-Saharan Africa, Southeast Asia, and Central Asia. Their economies are largely agriculturally based.
3. It is difficult to compare GDPs between countries due to differences in measurement and problems with converting to a common currency. Incomes adjusted for purchasing power parities can significantly improve the reliability of cross-country comparisons. All comparisons should be used with care, however, because GDP is an imperfect measure of the quality of life.
4. Economic development is a complex process that occurs over many generations. It is difficult to pinpoint a single variable that explains success or failure in any one country. Economic institutions and policies can aid or hinder this process.

The second section of the chapter explored four key determinants of economic growth in the developing countries: labor force participation, the saving rate and the link between savings and productive investment, the choice of production technologies, and the population growth rate.

5. Labor force participation is generally very high in the developing countries. These countries remain poor because labor is not very productive.

6. A country must raise its savings rate in order to invest more and increase its potential growth rate. However, numerous cultural, institutional, and political factors hinder the channeling of savings into productive investments in many developing countries.
7. A country can grow faster by acquiring savings from abroad in the form of direct foreign investment, loans, or gifts.
8. The choice of technology affects the efficiency of the capital used. Distorted factor prices for labor and capital often lead to the wrong market signals being sent and cause businesses in the developing countries to use technologies that are too capital-intensive. Inappropriate capital-intensive technologies drain scarce savings and lower the rate of growth.
9. Population growth is very rapid in the poorest developing countries. This puts severe strains on the limited savings that are available for investment. High population growth rates are the result of both a high supply of children and a high demand for children.

The third section of the chapter looked at the relationship between the distribution of income and economic development.

10. The distribution of income is often most equal in the very poor and very rich countries and most unequal in the middle-income countries that are undergoing rapid industrialization. The Asian NICs have demonstrated that rising inequality is not a necessary condition for economic growth, however.

The final section of Chapter 41 compared and contrasted the outward-oriented and inward-oriented strategies for economic growth and development.

11. The Asian NICs followed a labor-intensive, outward-oriented export strategy for economic development that is based on the principle of comparative advantage and that proved to be highly successful. This strategy also mitigated the tendency toward a more unequal distribution of income.
12. The Latin American countries followed an inward-oriented import-substituting industrialization (ISI) strategy in which they tried to produce the goods that they had previously imported. This proved to be very costly in terms of economic efficiency and generated a number of macroeconomic problems, including high inflation, large budget deficits, current account trade deficits, and huge foreign debts.
13. Many developing countries are undertaking economic reforms to correct these problems. Protecting those at the bottom of the income distribution remains a serious problem for the future, however.

KEY TERMS

capital flight
developed countries
developing countries (LDCs or third world countries)
export-enclave production
financial repression
import-substituting industrialization (ISI)
International Comparisons Program (ICP)
Kuznets curve
labor force participation rate
newly industrializing countries (NICs)
petrodollar recycling

QUESTIONS

1. What are the strengths and the weaknesses of using per capita gross domestic product as a measure of how well off a particular country's citizens are?
2. Why do governments in developing countries often impose interest rate ceilings? Are interest rate ceilings a good policy?
3. As a country's per capita income rises, will the population tend to rise or fall? Explain.
4. Describe some of the factors that hold down the rate of saving in developing countries or prevent the saving that does occur from financing productive investments.
5. a. Discuss the differences between the outward-oriented growth strategy used by the Asian NICs and the inward-oriented growth strategy used by many of the Latin American countries.
   b. Why did each set of countries choose the growth strategy that it did?
   c. Which type of strategy has worked out better in practice, and why?
6. Are the gross domestic products of different countries comparable when they are all converted to one currency by their exchange rate with that currency? If yes, why? If no, why not?
7. Discuss the advantages and the disadvantages of direct foreign investment for developing countries.
8. What is the Kuznets curve, and why is it hump-shaped?
9. a. Why does it make sense for developing countries to use labor-intensive technologies rather than capital-intensive technologies?
   b. What incentives lead businesses in developing countries to use capital-intensive technologies?
10. Comment on the following statement: The demand for children is higher in developed countries than in developing countries because parents in developed countries have more resources to take care of their children.

CASE

The "Flipper" Factor in International Trade*

Dolphins swim above schools of tuna in the eastern tropical Pacific Ocean. Therefore, when fishing vessels catch the tuna in their nets, they invariably catch and kill a large number of dolphins as well. The U.S. Marine Mammal Protection Act of 1972, as amended in 1988, set a maximum level of dolphin mortality for U.S. tuna vessels fishing in this area. The Act also stipulated that tuna are not to be imported from any country whose fisherman have destroyed more than 1.25 times as many dolphins as the American fishing fleet did in the same year (from 1990 on).

The United States banned the import of yellowfin tuna products from Mexico in February, 1991 at the urging of environmentalists, and extended the ban to Venezuelan yellowfin tuna products in March, 1991. The United States also imposed a secondary ban on imports of yellowfin tuna products from France, Italy, the U.K., and Spain if the products used tuna imported from Mexico and Venezuela.

Mexico protested the U.S. ban before the Council of the General Agreement on Trade and Tariffs (GATT). In September 1991, a GATT dispute-resolution panel ruled that both the primary ban and the secondary ban were in violation of GATT rules. The ruling was never formally adopted by the GATT Council, and the dispute died down when Mexico voluntarily took steps to protect the dolphins. Nonetheless, this episode illustrates a potential conflict between the enforcement of varying environmental standards in different countries and the promotion of free trade. Specifically, should a country be allowed by GATT to impose unilateral sanctions against its trading partners for having less stringent environmental standards? The killing of dolphins by tuna fishing vessels is a particularly interesting case in point.

Killing dolphins is objectionable to many Americans who have been brought up watching the "Flipper" television series, and who have enjoyed watching dolphins perform at dolphin shows such as Florida's Sea World. But is this an environmental issue that merits a trade embargo? The dolphin is not an endangered species and thus is not protected by the International Convention on Trade in Endangered Species. Also, how can Mexican tuna fishermen know in advance what the American dolphin kill will be? Finally, the GATT ruling against the United States was not arbitrary. It

*Provided by K. K. Fung, Memphis State University.

continued on next page

The "Flipper" Factor in International Trade (cont.)

was based on a reasonable principle that the way an imported product is produced is not a good reason to discriminate against it. Many U.S. health and enviornmental laws directly regulate production in order to promote safety in the workplace and to protect the environment. The GATT principle simply states that such laws cannot be applied unilaterally to other countries in restraint of trade.

To be generally applicable, GATT requires that health, safety, and environmental laws be necessary and least trade restrictive. This means that such laws should achieve their objectives with regulations that are least costly to comply with and that do not unduly impose higher compliance costs on foreign than domestic producers. The North American Free Trade Agreement (NAFTA) further specifies that these laws be based on scientific principles and risk assessment. The provisions of the Marine Mammal Protection Act on the killing of dolphins may be inconsistent with these GATT and NAFTA principles.

Non-tariff trade barriers have dominated discussions in the current Uruguay Round of GATT because they are the main form of trade restriction imposed by the industrialized nations. Many domestic policies which were never intended to protect domestic producers from foreign competition have inadvertently become significant non-tariff barriers to imports. The "flipper" dolphin-tuna incident is a notable example.

ECONOMIC ADVISOR'S REPORT

Suppose that you have been hired by GATT to advise them on the application of domestic environmental standards to international trade. They ask you the following questions. How would you respond?

1. If imports are cheaper because they have lower environmental costs, should nations be allowed to impose "anti-dumping" tariffs that reflect the higher environmental costs faced by domestic producers? Would your answer be the same if the imports were cheaper because of lower wages in the exporting country?
2. Environmental concerns were an important obstacle to the U.S. ratification of NAFTA. Mexico's conciliatory gesture in the dolphin/tuna dispute was largely designed to avoid jeopardizing NAFTA. If environmental safeguards are not built into NAFTA, will Mexico become a haven for heavily-polluting U.S. industries in search of lax environmental regulations?
3. In your opinion, what is the least trade-restrictive way for the United States to limit the importation of tuna products from Mexico that is consistent with the GATT principles on this issue?

SOURCES: "EC Spokesman Condemns U.S. For Marine Mammal Protection, Act," *ENA International Environment Daily*, February 19, 1992; "Environmentalists Against GATT," *Wall Street Journal*, March 19, 1993; "Free Trade vs. Law," *The National Law Journal*, March 29, 1993; "Mexico Announces a Dolphin Protection Plan," *Los Angeles Times*, September 25, 1993, D6; "The Greening of Protectionism," *The Economist*, February 27, 1993; "We Can Have Free Trade and Clean Environment," *The Houston Chronicle*, April 6, 1993, A13.

GLOSSARY

Ability to Trade The rate at which consumers can trade one good for another in their budgets, equal to the price ratio of the two goods.
Actual Budget Deficit The difference between government expenditures and government revenues.
Administrative Lag (Fiscal Policy) The time required to enact legislation to change government purchases, transfer payments, or taxes.
Administrative Lag (Monetary Policy) The time required to change the course of monetary policy once the Board of Governors decides to do so.
Adverse Selection In the context of insurance, arises when the insurance company is forced to set one premium because it cannot distinguish between high-risk and low-risk individuals, with the result that low-risk individuals cancel their policies.
Age-Earnings Profile The average earnings per person at each age within the population.
Aggregate Demand Curve A graph of the aggregate demand schedule that shows the quantity of national output demanded by the four sectors of the economy at each overall level of prices.
Aggregate Demand The total quantity of final goods and services demanded at each overall price level by all the final demanders in the economy; the aggregate demand curve, labeled *AD*, is a graph of aggregate demand.
Aggregate Demand Schedule A schedule that indicates the quantity of national output demanded by the four sectors of the economy at each overall level of prices.
Aggregate Demand Shock Any event that directly affects the total demand for goods and services at each overall price level.
Aggregate Desired Expenditures (Aggregate Demand for Expenditures) The relationship between the aggregate demand for final goods and services and national income, other things equal.
Aggregate Supply Curve A graph of the aggregate supply schedule that shows the quantity of national output supplied by all producers at each overall level of prices.
Aggregate Supply The total quantity of final goods and services supplied at each overall price level by all the producers in the economy; the aggregate supply curve, labeled *AS*, is a graph of aggregate supply.
Aggregate Supply Schedule A schedule that indicates the quantity of national output supplied by all producers at each overall level of prices.
Aggregate Supply Shock Any event that directly affects producers' costs of production or the quantity that they can supply to the market.
Allocational Efficiency Achieved in a product market when the quantity exchanged in the market maximizes the net value of producing and consuming a good; the market test is price equal to short-run marginal cost.
Allocational Policies Government economic policies that respond to market failures relating to the goal of achieving an efficient use of society's scarce resources.
Alternatives The part of the economic problem that refers to the necessity of making choices.
Appreciation (Currency) The value of a nation's currency rises relative to the value of other currencies.
Arbitrage The buying and selling of commodities whose prices are out of line in such a way as to guarantee a profit.
Arrow's Impossibility Theorem The proposition that individuals' preferences for particular government policies might not aggregate into a consistent set of social preferences for those policies under democratic voting rules.
Asset Something that is owned, real or financial; a claim against someone or some institution.
Automatic Stabilizer Any component of the economy that is related to the level of national income and lowers the value of the spending multiplier; automatic stabilizers make the economy less responsive to aggregate demand shocks.
Autonomous Capital Inflow (or Outflow) A capital inflow (or outflow) undertaken for its own sake and not as an offset to some other transaction in the balance of payments.
Average Fixed Cost At every output, the firm's fixed cost divided by its output.
Average Propensity to Consume The ratio of consumption demand to disposable income.
Average Propensity to Save The ratio of saving demand to disposable income.
Average Revenue Curve An individual firm's demand curve.
Average (Total) Cost At every output, the firm's total cost divided by its output.
Average Variable Cost At every output, the firm's variable cost divided by its output.

Balanced Budget Change An equal change in government expenditures and revenues.
Balanced Budget Multiplier The ratio that relates the change in the equilibrium level of national income to a balanced budget change in government purchases and taxes.
Balanced Inflation An inflation in which the prices of all goods and services, including all factors of production, are rising at exactly the same rate.
Balance of Goods and Services The sum of the balance of trade plus net exports of services plus net receipts of factor incomes.
Balance of Payments The double-entry accounting system that nations use to record their international transactions during the course of a year.
Balance of Trade The difference between the value of a nation's exports and the value of its imports (merchandise exports and imports only; excludes trade in services).
Balance-of-Trade Deficit The value of a nation's imports exceeds the value of its exports.
Balance-of-Trade Surplus The value of a nation's exports exceeds the value of its imports.
Balance Sheet A listing of a person's or an institution's assets, liabilities, and net worth.
Bank Run An attempt by large numbers of depositors to close their checking (and savings) accounts in exchange for currency.

Barrier to Entry or Exit Anything that restricts or prevents the free flow of resources into or out of an industry.
Barter An exchange of goods directly for other goods.
Beggar-Thy-Neighbor Policy A government policy that attempts to export domestic unemployment abroad by means of tariffs and other restrictions on imports.
Behavioral Barrier to Entry A strategic decision on the part of a firm that is specifically designed either to deter entry entirely or to accommodate entry by forcing new firms to enter on a smaller scale
Benefits-Received Principle A pricing principle for public services, which says that citizens should pay for public services in accordance with the benefits they receive from them.
Benefits Received Principle of Taxation The principle that the taxes and other means of payment for public services are fair if they bear a direct relationship to the benefits people receive from the public services.
Bilateral Monopoly A market situation consisting of one buyer confronting one seller.
Board of Governors (Federal Reserve) The seven-member governing body that oversees and controls the Federal Reserve Banking System.
Break-Even Level of Disposable Income The level of disposable income at which households' consumption demand equals their disposable income.
Break-Even Point A market situation in which a firm's total revenue equals its long-run total cost (price equals long-run average cost), so that economic profit is zero.
Budget Constraint The maximum combination of goods and services that a consumer is able to purchase, given the consumer's income and the prices of the goods and services.
Budget Deficit Exists when a government's expenditures exceed its revenues from taxes, direct user charges, and grants-in-aid.
Budget Line A graphical representation of the consumer's budget constraint.
Budget Surplus Exists when a government's revenues from taxes, direct user charges, and grants-in-aid exceed its expenditures.
Business Cycle The continuing pattern over time of expansions and contractions, booms and busts, in the circular flow of economic activity in capitalist economies.
Business Saving The portion of the profits that managers set aside to finance future investment projects; also called *retained earnings*.
Business Sector The sector of an economy that consists of all the private business firms and is the major producer of final goods and services.

Capital The plant and equipment required to produce goods and services; one of the primary factors of production.
Capital Account (Balance of Payments) The subaccount in the balance of payments that records capital inflows and outflows.
Capital Account Balance The difference between a nation's capital inflows and capital outflows.
Capital Consumption Allowance Funds that firms set aside to replace equipment and structures as they age and lose their productive capacity, equal in principle to the economic depreciation of capital.
Capital Flight The purchase of foreign currencies or securities by domestic residents as a hedge against rapid domestic inflation.
Capital Gain (Annual) The difference between the value of an asset at the end of the year and its value at the beginning of the year.
Capital Inflows Purchases of domestic financial securities or loans to domestic residents by foreign residents.
Capital Outflows Purchases of foreign financial securities or loans to foreign residents by domestic residents.
Capital/Output Ratio The amount of capital required to produce each unit of output.
Cartel An organization of some or all of the firms in an industry established for the purpose of maximizing the total profits of the cooperating firms.
Categorical Assistance Public assistance that is based on some personal characteristic of a family or unrelated individual in addition to low income, such as whether the person is living in a family headed by a single parent.
Centralized Economy An economic system in which an agency of the national government has authority over all economic decisions and full access to all relevant economic information.
Centrally Planned Socialism An economic system characterized by centralized decision making, the use of a national economic plan to process information and coordinate exchange, public ownership of capital and land, and the use of both moral and material incentives.
Change in Demand A shift in the entire demand curve.
Change in Quantity Demanded A movement along the demand curve as price changes, other things equal.
Change in Quantity Supplied A movement along the supply curve as price changes, other things equal.
Change in Supply A shift in the entire supply curve.
Circular Flow Diagram A graphical representation of the circular flow of economic activity through the nation's product and factor markets.
Circular Flow of Economic Activity The flow of goods and services and factors of production through the product and the factor markets of the economy that results from the interactions of individuals and business firms; the flow is circular because firms sell products to individuals in the product markets and individuals sell factors of production to firms in the factor markets.
Closed Shop A labor union rule that requires a worker to join an established union upon being hired.
Collective Bargaining A process in which elected union representatives bargain with management on behalf of the members of the union over pay and other terms of employment.
Common-Use Resource A resource such as water or air that no one owns.
Comparative Advantage The principle that a country should specialize its production in those goods that it can produce with lower opportunity costs than other countries and trade for those goods that other countries can produce with lower opportunity costs.
Compensation of Employees The payment to, and the income received by, labor, including wages, salaries, and in-kind fringe benefits.
Competitive Market A market in which a large number of firms sell very similar or identical products, consumers are well informed about the price that each firm charges for its product, and resources move easily into and out of the market in response to profits and losses.
Complements Products that are used together to provide a service; specifically, two goods whose relationship is such that a decrease in the price of one good increases the demand for the other.
Complete Ordering of Preferences The ability to provide an ordering of all alternative combinations of goods and services potentially available to the consumer.

Compounding The process of computing the equivalent future value of current dollars.
Comprehensive Tax Base A broad-based measure of the personal income subject to tax under a personal income tax that includes all income received from factors of production, all transfer payments received, and net capital gains on assets received during the year.
Conglomerate Merger A merger between firms operating in different product markets.
Constant Cost Industry An industry in which the minimum long-run average cost of the firms remains constant no matter how much output is supplied to the market, so that the long-run market supply curve is horizontal.
Constant Dollar (Real) Gross Domestic Product The value of the gross domestic product generated each year, evaluated at the prices that existed in a given base year.
Constant Returns to Scale
- *In terms of long-run total cost:* the region of the long-run total cost curve along which the percentage change in total cost is equal to the percentage change in output.
- *In terms of the production function:* an equal proportionate increase in all the firm's inputs by an amount *k* leads to a proportionate increase in the firm's output equal to *k* (for example, a doubling of all the firm's inputs leads to a doubling of the firm's output).

Constraints The part of the economic problem that refers to the limitations that prevent economic agents from achieving their objectives.
Consumer Durables Manufactured goods that typically last more than one year.
Consumer Equilibrium A situation in which the marginal rate of substitution between any two goods equals the ratio of their prices; the consumer is maximizing utility.
Consumer Nondurables Manufactured goods that typically last less than one year.
Consumer Price Index A price index based on a market basket of consumer goods and services purchased by the typical household.
Consumer Sovereignty The principle that individuals are best able to judge their own self-interests.
Consumer Surplus At any quantity exchanged in the market, the difference between the total value to consumers and the total market value.
Consumers Economic agents who consume goods and services and who supply the primary factors of production—labor, capital, and land—to producers.
Consumption Aggregate purchases of final goods and services by households.
Consumption Function The relationship that indicates how much households in the aggregate are willing and able to consume during the year at every level of total disposable income, other things equal; also called *consumption demand.*
Contestable Market A market structure in which the existing firm or firms have market power and are subject to the possibility of hit-and-run entry by new firms.
Contraction Phase (Business Cycle) The period of time during which economic activity is declining; commonly referred to as a *recession.*
Contractionary Fiscal Policy Decreases in government purchases or transfer payments, or increases in taxes, for the purpose of decreasing aggregate demand.
Contractionary Monetary Policy A decrease in the money supply undertaken by the Fed for the purpose of decreasing aggregate demand; the Fed sells Treasury securities on the Open Market.
Contractionary Policy A fiscal or monetary policy that decreases the level of aggregate demand.
Contrived Scarcity The market situation generated by a pure monopolist (or any firm with market power), in which the monopolist (firm) consciously reduces its output below the efficient level of output to maximize its profit.
Controlled Experiment The scientific method of analysis for determining cause-and-effect relationships that studies the effects of changing one element in an environment at a time while holding constant all the other elements in the environment.
Cooperative Behavior Collusion by two or more firms in which they explicitly agree not to compete with one another.
Core Rate of Inflation The rate of inflation that is based on a restricted market basket of goods and services, which excludes items that have highly volatile prices and that have significant weight in computing the overall rate of inflation.
Corporate Profit The difference between the value of sales and the cost of goods sold; the income received by the stockholders who own the firm.
Corporation A form of business that is a recognized legal entity distinct from the owners of the firm, allows owners to transfer their shares of stock, allows owners to delegate authority and responsibility to a group of managers, has a potentially unlimited life, and has limited liability for business losses.
Cost-Benefit Analysis The analysis of government investment projects.
Cost of Capital The annual cost to a firm of purchasing an additional unit of capital.
Countercyclical Policy A fiscal or monetary policy that counteracts the movements in aggregate demand whenever aggregate demand tends to move the economy away from the target level of national income.
CR4 The four-firm concentration ratio, equal to the percentage of total domestic sales accounted for by the four largest firms in the industry.
Craft Union A labor union in which every member of the union is engaged in one particular craft or trade.
Creative Destruction The process by which invention, innovation, and diffusion cause drastic changes in the economic environment, simultaneously destroying markets and bankrupting some firms while creating new markets and profitable opportunities for other firms.
Credit Crunch A condition of excess demand in the loan markets in which potential borrowers complain that they cannot get loans even when they are willing to pay the quoted interest rate for the loans.
Creditor Nation A nation for which the market value of the assets that its citizens hold abroad exceeds the market value of the assets that foreign citizens hold in the nation.
Cross-Price Elasticity of Demand The percentage change in the demand for one good divided by the percentage change in the price of a related good.
Crowding-Out Effect Changes in the demands for consumer durables, investment, and net exports that are induced by the change in interest rates following a change (shift) in aggregate demand, and that lower the value of the spending multiplier.
Currency The dollar bills and coins of various denominations circulating in the economy.
Current Account (Balance of Payments) The subaccount in the balance of payments that records the exports and the imports of goods and services, the receipts of factor incomes by domestic and foreign residents, and net unilateral transfers.
Current Account Balance The balance of goods and services minus net unilateral transfers.
Current Dollar (Nominal) Gross Domestic Product The actual dollar value of the gross domestic product generated

during the year.

Current Market Discrimination In the context of labor markets, unequal treatment of people on the basis of personal characteristics, such as race or gender, that are unrelated to differences in their productivity, taking the form of unequal pay for the same work, unequal access to jobs, and unequal access to training programs and promotions.

Current Population Survey An annual survey of approximately 60,000 families and unrelated individuals compiled by the U.S. Bureau of the Census, which is used to obtain information on income and other personal characteritics.

Cyclical Budget Deficit The component of the government's budget deficit that fluctuates with the state of the economy; the difference between the actual budget deficit and the structural budget deficit.

Cyclical Indicator A monthly or quarterly data series that contains reliable and significant information concerning the performance of the economy over time and that moves in a pattern consistent with the movement of the overall business cycle.

Cyclical Unemployment Unemployment that fluctuates with the state of the economy because wages are sticky.

Debtor Nation A nation for which the market value of the assets that its citizens hold abroad is less than the market value of the assets that foreign citizens hold in the nation.

Decreasing Cost Industry An industry in which the minimum long-run average cost of the firms decreases as output supplied to the market increases, so that the long-run market supply curve is downward sloping.

Deficit Agents Economic agents who are the borrowers or the users of funds in financial markets because they have less income than they desire to spend in any one year.

Demand The amount of a product that individuals are willing and able to buy over a certain period of time.

Demand for Money The average amount of money that a person or an institution wants to hold and not spend.

Demand Pull Inflation Price inflation resulting from the attempt to purchase more goods and services than the economy is capable of producing.

Depository Institution A financial institution that accepts deposit accounts of any kind.

Depository Institutions Deregulation and Monetary Control Act of 1980 (DIDMCA) An act of Congress that brought all depository institutions under the control of the Fed.

Depreciation The decline in the market value of the firm's stock of capital during the year.

Depreciation (Currency) The value of a nation's currency falls relative to the value of other currencies.

Derived Demand The principle that the demand for labor depends in part on the market for the product that the workers are producing; the higher the price of the product, the higher the wages, other things equal.

Developed Countries Countries that have achieved, on average, a high standard of living, with a per capita income of at least $7,620 (as of 1990).

Developing Countries Countries that range from the nearly developed to the very poor, with a per capita income of less than $7,620 (as of 1990); also called *less developed countries (LDCs).*

Diffusion The final post-research stage of the process of invention and innovation in which firms are actually using a new production technology or producing and selling a new product.

Direct Foreign Investment The purchase of domestic stock or other assets by foreign residents that give them a controlling interest in a domestic firm.

Discount Factor The factor by which future dollars are multiplied to determine their present value; it is equal to $1/(1 + r)^n$, where r is the discount rate and n is the time in the future when the dollars are received or spent.

Discount Rate The interest rate used to calculate the present value of future dollars; alternatively, the interest rate used to compound current dollars to their future value.

Discount Rate (Federal Reserve) The rate of interest that the Fed charges commercial banks for loans of reserves to help the banks meet their reserve requirements.

Discounting to Present Value The process of computing the current value of future dollars.

Discouraged Workers Those people who have become so discouraged trying to find an acceptable job that they have dropped out of the labor force.

Diseconomies of Scale

- *In terms of long-run total cost:* the region of the long-run total cost curve along which the percentage change in total cost is greater than the percentage change in output.
- *In terms of the production function:* an equal proportionate increase in all the firm's inputs by an amount k leads to a proportionate increase in the firm's output by less than k (for example, a doubling of all the firm's inputs leads to less than a doubling of the firm's output); also called decreasing returns to scale.

Disposable Income The income available to households for their own use, to be consumed or saved.

Distributional Policies Government economic policies that respond to market failures relating to the goals of achieving fair and evenhanded market exchanges and an acceptable distribution of income.

Dividends The portion of after-tax profits that managers of the firm pay to the stockholders.

Division of Labor As an economy grows and as business firms become larger, the process by which factors of production tend to become ever more specialized, performing highly specific tasks associated with only one small part of the production process.

Dynamic Efficiency The reduction in firms' costs of production over time due to technical change and increased productivity.

Economic Depreciation The decline in the market value of a firm's capital stock over a given period of time.

Economic Problem A three-part problem consisting of objectives, alternatives, and constraints.

Economic Profit The difference between total revenue and total (economic) cost.

Economic Rent The difference between the wage a worker receives and the wage required to attract the worker to the job.

Economic System The set of decision-making mechanisms, organizational arrangements, and rules for allocating society's scarce resources and determining the appropriate distribution of income.

Economics The study of the allocation of scarce resources through the process of exchange.

Economies of Scale

- *In terms of long-run total cost:* the region of the long-run total cost curve along which the percentage change in total cost is less than the percentage change in output.
- *In terms of the production function:* an equal proportionate increase in all the firm's inputs by an amount k leads to a proportionate increase in the firm's output by more than k (for example, a doubling

of all the firm's inputs leads to more than a doubling of the firm's output); also called increasing returns to scale.

Effectively Competitive Product Market A product market in which individual firms have very little control over price and other market outcomes.

Effective Market (Monopoly) Power The ability of a firm to maintain an economic profit in the long run

Efficiency A criterion for judging the solution to an economic problem that refers to making the choices that best meet the objectives; if the economic problem has a single objective, then efficiency means coming as close to the objective as possible; if the economic problem has more than one objective, then efficiency means that the Law of Substitution holds. A solution is efficient if moving closer to one objective requires moving farther away from at least one other objective.

Efficiency Wage A wage that is higher than necessary to retain the employees, but that firms are willing to pay to improve the morale of the employees so that they will remain happy and productive and not shirk their duties; alternatively, the wage at which the marginal benefits and the marginal costs to the firm of further increases in the wage are equal; the wage that maximizes the firm's profit within the range of wages it could pay.

Employed People who have worked for at least one hour during the week of the Bureau of Labor Statistics employment survey.

End-Results Equity A criterion for judging the solution to an economic problem that asks whether economic outcomes are fair.

Engel's Curve A graphical representation of the relationship between income and quantity demanded, other things equal.

Entrepreneurs Imaginative individuals who bring new ideas to the business world and who are willing to take the risks of starting new ventures or businesses.

Equality of Opportunity A principle of process equity that requires that individuals have equal access to whatever economic opportunities they are willing and able to pursue so that they can develop their economic potential to the fullest; in the context of product markets, all investors have equal access to profitable market opportunities because of the absence of barriers to entry and equal access to all relevant market information.

Equalizing Wage Differential A difference in the wages for different jobs that just compensates workers for the relative attractiveness of the jobs.

Equation of Exchange The measure of the circular flow of economic activity in terms of money; a national income accounting identity, which says that the dollar value of national income or national product equals the product of the money supply times the velocity of circulation.

Equilibrium A state of rest, or balance, due to the equal action of opposing forces or influences; in economics, a situation from which no one has any incentive to change.

Equilibrium Level of National Income The level of national income at which aggregate demand equals national income; alternatively, the level of national income at which saving demand equals investment demand.

Equity In the context of product markets, the presence of equality of opportunity and horizontal equity; the inability of firms to maintain economic profits in the long run.

Eurodollar Account Any dollar-denominated account in a foreign bank.

Excess Demand The amount by which quantity demanded exceeds quantity supplied when price is below the equilibrium price.

Excess Reserves The difference between a commercial bank's total reserves and its required reserves; the amount of reserves that a commercial bank can lend and still be able to satisfy the reserve requirement.

Excess Supply The amount by which quantity supplied exceeds quantity demanded when price is above the equilibrium price.

Exchange The trading of goods, services, and factors of production among the key players in the economy.

Exchange Rate Mechanism (ERM) The dominant feature of the European Monetary System (EMS),which pegged the currencies of the Western European nations to the German mark.

Exclusive Good A good whose benefits are received only by the person who consumes it.

Exhaustible Resource A resource available in a finite amount whose quantity diminishes as it is used in production, such as the natural resources.

Expansion Phase (Business Cycle) The period of time during which economic activity is increasing; commonly referred to as a *boom.*

Expansionary Fiscal Policy Increases in government purchases or transfer payments, or decreases in taxes, for the purpose of increasing aggregate demand.

Expansionary Monetary Policy An increase in the money supply undertaken by the Fed for the purpose of increasing aggregate demand; the Fed buys Treasury securities on the Open Market.

Expansionary Policy A fiscal or monetary policy that increases the level of aggregate demand.

Explicit Monetary (Operating) Costs The firm's out-of-pocket payments for its factors of production plus the general sales and excise taxes paid by the firm on the sale of its products.

Export-Enclave Production Refers to production by resource-using firms in the developing countries, typically multinational corporations, whose output is not consumed locally, but is exported to the First World, thereby earning foreign exchange and creating new jobs and export opportunities.

Exports Domestically produced goods and services, and factors of production, sold to foreign individuals, businesses, and governments.

Externality A third-party effect of a transaction that directly affects either consumers' satisfaction or firms' production possibilities.

External Debt (Public) Public debt that is held by foreign citizens, businesses, and governments.

Factor Endowments Model of International Trade A model developed to explain the pattern of international trade that is based on differences in factor endowments across countries; countries specialize their production in and export those goods that use factors of production that are relatively abundant, and they import those goods that use factors of production that are relatively scarce.

Factor Indivisibility The inability to use a fraction of a particular factor of production, as when a self-employed catering service owner has to use at least one truck.

Factors of Production The resources or inputs that producers use to produce goods and services, consisting of labor, capital, land, and material inputs.

Featherbedding A work rule in which firms are forced to hire workers who are of no value to them.

Federal Deposit Insurance Corporation (FDIC) A public agency established by Congress that insures deposit accounts at commercial banks (and other depository institutions).

Federal Funds Rate The rate of interest that banks charge other banks on loans of excess reserves.
Federal Open Market Committee (FOMC) A 12-member committee of the Fed that formulates and executes the Fed's purchases and sales of Treasury securities on the Open Market in the conduct of monetary policy.
Federal Reserve Act of 1913 An act of Congress that established the Federal Reserve Banking System, the first true central bank in the United States.
Federal Reserve Banking System The central bank of the United States, commonly referred to as the "Fed."
Federal Reserve Note A dollar bill of any denomination that is the paper currency of the United States.
Financial Intermediary Any institution involved in the process of transferring funds from suppliers to users that positions itself between the ultimate suppliers and the ultimate users of funds in financial markets, such as a commercial bank.
Financial Markets Markets that play the role of transferring money from surplus agents to deficit agents throughout the economy.
Financial Repression A reduction in the supply of savings caused by government policies, such as a government-imposed interest rate ceiling in financial markets.
Fine Tuning Using fiscal or monetary policies to keep the economy at or very near the target level of national income.
Firm's How Problem The goal of producing the maximum output for a given total cost spent on factors of production; alternatively, the goal of producing a given output for the minimum total cost spent on factors of production.
Fiscal Policy Changes in the federal budget made for the specific purpose of influencing the level and the composition of the circular flow of economic activity; includes changes in government spending on goods and services, changes in transfer payments, or changes in taxes.
Fisher Equation The relationship between observed, or nominal, interest rates and the underlying real interest rates that says that the observed interest rate on a financial security equals the real interest rate plus the expected rate of inflation.
Fixed Cost The cost associated with the fixed factors of production in the short run.
Fixed Exchange Rate An exchange rate that is set at a fixed value.
Flexible Exchange Rate An exchange rate that is determined by the Laws of Supply and Demand in the foreign exchange markets.
Flow Variable A variable that can be measured only with reference to a period of time.
For Whom or Distribution Question Asks who will receive the various goods and services that are produced; one of the four fundamental economic questions that every society must answer.
Foreign Exchange Markets The markets in which nations' currencies are exchanged and the exchange rates between all nations' currencies are established.
Foreign Saving The difference between imports and exports.
Formal Education Refers to all schooling received in institutions outside the labor force, from elementary school through graduate school, and includes general vocational training by institutions established for that purpose and not associated with any one business firm.
Free-Rider A person who consumes a nonexclusive (public) good without paying for any of the costs of the good.
Frictional Unemployment Unemployment caused by the continuously shifting employment opportunities from sector to sector that go on beneath the surface of the economy; gathering information about job opportunities and relocating take time and act as frictions in the economy that generate unemployment.
Full Employment The condition when all people who want to work have a job.
Full Faith and Credit Bond Government bonds issued to finance capital projects that are not expected to bring in revenues; the bonds are backed by the government's power to tax.
Full Price The price of a product plus the value of the time spent shopping for and actually consuming the product.
Fully Anticipated Inflation This exists if everyone knows what the inflation rate will be in all future years.
Fully Decentralized Economy An economic system in which individuals and business firms make all economic decisions and are responsible for generating and processing all relevant economic information.

Gains from Trade The amount that a nation gains through international trade relative to producing itself all the goods and the services that it consumes; alternatively, the increase in consumer surplus plus producer surplus resulting from international trade.
GDP Deflator A price index based on a market basket of consumption goods, investment goods, government purchases, and net exports; used to convert current dollar GDP into constant dollar GDP.
General Agreement on Tariffs and Trade (GATT) A treaty originally signed by 23 capitalist nations in 1947 that commits the signatories to reduce tariffs and other trade barriers; membership in GATT has grown to nearly 100 nations.
General Training In a labor market context, the training people receive that teaches basic skills—reading, writing, arithmetic, analytical thinking, familiarity with computers, and so forth—that are useful in a number of occupations and that workers can take with them whenever they change jobs.
GINI Coefficient A common measure of the degree of inequality of income or wealth, equal to the area between the Lorenz curve and the diagonal of the square containing the Lorenz curve, divided by the entire area beneath the diagonal.
Government Bond A promissory note issued by a government that pays the bondholder (the lender) an amount equal to the principal, or face value, of a bond at a specified future date.
Government Purchases of Goods and Services Aggregate purchases of final goods and services by the federal, state, and local governments; the services are primarily the labor services of government employees.
Government Saving The difference between government revenues and government expenditures.
Government Sector In the United States, the economic activities of the federal government, the state governments, and all local governments.
Gross Domestic Product (GDP) The value of final goods and services produced within a country during the year, whether by the country's own citizens or by the citizens of a foreign country.
Gross Investment The value of new capital put in place during the year, equal to the sum of purchases of new plant and equipment, increases in firms' inventories, and purchases of new homes.
Gross National Product (GNP) The value of the final goods and services produced by the citizens of the country during the year no matter where the citizens happen to live.
Gross-of-Tax Price The price including the tax, which is the price that the consumers pay under an excise or sales tax.

Herfindahl-Hirschman Index (HHI) An index of industry concentration, equal to the sum of the squares of each firm's market share within the industry.
Horizontal Differentiation A form of product differentiation in which a firm distinguishes its product from the products of other firms in the industry by choosing where to locate its place of business.
Horizontal Equity A principle of end-results equity that requires that equals receive equal treatment; in the context of product markets, all owners of firms earn the same return to their capital in the long run (standardizing for risk).
Horizontal Equity (Taxation) The principle that two people with equal levels of utility before a tax should have equal levels of utility after a tax.
Horizontal Merger A merger between firms selling the same product.
Household Sector The sector of the economy that consists of individuals in their dual roles as consumers of final goods and services and as suppliers of factors of production to business firms.
How or Input Question Asks how the economy produces its goods and services; one of the four fundamental economic questions that every society must answer.
Human Capital The market value of all accumulated knowledge and skills.
Human Capital Theory A theory that analyzes the relationship between education and earnings, on the assumption that education increases people's earnings by making them more productive.
Hyperinflation An inflation in which prices are increasing very rapidly, causing people to lose confidence in the currency.

Impact of a Tax Refers to the levying of the tax; that is, who actually writes the tax check to the government.
Imports Goods and services, and factors of production, purchased from foreign individuals and business firms for domestic use.
Import-Substituting Industrialization (ISI) A strategy for economic growth and development in which a developing country produces goods that it had previously been importing.
Incentive-Based Pay A method of payment used by employers that relates pay directly to the results of an employee's work, such as the commissions received by salespeople.
Incidence of a Tax Refers to the true burden of the tax; that is, how the burden of the tax is split between demanders and suppliers.
Income Effect (of a Price Change) The change in the quantity demanded of a good due to the effect that the change in its price has on an individual's purchasing power or real income.
Income Elasticity of Demand A measure of the responsiveness of quantity demanded to a change in income; specifically, the percentage change in quantity demanded divided by the percentage change in income.
Income Statement A record of the value of the output and income generated by the firm during the course of the year; a record of a firm's sales and the cost of goods sold.
Increasing Cost Industry An industry in which the minimum long-run average cost of the firms increases as output supplied to the market increases, so that the long-run market supply curve is upward sloping.
Index of Coincident Indicators An index of four cyclical indicators that is designed to track the expansion and the contraction phases of the business cycle, and its turning points, as they are occurring.
Index of Lagging Indicators An index of seven cyclical indicators that is designed to confirm the existence of the various phases of the business cycle and its turning points with a few months' delay.
Index of Leading Indicators An index of 11 cyclical indicators that is designed to forecast aggregate economic activity and predict the turning points of the business cycle.
Indifference Curve A graphical representation of the different combinations of goods and services that an individual is indifferent to because they yield the same level of utility.
Indifference Map The set of all the indifference curves.
Indirect Business Taxes Sales and excise taxes that firms pay on the sale of their products.
Individual Demand Curve A graphical representation of the individual demand schedule, showing the quantity of a good that an individual is willing and able to buy at each price, other things equal.
Individual Demand Schedule The quantity of a good that an individual is willing and able to buy at each price, other things equal.
Individual Firm's Supply Curve A graphical representation of the individual firm's supply schedule, showing the quantity that the firm is willing and able to supply at each price, other things equal; equal to a competitive firm's marginal cost curve above the minimum of its average variable cost curve.
Individual Firm's Supply Schedule The quantity that the firm is willing and able to supply at each price, other things equal.
Industrial Union A labor union organized according to industry rather than the tasks that the workers perform within the industry.
Industry The collection of all firms producing the same product.
Inexhaustible Resource A resource whose quantity does not diminish as it is used in production, such as land.
Inflation Continuing increases in the level of prices generally, usually expressed as a percentage rate of increase.
Inflationary Gap Exists when the equilibrium level of national income is greater than the full-employment level of national income; the size of the gap is the amount that aggregate demand has to decrease to bring the equilibrium level of national income to the full-employment level of national income.
In-Kind Gift A charitable donation or transfer in the form of a particular good or service.
Innovation The process of recognizing the practical uses of an invention and understanding the steps required to make it commercially viable.
Insider/Outsider Theory A theory of wage stickiness that says that the older, more experienced employees, the "insiders," have the decision-making power and use it to place all the risks of a business downturn on the younger, less experienced employees, the "outsiders."
Intangible A benefit or a cost that cannot be evaluated in dollar terms.
Interdependence The principle that economic decisions are interrelated such that the consequences of a decision always spread beyond the immediate objectives of the decision.
Internal Debt (Public) Public debt that is held by U.S. citizens, businesses, and government agencies.
Internal Labor Market A method of hiring and promotion in which firms hire new employees from outside the firm only into the lowest-level jobs within the corporate hierarchy and then promote from within to all higher-level jobs.
Internal Yield on an Investment The rate of discount that just sets the present value of an investment equal to zero.
International Comparisons Program (ICP) A program undertaken by the

United Nations to correct for the problem of converting a country's gross domestic product (GDP) to another currency; it solves this problem by calculating a purchasing power parity exchange rate for each country.
International Credit Any international transaction that gives rise to a demand for dollars in the foreign exchange markets, such as an export or a capital inflow.
International Debit Any international transaction that gives rise to a supply of dollars in the foreign exchange markets, such as an import or a capital outflow.
International Monetary Fund (IMF) An international agency established in 1947 by the capitalist countries that acts as a forum for resolving exchange rate and balance-of-payments problems.
Investment A flow variable that refers to the increase in the stock of capital during the year.
Investment in Human Capital Expenditures on education, both formal education received in school and on-the-job training provided by business firms.
Investment Tax Credit A tax credit under the federal corporation income tax that allows firms to deduct a portion of the total value of their investment during the year from their taxable profits.

Job Leavers Those people who have voluntarily quit their jobs and are actively looking for other jobs.
Job Losers Those people who have been laid off or fired by their employers.

Known Reserves The amount of a natural resource that the U.S. Geological Survey estimates is profitable to extract at current prices and with current production technologies.
Kuznets Curve A curve that shows the relationship between the income distribution and the per capita income for countries in different stages of economic development.

Labor A catch-all term referring to all the different kinds of skills and occupations found in the work force; one of the primary factors of production.
Labor Force All people, aged 16 and older, who are either employed or unemployed.
Labor Force Participation The percentage of the population that joins the labor force.
Labor Productivity The amount of output produced per worker.
Land The property on which business firms build their factories and office buildings; includes the fertile soil and natural resources contained within the land; one of the primary factors of production.
Law of Demand Other things equal, the lower the price of a product, the larger the quantity demanded; the higher the price of a product, the smaller the quantity demanded.
Law of Diminishing Marginal Rate of Substitution The more of a good that consumers have, the fewer units of another good they are willing to trade to consume an additional unit of the good.
Law of Diminishing Marginal Utility The marginal utility of consuming a product decreases as the amount of the product consumed increases.
Law of Diminishing Returns As increasing amounts of a variable factor of production are added to one or more fixed factors of production, the marginal product of the variable factor eventually declines.
Law of Diminishing (Marginal) Willingness to Trade For a consumer, the marginal willingness to trade one good for some other good decreases as more and more of the one good is exchanged for the other good.
Law of Large Numbers A property of statistics, which says that the average behavior of a large group of firms (or people) becomes highly predictable, even if the behavior of individual members of the group is highly unpredictable.
Law of Scarcity The principle that resources are not sufficient to achieve all the objectives, or goals, of an economic problem.
Law of Substitution A test of efficiency with more than one objective that says that moving closer to one objective is possible only by moving farther away from at least one other objective.
Law of Supply Other things equal, the lower the price of a product, the smaller the quantity supplied; the higher the price of a product, the larger the quantity supplied.
Lease-Cost Production Rule The solution to the firm's How problem, in which the firm equalizes the ratio of marginal product to price across all factors of production.
Legal Barrier to Entry Any government policy, such as an exclusive franchise or a patent, that restricts or prevents the free flow of resources into or out of an industry.
Levered Investment An investment that is financed in part with borrowed funds.
Liability Something that is owed; a claim against someone by some other person or institution.
Licensing A type of government regulation that restricts entry into an industry as a means of assuring service quality and standards or as a means of controlling the spread of socially undesirable activities.
Life-Cycle Hypothesis A theory of household consumption demand that attempts to explain the average pattern of lifetime income and consumption given by the age-earnings profile.
Liquid Asset A financial asset that is easily converted into money.
Long-Purse Theory The theory that, in the absence of perfect capital markets, large firms have an advantage over new entrants in undertaking investment, since they can finance their investment out of past profits retained by the firms, whereas new entrants have to borrow to invest; this advantage acts as a barrier to entry.
Long Run A period of time long enough that the firm is able to vary all factors of production and firms can enter or leave the industry.
Long-Run Economic Growth A persistent increase in the economy's potential for producing goods and services.
Long-Run Phillips Curve A curve representing the idea that the economy tends to the natural rate of unemployment in the long run and that there is no long-run trade-off between inflation and unemployment; shows that any rate of inflation is compatible with the natural rate of unemployment in the long run.
Long-Run Total Cost Curve The other things equal relationship between output and total cost in the long run.
Lorenz Curve A graph of the distribution of income that relates the cumulative percentage of all families, ordered by income from lowest to highest, to the cumulative percentage of the total income (wealth) that they receive.

Macroeconomic Policy An attempt to achieve the macroeconomic policy goals by intervening in some form in the operation of the economy.
Macroeconomics The study of the economy "in the large"; analyzes the overall performance of the economy.
Managed Exchange Rate ("Dirty" Float) A variation of a flexible exchange rate system in which an exchange rate is determined by the Laws of Supply and Demand within a band of values selected by

the central banks; alternatively, a variation of a flexible exchange rate system in which the central banks occasionally intervene in the foreign exchange markets in order to prevent their currencies from appreciating or depreciating "too much."

Margin Refers to the effects of a small change in an economic variable.

Marginal Benefit The additional benefit, in terms of the objectives, of the next unit of an activity.

Marginal Cost The addition to total cost of producing an additional unit of output; in general, the change in total cost divided by the change in output.

Marginal Cost Curve A graphical representation of marginal cost, showing at each output the addition to total cost of producing an additional unit of output.

Marginal Cost of Pollution The additional cost of pollution experienced by all third parties combined when a polluting activity is increased by one unit.

Marginal Efficiency of Capital The returns to capital from the last unit of capital put in place; also, the demand curve for capital.

Marginal (Physical) Product of Labor The additional output produced by each additional unit of labor.

Marginal Product of Labor The additional output produced by hiring one more unit of labor, holding all other factors of production constant.

Marginal Propensity to Consume The portion of each additional dollar of disposable income that households consume; the ratio of the change in consumption demand to the change in disposable income.

Marginal Propensity to Import The additional amount of import demand resulting from a $1 increase in national income; the ratio of the change in import demand to the change in national income.

Marginal Propensity to Save The portion of each additional dollar of disposable income that households save; the ratio of the change in saving demand to the change in disposable income.

Marginal Propensity to Spend The portion of the change in national income that feeds back into further changes in aggregate demand during each round of the multiplier process; the slope of the aggregate desired expenditures (*ADE*) line.

Marginal Rate of Substitution The rate at which an individual is willing to trade one good for another so as to leave utility unchanged; the slope of an indifference curve.

Marginal Revenue The increase in total revenue from selling one more unit of output; equal to price for a competitive firm.

Marginal Revenue Product of Labor The marginal revenue from hiring an additional worker, equal to the product of the marginal (physical) product of labor and the marginal revenue from selling the output produced by that labor.

Marginal Tax Rate The rate of tax applied to additional income received under a personal income tax.

Marginal Utility The increase in utility obtained from consuming one more unit of a good.

Marginal Value The value of the last good consumed by each consumer.

(Marginal) Willingness to Trade The rate of trade between any two goods that leaves the consumer's level of utility unchanged; also called the *marginal rate of substitution* between the two goods.

Market Any institutional arrangement through which buyers and sellers engage in the voluntary exchange of goods, services, and factors of production.

Market Demand Curve A graphical representation of the market demand schedule, showing the total quantity demanded of a good by all consumers at each price, other things equal; the horizontal summation of the individual demand curves.

Market Demand Schedule The total amount demanded of a good by all the consumers at each price, other things equal; the summation of the individual demand schedules.

Market Equilibrium The intersection of the market demand and the market supply curves at which the quantity demanded equals the quantity supplied.

Market Power (Monopoly Power) A market situation in which an individual firm faces a downward-sloping demand curve for its product.

Market Share The ratio of a firm's sales (total revenue) to the total industry sales.

Market Supply Curve A graphical representation of the market supply schedule, showing the total quantity that all firms in the market are willing and able to supply at each price, other things equal; equal to the horizontal summation of the individual firms' supply curves; also called the *industry supply curve.*

Market Supply Curve—Long run—the total quantity supplied by the firms in the market at each price, when each firm is producing at the MES, the minimum of its long-run average cost.

Market Supply Curve—Short run—the horizontal summation of the individual firms' supply or marginal cost curves, above the minimum of average variable cost.

Market Supply Schedule The total quantity that all firms in the market are willing and able to supply at each price, other things equal; the sum of the individual firms' supply schedules.

Marketable Permit (Pollution) A government-issued allowance to emit a certain amount of a pollutant that firms can buy and sell; used in the United States to control the emission of sulfur dioxide by the electric utilities under the Clean Air Act.

Mark-Up Pricing A rule-of-thumb method of pricing in which a firm sets its price at a constant percentage above its unit or average cost.

Material Incentives Incentives that appeal to economic self-interest by allowing individuals and business firms to keep the gains from their exchanges.

Material Inputs Semi-finished products purchased by firms and used as a factor of production.

Means-Tested Refers to public assistance that is given to families or individuals only if their incomes are below some predetermined amount.

Median Income The income of the family in the middle of the income distribution (half the families have incomes higher than the median and half have incomes lower than the median).

Medium of Exchange Anything that people are routinely willing to accept in exchange for goods and services (and factors of production).

Menu Costs The costs to producers of publishing new price catalogs and informing customers of price changes.

Merit Good A good that society considers a virtual necessity, but that is priced beyond the means of those with low incomes.

Microeconomics The study of the economy "in the small"; analyzes the economic problems of individual economic agents and the exchanges between them.

Minimum Efficient Scale of Operation (MES) The minimum of the long-run average cost curve; alternatively, the output at which economies of scale end and diseconomies of scale begin.

Minimum Wage (Federal) A wage floor legislated by the federal government, set at $4.25/hour in 1993, which is the lowest wage that firms can pay their workers.

Model A simplified description of some real-world situation that isolates one particular aspect of the situation and studies the effects on that one aspect as different elements are changed one at a time.

Momentary Run The period immediately following a change in supply or demand when producers cannot change their output supplied to the market.
Monetary Base The sum of Federal Reserve Notes plus bank reserves.
Monetary Policy Changes in the money supply made for the specific purpose of influencing the level and the composition of the circular flow of economic activity.
Money Anything that is routinely used to pay for goods and services or to pay off debts.
Money Multiplier The ratio that relates the total change in the money supply to the value of Treasury securities that the Fed purchases or sells on the Open Market.
Money Rain An abstract device used by economists to represent an increase in the money supply that imagines the new money falling from the sky.
Monopolistic Competition A product market characterized by a large number of firms producing slightly differentiated products, with easy entry and exit, and in which strategic behavior is unimportant.
Monopsony Power Market power in labor markets (or in any factor markets) such that firms are able to set the wage of the workers (or cost of the factors) they hire.
Moral Hazard In the context of insurance, arises when individuals who are being insured can influence the probability of the event being insured against, unbeknownst to the insurer.
Moral Incentives Incentives that encourage behavior for the good of society and may be enforced with legal sanctions.
Most-Favored-Nation Principle A fundamental principle of GATT that states that any reduction in tariffs or other trade restrictions that is negotiated between any two nations automatically applies to all nations.
Multinational Corporation A corporation that has offices and/or factories in more than one country.
Multiplier-Accelerator Model An internal model of the business cycle that is based on the instability of investment demand and its relationship to national income through both the demand side and the supply side of the economy.
M1 The narrowest definition of money, consisting of those financial securities that are routinely accepted for transactions; the sum of currency and balances in checking accounts with unlimited checking privileges.
M2 A definition of money, consisting of M1 plus limited-checking money market deposit accounts and various kinds of very highly liquid small savings accounts with balances under $100,000.
M3 A broad definition of money, consisting of M2 plus various kinds of large deposit accounts with balances exceeding $100,000, including institutional money market mutual funds and European accounts held by U.S. citizens.

National Banking Acts of 1933 and 1935 Acts of Congress that brought the 12 Federal Reserve Banks under the control of one governing body, the Board of Governors.
National Economic Plan A plan developed by the central authority that sets national economic objectives regarding the four fundamental economic questions and instructs lower-level decision-making units on how to carry out the plan.
National Income The value of the labor, capital, and land exchanged in the nation's factor markets during the year.
National Net Worth The net worth or wealth of an entire nation, equal to the market value of the nation's real, or tangible, assets plus the market value of its land, less any claims against these assets held by foreigners.
National Product The value of the final goods and services exchanged in the nation's product markets during the year.
National Saving The amount of saving generated by the domestic economy during the year, equal to the sum of saving by the private sector and saving by the government sector; the difference between total saving and foreign saving.
Natural Barrier to Entry Features inherent in production or supply, such as economies of scale and limited access to a vital factor of production, that restrict or prevent the free flow of resources into or out of an industry.
Natural Monopoly A market situation in which the MES (the minimum of the long-run average cost curve) of a single firm is at or beyond the entire market demand for the product.
Natural Rate of Unemployment The sum of frictional and search unemployment and structural unemployment; the rate of unemployment that corresponds to production on the production possibilities frontier and that cannot be reduced very much by fiscal and monetary policies. Also called the *non-accelerating inflationary rate of unemployment.*
Negative Income Tax A subsidy given to families or individuals whose income is below some predetermined amount and administered as part of the federal personal income tax.
Net Domestic Product (NDP) The difference between gross domestic product and the BEA's estimate of the capital consumption allowance (depreciation).
Net Exports The difference between exports and imports.
Net Interest The difference between interest paid and interest received by firms.
Net Investment The difference between gross investment and the BEA's estimate of the capital consumption allowance (depreciation).
Net-of-Tax Price The price excluding the tax, which is the price that producers receive to cover their costs under an excise or sales tax.
Net Value At any quantity exchanged in the market, the difference between the total value as perceived by the consumers and the total cost as experienced by the firms.
Net Worth The difference between a person's assets and liabilities; also called *wealth.*
Newly Industrializing Countries (NICs) Countries in East Asia that are rapidly industrializing and approaching or surpassing the living standards in the lower tier of developed countries.
New Entrants Those people who are seeking employment for the first time, having never worked before.
Non-Accelerating Inflationary Rate of Unemployment The minimum that the rate of unemployment can be without starting an ever-accelerating inflationary process; also called the *natural rate of unemployment.*
Noncompetitive Product Market A product market in which individual firms have considerable control over price and other market outcomes.
Noncooperative Behavior Independent decision making by firms in which they openly compete with one another.
Nonexclusive (Public) Good A good such as national defense that is consumed by everyone once any one person or the government buys it; no one can be excluded or exclude themselves from consuming the good.
Nonmonetary Operating Costs Costs of production that do not involve out-of-pocket payments for factors of production, the most important being an estimate of the depreciation of the firm's stock of capital.
Nonresidential Fixed Investment Purchases of new plant and equipment during the year.

Normal Good A good whose consumption rises as income rises, other things equal.
Normative Economic Analysis The study of what ought to be; attempts to determine appropriate norms or criteria for judging the results of economic behavior and activity.
Now Versus the Future Question Asks whether society will favor the current generation over future generations, or the reverse; one of the four fundamental economic questions that every society must answer.

Objectives The part of the economic problem that refers to the goals that economic agents try to achieve.
Official Settlements Account The subaccount in the balance of payments that records transactions between a nation's central bank and the central banks of other nations.
Official Settlements Account Balance The difference between international credit and debit transactions between a nation's central bank and the central banks of other nations.
Okun's Law An observed relationship between output growth and unemployment, which states that every 2.5-percentage-point increase in the rate of growth of output reduces the unemployment rate in the United States by 1 percentage point.
Oligopoly A product market dominated by a few large firms.
On-the-Job Training Training offered by firms to their employees that teaches them skills that make them more productive to the firm.
Open Market Operation A purchase or sale of Treasury securities by the Fed for the purpose of controlling the money supply.
Operating Expenses The total accounting costs incurred by the firm in producing and selling its output, including the explicit monetary costs and certain nonmonetary costs.
Operational Lag (Fiscal Policy) The time period from the passage of new legislation to the final change in the equilibrium level of national income.
Operational Lag (Monetary Policy) The time required for a change in the money supply to affect the equilibrium level of national income.
Opportunity Cost The economic meaning of cost; the value, in terms of the objectives, of the next best alternative.
Opportunity Cost of Capital The return that the owners of the firm could earn if the value of the capital they own were invested in their next best investment alternatives.
Opportunity Cost of Labor The wage or salary available to the employees of a firm in their next best employment alternatives.
Ordering of Preferences When faced with two combinations of goods and services, the ability to determine either that one combination is preferred to the other or that the two combinations give the same level of utility; an ordering must also satisfy the condition of transitivity.
Overvalued Currency The value of a nation's currency relative to other currencies is greater than its equilibrium value determined by the Laws of Supply and Demand in the foreign exchange markets.

Parity The ratio of prices received by farmers for their output to the prices farmers pay for their inputs.
Partnership A form of business with two or more owners who have total control over the operation of the business and who jointly determine how to transfer funds into and out of the business.
Payoff Matrix A listing of the present values or the internal yields of an investment under every possible future environment.
Peak (Business Cycle) A turning point in the business cycle when the expansion phase ends and the contraction phase begins.
Perfect Competition A product market characterized by a large number of firms, identical products, perfect information, no strategic behavior, a free flow of resources into and out of the industry, and prices and quantities determined by the Laws of Supply and Demand.
Personal Saving The portion of disposable income that households do not consume.
Petrodollar Recycling The practice among financial institutions of lending to the developing countries the funds that they receive from the oil-producing countries.
Political Business Cycle A theory that attributes the business cycle to attempts by the incumbent administration to manipulate the economy to increase its chances of re-election, consisting of expansionary pre-election policies and contractionary post-election policies.
Positive Economic Analysis The study of what is; attempts to determine what actually exists in the real world and to describe the consequences of economic decisions.
Poverty Gap The minimum total amount of income that all poor families and unrelated individuals would have to be given to reach the poverty line and escape poverty.
Poverty Line The amount of income that allows a family or unrelated individual to purchase the bare necessities for a minimally adequate standard of living; anyone with income below the poverty line is considered to be living in poverty.
Precautionary Demand for Money The motive for holding money to cover temporary and unexpected expenses or losses of income.
Predatory Pricing A strategy used by an incumbent firm to deter entry in which the firm sets its price so low that a new entrant could not possibly make a profit.
Present Value The equivalent current value of future dollars, equal to the future dollars multiplied by the relevant future discount factor.
Present Value of an Investment The difference between the discounted stream of net returns on the investment and the initial investment cost.
Pre-Market Discrimination Denying people equal opportunities to develop their natural abilities to the fullest extent possible in their formative years before they enter the labor market, as when children are denied access to the best schools because of their race or gender.
Price Ceiling A legislated amount above which the market price is not allowed to rise.
Price Discrimination Charging different customers different prices that are unrelated to differences in the cost of serving the customers.
(Price) Elasticity of Demand A measure of the responsiveness of quantity demanded to changes in the price of a product along a demand curve; specifically, the percentage change in quantity demanded divided by the percentage change in price in absolute value.
(Price) Elasticity of Supply A measure of the responsiveness of quantity supplied to a change in price along a supply curve; specifically, the percentage change in quantity supplied divided by the percentage change in price.
Price Floor A legislated amount below which the market price is not allowed to fall.
Price Inflation A persistent increase in

the prices of most goods and services.
Price Stability Prices in general are neither rising nor falling.
Price Taker A firm or individual who has no influence over the market price.
Principal-Agent Problem An informational problem in which one individual (the principal) tries to monitor and control the behavior of another individual (the agent), but does not have enough information to do so, and the two individuals have different goals.
Prisoners' Dilemma In the context of an industry cartel, a game played among the member firms in which the equilibrium outcome is for the firms to cheat and destroy the profits made possible by the cartel.
Private-Sector Saving The sum of personal saving and business saving.
Process Equity A criterion for judging economic activity that asks whether the rules under which the economy operates are fair.
Producer Price Index A price index that is designed to track changes in the cost of production over time; it has three components derived from three separate market baskets: crude materials; intermediate materials, supplies, and components purchased from other firms; and finished manufactured goods.
Producer Surplus At any quantity exchanged in the market, the difference between the total market value and the total cost of production.
Producers Economic agents who produce goods and services by receiving factors of production from consumers and other producers.
Product Differentiation A situation in which buyers distinguish or identify products by the firms that produce them; also refers to firms' attempts to distinguish their products from similar products produced by other firms in the industry, by either real or illusory means.
Product Differentiation/Economies of Scale Model of International Trade A model specifically developed to explain the two-way trade in similar products between the industrialized countries; based on the idea that multinational corporations compete with each other through the research and development of new products and successful products enjoy economies of scale, which gives them a niche in the international marketplace.
Production Function The relationship between a firm's outputs and its inputs that indicates the maximum output attainable from all possible combinations of inputs that the firm might use.
Production Possibilities The economy's capacity for producing goods and services, assuming that it produces them efficiently.
Production Possibilities Frontier A graphical representation of the economy's capacity for producing goods and services, assuming that it produces them efficiently.
Production Technology A blueprint or method for transforming inputs into outputs.
Production (Technical) Efficiency Achieved when the output supplied to the market uses the least amount of society's scarce resources; the market test is that each firm produces in the long run at the minimum of its long-run average cost curve, the minimum efficient scale of operation (MES).
Profit The difference between the revenue obtained from selling goods and services and the cost of producing them.
Profit-Maximizing Output Rule A firm produces the output at which marginal revenue equals marginal cost (and charges the price on its demand curve corresponding to this output).
Profit-Maximizing Supply Rule A perfectly competitive firm supplies the output at which price equals marginal cost as long as price is greater than (short-run) average variable cost.
Profit Satisficers Large corporations that are interested in profit only to the point of achieving a satisfactory level of profit and then pursue other objectives.
Progressive Tax A tax for which the average tax burden increases as the taxpayer's income increases.
Property Rights The ownership of the factors of production.
Proportional Tax A tax for which the average tax burden remains constant as the taxpayer's income increases.
Proprietors' Income Income or profit earned by unincorporated forms of business, principally partnerships and sole proprietorships.
Purchasing Power The amount of goods and services that consumers are able to buy with their limited incomes, given prices; also called *real income*.
Purchasing Power Parity The principle that the overall price index of one country must equal the overall price index of any other country multiplied by the exchange rate of the first country's currency to the second country's currency.
Pure Market Capitalism An economic system characterized by fully decentralized decision making, the use of markets to process economic information and coordinate exchange, private ownership of capital and land, and the use of material incentives.
Pure Monopoly A product market in which a single firm comprises the entire industry and has complete control over all supply decisions.
Pure Monopsony The limiting case of monopsony power in which one firm is the only buyer of a particular kind of labor (or of any factor).

Quota A government-imposed limit on the quantity of a good or a service that can be imported into a country.
Quota Rent The economic profit earned by foreign importers under a quota when the quota licenses are given away (or sold at less than their full market value).

Rational Expectations The assumption that rational individuals consider all relevant information (past, present, and future) currently available when forming expectations of the future.
Real Business Cycle Theory A theory to explain the business cycle developed by new classical economists that is based on outside shocks to the fundamental structure of the economy, which consists of household preferences, resources, and production technologies.
Real Price Change The actual rate of change in a price less the general rate of inflation.
Recessionary Gap Exists when the equilibrium level of national income is less than the full-employment level of national income; the size of the gap is the amount that aggregate demand has to increase to bring the equilibrium level of national income to the full-employment level of national income.
Recognition Lag (Fiscal or Monetary Policy) The time required for policy makers to realize that the economy is in trouble and needs a dose of countercyclical policy.
Re-Entrants Those people who were once employed, then dropped out of the labor force, and have now re-entered the labor force.
Regressive Tax A tax for which the average tax burden declines as the taxpayer's income increases.
Rent Control A price ceiling on the rents that landlords can charge low-income tenants.

Rent Seeking The pursuit of profitable market opportunities by entrepreneurs that is directed toward unproductive, socially wasteful ends.
Rental Payments to Persons The combined payments to land and to capital in the form of rents.
Required Reserves The minimum amount of reserves against deposit accounts that commercial banks (and other depository institutions) are required to keep in an account at the Fed; equal to the reserve requirement times the amount of deposit account balances.
Reserve Requirement The minimum average ratio of reserves to deposit account balances that commercial banks (and other depository institutions) must maintain over every two week period.
Reserves A non-interest-bearing account against deposits that commercial banks (and other depository institutions) must keep with the Fed; used by the Fed to control the amount of loans and deposits that banks can create.
Rest-of-World Sector The sector of an economy that consists of a country's economic relations with foreign countries.
Retained Earnings The portion of the accounting profits of the firm that is not paid out as taxes or as dividends to stockholders, but is set aside to help finance the continued expansion of the firm.
Revenue Bond Government bonds that are used to pay for self-financing capital projects.
Rivalry The name commonly used to describe nonprice competition among oligopolistic firms.

Sales Maximization The goal of maximizing total revenue or sales by producing the output at which marginal revenue is zero.
Saving Function The relationship that indicates how much households in the aggregate are willing and able to save during the year at every level of total disposable income, other things equal; also called *saving demand.*
Search Unemployment Unemployment caused by employees who leave their jobs voluntarily and are looking for other jobs, or by re-entrants or new entrants to the labor force who are looking for a job.
Segmentation Theory In the context of labor markets, the theory that businesses teach their employees all they need to know in order to perform the various tasks within a company, so that on-the-job training is the only form of investment in human capital that determines a worker's productivity.
Segmented Labor Market A labor market in which workers who are qualified for a particular job are denied access to that job.
Services Purchases by consumers that are not manufactured, but that provide them with something useful.
Short Run The period following a change in supply or demand over which firms can vary some of their factors of production, but not all of them.
Short-Run Phillips Curve A curve that shows how the rate of inflation and the unemployment rate respond to a change in aggregate demand in the short run.
Short-Run Total Cost Curve The other things equal relationship between output and total cost in the short run.
Shut-Down Point A market situation in which a firm's total revenue equals its variable cost (price equals average variable cost), so that the firm is indifferent between producing and not producing.
Single Proprietorship A form of business in which a single owner has total control over the operation of the business and has complete freedom to transfer funds into and out of the business.
Social Mobility The extent to which families change their position over time within the personal distribution of income.
Socialism An economic system with public ownership of capital and land.
Special Drawing Right (SDR) A reserve currency created by the IMF and accepted by all central banks as an international reserve in their official settlement accounts; countries can purchase SDRs with their own currency and then trade them to central banks for dollars and other major currencies as needed to settle current account deficits.
Specific Training In a labor market context, the skills that employees learn during on-the-job training that are useful only to the firm offering the training, such as learning how to operate highly specialized equipment used only by that firm.
Speculative Demand for Money The motive for holding money based on expectations of future interest rates.
Spending Multiplier The ratio that relates the change in the equilibrium level of national income to an initial change, or shift, in aggregate demand.
Stabilization Policies Government economic policies that respond to market failures relating to the macroeconomic policy goals of achieving long-run economic growth, full employment, price stability, and satisfactory economic relations with foreign countries.
Stable Dollar The value of the dollar remains constant relative to the currencies of other nations.
Stable Market Equilibrium A property of the market equilibrium such that the market automatically returns to the equilibrium from any other quantity-price combination.
Stagflation A period of increasing inflation, falling output, and rising unemployment that follows an adverse aggregate supply shock.
Statistical Discrimination Attributing to each member of a group the average characteristics of the entire group of people, which become the basis for hiring, training, or promoting any one individual within the group.
Sterilizing Transaction A transaction by a central bank that is designed to offset the effect on the money supply caused by any transaction on the official settlements account; an example is the Fed's sales of Treasury securities on the Open Market to offset its purchases of foreign currencies.
Stock Variable A variable that can be measured at a given point in time.
Store of Value A means of holding wealth from one period to the next.
Strategic Behavior Any decision by a firm that considers how other firms will react to the decision.
Strategic Tariff A tariff that is designed to protect domestic firms from competition while they are attempting to research and develop successful new products.
Structural Budget Deficit An estimate of what the government's budget deficit would be if the economy were at full employment (the natural rate of unemployment), regardless of where the economy actually is; it increases and decreases with discretionary changes in government spending on goods and services, transfer payments, or taxes; formerly referred to as the ***high-employment budget deficit.***
Structural Unemployment Unemployment caused by severe and lasting mismatches between people who are looking for work and the jobs that are available to them; the mismatches are typically geographic or skills-related.
Substitutes Products that provide the same general kind of services; specifically, two goods whose relationship is such that a decrease in the price of one good decreases the demand for the other good.
Substitution Effect (of a Price Change) The tendency to purchase more of those products that have become relatively cheaper and fewer of those products that

have become relatively more expensive when relative prices change.
Sunk Cost A firm's fixed cost in the short run, arising from decisions about factors of production that were made in the past.
Supply The amount of a product that a firm is willing and able to sell over a certain period of time.
Supply Rule for Maximizing Profit A competitive firm should produce the output at which price (marginal revenue) equals marginal cost.
Surplus Agents Economic agents who are the savers, or lenders, or the suppliers of funds in financial markets because they have more income than they desire to spend in any one year.

Tacit Collusion An implicit agreement among the large corporations in an oligopoly, most often in the form of an agreement not to compete in terms of prices.
Target Efficiency In the context of public assistance, transfer payments that are given only to the poor and remove them from poverty at the lowest possible expense.
Tariff A tax on a good or a service entering a country.
Tax Multiplier The ratio that relates the change in the equilibrium level of national income to a change in taxes on households.
Tax Structure The tax rates and the tax base of any particular tax.
Terms-of-Trade The rate of exchange between imported goods and exported goods; alternatively, the ratio of a nation's export prices to its import prices.
Theory of Public Choice A theory of government based on the premise that people behave in the same self-interested manner in the political arena as they do in the economic arena.
Time-Based Pay A method of payment used by employers that consists of a straight payment per unit of time independent of the results of the employee's work, such as a manager's annual salary.
Total Cost Curve The best possible relationship between a firm's total cost and its output; it indicates either the minimum total cost of producing each level of output the firm might choose to produce or the maximum output obtainable for each given amount of total cost.
Total Economic Cost For any given output, the total opportunity cost of the factors of production used in producing and selling that output.
Total Investment Demand The sum of the three components of investment demand: investment demand for plant and equipment, investment demand for inventory, and investment demand for housing.
Total Market Value The dollars exchanged between the consumers and the producers in the market, equal to the total expenditures paid by the consumers and the total revenues received by the firms.
Total Saving The sum of personal saving, business saving, government saving, and foreign saving.
Transactions Demand for Money The fundamental motive for holding money that derives from money's role as the medium of exchange; it says that the aggregate demand for money is directly related to real national income, directly related to the overall price level, and inversely related to interest rates and rates of return on other assets.
Transactions Deposit A checking account with unlimited checking privileges.
Transfer Mechanism (International Trade) A grant or a loan to a foreign country that is then used to buy exports from the country that gave the grant or the loan; in other words, a mechanism in which first the money flows and then the goods flow.
Transfer Multiplier The ratio that relates the change in the equilibrium level of national income to a change in government transfer payments.
Transfer Payment The redistribution of existing income from one economic agent to another.
Transitivity A condition on an ordering of consumer preferences requiring that all pairwise rankings of alternative combinations be consistent with one another.
Trigger Strategy A punishment strategy within the context of a tacit collusion to maintain prices above average cost, in which the rival firms threaten to cut their prices to average cost forever if one of the firms cheats on the pricing agreement.
Trough (Business Cycle) A turning point in the business cycle when the contraction phase ends and the expansion phase begins.

Ultimate Recovery Reserves The amount of a natural resource that the U.S. Geological Survey estimates could conceivably be profitable to extract at any time in the future.
Unanticipated Inflation This exists when people are unable to guess correctly what the rate of inflation will be in all future years.
Unbalanced Inflation An inflation in which the prices of individual goods and services are rising at different rates, some faster than and others slower than the overall rate of inflation.
Underemployed Workers who are counted as employed, but who are working below their full capacities, either part time when they want to work full time or at jobs below their skill levels.
Undervalued Currency The value of a nation's currency relative to other currencies is less than its equilibrium value determined by the Laws of Supply and Demand in the foreign exchange markets.
Unemployed Those people who are actively seeking employment, but are unable to find a job.
Unemployment The condition when people are actively looking for work, but are unable to find a suitable job.
Unemployment Rate The ratio of the unemployed to the labor force, expressed as a percentage.
Union Shop A labor union rule that requires a worker to join a union within 30 days after being hired.
Unit of Account The standard that defines the value of goods and services in exchange.
Utility The value that a consumer derives from the consumption of goods and services.
Utility-Maximizing Decision Rule Utility is maximized when the ratios of marginal utility to price are equal for all goods.

Value Added For a single producer, the difference between the value of sales and the cost of the intermediate goods that it buys from other producers; for the economy, the sum of the value added by each producer.
Value of Labor's Marginal Product The marginal revenue from hiring an additional unit of labor in a competitive labor market, equal to the marginal (physical) product of labor times the price of the good or service that the labor is producing.
Value of Marginal Product of Capital (VMP_K) The present value of the additional revenue received over time from adding one more unit of capital to the existing capital stock.
Variable Cost The cost associated with the variable factors of production.
Velocity of Circulation The ratio of the dollar value of national income or national product to the money supply; the number of times the money supply changes hands

during the year to buy final goods and services (or primary factors of production).

Vertical Differentiation A form of product differentiation in which a firm distinguishes its product from the products of other firms in the industry on the basis of quality.

Vertical Equity A principle of end-results equity that asks how unequals should be treated; specifically, how much redistribution should society undertake among people with different amounts of income or wealth.

Vertical Equity (Taxation) The principle that unequals may be treated unequally, that is, two people with different values of a tax base may legitimately pay different amounts of tax.

Vertical Merger A merger between firms that operate in different stages in the production and marketing of a single product.

Voluntary Export Restriction An agreement between two nations in which one nation voluntarily limits the quantity of its exports to the other nation.

Wage Stickiness The existence of impediments that prevent wages from moving to their equilibrium level at the intersection of the supply and demand curves for labor.

Wealth The difference between a person's assets and liabilities; also called *net worth*.

What or Output Question Asks what goods and services the economy will produce and in what quantities; one of the four fundamental economic questions that every society must answer.

Windfall (Excessive) Profit A return to capital over and above the opportunity cost of capital that society considers to be excessive.

Workfare A state-administered program in which the state welfare office identifies the poor who are able to work, helps them find a job, and then makes work a prerequisite for receiving public assistance.

INDEX

Definitions appear on bolded pages; footnotes are marked with an *n*.